British and American
vocabulary
vocabulaire britannique
et américain

information
about register
informations
sur le niveau de langue

cultural
or encyclopedic
information
informations
de nature culturelle
ou encyclopédique

Big Dipper ['-dipər] *n* **-1.** *Br* [rollercoaster] montagnes *fpl* russes. **-2.** *Am* ASTRON : **the ~** la Grande Ourse.

Black Maria [-məˈraɪə] *n inf* panier *m* à salade.

city [ˈsɪtɪ] (*pl* **-ies**) *n* ville *f*, cité *f*.

◆ **City** *n Br* : **the City** la City.

THE CITY:

La City, quartier financier de la capitale, est une circonscription administrative autonome de Londres ayant sa propre police. Le terme « The City » est souvent employé pour désigner le monde britannique de la finance.

pronunciation shown
in International
Phonetic Alphabet
transcriptions
dans l'alphabet
phonétique
international

extra information
about the translation
précisions
sur la traduction

civil list *n Br* liste *f* civile *(allouée à la famille royale par le parlement britannique)*.

gynaecological *Br*, **gynecological** *Am* [sitɪ] *adj* gynécologique.

hadn't [ˈhædnt] = **had not**.

information
on verb forms
précisions
sur la conjugaison

variant
spellings
variantes

make [meɪk] (*pt & pp* **made**) - *vt* **-1.** [gen - produce] faire; [-manufacture] faire, fabriquer; **to ~ a meal** préparer un repas; **to ~ a film** tourner OR réaliser un film. **-2.** [perform an action] faire.

explanation
of meaning where
no translation exists
explications
lorsqu'il n'y a pas
de traduction

parent [ˈpeərənt] *n* père *m*, mère *f*.

◆ **parents** *npl* parents *mpl*.

pluriel ayant
son propre sens
plural which has
its own
specific meaning

PAYE (*abbr of* **pay as you earn**) *n* en Grande-Bretagne, système de retenue à la source des impôts sur le revenu.

step [step] (*pt & pp* **-ped**, *cont* **-ping**) ◇ *n* **-1.** [pace] pas *m*; **in/out of ~ with** en accord/désaccord avec; **to watch one's ~** faire attention où l'on marche; *fig* faire attention à ce que l'on fait. **-2.** [action] mesure *f*. **-3.** [stage] étape *f*; **~ by ~** petit à petit, progressivement. **-4.** [stair] marche *f*. **-5.** [of ladder] barreau *m*, échelon *m*. **-6.** *Am* MUS ton *m*. ◇ *vi* **-1.** [move foot]: **to ~ forward** avancer; **to ~ off** or **down from sthg** descendre de qqch; **to ~ back** reculer. **-2.** [tread]: **to ~ on/in sthg** marcher sur/dans qqch.

meaning and context
clearly labelled
signalisation claire
des sens et du contexte

clearly structured
entries
structuration
claire de l'article

◆ **steps** *npl* **-1.** [stairs] marches *fpl*. **-2.** *Br* [stepladder] escabeau *m*.

◆ **step aside** *vi* **-1.** [move away] s'écarter. **-2.** [leave job] démissionner.

parts of speech
clearly marked
signalisation claire
des catégories
grammaticales

phrasal verbs
easy to identify
mise en relief
des « phrasal verbs »

DICTIONNAIRE COMPACT

FRANÇAIS-ANGLAIS

ANGLAIS-FRANÇAIS

CONCISE

FRENCH-ENGLISH

ENGLISH-FRENCH

DICTIONARY

LAROUSSE

DICTIONNAIRE COMPACT

FRANÇAIS-ANGLAIS
ANGLAIS-FRANÇAIS

LAROUSSE

ISBN 2-03-401644-0
Larousse-Bordas, Paris

ISBN 2-03-420301-1 (hardcover edition)
ISBN 2-03-420501-4 (paperback edition)
Diffusion/Sales Larousse Kingfisher Chambers Inc., New York

Library of Congress Catalog Card Number
97-70920

ISBN 2-03-430350-4
Diffusion/Sales Thomas Nelson & Sons Ltd, Surrey, England

LAROUSSE

CONCISE

FRENCH-ENGLISH

ENGLISH-FRENCH

DICTIONARY

LAROUSSE

Réalisé par / Produced by
LAROUSSE

Direction de l'ouvrage
General Editor

CATHERINE E. LOVE

Coordination éditoriale
Coordinating Editors

WENDY LEE   PATRICK WHITE   CATHERINE JULIA

Rédaction
Editors

FLORENCE MILLAR   HARRY CAMPBELL
SABINE CITRON   DONALD WATT
LILIANE CHARRIER   KAREN GEORGE
VALÉRIE DUPIN   MARGARET ROSS
VÉRONIQUE ATHUKORALA   HUW DAVIES
JEAN BERTRAND   SARA MONTGOMERY
FRANÇOISE FAUCHET   CALUM SHORT
CARINE LIPSKI   JANE GOLDIE
CAROLE COEN   CHARLOTTE BOYNTON
                        CALLUM BRINES

Informatique éditoriale
Data Management

GABINO ALONSO   CLAUDE NIMMO

Maquette
Design

FRÉDÉRIQUE LONGUÉPÉE

AU LECTEUR

La gamme COMPACT offre l'outil de travail idéal pour un large éventail de situations, qui vont du travail scolaire ou en auto-apprentissage au contexte quotidien du bureau.

Le COMPACT anglais & français vise à répondre rapidement et efficacement au plus grand nombre des questions posées par la lecture de l'anglais d'aujourd'hui, et par la rédaction de travaux, de lettres, de rapports en anglais.

Avec plus de 90 000 mots et expressions éclairés par plus de 120 000 traductions, ce dictionnaire permet de pleinement apprécier textes romanesques et documents, de mieux comprendre la presse quotidienne ou hebdomadaire, de déchiffrer prospectus et notices, de faire une traduction rapide ou une synthèse. De nombreux sigles et noms propres, les termes les plus courants des affaires et de l'informatique en font une référence particulièrement actuelle.

Par le traitement clair et détaillé du vocabulaire fondamental, les exemples de constructions grammaticales, les tournures idiomatiques, les indications de sens soulignant la ou les traductions appropriées, il permet de rédiger dans la langue étrangère sans risque de contresens et sans hésitation.

Une présentation et une typographie très étudiées concourent à rendre plus aisée la consultation. Pour l'usager qui n'est plus un vrai débutant sans prétendre être un spécialiste, le COMPACT est la référence recommandée pour être à l'aise en anglais.

N'hésitez pas à nous faire part de vos observations, questions ou critiques éventuelles, vous contribuerez ainsi à rendre cet ouvrage encore meilleur.

L'ÉDITEUR

TO OUR READERS

The Larousse CONCISE dictionary is the perfect companion for a wide variety of situations, from language learning at school and at home to everyday use in the office.

This French dictionary is designed to provide fast and efficient solutions to the various problems encountered when reading present-day French. It will also be an invaluable aid in preparing written work of all kinds, from schoolwork to letters and reports.

The CONCISE has over 90,000 references and 120,000 translations. It enables the user to read and enjoy a wide range of fiction and journalism, to understand trade literature, brochures and manuals, and to summarize and translate from French quickly and accurately. This entirely new dictionary also features up-to-date coverage of common abbreviations and acronyms, proper names, business terms and computing vocabulary.

Writing French accurately and confidently is no longer a problem thanks to the CONCISE's detailed coverage of essential vocabulary, and helpful sense-markers which guide the user to the most appropriate translation.

Careful thought has gone into the presentation of the entries, both in terms of layout and typography. For the user who has moved beyond beginners' level but is not intending to pursue French at an academic level, the CONCISE is the ideal reference work.

Send us your comments or queries - you will be helping us to make this dictionary an even better book in future.

THE PUBLISHER

ABBREVIATIONS _____ ABRÉVIATIONS

Grammatical, register and regional labels		Étiquettes grammaticales, stylistiques et dialectales
abbreviation	*abbr/abr*	abréviation
adjective	*adj*	adjectif
adverb	*adv*	adverbe
American English	*Am*	anglais américain
slang	*arg*	argot
article	*art*	article
Australian English	*Austr*	anglais australien
auxiliary	*aux*	auxiliaire
before noun	*avant n*	avant le nom

indicates that the translation is always used attributively, i.e. directly before the noun which it modifies — *appliqué à la traduction d'un adjectif français, indique l'emploi d'un nom anglais avec valeur d'adjectif ; souligne aussi les cas où la traduction d'un adjectif est nécessairement antéposée*

Belgian French	*Belg*	belgicisme
British English	*Br*	anglais britannique
Canadian English/French	*Can*	canadianisme
compound	*comp*	nom anglais utilisé en apposition

*a noun used to modify another noun, e.g. **gardening** in **gardening book** or **airforce** in **airforce base*** — *par exemple **gardening** dans **gardening book** ou **airforce** dans **airforce base***

comparative	*compar*	comparatif
conjunction	*conj*	conjonction
continuous	*cont*	progressif
definite	*def/déf*	défini
demonstrative	*dem/dém*	démonstratif
especially	*esp*	particulièrement
exclamation	*excl*	interjection
informal	*fam*	familier
figurative	*fig*	figuré
formal	*fml*	soutenu
inseparable	*fus*	non séparable

*shows that a phrasal verb is "fused", i.e. inseparable, e.g. **look after** where the object cannot come between the verb and the particle, e.g. I looked after him but not * I looked him after* — *indique qu'un verbe anglais à particule ("phrasal verb") ne peut pas être séparé de sa particule, c'est-à-dire qu'un complément d'objet ne peut être inséré entre les deux, par exemple I looked after him (et non * I looked him after)*

generally, in most cases	*gen/gén*	généralement
identifies the most common translation of a word		*indique la traduction la plus courante d'un mot*

Swiss French	*Helv*	helvétisme
humorous	*hum*	humoristique
indefinite	*indef/indéf*	indéfini
informal	*inf*	familier
infinitive	*infin*	infinitif
exclamation	*interj*	interjection
interrogative	*interr*	interrogatif
invariable	*inv*	invariable

applied to a noun to indicate that plural form same as singular, e.g. **garde-boue** m inv : *les* **garde-boue**, **sheep** pl inv : *four* **sheep** ; *applied to a French adjective to indicate that feminine and plural forms same as masculine, e.g.* **vieux jeu** inv : *ils sont/elle est* **vieux jeu**

avec un nom, signifie que la forme du pluriel est identique à la forme du singulier, par exemple **garde-boue** m inv : *les* **garde-boue**, **sheep** pl inv : *four* **sheep** ; *avec un adjectif, signifie que la forme du féminin et celle du pluriel sont identiques à la forme du masculin, par exemple* **vieux jeu** inv : *ils sont/elle est* **vieux jeu**

ironic	*iro/iron*	ironique
literal	*lit/litt*	littéral

in conjunction with fig, *shows that both a literal and figurative sense is being covered by the same translation*

conjointement à l'étiquette fig, *indique que la traduction donnée couvre à la fois le sens littéral et le sens figuré*

phrase(s)	*loc*	locution(s)
adjectival phrase	*loc adj*	locution adjectivale
adverbial phrase	*loc adv*	locution adverbiale
conjunctival phrase	*loc conj*	locution conjonctive
prepositional phrase	*loc prép*	locution prépositionnelle

adjectives, adverbs, conjunctions and prepositions consisting of more than one word, e.g. **d'affilée, par dépit, en dépit de, bien que**

adjectifs, adverbes, conjonctions et prépositions composés de plusieurs mots, par exemple **d'affilée, par dépit, en dépit de, bien que**

noun	*n*	nom
feminine noun	*nf*	nom féminin
masculine noun	*nm*	nom masculin
masculine or feminine noun	*nmf*	nom masculin ou féminin

depending on gender, e.g. **dentiste** nmf *where you would say "un dentiste" or "le dentiste" for a man and "une dentiste" or "la dentiste" for a woman*

dentiste nmf *pouvant être "un dentiste" ou "une dentiste", selon le sexe*

numeral	*num*	numéral
oneself	*o.s.*	
pejorative	*pej/péj*	péjoratif
implies disapproval, e.g. bimbo, catty, macho		*implique une nuance dépréciative, par exemple accoutré*
personal	*pers*	personnel
phrase(s)	*phr*	locution(s)
plural	*pl*	pluriel
possessive	*poss*	possessif
past participle	*pp*	participe passé
present participle	*ppr*	participe présent
preposition	*prep/prép*	préposition
pronoun	*pron*	pronom
past tense	*pt*	passé
	qqch	quelque chose
	qqn	quelqu'un
registered trademark	®	nom déposé
words considered to be trademarks have been designated in this dictionary by the symbol ®. However, neither the presence nor the absence of such designation should be regarded as affecting the legal status of any trademark.		*les noms de marque sont désignés dans ce dictionnaire par le symbole ®. Néanmoins, ni ce symbole ni son absence éventuelle ne peuvent être considérés comme susceptibles d'avoir une incidence quelconque sur le statut légal d'une marque.*
relative	*rel*	relatif
someone, somebody	*sb*	
Scottish English	*Scot*	anglais écossais
separable	*sep*	séparable
shows that a phrasal verb is separable, e.g. let in, help out where the object can come between the verb and the particle, I let her in, he helped me out		*indique qu'un verbe anglais à post-position ("phrasal verb") peut être séparé de sa particule, c'est-à-dire qu'un complément d'objet peut être inséré entre les deux, par exemple I let her in, I helped him out*
singular	*sg*	singulier
slang	*sl*	argot
formal	*sout*	soutenu
something	*sthg*	
subject	*subj/suj*	sujet
superlative	*superl*	superlatif
very informal	*tfam*	très familier

uncountable noun *i.e. an English noun which is never used in the plural or with "a"; used when the French word is or can be a plural, e.g.* **applause** *n* (U) *applaudissements* mpl, **battement** *nm beat, beating* (U)	U	substantif non comptable *désigne en anglais les noms qui ne sont jamais utilisés au pluriel, lorsque le terme français est un pluriel ou peut être mis au pluriel, par exemple* **applause** *n* (U) *applaudissements* mpl, **battement** *nm beat, beating* (U)
usually	*usu*	habituellement
link verb followed by a predicative adjective or noun	*v attr*	verbe suivi d'un attribut
verb	*vb/v*	verbe
intransitive verb	*vi*	verbe intransitif
impersonal verb (always used with the subject "it")	*v impers*	verbe impersonnel
very informal	*v inf*	très familier
pronominal verb	*vp*	verbe pronominal
transitive verb	*vt*	verbe transitif
vulgar, offensive	*vulg*	vulgaire, susceptible de choquer
cultural equivalent	≃	équivalence culturelle
introduces a new part of speech within an entry	◇	introduit une nouvelle catégorie grammaticale dans une entrée
introduces a sub-entry, such as a plural form with its own specific meaning or a set phrase containing the headword (e.g. a phrasal verb or adverbial phrase)	◆	introduit une sous-entrée, par exemple une forme plurielle ayant un sens propre, ou une locution (locution adverbiale, verbe pronominal, etc.)

FIELD LABELS ———————————— DOMAINES

English	Label	Domaines
Administration, administrative	ADMIN	Administration
Aeronautics, aviation	AERON/AÉRON	Aéronautique
Agriculture, farming	AGR(IC)	Agriculture
Anatomy	ANAT	Anatomie
Archaeology	ARCHAEOL/ARCHÉOL	Archéologie
Architecture	ARCHIT	Architecture
Astrology	ASTROL	Astrologie
Astronomy	ASTRON	Astronomie
Automobile, cars	AUT(OM)	Automobile
Biology	BIOL	Biologie
Botany	BOT	Botanique
Chemistry	CHEM/CHIM	Chimie
Cinema, film-making	CIN(EMA)	Cinéma
Commerce, business	COMM	Commerce
Computers, computer science	COMPUT	Informatique
Construction, building trade	CONSTR	Construction, bâtiment
Sewing	COUT	Couture
Culinary, cooking	CULIN	Cuisine, art culinaire
Ecology	ÉCOL	Écologie
Economics	ECON/ÉCON	Économie
Electricity	ELEC/ÉLECTR	Électricité
Electronics	ELECTRON/ÉLECTRON	Électronique
Finance, financial	FIN	Finances
Soccer	FTBL	Football
Geography, geographical	GEOGR/GÉOGR	Géographie
Geology, geological	GEOL/GÉOL	Géologie
Geometry	GEOM/GÉOM	Géométrie
Grammar	GRAM(M)	Grammaire
History	HIST	Histoire
Industry	IND	Industrie
Computers, computer science	INFORM	Informatique
Juridical, legal	JUR	Juridique
Linguistics	LING	Linguistique
Mathematics	MATH(S)	Mathématiques
Medicine	MED/MÉD	Médecine
Weather, meteorology, climatology	METEOR/MÉTÉOR	Météorologie
Military, armed forces, armaments	MIL	Domaine militaire
Music	MUS	Musique
Mythology	MYTH	Mythologie
Nautical, maritime	NAUT/NAVIG	Navigation
Pharmacology, pharmaceutics	PHARM	Pharmacologie
Philosophy	PHILO	Philosophie

Photography	PHOT	Photographie
Physics	PHYS	Physique
Politics	POL(IT)	Politique
Psychology, psychiatry	PSYCH(OL)	Psychologie
Railways	RAIL	Rail
Religion	RELIG	Religion
School	SCH/SCOL	Scolarité
Sociology	SOCIOL	Sociologie
Stock Exchange	ST EX	Bourse
Technology, technical	TECH(NOL)	Domaine technique et technologique
Telecommunications	TELEC/TÉLÉCOM	Télécommunications
Television	TV/TÉLÉ	Télévision
Printing, typography	TYPO	Typographie
University	UNIV	Université
Veterinary science	VETER	Médecine vétérinaire
Zoology	ZOOL	Zoologie

A Note on French Verbs ——————————— Verbes Français

French verbs have a number (from [1] to [116]) which refers to the conjugation table given at the back of the dictionary. This number is not repeated for reflexive verbs when these are sub-entries.

Les verbes français comportent une numérotation (de [1] à [116]) qui renvoie aux conjugaisons fournies en fin d'ouvrage. Ce chiffre n'est pas répété après les verbes pronominaux lorsqu'ils apparaissent comme sous-libellés.

A Note on English Compounds ——————— Mots composés anglais

A compound is a word or expression which has a single meaning but is made up of more than one word, e.g. point of order, kiss of life, virtual reality, World Series and International Monetary Fund. It is a feature of this dictionary that English compounds appear in the A-Z list in strict alphabetical order. The compound blood pressure will therefore come after bloodless which itself follows blood group.

On désigne par composés des entités lexicales ayant un sens autonome mais qui sont composées de plus d'un mot. Nous avons pris le parti de faire figurer les composés anglais dans l'ordre alphabétique général. Le composé blood pressure est ainsi présenté après bloodless, qui suit blood group.

PHONETIC TRANSCRIPTION ——————— TRANSCRIPTION PHONÉTIQUE

English Vowels
[ɪ] pit, big, rid
[e] pet, tend
[æ] pat, bag, mad
[ʌ] putt, cut
[ɒ] pot, log
[ʊ] put, full
[ə] mother, suppose

[iː] bean, weed
[ɑː] barn, car, laugh
[ɔː] born, lawn
[uː] loop, loose
[ɜː] burn, learn, bird

Voyelles françaises
[i] fille, île
[e] pays, année
[ɛ] bec, aime
[a] lac, papillon
[ɑ] âme
[ɔ] hotte
[o] drôle, aube
[u] outil, goût
[y] usage, lune
[ø] aveu, jeu
[œ] peuple, bœuf
[ə] le, je

English Diphthongs
[eɪ] bay, late, great
[aɪ] buy, light, aisle
[ɔɪ] boy, foil
[əʊ] no, road, blow
[aʊ] now, shout, town
[ɪə] peer, fierce, idea
[eə] pair, bear, share
[ʊə] poor, sure, tour

Nasales françaises
[ɛ̃] limbe, main
[ɑ̃] champ, ennui
[ɔ̃] ongle, mon
[œ̃] parfum, brun

Semi-vowels
you, spaniel   [j]
wet, why, twin   [w]
                                [ɥ]

Semi-voyelles
yeux, lieu
ouest, oui
lui, nuit

Consonants
pop, people   [p]
bottle, bib   [b]
train, tip   [t]
dog, did   [d]
come, kitchen   [k]
loch   [x]
gag, great   [g]
chain, wretched   [ʧ]
jig, fridge   [dʒ]
fib, physical   [f]
vine, livid   [v]
think, fifth   [θ]
this, with   [ð]

Consonnes
prendre, grippe
bateau, rosbif
théâtre, temps
dalle, ronde
coq, quatre

garder, épilogue

physique, fort
voir, rive

seal, peace	[s]	cela, savant
zip, his	[z]	fraise, zéro
sheep, machine	[ʃ]	charrue, schéma
usual, measure	[ʒ]	rouge, jabot
how, perhaps	[h]	
metal, comb	[m]	mât, drame
night, dinner	[n]	nager, trône
sung, parking	[ŋ]	dancing, smoking
	[ɲ]	agneau, peigner
little, help	[l]	halle, lit
right, carry	[r]	arracher, sabre

The symbol ['] has been used to represent the French "h aspiré", e.g. hachis [ˈaʃi].

Le symbole ['] représente le "h aspiré" français, p. ex. hachis [ˈaʃi].

The symbol [ˈ] indicates that the following syllable carries primary stress and the symbol [ˌ] that the following syllable carries secondary stress.

Les symboles [ˈ] et [ˌ] indiquent respectivement un accent primaire et un accent secondaire sur la syllabe suivante.

The symbol [ʳ] in English phonetics indicates that the final "r" is pronounced only when followed by a word beginning with a vowel. Note that it is nearly always pronounced in American English.

Le symbole [ʳ] indique que le "r" final d'un mot anglais ne se prononce que lorsqu'il forme une liaison avec la voyelle du mot suivant; le "r" final est presque toujours prononcé en anglais américain.

A phonetic transcription has been given where appropriate after every French headword (the main word which starts an entry). All one-word English headwords similarly have phonetics. For English compound headwords, whether hyphenated or of two or more words, phonetics are given for any element which does not appear elsewhere in the dictionary as a headword in its own right.

Une transcription phonétique - quand elle a été jugée nécessaire - suit chaque libellé (terme-vedette de l'entrée) français, ainsi que chaque libellé anglais écrit en un seul mot. Pour les mots composés anglais (avec ou sans trait d'union, et composés de deux éléments ou plus), la phonétique est présente pour ceux des éléments qui n'apparaissent pas dans le dictionnaire en tant que libellés à part entière.

FRANÇAIS–ANGLAIS
FRENCH–ENGLISH

a¹, A [a] *nm inv* a, A; **prouver par a + b** to prove conclusively; **de A à Z** from beginning to end.
◆ **A -1.** *abr de* **anticyclone. -2.** (*abr de* **ampère**) A, amp. **-3.** (*abr de* **autoroute**) M. **-4.** (*abr de* **angström**) A.

a² ◇ → **avoir.** ◇ (*abr de* **are**) a.

à [a] *prép* (*contraction de à + le = au, contraction de à + les = aux*) **-1.** [introduisant un complément d'objet indirect] to; **parler à qqn** to speak to sb; **donner qqch à qqn** to give sthg to sb, to give sb sthg; **penser à qqch** to think about sthg. **-2.** [introduisant un complément de lieu - situation] at, in; [- direction] to; **être à la maison/au bureau** to be at home/at the office; **il habite à Paris/à la campagne** he lives in Paris/in the country; **il vit au Pérou** he lives in Peru; **aller à Paris/à la campagne/au Pérou** to go to Paris/to the country/to Peru; **un voyage à Londres/aux Seychelles** a journey to London/to the Seychelles. **-3.** [introduisant un complément de temps]: **à onze heures** at eleven o'clock; **au mois de février** in the month of February; **à lundi!** see you (on) Monday!; **à plus tard!** see you later!; **de huit à dix heures** from eight to ten o'clock; **se situer à une heure de l'aéroport** to be situated an hour (away) from the airport. **-4.** [introduisant un complément de manière, de moyen]: **à haute voix** out loud, aloud; **rire aux éclats** to roar with laughter; **agir à son gré** to do as one pleases; **acheter à crédit** to buy on credit; **à pied/cheval** on foot/horseback. **-5.** [indiquant une caractéristique] with; **l'homme à l'imperméable** the man with the raincoat. **-6.** [introduisant un chiffre]: **ils sont venus à dix** ten of them came; **un livre à 30 francs** a 30-franc book, a

book costing 30 francs; **la vitesse est limitée à 50 km à l'heure** the speed limit is 50 km per OU an hour; **un groupe de 10 à 12 personnes** a group of 10 to 12 people, a group of between 10 and 12 people; **deux à deux** two by two. **-7.** [marque l'appartenance]: **c'est à moi/toi/lui/elle** it's mine/yours/his/hers; **ce vélo est à ma sœur** this bike is my sister's OU belongs to my sister; **une amie à moi** a friend of mine. **-8.** [introduit le but]: **coupe à champagne** champagne goblet; **le courrier à poster** the mail to be posted; **appartement à vendre/louer** apartment for sale/to let.

AB (*abr de* **assez bien**) fair grade (as assessment of schoolwork).

abaisser [abese] [4] *vt* **-1.** [rideau, voile] to lower; [levier, manette] to push OU pull down. **-2.** [diminuer] to reduce, to lower. **-3.** *sout* [avilir] to debase.
◆ **s'abaisser** *vp* **-1.** [descendre - rideau] to fall, to come down; [- terrain] to fall away. **-2.** [s'humilier] to demean o.s.; **s'~ à faire qqch** to lower o.s. to do sthg.

abandon [abɑ̃dɔ̃] *nm* **-1.** [désertion, délaissement] desertion; **à l'~** [jardin, maison] neglected, in a state of neglect. **-2.** [renonciation] abandoning, giving up. **-3.** [cession] renunciation, giving up; **faire ~ de qqch (au profit de qqn)** to make sthg over (to sb). **-4.** [nonchalance, confiance] abandon.

abandonner [abɑ̃dɔne] [3] *vt* **-1.** [quitter - femme, enfants] to abandon, to desert; [- voiture, propriété] to abandon; **~ son poste** to desert one's post. **-2.** [renoncer à] to give up, to abandon. **-3.** [se retirer de - course, concours] to withdraw from. **-4.** [céder]: **~ qqch à qqn** to leave sthg to sb, to leave sb sthg.

◆ **s'abandonner** *vp* **-1.** [se laisser aller]: **s'~ à qqch** to give o.s. up to sthg. **-2.** [s'épancher] to pour out one's feelings.

abasourdi, -e [abazurdi] *adj* stunned.

abasourdir [abazurdir] [32] *vt* to stun.

abat-jour [abaʒur] *nm inv* lampshade.

abats [aba] *nmpl* [d'animal] offal (*U*); [de volaille] giblets.

abattage [abataʒ] *nm* [d'arbre] felling.

abattement [abatmɑ̃] *nm* **-1.** [faiblesse physique] weakness. **-2.** [désespoir] dejection. **-3.** [déduction] reduction; **~ fiscal** tax allowance.

abattis [abati] *nmpl* giblets.

abattoir [abatwar] *nm* abattoir, slaughterhouse.

abattre [abatr] [83] *vt* **-1.** [faire tomber - mur] to knock down; [- arbre] to cut down, to fell; [- avion] to bring down. **-2.** [tuer - gén] to kill; [- dans un abattoir] to slaughter. **-3.** [épuiser] to wear out; [démoraliser] to demoralize.

◆ **s'abattre** *vp*: **s'~ (sur)** [toit, arbre] to crash down (on); [pluie] to beat down (on); [avion, insectes, rapaces] to swoop down (on); [maladie, fléau] to descend (on).

abattu, -e [abaty] ◇ *pp* → **abattre**. ◇ *adj* **-1.** [déprimé] demoralized, dejected. **-2.** [affaibli] very weak.

abbaye [abei] *nf* abbey.

abbé [abe] *nm* **-1.** [prêtre] priest. **-2.** [de couvent] abbot.

abc *nm* basics (*pl*).

abcès [apsɛ] *nm* abscess; **crever l'~** *fig* to root out the problem.

abdication [abdikasjɔ̃] *nf* abdication.

abdiquer [abdike] [3] ◇ *vt* **-1.** [renoncer à] to renounce. **-2.** [suj: roi] to abdicate. ◇ *vi* **-1.** [roi] to abdicate. **-2.** [renoncer] to give up.

abdomen [abdɔmɛn] *nm* abdomen.

abdominal, -e, -aux [abdɔminal, o] *adj* abdominal.

◆ **abdominaux** *nmpl* **-1.** [muscles] abdominal OU stomach muscles. **-2.** [exercices]: **faire des abdominaux** to do exercises for the stomach muscles.

abécédaire [abesedɛr] *nm* ABC (*book*).

abeille [abɛj] *nf* bee.

aberrant, -e [abɛrɑ̃, ɑ̃t] *adj* absurd.

aberration [abɛrasjɔ̃] *nf* aberration.

abhorrer [abɔre] [3] *vt sout* to abhor.

Abidjan [abidʒɑ̃] *n* Abidjan.

abîme [abim] *nm* abyss, gulf.

abîmer [abime] [3] *vt* [détériorer - objet] to damage; [- partie du corps, vue] to ruin.

◆ **s'abîmer** *vp* **-1.** [gén] to be damaged; [- fruits] to go bad. **-2.** *fig* [personne]: **s'~ dans** [lecture] to bury o.s. in; [pensées] to lose o.s. in.

abject, -e [abʒɛkt] *adj* despicable, contemptible.

abjurer [abʒyre] [3] *vt* RELIG to renounce.

ablatif [ablatif] *nm* ablative.

ablation [ablasjɔ̃] *nf* MÉD removal.

ablutions [ablysjɔ̃] *nfpl*: **faire ses ~** to perform one's ablutions.

abnégation [abnegasjɔ̃] *nf* selflessness.

aboie, aboies *etc* → **aboyer**.

aboiement [abwamɑ̃] *nm* bark, barking (*U*).

abois [abwa] *nmpl*: **être aux ~** *fig* to be in dire straits.

abolir [abɔlir] [32] *vt* to abolish.

abolition [abɔlisjɔ̃] *nf* abolition.

abominable [abɔminabl] *adj* appalling, awful.

abominablement [abɔminabləmɑ̃] *adv* **-1.** [très mal] abominably. **-2.** [extrêmement] awfully.

abomination [abɔminasjɔ̃] *nf* abomination.

abondamment [abɔ̃damɑ̃] *adv* **-1.** [beaucoup] plentifully. **-2.** [largement] extensively.

abondance [abɔ̃dɑ̃s] *nf* **-1.** [profusion] abundance; **en ~** in abundance. **-2.** [opulence] affluence; **vivre dans l'~** to live in affluence.

abondant, -e *adj* [abɔ̃dɑ̃, ɑ̃t] [gén] plentiful; [végétation, chevelure] luxuriant; [pluie] heavy.

abonder [abɔ̃de] [3] *vi* to abound, to be abundant; **~ en qqch** to be rich in sthg; **~ dans le sens de qqn** to be entirely of sb's opinion.

abonné, -e [abɔne] *nm, f* **-1.** [à un journal, à une chaîne de télé] subscriber; [à un théâtre] season-ticket holder. **-2.** [à un service public] consumer.

abonnement [abɔnmɑ̃] *nm* **-1.** [à un journal, à une chaîne de télé] subscription; [à un théâtre] season ticket. **-2.** [au téléphone] rental; [au gaz, à l'électricité] standing charge.

abonner [abɔne] [3]

◆ **s'abonner** *vp*: **s'~ à qqch** [journal, chaîne de télé] to take out a subscription to sthg; [service public] to get connected to sthg; [théâtre] to buy a season ticket for sthg.

abord [abɔr] *nm*: **être d'un ~ facile/difficile** to be very/not very approachable; **au premier ~, de prime ~** at first sight; **dès l'~** from the outset.

◆ **abords** *nmpl* [gén] surrounding area (*sg*); [de ville] outskirts.

◆ **d'abord** *loc adv* **-1.** [en premier lieu] first. **-2.** [avant tout]: **(tout) d'~** first (of all), in the first place.

abordable [abɔrdabl] *adj* [lieu] accessible; [personne] approachable; [de prix modéré] affordable.

abordage [abɔrdaʒ] *nm* boarding.

aborder [abɔrde] [3] ◇ *vi* to land. ◇ *vt* **-1.** [personne, lieu] to approach. **-2.** [question] to tackle.

aborigène [abɔriʒɛn] *adj* aboriginal.

◆ **Aborigène** *nmf* (Australian) aborigine.

abouti, -e [abuti] *adj* **-1.** [projet, démarche] successful. **-2.** [œuvre] accomplished.

aboutir [abutir] [32] *vi* **-1.** [chemin]: ~ à OU dans to end up in. **-2.** [négociation] to be successful; ~ à qqch to result in sthg.

aboutissement [abutismɑ̃] *nm* outcome.

aboyer [abwaje] [13] *vi* to bark.

abracadabrant, -e [abrakadabrɑ̃, ɑ̃t] *adj* preposterous.

abrasif, -ive [abrazif, iv] *adj* abrasive.

◆ **abrasif** *nm* abrasive.

abrégé, -e [abreʒe] *adj* abridged.

◆ **abrégé** *nm* résumé, summary; **en ~** in abbreviated form.

abréger [abreʒe] [22] *vt* [visite, réunion] to cut short; [discours] to shorten; [mot] to abbreviate.

abreuver [abrœve] [5] *vt* [animal] to water; ~ qqn de *fig* to shower sb with.

◆ **s'abreuver** *vp* to drink.

abreuvoir [abrœvwar] *nm* [lieu] watering place; [installation] drinking trough.

abréviation [abrevjasjɔ̃] *nf* abbreviation.

abri [abri] *nm* shelter; **à l'~ de** sheltered from; *fig* safe from; **se mettre à l'~ (de)** to shelter (from), to take shelter (from); ~ **antiatomique** nuclear fallout shelter.

abricot [abriko] *nm & adj inv* apricot.

abricotier [abrikɔtje] *nm* apricot tree.

abriter [abrite] [3] *vt* **-1.** [protéger]: ~ **qqn/qqch (de)** to shelter sb/sthg (from). **-2.** [héberger] to accommodate.

◆ **s'abriter** *vp*: **s'~ (de)** to shelter (from).

abroger [abrɔʒe] [17] *vt* to repeal.

abrupt, -e [abrypt] *adj* **-1.** [raide] steep. **-2.** [rude] abrupt, brusque.

abruti, -e [abryti] *fam* ◇ *adj* moronic. ◇ *nm, f* moron.

abrutir [abrytir] [32] *vt* **-1.** [abêtir]: ~ **qqn** to deaden sb's mind. **-2.** [accabler]: ~ **qqn de travail** to work sb silly. **-3.** [étourdir] to daze.

◆ **s'abrutir** *vp* **-1.** [s'épuiser]: **s'~ de travail** to work o.s. stupid. **-2.** [s'abêtir] to become moronic.

abrutissant, -e [abrytisɑ̃, ɑ̃t] *adj* **-1.** [bruit, travail] stupefying. **-2.** [jeu, feuilleton] moronic.

abrutissement [abrytismɑ̃] *nm* **-1.** [épuisement] exhaustion. **-2.** [intellectuel] mindless state.

ABS (*abr de* **Antiblockiersystem**) *nm* ABS.

absence [apsɑ̃s] *nf* **-1.** [de personne] absence; **en l'~ de** in the absence of. **-2.** [carence] lack.

absent, -e [apsɑ̃, ɑ̃t] ◇ *adj* **-1.** [personne]: ~ **(de)** [gén] away (from); [pour maladie] absent (from). **-2.** [regard, air] vacant, absent. **-3.** [manquant] lacking. ◇ *nm, f* absentee.

absentéisme [apsɑ̃teism] *nm* absenteeism.

absenter [apsɑ̃te] [3]

◆ **s'absenter** *vp*: **s'~ (de la pièce)** to leave (the room).

abside [apsid] *nf* apse.

absinthe [apsɛ̃t] *nf* [plante] wormwood; [boisson] absinth.

absolu, -e [apsɔly] *adj* [gén] absolute; [décision, jugement] uncompromising.

◆ **absolu** *nm*: **l'~** the Absolute; **dans l'~** in isolation.

absolument [apsɔlymɑ̃] *adv* absolutely.

absolution [apsɔlysjɔ̃] *nf* absolution.

absolutisme [apsɔlytism] *nm* absolutism.

absorbant, -e [apsɔrbɑ̃, ɑ̃t] *adj* **-1.** [matière] absorbent. **-2.** [occupation] absorbing.

absorber [apsɔrbe] [3] *vt* **-1.** [gén] to absorb. **-2.** [manger] to take. **-3.** [entreprise] to take over.

◆ **s'absorber** *vp*: **s'~ dans qqch** to get OU become absorbed in sthg.

absorption [apsɔrpsjɔ̃] *nf* **-1.** [gén] absorption. **-2.** ÉCON takeover.

abstenir [apstənir] [40]

◆ **s'abstenir** *vp* **-1.** [ne rien faire]: **s'~ (de qqch/de faire qqch)** to refrain (from sthg/from doing sthg). **-2.** [ne pas voter] to abstain.

abstention [apstɑ̃sjɔ̃] *nf* abstention.

abstentionnisme [apstɑ̃sjɔnism] *nm* abstaining.

abstenu, -e [apstəny] *pp* → **abstenir**.

abstiendrai, abstiendras *etc* → **abstenir**.

abstinence [apstinɑ̃s] *nf* abstinence; **faire ~** to abstain (*from eating meat*).

abstraction [apstraksjɔ̃] *nf* abstraction; **faire ~ de** to disregard.

abstrait, -e [apstrɛ, ɛt] *adj* abstract.

◆ **abstrait** *nm*: **l'~** the abstract.

absurde [apsyrd] ◇ *adj* absurd. ◇ *nm*: l'~ the absurd; **raisonnement par l'~** reductio ad absurdum.

absurdité [apsyrdite] *nf* absurdity; **dire des ~s** to talk nonsense (*U*).

abus [aby] *nm* abuse; **~ de confiance** breach of trust; **~ de pouvoir** abuse of power.

abuser [abyze] [3] ◇ *vi* **-1.** [dépasser les bornes] to go too far. **-2.** [user]: **~ de** [autorité, pouvoir] to overstep the bounds of; [temps] to take advantage of; [temps] to take up too much of; **~ de ses forces** to overexert o.s. ◇ *vt sout* to mislead.

◆ **s'abuser** *vp*: **s'~ sur** to delude o.s. about.

abusif, -ive [abyzif, iv] *adj* **-1.** [excessif] excessive. **-2.** [fautif] improper.

AC (*abr de* **appellation contrôlée**) *nf label guaranteeing quality of wine.*

acabit [akabi] *nm*: **du même ~** *péj* of the same type.

acacia [akasja] *nm* acacia.

académicien, -ienne [akademisjɛ̃, jɛn] *nm, f* academician; [de l'Académie française] member of the French Academy.

académie [akademi] *nf* **-1.** SCOL & UNIV ≃ regional education authority *Br*, school district *Am*. **-2.** [institut] academy; **l'Académie française** the French Academy (*learned society of leading men and women of letters*); **l'Académie Goncourt** *literary society whose members choose the winner of the Prix Goncourt.*

académique [akademik] *adj* **-1.** UNIV academic. **-2.** [conventionnel] conventional.

acajou [akaʒu] *nm & adj inv* mahogany.

acariâtre [akarjatr] *adj* bad-tempered, cantankerous.

acarien [akarjɛ̃] *nm* [gén] acarid; [de poussière] dust mite.

accablant, -e [akablɑ̃, ɑ̃t] *adj* **-1.** [soleil, chaleur] oppressive. **-2.** [preuve, témoignage] overwhelming.

accabler [akable] [3] *vt* **-1.** [surcharger]: **~ qqn de** [travail] to overwhelm sb with; **~ qqn d'injures** to shower sb with abuse. **-2.** [accuser] to condemn.

accalmie [akalmi] *nf litt* & *fig* lull.

accaparer [akapare] [3] *vt* to monopolize; **son travail l'accapare** his work takes up all his time.

◆ **s'accaparer** *vp*: **s'~ qqch** to seize sthg.

accéder [aksede] [18]

◆ **accéder à** *vt* **-1.** [pénétrer dans] to reach, to get to. **-2.** [parvenir à] to attain. **-3.** [consentir à] to comply with.

accélérateur [akseleratœr] *nm* accelerator.

accélération [akselerasjɔ̃] *nf* [de voiture, machine] acceleration; [de projet] speeding up.

accélérer [akselere] [18] ◇ *vt* to accelerate, to speed up. ◇ *vi* AUTOM to accelerate.

accent [aksɑ̃] *nm* **-1.** [gén] accent; **~ aigu/ grave/circonflexe** acute/grave/circumflex (accent). **-2.** [intonation] tone; **~ tonique** stress; **mettre l'~ sur** to stress, to emphasize.

accentuation [aksɑ̃tɥasjɔ̃] *nf* **-1.** [à l'écrit] accenting; [en parlant] stress. **-2.** [intensification] intensification.

accentuer [aksɑ̃tɥe] [7] *vt* **-1.** [insister sur, souligner] to emphasize, to accentuate. **-2.** [intensifier] to intensify. **-3.** [à l'écrit] to put the accents on; [en parlant] to stress.

◆ **s'accentuer** *vp* to become more pronounced.

acceptable [akseptabl] *adj* satisfactory, acceptable.

acceptation [akseptasjɔ̃] *nf* acceptance.

accepter [aksepte] [4] *vt* to accept; **~ de faire qqch** to agree to do sthg; **~ que** (+ *subjonctif*): **~ que qqn fasse qqch** to agree to sb doing sthg; **je n'accepte pas qu'il me parle ainsi** I won't have him talking to me like that.

acception [aksepsjɔ̃] *nf* sense.

accès [aksɛ] *nm* **-1.** [entrée] entry; **avoir/ donner ~ à** to have/to give access to; «**~ interdit**» "no entry"; «**~ réservé aux riverains**» "residents only". **-2.** [voie d'entrée] entrance. **-3.** [abord]: **être d'un ~ facile/ difficile** [personne] to be approachable/ unapproachable; [livre] to be easy/difficult (to read). **-4.** [crise] bout; **~ de colère** fit of anger.

accessible [aksesibl] *adj* **-1.** [lieu, livre] accessible; [personne] approachable; [prix, équipement] affordable. **-2.** [sensible]: **~ à** susceptible to.

accession [aksesjɔ̃] *nf*: **~ à** [trône, présidence] accession to; [indépendance] attainment of.

accessoire [akseswar] ◇ *nm* **-1.** [gén] accessory. **-2.** [de théâtre, cinéma] prop. ◇ *adj* secondary.

accessoirement [akseswarmɑ̃] *adv* if need be.

accident [aksidɑ̃] *nm* accident; **par ~** by chance, by accident; **~ de parcours** hiccup; **~ de la route/de voiture/du travail** road/ car/industrial accident; **~ de terrain** bump.

accidenté, -e [aksidɑ̃te] ◇ *adj* **-1.** [terrain, surface] uneven. **-2.** [voiture] damaged. **-3.** [vie] eventful. ◇ *nm, f* (*gén pl*): **~ de la route** accident victim.

accidentel, -elle [aksidɑ̃tɛl] *adj* accidental.

accidentellement [aksidɑ̃tɛlmɑ̃] *adv* [rencontrer] by chance, accidentally; [mourir] in an accident.

acclamation [aklamasjɔ̃] *nf* (*gén pl*) cheers (*pl*), cheering (*U*).

acclamer [aklame] [3] *vt* to cheer.

acclimatation [aklimatasjɔ̃] *nf* acclimatization.

acclimater [aklimate] [3] *vt* to acclimatize; *fig* to introduce.
◆ **s'acclimater** *vp*: **s'~ à** to become acclimatized to.

accointances [akwɛ̃tɑ̃s] *nfpl*: **avoir des ~ dans/avec** *péj* to have contacts in/with.

accolade [akɔlad] *nf* **-1.** TYPO brace. **-2.** [embrassade] embrace; **donner l'~ à qqn** to embrace sb.

accoler [akɔle] [3] *vt* **-1.** [par accolade] to bracket together. **-2.** [adjoindre]: **~ qqch à** to add sthg to.

accommodant, -e [akɔmɔdɑ̃, ɑ̃t] *adj* obliging.

accommodement [akɔmɔdmɑ̃] *nm* compromise.

accommoder [akɔmɔde] [3] *vt* **-1.** CULIN to prepare. **-2.** [mettre en accord]: **~ qqch à** to adapt sthg to.
◆ **s'accommoder** *vp*: **s'~ de** to put up with; **s'~ à** to adapt to.

accompagnateur, -trice [akɔ̃paɲatœr, tris] *nm, f* **-1.** MUS accompanist. **-2.** [guide] guide.

accompagnement [akɔ̃paɲmɑ̃] *nm* **-1.** MUS accompaniment. **-2.** CULIN side dish.

accompagner [akɔ̃paɲe] [3] *vt* **-1.** [personne] to go with, to accompany. **-2.** [agrémenter]: **~ qqch de** to accompany sthg with; **elle accompagna sa réponse d'un sourire** she answered with a smile. **-3.** MUS to accompany; **~ qqn au piano/à la guitare** to accompany sb on the piano/guitar.

accompli, -e [akɔ̃pli] *adj* accomplished.

accomplir [akɔ̃plir] [32] *vt* to carry out.
◆ **s'accomplir** *vp* to come about.

accomplissement [akɔ̃plismɑ̃] *nm* [d'apprentissage] completion; [de travail] fulfilment.

accord [akɔr] *nm* **-1.** [gén & LING] agreement; **en ~ avec** in harmony with; **d'un commun ~** with one accord; **~ à l'amiable** COMM out-of-court settlement, mutual agreement. **-2.** MUS chord. **-3.** [acceptation] approval; **donner son ~ à qqch** to approve sthg.
◆ **d'accord** ◇ *loc adv* OK, all right. ◇ *loc adj*: **être d'~ (avec)** to agree (with); **tomber**

OU **se mettre d'~** to come to an agreement, to agree.

accordéon [akɔrdeɔ̃] *nm* accordion; **avoir les chaussettes en ~** to have one's socks down around one's ankles.

accorder [akɔrde] [3] *vt* **-1.** [donner]: **~ qqch à qqn** to grant sb sthg. **-2.** [attribuer]: **~ qqch à qqch** to accord sthg to sthg; **~ de l'importance à** to attach importance to. **-3.** [harmoniser] to match. **-4.** GRAM: **~ qqch avec qqch** to make sthg agree with sthg. **-5.** MUS to tune.
◆ **s'accorder** *vp* **-1.** [gén]: **s'~ (pour faire qqch)** to agree (to do sthg); **s'~ à faire qqch** to be unanimous in doing sthg. **-2.** [être assorti] to match. **-3.** GRAM to agree.

accordeur [akɔrdœr] *nm* tuner.

accoster [akɔste] [3] ◇ *vt* **-1.** NAVIG to come alongside. **-2.** [personne] to accost. ◇ *vi* NAVIG to dock.

accotement [akɔtmɑ̃] *nm* [de route] shoulder; **~ stabilisé** hard shoulder; **~ non stabilisé** soft verge *Br,* soft shoulder *Am.*

accouchement [akuʃmɑ̃] *nm* childbirth; **~ sans douleur** natural childbirth.

accoucher [akuʃe] [3] *vi*: **~ (de)** to give birth (to).

accouder [akude] [3]
◆ **s'accouder** *vp* to lean on one's elbows; **s'~ à** to lean one's elbows on.

accoudoir [akudwar] *nm* armrest.

accouplement [akupləmɑ̃] *nm* mating, coupling.

accourir [akurir] [45] *vi* to run up, to rush up.

accours, accourt *etc* → accourir.

accouru, -e [akury] *pp* → accourir.

accoutré, -e [akutre] *adj péj*: **être bizarrement ~** to be oddly got up.

accoutrement [akutrəmɑ̃] *nm péj* getup.

accoutrer [akutre] [3]
◆ **s'accoutrer** *vp péj*: **s'~ bizarrement** to get o.s. up very strangely.

accoutumance [akutymɑ̃s] *nf* [adaptation] adaptation; MÉD addiction.

accoutumé, -e [akutyme] *adj* usual.
◆ **comme à l'accoutumée** *loc adv sout* as usual.

accoutumer [akutyme] [3] *vt*: **~ qqn à qqn/qqch** to get sb used to sb/sthg; **~ qqn à faire qqch** to get sb used to doing sthg.
◆ **s'accoutumer** *vp*: **s'~ à qqn/qqch** to get used to sb/sthg; **s'~ à faire qqch** to get used to doing sthg.

accréditation [akreditasjɔ̃] *nf* FIN accreditation.

accréditer [akredite] [3] *vt* [rumeur] to substantiate; ~ qqn auprès de to accredit sb to.

◆ **s'accréditer** *vp* to gain substance.

accro [akro] *fam* ◇ *adj*: ~ à hooked on. ◇ *nmf*: **c'est une** ~ **de la planche** she's hooked on windsurfing.

accroc [akro] *nm* **-1.** [déchirure] tear; **faire un** ~ **à** to tear. **-2.** [incident] hitch; **sans** ~ without a hitch.

accrochage [akrɔʃaʒ] *nm* **-1.** [accident] collision. **-2.** *fam* [dispute] row. **-3.** [mise en place] hanging; [- d'œuvres d'art] private viewing.

accroche [akrɔʃ] *nf* COMM catch line.

accrocher [akrɔʃe] [3] *vt* **-1.** [suspendre]: ~ qqch (à) to hang sthg up (on). **-2.** [déchirer]: ~ qqch (à) to catch sthg (on). **-3.** [attacher]: ~ qqch (à) to hitch sthg (to). **-4.** [heurter] to bump into. **-5.** [retenir l'attention de] to attract.

◆ **s'accrocher** *vp* **-1.** [s'agripper]: **s'**~ **(à)** to hang on (to); **s'**~ **à qqn** *fig* to cling to sb. **-2.** *fam* [se disputer] to row, to have a row. **-3.** *fam* [persévérer] to stick at it.

accrocheur, -euse [akrɔʃœr, øz] *adj* **-1.** [qui retient l'attention] eye-catching. **-2.** [opiniâtre] tenacious.

accroire [akrwar] *vt sout*: **en faire** ~ **à qqn** to take sb in.

accroissement [akrwasmɑ̃] *nm* increase, growth.

accroître [akrwatr] [94] *vt* to increase.

◆ **s'accroître** *vp* to increase, to grow.

accroupir [akrupir] [32]

◆ **s'accroupir** *vp* to squat.

accru, -e [akry] *pp* → **accroître**.

accu [aky] *nm*: **recharger ses** ~s *fam fig* to recharge one's batteries.

accueil [akœj] *nm* **-1.** [lieu] reception. **-2.** [action] welcome, reception.

accueillant, -e [akœjɑ̃, ɑ̃t] *adj* welcoming, friendly.

accueillir [akœjir] [41] *vt* **-1.** [gén] to welcome. **-2.** [loger] to accommodate.

acculer [akyle] [3] *vt* **-1.** [repousser]: ~ qqn contre/à to drive sb up against/into. **-2.** *fig*: ~ qqn à [ruine, désespoir] to drive sb to; [faute] to force sb into.

accumulateur [akymylatœr] *nm* accumulator, battery.

accumulation [akymylasjɔ̃] *nf* accumulation.

accumuler [akymyle] [3] *vt* to accumulate; *fig* to store up.

◆ **s'accumuler** *vp* to pile up.

accusateur, -trice [akyzatœr, tris] ◇ *adj* accusing. ◇ *nm, f* accuser.

accusation [akyzasjɔ̃] *nf* **-1.** [reproche] accusation. **-2.** JUR charge; **mettre en** ~ to indict; **l'**~ the prosecution.

accusé, -e [akyze] *nm, f* accused, defendant.

◆ **accusé de réception** *nm* acknowledgement (of receipt).

accuser [akyze] [3] *vt* **-1.** [porter une accusation contre]: ~ qqn (de qqch) to accuse sb (of sthg). **-2.** JUR: ~ qqn de qqch to charge sb with sthg. **-3.** [mettre en relief] to emphasize.

acerbe [asɛrb] *adj* acerbic.

acéré, -e [asere] *adj* sharp.

acétate [asetat] *nm* acetate.

acétone [asetɔn] *nf* acetone.

achalandé, -e [aʃalɑ̃de] *adj* [en marchandises]: **bien** ~ well-stocked.

acharné, -e [aʃarne] *adj* [combat] fierce; [travail] unremitting.

acharnement [aʃarnəmɑ̃] *nm* relentlessness.

acharner [aʃarne] [3]

◆ **s'acharner** *vp* **-1.** [combattre]: **s'**~ **contre** OU **après** OU **sur qqn** [ennemi, victime] to hound sb; [suj: malheur] to dog sb. **-2.** [s'obstiner]: **s'**~ **(à faire qqch)** to persist (in doing sthg).

achat [aʃa] *nm* purchase; **faire des** ~s to go shopping; ~ **d'espace** COMM buying of (advertising) space.

acheminer [aʃmine] [3] *vt* to dispatch.

◆ **s'acheminer** *vp*: **s'**~ **vers** [lieu, désastre] to head for; [solution, paix] to move towards.

acheter [aʃte] [28] *vt litt* & *fig* to buy; ~ qqch à OU pour qqn to buy sthg for sb, to buy sb sthg; ~ qqch à qqn [commerçant] to buy sthg from sb.

acheteur, -euse [aʃtœr, øz] *nm, f* buyer, purchaser.

achevé, -e [aʃve] *adj sout*: **d'un ridicule** ~ utterly ridiculous.

achèvement [aʃɛvmɑ̃] *nm* completion.

achever [aʃve] [19] *vt* **-1.** [terminer] to complete, to finish (off). **-2.** [tuer, accabler] to finish off.

◆ **s'achever** *vp* to end, to come to an end.

achoppement [aʃɔpmɑ̃] → **pierre**.

acide [asid] ◇ *adj* **-1.** [saveur] sour. **-2.** [propos] sharp, acid. **-3.** CHIM acid. ◇ *nm* **-1.** CHIM acid; ~ **acétique/chlorhydrique/sul-**

furique acetic/hydrochloric/sulphuric acid; ~ **aminé** amino acid. **-2.** *arg drogue* acid.

acidité [asidite] *nf* **-1.** CHIM acidity. **-2.** [saveur] sourness. **-3.** [de propos] sharpness.

acidulé, -e [asidyle] *adj* slightly acid; → **bonbon**.

acier [asje] *nm* steel; ~ **inoxydable** stainless steel.

aciérie [asjeri] *nf* steelworks (*sg*).

acné [akne] *nf* acne; ~ **juvénile** teenage acne.

acolyte [akɔlit] *nm péj* henchman.

acompte [akɔ̃t] *nm* deposit; **verser un** ~ to put down OU pay a deposit.

acoquiner [akɔkine] [3]
◆ **s'acoquiner** *vp*: **s'**~ **avec qqn** to gang up with sb.

à-côté [akote] (*pl* **à-côtés**) *nm* **-1.** [point accessoire] side issue. **-2.** [gain d'appoint] extra.

à-coup [aku] (*pl* **à-coups**) *nm* jerk; **par** ~**s** in fits and starts.

acoustique [akustik] ◇ *nf* **-1.** [science] acoustics (*U*). **-2.** [d'une salle] acoustics (*pl*). ◇ *adj* acoustic.

acquéreur [akerœr] *nm* buyer.

acquérir [akerir] [39] *vt* **-1.** [gén] to acquire. **-2.** [conquérir] to win.
◆ **s'acquérir** *vp*: **s'**~ **qqch** to win sthg, to gain sthg.

acquiers, acquiert *etc* → **acquérir**.

acquiescement [akjɛsmã] *nm* approval.

acquiescer [akjese] [21] *vi* to acquiesce; ~ **à** to agree to.

acquis, -e [aki, iz] ◇ *pp* → **acquérir**. ◇ *adj* **-1.** [caractère] acquired. **-2.** [droit, avantage] established.
◆ **acquis** *nm* knowledge.

acquisition [akizisjɔ̃] *nf* acquisition.

acquit [aki] *nm* receipt; **pour** ~ COMM received; **faire qqch par** ~ **de conscience** *fig* to do sthg to set one's mind at rest.

acquittement [akitmã] *nm* **-1.** [d'obligation] settlement. **-2.** JUR acquittal.

acquitter [akite] [3] *vt* **-1.** JUR to acquit. **-2.** [régler] to pay. **-3.** [libérer]: ~ **qqn de** to release sb from.
◆ **s'acquitter** *vp*: **s'**~ **de qqch** [payer] to settle sthg; *fig* to carry sthg out.

âcre [akr] *adj* **-1.** [saveur] bitter. **-2.** [fumée] acrid.

acrimonie [akrimɔni] *nf* acrimony.

acrobate [akrɔbat] *nmf* acrobat.

acrobatie [akrɔbasi] *nf* acrobatics (*U*); ~**s aériennes** aerobatics (*pl*).

acrobatique [akrɔbatik] *adj* acrobatic.

acronyme [akrɔnim] *nm* acronym.

acrylique [akrilik] *adj & nm* acrylic.

acte [akt] *nm* **-1.** [action] act, action; **faire** ~ **d'autorité** to exercise one's authority; **faire** ~ **de bonne volonté** to make a gesture of goodwill; **faire** ~ **de candidature** to submit an application. **-2.** THÉÂTRE act. **-3.** JUR deed; ~ **d'accusation** charge; ~ **de naissance/de mariage** birth/marriage certificate; ~ **notarié** deed executed by a notary; ~ **de vente** bill of sale. **-4.** RELIG certificate; ~ **de baptême** baptismal certificate. **-5.** *loc*: **faire** ~ **de présence** to put in an appearance; **prendre** ~ **de** to note, to take note of.
◆ **actes** *nmpl* [de colloque] proceedings.

acteur, -trice [aktœr, tris] *nm, f* actor (*f* actress).

actif, -ive [aktif, iv] *adj* [gén] active; **la population active** the working population.
◆ **actif** *nm* **-1.** FIN assets (*pl*). **-2.** *loc*: **avoir qqch à son** ~ to have sthg to one's credit.

action [aksjɔ̃] *nf* **-1.** [gén] action; **passer à l'**~ to go into action; MIL to go into battle; **sous l'**~ **de** under the effect of. **-2.** [acte] action, act; **bonne/mauvaise** ~ good/bad deed. **-3.** JUR action, lawsuit. **-4.** FIN share. **-5.** RELIG: ~ **de grâces** thanksgiving.

actionnaire [aksjɔnɛr] *nmf* FIN shareholder.

actionner [aksjɔne] [3] *vt* to work, to activate.

activement [aktivmã] *adv* actively.

activer [aktive] [3] *vt* to speed up.
◆ **s'activer** *vp* to bustle about.

activisme [aktivism] *nm* activism.

activiste [aktivist] *adj & nmf* activist.

activité [aktivite] *nf* [gén] activity; **en** ~ [volcan] active; ~ **d'éveil** early learning experience; ~ **professionnelle** job, profession.

actuaire [aktɥɛr] *nmf* actuary.

actualisation [aktɥalizasjɔ̃] *nf* [d'un texte] updating.

actualiser [aktɥalize] [3] *vt* to bring up to date.

actualité [aktɥalite] *nf* **-1.** [d'un sujet] topicality; **être d'**~ to be topical. **-2.** [événements]: **l'**~ **sportive/politique//littéraire** the current sports/political/literary scene.
◆ **actualités** *nfpl*: **les** ~**s** the news (*sg*).

actuel, -elle [aktɥɛl] *adj* **-1.** [contemporain, présent] current, present; **à l'heure** ~**le** at the present time. **-2.** [d'actualité] topical.

actuellement [aktɥɛlmã] *adv* at present, currently.

acuité [akɥite] *nf* acuteness; ~ **visuelle** keenness of sight.

acupuncture, acuponcture [akupɔ̃ktyr] *nf* acupuncture.

adage [adaʒ] *nm* adage, saying.

adaptable [adaptabl] *adj* adaptable.

adaptateur, -trice [adaptatœr, tris] *nm, f* adapter.

◆ **adaptateur** *nm* ÉLECTR adapter.

adaptation [adaptasjɔ̃] *nf* adaptation.

adapter [adapte] [3] *vt* **-1.** [gén] to adapt. **-2.** [fixer] to fit; ~ qqch à qqch to fit sthg to sthg.

◆ **s'adapter** *vp*: s'~ (à) to adapt (to).

ADD (*abr de* **analogique/digital/digital**) ADD.

additif, -ive [aditif, iv] *adj* additive.

◆ **additif** *nm* **-1.** [supplément] rider, additional clause. **-2.** [substance] additive.

addition [adisjɔ̃] *nf* **-1.** [ajout, calcul] addition. **-2.** [note] bill *Br*, check *Am*.

additionnel, -elle [adisjɔnɛl] *adj* extra, additional.

additionner [adisjɔne] [3] *vt* **-1.** [ajouter]: ~ qqch à qqch to add sthg to sthg; ~ une poudre d'eau to add water to a powder. **-2.** [calculer] to add up.

◆ **s'additionner** *vp* to add up.

adduction [adyksjɔ̃] *nf* [des eaux, du gaz] supply.

adepte [adɛpt] *nmf* follower.

adéquat, -e [adekwa, at] *adj* suitable, appropriate.

adhérence [aderɑ̃s] *nf* [de pneu] grip.

adhérent, -e [aderɑ̃, ɑ̃t] ◇ *adj*: ~ à which adheres OU sticks to. ◇ *nm, f*: ~ (à) member (of).

adhérer [adere] [18] *vi* **-1.** [coller] to stick, to adhere; ~ à [se fixer sur] to stick OU adhere to; [être d'accord avec] *fig* to support, to adhere to. **-2.** [être membre de] to belong to, to be a member of.

adhésif, -ive [adezif, iv] *adj* sticky, adhesive.

◆ **adhésif** *nm* adhesive.

adhésion [adezjɔ̃] *nf* **-1.** [à idée]: ~ (à) support (for). **-2.** [de pneu]: **une bonne ~ à la route** good road-holding (*U*). **-3.** [à parti]: ~ (à) membership (of).

adieu [adjø] ◇ *interj* goodbye!, farewell!; **dire ~ à qqch** *fig* to say goodbye to sthg. ◇ *nm* (*gén pl*) farewell; **faire ses ~x à qqn** to say one's farewells to sb.

adipeux, -euse [adipø, øz] *adj* [tissu] adipose; [personne] fat.

adjacent, -e [adʒasɑ̃, ɑ̃t] *adj* adjoining, adjacent.

adjectif [adʒɛktif] *nm* GRAM adjective; ~ **attribut** predicative adjective; ~ **épithète** attributive adjective.

adjoindre [adjwɛ̃dr] [82] *vt*: ~ qqch à qqch to add sthg to sthg.

◆ **s'adjoindre** *vp* to appoint, to take on.

adjoint, -e [adʒwɛ̃, ɛ̃t] ◇ *adj* deputy (*avant n*), assistant (*avant n*). ◇ *nm, f* deputy, assistant; ~ **au maire** deputy mayor.

adjonction [adʒɔ̃ksjɔ̃] *nf* addition; **sans ~ de sel/sucre/conservateurs** with no added salt/sugar/preservatives.

adjudant [adʒudɑ̃] *nm* [dans la marine] warrant officer; [dans l'armée] company sergeant major; ~ **chef** [dans la marine] warrant officer 1st class *Br*, chief warrant officer *Am*; [dans l'armée] regimental sergeant major.

adjudicataire [adʒydikatɛr] *nmf* successful bidder.

adjudication [adʒydikasjɔ̃] *nf* **-1.** [vente aux enchères] sale by auction. **-2.** ADMIN awarding.

adjuger [adʒyʒe] [17] *vt*: ~ qqch (à qqn) [aux enchères] to auction sthg (to sb); [décerner] to award sthg (to sb); **adjugé!** sold!

◆ **s'adjuger** *vp*: s'~ qqch to give o.s. sthg.

adjurer [adʒyre] [3] *vt sout* to implore, to beg.

adjuvant [adʒyvɑ̃] *nm* **-1.** [médicament] adjuvant. **-2.** [stimulant] stimulant.

admets *etc* → **admettre**.

admettre [admɛtr] [84] *vt* **-1.** [tolérer, accepter] to allow, to accept. **-2.** [supposer] to suppose, to assume; **admettons que** (+ *subjonctif*) supposing OU assuming (that). **-3.** [autoriser] to allow; **être admis à faire qqch** to be allowed to do sthg. **-4.** [accueillir, reconnaître] to admit.

administrateur, -trice [administratœr, tris] *nm, f* **-1.** [gérant] administrator; ~ **de biens** administrator of an estate; ~ **judiciaire** receiver. **-2.** [de conseil d'administration] director.

administratif, -ive [administratif, iv] *adj* administrative.

administration [administrasjɔ̃] *nf* **-1.** [service public]: **l'Administration** ≃ the Civil Service. **-2.** [gestion] administration.

administrer [administre] [3] *vt* **-1.** [gérer] to manage, to administer. **-2.** [médicament, sacrement] to administer.

admirable [admirabl] *adj* **-1.** [personne, comportement] admirable. **-2.** [paysage, spectacle] wonderful.

admirablement [admirabləmã] *adv* admirably.

admirateur, -trice [admiratœr, tris] *nm, f* admirer.

admiratif, -ive [admiratif, iv] *adj* admiring.

admiration [admirasjɔ̃] *nf* admiration; être en ~ devant qqn/qqch to be filled with admiration for sb/sthg.

admirer [admire] [3] *vt* to admire.

admis, -e [admi, iz] *pp* → **admettre**.

admissible [admisibl] ◇ *adj* -1. [attitude] acceptable. -2. SCOL eligible. ◇ *nmf* SCOL eligible candidate.

admission [admisjɔ̃] *nf* admission.

admonester [admɔnɛste] [3] *vt* sout to admonish.

ADN (*abr de* **acide désoxyribonucléique**) *nm* DNA.

ado [ado] (*abr de* **adolescent**) *nmf fam* teenager.

adolescence [adɔlesãs] *nf* adolescence.

adolescent, -e [adɔlesã, ãt] ◇ *adj* adolescent. ◇ *nm, f* adolescent, teenager.

adonis [adɔnis] *nm* Adonis.

adonner [adɔne] [3]
◆ **s'adonner** *vp*: **s'**~ à [sport, activité] to devote o.s. to; [vice] to take to.

adopter [adɔpte] [3] *vt* -1. [gén] to adopt. -2. [loi] to pass.

adoptif, -ive [adɔptif, iv] *adj* [famille] adoptive; [pays, enfant] adopted.

adoption [adɔpsjɔ̃] *nf* adoption; **d'**~ [pays, ville] adopted; [famille] adoptive.

adorable [adɔrabl] *adj* adorable, delightful.

adorateur, -trice [adɔratœr, tris] ◇ *adj* adoring, worshipping. ◇ *nm, f* -1. [de personne] admirer. -2. RELIG worshipper.

adoration [adɔrasjɔ̃] *nf* -1. [amour] adoration; être en ~ devant qqn to worship sb. -2. RELIG worship.

adorer [adɔre] [3] *vt* -1. [personne, chose] to adore. -2. RELIG to worship.

adosser [adose] [3] *vt*: ~ qqch à qqch to place sthg against sthg.
◆ **s'adosser** *vp*: **s'**~ à qqch to lean against sthg.

adoucir [adusir] [32] *vt* -1. [gén] to soften. -2. [chagrin, peine] to ease, to soothe.
◆ **s'adoucir** *vp* -1. [temps] to become OU get milder. -2. [personne] to mellow.

adoucissant, -e [adusisã, ãt] *adj* soothing.
◆ **adoucissant** *nm* softener.

adoucissement [adusismã] *nm* -1. [de température]: **il y a eu un** ~ **de la température** the weather has become milder. -2. [de peine] soothing, easing. -3. [de l'eau] softening.

adoucisseur [adusisœr] *nm*: ~ **d'eau** water softener.

adrénaline [adrenalin] *nf* adrenalin.

adresse [adrɛs] *nf* -1. [gén & INFORM] address; **ce restaurant est une bonne** ~ this restaurant is a good place to go; **à l'**~ **de** *fig* for the benefit of. -2. [habileté] skill. -3. [mot] headword.

adresser [adrese] [4] *vt* -1. [faire parvenir]: ~ qqch à qqn to address sthg to sb. -2. [envoyer]: ~ qqn à qqn to refer sb to sb.
◆ **s'adresser** *vp*: **s'**~ à [parler à] to speak to; [être destiné à] to be aimed at, to be intended for.

Adriatique [adriatik] *nf*: **l'**~ the Adriatic.

adroit, -e [adrwa, at] *adj* skilful.

adroitement [adrwatmã] *adv* skilfully.

aduler [adyle] [3] *vt* to adulate.

adulte [adylt] *nmf & adj* adult.

adultère [adyltɛr] ◇ *nm* [acte] adultery. ◇ *adj* adulterous.

adultérin, -e [adylterɛ̃, in] *adj* illegitimate.

advenir [advənir] [40] *v impers* to happen; **qu'advient-il de ...?** what is happening to ...?; **qu'est-il advenu de ...?** what has happened OU become of ...?; **advienne que pourra** come what may.

advenu, -e [advəny] *pp* → **advenir**.

adverbe [advɛrb] *nm* adverb.

adversaire [advɛrsɛr] *nmf* adversary, opponent.

adverse [advɛrs] *adj* [opposé] opposing; → **partie**.

adversité [advɛrsite] *nf* adversity.

advient → **advenir**.

advint → **advenir**.

AE (*abr de* **adjoint d'enseignement**) *nm non-certified teacher*.

AELE (*abr de* **Association européenne de libre-échange**) *nf* EFTA.

AEN (*abr de* **Agence pour l'énergie nucléaire**) *nf French nuclear energy agency*, ≈ AEA *Br*, ≈ AEC *Am*.

aération [aerasjɔ̃] *nf* [circulation d'air] ventilation; [action] airing.

aérer [aere] [18] *vt* -1. [pièce, chose] to air. -2. *fig* [présentation, mise en page] to lighten.
◆ **s'aérer** *vp* [sortir] to get some fresh air.

aérien, -ienne [aerjɛ̃, jɛn] *adj* -1. [grâce] ethereal; [démarche] light. -2. [dans l'air] overhead (*avant n*). -3. [aviation] air (*avant n*).

aérobic [aerɔbik] *nm* aerobics (*U*).

aérodrome [aerɔdroͅm] *nm* aerodrome.

aérodynamique [aerɔdinamik] ◇ *nf* aerodynamics (*U*). ◇ *adj* streamlined, aerodynamic.

aérogare [aerɔgar] *nf* -1. [aéroport] airport. -2. [gare] air terminal.

aéroglisseur [aeroglisœr] *nm* hovercraft.

aérogramme [aerɔgram] *nm* aerogramme.

aéromodélisme [aeromɔdelism] *nm* model aircraft making.

aéronautique [aerɔnotik] ◇ *nf* aeronautics (*U*). ◇ *adj* aeronautical.

aéronaval, -e, -als [aerɔnaval] *adj* air and sea (*avant n*).

aérophagie [aerɔfaʒi] *nf* abdominal wind.

aéroport [aerɔpɔr] *nm* airport.

aéroporté, -e [aerɔpɔrte] *adj* airborne.

aérosol [aerɔsɔl] *nm & adj inv* aerosol.

aérospatial, -e, -iaux [aerɔspasjal, jo] *adj* aerospace (*avant n*).

◆ **aérospatiale** *nf* aerospace industry.

AF ◇ *nfpl abr de* **allocations familiales**. ◇ *nf* (*abr de* **Assemblée fédérale**) (Swiss) Federal Assembly.

affabilité [afabilite] *nf* affability.

affable [afabl] *adj* -1. [personne] affable, agreeable. -2. [parole] kind.

affabulation [afabylasjɔ̃] *nf* fabrication.

affaiblir [afeblir] [32] *vt litt & fig* to weaken.

◆ **s'affaiblir** *vp litt & fig* to weaken, to become weaker.

affaiblissement [afeblismɑ̃] *nm* weakening.

affaire [afɛr] *nf* -1. [question] matter. -2. [situation, polémique] affair. -3. [marché] affair; **faire une ~** to get a bargain OU a good deal; **une ~ en** or a real bargain. -4. [entreprise] business. -5. [procès] case. -6. *loc:* **avoir ~ à qqn** to deal with sb; **vous aurez ~ à moi!** you'll have me to deal with!; **c'est l'~ d'une minute** it will only take a minute; **faire l'~** to do nicely; **j'en fais mon ~** leave it to me; **tirer qqn d'~** to get sb out of trouble.

◆ **affaires** *nfpl* -1. COMM business (*U*). -2. [objets personnels] things, belongings. -3. [activités] affairs; **les ~s de l'État** affairs of state; **les Affaires étrangères** ≃ the Foreign Office; **se mêler** OU **s'occuper de ses ~s** to mind one's own business; **toutes ~s cessantes** forthwith.

affairé, -e [afere] *adj* busy.

affairer [afere] [4]

◆ **s'affairer** *vp* to bustle about.

affairisme [aferism] *nm* racketeering.

affaissement [afɛsmɑ̃] *nm* GÉOGR subsidence.

affaisser [afɛse] [4]

◆ **s'affaisser** *vp* -1. [se creuser] to subside, to sink. -2. [tomber] to collapse.

affaler [afale] [3]

◆ **s'affaler** *vp* to collapse.

affamé, -e [afame] *adj* starving.

affectation [afɛktasjɔ̃] *nf* -1. [attribution]: ~ **de qqch à** allocation of sthg to. -2. [nomination] appointment, posting. -3. [manque de naturel] affectation.

affecter [afɛkte] [4] *vt* -1. [consacrer]: ~ **qqch à** to allocate sthg to. -2. [nommer]: ~ **qqn à** to appoint sb to. -3. [feindre] to feign. -4. [émouvoir] to affect, to move.

affectif, -ive [afɛktif, iv] *adj* emotional.

affection [afɛksjɔ̃] *nf* -1. [sentiment] affection; **avoir de l'~ pour** to be fond of. -2. [maladie] complaint.

affectionner [afɛksjɔne] [3] *vt* to be fond of.

affectivité [afɛktivite] *nf* emotions (*pl*).

affectueusement [afɛktɥøzmɑ̃] *adv* affectionately.

affectueux, -euse [afɛktɥø, øz] *adj* affectionate.

afférent, -e [aferɑ̃, ɑ̃t] *adj* -1. JUR: ~ **à qqch** pertaining OU relating to sthg. -2. ANAT afferent.

affermir [afɛrmir] [32] *vt* [gén] to strengthen; [chairs] to tone up.

◆ **s'affermir** *vp* -1. [matière] to be strengthened; [chairs] to be toned up. -2. [pouvoir] to be consolidated.

affichage [afiʃaʒ] *nm* -1. [d'affiche] putting up, displaying. -2. ÉLECTRON: ~ **à cristaux liquides** LCD, liquid crystal display; ~ **numérique** digital display.

affiche [afiʃ] *nf* [gén] poster; [officielle] notice; ~ **publicitaire** (advertising) poster; **être à l'~** *fig* to be on.

afficher [afiʃe] [3] *vt* -1. [liste, affiche] to put up; [vente, réglementation] to put up a notice about. -2. [laisser transparaître] to display, to exhibit.

◆ **s'afficher** *vp*: **s'~ avec qqn** to flaunt o.s. with sb.

affichette [afiʃɛt] *nf* small poster.

afficheur [afiʃœr] *nm* -1. [entreprise] billposter. -2. ÉLECTRON display.

affilée [afile]

◆ **d'affilée** *loc adv*: **trois jours d'~** three days running.

affiler [afile] [3] *vt* to sharpen.

affilié, -e [afilje] *adj*: ~ **à** affiliated to.

affiner [afine] [3] *vt litt & fig* to refine.

◆ **s'affiner** *vp* [silhouette] to become thinner; [devenir plus raffiné] to become more refined.

affinité [afinite] *nf* affinity; **avoir des ~s avec** to have an affinity with.

affirmatif, -ive [afirmatif, iv] *adj* **-1.** [réponse] affirmative. **-2.** [personne] positive.
◆ **affirmatif** *adv* affirmative.
◆ **affirmative** *nf*: **dans l'affirmative** if yes, if the answer is yes; **répondre par l'affirmative** to reply in the affirmative.

affirmation [afirmasjɔ̃] *nf* assertion.

affirmativement [afirmativmɑ̃] *adv*: **répondre ~** to answer in the affirmative.

affirmer [afirme] [3] *vt* **-1.** [certifier] to maintain, to claim. **-2.** [exprimer] to assert.
◆ **s'affirmer** *vp* to assert o.s.

affixe [afiks] *nm* affix.

affleurer [aflœre] [5] *vi* *fig* to rise to the surface.

affliction [afliksjɔ̃] *nf* affliction.

affligeant, -e [afliʒɑ̃, ɑ̃t] *adj* **-1.** [désolant] saddening, distressing. **-2.** [lamentable] appalling.

affliger [afliʒe] [17] *vt* *sout* **-1.** [attrister] to sadden, to distress. **-2.** [de défaut, de maladie]: **être affligé de** to be afflicted with.
◆ **s'affliger** *vp* *sout*: **s'~ de** to be distressed at OU about.

affluence [aflyɑ̃s] *nf* crowd, crowds (*pl*).

affluent [aflyɑ̃] *nm* tributary.

affluer [aflye] [3] *vi* **-1.** [choses] to pour in, to flood in. **-2.** [personnes] to flock. **-3.** [sang]: **~ (à)** to rush (to).

afflux [afly] *nm* **-1.** [de liquide, dons, capitaux] flow. **-2.** [de personnes] flood.

affolant, -e [afɔlɑ̃, ɑ̃t] *adj* **-1.** [inquiétant] frightening. **-2.** [troublant] disturbing.

affolé, -e [afɔle] *adj* horrified.

affolement [afɔlmɑ̃] *nm* panic.

affoler [afɔle] [3] *vt* **-1.** [inquiéter] to terrify. **-2.** [émouvoir] to drive mad.
◆ **s'affoler** *vp* [paniquer] to panic.

affranchi, -e [afrɑ̃ʃi] *adj* **-1.** [lettre - avec timbre] stamped; [- à la machine] franked. **-2.** [personne, esclave] liberated.

affranchir [afrɑ̃ʃir] [32] *vt* **-1.** [lettre - avec timbre] to stamp; [- à la machine] to frank. **-2.** *arg crime* [renseigner] to put in the picture, to fill in. **-3.** [libérer]: **~ qqn de qqch** to liberate OU free sb from sthg. **-4.** [esclave] to set free, to liberate.
◆ **s'affranchir** *vp*: **s'~ de qqch** [se libérer de] to free o.s. from sthg.

affranchissement [afrɑ̃ʃismɑ̃] *nm* **-1.** [de lettre - avec timbre] stamping; [- à la machine]

franking. **-2.** [libération] liberation, emancipation.

affres [afr] *nfpl* *littéraire* throes.

affréter [afrete] [18] *vt* to charter.

affreusement [afrøzmɑ̃] *adv* **-1.** [horriblement] horribly. **-2.** [énormément] awfully.

affreux, -euse [afrø, øz] *adj* **-1.** [repoussant] horrible. **-2.** [effrayant] terrifying. **-3.** [détestable] awful, dreadful.

affriolant, -e [afrijɔlɑ̃, ɑ̃t] *adj* enticing.

affront [afrɔ̃] *nm* insult, affront; **faire un ~ à qqn** to insult sb.

affrontement [afrɔ̃tmɑ̃] *nm* confrontation.

affronter [afrɔ̃te] [3] *vt* to confront.
◆ **s'affronter** *vp* to confront each other.

affubler [afyble] [3] *vt* *péj*: **être affublé de** to be got up in.
◆ **s'affubler** *vp*: **s'~ de qqch** *péj* to get o.s. up in sthg.

affût [afy] *nm*: **être à l'~ (de)** to be lying in wait (for); *fig* to be on the lookout (for).

affûter [afyte] [3] *vt* to sharpen.

afghan, -e [afgɑ̃, an] *adj* Afghan.
◆ **afghan** *nm* [langue] Afghan, Pashto.
◆ **Afghan, -e** *nm, f* Afghan.

Afghanistan [afganistɑ̃] *nm*: **l'~** Afghanistan.

afin [afɛ̃]
◆ **afin de** *loc prép* in order to.
◆ **afin que** *loc conj* (+ *subjonctif*) so that.

AFNOR, Afnor [afnɔr] (*abr de* **Association française de normalisation**) *nf* French industrial standards authority, ≃ BSI *Br*, ≃ ASA *Am*.

a fortiori [afɔrsjɔri] *adv* all the more.

AFP (*abr de* **Agence France-Presse**) *nf* French press agency.

africain, -e [afrikɛ̃, ɛn] *adj* African.
◆ **Africain, -e** *nm, f* African.

afrikaner [afrikanɛr], **afrikaander** [afrikɑ̃der] *adj* Afrikaner.
◆ **Afrikaner, Afrikaander** *nmf* Afrikaner.

Afrique [afrik] *nf*: **l'~** Africa; **l'~ australe** Southern Africa; **l'~ noire** sub-Saharan Africa; **l'~ du Nord** North Africa; **l'~ du Sud** South Africa.

after-shave [aftœrʃɛv] *nm inv & adj inv* aftershave.

ag. *abr de* **agence**.

AG (*abr de* **assemblée générale**) *nf* GM.

agaçant, -e [agasɑ̃, ɑ̃t] *adj* irritating.

agacement [agasmɑ̃] *nm* irritation.

agacer [agase] [16] *vt* to irritate.

agate [agat] *nf* agate.

âge [aʒ] *nm* age; **à l'~ de** at the age of; **en ~ de faire qqch** old enough to do sthg; **en bas ~** very young; **quel ~ as-tu?** how old are you?; **d'un certain ~** middle-aged; **prendre de l'~** to age; **l'~ adulte** adulthood; **l'~ ingrat** the awkward OU difficult age; **d'un ~ avancé** elderly; **~ de fer/de bronze** Iron/Bronze Age; **~ mental** mental age; **d'~ mûr** of mature years; **~ d'or** golden age; **~ de raison** age of reason; **le troisième ~** [personnes] the over-sixties.

âgé, -e [aʒe] *adj* old, elderly; **être ~ de 20 ans** to be 20 years old OU of age; **un enfant ~ de 3 ans** a 3-year-old child.

agence [aʒɑ̃s] *nf* agency; **~ immobilière** estate agent's *Br*, real estate agent's *Am*; **~ matrimoniale** marriage bureau; **Agence nationale pour l'emploi** ≃ job centre; **~ de publicité** advertising agency; **~ de voyages** travel agent's, travel agency.

agencement [aʒɑ̃smɑ̃] *nm* arrangement.

agencer [aʒɑ̃se] [16] *vt* to arrange; *fig* to put together.
◆ **s'agencer** *vp* to fit together.

agenda [aʒɛ̃da] *nm* diary.

agenouiller [aʒnuje] [3]
◆ **s'agenouiller** *vp* to kneel; **s'~ devant** *fig* to bow down before.

agent [aʒɑ̃] *nm* agent; **~ de change** stockbroker; **~ commercial** sales representative; **~ immobilier** estate agent *Br*, real estate agent *Am*; **~ de police** police officer; **~ de publicité** advertising agent; **~ secret** secret agent.

agglomérat [aglɔmera] *nm* GÉOL & *fig* agglomerate.

agglomération [aglɔmerasjɔ̃] *nf* **-1.** [amas] conglomeration. **-2.** [ville] conurbation; **l'~ parisienne** the Parisian urban area.

aggloméré [aglɔmere] *nm* chipboard.

agglomérer [aglɔmere] [18] *vt* to mix together.
◆ **s'agglomérer** *vp* **-1.** [surface] to bind. **-2.** [foule] to gather.

agglutiner [aglytine] [3] *vt* to stick together.
◆ **s'agglutiner** *vp* [foule] to gather, to congregate.

aggravation [agravasjɔ̃] *nf* worsening, aggravation.

aggraver [agrave] [3] *vt* to make worse.
◆ **s'aggraver** *vp* to get worse, to worsen.

agile [aʒil] *adj* agile, nimble.

agilement [aʒilmɑ̃] *adv* agilely.

agilité [aʒilite] *nf litt* & *fig* agility.

agios [aʒjo] *nmpl* FIN bank charges.

agir [aʒir] [32] *vi* **-1.** [faire, être efficace] to act. **-2.** [se comporter] to behave. **-3.** [influer]: **~ sur** to have an effect on.
◆ **s'agir** *v impers*: **il s'agit de ...** it's a matter of ...; **il s'agit de faire qqch** we/you *etc* must do sthg; **de quoi s'agit-il?** what's it about?; **de quoi s'agit-il dans ce film/cette lettre ?** what is this film/letter about?

agissements [aʒismɑ̃] *nmpl péj* schemes, intrigues.

agitateur, -trice [aʒitatœr, tris] *nm, f* POLIT agitator.

agitation [aʒitasjɔ̃] *nf* agitation; [politique, sociale] unrest.

agité, -e [aʒite] *adj* **-1.** [gén] restless; [enfant, classe] restless, fidgety; [journée, atmosphère] hectic. **-2.** [mer] rough.

agiter [aʒite] [3] *vt* **-1.** [remuer - flacon, objet] to shake; [- drapeau, bras] to wave; **«~ avant l'emploi»** "shake well before use". **-2.** [énerver] to perturb.
◆ **s'agiter** *vp* [personne] to move about, to fidget; [mer] to stir; [population] to get restless.

agneau [aɲo] *nm* **-1.** [animal, viande] lamb; **doux comme un ~** gentle as a lamb. **-2.** [cuir] lambskin.

agonie [agɔni] *nf* [de personne] mortal agony; *fig* death throes (*pl*); **être à l'~** to be at death's door.

agoniser [agɔnize] [3] *vi* [personne] to be in mortal agony; *fig* to decline, to go under.

agoraphobie [agɔrafɔbi] *nf* agoraphobia.

agrafe [agraf] *nf* **-1.** [de bureau] staple. **-2.** MÉD clip.

agrafer [agrafe] [3] *vt* [attacher] to fasten; *fam fig* to nab.

agrafeuse [agrafœz] *nf* stapler.

agraire [agrɛr] *adj* agrarian.

agrandir [agrɑ̃dir] [32] *vt* **-1.** [élargir - gén & PHOT] to enlarge; [- rue, écart] to widen. **-2.** *fig* [développer] to expand. **-3.** [faire paraître plus grand]: **~ qqch** to make sthg look bigger.
◆ **s'agrandir** *vp* **-1.** [s'étendre] to grow. **-2.** *fig* [se développer] to expand.

agrandissement [agrɑ̃dismɑ̃] *nm* **-1.** [gén & PHOT] enlargement. **-2.** *fig* [développement] expansion.

agréable [agreabl] *adj* pleasant, nice.

agréablement [agreabləmɑ̃] *adv* pleasantly.

agréé, -e [agree] *adj* [concessionnaire, appareil] authorized.

agréer [agree] [15] *vt sout* **-1.** [accepter]: **faire ~ qqch** to have sthg accepted; **veuillez ~ mes salutations distinguées** OU **l'expression**

de mes sentiments distingués yours faithfully. **-2.** [convenir]: ~ **à qqn** to suit OU please sb.

agrégat [agrega] *nm* **-1.** [aggloméré] aggregate. **-2.** *fig* & *péj* [amas] hotchpotch.

agrégation [agregasjɔ̃] *nf competitive examination for secondary school and university teachers.*

agrégé, -e [agreʒe] *nm, f holder of the agrégation.*

agrément [agremã] *nm* **-1.** [caractère agréable] attractiveness; **d'~** [jardin] ornamental; [voyage] pleasure *(avant n)*. **-2.** [approbation] consent, approval.

agrémenter [agremãte] [3] *vt:* ~ **qqch (de qqch)** to embellish sthg (with sthg).

◆ **s'agrémenter** *vp:* **s'~ de qqch** [vêtement] to be trimmed OU adorned with sthg.

agrès [agrɛ] *nmpl* SPORT gym apparatus *(U).*

agresser [agrese] [4] *vt* **-1.** [suj: personne] to attack. **-2.** *fig* [suj: bruit, pollution] to assault.

agresseur [agresœr] *nm* attacker.

agressif, -ive [agresif, iv] *adj* aggressive.

agression [agresjɔ̃] *nf* attack; MIL & PSYCHOL aggression.

agressivement [agresivmã] *adv* aggressively.

agressivité [agresivite] *nf* aggressiveness.

agricole [agrikɔl] *adj* agricultural.

agriculteur, -trice [agrikyltœr, tris] *nm, f* farmer.

agriculture [agrikyltyr] *nf* agriculture, farming.

agripper [agripe] [3] *vt* **-1.** [personne] to cling OU hang on to. **-2.** [objet] to grip, to clutch.

◆ **s'agripper** *vp:* **s'~ à qqn** to cling OU hang on to sb; **s'~ à qqch** to grip OU clutch sthg.

agronome [agrɔnɔm] *nmf* agronomist.

agronomie [agrɔnɔmi] *nf* agronomy.

agronomique [agrɔnɔmik] *adj* agronomic.

agrume [agrym] *nm* citrus fruit.

aguerrir [agerir] [32] *vt* to harden.

◆ **s'aguerrir** *vp:* **s'~ (contre)** to become hardened (to).

aguets [agɛ]
◆ **aux aguets** *loc adv:* **être/rester aux ~** to be OU keep on the lookout.

aguichant, -e [agiʃɑ̃, ɑ̃t] *adj* enticing.

ah [a] *interj* oh!, ah!; **ah bon?** really?; **ah, quelle bonne surprise!** what a nice surprise!

Ah *(abr de* **ampère-heure)** ah.

ahuri, -e [ayri] *adj:* **être ~ (par qqch)** to be taken aback (by sthg).

ahurir [ayrir] [32] *vt* [étonner] to astound.

ahurissant, -e [ayrisɑ̃, ɑ̃t] *adj* astounding.

ahurissement [ayrismɑ̃] *nm* astonishment.

ai → **avoir.**

aide [ɛd] ◇ *nf* **-1.** [gén] help; **à l'~!** help!; **appeler (qqn) à l'~** to call (to sb) for help; **venir en ~ à qqn** to come to sb's aid, to help sb; ~ **ménagère** home help. **-2.** [secours financier] aid; ~ **sociale** social security *Br*, welfare *Am*. ◇ *nmf* [adjoint] assistant; ~ **de camp** MIL aide-de-camp.

◆ **à l'aide de** *loc prép* with the help OU aid of.

aide-mémoire [ɛdmemwar] *nm inv* aide-mémoire; [pour examen] revision notes *(pl).*

aider [ede] [4] *vt* to help; ~ **qqn à faire qqch** to help sb to do sthg; ~ **qqn dans qqch** to help sb with sthg; **se faire ~ par** OU **de qqn** to be helped by sb, to get help from sb; ~ **à faire qqch** to help to do sthg.

◆ **s'aider** *vp* **-1.** [s'assister mutuellement] to help each other. **-2.** [avoir recours]: **s'~ de** to use, to make use of.

aide-soignant, -e [ɛdswaɲɑ̃, ɑ̃t] *(mpl* **aides-soignants,** *fpl* **aides-soignantes)** *nm, f* nursing auxiliary *Br*, nurse's aide *Am*.

aïe [aj] *interj* **-1.** [exprime la douleur] ow!, ouch! **-2.** [exprime le désagrément] oh dear!, oh no!

AIEA *(abr de* **Agence internationale de l'énergie atomique)** *nf* IAEA.

aïeul, -e [ajœl] *nm, f sout* grandparent, grandfather *(f* grandmother).

aïeux [ajø] *nmpl* ancestors.

aigle [ɛgl] *nm* eagle.

aiglon [ɛglɔ̃] *nm* eaglet.

aigre [ɛgr] *adj* **-1.** [gén] sour. **-2.** [propos] harsh.

aigre-doux, -douce [ɛgrədu, dus] *adj* **-1.** CULIN sweet-and-sour. **-2.** [propos] bittersweet.

aigrelet, -ette [ɛgrəlɛ, ɛt] *adj* **-1.** [vin] vinegary. **-2.** [voix] sharpish.

aigrement [ɛgrəmɑ̃] *adv* bitterly.

aigrette [ɛgrɛt] *nf* egret.

aigreur [ɛgrœr] *nf* **-1.** [d'un aliment] sourness. **-2.** [d'un propos] harshness.

◆ **aigreurs d'estomac** *nfpl* heartburn *(U).*

aigri, -e [egri] *adj* embittered.

aigrir [egrir] [32] *vt* **-1.** [aliment] to make sour. **-2.** [personne] to embitter.

◆ **s'aigrir** *vp* **-1.** [aliment] to turn sour. **-2.** [personne] to become bitter.

aigu, -uë [egy] *adj* **-1.** [son] high-pitched. **-2.** [objet, lame] sharp; [angle] acute. **-3.** [douleur] sharp, acute. **-4.** [conflit, grève] bitter. **-5.** [intelligence, sens] acute, keen.
◆ **aigu** *nm* high note.

aiguillage [eguijaʒ] *nm* [RAIL - manœuvre] shunting *Br,* switching *Am;* [- dispositif] points (*pl*) *Br,* switch *Am.*

aiguille [eguij] *nf* **-1.** [gén] needle; ~ **à tricoter** knitting needle; ~ **de pin** pine needle; **chercher une ~ dans une botte de foin** *fig* to look for a needle in a haystack. **-2.** [de pendule] hand. **-3.** GÉOGR peak.

aiguiller [eguije] [3] *vt* **-1.** RAIL to shunt *Br,* to switch *Am.* **-2.** [personne, conversation] to steer, to direct.

aiguilleur [eguijœr] *nm* **-1.** RAIL pointsman *Br,* switchman *Am.* **-2.** AÉRON: ~ **du ciel** air traffic controller.

aiguillon [eguijɔ̃] *nm* **-1.** [dard] sting. **-2.** [stimulant] spur, incentive.

aiguiser [egize] [3] *vt litt & fig* to sharpen; ~ **l'appétit** to whet the appetite.

aïkido, aikido [ajkido] *nm* aikido.

ail [aj] (*pl* **ails** OU **aulx** [o]) *nm* garlic (*U*).

aile [ɛl] *nf* **-1.** [gén] wing; **battre de l'~** to be in a bad way; **donner des ~s à qqn** to lend sb wings; **voler de ses propres ~s** to stand on one's own two feet. **-2.** [de moulin] sail.

aileron [ɛlrɔ̃] *nm* **-1.** [de requin] fin. **-2.** [d'avion] aileron.

ailier [elje] *nm* winger.

aille, ailles *etc* → **aller.**

ailleurs [ajœr] *adv* elsewhere, somewhere else; **elle avait l'esprit ~** *fig* her mind was on other things; **nulle part/partout ~** nowhere/everywhere else.
◆ **d'ailleurs** *loc adv* moreover, besides.
◆ **par ailleurs** *loc adv* moreover, furthermore.

ailloli, aïoli [ajɔli] *nm* garlic mayonnaise.

aimable [ɛmabl] *adj* kind, nice.

aimablement [ɛmabləmɑ̃] *adv* kindly.

aimant¹, -e [ɛmɑ̃, ɑ̃t] *adj* loving.

aimant² [ɛmɑ̃] *nm* magnet.

aimanter [ɛmɑ̃te] [3] *vt* to magnetize.

aimer [eme] [4] *vt* **-1.** [gén] to like; ~ **bien qqch/qqn** to like sthg/sb, to be fond of sthg/sb; ~ **bien faire qqch** to (really) like doing sthg; ~ **(à) faire qqch** to like to do sthg, to like doing sthg; **j'aime à croire que ...** I like to think that ...; **elle aime qu'on l'appelle par son surnom** she likes being called by her nickname; **je n'aime pas que tu rentres seule le soir** I don't like you

coming home alone at night; **j'aimerais (bien) que tu viennes avec moi** I'd like you to come with me; **j'aimerais bien une autre tasse de café** I wouldn't mind another cup of coffee; ~ **mieux qqch** to prefer sthg; ~ **mieux faire qqch** to prefer doing OU to do sthg. **-2.** [d'amour] to love.
◆ **s'aimer** *vp* **-1.** (*emploi réfléchi*) to like o.s. **-2.** (*emploi réciproque*) to love each other; **s'~ bien** to like each other.

aine [ɛn] *nf* groin.

aîné, -e [ene] ◇ *adj* [plus âgé] elder, older; [le plus âgé] eldest, oldest. ◇ *nm, f* [plus âgé] older OU elder child, older OU eldest son/daughter; [le plus âgé] oldest OU eldest child, oldest OU eldest son/daughter; **elle est mon ~e de deux ans** she is two years older than me.

aînesse [ɛnɛs] → **droit.**

ainsi [ɛ̃si] *adv* **-1.** [manière] in this way, like this. **-2.** [valeur conclusive] thus; ~ **donc** so; **et ~ de suite** and so on, and so forth; **pour ~ dire** so to speak; ~ **soit-il** so be it.
◆ **ainsi que** *loc conj* **-1.** [comme, de même que] as. **-2.** [et] as well as.

aïoli = **ailloli.**

air [ɛr] *nm* **-1.** [gén] air; **le grand ~** the fresh air; **à l'~ libre** in the open air; **en plein ~** (out) in the open air, outside; **prendre l'~** to get some (fresh) air; **en l'~** [projet] (up) in the air; *fig* [paroles] empty; ~ **comprimé** compressed air; ~ **conditionné** air-conditioning; **s'envoyer en l'~** *vulg* to get laid. **-2.** [apparence, mine] air, look; **il a l'~ triste** he looks sad; **il a l'~ de bouder** he looks like he's sulking; **il a l'~ de faire beau** it looks like being a nice day; **sans en avoir l'~** without showing it; **d'un ~ dégagé** in a casual manner; **n'avoir l'~ de rien** to look OU seem unremarkable, to look OU seem insignificant; **un ~ de famille** a family resemblance. **-3.** MUS tune.

aire [ɛr] *nf* **-1.** [gén] area; ~ **d'atterrissage** landing strip; ~ **de jeu** playground; ~ **de repos** lay-by. **-2.** [nid] eyrie.

airelle [ɛrɛl] *nf* bilberry.

aisance [ɛzɑ̃s] *nf* **-1.** [facilité] ease. **-2.** [richesse]: **il vit dans l'~** he has an affluent lifestyle.

aise [ɛz] ◇ *nf sout* pleasure; **être à l'~** OU **à son ~** [confortable] to feel comfortable; [financièrement] to be comfortably off; **mettez-vous à l'~** make yourself comfortable; **mettre qqn mal à l'~** to make sb feel ill at ease OU uneasy; **en prendre à son ~** to do as one likes; **à votre ~** please your-

self, as you wish. ◇ *adj*: **être bien** ~ **(de faire qqch)** to be delighted (to do sthg).
◆ **aises** *nfpl*: **aimer ses** ~**s** to like one's (home) comforts; **prendre ses** ~**s** to make o.s. comfortable.

aisé, -e [eze] *adj* **-1.** [facile] easy. **-2.** [riche] well-off.

aisément [ezemã] *adv* easily.

aisselle [ɛsɛl] *nf* armpit.

ajonc [aʒɔ̃] *nm* gorse (*U*).

ajournement [aʒurnəmã] *nm* adjournment, postponement.

ajourner [aʒurne] [3] *vt* **-1.** [reporter - décision etc] to postpone; [- réunion, procès] to adjourn. **-2.** [candidat] to refer.

ajout [aʒu] *nm* addition.

ajouter [aʒute] [3] *vt* to add; ~ **que** to add that; ~ **foi à qqch** *sout* to give credence to sthg.
◆ **s'ajouter** *vp*: **s'**~ **à qqch** to be in addition to sthg.

ajustage [aʒystaʒ] *nm* fitting.

ajusté, -e [aʒyste] *adj* [coupé] fitted, tailored.

ajuster [aʒyste] [3] *vt* **-1.** [monter]: ~ **qqch (à)** to fit sthg (to). **-2.** [régler] to adjust. **-3.** [vêtement] to alter. **-4.** [tir, coup] to aim. **-5.** [arranger - coiffure, cravate] to adjust.
◆ **s'ajuster** *vp* to be adaptable.

ajusteur [aʒystœr] *nm* fitter.

alaise, alèse [alɛz] *nf* undersheet.

alambiqué, -e [alãbike] *adj* convoluted.

alarmant, -e [alarmã, ãt] *adj* alarming.

alarme [alarm] *nf* alarm; **donner l'**~ to give OU raise the alarm.

alarmer [alarme] [3] *vt* to alarm.
◆ **s'alarmer** *vp* to get OU become alarmed.

alarmiste [alarmist] ◇ *nmf* scaremonger. ◇ *adj* alarmist.

albanais, -e [albanɛ, ɛz] *adj* Albanian.
◆ **albanais** *nm* [langue] Albanian.
◆ **Albanais, -e** *nm, f* Albanian.

Albanie [albani] *nf*: **l'**~ Albania.

albâtre [albatr] *nm* alabaster.

albatros [albatros] *nm* albatross.

albinos [albinos] *nmf & adj inv* albino.

album [albɔm] *nm* album; ~ **(de) photo** photo album.

albumine [albymin] *nf* albumin.

alcalin, -e [alkalɛ̃, in] *adj* alkaline.

alchimiste [alʃimist] *nmf* alchemist.

alcool [alkɔl] *nm* alcohol; ~ **à brûler** methylated spirits (*pl*); ~ **à 90 degrés** surgi-

cal spirit; ~ **de prune/poire** plum/pear brandy.

alcoolémie [alkɔlemi] *nf*: **taux d'**~ blood alcohol level.

alcoolique [alkɔlik] *nmf & adj* alcoholic.

alcoolisé, -e [alkɔlize] *adj* alcoholic.

alcoolisme [alkɔlism] *nm* alcoholism.

Alc(o)otest® [alkotɛst] *nm* ≈ Breathalyser®; **passer un** ~ to be breathalysed.

alcôve [alkov] *nf* recess; **secret d'**~ intimate secret.

aléa [alea] *nm* (*gén pl*) *sout* hazard.

aléatoire [aleatwar] *adj* **-1.** [avenir] uncertain. **-2.** [choix] random.

alémanique [alemanik] *adj*: **Suisse** ~ German-speaking (part of) Switzerland.

alentour [alãtur] *adv* around, round about.
◆ **alentours** *nmpl* surroundings; **les** ~**s de la ville** the outskirts of the city; **aux** ~**s de** [spatial] in the vicinity of; [temporel] around.

alerte [alɛrt] ◇ *adj* **-1.** [personne, esprit] agile, alert. **-2.** [style, pas] lively. ◇ *nf* alarm, alert; **donner l'**~ to sound OU give the alert; ~ **à la bombe** bomb scare; **fausse** ~ false alarm.

alerter [alɛrte] [3] *vt* to warn, to alert.

alèse = **alaise**.

alexandrin [alɛksãdrɛ̃] *nm* alexandrine.

algèbre [alʒɛbr] *nf* algebra.

Algérie [alʒeri] *nf*: **l'**~ Algeria.

algérien, -ienne [alʒerjɛ̃, jɛn] *adj* Algerian.
◆ **Algérien, -ienne** *nm, f* Algerian.

Alger [alʒe] *n* Algiers.

algue [alg] *nf* seaweed (*U*).

alias [aljas] *adv* alias.

alibi [alibi] *nm* alibi.

aliénation [aljenasjɔ̃] *nf* alienation; ~ **mentale** insanity.

aliéné, -e [aljene] ◇ *adj* **-1.** MÉD insane. **-2.** JUR alienated. ◇ *nm, f* MÉD insane person.

aliéner [aljene] [18] *vt* to alienate.

alignement [alinmã] *nm* alignment, lining up; ~ **sur** alignment with; **être dans l'**~ **de** to be in line with.

aligner [aline] [3] *vt* **-1.** [disposer en ligne] to line up, to align. **-2.** [présenter] to set out. **-3.** [adapter]: ~ **qqch sur** to align sthg with, to bring sthg into line with.
◆ **s'aligner** *vp* to line up; **s'**~ **sur** POLIT to align o.s. with.

aliment [alimã] *nm* [nourriture] food (*U*).

alimentaire [alimãtɛr] *adj* **-1.** [gén] food (*avant n*); **c'est juste un travail** ~ I'm doing this job just for the money. **-2.** JUR maintenance (*avant n*).

alimentation [alimɑ̃tasjɔ̃] *nf* **-1.** [nourriture] diet; **magasin d'**~ food store. **-2.** [approvisionnement]: ~ **(en)** supply OU supplying *(U)* (of).

alimenter [alimɑ̃te] [3] *vt* **-1.** [nourrir] to feed. **-2.** [approvisionner]: ~ **qqch en** to supply sthg with. **-3.** *fig* [entretenir] to keep going.
♦ **s'alimenter** *vp* to eat.

alinéa [alinea] *nm* **-1.** [retrait de ligne] indent. **-2.** [dans document officiel] paragraph.

aliter [alite] [3] *vt*: **être alité** to be bedridden.
♦ **s'aliter** *vp* to take to one's bed.

allaitement [alɛtmɑ̃] *nm* [d'enfant] breastfeeding; [d'animal] suckling.

allaiter [alete] [4] *vt* [enfant] to breast-feed; [animal] to suckle.

allant [alɑ̃] *nm*: **plein d'**~ dynamic.

allé, -e [ale] *pp* → **aller**.

alléchant, -e [aleʃɑ̃, ɑ̃t] *adj* mouthwatering, tempting.

allécher [aleʃe] [18] *vt*: **il a été alléché par l'odeur/la perspective** the smell/prospect made his mouth water.

allée [ale] *nf* **-1.** [dans un jardin] path; [dans une ville] avenue. **-2.** [passage] aisle. **-3.** [trajet]: ~**s et venues** comings and goings.

allégation [alegasjɔ̃] *nf* allegation.

allégé, -e [aleʒe] *adj* [régime, produit] lowfat.

allégeance [aleʒɑ̃s] *nf* allegiance.

alléger [aleʒe] [22] *vt* **-1.** [fardeau] to lighten. **-2.** [douleur] to soothe.

allégorie [alegɔri] *nf* allegory.

allègre [alɛgr] *adj* **-1.** [ton] cheerful. **-2.** [démarche] jaunty.

allégresse [alegrɛs] *nf* elation.

alléguer [alege] [18] *vt*: ~ **une excuse** to put forward an excuse; ~ **que** to plead (that).

Allemagne [alman] *nf*: **l'**~ Germany; **l'(ex-)**~ **de l'Est** (former) East Germany; **l'(ex-)**~ **de l'Ouest** (former) West Germany.

allemand, -e [almɑ̃, ɑ̃d] *adj* German.
♦ **allemand** *nm* [langue] German.
♦ **Allemand, -e** *nm, f* German; **un Allemand de l'Est/l'Ouest** an East/a West German.

aller [ale] [31] ◇ *nm* **-1.** [trajet] outward journey. **-2.** [billet] single ticket *Br*, oneway ticket *Am*.
◇ *vi* **-1.** [gén] to go; **allez!** come on!; **allez, au revoir!** bye then!; **vas-y!** go on!; **allons-y!** let's go! **-2.** (+ *infinitif*): ~ **faire qqch** to go and do sthg; ~ **chercher les enfants à** l'école to go and fetch the children from school; ~ **travailler/se promener** to go to work/for a walk. **-3.** [indiquant un état]: **comment vas-tu？** how are you？; **je vais bien** I'm very well, I'm fine; **comment ça va？** — **ça va** [santé] how are you？ — fine OU all right; [situation] how are things？ — fine OU all right; ~ **mieux** to be better. **-4.** [convenir]: **ce type de clou ne va pas pour ce travail** this kind of nail won't do OU isn't suitable for this job; ~ **avec** to go with; ~ **à qqn** to suit sb; [suj: vêtement, taille] to fit sb; **ces couleurs ne vont pas ensemble** these colours don't go well together. **-5.** *loc*: **cela va de soi, cela va sans dire** that goes without saying; **il y a là de votre vie!** your life is at stake!, your life depends on it!; **il en va de ..., comme ...** the same goes for ... as ...; **il en va de même pour lui** the same goes for him.
◇ *v aux* (+ *infinitif*) [exprime le futur proche] to be going to, will; **je vais arriver en retard** I'm going to arrive late, I'll arrive late; **nous allons bientôt avoir fini** we'll soon have finished.
♦ **s'en aller** *vp* **-1.** [partir] to go, to be off; **allez-vous en!** go away! **-2.** [disparaître] to go away.

allergie [alɛrʒi] *nf* allergy.

allergique [alɛrʒik] *adj*: ~ **(à)** allergic (to).

aller-retour [aleratur] *nm* return (ticket).

alliage [aljaʒ] *nm* alloy.

alliance [aljɑ̃s] *nf* **-1.** [union - stratégique] alliance; [- par le mariage] union, marriage; **cousin par** ~ cousin by marriage. **-2.** [bague] wedding ring. **-3.** [organisation]: **l'Alliance française** *organization promoting French language and culture abroad*.

allié, -e [alje] ◇ *adj*: ~ **(à)** allied (to). ◇ *nm, f* ally.
♦ **Alliés** *nmpl*: **les Alliés** the Allies.

allier [alje] [9] *vt* **-1.** [métaux] to alloy. **-2.** [associer] to combine.
♦ **s'allier** *vp* to become allies; **s'**~ **qqn** to win sb over as an ally; **s'**~ **à qqn** to ally with sb.

alligator [aligatɔr] *nm* alligator.

allitération [aliterasjɔ̃] *nf* alliteration.

allô [alo] *interj* hello!

allocation [alɔkasjɔ̃] *nf* **-1.** [attribution] allocation. **-2.** [aide financière]: ~ **chômage** unemployment benefit *(U)*; ~ **logement** housing benefit *(U)*; ~**s familiales** child benefit *(U)*.

allocution [alɔkysjɔ̃] *nf* short speech.

allongé, -e [alɔ̃ʒe] *adj* **-1.** [position]: **être** ~

to be lying down OU stretched out. **-2.**
[forme] elongated.

allongement [alɔ̃ʒmɑ̃] *nm* lengthening.

allonger [alɔ̃ʒe] [17] ◇ *vt* **-1.** [gén] to
lengthen, to make longer. **-2.** [jambe, bras]
to stretch (out). **-3.** [personne] to lay down.
-4. *fam* [argent] to dish out. **-5.** *fam* [coup]
to aim. ◇ *vi* [jours] to get longer.
◆ **s'allonger** *vp* **-1.** [gén] to get longer. **-2.**
[se coucher] to lie down. **-3.** [se déployer] to
stretch (out).

allopathique [alɔpatik] *adj* allopathic.

allouer [alwe] [6] *vt*: ~ **qqch à qqn** to allocate sthg to sb.

allumage [alymaʒ] *nm* **-1.** [de feu] lighting.
-2. [d'appareil électrique] switching OU turning on. **-3.** [de moteur] ignition.

allume-cigares [alymsigar] *nm inv* cigar
lighter.

allume-gaz [alymgaz] *nm inv* gas lighter.

allumer [alyme] [3] *vt* **-1.** [lampe, radio, télé-
vision] to turn OU switch on; **allume dans la
cuisine** turn the kitchen light on. **-2.** [gaz]
to light; [cigarette] to light (up). **-3.** *fam* [per-
sonne] to turn on.
◆ **s'allumer** *vp* **-1.** [gén] to light up; **s'~
de** *fig* [de joie, curiosité] to light up with. **-2.**
ÉLECTR to come OU go on.

allumette [alymɛt] *nf* match; **craquer une
~** to strike a match.

allumeuse [alymøz] *nf fam péj* tease.

allure [alyr] *nf* **-1.** [vitesse] speed; **à toute
~** as quickly OU fast as possible. **-2.** [prestan-
ce] presence; **avoir de l'~** to have style. **-3.**
[apparence générale] appearance; **avoir une
drôle d'~** to look odd; **avoir fière ~** to cut
a striking figure.

allusion [alyzjɔ̃] *nf* allusion; **faire ~ à** to refer OU allude to.

almanach [almana] *nm* almanac.

aloès [alɔɛs] *nm* aloe.

aloi [alwa] *nm*: **de bon ~** [mesure] of real
worth; **de mauvais ~** [gaîté] not genuine;
[plaisanterie] in bad taste.

alors [alɔr] *adv* **-1.** [jadis] then, at that time.
-2. [à ce moment-là] then. **-3.** [exprimant la
conséquence] then, so; **et ~, qu'est-ce qui
s'est passé?** so what happened?; **il va se
mettre en colère — et ~?** he'll be angry —
so what? **-4.** [emploi expressif] well (then);
~, qu'est-ce qu'on fait? well, what are we
doing?; **ça ~!** well fancy that!
◆ **d'alors** *loc adv* at that time.
◆ **jusqu'alors** *loc adv* (up) until then.
◆ **alors que** *loc conj* **-1.** [exprimant le temps]
while, when. **-2.** [exprimant l'opposition]
even though; **elle est sortie ~ que c'était**

interdit she went out even though it was
forbidden; **ils aiment le café ~ que nous,
nous buvons du thé** they like coffee
whereas we drink tea.

alouette [alwɛt] *nf* lark.

alourdir [alurdir] [32] *vt* **-1.** [gén] to weigh
down, to make heavy. **-2.** *fig* [impôts] to
increase.
◆ **s'alourdir** *vp*. **-1.** [taille] to get bigger.
-2. [paupières] to grow heavy.

aloyau [alwajo] *nm* sirloin.

alpage [alpaʒ] *nm* high mountain pasture.

Alpes [alp] *nfpl*: **les ~** the Alps.

alpestre [alpɛstr] *adj* alpine.

alphabet [alfabɛ] *nm* alphabet.

alphabétique [alfabetik] *adj* alphabetical.

alphabétisation [alfabetizasjɔ̃] *nf* teaching
of literacy.

alphabétiser [alfabetize] [3] *vt*: ~ **qqn** to
teach sb (how) to read and write; ~ **un
pays** to eliminate illiteracy in a country.

alpin, -e [alpɛ̃, in] *adj* alpine.

alpinisme [alpinism] *nm* mountaineering.

alpiniste [alpinist] *nmf* mountaineer.

alsacien, -ienne [alzasjɛ̃, jɛn] *adj* Alsatian.
◆ **alsacien** *nm* [dialecte] Alsatian.
◆ **Alsacien, -ienne** *nm, f* Alsatian.

altération [alterasjɔ̃] *nf* **-1.** [dégradation -
gén] alteration, distortion; [- de santé] deterioration. **-2.** MUS inflection.

altercation [altɛrkasjɔ̃] *nf* altercation.

alter ego [altɛrego] *nm inv* alter ego.

altérer [altere] [18] *vt* **-1.** [détériorer] to spoil.
-2. [amitié, santé] to harm, to affect; [vérité,
récit] to distort.
◆ **s'altérer** *vp* **-1.** [matière - métal] to deteriorate; [- aliment] to go off, to spoil. **-2.**
[santé] to deteriorate.

alternance [altɛrnɑ̃s] *nf* **-1.** [succession] alternation; **en ~** alternately. **-2.** POLIT
change of government party.

alternatif, -ive [alternatif, iv] *adj* **-1.** [pério-
dique] alternating. **-2.** [parallèle] alternative.
◆ **alternative** *nf* alternative.

alternativement [alternativmɑ̃] *adv* alternatively.

alterner [alterne] [3] ◇ *vt*: **(faire) ~ qqch et
qqch** to alternate sthg with sthg. ◇ *vi* [se
succéder]: ~ **(avec)** to alternate (with).

altesse [altɛs] *nf*: **Son Altesse** His/Her
Highness.

altier, -ière [altje, jɛr] *adj* haughty.

altimètre [altimɛtr] *nm* altimeter.

altiport [altipɔr] *nm* *airport at high altitude,
used especially to serve ski resorts.*

altitude [altityd] *nf* altitude, height; **en** ~ **at** (high) altitude; **monter en** ~ **to** climb to altitude; **prendre de l'**~ AÉRON to gain height OU altitude.

alto [alto] *nm* [MUS - voix] alto; [- instrument] viola.

aluminium [alyminjɔm] *nm* aluminium *Br*, aluminum *Am*.

alunir [alynir] [32] *vi* to land on the moon.

alunissage [alynisaʒ] *nm* moon landing.

alvéole [alveɔl] *nf* **-1.** [cavité] cavity; ~ **dentaire** tooth socket. **-2.** [de ruche, poumon] alveolus.

amabilité [amabilite] *nf* kindness; **avoir l'**~ **de faire qqch** to be so kind as to do sthg.

amadouer [amadwe] [6] *vt* [adoucir] to tame, to pacify; [persuader] to coax.
◆ **s'amadouer** *vp* to relent.

amaigrir [amegrir] [32] *vt* to make thin OU thinner.
◆ **s'amaigrir** *vp* to get thin OU thinner.

amaigrissant, -e [amegrisã, ãt] *adj* slimming (*avant n*) *Br*, reducing (*avant n*) *Am*.

amaigrissement [amegrismã] *nm* loss of weight.

amalgame [amalgam] *nm* **-1.** TECHNOL amalgam. **-2.** [de styles] mixture. **-3.** [d'idées, de notions]: **il ne faut pas faire l'**~ **entre ces deux questions** the two issues must not be confused.

amalgamer [amalgame] [3] *vt* to combine.
◆ **s'amalgamer** *vp*; **s'**~ **avec** OU **à** to be combined OU mixed with.

amande [amãd] *nf* almond; **en** ~ *fig* almond-shaped.

amandier [amãdje] *nm* almond tree.

amanite [amanit] *nf*: ~ **phalloïde** death-cap (mushroom).

amant, -e [amã, ãt] *nm, f* lover.

amarre [amar] *nf* rope, cable; **larguer les** ~**s** [bateau] to cast off; *fam fig* [partir] to hit the road.

amarrer [amare] [3] *vt* **-1.** NAVIG to moor. **-2.** [fixer] to tie down.

amaryllis [amarilis] *nf* amaryllis.

amas [ama] *nm* pile.

amasser [amase] [3] *vt* **-1.** [objets] to pile up. **-2.** [argent] to accumulate.
◆ **s'amasser** *vp* **-1.** [gén] to pile up. **-2.** [foule] to gather.

amateur [amatœr] *nm* **-1.** [connaisseur]: ~ **de** lover of. **-2.** [non-professionnel] amateur; **faire qqch en** ~ to do sthg as a hobby. **-3.** *péj* [dilettante] amateur.

amateurisme [amatœrism] *nm* **-1.** SPORT amateurism. **-2.** *péj* [dilettantisme] amateurishness.

amazone [amazon] *nf* horsewoman; **monter en** ~ to ride sidesaddle.

Amazone [amazon] *nf*: **l'**~ the Amazon (River).

Amazonie [amazɔni] *nf*: **l'**~ the Amazon (Basin).

amazonien, -ienne [amazɔnjɛ̃, jɛn] *adj* Amazonian; **la forêt** ~**ne** the Amazon rainforest.

ambages [ãbaʒ]
◆ **sans ambages** *loc adv sout* without beating about the bush.

ambassade [ãbasad] *nf* embassy.

ambassadeur, -drice [ãbasadœr, dris] *nm, f* ambassador.

ambiance [ãbjãs] *nf* atmosphere; **il y a de l'**~! there's a good atmosphere!

ambiant, -e [ãbjã, ãt] *adj*: **température** ~**e** room temperature.

ambidextre [ãbidɛkstr] ◇ *nmf* ambidextrous person. ◇ *adj* ambidextrous.

ambigu, -uë [ãbigy] *adj* ambiguous.

ambiguïté [ãbiguite] *nf* ambiguity; **sans** ~ [parler, répondre] unambiguously; [réponse, attitude] unambiguous.

ambitieux, -ieuse [ãbisjø, jøz] ◇ *nm, f* ambitious person. ◇ *adj* ambitious.

ambition [ãbisjõ] *nf* **-1.** *péj* [arrivisme] ambitiousness. **-2.** [désir] ambition; **avoir l'**~ **de faire qqch** to have an ambition to do sthg.

ambitionner [ãbisjone] [3] *vt*: ~ **qqch/de faire qqch** to seek sthg/to do sthg.

ambivalent, -e [ãbivalã, ãt] *adj* ambivalent.

ambre [ãbr] *nm* **-1.** [couleur] amber. **-2.** [matière]: ~ **(gris)** ambergris.

ambré, -e [ãbre] *adj* [couleur] amber.

ambulance [ãbylãs] *nf* ambulance.

ambulancier, -ière [ãbylãsje, jɛr] *nm, f* ambulanceman (*f* ambulancewoman).

ambulant, -e [ãbylã, ãt] *adj* travelling (*avant n*).

âme [ɑm] *nf* **-1.** [gén] soul; **dans l'**~ [par goût] at heart; [accompli] through and through; **avoir une** ~ **de comédien** to be a born actor; **une bonne** ~ *hum* a kind soul; ~ **sœur** soulmate; **être l'**~ **de qqch** to be the heart and soul of sthg. **-2.** [caractère] spirit, soul. **-3.** *loc*: **en mon** ~ **et conscience** in all honesty; **sans rencontrer** ~ **qui vive** without seeing a living soul; **rendre l'**~ to breathe one's last.

amélioration [ameljɔrasjõ] *nf* improvement.

améliorer [ameljɔre] [3] *vt* to improve.
◆ **s'améliorer** *vp* to improve.

amen [amɛn] *adv* amen.

aménagement [amenaʒmɑ̃] *nm* **-1.** [de lieu] fitting out; ~ **du territoire** development, planning. **-2.** [de programme] planning, organizing.

aménager [amenaʒe] [17] *vt* **-1.** [pièce] to fit out. **-2.** [programme] to plan, to organize.

amende [amɑ̃d] *nf* fine; **mettre qqn à l'~** to penalize sb; **faire ~ honorable** to admit one's mistake.

amendement [amɑ̃dmɑ̃] *nm* POLIT amendment.

amender [amɑ̃de] [3] *vt* **-1.** POLIT to amend. **-2.** AGRIC to enrich.

◆ **s'amender** *vp* to mend one's ways.

amène [amɛn] *adj sout* amiable, affable.

amener [amne] [19] *vt* **-1.** [mener] to bring. **-2.** [inciter]: ~ **qqn à faire qqch** [suj: circonstances] to lead sb to do sthg; [suj: personne] to get sb to do sthg. **-3.** [occasionner, préparer] to bring about.

◆ **s'amener** *vp fam* **-1.** [arriver] to turn up, to show up. **-2.** [venir] to come.

aménorrhée [amenɔre] *nf* MÉD amenorrhoea.

amenuiser [amənɥize] [3] *vt* [rendre plus petit]: **ses cheveux amenuisent son visage** her hair makes her face look thinner; [réduire] to diminish, to reduce.

◆ **s'amenuiser** *vp* to dwindle, to diminish.

amer, -ère [amɛr] *adj* bitter.

amèrement [amɛrmɑ̃] *adv* bitterly.

américain, -e [amerikɛ̃, ɛn] *adj* American.

◆ **américain** *nm* [langue] American English.

◆ **Américain, -e** *nm, f* American.

américanisme [amerikanism] *nm* Americanism.

Amérique [amerik] *nf*: **l'~** America; **l'~ centrale** Central America; **l'~ du Nord** North America; **l'~ du Sud** South America; **l'~ latine** Latin America.

amerrir [amerir] [32] *vi* [hydravion] to land (on the sea); [cabine spatiale] to splash down.

amertume [amɛrtym] *nf* bitterness.

améthyste [ametist] *nf* amethyst.

ameublement [amœblǝmɑ̃] *nm* [meubles] furniture; [action de meubler] furnishing.

ameublir [amœblir] [32] *vt* [sol] to break up.

ameuter [amœte] [3] *vt* [curieux] to draw a crowd of; [quartier, voisins] to bring out.

ami, -e [ami] ◇ *adj* friendly. ◇ *nm, f* **-1.** [camarade] friend; ~ **d'enfance** childhood friend; **petit** ~ boyfriend; **petite** ~**e** girlfriend. **-2.** [partisan] supporter, friend.

◆ **faux ami** *nm* false friend.

amiable [amjabl] *adj* [accord] friendly, informal.

◆ **à l'amiable** *loc adv & loc adj* out of court.

amiante [amjɑ̃t] *nm* asbestos.

amibe [amib] *nf* amoeba.

amibien, -ienne [amibjɛ̃, jɛn] *adj* amoebic.

◆ **amibien** *nm* amoeba.

amical, -e, -aux [amikal, o] *adj* friendly.

◆ **amicale** *nf* association, club *(for people with a shared interest).*

amicalement [amikalmɑ̃] *adv* **-1.** [de façon amicale] amicably, in a friendly way. **-2.** [dans une lettre] yours (ever), (with) best wishes.

amidon [amidɔ̃] *nm* starch.

amidonner [amidɔne] [3] *vt* to starch.

amincir [amɛ̃sir] [32] ◇ *vt*: ~ **qqn** to make sb look slimmer. ◇ *vi* to get slimmer OU thinner.

◆ **s'amincir** *vp fig* [diminuer] to dwindle, to diminish.

amincissant, -e [amɛ̃sisɑ̃, ɑ̃t] *adj* slimming.

amiral, -aux [amiral, o] *nm* admiral.

amitié [amitje] *nf* **-1.** [affection] affection; **prendre qqn en** ~ to befriend sb. **-2.** [rapports amicaux] friendship; **faire ses** ~**s à qqn** to give sb one's good OU best wishes.

AMM *(abr de* **Autorisation de mise sur le marché)** *nf* official authorization for marketing a pharmaceutical product.

ammoniac, -iaque [amɔnjak] *adj* CHIM ammoniac.

◆ **ammoniac** *nm* ammonia.

◆ **ammoniaque** *nf* ammonia (water).

amnésie [amnezi] *nf* amnesia.

amniocentèse [amnjɔsɛ̃tɛz] *nf* amniocentesis.

amnistie [amnisti] *nf* amnesty.

amnistier [amnistje] [9] *vt* to amnesty.

amocher [amɔʃe] [3] *vt fam* to mess up.

◆ **s'amocher** *vp fam* to mess o.s. up.

amoindrir [amwɛ̃drir] [32] *vt* to diminish.

◆ **s'amoindrir** *vp* to dwindle, to diminish.

amollir [amɔlir] [32] *vt* [personne] to make soft.

◆ **s'amollir** *vp* [personne] to go soft.

amonceler [amɔ̃sle] [24] *vt* to accumulate.

◆ **s'amonceler** *vp* to pile up, to accumulate.

amoncelle, amoncelles *etc* → **amonceler**.

amont [amɔ̃] *nm* upstream (water); **en ~ de** [rivière] upriver OU upstream from; *fig* prior to.

amoral, -e, -aux [amɔral, o] *adj* **-1.** [qui ignore la morale] amoral. **-2.** [débauché] immoral.

amorce [amɔrs] *nf* **-1.** [d'explosif] priming; [de cartouche, d'obus] cap. **-2.** PÊCHE bait. **-3.** *fig* [commencement] beginnings (*pl*), germ.

amorcer [amɔrse] [16] *vt* **-1.** [explosif] to prime. **-2.** PÊCHE to bait. **-3.** *fig* [commencer] to begin, to initiate.
◆ **s'amorcer** *vp* to begin.

amorphe [amɔrf] *adj* **-1.** [personne] lifeless. **-2.** [matériau] amorphous.

amortir [amɔrtir] [32] *vt* **-1.** [atténuer - choc] to absorb; [- bruit] to deaden, to muffle. **-2.** [dette] to pay off. **-3.** [achat] to write off.

amortissement [amɔrtismɑ̃] *nm* **-1.** [de choc] absorption; [de bruit] deadening, muffling. **-2.** [de dette] payment, paying off. **-3.** [d'achat] writing off.

amortisseur [amɔrtisœr] *nm* AUTOM shock absorber.

amour [amur] *nm* **-1.** [gén] love; **~ maternel/filial** maternal/filial love; **pour l'~ de** for the love of; **pour l'~ du ciel** for heaven's sake; **faire l'~** to make love; **filer le parfait ~** to live out love's dream. **-2.** [jolie chose]: **un ~ de** a darling (little). **-3.** [personne]: **un ~** an angel, a dear.
◆ **amours** *nfpl* [vie sentimentale] love-life; **à tes ~s!** [toast] here's to you!; [quand on éternue] bless you!

amouracher [amuraʃe] [3]
◆ **s'amouracher** *vp*: **s'~ de** to become infatuated with.

amourette [amurɛt] *nf* passing fancy, brief love affair.

amoureusement [amurøzmɑ̃] *adv* amorously.

amoureux, -euse [amurø, øz] ◇ *adj* **-1.** [personne] in love; **être/tomber ~ (de)** to be/fall in love (with). **-2.** [regard, geste] loving. ◇ *nm, f* **-1.** [prétendant] suitor. **-2.** [passionné]: **~ de** lover of; **un ~ de la nature** a nature lover.

amour-propre [amurprɔpr] *nm* pride, self-respect.

amovible [amɔvibl] *adj* **-1.** [déplaçable] detachable, removable. **-2.** [fonctionnaire] removable.

ampère [ɑ̃pɛr] *nm* amp, ampere.

amphétamine [ɑ̃fetamin] *nf* amphetamine.

amphi [ɑ̃fi] *nm fam* lecture hall OU theatre; **cours en** OU **d'amphi** lecture.

amphibie [ɑ̃fibi] ◇ *nm* amphibian. ◇ *adj* amphibious.

amphithéâtre [ɑ̃fiteatr] *nm* **-1.** HIST amphitheatre. **-2.** [d'université] lecture hall OU theatre.

ample [ɑ̃pl] *adj* **-1.** [vêtement - gén] loose-fitting; [- jupe] full. **-2.** [projet] extensive; **pour de plus ~s informations** for further details.

amplement [ɑ̃pləmɑ̃] *adv* [largement] fully, amply.

ampleur [ɑ̃plœr] *nf* **-1.** [de vêtement] fullness. **-2.** [d'événement, de dégâts] extent. **-3.** *loc*: **prendre toute son ~** to reach its height.

ampli [ɑ̃pli] *nm* amp.

amplificateur, -trice [ɑ̃plifikatœr, tris] *adj* ÉLECTR amplifying; **un phénomène ~ de la croissance** *fig* a phenomenon which increases growth.
◆ **amplificateur** *nm* **-1.** [gén] amplifier. **-2.** PHOT enlarger.

amplifier [ɑ̃plifje] [9] *vt* **-1.** [mouvement, son] to amplify; [image] to magnify, to enlarge. **-2.** [scandale] to increase; [événement, problème] to highlight.
◆ **s'amplifier** *vp* [son] to grow OU get louder; *fig* [revendications, phénomène] to grow.

amplitude [ɑ̃plityd] *nf* **-1.** [de geste] fullness. **-2.** [d'onde] amplitude. **-3.** [de température] range.

ampoule [ɑ̃pul] *nf* **-1.** [de lampe] bulb. **-2.** [sur la peau] blister. **-3.** [médicament] ampoule, phial.

ampoulé, -e [ɑ̃pule] *adj péj* pompous.

amputation [ɑ̃pytasjɔ̃] *nf* MÉD amputation.

amputer [ɑ̃pyte] [3] *vt* MÉD to amputate; *fig* [couper] to cut (back OU down); **son article a été amputé d'un tiers** his article was cut by a third.

amulette [amylɛt] *nf* amulet.

amusant, -e [amyzɑ̃, ɑ̃t] *adj* [drôle] funny; [distrayant] amusing; **c'est très ~** it's great fun.

amuse-gueule [amyzgœl] *nm inv fam* cocktail snack, (party) nibble.

amusement [amyzmɑ̃] *nm* amusement (*U*).

amuser [amyze] [3] *vt* to amuse, to entertain.
◆ **s'amuser** *vp* to have fun, to have a good time; **s'~ à faire qqch** to amuse o.s. (by) doing sthg.

amygdale [amidal] *nf* tonsil.

an [ɑ̃] *nm* year; **avoir sept ~s** to be seven (years old); **l'~ dernier/prochain** last/next year; **en l'~ 2000** in the year 2000; **le premier** OU **le jour de l'~** New Year's Day; **le nouvel ~** the New Year; **bon ~ mal ~** taking the good years with the bad.

anabolisant [anabolizɑ̃] *nm* anabolic steroid.

anachronique [anakrɔnik] *adj* anachronistic.

anagramme [anagram] *nf* anagram.

ANAH (*abr de* **Agence nationale pour l'amélioration de l'habitat**) *nf national agency responsible for housing projects and restoration grants.*

anal, -e, -aux [anal, o] *adj* anal; **stade ~** PSYCHOL anal phase.

analgésique [analʒezik] *nm & adj* analgesic.

anallergique [analɛrʒik] *adj* hypoallergenic.

analogie [analɔʒi] *nf* analogy.

analogique [analɔʒik] *adj* analogue.

analogue [analɔg] ◇ *nm* equivalent, analogue. ◇ *adj* analogous, comparable.

analphabète [analfabɛt] *nmf & adj* illiterate.

analyse [analiz] *nf* -1. [étude] analysis; **en dernière ~** in the final analysis. -2. CHIM & MÉD test, analysis. -3. [psychanalyse] analysis (*U*).

analyser [analize] [3] *vt* -1. [étudier, psychanalyser] to analyse. -2. CHIM & MÉD to test, to analyse.
◆ **s'analyser** *vp* to be analysed OU understood; **un tel comportement ne s'analyse pas facilement** such behaviour is not easy to understand.

analyste [analist] *nmf* analyst.

analyste-programmeur, -euse [analistprɔgramœr, øz] (*mpl* **analystes-programmeurs,** *fpl* **analystes-programmeuses**) *nm, f* systems analyst.

analytique [analitik] *adj* analytical.

ananas [anana(s)] *nm* pineapple.

anar [anar] *nmf & adj fam* anarchist.

anarchie [anarʃi] *nf* -1. POLIT anarchy. -2. [désordre] chaos, anarchy.

anarchique [anarʃik] *adj* anarchic.

anarchiste [anarʃist] *nmf & adj* anarchist.

anathème [anatɛm] *nm* anathema; **jeter l'~ sur** *fig & sout* to curse.

Anatolie [anatoli] *nf*: **l'~** Anatolia.

anatomie [anatɔmi] *nf* anatomy.

anatomique [anatɔmik] *adj* anatomical.

ancestral, -e, -aux [ɑ̃sɛstral, o] *adj* ancestral.

ancêtre [ɑ̃sɛtr] *nmf* [aïeul] ancestor; *fig* [forme première] forerunner, ancestor; *fig* [initiateur] father (*f* mother).

anchois [ɑ̃ʃwa] *nm* anchovy.

ancien, -ienne [ɑ̃sjɛ̃, jɛn] *adj* -1. [gén] old; **l'~ franc** the old franc. -2. (*avant n*) [précédent] former, old. -3. [qui a de l'ancienneté] senior. -4. [du passé] ancient; **l'Ancien Régime** the Ancien Régime.
◆ **ancien** *nm* [mobilier]: **l'~** antiques (*pl*).
◆ **anciens** *nmpl* elders.

anciennement [ɑ̃sjɛnmɑ̃] *adv* formerly, previously.

ancienneté [ɑ̃sjɛnte] *nf* -1. [d'une tradition] oldness. -2. [d'un employé] seniority.

ancre [ɑ̃kr] *nf* NAVIG anchor; **jeter l'~** to drop anchor; **lever l'~** to weigh anchor; *fam* [partir] to make tracks.

ancrer [ɑ̃kre] [3] *vt* [bateau] to anchor; *fig* [idée, habitude] to root.

Andalousie [ɑ̃daluzi] *nf*: **l'~** Andalusia.

Andes [ɑ̃d] *nfpl*: **les ~** the Andes; **la cordillère des ~** the Andes Mountain Ranges.

Andorre [ɑ̃dɔr] *nf*: **(la principauté d')~** (the principality of) Andorra.

andouille [ɑ̃duj] *nf* -1. [charcuterie] *type of sausage made of chitterlings (pig's intestines), eaten as an hors d'œuvre.* -2. *fam* [imbécile] prat, twit.

andouillette [ɑ̃dujɛt] *nf type of sausage made of chitterlings (pig's intestines) eaten hot.*

androgyne [ɑ̃drɔʒin] ◇ *nmf* androgynous person. ◇ *adj* androgynous.

âne [an] *nm* -1. ZOOL ass, donkey. -2. *fam* [imbécile] ass.

anéantir [aneɑ̃tir] [32] *vt* -1. [détruire] to annihilate; *fig* to ruin, to wreck. -2. [démoraliser] to crush, to overwhelm.
◆ **s'anéantir** *vp* [disparaître] to vanish.

anéantissement [aneɑ̃tismɑ̃] *nm* -1. [destruction] annihilation; *fig* wrecking, ruin. -2. [abattement] dejection.

anecdote [anɛkdɔt] *nf* anecdote.

anecdotique [anɛkdɔtik] *adj* anecdotal.

anémie [anemi] *nf* MÉD anaemia; *fig* enfeeblement.

anémié, -e [anemje] *adj* anaemic.

anémier [anemje] [9] *vt* MÉD to make anaemic; *fig* to weaken.
◆ **s'anémier** *vp* MÉD to become anaemic; *fig* to weaken.

anémique [anemik] *adj* anaemic.

anémone [anemɔn] *nf* anemone.

ânerie [anri] *nf fam* -1. [caractère] stupidity (*U*). -2. [parole, acte]: **dire/faire une ~** to say/do something stupid.

ânesse [anɛs] *nf* she-ass, she-donkey.

anesthésie [anɛstezi] *nf* anaesthesia; **sous ~** under (the) anaesthetic, under anaesthesia; ~ **locale/générale** local/general anaesthetic.

anesthésier [anestezje] [9] *vt* to anaesthetize.

anesthésique [anestezik] *nm* & *adj* anaesthetic.

anesthésiste [anestezist] *nmf* anaesthetist.

aneth [anɛt] *nm* dill.

anfractuosité [ɑ̃fraktɥozite] *nf* crevice.

ange [ɑ̃ʒ] *nm* angel; ~ **gardien** guardian angel; **être aux** ~**s** *fig* to be in one's seventh heaven.

angélique [ɑ̃ʒelik] ◇ *nf* angelica. ◇ *adj* angelic.

angélus [ɑ̃ʒelys] *nm* [sonnerie] angelus (bell).

angevin, -e [ɑ̃ʒvɛ̃, in] *adj* **-1.** [de l'Anjou] of/from Anjou. **-2.** [d'Angers] of/from Angers.
◆ **Angevin, -e** *nm, f* **-1.** [de l'Anjou] person from Anjou. **-2.** [d'Angers] person from Angers.

angine [ɑ̃ʒin] *nf* [pharyngite] pharyngitis; [amygdalite] tonsillitis; ~ **de poitrine** angina (pectoris).

anglais, -e [ɑ̃glɛ, ɛz] *adj* English.
◆ **anglais** *nm* [langue] English.
◆ **Anglais, -e** *nm, f* Englishman (*f* Englishwoman); **les Anglais** the English.
◆ **anglaises** *nfpl* ringlets.
◆ **à l'anglaise** *loc adv* CULIN boiled; **filer à l'**~**e** *fig* to make OU sneak off.

angle [ɑ̃gl] *nm* **-1.** [coin] corner; ~ **mort** [zone invisible] blind spot; **arrondir les** ~**s** *fig* to smooth things over. **-2.** MATHS angle; ~ **droit/aigu/obtus** right/acute/obtuse angle; **voir les choses sous un certain** ~ *fig* to see things from a certain point of view.

Angleterre [ɑ̃glətɛr] *nf*: **l'**~ England.

anglican, -e [ɑ̃glikɑ̃, an] *adj* & *nm, f* Anglican.

anglophone [ɑ̃glɔfɔn] ◇ *nmf* Englishspeaker. ◇ *adj* English-speaking, anglophone.

anglo-saxon, -onne [ɑ̃glosaksɔ̃, ɔn] *adj* Anglo-Saxon.
◆ **anglo-saxon** *nm* [langue] Anglo-Saxon, Old English.
◆ **Anglo-Saxon, -onne** *nm, f* Anglo-Saxon.

angoisse [ɑ̃gwas] *nf* anguish.

angoissé, -e [ɑ̃gwase] ◇ *adj* anguished. ◇ *nmf* neurotic.

angoisser [ɑ̃gwase] [3] *vt* [effrayer] to cause anxiety to.
◆ **s'angoisser** *vp* **-1.** [être anxieux] to be overcome with anxiety. **-2.** *fam* [s'inquiéter] to fret.

Angola [ɑ̃gola] *nm*: **l'**~ Angola.

angolais, -e [ɑ̃gɔlɛ, ɛz] *adj* Angolan.
◆ **Angolais, -e** *nm, f* Angolan.

angora [ɑ̃gɔra] *nm* & *adj* angora.

anguille [ɑ̃gij] *nf* eel; **il y a** ~ **sous roche** *fig* something's up, something's going on.

anguleux, -euse [ɑ̃gylø, øz] *adj* angular.

anicroche [anikrɔʃ] *nf* hitch.

animal, -e, -aux [animal, o] *adj* **-1.** [propre à l'animal] animal (*avant n*). **-2.** [instinctif] instinctive.
◆ **animal** *nm* **-1.** [bête] animal; ~ **en peluche** cuddly toy; ~ **sauvage/domestique** wild/domestic animal. **-2.** *péj* [personne] lout, oaf.

animateur, -trice [animatœr, tris] *nm, f* **-1.** RADIO & TÉLÉ presenter. **-2.** [socioculturel, sportif] activities organizer. **-3.** [de manifestation] organizer.

animation [animasjɔ̃] *nf* **-1.** [de rue] activity, life; [de conversation, visage] animation. **-2.** [publicitaire] demonstration, promotion. **-3.** [activités] activities (*pl*). **-4.** CIN animation.

animé, -e [anime] *adj* [rue] lively; [conversation, visage] animated; [objet] animate.

animer [anime] [3] *vt* **-1.** [mettre de l'entrain dans] to animate, to liven up. **-2.** [présenter] to present. **-3.** [organiser des activités pour] to organize activities for.
◆ **s'animer** *vp* **-1.** [visage] to light up. **-2.** [rue] to come to life, to liven up.

animisme [animism] *nm* animism.

animiste [animist] *nmf* & *adj* animist.

animosité [animozite] *nf* animosity.

anis [ani(s)] *nm* BOT anise; CULIN aniseed.

anisette [anizɛt] *nf* anisette.

ankylosé, -e [ɑ̃kiloze] *adj* [paralysé] stiff; [engourdi] numb.

annales [anal] *nfpl* **-1.** [revue] review (*sg*), journal (*sg*). **-2.** [d'examen] past papers; **les** ~ **du bac** ≃ A-level past papers. **-3.** [chronique annuelle] chronicle, annals (*pl*); **rester dans les** ~ *fig* to go down in history.

anneau, -x [ano] *nm* **-1.** [gén] ring. **-2.** [maillon] link. **-3.** [de reptile] coil.
◆ **anneaux** *nmpl* SPORT rings.

année [ane] *nf* year; **d'**~ **en** ~ from year to year; **souhaiter la bonne** ~ **à qqn** to wish sb a Happy New Year; ~ **bissextile** leap year; ~ **fiscale** financial OU fiscal OU tax year; ~**-lumière** light year; ~ **scolaire** school year.

antérieurement

annexe [anɛks] ◇ *nf* **-1.** [de dossier] appendix, annexe. **-2.** [de bâtiment] annexe. ◇ *adj* related, associated.

annexer [anɛkse] [4] *vt* **-1.** [incorporer]: ~ qqch (à qqch) to append OU annex sthg (to sthg). **-2.** [pays] to annex.
◆ **s'annexer** *vp* **-1.** [s'attribuer] to grab. **-2.** [s'ajouter]: **s'~ à qqch** to be associated with sthg.

annexion [anɛksjɔ̃] *nf* annexation.

annihiler [aniile] [3] *vt* [réduire à néant] to destroy, to wreck.
◆ **s'annihiler** *vp* to be destroyed, to be wrecked.

anniversaire [anivɛrsɛr] ◇ *nm* [de mariage, mort, événement] anniversary; [de naissance] birthday. ◇ *adj* anniversary (avant n).

annonce [anɔ̃s] *nf* **-1.** [déclaration] announcement; *fig* sign, indication. **-2.** [texte] advertisement; ~ **commerciale** display ad; **passer une** ~ to place an advert OU advertisement; **petite** ~ classified advertisement, small ad.

annoncer [anɔ̃se] [16] *vt* **-1.** [faire savoir] to announce. **-2.** [indiquer] to herald. **-3.** [prédire] to predict.
◆ **s'annoncer** *vp*: **s'~ bien/mal** to look promising/unpromising; **la crise s'annonce** there is a crisis looming.

annonceur, -euse [anɔ̃sœr, øz] *nm, f* advertiser.

annonciateur, -trice [anɔ̃sjatœr, tris] *adj*: ~ **de qqch** heralding sthg.

Annonciation [anɔ̃sjasjɔ̃] *nf* [événement] Annunciation; [jour] Annunciation (Day).

annoter [anɔte] [3] *vt* to annotate.

annuaire [anɥɛr] *nm* annual, yearbook; ~ **téléphonique** telephone directory, phone book.

annuel, -elle [anɥɛl] *adj* **-1.** [tous les ans] annual, yearly. **-2.** [d'une année] annual.

annuellement [anɥɛlmã] *adv* annually, yearly.

annuité [anɥite] *nf* **-1.** [paiement] annual payment OU instalment. **-2.** [année de service] year (of service).

annulaire [anɥlɛr] ◇ *nm* ring finger. ◇ *adj* ring-shaped, annular.

annulation [anylasjɔ̃] *nf* **-1.** [de rendez-vous, réservation] cancellation. **-2.** [de mariage] annulment.

annuler [anyle] [3] *vt* **-1.** [rendez-vous, réservation] to cancel. **-2.** [mariage] to annul. **-3.** [procédure] to declare invalid.
◆ **s'annuler** *vp* to cancel each other out.

anoblir [anɔblir] [32] *vt* to ennoble.

anodin, -e [anɔdɛ̃, in] *adj* **-1.** [blessure] minor. **-2.** [propos] harmless. **-3.** [détail, personne] insignificant.

anomalie [anɔmali] *nf* anomaly.

ânon [anɔ̃] *nm* young donkey OU ass.

ânonner [anɔne] [3] *vt & vi* to recite in a drone.

anonymat [anɔnima] *nm* anonymity; **garder l'~** to remain anonymous.

anonyme [anɔnim] ◇ *nm* anonymous author OU donor OU caller. ◇ *adj* anonymous.

anorak [anɔrak] *nm* anorak.

anorexie [anɔrɛksi] *nf* anorexia.

anormal, -e, -aux [anɔrmal, o] ◇ *adj* **-1.** [inhabituel] abnormal, not normal. **-2.** [intolérable, injuste] wrong, not right. **-3.** [arriéré] (mentally) subnormal. ◇ *nm, f* mental defective.

anormalement [anɔrmalmã] *adv* abnormally.

ANPE (abr de **Agence nationale pour l'emploi**) *nf* national employment agency, ≃ job centre Br; **s'inscrire à l'~** to register as unemployed.

anse [ãs] *nf* **-1.** [d'ustensile] handle. **-2.** GÉOGR cove.

antagonisme [ãtagɔnism] *nm* antagonism.

antagoniste [ãtagɔnist] ◇ *nmf* antagonist. ◇ *adj* antagonistic.

antan [ãtã]
◆ **d'antan** *loc adj littéraire* of old, of yesteryear.

antarctique [ãtarktik] *adj* Antarctic; **le cercle polaire** ~ the Antarctic Circle.
◆ **Antarctique** *nm* **-1.** [continent]: **l'~** Antarctica. **-2.** [océan]: **l'~** the Antarctic (Ocean).

antécédent [ãtesedã] *nm* **-1.** (gén pl) [passé] history (sg). **-2.** GRAM antecedent.

antédiluvien, -ienne [ãtedilyvjɛ̃, jɛn] *adj* antediluvian, ancient.

antenne [ãtɛn] *nf* **-1.** [d'insecte] antenna, feeler; **avoir des ~s** *fam fig* to have a sixth sense. **-2.** [de télévision, de radio] aerial Br, antenna; **être à l'~** to be on the air; **hors** ~ off the air. **-3.** [bâtiment] unit. **-4.** [succursale] branch, office.

antépénultième [ãtepenyltjɛm] ◇ *nf* LING antepenultimate (syllable). ◇ *adj* antepenultimate.

antérieur, -e [ãterjœr] *adj* **-1.** [dans le temps] earlier, previous; ~ **à** previous OU prior to. **-2.** [dans l'espace] front (avant n).

antérieurement [ãterjœrmã] *adv* earlier, previously; ~ **à** prior to.

anthologie [ɑ̃tɔlɔʒi] *nf* anthology.

anthracite [ɑ̃trasit] ◇ *nm* anthracite. ◇ *adj inv* charcoal (grey).

anthropologie [ɑ̃trɔpɔlɔʒi] *nf* anthropology.

anthropométrie [ɑ̃trɔpɔmetri] *nf* anthropometry.

anthropophage [ɑ̃trɔpɔfaʒ] ◇ *nmf* cannibal (*human*). ◇ *adj* cannibalistic (*of humans*).

antiaérien, -ienne [ɑ̃tiaerjɛ̃, jɛn] *adj* anti-aircraft.

anti-âge [ɑ̃tiaʒ] *adj*: **crème** ~ anti-ageing cream.

antialcoolique [ɑ̃tialkɔlik] *adj*: **ligue** ~ temperance league.

antibiotique [ɑ̃tibiɔtik] *nm & adj* antibiotic.

antibrouillard [ɑ̃tibrujar] *nm & adj inv*: (**phare** OU **feu**) ~ fog lamp *Br*, foglight *Am*.

antibruit [ɑ̃tibrɥi] *adj inv* anti-noise; **mur** ~ noise reduction barrier.

antibuée [ɑ̃tibɥe] → **dispositif**.

antichambre [ɑ̃tiʃɑ̃br] *nf* antechamber; **faire** ~ *fig* to wait patiently (*to see somebody*).

anticipation [ɑ̃tisipasjɔ̃] *nf* **-1.** FIN advance; **paiement par** ~ advance payment, payment in advance. **-2.** LITTÉRATURE: **roman d'**~ science fiction novel.

anticipé, -e [ɑ̃tisipe] *adj* early.

anticiper [ɑ̃tisipe] [3] ◇ *vt* to anticipate. ◇ *vi*: ~ (**sur qqch**) to anticipate (sthg).

anticléricalisme [ɑ̃tiklerikalism] *nm* anticlericalism.

anticolonialisme [ɑ̃tikɔlɔnjalism] *nm* anticolonialism.

anticolonialiste [ɑ̃tikɔlɔnjalist] *nmf & adj* anticolonialist.

anticommunisme [ɑ̃tikɔmynism] *nm* anticommunism.

anticonformiste [ɑ̃tikɔ̃fɔrmist] *adj & nmf* non-conformist.

anticonstitutionnel, -elle [ɑ̃tikɔ̃stitysjɔnɛl] *adj* unconstitutional.

anticorps [ɑ̃tikɔr] *nm* antibody.

anticyclone [ɑ̃tisiklon] *nm* anticyclone.

antidater [ɑ̃tidate] [3] *vt* to backdate.

antidépresseur [ɑ̃tidepresœr] *nm & adj m* antidepressant.

antidérapant, -e [ɑ̃tiderapɑ̃, ɑ̃t] *adj* [pneu] non-skid; [semelle, surface] non-slip.
◆ **antidérapant** *nm* [pneu] anti-skid tyre.

antidote [ɑ̃tidɔt] *nm* antidote.

anti-effraction [ɑ̃tiefraksjɔ̃] *adj inv* [dispositif] antitheft.

antigang [ɑ̃tigɑ̃g] ◇ *adj* → **brigade**. ◇ *nf* ≃ serious crime squad.

antigel [ɑ̃tiʒɛl] *nm inv & adj inv* antifreeze.

antillais, -e [ɑ̃tije, ɛz] *adj* West Indian.
◆ **Antillais, -e** *nm, f* West Indian.

Antilles [ɑ̃tij] *nfpl*: **les** ~ the West Indies; **aux** ~ in the West Indies.

antilope [ɑ̃tilɔp] *nf* antelope.

antimilitarisme [ɑ̃timilitarism] *nm* antimilitarism.

antimilitariste [ɑ̃timilitarist] *nmf & adj* antimilitarist.

antimite [ɑ̃timit] *adj inv*: **boule** ~ mothball.

antinucléaire [ɑ̃tinykleɛr] *adj* antinuclear.

Antiope [ɑ̃tjɔp] *n* information system available via the French television network, ≃ Teletext *Br*.

antiparasite [ɑ̃tiparazit] ◇ *nm* suppressor. ◇ *adj inv* anti-interference.

antipathie [ɑ̃tipati] *nf* antipathy, hostility.

antipathique [ɑ̃tipatik] *adj* unpleasant; **elle m'est** ~ I dislike her, I don't like her.

antipelliculaire [ɑ̃tipelikyler] *adj*: **shampooing** ~ anti-dandruff shampoo.

antiphrase [ɑ̃tifraz] *nf* antiphrasis.

antipode [ɑ̃tipɔd] *nm*: **être à l'**~ OU **aux** ~**s** (**de**) [lieu] to be on the other side of the world (from); *fig* to be diametrically opposed (to).

antipoison [ɑ̃tipwazɔ̃] → **centre**.

antiquaire [ɑ̃tiker] *nmf* antique dealer.

antique [ɑ̃tik] *adj* **-1.** [de l'antiquité - civilisation] ancient; [- vase, objet] antique. **-2.** [vieux] antiquated, ancient.

antiquité [ɑ̃tikite] *nf* **-1.** [époque]: **l'Antiquité** antiquity. **-2.** [ancienneté] great age, antiquity. **-3.** [objet] antique.

antirabique [ɑ̃tirabik] *adj*: **vaccin** ~ rabies vaccine.

antiraciste [ɑ̃tirasist] *adj & nmf* antiracist.

antireflet [ɑ̃tirəflɛ] *adj inv* [surface] non-reflecting.

antirides [ɑ̃tirid] *adj inv* anti-wrinkle.

antirouille [ɑ̃tiruj] *adj inv* [traitement] rust (*avant n*); [revêtement, peinture] rustproof.

antisèche [ɑ̃tiseʃ] *nm ou nf arg scol* crib *Br*, cheat sheet *Am*.

antisémite [ɑ̃tisemit] ◇ *nmf* anti-Semite. ◇ *adj* anti-Semitic.

antiseptique [ɑ̃tisɛptik] *nm & adj* antiseptic.

antisismique [ɑ̃tisismik] *adj* earthquake-proof.

antithèse [ɑ̃titɛz] *nf* antithesis.

antitussif, -ive [ãtitysif, iv] *adj* cough (*avant n*).
◆ **antitussif** *nm* cough mixture.

antiviral, -aux [ãtiviral, o] *nm* antivirus.

antivol [ãtivɔl] ◇ *nm inv* anti-theft device. ◇ *adj inv* anti-theft.

antre [ãtr] *nm* den, lair.

anus [anys] *nm* anus.

anxiété [ãksjete] *nf* anxiety; **être dans l'~** to be very worried OU anxious.

anxieusement [ãksjøzmã] *adv* anxiously.

anxieux, -ieuse [ãksjø, jøz] ◇ *adj* anxious, worried; **être ~ de qqch** to be worried OU anxious about sthg; **être ~ de faire qqch** to be anxious to do sthg. ◇ *nm, f* worrier.

AOC (*abr de* **appellation d'origine contrôlée**) *nf label guaranteeing quality of French wine.*

aorte [aɔrt] *nf* aorta.

août [u(t)] *nm* August; **le quinze août** Assumption Day; *voir aussi* **septembre**.

aoûtat [auta] *nm* harvest tick.

apaisement [apɛzmã] *nm* **-1.** [moral] comfort. **-2.** [de douleur] alleviation. **-3.** [de tension, de crise] calming.

apaiser [apɛze] [4] *vt* **-1.** [personne] to calm down, to pacify. **-2.** [conscience] to salve; [douleur] to soothe; [soif] to slake, to quench; [faim] to assuage; [passion] to calm.
◆ **s'apaiser** *vp* **-1.** [personne] to calm down. **-2.** [besoin, passion] to be assuaged; [tempête] to subside, to abate; [douleur] to die down; [scrupules] to be allayed.

apanage [apanaʒ] *nm sout* privilege; **être l'~ de qqn/qqch** to be the prerogative of sb/sthg.

aparté [aparte] *nm* **-1.** THÉÂTRE aside. **-2.** [conversation] private conversation; **prendre qqn en ~** to take sb aside.

apartheid [apartɛd] *nm* apartheid.

apathie [apati] *nf* apathy.

apathique [apatik] *adj* apathetic.

apatride [apatrid] ◇ *nmf* stateless person. ◇ *adj* stateless.

apercevoir [apɛrsəvwar] [52] *vt* **-1.** [voir] to see, to catch sight of. **-2.** [comprendre] to perceive.
◆ **s'apercevoir** *vp*: **s'~ de qqch** to notice sthg; **s'~ que** to notice (that).

aperçois, aperçoit *etc* → **apercevoir**.

aperçu, -e [apɛrsy] *pp* → **apercevoir**.
◆ **aperçu** *nm* general idea; **donner un ~ de qqch** to give a general idea of sthg.

apéritif, -ive [aperitif, iv] *adj* which whets the appetite.

◆ **apéritif** *nm* aperitif; **prendre l'~** to have an aperitif, to have drinks (*before a meal*).

apesanteur [apəzãtœr] *nf* weightlessness.

à-peu-près [apøprɛ] *nm inv* approximation.

aphasie [afazi] *nf* aphasia.

aphone [afɔn] *adj* voiceless.

aphorisme [afɔrism] *nm* aphorism.

aphrodisiaque [afrodizjak] *nm & adj* aphrodisiac.

aphte [aft] *nm* mouth ulcer.

API (*abr de* **alphabet phonétique international**) *nm* IPA.

apiculteur, -trice [apikyltœr, tris] *nm, f* beekeeper.

apiculture [apikyltyr] *nf* beekeeping.

apitoie, apitoies *etc* → **apitoyer**.

apitoiement [apitwamã] *nm* pity.

apitoyer [apitwaje] [13] *vt* to move to pity.
◆ **s'apitoyer** *vp* to feel pity; **s'~ sur** to feel sorry for.

ap. J.-C. (*abr de* **après Jésus-Christ**) AD.

APL (*abr de* **aide personnalisée au logement**) *nf housing benefit.*

aplanir [aplanir] [32] *vt* **-1.** [aplatir] to level. **-2.** *fig* [difficulté, obstacle] to smooth away, to iron out.
◆ **s'aplanir** *vp fig* [se résoudre] to be ironed out.

aplatir [aplatir] [32] *vt* [gén] to flatten; [couture] to press flat; [cheveux] to smooth down.
◆ **s'aplatir** *vp* **-1.** [s'écraser] to be flattened. **-2.** [s'étaler] to lie flat; **s'~ devant qqn** *fig* to grovel before sb.

aplomb [aplɔ̃] *nm* **-1.** [stabilité] balance. **-2.** [audace] nerve, cheek; **garder/perdre son ~** to keep/lose one's nerve.
◆ **d'aplomb** *loc adv* steady; **se tenir d'~** to be steady; **ne pas se sentir d'~** to feel out of sorts.

apnée [apne] *nf*: **plonger en ~** to dive without breathing apparatus.

apocalypse [apɔkalips] *nf* apocalypse.

apocalyptique [apɔkaliptik] *adj* apocalyptic.

apogée [apɔʒe] *nm* ASTRON apogee; *fig* peak.

apolitique [apɔlitik] *adj* apolitical, unpolitical.

apologie [apɔlɔʒi] *nf* justification, apology; **faire l'~ de qqn/qqch** to praise sb/sthg.

apoplexie [apɔplɛksi] *nf* apoplexy.

apostrophe [apɔstrɔf] *nf* **-1.** [signe graphique] apostrophe. **-2.** [interpellation] rude remark.

apostropher [apɔstrɔfe] [3] *vt*: ~ qqn to speak rudely to sb.

apothéose [apɔteoz] *nf* **-1.** [consécration] great honour. **-2.** [point culminant - d'un spectacle] grand finale; [- d'une carrière] crowning glory.

apôtre [apotr] *nm* apostle, disciple; **se faire l'~ de qqch** *fig* to be the OU an advocate of sth.

Appalaches [apalaʃ] *nmpl*: **les ~** the Appalachians.

apparaissais, apparaissions *etc* → **apparaître**.

apparaître [aparɛtr] [91] ◇ *vi* **-1.** [gén] to appear. **-2.** [se dévoiler] to come to light. ◇ *v impers*: **il apparaît que** it seems OU appears that.

apparat [apara] *nm* pomp; **d'~** [dîner, habit] ceremonial; **en grand ~** with great pomp and ceremony.

appareil [aparɛj] *nm* **-1.** [gén] device; [électrique] appliance; INFORM unit, device; **porter un ~ (auditif)/(dentaire)** to wear a hearing aid/a brace. **-2.** [téléphone] phone, telephone; **qui est à l'~?** who's speaking? **-3.** [avion] aircraft. **-4.** [structure] apparatus. **-5.** *loc*: **dans le plus simple ~** in one's birthday suit.
◆ **appareil digestif** *nm* digestive system.
◆ **appareil photo** *nm* camera.

appareillage [aparɛjaʒ] *nm* **-1.** [équipement] equipment. **-2.** NAVIG getting under way.

appareiller [aparɛje] [4] ◇ *vt* [assortir] to match up. ◇ *vi* NAVIG to get under way.

apparemment [aparamɑ̃] *adv* apparently.

apparence [aparɑ̃s] *nf* appearance; **malgré les** OU **en dépit des ~s** in spite of appearances; **sauver les ~s** to keep up appearances.
◆ **en apparence** *loc adv* seemingly, apparently.

apparent, -e [aparɑ̃, ɑ̃t] *adj* **-1.** [superficiel, illusoire] apparent. **-2.** [visible] visible; **coutures ~es** top-stitched seams. **-3.** [évident] obvious.

apparenté, -e [aparɑ̃te] *adj*: **~ à** [personne] related to; *fig* [ressemblant] similar to; [affilié] affiliated to.

appariteur [aparitœr] *nm* porter (*in university*).

apparition [aparisjɔ̃] *nf* **-1.** [gén] appearance; **faire son ~** to make one's appearance. **-2.** [vision - RELIG] vision; [- de fantôme] apparition.

appart [apart] (*abr de* **appartement**) *nm fam* flat *Br,* apartment *Am.*

appartement [apartəmɑ̃] *nm* flat *Br,* apartment *Am.*

appartenance [apartənɑ̃s] *nf*: **~ à** [famille] belonging to; [parti] membership of.

appartenir [apartənir] [40] *vi* **-1.** [être la propriété de]: **~ à qqn** to belong to sb. **-2.** [faire partie de]: **~ à qqch** to belong to sth, to be a member of sth; **il ne m'appartient pas de faire ...** *fig* & *sout* it's not up to me to do ....

appartenu [apartəny] *pp inv* → **appartenir**.

appartiendrai, appartiendrais *etc* → **appartenir**.

apparu, -e [apary] *pp* → **apparaître**.

appât [apa] *nm* PÊCHE bait, lure.

appâter [apate] [3] *vt litt* & *fig* to lure.

appauvrir [apovrir] [32] *vt* to impoverish.
◆ **s'appauvrir** *vp* to grow poorer, to become impoverished.

appel [apɛl] *nm* **-1.** [gén] call; **faire ~ à qqn** to appeal to sb; **faire ~ à qqch** [nécessiter] to call for sth; [avoir recours à] to call on sth; **~ (téléphonique)** (phone) call. **-2.** JUR appeal; **faire ~** JUR to appeal; **sans ~** final. **-3.** [pour vérifier - gén] roll-call; [- SCOL] registration; **manquer à l'~** to be absent. **-4.** COMM: **~ d'offre** invitation to tender. **-5.** [signe]: **faire un ~ de phares** to flash one's headlights.

appelé, -e [aple] *pp* → **appeler**.
◆ **appelé** *nm* conscript.

appeler [aple] [24] ◇ *vt* **-1.** [gén] to call; **~ au secours** OU **à l'aide** to call for help. **-2.** [téléphoner] to ring, to call. **-3.** [exiger] to call for. **-4.** [entraîner] to lead to. **-5.** [nommer]: **être appelé à un poste** to be appointed to a post. **-6.** [amener]: **~ qqn à faire qqch** to call on sb to do sth. ◇ *vi* [solliciter]: **en ~ à qqch** to appeal to sth.
◆ **s'appeler** *vp* **-1.** [se nommer] to be called; **comment cela s'appelle?** what is it called?; **il s'appelle Patrick** his name is Patrick, he's called Patrick. **-2.** [se téléphoner]: **on s'appelle demain?** shall we talk tomorrow?

appellation [apɛlasjɔ̃] *nf* designation, name; **~ contrôlée** *guarantee that a wine conforms to certain conditions of origin, strength and quality*; **~ d'origine** JUR label of origin.

appelle, appelles *etc* → **appeler**.

appendice [apɛ̃dis] *nm* appendix.

appendicite [apɛ̃disit] *nf* appendicitis.

appentis [apɑ̃ti] *nm* lean-to.

appesantir [apəzɑ̃tir] [32] *vt* [démarche] to slow down.

◆ **s'appesantir** *vp* **-1.** [s'alourdir] to become heavy. **-2.** [insister]: **s'~ sur qqch** to dwell on sthg.

appétissant, -e [apetisɑ̃, ɑ̃t] *adj* [nourriture] appetizing.

appétit [apeti] *nm* appetite; **~ de qqch/de faire qqch** *fig* appetite for sthg/for doing sthg; **bon ~!** enjoy your meal!; **couper/ouvrir l'~ à qqn** to spoil/whet sb's appetite; **manger de bon ~** to eat heartily.

applaudir [aplodir] [32] ◇ *vt* to applaud. ◇ *vi* to clap, to applaud; **~ à qqch** *fig* to applaud sthg; **~ à tout rompre** *fig* to bring the house down.

applaudissements [aplodismɑ̃] *nmpl* applause *(U)*, clapping *(U)*.

applicable [aplikabl] *adj*: **~ (à)** applicable (to).

application [aplikasjɔ̃] *nf* [gén & INFORM] application; **mettre qqch en ~** to apply sthg.

applique [aplik] *nf* wall lamp.

appliquer [aplike] [3] *vt* [gén] to apply; [loi] to enforce.

◆ **s'appliquer** *vp* **-1.** [s'étaler, se poser]: **cette peinture s'applique facilement** this paint goes on easily. **-2.** [concerner]: **s'~ à qqn/qqch** to apply to sb/sthg. **-3.** [se concentrer]: **s'~ (à faire qqch)** to apply o.s. (to doing sthg).

appoint [apwɛ̃] *nm* **-1.** [monnaie] change; **donner** OU **faire l'~** to give the right money. **-2.** [aide] help, support; **d'~** [salaire, chauffage] extra.

appointements [apwɛ̃təmɑ̃] *nmpl* salary *(sg)*.

apport [apɔr] *nm* **-1.** [gén & FIN] contribution. **-2.** [de chaleur] input.

apporter [apɔrte] [3] *vt* **-1.** [gén] to bring. **-2.** [raison, preuve] to provide, to give. **-3.** [contribuer à] to give, to bring; [provoquer] to bring about. **-4.** **~ qqch à** [enrichir] to be beneficial to. **-5.** [mettre - soin] to exercise; [- attention] to give.

apposer [apoze] [3] *vt* **-1.** [affiche] to put up. **-2.** [signature] to append.

apposition [apozisjɔ̃] *nf* GRAM apposition; **en ~** in apposition.

appréciable [apresjabl] *adj* **-1.** [notable] appreciable. **-2.** [précieux]: **un grand jardin, c'est ~!** I/we really appreciate having a big garden.

appréciation [apresjasjɔ̃] *nf* **-1.** [de valeur] valuation; [de distance, poids] estimation. **-2.** [jugement] judgment. **-3.** SCOL assessment.

apprécier [apresje] [9] *vt* **-1.** [gén] to appreciate. **-2.** [évaluer] to estimate, to assess.

◆ **s'apprécier** *vp* to like one other.

appréhender [apreɑ̃de] [3] *vt* **-1.** [arrêter] to arrest. **-2.** [craindre]: **~ qqch/de faire qqch** to dread sthg/doing sthg.

appréhension [apreɑ̃sjɔ̃] *nf* apprehension.

apprenais → **apprendre**.

apprendre [aprɑ̃dr] [79] *vt* **-1.** [gén] to learn; **~ à faire qqch** to learn (how) to do sthg; **~ qqch à qqn** to teach sb sthg; **~ à qqn à faire qqch** to teach sb (how) to do sthg. **-2.** [nouvelle] to hear of, to learn of; **~ que** to hear that, to learn that; **~ qqch à qqn** to tell sb of sthg.

apprenne → **apprendre**.

apprenti, -e [aprɑ̃ti] *nm, f* [élève] apprentice; *fig* beginner; **~ sorcier** *fig* sorcerer's apprentice.

apprentissage [aprɑ̃tisaʒ] *nm* **-1.** [de métier] apprenticeship. **-2.** [formation] learning; **~ de la vie** learning about life.

apprêter [aprete] [4] *vt* to prepare.

◆ **s'apprêter** *vp* **-1.** [être sur le point]: **s'~ à faire qqch** to get ready to do sthg. **-2.** [s'habiller]: **s'~ pour qqch** to dress up for sthg.

appris, -e [apri, iz] *pp* → **apprendre**.

apprivoiser [aprivwaze] [3] *vt* to tame.

◆ **s'apprivoiser** *vp* **-1.** [animal] to become tame. **-2.** [personne] to become more sociable.

approbateur, -trice [aprɔbatœr, tris] *adj* approving.

approbation [aprɔbasjɔ̃] *nf* approval.

approchant, -e [aprɔʃɑ̃, ɑ̃t] *adj* similar; **quelque chose d'~** something similar.

approche [aprɔʃ] *nf* [arrivée] approach; **à l'~ des fêtes** as the Christmas holidays draw near; **il a pressé le pas à l'~ de la maison** he quickened his step as he approached OU drew near the house.

◆ **approches** *nfpl* [abords] surrounding area *(sg)*.

approcher [aprɔʃe] [3] ◇ *vt* **-1.** [mettre plus près] to move near, to bring near; **~ qqch de qqn/qqch** to move sthg near (to) sb/sthg. **-2.** [aborder] to go up to, to approach. **-3.** [côtoyer] to mix with. ◇ *vi* to approach, to go/come near; **approchez!** come nearer!; **n'approchez pas!** keep OU stay away!; **~ de** [moment, fin] to approach.

◆ **s'approcher** *vp* to come/go near, to approach; **s'~ de qqn/qqch** to approach sb/sthg.

approfondir [aprɔfɔ̃dir] [32] *vt* **-1.** [creuser] to make deeper. **-2.** [développer] to go further into.

◆ **s'approfondir** *vp* -1. [se creuser] to become deeper. -2. [se compliquer] to deepen.

approprié, -e [aprɔprije] *adj*: ~ (à) appropriate (to).

approprier [aprɔprije] [10] *vt* -1. [adapter] to adapt. -2. *Belg* to clean.

◆ **s'approprier** *vp* [s'adjuger] to appropriate.

approuver [apruve] [3] *vt* -1. [gén] to approve of; ~ **qqn de faire qqch** to commend sb for doing qqch. -2. JUR to approve.

approvisionnement [aprɔvizjɔnmɑ̃] *nm* supplies (*pl*), stocks (*pl*).

approvisionner [aprɔvizjɔne] [3] *vt* -1. [compte en banque] to pay money into. -2. [magasin, pays] to supply.

◆ **s'approvisionner** *vp*: **s'~ chez/à** [suj: particulier] to shop at/in; [suj: commerçant] to get one's supplies from.

approximatif, -ive [aprɔksimatif, iv] *adj* approximate, rough.

approximation [aprɔksimasjɔ̃] *nf* approximation.

approximativement [aprɔksimativmɑ̃] *adv* approximately, roughly.

appt *abr de* **appartement**.

appui [apɥi] *nm* -1. [soutien] support; **à l'~ de** in support of. -2. [de fenêtre] sill.

appuie, appuies *etc* → **appuyer**.

appui-tête [apɥitɛt] (*pl* **appuis-tête**) *nm* headrest.

appuyer [apɥije] [14] ◇ *vt* -1. [poser]: ~ **qqch sur/contre qqch** to lean sthg on/against sthg, to rest sthg on/against sthg. -2. [presser]: ~ **qqch sur/contre** to press sthg on/against. -3. *fig* [soutenir] to support. ◇ *vi* -1. [reposer]: ~ **sur** to lean OU rest on. -2. [presser] to push; ~ **sur** [bouton] to press. -3. *fig* [insister]: ~ **sur** to stress. -4. [se diriger]: ~ **sur la** OU **à droite** to bear right.

◆ **s'appuyer** *vp* -1. [se tenir]: **s'~ contre/sur** to lean against/on, to rest against/on. -2. [se baser]: **s'~ sur** to rely on. -3. [compter]: **s'~ sur** to rely on, to count on. -4. *fam* [supporter, prendre en charge]: **s'~ qqn** to put up with sb; **s'~ qqch** to take sthg on, to take on sthg.

apr. *abr de* **après**.

âpre [apr] *adj* -1. [goût, discussion, combat] bitter. -2. [ton, épreuve, critique] harsh. -3. [concurrence] fierce.

âprement [aprəmɑ̃] *adv* bitterly, fiercely.

après [aprɛ] ◇ *prép* -1. [gén] after; ~ **avoir mangé, ils ...** after having eaten OU after they had eaten, they ...; ~ **cela** after that;

~ **quoi** after which. -2. [indiquant l'attirance, l'attachement, l'hostilité]: **soupirer** ~ **qqn** to yearn for sb; **aboyer** ~ **qqn** to bark at sb; **se fâcher** ~ **qqn** to get angry at OU with sb.

◇ *adv* -1. [temps] afterwards; ~, **je rentrerai à la maison** I'll go home afterwards; **un mois** ~ one month later; **le mois d'~** the following OU next month. -2. [lieu, dans un ordre, dans un rang]: **la rue d'~** the next street; **c'est ma sœur qui vient** ~ **my** sister's next.

◆ **et après** *loc adv* (*employée interrogativement*) -1. [questionnement sur la suite] and then what? -2. [exprime l'indifférence] so what?

◆ **après coup** *loc adv* afterwards, after the event.

◆ **après tout** *loc adv* after all.

◆ **d'après** *loc prép* according to; **d'~ moi** in my opinion; **d'~ lui** according to him.

◆ **après que** *loc conj* (+ *indicatif*) after; **je le verrai** ~ **qu'il aura fini** I'll see him after OU when he's finished; ~ **qu'ils eurent dîné, ...** after dinner OU after they had dined, ...

après-demain [apredmɛ̃] *adv* the day after tomorrow.

après-guerre [apregɛr] *nm* post-war years (*pl*); **d'~** post-war.

après-midi [apremidi] *nm inv* ou *nf inv* afternoon.

après-rasage [aprerazaʒ] (*pl* **après-rasages**) *nm* & *adj inv* aftershave.

après-ski [apreski] (*pl* **après-skis**) *nm* [chaussure] snow-boot.

après-soleil [apresɔlɛj] *adj inv* after-sun (*avant n*).

après-vente [aprevɑ̃t] → **service**.

âpreté [aprəte] *nf* -1. [de goût, discussion, combat] bitterness. -2. [de voix, épreuve, critique] harshness. -3. [de concurrence] ferocity.

à-propos [aprɔpo] *nm inv* [de remarque] aptness; **faire preuve d'~** to show presence of mind.

apte [apt] *adj*: ~ **à qqch/à faire qqch** capable of sthg/of doing sthg; ~ **(au service)** MIL fit (for service).

aptitude [aptityd] *nf*: ~ **(à** OU **pour qqch)** aptitude (for sthg); ~ **à** OU **pour faire qqch** ability to do OU for doing sthg.

aquarelle [akwarɛl] *nf* watercolour.

aquarium [akwarjɔm] *nm* aquarium.

aquatique [akwatik] *adj* [plante, animal] aquatic; [milieu, paysage] watery, marshy.

aqueduc [akdyk] *nm* aqueduct.

aqueux, -euse [akø, øz] *adj* watery.

aquilin [akilɛ̃] → **nez**.

Aquitaine [akitɛn] *nf*: l'~ Aquitaine.

AR ◇ *nm* **-1.** *abr de* **accusé de réception**. **-2.** (*abr de* **aller-retour**) RTN. ◇ *abr de* **arrière**.

arabe [arab] ◇ *adj* [peuple] Arab; [désert] Arabian. ◇ *nm* [langue] Arabic.
◆ **Arabe** *nmf* Arab.

arabesque [arabɛsk] *nf* **-1.** [ornement] arabesque. **-2.** [ligne sinueuse] flourish.

Arabie [arabi] *nf*: l'~ Arabia; l'~ **Saoudite** Saudi Arabia.

arachide [araʃid] *nf* **-1.** [plante] groundnut. **-2.** [graine] peanut, groundnut.

araignée [arɛɲe] *nf* spider; **avoir une ~ dans le** OU **au plafond** *fam fig* to have a screw loose.
◆ **araignée de mer** *nf* spider crab.

araser [araze] [3] *vt* GÉOL to erode.

arbalète [arbalɛt] *nf* crossbow.

arbitrage [arbitraʒ] *nm* **-1.** [SPORT - gén] refereeing; [- au tennis, cricket] umpiring. **-2.** JUR arbitration.

arbitraire [arbitrɛr] *adj* arbitrary.

arbitrairement [arbitrɛrmɑ̃] *adv* arbitrarily.

arbitre [arbitr] *nm* **-1.** [SPORT - gén] referee; [- au tennis, cricket] umpire. **-2.** [conciliateur] arbitrator.
◆ **libre arbitre** *nm* free will.

arbitrer [arbitre] [3] *vt* **-1.** [SPORT - gén] to referee; [- au tennis, cricket] to umpire. **-2.** [conflit] to arbitrate.

arborer [arbɔre] [3] *vt* **-1.** [exhiber] to display, to sport. **-2.** [expression] to wear.

arborescence [arbɔresɑ̃s] *nf* INFORM tree.

arboriculteur, -trice [arbɔtikyltœr, tris] *nm, f* tree grower.

arboriculture [arbɔrikyltyr] *nf* tree growing.

arbouse [arbuz] *nf* arbutus berry.

arbre [arbr] *nm* **-1.** BOT & *fig* tree; ~ **fruitier** fruit tree; ~ **généalogique** family tree; ~ **de Noël** Christmas tree. **-2.** [axe] shaft; ~ **de transmission** AUTOM drive shaft, propeller shaft.

arbrisseau [arbriso] *nm* shrub.

arbuste [arbyst] *nm* shrub.

arc [ark] *nm* **-1.** [arme] bow. **-2.** [courbe] arc; ~ **de cercle** arc of a circle. **-3.** ARCHIT arch.

arcade [arkad] *nf* **-1.** ARCHIT arch; ~s arcade (*sg*). **-2.** ANAT: ~ **sourcilière** arch of the eyebrows.

arc-bouter [arkbute] [3]
◆ **s'arc-bouter** *vp* to brace o.s.

arceau [arso] *nm* **-1.** ARCHIT arch. **-2.** [objet métallique] hoop.

arc-en-ciel [arkɑ̃sjɛl] (*pl* **arcs-en-ciel**) *nm* rainbow.

archaïque [arkaik] *adj* archaic.

arche [arʃ] *nf* ARCHIT arch.

archéologie [arkeɔlɔʒi] *nf* archaeology.

archéologique [arkeɔlɔʒik] *adj* archaeological.

archéologue [arkeɔlɔg] *nmf* archaeologist.

archer [arʃe] *nm* archer.

archet [arʃɛ] *nm* MUS bow.

archétype [arketip] *nm* archetype.

archevêché [arʃəveʃe] *nm* [charge] archbishopric; [logement] archbishop's palace.

archevêque [arʃəvɛk] *nm* archbishop.

archipel [arʃipɛl] *nm* archipelago.

architecte [arʃitɛkt] *nmf* architect.

architectural, -e, -aux [arʃitɛktyral, o] *adj* architectural.

architecture [arʃitɛktyr] *nf* architecture; *fig* structure.

archiver [arʃive] [3] *vt* to archive.

archives [arʃiv] *nfpl* [de bureau] records; [de musée] archives.

archiviste [arʃivist] *nmf* archivist.

arctique [arktik] *adj* Arctic; **le cercle polaire ~** the Arctic Circle.
◆ **Arctique** *nm*: l'~ the Arctic.

ardemment [ardamɑ̃] *adv* fervently, passionately.

ardent, -e [ardɑ̃, ɑ̃t] *adj* **-1.** [soleil] blazing. **-2.** [soif, fièvre] raging; [passion] burning. **-3.** [yeux, couleur] blazing.

ardeur [ardœr] *nf* **-1.** [vigueur] fervour, enthusiasm. **-2.** [chaleur] blazing heat.

ardoise [ardwaz] *nf* slate.

ardu, -e [ardy] *adj* **-1.** [travail] arduous; [problème] difficult. **-2.** [pente] steep.

are [ar] *nm* 100 square metres.

arène [arɛn] *nf* arena; l'~ **politique** the political arena.
◆ **arènes** *nfpl* amphitheatre (*sg*).

arête [arɛt] *nf* **-1.** [de poisson] bone. **-2.** [d'un toit, d'une montagne] ridge. **-3.** [du nez] bridge.

arg. *abr de* **argus**.

argent [arʒɑ̃] *nm* **-1.** [métal, couleur] silver. **-2.** [monnaie] money; ~ **comptant** cash; ~ **liquide** (ready) cash; ~ **de poche** pocket money; **en avoir pour son ~** to get one's money's worth.

argenté, -e [arʒɑ̃te] *adj* silvery, silver.

argenterie [arʒɑ̃tri] *nf* silverware.

argentin, -e [arʒɑ̃tɛ̃, in] *adj* **-1.** [son] silvery. **-2.** [d'Argentine] Argentinian.
◆ **Argentin, -e** *nm, f* Argentinian.

Argentine [arʒɑ̃tin] *nf*: **l'~** Argentina.

argile [arʒil] *nf* clay.

argileux, -euse [arʒilø, øz] *adj* clayey.

argot [argo] *nm* slang.

argotique [argɔtik] *adj* slang (*avant n*), slangy.

arguer [arɡɥe] [8] *vi sout* [prétexter]: **~ de qqch (pour)** to put sthg forward as a reason (for).

argument [argymɑ̃] *nm* argument; **tirer ~ de qqch** to use sthg as an argument; **~ de vente** COMM selling point.

argumentation [argymɑ̃tasjɔ̃] *nf* argumentation.

argus [argys] *nm*: **coté à l'~** *rated in the guide to secondhand car prices.*

aride [arid] *adj litt* & *fig* arid; [travail] thankless.

aridité [aridite] *nf* aridity.

aristocrate [aristɔkrat] *nmf* aristocrat.

aristocratie [aristɔkrasi] *nf* aristocracy.

aristocratique [aristɔkratik] *adj* aristocratic.

arithmétique [aritmetik] ◇ *nf* arithmetic. ◇ *adj* arithmetical.

armagnac [armaɲak] *nm* armagnac.

armateur [armatœr] *nm* ship owner.

armature [armatyr] *nf* **-1.** CONSTR & *fig* framework. **-2.** [de parapluie] frame; [de soutiengorge] underwiring. **-3.** MUS key signature.

arme [arm] *nf litt* & *fig* weapon; **~ blanche** blade; **~ à feu** firearm; **passer l'~ à gauche** *fam fig* to snuff it.
◆ **armes** *nfpl* **-1.** [armée]: **les ~s** the army. **-2.** [blason] coat of arms (*sg*). **-3.** *loc*: **faire ses premières ~s** [apprendre] to learn the ropes; **fourbir ses ~s** to prepare for battle; **partir avec ~s et bagages** to leave taking everything.

armée [arme] *nf* army; **l'~ de l'air** the airforce; **l'~ de terre** the army.
◆ **Armée du salut** *nf*: **l'Armée du salut** the Salvation Army.

armement [arməmɑ̃] *nm* **-1.** [MIL - de personne] arming; [- de pays] armament; [- ensemble d'armes] arms (*pl*); **la course aux ~s** the arms race. **-2.** [de fusil] cocking. **-3.** [d'appareil-photo] winding-on. **-4.** [de navire] fitting-out.

Arménie [armeni] *nf*: **l'~** Armenia.

arménien, -ienne [armenjɛ̃, jɛn] *adj* Armenian.
◆ **arménien** *nm* [langue] Armenian.
◆ **Arménien, -ienne** *nm, f* Armenian.

armer [arme] [3] *vt* **-1.** [pourvoir en armes] to arm; **être armé pour qqch/pour faire qqch** *fig* [préparé] to be equipped for sthg/to do sthg. **-2.** [fusil] to cock. **-3.** [appareil photo] to wind on. **-4.** [navire] to fit out.
◆ **s'armer** *vp litt* & *fig*: **s'~ (de)** to arm o.s. (with).

armistice [armistis] *nm* armistice.

armoire [armwar] *nf* [gén] cupboard *Br*, closet *Am*; [garde-robe] wardrobe; **~ à glace** wardrobe with a mirror; **c'est une ~ à glace!** *fam fig* he's built like a tank!; **~ à pharmacie** medicine cabinet.

armoiries [armwari] *nfpl* coat of arms (*sg*).

armure [armyr] *nf* armour.

armurerie [armyrri] *nf* [magasin] gunsmith's (shop).

armurier [armyrje] *nm* [d'armes à feu] gunsmith; [d'armes blanches] armourer.

ARN (*abr de* **acide ribonucléique**) *nm* RNA.

arnaque [arnak] *nf fam* rip-off.

arnaquer [arnake] [3] *vt fam* to do *Br*, to swindle; **se faire ~** to be had.

aromate [arɔmat] *nm* [épice] spice; [fine herbe] herb.

aromatique [arɔmatik] *adj* aromatic.

aromatiser [arɔmatize] [3] *vt* to flavour.

arôme [arom] *nm* **-1.** [gén] aroma; [de fleur, parfum] fragrance. **-2.** [goût] flavour.

arpège [arpɛʒ] *nm* arpeggio.

arpenter [arpɑ̃te] [3] *vt* **-1.** [marcher] to pace up and down. **-2.** [terrain] to survey.

arpenteur [arpɑ̃tœr] *nm* surveyor.

arqué, -e [arke] *adj* **-1.** [objet] curved. **-2.** [jambe] bow (*avant n*), bandy; [nez] hooked; [sourcil] arched.

arr. *abr de* **arrondissement**.

arraché [araʃe]
◆ **à l'arraché** *loc adv*: **gagner** OU **emporter la victoire à l'~** to snatch victory.

arrachement [araʃmɑ̃] *nm fig* wrench.

arrache-pied [araʃpje]
◆ **d'arrache-pied** *loc adv*: **travailler d'~** to work away furiously.

arracher [araʃe] [3] *vt* **-1.** [extraire - plante] to pull up OU out; [- dent] to extract. **-2.** [déchirer - page] to tear off OU out; [- chemise, bras] to tear off. **-3.** [prendre]: **~ qqch à qqn** to snatch sthg from sb; *fig* [extorquer] to extract sthg from sb; [susciter] to wring sthg from sb. **-4.** [soustraire]: **~ qqn à** [milieu, lieu] to drag sb away from; [lit, sommeil] to drag sb from; [habitude, torpeur] to force sb out of; [mort, danger] to snatch sb from.

◆ **s'arracher** *vp* **-1.** [se détacher]: **s'~ de** OU **à** [milieu, lieu] to drag o.s. away from; [lit, sommeil] to drag o.s. from. **-2.** [se disputer]: **s'~ qqn/qqch** to fight over sb/sthg. **-3.** *fam* [partir] to split, to beat it.

arraisonner [arɛzɔne] [3] *vt* [navire] to stop and inspect.

arrangeant, -e [arɑ̃ʒɑ̃, ɑ̃t] *adj* obliging.

arrangement [arɑ̃ʒmɑ̃] *nm* **-1.** [gén] arrangement. **-2.** [accord] agreement, arrangement.

arranger [arɑ̃ʒe] [17] *vt* **-1.** [gén] to arrange. **-2.** [convenir à] to suit. **-3.** [régler] to settle. **-4.** [améliorer] to sort out. **-5.** [réparer] to fix.
◆ **s'arranger** *vp* to come to an agreement; **s'~ pour faire qqch** to manage to do sthg; **arrangez-vous pour être là à cinq heures** make sure you're there at five o'clock; **cela va s'~** things will work out.

arrdt *abr de* **arrondissement**.

arrérages [areraʒ] *nmpl* arrears.

arrestation [arɛstasjɔ̃] *nf* arrest; **être en état d'~** to be under arrest.

arrêt [arɛ] *nm* **-1.** [d'un mouvement] stopping; **à l'~** [véhicule] stationary; [machine] (switched) off; **tomber en ~ devant qqch** to stop dead in front of sthg. **-2.** [interruption] interruption; **sans ~** [sans interruption] non-stop; [sans relâche] constantly, continually; **être en ~ maladie** to be on sick leave; **~ maladie** OU **de travail** doctor's certificate; **~ du travail** stoppage. **-3.** [station]: **~ (d'autobus)** (bus) stop; **~ facultatif** request stop. **-4.** JUR decision, judgment.

arrêté [arete] *nm* **-1.** FIN settlement. **-2.** ADMIN order, decree; **par ~ préfectoral** by order of the prefect.

arrêter [arete] [4] ◇ *vt* **-1.** [gén] to stop. **-2.** [cesser]: **~ de faire qqch** to stop doing sthg; **~ de fumer** to stop smoking. **-3.** [abandonner - gén] to give up; [- école] to leave. **-4.** [voleur] to arrest. **-5.** [fixer] to decide on. ◇ *vi* to stop.
◆ **s'arrêter** *vp* to stop; **s'~ à qqch**: **il ne s'arrête pas à ces détails** he's not going to dwell on these details; **s'~ de faire** to stop doing; **s'~ chez qqn** to stay with sb.

arrhes [ar] *nfpl* deposit (*sg*).

arriéré, -e [arjere] *adj* **-1.** [mentalité, pays] backward. **-2.** [dette] outstanding, overdue.
◆ **arriéré** *nm* arrears (*pl*).

arrière [arjer] ◇ *adj inv* back, rear; **roue ~** rear OU back wheel; **marche ~** reverse gear. ◇ *nm* **-1.** [partie postérieure] back; **à l'~** at the back *Br*, in back *Am*; **assurer ses ~s** *fig* to play safe. **-2.** SPORT back.

◆ **en arrière** *loc adv* **-1.** [dans la direction opposée] back, backwards; **faire un pas en ~** to take a step back OU backwards. **-2.** [derrière, à la traîne] behind; **rester en ~** to lag behind.

◆ **en arrière de** *loc prép* behind.

arrière-boutique [arjerbutik] (*pl* **arrière-boutiques**) *nf* back shop.

arrière-garde [arjergard] (*pl* **arrière-gardes**) *nf* rearguard; **combat d'~** *litt* & *fig* rearguard action.

arrière-goût [arjergu] (*pl* **arrière-goûts**) *nm* aftertaste.

arrière-grand-mère [arjergrɑ̃mɛr] (*pl* **arrière-grands-mères**) *nf* great-grandmother.

arrière-grand-père [arjergrɑ̃pɛr] (*pl* **arrière-grands-pères**) *nm* great-grandfather.

arrière-pays [arjerpei] *nm inv* hinterland.

arrière-pensée [arjerpɑ̃se] (*pl* **arrière-pensées**) *nf* **-1.** [raison intéressée] ulterior motive. **-2.** [réserve]: **sans ~** without reservation.

arrière-plan [arjerplɑ̃] (*pl* **arrière-plans**) *nm* background.

arrière-saison [arjersɛzɔ̃] (*pl* **arrière-saisons**) *nf* late autumn.

arrière-train [arjertrɛ̃] (*pl* **arrière-trains**) *nm* hindquarters (*pl*).

arrimer [arime] [3] *vt* **-1.** [attacher] to secure. **-2.** NAVIG to stow.

arrivage [arivaʒ] *nm* **-1.** [de marchandises] consignment, delivery. **-2.** [de touristes] influx.

arrivant, -e [arivɑ̃, ɑ̃t] *nm, f* [personne] arrival.

arrivée [arive] *nf* **-1.** [venue] arrival. **-2.** TECHNOL inlet.

arriver [arive] [3] ◇ *vi* **-1.** [venir] to arrive; **en ~ à faire qqch** *fig* to begin to do sthg; **j'arrive!** (I'm) coming!; **~ à Paris** to arrive in OU reach Paris; **l'eau m'arrivait aux genoux** the water came up to my knees. **-2.** [réussir dans la vie] to succeed, to get on. **-3.** [parvenir]: **~ à faire qqch** to manage to do sthg, to succeed in doing sthg; **il n'arrive pas à faire ses devoirs** he can't do his homework.
◇ *v impers* to happen; **il arrive que** (+ *subjonctif*): **il arrive qu'il soit en retard** he is sometimes late; **il arrive à tout le monde de se décourager** we all get fed up sometimes; **il arrive à tout le monde de se tromper** anyone can make a mistake; **il lui arrive d'oublier quel jour on est** he sometimes forgets what day it is; **quoi qu'il arrive** whatever happens.

arrivisme [arivism] *nm péj* ambition.

arrogance [arɔgɑ̃s] *nf* arrogance.

arrogant, -e [arɔgɑ̃, ɑ̃t] ◇ *adj* arrogant. ◇ *nm, f* arrogant person.

arroger [arɔʒe] [17]
◆ **s'arroger** *vp*: **s'~ le droit de faire qqch** to take it on o.s. to do sthg.

arrondi [arɔ̃di] *nm* [de jupe] hemline.

arrondir [arɔ̃dir] [32] *vt* **-1.** [forme] to make round. **-2.** [capital] to increase. **-3.** [chiffre - en haut] to round up; [- en bas] to round down.
◆ **s'arrondir** *vp* [corps, visage] to fill out.

arrondissement [arɔ̃dismɑ̃] *nm* **-1.** ADMIN arrondissement (*administrative division of a département or city*). **-2.** [de somme - en bas] rounding down; [- en haut] rounding up.

arrosage [arozaʒ] *nm* [de jardin] watering; [de rue] spraying.

arroser [aroze] [3] *vt* **-1.** [jardin] to water, to spray. **-2.** [couler à travers] to flow through. **-3.** *fam* [café]: **~ son café (avec)** to lace one's coffee (with). **-4.** *fam* [repas] to wash down. **-5.** *fam* [célébrer] to celebrate. **-6.** *fam* [soudoyer]: **~ qqn** to grease sb's palm.

arrosoir [arozwar] *nm* watering can.

arsenal, -aux [arsənal, o] *nm* **-1.** [de navires] naval dockyard. **-2.** [d'armes] arsenal; **~ de pêcheur** fishing gear.

arsenic [arsənik] *nm* arsenic.

art [ar] *nm* art; **l'~ de faire qqch** the art of doing sthg; **~ culinaire** art of cooking; **~ dramatique/graphique** dramatic/graphic art; **le septième ~** cinema; **~s appliqués** applied arts; **~s et métiers** *state-funded institution offering vocational courses by correspondence or evening classes*; **Salon des Arts ménagers** ≃ Ideal Home Exhibition *Br*.

art. *abr de* **article.**

artère [arter] *nf* **-1.** ANAT artery; **~ coronaire** coronary artery.
-2. [rue] arterial road.

artériel, -ielle [arterjel] *adj* arterial.

artériosclérose [arterjɔskleroz] *nf* arteriosclerosis.

arthrite [artrit] *nf* arthritis.

arthrose [artroz] *nf* osteoarthritis.

artichaut [artiʃo] *nm* artichoke.

article [artikl] *nm* **-1.** [gén] article; **~ défini/indéfini** definite/indefinite article; **~ de fond** feature; **~s de bureau** office supplies. **-2.** INFORM record. **-3.** *loc*: **faire l'~** to make a sales pitch; **à l'~ de la mort** at death's door.

articulation [artikylasjɔ̃] *nf* **-1.** ANAT & TECHNOL joint. **-2.** [prononciation] articulation. **-3.** [d'une démonstration] structure.

articulé, -e [artikyle] *adj* jointed.

articuler [artikyle] [3] *vt* **-1.** [prononcer] to articulate. **-2.** ANAT & TECHNOL to articulate, to joint. **-3.** JUR to set out.
◆ **s'articuler** *vp* to hang together; **s'~ sur/autour de qqch** [réflexion] to be based OU centred on sthg.

artifice [artifis] *nm* **-1.** [moyen astucieux] clever device OU trick. **-2.** [tromperie] trick.

artificiel, -ielle [artifisjel] *adj* artificial.

artificiellement [artifisjelmɑ̃] *adv* artificially.

artillerie [artijri] *nf* MIL artillery.

artisan, -e [artizɑ̃, an] *nm, f* craftsman (*f* craftswoman).
◆ **artisan** *nm* [responsable]: **être l'~ de** *fig* to be the architect of.

artisanal, -e, -aux [artizanal, o] *adj* craft (*avant n*); **fabrication ~e** cottage industry.

artisanat [artizana] *nm* [métier] craft; [classe] craftsmen.

artiste [artist] *nmf* **-1.** [créateur] artist. **-2.** [interprète] performer.
◆ **artiste-peintre** *nm* painter.

artistique [artistik] *adj* artistic.

as¹ [a] → **avoir.**

as² [as] *nm* **-1.** [carte] ace. **-2.** [premier] number one. **-3.** [champion] star, ace. **-4.** *loc*: **être fringué comme l'~ de pique** *fam* to look like a scarecrow; **passer à l'~** *fam* to go by the board; **être plein aux ~** *fam* to be rolling in it.

a/s (*abr de* **aux soins de**) c/o.

AS (*abr de* **association sportive**) *nf* sports association.

ASA, Asa [aza] (*abr de* **American Standards Association**) *nf* ASA.

asc. *abr de* **ascenseur.**

ascendant, -e [asɑ̃dɑ̃, ɑ̃t] *adj* rising.
◆ **ascendant** *nm* **-1.** [influence] influence, power; **avoir de l'~ sur qqn** to have influence over sb. **-2.** ASTROL ascendant.

ascenseur [asɑ̃sœr] *nm* lift.

ascension [asɑ̃sjɔ̃] *nf* **-1.** [de montagne] ascent. **-2.** [d'avion] climb. **-3.** [progression] rise.
◆ **Ascension** *nf*: **l'Ascension** Ascension (Day).

ascensionnel, -elle [asɑ̃sjɔnɛl] *adj* upward.

ascèse [asɛz] *nf* asceticism.

ascète [asɛt] *nmf* ascetic.

ASE (*abr de* **Agence spatiale européenne**) *nf* ESA.

aseptique [asɛptik] *adj* aseptic.

ashkénase [aʃkenaz] *adj & nmf*: **(Juif)** ~ Ashkenazi; **les** ~s the Ashkenazim.

asiatique [azjatik] *adj* **-1.** [de l'Asie en général] Asian. **-2.** [d'extrême-orient] oriental.
◆ **Asiatique** *nmf* Asian.

Asie [azi] *nf*: **l'**~ Asia; **l'**~ **centrale** Central Asia; **l'**~ **du Sud-Est** Southeast Asia.

asile [azil] *nm* **-1.** [refuge] refuge. **-2.** POLIT: **demander/accorder l'**~ **politique** to seek/to grant political asylum. **-3.** *vieilli* [psychiatrique] asylum.

asocial, -e, -iaux [asɔsjal, jo] ◇ *adj* antisocial. ◇ *nm, f* social misfit.

aspect [aspɛ] *nm* **-1.** [apparence] appearance; **d'**~ **agréable** nice-looking. **-2.** [angle & LING] aspect. **-3.** [vue]: **à l'**~ **de** *sout* at the sight of.

asperge [aspɛrʒ] *nf* [légume] asparagus.

asperger [aspɛrʒe] [17] *vt*: ~ **qqch de qqch** to spray sthg with sthg; ~ **qqn de qqch** [arroser] to spray sb with sthg; [éclabousser] to splash sb with sthg.
◆ **s'asperger** *vp*: **s'**~ **de qqch** to spray o.s. with sthg.

aspérité [asperite] *nf* [du sol] bump.

asphalte [asfalt] *nm* asphalt.

asphyxie [asfiksi] *nf* **-1.** MÉD asphyxia, suffocation. **-2.** *fig* [de l'économie] paralysis.

asphyxier [asfiksje] [9] *vt* **-1.** MÉD to asphyxiate, to suffocate. **-2.** *fig* [économie] to paralyse.
◆ **s'asphyxier** *vp* to suffocate.

aspic [aspik] *nm* [vipère] asp.

aspirant, -e [aspirã, ãt] *adj*: **hotte** ~**e** cooker hood *Br*, cooker range *Am*; **pompe** ~**e** suction pump.
◆ **aspirant** *nm* [armée] ≃ officer cadet; [marine] ≃ midshipman.

aspirateur [aspiratœr] *nm* Hoover® *Br*, vacuum cleaner; **passer l'**~ to do the vacuuming OU hoovering.

aspiration [aspirasjɔ̃] *nf* **-1.** [souffle] inhalation. **-2.** TECHNOL suction. **-3.** LING aspiration.
◆ **aspirations** *nfpl* aspirations.

aspirer [aspire] [3] *vt* **-1.** [air] to inhale; [liquide] to suck up. **-2.** TECHNOL to suck up, to draw up. **-3.** ~ **à qqch/à faire qqch** to aspire to sthg/to do sthg.

aspirine [aspirin] *nf* aspirin.

assagir [asaʒir] [32] *vt* to quieten down.
◆ **s'assagir** *vp* to quieten down.

assaillant, -e [asajã, ãt] ◇ *adj* attacking. ◇ *nm, f* assailant, attacker.

assaillir [asajir] [47] *vt* to attack, to assault;

~ **qqn de qqch** *fig* to assail OU bombard sb with sthg.

assainir [asenir] [32] *vt* **-1.** [logement] to clean up. **-2.** [eau] to purify. **-3.** ÉCON to rectify, to stabilize.

assainissement [asenismã] *nm* **-1.** [de quartier] cleaning up. **-2.** [d'eau] purification. **-3.** ÉCON stabilization.

assaisonnement [asɛzɔnmã] *nm* [sauce] dressing.

assaisonner [asɛzɔne] [3] *vt* **-1.** [salade] to dress; [viande, plat] to season. **-2.** [propos] to season. **-3.** *fam* [gronder] to tell off; **se faire** ~ **par qqn** to get a (good) telling-off from sb.

assassin, -e [asasɛ̃, in] *adj* provocative.
◆ **assassin** *nm* [gén] murderer; POLIT assassin.

assassinat [asasina] *nm* [gén] murder; POLIT assassination.

assassiner [asasine] [3] *vt* [tuer - gén] to murder; [- POLIT] to assassinate.

assaut [aso] *nm* **-1.** [attaque] assault, attack; **prendre d'**~ [lieu] to storm; [personne] to attack. **-2.** SPORT bout. **-3.** *loc*: **faire** ~ **de** to vie with each other in.

assécher [aseʃe] [18] *vt* to drain.
◆ **s'assécher** *vp* to become dry, to dry up.

ASSEDIC, Assedic [asedik] (*abr de* **Associations pour l'emploi dans l'industrie et le commerce**) *nfpl* French unemployment insurance scheme; **toucher les** ~ to get unemployment benefit *Br* OU welfare *Am*.

assemblage [asãblaʒ] *nm* **-1.** [gén] assembly. **-2.** INFORM: **langage d'**~ assembler OU assembly language.

assemblée [asãble] *nf* **-1.** [réunion] meeting. **-2.** [public] gathering. **-3.** ADMIN & POLIT assembly; ~ **constituante** constituent assembly; ~ **consultative** advisory body; **l'Assemblée nationale** the (French) National Assembly.

L'ASSEMBLÉE NATIONALE:
The French parliament has two chambers: the National Assembly and the Senate. The members of the National Assembly (the 'députés') are elected in the 'élections législatives' held every five years

assembler [asãble] *vt* **-1.** [monter] to put together. **-2.** [réunir - objets] to gather (together). **-3.** [associer] to connect. **-4.** [personnes - gén] to bring together, to assemble; [- députés] to convene.
◆ **s'assembler** *vp* to gather.

assener [asəne] [19], **asséner** [asene] [18] *vt*: ~ **un coup à qqn** [frapper] to strike sb, to deal sb a blow.

assentiment [asɑ̃timɑ̃] *nm* assent; **donner son** ~ **à qqch** to give one's assent to sthg.

asseoir [aswar] [65] *vt* **-1.** [sur un siège] to put; **faire** ~ **qqn** to seat sb, to ask sb to take a seat. **-2.** [fondations] to lay. **-3.** *fig* [réputation] to establish; ~ **qqch sur qqch** to base sthg on sthg; ~ **l'impôt sur le revenu** to base taxation on income.
◆ **s'asseoir** *vp* to sit (down).

assermenté, -e [asɛrmɑ̃te] *adj* **-1.** [fonctionnaire, expert] sworn. **-2.** [témoin] under oath.

assertion [asɛrsjɔ̃] *nf* assertion.

assesseur [asesœr] *nm* assessor.

asseyais, asseyions *etc* → asseoir.

asseyez, asseyons *etc* → asseoir.

assez [ase] *adv* **-1.** [suffisamment] enough; ~ **de** enough; ~ **de lait/chaises** enough milk/chairs; **il en reste juste** ~ there is/are just enough left; **en avoir** ~ **de qqn/qqch** to have had enough of sb/sthg, to be fed up with sb/sthg. **-2.** [plutôt] quite, rather.

assidu, -e [asidy] *adj* **-1.** [élève] diligent. **-2.** [travail] painstaking. **-3.** [empressé]: ~ **(auprès de qqn)** attentive (to sb).

assiduité [asidɥite] *nf* **-1.** [zèle] diligence. **-2.** [fréquence]: **avec** ~ regularly.
◆ **assiduités** *nfpl péj & sout* attentions; **poursuivre qqn de ses** ~**s** to press one's attentions on sb.

assidûment [asidymɑ̃] *adv* **-1.** [avec zèle] assiduously, diligently. **-2.** [fréquemment] regularly.

assiégeant, -e [asjeʒɑ̃, ɑ̃t] *adj* besieging.
◆ **assiégeant** *nm* besieger.

assiéger [asjeʒe] [22] *vt litt & fig* to besiege.

assiette [asjɛt] *nf* **-1.** [vaisselle] plate; ~ **creuse** OU **à soupe** soup plate; ~ **à dessert** dessert plate; ~ **plate** dinner plate. **-2.** [de cavalier] seat. **-3.** [d'impôt] base. **-4.** CULIN: ~ **anglaise** assorted cold meats (*pl*) *Br*, cold cuts (*pl*) *Am*; ~ **de crudités** *raw vegetables served as an hors-d'œuvre*. **-5.** *loc*: **ne pas être dans son** ~ to feel off colour.

assiettée [asjete] *nf* plate, plateful.

assignation [asiɲasjɔ̃] *nf* **-1.** [attribution]: ~ **de qqch à qqn** allocation of sthg to sb. **-2.** JUR summons.

assigner [asiɲe] [3] *vt* **-1.** [fonds, tâche]: ~ **qqch à qqn** to allocate OU assign sthg to sb. **-2.** [personne]: ~ **qqn à qqch** to assign sb to sthg. **-3.** JUR: ~ **qqn en justice** to issue a writ against sb.

assimilation [asimilasjɔ̃] *nf* assimilation; ~ **de qqch à qqch** assimilation of sthg with sthg; ~ **de qqn à qqn** comparison of sb to sb.

assimiler [asimile] [3] *vt* **-1.** [aliment, connaissances] to assimilate. **-2.** [confondre]: ~ **qqch (à qqch)** to liken sthg (to sthg); ~ **qqn à qqn** to compare sb to OU with sb.
◆ **s'assimiler** *vp* **-1.** [se comparer]: **s'**~ **à qqn** to be (able to be) compared to sb. **-2.** [s'intégrer] to integrate.

assis, -e [asi, iz] ◇ *pp* → asseoir. ◇ *adj*: **place** ~**e** seat.
◆ **assise** *nf* **-1.** [base] seat, seating. **-2.** BIOL & GÉOL stratum.
◆ **assises** *nfpl* **-1.** JUR assizes. **-2.** [congrès] conference (*sg*).

assistance [asistɑ̃s] *nf* **-1.** [aide] assistance; **prêter** ~ **à qqn** to lend assistance to sb; **l'Assistance publique** *French authority which manages the social services and state-owned hospitals*; **être à l'Assistance (publique)** to be in care; ~ **technique** technical aid. **-2.** [auditoire] audience.

assistant, -e [asistɑ̃, ɑ̃t] *nm, f* **-1.** [auxiliaire] assistant; ~**e sociale** social worker. **-2.** UNIV assistant lecturer.

assister [asiste] [3] ◇ *vi*: ~ **à qqch** to be at sthg, to attend sthg. ◇ *vt* to assist.

associatif, -ive [asɔsjatif, iv] *adj* **-1.** [mémoire] associative. **-2.** [vie] community (*avant n*).

association [asɔsjasjɔ̃] *nf* **-1.** [gén] association; ~ **d'idées** association of ideas. **-2.** [union] society, association; ~ **à but non lucratif** JUR non-profit-making organization; ~ **sportive** sports club. **-3.** COMM partnership.

associé, -e [asɔsje] ◇ *adj* associated. ◇ *nm, f* **-1.** [collaborateur] associate. **-2.** [actionnaire] partner.

associer [asɔsje] [9] *vt* **-1.** [personnes] to bring together. **-2.** [idées] to associate. **-3.** [faire participer]: ~ **qqn à qqch** [inclure] to bring sb in on sthg; [prendre pour partenaire] to make sb a partner in sthg.
◆ **s'associer** *vp* **-1.** [prendre part]: **s'**~ **à qqch** [participer] to join OU participate in sthg; [partager] to share sthg. **-2.** [collaborer]: **s'**~ **à** OU **avec qqn** to join forces with sb. **-3.** [se combiner]: **s'**~ **à qqch** to be combined with sthg.

assoiffé, -e [aswafe] *adj* thirsty; *fig*: ~ **de pouvoir** power-hungry.

assois → asseoir.

assombrir [asɔ̃brir] [32] *vt* **-1.** [plonger dans

l'obscurité] to darken. **-2.** *fig* [attrister] to cast a shadow over.

◆ **s'assombrir** *vp* **-1.** [devenir sombre] to grow dark. **-2.** *fig* [s'attrister] to darken.

assommant, -e [asɔmɑ̃, ɑ̃t] *adj péj* deadly boring.

assommer [asɔme] [3] *vt* **-1.** [frapper] to knock out. **-2.** [ennuyer] to bore stiff. **-3.** [de reproches] to overwhelm.

Assomption [asɔ̃psjɔ̃] *nf*: **l'~** the Assumption.

assorti, -e [asɔrti] *adj* **-1.** [accordé]: **bien ~** well-matched; **mal ~** ill-matched; **une cravate ~e au costume** a tie which matches the suit. **-2.** [varié] assorted.

assortiment [asɔrtimɑ̃] *nm* assortment, selection.

assortir [asɔrtir] [32] *vt* **-1.** [objets]: **~ qqch à qqch** to match sthg to OU with sthg. **-2.** [magasin] to stock.

◆ **s'assortir** *vp* to match; **s'~ de qqch** to be accompanied by OU with sthg.

assoupi, -e [asupi] *adj* **-1.** [endormi] dozing. **-2.** *fig & littéraire* [sens, intérêt] dulled; [passion, haine] spent; [querelle] dormant.

assoupir [asupir] [32] *vt* **-1.** *sout* [enfant] to send to sleep. **-2.** *fig & littéraire* [douleur] to soothe.

◆ **s'assoupir** *vp* **-1.** [s'endormir] to doze off. **-2.** *fig & littéraire* [douleur] to die down.

assoupissement [asupismɑ̃] *nm* **-1.** [sommeil] doze. **-2.** *fig & sout*: **l'~ culturel** cultural apathy.

assouplir [asuplir] [32] *vt* **-1.** [corps] to make supple. **-2.** [matière] to soften. **-3.** [règlement] to relax. **-4.** [caractère] to mellow.

◆ **s'assouplir** *vp* **-1.** [physiquement] to become supple. **-2.** [moralement] to mellow.

assouplissement [asuplismɑ̃] *nm* **-1.** [de corps] making supple. **-2.** [de matière] softening. **-3.** [de règlement] easing, relaxation. **-4.** [de caractère] mellowing.

assourdir [asurdir] [32] *vt* **-1.** [rendre sourd] to deafen. **-2.** [abrutir] to exhaust, to wear out. **-3.** [amortir] to deaden, to muffle.

assouvir [asuvir] [32] *vt* to satisfy.

◆ **s'assouvir** *vp littéraire* to be satisfied.

ASSU, Assu [asy] (*abr de* **Association du sport scolaire et universitaire**) *nf* former schools and university sports association.

assujetti, -e [asyʒeti] *adj*: **~ à l'impôt** subject to tax OU taxation.

assujettir [asyʒetir] [32] *vt* **-1.** [peuple] to subjugate. **-2.** [soumettre à]: **~ qqn à qqch** to subject sb to sthg. **-3.** [fixer] to secure.

◆ **s'assujettir** *vp*: **s'~ à qqch** to submit to sthg.

assumer [asyme] [3] *vt* **-1.** [fonction - exercer] to carry out; [- prendre] to take on. **-2.** [risque, responsabilité] to accept. **-3.** [condition] to come to terms with. **-4.** [frais] to meet.

◆ **s'assumer** *vp* to come to terms with o.s.

assurance [asyrɑ̃s] *nf* **-1.** [gén] assurance. **-2.** [contrat] insurance; **contracter** OU **prendre une ~** to take out insurance; **~ maladie** health insurance; **~ tous risques** AUTOM comprehensive insurance; **~-vie** life assurance.

assuré, -e [asyre] *nm, f* policy holder; **~ social** National Insurance *Br* OU Social Security *Am* contributor.

assurément [asyremɑ̃] *adv sout* certainly.

assurer [asyre] ◇ *vt* **-1.** [promettre]: **~ à qqn que** to assure sb (that); **~ qqn de qqch, ~ qqch à qqn** to assure sb of sthg. **-2.** [permanence, liaison] to provide. **-3.** [voiture] to insure. **-4.** [paix] to ensure. **-5.** [échelle] to secure, to fix.

◆ **s'assurer** *vp* **-1.** [vérifier]: **s'~ que** to make sure (that). **-2.** COMM: **s'~ (contre qqch)** to insure o.s. (against sthg). **-3.** [être sûr]: **s'~ de qqch** to ensure sthg, to make sure of sthg. **-4.** [obtenir]: **s'~ (de) qqch** to secure sthg. **-5.** [se stabiliser] to steady o.s.

Assyrie [asiri] *nf*: **l'~** Assyria.

assyrien, -ienne [asirjɛ̃, jɛn] *adj* Assyrian.

◆ **Assyrien, -ienne** *nm, f* Assyrian.

astérisque [asterisk] *nm* asterisk.

asthmatique [asmatik] *nmf & adj* asthmatic.

asthme [asm] *nm* MÉD asthma.

asticot [astiko] *nm* maggot.

astigmate [astigmat] *nmf & adj* astigmatic.

astiquer [astike] [3] *vt* to polish.

astrakan [astrakɑ̃] *nm* astrakhan.

astral, -e, -aux [astral, o] *adj* astral, star (*avant n*).

astre [astr] *nm* star.

astreignant, -e [astrɛɲɑ̃, ɑ̃t] *adj* demanding.

astreindre [astrɛ̃dr] [81] *vt*: **~ qqn à qqch** to subject sb to sthg; **~ qqn à faire qqch** to compel sb to do sthg.

◆ **s'astreindre** *vp*: **s'~ à qqch** to subject o.s. to sthg; **s'~ à faire qqch** to compel o.s. to do sthg.

astreint, -e [astrɛ̃, ɛ̃t] *pp* → **astreindre**.

astringent, -e [astrɛ̃ʒɑ̃, ɑ̃t] *adj* astringent.

◆ **astringent** *nm* astringent.

astrologie [astrɔlɔʒi] *nf* astrology.

astrologique [astrɔlɔʒik] *adj* astrological.

astrologue [astrɔlɔg] *nm* astrologer.

astronaute [astrɔnot] *nmf* astronaut.

astronautique [astrɔnotik] *nf* astronautics (U).

astronome [astrɔnɔm] *nmf* astronomer.

astronomie [astrɔnɔmi] *nf* astronomy.

astronomique [astrɔnɔmik] *adj* astronomical.

astrophysique [astrɔfizik] *nf* astrophysics (U).

astuce [astys] *nf* **-1.** [ruse] **(clever) trick. -2.** [ingéniosité] shrewdness (U). **-3.** [plaisanterie] wisecrack.

astucieux, -ieuse [astysjø, jøz] *adj* **-1.** [idée] clever. **-2.** [personne] shrewd.

asymétrique [asimetrik] *adj* asymmetric, asymmetrical.

atavisme [atavism] *nm* atavism.

atelier [atəlje] *nm* **-1.** [d'artisan] workshop. **-2.** [de peintre] studio.

atermoiement [atɛrmwamɑ̃] *nm* **-1.** [tergiversation] procrastination. **-2.** JUR postponement.

athée [ate] ◇ *nmf* atheist. ◇ *adj* atheistic.

athénée [atene] *nm Belg* secondary school.

Athènes [atɛn] *n* Athens.

athénien, -ienne [atenjɛ̃, jɛn] *adj* Athenian.
◆ **Athénien, -ienne** *nm, f* Athenian.

athlète [atlɛt] *nmf* athlete.

athlétique [atletik] *adj* athletic.

athlétisme [atletism] *nm* athletics (U).

Atlantide [atlɑ̃tid] *nf*: **l'~** Atlantis.

atlantique [atlɑ̃tik] *adj* Atlantic.
◆ **Atlantique** *nm*: **l'Atlantique** the Atlantic (Ocean).

atlas [atlas] *nm* atlas.

Atlas [atlas] *nm*: **l'~** the Atlas Mountains (*pl*).

atmosphère [atmɔsfɛr] *nf* atmosphere.

atmosphérique [atmɔsferik] *adj* atmospheric.

atoll [atɔl] *nm* atoll.

atome [atom] *nm* atom; **avoir des ~s crochus avec qqn** to be on the same wavelength as sb.

atomique [atomik] *adj* **-1.** [gén] nuclear. **-2.** CHIM & PHYS atomic.

atomiseur [atomizœr] *nm* spray.

atone [atɔn] *adj* **-1.** [inexpressif] lifeless. **-2.** MÉD atonic. **-3.** [voyelle] unstressed.

atours [atur] *nmpl littéraire*: **paré de** OU **dans ses plus beaux ~** in all one's finery.

atout [atu] *nm* **-1.** [carte] trump; **~ cœur/pique/trèfle/carreau** hearts/spades/clubs/diamonds are trumps. **-2.** *fig* [ressource] asset, advantage.

ATP ◇ *nf* (*abr de* **Association des tennismen professionnels**) ATP. ◇ *nfpl* (*abr de* **arts et traditions populaires**) arts and crafts; **musée des ~** arts and crafts museum.

âtre [atr] *nm littéraire* hearth.

atroce [atrɔs] *adj* **-1.** [crime] atrocious, dreadful. **-2.** [souffrance] horrific, atrocious. **-3.** [temps] terrible.

atrocement [atrɔsmɑ̃] *adv* **-1.** [horriblement] horribly, terribly. **-2.** [exagérément] terribly.

atrocité [atrɔsite] *nf* **-1.** [horreur] atrocity. **-2.** [calomnie] insult.

atrophie [atrɔfi] *nf* atrophy.

atrophier [atrɔfje] [9]
◆ **s'atrophier** *vp* to atrophy.

attabler [atable] [3]
◆ **s'attabler** *vp* to sit down (at the table); **s'~ devant qqch** to sit down to sthg.

attachant, -e [ataʃɑ̃, ɑ̃t] *adj* lovable.

attache [ataʃ] *nf* [lien] fastening.
◆ **attaches** *nfpl* links, connections.

attaché, -e [ataʃe] *nm, f* attaché; **~ d'ambassade** attaché; **~ commercial/culturel/militaire** commercial/cultural/military attaché; **~ de presse** [diplomatique] press attaché; [d'organisme, d'entreprise] press officer.

attaché-case [ataʃekɛz] (*pl* **attachés-cases**) *nm* attaché case.

attachement [ataʃmɑ̃] *nm* attachment.

attacher [ataʃe] [3] ◇ *vt* **-1.** [lier]: **~ qqch (à)** to fasten OU tie sthg (to); *fig* [associer] to attach sthg (to). **-2.** [paquet] to tie up. **-3.** [lacet] to do up; [ceinture de sécurité] to fasten. **-4.** *fig* [émotionnellement]: **~ qqn à** to bind sb to. ◇ *vi* CULIN: **~ (à)** to stick (to).
◆ **s'attacher** *vp* **-1.** [émotionnellement]: **s'~ à qqn/qqch** to become attached to sb/sthg. **-2.** [se fermer] to fasten; **s'~ avec** OU **par qqch** to do up OU fasten with sthg. **-3.** [s'appliquer]: **s'~ à qqch/à faire qqch** to devote o.s. to sthg/to doing sthg, to apply o.s. to sthg/to doing sthg.

attaquant, -e [atakɑ̃, ɑ̃t] ◇ *adj* attacking. ◇ *nm, f* attacker.

attaque [atak] *nf* **-1.** [offensive] attack; **~ à main armée** holdup; *fig*: **~ contre qqn/qqch** attack on sb/sthg. **-2.** MUS [de note] attack. **-3.** *loc*: **être d'~** to be on form; **être/se sentir d'~ pour faire qqch** to be/feel up to doing sthg.

attaquer [atake] [3] *vt* **-1.** [gén] to attack. **-2.** [JUR - personne] to take to court; [- jugement] to contest. **-3.** *fam* [plat] to tuck into. **-4.** [tâche] to tackle.

◆ **s'attaquer** *vp* **-1.** [combattre]: **s'~ à qqn** to attack sb. **-2.** *fig*: **s'~ à qqch** [tâche] to tackle sthg.

attardé, -e [atarde] ◇ *adj* **-1.** [idées] outdated. **-2.** [passants] late. **-3.** [enfant] backward. ◇ *nm, f* [enfant] backward child.

attarder [atarde] [3]
◆ **s'attarder** *vp*: **s'~ à qqch** to dwell on sthg; **s'~ à faire qqch** to stay on to do OU doing sthg, to stay behind to do OU doing sthg.

atteignais, atteignions *etc* → **atteindre**.

atteindre [atɛ̃dr] [81] *vt* **-1.** [gén] to reach. **-2.** [toucher] to hit. **-3.** [affecter] to affect.

atteint, -e [atɛ̃, ɛ̃t] ◇ *pp* → **atteindre**. ◇ *adj* **-1.** [malade]: **être ~ de** to be suffering from. **-2.** *fam* [fou] touched.

◆ **atteinte** *nf* **-1.** [préjudice]: **~ à** attack on; **porter ~e à** to undermine; **hors d'~e** [hors de portée] out of reach; [inattaquable] beyond reach. **-2.** [effet] effect.

attelage [atlaʒ] *nm* **-1.** [chevaux] team. **-2.** [harnachement] harnessing (*U*).

atteler [atle] [24] *vt* **-1.** [animaux, véhicules] to hitch up; [wagons] to couple. **-2.** [à une tâche]: **~ qqn à** to assign sb to.
◆ **s'atteler** *vp*: **s'~ à** to get down to.

attelle [atɛl] *nf* splint.

attenant, -e [atnɑ̃, ɑ̃t] *adj*: **~ (à qqch)** adjoining (sthg).

attendre [atɑ̃dr] [73] ◇ *vt* **-1.** [gén] to wait for; **le déjeuner nous attend** lunch is ready; **~ que** (+ *subjonctif*): **~ que la pluie s'arrête** to wait for the rain to stop; **faire ~ qqn** [personne] to keep sb waiting; **les résultats se font ~** we're all waiting for the results. **-2.** [espérer]: **~ qqch (de qqn/qqch)** to expect sthg (from sb/sthg). **-3.** [suj: surprise, épreuve] to be in store for. ◇ *vi* to wait; **attends!** hang on!
◆ **s'attendre** *vp*: **s'~ à** to expect.
◆ **en attendant** *loc adv* **-1.** [pendant ce temps] meanwhile, in the meantime. **-2.** [quand même] all the same.

attendrir [atɑ̃drir] [32] *vt* **-1.** [viande] to tenderize. **-2.** [personne] to move.
◆ **s'attendrir** *vp*: **s'~ (sur qqn/qqch)** to be moved (by sb/sthg).

attendrissant, -e [atɑ̃drisɑ̃, ɑ̃t] *adj* moving, touching.

attendrissement [atɑ̃drismɑ̃] *nm* pity.

attendrisseur [atɑ̃drisœr] *nm* meat tenderizer.

attendu, -e [atɑ̃dy] *pp* → **attendre**.
◆ **attendu** ◇ *nm* JUR reasoning (*U*). ◇ *prép* considering.

◆ **attendu que** *loc conj* since, considering that.

attentat [atɑ̃ta] *nm* attack; **~ à la bombe** bomb attack, bombing; **~ à la pudeur** JUR indecent assault.

attente [atɑ̃t] *nf* **-1.** [station] wait; **en ~** in abeyance. **-2.** [espoir] expectation; **contre toute ~** contrary to all expectations; **répondre aux ~s de qqn** to live up to sb's expectations.

attenter [atɑ̃te] [3] *vi*: **~ à** [liberté, droit] to violate; **~ à ses jours** to attempt suicide; **~ à la vie de qqn** to make an attempt on sb's life.

attentif, -ive [atɑ̃tif, iv] *adj* **-1.** [auditoire]: **~ (à qqch)** attentive (to sthg). **-2.** [soin] careful, scrupulous.

attention [atɑ̃sjɔ̃] ◇ *nf* attention; **à l'~ de** for the attention of; **faire ~ à** [prudence] to be careful of; [concentration] to pay attention to; **porter qqch à l'~ de qqn** to bring sthg to sb's attention. ◇ *interj* watch out!, be careful!; **«~ chien méchant»** "beware of the dog"; **~ à la marche** mind the step; **«~ peinture fraîche»** "wet paint".

attentionné, -e [atɑ̃sjɔne] *adj* thoughtful; **~ auprès de** attentive to.

attentisme [atɑ̃tism] *nm* [gén] waiting game; POLIT policy of wait-and-see.

attentivement [atɑ̃tivmɑ̃] *adv* attentively, carefully.

atténuante [atenɥɑ̃t] → **circonstance**.

atténuation [atenɥasjɔ̃] *nf* [de lumière] dimming; [de propos] toning down; [de douleur] easing; **~ de peine** JUR reduction in sentence.

atténuer [atenɥe] [7] *vt* [douleur] to ease; [propos, ton] to tone down; [lumière] to dim, to subdue; [bruit] to quieten.
◆ **s'atténuer** *vp* [lumière] to dim, to fade; [bruit] to fade; [douleur] to ease.

atterrer [atere] [4] *vt* to stagger.

atterrir [aterir] [32] *vi* to land; **~ dans qqch** *fig* to land up in sthg.

atterrissage [aterisaʒ] *nm* landing; **~ sans visibilité** blind landing; **~ forcé** emergency landing.

attestation [atɛstasjɔ̃] *nf* **-1.** [certificat] certificate. **-2.** [action] attestation. **-3.** [preuve] proof.

attester [atɛste] [3] *vt* **-1.** [confirmer] to vouch for, to testify. **-2.** [certifier] to attest.

attifer [atife] [3] *vt* to get up.
◆ **s'attifer** *vp* to get OU doll o.s. up.

attique [atik] *nm* penthouse.

attirail [atiraj] *nm fam* [équipement] gear.

attirance [atirɑ̃s] *nf* attraction; **avoir/ éprouver de l'~ pour** to be/to feel attracted to.

attirant, -e [atirɑ̃, ɑ̃t] *adj* attractive.

attirer [atire] [3] *vt* **-1.** [gén] to attract. **-2.** [amener vers soi]: ~ **qqn à/vers soi** to draw sb to/towards one. **-3.** [provoquer]: ~ **des ennuis à qqn** to cause trouble for sb.
◆ **s'attirer** *vp*: **s'~ qqch** to bring sthg on o.s.

attiser [atize] [3] *vt* **-1.** [feu] to poke. **-2.** *fig* [haine] to stir up.

attitré, -e [atitre] *adj* **-1.** [habituel] usual. **-2.** [titulaire - fournisseur] by appointment; [- représentant] accredited.

attitude [atityd] *nf* **-1.** [comportement, approche] attitude. **-2.** [posture] posture.

attouchement [atuʃmɑ̃] *nm* caress.

attractif, -ive [atraktif, iv] *adj* **-1.** [force] magnetic. **-2.** [prix] attractive.

attraction [atraksjɔ̃] *nf* **-1.** [gén] attraction. **-2.** [force]: ~ **magnétique** magnetic force; **l'~ terrestre** the earth's gravitational force.
◆ **attractions** *nfpl* **-1.** [jeux] amusements. **-2.** [spectacle] attractions.

attrait [atrɛ] *nm* **-1.** [séduction] appeal. **-2.** [intérêt] attraction.
◆ **attraits** *nmpl* attractions.

attrape [atrap] *nf* trick.

attrape-nigaud [atrapnigo] (*pl* **attrape-nigauds**) *nm* con.

attraper [atrape] [3] *vt* **-1.** [gén] to catch. **-2.** *fam* [gronder] to tell off; **se faire ~ (par qqn)** to get a telling-off (from sb). **-3.** [habitude, accent] to pick up. **-4.** *fam* [tromper] to take in.

attrayant, -e [atrɛjɑ̃, ɑ̃t] *adj* attractive.

attribuer [atribɥe] [7] *vt* **-1.** [tâche, part]: ~ **qqch à qqn** to assign OU allocate sthg to sb, to assign OU allocate sb sthg; [privilège] to grant sthg to sb, to grant sb sthg; [récompense] to award sthg to sb, to award sb sthg. **-2.** [faute]: ~ **qqch à qqn** to attribute sthg to sb, to put sthg down to sb.
◆ **s'attribuer** *vp* **-1.** [s'approprier] to appropriate (for o.s.). **-2.** [revendiquer] to claim (for o.s).

attribut [atriby] *nm* **-1.** [gén] attribute. **-2.** GRAM complement.

attribution [atribysjɔ̃] *nf* **-1.** [de prix] awarding, award. **-2.** [de part, tâche] allocation, assignment. **-3.** [d'avantage] bestowing.
◆ **attributions** *nfpl* [fonctions] duties.

attrister [atriste] [3] *vt* to sadden.
◆ **s'attrister** *vp* to be saddened.

attroupement [atrupmɑ̃] *nm* crowd.

attrouper [atrupe] [3]
◆ **s'attrouper** *vp* to form a crowd, to gather.

au [o] → **à**.

aubade [obad] *nf* dawn serenade.

aubaine [obɛn] *nf* piece of good fortune.

aube [ob] *nf* **-1.** [aurore] dawn, daybreak; **à l'~** at dawn; **à l'~ de** *fig* at the dawn of. **-2.** RELIG alb.

aubépine [obepin] *nf* hawthorn.

auberge [obɛrʒ] *nf* [hôtel] inn; ~ **de jeunesse** youth hostel; **on n'est pas sorti de l'~** *fam fig* we're not out of the woods yet.

aubergine [obɛrʒin] ◇ *nf* **-1.** BOT aubergine *Br*, eggplant *Am*. **-2.** *péj* [contractuelle] traffic warden *Br*, meter maid *Am*. ◇ *adj inv* [couleur] aubergine.

aubergiste [obɛrʒist] *nmf* innkeeper.

auburn [obœrn] *adj inv* auburn.

aucun, -e [okœ̃, yn] ◇ *adj* **-1.** [sens négatif]: **ne ... ~** no; **il n'y a ~e voiture dans la rue** there aren't any cars in the street, there are no cars in the street; **sans faire ~ bruit** without making a sound. **-2.** [sens positif] any; **il lit plus qu'~ autre enfant** he reads more than any other child.
◇ *pron* **-1.** [sens négatif] none; ~ **des enfants** none of the children; ~ **d'entre nous** none of us; ~ **(des deux)** neither (of them). **-2.** [sens positif]: **plus qu'~ de nous** more than any of us; **d'~s** *sout* some (people).

aucunement [okynmɑ̃] *adv* not at all, in no way.

audace [odas] *nf* **-1.** [hardiesse] daring, boldness. **-2.** [insolence] audacity; **avoir l'~ de faire qqch** to have the cheek OU audacity to do sthg. **-3.** [innovation] daring innovation.

audacieux, -ieuse [odasjø, jøz] ◇ *adj* **-1.** [projet] daring, bold. **-2.** [personne, geste] bold. ◇ *nm, f* daring person.

au-dedans [odədɑ̃] *loc adv* inside.
◆ **au-dedans de** *loc prép* inside.

au-dehors [odəɔr] *loc adv* outside.
◆ **au-dehors de** *loc prép* outside.

au-delà [odəla] ◇ *loc adv* **-1.** [plus loin] beyond. **-2.** [davantage, plus] more. ◇ *nm*: **l'~** RELIG the beyond, the afterlife.
◆ **au-delà de** *loc prép* beyond.

au-dessous [odsu] *loc adv* below, underneath.
◆ **au-dessous de** *loc prép* below, under.

au-dessus [odsy] *loc adv* above.
◆ **au-dessus de** *loc prép* above, over.

au-devant [odəvɑ̃] *loc adv* ahead.

◆ **au-devant de** *loc prép*: **aller ~ de** to go to meet; **aller ~ du danger** to court danger.

audible [odibl] *adj* audible.

audience [odjɑ̃s] *nf* **-1.** [public, entretien] audience. **-2.** JUR hearing.

Audimat® [odimat] *nm* audience rating.

AUDIMAT:

Viewing figures for French television are calculated using a device which is installed for a period of time in selected households

---

audionumérique [odjɔnymerik] *adj* digital audio.

audiovisuel, -elle [odjɔvizɥɛl] *adj* audiovisual.

◆ **audiovisuel** *nm* TV and radio.

audit [odit] *nm* audit; **~ marketing** COMM marketing audit.

auditeur, -trice [oditœr, tris] *nm, f* listener.

◆ **auditeur** *nm* **-1.** UNIV: **~ libre** *person allowed to attend lectures without being registered,* auditor *Am.* **-2.** FIN auditor.

auditif, -ive [oditif, iv] *adj* **-1.** [appareil] hearing (*avant n*). **-2.** [mémoire] auditory.

audition [odisjɔ̃] *nf* **-1.** [fait d'entendre] hearing. **-2.** JUR examination. **-3.** THÉÂTRE audition. **-4.** MUS recital.

auditionner [odisjɔne] [3] *vt & vi* to audition.

auditoire [oditwar] *nm* [public] audience; **~ cible** COMM target audience.

auditorium [oditɔrjɔm] *nm* [de concert] auditorium; [d'enregistrement] studio.

auge [oʒ] *nf* [pour animaux] trough.

augmentation [ogmɑ̃tasjɔ̃] *nf*: **~ (de)** increase (in); **~ (de salaire)** rise (in salary).

augmenter [ogmɑ̃te] [3] ◇ *vt* to increase; [prix, salaire] to raise; [personne] to give a rise *Br* OU raise *Am* to. ◇ *vi* to increase, to rise; **le froid augmente** it's getting colder; **la douleur augmente** the pain is getting worse.

augure [ogyr] *nm* [présage] omen; **être de bon/mauvais ~** to be a good/bad sign.

augurer [ogyre] [3] *vt*: **~ bien/mal de qqch** to augur well/ill for sthg.

auguste [ogyst] *adj* august.

aujourd'hui [oʒurdɥi] *adv* today.

aulx → **ail**.

aumône [omon] *nf*: **faire l'~ à qqn** to give alms to sb; **faire l'~ de qqch à qqn** *fig* to favour sb with sthg.

aumônier [omonje] *nm* RELIG chaplain.

auparavant [oparavɑ̃] *adv* **-1.** [tout d'abord] first (of all). **-2.** [avant] before, previously.

auprès [oprɛ]

◆ **auprès de** *loc prép* **-1.** [à côté de] beside, next to. **-2.** [dans l'opinion de] in the eyes of. **-3.** [comparé à] compared with. **-4.** [en s'adressant à] to.

auquel [okɛl] → **lequel**.

aurai, auras *etc* → **avoir**.

auréole [oreɔl] *nf* **-1.** ASTRON & RELIG halo. **-2.** [trace] ring.

auréoler [oreɔle] [3] *vt*: **être auréolé de** to be crowned with.

auriculaire [orikylɛr] *nm* little finger.

aurore [orɔr] *nf* dawn; **~ boréale** northern lights (*pl*), aurora borealis; **à l'~ de** *fig* at the dawn of.

ausculter [oskylte] [3] *vt* MÉD to sound.

auspice [ospis] *nm* (*gén pl*) sign, auspice; **sous d'heureux ~s** promisingly; **sous les ~s de qqn** under the auspices of sb.

aussi [osi] *adv* **-1.** [pareillement, en plus] also, too; **moi ~** me too; **j'y vais ~** I'm going too OU as well; **il parle anglais et ~ espagnol** he speaks English as well as Spanish. **-2.** [dans une comparaison]: **~ ... que** as ... as; **il n'est pas ~ intelligent que son frère** he's not as clever as his brother; **je n'ai jamais rien vu d'~ beau** I've never seen anything so beautiful; **~ léger qu'il soit, je ne pourrai pas le porter** even though it's light OU light though it is, I won't be able to carry it; **~ incroyable que cela paraisse** incredible though OU as it may seem. **-3.** *sout* [introduisant une explication] so.

◆ **(tout) aussi bien** *loc adv* just as easily, just as well; **j'aurais pu (tout) ~ bien refuser** I could just as easily have said no.

◆ **aussi bien ... que** *loc conj* as well ... as; **tu le sais ~ bien que moi** you know as well as I do.

aussitôt [osito] *adv* immediately.

◆ **aussitôt que** *loc conj* as soon as.

austère [ostɛr] *adj* **-1.** [personne, vie] austere. **-2.** [vêtement] severe; [paysage] harsh.

austérité [osterite] *nf* **-1.** [de personne, vie] austerity. **-2.** [de vêtement] severeness; [de paysage] harshness.

austral, -e [ostral] (*pl* **australs** OU **austraux** [ostro]) *adj* southern.

Australie [ostrali] *nf*: **l'~** Australia; **l'~-Méridionale** South Australia; **l'~-Occidentale** Western Australia.

australien, -ienne [ostraljɛ̃, jɛn] *adj* Australian.

◆ **Australien, -ienne** *nm, f* Australian.

autant [otɑ̃] *adv* **-1.** [comparatif]: **~ que** as much as; **ce livre coûte ~ que l'autre** this book costs as much as the other one; ~ **de** (**... que**) [quantité] as much (**... as**); [nombre] as many (**... as**); **il a dépensé ~ d'argent que moi** he spent as much money as I did; **il y a ~ de femmes que d'hommes** there are as many women as men; ~ **il est gentil avec moi ~ il est désagréable avec elle** he is as kind to me as he is unpleasant to her. **-2.** [à un tel point, en si grande quantité] so much; [en si grand nombre] so many; ~ **de patience** so much patience; ~ **de gens** so many people; **il ne peut pas en dire ~** he can't say the same; **en faire ~** to do likewise. **-3.** [il vaut mieux]: ~ **dire la vérité** we/you *etc* may as well tell the truth.

◆ **autant que** *loc conj*: (**pour**) ~ **que je sache** as far as I know; ~ **d'hommes ~ d'avis** each to his own opinion.

◆ **d'autant** *loc adv* accordingly, in proportion.

◆ **d'autant que** *loc conj*: **d'~** (**plus**) **que** all the more so since; **d'~ moins que** all the less so since.

◆ **d'autant mieux** *loc adv* all the better; **d'~ mieux que** all the better since.

◆ **pour autant** *loc adv* for all that.

autarcie [otarsi] *nf* autarky.

autel [otɛl] *nm* altar.

auteur [otœr] *nm* **-1.** [d'œuvre] author. **-2.** [inventeur] originator. **-3.** [responsable] perpetrator.

authenticité [otɑ̃tisite] *nf* authenticity, genuineness.

authentifier [otɑ̃tifje] [9] *vt* to authenticate.

authentique [otɑ̃tik] *adj* authentic, genuine.

autisme [otism] *nm* autism.

autiste [otist] ◇ *nmf* autistic person. ◇ *adj* autistic.

autistique [otistik] *adj* autistic.

auto [oto] *nf* car; ~ **tamponneuse** dodgem *Br*, bumper car.

autobiographie [otɔbjɔgrafi] *nf* autobiography.

autobiographique [otɔbjɔgrafik] *adj* autobiographical.

autobronzant, -e [otɔbrɔ̃zɑ̃, ɑ̃t] *adj* self-tanning; **lotion ~e** self-tanning lotion.

◆ **autobronzant** *nm* self-tanning product.

autobus [otɔbys] *nm* bus; ~ **à impériale** ≃ double-decker bus.

autocar [otɔkar] *nm* coach.

autochtone [otɔktɔn] *nmf & adj* native.

autocollant, -e [otɔkɔlɑ̃, ɑ̃t] *adj* self-adhesive, sticky.

◆ **autocollant** *nm* sticker.

auto-couchettes [otɔkuʃɛt] *adj inv*: **train ~** ≃ Motorail® train.

autocritique [otɔkritik] *nf* self-criticism.

autocuiseur [otɔkɥizœr] *nm* pressure cooker.

autodéfense [otɔdefɑ̃s] *nf* self-defence.

autodétermination [otɔdetɛrminasjɔ̃] *nf* self-determination.

autodétruire [otɔdetrɥir] [98]

◆ **s'autodétruire** *vp* **-1.** [machine] to self-destruct. **-2.** [personne] to destroy o.s.

autodidacte [otɔdidakt] ◇ *nmf* self-taught person. ◇ *adj* self-taught.

autodiscipline [otɔdisiplin] *nf* self-discipline.

auto-école [otoekɔl] (*pl* **auto-écoles**) *nf* driving school.

autofinancement [otɔfinɑ̃smɑ̃] *nm* self-financing.

autofocus [otɔfɔkys] *nm & adj inv* auto-focus.

autogène [otɔʒɛn] *adj*: **training ~** autogenic training.

autogéré, -e [otɔʒere] *adj* worker-controlled, self-managed.

autogestion [otɔʒɛstjɔ̃] *nf* workers' control.

autographe [otɔgraf] ◇ *nm* autograph. ◇ *adj* autograph (*avant n*).

autoguidé, -e [otɔgide] *adj* self-guided.

automate [otɔmat] *nm* [robot] automaton.

automatique [otɔmatik] ◇ *nm* **-1.** [pistolet] automatic. **-2.** TÉLÉCOM ≃ direct dialling. ◇ *adj* TÉLÉCOM automatic.

automatiquement [otɔmatikmɑ̃] *adv* automatically.

automatisation [otɔmatizasjɔ̃] *nf* automation.

automatisme [otɔmatism] *nm* **-1.** [de machine] automatic operation. **-2.** [réflexe] automatic reaction, automatism.

automédication [otɔmedikasjɔ̃] *nf* self-medication.

automitrailleuse [otɔmitrajøz] *nf* armoured vehicle.

automnal, -e, -aux [otɔnal, o] *adj* autumnal, autumn (*avant n*).

automne [otɔn] *nm* autumn; **être à l'~ de sa vie** *fig* to be in the autumn of one's life.

automobile [otɔmɔbil] ◇ *nf* car, automobile *Am*. ◇ *adj* [industrie, accessoires] car (*avant n*), automobile (*avant n*) *Am*; [véhicule] motor (*avant n*).

automobiliste [otɔmɔbilist] *nmf* motorist.

automoteur, -trice [otɔmɔtœr, tris] *adj* self-propelled.

◆ **automoteur** *nm* large self-propelled river barge.

◆ **automotrice** *nf* railcar.

autonettoyant, -e [otɔnɛtwajɑ̃, ɑ̃t] *adj* self-cleaning.

autonome [otɔnɔm] *adj* **-1.** [gén] autonomous, independent. **-2.** INFORM off-line. **-3.** [appareil] self-contained.

autonomie [otɔnɔmi] *nf* **-1.** [indépendance] autonomy, independence. **-2.** AUTOM & AVIAT range; ~ **de vol** AVIAT flight range. **-3.** POLIT autonomy, self-government.

autonomiste [otɔnɔmist] *nmf & adj* separatist.

autoportrait [otɔpɔrtrɛ] *nm* self-portrait.

autopropulsé, -e [otɔprɔpylse] *adj* self-propelled.

autopsie [otɔpsi] *nf* post-mortem, autopsy.

autoradio [otoradjo] *nm* car radio.

autorail [otoraj] *nm* railcar.

auto-reverse [otɔrivœrs] *adj inv* auto-reverse.

autorisation [otɔrizasjɔ̃] *nf* **-1.** [permission] permission, authorization; **avoir l'~ de faire qqch** to be allowed to do sthg; **demander/accorder l'~ de faire qqch** to request/grant permission to do sthg. **-2.** [attestation] pass, permit.

autorisé, -e [otɔrize] *adj* [personne] in authority; **milieux ~s** official circles.

autoriser [otɔrize] [3] *vt* to authorize, to permit; ~ **qqn à faire qqch** [permission] to give sb permission to do sthg; [possibilité] to permit OU allow sb to do sthg.

autoritaire [otɔritɛr] *nmf & adj* authoritarian.

autoritarisme [otɔritarism] *nm* authoritarianism.

autorité [otɔrite] *nf* authority; **faire ~** [ouvrage] to be authoritative; [personne] to be an authority; **faire qqch d'~** to do sthg out of hand.

autoroute [otorut] *nf* motorway *Br*, highway *Am*, freeway *Am*.

autoroutier, -ière [otorutje, jɛr] *adj* motorway (*avant n*) *Br*, freeway (*avant n*) *Am*.

auto-stop [otostɔp] *nm* hitchhiking, hitching; **faire de l'~** to hitchhike, to hitch; **prendre quelqu'un en ~** to pick up a hitchhiker.

auto-stoppeur, -euse [otostɔpœr, øz] *nm, f* hitchhiker, hitcher.

autosuggestion [otosygʒɛstjɔ̃] *nf* autosuggestion.

autour [otur] *adv* round, around.

◆ **autour de** *loc prép* **-1.** [sens spatial] round, around. **-2.** [sens temporel] about, around.

autre [otr] ◇ *adj indéf* **-1.** [distinct, différent] other, different; **je préfère une ~ marque de café** I prefer another OU a different brand of coffee; **l'un et l'~ projets** both projects; **ni l'une ni l'~ maison** neither house; ~ **chose** something else. **-2.** [supplémentaire] other; **tu veux une ~ tasse de café?** would you like another cup of coffee? **-3.** [qui est différent par une certaine supériorité]: **c'est un (tout) ~ homme que son père** he's not at all like his father, he's a different man from his father. **-4.** [qui reste] other, remaining; **les ~s passagers ont été rapatriés en autobus** the other OU remaining passengers were bussed home. ◇ *pron indéf*: **l'~** the other (one); **un ~** another (one); **les ~s** [personnes] the others; [objets] the others, the other ones; **l'un à côté de l'~** side by side; **d'une semaine à l'~** from one week to the next; **aucun ~**, **nul ~**, **personne d'~** no one else, nobody else; **quelqu'un d'~** somebody else, someone else; **rien d'~** nothing else; **l'une chante, l'~ danse** one sings and the other dances; **l'un et l'~ sont venus** they both came, both of them came; **l'un ou l'~ ira** one or other (of them) will go; **ni l'un ni l'~ n'est venu** neither (of them) came.

◆ **entre autres** *loc adv* among other things.

autrefois [otrəfwa] *adv* in the past, formerly.

autrement [otrəmɑ̃] *adv* **-1.** [différemment] otherwise, differently; **je n'ai pas pu faire ~ que d'y aller** I had no choice but to go; ~ **dit** in other words. **-2.** [sinon] otherwise. **-3.** *sout* [beaucoup plus] far more; **je n'en suis pas ~ étonné** it doesn't particularly surprise me.

Autriche [otriʃ] *nf*: **l'~** Austria.

autrichien, -ienne [otriʃjɛ̃, jɛn] *adj* Austrian.

◆ **Autrichien, -ienne** *nm, f* Austrian.

autruche [otryʃ] *nf* ostrich; **avoir un estomac d'~** *fig* to have a cast-iron stomach; **pratiquer la politique de l'~** *fig* to bury one's head in the sand.

autrui [otrɥi] *pron* others, other people.

auvent [ovɑ̃] *nm* canopy.

aux [o] → **à**.

auxiliaire [oksiljɛr] ◇ *nmf* [assistant] assistant; ~ **médical** medical auxiliary. ◇ *nm* GRAM auxiliary (verb). ◇ *adj* **-1.** [secondaire] auxiliary. **-2.** ADMIN assistant (*avant n*).

auxquels, auxquelles [okεl] → **lequel**.

av. *abr de* **avenue**.

AV ◇ *nm* (*abr de* **avis de virement**) *notification of bank transfer*. ◇ *abr de* **avant**.

avachi, -e [avaʃi] *adj* **-1.** [gén] misshapen. **-2.** [personne] listless; **il était ~ dans un fauteuil** he was slumped in an armchair.

aval, -als [aval] *nm* backing (*U*), endorsement.
◆ **en aval** *loc adv litt* & *fig* downstream.
◆ **en aval de** *loc prép litt* & *fig* downstream of.

avalanche [avalɑ̃ʃ] *nf litt* & *fig* avalanche.

avaler [avale] [3] *vt* **-1.** [gén] to swallow. **-2.** *fig* [supporter] to take; **dur à ~** difficult to swallow.

avaliser [avalize] [3] *vt* **-1.** [traite] to endorse. **-2.** [décision, projet] to back.

avance [avɑ̃s] *nf* **-1.** [progression, somme d'argent] advance. **-2.** [distance, temps] lead; **le train a dix minutes d'~** the train is ten minutes early; **le train a une ~ de dix minutes sur l'horaire** the train is running ten minutes ahead of schedule; **prendre de l'~ (dans qqch)** to get ahead (in sthg).
◆ **avances** *nfpl*: **faire des ~s à qqn** to make advances towards sb.
◆ **à l'avance** *loc adv* in advance.
◆ **d'avance** *loc adv* in advance.
◆ **en avance** *loc adv*: **être en ~** to be early; **être en ~ sur qqch** to be ahead of sthg.
◆ **par avance** *loc adv* in advance.

avancement [avɑ̃smɑ̃] *nm* **-1.** [développement] progress. **-2.** [promotion] promotion.

avancer [avɑ̃se] [16] ◇ *vt* **-1.** [objet, tête] to move forward; [date, départ] to bring forward; [main] to hold out. **-2.** [projet, travail] to advance. **-3.** [montre, horloge] to put forward. **-4.** [argent]: **~ qqch à qqn** to advance sb sthg.
◇ *vi* **-1.** [approcher] to move forward. **-2.** [progresser] to advance; **~ dans qqch** to make progress in sthg. **-3.** [faire saillie]: **~ (dans/sur)** to jut out (into/over), to project (into/over). **-4.** [montre, horloge]: **ma montre avance de dix minutes** my watch is ten minutes fast. **-5.** [servir]: **ça n'avance à rien** that won't get us/you anywhere.
◆ **s'avancer** *vp* **-1.** [s'approcher] to move forward; **s'~ vers qqn/qqch** to move towards sb/sthg. **-2.** [prendre de l'avance]: **s'~ (dans qqch)** to get ahead (in sthg). **-3.** [s'engager] to commit o.s.

avant [avɑ̃] ◇ *prép* before; **quelques jours ~** a few days earlier OU before; **le chemin se situe un peu ~** the path is a bit further on OU ahead; **bien ~** [spatial] well ahead; [temporel] well before OU beforehand. ◇ *adj inv* front; **les roues ~** the front wheels. ◇ *nm* **-1.** [partie antérieure] front. **-2.** SPORT forward.
◆ **avant de** *loc prép*: **~ de faire qqch** before doing sthg; **~ de partir** before leaving.
◆ **avant que** *loc conj* (+ *subjonctif*): **~ que nous partions, nous devons ...** before we leave, we must ....
◆ **avant tout** *loc adv* above all; **sa carrière passe ~ tout** his career comes first.
◆ **en avant** *loc adv* forward, forwards.
◆ **en avant de** *loc prép* in front of.

avantage [avɑ̃taʒ] *nm* [gén & TENNIS] advantage; **se montrer à son ~** to look one's best; **~s en nature** fringe benefits, perks; **~s sociaux** welfare benefits.

avantager [avɑ̃taʒe] [17] *vt* **-1.** [favoriser] to favour. **-2.** [mettre en valeur] to flatter.

avantageusement [avɑ̃taʒøzmɑ̃] *adv* favourably.

avantageux, -euse [avɑ̃taʒø, øz] *adj* **-1.** [attrayant] attractive. **-2.** [profitable] profitable, lucrative. **-3.** [économique - prix] reasonable. **-4.** [flatteur] flattering. **-5.** *sout* [présomptueux]: **prendre l'air ~** to look superior.

avant-bras [avɑ̃bra] *nm inv* forearm.

avant-centre [avɑ̃sɑ̃tr] (*pl* **avants-centres**) *nm* centre forward.

avant-coureur [avɑ̃kurœr] → **signe**.

avant-dernier, -ière [avɑ̃dεrnje, jεr] (*mpl* **avant-derniers**, *fpl* **avant-dernières**) *adj* second to last, penultimate.

avant-garde [avɑ̃gard] (*pl* **avant-gardes**) *nf* **-1.** MIL vanguard. **-2.** [idée] avant-garde; **d'~** avant-garde.

avant-goût [avɑ̃gu] (*pl* **avant-goûts**) *nm* foretaste.

avant-hier [avɑ̃tjεr] *adv* the day before yesterday.

avant-première [avɑ̃prəmjεr] (*pl* **avant-premières**) *nf* preview; **présenté en ~** [film, pièce] previewed.

avant-projet [avɑ̃prɔʒε] (*pl* **avant-projets**) *nm* draft.

avant-propos [avɑ̃prɔpo] *nm inv* foreword.

avant-veille [avɑ̃vεj] (*pl* **avant-veilles**) *nf*: **l'~** two days earlier.

avare [avar] ◇ *nmf* miser. ◇ *adj* miserly; **être ~ de qqch** *fig* to be sparing with sthg.

avarice [avaris] *nf* avarice.

avarie [avari] *nf* damage (*U*).

avarié, -e [avarje] *adj* rotting, bad.

avatar [avatar] *nm* [transformation] metamorphosis.
◆ **avatars** *nmpl* [mésaventures] misfortunes.

Ave (Maria) [ave (marja)] *nm inv* Hail Mary.

avec [avɛk] ◇ *prép* **-1.** [gén] with; ~ **respect** with respect, respectfully; **c'est fait ~ du cuir** it's made from leather; **et ~ ça?** *fam* [dans un magasin] anything else? **-2.** [vis-à-vis de] to, towards. ◇ *adv fam* with it/him *etc*; **tiens mon sac, je ne peux pas courir ~!** hold my bag, I can't run with it!

avenant, -e [avnɑ̃, ɑ̃t] *adj* pleasant.
◆ **avenant** *nm* JUR additional clause.
◆ **à l'avenant** *loc adv* in the same vein.

avènement [avɛnmɑ̃] *nm* **-1.** [d'un roi] accession. **-2.** *fig* [début] advent.

avenir [avnir] *nm* future; **avoir de l'~** to have a future; **d'~** [profession, concept] with a future, with prospects.
◆ **à l'avenir** *loc adv* in future.

Avent [avɑ̃] *nm*: **l'~** Advent.

aventure [avɑ̃tyr] *nf* **-1.** [gén] adventure. **-2.** [liaison amoureuse] affair. **-3.** *loc*: **dire la bonne ~** à qqn to tell sb's fortune.
◆ **d'aventure** *loc adv* by (any) chance.

aventurer [avɑ̃tyre] [3] *vt* **-1.** [risquer] to risk. **-2.** *sout* [remarque] to venture.
◆ **s'aventurer** *vp* to venture (out); **s'~ à faire qqch** *fig* to venture to do sthg.

aventureux, -euse [avɑ̃tyrø, øz] *adj* **-1.** [personne, vie] adventurous. **-2.** [projet] risky.

aventurier, -ière [avɑ̃tyrje, jɛr] *nm, f* adventurer.

avenu [avny] *adj*: **nul et non ~** JUR null and void.

avenue [avny] *nf* avenue.

avérer [avere] [18]
◆ **s'avérer** *vp*: **il s'est avéré (être) à la hauteur** he proved (to be) up to it; **il s'est avéré (être) un musicien accompli** he proved to be an accomplished musician.

averse [avɛrs] *nf* downpour.

aversion [avɛrsjɔ̃] *nf*: ~ **pour** aversion to, loathing for; **prendre qqn/qqch en ~** to take an intense dislike to sb/sthg; **avoir qqn/qqch en ~** to have an aversion to sb/sthg.

averti, -e [avɛrti] *adj* **-1.** [expérimenté] experienced. **-2.** [initié]: ~ **(de)** informed OU well-informed (about).

avertir [avɛrtir] [32] *vt* **-1.** [mettre en garde] to warn. **-2.** [prévenir] to inform; **avertissez-moi dès que possible** let me know as soon as possible.

avertissement [avɛrtismɑ̃] *nm* **-1.** [gén] warning. **-2.** [avis] notice, notification.

avertisseur, -euse [avɛrtisœr, øz] ◇ *adj* warning *(avant n)*. ◇ *nm* **-1.** [klaxon] horn, siren. **-2.** [d'incendie] alarm.

aveu, -x [avø] *nm* confession; **de l'~ de tout le monde, c'est lui le responsable** everyone agrees that he is responsible; **passer aux ~x** to make a confession.

aveuglant, -e [avœglɑ̃, ɑ̃t] *adj* **-1.** [lumière] blinding. **-2.** *fig* [vérité] blindingly obvious.

aveugle [avœgl] ◇ *nmf* blind person; **les ~s** the blind. ◇ *adj litt* & *fig* blind.

aveuglement [avœgləmɑ̃] *nm* blindness.

aveuglément [avœglemɑ̃] *adv* blindly.

aveugler [avœgle] [5] *vt* **-1.** *litt* & *fig* [priver de la vue] to blind. **-2.** [fenêtre] to board up.
◆ **s'aveugler** *vp*: **s'~ sur qqn** to be blind to sb's faults.

aveuglette [avœglɛt]
◆ **à l'aveuglette** *loc adv*: **marcher à l'~** to grope one's way; **avancer à l'~** *fig* to be in the dark.

aviateur, -trice [avjatœr, tris] *nm, f* aviator.

aviation [avjasjɔ̃] *nf* **-1.** [transport aérien] aviation. **-2.** MIL airforce.

aviculture [avikyltyr] *nf* [gén] bird-breeding; [de volailles] poultry farming.

avide [avid] *adj* **-1.** [vorace, cupide] greedy. **-2.** [désireux]: ~ **(de qqch/de faire qqch)** eager (for sthg/to do sthg).

avidement [avidmɑ̃] *adv* **-1.** [avec appétit, convoitise] greedily. **-2.** [avec intérêt] avidly. **-3.** [avec passion] eagerly.

avidité [avidite] *nf* **-1.** [voracité, cupidité] greed. **-2.** [passion] eagerness.

Avignon [aviɲɔ̃] *n* Avignon; **en ~** in Avignon; **le festival d'~** the Avignon festival.

LE FESTIVAL D'AVIGNON:
Founded by Jean Vilar in 1947 and held every summer in and around Avignon, this arts festival is a showcase for new theatre and dance performances

---

avilir [avilir] [32] *vt* **-1.** [personne] to degrade. **-2.** [monnaie, marchandise] to devalue.
◆ **s'avilir** *vp* **-1.** [personne] to demean o.s. **-2.** [monnaie, marchandise] to depreciate.

aviné, -e [avine] *adj* **-1.** [personne] inebriated. **-2.** [haleine] smelling of alcohol.

avion [avjɔ̃] *nm* plane, aeroplane, airplane *Am*; **en ~** by plane, by air; **par ~** [courrier] airmail; ~ **de ligne** airliner; ~ **à réaction** jet (plane).

aviron [avirɔ̃] *nm* **-1.** [rame] oar. **-2.** SPORT: **l'~** rowing.

avis [avi] *nm* **-1.** [opinion] opinion; **changer d'~** to change one's mind; **être d'~ que** to think that, to be of the opinion that; **à mon ~** in my opinion; **les ~ sont partagés** opinion is divided. **-2.** [conseil] advice (*U*). **-3.** [notification] notification, notice; **sauf ~ contraire** unless otherwise informed; **jusqu'à nouvel ~** until further notice; **~ de débit/crédit** debit/credit advice.

avisé, -e [avize] *adj* [sensé] sensible; **être bien/mal ~ de faire qqch** to be well-advised/ill-advised to do sthg.

aviser [avize] [3] ◇ *vt* **-1.** [informer]: **~ qqn de qqch** to inform sb of sthg. **-2.** *sout* [apercevoir] to notice. ◇ *vi* to reassess the situation.

◆ **s'aviser** *vp* **-1.** *sout* [s'apercevoir]: **s'~ de qqch** to notice sthg; **s'~ que** to notice (that). **-2.** [oser]: **s'~ de faire qqch** to take it into one's head to do sthg; **ne t'avise pas de répondre!** don't you dare answer me back!

av. J.-C. (*abr de* **avant Jésus-Christ**) B.C.

avocat, -e [avɔka, at] *nm, f* **-1.** JUR lawyer; **~ d'affaires** commercial lawyer; **~ de la défense** counsel for the defence *Br*, defense counsel *Am*; **~ général** ≃ counsel for the prosecution *Br*, prosecuting attorney *Am*. **-2.** [défenseur]: **se faire l'~ de qqch** to champion sthg; **se faire l'~ du diable** *fig* to play devil's advocate.

◆ **avocat** *nm* [fruit] avocado.

avoine [avwan] *nf* oats (*pl*).

avoir [avwar] [1] ◇ *nm* **-1.** [biens] assets (*pl*). **-2.** [document] credit note.

◇ *v aux* to have; **j'ai fini** I have finished; **il a attendu pendant deux heures** he waited for two hours.

◇ *vt* **-1.** [posséder] to have (got); **il a deux enfants/les cheveux bruns** he has (got) two children/brown hair; **la maison a un grand jardin** the house has (got) a large garden. **-2.** [être âgé de]: **il a 20 ans** he is 20 (years old); **il a deux ans de plus que son frère** he is two years older than his brother. **-3.** [obtenir] to get. **-4.** [éprouver] to have; **~ du chagrin** to feel sorrowful; **~ de la sympathie pour qqn** to have a liking for sb; *voir aussi* **faim, peur, soif** *etc*. **-5.** *loc*: **se faire ~** *fam* to be had *OU* conned; **en ~ assez de qqch/de faire qqch** to have had enough (of sthg/of doing sthg); **j'en ai pour cinq minutes** it'll take me five minutes; **tu n'as qu'à y aller toi-même** just go (there) yourself, why don't you just go (there) yourself?; **en ~ après qqn** to have (got) it in for sb.

◆ **avoir à** *vi + prép* [devoir]: **~ à faire qqch** to have to do sthg; **tu n'avais pas à lui par-** ler sur ce ton you had no need to speak to him like that, you shouldn't have spoken to him like that; **tu n'avais qu'à me demander** you only had to ask me.

◆ **il y a** *v impers* **-1.** [présentatif] there is/are; **il y a un problème** there's a problem; **il y a des problèmes** there are (some) problems; **qu'est-ce qu'il y a?** what's the matter?, what is it?; **il n'y a qu'à en finir** we'll/you'll *etc* just have to have done (with it). **-2.** [temporel]: **il y a trois ans** three years ago; **il y a longtemps de cela** that was a long time ago; **il y a longtemps qu'il est parti** he left a long time ago.

avoisinant, -e [avwazinɑ̃, ɑ̃t] *adj* **-1.** [lieu, maison] neighbouring. **-2.** [sens, couleur] similar.

Avoriaz [avɔrjaz] *n*: **le festival d'~** festival of science fiction and horror films held annually at *Avoriaz* in the French Alps.

avortement [avɔrtəmɑ̃] *nm* **-1.** MÉD abortion. **-2.** *fig* [d'un projet] abandonment.

avorter [avɔrte] [3] *vi* **-1.** MÉD: **(se faire) ~** to have an abortion. **-2.** [échouer] to fail.

avorton [avɔrtɔ̃] *nm péj* [nabot] runt.

avouer [avwe] [6] *vt* **-1.** [confesser] to confess (to). **-2.** [reconnaître] to admit. **-3.** [déclarer] to avow.

◆ **s'avouer** *vp* to admit (to being); **s'~ vaincu** to admit defeat.

avril [avril] *nm* April; *voir aussi* **septembre**.

AVS (*abr de* **assurance vieillesse et survivants**) *nf* Swiss pension scheme.

axe [aks] *nm* **-1.** GÉOM & PHYS axis. **-2.** [de roue] axle. **-3.** [route]: **les grands ~s** the major roads; **~ rouge** section of the Paris road system where parking is prohibited to avoid congestion. **-4.** [prolongement]: **dans l'~ de** directly in line with. **-5.** [de politique, de parti] line.

axer [akse] [3] *vt*: **~ qqch sur/autour de qqch** to centre sthg on/around sthg.

axial, -e, -iaux [aksjal, jo] *adj* axial.

axiome [aksjɔm] *nm* axiom.

ayant [ɛjɑ̃] *ppr* → **avoir**.

ayant droit [ɛjɑ̃drwa] (*pl* **ayants droit**) *nm* beneficiary.

ayatollah [ajatɔla] *nm* ayatollah.

azalée [azale] *nf* azalea.

azimut [azimyt]

◆ **tous azimuts** *loc adj* [défense, offensive] all-out.

azote [azɔt] *nm* nitrogen.

aztèque [aztɛk] *adj* Aztec.

◆ **Aztèque** *nmf* Aztec.

azur [azyr] *nm littéraire* **-1.** [couleur] azure. **-2.** [ciel] skies (*pl*).

azyme [azim] → **pain**.

B

b, B [be] *nm inv* b, B.
◆ **B** (*abr de* **bien**) *good grade (as assessment on schoolwork)*, ≃ B.

BA (*abr de* **bonne action**) *nf fam* good deed.

baba [baba] ◇ *nm* **-1.** CULIN: ~ **(au rhum)** rum baba. **-2.** [hippie] *person practising hippie lifestyle and values.* ◇ *adj inv fam*: **en rester** ~ to be flabbergasted.

babeurre [babœr] *nm* buttermilk.

babil [babil] *nm* [d'enfant] babble, babbling.

babiller [babije] [3] *vi* to babble.

babines [babin] *nfpl* chops; **se lécher les** ~ *fig* to lick one's lips.

babiole [babjɔl] *nf* **-1.** [objet] knick-knack. **-2.** [broutille] trifling matter.

bâbord [babɔr] *nm* port; **à** ~ to port, on the port side.

babouin [babwɛ̃] *nm* baboon.

baby-foot [babifut] *nm inv* table football.

baby-sitter [bebisitœr] (*pl* **baby-sitters**) *nmf* baby-sitter.

baby-sitting [bebisitiŋ] (*pl* **baby-sittings**) *nm*: **faire du** ~ to baby-sit.

bac [bak] *nm* **-1.** → **baccalauréat**. **-2.** [bateau] ferry. **-3.** [de réfrigérateur]: ~ **à glace** ice tray; ~ **à légumes** vegetable drawer. **-4.** [d'évier] sink.

baccalauréat [bakalɔrea] *nm school-leaving examinations leading to university entrance qualification.*

BACCALAURÉAT:

The baccalauréat or 'bac' is taken by pupils who have completed their final year at the 'lycée'; successful candidates may go to university. There are six types of 'bac', each corresponding to a specific field: 'bac A' (arts subjects), 'bac B' (economics), 'bac C' (maths and physics), 'bac D' (maths and natural sciences), 'bac D prime' (agriculture), and 'bac E' (science and technology)

bâche [baʃ] *nf* [toile] tarpaulin.

bachelier, -ière [baʃəlje, jɛr] *nm, f holder of the baccalauréat.*

bachot [baʃo] *vieilli* → **baccalauréat**.

bachotage [baʃɔtaʒ] *nm* cramming.

bacille [basil] *nm* bacillus.

bâcler [bakle] [3] *vt* to botch.

bacon [bekɔn] *nm* bacon.

bactéricide [bakterisid] *adj* bactericidal.

bactérie [bakteri] *nf* bacterium.

badaud, -e [bado, od] *nm, f* gawper.

badge [badʒ] *nm* badge.

badigeon [badiʒɔ̃] *nm* whitewash.

badigeonner [badiʒɔne] [3] *vt* **-1.** [mur] to whitewash. **-2.** [plaie] to paint. **-3.** [tarte, pain] to brush.

badin, -e [badɛ̃, in] *adj* playful.

badinage [badinaʒ] *nm sout* joking.

badiner [badine] [3] *vi sout* to joke; **ne pas** ~ **avec qqch** not to treat sthg lightly.

badminton [badmintɔn] *nm* badminton.

BAFA, Bafa [bafa] (*abr de* **brevet d'aptitude aux fonctions d'animation**) *nm diploma for youth leaders and workers.*

baffe [baf] *nf fam* slap.

baffle [bafl] *nm* baffle.

bafouer [bafwe] [6] *vt* **-1.** [principe] to trample upon. **-2.** [personne] to ridicule.

bafouille [bafuj] *nf fam* letter.

bafouiller [bafuje] [3] *vi & vt* to mumble.

bâfrer [bafre] [3] *fam* ◇ *vi* to guzzle. ◇ *vt* to wolf down.

bagage [bagaʒ] *nm* **-1.** (*gén pl*) [valises, sacs] luggage (*U*), baggage (*U*); **faire ses** ~**s** to pack; ~**s à main** hand luggage; **plier** ~ to pack one's bags (and leave). **-2.** [connaissances] (fund of) knowledge; ~ **intellectuel/culturel** intellectual/cultural baggage.

bagagiste [bagaʒist] *nmf* [chargement des avions] baggage handler; [à l'hôtel etc] porter; [fabricant] travel goods manufacturer.

bagarre [bagar] *nf* brawl, fight; **chercher la** ~ *fam* to look for a fight.

bagarrer [bagare] [3] *vi* to fight.
◆ **se bagarrer** *vp* to fight.

bagarreur, -euse [bagarœr, øz] ◇ *adj* aggressive, who likes a fight. ◇ *nm, f fig* fighter.

bagatelle [bagatɛl] *nf* **-1.** [objet] trinket. **-2.** [somme d'argent]: **acheter qqch pour une** ~ to buy sthg for next to nothing; **la** ~ **de X francs** *iron* a mere X francs. **-3.** [chose futile] trifle. **-4.** [sexe]: **être porté sur la** ~ to be quite a one for the ladies.

bagnard [baɲar] *nm* convict.

bagne [baɲ] *nm* **-1.** [prison] labour camp. **-2.** [sentence] hard labour; **c'est le ~ ici** *fig* it's slave labour here.

bagnole [baɲɔl] *nf fam* car.

bagou(t) [bagu] *nm* patter; **avoir du ~** to have the gift of the gab.

bague [bag] *nf* **-1.** [bijou, anneau] ring; **~ de fiançailles** engagement ring. **-2.** [de cigare] band. **-3.** **~ de serrage** clip.

baguer [bage] [3] *vt* [oiseau, arbre] to ring.

baguette [bagɛt] *nf* **-1.** [pain] French stick. **-2.** [petit bâton] stick; **~ magique** magic wand; **~ de tambour** drumstick; **mener qqn à la ~** to rule sb with a rod of iron. **-3.** [pour manger] chopstick. **-4.** [de chef d'orchestre] baton.

Bahamas [baamas] *nfpl*: **les ~** the Bahamas; **aux ~** in the Bahamas.

bahut [bay] *nm* **-1.** [buffet] sideboard. **-2.** [coffre] chest. **-3.** *arg scol* [lycée] secondary school. **-4.** *fam péj* [voiture] old banger.

baie [bɛ] *nf* **-1.** [fruit] berry. **-2.** GÉOGR bay. **-3.** [fenêtre]: **~ vitrée** picture window.

baignade [beɲad] *nf* [action] bathing (U) *Br*, swimming (U); **«~ interdite»** "no bathing/swimming".

baigner [beɲe] [4] ◇ *vt* **-1.** [donner un bain à] to bath. **-2.** [tremper, remplir] to bathe; **baigné de soleil** bathed in sunlight. ◇ *vi*: **~ dans le luxe** to be surrounded by wealth; **~ dans son sang** to lie in a pool of blood; **les tomates baignaient dans l'huile** the tomatoes were swimming in oil; **tout/ça baigne** *fam* everything's/it's great.
◆ **se baigner** *vp* **-1.** [dans la mer] to go swimming, to swim. **-2.** [dans une baignoire] to have a bath.

baigneur, -euse [bɛɲœr, øz] *nm, f* bather *Br*, swimmer.
◆ **baigneur** *nm* [poupée] baby doll.

baignoire [beɲwar] *nf* bath.

bail [baj] (*pl* **baux** [bo]) *nm* **-1.** JUR lease; **renouveler un ~** to renew a lease; **~ à loyer** residential lease; **~ reconductible** renewable lease. **-2.** *loc*: **ça fait un ~ que** *fam* it's ages since.

bâillement [bajmɑ̃] *nm* yawning (U), yawn.

bâiller [baje] [3] *vi* **-1.** [personne] to yawn. **-2.** [vêtement] to gape.

bailleur, -eresse [bajœr, bajrɛs] *nm, f* lessor; **~ de fonds** backer.

bâillon [bajɔ̃] *nm* gag.

bâillonner [bajɔne] [3] *vt* to gag.

bain [bɛ̃] *nm* **-1.** [gén] bath; **faire couler un ~** to run a bath; **prendre un ~** to have OU take a bath; **~ moussant** foaming bath oil; **~s-douches** public baths. **-2.** [dans mer, piscine] swim; **~ de mer** sea bathing *Br* OU swimming. **-3.** [de partie du corps]: **~ de bouche** mouthwash; **~ de pieds** foot-bath. **-4.** *loc*: **se mettre dans le ~** to get the hang of things; **prendre un ~ de foule** to go on a walkabout; **prendre un ~ de soleil** to sunbathe.

bain-marie [bɛ̃mari] (*pl* **bains-marie**) *nm*: **au ~** in a bain-marie.

baïonnette [bajɔnɛt] *nf* **-1.** [arme] bayonet. **-2.** ÉLECTR bayonet fitting.

baise [bɛz] *nf vulg* fucking.

baisemain [bɛzmɛ̃] *nm*: **faire le ~ à qqn** to kiss sb's hand.

baiser [beze] [4] ◇ *nm* kiss. ◇ *vt vulg* [avoir des relations sexuelles avec] to fuck. ◇ *vi vulg* to fuck.

baisse [bɛs] *nf* **-1.** [gén]: **~ (de)** drop (in), fall (in); **en ~** falling; **la tendance est à la ~** there is a downward trend. **-2.** INFORM: **~ de tension** brownout.

baisser [bese] [4] ◇ *vt* [gén] to lower; [radio] to turn down; **~ le ton** to modify one's tone; **~ les yeux** to look down. ◇ *vi* **-1.** [descendre] to go down; **le jour baisse** it's getting dark. **-2.** [santé, voix] to fail. **-3.** [prix] to fall. **-4.** [s'affaiblir - malade] to grow weaker; [- talent] to decline.
◆ **se baisser** *vp* to bend down.

bajoues [baju] *nfpl* jowls.

bakchich [bakʃiʃ] *nm* baksheesh.

bal [bal] *nm* ball; **~ masqué/costumé** masked/fancy-dress ball; **~ populaire** OU **musette** *popular old-fashioned dance accompanied by accordion.*

BAL, Bal (*abr de* **boîte aux lettres (électronique)**) *nf* E-mail.

balade [balad] *nf fam* stroll; **faire une ~** to go for a stroll.

balader [balade] [3] ◇ *vt* **-1.** *fam* [traîner avec soi] to trail around. **-2.** [emmener en promenade] to take for a walk. ◇ *vi*: **envoyer ~ qqn** to send sb packing.
◆ **se balader** *vp fam* **-1.** [se promener - à pied] to go for a walk; [- en voiture] to go for a drive. **-2.** [traîner] to be kicking around.

baladeur, -euse [baladœr, øz] *adj* wandering.
◆ **baladeur** *nm* personal stereo.
◆ **baladeuse** *nf* inspection lamp.

balafre [balafr] *nf* **-1.** [blessure] gash. **-2.** [cicatrice] scar.

balafré, -e [balafre] *adj* scarred.

balai [balɛ] *nm* **-1.** [de nettoyage] broom, brush; ~ **mécanique** carpet sweeper. **-2.** [d'essuie-glace] wiper blade. **-3.** *fam* [an]: **il a 50 ~s** he's 50 years old.

balai-brosse [balɛbrɔs] (*pl* **balais-brosses**) *nm* (long-handled) scrubbing brush.

balaie, balaies → **balayer**.

balance [balɑ̃s] *nf* **-1.** [instrument] scales (*pl*); **faire pencher la** ~ *fig* to tip the balance. **-2.** COMM & POLIT balance; ~ **des paiements/commerciale** balance of payments/of trade; ~ **des pouvoirs** balance of power.
◆ **Balance** *nf* ASTROL Libra; **être Balance** to be (a) Libra.

balancement [balɑ̃smɑ̃] *nm* [mouvement - d'objet, de hanches] swaying; [- de bras, de jambe] swinging; [- de navire] motion.

balancer [balɑ̃se] [16] ◇ *vt* **-1.** [bouger] to swing. **-2.** *fam* [lancer] to chuck. **-3.** *fam* [jeter] to chuck out. ◇ *vi* **-1.** *sout* [hésiter] to waver. **-2.** [osciller] to swing.
◆ **se balancer** *vp* **-1.** [sur une chaise] to rock backwards and forwards. **-2.** [sur une balançoire] to swing. **-3.** *fam*: **se ~ de qqch** not to give a damn about sthg.

balancier [balɑ̃sje] *nm* **-1.** [de pendule] pendulum. **-2.** [de funambule] pole.

balançoire [balɑ̃swar] *nf* [suspendue] swing; [bascule] see-saw.

balayage [balɛjaʒ] *nm* [gén] sweeping; TECHNOL scanning.

balayer [balɛje] [11] *vt* **-1.** [nettoyer] to sweep. **-2.** [chasser] to sweep away. **-3.** *fig* [écarter] to brush aside. **-4.** [suj: radar] to scan; [suj: projecteurs] to sweep (across).

balayette [balɛjɛt] *nf* small brush.

balayeur, -euse [balɛjœr, øz] *nm, f* roadsweeper *Br*, streetsweeper *Am*.
◆ **balayeuse** *nf* [machine] roadsweeper.

balayures [balɛjyr] *nfpl* sweepings.

balbutiement [balbysimɑ̃] *nm* **-1.** [bredouillement] stammering. **-2.** *fig*: ~**s** [débuts] infancy (*U*).

balbutier [balbysje] [9] ◇ *vi* **-1.** [bafouiller] to stammer. **-2.** *fig* [débuter] to be in its infancy. ◇ *vt* [bafouiller] to stammer (out).

balcon [balkɔ̃] *nm* **-1.** [de maison - terrasse] balcony; [- balustrade] parapet. **-2.** [de théâtre, de cinéma] circle.

balconnet [balkɔnɛ] *nm*: **soutien-gorge à** ~ half-cup bra.

baldaquin [baldakɛ̃] *nm* **-1.** ARCHIT canopy. **-2.** → **lit**.

Baléares [balear] *nfpl*: **les** ~ the Balearic Islands; **aux** ~ in the Balearic Islands.

baleine [balɛn] *nf* **-1.** [mammifère] whale. **-2.** [de corset] whalebone. **-3.** [de parapluie] rib.

baleinier, -ière [balɛnje, jɛr] *adj* whaling (*avant n*).
◆ **baleinier** *nm* whaler.
◆ **baleinière** *nf* [bateau] whaler.

Bali [bali] *n* Bali; **à** ~ in Bali.

balinais, -e [balinɛ, ɛz] *adj* Balinese.
◆ **Balinais, -e** *nm, f* Balinese (*inv*).

balisage [balizaʒ] *nm* **-1.** [action] marking out. **-2.** [signaux - NAVIG] markers (*pl*), marker buoys (*pl*); [- AÉRON] runway lights (*pl*); [- AUTOM] road signs (*pl*).

balise [baliz] *nf* **-1.** NAVIG marker (buoy). **-2.** AÉRON runway light. **-3.** AUTOM road sign. **-4.** INFORM tag.

baliser [balize] [3] ◇ *vt* to mark out. ◇ *vi* *fam* to be spooked.

balistique [balistik] ◇ *nf* ballistics (*U*). ◇ *adj* ballistic.

balivernes [balivɛrn] *nfpl* nonsense (*U*).

Balkans [balkɑ̃] *nmpl*: **les** ~ the Balkans.

ballade [balad] *nf* ballad.

ballant, -e [balɑ̃, ɑ̃t] *adj*: **les bras ~s** arms dangling.
◆ **ballant** *nm* [mouvement]: **avoir du** ~ to sway.

ballast [balast] *nm* **-1.** [chemin de fer] ballast. **-2.** NAVIG ballast tank.

balle [bal] *nf* **-1.** [d'arme à feu] bullet; ~ **perdue** stray bullet. **-2.** [de jeu] ball; ~ **de ping-pong/tennis** table-tennis/tennis ball. **-3.** [de marchandises] bale. **-4.** *fam* [argent] franc. **-5.** *loc*: **se renvoyer la** ~ to pass the buck; **saisir la** ~ **au bond** to jump at the chance.

ballerine [balrin] *nf* **-1.** [danseuse] ballerina. **-2.** [chaussure] ballet shoe.

ballet [balɛ] *nm* [gén] ballet; *fig* [activité intense] to-ing and fro-ing.

ballon [balɔ̃] *nm* **-1.** JEU & SPORT ball; ~ **de football** football; **le** ~ **ovale** rugby; **le** ~ **rond** football. **-2.** [montgolfière, de fête] balloon. **-3.** [verre de vin]: ~ **de rouge** glass of red (wine).

ballonné, -e [balɔne] *adj*: **avoir le ventre** ~, **être** ~ to be bloated.

ballot [balo] *nm* **-1.** [de marchandises] bundle. **-2.** *vieilli* [imbécile] twit.

ballottage [balɔtaʒ] *nm* POLIT second ballot; **en** ~ standing for a second ballot.

ballotter [balɔte] [3] ◇ *vt* to toss about;

être ballotté entre *fig* to be torn between. ◇ *vi* [chose] to roll around.

ballottine [balɔtin] *nf*: ~ **de foie gras** *type of galantine made with foie gras.*

ball-trap [baltrap] *nm* clay pigeon shooting.

balluchon = **baluchon**.

balnéaire [balneɛr] *adj*: **station** ~ seaside resort.

balourd, -e [balur, urd] ◇ *adj* clumsy. ◇ *nm, f* clumsy idiot.

balte [balt] *adj* Baltic.
◆ **Balte** *nmf* native of the Baltic states.

Baltique [baltik] *nf*: **la** ~ the Baltic (Sea).

baluchon, balluchon [balyʃɔ̃] *nm* bundle; **faire son** ~ *fam* to pack one's bags (and leave).

balustrade [balystrad] *nf* -**1.** [de terrasse] balustrade. -**2.** [rambarde] guardrail.

bambin [bɑ̃bɛ̃] *nm* kiddie.

bambou [bɑ̃bu] *nm* -**1.** [plante] bamboo; **pousse de** ~ bamboo shoot. -**2.** [matériau]: **en** ~ bamboo (*avant n*).

bamboula [bɑ̃bula] *nf*: **faire la** ~ *fam* to go out on the town.

ban [bɑ̃] *nm* -**1.** [de mariage]: **publier** OU **afficher les** ~**s** to publish OU display the banns. -**2.** [applaudissements] round of applause. -**3.** *loc*: **être/mettre qqn au** ~ (**de la société**) to be outlawed/to outlaw sb (from society); **le** ~ **et l'arrière-**~ the whole lot of them.

banal, -e, -als [banal] *adj* commonplace, banal; **pas** OU **peu** ~ unusual.

banaliser [banalize] [3] *vt*: **voiture banalisée** unmarked police car.
◆ **se banaliser** *vp* to become commonplace.

banalité [banalite] *nf* -**1.** [caractère banal] banality. -**2.** [cliché] commonplace; **échanger des** ~**s** to make small-talk.

banane [banan] *nf* -**1.** [fruit] banana. -**2.** [sac] bum-bag. -**3.** [coiffure] quiff.

bananier, -ière [bananje, jɛr] *adj* banana (*avant n*).
◆ **bananier** *nm* -**1.** [arbre] banana tree. -**2.** [cargo] banana boat.

banc [bɑ̃] *nm* [siège] bench; **le** ~ **des accusés** JUR the dock; ~ **d'essai** test-bed; **être au** ~ **d'essai** *fig* to be at the test stage; ~ **de poissons** shoal of fish; ~ **de sable** sand-bank.

bancaire [bɑ̃kɛr] *adj* bank (*avant n*), banking (*avant n*).

bancal, -e, -als [bɑ̃kal] *adj* -**1.** [personne] lame. -**2.** [meuble] wobbly. -**3.** [théorie, idée] unsound.

bandage [bɑ̃daʒ] *nm* [de blessé] bandage.

bande [bɑ̃d] *nf* -**1.** [de tissu, de papier] strip. -**2.** [bandage] bandage; ~ **Velpeau®** crepe bandage. -**3.** [de billard] cushion; **par la** ~ *fig* by a roundabout route. -**4.** [groupe] band; ~ **de ...!** *fam* bunch of ...!; **en** ~ in a group; **faire** ~ **à part** to keep to o.s. -**5.** [pellicule de film] film; ~ **dessinée** comic strip. -**6.** [d'enregistrement] tape; ~ **audionumérique** DAT tape; ~ **magnétique** (magnetic) tape; ~ **vidéo** video (tape). -**7.** [voie]: ~ **d'arrêt d'urgence** hard shoulder. -**8.** RADIO: ~ **de fréquence** waveband. -**9.** NAVIG: **donner de la** ~ to list.

bande-annonce [bɑ̃danɔ̃s] (*pl* **bandes-annonces**) *nf* trailer.

bandeau [bɑ̃do] *nm* -**1.** [sur les yeux] blindfold. -**2.** [dans les cheveux] headband.

bandelette [bɑ̃dlɛt] *nf* strip (of cloth).

bander [bɑ̃de] [3] ◇ *vt* -**1.** MÉD to bandage; ~ **les yeux de qqn** to blindfold sb. -**2.** [arc] to draw back. -**3.** [muscle] to flex. ◇ *vi vulg* to have a hard-on.

banderole [bɑ̃drɔl] *nf* streamer.

bande-son [bɑ̃dsɔ̃] (*pl* **bandes-son**) *nf* sound track.

bandit [bɑ̃di] *nm* -**1.** [voleur] bandit. -**2.** [personne sans scrupules] crook.

banditisme [bɑ̃ditism] *nm* serious crime.

bandoulière [bɑ̃duljɛr] *nf* bandolier; **en** ~ across the shoulder.

bangladais, -e [bɑ̃gladɛ, ɛz] *adj* Bangladeshi.
◆ **Bangladais, -e** *nm, f* Bangladeshi.

Bangladesh [bɑ̃gladɛʃ] *nm*: **le** ~ Bangladesh; **au** ~ in Bangladesh.

banlieue [bɑ̃ljø] *nf* suburbs (*pl*); **en** ~ in the suburbs; **la grande** ~ the outer suburbs; **la** ~ **parisienne** the Paris suburbs; **réseau de** ~ commuter OU suburban network.

banlieusard, -e [bɑ̃ljøzar, ard] *nm, f person living in the suburbs.*

bannière [banjɛr] *nf* [étendard] banner.

bannir [banir] [32] *vt*: ~ **qqn/qqch (de)** to banish sb/sthg (from).

banque [bɑ̃k] *nf* -**1.** [activité] banking. -**2.** [établissement, au jeu] bank; **Banque de France** Bank of France. -**3.** INFORM: ~ **de données** data bank. -**4.** MÉD: ~ **d'organes/ du sang/du sperme** organ/blood/sperm bank.

banqueroute [bɑ̃krut] *nf* bankruptcy; **faire** ~ to go bankrupt.

banquet [bɑ̃kɛ] *nm* (celebration) dinner; [de gala] banquet.

banquette [bɑ̃kɛt] *nf* seat; ~ **arrière** back seat.

banquier, -ière [bɑ̃kje, jɛr] *nm, f* banker.

banquise [bɑ̃kiz] *nf* ice field.

baobab [baɔbab] *nm* baobab.

baptême [batɛm] *nm* **-1.** RELIG baptism, christening. **-2.** [première fois]: ~ **de l'air** maiden flight; ~ **du feu** baptism of fire.

baptiser [batize] [3] *vt* to baptize, to christen.

baptismal, -e, -aux [batismal, o] *adj* baptismal; *voir aussi* fonts.

baquet [bakɛ] *nm* **-1.** [cuve] tub. **-2.** [siège] bucket seat.

bar [bar] *nm* **-1.** [café, unité de pression] bar; ~ **à café** *Helv* coffee bar; ~ **à vin** wine bar. **-2.** [poisson] bass.

baragouiner [baragwine] [3] *vt fam* **-1.** [langue]: **il baragouine le français** he speaks broken French. **-2.** [bredouiller] to gabble.

baraka [baraka] *nf fam*: **avoir la** ~ to be lucky.

baraque [barak] *nf* **-1.** [cabane] hut. **-2.** *fam* [maison] house. **-3.** [de forain] stall, stand.

baraqué, -e [barake] *adj fam* well-built.

baraquement [barakmɑ̃] *nm* camp (*of huts for refugees, workers etc*).

baratin [baratɛ̃] *nm fam* smooth talk; **faire du** ~ **à qqn** to sweet-talk sb.

baratiner [baratine] [3] *fam* ◇ *vt* [femme] to chat up; [client] to give one's sales pitch to. ◇ *vi* to be a smooth talker.

Barbade [barbad] *nf*: **la** ~ Barbados; **à la** ~ in Barbados.

barbant, -e [barbɑ̃, ɑ̃t] *adj fam* deadly dull OU boring.

barbare [barbar] ◇ *nm* barbarian. ◇ *adj* **-1.** *péj* [non civilisé] barbarous. **-2.** [cruel] barbaric.

barbarisme [barbarism] *nm* GRAM barbarism.

barbe [barb] *nf* beard; **se laisser pousser la** ~ to grow a beard; ~ **à papa** candy floss *Br*, cotton candy *Am*; **faire qqch au nez et à la** ~ **de qqn** *fig* to do sthg right under sb's nose; **quelle** OU **la** ~! *fam* what a drag!

barbecue [barbəkju] *nm* barbecue.

barbelé, -e [barbəle] *adj* barbed; **fil de fer** ~ barbed wire.
◆ **barbelé** *nm* barbed wire (*U*).

barber [barbe] [3] *vt fam* to bore stiff.
◆ **se barber** *vp fam* to be bored stiff.

barbiche [barbiʃ] *nf* goatee (beard).

barbiturique [barbityrik] *nm* barbiturate.

barboter [barbɔte] [3] ◇ *vi* to paddle. ◇ *vt fam* to nick.

barboteuse [barbɔtøz] *nf* romper-suit.

barbouillé, -e [barbuje] *adj*: **être** ~, **avoir l'estomac** ~ to feel sick.

barbouiller [barbuje] [3] *vt* **-1.** [salir]: ~ **qqch (de)** to smear sthg (with). **-2.** *péj* [peindre] to daub. **-3.** *fam* [écrire sur] to scribble on.

barbu, -e [barby] *adj* bearded.
◆ **barbu** *nm* bearded man.
◆ **barbue** *nf* [poisson] brill.

barda [barda] *nm* **-1.** *arg mil* kit. **-2.** *fam* [attirail] gear; **avec tout son** ~ with all his/her gear.

barde [bard] ◇ *nm* [poète] bard. ◇ *nf* CULIN bacon, bard.

bardé, -e [barde] *adj fig*: **il est** ~ **de diplômes** he's got heaps of diplomas.

barder [barde] [3] ◇ *vt* CULIN to bard. ◇ *vi fam*: **ça va** ~ there'll be trouble.

barème [barɛm] *nm* [de référence] table; [de salaires] scale.

barge [barʒ] *nf* [bateau] barge.

baril [baril] *nm* barrel; **un** ~ **de pétrole** a barrel of oil.

barillet [barije] *nm* **-1.** [petit baril] cask. **-2.** [de revolver, de serrure] cylinder.

bariolé, -e [barjɔle] *adj* multicoloured.

barjo(t) [barʒo] *adj inv fam* nuts.

barmaid [barmɛd] *nf* barmaid.

barman [barman] (*pl* **barmans** OU **barmen** [barmɛn]) *nm* barman.

baromètre [barɔmɛtr] *nm* barometer.

baron, -onne [barɔ̃, ɔn] *nm, f* baron (*f* baroness).
◆ **baron** *nm* [magnat] baron.

baroque [barɔk] ◇ *nm* ART: **le** ~ the Baroque style. ◇ *adj* **-1.** [style] baroque. **-2.** [bizarre] weird.

baroud [barud] *nm*: ~ **d'honneur** last stand.

barque [bark] *nf* small boat; **savoir mener sa** ~ *fig* to be well-organized.

barquette [barkɛt] *nf* **-1.** [tartelette] pastry boat. **-2.** [récipient - de fruits] punnet; [- de frites] carton; [- de crème glacée] tub.

barrage [baraʒ] *nm* **-1.** [de rue] roadblock. **-2.** CONSTR dam.

barre [bar] *nf* **-1.** [gén & JUR] bar; ~ **d'espacement** [sur machine à écrire] space bar; ~ **fixe** GYM high bar; ~ **des témoins** JUR witness box *Br* OU stand *Am*; **c'est le coup de** ~ *fam* it's a rip-off; **avoir un coup de** ~ *fam* to be shattered. **-2.** NAVIG helm; **être à la** ~

NAVIG & *fig* to be at the helm. **-3.** [trait] stroke.

barreau [baro] *nm* bar; **le ~** JUR the Bar.

barrer [bare] [3] *vt* **-1.** [rue, route] to block. **-2.** [mot, phrase] to cross out. **-3.** [bateau] to steer.

◆ **se barrer** *vp fam* to clear off.

barrette [barɛt] *nf* [pince à cheveux] **(hair) slide** *Br*, **barrette** *Am*.

barreur, -euse [barœr, øz] *nm, f* NAVIG helmsman; [à l'aviron] cox.

barricade [barikad] *nf* barricade; **monter sur les ~s** *fig* to man the barricades.

barricader [barikade] [3] *vt* to barricade.

◆ **se barricader** *vp* to barricade o.s.; **se ~ chez soi** to shut o.s. away (at home).

barrière [barjɛr] *nf litt & fig* barrier; **~ de dégel** *ban on heavy lorries on certain roads during a thaw.*

barrique [barik] *nf* barrel.

barrir [barir] [32] *vi* to trumpet.

baryton [baritɔ̃] *nm* baritone.

bas, basse [ba, baz *devant nm commençant par voyelle ou h muet,* bas] *adj* **-1.** [gén] low. **-2.** *péj* [vil] base, low. **-3.** MUS bass.

◆ **bas** ◇ *nm* **-1.** [partie inférieure] bottom, lower part; **avoir/connaître des hauts et des ~** to have/go through ups and downs. **-2.** [vêtement] stocking; **~ de laine** woollen stocking; *fig* nest egg. ◇ *adv* low; **à ~ ...!** down with ...!; **parler ~** to speak in a low voice, to speak softly; **mettre ~** [animal] to give birth.

◆ **en bas** *loc adv* at the bottom; [dans une maison] downstairs.

◆ **en bas de** *loc prép* at the bottom of; **attendre qqn en ~ de chez lui** to wait for sb downstairs.

◆ **bas de gamme** ◇ *adj* downmarket. ◇ *nm* bottom of the range.

basalte [bazalt] *nm* basalt.

basané, -e [bazane] *adj* tanned.

bas-bleu [bablø] (*pl* **bas-bleus**) *nm péj* bluestocking.

bas-côté [bakote] (*pl* **bas-côtés**) *nm* [de route] verge.

bascule [baskyl] *nf* **-1.** [balance] weighing machine. **-2.** [balançoire] seesaw.

basculer [baskyle] [3] ◇ *vi* to fall over, to overbalance; [benne] to tip up; **~ dans qqch** *fig* to tip over into sthg. ◇ *vt* to tip up, to tilt.

base [baz] *nf* **-1.** [partie inférieure] base; **la ~** [d'entreprise, de syndicat] the rank and file. **-2.** [principe fondamental] basis; **à ~ de** based on; **de ~** basic; **une boisson à ~**

d'orange an orange-based drink; **sur la ~ de** on the basis of. **-3.** INFORM: **~ de données** database. **-4.** [cosmétique]: **~ de maquillage** make-up base.

base-ball [bɛzbol] (*pl* **base-balls**) *nm* baseball.

baser [baze] [3] *vt* to base; **~ qqch sur** *fig* to base sthg on.

◆ **se baser** *vp*: **sur quoi vous basez-vous pour affirmer cela?** what are you basing this statement on?

bas-fond [bafɔ̃] (*pl* **bas-fonds**) *nm* [de l'océan] shallow.

◆ **bas-fonds** *nmpl fig* **-1.** [de la société] dregs. **-2.** [quartiers pauvres] slums.

basilic [bazilik] *nm* [plante] basil.

basilique [bazilik] *nf* basilica.

basique [bazik] *adj* basic.

basket [baskɛt] *nf* **-1.** [chaussure] trainer *Br*, sneaker *Am*; **lâche-moi les ~s!** *fig* get off my back! **-2.** = **basket-ball**.

basket-ball [baskɛtbol] *nm* basketball.

basque [bask] ◇ *adj* Basque; **le Pays ~** the Basque country. ◇ *nm* [langue] Basque. ◇ *nf* [vêtement] **tail** (*of coat*); **être toujours pendu aux ~s de qqn** *fig fam* to be always tagging along after sb.

◆ **Basque** *nmf* Basque.

bas-relief [barəljɛf] (*pl* **bas-reliefs**) *nm* bas-relief.

basse [bas] ◇ *adj* → **bas**. ◇ *nf* MUS bass.

basse-cour [baskur] (*pl* **basses-cours**) *nf* **-1.** [volaille] poultry. **-2.** [partie de ferme] farmyard.

bassement [basmɑ̃] *adv* despicably; **être ~ intéressé** to be motivated by petty self-interest.

bassesse [basɛs] *nf* **-1.** [mesquinerie] baseness, meanness. **-2.** [action vile] despicable act.

basset [basɛ] *nm* basset hound.

bassin [basɛ̃] *nm* **-1.** [cuvette] bowl. **-2.** [pièce d'eau] (ornamental) pond. **-3.** [de piscine]: **petit/grand ~** children's/main pool. **-4.** ANAT pelvis. **-5.** GÉOL basin; **~ houiller** coalfield; **le Bassin parisien** the Paris basin.

bassine [basin] *nf* bowl, basin.

bassiner [basine] [3] *vt* **-1.** [humecter] to bathe. **-2.** *fam* [importuner] to bore.

bassiste [basist] *nmf* bass player.

basson [basɔ̃] *nm* [instrument] bassoon; [personne] bassoonist.

bastide [bastid] *nf traditional farmhouse or country house in southern France; walled town (in south-west France).*

Bastille [bastij] *nf*: **la prise de la ~** the storming of the Bastille.

BASTILLE:
A state prison, the Bastille fell to the people of Paris on 14 July 1789 — today celebrated as Bastille Day. The square where the Bastille once stood is now the home of the new Paris opera house, known as 'l'Opéra-Bastille'

---

bastingage [bastɛ̃gaʒ] *nm* (ship's) rail.

bastion [bastjɔ̃] *nm litt & fig* bastion.

baston [bastɔ̃] *nf tfam* punch-up.

bas-ventre [bavɑ̃tr] (*pl* **bas-ventres**) *nm* stomach.

bât [ba] *nm* packsaddle; **c'est là que le ~ blesse** *fig* that's his/her *etc* weak point.

bataille [bataj] *nf* **-1.** MIL battle. **-2.** [bagarre] fight. **-3.** [jeu de cartes] ≃ beggar-my-neighbour. **-4.** *loc*: **en ~** [cheveux] dishevelled.

batailler [bataje] [3] *vi*: **~ pour qqch/pour faire qqch** to fight for sthg/to do sthg.

bataillon [batajɔ̃] *nm* MIL battalion; *fig* horde.

bâtard, -e [batar, ard] ◇ *adj* **-1.** [enfant] illegitimate. **-2.** *péj* [style, solution] hybrid. ◇ *nm, f* illegitimate child.
◆ **bâtard** *nm* **-1.** [pain] ≃ Vienna loaf. **-2.** [chien] mongrel.

batavia [batavja] *nf* Webb lettuce.

bateau [bato] *nm* **-1.** [embarcation - gén] boat; [- plus grand] ship; **~ à voile/moteur** sailing/motor boat; **~ de pêche** fishing boat; **mener qqn en ~** *fig* to take sb for a ride. **-2.** [de trottoir] driveway entrance (*low kerb*). **-3.** (*en apposition inv*) **encolure ~** boat neck. **-4.** (*en apposition inv*) [sujet, thème] well-worn; **c'est ~!** it's the same old stuff!

bateau-mouche [batomuʃ] (*pl* **bateaux-mouches**) *nm* riverboat (*on the Seine*).

bateleur, -euse [batlœr, øz] *nm, f* street acrobat.

bâti, -e [bati] *adj* **-1.** [terrain] developed. **-2.** [personne]: **bien ~** well-built.
◆ **bâti** *nm* **-1.** COUTURE tacking. **-2.** CONSTR frame, framework.

batifoler [batifɔle] [3] *vi* to frolic.

bâtiment [batimɑ̃] *nm* **-1.** [édifice] building. **-2.** IND: **le ~** the building trade. **-3.** NAVIG ship, vessel.

bâtir [batir] [32] *vt* **-1.** CONSTR to build. **-2.** *fig* [réputation, fortune] to build (up); [théorie, phrase] to construct. **-3.** COUTURE to tack.
◆ **se bâtir** *vp* to be built.

bâtisse [batis] *nf souvent péj* house.

bâton [batɔ̃] *nm* **-1.** [gén] stick; **~ de réglisse** liquorice stick; **~ de ski** ski pole. **-2.** *fam fig* 10 000 francs. **-3.** *loc*: **mettre des ~s dans les roues à qqn** to put a spoke in sb's wheel; **à ~s rompus** [conversation] rambling; **parler à ~s rompus** to talk of this and that.

bâtonnet [batɔnɛ] *nm* rod.

bâtonnier [batɔnje] *nm* JUR ≃ President of the Bar.

batracien [batrasjɛ̃] *nm* amphibian.

battage [bataʒ] *nm*: **~ (publicitaire OU médiatique)** (media) hype.

battant, -e [batɑ̃, ɑ̃t] ◇ *adj*: **sous une pluie ~e** in the pouring OU driving rain; **le cœur ~** with beating heart. ◇ *nm, f* fighter.
◆ **battant** *nm* **-1.** [de porte] door (*of double doors*); [de fenêtre] half (*of double window*). **-2.** [de cloche] clapper.

batte [bat] *nf* SPORT bat.

battement [batmɑ̃] *nm* **-1.** [mouvement - d'ailes] flap, beating (*U*); [- de cœur, pouls] beat, beating (*U*); [- de cils, paupières] flutter, fluttering (*U*). **-2.** [bruit - de porte] banging (*U*); [- de la pluie] beating (*U*). **-3.** [intervalle de temps] break; **une heure de ~** an hour free.

batterie [batri] *nf* **-1.** ÉLECTR & MIL battery; **recharger ses ~s** *fig* to recharge one's batteries. **-2.** [attirail]: **~ de cuisine** kitchen utensils (*pl*). **-3.** MUS drums (*pl*). **-4.** [série]: **une ~ de** a string of.

batteur [batœr] *nm* **-1.** MUS drummer. **-2.** CULIN beater, whisk. **-3.** [SPORT - de cricket] batsman; [- de base-ball] batter.

batteuse [batøz] *nf* AGRIC thresher.

battoir [batwar] *nm* **-1.** [à tapis] carpet beater. **-2.** *fig* [main] great mitt OU paw.

battre [batr] [83] ◇ *vt* **-1.** [gén] to beat; **~ en neige** [blancs d'œufs] to beat until stiff. **-2.** [parcourir] to scour. **-3.** [cartes] to shuffle. ◇ *vi* [gén] to beat; **~ des cils** to blink; **~ des mains** to clap (one's hands).
◆ **se battre** *vp* to fight; **se ~ contre qqn** to fight sb.

battu, -e [baty] ◇ *pp* → **battre**. ◇ *adj* **-1.** [tassé] hard-packed; **jouer sur terre ~e** TENNIS to play on clay. **-2.** [fatigué]: **avoir les yeux ~s** to have shadows under one's eyes.
◆ **battue** *nf* **-1.** [chasse] beat. **-2.** [chasse à l'homme] manhunt.

baud [bo] *nm* baud.

baudroie [bodrwa] *nf* monkfish.

baudruche [bodryʃ] *nf* **-1.** [ballon] balloon. **-2.** *fig* [personne] front man.

baume [bom] *nm litt* & *fig* balm; **mettre du ~ au cœur de qqn** to comfort sb.

bauxite [boksit] *nf* bauxite.

bavard, -e [bavar, ard] ◇ *adj* talkative. ◇ *nm, f* chatterbox; *péj* gossip.

bavardage [bavardaʒ] *nm* **-1.** [papotage] chattering. **-2.** (*gén pl*) [raconter] gossip (*U*).

bavarder [bavarde] [3] *vi* to chatter; *péj* to gossip.

bavarois, -e [bavarwa, waz] *adj* Bavarian.

◆ **bavarois** *nm*, **bavaroise** *nf* [gâteau] ≃ mousse.

◆ **Bavarois, -e** *nm, f* Bavarian.

bave [bav] *nf* **-1.** [salive] dribble. **-2.** [d'animal] slaver. **-3.** [de limace] slime.

baver [bave] [3] *vi* **-1.** [personne] to dribble. **-2.** [animal] to slaver. **-3.** [limace] to leave a trail. **-4.** [stylo] to leak. **-5.** *loc*: **en ~** *fam* to have a hard ou rough time of it.

bavette [bavɛt] *nf* **-1.** [bavoir, de tablier] bib. **-2.** [viande] flank. **-3.** *loc*: **tailler une ~ (avec qqn)** *fam* to have a natter *Br* (with sb).

baveux, -euse [bavø, øz] *adj* **-1.** [bébé] dribbling. **-2.** [lettre] blurred. **-3.** [omelette] runny.

Bavière [bavjɛr] *nf*: **la ~** Bavaria.

bavoir [bavwar] *nm* bib.

bavure [bavyr] *nf* **-1.** [tache] smudge. **-2.** [erreur] blunder.

bayer [baje] [3] *vi*: **~ aux corneilles** to stand gazing into space.

bazar [bazar] *nm* **-1.** [boutique] general store. **-2.** *fam* [désordre] jumble, clutter.

bazarder [bazarde] [3] *vt fam* to chuck out, to get rid of.

BCBG (*abr de* **bon chic bon genre**) *n & adj* term used to describe an upper-class lifestyle reflected especially in expensive but conservative clothes; **il est très ~** ≃ he's a real preppie type.

BCG (*abr de* **bacille Calmette-Guérin**) *nm* BCG.

bcp *abr de* **beaucoup**.

bd *abr de* **boulevard**.

BD, bédé [bede] (*abr de* **bande dessinée**) *nf*: **une ~** a comic strip; **la ~** comic strips (*pl*).

béant, -e [beɑ̃, ɑ̃t] *adj* [plaie, gouffre] gaping; [yeux] wide open.

béarnais, -e [bearnɛ, ɛz] *adj* of ou from the Béarn.

◆ **Béarnais, -e** *nm, f* native ou inhabitant of the Béarn.

◆ **béarnaise** *nf*: **(sauce) ~e** Béarnaise sauce.

béat, -e [bea, at] *adj* **-1.** [content de soi] smug. **-2.** [heureux] blissful.

béatement [beatmɑ̃] *adv* blissfully.

béatitude [beatityd] *nf* **-1.** RELIG beatitude. **-2.** [bonheur] bliss.

beau, belle, beaux [bo, bɛl] *adj* (**bel** *devant voyelle ou h muet*) **-1.** [joli - femme] beautiful, good-looking; [- homme] handsome, good-looking; [- chose] beautiful. **-2.** [temps] fine, good. **-3.** (*toujours avant le nom*) [important] fine, excellent; **une belle somme** a tidy sum (of money). **-4.** *iron* [mauvais]: **une belle grippe** a nasty dose of the flu; **un ~ travail** a fine piece of work. **-5.** (*sens intensif*): **un ~ jour** one fine day. **-6.** [noble] fine, noble. **-7.** *loc*: **elle a ~ jeu de dire** ça it's easy ou all very well for her to say that.

◆ **beau** ◇ *adv*: **il fait ~** the weather is good ou fine; **j'ai ~ essayer ...** however hard I try ..., try as I may ...; **j'ai ~ dire ...** whatever I say ....

◇ *nm*: **être au ~ fixe** to be set fair; **avoir le moral au ~ fixe** *fig* to have a sunny disposition; **faire le ~** [chien] to sit up and beg.

◆ **belle** *nf* **-1.** [femme] lady friend. **-2.** [dans un jeu] decider. **-3.** *loc*: **(se) faire la belle** to escape.

◆ **bel et bien** *loc adv* well and truly, actually.

◆ **de plus belle** *loc adv* more than ever.

beaucoup [boku] ◇ *adv* **-1.** [un grand nombre]: **~ de** a lot of, many; **il y en a ~** there are many ou a lot (of them). **-2.** [une grande quantité]: **~ de** a lot of; **~ d'énergie** a lot of energy; **il n'a pas ~ de temps** he hasn't a lot of ou much time; **il n'en a pas ~** he doesn't have much ou a lot (of it). **-3.** (*modifiant un verbe*) a lot; **il boit ~** he drinks a lot; **c'est ~ dire** that's saying a lot. **-4.** (*modifiant un adjectif comparatif*) much, a lot; **c'est ~ mieux** it's much ou a lot better; **~ trop vite** much too quickly.

◇ *pron inv* many; **nous sommes ~ à penser que ...** many of us think that ....

◆ **de beaucoup** *loc adv* by far.

beauf [bof] *nm* **-1.** *péj* stereotype of average Frenchman with narrow views. **-2.** *fam* [beau-frère] brother-in-law.

beau-fils [bofis] (*pl* **beaux-fils**) *nm* **-1.** [gendre] son-in-law. **-2.** [de remariage] stepson.

beau-frère [bofrɛr] (*pl* **beaux-frères**) *nm* brother-in-law.

beau-père [bopɛr] (*pl* **beaux-pères**) *nm* **-1.** [père du conjoint] father-in-law. **-2.** [de remariage] stepfather.

beauté [bote] *nf* beauty; **de toute** ~ absolutely beautiful; **en** ~ [magnifiquement] in great style; *sout* [femme] ravishing.

beaux-arts [bozar] *nmpl* fine art (*sg*).
◆ **Beaux-Arts** *nmpl*: **les Beaux-Arts** *the Paris art school.*

beaux-parents [boparɑ̃] *nmpl* **-1.** [de l'homme] husband's parents, in-laws. **-2.** [de la femme] wife's parents, in-laws.

bébé [bebe] *nm* baby; ~ **phoque** seal pup, baby seal. ◇ *adj inv* babyish.

bébé-éprouvette [bebeepruvɛt] (*pl* **bébés-éprouvette**) *nm* test-tube baby.

bébête [bebɛt] *adj* silly.

bec [bɛk] *nm* **-1.** [d'oiseau] beak. **-2.** [d'instrument de musique] mouthpiece. **-3.** [de casserole etc] lip; ~ **de gaz** [réverbère] gaslamp (*in street*); ~ **verseur** spout. **-4.** *fam* [bouche] mouth; **ouvrir le** ~ to open one's mouth; **clouer le** ~ **à qqn** to shut sb up.

bécane [bekan] *nf fam* **-1.** [moto, vélo] bike. **-2.** [ordinateur etc] machine.

bécasse [bekas] *nf* **-1.** [oiseau] woodcock. **-2.** *fam* [femme sotte] silly goose.

bécassine [bekasin] *nf* **-1.** [oiseau] snipe. **-2.** *fam* [jeune fille naïve] silly little goose.

bec-de-lièvre [bɛkdəljɛvr] (*pl* **becs-de-lièvre**) *nm* harelip.

béchamel [beʃamɛl] *nf*: **(sauce)** ~ béchamel sauce.

bêche [bɛʃ] *nf* spade.

bêcher [beʃe] [4] ◇ *vt* to dig. ◇ *vi fam* to show off, to pose.

bêcheur, -euse [beʃœr, øz] *nm, f fam* stuck-up person.

bécoter [bekɔte] [3] *vt fam* to snog *Br* OU smooch with.
◆ **se bécoter** *vp* to snog *Br*, to smooch.

becquée [beke] *nf*: **donner la** ~ **à** to feed.

becqueter, béqueter [bɛkte] [27] *vt* to peck at.

becter [bɛkte] [4] *vi fam* to eat.

bedaine [bədɛn] *nf* potbelly.

bédé = **BD**.

bedeau, -x [bədo] *nm* verger.

bedonnant, -e [bədɔnɑ̃, ɑ̃t] *adj* potbellied.

bédouin, -e [bedwɛ̃, in] *adj* Bedouin.
◆ **Bédouin, -e** *nm, f* Bedouin.

bée [be] *adj*: **bouche** ~ open-mouthed.

bégaiement [begɛmɑ̃] *nm* stammering.

bégayer [begeje] [11] ◇ *vi* to have a stutter OU stammer. ◇ *vt* to stammer (out).

bégonia [begɔnja] *nm* begonia.

bègue [bɛg] ◇ *adj*: **être** ~ to have a stutter OU stammer. ◇ *nmf* stutterer, stammerer.

bégueule [begœl] *fam péj* ◇ *adj* prudish. ◇ *nf* prude.

béguin [begɛ̃] *nm fam*: **avoir le** ~ **pour qqn** to have a crush on sb; **avoir le** ~ **pour qqch** to be mad keen on sthg.

beige [bɛʒ] *adj & nm* beige.

beigne [bɛɲ] *nf fam* slap.

beignet [bɛɲɛ] *nm* fritter.

bel [bɛl] → **beau**.

bêler [bele] [4] *vi* to bleat.

belette [bəlɛt] *nf* weasel.

belge [bɛlʒ] *adj* Belgian.
◆ **Belge** *nmf* Belgian.

belgicisme [bɛlʒisism] *nm* [mot] Belgian word; [tournure] Belgian expression.

Belgique [bɛlʒik] *nf*: **la** ~ Belgium.

bélier [belje] *nm* **-1.** [animal] ram. **-2.** [poutre] battering ram.
◆ **Bélier** *nm* ASTROL Aries; **être Bélier** to be (an) Aries.

Belize [beliz] *nm*: **le** ~ Belize; **au** ~ in Belize.

belladone [beladɔn] *nf* deadly nightshade.

bellâtre [bɛlatr] *nm péj* smoothie.

belle [bɛl] *adj & nf* → **beau**.

belle-famille [bɛlfamij] (*pl* **belles-familles**) *nf* **-1.** [de l'homme] husband's family, in-laws (*pl*). **-2.** [de la femme] wife's family, in-laws (*pl*).

belle-fille [bɛlfij] (*pl* **belles-filles**) *nf* **-1.** [épouse du fils] daughter-in-law. **-2.** [de remariage] stepdaughter.

belle-mère [bɛlmɛr] (*pl* **belles-mères**) *nf* **-1.** [mère du conjoint] mother-in-law. **-2.** [de remariage] stepmother.

belles-lettres [bɛllɛtr] *nfpl* (great) literature (*U*).

belle-sœur [bɛlsœr] (*pl* **belles-sœurs**) *nf* sister-in-law.

belligérant, -e [beliʒerɑ̃, ɑ̃t] *adj & nm, f* belligerent.

belliqueux, -euse [belikø, øz] *adj* [peuple] warlike; [humeur, tempérament] aggressive.

belote [bəlɔt] *nf French card game*.

belvédère [belvedɛr] *nm* **-1.** [construction] belvedere. **-2.** [terrasse] viewpoint.

bémol [bemɔl] *adj & nm* MUS flat.

bénédictin, -e [benediktɛ̃, in] ◇ *adj* Benedictine. ◇ *nm, f* Benedictine; **travail de** ~ *fig* painstaking task.
◆ **Bénédictine** *nf* [liqueur] Benedictine.

bénédiction [benediksjɔ̃] *nf* blessing; **donner sa ~ à** *fig* to give one's blessing to.

bénéfice [benefis] *nm* **-1.** [avantage] advantage, benefit; **àu ~ de** in aid of; **accorder à qqn le ~ du doute** to give sb the benefit of the doubt. **-2.** [profit] profit; **~ net/brut** net/gross profit; **intéressement aux ~s** profit-sharing; **rapport cours-~** price-earnings ratio; **~s commerciaux** trading profit (*sg*).

bénéficiaire [benefisjɛr] ◇ *nmf* [gén] beneficiary; [de chèque] **payee.** ◇ *adj* [marge] profit (*avant n*); [résultat, société] profit-making.

bénéficier [benefisje] [9] *vi:* **~ de** [profiter de] to benefit from; [jouir de] to have, to enjoy; [obtenir] to have, to get.

bénéfique [benefik] *adj* beneficial.

Bénélux [benelyks] *nm:* **le ~** Benelux; **les pays du ~** the Benelux countries.

benêt [bənɛ] ◇ *nm* clod. ◇ *adj (seulement masculin)* silly, simple.

bénévolat [benevɔla] *nm* voluntary work.

bénévole [benevɔl] ◇ *adj* voluntary. ◇ *nmf* volunteer, voluntary worker.

bénévolement [benevɔlmɑ̃] *adv* voluntarily, for nothing.

Bengale [bɛ̃gal] *nm:* **le ~** Bengal; **au ~** in Bengal.

bénin, -igne [benɛ̃, iɲ] *adj* **-1.** [maladie, accident] minor; [tumeur] benign. **-2.** *sout* [bienveillant] benign.

Bénin [benɛ̃] *nm:* **le ~** Benin; **au ~** in Benin.

béninois, -e [beninwa, waz] *adj* Beninese.
◆ **Béninois, -e** *nm, f* Beninese (*inv*).

bénir [benir] [32] *vt* **-1.** [gén] to bless. **-2.** [se réjouir de] to thank God for.

bénit, -e [beni, it] *adj* consecrated; **eau ~e** holy water.

bénitier [benitje] *nm* holy water font.

benjamin, -e [bɛ̃ʒamɛ̃, in] *nm, f* [de famille] youngest child; [de groupe] youngest member.

benne [bɛn] *nf* **-1.** [de camion] tipper. **-2.** [de téléphérique] car. **-3.** [pour déchets] skip.

benzine [bɛ̃zin] *nf* benzine.

béotien, -ienne [beɔsjɛ̃, jɛn] *nm, f* philistine.

BEP, Bep (*abr de* **brevet d'études professionnelles**) *nm* school-leaver's diploma (*taken at age 18*).

BEPC, Bepc (*abr de* **brevet d'études du premier cycle**) *nm* former school certificate (*taken at age 16*).

béqueter = **becqueter.**

béquille [bekij] *nf* **-1.** [pour marcher] crutch. **-2.** [d'un deux-roues] stand.

berbère [bɛrbɛr] *adj & nm* Berber.
◆ **Berbère** *nmf* Berber.

bercail [bɛrkaj] *nm* fold; **rentrer au ~** *fig* to return to the fold.

berceau, -x [bɛrso] *nm* cradle.

bercer [bɛrse] [16] *vt* **-1.** [bébé, bateau] to rock; **son enfance a été bercée de cette musique** he was brought up on this kind of music. **-2.** *fig* [tromper]: **~ qqn de** to delude sb with.
◆ **se bercer** *vp fig:* **se ~ de** to delude o.s. with; **se ~ d'illusions** to delude o.s.

berceuse [bɛrsøz] *nf* **-1.** [chanson] lullaby. **-2.** *Can* [fauteuil] rocking chair.

Bercy [bɛrsi] *n* **-1.** [ministère] *the French Ministry of Finance.* **-2.** [stade] *large sports and concert hall in Paris.*

BERD, Berd [bɛrd] (*abr de* **Banque européenne pour la reconstruction et le développement**) *nf* EBRD.

béret [berɛ] *nm* beret; **~ basque** (French) beret.

bergamote [bɛrgamɔt] *nf* bergamot orange.

berge [bɛrʒ] *nf* **-1.** [bord] bank. **-2.** *fam* [an]: **il a plus de 50 ~s** he's over 50.

berger, -ère [bɛrʒe, ɛr] *nm, f* shepherd (*f* shepherdess).
◆ **bergère** *nf* [canapé] wing chair.
◆ **berger allemand** *nm* alsatian *Br,* German shepherd.

bergerie [bɛrʒəri] *nf* sheepfold.

bergeronnette [bɛrʒərɔnɛt] *nf* wagtail.

Berlin [bɛrlɛ̃] *n* Berlin; **~-Est** East Berlin; **~-Ouest** West Berlin; **le mur de ~** the Berlin Wall.

berline [bɛrlin] *nf* saloon (car) *Br,* sedan *Am.*

berlingot [bɛrlɛ̃go] *nm* **-1.** [de lait etc] carton. **-2.** [bonbon] boiled sweet.

berlue [bɛrly] *nf:* **j'ai la ~!** I must be seeing things!

bermuda [bɛrmyda] *nm* bermuda shorts (*pl*).

Bermudes [bɛrmyd] *nfpl:* **les ~** Bermuda (*sg*); **aux ~** in Bermuda; **le triangle des ~** the Bermuda Triangle.

bernard-l'ermite [bɛrnarlɛrmit] *nm inv* hermit crab.

berne [bɛrn] *nf:* **en ~ ≃** at half-mast.

berner [bɛrne] [3] *vt* to fool.

berrichon, -onne [beriʃɔ̃, ɔn] *adj* of OU from the Berry.

besace [bəzas] *nf* pouch.

besicles [bezikl] *nfpl hum* specs.

besogne [bəzɔɲ] *nf* job, work (*U*); **aller vite en ~** *fig* to be a fast worker.

besoin [bəzwɛ̃] *nm* need; **avoir ~ de qqch/ de faire qqch** to need sthg/to do sthg; **au ~** if necessary, if need ou needs be; **être dans le ~** to be in need.

◆ **besoins** *nmpl* **-1.** [exigences] needs. **-2.** *loc*: **faire ses ~s** to relieve o.s.; **pour les ~s de la cause** for our purposes.

bestial, -e, -iaux [bɛstjal, jo] *adj* bestial, brutish.

bestiole [bɛstjɔl] *nf* (little) creature.

best-seller [bɛstselœr] (*pl* **best-sellers**) *nm* best-seller.

bétail [betaj] *nm* cattle (*pl*).

bête [bɛt] ◇ *nf* **-1.** [animal] animal; [insecte] insect; **~ à bon Dieu** ladybird; **~ féroce** wild animal; **~ de somme** beast of burden. **-2.** *loc*: **chercher la petite ~** to nit-pick; **c'est sa ~ noire** that's his/her pet hate. ◇ *adj* **-1.** [stupide] stupid. **-2.** [simple]: **c'est tout ~** there's nothing to it.

bêtement [bɛtmɑ̃] *adv* **-1.** [de façon bête] stupidly. **-2.** [simplement]: **tout ~** just, quite simply.

bêtifiant, -e [betifjɑ̃, ɑ̃t] *adj* idiotic.

bêtise [betiz] *nf* **-1.** [stupidité] stupidity. **-2.** [action, remarque] stupid thing; **faire/dire une ~** to do/say something stupid; **faire des ~s** to be stupid ou silly.

béton [betɔ̃] *nm* **-1.** [matériau] concrete; **~ armé** reinforced concrete. **-2.** *fig*: **en ~** [argument] cast-iron.

bétonner [betɔne] [3] ◇ *vt* to concrete. ◇ *vi* FOOTBALL to play defensively.

bétonnière [betɔnjɛr] *nf* cement mixer.

bette [bɛt], **blette** [blɛt] *nf* Swiss chard.

betterave [betrav] *nf* beetroot *Br*, beet *Am*; **~ fourragère** mangel-wurzel; **~ sucrière** ou **à sucre** sugar beet.

beuglement [bøɡləmɑ̃] *nm* **-1.** [de bovin] mooing (*U*), lowing (*U*). **-2.** [de radio] blaring (*U*).

beugler [bøɡle] [5] *vi* **-1.** [bovin] to moo, to low. **-2.** *fam* [personne] to bellow; [radio] to blare out.

beur [bœr] *nmf person born in France of North African immigrant parents.*

beurre [bœr] *nm* **-1.** [aliment] butter; **~ de cacahuètes** peanut butter; **~ de cacao** cocoa butter; **~ demi-sel** slightly-salted butter; **~ noir** brown butter sauce. **-2.** *loc*: **compter pour du ~** to count for nothing; **faire son ~** to make one's pile; **mettre du**

~ dans les épinards to make life a little more comfortable.

beurré, -e [bœre] *adj* **-1.** [couvert de beurre] buttered. **-2.** *fam* [ivre] plastered.

beurrer [bœre] [5] *vt* to butter.

beurrier, -ière [bœrje, jɛr] *adj* [industrie] butter (*avant n*); [région] butter-producing.

◆ **beurrier** *nm* butter dish.

beuverie [bœvri] *nf* drinking session.

bévue [bevy] *nf* blunder; **faire** ou **commettre une ~** to slip up.

Beyrouth [berut] *n* Beirut; **~-Est** East Beirut; **~-Ouest** West Beirut.

BHV (*abr de* **Bazar de l'Hôtel de Ville**) *nm large department store in central Paris.*

biais [bjɛ] *nm* **-1.** [ligne oblique] slant; **en** ou **de ~** [de travers] at an angle; *fig* indirectly. **-2.** COUTURE bias; **tailler un tissu dans le ~** to cut a piece of cloth on the bias. **-3.** [aspect] angle. **-4.** [moyen détourné] expedient; **par le ~ de** by means of.

biaiser [bjeze] [4] *vi fig* to dodge the issue.

bibelot [biblo] *nm* trinket, curio.

biberon [bibrɔ̃] *nm* baby's bottle; **nourrir au ~** to bottle-feed.

bible [bibl] *nf* bible.

bibliobus [biblijɔbys] *nm* mobile library.

bibliographie [biblijɔɡrafi] *nf* bibliography.

bibliographique [biblijɔɡrafik] *adj* bibliographical.

bibliophile [biblijɔfil] *nmf* book lover.

bibliothécaire [biblijɔtekɛr] *nmf* librarian.

bibliothèque [biblijɔtɛk] *nf* **-1.** [meuble] bookcase. **-2.** [édifice, collection] library; **~ municipale** public library; **la Bibliothèque nationale** *the French national library.*

BIBLIOTHÈQUE NATIONALE:
Situated in the rue de Richelieu in Paris, the Bibliothèque nationale or 'BN' is a large copyright deposit library comparable to the British Library and the Library of Congress

biblique [biblik] *adj* biblical.

Bic® [bik] *nm* ball-point pen.

bicarbonate [bikarbɔnat] *nm*: **~ (de soude)** bicarbonate of soda.

bicentenaire [bisɑ̃tnɛr] ◇ *adj* two-hundred-year-old (*avant n*). ◇ *nm* bicentenary, bicentennial.

biceps [bisɛps] *nm* biceps.

biche [biʃ] *nf* ZOOL hind, doe.

bichonner [biʃɔne] [3] *vt* [choyer] to cosset, to pamper.

◆ **se bichonner** *vp* to spruce o.s. up; [femme] to doll o.s. up.

bicolore [bikɔlɔr] *adj* two-coloured.

bicoque [bikɔk] *nf péj* house.

bicorne [bikɔrn] *nm* cocked hat.

bicyclette [bisiklɛt] *nf* bicycle; **rouler à** ~ **to** cycle.

bidasse [bidas] *nm fam* squaddie *Br*, grunt *Am*.

bide [bid] *nm fam* -1. [ventre] belly. -2. [échec] flop.

bidet [bidɛ] *nm* -1. [sanitaire] bidet. -2. *hum* [cheval] nag.

bidon [bidɔ̃] *nm* -1. [récipient] can. -2. *fam* [ventre] belly. -3. (*en apposition inv*) *fam* [faux] phoney. -4. *fam* [simulation]: **c'est du** ~ it's (a load of) rubbish.

bidonner [bidɔne] [3]
◆ **se bidonner** *vp fam* to laugh one's head off.

bidonville [bidɔ̃vil] *nm* shantytown.

bidouilleur [bidujœr] *nm* INFORM do-it-yourselfer.

bidule [bidyl] *nm fam* thing, thingy.

bielle [bjɛl] *nf* connecting rod.

biélorusse [bjelɔrys] *adj* Belorussian, Byelorussian.
◆ **Biélorusse** *nmf* Belorussian, Byelorussian.

Biélorussie [bjelɔrysi] *nf*: **la** ~ Belorussia, Byelorussia.

bien [bjɛ̃] (*compar & superl* **mieux**) ◇ *adj inv* -1. [satisfaisant] good; **il est** ~ **comme prof** he's a good teacher; **il est** ~, **ce bureau** this is a good office. -2. [en bonne santé] well; **je ne me sens pas** ~ I don't feel well. -3. [joli] good-looking; **tu ne trouves pas qu'elle est** ~ **comme ça?** don't you think she looks good OU nice like that? -4. [à l'aise] comfortable. -5. [convenable] respectable.
◇ *nm* -1. [sens moral]: **le** ~ good; **le** ~ **et le mal** good and evil. -2. [intérêt] good; **je te dis ça pour ton** ~ I'm telling you this for your own good. -3. [richesse, propriété] property, possession; ~**s de consommation** consumer goods. -4. *loc*: **faire du** ~ **à qqn** to do sb good; **dire du** ~ **de qqn/qqch** to speak well of sb/sthg; **mener à** ~ to bring to fruition, to complete; **en tout** ~ **tout honneur** with the best of intentions.
◇ *adv* -1. [de manière satisfaisante] well; **on mange** ~ **ici** the food's good here; **il ne s'est pas** ~ **conduit** he didn't behave well; **tu as** ~ **fait** you did the right thing; **tu ferais** ~ **d'y aller** you would be wise to go; **c'est** ~ **fait!** it serves him/her *etc* right! -2. [sens intensif] quite, really; ~ **souvent** quite often; **en es-tu** ~ **sûr?** are you quite sure (about it)?; **j'espère** ~ **que** ... I DO hope that ...; **on a** ~ **ri** we had a good laugh; **il a** ~ **de la chance** he's very OU really lucky; **il y a** ~ **trois heures que j'attends** I've been waiting for at least three hours; **c'est** ~ **aimable à vous** it's very kind OU good of you. -3. [renforçant un comparatif]: **il est parti** ~ **plus tard** he left much later; **on était** ~ **moins riches** we were a lot worse off OU poorer; **il était** ~ **aussi gentil que** ... he was just as kind as .... -4. [servant à conclure ou à introduire]: **bien, c'est fini pour aujourd'hui** well, that's it for today; ~, **je t'écoute** well, I'm listening; **très** ~, **je vais avec toi** all right then, I'll go with you. -5. [en effet]: **c'est** ~ **lui** it really IS him; **c'est** ~ **ce que je disais** that's just what I said.
◇ *interj*: **eh** ~! oh well!; **eh** ~, **qu'en penses-tu?** well, what do you think?

◆ **biens** *nmpl* property (*U*).

◆ **bien de, bien des** *loc adj*: ~ **des gens sont venus** quite a lot of people came; ~ **des fois** many times; **il a eu** ~ **de la peine à me convaincre** he had quite a lot of trouble convincing me.

◆ **bien entendu** *loc adv* of course.

◆ **bien que** *loc conj* (+ *subjonctif*) although, though.

◆ **bien sûr** *loc adv* of course, certainly.

bien-aimé, -e [bjɛ̃neme] (*mpl* **bien-aimés**, *fpl* **bien-aimées**) *adj & nm, f* beloved.

bien-être [bjɛ̃nɛtr] *nm inv* -1. [physique] wellbeing. -2. [matériel] wellbeing, comfort.

bienfaisance [bjɛ̃fəzɑ̃s] *nf* charity.

bienfaisant, -e [bjɛ̃fəzɑ̃, ɑ̃t] *adj* beneficial.

bienfait [bjɛ̃fɛ] *nm* -1. [effet bénéfique] benefit. -2. [faveur] kindness.

bienfaiteur, -trice [bjɛ̃fɛtœr, tris] *nm, f* benefactor.

bien-fondé [bjɛ̃fɔ̃de] (*pl* **bien-fondés**) *nm* validity.

bienheureux, -euse [bjɛ̃nørø, øz] *adj* -1. RELIG blessed. -2. [heureux] happy.

biennal, -e, -aux [bjenal, o] *adj* biennial.
◆ **biennale** *nf* biennial festival.

bien-pensant, -e [bjɛ̃pɑ̃sɑ̃, ɑ̃t] (*mpl* **bien-pensants**, *fpl* **bien-pensantes**) *adj & nm, f péj* conformist.

bienséance [bjɛ̃seɑ̃s] *nf* decorum.
◆ **bienséances** *nfpl* conventions.

bientôt [bjɛ̃to] *adv* soon; **à** ~! see you soon!

bienveillance [bjɛ̃vejɑ̃s] *nf* kindness.

bienveillant, -e [bjɛ̃vejɑ̃, ɑ̃t] *adj* kindly.

bienvenu, -e [bjɛ̃vəny] ◇ *adj* [qui arrive à

bis¹

propos] welcome. ◇ *nm, f*: être le ~/la ~e to be welcome; soyez le ~! welcome!

◆ **bienvenue** *nf* welcome; souhaiter la ~e à qqn to welcome sb.

bière [bjɛr] *nf* **-1.** [boisson] beer; ~ **blonde** lager; ~ **brune** brown ale; ~ **pression** draught beer. **-2.** [cercueil] coffin.

biffer [bife] [3] *vt sout* to cross out.

bifteck [biftɛk] *nm* steak.

bifurcation [bifyrkasjɔ̃] *nf* [embranchement] fork; *fig* new direction.

bifurquer [bifyrke] [3] *vi* **-1.** [route, voie ferrée] to fork. **-2.** [voiture] to turn off. **-3.** *fig* [personne] to branch off.

bigame [bigam] ◇ *adj* bigamous. ◇ *nmf* bigamist.

bigamie [bigami] *nf* bigamy.

bigarreau, -x [bigaro] *nm* cherry.

bigophone [bigɔfɔn] *nm fam vieilli* [téléphone] blower *Br*, horn *Am*.

bigorneau, -x [bigɔrno] *nm* winkle.

bigot, -e [bigo, ɔt] *péj* ◇ *adj* bigoted. ◇ *nm, f* bigot.

bigoudi [bigudi] *nm* curler.

bigrement [bigrəmɑ̃] *adv fam vieilli* [beaucoup] a lot; [très] very.

bijou, -x [biʒu] *nm* **-1.** [joyau] jewel. **-2.** *fig* [chef d'œuvre] gem.

bijouterie [biʒutri] *nf* **-1.** [magasin] jeweller's (shop). **-2.** [activité] jewellery-making. **-3.** [commerce] jewellery trade.

bijoutier, -ière [biʒutje, jɛr] *nm, f* jeweller.

bikini [bikini] *nm vieilli* bikini.

bilan [bilɑ̃] *nm* **-1.** FIN balance sheet; **déposer son** ~ to declare bankruptcy. **-2.** [état d'une situation] state of affairs; **faire le** ~ **(de)** to take stock (of); ~ **de santé** checkup.

bilatéral, -e, -aux [bilateral, o] *adj* **-1.** [stationnement] on both sides (of the road). **-2.** [contrat, accord] bilateral.

bile [bil] *nf* bile; **déverser sa** ~ to vent one's spleen; **se faire de la** ~ *fam* to worry.

biliaire [biljɛr] *adj* biliary; **calcul** ~ gallstone; **vésicule** ~ gall bladder.

bilieux, -ieuse [biljø, jøz] *adj* **-1.** [teint] bilious. **-2.** [tempérament] irascible.

bilingue [bilɛ̃g] ◇ *adj* bilingual. ◇ *nmf* [personne] bilingual person. ◇ *nm* [dictionnaire] bilingual dictionary.

bilinguisme [bilɛ̃gɥism] *nm* bilingualism.

billard [bijar] *nm* **-1.** [jeu] billiards (*U*). **-2.** [table de jeu] billiard table. **-3.** *loc*: passer OU monter sur le ~ *fam* to go under the knife.

bille [bij] *nf* **-1.** [d'enfant] marble. **-2.** [de

billard] ball. **-3.** *fam* [tête] face. **-4.** [de bois] block of wood.

billet [bijɛ] *nm* **-1.** [lettre] note; ~ **doux** love letter. **-2.** [argent]: ~ **(de banque)** (bank) note. **-3.** [ticket] ticket; ~ **de train/d'avion** train/plane ticket; ~ **de faveur** complimentary ticket; ~ **de loterie** lottery ticket.

billetterie [bijɛtri] *nf* **-1.** [à l'aéroport] ticket desk; [à la gare] booking office OU hall. **-2.** [bureau, service] ticket office. **-3.** BANQUE cash dispenser.

billion [biljɔ̃] *nm* billion *Br*, trillion *Am*.

bimensuel, -elle [bimɑ̃sɥɛl] *adj* fortnightly *Br*, twice monthly.

◆ **bimensuel** *nm* fortnightly review *Br*.

bimestriel, -ielle [bimɛstrijɛl] *adj* two-monthly.

bimoteur [bimɔtœr] ◇ *adj* twin-engined. ◇ *nm* twin-engined plane.

binaire [binɛr] *adj* binary.

biner [bine] [3] *vt* to hoe.

biniou [binju] *nm* (Breton) bagpipes (*pl*).

binocle [binɔkl] *nm* pince-nez.

◆ **binocles** *nmpl fam vieilli* specs.

bio [bjo] *adj inv* natural; **aliments** ~ wholefood, health food.

biocarburant [bjɔkarbyrɑ̃] *nm* biofuel.

biochimie [bjɔʃimi] *nf* biochemistry.

biodégradable [bjɔdegradabl] *adj* biodegradable.

biodiversité [bjɔdivɛrsite] *nf* biodiversity.

biographie [bjɔgrafi] *nf* biography.

biographique [bjɔgrafik] *adj* biographical.

biologie [bjɔlɔʒi] *nf* biology.

biologique [bjɔlɔʒik] *adj* **-1.** SCIENCE biological. **-2.** [naturel] organic.

biopsie [bjɔpsi] *nf* biopsy.

biorythme [bjɔritm] *nm* biorhythm.

bip [bip] *nm* tone, beep; **parler après le** ~ to start talking after the tone, to speak after the beep.

bipède [bipɛd] *nm & adj* biped.

biper [bipe] [3] *vt* to page.

bique [bik] *nf* **-1.** *fam* [chèvre] (nanny) goat. **-2.** *péj* [femme]: **vieille** ~ old bag.

BIRD [bœrd] (*abr de* **Banque internationale pour la reconstruction et le développement**) *nf* IBRD.

biréacteur [bireaktœr] *nm* twin-engined jet.

birman, -e [birmɑ̃, an] *adj* Burmese.

◆ **birman** *nm* [langue] Burmese.

◆ **Birman, -e** *nm, f* Burmese.

Birmanie [birmani] *nf*: **la** ~ Burma.

bis¹, -e [bi, biz] *adj* greyish-brown; **pain** ~ brown bread.

bis² [bis] ◇ *adv* **-1.** [dans adresse]: **5 ~ 5a.**
-2. [à la fin d'un spectacle] encore. ◇ *nm* encore.

bisannuel, -elle [bizanɥɛl] *adj* biennial.

bisbille [bizbij] *nf* squabble, tiff; être en ~ (avec) to be on bad terms (with).

biscornu, -e [biskɔrny] *adj* **-1.** [difforme] irregularly shaped. **-2.** [bizarre] weird.

biscotte [biskɔt] *nf toasted bread sold in packets and often eaten for breakfast.*

biscuit [biskɥi] *nm* **-1.** [sec] biscuit *Br*, cookie *Am*; [salé] cracker. **-2.** [gâteau] sponge.

bise [biz] *nf* **-1.** [vent] north wind. **-2.** *fam* [baiser] kiss.

biseau, -x [bizo] *nm* bevel; en ~ bevelled.

bison [bizɔ̃] *nm* bison.

bisou [bizu] *nm fam* kiss.

bisque [bisk] *nf thick soup, the ingredients of which have been pureed;* ~ de homard lobster bisque.

bissextile [bisɛkstil] → année.

bistouri [bisturi] *nm* lancet.

bistro(t) [bistro] *nm fam* cafe, bar.

BISTROT:

This word can refer either to a small cafe or to a cosy restaurant, especially one frequented by regulars. 'Le style bistrot' refers to a style of furnishing inspired by the chairs, tables and zinc countertops typical of the traditional 'bistrot'

---

bit [bit] *nm* INFORM bit.

BIT (*abr de* **Bureau international du travail**) *nm* ILO.

bit(t)e [bit] *nf vulg* cock.

bitume [bitym] *nm* **-1.** [revêtement] asphalt. **-2.** CHIM bitumen.

bivouac [bivwak] *nm* bivouac.

bizarre [bizar] *adj* strange, odd.

bizarrement [bizarmɑ̃] *adv* strangely, oddly.

bizarrerie [bizarri] *nf* strangeness.

bizutage [bizytaʒ] *nm practical jokes played on new arrivals in a school or college.*

BIZUTAGE:

In some French schools and colleges, students in fancy-dress take to the streets and play practical jokes (sometimes very cruel ones) on each other and on passers-by at the beginning of the school year. This is part of the traditional initiation ceremony known as 'bizutage'

---

blabla, bla-bla [blabla] *nm inv fam* waffle.

blackbouler [blakbule] [3] *vt* **-1.** [à une élection] to blackball. **-2.** *fam* [à un examen] to fail.

black-out [blakaut] *nm* blackout.

blafard, -e [blafar, ard] *adj* pale.

blague [blag] *nf* **-1.** [plaisanterie] joke; ~ à part joking apart; sans ~! no!, really? **-2.** [sac]: ~ à tabac tobacco pouch.

blaguer [blage] [3] *fam* ◇ *vi* to joke. ◇ *vt* to tease.

blagueur, -euse [blagœr, øz] *fam* ◇ *adj* jokey. ◇ *nm, f* joker.

blaireau, -x [blɛro] *nm* **-1.** [animal] badger. **-2.** [de rasage] shaving brush.

blairer [blɛre] [4] *vt fam*: je ne peux pas la ~ I can't stand her.

blâme [blam] *nm* **-1.** [désapprobation] disapproval. **-2.** [sanction] reprimand.

blâmer [blame] [3] *vt* **-1.** [désapprouver] to blame. **-2.** [sanctionner] to reprimand.

blanc, blanche [blɑ̃, blɑ̃ʃ] *adj* **-1.** [gén] white. **-2.** [non écrit] blank. **-3.** [pâle] pale.
◆ **blanc** *nm* **-1.** [couleur] white; ~ cassé off-white. **-2.** [personne] white (man). **-3.** [linge de maison]: le ~ the (household) linen. **-4.** [sur page] blank (space); en ~ [chèque] blank; laisser en ~ to leave blank. **-5.** [dans conversation] gap. **-6.** [de volaille] white meat. **-7.** [vin] white (wine); ~ de ~s *white wine from white grapes.* **-8.** *loc:* chauffé à ~ white-hot; tirer à ~ to shoot OU fire blanks.
◆ **blanche** *nf* **-1.** [personne] white (woman). **-2.** MUS minim.
◆ **blanc d'œuf** *nm* egg white.

blanc-bec [blɑ̃bɛk] (*pl* **blancs-becs**) *nm péj* & *vieilli* greenhorn.

blanchâtre [blɑ̃ʃɑtr] *adj* whitish.

blanche → blanc.

blancheur [blɑ̃ʃœr] *nf* whiteness.

blanchiment [blɑ̃ʃimɑ̃] *nm* **-1.** [décoloration] bleaching. **-2.** [coloration en blanc] whitewashing; ~ d'argent *fig* money laundering.

blanchir [blɑ̃ʃir] [32] ◇ *vt* **-1.** [mur] to whitewash. **-2.** [linge, argent] to launder. **-3.** [légumes] to blanch. **-4.** [sucre] to refine; [papier, tissu] to bleach. **-5.** *fig* [accusé]: ~ qqn de qqch to clear sb of sthg. ◇ *vi*: ~ (de) to go white (with).

blanchissage [blɑ̃ʃisaʒ] *nm* **-1.** [de linge] laundering. **-2.** [de sucre] refining.

blanchisserie [blɑ̃ʃisri] *nf* laundry.

blanquette [blɑ̃kɛt] *nf* **-1.** CULIN *stew of veal, lamb or chicken served in a white sauce;* ~ de

veau veal blanquette. **-2.** [vin]: ~ **de Limoux** *sparkling wine from Limoux.*

blasé, -e [blaze] ◇ *adj* blasé. ◇ *nm, f* blasé person.

blason [blazɔ̃] *nm* coat of arms.

blasphématoire [blasfematwar] *adj* blasphemous.

blasphème [blasfɛm] *nm* blasphemy.

blasphémer [blasfeme] [18] *vt & vi* to blaspheme.

blatte [blat] *nf* cockroach.

blazer [blazɛr] *nm* blazer.

blé [ble] *nm* **-1.** [céréale] wheat, corn; ~ **en herbe** unripe corn; ~ **noir** buckwheat; **blond comme les ~s** with corn-coloured hair. **-2.** *fam* [argent] dough.

bled [blɛd] *nm* **-1.** [brousse] *North African interior.* **-2.** *fam péj* [village isolé] godforsaken place.

blême [blɛm] *adj:* ~ **(de)** pale (with).

blêmir [blemir] [32] *vi* to go ou turn pale.

blennorragie [blenɔraʒi] *nf* gonorrhoea.

blessant, -e [blɛsɑ̃, ɑ̃t] *adj* hurtful.

blessé, -e [blese] *nm, f* wounded ou injured person; **un grand** ~ a badly wounded ou injured person.

blesser [blese] [4] *vt* **-1.** [physiquement - accidentellement] to injure, to hurt; [- par arme] to wound; [- suj: souliers] to hurt. **-2.** [moralement] to hurt.
◆ **se blesser** *vp* to injure o.s., to hurt o.s.

blessure [blesyr] *nf litt & fig* wound.

blet, blette [blɛ, blɛt] *adj* overripe.

blette = **bette**.

bleu, -e [blø] *adj* **-1.** [couleur] blue; ~ **pâle/pétrole/roi** pale/petrol/royal blue. **-2.** [viande] very rare.
◆ **bleu** *nm* **-1.** [couleur] blue. **-2.** [meurtrissure] bruise. **-3.** *fam* [novice - à l'armée] raw recruit; [- à l'université] freshman, fresher *Br.* **-4.** [fromage] blue cheese. **-5.** [antiseptique]: ~ **de méthylène** methylene blue. **-6.** [vêtement]: ~ **de travail** overalls *(pl).*

bleuet [bløɛ] *nm* cornflower.

bleuir [bløir] [32] *vt & vi* to turn blue.

bleuté, -e [bløte] *adj* bluish.

blindé, -e [blɛ̃de] *adj* **-1.** [véhicule] armoured; [porte, coffre] armour-plated. **-2.** *fam fig* [personne] hardened.
◆ **blindé** *nm* armoured car.

blinder [blɛ̃de] [3] *vt* **-1.** [véhicule] to armour; [porte, coffre] to armour-plate. **-2.** *fam* [endurcir] to harden.
◆ **se blinder** *vp fam fig* to harden o.s.

blizzard [blizar] *nm* blizzard.

bloc [blɔk] *nm* **-1.** [gén] block; **en** ~ wholesale; **faire** ~ to unite. **-2.** [assemblage] unit; ~ **d'alimentation** INFORM power pack; ~ **opératoire** operating theatre; ~ **sanitaire** toilet block.

blocage [blɔkaʒ] *nm* **-1.** ÉCON freeze, freezing *(U).* **-2.** [de roue] locking. **-3.** PSYCHOL (mental) block. **-4.** CONSTR rubble.

blockhaus [blɔkos] *nm* blockhouse.

bloc-moteur [blɔkmɔtœr] *(pl* **blocs-moteurs)** *nm* engine block.

bloc-notes [blɔknɔt] *(pl* **blocs-notes)** *nm* notepad.

blocus [blɔkys] *nm* blockade.

blond, -e [blɔ̃, blɔ̃d] ◇ *adj* fair, blond. ◇ *nm, f* fair-haired ou blond man *(f* fair-haired ou blonde woman).
◆ **blond** *nm:* ~ **cendré/vénitien/platine** ash/strawberry/platinum blond.
◆ **blonde** *nf* **-1.** [cigarette] Virginia cigarette. **-2.** [bière] lager.

blondeur [blɔ̃dœr] *nf* blondness, fairness.

blondir [blɔ̃dir] [32] *vi* to go ou turn blond; **faire** ~ CULIN to fry gently without browning.

bloquer [blɔke] [3] *vt* **-1.** [porte, freins] to jam; [roues] to lock. **-2.** [route, chemin] to block; [personne]: **être bloqué** to be stuck. **-3.** [prix, salaires, crédit] to freeze. **-4.** [regrouper] to combine. **-5.** PSYCHOL: **être bloqué** to have a (mental) block.
◆ **se bloquer** *vp* **-1.** [se coincer] to jam. **-2.** PSYCHOL: **se** ~ **contre** to have a (mental) block about.

blottir [blɔtir] [32]
◆ **se blottir** *vp:* **se** ~ **(contre)** to snuggle up (to).

blouse [bluz] *nf* **-1.** [de travail, d'écolier] smock. **-2.** [chemisier] blouse.

blouser [bluze] [3] ◇ *vi* to be full. ◇ *vt fam:* ~ **qqn** to pull a fast one on sb.

blouson [bluzɔ̃] *nm* bomber jacket, blouson; ~ **noir** ≃ teddy boy.

blue-jean [bludʒin] *(pl* **blue-jeans** [bludʒins]) *nm* jeans *(pl).*

blues [bluz] *nm inv* blues.

bluff [blœf] *nm* bluff.

bluffer [blœfe] [3] *fam vi & vt* to bluff.

blush [blœʃ] *nm* blusher.

BN *nf abr de* **Bibliothèque nationale**.

boa [bɔa] *nm* boa.

boat people [botpipœl] *nmpl* boat people.

bob [bɔb] *nm* SPORT bob.

bobard [bɔbar] *nm fam* fib.

bobine [bɔbin] *nf* **-1.** [cylindre] reel, spool. **-2.** ÉLECTR coil. **-3.** *fam vieilli* [visage] face.

bobo [bɔbo] *nm* (*langage enfantin*): **se faire ~** to hurt o.s.; **j'ai ~ à la tête** my head hurts.

bobsleigh [bɔbslɛg] *nm* bobsleigh.

bocage [bɔkaʒ] *nm* **-1.** [bois] grove. **-2.** GÉOGR bocage.

bocal, -aux [bɔkal, o] *nm* jar.

bock [bɔk] *nm* beer mug.

body-building [bɔdibɥildiŋ] *nm*: **le ~** body building (*U*).

bœuf [bœf, *pl* bø] *nm* **-1.** [animal] ox. **-2.** [viande] beef; **~ bourguignon** *beef stew in red-wine sauce*; **~ en daube** *beef braised in wine and stock*; **~ miroton** *slices of beef reheated in stock.*

bof [bɔf] *interj fam* [exprime le mépris] so what؟; [exprime la lassitude] I don't really care.

bohème [bɔɛm] ◇ *adj* bohemian. ◇ *nf*: **la ~** bohemia.

Bohême [bɔɛm] *nf*: **la ~** Bohemia.

bohémien, -ienne [bɔemjɛ̃, jɛn] ◇ *adj* **-1.** [tsigane] gipsy (*avant n*). **-2.** [non-conformiste] bohemian. ◇ *nm, f* **-1.** [tsigane] gipsy **-2.** [non-conformiste] bohemian.
◆ **Bohémien, -ienne** *nm, f* Bohemian.

boire [bwar] [108] ◇ *vt* **-1.** [s'abreuver] to drink. **-2.** [absorber] to soak up, to absorb. ◇ *vi* to drink.

bois [bwa] ◇ *nm* wood; **en ~** wooden; **~ mort** dead wood; **~ vert** green wood; **chèque en ~** *fig* rubber cheque; **petit ~** kindling; **toucher du ~** *fam fig* to touch wood *Br*, to knock on wood *Am*. ◇ *nmpl* **-1.** MUS woodwind (*U*). **-2.** [cornes] antlers.

boisé, -e [bwaze] *adj* wooded.

boiser [bwaze] [3] *vt* to afforest.

boiserie [bwazri] *nf* panelling (*U*).

boisson [bwasɔ̃] *nf* **-1.** [breuvage] drink; **~ chaude/froide** hot/cold drink; **être pris de ~** to be intoxicated. **-2.** [habitude] drink, drinking (*U*).

boîte [bwat] *nf* **-1.** [récipient] box; **en ~** tinned *Br*, canned; **~ de conserve** tin *Br*, can; **~ de dialogue** INFORM dialog box; **~ à gants** glove compartment; **~ aux lettres** [pour la réception] letterbox; [pour l'envoi] postbox *Br* mailbox *Am*; **~ à musique** musical box *Br*, music box *Am*; **~ noire** black box; **~ postale** post office box; **~ de vitesses** gearbox; **mettre qqn en ~** *fig* to pull sb's leg. **-2.** *fam* [entreprise] company, firm; [lycée] school. **-3.** *fam* [discothèque]: **~ (de nuit)** nightclub, club.

boiter [bwate] [3] *vi* **-1.** [personne] to limp. **-2.** [meuble] to wobble.

boiteux, -euse [bwatø, øz] ◇ *adj* **-1.** [personne] lame. **-2.** [meuble] wobbly. **-3.** *fig* [raisonnement] shaky. ◇ *nm, f* lame person.

boîtier [bwatje] *nm* **-1.** [boîte] case. **-2.** TECHNOL casing.

boitiller [bwatije] [3] *vi* to limp slightly.

bol [bɔl] *nm* **-1.** [récipient] bowl. **-2.** [contenu] bowl, bowlful. **-3.** *loc*: **avoir du ~** *fam* to be lucky; **prendre un ~ d'air** to get some fresh air.

bolet [bɔlɛ] *nm* boletus.

bolide [bɔlid] *nm* **-1.** [véhicule] racing car; **comme un ~** like a rocket. **-2.** ASTRON meteor.

Bolivie [bɔlivi] *nf*: **la ~** Bolivia.

bolivien, -ienne [bɔlivjɛ̃, jɛn] *adj* Bolivian.
◆ **Bolivien, -ienne** *nm, f* Bolivian.

bombance [bɔ̃bɑ̃s] *nf*: **faire ~** *fam* to have a feast.

bombardement [bɔ̃bardəmɑ̃] *nm* bombardment, bombing (*U*).

bombarder [bɔ̃barde] [3] *vt* **-1.** MIL to bomb. **-2.** [assaillir]: **~ qqn/qqch de** to bombard sb/sthg with. **-3.** *fam fig* [nommer]: **~ qqn chef de personnel** to pitchfork sb into the job of personnel manager.

bombardier [bɔ̃bardje] *nm* **-1.** [avion] bomber. **-2.** [aviateur] bombardier.

bombe [bɔ̃b] *nf* **-1.** [projectile] bomb; *fig* bombshell; **~ atomique** atomic bomb; **~ incendiaire** incendiary OU fire bomb; **~ à retardement** time bomb. **-2.** [casquette] riding hat. **-3.** [atomiseur] spray, aerosol. **-4.** CULIN: **~ glacée** (ice-cream) bombe. **-5.** *loc*: **faire la ~** to live it up.

bombé, -e [bɔ̃be] *adj* bulging, rounded.

bomber [bɔ̃be] [3] ◇ *vt* **-1.** [torse] to stick out. **-2.** *fam* [dessiner à la bombe] to spray. ◇ *vi* **-1.** [devenir convexe] to bulge. **-2.** *fam* [aller vite] to bomb along.

bon, bonne [bɔ̃, bɔn] *adj* (*compar* & *superl* **meilleur**) **-1.** [gén] good. **-2.** [généreux] good, kind. **-3.** [utilisable - billet, carte] valid. **-4.** [correct] right. **-5.** [dans l'expression d'un souhait]: **bonne année!** Happy New Year!; **bonne chance!** good luck!; **bonnes vacances!** have a nice holiday! **-6.** **être ~ pour qqch/pour faire qqch** *fam* to be fit for sthg/for doing sthg; **tu es ~ pour une contravention** you'll end up with OU you'll get a parking ticket; **~ à** (+ *infinitif*) fit to; **c'est ~ à savoir** that's worth knowing.
◆ **bon** ◇ *adv*: **à quoi ~ ...?** what's the use ...؟ **il fait ~** the weather's fine, it's fine; **sentir ~** to smell good; **tenir ~** to stand firm.

◇ *interj* **-1.** [marque de satisfaction] good! **-2.** [marque de surprise]: **ah ~! really?**

◇ *nm* **-1.** [constatant un droit] voucher; **~ de commande** order form; **~ du Trésor** FIN Treasury bill OU bond. **-2.** (*gén pl*) [personne]: **les ~s et les méchants** good people and wicked people. **-3.** [éléments valables] good (*U*).
◆ **pour de bon** *loc adv* seriously, really.

bonbon [bɔ̃bɔ̃] *nm* **-1.** [friandise] sweet *Br*, piece of candy *Am*; **~ acidulé** acid drop. **-2.** *Belg* [gâteau] biscuit.

bonbonne [bɔ̃bɔn] *nf* demijohn.

bonbonnière [bɔ̃bɔnjɛr] *nf* **-1.** [boîte] sweet-box *Br*, candy box *Am*. **-2.** *fig* [appartement] bijou flat *Br* OU apartment *Am*.

bond [bɔ̃] *nm* [d'animal, de personne] leap, bound; [de balle] bounce; **faire un ~** to leap (forward); **faire faux ~ à qqn** to let sb down.

bonde [bɔ̃d] *nf* **-1.** [d'évier] plug. **-2.** [trou] bunghole. **-3.** [bouchon] bung.

bondé, -e [bɔ̃de] *adj* packed.

bondieuserie [bɔ̃djøzri] *nf péj* **-1.** [bigoterie] religiosity. **-2.** [objet] religious trinket.

bondir [bɔ̃dir] [32] *vi* **-1.** [sauter] to leap, to bound; **~ sur qqn/qqch** to pounce on sb/sth. **-2.** [s'élancer] to leap forward. **-3.** *fig* [réagir violemment]: **~ (de)** to jump (with).

bonheur [bɔnœr] *nm* **-1.** [félicité] happiness. **-2.** [chance] (good) luck, good fortune; **par ~** happily, fortunately; **au petit ~** haphazardly; **porter ~** to be lucky, to bring good luck.

bonhomie [bɔnɔmi] *nf* good-naturedness, good nature.

bonhomme [bɔnɔm] (*pl* **bonshommes** [bɔ̃zɔm]) *nm* **-1.** *fam* [homme] fellow. **-2.** [petit garçon] fellow. **-3.** [représentation] man; **~ de neige** snowman. **-4.** *loc*: **aller son petit ~ de chemin** *fig* to jog along.

boniche [bɔniʃ] *nf péj* skivvy *Br*, servant.

bonification [bɔnifikasjɔ̃] *nf* **-1.** [de terre, de vin] improvement. **-2.** SPORT bonus points (*pl*).

bonifier [bɔnifje] [9] *vt* to improve.
◆ **se bonifier** *vp* to improve.

boniment [bɔnimɑ̃] *nm* **-1.** [baratin] sales talk (*U*). **-2.** [mensonge] (tall) story.

bonjour [bɔ̃ʒur] *nm* hello; [avant midi] good morning; [après midi] good afternoon; **simple comme ~** it's (as) easy as ABC.

bonne [bɔn] ◇ *nf* maid. ◇ *adj* → **bon**.

bonne-maman [bɔnmamɑ̃] (*pl* **bonnes-mamans**) *nf* granny, grandma.

bonnement [bɔnmɑ̃] *adv*: **tout ~** just, simply.

bonnet [bɔnɛ] *nm* **-1.** [coiffure] (woolly) hat; **~ d'âne** ≃ dunce's cap; **~ de bain** swimming cap; **~ de nuit** *fig* [personne] misery; **gros ~** *fig* [personne] big cheese; **~ phrygien** Phrygian cap (*worn by the sans-culottes during the French Revolution*). **-2.** [de soutien-gorge] cup. **-3.** *loc*: **~ blanc et blanc ~** six of one and half a dozen of the other.

bonneterie [bɔnɛtri] *nf* **-1.** [magasin] hosier's (shop). **-2.** [marchandise] hosiery (*U*). **-3.** [commerce] hosiery (business OU trade).

bon-papa [bɔ̃papa] (*pl* **bons-papas**) *nm* grandad, grandpa.

bonsoir [bɔ̃swar] *nm* [en arrivant] hello, good evening; [en partant] goodbye, good evening; [en se couchant] good night.

bonté [bɔ̃te] *nf* **-1.** [qualité] goodness, kindness; **avoir la ~ de faire qqch** *sout* to be so good OU kind as to do sthg. **-2.** (*gén pl*) [acte] act of kindness.

bonus [bɔnys] *nm* [prime d'assurance] no-claims bonus.

boom [bum] *nm* boom.

boomerang [bumrɑ̃g] *nm* boomerang.

borborygme [bɔrbɔrigm] *nm* rumbling (*U*).

bord [bɔr] *nm* **-1.** [de table, de vêtement] edge; [de verre, de chapeau] rim; **à ras ~s** to the brim. **-2.** [de rivière] bank; [de lac] edge, shore; **au ~ de la mer** at the seaside. **-3.** [de bois, jardin] edge; [de route] edge, side. **-4.** [d'un moyen de transport]: **passer par-dessus ~** to fall overboard; **virer de ~** NAVIG to tack. **-5.** *loc*: **être du même ~** *fig* to be on the same side.
◆ **à bord de** *loc prép*: **à ~ de qqch** on board sthg.
◆ **au bord de** *loc prép* at the edge of; *fig* on the verge of.

bordeaux [bɔrdo] ◇ *nm* **-1.** [vin] Bordeaux. **-2.** [couleur] claret. ◇ *adj inv* claret.

bordée [bɔrde] *nf* broadside; **~ d'injures** *fig* torrent of abuse.

bordel [bɔrdɛl] *nm vulg* **-1.** [maison close] brothel. **-2.** [désordre] shambles (*sg*).

border [bɔrde] [3] *vt* **-1.** [vêtement]: **~ qqch de** to edge sthg with. **-2.** [être en bordure de] to line. **-3.** [voile] to haul on. **-4.** [couverture, personne] to tuck in.

bordereau [bɔrdəro] *nm* **-1.** [liste] schedule. **-2.** [facture] invoice. **-3.** [relevé] statement; **~ de salaire** pay slip.

bordure [bɔrdyr] *nf* **-1.** [bord] edge; **en ~ de** on the edge of. **-2.** [de fleurs] border. **-3.** [de vêtement] edge, edging.

boréal, -e, -aux [bɔreal, o] *adj* northern.

borgne [bɔrɲ] ◇ *nmf* [personne] one-eyed person. ◇ *adj* -1. [personne] one-eyed. -2. [fenêtre] with an obstructed view. -3. *fig* [sordide] disreputable.

borne [bɔrn] *nf* -1. [marque] boundary marker; ~ **kilométrique** ≃ milestone. -2. *fam* [kilomètre] kilometre. -3. [limite] limit, bounds (*pl*); **dépasser les ~s** to go too far; **sans ~s** boundless. -4. ÉLECTR terminal.

borné, -e [bɔrne] *adj* -1. [horizon] limited. -2. [personne] narrow-minded; [esprit] narrow.

Bornéo [bɔrneo] *n* Borneo; **à ~** in Borneo.

borner [bɔrne] [3] *vt* [terrain] to limit; [projet, ambition] to limit, to restrict.

◆ **se borner** *vp*: **se ~ à qqch/à faire qqch** [suj: personne] to confine o.s. to sthg/to doing sthg.

Bosnie [bɔsni] *nf*: **la ~** Bosnia.

bosnien, -ienne [bɔsnjɛ̃, jɛn] *adj* Bosnian.

◆ **Bosnien, -ienne** *nm, f* Bosnian.

bosquet [bɔskɛ] *nm* copse.

bosse [bɔs] *nf* -1. [sur tête, sur route] bump. -2. [de bossu, chameau] hump. -3. *loc*: **avoir la ~ des maths** *fam* to have a good head for maths; **rouler sa ~** *fam* to knock around OU about.

bosseler [bɔsle] [24] *vt* -1. [cabosser] to dent. -2. [travailler] to emboss.

bosser [bɔse] [3] *vi fam* to work hard.

bosseur, -euse [bɔsœr, øz] *fam* ◇ *adj* hard-working. ◇ *nm, f* hard worker.

bossu, -e [bɔsy] ◇ *adj* hunchbacked. ◇ *nm, f* hunchback.

bot [bo] → **pied**.

botanique [bɔtanik] ◇ *adj* botanical. ◇ *nf*: **la ~** botany.

Botswana [bɔtswana] *nm*: **le ~** Botswana; **au ~** in Botswana.

botte [bɔt] *nf* -1. [chaussure] boot; **~ de caoutchouc** wellington (boot) *Br*, rubber boot *Am*; **lécher les ~s de qqn** *fam fig* to lick sb's boots; **en avoir plein les ~s** *fam fig* to have had a bellyful. -2. [de légumes] bunch. -3. [en escrime] thrust, lunge.

botter [bɔte] [3] *vt* -1. [chausser]: **être botté de cuir** to be wearing leather boots. -2. *fam* [donner un coup de pied à] to boot. -3. *fam vieilli* [plaire à]: **ça me botte** I dig it.

bottier [bɔtje] *nm* [de bottes] bootmaker; [de chaussures] shoemaker.

bottillon [bɔtijɔ̃] *nm* (ankle) boot.

Bottin® [bɔtɛ̃] *nm* phone book.

bottine [bɔtin] *nf* (ankle) boot.

bouc [buk] *nm* -1. [animal] (billy) goat; **~ émissaire** *fig* scapegoat. -2. [barbe] goatee.

boucan [bukɑ̃] *nm fam* row, racket.

bouche [buʃ] *nf* -1. [gén] mouth; **~ d'incendie** fire hydrant; **~ de métro** metro entrance OU exit. -2. *loc*: **garder qqch pour la bonne ~** to save sthg till last OU the end; **de ~ à oreille** by word of mouth; **faire la fine ~** to be awkward, to make difficulties.

bouché, -e [buʃe] *adj* -1. [en bouteille] bottled. -2. *fam* [personne] thick *Br*, dumb.

bouche-à-bouche [buʃabuʃ] *nm inv*: **faire du ~ à qqn** to give sb mouth-to-mouth resuscitation.

bouchée [buʃe] *nf* mouthful; **~ à la reine** CULIN chicken vol-au-vent; **pour une ~ de pain** *fig* for a song.

boucher¹ [buʃe] [3] *vt* -1. [fermer - bouteille] to cork; [- trou] to fill (in OU up). -2. [passage, vue] to block.

◆ **se boucher** *vp* to get blocked (up); **se ~ le nez** to hold one's nose.

boucher², -ère [buʃe, ɛr] *nm, f* butcher.

boucherie [buʃri] *nf* -1. [magasin] butcher's (shop); **~ chevaline** horse butcher's. -2. [commerce] butchery (trade). -3. *fig* [carnage] slaughter.

boucherie-charcuterie [buʃriʃarkytri] (*pl* **boucheries-charcuteries**) *nf* butcher's.

bouche-trou [buʃtru] (*pl* **bouche-trous**) *nm* -1. [personne]: **servir de ~** to make up (the) numbers. -2. [objet] stopgap.

bouchon [buʃɔ̃] *nm* -1. [pour obturer - gén] top; [- de réservoir] cap; [- de bouteille] cork; **~ de cire** buildup of wax in the ear. -2. [de canne à pêche] float. -3. [embouteillage] traffic jam.

bouchonner [buʃɔne] [3] ◇ *vt* -1. [cheval] to rub down. -2. [enfant] to pamper. ◇ *vi*: **ça bouchonne sur l'autoroute** there is a traffic jam on the motorway.

boucle [bukl] *nf* -1. [de ceinture, soulier] buckle. -2. [bijou]: **~ d'oreille** earring. -3. [de cheveux] curl. -4. [de fleuve, d'avion & INFORM] loop.

bouclé, -e [bukle] *adj* [cheveux] curly; [personne] curly-haired.

boucler [bukle] [3] *vt* -1. [attacher] to buckle; [ceinture de sécurité] to fasten. -2. [fermer] to shut. -3. *fam* [enfermer - voleur] to lock up; [- malade] to shut away. -4. [encercler] to seal off. -5. [terminer] to finish.

bouclier [buklije] *nm litt & fig* shield.

bouddha [buda] *nm* [statuette] buddha.

◆ **Bouddha** *nm* Buddha.

bouddhisme [budism] *nm* Buddhism.

bouddhiste [budist] *nmf & adj* Buddhist.

bouder [bude] [3] ◇ *vi* to sulk. ◇ *vt* [chose] to dislike; [personne] to shun; **elle me boude depuis que je lui ai fait faux-bond** she has cold-shouldered me ever since I let her down.

boudeur, -euse [budœr, øz] ◇ *adj* sulky. ◇ *nm, f* sulky person.

boudin [budɛ̃] *nm* **-1.** CULIN blood pudding; ~ **blanc/noir** white/black pudding. **-2.** *fam péj* [personne] podge.

boudiné, -e [budine] *adj* **-1.** [gros] podgy. **-2.** [serré]: **être ~ dans ses vêtements** to be squeezed into one's clothes.

boudoir [budwar] *nm* **-1.** [salon] boudoir. **-2.** [biscuit] sponge finger.

boue [bu] *nf* mud; **traîner qqn dans la ~, couvrir qqn de ~** *fig* to drag sb OU sb's name through the mud.

bouée [bwe] *nf* **-1.** [balise] buoy. **-2.** [pour flotter] rubber ring; ~ **de sauvetage** lifebelt.

boueux, -euse [buø, øz] *adj* muddy.

◆ **boueux** *nm fam* dustman *Br*, garbage man *Am*.

bouffant, -e [bufɑ̃, ɑ̃t] *adj* [manche, jupe] full; [cheveux] bouffant.

bouffe [buf] *nf fam* grub.

bouffée [bufe] *nf* **-1.** [de fumée] puff; [de parfum] whiff; [d'air] breath; ~**s de chaleur** (hot) flushes *Br*, hot flashes *Am*. **-2.** [accès] surge; ~**s délirantes** mad fits.

bouffer [bufe] [3] ◇ *vi* [manches] to puff out. ◇ *vt fam* [manger] to eat.

bouffi, -e [bufi] *adj*: ~ **(de)** swollen (with).

bouffon, -onne [bufɔ̃, ɔn] *adj* farcical.

◆ **bouffon** *nm* **-1.** HIST jester. **-2.** [pitre] clown.

bouge [buʒ] *nm péj* **-1.** [taudis] hovel. **-2.** [café] dive.

bougeoir [buʒwar] *nm* candlestick.

bougeotte [buʒɔt] *nf*: **avoir la ~** to have itchy feet.

bouger [buʒe] [17] ◇ *vt* [déplacer] to move. ◇ *vi* **-1.** [remuer] to move; **je ne bouge pas (de chez moi) aujourd'hui** I'm staying at home today. **-2.** [vêtement] to shrink. **-3.** [changer] to change. **-4.** [s'agiter]: **ça bouge partout dans le monde** there is unrest all over the world.

◆ **se bouger** *vp fam* **-1.** [faire des efforts] to move OU shift o.s. **-2.** [se déplacer] to move (over).

bougie [buʒi] *nf* **-1.** [chandelle] candle. **-2.** [de moteur] spark plug, sparking plug.

bougon, -onne [bugɔ̃, ɔn] ◇ *adj* grumpy. ◇ *nm, f* grumbler.

bougonner [bugɔne] [3] *vt & vi* to grumble.

bougre, -esse [bugr, -ɛs] *nm, f fam* [homme] bloke *Br*, guy; [femme] (old) girl.

◆ **bougre** *nm fam*: ~ **d'andouille!** you bloody fool! *Br*, you damned idiot!

boui-boui [bwibwi] (*pl* **bouis-bouis**) *nm fam péj* [café] caff.

bouillabaisse [bujabɛs] *nf* bouillabaisse (*Provençal fish soup*).

bouillant, -e [bujɑ̃, ɑ̃t] *adj* **-1.** [qui bout] boiling. **-2.** [très chaud] boiling (hot). **-3.** *fig* [ardent] fiery.

bouille [buj] *nf fam* [visage] face.

bouilleur [bujœr] *nm*: ~ **de cru** small-scale distiller.

bouillie [buji] *nf* baby's cereal; **réduire en ~** [légumes] to puree; [personne] to reduce to a pulp.

bouillir [bujir] [48] *vi* **-1.** [aliments] to boil; **faire ~** to boil. **-2.** *fig* [personne]: ~ **(de)** to seethe (with).

bouilloire [bujwar] *nf* kettle.

bouillon [bujɔ̃] *nm* **-1.** [soupe] stock. **-2.** [bouillonnement] bubble; **faire bouillir à gros ~s** to bring to a rolling boil. **-3.** [bactériologique]: ~ **de culture** culture medium.

bouillonner [bujɔne] [3] *vi* **-1.** [liquide] to bubble. **-2.** [torrent] to foam. **-3.** *fig* [personne] to seethe.

bouillotte [bujɔt] *nf* hot-water bottle.

boul. *abr de* **boulevard**.

boulanger, -ère [bulɑ̃ʒe, ɛr] ◇ *adj* bakery (*avant n*), baking (*avant n*). ◇ *nm, f* baker.

boulangerie [bulɑ̃ʒri] *nf* **-1.** [magasin] baker's (shop). **-2.** [commerce] bakery trade.

boulangerie-pâtisserie [bulɑ̃ʒripatisri] (*pl* **boulangeries-pâtisseries**) *nf* ≃ baker's (shop).

boule [bul] *nf* **-1.** [gén] ball; [- de loto] counter; [- de pétanque] bowl; ~ **de neige** snowball; **faire ~ de neige** to snowball. **-2.** *loc*: **se mettre en ~** *fam* to blow one's top; **perdre la ~** *fam* to lose one's marbles.

◆ **boules Quiès®** *nfpl* earplugs made of wax.

bouleau [bulo] *nm* silver birch.

bouledogue [buldɔg] *nm* bulldog.

boulet [bulɛ] *nm* **-1.** [munition]: ~ **de canon** cannonball; **tirer à ~s rouges sur qqn** *fig* to let fly at sb. **-2.** [de forçat] ball and chain. **-3.** *fig* [fardeau] millstone (round one's neck).

boulette [bulɛt] *nf* **-1.** [petite boule] pellet. **-2.** [de viande] meatball.

boulevard [bulvar] *nm* **-1.** [rue] boulevard; **les grands ~s** *Paris boulevards running from the Place de la République to la Madeleine*. **-2.** THÉÂTRE light comedy (*U*).

bouleversant, **-e** [bulvɛrsɑ̃, ɑ̃t] *adj* distressing.

bouleversement [bulvɛrsəmɑ̃] *nm* disruption.

bouleverser [bulvɛrse] [3] *vt* **-1.** [objets] to turn upside down. **-2.** [modifier] to disrupt. **-3.** [émouvoir] to distress.

boulier [bulje] *nm* abacus.

boulimie [bulimi] *nf* bulimia.

bouliste [bulist] *nmf* bowls player.

Boulle [bul] *n*: **l'école** ~ prestigious school training cabinetmakers.

boulon [bulɔ̃] *nm* bolt.

boulonner [bulɔne] [3] ◇ *vt* to bolt. ◇ *vi fam* to slog (away).

boulot¹, **-otte** [bulo, ɔt] *adj* dumpy.

boulot² [bulo] *nm fam* **-1.** [travail] work. **-2.** [emploi] job.

boum [bum] ◇ *interj* bang! ◇ *nm* **-1.** [bruit] bang; **faire** ~ to go bang. **-2.** ÉCON & *fig* boom. ◇ *nf fam vieilli* party.

bouquet [bukɛ] *nm* **-1.** [de fleurs - gén] bunch (of flowers); [- formel] bouquet. **-2.** [crevette] prawn. **-3.** [de vin] bouquet. **-4.** [de feu d'artifice] crowning piece. **-5.** CULIN: ~ **garni** bouquet garni. **-6.** *loc*: **ça c'est le** ~! *fam* that takes the cake OU biscuit *Br*!

bouquetin [buktɛ̃] *nm* ibex.

bouquin [bukɛ̃] *nm fam* book.

bouquiner [bukine] [3] *vi & vt fam* to read.

bouquiniste [bukinist] *nmf* secondhand bookseller.

bourbeux, **-euse** [burbø, øz] *adj* muddy.

bourbier [burbje] *nm* [lieu] quagmire, mire; *fig* mess.

bourbon [burbɔ̃] *nm* [whisky] bourbon.

bourde [burd] *nf* **-1.** [baliverne] rubbish (*U*). **-2.** *fam* [erreur] blunder.

bourdon [burdɔ̃] *nm* **-1.** [insecte] bumblebee. **-2.** [cloche] (large) bell. **-3.** [ton grave] drone. **-4.** *loc*: **avoir le** ~ *fam* to be (feeling) down.

bourdonnement [burdɔnmɑ̃] *nm* **-1.** [d'insecte, de voix] buzz (*U*). **-2.** [de moteur] hum (*U*). **-3.** *loc*: **avoir des** ~**s d'oreilles** to have a ringing in one's ears.

bourdonner [burdɔne] [3] *vi* **-1.** [insecte] to buzz. **-2.** [machine, voix] to hum. **-3.** [oreille] to ring.

bourg [bur] *nm* market town.

bourgade [burgad] *nf* village.

bourgeois, **-e** [burʒwa, az] ◇ *adj* **-1.** [valeur] middle-class. **-2.** [cuisine] plain. **-3.** *péj* [personne] bourgeois. ◇ *nm, f* bourgeois.

bourgeoisie [burʒwazi] *nf* middle classes (*pl*).

bourgeon [burʒɔ̃] *nm* bud.

bourgeonner [burʒɔne] [3] *vi* to bud.

bourgmestre [burgmɛstr] *nm* burgomaster.

bourgogne [burgɔɲ] *nm* Burgundy (*wine*).

Bourgogne [burgɔɲ] *nf*: **la** ~ Burgundy.

bourguignon, **-onne** [burgiɲɔ̃, ɔn] *adj* [de Bourgogne] Burgundian.

◆ **Bourguignon**, **-onne** *nm, f* Burgundian.

bourlinguer [burlɛ̃ge] [3] *vi* [voyager] to bum around the world.

bourrade [burad] *nf* thump.

bourrage [buraʒ] *nm* [de coussin] stuffing.

◆ **bourrage de crâne** *nm* **-1.** [bachotage] swotting. **-2.** [propagande] brainwashing.

bourrasque [burask] *nf* gust of wind.

bourratif, **-ive** [buratif, iv] *adj* stodgy.

bourre [bur] *nf* **-1.** [de coussin] stuffing. **-2.** [de laine] flock. **-3.** [de bourgeon] down. **-4.** *loc*: **être à la** ~ *fam* to be behind.

bourré, **-e** [bure] *adj fam* **-1.** [plein]: ~ **(de)** [salle] packed (with); *fig* chock-full (of). **-2.** [ivre] plastered.

bourreau [buro] *nm* **-1.** HIST executioner. **-2.** [personne cruelle] torturer; ~ **de travail** workaholic.

bourrelé [burle] → **remords**.

bourrelet [burlɛ] *nm* **-1.** [de graisse] roll of fat. **-2.** [de porte] draught excluder.

bourrer [bure] [3] *vt* **-1.** [remplir - coussin] to stuff; [- pipe] to fill; [- sac, armoire]: ~ **qqch (de)** to cram sthg full (with). **-2.** *fam* [gaver]: ~ **qqn (de)** to stuff sb (with). **-3.** *fam* [estomac]: **ça bourre!** it's really filling!

◆ **se bourrer** *vp fam* **-1.** [se gaver]: **se** ~ **(de qqch)** to stuff o.s. (with sthg). **-2.** [se soûler]: **se** ~ **la gueule** to get plastered.

bourricot [buriko] *nm* (small) donkey.

bourrique [burik] *nf* **-1.** [ânesse] she-ass; **faire tourner qqn en** ~ *fam fig* to drive sb up the wall. **-2.** *fam* [personne] pigheaded person.

bourru, **-e** [bury] *adj* [peu aimable] surly.

bourse [burs] *nf* **-1.** [porte-monnaie] purse; **sans** ~ **délier** without spending anything. **-2.** [d'études] grant.

◆ **Bourse** *nf* **-1.** [lieu] ≃ Stock Exchange *Br*, ≃ Wall Street *Am*. **-2.** [opérations]: **Bourse des valeurs** stock market, stock exchange; **Bourse de commerce** commodity market.

boursicoter [bursikɔte] [3] *vi* to dabble on the stock market.

boursier, **-ière** [bursje, jɛr] ◇ *adj* **-1.** [élève] on a grant. **-2.** FIN stock-market (*avant n*).

◇ *nm, f* **-1.** [étudiant] student on a grant. **-2.** FIN stockbroker.

boursouflé, -e [bursufle] *adj* **-1.** [enflé] swollen. **-2.** [emphatique] overblown.

boursoufler [bursufle] [3] *vt* to puff up, to swell.

◆ **se boursoufler** *vp* [peinture] to blister.

bous, bout *etc* → **bouillir.**

bousculade [buskylad] *nf* **-1.** [cohue] crush. **-2.** [agitation] rush.

bousculer [buskyle] [3] *vt* **-1.** [pousser] to shove. **-2.** [faire tomber] to knock over. **-3.** [presser] to rush. **-4.** [modifier] to overturn.

◆ **se bousculer** *vp* to jostle each other.

bouse [buz] *nf* : ~ **de vache** cow dung.

bousiller [buzije] [3] *vt fam* **-1.** [abîmer] to ruin, to knacker *Br.* **-2.** [bâcler] to botch.

boussole [busɔl] *nf* compass.

bout [bu] *nm* **-1.** [extrémité, fin] end; ~ **à** ~ end to end; **au** ~ **de after; d'un** ~ **à l'autre** [de ville etc] from one end to the other; [de livre] from beginning to end; ~ **filtre** filter tip. **-2.** [morceau] bit. **-3.** *loc* : **au** ~ **du compte** all things considered; **à tout** ~ **de champ** every five minutes; **être à** ~ to be exhausted; **il n'est pas au** ~ **de ses peines** his troubles are not over yet; **à** ~ **de souffle** out of breath, breathless; **être à** ~ **de forces** to have no strength left; **mener qqn par le** ~ **du nez** to lead sb by the nose; **à** ~ **portant** at point-blank range; **pousser qqn à** ~ to drive sb to distraction; **être au** ~ **du rouleau** to have come to the end of the road; **venir à** ~ **de** [personne] to get the better of; [difficulté] to overcome.

◆ **bout de chou** *nm fam* poppet.

boutade [butad] *nf* [plaisanterie] jest.

boute-en-train [butɑ̃trɛ̃] *nm inv* live wire; **il était le** ~ **de la soirée** he was the life and soul of the party.

bouteille [butɛj] *nf* bottle; **mettre en** ~ OU ~**s** to bottle; **prendre de la** ~ *fam fig* to be getting on a bit.

boutique [butik] *nf* [gén] shop; [de mode] boutique; ~ **hors-taxe** duty-free shop; **fermer** ~ to shut up shop; **parler** ~ to talk shop.

bouton [butɔ̃] *nm* **-1.** COUTURE button; ~ **de manchette** cuff link. **-2.** [sur la peau] spot. **-3.** [de porte] knob. **-4.** [commutateur] switch. **-5.** [bourgeon] bud.

bouton-d'or [butɔ̃dɔr] (*pl* **boutons-d'or**) *nm* buttercup.

boutonner [butɔne] [3] *vt* to button (up).

◆ **se boutonner** *vp* [vêtement] to button.

boutonneux, -euse [butɔnø, øz] *adj* spotty.

boutonnière [butɔnjɛr] *nf* [de vêtement] buttonhole.

bouton-pression [butɔ̃presjɔ̃] (*pl* **boutons-pression**) *nm* press-stud *Br*, snap fastener *Am.*

bouture [butyr] *nf* cutting.

bouvier [buvje] *nm* **-1.** [personne] herdsman. **-2.** [chien] sheepdog.

bouvreuil [buvrœj] *nm* bullfinch.

bovidé [bɔvide] *nm* bovine.

bovin, -e [bɔvɛ̃, in] *adj* bovine.

◆ **bovin** *nm* bovine.

bowling [buliŋ] *nm* **-1.** [jeu] bowling. **-2.** [lieu] bowling alley.

box [bɔks] (*pl* **boxes**) *nm* **-1.** [d'écurie] loose box. **-2.** [compartiment] cubicle; **le** ~ **des accusés** the dock. **-3.** [parking] lock-up garage.

boxe [bɔks] *nf* boxing.

boxer[1] [bɔkse] [3] ◇ *vi* to box. ◇ *vt fam* to thump.

boxer[2] [bɔksɛr] *nm* [chien] boxer.

boxeur [bɔksœr] *nm* SPORT boxer.

boyau [bwajo] *nm* **-1.** [chambre à air] inner tube. **-2.** [corde] catgut. **-3.** [galerie] narrow gallery.

◆ **boyaux** *nmpl* [intestins] guts.

boycott [bɔjkɔt] *nm* boycott.

boycotter [bɔjkɔte] [3] *vt* to boycott.

boy-scout [bɔjskut] (*pl* **boy-scouts**) *nm vieilli* boy scout.

BP (*abr de* **boîte postale**) *nf* P.O. Box.

BPF (*abr de* **bon pour francs**) *printed on cheques before space where amount is to be inserted.*

bracelet [braslɛ] *nm* **-1.** [bijou] bracelet. **-2.** [de montre] strap.

bracelet-montre [braslɛmɔ̃tr] (*pl* **bracelets-montres**) *nm* wristwatch.

braconnage [brakɔnaʒ] *nm* poaching.

braconner [brakɔne] [3] *vi* to go poaching, to poach.

braconnier [brakɔnje] *nm* poacher.

brader [brade] [3] *vt* [solder] to sell off; [vendre à bas prix] to sell for next to nothing.

braderie [bradri] *nf* clearance sale.

braguette [bragɛt] *nf* flies (*pl*).

braille [braj] *nm* Braille.

brailler [braje] [3] ◇ *vi* to bawl. ◇ *vt* to bawl (out).

braire [brɛr] [112] *vi* **-1.** [âne] to bray. **-2.** *fam* [personne] to bellow.

braise [brɛz] *nf* embers (*pl*); **cuire sous la** ~

to cook in the embers of a fire; **de** ~ *fig* fiery.

braiser [breze] [4] *vt* to braise.

bramer [brame] [3] *vi* [cerf] to bell.

brancard [brɑ̃kar] *nm* **-1.** [civière] stretcher. **-2.** [de charrette] shaft; **ruer dans les** ~**s** *fig* to rebel, to protest.

brancardier, -ière [brɑ̃kardje, jɛr] *nm, f* stretcher-bearer.

branchage [brɑ̃ʃaʒ] *nm* branches (*pl*).

branche [brɑ̃ʃ] *nf* **-1.** [gén] branch. **-2.** [de lunettes] side. **-3.** [de compas] leg.

branché, -e [brɑ̃ʃe] *adj* **-1.** ÉLECTR plugged in, connected. **-2.** *fam* [à la mode] trendy.

branchement [brɑ̃ʃmɑ̃] *nm* **-1.** [raccordement] connection, plugging in. **-2.** [bifurcation] branch.

brancher [brɑ̃ʃe] [3] *vt* **-1.** [raccorder & INFORM] to connect; ~ **qqch sur** ÉLECTR to plug sthg into. **-2.** *fam* [orienter] to steer; ~ **qqn sur qqch** to start sb off on sthg; ~ **la conversation sur** to steer the conversation towards. **-3.** *fam* [plaire] to appeal to.

branchies [brɑ̃ʃi] *nfpl* [de poisson] gills.

brandade [brɑ̃dad] *nf*: ~ **de morue** creamed salt cod.

brandir [brɑ̃dir] [32] *vt* to wave.

branlant, -e [brɑ̃lɑ̃, ɑ̃t] *adj* [escalier, mur] shaky; [meuble, dent] wobbly.

branle [brɑ̃l] *nm*: **mettre en** ~ to set in motion.

branle-bas [brɑ̃lba] *nm inv* pandemonium (*U*); ~ **de combat** action stations (*pl*).

branler [brɑ̃le] [3] ◇ *vt* **-1.** [hocher]: ~ **la tête** to shake one's head. **-2.** *tfam* [faire]: **qu'est-ce qu'il branle?** what is he playing at? ◇ *vi* [escalier, chaise] to be shaky; [dent, meuble] to be wobbly.
◆ **se branler** *vp vulg* to wank *Br*, to jerk off.

braquage [brakaʒ] *nm* **-1.** AUTOM lock. **-2.** [attaque] holdup.

braquer [brake] [3] ◇ *vt* **-1.** [diriger]: ~ **qqch sur** [arme] to aim sthg at; [télescope] to train sthg on; [regard] to fix sthg on. **-2.** [contrarier] to antagonize. **-3.** *fam* [attaquer] to hold up. ◇ *vi* to turn (the wheel).
◆ **se braquer** *vp* [personne] to take a stand.

bras [bra] *nm* **-1.** [gén] arm; ~ **dessus** ~ **dessous** arm in arm; **le** ~ **en écharpe** with one's arm in a sling; ~ **droit** right-hand man OU woman; ~ **de fer** [jeu] arm wrestling; *fig* trial of strength; **baisser les** ~ to throw in the towel; **en** ~ **de chemise** in one's shirtsleeves; **se croiser les** ~ just to

sit there; **avoir le** ~ **long** [avoir de l'influence] to have pull. **-2.** [main-d'œuvre] hand, worker. **-3.** [de cours d'eau] branch; ~ **de mer** arm of the sea.

brasier [brazje] *nm* [incendie] blaze, inferno.

Brasilia [brazilja] *n* Brasilia.

bras-le-corps [bralkɔr]
◆ **à bras-le-corps** *loc adv* bodily.

brassage [brasaʒ] *nm* **-1.** [de bière] brewing. **-2.** *fig* [mélange] mixing.

brassard [brasar] *nm* armband.

brasse [bras] *nf* [nage] breaststroke; ~ **coulée** breaststroke; ~ **papillon** butterfly (stroke).

brassée [brase] *nf* armful.

brasser [brase] [3] *vt* **-1.** [bière] to brew. **-2.** [mélanger] to mix. **-3.** *fig* [manier] to handle.

brasserie [brasri] *nf* **-1.** [usine] brewery. **-2.** [industrie] brewing (industry). **-3.** [café-restaurant] brasserie.

brasseur, -euse [brasœr, øz] *nm, f* **-1.** [de bière] brewer. **-2.** *fig*: ~ **d'affaires** wheeler-dealer. **-3.** [nageur] breaststroke swimmer.

brassière [brasjɛr] *nf* **-1.** [de bébé] (baby's) vest *Br* OU undershirt *Am*. **-2.** [gilet de sauvetage] life jacket. **-3.** *Can* [soutien-gorge] bra.

bravade [bravad] *nf* bravado; **par** ~ out of bravado.

brave [brav] ◇ *adj* **-1.** (*après n*) [courageux] brave. **-2.** (*avant n*) [honnête] decent. **-3.** [naïf et gentil] nice. ◇ *nmf*: **mon** ~ my good man.

bravement [bravmɑ̃] *adv* **-1.** [courageusement] bravely. **-2.** [résolument] determinedly.

braver [brave] [3] *vt* **-1.** [parents, règlement] to defy. **-2.** [mépriser] to brave.

bravo [bravo] *interj* bravo!
◆ **bravos** *nmpl* cheers.

bravoure [bravur] *nf* bravery.

BRB (*abr de* **Brigade de répression du banditisme**) *nf French serious crime squad*.

break [brɛk] *nm* **-1.** [voiture] estate (car) *Br*, station wagon *Am*. **-2.** [jazz] break. **-3.** [pause] break.

brebis [brəbi] *nf* ewe; ~ **galeuse** black sheep.

brèche [brɛʃ] *nf* **-1.** [de mur] gap. **-2.** MIL breach. **-3.** *loc*: **battre qqn en** ~ [attaquer] to knock sb down; **battre qqch en** ~ *fig* to demolish sthg; **être sur la** ~ to be hard at work.

bredouille [brəduj] *adj*: **être/rentrer collé** ~ to be/to return empty-handed.

bredouillement [brədujmɑ̃] *nm* stammering.

bredouiller [brəduje] [3] ◇ *vi* to stammer. ◇ *vt* to stammer (out).

bref, brève [brɛf, brɛv] *adj* **-1.** [gén] short, brief; **soyez ~!** make it brief!; **d'un ton ~** curtly. **-2.** LING short.
◆ **bref** *adv* in short, in a word; **en ~** briefly.
◆ **brève** *nf* PRESSE brief news item.

brelan [brəlɑ̃] *nm*: **un ~** three of a kind; **un ~ de valets** three jacks.

breloque [brələk] *nf* charm.

brème [brɛm] *nf* [poisson] bream.

Brésil [brezil] *nm*: **le ~** Brazil; **au ~** in Brazil.

brésilien, -ienne [breziljɛ̃, jɛn] *adj* Brazilian.
◆ **Brésilien, -ienne** *nm, f* Brazilian.

Bretagne [brətaɲ] *nf*: **la ~** Brittany.

bretelle [brətɛl] *nf* **-1.** [d'autoroute] slip road *Br*. **-2.** [de fusil] sling. **-3.** [de pantalon]: **~s** braces *Br*, suspenders *Am*. **-4.** [de bustier] strap.

breton, -onne [brətɔ̃, ɔn] *adj* Breton.
◆ **breton** *nm* [langue] Breton.
◆ **Breton, -onne** *nm, f* Breton.

breuvage [brœvaʒ] *nm* [boisson] beverage.

brève → bref.

brevet [brəvɛ] *nm* **-1.** [certificat] certificate; **~ de secouriste** first-aid certificate. **-2.** [diplôme] diploma. **-3.** [d'invention] patent; **déposer un ~** to file a patent. **-4.** *fig* [assurance] guarantee.

breveter [brəvte] [27] *vt* to patent; **faire ~ qqch** to take out a patent on sthg, to patent sthg.

bréviaire [brevjɛr] *nm* breviary.

bribe [brib] *nf* [fragment] scrap, bit; *fig* snippet; **~s de conversation** snatches of conversation.

bric [brik]
◆ **de bric et de broc** *loc adv* any old how.

bric-à-brac [brikabrak] *nm inv* bric-a-brac.

bricolage [brikɔlaʒ] *nm* **-1.** [travaux] do-it-yourself, DIY. **-2.** [réparation provisoire] patching up.

bricole [brikɔl] *nf* **-1.** [babiole] trinket. **-2.** [chose insignifiante] trivial matter.

bricoler [brikɔle] [3] ◇ *vi* to do odd jobs (around the house). ◇ *vt* **-1.** [réparer] to fix, to mend. **-2.** [fabriquer] to knock up *Br*.

bricoleur, -euse [brikɔlœr, øz] ◇ *adj* handy (about the house). ◇ *nm, f* home handyman (*f* handywoman).

bride [brid] *nf* **-1.** [de cheval] bridle; **à ~ abattue** at full tilt; **lâcher la ~ à qqn** to give sb his/her head. **-2.** [de chapeau] string. **-3.** COUTURE bride, bar. **-4.** TECHNOL flange.

bridé [bride] → œil.

brider [bride] [3] *vt* [cheval] to bridle; *fig* to rein (in).

bridge [bridʒ] *nm* bridge.

brie [bri] *nm* [fromage] Brie.

briefer [brife] [3] *vt* to brief.

briefing [brifiŋ] *nm* briefing.

brièvement [brijɛvmɑ̃] *adv* briefly.

brièveté [brijɛvte] *nf* brevity, briefness.

brigade [brigad] *nf* **-1.** [d'ouvriers, de soldats] brigade. **-2.** [détachement] squad; **~ anti-gang** *police squad concerned with combating terrorism and organized crime*; **~ des mœurs/des stups** vice/drugs squad; **~ volante** flying squad.

brigadier [brigadje] *nm* **-1.** MIL corporal. **-2.** [de police] sergeant.

brigand [brigɑ̃] *nm* **-1.** [bandit] bandit. **-2.** [homme malhonnête] crook.

brigandage [brigɑ̃daʒ] *nm* **-1.** [vol à main armée] armed robbery. **-2.** [action malhonnête] robbery.

briguer [brige] [3] *vt sout* to aspire to; **~ un second mandat** to seek re-election.

brillamment [brijamɑ̃] *adv* [gén] brilliantly; [réussir un examen] with flying colours.

brillant, -e [brijɑ̃, ɑ̃t] *adj* **-1.** [qui brille - gén] sparkling; [- cheveux] glossy; [- yeux] bright. **-2.** [remarquable] brilliant.
◆ **brillant** *nm* **-1.** [diamant] brilliant. **-2.** [éclat] shine.

brillantine [brijɑ̃tin] *nf* brilliantine.

briller [brije] [3] *vi* to shine.

brimade [brimad] *nf* **-1.** [vexation] harassment (*U*). **-2.** [de bizutage] bullying (*U*).

brimer [brime] [3] *vt* to victimize, to bully.

brin [brɛ̃] *nm* **-1.** [tige] twig; **~ d'herbe** blade of grass; **un beau ~ de fille** a fine figure of a girl. **-2.** [fil] strand. **-3.** [petite quantité]: **un ~ (de)** a bit (of); **faire un ~ de toilette** to have a quick wash.

brindille [brɛ̃dij] *nf* twig.

bringue [brɛ̃g] *nf fam* binge; **faire la ~** to go on a binge.

bringuebaler, brinquebaler [brɛ̃gbale] [3] *vi* [voiture] to jolt along.

brio [brijo] *nm* **-1.** MUS brio. **-2.** [talent]: **avec ~** brilliantly.

brioche [brijɔʃ] *nf* **-1.** [pâtisserie] brioche. **-2.** *fam* [ventre] paunch.

brioché, -e [brijɔʃe] *adj* [pain] brioche-style.

brique [brik] ◇ nf **-1.** [pierre] brick. **-2.** [emballage] carton. **-3.** fam [argent] 10,000 francs. ◇ adj inv brick red.

briquer [brike] [3] vt to scrub.

briquet [brikε] nm (cigarette) lighter.

briqueterie [brikεtri] nf brickworks (sg).

bris [bri] nm [destruction] breaking; ~ **de glace** broken windows.

brisant [brizɑ̃] nm [écueil] reef.
◆ **brisants** nmpl [récif] breakers.

brise [briz] nf breeze.

brisé, -e [brize] adj fig broken; ~ **de chagrin** overwhelmed by sorrow; ~ **de fatigue** exhausted.

brise-glace(s) [brizglas] nm inv [navire] icebreaker.

brise-jet [brizʒε] nm inv nozzle (for tap).

brise-lames [brizlam] nm inv breakwater.

brise-mottes [brizmɔt] nm inv harrow.

briser [brize] [3] vt **-1.** [gén] to break. **-2.** fig [carrière] to ruin; [conversation] to break off; [espérances] to shatter.
◆ **se briser** vp **-1.** [gén] to break. **-2.** fig [espoir] to be dashed; [efforts] to be thwarted.

briseur, -euse [brizœr, øz] nm, f: ~ **de grève** strike-breaker.

bristol [bristɔl] nm **-1.** [papier] Bristol board. **-2.** vieilli [carte de visite] visiting card.

britannique [britanik] adj British.
◆ **Britannique** nmf British person, Briton; **les Britanniques** the British.

broc [bro] nm jug.

brocante [brɔkɑ̃t] nf **-1.** [commerce] secondhand trade. **-2.** [objets] secondhand goods (pl).

brocanteur, -euse [brɔkɑ̃tœr, øz] nm, f dealer in secondhand goods.

brocart [brɔkar] nm brocade.

broche [brɔʃ] nf **-1.** [bijou] brooch. **-2.** CULIN spit; **cuire à la** ~ to spit-roast. **-3.** ÉLECTR & MÉD pin. **-4.** [de métier à filer] spindle.

broché, -e [brɔʃe] adj **-1.** [tissu] brocade (avant n), brocaded. **-2.** **livre** ~ paperback (book).

brochet [brɔʃε] nm pike.

brochette [brɔʃεt] nf **-1.** [ustensile] skewer. **-2.** [plat] kebab. **-3.** fam fig [groupe] string, row.

brochure [brɔʃyr] nf **-1.** [imprimé] brochure, booklet. **-2.** [de livre] binding. **-3.** [de tissu] brocaded pattern.

brocoli [brɔkɔli] nm broccoli (U).

brodequin [brɔdkɛ̃] nm boot.

broder [brɔde] [3] vt & vi to embroider.

broderie [brɔdri] nf **-1.** [art] embroidery. **-2.** [ouvrage] (piece of) embroidery.

broie, broies etc → **broyer.**

bromure [brɔmyr] nm bromide.

bronche [brɔ̃ʃ] nf bronchus; **j'ai des problèmes de** ~**s** I've got chest problems.

broncher [brɔ̃ʃe] [3] vi to stumble; **sans** ~ without complaining, uncomplainingly.

bronchite [brɔ̃ʃit] nf bronchitis (U).

bronzage [brɔ̃zaʒ] nm **-1.** [de peau] tan, suntan. **-2.** [de métal] bronzing.

bronzant, -e [brɔ̃zɑ̃, ɑ̃t] adj suntan (avant n).

bronze [brɔ̃z] nm bronze.

bronzé, -e [brɔ̃ze] adj tanned, suntanned.

bronzer [brɔ̃ze] [3] vi [peau] to tan; [personne] to get a tan.

brosse [brɔs] nf brush; ~ **à cheveux** hairbrush; ~ **à dents** toothbrush; ~ **à habits** clothes brush; **avoir les cheveux en** ~ to have a crew cut.

brosser [brɔse] [3] vt **-1.** [habits, cheveux] to brush. **-2.** [paysage, portrait] to paint.
◆ **se brosser** vp to brush one's clothes, to brush o.s. down; **se** ~ **les cheveux/les dents** to brush one's hair/teeth.

brou [bru]
◆ **brou de noix** nm **-1.** [liqueur] walnut liqueur. **-2.** [teinture] walnut stain.

brouet [bruε] nm gruel.

brouette [bruεt] nf wheelbarrow.

brouhaha [bruaa] nm hubbub.

brouillard [brujar] nm [léger] mist; [dense] fog; ~ **givrant** freezing fog; **être dans le** ~ fig to be lost.

brouille [bruj] nf quarrel.

brouillé, -e [bruje] adj **-1.** [fâché]: **être** ~ **avec qqn** to be on bad terms with sb; **être** ~ **avec qqch** fig to be hopeless OU useless at sthg. **-2.** [teint] muddy. **-3.** → **œuf.**

brouiller [bruje] [3] vt **-1.** [désunir] to set at odds, to put on bad terms. **-2.** [vue] to blur. **-3.** RADIO to cause interference to; [- délibérément] to jam. **-4.** [rendre confus] to muddle (up).
◆ **se brouiller** vp **-1.** [se fâcher] to fall out; **se** ~ **avec qqn (pour qqch)** to fall out with sb (over sthg). **-2.** [se troubler] to become blurred. **-3.** [devenir confus] to get muddled (up), to become confused. **-4.** MÉTÉOR to cloud over.

brouilleur [brujœr] nm INFORM scrambler.

brouillon, -onne [brujɔ̃, ɔn] adj careless, untidy.
◆ **brouillon** nm rough copy, draft.

broussaille [brusaj] *nf*: les ~s the under-growth; **en ~** *fig* [cheveux] untidy; [sourcils] bushy.

broussailleux, -euse [brusajø, øz] *adj* -1. [région] scrubby. -2. [sourcils] bushy.

brousse [brus] *nf* GÉOGR scrubland, bush.

brouter [brute] [3] ◇ *vt* to graze on. ◇ *vi* -1. [animal] to graze. -2. TECHNOL to judder.

broutille [brutij] *nf* trifle.

broyer [brwaje] [13] *vt* to grind, to crush.

broyeur [brwajœr] *nm*: **évier à ~** sink with waste disposal unit.

bru [bry] *nf sout* daughter-in-law.

brucelles [brysɛl] *nfpl* -1. [pince] (pair of) tweezers. -2. *Helv* [pince à épiler] (pair of) eyebrow tweezers.

brugnon [bryɲɔ̃] *nm* nectarine.

bruine [brɥin] *nf* drizzle.

bruire [brɥir] [105] *vi* [feuilles, étoffe] to rus-tle; [eau] to murmur.

bruissement [brɥismɑ̃] *nm* [de feuilles, d'étoffe] rustle, rustling (*U*); [d'eau] murmur, murmuring (*U*).

bruit [brɥi] *nm* -1. [son] noise, sound; ~ **de fond** background noise. -2. [vacarme & TECHNOL] noise; **faire du ~** to make a noise; **sans ~** silently, noiselessly. -3. [rumeur] ru-mour. -4. [retentissement] fuss; **faire du ~** to cause a stir.

bruitage [brɥitaʒ] *nm* sound-effects (*pl*).

brûlant, -e [brylɑ̃, ɑ̃t] *adj* -1. [gén] burning (hot); [liquide] boiling (hot); [plat] piping hot. -2. *fig* [amour, question] burning.

brûle-pourpoint [brylpurpwɛ̃]
◆ **à brûle-pourpoint** *loc adv* point-blank, straight out.

brûler [bryle] [3] ◇ *vt* -1. [gén] to burn; [suj: eau bouillante] to scald; **la fumée me brûle les yeux** the smoke is making my eyes sting. -2. [café] to roast. -3. [feu rouge] to drive through; [étape] to miss out, to skip. ◇ *vi* -1. [gén] to burn; [maison, forêt] to be on fire. -2. [être brûlant] to be burning (hot); ~ **de** *fig* to be consumed with; ~ **de faire qqch** to be longing OU dying to do sthg; ~ **de fièvre** to be running a high tempera-ture.
◆ **se brûler** *vp* to burn o.s.

brûlis [bryli] *nm* burn-off.

brûlure [brylyr] *nf* -1. [lésion] burn; ~ **au premier/troisième degré** first-degree/third-degree burn. -2. [sensation] burning (sensa-tion); **avoir des ~s d'estomac** to have heartburn.

brume [brym] *nf* mist.

brumeux, -euse [brymø, øz] *adj* misty; *fig* hazy.

brun, -e [brœ, bryn] ◇ *adj* brown; [cheveux] dark. ◇ *nm, f* dark-haired man (*f* woman).
◆ **brun** *nm* [couleur] brown.
◆ **brune** *nf* -1. [cigarette] *cigarette made of dark tobacco*. -2. [bière] brown ale.

brunâtre [brynatr] *adj* brownish.

brunir [brynir] [32] ◇ *vt* -1. [peau] to tan. -2. [métal] to polish, to burnish. ◇ *vi* [per-sonne] to get a tan; [peau] to tan.

brushing [brœʃiŋ] *nm*: **faire un ~ à qqn** to give sb a blow-dry, to blow-dry sb's hair.

brusque [brysk] *adj* abrupt.

brusquement [bryskəmɑ̃] *adv* abruptly.

brusquer [bryske] [3] *vt* to rush; [élève] to push.

brusquerie [bryskəri] *nf* abruptness.

brut, -e [bryt] *adj* -1. [pierre précieuse, bois] rough; [sucre] unrefined; [métal, soie] raw; [champagne] extra dry; (**pétrole**) ~ **crude** (oil). -2. *fig* [fait, idées] crude, raw. -3. ÉCON gross.
◆ **brute** *nf* brute.

brutal, -e, -aux [brytal, o] *adj* -1. [violent] violent, brutal; **être ~ avec qqn** to be bru-tal to sb. -2. [soudain] sudden. -3. [manière] blunt.

brutalement [brytalmɑ̃] *adv* -1. [violem-ment] brutally. -2. [soudainement] suddenly. -3. [sèchement] bluntly.

brutaliser [brytalize] [3] *vt* to mistreat.

brutalité [brytalite] *nf* -1. [violence] vio-lence, brutality. -2. [caractère soudain] sud-denness.
◆ **brutalités** *nfpl* brutality (*U*).

Bruxelles [bry(k)sɛl] *n* Brussels.

bruxellois, -e [brysɛlwa, az] *adj* of/from Brussels.
◆ **Bruxellois, -e** *nm, f* native OU inhab-itant of Brussels.

bruyamment [brɥijamɑ̃] *adv* noisily.

bruyant, -e [brɥijɑ̃, ɑ̃t] *adj* noisy.

bruyère [brɥjɛr] *nf* -1. [plante] heather. -2. [lande] heathland.

BT ◇ *nm* (*abr de* **brevet de technicien**) *voca-tional training certificate (taken at age 18)*. ◇ *nf* (*abr de* **basse tension**) LT.

BTA (*abr de* **brevet de technicien agricole**) *nm agricultural training certificate (taken at age 18)*.

BTP (*abr de* **bâtiments et travaux publics**) *nmpl building and public works sector*.

BTS (*abr de* **brevet de technicien supérieur**) *nm advanced vocational training certificate (taken at the end of a 2-year higher education course)*.

bu, -e [by] *pp* → **boire**.

BU (*abr de* **bibliothèque universitaire**) *nf* university library.

buanderie [byɑ̃dri] *nf* laundry.

buccal, -e, -aux [bykal, o] *adj* buccal; **par voie ~e** orally.

bûche [byʃ] *nf* **-1.** [bois] log; **~ de Noël** Yule log; **prendre** OU **ramasser une ~** *fam* to fall flat on one's face. **-2.** *fam* [personne] lump.

bûcher[1] [byʃe] *nm* **-1.** [supplice]: **le ~** the stake. **-2.** [funéraire] pyre.

bûcher[2] [byʃe] [3] ◇ *vi* to swot. ◇ *vt* to swot up.

bûcheron, -onne [byʃrɔ̃, ɔn] *nm, f* forestry worker.

bûcheur, -euse [byʃœr, øz] ◇ *adj* hardworking. ◇ *nm, f fam* swot.

bucolique [bykɔlik] *adj* pastoral.

budget [bydʒɛ] *nm* budget.

budgétaire [bydʒetɛr] *adj* budgetary; **année ~** financial year.

budgétiser [bydʒetize] [3] *vt* to budget for.

buée [bɥe] *nf* [sur vitre] condensation.

buffet [byfɛ] *nm* **-1.** [meuble] sideboard. **-2.** [repas] buffet. **-3.** [café-restaurant]: **~ de gare** station buffet.

buis [bɥi] *nm* box (wood).

buisson [bɥisɔ̃] *nm* bush.

buissonnière [bɥisɔnjɛr] → **école**.

bulbe [bylb] *nm* bulb.

bulgare [bulgar] *adj* Bulgarian.
◆ **bulgare** *nm* [langue] Bulgarian.
◆ **Bulgare** *nmf* Bulgarian.

Bulgarie [bylgari] *nf*: **la ~** Bulgaria.

bulldozer [byldozɛr] *nm* bulldozer.

bulle [byl] *nf* **-1.** [gén] bubble; **~ de savon** soap bubble. **-2.** [de bande dessinée] speech balloon. **-3.** RELIG [papal] bull.

bulletin [byltɛ̃] *nm* **-1.** [communiqué] bulletin; **~ (de la) météo** weather forecast; **~ de santé** medical bulletin. **-2.** [imprimé] form; **~ de vote** ballot paper. **-3.** SCOL report. **-4.** [certificat] certificate; **~ de consigne** left luggage ticket *Br*, luggage room OU checkroom ticket *Am*; **~ de salaire** OU **de paye** pay slip.

bulletin-réponse [byltɛ̃repɔ̃s] (*pl* **bulletins-réponse**) *nm* reply form.

bungalow [bœgalo] *nm* [maison] bungalow; [de vacances] chalet.

bunker [bunkœr] *nm* bunker.

buraliste [byralist] *nmf* **-1.** [d'un bureau de tabac] tobacconist. **-2.** [préposé] clerk.

bure [byr] *nf* **-1.** [étoffe] *coarse brown woollen cloth*. **-2.** [de moine] frock.

bureau [byro] *nm* **-1.** [gén] office; **~ d'aide sociale** social security office; **~ d'études** design office; **~ de poste** post office; **~ de tabac** tobacconist's; **~ de vote** polling station. **-2.** [meuble] desk. **-3.** [comité] committee.

bureaucrate [byrokrat] *nmf* bureaucrat.

bureaucratie [byrokrasi] *nf* bureaucracy.

bureaucratique [byrokratik] *adj péj* bureaucratic.

bureautique [byrotik] *nf* office automation.

burette [byrɛt] *nf* **-1.** [flacon] cruet. **-2.** [de chimiste] burette. **-3.** [de mécanicien] oilcan.

burin [byrɛ̃] *nm* **-1.** [outil] chisel. **-2.** [gravure] engraving.

buriné, -e [byrine] *adj* engraved; [visage, traits] lined.

Burkina [byrkina] *nm*: **le ~ Burkina Faso; au ~** in Burkina Faso.

burkinabé [byrkinabe] *adj* from Burkina Faso.
◆ **Burkinabé** *nmf* native OU inhabitant of Burkina Faso.

burlesque [byrlɛsk] ◇ *adj* **-1.** [comique] funny. **-2.** [ridicule] ludicrous, absurd. **-3.** THÉÂTRE burlesque. ◇ *nm*: **le ~** the burlesque.

burnous [byrnu] *nm* **-1.** [manteau] burnous. **-2.** [de bébé] hooded cape.

burundais, -e [burundɛ, ɛz] *adj* Burundian.
◆ **Burundais, -e** *nm, f* Burundian.

Burundi [burundi] *nm*: **le ~ Burundi; au ~** in Burundi.

bus [bys] *nm* bus.

buse [byz] *nf* **-1.** [oiseau] buzzard. **-2.** [tuyau] pipe, duct. **-3.** *fam fig* twit *Br*, idiot.

busqué [byske] → **nez**.

buste [byst] *nm* [torse] chest; [poitrine de femme, sculpture] bust.

bustier [bystje] *nm* [corsage] strapless top; [soutien-gorge] longline bra.

but [byt] *nm* **-1.** [point visé] target; **-2.** [objectif] goal, aim, purpose; **errer sans ~** to wander aimlessly; **il touche au ~** he's nearly there; **à ~ non lucratif** *Br*, non-profit *Am*; **aller droit au ~** to go straight to the point; **dans le ~ de faire qqch** with the aim OU intention of doing sthg. **-3.** SPORT goal; **marquer un ~** to score a goal. **-4.** *loc*: **de ~ en blanc** point-blank, straight out.

butane [bytan] *nm*: **(gaz) ~ butane**; [domestique] Calor gas® *Br*, butane.

buté, -e [byte] *adj* stubborn.

◆ **butée** *nf* **-1.** ARCHIT abutment. **-2.** TECHNOL stop.

buter [byte] [3] ◇ *vi* **-1.** [se heurter]: ~ **sur/contre qqch** to stumble on/over sthg, to trip on/over sthg; *fig* to run into/come up against sthg. **-2.** SPORT to score a goal. ◇ *vt* **-1.** [étayer] to support. **-2.** *tfam* [tuer] to do in, to bump off.

◆ **se buter** *vp* to dig one's heels in; **se ~ contre** *fig* to refuse to listen to.

butin [bytɛ̃] *nm* [de guerre] booty; [de vol] loot; [de recherche] finds (*pl*).

butiner [bytine] [3] ◇ *vi* to collect nectar. ◇ *vt* [suj: abeille] to collect nectar from; *fig* to gather.

butoir [bytwar] *nm* **-1.** [de porte] doorstop. **-2.** [de chemin de fer] buffer.

butte [byt] *nf* [colline] mound, rise; ~ **de tir** butts (*pl*); **être en ~ à** *fig* to be exposed to.

buvable [byvabl] *adj* [boisson] drinkable; [ampoule] (to be) taken orally.

buvard [byvar] *nm* [papier] blotting-paper; [sous-main] blotter.

buvette [byvɛt] *nf* **-1.** [café] refreshment room, buffet. **-2.** [de station thermale] pump room.

buveur, -euse [byvœr, øz] *nm, f* drinker.

buvez, buvons *etc* → **boire**.

BVA (*abr de* **Brulé Ville Associés**) *n* French market research company.

BVP (*abr de* **Bureau de vérification de la publicité**) *nm* French advertising standards authority, ≃ ASA *Br*.

Byzance [bizɑ̃s] *n* **-1.** HIST Byzantium. **-2.** *loc*: **c'est ~!** it's fantastic!

BZH (*abr de* **Breizh**) Brittany (as nationality sticker on a car).

C

c¹, C [se] *nm inv* c, C.

◆ **C -1.** (*abr de* **celsius, centigrade**) C. **-2.** (*abr de* **coulomb**) C. **-3.** *abr de* **code**.

c² *abr de* **centime**.

c' → **ce**.

ca *abr de* **centiare**.

ça [sa] *pron dém* **-1.** [pour désigner] that; [- plus près] this. **-2.** [sujet indéterminé] it, that; **comment ~ va?** how are you?, how are things?; ~ **ira comme ~** that will be fine; ~ **y est** that's it; **c'est ~** that's right. **-3.** [renforcement expressif] that; **où/qui ~?** where's/who's that?

çà [sa] *adv*: ~ **et là** here and there.

CA ◇ *nm* **-1.** *abr de* **chiffre d'affaires**. **-2.** *abr de* **conseil d'administration**. **-3.** *abr de* **corps d'armée**. ◇ *nf* (*abr de* **chambre d'agriculture**) *local government body responsible for agricultural matters*.

caban [kabɑ̃] *nm* reefer (jacket).

cabane [kaban] *nf* **-1.** [abri] cabin, hut; [remise] shed; ~ **à lapins** hutch. **-2.** *fam* [prison]: **en ~** in the clink.

cabanon [kabanɔ̃] *nm* **-1.** [à la campagne] cottage. **-2.** [sur la plage] chalet. **-3.** [cellule] padded cell. **-4.** [de rangement] shed.

cabaret [kabarɛ] *nm* cabaret.

cabas [kaba] *nm* shopping-bag.

cabillaud [kabijo] *nm* (fresh) cod.

cabine [kabin] *nf* **-1.** [de navire, d'avion, de véhicule] cabin. **-2.** [compartiment, petit local] cubicle; ~ **d'essayage** fitting room; ~ **téléphonique** phone box.

cabinet [kabinɛ] *nm* **-1.** [pièce]: ~ **de toilette** ≃ bathroom; ~ **de travail** study. **-2.** [toilettes] toilet. **-3.** [local professionnel] office; ~ **dentaire/médical** dentist's/doctor's surgery *Br*, dentist's/doctor's office *Am*. **-4.** [de ministre] advisers (*pl*).

◆ **cabinets** *nmpl* toilet (*sg*).

câble [kabl] *nm* cable; **télévision par ~** cable television.

câblé, -e [kable] *adj* TÉLÉ equipped with cable TV.

cabosser [kabɔse] [3] *vt* to dent.

cabot [kabo] ◇ *adj* theatrical. ◇ *nm* **-1.** [personne] poser. **-2.** *fam* [chien] mutt.

cabotage [kabɔtaʒ] *nm* coastal navigation.

caboteur [kabɔtœr] *nm* [navire] coaster.

cabotin, -e [kabɔtɛ̃, in] *péj* ◇ *adj* theatrical. ◇ *nm, f* **-1.** *fam* [acteur] ham (actor). **-2.** [frimeur] poser.

cabrer [kabre] [3]
◆ **se cabrer** *vp* **-1.** [cheval] to rear (up); [avion] to climb steeply. **-2.** *fig* [personne] to take offence.

cabri [kabri] *nm* kid.

cabriole [kabrijɔl] *nf* [bond] caper; [pirouette] somersault.

cabriolet [kabrijɔlɛ] *nm* convertible.

CAC, Cac [kak] (*abr de* **Compagnie des agents de change**) *nf:* **l'indice ~-40** *the French stock exchange shares index.*

caca [kaka] *nm fam* pooh; **faire ~** to do a pooh; **~ d'oie** greeny-yellow.

cacahouète [kakawɛt], **cacahuète** [kakaɥɛt] *nf* peanut.

cacao [kakao] *nm* **-1.** [poudre] cocoa (powder). **-2.** [boisson] cocoa. **-3.** [graine] cocoa bean.

cachalot [kaʃalo] *nm* sperm whale.

cache [kaʃ] ◇ *nf* [cachette] hiding place. ◇ *nm* **-1.** [masque] card (*for masking text etc*). **-2.** CIN & PHOT mask.

cache-cache [kaʃkaʃ] *nm inv:* **jouer à ~** to play hide and seek.

cache-col [kaʃkɔl] *nm inv* scarf.

cachemire [kaʃmir] *nm* **-1.** [laine] cashmere. **-2.** [dessin] paisley.

cache-nez [kaʃne] *nm inv* scarf.

cache-pot [kaʃpo] *nm inv* flowerpot-holder.

cacher [kaʃe] [3] *vt* **-1.** [gén] to hide; **je ne vous cache pas que ...** to be honest, ... **-2.** [vue] to mask.
◆ **se cacher** *vp:* **se ~ (de qqn)** to hide (from sb).

cache-sexe [kaʃsɛks] *nm inv* G-string.

cachet [kaʃɛ] *nm* **-1.** [comprimé] tablet, pill. **-2.** [marque] postmark. **-3.** [style] style, character; **avoir du ~** to have character. **-4.** [rétribution] fee. **-5.** [sceau] seal.

cacheter [kaʃte] [27] *vt* to seal.

cachette [kaʃɛt] *nf* hiding place; **en ~** secretly.

cachot [kaʃo] *nm* **-1.** [cellule] cell. **-2.** [punition] solitary confinement.

cachotterie [kaʃɔtri] *nf* little secret; **faire des ~s (à qqn)** to hide things (from sb).

cachottier, -ière [kaʃɔtje, jɛr] ◇ *adj* secretive. ◇ *nm, f* secretive person.

cachou [kaʃu] *nm* sweet taken to freshen the breath.

cacophonie [kakɔfɔni] *nf* din.

cactus [kaktys] *nm* cactus.

c.-à-d. (*abr de* **c'est-à-dire**) i.e.

cadastre [kadastr] *nm* [registre] ≃ land register; [service] ≃ land registry, land office *Am*.

cadavérique [kadaverik] *adj* deathly.

cadavre [kadavr] *nm* corpse, (dead) body; **un ~ ambulant** a walking skeleton.

caddie¹ [kadi] *nm* GOLF caddie.

Caddie²® [kadi] *nm* [chariot] trolley.

cadeau, -x [kado] ◇ *nm* present, gift; **faire ~ de qqch à qqn** to give sthg to sb (as a present); **~ d'anniversaire** birthday present; **il ne nous a pas fait de ~** *fam* he didn't do us any favours. ◇ *adj inv:* **idée ~** gift idea; **paquet ~** gift-wrapped parcel.

cadenas [kadna] *nm* padlock.

cadenasser [kadnase] [3] *vt* to padlock.
◆ **se cadenasser** *vp* to padlock.

cadence [kadɑ̃s] *nf* **-1.** [rythme musical] rhythm; **en ~** in time. **-2.** [de travail] rate.

cadencé, -e [kadɑ̃se] *adj* rhythmical.

cadet, -ette [kadɛ, ɛt] ◇ *adj* younger. ◇ *nm, f* **-1.** [de deux enfants] younger; [de plusieurs enfants] youngest; **il est mon ~ de deux ans** he's two years younger than me; **c'est le ~ de mes soucis** *fig* that's the least of my worries. **-2.** SPORT junior.

cadran [kadrɑ̃] *nm* dial; **~ solaire** sundial.

cadre [kadr] *nm* **-1.** [de tableau, de porte] frame. **-2.** [contexte] context; **dans le ~ de** as part of; [limite] within the limits OU scope of; **sortir du ~ de** to go beyond (the scope of). **-3.** [décor, milieu] surroundings (*pl*). **-4.** [responsable]: **~ moyen/supérieur** middle/senior manager; **jeune ~ dynamique** *iron* dynamic young executive; **être rayé des ~s** to be dismissed. **-5.** [sur formulaire] box.

cadrer [kadre] [3] ◇ *vi* to agree, to tally. ◇ *vt* CIN, PHOT & TÉLÉ to frame.

cadreur [kadrœr] *nm* cameraman.

caduc, caduque [kadyk] *adj* **-1.** [feuille] deciduous. **-2.** [qui n'est plus valide] obsolete.

CAF ◇ *nf* (*abr de* **Caisse d'allocations familiales**) family allowance office. ◇ (*abr de* **coût, assurance, fret**) cif.

cafard [kafar] *nm* **-1.** *fam* SCOL sneak; [à la police] grass. **-2.** [insecte] cockroach. **-3.** *fig* [mélancolie]: **avoir le ~** to feel low OU down.

cafarder [kafarde] [3] *vi* **-1.** [dénoncer - SCOL] to sneak; [- à la police] to grass. **-2.** [déprimer] to feel low OU down.

cafardeux, **-euse** [kafardø, øz] *adj* low, down.

café [kafe] ◇ *nm* **-1.** [plante, boisson] coffee; ~ **crème** white coffee (*with cream*); ~ **glacé** iced coffee; ~ **en grains** coffee beans; ~ **au lait** white coffee (*with hot milk*); ~ **liégeois** *coffee ice cream with whipped cream poured over*; ~ **moulu** ground coffee; ~ **noir** black coffee; ~ **en poudre** OU **soluble** instant coffee. **-2.** [lieu] bar, cafe. ◇ *adj inv* coffee-coloured.

CAFÉ:

In French cafes, a small cup of strong black coffee is called 'un (petit) café', 'un express' or, colloquially, 'un petit noir'. This may be served 'serré' (extra-strong), 'léger' (weak) or 'allongé' (diluted with hot water). An 'express' with a tiny amount of milk added is called 'une noisette'. A large cup of black coffee is 'un grand café', 'un double express' or, colloquially, 'un grand noir'. Coffee with frothy, steam-heated milk is called 'un (grand/petit) crème'. The term 'café au lait' is almost never used in cafes

---

caféine [kafein] *nf* caffeine; **sans** ~ caffeine-free.

cafétéria [kafeterja] *nf* cafeteria.

café-théâtre [kafeteatr] (*pl* **cafés-théâtres**) *nm* ≃ cabaret.

cafetier [kaftje] *nm* café owner.

cafetière [kaftjɛr] *nf* **-1.** [récipient] coffee-pot. **-2.** [appareil] percolator; [électrique] coffee-maker.

cafouiller [kafuje] [3] *vi fam* **-1.** [s'embrouiller] to get into a mess. **-2.** [moteur] to misfire; TÉLÉ to be on the blink.

cage [kaʒ] *nf* **-1.** [pour animaux] cage. **-2.** [dans une maison]: ~ **d'escalier** stairwell. **-3.** ANAT: ~ **thoracique** rib cage.

cageot [kaʒo] *nm* [caisse] crate.

cagibi [kaʒibi] *nm* boxroom *Br*.

cagneux, **-euse** [kaɲø, øz] *adj* knock-kneed.

cagnotte [kaɲɔt] *nf* **-1.** [caisse commune] kitty. **-2.** [économies] savings (*pl*).

cagoule [kagul] *nf* **-1.** [passe-montagne] bala-clava. **-2.** [de moine] cowl. **-3.** [de voleur, de pénitent] hood.

cahier [kaje] *nm* **-1.** [de notes] exercise book, notebook; ~ **de brouillon** rough book; ~ **de textes** homework book. **-2.** COMM: ~ **des charges** specification.

cahin-caha [kaɛ̃kaa] *adv*: **aller** ~ to be jogging along.

cahot [kao] *nm* bump, jolt.

cahoter [kaɔte] [3] ◇ *vi* to jolt around. ◇ *vt* **-1.** [secouer] to jolt. **-2.** *fig* [malmener] to knock around.

cahute [kayt] *nf* shack.

caïd [kaid] *nm* **-1.** [chef de bande] leader. **-2.** *fam* [homme fort] big shot.

caillasse [kajas] *nf fam* loose stones (*pl*).

caille [kaj] *nf* quail.

caillé, **-e** [kaje] *adj* [lait] curdled; [sang] clotted.

◆ **caillé** *nm* CULIN curds (*pl*).

cailler [kaje] [3] *vi* **-1.** [lait] to curdle; [sang] to clot. **-2.** *fam* [avoir froid] to be freezing.

◆ **se cailler** *vp* **-1.** [lait] to curdle; [sang] to clot. **-2.** *fam* [avoir froid]: **on se caille** it's freezing.

caillot [kajo] *nm* clot.

caillou, **-x** [kaju] *nm* **-1.** [pierre] stone, pebble. **-2.** *fam* [pierre précieuse] rock. **-3.** *fam* [crâne] head.

caillouteux, **-euse** [kajutø, øz] *adj* stony.

caïman [kaimɑ̃] *nm* cayman.

Caire [kɛr] *n*: **Le** ~ Cairo.

caisse [kɛs] *nf* **-1.** [boîte] crate, box; ~ à **outils** toolbox. **-2.** TECHNOL case. **-3.** MUS: **grosse** ~ bass drum. **-4.** [guichet] cash desk, till; [de supermarché] checkout, till; ~ **enregistreuse** cash register. **-5.** [recette] takings (*pl*); **tenir la** ~ *fig* to hold the purse-strings; ~ **noire** slush fund. **-6.** [organisme]: ~ **d'allocation** ≃ social security office; ~ **d'épargne** [fonds] savings fund; [établissement] savings bank; ~ **de prévoyance** contingency fund; ~ **de retraite** pension fund.

caissette [kɛsɛt] *nf* small box.

caissier, **-ière** [kesje, jɛr] *nm, f* cashier.

caisson [kɛsɔ̃] *nm* **-1.** MIL & TECHNOL caisson. **-2.** ARCHIT coffer.

cajoler [kaʒɔle] [3] *vt* to make a fuss of, to cuddle.

cajolerie [kaʒɔlri] *nf* cuddle.

cajou [kaʒu] → **noix**.

cake [kɛk] *nm* fruit-cake.

cal¹ [kal] *nm* callus.

cal² (*abr de* **calorie**) cal.

calamar [kalamar], **calmar** [kalmar] *nm* squid.

calaminé, **-e** [kalamine] *adj* coked up.

calamité [kalamite] *nf* disaster.

calandre [kalɑ̃dr] *nf* **-1.** [de voiture] radiator grille. **-2.** [machine] calender.

calanque [kalɑ̃k] *nf* rocky inlet.

calcaire [kalkɛr] ◇ *adj* [eau] hard; [sol] chalky; [roche] limestone (*avant n*). ◇ *nm* limestone.

calciner [kalsine] [3] *vt* to burn to a cinder.

calcium [kalsjɔm] *nm* calcium.

calcul [kalkyl] *nm* **-1.** [opération]: **le ~** arithmetic; **~ mental** mental arithmetic. **-2.** [compte] calculation. **-3.** *fig* [plan] plan; **agir par ~** to act out of self-interest. **-4.** MÉD: **~ (rénal)** kidney stone.

calculateur, -trice [kalkylatœr, tris] *adj péj* calculating.

◆ **calculateur** *nm* computer.

◆ **calculatrice** *nf* calculator; **calculatrice de poche** pocket calculator.

calculer [kalkyle] [3] ◇ *vt* **-1.** [déterminer] to calculate, to work out. **-2.** [prévoir] to plan; **mal/bien ~ qqch** to judge sthg badly/well. ◇ *vi* **-1.** [faire des calculs] to calculate. **-2.** *péj* [dépenser avec parcimonie] to count the pennies.

calculette [kalkylɛt] *nf* pocket calculator.

Calcutta [kalkyta] *n* Calcutta.

cale [kal] *nf* **-1.** [de navire] hold; **~ sèche** dry dock. **-2.** [pour immobiliser] wedge.

calé, -e [kale] *adj fam* **-1.** [personne] clever, brainy; **être ~ en** to be good at. **-2.** [problème] tough.

calebasse [kalbas] *nf* gourd.

calèche [kalɛʃ] *nf* (horse-drawn) carriage.

caleçon [kalsɔ̃] *nm* **-1.** [sous-vêtement masculin] boxer shorts (*pl*), pair of boxer shorts; **~ long** longjohns (*pl*), pair of longjohns. **-2.** [vêtement féminin] leggings (*pl*), pair of leggings.

Calédonie [kaledɔni] *nf*: **la ~** Caledonia.

calembour [kalɑ̃bur] *nm* pun, play on words.

calendes [kalɑ̃d] *nfpl*: **renvoyer qqch aux ~ grecques** to postpone sthg indefinitely.

calendrier [kalɑ̃drije] *nm* **-1.** [système, agenda, d'un festival] calendar. **-2.** [emploi du temps] timetable. **-3.** [d'un voyage] schedule.

cale-pied [kalpje] (*pl* **cale-pieds**) *nm* toeclip.

calepin [kalpɛ̃] *nm* notebook.

caler [kale] [3] ◇ *vt* **-1.** [avec cale] to wedge. **-2.** [stabiliser, appuyer] to prop up. **-3.** *fam* [remplir]: **ça cale (l'estomac)** it's filling. ◇ *vi* **-1.** [moteur, véhicule] to stall. **-2.** *fam* [personne] to give up.

calfeutrer [kalføtre] [3] *vt* to draughtproof.

◆ **se calfeutrer** *vp* to shut o.s. up OU away.

calibre [kalibr] *nm* **-1.** [de tuyau] diameter, bore; [de fusil] calibre; [de fruit, d'œuf] size; **de gros ~** large-calibre. **-2.** *fam fig* [envergure] calibre; **du même ~** of the same calibre.

calibrer [kalibre] [3] *vt* **-1.** [machine, fusil] to calibrate. **-2.** [fruit, œuf] to grade.

calice [kalis] *nm* **-1.** RELIG chalice. **-2.** BOT calyx.

calicot [kaliko] *nm* **-1.** [tissu] calico. **-2.** [banderole] banner.

Californie [kalifɔrni] *nf*: **la ~** California; **la Basse ~** Lower California.

californien, -ienne [kalifɔrnjɛ̃, jɛn] *adj* Californian.

◆ **Californien, -ienne** *nm, f* Californian.

califourchon [kalifurʃɔ̃]

◆ **à califourchon** *loc adv* astride; **être (assis) à ~ sur qqch** to sit astride sthg.

câlin, -e [kalɛ̃, in] *adj* affectionate.

◆ **câlin** *nm* cuddle; **faire un ~ à qqn** to give sb a cuddle.

câliner [kaline] [3] *vt* to cuddle.

calisson [kalisɔ̃] *nm small iced cake made with almond paste.*

calleux, -euse [kalø, øz] *adj* calloused.

call-girl [kɔlgœrl] (*pl* **call-girls**) *nf* call girl.

calligraphie [kaligrafi] *nf* calligraphy.

callosité [kalozite] *nf* callus.

calmant, -e [kalmɑ̃, ɑ̃t] *adj* soothing.

◆ **calmant** *nm* [pour la douleur] painkiller; [pour l'anxiété] tranquillizer, sedative.

calmar → **calamar**.

calme [kalm] ◇ *adj* quiet, calm. ◇ *nm* **-1.** [gén] calm, calmness; **dans le ~** quietly, calmly; **du ~!** calm down!; **rétablir le ~** to restore order; **le ~ plat** [de la mer] dead calm; **c'est le ~ plat en ce moment** *fig* things are very quiet at the moment. **-2.** [absence de bruit] peace (and quiet).

calmer [kalme] [3] *vt* **-1.** [apaiser] to calm (down). **-2.** [réduire - douleur] to soothe; [- inquiétude] to allay.

◆ **se calmer** *vp* **-1.** [s'apaiser - personne, discussion] to calm down; [- tempête] to abate; [- mer] to become calm. **-2.** [diminuer - douleur] to ease; [- fièvre, inquiétude, désir] to subside.

calomnie [kalɔmni] *nf* [écrits] libel; [paroles] slander.

calomnier [kalɔmnje] [9] *vt* [par écrit] to libel; [verbalement] to slander.

calomnieux, -ieuse [kalɔmnjø, jøz] *adj* [écrits] libellous; [propos] slanderous.

calorie [kalɔri] *nf* calorie.

calorifère [kalɔrifɛr] ◇ *nm* stove. ◇ *adj* heat-giving.

calorifique [kalɔrifik] *adj* calorific.

calorifuge [kalɔrifyʒ] ◇ *adj* insulating. ◇ *nm* insulation.

calorique [kalɔrik] *adj* calorific.

calot [kalo] *nm* **-1.** [de militaire] ≃ beret. **-2.** [bille] **(large)** marble.

calotte [kalɔt] *nf* **-1.** [bonnet] skullcap. **-2.** *fam* [gifle] slap. **-3.** GÉOGR: ~ **glaciaire** ice cap.

calque [kalk] *nm* **-1.** [dessin] tracing. **-2.** [papier]: **(papier)** ~ tracing paper. **-3.** *fig* [imitation] **(exact)** copy; **il est le ~ de son père** he's the spitting image of his father. **-4.** [traduction] calque, loan translation.

calquer [kalke] [3] *vt* **-1.** [carte] to trace. **-2.** [imiter] to copy exactly; ~ **qqch sur qqch** to model sthg on sthg. **-3.** [traduire littéralement] to translate literally.

calvados [kalvados] *nm* Calvados.

calvaire [kalvɛr] *nm* **-1.** [croix] wayside cross. **-2.** *fig* [épreuve] ordeal.
◆ **Calvaire** *nm*: **le Calvaire** Calvary.

calviniste [kalvinist] *adj & nmf* Calvinist.

calvitie [kalvisi] *nf* baldness; ~ **précoce** premature baldness.

camaïeu [kamajø] *nm* monochrome; **en ~** in monochrome, monochrome *(avant n)*.

camarade [kamarad] *nmf* **-1.** [compagnon, ami] friend; ~ **de classe** classmate; ~ **d'école** schoolfriend. **-2.** POLIT comrade.

camaraderie [kamaradri] *nf* **-1.** [familiarité, entente] friendship. **-2.** [solidarité] comradeship, camaraderie.

cambiste [kɑ̃bist] FIN ◇ *adj* foreign-exchange *(avant n)*. ◇ *nmf* foreign exchange dealer.

Cambodge [kɑ̃bɔdʒ] *nm*: **le ~** Cambodia; **au ~** in Cambodia.

cambodgien, -ienne [kɑ̃bɔdʒjɛ̃, jɛn] *adj* Cambodian.
◆ **Cambodgien, -ienne** *nm, f* Cambodian.

cambouis [kɑ̃bwi] *nm* dirty grease.

cambré, -e [kɑ̃bre] *adj* arched.

cambrer [kɑ̃bre] [3] *vt*: ~ **les reins** OU **la taille** to arch one's back.
◆ **se cambrer** *vp* [se redresser] to arch one's back.

cambriolage [kɑ̃brijɔlaʒ] *nm* burglary.

cambrioler [kɑ̃brijɔle] [3] *vt* to burgle *Br*, to burglarize *Am*.

cambrioleur, -euse [kɑ̃brijɔlœr, øz] *nm, f* burglar.

cambrousse [kɑ̃brus] *nf fam*: **en pleine ~** out in the sticks.

cambrure [kɑ̃bryr] *nf* **-1.** [de pied] instep; ~ **des reins** OU **du dos** small of the back. **-2.** [de poutre] curve; [de chaussure] arch.

came [kam] *nf* **-1.** TECHNOL cam. **-2.** *tfam* [drogue] stuff.

camé, -e [kame] *tfam* ◇ *adj* [drogué] stoned. ◇ *nm, f* junkie.

camée [kame] *nm* cameo.

caméléon [kamele5] *nm litt & fig* chameleon.

camélia [kamelja] *nm* camellia.

camelote [kamlɔt] *nf* [marchandise de mauvaise qualité] rubbish.

camembert [kamɑ̃bɛr] *nm* **-1.** [fromage] Camembert. **-2.** [graphique] pie chart.

caméra [kamera] *nf* **-1.** CIN & TÉLÉ camera. **-2.** [d'amateur] cinecamera.

cameraman [kameraman] *(pl* **cameramen** [kameramɛn] OU **cameramans)** *nm* cameraman.

Cameroun [kamrun] *nm*: **le ~** Cameroon; **au ~** in Cameroon.

camerounais, -e [kamryne, ɛz] *adj* Cameroonian.
◆ **Camerounais, -e** *nm, f* Cameroonian.

Caméscope® [kameskɔp] *nm* camcorder.

camion [kamjɔ̃] *nm* lorry *Br*, truck *Am*; ~ **de déménagement** removal van *Br*, moving van *Am*.

camion-citerne [kamjɔ̃sitɛrn] *(pl* **camions-citernes)** *nm* tanker *Br*, tanker truck *Am*.

camionnage [kamjɔnaʒ] *nm* road haulage *Br*, trucking *Am*.

camionnette [kamjɔnɛt] *nf* van.

camionneur [kamjɔnœr] *nm* **-1.** [conducteur] lorry-driver *Br*, truck-driver *Am*. **-2.** [entrepreneur] road haulier *Br*, trucker *Am*.

camisole [kamizɔl]
◆ **camisole de force** *nf* straitjacket.

camomille [kamɔmij] *nf* **-1.** [plante] camomile. **-2.** [tisane] camomile tea.

camouflage [kamuflaʒ] *nm* [déguisement] camouflage; *fig* [dissimulation] concealment.

camoufler [kamufle] [3] *vt* [déguiser] to camouflage; *fig* [dissimuler] to conceal, to cover up; ~ **qqch en qqch** to camouflage sthg as sthg.
◆ **se camoufler** *vp* [se cacher] to hide.

camouflet [kamufle] *nm littéraire* [affront] snub; **infliger un ~ à qqn** to snub sb.

camp [kɑ̃] *nm* **-1.** [gén] camp; ~ **de concentration** concentration camp; ~ **retranché** fortified camp, fortress; ~ **de vacances** holiday camp; ~ **volant** temporary camp; **ficher le ~** *fam* to get lost, to clear off; **lever le ~** to break camp; *fig* to clear off OU out. **-2.** SPORT half (of the field). **-3.** [parti] side.

campagnard, -e [kɑ̃paɲar, ard] ◇ *adj* **-1.** [de la campagne] country *(avant n)*. **-2.** [rustique] rustic. ◇ *nm, f* countryman (*f* countrywoman).

campagne [kɑ̃paɲ] *nf* -**1**. [régions rurales] country; **à la ~** in the country; **en rase ~** in open country; **battre la ~** [police] to comb the countryside; [divaguer] to wander. -**2**. MIL, POLIT & PUBLICITÉ campaign; **partir en ~** POLIT to start campaigning; **faire ~ pour/contre** to campaign for/against; **~ d'affichage** outdoor campaign, billposter campaign; **~ électorale** election campaign; **~ de presse** press campaign; **~ publicitaire** advertising campaign; **~ de vente** sales campaign.

campanule [kɑ̃panyl] *nf* bellflower, campanula.

campé, -e [kɑ̃pe] *adj*: **bien ~** [personnage] well-rounded; [récit] well-constructed; **être bien ~ (sur ses jambes)** to stand firmly on one's feet.

campement [kɑ̃pmɑ̃] *nm* camp, encampment.

camper [kɑ̃pe] [3] ◇ *vi* to camp. ◇ *vt* -**1**. [poser solidement] to place firmly. -**2**. *fig* [esquisser] to portray.
◆ **se camper** *vp*: **se ~ devant qqn/qqch** to plant o.s. in front of sb/sthg.

campeur, -euse [kɑ̃pœr, øz] *nm, f* camper.

camphre [kɑ̃fr] *nm* camphor.

camphré, -e [kɑ̃fre] *adj* camphorated.

camping [kɑ̃piŋ] *nm* -**1**. [activité] camping; **faire du ~** to go camping; **~ sauvage** unauthorized camping. -**2**. [terrain] campsite.

camping-car [kɑ̃piŋkar] (*pl* **camping-cars**) *nm* camper, Dormobile® *Br*.

Camping-Gaz® [kɑ̃piŋgaz] *nm inv* ≃ Primus® stove.

campus [kɑ̃pys] *nm* campus.

camus [kamy] → **nez**.

Canada [kanada] *nm*: **le ~** Canada; **au ~** in Canada.

Canadair® [kanadɛr] *nm plane equipped with water tanks to fight forest fires.*

canadianisme [kanadjanism] *nm* Canadianism.

canadien, -ienne [kanadjɛ̃, jɛn] *adj* Canadian.
◆ **canadienne** *nf* [veste] sheepskin jacket.
◆ **Canadien, -ienne** *nm, f* Canadian.

canaille [kanaj] ◇ *adj* -**1**. [coquin] roguish. -**2**. [vulgaire] crude. ◇ *nf* -**1**. [scélérat] scoundrel. -**2**. *hum* [coquin] little devil.

canal, -aux [kanal, o] *nm* -**1**. [gén] channel; **par le ~ de qqn** *fig* [par l'entremise de] through sb; **~ de distribution** distribution channel. -**2**. [voie d'eau] canal. -**3**. ANAT canal, duct.
◆ **Canal** *nm*: **Canal+** *French TV pay channel.*

CANAL+:
Canal+ broadcasts programmes that have to be unscrambled using a special decoding unit, although for part of the day its programmes can be seen without this device

canalisation [kanalizasjɔ̃] *nf* -**1**. [conduit] pipe. -**2**. *litt* & *fig* [action de canaliser] channelling.

canaliser [kanalize] [3] *vt* -**1**. [cours d'eau] to canalize. -**2**. *fig* [orienter] to channel.

canapé [kanape] *nm* -**1**. [siège] sofa; **~ convertible** sofa bed. -**2**. CULIN canapé.

canapé-lit [kanapeli] (*pl* **canapés-lits**) *nm* sofa bed.

canaque, kanak [kanak] *adj* Kanak.
◆ **Canaque** *nmf* Kanak.

canard [kanar] *nm* -**1**. [oiseau] duck. -**2**. [fausse note] wrong note. -**3**. *fam* [journal] rag.

canari [kanari] ◇ *nm* canary. ◇ *adj inv*: **jaune ~** canary yellow.

Canaries [kanari] *nfpl*: **les ~** the Canaries; **aux ~** in the Canaries.

Canberra [kɑ̃bera] *n* Canberra.

cancan [kɑ̃kɑ̃] *nm* -**1**. [ragot] piece of gossip; **dire des ~s sur qqn** to spread gossip about sb. -**2**. [danse] cancan.

cancaner [kɑ̃kane] [3] *vi* -**1**. [canard] to quack. -**2**. [médire] to spread gossip; **~ sur qqn** to spread gossip about sb.

cancanier, -ière [kɑ̃kanje, jɛr] ◇ *adj* gossipy. ◇ *nm, f* gossip.

cancer [kɑ̃sɛr] *nm* MÉD cancer.
◆ **Cancer** *nm* -**1**. ASTROL Cancer; **être Cancer** to be (a) Cancer. -**2**. GÉOGR: **le tropique du Cancer** the tropic of Cancer.

cancéreux, -euse [kɑ̃serø, øz] ◇ *adj* -**1**. [personne] suffering from cancer. -**2**. [tumeur] cancerous. ◇ *nm, f* [personne] cancer sufferer.

cancérigène [kɑ̃seriʒɛn] *adj* carcinogenic.

cancre [kɑ̃kr] *nm fam* dunce.

cancrelat [kɑ̃krəla] *nm* cockroach.

candélabre [kɑ̃delabr] *nm* candelabra.

candeur [kɑ̃dœr] *nf* ingenuousness.

candi [kɑ̃di] → **sucre**.

candidat, -e [kɑ̃dida, at] *nm, f*: **~ (à)** candidate (for).

candidature [kɑ̃didatyr] *nf* -**1**. [à un poste] application; **poser sa ~ pour qqch** to apply for sthg. -**2**. [à une élection] candidature.

candide [kɑ̃did] *adj* ingenuous.

cane [kan] *nf* (female) duck.

caneton [kantɔ̃] *nm* (male) duckling.

canette [kanɛt] *nf* **-1.** [de fil] spool. **-2.** [petite cane] (female) duckling. **-3.** [de boisson - bouteille] bottle; [- boîte] can.

canevas [kanva] *nm* **-1.** COUTURE canvas. **-2.** [plan] structure.

caniche [kaniʃ] *nm* poodle.

canicule [kanikyl] *nf* heatwave.

canif [kanif] *nm* penknife.

canin, -e [kanɛ̃, in] *adj* canine; **exposition ~e** dog show.
◆ **canine** *nf* canine (tooth).

caniveau [kanivo] *nm* gutter.

cannabis [kanabis] *nm* cannabis.

canne [kan] *nf* **-1.** [bâton] walking stick; **~ à pêche** cane] fishing rod. **-2.** *fam* [jambe] pin.
◆ **canne à sucre** *nf* sugar cane.

canné, -e [kane] *adj* cane (*avant n*).

cannelé, -e [kanle] *adj* fluted.

cannelle [kanɛl] ◇ *nf* **-1.** [aromate] cinnamon. **-2.** [robinet] tap *Br*, faucet *Am*. ◇ *adj inv* [couleur] cinnamon.

cannelure [kanlyr] *nf* **-1.** [de colonne] flute. **-2.** BOT & GÉOL striation.

Cannes [kan] *n* Cannes; **le festival de ~** the Cannes film festival.

cannibale [kanibal] *nmf & adj* cannibal.

cannibalisme [kanibalism] *nm* cannibalism.

canoë [kanɔe] *nm* canoe.

canoë-kayak [kanɔekajak] (*pl* **canoës-kayaks**) *nm* kayak.

canon [kanɔ̃] ◇ *nm* **-1.** [arme] gun; HIST cannon. **-2.** [tube d'arme] barrel. **-3.** *fam* [verre de vin] glass (of wine). **-4.** MUS: **chanter en ~** to sing in canon. **-5.** [norme & RELIG] canon. ◇ *adj* → **droit**.

canonique [kanɔnik] *adj* canonical; **d'un âge ~** *fig* of a venerable age.

canoniser [kanɔnize] [3] *vt* to canonize.

canot [kano] *nm* dinghy; **~ pneumatique** inflatable dinghy; **~ de sauvetage** lifeboat.

canotage [kanɔtaʒ] *nm* rowing, boating; **faire du ~** to go rowing OU boating.

canotier [kanɔtje] *nm* **-1.** [rameur] rower. **-2.** [chapeau] boater.

cantal [kɑ̃tal] *nm* semi-hard cheese from the Auvergne.

cantate [kɑ̃tat] *nf* cantata.

cantatrice [kɑ̃tatris] *nf* prima donna.

cantine [kɑ̃tin] *nf* **-1.** [réfectoire] canteen. **-2.** [malle] trunk.

cantique [kɑ̃tik] *nm* hymn.

canton [kɑ̃tɔ̃] *nm* **-1.** [en France] ≃ district. **-2.** [en Suisse] canton.

cantonade [kɑ̃tɔnad]
◆ **à la cantonade** *loc adv*: **parler à la ~** to speak to everyone (in general).

cantonais, -e [kɑ̃tɔnɛ, ɛz] *adj* Cantonese; **riz ~** egg fried rice.
◆ **cantonais** *nm* [langue] Cantonese.
◆ **Cantonais, -e** *nm, f* native OU inhabitant of Canton.

cantonal, -e, -aux [kɑ̃tɔnal, o] *adj* **-1.** [en France] ≃ district (*avant n*). **-2.** [en Suisse] cantonal.

cantonnement [kɑ̃tɔnmɑ̃] *nm* [MIL - action] billeting; [- lieu] billet.

cantonner [kɑ̃tɔne] [3] *vt* **-1.** MIL to quarter, to billet *Br*. **-2.** [maintenir] to confine; **~ qqn à** OU **dans** to confine sb to.
◆ **se cantonner** *vp*: **se ~ dans** to confine o.s. to.

cantonnier [kɑ̃tɔnje] *nm* roadman.

canular [kanylar] *nm fam* hoax.

CAO (*abr de* **conception assistée par ordinateur**) *nf* CAD.

caoutchouc [kautʃu] *nm* **-1.** [substance] rubber; **en ~** rubber (*avant n*); **~ mousse** foam rubber. **-2.** [plante] rubber plant. **-3.** [élastique] elastic OU rubber band.

caoutchouteux, -euse [kautʃutø, øz] *adj* rubbery.

cap [kap] *nm* **-1.** GÉOGR cape; **le cap de Bonne-Espérance** the Cape of Good Hope; **le cap Horn** Cape Horn; **passer le ~ de qqch** *fig* to get through sthg; **passer le ~ de la quarantaine** *fig* to turn forty. **-2.** [direction] course; **changer de ~** to change course; **mettre le ~ sur** to head for.
◆ **Cap** *nm*: **Le Cap** Cape Town.

CAP (*abr de* **certificat d'aptitude professionnelle**) *nm vocational training certificate (taken at secondary school)*.

capable [kapabl] *adj* **-1.** [apte]: **~ (de qqch/de faire qqch)** capable (of sthg/of doing sthg). **-2.** [à même]: **~ de faire qqch** likely to do sthg; **~ de réussir** likely to succeed. **-3.** JUR competent.

capacité [kapasite] *nf* **-1.** [de récipient] capacity. **-2.** [de personne] ability. **-3.** JUR [mentale] capacity. **-4.** UNIV: **~ en droit** [diplôme] *qualifying certificate in law gained by examination after 2 years' study*.

cape [kap] *nf* [vêtement] cloak; **rire sous ~** *fig* to laugh up one's sleeve.

CAPES, Capes [kapɛs] (*abr de* **certificat d'aptitude au professorat de l'enseignement du second degré**) *nm secondary school teaching certificate*.

capésien, **-ienne** [kapesjɛ̃, jɛn] *nm, f person holding a secondary school teaching qualification*.

CAPET, **Capet** [kapɛt] (*abr de* **certificat d'aptitude au professorat de l'enseignement technique**) *nm specialized teaching certificate*.

capharnaüm [kafarnaɔm] *nm* mess.

capillaire [kapilɛr] ◇ *adj* **-1.** [lotion] hair (*avant n*). **-2.** ANAT & BOT capillary. ◇ *nm* **-1.** BOT maidenhair fern. **-2.** ANAT capillary.

capillarité [kapilarite] *nf* PHYS capillarity.

capitaine [kapitɛn] *nm* captain; ~ **au long cours** NAVIG master mariner.

capitainerie [kapitɛnri] *nf* harbour master's office.

capital, -e, -aux [kapital, o] *adj* **-1.** [décision, événement] major. **-2.** JUR capital.

◆ **capital** *nm* FIN capital; ~ **d'exploitation** working capital; ~ **santé** *fig* reserves (*pl*) of health; ~ **social** authorized OU share capital.

◆ **capitale** *nf* [ville, lettre] capital.

◆ **capitaux** *nmpl* capital (*U*).

capitaliser [kapitalize] [3] ◇ *vt* FIN to capitalize; *fig* to accumulate. ◇ *vi* to save.

capitalisme [kapitalism] *nm* capitalism.

capitaliste [kapitalist] *nmf & adj* capitalist.

capiteux, -euse [kapitø, øz] *adj* **-1.** [vin] intoxicating; [parfum] heady. **-2.** [charme] alluring.

capitonné, -e [kapitɔne] *adj* padded; ~ **de cuir** with leather upholstery.

capituler [kapityle] [3] *vi* to surrender; ~ **devant qqn/qqch** to surrender to sb/sthg.

caporal, -aux [kapɔral, o] *nm* **-1.** MIL lance-corporal. **-2.** [tabac] caporal.

caporal-chef [kapɔralʃɛf] (*pl* **caporaux-chefs** [kapɔroʃɛf]) *nm* corporal.

capot [kapo] ◇ *adj inv* [aux jeux de cartes]: **mettre qqn** ~ to take all the tricks from sb. ◇ *nm* **-1.** [de voiture] bonnet *Br*, hood *Am*. **-2.** [de machine] (protective) cover.

capote [kapɔt] *nf* **-1.** [de voiture] hood *Br*, top *Am*. **-2.** [manteau] greatcoat, overcoat. **-3.** [chapeau] bonnet. **-4.** *fam* [préservatif]: ~ **(anglaise)** condom.

capoter [kapɔte] [3] *vi* **-1.** [se retourner] to overturn. **-2.** *Can* [perdre la tête] to lose one's head. **-3.** [échouer] to come to nothing.

câpre [kapr] *nf* caper.

caprice [kapris] *nm* whim; **les ~s de la météo** the vagaries of the weather; **faire des ~s** to be temperamental.

capricieux, -ieuse [kaprisjø, jøz] ◇ *adj*

[changeant] capricious; [coléreux] temperamental. ◇ *nm, f* temperamental person.

capricorne [kaprikɔrn] *nm* **-1.** ZOOL capricorn beetle.

◆ **Capricorne** *nm* **-1.** ASTROL Capricorn; **être Capricorne** to be (a) Capricorn. **-2.** GÉOGR: **le tropique du Capricorne** the tropic of Capricorn.

capsule [kapsyl] *nf* **-1.** [de bouteille] cap. **-2.** ASTRON, BOT & MÉD capsule.

capter [kapte] [3] *vt* **-1.** [recevoir sur émetteur] to pick up. **-2.** [source, rivière] to harness. **-3.** *fig* [attention, confiance] to gain, to win.

capteur [kaptœr] *nm* PHYS sensor; ~ **solaire** solar panel.

captieux, -ieuse [kapsjø, jøz] *adj* specious.

captif, -ive [kaptif, iv] ◇ *adj* captive; **être ~ de qqch** *fig* to be a slave to sthg. ◇ *nm, f* prisoner.

captivant, -e [kaptivɑ̃, ɑ̃t] *adj* [livre, film] enthralling; [personne] captivating.

captiver [kaptive] [3] *vt* to captivate.

captivité [kaptivite] *nf* captivity; **en ~** in captivity.

capture [kaptyr] *nf* **-1.** [action] capture. **-2.** [prise] catch.

capturer [kaptyre] [3] *vt* to catch, to capture.

capuche [kapyʃ] *nf* (detachable) hood.

capuchon [kapyʃɔ̃] *nm* **-1.** [bonnet - d'imperméable] hood; [- de religieux] cowl. **-2.** [bouchon] cap, top.

capucin [kapysɛ̃] *nm* RELIG Capuchin.

capucine [kapysin] *nf* [fleur] nasturtium.

capverdien, -ienne [kapvɛrdjɛ̃, jɛn] *adj* Cape Verdean.

◆ **Capverdien, -ienne** *nm, f* Cape Verdean.

Cap-Vert [kapvɛr] *nm* Cape Verde.

caquelon [kaklɔ̃] *nm* fondue dish.

caquet [kakɛ] *nm* **-1.** [de poule] cackling (*U*). **-2.** *péj* [bavardage] chatter (*U*); **rabattre le ~ à** OU **de qqn** to shut sb up.

caqueter [kakte] [27] *vi* **-1.** [poule] to cackle. **-2.** *péj* [personne] to chatter.

car¹ [kar] *nm* coach *Br*, bus *Am*.

car² [kar] *conj* for, because.

carabine [karabin] *nf* rifle.

carabiné, -e [karabine] *adj fam* [tempête] violent; [rhume] stinking; [amende] heavy.

Caracas [karakas] *n* Caracas.

caraco [karako] *nm* loose blouse.

caracoler [karakɔle] [3] *vi* **-1.** [cheval] to prance; [cavalier] to caracole. **-2.** *fig* [sautiller] to prance about.

caractère [karaktɛr] nm **-1.** [gén] character; **avoir du ~** to have character; **avoir mauvais ~** to be bad-tempered; **en petits/gros ~s** in small/large print; **~s d'imprimerie** block capitals. **-2.** [caractéristique] feature, characteristic.

caractériel, -ielle [karakterjɛl] ◇ adj [troubles] emotional; [personne] emotionally disturbed. ◇ nm, f emotionally disturbed person.

caractérisé, -e [karakterize] adj [net] clear; **être d'une grossièreté ~e** to be downright rude.

caractériser [karakterize] [3] vt to be characteristic of.
◆ **se caractériser** vp: **se ~ par qqch** to be characterized by sthg.

caractéristique [karakteristik] ◇ nf characteristic, feature. ◇ adj: **~ (de)** characteristic (of).

carafe [karaf] nf [pour vin, eau] carafe; [pour alcool] decanter; **rester en ~** fam to be left stranded.

carafon [karafɔ̃] nm small carafe.

caraïbe [karaib] adj Caribbean.
◆ **Caraïbe** nmf Carib.
◆ **Caraïbes** nfpl: **les Caraïbes** the Caribbean; **dans les Caraïbes** in the Caribbean.

carambolage [karɑ̃bɔlaʒ] nm pile-up.

caramel [karamɛl] ◇ nm **-1.** CULIN caramel. **-2.** [bonbon - dur] toffee, caramel; [- mou] fudge. ◇ adj inv [couleur] caramel.

caraméliser [karamelize] [3] vt [sucre] to caramelize; [gâteau] to coat with caramel.
◆ **se caraméliser** vp to caramelize.

carapace [karapas] nf shell; fig protection, shield.

carapater [karapate] [3]
◆ **se carapater** vp to scarper, to hop it.

carat [kara] nm carat; **or à 9 ~s** 9-carat gold.

caravane [karavan] nf **-1.** [de camping, de désert] caravan. **-2.** [groupe de personnes] procession.

caravaning [karavaniŋ] nm caravanning.

carbone [karbɔn] nm carbon; **(papier) ~** carbon paper.

carbonique [karbɔnik] adj: **gaz ~** carbon dioxide; **neige ~** dry ice.

carboniser [karbɔnize] [3] vt to burn to a cinder.

carbonnade [karbɔnad] nf CULIN type of stew.

carburant [karbyrɑ̃] ◇ adj m: **mélange ~** (fuel) mixture. ◇ nm fuel.

carburateur [karbyratœr] nm carburettor.

carbure [karbyr] nm carbide.

carburer [karbyre] [3] vi **-1.** [moteur]: **~ bien/mal** to be well/badly tuned. **-2.** fam [être en forme] to be fine.

carcan [karkɑ̃] nm HIST iron collar; fig yoke.

carcasse [karkas] nf **-1.** [d'animal] carcass. **-2.** [de bâtiment, navire] framework. **-3.** [de véhicule] shell.

carcéral, -e, -aux [karseral, o] adj prison (avant n).

carcinome [karsinɔm] nm carcinoma.

cardan [kardɑ̃] nm universal joint.

carder [karde] [3] vt to card.

cardiaque [kardjak] ◇ adj cardiac; **être ~** to have a heart condition; **crise ~** heart attack. ◇ nmf heart patient.

cardigan [kardigɑ̃] nm cardigan.

cardinal, -e, -aux [kardinal, o] adj cardinal.
◆ **cardinal** nm **-1.** RELIG cardinal. **-2.** [nombre] cardinal number.

cardiologue [kardjɔlɔg] nmf heart specialist, cardiologist.

cardio-vasculaire [kardjovaskylɛr] (pl **cardio-vasculaires**) adj cardiovascular.

Carême [karɛm] nm: **le ~** Lent.

carence [karɑ̃s] nf **-1.** [de personne, gouvernement] inadequacy, incompetence. **-2.** [manque]: **~ (en)** deficiency (in).

carène [karɛn] nf NAVIG hull.

caréner [karene] [18] vt **-1.** [navire] to careen. **-2.** [carrosserie] to streamline.

caressant, -e [karɛsɑ̃, ɑ̃t] adj affectionate.

caresse [karɛs] nf caress; **faire une ~ à qqn** to caress sb.

caresser [karese] [4] vt **-1.** [personne] to caress; [animal, objet] to stroke. **-2.** fig [espoir] to cherish.

car-ferry [karferi] (pl **car-ferries**) nm car ferry.

cargaison [kargezɔ̃] nf **-1.** TRANSPORT cargo. **-2.** fam [grande quantité] load, pile.

cargo [kargo] nm **-1.** [navire] freighter. **-2.** [avion] cargo plane.

cari = **curry**.

caribou [karibu] nm caribou.

caricatural, -e, -aux [karikatyral, o] adj [récit] exaggerated.

caricature [karikatyr] nf **-1.** [gén] caricature. **-2.** péj [personne] sight.

carie [kari] nf **-1.** MÉD caries. **-2.** BOT blight.

carillon [karijɔ̃] nm **-1.** [cloches] bells (pl). **-2.** [d'horloge, de porte] chime.

carillonner [karijɔne] [3] ◇ vi to ring. ◇ vt **-1.** [heure] to strike, to chime. **-2.** fig [nouvelle] to announce.

caritatif, -ive [karitatif, iv] *adj* charitable.

carlingue [karlɛ̃g] *nf* **-1.** [d'avion] cabin. **-2.** [de navire] keelson.

carmélite [karmelit] *nf* Carmelite (nun).

carmin [karmɛ̃] ◇ *adj inv* crimson. ◇ *nm* [couleur] crimson; [colorant] cochineal.

carnage [karnaʒ] *nm* slaughter, carnage.

carnassier, -ière [karnasje, jɛr] *adj* carnivorous.

◆ **carnassier** *nm* carnivore.

carnaval [karnaval] *nm* carnival.

carnet [karnɛ] *nm* **-1.** [petit cahier] notebook; ~ **d'adresses** address book; ~ **de notes** SCOL report card. **-2.** [bloc de feuilles] book; ~ **de chèques** cheque book; ~ **de tickets** book of tickets.

carnivore [karnivɔr] ◇ *adj* carnivorous. ◇ *nm* carnivore.

carotide [karɔtid] ANAT ◇ *adj* carotid. ◇ *nf* carotid artery.

carotte [karɔt] ◇ *nf* carrot; **~s râpées** grated carrots; **~s Vichy** glazed carrots; **les ~s sont cuites** *fam* they've/we've *etc* had it. ◇ *adj inv* [couleur] carroty.

carpe [karp] ◇ *nf* carp; **être muet comme une ~** *fig* not to say a word. ◇ *nm* ANAT carpus.

carpette [karpɛt] *nf* **-1.** [petit tapis] rug. **-2.** *fam péj* [personne] doormat.

carquois [karkwa] *nm* quiver.

carré, -e [kare] *adj* **-1.** [gén] square; **20 mètres ~s** 20 square metres. **-2.** [franc] straightforward.

◆ **carré** *nm* **-1.** [quadrilatère] square; **élever un nombre au ~** MATHS to square a number; ~ **blanc** TV *white square in the corner of the screen indicating that a television programme is not recommended for children;* ~ **de soie** [foulard] silk square. **-2.** [sur un navire] wardroom. **-3.** CARTES: **un ~ d'as** four aces. **-4.** CULIN: ~ **d'agneau** rack of lamb. **-5.** [petit terrain] patch, plot.

carreau [karo] *nm* **-1.** [carrelage] tile. **-2.** [sol] tiled floor; **rester sur le ~** *fig* to be knocked out. **-3.** [vitre] window pane. **-4.** [motif carré] check; **à ~x** [tissu] checked; [papier] squared. **-5.** CARTES diamond; **l'atout est ~** diamonds are trumps. **-6.** *loc*: **se tenir à ~** to watch one's step.

carrefour [karfur] *nm* **-1.** [de routes, de la vie] crossroads (*sg*). **-2.** [forum] forum, conference.

carrelage [karlaʒ] *nm* **-1.** [action] tiling. **-2.** [surface] tiles (*pl*).

carreler [karle] [24] *vt* to tile.

carrelet [karlɛ] *nm* **-1.** [poisson] plaice. **-2.** [filet de pêche] net.

carreleur [karlœr] *nm* tiler.

carrément [karemɑ̃] *adv* **-1.** [franchement] bluntly. **-2.** [complètement] completely, quite. **-3.** [sans hésiter] straight.

carrer [kare] [3]

◆ **se carrer** *vp*: **se ~ dans** to settle o.s. in.

carrière [karjɛr] *nf* **-1.** [profession] career; **embrasser une ~** to take up a career; **faire ~ dans qqch** to make a career (for o.s.) in sthg. **-2.** [gisement] quarry.

carriériste [karjerist] *nmf péj* careerist.

carriole [karjɔl] *nf* **-1.** [petite charrette] cart. **-2.** *Can* [traîneau] sleigh.

carrossable [karɔsabl] *adj* suitable for vehicles.

carrosse [karɔs] *nm* (horse-drawn) coach.

carrosserie [karɔsri] *nf* **-1.** [de voiture] bodywork, body. **-2.** [industrie] coachbuilding.

carrossier [karɔsje] *nm* coachbuilder.

carrousel [karuzɛl] *nm* ÉQUITATION carousel; ~ **d'avions** *fig* aerial display.

carrure [karyr] *nf* **-1.** [de personne] build; *fig* stature. **-2.** [de vêtement] width across the shoulders.

cartable [kartabl] *nm* schoolbag.

carte [kart] *nf* **-1.** [gén] card; ~ **bancaire** cash card *Br*; ~ **de crédit** credit card; ~ **d'étudiant** student card; ~ **graphique** IN-FORM graphics board; ~ **grise** ≃ (vehicle) registration document *Br*; ~ **d'identité** identity card; ~ **à mémoire** memory card; ~ **mère** INFORM motherboard; ~ **nominative** personal identity card; ~ **orange** season ticket *(for use on public transport in Paris)*; ~ **postale** postcard; ~ **privative** personal credit card; ~ **à puce** smart card; ~ **de séjour** residence permit; ~ **vermeil** *card entitling senior citizens to reduced rates in cinemas, on public transport etc*; ~ **de visite** visiting card *Br*, calling card *Am*; **donner ~ blanche à qqn** *fig* to give sb a free hand. **-2.** [de jeu]: ~ **(à jouer)** (playing) card; **abattre ses ~s** to lay down one's cards; *fig* to show one's hand; **battre les ~s** to shuffle the cards; **brouiller les ~s** *fig* to cloud OU obscure the issue; **tirer les ~s à qqn** to read sb's cards. **-3.** GÉOGR map; ~ **d'état-major** ≃ Ordnance Survey map *Br*; ~ **routière** road map. **-4.** [au restaurant] menu; **à la ~** [menu] à la carte; [horaires] flexible; ~ **des vins** wine list.

cartel [kartɛl] *nm* **-1.** ÉCON cartel. **-2.** POLIT coalition.

carter [kartɛr] *nm* **-1.** [de bicyclette] chain guard. **-2.** [de moteur] crankcase.

carte-réponse [kartrepɔ̃s] (*pl* **cartes-réponses**) *nf* reply card.

cartésien, -ienne [kartezjɛ̃, jɛn] ◇ *adj* **-1.** [rationnel] logical, rational. **-2.** [relatif à Descartes] Cartesian. ◇ *nm, f* Cartesian.

cartilage [kartilaʒ] *nm* cartilage.

cartilagineux, -euse [kartilaʒinø, øz] *adj* **-1.** [tissu] cartilaginous. **-2.** [viande] gristly.

cartographie [kartɔgrafi] *nf* cartography.

cartomancien, -ienne [kartɔmɑ̃sjɛ̃, jɛn] *nm, f* fortune-teller (*using cards*).

carton [kartɔ̃] *nm* **-1.** [matière] cardboard; **en** ~ cardboard; ~ **ondulé** corrugated cardboard. **-2.** [emballage] cardboard box; ~ **à dessin** portfolio. **-3.** [cible] target; **faire un** ~ *fam* to target-shoot; *fig* to take potshots. **-4.** [carte]: ~ **d'invitation** formal invitation.

cartonné, -e [kartɔne] *adj* [livre] hardback.

carton-pâte [kartɔ̃pat] (*pl* **cartons-pâtes**) *nm* pasteboard; **de** OU **en** ~ cardboard.

cartouche [kartuʃ] *nf* **-1.** [gén & INFORM] cartridge. **-2.** [de cigarettes] carton.

cas [ka] *nm* case; **au** ~ **où** in case; **auquel** ~ in which case; **dans** OU **en ce** ~ in that case; **en aucun** ~ under no circumstances; **en tout** ~ in any case, anyway; **en** ~ **de** in case of; **en** ~ **d'urgence** in an emergency; **en** ~ **de besoin** if need be; **c'est le** ~ **de le dire** you've hit the nail on the head; **le** ~ **échéant** if the need arises, if need be; ~ **de conscience** matter of conscience; ~ **de force majeure** emergency; ~ **social** person with social problems; **faire grand** ~ **de** to set great store by.

casanier, -ière [kazanje, jɛr] *adj & nm, f* stay-at-home.

casaque [kazak] *nf* **-1.** [veste] overblouse; **tourner** ~ *fig* to change sides. **-2.** HIPPISME blouse.

cascade [kaskad] *nf* **-1.** [chute d'eau] waterfall; *fig* stream, torrent; **en** ~ *fig* one after the other. **-2.** CIN stunt.

cascadeur, -euse [kaskadœr, øz] *nm, f* **-1.** [au cirque] acrobat. **-2.** CIN stuntman (*f* stuntwoman).

case [kaz] *nf* **-1.** [habitation] hut. **-2.** [de boîte, tiroir] compartment; [d'échiquier] square; [sur un formulaire] box.

casemate [kazmat] *nf* bunker.

caser [kaze] [3] *vt* **-1.** *fam* [trouver un emploi pour] to get a job for. **-2.** *fam* [loger] to put up. **-3.** *fam* [marier] to marry off. **-4.** [placer] to put.

◆ **se caser** *vp fam* **-1.** [trouver un emploi] to get (o.s.) a job. **-2.** [se marier] to get hitched. **-3.** [se loger] to find a place to live.

caserne [kazɛrn] *nf* barracks.

cash [kaʃ] *nm* cash; **payer** ~ to pay (in) cash.

casher → **kasher**.

casier [kazje] *nm* **-1.** [compartiment] compartment; [pour le courrier] pigeonhole. **-2.** [meuble - à bouteilles] rack; [- à courrier] set of pigeonholes. **-3.** PÊCHE lobster pot.

◆ **casier judiciaire** *nm* police record; ~ **judiciaire vierge** clean (police) record.

casino [kazino] *nm* casino.

Caspienne [kaspjɛn] *n*: **la** ~ the Caspian Sea.

casque [kask] *nm* **-1.** [de protection] helmet; ~ **intégral** crash helmet. **-2.** [séchoir] hairdryer. **-3.** [à écouteurs] headphones (*pl*).

◆ **Casques bleus** *nmpl*: **les Casques bleus** the UN peace-keeping force.

casqué, -e [kaske] *adj* wearing a helmet.

casquer [kaske] [3] *vi fam* to cough up.

casquette [kaskɛt] *nf* cap.

cassant, -e [kasɑ̃, ɑ̃t] *adj* **-1.** [fragile - verre] fragile; [- cheveux] brittle. **-2.** [dur] brusque.

cassation [kasasjɔ̃] → **cour**.

casse [kas] ◇ *nf* **-1.** [action] breakage. **-2.** *fam* [violence] aggro. **-3.** [de voitures] scrapyard. **-4.** TYPO: **haut/bas de** ~ upper/lower case. ◇ *nm fam* [cambriolage] break-in.

cassé, -e [kase] *adj* **-1.** [voûté, courbé] stooped. **-2.** [voix] trembling, breaking.

casse-cou [kasku] *nmf inv* [personne] daredevil.

casse-croûte [kaskrut] *nm inv* snack.

casse-noisettes [kasnwazɛt], **casse-noix** [kasnwa] *nm inv* nutcrackers (*pl*).

casse-pieds [kaspje] ◇ *adj inv fam* annoying. ◇ *nmf inv* pain (in the neck).

casser [kase] [3] ◇ *vt* **-1.** [briser] to break; **à tout** ~ *fam fig* [extraordinaire] fabulous, fantastic; [tout au plus] at (the) most. **-2.** JUR to quash. **-3.** COMM: ~ **les prix** to slash prices. ◇ *vi* to break.

◆ **se casser** *vp* **-1.** [se briser] to break. **-2.** [membre]: **se** ~ **un bras** to break one's arm. **-3.** *fam* [se fatiguer] to strain o.s. **-4.** *fam* [s'en aller] to hop it, to push off.

casserole [kasrɔl] *nf* **-1.** [ustensile] saucepan; **à la** ~ CULIN braised. **-2.** [voiture] (**old**) banger. **-3.** *fam* [instrument]: **être une vraie** ~ to sound tinny. **-4.** *loc*: **passer à la** ~ *fam* to be bumped off; [sexuellement] to get laid.

casse-tête [kastɛt] *nm inv* **-1.** *fig* [problème] headache. **-2.** [jeu] puzzle.

cassette [kasɛt] *nf* **-1.** [coffret] casket. **-2.** [de musique, vidéo] cassette. **-3.** INFORM: ~ **audionumérique** DAT tape.

casseur [kasœr] *nm* **-1.** [cambrioleur] burglar. **-2.** [manifestant] rioting demonstrator.

cassis [kasis] *nm* **-1.** [fruit] blackcurrant; [arbuste] blackcurrant bush; [liqueur] blackcurrant liqueur. **-2.** [sur la route] dip.

cassonade [kasɔnad] *nf* brown sugar.

cassoulet [kasulɛ] *nm stew of haricot beans and meat.*

cassure [kasyr] *nf* break.

castagnettes [kastaɲɛt] *nfpl* castanets.

caste [kast] *nf* caste.

casting [kastiŋ] *nm* [acteurs] cast; [sélection] casting; **aller à un ~** to go to an audition.

castor [kastɔr] *nm* beaver.

castration [kastrasjɔ̃] *nf* castration.

castrer [kastre] [3] *vt* to castrate; [chat] to neuter; [chatte] to spay.

cataclysme [kataklism] *nm* cataclysm.

catacombes [katakɔ̃b] *nfpl* catacombs.

catadioptre [katadjɔptr], **Cataphote®** [katafɔt] *nm* **-1.** [sur la route] cat's eye. **-2.** [de véhicule] reflector.

catalan, -e [katalɑ̃, an] *adj* Catalan, Catalonian.

◆ **catalan** *nm* [langue] Catalan.

◆ **Catalan, -e** *nm, f* Catalan, Catalonian.

Catalogne [katalɔɲ] *nf*: **la ~** Catalonia.

catalogue [katalɔg] *nm* catalogue.

cataloguer [katalɔge] [3] *vt* **-1.** [classer] to catalogue. **-2.** *péj* [juger] to label.

catalyseur [katalizœr] *nm* CHIM & *fig* catalyst.

catalytique [katalitik] → **pot**.

catamaran [katamarɑ̃] *nm* **-1.** [voilier] catamaran. **-2.** [d'hydravion] floats (*pl*).

Cataphote® = **catadioptre**.

cataplasme [kataplasm] *nm* poultice.

catapulter [katapylte] [3] *vt* to catapult.

cataracte [katarakt] *nf* cataract.

catarrhe [katar] *nm* catarrh.

catastrophe [katastrɔf] *nf* disaster, catastrophe; **atterrir en ~** to crashland; **partir en ~** to leave in a mad rush.

catastrophé, -e [katastrɔfe] *adj* shocked, upset.

catastrophique [katastrɔfik] *adj* disastrous, catastrophic.

catch [katʃ] *nm* wrestling.

catéchisme [kateʃism] *nm* catechism.

catégorie [kategɔri] *nf* [gén] category; ~ **socioprofessionnelle** ÉCON socio-economic

group; [de personnel] grade; [de viande, fruits] quality.

catégorique [kategɔrik] *adj* categorical.

catégoriquement [kategɔrikmɑ̃] *adv* categorically.

caténaire [katenɛr] *adj & nf* catenary.

cathédrale [katedral] *nf* cathedral.

cathode [katɔd] *nf* cathode.

cathodique [katɔdik] → **tube**.

catholicisme [katɔlisism] *nm* Catholicism.

catholique [katɔlik] *adj* Catholic; **pas (très) ~** *fig* dubious, dodgy.

catimini [katimini]

◆ **en catimini** *loc adv* secretly.

catogan [katɔgɑ̃] *nm* ribbon (*securing hair at the back of the neck*).

cauchemar [koʃmar] *nm litt & fig* nightmare.

cauchemardesque [koʃmardɛsk] *adj* nightmarish.

caudal, -e, -aux [kodal, o] *adj* caudal, tail (*avant n*).

causal, -e, -als OU **-aux** [kozal, o] *adj* causal.

causalité [kozalite] *nf* causality.

causant, -e [kozɑ̃, ɑ̃t] *adj*: **peu ~** not very chatty.

cause [koz] *nf* **-1.** [gén] cause; **gagner qqn à sa ~** to win sb over (to one's cause); **à ~ de** because of; **pour ~ de** on account of, because of; **et pour ~!** and for good reason!; **faire ~ commune avec qqn** to make common cause with sb. **-2.** JUR case. **-3.** *loc*: **être en ~** [intérêts] to be at stake; [honnêteté] to be in doubt OU in question; **être hors de ~** to be beyond suspicion; **remettre en ~** to challenge, to question.

causer [koze] [3] ◇ *vt*: ~ **qqch à qqn** to cause sb sthg. ◇ *vi* **-1.** [bavarder]: ~ **(de)** to chat (about). **-2.** [jaser]: ~ **(sur)** to gossip (about).

causerie [kozri] *nf* talk.

causette [kozɛt] *nf fam* chat; **faire la ~ avec qqn** to have a chat with sb.

causticité [kostisite] *nf* causticness, causticity.

caustique [kostik] *adj & nm* caustic.

cauteleux, -euse [kotlø, øz] *adj* sly.

cautériser [koterize] [3] *vt* to cauterize.

caution [kosjɔ̃] *nf* **-1.** [somme d'argent] guarantee; **libérer qqn sous ~** JUR to free sb on bail; **payer la ~ de qqn** to stand bail for sb. **-2.** [personne] guarantor; **se porter ~ pour qqn** to act as guarantor for sb. **-3.** [soutien] support, backing.

CAUTION:
When renting accommodation in France, the future tenant is usually required to pay a deposit (normally twice the monthly rent), returnable if the property is maintained in good condition. A 'caution solidaire' is a statement signed by a third party guaranteeing payment of rent in the event of non-payment by the tenant. The term 'caution parentale' is used when the guarantor is the tenant's mother or father

cautionner [kosjone] [3] *vt* **-1.** [se porter garant de] to guarantee. **-2.** *fig* [appuyer] to support, to back.

cavalcade [kavalkad] *nf* **-1.** [de cavaliers] cav- alcade. **-2.** [d'enfants] stampede.

cavale [kaval] *nf fam*: être en ~ to be on the run.

cavaler [kavale] [3] *vi fam* [courir] to run OU rush around; ~ après qqn/qqch to chase (after) sb/sthg.

cavalerie [kavalri] *nf* **-1.** MIL cavalry. **-2.** [de cirque] horses (*pl*).

cavalier, -ière [kavalje, jɛr] ◇ *adj* **-1.** [destiné aux cavaliers]: **allée cavalière** bridle path. **-2.** *sout* [impertinent] offhand. ◇ *nm, f* **-1.** [à cheval] rider. **-2.** [partenaire] partner; faire ~ seul *fig* to go it alone.
◆ **cavalier** *nm* [aux échecs] knight.

cavalièrement [kavaljɛrmɑ̃] *adv* in an off-hand manner.

cave [kav] ◇ *nf* **-1.** [sous-sol] cellar. **-2.** [de vins] (wine) cellar. **-3.** [cabaret] cellar night-club. ◇ *nm arg crime* outsider. ◇ *adj* [joues] hollow; [yeux] sunken.

caveau [kavo] *nm* **-1.** [petite cave] small cellar. **-2.** [cabaret] nightclub. **-3.** [sépulture] vault.

caverne [kavɛrn] *nf* cave.

caverneux, -euse [kavɛrnø, øz] → **voix**.

caviar [kavjar] *nm* caviar.

cavité [kavite] *nf* cavity.

CB (*abr de* **citizen's band, canaux banalisés**) *nf* CB.

cc -1. (*abr de* **cuillère à café**) tsp. **-2.** *abr de* **charges comprises**.

CC (*abr de* **corps consulaire**) CC.

CCE (*abr de* **Commission des communautés européennes**) *nf* ECC.

CCI (*abr de* **Chambre de commerce et d'industrie**) *nf* CCI.

CCP (*abr de* **compte chèque postal, compte courant postal**) *nm* post office account, ≃ Giro *Br*.

CD *nm* **-1.** (*abr de* **chemin départemental**) minor road. **-2.** (*abr de* **compact disc**) CD. **-3.** (*abr de* **comité directeur**) steering committee. **-4.** (*abr de* **corps diplomatique**) CD.

CDD (*abr de* **contrat à durée déterminée**) *nm* fixed term contract; elle est ~ she's on a fixed term contract.

CdF (*abr de* **Charbonnages de France**) *nmpl* French national coal board, ≃ NCB *Br*.

CDI *nm* **-1.** (*abr de* **centre de documentation et d'information**) school library. **-2.** (*abr de* **contrat à durée indéterminée**) permanent work contract; elle est ~ she's got a permanent work contract.

CD-Rom [sederɔm] (*abr de* **compact disc read only memory**) *nm* CD-Rom.

CDS (*abr de* **Centre des démocrates sociaux**) *nm* French political party.

CDU (*abr de* **Classification décimale universelle**) *nf* DDS.

ce [sə] ◇ *adj dém* (**cet** [sɛt] *devant voyelle ou h muet*, *f* **cette** [sɛt], *pl* **ces** [se]) [proche] this, (*pl*) these; [éloigné] that, (*pl*) those; ~ **mois**, ~ **mois-ci** this month; cette année, cette année-là that year; regarde de ~ côté-ci et pas de ~ côté-là look on this side, not that side.
◇ *pron dém* (**c'** *devant voyelle*): c'est it is, it's; ~ sont they are, they're; c'est mon bureau this is my office, it's my office; ~ sont mes enfants these are my children, they're my children; c'est à Paris it's in Paris; c'était hier it was yesterday; qui est-~? who is it?; ~ qui, ~ que what; ils ont eu ~ qui leur revenait they got what they deserved; ..., ~ qui est étonnant ..., which is surprising; elle n'achète même pas ~ dont elle a besoin she doesn't even buy what she needs; vous savez bien ~ à quoi je pense you know exactly what I'm thinking about; faites donc ~ pour quoi on vous paie do what you're paid to do.
◆ **n'est-ce pas?** *loc adv* isn't it?/aren't you? *etc*; ~ café est bon, n'est-~ pas? this coffee's good, isn't it?; tu connais Pierre, n'est-~ pas? you know Pierre, don't you?; elle est jolie, n'est-~ pas? she's pretty, isn't she?; n'est-~ pas que tu aimes la soupe? you like the soup, don't you?

CE ◇ *nm* **-1.** *abr de* **comité d'entreprise**. **-2.** (*abr de* **cours élémentaire**) ~1 second year of primary school; ~2 third year of primary school. ◇ *nf* (*abr de* **Communauté européenne**) EC.

CEA (*abr de* **Commissariat à l'énergie ato-**

mique) nm French atomic energy commission, ≃ AEA Br, ≃ AEC Am.

CECA, Ceca [seka] (abr de **Communauté européenne du charbon et de l'acier)** nf ECSC.

ceci [səsi] pron dém this; ~ **pour vous dire que ...** this is just to say (that) ...; ~ **n'explique pas cela** this doesn't explain that; ~ **(étant) dit** having said that; **à ~ près que** with the exception that, except that.

cécité [sesite] nf blindness.

céder [sede] [18] ◇ vt **-1.** [donner] to give up. **-2.** [revendre] to sell. ◇ vi **-1.** [personne]: ~ **(à)** to give in (to), to yield (to). **-2.** [chaise, plancher] to give way.

CEDEX, Cedex [sedɛks] (abr de **courrier d'entreprise à distribution exceptionnelle)** nm accelerated postal service for bulk users.

cédille [sedij] nf cedilla; **c ~ c** cedilla.

cèdre [sɛdr] nm cedar.

CEE (abr de **Communauté économique européenne)** nf EEC.

CEI (abr de **Communauté des États Indépendants)** nf CIS.

ceindre [sɛ̃dr] [81] vt **-1.** [entourer]: ~ **qqch de qqch** to put sthg around sthg. **-2.** [mettre] to put on.

ceinture [sɛ̃tyr] nf **-1.** [gén] belt; **attachez vos ~s** fasten your seat OU safety belts; ~ **à enrouleur** inertia-reel seat belt; ~ **noire** JUDO black belt; ~ **de sauvetage** life belt; ~ **de sécurité** safety OU seat belt; ~ **verte** green belt; **se serrer la ~** fig to tighten one's belt. **-2.** ANAT waist. **-3.** COUTURE waistband.

ceinturon [sɛ̃tyrɔ̃] nm belt.

cela [səla] pron dém that; ~ **ne vous regarde pas** it's OU that's none of your business; **il y a des années de ~** that was many years ago; **c'est ~** that's right; ~ **dit ...** having said that ...; **malgré ~** in spite of that, nevertheless.

célébration [selebrasjɔ̃] nf celebration.

célèbre [selɛbr] adj famous.

célébrer [selebre] [18] vt **-1.** [gén] to celebrate. **-2.** [faire la louange de] to praise.

célébrité [selebrite] nf **-1.** [renommée] fame. **-2.** [personne] celebrity.

céleri [sɛlri] nm celery; ~ **rémoulade** CULIN grated celeriac in mustard dressing.
◆ **céleri rave, céleri-rave** nm celeriac.

célérité [selerite] nf speed.

céleste [selɛst] adj heavenly.

célibat [seliba] nm celibacy.

célibataire [selibatɛr] ◇ adj single, unmar-

ried. ◇ nmf single person, single man (f woman); ~ **endurci** confirmed bachelor.

celle → **celui**.

celle-ci → **celui-ci**.

celle-là → **celui-là**.

celles → **celui**.

celles-ci → **celui-ci**.

celles-là → **celui-là**.

cellier [selje] nm storeroom.

Cellophane® [selɔfan] nf Cellophane®; **sous ~** (wrapped) in cellophane.

cellulaire [selyler] adj **-1.** BIOL & TÉLÉCOM cellular. **-2.** [destiné aux prisonniers]: **régime ~** solitary confinement; **voiture ~** prison van.

cellule [selyl] nf **-1.** [gén & INFORM] cell; ~ **photoélectrique** photoelectric cell. **-2.** [groupe] unit; ~ **de crise** [groupe] emergency committee; [réunion] emergency committee meeting.

cellulite [selylit] nf cellulite.

celluloïd [selylɔid] nm celluloid.

cellulose [selyloz] nf cellulose.

celte [sɛlt] adj Celtic.
◆ **Celte** nmf Celt.

celtique [sɛltik] ◇ adj Celtic. ◇ nm [langue] Celtic.

celui [səlɥi] (f **celle** [sɛl], mpl **ceux** [sø], fpl **celles** [sɛl]) pron dém **-1.** [suivi d'un complément prépositionnel] the one; **celle de devant** the one in front; **ceux d'entre vous qui ...** those of you who .... **-2.** [suivi d'un pronom relatif]: ~ **qui** [objet] the one which OU that; [personne] the one who; **c'est celle qui te va le mieux** that's the one which OU that suits you best; ~ **que vous voyez** the one (which OU that) you can see, the one whom you can see; **ceux que je connais** those I know. **-3.** [suivi d'un adjectif, d'un participe] the one.

celui-ci [səlɥisi] (f **celle-ci** [sɛlsi], mpl **ceux-ci** [søsi], fpl **celles-ci** [sɛlsi]) pron dém this one, these ones (pl).

celui-là [səlɥila] (f **celle-là** [sɛlla], mpl **ceux-là** [søla], fpl **celles-là** [sɛlla]) pron dém that one, those ones (pl); ~ **... celui-ci** the former ... the latter.

cénacle [senakl] nm [coterie] circle.

cendre [sɑ̃dr] nf ash; **réduire qqch en ~s** reduce sthg to ashes.
◆ **cendres** nfpl [restes des morts] ashes; **renaître de ses ~s** fig to rise from the ashes.
◆ **Cendres** nfpl: **le mercredi des Cendres** Ash Wednesday.

cendré, -e [sɑ̃dre] adj [chevelure]: **blond ~** ash blond.

cendrier [sãdrije] *nm* **-1.** [de fumeur] ashtray. **-2.** [de poêle] ashpan.

cène [sɛn] *nf* (Holy) Communion.
◆ **Cène** *nf*: **la Cène** the Last Supper.

censé, -e [sãse] *adj*: **être ~ faire qqch** to be supposed to do sthg.

censément [sãsemã] *adv sout* supposedly.

censeur [sãsœr] *nm* **-1.** SCOL ≃ deputy head *Br,* ≃ vice-principal *Am.* **-2.** CIN & PRESSE censor. **-3.** *fig* [juge] critic.

censure [sãsyr] *nf* **-1.** [CIN & PRESSE - contrôle] censorship; [- censeurs] censors (*pl*). **-2.** POLIT censure. **-3.** PSYCHOL censor.

censurer [sãsyre] [3] *vt* **-1.** CIN, PRESSE & PSYCHOL to censor. **-2.** [juger] to censure.

cent [sã] ◇ *adj num* one hundred, a hundred; *voir aussi* **six.** ◇ *nm* **-1.** [nombre] a hundred; *voir aussi* **six. -2.** [mesure de proportion]: **pour ~** per cent; **~ pour ~** a hundred per cent. **-3.** [monnaie] cent.

centaine [sãtɛn] *nf* **-1.** [cent unités] hundred. **-2.** [un grand nombre]: **une ~ de** about a hundred; **des ~s (de)** hundreds (of); **plusieurs ~s de** several hundred; **par ~s** in hundreds.

centenaire [sãtnɛr] ◇ *adj* hundred-year-old (*avant n*); **être ~** to be a hundred years old. ◇ *nmf* centenarian. ◇ *nm* [anniversaire] centenary.

centiare [sãtjar] *nm* square metre.

centième [sãtjɛm] ◇ *adj num, nm & nmf* hundredth; *voir aussi* **sixième.** ◇ *nf* THÉÂTRE hundredth performance.

centigrade [sãtigrad] → **degré.**

centigramme [sãtigram] *nm* centigram.

centilitre [sãtilitr] *nm* centilitre.

centime [sãtim] *nm* centime.

centimètre [sãtimɛtr] *nm* **-1.** [mesure] centimetre; **~ cube** cubic centimetre. **-2.** [ruban, règle] tape measure.

central, -e, -aux [sãtral, o] *adj* central.
◆ **central** *nm* **-1.** TENNIS centre court. **-2.** [de réseau]: **~ téléphonique** telephone exchange.
◆ **centrale** *nf* **-1.** [usine] power plant OU station; **~e hydroélectrique** hydroelectric power station; **~e nucléaire** nuclear power plant OU station. **-2.** [syndicale] *group of affiliated trade unions.* **-3.** COMM: **~e d'achat** buying group.
◆ **Centrale** *nf grande école training highly-qualified engineers.*

centralien, -ienne [sãtraljɛ̃, jɛn] *nm, f* engineering student.

centralisation [sãtralizasjɔ̃] *nf* centralization.

centraliser [sãtralize] [3] *vt* to centralize.

centre [sãtr] *nm* [gén] centre; **~ aéré** outdoor centre; **~ antipoison** poison centre; **~ commercial** shopping centre; **~ culturel** arts centre; **~ de documentation** reference library; **~ équestre** riding school; **~ de gravité** centre of gravity; **~ nerveux** nerve centre; **~ de rééducation** rehabilitation centre.

centrer [sãtre] [3] *vt* to centre.

centre-ville [sãtrəvil] (*pl* **centres-villes**) *nm* city centre, town centre.

centrifuge [sãtrifyʒ] → **force.**

centrifugeuse [sãtrifyʒøz] *nf* **-1.** TECHNOL centrifuge. **-2.** CULIN juice extractor.

centriste [sãtrist] POLIT ◇ *adj* centre (*avant n*). ◇ *nmf* centrist.

centuple [sãtypl] *nm*: **être le ~ de qqch** to be a hundred times sthg; **au ~** a hundredfold.

centupler [sãtyple] [3] *vt & vi* to increase a hundredfold.

cep [sɛp] *nm* stock.

CEP (*abr de* **certificat d'études primaires**) *nm school-leaving certificate formerly taken at end of primary education.*

cépage [sepaʒ] *nm* (type of) vine.

cèpe [sɛp] *nm* cep.

cependant [səpãdã] *conj* however, yet.

céramique [seramik] *nf* **-1.** [matière, objet] ceramic. **-2.** [art] ceramics (*U*), pottery.

cerbère [sɛrbɛr] *nm* strict caretaker OU doorkeeper.

cerceau [sɛrso] *nm* hoop.

cercle [sɛrkl] *nm* circle; **~ d'amis** circle of friends; **~ vicieux** vicious circle.

cerclé, -e [sɛrkle] *adj* ringed; **des lunettes ~es d'écaille** horn-rimmed glasses.

cercueil [sɛrkœj] *nm* coffin.

céréale [sereal] *nf* cereal.

cérébral, -e, -aux [serebral, o] ◇ *adj* **-1.** [du cerveau] cerebral. **-2.** [personne, activité] intellectual. ◇ *nm, f* intellectual.

cérémonial, -als [seremɔnjal] *nm* ceremonial.

cérémonie [seremɔni] *nf* ceremony; **sans ~** without ceremony, informally; **faire des ~s** to make a fuss.

cérémonieux, -ieuse [seremɔnjø, jøz] *adj* ceremonious.

CERES [seres] (*abr de* **Centre d'études, de recherches et d'éducation socialiste**) *nm formerly the intellectual section of the French socialist party.*

cerf [sɛr] *nm* stag.

cerfeuil [sɛrfœj] *nm* chervil.

cerf-volant [sɛrvɔlɑ̃] (*pl* **cerfs-volants**) *nm* **-1.** [jouet] kite. **-2.** [insecte] stag beetle.

cerise [səriz] *nf & adj inv* cherry.

cerisier [sərizje] *nm* [arbre] cherry (tree); [bois] cherry (wood).

CERN, Cern [sɛrn] (*abr de* **Conseil européen pour la recherche nucléaire**) *nm* CERN.

cerne [sɛrn] *nm* ring.

cerné [sɛrne] → **œil**.

cerner [sɛrne] [3] *vt* **-1.** [encercler] to surround. **-2.** [entourer d'un trait] to ring. **-3.** *fig* [sujet] to define.

certain, -e [sɛrtɛ̃, ɛn] ◇ *adj* certain; **c'est une chose ~e** there's no doubt about it; **être ~ de qqch** to be certain OU sure of sthg; **être ~ que** to be certain OU sure (that); **je suis pourtant ~ d'avoir mis mes clés là** but I'm certain OU sure I left my keys there.
◇ *adj indéf (avant n)* certain; **il a un ~ talent** he has some talent OU a certain talent; **à un ~ moment** at some point; **~s jours** some days; **un ~ temps** for a while; **dans une certaine mesure** to a certain extent; **avoir un ~ âge** to be getting on, to be past one's prime; **c'est un monsieur d'un ~ âge** he's getting on a bit; **un ~ M Lebrun** a Mr Lebrun.
◆ **certains** (*fpl* **certaines**) *pron indéf pl* some.

certainement [sɛrtɛnmɑ̃] *adv* certainly.

certes [sɛrt] *adv* of course.

certificat [sɛrtifika] *nm* **-1.** [attestation, diplôme] certificate; **~ d'aptitude professionnelle** vocational training certificate; **~ d'études** *primary school-leaving certificate*; **~ médical** medical certificate; **~ de scolarité** *certificate of regular attendance at school or university*. **-2.** [référence] reference.

certifié, -e [sɛrtifje] *adj*: **professeur ~** qualified teacher.

certifier [sɛrtifje] [9] *vt* **-1.** [assurer]: **~ qqch à qqn** to assure sb of sthg. **-2.** [authentifier] to certify.

certitude [sɛrtityd] *nf* certainty.

cérumen [serymɛn] *nm* wax, earwax.

cerveau [sɛrvo] *nm* brain.

cervelas [sɛrvəla] *nm* saveloy.

cervelle [sɛrvɛl] *nf* **-1.** ANAT brain. **-2.** [facultés mentales, aliment] brains (*pl*). **-3.** *loc*: **se brûler la ~** to blow one's brains out; **se creuser la ~** to rack one's brains.

cervical, -e, -aux [sɛrvikal, o] *adj* cervical; (**vertèbre**) **~e** cervical vertebra.

ces → **ce**.

CES (*abr de* **collège d'enseignement secondaire**) *nm former secondary school*.

César [sezar] *nm*: **les ~s** *French cinema awards*.

césarienne [sezarjɛn] *nf* caesarean (section).

cessante [sɛsɑ̃t] → **affaire**.

cessation [sɛsasjɔ̃] *nf* suspension.

cesse [sɛs] *nf*: **n'avoir de ~ que** (+ *subjonctif*) *sout* not to rest until.
◆ **sans cesse** *loc adv* continually, constantly.

cesser [sese] [4] ◇ *vi* to stop, to cease. ◇ *vt* to stop; **~ de faire qqch** to stop doing sthg.

cessez-le-feu [seselfø] *nm inv* cease-fire.

cession [sɛsjɔ̃] *nf* transfer.

c'est-à-dire [sɛtadir] *conj* **-1.** [en d'autres termes]: **~ (que)** that is (to say). **-2.** [introduit une restriction, précision, réponse]: **~ que** well ..., actually ....

cet [sɛt] → **ce**.

cétacé [setase] *nm* cetacean.

cette → **ce**.

ceux → **celui**.

ceux-ci → **celui-ci**.

ceux-là → **celui-là**.

cévenol, -e [sevnɔl] *adj* of/from the Cévennes region.

Ceylan [selɑ̃] *nm* Ceylon.

cf. (*abr de* **confer**) cf.

CFA ◇ *nf* (*abr de* **Communauté financière africaine**): **franc ~** *currency used in former French African colonies.* ◇ *nm* (*abr de* **centre de formation des apprentis**) *centre for apprenticeship training.*

CFAO (*abr de* **conception de fabrication assistée par ordinateur**) *nf* CAM.

CFC (*abr de* **chlorofluorocarbone**) *nm* CFC.

CFDT (*abr de* **Confédération française démocratique du travail**) *nf French trade union.*

CFES (*abr de* **certificat de fin d'études secondaires**) *nm school-leaving certificate.*

CFF (*abr de* **Chemins de fer fédéraux**) *nmpl Swiss railways.*

CFL (*abr de* **Chemins de fer luxembourgeois**) *nmpl Luxembourg railways.*

CFP (*abr de* **Compagnie française des pétroles**) *nf French oil company.*

CFTC (*abr de* **Confédération française des travailleurs chrétiens**) *nf French trade union.*

CGC (*abr de* **Confédération générale des cadres**) *nf French management union.*

CGT (*abr de* **Confédération générale du**

travail) *nf* French trade union *(affiliated to the Communist party).*

ch. -1. *abr de* **charges. -2.** *abr de* **chauffage. -3.** *abr de* **cherche.**

CH *(abr de* **Confédération helvétique)** *Switzerland (as nationality sticker on a car).*

chacal [ʃakal] *nm* jackal.

chacun, -e [ʃakœ̃, yn] *pron indéf* each (one); [tout le monde] everyone, everybody; ~ **de nous/de vous/d'eux** each of us/you/them; ~ **pour soi** every man for himself; **tout un** ~ every one of us/them.

chagrin, -e [ʃagrɛ̃, in] *adj* [personne] grieving; [caractère, humeur] morose.
◆ **chagrin** *nm* grief; **avoir du** ~ to grieve.

chagriner [ʃagrine] [3] *vt* **-1.** [peiner] to grieve, to distress. **-2.** [contrarier] to upset.

chahut [ʃay] *nm* uproar.

chahuter [ʃayte] [3] ◇ *vi* to cause an uproar. ◇ *vt* **-1.** [importuner - professeur] to rag, to tease; [- orateur] to heckle. **-2.** [bousculer] to jostle.

chahuteur, -euse [ʃaytœr, øz] ◇ *adj* disruptive, rowdy. ◇ *nm, f* **-1.** [enfant] disruptive child. **-2.** [manifestant] heckler.

chai [ʃɛ] *nm* wine and spirits store OU storehouse.

chaîne [ʃɛn] *nf* **-1.** [gén] chain; ~ **de montagnes** mountain range. **-2.** IND: ~ **de fabrication/de montage** production/assembly line; **travail à la** ~ production-line work; **produire qqch à la** ~ to mass-produce sthg. **-3.** TÉLÉ channel. **-4.** [appareil] stereo (system); ~ **hi-fi** hi-fi system.
◆ **chaînes** *nfpl fig* chains, bonds.

chaînette [ʃɛnɛt] *nf* small chain.

chaînon [ʃɛnɔ̃] *nm litt & fig* link.

chair [ʃɛr] ◇ *nf* flesh; **bien en** ~ plump; **en** ~ **et en os** in the flesh; ~ **à saucisse** sausage meat; **avoir la** ~ **de poule** *fig* to have goosepimples *Br,* to have goosebumps *Am.* ◇ *adj inv* flesh-coloured.

chaire [ʃɛr] *nf* **-1.** [estrade - de prédicateur] pulpit; [- de professeur] rostrum. **-2.** UNIV chair.

chaise [ʃɛz] *nf* chair; ~ **électrique** electric chair; ~ **haute** high chair; ~ **longue** deckchair; **être assis entre deux** ~**s** *fig* to be in an awkward situation.

chaland [ʃalɑ̃] *nm* [bateau] barge.

châle [ʃal] *nm* shawl.

chalet [ʃalɛ] *nm* **-1.** [de montagne] chalet. **-2.** *Can* [maison de campagne] (holiday) cottage.

chaleur [ʃalœr] *nf* heat; [agréable] warmth;

avec ~ [accueillir] warmly; **en** ~ [animal] on heat.

chaleureusement [ʃalœrøzmɑ̃] *adv* warmly.

chaleureux, -euse [ʃalœrø, øz] *adj* warm.

challenge [ʃalɑ̃ʒ] *nm* **-1.** SPORT tournament. **-2.** *fig* [défi] challenge.

challenger [tʃalɛndʒœr] *nm* SPORT & *fig* challenger.

chaloupe [ʃalup] *nf* rowing boat *Br,* rowboat *Am.*

chalumeau [ʃalymo] *nm* **-1.** TECHNOL blowlamp *Br,* blowtorch *Am.* **-2.** [paille] (drinking) straw.

chalutier [ʃalytje] *nm* **-1.** [bateau] trawler. **-2.** [pêcheur] trawlerman.

chamade [ʃamad] *nf*: **battre la** ~ [cœur] to pound.

chamailler [ʃamaje] [3]
◆ **se chamailler** *vp fam* to squabble.

chambardement [ʃɑ̃bardəmɑ̃] *nm fam* [bouleversement] upheaval.

chambarder [ʃɑ̃barde] [3] *vt fam* **-1.** [pièce] to turn upside down. **-2.** [projet] to upset.

chambouler [ʃɑ̃bule] [3] *vt fam* to make a mess of, to turn upside down.

chambranle [ʃɑ̃brɑ̃l] *nm* [de porte, fenêtre] frame; [de cheminée] mantelpiece.

chambre [ʃɑ̃br] *nf* **-1.** [où l'on dort]: ~ (**à coucher**) bedroom; **garder la** ~ to stay in one's room; **faire** ~ **à part** to sleep in separate rooms; ~ **à un lit,** ~ **pour une personne** single room; ~ **pour deux personnes** double room; ~ **à deux lits** twin-bedded room; ~ **d'amis** spare room; ~ **d'hôte** bed and breakfast. **-2.** [local] room; ~ **forte** strongroom; ~ **froide** cold store; ~ **noire** darkroom. **-3.** JUR division; ~ **d'accusation** court of criminal appeal. **-4.** POLIT chamber, house; **Chambre des députés** ≃ House of Commons *Br,* ≃ House of Representatives *Am.* **-5.** COMM: ~ **de commerce** chamber of commerce; ~ **des métiers** guild chamber. **-6.** TECHNOL chamber; ~ **à air** [de pneu] inner tube.

chambrée [ʃɑ̃bre] *nf* room, roomful; [de soldats] barrack room.

chambrer [ʃɑ̃bre] [3] *vt* **-1.** [vin] to bring to room temperature. **-2.** *fam* [se moquer] to wind up *Br.*

chameau, -x [ʃamo] *nm* **-1.** [mammifère] camel. **-2.** *fam injurieux* [homme] pig; [femme] cow.

chamois [ʃamwa] ◇ *nm* chamois; [peau] chamois (leather). ◇ *adj inv* [couleur] fawn.

champ [ʃɑ̃] nm -1. [gén & INFORM] field; ~ de bataille battlefield; ~ de courses racecourse; ~ magnétique magnetic field; fleurs des ~s wild flowers; ~ visuel field of vision OU view; laisser le ~ libre à qqn *fig* to leave the field open OU clear for sb. -2. [étendue] area; ~ d'action sphere of activity.

champagne [ʃɑ̃paɲ] nm champagne; ~ rosé pink champagne.

champagnisé [ʃɑ̃paɲize] → vin.

champenois, -e [ʃɑ̃pənwa, az] *adj*: méthode ~e champagne-style.

champêtre [ʃɑ̃pɛtr] *adj* rural.

champignon [ʃɑ̃piɲɔ̃] nm -1. BOT & MÉD fungus; pousser comme des ~s *fig* to mushroom. -2. [comestible] mushroom; ~ de Paris button mushroom; ~ vénéneux toadstool. -3. *fam* [accélérateur] accelerator; appuyer sur le ~ to put one's foot down *Br*, to step on the gas *Am*.

champion, -ionne [ʃɑ̃pjɔ̃, jɔn] ◇ nm, f champion; ~ du monde world champion. ◇ *adj fam* brilliant.

championnat [ʃɑ̃pjɔna] nm championship; ~ du monde world championship.

chance [ʃɑ̃s] nf -1. [bonheur] luck (U); avoir de la ~ to be lucky; ne pas avoir de ~ to be unlucky; bonne ~! good luck!; quelle ~! what luck!, how lucky!; porter ~ to bring good luck. -2. [probabilité, possibilité] chance, opportunity; avoir des ~s de faire qqch to have a chance of doing sthg; donner sa ~ à qqn to give sb a chance; il y a peu de ~s que ... there's not much chance that ....

chancelant, -e [ʃɑ̃slɑ̃, ɑ̃t] *adj* -1. [titubant, bancal] unsteady. -2. *fig* [mémoire, santé] shaky.

chanceler [ʃɑ̃sle] [24] *vi* [personne, gouvernement] to totter; [meuble] to wobble.

chancelier [ʃɑ̃səlje] nm -1. [premier ministre] chancellor. -2. [de consulat, d'ambassade] secretary.

◆ Chancelier nm: le Chancelier de l'Échiquier the Chancellor of the Exchequer.

chancellerie [ʃɑ̃sɛlri] nf -1. [ministère de la justice] chancery *Br*. -2. [en Allemagne] chancellor's office. -3: [de consulat, d'ambassade] chancery.

chanceux, -euse [ʃɑ̃sø, øz] *adj* lucky.

chancre [ʃɑ̃kr] nm -1. MÉD chancre. -2. BOT canker.

chandail [ʃɑ̃daj] nm (thick) sweater.

Chandeleur [ʃɑ̃dlœr] nf Candlemas.

chandelier [ʃɑ̃dəlje] nm [pour une bougie] candlestick; [à plusieurs branches] candelabra.

chandelle [ʃɑ̃dɛl] nf [bougie] candle; dîner aux ~s candlelit dinner; brûler la ~ par les deux bouts *fig* to burn the candle at both ends; devoir une fière ~ à qqn *fig* to play sb a big favour; tenir la ~ to play gooseberry; voir trente-six ~s *fam fig* to see stars.

change [ʃɑ̃ʒ] nm -1. [troc & FIN] exchange; donner le ~ à qqn to pull the wool over sb's eyes; gagner au ~ to be better off; perdre au ~ to lose out. -2. [couche de bébé] disposable nappy *Br*, diaper *Am*.

changeant, -e [ʃɑ̃ʒɑ̃, ɑ̃t] *adj* -1. [temps, humeur] changeable. -2. [reflet] shimmering.

changement [ʃɑ̃ʒmɑ̃] nm change; ~ de programme change of plan; ~ de vitesse gear lever *Br*, gearshift *Am*.

changer [ʃɑ̃ʒe] [17] ◇ *vt* -1. [gén] to change; ~ qqch contre to change OU exchange sthg for; ~ qqn en to change sb into. -2. [modifier] to change, to alter; ne rien ~ à qqch to not make any changes to sthg; ça me/te changera that will be a (nice) change for me/you.

◇ *vi* -1. [gén] to change; ~ de train (à) to change trains (at); ~ d'avis to change one's mind; ça changera! that'll make a change!; ~ de direction to change direction; ~ de place (avec qqn) to change places (with sb); ~ de vitesse AUTOM to change gear; ~ de voiture to change one's car; pour ~ for a change. -2. [modifier] to change, to alter; ~ de comportement to alter one's behaviour.

◆ se changer *vp* -1. [se rhabiller] to change, to get changed. -2. [se transformer]: se ~ en to change into.

changeur [ʃɑ̃ʒœr] nm -1. [personne] moneychanger. -2. [appareil]: ~ de monnaie change machine.

chanoine [ʃanwan] nm canon.

chanson [ʃɑ̃sɔ̃] nf song; c'est toujours la même ~ *fig* it's the same old story.

chansonnette [ʃɑ̃sɔnɛt] nf ditty.

chansonnier, -ière [ʃɑ̃sɔnje, jɛr] nm, f cabaret singer-songwriter.

chant [ʃɑ̃] nm -1. [chanson] song, singing (U); [sacré] hymn; ~ du cygne *fig* swansong; ~ grégorien Gregorian chant. -2. [art] singing.

chantage [ʃɑ̃taʒ] nm *litt* & *fig* blackmail; faire du ~ to use OU resort to blackmail; faire du ~ à qqn to blackmail sb.

chantant, -e [ʃɑ̃tɑ̃, ɑ̃t] *adj* -1. [accent, voix] lilting. -2. [musique, air] catchy.

chanter [ʃɑ̃te] [3] ◇ vt **-1.** [chanson] to sing. **-2.** fam [raconter] to tell. **-3.** littéraire [célébrer] to sing OU tell of; ~ **les louanges de qqn** to sing sb's praises. ◇ vi **-1.** [gén] to sing; ~ **juste** to sing in tune; ~ **faux** to sing off key. **-2.** loc: **faire** ~ **qqn** to blackmail sb; **si ça vous chante!** fam if you feel like OU fancy it!

chanterelle [ʃɑ̃trɛl] nf [champignon] chanterelle.

chanteur, -euse [ʃɑ̃tœr, øz] nm, f singer.

chantier [ʃɑ̃tje] nm **-1.** CONSTR (building) site; [sur la route] roadworks (pl); **en** ~ fig in progress; ~ **naval** shipyard, dockyard. **-2.** fig [désordre] shambles (sg), mess.

Chantilly [ʃɑ̃tiji] nf: **(crème)** ~ stiffly whipped cream sweetened and flavoured.

chantonner [ʃɑ̃tɔne] [3] vt & vi to hum.

chanvre [ʃɑ̃vr] nm hemp.

chaos [kao] nm chaos.

chaotique [kaɔtik] adj chaotic.

chap. (abr de chapitre) ch.

chaparder [ʃaparde] [3] vt to steal.

chapeau, -x [ʃapo] nm **-1.** [coiffure] hat; ~ **melon** bowler hat; **tirer son** ~ **à qqn** to take one's hat off to sb. **-2.** PRESSE introductory paragraph. **-3.** loc: ~**!** fam nice one!; **démarrer sur les** ~**x de roues** fam to take off like a bat out of hell.

chapeauter [ʃapote] [3] vt [service] to head; [personnes] to supervise.

chapelain [ʃaplɛ̃] nm chaplain.

chapelet [ʃaplɛ] nm **-1.** RELIG rosary; **dire son** ~ to say one's rosary, to tell one's beads. **-2.** [de saucisses, d'oignons] string. **-3.** fig [d'injures] string, torrent.

chapelier, -ière [ʃapəlje, jɛr] ◇ adj hat (avant n). ◇ nm, f [pour hommes] hatter; [pour femmes] milliner.

chapelle [ʃapɛl] nf **-1.** [petite église] chapel; [partie d'église] chapel; ~ **ardente** chapel of rest. **-2.** [coterie] clique.

chapelure [ʃaplyr] nf (dried) breadcrumbs (pl).

chaperon [ʃaprɔ̃] nm **-1.** LITTÉRATURE: **le Petit** ~ **Rouge** Little Red Riding Hood. **-2.** [personne] chaperone.

chapiteau, -x [ʃapito] nm **-1.** [de colonne] capital. **-2.** [de cirque] big top.

chapitre [ʃapitr] nm **-1.** [de livre & RELIG] chapter. **-2.** [de budget] head, item. **-3.** fig [sujet] subject.

chapitrer [ʃapitre] [3] vt sout to reprimand.

chapon [ʃapɔ̃] nm **-1.** [volaille] capon. **-2.** [en-cas] piece of bread rubbed with garlic and oil.

chaque [ʃak] adj indéf each, every; ~ **personne** each person, everyone; **j'ai payé ces livres 100 francs** ~ I paid 100 francs each for these books.

char [ʃar] nm **-1.** MIL: ~ **(d'assaut)** tank. **-2.** [charrette] cart, waggon. **-3.** [de carnaval] float. **-4.** Can [voiture] car. **-5.** HIST chariot.

charabia [ʃarabja] nm gibberish.

charade [ʃarad] nf charade.

charbon [ʃarbɔ̃] nm **-1.** [combustible] coal; ~ **de bois** charcoal; **être sur des** ~**s ardents** fig to be like a cat on hot bricks Br OU on a hot roof Am. **-2.** [maladie] anthrax.

charbonnage [ʃarbɔnaʒ] nm coalmining; **les** ~**s** collieries, coalmines.

charbonnier, -ière [ʃarbɔnje, jɛr] adj coal (avant n).
◆ **charbonnier** nm **-1.** [cargo] collier. **-2.** [vendeur] coal merchant; [livreur] coalman.

charcuterie [ʃarkytri] nf **-1.** [magasin] pork butcher's. **-2.** [produits] pork meat products. **-3.** [commerce] pork meat trade.

charcutier, -ière [ʃarkytje, jɛr] nm, f [commerçant] pork butcher.

chardon [ʃardɔ̃] nm **-1.** [plante] thistle. **-2.** [sur un mur] spikes (pl).

charentais, -e [ʃarɑ̃tɛ, ɛz] adj of/from Charente.
◆ **charentaise** nf (bedroom) slipper.

charge [ʃarʒ] nf **-1.** [fardeau] load. **-2.** [fonction] office. **-3.** [responsabilité] responsibility; **être à la** ~ **de** [personne] to be dependent on; **les travaux sont à la** ~ **du propriétaire** the owner is liable for the cost of the work; **prendre qqch en** ~ [payer] to pay (for) sthg; [s'occuper de] to take charge of sthg; **prendre qqn en** ~ to take charge of sb. **-4.** ÉLECTR, JUR & MIL charge; **revenir à la** ~ to return to the fray. **-5.** loc: **j'accepte, à** ~ **de revanche** I accept, provided that you'll let me do the same for you some time.
◆ **charges** nfpl **-1.** [d'appartement] service charge. **-2.** ÉCON expenses, costs; ~**s sociales** ≃ employer's contributions.

CHARGES:
Householders and tenants in blocks of flats are required to pay 'charges', a monthly contribution to pay for the general upkeep of the building. In estate agencies, rent is expressed either including this sum ('charges comprises' or 'cc') or excluding it ('hors charges' or 'charges en sus'). Sometimes the 'charges' include heating costs

chargé, -e [ʃaʁʒe] ◇ *adj* **-1.** [véhicule, personne]: ~ **(de)** loaded (with). **-2.** [responsable]: ~ **(de)** responsible (for). **-3.** [occupé] full, busy. ◇ *nm, f*: ~ **d'affaires** chargé d'affaires; ~ **de cours** ≃ lecturer; ~ **de mission** head of mission.

chargement [ʃaʁʒəmɑ̃] *nm* **-1.** [action] loading. **-2.** [marchandises] load.

charger [ʃaʁʒe] [17] *vt* **-1.** [gén & INFORM] to load. **-2.** [remplir] to fill. **-3.** ÉLECTR, JUR & MIL to charge. **-4.** [donner une mission à]: ~ **qqn de faire qqch** to put sb in charge of doing sthg.

◆ **se charger** *vp*: se ~ **de qqn/qqch** to take care of sb/sthg, to take charge of sb/sthg; se ~ **de faire qqch** to undertake to do sthg.

chargeur [ʃaʁʒœʁ] *nm* **-1.** ÉLECTR charger. **-2.** [d'arme] magazine. **-3.** [d'appareil photo] cartridge, cassette. **-4.** [personne - qui expédie une charge] shipper; [- qui charge] docker *Br*, longshoreman *Am*, stevedore *Am*.

chariot [ʃaʁjo] *nm* **-1.** [charrette] handcart. **-2.** [à bagages, dans un hôpital] trolley *Br*, wagon *Am*; ~ **élévateur** forklift truck. **-3.** [de machine à écrire] carriage.

charismatique [kaʁismatik] *adj* charismatic.

charisme [kaʁism] *nm* charisma.

charitable [ʃaʁitabl] *adj* charitable; [conseil] friendly.

charité [ʃaʁite] *nf* **-1.** [aumône & RELIG] charity; **faire la ~ à qqn** to give sb charity. **-2.** [bonté] kindness.

charivari [ʃaʁivaʁi] *nm* hullabaloo.

charlatan [ʃaʁlatɑ̃] *nm péj* charlatan.

charlotte [ʃaʁlɔt] *nf* CULIN charlotte.

charmant, -e [ʃaʁmɑ̃, ɑ̃t] *adj* charming.

charme [ʃaʁm] *nm* **-1.** [séduction] charm; **faire du ~ (à qqn)** to turn on the charm (for sb). **-2.** [enchantement] spell; **rompre le ~** to break the spell. **-3.** [arbre] ironwood, hornbeam. **-4.** *loc*: **se porter comme un ~** *fam* to be as fit as a fiddle.

charmer [ʃaʁme] [3] *vt* to charm; **être charmé de faire qqch** to be delighted to do sthg.

charmeur, -euse [ʃaʁmœʁ, øz] ◇ *adj* charming. ◇ *nm, f* charmer; ~ **de serpents** snake charmer.

charnel, -elle [ʃaʁnɛl] *adj* carnal.

charnier [ʃaʁnje] *nm* mass grave.

charnière [ʃaʁnjɛʁ] ◇ *nf* hinge; *fig* turning point. ◇ *adj* [période] transitional.

charnu, -e [ʃaʁny] *adj* fleshy.

charognard [ʃaʁɔɲaʁ] *nm litt & fig* vulture.

charogne [ʃaʁɔɲ] *nf* **-1.** [d'animal] carrion (*U*). **-2.** *tfam* [crapule - homme] bastard; [- femme] bitch.

charpente [ʃaʁpɑ̃t] *nf* **-1.** [de bâtiment, de roman] framework. **-2.** [ossature] frame.

charpenté, -e [ʃaʁpɑ̃te] *adj*: **être bien ~** [personne] to be well-built; [roman] to be well-constructed.

charpentier [ʃaʁpɑ̃tje] *nm* carpenter.

charretier, -ière [ʃaʁtje, jɛʁ] ◇ *adj* cart (*avant n*). ◇ *nm, f* carter; **jurer comme un ~** to swear like a trooper.

charrette [ʃaʁɛt] *nf* cart.

charrier [ʃaʁje] [9] ◇ *vt* **-1.** to carry. **-2.** *fam* [se moquer de]: ~ **qqn** to take sb for a ride. ◇ *vi fam* [exagérer] to go too far.

charrue [ʃaʁy] *nf* plough, plow *Am*; **mettre la ~ avant les bœufs** *fam fig* to put the cart before the horse.

charte [ʃaʁt] *nf* charter; **l'École nationale des ~s** *grande école for archivists and librarians*.

charter [ʃaʁtɛʁ] ◇ *nm* chartered plane. ◇ *adj inv* (*en apposition*) charter (*avant n*).

chartreuse [ʃaʁtʁøz] *nf* **-1.** RELIG Carthusian monastery. **-2.** [liqueur] Chartreuse.

Charybde [kaʁibd] *n* Charybdis; **tomber de ~ en Scylla** to go from the frying pan into the fire.

chas [ʃa] *nm* eye (*of needle*).

chasse [ʃas] *nf* **-1.** [action] hunting; **aller à la ~** to go hunting; ~ **à courre** hunting (*on horseback with hounds*). **-2.** [période]: **la ~ est ouverte/fermée** it's the open/close season. **-3.** [domaine]: ~ **gardée** private hunting OU shooting preserve; *fig* preserve. **-4.** [poursuite] chase; **faire la ~ à qqch** to chase sthg; **faire la ~ à qqn/qqch** *fig* to hunt (for) sb/sthg, to hunt sb/sthg down; **prendre qqn/qqch en ~** to give chase to sb/sthg; ~ **à l'homme** manhunt. **-5.** [des cabinets]: ~ **(d'eau)** flush; **tirer la ~** to flush the toilet.

chassé-croisé [ʃasekwaze] (*pl* **chassés-croisés**) *nm* toing and froing.

chasse-neige [ʃasnɛʒ] *nm inv* snowplough.

chasser [ʃase] [3] ◇ *vt* **-1.** [animal] to hunt. **-2.** [faire partir - personne] to drive OU chase away; [- odeur, souci] to dispel. ◇ *vi* **-1.** [aller à la chasse] to go hunting, to hunt. **-2.** [roues] to skid.

chasseur, -euse [ʃasœʁ, øz] *nm, f* hunter.

◆ **chasseur** *nm* **-1.** [d'hôtel] page, messenger. **-2.** MIL: ~ **alpin** *soldier specially trained for operations in mountainous terrain*. **-3.** [avion] fighter.

◆ **chasseur de têtes** *nm* headhunter.

châssis [ʃasi] *nm* **-1.** [de fenêtre, de porte, de machine] frame. **-2.** [de véhicule] chassis. **-3.** [de tableau] stretcher.

chaste [ʃast] *adj* chaste.

chasteté [ʃastəte] *nf* chastity.

chasuble [ʃazybl] ◇ *nf* chasuble. ◇ *adj* → robe.

chat, chatte [ʃa, ʃat] *nm, f* cat; ~ **de gouttière** ordinary cat, alley cat *Am*; ~ **persan/siamois** Persian/Siamese cat; **il n'y a pas un** ~ *fam* there's not a soul; **appeler un** ~ **un** ~ to call a spade a spade; **avoir d'autres** ~**s à fouetter** to have other fish to fry; **avoir un** ~ **dans la gorge** to have a frog in one's throat.

châtaigne [ʃatɛɲ] *nf* **-1.** [fruit] chestnut. **-2.** *fam* [coup] clout.

châtaignier [ʃatɛɲe] *nm* [arbre] chestnut (tree); [bois] chestnut.

châtain [ʃatɛ̃] *adj m & nm* chestnut, chestnut-brown.

château, -x [ʃato] *nm* **-1.** [forteresse]: ~ **(fort)** castle. **-2.** [résidence - seigneuriale] mansion; [- de monarque, d'évêque] palace; ~ **de cartes** *litt & fig* house of cards; ~ **de sable** sandcastle; **bâtir des** ~**x en Espagne** to build castles in Spain. **-3.** [vignoble] château, vineyard. **-4.** [réservoir]: ~ **d'eau** water tower.

chateaubriand, châteaubriant [ʃatobrijɑ̃] *nm thickest part of a fillet of beef.*

châtelain, -e [ʃatlɛ̃, ɛn] *nm, f* lord (*f* lady) of the manor.

châtier [ʃatje] [9] *vt sout* **-1.** [punir] to punish. **-2.** [polir] to refine, to hone.

chatière [ʃatjɛr] *nf* **-1.** [pour chat] cat-flap. **-2.** [d'aération] air vent.

châtiment [ʃatimɑ̃] *nm* punishment.

chaton [ʃatɔ̃] *nm* **-1.** [petit chat] kitten. **-2.** BOT catkin. **-3.** [de bague] setting. **-4.** [pierre] stone.

chatouiller [ʃatuje] [3] *vt* **-1.** [faire des chatouilles à] to tickle. **-2.** *fig* [titiller] to titillate.

chatouilles [ʃatuj] *nfpl* tickling (*U*).

chatouilleux, -euse [ʃatujø, øz] *adj* **-1.** [sensible aux chatouilles] ticklish. **-2.** *fig* [susceptible] touchy.

chatoyant, -e [ʃatwajɑ̃, ɑ̃t] *adj* [reflet, étoffe] shimmering; [bijou] sparkling.

chatoyer [ʃatwaje] [13] *vi* [reflet, étoffe] to shimmer; [bijou] to sparkle.

châtrer [ʃɑtre] [3] *vt* to castrate; [chat] to neuter; [chatte] to spay.

chatte → chat.

chatterton [ʃatɛrtɔ̃] *nm* ÉLECTR insulating tape.

chaud, -e [ʃo, ʃod] *adj* **-1.** [gén] warm; [de température très élevée, sensuel] hot. **-2.** *fig* [enthousiaste]: **être** ~ **pour qqch/pour faire qqch** to be keen on sthg/on doing sthg. **-3.** [animé] tense.

◆ **chaud** ◇ *adv*: **avoir** ~ to be warm OU hot; **il fait** ~ it's warm OU hot; **manger** ~ to have something hot (to eat); **tenir** ~ to keep warm; **j'ai eu** ~ [l'échapper belle] I had a narrow OU lucky escape; [avoir peur] I had a nasty shock OU fright. ◇ *nm* heat; **rester au** ~ to stay in the warm; **un** ~ **et froid** a chill.

chaudement [ʃodmɑ̃] *adv* warmly.

chaud-froid [ʃofrwa] (*pl* **chauds-froids**) *nm poultry or game served cold in a thick white sauce glazed with jelly.*

chaudière [ʃodjɛr] *nf* boiler.

chaudron [ʃodrɔ̃] *nm* cauldron.

chauffage [ʃofaʒ] *nm* **-1.** [action] heating. **-2.** [appareil] heating (system); ~ **central** central heating.

chauffant, -e [ʃofɑ̃, ɑ̃t] *adj* heating; **couverture** ~**e** electric blanket; **plaque** ~**e** hotplate.

chauffard [ʃofar] *nm péj* reckless driver.

chauffe-biberon [ʃofbibrɔ̃] (*pl* **chauffe-biberons**) *nm* bottle-warmer.

chauffe-eau [ʃofo] *nm inv* water-heater.

chauffe-plats [ʃofpla] *nm inv* hotplate, chafing dish.

chauffer [ʃofe] [3] ◇ *vt* [rendre chaud] to heat (up); ~ **à blanc** to heat until white-hot. ◇ *vi* **-1.** [devenir chaud] to heat up. **-2.** [moteur] to overheat. **-3.** *fam* [barder]: **ça va** ~ there's going to be trouble.

◆ **se chauffer** *vp*: **se** ~ **à qqch** to heat one's house with sthg.

chaufferette [ʃofrɛt] *nf* **-1.** [réchaud] hotplate, chafing dish. **-2.** [pour les pieds] foot-warmer.

chaufferie [ʃofri] *nf* boiler room.

chauffeur [ʃofœr] *nm* **-1.** AUTOM driver; ~ **du dimanche** Sunday driver; ~ **de taxi** taxi driver. **-2.** [de chaudière] stoker.

chaume [ʃom] *nm* **-1.** [paille] thatch. **-2.** [de céréales] stubble.

chaumière [ʃomjɛr] *nf* cottage.

chaussée [ʃose] *nf* road, roadway.

chausse-pied [ʃospje] (*pl* **chausse-pieds**) *nm* shoehorn.

chausser [ʃose] [3] ◇ *vt* **-1.** [chaussures, lunettes, skis] to put on; ~ **qqn** to put sb's shoes on. **-2.** [fournir] to supply shoes to. **-3.** [suj: chaussures] to fit. ◇ *vi*: ~ **du 39** to take size 39 (shoes).

◆ **se chausser** *vp* to put one's shoes on.

chausse-trape (*pl* **chausse-trapes**), **chausse-trappe** (*pl* **chausse-trappes**) [ʃostrap] *nf* trap.

chaussette [ʃosɛt] *nf* sock.

chausseur [ʃosœr] *nm* shoemaker.

chausson [ʃosɔ̃] *nm* **-1.** [pantoufle] slipper. **-2.** [de danse] ballet shoe. **-3.** [de bébé] bootee. **-4.** CULIN turnover; ~ **aux pommes** apple turnover.

chaussure [ʃosyr] *nf* **-1.** [soulier] shoe; ~ **basse** low-heeled shoe, flat shoe; ~ **à crampons** [pour football, rugby] studded boot; [pour athlétisme] spiked shoe; ~ **de marche** [de randonnée] hiking OU walking boot; [confortable] walking shoe; ~ **montante** (ankle) boot; ~ **de ski** ski boot; **trouver** ~ **à son pied** *fam fig* to find Mr/Miss Right. **-2.** [industrie] footwear industry.

chauve [ʃov] ◇ *adj* [sans cheveux] bald. ◇ *nm* bald man.

chauve-souris [ʃovsuri] (*pl* **chauves-souris**) *nf* bat.

chauvin, -e [ʃovɛ̃, in] ◇ *adj* chauvinistic. ◇ *nm, f* chauvinist.

chauvinisme [ʃovinism] *nm* chauvinism.

chaux [ʃo] *nf* lime; **blanchi à la** ~ whitewashed.

chavirer [ʃavire] [3] ◇ *vi* **-1.** [bateau] to capsize. **-2.** *fig* [tourner] to spin. **-3.** *fig* [échouer] to founder. ◇ *vt* **-1.** [bateau] to capsize. **-2.** [meuble] to tip over.

chéchia [ʃeʃja] *nf* fez.

check-up [tʃɛkœp] *nm inv* check-up.

chef [ʃɛf] *nm* **-1.** [d'un groupe] head, leader; [au travail] boss; **en** ~ **in chief;** ~ **de chantier** foreman; ~ **d'entreprise** company head; ~ **d'État** head of state; ~ **de fabrication** production manager; ~ **de famille** head of the family; ~ **de file** POLIT (party) leader; ~ **de gare** stationmaster; ~ **de marque** brand manager; ~ **d'orchestre** conductor; ~ **de produit** product manager; ~ **de projet** project manager; ~ **de rayon** departmental manager OU supervisor; ~ **de service** ADMIN departmental manager. **-2.** [cuisinier] chef. **-3.** *loc*: **de son propre** ~ on one's own initiative; **opiner du** ~ to nod agreement.

◆ **chef d'accusation** *nm* charge, count.

chef-d'œuvre [ʃedœvr] (*pl* **chefs-d'œuvre**) *nm* masterpiece.

chef-lieu [ʃefljø] (*pl* **chefs-lieux**) *nm* ≃ county town.

cheik [ʃɛk] *nm* sheikh.

chemin [ʃəmɛ̃] *nm* **-1.** [voie] path; ~ **de fer** railway; ~ **vicinal** byroad, minor road. **-2.** [parcours] way; *fig* road; **en** ~ on the way; **faire du** ~ to cover a lot of ground; *fig* to gain ground; **rebrousser** ~ to turn back; **le** ~ **de croix** the way of the cross; **prendre le** ~ **des écoliers** *fig* to go the long way round; **suivre le droit** ~ *fig* to stay on the straight and narrow.

cheminée [ʃəmine] *nf* **-1.** [foyer] fireplace. **-2.** [conduit d'usine] chimney. **-3.** [encadrement] mantelpiece. **-4.** [de paquebot, locomotive] funnel.

cheminement [ʃəminmɑ̃] *nm* [progression] advance; *fig* [d'idée] development.

cheminer [ʃəmine] [3] *vi* [avancer] to make one's way; *fig* [idée] to develop.

cheminot [ʃəmino] *nm* railwayman *Br*, railroad man *Am*.

chemise [ʃəmiz] *nf* **-1.** [d'homme] shirt; ~ **de nuit** [de femme] nightdress. **-2.** [dossier] folder.

chemiserie [ʃəmizri] *nf* [magasin] shirtmaker's; [industrie] shirtmaking.

chemisette [ʃəmizɛt] *nf* [d'homme] shortsleeved shirt; [de femme] short-sleeved blouse.

chemisier [ʃəmizje] *nm* **-1.** [vêtement] blouse. **-2.** [marchand, fabricant] shirtmaker.

chenal, -aux [ʃənal, o] *nm* [canal] channel.

chenapan [ʃənapɑ̃] *nm hum* rascal.

chêne [ʃɛn] *nm* [arbre] oak (tree); [bois] oak.

chenet [ʃənɛ] *nm* firedog.

chenil [ʃənil] *nm* [pour chiens] kennel.

chenille [ʃənij] *nf* **-1.** [insecte] caterpillar. **-2.** [courroie] caterpillar track.

chenu, -e [ʃəny] *adj littéraire* [tête, barbe] hoary.

cheptel [ʃɛptɛl] *nm* [bétail] livestock (*U*).

chèque [ʃɛk] *nm* cheque; **faire/toucher un** ~ to write/cash a cheque; ~ **(bancaire)** (bank) cheque; ~ **barré** crossed cheque; ~ **en blanc** blank cheque; ~ **postal** post office cheque; ~ **sans provision** bad cheque; ~ **de voyage** traveller's cheque.

chèque-cadeau [ʃɛkkado] (*pl* **chèques-cadeaux**) *nm* gift token.

chèque-repas [ʃɛkrəpa] (*pl* **chèques-repas**), **chèque-restaurant** [ʃɛkrɛstɔrɑ̃] (*pl* **chèques-restaurant**) *nm* luncheon voucher.

chéquier [ʃekje] *nm* cheque book.

cher, chère [ʃɛr] ◇ *adj* **-1.** [aimé]: ~ **(à qqn)** dear (to sb); **Cher Monsieur ...** [au début d'une lettre] Dear Sir; **Chère Madame ...** [au début d'une lettre] Dear Madam. **-2.** [pro-

duit, vie, commerçant] expensive. ◇ nm, f
hum: mon ~ dear.
◆ cher adv: valoir ~, coûter ~ to be expensive, to cost a lot; payer ~ to pay a lot;
je l'ai payé ~ litt & fig it cost me a lot.
◆ chère nf: aimer la bonne ~ sout to like
to eat well.
chercher [ʃɛrʃe] [3] ◇ vt -1. [gén] to look
for; vous l'aurez cherché! you're asking for
it! -2. [prendre]: aller/venir ~ qqn [à un
rendez-vous] to (go/come and) meet sb; [en
voiture] to (go/come and) pick sb up; aller/
venir ~ qqch to (go/come and) get sthg.
-3. fam [atteindre]: ça va ~ dans les 100
francs it will come to about 100 francs. ◇
vi: ~ à faire qqch to try to do sthg.
◆ se chercher vp to try to find o.s.
chercheur, -euse [ʃɛrʃœr, øz] ◇ adj -1.
[esprit] inquiring. -2. → tête. ◇ nm, f [scien-
tifique] researcher.
chèrement [ʃɛrmã] adv dearly.
chéri, -e [ʃeri] ◇ adj dear. ◇ nm, f darling.
chérir [ʃerir] [32] vt [personne] to love
dearly; [chose, idée] to cherish.
cherté [ʃɛrte] nf high cost.
chétif, -ive [ʃetif, iv] adj -1. [malingre]
sickly, weak. -2. [rabougri] stunted, puny.
-3. littéraire [insuffisant] meagre.
cheval, -aux [ʃəval, o] nm -1. [animal]
horse; être à ~ sur qqch [être assis] to be
sitting astride sthg; fig [siècles] to straddle
sthg; fig [tenir à] to be a stickler for sthg; ~
d'arçons horse (in gymnastics); ~ de bataille
fig hobby horse; ~ de course racehorse; ~
de trait draught horse; chevaux de bois
merry-go-round (sg); monter sur ses grands
chevaux to get on one's high horse. -2.
[équitation] riding, horse-riding; faire du ~
to ride. -3. AUTOM: ~, ~-vapeur horsepower.
chevaleresque [ʃəvalrɛsk] adj chivalrous.
chevalerie [ʃəvalri] nf -1. [institution] chivalry. -2. HIST knighthood.
chevalet [ʃəvalɛ] nm [de peintre] easel.
chevalier [ʃəvalje] nm knight; ~ servant
(faithful) admirer.
chevalière [ʃəvaljɛr] nf [bague] signet ring.
chevalin, -e [ʃəvalɛ̃, in] adj [de cheval] horse
(avant n); fig horsey.
chevauchée [ʃəvoʃe] nf -1. [course] ride,
horse-ride. -2. [cavalcade] cavalcade.
chevaucher [ʃəvoʃe] [3] vt [être assis] to sit
OU be astride.
◆ se chevaucher vp to overlap.
chevelu, -e [ʃəvly] adj hairy.
chevelure [ʃəvlyr] nf [cheveux] hair.

chevet [ʃəvɛ] nm head (of bed); être au ~ de
qqn to be at sb's bedside.
cheveu, -x [ʃəvø] nm [chevelure] hair; avoir
les ~x taillés en brosse to have a crew cut;
se faire couper les ~x to have one's hair
cut; s'arracher les ~x to tear one's hair
out; avoir un ~ sur la langue to have a
lisp; arriver comme un ~ sur la soupe to
come at an awkward moment; couper les
~x en quatre to split hairs; tiré par les ~x
far-fetched, contrived.
cheville [ʃəvij] nf -1. ANAT ankle; il ne t'arrive pas à la ~ fam fig he can't hold a candle to you. -2. [pour fixer une vis] Rawl-
plug®; ~ ouvrière AUTOM & fig kingpin.
chèvre [ʃɛvr] ◇ nf [animal] goat; ménager
la ~ et le chou to run with the hare and
hunt with the hounds. ◇ nm [fromage]
goat's cheese.
chevreau, -x [ʃəvro] nm kid.
chèvrefeuille [ʃɛvrəfœj] nm honeysuckle.
chevreuil [ʃəvrœj] nm -1. [animal] roe deer.
-2. CULIN venison.
chevron [ʃəvrɔ̃] nm -1. CONSTR rafter. -2.
[motif décoratif] chevron.
chevronné, -e [ʃəvrɔne] adj [expérimenté]
experienced.
chevrotant, -e [ʃəvrɔtã, ãt] adj tremulous.
chevrotine [ʃəvrɔtin] nf buckshot.
chewing-gum [ʃwiŋgɔm] (pl chewing-
gums) nm chewing gum (U).
chez [ʃe] prép -1. [dans la maison de]: il est
~ lui he's at home; il rentre ~ lui he's
going home; être ~ le coiffeur/médecin to
be at the hairdresser's/doctor's; aller ~ le
médecin/coiffeur to go to the hairdresser's/doctor's; il va venir ~ nous he is
going to come to our place OU house; il
habite ~ nous he lives with us. -2. [en ce
qui concerne]: ~ les jeunes among young
people; ~ les Anglais in England. -3. [dans
les œuvres de]: ~ Proust in (the works of)
Proust. -4. [dans le caractère de]: cette réaction est normale ~ lui this reaction is normal for OU with him; ce que j'apprécie ~
lui, c'est sa gentillesse what I like about
him is his kindness.
chez-soi [ʃeswa] nm inv home, place of
one's own.
chialer [ʃjale] [3] vi fam to blubber.
chiant, -e [ʃjã, ãt] adj tfam -1. [très en-
nuyeux] bloody Br OU damned boring. -2.
[contrariant] bloody Br OU damned annoying; c'est ~ it's a bloody Br OU damned
pain.
chic [ʃik] ◇ adj (inv en genre) -1. [élégant]
smart, chic. -2. vieilli [serviable] nice. ◇ nm

style; **bon ~ bon genre** ≈ Sloaney *Br,* ≈ preppie *Am;* **avoir le ~ pour faire qqch** to have the knack of doing sth. ◇ *interj:* ~ **(alors)!** great!

chicane [ʃikan] *nf* [querelle] squabble.

chicaner [ʃikane] [3] ◇ *vt:* ~ **qqn sur qqch** to quibble with sb over sthg. ◇ *vi* [contester]: ~ **(sur qqch)** to quibble (over OU about sthg).
◆ **se chicaner** *vp* to squabble, to bicker.

chiche [ʃiʃ] ◇ *adj* **-1.** [avare] mean; **être ~ de** to be sparing with. **-2.** [peu abondant] meagre, scanty. **-3.** *fam* [capable]: **il n'est pas ~ de le faire!** he wouldn't dare (do it)! ◇ *interj:* **~!** (you) want a bet?

chichement [ʃiʃmɑ̃] *adv* [pauvrement] meagrely.

chichi [ʃiʃi] *nm:* **faire des ~s** *fam* to make a fuss.

chicorée [ʃikɔre] *nf* [salade] endive; [à café] chicory; **~ frisée** curly endive.

chien [ʃjɛ̃] *nm* **-1.** [animal] dog; **~ d'aveugle** guide dog; **~ de chasse** [d'arrêt] gundog; **~ esquimau** husky; **~ de garde** guard dog; **~ policier/savant** police/performing dog; **avoir un mal de ~ à faire qqch** to have a lot of trouble doing sthg; **entre ~ et loup** at dusk OU twilight; **se regarder en ~s de faïence** to stare grimly at each other. **-2.** [d'arme] hammer. **-3.** *loc:* **en ~ de fusil** curled up; **avoir du ~** to have class OU style.

chiendent [ʃjɛ̃dɑ̃] *nm* couch grass.

chien-loup [ʃjɛ̃lu] (*pl* **chiens-loups**) *nm* Alsatian (dog).

chienne [ʃjɛn] *nf* bitch.

chier [ʃje] [9] *vi vulg* to shit; **faire ~ qqn** to get on sb's tits; **se faire ~** to be bored shitless.

chiffe [ʃif] *nf:* **c'est une ~ molle** he's spineless, he's a weed.

chiffon [ʃifɔ̃] *nm* [linge] **rag;** **parler ~s** to talk clothes.

chiffonné, -e [ʃifɔne] *adj* [visage, mine] worn.

chiffonner [ʃifɔne] [3] *vt* **-1.** [froisser - faire des plis] to crumple, to crease; [- déformer] to crumple. **-2.** *fam fig* [contrarier] to bother.

chiffonnier, -ière [ʃifɔnje, jɛr] *nm, f* rag-and-bone man (*f* woman).
◆ **chiffonnier** *nm* [meuble] chiffonier.

chiffre [ʃifr] *nm* **-1.** [caractère] figure, number; **~ arabe/romain** Arabic/Roman numeral. **-2.** [montant] sum; **~ d'affaires** COMM turnover; **~ rond** round number; **~ de ventes** sales figures (*pl*). **-3.** [code secret] code.

chiffrer [ʃifre] [3] ◇ *vt* **-1.** [numéroter] to number. **-2.** [évaluer] to calculate, to assess. **-3.** [coder] to encode. ◇ *vi fam* to mount up.
◆ **se chiffrer** *vp:* **se ~ à** to add up to.

chignole [ʃiɲɔl] *nf* drill.

chignon [ʃiɲɔ̃] *nm* bun (*in hair*); **se crêper le ~** *fig* to scratch each other's eyes out.

Chili [ʃili] *nm:* **le ~** Chile; **au ~** in Chile.

chilien, -ienne [ʃiljɛ̃, jɛn] *adj* Chilean.
◆ **Chilien, -ienne** *nm, f* Chilean.

chimère [ʃimɛr] *nf* **-1.** MYTH chimera. **-2.** [illusion] illusion, dream.

chimérique [ʃimerik] *adj* **-1.** [illusoire] illusory. **-2.** [rêveur] fanciful.

chimie [ʃimi] *nf* chemistry.

chimiothérapie [ʃimjɔterapi] *nf* chemotherapy.

chimique [ʃimik] *adj* chemical.

chimiquement [ʃimikmɑ̃] *adv* chemically.

chimiste [ʃimist] *nmf* chemist.

chimpanzé [ʃɛ̃pɑ̃ze] *nm* chimpanzee.

chinchilla [ʃɛ̃ʃila] *nm* chinchilla.

Chine [ʃin] *nf:* **la ~** China.

chiné, -e [ʃine] *adj* mottled.

chiner [ʃine] [3] *vi* to look for bargains.

chinois, -e [ʃinwa, waz] *adj* Chinese.
◆ **chinois** *nm* **-1.** [langue] Chinese; **c'est du ~** *fig* it's all Greek to me. **-2.** [passoire] conical sieve.
◆ **Chinois, -e** *nm, f* Chinese person; **les Chinois** the Chinese.

chinoiserie [ʃinwazri] *nf* [objet] Chinese curio, piece of chinoiserie; *fig* unnecessary complication.
◆ **chinoiseries** *nfpl* unnecessary complications, red tape (*sg*).

chiot [ʃjo] *nm* puppy.

chiottes [ʃjɔt] *nfpl vulg* shithouse (*sg*).

chiper [ʃipe] [3] *vt fam* [voler] to pinch, to nick *Br.*

chipie [ʃipi] *nf* vixen *péj.*

chipolata [ʃipɔlata] *nf* chipolata.

chipoter [ʃipɔte] [3] *vi:* ~ **(sur)** [nourriture] to pick (at); [contester] to quibble (over OU about).

chips [ʃips] *nfpl:* **(pommes) ~** (potato) crisps *Br,* (potato) chips *Am.*

chiqué [ʃike] *nm:* **c'est du ~** it's all sham.

chiquenaude [ʃiknod] *nf* flick.

chiquer [ʃike] [3] ◇ *vt* to chew. ◇ *vi* to chew tobacco.

chiromancien, -ienne [kirɔmɑ̃sjɛ̃, jɛn] *nm, f* palmist.

chiropraticien, **-ienne** [kiʀɔpʀatisjɛ̃, jɛn] *nm, f*, **chiropracteur** [kiʀɔpʀaktœʀ] *nm* chiropractor.

chirurgical, **-e**, **-aux** [ʃiʀyʀʒikal, o] *adj* surgical.

chirurgie [ʃiʀyʀʒi] *nf* surgery; ~ **esthétique** plastic surgery.

chirurgien [ʃiʀyʀʒjɛ̃] *nm* surgeon.

chirurgien-dentiste [ʃiʀyʀʒjɛ̃dɑ̃tist] (*pl* chirurgiens-dentistes) *nm* dental surgeon.

chiure [ʃjyʀ] *nf*: ~ (**de mouche**) flyspecks (*pl*).

ch.-l. *abr de* chef-lieu.

chlinguer = **schlinguer**.

chlore [klɔʀ] *nm* chlorine.

chloroforme [klɔʀɔfɔʀm] *nm* chloroform.

chlorophylle [klɔʀɔfil] *nf* chlorophyll.

chlorure [klɔʀyʀ] *nm* chloride.

chnoque = **schnock**.

choc [ʃɔk] *nm* **-1.** [heurt, coup] impact; **de** ~ *fig* shock (*avant n*). **-2.** [conflit] clash. **-3.** [émotion] shock; ~ **opératoire** post-operative shock. **-4.** (*en apposition*): **images-~s** shock pictures; **prix-~** amazing bargain.

chocolat [ʃɔkɔla] ◇ *nm* chocolate; ~ **au lait/noir** milk/plain chocolate; ~ **à cuire/à croquer** cooking/eating chocolate; ~ **Liégeois** *chocolate ice cream with Chantilly cream.* ◇ *adj inv* chocolate (brown).

chocolaté, **-e** [ʃɔkɔlate] *adj* chocolate (flavoured).

chocolatier, **-ière** [ʃɔkɔlatje, jɛʀ] ◇ *adj* chocolate (*avant n*). ◇ *nm, f* [fabricant] choco- late manufacturer; [commerçant] confectioner.

◆ **chocolatière** *nf* [récipient] chocolate pot.

chœur [kœʀ] *nm* **-1.** [chorale] choir; [d'opéra & *fig*] chorus; **chanter en** ~ to sing in chorus; **en** ~ *fig* all together. **-2.** [d'église] choir, chancel.

choir [ʃwaʀ] [72] *vt littéraire*: **laisser** ~ **qqch** to let sth fall; **laisser** ~ **qqn** *fig* & *littéraire* to let sb down; **se laisser** ~ **dans qqch** to drop OU fall into sthg.

choisi, **-e** [ʃwazi] *adj* selected; [termes, langage] carefully chosen.

choisir [ʃwaziʀ] [32] ◇ *vt*: ~ (**de faire qqch**) to choose (to do sthg). ◇ *vi* to choose.

choix [ʃwa] *nm* **-1.** [gén] choice; **le livre de ton** ~ any book you like; **au** ~ as you prefer; **avoir le** ~ to have the choice. **-2.** [qualité]: **de premier** ~ grade OU class one; **articles de second** ~ seconds.

choléra [kɔleʀa] *nm* cholera.

cholestérol [kɔlɛsteʀɔl] *nm* cholesterol.

chômage [ʃomaʒ] *nm* unemployment; **en** ~, **au** ~ unemployed; ~ **partiel** short time (working); **être mis au** ~ **technique** to be laid off.

chômé [ʃome] → **jour**.

chômer [ʃome] [3] ◇ *vt* to keep. ◇ *vi* to be unemployed; *fig* to be idle.

chômeur, **-euse** [ʃomœʀ, øz] *nm, f*: **les** ~**s** the unemployed.

chope [ʃɔp] *nf* tankard.

choper [ʃɔpe] [3] *vt fam* **-1.** [voler, arrêter] to nick *Br*, to pinch. **-2.** [attraper] to catch.

choquant, **-e** [ʃɔkɑ̃, ɑ̃t] *adj* shocking.

choquer [ʃɔke] [3] *vt* **-1.** [scandaliser] to shock. **-2.** [traumatiser] to shake (up).

choral, **-e**, **-als** OU **-aux** [kɔʀal, o] *adj* choral.

◆ **choral**, **-als** *nm* [chant] chorale.

◆ **chorale** *nf* [groupe] choir.

chorégraphie [kɔʀegʀafi] *nf* choreography.

choriste [kɔʀist] *nmf* chorister.

chose [ʃoz] ◇ *nf* thing; **c'est (bien) peu de** ~ it's nothing really; **c'est la moindre des** ~**s** it's the least I/we can do; **chaque** ~ **en son temps** everything in good time; **de deux** ~**s l'une** (it's got to be) one thing or the other; **dire bien des** ~**s à qqn** to give sb one's regards; **ne pas faire les** ~**s à moitié** not to do things by halves; **parler de** ~**s et d'autres** to talk of this and that; **regarder les** ~**s en face** to face up to things. ◇ *nm fam* **-1.** [truc] thingy, whatsit. **-2.** [personne] thingy, what's-his-name (*f* what's-her-name). ◇ *adj inv*: **se sentir (tout)** ~ to feel a bit peculiar.

chou, **-x** [ʃu] ◇ *nm* **-1.** [légume] cabbage; ~ **de Bruxelles** Brussels sprout; **faire** ~ **blanc** *fam fig* to draw a blank. **-2.** [pâtisserie] choux bun; ~ **à la crème** cream puff. **-3.** [personne]: **mon** ~ darling. ◇ *adj inv* sweet, cute.

choucas [ʃuka] *nm* jackdaw.

chouchou, **-oute** [ʃuʃu, ut] *nm, f* teacher's pet.

chouchouter [ʃuʃute] [3] *vt* to pet.

choucroute [ʃukʀut] *nf* sauerkraut; ~ **garnie** *sauerkraut with meat and potatoes.*

chouette [ʃwɛt] ◇ *nf* [oiseau] owl. ◇ *adj fam vieilli* smashing *Br*, great. ◇ *interj*: ~ (**alors**)! great!

chou-fleur [ʃuflœʀ] (*pl* choux-fleurs) *nm* cauliflower.

choyer [ʃwaje] [13] *vt sout* to pamper.

CHR (*abr de* centre hospitalier régional) *nm* regional hospital.

chrétien, -ienne [kretjɛ̃, jɛn] *adj & nm, f* Christian.

chrétienté [kretjɛ̃te] *nf* Christendom.

Christ [krist] *nm* Christ.

christianiser [kristjanize] [3] *vt* **-1.** [personne] to convert (to Christianity). **-2.** [pays] to christianize.

christianisme [kristjanism] *nm* Christianity.

chromatique [krɔmatik] *adj* **-1.** MUS & OPTIQUE chromatic. **-2.** BIOL chromosomal.

chrome [krom] *nm* **-1.** [de voiture] chrome. **-2.** CHIM chromium.

chromé, -e [krome] *adj* chrome-plated; **acier ~** chrome steel.

chromosome [krɔmozom] *nm* chromosome.

chronique [krɔnik] ◇ *nf* **-1.** [annales] chronicle; **défrayer la ~** to be the talk of the town. **-2.** PRESSE: **~ sportive** sports section. ◇ *adj* chronic.

chrono [krɔno] = **chronomètre.**

chronologie [krɔnɔlɔʒi] *nf* chronology.

chronologique [krɔnɔlɔʒik] *adj* chronological.

chronomètre [krɔnɔmɛtr] *nm* SPORT stopwatch.

chronométrer [krɔnɔmetre] [18] *vt* to time.

chrysalide [krizalid] *nf* chrysalis.

chrysanthème [krizɑ̃tɛm] *nm* chrysanthemum.

CHRYSANTHÈME:

Chrysanthemums are often associated with funerals in France, as they are traditionally used to decorate graves, especially on All Saints' Day

---

CHS (*abr de* **Comité d'hygiène et de sécurité**) *nm* health and safety committee.

chu, -e [ʃy] *pp*; → **choir.**

CHU (*abr de* **centre hospitalo-universitaire**) *nm* teaching hospital.

chuchotement [ʃyʃɔtmɑ̃] *nm* whisper.

◆ **chuchotements** *nmpl* whispering (*U*).

chuchoter [ʃyʃɔte] [3] *vt & vi* to whisper.

chuinter [ʃɥɛ̃te] [3] *vi* [siffler] to hiss.

chut [ʃyt] *interj* sh!, hush!

chute [ʃyt] *nf* **-1.** [gén] fall; **faire une ~** to (have OU take a) fall; **~ de cheveux** hair loss; **~ d'eau** waterfall; **~ libre** free fall; **~ de neige** snowfall; **~ de pierres** falling rocks; **~ de reins** small of the back. **-2.** [de tissu] scrap.

chuter [ʃyte] [3] *vi* **-1.** [baisser] to fall, to drop. **-2.** [tomber] to fall.

Chypre [ʃipr] *nf* Cyprus; **à ~** in Cyprus.

chypriote [ʃipriɔt], **cypriote** [sipriɔt] *adj* Cypriot.

◆ **Chypriote, Cypriote** *nmf* Cypriot.

ci [si] *adv* (*après n*): **ce livre-~** this book; **ces jours-~** these days.

Ci (*abr de* **curie**) Ci.

CIA (*abr de* **Central Intelligence Agency**) *nf* CIA.

ci-après [siaprɛ] *adv* below.

cibiste [sibist] *nmf* CB enthusiast.

cible [sibl] *nf litt & fig* target; **groupe ~** target group.

ciblé [sible] *adj* COMM targeted.

cibler [sible] [3] *vt* to target.

ciboire [sibwar] *nm* ciborium.

ciboulette [sibulɛt] *nf* chives (*pl*).

cicatrice [sikatris] *nf* scar.

cicatriser [sikatrize] [3] *vt litt & fig* to heal.

◆ **se cicatriser** *vp litt & fig* to heal.

ci-contre [sikɔ̃tr] *adv* opposite.

CICR (*abr de* **Comité international de la Croix-Rouge**) *nm* IRCC.

ci-dessous [sidəsu] *adv* below.

ci-dessus [sidəsy] *adv* above.

CIDEX, Cidex [sidɛks] (*abr de* **courrier individuel à distribution exceptionnelle**) *nm system grouping letter boxes in country areas.*

CIDJ (*abr de* **centre d'information et de documentation de la jeunesse**) *nm careers advisory service.*

cidre [sidr] *nm* cider; **~ bouché** *superior bottled cider*; **~ doux/brut** sweet/dry cider.

CIDUNaTI [sidynati] (*abr de* **Comité interprofessionnel d'information et de défense de l'union nationale des travailleurs indépendants**) *nm* union of self-employed craftsmen.

Cie (*abr de* **compagnie**) Co.

ciel, cieux [sjɛl, sjø] ◇ *nm* **-1.** [firmament] sky; **~ de plomb** leaden sky; **à ~ ouvert** open-air; **être au septième ~** to be in one's seventh heaven; **remuer ~ et terre (pour faire qqch)** to move heaven and earth (to do sthg); **tomber du ~** *fam* to be heavensent OU a godsend. **-2.** [paradis, providence] heaven; **c'est le ~ qui l'envoie!** he's heaven-sent! ◇ *interj hum & sout* good heavens!

◆ **cieux** *npl* heaven (*sg*).

CIEP (*abr de* **Centre international d'études pédagogiques**) *nm French centre for educational research.*

cierge [sjɛrʒ] *nm* RELIG (votive) candle.

cigale [sigal] *nf* cicada.

cigare [sigar] *nm* cigar.

cigarette [sigaʀɛt] *nf* cigarette; ~ **blonde/ brune** cigarette made from Virginia/dark tobacco.

cigarillo [sigaʀijo] *nm* cigarillo.

ci-gît [siʒi] *adv* here lies.

cigogne [sigɔɲ] *nf* stork.

ci-inclus, -e [siɛ̃kly, yz] *adj* enclosed.
◆ **ci-inclus** *adv* enclosed.

ci-joint, -e [siʒwɛ̃, ɛt] *adj* enclosed.
◆ **ci-joint** *adv*: **veuillez trouver** ~ ... please find enclosed ....

cil [sil] *nm* ANAT eyelash, lash.

ciller [sije] [3] *vi* to blink (one's eyes); **sans** ~ *fig* without blinking.

cimaise [simɛz] *nf* [de salle d'exposition] gallery wall.

cime [sim] *nf* [d'arbre, de montagne] top; *fig* height.

ciment [simã] *nm* cement.

cimenter [simãte] [3] *vt* to cement.

cimetière [simtjɛʀ] *nm* cemetery.

ciné [sine] *nm fam* cinema.

cinéaste [sineast] *nmf* film-maker.

ciné-club [sineklœb] (*pl* **ciné-clubs**) *nm* film club.

cinéma [sinema] *nm* **-1.** [salle, industrie] cinema; **aller au** ~ to go to the cinema. **-2.** [art] cinema, film; **un acteur de** ~ a film star; ~ **publicitaire** COMM cinema screen advertising; **faire du** ~ to be in film; *fig* to put on an act.

cinémathèque [sinematɛk] *nf* film archive; **la Cinémathèque française** the French film institute.

LA CINÉMATHÈQUE FRANÇAISE:
Founded in 1936, the 'Cinémathèque française' specializes in the conservation and restoration of films; it also screens films for public viewing

---

cinématographique [sinematɔgʀafik] *adj* cinematographic.

cinéphile [sinefil] *nmf* film buff.

cinétique [sinetik] ◇ *nf* kinetics (*U*). ◇ *adj* kinetic.

cinglant, -e [sɛ̃glã, ãt] *adj litt* & *fig* biting; [pluie] driving.

cinglé, -e [sɛ̃gle] *fam* ◇ *adj* nuts, nutty. ◇ *nm, f* nutcase.

cingler [sɛ̃gle] [3] ◇ *vt* to lash. ◇ *vi littéraire* [naviguer] to sail.

cinq [sɛ̃k] ◇ *adj num* five. ◇ *nm* five; **il était moins** ~ *fam* it was a near thing; *voir aussi* **six**.

cinquantaine [sɛ̃kãtɛn] *nf* **-1.** [nombre]: **une** ~ **de** about fifty. **-2.** [âge]: **avoir la** ~ to be in one's fifties.

cinquante [sɛ̃kãt] *adj num* & *nm* fifty; *voir aussi* **soixante**.

cinquantenaire [sɛ̃kãtnɛʀ] ◇ *nmf person in his/her fifties*. ◇ *nm* [de personne] fiftieth birthday; [d'événement] fiftieth anniversary; [d'institution] golden jubilee. ◇ *adj* fifty-year-old.

cinquantième [sɛ̃kãtjɛm] *adj num, nm* & *nmf* fiftieth; *voir aussi* **sixième**.

cinquième [sɛ̃kjɛm] ◇ *adj num, nm* & *nmf* fifth. ◇ *nf* second year (*of secondary school*); *voir aussi* **sixième**.

cinquièmement [sɛ̃kjɛmmã] *adv* fifthly, in the fifth place.

cintre [sɛ̃tʀ] *nm* **-1.** [pour vêtements] coat hanger. **-2.** ARCHIT arch, curve.

cintré, -e [sɛ̃tʀe] *adj* **-1.** COUTURE waisted. **-2.** ARCHIT arched, vaulted.

CIO (*abr de* **Comité international olympique**) *nm* IOC.

cirage [siʀaʒ] *nm* **-1.** [action] polishing. **-2.** [produit] shoe polish. **-3.** *loc*: **être dans le** ~ *fam* to be in a daze.

circoncision [siʀkɔ̃sizjɔ̃] *nf* circumcision.

circonférence [siʀkɔ̃feʀɑ̃s] *nf* **-1.** GÉOM circumference. **-2.** [pourtour] boundary.

circonflexe [siʀkɔ̃flɛks] → **accent**.

circonscription [siʀkɔ̃skʀipsjɔ̃] *nf* district; ~ **électorale** [nationale] constituency; [locale] ward.

circonscrire [siʀkɔ̃skʀiʀ] [99] *vt* **-1.** GÉOM to circumscribe. **-2.** [incendie, épidémie] to contain. **-3.** *fig* [sujet] to define.
◆ **se circonscrire** *vp*: **se** ~ **autour de** to be centred on OU around.

circonspect, -e [siʀkɔ̃spɛ, ɛkt] *adj* cautious.

circonspection [siʀkɔ̃spɛksjɔ̃] *nf* caution, wariness.

circonstance [siʀkɔ̃stɑ̃s] *nf* **-1.** [occasion] occasion. **-2.** (*gén pl*) [contexte, conjoncture] circumstance; ~**s atténuantes** JUR mitigating circumstances; **de** ~ appropriate.

circonstancié, -e [siʀkɔ̃stɑ̃sje] *adj* detailed.

circonstanciel, -ielle [siʀkɔ̃stɑ̃sjɛl] *adj* GRAM adverbial.

circuit [siʀkɥi] *nm* **-1.** [chemin] route. **-2.** [parcours touristique] tour; ~ **touristique** tourist route. **-3.** SPORT & TECHNOL circuit; **en** ~ **fermé** [en boucle] closed-circuit (*avant n*); *fig* within a limited circle; ~ **imprimé/ intégré** printed/integrated circuit. **-4.** ÉCON network.

circulaire [siʀkylɛʀ] *nf* & *adj* circular.

circulation [sirkylasjɔ̃] *nf* **-1.** [mouvement] circulation; **mettre en** ~ to circulate; **retirer de la** ~ to withdraw from circulation; ~ **(du sang)** circulation. **-2.** [trafic] traffic; **route à grande** ~ main road, trunk road *Br*; **«~ alternée»** "traffic control ahead"; **disparaître de la** ~ *fig* to disappear from the scene.

circulatoire [sirkylatwar] *adj* circulatory.

circuler [sirkyle] [3] *vi* **-1.** [sang, air, argent] to circulate; **faire** ~ **qqch** to circulate sthg. **-2.** [aller et venir] to move (along); **circulez!** move along!; **on circule mal en ville** the traffic is bad in town. **-3.** [train, bus] to run. **-4.** *fig* [rumeur, nouvelle] to spread.

cire [sir] *nf* **-1.** [matière] wax; ~ **d'abeilles** beeswax; ~ **à cacheter** sealing wax. **-2.** [encaustique] polish.

ciré, -e [sire] *adj* **-1.** [parquet] polished. **-2.** → **toile.**

◆ **ciré** *nm* oilskin.

cirer [sire] [3] *vt* to polish.

cireux, -euse [sirø, øz] *adj* **-1.** [pâle] waxen. **-2.** [matière] waxy.

◆ **cireuse** *nf* floor polisher.

cirque [sirk] *nm* **-1.** [gén] circus. **-2.** GÉOL cirque. **-3.** *fam fig* [désordre, chahut] chaos (*U*).

cirrhose [siroz] *nf* cirrhosis (*U*).

cisaille [sizaj] *nf* shears (*pl*).

cisaillement [sizajmɑ̃] *nm* [de métal] cutting; [de branches] pruning.

cisailler [sizaje] [3] *vt* [métal] to cut; [branches] to prune.

ciseau, -x [sizo] *nm* chisel.

◆ **ciseaux** *nmpl* scissors.

ciseler [sizle] [25] *vt* **-1.** [pierre, métal] to chisel. **-2.** [bijou] to engrave. **-3.** *fig* [parfaire] to polish (up).

ciselure [sizlyr] *nf* [bois] carving; [objet précieux] engraving.

Cisjordanie [sizʒɔrdani] *nf*: **la** ~ the West Bank.

cisjordanien, -ienne [sizʒɔrdanjɛ̃, jɛn] *adj* of/from the West Bank.

◆ **Cisjordanien, -ienne** *nm, f* native OU inhabitant of the West Bank.

cistercien, -ienne [sistersjɛ̃, jɛn] *adj* Cistercian.

◆ **cistercien** *nm* Cistercian.

citadelle [sitadɛl] *nf litt & fig* citadel.

citadin, -e [sitadɛ̃, in] ◇ *adj* city (*avant n*), urban. ◇ *nm, f* city dweller.

citation [sitasjɔ̃] *nf* **-1.** JUR summons. **-2.** [extrait] quote, quotation.

cité [site] *nf* **-1.** [ville] city. **-2.** [lotissement] housing estate; ~ **ouvrière** (workers') housing estate; ~ **universitaire** halls (*pl*) of residence.

cité-dortoir [sitedɔrtwar] (*pl* **cités-dortoirs**) *nf* dormitory town.

citer [site] [3] *vt* **-1.** [exemple, propos, auteur] to quote. **-2.** JUR [convoquer] to summon. **-3.** MIL: **être cité à l'ordre du jour** to be mentioned in dispatches.

citerne [sitɛrn] *nf* **-1.** [d'eau] water tank. **-2.** [cuve] tank; ~ **à mazout** oil tank.

cité U [sitey] *nf fam abr de* **cité universitaire.**

citoyen, -enne [sitwajɛ̃, ɛn] *nm, f* citizen.

citoyenneté [sitwajɛnte] *nf* citizenship.

citron [sitrɔ̃] ◇ *nm* lemon; ~ **pressé** fresh lemon juice; ~ **vert** lime. ◇ *adj inv* lemon yellow.

citronnade [sitrɔnad] *nf* (still) lemonade.

citronnelle [sitrɔnɛl] *nf* [plante] lemon balm.

citronnier [sitrɔnje] *nm* lemon tree.

citrouille [sitruj] *nf* pumpkin.

civet [sivɛ] *nm* stew; ~ **de lièvre** jugged hare.

civière [sivjɛr] *nf* stretcher.

civil, -e [sivil] ◇ *adj* **-1.** [gén] civil. **-2.** [non militaire] civilian. ◇ *nm, f* civilian; **dans le** ~ in civilian life; **policier en** ~ plain-clothes policeman (*f* policewoman); **soldat en** ~ soldier in civilian clothes.

civilement [sivilmɑ̃] *adv*: **se marier** ~ to get married at a registry office.

civilisation [sivilizasjɔ̃] *nf* civilization.

civilisé, -e [sivilize] *adj* civilized.

civiliser [sivilize] [3] *vt* to civilize.

◆ **se civiliser** *vp* to become civilized.

civilité [sivilite] *nf* civility.

◆ **civilités** *nfpl sout* compliments.

civique [sivik] *adj* civic; **instruction** ~ civics (*U*).

civisme [sivism] *nm* sense of civic responsibility.

cl (*abr de* **centilitre**) cl.

clac [klak] *interj* [porte] slam!; [taquets] click!

clafoutis [klafuti] *nm* [gâteau] *cake made from a batter poured over fruit.*

claie [klɛ] *nf* **-1.** [treillis] rack. **-2.** [clôture] hurdle.

clair, -e [klɛr] *adj* **-1.** [gén] clear; **c'est** ~ **et net** there's no two ways about it; **il est** ~ **que c'est impossible** it's clear that it's impossible, clearly it's impossible. **-2.** [lumineux] **bright. -3.** [pâle - couleur, teint] **light;** [- tissu, cheveux] **light-coloured.**

◆ **clair** ◇ *adv*: **voir ~ (dans qqch)** *fig* to have a clear understanding (of sthg). ◇ *nm*: **passer le plus ~ de son temps à faire qqch** to spend most OU the bulk of one's time doing sthg; **mettre** OU **tirer qqch au ~** to shed light upon sthg.

◆ **clair de lune** (*pl* **clairs de lune**) *nm* moonlight (U).

◆ **en clair** *loc adv* TÉLÉ unscrambled (*esp of a private TV channel*).

clairement [klɛrmɑ̃] *adv* clearly.

claire-voie [klɛrvwa]

◆ **à claire-voie** *loc adv* openwork (*avant n*).

clairière [klɛrjɛr] *nf* clearing.

clairon [klɛrɔ̃] *nm* bugle.

claironner [klɛrɔne] [3] ◇ *vi* to play the bugle. ◇ *vt fig* [crier]: **~ qqch** to shout sthg from the rooftops.

clairsemé, -e [klɛrsəme] *adj* [cheveux] thin; [arbres] **scattered;** [population] **sparse.**

clairvoyant, -e [klɛrvwajɑ̃, ɑ̃t] *adj* perceptive.

clamer [klame] [3] *vt* to proclaim.

clameur [klamœr] *nf* clamour.

clamser [klamse] [3] *vi tfam* to snuff it *Br.*

clan [klɑ̃] *nm* clan.

clandestin, -e [klɑ̃dɛstɛ̃, in] ◇ *adj* [journal, commerce] **clandestine;** [activité] **covert.** ◇ *nm, f* [étranger] **illegal immigrant** OU **alien;** [voyageur] **stowaway.**

clandestinité [klɑ̃dɛstinite] *nf* clandestine nature; **dans la ~** [travailler] clandestinely; [vivre] **underground.**

clapet [klapɛ] *nm* **-1.** TECHNOL **valve. -2.** *fam fig* [bouche] **trap.**

clapier [klapje] *nm* [à lapins] hutch.

clapotement [klapɔtmɑ̃], **clapotis** [klapɔti] *nm* [de vagues] lapping (U).

clapoter [klapɔte] [3] *vi* [vagues] to lap.

clapotis = **clapotement.**

claquage [klakaʒ] *nm* MÉD strain; **se faire un ~** to pull OU to strain a muscle.

claque [klak] *nf* **-1.** [gifle] **slap; donner une ~ à qqn** to slap sb. **-2.** THÉÂTRE **claque. -3.** *loc*: **en avoir sa ~ (de)** *fam* to be fed up to the back teeth (with).

claqué, -e [klake] *adj fam* [éreinté] **whacked** *Br*, **bushed.**

claquement [klakmɑ̃] *nm* **-1.** [de porte - qui se ferme] **slam, slamming** (U); [- mal fermée] **banging** (U). **-2.** [de doigts] **snap, snapping** (U).

claquemurer [klakmyre] [3]

◆ **se claquemurer** *vp* to shut o.s. up OU away.

claquer [klake] [3] ◇ *vt* **-1.** [fermer] to slam. **-2. faire ~** [langue] to click; [doigts] to snap; [fouet] to crack. **-3.** *fam* [gifler] to slap. **-4.** *fam* [dépenser] to blow. **-5.** *fam* [fatiguer] to wear out. ◇ *vi* **-1.** [porte, volet] to bang. **-2.** *fam* [personne] to snuff it *Br.* **-3.** *fam* [machine] to conk out. **-4.** [ampoule] to burn out, to go.

◆ **se claquer** *vp* **-1.** [se fatiguer] to wear o.s. out. **-2.** [se déchirer]: **se ~ un muscle** to pull OU tear a muscle.

claquettes [klakɛt] *nfpl* [danse] tap dancing (U).

clarification [klarifikasjɔ̃] *nf litt* & *fig* clarification.

clarifier [klarifje] [9] *vt litt* & *fig* to clarify.

◆ **se clarifier** *vp fig* to become clear.

clarinette [klarinɛt] *nf* [instrument] clarinet.

clarté [klarte] *nf* **-1.** [lumière] **brightness. -2.** [transparence] **clearness. -3.** [netteté] **clarity.**

classe [klas] *nf* **-1.** [gén] class; **de grande ~** first-class, high-class; **~ ouvrière** working class; **~ touriste** economy class. **-2.** SCOL: **aller en ~** to go to school; **~ de neige** skiing trip (*with school*); **~ de rattrapage** remedial class; **~ verte** field trip (*with school*). **-3.** [catégorie] **category, type. -4.** MIL **rank. -5.** *loc*: **la** OU **quelle ~!** *fam* first class!, fantastic!; **faire ses ~s** MIL to do one's training.

classé, -e [klase] *adj* [monument] **listed.**

classement [klasmɑ̃] *nm* **-1.** [rangement] **filing. -2.** [classification] **classification. -3.** [rang - SCOL] **position;** [- SPORT] **placing. -4.** [liste - SCOL] **class list;** [- SPORT] **final placings** (*pl*); **~ général** overall placings (*pl*).

classer [klase] [3] *vt* **-1.** [ranger] to file. **-2.** [plantes, animaux] to classify. **-3.** [cataloguer]: **~ qqn (parmi)** to label sb (as). **-4.** [attribuer un rang à] to rank.

◆ **se classer** *vp* to be classed, to rank; **se ~ troisième** to come third.

classeur [klasœr] *nm* **-1.** [meuble] **filing cabinet. -2.** [portefeuille] **file, folder. -3.** [d'écolier] **ring binder.**

classification [klasifikasjɔ̃] *nf* classification; **~ périodique des éléments** CHIM periodic table.

classique [klasik] ◇ *nm* **-1.** [auteur] **classical author; les grands ~s** the great classical authors. **-2.** [œuvre] **classic. -3.** ART & MUS: **le ~** [musique] **classical (music);** [architecture] **classical architecture;** [beaux-arts] **classical art.** ◇ *adj* **-1.** ART & MUS **classical. -2.** [sobre] **classic. -3.** [habituel] **classic; ça c'est l'histoire ~!** it's the usual story!

clause [kloz] *nf* clause.

claustrer [klostre] [3]
◆ **se claustrer** *vp sout* to shut o.s. away OU up.

claustrophobie [klostrɔfɔbi] *nf* claustrophobia.

clavecin [klavsɛ̃] *nm* harpsichord.

clavicule [klavikyl] *nf* collarbone.

clavier [klavje] *nm* keyboard.

clé, **clef** [kle] ◇ *nf* **-1.** [gén] key; **la ~ du mystère** the key to the mystery; **fermer qqch à ~** to lock sthg; **~s en main** [usine] turnkey; [logement] ready for immediate entry; **mettre qqn/qqch sous ~** to lock sb/ sthg up; **~ de contact** AUTOM ignition key; **mettre la ~ sous la porte** to clear out. **-2.** [outil]: **~ anglaise** OU **à molette** adjustable spanner *Br* OU wrench *Am*, monkey wrench. **-3.** MUS [signe] clef; **~ de sol/fa** treble/bass clef; **à la ~** *fig* at the end (of it all). ◇ *adj*: **industrie/rôle ~** key industry/role.
◆ **clé de voûte** *nf litt* & *fig* keystone.

clean [klin] *adj fam* [chose, lieu] neat; [personne] clean-living.

clef → **clé**.

clématite [klematit] *nf* clematis.

clémence [klemɑ̃s] *nf* **-1.** *sout* [indulgence] clemency. **-2.** *fig* [douceur] mildness.

clément, **-e** [klemɑ̃, ɑ̃t] *adj* **-1.** [indulgent] lenient. **-2.** *fig* [température] mild.

clémentine [klemɑ̃tin] *nf* clementine.

cleptomane → **kleptomane**.

clerc [klɛr] *nm* [assistant] clerk; **~ de notaire** lawyer's clerk.

clergé [klɛrʒe] *nm* clergy.

clérical, **-e**, **-aux** [klerikal, o] ◇ *adj* clerical. ◇ *nm*, *f* clericalist.

CLES, **Cles** [kles] (*abr de* **contrat local emploi-solidarité**) *nm* community work scheme for young unemployed people.

cliché [kliʃe] *nm* **-1.** PHOT negative. **-2.** [banalité] cliché.

client, **-e** [kliɑ̃, ɑ̃t] *nm*, *f* **-1.** [de notaire, d'agence] client; [de médecin] patient. **-2.** [acheteur] customer. **-3.** [habitué] regular (customer).

clientèle [kliɑ̃tɛl] *nf* **-1.** [ensemble des clients] customers (*pl*); [de profession libérale] clientele. **-2.** [fait d'être client]: **accorder sa ~ à** to give one's custom to.

cligner [kliɲe] [3] ◇ *vt*: **~ les yeux** to blink. ◇ *vi*: **~ de l'œil** to wink; **~ des yeux** to blink.

clignotant, **-e** [kliɲɔtɑ̃, ɑ̃t] *adj* [lumière] flickering.

◆ **clignotant** *nm* **-1.** AUTOM indicator; **mettre son ~** to indicate. **-2.** ÉCON & *fig* warning sign.

clignoter [kliɲɔte] [3] *vi* **-1.** [yeux] to blink. **-2.** [lumière] to flicker.

climat [klima] *nm litt* & *fig* climate.

climatique [klimatik] *adj* climatic.

climatisation [klimatizasjɔ̃] *nf* air-conditioning.

climatisé, **-e** [klimatize] *adj* air-conditioned.

clin [klɛ̃]
◆ **clin d'œil** *nm*: **faire un ~ d'œil (à)** to wink (at); **en un ~ d'œil** in a flash.

clinique [klinik] ◇ *nf* clinic. ◇ *adj* clinical.

clinquant, **-e** [klɛ̃kɑ̃, ɑ̃t] *adj litt* & *fig* flashy.
◆ **clinquant** *nm* **-1.** [faux bijou] imitation jewellery (*U*). **-2.** *fig* [éclat] gloss.

clip [klip] *nm* **-1.** [vidéo] pop video. **-2.** [boucle d'oreilles] clip-on earring.

clique [klik] *nf péj* clique.
◆ **cliques** *nfpl*: **prendre ses ~s et ses claques** *fam* to pack one's bags (and go).

cliquer [klike] [3] *vi* INFORM to click.

cliqueter [klikte] [27] *vi* **-1.** [pièces, clés, chaînes] to jingle, to jangle. **-2.** [verres] to clink.

cliquetis [klikti] *nm* **-1.** [de pièces, clés, chaînes] jingling (*U*), jangling (*U*). **-2.** [de verres] clinking (*U*).

clitoris [klitɔris] *nm* clitoris.

clivage [klivaʒ] *nm* **-1.** GÉOL cleavage. **-2.** *fig* [division] division.

cloaque [klɔak] *nm* [lieu] cesspit.

clochard, **-e** [klɔʃar, ard] *nm*, *f* tramp.

cloche [klɔʃ] ◇ *nf* **-1.** [d'église] bell. **-2.** [couvercle]: **~ à fromage** glass cover for cheese. **-3.** *fam* [idiot] clot *Br*. **-4.** (*en apposition*) [jupe] flared. ◇ *adj fam*: **ce qu'elle peut être ~, celle-là!** she can be a right idiot!

cloche-pied [klɔʃpje]
◆ **à cloche-pied** *loc adv* hopping; **sauter à ~** to hop.

clocher¹ [klɔʃe] *nm* [d'église] church tower.

clocher² [klɔʃe] [3] *vi*: **il y a quelque chose qui cloche** there's something wrong here.

clochette [klɔʃɛt] *nf* **-1.** [petite cloche] (little) bell. **-2.** [de fleur] bell.

clodo [klɔdo] *nmf* tramp.

cloison [klwazɔ̃] *nf* [mur] partition.

cloisonner [klwazɔne] [3] *vt* [pièce, maison] to partition (off); *fig* to compartmentalize.

cloître [klwatr] *nm* cloister.

cloîtrer [klwatre] [3] *vt* **-1.** RELIG to cloister. **-2.** [enfermer] to shut away (from the outside world).

◆ **se cloîtrer** *vp* **-1.** [s'enfermer] to shut o.s. away; **se ~ dans** *fig* to retreat into. **-2.** [RELIG - sœur] to enter a convent; [- moine] to enter a monastery.

clone [klɔn] *nm* INFORM clone.

clope [klɔp] *nm ou nf fam* fag *Br*.

clopin-clopant [klɔpɛ̃klɔpɑ̃] *adv*: **aller ~** [person] to hobble along; *fig* to struggle along.

clopiner [klɔpine] [3] *vi* to hobble along.

cloporte [klɔpɔrt] *nm* woodlouse.

cloque [klɔk] *nf* blister.

cloquer [klɔke] [3] *vi* to blister.

clore [klɔr] [113] *vt* to close; [négociations] to conclude; **~ une session** INFORM to log out.

clos, -e [klo, kloz] ◇ *pp* → **clore.** ◇ *adj* closed.

◆ **clos** *nm* **-1.** [terrain] enclosed field. **-2.** [vignoble] vineyard.

clôture [klotyr] *nf* **-1.** [haie] hedge; [de fil de fer] fence; **~ électrifiée** OU **électrique** electric fence. **-2.** [fermeture] closing, closure. **-3.** [fin] end, conclusion.

clôturer [klotyre] [3] *vt* **-1.** [terrain] to enclose. **-2.** [négociation] to close, to conclude.

clou [klu] *nm* **-1.** [pointe] nail; **~ de girofle** CULIN clove; **des ~s!** *fam* no chance!; **maigre comme un ~** as thin as a rake; **mettre au ~** [en gage] to pawn; [en prison] to put in the clink. **-2.** [attraction] highlight.

◆ **clous** *nmpl* pedestrian crossing (*sg*).

clouer [klue] [3] *vt* [fixer - couvercle, planche] to nail (down); [- tableau, caisse] to nail (up); *fig* [immobiliser]: **rester cloué sur place** to be rooted to the spot; **être cloué au lit (par)** *fam* to be laid up in bed (with).

clouté, -e [klute] *adj* [vêtement] studded.

clown [klun] *nm* clown; **faire le ~** to clown around, to act the fool.

CLT (*abr de* **Compagnie luxembourgeoise de télévision**) *nf* Luxembourg TV company.

club [klœb] *nm* club.

cm (*abr de* **centimètre**) cm.

CM ◇ *nf* (*abr de* **Chambre des métiers**) chamber of commerce for trades. ◇ *nm* (*abr de* **cours moyen**): **~ 1** fourth year of primary school; **~ 2** fifth year of primary school.

CNAC [knak] (*abr de* **Centre national d'art et de culture**) *nm* official name of the Pompidou Centre.

CNAM [knam] (*abr de* **Conservatoire national des arts et métiers**) *nm* science and technology school in Paris.

CNC *nm* **-1.** (*abr de* **Conseil national de la consommation**) official consumer protection organization. **-2.** (*abr de* **Centre national de la cinématographie**) national cinematographic organization.

CNDP (*abr de* **Centre national de documentation pédagogique**) *nm* national organization for educational resources.

CNE (*abr de* **Caisse nationale d'épargne**) *nf* national savings bank.

CNEC [knɛk] (*abr de* **Centre national de l'enseignement par correspondance**) *nm* national education body organizing correspondence courses, ≃ Open University *Br*.

CNES, Cnes [knɛs] (*abr de* **Centre national d'études spatiales**) *nm* French national space research centre.

CNIL [knil] *nf abr de* **Commission nationale de l'informatique et des libertés**.

CNIT, Cnit [knit] (*abr de* **Centre national des industries et des techniques**) *nm* exhibition centre at la Défense near Paris.

CNJA (*abr de* **Centre national des jeunes agriculteurs**) *nm* young farmers' union.

CNPF (*abr de* **Conseil national du patronat français**) *nm* national council of French employers, ≃ CBI *Br*.

CNRS (*abr de* **Centre national de la recherche scientifique**) *nm* national scientific research organization.

CNTS (*abr de* **Centre national de transfusion sanguine**) *nm* national blood transfusion centre.

CNUCED, Cnuced [knysɛd] (*abr de* **Conférence des Nations unies pour le commerce et l'industrie**) *nf* UNCTAD.

coaguler [kɔagyle] [3] ◇ *vt* **-1.** [sang] to clot. **-2.** [lait] to curdle. ◇ *vi* **-1.** [sang] to clot. **-2.** [lait] to curdle.

◆ **se coaguler** *vp* **-1.** [sang] to clot. **-2.** [lait] to curdle.

coaliser [kɔalize] [3] *vt* to group together, to unite.

◆ **se coaliser** *vp* **-1.** [s'allier] to form a coalition OU an alliance. **-2.** [s'unir] to unite.

coalition [kɔalisjɔ̃] *nf* coalition.

coasser [kɔase] [3] *vi* [grenouille] to croak.

COB, Cob [kɔb] (*abr de* **Commission des opérations de Bourse**) *nf* commission for supervision of stock exchange operations, ≃ SIB *Br*, ≃ SEC *Am*.

cobalt [kɔbalt] *nm* cobalt.

cobaye [kɔbaj] *nm litt* & *fig* guinea pig.

cobra [kɔbra] *nm* cobra.

coca [kɔka] ◇ *nm* **-1.** [boisson] Coke®. **-2.** BOT coca. ◇ *nf* coca extract.

cocagne [kɔkaɲ] → **mât, pays**.

cocaïne [kɔkain] *nf* cocaine.

cocaïnomane [kokainɔman] *nmf* cocaine addict.

cocarde [kɔkard] *nf* **-1.** [insigne] roundel. **-2.** [distinction] rosette.

cocardier, -ière [kɔkardje, jɛr] ◇ *adj* [chauvin] jingoistic. ◇ *nm, f* jingoist.

cocasse [kɔkas] *adj* funny.

coccinelle [kɔksinɛl] *nf* **-1.** [insecte] ladybird *Br*, ladybug *Am*. **-2.** [voiture] Beetle.

coccyx [kɔksis] *nm* coccyx.

coche [kɔʃ] *nm*: **manquer le ~** *fam fig* to miss the boat.

cocher¹ [kɔʃe] *nm* coachman.

cocher² [kɔʃe] [3] *vt* to tick (off) *Br*, to check (off) *Am*.

cochère [kɔʃɛr] → **porte**.

cochon, -onne [kɔʃɔ̃, ɔn] ◇ *adj* dirty, smutty. ◇ *nm, f fam péj* pig; **un tour de ~** a dirty trick.
◆ **cochon** *nm* pig; **~ d'Inde** guinea pig; **~ de lait** piglet.

cochonnaille [kɔʃɔnaj] *nf fam* [charcuterie] pork.

cochonner [kɔʃɔne] [3] *vt fam* to mess up.

cochonnerie [kɔʃɔnri] *nf fam* **-1.** [nourriture] muck (*U*). **-2.** [chose] rubbish (*U*). **-3.** [saleté] mess (*U*). **-4.** [obscénité] dirty joke, smut (*U*).

cochonnet [kɔʃɔnɛ] *nm* **-1.** [petit cochon] piglet. **-2.** JEU jack.

cocker [kɔkɛr] *nm* cocker spaniel.

cockpit [kɔkpit] *nm* cockpit.

cocktail [kɔktɛl] *nm* **-1.** [réception] cocktail party. **-2.** [boisson] cocktail. **-3.** *fig* [mélange] mixture; **~ Molotov** Molotov cocktail.

coco [kɔko] *nm* **-1.** → **noix. -2.** *fam péj* [individu] bloke *Br*, guy. **-3.** *péj* [communiste] commie.

cocon [kɔkɔ̃] *nm* ZOOL & *fig* cocoon.

cocooning [kɔkuniɲ] *nm*: **faire du ~** to cocoon o.s.

cocorico [kɔkɔriko] *nm* [du coq] cock-a-doodle-doo.

cocotier [kɔkɔtje] *nm* coconut tree.

cocotte [kɔkɔt] *nf* **-1.** [marmite] casserole (dish). **-2.** [poule] hen; **~ en papier** paper shape. **-3.** *péj* [courtisane] tart.

Cocotte-minute® [kɔkɔtminut] *nf* pressure cooker.

cocu, -e [kɔky] *nm, f & adj fam* cuckold.

code [kɔd] *nm* **-1.** [gén] code; **~ barres** bar code; **~ de caractères** INFORM character code; **~ civil** OU **Napoléon** civil code; **~ pénal** penal code; **~ postal** postcode *Br*, zip code *Am*; **~ de la route** highway code. **-2.**
[phares] dipped headlights (*pl*); **se mettre en ~s** to dip one's headlights.

codéine [kɔdein] *nf* codeine.

coder [kɔde] [3] *vt* to code.

codétenu, -e [kɔdetny] *nm, f* (fellow) prisoner.

codifier [kɔdifje] [9] *vt* to codify.

coefficient [kɔefisjɑ̃] *nm* coefficient; **~ d'erreur** margin of error.

COEFFICIENT:
In baccalauréat examinations, the grade for each subject is multiplied by a 'coefficient' which is determined by the type of baccalauréat chosen. For a 'bac C', which has a scientific bias, the 'coefficient' for maths will be higher than the philosophy 'coefficient', for example

coéquipier, -ière [kɔekipje, jɛr] *nm, f* teammate.

cœur [kœr] *nm* heart; **au ~ de l'hiver** in the depths of winter; **au ~ de l'été** at the height of summer; **au ~ du conflit** at the height of the conflict; **de bon ~** willingly; **de tout son ~** with all one's heart; **à ~ ouvert** MÉD open-heart; **parler à ~ ouvert à** qqn to have a heart-to-heart with sb; **apprendre par ~** to learn by heart; **avoir qqch à ~** to have one's heart set on sthg; **avoir bon ~** to be kind-hearted; **avoir le ~ sur la main** to be big-hearted; **avoir mal au ~** to feel sick; **avoir un ~ d'artichaut** to fall in love very easily; **en avoir le ~ net** to be clear in one's (own) mind; **avoir le ~ serré** OU **gros** to have a heavy heart; **briser** OU **fendre le ~ de** qqn to break sb's heart; **s'en donner à ~ joie** [prendre beaucoup de plaisir] to have a whale of a time; **manquer de ~, ne pas avoir de ~** to be heartless; **ne pas avoir le ~ de faire** qqch not to have the heart to do sthg; **serrer qqn contre son ~** to clasp sb to one's breast; **soulever le ~ à** qqn to make sb feel sick; **tenir à ~** to be close to one's heart.
◆ **cœur de pierre** *nm* heart of stone.

coexistence [kɔegzistɑ̃s] *nf* coexistence.

coexister [kɔegziste] [3] *vi* to coexist.

COFACE [kɔfas] (*abr de* **Compagnie française d'assurance pour le commerce extérieur**) *nf export insurance company*, ≃ ECGD.

coffrage [kɔfraʒ] *nm* [pour le béton] formwork (*U*); [charpente] coffering.

coffre [kɔfr] *nm* **-1.** [meuble] chest. **-2.** [de voiture] boot *Br*, trunk *Am*. **-3.** [coffre-fort] safe. **-4.** *loc*: **avoir du ~** *fam fig* to have a lot of puff.

coffre-fort [kɔfrəfɔr] (*pl* **coffres-forts**) *nm* safe.

coffrer [kɔfre] [3] *vt* **-1.** *fam* [emprisonner] to bang up. **-2.** TECHNOL to put up shuttering for.

coffret [kɔfrɛ] *nm* **-1.** [petit coffre] casket; ~ à bijoux jewellery box. **-2.** [de disques] boxed set.

cogestion [kɔʒɛstjɔ̃] *nf* joint management.

cogitation [kɔʒitasjɔ̃] *nf hum* cogitation.

cogiter [kɔʒite] [3] *vi hum* to cogitate.

cognac [kɔɲak] *nm* cognac, brandy.

cogner [kɔɲe] [3] ◇ *vt fam* to beat up. ◇ *vi* **-1.** [frapper - personne] to knock; [- chose] to bang. **-2.** [donner des coups] to hit. **-3.** [soleil] to beat down.

◆ **se cogner** *vp* **-1.** [se heurter] to bump o.s.; **se** ~ **à** OU **contre qqch** to bump into sthg; **se** ~ **la tête/le genou** to hit one's head/knee. **-2.** *fam* [se battre] to have a punch-up *Br*.

cohabitation [kɔabitasjɔ̃] *nf* **-1.** [de personnes] living together, cohabitation. **-2.** POLIT cohabitation.

cohabiter [kɔabite] [3] *vi* **-1.** [habiter ensemble] to live together. **-2.** POLIT to cohabit.

cohérence [kɔerɑ̃s] *nf* consistency, coherence.

cohérent, -e [kɔerɑ̃, ɑ̃t] *adj* **-1.** [logique] consistent, coherent. **-2.** [unifié] coherent.

cohéritier, -ière [kɔeritje, jɛr] *nm, f* joint heir (*f* heiress).

cohésion [kɔezjɔ̃] *nf* cohesion.

cohorte [kɔɔrt] *nf* [groupe] troop.

cohue [kɔy] *nf* **-1.** [foule] crowd. **-2.** [bousculade] crush.

coi, coite [kwa, kwat] *adj*: **rester** ~ *sout* to remain silent.

coiffe [kwaf] *nf* headdress.

coiffé, -e [kwafe] *adj*: **être bien/mal** ~ to have tidy/untidy hair; **être** ~ **d'une casquette** to be wearing a cap.

coiffer [kwafe] [3] *vt* **-1.** [mettre sur la tête]: ~ **qqn de qqch** to put sthg on sb's head. **-2.** [les cheveux]: ~ **qqn** to do sb's hair. **-3.** [recouvrir] to top, to cover. **-4.** [diriger] to head.

◆ **se coiffer** *vp* **-1.** [les cheveux] to do one's hair. **-2.** [mettre sur sa tête]: **se** ~ **de** to wear, to put on.

coiffeur, -euse [kwafœr, øz] *nm, f* hairdresser.

◆ **coiffeuse** *nf* [meuble] dressing table.

coiffure [kwafyr] *nf* **-1.** [chapeau] hat. **-2.** [cheveux] hairstyle. **-3.** [profession] hairdressing.

coin [kwɛ̃] *nm* **-1.** [angle] corner; **au** ~ **du feu** by the fireside; **du** ~ local; **dans le** ~ in the area; **envoyer qqn au** ~ to make sb stand in the corner; **à tous les** ~**s de rue** on every street corner; **regarder qqn du** ~ **de l'œil** [à la dérobée] to look at sb out of the corner of one's eye. **-2.** [parcelle, endroit] place, spot; **un** ~ **de ciel bleu** a patch of blue sky; *fig* **dans un** ~ **de ma mémoire** in a corner of my memory; ~ **cuisine** kitchen area; **le petit** ~ *fam* the little boys'/girls' room. **-3.** [outil] wedge. **-4.** [matrice] die.

coincé, -e [kwɛ̃se] *adj fam* [personne] hung up.

coincer [kwɛ̃se] [16] *vt* **-1.** [bloquer] to jam. **-2.** *fam* [prendre] to nab; *fig* to catch out. **-3.** [acculer] to corner, to trap.

◆ **se coincer** *vp* to get stuck.

coïncidence [kɔɛ̃sidɑ̃s] *nf* coincidence.

coïncider [kɔɛ̃side] [3] *vi* to coincide.

coing [kwɛ̃] *nm* [fruit] quince.

coït [kɔit] *nm* coitus.

coke [kɔk] ◇ *nf* [cocaïne] coke. ◇ *nm* [combustible] coke.

col [kɔl] *nm* **-1.** [de vêtement] collar; **faux** ~ detachable collar; ~ **roulé** polo neck *Br*, turtleneck *Am*. **-2.** [partie étroite] neck. **-3.** ANAT: ~ **du fémur** neck of the thighbone OU femur; ~ **de l'utérus** cervix, neck of the womb. **-4.** GÉOGR pass.

col. *abr de* **colonne.**

colchique [kɔlʃik] *nm* [plante] autumn crocus.

coléoptère [kɔleɔptɛr] *nm* beetle.

colère [kɔlɛr] *nf* **-1.** [irritation] anger; **être/se mettre en** ~ to be/get angry; **ravaler sa** ~ to keep one's temper; **piquer une** ~ to fly into a rage. **-2.** [accès d'humeur] fit of anger OU rage.

coléreux, -euse [kɔlerø, øz], **colérique** [kɔlerik] *adj* [tempérament] fiery; [personne] quick-tempered.

colifichet [kɔlifiʃɛ] *nm* [bijou] trinket.

colimaçon [kɔlimasɔ̃]

◆ **en colimaçon** *loc adv* spiral.

colin [kɔlɛ̃] *nm* [merlu] hake.

colin-maillard [kɔlɛmajar] (*pl* **colin-maillards**) *nm* blind man's buff.

colique [kɔlik] *nf* **-1.** (*gén pl*) [douleur] colic (U). **-2.** [diarrhée] diarrhoea.

colis [kɔli] *nm* parcel.

colistier, -ière [kɔlistje, jɛr] *nm, f* fellow candidate.

coll. -1. *abr de* **collection. -2.** (*abr de* **collaborateurs**): **et** ~ et al.

collabo [kɔlabo] *nmf* HIST & *péj* collaborator.

collaborateur, -trice [kɔlabɔratœr, tris] *nm, f* **-1.** [employé] colleague. **-2.** [de journal] contributor. **-3.** HIST collaborator.

collaboration [kɔlabɔrasjɔ̃] *nf* collaboration.

collaborer [kɔlabɔre] [3] *vi* **-1.** [coopérer, sous l'Occupation] to collaborate. **-2.** [participer]: ~ à to contribute to.

collage [kɔlaʒ] *nm* **-1.** [action] sticking, gluing. **-2.** ART collage.

collant, -e [kɔlɑ̃, ɑ̃t] *adj* **-1.** [substance] sticky. **-2.** [vêtement] close-fitting, tight-fitting. **-3.** *fam* [personne] clinging, clingy.
◆ **collant** *nm* tights (*pl*) *Br*, panty hose (*U*) *Am*.

collatéral, -e, -aux [kɔlateral, o] ◇ *adj* **-1.** ANAT collateral. **-2.** ARCHIT side (*avant n*). **-3.** JUR collateral. ◇ *nm, f* collateral.

collation [kɔlasjɔ̃] *nf* [repas] snack.

colle [kɔl] *nf* **-1.** [substance] glue. **-2.** [question] poser; **poser une ~ à qqn** to set sb a (real) poser. **-3.** [SCOL - interrogation] test; [- retenue] detention; **avoir une heure de ~** to get an hour's detention.

collecte [kɔlɛkt] *nf* collection.

collecteur, -trice [kɔlɛktœr, tris] ◇ *adj*: **égout ~** main sewer. ◇ *nm, f*: **~ de fonds** fundraiser; **~ d'impôts** tax collector.

collectif, -ive [kɔlɛktif, iv] *adj* **-1.** [responsabilité, travail] collective. **-2.** [billet, voyage] group (*avant n*).
◆ **collectif** *nm* **-1.** [équipe] team. **-2.** LING collective noun. **-3.** FIN: **~ budgétaire** collection of budgetary measures.

collection [kɔlɛksjɔ̃] *nf* **-1.** [d'objets, de livres, de vêtements] collection; **faire la ~ de** to collect. **-2.** COMM line.

collectionner [kɔlɛksjɔne] [3] *vt litt* & *fig* to collect.

collectionneur, -euse [kɔlɛksjɔnœr, øz] *nm, f* collector.

collectivité [kɔlɛktivite] *nf* community; **les ~s locales** ADMIN the local communities.

collège [kɔlɛʒ] *nm* **-1.** SCOL ≃ secondary school; **le Collège de France** the Collège de France. **-2.** [de personnes] college; **~ électoral** electoral college.

COLLÈGE DE FRANCE:
This place of learning near the Sorbonne holds public lectures given by prominent academics and specialists. It is not a university and does not confer degrees, although it is controlled by the Ministry of Education

---

collégial, -e, -iaux [kɔleʒjal, jo] *adj* collegial, collegiate.
◆ **collégiale** *nf* collegiate church.

collégien, -ienne [kɔleʒjɛ̃, jɛn] *nm, f* schoolboy (*f* schoolgirl).

collègue [kɔlɛg] *nmf* colleague.

coller [kɔle] [3] ◇ *vt* **-1.** [fixer - affiche] to stick (up); [- timbre] to stick; [- tasse, vase] to glue. **-2.** [appuyer] to press. **-3.** *fam* [mettre] to stick, to dump. **-4.** SCOL to give (a) detention to, to keep behind. **-5.** [embarrasser] to catch out. **-6.** *fam* [suivre] to cling to. **-7.** *fam* [donner]: **~ qqch à qqn** to give sthg to sb, to give sb sthg.
◇ *vi* **-1.** [adhérer] to stick. **-2.** [être adapté]: **~ à qqch** [vêtement] to cling to sthg; *fig* to fit in with sthg, to adhere to sthg. **-3.** *fam* [bien se passer] to be OU go OK. **-4.** [suivre]: **~ à** to stick close to.
◆ **se coller** *vp* **-1.** *fam* [subir] to get landed with. **-2.** [se plaquer]: **se ~ contre qqn/qqch** to press o.s. against sb/sthg.

collerette [kɔlrɛt] *nf* **-1.** [de vêtement] ruff. **-2.** [de tuyau] flange.

collet [kɔlɛ] *nm* **-1.** [de vêtement] collar; **mettre la main au ~ de qqn** to grab sb by the collar OU the scruff of the neck; **être ~ monté** [affecté, guindé] to be strait-laced. **-2.** [piège] snare.

collier [kɔlje] *nm* **-1.** [bijou] necklace; **~ de perles** pearl necklace. **-2.** [d'animal] collar. **-3.** [barbe] fringe of beard along the jawline.

collimateur [kɔlimatœr] *nm*: **avoir qqn dans le ~** *fam* to have sb in one's sights.

colline [kɔlin] *nf* hill.

collision [kɔlizjɔ̃] *nf* [choc] collision, crash; **entrer en ~ avec** to collide with; *fig* [opposition] clash.

colloque [kɔlɔk] *nm* colloquium.

collusion [kɔlyzjɔ̃] *nf* collusion.

collyre [kɔlir] *nm* eye lotion.

colmater [kɔlmate] [3] *vt* **-1.** [fuite] to plug, to seal off. **-2.** [brèche] to fill, to seal.

colombage [kɔlɔ̃baʒ] *nm* half-timbering; **à ~s** half-timbered.

colombe [kɔlɔ̃b] *nf* dove.

Colombie [kɔlɔ̃bi] *nf*: **la ~** Colombia.

colombien, -ienne [kɔlɔ̃bjɛ̃, jɛn] *adj* Colombian.
◆ **Colombien, -ienne** *nm, f* Colombian.

Colombo [kɔlɔ̃bo] *n* Colombo.

colon [kɔlɔ̃] *nm* settler.

côlon [kolɔ̃] *nm* colon.

colonel [kɔlɔnɛl] *nm* colonel.

colonelle [kɔlɔnɛl] *nf* colonel's wife.

colonial, -e, -iaux [kɔlɔnjal, jo] *adj* colonial.

colonialisme [kɔlɔnjalism] *nm* colonialism.

colonialiste [kɔlɔnjalist] *nmf & adj* colonialist.

colonie [kɔlɔni] *nf* **-1.** [territoire] colony. **-2.** [d'expatriés] community; **~ de vacances** holiday *Br* OU vacation *Am* camp (*for children*).

colonisation [kɔlɔnizasjɔ̃] *nf* colonization.

coloniser [kɔlɔnize] [3] *vt litt & fig* to colonize.

colonne [kɔlɔn] *nf* column; **en ~** in a line OU column.

◆ **colonne vertébrale** *nf* spine, spinal column.

colorant, -e [kɔlɔrɑ̃, ɑ̃t] *adj* colouring.

◆ **colorant** *nm* colouring; **~ alimentaire** food colouring.

coloration [kɔlɔrasjɔ̃] *nf* colour, colouring.

coloré, -e [kɔlɔre] *adj* **-1.** [de couleur] coloured. **-2.** *fig* [diversifié, imagé] colourful.

colorer [kɔlɔre] [3] *vt* [teindre] to colour; **~ qqch de** *fig* to colour sthg with.

◆ **se colorer** *vp* [les cheveux] to colour, to dye; **se ~ de** *fig* to be coloured with.

coloriage [kɔlɔrjaʒ] *nm* **-1.** [action] colouring. **-2.** [dessin] drawing.

colorier [kɔlɔrje] [9] *vt* to colour in.

coloris [kɔlɔri] *nm* shade.

colorisation [kɔlɔrizasjɔ̃] *nf* CIN colourization.

coloriser [kɔlɔrize] [3] *vt* CIN to colourize.

colossal, -e, -aux [kɔlɔsal, o] *adj* colossal, huge.

colosse [kɔlɔs] *nm* **-1.** [homme] giant. **-2.** [statue] colossus.

colportage [kɔlpɔrtaʒ] *nm* hawking.

colporter [kɔlpɔrte] [3] *vt* [marchandise] to hawk; [information] to spread.

◆ **se colporter** *vp* [information] to spread.

colporteur, -euse [kɔlpɔrtœr, øz] *nm, f* **-1.** [de marchandises] hawker. **-2.** [de ragots] gossip.

coltiner [kɔltine] [3]

◆ **se coltiner** *vp fam* to be landed with.

colza [kɔlza] *nm* rape (seed).

coma [kɔma] *nm* coma; **être dans le ~** to be in a coma.

comateux, -euse [kɔmatø, øz] ◇ *adj* comatose. ◇ *nm, f* person in a coma.

combat [kɔ̃ba] *nm* **-1.** [bataille] battle, fight; **mettre/être hors de ~** to put/be out of the fight; *fig* to put/be out of the game. **-2.** [lutte] **struggle. -3.** SPORT fight.

combatif, -ive [kɔ̃batif, iv] *adj* [humeur] fighting (*avant n*); [troupes] willing to fight.

combativité [kɔ̃bativite] *nf* fighting spirit.

combattant, -e [kɔ̃batɑ̃, ɑ̃t] ◇ *adj* fighting (*avant n*). ◇ *nm, f* [en guerre] combatant; [dans bagarre] fighter; **ancien ~** veteran.

combattre [kɔ̃batr] [83] ◇ *vt litt & fig* to fight (against). ◇ *vi* to fight.

combattu, -e [kɔ̃baty] *pp* → **combattre**.

combien [kɔ̃bjɛ̃] ◇ *conj* how much; **~ de** [nombre] how many; [quantité] how much; **~ de temps?** how long?; **ça fait ~?** [prix] how much is that?; [longueur, hauteur etc] how long/high *etc* is it? ◇ *adv* how (much). ◇ *nm inv:* **le ~ sommes-nous?** what date is it?; **tous les ~?** how often?

combientième [kɔ̃bjɛ̃tjɛm] ◇ *nmf:* **il est le ~?** where did he come? ◇ *adj:* **c'est le ~ examen qu'on passe?** that makes how many exams we've taken?

combinaison [kɔ̃binɛzɔ̃] *nf* **-1.** [d'éléments] combination. **-2.** [de femme] slip. **-3.** [vêtement - de mécanicien] boiler suit *Br*, overalls (*pl*) *Br*, overall *Am*; [- de ski] ski suit. **-4.** [coffre] combination. **-5.** [manœuvre] scheme.

combine [kɔ̃bin] *nf fam* trick.

combiné [kɔ̃bine] *nm* receiver.

combiner [kɔ̃bine] [3] *vt* **-1.** [arranger] to combine. **-2.** [organiser] to devise.

◆ **se combiner** *vp* to turn out.

comble [kɔ̃bl] ◇ *nm* height; **le ~ de** the height of; **c'est un OU le ~!** that beats everything!; **être au ~ du désespoir** to be in the depths of despair; **être au ~ du bonheur** to be overjoyed. ◇ *adj* packed.

◆ **combles** *nmpl* attic (*sg*), loft (*sg*); **loger sous les ~s** to live in an attic.

combler [kɔ̃ble] [3] *vt* **-1.** [gâter] to spoil; **~ qqn de** to shower sb with. **-2.** [boucher] to fill in. **-3.** [déficit] to make good; [lacune] to fill.

combustible [kɔ̃bystibl] ◇ *nm* fuel. ◇ *adj* combustible.

combustion [kɔ̃bystjɔ̃] *nf* combustion.

COMECON, Comecon [kɔmekɔn] (*abr de* **Council for Mutual Economic Assistance**) *nm* COMECON.

comédie [kɔmedi] *nf* **-1.** CIN & THÉÂTRE comedy; **la Comédie-Française** the Comédie Française; **~ musicale** musical; **jouer la ~** *fig* to put on an act. **-2.** [complication] palaver.

LA COMÉDIE-FRANÇAISE:

This state-subsidized company dates back to the seventeenth century; the theatre itself, officially called 'le Théâtre-Français' or 'le Français', is situated in the rue de Riche-lieu in Paris. Its repertoire consists mainly of classical works, although modern plays are sometimes staged

comédien, -ienne [kɔmedjɛ̃, jɛn] ◇ *nm, f* [acteur] actor (*f* actress); *fig* & *péj* sham. ◇ *adj fig* & *péj*: **être** ~ to be a sham.

COMES, Comes [kɔmɛs] (*abr de* **Commis-sariat à l'énergie solaire**) *nm* solar energy commission.

comestible [kɔmɛstibl] *adj* edible.
◆ **comestibles** *nmpl* food (*U*).

comète [kɔmɛt] *nf* comet; **tirer des plans sur la** ~ *fig* to count one's chickens (before they are hatched).

comice [kɔmis] *nm*: ~ **agricole** *local farmers' meeting*.

comique [kɔmik] ◇ *nm* **-1.** THÉÂTRE comic actor. **-2.** [genre]: **le** ~ comedy. ◇ *adj* **-1.** [style] comic. **-2.** [drôle] comical, funny.

comité [kɔmite] *nm* committee; **en petit** ~ *fig* with a few close friends; ~ **d'entreprise** works council.

COMITÉ D'ENTREPRISE:
The 'comité d'entreprise' or 'CE' looks after the general welfare of company employees and organizes subsidized leisure activities, outings, holidays etc

commandant [kɔmɑ̃dɑ̃] *nm* commander; ~ **de bord** AÉRON captain.

commande [kɔmɑ̃d] *nf* **-1.** [de marchandises] order; **passer une** ~ to place an order; **sur** ~ to order; **disponible sur** ~ available on request. **-2.** TECHNOL control; **être aux** ~**s (de), tenir les** ~**s (de)** [d'avion, de machine] to be at the controls (of); NAVIG & *fig* to be at the helm (of). **-3.** INFORM command; ~ **numérique** digital control.

commandement [kɔmɑ̃dmɑ̃] *nm* com-mand; **les dix** ~**s** RELIG the Ten Command-ments.

commander [kɔmɑ̃de] [3] ◇ *vt* **-1.** [ordon-ner] to order, to command. **-2.** MIL to com-mand. **-3.** [contrôler] to operate, to control. **-4.** COMM to order. ◇ *vi* to be in charge; ~ **à qqn de faire qqch** to order sb to do sthg.
◆ **se commander** *vp*: **ça ne se commande pas** *fig* it is uncontrollable.

commanditaire [kɔmɑ̃ditɛr] JUR ◇ *nm* back-er. ◇ *adj*: **(associé)** ~ sleeping partner *Br*, silent partner *Am*.

commanditer [kɔmɑ̃dite] [3] *vt* **-1.** [entre-prise] to finance. **-2.** [meurtre] to put up the money for.

commando [kɔmɑ̃do] *nm* commando (unit).

comme [kɔm] ◇ *conj* **-1.** [introduisant une comparaison] like; **il sera médecin** ~ **son père** he'll become a doctor (just) like his father; **nous nagerons** ~ **quand nous étions en Sicile** we'll go swimming as OU like we did when we were in Sicily; **il se mit à pleurer** ~ **pour m'émouvoir** he started to cry as though to move me. **-2.** [exprimant la manière] as; **fais** ~ **il te plaira** do as you wish; ~ **tu le dis** as you say; **il était** ~ **fou** he was like a madman; ~ **prévu/convenu** as planned/agreed; ~ **bon vous semble** as you think best. **-3.** [tel que] like, such as; **les arbres** ~ **le marronnier** trees such as OU like the chestnut. **-4.** [en tant que] as; ~ **professeur, il est nul** as a teacher he's hopeless. **-5.** [ainsi que]: **les filles** ~ **les gar-çons iront jouer au foot** both girls and boys will play football; **l'un** ~ **l'autre sont très gentils** the one is as kind as the other, they are equally kind. **-6.** [introduisant une cause] as, since; ~ **il pleuvait nous sommes rentrés** as it was raining we went back.
◇ *adv* **-1.** [marquant l'intensité] how; ~ **tu as grandi!** how you've grown!; ~ **c'est diffi-cile!** it's so difficult!; **regarde** ~ **il nage bien!** (just) look what a good swimmer he is!, (just) look how well he swims!
◆ **comme si** *loc conj* as if.
◆ **comme quoi** *loc adv* to the effect that; ~ **quoi, on ne peut pas tout prévoir** which just goes to show you can't think of everything.
◆ **quelque chose comme** *loc adv* [à peu près] something like; **cela fait quelque chose** ~ **10 000 francs** that comes to something like 10,000 francs.

commémoration [kɔmemɔrasjɔ̃] *nf* com-memoration.

commémorer [kɔmemɔre] [3] *vt* to com-memorate.

commencement [kɔmɑ̃smɑ̃] *nm* beginning, start; **au** ~ at first, in the beginning.

commencer [kɔmɑ̃se] [16] ◇ *vt* [entrepren-dre] to begin, to start; [être au début de] to begin. ◇ *vi* to start, to begin; ~ **à faire qqch** to begin OU start to do sthg, to begin OU start doing sthg; ~ **par faire qqch** to begin OU start by doing sthg; ~ **mal/bien** to start badly/well.

comment [kɔmɑ̃] ◇ *adv* how; ~? what?; ~ **ça va?** how are you?; ~ **cela?** how come? ◇ *interj*: ~ **donc!** of course!, sure thing!; **et** ~! *fam* and how!, absolutely! ◇ *nm inv* → **pourquoi**.

commentaire [kɔmɑ̃tɛr] *nm* **-1.** [explication] commentary. **-2.** [observation] comment; **sans ~!** enough said!

commentateur, -trice [kɔmɑ̃tatœr, tris] *nm, f* RADIO & TÉLÉ commentator; **~ sportif** sports commentator.

commenter [kɔmɑ̃te] [3] *vt* to comment on.

commérage [kɔmeraʒ] *nm péj* gossip (*U*).

commerçant, -e [kɔmɛrsɑ̃, ɑ̃t] *◇ adj* [rue] shopping (*avant n*); [quartier] commercial; [personne] business-minded. *◇ nm, f* shopkeeper; **petit ~** small trader.

commerce [kɔmɛrs] *nm* **-1.** [achat et vente] commerce, trade; **dans le ~** in the shops *Br* OU stores *Am*; **~ de gros/détail** wholesale/retail trade; **~ extérieur** foreign trade. **-2.** [magasin] business; **le petit ~** small shopkeepers (*pl*). **-3.** *loc:* **être d'un ~ agréable** *sout* to be easy to get on with.

commercial, -e, -iaux [kɔmɛrsjal, jo] *◇ adj* [entreprise, valeur] commercial; [politique] trade (*avant n*). *◇ nm, f* marketing man (*f* woman).

commercialisation [kɔmɛrsjalizasjɔ̃] *nf* marketing.

commercialiser [kɔmɛrsjalize] [3] *vt* to market.

commère [kɔmɛr] *nf péj* gossip.

commets → **commettre**.

commettre [kɔmɛtr] [84] *vt* to commit.
♦ **se commettre** *vp sout:* **se ~ avec** to become involved with.

commis, -e [kɔmi, iz] *pp* → **commettre**.
♦ **commis** *nm* assistant; **~ voyageur** commercial traveller.

commisération [kɔmizerasjɔ̃] *nf sout* commiseration.

commissaire [kɔmisɛr] *nm* commissioner; **~ aux comptes** auditor; **~ de police** (police) superintendent *Br*.

commissaire-priseur [kɔmisɛrprizœr] (*pl* **commissaires-priseurs**) *nm* auctioneer.

commissariat [kɔmisarja] *nm:* **~ de police** police station.

commission [kɔmisjɔ̃] *nf* **-1.** [délégation] commission, committee; **~ d'enquête** commission of inquiry; **la Commission nationale de l'informatique et des libertés** *watchdog committee supervising the application of data protection legislation*; **~ parlementaire** parliamentary committee. **-2.** [message] message. **-3.** [rémunération] commission.
♦ **commissions** *nfpl* shopping (*U*); **faire les ~s** to do the shopping.

commissionnaire [kɔmisjɔnɛr] *nm* [intermédiaire] **agent;** [d'un message] **messenger;** [d'un objet] **delivery boy** OU **man.**

commissure [kɔmisyr] *nf:* **la ~ des lèvres** the corner of the mouth.

commode [kɔmɔd] *◇ nf* chest of drawers. *◇ adj* **-1.** [pratique - système] convenient; [- outil] handy. **-2.** [aimable]: **pas ~** awkward. **-3.** [facile] easy.

commodité [kɔmɔdite] *nf* convenience.
♦ **commodités** *nfpl* [conforts] comforts.

commotion [kɔmosjɔ̃] *nf* MÉD shock; **~ cérébrale** concussion.

commuer [kɔmɥe] [7] *vt:* **~ qqch en** to commute sthg to.

commun, -e [kɔmœ̃, yn] *adj* **-1.** [gén] common; [- décision, effort] joint; [- salle] shared; **~ à** common to; **avoir qqch en ~** to have sthg in common; **faire qqch en ~** to do sthg together. **-2.** [méthode] usual, common.
♦ **commun** *nm:* **le ~** the ordinary; **hors du ~** out of the ordinary; **le ~ des mortels** ordinary people.
♦ **commune** *nf* town.
♦ **Commune** *nf* HIST Paris Commune.
♦ **communs** *nmpl* outhouses.

communal, -e, -aux [kɔmynal, o] *adj* [école] local; [bâtiments] council (*avant n*).

communautaire [kɔmynotɛr] *adj* community (*avant n*).

communauté [kɔmynote] *nf* **-1.** community; **vivre en ~** to live communally. **-2.** [de sentiments, d'idées] identity.
♦ **Communauté européenne** *nf:* **la Communauté européenne** the European Community.

communément [kɔmynemɑ̃] *adv* commonly.

communiant, -e [kɔmynjɑ̃, ɑ̃t] *nm, f* communicant; **premier ~** *child taking first communion*.

communicatif, -ive [kɔmynikatif, iv] *adj* **-1.** [rire, éternuement] infectious. **-2.** [personne] communicative.

communication [kɔmynikasjɔ̃] *nf* **-1.** [gén] communication; **~ en entreprise** communication; **~ de masse** mass media. **-2.** TÉLÉCOM: **~ (téléphonique)** (phone) call; **être en ~ avec qqn** to be talking to sb; **obtenir la ~** to get through; **recevoir/prendre une ~** to receive/take a (phone) call; **~ interurbaine** long-distance (phone) call.

communier [kɔmynje] [9] *vi* RELIG to take communion; **~ (dans)** *fig* to be united (in).

communion [kɔmynjɔ̃] *nf* RELIG communion; **être en ~ avec** *fig* & *littéraire* to commune with.

communiqué [kɔmynike] *nm* communiqué; ~ **de presse** press release.

communiquer [kɔmynike] [3] ◇ *vt*: ~ **qqch à** [information, sentiment] to pass on OU communicate sthg to; [chaleur] to transmit sthg to; [maladie] to pass sthg on to. ◇ *vi*: ~ **avec** to communicate with.
◆ **se communiquer** *vp* [se propager] to spread.

communisme [kɔmynism] *nm* communism.

communiste [kɔmynist] *nmf & adj* communist.

commutateur [kɔmytatœr] *nm* switch.

commutation [kɔmytasjɔ̃] *nf* **-1.** JUR: ~ **de peine** commutation of sentence. **-2.** TECHNOL switching.

Comores [kɔmɔr] *nfpl*: **les** ~ the Comoro Islands, the Comoros; **aux** ~ in the Comoro Islands.

comorien, **-ienne** [kɔmɔrjɛ̃, jɛn] *adj* Comoran, Comorian.
◆ **Comorien, -ienne** *nm, f* Comoran, Comorian.

compact, **-e** [kɔ̃pakt] *adj* **-1.** [épais, dense] dense. **-2.** [petit] compact.
◆ **compact** *nm* [disque laser] compact disc, CD.

compagne → compagnon.

compagnie [kɔ̃paɲi] *nf* **-1.** [gén & COMM] company; **fausser** ~ **à qqn** to slip away from sb; **tenir** ~ **à qqn** to keep sb company; **et** ~ and company; *iron* and the rest; ~ **aérienne** airline (company); ~ **d'assurances** insurance company; ~ **de navigation** shipping company; **en** ~ **de** in the company of. **-2.** [assemblée] gathering.

compagnon [kɔ̃paɲɔ̃], **compagne** [kɔ̃paɲ] *nm, f* companion.
◆ **compagnon** *nm* HIST journeyman.

comparable [kɔ̃parabl] *adj* comparable.

comparaison [kɔ̃parɛzɔ̃] *nf* [parallèle] comparison; **en** ~ **de**, **par** ~ **avec** compared with, in OU by comparison with.

comparaître [kɔ̃parɛtr] [91] *vi* JUR: ~ **(devant)** to appear (before).

comparatif, **-ive** [kɔ̃paratif, iv] *adj* comparative.
◆ **comparatif** *nm* GRAM comparative.

comparativement [kɔ̃parativmã] *adv* comparatively.

comparé, **-e** [kɔ̃pare] *adj* comparative; [mérites] relative.

comparer [kɔ̃pare] [3] *vt* **-1.** [confronter]: ~ **(avec)** to compare (with). **-2.** [assimiler]: ~ **qqch à** to compare OU liken sthg to.

comparse [kɔ̃pars] *nmf péj* stooge.

compartiment [kɔ̃partimã] *nm* compartment.

compartimenter [kɔ̃partimãte] [3] *vt* [meuble] to partition; *fig* [administration] to compartmentalize.

comparu, -e [kɔ̃pary] *pp* → comparaître.

comparution [kɔ̃parysjɔ̃] *nf* JUR appearance.

compas [kɔ̃pa] *nm* **-1.** [de dessin] pair of compasses, compasses (*pl*). **-2.** NAVIG compass.

compassé, **-e** [kɔ̃pase] *adj sout* staid, stuffy.

compassion [kɔ̃pasjɔ̃] *nf sout* compassion.

compatible [kɔ̃patibl] *adj*: ~ **(avec)** compatible (with).

compatir [kɔ̃patir] [32] *vi*: ~ **(à)** to sympathize (with).

compatissant, **-e** [kɔ̃patisɑ̃, ɑ̃t] *adj* sympathetic.

compatriote [kɔ̃patrijɔt] *nmf* compatriot, fellow countryman (*f* countrywoman).

compensation [kɔ̃pɑ̃sasjɔ̃] *nf* **-1.** [dédommagement] compensation; **en** ~ in compensation. **-2.** [équilibrage] balance.

compensé, **-e** [kɔ̃pɑ̃se] *adj* built-up.

compenser [kɔ̃pɑ̃se] [3] ◇ *vt* to compensate OU make up for. ◇ *vi* to compensate, to make up.

compétence [kɔ̃petɑ̃s] *nf* **-1.** [qualification] skill, ability. **-2.** JUR competence; **cela n'entre pas dans mes** ~**s** that's outside my scope.

compétent, **-e** [kɔ̃petɑ̃, ɑ̃t] *adj* **-1.** [connaisseur] skilled, expert. **-2.** ADMIN & JUR competent; **les autorités** ~**es** the relevant authorities.

compétitif, **-ive** [kɔ̃petitif, iv] *adj* competitive.

compétition [kɔ̃petisjɔ̃] *nf* competition; **faire de la** ~ to go in for competitive sport; ~ **automobile** motor race.

compétitivité [kɔ̃petitivite] *nf* competitiveness.

compilation [kɔ̃pilasjɔ̃] *nf* compilation.

complainte [kɔ̃plɛ̃t] *nf* lament.

complaire [kɔ̃plɛr] [110] *vi*: ~ **à qqn** *sout* to please sb.
◆ **se complaire** *vp*: **se** ~ **dans qqch/à faire qqch** to revel in sthg/in doing sthg.

complaisance [kɔ̃plɛzɑ̃s] *nf* **-1.** [obligeance] kindness. **-2.** [indulgence] indulgence. **-3.** [autosatisfaction]: **avec** ~ indulgently.

complaisant, **-e** [kɔ̃plɛzɑ̃, ɑ̃t] *adj* **-1.** [aimable] obliging, kind. **-2.** [indulgent] indulgent.

complément [kɔ̃plemɑ̃] *nm* **-1.** [gén & GRAM] complement; ~ **d'information** additional OU further information; ~ **du nom** possessive phrase; ~ **d'objet direct** direct object; ~ **d'objet indirect** indirect object. **-2.** [reste] remainder.

complémentaire [kɔ̃plemɑ̃tɛr] *adj* **-1.** [supplémentaire] supplementary. **-2.** [caractères, couleurs] complementary.

complet, -ète [kɔ̃plɛ, ɛt] *adj* **-1.** [gén] complete; **c'est ~!** *fam* that's all I/we need; **la famille au (grand) ~** the whole family. **-2.** [plein] full.

◆ **complet(-veston)** *nm* suit.

complètement [kɔ̃plɛtmɑ̃] *adv* **-1.** [vraiment] absolutely, totally. **-2.** [entièrement] completely.

compléter [kɔ̃plete] [18] *vt* [gén] to complete, to complement; [somme d'argent] to make up.

◆ **se compléter** *vp* to complement one another.

complexe [kɔ̃plɛks] ◇ *nm* **-1.** PSYCHOL complex; **avoir des ~s** to have hang-ups, to be hung up; **sans ~** OU **complexes** well-adjusted; ~ **d'infériorité/de supériorité** inferiority/superiority complex. **-2.** [ensemble] complex; ~ **hospitalier/scolaire/sportif** hospital/school/sports complex. ◇ *adj* complex, complicated.

complexé, -e [kɔ̃plɛkse] *adj* hung up, mixed up.

complexifier [kɔ̃plɛksifje] *vt* to make (more) complex.

complexité [kɔ̃plɛksite] *nf* complexity.

complication [kɔ̃plikasjɔ̃] *nf* intricacy, complexity.

◆ **complications** *nfpl* complications.

complice [kɔ̃plis] ◇ *nmf* accomplice. ◇ *adj* [sourire, regard, air] knowing.

complicité [kɔ̃plisite] *nf* complicity.

compliment [kɔ̃plimɑ̃] *nm* compliment.

complimenter [kɔ̃plimɑ̃te] [3] *vt* to compliment.

compliqué, -e [kɔ̃plike] *adj* [problème] complex, complicated; [personne] complicated.

compliquer [kɔ̃plike] [3] *vt* to complicate.

◆ **se compliquer** *vp* to get complicated.

complot [kɔ̃plo] *nm* plot.

comploter [kɔ̃plɔte] [3] *vt & vi litt & fig* to plot.

comportement [kɔ̃pɔrtəmɑ̃] *nm* behaviour.

comportemental, -e, -aux [kɔ̃pɔrtəmɑ̃tal, o] *adj* behavioural *Br,* behavioral *Am.*

comporter [kɔ̃pɔrte] [3] *vt* **-1.** [contenir] to include, to contain. **-2.** [être composé de] to consist of, to be made up of.

◆ **se comporter** *vp* to behave.

composant, -e [kɔ̃pozɑ̃, ɑ̃t] *adj* constituent, component.

◆ **composant** *nm* component.

◆ **composante** *nf* component.

composé, -e [kɔ̃poze] *adj* compound.

◆ **composé** *nm* **-1.** [mélange] combination. **-2.** CHIM & LING compound.

composer [kɔ̃poze] [3] ◇ *vt* **-1.** [constituer] to make up, to form; **être composé de** to be made up of. **-2.** [créer - roman, lettre, poème] to write; [- musique] to compose, to write. **-3.** [numéro de téléphone] to dial. ◇ *vi* to compromise.

◆ **se composer** *vp* [être constitué] : **se ~ de** to be composed of, to be made up of.

composite [kɔ̃pozit] ◇ *nm* composite. ◇ *adj* **-1.** [disparate - mobilier] assorted, of various types; [- foule] heterogeneous. **-2.** [matériau] composite.

compositeur, -trice [kɔ̃pozitœr, tris] *nm, f* **-1.** MUS composer. **-2.** TYPO typesetter.

composition [kɔ̃pozisjɔ̃] *nf* **-1.** [gén] composition; [de roman] writing, composition. **-2.** TYPO typesetting. **-3.** SCOL test; ~ **française** French composition. **-4.** [caractère] : **être de bonne ~** to be good-natured.

compost [kɔ̃pɔst] *nm* compost.

composter [kɔ̃pɔste] [3] *vt* [ticket, billet] to date-stamp.

compote [kɔ̃pɔt] *nf* compote; ~ **de pommes** stewed apple; **j'ai les jambes en ~** *fam fig* my legs feel like jelly.

compotier [kɔ̃pɔtje] *nm* fruit bowl.

compréhensible [kɔ̃preɑ̃sibl] *adj* [texte, parole] comprehensible; *fig* [réaction] understandable.

compréhensif, -ive [kɔ̃preɑ̃sif, iv] *adj* understanding.

compréhension [kɔ̃preɑ̃sjɔ̃] *nf* **-1.** [de texte] comprehension, understanding. **-2.** [indulgence] understanding.

comprenais, comprenions *etc* → comprendre.

comprendre [kɔ̃prɑ̃dr] [79] ◇ *vt* **-1.** [gén] to understand; **je comprends!** I see!; **se faire ~** to make o.s. understood; **mal ~** to misunderstand. **-2.** [comporter] to comprise, to consist of. **-3.** [inclure] to include. ◇ *vi* to understand.

◆ **se comprendre** *vp* to understand one another; **ça se comprend** that's understandable.

comprenne, comprennes *etc* → comprendre.

compresse [kɔ̃prɛs] *nf* compress.

compresseur [kɔ̃prɛsœr] → **rouleau**.

compression [kɔ̃presjɔ̃] *nf* [de gaz] compression; *fig* cutback, reduction.

comprimé, -e [kɔ̃prime] *adj* compressed.
◆ **comprimé** *nm* tablet; ~ **effervescent** effervescent tablet.

comprimer [kɔ̃prime] [3] *vt* **-1.** [gaz, vapeur] to compress. **-2.** [personnes]: **être comprimés dans** to be packed into.

compris, -e [kɔ̃pri, iz] ◇ *pp* → **comprendre**. ◇ *adj* **-1.** [situé] lying, contained. **-2.** [inclus]: **charges (non) comprises** (not) including bills, bills (not) included; **tout** ~ all inclusive, all in; **y** ~ including.

compromets → **compromettre**.

compromettant, -e [kɔ̃prɔmetɑ̃, ɑ̃t] *adj* compromising.

compromettre [kɔ̃prɔmetr] [84] *vt* to compromise.
◆ **se compromettre** *vp*: **se** ~ **(avec qqn/dans qqch)** to compromise o.s. (with sb/in sthg).

compromis, -e [kɔ̃prɔmi, iz] *pp* → **compromettre**.
◆ **compromis** *nm* compromise.

compromission [kɔ̃prɔmisjɔ̃] *nf* *péj* (dishonest) compromise.

comptabiliser [kɔ̃tabilize] [3] *vt* to enter in an account.

comptabilité [kɔ̃tabilite] *nf* [comptes] accounts (*pl*); [service]: **la** ~ accounts, the accounts department.

comptable [kɔ̃tabl] ◇ *nmf* accountant. ◇ *adj* accounting (*avant n*).

comptant [kɔ̃tɑ̃] ◇ *adj inv* cash, in cash. ◇ *adv*: **payer** OU **régler** ~ to pay cash.
◆ **au comptant** *loc adv*: **payer au** ~ to pay cash.

compte [kɔ̃t] *nm* **-1.** [action] count, counting (*U*); [total] number; ~ **à rebours** countdown; ~ **rond** round number. **-2.** BANQUE, COMM & COMPTABILITÉ account; **ouvrir un** ~ to open an account; **régler un** ~ to settle an account; ~ **bancaire** OU **en banque** bank account; ~ **courant** current account, checking account *Am*; ~ **créditeur** account in credit; ~ **débiteur** overdrawn account; **de dépôt** deposit account; ~ **d'épargne** savings account; ~ **d'exploitation** operating account; ~ **postal** post office account. **-3.** *loc*: **avoir son** ~ to have had enough; **être/se mettre à son** ~ to be/become self-employed; **prendre qqch en** ~, **tenir** ~ **de qqch** to take sthg into account; **régler son** ~ **à qqn** *fam fig* to sort sb out; **rendre** ~ **de** to account for; **se rendre** ~ **de qqch** to

realize sthg; **se rendre** ~ **que** to realize (that); **s'en tirer à bon** ~ to get off lightly; **tout** ~ **fait** all things considered.
◆ **comptes** *nmpl* accounts; **devoir des** ~**s à** to be accountable to; **faire ses** ~**s** to do one's accounts; **faire des** ~**s d'apothicaire** to account for every last penny; **régler ses** ~**s avec qqch** to come to terms with sthg; **régler ses** ~**s avec qqn** to have it out with sb.

compte-chèques (*pl* **comptes-chèques**), **compte chèque** (*pl* **comptes chèques**) [kɔ̃tʃɛk] *nm* current account, checking account *Am*.

compte-gouttes [kɔ̃tgut] *nm inv* dropper; **au** ~ *fig* sparingly.

compter [kɔ̃te] [3] ◇ *vt* **-1.** [dénombrer] to count. **-2.** [avoir l'intention de]: ~ **faire qqch** to intend to do sthg, to plan to do sthg. ◇ *vi* **-1.** [calculer] to count. **-2.** [être important] to count, to matter; ~ **pour** to count for. **-3.** ~ **sur** [se fier à] to rely OU count on. **-4.** ~ **avec** [tenir compte de] to reckon with, to take account of. **-5.** ~ **parmi** [faire partie de] to be included amongst, to rank amongst.
◆ **à compter de** *loc prép* as from, starting from.
◆ **sans compter** ◇ *loc prép* [excepté] not including. ◇ *loc adv*: **se dépenser sans** ~ *fig* to give unsparingly of o.s.
◆ **sans compter que** *loc conj* besides which.

compte rendu (*pl* **comptes rendus**), **compte-rendu** (*pl* **comptes-rendus**) [kɔ̃trɑ̃dy] *nm* report, account.

compte-tours [kɔ̃ttur] *nm inv* rev counter, tachometer.

compteur [kɔ̃tœr] *nm* meter.

comptine [kɔ̃tin] *nf* nursery rhyme.

comptoir [kɔ̃twar] *nm* **-1.** [de bar] bar; [de magasin] counter. **-2.** HIST trading post. **-3.** *Helv* [foire] trade fair.

compulser [kɔ̃pylse] [3] *vt* to consult.

comte [kɔ̃t] *nm* count.

comté [kɔ̃te] *nm* **-1.** [fromage] *type of cheese similar to Gruyère.* **-2.** ADMIN [au Canada] county. **-3.** HIST earldom.

comtesse [kɔ̃tɛs] *nf* countess.

con, conne [kɔ̃, kɔn] *tfam* ◇ *adj* bloody *Br* OU damned stupid. ◇ *nm, f* stupid bastard (*f* bitch).

Conakry [kɔnakri] *n* Conakry.

concasser [kɔ̃kase] [3] *vt* to crush; [poivre] to grind.

concave [kɔ̃kav] *adj* concave.

concéder [kɔsede] [18] *vt*: ~ **qqch à** [droit, terrain] to grant sthg to; [point, victoire] to concede sthg to; ~ **que** to admit (that), to concede (that).

concentration [kɔsɑ̃trasjɔ̃] *nf* concentration.

concentré, -e [kɔsɑ̃tre] *adj* **-1.** [gén] concentrated. **-2.** [personne] concentrating. **-3.** → **lait.**
◆ **concentré** *nm* concentrate; ~ **de tomates** CULIN tomato paste OU purée.

concentrer [kɔsɑ̃tre] [3] *vt* to concentrate.
◆ **se concentrer** *vp* **-1.** [se rassembler] to be concentrated. **-2.** [personne] to concentrate.

concentrique [kɔsɑ̃trik] *adj* concentric.

concept [kɔsɛpt] *nm* concept.

concepteur, -trice [kɔsɛptœr, tris] *nm, f* designer.

conception [kɔsɛpsjɔ̃] *nf* **-1.** [gén] conception. **-2.** [d'un produit, d'une campagne] design, designing (*U*).

concernant [kɔsɛrnɑ̃] *prép* regarding, concerning.

concerner [kɔsɛrne] [3] *vt* to concern; **être/se sentir concerné par qqch** to be/feel concerned by sthg; **en ce qui me concerne** as far as I'm concerned.

concert [kɔsɛr] *nm* **-1.** MUS concert. **-2.** [entente] accord; **de ~ avec qqn** together with sb.

concertation [kɔsɛrtasjɔ̃] *nf* consultation.

concerter [kɔsɛrte] [3] *vt* [organiser] to devise (jointly).
◆ **se concerter** *vp* to consult (each other).

concerto [kɔsɛrto] *nm* concerto.

concession [kɔsesjɔ̃] *nf* **-1.** [compromis & GRAM] concession; **faire des ~s (à qqn)** to make concessions (to sb). **-2.** [autorisation] rights (*pl*), concession.

concessionnaire [kɔsesjɔnɛr] ◇ *nmf* **-1.** [automobile] (car) dealer. **-2.** [qui possède une franchise] franchise holder. ◇ *adj* concessionary.

concevable [kɔsəvabl] *adj* conceivable.

concevoir [kɔsəvwar] [52] *vt* **-1.** [enfant, projet] to conceive. **-2.** [comprendre] to conceive of; **je ne peux pas ~ comment/pourquoi** I cannot conceive how/why. **-3.** *sout* [éprouver] to feel.
◆ **se concevoir** *vp* to be imagined.

concierge [kɔsjɛrʒ] *nmf* caretaker, concierge.

concile [kɔsil] *nm* council.

conciliabule [kɔsiljabyl] *nm* [discussion] consultation.

conciliant, -e [kɔsiljɑ̃, ɑ̃t] *adj* conciliating.

conciliation [kɔsiljasjɔ̃] *nf* **-1.** [règlement d'un conflit] reconciliation, reconciling. **-2.** [accord & JUR] conciliation.

concilier [kɔsilje] [9] *vt* **-1.** [mettre d'accord, allier] to reconcile; ~ **qqch et** OU **avec qqch** to reconcile sthg with sthg. **-2.** [gagner à sa cause]: ~ **qqn à** to win sb over to.
◆ **se concilier** *vp*: **se ~ qqn** to win sb over; **se ~ qqch** to gain sthg.

concis, -e [kɔsi, iz] *adj* [style, discours] concise; [personne] terse.

concision [kɔsizjɔ̃] *nf* conciseness, concision.

concitoyen, -yenne [kɔsitwajɛ̃, jɛn] *nm, f* fellow citizen.

conclu, -e [kɔkly] *pp* → **conclure.**

concluant, -e [kɔklyɑ̃, ɑ̃t] *adj* [convainquant] conclusive.

conclure [kɔklyr] [96] ◇ *vt* to conclude; ~ **de qqch que** to conclude from sthg that; **en ~ que** to deduce (that). ◇ *vi*: ~ **à qqch** to conclude (that); **les experts ont conclu à la folie** the experts concluded he/she was mad; **le tribunal a conclu au suicide** the court returned a verdict of suicide.

conclusion [kɔklyzjɔ̃] *nf* **-1.** [gén] conclusion; **en arriver à la ~ que** to come to the conclusion that. **-2.** [partie finale] close.

concocter [kɔkɔkte] [3] *vt* to concoct.

concombre [kɔkɔbr] *nm* cucumber.

concomitant, -e [kɔkɔmitɑ̃, ɑ̃t] *adj* concomitant.

concordance [kɔkɔrdɑ̃s] *nf* [conformité] agreement; ~ **des temps** GRAM sequence of tenses.

concorde [kɔkɔrd] *nf* concord.

Concorde® [kɔkɔrd] *nm* Concorde®.

concorder [kɔkɔrde] [3] *vi* **-1.** [coïncider] to agree, to coincide. **-2.** [être en accord]: ~ **(avec)** to be in accordance (with). **-3.** [avoir un même but] to coincide.

concourir [kɔkurir] [45] *vi* **-1.** [contribuer]: ~ **à** to work towards. **-2.** [participer à un concours] to compete.

concours [kɔkur] *nm* **-1.** [examen] competitive examination; ~ **de recrutement** competitive entry examination. **-2.** [compétition] competition, contest; **hors ~** [dans une compétition] ineligible; *fig* exceptional; ~ **hippique** horse show. **-3.** [collaboration] help; **avec le ~ de qqn** with sb's help OU assistance. **-4.** [coïncidence]: ~ **de circonstances** combination of circumstances.

concret, -ète [kɔkrɛ, ɛt] *adj* concrete.

concrètement [kɔ̃kretmɑ̃] *adv* [en réalité] in real OU practical terms.

concrétiser [kɔ̃kretize] [3] *vt* [projet] to give shape to; [rêve, espoir] to give solid form to.
◆ **se concrétiser** *vp* [projet] to take shape; [rêve, espoir] to materialize.

conçu, -e [kɔ̃sy] *pp* → **concevoir**.

concubin, -e [kɔ̃kybɛ̃, in] *nm, f* partner, common-law husband (*f* wife).

concubinage [kɔ̃kybinaʒ] *nm* living together, cohabitation.

concupiscent, -e [kɔ̃kypisɑ̃, ɑ̃t] *adj* concupiscent.

concurremment [kɔ̃kyramɑ̃] *adv* jointly.

concurrence [kɔ̃kyrɑ̃s] *nf* **-1.** [rivalité] rivalry. **-2.** ÉCON competition; ~ **déloyale** unfair competition; **des prix défiant toute** ~ unbeatable prices. **-3.** [montant]: **jusqu'à** ~ **de** to the amount of, not exceeding.

concurrent, -e [kɔ̃kyrɑ̃, ɑ̃t] ◇ *adj* rival, competing. ◇ *nm, f* competitor.

concurrentiel, -ielle [kɔ̃kyrɑ̃sjɛl] *adj* competitive.

condamnable [kɔ̃danabl] *adj* reprehensible.

condamnation [kɔ̃danasjɔ̃] *nf* **-1.** JUR sentence. **-2.** [dénonciation] condemnation.

condamné, -e [kɔ̃dane] *nm, f* convict, prisoner.

condamner [kɔ̃dane] [3] *vt* **-1.** JUR: ~ **qqn (à)** to sentence sb (to); ~ **qqn à une amende** to fine sb. **-2.** *fig* [obliger]: ~ **qqn à qqch** to condemn sb to sthg. **-3.** [malade]: **être condamné** to be terminally ill. **-4.** [interdire] to forbid. **-5.** [blâmer] to condemn. **-6.** [fermer] to fill in, to block up.

condensateur [kɔ̃dɑ̃satœr] *nm* condenser.

condensation [kɔ̃dɑ̃sasjɔ̃] *nf* condensation.

condensé [kɔ̃dɑ̃se] ◇ *nm* summary. ◇ *adj* → **lait**.

condenser [kɔ̃dɑ̃se] [3] *vt* to condense.
◆ **se condenser** *vp* to condense.

condescendant, -e [kɔ̃desɑ̃dɑ̃, ɑ̃t] *adj* condescending.

condescendre [kɔ̃desɑ̃dr] [73] *vi sout*: ~ **à qqch/à faire qqch** to condescend to sthg/to do sthg.

condescendu [kɔ̃desɑ̃dy] *pp inv* → **condescendre**.

condiment [kɔ̃dimɑ̃] *nm* condiment.

condisciple [kɔ̃disipl] *nm* fellow student.

condition [kɔ̃disjɔ̃] *nf* **-1.** [gén] condition; ~ **sine qua non** essential condition; **remplir une** ~ to fulfil a condition; **se mettre en** ~ [physiquement] to get into shape. **-2.** [place sociale] station; **la** ~ **des ouvriers** the workers' lot.

◆ **conditions** *nfpl* **-1.** [circonstances] conditions; ~**s de vie** living conditions; ~**s atmosphériques** atmospheric conditions. **-2.** [de paiement] terms.
◆ **à condition de** *loc prép* providing OU provided (that).
◆ **à condition que** *loc conj* (+ *subjonctif*) providing OU provided (that).
◆ **sans conditions** ◇ *loc adj* unconditional. ◇ *loc adv* unconditionally.

conditionné, -e [kɔ̃disjɔne] *adj* **-1.** [emballé]: ~ **sous vide** vacuum-packed. **-2.** → **air**.

conditionnel, -elle [kɔ̃disjɔnɛl] *adj* conditional.
◆ **conditionnel** *nm* GRAM conditional.

conditionnement [kɔ̃disjɔnmɑ̃] *nm* **-1.** [action d'emballer] packaging, packing. **-2.** [emballage] package. **-3.** PSYCHOL & TECHNOL conditioning.

conditionner [kɔ̃disjɔne] [3] *vt* **-1.** [déterminer] to govern. **-2.** PSYCHOL & TECHNOL to condition. **-3.** [emballer] to pack.

condoléances [kɔ̃dɔleɑ̃s] *nfpl* condolences.

conducteur, -trice [kɔ̃dyktœr, tris] ◇ *adj* conductive. ◇ *nm, f* [de véhicule] driver.
◆ **conducteur** *nm* ÉLECTR conductor.

conduire [kɔ̃dɥir] [98] ◇ *vt* **-1.** [voiture, personne] to drive. **-2.** [transmettre] to conduct. **-3.** *fig* [diriger] to manage. **-4.** *fig* [à la ruine, au désespoir]: ~ **qqn à** to drive sb to sthg. ◇ *vi* **-1.** AUTOM to drive. **-2.** [mener]: ~ **à** to lead to.
◆ **se conduire** *vp* to behave.

conduisais, conduisions *etc* → **conduire**.

conduit, -e [kɔ̃dɥi, it] *pp* → **conduire**.
◆ **conduit** *nm* **-1.** [tuyau] conduit, pipe. **-2.** ANAT duct, canal.
◆ **conduite** *nf* **-1.** [pilotage d'un véhicule] driving; ~ **à droite/gauche** right-hand/left-hand drive; ~ **en état d'ébriété** drunken driving. **-2.** [direction] running. **-3.** [comportement] behaviour (*U*). **-4.** [canalisation]: ~ **de gaz/d'eau** gas/water main, gas/water pipe.

cône [kon] *nm* GÉOM cone.

confection [kɔ̃fɛksjɔ̃] *nf* **-1.** [réalisation] making. **-2.** [industrie] clothing industry.

confectionner [kɔ̃fɛksjɔne] [3] *vt* to make.

confédéral, -e, -aux [kɔ̃federal, o] *adj* confederal.

confédération [kɔ̃federasjɔ̃] *nf* **-1.** [d'états] confederacy. **-2.** [d'associations] confederation.

conférence [kɔ̃ferɑ̃s] *nf* **-1.** [exposé] lecture. **-2.** [réunion] conference; ~ **de presse** press conference; ~ **au sommet** summit conference.

conférencier, -ière [kɔ̃ferɑ̃sje, jɛr] *nm, f* lecturer.

conférer [kɔ̃fere] [18] *vt* [accorder]: ~ **qqch à qqn** to confer sthg on sb.

confesse [kɔ̃fɛs] *nf*: **aller à** ~ to go to confession.

confesser [kɔ̃fese] [4] *vt* **-1.** [avouer] to confess. **-2.** RELIG: ~ **qqn** to hear sb's confession.
◆ **se confesser** *vp* to go to confession.

confession [kɔ̃fesjɔ̃] *nf* confession.

confessionnal, -aux [kɔ̃fesjɔnal, o] *nm* confessional.

confessionnel, -elle [kɔ̃fesjɔnɛl] *adj* RELIG denominational.

confetti [kɔ̃feti] *nm* confetti (*U*).

confiance [kɔ̃fjɑ̃s] *nf* confidence; **avoir** ~ **en** to have confidence OU faith in; **avoir** ~ **en soi** to be self-confident; **en toute** ~ with complete confidence; **de** ~ trustworthy; **faire** ~ **à qqn/qqch** to trust sb/sthg.

confiant, -e [kɔ̃fjɑ̃, ɑ̃t] *adj* **-1.** [sans méfiance] trusting. **-2.** [assuré]: ~ **(en qqch)** confident (of sthg).

confidence [kɔ̃fidɑ̃s] *nf* confidence; **en** ~ in confidence; **faire des** ~s **à qqn** to confide in sb; **être dans la** ~ to be in the know.

confident, -e [kɔ̃fidɑ̃, ɑ̃t] *nm, f* confidant (*f* confidante).

confidentiel, -ielle [kɔ̃fidɑ̃sjɛl] *adj* confidential.

confier [kɔ̃fje] [9] *vt* **-1.** [donner]: ~ **qqn/ qqch à qqn** to entrust sb/sthg to sb. **-2.** [dire]: ~ **qqch à qqn** to confide sthg to sb.
◆ **se confier** *vp*: **se** ~ **à qqn** to confide in sb.

configuration [kɔ̃figyrasjɔ̃] *nf* TECHNOL configuration; [conception] layout.

confiné, -e [kɔ̃fine] *adj* **-1.** [air] stale; [atmosphère] enclosed. **-2.** [enfermé] shut away.

confins [kɔ̃fɛ̃]
◆ **aux confins de** *loc prép* on the borders of.

confirmation [kɔ̃firmasjɔ̃] *nf* confirmation.

confirmer [kɔ̃firme] [3] *vt* [certifier] to confirm; ~ **qqn dans qqch** to confirm sb in sthg; **il n'a pas été confirmé dans ses fonctions** he was not retained in the post.
◆ **se confirmer** *vp* to be confirmed.

confiscation [kɔ̃fiskasjɔ̃] *nf* confiscation.

confiserie [kɔ̃fizri] *nf* **-1.** [magasin] sweet shop *Br*, candy store *Am*, confectioner's. **-2.** [sucreries] sweets (*pl*) *Br*, candy (*U*) *Am*, confectionery (*U*).

confiseur, -euse [kɔ̃fizœr, øz] *nm, f* confectioner.

confisquer [kɔ̃fiske] [3] *vt* to confiscate.

confit, -e [kɔ̃fi, it] *adj* → **fruit**.
◆ **confit** *nm* conserve.

confiture [kɔ̃fityr] *nf* jam.

conflagration [kɔ̃flagrasjɔ̃] *nf* cataclysm.

conflictuel, -elle [kɔ̃fliktɥɛl] *adj* conflicting.

conflit [kɔ̃fli] *nm* **-1.** [situation tendue] clash, conflict. **-2.** [entre États] conflict.

confluent [kɔ̃flyɑ̃] *nm* confluence; **au** ~ **de** at the confluence of.

confondre [kɔ̃fɔ̃dr] [75] *vt* **-1.** [ne pas distinguer] to confuse. **-2.** [accusé] to confound. **-3.** [stupéfier] to astound.
◆ **se confondre** *vp* **-1.** [se mêler] to merge. **-2.** *fig*: **se** ~ **en excuses** to apologize profusely; **il s'est confondu en remerciements** he thanked me/him *etc* profusely.

confondu, -e [kɔ̃fɔ̃dy] *pp* → **confondre**.

conformation [kɔ̃fɔrmasjɔ̃] *nf* structure.

conforme [kɔ̃fɔrm] *adj*: ~ **à** in accordance with.

conformé, -e [kɔ̃fɔrme] *adj*: **bien** ~ well-formed; **mal** ~ ill-formed.

conformément [kɔ̃fɔrmemɑ̃]
◆ **conformément à** *loc prép* in accordance with.

conformer [kɔ̃fɔrme] [3] *vt*: ~ **qqch à** to shape sthg according to.
◆ **se conformer** *vp*: **se** ~ **à** [s'adapter] to conform to; [obéir] to comply with.

conformiste [kɔ̃fɔrmist] ◇ *nmf* conformist. ◇ *adj* **-1.** [traditionaliste] conformist. **-2.** [Anglican] Anglican.

conformité [kɔ̃fɔrmite] *nf* **-1.** [ressemblance]: ~ **(à)** conformity (to). **-2.** [accord]: **être en** ~ **avec** to be in accordance with.

confort [kɔ̃fɔr] *nm* comfort; **tout** ~ with all mod cons *Br*.

confortable [kɔ̃fɔrtabl] *adj* comfortable.

confortablement [kɔ̃fɔrtabləmɑ̃] *adv* comfortably; ~ **payé** well-paid.

conforter [kɔ̃fɔrte] [3] *vt*: ~ **qqn (dans qqch)** to strengthen sb (in sthg).

confrère [kɔ̃frɛr], **consœur** [kɔ̃sœr] *nm, f* colleague.

confrérie [kɔ̃freri] *nf* brotherhood.

confrontation [kɔ̃frɔ̃tasjɔ̃] *nf* **-1.** [face à face] confrontation. **-2.** [comparaison] comparison.

confronter [kɔ̃frɔ̃te] [3] *vt* **-1.** [mettre face à face] to confront; *fig*: **être confronté à** to be confronted OU faced with. **-2.** [comparer] to compare.

confus, **-e** [kɔ̃fy, yz] *adj* **-1.** [indistinct, embrouillé] confused. **-2.** [gêné] embarrassed; **je suis vraiment** ~ I'm really very sorry.

confusément [kɔ̃fyzemɑ̃] *adj* **-1.** [pêle-mêle] in confusion. **-2.** [indistinctement] indistinctly. **-3.** [vaguement] vaguely.

confusion [kɔ̃fyzjɔ̃] *nf* **-1.** [gén] confusion. **-2.** [embarras] confusion, embarrassment.

congé [kɔ̃ʒe] *nm* **-1.** [arrêt de travail] leave (*U*); ~ **(de) maladie** sick leave; ~ **de maternité** maternity leave. **-2.** [vacances] holiday *Br*, vacation *Am*; **en** ~ on holiday; ~ **annuel** annual leave; ~**s payés** paid holiday (*U*) OU holidays OU leave (*U*) *Br*, paid vacation *Am*; **une journée/semaine de** ~ a day/week off. **-3.** [renvoi] notice; **donner son** ~ **à qqn** to give sb his/her notice; **prendre** ~ **(de qqn)** *sout* to take one's leave (of sb).

congédier [kɔ̃ʒedje] [9] *vt* to dismiss.

congé-formation [kɔ̃ʒefɔrmasjɔ̃] (*pl* **congés-formation**) *nm* training leave.

congélateur [kɔ̃ʒelatœr] *nm* freezer.

congeler [kɔ̃ʒle] [25] *vt* to freeze.

congénital, **-e**, **-aux** [kɔ̃ʒenital, o] *adj* congenital.

congère [kɔ̃ʒɛr] *nf* snowdrift.

congestion [kɔ̃ʒɛstjɔ̃] *nf* congestion; ~ **pulmonaire** pulmonary congestion.

conglomérat [kɔ̃glɔmera] *nm* conglomerate.

Congo [kɔ̃go] *nm*: **le** ~ the Congo; **au** ~ in the Congo.

congolais, **-e** [kɔ̃gɔlɛ, ɛz] *adj* Congolese.
◆ **congolais** *nm* CULIN coconut cake.
◆ **Congolais**, **-e** *nm*, *f* Congolese person.

congratuler [kɔ̃gratyle] [3] *vt* to congratulate.

congre [kɔ̃gr] *nm* conger eel.

congrégation [kɔ̃gregasjɔ̃] *nf* congregation.

congrès [kɔ̃grɛ] *nm* **-1.** [colloque] assembly. **-2.** HIST [réunion] congress.
◆ **Congrès** *nm* [parlement américain]: **le Congrès** Congress.

congressiste [kɔ̃gresist] *nmf* congress participant.

congrue [kɔ̃gry] → **portion**.

conifère [kɔnifɛr] *nm* conifer.

conique [kɔnik] *adj* conical.

conjecture [kɔ̃ʒɛktyr] *nf* conjecture; **se perdre en** ~**s** to lose o.s. in conjecture.

conjecturer [kɔ̃ʒɛktyre] [3] *vt & vi* to conjecture.

conjoint, **-e** [kɔ̃ʒwɛ̃, ɛt] ◇ *adj* joint. ◇ *nm*, *f* spouse.

conjointement [kɔ̃ʒwɛ̃tmɑ̃] *adv*: ~ **(avec qqn)** jointly (with sb).

conjonctif, **-ive** [kɔ̃ʒɔ̃ktif, iv] *adj* **-1.** → **tissu**. **-2.** GRAM conjunctive.

conjonction [kɔ̃ʒɔ̃ksjɔ̃] *nf* conjunction; ~ **de coordination/de subordination** GRAM coordinating/subordinating conjunction.

conjonctivite [kɔ̃ʒɔ̃ktivit] *nf* conjunctivitis (*U*).

conjoncture [kɔ̃ʒɔ̃ktyr] *nf* ÉCON situation, circumstances (*pl*).

conjoncturel, **-elle** [kɔ̃ʒɔ̃ktyrɛl] *adj* economic.

conjugaison [kɔ̃ʒygezɔ̃] *nf* **-1.** [union] uniting. **-2.** GRAM conjugation.

conjugal, **-e**, **-aux** [kɔ̃ʒygal, o] *adj* conjugal.

conjuguer [kɔ̃ʒyge] [3] *vt* **-1.** [unir] to combine. **-2.** GRAM to conjugate.

conjuration [kɔ̃ʒyrasjɔ̃] *nf* **-1.** [conspiration] conspiracy. **-2.** [exorcisme] exorcism.

conjurer [kɔ̃ʒyre] [3] *vt* **-1.** [supplier] to beg; **je vous en conjure!** *sout* I beg (of) you! **-2.** [exorciser] to exorcize. **-3.** [écarter] to avert.
◆ **se conjurer** *vp* to plot, to conspire.

connaissais, **connaissions** *etc* → **connaître**.

connaissance [kɔnɛsɑ̃s] *nf* **-1.** [savoir] knowledge (*U*); **à ma** ~ to (the best of) my knowledge; **en** ~ **de cause** with full knowledge of the facts; **prendre** ~ **de qqch** to study, to examine. **-2.** [personne] acquaintance; **une vieille** ~ an old acquaintance; **faire** ~ **(avec qqn)** to become acquainted (with sb); **faire la** ~ **de** to meet. **-3.** [conscience]: **perdre/reprendre** ~ to lose/regain consciousness; **sans** ~ unconscious.

connaisseur, **-euse** [kɔnɛsœr, øz] ◇ *adj* expert (*avant n*). ◇ *nm*, *f* connoisseur.

connaître [kɔnɛtr] [91] *vt* **-1.** [gén] to know; ~ **qqn de nom/de vue** to know sb by name/sight. **-2.** [éprouver] to experience.
◆ **se connaître** *vp* **-1.** **s'y** ~ **en** [être expert] to know about; **il s'y connaît** he knows what he's talking about/doing. **-2.** [soi-même] to know o.s.. **-3.** [se rencontrer] to meet (each other); **ils se connaissent** they've met (each other).

connecter [kɔnɛkte] [4] *vt* to connect.

connecteur [kɔnɛktœr] *nm*: ~ **à broche** INFORM pin connector.

connerie [kɔnri] *nf tfam* stupidity (*U*); **faire/dire des** ~**s** to do/to say something bloody stupid *Br*, to do/to say something damned stupid.

connexe [kɔnɛks] *adj* related.

connexion [kɔnɛksjɔ̃] *nf* connection.
connivence [kɔnivɑ̃s] *nf* connivance; **être de ~ (avec qqn)** to be in league (with sb).
connotation [kɔnɔtasjɔ̃] *nf* connotation.
connu, -e [kɔny] ◇ *pp* → **connaître**. ◇ *adj* **-1.** [célèbre] well-known, famous. **-2.** [su]: **~ de qqn** known to sb.
conquérant, -e [kɔ̃kerɑ̃, ɑ̃t] ◇ *adj* conquering. ◇ *nm, f* conqueror.
conquérir [kɔ̃kerir] [39] *vt* to conquer.
conquête [kɔ̃kɛt] *nf* conquest; **faire la ~ de qqch** to conquer sthg; **faire la ~ de qqn** to win sb over.
conquiers, conquiert *etc* → **conquérir**.
conquis, -e [kɔ̃ki, iz] *pp* → **conquérir**.
consacré, -e [kɔ̃sakre] *adj* **-1.** [habituel] established, accepted. **-2.** RELIG consecrated.
consacrer [kɔ̃sakre] [3] *vt* **-1.** RELIG to consecrate. **-2.** [employer]: **~ qqch à** to devote sthg to.
◆ **se consacrer** *vp*: **se ~ à** to dedicate o.s. to, to devote o.s. to.
consanguin, -e [kɔ̃sɑ̃gɛ̃, in] *adj*: **frère ~** half-brother; **sœur ~e** half-sister; *voir aussi* **mariage**.
consciemment [kɔ̃sjamɑ̃] *adv* knowingly, consciously.
conscience [kɔ̃sjɑ̃s] *nf* **-1.** [connaissance & PSYCHOL] consciousness; **avoir ~ de qqch** to be aware of sthg. **-2.** [morale] conscience; **agir selon sa ~** to follow one's conscience; **avoir qqch sur la ~** to have sthg on one's conscience; **bonne/mauvaise ~** clear/guilty conscience; **~ professionnelle** professional integrity, conscientiousness.
consciencieusement [kɔ̃sjɑ̃søzmɑ̃] *adv* conscientiously.
consciencieux, -ieuse [kɔ̃sjɑ̃sjø, jøz] *adj* conscientious.
conscient, -e [kɔ̃sjɑ̃, ɑ̃t] *adj* conscious; **être ~ de qqch** [connaître] to be conscious of sthg.
conscription [kɔ̃skripsjɔ̃] *nf* conscription, draft *Am*.
conscrit [kɔ̃skri] *nm* conscript, recruit, draftee *Am*.
consécration [kɔ̃sekrasjɔ̃] *nf* **-1.** [reconnaissance] recognition; [de droit, coutume] establishment. **-2.** RELIG consecration.
consécutif, -ive [kɔ̃sekytif, iv] *adj* **-1.** [successif & GRAM] consecutive. **-2.** [résultant]: **~ à** resulting from.
conseil [kɔ̃sɛj] *nm* **-1.** [avis] piece of advice, advice (*U*); **donner un ~** OU **des ~s (à qqn)** to give (sb) advice; **suivre le ~ de qqn** to take somebody's advice. **-2.** [personne]: **~**

(en) consultant (in). **-3.** [assemblée] council; **~ d'administration** board of directors; **~ de classe** staff meeting; **le Conseil constitutionnel** *French government body ensuring that laws, elections and referenda are constitutional*; **~ de discipline** disciplinary committee; **le Conseil d'État** the (French) Council of State; **le Conseil des ministres** ≃ the Cabinet; **~ municipal** town council *Br*, city council *Am*; **le Conseil supérieur de la magistrature** *French state body that appoints members of the judiciary*.

LE CONSEIL D'ÉTAT:
The French Council of State has 200 members. It acts both as the highest court to which the legal affairs of the state can be referred, and as a consultative body to which bills and rulings are submitted by the government prior to examination by the 'Conseil des ministres'

LE CONSEIL DES MINISTRES:
The President himself presides over the 'Conseil des ministres', which traditionally meets every Wednesday morning; strictly speaking, when ministers assemble in the sole presence of the Prime Minister, this is known as 'le Conseil du cabinet'

conseiller¹ [kɔ̃seje] [4] ◇ *vt* **-1.** [recommander] to advise; **~ qqch à qqn** to recommend sthg to sb. **-2.** [guider] to advise, to counsel. ◇ *vi* [donner un conseil]: **~ à qqn de faire qqch** to advise sb to do sthg.
conseiller², -ère [kɔ̃seje, ɛr] *nm, f* **-1.** [guide] counsellor; **~ matrimonial** marriage counsellor. **-2.** [d'un conseil] councillor; **~ municipal** town councillor *Br*, city councilman (*f* -woman) *Am*.
consensuel [kɔ̃sɑ̃sɥɛl] *adj* [contrat] consensual; **politique consensuelle** consensus politics.
consensus [kɔ̃sɛ̃sys] *nm* consensus.
consentement [kɔ̃sɑ̃tmɑ̃] *nm* consent.
consentir [kɔ̃sɑ̃tir] [37] ◇ *vt* **-1.** [accorder]: **~ qqch à qqn** to grant sb sthg. **-2.** [accepter]: **~ que** (+ *subjonctif*): **je consens qu'il vienne** I consent to his coming. ◇ *vi*: **~ à qqch** to consent to sthg.
conséquence [kɔ̃sekɑ̃s] *nf* consequence, result; **avoir des ~s (sur qqch)** to have consequences (for sthg); **sans ~** [sans importance] of no importance; **ne pas tirer à ~** to be of no consequence.
conséquent, -e [kɔ̃sekɑ̃, ɑ̃t] *adj* **-1.** [cohérent] consistent. **-2.** [important] sizeable, considerable.

◆ **par conséquent** *loc adv* therefore, consequently.

conservateur, **-trice** [kɔ̃sɛrvatœr, tris] ◇ *adj* conservative. ◇ *nm, f* **-1.** POLIT conservative. **-2.** [administrateur] curator.

◆ **conservateur** *nm* preservative.

conservation [kɔ̃sɛrvasjɔ̃] *nf* **-1.** [état, entretien] preservation. **-2.** [aliment] preserving.

conservatoire [kɔ̃sɛrvatwar] *nm* academy; ~ **de musique** music college; **le Conservatoire national supérieur d'art dramatique, le Conservatoire** *national drama school in Paris.*

conserve [kɔ̃sɛrv] *nf* tinned *Br* OU canned food; **en** ~ [en boîte] tinned, canned; [en bocal] preserved, bottled.

◆ **de conserve** *loc adv* together.

conserver [kɔ̃sɛrve] [3] *vt* **-1.** [garder, entretenir] to preserve. **-2.** [entreposer - en boîte] to can; [- en bocal] to bottle; «~ **au frais**» "keep in a cool place". **-3.** [personne]: **être bien conservé** to be well-preserved.

◆ **se conserver** *vp* to keep.

considérable [kɔ̃siderabl] *adj* considerable.

considération [kɔ̃siderasjɔ̃] *nf* **-1.** [réflexion, motivation] consideration; **en** ~ **de qqch** in consideration of sthg; **prendre qqch en** ~ to take sthg into consideration. **-2.** [estime] respect.

considérer [kɔ̃sidere] [18] *vt* to consider; **tout bien considéré** all things considered.

consigne [kɔ̃siɲ] *nf* **-1.** [ordre] orders (*pl*). **-2.** (*gén pl*) [instruction] instructions (*pl*). **-3.** [entrepôt de bagages] left-luggage office *Br*, checkroom *Am*, baggage room *Am*; ~ **automatique** left-luggage lockers (*pl*). **-4.** [somme d'argent] deposit.

consigné, **-e** [kɔ̃siɲe] *adj* returnable.

consigner [kɔ̃siɲe] [3] *vt* **-1.** [bagages] to leave in the left-luggage office *Br* OU checkroom *Am* OU baggage room *Am*. **-2.** *sout* [relater] to record, to set down. **-3.** MIL to confine to barracks. **-4.** *vieilli* SCOL: ~ **qqn** to give sb detention.

consistance [kɔ̃sistãs] *nf* [solidité] consistency; *fig* substance; **sans** ~ [fade] colourless.

consistant, **-e** [kɔ̃sistã, ãt] *adj* **-1.** [épais] thick. **-2.** [nourrissant] substantial. **-3.** [fondé] sound.

consister [kɔ̃siste] [3] *vi*: ~ **en** to consist of; ~ **à faire qqch** to consist in doing sthg.

consœur → **confrère**.

consolation [kɔ̃sɔlasjɔ̃] *nf* consolation.

console [kɔ̃sɔl] *nf* **-1.** [table] console (table).

-2. INFORM: ~ **de visualisation** VDU, visual display unit.

consoler [kɔ̃sɔle] [3] *vt* **-1.** [réconforter]: ~ **qqn (de qqch)** to comfort sb (in sthg). **-2.** [apaiser] to soothe.

◆ **se consoler** *vp*: **se** ~ **de qqch** to get over sthg.

consolider [kɔ̃sɔlide] [3] *vt litt* & *fig* to strengthen.

consommateur, **-trice** [kɔ̃sɔmatœr, tris] *nm, f* [acheteur] consumer; [d'un bar] customer.

consommation [kɔ̃sɔmasjɔ̃] *nf* **-1.** [utilisation] consumption; **faire une grande** OU **grosse** ~ **de** to use (up) a lot of. **-2.** [boisson] drink.

consommé, **-e** [kɔ̃sɔme] *adj sout* consummate.

◆ **consommé** *nm* consommé.

consommer [kɔ̃sɔme] [3] ◇ *vt* **-1.** [utiliser] to use (up). **-2.** [manger] to eat; «~ **avant le 5 juin 1994**» "best before OU use by 5/6/94". **-3.** [énergie] to consume, to use. ◇ *vi* **-1.** [boire] to drink. **-2.** [voiture]: **cette voiture consomme beaucoup** this car uses a lot of fuel.

consonance [kɔ̃sɔnãs] *nf* consonance; **un nom aux** ~**s harmonieuses** a beautiful name.

consonne [kɔ̃sɔn] *nf* consonant.

consort [kɔ̃sɔr] → **prince**.

◆ **consorts** *nmpl*: **et** ~**s** *péj* and his/their sort, and the like.

consortium [kɔ̃sɔrsjɔm] *nm* consortium.

conspirateur, **-trice** [kɔ̃spiratœr, tris] *nm, f* conspirator.

conspiration [kɔ̃spirasjɔ̃] *nf* conspiracy.

conspirer [kɔ̃spire] [3] ◇ *vt* [comploter] to plot. ◇ *vi* to conspire.

conspuer [kɔ̃spɥe] [7] *vt* to boo.

constamment [kɔ̃stamã] *adv* constantly.

constance [kɔ̃stãs] *nf* **-1.** [persévérance] perseverance; **avoir de la** ~ to be indefatigable. **-2.** [permanence, fidélité] constancy.

constant, **-e** [kɔ̃stã, ãt] *adj* constant.

constat [kɔ̃sta] *nm* **-1.** [procès-verbal] report; ~ **à l'amiable** joint insurance statement made by drivers after an accident; ~ **d'huissier** affidavit made before a bailiff. **-2.** [constatation] established fact; **faire le** ~ **de qqch** to note sthg; ~ **d'échec** acknowledgement of failure.

constatation [kɔ̃statasjɔ̃] *nf* **-1.** [révélation] observation. **-2.** [fait retenu] finding.

constater [kɔ̃state] [3] *vt* **-1.** [se rendre compte de] to see, to note. **-2.** [consigner - fait, infraction] to record; [- décès, authenticité] to certify.

constellation [kɔ̃stelasjɔ̃] *nf* ASTRON constellation.

consternation [kɔ̃stɛrnasjɔ̃] *nf* dismay.

consterner [kɔ̃stɛrne] [3] *vt* to dismay.

constipation [kɔ̃stipasjɔ̃] *nf* constipation.

constipé, -e [kɔ̃stipe] *adj* **-1.** MÉD constipated. **-2.** *fam fig* [manière, air] ill at ease.

constituant, -e [kɔ̃stitɥɑ̃, ɑ̃t] *adj* constituent; *voir aussi* **assemblée**.

constitué, -e [kɔ̃stitɥe] *adj* **-1.** [personne]: **normalement/bien** ~ of normal/sound constitution. **-2.** [composé]: ~ **de** consisting of, composed of. **-3.** [établi par la loi] constituted.

constituer [kɔ̃stitɥe] [7] *vt* **-1.** [élaborer] to set up. **-2.** [composer] to make up. **-3.** [représenter] to constitute. **-4.** [établir] to agree, to settle (on).
◆ **se constituer** *vp*: **se** ~ **de** to be made up of, to consist of; **se** ~ **en** to form; **se** ~ **prisonnier** to give o.s. up; **se** ~ **partie civile** JUR to sue privately for damages.

constitution [kɔ̃stitysjɔ̃] *nf* **-1.** [création] setting up. **-2.** [de pays, de corps] constitution. **-3.** [composition] composition. **-4.** [établissement] establishment.

constitutionnel, -elle [kɔ̃stitysjɔnɛl] *adj* constitutional.

constructeur [kɔ̃stryktœr] *nm* **-1.** [fabricant] manufacturer; [de navire] shipbuilder. **-2.** [bâtisseur] builder.

constructif, -ive [kɔ̃stryktif, iv] *adj* **-1.** [créateur] creative. **-2.** [positif] constructive.

construction [kɔ̃stryksjɔ̃] *nf* **-1.** IND building, construction; ~ **navale** shipbuilding. **-2.** [édifice] structure, building. **-3.** GRAM & *fig* construction.

construire [kɔ̃strɥir] [98] *vt* **-1.** [bâtir, fabriquer] to build. **-2.** [roman] to structure. **-3.** [théorie, phrase] to construct.

construisais, construisions *etc* → **construire**.

construit, -e [kɔ̃strɥi, it] *pp* → **construire**.

consul [kɔ̃syl] *nm* consul; ~ **honoraire** honorary consul.

consulat [kɔ̃syla] *nm* **-1.** [charge] consulship. **-2.** [résidence] consulate.

consultatif, -ive [kɔ̃syltatif, iv] *adj* consultative, advisory.

consultation [kɔ̃syltasjɔ̃] *nf* **-1.** [d'ouvrage]: **de** ~ **aisée** easy to use. **-2.** MÉD & POLIT consultation. **-3.** [d'expert] (professional) advice.

consulter [kɔ̃sylte] [3] ◇ *vt* **-1.** [compulser] to consult. **-2.** [interroger, demander conseil à] to consult, to ask. **-3.** [spécialiste] to consult, to see. ◇ *vi* [médecin] to take OU hold surgery; [avocat] to be available for consultation.
◆ **se consulter** *vp* to confer.

consumer [kɔ̃syme] [3] *vt* **-1.** *sout* [brûler] to burn, to destroy. **-2.** *fig* & *littéraire* [épuiser] to consume, to eat up.
◆ **se consumer** *vp* to waste away; **se** ~ **de qqch** *littéraire* to be eaten up OU consumed with sthg.

consumérisme [kɔ̃symerism] *nm* consumerism.

contact [kɔ̃takt] *nm* **-1.** [gén] contact; **le** ~ **du marbre est froid** marble is cold to the touch; **mettre qqn et qqn en** ~, **mettre qqn en** ~ **avec qqn** to put sb in touch with sb; **prendre** ~ **avec** to make contact with; **rester en** ~ **(avec)** to stay in touch (with); **au** ~ **de** on contact with; **au** ~ **des jeunes** through mixing OU associating with young people. **-2.** AUTOM ignition; **mettre/couper le** ~ to switch on/off the ignition.

contacter [kɔ̃takte] [3] *vt* to contact.

contagieux, -ieuse [kɔ̃taʒjø, jøz] ◇ *adj* MÉD contagious; *fig* infectious. ◇ *nm, f* contagious patient.

contagion [kɔ̃taʒjɔ̃] *nf* MÉD contagion; *fig* infectiousness.

container → **conteneur**.

contaminer [kɔ̃tamine] [3] *vt* [infecter] to contaminate; *fig* to contaminate, to infect.

conte [kɔ̃t] *nm* story; ~ **de fées** fairy tale.

contemplation [kɔ̃tɑ̃plasjɔ̃] *nf* contemplation; **rester en** ~ **devant** to gaze in contemplation at.

contempler [kɔ̃tɑ̃ple] [3] *vt* to contemplate.

contemporain, -e [kɔ̃tɑ̃pɔrɛ̃, ɛn] ◇ *adj*: ~ **(de)** contemporary (with). ◇ *nm, f* contemporary.

contenance [kɔ̃tnɑ̃s] *nf* **-1.** [capacité volumique] capacity. **-2.** [attitude]: **se donner une** ~ to give an impression of composure; **perdre** ~ to lose one's composure.

conteneur [kɔ̃tənœr], **container** [kɔ̃tɛnɛr] *nm* (freight) container.

contenir [kɔ̃tnir] [40] *vt* to contain, to hold, to take.
◆ **se contenir** *vp* to contain o.s., to control o.s.

content, -e [kɔ̃tɑ̃, ɑ̃t] *adj* **-1.** [joyeux] happy. **-2.** [satisfait]: ~ **(de qqn/qqch)** happy (with sb/sthg), content (with sb/sthg); ~ **de faire qqch** happy to do sthg.

◆ **content** *nm*: avoir son ~ de to have one's fill of.

contentement [kɔ̃tãtmã] *nm* satisfaction.

contenter [kɔ̃tãte] [3] *vt* to satisfy.

◆ **se contenter** *vp*: se ~ de qqch/de faire qqch to content o.s. with sthg/with doing sthg; se ~ de peu to be content with little.

contentieux [kɔ̃tãsjø] *nm* [litige] dispute; [service] legal department.

contenu, -e [kɔ̃tny] *pp* → **contenir**.

◆ **contenu** *nm* -1. [de récipient] contents (*pl*). -2. [de texte, discours] content.

conter [kɔ̃te] [3] *vt* to tell.

contestable [kɔ̃tɛstabl] *adj* questionable.

contestataire [kɔ̃tɛstatɛr] ◇ *nmf* anti-establishment figure. ◇ *adj* anti-establishment.

contestation [kɔ̃tɛstasjɔ̃] *nf* -1. [protestation] protest, dispute. -2. POLIT: la ~ anti-establishment activity.

conteste [kɔ̃tɛst]

◆ **sans conteste** *loc adv* unquestionably.

contester [kɔ̃tɛste] [3] ◇ *vt* to. dispute, to contest. ◇ *vi* to protest.

conteur, -euse [kɔ̃tœr, øz] *nm, f* storyteller.

contexte [kɔ̃tɛkst] *nm* context.

contiens, contient *etc* → **contenir**.

contigu, -uë [kɔ̃tigy] *adj*: ~ (à) adjacent (to).

continent [kɔ̃tinã] *nm* continent.

continental, -e, -aux [kɔ̃tinãtal, o] *adj* continental.

contingence [kɔ̃tẽʒãs] *nf* (*gén pl*) contingency.

contingent [kɔ̃tẽʒã] *nm* -1. MIL national service conscripts (*pl*), draft *Am*. -2. COMM quota.

contingenter [kɔ̃tẽʒãte] [3] *vt* to put a quota on.

continu, -e [kɔ̃tiny] *adj* continuous.

continuation [kɔ̃tinɥasjɔ̃] *nf* continuation.

continuel, -elle [kɔ̃tinɥɛl] *adj* -1. [continu] continuous. -2. [répété] continual.

continuellement [kɔ̃tinɥɛlmã] *adv* continually.

continuer [kɔ̃tinɥe] [7] ◇ *vt* -1. [poursuivre] to carry on with, to continue (with). -2. [prolonger] to continue. ◇ *vi* to continue, to go on; ~ à OU de faire qqch to continue to do OU doing sthg.

◆ **se continuer** *vp* to continue, to carry on.

continuité [kɔ̃tinɥite] *nf* continuity.

contondant, -e [kɔ̃tɔ̃dã, ãt] *adj* blunt.

contorsionner [kɔ̃tɔrsjɔne] [3]

◆ **se contorsionner** *vp* to contort (o.s.), to writhe.

contour [kɔ̃tur] *nm* -1. [limite] outline. -2. (*gén pl*) [courbe] bend.

contourner [kɔ̃turne] [3] *vt litt & fig* to bypass, to get round.

contraceptif, -ive [kɔ̃trasɛptif, iv] *adj* contraceptive.

◆ **contraceptif** *nm* contraceptive.

contraception [kɔ̃trasɛpsjɔ̃] *nf* contraception.

contracter [kɔ̃trakte] [3] *vt* -1. [muscle] to contract, to tense; [visage] to contort. -2. [maladie] to contract, to catch. -3. [engagement] to contract; [assurance] to take out. -4. [moralement] to make tense OU nervous. -5. [habitude] to pick up, to acquire.

contraction [kɔ̃traksjɔ̃] *nf* contraction; [état de muscle] tenseness; avoir des ~s to have contractions.

contractuel, -elle [kɔ̃traktɥɛl] ◇ *adj* contractual. ◇ *nm, f* traffic warden *Br*.

contradiction [kɔ̃tradiksjɔ̃] *nf* contradiction.

contradictoire [kɔ̃tradiktwar] *adj* contradictory; débat ~ open debate.

contraignais, contraignions *etc* → **contraindre**.

contraignant, -e [kɔ̃trɛɲã, ãt] *adj* restricting.

contraindre [kɔ̃trɛ̃dr] [80] *vt*: ~ qqn à faire qqch to compel OU force sb to do sthg; être contraint de faire qqch to be compelled OU forced to do sthg.

◆ **se contraindre** *vp* -1. *sout* [se maîtriser] to contain o.s., to control o.s. -2. [s'obliger]: se ~ à faire qqch to make o.s. do sthg, to force o.s. to do sthg.

contraint, -e [kɔ̃trɛ̃, ɛ̃t] ◇ *pp* → **contraindre**. ◇ *adj* forced; ~ et forcé under duress.

◆ **contrainte** *nf* constraint; sans ~e freely.

contraire [kɔ̃trɛr] ◇ *nm*: le ~ the opposite; je n'ai jamais dit le ~ I have never denied it. ◇ *adj* opposite; ~ à [non conforme à] contrary to; [nuisible à] harmful to, damaging to.

◆ **au contraire** *loc adv* on the contrary.

◆ **au contraire de** *loc prép* unlike.

contrairement [kɔ̃trɛrmã]

◆ **contrairement à** *loc prép* contrary to.

contrariant, -e [kɔ̃trarjã, ãt] *adj* -1. [personne] contrary, perverse. -2. [événement] annoying, tiresome.

contrarier [kɔ̃trarje] [9] *vt* -1. [contrecarrer] to thwart, to frustrate. -2. [irriter] to annoy.

◆ **se contrarier** *vp* to contrast.

contrepoison

contrariété [kɔ̃trarjete] *nf* annoyance.

contraste [kɔ̃trast] *nm* contrast; **faire ~ avec** to contrast with.

contraster [kɔ̃traste] [3] *vt & vi* to contrast.

contrat [kɔ̃tra] *nm* contract, agreement; **remplir son ~** *fig* to keep OU fulfil one's promise; **~ collectif** collective agreement; **~ à durée déterminée/indéterminée** fixed-term/permanent contract; **~ reconductible** renewable agreement.

contravention [kɔ̃travɑ̃sjɔ̃] *nf* [amende] fine; **~ pour stationnement interdit** parking ticket; **dresser une ~ à qqn** to give sb a parking ticket.

contre [kɔ̃tr] ◇ *prép* -**1.** [juxtaposition, opposition] against. -**2.** [proportion, comparaison]: **élu à 15 voix ~ 9** elected by 15 votes to 9; **parier à 10 ~ 1** to bet 10 to 1. -**3.** [échange] (in exchange) for. ◇ *adv* -**1.** [juxtaposition]: **prends la rampe et appuie-toi ~** take hold of the rail and lean against it. -**2.** [opposition]: **vous êtes pour ou ~?** are you for or against? ◇ *nm* → **pour.**
◆ **par contre** *loc adv* on the other hand.

contre-attaque [kɔ̃tratak] (*pl* **contre-attaques**) *nf* counterattack.

contrebalancer [kɔ̃trəbalɑ̃se] [16] *vt* to counterbalance, to offset.
◆ **se contrebalancer** *vp*: **se ~ de** *fam* not to give a damn about.

contrebande [kɔ̃trəbɑ̃d] *nf* [activité] smuggling; [marchandises] contraband; **passer qqch en ~** to smuggle sthg.

contrebandier, -ière [kɔ̃trəbɑ̃dje, jɛr] *nm, f* smuggler.

contrebas [kɔ̃trəba]
◆ **en contrebas** *loc adv* (down) below.

contrebasse [kɛ̃trəbas] *nf* -**1.** [instrument] (double) bass. -**2.** [musicien] (double) bass player.

contrecarrer [kɔ̃trəkare] [3] *vt* to thwart, to frustrate.

contrecœur [kɔ̃trəkœr]
◆ **à contrecœur** *loc adv* grudgingly.

contrecoup [kɔ̃trəku] *nm* consequence.

contre-courant [kɔ̃trəkurɑ̃]
◆ **à contre-courant** *loc adv* against the current.

contredire [kɔ̃trədir] [103] *vt* to contradict.
◆ **se contredire** *vp* -**1.** (emploi réciproque) to contradict (each other). -**2.** (emploi réfléchi) to contradict o.s.

contredit, -e [kɔ̃trədi] *pp* → **contredire.**

contrée [kɔ̃tre] *nf* [pays] land; [région] region.

contre-écrou [kɔ̃trekru] (*pl* **contre-écrous**) *nm* lock-nut.

contre-espionnage [kɔ̃trɛspjɔnaʒ] *nm* counterespionage.

contre-exemple [kɔ̃trɛgzɑ̃pl] (*pl* **contre-exemples**) *nm* example to the contrary.

contre-expertise [kɔ̃trɛkspertiz] (*pl* **contre-expertises**) *nf* second (expert) opinion.

contrefaçon [kɔ̃trəfasɔ̃] *nf* [activité] counterfeiting; [produit] forgery.

contrefaire [kɔ̃trəfɛr] [109] *vt* -**1.** [signature, monnaie] to counterfeit, to forge. -**2.** [voix] to disguise.

contrefait, -e [kɔ̃trəfɛ, ɛt] *adj* -**1.** [frauduleux] forged. -**2.** *sout* [difforme] deformed.

contreficher [kɔ̃trəfiʃe] [3]
◆ **se contreficher** *vp*: **se ~ de** *fam* not to give a damn about.

contre-filet [kɔ̃trəfilɛ] (*pl* **contre-filets**) *nm* sirloin.

contrefort [kɔ̃trəfɔr] *nm* -**1.** [pilier] buttress. -**2.** [de chaussure] back.
◆ **contreforts** *nmpl* foothills.

contre-indication [kɔ̃trɛ̃dikasjɔ̃] (*pl* **contre-indications**) *nf* contraindication.

contre-interrogatoire [kɔ̃trɛ̃tɛrɔgatwar] (*pl* **contre-interrogatoires**) *nm* cross-examination.

contre-jour [kɔ̃trəʒur]
◆ **à contre-jour** *loc adv* against the light.

contremaître, -esse [kɔ̃trəmɛtr, ɛs] *nm, f* foreman (f forewoman).

contremarque [kɛ̃trəmark] *nf* [pour sortir d'un spectacle] pass-out ticket.

contre-offensive [kɔ̃trɔfɑ̃siv] (*pl* **contre-offensives**) *nf* counteroffensive.

contre-OPA [kɔ̃trɔpea] *nf inv* counterbid.

contre-ordre = **contrordre.**

contrepartie [kɔ̃trəparti] *nf* -**1.** [compensation] compensation. -**2.** [contraire] opposing view.
◆ **en contrepartie** *loc adv* in return.

contre-performance [kɔ̃trəperfɔrmɑ̃s] (*pl* **contre-performances**) *nf* disappointing performance.

contrepèterie [kɔ̃trəpɛtri] *nf* spoonerism.

contre-pied [kɔ̃trəpje] *nm*: **prendre le ~ de** to do the opposite of.

contreplaqué, contre-plaqué [kɔ̃trəplake] *nm* plywood.

contrepoids [kɔ̃trəpwa] *nm litt & fig* counterbalance, counterweight.

contrepoint [kɔ̃trəpwɛ̃] *nm* counterpoint.

contrepoison [kɔ̃trəpwazɔ̃] *nm* antidote.

contre-pouvoir [kɔ̃trəpuvwar] (*pl* contre-pouvoirs) *nm* counterbalance.

contre-publicité [kɔ̃trəpyblisite] (*pl* contre-publicités) *nf* -1. [mauvaise publicité] adverse OU bad publicity (*U*). -2. [publicité offensive] negative advertising (*U*).

contrer [kɔ̃tre] [3] *vt* -1. [s'opposer à] to counter. -2. CARTES to double.

contresens [kɔ̃trəsɑ̃s] *nm* -1. [erreur - de traduction] mistranslation; [- d'interprétation] misinterpretation. -2. [absurdité] nonsense (*U*).
◆ **à contresens** *loc adv* *litt* & *fig* the wrong way.

contresigner [kɔ̃trəsiɲe] [3] *vt* to countersign.

contretemps [kɔ̃trətɑ̃] *nm* hitch, mishap.
◆ **à contretemps** *loc adv* MUS out of time; *fig* at the wrong moment.

contrevenant, -e [kɔ̃trəvnɑ̃, ɑ̃t] *nm, f* offender.

contrevenir [kɔ̃trəvnir] [40] *vi*: ~ à to contravene, to infringe.

contrevenu [kɔ̃trəvny] *pp inv* → **contrevenir**.

contribuable [kɔ̃tribɥabl] *nmf* taxpayer.

contribuer [kɔ̃tribɥe] [7] *vi*: ~ à to contribute to OU towards.

contribution [kɔ̃tribysjɔ̃] *nf*: ~ (à) contribution (to); **mettre qqn à ~** to call on sb's services.
◆ **contributions** *nfpl* taxes; ~s directes/indirectes direct/indirect taxation.

contrit, -e [kɔ̃tri, it] *adj* contrite.

contrôle [kɔ̃trol] *nm* -1. [vérification - de déclaration] check, checking (*U*); [- de documents, billets] inspection; ~ **d'identité** identity check; ~ **de qualité** quality control; ~ **radar** AUTOM radar speed-trap; ~ **de routine** routine inspection. -2. [maîtrise, commande] control; **perdre le ~ de qqch** to lose control of sth; ~ **des naissances** birth control; ~ **des prix** price control. -3. [salle] control room. -4. SCOL test; ~ **continu** UNIV continuous assessment. -5. [direction] running, supervision.

contrôler [kɔ̃trole] [3] *vt* -1. [vérifier - documents, billets] to inspect; [- déclaration] to check; [- connaissances] to test. -2. [maîtriser, diriger] to control. -3. TECHNOL to monitor, to control. -4. [superviser] to supervise.
◆ **se contrôler** *vp* to control o.s.

contrôleur, -euse [kɔ̃trolœr, øz] *nm, f* [de train] ticket inspector; [d'autobus] (bus) conductor (*f* conductress); ~ **aérien** air traffic controller.

contrordre, contre-ordre (*pl* contre-ordres) [kɔ̃trɔrdr] *nm* countermand; **sauf ~** unless otherwise instructed.

controverse [kɔ̃trɔvɛrs] *nf* controversy.

controversé, -e [kɔ̃trɔvɛrse] *adj* [personne, décision] controversial.

contumace [kɔ̃tymas] *nf* JUR: **condamné par ~** sentenced in absentia.

contusion [kɔ̃tyzjɔ̃] *nf* bruise, contusion.

conurbation [kɔnyrbasjɔ̃] *nf* conurbation.

convaincant, -e [kɔ̃vēkɑ̃, ɑ̃t] *adj* convincing.

convaincre [kɔ̃vēkr] [114] *vt* -1. [persuader]: ~ **qqn (de qqch)** to convince sb (of sth); ~ **qqn (de faire qqch)** to persuade sb (to do sth). -2. JUR: ~ **qqn de** to find sb guilty of, to convict sb of.

convaincu, -e [kɔ̃vēky] ◇ *pp* → **convaincre**. ◇ *adj* [partisan] committed; **d'un ton ~, d'un air ~** with conviction.

convainquais, convainquions *etc* → **convaincre**.

convainquant [kɔ̃vēkɑ̃] *participe présent* → **convaincre**.

convalescence [kɔ̃valesɑ̃s] *nf* convalescence; **être en ~** to be convalescing OU recovering.

convalescent, -e [kɔ̃valesɑ̃, ɑ̃t] *adj* & *nm, f* convalescent.

convenable [kɔ̃vnabl] *adj* -1. [manières, comportement] polite; [tenue, personne] decent, respectable. -2. [approprié] suitable. -3. [acceptable] adequate, acceptable.

convenablement [kɔ̃vnabləmɑ̃] *adv* -1. [s'habiller, se tenir] properly. -2. [être payé] decently. -3. [travailler] adequately.

convenance [kɔ̃vnɑ̃s] *nf*: **à ma/votre ~** to my/your convenience.
◆ **convenances** *nfpl* proprieties.

convenir [kɔ̃vnir] [40] *vi* -1. [décider]: ~ **de qqch/de faire qqch** to agree on sth/to do sth. -2. [plaire]: ~ **à qqn** to suit sb, to be convenient for sb. -3. [être approprié]: ~ **à** OU **pour** to be suitable for; **il convient de ...** it is advisable to .... -4. *sout* [admettre]: ~ **de qqch** to admit to sth; ~ **que** to admit (that); **j'en conviens** *sout* I admit it.

convention [kɔ̃vɑ̃sjɔ̃] *nf* -1. [règle, assemblée] convention. -2. [accord] agreement; ~ **collective** collective agreement.
◆ **conventions** *nfpl*: **les ~s** convention (*sg*).
◆ **de convention** *loc adj* conventional.

conventionné, -e [kɔ̃vɑ̃sjɔne] *adj* ≃ National Health (*avant n*) *Br*.

conventionnel, -elle [kɔ̃vɑ̃sjɔnɛl] *adj* conventional.

convenu, -e [kɔ̃vny] ◇ *pp* → **convenir**. ◇ *adj* **-1.** [décidé]: **comme ~** as agreed. **-2.** *péj* [stéréotypé] conventional.

convergent, -e [kɔ̃vɛrʒɑ̃, ɑ̃t] *adj* convergent.

converger [kɔ̃vɛrʒe] [17] *vi:* **~ (vers)** to converge (on).

conversation [kɔ̃vɛrsasjɔ̃] *nf* conversation; **détourner la ~** to change the subject; **être en grande ~ avec** to be deep in conversation with.

converser [kɔ̃vɛrse] [3] *vi sout:* **~ (avec)** to converse (with).

conversion [kɔ̃vɛrsjɔ̃] *nf* **-1.** [gén]: **~ (à/en)** conversion (to/into). **-2.** SKI kick turn.

converti, -e [kɔ̃vɛrti] *nm, f:* **prêcher un ~** *fig* to preach to the converted.

convertible [kɔ̃vɛrtibl] ◇ *nm* [canapé-lit] sofa-bed. ◇ *adj* convertible.

convertir [kɔ̃vɛrtir] [32] *vt:* **~ qqn (à)** to convert sb (to); **~ qqch (en)** to convert sthg (into).

◆ **se convertir** *vp:* **se ~ (à)** to be converted (to).

convexe [kɔ̃vɛks] *adj* convex.

conviction [kɔ̃viksjɔ̃] *nf* conviction; **avoir la ~ que** to be convinced (that).

conviendrai, conviendrons *etc* → **convenir**.

convier [kɔ̃vje] [9] *vt:* **~ qqn à** to invite sb to.

convive [kɔ̃viv] *nmf* guest (*at a meal*).

convivial, -e, -iaux [kɔ̃vivjal, jo] *adj* **-1.** [réunion] convivial. **-2.** INFORM user-friendly.

convocation [kɔ̃vɔkasjɔ̃] *nf* [avis écrit] summons (*sg*), notification to attend.

convoi [kɔ̃vwa] *nm* **-1.** [de véhicules] convoy; **~ exceptionnel** wide load. **-2.** [train] train.

convoiter [kɔ̃vwate] [3] *vt* to covet.

convoitise [kɔ̃vwatiz] *nf* covetousness.

convoler [kɔ̃vɔle] [3] → **noces**.

convoquer [kɔ̃vɔke] [3] *vt* **-1.** [assemblée] to convene. **-2.** [pour un entretien] to invite. **-3.** [subalterne, témoin] to summon. **-4.** [à un examen]: **~ qqn** to ask sb to attend.

convoyer [kɔ̃vwaje] [13] *vt* to escort.

convoyeur, -euse [kɔ̃vwajœr, øz] ◇ *adj* escort (*avant n*). ◇ *nm, f* escort; **~ de fonds** security guard.

convulser [kɔ̃vylse] [3] *vt* to convulse.

◆ **se convulser** *vp* to convulse.

convulsif, -ive [kɔ̃vylsif, iv] *adj* convulsive.

convulsion [kɔ̃vylsjɔ̃] *nf* convulsion.

cool [kul] *adj inv fam* [décontracté] laid-back, cool.

coopérant [kɔɔperɑ̃] *nm* **-1.** MIL *person engaged in voluntary work abroad as an alternative to military service*. **-2.** ÉCON *foreign expert working in developing country*.

coopératif, -ive [kɔɔperatif, iv] *adj* cooperative.

◆ **coopérative** *nf* [groupement] cooperative; **coopérative de consommation** consumers' cooperative.

coopération [kɔɔperasjɔ̃] *nf* **-1.** [collaboration] cooperation; **en ~ avec qqn** in collaboration with sb. **-2.** [aide]: **la ~** ≃ overseas development.

coopérer [kɔɔpere] [18] *vi:* **~ (à)** to cooperate (in).

cooptation [kɔɔptasjɔ̃] *nf* co-opting.

coordinateur, -trice [kɔɔrdinatœr, tris] ◇ *adj* coordinating. ◇ *nm, f* coordinator.

coordination [kɔɔrdinasjɔ̃] *nf* coordination; *voir aussi* **conjonction**.

coordonnée [kɔɔrdɔne] *nf* **-1.** LING coordinate clause. **-2.** MATHS coordinate.

◆ **coordonnées** *nfpl* **-1.** GÉOGR coordinates. **-2.** [adresse] address and phone number, details.

coordonner [kɔɔrdɔne] [3] *vt* to coordinate.

copain, -ine [kɔpɛ̃, in] ◇ *adj* friendly, matey; **être très ~s** to be great pals. ◇ *nm, f* friend, mate.

copeau, -x [kɔpo] *nm* [de bois] **(wood)** shaving.

Copenhague [kɔpenag] *n* Copenhagen.

copie [kɔpi] *nf* **-1.** [double, reproduction] copy; **~ (certifiée) conforme** certified copy. **-2.** [SCOL - de devoir] fair copy; [- d'examen] paper, script.

copier [kɔpje] [9] ◇ *vt* to copy. ◇ *vi:* **~ sur qqn** to copy from sb.

copieur, -ieuse [kɔpjœr, jøz] *nm, f* [étudiant] copier.

◆ **copieur** *nm* [photocopieur] copier, photocopier.

copieusement [kɔpjøzmɑ̃] *adv* copiously.

copieux, -ieuse [kɔpjø, jøz] *adj* copious.

copilote [kɔpilɔt] *nmf* copilot.

copine → **copain**.

coprocesseur [kɔprɔsɛsœr] *nm:* **~ mathématique** INFORM maths coprocessor.

coproducteur, -trice [kɔprɔdyktœr, tris] *nm, f* [pour spectacle] coproducer.

coproduction [kɔprɔdyksjɔ̃] *nf* coproduction; **en ~** coproduced.

copropriétaire [kɔprɔprijetɛr] *nmf* co-owner, joint owner.

copropriété [kɔprɔprijete] *nf* co-ownership, joint ownership.

copuler [kɔpyle] [3] *vi* to copulate.

copyright [kɔpirajt] *nm* copyright.

coq [kɔk] *nm* cock, cockerel; ~ **de bruyère** grouse; **le ~ gaulois** the French cockerel; **fier comme un ~** *fig* as proud as a peacock; **être comme un ~ en pâte** *fig* to be in clover.

LE COQ GAULOIS:
The cockerel is the symbol of France. Its cry, 'cocorico!', is sometimes used humorously to express national pride: 'trois médailles d'or pour la France - cocorico!'

---

coq-à-l'âne [kɔkalan] *nm inv*: **sauter** OU **passer du coq à l'âne** to jump from one subject to another.

coque [kɔk] *nf* **-1.** [de mollusque, œuf, noix] shell. **-2.** [de navire] hull.

coquelet [kɔklɛ] *nm* cockerel.

coquelicot [kɔkliko] *nm* poppy.

coqueluche [kɔklyʃ] *nf* whooping cough; **être la ~ de** *fig* to be the idol OU darling of.

coquet, -ette [kɔkɛ, ɛt] *adj* **-1.** [vêtements] smart, stylish; [ville, jeune fille] pretty. **-2.** (*avant n*) *hum* [important]: **la ~te somme de 100 livres** the tidy sum of £100.
◆ **coquette** *nf* flirt.

coquetier [kɔktje] *nm* eggcup.

coquetterie [kɔkɛtri] *nf* **-1.** [désir de plaire] coquettishness. **-2.** [élégance] smartness, stylishness.

coquillage [kɔkijaʒ] *nm* **-1.** [mollusque] shellfish. **-2.** [coquille] shell.

coquille [kɔkij] *nf* **-1.** [de mollusque, noix, œuf] shell; ~ **de noix** [embarcation] cockleshell; ~ **Saint-Jacques** scallop; **rentrer dans sa ~** *fig* to go back into one's shell. **-2.** TYPO misprint.

coquillettes [kɔkijɛt] *nfpl* pasta shells.

coquin, -e [kɔkɛ̃, in] ◇ *adj* [sous-vêtement] sexy, naughty; [regard, histoire] saucy. ◇ *nm, f* rascal.

cor [kɔr] *nm* **-1.** [instrument] horn; ~ **de chasse** hunting horn. **-2.** [au pied] corn.
◆ **à cor et à cri** *loc adv*: **réclamer qqch à ~ et à cri** to clamour for sthg.

corail, -aux [kɔraj, o] *nm* **-1.** [gén] coral. **-2.** RAIL: **train ~** ≃ express train.
◆ **corail** *adj inv* coral (pink).

Coran [kɔrɑ̃] *nm*: **le ~** the Koran.

coranique [kɔranik] *adj* Koranic.

corbeau [kɔrbo] *nm* **-1.** [oiseau] crow. **-2.** [délateur] writer of poison-pen letters.

corbeille [kɔrbɛj] *nf* **-1.** [panier] basket; ~ **à papier** waste paper basket. **-2.** THÉÂTRE (dress) circle. **-3.** [de Bourse] stockbrokers' enclosure (*at Paris Stock Exchange*).

corbillard [kɔrbijar] *nm* hearse.

cordage [kɔrdaʒ] *nm* **-1.** [de bateau] rigging (*U*). **-2.** [de raquette] strings (*pl*).

corde [kɔrd] *nf* **-1.** [filin] rope; ~ **à linge** washing OU clothes line; ~ **à sauter** skipping rope. **-2.** [d'instrument, arc] string; **avoir plus d'une ~ à son arc** *fig* to have more than one string to one's bow. **-3.** ANAT: ~ **vocale** vocal cord. **-4.** HIPPISME rails (*pl*); ATHLÉTISME inside (lane). **-5.** *loc*: **usé jusqu'à la ~** [vêtement] threadbare; [histoire] well-worn, hackneyed; **faire vibrer la ~ sensible** to strike the right chord.
◆ **cordes** *nfpl* **-1.** MUS strings. **-2.** BOXE: **les ~s** the ropes. **-3.** *loc*: **être dans les ~s de qqn** to be (in) sb's line; **il tombe** OU **pleut des ~s** it's raining cats and dogs.

cordeau [kɔrdo] *nm* [de jardinier] line; **tracé au ~** *fig* [route] dead straight.

cordée [kɔrde] *nf* ALPINISME roped party (*of mountaineers*).

cordelette [kɔrdəlɛt] *nf* string.

cordial, -e, -iaux [kɔrdjal, jo] *adj* warm, cordial.
◆ **cordial, -aux** *nm vieilli* tonic, pick-me-up.

cordialement [kɔrdjalmɑ̃] *adv* warmly, cordially.

cordialité [kɔrdjalite] *nf* warmth.

cordon [kɔrdɔ̃] *nm* string, cord; ~ **ombilical** umbilical cord; ~ **de police** police cordon.

cordon-bleu [kɔrdɔ̃blø] (*pl* **cordons-bleus**) *nm* cordon bleu cook.

cordonnerie [kɔrdɔnri] *nf* **-1.** [magasin] shoe repairer's, cobbler's. **-2.** [activité, commerce] shoe repairing.

cordonnier, -ière [kɔrdɔnje, jɛr] *nm, f* shoe repairer, cobbler.

Cordoue [kɔrdu] *n* Cordoba.

Corée [kɔre] *nf* Korea; **la ~ du Nord/du Sud** North/South Korea.

coréen, -enne [kɔreɛ̃, ɛn] *adj* Korean.
◆ **Coréen, -enne** *nm, f* Korean.

coreligionnaire [kɔreliʒɔnɛr] *nmf* fellow Jew/Christian *etc*.

coriace [kɔrjas] *adj litt & fig* tough.

coriandre [kɔrjɑ̃dr] *nf* coriander.

cormoran [kɔrmɔrɑ̃] *nm* cormorant.

corne [kɔrn] *nf* **-1.** [gén] horn; [de cerf] antler; ~ **d'abondance** *fig* horn of plenty; ~ **de brume** foghorn. **-2.** [callosité] hard skin (*U*), callus.

cornée [kɔrne] *nf* cornea.

corneille [kɔrnɛj] *nf* crow.

cornélien, -ienne [kɔrneljɛ̃, jɛn] *adj involving the conflict between love and duty.*

cornemuse [kɔrnəmyz] *nf* bagpipes (*pl*).

corner¹ [kɔrne] [3] ◇ *vi* [sirène] to blare (out). ◇ *vt* [page] to turn down the corner of.

corner² [kɔrnɛr] *nm* FOOTBALL corner (kick).

cornet [kɔrnɛ] *nm* **-1.** [d'aliment] cornet, cone. **-2.** [de jeu] (dice) shaker.

corniaud, corniot [kɔrnjo] *nm* **-1.** [chien] mongrel. **-2.** *fam* [imbécile] twit.

corniche [kɔrniʃ] *nf* **-1.** [route] cliff road. **-2.** [moulure] cornice.

cornichon [kɔrniʃɔ̃] *nm* **-1.** [condiment] gherkin. **-2.** *fam* [imbécile] twit.

corniot = **corniaud**.

Cornouailles [kɔrnwaj] *nf*: **la** ~ Cornwall.

corollaire [kɔrɔlɛr] *nm* corollary.

corolle [kɔrɔl] *nf* corolla.

coron [kɔrɔ̃] *nm* [village] mining village.

coronaire [kɔrɔnɛr] → **artère**.

corporation [kɔrpɔrasjɔ̃] *nf* corporate body.

corporel, -elle [kɔrpɔrɛl] *adj* **-1.** [physique - besoin] bodily; [- châtiment] corporal. **-2.** JUR tangible.

corps [kɔr] *nm* **-1.** [gén] body; **être au** ~ à ~ to fight hand-to-hand; **le** ~ **du délit** JUR corpus delicti; ~ **étranger** foreign body; ~ **gras** fat. **-2.** [groupe]: ~ **d'armée** (army) corps; ~ **diplomatique** diplomatic corps; **le** ~ **électoral** the electorate; ~ **enseignant** [profession] teaching profession; [d'école] teaching staff; ~ **expéditionnaire** task force; **le** ~ **législatif** the legislative body; **le** ~ **médical** the medical profession. **-3.** *loc*: **à mon** ~ **défendant** against my will; **faire** ~ **avec** to form (an integral) part of; **se dévouer** ~ **et âme à** to commit o.s. body and soul to; **se jeter** OU **se lancer à** ~ **perdu dans qqch** to throw o.s. (headlong) into sthg; **prendre** ~ to take shape; **sombrer** ~ **et biens** to go down with all hands.

corpulent, -e [kɔrpylɑ̃, ɑ̃t] *adj* corpulent, stout.

corpus [kɔrpys] *nm* corpus.

corpuscule [kɔrpyskyl] *nm* corpuscle.

correct, -e [kɔrɛkt] *adj* **-1.** [exact] correct, right. **-2.** [honnête] correct, proper. **-3.** [acceptable] decent; [travail] fair.

correctement [kɔrɛktəmɑ̃] *adv* **-1.** [sans faute] accurately. **-2.** [décemment] properly.

correcteur, -trice [kɔrɛktœr, tris] ◇ *adj* corrective. ◇ *nm, f* **-1.** [d'examen] examiner, marker *Br*, grader *Am*. **-2.** TYPO proofreader.

correctif, -ive [kɔrɛktif, iv] *adj* corrective.

◆ **correctif** *nm* rider; **apporter un** ~ **à qqch** to qualify sthg.

correction [kɔrɛksjɔ̃] *nf* **-1.** [d'erreur] correction. **-2.** [punition] punishment; **donner une** ~ **à qqn** to give sb a good hiding. **-3.** [modification] correction. **-4.** TYPO proofreading. **-5.** [notation] marking. **-6.** [qualité] correctness. **-7.** [bienséance] propriety.

correctionnel, -elle [kɔrɛksjɔnɛl] *adj* JUR: **tribunal** ~ ≃ magistrate's court; **peine** ~**le** *sentence of up to five years' imprisonment.*

◆ **correctionnelle** *nf* JUR ≃ magistrate's court; **passer en** ~**le** to appear before the magistrate.

corrélation [kɔrelasjɔ̃] *nf* correlation.

correspondance [kɔrɛspɔ̃dɑ̃s] *nf* **-1.** [gén] correspondence; **cours par** ~ correspondence course. **-2.** TRANSPORT connection; **assurer la** ~ **avec** to connect with.

correspondant, -e [kɔrɛspɔ̃dɑ̃, ɑ̃t] ◇ *adj* corresponding. ◇ *nm, f* **-1.** [par lettres] penfriend, correspondent. **-2.** [par téléphone]: **je vous passe votre** ~ I'll put you through. **-3.** PRESSE correspondent; **de notre** ~ **à New York** from our New York correspondent; ~ **de guerre/de presse** war/newspaper correspondent.

correspondre [kɔrɛspɔ̃dr] [75] *vi* **-1.** [être conforme]: ~ **à** to correspond to. **-2.** [communiquer] to communicate. **-3.** [par lettres]: ~ **avec** to correspond with.

◆ **se correspondre** *vp* [s'accorder] to correspond.

correspondu, -e [kɔrɛspɔ̃dy] *pp* → **correspondre**.

corrida [kɔrida] *nf* bullfight.

corridor [kɔridɔr] *nm* corridor.

corrigé [kɔriʒe] *nm* correct version.

corriger [kɔriʒe] [17] *vt* **-1.** TYPO to correct, to proofread. **-2.** [noter] to mark. **-3.** [modifier] to correct. **-4.** [guérir]: ~ **qqn de** to cure sb of. **-5.** [punir] to give sb a good hiding.

◆ **se corriger** *vp* **-1.** [d'un défaut]: **se** ~ **de** to cure o.s. of. **-2.** [devenir raisonnable] to mend one's ways.

corroborer [kɔrɔbɔre] [3] *vt* to corroborate.

corroder [kɔrode] [3] *vt* [ronger] to corrode; *fig* to erode.

corrompre [kɔrɔ̃pr] [78] *vt* **-1.** [soudoyer] to bribe. **-2.** [dépraver] to corrupt. **-3.** *fig* [gâter] to spoil.

corrompu, -e [kɔrɔ̃py] ◇ *pp* → **corrompre.**
◇ *adj* [fonctionnaire, âme] corrupt.

corrosif, -ive [kɔrozif, iv] *adj* **-1.** [acide] corrosive. **-2.** *fig* [ironie] biting.
◆ **corrosif** *nm* corrosive.

corrosion [kɔrozjɔ̃] *nf* corrosion.

corruption [kɔrypsjɔ̃] *nf* **-1.** [subornation] bribery; ~ **de fonctionnaire** bribery of a public official. **-2.** [dépravation] corruption. **-3.** [décomposition] decomposition. **-4.** [altération] debasing.

corsage [kɔrsaʒ] *nm* **-1.** [chemisier] blouse. **-2.** [de robe] bodice.

corsaire [kɔrsɛr] *nm* **-1.** [navire, marin] corsair, privateer. **-2.** [pantalon] pedal-pushers (*pl*).

corse [kɔrs] ◇ *adj* Corsican. ◇ *nm* [langue] Corsican. ◇ *nmf* Corsican.

Corse [kɔrs] *nf*: **la** ~ Corsica; **en** ~ in Corsica.

corsé, -e [kɔrse] *adj* [café] strong; [vin] full-bodied; [plat, histoire] spicy.

corser [kɔrse] [3] *vt* **-1.** [plat, sauce] to spice up. **-2.** [histoire] to liven up. **-3.** [vin] to strengthen.
◆ **se corser** *vp* [se compliquer] to get complicated; **ça se corse** things are getting serious.

corset [kɔrsɛ] *nm* corset; ~ **orthopédique** MÉD surgical corset.

cortège [kɔrtɛʒ] *nm* procession; ~ **funèbre** funeral procession, cortege.

cortisone [kɔrtizɔn] *nf* cortisone.

corvée [kɔrve] *nf* **-1.** MIL fatigue (duty). **-2.** [activité pénible] chore.

cosignataire [kɔsiɲatɛr] *nmf* JUR cosignatory.

cosinus [kɔsinys] *nm* cosine.

cosmétique [kɔsmetik] *nm & adj* cosmetic.

cosmique [kɔsmik] *adj* cosmic.

cosmonaute [kɔsmɔnot] *nmf* cosmonaut.

cosmopolite [kɔsmɔpɔlit] *adj* cosmopolitan.

cosmos [kɔsmos] *nm* **-1.** [univers] cosmos. **-2.** [espace] outer space.

cosse [kɔs] *nf* **-1.** [de légume] pod. **-2.** *fam vieilli* [paresse]: **avoir la** ~ to feel lazy.

cossu, -e [kɔsy] *adj* **-1.** [personne] wealthy, moneyed. **-2.** [maison] opulent.

Costa Rica [kɔstarika] *nm*: **le** ~ Costa Rica; **au** ~ in Costa Rica.

costaricien, -ienne [kɔstarisjɛ̃, jɛn] *adj* Costa Rican.
◆ **Costaricien, -ienne** *nm, f* Costa Rican.

costaud (*f* **costaud** OU **-e**) [kɔsto, od] *adj* sturdily built.
◆ **costaud** *nm* strapping man.

costume [kɔstym] *nm* **-1.** [folklorique, de théâtre] costume. **-2.** [vêtement d'homme] suit; ~ **trois-pièces** three-piece suit.

costumé, -e [kɔstyme] *adj* fancy-dress (*avant n*).

costumier, -ière [kɔstymje, jɛr] *nm, f* THÉÂTRE wardrobe master (*f* mistress).

cotation [kɔtasjɔ̃] *nf* FIN quotation; ~ **en Bourse** quoting on the stock exchange.

cote [kɔt] *nf* **-1.** [marque de classement] classification mark; [marque numérale] serial number. **-2.** FIN quotation. **-3.** [de valeur] valuation. **-4.** [de cheval] odds (*pl*). **-5.** [popularité] rating; **avoir la** ~ **(auprès de qqn)** *fam* to be popular (with sb). **-6.** [niveau] level; ~ **d'alerte** [de cours d'eau] danger level; *fig* crisis point.

coté, -e [kɔte] *adj* [estimé] popular; **être** ~ to be well thought of; **être bien/mal** ~ to be highly/poorly rated.

côte [kot] *nf* **-1.** [ANAT, BOT & de bœuf] rib; [de porc, mouton, agneau] chop; ~ **à** ~ side by side. **-2.** [pente] hill. **-3.** [littoral] coast; **la Côte d'Azur** the French Riviera. **-4.** [tissu]: **velours à** ~**s** corduroy.

côté [kote] *nm* **-1.** [gén] side; **être couché sur le** ~ to be lying on one's side; **être aux** ~**s de qqn** *fig* to be by sb's side; **d'un** ~ ..., **de l'autre** ~ ... on the one hand ..., on the other hand ...; **et** ~ **finances, ça va?** *fam* how are things moneywise? **-2.** [endroit, direction] direction, way; **de quel** ~ **est-il parti?** which way did he go?; **de l'autre** ~ **de** on the other side of; **de tous** ~**s** from all directions; **du** ~ **de** [près de] near; [direction] towards; [provenance] from.
◆ **à côté** *loc adv* **-1.** [lieu - gén] nearby; [- dans la maison adjacente] next door. **-2.** [cible]: **tirer à** ~ to shoot wide (of the target).
◆ **à côté de** *loc prép* **-1.** [proximité] beside, next to. **-2.** [en comparaison avec] beside, compared to. **-3.** [en dehors de]: **être à** ~ **du sujet** to be off the point.
◆ **de côté** *loc adv* **-1.** [se placer, marcher] sideways. **-2.** [en réserve] aside; **mettre/laisser qqch de** ~ to put/leave sthg aside.

coteau [kɔto] *nm* **-1.** [colline] hill. **-2.** [versant] slope.

Côte-d'Ivoire [kotdivwar] *nf*: **la** ~ the Ivory Coast.

côtelé, -e [kotle] *adj* ribbed; **velours** ~ corduroy.

côtelette [kotlɛt] *nf* [de porc, mouton, d'agneau] chop; [de veau] cutlet.

coter [kɔte] [3] *vt* **-1.** [marquer, noter] to mark. **-2.** FIN to quote. **-3.** [carte, plan] to mark spot heights on.

coterie [kɔtri] *nf péj & vieilli* set, clique.

côtier, -ière [kotje, jɛr] *adj* coastal.

cotisation [kɔtizasjɔ̃] *nf* [à club, parti] subscription; [à la Sécurité sociale] contribution.

cotiser [kɔtize] [3] *vi* [à un club, un parti] to subscribe; [à la Sécurité sociale] to contribute.
◆ **se cotiser** *vp* to club together.

coton [kɔtɔ̃] *nm* cotton; ~ **(hydrophile)** cotton wool; **filer un mauvais** ~ *fig* to be in a bad way.

cotonnade [kɔtɔnad] *nf* cotton fabric.

Coton-Tige® [kɔtɔ̃tiʒ] (*pl* **Coton-Tiges**) *nm* cotton bud.

côtoyer [kotwaje] [13] *vt* **-1.** [longer] to run alongside. **-2.** *fig* [frôler] to verge on. **-3.** *fig* [fréquenter] to mix with.

cotte [kɔt] *nf* HIST tunic; ~ **de mailles** coat of mail.

cou [ku] *nm* [de personne, bouteille] neck; **se jeter au ~ de qqn, sauter au ~ de qqn** to throw one's arms around sb's neck; **jusqu'au ~** *fig* up to one's eyes; **se pendre au ~ de qqn** to hang round sb's neck.

couac [kwak] *nm* false OU wrong note.

couard, -e [kwar, ard] *sout* ◇ *adj* cowardly. ◇ *nm, f* coward.

couchage [kuʃaʒ] *nm* sleeping arrangements (*pl*); → **sac.**

couchant [kuʃɑ̃] ◇ *adj* → **soleil.** ◇ *nm* west.

couche [kuʃ] *nf* **-1.** [de peinture, de vernis] coat, layer; [de poussière] film, layer. **-2.** [épaisseur] layer; ~ **d'ozone** ozone layer; **en avoir** OU **en tenir une** ~ *fam* to be (as) thick as two short planks. **-3.** [de bébé] nappy *Br,* diaper *Am.* **-4.** [classe sociale] stratum.
◆ **couches** *nfpl* childbirth (*U*), labour (*U*).
◆ **fausse couche** *nf* miscarriage.

couché, -e [kuʃe] *adj*: **être ~** [étendu] to be lying down; [au lit] to be in bed.

couche-culotte [kuʃkylɔt] (*pl* **couches-culottes**) *nf* disposable nappy *Br* OU diaper *Am.*

coucher¹ [kuʃe] [3] ◇ *vt* **-1.** [enfant] to put to bed. **-2.** [objet, blessé] to lay down. **-3.** *sout* [inscrire] to mention. ◇ *vi* **-1.** [dormir] to sleep. **-2.** [passer la nuit] to spend the night; **un nom à ~ dehors** *fam* an imposs-

ible name. **-3.** *fam* [avoir des rapports sexuels]: ~ **avec** to sleep with.
◆ **se coucher** *vp* **-1.** [s'allonger] to lie down. **-2.** [se mettre au lit] to go to bed. **-3.** [se courber] to bend over. **-4.** [astre] to set.

coucher² [kuʃe] *nm* [d'astre] setting; **au ~ du soleil** at sunset.

couchette [kuʃet] *nf* **-1.** [de train] couchette. **-2.** [de navire] berth.

coucheur [kuʃœr] *nm*: **mauvais ~** *fig* awkward customer.

couci-couça [kusikusa] *adv fam* so-so.

coucou [kuku] ◇ *nm* **-1.** [oiseau] cuckoo. **-2.** [pendule] cuckoo clock. **-3.** *péj* [avion] crate. ◇ *interj* peekaboo!

coude [kud] *nm* **-1.** [de personne, de vêtement] elbow; **être au ~ à ~** to be shoulder to shoulder; **jouer des ~s** to elbow people aside; **se serrer les ~s** to stick together. **-2.** [courbe] bend.

coudée [kude] *nf*: **avoir les ~s franches** to have room to move OU elbow room.

cou-de-pied [kudpje] (*pl* **cous-de-pied**) *nm* instep.

coudoyer [kudwaje] [13] *vt* to rub shoulders with.

coudre [kudr] [86] ◇ *vt* **-1.** [bouton] to sew on. **-2.** MÉD to sew up, to stitch. ◇ *vi* to sew.

coudrier [kudrije] *nm* hazel tree.

couenne [kwan] *nf* [de lard] rind.

couette [kwɛt] *nf* **-1.** [édredon] duvet. **-2.** [coiffure] bunches (*pl*).

couffin [kufɛ̃] *nm* **-1.** [berceau] Moses basket. **-2.** [cabas] basket.

couille [kuj] *nf* (*gén pl*) *vulg* ball.

couiner [kwine] [3] *vi* **-1.** [animal] to squeal. **-2.** [pleurnicher] to whine.

coulant, -e [kulɑ̃, ɑ̃t] *adj* **-1.** [fluide] runny. **-2.** [style] fluent. **-3.** *fam* [indulgent] easygoing, laid-back.

coulée [kule] *nf* **-1.** [de matière liquide]: ~ **de lave** lava flow; ~ **de boue** mudslide. **-2.** [de métal] casting.

couler [kule] [3] ◇ *vi* **-1.** [liquide] to flow. **-2.** [beurre, fromage, nez] to run. **-3.** [robinet] to drip; [tonneau, stylo] to leak. **-4.** [temps] to slip by. **-5.** [navire, entreprise] to sink. ◇ *vt* **-1.** [navire] to sink. **-2.** [métal, bronze] to cast. **-3.** *fam* [personne, entreprise] to ruin. **-4. faire ~ un bain** [remplir] to run a bath.
◆ **se couler** *vp* [se glisser] to slip; **se la ~ douce** *fam* to have an easy life.

couleur [kulœr] ◇ *nf* **-1.** [teinte, caractère] colour; **télévision en ~s** colour television; **haut en ~** [personne] high-coloured; [quartier, récit] colourful. **-2.** [linge] coloureds (*pl*). **-3.** CARTES suit. **-4.** [d'opinion] shade. **-5.** *loc*: **annoncer la ~** to state one's intentions; **en faire voir de toutes les ~s à qqn** to give sb a hard time; **sous ~ de qqch/de faire qqch** under the guise of sthg/of doing sthg. ◇ *adj inv* [télévision, pellicule] colour (*avant n*).

couleuvre [kulœvr] *nf* grass snake; **avaler des ~s** *fam fig* [être impassible] to swallow insults.

coulis [kuli] *nm* CULIN puree.

coulissant, -e [kulisɑ̃, ɑ̃t] *adj* sliding (*avant n*).

coulisse [kulis] *nf* **-1.** [glissière]: **fenêtre/ porte à ~** sliding window/door. **-2.** COUTURE hem.

◆ **coulisses** *nfpl* THÉÂTRE wings; **dans les ~s** *fig* behind the scenes.

coulisser [kulise] [3] *vi* to slide.

couloir [kulwar] *nm* **-1.** [corridor] corridor. **-2.** GÉOGR gully. **-3.** SPORT & TRANSPORT lane; **~ aérien** air lane; **~ d'autobus** bus lane.

coulommiers [kulɔmje] *nm* soft cheese made from cow's milk.

coulpe [kulp] *nf*: **battre sa ~** to repent one's sins openly.

coup [ku] *nm* **-1.** [choc - physique, moral] blow; **donner un ~ de coude à qqn** to nudge sb; **rouer qqn de ~s** to give sb a beating; **c'est un ~ bas!** *fig* that's below the belt!; **un ~ de couteau** stab (*with a knife*); **un ~ dur** *fig* a heavy blow; **donner un ~ de fouet à qqn** *fig* to give sb a shot in the arm; **~ de grâce** *litt* & *fig* coup de grâce, death-blow; **~ de pied** kick; **~ de poing** punch. **-2.** [action nuisible] trick; **faire un sale ~ à qqn** to play a dirty trick on sb; **~ fourré** stab in the back. **-3.** [SPORT - au tennis] stroke; [- en boxe] blow, punch; [- au football] kick; **~ franc** free kick. **-4.** [d'éponge, de chiffon] wipe; **un ~ de crayon** a pencil stroke; **donner un ~ de balai** to give the floor a sweep. **-5.** [bruit] noise; **~ de feu** shot, gunshot; **~ de sonnette** ring; **~ de tonnerre** thunderclap. **-6.** [action spectaculaire]: **~ d'éclat** feat; **~ d'état** coup (d'état); **~ de théâtre** *fig* dramatic turn of events. **-7.** *fam* [fois] time. **-8.** *loc*: **boire un ~** to have a drink; **donner un ~ de main à qqn** to give sb a helping hand; **être dans le ~** [être à la mode] to be up to date; [être au courant] to be in the know; **faire les quatre cents ~s** to lead a wild life; **frapper un grand ~** to strike a decisive blow; **jeter un ~ d'œil à** to glance at; **marquer le ~** to mark the occasion; **en prendre un ~** to take a knock; **tenir le ~** to hold out; **tenter**

le **~** to have a go; **valoir le ~** to be well worth it.

◆ **coup de fil** *nm* phone call.

◆ **coup de foudre** *nm* love at first sight.

◆ **coup du lapin** *nm* AUTOM whiplash (*U*).

◆ **coup de soleil** *nm* sunburn (*U*).

◆ **coup de téléphone** *nm* telephone OU phone call; **donner** OU **passer un ~ de téléphone à qqn** to telephone OU phone sb.

◆ **coup de vent** *nm* gust of wind; **partir en ~ de vent** to rush off.

◆ **après coup** *loc adv* afterwards.

◆ **du coup** *loc adv* as a result.

◆ **coup sur coup** *loc adv* one after the other.

◆ **du premier coup** *loc adv* first time, at the first attempt.

◆ **tout à coup** *loc adv* suddenly.

◆ **à coup sûr** *loc adv* definitely.

◆ **sous le coup de** *loc prép* **-1.** [sous l'action de]: **tomber sous le ~ de la loi** to be a statutory offence. **-2.** [sous l'effet de] in the grip of.

coupable [kupabl] ◇ *adj* **-1.** [personne, pensée] guilty; **plaider ~/non ~** JUR to plead guilty/not guilty. **-2.** [action, dessein] culpable, reprehensible; [négligence, oubli] sinful. ◇ *nmf* guilty person OU party.

coupant, -e [kupɑ̃, ɑ̃t] *adj* **-1.** [tranchant] cutting. **-2.** *fig* [sec] sharp.

coupe [kup] *nf* **-1.** [verre] glass; **~ de champagne** glass of champagne. **-2.** [à fruits] dish. **-3.** SPORT cup; **Coupe du monde** World Cup. **-4.** [d'arbres] felling. **-5.** [de vêtement, aux cartes] cut. **-6.** **~ (de cheveux)** haircut. **-7.** [plan, surface] (cross) section. **-8.** [de phrase] break. **-9.** [réduction] cut, cutback.

coupé, -e [kupe] *adj*: **bien/mal ~** well/ badly cut.

◆ **coupé** *nm* coupé.

coupe-circuit [kupsirkɥi] (*pl inv* OU **coupe-circuits**) *nm* circuit breaker.

coupe-faim [kupfɛ̃] *nm inv* appetite suppressant.

coupe-feu [kupfø] ◇ *nm inv* firebreak. ◇ *adj inv* fire (*avant n*).

coupe-gorge [kupgɔrʒ] *nm inv* dangerous place.

coupelle [kupɛl] *nf* dish.

coupe-ongles [kupɔ̃gl] *nm inv* nail clippers.

coupe-papier [kuppapje] (*pl inv* OU **coupe-papiers**) *nm* paper knife.

couper [kupe] [3] ◇ *vt* **-1.** [matériau, cheveux, blé] to cut. **-2.** [découper] to cut out. **-3.** [interrompre, trancher] to cut off. **-4.** [traverser] to cut across. **-5.** [pain, au tennis] to slice; [rôti] to **carve**. **-6.** [mélanger] to **dilute**. **-7.** [CARTES - avec atout] to **trump**; [- paquet] to **cut**. **-8.** [envie, appétit] to **take away**. ◇ *vi* **-1.** [gén] to **cut**. **-2.** [échapper]: ~ **à** to get out of. **-3.** *loc*: ~ **court à qqch** to cut sthg short.

◆ **se couper** *vp* **-1.** [se blesser] to cut o.s. **-2.** [se croiser] to **cross**. **-3.** [s'isoler]: **se ~ de** to cut o.s. off from.

couperet [kuprɛ] *nm* **-1.** [de boucher] **cleaver**. **-2.** [de guillotine] **blade**.

couperose [kuproz] *nf* [sur le visage] **blotchiness**.

couperosé, -e [kuproze] *adj* **blotchy**.

coupe-vent [kupvɑ̃] *nm inv* [vêtement] **windcheater** *Br,* **windbreaker** *Am*.

couple [kupl] *nm* [de personnes] **couple**; [d'animaux] **pair**.

couplé, -e [kuple] *adj* HIPPISME **doubled**.

◆ **couplé** *nm* HIPPISME **double**.

coupler [kuple] [3] *vt* [objets] to **couple**.

couplet [kuplɛ] *nm* **verse**.

coupole [kupɔl] *nf* ARCHIT **dome, cupola**.

coupon [kupɔ̃] *nm* **-1.** [d'étoffe] **remnant**. **-2.** FIN **coupon**. **-3.** [billet] **ticket**.

coupon-réponse [kupɔ̃repɔ̃s] (*pl* **coupons-réponse**) *nm* **reply coupon**.

coupure [kupyr] *nf* **-1.** [gén] **cut**; [billet de banque]: **petite ~** small denomination note; **~ de courant** ÉLECTR power cut; INFORM **blackout**; **~ de presse** (press) cutting, clipping; **une ~ publicitaire** commercial break. **-2.** *fig* [rupture] **break**.

cour [kur] *nf* **-1.** [espace] **courtyard**; **~ de récréation** playground. **-2.** [du roi, tribunal] **court**; *fig* & *hum* following; **~ d'assises** Crown Court *Br*; **Cour de cassation** Court of Appeal; **la Cour des comptes** the French *audit office*; **Haute ~ (de justice)** High Court; **~ martiale** court-martial. **-3.** *loc*: **faire la ~ à** [femme] to court; *fig* to charm, to woo.

LA COUR DES COMPTES:
This state body supervises the financial affairs of public bodies and local government, and monitors the way public funds are used

---

courage [kuraʒ] *nm* **courage**; **bon ~!** good luck!; **prendre son ~ à deux mains** to pluck up courage; **je n'ai pas le ~ de faire mes devoirs** I can't bring myself to do my homework.

courageusement [kuraʒøzmɑ̃] *adv* **courageously**.

courageux, -euse [kuraʒø, øz] *adj* **-1.**

[brave] **brave**. **-2.** [qui a de l'énergie] **energetic**. **-3.** [audacieux] **bold**.

couramment [kuramɑ̃] *adv* **-1.** [parler une langue] **fluently**. **-2.** [communément] **commonly**.

courant, -e [kurɑ̃, ɑ̃t] *adj* **-1.** [habituel] everyday (*avant n*). **-2.** [en cours] **present**.

◆ **courant** *nm* **-1.** [marin, atmosphérique, électrique] **current**; **couper le ~** to cut off the power; **~ d'air** draught; **~ alternatif** alternating current. **-2.** [d'idées] **current**. **-3.** [laps de temps]: **dans le ~ du mois/de l'année** in the course of the month/the year; **~ décembre** in the course of December.

◆ **au courant** *loc adv*: **être au ~** to know (about it); **mettre qqn au ~ (de)** to tell sb (about); **tenir qqn au ~ (de)** to keep sb informed (about); **se mettre/se tenir au ~ (de)** to get/keep up to date (with).

courbatu, -e [kurbaty] *adj* **aching**.

courbature [kurbatyr] *nf* **ache**.

courbaturé, -e [kurbatyre] *adj* **aching**.

courbe [kurb] ◇ *nf* **curve**; **~ de niveau** [sur une carte] contour (line); **~ de température** MÉD temperature curve. ◇ *adj* **curved**.

courber [kurbe] [3] ◇ *vt* **-1.** [tige] to **bend**. **-2.** [tête] to **bow**. ◇ *vi* to **bow**.

◆ **se courber** *vp* **-1.** [chose] to **bend**. **-2.** [personne] to **bow**, to bend down.

courbette [kurbet] *nf* [révérence] **bow**; **faire des ~s** *fig* to bow and scrape.

coureur, -euse [kurœr, øz] *nm, f* **-1.** SPORT runner; **~ cycliste** racing cyclist. **-2.** *fam fig* [amateur]: **~ (de jupons)** womanizer.

courge [kurʒ] *nf* **-1.** [légume] marrow *Br*, squash *Am*. **-2.** *fam* [imbécile] **dimwit**.

courgette [kurʒet] *nf* **courgette** *Br*, zucchini *Am*.

courir [kurir] [45] ◇ *vi* **-1.** [aller rapidement] to **run**; **~ après qqn/qqch** *fig* to chase after sb/sthg, to run after sb/sthg; **laisse ~!** *fig* let it go!; **faire ~ qqn** *fig* to pull sb's leg. **-2.** SPORT to **race**. **-3.** [se précipiter, rivière] to **rush**. **-4.** [se propager]: **le bruit court que ...** rumour has it that ...; **faire ~ un bruit** to spread a rumour.

◇ *vt* **-1.** SPORT to run in. **-2.** [parcourir] to roam (through). **-3.** [faire le tour de] to go round. **-4.** [fréquenter - bals, musées] to do the rounds of.

couronne [kurɔn] *nf* **-1.** [ornement, autorité] crown. **-2.** [de fleurs] wreath; **~ mortuaire** OU **funéraire** funeral wreath. **-3.** [monnaie - de Suède, d'Islande] **krona**; [- de Danemark, Norvège] **krone**; [- de Tchécoslovaquie] **crown**.

couronnement [kurɔnmɑ̃] *nm* **-1.** [de monarque] coronation. **-2.** [d'édifice] crown. **-3.** *fig* [apogée] crowning achievement.

couronner [kurɔne] [3] *vt* **-1.** [monarque] to crown. **-2.** [récompenser] to give a prize to; **être couronné de succès** *fig* to be crowned with success.

courrai, **courras** *etc* → **courir**.

courre [kur] → **chasse**.

courrier [kurje] *nm* mail, letters (*pl*); ~ **du cœur** agony column; ~ **direct** COMM direct mail shot; ~ **électronique** INFORM electronic mail, E-mail; ~ **des lecteurs** [rubrique] letters to the editor.

courroie [kurwa] *nf* TECHNOL belt; [attache] strap; ~ **de transmission** driving belt; ~ **de ventilateur** fanbelt.

courroucer [kuruse] [16] *vt littéraire* to anger.

courroux [kuru] *nm littéraire* wrath, rage.

cours [kur] ◇ → **courir**.
◇ *nm* **-1.** [écoulement] flow; ~ **d'eau** waterway; **donner** OU **laisser libre** ~ **à** *fig* to give free rein to. **-2.** [déroulement] course; **au** ~ **de** during, in the course of; **en** ~ [année, dossier] current; [affaires] in hand; **en** ~ **de route** on the way; **entraver le** ~ **de la justice** to hinder the course of justice; **suivre son** ~ to take its course. **-3.** FIN price; ~ **du change** exchange rate; **avoir** ~ [monnaie] to be legal tender. **-4.** [leçon] class, lesson; **donner des** ~ **(à qqn)** to teach (sb); ~ **intensifs** crash course (*sg*); ~ **magistral** lecture; ~ **de rattrapage/du soir** remedial/ evening class. **-5.** [classe]: ~ **élémentaire** *years two and three of primary school*; ~ **moyen** *last two years of primary school*; ~ **préparatoire** ≃ first-year infants *Br.* **-6.** [avenue] avenue.

course [kurs] *nf* **-1.** [action] running (*U*); **au pas de** ~ at a run; **être dans la** ~ *fig* to be in touch OU in the know. **-2.** [compétition] race; ~ **automobile/cycliste** car/cycle race; ~ **à pied** (foot) race. **-3.** [excursion] trip. **-4.** [en taxi] journey. **-5.** [mouvement] flight, course. **-6.** [commission] errand; **faire des** ~s to go shopping.

coursier, -ière [kursje, jɛr] *nm, f* messenger.

coursive [kursiv] *nf* gangway.

court, courte [kur, kurt] *adj* short.
◆ **court** ◇ → **courir**. ◇ *adv*: **être à** ~ **d'argent/d'idées/d'arguments** to be short of money/ideas/arguments; **prendre qqn de** ~ to catch sb unawares; **tourner** ~ to stop suddenly. ◇ *nm*: ~ **de tennis** tennis court.

court-bouillon [kurbujɔ̃] (*pl* **courts-bouillons**) *nm* court-bouillon.

court-circuit [kursirkчi] (*pl* **courts-circuits**) *nm* short circuit.

court-circuiter [kursirkчite] [3] *vt* ÉLECTR to short-circuit; *fig* to bypass.

courtier, -ière [kurtje, jɛr] *nm, f* broker.

courtisan, -e [kurtizɑ̃, an] *nm, f* **-1.** HIST courtier. **-2.** [flatteur] sycophant.
◆ **courtisane** *nf* courtesan.

courtiser [kurtize] [3] *vt* **-1.** [femme] to woo, to court. **-2.** *péj* [flatter] to flatter.

court-jus [kurʒy] (*pl* **courts-jus**) *nm fam* short.

court-métrage [kurmetraʒ] (*pl* **courts-métrages**) *nm* short (film).

courtois, -e [kurtwa, az] *adj* courteous.

courtoisie [kurtwazi] *nf* courtesy.

couru, -e [kury] ◇ *pp* → **courir**. ◇ *adj* popular; **c'est** ~ **(d'avance)** *fam fig* it's a foregone conclusion.

cousais, **cousions** *etc* → **coudre**.

couscous [kuskus] *nm* couscous.

cousin, -e [kuzɛ̃, in] *nm, f* cousin; ~ **germain** first cousin.

coussin [kusɛ̃] *nm* [de siège] cushion; ~ **d'air** air cushion.

coussinet [kusinɛ] *nm* **-1.** [coussin] small cushion. **-2.** [de patte d'animal] pad.

cousu, -e [kuzy] ◇ *pp* → **coudre**. ◇ *adj*: **c'est du** ~ **main** *fam fig* it's top-quality stuff; ~ **de fil blanc** *fig* obvious.

coût [ku] *nm* cost; **le** ~ **de la vie** the cost of living; ~s **de distribution** COMM distribution costs.

coûtant [kutɑ̃] → **prix**.

couteau, -x [kuto] *nm* **-1.** [gén] knife; ~ **à cran d'arrêt** flick knife; ~ **de cuisine** kitchen knife; **à couper au** ~ *fig* that you could cut with a knife; **avoir le** ~ **sous la gorge** *fig* to have a gun to one's head; **être à** ~x **tirés (avec qqn)** *fig* to be at daggers drawn (with sb). **-2.** [coquillage] razor-shell *Br*, razor clam *Am*.

coutelas [kutla] *nm* [grand couteau] large knife.

coutellerie [kutɛlri] *nf* [industrie, produits] cutlery; [atelier] cutlery factory; [magasin] cutler's (shop).

coûter [kute] [3] ◇ *vi* **-1.** [valoir] to cost; **ça coûte combien?** how much is it?; ~ **cher** to be expensive, to cost a lot; *fig* to be costly; ~ **cher à qqn** to cost sb a lot; *fig* to cost sb dear OU dearly. **-2.** *fig* [être pénible] to be difficult. ◇ *vt fig* to cost.
◆ **coûte que coûte** *loc adv* at all costs.

coûteux, -euse [kutø, øz] *adj* costly, expensive.

coutume [kutym] *nf* [gén & JUR] custom; avoir ~ de faire qqch to be in the habit of doing sthg; la ~ veut que ... tradition dictates that ....

coutumier, -ière [kutymje, jɛr] *adj* customary; il est ~ du fait he's always doing that.

couture [kutyr] *nf* **-1.** [action] sewing; faire de la ~ to sew. **-2.** [points] seam; ~ apparente topstitching, overstitching. **-3.** [activité] dressmaking; haute ~ haute couture.

couturier, -ière [kutyrje, jɛr] *nm, f* couturier; grand ~ fashion designer, couturier.

couvée [kuve] *nf* [d'œufs] clutch; [de poussins] brood.

couvent [kuvã] *nm* [de sœurs] convent; [de moines] monastery.

couver [kuve] [3] ◇ *vt* **-1.** [œufs] to sit on. **-2.** [dorloter] to mollycoddle. **-3.** [maladie] to be sickening for. ◇ *vi* [poule] to brood; *fig* [complot] to hatch.

couvercle [kuvɛrkl] *nm* [de casserole, boîte] lid, cover; [de flacon, bombe, aérosol] top, cap.

couvert, -e [kuvɛr, ɛrt] ◇ *pp* → couvrir. ◇ *adj* **-1.** [submergé] covered; ~ de covered with. **-2.** [habillé] dressed; être bien ~ to be well wrapped up. **-3.** [nuageux] overcast.
◆ **couvert** *nm* **-1.** [abri]: se mettre à ~ to take shelter; sous le ~ de l'amitié *fig* under a cloak of friendship. **-2.** [place à table] place (setting); mettre OU dresser le ~ to set OU lay the table.
◆ **couverts** *nmpl* cutlery (U).

couverture [kuvɛrtyr] *nf* **-1.** [gén] cover; ~ sociale social security cover. **-2.** [de lit] blanket; ~ chauffante electric blanket; tirer la ~ à soi *fam fig* to take (all) the credit (for o.s.). **-3.** [toit] roofing (U). **-4.** PRESSE coverage.

couveuse [kuvøz] *nf* **-1.** [poule] sitting hen. **-2.** [machine] incubator.

couvre-chef [kuvrəʃɛf] (*pl* couvre-chefs) *nm hum* hat.

couvre-feu [kuvrəfø] (*pl* couvre-feux) *nm* curfew.

couvre-lit [kuvrəli] (*pl* couvre-lits) *nm* bedspread.

couvre-pied (*pl* couvre-pieds) *nm*,
couvre-pieds *nm inv* [kuvrəpje] quilt, eiderdown.

couvreur [kuvrœr] *nm* roofer.

couvrir [kuvrir] [34] *vt* **-1.** [gén] to cover; ~ qqn/qqch de *litt* & *fig* to cover sb/sthg with. **-2.** [protéger] to shield. **-3.** [son] to drown (out).
◆ **se couvrir** *vp* **-1.** [se vêtir] to wrap up. **-2.** [se recouvrir]: se ~ de feuilles/de fleurs to come into leaf/blossom. **-3.** [ciel] to cloud over. **-4.** [se protéger] to cover o.s.

cover-girl [kɔvœrgœrl] (*pl* cover-girls) *nf* cover girl.

cow-boy [kɔbɔj] (*pl* cow-boys) *nm* cowboy.

coyote [kɔjɔt] *nm* coyote.

CP *nm abr de* cours préparatoire.

CPAM (*abr de* caisse primaire d'assurances maladie) *nf* national health insurance office.

cps (*abr de* caractères par seconde) cps.

cpt *abr de* comptant.

CQFD (*abr de* ce qu'il fallait démontrer) QED.

crabe [krab] *nm* crab.

crac [krak] *interj* crack!

crachat [kraʃa] *nm* spit (U).

craché, -e [kraʃe] *adj*: c'est son père tout ~ he's the spitting image of his father.

cracher [kraʃe] [3] ◇ *vi* **-1.** [personne] to spit. **-2.** [crépiter] to crackle. **-3.** *fam fig* [dénigrer]: ~ sur qqn to run sb down. **-4.** *fam* [dédaigner]: ne pas ~ sur qqch not to turn one's nose up at sthg. ◇ *vt* [sang] to spit (up); [lave, injures] to spit (out).

crachin [kraʃɛ̃] *nm* drizzle.

crachoir [kraʃwar] *nm* spittoon; tenir le ~ *fam fig* to monopolize the conversation.

crack [krak] *nm* **-1.** [cheval] top horse. **-2.** *fam* [as] star (performer); c'est un ~ en mathématiques he's a whizz at maths.

cradingue [kradɛ̃g] *adj fam* grotty *Br*.

craie [krɛ] *nf* chalk.

craignais, craignions *etc* → craindre.

craindre [krɛ̃dr] [80] *vt* **-1.** [redouter] to fear, to be afraid of; ~ de faire qqch to be afraid of doing sthg; je crains d'avoir oublié mes papiers I'm afraid I've forgotten my papers; ~ que (+ *subjonctif*) to be afraid (that); je crains qu'il oublie OU n'oublie I'm afraid he may forget. **-2.** [être sensible à] to be susceptible to.

craint, -e [krɛ̃, ɛ̃t] *pp* → craindre.

crainte [krɛ̃t] *nf* fear; de ~ de faire qqch for fear of doing sthg; de ~ que (+ *subjonctif*) for fear that; il a fui de ~ qu'on ne le voie he fled for fear that he might be seen OU for fear of being seen.

craintif, -ive [krɛ̃tif, iv] *adj* timid.

cramer [krame] [3] *vt* & *vi fam* to burn.
◆ **se cramer** *vp fam* to burn o.s.; se ~ le doigt to burn one's finger.

cramoisi, -e [kramwazi] *adj* crimson.

crampe [krãp] *nf* cramp.

crampon [krɑ̃pɔ̃] *nm* -1. [crochet - gén] clamp; [- pour alpinisme] crampon. -2. *fam* [personne] (persistent) bore.

cramponner [krɑ̃pɔne] [3] *vt* to clamp.

◆ **se cramponner** *vp* [s'agripper] to hang on; **se ~ à qqn/qqch** *litt* & *fig* to cling to sb/sthg.

cran [krɑ̃] *nm* -1. [entaille, degré] notch, cut. -2. (*U*) [audace] guts (*pl*); **avoir du ~** to have guts.

crâne [krɑn] *nm* skull; **se mettre qqch dans le ~** *fig* to get sthg into one's head.

crâner [krane] [3] *vi fam* to show off.

crâneur, -euse [krɑnœr, øz] *fam* ◇ *adj* boastful. ◇ *nm, f* show-off.

crânien, -ienne [krɑnjɛ̃, jɛn] *adj*: **boîte ~ne** skull; **traumatisme ~** head injury.

crapaud [krapo] *nm* toad.

crapule [krapyl] *nf* scum (*U*).

crapuleux, -euse [krapylø, øz] *adj* sordid.

craqueler [krakle] [24] *vt* to crack.

◆ **se craqueler** *vp* to crack.

craquelure [kraklyr] *nf* crack.

craquement [krakmɑ̃] *nm* crack, cracking (*U*).

craquer [krake] [3] *vi* -1. [produire un bruit] to crack; [plancher, chaussure] to creak; **faire ~ une allumette** to strike a match. -2. [se déchirer] to split. -3. [s'effondrer - personne] to crack up; [- régime, projet] to be falling apart. -4. [être séduit par]: **~ pour** to fall for.

crash [kraʃ] (*pl* **crashs** OU **crashes**) *nm* crash landing.

crasse [kras] ◇ *nf* -1. [saleté] dirt, filth. -2. *fam* [mauvais tour] dirty trick. ◇ *adj* crass.

crasseux, -euse [krasø, øz] *adj* filthy.

cratère [kratɛr] *nm* crater.

cravache [kravaʃ] *nf* riding crop.

cravacher [kravaʃe] [3] ◇ *vt* to whip. ◇ *vi fam fig* to pull out all the stops.

cravate [kravat] *nf* tie.

crawl [krol] *nm* crawl.

crayon [krɛjɔ̃] *nm* -1. [gén] pencil; **~ à bille** ballpoint (pen); **~ de couleur** crayon; **~ noir** pencil. -2. TECHNOL pen; **~ optique** light pen.

crayon-feutre [krɛjɔ̃føtr] (*pl* **crayons-feutres**) *nm* felt-tip (pen).

crayonner [krɛjɔne] [3] *vt* [dessin] to sketch.

CRDP (*abr de* **centre régional de documentation pédagogique**) *nm* local centre for educational resources.

créance [kreɑ̃s] *nf* COMM debt.

créancier, -ière [kreɑ̃sje, jɛr] *nm, f* creditor.

créateur, -trice [kreatœr, tris] ◇ *adj* creative. ◇ *nm, f* creator.

◆ **Créateur** *nm*: **le Créateur** the Creator.

créatif, -ive [kreatif, iv] *adj* creative.

◆ **créatif** *nm* ideas man, designer.

création [kreasjɔ̃] *nf* creation; **la ~ (du monde)** the Creation.

créativité [kreativite] *nf* creativity.

créature [kreatyr] *nf* creature.

crécelle [kresɛl] *nf* rattle.

crèche [krɛʃ] *nf* -1. [de Noël] crib. -2. [garderie] crèche.

crécher [kreʃe] [18] *vi fam* to crash, to kip down *Br*.

crédibiliser [kredibilize] *vt* [3] to make credible.

crédibilité [kredibilite] *nf* credibility.

crédible [kredibl] *adj* credible.

CREDIF, Crédif [kredif] (*abr de* **Centre de recherche et d'étude pour la diffusion du français**) *nm official body promoting use of the French language.*

crédit [kredi] *nm* -1. [gén] credit; **faire ~ à qqn** to give sb credit; **acheter/vendre qqch à ~** to buy/sell sthg on credit; **~ municipal** pawnshop; **~ relais** bridging loan. -2. *fig* & *sout* influence.

crédit-bail [kredibaj] (*pl* **crédits-bails**) *nm* leasing.

créditer [kredite] [3] *vt* [compte] to credit; *fig*: **~ qqn de qqch** to credit sb with sthg.

créditeur, -trice [kreditœr, tris] ◇ *adj* in credit. ◇ *nm, f* creditor.

credo [kredo] *nm* creed, credo.

crédule [kredyl] *adj* credulous.

crédulité [kredylite] *nf* credulity.

créer [kree] [15] *vt* -1. [RELIG & inventer] to create. -2. [fonder] to found, to start up. -3. [causer]: **~ des problèmes à qqn** to create trouble for sb.

crémaillère [kremajɛr] *nf* -1. [de cheminée] trammel; **pendre la ~** *fig* to have a house-warming (party). -2. TECHNOL rack.

crémation [kremasjɔ̃] *nf* cremation.

crématoire [krematwar] → **four**.

crématorium [krematɔrjɔm] *nm* crematorium.

crème [krɛm] ◇ *nf* -1. [gén] cream; **~ dépilatoire/à raser** depilatory/shaving cream; **~ fouettée/fraîche/glacée** whipped/fresh/ice cream; **café ~** white coffee *Br*; **~ anglaise** custard; **~ auto-bronzante** self-tanning cream; **~ de cassis** blackcurrant liqueur; **~ glacée** ice cream; **~ hydratante** moisturizer; **~ pâtissière** confectioner's custard; **~ renversée** custard

cream *Br*, cup custard *Am*. **-2.** [personne]: **la ~ des maris/des hommes** the best of husbands/of men.
◇ *adj inv* cream.

crémerie [kremri] *nf* dairy.

crémeux, -euse [kremø, øz] *adj* creamy.

crémier, -ière [kremje, jɛr] *nm, f* dairyman (*f* dairywoman).

créneau, -aux [kreno] *nm* **-1.** [de fortification] crenel. **-2.** [pour se garer]: **faire un ~** to reverse into a parking space. **-3.** [de marché] niche. **-4.** [horaire] window, gap.

crénelé, -e [krɛnle] *adj* crenelated.

créole [kreɔl] *adj & nm* creole.
◆ **créoles** *nfpl* dangly earrings.

crêpe [krɛp] ◇ *nf* CULIN pancake. ◇ *nm* [tissu] crepe.

crêper [krepe] [4] *vt* to backcomb.

crêperie [krɛpri] *nf* pancake restaurant.

crépi [krepi] *nm* roughcast.

crépinette [krepinɛt] *nf* flat sausage.

crépir [krepir] [32] *vt* to roughcast.

crépiter [krepite] [3] *vi* [feu, flammes] to crackle; [pluie] to patter.

crépon [krepɔ̃] ◇ *adj* → **papier**. ◇ *nm* seersucker.

CREPS, Creps [krɛps] (*abr de* **centre régional d'éducation physique et sportive**) *nm* regional sports centre.

crépu, -e [krepy] *adj* frizzy.

crépuscule [krepyskyl] *nm* [du jour] dusk, twilight; *fig* twilight; **au ~** at dusk, at twilight.

crescendo [kreʃɛndo, kreʃēdo] ◇ *adv* crescendo; **aller ~** *fig* [bruit] to get OU grow louder and louder; [dépenses, émotion] to grow apace. ◇ *nm inv* MUS & *fig* crescendo.

cresson [kresɔ̃] *nm* watercress.

crête [krɛt] *nf* **-1.** [de coq] comb. **-2.** [de montagne, vague, oiseau] crest.

Crète [krɛt] *nf*: **la ~** Crete.

crétin, -e [kretɛ̃, in] *fam* ◇ *adj* cretinous, idiotic. ◇ *nm, f* cretin, idiot.

crétois, -e [kretwa, az] *adj* Cretan.
◆ **Crétois, -e** *nm, f* Cretan.

cretonne [krətɔn] *nf* cretonne.

creuser [krøze] [3] *vt* **-1.** [trou] to dig. **-2.** [objet] to hollow out. **-3.** [taille, reins] to arch. **-4.** *fig* [approfondir] to go into deeply. **-5.** *loc*: **ça creuse!** *fam* that gives you an appetite!
◆ **se creuser** *vp* **-1.** [devenir creux] to become hollow. **-2.** *fam fig* [réfléchir] to rack

one's brains. **-3.** *fig* [s'élargir] to deepen, to widen.

creuset [krøzɛ] *nm* crucible; *fig* melting pot.

creux, creuse [krø, krøz] *adj* **-1.** [vide, concave] hollow. **-2.** [période - d'activité réduite] slack; [- à tarif réduit] off-peak. **-3.** [paroles] empty.
◆ **creux** *nm* **-1.** [concavité] hollow; **le ~ de la main** the hollow of one's hand. **-2.** [période] lull. **-3.** *loc*: **être au ~ de la vague** *fig* to be at a low point.

crevaison [krəvɛzɔ̃] *nf* puncture.

crevant, -e [krəvɑ̃, ɑ̃t] *adj fam* **-1.** [fatigant] knackering *Br*. **-2.** [amusant] hilarious.

crevasse [krəvas] *nf* [de mur] crevice, crack; [de glacier] crevasse; [sur la main] crack.

crève [krɛv] *nf fam* bad OU stinking cold; **attraper la ~** to catch one's death (of cold).

crève-cœur [krɛvkœr] *nm inv* heartbreak.

crever [krəve] [19] ◇ *vi* **-1.** [éclater] to burst. **-2.** *tfam* [mourir] to die; **~ de** *fig* [jalousie, santé, orgueil] to be bursting with. ◇ *vt* **-1.** [percer] to burst. **-2.** *fam* [épuiser] to wear out.
◆ **se crever** *vp fam* to wear o.s. out.

crevette [krəvɛt] *nf*: **~ (grise)** shrimp; **~ (rose)** prawn.

CRF (*abr de* **Croix-Rouge française**) *nf* French Red Cross.

cri [kri] *nm* **-1.** [de personne] cry, shout; [perçant] scream; [d'animal] cry; **pousser un ~** to cry (out), to shout; **pousser des ~s de joie** to shout for OU with joy; **pousser un ~ de douleur** to cry out in pain; **à grands ~s** *fig* loudly. **-2.** [appel] cry; **le dernier ~** *fig* the latest thing; **~ du cœur** cri de cœur.

criailler [kriaje] [3] *vi* to scream, to squawk.

criant, -e [krijɑ̃, ɑ̃t] *adj* [injustice] blatant.

criard, -e [krijar, ard] *adj* **-1.** [voix] strident, piercing. **-2.** [couleur] loud.

crible [kribl] *nm* [instrument] sieve; **passer qqch au ~** *fig* to examine sthg closely.

criblé, -e [krible] *adj* riddled; **être ~ de dettes** to be up to one's eyes in debt.

cric [krik] *nm* jack.

cricket [krikɛt] *nm* cricket.

criée [krije] → **vente**.

crier [krije] [10] ◇ *vi* **-1.** [jeter un cri] to shout (out), to yell. **-2.** [parler fort] to shout. **-3.** [protester]: **~ contre** OU **après qqn** to nag sb, to go on at sb. **-4.** *sout* [grincer] to creak. ◇ *vt* to shout (out).

crime [krim] *nm* **-1.** [délit] crime; **~ de**

lèse-majesté *fig* treason (*U*). **-2.** [meurtre] murder; ~ **passionnel** crime of passion.

Crimée [krime] *nf*: **la** ~ the Crimea; **la guerre de** ~ the Crimean War.

criminalité [kriminalite] *nf* criminality.

criminel, -elle [kriminɛl] ◇ *adj* criminal; ~ **de guerre** war criminal. ◇ *nm, f* criminal.

crin [krɛ̃] *nm* [d'animal] hair; **à tout** ~ *fig* dyed-in-the-wool.

crinière [krinjɛr] *nf* mane.

crique [krik] *nf* creek.

criquet [krikɛ] *nm* locust; [sauterelle] grasshopper.

crise [kriz] *nf* **-1.** MÉD attack; ~ **cardiaque** heart attack; ~ **de foie** bilious attack; ~ **de tétanie** muscle spasm. **-2.** [accès] fit; ~ **de larmes** fit of tears; ~ **de nerfs** attack of nerves; **piquer une** ~ *fam* to have a fit, to fly off the handle. **-3.** [élan] (sudden) urge. **-4.** [phase critique] crisis; **en** ~ in crisis.

crispant, -e [krispɑ̃, ɑ̃t] *adj* irritating, frustrating.

crispation [krispasjɔ̃] *nf* **-1.** [contraction] contraction. **-2.** [agacement] irritation.

crispé, -e [krispe] *adj* tense, on edge.

crisper [krispe] [3] *vt* **-1.** [contracter - visage] to tense; [- poing] to clench. **-2.** [agacer] to irritate.

◆ **se crisper** *vp* **-1.** [se contracter] to tense (up). **-2.** [s'irriter] to get irritated.

criss [kris] *nm* kris.

crisser [krise] [3] *vi* [pneu] to screech; [étoffe] to rustle.

cristal, -aux [kristal, o] *nm* crystal; **en** ~ crystal (*avant n*); ~ **de roche** quartz.

cristallin, -e [kristalɛ̃, in] *adj* **-1.** [limpide] crystal clear, crystalline. **-2.** [roche] crystalline.

◆ **cristallin** *nm* crystalline lens.

cristalliser [kristalize] [3] *vt litt* & *fig* to crystallize.

◆ **se cristalliser** *vp* to crystallize.

critère [kritɛr] *nm* criterion.

critérium [kriterjɔm] *nm* qualifier.

critiquable [kritikabl] *adj* [décision] debatable; [personne] open to criticism.

critique [kritik] ◇ *adj* critical. ◇ *nmf* critic; ~ **d'art** art critic; ~ **littéraire** literary critic. ◇ *nf* criticism; **la** ~ the critics (*pl*).

critiquer [kritike] [3] *vt* to criticize.

croasser [krɔase] [3] *vi* to croak, to caw.

croate [krɔat] *adj* Croat, Croatian.

◆ **Croate** *nmf* Croat, Croatian.

Croatie [krɔasi] *nf*: **la** ~ Croatia.

croc [kro] *nm* **-1.** [de chien] fang; **montrer les** ~**s** *fig* to bare one's teeth. **-2.** [crochet] hook.

croc-en-jambe [krɔkɑ̃ʒɑ̃b] (*pl* **crocs-en-jambe**) *nm*: **faire un** ~ **à qqn** to trip sb up.

croche [krɔʃ] *nf* quaver *Br*, eighth (note) *Am*.

croche-pied [krɔʃpje] (*pl* **croche-pieds**) *nm*: **faire un** ~ **à qqn** to trip sb up.

crochet [krɔʃɛ] *nm* **-1.** [de métal] hook; **vivre aux** ~**s de qqn** to live off sb. **-2.** TRICOT crochet hook. **-3.** TYPO square bracket. **-4.** [détour]: **faire un** ~ to make a detour. **-5.** BOXE: ~ **du gauche/du droit** left/right hook.

crocheter [krɔʃte] [28] *vt* to pick.

crochu, -e [krɔʃy] *adj* [doigts] claw-like; [nez] hooked.

croco [krɔko] *nm fam* crocodile (skin).

crocodile [krɔkɔdil] *nm* crocodile.

crocus [krɔkys] *nm* crocus.

croire [krwar] [107] ◇ *vt* **-1.** [chose, personne] to believe; **à l'en** ~, **on n'y arrivera jamais** to hear him talk, you'd think we'd never manage it. **-2.** [penser] to think; **tu crois?** do you think so?; **il te croyait parti** he thought you'd left; ~ **que** to think (that). ◇ *vi*: ~ **à** to believe in; ~ **en** to believe in, to have faith in.

◆ **se croire** *vp* **-1.** [prétendre être]: **il se croit plus fort que moi** he thinks he's stronger than me; **se** ~ **tout permis** to think one can get away with anything; **s'y** ~ *fam* to think one is it. **-2.** [penser se trouver]: **on se croirait au Japon** you'd think you were in Japan.

croisade [krwazad] *nf* HIST & *fig* crusade.

croisé, -e [krwaze] *adj* [veste] double-breasted.

◆ **croisé** *nm* HIST crusader.

◆ **croisée** *nf* **-1.** [fenêtre] casement, window. **-2.** [croisement]: **à la** ~**e des chemins** *litt* & *fig* at a crossroads.

croisement [krwazmɑ̃] *nm* **-1.** [intersection] junction, intersection. **-2.** BIOL crossbreeding.

croiser [krwaze] [3] ◇ *vt* **-1.** [jambes] to cross; [bras] to fold. **-2.** [passer à côté de] to pass. **-3.** [chemin] to cross, to cut across. **-4.** [métisser] to interbreed. ◇ *vi* NAVIG to cruise.

◆ **se croiser** *vp* [chemins] to cross, to intersect; [personnes] to pass; [lettres] to cross; [regards] to meet.

croisière [krwazjɛr] *nf* cruise.

croisillon [krwazijɔ̃] *nm*: **à** ~**s** lattice (*avant n*).

croissais, croissions *etc* → croître.

croissance [krwasɑ̃s] *nf* growth, development; ~ **économique** economic growth OU development.

croissant, -e [krwasɑ̃, ɑ̃t] *adj* increasing, growing.
◆ **croissant** *nm* **-1.** [de lune] crescent. **-2.** CULIN croissant.

croître [krwatr] [93] *vi* **-1.** [grandir] to grow. **-2.** [augmenter] to increase.

croix [krwa] *nf* cross; **en** ~ in the shape of a cross; ~ **gammée** swastika; **la Croix rouge** the Red Cross; **mettre** OU **faire une** ~ **sur qqch** *fig* to write sthg off; **la** ~ **et la bannière** *fig* the devil's own job.

croquant, -e [krɔkɑ̃, ɑ̃t] *adj* crisp, crunchy.
◆ **croquant** *nm vieilli* yokel.

croque-madame [krɔkmadam] *nm inv* *croque-monsieur with a fried egg*.

croque-mitaine [krɔkmitɛn] (*pl* **croque-mitaines**) *nm* bogeyman.

croque-monsieur [krɔkməsjø] *nm inv* *toasted cheese and ham sandwich*.

croque-mort [krɔkmɔr] (*pl* **croque-morts**) *nm fam* undertaker.

croquer [krɔke] [3] ◇ *vt* **-1.** [manger] to crunch. **-2.** [dessiner] to sketch; **(jolie) à** ~ *fig* pretty as a picture. ◇ *vi* to be crunchy.

croquette [krɔkɛt] *nf* croquette.

croquis [krɔki] *nm* sketch; **faire un** ~ to make a sketch.

cross [krɔs] *nm* [exercice] cross-country (running); [course] cross-country race.

crosse [krɔs] *nf* **-1.** [d'évêque] crozier. **-2.** [de fusil] butt. **-3.** HOCKEY hockey stick.

crotale [krɔtal] *nm* rattlesnake.

crotte [krɔt] *nf* [de lapin etc] droppings (*pl*); [de chien] dirt; ~! *fam* damn!

crottin [krɔtɛ̃] *nm* [de cheval] (horse) manure.

croulant, -e [krulɑ̃, ɑ̃t] ◇ *adj* crumbling. ◇ *nm, f fam* (old) fogy, wrinkly.

crouler [krule] [3] *vi* to crumble; ~ **sous** *litt & fig* to collapse under.

croupe [krup] *nf* rump; **monter en** ~ to ride pillion.

croupier [krupje] *nm* croupier.

croupion [krupjɔ̃] *nm* ZOOL rump; CULIN parson's nose.

croupir [krupir] [32] *vi litt & fig* to stagnate.

CROUS, Crous [krus] (*abr de* **centre régional des œuvres universitaires et scolaires**) *nm* *student representative body dealing with accommodation, catering etc*.

croustade [krustad] *nf* croustade.

croustillant, -e [krustijɑ̃, ɑ̃t] *adj* **-1.** [croquant - pain] crusty; [- biscuit] crunchy. **-2.** [grivois] spicy, juicy.

croustiller [krustije] [3] *vi* to be crusty.

croûte [krut] *nf* **-1.** [du pain, terrestre] crust; **casser la** ~ *fam fig* to have a bite to eat; **gagner sa** ~ *fam fig* to earn a crust. **-2.** CULIN: **en** ~ in piecrust OU pastry. **-3.** [de fromage] rind. **-4.** [de plaie] scab. **-5.** *fam péj* [tableau] daub.

croûton [krutɔ̃] *nm* **-1.** [bout du pain] crust. **-2.** [pain frit] crouton. **-3.** *fam péj* [personne] fuddy-duddy.

croyable [krwajabl] *adj* believable; **c'est pas** ~! it's unbelievable OU incredible!

croyais, croyions *etc* → croire.

croyance [krwajɑ̃s] *nf* belief.

croyant, -e [krwajɑ̃, ɑ̃t] ◇ *ppr* → croire. ◇ *adj*: **être** ~ to be a believer. ◇ *nm, f* believer.

CRS (*abr de* **Compagnie républicaine de sécurité**) *nm* *member of the French riot police*; **on a fait appel aux** ~ the riot police were called in.

cru, -e [kry] ◇ *pp* → croire. ◇ *adj* **-1.** [non cuit] raw. **-2.** [violent] harsh. **-3.** [direct] blunt. **-4.** [grivois] crude.
◆ **cru** *nm* [vin] wine; [vignoble] vineyard; **du** ~ *fig* local; **un grand** ~ a fine wine; **de son propre** ~ *fig* of one's own devising.

crû, -e [kry] *pp* → croître.

cruauté [kryote] *nf* cruelty.

cruche [kryʃ] *nf* **-1.** [objet] jug. **-2.** *fam péj* [personne niaise] twit.

crucial, -e, -iaux [krysjal, jo] *adj* crucial.

crucifix [krysifi] *nm* crucifix.

crucifixion [krysifiksjɔ̃] *nf* crucifixion.

cruciverbiste [krysivɛrbist] *nmf* crossword enthusiast.

crudité [krydite] *nf* crudeness.
◆ **crudités** *nfpl* crudités.

crue [kry] *nf* rise in the water level; **en** ~ in spate.

cruel, -elle [kryɛl] *adj* cruel.

cruellement [kryɛlmɑ̃] *adv* cruelly.

crûment [krymɑ̃] *adv* **-1.** [sans ménagement] bluntly. **-2.** [avec grossièreté] crudely.

crustacé [krystase] *nm* shellfish, crustacean; ~**s** shellfish (*U*).

crypte [kript] *nf* crypt.

cs (*abr de* **cuillère à soupe**) tbs, tbsp.

CSA (*abr de* **Conseil supérieur de l'audiovisuel**) *nm* *French broadcasting supervisory body*.

CSCE (*abr de* **Conférence sur la sécurité et la coopération en Europe**) *nf* CSCE.

CSEN (*abr de* **Confédération des syndicats de l'éducation nationale**) *nf confederation of teachers' unions.*

CSG (*abr de* **contribution sociale généralisée**) *nf income-related tax contribution.*

CSP (*abr de* **catégorie socio-professionnelle**) *nf socio-professional group.*

Cuba [kyba] *n* Cuba; **à ~** in Cuba.

cubain, -aine [kybɛ̃, ɛn] *adj* Cuban.
◆ **Cubain, -aine** *nm, f* Cuban.

cube [kyb] *nm* cube; **4 au ~ = 16** 4 cubed is 16; **élever au ~** MATHS to cube; **mètre ~** cubic metre.
◆ **gros cube** *nm* big motorbike.

cubique [kybik] *adj* cubic.

cubisme [kybism] *nm* cubism.

cubitus [kybitys] *nm* ulna.

cucu(l) [kyky] *adj inv fam* silly.

cueille, cueilles *etc* → **cueillir.**

cueillette [kœjɛt] *nf* picking, harvesting.

cueilli, -e [kœji] *pp* → **cueillir.**

cueillir [kœjir] [41] *vt* **-1.** [fruits, fleurs] to pick. **-2.** *fam* [personne] to catch, to nab.

cuillère, cuiller [kɥijɛr] *nf* spoonful; **~ à café** coffee spoon; CULIN teaspoon; **~ à dessert** dessertspoon; **~ à soupe** soup spoon; CULIN tablespoon; **petite ~** teaspoon.

cuillerée [kɥijere] *nf* spoonful; **~ à café** CULIN teaspoonful; **~ à soupe** CULIN tablespoonful.

cuir [kɥir] *nm* leather; [non tanné] hide; **en ~** leather (*avant n*); **~ chevelu** ANAT scalp.

cuirasse [kɥiras] *nf* [de chevalier] breastplate; *fig* armour.

cuirassé [kɥirase] *nm* battleship.

cuire [kɥir] [98] *vt* **-1.** [viande, œuf] to cook; [tarte, gâteau] to bake. **-2.** [briques, poterie] to fire. ◇ *vi* **-1.** [viande, œuf] to cook; [tarte, gâteau] to bake. **-2.** [personne] to roast, to be boiling; **il vous en cuira!** *fig* you'll suffer (for it)!, you'll regret it!

cuisais, cuisions *etc* → **cuire.**

cuisant, -e [kɥizɑ̃, ɑ̃t] *adj* [douloureux] stinging, smarting; *fig* bitter.

cuisine [kɥizin] *nf* **-1.** [pièce] kitchen. **-2.** [art] cooking, cookery; **faire la ~** to do the cooking, to cook; **~ bourgeoise** home cooking. **-3.** *fam* [combine] schemings (*pl*), schemes (*pl*); **~ électorale** electoral hanky-panky (*U*).

cuisiné, -e [kɥizine] *adj*: **plat ~** ready-cooked meal.

cuisiner [kɥizine] [3] ◇ *vt* **-1.** [aliment] to cook. **-2.** *fam* [personne] to grill. ◇ *vi* to cook; **bien/mal ~** to be a good/bad cook.

cuisinier, -ière [kɥizinje, jɛr] *nm, f* cook.
◆ **cuisinière** *nf* cooker; **cuisinière électrique/à gaz** electric/gas cooker.

cuissardes [kɥisard] *nfpl* [de pêcheur] waders; [de femme] thigh boots.

cuisse [kɥis] *nf* **-1.** ANAT thigh. **-2.** CULIN leg; **~s de grenouille** frog's legs.

cuisson [kɥisɔ̃] *nf* cooking.

cuissot [kɥiso] *nm* haunch; **~ de chevreuil** haunch of venison.

cuistot [kɥisto] *nm fam* cook.

cuistre [kɥistr] *littéraire* ◇ *nm* prig. ◇ *adj* priggish.

cuit, cuite [kɥi, kɥit] ◇ *pp* → **cuire.** ◇ *adj*: **bien ~** [steak] well-done; **trop ~** overcooked, overdone; **être ~** *fam fig* to have had it.
◆ **cuite** *nf fam*: **prendre une ~e** to get plastered OU smashed.

cuiter [kɥite] [3]
◆ **se cuiter** *vp fam* to get plastered OU smashed.

cuivre [kɥivr] *nm* **-1.** [métal]: **~ (rouge)** copper; **~ jaune** brass. **-2.** (*gén pl*) [objet] brass (object).
◆ **cuivres** *nmpl*: **les ~s** MUS the brass.

cuivré, -e [kɥivre] *adj* [couleur, reflet] coppery; [teint] bronzed.

cul [ky] *nm* **-1.** *tfam* [postérieur] bum; **avoir le ~ entre deux chaises** to be in an awkward position; **en avoir plein le ~ de qqch** *tfam* to have had it up to here with sthg; **être comme ~ et chemise** to be as thick as thieves. **-2.** [de bouteille] bottom; **faire ~ sec** *fam* to down one's drink in one.

culasse [kylas] *nf* **-1.** [d'arme à feu] breech. **-2.** AUTOM cylinder head.

culbute [kylbyt] *nf* **-1.** [saut] somersault. **-2.** [chute] tumble, fall.

culbuter [kylbyte] [3] ◇ *vt* [objet] to knock over. ◇ *vi* **-1.** [faire une chute] to (take a) tumble. **-2.** [se renverser] to (do a) somersault.

cul-de-jatte [kydʒat] (*pl* **culs-de-jatte**) *nm* legless cripple.

cul-de-sac [kydsak] (*pl* **culs-de-sac**) *nm* dead end.

culinaire [kylinɛr] *adj* culinary.

culminant [kylminɑ̃] → **point.**

culminer [kylmine] [3] *vi* [surplomber] to tower; **~ à** [s'élever à] to reach its highest point at; *fig* to peak at.

culot [kylo] *nm* **-1.** *fam* [toupet] cheek, nerve; **avoir le ~ de** to have the cheek OU nerve to; **avoir du ~** to have a lot of nerve. **-2.** [de cartouche, ampoule] cap.

culotte [kylɔt] *nf* **-1.** [sous-vêtement féminin] knickers (*pl*), panties (*pl*), pair of knickers OU panties. **-2.** [vêtement]: ~s **courtes/ longues** short/long trousers; **porter la** ~ *fam fig* to wear the trousers.

culotté, -e [kylɔte] *adj* [effronté]: **elle est** ~**e** she's got a nerve.

culpabiliser [kylpabilize] [3] ◇ *vt*: ~ **qqn** to make sb feel guilty. ◇ *vi* to feel guilty.

culpabilité [kylpabilite] *nf* guilt.

culte [kylt] *nm* **-1.** [vénération, amour] worship. **-2.** [religion] religion.

cultivateur, -trice [kyltivatœr, tris] *nm, f* farmer.

cultivé, -e [kyltive] *adj* [personne] educated, cultured.

cultiver [kyltive] [3] *vt* **-1.** [terre, goût, relation] to cultivate. **-2.** [plante] to grow.
◆ **se cultiver** *vp* to cultivate OU improve one's mind.

culture [kyltyr] *nf* **-1.** AGRIC cultivation, farming; **les** ~**s** cultivated land. **-2.** [savoir] culture, knowledge; ~ **générale** [connaissances] general knowledge; [éducation] general education; ~ **physique** physical training. **-3.** [civilisation] culture.

culturel, -elle [kyltyrɛl] *adj* cultural.

culturisme [kyltyrism] *nm* bodybuilding.

cumin [kymɛ̃] *nm* cumin.

cumul [kymyl] *nm* [de fonctions, titres] holding simultaneously; [de salaires] drawing simultaneously.

cumuler [kymyle] [3] *vt* [fonctions, titres] to hold simultaneously; [salaires] to draw simultaneously.

cumulus [kymylys] *nm* cumulus.

cupide [kypid] *adj* greedy.

cupidité [kypidite] *nf* greed, cupidity.

curaçao [kyraso] *nm* curaçao.

curatif, -ive [kyratif, iv] *adj* curative.

cure [kyr] *nf* (course of) treatment; **faire une** ~ **de fruits** to go on a fruit-based diet; ~ **d'amaigrissement** slimming course *Br*, reducing treatment *Am*; ~ **de désintoxication** [d'alcool] drying-out treatment; [de drogue] detoxification treatment; ~ **de sommeil** sleep therapy; **faire une** ~ **thermale** to take the waters.

curé [kyre] *nm* parish priest.

cure-dents [kyrdɑ̃] *nm inv* toothpick.

cure-pipes *nm inv*, **cure-pipe** (*pl* **cure- pipes**) [kyrpip] *nm* pipe cleaner.

curer [kyre] [3] *vt* to clean out.
◆ **se curer** *vp*: **se** ~ **les ongles** to clean one's nails.

curetage [kyrtaʒ] *nm* curettage.

curie [kyri] *nf* curia.

curieusement [kyrjøzmɑ̃] *adv* curiously, strangely.

curieux, -ieuse [kyrjø, jøz] ◇ *adj* **-1.** [intéressé] curious; ~ **de qqch/de faire qqch** curious about sthg/to do sthg. **-2.** [indiscret] inquisitive. **-3.** [étrange] strange, curious. ◇ *nm, f* busybody.

curiosité [kyrjozite] *nf* curiosity.
◆ **curiosités** *nfpl* interesting sights.

curiste [kyrist] *nmf person undergoing treatment at a spa.*

curling [kœrliŋ] *nm* curling.

curriculum vitae [kyrikylɔmvite] *nm inv* curriculum vitae.

curry [kyri], **carry** [kari], **cari** [kari] *nm* **-1.** [épice] curry powder. **-2.** [plat] curry.

curseur [kyrsœr] *nm* cursor.

cursus [kyrsys] *nm* degree course.

cutané, -e [kytane] *adj* cutaneous, skin (*avant n*).

cuti [kyti] *nf*: **virer sa** ~ *fam fig* to throw off one's shackles.

cuti-réaction (*pl* **cuti-réactions**), **cutiréaction** [kytireaksjɔ̃] *nf* skin test.

cutter [kœtœr] *nm* Stanley knife®.

cuve [kyv] *nf* **-1.** [citerne] tank. **-2.** [à vin] vat.

cuvée [kyve] *nf* **-1.** [récolte] vintage. **-2.** [contenu de cuve] vatful.

cuver [kyve] [3] *vt* **-1.** [faire séjourner en cuve] to put in a vat to ferment. **-2.** [alcool, déception]: ~ **qqch** to sleep sthg off.

cuvette [kyvɛt] *nf* **-1.** [récipient] basin, bowl. **-2.** [de lavabo] basin; [de W.-C.] bowl. **-3.** GÉOGR basin.

cv (*abr de* **cheval-vapeur**) [puissance] HP.

CV *nm* **-1.** (*abr de* **curriculum vitae**) CV; **ça fera bien dans ton** ~ it'll look good on your CV. **-2.** (*abr de* **cheval-vapeur**) hp; [puissance fiscale] *classification for scaling of car tax.*

CVS (*abr de* **corrigées des variations saisonnières**) *adj* seasonally adjusted.

cx *nm* [coefficient de pénétration dans l'air] drag coefficient.

cyanure [sjanyr] *nm* cyanide.

cyclable [siklabl] → **piste**.

Cyclades [siklad] *nfpl*: **les** ~ the Cyclades; **dans les** ~ in the Cyclades.

cyclamen [siklamɛn] *nm* cyclamen.

cycle [sikl] *nm* cycle; ~ **menstruel** menstrual cycle; **premier** ~ UNIV ≃ first and second year; SCOL middle school *Br*, junior high school *Am*; **second** ~ UNIV ≃ final year *Br*, ≃ senior year *Am*; SCOL upper school *Br*, high school *Am*; **troisième** ~ UNIV ≃ postgraduate year OU years.

cyclique [siklik] *adj* cyclic, cyclical.

cyclisme [siklism] *nm* cycling.

cycliste [siklist] ◇ *nmf* cyclist. ◇ *adj* cycle (*avant n*).

cyclo-cross [siklɔkrɔs] *nm inv* cyclo-cross.

cyclomoteur [siklɔmɔtœr] *nm* moped.

cyclone [siklon] *nm* cyclone.

cyclothymique [siklɔtimik] *nmf & adj* manic-depressive.

cyclotourisme [siklɔturism] *nm* cycle touring.

cygne [siɲ] *nm* swan.

cylindre [silɛ̃dr] *nm* **-1.** AUTOM & GÉOM cylinder. **-2.** [rouleau] roller.

cylindrée [silɛ̃dre] *nf* engine capacity.

cylindrique [silɛ̃drik] *adj* cylindrical.

cymbale [sɛ̃bal] *nf* cymbal.

cynique [sinik] ◇ *nmf* cynic. ◇ *adj* cynical.

cynisme [sinism] *nm* cynicism.

cyprès [siprɛ] *nm* cypress.

cypriote, Cypriote → **chypriote**.

cyrillique [sirilik] *adj* Cyrillic.

cystite [sistit] *nf* cystitis (*U*).

cytise [sitiz] *nm* laburnum.

D

d, D [de] *nm inv* d, D.

d' → **de**.

da (*abr de* **déca**) da.

d'abord [dabɔr] → **abord**.

Dacca [daka] *n* Dacca.

d'accord [dakɔr] *loc adv*: ~! all right!, OK!; **être** ~ **avec** to agree with.

dactylo [daktilo] *nf* [personne] typist; [procédé] typing.

dactylographier [daktilɔgrafje] [9] *vt* to type.

dada [dada] *nm* **-1.** [cheval] gee-gee. **-2.** *fam* [occupation] hobby. **-3.** *fam* [idée] hobby-horse. **-4.** ART Dadaism.

dadais [dadɛ] *nm* fool; **un grand** ~ a big OU great lump.

dahlia [dalja] *nm* dahlia.

Dahomey [daɔmɛ] *nm*: **le** ~ Dahomey; **au** ~ in Dahomey.

daigner [deɲe] [4] *vi* to deign.

daim [dɛ̃] *nm* **-1.** [animal] fallow deer. **-2.** [peau] suede.

dais [dɛ] *nm* canopy.

Dakar [dakar] *n* Dakar.

dal (*abr de* **décalitre**) dal.

dallage [dalaʒ] *nm* [action] paving; [dalles] pavement.

dalle [dal] *nf* [de pierre] slab; [de lino] tile; **avoir la** ~ *fam fig* to be famished OU starving; **que** ~! *fam fig* damn all!, not a (damn) thing!

dalmatien, -ienne [dalmasjɛ̃, jɛn] *nm, f* dalmatian.

daltonien, -ienne [daltɔnjɛ̃, jɛn] ◇ *adj* colour-blind. ◇ *nm, f* colour-blind person.

dam[1] [dam] *nm*: **au grand** ~ **de** [déplaisir] to the great displeasure of.

dam[2] (*abr de* **décamètre**) dam.

Damas [damas] *n* Damascus.

dame [dam] *nf* **-1.** [femme] lady. **-2.** CARTES & ÉCHECS queen.
◆ **dames** *nfpl* draughts *Br*, checkers *Am*.

dame-jeanne [damʒan] (*pl* **dames-jeannes**) *nf* demijohn.

damer [dame] [3] *vt* to pack down.

damier [damje] *nm* **-1.** [de jeu] draughtboard *Br*, checkerboard *Am*. **-2.** [motif]: **à** ~ checked.

damnation [danasjɔ̃] *nf* damnation.

damné, -e [dane] ◇ *adj fam* damned. ◇ *nm, f* damned person.

damner [dane] [3] *vt* to damn.
◆ **se damner** *vp* to be damned; **se** ~ **pour** *fig* to risk damnation for.

dancing [dɑ̃siŋ] *nm* dance hall.

dandiner [dɑ̃dine] [3]
◆ **se dandiner** *vp* to waddle.

dandy [dɑ̃di] *nm* dandy.

Danemark [danmark] *nm*: **le** ~ Denmark; **au** ~ in Denmark.

danger [dɑ̃ʒe] *nm* danger; **en** ~ in danger; **hors de** ~ out of danger; **courir un** ~ to run a risk; **narguer le** ~ to flout danger; ~ **public** public menace.

dangereusement [dɑ̃ʒrøzmɑ̃] *adv* dangerously.

dangereux, -euse [dɑ̃ʒrø, øz] *adj* dangerous.

danois, -e [danwa, az] *adj* Danish.
◆ **danois** *nm* **-1.** [langue] Danish. **-2.** [chien] Great Dane.

◆ **Danois, -e** nm, f Dane.

dans [dã] prép **-1.** [dans le temps] in; **je reviens ~ un mois** I'll be back in a month OU in a month's time. **-2.** [dans l'espace] in; **~ une boîte** in OU inside a box; **c'est ~ ma chambre/mon sac** it's in my room/my bag. **-3.** [avec mouvement] into; **entrer ~ une chambre** to come into a room, to enter a room. **-4.** [indiquant état, manière] in; **vivre ~ la misère** to live in poverty; **il est ~ le commerce** he's in business. **-5.** [environ]: **~ les ... about ...; ça coûte ~ les 200 francs** it costs about 200 francs.

dansant, -e [dãsã, ãt] adj litt & fig dancing; **soirée ~e** dance; **thé ~** tea dance.

danse [dãs] nf **-1.** [art] dancing; **~ classique/folklorique/moderne** ballet/folk/modern dancing; **~ du ventre** belly dance. **-2.** [musique] dance.

danser [dãse] [3] ◇ vi **-1.** [personne] to dance. **-2.** [bateau] to bob; [flammes] to flicker. ◇ vt to dance.

danseur, -euse [dãsœr, øz] nm, f dancer; **en danseuse** CYCLISME standing on the pedals; **~ étoile** principal dancer.

dantesque [dãtɛsk] adj Dantesque, Dantean.

DAO (abr de dessin assisté par ordinateur) nm CAD.

dard [dar] nm [d'animal] sting.

darder [darde] [3] vt to beat down; **~ un regard sur** fig to shoot a glance at.

dare-dare [dardar] adv fam like the clappers Br.

Dar es-Salaam [darɛssalam] n Dar es-Salaam.

darne [darn] nf [de poisson] steak.

dartre [dartr] nf sore.

DAT (abr de digital audio tape) DAT.

DATAR, Datar [datar] (abr de Délégation à l'aménagement du territoire et à l'action régionale) nf regional land development agency.

datation [datasjɔ̃] nf dating.

date [dat] nf **-1.** [jour+mois+année] date; **~ limite de vente/de consommation** sell-by/use-by date; **de longue ~** long-standing; **~ de naissance** date of birth. **-2.** [moment] event.

dater [date] [3] ◇ vt to date. ◇ vi **-1.** [marquer] to be OU mark a milestone. **-2.** fam [être démodé] to be dated.

◆ **à dater de** loc prép as of OU from.

dateur, -euse [datœr, øz] adj date (avant n).

◆ **dateur** nm [timbre] datestamp; [de montre] date indicator.

datif [datif] nm GRAM dative.

datte [dat] nf date.

dattier [datje] nm date palm.

daube [dob] nf CULIN ≃ stew.

dauphin [dofɛ̃] nm **-1.** [mammifère] dolphin. **-2.** HIST heir apparent.

dauphine [dofin] nf HIST heir apparent.

daurade, dorade [dɔrad] nf sea bream.

davantage [davãtaʒ] adv **-1.** [plus] more; **~ de** more. **-2.** [plus longtemps] (any) longer.

dB (abr de décibel) dB.

DB (abr de division blindée) nf armoured division.

DCA (abr de défense contre aéronefs) nf AA (anti-aircraft).

DCT (abr de diphtérie coqueluche tétanos) nm vaccine against diphtheria, tetanus and whooping cough.

DDA (abr de Direction départementale de l'agriculture) nf local offices of the Ministry of Agriculture.

DDASS, Ddass [das] (abr de Direction départementale d'action sanitaire et sociale) nf ≈ DSS Br, ≈ SSA Am; **un enfant de la ~** a state orphan.

DDD (abr de digital digital digital) DDD.

DDE (abr de Direction départementale de l'Équipement) nf local offices of the Ministry of the Environment.

DDT (abr de dichloro-diphényl-trichloréthane) nm DDT.

DDTAB (abr de diphtérie, tétanos, typhoïde, paratyphoïde A) nm vaccine against diphtheria, tetanus, typhoid and paratyphoid.

de [də] (contraction de de + le = **du** [dy], de + les = **des** [de]) ◇ prép **-1.** [provenance] from; **revenir ~ Paris** to come back OU return from Paris; **il est sorti ~ la maison** he left the house, he went out of the house. **-2.** [avec à]: **~ ... à** from ... to; **~ Paris à Tokyo** from Paris to Tokyo; **~ dix heures à midi** from ten o'clock to OU till midday; **il y avait ~ quinze à vingt mille spectateurs** there were between fifteen and twenty thousand spectators. **-3.** [appartenance] of; **la porte du salon** the door of the sitting room, the sitting-room door; **le frère ~ Pierre** Pierre's brother; **la maison ~ mes parents** my parents' house. **-4.** [indique la détermination, la qualité]: **un verre d'eau** a glass of water; **un peignoir ~ soie** a silk dressing gown; **un appartement ~ 60m²** a flat 60 metres square; **un bébé ~ trois jours** a three-day-old baby; **une ville ~ 500 000 habitants** a town with OU of 500,000 inhabitants.

◇ *article partitif* **-1.** [dans une phrase affirmative] some; **je voudrais du vin/du lait** I'd like (some) wine/(some) milk; **boire ~ l'eau** to drink (some) water; **acheter des légumes** to buy some vegetables. **-2.** [dans une interrogation ou une négation] any; **ils n'ont pas d'enfants** they don't have any children, they have no children; **avez-vous du pain?** do you have any bread?, have you got any bread?; **voulez-vous du thé?** would you like some tea?

dé [de] *nm* **-1.** [à jouer] dice, die. **-2.** [morceau] dice, cube; **couper en ~s** CULIN to dice. **-3.** COUTURE: ~ **(à coudre)** thimble.

DE (*abr de* **diplômé d'État**) *adj* qualified; **infirmière ~** qualified nurse, ≃ RGN *Br*.

DEA (*abr de* **diplôme d'études approfondies**) *nm* postgraduate diploma.

dealer¹ [dile] *vt* to deal.

dealer² [dilœr] *nm fam* dealer.

déambuler [deãbyle] [3] *vi* to stroll (around).

débâcle [debakl] *nf* [débandade] rout; *fig* collapse.

déballage [debalaʒ] *nm litt* unpacking.

déballer [debale] [3] *vt* to unpack; *fam fig* to pour out.

débandade [debãdad] *nf* dispersal.

débaptiser [debatize] [3] *vt* to rename.

débarbouiller [debarbuje] [3] *vt*: ~ **qqn** to wash sb's face.

◆ **se débarbouiller** *vp* to wash one's face.

débarcadère [debarkadɛr] *nm* landing stage.

débardeur [debardœr] *nm* **-1.** [ouvrier] docker. **-2.** [vêtement] slipover.

débarquement [debarkəmã] *nm* unloading; **le Débarquement** HIST the D-Day landings.

débarquer [debarke] [3] ◇ *vt* [marchandises] to unload; [passagers & MIL] to land. ◇ *vi* **-1.** [d'un bateau] to disembark. **-2.** MIL to land. **-3.** *fam* [arriver à l'improviste] to turn up; *fig* to know nothing.

débarras [debara] *nm* junk room; **bon ~!** *fig* good riddance!

débarrasser [debarase] [3] *vt* **-1.** [pièce] to clear up; [table] to clear. **-2.** [ôter]: ~ **qqn de qqch** to take sth from sb.

◆ **se débarrasser** *vp*: **se ~ de** to get rid of.

débat [deba] *nm* debate; **élargir le ~** to broaden OU widen the debate.

◆ **débats** *nmpl* debates, proceedings.

débattre [debatr] [83] ◇ *vt* to debate, to

discuss. ◇ *vi*: ~ **de qqch** to debate OU discuss sthg.

◆ **se débattre** *vp* to struggle; **se ~ avec** OU **contre** *fig* to struggle with OU against.

débattu, -e [debaty] *pp* → **débattre**.

débauche [deboʃ] *nf* debauchery; **une ~ de** *fig* a profusion of.

débauché, -e [deboʃe] ◇ *adj* debauched. ◇ *nm, f* debauched person.

débaucher [deboʃe] [3] *vt* **-1.** [corrompre] to debauch, to corrupt. **-2.** [licencier] to make redundant.

débile [debil] ◇ *nmf* **-1.** [attardé] retarded person; ~ **mental** mentally retarded person; ~ **profond** profoundly retarded person. **-2.** *fam* [idiot] moron. ◇ *adj fam* stupid.

débilitant, -e [debilitã, ãt] *adj* debilitating.

débilité [debilite] *nf* **-1.** [stupidité] stupidity. **-2.** [maladie] debility, deficiency.

débiner [debine] [3]

◆ **se débiner** *vp fam* to clear off.

débit [debi] *nm* **-1.** [de marchandises] (retail) sale. **-2.** [magasin]: ~ **de boissons** bar; ~ **de tabac** tobacconist's *Br*, tobacco shop *Am*. **-3.** [coupe] sawing up, cutting up. **-4.** [de liquide] (rate of) flow. **-5.** [élocution] delivery. **-6.** FIN debit; **avoir un ~ de 500 francs** to be 500 francs overdrawn.

débitant, -e [debitã, ãt] *nm, f* **-1.** [de boissons] licensed grocer. **-2.** [de tabac] tobacconist *Br*, tobacco dealer *Am*.

débiter [debite] [3] *vt* **-1.** [marchandises] to sell. **-2.** [arbre] to saw up; [viande] to cut up. **-3.** [suj: robinet] to have a flow of. **-4.** *fam fig* [prononcer] to spout. **-5.** FIN to debit.

débiteur, -trice [debitœr, tris] ◇ *adj* **-1.** [personne] debtor (*avant n*). **-2.** FIN debit (*avant n*), in the red. ◇ *nm, f* debtor.

déblaiement [deblɛmã], **déblayage** [deblɛjaʒ] *nm* clearing.

déblatérer [deblatere] [18] *vi fam* [médire]: ~ **contre** to rant on about.

déblayage = **déblaiement**.

déblayer [debleje] [11] *vt* [dégager] to clear; ~ **le terrain** *fig* to clear the ground.

débloquer [deblɔke] [3] ◇ *vt* **-1.** [machine] to get going again. **-2.** [crédit] to release. **-3.** [compte, salaires, prix] to unfreeze. ◇ *vi fam* to talk rubbish.

déboires [debwar] *nmpl* **-1.** [déceptions] disappointments. **-2.** [échecs] setbacks. **-3.** [ennuis] trouble (*U*), problems.

déboisement [debwazmã] *nm* deforestation.

déboiser [debwaze] [3] *vt* [région] to deforest; [terrain] to clear (of trees).
◆ **se déboiser** *vp* to become deforested.

déboîter [debwate] [3] ◇ *vt* **-1.** [objet] to dislodge; ~ **une porte** to take a door off its hinges. **-2.** [membre] to dislocate. ◇ *vi* AUTOM to pull out.
◆ **se déboîter** *vp* **-1.** [se démonter] to come apart; [porte] to come off its hinges. **-2.** [membre] to dislocate.

débonnaire [debɔnɛr] *adj* good-natured, easy-going.

débordant, -e [debɔrdɑ̃, ɑ̃t] *adj* **-1.** [activité] bustling. **-2.** [personne]: ~ **de** [joie, vie] overflowing with; [santé, énergie] bursting with.

débordement [debɔrdəmɑ̃] *nm* **-1.** [de fleuve, récipient] **overflowing. -2.** [de joie, tendresse] **outburst.**
◆ **débordements** *nmpl* excesses.

déborder [debɔrde] [3] ◇ *vi* [fleuve, liquide] to overflow; *fig* to flood; ~ **de** [vie, joie] to be bubbling with. ◇ *vt* [limite] to go beyond.

débouché [debuʃe] *nm* **-1.** [issue] end. **-2.** (*gén pl*) COMM outlet. **-3.** [de carrière] prospect, opening.

déboucher [debuʃe] [3] ◇ *vt* **-1.** [bouteille] to open. **-2.** [conduite, nez] to unblock. ◇ *vi*: ~ **sur** [arriver] to open out into; *fig* to lead to, to achieve.

débouler [debule] [3] ◇ *vi* [personne - arriver] to charge up; [animal] to bolt. ◇ *vt* to hurtle down.

déboulonner [debulɔne] [3] *vt* [statue] to dismantle.

débourser [deburse] [3] *vt* to pay out.

déboussoler [debusɔle] [3] *vt fam* to throw, to disorientate.

debout [dəbu] *adv* **-1.** [gén] **être** ~ [sur ses pieds] to be standing (up); [réveillé] to be up; [objet] to be standing up OU upright; **mettre qqch** ~ to stand sthg up; **se mettre** ~ to stand up; ~**!** get up!, on your feet! **-2.** *loc*: **tenir** ~ [bâtiment] to remain standing; [argument] to stand up; **il ne tient pas** ~ he's asleep on his feet.

débouter [debute] [3] *vt* JUR to dismiss.

déboutonner [debutɔne] [3] *vt* to unbutton, to undo.
◆ **se déboutonner** *vp* [défaire ses boutons] to undo one's buttons/one's jacket *etc*.

débraillé, -e [debraje] *adj* dishevelled.

débrancher [debrɑ̃ʃe] [3] *vt* **-1.** [appareil] to unplug. **-2.** [téléphone] to disconnect.

débrayage [debrɛjaʒ] *nm* **-1.** [AUTOM - pièce]

clutch; [- action] disengagement of the clutch. **-2.** [arrêt de travail] stoppage.

débrayer [debreje] [11] *vi* **-1.** AUTOM to disengage the clutch, to declutch. **-2.** [cesser le travail] to stop work.

débridé, -e [debride] *adj fig* & *sout* [imagination, sensualité] unbridled.

débris [debri] ◇ *nm* piece, fragment. ◇ *nmpl* **-1.** [restes] leftovers. **-2.** *fig* & *littéraire* [d'armée, fortune] remains; [d'un état] ruins.

débrouillard, -e [debrujar, ard] *fam* ◇ *adj* resourceful. ◇ *nm, f* resourceful person.

débrouillardise [debrujardiz] *nf fam* resourcefulness.

débrouiller [debruje] [3] *vt* **-1.** [démêler] to untangle. **-2.** *fig* [résoudre] to unravel, to solve.
◆ **se débrouiller** *vp*: **se** ~ **(pour faire qqch)** to manage (to do sthg); **se** ~ **en anglais/math** to get by in English/maths; **débrouille-toi!** you'll have to sort it out (by) yourself!

débroussailler [debrusaje] [3] *vt* [terrain] to clear; *fig* to do the groundwork for.

débusquer [debyske] [3] *vt* **-1.** [gibier] to drive out. **-2.** [personne] to flush out.

début [deby] *nm* beginning, start; **au** ~ at the start OU beginning; **dès le** ~ (right) from the start.
◆ **débuts** *nmpl* debut (*sg*).
◆ **au début de** *loc prép* at the beginning of.

débutant, -e [debytɑ̃, ɑ̃t] *nm, f* beginner.

débuter [debyte] [3] *vi* **-1.** [commencer]: ~ **(par)** to begin (with), to start (with). **-2.** [faire ses débuts] to start out.

deçà [dəsa]
◆ **deçà delà** *loc adv* here and there.
◆ **en deçà de** *loc prép* **-1.** [de ce côté-ci de] on this side of. **-2.** [en dessous de] short of.

décacheter [dekaʃte] [27] *vt* to open.

décade [dekad] *nf* period of ten days.

décadence [dekadɑ̃s] *nf* **-1.** [déclin] decline. **-2.** [débauche] decadence.

décadent, -e [dekadɑ̃, ɑ̃t] *adj* decadent.

décaféiné, -e [dekafeine] *adj* decaffeinated.
◆ **décaféiné** *nm* decaffeinated coffee.

décalage [dekalaʒ] *nm* gap; *fig* gulf, discrepancy; ~ **horaire** [entre zones] time difference; [après un vol] jet lag.

décalcification [dekalsifikasjɔ̃] *nf* decalcification.

décalcomanie [dekalkɔmani] *nf* transfer (*adhesive*).

décaler [dekale] [3] *vt* **-1.** [dans le temps -

avancer] to bring forward; [- retarder] to put back. **-2.** [dans l'espace] to move, to shift.
◆ **se décaler** *vp* to move.

décalquer [dekalke] [3] *vt* to trace.

décamper [dekɑ̃pe] [3] *vi fam* to clear off.

décan [dekɑ̃] *nm* ASTROL *one of three subdivisions of each star sign.*

décanter [dekɑ̃te] [3] ◇ *vt*: **laisser** ~ [liquide] to allow to settle; *fig* [idée] to allow to settle down OU become clearer. ◇ *vi* [liquide] to settle; *fig* [idées] to become clear.
◆ **se décanter** *vp* [idées] to become clear.

décapant, -e [dekapɑ̃, ɑ̃t] *adj* **-1.** [nettoyant] stripping. **-2.** *fig* [incisif] cutting, caustic.
◆ **décapant** *nm* (paint) stripper.

décaper [dekape] [3] *vt* to strip, to sand.

décapiter [dekapite] [3] *vt* [personne] to behead; [- accidentellement] to decapitate; [arbre] to cut the top off; *fig* to remove the leader OU leaders of.

décapotable [dekapɔtabl] *nf & adj* convertible.

décapsuler [dekapsyle] [3] *vt* to take the top off, to open.

décapsuleur [dekapsylœr] *nm* bottle opener.

décarcasser [dekarkase] [3]
◆ **se décarcasser** *vp fam*: **se** ~ (**à faire qqch**) to slog away (at doing sthg).

décédé, -e [desede] *adj* deceased.

décéder [desede] [18] *vi* to die.

déceler [desle] [25] *vt* **-1.** [révéler] to reveal. **-2.** [repérer] to detect.

décélération [deselerasjɔ̃] *nf* deceleration.

décembre [desɑ̃br] *nm* December; *voir aussi* **septembre**.

décemment [desamɑ̃] *adv* **-1.** [convenablement] properly. **-2.** [raisonnablement] reasonably.

décence [desɑ̃s] *nf* decency.

décennie [deseni] *nf* decade.

décent, -e [desɑ̃, ɑ̃t] *adj* decent.

décentralisation [desɑ̃tralizasjɔ̃] *nf* decentralization.

décentraliser [desɑ̃tralize] [3] *vt* to decentralize.

décentrer [desɑ̃tre] [3] *vt* to move off-centre OU away from the centre.

déception [desɛpsjɔ̃] *nf* disappointment.

décerner [desɛrne] [3] *vt*: ~ **qqch à** to award sthg to.

décès [desɛ] *nm* death.

décevant, -e [desəvɑ̃, ɑ̃t] *adj* disappointing.

décevoir [desəvwar] [52] *vt* to disappoint.

déchaîné, -e [deʃene] *adj* **-1.** [vent, mer] stormy, wild. **-2.** [passion] unrestrained; [opinion publique] raging. **-3.** [personne] wild.

déchaîner [deʃene] [4] *vt* [passion] to unleash; [rires] to cause an outburst of.
◆ **se déchaîner** *vp* **-1.** [éléments naturels] to erupt. **-2.** [personne] to fly into a rage.

déchanter [deʃɑ̃te] [3] *vi* to become disillusioned.

décharge [deʃarʒ] *nf* **-1.** JUR discharge. **-2.** ÉLECTR discharge; ~ **électrique** electric shock. **-3.** [reçu] receipt. **-4.** [dépotoir] rubbish tip OU dump *Br,* garbage dump *Am;* ~ **municipale** city/town refuse tip *Br.*

déchargement [deʃarʒəmɑ̃] *nm* unloading.

décharger [deʃarʒe] [17] *vt* **-1.** [véhicule, marchandises] to unload. **-2.** [arme - tirer] to fire, to discharge; [- enlever la charge] to unload. **-3.** [soulager - cœur] to unburden; [- conscience] to salve; [- colère] to vent. **-4.** [libérer]: ~ **qqn de** to release sb from.
◆ **se décharger** *vp* **-1.** ÉLECTR to go flat. **-2.** [se libérer]: **se** ~ **de qqch sur** to offload sthg onto. **-3.** [rivière]: **se** ~ **dans** to flow into.

décharné, -e [deʃarne] *adj* [maigre] emaciated.

déchausser [deʃose] [3] *vt*: ~ **qqn** to take sb's shoes off.
◆ **se déchausser** *vp* **-1.** [personne] to take one's shoes off. **-2.** [dent] to come loose.

dèche [dɛʃ] *nf fam*: **être dans la** ~ to be on one's uppers.

déchéance [deʃeɑ̃s] *nf* **-1.** [déclin] degeneration, decline. **-2.** [d'un souverain] dethronement. **-3.** JUR loss.

déchet [deʃɛ] *nm* [de matériau] scrap.
◆ **déchets** *nmpl* refuse (*U*), waste (*U*); ~**s radioactifs** radioactive waste.

déchiffrer [deʃifre] [3] *vt* **-1.** [inscription, hiéroglyphes] to decipher; [énigme] to unravel. **-2.** MUS to sight-read.

déchiqueter [deʃikte] [27] *vt* to tear to shreds.

déchirant, -e [deʃirɑ̃, ɑ̃t] *adj* heartrending.

déchirement [deʃirmɑ̃] *nm* **-1.** [division] rift, split. **-2.** [souffrance morale] heartbreak, distress.

déchirer [deʃire] [3] *vt* **-1.** [papier, tissu] to tear up, to rip up. **-2.** *fig* [diviser] to tear apart.
◆ **se déchirer** *vp* **-1.** [personnes] to tear each other apart. **-2.** [matériau, muscle] to tear.

déchirure [deʃiryr] *nf* tear; *fig* wrench; ~ **musculaire** MÉD torn muscle.

déchoir [deʃwar] [71] *vi sout* [s'abaisser] to demean o.s.

déchu, -e [deʃy] ◇ *pp* → **déchoir.** ◇ *adj* **-1.** [homme, ange] fallen; [souverain] deposed. **-2.** JUR: être ~ **de** to be deprived of.

deci [dəsi]
◆ **deci-delà** *adv sout* here and there.

décibel [desibɛl] *nm* decibel.

décidé, -e [deside] *adj* **-1.** [résolu] determined. **-2.** [arrêté] settled.

décidément [desidemɑ̃] *adv* really.

décider [deside] [3] *vt* **-1.** [prendre une décision]: ~ **(de faire qqch)** to decide (to do sthg); ~ **que** to decide (that). **-2.** [convaincre]: ~ **qqn à faire qqch** to persuade sb to do sthg. **-3.** [déterminer]: ~ **de qqch** to decide on sthg.
◆ **se décider** *vp* **-1.** [personne]: se ~ **(à faire qqch)** to make up one's mind (to do sthg). **-2.** [affaire] to be decided, to be settled. **-3.** [choisir]: se ~ **pour** to decide on, to settle on.

décideur [desidœr] *nm* decision-maker.

décilitre [desilitr] *nm* decilitre.

décimal, -e, -aux [desimal, o] *adj* decimal.
◆ **décimale** *nf* decimal.

décimer [desime] [3] *vt* to decimate.

décimètre [desimɛtr] *nm* **-1.** [dixième de mètre] decimetre. **-2.** [règle] ruler; **double ~** ≃ foot rule.

décisif, -ive [desizif, iv] *adj* decisive.

décision [desizjɔ̃] *nf* decision; **prendre une** ~ to take OU make a decision.

décisionnaire [desizjɔnɛr] *nmf* decision-maker.

déclamer [deklame] [3] *vt* to declaim.

déclaration [deklarasjɔ̃] *nf* **-1.** [orale] declaration, announcement; **faire une** ~ to make a statement; ~ **de guerre/d'amour** declaration of war/of love. **-2.** [écrite] report, declaration; [d'assurance] claim; ~ **de naissance/de décès** registration of birth/death; ~ **d'impôts** tax return; ~ **de revenus** statement of income.

DÉCLARATION D'IMPÔTS:
People in France are required to declare their taxable earnings at the beginning of the year. Quarterly tax payments ('tiers provisionnels') are based on estimated tax for the year, the payment for the final quarter being adjusted according to the actual tax owed

déclarer [deklare] [3] *vt* **-1.** [annoncer] to declare; ~ **que** to declare (that). **-2.** [signaler] to report; ~ **une naissance** to register a birth.
◆ **se déclarer** *vp* **-1.** [se prononcer]: se ~ **pour/contre qqch** to come out in favour of/against sthg. **-2.** [se manifester] to break out.

déclasser [deklase] [3] *vt* **-1.** [personne - gén] to downgrade; SPORT to relegate. **-2.** [objets] to get out of order.

déclenchement [deklɑ̃ʃmɑ̃] *nm* [de mécanisme] activating, setting off; *fig* launching.

déclencher [deklɑ̃ʃe] [3] *vt* [mécanisme] to activate, to set off; *fig* to launch.
◆ **se déclencher** *vp* [mécanisme] to go off, to be activated; *fig* to be triggered off.

déclic [deklik] *nm* **-1.** [mécanisme] trigger. **-2.** [bruit] click.

déclin [deklɛ̃] *nm* **-1.** [de civilisation, population, santé] decline; **une personnalité sur son** ~ *fig* a celebrity on the wane. **-2.** [fin] close.

déclinaison [deklinɛzɔ̃] *nf* GRAM declension.

décliner [dekline] [3] ◇ *vi* **-1.** [santé, population, popularité] to decline. **-2.** [jour] to draw to a close. ◇ *vt* **-1.** [offre, honneur] to decline; ~ **une invitation** to decline an invitation; ~ **toute responsabilité** to accept no responsibility. **-2.** GRAM to decline; *fig* [gamme de produits] to develop. **-3.** [énoncer] to state.
◆ **se décliner** *vp* GRAM to decline.

déclivité [deklivite] *nf* slope, incline.

décloisonner [deklwazɔne] [3] *vt fig* to decompartmentalize.

déclouer [deklue] [3] *vt* to take the nails out of.

décocher [dekɔʃe] [3] *vt litt & fig* to let fly; ~ **un regard** to shoot a glance.

décoction [dekɔksjɔ̃] *nf* decoction.

décodage [dekɔdaʒ] *nm* decoding.

décoder [dekɔde] [3] *vt* to decode.

décodeur [dekɔdœr] *nm* decoder.

décoiffer [dekwafe] [3] *vt* [cheveux] to mess up.
◆ **se décoiffer** *vp* **-1.** [cheveux] to be messed up. **-2.** [enlever son chapeau] to take off one's hat.

décoincer [dekwɛse] [16] *vt* **-1.** [chose] to loosen; [mécanisme] to unjam. **-2.** *fam* [personne] to loosen up.
◆ **se décoincer** *vp* **-1.** [mécanisme] to loosen. **-2.** *fam fig* [personne] to loosen up.

déçois, déçoit *etc* → **décevoir.**

décolérer [dekɔlere] [18] *vi*: **il n'a pas décoléré** he hasn't calmed down.

décollage [dekɔlaʒ] *nm litt & fig* takeoff.

décollé, -e [dekɔle] adj: **il a les oreilles ~es** his ears stick out.

décollement [dekɔlmɑ̃] nm: **~ de la rétine** MÉD detachment of the retina.

décoller [dekɔle] [3] ◇ vt [étiquette, timbre] to unstick; [papier peint] to strip (off). ◇ vi litt & fig to take off.
◆ **se décoller** vp [étiquette, timbre] to come unstuck; [papier peint] to peel off.

décolleté, -e [dekɔlte] adj [vêtement] low-cut.
◆ **décolleté** nm -1. [de personne] neck and shoulders (pl). -2. [de vêtement] neckline, neck.

décolonisation [dekɔlɔnizasjɔ̃] nf decolonization.

décolorant, -e [dekɔlɔrɑ̃, ɑ̃t] adj bleaching (avant n).
◆ **décolorant** nm bleach.

décoloration [dekɔlɔrasjɔ̃] nf bleaching.

décolorer [dekɔlɔre] [3] vt [par décolorant] to bleach, to lighten; [par usure] to fade.
◆ **se décolorer** vp -1. [se ternir] to fade. -2. [cheveux] to bleach.

décombres [dekɔ̃br] nmpl debris (U).

décommander [dekɔmɑ̃de] [3] vt to cancel.
◆ **se décommander** vp to cancel one's appointment.

décomposé, -e [dekɔ̃poze] adj -1. [pourri] decomposed. -2. [visage] haggard; [personne] in shock.

décomposer [dekɔ̃poze] [3] vt -1. [gén]: **~ (en)** to break down (into). -2. fig [troubler] to distort.
◆ **se décomposer** vp -1. [se putréfier] to rot, to decompose. -2. [se diviser]: **se ~ en** to be broken down into. -3. fig [s'altérer] to be distorted.

décomposition [dekɔ̃pozisjɔ̃] nf -1. [putréfaction] decomposition. -2. fig [analyse] breaking down, analysis.

décompresser [dekɔ̃prese] [4] ◇ vt TECHNOL to decompress. ◇ vi to unwind.

décompression [dekɔ̃presjɔ̃] nf decompression.

décompte [dekɔ̃t] nm -1. [calcul] breakdown (of an amount). -2. [réduction] deduction; **j'ai fait le ~ de ce que tu me dois** I've deducted OU taken off what you owe me.

décompter [dekɔ̃te] [3] vt to deduct.

déconcentrer [dekɔ̃sɑ̃tre] [3] vt -1. [disséminer] to decentralize. -2. [distraire] to distract.
◆ **se déconcentrer** vp to be distracted.

déconcertant, -e [dekɔ̃sɛrtɑ̃, ɑ̃t] adj disconcerting.

déconcerter [dekɔ̃sɛrte] [3] vt to disconcert.

déconfit, -e [dekɔ̃fi, it] adj crestfallen.

déconfiture [dekɔ̃fityr] nf collapse, ruin.

décongeler [dekɔ̃ʒle] [25] vt to defrost.

décongestionner [dekɔ̃ʒɛstjɔne] [3] vt to relieve congestion in; **~ la circulation** to reduce traffic.

déconnecter [dekɔnɛkte] [4] vt to disconnect; **être déconnecté** fam to be out of touch.
◆ **se déconnecter** vp INFORM to disconnect, to log off.

déconner [dekɔne] [3] vi tfam [dire] to talk rubbish; [faire] to muck around.

déconseillé, -e [dekɔ̃seje] adj: **c'est fortement ~** it's extremely inadvisable.

déconseiller [dekɔ̃seje] [4] vt: **~ qqch à qqn** to advise sb against sthg; **~ à qqn de faire qqch** to advise sb against doing sthg.

déconsidérer [dekɔ̃sidere] [18] vt to discredit.
◆ **se déconsidérer** vp to be discredited.

décontaminer [dekɔ̃tamine] [3] vt to decontaminate.

décontenancer [dekɔ̃tnɑ̃se] [16] vt to put out.
◆ **se décontenancer** vp to be put out.

décontracté, -e [dekɔ̃trakte] adj -1. [muscle] relaxed. -2. [détendu] casual, laid-back.

décontracter [dekɔ̃trakte] [3] vt to relax.
◆ **se décontracter** vp to relax.

déconvenue [dekɔ̃vny] nf disappointment.

décor [dekɔr] nm -1. [cadre] scenery. -2. [ornement] decoration. -3. THÉÂTRE scenery (U); CIN sets (pl), décor.

décorateur, -trice [dekɔratœr, tris] nm, f CIN & THÉÂTRE designer; **~ d'intérieur** interior decorator.

décoratif, -ive [dekɔratif, iv] adj decorative.

décoration [dekɔrasjɔ̃] nf decoration.

décorer [dekɔre] [3] vt to decorate.

décortiquer [dekɔrtike] [3] vt [noix] to shell; [graine] to husk; fig to analyse in minute detail.

décorum [dekɔrɔm] nm decorum.

découcher [dekuʃe] [3] vi to stay out all night.

découdre [dekudr] [86] vt COUTURE to unpick; **en ~** to come to blows.
◆ **se découdre** vp to come unstitched.

découler [dekule] [3] vi: **~ de** to follow from.

découpage [dekupaʒ] nm -1. [action] cutting out; [résultat] paper cutout. -2. CIN preparation of screenplay. -3. ADMIN: **~ (électoral)**

division into constituencies. **-4.** *fig* [de texte] cutting, editing.

découper [dekupe] [3] *vt* **-1.** [couper] to cut up. **-2.** *fig* [diviser] to cut out.

◆ **se découper** *vp fig*: **se ~ sur** to stand out against.

découplé, -e [dekuple] *adj*: **bien ~** well-proportioned.

découpure [dekupyr] *nf* [bord] indentations (*pl*), jagged outline.

décourageant, -e [dekuraʒɑ̃, ɑ̃t] *adj* discouraging.

découragement [dekuraʒmɑ̃] *nm* discouragement.

décourager [dekuraʒe] [17] *vt* to discourage; **~ qqn de qqch** to put sb off sthg; **~ qqn de faire qqch** to discourage sb from doing sthg.

◆ **se décourager** *vp* to lose heart.

décousu, -e [dekuzy] ◇ *pp* → **découdre**. ◇ *adj fig* [conversation] disjointed.

découvert, -e [dekuvɛr, ɛrt] ◇ *pp* → **découvrir**. ◇ *adj* [tête] bare; [terrain] exposed.

◆ **découvert** *nm* BANQUE overdraft; **être à ~ (de 6000 francs)** to be (6,000 francs) overdrawn.

◆ **découverte** *nf* discovery; **aller à la ~e de** to explore.

découvrir [dekuvrir] [34] *vt* **-1.** [trouver, surprendre] to discover. **-2.** [ôter ce qui couvre, mettre à jour] to uncover. **-3.** [laisser voir] to reveal.

◆ **se découvrir** *vp* **-1.** [se dévêtir] to take off one's clothes, to undress. **-2.** [ôter son chapeau] to take off one's hat. **-3.** [ciel] to clear. **-4.** [se trouver - cousin, penchant] to discover.

décrasser [dekrase] [3] *vt* to scrub.

décrépit, -e [dekrepi, it] *adj* decrepit.

décrépitude [dekrepityd] *nf* **-1.** [de personne] decrepitude. **-2.** [d'objet] dilapidation.

decrescendo [dekreʃɛndo] ◇ *nm inv* decrescendo. ◇ *adv* MUS decrescendo; **aller ~** *fig* to wane.

décret [dekrɛ] *nm* decree; **~ ministériel** order in council.

décréter [dekrete] [18] *vt* **-1.** ADMIN to decree. **-2.** [décider]: **~ que** to decide that.

décrier [dekrije] [10] *vt sout* to decry.

décrire [dekrir] [99] *vt* to describe.

décrit, -e [dekri, it] *pp* → **décrire**.

décrisper [dekrispe] [3] *vt* **-1.** [personne] to put at ease. **-2.** [atmosphère] to ease.

◆ **se décrisper** *vp* to relax.

décrochement [dekrɔʃmɑ̃] *nm* **-1.** GÉOL thrust fault. **-2.** [action] unhooking. **-3.** [partie en retrait] recess.

décrocher [dekrɔʃe] [3] ◇ *vt* **-1.** [enlever] to take down. **-2.** [téléphone] to pick up. **-3.** *fam* [obtenir] to land. ◇ *vi fam* [abandonner] to drop out.

◆ **se décrocher** *vp* to fall down.

décroiser [dekrwaze] [3] *vt* to unfold, to uncross.

décroissant, -e [dekrwasɑ̃, ɑ̃t] *adj* [courbe] decreasing; [influence] diminishing; **par ordre ~** in descending order.

décroître [dekrwatr] [94] *vi* to decrease, to diminish; [jours] to get shorter.

décrotter [dekrɔte] [3] *vt* to clean the mud off.

décru, -e [dekry] *pp* → **décroître**.

◆ **décrue** *nf* drop in the water level.

décrypter [dekripte] [3] *vt* to decipher.

déçu, -e [desy] ◇ *pp* → **décevoir**. ◇ *adj* disappointed.

déculotter [dekylɔte] [3] *vt*: **~ qqn** to take sb's trousers off.

◆ **se déculotter** *vp* to take off one's trousers.

déculpabiliser [dekylpabilize] [3] *vt*: **~ qqn** to free sb from guilt.

◆ **se déculpabiliser** *vp* to free o.s. from guilt.

décupler [dekyple] [3] *vt & vi* to increase tenfold.

dédaigner [dedɛɲe] [4] *vt* **-1.** [mépriser - personne] to despise; [- conseils, injures] to scorn. **-2.** [refuser]: **~ de faire qqch** *sout* to disdain to do sthg; **ne pas ~ qqch/de faire qqch** not to be above sthg/above doing sthg.

dédaigneusement [dedɛɲøzmɑ̃] *adv* disdainfully.

dédaigneux, -euse [dedɛɲø, øz] *adj* disdainful.

dédain [dedɛ̃] *nm* disdain, contempt.

dédale [dedal] *nm litt & fig* maze.

dedans [dədɑ̃] *adv & nm* inside.

◆ **de dedans** *loc adv* from inside, from within.

◆ **en dedans** *loc adv* inside, within.

◆ **en dedans de** *loc prép* inside, within; *voir aussi* **là-dedans**.

dédicace [dedikas] *nf* dedication.

dédicacer [dedikase] [16] *vt*: **~ qqch (à qqn)** to sign OU autograph sthg (for sb).

dédié, -e [dedje] *adj* INFORM dedicated.

dédier [dedje] [9] *vt*: **~ qqch (à qqn/à qqch)** to dedicate sthg (to sb/to sthg).

dédire [dedir] [103]
◆ **se dédire** *vp sout* to go back on one's word.

dédit [dedi] *nm* JUR penalty (clause).

dédommagement [dedɔmaʒmã] *nm* compensation.

dédommager [dedɔmaʒe] [17] *vt* **-1.** [indemniser] to compensate. **-2.** *fig* [remercier] to repay.

dédouanement [dedwanmã], **dédouanage** [dedwanaʒ] *nm* customs clearance.

dédouaner [dedwane] [3] *vt* [marchandises] to clear through customs.

dédoublement [dedublǝmã] *nm* halving, splitting (in two); ~ **de la personnalité** PSYCHOL & *fig* split personality.

dédoubler [deduble] [3] *vt* to halve, to split; [fil] to separate.
◆ **se dédoubler** *vp* **-1.** PSYCHOL & *fig* to have a split personality. **-2.** *fig & hum* [être partout] to be in two places at once.

dédramatiser [dedramatize] [3] *vt* [événement] to play down; [situation] to defuse.

déductible [dedyktibl] *adj* deductible.

déduction [dedyksjɔ̃] *nf* deduction.

déduire [dedɥir] [98] *vt*: ~ **qqch (de)** [ôter] to deduct sthg (from); [conclure] to deduce sthg (from).

déduisais, **déduisait** *etc* → **déduire**.

déduit, -e [dedɥi, ɥit] *pp* → **déduire**.

déesse [deɛs] *nf* goddess.

DEFA, Defa [defa] (*abr de* **diplôme d'État relatif aux fonctions d'animation**) *nm diploma for senior youth leaders.*

défaillance [defajãs] *nf* **-1.** [incapacité - de machine] failure; [- de personne, organisation] weakness. **-2.** [malaise] blackout, fainting fit; ~ **cardiaque** MÉD heart failure.

défaillant, -e [defajã, ãt] *adj* [faible] failing.

défaillir [defajir] [47] *vi* **-1.** [s'évanouir] to faint. **-2.** [faire défaut] to fail.

défaire [defɛr] [109] *vt* **-1.** [détacher] to undo; [valise] to unpack; [lit] to strip. **-2.** *sout* [vaincre] to defeat.
◆ **se défaire** *vp* **-1.** [ne pas tenir] to come undone. **-2.** *sout* [se séparer]: **se** ~ **de** *sout* to get rid of.

défaisais, **défaisions** *etc* → **défaire**.

défait, -e [defɛ, ɛt] ◇ *pp* → **défaire**. ◇ *adj fig* [épuisé] haggard.
◆ **défaite** *nf* defeat.

défaitisme [defetism] *nm* defeatism.

défaitiste [defetist] *nmf & adj* defeatist.

défalcation [defalkasjɔ̃] *nf* deduction.

défalquer [defalke] [3] *vt* to deduct.

défasse, **défasses** *etc* → **défaire**.

défaut [defo] *nm* **-1.** [imperfection] flaw; [- de personne] fault, shortcoming; ~ **de fabrication** manufacturing fault. **-2.** [manque] lack; à ~ **de** for lack of; **l'eau fait (cruellement)** ~ there is a serious water shortage; **par** ~ [être jugé] in one's absence; [calculer] to the nearest decimal point.

défaveur [defavœr] *nf* disfavour; **être/tomber en** ~ to be/fall out of favour.

défavorable [defavɔrabl] *adj* unfavourable.

défavoriser [defavɔrize] [3] *vt* to handicap, to penalize.

défectif, -ive [defɛktiv, iv] *adj* GRAM defective.

défection [defɛksjɔ̃] *nf* **-1.** [absence] absence. **-2.** [abandon] defection.

défectueux, -euse [defɛktɥø, øz] *adj* faulty, defective.

défendable [defãdabl] *adj litt & fig* defensible.

défendais, **défendions** *etc* → **défendre**.

défendeur, -eresse [defãdœr, rɛs] *nm, f* defendant.

défendre [defãdr] [73] *vt* **-1.** [personne, opinion, client] to defend. **-2.** [interdire] to forbid; ~ **qqch à qqn** to forbid sb sthg; ~ **à qqn de faire qqch** to forbid sb to do sthg; ~ **que qqn fasse qqch** to forbid sb to do sthg.
◆ **se défendre** *vp* **-1.** [se battre, se justifier] to defend o.s. **-2.** *fam* [se débrouiller]: **se** ~ **(en)** to get by (in). **-3.** [nier]: **se** ~ **de faire qqch** to deny doing sthg. **-4.** [thèse] to stand up.

défendu, -e [defãdy] ◇ *pp* → **défendre**. ◇ *adj*: «**il est** ~ **de jouer au ballon**» "no ball games".

défense [defãs] *nf* **-1.** [d'éléphant] tusk. **-2.** [interdiction] prohibition, ban; «~ **de fumer/de stationner/d'entrer**» "no smoking/parking/entry"; «~ **d'afficher**» "stick no bills". **-3.** [protection] defence; **prendre la** ~ **de** to stand up for; ~ **antiaérienne** MIL anti-aircraft defence; ~ **des consommateurs** consumer protection; **la** ~ **nationale** MIL national defence; **légitime** ~ JUR self-defence.

défenseur [defãsœr] *nm* **-1.** JUR counsel for the defence *Br*, defense attorney *Am*. **-2.** [partisan] champion.

défensif, -ive [defãsif, iv] *adj* defensive.
◆ **défensive** *nf*: **être sur la défensive** to be on the defensive.

déféquer [defeke] [18] *vi* to defecate.

déférence [deferãs] *nf* deference.

dégât

déférer [defere] [18] ◇ *vt* JUR to refer. ◇ *vi sout* [céder]: ~ à to defer to.

déferlement [defɛrləmã] *nm* [de vagues] breaking; *fig* surge, upsurge.

déferler [defɛrle] [3] *vi* [vagues] to break; *fig* to surge.

défi [defi] *nm* challenge; **mettre qqn au ~ de faire qqch** to challenge sb to do sthg; **relever le ~** to take up the challenge.

défiance [defjɑ̃s] *nf* distrust, mistrust.

défiant, -e [defjɑ̃, ɑ̃t] *adj* distrustful, mistrustful.

déficeler [defisle] [24] *vt* to untie.

déficience [defisjɑ̃s] *nf* deficiency.

déficient, -e [defisjɑ̃, ɑ̃t] *adj* deficient.

déficit [defisit] *nm* **-1.** FIN deficit; **être en ~** to be in deficit. **-2.** [manque] deficiency.

déficitaire [defisitɛr] *adj* in deficit.

défier [defje] [9] *vt* **-1.** [braver]: ~ **qqn de faire qqch** to defy sb to do sthg. **-2.** *vieilli* [provoquer]: ~ **(qqn à)** to challenge (sb to).
◆ **se défier** *vp littéraire*: **se ~ de qqn/qqch** to mistrust sb/sthg.

défigurer [defigyre] [3] *vt* **-1.** [blesser] to disfigure. **-2.** [enlaidir] to deface.

défilé [defile] *nm* **-1.** [parade] parade; ~ **de mode** fashion parade. **-2.** [couloir] defile, narrow pass.

défiler [defile] [3] *vi* **-1.** [dans une parade] to march past. **-2.** [se succéder] to pass.
◆ **se défiler** *vp fam* to back out.

défini, -e [defini] *adj* **-1.** [précis] clear, precise. **-2.** GRAM definite.

définir [definir] [32] *vt* to define.

définitif, -ive [definitif, iv] *adj* definitive, final.
◆ **en définitive** *loc adv* in the end.

définition [definisjɔ̃] *nf* definition; **par ~** by definition.

définitivement [definitivmã] *adv* for good, permanently.

défiscaliser [defiskalize] [3] *vt* to exempt from taxation.

déflagration [deflagrasjɔ̃] *nf* explosion.

déflation [deflasjɔ̃] *nf* deflation.

déflationniste [deflasjɔnist] *adj* deflationary, deflationist.

déflecteur [deflɛktœr] *nm* quarterlight.

déflorer [deflɔre] [3] *vt* [jeune fille] to deflower; *fig* to taint.

défonce [defɔ̃s] *nf arg drogue* high.

défoncé, -e [defɔ̃se] *adj* **-1.** [abîmé - route] with large potholes; [- chaise] broken, broken-down. **-2.** *arg drogue* [drogué] high, stoned.

défoncer [defɔ̃se] [16] *vt* [caisse, porte] to smash in; [route] to break up; [mur] to smash down; [chaise] to break.
◆ **se défoncer** *vp* **-1.** *arg drogue* to trip, to get high. **-2.** *fam* [se surpasser] to go all out, to work flat out.

déformant, -e [defɔrmã, ɑ̃t] *adj* distorting.

déformation [defɔrmasjɔ̃] *nf* **-1.** [d'objet, de théorie] distortion. **-2.** MÉD deformity; ~ **professionnelle** *mental conditioning caused by one's job.*

déformer [defɔrme] [3] *vt* to distort.
◆ **se déformer** *vp* [changer de forme] to be distorted, to be deformed; [se courber] to bend.

défoulement [defulmã] *nm* unwinding, letting off steam.

défouler [defule] [3] *vt fam* to unwind.
◆ **se défouler** *vp fam* to let off steam, to unwind.

défrayer [defreje] [11] *vt* [payer]: ~ **qqn** to pay sb's expenses OU costs.

défricher [defriʃe] [3] *vt* [terrain] to clear; *fig* [question] to do the groundwork for.

défriser [defrize] [3] *vt* **-1.** [cheveux] to straighten. **-2.** *fam fig* [déplaire] to bother.

défroisser [defrwase] [3] *vt* to smooth out.

défunt, -e [defœ̃, œt] ◇ *adj* [décédé] late. ◇ *nm, f* deceased.

dégagé, -e [degaʒe] *adj* **-1.** [ciel, vue] clear; [partie du corps] bare. **-2.** [désinvolte] casual, airy. **-3.** [libre]: ~ **de** free from.

dégagement [degaʒmã] *nm* **-1.** [passage] passage. **-2.** [émanation] emission. **-3.** [évacuation] freeing, extricating.

dégager [degaʒe] [17] ◇ *vt* **-1.** [odeur] to produce, to give off. **-2.** [délivrer - blessé] to free, to extricate. **-3.** [idée] to bring out. **-4.** [bénéfice] to show. **-5.** [budget] to release. **-6.** [pièce] to clear. **-7.** [libérer]: ~ **qqn de** to release sb from. ◇ *vi fam* [partir] to clear off.
◆ **se dégager** *vp* **-1.** [se délivrer]: **se ~ de qqch** to free o.s. from sthg; *fig* to get out of sthg. **-2.** [se désencombrer] to clear. **-3.** [émaner] to be given off. **-4.** [émerger] to emerge.

dégaine [degen] *nf fam* gawkiness (U).

dégainer [degene] [4] *vt* [épée, revolver] to draw.

dégarnir [degarnir] [32] *vt* to strip, to clear.
◆ **se dégarnir** *vp* [vitrine] to be cleared; [arbre] to lose its leaves; **sa tête se dégarnit, il se dégarnit** he's going bald.

dégât [dega] *nm litt* & *fig* damage (U); **faire**

des ~s to cause damage; **limiter les ~s** *fig* to call a halt before things get any worse.

dégel [deʒɛl] *nm* **-1.** [fonte des glaces] thaw. **-2.** FIN unfreezing.

dégeler [deʒle] [25] ◇ *vt* **-1.** [produit surgelé] to thaw. **-2.** FIN to unfreeze. **-3.** *fig* [dérider] to warm up. ◇ *vi* to thaw.
◆ **se dégeler** *vp fig* to thaw, to warm up.

dégénéré, -e [deʒenere] *adj & nm, f* degenerate.

dégénérer [deʒenere] [18] *vi* to degenerate; **~ en** to degenerate into.

dégénérescence [deʒeneresãs] *nf* degeneration, degeneracy.

dégingandé, -e [deʒɛ̃gãde] *adj fam* gangling.

dégivrer [deʒivre] [3] *vt* [pare-brise] to de-ice; [réfrigérateur] to defrost.

dégivreur [deʒivrœr] *nm* [de voiture, avion] de-icer; [de réfrigérateur] defroster.

déglinguer [deglɛ̃ge] [3] *vt fam* to smash (to pieces).
◆ **se déglinguer** *vp fam* to fall to pieces.

déglutition [deglytisjɔ̃] *nf* swallowing.

dégonflé, -e [degɔ̃fle] ◇ *adj* [pneu, roue] flat. ◇ *nm, f fam* [personne] chicken, yellow-belly.

dégonfler [degɔ̃fle] [3] ◇ *vt* to deflate, to let down. ◇ *vi* to go down; **faire ~** to reduce the swelling of.
◆ **se dégonfler** *vp* **-1.** [objet] to go down. **-2.** *fam* [personne] to chicken out.

dégorger [degɔrʒe] [17] ◇ *vt* **-1.** [tuyau] to clear (out). **-2.** [eau] to discharge. **-3.** [soie, laine] to purify. ◇ *vi* **-1.** [tissu] to run. **-2.** CULIN: **faire ~** to soak.

dégot(t)er [degɔte] [3] *vt fam* to dig up.
◆ **se dégot(t)er** *vp fam* to dig up for o.s.

dégouliner [deguline] [3] *vi* to trickle.

dégourdi, -e [degurdi] ◇ *adj* clever. ◇ *nm, f* clever person.

dégourdir [degurdir] [32] *vt* **-1.** [membres - ankylosés] to restore the circulation to; [- gelés] to warm up. **-2.** *fig* [déniaiser]: **~ qqn** to teach sb a thing or two.
◆ **se dégourdir** *vp* **-1.** [membres]: **se ~ les jambes** to stretch one's legs. **-2.** *fig* [acquérir de l'aisance] to learn a thing or two.

dégoût [degu] *nm* disgust, distaste; **le ~ de la vie** world-weariness; **ravaler son ~** to swallow one's distaste.

dégoûtant, -e [degutɑ̃, ɑ̃t] ◇ *adj* **-1.** [sale] filthy, disgusting. **-2.** [révoltant, grossier] disgusting. ◇ *nm, f* disgusting person.

dégoûté, -e [degute] ◇ *adj* [écœuré] dis-gusted; **~ de** sick of. ◇ *nm, f*: **faire le ~** to be fussy.

dégoûter [degute] [3] *vt* to disgust; **~ qqn de qqch/de faire qqch** to put sb off sthg/off doing sthg.

dégoutter [degute] [3] *vi*: **~ (de qqch)** to drip (with sthg).

dégradant, -e [degradɑ̃, ɑ̃t] *adj* degrading.

dégradation [degradasjɔ̃] *nf* **-1.** [de bâtiment] damage; [du sol] erosion. **-2.** [de moral] decline. **-3.** [de personne] degradation. **-4.** [de situation] deterioration.

dégradé, -e [degrade] *adj* [couleur] shading off.
◆ **dégradé** *nm* gradation; **un ~ de bleu** a blue shading.
◆ **en dégradé** *loc adv* [cheveux] layered.

dégrader [degrade] [3] *vt* **-1.** [officier] to degrade. **-2.** [abîmer] to damage; [- sol] to erode. **-3.** *fig* [avilir] to degrade, to debase.
◆ **se dégrader** *vp* **-1.** [bâtiment, santé] to deteriorate. **-2.** *fig* [personne] to degrade o.s.

dégrafer [degrafe] [3] *vt* to undo, to unfasten.
◆ **se dégrafer** *vp* to come undone.

dégraissage [degrɛsaʒ] *nm* **-1.** [de vêtement] dry-cleaning. **-2.** [de personnel] trimming, cutting back.

dégraisser [degrese] [4] *vt* **-1.** [vêtement] to dry-clean. **-2.** [personnel] to trim, to cut back.

degré [dəgre] *nm* **-1.** [gén] degree; **~s centi-grades** OU **Celsius** degrees centigrade OU Celsius; **~ de parenté** degree of kinship; **prendre qqn/qqch au premier ~** to take sb/sthg at face value. **-2.** *sout* [marche] step.

dégressif, -ive [degresif, iv] *adj*: **tarif ~** decreasing price scale.

dégrèvement [degrɛvmã] *nm* tax relief.

dégriffé, -e [degrife] *adj* ex-designer label (*avant n*).
◆ **dégriffé** *nm* ex-designer label garment.

dégringolade [degrɛ̃gɔlad] *nf litt* & *fig* tumble.

dégringoler [degrɛ̃gɔle] [3] *fam* ◇ *vt* to tumble down. ◇ *vi* [tomber] to tumble; *fig* to crash.

dégriser [degrize] [3] *vt sout* [désenivrer] to sober up; **~ qqn** *fig* to bring sb to his/her senses.

dégrossir [degrosir] [32] *vt* **-1.** [matériau] to rough-hew. **-2.** *fig* [affaire, question] to rough out. **-3.** *fig* [personne] to polish.
◆ **se dégrossir** *vp* [personne] to become more polished.

déguenillé, -e [degnije] *adj* ragged.

déguerpir [degɛrpir] [32] *vi* to clear off.

dégueulasse [degœlas] *tfam* ◇ *adj* **-1.** [très sale, grossier] filthy; **blague** ~ dirty joke. **-2.** [révoltant] dirty, rotten. ◇ *nmf* scum (*U*).

dégueuler [degœle] [5] *vi fam* to throw up.

déguisé, -e [degize] *adj* disguised; [pour s'amuser] in fancy dress.

déguisement [degizmã] *nm* disguise; [pour bal masqué] fancy dress.

déguiser [degize] [3] *vt* to disguise.

◆ **se déguiser** *vp*: **se** ~ **en** [pour tromper] to disguise o.s. as; [pour s'amuser] to dress up as.

dégustation [degystasjɔ̃] *nf* tasting, sampling; ~ **de vin** wine tasting.

déguster [degyste] [3] ◇ *vt* [savourer] to taste, to sample. ◇ *vi fam* [subir]: **il va** ~! he'll be for it!

déhancher [deɑ̃ʃe] [3]

◆ **se déhancher** *vp* [en marchant] to swing one's hips; [en restant immobile] to put all one's weight on one leg.

dehors [dəɔr] ◇ *adv* outside; **aller** ~ to go outside; **dormir** ~ to sleep out of doors, to sleep out; **jeter** OU **mettre qqn** ~ to throw sb out. ◇ *nm* outside. ◇ *nmpl*: **les** ~ [les apparences] appearances.

◆ **en dehors** *loc adv* outside, outwards; **se pencher en** ~ to lean out.

◆ **en dehors de** *loc prép* [excepté] apart from.

déjà [deʒa] *adv* **-1.** [dès cet instant] already. **-2.** [précédemment] already, before. **-3.** [au fait]: **quel est ton nom** ~? what did you say your name was? **-4.** [renforce une affirmation]: **ce n'est** ~ **pas si mal** that's not bad at all.

déjanter [deʒɑ̃te] [3] *vt*: ~ **un pneu** to take a tyre off the rim.

déjà-vu [deʒavy] *nm inv*: **c'est du** ~ it's old hat.

déjection [deʒɛksjɔ̃] *nf* [action] evacuation.

◆ **déjections** *nfpl* excrement (*U*).

déjeuner [deʒœne] [5] ◇ *vi* **-1.** [le matin] to have breakfast. **-2.** [à midi] to have lunch. ◇ *nm* **-1.** [repas de midi] lunch; ~ **d'affaires** business lunch. **-2.** *Can* [dîner] dinner.

déjouer [deʒwe] [6] *vt* to frustrate; ~ **la surveillance** to elude surveillance.

delà [dəla]

◆ **au-delà** *nm*: **l'au-**~ the hereafter.

◆ **au-delà de** *loc prép* beyond.

◆ **par delà** *loc prép* beyond.

délabré, -e [delabre] *adj* ruined.

délabrement [delabrəmã] *nm* **-1.** [de bâtiment] dilapidation, ruining. **-2.** [de personne] ruin.

délacer [delase] [16] *vt* to unlace, to undo.

délai [delɛ] *nm* **-1.** [temps accordé] period; **dans un** ~ **de** within (a period of); **dans les** ~**s impartis** by the deadline; **sans** ~ immediately, without delay; ~ **de livraison** delivery time, lead time. **-2.** [sursis] extension (of deadline).

délaissé, -e [delese] *adj* abandoned.

délaisser [delese] [4] *vt* **-1.** [abandonner] to leave. **-2.** [négliger] to neglect.

délassement [delasmã] *nm* relaxation.

délasser [delase] [3] *vt* to refresh.

◆ **se délasser** *vp* to relax.

délateur, -trice [delatœr, tris] *nm, f* informer.

délation [delasjɔ̃] *nf* informing.

délavé, -e [delave] *adj* faded.

délayage [delɛjaʒ] *nm* verbiage, waffle.

délayer [deleje] [11] *vt* **-1.** [diluer]: ~ **qqch dans qqch** to mix sthg with sthg. **-2.** *fig* [exposer longuement] to pad out.

Delco® [dɛlko] *nm* AUTOM distributor.

délectable [delɛktable] *adj sout* delectable.

délectation [delɛktasjɔ̃] *nf* [plaisir] delight; **avec** ~ in delight.

délecter [delɛkte] [4]

◆ **se délecter** *vp*: **se** ~ **de qqch/à faire qqch** to delight in sthg/in doing sthg.

délégation [delegasjɔ̃] *nf* delegation; **agir par** ~ to be delegated to act.

délégué, -e [delege] ◇ *adj* [personne] delegated. ◇ *nm, f* [représentant]: ~ **(à)** delegate (to); ~ **de classe/du personnel/syndical** class/staff/trade union representative.

déléguer [delege] [18] *vt*: ~ **qqn (à qqch)** to delegate sb (to sthg).

délestage [delɛstaʒ] *nm* **-1.** [de ballon, de navire] removal of ballast. **-2.** [de circulation] (temporary) diversion.

délester [delɛste] [3] *vt* **-1.** [ballon, navire] to remove ballast from. **-2.** [circulation routière] to set up a diversion on, to divert. **-3.** *fig* & *hum* [voler]: ~ **qqn de qqch** to relieve sb of sthg.

délibératif, -ive [deliberatif, iv] *adj*: **avoir voix délibérative** to have voting rights.

délibération [deliberasjɔ̃] *nf* deliberation.

délibéré, -e [delibere] *adj* **-1.** [intentionnel] deliberate. **-2.** [résolu] determined.

◆ **délibéré** *nm* JUR judge's deliberations (*pl*).

délibérément [deliberemã] *adv* **-1.** [en connaissance de cause] after deliberation OU due consideration. **-2.** [intentionnellement] deliberately, on purpose.

délibérer [delibere] [18] *vi*: ~ **(de** OU **sur)** to deliberate (on OU over).

délicat, -e [delika, at] *adj* **-1.** [gén] delicate. **-2.** [aimable] thoughtful, sensitive. **-3.** [exigeant] fussy, difficult; **faire le** ~ to be fussy.

délicatement [delikatmã] *adv* delicately.

délicatesse [delikatɛs] *nf* **-1.** [gén] delicacy. **-2.** [tact] delicacy, tact.

délice [delis] *nm* delight.

délicieusement [delisjøzmã] *adv* [agréablement] delightfully.

délicieux, -ieuse [delisjø, jøz] *adj* **-1.** [savoureux] delicious. **-2.** [agréable] delightful.

délictueux, -euse [deliktɥø, øz] *adj* criminal.

délié, -e [delje] *adj* [doigts] nimble.

délier [delje] [9] *vt* to untie; ~ **qqn de** *fig* & *sout* to release sb from.

délimitation [delimitasjɔ̃] *nf* **-1.** [de territoire] fixing of the boundaries. **-2.** [de fonction] demarcation. **-3.** *fig* [de sujet] definition.

délimiter [delimite] [3] *vt* [frontière] to fix; *fig* [question, domaine] to define, to demarcate.

délinquance [delɛ̃kɑ̃s] *nf* delinquency; ~ **juvénile** juvenile delinquency.

délinquant, -e [delɛ̃kɑ̃, ɑ̃t] ◇ *adj* delinquent. ◇ *nm, f* delinquent; **petit** ~ petty criminal.

déliquescent, -e [delikɛsɑ̃, ɑ̃t] *adj fam* [personne] feeble; *vieilli* [mœurs] decaying.

délirant, -e [delirɑ̃, ɑ̃t] *adj* **-1.** MÉD delirious. **-2.** [extravagant] frenzied. **-3.** *fam* [extraordinaire] crazy.

délire [delir] *nm* MÉD delirium; **en** ~ *fig* frenzied.

délirer [delire] [3] *vi* MÉD to be OU become delirious; *fam fig* to rave.

délit [deli] *nm* crime, offence; **en flagrant** ~ red-handed, in the act; ~ **de fuite** failure to stop (*after an accident*); ~**s d'initiés** FIN insider trading (*U*).

délivrance [delivrɑ̃s] *nf* **-1.** [libération] freeing, release. **-2.** [soulagement] relief. **-3.** [accouchement] delivery.

délivrer [delivre] [3] *vt* **-1.** [prisonnier] to free, to release. **-2.** [pays] to deliver, to free; ~ **de** to free from; *fig* to relieve from. **-3.** [remettre]: ~ **qqch (à qqn)** to issue sthg (to sb). **-4.** [marchandise] to deliver.

◆ **se délivrer** *vp* **-1.** [se libérer]: **se** ~ **(de)** to free o.s. (from). **-2.** [passeport] to be issued.

déloger [delɔʒe] [17] *vt*: ~ **(de)** to dislodge (from).

déloyal, -e, -aux [delwajal, o] *adj* **-1.** [infidèle] disloyal. **-2.** [malhonnête] unfair.

Delphes [dɛlf] *n* Delphi.

delta [dɛlta] *nm* delta.

delta-plane (*pl* **delta-planes**), **deltaplane** [dɛltaplan] *nm* hang glider.

déluge [delyʒ] *nm* **-1.** RELIG: **le Déluge** the Flood; **remonter au Déluge** *fig* to go back to the year dot. **-2.** [pluie] downpour, deluge; **un** ~ **de** *fig* a flood of.

déluré, -e [delyre] *adj* [malin] quick-witted; *péj* [dévergondé] saucy.

démagogie [demagɔʒi] *nf* pandering to public opinion, demagogy.

démagogique [demagɔʒik] *adj* demagogic.

démagogue [demagɔg] *nmf* demagogue.

demain [dəmɛ̃] ◇ *adv* **-1.** [le jour suivant] tomorrow; ~ **matin** tomorrow morning. **-2.** *fig* [plus tard] in the future. ◇ *nm* tomorrow; **à** ~! see you tomorrow!

demande [dəmɑ̃d] *nf* **-1.** [souhait] request; **à la** ~ **générale** by popular demand; **accéder à une** ~ to accede to a demand. **-2.** [démarche] proposal; ~ **en mariage** proposal of marriage. **-3.** [candidature] application; ~ **d'emploi** job application; «~**s d'emploi**» "situations wanted". **-4.** [commande] order. **-5.** ÉCON demand. **-6.** JUR petition.

demandé, -e [dəmɑ̃de] *adj* in demand.

demander [dəmɑ̃de] [3] ◇ *vt* **-1.** [réclamer, s'enquérir] to ask for; ~ **qqch à qqn** to ask sb for sthg. **-2.** [appeler] to call; **on vous demande à la réception/au téléphone** you're wanted at reception/ on the telephone; **qui demandez-vous?** who do you want? **-3.** [désirer] to ask, to want; **je ne demande pas mieux** I'd be only too pleased (to), I'd love to. **-4.** [exiger]: **tu m'en demandes trop** you're asking too much of me. **-5.** [nécessiter] to require. **-6.** [chercher] to look for, to require.

◇ *vi* **-1.** [réclamer]: ~ **à qqn de faire qqch** to ask sb to do sthg; **ne** ~ **qu'à** ... to be ready to .... **-2.** [nécessiter]: **ce projet demande à être étudié** this project requires investigation OU needs investigating.

◆ **se demander** *vp*: **se** ~ **(si)** to wonder (if OU whether).

demandeur[1], -euse [dəmɑ̃dœr, øz] *nm, f* [solliciteur]: ~ **d'asile** asylum-seeker; ~ **d'emploi** job-seeker.

demandeur[2], -eresse [dəmɑ̃dœr, drɛs] *nm, f* JUR plaintiff.

démangeaison [demɑ̃ʒezɔ̃] *nf* [irritation] itch, itching (*U*); *fam fig* urge.

démanger [demãʒe] [17] *vi* [gratter] to itch; **ça me démange de ...** *fig* I'm itching OU dying to ....

démanteler [demãtle] [25] *vt* [construction] to demolish; *fig* to break up.

démaquillant, -e [demakijã, ãt] *adj* make-up-removing (*avant n*).
◆ **démaquillant** *nm* make-up remover.

démaquiller [demakije] [3] *vt* to remove make-up from.
◆ **se démaquiller** *vp* to remove one's make-up.

démarcation [demarkasjõ] *nf* [frontière] demarcation; *fig* separation.

démarchage [demarʃaʒ] *nm*: ~ **à domicile** door-to-door selling.

démarche [demarʃ] *nf* **-1.** [manière de marcher] gait, walk. **-2.** [raisonnement] approach, method. **-3.** [requête] step; **faire les ~s pour faire qqch** to take the necessary steps to do sthg.

démarcheur, -euse [demarʃœr, øz] *nm, f* **-1.** [représentant] door-to-door salesman (*f* saleswoman). **-2.** [prospecteur] canvasser.

démarque [demark] *nf* [solde] marking down.

démarquer [demarke] [3] *vt* **-1.** [solder] to mark down. **-2.** SPORT not to mark.
◆ **se démarquer** *vp* **-1.** SPORT to shake off one's marker. **-2.** *fig* [se distinguer]: **se ~ (de)** to distinguish o.s. (from).

démarrage [demaraʒ] *nm* starting, start; ~ **en côte** hill start.

démarrer [demare] [3] ◇ *vi* **-1.** [véhicule] to start (up); [conducteur] to drive off. **-2.** SPORT to break away. **-3.** *fig* [affaire, projet] to get off the ground. ◇ *vt* **-1.** [véhicule] to start (up); **faire ~** to start. **-2.** *fam fig* [commencer]: ~ **qqch** to get sthg going.

démarreur [demarœr] *nm* starter.

démasquer [demaske] [3] *vt* **-1.** [personne] to unmask. **-2.** *fig* [complot, plan] to unveil.
◆ **se démasquer** *vp* to show one's true colours.

démêlant, -e [demelã, ãt] *adj* conditioning (*avant n*).
◆ **démêlant** *nm* conditioner.

démêlé [demele] *nm* quarrel; **avoir des ~s avec la justice** to get into trouble with the law.

démêler [demele] [4] *vt* [cheveux, fil] to untangle; *fig* to unravel.
◆ **se démêler** *vp*: **se ~ les cheveux** to comb out one's hair; **se ~ de** *fig* to extricate o.s. from.

démembrer [demãbre] [3] *vt* [animal] to dismember; *fig* [réseau] to break up.

déménagement [demenaʒmã] *nm* removal.

déménager [demenaʒe] [17] ◇ *vt* to move. ◇ *vi* to move (house).

déménageur [demenaʒœr] *nm* removal man *Br*, mover *Am*.

démence [demãs] *nf* MÉD dementia; [bêtise] madness.

démener [demne] [19]
◆ **se démener** *vp litt* & *fig* to struggle.

dément, -e [demã, ãt] ◇ *adj* MÉD demented; *fam* [extraordinaire, extravagant] crazy. ◇ *nm, f* demented person.

démenti [demãti] *nm* denial; **apporter un ~ à qqch** to deny sthg (formally).

démentiel, -ielle [demãsjɛl] *adj* MÉD demented; *fam* [incroyable] crazy.

démentir [demãtir] [37] *vt* **-1.** [réfuter] to deny. **-2.** [contredire] to contradict.
◆ **se démentir** *vp*: **ne pas se ~ sout** to remain unchanged.

démerder [demɛrde] [3]
◆ **se démerder** *vp tfam* [se débrouiller] to (know how to) look after o.s.

démériter [demerite] [3] *vi* **-1.** [être indigne]: ~ **de** to show o.s. (to be) unworthy of. **-2.** [être dévalorisé]: **en quoi a-t-il démérité?** what has he done wrong?; ~ **auprès de qqn** to come down in sb's eyes OU estimation.

démesure [deməzyr] *nf* excess, immoderation.

démesurément [deməzyremã] *adv* excessively.

démets *etc* → **démettre**.

démettre [demɛtr] [84] *vt* **-1.** MÉD to put out (of joint). **-2.** [congédier]: ~ **qqn de** to dismiss sb from.
◆ **se démettre** *vp* **-1.** MÉD: **se ~ l'épaule** to put one's shoulder out (of joint). **-2.** [démissionner]: **se ~ de ses fonctions** to resign.

demeurant [demœrã]
◆ **au demeurant** *loc adv* all things considered.

demeure [demœr] *nf* **-1.** *sout* [domicile, habitation] residence. **-2.** JUR: **mettre qqn en ~ (de faire qqch)** to order sb (to do sthg).
◆ **à demeure** ◇ *loc adj* permanent. ◇ *loc adv* permanently.

demeuré, -e [demœre] ◇ *adj* simple, half-witted. ◇ *nm, f* half-wit.

demeurer [demœre] [5] *vi* **-1.** (*aux: avoir*) [habiter] to live. **-2.** (*aux: être*) [rester] to remain.

demi, -e [dəmi] *adj* half; **un kilo et ~** one and a half kilos; **une heure et ~e** half past one; **à ~** half; **dormir à ~** to be nearly asleep; **ouvrir à ~** to half-open; **faire les choses à ~** to do things by halves.
◆ **demi** *nm* **-1.** [bière] beer, ≃ half-pint *Br*. **-2.** FOOTBALL midfielder; **~ de mêlée** RUGBY scrumhalf; **~ d'ouverture** RUGBY fly half, standoff (half).
◆ **demie** *nf*: **à la ~e** on the half-hour.

demi-bouteille [dəmibutɛj] (*pl* **demi-bouteilles**) *nf* half-bottle.

demi-cercle [dəmisɛrkl] (*pl* **demi-cercles**) *nm* semicircle; **en ~** semicircular.

demi-douzaine [dəmiduzɛn] (*pl* **demi-douzaines**) *nf* half-dozen; **une ~ (de)** half a dozen.

demi-fin, -e [dəmifɛ̃, in] (*mpl* **demi-fins**, *fpl* **demi-fines**) *adj* [haricots] medium.

demi-finale [dəmifinal] (*pl* **demi-finales**) *nf* semifinal.

demi-frère [dəmifrɛr] (*pl* **demi-frères**) *nm* half-brother.

demi-gros [dəmigro] *nm*: **(commerce de) ~** cash and carry.

demi-heure [dəmijœr] (*pl* **demi-heures**) *nf* half an hour, half-hour.

demi-jour [dəmiʒur] *nm* half-light.

demi-journée [dəmiʒurne] (*pl* **demi-journées**) *nf* half a day, half-day.

démilitariser [demilitarize] [3] *vt* to demilitarize.

demi-litre [dəmilitr] (*pl* **demi-litres**) *nm* half a litre, half-litre.

demi-mal [dəmimal] (*pl* **demi-maux**) *nm*: **ce n'est que ~** things OU it could have been worse.

demi-mesure [dəmiməzyr] (*pl* **demi-mesures**) *nf* **-1.** [quantité] half a measure. **-2.** [compromis] half-measure.

demi-mot [dəmimo]
◆ **à demi-mot** *loc adv*: **comprendre à ~** to understand without things having to be spelled out.

déminage [deminaʒ] *nm* [de sol] mine clearance; [d'eau] minesweeping.

déminer [demine] [3] *vt* to clear of mines.

demi-pension [dəmipɑ̃sjɔ̃] (*pl* **demi-pensions**) *nf* **-1.** [d'hôtel] half-board. **-2.** [d'école]: **être en ~** to take school dinners (*pl*).

demi-pensionnaire [dəmipɑ̃sjɔnɛr] (*pl* **demi-pensionnaires**) *nmf child who has school dinners.*

demi-place [dəmiplas] (*pl* **demi-places**) *nf*

-1. [pour spectacle] half-price ticket. **-2.** [dans transports publics] half-fare.

démis, -e [demi, iz] *pp* → **démettre**.

demi-saison [dəmisɛzɔ̃] *nf*: **une veste de ~** a spring/autumn jacket.

demi-sel [dəmisɛl] *adj inv* slightly salted.

demi-sœur [dəmisœr] (*pl* **demi-sœurs**) *nf* half-sister.

demi-soupir [dəmisupir] (*pl* **demi-soupirs**) *nm* quaver rest *Br,* eighth note rest *Am*.

démission [demisjɔ̃] *nf* resignation; **remettre sa ~** to hand in one's notice.

démissionnaire [demisjɔnɛr] ◇ *nmf* person resigning. ◇ *adj* resigning (*avant n*); [ministre] outgoing (*avant n*).

démissionner [demisjɔne] [3] ◇ *vi* [d'un emploi] to resign; *fig* to give up. ◇ *vt hum*: **~ qqn** to give sb the boot.

demi-tarif [dəmitarif] (*pl* **demi-tarifs**) ◇ *adj* half-price. ◇ *nm* **-1.** [tarification] half-fare. **-2.** [billet] half-price ticket.

demi-teinte [dəmitɛ̃t] (*pl* **demi-teintes**) *nf* halftone; **en ~, en ~s** *fig* subtle.

demi-ton [dəmitɔ̃] (*pl* **demi-tons**) *nm* semitone.

demi-tour [dəmitur] (*pl* **demi-tours**) *nm* [gén] half-turn; MIL about-turn; **faire ~** to turn back.

démobiliser [demɔbilize] [3] *vt* MIL to demobilize; **être démobilisé** *fig* to be demotivated.

démocrate [demɔkrat] ◇ *nmf* democrat. ◇ *adj* democratic.

démocrate-chrétien, -ienne [demɔkratkretjɛ̃, ɛn] (*mpl* **démocrates-chrétiens**, *fpl* **démocrates-chrétiennes**) ◇ *adj* Christian-Democratic. ◇ *nm, f* Christian Democrat.

démocratie [demɔkrasi] *nf* democracy; **les ~s occidentales** the Western democracies.

démocratique [demɔkratik] *adj* democratic.

démocratisation [demɔkratizasjɔ̃] *nf* democratization.

démocratiser [demɔkratize] [3] *vt* to democratize.

démodé, -e [demɔde] *adj* old-fashioned.

démographie [demɔgrafi] *nf* demography.

démographique [demɔgrafik] *adj* demographic.

demoiselle [dəmwazɛl] *nf* **-1.** [jeune fille] maid; **~ d'honneur** bridesmaid. **-2.** [libellule] dragonfly.

démolir [demɔlir] [32] *vt* **-1.** [gén] to demolish. **-2.** *fam* [frapper]: **~ qqn** to smash sb's face in; **se faire ~** to get one's face smashed in.

démolisseur [demɔlisœr] *nm* demolition worker.

démolition [demɔlisjɔ̃] *nf* demolition; **en ~** in the course of being demolished.

démon [demɔ̃] *nm* **-1.** [diable, personne] devil, demon; **le ~** RELIG the Devil. **-2.** *fig*: **le ~ de l'alcool/de la curiosité** the demon drink/curiosity; **le ~ de midi** middle-aged lust.

démoniaque [demɔnjak] *adj* **-1.** [diabolique] diabolical. **-2.** [possédé du démon] possessed.

démonstrateur, -trice [demɔ̃stratœr, tris] *nm, f* demonstrator.

démonstratif, -ive [demɔ̃stratif, iv] *adj* **-1.** [argument] convincing. **-2.** [personne & GRAM] demonstrative.

◆ **démonstratif** *nm* GRAM demonstrative.

démonstration [demɔ̃strasjɔ̃] *nf* **-1.** [gén] demonstration. **-2.** MIL show, demonstration.

démontable [demɔ̃tabl] *adj* collapsible.

démontage [demɔ̃taʒ] *nm* dismantling, taking to pieces; [de moteur] stripping down.

démonté, -e [demɔ̃te] *adj* [océan] raging.

démonte-pneu [demɔ̃tpnø] (*pl* **démonte-pneus**) *nm* tyre lever *Br*, tire iron *Am*.

démonter [demɔ̃te] [3] *vt* **-1.** [appareil] to dismantle, to take apart. **-2.** [troubler]: **~ qqn** to put sb out.

◆ **se démonter** *vp fam* to be put out.

démontrer [demɔ̃tre] [3] *vt* **-1.** [prouver] to prove, to demonstrate. **-2.** [témoigner de] to show, to demonstrate.

démoralisant, -e [demɔralizɑ̃, ɑ̃t] *adj* demoralizing.

démoraliser [demɔralize] [3] *vt* to demoralize.

◆ **se démoraliser** *vp* to lose heart.

démordre [demɔrdr] [76] *vt*: **ne pas ~ de** to stick to.

démordu [demɔrdy] *pp inv* → **démordre**.

démotiver [demɔtive] [3] *vt* to demotivate.

démouler [demule] [3] *vt* to turn out of a mould, to remove from a mould.

démultiplication [demyltiplikasjɔ̃] *nf* TECHNOL reduction in gear ratio.

démunir [demynir] [32] *vt* to deprive.

◆ **se démunir** *vp*: **se ~ de** to part with.

démystifier [demistifje] [9] *vt* **-1.** [concept] to demystify. **-2.** [personne] to disabuse.

dénatalité [denatalite] *nf* fall in the birth-rate.

dénationaliser [denasjɔnalize] [3] *vt* to denationalize.

dénaturé, -e [denatyre] *adj* **-1.** [parents] unfit. **-2.** [goût] unnatural. **-3.** TECHNOL denatured.

dénaturer [denatyre] [3] *vt* **-1.** [goût] to impair, to mar. **-2.** TECHNOL to denature. **-3.** [déformer] to distort.

dénégation [denegasjɔ̃] *nf* denial.

déneigement [denɛʒmɑ̃] *nm* snow clearance.

déni [deni] *nm* denial; **~ de justice** JUR denial of justice.

déniaiser [denjeze] [4] *vt hum & vieilli*: **~ qqn** to teach sb a thing or two.

dénicher [deniʃe] [3] *vt fig* **-1.** [personne] to flush out. **-2.** *fam* [objet] to unearth.

denier [dənje] *nm* denier (*coin*).

◆ **deniers** *nmpl*: **les ~s publics** the public purse (*sg*); **les ~s de l'État** the State coffers.

dénigrer [denigre] [3] *vt* to denigrate, to run down.

dénivelé [denivle] *nm* difference in level OU height.

dénivellation [denivɛlasjɔ̃] *nf* **-1.** [différence de niveau] difference in height OU level. **-2.** [de route] bumps (*pl*), unevenness (*U*). **-3.** [pente] slope.

dénombrer [denɔ̃bre] [3] *vt* [compter] to count; [énumérer] to enumerate.

dénominateur [denɔminatœr] *nm* denominator; **~ commun** MATHS & *fig* common denominator.

dénomination [denɔminasjɔ̃] *nf* name.

dénommé, -e [denɔme] *adj*: **un ~ Robert** someone by the name of Robert.

dénoncer [denɔ̃se] [16] *vt* **-1.** [gén] to denounce; **~ qqn à qqn** to denounce sb to sb, to inform on sb. **-2.** *fig* [trahir] to betray.

dénonciation [denɔ̃sjasjɔ̃] *nf* denunciation.

dénoter [denɔte] [3] *vt* to show, to indicate.

dénouement [denumɑ̃] *nm* **-1.** [d'intrigue] outcome. **-2.** CIN & THÉÂTRE denouement. **-3.** [issue] conclusion.

dénouer [denwe] [6] *vt* [nœud] to untie, to undo; *fig* to unravel.

dénoyauter [denwajote] [3] *vt* [fruit] to stone.

denrée [dɑ̃re] *nf* [produit] produce (*U*); **~s alimentaires** foodstuffs; **~ rare** *fig* rare commodity.

dense [dɑ̃s] *adj* **-1.** [gén] dense. **-2.** [style] condensed.

densité [dɑ̃site] *nf* density; **~ de population** population density; **double/haute ~** INFORM double/high density.

dent [dɑ̃] *nf* **-1.** [de personne, d'objet] tooth; **il claquait des** ~**s** his teeth were chattering; **faire ses** ~**s** to cut one's teeth, to teethe; **mordre à belles** ~**s dans** to get one's teeth into; ~ **de lait/de sagesse** milk/wisdom tooth; **en** ~**s de scie** jagged, serrated; **avoir les** ~**s longues** to have high hopes; **avoir une** ~ **contre qqn** to have it in for sb; **ne rien avoir à se mettre sous la** ~ to have nothing left to eat; **ne pas desserrer les** ~**s** not to open one's mouth; **grincer des** ~**s** to gnash one's teeth. **-2.** GÉOGR peak.

dentaire [dɑ̃tɛr] *adj* dental.

dental, -e, -aux [dɑ̃tal, o] *adj* LING dental.

denté, -e [dɑ̃te] *adj* **-1.** TECHNOL toothed; **roue** ~**e** cogwheel. **-2.** [feuille] dentate.

dentelé, -e [dɑ̃tle] *adj* serrated, jagged.

dentelle [dɑ̃tɛl] *nf* lace (*U*).

dentier [dɑ̃tje] *nm* **-1.** [dents] dentures (*pl*). **-2.** TECHNOL set of teeth, teeth (*pl*).

dentifrice [dɑ̃tifris] *nm:* **(pâte)** ~ toothpaste.

dentiste [dɑ̃tist] *nmf* dentist.

dentition [dɑ̃tisjɔ̃] *nf* teeth (*pl*), dentition.

dénuder [denyde] [3] *vt* to leave bare; [fil électrique] to strip.

◆ **se dénuder** *vp* to strip (off).

dénué, -e [denɥe] *adj sout:* ~ **de** devoid of.

dénuement [denymɑ̃] *nm* destitution (*U*).

dénutrition [denytrisjɔ̃] *nf* malnutrition.

déodorant, -e [deɔdɔrɑ̃, ɑ̃t] *adj* deodorant.

◆ **déodorant** *nm* deodorant.

déontologie [deɔ̃tɔlɔʒi] *nf* professional ethics (*pl*).

dép. -1. *abr de* **départ. -2.** *abr de* **département.**

dépannage [depanaʒ] *nm* repair.

dépanner [depane] [3] *vt* **-1.** [réparer] to repair, to fix. **-2.** *fam* [aider] to bail out.

dépanneur, -euse [depanœr, øz] *nm, f* repairman (*f* repairwoman).

◆ **dépanneuse** *nf* [véhicule] (breakdown) recovery vehicle.

dépareillé, -e [depareje] *adj* [ensemble] non-matching; [paire] odd.

déparer [depare] [3] *vt* to spoil.

départ [depar] *nm* **-1.** [de personne] departure, leaving; [de véhicule] departure; **les grands** ~**s** the holiday exodus (*sg*). **-2.** SPORT & *fig* start; **faux** ~ false start.

◆ **au départ** *loc adv* to start with.

départager [departaʒe] [17] *vt* **-1.** [concurrents, opinions] to decide between. **-2.** [lors d'une élection] to choose between. **-3.** [séparer] to separate.

département [departəmɑ̃] *nm* **-1.** [territoire] *territorial and administrative division of France.* **-2.** [service] department.

départemental, -e, -aux [departəmɑ̃tal, o] *adj* of a French département.

◆ **départementale** *nf* ≃ B road *Br.*

départir [departir] [32]

◆ **se départir** *vp:* **ne pas se** ~ **de** to retain.

dépassé, -e [depase] *adj* **-1.** [périmé] old-fashioned. **-2.** *fam* [déconcerté]: ~ **par** overwhelmed by.

dépassement [depasmɑ̃] *nm* **-1.** [en voiture] overtaking; ~ **sans visibilité** overtaking blind. **-2.** FIN overspending.

dépasser [depase] [3] ◇ *vt* **-1.** [doubler] to overtake. **-2.** [être plus grand que] to be taller than. **-3.** [être plus long que] to be longer than. **-4.** [excéder] to exceed, to be more than. **-5.** [durer plus longtemps que]: ~ **une heure** to go on for more than an hour. **-6.** [surpasser] to outshine. **-7.** [aller au-delà de] to exceed. **-8.** [franchir] to pass. **-9.** *loc:* **ça me dépasse** *fam* it's beyond me. ◇ *vi:* ~ **(de)** to stick out (from).

◆ **se dépasser** *vp* to excel o.s.

dépassionner [depasjɔne] [3] *vt* to take the heat out of.

dépaysement [depeizmɑ̃] *nm* change of scene, disorientation.

dépayser [depeize] [3] *vt* **-1.** [désorienter] to disorientate *Br*, to disorient *Am.* **-2.** [changer agréablement] to make a change of scene for.

dépecer [depəse] [29] *vt* **-1.** [découper] to chop up. **-2.** [déchiqueter] to tear apart.

dépêche [depɛʃ] *nf* dispatch.

dépêcher [depeʃe] [4] *vt sout* [envoyer] to dispatch.

◆ **se dépêcher** *vp* to hurry up; **se** ~ **de faire qqch** to hurry to do sthg.

dépeignais, dépeignions *etc* → **dépcindre.**

dépeindre [depɛ̃dr] [81] *vt* to depict, to describe.

dépeint, -e [depɛ̃, ɛ̃t] *pp* → **dépeindre.**

dépendance [depɑ̃dɑ̃s] *nf* **-1.** [de personne] dependence; **être sous la** ~ **de** to be dependent on. **-2.** [à la drogue] dependency. **-3.** [de bâtiment] outbuilding.

dépendant, -e [depɑ̃dɑ̃, ɑ̃t] *adj:* ~ **(de)** dependent (on).

dépendre [depɑ̃dr] [73] *vt* **-1.** [être soumis]: ~ **de** to depend on. **-2.** [appartenir]: ~ **de** to belong to. **-3.** [décrocher] to take down.

dépendu [depɑ̃dy] *pp inv* → **dépendre.**

dépens [depã] *nmpl* JUR costs; **aux ~ de qqn** at sb's expense; **je l'ai appris à mes ~** I learned that to my cost.

dépense [depãs] *nf* **-1.** [frais] expense. **-2.** FIN & *fig* expenditure (*U*); **les ~s publiques** public spending (*U*). **-3.** [consommation] consumption.

dépenser [depãse] [3] *vt* **-1.** [argent] to spend; **~ sans compter** to spend lavishly. **-2.** *fig* [énergie] to expend.
◆ **se dépenser** *vp litt* & *fig* to exert o.s.

dépensier, -ière [depãsje, jɛr] *adj* extravagant.

déperdition [depɛrdisjɔ̃] *nf* loss; **~ de chaleur** heat loss.

dépérir [deperir] [32] *vi* **-1.** [personne] to waste away. **-2.** [santé, affaire] to decline. **-3.** [plante] to wither.

dépêtrer [depetre] [4]
◆ **se dépêtrer** *vp*: **se ~ de** *fam* [se dégager de] to get out of; *fig* [se sortir de] to extricate o.s. from; *fig* [se débarrasser de] to get rid of.

dépeuplement [depœpləmã] *nm* **-1.** [de pays] depopulation. **-2.** [d'étang, de rivière, de forêt] emptying of wildlife.

dépeupler [depœple] [5] *vt* **-1.** [pays] to depopulate. **-2.** [étang, rivière, forêt] to drive the wildlife from.
◆ **se dépeupler** *vp* **-1.** [pays] to become depopulated. **-2.** [rivière, étang] to have a diminishing OU disappearing wildlife population.

déphasé, -e [defaze] *adj* ÉLECTR out of phase; *fam fig* out of touch.

dépiauter [depjote] [3] *vt fam* [animal] to skin; *fig* [texte] to pull to pieces.

dépilatoire [depilatwar] *adj*: **crème/lotion ~** depilatory cream/lotion.

dépistage [depistaʒ] *nm* **-1.** [de gibier, de voleur] tracking down. **-2.** [de maladie] screening; **~ du SIDA** AIDS testing.

dépister [depiste] [3] *vt* **-1.** [gibier, voleur] to track down. **-2.** [maladie] to screen for. **-3.** [déjouer] to throw off the scent. **-4.** *fig* [découvrir] to detect.

dépit [depi] *nm* pique, spite; **par ~** out of pique OU spite.
◆ **en dépit de** *loc prép* in spite of.

dépité, -e [depite] *adj* cross, annoyed.

déplacé, -e [deplase] *adj* **-1.** [propos, attitude, présence] out of place. **-2.** [personne] displaced.

déplacement [deplasmã] *nm* **-1.** [d'objet] moving; **~ de vertèbre** MÉD slipped disc. **-2.**

[voyage] travelling (*U*); **en ~** away on business; **valoir le ~** *fig* to be worth going.

déplacer [deplase] [16] *vt* **-1.** [objet] to move, to shift; *fig* [problème] to shift the emphasis of. **-2.** [muter] to transfer.
◆ **se déplacer** *vp* **-1.** [se mouvoir - animal] to move (around); [- personne] to walk. **-2.** [voyager] to travel. **-3.** MÉD: **se ~ une vertèbre** to slip a disc.

déplaire [deplɛr] [110] *vt* **-1.** [ne pas plaire]: **cela me déplaît** I don't like it. **-2.** [irriter] to displease; **n'en déplaise à mon patron** *hum* whether my boss likes it or not.

déplaisant, -e [deplɛzã, ãt] *adj sout* unpleasant.

déplaisir [deplezir] *nm sout* displeasure.

dépliant [deplijã] *nm* leaflet; **~ touristique** tourist brochure.

déplier [deplije] [10] *vt* to unfold.
◆ **se déplier** *vp* to unfold.

déploiement [deplwamã] *nm* **-1.** MIL deployment. **-2.** [d'ailes] spreading. **-3.** [de voile] unfurling, opening. **-4.** *fig* [d'efforts] display; **un grand ~ de** a major display of.

déplorable [deplɔrabl] *adj* deplorable.

déplorer [deplɔre] [3] *vt* **-1.** [regretter] to deplore. **-2.** [pleurer] to mourn.

déployer [deplwaje] [13] *vt* **-1.** [déplier - gén] to unfold; [- plan, journal] to open; [ailes] to spread. **-2.** MIL to deploy. **-3.** [mettre en œuvre] to expend. **-4.** [manifester] to display.

déplu [deply] *pp inv* → **déplaire.**

dépoitraillé, -e [depwatraje] *adj fam péj* with one's shirt wide open.

dépoli, -e [depɔli] *adj* [métal] tarnished; [verre] frosted.

dépolitiser [depɔlitize] [3] *vt* to depoliticize.

déportation [depɔrtasjɔ̃] *nf* **-1.** [exil] deportation. **-2.** [internement] transportation to a concentration camp.

déporté, -e [depɔrte] *nm, f* **-1.** [exilé] deportee. **-2.** [interné] prisoner (*in a concentration camp*).

déporter [depɔrte] [3] *vt* **-1.** [dévier] to carry off course. **-2.** [exiler] to deport. **-3.** [interner] to send to a concentration camp.

déposant, -e [depozã, ãt] *nm, f* **-1.** FIN depositor. **-2.** JUR deponent.

déposé, -e [depoze] *adj*: **marque ~e** registered trademark; **modèle ~** patented design.

déposer [depoze] [3] ◇ *vt* **-1.** [poser] to put down. **-2.** [personne, paquet] to drop. **-3.** [argent, sédiment] to deposit. **-4.** ADMIN to register. **-5.** JUR to file; **~ son bilan** FIN to go into liquidation. **-6.** [monarque] to depose.

-7. [moteur] to take out. ◇ *vi* **-1.** JUR to testify, to give evidence. **-2.** [sédiment] to form a deposit.

◆ **se déposer** *vp* to settle.

dépositaire [depozitɛr] *nmf* **-1.** COMM agent. **-2.** [d'objet] bailee; ~ **de** *fig* person entrusted with.

déposition [depozisjɔ̃] *nf* deposition.

déposséder [deposede] [18] *vt*: ~ **qqn de** to dispossess sb of.

dépôt [depo] *nm* **-1.** [d'objet, d'argent, de sédiment] deposit, depositing (*U*); **verser un** ~ **(de garantie)** to put down a deposit; ~ **d'ordures** (rubbish) dump *Br*, garbage dump *Am*. **-2.** ADMIN registration; ~ **légal** copyright registration. **-3.** [garage] depot. **-4.** [entrepôt] store, warehouse. **-5.** [prison] ≃ police cells (*pl*).

dépoter [depɔte] [3] *vt* [plante] to remove from the pot.

dépotoir [depɔtwar] *nm* **-1.** [décharge] (rubbish) dump *Br*, garbage dump *Am*; *fam fig* dump, tip. **-2.** [usine] sewage works, sewage reprocessing plant.

dépouille [depuj] *nf* **-1.** [peau] hide, skin. **-2.** [humaine] remains (*pl*); ~ **mortelle** mortal remains.

◆ **dépouilles** *nfpl* spoils.

dépouillement [depujmɑ̃] *nm* **-1.** [sobriété] austerity, sobriety. **-2.** [examen] perusal; ~ **de scrutin** counting of the votes.

dépouiller [depuje] [3] *vt* **-1.** [priver]: ~ **qqn (de)** to strip sb (of). **-2.** [examiner] to peruse; ~ **un scrutin** to count the votes.

◆ **se dépouiller** *vp*: **se** ~ **de** to divest o.s. of.

dépourvu, -e [depurvy] *adj*: ~ **de** without, lacking in.

◆ **au dépourvu** *loc adv*: **prendre qqn au** ~ to catch sb unawares.

dépoussiérer [depusjere] [18] *vt* to dust (off).

dépravation [depravasjɔ̃] *nf* depravity.

dépravé, -e [deprave] ◇ *adj* depraved. ◇ *nm, f* degenerate.

dépraver [deprave] [3] *vt* to deprave.

◆ **se dépraver** *vp* to become depraved.

dépréciation [depresjasjɔ̃] *nf* depreciation.

déprécier [depresje] [9] *vt* **-1.** [marchandise] to reduce the value of. **-2.** [œuvre] to disparage.

◆ **se déprécier** *vp* **-1.** [marchandise] to depreciate. **-2.** [personne] to put o.s. down.

dépressif, -ive [depresif, iv] ◇ *adj* depressive. ◇ *nm, f* depressive (person).

dépression [depresjɔ̃] *nf* depression; **faire de la** ~ to be depressed; ~ **nerveuse** nervous breakdown.

déprimant, -e [deprimɑ̃, ɑ̃t] *adj* depressing.

déprime [deprim] *nf fam*: **faire une** ~ to be (feeling) down.

déprimé, -e [deprime] *adj* depressed.

déprimer [deprime] [3] ◇ *vt* to depress. ◇ *vi fam* to be (feeling) down.

déprogrammer [deprɔgrame] [3] *vt* to remove from the schedule; TÉLÉ to take off the air.

dépuceler [depysle] [24] *vt fam*: ~ **qqn** to take sb's virginity.

depuis [dəpɥi] ◇ *prép* **-1.** [à partir d'une date ou d'un moment précis] since; **je ne l'ai pas vu** ~ **son mariage** I haven't seen him since he got married; **il est parti** ~ **hier** he's been away since yesterday; ~ **le début jusqu'à la fin** from beginning to end. **-2.** [exprimant une durée] for; **il est malade** ~ **une semaine** he has been ill for a week; ~ **10 ans/longtemps** for 10 years/a long time; ~ **toujours** for ever. **-3.** [dans l'espace] from; ~ **la route, on pouvait voir la mer** you could see the sea from the road; ~ **le premier jusqu'au dernier** from the first to the last. ◇ *adv* since (then); ~, **nous ne l'avons pas revu** we haven't seen him since (then).

◆ **depuis lors** *loc adv* since then.

◆ **depuis que** *loc conj* since; **je ne l'ai pas revu** ~ **qu'il s'est marié** I haven't seen him since he got married.

dépuratif, -ive [depyratif, iv] *adj* cleansing, eliminating.

◆ **dépuratif** *nm* depurative.

députation [depytasjɔ̃] *nf* **-1.** [délégation] deputation. **-2.** [fonction]: **candidat à la** ~ parliamentary candidate.

député [depyte] *nm* **-1.** [délégué] representative. **-2.** [au parlement] member of parliament *Br*, representative *Am*; ~ **européen** Euro-MP, MEP; ~**-maire** MP and mayor.

députer [depyte] [3] *vt* to send as representative.

déraciner [derasine] [3] *vt litt & fig* to uproot.

déraillement [derajmɑ̃] *nm* derailment.

dérailler [deraje] [3] *vi* **-1.** [train] to leave the rails, to be derailed. **-2.** *fam fig* [mécanisme] to go on the blink. **-3.** *fam fig* [personne] to go to pieces.

dérailleur [derajœr] *nm* [de bicyclette] derailleur.

déraison [derezɔ̃] *nf* lack of reason.

déraisonnable [derɛzɔnabl] *adj* unreasonable.

déraisonner [derɛzɔne] [3] *vi sout* to talk nonsense.

dérangement [derɑ̃ʒmɑ̃] *nm* trouble; **en ~** out of order.

déranger [derɑ̃ʒe] [17] ◇ *vt* -**1.** [personne] to disturb, to bother; **ça vous dérange si je fume?** do you mind if I smoke? -**2.** [plan] to disrupt. -**3.** [maison, pièce] to disarrange, to make untidy. ◇ *vi* to be disturbing.
◆ **se déranger** *vp* -**1.** [se déplacer] to move. -**2.** [se gêner] to put o.s. out.

dérapage [derapaʒ] *nm* [glissement] skid; *fig* excess; **~ contrôlé** controlled skid.

déraper [derape] [3] *vi* [glisser] to skid; *fig* to get out of hand.

dératé, -e [derate] *nm, f fam*: **courir comme un ~** to run flat out.

dératisation [deratizasjɔ̃] *nf* extermination of rats.

derechef [dərəʃɛf] *adv sout* once again.

dérèglement [derɛɡləmɑ̃] *nm* [de machine] malfunction; [de fonction corporelle] upset.

déréglementation [dereɡləmɑ̃tasjɔ̃] *nf* deregulation.

déréglementer [dereɡləmɑ̃te] [3] *vt* to deregulate.

dérégler [dereɡle] [18] *vt* [mécanisme] to put out of order; *fig* to upset.
◆ **se dérégler** *vp* [mécanisme] to go wrong; *fig* to be upset OU unsettled.

dérider [deride] [3] *vt fig*: **~ qqn** to cheer sb up.
◆ **se dérider** *vp* to cheer up.

dérision [derizjɔ̃] *nf* derision; **tourner qqch en ~** to hold sthg up to ridicule.

dérisoire [derizwar] *adj* derisory.

dérivatif, -ive [derivatif, iv] *adj* derivative.
◆ **dérivatif** *nm* distraction.

dérivation [derivasjɔ̃] *nf* -**1.** [de cours d'eau, circulation] diversion. -**2.** LING & MATHS derivation.

dérive [deriv] *nf* -**1.** [aileron] centreboard. -**2.** [mouvement] drift, drifting (*U*); **aller** OU **partir à la ~** *fig* to fall apart.

dérivé [derive] *nm* derivative.

dérivée [derive] *nf* MATHS derivative.

dériver [derive] [3] ◇ *vt* -**1.** [détourner] to divert. -**2.** LING to derive. ◇ *vi* -**1.** [aller à la dérive] to drift. -**2.** *fig* [découler]: **~ de** to derive from.

dériveur [derivœr] *nm* sailing dinghy (*with centreboard*).

dermato [dɛrmato] *nm, f fam* dermatologist.

dermatologie [dɛrmatɔlɔʒi] *nf* dermatology.

dermatologue [dɛrmatɔlɔɡ], **dermatologiste** [dɛrmatɔlɔʒist] *nmf* dermatologist.

dernier, -ière [dɛrnje, jɛr] ◇ *adj* -**1.** [gén] last; **samedi ~** last Saturday; **l'année dernière** last year. -**2.** [ultime] last, final. -**3.** [plus récent] latest. ◇ *nm, f* last; **ce ~** the latter; **petit ~** baby of the family.
◆ **en dernier** *loc adv* last.

dernièrement [dɛrnjɛrmɑ̃] *adv* recently, lately.

dernier-né, **dernière-née** [dɛrnjene, dɛrnjɛrne] (*mpl* **derniers-nés**, *fpl* **dernières-nées**) *nm, f* [bébé] youngest (child); *fig*: **la dernière-née de Fiat®** the new Fiat®.

dérobade [derɔbad] *nf* evasion, shirking (*U*).

dérobé, -e [derɔbe] *adj* -**1.** [volé] stolen. -**2.** [caché] hidden.
◆ **à la dérobée** *loc adv* surreptitiously.

dérober [derɔbe] [3] *vt sout* to steal.
◆ **se dérober** *vp* -**1.** [se soustraire]: **se ~ à qqch** to shirk sthg. -**2.** [s'effondrer] to give way.

dérogation [derɔɡasjɔ̃] *nf* [action] dispensation; [résultat] exception.

déroger [derɔʒe] [17] *vi*: **~ à** to depart from.

dérouiller [deruje] [3] *vt* -**1.** [nettoyer] to remove the rust from. -**2.** *fam* [frapper]: **~ qqn** to give sb a belting.
◆ **se dérouiller** *vp fig* to stretch (o.s.).

déroulement [derulmɑ̃] *nm* -**1.** [de bobine] unwinding. -**2.** *fig* [d'événement] development.

dérouler [derule] [3] *vt* [fil] to unwind; [papier, tissu] to unroll.
◆ **se dérouler** *vp* to take place.

déroutant, -e [derutɑ̃, ɑ̃t] *adj* disconcerting, bewildering.

déroute [derut] *nf* MIL rout; *fig* collapse; **mettre en ~** to rout.

dérouter [derute] [3] *vt* -**1.** [déconcerter] to disconcert, to put out. -**2.** [dévier] to divert.

derrick [derik] *nm* derrick.

derrière [dɛrjɛr] ◇ *prép & adv* behind. ◇ *nm* -**1.** [partie arrière] back; **la porte de ~** the back door. -**2.** [partie du corps] bottom, behind.

des [de] ◇ *art indéf* → **un**. ◇ *prép* → **de**.

dès [dɛ] *prép* from; **~ son arrivée** the minute he arrives/arrived, as soon as he arrives/arrived; **~ l'enfance** since childhood; **~ 1900** as far back as 1900, as early as 1900; ~ **maintenant** from now on; ~ **demain** starting OU from tomorrow.

◆ **dès lors** *loc adv* from then on.

◆ **dès lors que** *loc conj* [puisque] since.

◆ **dès que** *loc conj* as soon as.

désabusé, -e [dezabyse] *adj* disillusioned.

désaccord [dezakɔr] *nm* disagreement.

désaccordé, -e [dezakɔrde] *adj* out of tune.

désaccoutumer [dezakutyme] [3] *vt*: ~ **qqn de** to get sb out of the habit of.

◆ **se désaccoutumer** *vp*: se ~ **de qqch/de faire qqch** to become unaccustomed to sthg/to doing sthg.

désaffecté, -e [dezafɛkte] *adj* disused.

désaffection [dezafɛksjɔ̃] *nf* disaffection.

désagréable [dezagreabl] *adj* unpleasant.

désagréablement [dezagreabləmã] *adv* unpleasantly.

désagréger [dezagreʒe] [22] *vt* to break up.

◆ **se désagréger** *vp* to break up.

désagrément [dezagremã] *nm* annoyance.

désaltérant, -e [dezalterã, ãt] *adj* thirst-quenching.

désaltérer [dezaltere] [18] ◇ *vt* to quench the thirst of. ◇ *vi* to be thirst-quenching.

◆ **se désaltérer** *vp* to quench one's thirst.

désamorcer [dezamɔrse] [16] *vt* [arme] to remove the primer from; [bombe] to defuse; *fig* [complot] to nip in the bud.

désappointer [dezapwɛ̃te] [3] *vt* to disappoint.

désapprendre [dezaprãdr] [79] *vt* to forget.

désapprobateur, -trice [dezaprɔbatœr, tris] *adj* disapproving.

désapprobation [dezaprɔbasjɔ̃] *nf* disapproval.

désapprouver [dezapruve] [3] ◇ *vt* to disapprove of. ◇ *vi* to be disapproving.

désarçonner [dezarsɔne] [3] *vt litt & fig* to throw.

désargenté, -e [dezarʒãte] *adj* short (of money).

désarmant, -e [dezarmã, ãt] *adj* disarming.

désarmement [dezarməmã] *nm* disarmament.

désarmer [dezarme] [3] ◇ *vt* to disarm; [fusil] to unload. ◇ *vi* -**1.** [pays] to disarm. -**2.** *fig* [personne] to give up; [haine] to cease.

désarroi [desarwa] *nm* confusion.

désassorti, -e [dezasɔrti] *adj* [dépareillé] non-matching.

désastre [dezastr] *nm* disaster.

désastreux, -euse [dezastrø, øz] *adj* disastrous.

désavantage [dezavãtaʒ] *nm* disadvantage.

désavantager [dezavãtaʒe] [17] *vt* to disadvantage.

désavantageux, -euse [dezavãtaʒø, øz] *adj* unfavourable.

désaveu, -x [dezavø] *nm* -**1.** [reniement] denial. -**2.** [désapprobation] disapproval.

désavouer [dezavue] [6] *vt* to disown.

◆ **se désavouer** *vp* to go back on one's word.

désaxé, -e [dezakse] ◇ *adj* [mentalement] disordered, unhinged. ◇ *nm, f* unhinged person.

descendance [desãdãs] *nf* -**1.** [origine] descent. -**2.** [progéniture] descendants (*pl*).

descendant, -e [desãdã, ãt] *nm, f* [héritier] descendant.

descendre [desãdr] [73] ◇ *vt (aux: avoir)* -**1.** [escalier, pente] to go/come down; ~ **la rue en courant** to run down the street. -**2.** [rideau, tableau] to lower. -**3.** [apporter] to bring/take down. -**4.** *fam* [personne, avion] to shoot down.

◇ *vi (aux: être)* -**1.** [gén] to go/come down; [température, niveau] to fall. -**2.** [passager] to get off; ~ **d'un bus** to get off a bus; ~ **d'une voiture** to get out of a car. -**3.** [loger]: ~ **chez** to stay with; ~ **à l'hôtel** to stay in a hotel. -**4.** [être issu]: ~ **de** to be descended from. -**5.** [marée] to go out.

descendu, -e [desãdy] *pp* → **descendre**.

descente [desãt] *nf* -**1.** [action] descent. -**2.** [pente] downhill slope OU stretch. -**3.** *fam fig* [capacité à boire]: **il a une bonne** ~ he can certainly put it away. -**4.** [irruption] raid. -**5.** [tapis]: ~ **de lit** bedside rug.

descriptif, -ive [dɛskriptif, iv] *adj* descriptive.

◆ **descriptif** *nm* [de lieu] particulars (*pl*); [d'appareil] specification.

description [dɛskripsjɔ̃] *nf* description.

désemparé, -e [dezãpare] *adj* [personne] helpless; [avion, navire] disabled.

désemplir [dezãplir] [32] *vi*: **ce restaurant ne désemplit pas** this restaurant is always packed.

désencombrer [dezãkɔ̃bre] [3] *vt* to clear.

désendettement [dezãdɛtmã] *nm* degearing, debt reduction.

désenfler [dezãfle] [3] *vi* to go down, to become less swollen.

désengagement [dezãgaʒmã] *nm* disengagement.

désensibiliser [desãsibilize] [3] *vt* to desensitize.

déséquilibre [dezekilibr] *nm* imbalance.

déséquilibré, -e [dezekilibre] *nm, f* unbalanced person.

déséquilibrer [dezekilibre] [3] *vt* **-1.** [physiquement]: ~ **qqn** to throw sb off balance. **-2.** [perturber] to unbalance.

désert, -e [dezεr, εrt] *adj* [désertique - île] desert (*avant n*); [peu fréquenté] deserted.
◆ **désert** *nm* desert.

déserter [dezεrte] [3] ◇ *vt* to desert. ◇ *vi* MIL to desert.

déserteur [dezεrtœr] *nm* MIL deserter; *fig* & *péj* traitor.

désertification [dezεrtifikasjɔ̃], **désertisation** [desεrtizasjɔ̃] *nf* desertification; [de région] depopulation.

désertion [dezεrsjɔ̃] *nf* desertion.

désertique [dezεrtik] *adj* desert (*avant n*).

désertisation = **désertification**.

désespérant, -e [dezεsperɑ̃, ɑ̃t] *adj* **-1.** [déprimant] depressing. **-2.** [affligeant] hopeless.

désespéré, -e [dezεspere] *adj* **-1.** [regard] desperate. **-2.** [situation] hopeless.

désespérément [dezεsperemɑ̃] *adv* **-1.** [sans espoir] hopelessly. **-2.** [avec acharnement] desperately.

désespérer [dezεspere] [18] ◇ *vt* **-1.** [décourager]: ~ **qqn** to drive sb to despair. **-2.** [perdre espoir]: ~ **de faire qqch** to despair of doing sthg; ~ **que qqch arrive** to give up hope of sthg happening. ◇ *vi*: ~ **(de)** to despair (of).
◆ **se désespérer** *vp* to despair.

désespoir [dezεspwar] *nm* despair; **en** ~ **de cause** as a last resort; **faire le** ~ **de qqn** to be the despair of sb.

déshabillé [dezabije] *nm* negligee.

déshabiller [dezabije] [3] *vt* to undress.
◆ **se déshabiller** *vp* to undress, to get undressed.

déshabituer [dezabitɥe] [7] *vt*: ~ **qqn de faire qqch** to break sb of the habit of doing sthg.
◆ **se déshabituer** *vp*: se ~ **de qqch** to become unaccustomed to sthg.

désherbant, -e [dezεrbɑ̃, ɑ̃t] *adj* weedkilling.
◆ **désherbant** *nm* weedkiller.

désherber [dezεrbe] [3] *vt* & *vi* to weed.

déshérité, -e [dezerite] ◇ *adj* **-1.** [privé d'héritage] disinherited. **-2.** [pauvre] deprived. ◇ *nm, f* [pauvre] deprived person.

déshériter [dezerite] [3] *vt* to disinherit.

déshonneur [dezɔnœr] *nm* disgrace.

déshonorant, -e [dezɔnɔrɑ̃, ɑ̃t] *adj* dishonourable.

déshonorer [dezɔnɔre] [3] *vt* to disgrace, to bring disgrace on.
◆ **se déshonorer** *vp* to disgrace o.s.

déshumaniser [dezymanize] [3] *vt* to dehumanize.

déshydratation [dezidratasjɔ̃] *nf* dehydration.

déshydrater [dezidrate] [3] *vt* to dehydrate.
◆ **se déshydrater** *vp* to become dehydrated.

desiderata [deziderata] *nmpl* requirements.

design [dizajn] ◇ *adj inv* modern. ◇ *nm inv* modernism.

désignation [deziɲasjɔ̃] *nf* **-1.** [appellation] designation, name. **-2.** [nomination] appointment.

désigner [deziɲe] [3] *vt* **-1.** [choisir] to appoint. **-2.** [signaler] to point out. **-3.** [nommer] to designate.
◆ **se désigner** *vp*: se ~ **(volontaire) pour qqch/pour faire qqch** to volunteer for sthg/to do sthg.

désillusion [dezilyzjɔ̃] *nf* disillusion.

désillusionner [dezilyzjɔne] [3] *vt* to disillusion.

désincarné, -e [dezɛ̃karne] *adj* **-1.** RELIG disembodied. **-2.** [éthéré] unearthly.

désindustrialisation [dezɛ̃dystrializasjɔ̃] *nf* deindustrialization.

désinence [dezinɑ̃s] *nf* LING ending.

désinfectant, -e [dezɛ̃fεktɑ̃, ɑ̃t] *adj* disinfectant.
◆ **désinfectant** *nm* disinfectant.

désinfecter [dezɛ̃fεkte] [4] *vt* to disinfect.

désinflation [dezɛ̃flasjɔ̃] *nf* disinflation.

désinformation [dezɛ̃fɔrmasjɔ̃] *nf* disinformation.

désintégration [dezɛ̃tegrasjɔ̃] *nf* [désagrégation] disintegration; *fig* break-up.

désintégrer [dezɛ̃tegre] [18] to break up.
◆ **se désintégrer** *vp* to disintegrate, to break up.

désintéressé, -e [dezɛ̃terese] *adj* disinterested.

désintéresser [dezɛ̃terese] [4]
◆ **se désintéresser** *vp*: se ~ **de** to lose interest in.

désintérêt [dezɛ̃terε] *nm* lack of interest.

désintoxication [dezɛ̃tɔksikasjɔ̃] *nf* detoxification.

désinvolte [dezɛ̃vɔlt] *adj* **-1.** [à l'aise] casual. **-2.** *péj* [sans-gêne] offhand.

désinvolture [dezɛ̃vɔltyr] *nf* **-1.** [légèreté] casualness. **-2.** *péj* [sans-gêne] offhandedness; **avec** ~ in an offhand manner.

désir [dezir] *nm* **-1.** [souhait] desire, wish. **-2.** [charnel] desire.

désirable [dezirabl] *adj* desirable.

désirer [dezire] [3] *vt* **-1.** *sout* [chose]: ~ faire qqch to wish to do sthg; **vous désirez?** [dans un magasin] can I help you?; [dans un café] what can I get you? **-2.** [sexuellement] to desire. **-3.** *loc*: **laisser à** ~ to leave a lot to be desired.

désireux, -euse [dezirø, øz] *adj sout*: ~ **de faire qqch** anxious to do sthg.

désistement [dezistəmã] *nm*: ~ **(de)** withdrawal (from).

désister [deziste] [3]
◆ **se désister** *vp* **-1.** JUR: **se** ~ **de qqch** to withdraw sthg. **-2.** [se retirer] to withdraw, to stand down.

désobéir [dezɔbeir] [32] *vi*: ~ **(à qqn)** to disobey (sb).

désobéissance [dezɔbeisɑ̃s] *nf* disobedience.

désobéissant, -e [dezɔbeisɑ̃, ɑ̃t] *adj* disobedient.

désobligeant, -e [dezɔbliʒɑ̃, ɑ̃t] *adj sout* offensive.

désodorisant, -e [dezɔdɔrizɑ̃, ɑ̃t] *adj* deodorant.
◆ **désodorisant** *nm* deodorant.

désodoriser [dezɔdɔrize] [3] *vt* to deodorize.

désœuvré, -e [dezœvre] *adj* idle.

désœuvrement [dezœvrəmã] *nm* idleness.

désolant, -e [dezɔlɑ̃, ɑ̃t] *adj* disappointing.

désolation [dezɔlasjɔ̃] *nf* **-1.** [destruction] desolation. **-2.** *sout* [affliction] distress.

désolé, -e [dezɔle] *adj* **-1.** [ravagé] desolate. **-2.** [très affligé] distressed. **-3.** [contrarié] very sorry.

désoler [dezɔle] [3] *vt* **-1.** [affliger] to sadden. **-2.** [contrarier] to upset, to make sorry.
◆ **se désoler** *vp* [être contrarié] to be upset.

désolidariser [desɔlidarize] [3] *vt* **-1.** [choses]: ~ **qqch (de)** to disengage OU disconnect sthg (from). **-2.** [personnes] to estrange.
◆ **se désolidariser** *vp*: **se** ~ **de** to dissociate o.s. from.

désopilant, -e [dezɔpilɑ̃, ɑ̃t] *adj* hilarious.

désordonné, -e [dezɔrdɔne] *adj* [maison, personne] untidy; *fig* [vie] disorganized.

désordre [dezɔrdr] *nm* **-1.** [fouillis] untidiness; **en** ~ untidy; **dans le** ~ in random order. **-2.** *fig* [confusion] disorder. **-3.** [agitation] disturbances (*pl*), disorder (*U*).

désorganiser [dezɔrganize] [3] *vt* to disrupt.

◆ **se désorganiser** *vp* to become disorganized.

désorienté, -e [dezɔrjɑ̃te] *adj* disoriented, disorientated.

désorienter [dezɔrjɑ̃te] [3] *vt* [égarer] to disorient, to disorientate; *fig* [déconcerter] to bewilder.

désormais [dezɔrmɛ] *adv* from now on, in future.

désosser [dezɔse] [3] *vt* to bone.

despote [dɛspɔt] ◇ *nm* [chef d'état] despot; *fig* & *péj* tyrant. ◇ *adj* despotic.

despotique [dɛspɔtik] *adj* despotic.

despotisme [dɛspɔtism] *nm* [gouvernement] despotism; *fig* & *péj* tyranny.

desquels, desquelles [dekɛl] → **lequel**.

DESS (*abr de* **diplôme d'études supérieures spécialisées**) *nm postgraduate diploma*.

dessaisir [desezir] [32] *vt* JUR: ~ **qqn d'une affaire** to withdraw a case from sb.
◆ **se dessaisir** *vp sout*: **se** ~ **de qqch** to relinquish sthg.

dessaler [desale] [3] ◇ *vt* [poisson]: **faire** ~ to soak. ◇ *vi* NAVIG to capsize.

dessaouler, dessoûler [desule] [3] ◇ *vt* to sober up. ◇ *vi* to sober up; **ne pas** ~ *fam* to be permanently plastered.

dessécher [deseʃe] [18] *vt* [peau] to dry (out); *fig* [cœur] to harden.
◆ **se dessécher** *vp* [peau, terre] to dry out; [plante] to wither; *fig* to harden.

dessein [desɛ̃] *nm sout* intention.
◆ **à dessein** *loc adv* intentionally, on purpose.

desserrer [desere] [4] *vt* to loosen; [poing, dents] to unclench; [frein] to release.

dessert [desɛr] *nm* dessert.

desserte [desɛrt] *nf* **-1.** TRANSPORT (transport) service. **-2.** [meuble] sideboard.

desservir [desɛrvir] [38] *vt* **-1.** TRANSPORT to serve. **-2.** [table] to clear. **-3.** [désavantager] to do a disservice to.

dessin [desɛ̃] *nm* **-1.** [graphique] drawing; ~ **animé** cartoon (*film*); ~ **humoristique** cartoon (*drawing*); ~ **industriel** draughtsmanship. **-2.** *fig* [contour] outline.

dessinateur, -trice [desinatœr, tris] *nm* artist, draughtsman (*f* draughtswoman); ~ **industriel** draughtsman.

dessiner [desine] [3] ◇ *vt* [représenter] to draw; *fig* to outline. ◇ *vi* to draw.
◆ **se dessiner** *vp* [se former] to take shape; *fig* to stand out.

dessoûler = dessaouler.

dessous [dəsu] ◇ *adv* underneath. ◇ *prép* underneath, under.

◇ *nm* **-1.** [partie inférieure - gén] underside; [- d'un tissu] **wrong side. -2.** *loc*: **avoir le ~** to come off worst; **être au trente-sixième ~** to be in dire straits; **connaître le ~ des cartes (de)** to have inside information (on); **les ~ de la politique/la finance** the hidden side of politics/the financial world. ◇ *nmpl* [sous-vêtements féminins] **underwear** (U).

◆ **en dessous** *loc adv* underneath; [plus bas] below; **ils habitent l'appartement d'en ~** they live in the flat below OU downstairs; **agir par en ~** to act in an underhand way.

◆ **en dessous de** *loc prép* below.

dessous-de-plat [dəsudpla] *nm inv* tablemat.

dessous-de-table [dəsudtabl] *nm inv* backhander.

dessus [dəsy] ◇ *adv* on top; **n'oubliez pas d'inscrire l'adresse ~** don't forget to write the address on it; **faites attention à ne pas marcher ~** be careful not to walk on it. ◇ *nm* **-1.** [partie supérieure] **top. -2.** [étage supérieur] **upstairs; les voisins du ~** the upstairs neighbours. **-3.** *loc*: **avoir le ~** to have the upper hand; **reprendre le ~** to get over it; **sens ~ dessous** upside down.

◆ **en dessus** *loc adv* above.

dessus-de-lit [dəsydli] *nm inv* bedspread.

déstabilisateur, -trice [destabilizatœr, tris] *adj* destabilizing.

déstabilisation [destabilizasjɔ̃] *nf* destabilization.

déstabiliser [destabilize] [3] *vt* to destabilize.

destin [dɛstɛ̃] *nm* fate.

destinataire [dɛstinatɛr] *nmf* addressee.

destination [dɛstinasjɔ̃] *nf* **-1.** [direction] destination; **arriver à ~** to reach one's destination; **un avion à ~ de Paris** a plane to OU for Paris. **-2.** [rôle] purpose.

destinée [dɛstine] *nf* destiny.

destiner [dɛstine] [3] *vt* **-1.** [consacrer]: **~ qqch à** to intend sthg for, to mean sthg for. **-2.** [vouer]: **~ qqn à qqch/à faire qqch** [à un métier] to destine sb for sthg/to do sthg; [sort] to mark out for.

◆ **se destiner** *vp*: **se ~ à** to intend to go into.

destituer [dɛstitɥe] [7] *vt* to dismiss.

destitution [dɛstitysjɔ̃] *nf* dismissal.

destructeur, -trice [dɛstryktœr, tris] ◇ *adj* destructive. ◇ *nm, f* destroyer.

destruction [dɛstryksjɔ̃] *nf* destruction.

déstructuration [destryktyrasjɔ̃] *nf* breaking down.

déstructurer [destryktyre] [3] *vt* to break down.

désuet, -ète [dezɥɛ, ɛt] *adj* [expression, coutume] obsolete; [style, tableau] outmoded.

désuétude [dezɥetyd] *nf*: **tomber en ~** [expression, coutume] to become obsolete; [style, tableau] to become outmoded.

désuni, -e [dezyni] *adj* divided.

désunion [dezynjɔ̃] *nf* division, dissension.

désunir [dezynir] [32] *vt* [scinder] to divide, to separate; *fig* to divide.

◆ **se désunir** *vp* [athlète] to lose one's stride.

détachable [detaʃabl] *adj* detachable, removable.

détachage [detaʃaʒ] *nm* stain removal.

détachant, -e [detaʃɑ̃, ɑ̃t] *adj* stainremoving.

◆ **détachant** *nm* stain remover.

détaché, -e [detaʃe] *adj* detached; **~ à** OU **auprès de** seconded to.

détachement [detaʃmɑ̃] *nm* **-1.** [d'esprit] detachment. **-2.** [de fonctionnaire] secondment. **-3.** MIL detachment.

détacher [detaʃe] [3] *vt* **-1.** [enlever]: **~ qqch (de)** [objet] to detach sthg (from); *fig* to free sthg (from); **coupon à ~** tear-off coupon. **-2.** [nettoyer] to remove stains from, to clean. **-3.** [délier] to undo; [cheveux] to untie. **-4.** ADMIN: **~ qqn auprès de** to second sb to.

◆ **se détacher** *vp* **-1.** [tomber]: **se ~ (de)** to come off; *fig* to free o.s. (from). **-2.** [se défaire] to come undone. **-3.** [ressortir]: **se ~ sur** to stand out on. **-4.** [se désintéresser]: **se ~ de qqn** to drift apart from sb.

détail [detaj] *nm* **-1.** [précision] detail. **-2.** [description]: **faire le ~ de** to give a detailed breakdown OU description of. **-3.** COMM: **le ~** retail.

◆ **au détail** *loc adj & loc adv* retail.

◆ **en détail** *loc adv* in detail.

détaillant, -e [detajɑ̃, ɑ̃t] ◇ *adj* retail. ◇ *nm, f* retailer.

détaillé, -e [detaje] *adj* detailed.

détailler [detaje] [3] *vt* **-1.** [expliquer] to give details of. **-2.** [vendre] to retail.

détaler [detale] [3] *vi* **-1.** [personne] to clear out. **-2.** [animal] to bolt.

détartrant, -e [detartrɑ̃, ɑ̃t] *adj* descaling.

◆ **détartrant** *nm* descaling agent.

détartrer [detartre] [3] *vt* to scale, to descale.

détaxe [detaks] *nf*: ~ **(sur)** [suppression] removal of tax (from); [réduction] reduction in tax (on).

détecter [detɛkte] [4] *vt* to detect.

détecteur, -trice [detɛktœr, tris] *adj* detecting, detector (*avant n*).
◆ **détecteur** *nm* detector; ~ **de fumée** smoke detector.

détection [detɛksjɔ̃] *nf* detection.

détective [detɛktiv] *nm* detective; ~ **privé** private detective.

déteindre [detɛ̃dr] [81] ◇ *vt* to fade. ◇ *vi* to fade; ~ **sur** *fig* to rub off on; ~ **au lavage** to run (in the wash).

déteint, -e [detɛ̃, ɛ̃t] *pp* → **déteindre**.

dételer [detle] [24] ◇ *vt* -1. [cheval] to unharness. -2. [wagon] to unhitch. ◇ *vi fam fig*: **sans** ~ at a stretch.

détendre [detɑ̃dr] [73] *vt* -1. [corde] to loosen, to slacken; *fig* to ease. -2. [personne] to relax.
◆ **se détendre** *vp* -1. [se relâcher] to slacken; *fig* [situation] to ease; [atmosphère] to become more relaxed. -2. [se reposer] to relax.

détendu, -e [detɑ̃dy] ◇ *pp* → **détendre**. ◇ *adj* -1. [corde] loose, slack. -2. [personne] relaxed.

détenir [detnir] [40] *vt* -1. [objet] to have, to hold. -2. [personne] to detain, to hold.

détente [detɑ̃t] *nf* -1. [de ressort] release. -2. [repos] relaxation. -3. POLIT détente. -4. [d'athlète] thrust. -5. *loc*: **être dur à la** ~ to be slow on the uptake.

détenteur, -trice [detɑ̃tœr, tris] *nm* [d'objet, de secret] possessor; [de prix, record] holder.

détention [detɑ̃sjɔ̃] *nf* -1. [possession] possession. -2. [emprisonnement] detention; ~ **préventive** remand (in custody).

détenu, -e [detny] ◇ *pp* → **détenir**. ◇ *adj* detained. ◇ *nm, f* prisoner.

détergent, -e [detɛrʒɑ̃, ɑ̃t] *adj* detergent (*avant n*).
◆ **détergent** *nm* detergent.

détérioration [deterjɔrasjɔ̃] *nf* [de bâtiment] deterioration; [de situation] worsening.

détériorer [deterjɔre] [3] *vt* -1. [abîmer] to damage. -2. [altérer] to ruin.
◆ **se détériorer** *vp* -1. [bâtiment] to deteriorate; [situation] to worsen. -2. [s'altérer] to be spoiled.

déterminant, -e [detɛrminɑ̃, ɑ̃t] *adj* decisive, determining.
◆ **déterminant** *nm* -1. LING determiner. -2. MATHS determinant.

détermination [detɛrminasjɔ̃] *nf* -1. [définition] determining (*U*). -2. [fixation] determination. -3. [résolution] decision.

déterminé, -e [detɛrmine] *adj* -1. [quantité] given (*avant n*). -2. [expression] determined.

déterminer [detɛrmine] [3] *vt* -1. [préciser] to determine, to specify. -2. [provoquer] to bring about; ~ **qqn à faire qqch** to cause sb to do sthg.
◆ **se déterminer** *vp*: **se** ~ **à faire qqch** to decide to do sthg.

déterminisme [detɛrminism] *nm* determinism.

déterré, -e [detere] *adj*: **avoir une mine de** ~ to look like death warmed up.

déterrer [detere] [4] *vt* to dig up.

détersif, -ive [detɛrsif, iv] *adj* detergent (*avant n*).
◆ **détersif** *nm* detergent.

détestable [detɛstabl] *adj* dreadful.

détester [detɛste] [3] *vt* to detest.

détiendrai, détiendras *etc* → **détenir**.

détonant, -e [detɔnɑ̃, ɑ̃t] *adj* explosive.

détonateur [detɔnatœr] *nm* TECHNOL detonator; *fig* trigger.

détonation [detɔnasjɔ̃] *nf* detonation.

détoner [detɔne] [3] *vi* to detonate.

détonner [detɔne] [3] *vi* MUS to be out of tune; [couleur] to clash; [personne] to be out of place.

détour [detur] *nm* -1. [crochet] detour; **faire un** ~ **(par)** to make a detour (through). -2. [méandre] bend; **au** ~ **du chemin** at the bend in the road; **sans** ~ *fig* directly.

détourné, -e [deturne] *adj* [dévié] indirect; *fig* roundabout (*avant n*).

détournement [deturnəmɑ̃] *nm* diversion; ~ **d'avion** hijacking; ~ **de fonds** embezzlement; ~ **de mineur** corruption of a minor.

détourner [deturne] [3] *vt* -1. [dévier - gén] to divert; [- avion] to hijack. -2. [écarter]: ~ **qqn de** to distract sb from, to divert sb from. -3. [tourner ailleurs] to turn away. -4. [argent] to embezzle.
◆ **se détourner** *vp* to turn away; **se** ~ **de** *fig* to move away from.

détracteur, -trice [detraktœr, tris] *nm, f* detractor.

détraqué, -e [detrake] *fam* ◇ *adj* -1. [déréglé] on the blink. -2. [fou] nutty, loopy. ◇ *nm, f* nutter.

détraquer [detrake] [3] *vt fam* [dérégler] to break; *fig* to upset.
◆ **se détraquer** *vp fam* [se dérégler] to go wrong; *fig* to become unsettled.

détrempe [detrɑ̃p] *nf* ART tempera.

détremper [detrɑ̃pe] [3] *vt* **-1.** [sol] to soften. **-2.** [peinture] to thin.

détresse [detrɛs] *nf* distress; **en ~** in distress.

détriment [detrimɑ̃]
◆ **au détriment de** *loc prép* to the detriment of.

détritus [detrity(s)] *nm* detritus.

détroit [detrwa] *nm* strait; **le ~ de Bering** the Bering Strait; **le ~ de Gibraltar** the Strait of Gibraltar.

détromper [detrɔ̃pe] [3] *vt* to disabuse.
◆ **se détromper** *vp* to disabuse o.s.; **détrompez-vous!** think again!

détrôner [detrone] [3] *vt* [souverain] to dethrone; *fig* to oust.

détrousser [detruse] [3] *vt vieilli* to rob.

détruire [detrɥir] [98] *vt* **-1.** [démolir, éliminer] to destroy. **-2.** [massacrer] to wipe out. **-3.** *fig* [anéantir] to ruin.
◆ **se détruire** *vp* to destroy o.s.

détruisais, détruise *etc* → **détruire**.

détruit, -e [detrɥi, ɥit] *pp* → **détruire**.

dette [dɛt] *nf* debt; **avoir des ~s** to have debts; **la ~ publique** the national debt; **être criblé de ~s** to be crippled by debt.

DEUG, Deug [dœg] (*abr de* **diplôme d'études universitaires générales**) *nm university diploma taken after 2 years of arts courses.*

DEUG, DEUST:
In French universities, students take the courses. They may then take further courses leading to the 'licence' (the equivalent of a bachelor's degree)

deuil [dœj] *nm* [douleur, mort] bereavement; [vêtements, période] mourning (*U*); **en ~** in mourning; **porter le ~** to be in OU wear mourning; **faire son ~ de qqch** *fig* to wave sthg goodbye.

DEUST, Deust [dœst] (*abr de* **diplôme d'études universitaires scientifiques et techniques**) *nm university diploma taken after 2 years of science courses; voir aussi* **DEUG**.

deux [dø] ◇ *adj num* two; **ses ~ fils** both his sons, his two sons; **tous les ~ jours** every other day, every two days, every second day; **en moins de ~** *fam fig* in no time at all, in two ticks. ◇ *nm* two; **les ~** both; **par ~** in pairs; *voir aussi* **six**.

deuxième [døzjɛm] *adj num, nm & nmf* second; *voir aussi* **sixième**.

deuxièmement [døzjɛmmɑ̃] *adv* secondly.

deux-pièces [døpjɛs] *nm inv* **-1.** [appartement] two-room flat *Br* OU apartment *Am*. **-2.** [bikini] two-piece (swimming costume).

deux-points [døpwɛ̃] *nm inv* colon.

deux-roues [døru] *nm inv* two-wheeled vehicle.

deux-temps [døtɑ̃] *adj* **-1.** MUS: **mesure à ~** two/two time. **-2.** MÉCANIQUE: **moteur à ~** two-stroke engine.
◆ **deux-temps** *nm inv* MÉCANIQUE two-stroke (engine).

dévaler [devale] [3] ◇ *vt* to run down. ◇ *vi* to hurtle down.

dévaliser [devalize] [3] *vt* [cambrioler - maison] to ransack; [- personne] to rob; *fig* to strip bare.

dévalorisant, -e [devalɔrizɑ̃, ɑ̃t] *adj* demeaning.

dévalorisation [devalɔrizasjɔ̃] *nf* depreciation.

dévaloriser [devalɔrize] [3] *vt* **-1.** [monnaie] to devalue. **-2.** [personne] to run OU put down.
◆ **se dévaloriser** *vp* **-1.** [monnaie] to fall in value. **-2.** [personne] *fig* to run OU put o.s. down.

dévaluation [devalɥasjɔ̃] *nf* devaluation.

dévaluer [devalɥe] [7] ◇ *vt* to devalue. ◇ *vi* to devalue.
◆ **se dévaluer** *vp* to devalue.

devancer [dəvɑ̃se] [16] *vt* **-1.** [précéder] to arrive before. **-2.** [surpasser] to be in front of. **-3.** [anticiper] to anticipate.

devant [dəvɑ̃] ◇ *prép* **-1.** [en face de] in front of. **-2.** [en avant de] ahead of, in front of; **aller droit ~ soi** to go straight ahead OU on. **-3.** [en présence de, face à] in the face of. ◇ *adv* **-1.** [en face] in front. **-2.** [en avant] in front, ahead. ◇ *nm* front; **prendre les ~s** to make the first move.
◆ **de devant** *loc adj* [pattes, roues] front (*avant n*).

devanture [dəvɑ̃tyr] *nf* shop window; **à la ~ de** on display in.

dévastateur, -trice [devastatœr, tris] *adj* devastating.

dévastation [devastasjɔ̃] *nf* devastation.

dévaster [devaste] [3] *vt* to devastate.

déveine [devɛn] *nf fam* bad luck.

développement [devlɔpmɑ̃] *nm* **-1.** [gén] development. **-2.** PHOT developing. **-3.** [exposé] exposition.
◆ **développements** *nmpl* developments.

développer [devlɔpe] [3] *vt* to develop; [industrie, commerce] to expand.

◆ **se développer** *vp* **-1.** [s'épanouir] to spread. **-2.** ÉCON to grow, to expand.

devenir [dəvnir] [40] *vi* to become; **que devenez-vous?** *fig* how are you doing?

devenu, -e [dəvny] *pp* → **devenir.**

dévergondé, -e [devɛrgɔ̃de] ◇ *adj* shameless, wild. ◇ *nm, f* shameless person.

dévergonder [devɛrgɔ̃de] [3]

◆ **se dévergonder** *vp* to go to the bad, to get into bad ways.

déverrouiller [deveruje] [3] *vt* **-1.** [porte] to unbolt. **-2.** [arme] to release the catch of.

déverser [devɛrse] [3] *vt* **-1.** [liquide] to pour out. **-2.** [ordures] to tip (out). **-3.** [bombes] to unload, to drop. **-4.** *fig* [injures] to pour out.

◆ **se déverser** *vp*: **se ~ dans** to flow into.

déversoir [devɛrswar] *nm* overflow.

dévêtir [devetir] [44] *vt sout* to undress.

◆ **se dévêtir** *vp sout* to undress, to get undressed.

dévêtu, -e [devɛty] *pp* → **dévêtir.**

déviant, -e [devjɑ̃, ɑ̃t] *adj* deviant.

déviation [devjasjɔ̃] *nf* **-1.** [gén] deviation **-2.** [d'itinéraire] diversion.

dévider [devide] [3] *vt* [fil] to unwind.

deviendrai, deviendras *etc* → **devenir.**

devienne, devient → **devenir.**

dévier [devje] [9] ◇ *vi*: **~ de** to deviate from. ◇ *vt* to divert.

devin, devineresse [dəvɛ̃, dəvinrɛs] *nm, f*: **je ne suis pas ~!** I'm not psychic!

deviner [dəvine] [3] *vt* to guess.

◆ **se deviner** *vp* **-1.** [aller de soi] to just come naturally. **-2.** [se voir]: **ça se devine facilement** that's easy to see.

devinette [dəvinɛt] *nf* riddle.

devis [dəvi] *nm* estimate; **faire un ~** to (give an) estimate.

dévisager [devizaʒe] [17] *vt* to stare at.

devise [dəviz] *nf* **-1.** [formule] motto. **-2.** [monnaie] currency.

◆ **devises** *nfpl* [argent] currency (*U*).

deviser [dəvize] [3] *vi* **-1.** *sout* [parler]: **~ de** OU **sur** to converse about. **-2.** *Helv* [faire un devis] to estimate.

dévisser [devise] [3] ◇ *vt* to unscrew. ◇ *vi* ALPINISME to fall (off).

de visu [dəvizy] *adv*: **constater qqch ~** to see sthg with one's own eyes.

dévoiler [devwale] [3] *vt* to unveil; *fig* to reveal.

devoir [dəvwar] [53] ◇ *nm* **-1.** [obligation] duty; **faire son ~** to do one's duty. **-2.** SCOL

homework (*U*); **faire ses ~s** to do one's homework.

◇ *vt* **-1.** [argent, respect]: **~ qqch (à qqn)** to owe (sb) sthg. **-2.** [être redevable de]: **~ qqch à qqn** to owe sthg to sb; **je lui dois d'être ici** it's thanks to him that I'm here. **-3.** [marque l'obligation]: **~ faire qqch** to have to do sthg; **je dois partir à l'heure ce soir** I have to OU must leave on time tonight; **tu devrais faire attention** you should be OU ought to be careful; **il n'aurait pas dû mentir** he shouldn't have lied, he ought not to have lied. **-4.** [marque la probabilité]: **il doit faire chaud là-bas** it must be hot over there; **il a dû oublier** he must have forgotten. **-5.** [marque le futur, l'intention]: **~ faire qqch** to be (due) to do sthg, to be going to do sthg; **elle doit arriver à 6 heures** she's due to arrive at 6 o'clock; **je dois voir mes parents ce week-end** I'm seeing OU going to see my parents this weekend. **-6.** [être destiné à]: **il devait mourir trois ans plus tard** he was to die three years later; **cela devait arriver** it had to happen, it was bound to happen.

◆ **se devoir** *vp*: **se ~ de faire qqch** to be duty-bound to do sthg; **comme il se doit** as is proper.

dévolu, -e [devɔly] *adj sout*: **~ à** allotted to.

◆ **dévolu** *nm*: **jeter son ~ sur** to set one's sights on.

dévorer [devɔre] [3] *vt* to devour; **être dévoré de** *fig* to be eaten up by OU with.

dévot, -e [devo, ɔt] ◇ *adj* devout. ◇ *nm, f* devout person.

dévotion [devɔsjɔ̃] *nf* devotion; **avec ~** [prier] devoutly; [soigner, aimer] devotedly; **faire ses ~s** to perform one's devotions.

dévoué, -e [devwe] *adj* devoted.

dévouement [devumɑ̃] *nm* devotion.

dévouer [devwe] [6]

◆ **se dévouer** *vp* **-1.** [se consacrer]: **se ~ à** to devote o.s. to. **-2.** *fig* [se sacrifier]: **se ~ pour qqch/pour faire qqch** to sacrifice o.s. for sthg/to do sthg.

dévoyé, -e [devwaje] *adj & nm, f* delinquent.

dévoyer [devwaje] [13] *vt littéraire* to lead astray.

◆ **se dévoyer** *vp littéraire* to go astray.

devrai, devras *etc* → **devoir.**

dextérité [dɛksterite] *nf* dexterity, skill; **avec ~** skilfully.

dg (*abr de* **décigramme**) dg.

DG (*abr de* **directeur général**) *nm* GM.

DGE (*abr de* **dotation globale d'équipement**) *nf* state contribution to local government capital budget.

DGF (*abr de* **dotation globale de fonctionnement**) *nf* state contribution to local government revenue budget.

DGI (*abr de* **Direction générale des impôts**) *nf* central tax office.

DGSE (*abr de* **Direction générale de la sécurité extérieure**) *nf* French intelligence and espionage service, ≃ MI6 *Br*, ≃ CIA *Am*.

diabète [djabɛt] *nm* diabetes (*U*).

diabétique [djabetik] *nmf & adj* diabetic.

diable [djabl] *nm* devil; **au ~** [loin] miles from anywhere; **avoir le ~ au corps** to be a real handful; **tirer le ~ par la queue** to live from hand to mouth.

diablement [djabləmã] *adv vieilli* horribly.

diablesse [djablɛs] *nf* she-devil; [femme turbulente] shrew, vixen.

diablotin [djablɔtɛ̃] *nm* imp.

diabolique [djabɔlik] *adj* diabolical.

diabolo [djabɔlo] *nm* **-1.** [jouet] diabolo. **-2.** [boisson] fruit cordial and lemonade; **~ menthe** mint (cordial) and lemonade.

diacre [djakr] *nm* RELIG deacon.

diadème [djadɛm] *nm* diadem.

diagnostic [djagnɔstik] *nm* MÉD & *fig* diagnosis.

diagnostiquer [djagnɔstike] [3] *vt* MÉD & *fig* to diagnose.

diagonale [djagɔnal] *nf* diagonal; **en ~** diagonally; **lire en ~** *fig* to skim.

diagramme [djagram] *nm* graph.

dialecte [djalɛkt] *nm* dialect.

dialectique [djalɛktik] *nf & adj* dialectic.

dialogue [djalɔg] *nm* discussion; **c'est un ~ de sourds** they're/you're *etc* never going to agree.

◆ **dialogues** *nmpl* dialogue (*sg*).

dialoguer [djalɔge] [3] *vi* **-1.** [converser] to converse. **-2.** INFORM to interact.

dialyse [djaliz] *nf* dialysis.

diamant [djamã] *nm* [pierre] diamond.

diamétralement [diametralmã] *adv*: **~ opposé** diametrically opposed.

diamètre [djametr] *nm* diameter.

diantre [djãtr] *interj littéraire & vieilli* by Jove!

diapason [djapazɔ̃] *nm* [instrument] tuning fork; **se mettre au ~** *fig* to get on the same wavelength.

diaphane [djafan] *adj* [peau, teint] translucent; [tissu] diaphanous.

diaphragme [djafragm] *nm* diaphragm.

diapositive [djapozitiv] *nf* slide.

diarrhée [djare] *nf* diarrhoea.

diatribe [djatrib] *nf sout* diatribe.

dichotomie [dikɔtɔmi] *nf* dichotomy.

dico [diko] *nm fam* dictionary.

Dictaphone® [diktafɔn] *nm* Dictaphone®.

dictateur [diktatœr] *nm* dictator.

dictatorial, -e, -iaux [diktatɔrjal, jo] *adj* dictatorial.

dictature [diktatyr] *nf* dictatorship.

dictée [dikte] *nf* dictation.

dicter [dikte] [3] *vt* to dictate.

diction [diksjɔ̃] *nf* diction.

dictionnaire [diksjɔnɛr] *nm* dictionary; **~ bilingue/encyclopédique** bilingual/encyclopedic dictionary.

dicton [diktɔ̃] *nm* saying, dictum.

didactique [didaktik] *adj* didactic.

dièse [djɛz] ◇ *adj* sharp; **do/fa ~** C/F sharp. ◇ *nm* sharp.

diesel [djezɛl] *adj inv* diesel; **moteur ~** diesel engine.

diète [djɛt] *nf* diet; **être à la ~** to be on a diet.

diététicien, -ienne [djetetisjɛ̃, jɛn] *nm, f* dietician.

diététique [djetetik] ◇ *nf* dietetics (*U*). ◇ *adj* [considération, raison] dietary; [produit, magasin] health (*avant n*).

dieu, -x [djø] *nm* god; **comme un ~** *fig & hum* divinely.

◆ **Dieu** *nm* God; **mon Dieu!** my God!; **Dieu sait où/comment** God knows where/how; **Dieu merci!** thank God!

diffamation [difamasjɔ̃] *nf* [écrite] libel; [orale] slander; **attaquer qqn en ~** to sue sb for slander/libel.

diffamatoire [difamatwar] *adj* defamatory.

différant [diferã] *participe présent* → **différer**.

différé, -e [difere] *adj* recorded.

◆ **différé** *nm*: **en ~** TÉLÉ recorded; INFORM off-line.

différemment [diferamã] *adv* differently.

différence [diferãs] *nf* difference.

différencier [diferãsje] [9] *vt*: **~ qqch de qqch** to differentiate sthg from sthg.

◆ **se différencier** *vp*: **se ~ de** to be different from.

différend [diferã] *nm* [désaccord] difference of opinion; **avoir un ~ avec** to have a difference of opinion with.

différent, -e [diferã, ãt] *adj*: **~ (de)** different (from).

différentiel, -ielle [diferɑ̃sjɛl] *adj* differential.

différer [difere] [18] ◇ *vt* [retarder] to postpone. ◇ *vi*: ~ **de** to differ from, to be different from; ~ **(selon)** to vary (according to).

difficile [difisil] ◇ *adj* difficult. ◇ *nm*: **faire le/la** ~ to be hard to please.

difficilement [difisilmɑ̃] *adv* with difficulty.

difficulté [difikylte] *nf* **-1.** [complexité, peine] difficulty. **-2.** [obstacle] problem; **en** ~ in difficulty.

difforme [difɔrm] *adj* deformed.

difformité [difɔrmite] *nf* deformity.

diffraction [difraksjɔ̃] *nf* diffraction.

diffus, -e [dify, yz] *adj* diffused; *fig* vague.

diffuser [difyze] [3] *vt* **-1.** [lumière] to diffuse. **-2.** [émission] to broadcast. **-3.** [livres] to distribute.

diffuseur [difyzœr] *nm* **-1.** [appareil] diffuser. **-2.** [de livres] distributor.

diffusion [difyzjɔ̃] *nf* **-1.** [d'émission, d'onde] broadcast. **-2.** [de livres] distribution.

digérer [diʒere] [18] ◇ *vi* to digest. ◇ *vt* **-1.** [repas, connaissance] to digest. **-2.** *fam fig* [désagrément] to put up with.

digeste [diʒɛst] *adj* (easily) digestible.

digestible [diʒɛstibl] *adj* digestible.

digestif, -ive [diʒɛstif, iv] *adj* digestive.
◆ **digestif** *nm* liqueur.

digestion [diʒɛstjɔ̃] *nf* digestion.

digital, -e, -aux [diʒital, o] *adj* **-1.** TECHNOL digital. **-2.** → **empreinte**.
◆ **digitale** *nf* digitalis.

digne [diɲ] *adj* **-1.** [honorable] dignified. **-2.** [méritant]: ~ **de** worthy of; ~ **de foi** trustworthy.

dignement [diɲmɑ̃] *adv* with dignity.

dignitaire [diɲitɛr] *nm* dignitary; **haut** ~ mandarin.

dignité [diɲite] *nf* dignity; **se draper dans sa** ~ to stand on one's dignity.

digression [digresjɔ̃] *nf* digression.

digue [dig] *nf* dike.

diktat [diktat] *nm* diktat.

dilapider [dilapide] [3] *vt* to squander.

dilatation [dilatasjɔ̃] *nf* dilation.

dilater [dilate] [3] *vt* to dilate.
◆ **se dilater** *vp* to expand, to dilate.

dilatoire [dilatwar] *adj* delaying (*avant n*).

dilemme [dilɛm] *nm* dilemma.

dilettante [diletɑ̃t] *nmf* dilettante; **faire qqch en** ~ to dabble in sthg.

diligence [diliʒɑ̃s] *nf* HIST & *sout* diligence.

diligent, -e [diliʒɑ̃, ɑ̃t] *adj vieilli* diligent.

diluant [dilɥɑ̃] *nm* thinner.

diluer [dilɥe] [7] *vt* to dilute.

diluvien, -ienne [dilyvjɛ̃, jɛn] *adj* torrential.

dimanche [dimɑ̃ʃ] *nm* Sunday; ~ **des Rameaux** Palm Sunday; *voir aussi* **samedi**.

dimension [dimɑ̃sjɔ̃] *nf* **-1.** [mesure] dimension. **-2.** [taille] **dimensions** (*pl*), size. **-3.** *fig* [importance] magnitude; **à la** ~ **de** equal to.

diminué, -e [diminɥe] *adj* diminished.

diminuer [diminɥe] [7] ◇ *vt* [réduire] to diminish, to reduce. ◇ *vi* [intensité] to diminish, to decrease.
◆ **se diminuer** *vp* to put o.s. down.

diminutif, -ive [diminytif, iv] *adj* diminutive.
◆ **diminutif** *nm* diminutive.

diminution [diminysjɔ̃] *nf* diminution.

DIN, Din [din] (*abr de* **Deutsche Industrie Norm**) DIN.

dinde [dɛ̃d] *nf* **-1.** [animal] turkey. **-2.** *péj* [femme] stupid woman.

dindon [dɛ̃dɔ̃] *nm* turkey; **être le** ~ **de la farce** *fig* to be made a fool of.

dîner [dine] [3] ◇ *vi* to dine. ◇ *nm* dinner; ~. **d'affaires/aux chandelles** business/candlelit dinner.

dînette [dinɛt] *nf* doll's tea party; **faire la** ~ to have a snack; **jouer à la** ~ to have a doll's tea party.

dingue [dɛ̃g] *fam* ◇ *adj* **-1.** [personne] crazy. **-2.** [histoire] incredible. ◇ *nmf* loony.

dinosaure [dinozɔr] *nm* dinosaur.

diocèse [djɔsɛz] *nm* diocese.

diode [djɔd] *nf* diode.

dioptrie [djɔptri] *nf* dioptre.

diphasé, -e [difaze] *adj* two-phase.

diphtérie [difteri] *nf* diphtheria.

diphtongue [diftɔ̃g] *nf* diphthong.

diplomate [diplɔmat] ◇ *nmf* [ambassadeur] diplomat. ◇ *nm* [gâteau] ≈ trifle. ◇ *adj* diplomatic.

diplomatie [diplɔmasi] *nf* diplomacy.

diplomatique [diplɔmatik] *adj* diplomatic.

diplôme [diplom] *nm* diploma.

diplômé, -e [diplome] ◇ *adj*: **être** ~ **de/en** to be a graduate of/in. ◇ *nm, f* graduate.

dire [dir] [102] *vt*: ~ **qqch (à qqn)** [parole] to say sthg (to sb); [vérité, mensonge, secret] to tell (sb) sthg; ~ **à qqn qu'il fasse qqch** to tell sb to do sthg; **il m'a dit que ...** he told me (that) ...; **cela va sans** ~ that goes without saying; **c'est vite dit** *fam* that's easy (for you/him *etc*) to say; **c'est beaucoup** ~ that's saying a lot; **elle est vraiment difficile, et ce n'est pas peu dire** she's very difficult - and I mean difficult; **en** ~ **long** *fig* to speak volumes; **entre nous soit dit** between you and me; **la ville proprement dite** the actual town; **dire du bien/du mal (de)** to speak well/ill (of); **dire dirais-tu de ...?** what would you say to ...?; **qu'en dis-tu?** what do you think (of it)?; **on dit que ...** they say (that) ...; **on dirait que ...** it looks as if ...; **on dirait de la soie** it looks like silk, you'd think it was silk; **et ~ que je n'étais pas là!** and to think I wasn't there!; **ça ne me dit rien** I don't fancy that.

◆ **se dire** *vp* **-1.** [penser] to think (to o.s.). **-2.** [s'employer]: **ça ne se dit pas** [par décence] you mustn't say that; [par usage] people don't say that, nobody says that. **-3.** [se traduire]: **«chat» se dit «gato» en espagnol** the Spanish for "cat" is "gato".

◆ **au dire de** *loc prép* according to.

◆ **cela dit** *loc adv* having said that.

◆ **dis donc** *loc adv fam* so; [au fait] by the way; [à qqn qui exagère] look here!

◆ **pour ainsi dire** *loc adv* so to speak.

◆ **à vrai dire** *loc adv* to tell the truth.

direct, -e [dirɛkt] *adj* direct.

◆ **direct** *nm* **-1.** BOXE jab; **un ~ du gauche** a straight left. **-2.** [train] direct train. **-3.** RADIO & TÉLÉ: **le ~** live transmission (*U*); **en ~** live.

directement [dirɛktəmɑ̃] *adv* directly.

directeur, -trice [dirɛktœr, tris] ◇ *adj* **-1.** [dirigeant] leading; **comité ~** steering committee. **-2.** [central] guiding.

◇ *nm, f* director, manager; **~ commercial/du marketing** sales/marketing director, sales/marketing manager; **~ général** general manager, managing director *Br*, chief executive officer *Am*; **~ de la communication** director of communications; **~ du personnel** OU **des ressources humaines** personnel OU human resources manager; **~ de thèse** UNIV supervisor *Br*, reader *Am*; **~ des ventes** sales manager.

direction [dirɛksjɔ̃] *nf* **-1.** [gestion, ensemble des cadres] management; **sous la ~ de** under the management of. **-2.** [orientation] direction; **en** OU **dans la ~ de** in the direction of; **«toutes ~s»** "all routes". **-3.** AUTOM steering; **~ assistée** power steering.

directive [dirɛktiv] *nf* directive.

directorial, -e, -iaux [dirɛktɔrjal, jo] *adj* managerial.

directrice → **directeur**.

dirigeable [diriʒabl] *nm*: **(ballon) ~** airship.

dirigeant, -e [diriʒɑ̃, ɑ̃t] ◇ *adj* ruling. ◇ *nm, f* [de pays] leader; [d'entreprise] manager.

diriger [diriʒe] [17] *vt* **-1.** [mener - entreprise] to run, to manage; [- orchestre] to conduct; [- film, acteurs] to direct; [- recherches, projet] to supervise. **-2.** [conduire] to steer. **-3.** [orienter]: **~ qqch sur/vers** to aim sthg at/towards.

◆ **se diriger** *vp*: **se ~ vers** to go OU head towards.

dirigisme [diriʒism] *nm* interventionism.

disais, disions *etc* → **dire**.

discal, -e, -aux [diskal, o] → **hernie**.

discernement [disɛrnəmɑ̃] *nm* **-1.** [jugement] discernment. **-2.** *sout* [distinction] distinction.

discerner [disɛrne] [3] *vt* **-1.** [distinguer]: **~ qqch de** to distinguish sthg from. **-2.** [deviner] to discern.

disciple [disipl] *nmf* disciple.

disciplinaire [disiplinɛr] *adj* disciplinary; **mesure ~** disciplinary measure.

discipline [disiplin] *nf* discipline; **~ de fer** iron rule.

discipliné, -e [disipline] *adj* disciplined.

discipliner [discipline] [3] *vt* [personne] to discipline; [cheveux] to control.

disc-jockey [diskʒɔkɛ] (*pl* **disc-jockeys**) *nm* disc jockey.

disco [disko] ◇ *adj inv* disco (*avant n*). ◇ *nf* disco. ◇ *nm* disco (music).

discographie [diskɔgrafi] *nf* discography.

discontinu, -e [diskɔ̃tiny] *adj* [ligne] broken; [bruit, effort] intermittent.

discontinuer [diskɔ̃tinɥe] [7] *vi*: **sans ~** without interruption.

discordance [diskɔrdɑ̃s] *nf* discrepancy.

discordant, -e [diskɔrdɑ̃, ɑ̃t] *adj* discordant.

discorde [diskɔrd] *nf* discord.

discothèque [diskɔtɛk] *nf* **-1.** [boîte de nuit] discothèque. **-2.** [de prêt] record library.

discount [disk(a)unt] *nm* discount.

discourir [diskurir] [45] *vi* to talk at length; **~ sur** to hold forth on.

discours [diskur] *nm* **-1.** [allocution] speech; **faire un ~** to make a speech. **-2.** LING: **~ direct/indirect** direct/reported speech.

discouru, -e [diskyru] *pp* → **discourir**.

discrédit [diskredi] *nm* discredit, disrepute; **jeter le ~ sur** to bring disgrace on.

discréditer [diskredite] [3] *vt* to discredit.

◆ **se discréditer** *vp* to discredit o.s.

discret, -ète [diskrɛ, ɛt] *adj* [gén] discreet; [réservé] reserved.

discrètement [diskrɛtmɑ̃] *adv* discreetly.

discrétion [diskresjɔ̃] *nf* **-1.** [réserve, tact, silence] discretion. **-2.** [sobriété] **sobriety, simplicity; avec** ~ **discreetly.**

◆ **à discrétion** ◇ *loc adj* **unlimited.** ◇ *loc adv* **as much as you want.**

discrétionnaire [diskresjɔnɛr] *adj* discretionary.

discrimination [diskriminasjɔ̃] *nf* discrimination; **sans** ~ **indiscriminately.**

discriminatoire [diskriminatwar] *adj* discriminatory.

disculper [diskylpe] [3] *vt* **to exonerate.**

◆ **se disculper** *vp* **to exonerate o.s.**

discussion [diskysjɔ̃] *nf* **-1.** [conversation, examen] **discussion. -2.** [contestation, altercation] **argument; sans** ~ **without argument.**

discutable [diskytabl] *adj* **-1.** [contestable] **questionable. -2.** [douteux] **doubtful, questionable.**

discutailler [diskytaje] [3] *vi fam péj* **to argue over trivialities** OU **details.**

discuter [diskyte] [3] ◇ *vt* **-1.** [débattre]: ~ **(de) to discuss sthg. -2.** [contester] **to dispute.** ◇ *vi* **-1.** [parlementer] **to discuss. -2.** [converser] **to talk. -3.** [contester] **to argue.**

◆ **se discuter** *vp* **to be questionable** OU **debatable.**

disert, -e [dizɛr, ɛrt] *adj littéraire* **articulate.**

disette [dizɛt] *nf sout* [famine] **famine;** *fig* [manque] **shortage.**

diseur, -euse [dizœr, øz] *nm, f:* ~ **de bonne aventure fortune-teller.**

disgrâce [disgras] *nf* **disgrace.**

disgracieux, -ieuse [disgrasjø, jøz] *adj* **-1.** [sans grâce] **awkward, graceless. -2.** [laid] **plain.**

disjoindre [disʒwɛ̃dr] [82] *vt* [planches, tuiles] **to take apart;** *fig* **to separate, to distinguish.**

◆ **se disjoindre** *vp* **to come apart.**

disjoint, -e [disʒwɛ̃, ɛ̃t] *pp* → **disjoindre.**

disjoncteur [disʒɔ̃ktœr] *nm* **trip switch, circuit breaker.**

dislocation [dislɔkasjɔ̃] *nf* MÉD **dislocation.**

disloquer [dislɔke] [3] *vt* **-1.** MÉD **to dislocate. -2.** [machine, empire] **to dismantle.**

◆ **se disloquer** *vp* [machine] **to fall apart** OU **to pieces;** *fig* [empire] **to break up.**

disparaissais, disparaissions *etc* → **disparaître.**

disparaître [disparɛtr] [91] *vi* **-1.** [gén] **to disappear, to vanish; disparais! vanish!; faire** ~ [personne] **to get rid of;** [obstacle] **to remove. -2.** [mourir] **to die.**

disparate [disparat] *adj* [éléments] **disparate;** [couleurs, mobilier] **badly matched.**

disparité [disparite] *nf* **-1.** [écart] **disparity. -2.** [différence - d'éléments] **disparity;** [- de couleurs] **mismatch.**

disparition [disparisjɔ̃] *nf* **-1.** [gén] **disappearance;** [d'espèce] **extinction; en voie de** ~ **endangered. -2.** [mort] **passing.**

disparu, -e [dispary] ◇ *pp* → **disparaître.** ◇ *nm, f* **dead person, deceased.**

dispatcher [dispatʃe] [3] *vt* **to dispatch, to despatch.**

dispendieux, -ieuse [dispɑ̃djø, jøz] *adj sout* **expensive.**

dispensaire [dispɑ̃sɛr] *nm* **community clinic** *Br,* **free clinic** *Am.*

dispense [dispɑ̃s] *nf* **-1.** [exemption] **exemption;** ~ **d'âge special dispensation** (*in the matter of age*). **-2.** [certificat] **certificate of exemption.**

dispenser [dispɑ̃se] [3] *vt* **-1.** [distribuer] **to dispense. -2.** [exempter]: ~ **qqn de qqch** [corvée] **to excuse sb sthg, to let sb off sthg; je te dispense de tes réflexions!** *fig* **spare us the comments!, keep your comments to yourself!**

◆ **se dispenser** *vp:* **se** ~ **de qqch/de faire qqch to get out of sthg/of doing sthg.**

disperser [dispɛrse] [3] *vt* **to scatter (about** OU **around);** [collection, brume, foule] **to break up;** *fig* [efforts, forces] **to dissipate, to waste.**

◆ **se disperser** *vp* **-1.** [feuilles, cendres] **to scatter;** [brume, foule] **to break up, to clear. -2.** [personne] **to take on too much at once, to spread o.s. too thin.**

dispersion [dispɛrsjɔ̃] *nf* **scattering;** [de collection, brume, foule] **breaking up;** *fig* [d'efforts, de forces] **waste, squandering.**

disponibilité [dispɔnibilite] *nf* **-1.** [de choses] **availability. -2.** [de fonctionnaire] **leave of absence; en** ~ **on leave of absence. -3.** [d'esprit] **alertness, receptiveness.**

◆ **disponibilités** *nfpl* **available funds, liquid assets.**

disponible [dispɔnibl] *adj* **-1.** [place, personne] **available, free. -2.** [fonctionnaire] **on leave of absence.**

dispos, -e [dispo, oz] *adj* **fresh, full of energy.**

disposé, -e [dispoze] *adj:* **être** ~ **à faire qqch to be prepared** OU **willing to do sthg; être bien** ~ **envers qqn to be well-disposed towards** OU **to sb.**

disposer [dispoze] [3] ◇ *vt* **-1.** [arranger] **to arrange. -2.** [inciter]: ~ **qqn à faire qqch to lead** OU **move sb to do sthg.** ◇ *vi:* ~ **de** [moyens, argent] **to have available (to one), to have at one's disposal;** [chose] **to have**

the use of; [temps] to have free OU available; **vous pouvez** ~ *fig* & *sout* you may leave OU go.

◆ **se disposer** *vp*: **se** ~ **à qqch/à faire qqch** *sout* to prepare for sthg/to do sthg.

dispositif [dispozitif] *nm* [mécanisme] device, mechanism; ~ **antibuée** demister; ~ **antiparasite** suppressor; ~ **de sûreté** safety device.

disposition [dispozisjɔ̃] *nf* **-1.** [arrangement] arrangement. **-2.** [disponibilité]: **à la** ~ **de** at the disposal of, available to.

◆ **dispositions** *nfpl* **-1.** [mesures] arrangements, measures. **-2.** JUR provisions. **-3.** [dons]: **avoir des** ~**s pour** to have a gift for.

disproportion [disprɔpɔrsjɔ̃] *nf* disproportion.

disproportionné, -e [disprɔpɔrsjɔne] *adj* out of proportion.

dispute [dispyt] *nf* argument, quarrel.

disputer [dispyte] [3] *vt* **-1.** [SPORT - course] to run; [- match] to play. **-2.** [lutter pour] to fight for.

◆ **se disputer** *vp* **-1.** [se quereller] to quarrel, to fight. **-2.** SPORT [se played. **-3.** [lutter pour] to fight over OU for.

disquaire [disker] *nm* record dealer.

disqualification [diskalifikasjɔ̃] *nf* disqualification.

disqualifier [diskalifje] [9] *vt* to disqualify.

disque [disk] *nm* **-1.** MUS record; [vidéo] video disc; ~ **compact** OU **laser** compact disc. **-2.** ANAT disc. **-3.** INFORM disk; ~ **dur** hard disk. **-4.** SPORT discus.

◆ **disque de stationnement** *nm* parking disc.

disquette [disket] *nf* diskette, floppy disk; ~ **haute/double densité** high/double density disk; ~ **système** system diskette.

dissection [diseksjɔ̃] *nf* dissection.

dissemblable [disãblabl] *adj* dissimilar.

dissémination [diseminasjɔ̃] *nf* **-1.** [dispersion] scattering, spreading (out); *fig* dissemination, spreading. **-2.** [répartition] scattering.

disséminer [disemine] [3] *vt* [graines, maisons] to scatter, to spread (out); *fig* [idées] to disseminate, to spread.

dissension [disãsjɔ̃] *nf* dissent.

disséquer [diseke] [18] *vt* *litt* & *fig* to dissect.

dissertation [disertasjɔ̃] *nf* essay.

disserter [diserte] [3] *vi*: ~ **sur** [à l'écrit] to write on; [à l'oral] to speak on.

dissidence [disidãs] *nf* dissent, dissidence.

dissident, -e [disidã, ãt] *adj* & *nm, f* dissident.

dissimulation [disimylasjɔ̃] *nf* **-1.** [hypocrisie] duplicity. **-2.** [de la vérité] concealment.

dissimulé, -e [disimyle] *adj* [hypocrite] dissembling, duplicitous.

dissimuler [disimyle] [3] *vt* to conceal.

◆ **se dissimuler** *vp* **-1.** [se cacher] to conceal o.s., to hide. **-2.** [refuser de voir]: **se** ~ **qqch** to close one's eyes to sthg.

dissipation [disipasjɔ̃] *nf* **-1.** [dispersion] dispersal, breaking up; *fig* [de malentendu] clearing up; [de craintes] dispelling. **-2.** [indiscipline] indiscipline, misbehaviour. **-3.** [dilapidation] squandering. **-4.** [débauche] dissipation.

dissipé, -e [disipe] *adj* **-1.** [turbulent] unruly, badly behaved. **-2.** [frivole] dissipated, dissolute.

dissiper [disipe] [3] *vt* **-1.** [chasser] to break up, to clear; *fig* to dispel. **-2.** [dilapider, gâcher] to squander. **-3.** [distraire] to lead astray.

◆ **se dissiper** *vp* **-1.** [brouillard, fumée] to clear. **-2.** [élève] to misbehave. **-3.** *fig* [malaise, fatigue] to go away; [doute] to be dispelled.

dissocier [disɔsje] [9] *vt* **-1.** [séparer] to separate, to distinguish. **-2.** CHIM to dissociate.

dissolu, -e [disɔly] *adj* dissolute.

dissolution [disɔlysjɔ̃] *nf* **-1.** JUR dissolution. **-2.** [mélange] dissolving. **-3.** *sout* [débauche] dissipation.

dissolvais, dissolvions etc → **dissoudre**.

dissolvant, -e [disɔlvã, ãt] *adj* solvent.

◆ **dissolvant** *nm* [solvant] solvent; [pour vernis à ongles] nail varnish remover.

dissonance [disɔnãs] *nf* dissonance; *fig* clash, discord.

dissoudre [disudr] [87] *vt*: **(faire)** ~ to dissolve.

◆ **se dissoudre** *vp* **-1.** [substance] to dissolve. **-2.** JUR to be dissolved.

dissous, -oute [disu, ut] *pp* → **dissoudre**.

dissuader [disɥade] [3] *vt* to dissuade.

dissuasif, -ive [disɥazif, iv] *adj* deterrent.

dissuasion [disɥazjɔ̃] *nf* dissuasion; **force de** ~ deterrent (effect).

dissymétrique [disimetrik] *adj* dissymmetrical.

distance [distãs] *nf* **-1.** [éloignement] distance; **à** ~ at a distance; [télécommander] by remote control; **à une** ~ **de 300 mètres** 300 metres away; **se tenir à** ~ to keep one's distance; **garder ses** ~**s** to keep one's distance; **prendre ses ~s** *fig* to stand back OU aloof. **-2.** [intervalle] interval. **-3.** [écart] gap.

distancer [distãse] [16] *vt* to outstrip.

distanciation [distãsjasjɔ̃] *nf* distance.

distancier [distãsje] [9]

◆ **se distancier** *vp*: **se ~ de** to distance o.s. from.

distant, -e [distã, ãt] *adj* **-1.** [éloigné]: **une ville ~e de 10 km** a town 10 km away; **des villes ~es de 10 km** towns 10 km apart. **-2.** [froid] distant.

distendre [distãdr] [73] *vt* [ressort, corde] to stretch; [abdomen] to distend.

◆ **se distendre** *vp* to distend.

distendu, -e [distãdy] *pp* → **distendre**.

distillation [distilasjɔ̃] *nf* distilling, distillation.

distiller [distile] [3] *vt* [alcool] to distil; [pétrole] to refine; [miel] to secrete; *fig & littéraire* to exude.

distillerie [distilri] *nf* [industrie] distilling; [lieu] distillery.

distinct, -e [distɛ̃, ɛ̃kt] *adj* distinct.

distinctement [distɛ̃ktəmã] *adv* distinctly, clearly.

distinctif, -ive [distɛ̃ktif, iv] *adj* distinctive.

distinction [distɛ̃ksjɔ̃] *nf* distinction.

distingué, -e [distɛ̃ge] *adj* distinguished.

distinguer [distɛ̃ge] [3] *vt* **-1.** [différencier] to tell apart, to distinguish. **-2.** [percevoir] to make out, to distinguish. **-3.** [rendre différent]: **~ de** to distinguish from, to set apart from.

◆ **se distinguer** *vp* **-1.** [se différencier]: **se ~ (de)** to stand out (from). **-2.** [s'illustrer] to distinguish o.s. **-3.** [être perçu]: **au loin se distinguait la côte** you could make out the coast in the distance.

distraction [distraksjɔ̃] *nf* **-1.** [inattention] inattention, absent-mindedness; **par ~** absent-mindedly. **-2.** [passe-temps] leisure activity.

distraire [distrer] [112] *vt* **-1.** [déranger] to distract. **-2.** [divertir] to amuse, to entertain.

◆ **se distraire** *vp* to amuse o.s.

distrait, -e [distre, et] ◇ *pp* → **distraire**. ◇ *adj* absent-minded.

distraitement [distretmã] *adv* absent-mindedly, absently.

distrayais, distrayons *etc* → **distraire**.

distrayant, -e [distrejã, ãt] *adj* entertaining.

distribanque [distribãk] *nm* cash dispenser.

distribuer [distribɥe] [7] *vt* to distribute; [courrier] to deliver; [ordres] to give out; [cartes] to deal; [coups, sourires] to dispense.

distributeur, -trice [distribytœr, tris] *nm, f* distributor.

◆ **distributeur** *nm* **-1.** AUTOM & COMM distributor. **-2.** [machine]: **~ (automatique) de billets** BANQUE cash machine, cash dispenser; TRANSPORT ticket machine; **~ de boissons** drinks machine.

distribution [distribysjɔ̃] *nf* **-1.** [répartition, diffusion, disposition] distribution; **~ du courrier** postal delivery; **~ des prix** SCOL prize-giving. **-2.** [approvisionnement] supply. **-3.** CIN & THÉÂTRE cast.

district [distrikt] *nm* district.

dit, dite [di, dit] ◇ *pp* → **dire**. ◇ *adj* **-1.** [appelé] known as. **-2.** JUR said, above. **-3.** [fixé]: **à l'heure ~e** at the appointed time.

dites, dîtes → **dire**.

dithyrambique [ditirãbik] *adj* eulogistic.

DIU (*abr de* **dispositif intra-utérin**) *nm* IUD.

diurétique [djyretik] *nm & adj* diuretic.

diurne [djyrn] *adj* diurnal.

diva [diva] *nf* prima donna, diva.

divagation [divagasjɔ̃] *nf* wandering.

divaguer [divage] [3] *vi* to ramble.

divan [divã] *nm* divan (*seat*).

divergeant [diverʒã] *ppr* → **diverger**.

divergence [diverʒãs] *nf* divergence, difference; [d'opinions] difference.

divergent, -e [diverʒã, ãt] *adj* divergent.

diverger [diverʒe] [17] *vi* to diverge; [opinions] to differ.

divers, -e [diver, ers] *adj* **-1.** [différent] different, various. **-2.** [disparate] diverse. **-3.** (*avant n*) [plusieurs] various, several. **-4.** PRESSE: **«~»** "miscellaneous".

diversement [diversəmã] *adv* variously, in different ways.

diversification [diversifikasjɔ̃] *nf* diversification.

diversifier [diversifje] [9] *vt* to vary, to diversify.

◆ **se diversifier** *vp* to diversify.

diversion [diversjɔ̃] *nf* diversion; **créer une ~, faire ~** to create a diversion.

diversité [diversite] *nf* diversity.

divertir [divertir] [32] *vt* [distraire] to entertain, to amuse.

◆ **se divertir** *vp* to amuse o.s., to entertain o.s.

divertissant, -e [divertisã, ãt] *adj* entertaining, amusing.

divertissement [divertismã] *nm* **-1.** [passe-temps] form of relaxation. **-2.** MUS divertimento.

dividende [dividãd] *nm* dividend.

divin, -e [divɛ̃, in] *adj* divine.

divination [divinasjɔ̃] *nf* divination.

divinement [divinmɑ̃] *adv* divinely.

divinité [divinite] *nf* divinity.

diviser [divize] [3] *vt* **-1.** [gén] to divide, to split up; ~ **pour régner** *fig* divide and rule. **-2.** MATHS to divide; ~ **8 par 4** to divide 8 by 4.

♦ **se diviser** *vp* **-1.** [se séparer] to divide. **-2.** [diverger] to be divided.

divisible [divizibl] *adj* divisible.

division [divizjɔ̃] *nf* division; ~ **aéroportée** MIL airborne division.

divisionnaire [divizjɔnɛr] *adj* divisional.

divorce [divɔrs] *nm* **-1.** JUR divorce; **demander le** ~ to ask for a divorce, to sue for divorce. **-2.** *fig* [divergence] gulf, separation.

divorcé, -e [divɔrse] ◇ *adj* divorced. ◇ *nm, f* divorcee, divorced person.

divorcer [divɔrse] [16] *vi* to divorce.

divulgation [divylgasjɔ̃] *nf* disclosure.

divulguer [divylge] [3] *vt* to divulge.

dix [dis] *adj num & nm* ten; *voir aussi* **six.**

dix-huit [dizɥit] *adj num & nm* eighteen; *voir aussi* **six.**

dix-huitième [dizɥitjɛm] *adj num, nm & nmf* eighteenth; *voir aussi* **sixième.**

dixième [dizjɛm] *adj num, nm & nmf* tenth; *voir aussi* **sixième.**

dix-neuf [diznœf] *adj num & nm* nineteen; *voir aussi* **six.**

dix-neuvième [diznœvjɛm] *adj num, nm & nmf* nineteenth; *voir aussi* **sixième.**

dix-sept [disɛt] *adj num & nm* seventeen; *voir aussi* **six.**

dix-septième [disɛtjɛm] *adj num, nm & nmf* seventeenth; *voir aussi* **sixième.**

dizaine [dizɛn] *nf* **-1.** MATHS ten. **-2.** [environ dix]: **une** ~ **de** about ten; **par** ~**s** [en grand nombre] in their dozens.

Djakarta [dʒakarta] *n* Jakarta.

djellaba [dʒɛlaba] *nf* jellaba.

Djibouti [dʒibyti] ◇ *nm* [État]: **le** ~ Djibouti; **au** ~ in Djibouti. ◇ *n* [ville] Djibouti.

djiboutien, -ienne [dʒibytjɛ̃, jɛn] *adj* of/from Djibouti.

♦ **Djiboutien, -ienne** *nm, f* person from Djibouti.

dm (*abr de* **décimètre**) dm.

DM (*abr de* **deutschmark**) DM.

do¹ [do] *nm inv* MUS C; [dans la gamme] doh.

do² (*abr de* **dito**) do.

doberman [dɔbɛrman] *nm* Doberman (pinscher).

doc [dɔk] (*abr de* **documentation**) *nf* literature, brochures (*pl*); **pouvez-vous me donner de la** ~ **sur cet ordinateur?** could you

give me some literature about this computer?

doc. (*abr de* **document**) doc.

docile [dɔsil] *adj* **-1.** [obéissant] docile. **-2.** [cheveux] manageable.

docilement [dɔsilmɑ̃] *adv* meekly, obediently.

docilité [dɔsilite] *nf* obedience.

dock [dɔk] *nm* **-1.** [bassin] dock. **-2.** [hangar] warehouse.

docker [dɔkɛr] *nm* docker.

docte [dɔkt] *adj iron* professorial.

doctement [dɔktəmɑ̃] *adv* [savamment] learnedly.

docteur [dɔktœr] *nm* **-1.** [médecin] doctor; ~ **en médecine** doctor of medicine. **-2.** UNIV: ~ **ès lettres/sciences** ≃ PhD; ~ **honoris causa** ≃ Hon. PhD.

doctoral, -e, -aux [dɔktɔral, o] *adj péj* pompous, professorial.

doctorat [dɔktɔra] *nm* **-1.** [grade] doctorate; ~ **d'État** ≃ D. Litt., *higher doctorate awarded for aptitude for advanced research;* ~ **du troisième cycle** *doctorate awarded for two years' study and a work of research.* **-2.** [épreuve] doctoral exam.

doctoresse [dɔktɔrɛs] *nf* woman OU lady doctor.

doctrinaire [dɔktrinɛr] *adj* **-1.** [dogmatique] doctrinaire. **-2.** [sentencieux] sententious.

doctrine [dɔktrin] *nf* doctrine.

document [dɔkymɑ̃] *nm* document.

documentaire [dɔkymɑ̃tɛr] *nm & adj* documentary.

documentaliste [dɔkymɑ̃talist] *nmf* [d'archives] archivist; PRESSE & TÉLÉ researcher.

documentation [dɔkymɑ̃tasjɔ̃] *nf* **-1.** [travail] research. **-2.** [documents] paperwork, papers (*pl*). **-3.** [brochures] documentation.

documenté, -e [dɔkymɑ̃te] *adj* **-1.** [personne] well-informed. **-2.** [étude] well-documented.

documenter [dɔkymɑ̃te] [3] *vt* to document.

♦ **se documenter** *vp* to do some research.

dodeliner [dɔdəline] [3] *vi*: ~ **de la tête** to nod gently.

dodo [dɔdo] *nm fam* beddy-byes; **faire** ~ to sleep.

dodu, -e [dɔdy] *adj fam* [enfant, joue, bras] chubby; [animal] plump.

dogmatique [dɔgmatik] *adj* dogmatic.

dogme [dɔgm] *nm* dogma.

dogue [dɔg] *nm* mastiff.

doigt [dwa] *nm* finger; **un ~ de** (just) a drop OU finger of; **montrer qqch du ~** to point at sthg; **de pied** toe; **être à deux ~s de faire qqch** to be within an ace of doing sthg; **mettre le ~ dans l'engrenage** to embark on sthg, to get involved; **se mettre le ~ dans l'œil** *fam* to be kidding o.s.; **je m'en mords les ~s** I could kick myself (for it); **obéir à qqn au ~ et à l'œil** to obey sb's every whim, to be at sb's beck and call.

doigté [dwate] *nm* delicacy, tact.

dois → devoir.

doive → devoir.

doléances [dɔleɑ̃s] *nfpl sout* grievances.

dollar [dɔlar] *nm* dollar.

dolmen [dɔlmɛn] *nm* dolmen.

DOM [dɔm] (*abr de* **département d'outre-mer**) *nm* French overseas department.

domaine [dɔmɛn] *nm* **-1.** [propriété] estate. **-2.** [secteur, champ d'activité] field, domain; **tomber dans le ~ public** be out of copyright.

domanial, -e, -iaux [dɔmanjal, jo] *adj* national, state (*avant n*).

dôme [dom] *nm* **-1.** ARCHIT dome. **-2.** GÉOGR rounded peak.

domestication [dɔmɛstikasjɔ̃] *nf* domestication.

domestique [dɔmɛstik] ◇ *nmf* (domestic) servant. ◇ *adj* family (*avant n*); [travaux] household (*avant n*).

domestiquer [dɔmɛstike] [3] *vt* **-1.** [animal] to domesticate. **-2.** [éléments naturels] to harness.

domicile [dɔmisil] *nm* **-1.** [gén] (place of) residence; **travailler à ~** to work from OU at home; **ils livrent à ~** they do deliveries; **sans ~ fixe** of no fixed abode; **élire ~** to take up residence; **~ conjugal** JUR marital home. **-2.** [d'entreprise] (registered) address.

domiciliation [dɔmisiljasjɔ̃] *nf*: **~ bancaire** domiciliation.

domicilié, -e [dɔmisilje] *adj*: **~ à** (officially) resident in OU at.

dominant, -e [dɔminɑ̃, ɑ̃t] *adj* **-1.** [qui prévaut] dominant. **-2.** [qui surplombe] dominating.

◆ **dominante** *nf* **-1.** [caractéristique] dominant feature OU characteristic. **-2.** [couleur] dominant colour. **-3.** MUS dominant.

domination [dɔminasjɔ̃] *nf* **-1.** [autorité] domination, dominion. **-2.** [influence] influence.

dominer [dɔmine] [3] ◇ *vt* **-1.** [surplomber, avoir de l'autorité sur] to dominate. **-2.** [sur-

passer] to outclass. **-3.** [maîtriser] to control, to master. **-4.** *fig* [connaître] to master. ◇ *vi* **-1.** [régner] to dominate, to be dominant. **-2.** [prédominer] to predominate. **-3.** [triompher] to be on top, to hold sway.

◆ **se dominer** *vp* to control o.s.

dominicain, -e [dɔminikɛ̃, ɛn] *adj* Dominican.

◆ **Dominicain, -e** *nm, f* Dominican.

dominical, -e, -aux [dɔminikal, o] *adj* Sunday (*avant n*).

Dominique [dɔminik] *nf*: **la ~** Dominica.

domino [dɔmino] *nm* domino.

dommage [dɔmaʒ] *nm* **-1.** [préjudice] harm (*U*); **~s et intérêts, ~s-intérêts** damages; (**c'est**) **~!** what a shame OU pity!; **c'est ~ que** it's a pity OU shame (that). **-2.** [dégâts] damage (*U*).

dompter [dɔ̃te] [3] *vt* **-1.** [animal, fauve] to tame. **-2.** [rebelles, enfants] to subdue. **-3.** *fig* [maîtriser] to overcome, to control.

dompteur, -euse [dɔ̃tœr, øz] *nm, f* [de fauves] tamer.

DOM-TOM [dɔmtɔm] (*abr de* **départements d'outre-mer/territoires d'outre-mer**) *nmpl French overseas départements and territories*.

don [dɔ̃] *nm* **-1.** [cadeau] gift; **faire ~ de** to make a gift OU present of; **~ du sang** blood donation. **-2.** [aptitude] knack.

DON [dɔn] (*abr de* **disque optique numérique**) *nm digital optical disk*.

donateur, -trice [dɔnatœr, tris] *nm, f* donor.

donation [dɔnasjɔ̃] *nf* settlement.

donc [dɔ̃k] *conj* so; **je disais ~ ...** so as I was saying ...; **allons ~!** come on!; **tais-toi ~!** will you be quiet!

donjon [dɔ̃ʒɔ̃] *nm* keep.

donjuanisme [dɔ̃ʒyanism] *nm* womanizing.

donnant [dɔnɑ̃]

◆ **donnant donnant** *loc adv* fair's fair.

donne [dɔn] *nf* JEU deal.

donné, -e [dɔne] *adj* given; **c'est ~** it's a .gift; **c'est pas ~** it's not exactly cheap; **étant ~ que** given that, considering (that).

◆ **donnée** *nf* **-1.** INFORM & MATHS datum, piece of data; **données numériques** numerical data. **-2.** [élément] fact, particular.

donner [dɔne] [3] ◇ *vt* **-1.** [gén] to give; [se débarrasser de] to give away; **~ qqch à qqn** to give sb sthg, to give sthg to sb; **~ qqch à faire à qqn** to give sb sthg to do, to give sthg to sb to do; **~ sa voiture à réparer** to leave one's car to be repaired; **quel âge lui**

donnes-tu? how old do you think he/she is?; **ne rien ~** to be no use OU good, to be unproductive. **-2.** *fam* [dénoncer] to shop. **-3.** [occasionner] to give, to cause. ◇ *vi* **-1.** [tomber]: **~ dans** to fall into; *fig* to have a tendency towards. **-2.** [s'ouvrir]: **~ sur** to look out onto. **-3.** [produire] to produce, to yield. **-4.** [amener]: **~ à penser/ entendre que** to lead sb to think/ understand that.
◆ **se donner** *vp*: **-1.** [se consacrer]: **se ~ à qqch** to give OU devote o.s. to sthg. **-2.** [céder]: **se ~ à qqn** to give o.s. to sb.

donneur, -euse [dɔnœr, øz] *nm, f* **-1.** MÉD donor; **~ de sang** blood donor. **-2.** CARTES dealer.

dont [dɔ̃] *pron rel* **-1.** [complément de verbe ou d'adjectif]: **la personne ~ tu parles** the person you're speaking about, the person about whom you are speaking; **l'accident ~ il est responsable** the accident for which he is responsible; **c'est quelqu'un ~ on dit le plus grand bien** he's someone about whom people speak highly (*la traduction varie selon la préposition anglaise utilisée avec le verbe ou l'adjectif en question*). **-2.** [complément de nom ou de pronom - relatif à l'objet] of which, whose; [- relatif à personne] whose; **un meuble ~ le bois est vermoulu** a piece of furniture with woodworm; **la boîte ~ le couvercle est jaune** the box whose lid is yellow, the box with the yellow lid; **c'est quelqu'un ~ j'apprécie l'honnêteté** he's someone whose honesty I appreciate; **celui ~ les parents sont divorcés** the one whose parents are divorced. **-3.** [indiquant la partie d'un tout]: **plusieurs personnes ont téléphoné, ~ ton frère** several people phoned, one of which was your brother OU and among them was your brother; **j'ai vu plusieurs films ~ deux étaient particulièrement intéressants** I saw several films, two of which were particularly interesting.

dopage [dɔpaʒ] *nm* doping.

dopant, -e [dɔpɑ̃, ɑ̃t] *adj* stimulant.
◆ **dopant** *nm* dope (*U*).

dope [dɔp] *nf fam* dope.

doper [dɔpe] [3] *vt* to dope.
◆ **se doper** *vp* to take stimulants.

dorade = **daurade**.

doré, -e [dɔre] *adj* **-1.** [couvert de dorure] gilded, gilt; **~ sur tranche** gilt-edged. **-2.** [couleur] golden.

dorénavant [dɔrenavɑ̃] *adv* from now on, in future.

dorer [dɔre] [3] ◇ *vt* **-1.** [couvrir d'or] to gild. **-2.** [peau] to tan. **-3.** CULIN to glaze. ◇ *vi* CULIN: **faire ~** to brown.
◆ **se dorer** *vp* to tan.

dorloter [dɔrlɔte] [3] *vt* to pamper, to cosset.

dormant, -e [dɔrmɑ̃, ɑ̃t] *adj* [eau] still.

dormeur, -euse [dɔrmœr, øz] *nm, f* sleeper.

dormir [dɔrmir] [36] *vi* **-1.** [sommeiller] to sleep; **~ debout** to be asleep on one's feet; **à ~ debout** unbelievable, implausible. **-2.** [rester inactif - personne] to slack, to stand around (doing nothing); [- capitaux] to lie idle.

dorsal, -e, -aux [dɔrsal, o] *adj* dorsal.

dortoir [dɔrtwar] *nm* dormitory.

dorure [dɔryr] *nf* **-1.** [couche d'or] gilt. **-2.** [ce qui est doré] golden OU gilt decoration.

doryphore [dɔrifɔr] *nm* colorado beetle.

dos [do] *nm* back; **~ à ~** back to back; **de ~** from behind; **sur le ~** on one's back; **«voir au ~»** "see over"; **à ~ d'âne** (riding) on a mule; **ne rien avoir à se mettre sur le ~** to have nothing to wear; **tourner le ~ à** [être tourné] to have one's back to; *litt* & *fig* [se tourner] to turn one's back on; **~ crawlé** backstroke; **avoir bon ~** to be the one who always gets the blame; **en avoir plein le ~** *fam* to be fed up (to the back teeth), to have had it up to here; **se mettre qqn à ~** to put sb's back up.

DOS, Dos [dɔs] (*abr de* **Disk Operating System**) *nm* DOS.

dosage [dozaʒ] *nm* [de médicament] dose; [d'ingrédient] amount.

dos-d'âne [dodan] *nm* bump.

dose [doz] *nf* **-1.** [quantité de médicament] dose; **«ne pas dépasser la ~ prescrite»** "do not exceed the prescribed dose". **-2.** [quantité] share; **forcer la ~** *fam fig* to overdo it; **une (bonne) ~ de bêtise** *fam fig* a lot of silliness; **j'en ai eu ma ~** *fam fig* I've had enough.

doser [doze] [3] *vt* [médicament, ingrédient] to measure out; *fig* to weigh up.

doseur [dozœr] *nm* [appareil] measure; [de cuisine] measuring jug.

dossard [dosar] *nm* number (*on competitor's back*).

dossier [dosje] *nm* **-1.** [de fauteuil] back. **-2.** [documents] file, dossier; **~ suspendu** suspension file. **-3.** [classeur] file, folder. **-4.** *fig* [question] question.

dot [dɔt] *nf* dowry.

dotation [dɔtasjɔ̃] *nf* **-1.** JUR endowment. **-2.** ADMIN grant.

doter [dɔte] [3] *vt* [pourvoir]: ~ **de** [talent] to endow with; [machine] to equip with.

douairière [dwɛrjɛr] *nf* [veuve] dowager.

douane [dwan] *nf* **-1.** [service, lieu] customs (*pl*); **passer la** ~ to go through customs. **-2.** [taxe] (import) duty.

douanier, -ière [dwanje, jɛr] ◇ *adj* customs (*avant n*). ◇ *nm, f* customs officer.

doublage [dublaʒ] *nm* **-1.** [renforcement] lining. **-2.** [de film] dubbing. **-3.** [d'acteur] understudying.

double [dubl] ◇ *adj* double. ◇ *adv* double; **voir** ~ to see double, to have double vision. ◇ *nm* **-1.** [quantité]: **le** ~ double. **-2.** [copie] copy; **en** ~ in duplicate. **-3.** [d'une personne] double. **-4.** TENNIS doubles (*pl*).

doublé [duble] *nm* **-1.** [en orfèvrerie] rolled gold. **-2.** [réussite double] double.

doublement [dublǝmã] ◇ *adv* doubly. ◇ *nm* [de lettre] doubling.

doubler [duble] [3] ◇ *vt* **-1.** [multiplier] to double. **-2.** [plier] to (fold) double. **-3.** [renforcer]: ~ **(de)** to line (with). **-4.** [dépasser] to overtake. **-5.** [film, acteur] to dub. **-6.** *fam* [trahir] to con, to double-cross. **-7.** [augmenter] to double. ◇ *vi* **-1.** [véhicule] to overtake. **-2.** [augmenter] to double.

◆ **se doubler** *vp*: **se** ~ **de** to be coupled with.

doublure [dublyr] *nf* **-1.** [renforcement] lining. **-2.** CIN stand-in.

douce → **doux**.

douceâtre [dusatr] *adj* sickly (sweet), cloying.

doucement [dusmã] *adv* **-1.** [descendre] carefully; [frapper] gently; ~! gently OU easy (does it)! **-2.** [traiter] gently; [parler] softly. **-3.** [médiocrement] (only) so-so.

doucereux, -euse [dusrø, øz] *adj* **-1.** [saveur] sickly (sweet), cloying. **-2.** [mielleux] smooth, suave.

doucette [dusɛt] *nf* BOT lamb's lettuce.

douceur [dusœr] *nf* **-1.** [de saveur, parfum] sweetness. **-2.** [d'éclairage, de peau, de musique] softness. **-3.** [de climat] mildness. **-4.** [de caractère] gentleness. **-5.** [plaisir] pleasure.

◆ **douceurs** *nfpl* [friandises] sweets.

◆ **en douceur** ◇ *loc adv* smoothly. ◇ *loc adj* smooth.

douche [duʃ] *nf* **-1.** [appareil, action] shower; **prendre une** ~ to take OU have a shower. **-2.** *fam fig* [déception] letdown; ~ **écossaise** shock to the system.

doucher [duʃe] [3] *vt* **-1.** [donner une douche à]: ~ **qqn** to give sb a shower. **-2.** *fam fig* [décevoir] to let down.

◆ **se doucher** *vp* to take OU have a shower, to shower.

doudoune [dudun] *nf* quilted jacket.

doué, -e [due] *adj* talented; **être** ~ **pour** to have a gift for.

douer [due] [6] *vt*: ~ **qqn de** to endow sb with.

douille [duj] *nf* **-1.** [d'ampoule] socket. **-2.** [de cartouche] cartridge.

douillet, -ette [duje, ɛt] ◇ *adj* **-1.** [confortable] snug, cosy. **-2.** [sensible] soft. ◇ *nm, f* wimp.

douillettement [dujɛtmã] *adv* snugly.

douleur [dulœr] *nf litt & fig* pain; **se tordre de** ~ to writhe in pain; **nous avons la** ~ **de vous annoncer ...** it is with great sorrow that we announce ....

douloureux, -euse [dulurø, øz] *adj* **-1.** [physiquement] painful. **-2.** [moralement] distressing. **-3.** [regard, air] sorrowful.

doute [dut] *nm* doubt; **avoir des** ~**s sur** to have misgivings about; **mettre qqch en** ~ to cast doubt on sthg.

◆ **sans doute** *loc adv* no doubt; **sans aucun** ~ without (a) doubt.

douter [dute] [3] ◇ *vt* [ne pas croire]: ~ **que** (+ *subjonctif*) to doubt (that). ◇ *vi* [ne pas avoir confiance]: ~ **de qqn/qqch** to doubt sb/sthg, to have doubts about sb/sthg; **j'en doute** I doubt it.

◆ **se douter** *vp*: **se** ~ **de qqch** to suspect sthg; **je m'en doutais** I thought so; **je m'en doute** I'm not surprised.

douteux, -euse [dutø, øz] *adj* **-1.** [incertain] doubtful. **-2.** [contestable] questionable. **-3.** [péj] [mœurs] dubious; [vêtements, personne] dubious-looking.

douves [duv] *nfpl* [de château] moat (*sg*).

doux, douce [du, dus] *adj* **-1.** [éclairage, peau, musique] soft. **-2.** [saveur, parfum] sweet. **-3.** [climat, condiment] mild. **-4.** *sout* [agréable] pleasant. **-5.** [pente, regard, caractère] gentle.

◆ **doux** *loc adv*: **il fait** ~ the weather is mild.

◆ **en douce** *loc adv* secretly.

douzaine [duzɛn] *nf* **-1.** [douze] dozen. **-2.** [environ douze]: **une** ~ **de** about twelve.

douze [duz] *adj num & nm* twelve; *voir aussi* **six**.

douzième [duzjɛm] *adj num, nm & nmf* twelfth; *voir aussi* **sixième**.

doyen, -enne [dwajɛ̃, ɛn] *nm, f* [le plus ancien] most senior member.

DP (*abr de* **délégué du personnel**) *nm* staff representative.

DPLG (*abr de* **diplômé par le gouvernement**) *adj* holder of official certificate for architects, engineers etc.

dr. (*abr de* **droite**) R, r.

Dr (*abr de* **Docteur**) Dr.

draconien, -ienne [drakɔnjɛ̃, jɛn] *adj* draconian.

dragage [dragaʒ] *nm* dredging.

dragée [draʒe] *nf* **-1.** [confiserie] sugared almond; **tenir la ~ haute à qqn** to hold out against sb. **-2.** [comprimé] pill.

dragon [dragɔ̃] *nm* **-1.** [monstre, personne autoritaire] dragon. **-2.** [soldat] dragoon.

drague [drag] *nf* **-1.** TECHNOL dredger. **-2.** *fam fig* [flirt] picking up.

draguer [drage] [3] *vt* **-1.** [nettoyer] to dredge. **-2.** *fam* [personne] to chat up, to get off with.

dragueur, -euse [dragœr, øz] *nm, f fam* [homme] womanizer; **quelle dragueuse!** she's always chasing after men!
◆ **dragueur** *nm* [bateau] dredger.

drainage [drɛnaʒ] *nm* draining.

drainer [drene] [4] *vt* **-1.** [terrain, plaie] to drain. **-2.** *fig* [attirer] to drain off.

dramatique [dramatik] ◇ *nf* play. ◇ *adj* **-1.** THÉÂTRE dramatic. **-2.** [grave] tragic.

dramatisation [dramatizasjɔ̃] *nf* dramatization.

dramatiser [dramatize] [3] *vt* [exagérer] to dramatize.

drame [dram] *nm* **-1.** [catastrophe] tragedy; **faire un ~ de qqch** *fig* to make a drama of sthg. **-2.** LITTÉRATURE drama.

drap [dra] *nm* **-1.** [de lit] sheet. **-2.** [tissu] woollen cloth; **être dans de beaux ~s** to be in a real mess.

drapeau, -x [drapo] *nm* flag; **~ blanc** white flag; **le ~ tricolore** the tricolour, the French flag; **être sous les ~x** *fig* to be doing military service.

draper [drape] [3] *vt sout* to drape.
◆ **se draper** *vp*: **se ~ dans** to drape o.s. in.

draperie [drapri] *nf* **-1.** [tenture] drapery. **-2.** [industrie] cloth industry.

drap-housse [draus] (*pl* **draps-housses**) *nm* fitted sheet.

drapier, -ière [drapje, jɛr] ◇ *adj* clothing (*avant n*). ◇ *nm, f* **-1.** [fabricant] cloth manufacturer. **-2.** [marchand] draper.

drastique [drastik] *adj* drastic.

dressage [drɛsaʒ] *nm* [d'animal] training, taming.

dresser [drese] [4] *vt* **-1.** [lever] to raise. **-2.** [faire tenir] to put up. **-3.** *sout* [construire] to erect. **-4.** [acte, liste, carte] to draw up; [procès-verbal] to make out. **-5.** [dompter] to train. **-6.** *fig* [opposer]: **~ qqn contre qqn** to set sb against sb.
◆ **se dresser** *vp* **-1.** [se lever] to stand up. **-2.** [s'élever] to rise (up); *fig* to stand; **se ~ contre qqch** to rise up against.

dresseur, -euse [drɛsœr, øz] *nm, f* trainer.

dressoir [drɛswar] *nm* dresser.

DRH ◇ *nf* (*abr de* **direction des ressources humaines**) personnel department. ◇ *nm* (*abr de* **directeur des ressources humaines**) personnel manager.

dribbler [drible] [3] SPORT ◇ *vi* to dribble. ◇ *vt*: **~ qqn** to dribble past sb.

drille [drij] *nm*: **un joyeux ~** a cheery person.

driver [drajvœr] [3] GOLF ◇ *nm* driver. ◇ *vi* to drive.

drogue [drɔg] *nf* **-1.** [stupéfiant & *fig*] drug; **la ~** drugs (*pl*); **~ dure** hard drug. **-2.** [médicament] medicine.

drogué, -e [drɔge] ◇ *adj* drugged. ◇ *nm, f* drug addict.

droguer [drɔge] [3] *vt* [victime] to drug.
◆ **se droguer** *vp* [de stupéfiants] to take drugs.

droguerie [drɔgri] *nf* hardware shop.

droguiste [drɔgist] *nmf*: **chez le ~** at the hardware shop.

droit, -e [drwa, drwat] *adj* **-1.** [du côté droit] right. **-2.** [rectiligne, vertical, honnête] straight; **~ comme un i** straight as a ramrod, bolt upright.
◆ **droit** ◇ *adv* straight; **tout ~** straight ahead; **aller ~ au but** *fig* to go straight to the point.
◇ *nm* **-1.** JUR law; **~ canon** canon law; **~ civil** civil law; **~ coutumier** common law; **~ pénal** criminal law; **de ~ commun** common-law (*avant n*). **-2.** [prérogative] right; **avoir ~ à** to be entitled to; **avoir le ~ de faire qqch** to be allowed to do sthg; **être dans son ~** to be within one's rights; **être en ~ de faire qqch** to have a right to do sthg; **de quel ~?** by what right?; **~ d'aînesse** birthright; **~ d'asile** right of asylum; **~ de grâce** power of pardon; **~ de regard** right of access; **~ de visite** visiting rights (*pl*), access; **~ de vote** right to vote; **~s d'auteur** royalties; **~s de l'homme** human rights; **~s d'inscription** registration fees; **à qui de ~** to the proper authority.
◆ **droite** *nf* **-1.** [gén] right, right-hand side; **à ~e** on the right; **à ~e de** to the right of;

garder/serrer sa ~e to keep to the right. **-2.** POLIT: **la** ~e the right (wing); **de** ~e right-wing.

droitier, -ière [drwatje, jɛr] ◇ *adj* right-handed. ◇ *nm, f* right-handed person, right-hander.

droiture [drwatyr] *nf* straightforwardness.

drôle [drol] *adj* **-1.** [amusant] funny. **-2.** ~ **de** [bizarre] funny; *fam* [remarquable] amazing.

drôlement [drolmã] *adv* **-1.** *fam* [très] tremendously. **-2.** [bizarrement] in a strange way. **-3.** [de façon amusante] in a funny way.

drôlerie [drolri] *nf* humour.

dromadaire [drɔmadɛr] *nm* dromedary.

dru, -e [dry] *adj* thick.
◆ **dru** *adv*: **tomber** ~ to fall heavily.

drugstore [drœgstɔr] *nm* drugstore.

druide [drɥid] *nm* druid.

ds *abr de* **dans**.

DST (*abr de* **Direction de la surveillance du territoire**) *nf internal state security department*, ≃ MI5 *Br*.

DT (*abr de* **diphtérie, tétanos**) *nm vaccine against diphtheria and tetanus*.

D.T.COQ. (*abr de* **diphtérie, tétanos, coqueluche**) *nm vaccine against diphtheria, tetanus and whooping cough*.

du → **de**.

dû, due [dy] ◇ *pp* → **devoir**. ◇ *adj* due, owing.
◆ **dû** *nm* due; **réclamer son** ~ to demand one's due.

dualité [dɥalite] *nf* duality.

Dubayy [dybaj] *n* Dubai.

dubitatif, -ive [dybitatif, iv] *adj* doubtful.

Dublin [dyblɛ̃] *n* Dublin.

dublinois, -e [dyblinwa, waz], *adj* of/from Dublin.
◆ **Dublinois, -e** *nm, f* Dubliner.

duc [dyk] *nm* duke.

ducal, -e, -aux [dykal, o] *adj* ducal.

duché [dyʃe] *nm* duchy.

duchesse [dyʃɛs] *nf* duchess.

duel [dɥɛl] *nm* duel.

duffel-coat (*pl* **duffel-coats**), **duffle-coat** (*pl* **duffle-coats**) [dœfœlkot] *nm* duffel coat.

dûment [dymã] *adv* duly.

dumping [dœmpiŋ] *nm* COMM dumping.

dune [dyn] *nf* dune.

duo [dɥo] *nm* **-1.** MUS duet; **en** ~ in duet. **-2.** *fam* [couple] duo.

dupe [dyp] ◇ *nf* dupe. ◇ *adj* gullible; **être/ne pas être** ~ to be/not to be taken in.

duper [dype] [3] *vt sout* to dupe, to take sb in.

duplex [dyplɛks] *nm* **-1.** [appartement] split-level flat, maisonette *Br*, duplex *Am*. **-2.** RADIO & TÉLÉ link-up; **en** ~ link-up (*avant n*).

duplicata [dyplikata] *nm inv* duplicate.

duplicité [dyplisite] *nf* duplicity.

dupliquer [dyplike] [3] *vt* [document] to duplicate.

duquel [dykɛl] → **lequel**.

dur, -e [dyr] ◇ *adj* **-1.** [matière, personne, travail] hard; [carton] stiff. **-2.** [viande] tough. **-3.** [climat, punition, loi] harsh. ◇ *nm, f fam*: ~ **(à cuire)** tough nut.
◆ **dur** *adv* hard.
◆ **à la dure** *loc adv*: **coucher à la** ~e to sleep rough; **être élevé à la** ~e to have been brought up the hard way.

durable [dyrabl] *adj* lasting.

durablement [dyrabləmã] *adv* durably.

durant [dyrã] *prép* **-1.** [pendant] for. **-2.** [au cours de] during.

durcir [dyrsir] [32] ◇ *vt litt* & *fig* to harden. ◇ *vi* to harden, to become hard.
◆ **se durcir** *vp litt* & *fig* to harden.

durcissement [dyrsismã] *nm* hardening.

durée [dyre] *nf* length; **(de) longue** ~ long-lasting; **«**~ **de conservation ...»** "best before ..."

durement [dyrmã] *adv* **-1.** [violemment] hard, vigorously. **-2.** [péniblement] severely. **-3.** [méchamment] harshly.

durer [dyre] [3] *vi* to last.

dureté [dyrte] *nf* **-1.** [de matériau, de l'eau] hardness. **-2.** [de problème] difficulty. **-3.** [d'époque, de climat, de personne] harshness. **-4.** [de punition] severity.

durillon [dyrijɔ̃] *nm* [sur le pied] corn; [sur la main] callus.

dus, dut *etc* → **devoir**.

DUT (*abr de* **diplôme universitaire de technologie**) *nm university diploma in technology*.

duvet [dyvɛ] *nm* **-1.** [plumes, poils fins] down. **-2.** [sac de couchage] sleeping bag.

dynamique [dinamik] ◇ *nf* **-1.** PHYS dynamics (*U*). **-2.** *fig*: ~ **de groupe** group dynamics (*pl*). ◇ *adj* dynamic.

dynamiser [dinamize] [3] *vt* to inspire with energy.

dynamisme [dinamism] *nm* dynamism.

dynamite [dinamit] *nf* dynamite.

dynamiter [dinamite] [3] *vt* to dynamite.

dynamo [dinamo] *nf* dynamo.

dynamomètre [dinamɔmɛtr] *nm* dynamometer.

dynastie [dinasti] *nf* dynasty.

dysenterie [disɑ̃tri] *nf* dysentery.

dyslexique [disleksik] ◇ *nmf* dyslexic person. ◇ *adj* dyslexic.

dyspepsie [dispɛpsi] *nf* dyspepsia.

dz. (*abr de* **douzaine**) doz.

E

e, E [ə] *nm inv* e, E.
◆ **E** (*abr de* **est**) E.

EAO (*abr de* **enseignement assisté par ordinateur**) *nm* CAL.

eau, -x [o] *nf* water; **prendre l'~** to leak; ~ **douce/salée/de mer** fresh/salt/sea water; ~ **gazeuse/plate** fizzy/still water; ~ **bénite** holy water; ~ **courante** running water; ~ **distillée** distilled water; ~ **minérale** mineral water; ~ **oxygénée** hydrogen peroxide; ~ **de pluie** rainwater; ~ **de source** spring water; ~ **de toilette** toilet water; ~ **dormantes** still waters; **les Eaux et Forêts** ≃ the Forestry Commission; **les ~x territoriales** territorial waters; **les ~x usées** waste water (*U*); **à l'~ de rose** soppy, sentimental; **mettre** OU **faire venir l'~ à la bouche** to make one's mouth water; **mettre de l'~ dans son vin** to calm down, to tone it down a bit; **tomber à l'~** to fall through.

EAU (*abr de* **Émirats arabes unis**) *nmpl* UAE.

eau-de-vie [odvi] (*pl* **eaux-de-vie**) *nf* brandy.

eau-forte [ofɔrt] (*pl* **eaux-fortes**) *nf* etching.

ébahi, -e [ebai] *adj* staggered, astounded.

ébahissement [ebaismɑ̃] *nm* amazement.

ébats [eba] *nmpl littéraire* frolics; ~ **amoureux** lovemaking (*U*).

ébattre [ebatr] [83]
◆ **s'ébattre** *vp littéraire* to frolic.

ébauche [eboʃ] *nf* [esquisse] sketch; *fig* outline; **l'~ d'un sourire** the ghost of a smile.

ébaucher [eboʃe] [3] *vt* -**1.** [esquisser] to rough out. -**2.** *fig* [commencer]: ~ **un geste** to start to make a gesture.

ébène [ebɛn] *nf* ebony.

ébéniste [ebenist] *nm* cabinet-maker.

ébénisterie [ebenistəri] *nf* -**1.** [métier] cabinet-making. -**2.** [travail] cabinet work.

éberlué, -e [ebɛrlɥe] *adj* flabbergasted.

éblouir [ebluir] [32] *vt* to dazzle.

éblouissant, -e [ebluisɑ̃, ɑ̃t] *adj* dazzling.

éblouissement [ebluismɑ̃] *nm* -**1.** [aveuglement] glare, dazzle. -**2.** [vertige] dizziness. -**3.** [émerveillement] amazement.

ébonite [ebɔnit] *nf* vulcanite, ebonite.

éborgner [ebɔrɲe] [3] *vt*: ~ **qqn** to put sb's eye out.

éboueur [ebwœr] *nm* dustman *Br,* garbage collector *Am*.

ébouillanter [ebujɑ̃te] [3] *vt* to scald.
◆ **s'ébouillanter** *vp* to scald o.s.

éboulement [ebulmɑ̃] *nm* caving in, fall.

éboulis [ebuli] *nm* mass of fallen rocks.

ébouriffer [eburife] [3] *vt* -**1.** [cheveux] to ruffle. -**2.** *fam* [étonner] to amaze.

ébranler [ebrɑ̃le] [3] *vt* -**1.** [bâtiment, opinion] to shake. -**2.** [gouvernement, nerfs] to weaken.
◆ **s'ébranler** *vp* to move off.

ébrécher [ebreʃe] [18] *vt* [assiette, verre] to chip; *fam fig* to break into.

ébriété [ebrijete] *nf* drunkenness.

ébrouer [ebrue] [3]
◆ **s'ébrouer** *vp* [animal] to shake o.s.

ébruiter [ebrɥite] [3] *vt* to spread.
◆ **s'ébruiter** *vp* to become known.

ébullition [ebylisjɔ̃] *nf* -**1.** [de liquide] boiling point; **porter à** ~ CULIN to bring to the boil. -**2.** [effervescence]: **en** ~ *fig* in a state of agitation.

écaille [ekaj] *nf* -**1.** [de poisson, reptile] scale; [de tortue] shell. -**2.** [de plâtre, peinture, vernis] flake. -**3.** [matière] tortoiseshell; **en** ~ [lunettes] horn-rimmed.

écailler[1], **-ère** [ekaje, ɛr] *nm, f* oyster seller.

écailler[2] [ekaje] [3] *vt* -**1.** [poisson] to scale. -**2.** [huîtres] to open.
◆ **s'écailler** *vp* to flake OU peel off.

écarlate [ekarlat] *adj & nf* scarlet; **devenir** ~ to turn crimson OU scarlet.

écarquiller [ekarkije] [3] *vt*: ~ **les yeux** to stare wide-eyed.

écart [ekar] *nm* -**1.** [espace] space. -**2.** [temps] gap. -**3.** [différence] difference. -**4.** [déviation]: **faire un** ~ [personne] to step aside; [cheval] to shy; **être à l'~** to be in the background; *fig* **tenir qqn à l'~ de** to keep sb out of OU away from. -**5.** GYM: **grand** ~ splits (*pl*).

écarteler [ekartəle] [25] *vt fig* to tear apart.

écartement [ekartəmã] *nm*: ~ **de** space between.

écarter [ekarte] [3] *vt* **-1.** [bras, jambes] to open, to spread; ~ **qqch de** to move sthg away from. **-2.** [obstacle, danger] to brush aside. **-3.** [foule, rideaux] to push aside; [solution] to dismiss; ~ **qqn de** to exclude sb from.
◆ **s'écarter** *vp* **-1.** [se séparer] to part. **-2.** [se détourner]: **s'~ de** to deviate from.

ecchymose [ekimoz] *nf* bruise.

ecclésiastique [eklezjastik] ◇ *nm* clergyman. ◇ *adj* ecclesiastical.

écervelé, -e [esεrvəle] ◇ *adj* scatty, scatterbrained. ◇ *nm, f* scatterbrain.

échafaud [eʃafo] *nm* scaffold.

échafaudage [eʃafodaʒ] *nm* **-1.** CONSTR scaffolding. **-2.** [amas] pile.

échafauder [eʃafode] [3] ◇ *vt* **-1.** [empiler] to pile up. **-2.** [élaborer] to construct. ◇ *vi* to put up scaffolding.

échalas [eʃala] *nm* **-1.** [perche] stake, pole. **-2.** *péj* [personne] beanpole.

échalote [eʃalɔt] *nf* shallot.

échancré, -e [eʃãkre] *adj* **-1.** [vêtement] low-necked. **-2.** [côte] indented.

échancrure [eʃãkryr] *nf* **-1.** [de robe] low neckline. **-2.** [de côte] indentation.

échange [eʃãʒ] *nm* **-1.** [de choses] exchange; **en ~ (de)** in exchange (for); ~ **standard** *replacement of faulty goods with the same item;* ~ **de bons procédés** exchange of favours. **-2.** COMM: **les ~s** trade *(sg)*; **libre-~** free trade.

échangeable [eʃãʒabl] *adj* exchangeable.

échanger [eʃãʒe] [17] *vt* **-1.** [troquer] to swap, to exchange. **-2.** [marchandise]: ~ **qqch (contre)** to change sthg (for). **-3.** [communiquer] to exchange.

échangeur [eʃãʒœr] *nm* interchange.

échangisme [eʃãʒism] *nm* [de partenaires sexuels] partner-swapping.

échantillon [eʃãtijɔ̃] *nm* [de produit, de population] sample; *fig* example.

échantillonnage [eʃãtijɔnaʒ] *nm* [série d'échantillons] range of samples.

échappatoire [eʃapatwar] *nf* way out.

échappée [eʃape] *nf* **-1.** SPORT breakaway. **-2.** [vue] vista.

échappement [eʃapmã] *nm* **-1.** AUTOM exhaust. **-2.** → **pot. -3.** [d'horloge] escapement.

échapper [eʃape] [3] *vi* **-1.** ~ **à** [personne, situation] to escape from; [danger, mort] to escape; [suj: détail, parole, sens] to escape. **-2.** [glisser]: ~ **de** to slip from OU out of; **laisser**

~ **to let slip. -3.** *loc*: **l'~ belle** to have a narrow escape.
◆ **s'échapper** *vp*: ~ **(de)** to escape (from).

écharde [eʃard] *nf* splinter.

écharpe [eʃarp] *nf* scarf; **en ~** in a sling; **l'~ tricolore** *mayoral sash worn by French mayors at civic functions;* **prendre en ~** *fig* to hit on the side.

écharper [eʃarpe] [3] *vt* to rip to pieces OU shreds.

échasse [eʃas] *nf* [de berger, oiseau] stilt.

échassier [eʃasje] *nm* wader.

échauder [eʃode] [3] *vt* **-1.** [ébouillanter] to scald. **-2.** *fam fig* [enseigner]: ~ **qqn** to teach sb a lesson.

échauffement [eʃofmã] *nm* **-1.** [de moteur] overheating; [de terre] heating up. **-2.** SPORT warm-up. **-3.** [surexcitation] overheating. **-4.** MÉD inflammation.

échauffer [eʃofe] [3] *vt* **-1.** [chauffer] to overheat. **-2.** [exciter] to excite. **-3.** [énerver] to irritate.
◆ **s'échauffer** *vp* **-1.** SPORT to warm up. **-2.** *fig* [s'animer] to become heated.

échauffourée [eʃofure] *nf* brawl, skirmish.

échéance [eʃeãs] *nf* **-1.** [délai] expiry; **à courte** OU **brève ~** in the short term; **à longue ~** in the long term. **-2.** [date] payment date; **arriver à ~** to fall due.

échéancier [eʃeãsje] *nm* bill-book.

échéant [eʃeã] *adj*: **le cas ~** if necessary, if need be.

échec [eʃεk] *nm* failure; **un ~ cuisant** a bitter defeat; **essuyer un ~** to suffer a defeat; **tenir qqn en ~** to hold sb in check; **voué à l'~** doomed to failure.
◆ **échecs** *nmpl* chess *(U)*; ~ **et mat** checkmate.

échelle [eʃεl] *nf* **-1.** [objet] ladder; ~ **de corde** rope ladder; **faire la courte ~ à qqn** *litt* & *fig* to give sb a leg up. **-2.** [ordre de grandeur] scale; **à l'~ de** on the level of; **sur une grande ~** on a large scale.

échelon [eʃlɔ̃] *nm* **-1.** [barreau] rung. **-2.** *fig* [niveau] level; **gravir les ~s (de)** to climb the rungs (of).

échelonner [eʃlɔne] [3] *vt* [espacer] to spread out.
◆ **s'échelonner** *vp* to be spread out.

écheveau, -x [eʃvo] *nm* skein.

échevelé, -e [eʃəvle] *adj* **-1.** [ébouriffé] dishevelled. **-2.** [frénétique] wild.

échine [eʃin] *nf* ANAT spine; **courber l'~** *fig* to submit.

échiner [eʃine] [3]

◆ **s'échiner** *vp fam* [s'épuiser]: **s'~** (**à faire qqch**) to exhaust o.s. (doing sthg).

échiquier [eʃikje] *nm* **-1.** JEU chessboard. **-2.** *fig* [scène] scene; **l'~ politique** the political scene.

écho [eko] *nm* echo; **il se fait l'~ de la direction** he repeats what the managers say; **rester sans ~** to get no response.

échographie [ekɔgrafi] *nf* [examen] ultrasound (scan).

échoir [eʃwar] [70] *vi* **-1.** [être dévolu]: **~ à** to fall to. **-2.** [expirer] to fall due.

échoppe [eʃɔp] *nf* stall.

échouer [eʃwe] [6] *vi* **-1.** [ne pas réussir] to fail; **~ à un examen** to fail an exam. **-2.** [navire] to run aground. **-3.** *fam fig* [aboutir] to end up.

◆ **s'échouer** *vp* [navire] to run aground.

échu, -e [eʃy] *pp* → échoir.

éclabousser [eklabuse] [3] *vt* **-1.** [liquide] to spatter. **-2.** *fig* [compromettre] to compromise.

éclaboussure [eklabusyr] *nf* **-1.** [de liquide] splash. **-2.** *fig* blot (on one's reputation).

éclair [eklɛr] ◇ *nm* **-1.** [de lumière] flash of lightning. **-2.** *fig* [instant]: **~ de** flash of; **en un ~** in a flash. **-3.** [gâteau]: **~ au chocolat/café** chocolate/coffee éclair. ◇ *adj inv*: **visite ~** flying visit; **guerre ~** blitzkrieg.

éclairage [eklɛraʒ] *nm* **-1.** [lumière] lighting. **-2.** *fig* [point de vue] light.

éclaircie [eklɛrsi] *nf* bright interval, sunny spell.

éclaircir [eklɛrsir] [32] *vt* **-1.** [rendre plus clair] to lighten. **-2.** [rendre moins épais] to thin. **-3.** *fig* [clarifier] to clarify.

◆ **s'éclaircir** *vp* **-1.** [devenir plus clair] to clear. **-2.** [devenir moins épais] to thin. **-3.** [se clarifier] to become clearer.

éclaircissement [eklɛrsismɑ̃] *nm* [explication] explanation.

éclairer [eklere] [4] *vt* **-1.** [de lumière] to light up. **-2.** [expliquer] to clarify. **-3.** *littéraire* [renseigner]: **~ qqn sur qqch** to throw light on sthg for sb.

◆ **s'éclairer** *vp* **-1.** [de lumière] to light one's way. **-2.** [regard, visage] to light up. **-3.** [situation, idées] to become clear. **-4.** [rue, ville] to light up.

éclaireur [eklɛrœr] *nm* scout; **partir en ~** to have a scout around.

éclat [ekla] *nm* **-1.** [de verre, d'os] splinter; [de pierre] chip; **voler en ~s** to fly into pieces. **-2.** [de lumière] brilliance. **-3.** [de couleur] vividness. **-4.** [beauté] radiance. **-5.** [faste] splendour. **-6.** [bruit] break; **~ de rire**

burst of laughter; **~s de voix** shouts; **faire un ~** to cause a scandal. **-7.** *loc*: **rire aux ~s** to roar OU shriek with laughter.

éclatant, -e [eklatɑ̃, ɑ̃t] *adj* **-1.** [brillant, resplendissant] brilliant, bright; [teint, beauté] radiant; **~ de** bursting with. **-2.** [admirable] resounding. **-3.** [perçant] loud.

éclater [eklate] [3] *vi* **-1.** [exploser - pneu] to burst; [- verre] to shatter; [- obus] to explode; **faire ~** [ballon] to burst; [bombe] to explode; [pétard] to let off; **faire ~ qqn (de)** to make sb explode (with). **-2.** [incendie, rires] to break out. **-3.** [joie] to shine; **laisser ~** to give vent to. **-4.** [bijou] to sparkle, to glitter. **-5.** *fig* [nouvelles, scandale] to break.

◆ **s'éclater** *vp fam* to have a great time.

éclectique [eklɛktik] *nmf & adj* eclectic.

éclipse [eklips] *nf* **-1.** ASTRON eclipse; **~ de lune/soleil** eclipse of the moon/sun. **-2.** *fig* [période de défaillance] eclipse. **-3.** *fig* [disparition] disappearance.

éclipser [eklipse] [3] *vt* to eclipse.

◆ **s'éclipser** *vp* **-1.** ASTRON to go into eclipse. **-2.** *fam* [s'esquiver] to slip away.

éclopé, -e [eklɔpe] ◇ *adj* lame. ◇ *nm, f* lame person.

éclore [eklɔr] [113] *vi* **-1.** [s'ouvrir - fleur] to open out, to blossom; [- œuf] to hatch; **faire ~** [œuf] to hatch; *fig* [vocation] to develop. **-2.** *fig* [naître] to dawn.

éclos, -e [eklo, oz] *pp* → éclore.

éclosion [eklozjɔ̃] *nf* **-1.** [de fleur] blossoming. **-2.** [d'œuf] hatching. **-3.** *fig* [naissance] blossoming, birth.

écluse [eklyz] *nf* lock.

écluser [eklyze] [3] *vt* **-1.** [NAVIG - fleuve] to construct locks on; [- bateau] to take through a lock. **-2.** *fam* [boire] to knock back.

écœurant, -e [ekœrɑ̃, ɑ̃t] *adj* **-1.** [gén] disgusting. **-2.** [démoralisant] sickening.

écœurement [ekœrmɑ̃] *nm* **-1.** [nausée] nausea. **-2.** [répugnance] disgust. **-3.** [découragement] discouragement.

écœurer [ekœre] [5] *vt* **-1.** [dégoûter] to sicken, to disgust. **-2.** *fig* [indigner] to sicken. **-3.** [décourager] to discourage.

école [ekɔl] *nf* **-1.** [gén] school; **aller à l'~** to go to school; **~ communale** local primary Br OU grade Am school; **~ maternelle** nursery school; **~ normale** ≃ teacher training college Br, ≈ teachers college Am; **École normale supérieure** *grande école for secondary and university teachers*; **~ primaire/secondaire** primary/secondary school Br, grade/high school Am; **grande ~** *specialist training establishment, entered by competitive* *exam and highly prestigious*; **faire l'~ buisson-nière** to play truant *Br* OU **hooky** *Am*; **être à bonne ~** to be in good hands; **faire ~** to be accepted. **-2.** [éducation] **schooling**; **l'~ libre** education at an école libre (*Catholic school, partly state-funded*); **l'~ privée** private education.

GRANDE ÉCOLE:
The 'grandes écoles' are relatively small non-university establishments awarding highly-respected diplomas. Admission is usually only possible after two years of intensive preparatory studies and a competitive examination. Most have close links with industry. The 'grandes écoles' include l'École des hautes études commerciales (management), l'École polytechnique (engineering) and l'École normale supérieure (the humanities). A diploma from a 'grande école' is comparable in prestige to an Oxbridge degree in Britain

écolier, -ière [ekɔlje, jɛr] *nm, f* **-1.** [élève] **pupil. -2.** *fig* [novice] **beginner.**

écolo [ekɔlo] *nmf fam* **ecologist**; **les ~s** the **Greens.**

écologie [ekɔlɔʒi] *nf* **ecology.**

écologique [ekɔlɔʒik] *adj* **ecological.**

écologiste [ekɔlɔʒist] *nmf* **ecologist.**

éconduire [ekɔ̃dʮir] [98] *vt* [repousser - demande] to **dismiss**; [- visiteur, soupirant] to **show to the door.**

économat [ekɔnɔma] *nm* **-1.** [fonction] **bursarship. -2.** [magasin] **staff shop.**

économe [ekɔnɔm] ◇ *nmf* **bursar.** ◇ *adj* **careful, thrifty**; **être ~ de** to be sparing of.

économie [ekɔnɔmi] *nf* **-1.** [science] **economics** (*U*). **-2.** POLIT **economy**; **~ dirigée** state-controlled economy; **~ de marché** market economy; **~ mixte** mixed economy. **-3.** [parcimonie] **economy, thrift. -4.** *litt* & *fig* [épargne] **saving**; **~s d'énergie** energy savings. **-5.** (*gén pl*) [pécule] **savings** (*pl*); **faire des ~s** to save up.

économique [ekɔnɔmik] *adj* **-1.** ÉCON **economic. -2.** [avantageux] **economical.**

économiquement [ekɔnɔmikmɑ̃] *adv* **economically.**

économiser [ekɔnɔmize] [3] *vt litt* & *fig* to **save.**

économiste [ekɔnɔmist] *nmf* **economist.**

écoper [ekɔpe] [3] ◇ *vt* **-1.** NAVIG to **bale out. -2.** *fam* [sanction]: **~ (de) qqch** to get sthg. ◇ *vi fam* [être puni] to **get the blame.**

écoproduit [ekɔprɔdʮi] *nm* **green product.**

écorce [ekɔrs] *nf* **-1.** [d'arbre] **bark. -2.** [d'agrume] **peel**; **~ d'orange** orange peel. **-3.** GÉOL **crust.**

écorché [ekɔrʃe] *nm* **-1.** ANAT **cut-away anatomical figure. -2.** TECHNOL **cut-away. -3.** *loc*: **un ~ vif** a soul in torment.

écorcher [ekɔrʃe] [3] *vt* **-1.** [lapin] to **skin. -2.** [bras, jambe] to **scratch. -3.** *fig* [langue, nom] to **mispronounce.**
◆ **s'écorcher** *vp* to **graze o.s.**

écorchure [ekɔrʃyr] *nf* **graze, scratch.**

écorner [ekɔrne] [3] *vt* [endommager - meuble] to **damage**; [- page] to **dog-ear.**

écossais, -e [ekɔsɛ, ɛz] *adj* **-1.** [de l'Écosse] **Scottish**; [whisky] **Scotch. -2.** [tissu] **tartan.**
◆ **écossais** *nm* **-1.** [langue] **Scots. -2.** [tissu] **tartan.**
◆ **Écossais, -e** *nm, f* **Scot, Scotsman** (*f* **Scotswoman**).

Écosse [ekɔs] *nf*: **l'~** **Scotland.**

écosser [ekɔse] [3] *vt* to **shell.**

écosystème [ekɔsistɛm] *nm* **ecosystem.**

écot [eko] *nm* **share**; **payer son ~** to pay one's share.

écoulement [ekulmɑ̃] *nm* **-1.** [gén] **flow. -2.** [du temps] **passing. -3.** [de marchandises] **selling.**

écouler [ekule] [3] *vt* to **sell.**
◆ **s'écouler** *vp* **-1.** [eau] to **flow. -2.** [personnes] to **flow out. -3.** [temps] to **pass.**

écourter [ekurte] [3] *vt* to **shorten.**

écoute [ekut] *nf* **-1.** [action d'écouter] **listening**; **être à l'~ de** to be listening to. **-2.** [audience] **audience**; **heure de grande ~** RADIO **peak listening time**; TÉLÉ **peak viewing time. -3.** [surveillance]: **les ~s téléphoniques** **phone tapping** (*U*); **être sur table d'~** to have one's phone tapped.

écouter [ekute] [3] *vt* to **listen to.**
◆ **s'écouter** *vp fig* **-1.** [écouter soi-même] to **listen to o.s. -2.** [s'observer] to **coddle o.s.**

écouteur [ekutœr] *nm* [de téléphone] **earpiece**; [personne] **listener.**
◆ **écouteurs** *nmpl* [de radio] **headphones.**

écoutille [ekutij] *nf* **hatchway.**

écrabouiller [ekrabuje] [3] *vt fam* [écraser] to **crush, to squash.**

écran [ekrɑ̃] *nm* **-1.** [de protection] **shield**; **~ de fumée** **smoke screen. -2.** CIN & INFORM **screen**; **~ orientable** **tiltable screen**; **le petit ~** **television.**

écrasant, -e [ekrazɑ̃, ɑ̃t] *adj* **-1.** [lourd] **crushing. -2.** *fig* [accablant] **overwhelming.**

écraser [ekraze] [3] ◇ *vt* **-1.** [comprimer - cigarette] to **stub out**; [- pied] to **tread on**;

[- insecte, raisin] to crush. **-2.** [accabler]: ~
qqn (de) to burden sb (with). **-3.** [vaincre]
to crush. **-4.** [renverser] to run over. ◇ *vi*
fam: **en ~** to sleep like a log.
◆ **s'écraser** *vp* **-1.** [avion, automobile]: **s'~**
(contre) to crash (into). **-2.** [foule] to be
crushed. **-3.** *fam* [se taire] to shut up.
écrémer [ekreme] [18] *vt* **-1.** [lait] to skim.
-2. *fig* [bibliothèque, collection] to cream off
the best from.
écrevisse [ekrəvis] *nf* crayfish; **rouge**
comme une ~ (as) red as a beetroot.
écrier [ekrije] [10]
◆ **s'écrier** *vp* to cry out.
écrin [ekrɛ̃] *nm* case.
écrire [ekrir] [99] *vt* **-1.** [phrase, livre] to
write. **-2.** [orthographier] to spell.
écrit, -e [ekri, it] ◇ *pp* → **écrire.** ◇ *adj*
written; **bien/mal ~** well/badly written.
◆ **écrit** *nm* **-1.** [ouvrage] writing. **-2.** [exa-
men] written exam. **-3.** [document] piece of
writing.
◆ **par écrit** *loc adv* in writing.
écriteau, -x [ekrito] *nm* notice.
écriture [ekrityr] *nf* **-1.** [gén] writing. **-2.**
(*gén pl*) COMM [comptes] books (*pl*). **-3.** BIBLE:
l'Écriture sainte the Holy Scripture.
écrivain [ekrivɛ̃] *nm* writer, author; **~ pu-**
blic (public) letter-writer.
écrivais, écrivions *etc* → **écrire.**
écrou [ekru] *nm* TECHNOL nut.
écrouer [ekrue] [3] *vt* to imprison.
écroulement [ekrulmɑ̃] *nm* *litt* & *fig* collapse.
écrouler [ekrule] [3]
◆ **s'écrouler** *vp litt* & *fig* to collapse.
écru, -e [ekry] *adj* [naturel] unbleached.
ecstasy [ɛkstazi] *nm* [drogue] ecstasy.
ectoplasme [ɛktɔplasm] *nm* ectoplasm.
écu [eky] *nm* **-1.** [bouclier, armoiries] shield.
-2. [monnaie ancienne] crown. **-3.** = ECU.
ECU [eky] (*abr de* **European Currency Unit**)
nm ECU.
écueil [ekœj] *nm* **-1.** [rocher] reef. **-2.** *fig*
[obstacle] stumbling block.
écuelle [ekɥɛl] *nf* **-1.** [objet] bowl. **-2.**
[contenu] bowlful.
éculé, -e [ekyle] *adj* **-1.** [chaussure] down-
at-heel. **-2.** *fig* [plaisanterie] hackneyed.
écume [ekym] *nf* **-1.** [mousse, bave] foam.
-2. *fig* [lie] dregs (*pl*).
écumer [ekyme] [3] ◇ *vt* **-1.** [confiture] to
skim. **-2.** *fig* [mer, ville] to scour. ◇ *vi* **-1.**
[mer] to foam, to boil. **-2.** [animal] to foam
at the mouth. **-3.** *fig* [être furieux]: **~ (de)** to
boil (with).

écumoire [ekymwar] *nf* skimmer.
écureuil [ekyrœj] *nm* squirrel; **l'Écureuil**
*nickname for the Caisse d'Épargne (whose logo
is a squirrel).*
écurie [ekyri] *nf* **-1.** [pour chevaux & SPORT]
stable. **-2.** *fig* [local sale] pigsty.
écusson [ekysɔ̃] *nm* **-1.** [d'armoiries] coat-
of-arms. **-2.** MIL badge.
écuyer, -ère [ekɥije, jɛr] *nm, f* [de cirque] rider.
◆ **écuyer** *nm* [de chevalier] squire.
eczéma [ɛgzema] *nm* eczema.
éd. (*abr de* **édition**) ed., edit.
edelweiss [edɛlvɛs] *nm* edelweiss.
éden [edɛn] *nm:* **un ~** a garden of Eden;
l'Éden the garden of Eden.
édenté, -e [edɑ̃te] *adj* toothless.
EDF, Edf (*abr de* **Électricité de France**) *nf*
French national electricity company.
édifiant, -e [edifjɑ̃, ɑ̃t] *adj* edifying.
édification [edifikasjɔ̃] *nf* **-1.** [de temple, em-
pire] building. **-2.** *fig* [de fidèles] edification.
édifice [edifis] *nm* **-1.** [construction] building;
~ public public building. **-2.** *fig* [institution]:
l'~ social the fabric of society.
édifier [edifje] [9] *vt* **-1.** [ville, église] to
build. **-2.** *fig* [théorie] to construct. **-3.** [per-
sonne] to edify; *iron* to enlighten.
Édimbourg [edɛ̃bur] *n* Edinburgh.
édit [edi] *nm* edict.
édit. *abr de* **éditeur.**
éditer [edite] [3] *vt* to publish.
éditeur, -trice [editœr, tris] *nm, f* publisher.
édition [edisjɔ̃] *nf* **-1.** [profession] publishing. **-2.** [de journal, livre] edition; **dernière ~**
last edition; **~ originale** first edition.
édito [edito] *nm fam* editorial.
éditorial, -iaux [editɔrjal, jo] *nm* leader,
editorial.
éditorialiste [editɔrjalist] *nmf* leader writer,
editorialist.
édredon [edrədɔ̃] *nm* eiderdown.
éducateur, -trice [edykatœr, tris] ◇ *adj*
educational. ◇ *nm, f* teacher; **~ spécialisé**
*teacher of children with special educational
needs.*
éducatif, -ive [edykatif, iv] *adj* educational.
éducation [edykasjɔ̃] *nf* **-1.** [apprentissage]
education; **~ civique** civics (*U*); **l'Éducation**
nationale ≃ Department for Education *Br*;
~ physique physical education; **~ sexuelle**
sex education. **-2.** [parentale] upbringing.
-3. [savoir-vivre] breeding.
édulcorant [edylkɔrɑ̃, ɑ̃t] *nm:* **~ (de syn-**
thèse) (artificial) sweetener.

édulcorer [edylkɔre] [3] *vt* **-1.** *sout* [tisane] to sweeten. **-2.** *fig* [propos] to tone down.

éduquer [edyke] [3] *vt* to educate.

effacé, -e [efase] *adj* **-1.** [teinte] faded. **-2.** [modeste - rôle] **unobtrusive;** [- personne] self-effacing.

effacer [efase] [16] *vt* **-1.** [mot] to erase, to rub out; INFORM to delete. **-2.** [souvenir] to erase. **-3.** [réussite] to eclipse.

◆ **s'effacer** *vp* **-1.** [s'estomper] to fade (away). **-2.** *sout* [s'écarter] to move aside. **-3.** *fig* [s'incliner] to give way.

effarant, -e [efarɑ̃, ɑ̃t] *adj* frightening.

effaré, -e [efare] *adj* frightened, scared.

effarement [efarmɑ̃] *nm* fear, alarm.

effarer [efare] [3] *vt* to frighten, to scare.

effaroucher [efaruʃe] [3] *vt* **-1.** [effrayer] to scare off. **-2.** [intimider] to overawe.

effectif, -ive [efɛktif, iv] *adj* **-1.** [remède] effective. **-2.** [aide] positive.

◆ **effectif** *nm* **-1.** MIL strength. **-2.** [de groupe] total number.

effectivement [efɛktivmɑ̃] *adv* **-1.** [réellement] effectively. **-2.** [confirmation] in fact.

effectuer [efɛktɥe] [7] *vt* [réaliser - manœuvre] to carry out; [- trajet, paiement] to make.

◆ **s'effectuer** *vp* to be made.

efféminé, -e [efemine] *adj* effeminate.

effervescence [efɛrvesɑ̃s] *nf* **-1.** PHYS effervescence. **-2.** [agitation] turmoil; **en ~** in turmoil.

effervescent, -e [efɛrvesɑ̃, ɑ̃t] *adj* [boisson] effervescent; *fig* [pays] in turmoil.

effet [efɛ] *nm* **-1.** [gén] effect; **avoir pour ~ de faire qqch** to have the effect of doing sthg; **à ~ rétroactif** JUR retrospective; **rester sans ~** to be ineffective; **sous l'~ de** under the effects of; [alcool] under the influence of; **faire de l'~** to have an effect; **~ de serre** greenhouse effect. **-2.** [impression recherchée] impression; **faire son ~** to cause a stir. **-3.** COMM [titre] bill.

◆ **en effet** *loc adv* in fact, indeed.

◆ **à cet effet** *loc adv* with this end in view.

effeuiller [efœje] [5] *vt* [arbre] to remove the leaves from; [fleur] to remove the petals from.

◆ **s'effeuiller** *vp* [arbre] to lose its leaves; [fleur] to lose its petals.

efficace [efikas] *adj* **-1.** [remède, mesure] effective. **-2.** [personne, machine] efficient.

efficacité [efikasite] *nf* **-1.** [de remède, mesure] effectiveness. **-2.** [de personne, machine] efficiency.

efficience [efisjɑ̃s] *nf* efficiency.

effigie [efiʒi] *nf* effigy.

effilé, -e [efile] *adj* [doigt, silhouette] slim, slender; [lame] sharp; [voiture] streamlined.

effiler [efile] [3] *vt* **-1.** [tissu] to fray. **-2.** [lame] to sharpen. **-3.** [cheveux] to thin.

◆ **s'effiler** *vp* to fray.

effilocher [efiloʃe] [3] *vt* to fray.

◆ **s'effilocher** *vp* to fray.

efflanqué, -e [eflɑ̃ke] *adj* emaciated.

effleurer [eflœre] [5] *vt* **-1.** [visage, bras] to brush (against). **-2.** *fig* [problème, thème] to touch on. **-3.** *fig* [suj: pensée, idée] to cross one's mind.

effluve [eflyv] *nm* exhalation; *fig* [d'enfance, du passé] breath.

effondrement [efɔ̃drəmɑ̃] *nm* collapse.

effondrer [efɔ̃dre] [3]

◆ **s'effondrer** *vp litt* & *fig* to collapse.

efforcer [efɔrse] [16]

◆ **s'efforcer** *vp* to force o.s.; **s'~ de faire qqch** to make an effort to do sthg.

effort [efɔr] *nm* **-1.** [de personne] effort; **faire un ~** to make an effort; **faire l'~ de faire qqch** to make the effort to do sthg; **sans ~** [victoire] effortless; [gagner] effortlessly. **-2.** TECHNOL stress.

effraction [efraksjɔ̃] *nf* breaking in; **entrer par ~ dans** to break into.

effrayant, -e [efrɛjɑ̃, ɑ̃t] *adj* **-1.** [cauchemar] terrifying. **-2.** *fam* [appétit, prix] tremendous, awful.

effrayer [efrɛje] [11] *vt* **-1.** [terrifier] to frighten, to scare. **-2.** [rebuter] to alarm.

◆ **s'effrayer** *vp* to be frightened, to take fright.

effréné, -e [efrene] *adj* **-1.** [course] frantic. **-2.** [désir] unbridled.

effriter [efrite] [3] *vt* to cause to crumble.

◆ **s'effriter** *vp* **-1.** [mur] to crumble. **-2.** *fig* [majorité] to be eroded.

effroi [efrwa] *nm* fear, dread.

effronté, -e [efrɔ̃te] ◇ *adj* insolent. ◇ *nm, f* insolent person.

effrontément [efrɔ̃temɑ̃] *adv* insolently, brazenly.

effronterie [efrɔ̃tri] *nf* insolence.

effroyable [efrwajabl] *adj* **-1.** [catastrophe, misère] appalling. **-2.** [laideur] hideous.

effusion [efyzjɔ̃] *nf* **-1.** [de liquide] effusion; **sans ~ de sang** without bloodshed. **-2.** [de sentiments] effusiveness.

égal, -e, -aux [egal, o] ◇ *adj* **-1.** [équivalent] equal. **-2.** [régulier] even. **-3.** *fam* [indifférent]: **ça m'est ~, c'est ~** I don't mind. ◇ *nm, f* equal; **d'~ à ~** as an equal; **sans ~** unequalled.

également [egalmɑ̃] *adv* **-1.** [avec égalité] equally. **-2.** [aussi] as well, too.

égaler [egale] [3] *vt* **-1.** MATHS to equal. **-2.** [beauté] to match, to compare with.

égalisation [egalizasjɔ̃] *nf* equalization; SPORT equalizing *Br,* tying *Am.*

égaliser [egalize] [3] ◇ *vt* [haie, cheveux] to trim. ◇ *vi* SPORT to equalize *Br,* to tie *Am.*

égalitaire [egalitɛr] *adj* egalitarian.

égalitarisme [egalitarism] *nm* egalitarianism.

égalité [egalite] *nf* **-1.** [gén] equality; être à ~ to be level OU equal. **-2.** [d'humeur] evenness. **-3.** SPORT: être à ~ to be level.

égard [egar] *nm* consideration; à cet ~ in this respect; par ~ pour *sout* out of consideration for; eu ~ à considering.
◆ **à l'égard de** *loc prép* with regard to, towards.
◆ **à certains égards** *loc adv* in some respects.

égaré, -e [egare] *adj* **-1.** [perdu - voyageur] lost; [- animal] stray (*avant n*). **-2.** [regard, air] distraught.

égarement [egarmɑ̃] *nm* **-1.** [de jeunesse] wildness. **-2.** [de raisonnement] aberration.

égarer [egare] [3] *vt* **-1.** [objet] to mislay, to lose. **-2.** [personne] to mislead. **-3.** *fig* & *sout* [suj: passion] to lead astray.
◆ **s'égarer** *vp* **-1.** [lettre] to get lost, to go astray; [personne] to get lost, to lose one's way. **-2.** [discussion] to wander from the point. **-3.** *fig* & *sout* [personne] to stray from the point.

égayer [egeje] [11] *vt* **-1.** [personne] to cheer up. **-2.** [pièce] to brighten up.
◆ **s'égayer** *vp* to enjoy o.s.

égérie [eʒeri] *nf* mastermind.

égide [eʒid] *nf* protection; sous l'~ de *littéraire* under the aegis of.

églantier [eglɑ̃tje] *nm* wild rose (bush).

églantine [eglɑ̃tin] *nf* wild rose.

églefin, aiglefin [egləfɛ̃] *nm* haddock.

église [egliz] *nf* church; aller à l'~ to go to church.
◆ **Église** *nf*: l'Église the Church; l'Église catholique/protestante the Catholic/Protestant Church.

ego [ego] *nm* ego.

égocentrique [egɔsɑ̃trik] ◇ *nmf* self-centred person. ◇ *adj* self-centred, egocentric.

égocentrisme [egɔsɑ̃trism] *nm* self-centredness.

égoïsme [egɔism] *nm* selfishness, egoism.

égoïste [egɔist] ◇ *nmf* selfish person. ◇ *adj* selfish, egoistic.

égorger [egɔrʒe] [17] *vt* **-1.** [animal, personne] to cut the throat of. **-2.** *fig* [client] to bleed white.

égosiller [egɔzije] [3]
◆ **s'égosiller** *vp fam* **-1.** [crier] to bawl, to shout. **-2.** [chanter] to sing one's head off.

égout [egu] *nm* sewer.

égoutter [egute] [3] *vt* **-1.** [vaisselle] to leave to drain. **-2.** [légumes, fromage] to drain.
◆ **s'égoutter** *vp* to drip, to drain.

égouttoir [egutwar] *nm* **-1.** [à légumes] colander, strainer. **-2.** [à vaisselle] rack (*for washing-up*).

égratigner [egratiɲe] [3] *vt* to scratch; *fig* to have a go OU dig at.
◆ **s'égratigner** *vp*: s'~ la main to scratch one's hand.

égratignure [egratiɲyr] *nf* scratch, graze; *fig* dig.

égrener [egrəne] [19] *vt* **-1.** [détacher les grains de - épi, cosse] to shell; [- grappe] to pick grapes from. **-2.** [chapelet] to tell. **-3.** *fig* [marquer] to mark.
◆ **s'égrener** *vp* **-1.** [raisins] to drop off the bunch. **-2.** [personnes] to spread out.

égrillard, -e [egrijar, ard] *adj* ribald, bawdy.

Égypte [eʒipt] *nf*: l'~ Egypt.

égyptien, -ienne [eʒipsjɛ̃, jɛn] *adj* Egyptian.
◆ **égyptien** *nm* [langue] Egyptian.
◆ **Égyptien, -ienne** *nm, f* Egyptian.

égyptologie [eʒiptɔlɔʒi] *nf* Egyptology.

eh [e] *interj* hey!; ~ bien well.

éhonté, -e [eɔ̃te] ◇ *adj* shameless. ◇ *nm, f* shameless person.

éjaculation [eʒakylasjɔ̃] *nf* ejaculation; ~ précoce premature ejaculation.

éjectable [eʒɛktabl] *adj*: siège ~ ejector seat.

éjecter [eʒɛkte] [4] *vt* **-1.** [douille] to eject. **-2.** *fam* [personne] to kick out.

élaboration [elabɔrasjɔ̃] *nf* [de plan, système] working out, development.

élaboré, -e [elabɔre] *adj* elaborate.

élaborer [elabɔre] [3] *vt* [plan, système] to work out, to develop.

élagage [elagaʒ] *nm* *litt* & *fig* pruning.

élaguer [elage] [3] *vt* *litt* & *fig* to prune.

élan [elɑ̃] *nm* **-1.** ZOOL elk. **-2.** SPORT run-up; prendre son ~ to take a run-up, to gather speed. **-3.** *fig* [de joie] outburst.

élancé, -e [elɑ̃se] *adj* slender.

élancement [elɑ̃smɑ̃] *nm* [douleur] shooting pain.

élancer [elɑ̃se] [16] *vi* MÉD to give shooting pains.
◆ **s'élancer** *vp* **-1.** [se précipiter] to rush, to dash. **-2.** SPORT to take a run-up. **-3.** *fig* [s'envoler] to soar.

élargir [elaʀʒiʀ] [32] ◇ *vt* to widen; [vêtement] to let out; *fig* to expand. ◇ *vi fam* [forcir] to fill out.
◆ **s'élargir** *vp* **-1.** [s'agrandir] to widen; [vêtement] to stretch; *fig* to expand. **-2.** *fam* [grossir] to put on weight.

élargissement [elaʀʒismɑ̃] *nm* widening; [de vêtement] letting out; *fig* expansion.

élasticité [elastisite] *nf* **-1.** PHYS elasticity. **-2.** [de personne, corps] flexibility.

élastique [elastik] ◇ *nm* **-1.** [pour attacher] elastic band. **-2.** [matière] elastic. ◇ *adj* **-1.** PHYS elastic. **-2.** [corps] flexible. **-3.** *fig* [conscience] accommodating.

élastomère [elastɔmɛʀ] *nm* elastomer.

eldorado [ɛldɔrado] *nm* El Dorado.

électeur, -trice [elɛktœʀ, tʀis] *nm, f* voter, elector.

élection [elɛksjɔ̃] *nf* **-1.** [vote] election; ~ **partielle** by-election; ~ **présidentielle** presidential election; ~**s municipales** local elections. **-2.** *fig* [choix] choice; **d'**~ chosen.

électoral, -e, -aux [elɛktɔʀal, o] *adj* electoral; [campagne, réunion] election *(avant n)*.

électoralisme [elɛktɔʀalism] *nm* electioneering.

électorat [elɛktɔʀa] *nm* electorate.

électricien, -ienne [elɛktʀisjɛ̃, jɛn] *nm, f* electrician.

électricité [elɛktʀisite] *nf* electricity; **il y a de l'**~ **dans l'air** *fig* the atmosphere is electric.

électrification [elɛktʀifikasjɔ̃] *nf* electrification.

électrifier [elɛktʀifje] [9] *vt* to electrify.

électrique [elɛktʀik] *adj litt* & *fig* electric.

électriser [elɛktʀize] [3] *vt litt* & *fig* to electrify.

électroaimant [elɛktʀɔɛmɑ̃] *nm* electromagnet.

électrocardiogramme [elɛktʀɔkaʀdjɔgʀam] *nm* electrocardiogram.

électrochoc [elɛktʀɔʃɔk] *nm* electric shock treatment.

électrocuter [elɛktʀɔkyte] [3] *vt* to electrocute.

électrode [elɛktʀɔd] *nf* electrode.

électroencéphalogramme [elɛktʀɔɑ̃sefalɔgʀam] *nm* electroencephalogram.

électrogène [elɛktʀɔʒɛn] *adj*: **groupe** ~ generating unit.

électrolyse [elɛktʀɔliz] *nf* electrolysis.

électromagnétique [elɛktʀɔmaɲetik] *adj* electromagnetic.

électroménager [elɛktʀɔmenaʒe] ◇ *adj*: **appareil** ~ household electrical appliance. ◇ *nm* household electrical appliances *(pl)*.

électron [elɛktʀɔ̃] *nm* electron.

électronicien, -ienne [elɛktʀɔnisjɛ̃, jɛn] *nm, f* electronics specialist.

électronique [elɛktʀɔnik] ◇ *nf* SCIENCE electronics *(U)*. ◇ *adj* electronic; [microscope] electron *(avant n)*.

électrophone [elɛktʀɔfɔn] *nm* record player.

élégamment [elegamɑ̃] *adv* elegantly.

élégance [elegɑ̃s] *nf* **-1.** [de personne, style] elegance. **-2.** [délicatesse - de solution, procédé] elegance; [- de conduite] generosity.

élégant, -e [elegɑ̃, ɑ̃t] *adj* **-1.** [personne, style] elegant. **-2.** [délicat - solution, procédé] elegant; [- conduite] generous.

élément [elemɑ̃] *nm* **-1.** [gén] element; **les bons/mauvais** ~**s** the good/bad elements; **les quatre** ~**s** the four elements; **être dans son** ~ to be in one's element. **-2.** [de machine] component.

élémentaire [elemɑ̃tɛʀ] *adj* **-1.** [gén] elementary. **-2.** [installation, besoin] basic.

éléphant [elefɑ̃] *nm* elephant.

éléphantesque [elefɑ̃tɛsk] *adj fam* gigantic.

élevage [ɛlvaʒ] *nm* breeding, rearing; [installation] farm.

élévateur, -trice [elevatœʀ, tʀis] *adj* elevator *(avant n)*.
◆ **élévateur** *nm* lift *Br*, elevator *Am*.

élévation [elevasjɔ̃] *nf* **-1.** [gén] raising; ~ **à** MATHS raising to; *fig* elevation to. **-2.** [tertre] rise, mound. **-3.** [de sentiments] nobility.

élevé, -e [ɛlve] *adj* **-1.** [haut] high. **-2.** *fig* [sentiment, âme] noble. **-3.** [enfant]: **bien/mal** ~ well/badly brought up.

élève [elɛv] *nmf* **-1.** [écolier, disciple] pupil. **-2.** MIL cadet.

élever [ɛlve] [19] *vt* **-1.** [gén] to raise. **-2.** [fardeau] to lift, to raise. **-3.** [statue] to put up, to erect. **-4.** [à un rang supérieur] to elevate. **-5.** [esprit] to improve. **-6.** [enfant] to bring up. **-7.** [poulets] to rear, to breed.
◆ **s'élever** *vp* **-1.** [gén] to rise. **-2.** [montant]: **s'**~ **à** to add up to. **-3.** [protester]: **s'**~ **contre qqn/qqch** to protest against sb/sthg.

éleveur, -euse [ɛlvœʀ, øz] *nm, f* breeder.

elfe [ɛlf] *nm* elf.

élider [elide] [3] *vt* to elide.
◆ **s'élider** *vp* to be elided.

éligible [eliʒibl] *adj* eligible.

élimé, -e [elime] *adj* threadbare.

élimination [eliminasjɔ̃] *nf* elimination; **procéder par ~** to proceed by elimination.

éliminatoire [eliminatwar] ◇ *nf* (*gén pl*) SPORT qualifying heat OU round. ◇ *adj* qualifying (*avant n*).

éliminer [elimine] [3] *vt* to eliminate.

élire [elir] [106] *vt* to elect.

élisais, élisions *etc* → **élire**.

élision [elizjɔ̃] *nf* elision.

élite [elit] *nf* elite; **d'~** choice, select.

élitiste [elitist] *nmf & adj* elitist.

élixir [eliksir] *nm* elixir.

elle [ɛl] *pron pers* **-1.** [sujet - personne] she; [- animal] it, she; [- chose] it. **-2.** [complément - personne] her; [- animal] it, her; [- chose] it.
◆ **elles** *pron pers pl* **-1.** [sujet] they. **-2.** [complément] them.
◆ **elle-même** *pron pers* [personne] herself; [animal] itself, herself; [chose] itself.
◆ **elles-mêmes** *pron pers pl* themselves.

ellipse [elips] *nf* **-1.** GÉOM ellipse. **-2.** LING ellipsis.

elliptique [eliptik] *adj* elliptical.

élocution [elɔkysjɔ̃] *nf* delivery; **défaut d'~** speech defect.

éloge [elɔʒ] *nm* **-1.** [discours] eulogy. **-2.** [louange] praise; **faire l'~ de qqn/qqch** [louer] to speak highly of sb/sthg; **couvrir qqn d'~s** to shower sb with praise.

élogieux, -ieuse [elɔʒjø, jøz] *adj* laudatory.

éloigné, -e [elwaɲe] *adj* distant.

éloignement [elwaɲmã] *nm* **-1.** [mise à l'écart] removal. **-2.** [séparation] absence. **-3.** [dans l'espace, le temps] distance.

éloigner [elwaɲe] [3] *vt* **-1.** [écarter] to move away; **~ qqch de** to move sthg away from. **-2.** [détourner] to turn away. **-3.** [chasser] to dismiss.
◆ **s'éloigner** *vp* **-1.** [partir] to move OU go away. **-2.** *fig* [du sujet] to stray from the point. **-3.** [se détacher] to distance o.s.

élongation [elɔ̃gasjɔ̃] *nf* MÉD: **~ de muscle** pulled muscle.

éloquence [elɔkɑ̃s] *nf* **-1.** [d'orateur, d'expression] eloquence. **-2.** [de données] significance.

éloquent, -e [elɔkɑ̃, ɑ̃t] *adj* **-1.** [avocat, silence] eloquent. **-2.** [données] significant.

élu, -e [ely] ◇ *pp* → **élire**. ◇ *adj* POLIT elected. ◇ *nm, f* **-1.** POLIT elected representative. **-2.** RELIG chosen one; **l'~ de son cœur** *hum ou sout* one's heart's desire.

élucider [elyside] [3] *vt* to clear up.

élucubration [elykybrasjɔ̃] *nf* raving.

éluder [elyde] [3] *vt* to evade.

Élysée [elize] *nm*: **l'~** the Élysée Palace.

L'ÉLYSÉE:
This eighteenth-century palace near the Champs-Élysées is the official residence of the French President. The name is often used to refer to the presidency itself

émacié, -e [emasje] *adj littéraire* emaciated.

émail, -aux [emaj, emo] *nm* enamel; **en ~** enamel, enamelled.
◆ **émaux** *nmpl* enamelwork (*U*).

émanation [emanasjɔ̃] *nf* emanation; **être l'~ de** *fig* to emanate from.

émancipation [emɑ̃sipasjɔ̃] *nf* emancipation.

émanciper [emɑ̃sipe] [3] *vt* to emancipate.
◆ **s'émanciper** *vp* **-1.** [se libérer] to become free OU liberated. **-2.** *fam* [se dévergonder] to become emancipated.

émaner [emane] [3] *vi*: **~ de** to emanate from.

émarger [emarʒe] [17] ◇ *vt* **-1.** [signer] to sign. **-2.** [enlever la marge de] to trim the margins of. ◇ *vi* to sign.

émasculer [emaskyle] [3] *vt* to emasculate.

emballage [ɑ̃balaʒ] *nm* packaging.

emballement [ɑ̃balmã] *nm* **-1.** [enthousiasme] sudden craze. **-2.** [de moteur] racing (*U*).

emballer [ɑ̃bale] [3] *vt* **-1.** [objet] to pack (up), to wrap (up). **-2.** [moteur] to race. **-3.** *fam* [plaire] to thrill.
◆ **s'emballer** *vp* **-1.** [moteur] to race. **-2.** [cheval] to bolt. **-3.** *fam* [personne - s'enthousiasmer] to get carried away; [- s'emporter] to lose one's temper.

embarcadère [ɑ̃barkadɛr] *nm* landing stage.

embarcation [ɑ̃barkasjɔ̃] *nf* small boat.

embardée [ɑ̃barde] *nf* swerve; **faire une ~** to swerve.

embargo [ɑ̃bargo] *nm* embargo.

embarquement [ɑ̃barkəmã] *nm* **-1.** [de marchandises] loading. **-2.** [de passagers] boarding; **~ immédiat** immediate boarding.

embarquer [ɑ̃barke] [3] ◇ *vt* **-1.** [marchandises] to load. **-2.** [passagers] to (take on) board. **-3.** *fam* [dans une voiture] to take, to give a lift to. **-4.** *fam* [arrêter] to pick up. **-5.** *fam fig* [engager]: **~ qqn dans** to involve sb in. **-6.** *fam* [emmener] to cart off. ◇ *vi*: **~ (pour)** to sail (for).
◆ **s'embarquer** *vp* **-1.** [sur un bateau] to (set) sail. **-2.** *fig fam* [s'engager]: **s'~ dans** to get involved in.

embarras [ɑ̃bara] *nm* **-1.** [incertitude] **(state of) uncertainty; avoir l'~ du choix** to be spoilt for choice. **-2.** [situation difficile] **predicament; être dans l'~** to be in a predicament; **mettre qqn dans l'~** to place sb in an awkward position; **tirer qqn d'~** to get sb out of a tight spot. **-3.** [perplexité] confusion. **-4.** [gêne] embarrassment. **-5.** [souci] difficulty, worry.

embarrassant, -e [ɑ̃barasɑ̃, ɑ̃t] *adj* **-1.** [encombrant] cumbersome. **-2.** [délicat] embarrassing.

embarrassé, -e [ɑ̃barase] *adj* **-1.** [encombré - pièce, bureau] cluttered; **avoir les mains ~es** to have one's hands full. **-2.** [gêné] embarrassed. **-3.** [confus] confused.

embarrasser [ɑ̃barase] [3] *vt* **-1.** [encombrer - pièce] to clutter up; [- personne] to hamper. **-2.** [gêner] to put in an awkward position.
◆ **s'embarrasser** *vp* **-1.** [se charger] : **s'~ de qqch** to burden o.s. with sthg; *fig* to bother about sthg. **-2.** [s'empêtrer] : **s'~ dans** to get tangled up in.

embauche [ɑ̃boʃ] *nf*, **embauchage** [ɑ̃boʃaʒ] *nm* hiring, employment.

embaucher [ɑ̃boʃe] [3] *vt* **-1.** [employer] to employ, to take on. **-2.** *fam* [occuper] : **je t'embauche!** I need your help!

embaumer [ɑ̃bome] [3] ◇ *vt* **-1.** [cadavre] to embalm. **-2.** [parfumer] to scent. ◇ *vi* to be fragrant.

embellie [ɑ̃beli] *nf* [éclaircie] bright OU clear spell; *fig* (temporary) improvement.

embellir [ɑ̃belir] [32] ◇ *vt* **-1.** [agrémenter] to brighten up. **-2.** *fig* [enjoliver] to embellish. ◇ *vi* [devenir plus beau] to become more attractive; *fig & hum* to grow, to increase.

emberlificoter [ɑ̃berlifikɔte] [3] *vt fam fig* to sweet-talk.
◆ **s'emberlificoter** *vp fam* to get tangled up.

embêtant, -e [ɑ̃bɛtɑ̃, ɑ̃t] *adj fam* annoying.

embêtement [ɑ̃bɛtmɑ̃] *nm fam* trouble.

embêter [ɑ̃bɛte] [4] *vt fam* [contrarier, importuner] to annoy.
◆ **s'embêter** *vp fam* [s'ennuyer] to be bored.

emblée [ɑ̃ble]
◆ **d'emblée** *loc adv* right away.

emblème [ɑ̃blɛm] *nm* emblem.

embobiner [ɑ̃bɔbine] [3] *vt* **-1.** [fil] to wind. **-2.** *fam* [personne] to fool.

emboîter [ɑ̃bwate] [3] *vt* : **~ qqch dans qqch** to fit sthg into sthg; **~ le pas à qqn** [suivre] to follow close on sb's heels; *fig* to follow sb's lead.
◆ **s'emboîter** *vp* to fit together.

embolie [ɑ̃bɔli] *nf* embolism.

embonpoint [ɑ̃bɔ̃pwɛ̃] *nm* stoutness; **prendre de l'~** to get stout.

embouché, -e [ɑ̃buʃe] *adj fam* : **mal ~** foul-mouthed.

embouchure [ɑ̃buʃyr] *nf* **-1.** [d'instrument] mouthpiece. **-2.** [de fleuve] mouth; **l'~ du Rhône** the mouth of the Rhône.

embourber [ɑ̃burbe] [3]
◆ **s'embourber** *vp* [s'enliser] to get stuck in the mud; *fig* to get bogged down.

embourgeoisement [ɑ̃burʒwazmɑ̃] *nm* [de personne] adoption of middle-class values; [de quartier] gentrification.

embourgeoiser [ɑ̃burʒwaze] [3] *vt* [personne] to instil middle-class values in; [quartier] to gentrify.
◆ **s'embourgeoiser** *vp* [personne] to adopt middle-class values; [quartier] to become gentrified.

embout [ɑ̃bu] *nm* [protection] tip; [extrémité d'un tube] nozzle.

embouteillage [ɑ̃butɛjaʒ] *nm* **-1.** [circulation] traffic jam. **-2.** [mise en bouteilles] bottling.

embroutir [ɑ̃butir] [32] *vt* **-1.** *fam* [voiture] to crash into. **-2.** TECHNOL to stamp.

embranchement [ɑ̃brɑ̃ʃmɑ̃] *nm* **-1.** [carrefour] junction. **-2.** [division] branching (out); *fig* branch.

embraser [ɑ̃braze] [3] *vt* [incendier, éclairer] to set ablaze; *fig* [d'amour] to (set on) fire, to inflame.
◆ **s'embraser** *vp* [prendre feu, s'éclairer] to be ablaze; *fig & littéraire* to be inflamed.

embrassade [ɑ̃brasad] *nf* embrace.

embrasse [ɑ̃bras] *nf* tieback.

embrasser [ɑ̃brase] [3] *vt* **-1.** [donner un baiser à] to kiss. **-2.** [étreindre] to embrace. **-3.** *fig* [du regard] to take in.
◆ **s'embrasser** *vp* to kiss (each other).

embrasure [ɑ̃brazyr] *nf* : **dans l'~ de la fenêtre** in the window.

embrayage [ɑ̃brɛjaʒ] *nm* **-1.** [action] engaging the clutch. **-2.** [mécanisme] clutch.

embrayer [ɑ̃brɛje] [11] *vi* **-1.** AUTOM to engage the clutch. **-2.** *fam fig* [s'engager] : **~ sur** to get onto the subject of.

embrigader [ɑ̃brigade] [3] *vt* to recruit.
◆ **s'embrigader** *vp* to join.

embringuer [ɑ̃brɛ̃ge] [3] *vt fam* to involve.
◆ **s'embringuer** *vp fam* : **s'~ dans** to get mixed up in.

embrocher [ɑ̃brɔʃe] [3] *vt* to skewer.
◆ **s'embrocher** *vp fam* to stab o.s.

embrouillamini [ɑ̃brujamini] *nm fam* muddle.

embrouille [ãbruj] *nf fam* shenanigans (*pl*).

embrouiller [ãbruje] [3] *vt* **-1.** [mélanger] to mix (up), to muddle (up). **-2.** *fig* [compliquer] to confuse.

embruns [ãbr̃œ] *nmpl* spray (*U*).

embryologie [ãbrijɔlɔʒi] *nf* embryology.

embryon [ãbrijɔ̃] *nm litt* & *fig* embryo.

embryonnaire [ãbrijɔnɛr] *adj litt* & *fig* embryonic.

embûche [ãbyʃ] *nf* pitfall.

embuer [ãbɥe] [7] *vt* **-1.** [de vapeur] to steam up. **-2.** [de larmes] to mist (over).

embuscade [ãbyskad] *nf* ambush.

embusquer [ãbyske] [3] *vt* **-1.** [poster] to post away from the front line. **-2.** [mettre à l'abri] to position for an ambush.

◆ **s'embusquer** *vp* **-1.** [se poster] to be posted away from the front line. **-2.** [se mettre à l'abri] to lie in ambush.

éméché, -e [emeʃe] *adj fam* merry, tipsy.

émeraude [emrod] ◇ *nf* emerald. ◇ *adj inv* (*en apposition*): **vert** ~ emerald (green).

émergence [emɛrʒãs] *nf* emergence.

émerger [emɛrʒe] [17] *vi* **-1.** [gén] to emerge. **-2.** NAVIG & *fig* to surface.

émeri [emri] *nm*: **papier** OU **toile** ~ emery paper.

émérite [emerit] *adj* distinguished, eminent.

émerveillement [emɛrvejmã] *nm* wonder.

émerveiller [emɛrveje] [4] *vt* to fill with wonder.

◆ **s'émerveiller** *vp*: **s'**~ **(de)** to marvel (at).

émets → **émettre**.

émetteur, -trice [emetœr, tris] *adj* transmitting; **poste** ~ transmitter.

◆ **émetteur** *nm* [appareil] transmitter; **~-récepteur** transmitter-receiver.

émettre [emɛtr] [84] *vt* **-1.** [produire] to emit. **-2.** [diffuser] to transmit, to broadcast. **-3.** [mettre en circulation] to issue. **-4.** [exprimer] to express.

émeus, émeut *etc* → **émouvoir**.

émeute [emøt] *nf* riot.

émeutier, -ière [emøtje, jɛr] *nm, f* rioter.

émietter [emjete] [4] *vt* **-1.** [du pain] to crumble. **-2.** [morceler] to divide up.

émigrant, -e [emigrã, ãt] *adj & nm, f* emigrant.

émigration [emigrasjɔ̃] *nf* **-1.** [de personnes] emigration. **-2.** ZOOL migration.

émigré, -e [emigre] ◇ *adj* migrant. ◇ *nm, f* emigrant.

émigrer [emigre] [3] *vi* **-1.** [personnes] to emigrate. **-2.** [animaux] to migrate.

émincé, -e [emɛ̃se] *adj* sliced thinly.

◆ **émincé** *nm* *thin slices of meat served in a sauce.*

éminemment [eminamã] *adv* eminently.

éminence [eminãs] *nf* hill.

◆ **Éminence** *nf* Eminence; **Son Éminence** His Eminence.

◆ **éminence grise** *nf* éminence grise.

éminent, -e [eminã, ãt] *adj* eminent, distinguished.

émir [emir] *nm* emir.

émirat [emira] *nm* emirate.

◆ **Émirat** *nm*: **les Émirats arabes unis** the United Arab Emirates.

émis, -e [emi, iz] *pp* → **émettre**.

émissaire [emisɛr] ◇ *nm* **-1.** [envoyé] emissary, envoy. **-2.** TECHNOL outlet, drainage channel. ◇ *adj* **-1.** ANAT emissary. **-2.** → **bouc**.

émission [emisjɔ̃] *nf* **-1.** [de gaz, de son etc] emission. **-2.** [RADIO & TÉLÉ - transmission] transmission, broadcasting; [- programme] programme *Br*, program *Am*. **-3.** [mise en circulation] issue.

emmagasiner [ãmagazine] [3] *vt* **-1.** [stocker] to store. **-2.** [accumuler] to store up.

emmailloter [ãmajote] [3] *vt* to wrap up.

emmanchure [ãmãʃyr] *nf* armhole.

Emmaüs [emays] *n*: ~ **International** *charity organization which helps the poor and homeless.*

emmêler [ãmele] [4] *vt* **-1.** [fils] to tangle up. **-2.** *fig* [idées] to muddle up, to confuse.

◆ **s'emmêler** *vp* **-1.** [fils] to get into a tangle. **-2.** *fig* [personne] to get mixed up.

emménagement [ãmenaʒmã] *nm* moving in.

emménager [ãmenaʒe] [17] *vi* to move in.

emmener [ãmne] [19] *vt* to take.

emmerdant, -e [ãmɛrdã, ãt] *adj tfam* bloody *Br* OU damned annoying.

emmerdement [ãmɛrdəmã] *nm tfam* bloody *Br* OU damned nuisance; **avoir des** ~**s** to have problems.

emmerder [ãmɛrde] [3] *vt tfam* to piss off.

◆ **s'emmerder** *vp tfam* [s'embêter] to be bored stiff.

emmerdeur, -euse [ãmɛrdœr, øz] *nm, f tfam* pain (in the arse).

emmitoufler [ãmitufle] [3] *vt* to wrap up.

◆ **s'emmitoufler** *vp* to wrap o.s. up.

émoi [emwa] *nm* **-1.** *sout* [agitation] agitation, commotion; **en** ~ in turmoil. **-2.** [émotion] emotion.

émollient, -e [emɔljã, ãt] *adj* emollient.

◆ **émollient** *nm* emollient.

émotif, -ive [emɔtif, iv] ◇ *adj* emotional. ◇ *nm, f* emotional person.

émotion [emosjɔ̃] *nf* **-1.** [sentiment] emotion. **-2.** [peur] fright, shock; **donner des ~s à qqn** to give sb a fright OU shock.

émotionnel, -elle [emosjɔnel] *adj* emotional.

émotionner [emosjɔne] [3] *vt fam* to move (to the brink of tears).

émotivité [emɔtivite] *nf* emotionalism.

émoulu, -e [emuly] → **frais**.

émousser [emuse] [3] *vt litt & fig* to blunt.

◆ **s'émousser** *vp* [lame] to become blunt; *fig* to die down, to lessen.

émoustiller [emustije] [3] *vt* **-1.** [rendre gai] to liven up. **-2.** [exciter] to arouse, to excite.

émouvant, -e [emuvɑ̃, ɑ̃t] *adj* moving.

émouvoir [emuvwar] [55] *vt* **-1.** [troubler] to disturb, to upset. **-2.** [susciter la sympathie de] to move, to touch.

◆ **s'émouvoir** *vp* to show emotion, to be upset.

empailler [ɑ̃paje] [3] *vt* **-1.** [animal] to stuff. **-2.** [chaise] to upholster (with straw).

empaler [ɑ̃pale] [3] *vt*: **~ qqn/qqch sur** to impale sb/sthg on, to impale sb/sthg upon.

◆ **s'empaler** *vp*: **s'~ sur** to be impaled on OU upon.

empaqueter [ɑ̃pakte] [27] *vt* to pack (up), to wrap (up).

emparer [ɑ̃pare] [3]

◆ **s'emparer** *vp*: **s'~ de** [suj: personne] to seize; [suj: sentiment] to take hold of.

empâté, -e [ɑ̃pate] *adj* [visage, traits] bloated; [bouche, langue] coated.

empâter [ɑ̃pate] [3] *vt* **-1.** [visage, traits] to fatten out. **-2.** [bouche, langue] to coat, to fur up.

◆ **s'empâter** *vp* to put on weight.

empattement [ɑ̃patmɑ̃] *nm* **-1.** AUTOM wheelbase. **-2.** TYPO serif.

empêchement [ɑ̃peʃmɑ̃] *nm* obstacle; **j'ai un ~** something has come up.

empêcher [ɑ̃peʃe] [4] *vt* to prevent; **~ qqn/qqch de faire qqch** to prevent sb/sthg from doing sthg; **~ que qqn (ne) fasse qqch** to prevent sb from doing sthg; **(il) n'empêche que** nevertheless, all the same.

◆ **s'empêcher** *vp*: **s'~ de faire qqch** to stop o.s. doing sthg; **je ne peux pas m'~ de pleurer** I can't help crying.

empêcheur, -euse [ɑ̃peʃœr, øz] *nm, f fam*: **~ de tourner en rond** killjoy.

empeigne [ɑ̃pɛɲ] *nf* upper.

empereur [ɑ̃prœr] *nm* emperor.

empesé, -e [ɑ̃pəze] *adj* **-1.** [linge] starched. **-2.** *fig* [style] stiff.

empester [ɑ̃peste] [3] ◇ *vt* to stink out. ◇ *vi* to stink.

empêtrer [ɑ̃petre] [4] *vt*: **être empêtré dans** to be tangled up in.

◆ **s'empêtrer** *vp*: **s'~ (dans)** to get tangled up (in).

emphase [ɑ̃faz] *nf péj* pomposity.

emphatique [ɑ̃fatik] *adj péj* pompous.

empiècement [ɑ̃pjesmɑ̃] *nm* yoke.

empiéter [ɑ̃pjete] [18] *vi*: **~ sur** to encroach on.

empiffrer [ɑ̃pifre] [3]

◆ **s'empiffrer** *vp fam* to stuff o.s.

empilement [ɑ̃pilmɑ̃], **empilage** [ɑ̃pilaʒ] *nm* [action] piling up, stacking up; [pile] pile, stack.

empiler [ɑ̃pile] [3] *vt* **-1.** [entasser] to pile up, to stack up. **-2.** *tfam* [duper] to rip off.

◆ **s'empiler** *vp* to pile up.

empire [ɑ̃pir] *nm* **-1.** HIST & *fig* empire; **l'Empire** *the Empire under Napoleon I*; **le Second Empire** the Second Empire (*under Napoleon III*); **pour un ~** *fig* for the world. **-2.** *sout* [contrôle] influence; **sous l'~ de** [la boisson] under the influence of; [colère] gripped by.

empirer [ɑ̃pire] [3] *vi & vt* to worsen.

empirique [ɑ̃pirik] *adj* empirical.

empirisme [ɑ̃pirism] *nm* empiricism.

emplacement [ɑ̃plasmɑ̃] *nm* site, location.

emplâtre [ɑ̃platr] *nm* **-1.** [pommade] plaster. **-2.** *péj* [incapable] lazy lump.

emplette [ɑ̃plɛt] *nf* (*gén pl*) purchase; **faire des ~s** to go shopping; **faire l'~ de** to purchase.

emplir [ɑ̃plir] [32] *vt sout*: **~ (de)** to fill (with).

◆ **s'emplir** *vp*: **s'~ (de)** to fill (with).

emploi [ɑ̃plwa] *nm* **-1.** [utilisation] use; **faire double ~** to be unnecessary OU redundant; **~ du temps** timetable; **mode d'~** instructions (*pl*) (for use). **-2.** [travail] job.

employé, -e [ɑ̃plwaje] *nm, f* employee; **~ de bureau** office employee OU worker.

employer [ɑ̃plwaje] [13] *vt* **-1.** [utiliser] to use. **-2.** [salarier] to employ.

◆ **s'employer** *vp* to be used; **s'~ à qqch** to be working on sthg, to apply o.s. to sthg; **s'~ à faire qqch** to apply o.s. to doing sthg.

employeur, -euse [ɑ̃plwajœr, øz] *nm, f* employer.

empocher [ɑ̃pɔʃe] [3] *vt fam* to pocket.

empoignade [ɑ̃pwaɲad] *nf* row.

empoigne [ɑ̃pwaɲ] → **foire**.

empoigner [ɑ̃pwaɲe] [3] vt **-1.** [saisir] to grasp. **-2.** fig [émouvoir] to grip.

◆ **s'empoigner** vp fig to come to blows.

empoisonnant, -e [ɑ̃pwazɔnɑ̃, ɑ̃t] adj **-1.** [ennuyeux] boring. **-2.** [insupportable] irritating.

empoisonnement [ɑ̃pwazɔnmɑ̃] nm **-1.** [intoxication] poisoning. **-2.** fam fig [souci] trouble (U).

empoisonner [ɑ̃pwazɔne] [3] vt **-1.** [gén] to poison. **-2.** [empuantir] to stink out. **-3.** fam [ennuyer] to annoy, to bug.

emporté, -e [ɑ̃pɔrte] adj short-tempered.

emportement [ɑ̃pɔrtəmɑ̃] nm anger.

emporte-pièce [ɑ̃pɔrtəpjɛs] nm inv punch.

◆ **à l'emporte-pièce** loc adj incisive.

emporter [ɑ̃pɔrte] [3] vt **-1.** [emmener] to take (away); **à ~** [plats] to take away, to go Am. **-2.** [entraîner] to carry along. **-3.** [arracher] to tear off, to blow off. **-4.** [faire mourir] to carry off. **-5.** [gagner] to win. **-6.** [surpasser]: **l'~ sur** to get the better of.

◆ **s'emporter** vp to get angry, to lose one's temper.

empoté, -e [ɑ̃pɔte] fam ◇ adj clumsy. ◇ nm, f clumsy person.

empourprer [ɑ̃purpre] [3]

◆ **s'empourprer** vp littéraire to turn crimson.

empreinte [ɑ̃prɛ̃t] nf [trace] print; fig mark, trace; **~s digitales** fingerprints.

empressé, -e [ɑ̃prese] ◇ adj attentive. ◇ nm, f attentive person.

empressement [ɑ̃prɛsmɑ̃] nm **-1.** [zèle] attentiveness. **-2.** [enthousiasme] eagerness.

empresser [ɑ̃prese] [4]

◆ **s'empresser** vp: **s'~ de faire qqch** to hurry to do sthg; **s'~ auprès de qqn** to be attentive to sb.

emprise [ɑ̃priz] nf **-1.** [ascendant] influence; **sous l'~ de** [l'alcool] under the influence of; [la colère] gripped by. **-2.** JUR expropriation.

emprisonnement [ɑ̃prizɔnmɑ̃] nm imprisonment.

emprisonner [ɑ̃prizɔne] [3] vt **-1.** [voleur] to imprison. **-2.** [partie du corps] to fit tightly round.

emprunt [ɑ̃prœ̃] nm **-1.** FIN loan; **couvrir un ~** to guarantee a loan; **lancer un ~** to float a loan; **~ d'État** government loan. **-2.** LING & fig borrowing.

emprunté, -e [ɑ̃prœ̃te] adj awkward, self-conscious.

emprunter [ɑ̃prœ̃te] [3] vt **-1.** [gén] to borrow; **~ qqch à** to borrow sthg from. **-2.** [route] to take.

empuantir [ɑ̃pɥɑ̃tir] [32] vt to stink out.

EMT (abr de **éducation manuelle et technique**) nf practical sciences (pl).

ému, -e [emy] ◇ pp → **émouvoir**. ◇ adj [personne] moved, touched; [regard, sourire] emotional.

émulation [emylasjɔ̃] nf **-1.** [concurrence] rivalry. **-2.** [imitation] emulation.

émule [emyl] nmf **-1.** [imitateur] emulator. **-2.** [concurrent] rival.

émulsion [emylsjɔ̃] nf emulsion.

en [ɑ̃] ◇ prép **-1.** [temps] in; **~ 1994** in 1994; **~ hiver/septembre** in winter/September. **-2.** [lieu] in; [direction] to; **une maison ~ Suède** a house in Sweden; **habiter ~ Sicile/ville** to live in Sicily/town; **aller ~ Sicile/ville** to go to Sicily/town; **aller de ville ~ ville** to go from town to town. **-3.** [matière] made of; **c'est ~ métal** it's (made of) metal; **une théière ~ argent** a silver teapot. **-4.** [état, forme, manière]: **les arbres sont ~ fleurs** the trees are in blossom; **du sucre ~ morceaux** sugar cubes; **du lait ~ poudre** powdered milk; **je la préfère ~ vert** I prefer it in green; **agir ~ traître** to behave treacherously; **je l'ai eu ~ cadeau** I was given it as a present; **dire qqch ~ anglais** to say sthg in English; **~ vacances** on holiday. **-5.** [moyen] by; **~ avion/bateau/train** by plane/boat/train. **-6.** [mesure] in; **vous l'avez ~ 38?** do you have it in a 38?; **compter ~ dollars** to calculate in dollars. **-7.** [devant un participe présent]: **~ arrivant à Paris** on arriving in Paris, as he/she etc arrived in Paris; **~ faisant un effort** by making an effort; **~ mangeant** while eating; **elle répondit ~ souriant** she replied with a smile.

◇ pron adv **-1.** [complément de verbe, de nom, d'adjectif]: **il s'~ est souvenu** he remembered it; **nous ~ avons déjà parlé** we've already spoken about it; **on ~ meurt, de ce genre de maladie** people die from this sort of illness; **je m'~ porte garant** I'll vouch for him/her; **j'~ garde un très bon souvenir** I have very happy memories of it; **sa maison ~ est pleine** his house is full of them. **-2.** [avec un indéfini, exprimant une quantité]: **j'~ connais un/plusieurs** I know one/several of them; **j'ai du chocolat, tu ~ veux?** I've got some chocolate, do you want some?; **tu ~ as?** have you got any?, do you have any?; **il y ~ a plusieurs** there are several (of them). **-3.** [provenance] from there; **j'~ arrive à l'instant** I've just come from there.

ENA, **Ena** [ena] (*abr de* **École nationale d'administration**) *nf* prestigious grande école training future government officials.

énarque [enark] *nmf* graduate of the École nationale d'administration (ENA).

encablure [ākablyr] *nf* cable length.

encadrement [ākadrəmā] *nm* -1. [de tableau, porte] **frame.** -2. [dans une entreprise] managerial staff; [à l'armée] officers (*pl*); [à l'école] staff. -3. [du crédit] restriction.

encadrer [ākadre] [3] *vt* -1. [photo, visage] to **frame.** -2. [employés] to **supervise;** [soldats] to be in command of; [élèves] to teach. -3. [détenu] to flank. -4. *fam* [arbre] to crash into.

encadreur [ākadrœr] *nm* framer.

encaisse [ākɛs] *nf* ready cash.

encaissé, -e [ākese] *adj* [vallée] deep and narrow; [rivière] steep-banked.

encaisser [ākese] [4] *vt* -1. [argent, coups, insultes] to take. -2. [chèque] to cash. -3. *loc:* **ne pas pouvoir ~ qqn** *fam* not to be able to stand sb.

encanailler [ākanaje] [3]
◆ **s'encanailler** *vp* to slum it.

encart [ākar] *nm* insert; **~ publicitaire** advertising insert.

en-cas, encas [āka] *nm inv* snack.

encastrable [ākastrabl] *adj* that can be fitted (in).

encastrer [ākastre] [3] *vt* to fit.
◆ **s'encastrer** *vp* to fit (exactly).

encaustique [ākostik] *nf* -1. [cire] polish. -2. [peinture] encaustic.

encaustiquer [ākostike] [3] *vt* to polish.

enceinte [āsɛ̃t] ◇ *adj f* pregnant; **~ de 4 mois** 4 months pregnant. ◇ *nf* -1. [muraille] wall. -2. [espace]: **dans l'~ de** within (the confines of). -3. [baffle]: **~ (acoustique)** speaker.

encens [āsā] *nm* incense.

encenser [āsāse] [3] *vt* -1. [brûler de l'encens dans] to burn incense in. -2. *fig* [louer] to flatter.

encensoir [āsāswar] *nm* censer.

encercler [āserkle] [3] *vt* -1. [cerner, environner] to surround. -2. [entourer] to circle.

enchaînement [āʃɛnmā] *nm* -1. [succession] series. -2. [liaison] link. -3. MUS progression.

enchaîner [āʃene] [4] ◇ *vt* -1. [attacher] to chain up. -2. *fig* [asservir] to enslave. -3. [coordonner] to link. ◇ *vi:* **~ (sur)** to move on (to).
◆ **s'enchaîner** *vp* [se suivre] to follow on from each other.

enchanté, -e [āʃāte] *adj* -1. [ravi] delighted; **~ de faire votre connaissance** pleased to meet you. -2. [ensorcelé] enchanted.

enchantement [āʃātmā] *nm* -1. [sortilège] magic spell; **comme par ~** as if by magic. -2. *sout* [ravissement] delight. -3. [merveille] wonder.

enchanter [āʃāte] [3] *vt* -1. [ensorceler, charmer] to enchant. -2. [ravir] to delight.

enchanteur, -eresse [āʃātœr, trɛs] ◇ *adj* enchanting. ◇ *nm, f* -1. [magicien] enchanter. -2. [charmeur] charmer.

enchâsser [āʃase] [3] *vt* -1. [encastrer] to fit. -2. [sertir] to set.

enchère [āʃɛr] *nf* bid; **faire monter les ~s** to raise the bidding; **vendre qqch aux ~s** to sell sthg at OU by auction.

enchérir [āʃerir] [32] *vi:* **~ sur** to bid higher than; *fig & littéraire* [dépasser] to go beyond.

enchevêtrer [āʃvɛtre] [4] *vt* [emmêler] to tangle up; *fig* to muddle, to confuse.

enclave [āklav] *nf* enclave.

enclencher [āklāʃe] [3] *vt* -1. [mécanisme] to engage. -2. *fig* [projet] to set in motion.
◆ **s'enclencher** *vp* -1. TECHNOL to engage. -2. *fig* [commencer] to begin.

enclin, -e [āklɛ̃, in] *adj:* **~ à qqch/à faire qqch** inclined to sthg/to do sthg.

enclore [āklɔr] [113] *vt* to fence in, to enclose.

enclos, -e [āklo, oz] *pp* → **enclore.**
◆ **enclos** *nm* enclosure.

enclume [āklym] *nf* anvil.

encoche [ākɔʃ] *nf* notch.

encoder [ākɔde] [3] *vt* to encode.

encodeur [ākɔdœr] *nm* INFORM encoder.

encoignure [ākwaɲyr, ākɔɲyr] *nf* -1. [coin] corner. -2. [meuble] corner cupboard.

encolure [ākɔlyr] *nf* neck.

encombrant, -e [ākɔ̃brā, āt] cumbersome; *fig* [personne] undesirable.

encombre [ākɔ̃br]
◆ **sans encombre** *loc adv* without a hitch.

encombré, -e [ākɔ̃bre] *adj* [lieu] busy, congested; *fig* saturated.

encombrement [ākɔ̃brəmā] *nm* -1. [d'une pièce] clutter. -2. [d'un objet] overall dimensions (*pl*). -3. [embouteillage] traffic jam. -4. INFORM footprint.

encombrer [ākɔ̃bre] [3] *vt* to clutter (up).
◆ **s'encombrer** *vp fam:* **s'~ de qqn** to be lumbered with sb *Br;* **s'~ de qqch** to burden o.s. with sthg; *fig* to bother about sthg.

encontre [ãkɔ̃tr]
◆ **à l'encontre de** loc prép: **aller à l'~ de** to go against, to oppose.

encorbellement [ãkɔrbɛlmã] nm corbelled structure; **en ~** corbelled.

encorder [ãkɔrde] [3]
◆ **s'encorder** vp to rope up.

encore [ãkɔr] adv **-1.** [toujours] still; **il dort ~** he's still asleep; **~ un mois** one more month; **pas ~** not yet; **elle ne travaille pas ~** she's not working yet. **-2.** [de nouveau] again; **il m'a ~ menti** he's lied to me again; **quoi ~?** what now?; **l'ascenseur est en panne - ~!** the lift's out of order - not again!; **~ une fois** once more, once again. **-3.** [marque le renforcement] even; **~ mieux/pire** even better/worse. **-4.** [marque une restriction]: **il ne suffit pas d'être beau, ~ faut-il être intelligent** it's not enough to be good-looking, you have to be intelligent too.
◆ **et encore** loc adv: **j'ai eu le temps de prendre un sandwich, et ~!** I had time for a sandwich, but only just!; **ça vaut 100 francs, et ~** it's worth 100 francs, if that.
◆ **mais encore** loc adv what else?
◆ **si encore** loc adv if only.
◆ **encore que** loc conj although.

encourageant, -e [ãkuraʒã, ãt] adj encouraging.

encouragement [ãkuraʒmã] nm **-1.** [parole] (word of) encouragement. **-2.** [action] encouragement.

encourager [ãkuraʒe] [17] vt to encourage; **~ qqn à faire qqch** to encourage sb to do sthg.

encourir [ãkurir] [45] vt sout to incur.

encouru, -e [ãkyry] pp → **encourir**.

encrasser [ãkrase] [3] vt **-1.** TECHNOL to clog up. **-2.** fam [salir] to make dirty OU filthy.
◆ **s'encrasser** vp **-1.** TECHNOL to clog up. **-2.** fam [se salir] to get dirty OU filthy.

encre [ãkr] nf ink; **~ de Chine** Indian ink.

encrer [ãkre] [3] vt to ink.

encreur [ãkrœr] → **tampon, rouleau**.

encrier [ãkrije] nm inkwell.

encroûter [ãkrute] [3]
◆ **s'encroûter** vp fam to get into a rut; **s'~ dans ses habitudes** to become set in one's ways.

enculé [ãkyle] nm vulg arsehole Br, asshole Am.

enculer [ãkyle] [3] vt vulg to bugger.

encyclique [ãsiklik] nf RELIG encyclical.

encyclopédie [ãsiklɔpedi] nf encyclopedia.

encyclopédique [ãsiklɔpedik] adj encyclopedic.

endémique [ãdemik] adj endemic.

endettement [ãdɛtmã] nm debt.

endetter [ãdete] [4]
◆ **s'endetter** vp to get into debt.

endeuiller [ãdœje] [5] vt to plunge into mourning.

endiablé, -e [ãdjable] adj [frénétique] frantic, frenzied.

endiguer [ãdige] [3] vt **-1.** [fleuve] to dam. **-2.** fig [réprimer] to stem.

endimanché, -e [ãdimãʃe] adj in one's Sunday best.

endimancher [ãdimãʃe] [3]
◆ **s'endimancher** vp to dress in one's Sunday best.

endive [ãdiv] nf chicory (U).

endocrine [ãdɔkrin] → **glande**.

endoctrinement [ãdɔktrinmã] nm indoctrination.

endoctriner [ãdɔktrine] [3] vt to indoctrinate.

endommager [ãdɔmaʒe] [17] vt to damage.

endormi, -e [ãdɔrmi] adj **-1.** [personne] sleeping, asleep. **-2.** fig [village] sleepy; [jambe] numb; [passion] dormant; fam [apathique] sluggish.

endormir [ãdɔrmir] [36] vt **-1.** [assoupir, ennuyer] to send to sleep. **-2.** [anesthésier - patient] to anaesthetize; [- douleur] to ease. **-3.** fig [tromper] to allay. **-4.** fig [affaiblir] to dull.
◆ **s'endormir** vp **-1.** [s'assoupir] to fall asleep. **-2.** [s'affaiblir] to be allayed. **-3.** fig [jambe] to go to sleep.

endoscopie [ãdɔskɔpi] nf endoscopy.

endosser [ãdose] [3] vt **-1.** [vêtement] to put on. **-2.** FIN & JUR to endorse; **~ un chèque** to endorse a cheque. **-3.** fig [responsabilité] to take on.

endroit [ãdrwa] nm **-1.** [lieu, point] place; **à quel ~?** where? **-2.** [passage] part. **-3.** [côté] right side; **à l'~** the right way round.
◆ **à l'endroit de** prép littéraire with regard to.

enduire [ãdɥir] [98] vt: **~ qqch (de)** to coat sthg (with).

enduisais, enduisions etc → **enduire**.

enduit, -e [ãdɥi, ɥit] pp → **enduire**.
◆ **enduit** nm coating.

endurance [ãdyrãs] nf endurance.

endurant, -e [ãdyrã, ãt] adj tough, resilient.

endurci, -e [ãdyrsi] adj **-1.** [aguerri] hardened. **-2.** fig [insensible] hard.

endurcir [ãdyrsir] [32] *vt* to harden.
◆ **s'endurcir** *vp*: **s'~ à** to become hardened to.

endurer [ãdyre] [3] *vt* to endure.

énergétique [enɛrʒetik] *adj* **-1.** [ressource] energy (*avant n*). **-2.** [aliment] energy-giving.

énergie [enɛrʒi] *nf* energy; **~ nucléaire/ solaire** nuclear/solar energy; **~ éolienne** wind power.

énergique [enɛrʒik] *adj* [gén] energetic; [remède] powerful; [mesure] drastic.

énergiquement [enɛrʒikmã] *adv* energetically.

énergisant, -e [enɛrʒizã, ãt] *adj* stimulating.
◆ **énergisant** *nm* tonic.

énergumène [enɛrgymɛn] *nmf* rowdy character.

énervant, -e [enɛrvã, ãt] *adj* annoying, irritating.

énervé, -e [enɛrve] *adj* **-1.** [irrité] annoyed, irritated. **-2.** [surexcité] overexcited.

énervement [enɛrvəmã] *nm* **-1.** [irritation] irritation. **-2.** [surexcitation] excitement.

énerver [enɛrve] [3] *vt* to irritate, to annoy.
◆ **s'énerver** *vp* to get annoyed; **ne vous énervez pas!** don't get excited!

enfance [ãfãs] *nf* **-1.** [âge] childhood; **retomber en ~** to lapse into one's second childhood. **-2.** [enfants] children (*pl*). **-3.** *fig* [débuts] infancy; [de civilisation, de l'humanité] dawn; **l'~ de l'art** *fig* child's play.

enfant [ãfã] *nmf* **-1.** [gén] child; **~ illégitime** OU **naturel** illegitimate child; **~ martyr** abused child; **~ prodige** child prodigy; **attendre un ~** to be expecting a baby. **-2.** [originaire] native; **c'est un ~ de la balle** his/her parents were in the theatre/circus *etc*.
◆ **bon enfant** *loc adj* good-natured.

enfantement [ãfãtmã] *nm littéraire* childbirth; *fig* creation.

enfanter [ãfãte] [3] *vt littéraire* to give birth to.

enfantillage [ãfãtijaʒ] *nm* childishness (*U*).

enfantin, -e [ãfãtɛ̃, in] *adj* **-1.** [propre à l'enfance] childlike; *péj* childish; [jeu, chanson] children's (*avant n*). **-2.** [facile] childishly simple.

enfer [ãfɛr] *nm* **-1.** RELIG & *fig* hell; **d'~** *fig* hellish, infernal. **-2.** [de bibliothèque] restricted books department.
◆ **Enfers** *nmpl*: **les Enfers** the Underworld (*sg*).

enfermer [ãfɛrme] [3] *vt* **-1.** [séquestrer, ran-ger] to shut away. **-2.** *littéraire* [enclore] to enclose.
◆ **s'enfermer** *vp* to shut o.s. away OU up; **s'~ dans** *fig* to retreat into.

enfilade [ãfilad] *nf* row; **en ~** in a row.

enfiler [ãfile] [3] *vt* **-1.** [aiguille, sur un fil] to thread. **-2.** [vêtements] to slip on.
◆ **s'enfiler** *vp fam* [ingurgiter] to put away.

enfin [ãfɛ̃] *adv* **-1.** [en dernier lieu] finally, at last; [dans une liste] lastly. **-2.** [avant une récapitulation] in a word, in short. **-3.** [introduit une rectification] that is, well. **-4.** [introduit une concession] anyway.

enflammé, -e [ãflame] *adj* **-1.** [en flammes] burning. **-2.** *fig* [déclaration, discours] passionate; [discussion] heated.

enflammer [ãflame] [3] *vt* **-1.** [bois] to set fire to. **-2.** *fig* [exalter] to inflame.
◆ **s'enflammer** *vp* **-1.** [bois] to catch fire. **-2.** *fig* [s'exalter] to flare up.

enflé, -e [ãfle] *adj* [style] turgid.

enfler [ãfle] [3] *vi* to swell (up).

enflure [ãflyr] *nf* [de corps] swelling.

enfoncé, -e [ãfɔ̃se] *adj* deep-set.

enfoncer [ãfɔ̃se] [16] *vt* **-1.** [faire pénétrer] to drive in; **~ qqch dans qqch** to drive sthg into sthg. **-2.** [enfouir]: **~ ses mains dans ses poches** to thrust one's hands into one's pockets. **-3.** [défoncer] to break down. **-4.** *fam* [vaincre] to hammer, to thrash.
◆ **s'enfoncer** *vp* **-1.** **s'~ dans** [eau, boue] to sink into; [bois, ville] to disappear into. **-2.** [céder] to give way.

enfouir [ãfwir] [32] *vt* **-1.** [cacher] to hide. **-2.** [ensevelir] to bury.
◆ **s'enfouir** *vp* to bury o.s.

enfourcher [ãfurʃe] [3] *vt* to get on, to mount.

enfourner [ãfurne] [3] *vt* **-1.** [pain] to put in the oven. **-2.** *fam* [avaler] to gobble up.

enfreignais, enfreignions *etc* → **enfreindre**.

enfreindre [ãfrɛ̃dr] [81] *vt* to infringe.

enfreint, -e [ãfrɛ̃, ɛ̃t] *pp* → **enfreindre**.

enfuir [ãfɥir] [35]
◆ **s'enfuir** *vp* **-1.** [fuir] to run away. **-2.** *littéraire* [passer] to slip away.

enfumer [ãfyme] [3] *vt* to fill with smoke.

enfuyais, enfuyions *etc* → **enfuir**.

engagé, -e [ãgaʒe] *adj* committed.

engageant, -e [ãgaʒã, ãt] *adj* engaging.

engagement [ãgaʒmã] *nm* **-1.** [promesse] commitment; **sans ~** COMM without obligation. **-2.** JUR contract. **-3.** [embauche] engagement, taking on. **-4.** [MIL - de soldats] enlistment; [- combat] engagement. **-5.**

FOOTBALL & RUGBY kick-off. **-6.** [encouragement] encouragement.

engager [ãgaʒe] [17] ◇ *vt* **-1.** [lier] to commit. **-2.** [embaucher] to take on, to engage. **-3.** [faire entrer]: ~ **qqch dans** to insert sthg into. **-4.** [commencer] to start. **-5.** [impliquer] to involve. **-6.** [encourager]: ~ **qqn à faire qqch** to urge sb to do sthg. ◇ *vi* **-1.** FOOTBALL & RUGBY to kick off. **-2.** [lier]: **cela n'engage à rien** there is no obligation.
◆ **s'engager** *vp* **-1.** [promettre]: **s'~ à qqch/à faire qqch** to commit o.s. to sthg/to doing sthg. **-2.** MIL: **s'~ (dans)** to enlist (in). **-3.** [pénétrer]: **s'~ dans** to enter. **-4.** *fig* [débuter] to begin. **-5.** [militer] to be committed.

engeance [ãʒãs] *nf littéraire* riffraff.

engelure [ãʒlyr] *nf* chilblain.

engendrer [ãʒãdre] [3] *vt* **-1.** *littéraire* to father. **-2.** MATHS to generate. **-3.** *fig* [produire] to cause, to give rise to; [sentiment] to engender.

engin [ãʒẽ] *nm* **-1.** [machine] machine. **-2.** MIL missile. **-3.** *fam péj* [objet] thing.

engineering [ɛnʒiniriŋ] *nm* engineering.

englober [ãglɔbe] [3] *vt* to include.

engloutir [ãglutir] [32] *vt* **-1.** [dévorer] to gobble up. **-2.** [faire disparaître] to engulf. **-3.** *fig* [dilapider] to squander.
◆ **s'engloutir** *vp* to be engulfed.

engluer [ãglɥe] [3] *vt* **-1.** [oiseau] to catch (using birdlime). **-2.** [piège] to smear with birdlime.
◆ **s'engluer** *vp*: **s'~ (de)** to get sticky (with); **s'~ (dans)** *fig* to become bogged down (in).

engorgement [ãgɔrʒəmã] *nm* **-1.** MÉD engorgement. **-2.** *fig* [de marché] glutting, swamping.

engorger [ãgɔrʒe] [17] *vt* **-1.** [obstruer] to block, to obstruct. **-2.** MÉD to engorge.
◆ **s'engorger** *vp* to become blocked.

engouement [ãgumã] *nm* **-1.** [enthousiasme] infatuation. **-2.** MÉD strangulation (of hernia).

engouer [ãgue] [6]
◆ **s'engouer** *vp*: **s'~ de** to become infatuated with.

engouffrer [ãgufre] [3] *vt fam* **-1.** [dévorer] to wolf down. **-2.** [dilapider] to squander.
◆ **s'engouffrer** *vp*: **s'~ dans** to rush into.

engourdi, -e [ãgurdi] *adj* numb; *fig* dull.

engourdir [ãgurdir] [32] *vt* to numb; *fig* to dull.
◆ **s'engourdir** *vp* to go numb.

engourdissement [ãgurdismã] *nm* **-1.** [raideur] numbness. **-2.** [torpeur] torpor.

engrais [ãgrɛ] *nm* fertilizer; ~ **chimique** chemical fertilizer.

engraisser [ãgrese] [4] ◇ *vt* **-1.** [animal] to fatten. **-2.** [terre] to fertilize. ◇ *vi* to put on weight.
◆ **s'engraisser** *vp fam fig* to grow fat.

engranger [ãgrãʒe] [17] *vt* **-1.** [foin] to bring in. **-2.** *fig* [accumuler] to store up.

engrenage [ãgrənaʒ] *nm* **-1.** TECHNOL gears (*pl*). **-2.** *fig* [circonstances]: **être pris dans l'~** to be caught up in the system.

engrosser [ãgrose] [3] *vt fam* to get pregnant.

engueulade [ãgœlad] *nf fam* bawling out.

engueuler [ãgœle] [5] *vt fam*: ~ **qqn** to bawl sb out.
◆ **s'engueuler** *vp fam* to have a slanging match *Br*.

enguirlander [ãgirlãde] [3] *vt* **-1.** *fam* [gronder] to tell off. **-2.** *littéraire* [décorer] to decorate.

enhardir [ãardir] [32] *vt* to make bold.
◆ **s'enhardir** *vp* to pluck up one's courage.

ENI [eni] (*abr de* **École normale d'instituteurs**) *nf* training college for primary school teachers.

énième [enjɛm] *adj fam*: **la ~ fois** the nth time.

énigmatique [enigmatik] *adj* enigmatic.

énigme [enigm] *nf* **-1.** [mystère] enigma. **-2.** [jeu] riddle.

enivrant, -e [ãnivrã, ãt] *adj litt* & *fig* intoxicating.

enivrer [ãnivre] [3] *vt litt* to get drunk; *fig* to intoxicate.
◆ **s'enivrer** *vp*: **s'~ (de)** to get drunk (on); *fig* to become intoxicated (with).

enjambée [ãʒãbe] *nf* stride; **marcher à grandes ~s** to stride (along).

enjamber [ãʒãbe] [3] ◇ *vt* **-1.** [obstacle] to step over. **-2.** [cours d'eau] to straddle. ◇ *vi* [empiéter]: ~ **sur** to encroach on.

enjeu [ãʒø] *nm* [mise] stake; **quel est l'~ ici?** *fig* what's at stake here?

enjoignais, enjoignions *etc* → enjoindre.

enjoindre [ãʒwẽdr] [82] *vt littéraire*: ~ **à qqn de faire qqch** to enjoin sb to do sthg.

enjoint [ãʒwẽ] *pp inv* → enjoindre.

enjôler [ãʒole] [3] *vt* to coax.

enjôleur, -euse [ãʒolœr, øz] ◇ *adj* wheedling. ◇ *nm, f* wheedler.

enjoliver [ãʒɔlive] [3] *vt* to embellish.

enjoliveur [ãʒɔlivœr] *nm* [de roue] hubcap; [de calandre] badge.

enjoué, -e [ãʒwe] *adj* cheerful.

enlacer [ãlase] [16] *vt* -1. [prendre dans ses bras] to embrace, to hug. -2. [entourer] to wind round.

◆ **s'enlacer** *vp* -1. [s'entrelacer] to intertwine. -2. [s'embrasser] to embrace, to hug.

enlaidir [ãledir] [32] ◇ *vt* to make ugly. ◇ *vi* to become ugly.

enlevé, -e [ãlve] *adj*: (bien) ~ spirited.

enlèvement [ãlɛvmã] *nm* -1. [action d'enlever] removal; l'~ **des ordures (ménagères)** refuse collection. -2. [rapt] abduction.

enlever [ãlve] [19] *vt* -1. [gén] to remove; [vêtement] to take off. -2. [prendre]: ~ **qqch à qqn** to take sthg away from sb. -3. [obtenir] to win. -4. [kidnapper] to abduct. -5. *littéraire* [faire mourir] to carry off.

◆ **s'enlever** *vp* to be removable.

enliser [ãlize] [3]

◆ **s'enliser** *vp* -1. [s'embourber] to sink, to get stuck. -2. *fig* [piétiner]: **s'~ dans qqch** to get bogged down in sthg.

enluminure [ãlyminyr] *nf* illumination.

ENM (*abr de* **École nationale de la magistrature**) *nf* grande école training lawyers.

enneigé, -e [ãneʒe] *adj* snow-covered.

enneigement [ãnɛʒmã] *nm* snow cover; **bulletin d'~** snow report.

ennemi, -e [ɛnmi] ◇ *adj* enemy (*avant n*). ◇ *nm, f* enemy; **passer à l'~** to defect; ~ **juré** sworn enemy; ~ **public** public enemy.

ennui [ãnyi] *nm* -1. [lassitude] boredom. -2. [contrariété] annoyance; **l'~, c'est que ...** the annoying thing is that .... -3. [problème] trouble (*U*); **attirer des ~s à qqn** to cause trouble for sb; **s'attirer des ~s** to cause trouble for o.s.; **avoir des ~s** to have problems.

ennuyer [ãnyije] [14] *vt* -1. [agacer, contrarier] to annoy; **cela t'ennuierait de venir me chercher?** would you mind picking me up? -2. [lasser] to bore. -3. [inquiéter] to bother.

◆ **s'ennuyer** *vp* -1. [se morfondre] to be bored. -2. [déplorer l'absence]: **s'~ de qqn/qqch** to miss sb/sthg.

ennuyeux, -euse [ãnyijø, øz] *adj* -1. [lassant] boring. -2. [contrariant] annoying.

énoncé [enɔse] *nm* -1. [libellé] wording. -2. LING utterance.

énoncer [enɔse] [16] *vt* -1. [libeller] to word. -2. [exposer] to expound; [théorème] to set forth.

énonciation [enɔsjasjɔ̃] *nf* -1. [libellé] wording. -2. LING utterance.

enorgueillir [ãnɔrgœjir] [32]

◆ **s'enorgueillir** *vp*: **s'~ de qqch/de faire qqch** to pride o.s. on sthg/on doing sthg.

énorme [enɔrm] *adj* -1. *litt* & *fig* [immense] enormous. -2. *fam fig* [incroyable] farfetched.

énormément [enɔrmemã] *adv* enormously; ~ **de** a great deal of.

énormité [enɔrmite] *nf* -1. [gigantisme] enormity. -2. [absurdité]: **dire des ~s** to say the most awful things.

enquérir [ãkerir] [39]

◆ **s'enquérir** *vp sout*: **s'~ de qqn** to ask after sb; **s'~ de qqch** to inquire about sthg.

enquête [ãkɛt] *nf* -1. [de police, recherches] investigation; ~ **de routine** routine inquiry. -2. [sondage] survey.

enquêter [ãkete] [4] *vi* -1. [police, chercheur] to investigate. -2. [sonder] to conduct a survey.

enquêteur, -euse, -trice [ãkɛtœr, øz, tris] *nm, f* investigator.

enquiers, enquiert *etc* → **enquérir**.

enquiquinant, -e [ãkikinã, ãt] *adj fam* annoying.

enquis, -e [ãki, iz] *pp* → **enquérir**.

enraciner [ãrasine] [3] *vt* -1. [planter] to dig in. -2. *fig* [idée, préjugé] to implant.

◆ **s'enraciner** *vp* -1. [plante, idée] to take root. -2. [personne] to put down roots.

enragé, -e [ãraʒe] ◇ *adj* -1. [chien] rabid, with rabies. -2. *fig* [invétéré] keen. ◇ *nm, f*: **c'est un ~ de football** he's mad about OU on football.

enrageant, -e [ãraʒã, ãt] *adj* infuriating.

enrager [ãraʒe] [17] *vi* to be furious; **faire ~ qqn** to infuriate sb.

enrayer [ãreje] [11] *vt* -1. [épidémie] to check, to stop. -2. [mécanisme] to jam.

◆ **s'enrayer** *vp* [mécanisme] to jam.

enrégimenter [ãreʒimãte] [3] *vt* [dans l'armée] to enlist; [dans un groupe] to enrol.

enregistrement [ãrəʒistrəmã] *nm* -1. [de son, d'images, d'informations] recording; ~ **pirate** pirate recording. -2. [inscription] registration. -3. [à l'aéroport] check-in; ~ **des bagages** baggage registration.

enregistrer [ãrəʒistre] [3] *vt* -1. [son, images, informations] to record. -2. INFORM to store. -3. [inscrire] to register. -4. [à l'aéroport] to check in. -5. *fam* [mémoriser] to make a mental note of.

enregistreur, -euse [ãrəʒistrœr, øz] *adj* recording (*avant n*); **caisse enregistreuse** cash register.

enrhumé, **-e** [ɑ̃ryme] *adj*: **je suis ~** I have a cold.

enrhumer [ɑ̃ryme] [3]
◆ **s'enrhumer** *vp* to catch (a) cold.

enrichi, **-e** [ɑ̃riʃi] *adj* **-1.** [personne] nouveau riche. **-2.** [matériau] enriched. **-3.** *fig* [orné]: **~ de** enhanced by.

enrichir [ɑ̃riʃir] [32] *vt* **-1.** [financièrement] to make rich. **-2.** [terre & *fig*] to enrich.
◆ **s'enrichir** *vp* **-1.** [financièrement] to grow rich. **-2.** [sol & *fig*] to become enriched.

enrichissant, **-e** [ɑ̃riʃisɑ̃, ɑ̃t] *adj* enriching.

enrichissement [ɑ̃riʃismɑ̃] *nm* **-1.** [gén] enrichment. **-2.** [financier] increased wealth.

enrobé, **-e** [ɑ̃rɔbe] *adj* **-1.** [recouvert]: **~ de** coated with. **-2.** *fam* [grassouillet] plump.

enrober [ɑ̃rɔbe] [3] *vt* **-1.** [recouvrir]: **~ qqch de** to coat sthg with. **-2.** *fig* [requête, nouvelle] to wrap up.
◆ **s'enrober** *vp* to put on weight.

enrôlement [ɑ̃rolmɑ̃] *nm* enrolment.

enrôler [ɑ̃role] [3] *vt* to enrol; MIL to enlist.
◆ **s'enrôler** *vp* to enrol; MIL to enlist.

enroué, **-e** [ɑ̃rwe] *adj* hoarse.

enrouer [ɑ̃rwe] [6]
◆ **s'enrouer** *vp* to become hoarse.

enroulement [ɑ̃rulmɑ̃] *nm* rolling up.

enrouler [ɑ̃rule] [3] *vt* to roll up; **~ qqch autour de qqch** to wind sthg round sthg.
◆ **s'enrouler** *vp* **-1.** [entourer]: **s'~ sur** OU **autour de qqch** to wind around sthg. **-2.** [se pelotonner]: **s'~ dans qqch** to wrap o.s. up in sthg.

enrouleur, **-euse** [ɑ̃rulœr, øz] *adj* winding.

ENS (*abr de* **École normale supérieure**) *nf* grande école training secondary school teachers.

ensabler [ɑ̃sable] [3] *vt* to silt up.
◆ **s'ensabler** *vp* to silt up.

ENSAD, **Ensad** [ensad] (*abr de* **École nationale supérieure des arts décoratifs**) *nf* grande école for applied arts.

ENSAM, **Ensam** [ensam] (*abr de* **École nationale supérieure des arts et métiers**) *nf* grande école for engineering.

enseignant, **-e** [ɑ̃seɲɑ̃, ɑ̃t] ◇ *adj* teaching (avant n). ◇ *nm, f* teacher.

enseigne [ɑ̃seɲ] *nf* **-1.** [de commerce] sign; **~ lumineuse** neon sign. **-2.** [drapeau, soldat] ensign. **-3.** *loc*: **être logé à la même ~** to be in the same boat.
◆ **à telle enseigne que** *loc conj* so much so that.

enseignement [ɑ̃seɲmɑ̃] *nm* **-1.** [gén] teaching; **~ primaire/secondaire** primary/secondary education. **-2.** [leçon] lesson.

enseigner [ɑ̃seɲe] [4] *vt litt* & *fig* to teach; **~ qqch à qqn** to teach sb sthg, to teach sthg to sb.

ensemble [ɑ̃sɑ̃bl] ◇ *adv* together; **aller ~** to go together. ◇ *nm* **-1.** [totalité] whole; **l'~ de** all of; **idée d'~** general idea; **dans l'~** on the whole. **-2.** [harmonie] unity. **-3.** [vêtement] outfit. **-4.** [série] collection. **-5.** MATHS set. **-6.** ARCHIT development; **grand ~** housing estate. **-7.** MUS ensemble.

ensemblier [ɑ̃sɑ̃blije] *nm* interior decorator; CIN & TÉLÉ set designer.

ensemencer [ɑ̃smɑ̃se] [16] *vt* **-1.** [terre] to sow. **-2.** [rivière] to stock.

enserrer [ɑ̃sere] [4] *vt* [entourer] to encircle; *fig* to imprison.

ENSET, **Enset** [enset] (*abr de* **École nationale supérieure de l'enseignement technique**) *nf* grande école training science and technology teachers.

ensevelir [ɑ̃səvlir] [32] *vt litt* & *fig* to bury.
◆ **s'ensevelir** *vp* to bury o.s. (away).

ensoleillé, **-e** [ɑ̃sɔleje] *adj* sunny.

ensoleillement [ɑ̃sɔlɛjmɑ̃] *nm* sunshine.

ensommeillé, **-e** [ɑ̃sɔmeje] *adj* sleepy.

ensorceler [ɑ̃sɔrsəle] [24] *vt* to bewitch.

ensorcellement [ɑ̃sɔrsɛlmɑ̃] *nm* bewitching.

ensuite [ɑ̃sɥit] *adv* **-1.** [après, plus tard] after, afterwards, later. **-2.** [puis] then, next, after that; **et ~ what then?**, what next?

ensuivre [ɑ̃sɥivr] [89]
◆ **s'ensuivre** *vp* to follow; **il s'ensuit que** it follows that; **et tout ce qui s'ensuit** and all that that entails.

entaille [ɑ̃taj] *nf* cut.

entailler [ɑ̃taje] [3] *vt* to cut.
◆ **s'entailler** *vp*: **s'~ le doigt** to cut one's finger.

entame [ɑ̃tam] *nf* first slice.

entamer [ɑ̃tame] [3] *vt* **-1.** [commencer] to start (on); [- bouteille] to start, to open. **-2.** [capital] to dip into. **-3.** [cuir, réputation] to damage. **-4.** [courage] to shake.

entartrer [ɑ̃tartre] [3] *vt* to fur up.
◆ **s'entartrer** *vp* to fur up.

entassement [ɑ̃tasmɑ̃] *nm* **-1.** [d'objets] pile; [action] piling up. **-2.** [de personnes] squeezing.

entasser [ɑ̃tase] [3] *vt* **-1.** [accumuler, multiplier] to pile up. **-2.** [serrer] to squeeze.
◆ **s'entasser** *vp* **-1.** [objets] to pile up. **-2.** [personnes]: **s'~ dans** to squeeze into.

entendement [ɑ̃tɑ̃dmɑ̃] *nm* understanding; **dépasser l'~ (de qqn)** to be beyond (sb's) comprehension.

entendeur [ɑ̃tɑ̃dœr] *nm*: **à bon ~ salut!** so be warned!

entendre [ɑ̃tɑ̃dr] [73] *vt* **-1.** [percevoir, écouter] to hear; **~ dire que** to hear (that); **~ parler de qqch** to hear of OU about sthg; **à l'~ ...** to hear him/her talk ...; **qu'est-ce qu'il ne faut pas entendre!** *fam* give me a break! **-2.** *sout* [comprendre] to understand; **laisser ~ que** to imply that; **ne rien y ~ à qqch** not to know the first thing about sthg. **-3.** *sout* [vouloir]: **~ faire qqch** to intend to do sthg. **-4.** [vouloir dire] to mean.
◆ **s'entendre** *vp* **-1.** [sympathiser]: **s'~ avec qqn** to get on with sb. **-2.** [s'accorder] to agree. **-3.** [savoir]: **s'~ en qqch/à faire qqch** to be very good at sthg/at doing sthg; **s'y ~** to know all about it. **-4.** [être compris] to be understood; **cela s'entend** that is understood. **-5.** [s'écouter]: **on ne s'entend plus** we can't hear ourselves think.

entendu, -e [ɑ̃tɑ̃dy] ◇ *pp* → **entendre.** ◇ *adj* **-1.** [compris] agreed, understood; **~!** right!, O.K.! **-2.** [complice] knowing.
◆ **bien entendu** *loc adv* of course.

entente [ɑ̃tɑ̃t] *nf* **-1.** [harmonie] understanding. **-2.** [accord] agreement. **-3.** [compréhension]: **à double ~** with a double meaning.

entériner [ɑ̃terine] [3] *vt* to ratify.

entérite [ɑ̃terit] *nf* enteritis (*U*).

enterrement [ɑ̃tɛrmɑ̃] *nm* burial.

enterrer [ɑ̃tɛre] [4] *vt litt & fig* to bury.
◆ **s'enterrer** *vp fig* to bury o.s. (away).

entêtant, -e [ɑ̃tɛtɑ̃, ɑ̃t] *adj* heady.

entêté, -e [ɑ̃tete] ◇ *adj* stubborn. ◇ *nm, f* stubborn person.

en-tête [ɑ̃tɛt] (*pl* **en-têtes**) *nm* heading.

entêtement [ɑ̃tɛtmɑ̃] *nm* stubbornness.

entêter [ɑ̃tete] [4]
◆ **s'entêter** *vp* to persist; **s'~ à faire qqch** to persist in doing sthg; **s'~ dans qqch** to persist in sthg.

enthousiasme [ɑ̃tuzjasm] *nm* enthusiasm.

enthousiasmer [ɑ̃tuzjasme] [3] *vt* to fill with enthusiasm.
◆ **s'enthousiasmer** *vp*: **s'~ de** OU **pour** to be enthusiastic about.

enthousiaste [ɑ̃tuzjast] ◇ *nmf* enthusiast. ◇ *adj* enthusiastic.

enticher [ɑ̃tiʃe] [3]
◆ **s'enticher** *vp*: **s'~ de qqn/qqch** to become obsessed with sb/sthg.

entier, -ière [ɑ̃tje, jɛr] *adj* whole, entire.
◆ **en entier** *loc adv* in its entirety.

entièrement [ɑ̃tjɛrmɑ̃] *adv* **-1.** [complètement] fully. **-2.** [pleinement] wholly, entirely.

entité [ɑ̃tite] *nf* entity.

entomologie [ɑ̃tɔmɔlɔʒi] *nf* entomology.

entonner [ɑ̃tɔne] [3] *vt* [chant] to strike up.

entonnoir [ɑ̃tɔnwar] *nm* **-1.** [instrument] funnel. **-2.** [cavité] crater.

entorse [ɑ̃tɔrs] *nf* MÉD sprain; **se faire une ~ à la cheville/au poignet** to sprain one's ankle/wrist; **faire une ~ à** *fig* [loi, règlement] to bend.

entortiller [ɑ̃tɔrtije] [3] *vt* **-1.** [entrelacer] to twist. **-2.** [envelopper]: **~ qqch autour de qqch** to wrap sthg round sthg. **-3.** *fam fig* [personne] to sweet-talk.

entourage [ɑ̃turaʒ] *nm* **-1.** [milieu] entourage. **-2.** [clôture] surround.

entouré, -e [ɑ̃ture] *adj* **-1.** [enclos] surrounded. **-2.** [soutenu] popular.

entourer [ɑ̃ture] [3] *vt* **-1.** [enclore, encercler]: **~ (de)** to surround (with). **-2.** *fig* [soutenir] to rally round.
◆ **s'entourer** *vp*: **s'~ de** to surround o.s. with.

entourloupette [ɑ̃turlupɛt] *nf fam* dirty trick.

entournure [ɑ̃turnyr] *nf*: **être gêné aux ~s** *fig* [financièrement] to feel the pinch; [être mal à l'aise] to feel awkward.

entracte [ɑ̃trakt] *nm* interval; *fig* interlude.

entraide [ɑ̃trɛd] *nf* mutual assistance.

entraider [ɑ̃trede] [4]
◆ **s'entraider** *vp* to help each other.

entrailles [ɑ̃traj] *nfpl* **-1.** [intestins] entrails. **-2.** *sout* [profondeurs] depths. **-3.** *fig* [siège des sentiments] soul (*sg*).

entrain [ɑ̃trɛ̃] *nm* drive.

entraînement [ɑ̃trɛnmɑ̃] *nm* **-1.** [mécanisme] drive. **-2.** [préparation] practice; SPORT training; **manquer d'~** to be out of training; *fig* to be out of practice.

entraîner [ɑ̃trene] [4] *vt* **-1.** TECHNOL to drive. **-2.** [tirer] to pull. **-3.** [susciter] to lead to. **-4.** SPORT to coach. **-5.** [emmener] to take along. **-6.** [séduire] to influence; **~ qqn à faire qqch** to talk sb into sthg.
◆ **s'entraîner** *vp* to practise; SPORT to train; **s'~ à faire qqch** to practise doing sthg.

entraîneur, -euse [ɑ̃trɛnœr, øz] *nm, f* trainer, coach.
◆ **entraîneuse** *nf* [dans un cabaret etc] hostess.

entrant, -e [ɑ̃trɑ̃, ɑ̃t] *adj* incoming.

entrapercevoir, entr'apercevoir [ɑ̃trapɛrsəvwar] [52] *vt* to glimpse.

entrave [ɑ̃trav] *nf* hobble; *fig* obstruction.

entraver [ɑ̃trave] [3] *vt* to hobble; *fig* to hinder.

entre [ãtr] *prép* **-1.** [gén] between; ~ **nous** between you and me, between ourselves. **-2.** [parmi] among; **l'un d'~ nous** ira one of us will go; **généralement ils restent ~ eux** they tend to keep themselves to themselves; **ils se battent entre ~** they're fighting among OU amongst themselves.
◆ **entre autres** *loc prép*: ~ **autres (choses)** among other things; ~ **autres (personnes)** among others.

entrebâillement [ãtrəbajmã] *nm* opening; **dans l'~ de la porte** through the half-open door.

entrebâiller [ãtrəbaje] [3] *vt* to open slightly.

entrechat [ãtrəʃa] *nm* **-1.** DANSE entrechat. **-2.** [saut] leap; **faire des ~s** to leap about.

entrechoquer [ãtrəʃɔke] [3] *vt* to bang together.
◆ **s'entrechoquer** *vp* to bang into each other.

entrecôte [ãtrəkot] *nf* entrecôte.

entrecoupé, -e [ãtrəkupe] *adj*: ~ **de** interspersed with.

entrecouper [ãtrəkupe] [3] *vt* to intersperse.

entrecroiser [ãtrəkrwaze] [3] *vt* to interlace.
◆ **s'entrecroiser** *vp* to intersect.

entre-déchirer [ãtrədeʃire] [3]
◆ **s'entre-déchirer** *vp* to tear each other to pieces.

entre-deux [ãtrədø] *nm inv* gap, space; **dans l'~** *fig* in the interim.

entre-deux-guerres [ãtrədøgɛr] *nm inv* inter-war years.

entrée [ãtre] *nf* **-1.** [arrivée, accès] entry, entrance; **«~ interdite»** "no admittance"; **«~ libre»** [dans musée] "admission free"; [dans boutique] "browsers welcome"; ~ **en scène** entrance. **-2.** [porte] entrance; ~ **des artistes** stage door; ~ **de service** tradesmen's entrance. **-3.** [vestibule] (entrance) hall. **-4.** [billet] ticket. **-5.** [plat] starter, first course. **-6.** [début] onset; ~ **en matière** introduction. **-7.** [rubrique] entry. **-8.** INFORM input, entry. **-9.** *loc*: **d'~ de jeu** from the outset; **avoir ses ~s chez qqn** to have sb's ear.

entrefaites [ãtrəfɛt] *nfpl*: **sur ces ~** just at that moment.

entrefilet [ãtrəfilɛ] *nm* paragraph.

entregent [ãtrəʒã] *nm*: **avoir de l'~** to know how to behave.

entrejambe, entre-jambes [ãtrəʒãb] *nm* crotch.

entrelacer [ãtrəlase] [16] *vt* to intertwine.

◆ **s'entrelacer** *vp* to intertwine.

entrelarder [ãtrəlarde] [3] *vt* **-1.** CULIN to lard. **-2.** *fam fig* [discours]: ~ **de** to lace with.

entremêler [ãtrəmele] [4] *vt* to mix; ~ **de** to mix with.
◆ **s'entremêler** *vp* to mingle.

entremets [ãtrəmɛ] *nm* dessert.

entremettais, entremettions *etc* → **entremettre**.

entremetteur, -euse [ãtrəmɛtœr, øz] *nm, f* mediator.
◆ **entremetteuse** *nf péj* go-between.

entremettre [ãtrəmɛtr] [84]
◆ **s'entremettre** *vp*: **s'~ (dans)** to mediate (in).

entremis, -e [ãtrəmi, iz] *pp* → **entremettre**.

entremise [ãtrəmiz] *nf* intervention; **par l'~ de** through.

entrepont [ãtrəpɔ̃] *nm* steerage.

entreposer [ãtrəpoze] [3] *vt* to store.

entrepôt [ãtrəpo] *nm* warehouse.

entreprenais, entreprenions *etc* → **entreprendre**.

entreprenant, -e [ãtrəprənã, ãt] *adj* enterprising; [auprès des femmes] forward.

entreprendre [ãtrəprãdr] [79] *vt* to undertake; [commencer] to start; ~ **de faire qqch** to undertake to do sthg; ~ **qqn sur** to engage sb in conversation about.

entrepreneur, -euse [ãtrəprənœr, øz] *nm, f* **-1.** [de services & CONSTR] contractor. **-2.** [patron] businessman (*f* businesswoman).

entreprenne, entreprennes *etc* → **entreprendre**.

entrepris, -e [ãtrəpri, iz] *pp* → **entreprendre**.

entreprise [ãtrəpriz] *nf* **-1.** [travail, initiative] enterprise; **libre ~** ÉCON free enterprise. **-2.** [société] company; ~ **nationalisée** nationalized industry.

entrer [ãtre] [3] ◇ *vi* **-1.** [pénétrer] to enter, to go/come in; ~ **dans** [gén] to enter; [pièce] to go/come into; [bain, voiture] to get into; *fig* [sujet] to go into; ~ **dans un mur** to crash into a wall; ~ **par** to go in OU enter by; **entrez!** come in! **-2.** [être admis, devenir membre]: ~ **dans** to go into, to be part of. **-3.** [être admis, devenir membre]: ~ **à** [club, parti] to join; ~ **dans** [les affaires, l'enseignement] to go into; [la police, l'armée] to join; ~ **en politique** to go into politics; ~ **à l'université** to enter university; ~ **à l'hôpital** to go into hospital. **-4.** [être au début]: ~ **en** to start, to begin.

◇ *vt* **-1.** [gén] to bring in; **faire ~ qqn** to show sb in; **faire ~ qqch** to bring sthg in. **-2.** INFORM to enter, to input.

entresol [ãtrəsɔl] *nm* mezzanine.

entre-temps [ãtrətã] *adv* meanwhile.

entretenir [ãtrətnir] [40] *vt* **-1.** [faire durer] to keep alive. **-2.** [cultiver] to maintain. **-3.** [soigner] to look after. **-4.** [personne, famille] to support. **-5.** [parler]: **~ qqn de qqch** to speak to sb about sthg.
◆ **s'entretenir** *vp* **-1.** [se parler] to talk. **-2.** [prendre soin de soi] to look after o.s.

entretenu, -e [ãtrətny] ◇ *pp* → **entretenir.**
◇ *adj* **-1.** [soigné] well-kept; **bien/mal ~** well-/badly kept. **-2.** [femme] kept (*avant n*).

entretien [ãtrətjɛ̃] *nm* **-1.** [de voiture, jardin] maintenance, upkeep. **-2.** [conversation] discussion; [colloque] debate; **~ d'embauche** job interview.

entretiendrai, entretiendras *etc* → **entretenir.**

entre-tuer [ãtrətɥe] [7]
◆ **s'entre-tuer** *vp* to kill each other.

entreverrai, entreverras *etc* → **entrevoir.**

entrevoir [ãtrəvwar] [62] *vt* **-1.** [distinguer] to make out. **-2.** [voir rapidement] to see briefly. **-3.** *fig* [deviner] to glimpse.
◆ **s'entrevoir** *vp* **-1.** [se voir] to see each other briefly. **-2.** [se profiler] to be visible.

entrevoyais, entrevoyions *etc* → **entrevoir.**

entrevu, -e [ãtrəvy] *pp* → **entrevoir.**

entrevue [ãtrəvy] *nf* meeting.

entrouvert, -e [ãtruvɛr, ɛrt] ◇ *pp* → **entrouvrir.** ◇ *adj* half-open.

entrouvrir [ãtruvrir] [34] *vt* to open partly.
◆ **s'entrouvrir** *vp* to open partly.

énumération [enymerasjɔ̃] *nf* enumeration.

énumérer [enymere] [18] *vt* to enumerate.

env. *abr de* environ.

envahir [ãvair] [32] *vt* **-1.** [gén & MIL] to invade. **-2.** *fig* [suj: sommeil, doute] to overcome. **-3.** *fig* [déranger] to intrude on.

envahissant, -e [ãvaisã, ãt] *adj* **-1.** [herbes] invasive. **-2.** [personne] intrusive.

envahissement [ãvaismã] *nm* invasion.

envahisseur [ãvaisœr] *nm* invader.

enveloppe [ãvlɔp] *nf* **-1.** [de lettre] envelope; **mettre sous ~** to put in an envelope; **~ à fenêtre** window envelope; **~ timbrée** stamped addressed envelope. **-2.** [d'emballage] covering. **-3.** [membrane] membrane; [de graine] husk. **-4.** *fig & littéraire* [apparence] exterior.
◆ **enveloppe budgétaire** *nf* budget.

envelopper [ãvlɔpe] [3] *vt* **-1.** [emballer] to wrap (up). **-2.** [suj: brouillard] to envelop. **-3.** [déguiser] to mask.
◆ **s'envelopper** *vp*: **s'~ dans** to wrap o.s. up in.

envenimer [ãvnime] [3] *vt* **-1.** [blessure] to infect. **-2.** *fig* [querelle] to poison.
◆ **s'envenimer** *vp* **-1.** [s'infecter] to become infected. **-2.** *fig* [se détériorer] to become poisoned.

envergure [ãvɛrgyr] *nf* **-1.** [largeur] span; [d'oiseau, d'avion] wingspan. **-2.** *fig* [qualité] calibre. **-3.** *fig* [importance] scope; **prendre de l'~** to expand.

enverrai, enverras *etc* → **envoyer.**

envers¹ [ãvɛr] *prép* towards; **~ et contre tous** in spite of all opposition.

envers² [ãvɛr] *nm* **-1.** [de tissu] wrong side; [de feuillet etc] back; [de médaille] reverse. **-2.** [face cachée] other side; **l'~ du décor** *fig* behind the scenes.
◆ **à l'envers** *loc adv* [vêtement] inside out; [portrait, feuille] upside down; *fig* the wrong way.

envi [ãvi]
◆ **à l'envi** *loc adv littéraire* trying to outdo each other.

enviable [ãvjabl] *adj* enviable.

envie [ãvi] *nf* **-1.** [désir] desire; **avoir ~ de qqch/de faire qqch** to feel like sthg/like doing sthg, to want sthg/to do sthg; **mourir d'~ de faire qqch** to be dying to do sthg. **-2.** [convoitise] envy; **ce tailleur me fait ~** I covet that suit.

envier [ãvje] [9] *vt* to envy; **n'avoir rien à ~ à qqn/à qqch** to have no reason to envy sb/sthg.

envieux, -ieuse [ãvjø, jøz] ◇ *adj* envious. ◇ *nm, f* envious person; **faire des ~** to make other people envious.

environ [ãvirɔ̃] *adv* [à peu près] about.

environnant, -e [ãvironã, ãt] *adj* surrounding.

environnement [ãvironmã] *nm* environment.

environner [ãvirone] [3] *vt* to surround.

environs [ãvirɔ̃] *nmpl* (surrounding) area (*sg*); **dans les ~ de** in the vicinity of; **aux ~ de** [lieu] near; [époque] round about, around.

envisager [ãvizaʒe] [17] *vt* to consider; **~ de faire qqch** to be considering doing sthg.

envoi [ãvwa] *nm* **-1.** [action] sending, dispatch; **~ contre remboursement** cash on delivery. **-2.** [colis] parcel.

envoie, envoies *etc* → **envoyer.**

envol [ãvɔl] *nm* takeoff.

envolée [ãvɔle] *nf* **-1.** [d'oiseaux & *fig*] flight. **-2.** [augmentation]: **l'~ du dollar** the rapid rise in the value of the dollar.

envoler [ãvɔle] [3]
◆ **s'envoler** *vp* **-1.** [oiseau] to fly away. **-2.** [avion] to take off. **-3.** [disparaître] to disappear into thin air. **-4.** [se disperser] to blow away.

envoûtement [ãvutmã] *nm* enchantment.

envoûter [ãvute] [3] *vt* to bewitch.

envoyé, -e [ãvwaje] ◇ *adj*: **bien ~** well-aimed. ◇ *nm, f* envoy; **~ spécial** special correspondent.

envoyer [ãvwaje] [30] *vt* to send; **~ qqch à qqn** [expédier] to send sb sthg, to send sthg to sb; [jeter] to throw sb sthg, to throw sthg to sb; **~ qqn faire qqch** to send sb to do sthg; **~ chercher qqn/qqch** to send for sb/sthg; **~ promener qqn** *fam fig* to send sb packing.

envoyeur, -euse [ãvwajœr, øz] *nm, f* sender.

enzyme [ãzym] *nm ou nf* enzyme.

éolien, -ienne [eɔljɛ̃, jɛn] *adj* wind (*avant n*).
◆ **éolienne** *nf* windmill (*for generating power*), wind turbine.

épagneul [epaɲœl] *nm* spaniel.

épais, épaisse [epɛ, ɛs] *adj* **-1.** [large, dense] thick. **-2.** [trapu] thickset. **-3.** [grossier] crude.

épaisseur [epɛsœr] *nf* **-1.** [largeur, densité] thickness. **-2.** *fig* [consistance] depth.

épaissir [epesir] [32] *vt & vi* to thicken.
◆ **s'épaissir** *vp* **-1.** [liquide] to thicken. **-2.** *fig* [mystère] to deepen.

épanchement [epãʃmã] *nm* **-1.** [effusion] outpouring. **-2.** MED effusion; **~ de synovie** water on the knee.

épancher [epãʃe] [3] *vt* to pour out.
◆ **s'épancher** *vp* [se confier] to pour one's heart out.

épanoui, -e [epanwi] *adj* **-1.** [fleur] in full bloom. **-2.** [expression] radiant. **-3.** [corps] fully formed; **aux formes ~s** well-rounded.

épanouir [epanwir] [32] *vt* [personne] to make happy.
◆ **s'épanouir** *vp* **-1.** [fleur] to open. **-2.** [visage] to light up. **-3.** [corps] to fill out. **-4.** [personnalité] to blossom.

épanouissement [epanwismã] *nm* **-1.** [de fleur] blooming, opening. **-2.** [de visage] brightening. **-3.** [de corps] filling out. **-4.** [de personnalité] flowering.

épargnant, -e [eparɲã, ãt] ◇ *adj* thrifty. ◇ *nm, f* saver; **les petits ~s** small savers.

épargne [eparɲ] *nf* **-1.** [action, vertu] saving. **-2.** [somme] savings (*pl*); **~ logement** savings account (*to buy property*).

épargner [eparɲe] [3] *vt* **-1.** [gén] to spare; **~ qqch à qqn** to spare sb sthg. **-2.** [économiser] to save.
◆ **s'épargner** *vp* to save OU spare o.s.

éparpiller [eparpije] [3] *vt* **-1.** [choses, personnes] to scatter. **-2.** *fig* [forces] to dissipate.
◆ **s'éparpiller** *vp* **-1.** [se disperser] to scatter. **-2.** *fig* [perdre son temps] to lack focus.

épars, -e [epar, ars] *adj sout* [objets] scattered; [végétation, cheveux] sparse.

épatant, -e [epatã, ãt] *adj fam* great.

épate [epat] *nf fam*: **faire de l'~** to show off.

épaté, -e [epate] *adj* **-1.** [nez] flat. **-2.** *fam* [étonné] amazed.

épater [epate] [3] *vt fam* [étonner] to amaze.

épaule [epol] *nf* shoulder; **hausser les ~s** to shrug (one's shoulders); **~ d'agneau** CULIN shoulder of lamb.

épaulement [epolmã] *nm* **-1.** [mur] retaining wall. **-2.** GÉOL escarpment.

épauler [epole] [3] ◇ *vi* to raise one's rifle. ◇ *vt* to support, to back up.

épaulette [epolɛt] *nf* **-1.** MIL epaulet. **-2.** [rembourrage] shoulder pad.

épave [epav] *nf* wreck.

épée [epe] *nf* sword; **~ de Damoclès** sword of Damocles; **coup d'~ dans l'eau** *fig* wasted effort.

épeler [eple] [24] *vt* to spell.

épépiner [epepine] [3] *vt* to seed.

éperdu, -e [eperdy] *adj* [sentiment] passionate; **~ de** [personne] overcome with.

éperdument [eperdymã] *adv* **-1.** [travailler] frantically. **-2.** [aimer] passionately.

éperlan [eperlã] *nm* smelt.

éperon [eprɔ̃] *nm* [de cavalier, de montagne] spur; [de navire] ram; **~ rocheux** rocky outcrop.

éperonner [eprɔne] [3] *vt* to spur on.

épervier [epɛrvje] *nm* sparrowhawk.

éphèbe [efɛb] *nm* [beau jeune homme] Adonis.

éphémère [efemɛr] ◇ *adj* [bref] ephemeral, fleeting. ◇ *nm* ZOOL mayfly.

éphéméride [efemerid] *nf* tear-off calendar.

épi [epi] *nm* **-1.** [de céréale] ear; **~ de maïs** CULIN corn on the cob. **-2.** [cheveux] tuft; **~ rebelle** unruly tuft of hair.

épice [epis] *nf* spice.

épicé, -e [epise] *adj* spicy.

épicéa [episea] *nm* spruce.

épicentre [episɑ̃tr] *nm* epicentre.

épicer [epise] [16] *vt* **-1.** [plat] to spice. **-2.** [récit] to spice up.

épicerie [episri] *nf* **-1.** [magasin] grocer's (shop). **-2.** [denrées] groceries (*pl*); ~ **fine** delicatessen.

épicier, -ière [episje, jɛr] *nm, f* grocer.

épicurien, -ienne [epikyrjɛ̃, jɛn] ◇ *adj* epicurean. ◇ *nm, f* epicure.

épidémie [epidemi] *nf* epidemic.

épidémique [epidemik] *adj* contagious.

épiderme [epidɛrm] *nm* epidermis.

épidermique [epidɛrmik] *adj* [de l'épiderme] skin (*avant n*); **réaction** ~ *fig* kneejerk reaction.

épier [epje] [9] *vt* **-1.** [espionner] to spy on. **-2.** [observer] to look for.

épieu [epjø] *nm* **-1.** [de guerre] pike. **-2.** [de chasse] spear.

épigramme [epigram] *nf* epigram.

épilation [epilasjɔ̃] *nf* hair removal; ~ **à la cire** waxing.

épilepsie [epilɛpsi] *nf* epilepsy.

épileptique [epilɛptik] *nmf & adj* epileptic.

épiler [epile] [3] *vt* [jambes] to remove hair from; [sourcils] to pluck.
◆ **s'épiler** *vp*: **s'**~ **les jambes** to remove the hair from one's legs; **s'**~ **les sourcils** to pluck one's eyebrows.

épilogue [epilɔg] *nm* **-1.** [de roman] epilogue. **-2.** [d'affaire] outcome.

épiloguer [epilɔge] [3] *vi* to hold forth.

épinards [epinar] *nmpl* spinach (*U*); ~**s en branches** leaf spinach.

épine [epin] *nf* **-1.** [arbrisseau] thorn bush. **-2.** [piquant - de rosier] **thorn**; [- de hérisson] spine; **tirer une** ~ **du pied à qqn** *fig* to get sb out of a tight corner.
◆ **épine dorsale** *nf* backbone, spine.

épineux, -euse [epinø, øz] *adj* thorny.

épingle [epɛ̃gl] *nf* [instrument] pin; ~ **à cheveux** hairpin; ~ **à nourrice** OU **de sûreté** safety pin; **monter qqch en** ~ *fig* to blow sthg up; **tirer son** ~ **du jeu** *fig* to extricate o.s.; **tiré à quatre** ~**s** *fig* impeccably turned out.

épingler [epɛ̃gle] [3] *vt* **-1.** [fixer] to pin (up). **-2.** *fam fig* [arrêter] to nick *Br*.

épinière [epinjɛr] → **moelle**.

Épiphanie [epifani] *nf* Epiphany.

épique [epik] *adj* epic.

épiscopal, -e, -aux [episkɔpal, o] *adj* episcopal.

épiscopat [episkɔpa] *nm* episcopate.

épisiotomie [epizjɔtɔmi] *nf* episiotomy.

épisode [epizɔd] *nm* episode.

épisodique [epizɔdik] *adj* **-1.** [occasionnel] occasional. **-2.** [secondaire] minor.

épistémologie [epistemɔlɔʒi] *nf* epistemology.

épistolaire [epistɔlɛr] *adj* **-1.** [échange] of letters; **être en relations** ~**s avec qqn** to be in (regular) correspondence with sb. **-2.** [roman] epistolary.

épitaphe [epitaf] *nf* epitaph.

épithète [epitɛt] ◇ *nf* **-1.** GRAM attribute. **-2.** [qualificatif] term. ◇ *adj* attributive.

épître [epitr] *nf* epistle.

éploré, -e [eplɔre] *adj* [personne] in tears; [visage, air] tearful.

épluchage [eplyʃaʒ] *nm* **-1.** [de légumes] peeling. **-2.** [de textes] dissection; [de comptes] scrutiny.

épluche-légume [eplyʃlegym] *nm inv* potato peeler.

éplucher [eplyʃe] [3] *vt* **-1.** [légumes] to peel. **-2.** [textes] to dissect; [comptes] to scrutinize.

épluchure [eplyʃyr] *nf* peelings (*pl*).

éponge [epɔ̃ʒ] *nf* sponge; **jeter l'**~ *fig* to throw in the towel; **passer l'**~ *fig* to wipe the slate clean.

éponger [epɔ̃ʒe] [17] *vt* **-1.** [liquide, déficit] to mop up. **-2.** [visage] to mop, to wipe.
◆ **s'éponger** *vp* [personne] to mop o.s.; **s'**~ **le front** to mop one's brow.

épopée [epɔpe] *nf* epic.

époque [epɔk] *nf* **-1.** [de l'année] time. **-2.** [de l'histoire] period; **à l'**~ at the time; **d'**~ period; **la Belle Époque** ≃ the Edwardian era. **-3.** GÉOL period, age.

épouiller [epuje] [3] *vt* to delouse.

époumoner [epumɔne] [3]
◆ **s'époumoner** *vp* to shout o.s. hoarse.

épouse → **époux**.

épouser [epuze] [3] *vt* **-1.** [personne] to marry. **-2.** [forme] to hug. **-3.** *fig* [idée, principe] to espouse.

épousseter [epuste] [27] *vt* to dust.

époustouflant, -e [epustuflɑ̃, ɑ̃t] *adj fam* amazing.

époustoufler [epustufle] [3] *vt fam* to flabbergast, to amaze.

épouvantable [epuvɑ̃tabl] *adj* dreadful.

épouvantail [epuvɑ̃taj] *nm* [à moineaux] scarecrow; *fig* bogeyman.

épouvante [epuvɑ̃t] *nf* terror, horror; **film d'~** horror film.

épouvanter [epuvɑ̃te] [3] *vt* to terrify.

époux, épouse [epu, epuz] *nm, f* spouse; **prendre pour ~** to marry.

éprendre [eprɑ̃dr] [79]
◆ **s'éprendre** *vp sout*: **s'~ de** to fall in love with.

épreuve [eprœv] *nf* **-1.** [essai, examen] test; **à l'~ du feu** fireproof; **à l'~ des balles** bullet-proof; **mettre à l'~** to put to the test; **à toute ~** unfailing; **~ écrite/orale** written/oral test; **~ de force** *fig* trial of strength. **-2.** [malheur] ordeal. **-3.** SPORT event. **-4.** TYPO proof. **-5.** PHOT print.

épris, -e [epri, iz] ◇ *pp* → **éprendre**. ◇ *adj sout*: **~ de** in love with.

éprouvant, -e [epruvɑ̃, ɑ̃t] *adj* testing, trying.

éprouvé, -e [epruve] *adj* **-1.** [méthode] tried and tested. **-2.** [personne] sorely tried.

éprouver [epruve] [3] *vt* **-1.** [tester] to test. **-2.** [ressentir] to feel. **-3.** [faire souffrir] to distress; **être éprouvé par** to be afflicted by. **-4.** [difficultés, problèmes] to experience.

éprouvette [epruvɛt] *nf* **-1.** [tube à essai] test tube. **-2.** [échantillon] sample.

EPS (*abr de* **éducation physique et sportive**) *nf* PE.

épuisant, -e [epɥizɑ̃, ɑ̃t] *adj* exhausting.

épuisé, -e [epɥize] *adj* **-1.** [personne, corps] exhausted; **~ de fatigue** exhausted. **-2.** [marchandise] sold out, out of stock; [livre] out of print.

épuisement [epɥizmɑ̃] *nm* exhaustion; **jusqu'à ~ des stocks** while stocks last.

épuiser [epɥize] [3] *vt* to exhaust.

épuisette [epɥizɛt] *nf* landing net.

épuration [epyrasjɔ̃] *nf* **-1.** [des eaux] purification. **-2.** POLIT purge.

épure [epyr] *nf* technical drawing.

épurer [epyre] [3] *vt* **-1.** [eau, huile] to purify. **-2.** POLIT to purge. **-3.** *fig* [langage] to refine.

équarrir [ekarir] [32] *vt* **-1.** [animal] to cut up. **-2.** [poutre] to square. **-3.** *fig* [personne]: **mal équarri** rough, crude.

équateur [ekwatœr] *nm* equator.

Équateur [ekwatœr] *nm*: **l'~** Ecuador.

équation [ekwasjɔ̃] *nf* equation; **~ du premier/second degré** simple/quadratic equation.

équatorial, -e, -iaux [ekwatɔrjal, jo] *adj* equatorial.

équatorien, -ienne [ekwatɔrjɛ̃, jɛn] *adj* Ecuadoran, Ecuadorian.

◆ **Équatorien, -ienne** *nm, f* Ecuadoran, Ecuadorian.

équerre [ekɛr] *nf* [instrument] set square; [- en T] T-square; **en ~** at right angles.

équestre [ekɛstr] *adj* equestrian.

équeuter [ekøte] [3] *vt* to remove the stalk OU stalks from.

équidistance [ekɥidistɑ̃s] *nf* equidistance; **à ~ de ... et de ...** equidistant between ... and ....

équidistant, -e [ekɥidistɑ̃, ɑ̃t] *adj* equidistant.

équilatéral, -e, -aux [ekɥilateral, o] *adj* equilateral.

équilibre [ekilibr] *nm* **-1.** [gén] balance; **en ~ balanced; perdre l'~** to lose one's balance. **-2.** [psychique] stability.

équilibré, -e [ekilibre] *adj* **-1.** [personne] well-balanced. **-2.** [vie] stable. **-3.** [proportions] well-proportioned.

équilibrer [ekilibre] [3] *vt* to balance.

◆ **s'équilibrer** *vp* to balance each other out.

équilibriste [ekilibrist] *nmf* tightrope walker.

équipage [ekipaʒ] *nm* crew.

équipe [ekip] *nf* team; **d'~** team (*avant n*); **faire ~ avec** to team up with; **travailler en ~** to work together OU as a team; **~ de secours** rescue team.

équipée [ekipe] *nf* **-1.** [aventure] venture. **-2.** [promenade] outing.

équipement [ekipmɑ̃] *nm* **-1.** [matériel] equipment. **-2.** [aménagement] facilities (*pl*); **plan d'~ national** national development plan; **~s sportifs/scolaires** sports/educational facilities.

équiper [ekipe] [3] *vt* **-1.** [navire, armée] to equip. **-2.** [personne, local] to equip, to fit out; **~ qqn/qqch de** to equip sb/sthg with, to fit sb/sthg out with.

◆ **s'équiper** *vp*: **s'~ de** to equip o.s. (with).

équipier, -ière [ekipje, jɛr] *nm, f* team member.

équitable [ekitabl] *adj* fair.

équitablement [ekitabləmɑ̃] *adv* fairly.

équitation [ekitasjɔ̃] *nf* riding, horse-riding; **faire de l'~** to go riding OU horse-riding, to ride.

équité [ekite] *nf* fairness.

équivalent, -e [ekivalɑ̃, ɑ̃t] *adj* equivalent.

◆ **équivalent** *nm* equivalent.

équivaloir [ekivalwar] [60] *vi*: **~ à** to be equivalent to.

équivalu [ekivaly] *pp inv* → **équivaloir**.

équivaut → équivaloir.

équivoque [ekivɔk] ◇ *adj* **-1.** [ambigu] ambiguous. **-2.** [mystérieux] dubious. ◇ *nf* ambiguity; **sans** ~ unequivocal (*adj*), unequivocally (*adv*).

érable [erabl] *nm* maple.

éradication [eradikasjɔ̃] *nf* **-1.** [suppression] eradication. **-2.** [ablation] removal.

éradiquer [eradike] [3] *vt* to eradicate.

érafler [erafle] [3] *vt* **-1.** [peau] to scratch. **-2.** [mur, voiture] to scrape.
◆ **s'érafler** *vp* to scratch o.s.

éraflure [eraflyr] *nf* **-1.** [de peau] scratch. **-2.** [de mur, voiture] scrape.

éraillé, -e [eraje] *adj* [voix] hoarse.

ère [ɛr] *nf* era; **l'an 813 de notre** ~ the year 813 A.D.

érection [erɛksjɔ̃] *nf* erection; **en** ~ erect.

éreintant, -e [erɛ̃tɑ̃, ɑ̃t] *adj* exhausting.

éreinter [erɛ̃te] [3] *vt* **-1.** [fatiguer] to exhaust. **-2.** [critiquer] to pull to pieces.

érémiste [eremist] *nmf fam person entitled to RMI benefit.*

ergonomique [ɛrgɔnɔmik] *adj* ergonomic.

ergot [ɛrgo] *nm* **-1.** [de coq] spur; **se dresser sur ses** ~**s** to get one's hackles up. **-2.** [de mammifère] dewclaw. **-3.** [de blé] ergot.

ergoter [ɛrgɔte] [3] *vi* to quibble.

ergothérapie [ɛrgɔterapi] *nf* occupational therapy.

ériger [eriʒe] [17] *vt* **-1.** [monument] to erect. **-2.** [tribunal] to set up. **-3.** *fig* [transformer]: ~ **qqn en** to set sb up as.
◆ **s'ériger** *vp*: **s'** ~ **en** to set o.s. up as.

ermite [ɛrmit] *nm* hermit.

éroder [erɔde] [3] *vt* to erode.

érogène [erɔʒɛn] *adj* erogenous.

érosion [erozjɔ̃] *nf* erosion.

érotique [erɔtik] *adj* erotic.

érotisme [erɔtism] *nm* eroticism.

errance [erɑ̃s] *nf* wandering.

errant, -e [erɑ̃, ɑ̃t] *adj* [chien, chat] stray (*avant n*).

erratum [eratɔm] `(pl errata [erata]) nm` erratum.

errements [ermɑ̃] *nmpl* bad habits.

errer [ere] [4] *vi* to wander.

erreur [erœr] *nf* mistake; **par** ~ by mistake; **sauf** ~ **de ma part** unless I'm mistaken; **faire** ~ to be mistaken; **faire une** ~ to make a mistake; ~ **judiciaire** miscarriage of justice.

erroné, -e [erɔne] *adj sout* wrong.

ersatz [ɛrzats] *nm inv* ersatz.

éructer [erykte] [3] *vi* to belch.

érudit, -e [erydi, it] ◇ *adj* erudite, learned. ◇ *nm, f* learned person.

érudition [erydisjɔ̃] *nf* learning, erudition.

éruption [erypsjɔ̃] *nf* **-1.** MÉD rash. **-2.** [de volcan] eruption.

es → être.

ès [ɛs] *prép* of (*in certain titles*); **docteur** ~ **lettres** ≃ PhD, doctor of philosophy.

E/S (*abr de* **entrée/sortie**) I/O.

ESA, Esa [ɛza] (*abr de* **European Space Agency**) *nf* ESA.

esbroufe [ɛzbruf] *nf fam* showing-off; **faire de l'** ~ to show off.

escabeau, -x [ɛskabo] *nm* **-1.** [échelle] stepladder. **-2.** *vieilli* [tabouret] stool.

escadre [ɛskadr] *nf* **-1.** [navires] fleet. **-2.** [avions] wing.

escadrille [ɛskadrij] *nf* **-1.** [navires] flotilla. **-2.** [avions] flight.

escadron [ɛskadrɔ̃] *nm* squadron.

escalade [ɛskalad] *nf* **-1.** [de montagne, grille] climbing. **-2.** [des prix, de violence] escalation.

escalader [ɛskalade] [3] *vt* to climb.

escale [ɛskal] *nf* **-1.** [lieu - pour navire] port of call; [- pour avion] stopover; **faire** ~ **à** [navire] to put in at, to call at; [avion] to stop over at. **-2.** [arrêt - de navire] call; [- d'avion] stopover, stop; ~ **technique** refuelling stop.

escalier [ɛskalje] *nm* stairs (*pl*); **descendre/monter l'** ~ to go downstairs/upstairs; ~ **en colimaçon** spiral staircase; ~ **de secours** fire escape; ~ **de service** backstairs; ~ **roulant** OU **mécanique** escalator.

escalope [ɛskalɔp] *nf* escalope; ~ **panée** escalope in breadcrumbs.

escamotable [ɛskamɔtabl] *adj* **-1.** [train d'atterrissage] retractable; [antenne] telescopic. **-2.** [table] folding.

escamoter [ɛskamɔte] [3] *vt* **-1.** [faire disparaître] to make disappear. **-2.** [voler] to lift. **-3.** [rentrer] to retract. **-4.** [phrase, mot] to swallow. **-5.** [éluder - question] to evade; [- objection] to get round.

escampette [ɛskɑ̃pɛt] → poudre.

escapade [ɛskapad] *nf* **-1.** [voyage] outing. **-2.** [fugue] escapade.

escarbille [ɛskarbij] *nf* cinder.

escargot [ɛskargo] *nm* snail; **comme un** ~ [très lentement] at a snail's pace.

escarmouche [ɛskarmuʃ] *nf* skirmish.

escarpé, -e [ɛskarpe] *adj* steep.

escarpement [ɛskarpəmɑ̃] *nm* **-1.** [de pente] steep slope. **-2.** GÉOGR escarpment.

escarpin [ɛskarpɛ̃] *nm* court shoe *Br*.

escarre [ɛskar] *nf* bedsore, pressure sore.

Escaut [ɛsko] *nm*: l'~ the River Scheldt.

escient [ɛsjɑ̃] *nm*: **à bon** ~ advisedly; **à mauvais** ~ ill-advisedly.

esclaffer [ɛsklafe] [3]
◆ **s'esclaffer** *vp* to burst out laughing.

esclandre [ɛsklɑ̃dr] *nm sout* scene; **faire un** ~ to make a scene.

esclavage [ɛsklavaʒ] *nm* slavery.

esclavagisme [ɛsklavaʒism] *nm* slavery.

esclave [ɛsklav] ◇ *nmf* slave. ◇ *adj*: **être** ~ **de** to be a slave to.

escogriffe [ɛskɔgrif] *nm fam*: **un grand** ~ a beanpole.

escompte [ɛskɔ̃t] *nm* discount.

escompter [ɛskɔ̃te] [3] *vt* **-1.** [prévoir] to count on. **-2.** FIN to discount.

escorte [ɛskɔrt] *nf* escort.

escorter [ɛskɔrte] [3] *vt* to escort.

escouade [ɛskwad] *nf* squad.

escrime [ɛskrim] *nf* fencing.

escrimer [ɛskrime] [3]
◆ **s'escrimer** *vp*: **s'**~ **à faire qqch** to work (away) at doing sthg.

escroc [ɛskro] *nm* swindler.

escroquer [ɛskrɔke] [3] *vt* to swindle; ~ **qqch à qqn** to swindle sb out of sthg.

escroquerie [ɛskrɔkri] *nf* swindle, swindling (*U*).

eskimo, Eskimo → esquimau.

ésotérique [ezɔterik] *adj* esoteric.

espace [ɛspas] *nm* space; ~ **publicitaire** advertising space; ~ **vert** green space, green area; ~ **vital** living space.

espacement [ɛspasmɑ̃] *nm* **-1.** [spatial] spacing. **-2.** [temporel] spacing out.

espacer [ɛspase] [16] *vt* **-1.** [dans l'espace] to space out. **-2.** [dans le temps - visites] to space out; [- paiements] to spread out.
◆ **s'espacer** *vp* to become less frequent.

espadon [ɛspadɔ̃] *nm* **-1.** [poisson] swordfish. **-2.** [épée] two-handed sword.

espadrille [ɛspadrij] *nf* espadrille.

Espagne [ɛspaɲ] *nf*: l'~ Spain.

espagnol, -e [ɛspaɲɔl] *adj* Spanish.
◆ **espagnol** *nm* [langue] Spanish.
◆ **Espagnol, -e** *nm, f* Spaniard; **les Espagnols** the Spanish.

espagnolette [ɛspaɲɔlɛt] *nf* latch (*for window or shutter*).

espalier [ɛspalje] *nm* **-1.** [arbre] espalier. **-2.** SPORT wall bars (*pl*).

espèce [ɛspɛs] *nf* **-1.** BIOL, BOT & ZOOL species. **-2.** [sorte] kind, sort; ~ **d'idiot!** you

stupid fool! **-3.** [circonstance]: **en l'**~ *littéraire* in the case in point.
◆ **espèces** *nfpl* cash; **payer en** ~**s** to pay (in) cash.

espérance [ɛsperɑ̃s] *nf* hope; ~ **de vie** life expectancy.

espéranto [ɛsperɑ̃to] *nm* Esperanto.

espérer [ɛspere] [18] ◇ *vt* to hope for; ~ **que** to hope (that); ~ **faire qqch** to hope to do sthg. ◇ *vi* to hope; ~ **en qqn/qqch** to trust in sb/sthg.

espiègle [ɛspjɛgl] ◇ *nmf* little monkey. ◇ *adj* mischievous.

espièglerie [ɛspjɛgləri] *nf* **-1.** [malice] mischievousness. **-2.** [tour, farce] prank.

espion, -ionne [ɛspjɔ̃, jɔn] *nm, f* spy.

espionnage [ɛspjɔnaʒ] *nm* spying; ~ **industriel** industrial espionage.

espionner [ɛspjɔne] [3] *vt* to spy on.

esplanade [ɛsplanad] *nf* esplanade.

espoir [ɛspwar] *nm* hope; **avoir bon** ~ **que** to be confident that; **nourrir l'**~ **de faire qqch** to live in hope of doing sthg; **sans** ~ hopeless; **sans** ~ **de** without hope of.

esprit [ɛspri] *nm* **-1.** [entendement, personne, pensée] mind; **avoir l'**~ **mal tourné** to have a dirty OU filthy mind; **être large d'**~ to be broad-minded; **ouvrir l'**~ **de qqn** to open sb's eyes; **reprendre ses** ~**s** to recover; **venir à l'**~ **de qqn** to cross sb's mind. **-2.** [attitude] spirit; ~ **de caste** class consciousness; ~ **de compétition** competitive spirit; ~ **de contradiction** argumentative nature, contrariness; ~ **critique** critical acumen; ~ **d'équipe** team spirit; ~ **maison** company spirit. **-3.** [humour] wit; **faire de l'**~ to try to be funny. **-4.** [fantôme] spirit, ghost.

esquif [ɛskif] *nm littéraire* skiff.

esquimau, -aude, -aux, eskimo [ɛskimo, od] *adj* Eskimo.
◆ **esquimau, eskimo** *nm* [langue] Eskimo.
◆ **Esquimau, -aude** *nm, f*, **Eskimo** *nmf* Eskimo.

Esquimau® [ɛskimo] *nm inv*: ~ **(glacé)** *ice-cream on a stick*.

esquinter [ɛskɛ̃te] [3] *vt fam* **-1.** [abîmer] to ruin. **-2.** [critiquer] to slate *Br*, to pan.
◆ **s'esquinter** *vp*: **s'**~ **à faire qqch** to kill o.s. doing sthg.

esquisse [ɛskis] *nf* [croquis] sketch; *fig* [de projet] outline; *fig* [de geste, sourire] trace.

esquisser [ɛskise] [3] *vt* to sketch; ~ **un sourire** *fig* to give a half-smile.
◆ **s'esquisser** *vp* to take shape.

esquiver [ɛskive] [3] *vt* to dodge.
◆ **s'esquiver** *vp* to slip away.

essai [esɛ] *nm* **-1.** [vérification] test, testing; à l'~ on trial. **-2.** [tentative] attempt. **-3.** [étude]: ~ (**sur**) essay (on). **-4.** RUGBY try.

essaie, essaies *etc* → essayer.

essaim [esɛ̃] *nm litt* & *fig* swarm.

essaimer [eseme] [4] *vi* to swarm; *fig* to spread.

essayage [esɛjaʒ] *nm* fitting.

essayer [eseje] [11] *vt* to try; ~ **de faire qqch** to try to do sthg; **essaie un peu, pour voir!** go on then, why don't you try◊
◆ **s'essayer** *vp*: **s'~ à qqch/à faire qqch** to try one's hand at sthg/at doing sthg.

ESSEC, Essec [esɛk] (*abr de* École supérieure des sciences économiques et commerciales) *nf grande école for management and business studies.*

essence [esɑ̃s] *nf* **-1.** [fondement, de plante] essence; **par** ~ **sout** in essence. **-2.** [carburant] petrol *Br*, gas *Am*; **prendre de l'**~ to get some petrol. **-3.** [d'arbre] species.

essentiel, -ielle [esɑ̃sjɛl] *adj* **-1.** [indispensable] essential. **-2.** [fondamental] basic.
◆ **essentiel** *nm* **-1.** [point]: **l'**~ [le principal] the essential OU main thing; [objets] the essentials (*pl*); **l'**~ **est que** (+ *subjonctif*) the essential OU main thing is that. **-2.** [quantité]: **l'**~ **de** the main OU greater part of.

essentiellement [esɑ̃sjɛlmɑ̃] *adv* **-1.** [avant tout] above all. **-2.** [par essence] essentially.

esseulé, -e [esœle] *adj littéraire* forsaken.

essieu [esjø] *nm* axle.

essor [esɔr] *nm* flight, expansion, boom; **en plein** ~ booming; **prendre son** ~ to take flight; *fig* to take off.

essorage [esɔraʒ] *nm* [manuel, à rouleaux] wringing (out); [à la machine] spin-drying.

essorer [esɔre] [3] *vt* [à la main, à rouleaux] to wring out; [à la machine] to spin-dry; [salade] to spin, to dry.

essoreuse [esɔrøz] *nf* [à rouleaux] mangle; [électrique] spin-dryer; [à salade] salad spinner.

essouffler [esufle] [3] *vt* to make breathless.
◆ **s'essouffler** *vp* to be breathless OU out of breath; *fig* to run out of steam.

essuie, essuies *etc* → essuyer.

essuie-glace [esɥiglas] (*pl* essuie-glaces) *nm* windscreen wiper *Br*, windshield wiper *Am*.

essuie-mains [esɥimɛ̃] *nm inv* hand towel.

essuie-tout [esɥitu] *nm inv* kitchen roll.

essuyer [esɥije] [14] *vt* **-1.** [sécher] to dry. **-2.** [nettoyer] to dust. **-3.** *fig* [subir] to suffer.
◆ **s'essuyer** *vp* to dry o.s.

est¹ [ɛst] ◊ *nm* east; **un vent d'**~ an easterly wind; **le vent d'**~ the east wind; **à l'**~ in the east; **à l'**~ (**de**) to the east (of). ◊ *adj inv* east; [province, région] eastern.

est² [ɛ] → être.

establishment [ɛstabliʃmɛnt] *nm*: **l'**~ the Establishment.

estafette [ɛstafɛt] *nf* dispatch-rider; MIL liaison officer.

estafilade [ɛstafilad] *nf* slash, gash.

est-allemand, -e [ɛstalmɑ̃, ɑ̃d] *adj* East German.

estaminet [ɛstaminɛ] *nm* ≃ inn.

estampe [ɛstɑ̃p] *nf* print.

estamper [ɛstɑ̃pe] [3] *vt* **-1.** [monnaie] to mint. **-2.** *fam* [escroquer] to fleece.

estampille [ɛstɑ̃pij] *nf* stamp.

est-ce que [ɛskə] *adv interrogatif*: **est-ce-qu'il fait beau**◊ is the weather good◊; ~ **vous aimez l'accordéon**◊ do you like the accordion◊; **où** ~ **tu es**◊ where are you◊

esthète [ɛstɛt] ◊ *nmf* aesthete. ◊ *adj* aesthetic.

esthéticien, -ienne [ɛstetisjɛ̃, jɛn] *nm, f* **-1.** [spécialiste] beautician. **-2.** PHILO aesthetician.

esthétique [ɛstetik] ◊ *nf*: **l'**~ aesthetics (U). ◊ *adj* **-1.** [relatif à la beauté] aesthetic. **-2.** [harmonieux] attractive.

estimable [ɛstimabl] *adj* **-1.** [digne d'estime] honorable, respected. **-2.** [évaluable]: **facilement/difficilement** ~ easy/difficult to estimate.

estimatif, -ive [ɛstimatif, iv] *adj* estimated.

estimation [ɛstimasjɔ̃] *nf* estimate, estimation.

estime [ɛstim] *nf* respect, esteem; **avoir de l'**~ **pour qqn** to respect sb.

estimer [ɛstime] [3] *vt* **-1.** [expertiser] to value. **-2.** [évaluer] to estimate; **j'estime la durée du voyage à 2 heures** I reckon the journey time is 2 hours. **-3.** [respecter] to respect. **-4.** [penser]: ~ **que** to feel (that).
◆ **s'estimer** *vp* to consider o.s.

estival, -e, -aux [ɛstival, o] *adj* summer (*avant n*).

estivant, -e [ɛstivɑ̃, ɑ̃t] *nm, f* (summer) holiday-maker *Br* OU vacationer *Am*.

estocade [ɛstɔkad] *nf* death blow.

estomac [ɛstɔma] *nm* **-1.** ANAT stomach; **avoir l'**~ **barbouillé** to feel sick; **avoir un** ~ **d'autruche** *fig* to have a cast-iron digestion; **avoir l'**~ **dans les talons** *fig* to be starving. **-2.** [culot, cran] nerve.

estomaquer [ɛstɔmake] [3] *vt fam* to stagger.

estomper [ɛstɔ̃pe] [3] *vt* to blur; *fig* [douleur] to lessen.

◆ **s'estomper** *vp* to be/become blurred; *fig* [douleur] to lessen.

Estonie [ɛstɔni] *nf*: l'~ Estonia.

estonien, -ienne [ɛstɔnjɛ̃, jɛn] *adj* Estonian.

◆ **estonien** *nm* [langue] Estonian.

◆ **Estonien, -ienne** *nm, f* Estonian.

estrade [ɛstrad] *nf* dais.

estragon [ɛstragɔ̃] *nm* tarragon.

estropié, -e [ɛstrɔpje] ◇ *adj* crippled. ◇ *nm, f* cripple.

estropier [ɛstrɔpje] [9] *vt* [personne] to cripple; *fig* [nom, mot] to mispronounce.

◆ **s'estropier** *vp* to cripple o.s.

estuaire [ɛstɥɛr] *nm* estuary.

estudiantin, -e [ɛstydjɑ̃tɛ̃, in] *adj* student (*avant n*).

esturgeon [ɛstyrʒɔ̃] *nm* sturgeon.

et [e] *conj* -1. [gén] and; ~ moi? what about me? -2. [dans les fractions et les nombres composés]: **vingt** ~ **un** twenty-one; **il y a deux ans** ~ **demi** two and a half years ago; **à deux heures** ~ **demie** at half past two.

ét. (*abr de* **étage**) fl.

ETA (*abr de* **Euzkadi ta Askatsuna**) *nf* ETA.

étable [etabl] *nf* cowshed.

établi [etabli] *nm* workbench.

établir [etablir] [32] *vt* -1. [gén] to establish; [record] to set. -2. [dresser] to draw up.

◆ **s'établir** *vp* -1. [s'installer] to settle. -2. [créer son entreprise] to set o.s. up. -3. [s'instaurer] to become established.

établissement [etablismɑ̃] *nm* establishment; ~ **hospitalier** hospital; ~ **public** public body; ~ **scolaire** educational establishment.

étage [etaʒ] *nm* -1. [de bâtiment] storey, floor; **à l'**~ upstairs; **un immeuble à quatre** ~**s** a four-storey block of flats; **au premier** ~ on the first floor *Br*, on the second floor *Am*. -2. [de fusée] stage. -3. [de terrain, placard] level. -4. [condition]: **de bas** ~ second-rate.

étager [etaʒe] [17] *vt* to arrange in tiers.

◆ **s'étager** *vp* to be terraced.

étagère [etaʒɛr] *nf* -1. [rayon] shelf. -2. [meuble] shelves (*pl*), set of shelves.

étain [etɛ̃] *nm* -1. [métal] tin; [alliage] pewter. -2. [objet] piece of pewter.

étais, était *etc* → **être**.

étal [etal] (*pl* **-s** OU **étaux** [eto]) *nm* -1. [éventaire] stall. -2. [de boucher] butcher's block.

étalage [etalaʒ] *nm* -1. [action, ensemble d'objets] display; **faire** ~ **de** *fig* to flaunt. -2. [devanture] window display.

étalagiste [etalaʒist] *nmf* -1. [décorateur] window-dresser. -2. [vendeur] stall-holder.

étalement [etalmɑ̃] *nm* -1. [dans l'espace] spreading out. -2. [dans le temps] staggering.

étaler [etale] [3] *vt* -1. [exposer] to display. -2. [étendre] to spread out. -3. [dans le temps] to stagger. -4. [mettre une couche de] to spread. -5. [exhiber] to parade.

◆ **s'étaler** *vp* -1. [s'étendre] to spread. -2. [dans le temps]: **s'**~ **(sur)** to be spread (over). -3. *fam* [s'avachir] to sprawl. -4. *fam* [tomber] to come a cropper *Br*, to fall flat on one's face.

étalon [etalɔ̃] *nm* -1. [cheval] stallion. -2. [mesure] standard; ~**-or** gold standard.

étalonner [etalɔne] [3] *vt* [graduer] to calibrate.

étamine [etamin] *nf* -1. [de fleur] stamen. -2. [tissu] muslin.

étanche [etɑ̃ʃ] *adj* watertight; [montre] waterproof.

étanchéité [etɑ̃ʃeite] *nf* watertightness.

étancher [etɑ̃ʃe] [3] *vt* -1. [sang, larmes] to stem (the flow of). -2. [rendre étanche] to make watertight. -3. [assouvir] to quench.

étang [etɑ̃] *nm* pond.

étant *participe présent* → **être**.

étape [etap] *nf* -1. [gén] stage; **brûler les** ~**s** *fig* to race ahead. -2. [halte] stop; **faire** ~ **à** to break one's journey at.

état [eta] *nm* -1. [manière d'être] state; **être en** ~ /**hors d'**~ **de faire qqch** to be in a/in no fit state to do sthg; **en bon/mauvais** ~ in good/poor condition; **en** ~ **d'ivresse** under the influence of alcohol; **en** ~ **de marche** in working order; **laisser les choses en l'**~ to leave things as they stand; **remettre en** ~ to repair; ~ **d'âme** mood; ~ **d'esprit** state of mind; ~ **de santé** (state of) health; **être dans un** ~ **second** to be in a daze; ~ **de siège** state of siege; ~ **stationnaire** stable condition; ~ **d'urgence** state of emergency; **être dans tous ses** ~**s** *fig* to be in a state. -2. [métier, statut] status; **de son** ~ by profession; ~ **civil** ADMIN ≃ marital status. -3. [inventaire] inventory; [- de dépenses] statement; **faire** ~ **de qqch** to give an account of sthg; ~ **des lieux** *inventory and inspection of rented property.*

◆ **État** *nm* [nation] state; **l'État** the State; **État membre** member state; **les États du Golfe** the Gulf States.

◆ **en tout état de cause** *loc adv* in any case.

étatique [etatik] *adj* state (*avant n*).

étatiser [etatize] [3] *vt* to bring under state control.

étatisme [etatism] *nm* state control.

état-major [etamaʒɔr] (*pl* **états-majors**) *nm* **-1.** ADMIN & MIL staff; [de parti] leadership. **-2.** [lieu] headquarters (*pl*).

États-Unis [etazyni] *nmpl*: **les ~ (d'Amérique)** the United States (of America); **aux ~** in the United States.

étau [eto] *nm* vice.

étayer [eteje] [11] *vt* to prop up; *fig* to back up.

etc. (*abr de* **et cætera**) etc.

été [ete] ◇ *pp inv* → **être**. ◇ *nm* summer; **en ~** in (the) summer; **~ indien** Indian summer.

éteignais, **éteignions** *etc* → **éteindre**.

éteindre [etɛ̃dr] [81] *vt* **-1.** [incendie, bougie, cigarette] to put out; [radio, chauffage, lampe] to turn off, to switch off. **-2.** [soif] to quench. **-3.** JUR [annuler] to extinguish.
◆ **s'éteindre** *vp* **-1.** [feu, lampe] to go out. **-2.** [bruit, souvenir] to fade (away). **-3.** *fig* & *littéraire* [personne] to pass away. **-4.** [race] to die out.

éteint, -e [etɛ̃, ɛ̃t] ◇ *pp* → **éteindre**. ◇ *adj* **-1.** [couleur] faded. **-2.** [voix] faint; [regard] dull.

étendage [etɑ̃daʒ] *nm* hanging out.

étendard [etɑ̃dar] *nm* standard.

étendre [etɑ̃dr] [73] *vt* **-1.** [déployer] to stretch; [journal, linge] to spread (out). **-2.** [coucher] to lay. **-3.** [appliquer] to spread. **-4.** [accroître] to extend. **-5.** *fam fig* [candidat] to fail. **-6.** [diluer] to dilute; [sauce] to thin.
◆ **s'étendre** *vp* **-1.** [se coucher] to lie down. **-2.** [s'étaler au loin]: **s'~ (de/jusqu'à)** to stretch (from/as far as). **-3.** [croître] to spread. **-4.** [s'attarder]: **s'~ sur** to elaborate on.

étendu, -e [etɑ̃dy] ◇ *pp* → **étendre**. ◇ *adj* **-1.** [bras, main] outstretched. **-2.** [plaine, connaissances] extensive.
◆ **étendue** *nf* **-1.** [surface] area, expanse. **-2.** [durée] length. **-3.** [importance] extent. **-4.** MUS range.

éternel, -elle [etɛrnɛl] *adj* eternal; **ce ne sera pas ~** this won't last for ever.
◆ **Éternel** *nm*: **l'Éternel** the Eternal.

éternellement [etɛrnɛlmɑ̃] *adv* eternally.

éterniser [etɛrnize] [3] *vt* [prolonger] to drag out.
◆ **s'éterniser** *vp* **-1.** [se prolonger] to drag out. **-2.** *fam* [rester] to stay for ever.

éternité [etɛrnite] *nf* eternity; **il y a une ~**

que je ne t'ai pas vu I haven't seen you for ages.

éternuement [etɛrnymɑ̃] *nm* sneeze.

éternuer [etɛrnɥe] [7] *vi* to sneeze.

êtes → **être**.

étêter [etete] [4] *vt* to cut the head off.

éther [etɛr] *nm* ether.

éthéré, -e [etere] *adj* ethereal.

Éthiopie [etjɔpi] *nf*: **l'~** Ethiopia.

éthiopien, -ienne [etjɔpjɛ̃, jɛn] *adj* Ethiopian.
◆ **Éthiopien, -ienne** *nm, f* Ethiopian.

éthique [etik] ◇ *nf* ethics (*U ou pl*). ◇ *adj* ethical.

ethnie [ɛtni] *nf* ethnic group.

ethnique [ɛtnik] *adj* ethnic.

ethnographie [ɛtnɔgrafi] *nf* ethnography.

ethnologie [ɛtnɔlɔʒi] *nf* ethnology.

ethnologue [ɛtnɔlɔg] *nmf* ethnologist.

éthologie [etɔlɔʒi] *nf* ethology.

éthylique [etilik] ◇ *nmf* alcoholic. ◇ *adj* alcoholic; **alcool ~** ethyl alcohol, ethanol.

éthylisme [etilism] *nm* alcoholism.

étiez, étions *etc* → **être**.

étincelant, -e [etɛ̃slɑ̃, ɑ̃t] *adj* sparkling.

étinceler [etɛ̃sle] [24] *vi* to sparkle.

étincelle [etɛ̃sɛl] *nf* spark.

étioler [etjɔle] [3]
◆ **s'étioler** *vp* [plante] to wilt; [personne] to weaken; [mémoire] to go.

étique [etik] *adj littéraire* [plante] stunted; [personne] skinny.

étiqueter [etikte] [27] *vt litt* & *fig* to label.

étiquette [etikɛt] *nf* **-1.** [marque & *fig*] label. **-2.** [protocole] etiquette.

étirer [etire] [3] *vt* to stretch.
◆ **s'étirer** *vp* to stretch.

Etna [ɛtna] *nm*: **l'~** Mount Etna.

étoffe [etɔf] *nf* fabric, material; **avoir l'~ de** *fig* to have the makings of.

étoffer [etɔfe] [3] *vt* to flesh out.
◆ **s'étoffer** *vp* to fill out.

étoile [etwal] *nf* star; **l'~ du berger** the evening star; **~ filante** shooting star; **un trois ~s** a three-star hotel; **à la belle ~** *fig* under the stars; **être né sous une bonne ~** *fig* to be born under a lucky star.
◆ **étoile de mer** *nf* starfish.

étoilé, -e [etwale] *adj* **-1.** [ciel, nuit] starry; **la bannière ~e** the Star-Spangled Banner. **-2.** [vitre, pare-brise] shattered.

étole [etɔl] *nf* stole.

étonnamment [etɔnamɑ̃] *adv* astonishingly.

étonnant, -e [etɔnɑ̃, ɑ̃t] *adj* astonishing.

étonné, -e [etɔne] *adj* surprised, astonished.

étonnement [etɔnmɑ̃] *nm* astonishment, surprise; **au grand ~ de** to the great astonishment of.

étonner [etɔne] [3] *vt* to surprise, to astonish; **ça m'étonnerait!** I'd be (very) surprised!
◆ **s'étonner** *vp*: **s'~ (de)** to be surprised (by); **s'~ que** (+ *subjonctif*) to be surprised (that).

étouffant, -e [etufɑ̃, ɑ̃t] *adj* stifling.

étouffée [etufe]
◆ **à l'étouffée** *loc adv* steamed; [viande] braised; **faire cuire à l'~** to steam; [viande] to braise.

étouffement [etufmɑ̃] *nm* -1. [asphyxie] suffocation. -2. [répression] suppression.

étouffer [etufe] [3] ◇ *vt* -1. [gén] to stifle. -2. [asphyxier] to suffocate. -3. [feu] to smother. -4. [scandale, révolte] to suppress.
◇ *vi* to suffocate.
◆ **s'étouffer** *vp* -1. [s'étrangler] to choke. -2. *fig* [se presser, s'écraser] to stifle.

étouffoir [etufwar] *nm fam* oven.

étourderie [eturdəri] *nf* -1. [distraction] thoughtlessness. -2. [bévue] careless mistake; [acte irréfléchi] thoughtless act.

étourdi, -e [eturdi] ◇ *adj* scatterbrained. ◇ *nm, f* scatterbrain.

étourdiment [eturdimɑ̃] *adv* without thinking.

étourdir [eturdir] [32] *vt* -1. [assommer] to daze. -2. [fatiguer] to wear out.
◆ **s'étourdir** *vp* to be OU become dazed; **s'~ de** to get drunk on.

étourdissant, -e [eturdisɑ̃, ɑ̃t] *adj* -1. [fatigant] wearing. -2. [sensationnel] stunning.

étourdissement [eturdismɑ̃] *nm* dizzy spell.

étourneau, -x [eturno] *nm* starling.

étrange [etrɑ̃ʒ] *adj* strange.

étrangement [etrɑ̃ʒmɑ̃] *adv* strangely.

étranger, -ère [etrɑ̃ʒe, ɛr] ◇ *adj* -1. [gén] foreign. -2. [différent, isolé] unknown, unfamiliar; **être ~ à qqn** to be unknown to sb; **être ~ à qqch** to have no connection with sthg; **se sentir ~** to feel like an outsider. ◇ *nm, f* -1. [de nationalité différente] foreigner. -2. [inconnu] stranger. -3. [exclu] outsider.
◆ **étranger** *nm*: **l'~** foreign countries (*pl*); **à l'~** abroad.

étrangeté [etrɑ̃ʒte] *nf* strangeness.

étranglement [etrɑ̃gləmɑ̃] *nm* -1. [strangula-tion] strangulation. -2. [rétrécissement] constriction.

étrangler [etrɑ̃gle] [3] *vt* -1. [gén] to choke. -2. [stranguler] to strangle. -3. [réprimer] to stifle. -4. [serrer] to constrict.
◆ **s'étrangler** *vp* -1. [s'étouffer] to choke. -2. [sanglots] to catch.

étrave [etrav] *nf* stem.

être [etr] [2] ◇ *nm* being; **les ~s vivants/ humains** living/human beings.
◇ *v aux* -1. [pour les temps composés] to have/to be; **il est parti hier** he left yesterday; **il est déjà arrivé** he has already arrived; **il est né en 1952** he was born in 1952. -2. [pour le passif] to be; **la maison a été vendue** the house has been OU was sold.
◇ *v attr* -1. [état] to be; **il est grand/ heureux** he's tall/happy; **la maison est blanche** the house is white; **il est médecin** he's a doctor; **sois sage!** be good! -2. [possession]: **~ à qqn** to be sb's, to belong to sb; **c'est à vous, cette voiture?** is this your car?, is this car yours?; **cette maison est à lui/eux** this house is his/theirs, this is his/ their house.
◇ *v impers* -1. [exprimant le temps]: **quelle heure est-il?** what time is it?, what's the time?; **il est dix heures dix** it's ten past Br OU after Am ten. -2. [suivi d'un adjectif]: **il est...**, it is ...; **il est inutile de** it's useless to; **il serait bon de/que** it would be good to/if, it would be a good idea to/if.
◇ *vi* -1. [exister] to be; **n'~ plus** *sout* [être décédé] to be no more. -2. [indique une situation, un état] to be; **il est à Paris** he's in Paris; **nous sommes au printemps/en été** it's spring/summer. -3. [indiquant une origine]: **il est de Paris** he's from Paris.
◆ **être à** *v + prép* -1. [indiquant une obligation]: **c'est à vérifier** it needs to be checked; **cette chemise est à laver** this shirt needs washing; **c'est à voir** that remains to be seen. -2. [indiquant une continuité]: **il est toujours à ne rien faire** he never does a thing; **il est toujours à s'inquiéter** he's always worrying.

étreindre [etrɛ̃dr] [81] *vt* -1. [embrasser] to hug, to embrace. -2. *fig* [tenailler] to grip, to clutch.
◆ **s'étreindre** *vp* to embrace each other.

étreinte [etrɛ̃t] *nf* -1. [enlacement] embrace. -2. [pression] stranglehold.

étrenner [etrene] [4] *vt* to use for the first time.

étrennes [etrɛn] *nfpl* Christmas box (*sg*).

étrier [etrije] *nm* stirrup.

étriller [etrije] [3] *vt* **-1.** [cheval] to curry. **-2.** [personne] to wipe the floor with; [film] to tear to pieces.

étriper [etripe] [3] *vt* **-1.** [animal] to disembowel. **-2.** *fam fig* [tuer] to murder.

◆ **s'étriper** *vp fam* to tear each other to pieces.

étriqué, -e [etrike] *adj* **-1.** [vêtement] tight; [appartement] cramped. **-2.** [mesquin] narrow.

étroit, -e [etrwa, at] *adj* **-1.** [gén] narrow; **être à l'~** to be cramped. **-2.** [intime] close. **-3.** [serré] tight.

étroitement [etrwatmã] *adv* closely.

étroitesse [etrwatɛs] *nf* narrowness; **~ d'esprit** *fig* narrow-mindedness.

étude [etyd] *nf* **-1.** [gén] study; **à l'~** under consideration; **~ de faisabilité** feasibility study; **~ médias** media research; **~ de marché** market research (U). **-2.** [de notaire - local] office; [- charge] practice. **-3.** MUS étude.

◆ **études** *nfpl* studies; **faire des ~s** to study; **~s primaires/secondaires** primary/secondary education (U).

étudiant, -e [etydjã, ãt] ◇ *adj* student (avant n). ◇ *nm, f* student.

étudié, -e [etydje] *adj* studied.

étudier [etydje] [9] *vt* to study.

étui [etɥi] *nm* case; **~ à cigarettes/lunettes** cigarette/glasses case.

étuve [etyv] *nf* **-1.** [local] steam room; *fig* oven. **-2.** [appareil] sterilizer.

étuvée [etyve]

◆ **à l'étuvée** *loc adv* braised; **faire cuire à l'~** to braise.

étymologie [etimɔlɔʒi] *nf* etymology.

étymologique [etimɔlɔʒik] *adj* etymological.

eu, -e [y] *pp* → avoir.

E-U, E-U A (abr de États-Unis (d'Amérique)) *nmpl* US, USA.

eucalyptus [økaliptys] *nm* eucalyptus.

eucharistie [økaristi] *nf* Eucharist.

euh [ø] *interj* er.

eunuque [ønyk] *nm* eunuch.

euphémisme [øfemism] *nm* euphemism; **par ~** euphemistically.

euphorie [øfɔri] *nf* euphoria.

euphorique [øfɔrik] *adj* euphoric.

euphorisant, -e [øfɔrizã, ãt] *adj* exhilarating.

◆ **euphorisant** *nm* antidepressant.

eurasien, -ienne [ørazjɛ̃, jɛn] *adj* Eurasian.

◆ **Eurasien, -ienne** *nm, f* Eurasian.

eurent → avoir.

eurocentrisme [ørɔsãtrism] *nm* Eurocentrism.

eurocrate [ørɔkrat] *nmf* Eurocrat.

eurodevise [ørɔdəviz] *nf* Eurocurrency.

eurodollar [ørɔdɔlar] *nm* Eurodollar.

euromissile [ørɔmisil] *nm* Euromissile.

Europe [ørɔp] *nf:* **l'~** Europe; **l'~ centrale** Central Europe; **l'~ de l'Est** Eastern Europe; **ils ont parlé de l'~ verte** they discussed agriculture in the EC.

européen, -enne [ørɔpeɛ̃, ɛn] *adj* European.

◆ **Européen, -enne** *nm, f* European.

Eurovision® [ørovizjɔ̃] *nf inv* Eurovision®.

eus, eut *etc* → avoir.

eût → avoir.

euthanasie [øtanazi] *nf* euthanasia.

eux [ø] *pron pers* **-1.** [sujet] they; **ce sont ~ qui me l'ont dit** they're the ones who told me. **-2.** [complément] them.

◆ **eux-mêmes** *pron pers* themselves.

eV (abr de électron-volt) eV.

évacuation [evakɥasjɔ̃] *nf* **-1.** [gén] evacuation. **-2.** [de liquide] draining.

évacuer [evakɥe] [7] *vt* **-1.** [gén] to evacuate. **-2.** [liquide] to drain.

évadé, -e [evade] *nm, f* escaped prisoner.

évader [evade] [3]

◆ **s'évader** *vp:* **s'~ (de)** to escape (from).

évaluation [evalɥasjɔ̃] *nf* [action] valuation; [résultat] estimate.

évaluer [evalɥe] [7] *vt* [distance] to estimate; [tableau] to value; [risque] to assess.

évanescent, -e [evanesã, ãt] *adj* fleeting.

évangélique [evãʒelik] *adj* evangelical.

évangélisation [evãʒelizasjɔ̃] *nf* evangelizing.

évangéliser [evãʒelize] [3] *vt* to evangelize.

évangéliste [evãʒelist] *nm* **-1.** [auteur] Evangelist. **-2.** [prédicateur] evangelist.

évangile [evãʒil] *nm* gospel; **l'Évangile selon Saint Jean** the Gospel according to St. John.

évanouir [evanwir] [32]

◆ **s'évanouir** *vp* **-1.** [défaillir] to faint. **-2.** [disparaître] to fade.

évanouissement [evanwismã] *nm* **-1.** [syncope] fainting fit. **-2.** [disparition] fading.

évaporation [evaporasjɔ̃] *nf* evaporation.

évaporer [evapore] [3]

◆ **s'évaporer** *vp* to evaporate.

évasé, -e [evaze] *adj* flared.

évaser [evaze] [3] *vt* to flare.

◆ **s'évaser** *vp* to flare.

évasif, -ive [evazif, iv] *adj* evasive.

évasion [evazjɔ̃] *nf* escape.

évasivement [evazivmɑ̃] *adv* evasively.

évêché [eveʃe] *nm* [territoire] diocese; [résidence] bishop's palace.

éveil [evɛj] *nm* awakening; **en ~** on the alert.

éveillé, -e [eveje] *adj* -1. [qui ne dort pas] wide awake. -2. [vif, alerte] alert.

éveiller [eveje] [4] *vt* to arouse; [intelligence, dormeur] to awaken. ◆ **s'éveiller** *vp* -1. [dormeur] to wake, to awaken. -2. [curiosité] to be aroused. -3. [esprit, intelligence] to be awakened. -4. [s'ouvrir]: **s'~ à qqch** to discover sthg.

événement [evɛnmɑ̃] *nm* event.

événementiel, -ielle [evɛnmɑ̃sjɛl] *adj* [histoire] factual.

éventail [evɑ̃taj] *nm* -1. [objet] fan; **en ~** fan-shaped. -2. [choix] range.

éventaire [evɑ̃tɛr] *nm* -1. [étalage] stall, stand. -2. [corbeille] tray.

éventé, -e [evɑ̃te] *adj* stale.

éventer [evɑ̃te] [3] *vt* -1. [rafraîchir] to fan. -2. [divulguer] to give away. ◆ **s'éventer** *vp* -1. [se rafraîchir] to fan o.s. -2. [parfum, vin] to go stale.

éventrer [evɑ̃tre] [3] *vt* -1. [étriper] to disembowel. -2. [fendre] to rip open.

éventualité [evɑ̃tɥalite] *nf* -1. [possibilité] possibility. -2. [circonstance] eventuality; **dans l'~ de** in the event of; **parer à toute ~** to be ready for any eventuality.

éventuel, -elle [evɑ̃tɥɛl] *adj* possible.

éventuellement [evɑ̃tɥɛlmɑ̃] *adv* possibly.

évêque [evɛk] *nm* bishop.

évertuer [evɛrtɥe] [7] ◆ **s'évertuer** *vp*: **s'~ à faire qqch** to strive to do sthg.

éviction [eviksjɔ̃] *nf* eviction.

évidemment [evidamɑ̃] *adv* obviously.

évidence [evidɑ̃s] *nf* [caractère] evidence; [fait] obvious fact; **à l'~** obviously; **mettre en ~** to emphasize, to highlight; **se rendre à l'~** to face facts.

évident, -e [evidɑ̃, ɑ̃t] *adj* obvious; **ce n'est pas ~** it's not that easy.

évider [evide] [3] *vt* to hollow out.

évier [evje] *nm* sink.

évincer [evɛ̃se] [16] *vt*: **~ qqn (de)** to oust sb (from).

éviter [evite] [3] *vt* -1. [esquiver] to avoid. -2. [s'abstenir]: **~ de faire qqch** to avoid doing sthg. -3. [épargner]: **~ qqch à qqn** to save sb sthg.

◆ **s'éviter** *vp* -1. [se bouder] to avoid each other. -2. [s'épargner] to spare o.s.

évocateur, -trice [evɔkatœr, tris] *adj* -1. [film, roman]: **~ (de)** evocative (of). -2. [geste, regard] meaningful.

évocation [evɔkasjɔ̃] *nf* evocation.

évolué, -e [evolɥe] *adj* -1. [développé] developed. -2. [libéral, progressiste] broad-minded.

évoluer [evolɥe] [7] *vi* -1. [changer] to evolve; [personne] to change. -2. [se mouvoir] to move about.

évolutif, -ive [evolytif, iv] *adj* -1. [système] evolutionary. -2. MÉD progressive. -3. [travail]: **un poste ~** a job with prospects.

évolution [evolysjɔ̃] *nf* -1. [transformation] development. -2. BIOL evolution. -3. MÉD progress.

◆ **évolutions** *nfpl* movements.

évoquer [evɔke] [3] *vt* -1. [souvenir] to evoke; **son nom ne m'évoque rien** his name means nothing to me. -2. [problème] to refer to. -3. [esprits, démons] to call up.

ex [ɛks] *nmf* ex.

ex- [ɛks] *préfixe* ex-.

exacerbé, -e [ɛgzasɛrbe] *adj* exacerbated.

exacerber [ɛgzasɛrbe] [3] *vt* to heighten.

exact, -e [ɛgzakt] *adj* -1. [calcul] correct. -2. [récit, copie] exact. -3. [ponctuel] punctual.

exactement [ɛgzaktəmɑ̃] *adv* exactly.

exaction [ɛgzaksjɔ̃] *nf* extortion.

exactitude [ɛgzaktityd] *nf* -1. [de calcul, montre] accuracy. -2. [ponctualité] punctuality.

ex æquo [ɛgzeko] ◇ *adj inv & nmf inv* equal. ◇ *adv* equal; **troisième ~** third equal.

exagération [ɛgzaʒerasjɔ̃] *nf* exaggeration.

exagéré, -e [ɛgzaʒere] *adj* exaggerated.

exagérément [ɛgzaʒeremɑ̃] *adv* exaggeratedly.

exagérer [ɛgzaʒere] [18] *vt & vi* to exaggerate.

◆ **s'exagérer** *vp* to exaggerate.

exaltant, -e [ɛgzaltɑ̃, ɑ̃t] *adj* exhilarating.

exalté, -e [ɛgzalte] ◇ *adj* [sentiment] elated; [tempérament] over-excited; [imagination] vivid. ◇ *nm, f* fanatic.

exalter [ɛgzalte] [3] *vt* to excite. ◆ **s'exalter** *vp* to get carried away.

examen [ɛgzamɛ̃] *nm* examination; SCOL exam, examination; **~ médical** medical (examination).

examinateur, -trice [ɛgzaminatœr, tris] *nm, f* examiner.

examiner [ɛgzamine] [3] *vt* to examine.

exaspérant, -e [ɛgzasperɑ̃, ɑ̃t] *adj* exasperating.

exaspération [ɛgzasperasjɔ̃] *nf* exasperation.

exaspérer [ɛgzaspere] [18] *vt* to exasperate.

exaucer [ɛgzose] [16] *vt* to grant; ~ **qqn** to answer sb's prayers.

ex cathedra [ɛkskatedra] *loc adv* with authority.

excédant, -e [ɛksedɑ̃, ɑ̃t] *adj* exasperating.

excédent [ɛksedɑ̃] *nm* surplus; **en** ~ surplus (*avant n*); ~ **de bagages** [dans l'avion] excess luggage OU baggage; ~ **commercial** trade surplus.

excédentaire [ɛksedɑ̃tɛr] *adj* surplus (*avant n*).

excéder [ɛksede] [18] *vt* **-1.** [gén] to exceed. **-2.** [exaspérer] to exasperate.

excellemment [ɛkselamɑ̃] *adv* excellently.

excellence [ɛkselɑ̃s] *nf* excellence; **par** ~ par excellence.
◆ **Excellence** *nf*: **Son Excellence** His/Her Excellency.

excellent, -e [ɛkselɑ̃, ɑ̃t] *adj* excellent.

exceller [ɛksele] [4] *vi*: ~ **en** OU **dans qqch** to excel at OU in sthg; ~ **à faire qqch** to excel at doing sthg.

excentré, -e [ɛksɑ̃tre] *adj*: **c'est très excentré** it's quite a long way out.

excentrique [ɛksɑ̃trik] ◇ *nmf* eccentric. ◇ *adj* **-1.** [gén] eccentric. **-2.** [quartier] outlying.

excepté, -e [ɛksɛpte] *adj*: **tous sont venus, lui** ~ everyone came except (for) him.
◆ **excepté** *prép* apart from, except.

exception [ɛksɛpsjɔ̃] *nf* exception; **faire** ~ to be an exception; **d'**~ exceptional; **à l'**~ **de** except for.

exceptionnel, -elle [ɛksɛpsjɔnɛl] *adj* exceptional.

exceptionnellement [ɛksɛpsjɔnɛlmɑ̃] *adv* **-1.** [par exception] in this (one) instance. **-2.** [extrêmement] exceptionally.

excès [ɛksɛ] ◇ *nm* excess; ~ **de vitesse** speeding; ~ **de zèle** overzealousness; **à l'**~ to excess, excessively; **sans** ~ moderately. ◇ *nmpl* excesses.

excessif, -ive [ɛksesif, iv] *adj* **-1.** [démesuré] excessive. **-2.** [extrême] extreme.

excessivement [ɛksesivmɑ̃] *adv* **-1.** [démesurément] excessively. **-2.** [extrêmement] extremely.

excipient [ɛksipjɑ̃] *nm* excipient.

excision [ɛksizjɔ̃] *nf* excision.

excitant, -e [ɛksitɑ̃, ɑ̃t] *adj* **-1.** [stimulant, passionnant] exciting. **-2.** MÉD stimulating.
◆ **excitant** *nm* stimulant.

excitation [ɛksitasjɔ̃] *nf* **-1.** [énervement] excitement. **-2.** [stimulation] encouragement. **-3.** MÉD stimulation.

excité, -e [ɛksite] ◇ *adj* [énervé] excited. ◇ *nm, f* hothead.

exciter [ɛksite] [3] *vt* **-1.** [gén] to excite. **-2.** [inciter]: ~ **qqn (à qqch/à faire qqch)** to incite sb (to sthg/to do sthg). **-3.** MÉD to stimulate.
◆ **s'exciter** *vp*: **s'**~ **(sur)** to lose one's temper (with).

exclamation [ɛksklamasjɔ̃] *nf* exclamation.

exclamer [ɛksklame] [3]
◆ **s'exclamer** *vp*: **s'**~ **(devant)** to exclaim (at OU over).

exclu, -e [ɛkskly] ◇ *pp* → **exclure**. ◇ *adj* excluded. ◇ *nm, f* outsider.

exclure [ɛsklyr] [96] *vt* to exclude; [expulser] to expel.

exclusif, -ive [ɛksklyzif, iv] *adj* exclusive; ~ **de** exclusive of.

exclusion [ɛksklyzjɔ̃] *nf* expulsion; **à l'**~ **de** to the exclusion of.

exclusivement [ɛksklyzivmɑ̃] *adv* **-1.** [uniquement] exclusively. **-2.** [non inclus] exclusive.

exclusivité [ɛksklyzivite] *nf* **-1.** COMM exclusive rights (*pl*); **avoir l'**~ **(de)** to have exclusive rights (to). **-2.** CIN sole screening rights (*pl*); **en** ~ exclusively. **-3.** [de sentiment] exclusiveness.

excommunier [ɛkskɔmynje] [9] *vt* to excommunicate.

excrément [ɛkskremɑ̃] *nm* (*gén pl*) excrement (*U*).

excroissance [ɛkskrwasɑ̃s] *nf* excrescence.

excursion [ɛkskyrsjɔ̃] *nf* excursion; **faire une** ~ to go on a trip.

excursionniste [ɛkskyrsjɔnist] *nmf* daytripper *Br*.

excusable [ɛkskyzabl] *adj* excusable.

excuse [ɛkskyz] *nf* excuse; **avoir une** ~ to have an excuse; **se confondre en** ~**s** to apologize profusely; **présenter ses** ~**s à qqn** to apologize to sb.

excuser [ɛkskyze] [3] *vt* to excuse; **excusez-moi** [pour réparer] I'm sorry; [pour demander] excuse me; **se faire** ~ to ask to be excused.
◆ **s'excuser** *vp* [demander pardon] to apologize; **s'**~ **de qqch/de faire qqch** to apologize for sthg/for doing sthg.

exécrable [ɛgzekrabl] *adj* atrocious.

exécrer [ɛgzekre] [18] *vt* to loathe.

exécutant, -e [ɛgzekytɑ̃, ɑ̃t] *nm, f* **-1.** [personne] underling. **-2.** MUS performer.

exécuter [ɛgzekyte] [3] *vt* **-1.** [réaliser] to carry out; [tableau] to paint. **-2.** MUS to play, to perform. **-3.** [mettre à mort] to execute.
◆ **s'exécuter** *vp* to comply.

exécuteur, -trice [ɛgzekytœr, tris] *nm, f:* ~ **testamentaire** executor.

exécutif, -ive [ɛgzekytif, iv] *adj* executive.
◆ **exécutif** *nm*: **l'**~ the executive.

exécution [ɛgzekysjɔ̃] *nf* **-1.** [réalisation] carrying out; [de tableau] painting; **mettre à** ~ to carry out. **-2.** MUS performance. **-3.** [mise à mort] execution.

exécutoire [ɛgzekytwar] *adj* binding.

exégèse [ɛgzeʒɛz] *nf* exegesis.

exemplaire [ɛgzɑ̃plɛr] ◇ *nm* copy. ◇ *adj* exemplary.

exemple [ɛgzɑ̃pl] *nm* example; **par** ~ for example, for instance; **ça, par** ~! [exprime la surprise] well, well!, good heavens!; **pour l'**~ as an example; **citer qqn en** ~ to quote sb as an example; **montrer l'**~ to set an example; **prendre** ~ **sur qqn** to take a leaf out of sb's book; **à l'**~ **de** following in the footsteps of.

exempt, -e [ɛgzɑ̃, ɑ̃t] *adj*: ~ **de** [dispensé de] exempt from; [dépourvu de] free of; ~ **de taxes** tax-free.

exempté, -e [ɛgzɑ̃te] *adj*: ~ **(de)** exempt (from).

exemption [ɛgzɑ̃psjɔ̃] *nf* exemption.

exercer [ɛgzɛrse] [16] *vt* **-1.** [entraîner, mettre en usage] to exercise; [autorité, influence] to exert. **-2.** [métier] to carry on; [médecine] to practise.
◆ **s'exercer** *vp* **-1.** [s'entraîner] to practise; **s'**~ **à qqch/à faire qqch** to practise sthg/doing sthg. **-2.** [se manifester]: **s'**~ **(sur** OU **contre)** to be exerted (on).

exercice [ɛgzɛrsis] *nm* **-1.** [gén] exercise; ~**s d'assouplissement** keep-fit exercises. **-2.** [entraînement] practice. **-3.** [de métier, fonction] carrying out; **dans l'**~ **de ses fonctions** in the execution of one's duties; **en** ~ in office. **-4.** FIN financial year *Br*, fiscal year *Am*.

exergue [ɛgzɛrg] *nm* inscription; **mettre qqch en** ~ to emphasize sthg.

exhalaison [ɛgzalɛzɔ̃] *nf* odour.

exhaler [ɛgzale] [3] *vt littéraire* **-1.** [odeur] to give off. **-2.** *fig* [colère, rage] to vent. **-3.** [plainte, soupir] to utter.
◆ **s'exhaler** *vp* **-1.** [odeur] to rise. **-2.** [plainte, soupir]: **s'**~ **de** to rise from.

exhausser [ɛgzose] [3] *vt* to raise.

exhaustif, -ive [ɛgzostif, iv] *adj* exhaustive.

exhiber [ɛgzibe] [3] *vt* [présenter] to show; [faire étalage de] to show off.
◆ **s'exhiber** *vp* to make an exhibition of o.s.

exhibitionniste [ɛgzibisjɔnist] *nmf* exhibitionist.

exhortation [ɛgzɔrtasjɔ̃] *nf* exhortation.

exhorter [ɛgzɔrte] [3] *vt*: ~ **qqn à qqch/à faire qqch** to urge sb to sthg/to do sthg.

exhumer [ɛgzyme] [3] *vt* to exhume; *fig* to unearth, to dig up.

exigeant, -e [ɛgziʒɑ̃, ɑ̃t] *adj* demanding.

exigence [ɛgziʒɑ̃s] *nf* **-1.** [caractère] demanding nature. **-2.** [demande] demand.

exiger [ɛgziʒe] [17] *vt* **-1.** [demander] to demand; ~ **que** (+ *subjonctif*) to demand that; ~ **qqch de qqn** to demand sthg from sb. **-2.** [nécessiter] to require.

exigible [ɛgziʒibl] *adj* payable.

exigu, -ë [ɛgzigy] *adj* cramped.

exiguïté [ɛgziɡɥite] *nf* lack of space.

exil [ɛgzil] *nm* exile; **en** ~ exiled.

exilé, -e [ɛgzile] *nm, f* exile.

exiler [ɛgzile] [3] *vt* to exile.
◆ **s'exiler** *vp* **-1.** POLIT to go into exile. **-2.** *fig* [partir] to go into seclusion.

existence [ɛgzistɑ̃s] *nf* existence.

existentialisme [ɛgzistɑ̃sjalism] *nm* existentialism.

existentiel, -ielle [ɛgzistɑ̃sjɛl] *adj* existentiel.

exister [ɛgziste] [3] *vi* to exist.

exode [ɛgzɔd] *nm* exodus; ~ **rural** rural depopulation.

exonération [ɛgzɔnerasjɔ̃] *nf* exemption; ~ **de qqch** exemption from sthg; ~ **d'impôts** tax exemption.

exonérer [ɛgzɔnere] [18] *vt*: ~ **qqn de qqch** to exempt sb from sthg.

exorbitant, -e [ɛgzɔrbitɑ̃, ɑ̃t] *adj* exorbitant.

exorbité, -e [ɛgzɔrbite] → **œil**.

exorciser [ɛgzɔrsize] [3] *vt* to exorcize.

exotique [ɛgzɔtik] *adj* exotic.

exotisme [ɛgzɔtism] *nm* exoticism.

expansé, -e [ɛkspɑ̃se] *adj* expanded.

expansif, -ive [ɛkspɑ̃sif, iv] *adj* expansive.

expansion [ɛkspɑ̃sjɔ̃] *nf* expansion; ~ **démographique** population growth.

expansionniste [ɛkspɑ̃sjɔnist] *nmf & adj* expansionist.

expatrié, -e [ɛkspatrije] *adj & nm, f* expatriate.

expatrier [ɛkspatrije] [10] *vt* to expatriate.
◆ **s'expatrier** *vp* to leave one's country.
expectative [ɛkspɛktativ] *nf*: être dans l'~ to wait and see.
expectorant, -e [ɛkspɛktɔrɑ̃, ɑ̃t] *adj* expectorant.
◆ **expectorant** *nm* expectorant.
expédient [ɛkspedjɑ̃] *nm* expedient; vivre d'~s to live by one's wits.
expédier [ɛkspedje] [9] *vt* -**1.** [lettre, marchandise] to send, to dispatch. -**2.** [personne] to get rid of; [question] to dispose of. -**3.** [travail] to dash off.
expéditeur, -trice [ɛkspeditœr, tris] ◇ *adj* dispatching (*avant n*). ◇ *nm, f* sender.
expéditif, -ive [ɛkspeditif, iv] *adj* quick, expeditious.
expédition [ɛkspedisjɔ̃] *nf* -**1.** [envoi] sending. -**2.** [voyage, campagne militaire] expedition; ~ punitive punitive raid.
expéditionnaire [ɛkspedisjɔnɛr] → corps.
expérience [ɛksperjɑ̃s] *nf* -**1.** [pratique] experience; avoir de l'~ to have experience, to be experienced. -**2.** [essai] experiment; faire l'~ de qqch to experience OU try sthg; tenter l'~ to try.
expérimental, -e, -aux [ɛksperimɑ̃tal, o] *adj* experimental.
expérimentation [ɛksperimɑ̃tasjɔ̃] *nf* experimentation.
expérimenté, -e [ɛksperimɑ̃te] *adj* experienced.
expérimenter [ɛksperimɑ̃te] [3] *vt* to test.
expert, -e [ɛkspɛr, ɛrt] *adj* expert; être ~ (en la matière) to be an expert (on the subject).
◆ **expert** *nm* expert.
expert-comptable [ɛkspɛrkɔ̃tabl] (*pl* experts-comptables) *nm* chartered accountant *Br,* certified public accountant *Am.*
expertise [ɛkspɛrtiz] *nf* -**1.** [examen] expert appraisal; [estimation] (expert) valuation. -**2.** [compétence] expertise.
expertiser [ɛkspɛrtize] [3] *vt* to value; [dégâts] to assess.
expiation [ɛkspjasjɔ̃] *nf* atonement.
expier [ɛkspje] [9] *vt* to pay for.
expiration [ɛkspirasjɔ̃] *nf* -**1.** [d'air] exhalation. -**2.** [de contrat] expiry.
expirer [ɛkspire] [3] ◇ *vt* to breathe out. ◇ *vi* -**1.** [personne] to pass away. -**2.** [contrat] to expire.
explicable [ɛksplikabl] *adj* explicable.
explicatif, -ive [ɛksplikatif, iv] *adj* explanatory.

explication [ɛksplikasjɔ̃] *nf* explanation; demander des ~s à qqn to demand an explanation from sb; ~ de texte (literary) criticism.
explicite [ɛksplisit] *adj* explicit.
explicitement [ɛksplisitmɑ̃] *adv* explicitly.
expliciter [ɛksplisite] [3] *vt* to make explicit.
expliquer [ɛksplike] [3] *vt* -**1.** [gén] to explain. -**2.** [texte] to criticize.
◆ **s'expliquer** *vp* -**1.** [se justifier] to explain o.s. -**2.** [comprendre] to understand. -**3.** [discuter] to have it out. -**4.** [devenir compréhensible] to be explained, to become clear.
exploit [ɛksplwa] *nm* exploit, feat; *iron* [maladresse] achievement.
exploitable [ɛksplwatabl] *adj* [gisement] exploitable; [renseignement] usable; INFORM machine-readable.
exploitant, -e [ɛksplwatɑ̃, ɑ̃t] *nm, f* farmer.
exploitation [ɛksplwatasjɔ̃] *nf* -**1.** [mise en valeur] running; [de mine] working. -**2.** [entreprise] operation, concern; ~ agricole farm. -**3.** [d'une personne] exploitation.
exploiter [ɛksplwate] [3] *vt* -**1.** [gén] to exploit. -**2.** [entreprise] to operate, to run.
exploiteur, -euse [ɛksplwatœr, øz] *nm, f* exploiter.
explorateur, -trice [ɛksplɔratœr, tris] *nm, f* explorer.
exploration [ɛksplɔrasjɔ̃] *nf* exploration.
exploratoire [ɛksplɔratwar] *adj* exploratory.
explorer [ɛksplɔre] [3] *vt* to explore.
exploser [ɛksploze] [3] *vi* to explode.
explosif, -ive [ɛksplozif, iv] *adj* explosive.
◆ **explosif** *nm* explosive.
explosion [ɛksplozjɔ̃] *nf* explosion; [de colère, joie] outburst.
exponentiel, -ielle [ɛkspɔnɑ̃sjɛl] *adj* exponential.
exportateur, -trice [ɛkspɔrtatœr, tris] ◇ *adj* exporting. ◇ *nm, f* exporter.
exportation [ɛkspɔrtasjɔ̃] *nf* export.
exporter [ɛkspɔrte] [3] *vt* to export.
exposant, -e [ɛkspozɑ̃, ɑ̃t] *nm, f* exhibitor.
◆ **exposant** *nm* exponent.
exposé, -e [ɛkspoze] *adj* -**1.** [orienté]: bien ~ facing the sun. -**2.** [vulnérable] exposed.
◆ **exposé** *nm* account; SCOL talk.
exposer [ɛkspoze] [3] *vt* -**1.** [orienter, mettre en danger] to expose; ~ sa vie to risk one's life. -**2.** [présenter] to display; [- tableaux] to show, to exhibit. -**3.** [expliquer] to explain, to set out.
◆ **s'exposer** *vp*: s'~ à qqch to expose o.s. to sthg.

exposition [ɛkspozisjɔ̃] *nf* **-1.** [présentation] exhibition. **-2.** [orientation] aspect. **-3.** [explication] exposition.

exposition-vente [ɛkspozisjɔ̃vɑ̃t] (*pl* **expositions-ventes**) *nf* exhibition (*where purchases can be made*).

exprès¹, -esse [ɛksprɛ, ɛs] *adj* **-1.** [formel] formal, express. **-2.** (*inv*) [urgent] express; **en ~** by express delivery.

exprès² [ɛksprɛ] *adv* on purpose; **faire ~ de faire qqch** to do sthg deliberately OU on purpose.

express [ɛksprɛs] ◇ *nm inv* **-1.** [train] express. **-2.** [café] espresso. ◇ *adj inv* express.

expressément [ɛkspresemɑ̃] *adv* expressly.

expressif, -ive [ɛkspresif, iv] *adj* expressive.

expression [ɛkspresjɔ̃] *nf* expression; **~ idiomatique** idiom, idiomatic expression; **réduire qqch à sa plus simple ~** *fig* to reduce sthg to its simplest form; **selon l'~ consacrée** as the saying goes.

expressionnisme [ɛkspresjɔnism] *nm* expressionism.

expressivité [ɛkspresivite] *nf* expressiveness.

exprimable [ɛksprimabl] *adj* which can be expressed; **difficilement ~** difficult to express.

exprimer [ɛksprime] [3] *vt* [pensées, sentiments] to express; **~ qqch par qqch** to express sthg with sthg.
◆ **s'exprimer** *vp* to express o.s.

expropriation [ɛksprɔprijasjɔ̃] *nf* expropriation.

exproprier [ɛksprɔprije] [10] *vt* to expropriate.

expulser [ɛkspylse] [3] *vt*: **~ (de)** to expel (from); [locataire] to evict (from).

expulsion [ɛkspylsjɔ̃] *nf* expulsion; [de locataire] eviction.

expurger [ɛkspyrʒe] [17] *vt* to expurgate.

exquis, -e [ɛkski, iz] *adj* **-1.** [délicieux] exquisite. **-2.** [distingué, agréable] delightful.

exsangue [ɛksɑ̃g] *adj* [blême] deathly pale.

extase [ɛkstaz] *nf* ecstasy; **tomber en ~ devant** to go into ecstasies over.

extasier [ɛkstazje] [9]
◆ **s'extasier** *vp* to be ecstatic; **s'~ devant** to go into ecstasies over.

extatique [ɛkstatik] *adj* ecstatic.

extenseur [ɛkstɑ̃sœr] ◇ *nm* GYM chest expander. ◇ *adj* → **muscle**.

extensible [ɛkstɑ̃sibl] *adj* stretchable.

extensif, -ive [ɛkstɑ̃sif, iv] *adj* extensive.

extension [ɛkstɑ̃sjɔ̃] *nf* **-1.** [étirement] stretching. **-2.** [développement] spread. **-3.** [élargissement] extension; **par ~** by extension; **~ de nom de fichier** INFORM (filename) extension.

exténuant, -e [ɛkstenɥɑ, ɑ̃t] *adj* exhausting.

exténuer [ɛkstenɥe] [7] *vt* to exhaust.

extérieur, -e [ɛksterjœr] *adj* [au dehors] outside; [étranger] external; [apparent] outward.
◆ **extérieur** *nm* **-1.** [dehors] outside; [de maison] exterior; **à l'~ de qqch** outside sthg. **-2.** ÉCON & POLIT: **l'~** foreign countries (*pl*).

extérieurement [ɛksterjœrmɑ̃] *adv* **-1.** [à l'extérieur] on the outside, externally. **-2.** [en apparence] outwardly.

extérioriser [ɛksterjɔrize] [3] *vt* to show.
◆ **s'extérioriser** *vp* to show one's feelings.

extermination [ɛkstɛrminasjɔ̃] *nf* extermination.

exterminer [ɛkstɛrmine] [3] *vt* to exterminate.

externat [ɛkstɛrna] *nm* **-1.** SCOL day school. **-2.** MÉD *non-resident medical studentship*.

externe [ɛkstɛrn] ◇ *nmf* **-1.** SCOL day pupil. **-2.** MÉD *non-resident medical student*, ≈ extern *Am*. ◇ *adj* outer, external; **~ à qqch** outside sthg.

extincteur [ɛkstɛ̃ktœr] *nm* (fire) extinguisher.

extinction [ɛkstɛ̃ksjɔ̃] *nf* **-1.** [action d'éteindre] putting out, extinguishing; **~ des feux** lights out. **-2.** *fig* [disparition] extinction; **~ de voix** loss of one's voice.

extirper [ɛkstirpe] [3] *vt*: **~ (de)** [épine, réponse, secret] to drag (out of); [plante] to uproot (from); [erreur, préjugé] to root out (of).
◆ **s'extirper** *vp*: **s'~ de qqch** to struggle out of sthg.

extorquer [ɛkstɔrke] [3] *vt*: **~ qqch à qqn** to extort sthg from sb.

extorsion [ɛkstɔrsjɔ̃] *nf* extortion; **~ de fonds** extortion of money.

extra [ɛkstra] ◇ *nm inv* **-1.** [employé] extra help (*U*). **-2.** [chose inhabituelle] (special) treat. ◇ *adj inv* **-1.** [de qualité] top-quality. **-2.** *fam* [génial] great, fantastic.

extraction [ɛkstraksjɔ̃] *nf* extraction.

extrader [ɛkstrade] [3] *vt* to extradite.

extradition [ɛkstradisjɔ̃] *nf* extradition.

extraire [ɛkstrɛr] [112] *vt*: **~ (de)** to extract (from).

extrait, -e [ɛkstrɛ, ɛt] *pp* → **extraire**.
◆ **extrait** *nm* extract; **~ de café** coffee extract; **~ de naissance** birth certificate.

extralucide [εkstralysid] → **voyante**.

extraordinaire [εkstraɔrdinεr] *adj* extraordinary.

extraplat, -e [εkstrapla, at] *adj* wafer-thin.

extrapoler [εkstrapɔle] [3] *vt & vi* to extrapolate.

extraterrestre [εkstratεrεstr] *nmf & adj* extraterrestrial.

extravagance [εkstravagãs] *nf* extravagance.

extravagant, -e [εkstravagã, ãt] *adj* extravagant; [idée, propos] wild.

extraverti, -e [εkstravεrti] ◇ *adj* extrovert. ◇ *nm, f* extrovert.

extrême [εkstrεm] ◇ *nm* extreme; **d'un ~ à l'autre** from one extreme to the other. ◇ *adj* extreme; [limite] furthest.

extrêmement [εkstrεmmã] *adv* extremely.

extrême-onction [εkstrεmɔ̃ksjɔ̃] (*pl* **extrêmes-onctions**) *nf* last rites (*pl*), extreme unction.

Extrême-Orient [εkstrεmɔrjã] *nm*: **l'~** the Far East.

extrémiste [εkstremist] *nmf & adj* extremist.

extrémité [εkstremite] *nf* -1. [bout] end. -2. [situation critique] straights (*pl*); **à la dernière ~** *fig* at death's door.

exubérant, -e [εgzyberã, ãt] *adj* -1. [personne] exuberant. -2. [végétation] luxuriant.

exulter [εgzylte] [3] *vi* to exult.

exutoire [εgzytwar] *nm* outlet.

ex-voto [εksvɔto] *nm inv* votive offering.

eye-liner [ajlajnœr] (*pl* **eye-liners**) *nm* eyeliner.

F

f, F [εf] *nm inv* f, F; **F3** three-room flat *Br* OU apartment *Am*.
◆ **F -1.** *abr de* **femme**. **-2.** *abr de* **féminin**. **-3.** (*abr de* **Fahrenheit**) F. **-4.** (*abr de* **franc**) F, Fr.

fa [fa] *nm inv* F; [dans la gamme] fa.

FAB [fab] (*abr de* **franco à bord**) FOB, fob.

fable [fabl] *nf* fable.

fabricant, -e [fabrikã, ãt] *nm, f* manufacturer.

fabrication [fabrikasjɔ̃] *nf* manufacture, manufacturing; **de ~ artisanale** hand-made.

fabrique [fabrik] *nf* [usine] factory.

fabriquer [fabrike] [3] *vt* -1. [confectionner] to manufacture, to make; **fabriqué en France** made in France. -2. *fam* [faire]: **qu'est-ce que tu fabriques?** what are you up to? -3. [inventer] to fabricate.

fabulation [fabylasjɔ̃] *nf* fabrication.

fabuleusement [fabyløzmã] *adv* fabulously.

fabuleux, -euse [fabylø, øz] *adj* fabulous.

fac [fak] *nf fam* college, uni *Br*.

FAC (*abr de* **franc d'avarie commune**) *adj* FGA, fga.

façade [fasad] *nf litt & fig* facade.

face [fas] *nf* -1. [visage] face; **perdre la ~** to lose face; **sauver la ~** to save face. -2. [côté] side; **faire ~ à qqch** [maison] to face sthg, to be opposite sthg; *fig* [affronter] to face up to sthg; **de ~** from the front; **en ~ de qqn/qqch** opposite sb/sthg; **d'en ~** across the street, opposite; **~ à** facing; **~ à qqch** [situation] faced with sthg; **~ à ~** face to face; **regarder qqch en ~** *fig* to face up to sthg.

face-à-face [fasafas] *nm inv* debate.

facétie [fasesi] *nf* practical joke.

facétieux, -ieuse [fasesjø, jøz] ◇ *adj* playful. ◇ *nm, f* joker.

facette [fasεt] *nf litt & fig* facet.

fâché, -e [faʃe] *adj* -1. [en colère] angry; [contrarié] annoyed. -2. [brouillé] on bad terms.

fâcher [faʃe] [3] vt [mettre en colère] to anger, to make angry; [contrarier] to annoy, to make annoyed.
◆ **se fâcher** vp -1. [se mettre en colère]: se ~ (contre qqn) to get angry (with sb). -2. [se brouiller]: se ~ (avec qqn) to fall out (with sb).

fâcherie [faʃri] nf disagreement.

fâcheux, -euse [faʃø, øz] adj unfortunate.

facho [faʃo] nmf & adj fam fascist.

facial, -e, -iaux [fasjal, jo] adj facial.

faciès [fasjɛs] nm péj [visage] features (pl).

facile [fasil] adj -1. [aisé] easy; ~ à faire/prononcer easy to do/pronounce. -2. [peu subtil] facile. -3. [conciliant] easy-going; ~ à vivre easy to get on with.

facilement [fasilmɑ̃] adv easily.

facilité [fasilite] nf -1. [de tâche, problème] easiness. -2. [capacité] ease. -3. [dispositions] aptitude. -4. COMM: ~s de paiement easy (payment) terms; ~s de crédit credit facilities.

faciliter [fasilite] [3] vt to make easier.

façon [fasɔ̃] nf -1. [manière] way; ~ de parler figure of speech. -2. [travail] work; COUTURE making-up. -3. [imitation]: ~ cuir imitation leather.
◆ **façons** nfpl manner (sg), ways; faire des ~s to make a fuss.
◆ **de façon à** loc prép so as to.
◆ **de façon que** loc conj (+ subjonctif) so that.
◆ **de toute façon** loc adv anyway, in any case.
◆ **sans façon** ◇ loc adj unpretentious. ◇ loc adv [sincèrement] really, honestly; [accepter] without fuss.

façonner [fasɔne] [3] vt -1. [travailler, former] to shape. -2. [fabriquer] to manufacture, to make.

fac-similé [faksimile] (pl fac-similés) nm facsimile.

facteur, -trice [faktœr, tris] nm, f [des postes] postman (f postwoman) Br, mailman (f mailwoman) Am.
◆ **facteur** nm -1. MUS [fabricant] maker; ~ d'orgues organ-builder. -2. [élément & MATHS] factor; ~ rhésus MÉD Rhesus factor.

factice [faktis] adj artificial.

faction [faksjɔ̃] nf -1. [groupe] faction. -2. MIL: être en OU de ~ to be on guard (duty) OU on sentry duty.

factotum [faktotɔm] nm odd-job man.

factuel, -elle [faktɥɛl] adj factual.

facturation [faktyrasjɔ̃] nf -1. [action] invoicing. -2. [bureau] invoice office.

facture [faktyr] nf -1. COMM invoice; [de gaz, d'électricité] bill. -2. ART technique. -3. MUS [fabrication] making.

facturer [faktyre] [3] vt COMM to invoice.

facultatif, -ive [fakyltatif, iv] adj optional.

facultativement [fakyltativmɑ̃] adv optionally.

faculté [fakylte] nf -1. [don & UNIV] faculty; ~ de lettres/de droit/de médecine Faculty of Arts/Law/Medicine. -2. [possibilité] freedom. -3. [pouvoir] power.
◆ **facultés** nfpl (mental) faculties.

fada [fada] fam ◇ nm nutcase. ◇ adj nuts.

fadaises [fadɛz] nfpl drivel (U).

fade [fad] adj -1. [sans saveur] bland. -2. [sans intérêt] insipid.

fagot [fago] nm bundle of sticks; de derrière les ~s fig kept for a special occasion.

fagoté, -e [fagɔte] adj fam dressed.

fagoter [fagɔte] [3] vt fam to dress up.
◆ **se fagoter** vp fam to dress o.s. up.

Fahrenheit [farenajt] n inv Fahrenheit.

faible [fɛbl] ◇ adj -1. [gén] weak. -2. [petit - montant, proportion] small; [- revenu] low. -3. [lueur, bruit] faint. ◇ nmf weak person; ~ d'esprit feeble-minded person. ◇ nm weakness; avoir un ~ pour to have a weakness for.

faiblement [fɛbləmɑ̃] adv -1. [mollement] weakly, feebly. -2. [imperceptiblement] faintly. -3. [peu] slightly.

faiblesse [fɛblɛs] nf -1. [gén] weakness; ~ d'esprit feeble-mindedness. -2. [petitesse] smallness.

faiblir [feblir] [32] vi -1. [personne, monnaie] to weaken. -2. [forces] to diminish, to fail. -3. [tempête, vent] to die down.

faïence [fajɑ̃s] nf earthenware.

faignant, -e = fainéant.

faille [faj] ◇ → falloir. ◇ nf -1. GÉOL fault. -2. [défaut] flaw.

faillible [fajibl] adj fallible.

faillir [fajir] [46] vi -1. [manquer]: ~ à [promesse] not to keep; [devoir] not to do. -2. [être sur le point de]: ~ faire qqch to nearly OU almost do sthg.

faillite [fajit] nf FIN bankruptcy; faire ~ to go bankrupt; en ~ bankrupt.

faim [fɛ̃] nf hunger; avoir ~ to be hungry; avoir ~ de fig to hunger for; mourir de ~ to be starving; ne pas manger à sa ~ not to eat one's fill; rester sur sa ~ to be still hungry; fig to be unsatisfied OU disappointed; avoir une ~ de loup to be starving.

fainéant, -e [feneã, ãt], **feignant, -e, faignant, -e** [fɛɲã, ãt] ◇ *adj* lazy, idle. ◇ *nm, f* lazybones.

fainéanter [feneãte] [3] *vi* to laze about.

faire [fɛr] [109] ◇ *vt* -1. [fabriquer, préparer] to make; ~ **une maison** to build a house; ~ **une tarte/du café/un film** to make a tart/coffee/a film; ~ **qqch de qqch** [transformer] to make sthg into sthg; ~ **qqch de qqn** *fig* to make sthg of sb; **il veut en ~ un avocat** he wants him to be a lawyer, he wants to make a lawyer of him. -2. [s'occuper à] to do; **qu'est-ce qu'il fait dans la vie?** what does he do (for a living)?; **que fais-tu dimanche?** what are you doing on Sunday? -3. [entreprendre] to do; **qu'est-ce que je peux ~ pour vous aider?** what can I do to help you? -4. [étudier] to do; ~ **de l'anglais/des maths/du droit** to do English/maths/law. -5. [sport, musique] to play; ~ **du football/de la clarinette** to play football/the clarinet. -6. [effectuer] to do; ~ **le ménage** to do the housework; ~ **la cuisine** to cook, to do the cooking; ~ **la lessive** to do the washing. -7. [occasionner]: ~ **de la peine à qqn** to hurt sb; ~ **du mal à** to harm; ~ **du bruit** to make a noise; **ça m'a fait quelque chose** that had an effect on me; **ça ne fait rien** it doesn't matter. -8. [tenir le rôle de] to be, to play. -9. [imiter]: ~ **le sourd/l'innocent** to act deaf/(the) innocent. -10. [calcul, mesure]: **un et un font deux** one and one are OU make two; **ça fait combien (de kilomètres) jusqu'à la mer?** how far is it to the sea?; **la table fait 2 mètres de long** the table is 2 metres long. -11. [dire]: «**tiens**», **fit-elle** "really", she said. -12. **ne ~ que** [faire sans cesse] to do nothing but; **elle ne fait que bavarder** she does nothing but gossip, she's always gossiping; **je ne fais que passer** I've just popped in.

◇ *vi* [agir] to do, to act; ~ **vite** to act quickly; **tu ferais bien d'aller voir ce qui se passe** you ought to OU you'd better go and see what's happening; ~ **comme chez soi** to make o.s. at home.

◇ *v attr* [avoir l'air] to look; ~ **démodé/joli** to look old-fashioned/pretty; **ça fait jeune** it makes you look young.

◇ *v substitut* to do; **je lui ai dit de prendre une échelle mais il ne l'a pas fait** I told him to use a ladder but he didn't; **faites!** please do!

◇ *v impers* -1. [climat, temps]: **il fait beau/froid** it's fine/cold; **il fait 20 degrés** it's 20 degrees; **il fait jour/nuit** it's light/dark; **il fait bon se reposer** it's OU it feels good to have a rest. -2. [exprime la durée, la distance]: **ça fait six mois que je ne l'ai pas vu** it's six months since I last saw him; **ça fait six mois que je fais du portugais** I've been going to Portuguese classes for six months; **ça fait 30 kilomètres qu'on roule sans phares** we've been driving without lights for 30 kilometres.

◇ *v auxiliaire* -1. [à l'actif] to make; ~ **démarrer une voiture** to start a car; ~ **tomber qqch** to make sthg fall; ~ **travailler qqn** to make sb work; ~ **traverser la rue à un aveugle** to help a blind man cross the road. -2. [au passif]: ~ **faire qqch (par qqn)** to have sthg done (by sb); ~ **réparer sa voiture/nettoyer ses vitres** to have one's car repaired/one's windows cleaned.

◆ **se faire** *vp* -1. [avoir lieu] to take place. -2. [être à la mode] to be in. -3. [être convenable]: **ça ne se fait pas (de faire qqch)** it's not done (to do sthg). -4. [devenir]: **se ~** (+ *adjectif*) to get, to become; **il se fait tard** it's getting late; **se ~ beau** to make o.s. beautiful. -5. [causer] (+ *nom*): **se ~ mal** to hurt o.s.; **se ~ des amis** to make friends; **se ~ une idée sur qqch** to get some idea about sthg. -6. (+ *infinitif*): **se ~ écraser** to get run over; **se ~ opérer** to have an operation; **se ~ aider (par qqn)** to get help (from sb); **se ~ faire un costume** to have a suit made (for o.s.). -7. *loc*: **comment se fait-il que ...?** how is it that ...?, how come ...?; **s'en ~** to worry.

◆ **se faire à** *vp* + *prép* to get used to.

faire-part [fɛrpar] *nm inv* announcement; ~ **de naissance/mariage** birth/wedding announcement.

faire-valoir [fɛrvalwar] *nm inv* [personne] foil.

fair-play [fɛrplɛ] *adj inv* sporting; **se montrer ~** to be sporting.

fais, fait *etc* → **faire**.

faisable [fəzabl] *adj* feasible.

faisan [fəzã, ɑn] *nm, f* pheasant.

faisandé, -e [fəzãde] *adj* CULIN high.

faisceau [fɛso] *nm* -1. [rayon] beam; ~ **lumineux** beam of light. -2. [fagot] bundle.

faiseur, -euse [fəzœr, øz] *nm, f* maker; ~ **d'embarras** fusspot.

faisons → **faire**.

fait, faite [fɛ, fɛt] ◇ *pp* → **faire**.
◇ *adj* -1. [fabriqué] made; **être ~ pour** *litt* & *fig* to be made OU meant for; **il n'est pas ~ pour mener cette vie** he's not cut out for this kind of life; **ils sont ~s l'un pour l'autre** they are made for each other; ~ **sur mesure** made to measure. -2. [physique]: **bien ~** well-built. -3. [fromage] ripe. -4. *loc*:

c'est bien ~ pour lui (it) serves him right; c'en est ~ de nous we're done for.

◆ **fait** *nm* **-1.** [acte] act; **mettre qqn devant le ~ accompli** to present sb with a fait accompli; **prendre qqn sur le ~** to catch sb in the act; **~s et gestes** doings, actions. **-2.** [événement] event; **~s divers** news in brief. **-3.** [réalité] fact; **le ~ est que ...** the fact is (that) ....

◆ **au fait** *loc adv* by the way.

◆ **en fait** *loc adv* in (actual) fact.

◆ **en fait de** *loc prép* by way of.

◆ **tout à fait** *loc adv* completely, quite.

faîte [fɛt] *nm* **-1.** [de toit] ridge. **-2.** [d'arbre] top. **-3.** *fig* [sommet] pinnacle.

faites → **faire**.

faîtière [fɛtjɛr] *nf* skylight.

fait-tout (*pl inv*), **faitout** (*pl faitouts*) [fɛtu] *nm* stewpan.

fakir [fakir] *nm* fakir.

falaise [falɛz] *nf* cliff.

falbalas [falbala] *nmpl* furbelows.

fallacieux, -ieuse [falasjø, jøz] *adj* **-1.** [promesse] false. **-2.** [argument] fallacious.

falloir [falwar] [69] *v impers*: **il me faut du temps** I need (some) time; **il lui faudra de l'énergie** he'll need (a lot of) energy; **il te faut un peu de repos** you need some rest; **il faut que tu partes** you must go OU leave, you'll have to go OU leave; **il faut toujours qu'elle intervienne!** she always has to interfere!; **il faut agir** we/you *etc* must act; **il faut faire attention** we/you *etc* must be careful, we'll/you'll *etc* have to be careful; **s'il le faut** if necessary.

◆ **s'en falloir** *v impers*: **il s'en faut de peu pour qu'il puisse acheter cette maison** he can almost buy the house; **il s'en faut de 20 cm pour que l'armoire tienne dans le coin** the cupboard is 20 cm too big to fit into the corner; **il s'en faut de beaucoup pour qu'il ait l'examen** it'll take a lot for him to pass the exam; **peu s'en ait fallu qu'il démissionne** he very nearly resigned, he came close to resigning; **tant s'en faut** far from it, on the contrary.

fallu [faly] *pp inv* → **falloir**.

falot, -e [falo, ɔt] *adj* dull.

◆ **falot** *nm* lantern.

falsification [falsifikasjɔ̃] *nf* **-1.** [de document] forgery; [de monnaie] **counterfeiting**. **-2.** [de produit alimentaire] **adulteration**.

falsifier [falsifje] [9] *vt* **-1.** [document, signature, faits] to falsify. **-2.** [pensée, paroles] to misrepresent. **-3.** [produit alimentaire] to adulterate.

famé, -e [fame] *adj*: **mal ~** with a (bad) reputation.

famélique [famelik] *adj* half-starved.

fameusement [famøzmɑ̃] *adv fam* really.

fameux, -euse [famø, øz] *adj* **-1.** [célèbre] famous. **-2.** *fam* [remarquable] great; **pas ~** not up to much, nothing great.

familial, -e, -iaux [familjal, jo] *adj* family (*avant n*).

◆ **familiale** *nf* estate car *Br,* station wagon *Am*.

familiariser [familjarize] [3] *vt*: **~ qqn avec** to familiarize sb with.

◆ **se familiariser** *vp*: **se ~ avec** to get used to.

familiarité [familjarite] *nf* familiarity.

◆ **familiarités** *nfpl* liberties.

familier, -ière [familje, jɛr] *adj* familiar.

◆ **familier** *nm* regular (customer).

famille [famij] *nf* family; [ensemble des parents] relatives, relations; **de bonne ~** of good family; **fonder une ~** to start a family; **~ nombreuse** large family.

famine [famin] *nf* famine; **crier ~** *fig* to complain of one's poverty.

fan [fan] *nmf fam* fan.

fanal, -aux [fanal, o] *nm* **-1.** [de phare] beacon. **-2.** [de train] headlight. **-3.** [lanterne] lantern.

fanatique [fanatik] ◇ *nmf* fanatic. ◇ *adj* fanatical.

fanatiser [fanatize] [3] *vt* to make fanatics out of.

fanatisme [fanatism] *nm* fanaticism.

fane [fan] *nf* **-1.** [de carotte] top. **-2.** [d'arbre] fallen leaf.

faner [fane] [3] ◇ *vt* [altérer] to fade. ◇ *vi* **-1.** [fleur] to wither. **-2.** [beauté, couleur] to fade.

◆ **se faner** *vp* **-1.** [fleur] to wither. **-2.** [beauté, couleur] to fade.

fanfare [fɑ̃far] *nf* **-1.** [orchestre] brass band. **-2.** [musique] fanfare; **en ~** noisy.

fanfaron, -onne [fɑ̃farɔ̃, ɔn] ◇ *adj* boastful. ◇ *nm, f* braggart.

fanfaronnade [fɑ̃farɔnad] *nf* boasting (*U*).

fanfreluche [fɑ̃frəlyʃ] *nf* trimming.

fange [fɑ̃ʒ] *nf littéraire* mire; **traîner qqn dans la ~** to drag sb through the mire.

fanion [fanjɔ̃] *nm* pennant.

fantaisie [fɑ̃tezi] ◇ *nf* **-1.** [caprice] whim. **-2.** (*U*) [goût] fancy. **-3.** [imagination] imagination; **de ~** imaginary. **-4.** MUS fantasia. ◇ *adj*: **chapeau ~** fancy hat; **bijoux ~** fake jewellery.

fantaisiste [fɑ̃tezist] ◇ *nmf* entertainer. ◇ *adj* **-1.** [fumiste] dilettante. **-2.** [bizarre] fanciful.

fantasmagorique [fɑ̃tasmagɔrik] *adj* phantasmagorical, extraordinary.

fantasme [fɑ̃tasm] *nm* fantasy.

fantasmer [fɑ̃tasme] [3] *vi* to fantasize.

fantasque [fɑ̃task] *adj* **-1.** [personne] whimsical. **-2.** [humeur] capricious. **-3.** [chose] fantastic.

fantassin [fɑ̃tasɛ̃] *nm* infantryman.

fantastique [fɑ̃tastik] ◇ *adj* fantastic. ◇ *nm*: **le ~** the fantastic.

fantoche [fɑ̃tɔʃ] ◇ *adj* puppet (*avant n*). ◇ *nm* puppet.

fantomatique [fɑ̃tɔmatik] *adj* ghostly.

fantôme [fɑ̃tom] ◇ *nm* ghost. ◇ *adj* **-1.** [spectral] ghostly. **-2.** [inexistant] phantom.

FAO *nf* **-1.** (*abr de* **fabrication assistée par ordinateur**) CAM. **-2.** (*abr de* **Food and Agriculture Organisation**) FAO.

faon [fɑ̃] *nm* fawn.

FAP (*abr de* **franc d'avarie particulière**) *adj* FPA, fpa.

far [far] *nm*: **~ breton** *sweet flan containing plums.*

faramineux, -euse [faraminø, øz] *adj fam* **-1.** [prix] astronomical. **-2.** [génial] fantastic.

farandole [farɑ̃dɔl] *nf* farandole.

farce [fars] *nf* **-1.** CULIN stuffing. **-2.** [blague] (practical) joke; **faire une ~ à qqn** to play a (practical) joke on sb; **~s et attrapes** jokes and novelties. **-3.** LITTÉRATURE farce.

farceur, -euse [farsœr, øz] *nm, f* (practical) joker.

farci, -e [farsi] *adj* **-1.** CULIN stuffed. **-2.** *fig* [plein] stuffed, crammed.

farcir [farsir] [32] *vt* **-1.** CULIN to stuff. **-2.** [remplir]: **~ qqch de** to stuff OU cram sthg with.

◆ **se farcir** *vp fam* **-1.** [faire]: **se ~ qqch** to get stuck with sthg. **-2.** [supporter]: **se ~ qqn** to put up with sb. **-3.** [manger]: **se ~ qqch** to scoff sthg.

fard [far] *nm* make-up; **~ à joues** blusher; **~ à paupières** eyeshadow; **piquer un ~** *fam fig* to blush.

fardeau, -x [fardo] *nm* [poids] load; *fig* burden.

farder [farde] [3] *vt* **-1.** [maquiller] to make up. **-2.** *fig* [masquer] to disguise.

◆ **se farder** *vp* to make o.s. up, to put on one's make-up.

farfadet [farfadɛ] *nm* sprite.

farfelu, -e [farfəly] *fam* ◇ *adj* weird. ◇ *nm, f* weirdo.

farfouiller [farfuje] [3] *vi fam* to rummage.

farine [farin] *nf* flour; **rouler qqn dans la ~** *fig* to take sb for a ride.

farineux, -euse [farinø, øz] *adj* **-1.** [aspect, goût] floury. **-2.** [aliment] farinaceous.

◆ **farineux** *nm* starchy food.

farniente [farnjɛnte] *nm* idleness.

farouche [faruʃ] *adj* **-1.** [animal] wild, not tame; [personne] shy, withdrawn. **-2.** [sentiment] fierce.

farouchement [faruʃmɑ̃] *adv* fiercely.

fart [far(t)] *nm* (ski) wax.

farter [farte] [3] *vt* to wax.

fascicule [fasikyl] *nm* part, instalment.

fascinant, -e [fasinɑ̃, ɑ̃t] *adj* **-1.** [regard] alluring, captivating. **-2.** [personne, histoire] fascinating.

fascination [fasinasjɔ̃] *nf* fascination.

fasciner [fasine] [3] *vt* to fascinate.

fascisant, -e [faʃizɑ̃, ɑ̃t] *adj* fascistic.

fascisme [faʃism] *nm* fascism.

fasciste [faʃist] *nmf & adj* fascist.

fasse, fassions *etc* → **faire**.

faste [fast] ◇ *nm* splendour. ◇ *adj* [favorable] lucky.

fast-food [fastfud] (*pl* **fast-foods**) *nm* fast food.

fastidieux, -ieuse [fastidjø, jøz] *adj* boring.

fastueux, -euse [fastɥø, øz] *adj* luxurious.

fatal, -e [fatal] *adj* **-1.** [mortel, funeste] fatal. **-2.** [inévitable] inevitable.

fatalement [fatalmɑ̃] *adv* inevitably.

fataliste [fatalist] ◇ *nmf* fatalist. ◇ *adj* fatalistic.

fatalité [fatalite] *nf* **-1.** [destin] fate. **-2.** [inéluctabilité] inevitability.

fatidique [fatidik] *adj* fateful.

fatigant, -e [fatigɑ̃, ɑ̃t] *adj* **-1.** [épuisant] tiring. **-2.** [ennuyeux] tiresome.

fatiguant [fatigɑ̃] *participe présent* → **fatiguer**.

fatigue [fatig] *nf* tiredness; **tomber de ~, être mort de ~** to be dead tired.

fatigué, -e [fatige] *adj* tired; [cœur, yeux] strained.

fatiguer [fatige] [3] ◇ *vt* **-1.** [épuiser, affecter] to tire; [- cœur, yeux] to strain. **-2.** [ennuyer] to wear out. ◇ *vi* **-1.** [personne] to grow tired. **-2.** [moteur] to strain.

◆ **se fatiguer** *vp* to get tired; **se ~ de qqch** to get tired of sthg; **se ~ à faire qqch** to wear o.s. out doing sthg.

fatras [fatra] *nm* jumble.

fatuité [fatɥite] *nf littéraire* complacency.

faubourg [fobur] *nm* suburb.

fauché, -e [foʃe] *adj fam* broke, hard-up.

faucher [foʃe] [3] *vt* **-1.** [couper - herbe, blé] to cut. **-2.** *fam* [voler]: ~ **qqch à qqn** to pinch sthg from sb. **-3.** [piéton] to run over. **-4.** *fig* [suj: mort, maladie] to cut down.

faucille [fosij] *nf* sickle.

faucon [fokɔ̃] *nm* hawk.

faudra → **falloir**.

faufil [fofil] *nm* tacking OU basting thread.

faufiler [fofile] [3] *vt* to tack, to baste.

◆ **se faufiler** *vp*: **se ~ dans** to slip into; **se ~ entre** to thread one's way between.

faune [fon] ◇ *nf* **-1.** [animaux] fauna. **-2.** *péj* [personnes]: **la ~ qui fréquente ce bar** the sort of people who hang round that bar. ◇ *nm* MYTH faun.

faussaire [foser] *nmf* forger.

faussement [fosmɑ̃] *adv* **-1.** [à tort] wrongly. **-2.** [prétendument] falsely.

fausser [fose] [3] *vt* **-1.** [déformer] to bend. **-2.** [rendre faux] to distort.

◆ **se fausser** *vp* [voix] to become strained.

fausset [fosɛ] → **voix**.

fausseté [foste] *nf* **-1.** [hypocrisie] duplicity. **-2.** [de jugement, d'idée] falsity.

faute [fot] *nf* **-1.** [erreur] mistake, error; **faire une ~** to make a mistake OU an error; **~ de calcul** arithmetical error; **~ de frappe** [à la machine à écrire] typing error; [a l'ordinateur] keying error; **~ de goût** error of taste; **~ d'inattention** careless mistake; **~ d'orthographe** spelling mistake. **-2.** [méfait, infraction] offence; **prendre qqn en ~** to catch sb out; **~ professionnelle** professional misdemeanour. **-3.** TENNIS fault; FOOTBALL foul. **-4.** [responsabilité] fault; **de ma/ta** *etc* **~** my/your *etc* fault; **par la ~ de qqn** because of sb; **rejeter la ~ sur qqn** to shift the blame onto sb.

◆ **faute de** *loc prép* for want OU lack of; **~ de mieux** for want OU lack of anything better.

◆ **sans faute** ◇ *loc adv* without fail. ◇ *loc adj* faultless.

fauteuil [fotœj] *nm* **-1.** [siège] armchair; **~ à bascule** rocking chair; **~ roulant** wheelchair. **-2.** [de théâtre] seat; **~ d'orchestre** stall seat *Br*, seat in the stalls *Br* OU orchestra *Am*. **-3.** [de président] chair; [d'académicien] seat.

fauteur, -trice [fotœr, tris] *nm, f*: **~ de troubles** troublemaker.

fautif, -ive [fotif, iv] ◇ *adj* **-1.** [coupable] guilty. **-2.** [défectueux] faulty. ◇ *nm, f* guilty party.

fauve [fov] ◇ *nm* **-1.** [animal] big cat. **-2.** [couleur] fawn. **-3.** ART Fauve. ◇ *adj* **-1.** [animal] wild. **-2.** [cuir, cheveux] tawny. **-3.** ART Fauvist.

fauvette [fovɛt] *nf* warbler.

faux, fausse [fo, fos] *adj* **-1.** [incorrect] wrong. **-2.** [postiche, mensonger, hypocrite] false; **~ témoignage** JUR perjury. **-3.** [monnaie, papiers] forged, fake; [bijou, marbre] imitation, fake. **-4.** [injustifié]: **fausse alerte** false alarm; **c'est un ~ problème** that's not an issue (here).

◆ **faux** ◇ *nm* [document, tableau] forgery, fake. ◇ *nf* scythe. ◇ *adv*: **chanter/jouer ~** MUS to sing/play out of tune; **sonner ~** *fig* not to ring true.

faux-filet (*pl* **faux-filets**), **faux filet** (*pl* **faux filets**) [fofilɛ] *nm* sirloin.

faux-fuyant [fofɥijɑ̃] (*pl* **faux-fuyants**) *nm* excuse.

faux-monnayeur [fomɔnɛjœr] (*pl* **faux-monnayeurs**) *nm* counterfeiter.

faux-semblant [fosɑ̃blɑ̃] (*pl* **faux-semblants**) *nm* pretence.

faux-sens [fosɑ̃s] *nm inv* mistranslation.

faveur [favœr] *nf* favour; **faire une ~ à qqn** to do sb a favour; **intercéder ~ de qqn** to intercede on sb's behalf OU in sb's favour.

◆ **à la faveur de** *loc prép* thanks to.

◆ **en faveur de** *loc prép* in favour of.

favorable [favɔrabl] *adj*: **~ (à)** favourable (to).

favorablement [favɔrabləmɑ̃] *adv* favourably.

favori, -ite [favɔri, it] *adj & nm, f* favourite.

◆ **favoris** *nmpl* side whiskers.

favoriser [favɔrize] [3] *vt* **-1.** [avantager] to favour. **-2.** [contribuer à] to promote. **-3.** [aider] to assist.

favoritisme [favɔritism] *nm* favouritism.

faxer [fakse] [3] *vt* to fax.

fayot [fajo] *nm fam* creep, crawler.

FB (*abr de* **franc belge**) BF.

FBI [ɛfbiaj] (*abr de* **Federal Bureau of Investigation**) *nm* FBI.

FC (*abr de* **Football club**) *nm* FC.

FCFA (*abr de* **franc CFA**) *currency still used in former French colonies in Africa.*

FCFP (*abr de* **franc CFP**) *currency still used in former French colonies in the Pacific.*

fébrile [febril] *adj* feverish.

fébrilement [febrilmɑ̃] *adv* feverishly.

fécal, -e, -aux [fekal, o] → **matière**.

fécond, -e [fekɔ̃, 5d] *adj* **-1.** [femelle, terre,

esprit] fertile. **-2.** [écrivain] prolific. **-3.** [histoire, situation]: ~ **en qqch** rich in sthg.

fécondation [fekɔ̃dasjɔ̃] *nf* fertilization; ~ **in vitro** in vitro fertilization.

féconder [fekɔ̃de] [3] *vt* **-1.** [ovule] to fertilize. **-2.** [femme, femelle] to impregnate. **-3.** *littéraire* [fertiliser] to make fertile.

fécondité [fekɔ̃dite] *nf* **-1.** [gén] fertility. **-2.** [d'écrivain] productiveness.

fécule [fekyl] *nf* starch.

féculent, -e [fekylɑ̃, ɑ̃t] *adj* starchy.
◆ **féculent** *nm* starchy food.

fédéral, -e, -aux [federal, o] *adj* federal.

fédéralisme [federalism] *nm* federalism.

fédératif, -ive [federatif, iv] *adj* federative.

fédération [federasjɔ̃] *nf* federation.

fée [fe] *nf* fairy; ~ **du logis** model housekeeper.

feed-back [fidbak] *nm inv* feedback.

féerie [fe(e)ri] *nf* **-1.** THÉÂTRE spectacular; CIN fantasy. **-2.** [de lieu] enchantment; [de vision] enchanting sight.

féerique [fe(e)rik] *adj* [enchanteur] enchanting.

feignais, feignions *etc* → **feindre**.

feignant, -e = **fainéant**.

feindre [fɛ̃dr] [81] ◇ *vt* to feign; ~ **de faire qqch** to pretend to do sthg. ◇ *vi* to pretend.

feint, -e [fɛ̃, fɛ̃t] *pp* → **feindre**.

feinte [fɛ̃t] *nf* **-1.** [ruse] ruse. **-2.** FOOTBALL dummy; BOXE feint.

fêlé, -e [fele] ◇ *adj* **-1.** [assiette] cracked. **-2.** *fam* [personne] cracked, loony. ◇ *nm, f fam* freak, nutter.

fêler [fele] [4] *vt* to crack.
◆ **se fêler** *vp* to crack.

félicitations [felisitasjɔ̃] *nfpl* congratulations; **avec les** ~ **du jury** highly commended.

féliciter [felisite] [3] *vt* to congratulate.
◆ **se féliciter** *vp*: **se** ~ **de** to congratulate o.s. on.

félin, -e [felɛ̃, in] *adj* feline.
◆ **félin** *nm* big cat.

félon, -onne [felɔ̃, ɔn] *littéraire* ◇ *adj* traitorous. ◇ *nm, f* traitor.

fêlure [felyr] *nf* crack.

femelle [fəmɛl] *nf & adj* female.

féminin, -e [feminɛ̃, in] *adj* **-1.** [gén] feminine. **-2.** [revue, équipe] women's *(avant n)*.
◆ **féminin** *nm* GRAM feminine.

féminiser [feminize] [3] *vt* **-1.** [efféminer] to make effeminate. **-2.** BIOL to feminize.

◆ **se féminiser** *vp* **-1.** [institution] to attract more women. **-2.** [homme] to become effeminate.

féminisme [feminism] *nm* feminism.

féministe [feminist] *nmf & adj* feminist.

féminité [feminite] *nf* femininity.

femme [fam] *nf* **-1.** [personne de sexe féminin] woman; **bonne** ~ *péj* woman; **contes/ remèdes de bonne** ~ old wives' tales/ remedies; ~ **d'affaires** businesswoman; ~ **de chambre** chambermaid; ~ **fatale** femme fatale; ~ **au foyer** housewife; ~ **de ménage** cleaning woman; ~ **du monde** society woman; ~ **de tête** forceful woman. **-2.** [épouse] wife; **prendre** ~ *vieilli* to take a wife.

femmelette [famlɛt] *nf péj* weakling.

fémur [femyr] *nm* femur.

FEN [fɛn] *(abr de Fédération de l'éducation nationale) nf* teachers' trade union.

fenaison [fənɛzɔ̃] *nf* haymaking.

fendiller [fɑ̃dije] [3] *vt* to crack.
◆ **se fendiller** *vp* to crack.

fendre [fɑ̃dr] [73] *vt* **-1.** [bois] to split. **-2.** [foule, flots] to cut through.
◆ **se fendre** *vp* **-1.** [se crevasser] to crack. **-2.** *fam* [d'une somme]: **se** ~ **de qqch** to part with sthg.

fendu, -e [fɑ̃dy] *pp* → **fendre**.

fenêtre [fənɛtr] *nf* [gén & INFORM] window; ~ **à guillotine** sash window.

fenouil [fənuj] *nm* fennel.

fente [fɑ̃t] *nf* **-1.** [fissure] crack. **-2.** [interstice, de vêtement] slit.

féodal, -e, -aux [feodal, o] *adj* feudal.
◆ **féodal, -aux** *nm* feudal lord.

féodalité [feodalite] *nf* feudalism.

fer [fɛr] *nm* iron; **en** ~, **de** ~ iron *(avant n)*; ~ **à cheval** horseshoe; ~ **forgé** wrought iron; ~ **de lance** spearhead; ~ **à repasser** iron; ~ **à souder** soldering iron; **les quatre** ~**s en l'air** flat on one's back; **croire qqch dur comme** ~ to firmly believe sthg; **il faut battre le** ~ **quand il est chaud** strike while the iron is hot; **marquer qqn au** ~ **rouge** to brand sb.

ferai, feras *etc* → **faire**.

fer-blanc [fɛrblɑ̃] *(pl* **fers-blancs)** *nm* tinplate, tin; **en** ~ tin *(avant n)*.

ferblanterie [fɛrblɑ̃tri] *nf* **-1.** [commerce] tin industry. **-2.** [ustensiles] tinware.

férié, -e [ferje] → **jour**.

férir [ferir] *vt*: **sans coup** ~ without meeting any resistance OU obstacle.

ferme¹ [fɛrm] *nf* farm.

ferme² [fɛrm] ◇ *adj* firm; **être** ~ **sur ses jambes** to be steady on one's feet. ◇ *adv*

-1. [beaucoup] a lot. **-2.** [définitivement]: **acheter/vendre** ~ **to make a firm purchase/sale. -3.** loc: **tenir** ~ to stand firm.

fermement [fɛrməmɑ̃] adv firmly.

ferment [fɛrmɑ̃] nm **-1.** [levure] ferment. **-2.** fig [germe] seed, seeds (pl).

fermentation [fɛrmɑ̃tasjɔ̃] nf CHIM fermentation; fig ferment.

fermenter [fɛrmɑ̃te] [3] vi CHIM & fig to ferment.

fermer [fɛrme] [3] ◇ vt **-1.** [porte, tiroir, yeux] to close, to shut; [rideaux] to close, to draw; [store] to pull down; [enveloppe] to seal. **-2.** [bloquer] to close; ~ **son esprit à qqch** to close one's mind to sthg. **-3.** [gaz, lumière] to turn off. **-4.** [vêtement] to do up. **-5.** [entreprise] to close down. **-6.** [interdire]: ~ **qqch à qqn** to close sthg to sb. **-7.** loc: **la ferme!, ferme-la!** fam shut it!
◇ vi **-1.** [gén] to shut, to close. **-2.** [vêtement] to do up. **-3.** [entreprise] to close down.
◆ **se fermer** vp **-1.** [porte] to close, to shut. **-2.** [plaie] to close up. **-3.** [vêtement] to do up. **-4.** fig [s'endurcir]: **se** ~ **(à qqch)** to close o.s. off (from sthg).

fermeté [fɛrməte] nf firmness.

fermeture [fɛrmətyr] nf **-1.** [de porte] closing; «~ **automatique des portes»** doors close automatically. **-2.** [de vêtement, sac] fastening; ~ **Éclair®** zip Br, zipper Am. **-3.** [d'établissement - temporaire] closing; [- définitive] closure; ~ **hebdomadaire/annuelle** weekly/annual closing.

fermier, -ière [fɛrmje, jɛr] ◇ adj farm (avant n). ◇ nm, f farmer.

fermoir [fɛrmwar] nm clasp.

féroce [ferɔs] adj [animal, appétit] ferocious; [personne, désir] fierce.

férocement [ferɔsmɑ̃] adv fiercely.

férocité [ferɔsite] nf ferocity.

Féroé [ferɔe] nfpl: **les îles** ~ the Faeroes; **aux îles** ~ in the Faeroes.

ferraille [fɛraj] nf **-1.** [vieux fer] scrap iron (U); **bon à mettre à la** ~ fit for the scrap heap. **-2.** fam [monnaie] loose change.

ferré, -e [fɛre] adj **-1.** [soulier] hobnailed. **-2.** fam fig [calé]: **être** ~ **en** to be well up on.

ferrer [fɛre] [4] vt **-1.** [cheval] to shoe. **-2.** [poisson] to strike. **-3.** [soulier] to put hobnails on.

ferreux, -euse [fɛrø øz] adj ferrous.

ferronnerie [fɛrɔnri] nf **-1.** [objet, métier] ironwork (U). **-2.** [atelier] ironworks (sg).

ferroviaire [fɛrɔvjɛr] adj rail (avant n).

ferrugineux, -euse [fɛryʒinø, øz] adj ferruginous.

ferrure [fɛryr] nf **-1.** [de porte] fitting. **-2.** [de cheval] shoeing.

ferry-boat [fɛribot] (pl ferry-boats) nm ferry.

fertile [fɛrtil] adj litt & fig fertile; ~ **en** fig filled with, full of.

fertilisant, -e [fɛrtilizɑ̃, ɑ̃t] adj fertilizing.

fertiliser [fɛrtilize] [3] vt to fertilize.

fertilité [fɛrtilite] nf fertility.

féru, -e [fery] adj sout [passionné]: **être** ~ **de qqch** to have a passion for sthg.

férule [feryl] nf: **(être) sous la** ~ **de qqn** sout (to be) under sb's iron rule.

fervent, -e [fɛrvɑ̃, ɑ̃t] ◇ adj [chrétien] fervent; [amoureux, démocrate] ardent. ◇ nm, f devotee.

ferveur [fɛrvœr] nf **-1.** [dévotion] fervour. **-2.** [zèle] zeal.

fesse [fɛs] nf buttock.

fessée [fese] nf spanking, smack (on the bottom).

fessier, -ière [fesje, jɛr] adj buttock (avant n).
◆ **fessier** nm buttocks (pl).

festin [fɛstɛ̃] nm banquet, feast.

festival, -als [fɛstival] nm festival.

festivités [fɛstivite] nfpl festivities.

feston [fɛstɔ̃] nm **-1.** ARCHIT festoon. **-2.** COUTURE scallop.

festoyer [fɛstwaje] [13] vi to feast.

fêtard, -e [fɛtar, ard] nm, f fun-loving person.

fête [fɛt] nf **-1.** [congé] holiday; **les** ~s **(de fin d'année)** the Christmas holidays; ~ **légale** public holiday; ~ **nationale** national holiday. **-2.** [réunion, réception] celebration; ~ **de famille** family celebration. **-3.** [kermesse] fair; **en** ~ in festive mood; ~ **foraine** funfair; **la** ~ **de l'Humanité** annual festival organized by the Communist daily newspaper 'l'Humanité'; **la** ~ **de la Musique** annual music festival which takes place in the streets. **-4.** [jour de célébration - de personne] saint's day; [- de saint] feast (day); ~ **des mères/des pères** Mother's/Father's Day. **-5.** [soirée] party. **-6.** loc: **ça va être ta** ~ fam you'll get it in the neck; **faire** ~ **à qqn** to make a fuss of sb; **faire la** ~ to have a good time.

FÊTE:
The French traditionally wish 'bonne fête' to the person who has the same name as the saint commemorated on a particular day

Fête-Dieu [fɛtdjø] (*pl inv* OU **Fêtes-Dieu**) *nf*
Corpus Christi.

fêter [fete] [4] *vt* [événement] to celebrate;
[personne] to have a party for.

fétiche [fetiʃ] *nm* **-1.** [objet de culte] fetish.
-2. [mascotte] mascot.

fétichisme [fetiʃism] *nm* **-1.** [culte, perver-
sion] fetishism. **-2.** [vénération] idolatry.

fétide [fetid] *adj* fetid.

fétu [fety] *nm*: ~ **(de paille)** wisp (of straw).

feu, -e [fø] *adj*: ~ **M. X** the late Mr X; ~
mon mari my late husband.

◆ **feu, -x** *nm* **-1.** [flamme, incendie] fire; **au**
~! fire!; **en ~** *litt* & *fig* on fire; **avez-vous**
du ~? have you got a light?; **faire ~** MIL to
fire; **mettre le ~ à qqch** to set fire to sthg,
to set sthg on fire; **prendre ~** to catch fire;
~ **de bois** wood fire; ~ **de camp** camp fire;
~ **de cheminée** chimney fire; ~ **follet** will-
o'-the-wisp; ~ **de joie** bonfire; **être pris entre deux ~x** to be caught in the crossfire;
jouer avec le ~ to play with fire; **mettre à**
~ **et à sang** to ravage. **-2.** [signal] light; **tous**
~x éteints without any lights; ~ **rouge/**
vert red/green light; **~x de croisement**
dipped headlights; **~x de position** side-
lights; **~x de route** headlights on full
beam; **~x de stationnement** parking lights;
donner son OU **le ~ vert (à qqn)** to give
(sb) the go-ahead. **-3.** CULIN ring *Br*, burner
Am; **à ~ doux/vif** on a low/high flame; **à**
petit ~ gently. **-4.** CIN & THÉÂTRE light (*U*).
-5. *loc*: **ne pas faire long ~** not to last long.

◆ **feu d'artifice** *nm* firework.

feuillage [fœjaʒ] *nm* foliage.

feuille [fœj] *nf* **-1.** [d'arbre] leaf; ~ **morte**
dead leaf; ~ **de vigne** BOT vine leaf; CULIN
stuffed vine leaf. **-2.** [page] sheet; ~ **blanche** blank sheet; ~ **de papier** sheet of paper; ~ **volante** loose leaf. **-3.** [document]
form; ~ **de soins** *claim form for reimbursement*
of medical expenses. **-4.** [journal] paper; ~ **de**
chou *fam péj* rag.

feuillet [fœjɛ] *nm* page.

feuilleté, -e [fœjte] *adj* **-1.** CULIN: **pâte ~e**
puff pastry. **-2.** GÉOL foliated.

◆ **feuilleté** *nm* pastry.

feuilleter [fœjte] [27] *vt* to flick through.

feuilleton [fœjtɔ̃] *nm* serial; ~ **télévisé** soap
opera.

feuillu, -e [fœjy] *adj* leafy.

◆ **feuillu** *nm* broad-leaved tree.

feutre [føtr] *nm* **-1.** [étoffe] felt. **-2.** [chapeau]
felt hat. **-3.** [crayon] felt-tip pen.

feutré, -e [føtre] *adj* **-1.** [garni de feutre]
trimmed with felt; [qui a l'aspect du feutre]
felted. **-2.** [bruit, cri] muffled.

feutrer [føtre] [3] ◇ *vt* **-1.** [garnir de feutre]
to trim with felt. **-2.** [bruit, cri] to muffle. ◇
vi to felt (up).

◆ **se feutrer** *vp* to felt (up).

feutrine [føtrin] *nf* lightweight felt.

fève [fɛv] *nf* broad bean.

février [fevrije] *nm* February; *voir aussi* **septembre**.

FF (*abr de* **francs français**) FF.

FFI (*abr de* **Forces françaises de l'intérieur**)
nfpl French Resistance forces operating within
France during World War II.

FFL (*abr de* **Forces françaises libres**) *nfpl* free
French Army during World War II.

FFR (*abr de* **Fédération française de rugby**)
nf French rugby federation.

fg *abr de* **faubourg**.

FGEN (*abr de* **Fédération générale de l'éducation nationale**) *nf teachers' trade union*.

fi [fi] *interj*: **faire ~ de** to scorn.

fiabilité [fjabilite] *nf* reliability.

fiable [fjabl] *adj* reliable.

FIAC [fjak] (*abr de* **Foire internationale**
d'art contemporain) *nf international contemporary art fair held annually in Paris*.

fiacre [fjakr] *nm* hackney carriage.

fiançailles [fjãsaj] *nfpl* engagement (*sg*).

fiancé, -e [fjãse] *nm, f* fiancé (*f* fiancée).

fiancer [fjãse] [16]

◆ **se fiancer** *vp*: **se ~ (avec)** to get engaged (to).

fiasco [fjasko] *nm* fiasco; **faire ~** to be a
fiasco.

fibre [fibr] *nf* **-1.** ANAT, BIOL & TECHNOL fibre;
~ **optique** fibre optics (*U*); ~ **de verre**
fibreglass, glass fibre. **-2.** *fig* [sentiment] feeling; **avoir la ~ maternelle** to have the maternal instinct.

fibreux, -euse [fibrø, øz] *adj* fibrous; [viande]
stringy.

fibrome [fibrom] *nm* fibroma.

ficelé, -e [fisle] *adj fam* dressed; **être mal ~**
to be scruffy.

ficeler [fisle] [24] *vt* [lier] to tie up.

ficelle [fisɛl] *nf* **-1.** [fil] string; **tirer les ~s** to
pull the strings. **-2.** [pain] *thin French stick*.
-3. (*gén pl*) [truc] trick.

fiche [fiʃ] *nf* **-1.** [document] card; ~ **de paie**
pay slip; ~ **signalétique** identification
sheet; ~ **technique** technical data sheet.
-2. ÉLECTR & TECHNOL pin.

ficher [fiʃe] [3] (*pp sens 1 & 2* **fiché**, *pp sens*
3 & 4 **fichu**) *vt* **-1.** [enfoncer]: ~ **qqch dans**
to stick sthg into. **-2.** [inscrire] to put on
file. **-3.** *fam* [faire]: **qu'est-ce qu'il fiche?**

what's he doing? **-4.** *fam* [mettre] to put; ~ qqn par terre to send sb flying; ~ qqch par terre *fig* to mess OU muck sth up; ~ qqn dehors OU à la porte to throw sb out.
◆ **se ficher** *vp* **-1.** [s'enfoncer - suj: clou, pique] **se ~ dans** to go into. **-2.** *fam* [se moquer]: **se ~ de** to make fun of. **-3.** *fam* [ne pas tenir compte]: **se ~ de** not to give a damn about. **-4.** *loc*: **se ~ dedans** *fam* to get it all wrong.

fichier [fiʃje] *nm* file.

fichu, -e [fiʃy] *adj* **-1.** *fam* [cassé, fini] done for. **-2.** (*avant n*) [désagréable] nasty. **-3.** *loc*: **être mal ~** *fam* [personne] to feel rotten; [objet] to be badly made; **il n'est même pas ~ de faire son lit** *fam* he can't even make his own bed.
◆ **fichu** *nm* scarf.

fictif, -ive [fiktif, iv] *adj* **-1.** [imaginaire] imaginary. **-2.** [faux] false. **-3.** [valeur] face (*avant n*).

fiction [fiksjɔ̃] *nf* **-1.** LITT fiction. **-2.** [monde imaginaire] dream world.

ficus [fikys] *nm* fig-tree.

fidèle [fidɛl] ◇ *nmf* **-1.** RELIG believer. **-2.** [adepte] fan. ◇ *adj* **-1.** [loyal, exact, semblable]: ~ **(à)** faithful (to); ~ **à la réalité** accurate. **-2.** [habitué] regular.

fidèlement [fidɛlmɑ̃] *adv* **-1.** [loyalement, exactement] faithfully. **-2.** [régulièrement] regularly.

fidéliser [fidelize] [3] *vt* to attract and keep.

fidélité [fidelite] *nf* faithfulness.

Fidji [fidʒi] *n* Fiji; **à ~** in Fiji.

fidjien, -ienne [fidʒjɛ̃, jɛn] *adj* Fijian.
◆ **Fidjien, -ienne** *nm, f* Fijian.

fief [fjɛf] *nm* fief; *fig* stronghold.

fieffé, -e [fjefe] *adj* arrant.

fiel [fjɛl] *nm* *litt* & *fig* gall.

fiente [fjɑ̃t] *nf* droppings (*pl*).

fier¹, fière [fjɛr] *adj* **-1.** [gén] proud; ~ **de qqn/qqch** proud of sb/sth; ~ **de faire qqch** proud to be doing sth. **-2.** [noble] noble.

fier² [fje] [9]
◆ **se fier** *vp*: **se ~ à** to trust, to rely on.

fièrement [fjɛrmɑ̃] *adv* proudly.

fierté [fjɛrte] *nf* **-1.** [satisfaction, dignité] pride. **-2.** [arrogance] arrogance.

fièvre [fjɛvr] *nf* **-1.** MÉD fever; **avoir de la ~** to have a fever; **avoir 40 de ~** to have a temperature of 105 (degrees). **-2.** *fig* [excitation] excitement.

fiévreusement [fjevrøzmɑ̃] *adv* feverishly.

fiévreux, -euse [fjevrø, øz] *adj* *litt* & *fig* feverish.

fig. *abr de* **figure**.

figé, -e [fiʒe] *adj* fixed.

figer [fiʒe] [17] *vt* to paralyse; **être figé sur place** to be rooted to the spot.
◆ **se figer** *vp* **-1.** [s'immobiliser] to freeze. **-2.** [se solidifier] to congeal.

fignoler [fiɲɔle] [3] *vt* to put the finishing touches to.

figue [fig] *nf* fig.

figuier [figje] *nm* fig-tree.

figurant, -e [figyrɑ̃, ɑ̃t] *nm, f* extra.

figuratif, -ive [figyratif, iv] *adj* figurative.

figuration [figyrasjɔ̃] *nf* CIN & THÉÂTRE: **faire de la ~** to work as an extra.

figure [figyr] *nf* **-1.** [gén] figure; **faire ~ de** to look like; ~**s imposées/libres** SPORT compulsory/freestyle section; ~ **de proue** figurehead; *fig* leading light; ~ **de rhétorique** LING figure of speech; ~ **de style** LING stylistic device. **-2.** [visage] face; **faire bonne ~** *fig* to put on a good face.

figuré, -e [figyre] *adj* [sens] figurative.
◆ **figuré** *nm*: **au ~** in the figurative sense.

figurer [figyre] [3] ◇ *vt* to represent. ◇ *vi*: ~ **dans/parmi** to figure in/among.

figurine [figyrin] *nf* figurine.

fil [fil] *nm* **-1.** [brin] thread; ~ **à plomb** plumb line; ~ **conducteur** *fig* main idea; **c'est cousu de ~ blanc** it doesn't fool anybody; **de ~ en aiguille** gradually; **donner du ~ à retordre** *fig* to make life difficult; **perdre le ~ (de qqch)** *fig* to lose the thread (of sth); **ne tenir qu'à un ~** *fig* to hang by a thread. **-2.** [câble] wire; ~ **de fer** wire; **avoir qqn au bout du ~** to have sb on the line. **-3.** [cours] course; **au ~ de** in the course of. **-4.** [tissu] linen. **-5.** [tranchant] edge.

filament [filamɑ̃] *nm* **-1.** ANAT & ÉLECTR filament. **-2.** [végétal] fibre. **-3.** [de colle, bave] thread.

filandreux, -euse [filɑ̃drø, øz] *adj* [viande] stringy.

filant, -e [filɑ̃, ɑ̃t] → **étoile**.

filasse [filas] ◇ *nf* tow. ◇ *adj inv* flaxen.

filature [filatyr] *nf* **-1.** [usine] mill; [fabrication] spinning. **-2.** [poursuite] tailing; **prendre qqn en ~** to tail sb.

file [fil] *nf* line; **à la ~** in a line; **en double ~** in two lines; **se garer en double ~** to double-park; **en ~ indienne** in single OU Indian file; **se mettre en ~** to line up; ~ **d'attente** queue *Br*, line *Am*.

filer [file] [3] ◇ *vt* **-1.** [soie, coton] to spin. **-2.** [personne] to tail. **-3.** *fam* [donner]: ~ **qqch à qqn** to slip sth to sb, to slip sb sth. ◇ *vi* **-1.** [bas] to ladder *Br*, to run *Am*.

-2. [aller vite - temps, véhicule] to fly (by). **-3.** *fam* [partir] to dash off. **-4.** *loc:* ~ **doux** to behave nicely.

filet [filɛ] *nm* **-1.** [à mailles] net; ~ **à papillons** butterfly net; ~ **de pêche** fishing net; ~ **à provisions** string bag; **travailler sans** ~ *fig* to take risks; **tendre un** ~ *fig* to set a trap. **-2.** CULIN fillet; ~ **de bœuf/de sole** fillet of beef/sole. **-3.** [de liquide] drop, dash; [de lumière] shaft. **-4.** [de vis] thread.

filial, -e, **-iaux** [filjal, jo] *adj* filial.
◆ **filiale** *nf* ÉCON subsidiary.

filiation [filjasjɔ̃] *nf* **-1.** [lien de parenté] line. **-2.** *fig* [enchaînement] logical relationship.

filière [filjɛr] *nf* **-1.** [voie]: **suivre la** ~ [professionnelle] to work one's way up; **suivre la** ~ **hiérarchique** to go through the right channels. **-2.** [réseau] network.

filiforme [filifɔrm] *adj* skinny.

filigrane [filigran] *nm* [dessin] watermark; **en** ~ *fig* between the lines.

filin [filɛ̃] *nm* rope.

fille [fij] *nf* **-1.** [enfant] daughter. **-2.** [femme] girl; **jeune** ~ girl; ~ **de joie** prostitute; ~ **mère** *péj* single mother; **petite-**~ granddaughter; **vieille** ~ *péj* spinster; **courir les** ~**s** *fig* to chase women.

fillette [fijɛt] *nf* little girl.

filleul, -e [fijœl] *nm, f* godchild.

film [film] *nm* **-1.** [gén] film; ~ **d'action** action film; ~**-culte** cult film *Br*, cult movie *Am*; ~ **d'épouvante** horror film; ~ **noir** film noir; ~ **policier** detective film. **-2.** *fig* [déroulement] course.

film-catastrophe [filmkatastrɔf] *nm* disaster movie.

filmer [filme] [3] *vt* to film.

filmographie [filmɔɡrafi] *nf* filmography, films (pl).

filon [filɔ̃] *nm* **-1.** [de mine] vein. **-2.** *fam fig* [possibilité] cushy number.

filou [filu] *nm* rogue.

filouterie [filutri] *nf* fraud.

fils [fis] *nm* son; ~ **de famille** boy from a privileged background; ~ **à papa** *péj* daddy's boy; **le** ~ **prodigue** the prodigal son.

filtrage [filtraʒ] *nm* filtering; *fig* screening.

filtrant, -e [filtrɑ̃, ɑ̃t] *adj* [verre] tinted.

filtre [filtr] *nm* filter; ~ **à air** AUTOM air filter; ~ **à café** coffee filter.

filtrer [filtre] [3] ◇ *vt* to filter; *fig* to screen. ◇ *vi* to filter; *fig* to filter through.

fin, fine [fɛ̃, fin] ◇ *adj* **-1.** [gén] fine. **-2.** [partie du corps] slender; [couche, papier] thin. **-3.** [subtil] shrewd. **-4.** [ouïe, vue] keen. **-5.**

(avant n) [spécialiste] expert. ◇ *adv* finely; ~ **prêt** quite ready.
◆ **fin** *nf* end; ~ **mars** at the end of March; **mettre** ~ **à** to put a stop OU an end to; **prendre** ~ to come to an end; **tirer** OU **toucher à sa** ~ to draw to a close; ~ **de citation** (quote) unquote; ~ **de saison** end of season; **arrondir ses** ~**s de mois** to make ends meet; **arriver** OU **parvenir à ses** ~**s** to achieve one's ends OU aims; **c'est la** ~ **des haricots** it's the last straw; **mener à bonne** ~ to bring to a successful conclusion; **mettre** ~ **à ses jours** to put an end to one's life; **à toutes** ~**s utiles** just in case.
◆ **fin de non-recevoir** *nf* objection; [refus] refusal.
◆ **fin de série** *nf* oddment.
◆ **à la fin** *loc adv*: **tu vas m'écouter, à la** ~? will you listen to me?
◆ **à la fin de** *loc prép* at the end of.
◆ **en fin de** *loc prép* at the end of.
◆ **sans fin** *loc adj* endless.

final, -e [final] (pl **finals** OU **finaux**) *adj* final.
◆ **final(e)** *nm* MUS finale.
◆ **finale** *nf* **-1.** SPORT final. **-2.** [de mot] last syllable.

finalement [finalmɑ̃] *adv* finally.

finaliser [finalize] [3] *vt* to finalize.

finaliste [finalist] *nmf & adj* finalist.

finalité [finalite] *nf sout* [fonction] purpose.

finance [finɑ̃s] *nf* finance; **la haute** ~ high finance.
◆ **finances** *nfpl* finances.
◆ **Finances** *nfpl*: **les Finances** ≃ the Treasury, the Exchequer *Br*.

financement [finɑ̃smɑ̃] *nm* financing, funding.

financer [finɑ̃se] [16] *vt* to finance, to fund.

financier, -ière [finɑ̃sje, jɛr] *adj* financial.
◆ **financier** *nm* financier.

financièrement [finɑ̃sjɛrmɑ̃] *adv* financially.

finasser [finase] [3] *vi fam* to resort to tricks.

finaud, -e [fino, od] *adj* wily, crafty.

fine [fin] *nf type of brandy*.

finement [finmɑ̃] *adv* **-1.** [délicatement] finely. **-2.** [adroitement] cleverly. **-3.** [subtilement] subtly.

finesse [fines] *nf* **-1.** [gén] fineness. **-2.** [minceur] slenderness. **-3.** [perspicacité] shrewdness. **-4.** [subtilité] subtlety.

fini, -e [fini] *adj* **-1.** *péj* [fieffé]: **un crétin** ~ a complete idiot. **-2.** *fam* [usé, diminué] finished. **-3.** [limité] finite.
◆ **fini** *nm* [d'objet] finish.

finir [finir] [32] ◇ *vt* **-1.** [gén] to finish, to end. **-2.** [vider] to empty. **-3.** *fam* [user] to wear out. ◇ *vi* **-1.** [gén] to finish, to end; ~ par faire qqch to do sthg eventually; **tu finis par m'énerver!** you're starting to get on my nerves!; **mal** ~ to end badly. **-2.** [arrêter]: ~ **de faire qqch** to stop doing sthg; **en** ~ **(avec)** to finish (with); **à n'en plus** ~ never-ending.

finish [finiʃ] *nm* finish; **au** ~ to the finish.

finition [finisjɔ̃] *nf* **-1.** [action] finishing. **-2.** [d'objet] finish.

finlandais, -e [fɛ̃lɑ̃dɛ, ɛz] *adj* Finnish.
◆ **Finlandais, -e** *nm, f* Finn.

Finlande [fɛ̃lɑ̃d] *nf*: **la** ~ Finland.

finnois, -e [finwa, az] *adj* Finnish.
◆ **finnois** *nm* [langue] Finnish.
◆ **Finnois, -e** *nm, f* Finn.

FINUL, Finul [finyl] (*abr de* **Forces intérimaires des Nations unies au Liban**) *nfpl* UNIFIL.

fiole [fjɔl] *nf* flask.

fioriture [fjorityr] *nf* flourish.

fioul = **fuel**.

FIP [fip] (*abr de* **France Inter Paris**) *nf French national radio station broadcasting light music.*

firmament [firmamɑ̃] *nm* firmament.

firme [firm] *nf* firm.

fis, fit *etc* → **faire**.

FIS [fis] (*abr de* **Front islamique du salut**) *nm*: **le** ~ the Islamic Salvation Front.

fisc [fisk] *nm* ≃ Inland Revenue *Br*, ≃ Internal Revenue *Am*.

fiscal, -e, -aux [fiskal, o] *adj* tax (*avant n*), fiscal.

fiscaliser [fiskalize] [3] *vt* to (make) subject to tax.

fiscalité [fiskalite] *nf* tax system.

fissure [fisyr] *nf litt* & *fig* crack.

fissurer [fisyre] [3] *vt* [fendre] to crack; *fig* to split.
◆ **se fissurer** *vp* to crack.

fiston [fistɔ̃] *nm fam* son.

FIV (*abr de* **fécondation in vitro**) *nf* IVF.

FIVETE, Fivete [fivet] (*abr de* **fécondation in vitro et transfert d'embryon**) *nf* GIFT; **une** ~ a test-tube baby.

fixateur, -trice [fiksatœr, tris] *adj* **-1.** PHOT fixing (*avant n*). **-2.** [lotion, crème] setting (*avant n*).
◆ **fixateur** *nm* PHOT fixer.

fixatif [fiksatif] *nm* fixative.

fixation [fiksasjɔ̃] *nf* **-1.** [action de fixer] fixing. **-2.** [attache] fastening, fastener; [de ski] binding. **-3.** PSYCHOL fixation.

fixe [fiks] *adj* fixed; [encre] permanent; **à heure** ~ at set OU fixed times.
◆ **fixe** *nm* fixed salary.

fixement [fiksəmɑ̃] *adv* fixedly; **regarder** ~ **qqn/qqch** to stare at sb/sthg.

fixer [fikse] [3] *vt* **-1.** [gén] to fix; [règle] to set; ~ **son choix sur** to decide on. **-2.** [monter] to hang. **-3.** [regarder] to stare at. **-4.** [renseigner]: ~ **qqn sur qqch** to put sb in the picture about sthg; **être fixé sur qqch** to know all about sthg.
◆ **se fixer** *vp* to settle; **se** ~ **sur** [suj: choix, personne] to settle on; [suj: regard] to rest on.

fixité [fiksite] *nf* steadiness.

fjord [fjord] *nm* fjord.

fl. (*abr de* **fleuve**) R.

FL (*abr de* **florin**) Fl, F, G.

flacon [flakɔ̃] *nm* small bottle.

flageller [flaʒele] [4] *vt* **-1.** [fouetter] to flagellate. **-2.** *fig* [fustiger] to denounce.

flageoler [flaʒɔle] [3] *vi* to tremble.

flageolet [flaʒɔlɛ] *nm* **-1.** [haricot] flageolet bean. **-2.** MUS flageolet.

flagornerie [flagornəri] *nf* flattery.

flagrant, -e [flagrɑ̃, ɑ̃t] *adj* flagrant; → **délit**.

flair [flɛr] *nm* sense of smell; *fig*: **avoir du** ~ *fig* to be intuitive.

flairer [flɛre] [4] *vt* to sniff, to smell; *fig* to scent.

flamand, -e [flamɑ̃, ɑ̃d] *adj* Flemish.
◆ **flamand** *nm* [langue] Flemish.
◆ **Flamand, -e** *nm, f* Flemish person, Fleming.

flamant [flamɑ̃] *nm* flamingo; ~ **rose** pink flamingo.

flambant, -e [flɑ̃bɑ̃, ɑ̃t] *adj*: ~ **neuf** brand new.

flambeau, -x [flɑ̃bo] *nm* torch; *fig* flame; **se passer le** ~ *fig* to hand on the torch.

flambée [flɑ̃be] *nf* **-1.** [feu] blaze. **-2.** *fig* [de colère] outburst; [de violence] outbreak; **il y a eu une** ~ **des prix** prices have skyrocketed.

flamber [flɑ̃be] [3] ◇ *vi* **-1.** [brûler] to blaze. **-2.** *fam* JEU to play for high stakes. ◇ *vt* **-1.** [crêpe] to flambé. **-2.** [volaille] to singe.

flamboie, flamboies *etc* → **flamboyer**.

flamboyant, -e [flɑ̃bwajɑ̃, ɑ̃t] *adj* **-1.** [ciel, regard] blazing; [couleur] flaming. **-2.** ARCHIT flamboyant.

flamboyer [flɑ̃bwaje] [13] *vi* to blaze.

flamingant, -e [flamɛ̃gɑ̃, ɑ̃t] *adj* **-1.** [nationaliste] Flemish-nationalist. **-2.** [de langue] Flemish-speaking.

◆ **Flamingant**, **-e** *nm, f* **-1.** [nationaliste] Flemish nationalist. **-2.** [de langue] Flemish speaker.

flamme [flam] *nf* flame; *fig* fervour, fire.

flan [flɑ̃] *nm* baked custard.

flanc [flɑ̃] *nm* [de personne, navire, montagne] side; [d'animal, d'armée] flank; **à ~ de coteau** on the hillside; **être sur le ~** *fig* to feel washed out; **tirer au ~** *fam fig* to skive *Br*.

flancher [flɑ̃ʃe] [3] *vi fam* to give up.

flanelle [flanɛl] *nf* flannel.

flâner [flane] [3] *vi* **-1.** [se promener] to stroll. **-2.** [s'attarder] to hang about, to lounge about.

flânerie [flɑnri] *nf* stroll.

flâneur, **-euse** [flɑnœr, øz] *nm, f* stroller.

flanquer [flɑ̃ke] [3] *vt* **-1.** *fam* [jeter]: **~ qqch par terre** to fling sthg to the ground; **~ qqn dehors** to chuck OU fling sb out. **-2.** *fam* [donner]: **~ une gifle à qqn** to clout sb round the ear; **~ la frousse à qqn** to put the wind up sb. **-3.** [accompagner]: **être flanqué de** to be flanked by.

◆ **se flanquer** *vp fam*: **se ~ par terre** to fall flat on one's face.

flapi, **-e** [flapi] *adj fam* dead beat.

flaque [flak] *nf* pool; **~ (d'eau)** puddle.

flash [flaʃ] *nm* **-1.** PHOT flash. **-2.** RADIO & TÉLÉ: **~ (d'information)** newsflash; **~ de publicité** commercial.

flash-back [flaʃbak] (*pl inv* OU **flash-backs**) *nm* CIN flashback.

flasher [flaʃe] [3] *vi fam*: **~ sur qqn/qqch** to be turned on by sb/sthg; **faire ~ qqn** to turn sb on.

flasque [flask] ◇ *nf* flask. ◇ *adj* flabby, limp.

flatter [flate] [3] *vt* **-1.** [louer] to flatter. **-2.** [caresser] to stroke.

◆ **se flatter** *vp* to flatter o.s.; **je me flatte de le convaincre** I flatter myself that I can convince him; **se ~ de faire qqch** to pride o.s. on doing sthg.

flatterie [flatri] *nf* flattery.

flatteur, **-euse** [flatœr, øz] ◇ *adj* flattering. ◇ *nm, f* flatterer.

flatulence [flatylɑ̃s] *nf* flatulence, wind.

FLE, **fle** [flə] (*abr de* **français langue étrangère**) *nm* French as a foreign language.

fléau, **-x** [fleo] *nm* **-1.** *litt* & *fig* [calamité] scourge. **-2.** [instrument] flail.

flèche [flɛʃ] *nf* **-1.** [gén] arrow. **-2.** [d'église] spire. **-3.** *fig* [critique] shaft. **-4.** *loc*: **monter en ~** to shoot up; **partir comme une ~** to shoot off.

flécher [fleʃe] [18] *vt* to mark (with arrows).

fléchette [fleʃɛt] *nf* dart.

◆ **fléchettes** *nfpl* darts (*sg*).

fléchir [fleʃir] [32] ◇ *vt* to bend, to flex; *fig* to sway. ◇ *vi* to bend; *fig* to weaken.

fléchissement [fleʃismɑ̃] *nm* flexing, bending; *fig* weakening.

flegmatique [flɛgmatik] *adj* phlegmatic.

flegme [flɛgm] *nm* composure.

flemmard, **-e** [flɛmar, ard] *fam* ◇ *adj* lazy. ◇ *nm, f* lazybones (*sg*), idler.

flemmarder [flɛmarde] [3] *vi fam* to lounge about.

flemme [flɛm] *nf fam* laziness; **avoir la ~** to laze about.

flétan [fletɑ̃] *nm* halibut.

flétrir [fletrir] [32] *vt* [fleur, visage] to wither.

◆ **se flétrir** *vp* to wither.

fleur [flœr] *nf* BOT & *fig* flower; **en ~**, **en ~s** [arbre] in flower, in blossom; **à ~s** [motif] flowered; **la fine ~ de** *fig* the flower OU the cream of; **~ de lys** fleur-de-lis; **dans la ~ de l'âge** in the prime of life; **être ~ bleue** to be a romantic, to be sentimental; **faire une ~ à qqn** *fam* to do sb a good turn; **avoir les nerfs à ~ de peau** to be all on edge.

fleurer [flœre] [5] *vt*: **~ bon la vanille** to have a pleasant smell of vanilla.

fleuret [flœrɛ] *nm* foil.

fleurette [flœrɛt] *nf*: **conter ~ à qqn** *vieilli ou hum* to whisper sweet nothings to sb.

fleuri, **-e** [flœri] *adj* **-1.** [jardin, pré] in flower; [vase] of flowers; [tissu] flowered; [table, appartement] decorated with flowers. **-2.** *fig* [style] flowery.

fleurir [flœrir] [32] ◇ *vi* to blossom; *fig* to flourish. ◇ *vt* [maison] to decorate with flowers; [tombe] to lay flowers on.

fleuriste [flœrist] *nmf* florist.

fleuron [flœrɔ̃] *nm fig* jewel.

fleuve [flœv] *nm* **-1.** [cours d'eau] river. **-2.** (*en apposition*) [interminable] lengthy, interminable; **un discours-~** an interminable speech.

flexible [flɛksibl] *adj* flexible.

flexion [flɛksjɔ̃] *nf* **-1.** [de genou, de poutre] bending. **-2.** LING inflexion.

flibustier [flibystje] *nm* buccaneer.

flic [flik] *nm fam* cop.

flingue [flɛ̃g] *nm fam* gun.

flinguer [flɛ̃ge] [3] *vt fam* to gun down.

◆ **se flinguer** *vp fam* to blow one's brains out.

fœtal

flipper¹ [flipœ] *nm* pin-ball machine.

flipper² [flipe] [3] *vi fam* **-1.** [être déprimé] to feel down. **-2.** [planer] to freak out.

flirt [flœrt] *nm* **-1.** [amourette] flirtation. **-2.** [personne] boyfriend (*f* girlfriend).

flirter [flœrte] [3] *vi*: ~ (**avec qqn**) to flirt (with sb); ~ **avec qqch** *fig* to flirt with sthg.

FLN (*abr de* **Front de libération nationale**) *nm Algerian national liberation front.*

FLNC (*abr de* **Front de libération nationale corse**) *nm Corsican national liberation front.*

FLNKS (*abr de* **Front de libération nationale kanak et socialiste**) *nm political movement in New Caledonia.*

flocon [flɔkɔ̃] *nm* flake; ~ **de neige** snowflake; ~**s d'avoine** oat flakes.

flonflon [flɔ̃flɔ̃] *nm* (*gén pl*) blare.

flop [flɔp] *nm* [échec] flop, failure.

flopée [flɔpe] *nf fam*: **une** ~ **de** heaps of, masses of.

floraison [flɔrɛzɔ̃] *nf litt* & *fig* flowering, blossoming.

floral, -e, -aux [flɔral, o] *adj* floral.

floralies [flɔrali] *nfpl* flower show (*sg*).

flore [flɔr] *nf* flora.

Florence [flɔrɑ̃s] *n* Florence.

Floride [flɔrid] *nf*: **la** ~ Florida.

florilège [flɔrilɛʒ] *nm* anthology.

florissant, -e [flɔrisɑ̃, ɑ̃t] *adj* [santé] blooming; [économie] flourishing.

flot [flo] *nm* flood, stream; **être à** ~ [navire] to be afloat; *fig* to be back to normal; **couler à** ~**s** *fig* to flow like water.

♦ **flots** *nmpl littéraire* waves.

flottage [flɔtaʒ] *nm* floating (*of logs*).

flottaison [flɔtɛzɔ̃] *nf* floating.

flottant, -e [flɔtɑ̃, ɑ̃t] *adj* **-1.** [gén] floating; [esprit] irresolute. **-2.** [robe] loose-fitting.

flotte [flɔt] *nf* **-1.** AÉRON & NAVIG fleet; ~ **aérienne** air fleet. **-2.** *fam* [eau] water. **-3.** *fam* [pluie] rain.

flottement [flɔtmɑ̃] *nm* **-1.** [de drapeau] fluttering. **-2.** [indécision] hesitation, wavering. **-3.** [de monnaie] floating.

flotter [flɔte] [3] ◇ *vi* **-1.** [sur l'eau] to float. **-2.** [drapeau] to flap; [brume, odeur] to drift. **-3.** [dans un vêtement] : **tu flottes dedans** it's baggy on you. ◇ *v impers fam*: **il flotte** it's raining.

flotteur [flɔtœr] *nm* [de ligne de pêche, d'hydravion] float; [de chasse d'eau] ballcock.

flou, -e [flu] *adj* **-1.** [couleur, coiffure] soft. **-2.** [photo] blurred, fuzzy. **-3.** [pensée] vague, woolly.

♦ **flou** *nm* [de photo] fuzziness; [de décision] vagueness; **le** ~ **artistique** CIN & PHOT soft focus; *fig* vagueness.

flouer [flue] [3] *vt fam* to do, to swindle.

fluctuant, -e [flyktɥɑ̃, ɑ̃t] *adj* fluctuating.

fluctuation [flyktɥasjɔ̃] *nf* fluctuation.

fluctuer [flyktɥe] [3] *vi* to fluctuate.

fluet, -ette [flɥɛ, ɛt] *adj* [personne] thin, slender; [voix] thin.

fluide [flɥid] ◇ *nm* **-1.** [matière] fluid. **-2.** *fig* [pouvoir] (occult) power. ◇ *adj* [matière] fluid; [circulation] flowing freely.

fluidifier [flɥidifje] [9] *vt* [trafic] to improve the flow of.

fluidité [flɥidite] *nf* [gén] fluidity; [de circulation] easy flow.

fluor [flyɔr] *nm* fluorine.

fluorescent, -e [flyɔresɑ̃, ɑ̃t] *adj* fluorescent.

flûte [flyt] ◇ *nf* **-1.** MUS flute; ~ **à bec** recorder; ~ **traversière** flute. **-2.** [verre] flute (glass); ~ **à champagne** champagne flute. **-3.** [pain] French stick. ◇ *interj fam* bother!

flûtiste [flytist] *nmf* flautist.

fluvial, -e, -iaux [flyvjal, jo] *adj* [eaux, pêche] river (*avant n*); [alluvions] fluvial.

flux [fly] *nm* **-1.** [écoulement] flow; **un** ~ **de** *fig* a flood of. **-2.** [marée] flood tide; **le** ~ **et le reflux** the ebb and flow. **-3.** PHYS flux.

fluxion [flyksjɔ̃] *nf* inflammation; ~ **de poitrine** pneumonia.

FM (*abr de* **frequency modulation**) *nf* FM.

FMI (*abr de* **Fonds monétaire international**) *nm* IMF.

FN (*abr de* **Front national**) *nm extreme right-wing French political party,* ≃ National Front *Br.*

FNAC, Fnac [fnak] (*abr de* **Fédération nationale des achats des cadres**) *nf chain of large stores selling books, records, audio and video equipment etc.*

FNEF, Fnef [fnɛf] (*abr de* **Fédération nationale des étudiants de France**) *nf students' union.*

FNSEA (*abr de* **Fédération nationale des syndicats d'exploitants agricoles**) *nf farmers' union.*

FO (*abr de* **Force ouvrière**) *nf workers' trade union.*

foc [fɔk] *nm* jib.

focal, -e, -aux [fɔkal, o] *adj* focal.

focaliser [fɔkalize] [3] *vt* to focus.

♦ **se focaliser** *vp fig*: **se** ~ **sur qqch** to focus on sthg.

fœtal, -e, -aux [fetal, o] *adj* foetal.

fœtus [fetys] *nm* foetus.

foi [fwa] *nf* **-1.** RELIG faith. **-2.** [confiance] trust; **avoir ~ en qqn/qqch** to trust sb/sthg, to have faith in sb/sthg. **-3.** *loc*: **ajouter ~ à** *sout* to lend credence to; **faire ~** to serve as proof; **être de bonne/mauvaise ~** to be in good/bad faith; **ma ~ ... well ...; sur la ~ de** on the strength of.

foie [fwa] *nm* ANAT & CULIN liver; **~ de veau/de volaille** calf's/chicken liver; **~ gras** foie gras; **avoir les ~s** *fam fig* to be scared out of one's wits.

foin [fwɛ̃] *nm* hay; **faire les ~s** to make hay; **faire du ~** *fam fig* to make a din.

foire [fwar] *nf* **-1.** [fête] funfair. **-2.** [exposition, salon] trade fair. **-3.** *fam* [agitation] circus; **~ d'empoigne** free-for-all; **faire la ~** *fam fig* to have a wild time.

foirer [fware] [3] *vi fam* [projet] to fall through.

foireux, -euse [fwarø, øz] *adj fam* [raté] disastrous; [qui va rater] doomed.

fois [fwa] *nf* time; **une ~** once; **deux ~** twice; **trois/quatre ~** three/four times; **deux ~ plus long** twice as long; **neuf ~ sur dix** nine times out of ten; **deux ~ trois** two times three; **cette ~** this time; **il était une ~ ...** once upon a time there was ...; **pour une ~ (que)** for once; **pour la énième ~** for the umpteenth time; **une autre ~** another time; **une (bonne) ~ pour toutes** once and for all; **une ~ n'est pas coutume** just the once won't hurt.

◆ **à la fois** *loc adv* at the same time, at once.

◆ **des fois** *loc adv* [parfois] sometimes; **non, mais des ~!** *fam* look here!

◆ **si des fois** *loc conj fam* if ever.

◆ **une fois que** *loc conj* once.

foison [fwazɔ̃]

◆ **à foison** *loc adv* in abundance.

foisonnement [fwazɔnmɑ̃] *nm* abundance.

foisonner [fwazɔne] [3] *vi* to abound; **~ en** OU **de** to abound in.

folâtre [fɔlatr] *adj* playful.

folâtrer [fɔlatre] [3] *vi* to romp (about).

folichon, -onne [fɔliʃɔ̃, ɔn] *adj*: **ça n'est pas ~** *fam* it's not much fun.

folie [fɔli] *nf litt* & *fig* madness; **à la ~** madly; **c'est de la ~** it's madness OU lunacy; **avoir la ~ des grandeurs** to have delusions of grandeur; **faire des ~s** *fig* to be extravagant.

folio [fɔljo] *nm* folio.

folk [fɔlk] ◇ *nm* folk music. ◇ *adj inv* folk; **la musique ~** folk music.

folklore [fɔlklɔr] *nm* [de pays] folklore; **c'est du ~** *fig* you can't take it seriously.

folklorique [fɔlklɔrik] *adj* **-1.** [danse] folk. **-2.** *fig* [situation, personne] bizarre, quaint.

folle → **fou.**

follement [fɔlmɑ̃] *adv* madly, wildly; **~ amoureux** madly in love.

follet [fɔlɛ] → **feu.**

fomenter [fɔmɑ̃te] [3] *vt* to foment.

foncé, -e [fɔ̃se] *adj* dark.

foncer [fɔ̃se] [16] ◇ *vt* to darken, to make darker. ◇ *vi* **-1.** [teinte] to darken. **-2.** [se ruer]: **~ sur** to rush at. **-3.** *fam* [se dépêcher] to get a move on.

fonceur, -euse [fɔ̃sœr, øz] ◇ *adj* dynamic, go-ahead. ◇ *nm, f* dynamic person.

foncier, -ière [fɔ̃sje, jɛr] *adj* **-1.** [impôt] land *(avant n)*; **propriétaire ~** landowner. **-2.** [fondamental] basic, fundamental.

foncièrement [fɔ̃sjɛrmɑ̃] *adv* basically.

fonction [fɔ̃ksjɔ̃] *nf* **-1.** [gén] function; **faire ~ de** to act as. **-2.** [profession] post; **se démettre de ses ~s** to resign; **entrer en ~** to take up one's post OU duties; **la ~ publique** the civil service.

◆ **en fonction de** *loc prép* according to.

fonctionnaire [fɔ̃ksjɔnɛr] *nmf* [de l'État] state employee; [dans l'administration] civil servant; **haut ~** senior civil servant.

fonctionnariat [fɔ̃ksjɔnarja] *nm* employment by the state.

fonctionnariser [fɔ̃ksjɔnarize] [3] *vt* **-1.** [personne] to make an employee of the state. **-2.** [service] to take into the public sector.

fonctionnel, -elle [fɔ̃ksjɔnɛl] *adj* functional.

fonctionnement [fɔ̃ksjɔnmɑ̃] *nm* working, functioning.

fonctionner [fɔ̃ksjɔne] [3] *vi* to work, to function.

fond [fɔ̃] *nm* **-1.** [de récipient, puits, mer] bottom; [de pièce] back; **un ~** [petite quantité] a drop; **sans ~** bottomless; **au fin ~ de** in the depths of; **de ~ en comble** from top to bottom. **-2.** [substance, essentiel] heart, root; **avoir un très bon ~** to be a good person at heart; **le ~ de ma pensée** what I really think; **le ~ et la forme** content and form; **aller au ~ des choses** to go to the heart OU root of things. **-3.** [arrière-plan] background; **~ sonore** background music.

◆ **fond d'artichaut** *nm* artichoke heart.

◆ **fond de bouteille** *nm* lees *(pl)*, dregs *(pl)*.

◆ **fond de teint** *nm* foundation.

◆ **à fond** *loc adv* **-1.** [entièrement] thoroughly; **se donner à ~** to give one's all. **-2.** [très vite] at top speed.

◆ **au fond** *loc adv* basically.

◆ **au fond de** *loc prép*: **au ~ de moi-même/lui-même** *etc* at heart, deep down.

◆ **dans le fond** *loc adv* basically, really.

fondais, fondions *etc* → **fondre**.

fondamental, -e, -aux [fɔ̃damɑ̃tal, o] *adj* fundamental.

fondamentalement [fɔ̃damɑ̃talmɑ̃] *adv* fundamentally.

fondamentaliste [fɔ̃damɑ̃talist] *nmf & adj* fundamentalist.

fondant, -e [fɔ̃dɑ̃, ɑ̃t] *adj* [neige, glace] melting; [aliment] which melts in the mouth.

◆ **fondant** *nm* [gâteau] fondant.

fondateur, -trice [fɔ̃datœr, tris] *nm, f* founder.

fondation [fɔ̃dasjɔ̃] *nf* foundation.

◆ **fondations** *nfpl* CONSTR foundations.

fondé, -e [fɔ̃de] *adj* [craintes, reproches] justified, well-founded; **non ~** unfounded; **être ~ à faire qqch** to have good reason to do sthg.

◆ **fondé de pouvoir** *nm* authorized representative.

fondement [fɔ̃dmɑ̃] *nm* [base, motif] foundation; **sans ~** groundless, without foundation.

fonder [fɔ̃de] [3] *vt* **-1.** [créer] to found. **-2.** [baser]: **~ qqch sur** to base sthg on; **~ de grands espoirs sur qqn** to pin one's hopes on sb.

◆ **se fonder** *vp*: **se ~ sur** [suj: personne] to base o.s. on; [suj: argument] to be based on.

fonderie [fɔ̃dri] *nf* [usine] foundry.

fondre [fɔ̃dr] [75] ◇ *vt* **-1.** [beurre, neige] to melt; [sucre, sel] to dissolve; [métal] to melt down. **-2.** [mouler] to cast. **-3.** [mêler] to blend. ◇ *vi* **-1.** [beurre, neige] to melt; [sucre, sel] to dissolve; *fig* to melt away. **-2.** [maigrir] to lose weight. **-3.** [se ruer]: **~ sur** to swoop down on.

◆ **se fondre** *vp*: **se ~ dans la brume/la foule** to melt away into the fog/the crowd.

fonds [fɔ̃] ◇ *nm* **-1.** [ressources] fund; **le Fonds monétaire international** the International Monetary Fund; **~ de roulement** working capital. **-2.** [bien immobilier]: **~ (de commerce)** business. ◇ *nmpl* funds; **~ publics/secrets** public/secret funds.

fondu, -e [fɔ̃dy] *pp* → **fondre**.

◆ **fondu** *nm* **-1.** [CIN - ouverture] fade-in; [- fermeture] fade-out; **~ enchaîné** dissolve. **-2.** [de couleurs] blend.

◆ **fondue** *nf* fondue; **~ au fromage** OU **savoyarde** cheese fondue; **~ bourguignonne** meat fondue.

fongicide [fɔ̃ʒisid] ◇ *nm* fungicide. ◇ *adj* fungicidal.

font → **faire**.

fontaine [fɔ̃tɛn] *nf* [naturelle] spring; [publique] fountain.

fonte [fɔ̃t] *nf* **-1.** [de glace, beurre] melting; [de métal] melting down; **la ~ des neiges** the thaw. **-2.** [alliage] cast iron; **en ~** cast-iron.

fonts [fɔ̃] *nmpl*: **~ baptismaux** (baptismal) font (*sg*).

foot [fut] = **football**.

football [futbol] *nm* football *Br*, soccer; **~ américain** American football *Br*, football *Am*.

footballeur, -euse [futbolœr, øz] *nm, f* footballer *Br*, soccer player.

footing [futiŋ] *nm* jogging; **faire du ~** to go jogging.

for [fɔr] *nm*: **dans son ~ intérieur** in his/her heart of hearts.

FOR (*abr de* **forint**) F, Ft.

forage [fɔraʒ] *nm* drilling.

forain, -e [fɔrɛ̃, ɛn] *adj* → **fête**.

◆ **forain** *nm* stallholder.

forban [fɔrbɑ̃] *nm* **-1.** [corsaire] pirate. **-2.** [escroc] crook.

forçat [fɔrsa] *nm* convict.

force [fɔrs] *nf* **-1.** [vigueur] strength; **avoir de la ~** to be strong; **en ~** [passer] by (physical) effort; [arriver] in force; **être une ~ de la nature** to be a human dynamo; **être de ~ à faire qqch** to be up to doing sthg; **c'est ce qui fait sa ~** that's where his strength lies; **~ de caractère** strength of character; **dans la ~ de l'âge** *fig* in the prime of life. **-2.** [violence, puissance, MIL & PHYS] force; **faire faire qqch à qqn de ~** to force sb to do sthg; **par la ~ des choses** by force of circumstances; **avoir ~ de loi** to have force of law; **obtenir qqch par la ~** to obtain sthg by force; **~ centrifuge** PHYS centrifugal force; **~ de dissuasion** deterrent power; **~ de frappe** strike force; **~ d'inertie** PHYS force of inertia; **~ de vente** COMM sales force.

◆ **forces** *nfpl* **-1.** [physique] strength (*sg*); **être à bout de ~s** to have no strength left; **de toutes ses ~s** with all his/her strength; **recouvrer ses ~s** to get one's strength back; **reprendre des ~s** to recover one's strength. **-2.** [organisation]: **les ~s armées** the armed forces; **~s d'intervention** rapid deployment force (*sg*); **les ~s de l'ordre** the

police (sg); les ~s de police the police force (sg).
◆ à force de loc prép by dint of.
forcé, -e [fɔrse] adj forced.
forcément [fɔrsemɑ̃] adv inevitably.
forcené, -e [fɔrsəne] ◇ adj [haine, critique] frenzied; [partisan] fanatical. ◇ nm, f maniac.
forceps [fɔrsɛps] nm forceps (pl).
forcer [fɔrse] [16] ◇ vt -1. [gén] to force; ~ qqn à qqch/à faire qqch to force sb into sthg/to do sthg. -2. [admiration, respect] to compel, to command. -3. [talent, voix] to strain. ◇ vi: ça ne sert à rien de ~, ça ne passe pas there's no point in forcing it, it won't go through; ~ sur qqch to overdo sthg.
◆ se forcer vp [s'obliger]: se ~ à faire qqch to force o.s. to do sthg.
forcing [fɔrsiŋ] nm SPORT & fig pressure; faire du ~ to push o.s.
forcir [fɔrsir] [32] vi to put on weight.
forer [fɔre] [3] vt to drill.
forestier, -ière [fɔrɛstje, jɛr] adj forest (avant n).
◆ forestier nm forestry worker.
forêt [fɔrɛ] nf forest.
foreuse [fɔrøz] nf drill.
forfait [fɔrfɛ] nm -1. [prix fixe] fixed price; être au ~ [pour l'imposition] to pay an estimated amount of tax. -2. SPORT: déclarer ~ [abandonner] to withdraw; fig to give up. -3. littéraire [crime] heinous crime.
forfaitaire [fɔrfetɛr] adj inclusive.
forfait-vacances [fɔrfevakɑ̃s] (pl forfaits-vacances) nm package holiday.
forfanterie [fɔrfɑ̃tri] nf bragging.
forge [fɔrʒ] nf forge.
forger [fɔrʒe] [17] vt -1. [métal] to forge. -2. fig [caractère] to form. -3. [plan, excuse] to concoct.
forgeron [fɔrʒərɔ̃] nm blacksmith.
formaliser [fɔrmalize] [3] vt to formalize.
◆ se formaliser vp: se ~ (de) to take offence (at).
formalisme [fɔrmalism] nm formality.
formaliste [fɔrmalist] ◇ nmf formalist. ◇ adj [milieu] conventional; [personne]: être ~ to be a stickler for the rules.
formalité [fɔrmalite] nf formality; les ~s d'usage the usual formalities.
format [fɔrma] nm -1. [dimension] size; grand/petit ~ large/small size. -2. INFORM format.
formatage [fɔrmataʒ] nm INFORM formatting.

formater [fɔrmate] [3] vt INFORM to format.
formateur, -trice [fɔrmatœr, tris] ◇ adj formative. ◇ nm, f trainer.
formation [fɔrmasjɔ̃] nf -1. [gén] formation. -2. [apprentissage] training; ~ continue continuing education; ~ professionnelle vocational training.
forme [fɔrm] nf -1. [aspect] shape, form; en ~ de in the shape of; sous ~ de in the form of; sous toutes ses ~s in all its forms; prendre ~ to take shape. -2. [état] form; être en (pleine) ~ to be in (great) shape, to be on (top) form. -3. loc: en bonne et due ~ in due form; faire qqch dans les ~s to do sthg in the correct way; pour la ~ for form's sake; sans autre ~ de procès without further ado.
◆ formes nfpl figure (sg).
formel, -elle [fɔrmɛl] adj -1. [définitif, ferme] positive, definite. -2. [poli] formal.
formellement [fɔrmɛlmɑ̃] adv -1. [refuser] positively; [promettre] definitely. -2. [raisonner] formally.
former [fɔrme] [3] vt -1. [gén] to form. -2. [personnel, élèves] to train. -3. [goût, sensibilité] to develop.
◆ se former vp -1. [se constituer] to form. -2. [s'instruire] to train o.s.
Formica® [fɔrmika] nm inv Formica®.
formidable [fɔrmidabl] adj -1. [épatant] great, tremendous. -2. [incroyable] incredible.
formol [fɔrmɔl] nm formalin.
formosan, -e [fɔrmɔzɑ̃, an] adj Formosan.
◆ Formosan, -e nm, f Formosan.
Formose [fɔrmoz] n Formosa; à ~ in Formosa.
formulaire [fɔrmylɛr] nm form; remplir un ~ to fill in a form.
formulation [fɔrmylasjɔ̃] nf wording, formulation.
formule [fɔrmyl] nf -1. [expression] expression; ~ de politesse [orale] polite phrase; [épistolaire] letter ending. -2. CHIM & MATHS formula. -3. [méthode] way, method; nouvelle ~ new style of show/restaurant etc. -4. [slogan]: ~ publicitaire advertising slogan.
◆ formule 1 nf Formula One.
formuler [fɔrmyle] [3] vt to formulate, to express.
forniquer [fɔrnike] [3] vi to fornicate.
forsythia [fɔrsisja] nm forsythia.
fort, -e [fɔr, fɔrt] ◇ adj -1. [gén] strong; et le plus ~, c'est que ... and the most amazing thing about it is ...; c'est un peu ~! fam

that's a bit much!; **c'est plus ~ que moi** I can't help it. **-2.** [corpulent] heavy, big. **-3.** [doué] gifted; **être ~ en qqch** to be good at sthg. **-4.** [puissant - voix] loud; [- vent, lumière, accent] strong. **-5.** [considérable] large; **il y a de ~es chances qu'il gagne** there's a good chance he'll win.
◇ *adv* **-1.** [frapper, battre] hard; [sonner, parler] loud, loudly. **-2.** *sout* [très] very; **avoir ~ à faire (avec qqn)** to have a hard job (with sb).
◇ *nm* **-1.** [château] fort. **-2.** [personne]: **un ~ en qqch** a person who is good at sthg. **-3.** [spécialité]: **ce n'est pas mon ~** it's not my strong point OU forte.
◆ **au plus fort de** *loc prép* [hiver] in the depths of; [tempête, dispute] at the height of.

fortement [fɔrtəmã] *adv* **-1.** [avec force] hard. **-2.** [très, beaucoup - intéressé, ému] deeply; [- bégayer, loucher] badly.

forteresse [fɔrtərɛs] *nf* fortress.

fortifiant, -e [fɔrtifjã, ãt] *adj* fortifying.
◆ **fortifiant** *nm* tonic.

fortification [fɔrtifikasjɔ̃] *nf* fortification.

fortifier [fɔrtifje] [9] *vt* [personne, ville] to fortify; **~ qqn dans qqch** *fig* to strengthen sb in sthg.

fortuit, -e [fɔrtɥi, it] *adj* chance (*avant n*), fortuitous.

fortune [fɔrtyn] *nf* **-1.** [richesse] fortune; **faire ~** to make one's fortune. **-2.** [hasard] luck, fortune.

fortuné, -e [fɔrtyne] *adj* **-1.** [riche] wealthy. **-2.** [chanceux] fortunate, lucky.

forum [fɔrɔm] *nm* forum.

fosse [fos] *nf* **-1.** [trou] pit; **~ septique** septic tank; **~ aux lions** lions' den; **~ d'orchestre** orchestra pit. **-2.** [tombe] grave; **~ commune** common grave.

fossé [fose] *nm* ditch; *fig* gap.

fossette [fosɛt] *nf* dimple.

fossile [fosil] ◇ *adj* fossil (*avant n*), fossilized. ◇ *nm* **-1.** [de plante, d'animal] fossil. **-2.** *fig péj* [personne] fossil, fogy.

fossoyeur, -euse [foswajœr, øz] *nm, f* gravedigger.

fou, folle [fu, fɔl] ◇ *adj* (**fol** *devant voyelle ou h muet*) mad, insane; [prodigieux] tremendous; **être ~ de qqn/qqch** to be mad about sb/sthg; **être ~ de joie** to be deliriously happy; **~ à lier** raving mad. ◇ *nm, f* madman (*f* madwoman); **~ furieux** manic; **faire le ~** *fig* to act the fool.

foudre [fudr] *nf* lightning; **encourir** OU **s'attirer les ~s de qqn** *fig* to bring down sb's wrath on o.s.

foudroyant, -e [fudrwajã, ãt] *adj* **-1.** [progrès, vitesse] lightning (*avant n*); [succès] stunning. **-2.** [nouvelle] devastating; [regard] withering.

foudroyer [fudrwaje] [13] *vt* **-1.** [suj: foudre] to strike; **l'arbre a été foudroyé** the tree was struck by lightning. **-2.** *fig* [abattre] to strike down, to kill; **~ qqn du regard** to glare at sb.

fouet [fwɛ] *nm* **-1.** [en cuir] whip; **de plein ~ direct**; **il prit la pluie de plein ~** the rain hit him full in the face. **-2.** [CULIN] whisk.

fouetter [fwete] [4] *vt* **-1.** [gén] to whip; [suj: pluie] to lash (against). **-2.** [stimuler] to stimulate.

fougasse [fugas] *nf* type of unleavened bread.

fougère [fuʒɛr] *nf* fern.

fougue [fug] *nf* ardour.

fougueux, -euse [fugø, øz] *adj* ardent, spirited.

fouille [fuj] *nf* **-1.** [de personne, maison] search. **-2.** [du sol] dig, excavation.
◆ **fouilles** *nfpl fam* pockets.

fouiller [fuje] [3] ◇ *vt* **-1.** [gén] to search. **-2.** *fig* [approfondir] to examine closely. ◇ *vi*: **~ dans** to go through.

fouillis [fuji] *nm* jumble, muddle.

fouine [fwin] *nf* stone-marten.

fouiner [fwine] [3] *vi* to ferret about.

foulard [fular] *nm* scarf.

foule [ful] *nf* **-1.** [de gens] crowd; **en ~** in great numbers; **attirer les ~s** *fig* to draw the crowds. **-2.** *péj* [peuple]: **la ~** the masses (*pl*). **-3.** *fig* [multitude]: **une ~ de** masses of.

foulée [fule] *nf* [de coureur] stride; **je suis sorti faire des courses et dans la ~ ...** I went out to do some shopping and while I was at it ....

fouler [fule] [3] *vt* [raisin] to press; [sol] to walk on.
◆ **se fouler** *vp* **-1.** MÉD: **se ~ le poignet/la cheville** to sprain one's wrist/ankle. **-2.** *fam fig* [se fatiguer]: **ne pas se ~** not to strain o.s.

foulure [fulyr] *nf* sprain.

four [fur] *nm* **-1.** [de cuisson] oven; **cuit au ~** baked; **~ électrique/à micro-ondes** electric/microwave oven; **~ crématoire** [dans camp de concentration] oven; **je ne peux pas être (à la fois) au ~ et au moulin** *fig* I haven't got two pairs of hands, I can't be in two places at once; **noir comme dans un ~** *fig* black as pitch. **-2.** THÉÂTRE flop; **faire un ~** to flop.

fourbe [furb] ◇ *adj* treacherous, deceitful. ◇ *nmf* rogue.

fourbi [furbi] *nm fam* **-1.** [attirail] gear. **-2.** [fouillis] mess.

fourbir [furbir] [32] *vt litt & fig* to polish.

fourbu, -e [furby] *adj* tired out, exhausted.

fourche [furʃ] *nf* **-1.** [outil] pitchfork. **-2.** [de vélo, route] fork. **-3.** *Belg* SCOL free period.

fourcher [furʃe] [3] *vi* **-1.** [cheveux] to split. **-2.** *loc*: sa langue a fourché he made a slip of the tongue.

fourchette [furʃɛt] *nf* **-1.** [couvert] fork. **-2.** [écart] range, bracket.

fourchu, -e [furʃy] *adj* forked.

fourgon [furgɔ̃] *nm* **-1.** [camionnette] van; ~ cellulaire police van *Br*, patrol wagon *Am*; ~ mortuaire hearse. **-2.** [ferroviaire]: ~ à bestiaux cattle truck; ~ postal mail van.

fourgonnette [furgɔnɛt] *nf* small van.

fourguer [furge] [3] *vt fam*: ~ qqch à qqn to palm sthg off on sb.

fourmi [furmi] *nf* [insecte] ant; *fig* hard worker; **avoir des ~s dans les bras/les jambes** to have pins and needles in one's arms/legs.

fourmilière [furmiljɛr] *nf* anthill.

fourmillement [furmijmɑ̃] *nm* **-1.** [d'insectes, de personnes] swarming. **-2.** [picotement] pins and needles (*pl*).

fourmiller [furmije] [3] *vi* [pulluler] to swarm; ~ de *fig* to be swarming with.

fournaise [furnɛz] *nf* furnace.

fourneau, -x [furno] *nm* **-1.** [cuisinière, poêle] stove. **-2.** [de fonderie] furnace; **haut ~** blast furnace. **-3.** [de pipe] bowl.

fournée [furne] *nf* batch.

fourni, -e [furni] *adj* [barbe, cheveux] thick.

fournil [furnil] *nm* bakery.

fournir [furnir] [32] ◇ *vt* **-1.** [procurer]: ~ qqch à qqn to supply sb with sthg. **-2.** [produire]: ~ un effort to make an effort. **-3.** [approvisionner]: ~ qqn (en) to supply sb (with). ◇ *vi*: ~ à to provide for.
◆ **se fournir** *vp*: se ~ chez/en to get supplies from/of.

fournisseur, -euse [furnisœr, øz] *nm, f* supplier.

fourniture [furnityr] *nf* supply, supplying (*U*).
◆ **fournitures** *nfpl*: ~s de bureau office supplies; ~s scolaires school supplies.

fourrage [furaʒ] *nm* fodder.

fourrager¹, -ère [furaʒe, ɛr] *adj* fodder (*avant n*).

fourrager² [furaʒe] [17] *vi fam*: ~ dans qqch to rummage through sthg.

fourré [fure] *nm* thicket.

fourreau, -x [furo] *nm* **-1.** [d'épée] sheath; [de parapluie] cover. **-2.** [robe] sheath dress.

fourrer [fure] [3] *vt* **-1.** CULIN to stuff, to fill. **-2.** *fam* [mettre]: ~ qqch (dans) to stuff sthg (into).
◆ **se fourrer** *vp*: se ~ dans le pétrin to get into a mess; se ~ une idée dans la tête to get an idea into one's head; je ne savais plus où me ~ I didn't know where to put myself.

fourre-tout [furtu] *nm inv* **-1.** [pièce] lumber room *Br*, junk room *Am*. **-2.** [sac] holdall. **-3.** *fig & péj* [d'idées] hotch-potch.

fourreur [furœr] *nm* furrier.

fourrière [furjɛr] *nf* pound; **mettre à la ~** [voiture] to tow away.

fourrure [furyr] *nf* fur; **un manteau en fausse ~** a fake fur coat.

fourvoyer [furvwaje] [13]
◆ **se fourvoyer** *vp sout* [s'égarer] to lose one's way; [se tromper] to go off on the wrong track.

foutaise [futɛz] *nf fam* crap (*U*).

foutoir [futwar] *nm fam* pigsty.

foutre [futr] [116] *vt tfam* **-1.** [mettre] to shove, to stick; ~ qqn dehors OU à la porte to chuck sb out. **-2.** [donner]: ~ la trouille à qqn to put the wind up sb; **il lui a foutu une baffe** he thumped him one. **-3.** [faire] to do; **ne rien ~ de la journée** to do damn all day; **j'en ai rien à ~** I don't give a toss.
◆ **se foutre** *vp tfam* **-1.** [se mettre]: se ~ dans [situation] to get o.s. into. **-2.** [se moquer]: se ~ de (la gueule de) qqn to take the mickey out of sb *Br*. **-3.** [ne pas s'intéresser]: **je m'en fous** I don't give a damn about it.

foutu, -e [futy] *adj fam* **-1.** [maudit] bloody *Br*, damned; [caractère] nasty. **-2.** [fait, conçu]: **bien ~** [projet, maison] great; **elle est bien ~e, celle-là** [femme] she's a real stunner. **-3.** [perdu]: **il est ~** he's/it's had it. **-4.** [capable]: **être ~ de faire qqch** to be liable OU quite likely to do sthg.

fox-terrier [fɔkstɛrje] (*pl* fox-terriers) *nm* fox terrier.

foyer [fwaje] *nm* **-1.** [maison] home; **rentrer au ~** to go home. **-2.** [famille] family; **fonder un ~** to set up home. **-3.** [résidence] home, hostel. **-4.** [point central] centre. **-5.** [de lunettes] focus; **verres à double ~** bifocals.

FP (*abr de* franchise postale) PP.

FPA (*abr de* **formation professionnelle des adultes**) *nf state-run adult training scheme.*

FPLP (*abr de* **Front populaire de libération de la Palestine**) *nm* PFLP.

frac [frak] *nm* tails (*pl*).

fracas [fraka] *nm* roar.

fracassant, **-e** [frakasɑ̃, ɑ̃t] *adj* [bruyant] thunderous; *fig* staggering, sensational.

fracasser [frakase] [3] *vt* to smash, to shatter.

◆ **se fracasser** *vp*: **se ~ contre/sur** to crash against/into.

fraction [fraksjɔ̃] *nf* fraction.

fractionner [fraksjɔne] [3] *vt* to divide (up), to split up.

◆ **se fractionner** *vp* to split up.

fracture [fraktyr] *nf* MÉD fracture; **~ du crâne** fractured skull.

fracturer [fraktyre] [3] *vt* **-1.** MÉD to fracture. **-2.** [coffre, serrure] to break open.

◆ **se fracturer** *vp* to break, to fracture.

fragile [fraʒil] *adj* [gén] fragile; [peau, santé] delicate.

fragiliser [fraʒilize] [3] *vt* to weaken.

fragilité [fraʒilite] *nf* fragility.

fragment [fragmɑ̃] *nm* **-1.** [morceau] fragment. **-2.** [extrait - d'œuvre] extract; [- de conversation] snatch.

fragmentaire [fragmɑ̃tɛr] *adj* fragmentary.

fragmenter [fragmɑ̃te] [3] *vt* to fragment, to break up.

◆ **se fragmenter** *vp* to fragment, to break up.

fraîche → **frais**.

fraîchement [frɛʃmɑ̃] *adv* **-1.** [récemment] recently. **-2.** [froidement] coolly.

fraîcheur [frɛʃœr] *nf* **-1.** [d'air, d'accueil] coolness. **-2.** [de teint, d'aliment] freshness.

fraîchir [frɛʃir] [32] *vi* to freshen.

frais, **fraîche** [frɛ, frɛʃ] *adj* **-1.** [air, accueil] cool; «**servir ~**» "serve chilled". **-2.** [récent - trace] fresh; [- encre] wet; **~ émoulu (de)** fresh (from). **-3.** [teint] fresh, clear; **~ et dispos** hale and hearty.

◆ **frais** ◇ *nm*: **mettre qqch au ~** to put sthg in a cool place; **prendre le ~** to take a breath of fresh air.

◇ *nmpl* [dépenses] expenses, costs; **aux ~ de la maison** at the company's expense; **faire des ~** to spend a lot of money; **rentrer dans ses ~** to cover one's expenses; **faux ~** incidentals; **~ d'entretien** upkeep; **~ d'équipement** capital expenditure; **~ généraux** overheads; **~ de justice** legal costs; **~ de représentation** entertainment allowance; **à grands ~** at a high price; **à peu de**

~ cheaply; **faire les ~ de qqch** to bear the brunt of sthg.

◇ *adv*: **il fait ~** it's cool.

fraise [frɛz] *nf* **-1.** [fruit] strawberry; **~ des bois** wild strawberry. **-2.** [de dentiste] drill; [de menuisier] bit.

fraiser [frɛze] [4] *vt* to countersink.

fraiseuse [frɛzøz] *nf* milling machine.

fraisier [frɛzje] *nm* **-1.** [plante] strawberry plant. **-2.** [gâteau] strawberry sponge.

framboise [frɑ̃bwaz] *nf* **-1.** [fruit] raspberry. **-2.** [liqueur] raspberry liqueur.

framboisier [frɑ̃bwazje] *nm* **-1.** [plante] raspberry bush. **-2.** [gâteau] raspberry sponge.

franc, franche [frɑ̃, frɑ̃ʃ] *adj* **-1.** [sincère] frank. **-2.** [net] clear, definite.

◆ **franc** *nm* franc; **ancien/nouveau ~** old/new franc; **~ français/belge/suisse** French/Belgian/Swiss franc.

français-e [frɑ̃sɛ, ɛz], *adj* French.

◆ **français** *nm* [langue] French.

◆ **Français**, **-e** *nm, f* Frenchman (*f* Frenchwoman); **les Français** the French; **le Français moyen** the average Frenchman.

France [frɑ̃s] *nf*: **la ~** France; **~ 2, 3** TÉLÉ *French state-owned television channels*; **~-Inter** RADIO *radio station broadcasting mainly current affairs programmes, interviews and debates.*

franche → **franc**.

franchement [frɑ̃ʃmɑ̃] *adv* **-1.** [sincèrement] frankly. **-2.** [nettement] clearly. **-3.** [tout à fait] completely, downright.

franchir [frɑ̃ʃir] [32] *vt* **-1.** [obstacle] to get over. **-2.** [porte] to go through; [seuil] to cross. **-3.** [distance] to cover.

franchise [frɑ̃ʃiz] *nf* **-1.** [sincérité] frankness. **-2.** COMM franchise; **agent en ~** franchise holder. **-3.** [d'assurance] excess. **-4.** [détaxe] exemption.

franciscain, **-e** [frɑ̃siskɛ̃, ɛn] *adj & nm, f* Franciscan.

franciser [frɑ̃size] [3] *vt* to frenchify.

franc-jeu [frɑ̃ʒø] *nm*: **jouer ~** to play fair.

franc-maçon, **-onne** [frɑ̃masɔ̃, ɔn] (*mpl* **francs-maçons**, *fpl* **franc-maçonnes**) *adj* masonic.

◆ **franc-maçon** *nm* freemason.

franc-maçonnerie [frɑ̃masɔnri] (*pl* **franc-maçonneries**) *nf* freemasonry (*U*).

franco [frɑ̃ko] *adv* **-1.** *fam* [franchement]: **y aller ~** to go straight to the point. **-2.** COMM: **~ à bord** free on board; **~ de port** carriage paid.

francophile [frɑ̃kɔfil] *nmf & adj* francophile.

francophone [frãkɔfɔn] ◇ *adj* French-speaking. ◇ *nmf* French speaker.
francophonie [frãkɔfɔni] *nf*: **la ~** French-speaking nations (*pl*).

FRANCOPHONIE:
This is a wide-ranging cultural and political concept involving the promotion of French-speaking communities around the world, with a view to creating a 'French Commonwealth' with a strong identity

---

franc-parler [frãparle] (*pl* **francs-parlers**) *nm*: **avoir son ~** to speak one's mind.
franc-tireur [frãtirœr] (*pl* **francs-tireurs**) *nm* **-1.** MIL irregular. **-2.** *fig* [indépendant] freelance; **agir en ~** to act independently.
frange [frãʒ] *nf* fringe.
frangin, -e [frãʒɛ̃, in] *nm, f fam* brother (*f* sister).
frangipane [frãʒipan] *nf* almond paste.
franglais [frãglɛ] *nm* Franglais.
franquette [frãkɛt]
◆ **à la bonne franquette** *loc adv* informally, without any ceremony.
frappant, -e [frapã, ãt] *adj* striking.
frappe [frap] *nf* **-1.** [de monnaie] minting, striking. **-2.** [à la machine] typing; INFORM keying. **-3.** [de boxeur] punch. **-4.** *péj* [voyou] lout, yob *Br*.
frappé, -e [frape] *adj* **-1.** [champagne] chilled. **-2.** *fam* [personne] crazy, nutty.
frapper [frape] [3] ◇ *vt* **-1.** [gén] to strike. **-2.** [boisson] to chill. ◇ *vi* to knock.
frasques [frask] *nfpl* pranks, escapades.
fraternel, -elle [fratɛrnɛl] *adj* fraternal, brotherly.
fraterniser [fratɛrnize] [3] *vi* to fraternize.
fraternité [fratɛrnite] *nf* brotherhood.
fratricide [fratrisid] ◇ *nmf* fratricide. ◇ *adj* fratricidal.
fraude [frod] *nf* fraud; **passer qqch en ~** to smuggle sthg in; **~ électorale** ballot-rigging; **~ fiscale** tax evasion; **~ informatique** computer crime.
frauder [frode] [3] *vt & vi* to cheat.
fraudeur, -euse [frodœr, øz] *nm, f* cheat.
frauduleux, -euse [frodylø, øz] *adj* fraudulent.
frayer [frɛje] [11] ◇ *vt*: **~ la voie à qqn** to clear the way for sb. ◇ *vi* [fréquenter]: **~ avec** to associate OU mix with.
◆ **se frayer** *vp*: **se ~ un chemin (à travers une foule)** to force one's way through (a crowd).
frayeur [frɛjœr] *nf* fright, fear.

fredaines [frədɛn] *nfpl* pranks.
fredonner [frədɔne] [3] *vt & vi* to hum.
freezer [frizœr] *nm* freezer compartment.
frégate [fregat] *nf* **-1.** [bateau] frigate. **-2.** [oiseau] frigate-bird.
frein [frɛ̃] *nm* **-1.** AUTOM brake; **~ à main** handbrake; **~ moteur** engine brake. **-2.** *fig* [obstacle] brake, check; **mettre un ~ à** to curb. **-3.** *loc*: **ronger son ~** *fig* to champ at the bit.
freinage [frɛnaʒ] *nm* braking.
freiner [frene] [4] ◇ *vt* **-1.** [mouvement, véhicule] to slow down; [inflation, dépenses] to curb. **-2.** [personne] to restrain. ◇ *vi* to brake.
frelaté, -e [frəlate] *adj* [vin] adulterated; *fig* corrupt.
frêle [frɛl] *adj* **-1.** [enfant, voix] frail. **-2.** [construction] flimsy, fragile.
frelon [frəlɔ̃] *nm* hornet.
freluquet [frəlykɛ] *nm péj* whippersnapper.
frémir [fremir] [32] *vi* **-1.** [corps, personne] to tremble. **-2.** [eau] to simmer.
frémissement [fremismã] *nm* **-1.** [de corps, personne] shiver, trembling (*U*). **-2.** [d'eau] simmering.
frêne [frɛn] *nm* ash.
frénésie [frenezi] *nf* frenzy.
frénétique [frenetik] *adj* frenzied.
frénétiquement [frenetikmã] *adv* [applaudir] furiously.
fréquemment [frekamã] *adv* frequently.
fréquence [frekãs] *nf* frequency.
fréquent, -e [frekã, ãt] *adj* frequent.
fréquentable [frekãtabl] *adj* respectable.
fréquentation [frekãtasjɔ̃] *nf* **-1.** [d'endroit] frequenting. **-2.** [de personne] association.
◆ **fréquentations** *nfpl* company (*U*); **avoir de mauvaises ~s** to keep bad company.
fréquenté, -e [frekãte] *adj*: **très ~** busy; **c'est très bien/mal ~** the right/wrong sort of people go there.
fréquenter [frekãte] [3] *vt* **-1.** [endroit] to frequent. **-2.** [personne] to associate with; [petit ami] to go out with, to see.
frère [frɛr] ◇ *nm* brother; **faux ~** false friend; **~ de lait** foster brother; **grand ~** big brother. ◇ *adj* [parti, pays] sister (*avant n*).
fresque [frɛsk] *nf* fresco.
fret [frɛ] *nm* freight.
frétiller [fretije] [3] *vi* [poisson, personne] to wriggle; **~ de joie** *fig* to quiver with delight.

fretin [frətɛ̃] *nm*: **le menu** ~ the small fry.

freudien, -ienne [frødjɛ̃, jɛn] *adj* Freudian.

friable [frijabl] *adj* crumbly.

friand, -e [frijɑ̃, ɑ̃d] *adj*: **être ~ de** to be partial to.
◆ **friand** *nm* savoury tartlet.

friandise [frijɑ̃diz] *nf* delicacy.

fric [frik] *nm fam* cash.

fricassée [frikase] *nf* fricassee.

fric-frac [frikfrak] *nm inv fam* break-in.

friche [friʃ] *nf* fallow land; **en** ~ fallow.

fricoter [frikɔte] [3] *vt litt & fig* to cook up.

friction [friksjɔ̃] *nf* **-1.** [massage] massage. **-2.** *fig* [désaccord] friction.

frictionner [friksjɔne] [3] *vt* to rub.

frigidaire® [friʒidɛr] *nm* fridge, refrigerator.

frigide [friʒid] *adj* frigid.

frigidité [friʒidite] *nf* frigidity.

frigo [frigo] *nm fam* fridge.

frigorifié, -e [frigɔrifje] *adj fam* frozen.

frigorifique [frigɔrifik] *adj* refrigerated.

frileux, -euse [frilø, øz] *adj* **-1.** [craignant le froid] sensitive to the cold. **-2.** [prudent] unadventurous.

frimas [frima] *nm littéraire* foggy winter weather.

frime [frim] *nf fam* showing off.

frimer [frime] [3] *vi fam* [bluffer] to pretend; [se mettre en valeur] to show off.

frimeur, -euse [frimœr, øz] *nmf* show-off.

frimousse [frimus] *nf fam* dear little face.

fringale [frɛ̃gal] *nf fam*: **avoir la** ~ to be starving.

fringant, -e [frɛ̃gɑ̃, ɑ̃t] *adj* high-spirited.

fringuer [frɛ̃ge] [3] *vt* to dress.
◆ **se fringuer** *vp fam* to get dressed.

fringues [frɛ̃g] *nfpl fam* clothes.

fripe [frip] *nf*: **les** ~**s** secondhand clothes.

friper [fripe] [3] *vt* to crumple.
◆ **se friper** *vp* to crumple.

fripier, -ière [fripje, jɛr] *nm, f* secondhand clothes dealer.

fripon, -onne [fripɔ̃, ɔn] ◇ *nm, f fam vieilli* rogue, rascal. ◇ *adj* mischievous, cheeky.

fripouille [fripuj] *nf fam* scoundrel; **petite** ~ little devil.

frire [frir] [115] ◇ *vt* to fry. ◇ *vi* to fry; **faire** ~ to fry.

Frisbee® [frizbi] *nm* Frisbee®.

frise [friz] *nf* ARCHIT frieze.

frisé, -e [frize] *adj* [cheveux] curly; [personne] curly-haired.
◆ **frisée** *nf* [salade] curly endive.

friser [frize] [3] ◇ *vt* **-1.** [cheveux] to curl. **-2.** *fig* [ressembler à] to border on. ◇ *vi* to curl.

frisette [frizɛt] *nf* curl.

frisotter [frizɔte] [3] ◇ *vt* to crimp, to frizz. ◇ *vi* to be frizzy.

frisquet [friskɛ] *adj m*: **il fait** ~ it's chilly.

frisson [frisɔ̃] *nm* [gén] shiver; [de dégoût] shudder.

frissonner [frisɔne] [3] *vi* **-1.** [trembler] to shiver; [de dégoût] to shudder. **-2.** [s'agiter - eau] to ripple; [- feuillage] to tremble.

frit, -e [fri, frit] *pp* → **frire**.

frite [frit] *nf* chip *Br,* (French) fry *Am*.

friterie [fritri] *nf* ≃ chip shop *Br*.

friteuse [fritøz] *nf* deep fat fryer.

friture [frityr] *nf* **-1.** [action de frire] frying. **-2.** [poisson] fried fish; **petite** ~ fried whitebait. **-3.** *fam* RADIO crackle.

frivole [frivɔl] *adj* frivolous.

frivolité [frivɔlite] *nf* frivolity.

froc [frɔk] *nm* **-1.** RELIG habit. **-2.** *fam* [pantalon] trousers *(pl) Br,* pants *(pl) Am*.

froid, froide [frwa, frwad] *adj litt & fig* cold; **rester** ~ to keep OU stay cool.
◆ **froid** ◇ *nm* **-1.** [température] cold; **prendre** ~ to catch (a) cold; **crever de** ~ *fam* to be freezing to death; **grand** ~ intense cold; **il fait un** ~ **de canard** it's freezing cold; **n'avoir pas** ~ **aux yeux** *fig* to be bold OU adventurous. **-2.** [tension] coolness; **être en** ~ **(avec qqn)** to be on bad terms (with sb). ◇ *adv*: **il fait** ~ it's cold; **avoir** ~ to be cold; **manger** ~ to have something cold (to eat).
◆ **à froid** *loc adv* [dire, faire] coolly, unemotionally.

froidement [frwadmɑ̃] *adv* **-1.** [accueillir] coldly. **-2.** [écouter, parler] coolly. **-3.** [tuer] cold-bloodedly.

froideur [frwadœr] *nf* **-1.** [indifférence] coldness. **-2.** [impassibilité] coolness.

froisser [frwase] [3] *vt* **-1.** [tissu, papier] to crumple, to crease. **-2.** *fig* [offenser] to offend.
◆ **se froisser** *vp* **-1.** [tissu] to crumple, to crease. **-2.** MÉD: **se** ~ **un muscle** to strain a muscle. **-3.** [se vexer] to take offence.

frôler [frole] [3] *vt* to brush against; *fig* to have a brush with, to come close to.

fromage [frɔmaʒ] *nm* cheese; ~ **à pâte molle/dure** soft/hard cheese; ~ **de chèvre** goat's cheese; ~ **de tête** brawn *Br,* headcheese *Am*.

fromager, -ère [frɔmaʒe, ɛr] ◇ *adj* cheese *(avant n)*. ◇ *nm, f* cheesemaker.

fromagerie [frɔmaʒri] *nf* cheese-dairy.

froment [frɔmã] *nm* wheat.

fronce [frɔ̃s] *nf* gather.

froncement [frɔ̃smã] *nm:* ~ **de sourcils** frown.

froncer [frɔ̃se] [16] *vt* **-1.** COUTURE to gather. **-2.** [plisser]: ~ **les sourcils** to frown.

frondaison [frɔ̃dɛzɔ̃] *nf* **-1.** [phénomène] foliation. **-2.** [feuillage] foliage.

fronde [frɔ̃d] *nf* **-1.** [arme] sling; [jouet] catapult *Br*, slingshot *Am*. **-2.** [révolte] rebellion.

frondeur, -euse [frɔ̃dœr, øz] ◇ *nm, f* rebel. ◇ *adj* rebellious.

front [frɔ̃] *nm* **-1.** ANAT forehead. **-2.** *fig* [audace] cheek; **avoir le** ~ **de faire qqch** to have the cheek to do sthg. **-3.** [avant] front; [de bâtiment] front, façade; ~ **de mer** (sea) front; **de** ~ [attaquer] head on. **-4.** MÉTÉOR, MIL & POLIT front. **-5.** *loc:* **faire** ~ **à** to face up to; **mener plusieurs activités de** ~ to do several things at the same time.

frontal, -e, -aux [frɔ̃tal, o] *adj* **-1.** ANAT frontal. **-2.** [collision, attaque] head-on.

frontalier, -ière [frɔ̃talje, jɛr] ◇ *adj* frontier (*avant n*); **travailleur** ~ *person who lives on one side of the border and works on the other.* ◇ *nm, f* inhabitant of border area.

frontière [frɔ̃tjɛr] ◇ *adj* border (*avant n*). ◇ *nf* frontier, border; *fig* frontier.

frontispice [frɔ̃tispis] *nm* frontispiece.

fronton [frɔ̃tɔ̃] *nm* **-1.** ARCHIT pediment. **-2.** SPORT *upper part of the wall in the game of pelota.*

frottement [frɔtmã] *nm* **-1.** [action] rubbing. **-2.** [contact, difficulté] friction.

frotter [frɔte] [3] ◇ *vt* to rub; [parquet] to scrub. ◇ *vi* to rub, to scrape.

◆ **se frotter** *vp* **-1.** [se blottir]: **se** ~ **contre** OU **à** to rub (up) against; **il ne faut pas s'y** ~ *fig* don't swap swords with him. **-2.** [se laver] to rub o.s.

frottis [frɔti] *nm* smear; ~ **vaginal** cervical smear.

froufrou, -s [frufru] *nm* rustle, swish.

◆ **froufrous** *nmpl* [de robe] frills.

froussard, -e [frusar, ard] *adj & nm, f fam* chicken.

frousse [frus] *nf fam* fright; **avoir la** ~ to be scared stiff.

fructifier [fryktifje] [9] *vi* **-1.** [investissement] to give OU yield a profit; **faire** ~ **son argent** to make one's money grow. **-2.** [terre] to be productive. **-3.** [arbre, idée] to bear fruit.

fructose [fryktoz] *nm* fructose.

fructueux, -euse [fryktɥø, øz] *adj* fruitful, profitable.

frugal, -e, -aux [frygal, o] *adj* frugal.

fruit [frɥi] *nm litt & fig* fruit (*U*); ~ **confit** candied fruit; **le** ~ **défendu** the forbidden fruit; ~ **sec** dried fruit (*U*); ~**s de mer** seafood (*U*).

fruité, -e [frɥite] *adj* fruity.

fruitier, -ière [frɥitje, jɛr] ◇ *adj* [arbre] fruit (*avant n*). ◇ *nm, f* fruiterer.

◆ **fruitier** *nm* [local] store-room for fruit.

frusques [frysk] *nfpl* gear (*U*), clobber (*U*).

fruste [fryst] *adj* uncouth.

frustrant, -e [frystrã, ãt] *adj* frustrating.

frustration [frystrasjɔ̃] *nf* frustration.

frustré, -e [frystre] ◇ *adj* frustrated. ◇ *nm, f* frustrated person.

frustrer [frystre] [3] *vt* **-1.** [priver]: ~ **qqn de** to deprive sb of. **-2.** [décevoir] to frustrate.

FS (*abr de* franc suisse) SFr.

FTP (*abr de* **francs-tireurs et partisans**) *nmpl* Communist Resistance forces during World War II.

fuchsia [fyʃja] *nm* fuchsia.

fuel, fioul [fjul] *nm* **-1.** [de chauffage] fuel. **-2.** [carburant] fuel oil.

fugace [fygas] *adj* fleeting.

fugitif, -ive [fyʒitif, iv] ◇ *adj* fleeting. ◇ *nm, f* fugitive.

fugue [fyg] *nf* **-1.** [de personne] flight; **faire une** ~ to run away. **-2.** MUS fugue.

fuguer [fyge] [3] *vi* to run off OU away.

fugueur, -euse [fygœr, øz] *adj & nm, f* runaway.

fui [fɥi] *pp inv* → **fuir**.

fuir [fɥir] [35] ◇ *vi* **-1.** [détaler] to flee. **-2.** [tuyau] to leak. **-3.** *fig* [s'écouler] to fly by. ◇ *vt* [éviter] to avoid, to shun.

fuis, fuit *etc* → **fuire**.

fuite [fɥit] *nf* **-1.** [de personne] escape, flight; **en** ~ on the run; **prendre la** ~ to take flight; **mettre qqn en** ~ to put sb to flight. **-2.** [écoulement, d'information] leak.

fulgurant, -e [fylgyrã, ãt] *adj* **-1.** [découverte] dazzling. **-2.** [vitesse] lightning (*avant n*). **-3.** [douleur] searing. **-4.** *littéraire* [regard] of thunder.

fulminant, -e [fylminã, ãt] *adj* [menaçant] threatening.

fulminer [fylmine] [3] *vi* **-1.** [personne]: ~ **(contre)** to fulminate (against). **-2.** CHIM to detonate.

fumant, -e [fymã, ãt] *adj* **-1.** [cheminée] smoking. **-2.** [plat] steaming.

fumé, -e [fyme] *adj* **-1.** CULIN smoked. **-2.** [verres] tinted.

fumée [fyme] *nf* **-1.** [de combustion] smoke; **partir en ~** *fig* to go up in smoke. **-2.** [vapeur] steam.

◆ **fumées** *nfpl littéraire* fumes.

fumer [fyme] [3] ◇ *vi* **-1.** [personne, cheminée] to smoke. **-2.** [bouilloire, plat] to steam. **-3.** *fam* [être furieux] to fume, to rage. ◇ *vt* **-1.** [cigarette, aliment] to smoke. **-2.** AGRIC to spread manure on.

fumet [fymɛ] *nm* **-1.** [odeur] aroma. **-2.** CULIN greatly reduced stock.

fumeur, -euse [fymœr, øz] *nm, f* smoker.

fumeux, -euse [fymø, øz] *adj* confused, woolly.

fumier [fymje] *nm* **-1.** AGRIC dung, manure. **-2.** *vulg* [salaud] shit.

fumigation [fymigasjɔ̃] *nf* fumigation.

fumiste [fymist] *nmf péj* skiver *Br*, shirker.

fumisterie [fymistəri] *nf fam* skiving *Br*, shirking.

fumoir [fymwar] *nm* **-1.** [pour aliments] smokehouse. **-2.** [pièce] smoking room.

funambule [fynãbyl] *nmf* tightrope walker.

funèbre [fynebr] *adj* **-1.** [de funérailles] funeral (*avant n*). **-2.** [lugubre] funereal; [sentiments] dismal.

funérailles [fyneraj] *nfpl* funeral (*sg*).

funéraire [fynerɛr] *adj* funeral (*avant n*).

funeste [fynɛst] *adj* **-1.** [accident] fatal. **-2.** [initiative, erreur] disastrous. **-3.** [présage] of doom.

funiculaire [fynikylɛr] *nm* funicular railway.

FUNU, Funu [fyny] (*abr de* **Force d'urgence des Nations unies**) *nf* UNEF.

fur [fyr]

◆ **au fur et à mesure** *loc adv* as I/you *etc* go along; **au ~ et à mesure des besoins** as (and when) needed.

◆ **au fur et à mesure que** *loc conj* as (and when).

furax [fyraks] *adj inv fam* hopping mad.

furet [fyrɛ] *nm* **-1.** [animal] ferret. **-2.** [personne] nosy parker. **-3.** [jeu] hunt-the-slipper.

fureter [fyrte] [28] *vi* **-1.** [fouiller] to ferret around. **-2.** [chasser] to go ferreting.

fureur [fyrœr] *nf* **-1.** [colère] fury. **-2.** [passion] passion; **faire ~** to be all the rage.

furibard, -e [fyribar, ard] *adj fam* furious.

furibond, -e [fyribɔ̃, ɔ̃d] *adj* furious.

furie [fyri] *nf* **-1.** [colère, agitation] fury; **en ~** [personne] infuriated; [éléments] raging. **-2.** *fig* [femme] shrew. **-3.** [passion] passion.

furieusement [fyrjøzmã] *adv* **-1.** [avec fureur] furiously. **-2.** [extrêmement] tremendously.

furieux, -ieuse [fyrjø, jøz] **-1.** [personne] furious. **-2.** [violent] violent. **-3.** [énorme] tremendous.

furoncle [fyrɔ̃kl] *nm* boil.

furtif, -ive [fyrtif, iv] *adj* furtive.

furtivement [fyrtivmã] *adv* furtively.

fus, fut *etc* → être.

fusain [fyzɛ̃] *nm* **-1.** [crayon] charcoal. **-2.** [dessin] charcoal drawing. **-3.** [arbre] spindle tree.

fuseau, -x [fyzo] *nm* **-1.** [outil] spindle. **-2.** [pantalon] ski-pants (*pl*).

◆ **fuseau horaire** *nm* time zone.

fusée [fyze] *nf* **-1.** [pièce d'artifice & AÉRON] rocket. **-2.** TECHNOL spindle; AUTOM stub axle.

fuselage [fyzlaʒ] *nm* fuselage.

fuselé, -e [fyzle] *adj* [doigts] tapering; [jambes] slender.

fuser [fyze] [3] *vi* [cri, rire] to burst forth OU out.

fusible [fyzibl] *nm* fuse.

fusil [fyzi] *nm* **-1.** [arme] gun; **changer son ~ d'épaule** *fig* to change one's approach. **-2.** [personne] marksman.

fusillade [fyzijad] *nf* **-1.** [combat] gunfire (*U*), fusillade. **-2.** [exécution] shooting.

fusiller [fyzije] [3] *vt* **-1.** [exécuter] to shoot; **~ qqn du regard** *fig* to look daggers at sb. **-2.** *fam* [bousiller] to muck up, to ruin.

fusil-mitrailleur [fyzimitrajœr] (*pl* **fusils-mitrailleurs**) *nm* machine gun.

fusion [fyzjɔ̃] *nf* **-1.** [gén] fusion. **-2.** [fonte] smelting; **en ~** molten. **-3.** ÉCON & POLIT merger.

fusionner [fyzjɔne] [3] *vt & vi* to merge.

fustiger [fystiʒe] [17] *vt* to castigate.

fût [fy] ◇ → être. ◇ *nm* **-1.** [d'arbre] trunk. **-2.** [tonneau] barrel, cask. **-3.** [d'arme] stock. **-4.** [de colonne] shaft.

futaie [fytɛ] *nf* wood.

futé, -e [fyte] *fam* ◇ *adj* cunning. ◇ *nm, f* sharp cookie.

futile [fytil] *adj* **-1.** [insignifiant] futile. **-2.** [frivole] frivolous.

futilité [fytilite] *nf* **-1.** [d'action] futility. **-2.** [vétille] triviality.

futur, -e [fytyr] ◇ *adj* future (*avant n*); **la vie ~** RELIG the life to come; **~s mariés** bride- and groom-to-be. ◇ *nm, f* [fiancé] intended.

◆ **futur** *nm* future; ~ **antérieur** LING future perfect.

futuriste [fytyrist] ◇ *nmf* futurist. ◇ *adj* futuristic.

futurologue [fytyrɔlɔg] *nmf* futurologist.

fuyant, -e [fɥijɑ̃, ɑ̃t] *adj* **-1.** [perspective, front] receding (*avant n*). **-2.** [regard] evasive.

fuyard, -e [fɥijar, ard] *nm, f* runaway.

fuyez, fuyons *etc* → **fuir.**

FV (*abr de* **fréquence vocale**) VF.

G

g¹, G [ʒe] *nm inv* g, G.

g² (*abr de* **gauche**) L, l.

◆ **G** (*abr de* **giga**) G.

GAB [gab] (*abr de* **guichet automatique de banque**) *nm* cash dispenser, ATM *Am*.

gabardine [gabardin] *nf* gabardine.

gabarit [gabari] *nm* **-1.** [appareil de mesure] gauge. **-2.** [dimension] size. **-3.** [valeur] calibre; **du même ~** of the same calibre.

gabegie [gabʒi] *nf* muddle, disorder.

Gabon [gabɔ̃] *nm*: **le ~** Gabon; **au ~** in Gabon.

gabonais, -e [gabɔnɛ, ɛz] *adj* Gabonese.

◆ **Gabonais, -e** *nm, f* Gabonese.

gâche [gɑʃ] *nf* **-1.** [de serrure] striking plate. **-2.** [outil] trowel.

gâcher [gɑʃe] [3] *vt* **-1.** [gaspiller] to waste. **-2.** [gâter] to spoil. **-3.** CONSTR to mix.

gâchette [gɑʃɛt] *nf* trigger; **appuyer sur la ~** to pull the trigger.

gâchis [gɑʃi] *nm* **-1.** [gaspillage] waste (*U*). **-2.** [désordre] mess. **-3.** CONSTR mortar.

gadget [gadʒɛt] *nm* gadget.

gadoue [gadu] *nf fam* [boue] mud; [engrais] sludge.

gaélique [gaelik] ◇ *adj* Gaelic. ◇ *nm* Gaelic; ~ **d'Écosse** Scots Gaelic; ~ **d'Irlande** Irish Gaelic.

gaffe [gaf] *nf* **-1.** *fam* [maladresse] clanger; **faire une ~** to drop a clanger. **-2.** [outil] boat hook. **-3.** *loc*: **faire ~** *fam* to take care.

gaffer [gafe] [3] ◇ *vt* to hook. ◇ *vi fam* to put one's foot in it.

gaffeur, -euse [gafœr, øz] *fam* ◇ *adj* blundering. ◇ *nm, f* blunderer.

gag [gag] *nm* gag.

gaga [gaga] *adj fam* gaga, doddering.

gage [gaʒ] *nm* **-1.** [dépôt] pledge; **mettre qqch en ~** to pawn sthg. **-2.** [assurance, preuve] proof; **en ~ de** as a token of. **-3.** [dans jeu] forfeit.

gager [gaʒe] [17] *vt*: ~ **que** to bet (that).

gageure [gaʒyr] *nf* challenge.

gagnant, -e [gaɲɑ̃, ɑ̃t] ◇ *adj* winning (*avant n*). ◇ *nm, f* winner.

gagne-pain [gaɲpɛ̃] *nm inv* livelihood.

gagne-petit [gaɲpəti] *nm inv* person earning a pittance.

gagner [gaɲe] [3] ◇ *vt* **-1.** [salaire, argent, repos] to earn. **-2.** [course, prix, affection] to win. **-3.** [obtenir, économiser] to gain; ~ **du temps/de la place** to gain time/space. **-4.** [vaincre]: ~ **qqn de vitesse** to outpace sb. **-5.** [atteindre] to reach; [- suj: feu, engourdissement] to spread to; [- suj: sommeil, froid] to overcome. **-6.** [se concilier] to win over.
◇ *vi* **-1.** [être vainqueur] to win. **-2.** [bénéficier] to gain; ~ **à faire qqch** to be better off doing sthg; **qu'est-ce que j'y gagne?** what do I get out of it? **-3.** [s'améliorer]: ~ **en** to increase in; ~ **à être connu** to improve on acquaintance.

gagneur, -euse [gaɲœr, øz] *nm, f* winner.

gai, -e [ge] *adj* **-1.** [joyeux] cheerful, happy. **-2.** [vif, plaisant] bright.

gaiement [gemɑ̃] *adv* cheerfully.

gaieté [gete] *nf* **-1.** [joie] cheerfulness; **de ~ de cœur** enthusiastically. **-2.** [vivacité] brightness.

gaillard, -e [gajar, ard] ◇ *adj* **-1.** [alerte] sprightly, spry. **-2.** [licencieux] ribald. ◇ *nm, f* strapping individual.

gain [gɛ̃] *nm* **-1.** [profit] gain, profit. **-2.** [succès] winning; **avoir** OU **obtenir ~ de cause** to win one's case. **-3.** [économie] saving.

◆ **gains** *nmpl* earnings.

gaine [gɛn] *nf* **-1.** [étui, enveloppe] sheath. **-2.** [sous-vêtement] girdle, corset.

gaine-culotte [gɛnkylɔt] (*pl* **gaines-culottes**) *nf* panty girdle.

gainer [gene] [4] *vt* to sheathe.

gala [gala] *nm* gala, reception; **de ~ gala** (*avant n*).

galamment [galamɑ̃] *adv* politely, gallantly.

galant, -e [galɑ̃, ɑ̃t] *adj* **-1.** [courtois] gallant. **-2.** [amoureux] flirtatious.

◆ **galant** *nm* admirer.

galanterie [galɑ̃tri] *nf* **-1.** [courtoisie] gallantry, politeness. **-2.** [flatterie] compliment.

galantine [galãtin] *nf boned meat or poultry pressed into a loaf shape.*

galaxie [galaksi] *nf* galaxy.

galbe [galb] *nm* curve.

galbé, -e [galbe] *adj* -1. [objet] curved. -2. [jambe] shapely.

gale [gal] *nf* MÉD scabies (*U*).

galère [galɛr] *nf* NAVIG galley; **quelle ~!** *fig* what a hassle!, what a drag!

galérer [galere] [18] *vi fam* to have a hard time.

galerie [galri] *nf* -1. [gén] gallery; **~ marchande** shopping arcade; **~ de peinture** picture gallery. -2. THÉÂTRE circle; **amuser la ~** *fig* to play to the gallery. -3. [porte-bagages] roof rack.

galet [galɛ] *nm* -1. [caillou] pebble. -2. TECHNOL wheel, roller.

galette [galɛt] *nf* -1. CULIN pancake (*made from buckwheat flour*); **~ des Rois** *cake eaten on Twelfth Night.* -2. *fam* [argent] dough, cash.

galeux, -euse [galø, øz] ◇ *adj* -1. MÉD scabious. -2. → **brebis.** ◇ *nm, f* scruffy person.

galimatias [galimatja] *nm* gibberish (*U*).

galipette [galipɛt] *nf fam* somersault; **faire des ~s** to do somersaults.

Galles → **pays.**

gallicisme [galisism] *nm* [expression] French idiom; [dans une langue étrangère] gallicism.

gallinacé, -e [galinase] *adj* domestic.
◆ **gallinacé** *nm* domestic fowl.

gallois, -e [galwa, az] *adj* Welsh.
◆ **gallois** *nm* [langue] Welsh.
◆ **Gallois, -e** *nm, f* Welshman (*f* Welshwoman); **les Gallois** the Welsh.

gallo-romain, -e [galɔrɔmɛ̃, ɛn] (*mpl* **gallo-romains**, *fpl* **gallo-romaines**) *adj* Gallo-Roman.
◆ **Gallo-Romain, -e** *nm, f* Gallo-Roman.

galoche [galɔʃ] *nf* clog.

galon [galɔ̃] *nm* -1. COUTURE braid (*U*). -2. MIL stripe; **prendre du ~** *fig* to be promoted.

galop [galo] *nm* [allure] gallop; **au ~** [cheval] at a gallop; *fig* at the double.

galopade [galɔpad] *nf* -1. [de cheval] gallop. -2. [de personne] stampede.

galopant, -e [galɔpã, ãt] *adj fig* galloping, runaway.

galoper [galɔpe] [3] *vi* -1. [cheval] to gallop. -2. [personne] to run about. -3. [imagination] to run riot.

galopin [galɔpɛ̃] *nm fam* brat.

galvaniser [galvanize] [3] *vt litt* & *fig* to galvanize.

galvauder [galvode] [3] *vt* [ternir] to tarnish.
◆ **se galvauder** *vp* to demean o.s.

gambade [gãbad] *nf* leap.

gambader [gãbade] [3] *vi* [sautiller] to leap about; [agneau] to gambol.

gamberger [gãbɛrʒe] [17] *vi fam* to think hard.

gambette [gãbɛt] *nf fam* leg, pin.

Gambie [gãbi] *nf*: **la ~** Gambia.

gambien, -ienne [gãbjɛ̃, jɛn] *adj* Gambian.
◆ **Gambien, -ienne** *nm, f* Gambian.

gamelle [gamɛl] *nf* -1. [plat] mess tin *Br*, kit *Am*. -2. *fam* [chute]: **se ramasser une ~** to come a cropper.

gamin, -e [gamɛ̃, in] ◇ *adj* -1. [espiègle] lively, mischievous. -2. [puéril] childish. ◇ *nm, f* -1. *fam* [enfant] kid. -2. [des rues] street urchin.

gaminerie [gaminri] *nf* -1. [espièglerie] mischievousness. -2. [enfantillage] childishness; **faire des ~s** to be childish.

gamme [gam] *nf* -1. [série] range; **~ de produits** product range; **haut/bas de ~** at the top/bottom of the range. -2. MUS scale.

Gand [gã] *n* Ghent.

gang [gãg] *nm* gang.

Gange [gãz] *nm*: **le ~** the (River) Ganges.

ganglion [gãglijɔ̃] *nm* ganglion.

gangrène [gãgrɛn] *nf* gangrene; *fig* corruption, canker.

gangster [gãgstɛr] *nm* gangster; *fig* crook.

gangue [gãg] *nf* -1. [de minerai] gangue. -2. *fig* [carcan] straitjacket.

gant [gã] *nm* glove; **~ de boxe** boxing glove; **~ de caoutchouc** rubber glove; **~ de crin** friction glove; **~ de toilette** face cloth, flannel *Br*; **aller comme un ~ à qqn** to fit sb like a glove; **prendre des ~s** to be cautious; **prendre des ~s avec qqn** to handle sb with kid gloves.

garage [garaʒ] *nm* garage.

garagiste [garaʒist] *nmf* [propriétaire] garage owner; [réparateur] garage mechanic.

garant, -e [garã, ãt] *nm, f* [responsable] guarantor; **se porter ~ de** to vouch for.
◆ **garant** *nm* [garantie] guarantee.

garantie [garãti] *nf* -1. [gén] guarantee. -2. [de police d'assurance] cover.

garantir [garãtir] [32] *vt* -1. [assurer & COMM] to guarantee; **~ à qqn que** to assure OU guarantee sb that. -2. [protéger]: **~ qqch (de)** to protect sthg (from).

garce [gars] *nf* bitch.

garçon [garsɔ̃] *nm* **-1.** [enfant] boy; ~ **man-qué** tomboy. **-2.** [célibataire]: **vieux ~** confirmed bachelor. **-3.** [serveur]: ~ **(de café)** waiter; ~**!** waiter!

garçonne [garsɔn] *nf*: **coiffure à la ~** urchin cut.

garçonnet [garsɔnɛ] *nm* little boy.

garçonnière [garsɔnjɛr] *nf* bachelor flat *Br* OU apartment *Am*.

garde [gard] ◇ *nf* **-1.** [surveillance] protection. **-2.** [veille]: **de ~** on duty; **pharmacie de ~** duty chemist; **~ de nuit** night duty. **-3.** MIL guard; **monter la ~** to go on guard. **-4.** JUR: **avoir la ~ d'un enfant** to have custody of a child; **~ à vue** ≃ police custody. **-5.** *loc*: **être/se tenir sur ses ~s** to be/stay on one's guard; **mettre qqn en ~ contre qqch** to put sb on their guard about sthg; **prendre ~ à qqch** to watch out for sthg; **prendre ~ à ne pas faire qqch** to take care not to do sthg; **prendre ~ que** (+ *subjonctif*) to take care that. ◇ *nmf* keeper; **~ du corps** bodyguard; **~ d'enfants** childminder; **~ forestier** forest ranger; **le ~ des Sceaux** the Minister of Justice, ≃ Lord Chancellor *Br*, ≃ Attorney General *Am*.

◆ **Garde** *nf*: **la Garde républicaine** the Republican Guard.

garde-à-vous [gardavu] *nm inv* attention; **se mettre au ~** to stand to attention.

garde-barrière [gardəbarjɛr] (*pl* **gardes-barrière** OU **gardes-barrières**) *nmf* level-crossing keeper.

garde-boue [gardəbu] *nm inv* mudguard *Br*, fender *Am*.

garde-chasse [gardəʃas] (*pl* **gardes-chasse** OU **gardes-chasses**) *nm* gamekeeper.

garde-chiourme [gardəʃjurm] (*pl* **gardes-chiourme** OU **gardes-chiourmes**) *nm* warder; *fig* slavedriver.

garde-fou [gardəfu] (*pl* **garde-fous**) *nm* railing, parapet.

garde-malade [gardəmalad] (*pl* **gardes-malades**) *nmf* nurse.

garde-manger [gardəmɑ̃ʒe] *nm inv* [pièce] pantry, larder; [armoire] meat safe *Br*, cooler *Am*.

garde-meuble [gardəmœbl] (*pl inv* OU **garde-meubles**) *nm* warehouse.

gardénia [gardenja] *nm* gardenia.

garde-pêche [gardəpɛʃ] (*pl* **gardes-pêche**) ◇ *nm* [personne] water bailiff *Br*, fishwarden *Am*. ◇ *nm inv* [bateau] fishery protection vessel.

garder [garde] [3] *vt* **-1.** [gén] to keep; [vêtement] to keep on. **-2.** [surveiller] to mind, to look after; [défendre] to guard. **-3.** [protéger]: **~ qqn de qqch** to save sb from sthg.

◆ **se garder** *vp* **-1.** [se conserver] to keep. **-2.** [se méfier]: **se ~ de qqn/qqch** to beware of sb/sthg. **-3.** [s'abstenir]: **se ~ de faire qqch** to take care not to do sthg.

garderie [gardəri] *nf*: **~ (d'enfants)** crèche *Br*, day nursery *Br*, day-care center *Am*.

garde-robe [gardərɔb] (*pl* **garde-robes**) *nf* wardrobe.

gardien, -ienne [gardjɛ̃, jɛn] *nm, f* **-1.** [surveillant] guard, keeper; **~ de but** goalkeeper; **~ de nuit** night watchman; **~ de prison** prison warder OU officer. **-2.** *fig* [défenseur] protector, guardian. **-3.** [agent]: **~ (de la paix)** policeman.

gardiennage [gardjɛnaʒ] *nm* caretaking.

gardon [gardɔ̃] *nm* roach; **frais comme un ~** *fig* fresh as a daisy.

gare¹ [gar] *nf* station; **~ maritime** harbour station; **~ routière** [de marchandises] road haulage depot; [pour passagers] bus station; **~ de triage** marshalling yard.

gare² [gar] *interj* **-1.** [attention] watch out!; **~ aux voleurs** watch out for pickpockets; **sans crier ~** *fig* without warning. **-2.** [menace]: **~ à toi!** watch out!, watch it!

garer [gare] [3] *vt* **-1.** [ranger] to park. **-2.** [mettre à l'abri] to put in a safe place.

◆ **se garer** *vp* **-1.** [stationner] to park. **-2.** [se ranger] to pull over. **-3.** [éviter]: **se ~ de qqch** to avoid sthg.

gargariser [gargarize] [3]

◆ **se gargariser** *vp* **-1.** [se rincer] to gargle. **-2.** *péj* [se délecter]: **se ~ de** to delight OU revel in.

gargarisme [gargarism] *nm* gargle.

gargote [gargɔt] *nf* cheap restaurant, greasy spoon.

gargouille [garguj] *nf* gargoyle.

gargouillement [gargujmɑ̃] *nm* gurgling (*U*).

gargouiller [garguje] [3] *vi* **-1.** [eau] to gurgle. **-2.** [intestins] to rumble.

garnement [garnəmɑ̃] *nm* rascal, pest.

garni [garni] *nm vieilli* furnished accommodation (*U*).

garnir [garnir] [32] *vt* **-1.** [équiper] to fit out, to furnish. **-2.** [couvrir]: **~ qqch (de)** to cover sthg (with). **-3.** [remplir] to fill. **-4.** [orner]: **~ qqch de** to decorate sthg with; COUTURE to trim sthg with.

◆ **se garnir** *vp* to fill up.

garnison [garnizɔ̃] *nf* garrison.

garniture [garnityr] *nf* **-1.** [ornement] trimming; [de lit] bed linen. **-2.** AUTOM: **~ de**

frein brake lining; ~ **(intérieure)** upholstery. **-3.** [CULIN - pour accompagner] garnish
Br, fixings (*pl*) *Am;* [- pour remplir] filling; ~
de légumes vegetables (*pl*).

garrigue [garig] *nf* scrub.

garrot [garo] *nm* **-1.** [de cheval] withers (*pl*).
-2. MÉD tourniquet. **-3.** [de torture] garrotte.

garrotter [garɔte] [3] *vt* **-1.** [attacher] to tie
up. **-2.** *fig* [museler] to muzzle.

gars [ga] *nm fam* **-1.** [garçon, homme] lad.
-2. [type] guy, bloke *Br.*

gascon, -onne [gaskɔ̃, ɔn] *adj* Gascon.
◆ **Gascon, -onne** *nm, f* Gascon.

gas-oil [gazɔjl, gazwal], **gazole** [gazɔl] *nm*
diesel oil.

gaspillage [gaspijaʒ] *nm* waste.

gaspiller [gaspije] [3] *vt* to waste.

gastrique [gastrik] *adj* gastric.

gastrite [gastrit] *nf* gastritis (*U*).

gastro-entérite [gastroãterit] (*pl* **gastro-
entérites**) *nf* gastroenteritis (*U*).

gastronome [gastrɔnɔm] *nmf* gourmet.

gastronomie [gastrɔnɔmi] *nf* gastronomy.

gastronomique [gastrɔnɔmik] *adj* gastronomic.

gâteau, -x [gato] *nm* cake; ~ **d'anniversaire**
birthday cake; ~ **de miel** honeycomb; ~
sec biscuit *Br,* cookie *Am;* **c'est du ~** *fam*
it's a piece of cake.

gâter [gate] [3] *vt* **-1.** [gén] to spoil; [vacan-
ces, affaires] to ruin, to spoil. **-2.** *iron*
[combler] to be too good to sb; **on est gâté!**
just marvellous!
◆ **se gâter** *vp* **-1.** [aliments] to spoil, to go
off. **-2.** [temps] to change for the worse. **-3.**
[situation] to take a turn for the worse.

gâterie [gatri] *nf* treat.

gâteux, -euse [gatø, øz] ◇ *adj* senile; **être**
~ **de** *fig* to be daft about OU besotted with.
◇ *nm, f* **-1.** [sénile] doddering old man (*f*
woman). **-2.** [radoteur] old bore.

gâtisme [gatism] *nm* **-1.** [vieillissement] senility. **-2.** [stupidité] stupidity.

GATT, Gatt [gat] (*abr de* **General Agreement on Tariffs and Trade**) *nm* GATT.

gauche [goʃ] ◇ *nf* **-1.** [côté] left, left-hand
side; **rouler sur la** ~ to drive on the left; **à**
~ **(de)** on the left (of); **à ma/ta** *etc* ~ on
my/your *etc* left; **de** ~ on the left. **-2.** POLIT:
la ~ the left (wing); **de** ~ left-wing. ◇ *nm*
BOXE left. ◇ *adj* **-1.** [côté] left. **-2.** [personne]
clumsy.

gauchement [goʃmã] *adv* clumsily.

gaucher, -ère [goʃe, ɛr] ◇ *adj* left-handed.
◇ *nm, f* left-handed person.

gauchir [goʃir] [32] ◇ *vi* to warp. ◇ *vt fig*
to distort.

gauchisant, -e [goʃizã, ãt] *adj* leftist.

gauchisme [goʃism] *nm* leftism.

gauchiste [goʃist] ◇ *nmf* leftist. ◇ *adj* left-
wing.

gaufre [gofr] *nf* waffle.

gaufrer [gofre] [3] *vt* to emboss.

gaufrette [gofrɛt] *nf* wafer.

gaule [gol] *nf* **-1.** [perche] pole. **-2.** [canne à
pêche] fishing rod.

gauler [gole] [3] *vt* to bring OU shake
down.

gaulliste [golist] *nmf & adj* Gaullist.

gaulois, -e [golwa, az] *adj* **-1.** [de Gaule]
Gallic. **-2.** [osé] ribald.
◆ **Gaulois, -e** *nm, f* Gaul.

gauloiserie [golwazri] *nf* bawdy story.

gausser [gose] [3]
◆ **se gausser** *vp*: **se** ~ **de** *littéraire* to make
fun of.

gaver [gave] [3] *vt* **-1.** [animal] to force-feed.
-2. [personne]: ~ **qqn de** to feed sb full of.
◆ **se gaver** *vp*: **se** ~ **de** to gorge o.s. on.

gay [gɛ] *adj inv & nm* gay.

gaz [gaz] *nm inv* gas; **à pleins** ~ *fam* AUTOM
flat out; ~ **carbonique** carbon dioxide; ~
lacrymogène tear gas; ~ **naturel** natural
gas.

Gaza [gaza] *n* Gaza; **la bande de** ~ the
Gaza Strip.

gaze [gaz] *nf* gauze.

gazelle [gazɛl] *nf* gazelle.

gazer [gaze] [3] ◇ *vt* to gas. ◇ *vi fam* to go
at top speed; **ça gaze!** everything's great!;
ça gaze¿ how are things¿

gazette [gazɛt] *nf* newspaper, gazette.

gazeux, -euse [gazø, øz] *adj* **-1.** CHIM gaseous. **-2.** [boisson] fizzy.

gazoduc [gazodyk] *nm* gas pipeline.

gazole → **gas-oil.**

gazomètre [gazɔmɛtr] *nm* gasometer.

gazon [gazɔ̃] *nm* [herbe] grass; [terrain] lawn.

gazouiller [gazuje] [3] *vi* **-1.** [oiseau] to
chirp, to twitter. **-2.** [bébé] to gurgle.

gazouillis [gazuji] *nm* **-1.** [d'oiseau] chirping, twittering. **-2.** [de bébé] gurgling.

GB, G-B (*abr de* **Grande-Bretagne**) *nf* GB.

gd *abr de* **grand.**

GDF, Gdf (*abr de* **Gaz de France**) *French national gas company.*

geai [ʒɛ] *nm* jay.

géant, -e [ʒeã, ãt] ◇ *adj* gigantic, giant. ◇
nm, f giant.

geignement [ʒɛɲəmɑ̃] *nm* moaning.

geindre [ʒɛ̃dr] [81] *vi* **-1.** [gémir] to moan. **-2.** *fam* [pleurnicher] to whine.

gel [ʒɛl] *nm* **-1.** MÉTÉOR frost. **-2.** [d'eau] freezing. **-3.** [cosmétique] gel.

gélatine [ʒelatin] *nf* gelatine.

gélatineux, -euse [ʒelatinø, øz] *adj* gelatinous.

gelée [ʒəle] *nf* **-1.** MÉTÉOR frost; ~ **blanche** hoarfrost. **-2.** CULIN jelly; **en** ~ in jelly; ~ **royale** royal jelly.

geler [ʒəle] [25] *vt & vi* **-1.** [gén] to freeze. **-2.** [projet] to halt.

◆ **se geler** *vp fam* to freeze.

gélule [ʒelyl] *nf* capsule.

Gémeaux [ʒemo] *nmpl* ASTROL Gemini; **être** ~ to be a(a) Gemini.

gémir [ʒemir] [32] *vi* **-1.** [gén] to moan. **-2.** [par déception] to groan.

gémissement [ʒemismɑ̃] *nm* **-1.** [gén] moan; [du vent] moaning (*U*). **-2.** [de déception] groan.

gemme [ʒɛm] *nf* gem, precious stone.

gênant, -e [ʒenɑ̃, ɑ̃t] *adj* **-1.** [encombrant] in the way. **-2.** [embarrassant] awkward, embarrassing. **-3.** [énervant]: **être** ~ to be a nuisance.

gencive [ʒɑ̃siv] *nf* gum.

gendarme [ʒɑ̃darm] *nm* policeman.

gendarmerie [ʒɑ̃darməri] *nf* **-1.** [corps] police force. **-2.** [lieu] police station.

gendre [ʒɑ̃dr] *nm* son-in-law.

gène [ʒɛn] *nm* gene.

gêne [ʒɛn] *nf* **-1.** [physique] difficulty. **-2.** [psychologique] embarrassment; **être sans** ~ *fam* to be a cool customer. **-3.** [financière] difficulty; **être dans la** ~ to be in financial difficulties.

gêné, -e [ʒene] *adj* **-1.** [physiquement]: **être** ~ **pour marcher** to have difficulty walking. **-2.** [psychologiquement] embarrassed. **-3.** [financièrement] in financial difficulties.

généalogie [ʒenealɔʒi] *nf* genealogy.

généalogique [ʒenealɔʒik] *adj* genealogical; **arbre** ~ family tree.

gêner [ʒene] [4] *vt* **-1.** [physiquement - gén] to be too tight for; [- suj: chaussures] to pinch. **-2.** [moralement] to embarrass. **-3.** [incommoder] to bother. **-4.** [encombrer] to hamper.

◆ **se gêner** *vp* to put o.s. out; **ne pas se** ~ **pour faire qqch** to feel free to do sthg; *hum* to make no bones about doing sthg; **ne vous gênez pas!** *hum* don't mind me!

général, -e, -aux [ʒeneral, o] *adj* general; **en** ~ generally, in general; **répétition** ~**e** dress rehearsal.

◆ **général** *nm* MIL general.

◆ **générale** *nf* **-1.** THÉÂTRE dress rehearsal. **-2.** MIL alarm.

généralement [ʒeneralmɑ̃] *adv* generally.

généralisation [ʒeneralizasjɔ̃] *nf* generalization.

généraliser [ʒeneralize] [3] *vt & vi* to generalize.

◆ **se généraliser** *vp* to become general OU widespread.

généraliste [ʒeneralist] ◇ *nmf* GP *Br*, family doctor. ◇ *adj* general.

généralité [ʒeneralite] *nf* **-1.** [idée] generality. **-2.** [universalité] general nature.

◆ **généralités** *nfpl* generalities.

générateur, -trice [ʒeneratœr, tris] *adj* generating.

◆ **générateur** *nm* TECHNOL generator.

◆ **génératrice** *nf* ÉLECTR generator.

génération [ʒenerasjɔ̃] *nf* generation; **la nouvelle** ~ the younger generation; ~ **spontanée** SCIENCE spontaneous generation.

générer [ʒenere] [18] *vt* to generate.

généreusement [ʒenerøzmɑ̃] *adv* generously.

généreux, -euse [ʒenerø, øz] *adj* generous; [terre] fertile.

générique [ʒenerik] ◇ *adj* generic. ◇ *nm* credits (*pl*).

générosité [ʒenerozite] *nf* generosity.

genèse [ʒənɛz] *nf* [création] genesis.

◆ **Genèse** *nf* BIBLE Genesis.

genêt [ʒənɛ] *nm* broom.

génétique [ʒenetik] ◇ *adj* genetic. ◇ *nf* genetics (*U*).

gêneur, -euse [ʒenœr, øz] *nm, f* nuisance.

Genève [ʒənɛv] *n* Geneva.

genevois, -e [ʒənvwa, az] *adj* Genevan.

génial, -e, -iaux [ʒenjal, jo] *adj* **-1.** [personne] of genius. **-2.** [idée, invention] inspired. **-3.** *fam* [formidable]: **c'est** ~! that's great!, that's terrific!

génie [ʒeni] *nm* **-1.** [personne, aptitude] genius; **avoir du** ~ to be a genius. **-2.** MYTH spirit, genie. **-3.** TECHNOL engineering; **le** ~ MIL ≃ the Royal Engineers *Br*; ~ **civil** civil engineering; ~ **maritime** [corps] marine architects.

genièvre [ʒənjɛvr] *nm* juniper.

génisse [ʒenis] *nf* heifer.

génital, -e, -aux [ʒenital, o] *adj* genital.

géniteur, -trice [ʒenitœr, tris] *nm, f* parent; [d'animal] sire (*f* dam).

génitif [ʒenitif] *nm* genitive (case).

génocide [ʒenɔsid] *nm* genocide.

génoise [ʒenwaz] *nf* sponge cake.

genou, -x [ʒɔnu] *nm* knee; à ~x on one's knees, kneeling; **se mettre à ~x** to kneel (down); **tenir** OU **avoir qqn sur ses ~x** to hold sb in one's lap OU on one's knee; **être à ~x devant qqn** *fig* to worship sb; **être sur les ~x** *fam fig* to be worn out, to be on one's last legs.

genouillère [ʒɔnujɛr] *nf* -1. [bandage] knee bandage. -2. SPORT kneepad.

genre [ʒɑ̃r] *nm* -1. [type] type, kind; **en tous ~s** of all kinds; **le ~ humain** the human race. -2. LITTÉRATURE genre. -3. [style de personne] style; **avoir mauvais ~** to be coarse-looking. -4. GRAM gender.

gens [ʒɑ̃] *nmpl* people.

gentiane [ʒɑ̃sjan] *nf* gentian.

gentil, -ille [ʒɑ̃ti, ij] *adj* -1. [agréable] nice. -2. [aimable] kind, nice; **être ~ avec qqn** to be nice OU kind to sb.

gentilhomme [ʒɑ̃tijɔm] (*pl* **gentilshommes**) *nm* gentleman.

gentillesse [ʒɑ̃tijɛs] *nf* kindness; **avoir la ~ de faire qqch** to be so kind as to do sthg.

gentillet, -ette [ʒɑ̃tijɛ, ɛt] *adj* -1. [petit et gentil] nice little. -2. *péj* [assez agréable] nice enough.

gentiment [ʒɑ̃timɑ̃] *adv* -1. [sagement] nicely. -2. [aimablement] kindly, nicely. -3. *Helv* [tranquillement] calmly, quietly.

gentleman [dʒɛntləman] (*pl* **gentlemen** [dʒɛntləmɛn]) *nm* gentleman.

génuflexion [ʒenyflɛksjɔ̃] *nf* genuflexion.

géographe [ʒeɔgraf] *nmf* geographer.

géographie [ʒeɔgrafi] *nf* geography.

géographique [ʒeɔgrafik] *adj* geographical.

geôlier, -ière [ʒolje, jɛr] *nm, f* gaoler.

géologie [ʒeɔlɔʒi] *nf* geology.

géologique [ʒeɔlɔʒik] *adj* geological.

géologue [ʒeɔlɔg] *nmf* geologist.

géomètre [ʒeɔmɛtr] *nmf* -1. [spécialiste] geometer, geometrician. -2. [technicien] surveyor.

géométrie [ʒeɔmetri] *nf* geometry.

géométrique [ʒeɔmetrik] *adj* geometric.

géophysique [ʒeɔfizik] ◇ *nf* geophysics (U). ◇ *adj* geophysical.

géopolitique [ʒeɔpɔlitik] ◇ *nf* geopolitics (U). ◇ *adj* geopolitical.

géosphère [ʒeɔsfɛr] *nf* geosphere.

gérance [ʒerɑ̃s] *nf* management.

géranium [ʒeranjɔm] *nm* geranium.

gérant, -e [ʒerɑ̃, ɑ̃t] *nm, f* manager.

gerbe [ʒɛrb] *nf* -1. [de blé] sheaf; [de fleurs] spray. -2. [d'étincelles, d'eau] shower.

gerber [ʒɛrbe] [3] ◇ *vt* -1. [blé] to bind into sheaves. -2. [sacs, caisses] to pile (up). ◇ *vi* -1. [fusée] to burst in a shower of sparks. -2. *tfam* [vomir] to puke.

gerboise [ʒɛrbwaz] *nf* jerboa.

gercer [ʒɛrse] [16] *vt & vi* to crack, to chap.
◆ **se gercer** *vp* to crack, to chap.

gérer [ʒere] [18] *vt* to manage.

gériatrie [ʒerjatri] *nf* geriatrics (U).

gériatrique [ʒerjatrik] *adj* geriatric.

germain, -e [ʒɛrmɛ̃, ɛn] → **cousin**.

germanique [ʒɛrmanik] *adj* Germanic.

germaniste [ʒɛrmanist] *nmf* -1. [spécialiste] German specialist. -2. [étudiant] German student, student of German.

germe [ʒɛrm] *nm* -1. BOT & MÉD germ; [de pomme de terre] eye; **~s de soja** beansprouts. -2. *fig* [origine] seed, cause.

germer [ʒɛrme] [3] *vi* to germinate.

germination [ʒɛrminasjɔ̃] *nf* germination.

gérondif [ʒerɔ̃dif] *nm* [latin] gerundive; [français] gerund.

gérontologie [ʒerɔ̃tɔlɔʒi] *nf* gerontology.

gésier [ʒezje] *nm* gizzard.

gésir [ʒezir] [49] *vi littéraire* to lie.

gestation [ʒɛstasjɔ̃] *nf* gestation; **en ~** *fig* in gestation.

geste [ʒɛst] *nm* -1. [mouvement] gesture. -2. [acte] act, deed; **faire un ~** *fig* to make a gesture.

gesticuler [ʒɛstikyle] [3] *vi* to gesticulate.

gestion [ʒɛstjɔ̃] *nf* management; JUR administration; **~ d'entreprise** business administration; **~ de fichiers** INFORM file management.

gestionnaire [ʒɛstjɔnɛr] ◇ *nmf* [personne] manager. ◇ *adj* management (*avant n*). ◇ *nm* INFORM: **~ de données** data manager.

gestuel, -elle [ʒɛstɥɛl] *adj* [langage] sign (*avant n*).

Ghana [gana] *nm*: **le ~** Ghana.

ghanéen, -enne [ganeɛ̃, ɛn] *adj* Ghanaian.
◆ **Ghanéen, -enne** *nm, f* Ghanaian.

ghetto [geto] *nm litt & fig* ghetto.

ghettoïsation [getoizasjɔ̃] *nf* ghettoization.

gibecière [ʒibsjɛr] *nf* game bag; [d'écolier] satchel.

gibelotte [ʒiblɔt] *nf rabbit cooked in white wine*.

gibet [ʒibɛ] *nm* gallows (*sg*), gibbet.

gibier [ʒibje] *nm* game; *fig* [personne] prey; **du gros ~** big game; *fig* [personne] important catch.

giboulée [ʒibule] *nf* sudden shower.

giboyeux, -euse [ʒibwajø, øz] *adj* abounding in game.

Gibraltar [ʒibraltar] *nm* Gibraltar; **à ~ in** Gibraltar.

GIC (*abr de* **Groupe interministériel de contrôle**) *nm official body controlling the use of telephone tapping.*

giclée [ʒikle] *nf* squirt, spurt.

gicler [ʒikle] [3] *vi* to squirt, to spurt.

gicleur [ʒiklœr] *nm* jet.

gifle [ʒifl] *nf* slap; **donner une ~ à qqn** to slap sb.

gifler [ʒifle] [3] *vt* to slap; *fig* [suj: vent, pluie] to whip, to lash.

GIG (*abr de* **grand invalide de guerre**) *nm* war invalid.

gigantesque [ʒigɑ̃tɛsk] *adj* gigantic.

giga-octet [ʒigaɔktɛ] *nm* INFORM gigabyte.

GIGN (*abr de* **Groupe d'intervention de la gendarmerie nationale**) *nm special crack force of the French police,* ≃ SAS *Br,* ≃ SWAT *Am.*

gigogne [ʒigɔɲ] → **lit, table.**

gigolo [ʒigɔlo] *nm* gigolo.

gigot [ʒigo] *nm* CULIN leg.

gigoter [ʒigɔte] [3] *vi* to squirm, to wriggle.

gilet [ʒilɛ] *nm* **-1.** [cardigan] cardigan. **-2.** [sans manches] waistcoat *Br*, vest *Am*; **~ pare-balles** bulletproof vest; **~ de sauvetage** life jacket.

gin [dʒin] *nm* gin.

gingembre [ʒɛ̃ʒɑ̃br] *nm* ginger.

gingivite [ʒɛ̃ʒivit] *nf* inflammation of the gums, gingivitis (*U*).

girafe [ʒiraf] *nf* giraffe.

giratoire [ʒiratwar] *adj* gyrating; **sens ~** roundabout *Br*, traffic circle *Am*.

girofle [ʒirɔfl] → **clou.**

giroflée [ʒirɔfle] *nf* stock.

girolle [ʒirɔl] *nf* chanterelle.

giron [ʒirɔ̃] *nm* lap; **le ~ familial** *fig* the bosom of one's family.

girouette [ʒirwɛt] *nf* weathercock.

gisait, gisions *etc* → **gésir.**

gisant [ʒizɑ̃] ◇ *participe présent* → **gésir.** ◇ *nm* recumbent figure (*on tomb*).

gisement [ʒizmɑ̃] *nm* deposit.

gît → **gésir.**

gitan, -e [ʒitɑ̃, an] *adj* Gipsy (*avant n*).
◆ **Gitan, -e** *nm, f* Gipsy.

Gitane® [ʒitan] *nf* [cigarette] Gitane®.

gîte [ʒit] *nm* **-1.** [logement]: **~ (rural)** gîte, *self-catering accommodation in the country.* **-2.** *littéraire* [abri] lodging; **le ~ et le couvert**

board and lodging. **-3.** [du lièvre] form. **-4.** [du bœuf] shin *Br*, shank *Am*.

gîter [ʒite] [3] *vi* **-1.** [lièvre] to lie. **-2.** [bateau] to list.

givrant, -e [ʒivrɑ̃, ɑ̃t] *adj* freezing.`

givre [ʒivr] *nm* frost.

givré, -e [ʒivre] *adj* **-1.** CULIN: **orange** *etc* **~e** orange *etc* sorbet (*served in the hollowed-out fruit*). **-2.** *fam* [personne] round the twist.

glabre [glabr] *adj* hairless.

glaçage [glasaʒ] *nm* **-1.** [de gâteau] icing *Br*, frosting *Am*. **-2.** [de tissu] glazing.

glaçant, -e [glasɑ̃, ɑ̃t] *adj* cold.

glace [glas] *nf* **-1.** [eau congelée] ice; **rester de ~** *fig* to be unmoved; **rompre la ~** *fig* to break the ice. **-2.** [crème glacée] ice cream. **-3.** [vitre] pane; [- de voiture] window. **-4.** [miroir] mirror; **~ sans tain** two-way mirror.
◆ **glaces** *nfpl* ice floes.

glacé, -e [glase] *adj* **-1.** [gelé] frozen. **-2.** [très froid] freezing. **-3.** *fig* [hostile] cold. **-4.** [fruit] glacé.

glacer [glase] [16] *vt* **-1.** [geler, paralyser] to chill. **-2.** [étoffe, papier] to glaze. **-3.** [gâteau] to ice *Br*, to frost *Am*.
◆ **se glacer** *vp* [sang] to run cold.

glaciaire [glasjɛr] *adj* glacial.

glacial, -e, -iaux [glasjal, jo] *litt* & *fig* icy.

glacier [glasje] *nm* **-1.** GÉOGR glacier. **-2.** [marchand] ice cream seller OU man.

glacière [glasjɛr] *nf* icebox.

glaçon [glasɔ̃] *nm* **-1.** [dans boisson] ice cube. **-2.** [sur toit] icicle. **-3.** *fam* *fig* [personne] iceberg.

glaïeul [glajœl] *nm* gladiolus.

glaire [glɛr] *nf* **-1.** MÉD phlegm. **-2.** [d'œuf] white.

glaise [glɛz] *nf* clay.

glaive [glɛv] *nm* sword.

gland [glɑ̃] *nm* **-1.** [de chêne] acorn. **-2.** [ornement] tassel. **-3.** ANAT glans.

glande [glɑ̃d] *nf* gland.

glander [glɑ̃de] [3] *vi* *tfam* to bugger about.

glaner [glane] [3] *vt* to glean.

glapir [glapir] [32] *vi* to yelp, to yap.

glapissement [glapismɑ̃] *nm* yelping, yapping.

glas [gla] *nm* knell; **sonner le ~** to toll the bell; **sonner le ~ de** *fig* to sound the death knell for.

glaucome [glokom] *nm* glaucoma.

glauque [glok] *adj* **-1.** [couleur] bluey-green. **-2.** *fam* [lugubre] gloomy. **-3.** *fam* [sordide] sordid.

glissade [glisad] *nf* slip; **faire des** ~**s** to slide.

glissant, -e [glisã, ãt] *adj* slippery.

glissement [glismã] *nm* **-1.** [action de glisser] gliding, sliding; ~ **de terrain** landslip, landslide. **-2.** *fig* [électoral] swing, shift.

glisser [glise] [3] ◇ *vi* **-1.** [se déplacer]: ~ **(sur)** to glide (over), to slide (over). **-2.** [déraper]: ~ **(sur)** to slip (on). **-3.** *fig* [passer rapidement]: ~ **sur** to skate over. **-4.** [surface] to be slippery. **-5.** [progresser] to slip; ~ **dans/vers** to slip into/towards, to slide into/towards. ◇ *vt* to slip; ~ **un regard à qqn** *fig* to give sb a sidelong glance.
◆ **se glisser** *vp* to slip; **se** ~ **dans** [lit] to slip OU slide into; *fig* to slip OU creep into.

glissière [glisjɛr] *nf* runner; **à** ~ sliding; ~ **de sécurité** crash barrier.

glissoire [gliswar] *nf* slide.

global, -e, -aux [glɔbal, o] *adj* global.

globalement [glɔbalmã] *adv* on the whole.

globalisation [glɔbalizasjɔ̃] *nf* [d'un marché] globalization.

globalité [glɔbalite] *nf* entirety.

globe [glɔb] *nm* **-1.** [sphère, terre] globe; **le** ~ **terrestre** the globe. **-2.** [de verre] glass cover.

globe-trotter [glɔbtrɔtɛr] (*pl* **globe-trotters**) *nmf* globe-trotter.

globule [glɔbyl] *nm* globule; ~ **blanc/rouge** white/red corpuscle.

globuleux [glɔbylø] → **œil.**

gloire [glwar] *nf* **-1.** [renommée] glory; [de vedette] fame, stardom. **-2.** [mérite] credit; **à la** ~ **de** in praise of.

glorieux, -ieuse [glɔrjø, jøz] *adj* [mort, combat] glorious; [héros, soldat] renowned.

glorifier [glɔrifje] [9] *vt* to glorify, to praise.
◆ **se glorifier** *vp*: **se** ~ **de** to glory in.

gloriole [glɔrjɔl] *nf* vainglory.

glose [gloz] *nf* gloss.

gloser [gloze] [3] ◇ *vi*: ~ **sur** to gossip about. ◇ *vt* to gloss.

glossaire [glɔsɛr] *nm* glossary.

glotte [glɔt] *nf* glottis.

glouglou [gluglu] *nm* **-1.** *fam* [de liquide] gurgling. **-2.** [de dindon] gobbling.

gloussement [glusmã] *nm* **-1.** [de poule] cluck, clucking (*U*). **-2.** *fam* [de personne] chortle, chuckle.

glousser [gluse] [3] *vi* **-1.** [poule] to cluck. **-2.** *fam* [personne] to chortle, to chuckle.

glouton, -onne [glutɔ̃, ɔn] ◇ *adj* greedy. ◇ *nm, f* glutton.

gloutonnerie [glutɔnri] *nf* gluttony, greed.

glu [gly] *nf* **-1.** [colle] glue. **-2.** *fam fig* [personne] limpet, leech.

gluant, -e [glyã, ãt] *adj* sticky.

glucide [glysid] *nm* glucide.

glucose [glykoz] *nm* glucose.

gluten [glytɛn] *nm* gluten.

glycémie [glisemi] *nf* glycaemia.

glycérine [gliserin] *nf* glycerine.

glycine [glisin] *nf* wisteria.

GMT (*abr de* **Greenwich Mean Time**) GMT.

gnangnan [ɲãɲã] *adj inv fam* spineless, wet.

GNL (*abr de* **gaz naturel liquéfié**) *nm* LNG.

gnôle [ɲol] *nf* brandy.

gnome [gnom] *nm* gnome.

gnon [ɲɔ̃] *nm fam* thump.

go [go]
◆ **tout de go** *loc adv* straight.

GO (*abr de* **grandes ondes**) *nfpl* LW.

goal [gol] *nm* goalkeeper.

gobelet [gɔblɛ] *nm* beaker, tumbler.

gober [gɔbe] [3] *vt* **-1.** [avaler] to gulp down. **-2.** *fam* [croire] to swallow. **-3.** *fam* [aimer]: **je ne peux pas la** ~ I can't stand her.

goberger [gɔbɛrʒe] [17]
◆ **se goberger** *vp fam* **-1.** [manger] to stuff o.s. **-2.** [se prélasser] to take it easy.

godasse [gɔdas] *nf fam* shoe.

godet [gɔdɛ] *nm* **-1.** [récipient] jar, pot. **-2.** COUTURE flare.

godiller [gɔdije] [3] *vi* **-1.** [rameur] to scull. **-2.** [skieur] to wedeln.

goéland [gɔelã] *nm* gull, seagull.

goélette [gɔelɛt] *nf* schooner.

goémon [gɔemɔ̃] *nm* wrack.

gogo [gogo]
◆ **à gogo** *loc adv fam* galore.

goguenard, -e [gɔgnar, ard] *adj* mocking.

goguette [gɔgɛt]
◆ **en goguette** *loc adv fam* a bit tight OU tipsy.

goinfre [gwɛ̃fr] *nmf fam* pig.

goinfrer [gwɛ̃fre] [3]
◆ **se goinfrer** *vp*: **se** ~ **de** *fam* to stuff OU pig o.s. with.

goitre [gwatr] *nm* goitre.

golden [gɔldɛn] *nf inv* Golden Delicious.

golf [gɔlf] *nm* [sport] golf; [terrain] golf course.

golfe [gɔlf] *nm* gulf, bay; **le** ~ **de Gascogne** the Bay of Biscay; **le** ~ **Persique** the (Persian) Gulf.

gommage [gɔmaʒ] *nm* **-1.** [d'écriture] erasing, rubbing out. **-2.** [cosmétique] face scrub.

gomme [gɔm] *nf* **-1.** [substance, bonbon] gum. **-2.** [pour effacer] rubber *Br*, eraser *Am*. **-3.** *loc*: à la ~ *fam* hopeless, useless.

gommé, -e [gɔme] *adj* gummed.

gommer [gɔme] [3] *vt* to rub out, to erase; *fig* to erase.

gond [gɔ̃] *nm* hinge; **sortir de ses ~s** *fam fig* to fly off the handle.

gondole [gɔ̃dɔl] *nf* gondola.

gondoler [gɔ̃dɔle] [3] *vi* [bois] to warp; [carton] to curl.

◆ **se gondoler** *vp* **-1.** [bois] to warp. **-2.** *fam* [rire] to split one's sides laughing.

gonflable [gɔ̃flabl] *adj* inflatable.

gonfler [gɔ̃fle] [3] ◇ *vt* **-1.** [ballon, pneu] to blow up, to inflate; [rivière, poitrine, yeux] to swell; [joues] to blow out. **-2.** *fig* [grossir] to exaggerate. **-3.** *loc*: **être gonflé** *fam* [être courageux] to have guts; [exagérer] to have a cheek OU a nerve. ◇ *vi* to swell.

◆ **se gonfler** *vp* **-1.** [se distendre] to swell. **-2.** [être envahi]: **se ~ de** [orgueil] to swell with; [espoir] to be filled with.

gonflette [gɔ̃flɛt] *nf fam*: **faire de la ~** to pump iron.

gonfleur [gɔ̃flœr] *nm* pump.

gong [gɔ̃g] *nm* gong.

gonzesse [gɔ̃zɛs] *nf tfam* bird, chick.

goret [gɔrɛ] *nm* **-1.** [cochon] piglet. **-2.** *fam* [garçon] dirty little pig.

gorge [gɔrʒ] *nf* **-1.** [gosier, cou] throat; **avoir la ~ serrée** to have a lump in one's throat; **s'éclaircir la ~** to clear one's throat; **faire des ~s chaudes de qqch** to laugh sthg to scorn; **prendre qqn à la ~** to put sb in a difficult situation; **rire à ~ déployée** to laugh heartily. **-2.** *littéraire* [poitrine] breast, bosom. **-3.** *(gén pl)* [vallée] gorge.

gorgée [gɔrʒe] *nf* mouthful; **à petites ~s** in sips.

gorger [gɔrʒe] [17] *vt*: **~ qqn de qqch** [gaver] to stuff sb with sthg; [combler] to heap sthg on sb; **~ qqch de** to fill sthg with.

◆ **se gorger** *vp*: **se ~ de** to gorge o.s. on.

gorille [gɔrij] *nm* **-1.** [animal] gorilla. **-2.** *fam* [personne] bodyguard.

gosier [gozje] *nm* throat, gullet.

gosse [gɔs] *nmf fam* kid.

gothique [gɔtik] *adj* **-1.** ARCHIT Gothic. **-2.** TYPO: **écriture ~** Gothic script.

◆ **gothique** *nm*: **le ~** the Gothic style.

gouache [gwaʃ] *nf* gouache.

gouaille [gwaj] *nf* cheek.

goudron [gudrɔ̃] *nm* tar.

goudronner [gudrɔne] [3] *vt* to tar.

gouffre [gufr] *nm* abyss; **le ~ de l'oubli/du désespoir** the depths of oblivion/despair; **au bord du ~** *fig* on the edge of the abyss.

goujat [guʒa] *nm* boor.

goujaterie [guʒatri] *nf* boorishness.

goujon [guʒɔ̃] *nm* [poisson] gudgeon; **taquiner le ~** to do a bit of fishing.

goulet [gulɛ] *nm* narrows *(pl)*; **~ d'étranglement** bottleneck.

goulot [gulo] *nm* neck; **boire au ~** to drink straight from the bottle.

goulu, -e [guly] ◇ *adj* greedy, gluttonous. ◇ *nm, f* glutton.

goulûment [gulymɑ̃] *adv* greedily.

goupille [gupij] *nf* pin.

goupiller [gupije] [3] *vt fam* to fix.

◆ **se goupiller** *vp fam* to work out.

goupillon [gupijɔ̃] *nm* **-1.** RELIG (holy water) sprinkler. **-2.** [à bouteille] bottle brush.

gourd, -e [gur, gurd] *adj* numb.

gourde [gurd] ◇ *nf* **-1.** [récipient] flask, waterbottle. **-2.** *fam* [personne] clot *Br*. ◇ *adj fam* thick.

gourdin [gurdɛ̃] *nm* club.

gourer [gure] [3]

◆ **se gourer** *vp fam* to slip up.

gourmand, -e [gurmɑ̃, ɑ̃d] ◇ *adj* greedy; **~ de** fond of. ◇ *nm, f* glutton.

gourmandise [gurmɑ̃diz] *nf* **-1.** [caractère] greed, greediness. **-2.** [sucrerie] sweet thing.

gourme [gurm] *nf* **-1.** MÉD impetigo. **-2.** [maladie du cheval] strangles *(U)*. **-3.** *loc*: **jeter sa ~** *vieilli* to sow one's wild oats.

gourmet [gurmɛ] *nm*: **(fin) ~** gourmet.

gourmette [gurmɛt] *nf* chain bracelet.

gourou [guru] *nm* guru.

gousse [gus] *nf* pod; **~ d'ail** clove of garlic.

gousset [gusɛ] *nm* [de gilet] fob pocket.

goût [gu] *nm* taste; **au ~ du jour** fashionable; **avoir du ~** to have taste; **avoir le ~ de qqch** to have a taste OU liking for sthg; **de bon ~** [élégant] tasteful, in good taste; *hum* [bienséant] advisable; **de mauvais ~** tasteless, in bad taste; **il n'a ~ à rien** he doesn't feel like doing anything; **prendre ~ à qqch** to take a liking to sthg; **chacun ses ~s** each to his own.

goûter [gute] [3] ◇ *vt* **-1.** [déguster] to taste. **-2.** [savourer] to enjoy. **-3.** *littéraire* [estimer] to appreciate. ◇ *vi* to have (afternoon) tea *Br*; **~ à** to taste; **~ de** *litt & fig* to have a taste of. ◇ *nm afternoon snack for children, typi-*

cally consisting of bread, butter, chocolate and a drink.

goutte [gut] ◇ *nf* **-1.** [de pluie, d'eau] drop; **la ~ (d'eau) qui fait déborder le vase** *fig* the last straw; **une ~ dans l'océan** a drop in the ocean; **(se) ressembler comme deux ~s d'eau** to be as like as two peas in a pod. **-2.** *fam* [alcool]: **la ~ the hard stuff. -3.** MÉD [maladie] gout. ◇ *adv (de négation) littéraire*: **ne ... ~** not a thing, nothing; **je n'y vois ~** I can't see a thing.
◆ **gouttes** *nfpl* MÉD drops.

goutte-à-goutte [gutagut] *nm inv* (intravenous) drip *Br*, IV *Am*.

gouttelette [gutlɛt] *nf* droplet.

gouttière [gutjɛr] *nf* **-1.** [CONSTR - horizontale] gutter; [- verticale] drainpipe. **-2.** MÉD splint.

gouvernail [guvɛrnaj] *nm* rudder.

gouvernante [guvɛrnãt] *nf* **-1.** [d'enfants] governess. **-2.** [de maison] housekeeper.

gouverne [guvɛrn] *nf* AÉRON control surface; **~ de direction** rudder; **pour ma/ta ~** *fig* for my/your guidance.

gouvernement [guvɛrnəmã] *nm* government.

gouvernemental, -e, -aux [guvɛrnəmãtal, o] *adj* [politique, organisation] government *(avant n)*; [journal] pro-government.

gouverner [guvɛrne] [3] *vt* to govern.

gouverneur [guvɛrnœr] *nm* governor.

GPL *(abr de* **gaz de pétrole liquéfié)** *nm* LPG.

GQG *(abr de* **grand quartier général)** *nm* GHQ.

gr *abr de* **grade.**

GR *(abr de* **(sentier de) grande randonnée)** *nm long-distance hiking path.*

grabataire [grabatɛr] ◇ *nmf* invalid. ◇ *adj* bedridden.

grabuge [grabyʒ] *nm fam* trouble.

grâce [gras] *nf* **-1.** [charme] grace; **de bonne ~** with good grace, willingly; **de mauvaise ~** with bad grace, reluctantly. **-2.** [faveur] favour; **être dans les bonnes ~s de qqn** to be in sb's good books; **faire ~ de qqch à qqn** to spare sb sthg. **-3.** [miséricorde] mercy; **rendre ~ à** *littéraire* to give thanks to.
◆ **de grâce** *interj* for heaven's sake!
◆ **grâce à** *loc prép* thanks to.

gracier [grasje] [9] *vt* to pardon.

gracieusement [grasjøzmã] *adv* **-1.** [avec grâce] graciously. **-2.** [gratuitement] free (of charge).

gracieux, -ieuse [grasjø, jøz] *adj* **-1.** [charmant] graceful. **-2.** [gratuit] free.

gracile [grasil] *adj* slender.

gradation [gradasjɔ̃] *nf* gradation.

grade [grad] *nm* [échelon] rank; [universitaire] qualification; **monter en ~** to be promoted; **en prendre pour son ~** to get hauled over the coals.

gradé, -e [grade] ◇ *adj* non-commissioned. ◇ *nm, f* non-commissioned officer, NCO.

gradin [gradɛ̃] *nm* [de stade, de théâtre] tier; [de terrain] terrace; **en ~s** terraced.

graduation [gradɥasjɔ̃] *nf* graduation.

gradué, -e [gradɥe] *Belg* ◇ *adj* [étudiant] college *(avant n)*. ◇ *nm, f* college graduate.

graduel, -elle [gradɥɛl] *adj* gradual; [difficultés] increasing.

graduellement [gradɥɛlmã] *adv* gradually.

graduer [gradɥe] [7] *vt* **-1.** [récipient, règle] to graduate. **-2.** *fig* [effort, travail] to increase gradually.

graffiti [grafiti] *nm inv* graffiti *(U)*.

grailler [graje] [3] *vi fam* to nosh *Br*, to chow down *Am*.

graillon [grajɔ̃] *nm péj* burnt fat.

grain [grɛ̃] *nm* **-1.** [gén] grain; [de moutarde] seed; [de café] bean; **~ de raisin** grape. **-2.** [point]: **~ de beauté** beauty spot. **-3.** [averse] squall. **-4.** *fig* [petite quantité]: **un ~ de** a touch of; **un ~ de bon sens** an ounce of common sense. **-5.** *loc*: **avoir un ~** *fam* to be a bit touched; **mettre son ~ de sel** *péj* to put one's oar in; **veiller au ~** to be on one's guard.

graine [grɛn] *nf* **-1.** BOT seed; **mauvaise ~** *fig* bad lot. **-2.** *loc*: **être de la ~ de voleur** to be a thief in the making; **en prendre de la ~** *fam* to follow my/his *etc* example; **monter en ~** [salade] to bolt, to run to seed; *fig* to shoot up.

grainetier, -ière [grɛntje, jɛr] *nm, f* seed merchant.

graissage [grɛsaʒ] *nm* lubrication.

graisse [grɛs] *nf* **-1.** ANAT & CULIN fat. **-2.** [pour lubrifier] grease.

graisser [grɛse] [4] *vt* **-1.** [machine] to grease, to lubricate. **-2.** [vêtements] to get grease on.

graisseux, -euse [grɛsø, øz] *adj* **-1.** [papier] greasy. **-2.** [bourrelet] of fat.

grammaire [gramɛr] *nf* grammar.

grammatical, -e, -aux [gramatikal, o] *adj* grammatical.

grammaticalement [gramatikalmã] *adv* grammatically.

gramme [gram] *nm* gram, gramme; **il n'a pas un ~ de jugeote** he hasn't got an ounce of common sense.

grand, -e [grɑ̃, grɑ̃d] ◇ *adj* **-1.** [en hauteur] tall; [en dimensions] big, large; [en quantité, nombre] large, great; **une ~e partie de** a large OU great proportion of; **un ~ nombre de** a large OU great number of; **en ~** [dimension] full-size. **-2.** [âgé] grown-up; **les ~es personnes** grown-ups; **~ frère** big OU older brother; **~e sœur** big OU older sister; **il est assez ~ pour ...** he's old enough to .... **-3.** [puissant] big, leading. **-4.** [important, remarquable] great; **un ~ homme** a great man. **-5.** [intense]: **un grand blessé/brûlé** a person with serious wounds/burns; **un ~ buveur/fumeur** a heavy drinker/smoker. ◇ *nm, f* (*gén pl*) **-1.** [personnage] great man (*f* woman); **c'est l'un des ~s de l'électroménager** he's one of the big names in electrical appliances. **-2.** [enfant] older OU bigger boy (*f* girl).
◆ **grand** *adv*: **voir ~** to think big.

grand-angle [grɑ̃tɑ̃gl] (*pl* **grands-angles**), **grand-angulaire** [grɑ̃tɑ̃gylɛr] (*pl* **grands-angulaires**) ◇ *adj* wide-angle. ◇ *nm* wide-angle lens.

grand-chose [grɑ̃ʃoz]
◆ **pas grand-chose** ◇ *pron indéf* not much. ◇ *nmf inv fam* worthless person.

grand-duché [grɑ̃dyʃe] (*pl* **grands-duchés**) *nm* grand duchy.

Grande-Bretagne [grɑ̃dbrətaɲ] *nf*: **la ~** Great Britain.

grandement [grɑ̃dmɑ̃] *adv* **-1.** [beaucoup] greatly. **-2.** [largement] a lot; **avoir ~ de quoi vivre** to have plenty to live on.

grandeur [grɑ̃dœr] *nf* **-1.** [taille] size; **~ nature** life-size, life-sized. **-2.** [apogée & *fig*] greatness; **~ d'âme** *fig* magnanimity.

grand-guignolesque [grɑ̃giɲɔlɛsk] *adj* bloodthirsty and melodramatic.

grandiloquent, -e [grɑ̃dilɔkɑ̃, ɑ̃t] *adj* grandiloquent.

grandiose [grɑ̃djoz] *adj* imposing.

grandir [grɑ̃dir] [32] ◇ *vt*: **~ qqn** [suj: chaussures] to make sb look taller; *fig* to increase sb's standing. ◇ *vi* [personne, plante] to grow; [obscurité, bruit] to increase, to grow; **~ dans l'estime de qqn** to go up in sb's estimation.
◆ **se grandir** *vp* to make o.s. (appear) taller; *fig* to increase one's standing.

grandissant, -e [grɑ̃disɑ̃, ɑ̃t] *adj* growing.

grand-maman [grɑ̃mamɑ̃] (*pl* **grand-mamans** OU **grands-mamans**) *nf* granny, grandma.

grand-mère [grɑ̃mɛr] (*pl* **grand-mères** OU **grands-mères**) *nf* grandmother; *fam fig* old biddy; **~ maternelle/paternelle** maternal/paternal grandmother.

grand-messe [grɑ̃mɛs] (*pl* **grand-messes** OU **grands-messes**) *nf* high mass.

grand-oncle [grɑ̃tɔ̃kl] (*pl* **grands-oncles**) *nm* great-uncle.

grand-papa [grɑ̃papa] (*pl* **grands-papas**) *nm* grandpa, grandad.

grand-peine [grɑ̃pɛn]
◆ **à grand-peine** *loc adv* with great difficulty.

grand-père [grɑ̃pɛr] (*pl* **grands-pères**) *nm* grandfather; *fam fig* old geezer; **~ maternel/paternel** maternal/paternal grandfather.

grands-parents [grɑ̃parɑ̃] *nmpl* grandparents.

grand-tante [grɑ̃tɑ̃t] (*pl* **grand-tantes** OU **grands-tantes**) *nf* great-aunt.

grand-voile [grɑ̃vwal] (*pl* **grands-voiles**) *nf* mainsail.

grange [grɑ̃ʒ] *nf* barn.

granit(e) [granit] *nm* granite.

granité, -e [granite] *adj* [tissu] pebble-weave.
◆ **granité** *nm* **-1.** [tissu] pebble weave. **-2.** [glace] granita.

granule [granyl] *nm* **-1.** [grain] granule. **-2.** MÉD pill.

granulé, -e [granyle] *adj* [surface] granular.
◆ **granulé** *nm* tablet.

granuleux, -euse [granylø, øz] *adj* granular.

grape-fruit [grɛpfrut] (*pl* **grape-fruits**) *nm* grapefruit.

graphe [graf] *nm* graph.

graphie [grafi] *nf* spelling.

graphique [grafik] ◇ *nm* diagram; [graphe] graph. ◇ *adj* graphic.

graphisme [grafism] *nm* **-1.** [écriture] handwriting. **-2.** ART style of drawing.

graphiste [grafist] *nmf* graphic artist.

graphologie [grafɔlɔʒi] *nf* graphology.

graphologue [grafɔlɔg] *nmf* graphologist, handwriting expert.

grappe [grap] *nf* **-1.** [de fruits] bunch; [de fleurs] stem; **~ de raisin** bunch of grapes. **-2.** *fig* [de gens] knot.

grappiller [grapije] [3] ◇ *vt litt & fig* to gather, to pick up. ◇ *vi* [financièrement] to make money.

grappin [grapɛ̃] *nm* [ancre] grapnel; **mettre**

le ~ sur qqn *fig* & *péj* to get one's claws into sb.

gras, grasse [gra, gras] *adj* **-1.** [personne, animal] fat. **-2.** [plat, aliment] fatty; **matières grasses** fats. **-3.** [cheveux, mains] greasy. **-4.** [sol] clayey; [crayon] soft. **-5.** *fig* [plaisanterie] crude. **-6.** *fig* [rire] throaty; [toux] phlegmy. **-7.** *fig* [plante] succulent.
◆ **gras** ◇ *nm* **-1.** [du jambon] fat. **-2.** [de jambe] soft OU fleshy part. **-3.** TYPO bold (type). ◇ *adv*: **manger ~** to eat fatty foods; **tousser ~** to have a loose cough.

gras-double [gradubl] (*pl* **gras-doubles**) *nm* tripe.

grassement [grasmɑ̃] *adv* **-1.** [rire] coarsely. **-2.** [payer] a lot.

grassouillet, -ette [grasujɛ, ɛt] *adj fam* plump.

gratifiant, -e [gratifjɑ̃, ɑ̃t] *adj* gratifying.

gratification [gratifikasjɔ̃] *nf* **-1.** [en argent] bonus. **-2.** [psychologique] gratification.

gratifier [gratifje] [9] *vt* **-1.** [accorder]: ~ qqn de qqch to present sb with sthg, to present sthg to sb; *fig* to reward sb with sthg. **-2.** [stimuler] to gratify.

gratin [gratɛ̃] *nm* **-1.** CULIN dish sprinkled with breadcrumbs or cheese and browned; ~ **dauphinois** sliced potatoes baked in cream. **-2.** *fam fig* [haute société] upper crust.

gratiné, -e [gratine] *adj* **-1.** CULIN sprinkled with breadcrumbs or cheese and browned. **-2.** *fam fig* [ardu] stiff. **-3.** *fam fig* [déroutant] weird.
◆ **gratinée** *nf* onion soup sprinkled with cheese and browned.

gratiner [gratine] [3] *vt* to sprinkle with breadcrumbs or cheese and then brown.

gratis [gratis] *adv* free.

gratitude [gratityd] *nf*: ~ **(envers)** gratitude (to OU towards).

gratte-ciel [gratsjɛl] *nm inv* skyscraper.

grattement [gratmɑ̃] *nm* scratching.

gratte-papier [gratpapje] *nm inv fam* pen-pusher.

gratter [grate] [3] ◇ *vt* **-1.** [gén] to scratch; [pour enlever] to scrape off. **-2.** *fam* [gagner] to make. **-3.** *fam* [devancer] to overtake. ◇ *vi* **-1.** [démanger] to itch, to be itchy. **-2.** *fam* [écrire] to scribble. **-3.** [frapper]: ~ **à la porte** to tap at the door. **-4.** *fam* [travailler] to slave, to slog. **-5.** *fam* [jouer]: ~ **de** [violon] to scrape away at; [guitare] to strum on.
◆ **se gratter** *vp* to scratch.

grattoir [gratwar] *nm* **-1.** [outil] scraper. **-2.** [de boîte d'allumettes] striking surface.

gratuit, -e [gratɥi, it] *adj* **-1.** [entrée] free. **-2.** [hypothèse] unwarranted. **-3.** [violence] gratuitous.

gratuité [gratɥite] *nf* **-1.** [d'entrée] free nature. **-2.** [d'hypothèse] unwarranted nature.

gratuitement [gratɥitmɑ̃] *adv* **-1.** [sans payer] free, for nothing. **-2.** [sans raison] gratuitously.

gravats [grava] *nmpl* rubble (*U*).

grave [grav] ◇ *adj* **-1.** [attitude, faute, maladie] serious, grave; **ce n'est pas ~** [ce n'est rien] don't worry about it. **-2.** [voix] deep. **-3.** LING: **accent ~** grave accent. ◇ *nm* (*gén pl*) MUS low register.

graveleux, -euse [gravlø, øz] *adj* **-1.** [sol] gravelly. **-2.** [fruit] gritty. **-3.** [propos] crude.

gravement [gravmɑ̃] *adv* gravely, seriously.

graver [grave] [3] *vt* **-1.** [gén] to engrave. **-2.** [bois] to carve. **-3.** [disque] to cut.

graveur, -euse [gravœr, øz] *nm, f* engraver.

gravier [gravje] *nm* gravel (*U*).

gravillon [gravijɔ̃] *nm* fine gravel (*U*).

gravir [gravir] [32] *vt* to climb.

gravité [gravite] *nf* **-1.** [importance] seriousness, gravity; **sans ~** not serious. **-2.** PHYS gravity.

graviter [gravite] [3] *vi* **-1.** [astre] to revolve. **-2.** *fig* [évoluer] to gravitate.

gravure [gravyr] *nf* **-1.** [technique]: ~ **(sur)** engraving (on); ~ **sur bois** woodcutting. **-2.** [reproduction] print; [dans livre] plate.

gré [gre] *nm* **-1.** [goût]: **à mon/son ~** for my/his taste, for my/his liking. **-2.** [volonté]: **bon ~ mal ~** willy nilly; **contre mon/son ~** against my/his will; **de ~ ou de force** *fig* whether you/they *etc* like it or not; **de mon/son plein ~** of my/his own free will; **au ~ de qqn/qqch** at the will of sb/sthg, at the pleasure of sb/sthg. **-3.** [gratitude]: **je vous saurais ~ de bien vouloir ...** *littéraire* I should be grateful if you would ....

grec, grecque [grɛk] *adj* Greek.
◆ **grec** *nm* [langue] Greek; ~ **ancien/moderne** ancient/modern Greek.
◆ **grecque** *nf* CULIN: **à la grecque** stewed in oil (with tomatoes) and served cold.
◆ **Grec, Grecque** *nm, f* Greek.

Grèce [grɛs] *nf*: **la ~** Greece.

gredin, -e [grədɛ̃, in] *nm, f* rogue.

gréement [gremɑ̃] *nm* rigging.

green [grin] *nm* GOLF green.

Greenwich *n* [grinwitʃ] Greenwich; **le méridien de ~** the Greenwich Meridian.

gréer [gree] [15] *vt* to rig.

greffe [grɛf] ◇ nf -1. MÉD transplant; [de peau] graft; ~ **du cœur** heart transplant. -2. BOT graft. ◇ nm JUR: ~ **(du tribunal)** office of the clerk of court.

greffer [grɛfe] [4] vt -1. MÉD to transplant; [peau] to graft; ~ **un rein/un cœur à qqn** to give sb a kidney/heart transplant. -2. BOT to graft.
◆ **se greffer** vp: **se** ~ **sur qqch** to be added to sthg.

greffier [grɛfje] nm clerk of the court.

grégaire [gregɛr] adj gregarious.

grège [grɛʒ] → **soie.**

grégorien, -ienne [gregɔrjɛ̃, jɛn] adj Gregorian.

grêle [grɛl] ◇ nf hail. ◇ adj -1. [jambes] spindly. -2. [son] shrill.

grêlé, -e [grele] adj pockmarked.

grêler [grele] [4] ◇ v impers to hail; **il grêle** it's hailing. ◇ vt to devastate by hail.

grêlon [grɛlɔ̃] nm hailstone.

grelot [grəlo] nm bell.

grelotter [grəlɔte] [3] vi: ~ **(de)** to shiver (with).

grenade [grənad] nf -1. [fruit] pomegranate. -2. MIL grenade; ~ **lacrymogène** tear-gas grenade.

Grenade [grənad] ◇ nf [île]: **la** ~ Grenada; **à la** ~ in Grenada. ◇ n [ville d'Espagne] Granada.

grenadier [grənadje] nm -1. [arbre] pomegranate tree. -2. MIL grenadier.

grenadine [grənadin] nf grenadine (pomegranate syrup).

grenat [grəna] ◇ nm garnet. ◇ adj inv dark red.

grenier [grənje] nm -1. [de maison] attic. -2. [à foin] loft. -3. fig [région] breadbasket.

grenouille [grənuj] nf frog; ~ **de bénitier** fig fanatical churchgoer.

grenouillère [grənujɛr] nf [de bébé] all-in-one.

grenu, -e [grəny] adj -1. [cuir] grained. -2. [roche] granular.

grès [grɛ] nm -1. [roche] sandstone. -2. [poterie] stoneware.

grésil [grezil] nm hail.

grésillement [grezijmɑ̃] nm [de friture] sizzling; [de feu] crackling.

grésiller [grezije] [3] vi -1. [friture] to sizzle; [feu] to crackle. -2. [radio] to crackle.

grève [grɛv] nf -1. [arrêt du travail] strike; **être en** ~ to be on strike; **faire** ~ to strike, to go on strike; ~ **de la faim** hunger strike; ~ **générale** general strike; ~ **sauvage** wild-

cat strike; ~ **sur le tas** sit-down strike; ~ **tournante** rotating strike; ~ **du zèle** work-to-rule. -2. [rivage] shore.

grever [grəve] [19] vt to burden; [budget] to put a strain on.

gréviste [grevist] ◇ nmf striker. ◇ adj striking.

GRH (abr de **gestion des ressources humaines**) nf personnel management.

gribouillage [gribujaʒ] nm -1. [écriture] scrawl. -2. [dessin] doodle.

gribouiller [gribuje] [3] vt & vi -1. [écrire] to scrawl. -2. [dessiner] to doodle.

gribouillis [gribuji] = **gribouillage.**

grief [grijɛf] nm grievance; **faire** ~ **de qqch à qqn** to hold sthg against sb.

grièvement [grijɛvmɑ̃] adv seriously.

griffe [grif] nf -1. [d'animal] claw; **montrer les** ~s litt & fig to bare OU show one's claws; **tomber dans les** ~s **de qqn** fig to fall into sb's clutches. -2. [de créateur] hallmark; [de couturier] label. -3. Belg [éraflure] scratch.

griffer [grife] [3] vt -1. [suj: chat etc] to claw. -2. [suj: créateur] to put one's name to.

griffonner [grifɔne] [3] ◇ vt -1. [écrire] to scrawl. -2. [dessiner] to make a rough sketch of. ◇ vi -1. [écrire] to scrawl. -2. [dessiner] to make a rough sketch.

griffure [grifyr] nf scratch.

grignoter [griɲɔte] [3] ◇ vt -1. [manger] to nibble. -2. fam fig [réduire - capital] to eat away (at). -3. fam fig [gagner - avantage] to gain. ◇ vi -1. [manger] to nibble. -2. fam fig [prendre]: ~ **sur** to nibble away at.

grigou [grigu] nm fam skinflint.

gri-gri (pl **gris-gris**), **grigri** (pl **grigris**) [grigri] nm talisman, charm.

gril [gril] nm grill; **sur le** ~ on the grill; **être sur le** ~ fig to be like a cat on hot bricks.

grillade [grijad] nf CULIN grilled meat.

grillage [grijaʒ] nm -1. [de porte, de fenêtre] wire netting. -2. [clôture] wire fence.

grillager [grijaʒe] [17] vt to put wire netting on.

grille [grij] nf -1. [portail] gate. -2. [d'orifice, de guichet] grille; [de fenêtre] bars (pl). -3. [de mots croisés, de loto] grid. -4. [tableau] table; ~ **des programmes** programme listings (pl); ~ **des salaires** salary scale.

grille-pain [grijpɛ̃] nm inv toaster.

griller [grije] [3] ◇ vt -1. [viande] to grill Br, to broil Am; [pain] to toast; [café, marrons] to roast; ~ **une cigarette** fam to have a fag. -2. fig [au soleil - personne] to burn; [- végétation] to shrivel. -3. [ampoule] to blow. -4.

[moteur] to burn out. **-5.** *fam fig* [dépasser concurrents] to outstrip; ~ **un feu rouge** to jump the lights; ~ **une étape** to rush ahead. **-6.** *fig* [compromettre] to ruin; **être grillé** to be done for.
◇ *vi* **-1.** [viande] to grill *Br*, to broil *Am*. **-2.** [personne]: ~ **de** [envie, impatience] to be burning with; ~ **de faire qqch** to be longing to do sthg.
◆ **se griller** *vp fam* to be done for; **se ~ auprès de qqn** to blow it with sb.

grillon [grijɔ̃] *nm* [insecte] cricket.

grimace [grimas] *nf* grimace; **faire des ~s** to pull faces; **faire la ~** to pull a face.

grimacer [grimase] [16] *vi* to grimace.

grimer [grime] [3] *vt* CIN & THÉÂTRE to make up.
◆ **se grimer** *vp* CIN & THÉÂTRE to make (o.s.) up.

grimoire [grimwar] *nm* [de sorcier] book of spells.

grimpant, -e [grɛ̃pɑ̃, ɑ̃t] *adj* climbing (*avant n*).

grimper [grɛ̃pe] [3] ◇ *vt* to climb. ◇ *vi* to climb; ~ **à un arbre/une échelle** to climb a tree/a ladder.

grimpeur, -euse [grɛ̃pœr, øz] ◇ *adj* climbing (*avant n*). ◇ *nm, f* climber.

grinçant, -e [grɛ̃sɑ̃, ɑ̃t] *adj* **-1.** [charnière] squeaking; [porte, plancher] creaking. **-2.** *fig* [ironie] jarring.

grincement [grɛ̃smɑ̃] *nm* [de charnière] squeaking; [de porte, plancher] creaking; **~s de dents** *fig* gnashing of teeth.

grincer [grɛ̃se] [16] *vi* [charnière] to squeak; [porte, plancher] to creak.

grincheux, -euse [grɛ̃ʃø, øz] ◇ *adj* grumpy. ◇ *nm, f* moaner, grumbler.

gringalet [grɛ̃galɛ] *nm* weakling.

griotte [grijɔt] *nf* morello (cherry).

grippe [grip] *nf* MÉD flu (*U*); **avoir la ~** to have flu; ~ **intestinale** gastric flu; **prendre qqn/qqch en ~** *fig* to take a sudden dislike to sb/sthg.

grippé, -e [gripe] *adj* [malade]: **être ~** to have flu.

gripper [gripe] [3] *vi* **-1.** [mécanisme] to jam. **-2.** *fig* [processus] to stall.
◆ **se gripper** *vp* **-1.** [mécanisme] to jam. **-2.** *fig* [système] to seize up.

grippe-sou [gripsu] (*pl inv* OU **grippe-sous**) *nm fam* skinflint.

gris, -e [gri, griz] *adj* **-1.** [couleur] grey. **-2.** *fig* [morne] dismal. **-3.** [saoul] tipsy.
◆ **gris** *nm* **-1.** [couleur] grey. **-2.** [tabac] shag.

grisaille [grizaj] *nf* **-1.** [de ciel] greyness. **-2.** *fig* [de vie] dullness.

grisant, -e [grizɑ̃, ɑ̃t] *adj* intoxicating.

grisâtre [grizatr] *adj* greyish.

grisé [grize] *nm* (grey) shading.

griser [grize] [3] *vt* to intoxicate.
◆ **se griser** *vp*: **se ~ de** [vin] to get tipsy on; [air, succès] to get drunk on.

grisonnant, -e [grizɔnɑ̃, ɑ̃t] *adj* greying.

grisonner [grizɔne] [3] *vi* to turn grey.

grisou [grizu] *nm* firedamp.

grive [griv] *nf* thrush.

grivois, -e [grivwa, az] *adj* ribald.

Groenland [grɔɛnlɑ̃d] *nm*: **le ~** Greenland; **au ~** in Greenland.

grog [grɔg] *nm* (hot) toddy.

groggy [grɔgi] *adj inv* **-1.** [boxeur] groggy. **-2.** *fig* [assommé] stunned.

grogne [grɔɲ] *nf* discontent, grumbling.

grognement [grɔɲmɑ̃] *nm* **-1.** [son] grunt; [d'ours, de chien] growl. **-2.** [protestation] grumble.

grogner [grɔɲe] [3] *vi* **-1.** [émettre un son] to grunt; [ours, chien] to growl. **-2.** [protester] to grumble.

grognon, -onne [grɔɲɔ̃, ɔn] *adj* grumpy.

groin [grwɛ̃] *nm* snout.

grommeler [grɔmle] [24] *vt & vi* to mutter.

grondement [grɔ̃dmɑ̃] *nm* [d'animal] growl; [de tonnerre, de train] rumble; [de torrent] roar.

gronder [grɔ̃de] [3] ◇ *vi* **-1.** [animal] to growl; [tonnerre] to rumble. **-2.** *littéraire* [grommeler] to mutter. ◇ *vt* to scold.

groom [grum] *nm* page.

gros, grosse [gro, gros] ◇ *adj* (*gén avant n*) **-1.** [gén] large, big; *péj* big. **-2.** (*avant ou après n*) [corpulent] fat. **-3.** [grossier] coarse. **-4.** [fort, sonore] loud. **-5.** [important, grave] serious; [dépense] major. **-6.** [plein]: ~ **de** full of. ◇ *nm, f* **-1.** [personne corpulente] fat person. **-2.** [personnage important] big shot.
◆ **gros** ◇ *adv* [beaucoup] a lot; **en avoir ~ sur le cœur** to be upset. ◇ *nm* **-1.** [partie]: **le (plus) ~ (de qqch)** the main part (of sthg); **le (plus) ~ du travail** the bulk of the work. **-2.** COMM: **le ~** wholesale.
◆ **de gros** *loc adj* COMM wholesale.
◆ **en gros** *loc adv & loc adj* **-1.** COMM wholesale. **-2.** [en grands caractères] in large letters. **-3.** [grosso modo] roughly.

groseille [grozɛj] ◇ *nf* currant; ~ **blanche** white currant; ~ **à maquereau** gooseberry; ~ **rouge** redcurrant. ◇ *adj inv* red.

groseillier [grozeje] *nm* currant bush.

gros-porteur [gʀopɔʀtœʀ] (*pl* **gros-porteurs**) *nm* jumbo (jet).

grosse [gʀos] ◇ *nf* **-1.** [douze douzaines] gross. **-2.** JUR engrossment. ◇ *adj* → **gros**.

grossesse [gʀosɛs] *nf* pregnancy; ~ **extra-utérine** ectopic pregnancy; ~ **nerveuse** phantom pregnancy.

grosseur [gʀosœʀ] *nf* **-1.** [dimension, taille] size. **-2.** [corpulence] fatness. **-3.** MÉD lump.

grossier, -ière [gʀosje, jɛʀ] *adj* **-1.** [matière] coarse. **-2.** [sommaire] rough. **-3.** [insolent] rude. **-4.** [vulgaire] crude. **-5.** [erreur] crass.

grossièrement [gʀosjɛʀmɑ̃] *adv* **-1.** [sommairement] roughly. **-2.** [vulgairement] crudely.

grossièreté [gʀosjɛʀte] *nf* **-1.** [vulgarité] crudeness. **-2.** [parole grossière] crude remark. **-3.** [superficialité] superficiality.

grossir [gʀosiʀ] [32] ◇ *vi* **-1.** [prendre du poids] to put on weight. **-2.** [augmenter] to grow. **-3.** [s'intensifier] to increase. **-4.** [cours d'eau] to swell. ◇ *vt* **-1.** [suj: microscope, verre] to magnify. **-2.** [suj: vêtement]: ~ **qqn** to make sb look fatter. **-3.** [exagérer] to exaggerate.

grossissant, -e [gʀosisɑ̃, ɑ̃t] *adj* [verre] magnifying.

grossissement [gʀosismɑ̃] *nm* **-1.** [de personne] increase in weight. **-2.** [de loupe, de microscope] magnification. **-3.** [exagération] exaggeration.

grossiste [gʀosist] *nmf* wholesaler.

grosso modo [gʀosomɔdo] *adv* roughly.

grotesque [gʀɔtɛsk] ◇ *adj* grotesque, ludicrous. ◇ *nm*: **le** ~ the grotesque.

grotte [gʀɔt] *nf* cave.

grouillant, -e [gʀujɑ̃, ɑ̃t] *adj* **-1.** [foule] milling. **-2.** [lieu]: ~ **(de)** swarming (with).

grouiller [gʀuje] [3] *vi*: ~ **(de)** to swarm (with).

◆ **se grouiller** *vp fam* to get a move on; se ~ **de faire qqch** to rush to do sthg.

groupage [gʀupaʒ] *nm* bulking.

groupe [gʀup] *nm* group; **en** ~ as a group; ~ **de pression** pressure group.

◆ **groupe électrogène** *nm* generator.

◆ **groupe sanguin** *nm* blood group.

groupement [gʀupmɑ̃] *nm* **-1.** [action] grouping. **-2.** [groupe] group.

grouper [gʀupe] [3] *vt* to group.

◆ **se grouper** *vp* to come together.

groupie [gʀupi] *nmf* groupie.

groupuscule [gʀupyskyl] *nm* faction.

gruau [gʀyo] *nm* [farine] wheat flour.

grue [gʀy] *nf* TECHNOL & ZOOL crane; **faire le pied de** ~ *fig* to stand about.

gruger [gʀyʒe] [17] *vt littéraire* to dupe.

grumeau, -x [gʀymo] *nm* lump.

grumeleux -euse [gʀymlø, øz], *adj* **-1.** [pâte] lumpy. **-2.** [fruit] gritty. **-3.** [peau] bumpy.

gruyère [gʀyjɛʀ] *nm* Gruyère (cheese).

Guadeloupe [gwadlup] *nf*: **la** ~ Guadeloupe; **à la** ~ in Guadeloupe.

guadeloupéen, -enne [gwadlupeɛ̃, ɛn] *adj* of/from Guadeloupe.

◆ **Guadeloupéen, -enne** *nm, f* native OU inhabitant of Guadeloupe.

Guatemala [gwatemala] *nm*: **le** ~ Guatemala; **au** ~ in Guatemala.

guatémaltèque [gwatemaltɛk] *adj* Guatemalan.

◆ **Guatémaltèque** *nmf* Guatemalan.

gué [ge] *nm* ford; **traverser à** ~ to ford.

guenilles [gənij] *nfpl* rags.

guenon [gənɔ̃] *nf* female monkey.

guépard [gepaʀ] *nm* cheetah.

guêpe [gɛp] *nf* wasp.

guêpier [gepje] *nm* wasp's nest; *fig* hornet's nest; **aller se fourrer dans un** ~ to stir up a hornet's nest.

guère [gɛʀ] *adv* [peu] hardly; **ne** (+ *verbe*) ~ [peu] hardly; **il ne l'aime** ~ he doesn't like him/her very much; **l'appel n'a** ~ **eu de succès** the appeal met with very little success; **ne** (+ *verbe*) **plus** ~: **il ne m'écrit plus** ~ he hardly (ever) writes (to me) now OU any more; **il n'y a** ~ **plus de six ans** it's barely more than six years ago; **il n'y a** ~ **de** there are hardly any.

guéridon [geʀidɔ̃] *nm* pedestal table.

guérilla [geʀija] *nf* guerrilla warfare.

guérir [geʀiʀ] [32] ◇ *vt* to cure; ~ **qqn de** *litt* & *fig* to cure sb of. ◇ *vi* to recover, to get better.

guérison [geʀizɔ̃] *nf* **-1.** [de malade] recovery. **-2.** [de maladie] cure.

guérissable [geʀisabl] *adj* curable.

guérisseur, -euse [geʀisœʀ, øz] *nm, f* healer.

guérite [geʀit] *nf* MIL sentry box.

Guernesey [gɛʀnəzɛ] *n* Guernsey; **à** ~ on Guernsey.

guerre [gɛʀ] *nf* **-1.** MIL & *fig* war; **en** ~ at war; **déclarer la** ~ to declare war; **faire la** ~ **à un pays** to make OU wage war on a country; **faire la** ~ **à qqch** to wage war on sthg; **Première/Seconde Guerre mondiale** First/Second World War; ~ **civile** civil war; ~ **économique** trade war; ~ **froide** cold war; ~ **des nerfs** war of nerves; ~ **sainte** holy war. **-2.** [technique] warfare (*U*). **-3.** *loc*: **à la** ~ **comme à la** ~ you'll/we'll *etc* just have to make the best of things; **c'est de bonne ~** that's fair enough OU perfectly fair; **de ~ lasse** for the sake of peace.

guerrier, -ière [gɛʁje, jɛʁ] *adj* **-1.** [de guerre] war (*avant n*). **-2.** [peuple] warlike.
♦ **guerrier** *nm* warrior.

guerroyer [gɛʁwaje] [13] *vi littéraire* to wage war.

guet [gɛ] *nm*: **faire le ~** to be on the lookout.

guet-apens [gɛtapɑ̃] (*pl* **guets-apens**) *nm* ambush; *fig* trap; **tomber dans un ~** to fall into an ambush OU a trap.

guêtre [gɛtʁ] *nf* gaiter; **traîner ses ~s** *fam* to lounge about.

guetter [gete] [4] *vt* **-1.** [épier] to lie in wait for. **-2.** [attendre] to be on the look-out for, to watch for. **-3.** [menacer] to threaten.

gueulante [gœlɑ̃t] *nf fam* uproar; **pousser une ~** to yell (one's head off).

gueulard, -e [gœlar, ard] *fam* ◇ *adj* who shouts a lot. ◇ *nm, f* person who shouts a lot.
♦ **gueulard** *nm* TECHNOL throat.

gueule [gœl] *nf* **-1.** [d'animal, ouverture] mouth. **-2.** *tfam* [bouche de l'homme] gob *Br*; **ta ~!** shut your gob!, shut it!; **c'est une grande ~** he/she is all mouth. **-3.** *fam* [visage] face. **-4.** *loc*: **avoir la ~ de bois** to have a hangover; **casser la ~ à qqn** to smash sb's face in; **se casser la ~** *fam* [tomber] to fall flat on one's face; **faire la ~** *fam* to pull a long face; **se jeter dans la ~ du loup** to enter the lion's den.

gueule-de-loup [gœldəlu] (*pl* **gueules-de-loup**) *nf* snapdragon.

gueuler [gœle] [5] *fam* ◇ *vt* to yell. ◇ *vi* **-1.** [crier] to yell. **-2.** [protester] to kick up a stink, to scream and shout.

gueuleton [gœltɔ̃] *nm fam* blow-out *Br*.

gueux, gueuse [gø, gøz] *nm, f littéraire* beggar.

gui [gi] *nm* mistletoe.

guichet [giʃɛ] *nm* counter; [de gare, de théâtre] ticket office; **jouer à ~s fermés** *fig* to be sold out.

guide [gid] ◇ *nm* **-1.** [gén] guide; **~ de montagne** mountain guide. **-2.** [livre] guidebook. ◇ *nf* Girl Guide *Br*, Girl Scout *Am*.
♦ **guides** *nfpl* reins.

guider [gide] [3] *vt* to guide.

guidon [gidɔ̃] *nm* handlebars (*pl*).

guigne [giɲ] *nf fam* bad OU rotten luck.

guigner [giɲe] [3] *vt fam* **-1.** [regarder] to eye. **-2.** [convoiter] to have one's eye on.

guignol [giɲɔl] *nm* **-1.** [marionnette] glove puppet. **-2.** [théâtre] ≃ Punch and Judy show; **faire le ~** *fig* to act OU play the fool.

guillemet [gijmɛ] *nm* inverted comma, quotation mark; **entre ~s** in inverted commas OU quotation marks; **ouvrir/fermer les ~s** to open/close quotation marks.

guilleret, -ette [gijʁɛ, ɛt] *adj* perky.

guillotine [gijɔtin] *nf* **-1.** [instrument] guillotine. **-2.** [de fenêtre] sash.

guillotiner [gijɔtine] [3] *vt* to guillotine.

guimauve [gimov] *nf* **-1.** [confiserie, plante] marshmallow. **-2.** *fam* [sentimentalité] mush.

guimbarde [gɛ̃baʁd] *nf* **-1.** MUS Jew's harp. **-2.** *fam* [voiture] jalopy.

guindé, -e [gɛ̃de] *adj* stiff.

Guinée [gine] *nf*: **la ~** Guinea; **la ~-Bissau** Guinea-Bissau; **la ~-Équatoriale** Equatorial Guinea.

guinéen, -enne [gineɛ̃, ɛn] *adj* Guinean.
♦ **Guinéen, -enne** *nm, f* Guinean.

guingois [gɛ̃gwa]
♦ **de guingois** *adv sout* lopsidedly.

guinguette [gɛ̃gɛt] *nf* open-air dance floor.

guirlande [giʁlɑ̃d] *nf* **-1.** [de fleurs] garland. **-2.** [de papier] chain; [de Noël] tinsel (*U*).

guise [giz] *nf*: **à ma ~** as I please OU like; **en ~ de** by way of.

guitare [gitaʁ] *nf* guitar; **~ électrique** electric guitar.

guitariste [gitaʁist] *nmf* guitarist.

Gulf Stream [gœlfstʁim] *nm*: **le ~** the Gulf Stream.

gustatif, -ive [gystatif, iv] *adj*: **sensibilité gustative** sense of taste.

guttural, -e, -aux [gytyʁal, o] *adj* guttural.

Guyana [gɥijana] *nf*: **la ~** Guyana.

gym [ʒim] *nf* gym (*U*).

gymkhana [ʒimkana] *nm* rally.

gymnase [ʒimnaz] *nm* gymnasium.

gymnaste [ʒimnast] *nmf* gymnast.

gymnastique [ʒimnastik] *nf* SPORT & *fig* gymnastics (*U*); **faire de la ~** to do gymnastics; **~ corrective** remedial gymnastics.

gynéco [ʒineko] *nmf fam* gynaecologist.

gynécologie [ʒinekɔlɔʒi] *nf* gynaecology.

gynécologique [ʒinekɔlɔʒik] *adj* gynaecological.

gynécologue [ʒinekɔlɔg] *nmf* gynaecologist.

gypse [ʒips] *nm* gypsum.

gyrophare [ʒiʁɔfaʁ] *nm* flashing light.

h¹, H [aʃ] *nm inv* h, H; ~ **aspiré/muet** aspirate/silent h.

h² **-1.** (*abr de* **heure**) hr. **-2.** (*abr de* **hecto**) h.

◆ **H** **-1.** *abr de* **homme**. **-2.** (*abr de* **hydrogène**) H.

ha (*abr de* **hectare**) ha.

hab. *abr de* **habitant**.

habile [abil] *adj* skilful; [démarche] clever.

habilement [abilmã] *adv* skilfully; [manœuvrer] cleverly.

habileté [abilte] *nf* skill.

habiliter [abilite] [3] *vt* to authorize; **être habilité à faire qqch** to be authorized to do sthg.

habillage [abijaʒ] *nm* **-1.** [action] dressing. **-2.** [enveloppe, protection] covering.

habillé, -e [abije] *adj* [tenue] dressy; [réception] smart.

habillement [abijmã] *nm* **-1.** [action] clothing. **-2.** [tenue] outfit. **-3.** [profession] clothing trade.

habiller [abije] [3] *vt* **-1.** [vêtir]: ~ **qqn (de)** to dress sb (in). **-2.** [suj: fournisseur] to provide with clothing; [suj: fabricant] to make clothes for. **-3.** [recouvrir] to cover.

◆ **s'habiller** *vp* **-1.** [se vêtir] to dress, to get dressed; **s'~ de** to dress in. **-2.** [se vêtir élégamment] to dress (up). **-3.** [se fournir en vêtements] to buy one's clothes.

habilleur, -euse [abijœr, øz] *nm, f* dresser.

habit [abi] *nm* **-1.** [costume] suit; ~ **de soirée** evening dress. **-2.** RELIG habit.

◆ **habits** *nmpl* [vêtements] clothes.

habitable [abitabl] *adj* habitable.

habitacle [abitakl] *nm* [d'avion] cockpit; [de voiture] passenger compartment.

habitant, -e [abitã, ãt] *nm, f* **-1.** [de pays] inhabitant; **loger chez l'~** to stay with local people. **-2.** [d'immeuble] occupant. **-3.** *Can* [paysan] farmer.

habitat [abita] *nm* **-1.** [conditions de logement] housing conditions (*pl*). **-2.** [mode de peuplement] settlement. **-3.** [d'animal] habitat.

habitation [abitasjɔ̃] *nf* **-1.** [fait d'habiter] housing. **-2.** [résidence] house, home.

habiter [abite] [3] ◇ *vt* **-1.** [résider] to live in. **-2.** [suj: passion, sentiment] to dwell within. ◇ *vi* to live.

habitude [abityd] *nf* **-1.** [façon de faire] habit; **avoir l'~ de faire qqch** to be in the habit of doing sthg; **d'~** usually; **comme d'~** as usual; **par ~** out of habit. **-2.** [coutume] custom.

habitué, -e [abitye] *nm, f* regular.

habituel, -elle [abitɥɛl] *adj* **-1.** [coutumier] usual, customary. **-2.** [caractéristique] typical.

habituellement [abitɥɛlmã] *adv* usually.

habituer [abitɥe] [7] *vt*: ~ **qqn à qqch/à faire qqch** to get sb used to sthg/to doing sthg.

◆ **s'habituer** *vp*: **s'~ à qqch/à faire qqch** to get used to sthg/to doing sthg.

hâbleur, -euse ['ablœr, øz] *littéraire* ◇ *adj* boastful. ◇ *nm, f* braggart.

hache ['aʃ] *nf* axe; **enterrer la ~ de guerre** *fig* to bury the hatchet.

haché, -e ['aʃe] *adj* **-1.** [coupé - gén] finely chopped; [- viande] minced *Br*, ground *Am*. **-2.** [entrecoupé] jerky.

hacher ['aʃe] [3] *vt* **-1.** [couper - gén] to chop finely; [- viande] to mince *Br*, to grind *Am*. **-2.** [entrecouper] to interrupt.

hachette ['aʃɛt] *nf* hatchet.

hachis ['aʃi] *nm*: **un ~ de persil** finely chopped parsley; **un ~ de porc** minced pork *Br*, ground pork *Am*; ~ **Parmentier** ≃ shepherd's pie, ≃ cottage pie.

hachisch = **haschisch**.

hachoir ['aʃwar] *nm* **-1.** [couteau] chopper. **-2.** [appareil] mincer *Br*, grinder *Am*. **-3.** [planche] chopping-board.

hachure ['aʃyr] *nf* hatching.

hachurer ['aʃyre] [3] *vt* to hatch.

haddock ['adɔk] *nm* smoked haddock.

hagard, -e ['agar, ard] *adj* haggard.

hagiographie [aʒjɔgrafi] *nf* hagiography.

haï, -e ['ai] *pp* → **haïr**.

haie ['ɛ] *nf* **-1.** [d'arbustes] hedge. **-2.** [de personnes] row; [de soldats, d'agents de police] line; ~ **d'honneur** guard of honour. **-3.** SPORT hurdle; **400 mètres ~s** 400 metres hurdles.

haillons ['ajɔ] *nmpl* rags.

haine ['ɛn] *nf* hatred.

haineusement ['ɛnøzmã] *adv* with hatred.

haineux, -euse ['ɛnø, øz] *adj* full of hatred.

haïr ['air] [33] *vt* to hate.

hais, **hait** *etc* → **haïr**.
haïssable ['aisabl] *adj* hateful.
haïssais, **haïssions** *etc* → **haïr**.
Haïti *n* [aiti] Haiti; **à** ~ in Haiti.
haïtien, **-ienne** [aisjɛ̃, jɛn] *adj* Haitian.
◆ **Haïtien**, **-ienne** *nm, f* Haitian.
hâle ['al] *nm* tan.
hâlé, **-e** ['ale] *adj* tanned.
haleine [alɛn] *nf* breath; **avoir l'**~ **forte**, **avoir mauvaise** ~ to have bad breath; **courir à perdre** ~ to run until one is breathless; **hors d'**~ out of breath; **de longue** ~ exacting and time-consuming; **reprendre** ~ to catch one's breath; **tenir qqn en** ~ to keep sb in suspense.
haler ['ale] [3] *vt* **-1.** [tirer] to haul in. **-2.** [remorquer] to tow.
haletant, **-e** ['altɑ̃, ɑ̃t] *adj* panting.
halètement ['alɛtmɑ̃] *nm* panting.
haleter ['alte] [28] *vi* to pant.
hall ['ol] *nm* **-1.** [vestibule, entrée] foyer, lobby. **-2.** [salle publique] concourse; ~ **d'arrivée/de départ** arrival/departure hall.
halle ['al] *nf* covered market.
◆ **halles** *nfpl* wholesale food market (*sg*).
hallucinant, **-e** [alysinɑ̃, ɑ̃t] *adj* **-1.** [incroyable] extraordinary. **-2.** [grandiose] impressive.
hallucination [alysinasjɔ̃] *nf* hallucination.
halluciné, **-e** [alysine] ◇ *adj* crazed. ◇ *nm, f* lunatic.
hallucinogène [alysinɔʒɛn] ◇ *nm* hallucinogen. ◇ *adj* hallucinogenic.
halo ['alo] *nm* **-1.** [cercle lumineux] halo. **-2.** *fig* [rayonnement] aura.
halogène [alɔʒɛn] *nm & adj* halogen.
halte ['alt] ◇ *nf* stop; **faire** ~ to stop. ◇ *interj* stop!
haltère [altɛr] *nm* dumbbell.
haltérophile [alterɔfil] ◇ *nmf* weight-lifter. ◇ *adj* weight-lifting (*avant n*).
haltérophilie [alterɔfili] *nf* weight-lifting.
hamac ['amak] *nm* hammock.
hamburger ['ɑ̃burgœr] *nm* hamburger.
hameau, **-x** ['amo] *nm* hamlet.
hameçon [amsɔ̃] *nm* fish-hook; **mordre à l'**~ *fig* to rise to the bait.
hammam ['amam] *nm* Turkish baths (*pl*).
hampe ['ɑ̃p] *nf* [de drapeau] pole.
hamster ['amstɛr] *nm* hamster.
hanche ['ɑ̃ʃ] *nf* hip; **rouler des** ~s to swing one's hips.
handball ['ɑ̃dbal] *nm* handball.
handicap ['ɑ̃dikap] *nm* handicap.

handicapé, **-e** ['ɑ̃dikape] ◇ *adj* handicapped; **être** ~ **par qqch** *fig* to be handicapped by sthg. ◇ *nm, f* handicapped person; ~ **mental** mentally handicapped person; ~ **moteur** spastic.
handicaper ['ɑ̃dikape] [3] *vt* to handicap.
hangar ['ɑ̃gar] *nm* shed; AÉRON hangar.
hanneton ['antɔ̃] *nm* cockchafer.
Hanoi ['anɔj] *n* Hanoi.
hanter ['ɑ̃te] [3] *vt* to haunt.
hantise ['ɑ̃tiz] *nf* obsession; **avoir la** ~ **de qqch/de faire qqch** to be obsessed by the fear of sthg/of doing sthg.
happer ['ape] [3] *vt* **-1.** [attraper] to snap up. **-2.** [accrocher] to strike.
hara-kiri ['arakiri] *nm*: **(se) faire** ~ to commit hara-kiri.
harangue ['arɑ̃g] *nf* harangue.
haranguer ['arɑ̃ge] [3] *vt* to harangue.
haras ['ara] *nm* stud (farm).
harassant, **-e** ['arasɑ̃, ɑ̃t] *adj* exhausting.
harasser ['arase] [3] *vt* to exhaust.
harcèlement ['arsɛlmɑ̃] *nm* harassment; ~ **sexuel** sexual harassment.
harceler ['arsəle] [25] *vt* **-1.** [relancer] to harass. **-2.** MIL to harry. **-3.** [importuner]: ~ **qqn (de)** to pester sb (with).
hardes ['ard] *nfpl* old clothes.
hardi, **-e** ['ardi] *adj* bold, daring.
hardiesse ['ardjes] *nf* boldness, daring.
hardware ['ardwɛr] *nm* INFORM hardware.
harem ['arɛm] *nm* harem.
hareng ['arɑ̃] *nm* herring; ~ **saur** kipper.
hargne ['arɲ] *nf* spite (*U*), bad temper.
hargneux, **-euse** ['arɲø, øz] *adj* [personne] spiteful, bad-tempered; [remarque] spiteful, vicious.
haricot ['ariko] *nm* bean; ~s **verts/blancs/rouges** green/haricot/kidney beans.
harmonica [armɔnika] *nm* harmonica, mouth organ.
harmonie [armɔni] *nf* **-1.** [gén] harmony; **vivre en** ~ **(avec qqn)** to live in harmony (with sb). **-2.** [de visage] symmetry. **-3.** [fanfare] wind band.
harmonieusement [armɔnjøzmɑ̃] *adv* harmoniously.
harmonieux, **-ieuse** [armɔnjø, jøz] *adj* **-1.** [gén] harmonious. **-2.** [voix] melodious. **-3.** [traits, silhouette] regular.
harmonique [armɔnik] *adj* harmonic.
harmonisation [armɔnizasjɔ̃] *nf* **-1.** [coordination] harmonization. **-2.** MUS harmonizing.

harmoniser [armɔnize] [3] *vt* MUS & *fig* to harmonize; [salaires] to bring into line.

harmonium [armɔnjɔm] *nm* harmonium.

harnachement ['arnaʃmã] *nm* **-1.** [équipement de cheval] harness. **-2.** [action] harnessing. **-3.** *fig* [attirail] gear.

harnacher ['arnaʃe] [3] *vt* [cheval] to harness; **être harnaché** *fig* to be got up.

harnais ['arnɛ] *nm* **-1.** [de cheval, de parachutiste] harness. **-2.** TECHNOL train.

haro ['aro] *nm sout*: **crier ~ sur** to rail against.

harpagon [arpagɔ̃] *nm* ≃ Scrooge.

harpe ['arp] *nf* harp.

harpie ['arpi] *nf* harpy.

harpon ['arpɔ̃] *nm* harpoon.

harponner ['arpɔne] [3] *vt* **-1.** [poisson] to harpoon. **-2.** *fam* [personne] to waylay.

hasard ['azar] *nm* chance; **au ~** at random; **à tout ~** on the off chance; **par ~** by accident, by chance; **comme par ~** *iron* as if by chance; **si par ~** if by chance.

hasarder ['azarde] [3] *vt* **-1.** [tenter] to venture. **-2.** [risquer] to hazard.

◆ **se hasarder** *vp*: **se ~ à faire qqch** to risk doing sthg.

hasardeux, -euse ['azardø, øz] *adj* risky.

haschisch, haschich, hachisch ['aʃiʃ] *nm* hashish.

hâte ['at] *nf* haste; **à la ~, en ~** hurriedly, hastily; **avoir ~ de faire qqch** to be eager to do sthg.

hâter ['ate] [3] *vt* **-1.** [activer] to hasten. **-2.** [avancer] to bring forward.

◆ **se hâter** *vp* to hurry; **se ~ de faire qqch** to hurry to do sthg.

hâtif, -ive ['atif, iv] *adj* [précipité] hurried, hasty.

hauban ['obã] *nm* NAUT shroud.

hausse ['os] *nf* [augmentation] rise, increase; **à la ~, en ~** rising.

haussement ['osmã] *nm*: **~ d'épaules** shrug (of the shoulders).

hausser ['ose] [3] *vt* to raise.

haut, -e [o, ot] *adj* **-1.** [gén] high; **~ de 20 m** 20 m high. **-2.** [classe sociale, pays, région] upper. **-3.** [responsable] senior.

◆ **haut** ◇ *adv* **-1.** [gén] high; [placé] highly. **-2.** [fort] loudly; **dire bien ~ ce que l'on pense tout bas** to say out loud what everyone else is thinking. ◇ *nm* **-1.** [hauteur] height; **faire 2 m de ~** to be 2 m high OU in height. **-2.** [sommet, vêtement] top. **-3.** *loc*: **avoir OU connaître des ~s et des bas** to have one's ups and downs.

◆ **de haut** *loc adv* haughtily; **le prendre de ~** to react haughtily.

◆ **de haut en bas** *loc adv* from top to bottom.

◆ **du haut de** *loc prép* from the top of.

◆ **en haut de** *loc prép* at the top of.

◆ **là-haut** *loc adv* up there.

hautain, -e ['otɛ̃, ɛn] *adj* haughty.

hautbois ['obwa] *nm* oboe.

haut-de-forme ['odfɔrm] (*pl* **hauts-de-forme**) *nm* top hat.

haut de gamme [odgam] ◇ *adj* upmarket; **une chaîne ~** a state-of-the-art hi-fi system. ◇ *nm* top of the range.

haute-fidélité [otfidelite] (*pl* **hautes-fidélités**) *nf* high fidelity, hi-fi.

hautement ['otmã] *adv* highly.

hauteur ['otœr] *nf* height; **à ~ d'épaule** at shoulder level OU height; **ne pas être à la ~ de qqch** not to be up to sthg.

Haute-Volta [otvɔlta] *nf*: **la ~** Upper Volta.

haut-fond ['ofɔ̃] (*pl* **hauts-fonds**) *nm* shallows (*pl*).

haut-fourneau ['ofurno] (*pl* **hauts-fourneaux**) *nm* blast furnace.

haut-le-cœur ['olkœr] *nm inv* retch; **avoir des ~** to retch.

haut-le-corps ['olkɔr] *nm inv*: **avoir un ~** to start, to jump.

haut-parleur ['oparlœr] (*pl* **haut-parleurs**) *nm* loudspeaker.

havane ['avan] ◇ *nm* Havana cigar. ◇ *adj inv* tobacco-coloured.

Havane ['avan] *n*: **La ~** Havana.

hâve ['av] *adj littéraire* haggard.

havre ['avr] *nm* [refuge] haven.

Hawaii ['awaj] *n* Hawaii; **à ~** in Hawaii.

hawaiien, -ienne ['awajɛ̃, jɛn] *adj* Hawaiian.

◆ **Hawaiien, -ienne** *nm, f* Hawaiian.

Haye ['ɛ] *n*: **La ~** the Hague.

hayon ['ajɔ̃] *nm* hatchback.

hé ['e] *interj* hey!

hebdo [ɛbdo] *nm fam* weekly.

hebdomadaire [ɛbdɔmadɛr] *nm & adj* weekly.

hébergement [ebɛrʒəmã] *nm* accommodation.

héberger [ebɛrʒe] [17] *vt* **-1.** [loger] to put up. **-2.** [suj: hôtel] to take in.

hébété, -e [ebete] *adj* dazed.

hébétement [ebɛtmã] *nm* stupor.

hébétude [ebetyd] *nf littéraire* stupor.

hébraïque [ebraik] *adj* Hebrew.

hébreu, -x [ebrø] *adj* Hebrew.

◆ **hébreu** *nm* [langue] Hebrew.

◆ **Hébreu, -x** *nm* Hebrew.

Hébrides [ebrid] *nfpl*: **les ~** the Hebrides; **aux ~** in the Hebrides.

HEC (*abr de* **(école des) Hautes études commerciales**) *n grande école for management and business studies.*

hécatombe [ekatɔ̃b] *nf litt* & *fig* slaughter.

hectare [ɛktar] *nm* hectare.

hectolitre [ɛktɔlitr] *nm* hectolitre.

hédonisme [edɔnism] *nm* hedonism.

hédoniste [edɔnist] ◇ *nmf* hedonist. ◇ *adj* hedonistic.

hégémonie [eʒemɔni] *nf* hegemony.

hégire [eʒir] *nf* hegira.

hein ['ɛ̃] *interj fam* eh?, what?; **tu m'en veux, ~?** you're cross with me, aren't you?

hélas [elas] *interj* unfortunately, alas.

héler ['ele] [18] *vt sout* to hail.

hélice [elis] *nf* **-1.** [d'avion, de bateau] propeller. **-2.** MATHS helix.

hélicoïdal, -e, -aux [elikɔidal, o] *adj* **-1.** [forme] spiral, helical. **-2.** MATHS helical.

hélicoptère [elikɔptɛr] *nm* helicopter.

héliomarin, -e [eljɔmarɛ̃, in] *adj* MÉD [cure] using sun and sea air.

héliport [elipɔr] *nm* heliport.

héliporté, -e [elipɔrte] *adj* [troupes, fournitures] transported by helicopter; [opération] helicopter (*avant n*).

hélium [eljɔm] *nm* helium.

Helsinki ['ɛlzinki] *n* Helsinki.

helvétisme [ɛlvetism] *nm* Swiss expression.

hem ['ɛm] *interj* [indique le doute] hmm.

hématologie [ematɔlɔʒi] *nf* haematology.

hématome [ematom] *nm* MÉD haematoma.

hémicycle [emisikl] *nm* POLIT: **l'~** the Assemblée Nationale.

hémiplégique [emipleʒik] *nmf* & *adj* hemiplegic.

hémisphère [emisfɛr] *nm* hemisphere; **l'~ nord/sud** northern/southern hemisphere; **~ cérébral** ANAT cerebral hemisphere.

hémoglobine [emɔglɔbin] *nf* haemoglobin.

hémophile [emɔfil] ◇ *nmf* haemophiliac. ◇ *adj* haemophilic.

hémorragie [emɔraʒi] *nf* **-1.** MÉD haemorrhage; **~ cérébrale** brain haemorrhage; **interne** internal bleeding (*U*). **-2.** *fig* [perte, fuite] loss.

hémorroïdes [emɔrɔid] *nfpl* haemorrhoids, piles.

henné ['ene] *nm* henna.

hennir ['enir] [32] *vi* to neigh, to whinny.

hennissement ['enismɑ̃] *nm* neigh, whinny.

hep ['ɛp] *interj* hey!

hépatique [epatik] ◇ *nmf* person with liver problems. ◇ *adj* liver (*avant n*).

hépatite [epatit] *nf* MÉD hepatitis; **~ B** hepatitis B; **~ virale** viral hepatitis.

heptagone [ɛptagɔn] *nm* heptagon.

herbacé, -e [ɛrbase] *adj* herbaceous.

herbage [ɛrbaʒ] *nm* pasture.

herbe [ɛrb] *nf* **-1.** BOT grass; **mauvaise ~** weed. **-2.** CULIN & MÉD herb; **fines ~s** herbs. **-3.** *fam* [marijuana] grass. **-4.** *loc*: **en ~** budding; **couper l'~ sous les pieds de qqn** to cut the ground from under sb's feet.

herbeux, -euse [ɛrbø, øz] *adj* grassy.

herbicide [ɛrbisid] ◇ *nm* weedkiller, herbicide. ◇ *adj* herbicidal.

herbier [ɛrbje] *nm* herbarium.

herbivore [ɛrbivɔr] ◇ *nm* herbivore. ◇ *adj* herbivorous.

herboriste [ɛrbɔrist] *nmf* herbalist.

herboristerie [ɛrbɔristəri] *nf* herbalist's (shop).

herculéen, -enne [ɛrkyleɛ̃, ɛn] *adj* Herculean.

hère ['ɛr] *nm*: **pauvre ~** poor wretch.

héréditaire [ereditɛr] *adj* hereditary.

hérédité [eredite] *nf* **-1.** [génétique] heredity. **-2.** [de biens, de titre] inheritance.

hérésie [erezi] *nf* heresy.

hérétique [eretik] ◇ *nmf* heretic. ◇ *adj* heretical.

hérisser ['erise] [3] *vt* **-1.** [dresser]: **~ son poil** to bristle. **-2.** [garnir]: **être hérissé de** [de clous] to be studded with; *fig* [de difficultés] to be fraught with. **-3.** [irriter]: **~ qqn** to get sb's back up.

hérisson ['erisɔ̃] *nm* **-1.** ZOOL hedgehog. **-2.** [brosse] chimney sweep's brush.

héritage [eritaʒ] *nm* **-1.** [de biens] inheritance; **faire un ~** to come into an inheritance; **en ~** as an inheritance. **-2.** [culturel] heritage.

hériter [erite] [3] ◇ *vi* to inherit; **~ de qqch** to inherit sthg. ◇ *vt*: **~ qqch de qqn** *litt* & *fig* to inherit sthg from sb.

héritier, -ière [eritje, jɛr] *nm, f* heir (*f* heiress).

hermaphrodite [ɛrmafrɔdit] *nmf* & *adj* hermaphrodite.

hermétique [ɛrmetik] *adj* **-1.** [étanche] hermetic. **-2.** [incompréhensible] inaccessible, impossible to understand. **-3.** [impénétrable] impenetrable.

hermétiquement [ɛrmetikmɑ̃] *adv* hermetically.

hermétisme [ɛrmetism] *nm* [de texte] obscurity.

hermine [ɛrmin] *nf* -1. [animal] stoat. -2. [fourrure] ermine.

hernie ['ɛrni] *nf* hernia; ~ **discale** slipped disc.

héroïne [erɔin] *nf* -1. [personne] heroine. -2. [drogue] heroin.

héroïnomane [erɔinɔman] *nmf* heroin addict.

héroïque [erɔik] *adj* heroic.

héroïquement [erɔikmɑ̃] *adv* heroically.

héroïsme [erɔism] *nm* heroism.

héron ['erɔ̃] *nm* heron.

héros ['ero] *nm* hero.

herpès [ɛrpɛs] *nm* herpes.

herse ['ɛrs] *nf* -1. AGRIC harrow. -2. [grille] portcullis.

hertz ['ɛrts] *nm inv* hertz.

hésitant, -e [ezitɑ̃, ɑ̃t] *adj* hesitant.

hésitation [ezitasjɔ̃] *nf* hesitation; **avec** ~ hesitantly; **sans** ~ without hesitation, unhesitatingly.

hésiter [ezite] [3] ◇ *vi* to hesitate; ~ **entre/sur** to hesitate between/over. ◇ *vt*: ~ **à faire qqch** to hesitate to do sthg.

hétéro [etero] *adj & nmf* hetero.

hétéroclite [eterɔklit] *adj* motley.

hétérogène [eterɔʒɛn] *adj* heterogeneous.

hétérogénéité [eterɔʒeneite] *nf* heterogeneity.

hétérosexuel, -elle [eterɔsɛksyɛl] *adj & nm, f* heterosexual.

hêtre ['ɛtr] *nm* beech.

heure [œr] *nf* -1. [unité de temps] hour; **250 km à l'**~ 250 km per OU an hour; **faire des** ~**s supplémentaires** to work overtime. -2. [moment du jour] time; **il est deux** ~**s** it's two o'clock; **donner/demander l'**~ **à qqn** to tell/ask sb the time; **quelle** ~ **est-il?** what time is it?; **être à l'**~ to be on time; **mettre à l'**~ [montre, pendule] to put right; ~ **d'affluence** [dans les transports] rush hour; [au magasin] peak time; ~ **de battement** break; ~ **creuse** off-peak time, slack period; ~ **d'ouverture/de fermeture** opening/closing time; ~ **de pointe** rush hour; ~**s de bureau** office hours; ~**s de réception** office/surgery *etc* hours. -3. SCOL class, period. -4. *loc*: **à** ~ **fixe** at a set time; **à l'**~ **actuelle** at the present time; **à l'**~ **qu'il est** at this moment in time; **à la bonne** ~! that's wonderful!; **à la première** ~ at the crack of dawn; **à toute** ~ at any time; **c'est l'**~ (**de faire qqch**) it's time (to do sthg); **de bonne** ~ early; **de la première** ~ right from the start; **sur l'**~ at once.

heureusement [œrøzmɑ̃] *adv* -1. [par chance] luckily, fortunately. -2. [favorablement] successfully.

heureux, -euse [œrø, øz] ◇ *adj* -1. [gén] happy; [favorable] fortunate; **être** ~ **de faire qqch** to be happy to do sthg. -2. [réussi] successful, happy. -3. *loc*: **encore** ~ (**que**) (+ *subjonctif*) ... *fam* it's just as well (that) .... ◇ *nm, f*: **faire un** ~ to make somebody's day.

heurt ['œr] *nm* -1. [choc] collision, impact. -2. [désaccord] clash; **sans** ~**s** smoothly.

heurter ['œrte] [3] ◇ *vt* -1. [rentrer dans - gén] to hit; [- suj: personne] to bump into. -2. [offenser - personne, sensibilité] to offend. -3. [bon sens, convenances] to go against. ◇ *vi*: ~ **contre qqch** to bump into sthg. ◆ **se heurter** *vp* -1. [gén]: **se** ~ (**contre**) to collide (with). -2. [rencontrer]: **se** ~ **à qqch** to come up against sthg.

heurtoir ['œrtwar] *nm* knocker.

hexagonal, -e, -aux [ɛgzagɔnal, o] *adj* -1. GÉOM hexagonal. -2. [français] French.

hexagone [ɛgzagɔn] *nm* GÉOM hexagon. ◆ **Hexagone** *nm*: **l'Hexagone** (mainland) France.

HF (*abr de* **hautes fréquences**) HF.

hiatus [jatys] *nm inv* hiatus.

hibernation [ibɛrnasjɔ̃] *nf* hibernation.

hiberner [ibɛrne] [3] *vi* to hibernate.

hibiscus [ibiskys] *nm* hibiscus.

hibou, -x ['ibu] *nm* owl.

hic ['ik] *nm fam* snag.

hideux, -euse ['idø, øz] *adj* hideous.

hier [ijɛr] *adv* yesterday; ~ **matin/soir** yesterday morning/evening.

hiérarchie ['jerarʃi] *nf* hierarchy.

hiérarchique ['jerarʃik] *adj* hierarchical.

hiéroglyphe [jerɔglif] *nm* hieroglyph, hieroglyphic. ◆ **hiéroglyphes** *nmpl* hieroglyphics.

hilarant, -e [ilarɑ̃, ɑ̃t] *adj* hilarious.

hilare [ilar] *adj* beaming.

hilarité [ilarite] *nf* hilarity; **provoquer l'**~ **générale** to give rise to general hilarity.

Himalaya [imalaja] *nm*: **l'**~ the Himalayas (*pl*).

himalayen, -enne [imalajɛ̃, jɛn] *adj* Himalayan.

hindi ['indi] *nm* [langue] Hindi.

hindou, -e [ɛ̃du] *adj* Hindu. ◆ **Hindou, -e** *nm, f* Hindu.

hindouisme [ɛ̃duism] *nm* Hinduism.

hippie, hippy ['ipi] (*pl* **hippies**) *nmf & adj* hippy.

hippique [ipik] *adj* horse (*avant n*).

hippisme [ipism] *nm* (horse) riding.

hippocampe [ipɔkɑ̃p] *nm* seahorse.

hippodrome [ipɔdrom] *nm* race-course.

hippopotame [ipɔpɔtam] *nm* hippopotamus.

hirondelle [irɔ̃dɛl] *nf* swallow.

hirsute [irsyt] *adj* [chevelure, barbe] shaggy.

hispanique [ispanik] *adj* **-1.** [gén] Hispanic. **-2.** [aux États-Unis] Spanish-American.
◆ **Hispanique** *nmf* [aux États-Unis] Spanish American.

hispano-américain, -e [ispanɔamerikɛ̃, ɛn] (*mpl* **hispano-américains**, *fpl* **hispano-américaines**) *adj* Spanish-American.
◆ **Hispano-Américain, -e** *nm, f* Spanish-American, Hispanic.

hispanophone [ispanɔfɔn] ◇ *nmf* Spanish-speaker. ◇ *adj* Spanish-speaking.

hisser ['ise] [3] *vt* **-1.** [voile, drapeau] to hoist. **-2.** [charge] to heave, to haul.
◆ **se hisser** *vp* **-1.** [grimper]: se ~ (**sur**) to heave OU haul o.s. up (onto). **-2.** *fig* [s'élever]: se ~ **à** to pull o.s. up to.

histoire [istwar] *nf* **-1.** [science] history; ~ **ancienne/moderne/contemporaine** ancient/modern/contemporary history; ~ **de l'art** art history; ~ **de France** French history; ~ **sainte** Biblical history; ~ **sociale/économique** social/economic history. **-2.** [récit, mensonge] story; **c'est une autre** ~ that's another story; ~ **à dormir debout** tall story. **-3.** [aventure] funny OU strange thing. **-4.** (*gén pl*) [ennui] trouble (*U*); **faire des** ~s *fam* to make a fuss.

historien, -ienne [istɔrjɛ̃, jɛn] *nm, f* historian.

historique [istɔrik] *adj* **-1.** [roman, recherches] historical. **-2.** [monument, événement] historic.

historiquement [istɔrikmɑ̃] *adv* historically.

hit-parade ['itparad] (*pl* **hit-parades**) *nm*: **le** ~ **the charts** (*pl*).

hiver [ivɛr] *nm* winter; **en** ~ in (the) winter.

hivernal, -e, -aux [ivɛrnal, o] *adj* winter (*avant n*).

hiverner [ivɛrne] [3] *vi* to (spend the) winter.

hl (*abr de* **hectolitre**) hl.

HLM (*abr de* **habitation à loyer modéré**) *nm*

ou nf low-rent, state-owned housing, ≃ council house/flat *Br*, ≃ public housing unit *Am*.

hm (*abr de* **hectomètre**) hm.

ho ['o] *interj* oh!

hobby ['ɔbi] (*pl* **hobbies**) *nm* hobby.

hochement ['ɔʃmɑ̃] *nm*: ~ **de tête** [affirmatif] nod (of the head); [négatif] shake of the head.

hocher ['ɔʃe] [3] *vt*: ~ **la tête** [affirmativement] to nod (one's head); [négativement] to shake one's head.

hochet ['ɔʃɛ] *nm* rattle.

hockey ['ɔkɛ] *nm* hockey; ~ **sur glace** ice hockey *Br*, hockey *Am*; ~ **sur gazon** field hockey.

holà ['ɔla] ◇ *interj* **-1.** [pour appeler] hey! **-2.** [pour arrêter] hold on! ◇ *nm*: **mettre le** ~ **à qqch** *fam* to put a stop to sthg.

holding ['ɔldiŋ] *nm ou nf* holding company.

hold-up ['ɔldœp] *nm inv* hold-up.

hollandais, -e ['ɔlɑ̃dɛ, ɛz] *adj* Dutch.
◆ **hollandais** *nm* [langue] Dutch.
◆ **Hollandais, -e** *nm, f* Dutchman (*f* Dutchwoman).

Hollande ['ɔlɑ̃d] *nf*: **la** ~ Holland; **en** ~ in Holland.

holocauste [ɔlɔkost] *nm* holocaust.

hologramme [ɔlɔgram] *nm* hologram.

homard ['ɔmar] *nm* lobster; ~ **à l'armoricaine** OU **l'américaine** lobster *sautéed in oil with white wine, garlic and tomatoes*.

home ['om] *nm*: ~ **d'enfants** holiday centre for children.

homélie [ɔmeli] *nf* homily.

homéopathe [ɔmeɔpat] ◇ *nmf* homeopath. ◇ *adj* homeopathic.

homéopathie [ɔmeɔpati] *nf* homeopathy.

homéopathique [ɔmeɔpatik] *adj* homeopathic.

homicide [ɔmisid] ◇ *nm* [meurtre] murder; ~ **involontaire** manslaughter; ~ **volontaire** murder. ◇ *adj* homicidal.

hommage [ɔmaʒ] *nm* [témoignage d'estime] tribute; **rendre** ~ **à qqn/qqch** to pay tribute to sb/sthg.
◆ **hommages** *nmpl* [salutations] respects; **mes** ~ *sout* my respects.

hommasse [ɔmas] *adj péj* mannish, butch.

homme [ɔm] *nm* man; **vêtements d'**~ menswear (*U*); **grand** ~ great man; ~ **d'affaires** businessman; ~ **d'État** statesman; ~ **de main** hired man; ~ **du monde** man about town; ~ **de paille** stooge; **d'**~ **à** ~ man to man; **comme un seul** ~ as one (man).

homme-grenouille [ɔmgrənuj] (*pl* **hommes-grenouilles**) *nm* frogman.

homme-orchestre [ɔmɔrkɛstr] (*pl* **hommes-orchestres**) *nm* one-man band.

homme-sandwich [ɔmsɑ̃dwitʃ] (*pl* **hommes-sandwiches**) *nm* sandwich man.

homogène [ɔmɔʒɛn] *adj* homogeneous.

homogénéisé, -e [ɔmɔʒeneize] *adj* homogenized.

homogénéité [ɔmɔʒeneite] *nf* homogeneity.

homologue [ɔmɔlɔg] ◇ *nm* counterpart, opposite number. ◇ *adj* equivalent.

homologuer [ɔmɔlɔge] [3] *vt* [ratifier] to approve; SPORT to recognize, to ratify.

homonyme [ɔmɔnim] *nm* **-1.** LING homonym. **-2.** [personne, ville] namesake.

homosexualité [ɔmɔsɛksyalite] *nf* homosexuality.

homosexuel, -elle [ɔmɔsɛksyɛl] *adj & nm, f* homosexual.

Honduras [ˈɔdyras] *nm*: **le ~** Honduras; **au ~** in Honduras; **le ~ britannique** British Honduras.

hondurien, -ienne [ˈɔdyrjɛ̃, jɛn] *adj* Honduran.
◆ **Hondurien, -ienne** *nm, f* Honduran.

Hongkong, Hong Kong [ˈɔgkɔ̃g] *n* Hong Kong.

Hongrie [ˈɔgri] *nf*: **la ~** Hungary.

hongrois, -e [ˈɔgrwa, az] *adj* Hungarian.
◆ **hongrois** *nm* [langue] Hungarian.
◆ **Hongrois, -e** *nm, f* Hungarian.

honnête [ɔnɛt] *adj* **-1.** [intègre] honest. **-2.** [correct] honourable. **-3.** [convenable - travail, résultat] reasonable.

honnêtement [ɔnɛtmɑ̃] *adv* **-1.** [de façon intègre, franchement] honestly. **-2.** [correctement] honourably.

honnêteté [ɔnɛtte] *nf* honesty.

honneur [ɔnœr] *nm* honour; **en l'~ de** in honour of; **être à l'~** to be in favour; **à qui ai-je l'~? ~?** *sout* to whom do I have the honour of speaking?; **faire ~ à qqn/à qqch** to be a credit to sb/to sthg; **faire ~ à un repas** *fig* to do justice to a meal; **sauver l'~** to save one's honour.
◆ **honneurs** *nmpl* honours.

Honolulu [ˈonolyly] *n* Honolulu.

honorable [ɔnɔrabl] *adj* **-1.** [digne] honourable. **-2.** [convenable] respectable.

honorablement [ɔnɔrabləmɑ̃] *adv* honourably.

honoraire [ɔnɔrɛr] *adj* honorary.
◆ **honoraires** *nmpl* fee (*sg*), fees.

honorer [ɔnɔre] [3] *vt* **-1.** [vénérer, gratifier]: **~ qqn (de)** to honour sb (with). **-2.** [faire honneur à] to be a credit to. **-3.** [payer] to honour.
◆ **s'honorer** *vp*: **s'~ de qqch** to pride o.s. on sthg.

honorifique [ɔnɔrifik] *adj* honorary *Br*, ceremonial *Am*.

honte [ˈɔt] *nf* **-1.** [sentiment] shame; **avoir ~ de qqn/qqch** to be ashamed of sb/sthg; **avoir ~ de faire qqch** to be ashamed of doing sthg; **faire ~ à qqn** to make sb (feel) ashamed. **-2.** [action scandaleuse]: **c'est une ~!** it's a disgrace!

honteusement [ˈɔtøzmɑ̃] *adv* shamefully.

honteux, -euse [ˈɔtø, øz] *adj* shameful; [personne] ashamed.

hop [ˈɔp] *interj* **-1.** [pour faire sauter] hup! **-2.** [pour stimuler] off you go!

hôpital, -aux [ɔpital, o] *nm* hospital; **~ militaire/psychiatrique** military/psychiatric hospital; **~ de jour** outpatients unit.

hoquet [ˈɔkɛ] *nm* hiccup; **avoir le ~** to have (the) hiccups.

hoqueter [ˈɔkte] [27] *vi* to hiccup.

horaire [ɔrɛr] ◇ *nm* **-1.** [de départ, d'arrivée] timetable. **-2.** [de travail] hours (*pl*) (of work); **~ mobile** OU **flexible** OU **à la carte** flexitime. ◇ *adj* hourly.

horde [ˈɔrd] *nf* horde.

horions [ˈɔrjɔ̃] *nmpl littéraire* blows.

horizon [ɔrizɔ̃] *nm* **-1.** [ligne, perspective] horizon; **à l'~** *litt & fig* on the horizon. **-2.** [panorama] view.

horizontal, -e, -aux [ɔrizɔtal, o] *adj* horizontal.
◆ **horizontale** *nf* MATHS horizontal; **à l'~e** horizontal, in a horizontal position; [couché] flat out.

horizontalement [ɔrizɔtalmɑ̃] *adv* horizontally.

horloge [ɔrlɔʒ] *nf* clock; **~ parlante** speaking clock *Br*, Time *Am*.

horloger, -ère [ɔrlɔʒe, ɛr] ◇ *adj* clock/watch making (*avant n*). ◇ *nm, f* clock maker, watchmaker.

horlogerie [ɔrlɔʒri] *nf* clock/watch making.

hormis [ˈɔrmi] *prép* save.

hormonal, -e, -aux [ɔrmɔnal, o] *adj* hormonal.

hormone [ɔrmɔn] *nf* hormone.

horodateur [ɔrɔdatœr] *nm* [à l'usine] clock; [au parking] ticket machine.

horoscope [ɔrɔskɔp] *nm* horoscope.

horreur [ɔrœr] *nf* horror; **avoir ~ de qqn/qqch** to hate sb/sthg; **avoir ~ de faire qqch**

to hate doing sthg; **avoir qqn/qqch en** ~ **to**
hate sb/sthg; **faire** ~ **à qqn** to disgust sb;
quelle ~! how dreadful!, how awful!

horrible [ɔribl] *adj* **-1.** [affreux] horrible. **-2.**
fig [terrible] terrible, dreadful.

horriblement [ɔribləmã] *adv* horribly.

horrifiant, -e [ɔrifjã, ãt] *adj* horrifying.

horrifier [ɔrifje] [9] *vt* to horrify.

horripilant, -e [ɔripilã, ãt] *adj* exasperating.

horripiler [ɔripile] [3] *vt* to exasperate.

hors [ɔr] *prép*: ~ **pair** outstanding.
◆ **hors de** *loc prép* outside; ~ **d'ici!** get out
of here!; **être** ~ **de soi** to be beside o.s.

hors-bord [ɔrbɔr] *nm inv* speedboat.

hors-d'œuvre [ɔrdœvr] *nm inv* hors
d'oeuvre, starter.

hors-jeu [ɔrʒø] *nm inv & adj inv* offside.

hors-la-loi [ɔrlalwa] *nm inv* outlaw.

hors-piste [ɔrpist] *nm inv* off-piste skiing.

hortensia [ɔrtãsja] *nm* hydrangea.

horticole [ɔrtikɔl] *adj* horticultural.

horticulteur, -trice [ɔrtikyltœr, tris] *nm, f*
horticulturalist.

horticulture [ɔrtikyltyr] *nf* horticulture.

hospice [ɔspis] *nm* home.

hospitalier, -ière [ɔspitalje, jɛr] *adj* **-1.** [ac-
cueillant] hospitable. **-2.** [relatif aux hôpitaux]
hospital (*avant n*).

hospitalisation [ɔspitalizasjõ] *nf* hospitali-
zation.

hospitaliser [ɔspitalize] [3] *vt* to hospitalize.

hospitalité [ɔspitalite] *nf* hospitality.

hostie [ɔsti] *nf* host.

hostile [ɔstil] *adj*: ~ **(à)** hostile (to).

hostilité [ɔstilite] *nf* hostility.
◆ **hostilités** *nfpl* hostilities.

hôte, hôtesse [ot, otɛs] *nm, f* host (*f* hostess); **hôtesse d'accueil** receptionist; **hôtesse
de l'air** air hostess.
◆ **hôte** *nmf* [invité] guest.

hôtel [otɛl] *nm* **-1.** [d'hébergement] hotel;
descendre à l'~ to stay at a hotel; ~ **trois
étoiles** three-star hotel. **-2.** [demeure]: ~
(particulier) mansion. **-3.** [établissement pu-
blic] public building; ~ **de ville** town hall.

hôtelier, -ière [otəlje, jɛr] ◇ *adj* hotel
(*avant n*). ◇ *nm, f* hotelier.

hôtellerie [otɛlri] *nf* **-1.** [métier] hotel trade.
-2. [hôtel-restaurant] inn.

hotte [ɔt] *nf* **-1.** [panier] basket. **-2.** [d'aéra-
tion] hood; ~ **aspirante** extractor hood.

houblon [ublõ] *nm* **-1.** BOT hop. **-2.** [de la
bière] hops (*pl*).

houe [u] *nf* hoe.

houille [uj] *nf* coal; ~ **blanche** hydroelectric power.

houiller, -ère [uje, ɛr] *adj* coal (*avant n*).
◆ **houillère** *nf* coalmine.

houle [ul] *nf* swell.

houlette [ulɛt] *nf sout*: **sous la** ~ **de qqn**
under the guidance of sb.

houleux, -euse [ulø, øz] *adj litt & fig* turbulent.

houppe [up] *nf* **-1.** [à poudre] powder puff.
-2. [de cheveux] tuft.

houppette [upɛt] *nf* powder puff.

hourra, hurrah [ura] ◇ *nm* cheer. ◇ *interj*
hurrah!

houspiller [uspije] [3] *vt* to tell off.

housse [us] *nf* cover; ~ **de couette** duvet
cover.

houx [u] *nm* holly.

HS (*abr de* **hors service**) *adj* out of order; **la
télé est complètement** ~ *fam* the telly's on
the blink; **je suis** ~ *fam* I'm completely
washed out.

HT ◇ *adj abr de* **hors taxe**. ◇ *nf* (*abr de*
haute tension) HT.

hublot [yblo] *nm* **-1.** [de bateau] porthole.
-2. [de four, cuisinière] window.

huche [yʃ] *nf*: ~ **à pain** bread bin.

hue [y] *interj* gee up!, giddy up!

huées [ye] *nfpl* boos.

huer [ye] [7] ◇ *vt* [siffler] to boo. ◇ *vi*
[chouette, hibou] to hoot.

huile [ɥil] *nf* **-1.** [gén] oil; ~ **d'arachide/
d'olive** groundnut/olive oil; ~ **de coude**
fam fig elbow grease; ~ **essentielle** essential oil; ~ **de foie de morue** cod-liver oil; ~
de paraffine paraffin *Br*, kerosene *Am*; ~
solaire suntan oil/lotion; **jeter de l'**~ **sur le
feu** to add fuel to the flames. **-2.** [peinture]
oil painting. **-3.** *fam* [personnalité] bigwig.

huiler [ɥile] [3] *vt* to oil.

huileux, -euse [ɥilø, øz] *adj* oily.

huilier [ɥilje] *nm* **-1.** [accessoire] oil and vinegar set. **-2.** [fabricant] oil producer.

huis [ɥi] *nm littéraire* door; **à** ~ **clos** JUR in
camera.

huissier [ɥisje] *nm* **-1.** [appariteur] usher. **-2.**
JUR bailiff.

huit [ɥit] ◇ *adj num* eight. ◇ *nm* eight;
lundi en ~ a week on *Br* OU from *Am*
Monday, Monday week *Br*; *voir aussi* **six**.

huitaine [ɥitɛn] *nf*: **sous** OU **à** ~ in a
week's time, a week today.

huitième [ɥitjɛm] ◇ *adj num, nm & nmf*
eighth. ◇ *nf* **-1.** [championnat]: **la** ~ **de fi-**

nale *round before the quarterfinal.* **-2.** [classe] ≃ fourth year primary *Br,* ≃ fourth grade *Am; voir aussi* **sixième.**

huître [ɥitr] *nf* oyster.

hululement = ululement.

hululer = ululer.

hum ['œm] *interj* **-1.** [marque le doute] hmm! **-2.** [pour attirer l'attention] ahem!

humain, -e [ymɛ̃, ɛn] *adj* **-1.** [gén] human. **-2.** [sensible] humane.

◆ **humain** *nm* [être humain] human (being).

humainement [ymɛnmɑ̃] *adv* **-1.** [matériellement] humanly. **-2.** [avec bonté] humanely.

humaniser [ymanize] [3] *vt* to humanize.

◆ **s'humaniser** *vp* to become more human.

humaniste [ymanist] ◇ *nmf* **-1.** [philosophe] humanist. **-2.** [lettré] classicist. ◇ *adj* humanistic.

humanitaire [ymanitɛr] *adj* humanitarian.

humanité [ymanite] *nf* humanity.

◆ **humanités** *nfpl Belg* humanities.

humanoïde [ymanɔid] *nmf & adj* humanoid.

humble [œ̃bl] *adj* humble.

humblement [œ̃bləmɑ̃] *adv* humbly.

humecter [ymɛkte] [4] *vt* to moisten.

◆ **s'humecter** *vp* to moisten.

humer ['yme] [3] *vt* to smell.

humérus [ymerys] *nm* humerus.

humeur [ymœr] *nf* **-1.** [disposition] mood; être de bonne/mauvaise ~ to be in a good/bad mood. **-2.** [caractère] nature. **-3.** *sout* [irritation] temper; avec ~ angrily. **-4.** ANAT & *vieilli* [liquide] humour.

humide [ymid] *adj* [air, climat] humid; [terre, herbe, mur] wet, damp; [saison] rainy; [front, yeux] moist.

humidificateur [ymidifikatœr] *nm* humidifier.

humidifier [ymidifje] [9] *vt* to humidify.

humidité [ymidite] *nf* [de climat, d'air] humidity; [de terre, mur] dampness.

humiliant, -e [ymiljɑ̃, ɑ̃t] *adj* humiliating.

humiliation [ymiljasjɔ̃] *nf* humiliation.

humilier [ymilje] [9] *vt* to humiliate.

◆ **s'humilier** *vp*: **s'~ devant qqn** to grovel to sb.

humilité [ymilite] *nf* humility.

humoriste [ymɔrist] ◇ *nmf* humorist. ◇ *adj* humoristic.

humoristique [ymɔristik] *adj* humorous.

humour [ymur] *nm* humour; **avoir de l'~** to have a sense of humour; **manquer d'~**

to have no sense of humour; ~ **noir** black humour.

humus [ymys] *nm* humus.

huppé, -e ['ype] *adj* **-1.** *fam* [société] upper-crust. **-2.** [oiseau] crested.

hurlant, -e ['yrlɑ̃, ɑ̃t] *adj* **-1.** [gén] howling. **-2.** *fig* [couleurs] clashing.

hurlement ['yrləmɑ̃] *nm* howl.

hurler ['yrle] [3] *vi* **-1.** [gén] to howl. **-2.** [couleurs] to clash.

hurluberlu, -e [yrlybɛrly] *nm, f fam* crank.

hurrah = hourra.

hussard ['ysar] *nm* hussar.

◆ **hussarde** *nf*: à la ~e brutally.

hutte ['yt] *nf* hut.

hybride [ibrid] *nm & adj* hybrid.

hydratant, -e [idratɑ̃, ɑ̃t] *adj* moisturizing.

◆ **hydratant** *nm* moisturizer.

hydratation [idratasjɔ̃] *nf* **-1.** CHIM hydration. **-2.** [de peau] moisturizing.

hydrate [idrat] *nm* hydrate; ~ **de carbone** carbohydrate.

hydrater [idrate] [3] *vt* **-1.** CHIM to hydrate. **-2.** [peau] to moisturize.

hydraulique [idrolik] ◇ *nf* hydraulics (*U*). ◇ *adj* hydraulic.

hydravion [idravjɔ̃] *nm* seaplane, hydroplane.

hydre [idr] *nf* hydra.

hydrocarbure [idrɔkarbyr] *nm* hydrocarbon.

hydrocution [idrɔkysjɔ̃] *nf* immersion syncope.

hydroélectrique [idrɔelɛktrik] *adj* hydroelectric.

hydrogène [idrɔʒɛn] *nm* hydrogen.

hydrogéné, -e [idrɔʒene] *adj* hydrogenated.

hydroglisseur [idrɔglisœr] *nm* jetfoil, hydroplane.

hydrographie [idrɔgrafi] *nf* hydrography.

hydrologie [idrɔlɔʒi] *nf* hydrology.

hydrophile [idrɔfil] *adj* **-1.** [qui absorbe] absorbent. **-2.** → **coton.**

hyène [jɛn] *nf* hyena.

hygiène [iʒjɛn] *nf* hygiene; ~ **dentaire/ intime** dental/personal hygiene.

hygiénique [iʒjenik] *adj* **-1.** [sanitaire] hygienic. **-2.** [bon pour la santé] healthy.

hymen [imɛn] *nm* **-1.** ANAT hymen. **-2.** *littéraire* [mariage] marriage.

hymne [imn] *nm* hymn; ~ **national** national anthem.

hyperbole [ipɛrbɔl] *nf* **-1.** MATHS hyperbola. **-2.** LING hyperbole.

hyperglycémie [iperglisemi] *nf* hyperglycaemia.

hypermarché [ipermarʃe] *nm* hypermarket.

hypermétrope [ipermetrɔp] ◇ *nmf* longsighted person. ◇ *adj* longsighted.

hypersensible [ipersɑ̃sibl] ◇ *nmf* hypersensitive person. ◇ *adj* hypersensitive.

hypertension [ipertɑ̃sjɔ̃] *nf* high blood pressure, hypertension; **faire de l'~** to have high blood pressure.

hypertexte [ipertɛkst] *nm* hypertext.

hypertrophié [ipertrɔfje] *adj* hypertrophic; *fig* exaggerated.

hypnose [ipnoz] *nf* hypnosis.

hypnotique [ipnɔtik] *nm & adj* hypnotic.

hypnotiser [ipnɔtize] [3] *vt* to hypnotize; *fig* to mesmerize.

◆ **s'hypnotiser** *vp*: **s'~ sur qqch** to be mesmerized by sthg.

hypocondriaque [ipɔkɔ̃drijak] *nmf & adj* hypochondriac.

hypocrisie [ipɔkrizi] *nf* hypocrisy.

hypocrite [ipɔkrit] ◇ *nmf* hypocrite. ◇ *adj* hypocritical.

hypocritement [ipɔkritmɑ̃] *adv* hypocritically.

hypodermique [ipɔdɛrmik] *adj* hypodermic.

hypoglycémie [ipɔglisemi] *nf* hypoglycaemia.

hypokhâgne [ipɔkaɲ] *nf first year of a two-year preparatory arts course taken prior to the competitive examination for entry to the École normale supérieure.*

hypophyse [ipɔfiz] *nf* pituitary gland.

hypotension [ipɔtɑ̃sjɔ̃] *nf* low blood pressure; **faire de l'~** to have low blood pressure.

hypoténuse [ipɔtenyz] *nf* hypotenuse.

hypothécaire [ipɔtekɛr] *adj* [prêt, contrat] mortgage (*avant n*).

hypothèque [ipɔtɛk] *nf* mortgage; **grevé d'~s** [maison] heavily mortgaged.

hypothéquer [ipɔteke] [18] *vt* to mortgage.

hypothèse [ipɔtɛz] *nf* hypothesis; **dans l'~ où** assuming.

hypothétique [ipɔtetik] *adj* hypothetical.

hystérie [isteri] *nf* hysteria; **~ collective** mass hysteria.

hystérique [isterik] ◇ *nmf* hysterical person. ◇ *adj* hysterical.

Hz (*abr de* **hertz**) Hz.

I

i, I [i] *nm inv* i, I; **mettre les points sur les i** to dot the i's and cross the t's.

IA (*abr de* **intelligence artificielle**) *nf* AI.

IAC (*abr de* **insémination artificielle entre conjoints**) *nf* AIH.

IAD (*abr de* **insémination artificielle par donneur extérieur**) *nf* AID.

ibérique [iberik] *adj*: **la péninsule ~** the Iberian Peninsula.

ibid. (*abr de* **ibidem**) ibid.

iceberg [ajsbɛrg] *nm* iceberg.

ici [isi] *adv* **-1.** [lieu] here; **d'~** from around here; **~ même** on this very spot; **par ~** [direction] this way; [alentour] around here; **~-bas** here below. **-2.** [temps] now; **d'~ (à)** jeudi between now and Thursday; **d'~ là** by then; **d'~ peu** soon. **-3.** [au téléphone]: **~ Marie-Anne** this is Marie-Anne.

icône [ikon] *nf* INFORM & RELIG icon.

iconique [ikɔnik] *adj* iconic.

iconoclaste [ikɔnɔklast] ◇ *nmf* iconoclast. ◇ *adj* iconoclastic.

iconographie [ikɔnɔgrafi] *nf* iconography.

id. (*abr de* **idem**) id.

idéal, -e [ideal] (*pl* **idéals** OU **idéaux** [ideo]) *adj* ideal.

◆ **idéal** *nm* ideal.

idéalement [idealmɑ̃] *adv* ideally.

idéalisation [idealizasjɔ̃] *nf* idealization.

idéaliser [idealize] [3] *vt* to idealize.

idéalisme [idealism] *nm* idealism.

idéaliste [idealist] ◇ *nmf* idealist. ◇ *adj* idealistic.

idée [ide] *nf* idea; **à l'idée de/que** at the idea of/that; **avoir dans l'~ que ...** to have a feeling that ...; **changer d'~** to change one's mind; **ne pas avoir la moindre ~ (de)** not to have the slightest idea (about); **se faire des ~s** to imagine things; **se faire des ~s sur qqn/qqch** to get ideas about sb/sthg; **se faire une ~ de** to get an idea of; **cela ne m'est jamais venu à l'~** it never occurred to me; **~ fixe** obsession; **~ de génie** brainwave; **~s noires** black thoughts; **~s**

reçues assumptions; **se rafraîchir les** ~**s** to refresh one's memory.

idem [idɛm] *adv* idem.

identification [idɑ̃tifikasjɔ̃] *nf*: ~ **(à)** identification (with).

identifier [idɑ̃tifje] [9] *vt* to identify; ~ **qqn à qqch** to identify sb with sthg.

◆ **s'identifier** *vp*: **s'**~ **à qqn/qqch** to identify with sb/sthg.

identique [idɑ̃tik] *adj*: ~ **(à)** identical (to).

identité [idɑ̃tite] *nf* identity.

idéologie [ideɔlɔʒi] *nf* ideology.

idéologique [ideɔlɔʒik] *adj* ideological.

idiomatique [idjɔmatik] *adj* idiomatic.

idiome [idjom] *nm* idiom.

idiot, -e [idjo, ɔt] ◇ *adj* idiotic; MÉD idiot (*avant n*). ◇ *nm, f* idiot.

idiotie [idjɔsi] *nf* **-1.** [stupidité] idiocy. **-2.** [action, parole] idiotic thing.

idoine [idwan] *adj sout* appropriate.

idolâtrer [idɔlatre] [3] *vt* to idolize.

idole [idɔl] *nf* idol.

IDS (*abr de* **initiative de défense stratégique**) *nf* SDI.

idylle [idil] *nf* **-1.** [amour] romance. **-2.** [poème] idyll.

idyllique [idilik] *adj* [idéal] idyllic.

if [if] *nm* yew.

IFOP, Ifop [ifɔp] (*abr de* **Institut français d'opinion publique**) *nm French market research institute.*

Ifremer [ifrəmɛr] (*abr de* **Institut français de recherche pour l'exploitation de la mer**) *nm research establishment for marine resources.*

IGF (*abr de* **impôt sur les grandes fortunes**) *nm former wealth tax.*

IGH (*abr de* **immeuble de grande hauteur**) *nm very high building.*

igloo, iglou [iglu] *nm* igloo.

IGN (*abr de* **Institut géographique national**) *nm national geographical institute,* ≃ Ordnance Survey *Br.*

ignare [iɲar] ◇ *nmf* ignoramus. ◇ *adj* ignorant.

ignifuge [iɲify3] ◇ *nm* fireproofing material. ◇ *adj* fireproof.

ignoble [iɲɔbl] *adj* **-1.** [abject] base. **-2.** [hideux] vile.

ignominie [iɲɔmini] *nf* **-1.** [état] disgrace. **-2.** [action] disgraceful act.

ignominieux, -ieuse [iɲɔminjø, jøz] *adj* ignominious.

ignorance [iɲɔrɑ̃s] *nf* ignorance; **dans l'**~ **de** in the dark about, in ignorance of.

ignorant, -e [iɲɔrɑ̃, ɑ̃t] ◇ *adj* ignorant; ~ **en/de qqch** ignorant of sthg. ◇ *nm, f* ignoramus.

ignoré, -e [iɲɔre] *adj* unknown.

ignorer [iɲɔre] [3] *vt* **-1.** [ne pas savoir] not to know, to be unaware of; ~ **que** not to know that. **-2.** [ne pas tenir compte de] to ignore. **-3.** [ne pas connaître] to have no experience of.

◆ **s'ignorer** *vp* **-1.** [se bouder] to ignore each other. **-2.** [méconnaître ses possibilités] to be unaware of one's talent.

IGPN (*abr de* **Inspection générale de la police nationale**) *nf police disciplinary body.*

IGS (*abr de* **Inspection générale des services**) *nf police disciplinary body for Paris.*

il [il] *pron pers* **-1.** [sujet - personne] he; [- animal] it, he; [- chose] it. **-2.** [sujet d'un verbe impersonnel] it; ~ **pleut** it's raining.

◆ **ils** *pron pers pl* they.

île [il] *nf* island; **les** ~**s Anglo-Normandes** the Channel Islands; **les** ~**s Baléares** the Balearic Islands; **les** ~**s Britanniques** the British Isles; **les** ~**s Canaries** the Canary Islands; **les** ~**s Malouines** the Falkland Islands; **l'**~ **de Man** the Isle of Man; **l'**~ **Maurice** Mauritius.

illégal, -e, -aux [ilegal, o] *adj* illegal.

illégalité [ilegalite] *nf* **-1.** [fait d'être illégal] illegality. **-2.** [action illégale] illegal act.

illégitime [ileʒitim] *adj* **-1.** [enfant] illegitimate; [union] unlawful. **-2.** [non justifié] unwarranted.

illettré, -e [iletre] *adj & nm, f* illiterate.

illicite [ilisit] *adj* illicit.

illico [iliko] *adv fam* right away, pronto.

illimité, -e [ilimite] *adj* **-1.** [sans limites] unlimited. **-2.** [indéterminé] indefinite.

illisible [ilizibl] *adj* **-1.** [indéchiffrable] illegible. **-2.** [incompréhensible & INFORM] unreadable.

illogique [ilɔʒik] *adj* illogical.

illumination [ilyminasjɔ̃] *nf* **-1.** [éclairage] lighting. **-2.** [idée soudaine] inspiration.

◆ **illuminations** *nfpl* illuminations.

illuminé, -e [ilymine] ◇ *adj* illuminated. ◇ *nm, f péj* crank.

illuminer [ilymine] [3] *vt* to light up; [bâtiment, rue] to illuminate.

◆ **s'illuminer** *vp*: **s'**~ **de joie** to light up with joy.

illusion [ilyzjɔ̃] *nf* illusion; **se faire des** ~**s** to fool o.s.; ~ **d'optique** optical illusion; **se bercer d'**~**s** to live in cloud cuckoo land.

illusionner [ilyzjɔne] [3] *vt* to delude.

◆ **s'illusionner** *vp* to delude o.s.

illusionniste [ilyzjɔnist] *nmf* conjurer.

illusoire [ilyzwar] *adj* illusory.

illustrateur, -trice [ilystratœr, tris] *nm, f* illustrator.

illustration [ilystrasjɔ̃] *nf* illustration.

illustre [ilystr] *adj* illustrious.

illustré, -e [ilystre] *adj* illustrated.

◆ **illustré** *nm* illustrated magazine.

illustrer [ilystre] [3] *vt* -**1.** [gén] to illustrate. -**2.** [rendre célèbre] to make famous.

◆ **s'illustrer** *vp* to distinguish o.s.

îlot *nm* -**1.** [île] small island, islet. -**2.** [de maisons] block. -**3.** [lieu isolé] island. -**4.** *fig* [de résistance] pocket.

ils → **il**.

IMA [ima] (*abr de* **Institut du monde arabe**) *nm Paris exhibition centre for Arab culture and art.*

image [imaʒ] *nf* -**1.** [vision mentale, comparaison, ressemblance] image; **être l'~ de qqn** to be the image of sb; **~ de marque** [de personne] image; [d'entreprise] corporate image. -**2.** [dessin] picture; **~ d'Épinal** sentimental picture; *fig* simplistic argument/theory; **sage comme une ~** as good as gold.

imagé, -e [imaʒe] *adj* full of imagery.

imaginable [imaʒinabl] *adj* imaginable.

imaginaire [imaʒinɛr] ◇ *nm*: **l'~** the imaginary. ◇ *adj* imaginary.

imaginatif, -ive [imaʒinatif, iv] *adj* imaginative.

imagination [imaʒinasjɔ̃] *nf* imagination; **avoir de l'~** to be imaginative.

◆ **imaginations** *nfpl littéraire* & *péj* [chimères] fancies.

imaginer [imaʒine] [3] *vt* -**1.** [supposer, croire] to imagine. -**2.** [trouver] to think of.

◆ **s'imaginer** *vp* -**1.** [se voir] to see o.s. -**2.** [croire] to imagine.

imam [imam] *nm* imam.

imbattable [ɛ̃batabl] *adj* unbeatable.

imbécile [ɛ̃besil] ◇ *nmf* imbecile. ◇ *adj* idiotic.

imbécillité [ɛ̃besilite] *nf* -**1.** [manque d'intelligence] imbecility. -**2.** [acte, parole] stupid thing.

imberbe [ɛ̃bɛrb] *adj* beardless.

imbiber [ɛ̃bibe] [3] *vt*: **~ qqch de qqch** to soak sthg with OU in sthg.

◆ **s'imbiber** *vp*: **s'~ de** to soak up.

imbriqué, -e [ɛ̃brike] *adj* overlapping.

imbriquer [ɛ̃brike] [3]

◆ **s'imbriquer** *vp* [se chevaucher] to overlap; *fig* to intertwine.

imbroglio [ɛ̃brɔljo] *nm* imbroglio.

imbu, -e [ɛ̃by] *adj*: **être ~ de** to be full of; **être ~ de soi-même** to be full of oneself.

imbuvable [ɛ̃byvabl] *adj* -**1.** [eau] undrinkable. -**2.** *fam* [personne] unbearable.

imitateur, -trice [imitatœr, tris] *nm, f* -**1.** [comique] impersonator. -**2.** *péj* [copieur] imitator.

imitation [imitasjɔ̃] *nf* imitation; **~ cuir** imitation leather; **à l'~ de** in imitation of.

◆ **en imitation** *loc adj* imitation.

imiter [imite] [3] *vt* -**1.** [s'inspirer de, contrefaire] to imitate. -**2.** [reproduire l'aspect de] to look (just) like.

immaculé, -e [imakyle] *adj* immaculate; **L'Immaculée Conception** The Immaculate Conception.

immanent, -e [imanɑ̃, ɑ̃t] *adj* immanent; **~ à** inherent in.

immangeable [ɛ̃mɑ̃ʒabl] *adj* inedible.

immanquable [ɛ̃mɑ̃kabl] *adj* impossible to miss; [sort, échec] inevitable.

immanquablement [ɛ̃mɑ̃kabləmɑ̃] *adv* inevitably.

immatériel, -ielle [imaterjel] *adj* -**1.** PHILO immaterial. -**2.** [beauté] unreal. -**3.** [investissement] intangible.

immatriculation [imatrikylasjɔ̃] *nf* registration.

IMMATRICULATION:
The last two numbers on French licence plates refer to the 'département' where the car was registered. Cars from Val-de-Marne, for example, bear the number 94

immatriculer [imatrikyle] [3] *vt* to register.

immature [imatyr] *adj* immature.

immaturité [imatyrite] *nf* immaturity.

immédiat, -e [imedja, at] ◇ *adj* immediate. ◇ *nm*: **dans l'~** for the time being.

immédiatement [imedjatmɑ̃] *adv* immediately.

immémorial, -e, -iaux [imemɔrjal, jo] *adj* ancient.

immense [imɑ̃s] *adj* immense.

immensément [imɑ̃semɑ̃] *adv* immensely.

immensité [imɑ̃site] *nf* immensity, vastness.

immerger [imɛrʒe] [17] *vt* to submerge.

◆ **s'immerger** *vp* to submerge o.s.

immérité, -e [imerite] *adj* undeserved.

immersion [imɛrsjɔ̃] *nf* immersion.

immettable [ɛ̃metabl] *adj* unwearable.

immeuble [imœbl] ◇ *nm* building. ◇ *adj* JUR real.

immigrant, -e [imigrɑ̃, ɑ̃t] *nm, f* immigrant.

immigration [imigrasjɔ̃] *nf* immigration.

immigré, -e [imigre] *adj & nm, f* immigrant.

immigrer [imigre] [3] *vi* to immigrate.

imminence [iminɑ̃s] *nf* imminence.

imminent, -e [iminɑ̃, ɑ̃t] *adj* imminent.

immiscer [imise] [16]
♦ **s'immiscer** *vp*: **s'~ dans** to interfere in OU with.

immixtion [imiksjɔ̃] *nf* interference.

immobile [imɔbil] *adj* **-1.** [personne, visage] motionless. **-2.** [mécanisme] fixed, stationary. **-3.** *fig* [figé] immovable.

immobilier, -ière [imɔbilje, jɛr] *adj*: **biens ~s** property *Br*, real estate *Am* (U); **société immobilière** property *Br* OU real estate *Am* company.
♦ **immobilier** *nm*: **l'~** property *Br*, real estate *Am*.

immobilisation [imɔbilizasjɔ̃] *nf* immobilization.
♦ **immobilisations** *nfpl* FIN fixed assets.

immobiliser [imɔbilize] [3] *vt* to immobilize.
♦ **s'immobiliser** *vp* to stop.

immobilisme [imɔbilism] *nm péj* opposition to progress.

immobilité [imɔbilite] *nf* immobility; [de paysage, de lac] stillness.

immodéré, -e [imɔdere] *adj* inordinate.

immoler [imɔle] [3] *vt* to sacrifice; RELIG to immolate; **~ qqn/qqch à** to sacrifice sb/sthg to.
♦ **s'immoler** *vp* to immolate o.s.

immonde [imɔ̃d] *adj* **-1.** [sale] foul. **-2.** [abject] vile.

immondices [imɔ̃dis] *nfpl* waste (U), refuse (U).

immoral, -e, -aux [imɔral, o] *adj* immoral.

immoralité [imɔralite] *nf* **-1.** [dépravation] immorality. **-2.** [obscénité] obscenity.

immortaliser [imɔrtalize] [3] *vt* to immortalize.
♦ **s'immortaliser** *vp* to gain immortality.

immortalité [imɔrtalite] *nf* immortality.

immortel, -elle [imɔrtɛl] *adj* immortal.
♦ **immortel** *nm fam member of the Académie française.*
♦ **immortelle** *nf* BOT everlasting flower.

immuable [imɥabl] *adj* **-1.** [éternel - loi] immutable. **-2.** [constant] unchanging.

immunisation [imynizasjɔ̃] *nf* immunization.

immuniser [imynize] [3] *vt* **-1.** [vacciner] to immunize. **-2.** *fig* [garantir]: **~ qqn contre qqch** to make sb immune to sthg.

immunitaire [imynitɛr] *adj* immune (*avant n*).

immunité [imynite] *nf* immunity; **~ diplomatique/parlementaire** *fig* diplomatic/parliamentary immunity.

immunologique [imynɔlɔʒik] *adj* immunological.

impact [ɛ̃pakt] *nm* impact; **avoir de l'~ sur** to have an impact on; **étude d'~** impact study.

impair, -e [ɛ̃pɛr] *adj* odd.
♦ **impair** *nm* [faux-pas] gaffe.

imparable [ɛ̃parabl] *adj* **-1.** [coup] unstoppable. **-2.** [argument] unanswerable.

impardonnable [ɛ̃pardɔnabl] *adj* unforgivable.

imparfait, -e [ɛ̃parfɛ, ɛt] *adj* **-1.** [défectueux] imperfect. **-2.** [inachevé] incomplete.
♦ **imparfait** *nm* GRAM imperfect (tense).

imparfaitement [ɛ̃parfɛtmɑ̃] *adv* imperfectly.

impartial, -e, -iaux [ɛ̃parsjal, jo] *adj* impartial.

impartialité [ɛ̃parsjalite] *nf* impartiality.

impartir [ɛ̃partir] [32] *vt*: **~ qqch à qqn** *littéraire* [délai, droit] to grant sthg to sb; [don] to bestow sthg upon sb; [tâche] to assign sthg to sb.

impasse [ɛ̃pas] *nf* **-1.** [rue] dead end. **-2.** *fig* [difficulté] impasse, deadlock; **être dans une ~** OU **dans l'~** to be at an impasse, to be deadlocked. **-3.** SCOL & UNIV: **faire une ~ sur un sujet** *to give a subject a miss when revising for an exam.* **-4.** JEU: **faire une ~** to finesse. **-5.** FIN: **~ budgétaire** budget deficit.

impassibilité [ɛ̃pasibilite] *nf* impassivity.

impassible [ɛ̃pasibl] *adj* impassive; **rester ~** to be OU remain impassive.

impatiemment [ɛ̃pasjamɑ̃] *adv* impatiently.

impatience [ɛ̃pasjɑ̃s] *nf* impatience; **bouillir d'~** to be burning with impatience.

impatient, -e [ɛ̃pasjɑ̃, ɑ̃t] ◇ *adj* impatient; **être ~ de faire qqch** to be impatient OU longing to do sthg. ◇ *nm, f* impatient person.

impatienter [ɛ̃pasjɑ̃te] [3] *vt* to annoy.
♦ **s'impatienter** *vp*: **s'~ (de/contre)** to get impatient (at/with).

impayable [ɛ̃pɛjabl] *adj fam* priceless.

impayé, -e [ɛ̃pɛje] *adj* unpaid, outstanding.
♦ **impayé** *nm* outstanding payment.

impeccable [ɛ̃pekabl] *adj* **-1.** [parfait] impeccable, fau**l**tless. **-2.** [propre] spotless, immaculate.

impénétrable [ɛ̃penetrabl] *adj* impenetrable.

impénitent, -e [ɛ̃penitɑ̃, ɑ̃t] *adj* unrepentant.

impensable [ɛ̃pɑ̃sabl] *adj* unthinkable.

imper [ɛ̃pɛr] *nm fam* mac.

impératif, -ive [ɛ̃peratif, iv] *adj* **-1.** [ton, air] imperious. **-2.** [besoin] imperative, essential.
◆ **impératif** *nm* GRAM imperative.

impérativement [ɛ̃perativmɑ̃] *adv*: **il faut ~ faire qqch** it is imperative to do sthg.

impératrice [ɛ̃peratris] *nf* empress.

imperceptible [ɛ̃pɛrsɛptibl] *adj* imperceptible.

imperceptiblement [ɛ̃pɛrsɛptiblǝmɑ̃] *adv* imperceptibly.

imperfection [ɛ̃pɛrfɛksjɔ̃] *nf* imperfection.

impérial, -e, -iaux [ɛ̃perjal, jo] *adj* impérial.
◆ **impériale** *nf* top deck.

impérialisme [ɛ̃perjalism] *nm* POLIT imperialism; *fig* dominance.

impérialiste [ɛ̃perjalist] *nmf & adj* imperialist.

impérieusement [ɛ̃perjøzmɑ̃] *adv* imperiously.

impérieux, -ieuse [ɛ̃perjø, jøz] *adj* **-1.** [ton, air] imperious. **-2.** [nécessité] urgent.

impérissable [ɛ̃perisabl] *adj* undying.

imperméabilisation [ɛ̃pɛrmeabilizasjɔ̃] *nf* waterproofing.

imperméabiliser [ɛ̃pɛrmeabilize] [3] *vt* to waterproof.

imperméable [ɛ̃pɛrmeabl] ◇ *adj* waterproof; **~ à** [étanche] impermeable to; *fig* impervious OU immune to. ◇ *nm* raincoat.

impersonnel, -elle [ɛ̃pɛrsɔnɛl] *adj* impersonal.

impertinence [ɛ̃pɛrtinɑ̃s] *nf* impertinence (U).

impertinent, -e [ɛ̃pɛrtinɑ̃, ɑ̃t] ◇ *adj* impertinent. ◇ *nm, f* impertinent person.

imperturbable [ɛ̃pɛrtyrbabl] *adj* imperturbable.

impétigo [ɛ̃petigo] *nm* impetigo.

impétueux, -euse [ɛ̃petɥø, øz] *adj* **-1.** [personne, caractère] impetuous. **-2.** *littéraire* [vent, torrent] raging.

impétuosité [ɛ̃petɥozite] *nf* impetuousness.

impie [ɛ̃pi] ◇ *nmf* ungodly person. ◇ *adj littéraire* & *vieilli* impious.

impiété [ɛ̃pjete] *nf littéraire* & *vieilli* impiety.

impitoyable [ɛ̃pitwajabl] *adj* merciless, pitiless.

impitoyablement [ɛ̃pitwajablǝmɑ̃] *adv* mercilessly, pitilessly.

implacable [ɛ̃plakabl] *adj* implacable.

implant [ɛ̃plɑ̃] *nm* MÉD implant.

implantation [ɛ̃plɑ̃tasjɔ̃] *nf* **-1.** [d'usine, de système] establishment. **-2.** [de cheveux] implant.

implanter [ɛ̃plɑ̃te] [3] *vt* **-1.** [entreprise, système] to establish. **-2.** *fig* [préjugé] to implant.
◆ **s'implanter** *vp* to be established in.

implication [ɛ̃plikasjɔ̃] *nf* **-1.** [participation]: **~ (dans)** involvement (in). **-2.** (*gén pl*) [conséquence] implication.

implicite [ɛ̃plisit] *adj* implicit.

implicitement [ɛ̃plisitmɑ̃] *adv* implicitly.

impliquer [ɛ̃plike] [3] *vt* **-1.** [compromettre]: **~ qqn dans** to implicate sb in. **-2.** [requérir, entraîner] to imply.
◆ **s'impliquer** *vp*: **s'~ dans** *fam* to become involved in.

implorer [ɛ̃plɔre] [3] *vt* to beseech.

imploser [ɛ̃plɔze] [3] *vi* to implode.

implosion [ɛ̃plɔzjɔ̃] *nf* implosion.

impoli, -e [ɛ̃pɔli] *adj* rude, impolite.

impoliment [ɛ̃pɔlimɑ̃] *adv* rudely, impolitely.

impolitesse [ɛ̃pɔlitɛs] *nf* rudeness, impoliteness.

impondérable [ɛ̃pɔ̃derabl] *adj* imponderable.
◆ **impondérables** *nmpl* imponderables.

impopulaire [ɛ̃pɔpylɛr] *adj* unpopular.

import [ɛ̃pɔr] *nm* **-1.** COMM import. **-2.** *Belg* [montant] total.

importance [ɛ̃pɔrtɑ̃s] *nf* **-1.** [gén] importance; [de problème, montant] magnitude; **attacher de l'~ à** to attach importance to; **avoir de l'~** to be important; **d'~** [non négligeable] of some importance; **sans ~** unimportant; [accident] minor. **-2.** [de dommages] extent. **-3.** [de ville] size.

important, -e [ɛ̃pɔrtɑ̃, ɑ̃t] ◇ *adj* **-1.** [gén] important. **-2.** [considérable] considerable, sizeable; [- dommages] extensive. ◇ *nm, f*: **faire l'~** *péj* to act important.
◆ **important** *nm*: **l'~** the (most) important thing, the main thing.

importateur, -trice [ɛ̃pɔrtatœr, tris] *adj* importing (*avant n*).
◆ **importateur** *nm* importer.

importation [ɛ̃pɔrtasjɔ̃] *nf* COMM & *fig* import.

importer [ɛ̃pɔrte] [3] ◇ *vt* to import. ◇ *v impers*: ~ **(à)** to matter (to); **il importe de/ que** it is important to/that; **qu'importe!, peu importe!** it doesn't matter!; **n'importe qui** anyone (at all); **n'importe quoi** anything (at all); **n'importe où** anywhere (at all); **n'importe quand** at any time (at all); **n'importe comment** anyhow.

import-export [ɛ̃pɔrɛkspɔr] (*pl* **imports-exports**) *nm* import-export.

importun, -e [ɛ̃pɔrtœ̃, yn] ◇ *adj* -**1.** [indiscret] irksome, troublesome. -**2.** [embarrassant] awkward. ◇ *nm, f vieilli* intruder.

importuner [ɛ̃pɔrtyne] [3] *vt* to irk.

imposable [ɛ̃pozabl] *adj* taxable.

imposant, -e [ɛ̃pozɑ̃, ɑ̃t] *adj* imposing.

imposé, -e [ɛ̃poze] ◇ *adj* -**1.** [contribuable] taxed. -**2.** SPORT [figure] compulsory. ◇ *nm, f* [contribuable] taxpayer.

imposer [ɛ̃poze] [3] *vt* -**1.** [gén]: ~ **qqch/ qqn à qqn** to impose sthg/sb on sb. -**2.** [impressionner]: **en ~ à qqn** to impress sb. -**3.** [taxer] to tax.
◆ **s'imposer** *vp* -**1.** [être nécessaire] to be essential OU imperative. -**2.** [forcer le respect] to stand out. -**3.** [avoir pour règle]: **s'~ de faire qqch** to make it a rule to do sthg.

imposition [ɛ̃pozisjɔ̃] *nf* -**1.** FIN taxation. -**2.** RELIG laying on.

impossibilité [ɛ̃pɔsibilite] *nf* impossibility; **être dans l'~ de faire qqch** to find it impossible to OU to be unable to do sthg.

impossible [ɛ̃pɔsibl] ◇ *adj* impossible. ◇ *nm*: **tenter l'~** to attempt the impossible.

imposteur [ɛ̃pɔstœr] *nm* impostor.

imposture [ɛ̃pɔstyr] *nf* imposture.

impôt [ɛ̃po] *nm* tax; ~ **direct/indirect** direct/indirect tax; ~**s locaux** rates *Br*, local tax *Am*; ~ **sur les grandes fortunes** wealth tax; ~ **sur les plus-values** capital gains tax; ~ **sur le revenu** income tax; **être assujetti à l'~** to be subject to tax.

impotence [ɛ̃pɔtɑ̃s] *nf* infirmity.

impotent, -e [ɛ̃pɔtɑ̃, ɑ̃t] ◇ *adj* disabled. ◇ *nm, f* disabled person.

impraticable [ɛ̃pratikabl] *adj* -**1.** [inapplicable] impracticable. -**2.** [inaccessible] impassable.

imprécation [ɛ̃prekasjɔ̃] *nf littéraire* imprecation.

imprécis, -e [ɛ̃presi, iz] *adj* imprecise.

imprécision [ɛ̃presizjɔ̃] *nf* imprecision.

imprégner [ɛ̃preɲe] [18] *vt* [imbiber]: ~

qqch de qqch to soak sthg in sthg; ~ **qqn de qqch** *fig* to fill sb with sthg.
◆ **s'imprégner** *vp*: **s'~ de qqch** [s'imbiber] to soak sthg up; *fig* to soak sthg up, to steep o.s. in sthg.

imprenable [ɛ̃prənabl] *adj* -**1.** [forteresse] impregnable. -**2.** [vue] unimpeded.

imprésario, impresario [ɛ̃presarjo] *nm* impresario.

impression [ɛ̃presjɔ̃] *nf* -**1.** [gén] impression; **avoir l'~ que** to have the impression OU feeling that; **faire (une) bonne/ mauvaise ~ (à)** to make a good/bad impression (on). -**2.** [de livre, tissu] printing. -**3.** PHOT print.

impressionnable [ɛ̃presjɔnabl] *adj* -**1.** [émotif] impressionable. -**2.** PHOT sensitive.

impressionnant, -e [ɛ̃presjɔnɑ̃, ɑ̃t] *adj* -**1.** [imposant] impressive. -**2.** [effrayant] frightening.

impressionner [ɛ̃presjɔne] [3] *vt* -**1.** [frapper] to impress. -**2.** [choquer] to shock, to upset. -**3.** [intimider] to frighten. -**4.** PHOT to expose.

impressionnisme [ɛ̃presjɔnism] *nm* impressionism.

impressionniste [ɛ̃presjɔnist] *nmf & adj* impressionist.

imprévisible [ɛ̃previzibl] *adj* unforeseeable.

imprévoyance [ɛ̃prevwajɑ̃s] *nf* lack of foresight, improvidence.

imprévoyant, -e [ɛ̃prevwajɑ̃, ɑ̃t] *adj* improvident.

imprévu, -e [ɛ̃prevy] *adj* unforeseen.
◆ **imprévu** *nm* unforeseen situation; **sauf** ~ barring unforeseen circumstances.

imprimante [ɛ̃primɑ̃t] *nf* printer; ~ **laser/à jet d'encre/matricielle** laser/ink-jet/dot-matrix printer.

imprimé, -e [ɛ̃prime] *adj* printed.
◆ **imprimé** *nm* -**1.** POSTES printed matter (U). -**2.** [formulaire] printed form. -**3.** [tissu] print.

imprimer [ɛ̃prime] [3] *vt* -**1.** [texte, tissu] to print. -**2.** [mouvement] to impart. -**3.** [marque, empreinte] to leave.

imprimerie [ɛ̃primri] *nf* -**1.** [technique] printing. -**2.** [usine] printing works (*sg*).

imprimeur [ɛ̃primœr] *nm* printer.

improbable [ɛ̃prɔbabl] *adj* improbable.

improductif, -ive [ɛ̃prɔdyktif, iv] *adj* unproductive.

impromptu, -e [ɛ̃prɔ̃pty] *adj* impromptu.
◆ **impromptu** ◇ *adv* impromptu. ◇ *nm* impromptu.

imprononçable [ɛ̃prɔnɔ̃sabl] *adj* unpronounceable.

impropre [ɛ̃prɔpr] *adj* **-1.** GRAM incorrect. **-2.** [inadapté]: ~ à unfit for.

impropriété [ɛ̃prɔprijete] *nf* [emploi erroné] incorrectness; [expression] **(language) error.**

improvisation [ɛ̃prɔvizasjɔ̃] *nf* improvisation.

improviser [ɛ̃prɔvize] [3] *vt* to improvise.
◆ **s'improviser** *vp* **-1.** [s'organiser] to be improvised. **-2.** [devenir]: s'~ **metteur en scène** to act as director.

improviste [ɛ̃prɔvist]
◆ **à l'improviste** *loc adv* unexpectedly, without warning.

imprudemment [ɛ̃prydamɑ̃] *adv* rashly.

imprudence [ɛ̃prydɑ̃s] *nf* **-1.** [de personne, d'acte] rashness. **-2.** [acte] rash act.

imprudent, -e [ɛ̃prydɑ̃, ɑ̃t] ◇ *adj* rash. ◇ *nm, f* rash person.

impubère [ɛ̃pybɛr] ◇ *adj* [avant la puberté] pre-pubescent. ◇ *nmf* JUR ≃ minor.

impudence [ɛ̃pydɑ̃s] *nf* **-1.** [de personne, propos] impudence. **-2.** [propos] impudent remark.

impudent, -e [ɛ̃pydɑ̃, ɑ̃t] ◇ *adj* impudent. ◇ *nm, f* impudent person.

impudeur [ɛ̃pydœr] *nf* shamelessness.

impudique [ɛ̃pydik] *adj* shameless.

impuissance [ɛ̃pɥisɑ̃s] *nf* **-1.** [incapacité]: ~ **(à faire qqch)** powerlessness (to do sthg). **-2.** [sexuelle] impotence.

impuissant, -e [ɛ̃pɥisɑ̃, ɑ̃t] *adj* **-1.** [incapable]: ~ **(à faire qqch)** powerless to do sthg. **-2.** [homme, fureur] impotent.
◆ **impuissant** *nm* impotent man.

impulsif, -ive [ɛ̃pylsif, iv] ◇ *adj* impulsive. ◇ *nm, f* impulsive person.

impulsion [ɛ̃pylsjɔ̃] *nf* **-1.** [poussée, essor] impetus. **-2.** [instinct] impulse, instinct. **-3.** *fig*: **sous l'~ de qqn** [influence] at the prompting OU instigation of sb; **sous l'~ de qqch** [effet] impelled by sthg.

impulsivement [ɛ̃pylsivmɑ̃] *adv* impulsively.

impulsivité [ɛ̃pylsivite] *nf* impulsiveness.

impunément [ɛ̃pynemɑ̃] *adv* with impunity.

impuni, -e [ɛ̃pyni] *adj* unpunished.

impunité [ɛ̃pynite] *nf* impunity; **en toute** ~ with impunity.

impur, -e [ɛ̃pyr] *adj* impure.

impureté [ɛ̃pyrte] *nf* impurity.

imputable [ɛ̃pytabl] *adj* **-1.** [accident, erreur]:

~ à attributable to. **-2.** FIN: ~ à OU **sur** chargeable to.

imputation [ɛ̃pytasjɔ̃] *nf* **-1.** [accusation] charge. **-2.** FIN charging.

imputer [ɛ̃pyte] [3] *vt*: ~ **qqch à qqn/à qqch** to attribute sthg to sb/to sthg; ~ **qqch à qqch** FIN to charge sthg to sthg.

imputrescible [ɛ̃pytresibl] *adj* [bois] rotproof; [déchets] non-degradable.

in [in] *adj inv vieilli* in, with it.

INA [ina] (*abr de* **Institut national de l'audiovisuel**) *nm national television archive.*

inabordable [inabɔrdabl] *adj* **-1.** [prix] prohibitive. **-2.** GÉOGR inaccessible (*by boat*). **-3.** [personne] unapproachable.

inacceptable [inaksɛptabl] *adj* unacceptable.

inaccessible [inaksesibl] *adj* [destination, domaine, personne] inaccessible; [objectif, poste] unattainable; ~ à [sentiment] impervious to.

inaccoutumé, -e [inakutyme] *adj* unaccustomed.

inachevé, -e [inaʃve] *adj* unfinished, uncompleted.

inactif, -ive [inaktif, iv] *adj* **-1.** [sans occupation, non utilisé] idle. **-2.** [sans effet] ineffective. **-3.** [sans emploi] non-working.

inaction [inaksjɔ̃] *nf* inaction.

inactivité [inaktivite] *nf* **-1.** [oisiveté] inactivity. **-2.** ADMIN: **en** ~ out of active service.

inadapté, -e [inadapte] ◇ *adj* **-1.** [non adapté]: ~ **(à)** unsuitable (for), unsuited (to). **-2.** [asocial] maladjusted. ◇ *nm, f* maladjusted person.

inadéquat, -e [inadekwa, at] *adj*: ~ **(à)** inadequate (for).

inadéquation [inadekwasjɔ̃] *nf*: ~ **(à)** inadequacy (for).

inadmissible [inadmisibl] *adj* [conduite] unacceptable.

inadvertance [inadvɛrtɑ̃s] *nf littéraire* oversight; **par** ~ inadvertently.

inaliénable [inaljenabl] *adj* inalienable.

inaltérable [inalterabl] *adj* **-1.** [matériau] stable. **-2.** [sentiment] unfailing.

inamical, -e, -aux [inamikal, o] *adj* unfriendly.

inamovible [inamɔvibl] *adj* fixed.

inanimé, -e [inanime] *adj* **-1.** [sans vie] inanimate. **-2.** [inerte, évanoui] senseless.

inanité [inanite] *nf* futility.

inanition [inanisjɔ̃] *nf*: **tomber/mourir d'**~ to faint with/die of hunger.

inaperçu, -e [inapɛrsy] *adj* unnoticed; **passer** ~ to go OU pass unnoticed.

inapplicable [inaplikabl] *adj* inapplicable.

inappliqué, -e [inaplike] *adj* **-1.** [étourdi] lazy, lacking in application. **-2.** [inemployé] not applied OU practised.

inappréciable [inapresjabl] *adj* **-1.** [infime] imperceptible. **-2.** [précieux] invaluable.

inapprochable [inapraʃabl] *adj*: **il est vraiment ~ en ce moment** you can't say anything to him at the moment.

inapproprié, -e [inaproprije] *adj*: **~ à** not appropriate for.

inapte [inapt] *adj* **-1.** [incapable]: **~ à qqch/à faire qqch** incapable of sthg/of doing sthg. **-2.** MIL unfit.

inaptitude [inaptityd] *nf* **-1.** [incapacité]: **~ à qqch/à faire qqch** incapacity for sthg/for doing sthg. **-2.** MIL unfitness.

inarticulé, -e [inartikyle] *adj* inarticulate.

inassouvi, -e [inasuvi] *adj* [faim] unsatisfied; [soif] unquenched; *fig* [sentiment] unsatisfied, unfulfilled.

inattaquable [inatakabl] *adj* **-1.** [imprenable] impregnable. **-2.** [irréprochable] irreproachable, beyond reproach. **-3.** [irréfutable] irrefutable.

inattendu, -e [inatɑ̃dy] *adj* unexpected.

inattentif, -ive [inatɑ̃tif, iv] *adj*: **~ à** inattentive to.

inattention [inatɑ̃sjɔ̃] *nf* inattention; **faute d'~** careless mistake.

inaudible [inodibl] *adj* **-1.** [impossible à entendre] inaudible. **-2.** [inécoutable] impossible to listen to.

inaugural, -e, -aux [inogyral, o] *adj* inaugural (*avant n*), opening (*avant n*).

inauguration [inogyrasjɔ̃] *nf* **-1.** [cérémonie] inauguration, opening (ceremony). **-2.** [début] dawn.

inaugurer [inogyre] [3] *vt* **-1.** [monument] to unveil; [installation, route] to open; [procédé, édifice] to inaugurate. **-2.** [époque] to usher in.

inavouable [inavwabl] *adj* unmentionable.

inavoué, -e [inavwe] *adj* unconfessed.

INC (*abr de* **Institut national de la consommation**) *nm consumer research organization*.

inca [ɛ̃ka] *adj* Inca.
◆ **Inca** *nmf* Inca.

incalculable [ɛ̃kalkylabl] *adj* incalculable.

incandescence [ɛ̃kɑ̃desɑ̃s] *nf* incandescence.

incandescent, -e [ɛ̃kɑ̃desɑ̃, ɑ̃t] *adj* incandescent.

incantation [ɛ̃kɑ̃tasjɔ̃] *nf* incantation.

incapable [ɛ̃kapabl] ◇ *nmf* **-1.** [raté] incompetent. **-2.** JUR incapable person. ◇ *adj*: **~ de faire qqch** [inapte à] incapable of doing sthg; [dans l'impossibilité de] unable to do sthg.

incapacité [ɛ̃kapasite] *nf* **-1.** [impossibilité]: **~ à OU de faire qqch** inability to do sthg; **être dans l'~ de** to be unable to. **-2.** [invalidité] disability; **~ de travail** industrial disability. **-3.** JUR incapacity. **-4.** [incompétence] incompetence.

incarcération [ɛ̃karserasjɔ̃] *nf* incarceration.

incarcérer [ɛ̃karsere] [18] *vt* to incarcerate.

incarnation [ɛ̃karnasjɔ̃] *nf* incarnation.

incarné, -e [ɛ̃karne] *adj* incarnate.

incarner [ɛ̃karne] [3] *vt* **-1.** [personnifier] to be the incarnation of. **-2.** CIN & THÉÂTRE to play.
◆ **s'incarner** *vp* **-1.** RELIG to be OU become incarnate. **-2.** [se réaliser] to be incarnated. **-3.** MÉD [ongle] to become ingrown.

incartade [ɛ̃kartad] *nf* misdemeanour.

incassable [ɛ̃kasabl] *adj* unbreakable.

incendiaire [ɛ̃sɑ̃djer] ◇ *nmf* arsonist. ◇ *adj* [bombe] incendiary; *fig* inflammatory.

incendie [ɛ̃sɑ̃di] *nm* fire; *fig* flames (*pl*); **~ de forêt** forest fire.

incendier [ɛ̃sɑ̃dje] [9] *vt* **-1.** [mettre le feu à] to set alight, to set fire to. **-2.** *fig* [faire rougir] to make burn. **-3.** *fam* [réprimander] to tear a strip off.

incertain, -e [ɛ̃sɛrtɛ̃, ɛn] *adj* **-1.** [gén] uncertain; [temps] unsettled. **-2.** [vague - lumière] dim; [- contour] blurred.

incertitude [ɛ̃sɛrtityd] *nf* uncertainty; **être dans l'~** to be uncertain.

incessamment [ɛ̃sesamɑ̃] *adv* at any moment, any moment now.

incessant, -e [ɛ̃sesɑ̃, ɑ̃t] *adj* incessant.

incessible [ɛ̃sesibl] *adj* inalienable.

inceste [ɛ̃sɛst] *nm* incest.

incestueux, -euse [ɛ̃sɛstɥø, øz] ◇ *adj* **-1.** [liaison, parent] incestuous. **-2.** [enfant] born of incest. ◇ *nm, f* incestuous person.

inchangé, -e [ɛ̃ʃɑ̃ʒe] *adj* unchanged.

incidemment [ɛ̃sidamɑ̃] *adv* **-1.** [accidentellement] accidentally. **-2.** [entre parenthèses] in passing.

incidence [ɛ̃sidɑ̃s] *nf* **-1.** [conséquence] effect, impact (*U*). **-2.** FIN & PHYS incidence.

incident, -e [ɛ̃sidɑ̃, ɑ̃t] *adj* [accessoire] incidental.
◆ **incident** *nm* **-1.** [gén] incident; [ennui] hitch; **sans ~** without incident OU a hitch; **~ diplomatique** diplomatic incident; **~ de**

parcours (minor) setback. **-2.** JUR point of law.

incinérateur [ɛ̃sineratœr] *nm* incinerator.

incinération [ɛ̃sinerasjɔ̃] *nf* **-1.** [de corps] cremation. **-2.** [d'ordures] incineration.

incinérer [ɛ̃sinere] [18] *vt* **-1.** [corps] to cremate. **-2.** [ordures] to incinerate.

incise [ɛ̃siz] *nf* LING interpolated clause.

inciser [ɛ̃size] [3] *vt* to incise, to make an incision in.

incisif, -ive [ɛ̃sizif, iv] *adj* incisive.

◆ **incisive** *nf* incisor.

incision [ɛ̃sizjɔ̃] *nf* incision.

incitation [ɛ̃sitasjɔ̃] *nf* **-1.** [provocation]: ~ à qqch/à faire qqch incitement to sthg/to do sthg. **-2.** [encouragement]: ~ à qqch/à faire qqch incentive to sthg/to do sthg.

inciter [ɛ̃site] [3] *vt* **-1.** [provoquer]: ~ qqn à qqch/à faire qqch to incite sb to sthg/to do sthg. **-2.** [encourager]: ~ qqn à faire qqch to encourage sb to do sthg.

inclassable [ɛ̃klasabl] *adj* unclassifiable.

inclinable [ɛ̃klinabl] *adj* reclinable, reclining.

inclinaison [ɛ̃klinɛzɔ̃] *nf* **-1.** [pente] incline. **-2.** [de tête, chapeau] angle, tilt.

inclination [ɛ̃klinasjɔ̃] *nf* **-1.** [salut - de tête] nod; [- du corps entier] bow. **-2.** [tendance] inclination; avoir une ~ à to have an inclination OU a tendency to; avoir une ~ pour [aimer] to have a liking for. **-3.** *littéraire* [amour] (romantic) attachment.

incliner [ɛ̃kline] [3] ◇ *vt* **-1.** [pencher] to tilt, to lean. **-2.** [pousser]: ~ qqn à qqch/à faire qqch to incline sb to sthg/to do sthg. ◇ *vi:* ~ à qqch/à faire qqch to be inclined to sthg/to do sthg.

◆ **s'incliner** *vp* **-1.** [se pencher] to tilt, to lean. **-2.** [céder]: s'~ (devant) to give in (to), to yield (to). **-3.** [respecter]: s'~ devant to bow down before.

inclure [ɛ̃klyr] [96] *vt* [mettre dedans]: ~ qqch dans qqch to include sthg in sthg; [joindre] to enclose sthg with sthg.

inclus, -e [ɛ̃kly, yz] ◇ *pp* → **inclure.** ◇ *adj* **-1.** [compris - taxe, frais] included; [joint - lettre] enclosed; [y compris]: **jusqu'à la page 10** ~e up to and including page 10. **-2.** [dent] impacted. **-3.** MATHS: **être** ~ **dans** to be a subset of.

inclusion [ɛ̃klyzjɔ̃] *nf* inclusion.

inclusivement [ɛ̃klyzivmɑ̃] *adv* inclusive.

incoercible [ɛ̃kɔɛrsibl] *adj* *sout* uncontrollable.

incognito [ɛ̃kɔɲito] ◇ *adv* incognito. ◇ *nm:* **garder l'**~ to remain incognito.

incohérence [ɛ̃kɔerɑ̃s] *nf* [de paroles] incoherence; [d'actes] inconsistency.

incohérent, -e [ɛ̃kɔerɑ̃, ɑ̃t] *adj* [paroles] incoherent; [actes] inconsistent.

incollable [ɛ̃kɔlabl] *adj* **-1.** [riz] nonstick. **-2.** *fam* [imbattable] unbeatable.

incolore [ɛ̃kɔlɔr] *adj* colourless.

incomber [ɛ̃kɔ̃be] [3] *vi:* ~ à qqn to be sb's responsibility; **il incombe à qqn de faire qqch** (*emploi impersonnel*) it falls to sb OU it is incumbent on sb to do sthg.

incombustible [ɛ̃kɔ̃bystibl] *adj* incombustible.

incommensurable [ɛ̃kɔmɑ̃syrabl] *adj* **-1.** [immense] immeasurable. **-2.** MATHS: ~ **avec** incommensurable with.

incommodant, -e [ɛ̃kɔmɔdɑ̃, ɑ̃t] *adj* unpleasant.

incommode [ɛ̃kɔmɔd] *adj* **-1.** [heure, lieu] inconvenient. **-2.** [position, chaise] uncomfortable.

incommoder [ɛ̃kɔmɔde] [3] *vt sout* to trouble.

incommodité [ɛ̃kɔmɔdite] *nf* **-1.** [d'installation] impracticality. **-2.** [malaise] indisposition. **-3.** [de situation] awkwardness.

incommunicable [ɛ̃kɔmynikabl] *adj* **-1.** [indicible] inexpressible. **-2.** JUR nontransferable.

incomparable [ɛ̃kɔ̃parabl] *adj* **-1.** [différent] not comparable. **-2.** [sans pareil] incomparable.

incomparablement [ɛ̃kɔ̃parabləmɑ̃] *adv* incomparably.

incompatibilité [ɛ̃kɔ̃patibilite] *nf* incompatibility; ~ **d'humeur** (mutual) incompatibility.

incompatible [ɛ̃kɔ̃patibl] *adj* incompatible.

incompétence [ɛ̃kɔ̃petɑ̃s] *nf* **-1.** [incapacité] incompetence. **-2.** [ignorance]: ~ **en qqch** ignorance about sthg.

incompétent, -e [ɛ̃kɔ̃petɑ̃, ɑ̃t] *adj* **-1.** [incapable] incompetent. **-2.** [ignorant]: ~ **en qqch** ignorant about sthg.

incomplet, -ète [ɛ̃kɔ̃plɛ, ɛt] *adj* incomplete.

incomplètement [ɛ̃kɔ̃plɛtmɑ̃] *adv* incompletely.

incompréhensible [ɛ̃kɔ̃preɑ̃sibl] *adj* incomprehensible.

incompréhensif, -ive [ɛ̃kɔ̃preɑ̃sif, iv] *adj* unsympathetic.

incompréhension [ɛ̃kɔ̃preɑ̃sjɔ̃] *nf* lack of understanding.

incompressible [ɛ̃kɔ̃presibl] *adj* **-1.** TECHNOL incompressible. **-2.** *fig* [dépenses] impossible to reduce. **-3.** JUR → **peine.**

incompris, -e [ɛ̃kɔ̃pri, iz] ◇ *adj* misunderstood, not appreciated. ◇ *nm, f* misunderstood person.

inconcevable [ɛ̃kɔ̃svabl] *adj* unimaginable.

inconciliable [ɛ̃kɔ̃siljabl] *adj* irreconcilable.

inconditionnel, -elle [ɛ̃kɔ̃disjɔnɛl] ◇ *adj* -1. [total] unconditional. -2. [fervent] ardent. ◇ *nm, f* ardent supporter OU admirer.

inconditionnellement [ɛ̃kɔ̃disjɔnɛlmɑ̃] *adv* unconditionally.

inconduite [ɛ̃kɔ̃dɥit] *nf littéraire* scandalous behaviour.

inconfort [ɛ̃kɔ̃fɔr] *nm* discomfort.

inconfortable [ɛ̃kɔ̃fɔrtabl] *adj* uncomfortable.

incongru, -e [ɛ̃kɔ̃gry] *adj* -1. [malséant] unseemly, inappropriate. -2. [bizarre] incongruous.

incongruité [ɛ̃kɔ̃gryite] *nf* -1. [qualité bizarre] incongruity (U). -2. [parole malséante] unseemly remark.

inconnu, -e [ɛ̃kɔny] ◇ *adj* unknown. ◇ *nm, f* stranger; **la personne qui a eu le prix Goncourt cette année est un illustre ~ hum** no one has ever heard of the renowned winner of the prix Goncourt this year.

◆ **inconnue** *nf* -1. MATHS unknown. -2. [variable] unknown (factor).

inconsciemment [ɛ̃kɔ̃sjamɑ̃] *adv* -1. [sans en avoir conscience] unconsciously, unwittingly. -2. [à la légère] thoughtlessly.

inconscience [ɛ̃kɔ̃sjɑ̃s] *nf* -1. [évanouissement] unconsciousness. -2. [légèreté] thoughtlessness.

inconscient, -e [ɛ̃kɔ̃sjɑ̃, ɑ̃t] *adj* -1. [évanoui, machinal] unconscious. -2. [irresponsable] thoughtless.

◆ **inconscient** *nm*: l'~ the unconscious.

inconséquence [ɛ̃kɔ̃sekɑ̃s] *nf* inconsistency.

inconséquent, -e [ɛ̃kɔ̃sekɑ̃, ɑ̃t] *adj* inconsistent.

inconsidéré, -e [ɛ̃kɔ̃sidere] *adj* ill-considered, thoughtless.

inconsistant, -e [ɛ̃kɔ̃sistɑ̃, ɑ̃t] *adj* -1. [aliment] thin, watery. -2. [caractère] frivolous.

inconsolable [ɛ̃kɔ̃sɔlabl] *adj* inconsolable.

inconstance [ɛ̃kɔ̃stɑ̃s] *nf* fickleness.

inconstant, -e [ɛ̃kɔ̃stɑ̃, ɑ̃t] ◇ *adj* fickle. ◇ *nm, f vieilli* fickle heart.

incontestable [ɛ̃kɔ̃tɛstabl] *adj* unquestionable, indisputable.

incontestablement [ɛ̃kɔ̃tɛstabləmɑ̃] *adv* unquestionably, indisputably.

incontesté, -e [ɛ̃kɔ̃tɛste] *adj* uncontested, unchallenged.

incontinence [ɛ̃kɔ̃tinɑ̃s] *nf* -1. MÉD incontinence. -2. [excès] lack of restraint.

incontinent, -e [ɛ̃kɔ̃tinɑ̃, ɑ̃t] *adj* -1. MÉD incontinent. -2. [sans retenue] unrestrained.

◆ **incontinent** *adv littéraire* forthwith.

incontournable [ɛ̃kɔ̃turnabl] *adj* unavoidable.

inconvenance [ɛ̃kɔ̃vnɑ̃s] *nf* impropriety.

inconvenant, -e [ɛ̃kɔ̃vnɑ̃, ɑ̃t] *adj* improper, unseemly.

inconvénient [ɛ̃kɔ̃venjɑ̃] *nm* -1. [obstacle] problem; **si vous n'y voyez pas d'~** if that is convenient (for you), if you have no objection. -2. [désavantage] disadvantage, drawback. -3. [risque] risk.

incorporation [ɛ̃kɔrpɔrasjɔ̃] *nf* -1. [intégration] incorporation; CULIN mixing, blending. -2. [MIL] enlistment.

incorporé, -e [ɛ̃kɔrpɔre] *adj* [integré] built-in.

incorporel, -elle [ɛ̃kɔrpɔrɛl] *adj* -1. [immatériel] incorporeal. -2. JUR intangible.

incorporer [ɛ̃kɔrpɔre] [3] *vt* -1. [gén] to incorporate; ~ **qqch dans** to incorporate sthg into; ~ **qqch à** CULIN to mix OU blend sthg into. -2. MIL to enlist.

◆ **s'incorporer** *vp*: **s'~ à qqch** to become part of sthg.

incorrect, -e [ɛ̃kɔrɛkt] *adj* -1. [faux] incorrect. -2. [inconvenant] inappropriate; [impoli] rude. -3. [déloyal] unfair; **être ~ avec qqn** to treat sb unfairly.

incorrection [ɛ̃kɔrɛksjɔ̃] *nf* -1. [impolitesse] impropriety. -2. [de langage] grammatical mistake. -3. [malhonnêteté] dishonesty.

incorrigible [ɛ̃kɔriʒibl] *adj* incorrigible.

incorruptible [ɛ̃kɔryptibl] *adj* incorruptible.

incrédule [ɛ̃kredyl] ◇ *nmf* -1. [sceptique] sceptic. -2. RELIG unbeliever. ◇ *adj* -1. [sceptique] incredulous, sceptical. -2. RELIG unbelieving.

incrédulité [ɛ̃kredylite] *nf* -1. [scepticisme] incredulity, scepticism. -2. RELIG unbelief, lack of belief.

increvable [ɛ̃krəvabl] *adj* -1. [ballon, pneu] puncture-proof. -2. *fam fig* [personne] tireless; [machine] that will withstand rough treatment.

incriminer [ɛ̃krimine] [3] *vt* -1. [personne] to incriminate. -2. [conduite] to condemn.

incroyable [ɛ̃krwajabl] *adj* incredible, unbelievable.

incroyablement [ɛ̃krwajabləmɑ̃] *adv* incredibly, unbelievably.

incroyant, -e [ɛ̃krwajɑ̃, ɑ̃t] ◇ *adj* unbelieving. ◇ *nm, f* unbeliever.

incrustation [ɛ̃krystasjɔ̃] *nf* **-1.** [ornement] inlay. **-2.** [dépôt] deposit, fur (*U*).

incruster [ɛ̃kryste] [3] *vt* **-1.** [insérer]: ~ qqch dans qqch to inlay sthg into sthg. **-2.** [décorer]: ~ qqch de qqch to inlay sthg with sthg. **-3.** [couvrir d'un dépôt] to fur up. ◆ **s'incruster** *vp* **-1.** [s'insérer]: s'~ dans qqch to become embedded in sthg. **-2.** [chaudière] to fur up. **-3.** *fam fig* [personne] to take root.

incubateur, -trice [ɛ̃kybatœr, tris] *adj* incubating. ◆ **incubateur** *nm* incubator.

incubation [ɛ̃kybasjɔ̃] *nf* [d'œuf, de maladie] incubation; *fig* hatching.

inculpation [ɛ̃kylpasjɔ̃] *nf* charge; sous l'~ de on a charge of.

inculpé, -e [ɛ̃kylpe] *nm, f:* l'~ the accused.

inculper [ɛ̃kylpe] [3] *vt* to charge; ~ qqn de to charge sb with.

inculquer [ɛ̃kulke] [3] *vt:* ~ qqch à qqn to instil sthg in sb.

inculte [ɛ̃kylt] *adj* **-1.** [terre] uncultivated. **-2.** [barbe] unkempt. **-3.** *péj* [personne] uneducated.

inculture [ɛ̃kyltyr] *nf* **-1.** [intellectuelle] lack of education. **-2.** [de terre] lack of cultivation.

incurable [ɛ̃kyrabl] ◇ *nmf* incurably ill person. ◇ *adj* incurable.

incurie [ɛ̃kyri] *nf* negligence.

incursion [ɛ̃kyrsjɔ̃] *nf* incursion, foray.

incurver [ɛ̃kyrve] [3] *vt* to curve. ◆ **s'incurver** *vp* to curve, to bend.

Inde [ɛ̃d] *nf:* l'~ India.

indéboulonnable [ɛ̃debylɔnabl] *adj:* il est ~ *hum* they'll never be able to sack him.

indécence [ɛ̃desɑ̃s] *nf* **-1.** [impudeur, immoralité] indecency. **-2.** [propos] indecent remark; [action] indecent act.

indécent, -e [ɛ̃desɑ̃, ɑ̃t] *adj* **-1.** [impudique] indecent. **-2.** [immoral] scandalous.

indéchiffrable [ɛ̃deʃifrabl] *adj* **-1.** [texte, écriture] indecipherable. **-2.** [énigme] inexplicable. **-3.** *fig* [regard] inscrutable, impenetrable.

indéchirable [ɛ̃deʃirabl] *adj* tear-proof.

indécis, -e [ɛ̃desi, iz] ◇ *adj* **-1.** [personne - sur le moment] undecided; [- de nature] indecisive. **-2.** [sourire] vague. **-3.** [résultat] uncertain. ◇ *nm, f* indecisive person. ◆ **indécis** *nmpl* [dans sondage] don't knows.

indécision [ɛ̃desizjɔ̃] *nf* indecision; [perpétuelle] indecisiveness.

indécrottable [ɛ̃dekrɔtabl] *adj fam* **-1.** [borné] incredibly dumb. **-2.** [incorrigible] hopeless.

indéfectible [ɛ̃defɛktibl] *adj* indestructible.

indéfendable [ɛ̃defɑ̃dabl] *adj* indefensible.

indéfini, -e [ɛ̃defini] *adj* **-1.** [quantité, pronom] indefinite. **-2.** [sentiment] vague. ◆ **indéfini** *nm* GRAM indefinite.

indéfiniment [ɛ̃definimɑ̃] *adv* indefinitely.

indéfinissable [ɛ̃definisabl] *adj* indefinable.

indéformable [ɛ̃defɔrmabl] *adj* that retains its shape.

indélébile [ɛ̃delebil] *adj* indelible.

indélicat, -e [ɛ̃delika, at] *adj* **-1.** [mufle] indelicate. **-2.** [malhonnête] dishonest.

indémaillable [ɛ̃demajabl] ◇ *nm* run-resistant material. ◇ *adj* run-resistant.

indemne [ɛ̃dɛmn] *adj* unscathed, unharmed; sortir ~ de qqch to come out of sthg unscathed ou unharmed.

indemnisation [ɛ̃dɛmnizasjɔ̃] *nf* compensation.

indemniser [ɛ̃dɛmnize] [3] *vt:* ~ qqn de qqch [perte, préjudice] to compensate sb for sthg; [frais] to reimburse sb for sthg.

indemnité [ɛ̃dɛmnite] *nf* **-1.** [de perte, préjudice] compensation; ~ de licenciement redundancy payment. **-2.** [de frais] allowance; ~ journalière daily allowance; ~ de logement accommodation allowance. **-3.** [allocation]: ~ parlementaire MP's *Br* ou Congressman's *Am* salary.

indémodable [ɛ̃demɔdabl] *adj:* ce style est indémodable this style doesn't date.

indéniable [ɛ̃denjabl] *adj* undeniable.

indéniablement [ɛ̃denjablemɑ̃] *adv* undeniably.

indépendamment [ɛ̃depɑ̃damɑ̃] *adv:* ~ de [abstraction faite de] regardless ou irrespective of; [outre] apart from; [sans rapport avec] independently of.

indépendance [ɛ̃depɑ̃dɑ̃s] *nf* independence; accéder à l'~ to gain independence.

indépendant, -e [ɛ̃depɑ̃dɑ̃, ɑ̃t] *adj* **-1.** [gén] independent; [entrée] separate; ~ de indépendent of; ~ de ma volonté beyond my control. **-2.** [travailleur] self-employed.

indépendantiste [ɛ̃depɑ̃dɑ̃tist] ◇ *nmf* advocate of political independence. ◇ *adj* independence (*avant n*).

indéracinable [ɛ̃derasinabl] *adj* [arbre] impossible to uproot; *fig* ineradicable.

indescriptible [ɛ̃dɛskriptibl] *adj* indescribable.

indésirable [ɛ̃dezirabl] *nmf & adj* undesirable.

indestructible [ɛ̃dɛstryktibl] *adj* indestructible.

indéterminé, -e [ɛ̃detɛrmine] *adj* **-1.** [indéfini] indeterminate, indefinite. **-2.** [vague] vague. **-3.** [personne] undecided.

indétrônable [ɛ̃detronabl] *adj* inoustable.

index [ɛ̃dɛks] *nm* **-1.** [doigt] index finger. **-2.** [aiguille] pointer, needle. **-3.** [registre] index; **mettre à l'~** *fig* to blacklist.

indexation [ɛ̃dɛksasjɔ̃] *nf* indexing.

indexer [ɛ̃dɛkse] [4] *vt* **-1.** ÉCON: **~** qqch sur qqch to index sthg to sthg. **-2.** [livre] to index.

indicateur, -trice [ɛ̃dikatœr, tris] *adj*: **poteau ~** signpost; **panneau ~** road sign.
◆ **indicateur** *nm* **-1.** [guide] directory, guide; **~ des chemins de fer** railway timetable. **-2.** TECHNOL gauge; **~ d'altitude** altimeter; **~ de vitesse** speedometer. **-3.** ÉCON indicator. **-4.** [de police] informer.

indicatif, -ive [ɛ̃dikatif, iv] *adj* indicative.
◆ **indicatif** *nm* **-1.** RADIO & TÉLÉ signature tune. **-2.** [code]: **~ (téléphonique)** dialling code *Br*, dial code *Am*. **-3.** GRAM: **l'~** the indicative.

indication [ɛ̃dikasjɔ̃] *nf* **-1.** [mention] indication. **-2.** [renseignement] information (U). **-3.** [directive] instruction; THÉÂTRE direction; **sauf ~ contraire** unless otherwise instructed.

indice [ɛ̃dis] *nm* **-1.** [signe] sign. **-2.** [dans une enquête] clue. **-3.** [taux] rating; **~ du coût de la vie** ÉCON cost-of-living index; **~ des prix** ÉCON price index. **-4.** MATHS index.

indicible [ɛ̃disibl] *adj* inexpressible.

indien, -ienne [ɛ̃djɛ̃, jɛn] *adj* **-1.** [d'Inde] Indian. **-2.** [d'Amérique] American Indian, Native American.
◆ **Indien, -ienne** *nm, f* **-1.** [d'Inde] Indian. **-2.** [d'Amérique] American Indian, Native American.

indifféremment [ɛ̃diferamɑ̃] *adv* indifferently.

indifférence [ɛ̃diferɑ̃s] *nf* indifference.

indifférencié, -e [ɛ̃diferɑ̃sje] *adj* undifferentiated.

indifférent, -e [ɛ̃diferɑ̃, ɑ̃t] ◇ *adj* **-1.** [gén]: **~ à** indifferent to. **-2.** *sout* [égal] immaterial. ◇ *nm, f* unconcerned person.

indifférer [ɛ̃difere] [18] *vt* to be a matter of indifference to.

indigence [ɛ̃diʒɑ̃s] *nf* poverty.

indigène [ɛ̃diʒɛn] ◇ *nmf* native. ◇ *adj* [peuple] native; [faune, flore] indigenous.

indigent, -e [ɛ̃diʒɑ̃, ɑ̃t] ◇ *adj* [pauvre] destitute, poverty-stricken; *fig* [intellectuellement]

impoverished. ◇ *nm, f* poor person; **les ~s** the poor, the destitute.

indigeste [ɛ̃diʒɛst] *adj* indigestible.

indigestion [ɛ̃diʒɛstjɔ̃] *nf* **-1.** [alimentaire] indigestion; **avoir une ~** to have indigestion. **-2.** *fig* [saturation] surfeit; **avoir une ~ de** to have had one's fill of.

indignation [ɛ̃diɲasjɔ̃] *nf* indignation.

indigne [ɛ̃diɲ] *adj*: **~ (de)** unworthy (of).

indigné, -e [ɛ̃diɲe] *adj* indignant.

indigner [ɛ̃diɲe] [3] *vt* to make indignant.
◆ **s'indigner** *vp*: **s'~ de** OU **contre qqch** to get indignant about sthg; **s'~ que** (+ *subjonctif*) to be indignant that.

indigo [ɛ̃digo] ◇ *nm* indigo. ◇ *adj inv* indigo (blue).

indiqué, -e [ɛ̃dike] *adj* **-1.** [convenable] appropriate. **-2.** [recommandé] advisable; **ce n'est pas très ~** it's not very advisable. **-3.** [fixé] appointed.

indiquer [ɛ̃dike] [3] *vt* **-1.** [désigner] to indicate, to point out; **~ qqn/qqch du doigt** to point at sb/sthg, to point sb/sthg out; **~ qqn/qqch du regard** to glance towards sb/sthg. **-2.** [afficher, montrer - suj: carte, pendule, aiguille] to show, to indicate. **-3.** [recommander]: **~ qqn/qqch à qqn** to tell sb of sb/sthg, to suggest sb/sthg to sb. **-4.** [dire, renseigner sur] to tell; **~ à qqn comment faire qqch** to tell sb how to do sthg; **pourriez-vous m'~ l'heure?** could you tell me the time? **-5.** [fixer - heure, date, lieu] to name, to indicate. **-6.** [dénoter] to indicate, to point to.

indirect, -e [ɛ̃dirɛkt] *adj* [gén] indirect; [itinéraire] roundabout.

indirectement [ɛ̃dirɛktəmɑ̃] *adv* indirectly.

indiscipline [ɛ̃disiplin] *nf* lack of discipline.

indiscipliné, -e [ɛ̃disipline] *adj* **-1.** [écolier, esprit] undisciplined, unruly. **-2.** *fig* [mèches de cheveux] unmanageable.

indiscret, -ète [ɛ̃diskrɛ, ɛt] ◇ *adj* indiscreet; [curieux] inquisitive. ◇ *nm, f* indiscreet person.

indiscrètement [ɛ̃diskrɛtmɑ̃] *adv* indiscreetly; [avec curiosité] inquisitively.

indiscrétion [ɛ̃diskresjɔ̃] *nf* indiscretion; [curiosité] curiosity; **sans ~** ... without wishing to be indiscreet ....

indiscutable [ɛ̃diskytabl] *adj* unquestionable, indisputable.

indiscutablement [ɛ̃diskytabləmɑ̃] *adv* unquestionably, indisputably.

indiscuté, -e [ɛ̃diskyte] *adj* undisputed, unquestioned.

indispensable [ɛ̃dispɑ̃sabl] ◇ *adj* indispensable, essential; ~ à indispensable to, essential to; **il est** ~ **que** (+ *subjonctif*) it is essential OU vital that; **il est** ~ **de faire qqch** it is essential OU vital to do sthg. ◇ *nm*: **l'**~ the essentials (*pl*).

indisponibilité [ɛ̃dispɔnibilite] *nf* unavailability.

indisponible [ɛ̃dispɔnibl] *adj* unavailable.

indisposé, -e [ɛ̃dispoze] *adj* [malade] unwell; **être** ~**e** [femme] to be indisposed.

indisposer [ɛ̃dispoze] [3] *vt* **-1.** *sout* [rendre malade] to indispose. **-2.** *littéraire* [fâcher] to vex.

indisposition [ɛ̃dispozisjɔ̃] *nf* **-1.** [malaise] indisposition. **-2.** [règles] period.

indissociable [ɛ̃disɔsjabl] *adj* indissociable.

indissoluble [ɛ̃disɔlybl] *adj* indissoluble.

indistinct, -e [ɛ̃distɛ̃(kt), ɛ̃kt] *adj* indistinct; [souvenir] hazy.

indistinctement [ɛ̃distɛ̃ktəmɑ̃] *adv* **-1.** [confusément] indistinctly. **-2.** [indifféremment] equally well.

individu [ɛ̃dividy] *nm* individual.

individualiste [ɛ̃dividɥalist] ◇ *nmf* individualist. ◇ *adj* individualistic.

individualité [ɛ̃dividɥalite] *nf* **-1.** [personne] individual. **-2.** [unicité, originalité] individuality.

individuel, -elle [ɛ̃dividɥɛl] *adj* individual.

individuellement [ɛ̃dividɥɛlmɑ̃] *adv* individually.

indivis, -e [ɛ̃divi, iz] *adj* **-1.** [propriété] undivided. **-2.** [héritier] joint; **par** ~ jointly.

indivisible [ɛ̃divizibl] *adj* indivisible.

Indochine [ɛ̃dɔʃin] *nf*: **l'**~ Indochina; **la guerre d'**~ the Indochinese War.

indo-européen, -enne [ɛ̃dɔœrɔpeɛ̃, ɛn] (*mpl* **indo-européens,** *fpl* **indo-européennes**) *adj* Indo-European.

indolence [ɛ̃dɔlɑ̃s] *nf* **-1.** [de personne] indolence, lethargy. **-2.** [d'organisation] apathy. **-3.** [de geste, regard] languidness.

indolent, -e [ɛ̃dɔlɑ̃, ɑ̃t] *adj* **-1.** [personne] indolent, lethargic. **-2.** [geste, regard] languid.

indolore [ɛ̃dɔlɔr] *adj* painless.

indomptable [ɛ̃dɔ̃tabl] *adj* **-1.** [animal] untamable. **-2.** [personne] indomitable. **-3.** [sentiment] uncontrollable.

Indonésie [ɛ̃dɔnezi] *nf* Indonesia.

indonésien, -ienne [ɛ̃dɔnezjɛ̃, jɛn] *adj* Indonesian.

◆ **indonésien** *nm* [langue] Indonesian.

◆ **Indonésien, -ienne** *nm, f* Indonesian.

indu, -e [ɛ̃dy] *adj* **-1.** [heure] ungodly, unearthly. **-2.** [dépenses, remarque] unwarranted.

indubitable [ɛ̃dybitabl] *adj* indubitable, undoubted; **il est** ~ **que** it is disputable OU beyond doubt that.

indubitablement [ɛ̃dybitabləmɑ̃] *adv* undoubtedly, indubitably.

induction [ɛ̃dyksjɔ̃] *nf* induction; **par** ~ by induction.

induire [ɛ̃dɥir] [98] *vt* to induce; ~ **qqn à faire qqch** to induce sb to do sthg; ~ **qqn en erreur** to mislead sb; **en** ~ **que** to infer OU gather that.

induit, -e [ɛ̃dɥi, ɥit] ◇ *pp* → **induire.** ◇ *adj* **-1.** [consécutif] resulting. **-2.** ÉLECTR induced.

indulgence [ɛ̃dylʒɑ̃s] *nf* [de juge] leniency; [de parent] indulgence; **avec** ~ leniently/indulgently.

indulgent, -e [ɛ̃dylʒɑ̃, ɑ̃t] *adj* [juge] lenient; [parent] indulgent.

indûment [ɛ̃dymɑ̃] *adv* unduly.

industrialisation [ɛ̃dystrijalizasjɔ̃] *nf* industrialization.

industrialiser [ɛ̃dystrijalize] [3] *vt* to industrialize.

◆ **s'industrialiser** *vp* to become industrialized.

industrie [ɛ̃dystri] *nf* industry; ~ **alimentaire** food industry; ~ **automobile** car industry; ~ **chimique** chemical industry; ~ **lourde** heavy industry.

industriel, -ielle [ɛ̃dystrijɛl] *adj* industrial.

◆ **industriel** *nm* industrialist.

industrieux, -ieuse [ɛ̃dystrijø, jøz] *adj* *littéraire* industrious.

inébranlable [inebrɑ̃labl] *adj* **-1.** [roc] solid, immovable. **-2.** *fig* [conviction] unshakeable.

INED, Ined [inɛd] (*abr de* **Institut national d'études démographiques**) *nm national institute for demographic research.*

inédit, -e [inedi, it] *adj* **-1.** [texte] unpublished. **-2.** [trouvaille] novel, original.

◆ **inédit** *nm* unpublished work.

ineffable [inefabl] *adj* ineffable.

ineffaçable [inefasabl] *adj* indelible.

inefficace [inefikas] *adj* **-1.** [personne, machine] inefficient. **-2.** [solution, remède, mesure] ineffective.

inefficacité [inefikasite] *nf* **-1.** [de personne, machine] inefficiency. **-2.** [de solution, remède, mesure] ineffectiveness.

inégal, -e, -aux [inegal, o] *adj* **-1.** [différent, disproportionné] unequal. **-2.** [irrégulier] uneven. **-3.** [changeant] changeable; [artiste, travail] erratic.

inégalable [inegalabl] *adj* matchless.

inégalé, -e [inegale] *adj* unequalled.

inégalement [inegalmã] *adv* [gén] unequally; [irrégulièrement] unevenly.

inégalité [inegalite] *nf* -1. [injustice, disproportion] inequality; ~s sociales social inequalities. -2. [différence] difference, disparity. -3. [irrégularité] unevenness. -4. [d'humeur] changeability.

inélégant, -e [inelegã, ãt] *adj* -1. [dans l'habillement] inelegant. -2. *fig* [indélicat] discourteous.

inéligible [ineliʒibl] *adj* ineligible.

inéluctable [inelyktabl] *adj* inescapable.

inéluctablement [inelyktabləmã] *adv* inescapably.

inénarrable [inenarabl] *adj* very funny.

inepte [inɛpt] *adj* inept.

ineptie [inɛpsi] *nf* -1. [bêtise] ineptitude. -2. [chose idiote] nonsense (*U*); **dire des ~s** to talk nonsense.

inépuisable [inepɥizabl] *adj* inexhaustible.

inerte [inɛrt] *adj* -1. [corps, membre] lifeless. -2. [personne] passive, inert. -3. PHYS inert.

inertie [inɛrsi] *nf* -1. [manque de réaction] apathy, inertia. -2. PHYS inertia.

inespéré, -e [inɛspere] *adj* unexpected, unhoped-for.

inesthétique [inɛstetik] *adj* unaesthetic.

inestimable [inɛstimabl] *adj*: **d'une valeur ~** priceless; *fig* invaluable.

inévitable [inevitabl] *adj* [obstacle] unavoidable; [conséquence] inevitable.

inévitablement [inevitabləmã] *adv* inevitably.

inexact, -e [inegza(kt), akt] *adj* -1. [faux, incomplet] inaccurate, inexact. -2. [en retard] unpunctual.

inexactitude [inɛgzaktityd] *nf* -1. [erreur, imprécision] inaccuracy. -2. [retard] unpunctuality.

inexcusable [inɛkskyzabl] *adj* unforgivable, inexcusable.

inexistant, -e [inɛgzistã, ãt] *adj* nonexistent.

inexistence [inɛgzistãs] *nf* nonexistence.

inexorable [inɛgzɔrabl] *adj* inexorable.

inexorablement [inɛgzɔrabləmã] *adv* inexorably.

inexpérience [inɛksperjãs] *nf* lack of experience, inexperience.

inexpérimenté, -e [inɛksperimãte] *adj* -1. [personne] inexperienced. -2. [gestes] inexpert. -3. [produit] untested.

inexplicable [inɛksplikabl] *adj* inexplicable, unexplainable.

inexpliqué, -e [inɛksplike] *adj* unexplained.

inexploré, -e [inɛksplɔre] *adj litt* & *fig* unexplored; [mers] uncharted.

inexpressif, -ive [inɛkspresif, iv] *adj* inexpressive.

inexprimable [inɛksprimabl] *adj* inexpressible.

inexprimé, -e [inɛksprime] *adj* unexpressed.

inexpugnable [inɛkspygnabl] *adj* impregnable.

inextensible [inɛkstãsibl] *adj* -1. [matériau] unstretchable. -2. [étoffe] non-stretch.

inextinguible [inɛkstɛ̃gibl] ·*adj* [passion] inextinguishable; [soif] unquenchable; [rire] uncontrollable.

in extremis [inɛkstremis] *adv* at the last minute.

inextricable [inɛkstrikabl] *adj* -1. [fouillis] inextricable. -2. *fig* [affaire, mystère] that cannot be unravelled.

inextricablement [inɛkstrikabləmã] *adv* inextricably.

infaillible [ɛ̃fajibl] *adj* [personne, méthode] infallible; [instinct] unerring.

infaisable [ɛ̃fəzabl] *adj* unfeasible.

infamant, -e [ɛ̃famã, ãt] *adj* [marché] dishonourable; [propos] defamatory.

infâme [ɛ̃fam] *adj* -1. [ignoble] despicable. -2. *hum* & *littéraire* [dégoûtant] vile.

infamie [ɛ̃fami] *nf* infamy.

infanterie [ɛ̃fãtri] *nf* infantry.

infanticide [ɛ̃fãtisid] ◇ *nmf* infanticide, child-killer. ◇ *adj* infanticidal.

infantile [ɛ̃fãtil] *adj* -1. [maladie] childhood (*avant n*). -2. [médecine] for children. -3. [comportement] infantile.

infantiliser [ɛ̃fãtilize] [3] *vt* to treat like a child.

infarctus [ɛ̃farktys] *nm* infarction, infarct; ~ **du myocarde** coronary thrombosis, myocardial infarction.

infatigable [ɛ̃fatigabl] *adj* -1. [personne] tireless. -2. [attitude] untiring.

infatué, -e [ɛ̃fatɥe] *adj péj* & *sout*: ~ **de** conceited about; ~ **de soi-même** self-important.

infect, -e [ɛ̃fɛkt] *adj* -1. [dégoûtant] vile. -2. *littéraire* [marais] foul.

infecter [ɛ̃fɛkte] [4] *vt* -1. [eau] to contaminate. -2. [plaie] to infect. -3. [empoisonner] to poison.

◆ **s'infecter** *vp* to become infected, to turn septic.

infectieux, **-ieuse** [ɛ̃fɛksjø, jøz] *adj* infectious.

infection [ɛ̃fɛksjɔ̃] *nf* **-1.** MÉD infection. **-2.** *fig* & *péj* [puanteur] stench.

inféoder [ɛ̃feɔde] [3]
◆ **s'inféoder** *vp*: **s'~** à to pledge one's allegiance to.

inférer [ɛ̃fere] [18] *vt littéraire*: ~ qqch de qqch to infer sthg from sthg.

inférieur, **-ieure** [ɛ̃ferjœr] ◇ *adj* **-1.** [qui est en bas] **lower. -2.** [dans une hiérarchie] inferior; ~ à [qualité] inferior to; [quantité] less than; ~ **ou égal à 8** MATHS less than or equal to 8. ◇ *nm*, *f* inferior.

infériorité [ɛ̃ferjɔrite] *nf* inferiority.

infernal, **-e**, **-aux** [ɛ̃fɛrnal, o] *adj* **-1.** [personne] fiendish. **-2.** *fig* [bruit, chaleur, rythme] infernal; [vision] diabolical.

infester [ɛ̃fɛste] [3] *vt* to infest; être infesté de [rats, moustiques] to be infested with; [touristes] to be overrun by.

infidèle [ɛ̃fidɛl] ◇ *adj* **-1.** [mari, femme, ami]: ~ (à) unfaithful (to). **-2.** [traducteur, historien] inaccurate. **-3.** RELIG & *vieilli* infidel. ◇ *nmf* RELIG & *vieilli* infidel.

infidélité [ɛ̃fidelite] *nf* **-1.** [trahison] infidelity; faire des ~s à to be unfaithful to. **-2.** [de traduction] inaccuracy. **-3.** [de mémoire] unreliability.

infiltration [ɛ̃filtrasjɔ̃] *nf* infiltration.

infiltrer [ɛ̃filtre] [3] *vt* to infiltrate.
◆ **s'infiltrer** *vp* **-1.** [pluie, lumière]: **s'~ par/dans** to filter through/into. **-2.** [hommes, idées] to infiltrate.

infime [ɛ̃fim] *adj* minute, infinitesimal.

infini, **-e** [ɛ̃fini] *adj* **-1.** [sans bornes] infinite, boundless. **-2.** MATHS, PHILO & RELIG infinite. **-3.** *fig* [interminable] endless, interminable.
◆ **infini** *nm* infinity.
◆ **à l'infini** *loc adv* **-1.** MATHS to infinity. **-2.** [discourir] ad infinitum, endlessly.

infiniment [ɛ̃finimɑ̃] *adv* extremely, immensely.

infinité [ɛ̃finite] *nf* infinity, infinite number.

infinitésimal, **-e**, **-aux** [ɛ̃finitezimal, o] *adj* infinitesimal.

infinitif, **-ive** [ɛ̃finitif, iv] *adj* infinitive.
◆ **infinitif** *nm* infinitive.

infirme [ɛ̃firm] ◇ *adj* [handicapé] disabled; [avec l'âge] infirm. ◇ *nmf* disabled person; ~ de guerre disabled ex-serviceman (*f* ex-servicewoman).

infirmer [ɛ̃firme] [3] *vt* **-1.** [démentir] to invalidate. **-2.** JUR to annul.

infirmerie [ɛ̃firmɔri] *nf* infirmary.

infirmier, **-ière** [ɛ̃firmje, jɛr] *nm*, *f* nurse; ~ diplômé ≃ state-registered nurse.

infirmité [ɛ̃firmite] *nf* [handicap] disability; [de vieillesse] infirmity.

inflammable [ɛ̃flamabl] *adj* inflammable, flammable.

inflammation [ɛ̃flamasjɔ̃] *nf* inflammation.

inflation [ɛ̃flasjɔ̃] *nf* ÉCON inflation; *fig* increase.

inflationniste [ɛ̃flasjɔnist] *adj* & *nmf* inflationist.

infléchir [ɛ̃fleʃir] [32] *vt fig* [politique] to modify.
◆ **s'infléchir** *vp* **-1.** [route] to bend. **-2.** *fig* [politique] to shift.

inflexible [ɛ̃flɛksibl] *adj* inflexible.

inflexion [ɛ̃flɛksjɔ̃] *nf* **-1.** [de tête] nod. **-2.** [de voix] inflection. **-3.** [de route] bend. **-4.** *fig* [de politique] shift.

infliger [ɛ̃fliʒe] [17] *vt*: ~ qqch à qqn to inflict sthg on sb; [amende] to impose sthg on sb.

influençable [ɛ̃flyɑ̃sabl] *adj* easily influenced.

influence [ɛ̃flyɑ̃s] *nf* influence; [de médicament] effect; avoir de l'~ sur qqn to have an influence on sb; avoir une bonne/mauvaise ~ sur [suj: personne] to have a good/bad influence on, to be a good/bad influence on; [suj: chose] to have a good/bad effect on; agir sous l'~ de qqch to act under the influence of sthg.

influencer [ɛ̃flyɑ̃se] [16] *vt* to influence.

influent, **-e** [ɛ̃flyɑ̃, ɑ̃t] *adj* influential.

influer [ɛ̃flye] [3] *vi*: ~ sur qqch to influence sthg, to have an effect on sthg.

infographie [ɛ̃fɔgrafi] *nf* computer graphics (*U*).

informateur, **-trice** [ɛ̃fɔrmatœr, tris] *nm*, *f* **-1.** [qui renseigne] informant. **-2.** [de police] informer.

informaticien, **-ienne** [ɛ̃fɔrmatisjɛ̃, jɛn] *nm*, *f* computer scientist.

information [ɛ̃fɔrmasjɔ̃] *nf* **-1.** [renseignement] piece of information. **-2.** [renseignements & INFORM] information (*U*). **-3.** [nouvelle] piece of news. **-4.** JUR inquiry.
◆ **informations** *nfpl* MÉDIA news (*sg*).

informatique [ɛ̃fɔrmatik] ◇ *nf* **-1.** [technique] data-processing; ~ de gestion business applications (*pl*). **-2.** [science] computer science. ◇ *adj* data-processing (*avant n*), computer (*avant n*).

informatisation [ɛ̃fɔrmatizasjɔ̃] *nf* computerization.

informatiser [ɛ̃fɔrmatize] [3] *vt* to computerize.

◆ **s'informatiser** *vp* to become computerized.

informe [ɛ̃fɔrm] *adj* **-1.** [masse, vêtement, silhouette] shapeless. **-2.** *fig* [projet] sketchy, rough.

informé, -e [ɛ̃fɔrme] *adj* informed; **bien/mal ~** well/badly informed.

◆ **informé** *nm*: **jusqu'à plus ample ~** pending further information.

informel, -elle [ɛ̃fɔrmɛl] *adj* informal.

informer [ɛ̃fɔrme] [3] ◇ *vt* to inform; **~ qqn sur** OU **de qqch** to inform sb about sthg. ◇ *vi* JUR: **~ contre qqn/sur qqch** to investigate sb/sthg.

◆ **s'informer** *vp* to inform o.s.; **s'~ de qqch** to ask about sthg; **s'~ sur qqch** to find out about sthg.

infortune [ɛ̃fɔrtyn] *nf* misfortune.

infortuné, -e [ɛ̃fɔrtyne] *littéraire* & *vieilli* ◇ *adj* wretched. ◇ *nm, f* (*gén pl*) unfortunate.

infos [ɛ̃fo] (*abr de* **informations**) *nfpl fam*: **les ~** the news (*sg*).

infraction [ɛ̃fraksjɔ̃] *nf*: **~ à** infringement OU breach of; **être en ~** to be in breach of the law.

infranchissable [ɛ̃frɑ̃ʃisabl] *adj* insurmountable.

infrarouge [ɛ̃fraruʒ] *nm & adj* infrared.

infrastructure [ɛ̃frastryktyr] *nf* infrastructure; **~ hôtelière** hotel facilities (*pl*).

infréquentable [ɛ̃frekɑ̃tabl] *adj* **-1.** [personne]: **il est ~** you shouldn't mix with him. **-2.** [lieu]: **ce café est ~** it's not the kind of café you should go to.

infroissable [ɛ̃frwasabl] *adj* creaseresistant.

infructueux, -euse [ɛ̃fryktɥø, øz] *adj* fruitless.

infuse [ɛ̃fyz] → **science**.

infuser [ɛ̃fyze] [3] ◇ *vt* **-1.** [tisane] to infuse; [thé] to brew; **laisser ~** to leave to infuse OU brew. **-2.** *fig* & *littéraire*: **~ qqch à qqn/qqch** to infuse sb/sthg with sthg. ◇ *vi* [tisane] to infuse; [thé] to brew.

infusion [ɛ̃fyzjɔ̃] *nf* infusion.

ingambe [ɛ̃gɑ̃b] *adj* spry.

ingénier [ɛ̃ʒenje] [9]

◆ **s'ingénier** *vp*: **s'~ à faire qqch** to try hard to do sthg.

ingénierie [ɛ̃ʒeniri] *nf* engineering.

ingénieur [ɛ̃ʒenjœr] *nm* engineer; **~ agronome/chimiste/électronicien** agricultural/chemical/electronics engineer; **~ des mines** mining engineer; **~ des ponts et chaus-**

sées civil engineer; **~ du son** sound engineer; **~ des travaux publics** civil engineer.

ingénieux, -ieuse [ɛ̃ʒenjø, jøz] *adj* ingenious.

ingéniosité [ɛ̃ʒenjozite] *nf* ingenuity.

ingénu, -e [ɛ̃ʒeny] ◇ *adj littéraire* [candide] artless; *hum* & *péj* [trop candide] naïve. ◇ *nm, f littéraire* [candide] naïve person; THÉÂTRE **ingénue**; **jouer les ~s** THÉÂTRE to play ingénue roles; [dans la vie] to act the sweet young thing.

ingénuité [ɛ̃ʒenɥite] *nf* naïvety.

ingénument [ɛ̃ʒenymɑ̃] *adv* naïvely.

ingérable [ɛ̃ʒerabl] *adj* unmanageable.

ingérence [ɛ̃ʒerɑ̃s] *nf*: **~ dans** interference in.

ingérer [ɛ̃ʒere] [18] *vt* to ingest.

◆ **s'ingérer** *vp*: **s'~ dans** to interfere in.

ingrat, -e [ɛ̃gra, at] ◇ *adj* **-1.** [personne] ungrateful. **-2.** [métier] thankless, unrewarding. **-3.** [sol] barren. **-4.** [physique] unattractive. ◇ *nm, f* ungrateful wretch.

ingratitude [ɛ̃gratityd] *nf* ingratitude.

ingrédient [ɛ̃gredjɑ̃] *nm* ingredient.

inguérissable [ɛ̃gerisabl] *adj* incurable.

ingurgiter [ɛ̃gyrʒite] [3] *vt* **-1.** [avaler] to swallow. **-2.** *fig* [connaissances] to absorb.

inhabitable [inabitabl] *adj* uninhabitable.

inhabité, -e [inabite] *adj* uninhabited.

inhabituel, -elle [inabitɥel] *adj* unusual.

inhalateur, -trice [inalatœr, tris] *adj*: **appareil ~** inhaler.

◆ **inhalateur** *nm* inhaler.

inhalation [inalasjɔ̃] *nf* inhalation.

inhaler [inale] [3] *vt* to inhale, to breathe in.

inhérent, -e [inerɑ̃, ɑ̃t] *adj*: **~ à** inherent in.

inhiber [inibe] [3] *vt* to inhibit.

inhibition [inibisjɔ̃] *nf* inhibition.

inhospitalier, -ière [inɔspitalje, jɛr] *adj* inhospitable.

inhumain, -e [inymɛ̃, ɛn] *adj* inhuman.

inhumation [inymasjɔ̃] *nf* burial.

inhumer [inyme] [3] *vt* to bury.

inimaginable [inimaʒinabl] *adj* incredible, unimaginable.

inimitable [inimitabl] *adj* inimitable.

inimitié [inimitje] *nf*: **~ (contre** OU **à l'égard de)** enmity (towards).

ininflammable [inɛ̃flamabl] *adj* nonflammable.

inintelligible [inɛ̃teliʒibl] *adj* unintelligible.

inintéressant, -e [inɛ̃teresɑ̃, ɑ̃t] *adj* uninteresting.

ininterrompu, -e [inɛ̃tɛrɔ̃py] *adj* [file, vacarme] uninterrupted; [ligne, suite] unbroken; [travail, effort] continuous.

inique [inik] *adj* iniquitous.

iniquité [inikite] *nf* iniquity.

initial, -e, -iaux [inisjal, jo] *adj* [lettre] initial.

♦ **initiale** *nf* initial.

initialement [inisjalmã] *adv* initially.

initialiser [inisjalize] [3] *vt* INFORM to initialize.

initiateur, -trice [inisjatœr, tris] ◇ *adj* innovative. ◇ *nm, f* **-1.** [maître] initiator. **-2.** [précurseur] innovator.

initiation [inisjasjɔ̃] *nf*: ~ **(à)** [discipline] introduction (to); [rituel] initiation (into).

initiatique [inisjatik] *adj* [rite] initiation (*avant n*).

initiative [inisjativ] *nf* initiative; **avoir de l'~** to have initiative; **prendre l'~ de qqch/de faire qqch** to take the initiative for sthg/in doing sthg; **de sa propre ~** on one's own initiative.

initié, -e [inisje] ◇ *adj* initiated. ◇ *nm, f* initiate.

initier [inisje] [9] *vt*: ~ **qqn à** to initiate sb into.

♦ **s'initier** *vp*: **s'~ à** to familiarize o.s. with.

injecté, -e [ɛ̃ʒɛkte] *adj*: **yeux ~s de sang** bloodshot eyes.

injecter [ɛ̃ʒɛkte] [4] *vt* to inject.

♦ **s'injecter** *vp* [yeux]: **s'~ (de sang)** to become bloodshot.

injection [ɛ̃ʒɛksjɔ̃] *nf* injection.

injoignable [ɛ̃ʒwaɲabl] *adj*: **j'ai essayé de lui téléphoner mais il est** ~ I tried to phone him but I couldn't get through to him OR reach him OR get hold of him.

injonction [ɛ̃ʒɔ̃ksjɔ̃] *nf* injunction.

injure [ɛ̃ʒyr] *nf* insult; **abreuver qqn d'~s** to hurl insults at sb.

injurier [ɛ̃ʒyrje] [9] *vt* to insult.

injurieux, -ieuse [ɛ̃ʒyrjø, jøz] *adj* abusive, insulting.

injuste [ɛ̃ʒyst] *adj* unjust, unfair.

injustement [ɛ̃ʒystəmã] *adv* unjustly, unfairly.

injustice [ɛ̃ʒystis] *nf* injustice.

injustifiable [ɛ̃ʒystifjabl] *adj* unjustifiable.

injustifié, -e [ɛ̃ʒystifje] *adj* unjustified.

inlassable [ɛ̃lasabl] *adj* tireless.

inlassablement [ɛ̃lasabləmã] *adv* tirelessly.

inné, -e [ine] *adj* innate.

innocemment [inɔsamã] *adv* innocently.

innocence [inɔsãs] *nf* innocence.

innocent, -e [inɔsã, ãt] ◇ *adj* innocent. ◇ *nm, f* **-1.** JUR innocent person. **-2.** [inoffensif, candide] innocent; **faire l'~** *fig* to play the innocent. **-3.** *vieilli* [idiot] simpleton.

innocenter [inɔsãte] [3] *vt* **-1.** JUR to clear. **-2.** *fig* [excuser] to justify.

innocuité [inɔkɥite] *nf* harmlessness, innocuousness.

innombrable [inɔ̃brabl] *adj* innumerable; [foule] vast.

innovateur, -trice [inɔvatœr, tris] ◇ *adj* innovatory. ◇ *nm, f* innovator.

innovation [inɔvasjɔ̃] *nf* innovation.

innover [inɔve] [3] *vi* to innovate; ~ **en matière de** to innovate in the field of.

inobservation [inɔpsɛrvasjɔ̃] *nf* inobservance.

inoccupé, -e [inɔkype] *adj* **-1.** [lieu] empty, unoccupied. **-2.** [personne, vie] idle.

inoculation [inɔkylasjɔ̃] *nf* [volontaire] inoculation; [accidentelle] infection.

inoculer [inɔkyle] [3] *vt* MÉD: ~ **qqch à qqn** [volontairement] to inoculate sb with sthg; [accidentellement] to infect sb with sthg.

inodore [inɔdɔr] *adj* odourless.

inoffensif, -ive [inɔfãsif, iv] *adj* harmless.

inondation [inɔ̃dasjɔ̃] *nf* **-1.** [action] flooding. **-2.** [résultat] flood.

inonder [inɔ̃de] [3] *vt* to flood; ~ **de** *fig* to flood with.

inopérable [inɔperabl] *adj* inoperable.

inopérant, -e [inɔperã, ãt] *adj* ineffective.

inopiné, -e [inɔpine] *adj* unexpected.

inopinément [inɔpinemã] *adv* unexpectedly.

inopportun, -e [inɔpɔrtœ̃, yn] *adj* inopportune.

inorganisé, -e [inɔrganize] ◇ *adj* **-1.** [sans organisation] disorganized. **-2.** [politiquement] independent; [syndicalement] non-union (*avant n*). ◇ *nm, f* [politiquement] independent; [syndicalement] non-union member.

inoubliable [inublijabl] *adj* unforgettable.

inouï, -e [inwi] *adj* incredible, extraordinary.

Inox® [inɔks] *nm inv & adj inv* stainless steel.

inoxydable [inɔksidabl] ◇ *adj* stainless; [casserole] stainless steel (*avant n*). ◇ *nm* stainless steel.

inqualifiable [ɛ̃kalifjabl] *adj* unspeakable.

inquiet, -iète [ɛ̃kjɛ, jɛt] ◇ *adj* **-1.** [gén] anxious. **-2.** [tourmenté] feverish. ◇ *nm, f* worrier.

inquiétant, -e [ɛ̃kjetɑ̃, ɑ̃t] *adj* disturbing, worrying.

inquiéter [ɛ̃kjete] [18] *vt* **-1.** [donner du souci à] to worry. **-2.** [déranger] to disturb.

◆ **s'inquiéter** *vp* **-1.** [s'alarmer] to be worried. **-2.** [se préoccuper]: **s'~ de** [s'enquérir de] to enquire about; [se soucier de] to worry about.

inquiétude [ɛ̃kjetyd] *nf* anxiety, worry.

inquisiteur, -trice [ɛ̃kizitœr, tris] *adj* prying.

INR (*abr de* **Institut national de radiodiffusion**) *nm* Belgian broadcasting company.

INRA, Inra [inra] (*abr de* **Institut national de la recherche agronomique**) *nm national institute for agronomic research.*

insaisissable [ɛ̃sezisabl] *adj* **-1.** [personne] elusive. **-2.** *fig* [nuance] imperceptible.

insalubre [ɛ̃salybr] *adj* unhealthy.

insalubrité [ɛ̃salybrite] *nf* unhealthiness.

insanité [ɛ̃sanite] *nf* **-1.** [déraison] insanity, madness. **-2.** [propos]: **dire** OU **proférer des ~s** to say insane things. **-3.** [acte] insane act.

insatiable [ɛ̃sasjabl] *adj* insatiable.

insatisfait, -e [ɛ̃satisfɛ, ɛt] ◇ *adj* **-1.** [personne] dissatisfied. **-2.** [sentiment] unsatisfied. ◇ *nm, f* malcontent.

inscription [ɛ̃skripsjɔ̃] *nf* **-1.** [action, écrit] inscription. **-2.** [enregistrement] enrolment, registration. **-3.** JUR registration.

inscrire [ɛ̃skrir] [99] *vt* **-1.** [écrire] to write down; [- sur la pierre, le métal] to inscribe. **-2.** [personne]: **~ qqn à qqch** to enrol OU register sb for sthg; **~ qqn sur qqch** to put sb's name down on sthg. **-3.** SPORT [but] to score.

◆ **s'inscrire** *vp* **-1.** [personne]: **s'~ à qqch** to enrol OU register for sthg; **s'~ sur qqch** to put one's name down on sthg. **-2.** [s'insérer]: **s'~ dans** to come within the scope of. **-3.** *loc*: **s'~ en faux contre qqch** to deny sthg vigorously.

inscrit, -e [ɛ̃skri, it] ◇ *pp* → **inscrire.** ◇ *adj* [sur liste] registered; **être ~ sur une liste** to have one's name on a list. ◇ *nm, f* registered person.

inscrivais, inscrivions *etc* → **inscrire.**

INSEAD [insead] (*abr de* **Institut européen d'administration**) *nm European business school in Fontainebleau.*

insecte [ɛ̃sɛkt] *nm* insect.

insecticide [ɛ̃sɛktisid] *nm & adj* insecticide.

insectivore [ɛ̃sɛktivɔr] ◇ *adj* insectivorous. ◇ *nm* insectivore.

insécurité [ɛ̃sekyrite] *nf* insecurity.

INSEE, Insee [inse] (*abr de* **Institut national de la statistique et des études économiques**) *nm national institute of statistics and information about the economy.*

insémination [ɛ̃seminasjɔ̃] *nf* insemination; **~ artificielle** artificial insemination.

insensé, -e [ɛ̃sɑ̃se] *adj* **-1.** [déraisonnable] insane. **-2.** [incroyable, excentrique] extraordinary.

insensibiliser [ɛ̃sɑ̃sibilize] [3] *vt* to anaesthetize; **~ qqn (à)** *fig* to make sb insensitive (to).

insensibilité [ɛ̃sɑ̃sibilite] *nf*: **~ (à)** insensitivity (to).

insensible [ɛ̃sɑ̃sibl] *adj* **-1.** [gén]: **~ (à)** insensitive (to). **-2.** [imperceptible] imperceptible.

insensiblement [ɛ̃sɑ̃sibləmɑ̃] *adv* imperceptibly.

inséparable [ɛ̃separabl] *adj*: **~ (de)** inseparable (from).

◆ **inséparables** *nmpl* [perruches] lovebirds.

insérer [ɛ̃sere] [18] *vt* to insert; **~ une annonce dans un journal** to put an advertisement in a newspaper.

◆ **s'insérer** *vp* **-1.** [s'intégrer]: **s'~ dans** to fit into. **-2.** [s'attacher] to be attached.

INSERM, Inserm [insɛrm] (*abr de* **Institut national de la santé et de la recherche médicale**) *nm national institute for medical research.*

insertion [ɛ̃sɛrsjɔ̃] *nf* **-1.** [d'objet, de texte] insertion. **-2.** [de personne] integration.

insidieux, -ieuse [ɛ̃sidjø, jøz] *adj* insidious.

insigne [ɛ̃siɲ] ◇ *nm* badge. ◇ *adj* **-1.** *littéraire* [honneur] distinguished. **-2.** *hum* [maladresse] remarkable.

insignifiant, -e [ɛ̃siɲifjɑ̃, ɑ̃t] *adj* insignificant.

insinuant, -e [ɛ̃sinɥɑ̃, ɑ̃t] *adj* ingratiating.

insinuation [ɛ̃sinɥasjɔ̃] *nf* insinuation, innuendo.

insinuer [ɛ̃sinɥe] [7] *vt* to insinuate, to imply.

◆ **s'insinuer** *vp*: **s'~ dans** [eau, humidité, odeur] to seep into; *fig* [personne] to insinuate o.s. into.

insipide [ɛ̃sipid] *adj* [aliment] insipid, tasteless; *fig* insipid.

insistance [ɛ̃sistɑ̃s] *nf* insistence; **avec ~** insistently.

insistant, -e [ɛ̃sistɑ̃, ɑ̃t] *adj* insistent.

insister [ɛ̃siste] [3] *vi* to insist; **~ sur** to insist on; **~ pour faire qqch** to insist on doing sthg.

insolation [ɛ̃sɔlasjɔ̃] *nf* **-1.** [malaise] sun-stroke (*U*). **-2.** [ensoleillement] sunshine.

insolence [ɛ̃sɔlɑ̃s] *nf* insolence (*U*).

insolent, -e [ɛ̃sɔlɑ̃, ɑ̃t] ◇ *adj* **-1.** [personne, acte] insolent. **-2.** [joie, succès] unashamed, blatant. ◇ *nm, f* insolent person.

insolite [ɛ̃sɔlit] *adj* unusual.

insoluble [ɛ̃sɔlybl] *adj* insoluble.

insolvable [ɛ̃sɔlvabl] ◇ *adj* insolvent. ◇ *nmf* bankrupt.

insomniaque [ɛ̃sɔmnjak] *nmf & adj* insomniac.

insomnie [ɛ̃sɔmni] *nf* insomnia (*U*); **avoir des ~s** to suffer from insomnia.

insondable [ɛ̃sɔ̃dabl] *adj* [gouffre, mystère] unfathomable; [bêtise] abysmal.

insonore [ɛ̃sɔnɔr] *adj* soundproof.

insonorisation [ɛ̃sɔnɔrizasjɔ̃] *nf* sound-proofing.

insonoriser [ɛ̃sɔnɔrize] [3] *vt* to sound-proof.

insouciance [ɛ̃susjɑ̃s] *nf* **-1.** [inconscience]: **~ (de)** lack of concern (about). **-2.** [légèreté] carefree attitude.

insouciant, -e [ɛ̃susjɑ̃, ɑ̃t] *adj* **-1.** [sans-souci] carefree. **-2.** [inconscient]: **~ (de)** un-concerned (about).

insoumis, -e [ɛ̃sumi, iz] *adj* **-1.** [caractère] rebellious. **-2.** [peuple] unsubjugated. **-3.** [soldat] deserting.

◆ **insoumis** *nm* deserter.

insoumission [ɛ̃sumisjɔ̃] *nf* **-1.** [caractère rebelle] rebelliousness. **-2.** MIL desertion.

insoupçonné, -e [ɛ̃supsɔne] *adj* unsus-pected.

insoutenable [ɛ̃sutnabl] *adj* **-1.** [rythme] un-sustainable. **-2.** [scène, violence] unbearable. **-3.** [théorie] untenable.

inspecter [ɛ̃spɛkte] [4] *vt* to inspect.

inspecteur, -trice [ɛ̃spɛktœr, tris] *nm, f* in-spector; **~ des finances** ≃ tax inspector *Br*, ≃ Internal Revenue Service agent *Am*; **~ de police** police inspector.

inspection [ɛ̃spɛksjɔ̃] *nf* **-1.** [contrôle] in-spection; **faire l'~ de qqch** to inspect sthg. **-2.** [fonction] inspectorate; **~ générale des Finances** ≃ Inland Revenue *Br*, ≃ Internal Revenue Service *Am*.

inspiration [ɛ̃spirasjɔ̃] *nf* **-1.** [gén] inspira-tion; [idée] bright idea, brainwave; **avoir de l'~** to be inspired; **avoir une bonne/mauvaise ~** to have a good/bad idea. **-2.** [d'air] breathing in.

inspiré, -e [ɛ̃spire] *adj* inspired; **être bien ~ de faire qqch** be well-advised to do sthg.

inspirer [ɛ̃spire] [3] *vt* **-1.** [gén] to inspire; **~ qqch à qqn** to inspire sb with sthg. **-2.** [air] to breathe in, to inhale.

◆ **s'inspirer** *vp* [prendre modèle sur]: **s'~ de qqn/qqch** to be inspired by sb/sthg.

instabilité [ɛ̃stabilite] *nf* **-1.** [gén] instability. **-2.** [du temps] unsettled nature.

instable [ɛ̃stabl] ◇ *adj* **-1.** [gén] unstable. **-2.** [vie, temps] unsettled. ◇ *nmf* unstable person.

installateur, -trice [ɛ̃stalatœr, tris] *nm, f* fitter.

installation [ɛ̃stalasjɔ̃] *nf* **-1.** [de gaz, eau, électricité] installation. **-2.** [de personne - comme médecin, artisan] setting up; [- dans appartement] settling in. **-3.** [d'appartement] fitting out. **-4.** [de rideaux, étagères] putting up; [de meubles] putting in. **-5.** (*gén pl*) [équi-pement] installations (*pl*), fittings (*pl*); [indus-triel] plant (*U*); [de loisirs] facilities (*pl*); **~ électrique** wiring; **~s sanitaires** plumbing (*U*).

installer [ɛ̃stale] [3] *vt* **-1.** [gaz, eau, électrici-té] to install, to put in. **-2.** [appartement] to fit out. **-3.** [rideaux, étagères] to put up; [meubles] to put in. **-4.** [personne]: **~ qqn** to get sb settled, to install sb.

◆ **s'installer** *vp* **-1.** [comme médecin, artisan etc] to set (o.s.) up. **-2.** [emménager] to set-tle in; **s'~ chez qqn** to move in with sb. **-3.** [dans fauteuil] to settle down. **-4.** *fig* [maladie, routine] to set in.

instamment [ɛ̃stamɑ̃] *adv* insistently.

instance [ɛ̃stɑ̃s] *nf* **-1.** [autorité] authority. **-2.** JUR proceedings (*pl*). **-3.** [insistance] en-treaties (*pl*); **sur les ~s de** on the insistence of.

◆ **en instance** *loc adj* pending.

◆ **en instance de** *loc adv* on the point of; **en ~ de divorce** waiting for a divorce.

instant [ɛ̃stɑ̃] *nm* instant; **à l'~** [il y a peu de temps] a moment ago; [immédiatement] this minute; **à l'~ où** (just) as; **à tout ~** [en per-manence] at all times; [d'un moment à l'autre] at any moment; **pour l'~** for the moment; **dans un ~** in a moment OU minute; **dès l'~ où** from the moment (when); **un ~!** one moment!; **en un ~** in a flash OU an in-stant; **ne pas avoir un ~ de répit** not to have a moment's respite.

instantané, -e [ɛ̃stɑ̃tane] *adj* **-1.** [immédiat] instantaneous. **-2.** [soluble] instant.

◆ **instantané** *nm* snapshot.

instantanément [ɛ̃stɑ̃tanemɑ̃] *adv* instan-taneously, at once.

instar [ɛ̃star]

◆ **à l'instar de** *loc prép* following the example of.

instaurer [ɛ̃stɔre] [3] *vt* [instituer] to establish; *fig* [peur, confiance] to instil.

instigateur, -trice [ɛ̃stigatœr, tris] *nm, f* instigator.

instigation [ɛ̃stigasjɔ̃] *nf* instigation.

◆ **à l'instigation de, sur l'instigation de** *loc prép* at the instigation of.

instiller [ɛ̃stile] [3] *vt* **-1.** [substance] to drip. **-2.** [sentiment] to instil.

instinct [ɛ̃stɛ̃] *nm* instinct; **d'~** instinctively; **~ de conservation** instinct for self-preservation; **~ grégaire** herd instinct; **~ maternel** maternal instinct.

instinctif, -ive [ɛ̃stɛ̃ktif, iv] ◇ *adj* instinctive. ◇ *nm, f* instinctive person.

instinctivement [ɛ̃stɛ̃ktivmɑ̃] *adv* instinctively.

instituer [ɛ̃stitɥe] [7] *vt* **-1.** [pratique] to institute. **-2.** JUR [personne] to appoint.

◆ **s'instituer** *vp* to be set up OU established.

institut [ɛ̃stity] *nm* **-1.** [gén] institute; **l'Institut (de France)** the Institut de France; **~ médico-légal** mortuary; **l'~ Pasteur** the Institut Pasteur. **-2.** [de soins]: **~ de beauté** beauty salon; **~ dentaire** ≃ dental hospital.

L'INSTITUT DE FRANCE:
'L'Institut', as it is commonly known, is the learned society which includes the five 'Académies' (the 'Académie française' being one of them). Its headquarters are in the building of the same name on the banks of the Seine in Paris

L'INSTITUT PASTEUR:
This is a major research and teaching establishment specializing in microbiology and bacteriology. Its headquarters are in Paris but it has branches all over the world

instituteur, -trice [ɛ̃stitytœr, tris] *nm, f* primary *Br* OU grade *Am* school teacher.

institution [ɛ̃stitysjɔ̃] *nf* **-1.** [gén] institution. **-2.** [école privée] private school. **-3.** JUR nomination.

◆ **institutions** *nfpl* POLIT institutions.

institutionnaliser [ɛ̃stitysjɔnalize] [3] *vt* to institutionalize.

◆ **s'institutionnaliser** *vp* to become institutionalized.

instructeur [ɛ̃stryktœr] ◇ *nm* instructor. ◇ *adj* MIL: **sergent ~** drill sergeant.

instructif, -ive [ɛ̃stryktif, iv] *adj* instructive, educational.

instruction [ɛ̃stryksjɔ̃] *nf* **-1.** [enseignement, savoir] education; **avoir de l'~** to be educated; **~ civique** civics (U); **~ publique** state education; **~ religieuse** religious education. **-2.** [formation] training. **-3.** [directive] order. **-4.** JUR (pre-trial) investigation.

◆ **instructions** *nfpl* instructions.

instruire [ɛ̃strɥir] [98] *vt* **-1.** [éduquer] to teach, to instruct. **-2.** *sout* [informer] to inform. **-3.** JUR [affaire] to investigate; **~ contre qqn** to investigate sb.

◆ **s'instruire** *vp* **-1.** [se former] to learn. **-2.** *sout* [s'informer]: **s'~ de qqch auprès de qqn** to find out about sthg from sb.

instruisais, instruisions *etc* → **instruire**.

instruit, -e [ɛ̃strɥi, ɥit] ◇ *pp* → **instruire**. ◇ *adj* educated.

instrument [ɛ̃strymɑ̃] *nm* instrument; **~ à cordes/percussion/vent** stringed/percussion/wind instrument; **~ contondant** blunt instrument; **~ de musique** musical instrument; **~ de travail** tool.

instrumental, -e, -aux [ɛ̃strymɑ̃tal, o] *adj* instrumental.

◆ **instrumental** *nm* instrumental.

instrumentation [ɛ̃strymɑ̃tasjɔ̃] *nf* instrumentation.

instrumentiste [ɛ̃strymɑ̃tist] *nmf* instrumentalist.

insu [ɛ̃sy]

◆ **à l'insu de** *loc prép*: **à l'~ de qqn** without sb knowing; **à mon/ton** *etc* **~** without my/your *etc* realizing (it).

insubmersible [ɛ̃sybmɛrsibl] *adj* unsinkable.

insubordination [ɛ̃sybɔrdinasjɔ̃] *nf* insubordination.

insubordonné, -e [ɛ̃sybɔrdɔne] *adj* insubordinate.

insuccès [ɛ̃syksɛ] *nm* failure.

insuffisamment [ɛ̃syfizamɑ̃] *adv* insufficiently, inadequately.

insuffisance [ɛ̃syfizɑ̃s] *nf* **-1.** [manque] insufficiency. **-2.** MÉD deficiency; **~ cardiaque** cardiac insufficiency.

◆ **insuffisances** *nfpl* [faiblesses] shortcomings.

insuffisant, -e [ɛ̃syfizɑ̃, ɑ̃t] *adj* **-1.** [en quantité] insufficient. **-2.** [en qualité] inadequate, unsatisfactory.

insuffler [ɛ̃syfle] [3] *vt* **-1.** [air] to blow. **-2.** *fig* [sentiment]: **~ qqch à qqn** to inspire sb with sthg.

insulaire [ɛ̃sylɛr] ◇ *nmf* islander. ◇ *adj* **-1.** GÉOGR island (*avant n*). **-2.** *fig* [attitude] insular.

insularité [ɛ̃sylarite] *nf* insularity.
insuline [ɛ̃sylin] *nf* insulin.
insultant, -e [ɛ̃syltɑ̃, ɑ̃t] *adj* insulting.
insulte [ɛ̃sylt] *nf* insult.
insulter [ɛ̃sylte] [3] *vt* to insult.
◆ **s'insulter** *vp* to insult each other.
insupportable [ɛ̃sypɔrtabl] *adj* unbearable.
insurgé, -e [ɛ̃syrʒe] *adj & nm, f* insurgent, rebel.
insurger [ɛ̃syrʒe] [17]
◆ **s'insurger** *vp* to rebel, to revolt; **s'~ contre qqn** to rebel OU rise up against sb; **s'~ contre qqch** to protest against sthg.
insurmontable [ɛ̃syrmɔ̃tabl] *adj* [difficulté] insurmountable; [dégoût] uncontrollable.
insurrection [ɛ̃syrɛksjɔ̃] *nf* insurrection.
insurrectionnel, -elle [ɛ̃syrɛksjɔnɛl] *adj* insurrectionary.
intact, -e [ɛ̃takt] *adj* intact.
intangible [ɛ̃tɑ̃ʒibl] *adj* **-1.** *littéraire* [impalpable] intangible. **-2.** [sacré] inviolable.
intarissable [ɛ̃tarisabl] *adj* inexhaustible; **il est ~** he could go on talking for ever.
intégral, -e, -aux [ɛ̃tegral, o] *adj* **-1.** [paiement] in full; [texte] unabridged, complete; **bronzage ~** all-over tan. **-2.** MATHS: **calcul ~ intégral** calculus.
◆ **intégrale** *nf* **-1.** MUS complete works (*pl*). **-2.** MATHS integral.
intégralement [ɛ̃tegralmɑ̃] *adv* fully, in full.
intégralité [ɛ̃tegralite] *nf* whole; **dans son ~** in full.
intégrant, -e [ɛ̃tegrɑ̃, ɑ̃t] → **partie**.
intégration [ɛ̃tegrasjɔ̃] *nf* integration.
intègre [ɛ̃tɛgr] *adj* honest, of integrity.
intégré, -e [ɛ̃tegre] *adj* **-1.** [logiciel] integrated. **-2.** [élément] built-in.
intégrer [ɛ̃tegre] [18] *vt* [assimiler]: **~ (à OU dans)** to integrate (into).
◆ **s'intégrer** *vp* **-1.** [s'incorporer]: **s'~ dans** OU **à** to fit into. **-2.** [s'adapter] to integrate.
intégrisme [ɛ̃tegrism] *nm* fundamentalism.
intégriste [ɛ̃tegrist] *nmf & adj* fundamentalist.
intégrité [ɛ̃tegrite] *nf* **-1.** [totalité] entirety. **-2.** [honnêteté] integrity.
intellect [ɛ̃telɛkt] *nm* intellect.
intellectualisme [ɛ̃telɛktɥalism] *nm* intellectualism.
intellectuel, -elle [ɛ̃telɛktɥɛl] *adj & nm, f* intellectual.
intellectuellement [ɛ̃telɛktɥɛlmɑ̃] *adv* intellectually.
intelligemment [ɛ̃teliʒamɑ̃] *adv* intelligently.

intelligence [ɛ̃teliʒɑ̃s] *nf* **-1.** [facultés mentales] intelligence; **~ artificielle** artificial intelligence. **-2.** [personne] brain. **-3.** [compréhension, complicité] understanding; **agir d'~ avec qqn** to act in complicity with sb.
◆ **intelligences** *nfpl* secret contacts.
intelligent, -e [ɛ̃teliʒɑ̃, ɑ̃t] *adj* intelligent.
intelligentsia [ɛ̃teligɛnsja] *nf* intelligentsia.
intelligible [ɛ̃teliʒibl] *adj* **-1.** [voix] clear. **-2.** [concept, texte] intelligible.
intello [ɛ̃tɛlo] *adj inv & nmf péj* highbrow.
intempérance [ɛ̃tɑ̃perɑ̃s] *nf* **-1.** [abus] excessiveness. **-2.** [excès de plaisirs] overindulgence.
intempéries [ɛ̃tɑ̃peri] *nfpl* bad weather (*U*).
intempestif, -ive [ɛ̃tɑ̃pestif, iv] *adj* untimely.
intemporel, -elle [ɛ̃tɑ̃pɔrɛl] *adj* **-1.** [sans durée] timeless. **-2.** *littéraire* [immatériel] immaterial.
intenable [ɛ̃tənabl] *adj* **-1.** [chaleur, personne] unbearable. **-2.** [position] untenable, indefensible.
intendance [ɛ̃tɑ̃dɑ̃s] *nf* **-1.** MIL commissariat; SCOL & UNIV bursar's office. **-2.** *fig* [questions matérielles] housekeeping.
intendant, -e [ɛ̃tɑ̃dɑ̃, ɑ̃t] *nm, f* **-1.** SCOL & UNIV bursar. **-2.** [de manoir] steward.
◆ **intendant** *nm* MIL quartermaster.
intense [ɛ̃tɑ̃s] *adj* **-1.** [gén] intense. **-2.** [circulation] dense.
intensément [ɛ̃tɑ̃semɑ̃] *adv* intensely.
intensif, -ive [ɛ̃tɑ̃sif, iv] *adj* intensive.
intensification [ɛ̃tɑ̃sifikasjɔ̃] *nf* intensification.
intensifier [ɛ̃tɑ̃sifje] [9] *vt* to intensify.
◆ **s'intensifier** *vp* to intensify.
intensité [ɛ̃tɑ̃site] *nf* intensity.
intenter [ɛ̃tɑ̃te] [3] *vt* JUR: **~ qqch contre** OU **à qqn** to bring sthg against sb.
intention [ɛ̃tɑ̃sjɔ̃] *nf* intention; **avoir l'~ de faire qqch** to intend to do sthg; **~ d'achat** COMM purchasing intention; **agir dans une bonne ~** to act with good intentions.
◆ **à l'intention de** *loc prép* for.
intentionné, -e [ɛ̃tɑ̃sjɔne] *adj*: **bien ~** well-meaning; **mal ~** ill-disposed.
intentionnel, -elle [ɛ̃tɑ̃sjɔnɛl] *adj* intentional.
intentionnellement [ɛ̃tɑ̃sjɔnɛlmɑ̃] *adv* intentionally.
inter [ɛ̃tɛr] *nm* **-1.** *vieilli* = **interurbain**. **-2.** SPORT: **~ gauche/droit** inside left/right.
interactif, -ive [ɛ̃tɛraktif, iv] *adj* interactive.

interaction [ɛ̃teraksjɔ̃] *nf* interaction.

interbancaire [ɛ̃tɛrbɑ̃kɛr] *adj* interbank (*avant n*).

intercalaire [ɛ̃tɛrkalɛr] ◇ *nm* insert. ◇ *adj*: **feuillet** ~ insert; **jour** ~ *extra day in a leap year.*

intercaler [ɛ̃tɛrkale] [3] *vt*: ~ **qqch dans qqch** [feuillet, citation] to insert sthg in sthg; [dans le temps] to fit sthg into sthg.
◆ **s'intercaler** *vp*: **s'**~ **entre** to come between.

intercéder [ɛ̃tɛrsede] [18] *vi*: ~ **pour** OU **en faveur de qqn auprès de qqn** to intercede with sb on behalf of sb.

intercepter [ɛ̃tɛrsɛpte] [4] *vt* **-1.** [lettre, ballon] to intercept. **-2.** [chaleur] to block.

intercession [ɛ̃tɛrsesjɔ̃] *nf* intercession.

interchangeable [ɛ̃tɛrʃɑ̃ʒabl] *adj* interchangeable.

interclasse [ɛ̃tɛrklas] *nm* break.

intercommunal, -e, -aux [ɛ̃tɛrkɔmynal, o] *adj* intermunicipal.

intercontinental, -e, -aux [ɛ̃tɛrkɔ̃tinɑ̃tal, o] *adj* intercontinental.

interdépartemental, -e, -aux [ɛ̃tɛrdepartəmɑ̃tal, o] *adj* interdepartmental.

interdépendance [ɛ̃tɛrdepɑ̃dɑ̃s] *nf* interdependence.

interdépendant, -e [ɛ̃tɛrdepɑ̃dɑ̃, ɑ̃t] *adj* interdependent.

interdiction [ɛ̃tɛrdiksjɔ̃] *nf* **-1.** [défense]: «~ **absolue de stationner**» "strictly no parking"; «~ **de fumer**» "no smoking". **-2.** [prohibition, suspension]: ~ **(de)** ban (on), banning (of); **enfreindre/lever une** ~ to break/lift a ban; ~ **de séjour** *order banning released prisoner from living in certain areas.*

interdire [ɛ̃tɛrdir] [103] *vt* **-1.** [prohiber]: ~ **qqch à qqn** to forbid sb sthg; ~ **à qqn de faire qqch** to forbid sb to do sthg. **-2.** [empêcher] to prevent; ~ **à qqn de faire qqch** to prevent sb from doing sthg. **-3.** [d'exercer] to ban. **-4.** [bloquer] to block.
◆ **s'interdire** *vp*: **s'**~ **qqch/de faire qqch** to refrain from sthg/from doing sthg.

interdisais, interdisions *etc* → **interdire**.

interdisciplinaire [ɛ̃tɛrdisiplinɛr] *adj* interdisciplinary.

interdise, interdises *etc* → **interdire**.

interdit, -e [ɛ̃tɛrdi, it] ◇ *pp* → **interdire**. ◇ *adj* **-1.** [défendu] forbidden. **-2.** [ébahi]: **rester** ~ to be stunned. **-3.** [privé]: **être** ~ **de chéquier** to have had one's cheque book facilities withdrawn; ~ **de séjour** banned from entering the country.

◆ **interdit** *nm*: **jeter l'**~ **sur qqn** to bar sb; **lever un** ~ to lift a ban; «**film** ~ **aux moins de 18 ans**» ≃ "(18)".

intéressant, -e [ɛ̃teresɑ̃, ɑ̃t] ◇ *adj* **-1.** [captivant] interesting. **-2.** [avantageux] advantageous, good. ◇ *nm, f*: **faire l'**~ *péj* to show off.

intéressé, -e [ɛ̃terese] ◇ *adj* [concerné] concerned, involved; *péj* [motivé] self-interested. ◇ *nm, f* person concerned; **le principal** ~ the main person concerned.

intéressement [ɛ̃teresmɑ̃] *nm* profit-sharing (scheme).

intéresser [ɛ̃terese] [4] *vt* **-1.** [captiver] to interest; ~ **qqn à qqch** to interest sb in sthg. **-2.** COMM [faire participer]: ~ **les employés (aux bénéfices)** to give one's employees a share in the profits; ~ **qqn dans son commerce** to give sb a financial interest in one's business. **-3.** [concerner] to concern.
◆ **s'intéresser** *vp*: **s'**~ **à qqn/qqch** to take an interest in sb/sthg, to be interested in sb/sthg.

intérêt [ɛ̃terɛ] *nm* **-1.** [gén] interest; ~ **pour** interest in; **agir par** ~ to act in one's own interest; **avoir** ~ **à faire qqch** to be well advised to do sthg; **dans l'**~ **général** in everyone's interest. **-2.** [importance] significance. **-3.** [avantage] advantage.
◆ **intérêts** *nmpl* **-1.** FIN interest (*sg*); ~**s moratoires** interest on overdue payment. **-2.** COMM: **avoir des** ~**s dans** to have a stake in.

interface [ɛ̃tɛrfas] *nf* INFORM interface; ~ **graphique** graphic interface.

interférence [ɛ̃tɛrferɑ̃s] *nf* **-1.** PHYS & POLIT interference. **-2.** *fig* [conjonction] convergence.

interférer [ɛ̃tɛrfere] [18] *vi* **-1.** PHYS to interfere. **-2.** *fig* [se rencontrer] to converge. **-3.** *fig* [s'immiscer]: ~ **dans qqch** to interfere in sthg.

intergalactique [ɛ̃tɛrgalaktik] *adj* intergalactic.

intérieur, -e [ɛ̃terjœr] *adj* **-1.** [gén] inner. **-2.** [de pays] domestic.
◆ **intérieur** *nm* **-1.** [gén] inside; **de l'**~ from the inside; **à l'**~ **de soi-même** *fig* & *littéraire* inwardly; **à l'**~ **(de qqch)** inside (sthg). **-2.** [de pays] interior.

intérieurement [ɛ̃terjœrmɑ̃] *adv* inwardly.

intérim [ɛ̃terim] *nm* **-1.** [période] interim period; **assurer l'**~ **(de qqn)** to deputize (for sb); **par** ~ acting. **-2.** [travail temporaire] temporary OU casual work; [dans bureau] temping; **faire de l'**~, **travailler en** ~ to temp.

intérimaire [ēterimɛr] ◇ adj **-1.** [ministre, directeur] acting (avant n). **-2.** [employé, fonctions] temporary. ◇ nmf **-1.** [ministre] acting minister. **-2.** [employé] temp.

intérioriser [ēterjɔrize] [3] vt to internalize.

interjection [ēterʒeksjɔ̃] nf **-1.** LING interjection. **-2.** JUR lodging of an appeal.

interjeter [ēterʒəte] [27] vt JUR: ~ appel to lodge an appeal.

interligne [ēterliɲ] ◇ nm space between the lines; **simple/double** ~ single/double spacing. ◇ nf TYPO lead, leading.

interlocuteur, -trice [ēterlɔkytœr, tris] nm, f **-1.** [dans conversation] speaker; **mon** ~ the person to whom I am/was speaking. **-2.** [dans négociation] negotiator.

interlope [ēterlɔp] adj **-1.** [illégal] illegal. **-2.** fig [louche] suspect, shady.

interloquer [ēterlɔke] [3] vt to disconcert.

interlude [ēterlyd] nm interlude.

intermède [ētermɛd] nm interlude.

intermédiaire [ētermedjɛr] ◇ nm intermediary, go-between; **sans** ~ without an intermediary; **par l'**~ **de qqn/qqch** through sb/sthg. ◇ adj intermediate.

interminable [ēterminabl] adj never-ending, interminable.

interministériel, -ielle [ēterministerjɛl] adj interdepartmental.

intermittence [ētermitɑ̃s] nf [discontinuité]: **par** ~ intermittently, off and on.

intermittent, -e [ētermitɑ̃, ɑ̃t] adj intermittent.

internat [ēterna] nm **-1.** [SCOL - établissement] boarding school; [- système] boarding. **-2.** [MÉD & UNIV - concours] entrance examination; [- période de stage] period spent as a houseman Br OU an intern Am.

international, -e, -aux [ēternasjɔnal, o] adj international. ◇ nm, f SPORT international.

◆ **Internationale** nf **-1.** [association] International. **-2.** [hymne] Internationale.

internationalisation [ēternasjɔnalizasjɔ̃] nf internationalization.

interne [ētern] ◇ nmf **-1.** [élève] boarder. **-2.** MÉD & UNIV houseman Br, intern Am. ◇ adj **-1.** ANAT internal; [oreille] inner. **-2.** [du pays] domestic.

interné, -e [ēterne] nm, f **-1.** [prisonnier] internee. **-2.** MÉD inmate (of psychiatric hospital).

internement [ēternəmɑ̃] nm **-1.** POLIT internment. **-2.** MÉD confinement (to psychiatric hospital).

interner [ēterne] [3] vt **-1.** POLIT to intern. **-2.** MÉD to confine (to psychiatric hospital).

interpeller [ēterpəle] [26] vt **-1.** [apostropher] to call OU shout out to. **-2.** [interroger] to question.

◆ **s'interpeller** vp to exchange insults.

interphone [ēterfɔn] nm intercom; [d'un immeuble] entry phone.

interplanétaire [ēterplanetɛr] adj interplanetary.

interpoler [ēterpɔle] [3] vt to interpolate.

interposer [ēterpoze] [3] vt to interpose.

◆ **s'interposer** vp: **s'**~ **dans qqch** to intervene in sthg; **s'**~ **entre qqn et qqn** to intervene OU come between sb and sb.

interprétariat [ēterpretarja] nm interpreting.

interprétation [ēterpretasjɔ̃] nf interpretation.

interprète [ēterprɛt] nmf **-1.** [gén] interpreter. **-2.** [porte-parole] spokesperson. **-3.** CIN, MUS & THÉÂTRE performer.

interpréter [ēterprete] [18] vt to interpret.

interprofessionnel, -elle [ēterprɔfesjɔnɛl] adj interprofessional.

interrogateur, -trice [ēterɔgatœr, tris] ◇ adj inquiring (avant n). ◇ nm, f SCOL & UNIV oral examiner.

interrogatif, -ive [ēterɔgatif, iv] adj **-1.** GRAM interrogative. **-2.** [air, ton] inquiring (avant n).

◆ **interrogatif** nm GRAM interrogative.

interrogation [ēterɔgasjɔ̃] nf **-1.** [de prisonnier] interrogation; [de témoin] questioning. **-2.** [question] question; ~ **directe/indirecte** GRAM direct/indirect question. **-3.** SCOL test.

interrogatoire [ēterɔgatwar] nm **-1.** [de police, juge] questioning. **-2.** [procès-verbal] statement.

interrogeable [ēterɔʒabl] adj: **répondeur** ~ **à distance** answerphone with remote playback facility.

interroger [ēterɔʒe] [17] vt **-1.** [questionner] to question; [accusé, base de données] to interrogate; ~ **qqn (sur qqch)** to question sb (about sthg). **-2.** [faits, conscience] to examine.

◆ **s'interroger** vp: **s'**~ **sur** to wonder about.

interrompre [ēterɔ̃pr] [78] vt to interrupt.

◆ **s'interrompre** vp to break off; **s'**~ **de faire qqch** to break off doing sthg.

interrompu, -e [ēterɔ̃py] pp → interrompre.

interrupteur [ēteryptœr] nm switch; ~ **à bascule** toggle switch.

interruption [ɛ̃terypsjɔ̃] *nf* **-1.** [arrêt] break; **sans ~** without a break. **-2.** [action] interruption.

intersection [ɛ̃tɛrsɛksjɔ̃] *nf* intersection.

intersidéral, -e, -aux [ɛ̃tɛrsideral, o] *adj* interstellar.

interstice [ɛ̃tɛrstis] *nm* chink, crack.

intersyndical, -e, -aux [ɛ̃tɛrsɛ̃dikal, o] *adj* interunion.

intertitre [ɛ̃tɛrtitr] *nm* **-1.** PRESSE subheading. **-2.** CIN intertitle.

interurbain, -e [ɛ̃tɛryrbɛ̃, ɛn] *adj* long-distance.
◆ interurbain *nm*: **l'~** the long-distance telephone service.

intervalle [ɛ̃tɛrval] *nm* **-1.** [spatial] space, gap. **-2.** [temporel] interval, period (of time); **à 6 jours d'~** after 6 days; **dans l'~** in the meantime. **-3.** MUS interval.

intervenant, -e [ɛ̃tɛrvənɑ̃, ɑ̃t] *nm, f* **-1.** [orateur] speaker. **-2.** JUR intervening party.

intervenir [ɛ̃tɛrvənir] [40] *vi* **-1.** [personne] to intervene; **~ auprès de qqn** to intervene with sb; **~ dans qqch** to intervene in sthg; **faire ~ qqn** to bring OU call in sb. **-2.** [événement] to take place.

intervention [ɛ̃tɛrvɑ̃sjɔ̃] *nf* **-1.** [gén] intervention. **-2.** MÉD operation; **subir une ~ chirurgicale** to have an operation, to have surgery. **-3.** [discours] speech.

interventionniste [ɛ̃tɛrvɑ̃sjɔnist] *nmf & adj* interventionist.

intervenu, -e [ɛ̃tɛrvəny] *pp* → **intervenir**.

intervertir [ɛ̃tɛrvɛrtir] [32] *vt* to reverse, to invert.

interviendrai, interviendras *etc* → **intervenir**.

intervienne, interviennes *etc* → **intervenir**.

interviens, intervient *etc* → **intervenir**.

interview [ɛ̃tɛrvju] *nf* interview; **accorder une ~ à qqn** to give OU grant an interview to sb.

interviewer¹ [ɛ̃tɛrvjuve] [3] *vt* to interview.

interviewer² [ɛ̃tɛrvjuvœr] *nm* interviewer.

intestat [ɛ̃tɛsta] JUR ◇ *nmf person who dies intestate*. ◇ *adj* intestate.

intestin, -e [ɛ̃tɛstɛ̃, in] *adj sout* internal.
◆ intestin *nm* intestine; **~ grêle** small intestine; **gros ~** large intestine.

intestinal, -e, -aux [ɛ̃tɛstinal, o] *adj* intestinal.

intime [ɛ̃tim] ◇ *nmf* close friend. ◇ *adj* [gén] intimate; [vie, journal] private.

intimement [ɛ̃timmɑ̃] *adv* **-1.** [persuadé] firmly. **-2.** [lié] intimately.

intimer [ɛ̃time] [3] *vt* **-1.** [enjoindre]: **~ qqch à qqn** to notify sb of sthg. **-2.** JUR to summon.

intimidant, -e [ɛ̃timidɑ̃, ɑ̃t] *adj* intimidating.

intimidation [ɛ̃timidasjɔ̃] *nf* intimidation.

intimider [ɛ̃timide] [3] *vt* to intimidate.

intimiste [ɛ̃timist] *adj* ART & LITT intimist.

intimité [ɛ̃timite] *nf* **-1.** [secret] depths (*pl*). **-2.** [familiarité, confort] intimacy. **-3.** [vie privée] privacy; **dans l'~** amongst friends, in private; **dans la plus stricte ~** in complete privacy, in private.

intitulé [ɛ̃tityle] *nm* [titre] title; [de paragraphe] heading.

intituler [ɛ̃tityle] [3] *vt* to call, to entitle.
◆ s'intituler *vp* **-1.** [ouvrage] to be called OU entitled. **-2.** [personne] to call o.s.

intolérable [ɛ̃tɔlerabl] *adj* intolerable.

intolérance [ɛ̃tɔlerɑ̃s] *nf* **-1.** [religieuse, politique] intolerance. **-2.** [de l'organisme]: **~ à qqch** inability to tolerate sthg.

intolérant, -e [ɛ̃tɔlerɑ̃, ɑ̃t] *adj* intolerant.

intonation [ɛ̃tɔnasjɔ̃] *nf* intonation.

intouchable [ɛ̃tuʃabl] *nmf & adj* untouchable.

intoxication [ɛ̃tɔksikasjɔ̃] *nf* **-1.** [empoisonnement] poisoning; **~ alimentaire** food poisoning. **-2.** *fig* [propagande] brainwashing.

intoxiqué, -e [ɛ̃tɔksike] ◇ *adj*: **~ (de)** addicted (to). ◇ *nm, f* addict.

intoxiquer [ɛ̃tɔksike] [3] *vt*: **~ qqn par** [empoisonner] to poison sb with; *fig* to indoctrinate sb with.
◆ s'intoxiquer *vp* to poison o.s.

intraduisible [ɛ̃tradɥizibl] *adj* **-1.** [texte] untranslatable. **-2.** [sentiment] inexpressible.

intraitable [ɛ̃tretabl] *adj*: **~ (sur)** inflexible (about).

intransigeance [ɛ̃trɑ̃ziʒɑ̃s] *nf* intransigence.

intransigeant, -e [ɛ̃trɑ̃ziʒɑ̃, ɑ̃t] *adj* intransigent.

intransitif, -ive [ɛ̃trɑ̃zitif, iv] *adj* intransitive.

intransportable [ɛ̃trɑ̃spɔrtabl] *adj*: **il est ~** he/it cannot be moved.

intraveineux, -euse [ɛ̃travɛnø, øz] *adj* intravenous.

intrépide [ɛ̃trepid] *adj* bold, intrepid.

intrépidité [ɛ̃trepidite] *nf* boldness.

intrigant, -e [ɛ̃trigɑ̃, ɑ̃t] ◇ *adj* scheming. ◇ *nm, f* schemer.

intrigue [ɛ̃trig] *nf* **-1.** [liaison amoureuse] intrigue, affair. **-2.** [manœuvre] intrigue. **-3.** CIN, LITTÉRATURE & THÉÂTRE plot.

intriguer [ɛ̃trige] [3] ◇ *vt* to intrigue. ◇ *vi* to scheme, to intrigue.

intrinsèque [ɛ̃trɛ̃sɛk] *adj* intrinsic.

introductif, -ive [ɛ̃trɔdyktif, iv] *adj* JUR introductory.

introduction [ɛ̃trɔdyksjɔ̃] *nf* **-1.** [gén]: ~ (à) introduction (to). **-2.** [insertion] insertion.

introduire [ɛ̃trɔdɥir] [98] *vt* **-1.** [gén] to introduce. **-2.** [faire entrer] to show in. **-3.** [insérer] to insert. **-4.** INFORM to input, to enter.

◆ **s'introduire** *vp* **-1.** [pénétrer] to enter; s'~ dans une maison [cambrioleur] to get into OU enter a house. **-2.** [s'implanter] to be introduced.

introduisais, introduisions *etc* → **introduire**.

introduit, -e [ɛ̃trɔdɥi, it] *pp* → **introduire**.

intronisation [ɛ̃trɔnizasjɔ̃] *nf* RELIG enthronement; *fig* establishment.

introspection [ɛ̃trɔspɛksjɔ̃] *nf* introspection.

introuvable [ɛ̃truvabl] *adj* nowhere to be found.

introverti, -e [ɛ̃trɔvɛrti] ◇ *adj* introverted. ◇ *nm, f* introvert.

intrus, -e [ɛ̃try, yz] ◇ *adj* intrusive. ◇ *nm, f* intruder.

intrusion [ɛ̃tryzjɔ̃] *nf* **-1.** [gén & GÉOL] intrusion. **-2.** [ingérence] interference.

intuitif, -ive [ɛ̃tɥitif, iv] ◇ *adj* intuitive. ◇ *nm, f* intuitive person.

intuition [ɛ̃tɥisjɔ̃] *nf* intuition; avoir de l'~ to be intuitive, to have intuition; avoir l'~ de qqch to have an intuition about sthg.

intuitivement [ɛ̃tɥitivmɑ̃] *adv* intuitively.

inusable [inyzabl] *adj* hardwearing.

inusité, -e [inyzite] *adj* unusual, uncommon.

inutile [inytil] *adj* [objet, personne] useless; [effort, démarche] pointless; ~ d'insister it's pointless insisting.

inutilement [inytilmɑ̃] *adv* needlessly, unnecessarily.

inutilisable [inytilizabl] *adj* unusable.

inutilisé, -e [inytilize] *adj* unused.

inutilité [inytilite] *nf* [de personne, d'objet] uselessness; [de démarche, d'effort] pointlessness.

inv. (*abr de* **invariable**) inv.

invaincu, -e [ɛ̃vɛ̃ky] *adj* **-1.** SPORT unbeaten. **-2.** [peuple] unconquered.

invalide [ɛ̃valid] ◇ *nmf* disabled person; ~ de guerre disabled soldier; ~ du travail industrially disabled person. ◇ *adj* disabled.

invalider [ɛ̃valide] [3] *vt* to invalidate.

invalidité [ɛ̃validite] *nf* **-1.** JUR invalidity. **-2.** MÉD disability.

invariable [ɛ̃varjabl] *adj* **-1.** [immuable] unchanging. **-2.** GRAM invariable.

invariablement [ɛ̃varjabləmɑ̃] *adv* invariably.

invasion [ɛ̃vazjɔ̃] *nf* invasion.

invective [ɛ̃vɛktiv] *nf* invective, abuse.

invectiver [ɛ̃vɛktive] [3] *vt* to abuse.

◆ **s'invectiver** *vp* to hurl abuse at each other.

invendable [ɛ̃vɑ̃dabl] *adj* unsaleable, unsellable.

invendu, -e [ɛ̃vɑ̃dy] *adj* unsold.

◆ **invendu** *nm* (*gén pl*) remainder.

inventaire [ɛ̃vɑ̃tɛr] *nm* **-1.** [gén] inventory; faire l'~ de qqch to make an inventory of sthg. **-2.** [COMM - activité] stocktaking *Br*, inventory *Am*; [- liste] list.

inventer [ɛ̃vɑ̃te] [3] *vt* to invent.

inventeur, -trice [ɛ̃vɑ̃tœr, tris] *nm, f* **-1.** [de machine] inventor. **-2.** JUR [de trésor] finder.

inventif, -ive [ɛ̃vɑ̃tif, iv] *adj* inventive.

invention [ɛ̃vɑ̃sjɔ̃] *nf* **-1.** [découverte, mensonge] invention. **-2.** [imagination] inventiveness.

inventorier [ɛ̃vɑ̃tɔrje] [9] *vt* to make an inventory of.

invérifiable [ɛ̃verifjabl] *adj* unverifiable.

inverse [ɛ̃vɛrs] ◇ *nm* opposite, reverse; à l'~ de contrary to. ◇ *adj* **-1.** [sens] opposite; [ordre] reverse; en sens ~ (de) in the opposite direction (to). **-2.** [rapport] inverse.

inversement [ɛ̃vɛrsəmɑ̃] *adv* **-1.** MATHS inversely; ~ proportionnel à in inverse proportion to. **-2.** [au contraire] on the other hand. **-3.** [vice versa] vice versa.

inverser [ɛ̃vɛrse] [3] *vt* to reverse.

inversion [ɛ̃vɛrsjɔ̃] *nf* reversal.

invertébré, -e [ɛ̃vɛrtebre] *adj* invertebrate.

◆ **invertébré** *nm* invertebrate.

investigation [ɛ̃vɛstigasjɔ̃] *nf* investigation.

investir [ɛ̃vɛstir] [32] *vt* to invest; ~ qqn d'une fonction to invest OU vest sb with an office.

investissement [ɛ̃vɛstismɑ̃] *nm* investment.

investisseur, -euse [ɛ̃vɛtisœr, øz] *nm, f* investor; ~ institutionnel institutional investor.

investiture [ɛ̃vɛstityr] *nf* investiture.

invétéré, -e [ɛ̃vetere] *adj* *péj* inveterate.

invincible [ɛ̃vɛ̃sibl] *adj* [gén] invincible; [difficulté] insurmountable; [charme] irresistible.

inviolabilité [ɛ̃vjɔlabilite] *nf* **-1.** JUR inviolability. **-2.** [de parlementaire] immunity. **-3.** [de coffre] impregnability.

inviolable [ɛ̃vjɔlabl] *adj* **-1.** JUR inviolable. **-2.** [parlementaire] immune. **-3.** [coffre] impregnable.

invisible [ɛ̃vizibl] *adj* invisible; **rester ~** [personne] to stay out of sight.

invitation [ɛ̃vitasjɔ̃] *nf*: **~ (à)** invitation (to); **à** OU **sur l'~ de qqn** at sb's invitation; **sur ~** by invitation; **décliner une ~** to turn down an invitation.

invite [ɛ̃vit] *nf* invitation.

invité, -e [ɛ̃vite] ◇ *adj* [hôte] invited; [professeur, conférencier] guest (*avant n*). ◇ *nm, f* guest.

inviter [ɛ̃vite] [3] *vt* to invite; **~ qqn à faire qqch** to invite sb to do sthg; *fig* [suj: chose] to be an invitation to sb to do sthg; [ordonner] to urge sb to do sthg; **le beau temps invite à la promenade** this fine weather puts one in the mood for a walk.

in vitro [invitro] → **fécondation**.

invivable [ɛ̃vivabl] *adj* unbearable.

invocation [ɛ̃vɔkasjɔ̃] *nf* invocation; **~ à** call for.

involontaire [ɛ̃vɔlɔ̃tɛr] *adj* **-1.** [acte] involuntary. **-2.** [personne] unwilling.

involontairement [ɛ̃vɔlɔ̃tɛrmɑ̃] *adv* involuntarily, unintentionally.

invoquer [ɛ̃vɔke] [3] *vt* **-1.** [alléguer] to put forward. **-2.** [citer, appeler à l'aide] to invoke; [paix] to call for.

invraisemblable [ɛ̃vrɛsɑ̃blabl] *adj* **-1.** [incroyable] unlikely, improbable. **-2.** [extravagant] incredible.

invraisemblance [ɛ̃vrɛsɑ̃blɑ̃s] *nf* improbability.

invulnérable [ɛ̃vylnerabl] *adj* invulnerable.

iode [jɔd] *nm* iodine.

iodé, -e [jɔde] *adj* containing iodine.

ion [jɔ̃] *nm* ion.

IPC (*abr de* **indice des prix à la consommation**) *nm* CPI.

Ipsos [ipsos] *n French market research institute.*

IR (*abr de* **infra-rouge**) *adj* IR.

IRA [ira] (*abr de* **Irish Republican Army**) *nf* IRA.

irai, iras *etc* → **aller**.

Irak, Iraq [irak] *nm*: **l'~** Iraq.

irakien, -ienne, iraqien, -ienne [irakjɛ̃, jɛn] *adj* Iraqi.
◆ **irakien, iraqien** *nm* [langue] Iraqi.
◆ **Irakien, -ienne, Iraqien, -ienne** *nm, f* Iraqi.

Iran [irɑ̃] *nm*: **l'~** Iran.

iranien, -ienne [iranjɛ̃, jɛn] *adj* Iranian.
◆ **iranien** *nm* [langue] Iranian.
◆ **Iranien, -ienne** *nm, f* Iranian.

Iraq = Irak.

iraqien = irakien.

irascible [irasibl] *adj* irascible.

iris [iris] *nm* ANAT & BOT iris.

irisé, -e [irize] *adj* iridescent.

irlandais, -e [irlɑ̃dɛ, ɛz] *adj* Irish.
◆ **irlandais** *nm* [langue] Irish.
◆ **Irlandais, -e** *nm, f* Irishman (*f* Irishwoman).

Irlande [irlɑ̃d] *nf*: **l'~** Ireland; **l'~ du Nord/Sud** Northern/Southern Ireland.

ironie [irɔni] *nf* irony; **~ du sort** twist of fate.

ironique [irɔnik] *adj* ironic.

ironiquement [irɔnikmɑ̃] *adv* ironically.

ironiser [irɔnize] [3] *vi* to speak ironically.

IRPP (*abr de* **impôt sur le revenu des personnes physiques**) *nm* income tax.

irradiation [iradjasjɔ̃] *nf* [rayons] radiation; [action] irradiation.

irradier [iradje] [9] ◇ *vi* to radiate. ◇ *vt* to irradiate.

irraisonné, -e [irɛzɔne] *adj* irrational.

irrationnel, -elle [irasjɔnɛl] *adj* irrational.

irréalisable [irealizabl] *adj* unrealizable.

irréaliste [irealist] *adj* unrealistic.

irréalité [irealite] *nf* unreality.

irrecevable [irəsəvabl] *adj* inadmissible.

irréconciliable [irekɔ̃siljabl] *adj* irreconcilable.

irrécupérable [irekyperabl] *adj* **-1.** [irrécouvrable] irretrievable. **-2.** [irréparable] beyond repair. **-3.** *fam* [personne] beyond hope.

irrécusable [irekyzabl] *adj* unimpeachable.

irréductible [iredyktibl] ◇ *nmf* diehard. ◇ *adj* **-1.** CHIM, MATHS & MÉD irreducible. **-2.** *fig* [volonté] indomitable; [personne] implacable; [communiste] diehard (*avant n*).

irréel, -elle [ireɛl] *adj* unreal.

irréfléchi, -e [irefleʃi] *adj* unthinking.

irréfutable [irefytabl] *adj* irrefutable.

irrégularité [iregylarite] *nf* **-1.** [gén] irregularity. **-2.** [de terrain, performance] unevenness.

irrégulier, -ière [iregylje, jɛr] *adj* **-1.** [gén] irregular. **-2.** [terrain, surface] uneven, irregular. **-3.** [employé, athlète] erratic.

irrégulièrement [iregyljɛrmɑ̃] *adv* irregularly.

irrémédiable [iremedjabl] *adj* **-1.** [irréparable] irreparable. **-2.** [incurable] incurable.

irrémédiablement [iremedjabləmɑ̃] *adv* irreparably.

irremplaçable [irɑ̃plasabl] *adj* irreplaceable.

irréparable [ireparabl] ◇ *nm*: **commettre l'~** to do the unforgivable. ◇ *adj* **-1.** [objet] beyond repair. **-2.** *fig* [perte, erreur] irreparable.

irrepressible [irepresibl] *adj* irrepressible.

irréprochable [irepfoʃabl] *adj* irreproachable.

irrésistible [irezistibl] *adj* **-1.** [tentation, femme] irresistible. **-2.** [amusant] entertaining.

irrésistiblement [irezistibləmɑ̃] *adv* irresistibly.

irrésolu, -e [irezɔly] *adj* **-1.** [indécis] irresolute. **-2.** [sans solution] unresolved.

irrespirable [irɛspirabl] *adj* **-1.** [air] unbreathable. **-2.** *fig* [oppressant] oppressive.

irresponsable [irɛspɔ̃sabl] ◇ *nmf* irresponsible person. ◇ *adj* irresponsible.

irrévérencieux, -ieuse [ireverɑ̃sjø, jøz] *adj* irreverent.

irréversible [ireversibl] *adj* irreversible.

irrévocable [irevɔkabl] *adj* irrevocable.

irrévocablement [irevɔkabləmɑ̃] *adv* irrevocably.

irrigation [irigasjɔ̃] *nf* irrigation.

irriguer [irige] [3] *vt* to irrigate.

irritabilité [iritabilite] *nf* irritability.

irritable [iritabl] *adj* irritable.

irritant, -e [iritɑ̃, ɑ̃t] *adj* **-1.** [agaçant] irritating, annoying. **-2.** MÉD irritant.

irritation [iritasjɔ̃] *nf* irritation.

irriter [irite] [3] *vt* **-1.** [exaspérer] to irritate, to annoy. **-2.** MÉD to irritate.
◆ **s'irriter** *vp* to get irritated; **s'~ contre qqn/de qqch** to get irritated with sb/at sthg.

irruption [irypsjɔ̃] *nf* **-1.** [invasion] invasion. **-2.** [entrée brusque] irruption; **faire ~ dans** to burst into.

ISBN (*abr de* **International standard book number**) *nm* ISBN.

ISF (*abr de* **impôt de solidarité sur la fortune**) *nm* wealth tax.

islam [islam] *nm* Islam.

islamique [islamik] *adj* Islamic.

islamisation [islamizasjɔ̃] *nf* Islamization.

islamiser [islamize] [3] *vt* to Islamize.

islandais, -e [islɑ̃dɛ, ɛz] *adj* Icelandic.
◆ **islandais** *nm* [langue] Icelandic.
◆ **Islandais, -e** *nm, f* Icelander.

Islande [islɑ̃d] *nf*: **l'~** Iceland.

isocèle [izɔsɛl] *adj* isoceles.

isolant, -e [izɔlɑ̃, ɑ̃t] *adj* insulating.
◆ **isolant** *nm* insulator, insulating material.

isolateur, -trice [izɔlatœr, tris] *adj* insulating.
◆ **isolateur** *nm* insulator.

isolation [izɔlasjɔ̃] *nf* insulation; **~ phonique** soundproofing; **~ thermique** thermal insulation.

isolationnisme [izɔlasjɔnism] *nm* isolationism.

isolé, -e [izɔle] *adj* isolated.

isolement [izɔlmɑ̃] *nm* **-1.** [gén] isolation. **-2.** CONSTR & ÉLECTR insulation.

isolément [izɔlemɑ̃] *adv* individually.

isoler [izɔle] [3] *vt* **-1.** [séparer] to isolate; **~ qqch de qqch** to isolate sthg from sthg. **-2.** CONSTR & ÉLECTR to insulate; **~ qqch du froid** to insulate sthg (against the cold); **~ qqch du bruit** to soundproof sthg.
◆ **s'isoler** *vp*: **s'~ (de)** to isolate o.s. (from).

isoloir [izɔlwar] *nm* polling booth.

isotherme [izɔtɛrm] ◇ *nf* isotherm. ◇ *adj* isothermal.

Israël [izraɛl] *nm* Israel.

israélien, -ienne [israeljɛ̃, jɛn] *adj* Israeli.
◆ **Israélien, -ienne** *nm, f* Israeli.

israélite [israelit] *adj* Jewish.
◆ **Israélite** *nmf* Jew.

issu, -e [isy] *adj*: **~ de** [résultant de] emerging OU stemming from; [personne] descended from.
◆ **issue** *nf* **-1.** [sortie] exit; **~e de secours** emergency exit. **-2.** *fig* [solution] way out, solution; **sans ~e** hopeless. **-3.** [terme] outcome; **à l'~e de** at the end OU close of.

Istanbul [istaɑ̃bul] *n* Istanbul.

isthme [ism] *nm* isthmus.

Italie [itali] *nf*: **l'~** Italy.

italien, -ienne [italjɛ̃, jɛn] *adj* Italian.
◆ **italien** *nm* [langue] Italian.
◆ **Italien, -ienne** *nm, f* Italian.

italique [italik] ◇ *nm* **-1.** HIST & LING Italic. **-2.** TYPO italics (*pl*); **en ~** in italics. ◇ *adj* **-1.** HIST & LING Italic. **-2.** TYPO italic.

itinéraire [itinerɛr] *nm* itinerary, route.

itinérant, -e [itinerɑ̃, ɑ̃t] *adj* **-1.** [spectacle, troupe] itinerant. **-2.** [ambassadeur] roving (*avant n*).

itou [itu] *adv fam* as well.

ITP (*abr de* **ingénieur des travaux publics**) *nm* civil engineer.

IUFM (*abr de* **institut universitaire de formation des maîtres**) *nm* ≃ teacher training college *Br*, ≃ teachers college *Am*.

IUP (*abr de* **institut universitaire profes-sionnel**) *nm* business school.

IUT (*abr de* **institut universitaire de tech-nologie**) *nm* ≃ technical college.

IVG (*abr de* **interruption volontaire de grossesse**) *nf* abortion.

ivoire [ivwar] *nm* ivory.

ivoirien, -ienne [ivwarjɛ̃, jɛn] *adj* of/from the Ivory Coast.
◆ **Ivoirien, -ienne** *nm, f* native OU inhabi-tant of the Ivory Coast.

ivre [ivr] *adj* drunk; ~ **de colère** wild with anger; ~ **de joie** drunk OU mad with joy; ~ **mort** dead drunk.

ivresse [ivrɛs] *nf* drunkenness; [extase] rap-ture.

ivrogne [ivrɔɲ] *nmf* drunkard.

ivrognerie [ivrɔɲri] *nf* drunkenness.

j, J [ʒi] *nm inv* j, J.
◆ **J -1.** (*abr de* **joule**) J. **-2.** *abr de* **jour**.

j' → **je**.

jabot [ʒabo] *nm* **-1.** [d'oiseau] crop. **-2.** [de chemise] frill.

jacassement [ʒakasmɑ̃] *nm péj* chattering, jabbering.

jacasser [ʒakase] [3] *vi péj* to chatter, to jabber.

jachère [ʒaʃɛr] *nf*: **en** ~ fallow.

jacinthe [ʒasɛ̃t] *nf* hyacinth.

jacobin, -e [ʒakɔbɛ̃, in] *adj* Jacobin.
◆ **Jacobin** *nm* HIST Jacobin.

Jacuzzi® [ʒakyzi] *nm* Jacuzzi®.

jade [ʒad] *nm* jade.

jadis [ʒadis] *adv* formerly, in former times.

jaguar [ʒagwar] *nm* jaguar.

jaillir [ʒajir] [32] *vi* **-1.** [liquide] to gush; [flammes] to leap. **-2.** [cri] to ring out. **-3.** [personne] to spring out.

jais [ʒɛ] *nm* jet; **noir comme le** ~, **noir de** ~ jet-black.

Jakarta = **Djakarta**.

jalon [ʒalɔ̃] *nm* marker pole; **poser les (pre-miers)** ~s **de** *fig* to pave the way for.

jalonner [ʒalɔne] [3] *vt* to mark (out); **jalon-né de** [bordé de] lined with; *fig* punctuated with.

jalousement [ʒaluzmɑ̃] *adv* jealously.

jalouser [ʒaluze] [3] *vt* to be jealous of.

jalousie [ʒaluzi] *nf* **-1.** [envie] jealousy; **être malade** OU **crever de** ~ *fig* to be green with envy. **-2.** [store] blind.

jaloux, -ouse [ʒalu, uz] *adj*: ~ **(de)** jealous (of).

jamaïquain, -e, jamaïcain, -e [ʒamaikɛ̃, ɛn] *adj* Jamaican.
◆ **Jamaïquain, -e, Jamaïcain, -e** *nm, f* Ja-maican.

Jamaïque [ʒamaik] *nf*: **la** ~ Jamaica.

jamais [ʒamɛ] *adv* **-1.** [sens négatif] never; **ne ... ~**, ~ **ne** never; **je ne reviendrai** ~, ~ **je ne reviendrai** I'll never come back; **(ne) ... ~ plus, plus ~ (ne)** never again; **je ne viendrai ~ plus, plus ~ je ne viendrai** I'll never come here again; **plus ~!** never again! **-2.** [sens positif]: **plus que** ~ more than ever; **elle l'aimait plus que** ~ she loved him more than ever; **il est plus triste que** ~ he's sadder than ever; **si** ~ **tu le vois** if you should happen to see him, should you happen to see him.
◆ **à jamais** *loc adv* for ever.
◆ **pour jamais** *loc adv* for ever.

jambage [ʒɑ̃baʒ] *nm* [de lettre] downstroke.

jambe [ʒɑ̃b] *nf* leg; **courir à toutes** ~s to run flat out; **il s'enfuit à toutes** ~s he ran away as fast as his legs would carry him; **prendre ses** ~s **à son cou** to take to one's heels; **tenir la** ~ **à qqn** *fam fig* to keep sb talking; **ça me fait une belle** ~! *fam fig* that's no good to me!

jambières [ʒɑ̃bjɛr] *nfpl* [de football] shin pads; [de cricket] pads.

jambon [ʒɑ̃bɔ̃] *nm* ham; ~ **blanc** ham; ~ **fumé** smoked ham.

jambonneau, -x [ʒɑ̃bɔno] *nm* knuckle of ham.

jante [ʒɑ̃t] *nf* (wheel) rim.

janvier [ʒɑ̃vje] *nm* January; *voir aussi* **sep-tembre**.

Japon [ʒapɔ̃] *nm*: **le** ~ Japan; **au** ~ in Japan.

japonais, -e [ʒaponɛ, ɛz] *adj* Japanese.
◆ **japonais** *nm* [langue] Japanese.
◆ **Japonais, -e** *nm, f* Japanese (person); **les Japonais** the Japanese.

jappement [ʒapmɑ̃] *nm* yap, yapping (U).

japper [ʒape] [3] *vi* to yap.

jaquette [ʒakɛt] *nf* **-1.** [vêtement] jacket. **-2.** [de livre] (dust) jacket.

jardin [ʒardɛ̃] *nm* garden; ~ **d'enfants** nursery school, kindergarten; ~ **public** park; ~ **zoologique** zoo.

jardinage [ʒardinaʒ] *nm* gardening.

jardiner [ʒardine] [3] *vi* to garden.

jardinet [ʒardinɛ] *nm* small garden.

jardinier, -ière [ʒardinje, jɛr] *nm, f* gardener.

◆ **jardinière** *nf* -1. [bac à fleurs] window box. -2. CULIN: **jardinière de légumes** mixed vegetables (*pl*).

jargon [ʒargɔ̃] *nm* -1. [langage spécialisé] jargon. -2. *fam* [charabia] gibberish.

jarret [ʒarɛ] *nm* -1. ANAT back of the knee. -2. CULIN knuckle of veal.

jarretelle [ʒartɛl] *nf* suspender *Br*, garter *Am*.

jarretière [ʒartjɛr] *nf* garter.

jars [ʒar] *nm* gander.

jaser [ʒaze] [3] *vi* [bavarder] to gossip.

jasmin [ʒasmɛ̃] *nm* jasmine.

jatte [ʒat] *nf* bowl.

jauge [ʒoʒ] *nf* [instrument] gauge; ~ **de niveau d'huile** dipstick.

jauger [ʒoʒe] [17] *vt* to gauge.

jaunâtre [ʒonatr] *adj* yellowish.

jaune [ʒon] ◇ *nm* [couleur] yellow. ◇ *adj* yellow. ◇ *adv*: **rire** ~ *fig* to force o.s. to laugh.

◆ **jaune d'œuf** *nm* (egg) yolk.

jaunir [ʒonir] [32] *vt & vi* to turn yellow.

jaunisse [ʒonis] *nf* MÉD jaundice; **en faire une** ~ *fam fig* [de jalousie] to be green with envy; [de déception] to take it badly.

jaunissement [ʒonismɑ̃] *nm* yellowing.

java [ʒava] *nf type of popular dance*; **faire la** ~ *fam fig* to live it up.

Java [ʒava] *n* Java; **à** ~ in Java.

javanais, -e [ʒavanɛ, ɛz] *adj* Javanese.

◆ **javanais** *nm* [langue] Javanese.

◆ **Javanais, -e** *nm, f* Javanese (person); **les Javanais** the Javanese.

javel [ʒavɛl]

◆ **(eau de) Javel** *nf* bleach.

javelliser [ʒavelize] [3] *vt* to chlorinate.

javelot [ʒavlo] *nm* javelin.

jazz [dʒaz] *nm* jazz.

J.-C. (*abr de* **Jésus-Christ**) J.C.

je [ʒə], **j'** (*devant voyelle et h muet*) *pron pers* I.

jean [dʒin], **jeans** [dʒins] *nm* jeans (*pl*), pair of jeans.

Jeanne d'Arc [ʒandark]

◆ **coiffure à la Jeanne d'Arc** *nf* page boy (haircut).

Jeep® [dʒip] *nf* Jeep®.

je-m'en-foutisme [ʒmɑ̃futism] *nm* couldn't- give-a-damn attitude.

jérémiades [ʒeremjad] *nfpl* moaning (*U*), whining (*U*).

jerrycan, jerricane [ʒerikan] *nm* jerry can.

jersey [ʒɛrzɛ] *nm* jersey; **point de** ~ stocking stitch.

Jersey [ʒɛrzɛ] *n* Jersey; **à** ~ on Jersey.

Jérusalem [ʒeryzalɛm] *n* Jerusalem.

jésuite [ʒezɥit] ◇ *nm* Jesuit. ◇ *adj* Jesuit; *péj* jesuitical.

Jésus-Christ [ʒezykri] *nm* Jesus Christ.

jet¹ [ʒɛ] *nm* -1. [action de jeter] throw; **d'un seul** ~ *fig* in one go. -2. [de liquide] jet; ~ **d'eau** fountain. -3. [esquisse]: **premier** ~ rough outline OU draft.

jet² [dʒɛt] *nm* [avion] jet.

jetable [ʒətabl] *adj* disposable.

jetais, jetions *etc* → **jeter**.

jeté, -e [ʒəte] *pp* → **jeter**.

jetée [ʒəte] *nf* jetty.

jeter [ʒəte] [27] *vt* to throw; [se débarrasser de] to throw away; ~ **qqch à qqn** [lancer] to throw sthg to sb, to throw sb sthg; [pour faire mal] to throw sthg at sb; ~ **qqn dehors** to throw sb out; ~ **un coup d'œil (à)** to take a look (at).

◆ **se jeter** *vp*: **se** ~ **sur** to pounce on; **se** ~ **dans** [suj: rivière] to flow into; **se** ~ **dans les bras de qqn** to throw o.s. into sb's arms; **se** ~ **à l'eau** *fig* to take the plunge.

jeton [ʒətɔ̃] *nm* -1. [de jeu] counter; [de téléphone] token. -2. *loc*: **avoir les** ~s *fam* to have the jitters.

◆ **faux-jeton** *nm* hypocrite.

◆ **jeton de présence** *nm* fees paid to non-executive directors of a company.

jette, jettes *etc* → **jeter**.

jetterai, jetteras *etc* → **jeter**.

jeu, -x [ʒø] *nm* -1. [divertissement] play (*U*), playing (*U*); **par** ~ for fun; ~ **de mots** play on words, pun. -2. [régi par des règles] game; **en** ~ in (play); **hors** ~ out (of play); **mettre un joueur hors** ~ to put a player offside; ~ **de l'oie** ≃ snakes and ladders; ~ **de société** parlour game; ~ **télévisé** game show. -3. [d'argent]: **le** ~ gambling; ~ **de hasard** game of chance. -4. [d'échecs, de clés] set; ~ **de cartes** pack of cards. -5. [manière de jouer - MUS] playing; [- THÉÂTRE] acting; [- SPORT] game. -6. [TECHNOL] play; **il y a du** ~ there's a bit of play, it's rather loose. -7. *loc*: **cacher son** ~ to play one's cards close to one's chest; **être en** ~ to be at stake; **entrer en** ~ to come into play; **entrer dans le** ~ **de qqn** to play sb's game.

◆ **Jeux Olympiques** *nmpl*: **les Jeux Olym-piques** the Olympic Games.

jeudi [ʒødi] *nm* Thursday; ~ **saint** Maundy Thursday; *voir aussi* **samedi**.

jeun [ʒœ̃]

◆ **à jeun** *loc adv* on an empty stomach.

jeune [ʒœn] ◇ *adj* young; [style, apparence] youthful; ~ **homme/femme** young man/ woman; ~ **fille** girl; ~**s gens** [gén] young people; [garçons] young men. ◇ *adv*: **faire** ~ to look young. ◇ *nm* young person; **les** ~**s** young people.

jeûne [ʒøn] *nm* fast.

jeûner [ʒøne] [3] *vi* to fast.

jeunesse [ʒœnɛs] *nf* **-1.** [âge] youth; [de style, apparence] youthfulness. **-2.** [jeunes gens] young people (*pl*).

JF, jf *abr de* **jeune fille**.

JH *abr de* **jeune homme**.

jingle [dʒingəl] *nm* jingle.

JO ◇ *nm* (*abr de* **Journal officiel**) *bulletin giving details of laws and official announcements.* ◇ *nmpl* (*abr de* **Jeux Olympiques**) *Olympic Games.*

joaillerie [ʒɔajri] *nf* **-1.** [métier] jewel trade. **-2.** [magasin] jeweller's (shop).

joaillier, -ière [ʒɔaje, jɛr] *nm, f* jeweller.

job [dʒɔb] *nm fam* job.

jobard, -e [ʒɔbar, ard] *adj fam* gullible.

jockey [ʒɔkɛ] *nm* jockey.

jogging [dʒɔgiŋ] *nm* **-1.** [activité] jogging; **faire du** ~ to go jogging, to go for a jog. **-2.** [vêtement] tracksuit, jogging suit.

joie [ʒwa] *nf* joy; **avec** ~ with pleasure; ~ **de vivre** joie de vivre, joy of living.

joignable [ʒwaɲabl] *adj* contactable.

joignais, joignions *etc* → **joindre**.

joindre [jwɛ̃dr] [82] *vt* **-1.** [rapprocher] to join; [mains] to put together; **(ne pas) arriver à** ~ **les deux bouts** *fam fig* (to be unable) to make ends meet. **-2.** [ajouter]: ~ **qqch (à)** to attach sthg (to); [adjoindre] to enclose sthg (with). **-3.** [par téléphone] to contact, to reach.

◆ **se joindre** *vp*: **se** ~ **à qqn** to join sb; **se** ~ **à qqch** to join in sthg.

joint, -e [ʒwɛ̃, ɛ̃t] *pp* → **joindre**.

◆ **joint** *nm* **-1.** [d'étanchéité] seal. **-2.** *fam* [drogue] joint.

◆ **joint de culasse** *nm* cylinder head gasket.

jointure [ʒwɛ̃tyr] *nf* ANAT joint.

joker [ʒɔkɛr] *nm* joker.

joli, -e [ʒɔli] *adj* **-1.** [femme, chose] pretty, attractive. **-2.** [somme, situation] nice. **-3.** *loc*: **c'est bien** ~, **mais ...** that's all very well, but ...; **c'est du** ~ **travail!** *iron* well done!

joliment [ʒɔlimɑ̃] *adv* **-1.** [bien] prettily, attractively; *iron* nicely. **-2.** *fam* [beaucoup] really.

jonc [ʒɔ̃] *nm* rush, bulrush.

joncher [ʒɔ̃ʃe] [3] *vt* to strew; **être jonché de** to be strewn with.

jonction [ʒɔ̃ksjɔ̃] *nf* [de routes] junction.

jongler [ʒɔ̃gle] [3] *vi* to juggle.

jongleur, -euse [ʒɔ̃glœr, øz] *nm, f* juggler.

jonquille [ʒɔ̃kij] *nf* daffodil.

Jordanie [ʒɔrdani] *nf*: **la** ~ Jordan.

jordanien, -ienne [ʒɔrdanjɛ̃, jɛn] *adj* Jordanian.

◆ **Jordanien, -ienne** *nm, f* Jordanian.

jouable [ʒwabl] *adj* **-1.** SPORT playable. **-2.** [situation] feasible.

joual [ʒwal] *nm Can French-Canadian dialect.*

joue [ʒu] *nf* cheek; **tenir** OU **mettre qqn en** ~ *fig* to take aim at sb.

jouer [ʒwe] [6] ◇ *vi* **-1.** [gén] to play; ~ **avec qqn/qqch** to play with sb/sthg; ~ **à qqch** [jeu, sport] to play sthg; ~ **de** MUS to play; **à toi de** ~! (it's) your turn!; *fig* your move! **-2.** CIN & THÉÂTRE to act. **-3.** [parier] to gamble. **-4.** [s'appliquer] to apply. **-5.** *loc*: ~ **des coudes** to use one's elbows; ~ **de malchance** to be dogged by bad luck; ~ **sur les mots** to play with words.

◇ *vt* **-1.** [carte, partie] to play. **-2.** [somme d'argent] to bet, to wager; *fig* to gamble with. **-3.** [THÉÂTRE - personnage, rôle] to play; [- pièce] to put on, to perform. **-4.** CIN to show. **-5.** MUS to perform, to play. **-6.** *loc*: ~ **la comédie** to put on an act; ~ **le jeu** to play the game; ~ **un tour à qqn** to play a trick on sb.

◆ **se jouer** *vp*: **se** ~ **de qqch** to make light of sthg; **se** ~ **de qqn** to deceive sb.

jouet [ʒwɛ] *nm* toy; **être le** ~ **de** *fig* to be the victim of.

joueur, -euse [ʒwœr, øz] *nm, f* **-1.** SPORT player; ~ **de football** footballer, football player; **être beau/mauvais** ~ to be a good/ bad loser. **-2.** [du jeu] gambler.

joufflu, -e [ʒufly] *adj* [personne] chubby-cheeked.

joug [ʒu] *nm* yoke.

jouir [ʒwir] [32] *vi* **-1.** [profiter]: ~ **de** to enjoy. **-2.** [sexuellement] to have an orgasm.

jouissance [ʒwisɑ̃s] *nf* **-1.** JUR [d'un bien] use. **-2.** [sexuelle] orgasm.

joujou, -x [ʒuʒu] *nm* toy.

jour [ʒur] *nm* **-1.** [unité de temps] day; **huit** ~**s** a week; **quinze** ~**s** a fortnight *Br*, two weeks; **tous les ~s** every day; **l'autre ~** the other day; **de ~ en ~** day by day; **~ après ~** day after day; **au ~ le ~** from day to day; **~ et nuit** night and day; **du ~ au lendemain** overnight; **~ pour ~** to the day; **le ~ de l'an** New Year's Day; **~ de congé** day off; **~ férié** public holiday; **~ de fête** holiday; **le ~ J** D-Day; **~ ouvrable** working day. **-2.** [lumière] daylight; **de ~** in the daytime, by day; **il fait ~** it's light; **au petit ~** at the crack of dawn; **au grand ~** in broad daylight. **-3.** [époque] day; **le ~ où** the day (that); **un beau ~** one fine day; **un de ces ~s** one of these days. **-4.** *loc*: **être à ~** to be up-to-date; **mettre qqch à ~** to update sthg, to bring sthg up to date; **de nos ~s** these days, nowadays; **se faire ~** to become clear; **sous un ~ nouveau** in a new light.

journal, -aux [ʒurnal, o] *nm* **-1.** [publication] newspaper, paper; **le ~ officiel de la République française** *official publication in which public notices appear.* **-2.** TÉLÉ: **~ télévisé** television news. **-3.** [écrit]: **~ (intime)** diary, journal; **~ de bord** NAVIG ship's log; INFORM log.

---

journalier, -ière [ʒurnalje, jɛr] *adj* daily.

journalisme [ʒurnalism] *nm* journalism.

journaliste [ʒurnalist] *nmf* journalist, reporter.

journalistique [ʒurnalistik] *adj* journalistic.

journée [ʒurne] *nf* day; **faire la ~ continue** to work through lunch.

journellement [ʒurnɛlmɑ̃] *adv* daily.

joute [ʒut] *nf* joust; *fig* duel.

jouxter [ʒukste] [3] *vt* to adjoin.

jovial, -e, -iaux [ʒɔvjal, jo] *adj* jovial, jolly.

jovialité [ʒɔvjalite] *nf* joviality, jolliness.

joyau, -x [ʒwajo] *nm* jewel.

joyeusement [ʒwajøzmɑ̃] *adv* joyfully.

joyeux, -euse [ʒwajø, øz] *adj* joyful, happy; **~ Noël!** Merry Christmas!

JT (*abr de* **journal télévisé**) *nm* television news.

jubilation [ʒybilasjɔ̃] *nf* jubilation.

jubilé [ʒybile] *nm* jubilee.

jubiler [ʒybile] [3] *vi fam* to be jubilant.

jucher [ʒyʃe] [3] *vt*: **~ qqn sur qqch** to perch sb on sthg.

◆ **se jucher** *vp*: **se ~ sur qqch** to perch on sthg.

judaïque [ʒydaik] *adj* [loi] Judaic; [tradition, religion] Jewish.

judaïsme [ʒydaism] *nm* Judaism.

judas [ʒyda] *nm* [ouverture] peephole.

Judée [ʒyde] *nf*: **la ~** Judaea, Judea.

judéo-chrétien, -ienne [ʒydeɔkretjɛ̃, jɛn] (*mpl* **judéo-chrétiens**, *fpl* **judéo-chrétiennes**) *adj* Judaeo-Christian.

judiciaire [ʒydisjɛr] *adj* judicial.

judicieusement [ʒydisjøzmɑ̃] *adv* judiciously.

judicieux, -ieuse [ʒydisjø, jøz] *adj* judicious.

judo [ʒydo] *nm* judo.

juge [ʒyʒ] *nm* judge; **~ d'instruction** examining magistrate; **~ de ligne** TENNIS line judge; **~ de paix** justice of the peace; **~ de touche** FOOTBALL linesman; RUGBY touch judge.

jugé [ʒyʒe]

◆ **au jugé** *loc adv* by guesswork; **tirer au ~** to fire blind.

jugement [ʒyʒmɑ̃] *nm* judgment; **prononcer un ~** to pass sentence; **~ de valeur** value judgment.

◆ **Jugement** *nm*: **le Jugement dernier** the Last Judgment.

jugeote [ʒyʒɔt] *nf fam* common sense; **manquer de ~** to have no common sense.

juger [ʒyʒe] [17] ◇ *vt* to judge; [accusé] to try; **~ que** to judge (that), to consider (that); **~ qqn/qqch inutile** to consider sb/sthg useless; **~ bon de faire qqch** to consider it appropriate to do sthg. ◇ *vi* to judge; **~ de qqch** to judge sthg; **si j'en juge d'après mon expérience** judging from my experience; **jugez de ma surprise!** imagine my surprise!

juguler [ʒygyle] [3] *vt* [maladie] to halt; [révolte] to put down; [inflation] to curb.

juif, juive [ʒɥif, ʒɥiv] *adj* Jewish.

◆ **Juif, Juive** *nm, f* Jew.

juillet [ʒɥijɛ] *nm* July; **la fête du 14 Juillet** *the fourteenth of July celebrations; voir aussi* **septembre**.

---

the morning and a firework display in the evening

juin [ʒɥɛ̃] *nm* June; *voir aussi* **septembre**.

juke-box [dʒukbɔks] *nm inv* jukebox.

julienne [ʒyljɛn] *nf*: ~ **de légumes** *(clear soup with) very thin strips of vegetable*.

jumeau, -elle, **-x** [ʒymo, ɛl, o] ◇ *adj* twin *(avant n)*. ◇ *nm, f* twin; **vrais/faux ~x** identical/fraternal twins.

◆ **jumelles** *nfpl* OPTIQUE binoculars.

jumelage [ʒymlaʒ] *nm* twinning.

jumelé, -e [ʒymle] *adj* [villes] twinned; [maisons] semidetached; **roues ~es** double wheels.

jumeler [ʒymle] [24] *vt* to twin.

jumelle → **jumeau**.

jument [ʒymɑ̃] *nf* mare.

jungle [ʒœ̃gl] *nf* jungle.

junior [ʒynjɔr] *adj & nm, f* SPORT junior.

junte [ʒœ̃t] *nf* junta.

jupe [ʒyp] *nf* skirt.

jupe-culotte [ʒypkylɔt] *(pl* **jupes-culottes**) *nf* culottes *(pl)*.

jupon [ʒypɔ̃] *nm* petticoat, slip.

Jura [ʒyra] *nm*: **le ~** the Jura (Mountains).

juré, -e [ʒyre] ◇ *adj*: **ennemi ~** sworn enemy. ◇ *nm, f* JUR juror.

jurer [ʒyre] [3] ◇ *vt*: ~ **qqch à qqn** to swear OU pledge sthg to sb; ~ **(à qqn) que** ... to swear (to sb) that ...; ~ **de faire qqch** to swear OU vow to do sthg; **je le jure** I swear; **je vous jure!** *fam* honestly!; **ne plus** ~ **que par** to swear by. ◇ *vi* **-1.** [blasphémer] to swear, to curse. **-2.** [ne pas aller ensemble]: ~ **(avec)** to clash (with).

◆ **se jurer** *vp*: **se ~ de faire qqch** to swear OU vow to do sthg.

juridiction [ʒyridiksjɔ̃] *nf* jurisdiction.

juridictionnel, -elle [ʒyridiksjɔnɛl] *adj* jurisdictional.

juridique [ʒyridik] *adj* legal.

juridiquement [ʒyridikmɑ̃] *adv* legally.

jurisprudence [ʒyrisprydɑ̃s] *nf* jurisprudence; **faire ~** to set a precedent.

juriste [ʒyrist] *nmf* lawyer.

juron [ʒyrɔ̃] *nm* swearword, oath.

jury [ʒyri] *nm* **-1.** JUR jury. **-2.** [SCOL - d'examen] examining board; [- de concours] admissions board.

jus [ʒy] *nm* **-1.** [de fruits, légumes] juice; ~ **d'orange/de pomme** orange/apple juice. **-2.** [de viande] gravy.

jusqu'au-boutiste [ʒyskobutist] *nmf* hard-liner.

jusque, jusqu' [ʒysk(ə)]

◆ **jusqu'à** *loc prép* **-1.** [sens temporel] until, till; **jusqu'à nouvel ordre** until further notice; **jusqu'à présent** up until now, so far. **-2.** [sens spatial] as far as; **jusqu'au bout** to the end. **-3.** [même] even; **aller jusqu'à faire qqch** *fig* to go so far as to do sthg.

◆ **jusqu'à ce que** *loc conj* until, till.

◆ **jusqu'en** *loc prép* up until.

◆ **jusqu'ici** *loc adv* [lieu] up to here; [temps] up until now, so far.

◆ **jusque-là** *loc adv* [lieu] up to there; [temps] up until then.

justaucorps [ʒystokɔr] *nm* [maillot] leotard.

juste [ʒyst] ◇ *adj* **-1.** [équitable] fair. **-2.** [exact] right, correct. **-3.** [trop petit] tight. ◇ *adv* **-1.** [bien] correctly, right. **-2.** [exactement, seulement] just.

◆ **au juste** *loc adv* exactly.

◆ **tout juste** *loc adv* only just.

justement [ʒystəmɑ̃] *adv* **-1.** [avec raison] rightly. **-2.** [précisément] exactly, precisely.

justesse [ʒystɛs] *nf* [de remarque] aptness; [de raisonnement] soundness.

◆ **de justesse** *loc adv* only just.

justice [ʒystis] *nf* **-1.** JUR justice; **se faire ~** [se suicider] to take one's life; **passer en ~** to stand trial; **rendre la ~** to dispense justice; **rendre ~ à qqn/qqch** to do justice to sb/sthg. **-2.** [équité] fairness.

justiciable [ʒystisjabl] *adj*: **être ~ de** JUR to be answerable to.

justicier, -ière [ʒystisje, jɛr] *nm, f* righter of wrongs.

justifiable [ʒystifjabl] *adj* justifiable.

justificatif, -ive [ʒystifikatif, iv] *adj* supporting.

◆ **justificatif** *nm* written proof *(U)*.

justification [ʒystifikasjɔ̃] *nf* justification.

justifier [ʒystifje] [9] *vt* **-1.** [gén] to justify. **-2.** TYPO: ~ **à gauche/à droite** to left-/right-justify.

◆ **se justifier** *vp* to justify o.s.

jute [ʒyt] *nm* jute.

juter [ʒyte] [3] *vi* [fruit] to be juicy.

juteux, -euse [ʒytø, øz] *adj* juicy; **une affaire juteuse** *fam* a nice little earner.

juvénile [ʒyvenil] *adj* youthful.

juxtaposé, -e [ʒykstapoze] *adj* juxtaposed.

juxtaposer [ʒykstapoze] [3] *vt* to juxtapose.

juxtaposition [ʒykstapozisjɔ̃] *nf* juxtaposition.

K

k, K [ka] *nm inv* k, K.
K7 [kasɛt] (*abr de* **cassette**) *nf* cassette;
radio-~ radiocassette.
Kaboul [kabul] *n* Kabul.
kabyle [kabil] ◇ *adj* Kabyle. ◇ *nm* [langue]
Kabyle.
◆ **Kabyle** *nmf* Kabyle.
Kabylie [kabili] *nf:* **la ~** Kabylia.
kaki [kaki] ◇ *nm* **-1.** [couleur] khaki. **-2.**
[fruit] persimmon. ◇ *adj inv* khaki.
kaléidoscope [kaleidɔskɔp] *nm* kaleidoscope.
kamikaze [kamikaz] *nm* kamikaze pilot.
Kampuchéa [kɑ̃pyʃea] *nm:* **le ~** Kampuchea.
kanak = **canaque**.
kangourou [kɑ̃guru] *nm* kangaroo.
kapok [kapɔk] *nm* kapok.
karaoké [karaɔke] *nm* karaoke.
karaté [karate] *nm* karate.
karité [karite] *nm* shea.
kart [kart] *nm* go-kart.
karting [kartiŋ] *nm* go-karting.
kas(c)her, **cascher** [kaʃɛr] *adj inv* kosher;
manger ~ to eat kosher food.
Katar = **Qatar**.
Katmand(o)u [katmɑ̃du] *n* Katmandu.
kayak [kajak] *nm* kayak.
KCS (*abr de* **couronne tchécoslovaque**) Kcs.
Kenya [kenja] *nm:* **le ~** Kenya; **au ~** in
Kenya.
kenyan, -e [kenjɑ̃, an] *adj* Kenyan.
◆ **Kenyan, -e en, f** Kenyan.
képi [kepi] *nm* kepi.
kératine [keratin] *nf* keratin.
kermesse [kɛrmɛs] *nf* **-1.** [foire] fair. **-2.**
[fête de bienfaisance] fête.
kérosène [kerɔzɛn] *nm* kerosene.
ketchup [kɛtʃœp] *nm* ketchup.
KF -1. *abr de* **kilofranc. -2.** *abr de* **café**.
kg (*abr de* **kilogramme**) kg.
KGB (*abr de* **Komitet Gossoudarstvennoï
Bezopasnosti**) *nm* KGB.

khâgne [kaɲ] *nf* second year of a two-year
preparatory arts course taken prior to the competitive examination for entry to the École normale
supérieure.
Khartoum [kartum] *n* Khartoum.
khmer, -ère [kmɛr] *adj* Khmer.
◆ **khmer** *nm* [langue] Khmer.
◆ **Khmer, -ère** *nm, f* Khmer.
khôl [kol], **kohol** [kɔɔl] *nm* kohl.
kibboutz [kibutz] *nm inv* kibbutz.
kidnapper [kidnape] [3] *vt* to kidnap.
kidnapping [kidnapiŋ] *nm* kidnap.
kif-kif [kifkif] *adj inv fam:* **c'est ~** it makes
no odds *Br*, it's all the same.
kilo [kilo] *nm* kilo.
kilofranc [kilofrɑ̃] *nm* one thousand francs.
kilogramme [kilɔgram] *nm* kilogram.
kilométrage [kilɔmetraʒ] *nm* **-1.** [de voiture]
≃ mileage; **~ illimité** ≃ unlimited mileage.
-2. [distance] distance.
kilomètre [kilɔmɛtr] *nm* kilometre.
kilométrique [kilɔmetrik] *adj* kilometric.
kilo-octet [kilɔɔktɛ] *nm* INFORM kilobyte.
kilowatt [kilɔwat] *nm* kilowatt.
kilowatt-heure [kilɔwatœr] (*pl* **kilowatts-
heures**) *nm* kilowatt-hour.
kilt [kilt] *nm* kilt.
kimono [kimɔno] *nm* kimono.
kinésithérapeute [kineziterapøt] *nmf*
physiotherapist.
Kinshasa [kinʃasa] *n* Kinshasa.
kiosque [kjɔsk] *nm* **-1.** [de vente] kiosk; **~ à
journaux** newspaper kiosk. **-2.** [pavillon]
pavilion. **-3.** [de navire] pilot house, wheel-
house.
kir [kir] *nm* mixture of white wine and blackcurrant liqueur.
kirsch [kirʃ] *nm* cherry brandy.
kit [kit] *nm* kit; **en ~** in kit form.
kitchenette [kitʃɛnɛt] *nf* kitchenette.
kitsch [kitʃ] *adj inv* kitsch.
kiwi [kiwi] *nm* **-1.** [oiseau] kiwi. **-2.** [fruit]
kiwi, kiwi fruit (*U*).
Klaxon® [klaksɔ] *nm* horn.
klaxonner [klaksɔne] [3] *vi* to hoot.
kleptomane, **cleptomane** [klɛptɔman] *nmf*
kleptomaniac.
kleptomanie [klɛptɔmani] *nf* kleptomania.
km (*abr de* **kilomètre**) km.
km/h (*abr de* **kilomètre par heure**) kph.
Ko (*abr de* **kilo-octet**) K.
K.O. [kao] *nm:* **mettre qqn ~** to knock sb
out.
koala [kɔala] *nm* koala (bear).

kohol = khôl.

Kosovo [kɔsɔvɔ] *nm*: **le** ~ Kosovo-Metohija; **au** ~ in Kosovo-Metohija.

kouglof, **kugelhof** [kuglɔf] *nm cake made with dried fruit and almonds.*

Koweït [kɔwɛt] *nm*: **le** ~ Kuwait; **au** ~ in Kuwait.

Koweït City [kɔwɛtsiti] *n* Kuwait.

koweïtien, -ienne [kɔwɛtjɛ̃, jɛn] *adj* Kuwaiti.
◆ **Koweïtien, -ienne** *nm, f* Kuwaiti.

krach [krak] *nm* crash; ~ **boursier** stock market crash.

kraft [kraft] *nm* kraft; **papier** ~ brown paper.

KRD (*abr de* **couronne danoise**) Kr, DKr.

KRN (*abr de* **couronne norvégienne**) Kr, NKr.

KRS (*abr de* **couronne suédoise**) Kr, Skr.

Kuala Lumpur [kyalalympyr] *n* Kuala Lumpur.

kugelhof = **kouglof**.

kumquat [kumkwat] *nm* kumquat.

kung-fu [kuŋfu] *nm* kung fu.

kurde [kyrd] ◇ *adj* Kurdish. ◇ *nm* [langue] Kurdish.
◆ **Kurde** *nmf* Kurd.

Kurdistan [kyrdistɑ̃] *nm*: **le** ~ Kurdistan; **au** ~ in Kurdistan.

kWh (*abr de* **kilowatt-heure**) kW/hr.

Kyoto [kiɔtɔ] *n* Kyoto.

kyrielle [kirjɛl] *nf fam* stream; [d'enfants] horde.

kyste [kist] *nm* cyst.

L

l, L [ɛl] ◇ *nm inv* l, L. ◇ (*abr de* **litre**) l.

la¹ [la] *art déf & pron déf* → **le**.

la² [la] *nm inv* MUS A; [dans la gamme] la.

là [la] *adv* **-1.** [lieu] there; **à 3 kilomètres de** ~ 3 kilometres from there; **passe par** ~ go that way; **c'est** ~ **que je travaille** that's where I work; **je suis** ~ I'm here; **les faits sont** ~ those are the facts. **-2.** [temps] then; **à quelques jours de** ~ a few days later, a few days after that. **-3.** [dans cela]: **la santé, tout est** ~ (good) health is everything; ~ **est le vrai problème** that's the real problem. **-4.** [avec une proposition relative]: ~ **où** [lieu] where; [temps] when. **-5.** *loc*: **de** ~ **à dire qu'elle est sympathique, il y a loin!** there's a big difference between saying that and saying that she's a nice person; **nous en sommes** ~ that's the stage we've reached; **s'en tenir** ~ to call a halt (there); *voir aussi* **ce, là-bas, là-dedans** *etc*.

là-bas [laba] *adv* (over) there.

label [labɛl] *nm* **-1.** [étiquette]: ~ **de qualité** label guaranteeing quality. **-2.** [commerce] label, brand name.

labeur [labœr] *nm sout* labour.

labial, -e, -iaux [labjal, jo] *adj* labial.

labo [labo] (*abr de* **laboratoire**) *nm fam* lab.

laborantin, -e [labɔrɑ̃tɛ̃, in] *nm, f* laboratory assistant.

laboratoire [labɔratwar] *nm* laboratory; ~ **d'analyses** test laboratory; ~ **de langues** language laboratory.

laborieusement [labɔrjøzmɑ̃] *adv* laboriously.

laborieux, -ieuse [labɔrjø, jøz] *adj* **-1.** [difficile] laborious. **-2.** [travailleur] industrious; **les classes laborieuses** the working class (*sg*).

labour [labur] *nm* **-1.** [labourage] ploughing. **-2.** (*gén pl*) [terres] ploughed field.

labourage [laburaʒ] *nm* ploughing.

labourer [labure] [3] *vt* **-1.** AGRIC to plough. **-2.** *fig* [creuser] to make a gash in.

laboureur [laburœr] *nm* ploughman.

labrador [labradɔr] *nm* labrador.

labyrinthe [labirɛ̃t] *nm* labyrinth.

lac [lak] *nm* lake; **les Grands Lacs** the Great Lakes; **le ~ Léman** Lake Geneva; **le ~ Majeur** Lake Maggiore.

lacer [lase] [16] *vt* to tie.

lacérer [lasere] [18] *vt* -1. [déchirer] to shred. -2. [blesser, griffer] to slash.

lacet [lasɛ] *nm* -1. [cordon] lace. -2. [de route] bend. -3. [piège] snare.

lâche [laʃ] ◇ *nmf* coward. ◇ *adj* -1. [nœud] loose. -2. [personne, comportement] cowardly.

lâchement [laʃmɑ̃] *adv* like a coward/cowards.

lâcher [laʃe] [3] ◇ *vt* -1. [libérer - bras, objet] to let go of; [- animal] to let go, to release; *fig* [- mot] to let slip. -2. [laisser tomber]: ~ **qqch** to drop sthg. -3. *fam* [plaquer - ami] ~ **qqn** to drop sb. ◇ *vi* to give way. ◇ *nm*: **un ~ de** a release of.

lâcheté [laʃte] *nf* -1. [couardise] cowardice. -2. [acte] cowardly act.

lâcheur, -euse [laʃœr, øz] *nm, f fam* unreliable person.

lacis [lasi] *nm* [labyrinthe] maze.

laconique [lakɔnik] *adj* laconic.

laconiquement [lakɔnikmɑ̃] *adv* laconically.

lacrymal, -e, -aux [lakrimal, o] *adj* lacrimal.

lacrymogène [lakrimɔʒɛn] *adj* tear (*avant n*).

lactation [laktasjɔ̃] *nf* lactation.

lacté, -e [lakte] *adj* [régime] milk (*avant n*).

lactique [laktik] *adj* lactic.

lacunaire [lakynɛr] *adj* [insuffisant] incomplete.

lacune [lakyn] *nf* [manque] gap.

lacustre [lakystr] *adj* [faune, plante] lake (*avant n*); [cité, village] lakeside (*avant n*).

lad [lad] *nm* stable lad.

là-dedans [ladədɑ̃] *adv* inside, in there; **il y a quelque chose qui m'intrigue ~** there's something in that which intrigues me.

là-dessous [ladsu] *adv* underneath, under there; *fig* behind that.

là-dessus [ladsy] *adv* on that; **~, il partit** at that point OU with that, he left; **je suis d'accord ~** I agree about that.

ladite → **ledit**.

lagon [lagɔ̃] *nm*, **lagune** [lagyn] *nf* lagoon.

Lagos [lagos] *nm*: **le ~** Lagos.

là-haut [lao] *adv* up there.

laïc (*f* **laïque**), **laïque** [laik] ◇ *adj* lay (*avant*

n); [juridiction] civil (*avant n*); [école] state (*avant n*). ◇ *nm, f* layman (*f* laywoman).

laïcisation [laisizasjɔ̃] *nf* secularization.

laid, -e [lɛ, lɛd] *adj* -1. [esthétiquement] ugly. -2. [moralement] wicked.

laideron [lɛdrɔ̃] *nm* ugly woman.

laideur [lɛdœr] *nf* -1. [physique] ugliness. -2. [morale] wickedness.

laie [lɛ] *nf* ZOOL wild sow.

lainage [lɛnaʒ] *nm* [étoffe] woollen material; [vêtement] woolly OU woollen garment.

laine [lɛn] *nf* wool; **~ de verre** glass wool; **pure ~ vierge** pure new wool.

laineux, -euse [lɛnø, øz] *adj* woolly.

lainier, -ière [lɛnje, jɛr] ◇ *adj* wool (*avant n*). ◇ *nm, f* [marchand] wool merchant; [ouvrier] wool worker.

laïque → **laïc**.

laisse [lɛs] *nf* [corde] lead, leash; **tenir en ~** [chien] to keep on a lead OU leash; **tenir qqn en ~** *fig* to keep sb on a short lead.

laissé-pour-compte, **laissée-pour-compte** [lesepurkɔ̃t] (*mpl* **laissés-pour-compte,** *fpl* **laissées-pour-compte**) *adj* -1. [article] unsold. -2. *fig* [personne] rejected.

◆ **laissé-pour-compte** *nm* -1. [article] unsold item. -2. [personne] reject.

laisser [lese] [4] ◇ *v aux* (+ *infinitif*): **~ qqn faire qqch** to let sb do sthg; **laisse-le faire** leave him alone, don't interfere; **~ tomber qqch** *litt* & *fig* to drop sthg; **~ tomber qqn** *fam* to drop OU ditch sb; **laisse tomber!** *fam* drop it!

◇ *vt* -1. [gén] to leave; **~ qqch à qqn** [léguer] to leave sthg to sb, to leave sb sthg; **~ qqn/qqch à qqn** [confier] to leave sb/sthg with sb. -2. [céder]: **~ qqch à qqn** to let sb have sthg. -3. *loc*: **~ qqn tranquille** to leave sb in peace OU alone; **~ à désirer** to leave something to be desired.

◆ **se laisser** *vp*: **se ~ faire** to let o.s. be persuaded; **se ~ aller** to relax; [dans son apparence] to let o.s. go; **se ~ aller dans un fauteuil** to collapse into an armchair; **se ~ aller à qqch** to indulge in sthg; **se ~ tenter par** to be tempted by.

laisser-aller [leseale] *nm inv* carelessness.

laisser-passer [lesepase] *nm inv* pass.

lait [lɛ] *nm* -1. [gén] milk; **~ de chèvre/vache** goat's/cow's milk; **~ entier/écrémé** whole/skimmed milk; **~ concentré** OU **condensé** [sucré] condensed milk; [non sucré] evaporated milk; **~ maternel** mother's milk; **~ en poudre** powdered milk; **~ de poule** egg flip. -2. [cosmétique]: **~ démaquillant** cleansing milk OU lotion.

laitage [lɛtaʒ] *nm* milk product.

laiterie [lɛtri] *nf* dairy.

laiteux, -euse [lɛtø, øz] *adj* milky.

laitier, -ière [lɛtje, jɛr] ◇ *adj* dairy (*avant n*). ◇ *nm, f* milkman (*f* milkwoman).
◆ **laitier** *nm* TECHNOL slag.

laiton [lɛtɔ̃] *nm* brass.

laitue [lety] *nf* lettuce.

laïus [lajys] *nm* long speech.

lama [lama] *nm* **-1.** ZOOL llama. **-2.** RELIG lama.

lambeau, -x [lɑ̃bo] *nm* **-1.** [morceau] shred; **mettre qqch en ~x** to tear sthg to pieces OU shreds. **-2.** *fig* [fragment] fragment.

lambiner [lɑ̃bine] [3] *vi fam* to dawdle.

lambris [lɑ̃bri] *nm* panelling.

lambswool [lɑ̃bswul] *nm* lambswool.

lame [lam] *nf* **-1.** [fer] blade. **-2.** [lamelle] strip; **~ de rasoir** razor blade. **-3.** [vague] wave; **~ de fond** groundswell.

lamé, -e [lame] *adj* lamé; **~ or/argent** gold/silver lamé.
◆ **lamé** *nm* lamé; **de** OU **en ~** lamé.

lamelle [lamɛl] *nf* **-1.** [de champignon] gill. **-2.** [tranche] thin slice. **-3.** [de verre] slide.

lamentable [lamɑ̃tabl] *adj* **-1.** [résultats, sort] appalling. **-2.** [ton] plaintive.

lamentablement [lamɑ̃tabləmɑ̃] *adv* miserably.

lamentation [lamɑ̃tasjɔ̃] *nf* **-1.** [plainte] lamentation. **-2.** (*gén pl*) [jérémiade] moaning (*U*).

lamenter [lamɑ̃te] [3]
◆ **se lamenter** *vp* to complain; **se ~ sur qqch** to bemoan sthg; **se ~ d'avoir fait qqch** to complain about having done sthg.

laminage [laminaʒ] *nm* lamination.

laminer [lamine] [3] *vt* IND to laminate; *fig* [personne, revenus] to eat away at.

laminoir [laminwar] *nm* rolling mill.

lampadaire [lɑ̃padɛr] *nm* [dans maison] standard lamp *Br*, floor lamp *Am*; [de rue] street lamp OU light.

lampe [lɑ̃p] *nf* lamp, light; **~ à bronzer** sunlamp; **~ de chevet** bedside lamp; **~ halogène** halogen light; **~ à incandescence** incandescent lamp; **~ à pétrole** oil lamp; **~ de poche** torch *Br*, flashlight *Am*; **~ à souder** blowlamp; **~ témoin** pilot light; **s'en mettre plein la ~** *fam fig* to stuff o.s.

lampée [lɑ̃pe] *nf fam* swig.

lampion [lɑ̃pjɔ̃] *nm* Chinese lantern.

lampiste [lɑ̃pist] *nm* [employé, subalterne] dogsbody *Br*.

lance [lɑ̃s] *nf* **-1.** [arme] spear. **-2.** [de tuyau] nozzle; **~ d'incendie** fire hose.

lancée [lɑ̃se] *nf*: **continuer sur sa ~** to keep going.

lance-flammes [lɑ̃sflam] *nm inv* flame-thrower.

lancement [lɑ̃smɑ̃] *nm* **-1.** [d'entreprise, produit, navire] launching. **-2.** [de javelot, projectile] throwing.

lance-pierres [lɑ̃spjɛr] *nm inv* catapult.

lancer [lɑ̃se] [16] ◇ *vt* **-1.** [pierre, javelot] to throw; **~ qqch sur qqn** to throw sthg at sb. **-2.** [fusée, produit, style] to launch. **-3.** [émettre] to give off; [cri] to let out; [injures] to hurl; [ultimatum] to issue. **-4.** [moteur] to start up. **-5.** [INFORM - programme] to start; [- système] to boot (up). **-6.** *fig* [sur un sujet]: **~ qqn sur qqch** to get sb started on sthg.
◇ *nm* **-1.** PÊCHE casting. **-2.** SPORT throwing; **~ du poids** shotput.
◆ **se lancer** *vp* **-1.** [débuter] to make a name for o.s. **-2.** [s'engager]: **se ~ dans** [dépenses, explication, lecture] to embark on.

lanceur, -euse [lɑ̃sœr, øz] *nm, f* SPORT thrower.
◆ **lanceur** *nm* AÉRON launcher.

lancinant, -e [lɑ̃sinɑ̃, ɑ̃t] *adj* **-1.** [douleur] shooting. **-2.** *fig* [obsédant] haunting. **-3.** [monotone] insistent.

lanciner [lɑ̃sine] [3] ◇ *vi* to throb. ◇ *vt fig* to haunt.

landau [lɑ̃do] *nm* **-1.** [d'enfant] pram. **-2.** [carrosse] landau.

lande [lɑ̃d] *nf* moor.

langage [lɑ̃gaʒ] *nm* language; **~ machine** INFORM machine language.

lange [lɑ̃ʒ] *nm* nappy *Br*, diaper *Am*.

langer [lɑ̃ʒe] [17] *vt* to change.

langoureusement [lɑ̃gurøzmɑ̃] *adv* languorously.

langoureux, -euse [lɑ̃gurø, øz] *adj* languorous.

langouste [lɑ̃gust] *nf* crayfish.

langoustine [lɑ̃gustin] *nf* langoustine.

langue [lɑ̃g] *nf* **-1.** ANAT & *fig* tongue; **tirer la ~ à qqn** to stick out one's tongue at sb; **~ de bœuf** CULIN ox tongue; **mauvaise ~** *fig* gossip; **avoir la ~ bien pendue** to be a chatterbox; **donner sa ~ au chat** to give up; **ne pas avoir sa ~ dans sa poche** never to be at a loss for words; **tenir sa ~** *fig* to hold one's tongue. **-2.** LING language; **de ~ française** [livre] French; [personne] French-speaking; **les politiciens qui parlent la ~ de bois** politicians who mouth clichés; **~ ma-**

ternelle mother tongue; ~ **morte/vivante** dead/modern language.

langue-de-chat [lãgdəʃa] (*pl* **langues-de-chat**) *nf* light *finger-biscuit*.

languette [lãget] *nf* tongue.

langueur [lãgœr] *nf* -1. [dépérissement, mélancolie] languor. -2. [apathie] apathy.

languir [lãgir] [32] *vi* -1. [dépérir]: ~ **(de)** to languish (with). -2. *sout* [attendre] to wait; **faire** ~ **qqn** to keep sb waiting. -3. *littéraire* [désirer]: ~ **après** to pine for.

lanière [lanjɛr] *nf* strip.

lanoline [lanɔlin] *nf* lanolin.

lanterne [lãtɛrn] *nf* -1. [éclairage] lantern. -2. [phare] light. -3. *loc*: **éclairer la ~ de qqn** *fig* to put sb in the know; **être la ~ rouge** *fam fig* to bring up the rear.

lanterner [lãtɛrne] [3] *vi fam* to dawdle; **faire** ~ **qqn** to keep sb hanging around.

Laos [laɔs] *nm*: **le** ~ Laos; **au** ~ in Laos.

laotien, -ienne [laosjɛ̃, jɛn] *adj* Laotian.
◆ **laotien** *nm* [langue] Laotian.
◆ **Laotien, -ienne** *nm, f* Laotian.

lapalissade [lapalisad] *nf* statement of the obvious.

La Paz [lapaz] *n* La Paz.

laper [lape] [3] *vt & vi* to lap.

lapereau, -x [lapro] *nm* baby rabbit.

lapidaire [lapidɛr] ◇ *nm* lapidary. ◇ *adj* lapidary; *fig* [style] terse.

lapider [lapide] [3] *vt* [tuer] to stone.

lapin, -e [lapɛ̃, in] *nm, f* -1. CULIN & ZOOL rabbit; ~ **de garenne** wild rabbit. -2. [fourrure] rabbit fur. -3. *fam* [personne]: **mon** ~ my darling; **chaud** ~ stud. -4. *loc*: **poser un** ~ **à qqn** *fam* to stand sb up.

lapon, -onne OU **-one** [lapɔ̃, ɔn] *adj* Lapp.
◆ **lapon** *nm* [langue] Lapp.
◆ **Lapon, -onne** OU **-one** *nm, f* Lapp, Laplander.

Laponie [lapɔni] *nf*: **la** ~ Lapland.

laps [laps] *nm*: **(dans) un** ~ **de temps** (in) a while.

lapsus [lapsys] *nm* slip (of the tongue/pen); **faire un** ~ to make a slip (of the tongue/pen).

laquais [lakɛ] *nm* lackey.

laque [lak] *nf* -1. [vernis, peinture] lacquer. -2. [pour cheveux] hair spray, lacquer.

laqué, -e [lake] *adj* lacquered.

laquelle → **lequel**.

laquer [lake] [3] *vt* to lacquer.

larbin [larbɛ̃] *nm* -1. [domestique] servant. -2. [personne servile] yes-man.

larcin [larsɛ̃] *nm* -1. [vol] larceny, theft. -2. [butin] spoils (*pl*).

lard [lar] *nm* -1. [graisse de porc] lard. -2. [viande] bacon. -3. *fam* [graisse d'homme] blubber.

larder [larde] [3] *vt* -1. CULIN to lard. -2. *fig* [piquer]: ~ **qqn de coups/d'injures** to rain blows/insults on sb. -3. *fig* [truffer]: ~ **qqch de** to cram sthg with.

lardon [lardɔ̃] *nm* -1. CULIN cube or strip of bacon. -2. *fam* [enfant] kid.

large [larʒ] ◇ *adj* -1. [étendu, grand] wide; ~ **de 5 mètres** 5 metres wide; **être** ~ **de hanches/d'épaules** to have broad hips/shoulders. -2. [important, considérable] large, big. -3. [esprit, sourire] broad. -4. [généreux - personne] generous.
◇ *adv* amply; **voir** ~ to think big; **ne pas en mener** ~ *fig* to be afraid.
◇ *nm* -1. [largeur]: **5 mètres de** ~ 5 metres wide. -2. [mer]: **le** ~ the open sea; **au** ~ **de la côte française** off the French coast; **prendre le** ~ [navire] to put to sea; *fig* to be off.

largement [larʒəmã] *adv* -1. [diffuser, répandre] widely; **la porte était** ~ **ouverte** the door was wide open. -2. [donner, payer] generously; [dépasser] considerably; [récompenser] amply; **avoir** ~ **le temps** to have plenty of time. -3. [au moins] easily.

largesse [larʒɛs] *nf* -1. [générosité] generosity. -2. (*gén pl*) [don] gift.

largeur [larʒœr] *nf* -1. [d'avenue, de cercle] width. -2. *fig* [d'idées, d'esprit] breadth.

largué, -e [large] *adj*: **être** ~ to be all at sea.

larguer [large] [3] *vt* -1. [voile] to unfurl. -2. [bombe, parachutiste] to drop. -3. *fam fig* [abandonner] to chuck; **se faire** ~ to be chucked.

larme [larm] *nf* -1. [pleur] tear; **être en** ~**s** to be in tears; **fondre en** ~**s** to burst into tears; **pleurer à chaudes** ~**s** to cry bitterly; **ravaler ses** ~**s** to hold back one's tears; **rire aux** ~**s** to laugh until one cries; ~**s de crocodile** *fig* crocodile tears. -2. *fam* [goutte]: **une** ~ **de** a drop of.

larmoyant, -e [larmwajã, ãt] *adj* -1. [yeux, personne] tearful. -2. *péj* [histoire] tearjerking.

larmoyer [larmwaje] [13] *vi* -1. [pleurer - personne] to weep; [- yeux] to water. -2. *péj* [se lamenter] to moan.

larron [larɔ̃] *nm vieilli* [voleur] thief.

larve [larv] *nf* -1. ZOOL larva. -2. *péj* [personne] wimp.

larvé, -e [larve] *adj* **-1.** MÉD larvate. **-2.** [latent] latent.

laryngite [larẽʒit] *nf* laryngitis (U).

larynx [larɛ̃ks] *nm* larynx.

las, lasse [la, las] *adj littéraire* **-1.** [fatigué] weary. **-2.** [dégoûté, ennuyé] tired; ~ **de faire qqch** tired of doing sthg; ~ **de qqn/ qqch** tired of sb/sthg.
◆ **las** *interj* alas!

lascar [laskar] *nm* **-1.** [homme louche] shady character; [homme rusé] rogue. **-2.** *fam* [enfant] rascal.

lascif, -ive [lasif, iv] *adj* lascivious.

laser [lazɛr] ◇ *nm* laser. ◇ *adj* laser (*avant n*).

lassant, -e [lasɑ̃, ɑ̃t] *adj* tiresome.

lasser [lase] [3] *vt sout* [personne] to weary; [patience] to try.
◆ **se lasser** *vp* to weary; **ne pas se** ~ **de qqch/de faire qqch** not to weary of sthg/of doing sthg.

lassitude [lasityd] *nf* lassitude.

lasso [laso] *nm* lasso.

lat. (*abr de* **latitude**) lat.

latent, -e [latɑ̃, ɑ̃t] *adj* latent.

latéral, -e, -aux [lateral, o] *adj* lateral.

latex [latɛks] *nm inv* latex.

latin, -e [latɛ̃, in] *adj* Latin.
◆ **latin** *nm* [langue] Latin; **y perdre son** ~ *fig* to be at a loss.

latiniste [latinist] *nmf* [spécialiste] Latinist; [étudiant] Latin student.

latino-américain, -e [latinoamerikɛ̃, ɛn], (*mpl* **latino-américains**, *fpl* **latino-américaines**) *adj* Latin-American, Hispanic.

latitude [latityd] *nf litt* & *fig* latitude.

latrines [latrin] *nfpl* latrines.

latte [lat] *nf* lath, slat.

lattis [lati] *nm* lathwork.

laudatif, -ive [lodatif, iv] *adj* laudatory.

lauréat, -e [lɔrea, at] ◇ *adj* prizewinning, winning. ◇ *nm, f* prizewinner, winner.

laurier [lɔrje] *nm* BOT laurel.
◆ **lauriers** *nmpl* [gloire] laurels; **s'endormir** OU **se reposer sur ses** ~**s** to rest on one's laurels.

laurier-rose [lɔrjeroz] (*pl* **lauriers-roses**) *nm* oleander.

laurier-sauce [lɔrjesos] (*pl* **lauriers-sauce**) *nm* bay (tree).

Lausanne [lozan] *n* Lausanne.

lavable [lavabl] *adj* washable.

lavabo [lavabo] *nm* **-1.** [cuvette] basin. **-2.** (*gén pl*) [local] toilet.

lavage [lavaʒ] *nm* washing; ~ **à la main/en machine** hand/machine washing; ~ **de cerveau** *fig* brainwashing; **subir un** ~ **d'estomac** MÉD to have one's stomach pumped.

lavande [lavɑ̃d] ◇ *nf* **-1.** BOT lavender. **-2.** [eau] lavender water. ◇ *adj inv* lavender (*avant n*).

lavasse [lavas] *nf fam* dishwater (U).

lave [lav] *nf* lava.

lave-glace [lavglas] (*pl* **lave-glaces**) *nm* windscreen washer *Br*, windshield washer *Am*.

lave-linge [lavlɛ̃ʒ] *nm inv* washing machine.

lavement [lavmɑ̃] *nm* enema.

laver [lave] [3] *vt* **-1.** [nettoyer] to wash. **-2.** *fig* [disculper]: ~ **qqn de qqch** to clear sb of sthg.
◆ **se laver** *vp* **-1.** [se nettoyer] to wash o.s., to have a wash; **se** ~ **les mains/les cheveux** to wash one's hands/hair. **-2.** [se disculper]: **se** ~ **(de)** to clear o.s. (of).

laverie [lavri] *nf* [commerce] laundry; ~ **automatique** launderette.

lavette [lavɛt] *nf* **-1.** [brosse] washing-up brush; [en tissu] dishcloth. **-2.** *fam* [homme] drip.

laveur, -euse [lavœr, øz] *nm, f* washer; ~ **de carreaux** window cleaner (*person*).

lave-vaisselle [lavvesɛl] *nm inv* dishwasher.

lavis [lavi] *nm* [procédé] washing; [dessin] wash (painting).

lavoir [lavwar] *nm* **-1.** [lieu] laundry. **-2.** [bac] washtub.

laxatif, -ive [laksatif, iv] *adj* laxative.
◆ **laxatif** *nm* laxative.

laxisme [laksism] *nm* laxity.

laxiste [laksist] ◇ *nmf* person who is lax. ◇ *adj* lax.

layette [lɛjɛt] *nf* layette.

le [lə], **l'** (*devant voyelle ou h muet*) (*f* **la** [la], *pl* **les** [le]) ◇ *art déf* **-1.** [gén] the; ~ **lac** the lake; **la fenêtre** the window; **l'homme** the man; **les enfants** the children. **-2.** [devant les noms abstraits]: **l'amour** love; **la liberté** freedom; **la vieillesse** old age. **-3.** [devant les noms géographiques]: **la France** France; **les États-Unis** America, the United States (of America); **la Seine** the Seine; **les Alpes** the Alps. **-4.** [temps]: ~ **15 janvier 1993** 15th January 1993; **je suis arrivé** ~ **15 janvier 1993** I arrived on the 15th of January 1993; ~ **lundi** [habituellement] on Mondays; [jour précis] on (the) Monday. **-5.** [possession]: **se laver les mains** to wash one's hands; **secouer la tête** to shake one's head;

avoir les cheveux blonds to have fair hair. **-6.** [distributif] per, a; **10 francs ~ mètre** 10 francs per OU a metre.

◇ *pron pers* **-1.** [personne] him (*f* her); [chose] it; [animal] it, him (*f* her); **je ~/la/les connais bien** I know him/her/them well; **tu dois avoir la clé, donne-la moi** you must have the key, give it to me. **-2.** [représente une proposition]: **je ~ sais bien** I know, I'm well aware (of it); **je te l'avais bien dit!** I told you so!

LEA (*abr de* **langues étrangères appliquées**) *nfpl* modern languages department.

leader [lidœr] ◇ *nm* [de parti, course] leader. ◇ *adj* leading.

leadership [lidœrʃip] *nm* leadership.

lèche [lɛʃ] *nf* tfam bootlicking; **faire de la ~ à qqn** to lick sb's boots.

léché, -e [leʃe] *adj* fam [fignolé] polished.

lèchefrite [lɛʃfrit] *nf* dripping-pan.

lécher [leʃe] [18] *vt* **-1.** [passer la langue sur, effleurer] to lick; [suj: vague] to wash against. **-2.** *fam* [fignoler] to polish (up).
◆ **se lécher** *vp*: **se ~ les doigts** *fam* to lick one's fingers.

lèche-vitrines [lɛʃvitrin] *nm inv* window-shopping; **faire du ~** to go window-shopping.

leçon [ləsɔ̃]ˊ *nf* **-1.** [gén] lesson; **~s de conduite** driving lessons; **~s particulières** private lessons OU classes. **-2.** [conseil] advice (*U*); **faire la ~ à qqn** to lecture sb.

lecteur, -trice [lɛktœr, tris] *nm, f* **-1.** [de livres] reader. **-2.** UNIV foreign language assistant.
◆ **lecteur** *nm* **-1.** [gén] head; **~ de cassettes/CD** cassette/CD player; **~ laser universel** audio-video CD player. **-2.** INFORM reader; **~ de disques** disk drive.

lecture [lɛktyr] *nf* reading.

LED (*abr de* **light emitting diode**) *nf* LED.

ledit, ladite [lədi, ladit] (*mpl* **lesdits** [ledi], *fpl* **lesdites** [ledit]) *adj* the said, the aforementioned.

légal, -e, -aux [legal, o] *adj* legal.

légalement [legalmɑ̃] *adv* legally.

légalisation [legalizasjɔ̃] *nf* **-1.** [légitimation] legalization. **-2.** [authentification] authentication.

légaliser [legalize] [3] *vt* **-1.** [rendre légal] to legalize. **-2.** [certifier authentique] to authenticate.

légalisme [legalism] *nm* legalism.

légalité [legalite] *nf* **-1.** [de contrat, d'acte] legality, lawfulness. **-2.** [loi] law.

légataire [legatɛr] *nmf* legatee; **~ universel** sole legatee.

légation [legasjɔ̃] *nf* legation.

légendaire [leʒɑ̃dɛr] *adj* legendary.

légende [leʒɑ̃d] *nf* **-1.** [fable] legend. **-2.** *péj* [invention] story. **-3.** [explication] key.

léger, -ère [leʒe, ɛr] *adj* **-1.** [objet, étoffe, repas] light. **-2.** [bruit, différence, odeur] slight. **-3.** [alcool, tabac] low-strength. **-4.** [esprit & SPORT] lightweight. **-5.** [personne] flighty.
◆ **à la légère** *loc adv* lightly, thoughtlessly.

légèrement [leʒɛrmɑ̃] *adv* **-1.** [s'habiller, poser] lightly. **-2.** [agir] thoughtlessly. **-3.** [blesser, remuer] slightly.

légèreté [leʒɛrte] *nf* **-1.** [d'objet, de repas, de punition] lightness. **-2.** [de style] gracefulness. **-3.** [de conduite] thoughtlessness. **-4.** [de personne] flightiness.

légiférer [leʒifere] [18] *vi* to legislate.

légion [leʒjɔ̃] *nf* **-1.** MIL legion; **la Légion étrangère** the Foreign Legion. **-2.** [grand nombre]: **une ~ de** a host of; **être ~** *fig* to be legion.
◆ **Légion** *nf*: **la Légion d'honneur** the Legion of Honour.

légionnaire [leʒjɔnɛr] *nm* legionary.

législatif, -ive [leʒislatif, iv] *adj* legislative.
◆ **législatif** *nm* legislature.
◆ **législatives** *nfpl*: **les législatives** the legislative elections, ≈ the general election (*sg*) *Br*.

législation [leʒislasjɔ̃] *nf* legislation.

législature [leʒislatyr] *nf* **-1.** [période] term of office. **-2.** [corps] legislature.

légiste [leʒist] *adj* **-1.** [juriste] jurist. **-2.** → **médecin**.

légitimation [leʒitimasjɔ̃] *nf* **-1.** [d'enfant] legitimization. **-2.** *littéraire* [justification] justification.

légitime [leʒitim] *adj* legitimate.

légitimement [leʒitimmɑ̃] *adv* **-1.** [légalement] legitimately. **-2.** [justement] fairly.

légitimer [leʒitime] [3] *vt* **-1.** [reconnaître] to recognize; [enfant] to legitimize. **-2.** [justifier] to justify.

légitimité [leʒitimite] *nf* **-1.** [de pouvoir, d'enfant] legitimacy. **-2.** [de récompense] fairness.

legs [lɛg] *nm* legacy.

léguer [lege] [18] *vt*: **~ qqch à qqn** JUR to bequeath sthg to sb; *fig* to pass sthg on to sb.

légume [legym] ◇ *nm* vegetable. ◇ *nf fam*: **une grosse ~** a bigwig.

leitmotiv [lajtmɔtif, lɛtmɔtif] *nm* leitmotif.

Léman [lemã] → **lac.**

lendemain [lɑ̃dmɛ̃] *nm* **-1.** [jour] day after; **le ~ matin** the next morning; **au ~ de** after, in the days following. **-2.** [avenir] tomorrow; **sans ~** short-lived.

lénifiant, -e [lenifjɑ̃, ɑ̃t] *adj litt* & *fig* soothing.

léniniste [leninist] *nmf* & *adj* Leninist.

lent, -e [lɑ̃, lɑ̃t] *adj* slow; **~ à faire qqch** slow to do sthg.

lente [lɑ̃t] *nf* nit.

lentement [lɑ̃tmɑ̃] *adv* slowly.

lenteur [lɑ̃tœr] *nf* slowness (*U*).

lentille [lɑ̃tij] *nf* **-1.** BOT & CULIN lentil. **-2.** [d'optique] lens; **~s de contact** contact lenses.

léonin, -e [leonɛ̃, in] *adj* **-1.** [du lion] leonine. **-2.** [injuste] one-sided.

léopard [leopar] *nm* leopard.

LEP, Lep (*abr de* **lycée d'enseignement professionnel**) *nm* former secondary school for vocational training.

lèpre [lɛpr] *nf* **-1.** MÉD leprosy. **-2.** *fig* [mal] disease.

lépreux, -euse [leprø, øz] ◇ *adj* **-1.** MÉD leprous. **-2.** *fig* [mur, maison] peeling. ◇ *nm, f* leper.

lequel [ləkɛl] (*f* **laquelle** [lakɛl], *mpl* **lesquels** [lekɛl], *fpl* **lesquelles** [lekɛl]) (*contraction de à* + *lequel* = **auquel**, *de* + *lequel* = **duquel**, *à* + *lesquels/lesquelles* = **auxquels/auxquelles**, *de* + *lesquels/lesquelles* = **desquels/desquelles**) ◇ *pron relatif* **-1.** [complément personne] whom; [- chose] which. **-2.** [sujet - personne] who; [- chose] which. ◇ *pron interr:* **~?** which (one)?

les → **le.**

lesbienne [lɛsbjɛn] *nf* lesbian.

lesdits, lesdites → **ledit.**

lèse-majesté [lɛzmaʒɛste] *nf inv* lese-majesty.

léser [leze] [18] *vt* **-1.** [frustrer] to wrong. **-2.** MÉD to injure, to damage.

lésiner [lezine] [3] *vi* to skimp; **ne pas ~ sur** not to skimp on.

lésion [lezjɔ̃] *nf* lesion.

Lesotho [lesɔtɔ] *nm:* **le ~** Lesotho.

lesquels, lesquelles → **lequel.**

lessive [lesiv] *nf* **-1.** [nettoyage, linge] washing. **-2.** [produit] washing powder.

lessiver [lesive] [3] *vt* **-1.** [nettoyer] to wash. **-2.** CHIM to leach. **-3.** *fam* [épuiser] to wipe out.

lest [lɛst] *nm* ballast; **lâcher du ~** to jettison ballast; *fig* to make concessions.

leste [lɛst] *adj* **-1.** [agile] nimble, agile. **-2.** [licencieux] crude.

lestement [lɛstəmɑ̃] *adv* **-1.** [agilement] nimbly, agilely. **-2.** [grivoisement] crudely.

lester [lɛste] [3] *vt* **-1.** [garnir de lest] to ballast. **-2.** *fam* [charger] to fill, to cram.

letchi = **litchi.**

léthargie [letarʒi] *nf litt* & *fig* lethargy; **tomber en ~** to become lethargic.

léthargique [letarʒik] *adj* lethargic.

letton, -onne [lɛtɔ̃, ɔn] *adj* Latvian.
◆ **letton** *nm* [langue] Latvian.
◆ **Letton, -onne** *nm, f* Latvian.

Lettonie [letɔni] *nf:* **la ~** Latvia.

lettre [lɛtr] *nf* **-1.** [gén] letter; **en toutes ~s** in words, in full; **~ d'amour** love letter; **~ de couverture** cover note; **~ ouverte** open letter; **~ piégée** letter bomb; **~ de rappel** reminder; **~ de recommandation** (letter of) recommendation; **passer comme une ~ à la poste** *fam* [entretien, examen] to go smoothly; [personne] to get through easily. **-2.** [sens des mots]: **à la ~** to the letter.
◆ **lettres** *nfpl* **-1.** [culture littéraire] letters. **-2.** UNIV arts; **~s classiques** classics; **~s modernes** French language and literature. **-3.** [titre]: **~s de noblesse** letters patent of nobility.
◆ **lettre de change** *nf* bill of exchange.

leucémie [løsemi] *nf* leukemia.

leucocyte [løkɔsit] *nm* leucocyte.

leucorrhée [løkɔre] *nf* leucorrhoea.

leur [lœr] *pron pers inv* (to) them; **je voudrais ~ parler** I'd like to speak to them; **je ~ ai donné la lettre** I gave them the letter, I gave the letter to them.
◆ **leur** (*pl* **leurs**) *adj poss* their; **c'est ~ tour** it's their turn; **~s enfants** their children.
◆ **le leur** (*f* **la leur**, *pl* **les leurs**) *pron poss* theirs; **il faudra qu'ils y mettent du ~** they've got to pull their weight.

leurre [lœr] *nm* **-1.** [appât] lure. **-2.** *fig* [illusion] illusion. **-3.** *fig* [tromperie] deception, trap.

leurrer [lœre] [5] *vt* to deceive.
◆ **se leurrer** *vp* to deceive o.s.

levain [ləvɛ̃] *nm* **-1.** CULIN: **pain au ~/sans ~** leavened/unleavened bread. **-2.** *fig* [germe] seeds (*pl*), germ.

levant [ləvɑ̃] ◇ *nm* east. ◇ *adj* → **soleil.**

levé, -e [ləve] *adj* [debout] up.
◆ **levée** *nf* **-1.** [de scellés, difficulté] removal; [de blocus, de siège, d'interdiction] lifting. **-2.** [de séance] close, closing. **-3.** [d'impôts, du

courrier] collection. **-4.** [d'armée] raising. **-5.** [remblai] dyke. **-6.** CARTES trick.

◆ **levée de boucliers** *nf* (general) outcry.

lever [ləve] [19] ◇ *vt* **-1.** [objet, blocus, interdiction] to lift. **-2.** [main, tête, armée] to raise. **-3.** [scellés, difficulté] to remove. **-4.** [séance] to close, to end. **-5.** [impôts, courrier] to collect. **-6.** [plan, carte] to draw (up). **-7.** [enfant, malade]: ~ **qqn** to get sb up.
◇ *vi* **-1.** [plante] to come up. **-2.** [pâte] to rise.
◇ *nm* **-1.** [d'astre] rising, rise; ~ **du jour** daybreak; ~ **du soleil** sunrise. **-2.** [de personne]: **il est toujours de mauvaise humeur au** ~ he's always in a bad mood when he gets up. **-3.** THÉÂTRE: ~ **de rideau** curtain, curtain-up; *fig* curtain-raiser.

◆ **se lever** *vp* **-1.** [personne] to get up, to rise; [vent] to get up. **-2.** [soleil, lune] to rise; [jour] to break. **-3.** [temps] to clear.

lève-tard [lɛvtar] *nmf inv* late riser.

lève-tôt [lɛvto] *nmf inv* early riser.

levier [ləvje] *nm litt* & *fig* lever; ~ **de vitesses** gear lever *Br*, gear shift *Am*.

lévitation [levitasjɔ̃] *nf* levitation.

lèvre [lɛvr] *nf* **-1.** ANAT lip; [de vulve] labium; **être suspendu aux** ~**s de qqn** *fig* to hang on sb's every word; **se mordre les** ~**s** *fig* to bite one's lip. **-2.** [bord] edge.

lévrier, levrette [levrie, ləvrɛt] *nm, f* greyhound.

levure [ləvyr] *nf* yeast; ~ **chimique** baking powder.

lexical, -e, -aux [lɛksikal, -o] *adj* lexical.

lexicographie [lɛksikɔgrafi] *nf* lexicography.

lexique [lɛksik] *nm* **-1.** [dictionnaire] glossary. **-2.** [vocabulaire] vocabulary.

lézard [lezar] *nm* **-1.** [animal] lizard; **faire le** ~ *fam fig* to bask in the sun. **-2.** [peau] lizard (skin).

lézarde [lezard] *nf* crack.

lézarder [lezarde] [3] ◇ *vt* to crack. ◇ *vi fam* [paresser] to bask.
◆ **se lézarder** *vp* to crack.

Lhassa [lasa] *n* Lhasa.

liaison [ljezɔ̃] *nf* **-1.** [jonction, enchaînement] connection. **-2.** CULIN & LING liaison. **-3.** [contact, relation] contact; **avoir une** ~ to have an affair; **être/entrer en** ~ **avec** to in/establish contact with; **par** ~ **radio** by radio link. **-4.** TRANSPORT link.

liane [ljan] *nf* creeper.

liant, -e [ljɑ̃, ɑ̃t] *adj* sociable.
◆ **liant** *nm* **-1.** [substance] binder. **-2.** [élasticité] elasticity.

liasse [ljas] *nf* bundle; [de billets de banque] wad.

Liban [libɑ̃] *nm*: **le** ~ Lebanon; **au** ~ in Lebanon.

libanais, -e [libanɛ, ɛz] *adj* Lebanese.
◆ **Libanais, -e** *nm, f* Lebanese (person); **les Libanais** the Lebanese.

Libé [libe] (*abr de* **Libération**) *nm* French left-of-centre newspaper.

libelle [libɛl] *nm* lampoon.

libellé [libele] *nm* wording.

libeller [libele] [4] *vt* **-1.** [chèque] to make out. **-2.** [lettre] to word.

libellule [libelyl] *nf* dragonfly.

libéral, -e, -aux [liberal, o] ◇ *adj* [attitude, idée, parti] liberal. ◇ *nm, f* POLIT liberal.

libéralement [liberalmɑ̃] *adv* liberally.

libéralisation [liberalizasjɔ̃] *nf* liberalization.

libéraliser [liberalize] [3] *vt* to liberalize.

libéralisme [liberalism] *nm* liberalism.

libéralité [liberalite] *nf* **-1.** [générosité] generosity. **-2.** (*gén pl*) [don] generous gift.

libérateur, -trice [liberatœr, tris] ◇ *adj* [rire] liberating; **guerre libératrice** war of liberation. ◇ *nm, f* liberator.

libération [liberasjɔ̃] *nf* **-1.** [de prisonnier] release, freeing. **-2.** [de pays, de la femme] liberation; **la Libération** HIST the Liberation. **-3.** [d'énergie] release.

libéré, -e [libere] *nm, f* freed prisoner.

libérer [libere] [18] *vt* **-1.** [prisonnier, fonds] to release, to free. **-2.** [pays, la femme] to liberate; ~ **qqn de qqch** to free sb from sthg. **-3.** [passage] to clear. **-4.** [énergie] to release. **-5.** [instincts, passions] to give free rein to.
◆ **se libérer** *vp* **-1.** [se rendre disponible] to get away. **-2.** [se dégager]: **se** ~ **de** [lien] to free o.s. from; [engagement] to get out of.

Liberia [liberja] *nm*: **le** ~ Liberia; **au** ~ in Liberia.

libérien, -ienne [liberjɛ̃, jɛn] *adj* Liberian.
◆ **Libérien, -ienne** *nm, f* Liberian.

libertaire [libɛrtɛr] *nmf & adj* libertarian.

liberté [libɛrte] *nf* **-1.** [gén] freedom; **en** ~ free; **Liberté, Égalité, Fraternité** Liberty, Equality, Fraternity; **parler en toute** ~ to speak freely; **vivre en** ~ to live in freedom; ~ **d'expression** freedom of expression; ~ **d'opinion** freedom of thought. **-2.** JUR release; ~ **conditionnelle** parole; ~ **provisoire** bail; ~ **surveillée** probation. **-3.** [loisir] free time.

libertin, -e [libɛrtɛ̃, in] ◇ *adj* [dissolu] dissolute; [propos, livre] lewd. ◇ *nm, f* libertine.

libertinage [libɛrtinaʒ] *nm* [débauche] dissoluteness; [de propos, livre] lewdness.

libidineux, -euse [libidinø, øz] *adj* lecherous.

libido [libido] *nf* libido.

libraire [librɛr] *nmf* bookseller.

librairie [libreri] *nf* -1. [magasin] bookshop. -2. [commerce, activité] book trade.

librairie-papeterie [libreri-pəpɛtri] (*pl* **librairies-papeteries**) *nf* bookseller's and stationer's.

libre [libr] *adj* -1. [gén] free; ~ **de qqch** free from sthg; **être ~ de faire qqch** to be free to do sthg. -2. [école, secteur] private. -3. [passage] clear.

libre-échange [libreʃãʒ] (*pl* **libres-échanges**) *nm* free trade (*U*).

librement [librəmã] *adv* freely.

libre-penseur, -euse [librəpãsœr, øz] (*mpl* **libres-penseurs**, *fpl* **libres-penseuses**) *nm, f* free-thinker.

libre-service [librəsɛrvis] (*pl* **libres-services**) *nm* -1. [système]: **le ~** self-service. -2. [magasin] self-service store OU shop; [restaurant] self-service restaurant.

librettiste [librɛtist] *nmf* librettist.

Libreville [librəvil] *n* Libreville.

Libye [libi] *nf*: **la ~** Libya.

libyen, -yenne [libjɛ̃, jɛn] *adj* Libyan.
◆ **Libyen, -yenne** *nm, f* Libyan.

lice [lis] *nf*: **en ~** *fig* in the fray; **entrer en ~** *fig* to join the fray.

licence [lisãs] *nf* -1. [permis] permit; COMM licence. -2. UNIV (first) degree; ~ **ès lettres/ en droit** ≃ Bachelor of Arts/Law. -3. *littéraire* [liberté] licence; ~ **poétique** poetic licence.

licencié, -e [lisãsje] ◇ *adj* -1. UNIV graduate (*avant n*). -2. [autorisé] permit-holding (*avant n*); COMM licensed. ◇ *nm, f* -1. UNIV graduate. -2. [titulaire d'un permis] permit-holder; COMM licence-holder.

licenciement [lisãsimã] *nm* dismissal; [économique] redundancy *Br*.

licencier [lisãsje] [9] *vt* to dismiss; [pour cause économique] to make redundant *Br*.

licencieux, -ieuse [lisãsjø, jøz] *adj* licentious.

lichen [likɛn] *nm* lichen.

licite [lisit] *adj* lawful, legal.

licol [likɔl], **licou** [liku] *nm* halter.

licorne [likɔrn] *nf* unicorn.

licou = **licol**.

lie [li] *nf* [dépôt] dregs (*pl*), sediment; **la ~** de la société *fig* & *littéraire* the dregs (*pl*) of society.

◆ **lie-de-vin** *adj inv* burgundy, wine-coloured.

lié, -e [lje] *adj* -1. [mains] bound. -2. [amis]: **être très ~ avec** to be great friends with.

Liechtenstein [liʃtənʃtajn] *nm*: **le ~** Liechtenstein; **au ~** in Liechtenstein.

liechtensteinois, -e [liʃtənʃtajnwa, az] *adj* from Liechtenstein.
◆ **Liechtensteinois, -e** *nm, f* Liechtensteiner.

liège [ljɛʒ] *nm* cork; **en** OU **de ~** cork (*avant n*).

liégeois, -e [ljeʒwa, az] *adj* -1. GÉOGR of/ from Liège. -2. CULIN: **café/chocolat ~** *coffee or chocolate ice cream topped with whipped cream.*

lien [ljɛ̃] *nm* -1. [sangle] bond. -2. [relation, affinité] bond, tie; **avoir des ~s de parenté avec** to be related to. -3. *fig* [enchaînement] connection, link.

lier [lje] [9] *vt* -1. [attacher] to tie (up); ~ **qqn/qqch à** to tie sb/sthg to. -2. [suj: contrat, promesse] to bind; ~ **qqn/qqch par** to bind sb/sthg by. -3. [relier par la logique] to link, to connect; ~ **qqch à** to link sthg to, to connect sthg with. -4. [commencer]: ~ **connaissance/conversation avec** to strike up an acquaintance/a conversation with. -5. [suj: sentiment, intérêt] to unite. -6. CULIN to thicken.

◆ **se lier** *vp* -1. [s'attacher]: **se ~ (d'amitié) avec qqn** to make friends with sb. -2. [s'astreindre]: **se ~ par une promesse** to be bound by a promise.

lierre [ljɛr] *nm* ivy.

liesse [ljɛs] *nf* jubilation.

lieu, -x [ljø] *nm* -1. [endroit] place; **en ~ sûr** in a safe place; ~ **de naissance** birthplace; ~ **de perdition** den of vice; ~ **saint** holy place; **haut ~ de qqch** *fig* centre of sthg; **en haut ~** *fig* in high places. -2. *loc*: **avoir ~** to take place; **avoir ~ de faire qqch** to have grounds for doing sthg; **donner ~ à** to give rise to; **tenir ~ de** to take the place of.

◆ **lieux** *nmpl* -1. [scène] scene (*sg*), spot (*sg*); **sur les ~x (d'un crime/d'un accident)** at the scene (of a crime/an accident). -2. [domicile] premises.

◆ **lieu commun** (*pl* **lieux communs**) *nm* commonplace.

◆ **lieu-dit** (*pl* **lieux-dits**) *nm* locality, place.

◆ **au lieu de** *loc prép*: **au ~ de qqch/de faire qqch** instead of sthg/of doing sthg.

◆ **en dernier lieu** *loc adv* lastly.

◆ **en premier lieu** *loc adv* in the first place.

◆ **en second lieu** *loc adv* in the second place.

lieue [ljø] *nf* league; **j'étais à cent ~s de penser cela** *fig* I never thought that for a moment.

lieutenant [ljøtenã] *nm* lieutenant.

lieutenant-colonel [ljøtnãkɔlɔnɛl] (*pl* **lieutenants-colonels**) *nm* lieutenant-colonel.

lièvre [ljɛvr] *nm* hare; **courir deux ~s à la fois** *fig* to do more than one thing at a time; **lever un ~** *fig* to ask an awkward question.

lifter [lifte] [3] *vt* TENNIS to spin, to put a spin on.

lifting [liftiŋ] *nm* face-lift.

ligament [ligamã] *nm* ligament.

ligature [ligatyr] *nf* [MÉD - lien] ligature; [- opération] ligation, ligature; **~ des trompes** MÉD tying the tubes.

ligaturer [ligatyre] [3] *vt* **-1.** MÉD to ligature, to ligate. **-2.** AGRIC to bind.

lige [liʒ] *adj*: **homme ~** liege man.

ligne [liɲ] *nf* **-1.** [gén] line; **à la ~** new line OU paragraph; **en ~** [personnes] in a line; IN-FORM on line; **en ~ droite** as the crow flies; **lire entre les ~s** *fig* to read between the lines; **dans sa ~ de mire** in one's line of sight; **~ de départ/d'arrivée** starting/finishing line; **~ aérienne** airline; **~ de commande** INFORM command line; **~ de conduite** line of conduct; **~ de démarcation** demarcation line; **~ directrice** guideline; **~ de flottaison** water line; **~s de la main** lines of the hand. **-2.** [forme - de voiture, meuble] lines (*pl*). **-3.** [silhouette]: **avoir la ~** to have a good figure; **garder la ~** to keep one's figure; **surveiller sa ~** to watch one's waistline. **-4.** [de pêche] fishing line; **pêcher à la ~** to go angling. **-5.** *loc*: **dans les grandes ~s** in outline; **entrer en ~ de compte** to be taken into account.

lignée [liɲe] *nf* [famille] descendants (*pl*); **dans la ~ de** *fig* [d'écrivains, d'artistes] in the tradition of.

lignite [liɲit] *nm* lignite.

ligoter [ligɔte] [3] *vt* **-1.** [attacher] to tie up; **~ qqn à qqch** to tie sb to sthg. **-2.** *fig* [entraver] to bind.

ligue [lig] *nf* league.

liguer [lige] [3] *vt* to bring together, to unite; **être ligué avec** to be in league with.

◆ **se liguer** *vp* to form a league; **se ~ contre** to conspire against.

lilas [lila] *nm & adj inv* lilac.

limace [limas] *nf* **-1.** ZOOL slug. **-2.** *fig* [personne] slowcoach *Br*, slowpoke *Am*.

limaille [limaj] *nf* filings (*pl*).

limande [limãd] *nf* dab.

limbes [lɛ̃b] *nmpl* RELIG limbo (*sg*); **être dans les ~** *fig* to be in limbo.

lime [lim] *nf* **-1.** [outil] file; **~ à ongles** nail file. **-2.** BOT lime.

limer [lime] [3] *vt* [ongles] to file; [aspérités] to file down; [barreau] to file through.

limier [limje] *nm* **-1.** [chien] bloodhound. **-2.** [détective] sleuth; **fin ~** first-rate detective.

liminaire [liminɛr] *adj* introductory.

limitatif, -ive [limitatif, iv] *adj* restrictive.

limitation [limitasjɔ̃] *nf* limitation; [de naissances] control; **~ de vitesse** speed limit.

limite [limit] ◇ *nf* **-1.** [gén] limit; **à la ~** [au pire] at worst; **à la ~, j'accepterais de le voir** if pushed, I'd agree to see him. **-2.** [terme, échéance] deadline; **~ d'âge** age limit. ◇ *adj* [extrême] maximum (*avant n*); **cas ~** borderline case; **date ~** deadline; **date ~ de vente/consommation** sell-by/use-by date.

◆ **limites** *nfpl*: **sans ~s** limitless.

limité, -e [limite] *adj* [peu important] limited.

limiter [limite] [3] *vt* **-1.** [borner] to border, to bound. **-2.** [restreindre] to limit.

◆ **se limiter** *vp* **-1.** [se restreindre]: **se ~ à qqch/à faire qqch** to limit o.s. to sthg/to doing sthg. **-2.** [se borner]: **se ~ à** to be limited to.

limitrophe [limitrɔf] *adj* **-1.** [frontalier] border (*avant n*); **être ~ de** to border on. **-2.** [voisin] adjacent.

limogeage [limɔʒaʒ] *nm* dismissal.

limoger [limɔʒe] [17] *vt* to dismiss.

limon [limɔ̃] *nm* **-1.** GÉOL alluvium, silt. **-2.** CONSTR stringboard.

limonade [limɔnad] *nf* lemonade.

limpide [lɛ̃pid] *adj* **-1.** [eau] limpid. **-2.** [ciel, regard] clear. **-3.** [explication, style] clear, lucid.

limpidité [lɛ̃pidite] *nf* **-1.** [d'eau] limpidity. **-2.** [du ciel, de regard] clearness. **-3.** [d'explication, de style] clarity, lucidity.

lin [lɛ̃] *nm* **-1.** BOT flax. **-2.** [tissu] linen.

linceul [lɛ̃sœl] *nm* shroud.

linéaire [lineɛr] *adj* **-1.** [mesure, perspective] linear. **-2.** *fig* [récit] one-dimensional.

linge [lɛ̃ʒ] *nm* **-1.** [lessive] washing. **-2.** [de lit, de table] linen. **-3.** [sous-vêtements] underwear; **~ sale** dirty washing; **laver son ~ sale en famille** not to wash one's dirty linen in public. **-4.** [morceau de tissu] cloth.

-5. *loc*: **blanc** OU **pâle comme un** ~ as white as a sheet.

lingerie [lɛ̃ʒri] *nf* **-1.** [local] linen room. **-2.** [sous-vêtements] lingerie.

lingot [lɛ̃go] *nm* ingot; ~ **d'or** gold ingot.

linguiste [lɛ̃gɥist] *nmf* linguist.

linguistique [lɛ̃gɥistik] ◇ *nf* linguistics (*U*). ◇ *adj* linguistic.

linoléum [linɔleɔm] *nm* lino, linoleum.

linotte [linɔt] *nf* ZOOL linnet; **tête de** ~ *fig* featherbrain.

linteau, -x [lɛ̃to] *nm* lintel.

lion, lionne [ljɔ̃, ljɔn] *nm, f* lion (*f* lioness).
◆ **Lion** *nm* ASTROL Leo; **être Lion** to be (a) Leo.

lionceau, -x [ljɔ̃so] *nm* lion cub.

lipide [lipid] *nm* lipid.

lippu, -e [lipy] *adj* thick-lipped.

liquéfier [likefje] [9] *vt* to liquefy.
◆ **se liquéfier** *vp* **-1.** [matière] to liquefy. **-2.** *fig* [personne] to turn to jelly.

liqueur [likœr] *nf* liqueur.

liquidation [likidasjɔ̃] *nf* **-1.** [de compte & BOURSE] settlement. **-2.** [de société, stock] liquidation. **-3.** *arg crime* [de témoin] liquidation, elimination. **-4.** *fam fig* [de problème] elimination.

liquide [likid] ◇ *nm* **-1.** [substance] liquid. **-2.** [argent] cash; **en** ~ in cash. ◇ *nf* LING liquid. ◇ *adj* **-1.** [corps & LING] liquid. **-2.** [en argent] cash (*avant n*).

liquider [likide] [3] *vt* **-1.** [compte & BOURSE] to settle. **-2.** [société, stock] to liquidate. **-3.** *fam* [importun] to get rid of. **-4.** *arg crime* [témoin] to liquidate, to eliminate; *fig* [problème] to eliminate, to get rid of.

liquidité [likidite] *nf* liquidity.
◆ **liquidités** *nfpl* liquid assets.

liquoreux, -euse [likɔrø, øz] *adj* syrupy, sugary.

lire[1] [lir] [106] *vt* to read; **lu et approuvé** read and approved.

lire[2] [lir] *nf* lira.

lis, lys [lis] *nm* lily.

lisais, lisions *etc* → lire.

Lisbonne [lizbɔn] *n* Lisbon.

lise, lises *etc* → lire.

liseré [lizre], **liséré** [lizere] *nm* **-1.** [ruban] binding. **-2.** [bande] border, edging.

liseron [lizrɔ̃] *nm* bindweed.

liseuse [lizøz] *nf* **-1.** [couvre-livre] book cover. **-2.** [signet] paper knife (*cum bookmark*). **-3.** [vêtement] bedjacket. **-4.** [lampe] reading light.

lisible [lizibl] *adj* **-1.** [écriture] legible. **-2.** [roman] readable.

lisiblement [lizibləmɑ̃] *adv* legibly.

lisière [lizjer] *nf* **-1.** [limite] edge. **-2.** COUTURE selvage.

lisse [lis] ◇ *nf* **-1.** [rambarde] handrail. **-2.** NAVIG rib. ◇ *adj* **-1.** [surface, peau] smooth. **-2.** [cheveux] straight.

lisser [lise] [3] *vt* **-1.** [papier, vêtements] to smooth (out). **-2.** [moustache, cheveux] to smooth (down). **-3.** [plumes] to preen.

listage [lista3] *nm* listing.

liste [list] *nf* list; ~ **d'attente** waiting list; ~ **électorale** electoral roll; ~ **de mariage** wedding present list; ~ **noire** blacklist; **être sur la** ~ **rouge** to be ex-directory.

lister [liste] [3] *vt* to list.

listing [listiŋ] *nm* listing.

lit [li] *nm* **-1.** [gén] bed; **faire son** ~ to make one's bed; **garder le** ~ to stay in bed; **se mettre au** ~ to go to bed; ~ **à baldaquin** four-poster bed; ~ **de camp** camp bed; ~ **d'enfant** cot *Br*, crib *Am*; ~ **gigogne** pull-out bed; ~ **nuptial** marriage bed; ~**s jumeaux/superposés** twin/bunk beds. **-2.** JUR marriage; **d'un premier** ~ of a first marriage.

LIT (*abr de* **lire italienne**) L, Lit.

litanie [litani] *nf* litany.

litchi [litʃi], **letchi** [letʃi] *nm* lychee.

literie [litri] *nf* bedding.

lithographie [litɔgrafi] *nf* **-1.** [procédé] lithography. **-2.** [image] lithograph.

litière [litjer] *nf* litter.

litige [liti3] *nm* **-1.** JUR lawsuit. **-2.** [désaccord] dispute.

litigieux, -ieuse [liti3jø, jøz] *adj* **-1.** JUR litigious. **-2.** [douteux] disputed.

litote [litɔt] *nf* understatement, litotes.

litre [litr] *nm* **-1.** [mesure, quantité] litre, = 1.76 pints. **-2.** [récipient] litre bottle.

litron [litrɔ̃] *nm tfam* litre of wine.

littéraire [literer] ◇ *nmf person who is strong in arts subjects.* ◇ *adj* literary.

littéral, -e, -aux [literal, o] *adj* **-1.** [gén] literal. **-2.** [écrit] written.

littéralement [literalmɑ̃] *adv* literally.

littérature [literatyr] *nf* **-1.** [gén] literature; ~ **comparée** comparative literature. **-2.** [profession] writing.

littoral, -e, -aux [litɔral, o] *adj* coastal.
◆ **littoral** *nm* coast, coastline.

Lituanie [litɥani] *nf*: **la** ~ Lithuania.

lituanien, -ienne [litɥanjɛ̃, jɛn] *adj* Lithuanian.

◆ **lituanien** *nm* [langue] Lithuanian.
◆ **Lituanien, -ienne** *nm, f* Lithuanian.
liturgie [lityrʒi] *nf* liturgy.
liturgique [lityrʒik] *adj* liturgical.
livide [livid] *adj* [blême] pallid.
livrable [livrabl] *adj* which can be delivered.
livraison [livrɛzɔ̃] *nf* [de marchandise] delivery; ~ **à domicile** home delivery.
livre [livr] ◇ *nm* **-1.** [gén] book; ~ **de bord** log, logbook; ~ **de cuisine** cookery book; ~ **d'images** picture book; ~ **de messe** missal; ~ **d'or** visitors' book; ~ **de poche** paperback; **à ~ ouvert** *fig* at sight. **-2.** [industrie] book trade. ◇ *nf* pound; ~ **sterling** pound sterling.
livre-cassette [livrəkasɛt] *nm* spoken word cassette.
livrée [livre] *nf* [uniforme] livery.
livrer [livre] [3] *vt* **-1.** COMM to deliver; ~ **qqch à qqn** [achat] to deliver sthg to sb; *fig* [secret] to reveal OU give away sthg to sb. **-2.** [coupable, complice]: ~ **qqn à qqn** to hand sb over to sb. **-3.** [abandonner]: ~ **qqch à qqch** to give sthg over to sthg; ~ **qqn à lui-même** to leave sb to his own devices; ~ **passage à qqn** *fig* to let sb pass.
◆ **se livrer** *vp* **-1.** [se rendre]: **se ~ à** [police, ennemi] to give o.s. up to; [amant] to give o.s. to. **-2.** [se confier]: **se ~ à** [ami] to open up to, to confide in. **-3.** [se consacrer]: **se ~ à** [occupation] to devote o.s. to; [excès] to indulge in.
livresque [livrɛsk] *adj* bookish.
livret [livrɛ] *nm* **-1.** [carnet] booklet; ~ **de caisse d'épargne** passbook, bankbook; ~ **de famille** *official family record book, given by registrar to newlyweds*; ~ **scolaire** ≃ school report. **-2.** [catalogue] catalogue. **-3.** MUS book, libretto.
livreur, -euse [livrœr, øz] *nm, f* delivery man (*f* woman).
Ljubljana [ljubljana] *n* Ljubljana.
lm (*abr de* **lumen**) lm.
LO (*abr de* **Lutte ouvrière**) *nf* left-wing political party.
lobby [lɔbi] (*pl* **lobbies**) *nm* lobby.
lobe [lɔb] *nm* **-1.** ANAT & BOT lobe. **-2.** ARCHIT foil.
lober [lɔbe] [3] *vt* TENNIS to lob.
local, -e, -aux [lɔkal, o] *adj* local; [douleur] localized.
◆ **local** *nm* room, premises (*pl*).
◆ **locaux** *nmpl* premises, offices.
localement [lɔkalmɑ̃] *adv* locally.

localisation [lɔkalizasjɔ̃] *nf* **-1.** [d'avion, de bruit] location. **-2.** [d'épidémie, de conflit] localization.
localiser [lɔkalize] [3] *vt* **-1.** [avion, bruit] to locate. **-2.** [épidémie, conflit] to localize.
◆ **se localiser** *vp* to be confined.
localité [lɔkalite] *nf* (small) town.
locataire [lɔkatɛr] *nmf* tenant.
locatif, -ive [lɔkatif, iv] *adj* [relatif à la location] rental (*avant n*).
◆ **locatif** *nm* GRAM locative.
location [lɔkasjɔ̃] *nf* **-1.** [de propriété - par propriétaire] letting *Br*, renting *Am*; [- par locataire] renting; [de machine] leasing; ~ **de voitures/vélos** car/bicycle hire *Br*, car/bicycle rent *Am*. **-2.** [bail] lease. **-3.** [maison, appartement] rented property.
location-vente [lɔkasjɔ̃vɑ̃t] (*pl* **locations-ventes**) *nf* ≃ hire purchase *Br*, ≃ installment plan *Am*.
loc. cit. (*abr de* **loco citato**) loc. cit.
lock-out [lɔkaut] *nm inv* lockout.
locomoteur, -trice [lɔkɔmɔtœr, tris] *adj* locomotive (*avant n*).
locomotion [lɔkɔmɔsjɔ̃] *nf* locomotion.
locomotive [lɔkɔmɔtiv] *nf* **-1.** [machine] locomotive. **-2.** *fig* [leader] moving force.
locuteur, -trice [lɔkytœr, tris] *nm, f* speaker.
locution [lɔkysjɔ̃] *nf* expression, phrase.
loden [lɔdɛn] *nm* [étoffe] loden; [vêtement] loden overcoat.
loft [lɔft] *nm* (converted) loft.
logarithme [lɔgaritm] *nm* logarithm.
loge [lɔʒ] *nf* **-1.** [de concierge, de francs-maçons] lodge. **-2.** [d'acteur] dressing room. **-3.** [de spectacle] box; **être aux premières ~s** *fig* to have a ringside seat. **-4.** [d'écurie] loose box. **-5.** ARCHIT loggia.
logement [lɔʒmɑ̃] *nm* **-1.** [hébergement] accommodation. **-2.** [appartement] flat *Br*, apartment *Am*; ~ **de fonction** company flat *Br* OU apartment *Am*.
loger [lɔʒe] [17] ◇ *vi* [habiter] to live. ◇ *vt* **-1.** [amis, invités] to put up. **-2.** [clé] to put. **-3.** [suj: hôtel, maison] to accommodate, to take.
◆ **se loger** *vp* **-1.** [trouver un logement] to find accommodation. **-2.** [se placer - ballon, balle]: **se ~ dans** to lodge in, to stick in; **se ~ dans** *fig* [angoisse] to take hold of.
loggia [lɔdʒja] *nf* loggia.
logiciel [lɔʒisjɛl] *nm* software (*U*); ~ **intégré** integrated software.
logique [lɔʒik] ◇ *nf* logic. ◇ *adj* logical.
logiquement [lɔʒikmɑ̃] *adv* logically.

logis [lɔʒi] *nm* abode.

logistique [lɔʒistik] ◇ *nf* logistics (*pl*). ◇ *adj* logistic.

logo [logo] *nm* logo.

logorrhée [logɔre] *nf* logorrhoea.

loi [lwa] *nf* **-1.** [gén] law; **faire la ~** to lay down the law; **la ~ du plus fort** might is right; **~ de l'offre et de la demande** law of supply and demand; **la ~ du talion** an eye for an eye; **la ~ de 1901** *law concerning the setting up of non-profit-making organizations.* **-2.** [convention] rule.

loin [lwɛ̃] *adv* **-1.** [dans l'espace] far; **plus ~** further. **-2.** [dans le temps - passé] a long time ago; [- futur] a long way off.
◆ **au loin** *loc adv* in the distance, far off.
◆ **de loin** *loc adv* **-1.** [depuis une grande distance] from a distance; **de très ~** from a great distance; **de plus ~** from further away. **-2.** [assez peu] from a distance, from afar. **-3.** [de beaucoup] by far.
◆ **de loin en loin** *loc adv* **-1.** [dans l'espace] here and there. **-2.** [dans le temps] every now and then, from time to time.
◆ **loin de** *loc prép* **-1.** [gén] far from; **~ de là!** *fig* far from it! **-2.** [dans le temps]: **il n'est pas ~ de 9 h** it's nearly 9 o'clock, it's not far off 9 o'clock.

lointain, -e [lwɛ̃tɛ̃, ɛn] *adj* **-1.** [pays, avenir, parent] distant. **-2.** [ressemblance] vague.
◆ **lointain** *nm*: **au** OU **dans le ~** in the distance.

loir [lwar] *nm* dormouse; **dormir comme un ~** *fig* to sleep like a log.

loisible [lwazibl] *adj*: **il m'est ~ de participer** I am at liberty to take part.

loisir [lwazir] *nm* **-1.** [temps libre] leisure; **avoir le ~ de faire qqch** *sout* to have the time to do sthg; **à ~** [à satiété] as much as one likes; [sans hâte] at leisure. **-2.** (*gén pl*) [distractions] leisure activities (*pl*).

lombago = **lumbago**.

lombaire [lɔ̃bɛr] ◇ *nf* lumbar vertebra. ◇ *adj* lumbar.

lombes [lɔ̃b] *nfpl* loins.

Lomé [lome] *n* Lomé.

londonien, -ienne [lɔ̃dɔnjɛ̃, jɛn] *adj* London (*avant n*).
◆ **Londonien, -ienne** *nm, f* Londoner.

Londres [lɔ̃dr] *n* London.

long, longue [lɔ̃, lɔ̃g] *adj* **-1.** [gén] long. **-2.** [lent] slow; **être ~ à faire qqch** to take a long time doing sthg.
◆ **long** ◇ *nm* **-1.** [longueur]: **4 mètres de ~** 4 metres long OU in length; **de ~ en large** up and down, to and fro; **en ~ et en large** in great detail; **(tout) le ~ de** [espace] all

along; **tout le ~ du jour** the whole day long; **tout au ~ de** [année, carrière] throughout; **tomber de tout son ~** to go full length. **-2.** [vêtement]: **le ~** long clothes (*pl*). ◇ *adv* **-1.** [beaucoup]: **en savoir ~ sur qqch** to know a lot about sthg. **-2.** [s'habiller]: **elle est habillée trop ~** her clothes are too long.
◆ **longue** *nf* **-1.** LING long vowel. **-2.** MUS long note. **-3.** CARTES long suit.
◆ **à la longue** *loc adv* in the end.

long. (*abr de* **longitude**) long.

long-courrier [lɔ̃kurje] (*pl* **long-courriers**) ◇ *nm* NAVIG ocean liner; AÉRON long-haul aircraft. ◇ *adj* NAVIG ocean-going; AÉRON long-haul.

longe [lɔ̃ʒ] *nf* **-1.** [courroie] halter. **-2.** [viande] loin.

longer [lɔ̃ʒe] [17] *vt* **-1.** [border] to go along OU alongside. **-2.** [marcher le long de] to walk along; [raser] to stay close to, to hug.

longévité [lɔ̃ʒevite] *nf* longevity.

longiligne [lɔ̃ʒiliɲ] *adj* long-limbed.

longitude [lɔ̃ʒityd] *nf* longitude.

longitudinal, -e, -aux [lɔ̃ʒitydinal, o] *adj* longitudinal.

longtemps [lɔ̃tɑ̃] *adv* (for) a long time; **avant ~** before long; **il ne reviendra pas avant ~** he won't be back for some time; **depuis ~** (for) a long time; **il y a ~ que ...** it's been a long time since ...; **mettre ~ à faire qqch** to take a long time to do sthg; **je n'en ai pas pour ~** I won't be long.

longue → **long**.

longuement [lɔ̃gmɑ̃] *adv* **-1.** [longtemps] for a long time. **-2.** [en détail] at length.

longuet, -ette [lɔ̃gɛ, ɛt] *adj fam* longish, a bit long.

longueur [lɔ̃gœr] *nf* length; **faire 5 mètres de ~** to be 5 metres long; **disposer qqch en ~** to put sthg lengthways; **à ~ de journée/temps** the entire day/time; **à ~ d'années** all year long; **être sur la même ~ d'onde** *fig* to be on the same wavelength.
◆ **longueurs** *nfpl* [de film, de livre] boring parts.

longue-vue [lɔ̃gvy] (*pl* **longues-vues**) *nf* telescope.

look [luk] *nm* look; **avoir un ~** to have a style.

looping [lupiŋ] *nm* loop the loop.

lopin [lɔpɛ̃] *nm*: **~ (de terre)** patch OU plot of land.

loquace [lɔkas] *adj* loquacious.

loquacité [lɔkasite] *nf* loquacity.

loque [lɔk] *nf* **-1.** [lambeau] **rag; en ~s in rags. -2.** *fig* [personne] **wreck.**

loquet [lɔkɛ] *nm* **latch.**

lorgner [lɔrɲe] [3] *vt fam* **-1.** [observer] to **eye. -2.** [guigner] to **have one's eye on.**

lorgnette [lɔrɲɛt] *nf* **opera glasses** (*pl*).

lorgnon [lɔrɲɔ̃] *nm* **lorgnette.**

lors [lɔr] *adv*: **depuis ~** since that time; **~ de** at the time of.

lorsque [lɔrsk(ə)] *conj* **when.**

losange [lɔzɑ̃ʒ] *nm* **lozenge.**

lot [lo] *nm* **-1.** [part] **share;** [de terre] **plot. -2.** [stock] **batch. -3.** [prix] **prize; le gros ~** the jackpot. **-4.** *fig* [destin] **fate, lot.**

loterie [lɔtri] *nf* **lottery; la Loterie nationale** the National Lottery.

loti, -e [lɔti] *adj*: **être bien/mal ~** to be well/badly off.

lotion [losjɔ̃] *nf* **lotion; ~ après-rasage** aftershave (lotion).

lotir [lɔtir] [32] *vt* to **divide up; ~ qqn de qqch** to allot sthg to sb.

lotissement [lɔtismɑ̃] *nm* **-1.** [terrain] **plot. -2.** [division - de terrain] **parcelling out.**

loto [lɔto] *nm* **-1.** [jeu de société] **lotto. -2.** [loterie] **lottery.**

LOTO:

Loto is a popular game of chance with large cash prizes. Printed grids ('bulletins') are available at tobacconists or special kiosks. Players mark seven numbers on the grid and pay a fee. The twice-weekly prize draw is broadcast on television.

'Loto sportif' is a version of Loto in which players bet on the football results

lotte [lɔt] *nf* **monkfish.**

lotus [lɔtys] *nm* **lotus.**

louable [lwabl] *adj* **-1.** [méritoire] **praise-worthy. -2.** [location]: **facilement/ difficilement ~** easy/difficult to let *Br,* easy/difficult to rent *Am.*

louage [lwaʒ] *nm* **hire** *Br,* **rental** *Am;* **voi-ture de ~** hire *Br* OU rental *Am* car.

louange [lwɑ̃ʒ] *nf* **praise; chanter les ~s de qqn** *fig* to sing sb's praises.

loubar(d) [lubar] *nm fam* **hooligan.**

louche¹ [luʃ] *nf* **ladle.**

louche² [luʃ] *adj fam* [personne, histoire] **sus-picious.**

loucher [luʃe] [3] *vi* **-1.** [être atteint de stra-bisme] to **squint. -2.** *fam fig* [lorgner]: **~ sur** to have one's eye on.

louer [lwe] [6] *vt* **-1.** [glorifier] to **praise; ~ qqn de qqch** to praise sb for sthg. **-2.** [don-

ner en location - voiture] to **hire (out)** *Br,* to **rent (out);** [- machine] to **hire (out)** *Br;* [- ap-partement] to **rent out,** to **let** *Br;* **à ~** for **hire** *Br,* for rent *Am.* **-3.** [prendre en location - voiture] to **rent,** to **hire** *Br;* [- machine] to **hire** *Br;* [- appartement] to **rent. -4.** [réserver] to **book.**

◆ **se louer** *vp* **-1.** *sout* [se féliciter]: **se ~ de qqch/de faire qqch** to be very pleased about sthg/about doing sthg. **-2.** [apparte-ment] to be to let *Br* OU for rent *Am.* **-3.** *péj* [se vanter] to sing one's own praises.

loufoque [lufɔk] *fam* ◇ *nmf* **nutter.** ◇ *adj* **nuts, crazy.**

loup [lu] *nm* **-1.** [carnassier] **wolf. -2.** [pois-son] **bass. -3.** [masque] **mask. -4.** *fig* [per-sonne]: **(vieux) ~ de mer** (old) sea dog.

loupe [lup] *nf* **-1.** [optique] **magnifying glass; regarder qqch à la ~** *fig* to put sthg under the microscope. **-2.** BOT **burr.**

louper [lupe] [3] *vt fam* [travail] to **make a mess of;** [train] to **miss.**

loup-garou [lugaru] (*pl* **loups-garous**) *nm* **werewolf.**

loupiot, -iotte [lupjo, jɔt] *nm, f fam* **kid.**

lourd, -e [lur, lurd] *adj* **-1.** [gén] **heavy; ~ de** *fig* **full of. -2.** [tâche] **difficult;** [faute] se-rious. **-3.** [maladroit] **clumsy, heavy-handed. -4.** MÉTÉOR **close. -5.** [esprit] **slow.**

◆ **lourd** *adv*: **peser ~** to be heavy, to weigh a lot; **il n'en fait pas ~** *fam* he doesn't do much.

lourdaud, -e [lurdo, od] ◇ *adj* **clumsy.** ◇ *nm, f* **oaf.**

lourdement [lurdəmɑ̃] *adv* **-1.** [pesamment] **heavily. -2.** [maladroitement] **heavily, clum-sily;** [insister] **strenuously.**

lourdeur [lurdœr] *nf* **-1.** [gén] **heaviness. -2.** MÉTÉOR **closeness. -3.** [d'esprit] **slowness.**

loustic [lustik] *nm fam* **-1.** [enfant] **kid. -2.** [farceur] **joker. -3.** *péj* [type] **guy.**

loutre [lutr] *nf* **otter.**

louve [luv] *nf* **she-wolf.**

louveteau, -x [luvto] *nm* **-1.** ZOOL **wolf cub. -2.** [scout] **cub.**

louvoyer [luvwaje] [13] *vi* **-1.** NAVIG to **tack. -2.** *fig* [tergiverser] to **beat about the bush.**

Louvre [luvr] *n*: **le ~** the Louvre (museum); **l'école du ~** art school in Paris.

L'ÉCOLE DU LOUVRE:

This prestigious art school in the Louvre teaches art history and archaeology, and trains specialist museum staff

lover [lɔve] [3] *vt* to coil.
◆ **se lover** *vp* [serpent] to coil up.

loyal, -e, -aux [lwajal, o] *adj* -1. [fidèle] loyal. -2. [honnête] fair.

loyalement [lwajalmã] *adv* -1. [fidèlement] loyally. -2. [honnêtement] fairly.

loyauté [lwajote] *nf* -1. [fidélité] loyalty. -2. [honnêteté] fairness.

loyer [lwaje] *nm* rent.

LP (*abr de* **lycée professionnel**) *nm secondary school for vocational training.*

LSD (*abr de* **Lysergic acid diethylamide**) *nm* LSD.

lu, -e [ly] *pp* → lire.

Luanda [lyãda] *n* Luanda.

lubie [lybi] *nf fam* whim.

lubricité [lybrisite] *nf* lechery.

lubrifiant, -e [lybrifjã, ãt] *adj* lubricating.
◆ **lubrifiant** *nm* lubricant.

lubrification [lybrifikasjɔ̃] *nf* lubrication.

lubrifier [lybrifje] [9] *vt* to lubricate.

lubrique [lybrik] *adj* lewd.

lucarne [lykarn] *nf* -1. [fenêtre] skylight. -2. FOOTBALL top corner of the net.

lucide [lysid] *adj* lucid.

lucidement [lysidmã] *adv* lucidly.

lucidité [lysidite] *nf* lucidity.

luciole [lysjɔl] *nf* firefly.

lucratif, -ive [lykratif, iv] *adj* lucrative.

lucre [lykr] *nm péj* lucre.

ludique [lydik] *adj* play (*avant n*).

ludothèque [lydɔtɛk] *nf* toy library.

luette [lɥɛt] *nf* uvula.

lueur [lɥœr] *nf* -1. [de bougie, d'étoile] light; à la ~ de by the light of. -2. *fig* [de colère] gleam; [de raison] spark; ~ **d'espoir** glimmer of hope.

luge [lyʒ] *nf* toboggan.

lugubre [lygybr] *adj* lugubrious.

lui¹ [lɥi] *pp inv* → luire.

lui² [lɥi] *pron pers* -1. [complément d'objet indirect - homme] (to) him; [- femme] (to) her; [- animal, chose] (to) it; **je ~ ai parlé** I've spoken to him/to her; **il le ~ a présenté** he introduced him to her; **il ~ a serré la main** he shook his/her hand. -2. [sujet, en renforcement de «il»] he; **qui t'accompagnera? - lui** who will go with you? - he will; **il sait de quoi je parle, ~ HE** knows what I'm talking about. -3. [objet, après préposition, comparatif - personne] him; [- animal, chose] it; **je n'ai vu que ~** I saw no one else but him; **si j'étais ~ ...** if I were him ...; **~, tout le monde le connaît** everyone knows HIM;

sans ~ without him; **je vais chez ~** I'm going to his place; **elle est plus jeune que ~** she's younger than him OU than he is. -4. [remplaçant soi en fonction de pronom réfléchi - personne] himself; [- animal, chose] itself; **il est content de ~** he's pleased with himself.
◆ **lui-même** *pron pers* [personne] himself; [animal, chose] itself.

luire [lɥir] [97] *vi* [soleil, métal] to shine; *fig* [espoir] to glow, to glimmer.

luisais, luisions *etc* → luire.

luisant, -e [lɥizã, ãt] *adj* gleaming.
◆ **luisant** *nm* sheen.

lumbago, lombago [lɔ̃bago] *nm* lumbago.

lumière [lymjɛr] *nf* -1. [éclairage & *fig*] light; ~ **tamisée** subdued light; **à la ~ de** by the light of; **faire toute la ~ sur qqch** to make sthg clear; **mettre qqch en ~** to highlight sthg. -2. [personne] leading light; **ce n'est pas une ~** *fam* he's/she's not very bright.

luminaire [lyminer] *nm* light.

luminescent, -e [lyminesã, ãt] *adj* luminescent.

lumineux, -euse [lyminø, øz] *adj* -1. [couleur, cadran] luminous. -2. *fig* [visage] radiant; [idée] brilliant. -3. [explication] clear.

luminosité [lyminozite] *nf* -1. [du regard, ciel] radiance. -2. PHYS & SCIENCE luminosity.

lump [lœp] *nm*: **œufs de ~** lumpfish roe.

lunaire [lyner] *adj* -1. ASTRON lunar. -2. *fig* [visage] moon (*avant n*); [paysage] lunar.

lunatique [lynatik] ◇ *nmf* temperamental person. ◇ *adj* temperamental.

lunch [lœ̃ʃ] *nm* buffet lunch.

lundi [lœ̃di] *nm* Monday; ~ **de Pâques/Pentecôte** Easter/Whit Monday; *voir aussi* **samedi.**

lune [lyn] *nf* -1. ASTRON moon; **nouvelle ~** new moon; **pleine ~** full moon; ~ **de miel** *fig* honeymoon; **dans la ~** *fig* in the clouds; **décrocher la ~** *fig* to move heaven and earth; **promettre la ~** *fig* to promise the earth. -2. *fam fig* [derrière] backside.

luné, -e [lyne] *adj*: **être bien/mal ~** to be in a good/bad mood.

lunetier, -ière [lyntje, jɛr] ◇ *adj* spectacle-making (*avant n*). ◇ *nm, f* optician.

lunette [lynɛt] *nf* -1. [ouverture]: **la ~ des W.-C.** [cuvette] the toilet bowl; ~ **arrière** rear window. -2. ASTRON telescope.
◆ **lunettes** *nfpl* glasses; ~**s noires** dark glasses; ~**s de soleil** sunglasses.

lunule [lynyl] *nf* [d'ongle] half-moon.

lupanar [lypanar] *nm sout* brothel.

lupin [lypɛ̃] *nm* lupin.

lurette [lyrɛt] *nf*: **il y a belle ~ que ...** *fam* it's been ages since ....

luron, -onne [lyrɔ̃, ɔn] *nm, f fam*: **un joyeux ~** a bit of a lad.

Lusaka [lyzaka] *n* Lusaka.

lusophone [lyzɔfɔn] *adj* Portuguese-speaking.

lustre [lystr] *nm* **-1.** [luminaire] chandelier. **-2.** [éclat] sheen, shine; *fig* reputation. **-3.** *littéraire* [cinq ans] period of five years; **ça fait des ~s que ...** *fig* it's been ages since ....

lustrer [lystre] [3] *vt* **-1.** [faire briller] to make shine. **-2.** [user] to wear.

luth [lyt] *nm* lute.

luthérien, -ienne [lyterjɛ̃, jɛn] *adj & nm, f* Lutheran.

luthier [lytje] *nm* maker of stringed instruments.

lutin, -e [lytɛ̃, in] *adj* mischievous.
◆ **lutin** *nm* imp.

lutrin [lytrɛ̃] *nm* lectern.

lutte [lyt] *nf* **-1.** [combat] fight, struggle; **de haute ~** with a hard-fought struggle; **la ~ des classes** class struggle; **~ d'influence** power struggle. **-2.** SPORT wrestling.

lutter [lyte] [3] *vi* to fight, to struggle; **~ contre** to fight (against).

lutteur, -euse [lytœr, øz] *nm, f* SPORT wrestler; *fig* fighter.

luxation [lyksasjɔ̃] *nf* dislocation.

luxe [lyks] *nm* luxury; **de ~** luxury; **ce n'est pas un** OU **du ~** *fig* it is a necessity; **s'offrir** OU **se payer le ~ de** *fig* to afford the luxury of.

Luxembourg [lyksãbur] *nm* **-1.** [pays]: **le ~** Luxembourg; **au ~** in Luxembourg. **-2.** [ville] Luxembourg; **à ~** in (the city of) Luxembourg. **-3.** [jardins]: **le ~** the Luxembourg Gardens.

luxembourgeois, -e [lyksãburʒwa, az] *adj* of/from Luxembourg.
◆ **Luxembourgeois, -e** *nm, f* native OU inhabitant of Luxembourg.

luxer [lykse] [3] *vt* to dislocate.
◆ **se luxer** *vp*: **se ~ l'épaule** to dislocate one's shoulder.

luxueux, -euse [lyksɥø, øz] *adj* luxurious.

luxure [lyksyr] *nf* lust.

luxuriant, -e [lyksyrjã, ãt] *adj* luxuriant.

luzerne [lyzɛrn] *nf* lucerne, alfalfa.

lx (*abr de* **lux**) lx.

lycée [lise] *nm* ≃ secondary school *Br*, ≃ high school *Am*; **~ technique/professionnel** ≃ technical/training college; **~ pilote** experimental school.

lycéen, -enne [liseɛ̃, ɛn] *nm, f* secondary school pupil *Br*, high school pupil *Am*.

lymphatique [lɛ̃fatik] *adj* **-1.** MÉD lymphatic. **-2.** *fig* [apathique] sluggish.

lymphe [lɛ̃f] *nf* lymph.

lyncher [lɛ̃ʃe] [3] *vt* to lynch.

lynx [lɛ̃ks] *nm* lynx.

Lyon [ljɔ̃] *n* Lyons.

lyonnais, -e [ljɔnɛ, ɛz] *adj* of/from Lyons.
◆ **Lyonnais, -e** *nm, f* native OU inhabitant of Lyons.

lyre [lir] *nf* lyre.

lyrique [lirik] *adj* [poésie & *fig*] lyrical; [drame, chanteur, poète] lyric.

lyrisme [lirism] *nm* **-1.** [poésie] lyricism. **-2.** [exaltation] enthusiasm.

lys = **lis**.

m¹, M [ɛm] *nm inv* m, M.
◆ **M -1.** (*abr de* **maxwell**) Mx. **-2.** (*abr de* **mille (marin)**) nm. **-3.** (*abr de* **méga**) M. **-4.** (*abr de* **Major**) M. **-5.** (*abr de* **Monsieur**) Mr. **-6.** (*abr de* **million**) M. **-7.** *abr de* **masculin.**

m² (*abr de* **milli**) m.

M6 *n* private television channel broadcasting a high proportion of music and aimed at a younger audience.

ma → **mon.**

MA (*abr de* **maître auxiliaire**) *nm* teacher on short-term contract.

Maastricht [mastriʃt] *n* Maastricht; **le traité de ~** the Maastricht treaty.

maboul, -e [mabul] *fam* ◇ *adj* crazy. ◇ *nm, f* nutter.

macabre [makabr] *adj* macabre.

macadam [makadam] *nm* [revêtement] macadam; [route] road.

Macao [makao] *n* Macao; **à ~** in Macao.

macaque [makak] *nm* **-1.** ZOOL macaque. **-2.** *fam* [personne] ape.

macareux [makarø] *nm* puffin.

macaron [makarɔ̃] *nm* **-1.** [pâtisserie] maca-roon. **-2.** [coiffure] coil. **-3.** [autocollant] sticker.

macaroni [makarɔni] *nm* **-1.** CULIN macaro-ni. **-2.** *tfam* [Italien] *offensive term used with re-ference to Italians*, ≃ Eyetie.

macchabée [makabe] *nm tfam* stiff.

macédoine [masedwan] *nf* **-1.** CULIN: ~ de fruits fruit salad; ~ de légumes mixed vegetables. **-2.** *fig* [mélange] jumble.

macérer [masere] [18] ◇ *vt* to steep. ◇ *vi* **-1.** [mariner] to steep; faire ~ to steep. **-2.** *fig* & *péj* [personne] to wallow.

mâche [maʃ] *nf* lamb's lettuce.

mâcher [maʃe] [3] *vt* **-1.** [mastiquer] to chew. **-2.** TECHNOL to chew up.

machiavélique [makjavelik] *adj* Machiavel-lian.

mâchicoulis [maʃikuli] *nm* machicolation.

machin, -e, [maʃɛ̃, in] *nm, f fam* [personne] what's his name (*f* what's her name).

◆ **Machin, -ine** *nm, f* [chose] thing, thingamajig.

machinal, -e, -aux [maʃinal, o] *adj* me-chanical.

machinalement [maʃinalmɑ̃] *adv* mechani-cally.

machination [maʃinasjɔ̃] *nf* machination.

machine [maʃin] *nf* **-1.** TECHNOL machine; ~ à coudre sewing machine; ~ à écrire type-writer; ~ à laver washing machine; ~ à sous fruit machine *Br*, one-armed bandit *Am*; ~ à tricoter knitting machine. **-2.** [or-ganisation] machinery (*U*). **-3.** NAVIG engine; faire ~ arrière to reverse engines; *fig* to back-pedal. **-4.** [locomotive] engine, loco-motive.

machine-outil [maʃinuti] (*pl* machines-outils) *nf* machine tool.

machiner [maʃine] [3] *vt* to plot.

machiniste [maʃinist] *nm* **-1.** CIN & THÉÂTRE scene shifter. **-2.** TRANSPORT driver.

machisme [matʃism] *nm* machismo.

macho [matʃo] *péj* ◇ *nm* macho man. ◇ *adj inv* macho.

mâchoire [maʃwar] *nf* jaw; ~ supérieure/inférieure upper/lower jaw.

mâchonner [maʃɔne] [3] *vt* **-1.** [mâcher, mordiller] to chew. **-2.** [marmonner] to mut-ter.

mâchouiller [maʃuje] [3] *vt fam* to chew.

maçon [masɔ̃] *nm* mason.

maçonner [masɔne] [3] *vt* [construire] to build; [revêtir] to face; [boucher] to brick up.

maçonnerie [masɔnri] *nf* [travaux] building; [construction] masonry; [franc-maçonnerie] freemasonry.

maçonnique [masɔnik] *adj* masonic.

macramé [makrame] *nm* macramé.

macrobiotique [makrɔbjɔtik] ◇ *nf* macro-biotics (*U*). ◇ *adj* macrobiotic.

macroéconomie [makrɔekɔnɔmi] *nf* macro-economy.

maculer [makyle] [3] *vt* to stain.

Madagascar [madagaskar] *n* Madagascar; à ~ in Madagascar.

madame [madam] (*pl* mesdames [medam]) *nf* **-1.** [titre]: ~ X Mrs X; bonjour ~! good morning!; [dans hôtel, restaurant] good morn-ing, madam!; bonjour mesdames! good morning (ladies)!; Madame le Ministre n'est pas là the Minister is out. **-2.** HIST Madame (*title given to the wife of the brother of the King of France*).

madeleine [madlɛn] *nf small sponge cake.*

◆ **Madeleine** *nf*: pleurer comme une Ma-deleine to cry one's eyes out.

mademoiselle [madmwazɛl] (*pl* mesdemoi-selles [medmwazɛl]) *nf* **-1.** [titre]: ~ X Miss X; bonjour ~! good morning!; [à l'école, dans hôtel] good morning, miss; bonjour mesdemoiselles! good morning (ladies)! **-2.** HIST Mademoiselle (*title given to a Princess of France*).

madère [madɛr] *nm* Madeira (wine).

Madère [madɛr] *nf* Madeira; à ~ in Ma-deira.

madone [madɔn] *nf* **-1.** ART & RELIG Madon-na. **-2.** *fig* [jolie femme] beautiful woman.

Madrid [madrid] *n* Madrid.

madrier [madrije] *nm* beam.

madrilène [madrilɛn] *adj* of/from Madrid.

◆ **Madrilène** *nmf* native OU inhabitant of Madrid.

maestria [maɛstrija] *nf* mastery; avec ~ brilliantly.

maf(f)ia [mafja] *nf* Mafia.

magasin [magazɛ̃] *nm* **-1.** [boutique] shop *Br*, store *Am*; en ~ in stock; grand ~ de-partment store; faire les ~s *fig* to go round the shops *Br* OU stores *Am*. **-2.** [entrepôt] warehouse. **-3.** [d'arme, d'appareil photo] magazine.

magasinage [magazinaʒ] *nm* warehousing, storing.

magasinier [magazinje] *nm* warehouseman, storeman.

magazine [magazin] *nm* magazine.

mage [maʒ] *nm*: les trois Rois ~s the Three Wise Men.

Maghreb [magrɛb] *nm*: **le** ~ the Maghreb.

maghrébin, **-e** [magrebɛ̃, in] *adj* North African.

◆ **Maghrébin**, **-e** *nm*, *f* North African.

magicien, **-ienne** [maʒisjɛ̃, jɛn] *nm*, *f* magician.

magie [maʒi] *nf* magic; **comme par** ~ as if by magic; ~ **noire** black magic.

magique [maʒik] *adj* **-1.** [occulte] magic. **-2.** [merveilleux] magical.

magistère [maʒistɛr] *nm* authority.

magistral, **-e**, **-aux** [maʒistral, o] *adj* **-1.** [œuvre, habileté] masterly. **-2.** [dispute, fessée] enormous. **-3.** [attitude, ton] authoritative.

magistralement [maʒistralmɑ̃] *adv* authoritatively, brilliantly.

magistrat [maʒistra] *nm* magistrate.

magistrature [maʒistratyr] *nf* magistracy, magistrature.

magma [magma] *nm* **-1.** GÉOL magma. **-2.** *fig* [mélange] muddle.

magnanerie [maɲanri] *nf* **-1.** [bâtiment] silk farm. **-2.** [sériciculture] silkworm breeding, sericulture.

magnanime [maɲanim] *adj* magnanimous.

magnanimité [maɲanimite] *nf* magnanimity.

magnat [maɲa] *nm* magnate, tycoon.

magner [maɲe] [3]

◆ **se magner** *vp fam* to get a move on.

magnésium [maɲezjɔm] *nm* magnesium.

magnétique [maɲetik] *adj* magnetic.

magnétiser [maɲetize] [3] *vt* **-1.** PHYS to magnetize. **-2.** [hypnotiser, fasciner] to hypnotize.

magnétisme [maɲetism] *nm* **-1.** [PHYS & fascination] magnetism. **-2.** [hypnotisme] hypnotism.

magnéto(phone) [maɲeto(fɔn)] *nm* tape recorder.

magnétoscope [maɲetoskɔp] *nm* videorecorder.

magnificence [maɲifisɑ̃s] *nf* magnificence.

magnifier [maɲifje] [9] *vt* to magnify.

magnifique [maɲifik] *adj* magnificent.

magnifiquement [maɲifikmɑ̃] *adv* magnificently.

magnitude [maɲityd] *nf* magnitude.

magnolia [maɲɔlja] *nm* magnolia.

magnum [magnɔm] *nm* magnum.

magot [mago] *nm fam* tidy sum, packet.

magouille [maguj] *nf fam* plot, scheme.

magouiller [maguje] [3] *vi fam* to plot, to scheme.

magret [magrɛ] *nm* filet *Am*, fillet *Br*; ~ **de canard** breast of duck.

magyar, **-e** [magjar] *adj* Magyar.

mai [mɛ] *nm* May; **le premier** ~ May Day; **(les événements de)** ~ **1968** May 1968; *voir aussi* **septembre**.

MAI 68:

The events of May 1968 came about when student protests, coupled with widespread industrial unrest, culminated in a general strike and rioting. De Gaulle's government survived the crisis, but the issues raised made the events a turning point in French social history

---

maigre [mɛgr] ◇ *adj* **-1.** [très mince] thin. **-2.** [aliment] low-fat; [viande] lean. **-3.** [peu important] meager *Am*, meagre *Br*; [végétation] sparse. ◇ *adv*: **faire** ~ not to eat meat. ◇ *nmf* thin person. ◇ *nm* lean meat.

maigrelet, **-ette** [mɛgrəlɛ, ɛt] *adj* scrawny.

maigreur [mɛgrœr] *nf* thinness.

maigrir [megrir] [32] ◇ *vi* to lose weight. ◇ *vt*: ~ **qqn** to make sb look thinner OU slimmer.

mailing [mɛliŋ] *nm* mailing, mailshot.

maille [maj] *nf* **-1.** [de tricot] stitch; ~ **à l'endroit/l'envers** plain/purl stitch. **-2.** [de filet] mesh. **-3.** *loc*: **avoir** ~ **à partir avec** to have a set-to with.

maillet [majɛ] *nm* mallet.

maillon [majɔ̃] *nm* link.

maillot [majo] *nm* [de sport] shirt, jersey; ~ **de bain** swimsuit; ~ **de corps** undershirt *Am*, vest *Br*.

main [mɛ̃] *nf* hand; **à la** ~ by hand; **à pleines** ~**s** by the handful; **de première** ~ firsthand; **de seconde** ~ secondhand; **à quatre** ~**s** fourhanded, for four hands; **de** ~ **de maître** in a masterly fashion; **en sous** ~ secretly; **la** ~ **dans la** ~ hand in hand; **attaque à** ~ **armée** armed attack; ~ **courante** handrail, banister; **avoir la** ~ **leste** to be quick with one's hands; **avoir/prendre qqch en** ~ to have/to take sthg in hand; **avoir qqch sous la** ~ to have sthg at hand; **demander la** ~ **de qqn** to ask for sb's hand (in marriage); **donner la** ~ **à qqn** to take sb's hand; **faire** ~ **basse sur qqch** to help oneself to sthg; **forcer la** ~ **à qqn** to force sb's hand; **se frotter les** ~**s** to rub one's hands; **haut la** ~ effortlessly, hands down; **haut les** ~**s!** hands up!; **se laver les** ~**s de qqch** to wash one's hands of sthg; **mettre la dernière** ~ **à** to put the finishing touches to; **mettre la** ~ **à la pâte** to lend a helping hand; **ne pas y aller de** ~ **morte** not to pull one's punches; **passer la** ~ CARTES to pass the deal; **perdre la** ~ *fig* to lose one's touch; **remettre en** ~s **propres** to hand over personally; **en venir aux** ~s to come to blows.

main-d'œuvre [mɛ̃dœvr] *nf* labor *Am*, labour *Br*, workforce.

main-forte [mɛ̃fɔrt] *nf*: **prêter** ~ **à qqn** to come to sb's assistance.

mainmise [mɛ̃miz] *nf* seizure.

maint, -e [mɛ̃, mɛ̃t] *adj littéraire* many a; ~s many; ~es **fois** time and time again.

maintenance [mɛ̃tnɑ̃s] *nf* maintenance.

maintenant [mɛ̃tnɑ̃] *adv* now.

◆ **maintenant que** *loc prép* now that.

maintenir [mɛ̃tnir] [40] *vt* **-1.** [soutenir] to support; ~ **qqn à distance** to keep sb away. **-2.** [garder, conserver] to maintain. **-3.** [affirmer]: ~ **que** to maintain (that).

◆ **se maintenir** *vp* **-1.** [durer] to last. **-2.** [rester] to remain.

maintenu, -e [mɛ̃tny] *pp* → **maintenir**.

maintien [mɛ̃tjɛ̃] *nm* **-1.** [conservation] maintenance; [de tradition] upholding; **le** ~ **de l'ordre** the maintenance of law and order. **-2.** [tenue] posture.

maintiendrai, maintiendras *etc* → **maintenir**.

maire [mɛr] *nm* mayor.

mairie [meri] *nf* **-1.** [bâtiment] city hall *Am*, town hall *Br*. **-2.** [administration] city hall *Am*, town council *Br*.

mais [mɛ] ◇ *conj* but; ~ **non!** of course not!; ~ **alors, tu l'as vu ou non?** so did you see him or not?; **il a pleuré,** ~ **pleuré!** he cried, and how!; **non** ~ **ça ne va pas!** that's just not on!

◇ *adv* but; **vous êtes prêts?** - ~ **bien sûr!** are you ready? - but of course!; ~ **certainement** but of course; ~ **enfin** but after all; [marquant l'impatience] really!

◇ *nm*: **il y a un** ~ there's a hitch OU a snag; **il n'y a pas de** ~ (there are) no buts.

◆ **non seulement ... mais (encore)** *loc corrél* not only ... but (also).

maïs [mais] *nm* corn *Am*, maize *Br*.

maison [mɛzɔ̃] *nf* **-1.** [habitation, lignée & ASTROL] house; ~ **de campagne** house in the country; ~ **individuelle** detached house; ~s **mitoyennes** semidetached houses. **-2.** [foyer] home; [famille] family; **à la** ~ [au domicile] at home; [dans la famille] in my/your *etc* family. **-3.** COMM company; ~ **mère** parent company. **-4.** [institut]: ~ **d'arrêt** prison; ~ **de la culture** arts center *Am* OU centre *Br*; ~ **de quartier** ≃ community center *Am*

OU centre *Br*; ~ **de retraite** old people's home. **-5.** (*en apposition*) [artisanal] homemade; [dans restaurant - vin] house (*avant n*).

Maison-Blanche [mɛzɔ̃blɑ̃ʃ] *nf*: **la** ~ the White House.

maisonnée [mɛzɔne] *nf* household.

maisonnette [mɛzɔnɛt] *nf* small house.

maître, -esse [mɛtr, mɛtrɛs] *nm, f* **-1.** [professeur] teacher; ~ **auxiliaire** substitute teacher *Am*, supply teacher *Br*; ~ **de conférences** UNIV ≃ senior lecturer; ~ **d'école** schoolteacher; ~ **nageur** swimming instructor. **-2.** [modèle, artiste & *fig*] master; **les grands** ~s the Old Masters; ~ **à penser** mentor; **passer** ~ **dans l'art de faire qqch** to be a past master in the art of doing sthg. **-3.** [dirigeant] ruler; [d'animal] master (*f* mistress); ~ **d'hôtel** head waiter; ~ **de maison** host; ~ **d'œuvre** CONSTR project manager; *fig* artisan, architect; **être** ~ **de soi** to be in control of oneself, to have self-control. **-4.** (*en apposition*) [principal] main, principal.

◆ **Maître** *nm* *form of address for lawyers.*

◆ **maîtresse** *nf* [amie] mistress.

maître-assistant, -e [mɛtrasistɑ̃, ɑ̃t] (*mpl* **maîtres-assistants,** *fpl* **maîtres-assistantes**) *nm, f* ≃ assistant professor *Am*, ≃ lecturer *Br*.

maître-autel [mɛtrotɛl] (*pl* **maîtres-autels**) *nm* high altar.

maîtresse → **maître**.

maîtrisable [metrizabl] *adj* controllable.

maîtrise [metriz] *nf* **-1.** [sang-froid, domination] control; ~ **de soi** self-control. **-2.** [connaissance] mastery, command; [habileté] skill. **-3.** UNIV ≃ master's degree.

maîtriser [metrize] [3] *vt* **-1.** [animal, forcené] to subdue. **-2.** [émotion, réaction] to control, to master. **-3.** [incendie] to bring under control. **-4.** [dépenses] to curb.

◆ **se maîtriser** *vp* to control o.s.

majesté [maʒɛste] *nf* majesty.

◆ **Majesté** *nf*: **Sa Majesté** His/Her Majesty.

majestueux, -euse [maʒɛstɥø, øz] *adj* majestic.

majeur, -e [maʒœr] *adj* **-1.** [gén] major. **-2.** [personne] of age.

◆ **majeur** *nm* middle finger.

Majeur [maʒœr] → **lac**.

major [maʒɔr] *nm* **-1.** MIL ≃ adjutant. **-2.** SCOL: ~ **(de promotion)** first in OU top of one's year group.

majoration [maʒɔrasjɔ̃] *nf* increase.

majordome [maʒɔrdɔm] *nm* majordomo.

majorer [maʒɔre] [3] *vt* to increase.

majorette [maʒɔrɛt] *nf* majorette.

majoritaire [maʒɔritɛr] ◇ *nmf* member of majority group. ◇ *adj* majority (*avant n*); **être ~** to be in the majority.

majorité [maʒɔrite] *nf* majority; **en (grande) ~** in the majority; **~ absolue/relative** POLIT absolute/relative majority; **~ civile** voting age.

Majorque [majɔrk] *n* Majorca; **à ~** in Majorca.

majorquin, -e [maʒɔrkɛ̃, in] *adj* Majorcan.

◆ **Majorquin, -e** *nm, f* Majorcan.

majuscule [maʒyskyl] ◇ *nf* capital (letter); **en ~s** in capitals, in capital letters. ◇ *adj* capital (*avant n*).

mal, maux [mal, mo] *nm* **-1.** [ce qui est contraire à la morale] evil; **dire du ~ de qqn** to say bad things about sb. **-2.** [souffrance physique] pain; **avoir ~ au cœur** to feel sick; **avoir ~ au dos** to have backache; **avoir ~ à la gorge** to have a sore throat; **avoir le ~ de mer** to be seasick; **avoir ~ à la tête** to have a headache; **avoir des maux de tête** to get headaches; **avoir le ~ des transports** to be travelsick; **avoir ~ au ventre** to have stomachache; **faire ~ à qqn** to hurt sb; **ça fait ~** it hurts; **se faire ~** to hurt o.s. **-3.** [difficulté] difficulty; **avoir du ~ à faire qqch** to have difficulty doing sthg; **se donner du ~ (pour faire qqch)** to take trouble (to do sthg). **-4.** [douleur morale] pain, suffering (*U*); **avoir le ~ du pays** to be OU feel homesick; **être en ~ de qqch** to long for sthg; **faire du ~ (à qqn)** to hurt (sb); **c'est un moindre ~** it's the lesser of two evils.

◆ **mal** *adv* **-1.** [malade] ill; **aller ~** not to be well; **se sentir ~** to feel ill; **être au plus ~** to be extremely ill. **-2.** [respirer] with difficulty. **-3.** [informé, se conduire] badly; **être ~ reçu** to get a poor welcome; **~ prendre qqch** to take sthg badly; **~ tourner** to go wrong. **-4.** *loc*: **de ~ en pis** from bad to worse; **~ à propos** inappropriate; **pas ~** not bad (*adj*), not badly (*adv*); **pas ~ de** quite a lot of.

malabar [malabar] *nm fam* big lad, well-built fellow.

malade [malad] ◇ *nmf* invalid, sick person; **~ mental** mentally ill person. ◇ *adj* **-1.** [souffrant - personne] ill, sick; [- organe] bad; **tomber ~** to fall ill OU sick; **être ~ du cœur/des reins** to have heart/kidney trouble; **être ~ d'inquiétude** *fig* to be sick with worry. **-2.** *fam* [fou] crazy. **-3.** *fig* [en mauvais état] in a bad way.

maladie [maladi] *nf* **-1.** MÉD illness; **~ de Creutzfeldt-Jakob** Creutzfeldt-Jakob disease, CJD; **il en fait une ~** he's really worked up about it. **-2.** [passion, manie] mania.

maladif, -ive [maladif, iv] *adj* **-1.** [enfant] sickly. **-2.** [pâleur & *fig*] unhealthy.

maladresse [maladrɛs] *nf* **-1.** [inhabileté] clumsiness. **-2.** [bévue] blunder.

maladroit, -e [maladrwa, at] ◇ *adj* clumsy. ◇ *nm, f* clumsy person.

maladroitement [maladrwatmɑ̃] *adv* clumsily.

mal-aimé, -e [malɛme] (*mpl* **mal-aimés,** *fpl* **mal-aimées**) *nm, f* unloved person.

malais, -e [malɛ, ɛz] *adj* Malay, Malaysian; **la presqu'île Malaise** the Malay Peninsula.

◆ **malais** *nm* [langue] Malay.

◆ **Malais, -e** *nm, f* Malay, Malaysian.

malaise [malɛz] *nm* **-1.** [indisposition] discomfort; **avoir un ~** to feel faint. **-2.** [trouble] unease (*U*). **-3.** [crise] discontent (*U*).

malaisé, -e [maleze] *adj* difficult.

Malaisie [malɛzi] *nf*: **la ~** Malaya; **en ~** in Malaya.

malappris, -e [malapri, iz] ◇ *adj* uncouth, ill-mannered. ◇ *nm, f* lout.

malaria [malarja] *nf* malaria.

malavisé, -e [malavize] *adj littéraire* ill-advised, unwise.

malaxer [malakse] [3] *vt* to knead.

Malaysia [malɛzja] *nf*: **la ~** Malaysia; **la ~ occidentale** Malaya.

malchance [malʃɑ̃s] *nf* bad luck (*U*); **jouer de ~** to be dogged by bad luck.

malchanceux, -euse [malʃɑ̃sø, øz] ◇ *adj* unlucky. ◇ *nm, f* unlucky person.

malcommode [malkɔmɔd] *adj* inconvenient; [meuble] impractical.

Maldives [maldiv] *nfpl*: **les (îles) ~** the Maldives.

maldonne [maldɔn] *nf* misdeal; **il y a ~** the cards have been misdealt; *fig* there's been a misunderstanding.

mâle [mal] ◇ *adj* **-1.** [enfant, animal, hormone] male. **-2.** [voix, assurance] manly. **-3.** ÉLECTR male. ◇ *nm* male.

malédiction [malediksjɔ̃] *nf* curse.

maléfice [malefis] *nm sout* evil spell.

maléfique [malefik] *adj sout* evil.

malencontreusement [malɑ̃kɔ̃trøzmɑ̃] *adv* inopportunely.

malencontreux, -euse [malɑ̃kɔ̃trø, øz] *adj* [hasard, rencontre] unfortunate.

mal-en-point, mal en point [malɑ̃pwɛ̃] *adj inv* in a bad way OU sorry state.

malentendant, -e [malɑ̃tɑ̃dɑ̃, ɑ̃t] ◇ *adj* hard of hearing. ◇ *nm, f* person who is hard of hearing.

malentendu [malɑ̃tɑ̃dy] *nm* misunderstanding.

malfaçon [malfasɔ̃] *nf* defect.

malfaisant, -e [malfəzɑ̃, ɑ̃t] *adj* harmful.

malfaiteur [malfɛtœr] *nm* criminal.

malfamé, -e, mal famé, -e [malfame] *adj* disreputable.

malformation [malfɔrmasjɔ̃] *nf* malformation.

malfrat [malfra] *nm fam* crook.

malgache [malgaʃ] *adj* Madagascan, Malagasy.
◆ **malgache** *nm* [langue] Malagasy.
◆ **Malgache** *nmf* Madagascan, Malagasy.

malgré [malgre] *prép* in spite of; ~ **tout** [quoi qu'il arrive] in spite of everything; [pourtant] even so, yet.
◆ **malgré que** *loc conj* (+ *subjonctif*) *fam* although, in spite of the fact that.

malhabile [malabil] *adj* clumsy.

malheur [malœr] *nm* misfortune; **le** ~ misfortune, bad luck; **par** ~ unfortunately; **porter** ~ **à qqn** to bring sb bad luck; ~ **à toi!** woe betide you!; **faire un** ~ *fam fig* [faire un éclat] to do some damage; [avoir du succès] to be a great hit.

malheureusement [malœrøzmɑ̃] *adv* unfortunately.

malheureux, -euse [malœrø, øz] ◇ *adj* **-1.** [triste] unhappy. **-2.** [désastreux, regrettable] unfortunate. **-3.** [malchanceux] unlucky. **-4.** (*avant n*) [sans valeur] pathetic, miserable. ◇ *nm, f* **-1.** [infortuné] poor soul. **-2.** [indigent] poor person.

malhonnête [malɔnɛt] ◇ *nmf* dishonest person. ◇ *adj* **-1.** [personne, affaire] dishonest. **-2.** *hum* [proposition, propos] indecent.

malhonnêteté [malɔnɛtte] *nf* **-1.** [de personne] dishonesty. **-2.** [action] dishonest action.

Mali [mali] *nm*: **le** ~ Mali; **au** ~ in Mali.

malice [malis] *nf* mischief; **sans** ~ without malice.

malicieux, -ieuse [malisjø, jøz] ◇ *adj* mischievous. ◇ *nm, f* mischievous person.

malien, -ienne [maljɛ̃, jɛn] *adj* Malian.
◆ **Malien, -ienne** *nm, f* Malian.

malignité [maliɲite] *nf* **-1.** [méchanceté] malice, spite. **-2.** MÉD malignancy.

malin, -igne [malɛ̃, iɲ] ◇ *adj* **-1.** [rusé] crafty, cunning; **ce n'est pas** ~! *fig* that's not very clever!; [regard, sourire] knowing. **-2.** [méchant] malicious, spiteful. **-3.** MÉD malignant. ◇ *nm, f* cunning OU crafty person; **faire le** ~ to show off.

malingre [malɛ̃gr] *adj* sickly.

malle [mal] *nf* [coffre] trunk; [de voiture] trunk *Am*, boot *Br*; **se faire la** ~ *fam fig* to beat it.

malléable [maleabl] *adj* malleable.

mallette [malɛt] *nf* briefcase.

mal-logé, -e [malloʒe] (*mpl* **mal-logés**, *fpl* **mal-logées**) *nm, f person living in poor accommodation.*

malmener [malməne] [19] *vt* **-1.** [brutaliser] to handle roughly, to ill-treat. **-2.** [dominer] to have the better of.

malnutrition [malnytrisjɔ̃] *nf* malnutrition.

malodorant, -e [malɔdɔrɑ̃, ɑ̃t] *adj* smelly.

malotru, -e [malɔtry] *nm, f* lout.

Malouines [malwin] *nfpl*: **les (îles)** ~ the Falkland Islands, the Falklands.

malpoli, -e [malpɔli] *adj* rude.

malpropre [malprɔpr] *adj* [sale] dirty.

malpropreté [malprɔprəte] *nf* [saleté] dirtiness.

malsain, -e [malsɛ̃, ɛn] *adj* unhealthy.

malséant, -e [malseɑ̃, ɑ̃t] *adj* unbecoming.

malt [malt] *nm* **-1.** [céréale] malt. **-2.** [whisky] malt (whisky).

maltais, -e [maltɛ, ɛz] *adj* Maltese.
◆ **maltais** *nm* [langue] Maltese.
◆ **Maltais, -e** *nm, f* Maltese (person); **les Maltais** the Maltese.

Malte [malt] *n* Malta; **à** ~ in Malta.

maltraiter [maltrete] [4] *vt* to ill-treat; [en paroles] to attack, to run down.

malus [malys] *nm increase in car insurance charges, due to loss of no-claims bonus.*

malveillance [malvejɑ̃s] *nf* spite.

malveillant, -e [malvejɑ̃, ɑ̃t] *adj* spiteful.

malvenu, -e [malvəny] *adj* out of place; **être** ~ **de faire qqch** *sout* to be wrong to do sthg.

malversation [malvɛrsasjɔ̃] *nf* embezzlement.

malvoyant, -e [malvwajɑ̃, ɑ̃t] ◇ *adj* partially sighted. ◇ *nm, f person who is partially sighted.*

maman [mamɑ̃] *nf* mummy.

mamelle [mamɛl] *nf* teat; [de vache] udder.

mamelon [mamlɔ̃] *nm* **-1.** [du sein] nipple. **-2.** [butte] hillock.

mamie, mamy [mami] *nf* granny, grandma.

mammifère [mamifɛr] *nm* mammal.

mammographie [mamɔgrafi] *nf* mammography.

mammouth [mamut] *nm* mammoth.

mamours [mamur] *nmpl fam* billing and cooing (*U*); **se faire des** ~ to bill and coo.

mamy = mamie.

Man [man] → **île.**

management [manadʒmɛnt] *nm* management.

manager[1] [manadʒɛr] *nm* manager.

manager[2] [manadʒe] [17] *vt* to manage.

Managua [managwa] *n* Managua.

manche [mɑ̃ʃ] ◇ *nf* **-1.** [de vêtement] sleeve; **sans ~s** sleeveless; **~s courtes/ longues** short/long sleeves; **~s raglan** raglan sleeves; **être en ~s de chemise** to be in one's shirtsleeves. **-2.** [de jeu] round, game; TENNIS set. **-3.** *loc*: **faire la ~** *fam* to pass the hat round. ◇ *nm* **-1.** [d'outil] handle; **~ à balai** broomstick; [d'avion] joystick. **-2.** MUS neck.

Manche [mɑ̃ʃ] *nf* **-1.** [Normandie]: **la ~** the Manche (region). **-2.** [mer]: **la ~** the English Channel. **-3.** [en Espagne]: **la ~** La Mancha.

manchette [mɑ̃ʃɛt] *nf* **-1.** [de chemise] cuff. **-2.** [de journal] headline. **-3.** [coup] forearm blow.

manchon [mɑ̃ʃɔ̃] *nm* **-1.** [en fourrure] muff. **-2.** TECHNOL casing, sleeve.

manchot, -ote [mɑ̃ʃo, ɔt] ◇ *adj* one-armed. ◇ *nm, f* one-armed person.

◆ **manchot** *nm* penguin.

mandarin [mɑ̃darɛ̃] *nm* **-1.** [en Chine] mandarin. **-2.** *péj* [personnage important] mandarin. **-3.** [langue] Mandarin.

mandarine [mɑ̃darin] *nf* mandarin (orange).

mandat [mɑ̃da] *nm* **-1.** [pouvoir, fonction] mandate. **-2.** JUR warrant; **~ d'amener** summons; **~ d'arrêt** ≃ arrest warrant; **~ de perquisition** search warrant. **-3.** [titre postal] money order; **~ postal** money order *Am*, postal order *Br*.

mandataire [mɑ̃datɛr] *nmf* proxy, representative.

mandat-carte [mɑ̃dakart] (*pl* **mandats-cartes**) *nm* money order *Am*, postal order *Br*.

mandater [mɑ̃date] [3] *vt* **-1.** [personne] to appoint. **-2.** [somme] to pay by money order.

mandat-lettre [mɑ̃dalɛtr] (*pl* **mandats-lettres**) *nm* money order *Am*, postal order *Br*.

mandibule [mɑ̃dibyl] *nf* mandible.

mandoline [mɑ̃dɔlin] *nf* mandolin.

mandrill [mɑ̃dril] *nm* mandrill.

mandrin [mɑ̃drɛ̃] *nm* [de serrage] chuck; [de perçage] punch.

manège [manɛʒ] *nm* **-1.** [attraction] carousel *Am*, roundabout *Br*. **-2.** [de chevaux - lieu] riding school. **-3.** [manœuvre] scheme, game.

manette [manɛt] *nf* lever.

manganèse [mɑ̃ganɛz] *nm* manganese.

mangeable [mɑ̃ʒabl] *adj* edible.

mangeoire [mɑ̃ʒwar] *nf* manger.

manger [mɑ̃ʒe] [17] ◇ *vt* **-1.** [nourriture] to eat. **-2.** [étoffe, fer] to eat away. **-3.** [fortune] to get through, to squander. ◇ *vi* to eat.

mange-tout [mɑ̃ʒtu] ◇ *adj inv*: **haricots ~** string beans *Am*, runner beans *Br*. ◇ *nm inv* [haricot] string bean *Am*, runner bean *Br*; [pois] snow pea *Am*, mangetout *Br*.

mangeur, -euse [mɑ̃ʒœr, øz] *nm, f* eater; **gros ~** big eater.

mangue [mɑ̃g] *nf* mango.

maniable [manjabl] *adj* **-1.** [instrument] manageable. **-2.** [personne] easily influenced.

maniaque [manjak] ◇ *nmf* **-1.** [méticuleux] fusspot. **-2.** [fou] maniac. ◇ *adj* **-1.** [méticuleux] fussy. **-2.** [fou] maniacal.

maniaquerie [manjakri] *nf* fussiness.

manichéisme [manikeism] *nm* Manicheism.

manie [mani] *nf* **-1.** [habitude] funny habit; **avoir la ~ de qqch/de faire qqch** to have a mania for sthg/for doing sthg. **-2.** [obsession] mania.

maniement [manimɑ̃] *nm* handling.

manier [manje] [9] *vt* [manipuler, utiliser] to handle; *fig* [ironie, mots] to handle skilfully.

manière [manjɛr] *nf* **-1.** [méthode] manner, way; **recourir à la ~ forte** to resort to strong-arm tactics; **de toute ~** at any rate; **d'une ~ générale** generally speaking; **c'est une ~ de parler** it's just my/his *etc* way of putting it. **-2.** [style propre à un artiste] style; **à la ~ de** in the style of.

◆ **manières** *nfpl* manners; **les bonnes ~s** good manners; **faire des ~s** *fig* to pussyfoot around.

◆ **de manière à** *loc conj* (in order) to; **de ~ à ce que** (+ *subjonctif*) so that.

◆ **de manière que** *loc conj* (+ *subjonctif*) in such a way that.

maniéré, -e [manjere] *adj* affected.

maniérisme [manjerism] *nm* mannerism.

manif [manif] *nf fam* demo.

manifestant, -e [manifɛstɑ̃, ɑ̃t] *nm, f* demonstrator.

manifestation [manifɛstasjɔ̃] *nf* **-1.** [témoignage] expression. **-2.** [mouvement collectif] demonstration. **-3.** [apparition - de maladie] appearance.

manifeste [manifɛst] ◇ *nm* [déclaration] manifesto. ◇ *adj* obvious.

manifestement [manifɛstəmɑ̃] *adv* obviously.

manifester [manifɛste] [3] ◇ *vt* to show, to express. ◇ *vi* to demonstrate.

◆ **se manifester** *vp* **-1.** [apparaître] to show OU manifest itself. **-2.** [se montrer] to turn up, to appear.

manigance [manigɑ̃s] *nf fam* scheme, intrigue.

manigancer [manigɑ̃se] [16] *vt fam* to plot.

Manille [manij] *n* Manila.

manioc [manjɔk] *nm* manioc.

manipulateur, -trice [manipylatœr, tris] *nm, f* **-1.** [opérateur] technician. **-2.** *fig* & *péj* [de personnes] manipulator.

◆ **manipulateur** *nm* TÉLÉCOM key.

manipulation [manipylasjɔ̃] *nf* **-1.** [de produits, d'explosifs] handling; ~s **génétiques** genetic engineering. **-2.** *fig* & *péj* [manœuvre] manipulation (*U*).

manipuler [manipyle] [3] *vt* **-1.** [colis, appareil] to handle. **-2.** [statistiques, résultats] to falsify, to rig. **-3.** [personne] to manipulate.

manivelle [manivɛl] *nf* crank.

manne [man] *nf* RELIG manna; *fig* godsend.

mannequin [mankɛ̃] *nm* **-1.** [forme humaine] model, dummy. **-2.** [personne] model, mannequin.

manœuvre [manœvr] ◇ *nf* **-1.** [d'appareil, de véhicule] driving, handling; **fausse** ~ driver error; *fig* false move. **-2.** MIL maneuver *Am*, manoeuvre *Br*, exercise. **-3.** [machination] ploy, scheme. ◇ *nm* laborer *Am*, labourer *Br*.

manœuvrer [manœvre] [5] ◇ *vi* to maneuver *Am*, to manoeuvre *Br*. ◇ *vt* **-1.** [faire fonctionner] to operate, to work; [voiture] to maneuver *Am*, to manoeuvre *Br*. **-2.** [influencer] to manipulate.

manoir [manwar] *nm* manor, country house.

manomètre [manɔmɛtr] *nm* manometer.

manquant, -e [mɑ̃kɑ̃, ɑ̃t] *adj* missing.

manque [mɑ̃k] *nm* **-1.** [pénurie] lack, shortage; **par** ~ **de** for want of. **-2.** [de toxicomane] withdrawal symptoms (*pl*); **être en (état de)** ~ to have OU experience withdrawal symptoms. **-3.** [lacune] gap; ~ **à gagner** COMM loss of earnings.

◆ **à la manque** *loc adj fam* second-rate.

manqué, -e [mɑ̃ke] *adj* [raté] failed; [rendezvous] missed.

manquement [mɑ̃kmɑ̃] *nm*: ~ **(à)** breach (of).

manquer [mɑ̃ke] [3] ◇ *vi* **-1.** [faire défaut] to be lacking, to be missing; **l'argent/le temps me manque** I don't have enough money/time; **tu me manques** I miss you. **-2.** [être absent]: ~ **(à)** to be absent (from), to be missing (from). **-3.** [échouer] to fail. **-4.** [ne pas avoir assez]: ~ **de qqch** to lack sthg, to be short of sthg. **-5.** [faillir]: **il a manqué de se noyer** he nearly OU almost drowned, ne **manquez pas de lui dire** don't forget to tell him; **je n'y manquerai pas** I certainly will, I'll definitely do it. **-6.** [ne pas respecter]: ~ **à** [devoir] to fail in; ~ **à sa parole** to break one's word.

◇ *vt* **-1.** [gén] to miss. **-2.** [échouer à] to bungle, to botch.

◇ *v impers*: **il manque quelqu'un** somebody is missing; **il me manque 20 francs** I'm 20 francs short; **il ne manquait plus que ça** *fig* that's all I/you *etc* needed.

mansarde [mɑ̃sard] *nf* attic.

mansardé, -e [mɑ̃sarde] *adj* attic (*avant n*).

mansuétude [mɑ̃sɥetyd] *nf littéraire* indulgence.

mante [mɑ̃t] *nf* HIST mantle.

◆ **mante religieuse** *nf* praying mantis.

manteau, -x [mɑ̃to] *nm* **-1.** [vêtement] coat; **sous le** ~ *fig* secretly, clandestinely. **-2.** *fig* [de neige] mantle, blanket.

manucure [manykyr] *nmf* manicurist.

manuel, -elle [manɥɛl] ◇ *adj* manual. ◇ *nm, f* manual worker.

◆ **manuel** *nm* manual.

manufacture [manyfaktyr] *nf* [fabrique] factory.

manuscrit, -e [manyskri, it] *adj* handwritten.

◆ **manuscrit** *nm* manuscript.

manutention [manytɑ̃sjɔ̃] *nf* handling.

manutentionnaire [manytɑ̃sjɔnɛr] *nmf* packer.

MAP (*abr de* **mise au point**) *nf* focusing.

mappemonde [mapmɔ̃d] *nf* **-1.** [carte] map of the world. **-2.** [sphère] globe.

Maputo [mapyto] *n* Maputo.

maquereau, -elle, -x [makro, ɛl, o] *nm, f fam* pimp (*f* madam).

◆ **maquereau** *nm* mackerel.

maquette [makɛt] *nf* **-1.** [ébauche] paste-up. **-2.** [modèle réduit] model.

maquettiste [makɛtist] *nmf* model maker.

maquignon [makiɲɔ̃] *nm* **-1.** [marchand de chevaux] horse dealer. **-2.** *péj* [homme d'affaires] crook.

maquillage [makijaʒ] *nm* **-1.** [action, produits] make-up. **-2.** [falsification] disguising;

[- de chiffres] doctoring; [- de passeport] falsification.

maquiller [makije] [3] *vt* **-1.** [farder] to make up. **-2.** [fausser] to disguise; [- passeport] to falsify; [- chiffres] to doctor.

◆ **se maquiller** *vp* to make up, to put on one's make-up.

maquilleur, -euse [makijœr, øz] *nm, f* make-up artist.

maquis [maki] *nm* **-1.** [végétation] scrub, brush. **-2.** HIST Maquis; **prendre le ~** to join the Maquis. **-3.** *fig* [méli-mélo] maze.

maquisard [makizar] *nm* member of the Resistance.

marabout [marabu] *nm* **-1.** ZOOL marabou. **-2.** [guérisseur] marabout.

maraîcher, -ère [mareʃe, ɛr] ◇ *adj* truck farming (*avant n*) *Am*, market garden (*avant n*) *Br*. ◇ *nm, f* truck farmer *Am*, market gardener *Br*.

marais [marɛ] *nm* [marécage] marsh, swamp; **~ salant** saltpan; **le Marais** *historic district in central Paris*.

LE MARAIS:
The Marais includes the place des Vosges and the predominantly Jewish quarter around the rue des Rosiers. Typical flats in the Marais feature exposed beams and 'tomettes' (red hexagonal floor tiles)

---

marasme [marasm] *nm* **-1.** [récession] stagnation. **-2.** [accablement] depression.

marathon [maratɔ̃] *nm* marathon.

marâtre [maratr] *nf vieilli* **-1.** [mauvaise mère] bad mother. **-2.** [belle-mère] stepmother.

maraude [marod] *nf*, **maraudage** [marodaʒ] *nm* pilfering.

marbre [marbr] *nm* **-1.** [roche, objet] marble; **en** OU **de ~** marble (*avant n*); **rester de ~** *fig* to remain impassive. **-2.** [dans imprimerie] stone. **-3.** *Can* BASE-BALL home base OU plate.

marbré, -e [marbre] *adj* **-1.** [gâteau] marble (*avant n*). **-2.** [peau, teint] mottled.

marbrier [marbrije] *nm* monumental mason.

marbrure [marbryr] *nf* **-1.** [imitation du marbre] marbling. **-2.** [sur la peau] mottling.

marc [mar] *nm* **-1.** [eau-de-vie] *spirit distilled from grape residue*. **-2.** [de fruits] residue; [de thé] leaves; **~ de café** grounds (*pl*).

marcassin [markasɛ̃] *nm* young wild boar.

marchand, -e [marʃɑ̃, ɑ̃d] ◇ *adj* [valeur] market (*avant n*); [prix] trade (*avant n*). ◇ *nm, f* [commerçant] merchant; [détaillant]

storekeeper *Am*, shopkeeper *Br*; **~ de journaux** newsdealer *Am*, newsagent *Br*; **~ des quatre-saisons** street trader (*selling fruit and vegetables*).

◆ **marchand de sable** *nm fig* sandman.

marchandage [marʃɑ̃daʒ] *nm* bargaining.

marchander [marʃɑ̃de] [3] ◇ *vt* **-1.** [prix] to haggle over. **-2.** [appui] to begrudge. ◇ *vi* to bargain, to haggle.

marchandise [marʃɑ̃diz] *nf* merchandise (*U*), goods (*pl*).

marche [marʃ] *nf* **-1.** [d'escalier] step. **-2.** [de personne] walking; [promenade] walk; **être à deux heures de ~ (de)** to be two hours' walk OU a two-hour walk (from); **fermer la ~** to bring up the rear; **ouvrir la ~** to lead the way; **~ à pied** walking; **~ à suivre** *fig* correct procedure. **-3.** MUS march; **~ funèbre/nuptiale** funeral/wedding march. **-4.** [déplacement - du temps, d'astre] course; **assis dans le sens de la ~** [en train] sitting facing the engine; **en ~ arrière** in reverse; **faire ~ arrière** to reverse; *fig* to backpedal, to backtrack. **-5.** [fonctionnement] running, working; **en ~** running; **se mettre en ~** to start (up); **mettre qqch en ~** to start sthg (up).

marché [marʃe] *nm* **-1.** [gén] market; **faire son ~** to go shopping, to do one's shopping; **le ~ du travail** the labor *Am* OU labour *Br* market; **~ cible** target market; **~ noir** black market; **~ aux puces** flea market. **-2.** [contrat] bargain, deal; **(à) bon ~** cheap; **meilleur ~** cheaper; **par-dessus le ~** *fam fig* into the bargain.

◆ **Marché commun** *nm*: **le Marché commun** the Common Market.

marchepied [marʃəpje] *nm* [de train] step; [escabeau] stepladder; *fig* stepping-stone.

marcher [marʃe] [3] *vi* **-1.** [aller à pied] to walk. **-2.** [poser le pied] to step. **-3.** [avancer]: **~ sur** [ville, ennemi] to march on OU upon. **-4.** [fonctionner, tourner] to work; **son affaire marche bien** his business is doing well. **-5.** *fam* [accepter] to agree. **-6.** *loc*: **faire ~ qqn** *fam* to take sb for a ride.

marcheur, -euse [marʃœr, øz] *nm, f* walker.

marcottage [markɔtaʒ] *nm* layering.

mardi [mardi] *nm* Tuesday; **~ gras** Shrove Tuesday; *voir aussi* **samedi.**

mare [mar] *nf* pool.

marécage [marekaʒ] *nm* marsh, bog.

marécageux, -euse [marekaʒø, øz] *adj* **-1.** [terrain] marshy, boggy. **-2.** [plante] marsh (*avant n*).

maréchal, -aux [mareʃal, o] *nm* marshal.

◆ **maréchal des logis** *nm* sergeant.

maréchal-ferrant [mareʃalferɑ̃] (*pl* **maréchaux-ferrants** [mareʃoferɑ̃]) *nm* black-smith.

maréchaussée [mareʃose] *nf vieilli* con-stabulary.

marée [mare] *nf* **-1.** [de la mer] tide; **(à)** ~ **haute/basse** (at) high/low tide. **-2.** *fig* [de personnes] wave, surge. **-3.** [poissons] sea-food.

◆ **marée noire** *nf* oil slick.

marelle [marɛl] *nf* hopscotch.

marémoteur, -trice [maremɔtœr, tris] *adj* [énergie] tidal; [usine] tidal power (*avant n*).

mareyeur, -euse [marɛjœr, øz] *nm, f* wholesale fish merchant.

margarine [margarin] *nf* margarine.

marge [marʒ] *nf* **-1.** [espace] margin; **vivre en** ~ **de la société** *fig* to live on the fringes of society. **-2.** [latitude] leeway; ~ **d'erreur** margin of error; ~ **de sécurité** safety margin. **-3.** COMM margin; ~ **bénéficiaire** profit margin; ~ **commerciale** gross margin.

margelle [marʒɛl] *nf* coping.

marginal, -e, -aux [marʒinal, o] ◇ *adj* **-1.** [gén] marginal. **-2.** [groupe] dropout (*avant n*). ◇ *nm, f* dropout.

marginaliser [marʒinalize] [3] *vt* to margin-alize.

marginalité [marʒinalite] *nf* living on the fringes of society.

margoulin [margulɛ̃] *nm fam* shark, con-man.

marguerite [margərit] *nf* **-1.** BOT daisy. **-2.** [d'imprimante] daisy wheel.

mari [mari] *nm* husband.

mariage [marjaʒ] *nm* **-1.** [union, institution] marriage; **donner qqn en** ~ to give sb away; ~ **d'amour** love match; ~ **blanc** un-consummated marriage; ~ **consanguin** marriage between blood relations; ~ **de raison** marriage of convenience. **-2.** [céré-monie] wedding; ~ **civil/religieux** civil/church wedding. **-3.** *fig* [de choses] blend.

Marianne [marjan] *n symbol of the French Re-public.*

MARIANNE:
Marianne is the personification of the French Republic; there is a bust of her in every town hall in France, and her portrait appears on French stamps. Her face has changed over the centuries, but she can al-ways be recognized by the 'bonnet phry-gien' she wears

marié, -e [marje] ◇ *adj* married. ◇ *nm, f* groom, bridegroom (*f* bride); **jeunes** ~**s** newlyweds.

marier [marje] [9] *vt* **-1.** [personne] to marry. **-2.** *fig* [couleurs] to blend.

◆ **se marier** *vp* **-1.** [personnes] to get mar-ried; **se** ~ **avec qqn** to marry sb. **-2.** *fig* [couleurs] to blend.

marihuana [marirwana], **marijuana** [mariʒɥana] *nf* marijuana.

marin, -e [marɛ̃, in] *adj* **-1.** [de la mer] sea (*avant n*); [faune, biologie] marine. **-2.** NAVIG [carte, mille] nautical.

◆ **marin** *nm* **-1.** [navigateur] seafarer. **-2.** [matelot] sailor; ~ **pêcheur** deep-sea fisher-man.

◆ **marine** ◇ *nf* **-1.** [navigation] seaman-ship, navigation. **-2.** [navires] navy; ~**e mar-chande** merchant marine *Am* OU navy *Br*; ~**e nationale** navy. ◇ *nm* **-1.** MIL marine. **-2.** [couleur] navy (blue). ◇ *adj inv* navy (blue).

marinade [marinad] *nf* marinade.

mariner [marine] [3] ◇ *vt* to marinate. ◇ *vi* **-1.** [aliment] to marinate; **faire** ~ **qqch** to marinate sthg. **-2.** *fam fig* [attendre] to hang around; **faire** ~ **qqn** to let sb stew.

marinier [marinje] *nm* bargeman *Am*, bar-gee *Br*.

marinière [marinjɛr] *nf* smock.

marionnette [marjɔnɛt] *nf* puppet.

marital, -e, -aux [marital, o] *adj*: **autorisa-tion** ~**e** husband's permission.

maritalement [maritalmɑ̃] *adv*: **vivre** ~ to cohabit.

maritime [maritim] *adj* [navigation] mari-time; [ville] coastal.

marivaudage [marivodaʒ] *nm littéraire* ban-ter.

marjolaine [marʒɔlɛn] *nf* marjoram.

mark [mark] *nm* [monnaie] mark.

marketing [markɛtiŋ] *nm* marketing; ~ **té-léphonique** telemarketing.

marmaille [marmaj] *nf fam* brood (of kids).

marmelade [marmələd] *nf* stewed fruit; **en** ~ cooked to a pulp; *fam fig* [nez] smashed to a pulp; ~ **d'oranges** marmalade.

marmite [marmit] *nf* [casserole] pot; **faire bouillir la** ~ *fig* to be the breadwinner.

marmiton [marmitɔ̃] *nm* kitchen boy.

marmonner [marmɔne] [3] *vt & vi* to mut-ter, to mumble.

marmot [marmo] *nm fam* kid.

marmotte [marmɔt] *nf* marmot.

marmotter [marmɔte] [3] *vt* to mutter, to mumble.

marner [marne] [3] *vi fam* to slog.

Maroc [marɔk] *nm*: **le** ~ Morocco; **au** ~ in Morocco.

marocain, -e [marɔkɛ̃, ɛn] *adj* Moroccan.
◆ **Marocain, -e** *nm, f* Moroccan.

maroquin [marɔkɛ̃] *nm* morocco (leather).

maroquinerie [marɔkinri] *nf* **-1.** [fabrication] fine-leather production; [commerce] fine-leather trade. **-2.** [magasin] leather-goods store *Am* OU shop *Br*.

maroquinier [marɔkinje] *nm* **-1.** [artisan] leatherworker. **-2.** [commerçant] leather-goods dealer.

marotte [marɔt] *nf* [dada] craze.

marquant, -e [markɑ̃, ɑ̃t] *adj* outstanding.

marque [mark] *nf* **-1.** [signe, trace] mark; *fig* stamp, mark. **-2.** [label, fabricant] make, brand; **de** ~ designer (*avant n*); *fig* important; **une grande** ~ a well-known make OU brand; ~ **déposée** registered trademark; ~ **de fabrique** trademark. **-3.** SPORT score; **à vos** ~s, **prêts, partez!** on your marks, get set, go! **-4.** [insigne] badge. **-5.** [témoignage] sign, token; ~ **d'affection** sign OU token of affection.

marqué, -e [marke] *adj* **-1.** [net] marked, pronounced. **-2.** [personne, visage] marked.

marquer [marke] [3] ◇ *vt* **-1.** [gén] to mark. **-2.** *fam* [écrire] to write down, to note down. **-3.** [indiquer, manifester] to show. **-4.** [SPORT - but, point] to score; [- joueur] to mark; ~ **les points** to keep the score. ◇ *vi* **-1.** [événement, expérience] to leave its mark. **-2.** SPORT to score.

marqueterie [markɛtri] *nf* marquetry.

marqueur [markœr] *nm* **-1.** [crayon] marker (pen). **-2.** SPORT scorer.

marqueuse [markøz] *nf* labelling machine.

marquis, -e [marki, iz] *nm, f* marquis (*f* marchioness).
◆ **marquise** *nf* [auvent] canopy.

Marquises [markiz] *nfpl*: **les** ~ the Marquesas Islands.

marraine [marɛn] *nf* **-1.** [de filleul] godmother. **-2.** [de navire] christener.

marrant, -e [marɑ̃, ɑ̃t] *adj fam* funny.

marre [mar] *adv*: **en avoir** ~ **(de)** *fam* to be fed up (with).

marrer [mare] [3]
◆ **se marrer** *vp fam* to split one's sides.

marron, -onne [marɔ̃, ɔn] *adj péj* [médecin] quack (*avant n*); [avocat] crooked.
◆ **marron** ◇ *nm* **-1.** [fruit] chestnut; ~ **glacé** candied chestnut; ~ **d'Inde** horse chestnut. **-2.** [couleur] brown. **-3.** *fam* [coup de poing] thump. ◇ *adj inv* brown.

marronnier [marɔnje] *nm* chestnut tree.

mars [mars] *nm* March; *voir aussi* **septembre**.

marseillais, -e [marsɛjɛ, ɛz] *adj* of/from Marseilles.
◆ **Marseillais, -e** *nm, f* native OU inhabitant of Marseilles.
◆ **Marseillaise** *nf*: **la Marseillaise** French national anthem.

Marseille [marsɛj] *n* Marseilles.

marsouin [marswɛ̃] *nm* porpoise.

marsupial, -e, -iaux [marsypjal, jo] *adj* marsupial.
◆ **marsupial** *nm* marsupial.

marte = **martre**.

marteau, -x [marto] ◇ *nm* **-1.** [gén] hammer; ~ **piqueur**, ~ **pneumatique** pneumatic drill. **-2.** [heurtoir] knocker. ◇ *adj fam* barmy.

marteau-pilon [martopilɔ̃] (*pl* **marteaux-pilons**) *nm* power hammer.

marteau-piqueur [martopikœr] (*pl* **marteaux-piqueurs**) *nm* pneumatic drill.

martel [martɛl] *nm*: **se mettre** ~ **en tête** to get worked up.

marteler [martəle] [25] *vt* **-1.** [pieu] to hammer; [table, porte] to hammer on, to pound. **-2.** [phrase] to rap out.

martial, -e, -iaux [marsjal, jo] *adj* martial.

martien, -ienne [marsjɛ̃, jɛn] *adj & nm, f* Martian.

martinet [martinɛ] *nm* **-1.** ZOOL swift. **-2.** [fouet] whip.

martingale [martɛ̃gal] *nf* **-1.** [de vêtement] half-belt. **-2.** JEU winning system.

martini [martini] *nm* martini.

martiniquais, -e [martinikɛ, ɛz] *adj* of/from Martinique.
◆ **Martiniquais, -e** *nm, f* native OU inhabitant of Martinique.

Martinique [martinik] *nf*: **la** ~ Martinique; **à la** ~ in Martinique.

martin-pêcheur [martɛ̃pɛʃœr] (*pl* **martins-pêcheurs**) *nm* kingfisher.

martre [martr], **marte** [mart] *nf* marten.

martyr, -e [martir] ◇ *adj* martyred. ◇ *nm, f* martyr.
◆ **martyre** *nm* martyrdom; **souffrir le** ~**e** to suffer agonies.

martyriser [martirize] [3] *vt* to torment.

marxisme [marksism] *nm* Marxism.

marxiste [marksist] *nmf & adj* Marxist.

mas [mas] *nm country house or farm in the South of France*.

mascara [maskara] *nm* mascara.

mascarade [maskarad] *nf* **-1.** [mise en scène] masquerade. **-2.** [accoutrement] getup.

mascotte [maskɔt] *nf* mascot.

masculin, -e [maskylɛ̃, in] *adj* [apparence & GRAM] masculine; [métier, population, sexe] male.
◆ **masculin** *nm* GRAM masculine.

maso [mazo] *fam* ◇ *nm* masochist. ◇ *adj* masochistic.

masochisme [mazɔʃism] *nm* masochism.

masochiste [mazɔʃist] ◇ *nmf* masochist. ◇ *adj* masochistic.

masque [mask] *nm* **-1.** [gén] mask; ~ **à gaz** gas mask; ~ **de plongée** diving mask. **-2.** [crème]: ~ **(de beauté)** face pack. **-3.** *fig* [façade] front, façade; **lever le** ~ *fig* to show one's true colours.

masqué, -e [maske] *adj* masked.

masquer [maske] [3] *vt* **-1.** [vérité, crime, problème] to conceal. **-2.** [maison, visage] to conceal, to hide.

massacrant, -e [masakrɑ̃, ɑ̃t] *adj*: **être d'une humeur** ~**e** to be in a foul temper.

massacre [masakr] *nm litt* & *fig* massacre.

massacrer [masakre] [3] *vt* to massacre; [voiture] to smash up.

massage [masaʒ] *nm* massage; **faire un** ~ **à qqn** to give sb a massage.

masse [mas] *nf* **-1.** [de pierre] block; [d'eau] volume; **tomber comme une** ~ *fig* to drop like a stone. **-2.** [de gens]: **la** ~ the majority; **les** ~**s** the masses. **-3.** [grande quantité]: **une** ~ **de masses** (*pl*) OU **loads** (*pl*) **of. -4.** PHYS mass; ~ **molaire** molar weight; ~ **moléculaire** molecular weight. **-5.** ÉLECTR ground *Am*, earth *Br*. **-6.** [maillet] sledgehammer.
◆ **masse monétaire** *nf* FIN money supply.
◆ **masse salariale** *nf* payroll.
◆ **en masse** *loc adv* [venir] en masse, all together; *fam* [acheter] in bulk.

massepain [maspɛ̃] *nm* marzipan.

masser [mase] [3] *vt* **-1.** [assembler] to assemble. **-2.** [frotter] to massage.
◆ **se masser** *vp* **-1.** [s'assembler] to assemble, to gather. **-2.** [se frotter]: **se** ~ **le bras** to massage one's arm.

masseur, -euse [masœr, øz] *nm, f* [personne] masseur (*f* masseuse).
◆ **masseur** *nm* [appareil] massager.

massicot [masiko] *nm* guillotine.

massif, -ive [masif, iv] *adj* **-1.** [monument, personne, dose] massive. **-2.** [or, chêne] solid.
◆ **massif** *nm* **-1.** [de plantes] clump. **-2.** [de montagnes] massif; **le Massif central** the Massif Central.

massivement [masivmɑ̃] *adv* **-1.** [construit] massively. **-2.** [répondre] en masse.

massue [masy] ◇ *adj inv* crushing. ◇ *nf* club.

mastic [mastik] *nm* mastic, putty.

mastiquer [mastike] [3] *vt* **-1.** [mâcher] to chew. **-2.** [coller] to putty.

mastoc [mastɔk] *adj inv* *péj* hulking.

mastodonte [mastɔdɔ̃t] *nm* **-1.** [mammifère] mastodon. **-2.** *fam* [personne] hulk.

masturbation [mastyrbasjɔ̃] *nf* masturbation.

masturber [mastyrbe] [3]
◆ **se masturber** *vp* to masturbate.

m'as-tu-vu [matyvy] *nmf inv* show-off.

masure [mazyr] *nf* hovel.

mat, -e [mat] *adj* **-1.** [peinture, surface] matte *Am*, matt *Br*. **-2.** [peau, personne] dusky. **-3.** [bruit, son] dull. **-4.** [aux échecs] checkmated.
◆ **mat** *nm* checkmate.

mât [ma] *nm* **-1.** NAVIG mast. **-2.** [poteau] pole, post; ~ **de cocagne** greasy pole.

match [matʃ] (*pl* **matches** OU **matchs**) *nm* match; **(faire)** ~ **nul** (to) draw; ~ **aller/retour** first/second leg.

matelas [matla] *nm inv* [de lit] mattress; ~ **de crin** horsehair mattress; ~ **pneumatique** airbed.

matelassé, -e [matlase] *adj* padded.

matelot [matlo] *nm* sailor.

mater [mate] [3] *vt* **-1.** [soumettre, neutraliser] to subdue. **-2.** *fam* [regarder] to eye up.

matérialiser [materjalize] [3]
◆ **se matérialiser** *vp* [aspirations] to be realized.

matérialisme [materjalism] *nm* materialism.

matérialiste [materjalist] ◇ *nmf* materialist. ◇ *adj* materialistic.

matériau, -x [materjo] *nm* material.
◆ **matériaux** *nmpl* **-1.** CONSTR material (*U*), materials; ~**x de construction** building material OU materials. **-2.** [documents] material (*U*).

matériel, -ielle [materjɛl] *adj* **-1.** [être, substance] material, physical; [confort, avantage, aide] material. **-2.** [considération] practical.
◆ **matériel** *nm* **-1.** [gén] equipment (*U*); ~ **d'exploitation** plant (*U*); ~ **roulant** rolling stock (*U*). **-2.** INFORM hardware (*U*).

matériellement [materjɛlmɑ̃] *adv* materially.

maternel, -elle [matɛrnɛl] *adj* maternal; [langue] mother (*avant n*); **lait** ~ mother's milk.
◆ **maternelle** *nf* nursery school.

materner [matɛrne] [3] *vt* to mother.

maternité [maternite] *nf* **-1.** [qualité] maternity, motherhood. **-2.** [hôpital] maternity hospital.

mathématicien, -ienne [matematisjɛ̃, jɛn] *nm, f* mathematician.

mathématique [matematik] *adj* mathematical.

◆ **mathématiques** *nfpl* mathematics (U).

matheux, -euse [matø, øz] *nm, f fam* mathematician.

maths [mat] *nfpl fam* math *Am*, maths *Br*.

matière [matjɛr] *nf* **-1.** [substance] matter; ~s fécales feces *Am*, faeces *Br*; ~s grasses fats; ~ grise gray *Am* OU grey *Br* matter. **-2.** [matériau] material; ~ plastique plastic; ~s premières raw materials. **-3.** [discipline, sujet] subject; **en ~ de sport/littérature** as far as sport/literature is concerned. **-4.** *loc*: **donner ~ à** to give cause for.

MATIF, Matif [matif] (*abr de* **Marché à terme international de France**) *nm body regulating activities on the French stock exchange.*

Matignon [matiɲɔ̃] *n*: **(l'hôtel) ~** *building in Paris which houses the offices of the Prime Minister.*

MATIGNON:
This term is often used to refer to the Prime Minister and his or her administrative staff:
'Matignon ne semble pas être d'accord'

---

matin [matɛ̃] *nm* morning; **le ~** in the morning; **ce ~** this morning; **à trois heures du ~** at 3 o'clock in the morning; **de bon** OU **de grand ~** early in the morning; **du ~ au soir** *fig* from dawn to dusk.

matinal, -e, -aux [matinal, o] *adj* **-1.** [gymnastique, émission] morning (*avant n*). **-2.** [personne]: **être ~** to be an early riser.

mâtiné, -e [matine] *adj*: **~ de** [chien] crossed with; *fig* [mélangé de] mixed with.

matinée [matine] *nf* **-1.** [matin] morning; **faire la grasse ~** to have a lie in. **-2.** [spectacle] matinée, afternoon performance.

matines [matin] *nfpl* matins.

matois, -e [matwa, az] *littéraire* ◇ *adj* wily. ◇ *nm, f* wily person.

maton, -onne [matɔ̃, ɔn] *nm, f fam arg crime* screw.

matou [matu] *nm* tom, tomcat.

matraquage [matrakaʒ] *nm* **-1.** [bastonnade] beating, clubbing. **-2.** *fig* [intoxication] bombardment; **~ publicitaire** bombardment with adverts.

matraque [matrak] *nf* truncheon.

matraquer [matrake] [3] *vt* **-1.** [frapper] to beat, to club. **-2.** *fig* [intoxiquer] to bombard.

matriarcal, -e, -aux [matrijarkal, o] *adj* matriarchal.

matriarcat [matrijarka] *nm* matriarchy.

matrice [matris] *nf* **-1.** [moule] mould. **-2.** MATHS matrix. **-3.** ANAT womb.

matricule [matrikyl] ◇ *nm*: **(numéro) ~** number. ◇ *nf* register.

matrimonial, -e, -iaux [matrimɔnjal, jo] *adj* matrimonial.

matrone [matrɔn] *nf péj* old bag.

maturation [matyrasjɔ̃] *nf* maturing.

mature [matyr] *adj* mature.

mâture [matyr] *nf* masts (*pl*).

maturité [matyrite] *nf* maturity; [de fruit] ripeness.

maudire [modir] [104] *vt* to curse.

maudit, -e [modi, it] ◇ *pp* → **maudire**. ◇ *adj* **-1.** [réprouvé] accursed. **-2.** (*avant n*) [exécrable] damned. ◇ *nm, f* person who is damned.

maugréer [mogree] [15] ◇ *vt* to mutter. ◇ *vi*: **~ (contre)** to grumble (about).

maure, more [mor] *adj* Moorish.
◆ **Maure, More** *nmf* Moor.

mauresque, moresque [morɛsk] *adj* Moorish.
◆ **Mauresque, Moresque** *nf* Moorish woman.

Maurice [moris] → **île**.

mauricien, -ienne [morisjɛ̃, jɛn] *adj* Mauritian.
◆ **Mauricien, -ienne** *nm, f* Mauritian.

Mauritanie [moritani] *nf*: **la ~** Mauritania.

mauritanien, -ienne [moritanjɛ̃, jɛn] *adj* Mauritanian.
◆ **Mauritanien, -ienne** *nm, f* Mauritanian.

mausolée [mozole] *nm* mausoleum.

maussade [mosad] *adj* **-1.** [personne, air] sullen. **-2.** [temps] gloomy.

mauvais, -e [movɛ, ɛz] *adj* **-1.** [gén] bad. **-2.** [moment, numéro, réponse] wrong. **-3.** [mer] rough. **-4.** [personne, regard] nasty.
◆ **mauvais** *adv*: **il fait ~** the weather is bad; **sentir ~** to smell bad.

mauve [mov] *nm & adj* mauve.

mauviette [movjɛt] *nf fam* **-1.** [physiquement] weakling. **-2.** [moralement] coward, wimp.

maux → **mal**.

max [maks] (*abr de* **maximum**) *nm fam*: **un**

~ **de fric** loads of money; **il en a rajouté un** ~ he went completely overboard.

max. (*abr de* **maximum**) max.

maxillaire [maksilɛr] *nm* jawbone.

maximal, -e, -aux [maksimal, o] *adj* maximum; [degré] highest.

maxime [maksim] *nf* maxim.

maximum [maksimɔm] (*pl* **maxima** [maksima]) ◇ *nm* maximum; **le** ~ **de vitesse/capacité** *etc* maximum speed/capacity *etc*; **le** ~ **de personnes** the greatest (possible) number of people; **au** ~ at the most. ◇ *adj* maximum.

maya [maja] *adj* Mayan.
◆ **Maya** *nmf*: **les Mayas** the Maya.

mayonnaise [majɔnɛz] *nf* mayonnaise.

Mazarine [mazarin] *n*: **la bibliothèque** ~ *public library in Paris.*

LA BIBLIOTHÈQUE MAZARINE:
This library opened to the public in 1643, and is the oldest in France. It specializes in French history, especially local history

mazout [mazut] *nm* fuel oil.

mazouté, -e [mazute] *adj* polluted with oil.

MDM *nmpl abr de* **Médecins du monde.**

me [mə], **m'** (*devant voyelle ou h muet*) *pron pers* **-1.** [complément d'objet direct] me. **-2.** [complément d'objet indirect] (to) me. **-3.** [réfléchi] myself. **-4.** [avec un présentatif]: ~ **voici** here I am.

Me (*abr de* **maître**) *title for barristers*, ≃ QC *Br.*

mea culpa [meakulpa] *nm inv*: **faire son** ~ *fig* to admit one's mistake.

méandre [meɑ̃dr] *nm* [de rivière] meander, bend.
◆ **méandres** *nmpl* [détours sinueux] meanderings (*pl*).

mec [mɛk] *nm fam* guy, bloke.

mécanicien, -ienne [mekanisjɛ̃, jɛn] ◇ *adj* mechanized. ◇ *nm, f* **-1.** [de garage] mechanic. **-2.** [conducteur de train] engineer *Am*, train driver *Br*.

mécanique [mekanik] ◇ *nf* **-1.** TECHNOL mechanical engineering. **-2.** MATHS & PHYS mechanics (*U*). **-3.** [mécanisme] mechanism. ◇ *adj* mechanical.

mécaniquement [mekanikmɑ̃] *adv* mechanically.

mécanisation [mekanizasjɔ̃] *nf* mechanization.

mécaniser [mekanize] [3] *vt* to mechanize.

mécanisme [mekanism] *nm* mechanism.

mécano [mekano] *nm fam* mechanic.

mécénat [mesena] *nm* patronage.

mécène [mesɛn] *nm* patron.

méchamment [meʃamɑ̃] *adv* **-1.** [cruellement] nastily. **-2.** *fam* [beaucoup] really, terribly.

méchanceté [meʃɑ̃ste] *nf* **-1.** [attitude] nastiness. **-2.** *fam* [rosserie] nasty thing.

méchant, -e [meʃɑ̃, ɑ̃t] ◇ *adj* **-1.** [malveillant, cruel] nasty, wicked; [animal] vicious. **-2.** [désobéissant] naughty. ◇ *nm, f* **-1.** [moralement] wicked person. **-2.** [en langage enfantin] baddy.

mèche [mɛʃ] *nf* **-1.** [de bougie] wick. **-2.** [de cheveux] lock; ~ **rebelle** cowlick. **-3.** [de bombe] fuse. **-4.** [de perceuse] bit. **-5.** *loc*: **être de** ~ **avec qqn** to be hand in glove with sb; **vendre la** ~ to give the game away.

méchoui [meʃwi] *nm whole roast sheep.*

méconnaissable [mekɔnɛsabl] *adj* unrecognizable.

méconnaissance [mekɔnɛsɑ̃s] *nf* ignorance.

méconnu, -e [mekɔny] *adj* unrecognized.

mécontent, -e [mekɔ̃tɑ̃, ɑ̃t] ◇ *adj* unhappy. ◇ *nm, f* malcontent.

mécontentement [mekɔ̃tɑ̃tmɑ̃] *nm* displeasure, annoyance.

mécontenter [mekɔ̃tɑ̃te] [3] *vt* to displease.

Mecque [mɛk] *n*: **La** ~ Mecca.

mécréant, -e [mekreɑ̃, ɑ̃t] *nm, f* nonbeliever.

méd. *abr de* **médecin.**

médaille [medaj] *nf* **-1.** [pièce, décoration] medal. **-2.** [bijou] medallion. **-3.** [de chien] identification disk *Am* OU disc *Br*, tag.

médaillé, -e [medaje] ◇ *adj* MIL decorated; SPORT medal-winning (*avant n*). ◇ *nm, f* MIL holder of a medal; SPORT medal-winner, medalist *Am*, medallist *Br*.

médaillon [medajɔ̃] *nm* **-1.** [bijou] locket. **-2.** PRESSE: **en** ~ inset. **-3.** ART & CULIN medallion.

médecin [medsɛ̃] *nm* doctor; ~ **de famille** family doctor, GP *Br*; ~ **de garde** doctor on duty, duty doctor; ~ **légiste** medical examiner *Am*, forensic scientist *Br*; ~ **traitant** consulting physician.
◆ **Médecins** *nmpl*: **Médecins du monde, Médecins sans frontières** *organizations providing medical aid to victims of war and disasters, especially in the Third World.*

médecine [medsin] *nf* medicine; ~ **générale** general medicine.

média [medja] *nm*: **les** ~**s** the (mass) media.

médian, -e [medjɑ̃, an] *adj* median.
◆ **médiane** *nf* median.

médiateur, **-trice** [medjatœr, tris] ◇ *adj* mediating (*avant n*). ◇ *nm, f* mediator; [dans conflit de travail] arbitrator.
◆ **médiateur** *nm* ADMIN ombudsman.
◆ **médiatrice** *nf* median.

médiathèque [medjatɛk] *nf* media library.

médiation [medjasjɔ̃] *nf* mediation; [dans conflit de travail] arbitration.

médiatique [medjatik] *adj* media (*avant n*).

médiatisation [medjatizasjɔ̃] *nf* saturation media coverage.

médiatiser [medjatize] [3] *vt péj* to turn into a media event.

médical, **-e**, **-aux** [medikal, o] *adj* medical.

médicalisation [medikalizasjɔ̃] *nf* [d'établissement, de service] provision of medical equipment; [de population] provision of medical care.

médicament [medikamɑ̃] *nm* medicine, drug.

médicamenteux, **-euse** [medikamɑ̃tø, øz] *adj* medicinal.

médication [medikasjɔ̃] *nf* (course of) treatment.

médicinal, **-e**, **-aux** [medisinal, o] *adj* medicinal.

Médicis [medisis] *n*: **le prix ~** French literary *prize*.

médico-légal, **-e**, **-aux** [medikɔlegal, o] *adj* forensic.

médico-social, **-e**, **-iaux** [medikɔsɔsjal, jo] *adj* public health (*avant n*).

médiéval, **-e**, **-aux** [medjeval, o] *adj* medieval.

médiocre [medjɔkr] ◇ *nmf* mediocre person. ◇ *adj* mediocre.

médiocrité [medjɔkrite] *nf* mediocrity.

médire [medir] [103] *vi* to gossip; **~ de qqn** to speak ill of sb.

médisance [medizɑ̃s] *nf* **-1.** [calomnie] slander. **-2.** [ragot] piece of gossip.

médisant, **-e** [medizɑ̃, ɑ̃t] ◇ *adj* slanderous. ◇ *nm, f* slanderer, scandalmonger.

médit [medi] *pp inv* → **médire**.

méditatif, **-ive** [meditatif, iv] ◇ *adj* thoughtful, reflective. ◇ *nm, f* thoughtful person.

méditation [meditasjɔ̃] *nf* meditation.

méditer [medite] [3] ◇ *vt* **-1.** [projeter] to plan; **~ de faire qqch** to plan to do sthg. **-2.** [approfondir] to meditate on. ◇ *vi*: **~ (sur)** to meditate (on).

Méditerranée [mediterane] *nf*: **la ~** the Mediterranean (Sea).

méditerranéen, **-enne** [mediteraneɛ̃, ɛn] *adj* Mediterranean.
◆ **Méditerranéen**, **-enne** *nm, f* person from the Mediterranean.

médium [medjɔm] *nm* **-1.** [personne] medium. **-2.** MUS middle register.

médius [medjys] *nm* middle finger.

méduse [medyz] *nf* jellyfish.

méduser [medyze] [3] *vt* to dumbfound.

meeting [mitiŋ] *nm* meeting; **~ aérien** air show.

méfait [mefɛ] *nm* misdemeanor *Am*, misdemeanour *Br*, misdeed.
◆ **méfaits** *nmpl* [du temps] ravages.

méfiance [mefjɑ̃s] *nf* suspicion, distrust.

méfiant, **-e** [mefjɑ̃, ɑ̃t] *adj* suspicious, distrustful.

méfier [mefje] [9]
◆ **se méfier** *vp* to be wary OU careful; **se ~ de qqn/qqch** to distrust sb/sthg.

méga [mega] *adj* mega.

mégalo [megalo] *nmf & adj fam* megalomaniac; **il est complètement ~** he thinks he's God.

mégalomane [megalɔman] *nmf & adj* megalomaniac.

mégalomanie [megalɔmani] *nf* megalomania.

mega-octet [megaɔktɛ] *nm* megabyte.

mégaphone [megafɔn] *nm* megaphone, bullhorn *Am*.

mégapole [megapɔl] *nf* megalopolis, megacity.

mégarde [megard]
◆ **par mégarde** *loc adv* by mistake.

mégère [meʒɛr] *nf péj* shrew.

mégot [mego] *nm fam* butt *Am*, fag-end *Br*.

mégoter [megote] [3] *vi fam*: **sur qqch** to skimp on sthg.

meilleur, **-e** [mɛjœr] ◇ *adj* (*compar*) better; (*superl*) best. ◇ *nm, f* best; **c'est la ~e!** that takes the cake OU biscuit!
◆ **meilleur** ◇ *nm*: **le ~** the best. ◇ *adv* better.

méjuger [meʒyʒe] [17] ◇ *vt* to misjudge. ◇ *vi*: **~ de qqn/qqch** to underestimate sb/sthg.
◆ **se méjuger** *vp littéraire* to underestimate o.s.

mélancolie [melɑ̃kɔli] *nf* melancholy.

mélancolique [melɑ̃kɔlik] *adj* melancholy.

Mélanésie [melanezi] *nf*: **la ~** Melanesia.

mélanésien, **-ienne** [melanezjɛ̃, jɛn] *adj* Melanesian.
◆ **Mélanésien**, **-ienne** *nm, f* Melanesian.

mélange [melɑ̃ʒ] *nm* **-1.** [action] mixing; **sans ~** *fig* unadulterated. **-2.** [mixture] mixture.

mélanger [melɑ̃ʒe] [17] *vt* **-1.** [mettre ensemble] to mix. **-2.** [déranger] to mix up, to muddle up.

◆ **se mélanger** *vp* **-1.** [se mêler] to mix. **-2.** [se brouiller] to get mixed up.

mélangeur [melɑ̃ʒœr] *nm* **-1.** CIN mixer. **-2.** (robinet) ~ mixing tap *Am*, mixer tap *Br*.

mélasse [melas] *nf* **-1.** [liquide] molasses (*U*) *Am*, treacle *Br*. **-2.** *fam* [mélange] mess; **être dans la ~** *fig* to be in a fix.

mêlée [mele] *nf* **-1.** [combat] fray. **-2.** RUGBY scrum; ~ **ouverte** ruck.

mêler [mele] [4] *vt* **-1.** [mélanger] to mix. **-2.** [déranger] to muddle up, to mix up. **-3.** [impliquer]: ~ **qqn à qqch** to involve sb in sthg. **-4.** [joindre]: ~ **qqch à qqch** to mix OU combine sthg with sthg.

◆ **se mêler** *vp* **-1.** [se joindre]: **se ~ à** [groupe] to join. **-2.** [s'ingérer]: **se ~ de qqch** to get mixed up in sthg; **mêlez-vous de ce qui vous regarde!** mind your own business!

mélèze [melɛz] *nm* larch.

méli-mélo [melimelo] (*pl* **mélis-mélos**) *nm* muddle; [d'objets] jumble.

mélo [melo] *nm fam* melodrama.

mélodie [melɔdi] *nf* melody.

mélodieux, -ieuse [melɔdjø, jøz] *adj* melodious, tuneful.

mélodique [melɔdik] *adj* melodic.

mélodramatique [melɔdramatik] *adj* melodramatic.

mélodrame [melɔdram] *nm* melodrama.

mélomane [melɔman] ◇ *nmf* music lover. ◇ *adj* music-loving.

melon [məlɔ̃] *nm* **-1.** [fruit] melon. **-2.** [chapeau] bowler (hat).

melting-pot [mɛltiŋpɔt] *nm* melting pot.

membrane [mɑ̃bran] *nf* membrane.

membre [mɑ̃br] ◇ *nm* **-1.** [du corps] limb; ~**s supérieurs/inférieurs** upper/lower limbs; ~**s antérieurs/postérieurs** front/back legs; ~ **(viril)** male member. **-2.** [personne, pays, partie] member; ~ **fondateur** founder member. ◇ *adj* member (*avant n*).

mémé = **mémère**.

même [mɛm] ◇ *adj indéf* **-1.** [indique une identité ou une ressemblance] same; **il a le ~ âge que moi** he's the same age as me. **-2.** [sert à souligner]: **ce sont ses paroles ~s** those are his very words; **elle est la bonté ~** she's kindness itself.

◇ *pron indéf*: **le/la ~** the same one; **ce sont toujours les ~s qui gagnent** it's always the same people who win; **elle est toujours la ~** she's always the same.

◇ *adv* even; **il n'est ~ pas diplômé** he isn't even qualified; **elle ne va ~ plus au cinéma** she doesn't even go to the cinema any more.

◆ **de même** *loc adv* similarly, likewise; **il en va de ~ pour lui** the same goes for him.

◆ **de même que** *loc conj* just as.

◆ **tout de même** *loc adv* all the same.

◆ **à même** *loc prép*: **il boit à ~ la bouteille** he drinks (straight) from the bottle; **s'asseoir à ~ le sol** to sit on the bare ground.

◆ **à même de** *loc prép*: **être à ~ de faire qqch** to be able to do sthg, to be in a position to do sthg.

◆ **même si** *loc conj* even if.

mémento [memɛ̃to] *nm* **-1.** [agenda] pocket diary. **-2.** [ouvrage] notes (*title of school textbook*).

mémère [memɛr], **mémé** [meme] *nf fam* **-1.** [grand-mère] granny. **-2.** *péj* [vieille femme] old biddy.

mémoire [memwar] ◇ *nf* [gén & INFORM] memory; **de ~** from memory; **avoir bonne/mauvaise ~** to have a good/bad memory; **avoir de la ~** to have a good memory; **avoir la ~ des chiffres/noms** to have a good memory for figures/names; **perdre la ~** to lose one's memory; **se rafraîchir la ~** to refresh one's memory; **mettre en ~** INFORM to store; ~ **tampon** INFORM buffer; ~ **virtuelle** INFORM virtual memory; ~ **vive** INFORM random access memory; **à la ~ de** in memory of; **de ~ d'homme** in living memory; **pour ~** for the record.

◇ *nm* **-1.** ADMIN memorandum, report. **-2.** UNIV dissertation, paper.

◆ **mémoires** *nmpl* memoirs.

mémorable [memɔrabl] *adj* memorable.

mémorandum [memɔrɑ̃dɔm] *nm* **-1.** [note diplomatique] memorandum. **-2.** [carnet] notebook.

mémorial, -iaux [memɔrjal, jo] *nm* [monument] memorial.

mémorisable [memɔrizabl] *adj* INFORM storable.

mémoriser [memɔrize] [3] *vt* **-1.** [suj: personne] to memorize. **-2.** INFORM to store.

menaçant, -e [mənasɑ̃, ɑ̃t] *adj* threatening.

menace [mənas] *nf*: ~ **(pour)** threat (to).

menacer [mənase] [16] ◇ *vt* to threaten; ~ **de faire qqch** to threaten to do sthg; ~ **qqn de qqch** to threaten sb with sthg. ◇ *vi*: **la pluie menace** it looks like rain.

ménage [menaʒ] *nm* **-1.** [nettoyage] house-work (*U*); **faire le** ~ to do the housework; **faire des** ~**s** to work as a cleaner. **-2.** [couple] couple; **se mettre en** ~ to set up house together; ~ **à trois** ménage à trois. **-3.** ÉCON household. **-4.** *loc*: **faire bon** ~ (**avec**) to get on well (with).

ménagement [menaʒmɑ̃] *nm* [égards] con-sideration; **sans** ~ brutally.

ménager¹, -ère [menaʒe, ɛr] *adj* household (*avant n*), domestic.
◆ **ménagère** *nf* **-1.** [femme] housewife. **-2.** [de couverts] canteen.

ménager² [menaʒe] [17] *vt* **-1.** [bien traiter] to treat gently. **-2.** [économiser - sucre, réser-ves] to use sparingly; [- argent, temps] to use carefully; ~ **ses forces** to conserve one's strength; ~ **sa santé** to take care of one's health. **-3.** [préparer] to arrange. **-4.** [prati-quer - espace] to make.
◆ **se ménager** *vp* to take care of o.s., to look after o.s.

ménagerie [menaʒri] *nf* menagerie.

mendiant, -e [mɑ̃djɑ̃, ɑ̃t] *nm, f* beggar.

mendicité [mɑ̃disite] *nf* begging.

mendier [mɑ̃dje] [9] ◇ *vt* [argent] to beg for. **-2.** [éloges] to seek. ◇ *vi* to beg.

menées [məne] *nfpl* scheming (*U*).

mener [məne] [19] ◇ *vt* **-1.** [emmener] to take. **-2.** [diriger - débat, enquête] to conduct; [- affaires] to manage, to run; ~ **qqch à bonne fin** OU **à bien** to see sthg through, to bring sthg to a successful conclusion. **-3.** [être en tête de] to lead. ◇ *vi* to lead.

meneur, -euse [mənœr, øz] *nm, f* [chef] ring-leader; ~ **d'hommes** born leader; ~ **de jeu** host.

menhir [menir] *nm* standing stone.

méninge [menɛ̃ʒ] *nf* meninx.
◆ **méninges** *nfpl fam* brains.

méningite [menɛ̃ʒit] *nf* meningitis (*U*).

ménisque [menisk] *nm* meniscus.

ménopause [menopoz] *nf* menopause.

menotte [mənɔt] *nf* [main] little hand.
◆ **menottes** *nfpl* handcuffs; **passer les** ~**s à qqn** to handcuff sb.

mens → mentir.

mensonge [mɑ̃sɔ̃ʒ] *nm* **-1.** [propos] lie; **un pieux** ~ a white lie. **-2.** [acte] lying.

mensonger, -ère [mɑ̃sɔ̃ʒe, ɛr] *adj* false.

menstruation [mɑ̃stryasjɔ̃] *nf* menstrua-tion.

menstruel, -elle [mɑ̃stryɛl] *adj* men-strual.

mensualiser [mɑ̃sɥalize] [3] *vt* to pay monthly.

mensualité [mɑ̃sɥalite] *nf* **-1.** [traite] month-ly installment *Am*, instalment *Br*. **-2.** [sa-laire] (monthly) salary.

mensuel, -elle [mɑ̃sɥɛl] ◇ *adj* monthly. ◇ *nm, f* salaried employee.
◆ **mensuel** *nm* monthly (magazine).

mensuellement [mɑ̃sɥɛlmɑ̃] *adv* monthly, every month.

mensuration [mɑ̃syrasjɔ̃] *nf* measuring.
◆ **mensurations** *nfpl* measurements.

ment → mentir.

mental, -e, -aux [mɑ̃tal, o] *adj* mental.

mentalement [mɑ̃talmɑ̃] *adv* mentally.

mentalité [mɑ̃talite] *nf* mentality.

menteur, -euse [mɑ̃tœr, øz] ◇ *adj* false. ◇ *nm, f* liar.

menthe [mɑ̃t] *nf* mint; ~ **à l'eau** pepper-mint cordial.

mentholé, -e [mɑ̃tɔle] *adj* mentholated, menthol (*avant n*).

menti [mɑ̃ti] *pp inv* → mentir.

mention [mɑ̃sjɔ̃] *nf* **-1.** [citation] mention; **faire** ~ **de qqch** to mention sthg. **-2.** [note] note; «**rayer la** ~ **inutile**» "delete as ap-propriate". **-3.** UNIV: **avec** ~ with distinc-tion; **avec la** ~ **très bien/bien/passable** ≃ with First/Second/Third Class Honours.

mentionner [mɑ̃sjɔne] [3] *vt* to mention.

mentir [mɑ̃tir] [37] *vi*: ~ (**à**) to lie (to); **sans** ~ honestly.

menton [mɑ̃tɔ̃] *nm* chin; ~ **en galoche** prominent chin; **double** ~ double chin.

menu, -e [məny] *adj* [très petit] tiny; [mince] thin.
◆ **menu** ◇ *adv*: **hacher** ~ to chop finely. ◇ *nm* [gén & INFORM] menu; [repas à prix fixe] set menu; ~ **gastronomique/touristique** gourmet/tourist menu.

menuiserie [mənɥizri] *nf* **-1.** [métier] join-ery, carpentry. **-2.** [atelier] joinery (work-shop). **-3.** [ouvrages] joinery (*U*), carpentry (*U*).

menuisier [mənɥizje] *nm* joiner, carpenter.

méprenais, méprenions *etc* → mépren-dre.

méprendre [meprɑ̃dr] [79]
◆ **se méprendre** *vp littéraire*: **se** ~ **sur** to be mistaken about; **se ressembler à s'y** ~ to be as like as two peas in a pod.

mépris, -e [mepri, iz] *pp* → méprendre.
◆ **mépris** *nm* **-1.** [dédain]: ~ (**pour**) con-tempt (for), scorn (for). **-2.** [indifférence]: ~ **de** disregard for.
◆ **au mépris de** *loc prép* regardless of.

méprisable [meprizabl] *adj* contemptible, despicable.

méprisant, **-e** [meprizɑ̃, ɑ̃t] *adj* contemptuous, scornful.

méprise [mepriz] *nf* mistake, error.

mépriser [meprize] [3] *vt* to despise; [danger, offre] to scorn.

mer [mɛr] *nf* sea; **en ~** at sea; **prendre la ~** to put to sea; **haute** OU **pleine ~** open sea; **ce n'est pas la ~ à boire** it's no big deal; **la ~ Adriatique** the Adriatic; **la ~ Baltique** the Baltic Sea; **la ~ d'Irlande** the Irish Sea; **la ~ Morte** the Dead Sea; **la ~ Noire** the Black Sea; **la ~ du Nord** the North Sea.

mercantile [merkɑ̃til] *adj péj* mercenary.

mercenaire [mɛrsənɛr] *nm & adj* mercenary.

mercerie [mɛrsəri] *nf* **-1.** [articles] notions (*pl*) *Am*, haberdashery *Br*. **-2.** [boutique] notions store *Am*, haberdasher's shop *Br*.

merci [mɛrsi] ◇ *interj* thank you!, thanks!; **~ beaucoup!** thank you very much! ◇ *nm*: **~ (de** OU **pour)** thank you (for); **dire ~ à qqn** to thank sb, to say thank you to sb. ◇ *nf* mercy; **sans ~** merciless; **être à la ~ de** to be at the mercy of.

mercier, **-ière** [mɛrsje, jɛr] *nm, f* notions dealer *Am*, haberdasher *Br*.

mercredi [mɛrkrədi] *nm* Wednesday; **~ des Cendres** Ash Wednesday; *voir aussi* **samedi**.

mercure [mɛrkyr] *nm* mercury.

merde [mɛrd] *tfam* ◇ *nf* shit. ◇ *interj* shit!

merdier [mɛrdje] *nm tfam*: **on est dans un ~** we're in the shit.

mère [mɛr] *nf* mother; **~ célibataire** single OU unmarried mother; **~ de famille** mother; **~ indigne** unfit mother; **~ poule** mother hen; **~ supérieure** mother superior.

merguez [mɛrgɛz] *nf inv* North African spiced sausage.

méridien, **-ienne** [meridjɛ̃, jɛn] *adj* [ligne] meridian.

◆ **méridien** *nm* meridian.

méridional, **-e**, **-aux** [meridjɔnal, o] *adj* southern; [du sud de la France] Southern (French).

◆ **Méridional**, **-e**, **-aux** *nm, f* person from the Mediterranean; [du sud de la France] person from the South (of France).

meringue [mərɛ̃g] *nf* meringue.

mérinos [merinos] *nm* merino.

merisier [mərizje] *nm* **-1.** [arbre] wild cherry (tree). **-2.** [bois] cherry.

méritant, **-e** [meritɑ̃, ɑ̃t] *adj* deserving.

mérite [merit] *nm* merit; **il a du ~ à y prendre part** it is to his credit that he is taking part.

mériter [merite] [3] *vt* **-1.** [être digne de, encourir] to deserve. **-2.** [valoir] to be worth, to merit.

méritoire [meritwar] *adj* commendable.

merlan [mɛrlɑ̃] *nm* whiting.

merle [mɛrl] *nm* blackbird.

merveille [mɛrvɛj] *nf* marvel, wonder; **à ~** marvelously *Am*, marvellously *Br*, wonderfully.

merveilleusement [mɛrvɛjøzmɑ̃] *adv* marvelously *Am*, marvellously *Br*, wonderfully.

merveilleux, **-euse** [mɛrvɛjø, øz] *adj* **-1.** [remarquable, prodigieux] marvelous *Am*, marvellous *Br*, wonderful. **-2.** [magique] magic, magical.

◆ **merveilleux** *nm*: **le ~** the supernatural.

mes → **mon**.

mésalliance [mezaljɑ̃s] *nf* unsuitable marriage, misalliance.

mésange [mezɑ̃ʒ] *nf* ZOOL tit; **~ bleue/charbonnière** blue/coal tit.

mésaventure [mezavɑ̃tyr] *nf* misfortune.

mesdames → **madame**.

mesdemoiselles → **mademoiselle**.

mésentente [mezɑ̃tɑ̃t] *nf* disagreement.

mésestimer [mezɛstime] [3] *vt littéraire* to underestimate.

mesquin, **-e** [mɛskɛ̃, in] *adj* mean, petty.

mesquinerie [mɛskinri] *nf* **-1.** [étroitesse d'esprit] meanness, pettiness. **-2.** [action mesquine] petty act.

mess [mɛs] *nm* mess.

message [mesaʒ] *nm* message; **laisser un ~ à qqn** to leave a message for sb; **~ publicitaire** commercial, spot.

messager, **-ère** [mesaʒe, ɛr] *nm, f* messenger.

messagerie [mesaʒri] *nf* **-1.** (*gén pl*) [transport de marchandises] freight (*U*); **les ~s aériennes** air freight company (*sg*). **-2.** INFORM: **~ électronique** electronic mail; **~ rose** *computerized dating service*; **~ vocale électronique** INFORM voice messaging.

messe [mɛs] *nf* mass; **aller à la ~** to go to mass; **~ de minuit** midnight mass; **faire des ~s basses** *fam* to mutter.

messie [mesi] *nm* Messiah; *fig* savior *Am*, saviour *Br*.

messieurs → **monsieur**.

mesure [məzyr] *nf* **-1.** [disposition, acte] measure, step; **prendre des ~s** to take measures OU steps; **~s d'austérité** austerity measures; **~s de rétorsion** retaliatory measures. **-2.** [évaluation, dimension] measurement; **prendre les ~s de qqn/qqch** to measure sb/sthg. **-3.** [étalon, récipient] measure. **-4.** MUS time, tempo; **battre la ~** to

beat time. **-5.** [modération] moderation. **-6.** *loc:* **dans la ~ du possible** as far as possible; **être en ~ de** to be in a position to; **c'est sans commune ~** there's no possible comparison.
◆ **à la mesure de** *loc prép* worthy of.
◆ **à mesure que** *loc conj* as.
◆ **outre mesure** *loc adv* excessively.
◆ **sur mesure** *loc adj* custom-made; [costume] made-to-measure.

mesuré, -e [məzyre] *adj* [modéré] measured.

mesurer [məzyre] [3] *vt* **-1.** [gén] to measure; **elle mesure 1, 50 m** she's 5 feet tall; **la table mesure 1, 50 m** the table is 5 feet long. **-2.** [risques, portée, ampleur] to weigh up; **~ ses paroles** to weigh one's words. **-3.** [limiter] to limit. **-4.** [proportionner]: **~ qqch à qqch** to match sthg to sthg.
◆ **se mesurer** *vp:* **se ~ avec** OU **à qqn** to pit o.s. against sb.

métabolisme [metabɔlism] *nm* metabolism.

métairie [metɛri] *nf* sharecropping farm.

métal, -aux [metal, o] *nm* metal.

métallique [metalik] *adj* **-1.** [en métal] metal (*avant n*). **-2.** [éclat, son] metallic.

métallo [metalo] *nm fam* metalworker.

métallurgie [metalyrʒi] *nf* **-1.** [industrie] metallurgical industry. **-2.** [technique] metallurgy.

métallurgique [metalyrʒik] *adj* metallurgical.

métallurgiste [metalyrʒist] *nm* **-1.** [ouvrier] metalworker. **-2.** [industriel] metallurgist.

métamorphose [metamɔrfoz] *nf* metamorphosis.

métamorphoser [metamɔrfoze] [3] *vt:* **~ qqn/qqch (en)** to transform sb/sthg (into).
◆ **se métamorphoser** *vp* BIOL to metamorphose; *fig:* **se ~ (en)** to be transformed (into).

métaphore [metafɔr] *nf* metaphor.

métaphorique [metafɔrik] *adj* metaphorical.

métaphysique [metafizik] ◇ *nf* metaphysics (*U*). ◇ *adj* metaphysical.

métayer, -ère [meteje, metɛjer] *nm, f* tenant farmer.

météo [meteo] *nf* **-1.** [bulletin] weather forecast. **-2.** [service] ≃ National Weather Service *Am*, ≃ Met Office *Br*.

météore [meteɔr] *nm* meteor.

météorite [meteɔrit] *nm ou nf* meteorite.

météorologie [meteɔrɔlɔʒi] *nf* **-1.** SCIENCE meteorology. **-2.** [service] ≃ National Weather Service *Am*, ≃ Meteorological Office *Br*.

météorologique [meteɔrɔlɔʒik] *adj* meteorological, weather (*avant n*).

métèque [metɛk] *nm vulg racist term used with reference to people from Mediterranean countries*.

méthane [metan] *nm* methane.

méthode [metɔd] *nf* **-1.** [gén] method. **-2.** [ouvrage - gén] manual; [- de lecture, de langue] primer.

méthodique [metɔdik] *adj* methodical.

méthodiquement [metɔdikmɑ̃] *adv* methodically.

méthodiste [metɔdist] *nmf & adj* Methodist.

méthodologie [metɔdɔlɔʒi] *nf* methodology.

méthylène [metilɛn] *nm* **-1.** [alcool] methanol. **-2.** CHIM methylene.

méticuleusement [metikyløzmɑ̃] *adv* meticulously.

méticuleux, -euse [metikylø, øz] *adj* meticulous.

métier [metje] *nm* **-1.** [profession - manuelle] occupation, trade; [- intellectuelle] occupation, profession; **de son ~** by trade; **il est du ~** he's in the same trade OU same line of work; **avoir du ~** to have experience. **-2.** [machine]: **~ (à tisser)** loom.

métis, -isse [metis] ◇ *adj* **-1.** [personne] half-caste, half-breed. **-2.** [tissu] cotton and linen. ◇ *nm, f* half-caste, half-breed.
◆ **métis** *nm* [tissu] cotton-linen mix.

métissage [metisaʒ] *nm* [de personnes] interbreeding.

métisser [metise] [3] *vt* to cross, to crossbreed.

métrage [metraʒ] *nm* **-1.** [mesure] measurement, measuring. **-2.** [COUTURE - coupon] length. **-3.** CIN footage; **long ~** feature film; **court ~** short (film).

mètre [mɛtr] *nm* **-1.** LITTÉRATURE & MATHS meter *Am*, metre *Br*; **~ carré** square meter *Am* OU metre *Br*; **~ cube** cubic meter *Am* OU metre *Br*. **-2.** [instrument] rule.

métrer [metre] [18] *vt* [terrain] to survey; [tissu] to measure out.

métreur, -euse [metrœr, øz] *nm, f* surveyor.

métrique [metrik] ◇ *nf* LITTÉRATURE metrics (*U*). ◇ *adj* **-1.** MATHS metric. **-2.** LITTÉRATURE metrical.

métro [metro] *nm* subway *Am*, underground *Br*.

métronome [metrɔnɔm] *nm* metronome.

métropole [metrɔpɔl] *nf* **-1.** [ville] metropolis. **-2.** [pays] home country.

métropolitain, -e [metʀɔpɔlitɛ̃, ɛn] *adj* metropolitan.

mets [mɛ] ◇ → **mettre**. ◇ *nm* CULIN dish.

mettable [mɛtabl] *adj* wearable.

mette → **mettre**.

metteur [mɛtœʀ] *nm*: ~ **en ondes** RADIO producer; ~ **en scène** THÉÂTRE producer; CIN director.

mettre [mɛtʀ] [84] *vt* **-1.** [placer] to put; ~ **de l'eau à bouillir** to put some water on to boil. **-2.** [revêtir] to put on; **mets ta robe noire** put your black dress on; **je ne mets plus ma robe noire** I don't wear my black dress any more. **-3.** [consacrer - temps] to take; [- argent] to spend; ~ **longtemps à faire qqch** to take a long time to do sthg. **-4.** [allumer - radio, chauffage] to put on, to switch on. **-5.** [installer] to put in; **faire** ~ **l'électricité** to have electricity put in; **faire** ~ **de la moquette** to have a carpet put down OU fitted. **-6.** [inscrire] to put (down). **-7.** *loc*: ~ **bas** [animal] to drop, to give birth; **y** ~ **du sien** to do one's bit.
♦ **se mettre** *vp* **-1.** [se placer]: **où est-ce que ça se met?** where does this go?; **se** ~ **au lit** to get into bed; **se** ~ **à côté de qqn** to sit/stand near to sb. **-2.** [devenir]: **se** ~ **en colère** to get angry. **-3.** [commencer]: **se** ~ **à qqch/à faire qqch** to start sthg/ doing sthg. **-4.** [revêtir] to put on; **je n'ai rien à me** ~ I haven't got a thing to wear. **-5.** *fam* [se donner des coups]: **qu'est-ce qu'ils se sont mis!** they really set about each other!

meuble [mœbl] ◇ *nm* piece of furniture; ~**s** furniture (*U*); ~**s de bureau/jardin** office/garden furniture (*U*); **sauver les** ~**s** *fig* not to lose everything. ◇ *adj* **-1.** [terre, sol] easily worked. **-2.** JUR movable.

meublé, -e [mœble] *adj* furnished.
♦ **meublé** *nm* furnished apartment *Am*, furnished room/flat *Br*.

meubler [mœble] [5] ◇ *vt* **-1.** [pièce, maison] to furnish. **-2.** *fig* [occuper]: ~ **qqch (de)** to fill sthg (with). ◇ *vi* to be decorative.
♦ **se meubler** *vp* to furnish one's home.

meugler [møgle] [5] *vi* to moo.

meule [møl] *nf* **-1.** [à moudre] millstone. **-2.** [à aiguiser] grindstone. **-3.** [de fromage] round. **-4.** AGRIC stack; ~ **de foin** haystack.

meunier, -ière [mønje, jɛʀ] ◇ *adj* **-1.** [industrie] milling (*avant n*). **-2.** CULIN *coated in flour and fried*. ◇ *nm, f* miller (*f* miller's wife).

meurs, meurt *etc* → **mourir**.

meurtre [mœʀtʀ] *nm* murder.

meurtrier, -ière [mœʀtʀije, jɛʀ] ◇ *adj* [épidémie, arme] deadly; [fureur] murderous; [combat] bloody. ◇ *nm, f* murderer.
♦ **meurtrière** *nf* ARCHIT loophole.

meurtrir [mœʀtʀiʀ] [32] *vt* **-1.** [contusionner] to bruise. **-2.** *fig* [blesser] to wound.

meurtrissure [mœʀtʀisyʀ] *nf* **-1.** [marque] bruise. **-2.** *fig* [blessure] wound.

meute [møt] *nf* pack.

mévente [mevɑ̃t] *nf* poor sales (*pl*).

mexicain, -e [mɛksikɛ̃, ɛn] *adj* Mexican.
♦ **Mexicain, -e** *nm, f* Mexican.

Mexico [mɛksiko] *n* Mexico City.

Mexique [mɛksik] *nm*: **le** ~ Mexico; **au** ~ in Mexico.

mezzanine [mɛdzanin] *nf* mezzanine.

mezzo-soprano [mɛdzosɔpʀano] (*pl* **mezzo-sopranos**) *nmf* mezzo-soprano.

MF ◇ *nf* (*abr de* **modulation de fréquence**) FM. ◇ **-1.** (*abr de* **mark finlandais**) Mk, Fmk. **-2.** *abr de* **million de francs**.

Mgr (*abr de* **Monseigneur**) Mgr.

mi [mi] *nm inv* E; [dans la gamme] mi.

mi- [mi] ◇ *adj inv* half; **à la ~juin** in mid-June. ◇ *adv* half-.

miaou [mjau] *nm* meow *Am*, miaow *Br*.

miasme [mjasm] *nm* (*gén pl*) putrid OU foul smell.

miaulement [mjolmɑ̃] *nm* meowing *Am*, miaowing *Br*.

miauler [mjole] [3] *vi* to meow *Am*, to miaow *Br*.

mi-bas [miba] *nm inv* knee-sock.

mica [mika] *nm* mica.

mi-carême [mikaʀɛm] *nf feast day on third Thursday in Lent.*

miche [miʃ] *nf* [de pain] *large round loaf.*
♦ **miches** *nfpl fam* **-1.** [fesses] butt (*sg*) *Am*, bum (*sg*) *Br*. **-2.** [seins] boobs.

mi-chemin [miʃmɛ̃]
♦ **à mi-chemin** *loc adv* halfway (there).

mi-clos, -e [miklo, oz] *adj* half-closed.

micmac [mikmak] *nm fam* **-1.** [manigance] game, scheme. **-2.** [embrouillamini] muddle.

mi-côte [mikot]
♦ **à mi-côte** *loc adv* halfway up/down the hill.

micro [mikʀo] ◇ *nm* **-1.** [microphone] mike. **-2.** [ordinateur] micro. ◇ *nf* microcomputing.

microbe [mikʀɔb] *nm* **-1.** MÉD microbe, germ. **-2.** *péj* [avorton] (little) runt.

microbien, -ienne [mikʀɔbjɛ̃, jɛn] *adj* bacterial.

microbiologie [mikʀɔbjɔlɔʒi] *nf* microbiology.

microchirurgie [mikrɔʃiryrʒi] *nf* microsurgery.

microclimat [mikrɔklima] *nm* microclimate.

microcosme [mikrɔkɔsm] *nm* microcosm.

micro-édition [mikrɔedisjɔ̃] *nf* desktop publishing.

micro-électronique [mikrɔelɛktrɔnik] ◇ *nf* microelectronics (U). ◇ *adj* microelectronic.

microfiche [mikrɔfiʃ] *nf* microfiche.

microfilm [mikrɔfilm] *nm* microfilm.

micron [mikrɔ̃] *nm* micron.

Micronésie [mikronezi] *nf*: **la ~** Micronesia; **les États fédérés de ~** Federated States of Micronesia.

micro-ondes [mikrɔɔ̃d] *nfpl* microwaves; **four à ~** microwave (oven).

micro-ordinateur [mikrɔɔrdinatœr] (*pl* **micro-ordinateurs**) *nm* micro, microcomputer.

micro-organisme [mikrɔɔrganism] (*pl* **micro-organismes**) *nm* micro-organism.

microphone [mikrɔfɔn] *nm* microphone.

microprocesseur [mikrɔprɔsesœr] *nm* microprocessor.

microprogramme [mikrɔprɔgram] *nm* IN-FORM firmware.

microscope [mikrɔskɔp] *nm* microscope; **~ électronique** electron microscope.

microscopique [mikrɔskɔpik] *adj* microscopic.

microsillon [mikrɔsijɔ̃] *nm* LP, long-playing record.

MIDEM, Midem [midɛm] (*abr de* **Marché international du disque et de l'édition musicale**) *nm music industry trade fair*.

midi [midi] *nm* **-1.** [période du déjeuner] lunchtime. **-2.** [heure] midday, noon; **chercher ~ à quatorze heures** to look for complications. **-3.** [sud] south.
◆ **Midi** *nm*: **le Midi** the South of France.

midinette [midinɛt] *nf péj* empty-headed girl.

mie [mi] *nf* **-1.** [de pain] soft part, inside. **-2.** *vieilli* [bien-aimée]: **ma ~** sweetheart.

miel [mjɛl] *nm* honey.

mielleux, -euse [mjɛlø, øz] *adj* [personne] unctuous; [paroles, air] honeyed.

mien [mjɛ̃]
◆ **le mien** (*f* **la mienne** [lamjɛn], *mpl* **les miens** [lemjɛ̃], *fpl* **les miennes** [lemjɛn]) *pron poss* mine; **les ~s** my family; **j'y mets du ~** I put in a lot of effort.

miette [mjɛt] *nf* **-1.** [de pain] crumb, bread-

crumb. **-2.** (*gén pl*) [débris] shreds (*pl*); **en ~s** in bits OU pieces.

mieux [mjø] ◇ *adv* **-1.** [comparatif]: **~ (que)** better (than); **il travaille ~** he's working better; **il pourrait ~ faire** he could do better; **il va ~** he's better; **faire ~ de faire qqch** to do better to do sthg; **vous feriez ~ de vous taire** you would do better to keep quiet, you would be well-advised to keep quiet; **~ je le comprends, plus/moins j'ai envie de le lire** the better I understand it, the more/less I want to read it. **-2.** [superlatif] best; **il est le ~ payé du service** he's the best OU highest paid member of the department; **le ~ qu'il peut** as best he can. ◇ *adj* better.
◇ *nm* **-1.** (*sans déterminant*): **j'espérais ~** I was hoping for something better; **faute de ~** for lack of anything better. **-2.** (*avec déterminant*) best; **il y a un OU du ~** there's been an improvement; **faire de son ~** to do one's best.
◆ **au mieux** *loc adv* at best.
◆ **des mieux** *loc adv*: **un appareil des ~ conçus** one of the best-designed devices.
◆ **pour le mieux** *loc adv* for the best.
◆ **on ne peut mieux** *loc adv*: **c'est on ne peut ~** it couldn't be better.
◆ **de mieux en mieux** *loc adv* better and better.
◆ **à qui mieux mieux** *loc adv*: **on criait à qui ~ ~** it was a case of who could shout (the) loudest.

mieux-être [mjøzɛtr] *nm inv* improvement.

mièvre [mjɛvr] *adj* insipid.

mièvrerie [mjɛvrəri] *nf* insipidness.

mignon, -onne [miɲɔ̃, ɔn] ◇ *adj* **-1.** [charmant] sweet, cute. **-2.** [gentil] nice. ◇ *nm, f* darling, sweetheart.
◆ **mignon** *nm vieilli* favorite *Am*, favourite *Br*.

migraine [migrɛn] *nf* headache; MÉD migraine.

migrant, -e [migrɑ̃, ɑ̃t] ◇ *adj* migrant (*avant n*). ◇ *nm, f* migrant.

migrateur, -trice [migratœr, tris] *adj* migratory.
◆ **migrateur** *nm* migratory bird.

migration [migrasjɔ̃] *nf* migration.

mijaurée [miʒore] *nf* affected woman; **faire la ~** to put on airs.

mijoter [miʒɔte] [3] ◇ *vt* **-1.** CULIN to simmer. **-2.** *fam* [tramer] to cook up. ◇ *vi* CULIN to simmer.

mi-journée [miʒurne] *nf*: **les informations de la ~** the lunchtime news.

mil¹ [mij] *nm* millet.

mil² *adj* = **mille**.

milan [milɑ̃] *nm* kite (*bird*).

mildiou [mildju] *nm* mildew.

milice [milis] *nf* militia.

milicien, -ienne [milisjɛ̃, jɛn] *nm, f* militiaman (*f* militiawoman).

milieu, -x [miljø] *nm* **-1.** [centre] middle; **au ~ de** [au centre de] in the middle of; [parmi] among, surrounded by; **au beau** OU **en plein ~ de qqch** right in the middle of sthg. **-2.** [stade intermédiaire] middle course; **juste ~** happy medium. **-3.** BIOL & SOCIOL environment; **~ familial** family background; **dans les ~x autorisés** in official circles. **-4.** [pègre]: **le ~** the underworld. **-5.** FOOTBALL: **~ de terrain** midfielder.

militaire [militɛr] ◇ *nm* soldier; **~ de carrière** professional soldier. ◇ *adj* military.

militant, -e [militɑ̃, ɑ̃t] *adj & nm, f* militant.

militantisme [militɑ̃tism] *nm* militancy.

militariste [militarist] ◇ *nmf* militarist. ◇ *adj* militaristic.

militer [milite] [3] *vi* to be active; **~ pour** to militate in favor *Am* OU favour *Br* of; **~ contre** to militate against.

milk-shake [milkʃɛk] (*pl* **milk-shakes**) *nm* milk shake.

mille, mil [mil] ◇ *nm inv* **-1.** [unité] a OU one thousand. **-2.** [de cible] bull's-eye; **dans le ~** on target. **-3.** NAVIG: **~ marin** nautical mile. **-4.** *Can* [distance] mile. **-5.** *loc*: **des ~ et des cents** *fam* pots OU loads of money. ◇ *adj inv* thousand; **c'est ~ fois trop** it's far too much; **je lui ai dit ~ fois** I've told him/her a thousand times; *voir aussi* **six.**

mille-feuille [milfœj] (*pl* **mille-feuilles**) *nm* ≃ napoleon *Am*, ≃ vanilla slice *Br*.

millénaire [milenɛr] ◇ *nm* millennium, thousand years (*pl*). ◇ *adj* thousand-year-old (*avant n*).

mille-pattes [milpat] *nm inv* centipede, millipede.

millésime [milezim] *nm* **-1.** [de pièce] date. **-2.** [de vin] vintage, year.

millésimé, -e [milezime] *adj* [vin] vintage (*avant n*).

millet [mije] *nm* millet.

milliard [miljar] *nm* billion *Am*, thousand million *Br*; **par ~s** *fig* in (their) millions.

milliardaire [miljardɛr] *nmf* billionaire *Am*, multimillionaire *Br*.

millième [miljɛm] *adj, nm & nmf* thousandth; *voir aussi* **sixième.**

millier [milje] *nm* thousand; **un ~ de francs/personnes** about a thousand francs/people; **des ~s de** thousands of; **par ~s** in (their) thousands.

milligramme [miligram] *nm* milligram, milligramme.

millilitre [mililitr] *nm* milliliter *Am*, millilitre *Br*.

millimètre [milimɛtr] *nm* millimeter *Am*, millimetre *Br*.

millimétrique [milimetrik] *adj*: **papier ~** graph paper.

million [miljɔ̃] *nm* million; **un ~ de francs** a million francs.

millionième [miljɔnjɛm] *adj, nm & nmf* millionth.

millionnaire [miljɔnɛr] *nmf* millionaire.

mime [mim] ◇ *nm* mime. ◇ *nmf* mime (artist).

mimer [mime] [3] *vt* **-1.** [exprimer sans parler] to mime. **-2.** [imiter] to mimic.

mimétisme [mimetism] *nm* mimicry.

mimique [mimik] *nf* **-1.** [grimace] face. **-2.** [geste] sign language (*U*).

mimosa [mimɔza] *nm* mimosa.

min (*abr de* **minute**) min.

min. (*abr de* **minimum**) min.

MIN (*abr de* **marché d'intérêt national**) *nm wholesale market for agricultural produce.*

minable [minabl] *adj fam* **-1.** [misérable] seedy, shabby. **-2.** [médiocre] pathetic.

minaret [minarɛ] *nm* minaret.

minauder [minode] [3] *vi* to simper.

mince [mɛ̃s] ◇ *adj* **-1.** [maigre - gén] thin; [- personne, taille] slender, slim. **-2.** *fig* [faible] small, meager *Am*, meagre *Br*. ◇ *interj fam*: **~ alors!** drat!

minceur [mɛ̃sœr] *nf* **-1.** [gén] thinness; [de personne] slenderness, slimness. **-2.** *fig* [insuffisance] meagerness *Am*, meagreness *Br*.

mincir [mɛ̃sir] [32] *vi* to get thinner OU slimmer.

mine [min] *nf* **-1.** [expression] look; **avoir bonne/mauvaise ~** to look well/ill; **avoir une ~ de déterré** *fam* to look like death warmed up; **faire grise ~** to look annoyed. **-2.** [apparence] appearance; **faire ~ de faire qqch** to make as if to do sthg; [faire semblant] to pretend to do sthg; **~ de rien, il est très costaud** *fam* he's very strong, though he doesn't look it; **ne pas payer de ~** to be not much to look at. **-3.** [gisement & *fig*] mine; [exploitation] mining; **~ de charbon** coalmine. **-4.** [explosif] mine. **-5.** [de crayon] lead.

miner [mine] [3] *vt* **-1.** MIL to mine. **-2.** [ronger] to undermine; *fig* to wear down.

◆ **se miner** *vp* to worry o.s. sick.

minerai [minrɛ] *nm* ore.

minéral, -e, -aux [mineral, o] *adj* **-1.** CHIM inorganic. **-2.** [eau, source] mineral (*avant n*).
◆ **minéral** *nm* mineral.

minéralisé, -e [mineralize] *adj* mineralized.

minéralogie [mineralɔʒi] *nf* mineralogy.

minéralogique [mineralɔʒik] *adj* **-1.** AUTOM: numéro ~ license number *Am*, registration number *Br*; plaque ~ license plate *Am*, numberplate *Br*. **-2.** GÉOL mineralogical.

minet, -ette [minɛ, ɛt] *nm, f fam* **-1.** [chat] pussycat, pussy. **-2.** [personne] trendy.

mineur, -e [minœr] ◇ *adj* minor. ◇ *nm, f* JUR minor.
◆ **mineur** *nm* [ouvrier] miner; ~ **de fond** face worker.

mini *abr de* minimum.

miniature [minjatyr] ◇ *nf* miniature; **en** ~ in miniature. ◇ *adj* miniature.

miniaturiser [minjatyrize] [3] *vt* to miniaturize.

minibus [minibys] *nm* minibus.

minichaîne [miniʃɛn] *nf* portable hi-fi.

minier, -ière [minje, jɛr] *adj* mining (*avant n*).

minijupe [miniʒyp] *nf* miniskirt.

minimal, -e, -aux [minimal, o] *adj* minimum.

minimalisme [minimalism] *nm* minimalism.

minime [minim] ◇ *nmf* SPORT ≃ junior. ◇ *adj* minimal.

minimiser [minimize] [3] *vt* to minimize.

minimum [minimɔm] (*pl* **minimums** OU **minima** [minima]) ◇ *nm* **-1.** [gén & MATHS] minimum; **au** ~ at least; **le strict** ~ the bare minimum; **le** ~ **vital** a living wage. **-2.** JUR minimum penalty. ◇ *adj* minimum.

mini-ordinateur [miniɔrdinatœr] (*pl* **mini-ordinateurs**) *nm* minicomputer.

ministère [ministɛr] *nm* **-1.** [département] department, ministry *Br*. **-2.** [cabinet] government. **-3.** RELIG ministry.
◆ **ministère public** *nm* ≃ District Attorney's office *Am*, ≃ Crown Prosecution Service *Br*.

ministériel, -ielle [ministerjɛl] *adj* **-1.** [du ministère] departmental, ministerial *Br*. **-2.** [pro-gouvernemental] pro-government.

ministre [ministr] *nm* secretary, minister *Br*; ~ **délégué à** secretary for, minister of *Br*; ~ **des Affaires étrangères** ≃ Secretary of State *Am*, ≃ Foreign Secretary *Br*; ~ **des Affaires sociales** ≃ Social Services Secretary; ~ **de l'Éducation nationale** ≃ Education Secretary; ~ **d'État** secretary of state, cabinet minister *Br*; ~ **des Finances** ≃ Secretary of the Treasury *Am*, ≃ Chancellor of the Exchequer *Br*; ~ **de l'Intérieur** ≃ Secretary of the Interior *Am*, ≃ Home Secretary *Br*; ~ **de la Santé** ≃ Health Secretary; **premier** ~ prime minister.

Minitel® [minitɛl] *nm French teletext system.*

MINITEL®:

The domestic viewdata service run by France Télécom has become a familiar part of French life. The basic monitor and keyboard are given free of charge, and the subscriber is charged for the services used on his or her ordinary telephone bill. The subscriber dials a four-figure number (typically 3615); a code word then gives access to the particular service required. Some Minitel® services are purely informative (the weather, road conditions, news etc); others are interactive (enabling users to carry out bank transactions, book tickets for travel or, on the 'Minitel Rose', to look for companionship, for example). The Minitel® also serves as an electronic telephone directory.

---

minitéliste [minitelist] *nmf* Minitel® user.

minois [minwa] *nm* sweet (little) face.

minorer [minɔre] [3] *vt* to reduce.

minoritaire [minɔritɛr] ◇ *nmf* member of a minority. ◇ *adj* minority (*avant n*); **être** ~ to be in the minority.

minorité [minɔrite] *nf* minority; **en** ~ in the minority; ~ **ethnique** ethnic minority.

Minorque [minɔrk] *n* Minorca; **à** ~ in Minorca.

minorquin, -e [minɔrkɛ̃, in] *adj* Minorcan.
◆ **Minorquin, -e** *nm, f* Minorcan.

minoterie [minɔtri] *nf* **-1.** [moulin] flourmill. **-2.** [industrie] (flour) milling industry.

minuit [minɥi] *nm* midnight.

minuscule [minyskyl] ◇ *nf* [lettre] small letter; **en** ~**s** in small letters. ◇ *adj* **-1.** [lettre] small. **-2.** [très petit] tiny, minuscule.

minutage [minytaʒ] *nm* (precise) timing.

minute [minyt] ◇ *nf* minute; **à la** ~ at once; **dans une** ~ in a minute; **d'une** ~ **à l'autre** in next to no time. ◇ *interj fam* hang on (a minute)!

minuter [minyte] [3] *vt* **-1.** [chronométrer] to time (precisely). **-2.** JUR to draw up.

minuterie [minytri] *nf* [d'éclairage] time switch, timer.

minuteur [minytœr] *nm* timer.

minutie [minysi] *nf* [soin] meticulousness; [précision] attention to detail; **avec** ~ [avec soin] meticulously; [dans le détail] in minute detail.

minutieusement [minysjøzmɑ̃] *adv* [avec soin] meticulously; [dans le détail] minutely, in minute detail.

minutieux, -ieuse [minysjø, jøz] *adj* [méticuleux] meticulous; [détaillé] minutely detailed; **un travail** ~ a job requiring great attention to detail.

mioche [mjɔʃ] *nmf fam* kiddy.

mirabelle [mirabɛl] *nf* **-1.** [fruit] mirabelle (plum). **-2.** [alcool] plum brandy.

miracle [mirakl] *nm* miracle; **par** ~ by some OU a miracle, miraculously; **croire aux** ~**s** to believe in miracles.

miraculé, -e [mirakyle] ◇ *adj* lucky to be alive. ◇ *nm, f person who is lucky to be alive.*

miraculeusement [mirakyløzmɑ̃] *adv* miraculously.

miraculeux, -euse [mirakylø, øz] *adj* miraculous.

mirador [miradɔr] *nm* MIL watchtower.

mirage [miraʒ] *nm* mirage.

mire [mir] *nf* **-1.** TÉLÉ test card. **-2.** [visée]: **ligne de** ~ line of sight.

mirer [mire] [3] *vt* **-1.** [œuf] to candle. **-2.** *littéraire* [refléter] to reflect.

◆ **se mirer** *vp littéraire* **-1.** [se regarder] to gaze at o.s. **-2.** [se refléter] to be reflected OU mirrored.

mirifique [mirifik] *adj* fabulous.

mirobolant, -e [mirɔbɔlɑ̃, ɑ̃t] *adj* fabulous, fantastic.

miroir [mirwar] *nm* mirror; ~ **aux alouettes** *fig* lure; ~ **de poche** handbag mirror.

miroiter [mirwate] [3] *vi* to sparkle, to gleam; **faire** ~ **qqch à qqn** to hold out the prospect of sthg to sb.

miroiterie [mirwatri] *nf* **-1.** [industrie] mirror manufacturing. **-2.** [atelier] mirror workshop.

miroton [mirɔtɔ̃] *nm boiled beef in an onion sauce.*

mis, mise [mi, miz] *pp* → **mettre**.

misaine [mizɛn] *nf* foresail.

misanthrope [mizɑ̃trɔp] ◇ *nmf* misanthropist, misanthrope. ◇ *adj* misanthropic.

mise [miz] *nf* **-1.** [action] putting; ~ **en demeure** formal notice; ~ **à jour** updating; ~ **en liberté provisoire** JUR freeing on bail; ~ **en page** making up, composing; ~ **en plis** [coiffure] set; ~ **au point** PHOT focusing; TECHNOL adjustment; *fig* clarification; ~ **en scène** production; ~ **en service** putting into operation. **-2.** [d'argent] stake; **sauver la** ~ **à qqn** *fig* to get sb out of a tight corner; ~ **de fonds** capital investment. **-3.** [tenue]

clothing. **-4.** *loc*: **ne pas être de** ~ to be unacceptable.

miser [mize] [3] ◇ *vt* to bet. ◇ *vi*: ~ **sur** to bet on; *fig* to count on.

misérabilisme [mizerabilism] *nm* realism.

misérable [mizerabl] ◇ *nmf* **-1.** [pauvre] poor person. **-2.** [coquin] wretch. ◇ *adj* **-1.** [pauvre] poor, wretched. **-2.** [déplorable] pitiful. **-3.** [sans valeur] paltry, miserable.

misérablement [mizerabləmɑ̃] *adv* **-1.** [pauvrement] in poverty, wretchedly. **-2.** [pitoyablement] miserably.

misère [mizɛr] *nf* **-1.** [indigence] poverty; ~ **noire** utter destitution. **-2.** [infortune] misery. **-3.** *fig* [bagatelle] trifle.

◆ **misères** *nfpl* [ennuis] woes (*pl*), miseries (*pl*); **faire des** ~**s à qqn** *fam* to put sb through it.

miséreux, -euse [mizerø, øz] ◇ *adj* poverty-stricken. ◇ *nm, f* down-and-out.

miséricorde [mizerikɔrd] ◇ *nf* [clémence] mercy. ◇ *interj* mercy (me)!

miséricordieux, -ieuse [mizerikɔrdjø, jøz] *adj* merciful.

misogyne [mizɔʒin] ◇ *nmf* misogynist. ◇ *adj* misogynous.

misogynie [mizɔʒini] *nf* misogyny.

missel [misɛl] *nm* missal.

missile [misil] *nm* missile; ~ **balistique** ballistic missile.

mission [misjɔ̃] *nf* mission; **en** ~ on a mission.

missionnaire [misjɔnɛr] ◇ *nmf* missionary. ◇ *adj* missionary (*avant n*).

missive [misiv] *nf* letter.

mistral [mistral] *nm* mistral.

mitaine [mitɛn] *nf* fingerless glove.

mite [mit] *nf* (clothes) moth.

mité, -e [mite] *adj* moth-eaten.

mi-temps [mitɑ̃] ◇ *nf inv* [SPORT - période] half; [- pause] half-time; **à la** ~ at half-time; **première/seconde** ~ first/second half. ◇ *nm* part-time work.

◆ **à mi-temps** *loc adj & loc adv* part-time.

miteux, -euse [mitø, øz] *fam* ◇ *adj* seedy, dingy. ◇ *nm, f* shabby person.

mitigé, -e [mitiʒe] *adj* **-1.** [tempéré] lukewarm. **-2.** *fam* [mélangé] mixed.

mitonner [mitɔne] [3] ◇ *vt* **-1.** [faire cuire] to simmer. **-2.** [préparer avec soin] to prepare lovingly. **-3.** *fig* [affaire] to plot, to cook up. ◇ *vi* CULIN to simmer.

◆ **se mitonner** *vp*: **se** ~ **qqch** to cook sthg up for o.s.

mitoyen, -enne [mitwajɛ̃, ɛn] *adj* party (*avant n*), common.

mitrailler [mitraje] [3] *vt* **-1.** MIL to machinegun. **-2.** *fam* [photographier] to click away at. **-3.** *fig* [assaillir]: ~ **qqn (de)** to bombard sb (with).

mitraillette [mitrajɛt] *nf* submachine gun.

mitrailleur [mitrajœr] *nm* machinegunner.

mitrailleuse [mitrajøz] *nf* machinegun.

mitre [mitr] *nf* **-1.** [d'évêque] miter *Am*, mitre *Br*. **-2.** [de cheminée] cowl.

mi-voix [mivwa]
♦ **à mi-voix** *loc adv* in a low voice.

mixage [miksaʒ] *nm* CIN & RADIO (sound) mixing.

mixer[1], **mixeur** [miksœr] *nm* (food) mixer.

mixer[2] [mikse] [3] *vt* to mix.

mixité [miksite] *nf* coeducation.

mixte [mikst] *adj* mixed.

mixture [mikstyr] *nf* **-1.** CHIM & CULIN mixture. **-2.** *péj* [mélange] concoction.

MJC (*abr de* **maison des jeunes et de la culture**) *nf youth and cultural centre*.

ml (*abr de* **millilitre**) ml.

MLF (*abr de* **Mouvement de libération de la femme**) *nm women's movement*, ≃ NOW *Am*.

Mlle (*abr de* **Mademoiselle**) Miss.

mm (*abr de* **millimètre**) mm.

MM (*abr de* **Messieurs**) Messrs.

Mme (*abr de* **Madame**) Mrs.

mn (*abr de* **minute**) min.

mnémotechnique [mnemotɛknik] *adj* mnemonic.

MNS (*abr de* **maître nageur sauveteur**) *nm* lifeguard.

Mo (*abr de* **méga-octet**) Mb.

mobile [mɔbil] ◇ *nm* **-1.** [objet] mobile. **-2.** [motivation] motive. ◇ *adj* **-1.** [gén] movable, mobile; [partie, pièce] moving. **-2.** [population, main-d'œuvre] mobile. **-3.** [fête] movable; [échelle] sliding.

mobilier, -ière [mɔbilje, jɛr] *adj* JUR movable.
♦ **mobilier** *nm* furniture.

mobilisation [mɔbilizasjɔ̃] *nf* mobilization; ~ **générale** MIL general mobilization.

mobiliser [mɔbilize] [3] *vt* **-1.** [gén] to mobilize. **-2.** [moralement] to rally.
♦ **se mobiliser** *vp* to mobilize, to rally.

mobilité [mɔbilite] *nf* mobility.

Mobylette® [mɔbilɛt] *nf* moped.

mocassin [mɔkasɛ̃] *nm* moccasin.

moche [mɔʃ] *adj fam* **-1.** [laid] ugly. **-2.** [triste, méprisable] lousy, rotten.

modalité [mɔdalite] *nf* **-1.** [convention] form;

~s **de paiement** methods of payment. **-2.** JUR clause.

mode [mɔd] ◇ *nf* **-1.** [gén] fashion; **à la** ~ in fashion, fashionable; **lancer une** ~ to start'a fashion; **lancer la** ~ **de qqch** to start the fashion for sthg; **passé de** ~ out of fashion. **-2.** [coutume] custom, style; **à la** ~ **de** in the style of. ◇ *nm* **-1.** [manière] mode, form; ~ **de vie** way of life. **-2.** [méthode] method; ~ **d'emploi** instructions (for use). **-3.** GRAM mood. **-4.** MUS mode.

modelage [mɔdlaʒ] *nm* [action] modelling.

modelé [mɔdle] *nm* **-1.** [de visage] contours (*pl*). **-2.** ART & GÉOGR relief.

modèle [mɔdɛl] *nm* **-1.** [gén] model; **sur le** ~ **de** on the model of; ~ **déposé** patented design; ~ **réduit** scale model. **-2.** (*en apposition*) [exemplaire] model (*avant n*).

modeler [mɔdle] [25] *vt* to shape; ~ **qqch sur qqch** *fig* to model sthg on sthg.
♦ **se modeler** *vp littéraire*: **se** ~ **sur** *fig* to model o.s. on.

modélisme [mɔdelism] *nm* modelling (*of scale models*).

modem [mɔdɛm] *nm* modem; ~ **d'appel** dial-in modem; ~ **fax** fax modem.

modérateur, -trice [mɔderatœr, tris] *adj* moderating.
♦ **modérateur** *nm* **-1.** [personne] moderator. **-2.** [mécanisme] regulator.

modération [mɔderasjɔ̃] *nf* moderation.

modéré, -e [mɔdere] *adj & nm, f* moderate.

modérément [mɔderemɑ̃] *adv* in moderation, moderately.

modérer [mɔdere] [18] *vt* to moderate.
♦ **se modérer** *vp* to restrain o.s., to control o.s.

moderne [mɔdɛrn] ◇ *nm*: **le** ~ modern things (*pl*), (the) modern style. ◇ *adj* modern; [mathématiques] new.

modernisation [mɔdɛrnizasjɔ̃] *nf* modernization.

moderniser [mɔdɛrnize] [3] *vt* to modernize.
♦ **se moderniser** *vp* to become (more) modern.

modernisme [mɔdɛrnism] *nm* [style] modernism.

modernité [mɔdɛrnite] *nf* modernity.

modeste [mɔdɛst] *adj* modest; [origine] humble.

modestement [mɔdɛstəmɑ̃] *adv* modestly.

modestie [mɔdɛsti] *nf* modesty; **fausse** ~ false modesty.

modicité [mɔdisite] *nf* [de prix, salaire] lowness, moderateness.

modifiable [mɔdifjabl] *adj* modifiable, alterable.

modification [mɔdifikasjɔ̃] *nf* alteration, modification.

modifier [mɔdifje] [9] *vt* to alter, to modify.
◆ **se modifier** *vp* to alter.

modique [mɔdik] *adj* modest.

modiste [mɔdist] *nf* milliner.

modulation [mɔdylasjɔ̃] *nf* modulation.

module [mɔdyl] *nm* module.

moduler [mɔdyle] [3] *vt* **-1.** [air] to warble. **-2.** [structure] to adjust. **-3.** RADIO to modulate.

modus vivendi [mɔdysvivɛ̃di] *nm inv* modus vivendi.

moelle [mwal] *nf* ANAT marrow; ~ **osseuse** bone marrow; **jusqu'à la** ~ *fig* to the core.
◆ **moelle épinière** *nf* spinal cord.

moelleux, -euse [mwalø, øz] *adj* **-1.** [canapé, tapis] soft. **-2.** [fromage, vin] mellow.

moellon [mwalɔ̃] *nm* rubble stone.

mœurs [mœr(s)] *nfpl* **-1.** [morale] morals. **-2.** [coutumes] customs, habits. **-3.** ZOOL behavior (*U*) *Am*, behaviour (*U*) *Br*.

mohair [mɔɛr] *nm* mohair.

moi [mwa] ◇ *pron pers* **-1.** [objet, après préposition, comparatif] me; **aide-**~ help me; **il me l'a dit, à** ~ he told ME; **c'est pour** ~ it's for me; **plus âgé que** ~ older than me OU than I (am). **-2.** [sujet] I; ~ **non plus, je n'en sais rien** I don't know anything about it either; **qui est là? - (c'est)** ~ who's there? - it's me; **je l'ai vu hier -** ~ **aussi** I saw him yesterday - me too; **c'est** ~ **qui lui ai dit de venir** I was the one who told him to come; ~, **je n'ai rien dit!** I didn't say anything! ◇ *nm:* **le** ~ the ego, the self.
◆ **moi-même** *pron pers* myself.

moignon [mwaɲɔ̃] *nm* stump.

moindre [mwɛ̃dr] ◇ *adj superl:* **le/la** ~ the least; *(avec négation)* the least OU slightest; **les** ~**s détails** the smallest details; **sans la** ~ **difficulté** without the slightest problem; **c'est la** ~ **des choses** it's the least I/you *etc* could do. ◇ *adj compar* less; [prix] lower; **à un** ~ **degré** to a lesser extent.

moine [mwan] *nm* monk.

moineau, -x [mwano] *nm* sparrow.

moins [mwɛ̃] ◇ *adv* **-1.** [quantité] less; ~ **de** less (than); ~ **de lait** less milk; ~ **de gens** fewer people; ~ **de dix** less than ten; **il est un peu** ~ **de 10 heures** it's nearly 10 o'clock. **-2.** [comparatif]: ~ **(que)** less (than); **il est** ~ **vieux que ton frère** he's not as old as your brother, he's younger than your

brother; **il vient** ~ **souvent que Pierre** he doesn't come as often as Pierre, he comes less often than Pierre; **bien** ~ **grand que** much smaller than; ~ **il mange,** ~ **il travaille** the less he eats, the less he works. **-3.** [superlatif]: **le** ~ (the) least; **le** ~ **riche des hommes** the poorest man; **il est le** ~ **fort** he's the least strong, he's the weakest; **c'est lui qui vient le** ~ **souvent** he comes (the) least often; **c'est lui qui travaille le** ~ he works (the) least; **le** ~ **possible** as little as possible; **pas le** ~ **du monde** not in the least.
◇ *prép* **-1.** [gén] minus; **dix** ~ **huit font deux** ten minus eight is two, ten take away eight is two; **il fait** ~ **vingt** it's twenty below, it's minus twenty. **-2.** [servant à indiquer l'heure]: **il est 3 heures** ~ **le quart** it's quarter to 3; **il est** ~ **dix** it's ten to.
◇ *nm* **-1.** [signe] minus (sign). **-2.** *loc:* **le** ~ **qu'on puisse dire, c'est que ...** it's an understatement to say ....
◆ **à moins de** *loc prép:* **à** ~ **de battre le record** unless I/you beat the record.
◆ **à moins que** *loc conj* (+ *subjonctif*) unless.
◆ **au moins** *loc adv* at least.
◆ **de moins en moins** *loc adv* less and less.
◆ **du moins** *loc adv* at least.
◆ **en moins** *loc adv:* **il a une dent en** ~ he's missing OU minus a tooth; **c'était le paradis, les anges en** ~ it was heaven, minus the angels.
◆ **en moins de** *loc prép* in less than; **en** ~ **de rien** in less than no time.
◆ **on ne peut moins** *loc adv* far from.
◆ **pour le moins** *loc adv* at (the very) least.
◆ **tout au moins** *loc adv* at (the very) least.

moins-value [mwɛ̃valy] (*pl* **moins-values**) *nf* capital loss.

moire [mwar] *nf* [étoffe] moiré.

moiré, -e [mware] *adj* **-1.** [tissu] watered. **-2.** *littéraire* [reflet] shimmering.

mois [mwa] *nm* **-1.** [laps de temps] month. **-2.** [salaire] (monthly) salary; **le treizième** ~ extra month's salary. **-3.** *fam* [loyer] month's rent.

moïse [mɔiz] *nm* wicker cradle.

moisi, -e [mwazi] *adj* moldy *Am*, mouldy *Br*.
◆ **moisi** *nm* mold *Am*, mould *Br*.

moisir [mwazir] [32] *vi* **-1.** [pourrir] to go moldy *Am* OU mouldy *Br*. **-2.** *fig* [personne] to rot.

moisissure [mwazisyr] *nf* mold *Am*, mould *Br*.

moisson [mwasɔ̃] *nf* **-1.** [récolte] harvest; **faire la ~** OU **les ~s** to harvest, to bring in the harvest. **-2.** *fig* [d'idées, de projets] wealth.

moissonner [mwasɔne] [3] *vt* to harvest, to gather (in); *fig* to collect, to gather.

moissonneur, -euse [mwasɔnœr, øz] *nm, f* [personne] harvester.
◆ **moissonneuse** *nf* [machine] harvester.

moissonneuse-batteuse [mwasɔnøzbatøz] (*pl* **moissonneuses-batteuses**) *nf* combine (harvester).

moite [mwat] *adj* [peau, mains] moist, sweaty; [atmosphère] muggy.

moiteur [mwatœr] *nf* [de peau, mains] moistness; [d'atmosphère] mugginess.

moitié [mwatje] *nf* **-1.** [gén] half; **à ~ vide** half-empty; **faire qqch à ~** to half-do sthg; **la ~ du temps** half the time; **à la ~ de qqch** halfway through sthg; **faire ~-~** to go halves. **-2.** [épouse, époux]: **ma/ta ~** *fam hum* my/your better half.

moka [mɔka] *nm* **-1.** [café] mocha (coffee). **-2.** [gâteau] coffee cake.

mol → **mou**.

molaire [mɔlɛr] *nf* molar.

Moldavie [mɔldavi] *nf*: **la ~** Moldavia.

mole [mɔl] *nf* CHIM mole.

môle [mol] *nm* [quai] jetty.

moléculaire [mɔlekyler] *adj* molecular.

molécule [mɔlekyl] *nf* molecule.

moleskine [mɔlɛskin] *nf* imitation leather.

molester [mɔlɛste] [3] *vt* to manhandle.

molette [mɔlɛt] *nf* **-1.** [de réglage] knurled wheel. **-2.** [outil] glasscutter.

mollasse [mɔlas] *adj fam* **-1.** [mou] flabby. **-2.** *fig* [personne] lethargic.

mollasson, -onne [mɔlasɔ̃, ɔn] *nm, f fam* (lazy) lump.

molle → **mou**.

mollement [mɔlmɑ̃] *adv* **-1.** [faiblement] weakly, feebly. **-2.** *littéraire* [paresseusement] sluggishly, lethargically.

mollesse [mɔlɛs] *nf* **-1.** [de chose] softness. **-2.** [de personne] lethargy.

mollet [mɔlɛ] ◇ *nm* calf. ◇ *adj* → **œuf**.

molletière [mɔltjɛr] *adj*: **bande ~** puttee.

molleton [mɔltɔ̃] *nm* flannelette; [pour table] felt.

mollir [mɔlir] [32] *vi* **-1.** [physiquement, moralement] to give way. **-2.** [matière] to soften, to go soft. **-3.** [vent] to drop, to die down.

mollo [mɔlo] *adv fam* easy; **y aller ~** to go easy, to take it easy.

mollusque [mɔlysk] *nm* **-1.** ZOOL mollusc. **-2.** *fam fig* [personne] (lazy) lump.

molosse [mɔlɔs] *nm* **-1.** [chien] *large ferocious dog*. **-2.** *fig* & *péj* [personne] hulking great brute OU fellow.

môme [mom] *fam* ◇ *nmf* [enfant] kid, youngster. ◇ *nf* [jeune fille] chick, bird *Br*.

moment [mɔmɑ̃] *nm* **-1.** [gén] moment; **au ~ de l'accident** at the time of the accident, when the accident happened; **au ~ de partir** just as we/you *etc* were leaving; **au ~ où** just as; **dans un ~** in a moment; **d'un ~ à l'autre** (at) any moment, any moment now; **ne pas avoir un ~ à soi** not to have a moment to oneself; **à un ~ donné** at a given moment; **par ~s** at times, now and then; **sur le ~** at the time; **à tout ~** (at) any moment, any moment now; **en ce ~** at the moment; **pour le ~** for the moment. **-2.** [durée] (short) time; **avoir de bons ~s avec qqn** to have (some) good times with sb; **passer un mauvais ~** to have a bad time. **-3.** [occasion] time; **ce n'est pas le ~ (de faire qqch)** this is not the time (to do sthg); **c'est le ~ ou jamais** it's now or never.
◆ **du moment que** *loc prép* since, as.

momentané, -e [mɔmɑ̃tane] *adj* temporary.

momentanément [mɔmɑ̃tanemɑ̃] *adv* temporarily.

momie [mɔmi] *nf* mummy.

mon [mɔ̃] (*f* **ma** [ma], *pl* **mes** [me]) *adj poss* my.

monacal, -e, -aux [mɔnakal, o] *adj* monastic.

Monaco [mɔnako] *n*: **(la principauté de) ~** (the principality of) Monaco.

monarchie [mɔnarʃi] *nf* monarchy; **~ absolue/constitutionnelle** absolute/constitutional monarchy.

monarchique [mɔnarʃik] *adj* monarchical.

monarchiste [mɔnarʃist] *nmf & adj* monarchist.

monarque [mɔnark] *nm* monarch.

monastère [mɔnastɛr] *nm* monastery.

monastique [mɔnastik] *adj* monastic.

monceau, -x [mɔ̃so] *nm* **-1.** [tas] heap. **-2.** *fig* [de fautes, de bêtises] mass.

mondain, -e [mɔ̃dɛ̃, ɛn] ◇ *adj* **-1.** [chronique, journaliste] society (*avant n*). **-2.** *péj* [futile] frivolous, superficial. ◇ *nm, f* socialite.

mondanités [mɔ̃danite] *nfpl* **-1.** [événements] society life (*U*). **-2.** [paroles] small talk (*U*); [comportements] formalities.

monde [mɔ̃d] *nm* **-1.** [gén] world; **le/la plus ... au ~, le/la plus ... du ~** the most ... in

the world; **pour rien au** ~ not for the world, not for all the tea in China; **mettre un enfant au** ~ to bring a child into the world; **venir au** ~ to come into the world; **en ce bas** ~ RELIG in this world; **l'autre** ~ RELIG the other world; **le quart** ~ the Fourth World. **-2.** [gens] people (*pl*); **beaucoup/peu de** ~ a lot of/not many people; **tout le** ~ everyone, everybody. **-3.** *loc:* **c'est un** ~! that's really the limit!; **se faire un** ~ **de qqch** to make too much of sthg; **se moquer du** ~ to have a nerve; **noir de** ~ packed with people; **tromper son** ~ not to be what one seems.
◆ **Monde** *nm:* **le Nouveau Monde** the New World.

mondial, -e, -iaux [mɔ̃djal, jo] *adj* world (*avant n*).

mondialement [mɔ̃djalmɑ̃] *adv* throughout OU all over the world.

monégasque [mɔnegask] *adj* of/from Monaco.
◆ **Monégasque** *nmf* native OU inhabitant of Monaco.

monétaire [mɔnetɛr] *adj* monetary.

monétarisme [mɔnetarism] *nm* monetarism.

mongol, -e [mɔ̃gɔl] *adj* Mongolian.
◆ **mongol** *nm* [langue] Mongolian.
◆ **Mongol, -e** *nm, f* Mongolian.

Mongolie [mɔ̃gɔli] *nf:* **la** ~ Mongolia; **la ~-Extérieure** Outer Mongolia; **la ~-Intérieure** Inner Mongolia.

mongolien, -ienne [mɔ̃gɔljɛ̃, jɛn] *vieilli* ◇ *adj* Mongol (*avant n*). ◇ *nm, f* Mongol.

mongolisme [mɔ̃gɔlism] *nm vieilli* Mongolism.

mongoloïde [mɔ̃gɔlɔid] *adj vieilli* Mongol (*avant n*).

moniteur, -trice [mɔnitœr, tris] *nm, f* **-1.** [enseignant] instructor, coach; ~ **d'auto-école** driving instructor; ~ **de ski** ski instructor. **-2.** [de colonie de vacances] supervisor, leader.
◆ **moniteur** *nm* [appareil & INFORM] monitor.

monnaie [mɔnɛ] *nf* **-1.** [moyen de paiement] money; **fausse** ~ forged currency, counterfeit money; ~ **d'échange** *fig* currency; **c'est** ~ **courante** *fig* it's commonplace, it's common practice. **-2.** [de pays] currency. **-3.** [pièces] change; **avoir de la** ~ to have change; **avoir la** ~ to have the change; **rendre la** ~ **à qqn** to give sb his/her change; **avoir la** ~ **de 100 francs** to have change of OU for 100 francs; **faire (de) la** ~

to get (some) change; **menue** ~ small OU loose change.

monnayable [mɔnejabl] *adj* convertible (into cash); *fig* valuable.

monnayer [mɔneje] [11] *vt* **-1.** [biens] to convert into cash. **-2.** *fig* [silence] to buy.

monnayeur [mɔnejœr] → **faux**.

monochrome [mɔnɔkrom] *adj* monochrome, monochromatic.

monocle [mɔnɔkl] *nm* monocle.

monocoque [mɔnɔkɔk] *nm & adj* [bateau] monohull.

monocorde [mɔnɔkɔrd] *adj* **-1.** MUS single-stringed. **-2.** [monotone] monotonous.

monoculture [mɔnɔkyltyr] *nf* monoculture.

monogame [mɔnɔgam] *adj* monogamous.

monogamie [mɔnɔgami] *nf* monogamy.

monogramme [mɔnɔgram] *nm* monogram.

monolingue [mɔnɔlɛ̃g] *adj* monolingual.

monolithique [mɔnɔlitik] *adj* monolithic.

monologue [mɔnɔlɔg] *nm* **-1.** THÉÂTRE soliloquy. **-2.** [discours individuel] monologue; ~ **intérieur** stream of consciousness.

monologuer [mɔnɔlɔge] [3] *vi* **-1.** THÉÂTRE to soliloquize. **-2.** *fig & péj* [parler] to talk away.

monôme [mɔnom] *nm* **-1.** MATHS monomial. **-2.** *arg scol* [procession] ≃ rag day procession.

mononucléose [mɔnɔnykleoz] *nf:* ~ **infectieuse** glandular fever.

monoparental, -e, -aux [mɔnɔparɑ̃tal, o] *adj* single-parent (*avant n*).

monophasé, -e [mɔnɔfaze] *adj* ÉLECTR single-phase.
◆ **monophasé** *nm* single-phase current.

monoplace [mɔnɔplas] ◇ *nm* single-seater (plane). ◇ *adj* single-seater (*avant n*).

monopole [mɔnɔpɔl] *nm* monopoly; **avoir le** ~ **de qqch** *litt & fig* to have a monopoly of OU on sthg; ~ **d'État** state monopoly.

monopoliser [mɔnɔpɔlize] [3] *vt* to monopolize.

monorail [mɔnɔraj] ◇ *nm* monorail. ◇ *adj inv* monorail (*avant n*).

monoski [mɔnɔski] *nm* **-1.** [objet] monoski. **-2.** SPORT monoskiing.

monosyllabe [mɔnɔsilab] ◇ *nm* monosyllable. ◇ *adj* monosyllabic.

monosyllabique [mɔnɔsilabik] *adj* monosyllabic.

monothéisme [mɔnɔteism] *nm* monotheism.

monotone [mɔnɔtɔn] *adj* monotonous.

monotonie [mɔnɔtɔni] *nf* monotony; **rompre la** ~ to break the monotony.

Monrovia [mɔ̃rɔvja] *n* Monrovia.

monseigneur [mɔ̃sɛɲœr] (*pl* **messeigneurs** [mɛsɛɲœr]) *nm* **-1.** [titre - d'évêque, de duc] His Grace; [- de cardinal] His Eminence; [- de prince] His (Royal) Highness. **-2.** [formule d'adresse - à évêque, à duc] Your Grace; [- à cardinal] Your Eminence; [- à prince] Your (Royal) Highness.

monsieur [məsjø] (*pl* **messieurs** [mesjø]) *nm* **-1.** [titre]: ~ **X** Mr X; **bonjour** ~ good morning; [dans hôtel, restaurant] good morning, sir; **bonjour messieurs** good morning (gentlemen); **Monsieur le Ministre n'est pas là** the Minister is out. **-2.** [homme quelconque] gentleman.

monstre [mɔ̃str] *nm* **-1.** [gén] monster; ~ **marin** sea monster; ~ **sacré** idol. **-2.** (*en apposition*) *fam* [énorme] colossal.

monstrueusement [mɔ̃stryøzmɑ̃] *adv* [gros, laid] monstrously; [intelligent] prodigiously.

monstrueux, -euse [mɔ̃stryø, øz] *adj* **-1.** [gén] monstrous. **-2.** *fig* [erreur] terrible.

monstruosité [mɔ̃stryozite] *nf* monstrosity.

mont [mɔ̃] *nm* **-1.** *littéraire* [montagne] mountain; **par** ~**s et par vaux** *fig* up hill and down dale; **promettre** ~**s et merveilles** to promise the earth. **-2.** GÉOGR Mount; **le** ~ **Blanc** Mont Blanc; **le** ~ **Cervin** the Matterhorn. **-3.** ANAT: ~ **de Vénus** mons veneris.

montage [mɔ̃taʒ] *nm* **-1.** [assemblage] assembly; [de bijou] setting. **-2.** PHOT photomontage. **-3.** CIN editing. **-4.** ÉLECTR wiring.

montagnard, -e [mɔ̃taɲar, ard] ◇ *adj* mountain (*avant n*). ◇ *nm, f* mountain dweller.

montagne [mɔ̃taɲ] *nf* **-1.** [gén] mountain; **les** ~**s Rocheuses** the Rocky Mountains. **-2.** [région]: **la** ~ the mountains (*pl*); **à la** ~ in the mountains; **en haute** ~ at high altitudes; **faire de la haute** ~ to go mountain climbing. **-3.** *loc*: **se faire une** ~ **de qqch** to make a great song and dance about sthg.
◆ **montagnes russes** *nfpl* big dipper (*sg*), roller coaster (*sg*).

montagneux, -euse [mɔ̃taɲø, øz] *adj* mountainous.

montant, -e [mɔ̃tɑ̃, ɑ̃t] *adj* **-1.** [mouvement] rising. **-2.** [vêtement] high-necked.
◆ **montant** *nm* **-1.** [pièce verticale] upright. **-2.** [somme] total (amount).

mont-blanc [mɔ̃blɑ̃] (*pl* **monts-blancs**) *nm* *pureed chestnuts with whipped cream.*

mont-de-piété [mɔ̃dpjete] (*pl* **monts-de-piété**) *nm* pawnshop.

monté, -e [mɔ̃te] *adj*: **être** ~ **en qqch** to be well off for sthg.

monte-charge [mɔ̃tʃarʒ] *nm inv* service elevator *Am*, goods lift *Br*.

montée [mɔ̃te] *nf* **-1.** [de montagne] climb, ascent. **-2.** [de prix] rise. **-3.** [relief] slope, gradient.

Monténégro [mɔ̃tenegro] *nm*: **le** ~ Montenegro.

monte-plats [mɔ̃tpla] *nm inv* dumbwaiter.

monter [mɔ̃te] [3] ◇ *vi* (*aux: être*) **-1.** [personne] to come/go up; [température, niveau] to rise; [route, avion] to climb; ~ **sur qqch** to climb onto sthg. **-2.** [passager] to get on; ~ **dans un bus** to get on a bus; ~ **dans une voiture** to get into a car. **-3.** [cavalier] to ride; ~ **à cheval** to ride; ~ **à cheval sur qqch** *fig* to straddle sthg. **-4.** [marée] to go/come in.
◇ *vt* (*aux: avoir*) **-1.** [escalier, côte] to climb, to come/go up; ~ **la rue en courant** to run up the street. **-2.** [chauffage, son] to turn up. **-3.** [valise] to take/bring up. **-4.** [meuble] to assemble; COUTURE to assemble, to put OU sew together; [tente] to put up. **-5.** CIN to edit, to cut (together). **-6.** [cheval] to mount. **-7.** [dispositif] to assemble. **-8.** THÉÂTRE to put on. **-9.** [société, club] to set up. **-10.** CULIN to beat, to whisk (up). **-11.** *loc*: ~ **qqn contre qqn** to set sb against sb.
◆ **se monter** *vp* **-1.** [s'assembler]: **se** ~ **facilement** to be easy to assemble. **-2.** [atteindre]: **se** ~ **à** to amount to, to add up to.

monteur, -euse [mɔ̃tœr, øz] *nm, f* **-1.** TECHNOL fitter. **-2.** CIN editor.

monticule [mɔ̃tikyl] *nm* mound; *Can* BASEBALL pitcher's mound.

montre [mɔ̃tr] *nf* watch; ~ **à quartz** quartz watch; ~ **en main** to the minute, exactly; **contre la** ~ [sport] time-trialling; [épreuve] time trial; **une course contre la** ~ *fig* a race against time.

Montréal [mɔ̃real] *n* Montreal.

montre-bracelet [mɔ̃trəbraslɛ] (*pl* **montres-bracelets**) *nf* wristwatch.

montrer [mɔ̃tre] [3] *vt* **-1.** [gén] to show; ~ **qqch à qqn** to show sb sthg, to show sthg to sb. **-2.** [désigner] to show, to point out; ~ **qqch du doigt** to point at OU to sthg.
◆ **se montrer** *vp* **-1.** [se faire voir] to appear. **-2.** *fig* [se présenter] to show o.s. **-3.** *fig* [se révéler] to prove (to be).

montreur, -euse [mɔ̃trœr, øz] *nm, f*: ~ **de marionnettes** puppeteer.

monture [mɔ̃tyr] *nf* **-1.** [animal] mount. **-2.** [de lunettes] frame. **-3.** [de bijou] setting.

monument [mɔnymɑ̃] *nm* **-1.** [gén]: ~ (à) monument (to); ~ **aux morts** war memorial. **-2.** *fig* & *hum* [chef-d'œuvre] masterpiece.

monumental, -e, -aux [mɔnymɑ̃tal, o] *adj* monumental.

moquer [mɔke] [3]

◆ **se moquer** *vp*: **se** ~ **de** [plaisanter sur] to make fun of, to laugh at; [ne pas se soucier de] not to give a damn about; **ne vous moquez pas!** don't mock!, don't laugh!

moquerie [mɔkri] *nf* mockery (*U*), jibe.

moquette [mɔkɛt] *nf* (fitted) carpet.

moqueur, -euse [mɔkœr, øz] ◇ *adj* mocking. ◇ *nm, f* mocker.

moraine [mɔrɛn] *nf* moraine.

moral, -e, -aux [mɔral, o] *adj* moral.

◆ **moral** *nm* **-1.** [mental]: **au** ~ **comme au physique** mentally as well as physically. **-2.** [état d'esprit] morale, spirits (*pl*); **avoir/ ne pas avoir le** ~ to be in good/bad spirits; **remonter le** ~ **à qqn** to cheer sb up; **se remonter le** ~ to cheer (o.s.) up.

◆ **morale** *nf* **-1.** [science] moral philosophy, morals (*pl*). **-2.** [règle] morality. **-3.** [mœurs] morals (*pl*). **-4.** [leçon] moral; **faire la** ~**e à qqn** to preach at OU lecture sb.

moralement [mɔralmɑ̃] *adv* morally.

moralisateur, -trice [mɔralizatœr, tris] ◇ *adj* moralizing. ◇ *nm, f* moralizer.

moralisme [mɔralism] *nm* morality.

moraliste [mɔralist] ◇ *nmf* moralist. ◇ *adj* moralistic.

moralité [mɔralite] *nf* **-1.** [gén] morality. **-2.** [enseignement] moral.

moratoire [mɔratwar] *nm* moratorium.

morbide [mɔrbid] *adj* morbid.

morbidité [mɔrbidite] *nf* morbidity.

morceau, -x [mɔrso] *nm* **-1.** [gén] piece; **manger un** ~ *fam* to have a bite to eat; **mettre en** ~**x** to pull OU tear to pieces; **cracher le** ~ *fam fig* to spill the beans; **emporter le** ~ *fam* to carry it off. **-2.** [de poème, de film] passage; **un** ~ **de bravoure** a purple passage.

morceler [mɔrsəle] [24] *vt* to break up, to split up.

◆ **se morceler** *vp* to break up.

morcellement [mɔrsɛlmɑ̃] *nm* breaking up, splitting up.

mordant, -e [mɔrdɑ̃, ɑ̃t] *adj* biting.

◆ **mordant** *nm* [vivacité] keenness, bite.

mordicus [mɔrdikys] *adv fam* stubbornly, stoutly.

mordiller [mɔrdije] [3] *vt* to nibble.

mordoré, -e [mɔrdɔre] *adj* bronze.

mordre [mɔrdr] [76] ◇ *vt* **-1.** [blesser] to bite. **-2.** [dépasser] to go over. **-3.** *fig* [entamer, ronger] to eat into OU away. ◇ *vi* **-1.** [saisir avec les dents]: ~ **à** to bite. **-2.** [croquer]: ~ **dans qqch** to bite into sthg. **-3.** SPORT: ~ **sur la ligne** to step over the line.

mordu, -e [mɔrdy] ◇ *pp* → **mordre**. ◇ *adj* [amoureux] hooked. ◇ *nm, f*: ~ **de foot/ski** *etc* football/ski *etc* addict.

more = **maure**.

moresque = **mauresque**.

morfondre [mɔrfɔ̃dr] [75]

◆ **se morfondre** *vp* to mope.

morgue [mɔrg] *nf* **-1.** [attitude] pride. **-2.** [lieu] morgue.

moribond, -e [mɔribɔ̃, ɔ̃d] ◇ *adj* dying. ◇ *nm, f* dying person.

morigéner [mɔriʒene] [18] *vt littéraire* to rebuke.

morille [mɔrij] *nf* morel.

mormon, -e [mɔrmɔ̃, ɔn] *adj* & *nm, f* Mormon.

morne [mɔrn] *adj* [personne, visage] gloomy; [paysage, temps, ville] dismal, dreary.

Moroni [mɔroni] *n* Moroni.

morose [mɔroz] *adj* gloomy.

morosité [mɔrozite] *nf* gloominess.

morphine [mɔrfin] *nf* morphine.

morphologie [mɔrfɔlɔʒi] *nf* morphology.

morphologique [mɔrfɔlɔʒik] *adj* morphological.

morpion [mɔrpjɔ̃] *nm* **-1.** *fam* MÉD crab. **-2.** *fam* [enfant] brat. **-3.** [jeu] ≃ tick-tack-toe *Am*, ≃ noughts and crosses *Br*.

mors [mɔr] *nm* bit; **prendre le** ~ **aux dents** to get the bit between one's teeth.

morse [mɔrs] *nm* **-1.** ZOOL walrus. **-2.** [code] Morse (code).

morsure [mɔrsyr] *nf* bite.

mort, -e [mɔr, mɔrt] ◇ *pp* → **mourir**. ◇ *adj* dead; **raide** ~ stone dead; ~ **ou vif** dead or alive; ~ **de fatigue** *fig* dead tired; ~ **de peur** *fig* frightened to death. ◇ *nm, f* **-1.** [cadavre] corpse, dead body. **-2.** [défunt] dead person.

◆ **mort** ◇ *nm* **-1.** [victime] fatality. **-2.** CARTES dummy.

◇ *nf litt* & *fig* death; **de** ~ [silence] deathly; **condamner qqn à** ~ JUR to sentence sb to death; **se donner la** ~ to take one's own life, to commit suicide; **jusqu'à ce que** ~ **s'ensuive** to death; **en vouloir à** ~ **à qqn** to hate sb's guts; ~ **naturelle/violente** natural/violent death; **la** ~ **dans l'âme** sick at heart, with a heavy heart; **pâle comme la** ~ deathly pale.

mortadelle [mɔrtadɛl] *nf* mortadella.

mortalité [mɔrtalite] *nf* mortality, death rate; ~ **infantile** infant mortality.

mort-aux-rats [mɔrora] *nf inv* rat poison.

mortel, -elle [mɔrtɛl] ◇ *adj* **-1.** [humain] mortal. **-2.** [accident, maladie] fatal. **-3.** *fig* [ennuyeux] deadly (dull). ◇ *nm, f* mortal.

mortellement [mɔrtɛlmã] *adv* **-1.** [à mort] fatally. **-2.** [extrêmement] mortally, deeply; **s'ennuyer** ~ to be bored to death.

morte-saison [mɔrtsezɔ̃] (*pl* **mortes-saisons**) *nf* slack season, off-season.

mortier [mɔrtje] *nm* mortar.

mortifier [mɔrtifje] [9] *vt* to mortify.

mort-né, -e [mɔrne] (*mpl* **mort-nés**, *fpl* **mort-nées**) ◇ *adj* [enfant] still-born; *fig* [projet] abortive. ◇ *nm, f* still-born child.

mortuaire [mɔrtɥɛr] *adj* funeral (*avant n*).

morue [mɔry] *nf* **-1.** ZOOL cod. **-2.** *injurieux* [prostituée] whore.

morve [mɔrv] *nf* snot.

morveux, -euse [mɔrvø, øz] ◇ *adj* runny-nosed, snotty. ◇ *nm, f fam* brat.

mosaïque [mɔzaik] *nf litt* & *fig* mosaic.

Moscou [mɔsku] *n* Moscow.

moscovite [mɔskɔvit] *adj* of/from Moscow.

◆ **Moscovite** *nmf* Muscovite.

mosquée [mɔske] *nf* mosque.

mot [mo] *nm* **-1.** [gén] word; **avoir toujours le ~ pour rire** to be always able to raise a laugh; **au bas ~** at the lowest estimate; **à ~s couverts** in veiled terms; **le fin ~ de l'histoire** the real story; **~ d'esprit** witty remark; **~ d'excuse** SCOL note from one's parents; **gros ~** swearword; **~ d'ordre** watchword; **~ de passe** password; **~s croisés** crossword (puzzle) (*sg*); **~ à ~, ~ pour ~** word for word; **en un ~** in a word; **avoir son ~ à dire** to have one's say; **avoir des ~s avec qqn** to have words with sb; **avoir le dernier ~** to have the last word; **avoir deux ~s à dire à qqn** *fam* to give sb a piece of one's mind; **ne pas mâcher ses ~s** not to mince one's words; **prendre qqn au ~** to take sb at his/her word; **en toucher un ~ à qqn** *fam* to have a word with sb. **-2.** [message] note, message.

motard [mɔtar] *nm* **-1.** [motocycliste] motorcyclist. **-2.** [policier] motorcycle policeman.

motel [mɔtɛl] *nm* motel.

moteur, -trice [mɔtœr, tris] *adj* **-1.** [force, énergie] driving (*avant n*); **à quatre roues motrices** AUTOM with four-wheel drive. **-2.** [muscles, nerfs] motor (*avant n*).

◆ **moteur** *nm* TECHNOL motor, engine; *fig* driving force; **~ électrique** electric motor;

~ **à explosion** combustion engine; ~ **à injection** fuel-injection engine; ~ **à réaction** jet engine.

◆ **motrice** *nf* RAIL motor car *Am*, motor coach *Br*.

motif [mɔtif] *nm* **-1.** [raison] motive, grounds (*pl*). **-2.** [dessin, impression] motif.

motion [mɔsjɔ̃] *nf* POLIT motion; ~ **de censure** motion of censure.

motivant, -e [mɔtivã, ãt] *adj* motivating.

motivation [mɔtivasjɔ̃] *nf* motivation.

motiver [mɔtive] [3] *vt* **-1.** [stimuler] to motivate. **-2.** [justifier] to justify.

moto [mɔto] *nf* motorbike.

motocross [mɔtokrɔs] *nm* motocross.

motoculteur [mɔtokyltœr] *nm* ≃ Rotavator®.

motocyclette [mɔtosiklɛt] *nf* motorcycle, motorbike.

motocyclisme [mɔtosiklism] *nm* motorcyle racing.

motocycliste [mɔtosiklist] *nmf* motorcyclist.

motomarine [mɔtomarin] *nf Can* jet ski, aquaskooter *Am*.

motoneige [mɔtonɛʒ] *nf Can* snowmobile.

motorisé, -e [mɔtorize] *adj* motorized; **être ~** *fam* to have a car, to have wheels.

motrice → **moteur**.

motricité [mɔtrisite] *nf* motor functions (*pl*).

motte [mɔt] *nf*: ~ **(de terre)** clod, lump of earth; ~ **de beurre** slab of butter.

motus [mɔtys] *interj* not a word!; ~ **et bouche cousue!** mum's the word!

mou, molle [mu, mɔl] *adj* (**mol** *devant voyelle ou h muet*) **-1.** [gén] soft. **-2.** [faible] weak. **-3.** [résistance, protestation] half-hearted. **-4.** *fam* [de caractère] wet, wimpy.

◆ **mou** *nm* **-1.** [de corde]: **avoir du ~** to be slack. **-2.** [abats] lungs (*pl*), lights (*pl*).

mouchard, -e [muʃar, ard] *nm, f fam* [personne] sneak.

◆ **mouchard** *nm fam* [dans camion, train] spy in the cab.

moucharder [muʃarde] [3] *vi fam* to sneak.

mouche [muʃ] *nf* **-1.** ZOOL fly; ~ **tsé-tsé** tsetse fly; **fine ~** *fig* shrewd individual. **-2.** [accessoire féminin] beauty spot. **-3.** *loc*: **faire ~** to hit the bull's eye.

moucher [muʃe] [3] *vt* **-1.** [nez] to wipe; ~ **un enfant** to wipe a child's nose. **-2.** [chandelle] to snuff out. **-3.** *fam fig* [personne]: ~ **qqn** to put sb in his/her place.

◆ **se moucher** *vp* to blow OU wipe one's nose.

moucheron [muʃrɔ̃] *nm* [insecte] gnat.

moucheté, -e [muʃte] *adj* **-1.** [laine] flecked. **-2.** [animal] spotted, speckled.

mouchoir [muʃwar] *nm* handkerchief; **~ en papier** paper handkerchief, tissue; **grand comme un ~ de poche** *fig* no bigger than a pocket handkerchief.

moudre [mudr] [85] *vt* to grind.

mouds → **moudre**.

moue [mu] *nf* pout; **faire la ~** to pull a face.

mouette [mwɛt] *nf* seagull.

moufle [mufl] *nf* mitten.

mouflet, -ette [mufle, ɛt] *nm, f fam* kid, brat.

mouflon [muflɔ̃] *nm* wild sheep.

mouillage [mujaʒ] *nm* **-1.** [coupage] watering (down). **-2.** [NAVIG - emplacement] anchorage, moorings (*pl*); [- manœuvre] anchoring, mooring.

mouillé, -e [muje] *adj* wet.

mouiller [muje] [3] ◇ *vt* **-1.** [personne, objet] to wet; **se faire ~** to get wet OU soaked. **-2.** [vin, lait] to water down; CULIN to add liquid to. **-3.** NAVIG: **~ l'ancre** to drop anchor. **-4.** LING to palatalize. **-5.** *fam fig* [compromettre] to involve. ◇ *vi* NAVIG to anchor.

◆ se mouiller *vp* **-1.** [se tremper] to get wet. **-2.** *fam fig* [prendre des risques] to stick one's neck out.

mouillette [mujɛt] *nf* finger of bread, soldier.

mouise [mwiz] *nf*: **être dans la ~** *fam* to be broke.

moulage [mulaʒ] *nm* **-1.** [action] molding *Am*, moulding *Br*, casting. **-2.** [objet] cast.

moulant, -e [mulɑ̃, ɑ̃t] *adj* close-fitting.

moule [mul] ◇ *nm* mold *Am*, mould *Br*; **~ à gâteau** cake pan *Am* OU tin *Br*; **~ à gaufre** waffle-iron; **~ à tarte** flan dish. ◇ *nf* ZOOL mussel; **~s marinières** CULIN *mussels cooked in white wine*.

mouler [mule] [3] *vt* **-1.** [objet] to mold *Am*, to mould *Br*. **-2.** [forme] to make a cast of. **-3.** [corps] to hug.

moulin [mulɛ̃] *nm* mill; **~ à café** coffee mill; **~ à eau** watermill; **~ à paroles** *fig* chatterbox; **~ à poivre** peppermill; **~ à scie** *Can* sawmill; **~ à vent** windmill.

mouliner [muline] [3] *vt* [aliments] to put through a food mill.

moulinet [mulinɛ] *nm* **-1.** PÊCHE reel. **-2.** [mouvement]: **faire des ~s** to whirl one's arms around.

Moulinette® [mulinɛt] *nf* food mill; **passer qqn à la ~** *fam fig* to tear sb to pieces.

moult [mult] *adv vieilli* many.

moulu, -e [muly] *adj* **-1.** [en poudre] ground. **-2.** *fig* [brisé]: **être ~ (de fatigue)** to be worn out.

moulure [mulyr] *nf* moulding.

mourais, mourions *etc* → **mourir**.

mourant, -e [murɑ̃, ɑ̃t] ◇ *adj* **-1.** [moribond] dying. **-2.** *fig* [voix] faint. ◇ *nm, f* dying person.

mourir [murir] [42] *vi* **-1.** [personne] to die; **~ de froid/soif** *fig* to be dying of cold/thirst; **s'ennuyer à ~** to be bored to death; **c'est à ~ de rire** it's a scream. **-2.** [civilisation] to die out. **-3.** [feu] to die down.

mouroir [murwar] *nm péj* old dears' home.

mouron [murɔ̃] *nm* BOT pimpernel; **se faire du ~** *fam fig* to worry o.s. sick.

mourrai, mourras *etc* → **mourir**.

mousquetaire [muskətɛr] *nm* musketeer.

moussant, -e [musɑ̃, ɑ̃t] *adj* foaming.

mousse [mus] ◇ *nf* **-1.** BOT moss. **-2.** [substance] foam; **~ carbonique** foam (*for extinguishing fires*); **~ à raser** shaving foam. **-3.** CULIN mousse; **~ au chocolat** chocolate mousse. **-4.** [matière plastique] foam rubber. ◇ *nm* NAVIG cabin boy.

mousseline [muslin] ◇ *nf* muslin. ◇ *adj inv* lightened with cream or milk.

mousser [muse] [3] *vi* to foam, to lather; **se faire ~** *fam fig* to blow one's own trumpet.

mousseux, -euse [musø, øz] *adj* **-1.** [shampooing] foaming, frothy. **-2.** [vin, cidre] sparkling.

◆ mousseux *nm* sparkling wine.

mousson [musɔ̃] *nf* monsoon.

moussu, -e [musy] *adj* mossy.

moustache [mustaʃ] *nf* mustache *Am*, moustache *Br*.

◆ moustaches *nfpl* [d'animal] whiskers.

moustachu, -e [mustaʃy] *adj* with a mustache *Am* OU moustache *Br*.

◆ moustachu *nm* man with a moustache.

moustiquaire [mustikɛr] *nf* mosquito net.

moustique [mustik] *nm* mosquito.

moutard [mutar] *nm fam* kid.

moutarde [mutard] ◇ *nf* mustard; **la ~ me monte au nez** *fig* I'm losing my temper. ◇ *adj inv* mustard (*avant n*).

mouton [mutɔ̃] *nm* **-1.** ZOOL & *fig* sheep. **-2.** [viande] mutton. **-3.** *fam* [poussière] piece of fluff, fluff (*U*). **-4.** *loc*: **revenons à nos ~s** let's get back to the subject in hand.

◆ moutons *nmpl* [vagues] white horses.

mouture [mutyr] *nf* **-1.** [de céréales, de café] grinding. **-2.** [de thème, d'œuvre] rehash.

mouvance [muvɑ̃s] *nf* [domaine] sphere of influence.

mouvant, -e [muvɑ̃, ɑ̃t] *adj* **-1.** [terrain] unstable. **-2.** [situation] uncertain.

mouvement [muvmɑ̃] *nm* **-1.** [gén] movement; **en ~** on the move; **faux ~** clumsy OU awkward movement; **~ alternatif** TECHNOL reciprocating movement. **-2.** [de colère, d'indignation] burst, fit; **~ d'humeur** fit of bad temper.

mouvementé, -e [muvmɑ̃te] *adj* **-1.** [terrain] rough. **-2.** [réunion, soirée] eventful.

mouvoir [muvwar] [54] *vt* to move.

◆ **se mouvoir** *vp* to move.

moyen, -enne [mwajɛ̃, ɛn] *adj* **-1.** [intermédiaire] medium. **-2.** [médiocre, courant] average.

◆ **moyen** *nm* means (*sg*), way; **par tous les ~s** by any means possible; **y a-t-il ~ de ...?** is there any way of ...?; **~ de communication** means of communication; **~ d'expression** means of expression; **~ de locomotion** OU **transport** means of transport; **employer les grands ~s** to resort to extreme measures.

◆ **moyenne** *nf* average; **en moyenne** on average; **la moyenne** SCOL the passmark; **la moyenne d'âge** the average age.

◆ **moyens** *nmpl* **-1.** [ressources] means; **avoir les ~s** to be comfortably off; **avoir les ~s de faire qqch** to have the means to do sthg; **avec les ~s du bord** with the means at one's disposal. **-2.** [capacités] powers, ability; **faire qqch par ses propres ~s** to do sthg on one's own; **perdre tous ses ~s** to panic.

◆ **au moyen de** *loc prép* by means of.

Moyen Âge [mwajɛnaʒ] *nm*: **le ~** the Middle Ages (*pl*).

moyenâgeux, -euse [mwajɛnaʒø, øz] *adj* medieval.

moyen-courrier [mwajɛ̃kurje] (*pl* **moyens-courriers**) ◇ *nm* medium-haul aircraft. ◇ *adj* medium-haul (*avant n*).

moyennant [mwajɛnɑ̃] *prép* for, in return for.

moyennement [mwajɛnmɑ̃] *adv* moderately, fairly.

Moyen-Orient [mwajɛnɔrjɑ̃] *nm*: **le ~** the Middle East; **au ~** in the Middle East.

moyen-oriental, -e [mwajɛnɔrjɑ̃tal] *adj* Middle Eastern.

moyeu, -x [mwajø] *nm* hub.

mozambicain, -e [mɔzɑ̃bikɛ̃, ɛn] *adj* Mozambican.

◆ **Mozambicain, -e** *nm, f* Mozambican.

Mozambique [mɔzɑ̃bik] *nm*: **le ~** Mozambique; **au ~** in Mozambique.

MRAP [mrap] (*abr de* **Mouvement contre le racisme, l'antisémitisme et pour la paix**) *nm pacifist anti-racist organization.*

MRG (*abr de* **Mouvement des radicaux de gauche**) *nm centre-left political party.*

ms (*abr de* **manuscrit**) ms.

MSF (*abr de* **Médecins sans frontières**) *nmpl medical association for aid to third-world countries.*

MST *nf* **-1.** (*abr de* **maladie sexuellement transmissible**) STD. **-2.** (*abr de* **maîtrise de sciences et techniques**) *masters degree in science and technology.*

MT (*abr de* **moyenne tension**) MT.

mû, mue [my] *pp* → **mouvoir**.

mucosité [mykozite] *nf* mucus (*U*).

mucus [mykys] *nm* mucus (*U*).

mue [my] *nf* **-1.** [de pelage] moulting. **-2.** [de serpent] skin, slough. **-3.** [de voix] breaking.

muer [mɥe] [7] *vi* **-1.** [mammifère] to moult. **-2.** [serpent] to slough its skin. **-3.** [voix] to break; [jeune homme]: **il mue** his voice is breaking.

◆ **se muer** *vp littéraire*: **se ~ en** to turn into.

muesli [mysli] *nm* muesli.

muet, muette [mɥe, ɛt] ◇ *adj* **-1.** MÉD dumb. **-2.** [silencieux] silent; **~ d'admiration/d'étonnement** speechless with admiration/surprise. **-3.** LING silent, mute. ◇ *nm, f* mute, dumb person.

◆ **muet** *nm*: **le ~** CIN silent films (*pl*).

muezzin [mɥedzin] *nm* muezzin.

mufle [myfl] *nm* **-1.** [d'animal] muzzle, snout. **-2.** *fig* [goujat] lout.

muflerie [myfləri] *nf* loutishness.

mufti, muphti [myfti] *nm* mufti.

mugir [myʒir] [32] *vi* **-1.** [vache] to moo. **-2.** [vent, sirène] to howl.

mugissement [myʒismɑ̃] *nm* **-1.** [de vache] mooing. **-2.** [de vent, sirène] howling.

muguet [myge] *nm* **-1.** [fleur] lily of the valley. **-2.** MÉD thrush.

MUGUET:
On May Day in France, bunches of lily of the valley are sold in the streets and given as presents. The flowers are supposed to bring good luck

---

mulâtre, mulâtresse [mylatr, trɛs] *nm, f* mulatto.

◆ **mulâtre** *adj* mulatto.

mule [myl] *nf* mule.

mulet [mylɛ] *nm* **-1.** [âne] mule. **-2.** [poisson] mullet.

muletier, -ière [myltje, jɛʀ] *adj* mule (*avant n*).
◆ **muletier** *nm* muleteer.

mulot [mylo] *nm* field mouse.

multicolore [myltikɔlɔʀ] *adj* multicoloured.

multifonction [myltifɔ̃ksjɔ̃] *adj inv* multifunction.

multiforme [myltifɔʀm] *adj* multiform.

multilatéral, -e, -aux [myltilateral, o] *adj* multilateral.

multi-media [myltimedja] *adj* INFORM multimedia.

multimillionnaire [myltimiljɔnɛʀ] *nmf & adj* multimillionaire.

multinational, -e, -aux [myltinasjɔnal, o] *adj* multinational.
◆ **multinationale** *nf* multinational (company).

multiple [myltipl] ◇ *nm* multiple. ◇ *adj* **-1.** [nombreux] multiple, numerous. **-2.** [divers] many, various.

multiplication [myltiplikasjɔ̃] *nf* multiplication.

multiplicité [myltiplisite] *nf* multiplicity.

multiplier [myltiplije] [10] *vt* **-1.** [accroître] to increase. **-2.** MATHS to multiply; **X multiplié par Y égale Z** X multiplied by OU times Y equals Z.
◆ **se multiplier** *vp* to multiply.

multipropriété [myltiprɔprijete] *nf* timeshare.

multiracial, -e, -iaux [myltirasjal, jo] *adj* multiracial.

multirisque [myltirisk] *adj* comprehensive.

multitude [myltityd] *nf*: ~ **(de)** multitude (of).

municipal, -e, -aux [mynisipal, o] *adj* municipal.
◆ **municipales** *nfpl*: **les ~es** the local government elections.

municipalité [mynisipalite] *nf* **-1.** [commune] municipality. **-2.** [conseil] town council.

munir [mynir] [32] *vt*: ~ **qqn/qqch de** to equip sb/sthg with.
◆ **se munir** *vp*: **se ~ de** to equip o.s. with.

munitions [mynisjɔ̃] *nfpl* ammunition (U), munitions.

munster [mœ̃stɛr] *nm* strong semi-hard cheese.

muphti = **mufti**.

muqueuse [mykøz] *nf* mucous membrane.

mur [myr] *nm* **-1.** [gén] wall; ~ **antibruit** soundproof wall; ~ **mitoyen** party wall; **raser les ~s** to hug the walls; *fig* to tread warily. **-2.** *fig* [obstacle] barrier, brick wall; ~ **du son** AÉRON sound barrier.

mûr, mûre [myr] *adj* ripe; [personne] mature; **après ~e réflexion** *fig* after careful consideration.
◆ **mûre** *nf* **-1.** [de mûrier] mulberry. **-2.** [de ronce] blackberry, bramble.

muraille [myraj] *nf* wall.

mural, -e, -aux [myral, o] *adj* wall (*avant n*).

mûrement [myrmɑ̃] *adv*: **après avoir ~ réfléchi** after careful consideration.

murène [myrɛn] *nf* moray eel.

murer [myre] [3] *vt* **-1.** [boucher] to wall up, to block up. **-2.** [enfermer] to wall in.
◆ **se murer** *vp* to shut o.s. up OU away; **se ~ dans** *fig* to retreat into.

muret [myrɛ] *nm* low wall.

mûrier [myrje] *nm* **-1.** [arbre] mulberry tree. **-2.** [ronce] blackberry bush, bramble bush.

mûrir [myrir] [32] *vi* **-1.** [fruits, légumes] to ripen. **-2.** *fig* [idée, projet] to develop. **-3.** [personne] to mature.

murmure [myrmyr] *nm* murmur.

murmurer [myrmyre] [3] *vt & vi* to murmur.

musaraigne [myzarɛɲ] *nf* shrew.

musarder [myzarde] [3] *vi fam* to dawdle.

musc [mysk] *nm* musk.

muscade [myskad] *nf* nutmeg.

muscadet [myskadɛ] *nm* dry white wine.

muscat [myska] *nm* **-1.** [raisin] muscat grape. **-2.** [vin] sweet wine.

muscle [myskl] *nm* muscle; ~ **extenseur** extensor muscle.

musclé, -e [myskle] *adj* **-1.** [personne] muscular. **-2.** *fig* [mesure, décision] forceful.

muscler [myskle] [3] *vt*: ~ **son corps** to build up one's muscles.
◆ **se muscler** *vp* to build up one's muscles.

musculaire [myskylɛr] *adj* muscular.

musculation [myskylasjɔ̃] *nf*: **faire de la ~** to do muscle-building exercises.

musculature [myskylatyr] *nf* musculature.

muse [myz] *nf* muse.

museau [myzo] *nm* **-1.** [d'animal] muzzle, snout. **-2.** *fam* [de personne] face.

musée [myze] *nm* museum; [d'art] art gallery.

museler [myzle] [24] *vt litt & fig* to muzzle.

muselière [myzəljɛr] *nf* muzzle.

musette [myzɛt] ◇ *nf* haversack; [d'écolier] satchel. ◇ *nm*: **le ~** dance music played on the accordion.

muséum [myzeɔm] *nm* museum.

musical, -e, -aux [myzikal, o] *adj* **-1.** [son] musical. **-2.** [émission, critique] music (*avant n*).

music-hall [myzikol] (*pl* **music-halls**) *nm* music-hall.

musicien, -ienne [myzisjɛ̃, jɛn] ◇ *adj* musical. ◇ *nm, f* musician.

musicographie [myzikɔgrafi] *nf* musicography.

musicologue [myzikɔlɔg] *nmf* musicologist.

musique [myzik] *nf* music; ~ **de chambre** chamber music; ~ **de film** movie *Am* OU film *Br* score; **connaître la** ~ *fam fig* to know the score.

musqué, -e [myske] *adj* **-1.** [parfum] musky. **-2.** [animal]: **rat** ~ muskrat.

must [mœst] *nm fam* must.

musulman, -e [myzylmɑ̃, an] *adj & nm, f* Muslim.

mutant, -e [mytɑ̃, ɑ̃t] *adj & nm, f* mutant.

mutation [mytasjɔ̃] *nf* **-1.** BIOL mutation. **-2.** *fig* [changement] transformation; **en pleine** ~ undergoing a (complete) transformation. **-3.** [de fonctionnaire] transfer.

muter [myte] [3] *vt* to transfer.

mutilation [mytilasjɔ̃] *nf* mutilation.

mutilé, -e [mytile] *nm, f* disabled person.

mutiler [mytile] [3] *vt* to mutilate; **il a été mutilé du bras droit** he lost his right arm.

mutin, -e [mytɛ̃, in] *adj littéraire* impish.
◆ **mutin** *nm* rebel; MIL & NAVIG mutineer.

mutiner [mytine] [3]
◆ **se mutiner** *vp* to rebel; MIL & NAVIG to mutiny.

mutinerie [mytinri] *nf* rebellion; MIL & NAVIG mutiny.

mutisme [mytism] *nm* silence.

mutualiste [mytɥalist] ◇ *nmf* mutualist. ◇ *adj*: **société** ~ mutual insurance company.

mutualité [mytɥalite] *nf* [assurance] mutual insurance.

mutuel, -elle [mytɥɛl] *adj* mutual.
◆ **mutuelle** *nf* mutual insurance company.

mutuellement [mytɥɛlmɑ̃] *adv* mutually.

mycose [mikoz] *nf* mycosis, fungal infection.

myocarde [mjɔkard] *nm* myocardium.

myopathie [mjɔpati] *nf* myopathy.

myope [mjɔp] ◇ *nmf* shortsighted person. ◇ *adj* shortsighted, myopic.

myopie [mjɔpi] *nf* shortsightedness, myopia.

myosotis [mjozɔtis] *nm* forget-me-not.

myriade [mirjad] *nf*: **une** ~ **de** a myriad of.

myrtille [mirtij] *nf* blueberry *Am*, bilberry *Br*.

mystère [mistɛr] *nm* **-1.** [gén] mystery. **-2.** CULIN *ice cream covered in meringue and flaked almonds*.

mystérieusement [misterjøzmɑ̃] *adv* mysteriously.

mystérieux, -ieuse [misterjø, jøz] *adj* mysterious.

mysticisme [mistisism] *nm* mysticism.

mystification [mistifikasjɔ̃] *nf* [tromperie] hoax, practical joke.

mystifier [mistifje] [9] *vt* [duper] to take in.

mystique [mistik] ◇ *nmf* mystic. ◇ *adj* mystic, mystical.

mythe [mit] *nm* myth.

mythifier [mitifje] [9] *vt* to mythicize.

mythique [mitik] *adj* mythical.

mytho [mito] *adj fam*: **il est complètement** ~ you can't believe anything he says.

mythologie [mitɔlɔʒi] *nf* mythology.

mythologique [mitɔlɔʒik] *adj* mythological.

mythomane [mitɔman] *nmf* pathological liar.

n, N [ɛn] *nm inv* [lettre] n, N.
◆ **N -1.** (*abr de* **newton**) N. **-2.** (*abr de* **nord**) N.

n° (*abr de* **numéro**) no.

nabot, -e [nabo, ɔt] *nm, f péj* midget.

nacelle [nasɛl] *nf* [de montgolfière] basket.

nacre [nakr] *nf* mother-of-pearl.

nacré, -e [nakre] *adj* pearly.

nage [naʒ] *nf* **-1.** [natation] swimming; ~ **indienne** side stroke; ~ **papillon** butterfly (stroke); **à la** ~ CULIN *poached in wine and herbs*; **traverser à la** ~ to swim across. **-2.** *loc*: **en** ~ bathed in sweat.

nageoire [naʒwar] *nf* fin.

nager [naʒe] [17] ◇ *vi* **-1.** [se baigner] to swim. **-2.** [flotter] to float. **-3.** *fig* [dans vêtement]: ~ **dans** to be lost in; ~ **dans la joie** to be incredibly happy. ◇ *vt* to swim.

nageur, -euse [naʒœr, øz] *nm, f* swimmer.

naguère [nagɛr] *adv littéraire* a short time ago.

naïade [najad] *nf* water nymph.

naïf, naïve [naif, iv] ◇ *adj* **-1.** [ingénu, art] naive. **-2.** *péj* [crédule] gullible. ◇ *nm, f* **-1.** *péj* [niais] fool. **-2.** [peintre] naive painter.

nain, -e [nɛ̃, nɛn] ◇ *adj* dwarf (*avant n*). ◇ *nm, f* dwarf.

Nairobi [nɛrɔbi] *n* Nairobi.

naissais, naissions *etc* → **naître**.

naissance [nɛsɑ̃s] *nf* **-1.** [de personne] birth; **donner** ~ **à** to give birth to; **de** ~ [aveugle] from birth; **le contrôle des** ~**s** birth control. **-2.** [endroit] source; [du cou] nape. **-3.** *fig* [de science, nation] birth; **donner** ~ **à** to give rise to; **prendre** ~ **dans** to originate in.

naissant, -e [nɛsɑ̃, ɑ̃t] *adj* **-1.** [brise] rising; [jour] dawning. **-2.** [barbe] incipient.

naître [nɛtr] [92] *vi* **-1.** [enfant] to be born; **elle est née en 1965** she was born in 1965. **-2.** [espoir] to spring up; ~ **de** to arise from; **faire** ~ **qqch** to give rise to sthg.

naïvement [naivmɑ̃] *adv* naively.

naïveté [naivte] *nf* **-1.** [candeur] innocence. **-2.** *péj* [crédulité] gullibility.

naja [naʒa] *nm* cobra.

Namibie [namibi] *nf*: **la** ~ Namibia.

namibien, -ienne [namibjɛ̃, jɛn] *adj* Namibian.
◆ **Namibien, -ienne** *nm, f* Namibian.

nana [nana] *nf fam* [jeune fille] girl.

nanti, -e [nɑ̃ti] ◇ *adj* wealthy. ◇ *nm, f* wealthy person; **les** ~**s** the rich.

nantir [nɑ̃tir] [32] *vt littéraire*: ~ **qqn de** to provide sb with.
◆ **se nantir** *vp littéraire*: **se** ~ **de** to provide o.s. with.

NAP [nap] (*abr de* Neuilly Auteuil Passy) ◇ *adj* ≃ preppie *Am*, ≃ Sloany *Br*. ◇ *nf* ≃ preppie type *Am*, ≃ Sloane *Br*.

naphtaline [naftalin] *nf* mothballs (*pl*).

nappage [napaʒ] *nm* CULIN coating.

nappe [nap] *nf* **-1.** [de table] tablecloth, cloth. **-2.** *fig* [étendue - gén] sheet; [- de brouillard] blanket. **-3.** [couche] layer; ~ **de mazout** OU **pétrole** oil slick.

napper [nape] [3] *vt* CULIN to coat.

napperon [naprɔ̃] *nm* tablemat.

naquis, naquit *etc* → **naître**.

narcisse [narsis] *nm* BOT narcissus.

narcissique [narsisik] ◇ *nmf* narcissist. ◇ *adj* narcissistic.

narcissisme [narsisism] *nm* narcissism.

narcodollars [narkodɔlar] *nmpl* narcodollars.

narcotique [narkɔtik] *nm & adj* narcotic.

narguer [narge] [3] *vt* [danger] to flout; [personne] to scorn, to scoff at.

narine [narin] *nf* nostril.

narquois, -e [narkwa, az] *adj* sardonic.

narrateur, -trice [naratœr, tris] *nm, f* narrator.

narratif, -ive [naratif, iv] *adj* narrative.

narration [narasjɔ̃] *nf* **-1.** [récit] narration. **-2.** SCOL essay.

narrer [nare] [3] *vt littéraire* to narrate.

NASA, Nasa [naza] (*abr de* National Aeronautics and Space Administration) *nf* NASA.

nasal, -e, -aux [nazal, o] *adj* nasal.

nasaliser [nazalize] [3] *vt* to nasalize.

naseau, -x [nazo] *nm* nostril.

nasillard, -e [nazijar, ard] *adj* nasal.

nasiller [nazije] [3] *vi* **-1.** [personne] to speak through one's nose. **-2.** [machine] to whine.

nasse [nas] *nf* keep net.

natal, -e, -als [natal] *adj* [d'origine] native.

natalité [natalite] *nf* birth rate.

natation [natasjɔ̃] *nf* swimming; **faire de la** ~ to swim.

natif, -ive [natif, iv] ◇ *adj* **-1.** [originaire] native (*avant n*); ~ **de** native of. **-2.** [inné] innate. ◇ *nm, f* native.

nation [nasjɔ̃] *nf* nation.
◆ **Nations unies** *nfpl*: **les Nations unies** the United Nations.

national, -e, -aux [nasjɔnal, o] *adj* national.
◆ **nationale** *nf*: (**route**) ~**e** ≃ state highway *Am*, ≃ A road *Br*.

nationalisation [nasjɔnalizasjɔ̃] *nf* nationalization.

nationaliser [nasjɔnalize] [3] *vt* to nationalize.

nationalisme [nasjɔnalism] *nm* nationalism.

nationaliste [nasjɔnalist] *nmf & adj* nationalist.

nationalité [nasjɔnalite] *nf* nationality; **de** ~ **française** of French nationality; **double** ~ dual nationality.

nativité [nativite] *nf* nativity.

natte [nat] *nf* **-1.** [tresse] plait. **-2.** [tapis] mat.

natter [nate] [3] *vt* to plait.

naturalisation [natyralizasjɔ̃] *nf* **-1.** [de personne, de plante] naturalization. **-2.** [taxidermie] stuffing.

naturalisé, -e [natyralize] ◇ *adj* **-1.** [personne, plante] naturalized. **-2.** [empaillé] stuffed. ◇ *nm, f* naturalized person.

naturaliser [natyralize] [3] *vt* **-1.** [personne, plante] to naturalize; **se faire ~** to become naturalized. **-2.** [empailler] to stuff.

naturaliste [natyralist] ◇ *nmf* **-1.** LITTÉRATURE & ZOOL naturalist. **-2.** [empailleur] taxidermist. ◇ *adj* naturalistic.

nature [natyr] ◇ *nf* nature; **par ~** by nature; **payer en ~** to pay in kind. ◇ *adj inv* **-1.** [simple] plain. **-2.** *fam* [spontané] natural.
◆ **nature morte** *nf* still life.

naturel, -elle [natyrɛl] *adj* natural.
◆ **naturel** *nm* **-1.** [tempérament] nature; **être d'un ~ affable/sensible** *etc* to be affable/sensitive *etc* by nature. **-2.** [aisance, spontanéité] naturalness. **-3.** CULIN: **thon au ~** tuna in brine.

naturellement [natyrɛlmɑ̃] *adv* **-1.** [gén] naturally. **-2.** [logiquement] rationally.

naturisme [natyrism] *nm* naturism.

naturiste [natyrist] ◇ *nmf* naturist. ◇ *adj* naturist (*avant n*), nudist (*avant n*).

naufrage [nofraʒ] *nm* **-1.** [navire] shipwreck; **faire ~** to be wrecked. **-2.** *fig* [effondrement] collapse.

naufragé, -e [nofraʒe] ◇ *adj* shipwrecked. ◇ *nm, f* shipwrecked person.

nauséabond, -e [nozeabɔ̃, ɔ̃d] *adj* nauseating.

nausée [noze] *nf* **-1.** MÉD nausea; **avoir la ~** to feel nauseous OU sick; **donner la ~ à qqn** *litt* & *fig* to make sb (feel) sick. **-2.** [dégoût] disgust.

nautique [notik] *adj* nautical; [ski, sport] water (*avant n*).

nautisme [notism] *nm* water sports (*pl*).

naval, -e, -als [naval] *adj* naval.

navarin [navarɛ̃] *nm* lamb stew.

navet [navɛ] *nm* **-1.** BOT turnip. **-2.** *fam péj* [œuvre] load of rubbish.

navette [navɛt] *nf* shuttle; **~ spatiale** AÉRON space shuttle; **faire la ~** to shuttle.

navigable [navigabl] *adj* navigable.

navigant, -e [navigɑ̃, ɑ̃t] ◇ *adj* navigation (*avant n*). ◇ *nm, f*: **les ~s** the flight crew.

navigateur, -trice [navigatœr, tris] *nm, f* navigator.

navigation [navigasjɔ̃] *nf* navigation; COMM shipping; **~ aérienne/spatiale** air/space travel.

naviguer [navige] [3] *vi* **-1.** [voguer] to sail. **-2.** *fam* [voyager] to travel. **-3.** [piloter] to navigate.

navire [navir] *nm* ship; **~ de guerre** warship; **~ marchand** merchant ship.

navrant, -e [navrɑ̃, ɑ̃t] *adj* **-1.** [triste] upsetting, distressing. **-2.** [regrettable, mauvais] unfortunate.

navrer [navre] [3] *vt* to upset; **être navré de qqch/de faire qqch** to be sorry about sthg/to do sthg.

nazi, -e [nazi] ◇ *adj* Nazi (*avant n*). ◇ *nm, f* Nazi.

nazisme [nazism] *nm* Nazism.

NB (*abr de* **Nota Bene**) NB.

NBC (*abr de* **nucléaire, bactériologique, chimique**) *adj* NBC.

nbreuses *abr de* **nombreuses**.

nbrx *abr de* **nombreux**.

n.c. -1. (*abr de* **non communiqué**) n.a. **-2.** (*abr de* **non connu**) n.a.

n.d. -1. (*abr de* **non daté**) n.d. **-2.** (*abr de* **non disponible**) n.a.

N-D (*abr de* **Notre-Dame**) OL.

NDA (*abr de* **note de l'auteur**) author's note.

N'Djamena [ndʒamena] *n* N'Djamena.

NDLR (*abr de* **note de la rédaction**) editor's note.

NDT (*abr de* **note du traducteur**) translator's note.

ne [nə], **n'** (*devant voyelle ou h muet*) *adv* **-1.** [négation] → **pas, plus, rien** *etc*. **-2.** [négation implicite]: **il se porte mieux que je ~ (le) croyais** he's in better health than I thought (he would be). **-3.** [avec verbes ou expressions marquant la crainte, la crainte *etc*]: **je crains qu'il n'oublie** I'm afraid he'll forget; **j'ai peur qu'il n'en parle** I'm frightened he'll talk about it.

né, -e [ne] *adj* born; **~ en 1965** born in 1965; **~ le 17 juin** born on the 17th June; **~ de** born to OU of; **Mme X, ~e Y** Mrs X née Y; **je ne suis pas ~ d'hier** I wasn't born yesterday.

néanmoins [neɑ̃mwɛ̃] *adv* nevertheless.

néant [neɑ̃] *nm* **-1.** [absence de valeur] worthlessness. **-2.** [absence d'existence] nothingness; **réduire à ~** to reduce to nothing.

nébuleux, -euse [nebylø, øz] *adj* **-1.** [ciel] cloudy. **-2.** [idée, projet] nebulous.
◆ **nébuleuse** *nf* **-1.** ASTRON nebula. **-2.** *fig* [groupe] nebulous group.

nécessaire [nesesɛr] ◇ *adj* necessary; **~ à** necessary for; **il est ~ de faire qqch** it is necessary to do sthg; **il est ~ que** (+ *subjonctif*): **il est ~ qu'elle vienne** she must come.

◇ *nm* **-1.** [biens] necessities (*pl*); **le strict ~** the bare essentials (*pl*). **-2.** [mesures]: **faire le ~** to do the necessary. **-3.** [trousse] bag; **~ de couture** sewing kit; **~ de toilette** toilet bag.

nécessairement [nesesɛrmɑ̃] *adv* **-1.** [fatalement] necessarily, of necessity. **-2.** [absolument] absolutely, positively.

nécessité [nesesite] *nf* **-1.** [obligation, situation] necessity; **être dans la ~ de faire qqch** to have no choice OU alternative but to do sthg. **-2.** [besoin] need.
◆ **nécessités** *nfpl* necessities.

nécessiter [nesesite] [3] *vt* to necessitate.

nec plus ultra [nɛkplyzyltra] *nm inv*: **le ~ de** the last word in.

nécrologie [nekrɔlɔʒi] *nf* [notice] obituary; [rubrique] deaths (*pl*).

nécrologique [nekrɔlɔʒik] *adj* obituary (*avant n*).

nécromancien, -ienne [nekrɔmɑ̃sjɛ̃, jɛn] *nm, f* necromancer.

nécrose [nekroz] *nf* necrosis.

nectar [nɛktar] *nm* nectar; **~ d'abricot/de pêche** apricot/peach nectar.

nectarine [nɛktarin] *nf* nectarine.

néerlandais, -e [neerlɑ̃dɛ, ɛz] *adj* Dutch.
◆ **néerlandais** *nm* [langue] Dutch.
◆ **Néerlandais, -e** *nm, f* Dutchman (*f* Dutchwoman); **les Néerlandais** the Dutch.

nef [nɛf] *nf* [d'église] nave.

néfaste [nefast] *adj* **-1.** [jour, événement] fateful. **-2.** [influence] harmful.

nèfle [nɛfl] *nf* medlar.

néflier [nɛflije] *nm* medlar tree.

négatif, -ive [negatif, iv] *adj* negative.
◆ **négatif** *nm* PHOT negative.
◆ **négative** *nf*: **répondre par la négative** to reply in the negative.

négation [negasjɔ̃] *nf* **-1.** [rejet] denial. **-2.** GRAM negative.

négativement [negativmɑ̃] *adv* negatively.

négligé, -e [negliʒe] *adj* **-1.** [travail, tenue] untidy. **-2.** [ami, jardin] neglected.
◆ **négligé** *nm* **-1.** [laisser-aller] untidiness. **-2.** [déshabillé] negligee.

négligeable [negliʒabl] *adj* negligible.

négligemment [negliʒamɑ̃] *adv* **-1.** [sans soin] carelessly. **-2.** [avec indifférence] casually.

négligence [negliʒɑ̃s] *nf* **-1.** [laisser-aller] carelessness. **-2.** [omission] negligence; **par ~** out of negligence.

négligent, -e [negliʒɑ̃, ɑ̃t] ◇ *adj* **-1.** [sans

soin] careless. **-2.** [indifférent] casual. ◇ *nm, f* casual person.

négliger [negliʒe] [17] *vt* **-1.** [ami, jardin] to neglect; **~ de faire qqch** to fail to do sthg. **-2.** [avertissement] to ignore.
◆ **se négliger** *vp* to neglect o.s.

négoce [negɔs] *nm* business.

négociable [negɔsjabl] *adj* negotiable.

négociant, -e [negɔsjɑ̃, ɑ̃t] *nm, f* dealer.

négociateur, -trice [negɔsjatœr, tris] *nm, f* negotiator.

négociation [negɔsjasjɔ̃] *nf* negotiation; **~s de paix** peace negotiations; **~s au sommet** summit meeting (*sg*).

négocier [negɔsje] [9] *vt* to negotiate.

nègre, négresse [negr, negrɛs] *nm, f* negro (*f* negress) (*beware: the terms 'nègre' and 'négresse' are considered racist*).
◆ **nègre** ◇ *nm fam* ghost writer. ◇ *adj* negro (*avant n*) (*beware: the term 'nègre' is considered racist*).

négrier [negrije] *nm* **-1.** [esclavagiste] slave trader. **-2.** *fig* [exploiteur] slave driver.

négro [negro] *nm* racist term used with reference to black people.

neige [nɛʒ] *nf* **-1.** [flocons] snow; **aller à la ~** ≃ to go skiing; **blanc comme ~** as white as snow; *fig* pure as the driven snow; **~ fabriquée** *Can* artificial snow. **-2.** *loc*: **battre en ~** CULIN to beat OU whip until stiff.
◆ **neige carbonique** *nf* dry ice.

neiger [neʒe] [23] *v impers*: **il neige** it is snowing.

neigeux, -euse [nɛʒø, øz] *adj* snowy.

nénuphar [nenyfar] *nm* water-lily.

néo-calédonien, -ienne [neɔkaledɔnjɛ̃, jɛn] (*mpl* **néo-calédoniens**, *fpl* **néo-calédoniennes**) *adj* New Caledonian.
◆ **Néo-Calédonien, -ienne** *nm, f* New Caledonian.

néo-colonialiste [neɔkɔlɔnjalist] (*pl* **néo-colonialistes**) *nmf & adj* neo-colonialist.

néologisme [neɔlɔʒism] *nm* neologism.

néon [neɔ̃] *nm* **-1.** [gaz] neon. **-2.** [enseigne] neon light.

néonatal, -e, -als [neɔnatal] *adj* neonatal.

néophyte [neɔfit] ◇ *nmf* novice. ◇ *adj* novice (*avant n*).

néo-zélandais, -e [neɔzelɑ̃dɛ, ɛz] (*mpl inv*, *fpl* **néo-zélandaises**) *adj* New Zealand (*avant n*).
◆ **Néo-Zélandais, -e** *nm, f* New Zealander.

Népal [nepal] *nm*: **le ~** Nepal; **au ~** in Nepal.

népalais, -e [nepalɛ, ɛz] *adj* Nepalese.

◆ **népalais** *nm* [langue] Nepali, Nepalese.

◆ **Népalais, -e** *nm, f* Nepalese (person); **les Népalais** the Nepalese.

néphrite [nefrit] *nf* nephritis.

népotisme [nepɔtism] *nm* nepotism.

nerf [nɛr] *nm* **-1.** ANAT nerve; ~ **optique/ rachidien** optic/spinal nerve. **-2.** *fig* [vigueur] spirit.

◆ **nerfs** *nmpl* nerves; **avoir les ~s solides/ d'acier** to have strong nerves/nerves of steel; **être à bout de ~s** to be at the end of one's tether; **être sur les ~s** to be tense; **taper sur les ~s de qqn** *fam* to get on sb's nerves.

nerveusement [nɛrvøzmɑ̃] *adv* nervously.

nerveux, -euse [nɛrvø, øz] ◇ *adj* **-1.** [gén] nervous. **-2.** [viande] stringy. **-3.** [style] vigorous; [voiture] nippy. ◇ *nm, f* nervous person.

nervosité [nɛrvozite] *nf* nervousness.

nervure [nɛrvyr] *nf* **-1.** [de feuille, d'aile] vein. **-2.** [de voûte] rib.

n'est-ce pas [nɛspa] *adv*: **vous me croyez, ~?** you believe me, don't you?; **c'est délicieux, ~?** it's delicious, isn't it?; ~ **que vous vous êtes bien amusés?** you enjoyed yourselves, didn't you?

net, nette [nɛt] *adj* **-1.** [écriture, image, idée] clear. **-2.** [propre, rangé] clean, neat. **-3.** COMM & FIN net; ~ **d'impôt** tax-exempt *Am*, tax-free *Br*. **-4.** [visible, manifeste] definite, distinct.

◆ **net** *adv* **-1.** [sur le coup] on the spot; **s'arrêter ~** to stop dead; **se casser ~** to break clean off. **-2.** [franchement - parler] plainly.

Net [nɛt] *nm fam*: **le ~** the Net; **surfer sur le ~** to surf the Net.

nettement [nɛtmɑ̃] *adv* **-1.** [clairement] clearly. **-2.** [incontestablement] definitely; ~ **mieux** definitely better; ~ **plus/moins** much more/less.

netteté [nɛtte] *nf* clearness.

nettoie, nettoies *etc* → **nettoyer**.

nettoyage [netwajaʒ] *nm* [de vêtement] cleaning; ~ **à sec** dry cleaning.

nettoyant [netwajɑ̃] *nm* cleaning fluid.

nettoyer [netwaje] [13] *vt* **-1.** [gén] to clean. **-2.** [grenier] to clear out. **-3.** [suj: police, soldats] to clean up.

neuf¹, neuve [nœf, nœv] *adj* new; **flambant ~** brand new.

◆ **neuf** *nm*: **vêtu de ~** wearing new clothes; **quoi de ~?** what's new?; **rien de ~** nothing new; **refaire** OU **remettre à ~** to make as good as new, to refurbish.

neuf² [nœf] *adj num & nm* nine; *voir aussi* **six**.

neurasthénie [nørasteni] *nf* depression.

neurasthénique [nørastenik] *nmf & adj* depressive.

neurochirurgie [nøroʃiryrʒi] *nf* neurosurgery.

neuroleptique [nørɔlɛptik] ◇ *nm* neuroleptic drug. ◇ *adj* neuroleptic.

neurologie [nørɔlɔʒi] *nf* neurology.

neurologique [nørɔlɔʒik] *adj* neurological.

neurologue [nørɔlɔg] *nmf* neurologist.

neurovégétatif, -ive [nøroveʒetatif, iv] *adj*: **système ~** nervous system.

neutralisation [nøtralizasjɔ̃] *nf* neutralization.

neutraliser [nøtralize] [3] *vt* to neutralize.

neutralité [nøtralite] *nf* neutrality.

neutre [nøtr] ◇ *nm* LING neuter. ◇ *adj* **-1.** [gén] neutral. **-2.** LING neuter.

neutron [nøtrɔ̃] *nm* neutron.

neuve → **neuf**.

neuvième [nœvjɛm] ◇ *adj num, nm & nmf* ninth; *voir aussi* **sixième**. ◇ *nf* SCOL ≃ third grade *Am*, ≃ first year OU form *(at junior school) Br*.

névé [neve] *nm* snowbank.

neveu, -x [nəvø] *nm* nephew.

névralgie [nevralʒi] *nf* **-1.** MÉD neuralgia. **-2.** [mal de tête] headache.

névralgique [nevralʒik] *adj* **-1.** [douloureux] neuralgic. **-2.** *fig* [sensible] sensitive.

névrose [nevroz] *nf* neurosis.

névrosé, -e [nevroze] *adj & nm, f* neurotic.

névrotique [nevrɔtik] *adj* neurotic.

New Delhi [njudeli] *n* New Delhi.

New York [njujɔrk] *n* **-1.** [ville] New York (City); **à ~** in New York (City). **-2.** [état] New York State; **dans l'État de ~** in New York State.

new-yorkais, -e [njujɔrkɛ, ɛz] *(mpl* **new-yorkais,** *fpl* **new-yorkaises)** *adj* from New York.

◆ **New-Yorkais, -e** *nm, f* New Yorker.

nez [ne] *nm* nose; **saigner du ~** to have a nosebleed; ~ **aquilin** aquiline nose; ~ **busqué** hooked nose; ~ **camus** pug nose; ~ **retroussé** snub nose; **avoir le ~ fin** to have a good sense of smell; *fig* to have foresight; ~ **à ~** face to face; **ça lui pend au ~** *fam* he's got it coming to him; **faire qqch au ~ et à la barbe de qqn** to do sthg (right) under sb's nose; **mettre le ~ dehors** to put one's nose outside; **mettre le ~ à la fenêtre** to show one's face at the window; **raccro-**

cher au ~ de qqn to hang up on sb; **rire au ~ de qqn** to laugh in sb's face.

NF (*abr de* **Norme française**) *French industrial standard*, ≃ BS *Br*.

ni [ni] *conj*: **sans pull ~ écharpe** without a sweater or a scarf; **je ne peux ~ ne veux venir** I neither can nor want to come.

◆ **ni ... ni** *loc corrélative* neither ... nor; **~ lui ~ moi** neither of us; **~ l'un ~ l'autre n'a parlé** neither of them spoke; **je ne les aime ~ l'un ~ l'autre** I don't like either of them.

niable [njabl] *adj* deniable.

Niagara [njagara] *nm*: **les chutes du ~** Niagara Falls.

niais, -e [njɛ, njɛz] ◇ *adj* silly, foolish. ◇ *nm, f* fool.

niaisement [njɛzmɑ̃] *adv* foolishly.

niaiserie [njɛzri] *nf* foolishness (*U*); **dire des ~s** to talk rubbish.

Niamey [njamɛ] *n* Niamey.

Nicaragua [nikaragwa] *nm*: **le ~** Nicaragua; **au ~** in Nicaragua.

nicaraguayen, -enne [nikaragwajɛ̃, jɛn] *adj* Nicaraguan.

◆ **Nicaraguayen, -enne** *nm, f* Nicaraguan.

niche [niʃ] *nf* **-1.** [de chien] kennel. **-2.** [de statue] niche. **-3.** *fam* [farce] trick.

nicher [niʃe] [3] *vi* **-1.** [oiseaux] to nest. **-2.** *fam* [personne] to live.

◆ **se nicher** *vp* to hide.

nickel [nikɛl] ◇ *nm* nickel. ◇ *adj inv fam* spotless, spick and span.

niçois, -e [niswa, az] *adj* of/from Nice; **salade ~e** *salad made out of lettuce, green peppers, tuna fish, tomatoes, anchovy and hard-boiled egg*.

◆ **Niçois, -e** *nm, f* native OU inhabitant of Nice.

Nicosie [nikɔzi] *n* Nicosia.

nicotine [nikɔtin] *nf* nicotine.

nid [ni] *nm* nest; **~-d'abeilles** [tissu] waffle cloth; **~ à poussière** *fig* dust trap.

◆ **nid de poule** *nm* pothole.

nièce [njɛs] *nf* niece.

nier [nje] [9] *vt* to deny.

nigaud, -e [nigo, od] ◇ *adj* silly. ◇ *nm, f* simpleton.

Niger [niʒɛr] *nm* **-1.** [fleuve]: **le ~** the River Niger. **-2.** [État]: **le ~** Niger; **au ~** in Niger.

Nigeria [niʒerja] *nm*: **le ~** Nigeria; **au ~** in Nigeria.

nigérian, -e [niʒerjɑ̃, an] *adj* Nigerian.

◆ **Nigérian, -e** *nm, f* Nigerian.

nigérien, -ienne [niʒerjɛ̃, jɛn] *adj* Nigerien.

◆ **Nigérien, -ienne** *nm, f* Nigerien.

night-club [najtklœb] (*pl* **night-clubs**) *nm* nightclub.

Nil [nil] *nm*: **le ~** the Nile; **le ~ Blanc** the White Nile; **le ~ Bleu** the Blue Nile.

n'importe → **importer**.

nippes [nip] *nfpl fam* gear (*U*).

nippon, -one [nipɔ̃, ɔn] *adj* Japanese.

◆ **Nippon, -one** *nm, f* Japanese (person); **les Nippons** the Japanese.

nirvana [nirvana] *nm* nirvana.

nitrate [nitrat] *nm* nitrate.

nitrique [nitrik] *adj* nitric.

nitroglycérine [nitrɔgliserin] *nf* nitroglycerine.

niveau, -x [nivo] *nm* **-1.** [gén] level; **de même ~** *fig* of the same standard; **~ à bulle** spirit level; **au-dessus du ~ de la mer** above sea level; **~ scolaire** standard of education; **~ de vie** standard of living; **au ~ de** at the level of; *fig* [en ce qui concerne] as regards. **-2.** LING: **~ de langue** register.

niveler [nivle] [24] *vt* to level; *fig* to level out.

nivellement [nivɛlmɑ̃] *nm* levelling; *fig* levelling out; **~ par le bas** levelling down.

NN (*abr de* **nouvelle norme**) *revised standard of hotel classification*.

noble [nɔbl] ◇ *nmf* nobleman (*f* noblewoman). ◇ *adj* noble.

noblement [nɔblәmɑ̃] *adv* nobly.

noblesse [nɔblɛs] *nf* nobility.

noce [nɔs] *nf* **-1.** [mariage] wedding. **-2.** [invités] wedding party. **-3.** *loc*: **faire la ~** *fam* to live it up.

◆ **noces** *nfpl* wedding (*sg*); **convoler en justes ~s** to be married; **elle l'a épousé en secondes ~s** is her second husband; **~s d'or/d'argent** golden/silver wedding (anniversary).

nocif, -ive [nɔsif, iv] *adj* **-1.** [produit, gaz] noxious. **-2.** *fig* [théorie, doctrine] harmful.

nocivité [nɔsivite] *nf* **-1.** [de produit, gaz] noxiousness. **-2.** *fig* [de théorie, doctrine] harmfulness.

noctambule [nɔktɑ̃byl] *nmf* night bird.

nocturne [nɔktyrn] ◇ *nm* **-1.** MUS nocturne. **-2.** ZOOL night hunter. ◇ *nm ou nf* **-1.** [d'un magasin] late opening; **ouvert en ~** open late. **-2.** SPORT: **match en ~** evening game. ◇ *adj* **-1.** [émission, attaque] night (*avant n*). **-2.** [animal] nocturnal.

nodule [nɔdyl] *nm* nodule.

Noël [nɔɛl] *nm* Christmas; **joyeux ~!** happy OU merry Christmas!

nœud [nø] *nm* **-1.** [de fil, de bois] knot; ~ **coulant** slipknot; **double** ~ double knot. **-2.** NAVIG knot; **filer à X** ~**s** NAVIG to do X knots. **-3.** *fig* & *littéraire* [attachement] bond. **-4.** [de l'action, du problème] crux. **-5.** [ornement] bow; ~ **de cravate** knot (*in one's tie*); ~ **papillon** bow tie. **-6.** ANAT, ASTRON, ÉLECTR & RAIL node.

noie, noies *etc* → noyer.

noierai, noieras *etc* → noyer.

noir, -e [nwar] *adj* **-1.** [gén] black; ~ **de** [poussière, suie] black with. **-2.** [pièce, couloir] dark. **-3.** *fig* [pressentiment] sombre *Am*, sombre *Br*. **-4.** *fig* [ivre] drunk.
◆ **Noir, -e** *nm, f* black.
◆ **noir** *nm* **-1.** [couleur] black; ~ **sur blanc** *fig* in black and white. **-2.** [obscurité] dark. **-3.** *loc*: **acheter qqch au** ~ to buy sthg on the black market; **broyer du** ~ to be down in the dumps; **travail au** ~ moonlighting; **travailler au** ~ to moonlight; **voir tout en** ~ to see the dark side of everything.
◆ **noire** *nf* quarter note *Am*, crotchet *Br*.

noirâtre [nwaratr] *adj* blackish.

noiraud, -e [nwaro, od] ◇ *adj* swarthy. ◇ *nm, f* swarthy person.

noirceur [nwarsœr] *nf* **-1.** *littéraire* [couleur] blackness. **-2.** *fig* [méchanceté] wickedness.

noircir [nwarsir] [32] ◇ *vi* to darken. ◇ *vt* *litt* & *fig* to blacken.
◆ **se noircir** *vp* [devenir noir] to darken.

Noire → mer.

noise [nwaz] *nf littéraire*: **chercher** ~ **à qqn** to pick a quarrel with sb.

noisetier [nwaztje] *nm* hazel tree.

noisette [nwazɛt] ◇ *nf* **-1.** [fruit] hazelnut. **-2.** [petite quantité]: **une** ~ **de beurre** a knob of butter. ◇ *adj inv* hazel.

noix [nwa] *nf* **-1.** [fruit] walnut; ~ **de cajou** cashew (nut); ~ **de coco** coconut; ~ **de muscade** nutmeg. **-2.** [de viande]: ~ **de veau** cushion of veal. **-3.** *loc*: **à la** ~ *fam* dreadful.

nom [nɔ̃] *nm* **-1.** [gén] name; **au** ~ **de** in the name of; ~ **de Dieu!** *tfam* God damn it!, bloody hell! *Br*; ~ **d'un chien** OU **d'une pipe!** *fam* drat!; **faux** ~ false name; ~ **déposé** trade name; ~ **d'emprunt** assumed name; ~ **de famille** surname; ~ **de fichier** INFORM filename; ~ **de jeune fille** maiden name; **traiter qqn de tous les** ~**s** to call sb all the names under the sun. **-2.** [prénom] (first) name. **-3.** GRAM noun; ~ **composé** compound noun; ~ **propre/commun** proper/common noun.

nomade [nɔmad] ◇ *nmf* nomad. ◇ *adj* nomadic.

nombre [nɔ̃br] *nm* number; **au** ~ **de** among; **bon** ~ **de** a large number of, a good many; **un bon** ~ **d'entre nous/eux** many of us/them; **venir en** ~ to come in large numbers; ~ **pair/impair** even/odd number.

nombreux, -euse [nɔ̃brø, øz] *adj* **-1.** [famille, foule] large. **-2.** [erreurs, occasions] numerous; **peu** ~ few.

nombril [nɔ̃bril] *nm* navel; **il se prend pour le** ~ **du monde** he thinks the world revolves around him.

nombrilisme [nɔ̃brilism] *nm fam péj* navelgazing.

nomenclature [nɔmɑ̃klatyr] *nf* **-1.** [terminologie] nomenclature. **-2.** [liste] word list.

nominal, -e, -aux [nɔminal, o] *adj* **-1.** [liste] of names. **-2.** [valeur, autorité] nominal. **-3.** GRAM noun (*avant n*).

nominalement [nɔminalmɑ̃] *adv* **-1.** [désigner] by name. **-2.** GRAM nominally.

nominatif, -ive [nɔminatif, iv] *adj* [liste] of names.
◆ **nominatif** *nm* GRAM nominative.

nomination [nɔminasjɔ̃] *nf* nomination, appointment.

nommé, -e [nɔme] ◇ *adj* **-1.** [désigné] named. **-2.** [choisi] appointed. ◇ *nm, f* aforementioned.

nommément [nɔmemɑ̃] *adv* [citer] by name.

nommer [nɔme] [3] *vt* **-1.** [appeler] to name, to call. **-2.** [qualifier] to call. **-3.** [promouvoir] to appoint, to nominate. **-4.** [dénoncer, mentionner] to name.
◆ **se nommer** *vp* **-1.** [s'appeler] to be called. **-2.** [se désigner] to give one's name.

non [nɔ̃] ◇ *adv* **-1.** [réponse négative] no. **-2.** [se rapportant à une phrase précédente] not; **moi** ~ not me; **moi** ~ **plus** (and) neither am/do *etc* I; **elle ne travaille pas aujourd'hui, moi** ~ **plus** she's not working today and neither am I. **-3.** [sert à demander une confirmation]: **c'est une bonne idée,** ~? it's a good idea, isn't it? **-4.** [modifie un adjectif ou un adverbe] not; ~ **loin d'ici** not far from here; **une difficulté** ~ **négligeable** a not inconsiderable problem.
◇ *nm inv* no.
◆ **non moins** *loc adv* no less.
◆ **non (pas) ... mais** *loc corrélative* not ... but; ~ **pas maigre, mais mince** not skinny but slim.
◆ **non plus ... mais** *loc corrélative* no longer ... but.
◆ **non (pas) que ... mais** *loc corrélative* not that ... but.

◆ **non seulement ... mais (encore)** *loc corrélative* not only ... but also.

nonagénaire [nɔnaʒenɛr] *nmf & adj* nonagenarian.

non-agression [nɔnagresjɔ̃] *nf* non-aggression.

non-aligné, -e [nɔnaliɲe] *adj* non-aligned; **les pays ~s** the non-aligned countries.

nonante [nɔnɑ̃t] *adj num Belg & Helv* ninety.

non-assistance [nɔnasistɑ̃s] *nf* non-assistance; **~ à personne en danger** failure to give assistance to a person in danger.

nonchalance [nɔ̃ʃalɑ̃s] *nf* nonchalance, casualness.

nonchalant, -e [nɔ̃ʃalɑ̃, ɑ̃t] *adj* nonchalant, casual.

non-combattant, -e [nɔ̃kɔ̃batɑ̃, ɑ̃t] ◇ *adj* noncombatant. ◇ *nm, f* noncombatant.

non-conformiste [nɔ̃kɔ̃fɔrmist] ◇ *nmf* nonconformist. ◇ *adj* unconventional.

non-conformité [nɔ̃kɔ̃fɔrmite] *nf* nonconformity.

non-dit [nɔ̃di] *nm* unvoiced feeling.

non-fumeur, -euse [nɔ̃fymœr, øz] ◇ *nm, f* non-smoker. ◇ *adj* non-smoking (*avant n*).

non-ingérence [nɔnɛ̃ʒerɑ̃s] *nf* noninterference.

non-inscrit, -e [nɔnɛ̃skri, it] *adj & nm, f* POLIT independent.

non-intervention [nɔnɛ̃tɛrvɑ̃sjɔ̃] *nf* nonintervention.

non-lieu [nɔ̃ljø] (*pl* **non-lieux**) *nm* JUR dismissal through lack of evidence; **rendre un ~** to dismiss a case for lack of evidence.

nonne [nɔn] *nf* nun.

nonobstant [nɔnɔpstɑ̃] *sout* ◇ *prép* notwithstanding. ◇ *adv* nevertheless.

non-paiement [nɔ̃pɛmɑ̃] *nm* nonpayment.

non-recevoir [nɔ̃rəsəvwar]
◆ **fin de non-recevoir** *nf* JUR objection.

non-résident [nɔ̃rezidɑ̃] *nm* nonresident.

non-retour [nɔ̃rətur]
◆ **point de non-retour** *nm* point of no return.

non-sens [nɔ̃sɑ̃s] *nm inv* **-1.** [absurdité] nonsense. **-2.** [contresens] meaningless word.

non-stop [nɔnstɔp] *adj inv* non-stop.

non-violence [nɔ̃vjɔlɑ̃s] *nf* non-violence.

non-voyant, -e [nɔ̃vwajɑ̃, ɑ̃t] *nm, f* visually handicapped.

nord [nɔr] ◇ *nm* north; **un vent du ~** a northerly wind; **le vent du ~** the north wind; **au ~** in the north; **au ~ (de)** to the north (of); **le grand Nord** the frozen North;

perdre le ~ *fam fig* to lose one's head. ◇ *adj inv* north; [province, région] northern.

nord-africain, -e [nɔrafrikɛ̃, ɛn] (*mpl* **nord-africains**, *fpl* **nord-africaines**) *adj* North African.
◆ **Nord-Africain, -e** *nm, f* North African.

nord-américain, -e [nɔramerikɛ̃, ɛn] (*mpl* **nord-américains**, *fpl* **nord-américaines**) *adj* North American.
◆ **Nord-Américain, -e** *nm, f* North American.

nord-coréen, -enne [nɔrkɔreɛ̃, ɛn] *adj* (*mpl* **nord-coréens**, *fpl* **nord-coréennes**) North Korean.
◆ **Nord-Coréen, -enne** *nm, f* North Korean.

nord-est [nɔrɛst] *nm & adj inv* north-east.

nordicité [nɔrdisite] *nf Can* northerliness.

nordique [nɔrdik] *adj* Nordic, Scandinavian.
◆ **Nordique** *nmf* **-1.** [Scandinave] Scandinavian. **-2.** *Can* North Canadian.

nord-ouest [nɔrwɛst] *nm & adj inv* north-west.

normal, -e, -aux [nɔrmal, o] *adj* normal.
◆ **normale** *nf* **-1.** [moyenne]: **la ~e** the norm. **-2.** *Can* GOLF par.

normalement [nɔrmalmɑ̃] *adv* normally, usually; **~ il devrait déjà être arrivé** he should have arrived by now.

normalien, -ienne [nɔrmaljɛ̃, jɛn] *nm, f* student at teachers college *Am* OU teacher training college *Br*.

normalisation [nɔrmalizasjɔ̃] *nf* **-1.** [stabilisation] normalization. **-2.** [standardisation] standardization.

normaliser [nɔrmalize] [3] *vt* **-1.** [situation] to normalize. **-2.** [produit] to standardize.
◆ **se normaliser** *vp* to return to normal.

normalité [nɔrmalite] *nf* normality.

normand, -e [nɔrmɑ̃, ɑ̃d] *adj* Norman.
◆ **Normand, -e** *nm, f* Norman.

Normandie [nɔrmɑ̃di] *nf*: **la ~** Normandy.

normatif, -ive [nɔrmatif, iv] *adj* prescriptive.

norme [nɔrm] *nf* **-1.** [gén] standard, norm; **être hors ~s** to be non-standard. **-2.** [critère] criterion.

Norvège [nɔrvɛʒ] *nf*: **la ~** Norway.

norvégien, -ienne [nɔrveʒjɛ̃, jɛn] *adj* Norwegian.
◆ **norvégien** *nm* [langue] Norwegian.
◆ **Norvégien, -ienne** *nm, f* Norwegian.

nos → **notre**.

nostalgie [nɔstalʒi] *nf* nostalgia; **avoir la ~ de** to feel nostalgia for.

nostalgique [nɔstalʒik] *adj* nostalgic.

nota bene [nɔtabene] *nm inv* nota bene.

notable [nɔtabl] ◇ *adj* noteworthy, notable. ◇ *nm* notable.

notablement [nɔtabləmɑ̃] *adv* notably.

notaire [nɔtɛr] *nm* ≃ lawyer, ≃ solicitor *Br*.

notamment [nɔtamɑ̃] *adv* in particular.

notarial, -e, -iaux [nɔtarjal, jo] *adj* notarial.

notarié, -e [nɔtarje] *adj* ≃ drawn up by a lawyer OU solicitor *Br*.

notation [nɔtasjɔ̃] *nf* -1. [système] notation. -2. [remarque] note. -3. SCOL marking, grading *Am*.

note [nɔt] *nf* -1. [gén & MUS] note; **prendre des ~s** to take notes; **prendre qqch en ~** to make a note of sthg; **fausse ~** MUS false note; *fig* sour note; **~ de bas de page** footnote; **~ de service** memo. -2. SCOL & UNIV mark, grade *Am*; **avoir une bonne/mauvaise ~** to have a good/bad mark. -3. [facture] bill; **une ~ salée** *fam* a hefty OU steep bill.

noter [nɔte] [3] *vt* -1. [écrire] to note down. -2. [constater] to note, to notice. -3. SCOL & UNIV to mark, to grade *Am*. -4. [marquer] to mark.

notice [nɔtis] *nf* instructions (*pl*); **~ explicative** directions for use.

notification [nɔtifikasjɔ̃] *nf* notification.

notifier [nɔtifje] [9] *vt*: **~ qqch à qqn** to notify sb of sthg.

notion [nɔsjɔ̃] *nf* -1. [conscience, concept] notion, concept. -2. (*gén pl*) [rudiment] smattering (*U*).

notoire [nɔtwar] *adj* [fait] well-known; [criminel] notorious.

notoirement [nɔtwarmɑ̃] *adv* notoriously.

notoriété [nɔtɔrjete] *nf* -1. [de fait] notoriety; **être de ~ publique** to be common OU public knowledge. -2. [célébrité] fame.

notre [nɔtr] (*pl* **nos** [no]) *adj poss* our.

nôtre [notr]
◆ **le nôtre** (*f* **la nôtre**, *pl* **les nôtres**) *pron poss* ours; **les ~s** our family (*sg*); **serez-vous des ~s demain?** will you be joining us tomorrow?; **il faut y mettre du ~** we'll all have to pull our weight.

Nouakchott [nuakʃɔt] *n* Nouakchott.

nouba [nuba] *nf*: **faire la ~** *fam* to paint the town red.

nouer [nwe] [6] *vt* -1. [corde, lacet] to tie; [bouquet] to tie up. -2. *fig* [gorge, estomac] to knot. -3. *sout* [alliance, amitié] to make, to form.
◆ **se nouer** *vp* -1. [gorge] to tighten up.

-2. [alliance, amitié] to be formed. -3. [intrigue] to start.

noueux, -euse [nwø, øz] *adj* [bois] knotty; [mains] gnarled.

nougat [nuga] *nm* nougat.

nouille [nuj] *nf fam péj* idiot.
◆ **nouilles** *nfpl* [pâtes] pasta (*U*), noodles (*pl*).

Nouméa [numea] *n* Nouméa.

nounou [nunu] *nf* nanny.

nourrice [nuris] *nf* -1. [garde d'enfants] nanny, child-minder; [qui allaite] wet nurse. -2. [réservoir] can *Am*, jerrycan *Br*.

nourrir [nurir] [32] *vt* -1. [gén] to feed; **nourri-logé-blanchi** board, lodging and laundry. -2. [sentiment, projet] to nurture. -3. [style, esprit] to improve.
◆ **se nourrir** *vp* to eat; **se ~ de qqch** *litt & fig* to live on sthg.

nourrissant, -e [nurisɑ̃, ɑ̃t] *adj* nutritious, nourishing.

nourrisson [nurisɔ̃] *nm* infant.

nourriture [nurityr] *nf* food.

nous [nu] *pron pers* -1. [sujet] we. -2. [objet] us.
◆ **nous-mêmes** *pron pers* ourselves.

nouveau, -elle, -x [nuvo, nuvɛl, nuvo] (**nouvel** *devant voyelle et h muet*) ◇ *adj* new; **~x mariés** newlyweds. ◇ *nm, f* new boy (*f* new girl).
◆ **nouveau** *nm*: **il y a du ~** there's something new.
◆ **nouvelle** *nf* -1. [information] (piece of) news (*U*). -2. [court récit] short story.
◆ **nouvelles** *nfpl* news; **les nouvelles** MÉDIA the news (*sg*); **il a donné de ses nouvelles** I/we *etc* have heard from him; **être sans nouvelles de qqn/qqch** to have no news of sb/sthg; **aux dernières nouvelles ...** the latest is ....
◆ **à nouveau** *loc adv* -1. [encore] again. -2. [de manière différente] afresh, anew.
◆ **de nouveau** *loc adv* again.

nouveau-né, -e [nuvone] (*mpl* **nouveau-nés**, *fpl* **nouveau-nées**) ◇ *adj* newborn. ◇ *nm, f* newborn baby.

nouveauté [nuvote] *nf* -1. [actualité] novelty. -2. [innovation] something new. -3. [ouvrage] new book/film *etc*.

nouvel, nouvelle → nouveau.

Nouvelle-Calédonie [nuvɛlkaledɔni] *nf*: **la ~** New Caledonia.

Nouvelle-Écosse [nuvɛlekɔs] *nf*: **la ~** Nova Scotia.

Nouvelle-Guinée [nuvɛlgine] *nf*: **la ~** New Guinea.

nouvellement [nuvɛlmɑ̃] *adv* recently.

Nouvelle-Orléans [nuvɛlɔrleɑ̃] *n*: **La ~** New Orleans.

Nouvelle-Zélande [nuvɛlzelɑ̃d] *nf*: **la ~** New Zealand.

novateur, -trice [nɔvatœr, tris] ◇ *adj* innovative. ◇ *nm, f* innovator.

novembre [nɔvɑ̃br] *nm* November; *voir aussi* **septembre**.

novice [nɔvis] ◇ *nmf* novice. ◇ *adj* inexperienced.

noyade [nwajad] *nf* drowning.

noyau, -x [nwajo] *nm* **-1.** [de fruit] stone, pit. **-2.** ASTRON, BIOL & PHYS nucleus. **-3.** *fig* [d'amis] group, circle; [d'opposants, de résistants] cell; **~ dur** hard core. **-4.** *fig* [centre] core.

noyauter [nwajote] [3] *vt* to infiltrate.

noyé, -e [nwaje] ◇ *adj* **-1.** [personne] drowned. **-2.** [inondé] flooded; **yeux ~s de larmes** eyes swimming with tears. ◇ *nm, f* drowned person.

noyer [nwaje] [13] *vt* **-1.** [animal, personne] to drown; **~ son chagrin** to drown one's sorrows. **-2.** [terre, moteur] to flood. **-3.** [estomper, diluer] to swamp; [contours] to blur. ◆ **se noyer** *vp* **-1.** [personne] to drown. **-2.** *fig* [se perdre]: **se ~ dans** to become bogged down in. **-3.** [s'estomper] to be swamped.

N/Réf (*abr de* **Notre référence**) O/Ref.

NRF (*abr de* **Nouvelle Revue Française**) *nf* **-1.** [revue] literary review. **-2.** [mouvement] literary movement.

nu, -e [ny] *adj* **-1.** [personne] naked. **-2.** [paysage, fil électrique] bare. **-3.** [style, vérité] plain. ◆ **nu** *nm* nude; **à ~** stripped, bare; **mettre à ~** to strip bare.

nuage [nɥaʒ] *nm* **-1.** [gén] cloud; **être dans les ~s** *fig* to have one's head in the clouds. **-2.** [petite quantité]: **un ~ de lait** a drop of milk. **-3.** *Can* [foulard] scarf.

nuageux, -euse [nɥaʒø, øz] *adj* **-1.** [temps, ciel] cloudy. **-2.** *fig* [esprit] hazy.

nuance [nɥɑ̃s] *nf* **-1.** [de couleur] shade; [de son, de sens] nuance; **tout en ~s** extremely subtle. **-2.** [touche]: **~ de** touch of, trace of.

nuancer [nɥɑ̃se] [16] *vt* **-1.** [couleurs] to shade. **-2.** [pensée] to qualify.

nubile [nybil] *adj* nubile.

nucléaire [nykleɛr] ◇ *nm* nuclear energy. ◇ *adj* nuclear.

nudisme [nydism] *nm* nudism, naturism.

nudiste [nydist] *nmf & adj* nudist.

nudité [nydite] *nf* **-1.** [de personne] nudity, nakedness. **-2.** [de lieu, style] bareness.

nuée [nɥe] *nf* **-1.** [multitude]: **une ~ de** a horde of. **-2.** *littéraire* [nuage] cloud.

nues [ny] *nfpl*: **tomber des ~** to be completely taken aback.

nui [nɥi] *pp inv* → **nuire**.

nuire [nɥir] [97] *vi*: **~ à** to harm, to injure. ◆ **se nuire** *vp* to harm o.s.

nuisais, nuisions *etc* → **nuire**.

nuisance [nɥizɑ̃s] *nf* nuisance (*U*), harm (*U*); **~s sonores** noise pollution.

nuise, nuises *etc* → **nuire**.

nuisette [nɥizɛt] *nf* short nightgown, babydoll nightgown.

nuisible [nɥizibl] *adj* harmful.

nuit [nɥi] *nf* **-1.** [laps de temps] night; **cette ~** [la nuit dernière] last night; [la nuit prochaine] tonight; **de ~** at night; **bateau/vol de ~** night ferry/flight; **passer la ~ à l'hôtel** to spend the night in a hotel; **~ blanche** sleepless night. **-2.** [obscurité] darkness, night; **il fait ~** it's dark; **perdu dans la ~ des temps** lost in the mists of time.

nuitamment [nɥitamɑ̃] *adv littéraire* by night.

nuitée [nɥite] *nf* overnight stay.

nul, nulle [nyl] ◇ *adj indéf* (*avant n*) *littéraire* no. ◇ *adj* (*après n*) **-1.** [égal à zéro] nil. **-2.** [sans valeur] useless, hopeless; **c'est ~!** *fam* it's rubbish! **-3.** [sans résultat]: **match ~** draw. **-4.** [caduc]: **~ et non avenu** JUR null and void. ◇ *nm, f péj* nonentity. ◇ *pron indéf* *sout* no one, nobody. ◆ **nulle part** *adv* no-place *Am*, nowhere *Br*.

nullement [nylmɑ̃] *adv* by no means.

nullité [nylite] *nf* **-1.** [médiocrité] incompetence. **-2.** *péj* [personne] nonentity. **-3.** JUR invalidity, nullity.

numéraire [nymerɛr] ◇ *nm* cash. ◇ *adj* [espèces] legal.

numéral, -e, -aux [nymeral, o] *adj* numeral. ◆ **numéral, -aux** *nm* numeral.

numérateur [nymeratœr] *nm* numerator.

numération [nymerasjɔ̃] *nf* **-1.** MATHS numeration. **-2.** MÉD: **~ globulaire** blood count.

numérique [nymerik] *adj* **-1.** [gén] numerical. **-2.** INFORM digital.

numériquement [nymerikmɑ̃] *adv* numerically.

numéro [nymero] *nm* **-1.** [gén] number; **composer** OU **faire un ~** to dial a number; **faire un faux ~** to dial a wrong number; **~ minéralogique** OU **d'immatriculation** license *Am* OU registration *Br* number; **~ azur** *telephone number for which calls are charged at the* *local rate irrespective of the actual distance covered;* ~ **de téléphone** telephone number; ~ **vert** ≃ freefone number; **tirer le mauvais** ~ *fig* to get a raw deal. **-2.** [de spectacle] act, turn; **faire son** ~ *fig* to do one's little act. **-3.** *fam* [personne]: **quel** ~! what a character!

numéroter [nymerɔte] [3] *vt* to number.

numerus clausus [nymerysklozys] *nm* restricted intake of students.

numismatique [nymismatik] ◇ *nf* numismatics (*U*). ◇ *adj* numismatic.

nu-pieds [nypje] *nm inv* [sandale] sandal.

nuptial, -e, -iaux [nypsjal, jo] *adj* nuptial.

nuque [nyk] *nf* nape.

nurse [nœrs] *nf* children's nurse, nanny.

nutritif, -ive [nytritif, iv] *adj* nutritious.

nutritionniste [nytrisjɔnist] *nmf* nutritionist, dietician.

Nylon® [nilɔ̃] *nm* nylon.

nymphe [nɛ̃f] *nf* nymph.

nymphomane [nɛ̃fɔman] *nf & adj* nymphomaniac.

o, O [o] *nm inv* [lettre] o, O.

◆ **O** (*abr de* **Ouest**) W.

ô [o] *interj* oh!, O!

OACI (*abr de* **Organisation de l'aviation civile internationale**) *nf* ICAO.

OAS (*abr de* **Organisation de l'armée secrète**) *nf organization opposed to independence in Algeria in the 1960s.*

oasis [ɔazis] *nf* **-1.** [dans désert] oasis. **-2.** *fig* [de calme] haven, oasis.

obédience [ɔbedjɑ̃s] *nf* [appartenance] allegiance, persuasion; **être d'**~ **marxiste/catholique** to be a Marxist/Catholic.

obéir [ɔbeir] [32] *vi* **-1.** [personne]: ~ **à qqn/qqch** to obey sb/sthg. **-2.** [freins] to respond.

obéissance [ɔbeisɑ̃s] *nf* obedience; **devoir** ~ **à qqn** to owe sb allegiance.

obéissant, -e [ɔbeisɑ̃, ɑ̃t] *adj* obedient.

obélisque [ɔbelisk] *nm* obelisk.

obèse [ɔbɛz] ◇ *nmf* obese person. ◇ *adj* obese.

obésité [ɔbezite] *nf* obesity.

objecter [ɔbʒɛkte] [4] *vt* **-1.** [répliquer] to raise as an objection; ~ **que** to object that. **-2.** [prétexter]: ~ **qqch (à qqn)** to put forward sthg as an excuse (to sb).

objecteur [ɔbʒɛktœr] *nm* objector; ~ **de conscience** conscientious objector.

objectif, -ive [ɔbʒɛktif, iv] *adj* objective.

◆ **objectif** *nm* **-1.** PHOT lens. **-2.** [but, cible] objective, target.

objection [ɔbʒɛksjɔ̃] *nf* objection; **faire** ~ **à** to object to.

objectivement [ɔbʒɛktivmɑ̃] *adv* objectively.

objectivité [ɔbʒɛktivite] *nf* objectivity.

objet [ɔbʒɛ] *nm* **-1.** [chose] object; ~ **d'art** object d'art; ~**s trouvés** lost and found (*office*) *Am,* lost property office *Br.* **-2.** [sujet] subject; **être** OU **faire l'**~ **de** to be the subject of. **-3.** [but] aim, object; **cette réunion a pour** ~ **de ...** the aim of this meeting is to ...; **sans** ~ pointless.

objurgations [ɔbʒyrgasjɔ̃] *nfpl* **-1.** [remontrances] objurgations. **-2.** [prières] pleas.

obligation [ɔbligasjɔ̃] *nf* **-1.** [gén] obligation; **être dans l'**~ **de faire qqch** to be obliged to do sthg; **sans** ~ **d'achat** COMM (with) no obligation to buy; **avoir une** ~ **envers qqn** to be under an obligation to sb. **-2.** FIN bond, debenture.

◆ **obligations** *nfpl* obligations, duties; **avoir des** ~**s** to have obligations, to have a duty; ~**s militaires** military duties.

obligatoire [ɔbligatwar] *adj* **-1.** [imposé] compulsory, obligatory. **-2.** *fam* [inéluctable] inevitable.

obligeance [ɔbliʒɑ̃s] *nf sout* obligingness; **avoir l'**~ **de faire qqch** to be good OU kind enough to do sthg.

obligeant, -e [ɔbliʒɑ̃, ɑ̃t] *adj* helpful, obliging.

obliger [ɔbliʒe] [17] *vt* **-1.** [forcer]: ~ **qqn à qqch** to impose sthg on sb; ~ **qqn à faire qqch** to force sb to do sthg; **être obligé de faire qqch** to be obliged to do sthg. **-2.** JUR to bind. **-3.** [rendre service à] to oblige.

◆ **s'obliger** *vp*: **s'**~ **à qqch** to impose sthg on o.s.; **s'**~ **à faire qqch** to force o.s. to do sthg.

oblique [ɔblik] ◇ *adj* oblique; **en** ~ diagonally. ◇ *nf* oblique line.

obliquer [ɔblike] [3] *vi* to turn off.

oblitérer [ɔblitere] [18] *vt* **-1.** [tamponner] to

cancel. **-2.** MÉD to obstruct. **-3.** [effacer] to obliterate.

oblong, oblongue [ɔblɔ̃, ɔ̃g] *adj* oblong.

obnubiler [ɔbnybile] [3] *vt* to obsess; **être obnubilé par** to be obsessed with OU by.

obole [ɔbɔl] *nf* small contribution.

obscène [ɔpsɛn] *adj* obscene.

obscénité [ɔpsenite] *nf* obscenity.

obscur, -e [ɔpskyr] *adj* **-1.** [sombre] dark. **-2.** [confus] vague. **-3.** [inconnu, douteux] obscure.

obscurantisme [ɔpskyrɑ̃tism] *nm* obscurantism.

obscurcir [ɔpskyrsir] [32] *vt* **-1.** [assombrir] to darken. **-2.** [embrouiller] to confuse.
◆ **s'obscurcir** *vp* **-1.** [s'assombrir] to grow dark. **-2.** [s'embrouiller] to become confused.

obscurément [ɔpskyremɑ̃] *adv* obscurely.

obscurité [ɔpskyrite] *nf* **-1.** [nuit] darkness. **-2.** [anonymat] obscurity. **-3.** [hermétisme] abstruseness.

obsédant, -e [ɔpsedɑ̃, ɑ̃t] *adj* haunting.

obsédé, -e [ɔpsede] ◇ *adj* obsessed. ◇ *nm, f* obsessive; **~ sexuel** sex maniac.

obséder [ɔpsede] [18] *vt* to obsess, to haunt.

obsèques [ɔpsɛk] *nfpl* funeral (*sg*).

obséquieux, -ieuse [ɔpsekjø, jøz] *adj* obsequious.

obséquiosité [ɔpsekjozite] *nf* obsequiousness.

observance [ɔpsɛrvɑ̃s] *nf* observance.

observateur, -trice [ɔpsɛrvatœr, tris] ◇ *adj* observant. ◇ *nm, f* observer.

observation [ɔpsɛrvasjɔ̃] *nf* **-1.** [gén] observation; **être en ~** MÉD to be under observation. **-2.** [critique] remark. **-3.** [conformité] observance.

observatoire [ɔpsɛrvatwar] *nm* **-1.** ASTRON observatory. **-2.** [lieu de surveillance] observation post.

observer [ɔpsɛrve] [3] *vt* **-1.** [regarder, remarquer, respecter] to observe. **-2.** [épier] to watch. **-3.** [constater]: **~ que** to note that; **faire ~ qqch à qqn** to point sthg out to sb. **-4.** *sout* [attitude] to keep, to maintain.
◆ **s'observer** *vp* **-1.** [se surveiller] to be careful of one's behavior *Am* OU behaviour *Br*. **-2.** [s'épier] to watch each other.

obsession [ɔpsesjɔ̃] *nf* obsession.

obsessionnel, -elle [ɔpsesjɔnɛl] *adj* obsessional.

obsolète [ɔpsɔlɛt] *adj* obsolete.

obstacle [ɔpstakl] *nm* **-1.** [entrave] obstacle. **-2.** *fig* [difficulté] hindrance; **faire ~ à qqch/qqn** to hinder sthg/sb; **rencontrer un ~** to meet an obstacle.

obstétricien, -ienne [ɔpstetrisjɛ̃, jɛn] *nm, f* obstetrician.

obstétrique [ɔpstetrik] *nf* obstetrics (*U*).

obstination [ɔpstinasjɔ̃] *nf* stubbornness, obstinacy.

obstiné, -e [ɔpstine] ◇ *adj* **-1.** [entêté] stubborn, obstinate. **-2.** [acharné] dogged. ◇ *nm, f* stubborn OU obstinate person.

obstinément [ɔpstinemɑ̃] *adv* **-1.** [refuser] obstinately. **-2.** [travailler] doggedly.

obstiner [ɔpstine] [3]
◆ **s'obstiner** *vp* to insist; **s'~ à faire qqch** to persist stubbornly in doing sthg; **s'~ dans qqch** to cling stubbornly to sthg.

obstruction [ɔpstryksjɔ̃] *nf* **-1.** MÉD obstruction, blockage. **-2.** POLIT & SPORT obstruction.

obstructionniste [ɔpstryksjɔnist] *nmf & adj* POLIT obstructionist.

obstruer [ɔpstrye] [3] *vt* to block, to obstruct.
◆ **s'obstruer** *vp* to become blocked.

obtempérer [ɔptɑ̃pere] [18] *vi*: **~ à** to comply with.

obtenir [ɔptənir] [40] *vt* to get, to obtain; **~ qqch de qqn** to get sthg from sb; **~ de faire qqch** to get permission to do sthg; **~ qqch** OU **pour qqn** to obtain sthg for sb.

obtention [ɔptɑ̃sjɔ̃] *nf* obtaining.

obtenu, -e [ɔptəny] *pp* → **obtenir**.

obtiendrai, obtiendras *etc* → **obtenir**.

obtienne, obtiennes *etc* → **obtenir**.

obturateur, -trice [ɔptyratœr, tris] *adj* closing (*avant n*).
◆ **obturateur** *nm* **-1.** [valve] stop valve. **-2.** PHOT shutter.

obturation [ɔptyrasjɔ̃] *nf* closing, sealing.

obturer [ɔptyre] [3] *vt* to close, to seal; [dent] to fill.

obtus, -e [ɔpty, yz] *adj* obtuse.

obus [ɔby] *nm* shell.

OC (*abr de* **ondes courtes**) SW.

occasion [ɔkazjɔ̃] *nf* **-1.** [possibilité, chance] opportunity, chance; **saisir l'~ (de faire qqch)** to seize OU grab the chance (to do sthg); **rater une ~ (de faire qqch)** to miss a chance (to do sthg); **être l'~ de** to give rise to; **à l'~** some time; [de temps en temps] sometimes, on occasion; **à la première ~** at the first opportunity. **-2.** [circonstance] occasion; **à l'~ de** on the occasion of; **dans les**

grandes ~s on important occasions. **-3.** [bonne affaire] bargain.

◆ **d'occasion** *loc adv & loc adj* second-hand.

occasionnel, -elle [ɔkazjɔnɛl] *adj* [irrégulier - visite, problème] occasional; [- travail] casual.

occasionner [ɔkazjɔne] [3] *vt* to cause.

occident [ɔksidɑ̃] *nm* west.

◆ **Occident** *nm*: l'Occident the West.

occidental, -e, -aux [ɔksidɑ̃tal, o] *adj* western.

◆ **Occidental, -e, -aux** *nm, f* Westerner.

occiput [ɔksipyt] *nm* back of the head.

occitan, -e [ɔksitɑ̃, an] *adj* Provençal French.

◆ **occitan** *nm* [langue] Provençal French.

◆ **Occitan, -e** *nm, f* speaker of Provençal French.

occlusion [ɔklyzjɔ̃] *nf* **-1.** MÉD blockage, obstruction. **-2.** LING & CHIM occlusion.

occulte [ɔkylt] *adj* occult.

occulter [ɔkylte] [3] *vt* [sentiments] to conceal.

occupant, -e [ɔkypɑ̃, ɑ̃t] ◇ *adj* occupying. ◇ *nm, f* occupant, occupier.

◆ **occupant** *nm*: l'~ the occupying power OU forces (*pl*).

occupation [ɔkypasjɔ̃] *nf* **-1.** [activité] occupation, job; **vaquer à ses** ~s to go about one's business. **-2.** MIL occupation. **-3.** JUR occupancy.

◆ **Occupation** *nf*: l'Occupation the Occupation (of France).

occupé, -e [ɔkype] *adj* **-1.** [personne] busy; **être** ~ **à qqch** to be busy with sthg. **-2.** [appartement, zone] occupied. **-3.** [place] taken; [toilettes] engaged; **c'est** ~ [téléphone] it's busy *Am* OU engaged *Br*.

occuper [ɔkype] [3] *vt* **-1.** [gén] to occupy. **-2.** [espace] to take up. **-3.** [fonction, poste] to hold. **-4.** [ouvriers] to employ.

◆ **s'occuper** *vp* **-1.** [s'activer] to keep o.s. busy; **s'**~ **à qqch/à faire qqch** to be busy with sthg/doing sthg. **-2.** **s'**~ **de qqch** [se charger de] to take care of sthg, to deal with sthg; [s'intéresser à] to take an interest in, to be interested in; **occupez-vous de vos affaires!** mind your own business! **-3.** [prendre soin]: **s'**~ **de qqn** to take care of sb, to look after sb.

occurrence [ɔkyrɑ̃s] *nf* **-1.** [circonstance]: **en l'**~ in this case. **-2.** LING occurrence.

OCDE (*abr de* **Organisation de coopération et de développement économique**) *nf* OECD.

océan [ɔseɑ̃] *nm* ocean; l'~ **Antarctique** the Antarctic Ocean; l'~ **Arctique** the Arctic Ocean; l'~ **Atlantique** the Atlantic Ocean; l'~ **Indien** the Indian Ocean; l'~ **Pacifique** the Pacific Ocean.

Océanie [ɔseani] *nf*: l'~ Oceania.

océanien, -ienne [ɔseanjɛ̃, jɛn] *adj* Oceanian.

◆ **Océanien, -ienne** *nm, f* Oceanian.

océanique [ɔseanik] *adj* ocean (*avant n*).

océanographie [ɔseanɔgrafi] *nf* oceanography.

ocelot [ɔslo] *nm* ocelot.

ocre [ɔkr] *adj inv & nf* ocher *Am*, ochre *Br*.

octante [ɔktɑ̃t] *adj num* *Belg & Helv* eighty.

octave [ɔktav] *nf* octave.

octet [ɔktɛ] *nm* INFORM byte.

octobre [ɔktɔbr] *nm* October; *voir aussi* **septembre**.

octogénaire [ɔktɔʒenɛr] *nmf & adj* octogenarian.

octogone [ɔktɔgɔn] *nm* octagon.

octroie, octroies *etc* → **octroyer**.

octroyer [ɔktrwaje] [13] *vt*: ~ **qqch à qqn** to grant sb sthg, to grant sthg to sb.

◆ **s'octroyer** *vp* to grant o.s., to treat o.s. to.

oculaire [ɔkylɛr] ◇ *nm* eyepiece. ◇ *adj* ocular, eye (*avant n*); **témoin** ~ eyewitness.

oculiste [ɔkylist] *nmf* ophthalmologist.

ode [ɔd] *nf* ode.

odeur [ɔdœr] *nf* smell; **ne pas être en** ~ **de sainteté (auprès de)** *fig* to be out of favor *Am* OU favour *Br* (with).

odieusement [ɔdjøzmɑ̃] *adv* abominably.

odieux, -euse [ɔdjø, jøz] *adj* **-1.** [crime] odious, abominable. **-2.** [personne, attitude] unbearable, obnoxious.

odorant, -e [ɔdɔrɑ̃, ɑ̃t] *adj* sweet-smelling, fragrant.

odorat [ɔdɔra] *nm* (sense of) smell.

odoriférant, -e [ɔdɔriferɑ̃, ɑ̃t] *adj* sweet-smelling, fragrant.

odyssée [ɔdise] *nf* odyssey.

OEA (*abr de* **Organisation des États américains**) *nf* OAS.

œdème [edɛm] *nm* oedema.

œil [œj] (*pl* **yeux** [jø]) *nm* **-1.** [gén] eye; **yeux bridés/exorbités/globuleux** slanting/bulging/protruding eyes; **avoir les yeux cernés** to have bags under one's eyes; **baisser/lever les yeux** to look down/up, to lower/raise one's eyes; **du coin de l'**~ out of the corner of one's eye; **écarquiller les**

yeux to stare wide-eyed; **à l'~ nu** to the naked eye; **sous mes/tes** *etc* **yeux** before my/your *etc* very eyes; **à vue d'~** visibly. **-2.** [bulle de graisse] blob of grease OU fat. **-3.** *loc*: **avoir qqch/qqn à l'~** to have one's eye on sthg/sb; **avoir un ~ au beurre noir** to have a black eye; **n'avoir pas froid aux yeux** not to be afraid of anything, to have plenty of nerve; **avoir des yeux de lynx** to have eyes like a hawk; **ne pas avoir les yeux dans sa poche** to be very observant; **couver qqch/qqn des yeux** to look fondly at sthg/sb, to look lovingly at sthg/sb; **ça crève les yeux** *fam* it's staring you in the face, it's as plain as the nose on your face; **ne pas en croire ses yeux** not to believe one's eyes; **dévorer qqn/qqch des yeux** [avec insistance] to eye sb/sthg intently; [avec convoitise] to eye sb/sthg greedily; **faire de l'~ à qqn** *fam* to eye sb up; **faire les gros yeux à qqn** to glare at sb; **fermer les yeux sur qqch** to close one's eyes to sthg; **mon ~!** *fam* like hell!; **ouvrir l'~** to keep one's eyes open; **se rincer l'~** *fam* to get an eyeful; **cela saute aux yeux** it's obvious; **tourner de l'~** *fam* to pass out.

œil-de-bœuf [œjdəbœf] (*pl* **œils-de-bœuf**) *nm* bull's eye window.

œillade [œjad] *nf* wink; **lancer une ~ à qqn** to wink at sb.

œillère [œjɛr] *nf* eyebath.

◆ **œillères** *nfpl* blinders *Am*, blinkers *Br*; **avoir des ~s** *fam fig* to be blinkered.

œillet [œjɛ] *nm* **-1.** [fleur] carnation. **-2.** [de chaussure] eyelet.

œnologie [enɔlɔʒi] *nf* wine appreciation.

œnologue [enɔlɔg] *nmf* wine expert.

œsophage [ezɔfaʒ] *nm* esophagus *Am*, oesophagus *Br*.

œstrogène [ɛstrɔʒɛn] *nm* estrogen *Am*, œstrogen *Br*.

œuf [œf] *nm* egg; **~ à la coque/au plat/poché** boiled/fried/poached egg; **~ mollet/dur** soft-boiled/hard-boiled egg; **~ de Pâques** Easter egg; **~s brouillés** scrambled eggs; **~s en** OU **à la neige** whipped egg whites; **dans l'~** *fig* in the bud.

œuvre [œvr] ◇ *nf* **-1.** [travail] work; **être à l'~** to be working OU at work; **se mettre à l'~** to get down to work; **mettre qqch en ~** to make use of sthg; [loi, accord, projet] to implement sthg. **-2.** [d'artiste] work; [~ ensemble de sa production] works (*pl*); **~ d'art** work of art. **-3.** [organisation] charity; **~ de bienfaisance** charity, charitable organization. ◇ *nm* **-1.** [d'artiste] works (*pl*), work. **-2.** [de bâtiment]: **le gros ~** the shell.

œuvrer [œvre] [5] *vi littéraire*: **~ (pour)** to work (for).

OFCE (*abr de* **Observatoire français des conjonctures économiques**) *nm economic research institute*.

off [ɔf] *adj inv* **-1.** CIN [voix, son] off. **-2.** [festival] fringe (*avant n*).

offensant, -e [ɔfɑ̃sɑ̃, ɑ̃t] *adj* offensive.

offense [ɔfɑ̃s] *nf* **-1.** [insulte] insult. **-2.** RELIG trespass.

offenser [ɔfɑ̃se] [3] *vt* **-1.** [personne] to offend. **-2.** [bon goût] to offend against.

◆ **s'offenser** *vp*: **s'~ de** to take offense *Am* OU offence *Br* at, to be offended by.

offenseur [ɔfɑ̃sœr] *nm* offender, offending party.

offensif, -ive [ɔfɑ̃sif, iv] *adj* offensive.

◆ **offensive** *nf* **-1.** MIL offensive; **passer à l'offensive** to go on the offensive; **prendre l'offensive** to take the offensive. **-2.** *fig* [du froid] (sudden) onset.

offert, -e [ɔfɛr, ɛrt] *pp* → **offrir**.

offertoire [ɔfɛrtwar] *nm* offertory.

office [ɔfis] *nm* **-1.** [bureau] office, agency; **~ du tourisme** tourist office. **-2.** [fonction]: **faire ~ de** to act as; **remplir son ~** to do its job, to fulfil its function. **-3.** RELIG service. **-4.** *loc*: **recourir aux ~s de qqn** to turn to sb for help.

◆ **d'office** *loc adv* automatically, as a matter of course; **commis d'~** officially appointed.

officialiser [ɔfisjalize] [3] *vt* to make official.

officiel, -ielle [ɔfisjɛl] *adj & nm, f* official.

officiellement [ɔfisjɛlmɑ̃] *adv* officially.

officier[1] [ɔfisje] [9] *vi* to officiate.

officier[2] [ɔfisje] *nm* officer; **~ d'ordonnance** aide-de-camp.

officieusement [ɔfisjøzmɑ̃] *adv* unofficially.

officieux, -ieuse [ɔfisjø, jøz] *adj* unofficial.

officine [ɔfisin] *nf* **-1.** [pharmacie] pharmacy. **-2.** *péj* [repaire] agency.

offrande [ɔfrɑ̃d] *nf* **-1.** [don] offering. **-2.** RELIG offertory.

offrant [ɔfrɑ̃] *nm*: **au plus ~** to the highest bidder.

offre [ɔfr] *nf* **-1.** [proposition] offer; [aux enchères] bid; [pour contrat] tender; «**~s d'emploi**» "situations vacant", "vacancies"; **~ d'essai** trial offer; **~ de lancement** introductory offer; **~ publique d'achat** takeover bid. **-2.** ÉCON supply; **la loi de l'~ et de la demande** the law of supply and demand.

offrir [ɔfrir] [34] *vt* **-1.** [faire cadeau]: **~ qqch à qqn** to give sb sthg, to give sthg to sb. **-2.** [proposer]: **~ qqch à qqn** to offer sb

sthg OU sthg to sb; ~ (à qqn) de faire qqch to offer to do sthg (for sb). **-3.** [présenter] to offer, to present; **son visage n'offrait rien d'accueillant** his/her face showed no sign of welcome.
◆ **s'offrir** *vp* **-1.** [croisière, livre] to treat o.s. to. **-2.** [se présenter] to present itself. **-3.** [s'exposer]: **s'~ à qqch** to expose o.s. to sthg. **-4.** [se proposer] to offer one's services, to offer o.s.; **s'~ à faire qqch** to offer to do sthg.

offset [ɔfsɛt] ◇ *adj inv* offset. ◇ *nm inv* offset (lithography). ◇ *nf inv* offset press.

offshore [ɔfʃɔr] ◇ *adj inv* **-1.** [exploitation] offshore. **-2.** SPORT speedboat (*avant n*); **bateau** ~ speedboat. ◇ *nm* SPORT speedboat racing.

offusquer [ɔfyske] [3] *vt* to offend.
◆ **s'offusquer** *vp*: **s'~ (de)** to take offense *Am* OU offence *Br* (at).

ogive [ɔʒiv] *nf* **-1.** ARCHIT ogive; **en** ~ ribbed. **-2.** MIL [d'obus] head; [de fusée] nosecone; ~ **nucléaire** nuclear warhead.

ogre, ogresse [ɔgr, ɔgrɛs] *nm, f* ogre (*f* ogress).

oh [o] ◇ *interj* oh!; ~ **la la!** dear oh dear! ◇ *nm inv*: **pousser des** ~ **et des ah** to ooh and ah.

ohé [ɔe] *interj* hey!

OHQ (*abr de* **ouvrier hautement qualifié**) *nm* highly skilled worker.

oie [wa] *nf* goose; ~ **blanche** *fig* innocent young girl.

oignon [ɔɲɔ̃] *nm* **-1.** [plante] onion; **mêle-toi de tes** ~s *fam fig* mind your own business; **soigner qqn aux petits** ~s *fam fig* to take care of sb's every need. **-2.** [bulbe] bulb. **-3.** MÉD bunion.

oindre [wɛ̃dr] [82] *vt littéraire* **-1.** [corps] to (rub with) oil. **-2.** RELIG to anoint.

oiseau, -x [wazo] *nm* **-1.** ZOOL bird; ~ **de proie** bird of prey. **-2.** *fam péj* [individu] character.

oiseau-mouche [wazomuʃ] (*pl* **oiseaux-mouches**) *nm* hummingbird.

oiseleur [waslœr] *nm* bird-catcher.

oiseux, -euse [wazø, øz] *adj* pointless.

oisif, -ive [wazif, iv] ◇ *adj* idle. ◇ *nm, f* man of leisure (*f* woman of leisure).

oisillon [wazijɔ̃] *nm* fledgling.

oisiveté [wazivte] *nf* idleness.

oison [wazɔ̃] *nm* gosling.

OIT (*abr de* **Organisation internationale du travail**) *nf* ILO.

O.K. [ɔke] *interj fam* okay.

OL (*abr de* **ondes longues**) LW.

oléagineux, -euse [ɔleaʒinø, øz] *adj* oleaginous. ◆ **oléagineux** *nm* oleaginous plant.

oléoduc [ɔleɔdyk] *nm* (oil) pipeline.

olfactif, -ive [ɔlfaktif, iv] *adj* olfactory.

oligo-élément [ɔligɔelemɑ̃] (*pl* **oligo-éléments**) *nm* trace element.

olivâtre [ɔlivatr] *adj* [verdâtre] olive-colored *Am*, olive-coloured *Br*; [teint] sallow.

olive [ɔliv] ◇ *nf* olive. ◇ *adj inv* olive, olive-green.

oliveraie [ɔlivrɛ] *nf* olive grove.

olivier [ɔlivje] *nm* [arbre] olive tree; [bois] olive wood.

OLP (*abr de* **Organisation de libération de la Palestine**) *nf* PLO.

olympiade [ɔlɛ̃pjad] *nf* (*gén pl*) olympiad (*sg*).

olympien, -ienne [ɔlɛ̃pjɛ̃, jɛn] *adj* Olympian.

olympique [ɔlɛ̃pik] *adj* Olympic (*avant n*).

OM ◇ *nm* (*abr de* **Olympique de Marseille**) *Marseilles football team.* ◇ (*abr de* **ondes moyennes**) MW.

Oman [ɔman] *n* Oman; **le sultanat d'**~ the Sultanate of Oman.

ombilic [ɔ̃bilik] *nm* **-1.** [de personne] navel. **-2.** BOT navelwort.

ombilical, -e, -aux [ɔ̃bilikal, o] *adj* umbilical.

ombrage [ɔ̃braʒ] *nm* shade; **porter** ~ **à qqn** *fig* to offend sb; **prendre** ~ **de qqch** *fig* to take offense *Am* OU offence *Br* at sthg, to take umbrage at sthg.

ombragé, -e [ɔ̃braʒe] *adj* shady.

ombrageux, -euse [ɔ̃braʒø, øz] *adj* **-1.** [personne] touchy, prickly. **-2.** [cheval] nervous, skittish.

ombre [ɔ̃br] *nf* **-1.** [zone sombre] shade; **faire de l'**~ **à qqn** to get in sb's light; **à l'**~ **de** [arbre] in the shade of; [personne] in the shadow of; **rester dans l'**~ **de qqn** *fig* to live in sb's shadow; **laisser qqch dans l'**~ *fig* to deliberately ignore sthg; **vivre dans l'**~ *fig* to live in obscurity. **-2.** [forme, fantôme] shadow; ~s **chinoises** [spectacle] shadow play OU pantomime (*sg*); [jeu] Chinese shadows. **-3.** [trace] hint; **ça ne fait pas l'**~ **d'un doute** there's not the shadow of a doubt. **-4.** [cosmétique]: ~ **à paupières** eye shadow.

ombrelle [ɔ̃brɛl] *nf* parasol.

ombrer [ɔ̃bre] [3] *vt* **-1.** [paupières] to put eye shadow on. **-2.** [dessin] to shade (in).

omelette [ɔmlɛt] *nf* omelette; ~ **norvégienne** baked Alaska.

omets → **omettre**.

omettre [ɔmɛtr] [84] *vt* to omit; ~ **de faire qqch** to omit to do sthg.

OMI (*abr de* **Organisation maritime internationale**) *nf* IMO.

omis, -e [ɔmi, iz] *pp* → **omettre**.

omission [ɔmisjɔ̃] *nf* omission; **par** ~ by omission.

OMM (*abr de* **Organisation météorologique mondiale**) *nf* WMO.

omnibus [ɔmnibys] ◇ *nm* stopping OU local train. ◇ *adj inv*: **ce train est** ~ **pour ...** this train stops at all stations to ....

omnipotent, -e [ɔmnipɔtɑ̃, ɑ̃t] *adj* omnipotent.

omniprésence [ɔmniprezɑ̃s] *nf* omnipresence.

omniprésent, -e [ɔmniprezɑ̃, ɑ̃t] *adj* omnipresent.

omniscient, -e [ɔmnisjɑ̃, ɑ̃t] *adj* omniscient.

omnisports [ɔmnispɔr] *adj inv* sports (*avant n*).

omnivore [ɔmnivɔr] ◇ *nm* omnivore. ◇ *adj* omnivorous.

omoplate [ɔmɔplat] *nf* [os] shoulder blade; [épaule] shoulder.

OMS (*abr de* **Organisation mondiale de la santé**) *nf* WHO.

on [ɔ̃] *pron pers indéf* **-1.** [indéterminé] you, one; ~ **n'a pas le droit de fumer ici** you're not allowed OU one isn't allowed to smoke here, smoking isn't allowed here. **-2.** [les gens, l'espèce humaine] they, people; ~ **vit de plus en plus vieux en Europe** people in Europe are living longer and longer. **-3.** [quelqu'un] someone; ~ **vous a appelé au téléphone ce matin** there was a telephone call for you this morning. **-4.** *fam* [nous] we; ~ **s'en va** we're off, we're going.

onanisme [ɔnanism] *nm* onanism.

once [ɔ̃s] *nf*: **une** ~ **(de)** an ounce (of).

oncle [ɔ̃kl] *nm* uncle.

onction [ɔ̃ksjɔ̃] *nf* unction.

onctueux, -euse [ɔ̃ktɥø, øz] *adj* smooth.

onctuosité [ɔ̃ktɥozite] *nf* smoothness.

onde [ɔ̃d] *nf* **-1.** PHYS wave. **-2.** *littéraire* [eau]: **l'**~ **the waters** (*pl*).
◆ **ondes** *nfpl* [radio] air (*sg*).

ondée [ɔ̃de] *nf* shower (of rain).

on-dit [ɔ̃di] *nm inv* rumor *Am*, rumour *Br*, hearsay (*U*).

ondoyant, -e [ɔ̃dwajɑ̃, ɑ̃t] *adj* [ondulant] rippling; [démarche] swaying.

ondoyer [ɔ̃dwaje] [13] *vi* to ripple.

ondulant, -e [ɔ̃dylɑ̃, ɑ̃t] *adj* [ondoyant] undulating, wavy; [démarche] swaying.

ondulation [ɔ̃dylasjɔ̃] *nf* **-1.** [mouvement] rippling; [de sol, terrain] undulation. **-2.** [de coiffure] wave.

ondulé, -e [ɔ̃dyle] *adj* [surface] undulating; [chevelure] wavy; [tôle, carton] corrugated.

onduler [ɔ̃dyle] [3] *vi* [drapeau] to ripple, to wave; [cheveux] to be wavy.

one-man-show [wanmanʃo] *nm inv* one-man show.

onéreux, -euse [ɔnerø, øz] *adj* costly.

ONF (*abr de* **Office national des forêts**) *nm French national forestry agency,* ≃ National Forestry Service *Am*, ≃ Forestry Commission *Br*.

ONG (*abr de* **organisation non gouvernementale**) *nf* NGO.

ongle [ɔ̃gl] *nm* **-1.** [de personne] fingernail, nail; **se faire les** ~**s** to do one's nails; **se ronger les** ~**s** to bite one's nails. **-2.** [d'animal] claw.

onglée [ɔ̃gle] *nf*: **j'ai l'**~ my fingers are numb with cold.

onglet [ɔ̃glɛ] *nm* **-1.** [de reliure] tab. **-2.** [de lame] thumbnail groove. **-3.** CULIN top skirt.

onguent [ɔ̃gɑ̃] *nm* ointment.

onirique [ɔnirik] *adj* [relatif au rêve] dream (*avant n*); [semblable au rêve] dreamlike.

onomastique [ɔnɔmastik] ◇ *nf* onomastics (*sg*). ◇ *adj* onomastic.

onomatopée [ɔnɔmatope] *nf* onomatopoeia.

ont → **avoir**.

ONU, Onu [ɔny] (*abr de* **Organisation des Nations unies**) *nf* UN, UNO.

ONUDI, Onudi [ɔnydi] (*abr de* **Organisation des Nations unies pour le développement industriel**) *nf* UNIDO.

onyx [ɔniks] *nm* onyx.

onze [ɔ̃z] ◇ *adj num* eleven; *voir aussi* **six**. ◇ *nm* [chiffre & SPORT] eleven; *voir aussi* **six**.

onzième [ɔ̃zjɛm] ◇ *adj num, nm & nmf* eleventh; *voir aussi* **sixième**. ◇ *nf* [classe] = first grade *Am*, ≃ second year OU form (*at primary school*) *Br*; *voir aussi* **sixième**.

OP (*abr de* **ouvrier professionnel**) *nm* skilled worker.

OPA (*abr de* **offre publique d'achat**) *nf* takeover bid.

opacité [ɔpasite] *nf* opacity.

opale [ɔpal] *nf & adj inv* opal.

opaline [ɔpalin] *nf* opaline.

opaque [ɔpak] *adj*: ~ **(à)** opaque (to).

op. cit. (*abr de* **opere citato**) op. cit.

OPE (*abr de* **offre publique d'échange**) *nf* take-over bid where bidder offers to exchange shares.

OPEP, **Opep** (*abr de* **Organisation des pays exportateurs de pétrole**) *nf* OPEC.

opéra [ɔpera] *nm* **-1.** MUS opera. **-2.** [théâtre] opera house; **l'Opéra Bastille** *opera house built on the site of the Bastille;* **l'Opéra de Paris** the Paris Opera (House).

opérable [ɔperabl] *adj* operable.

opéra-bouffe [ɔperabuf] (*pl* **opéras-bouffes**) *nm* comic opera.

opéra-comique [ɔperakɔmik] (*pl* **opéras-comiques**) *nm* light opera.

opérateur, **-trice** [ɔperatœr, tris] *nm, f* operator; ~ **de saisie** keyboarder.

opération [ɔperasjɔ̃] *nf* **-1.** [gén] operation. **-2.** COMM deal, transaction.

opérationnel, **-elle** [ɔperasjɔnɛl] *adj* operational.

opératoire [ɔperatwar] *adj* MÉD operating (*avant n*); **choc** ~ post-operative shock.

opérer [ɔpere] [18] ◇ *vt* **-1.** MÉD to operate on. **-2.** [exécuter] to carry out, to implement; [choix, tri] to make. ◇ *vi* [agir] to take effect; [personne] to operate, to proceed.
◆ **s'opérer** *vp* to come about, to take place.

opérette [ɔperɛt] *nf* operetta.

ophtalmique [ɔftalmik] *adj* ophthalmic.

ophtalmologiste [ɔftalmɔlɔʒist] *nmf* ophthalmologist.

Opinel® [ɔpinɛl] *nm folding knife used especially for outdoor activities, scouting etc.*

opiner [ɔpine] [3] *vi sout:* ~ **à qqch** to give one's consent to sthg.

opiniâtre [ɔpinjatr] *adj* **-1.** [caractère, personne] stubborn, obstinate. **-2.** [effort] dogged; [travail] unrelenting; [fièvre, toux] persistent.

opiniâtreté [ɔpinjatrəte] *nf* [de caractère, personne] stubbornness, obstinacy.

opinion [ɔpinjɔ̃] *nf* opinion; **conforter** OU **renforcer qqn dans son** ~ to confirm sb's opinion; **avoir (une) bonne/mauvaise** ~ **de** to have a good/bad opinion of; **l'**~ **publique** public opinion.

opium [ɔpjɔm] *nm* opium.

opportun, **-e** [ɔpɔrtœ̃, yn] *adj* opportune, timely.

opportunément [ɔpɔrtynemɑ̃] *adv* opportunely.

opportunisme [ɔpɔrtynism] *nm* opportunism.

opportuniste [ɔpɔrtynist] ◇ *nmf* opportunist. ◇ *adj* opportunistic.

opportunité [ɔpɔrtynite] *nf* **-1.** [à-propos] opportuneness, timeliness. **-2.** [occasion] opportunity.

opposant, **-e** [ɔposɑ̃, ɑ̃t] ◇ *adj* opposing. ◇ *nm, f:* ~ **(à)** opponent (of).

opposé, **-e** [ɔpoze] *adj* **-1.** [direction, côté, angle] opposite. **-2.** [intérêts, opinions] conflicting; [forces] opposing. **-3.** [hostile]: ~ **à** opposed to.
◆ **opposé** *nm:* **l'**~ the opposite; **à l'**~ **de** in the opposite direction from; *fig* unlike, contrary to.

opposer [ɔpoze] [3] *vt* **-1.** [mettre en opposition - choses, notions]: ~ **qqch (à)** to contrast sthg (with). **-2.** [mettre en présence - personnes, armées] to oppose; ~ **deux équipes** to bring two teams together; ~ **qqn à qqn** to pit OU set sb against sb. **-3.** [refus, protestation, objection] to put forward; ~ **une objection à qqn** to raise an objection with sb, to put forward an objection to sb. **-4.** [diviser] to divide.
◆ **s'opposer** *vp* **-1.** [contraster] to contrast. **-2.** [entrer en conflit] to clash. **-3.** **s'**~ **à** [se dresser contre] to oppose, to be opposed to; **s'**~ **à ce que qqn fasse qqch** to be opposed to sb's doing sthg.

opposition [ɔpozisjɔ̃] *nf* **-1.** [gén] opposition; **faire** ~ **à** [décision, mariage] to oppose; [chèque] to stop; **entrer en** ~ **avec** to come into conflict with. **-2.** JUR: ~ **(à)** objection (to). **-3.** [contraste] contrast; **par** ~ **à** in contrast with, as opposed to.

oppressant, **-e** [ɔpresɑ̃, ɑ̃t] *adj* oppressive.

oppresser [ɔprese] [4] *vt* **-1.** [étouffer] to suffocate, to stifle. **-2.** *fig* [tourmenter] to oppress.

oppresseur [ɔpresœr] ◇ *nm* oppressor. ◇ *adj* oppressive.

oppressif, **-ive** [ɔpresif, iv] *adj* oppressive.

oppression [ɔpresjɔ̃] *nf* **-1.** [asservissement] oppression. **-2.** [malaise] tightness of the chest.

opprimé, **-e** [ɔprime] ◇ *adj* oppressed. ◇ *nm, f* oppressed person.

opprimer [ɔprime] [3] *vt* **-1.** [asservir] to oppress. **-2.** [étouffer] to stifle.

opprobre [ɔprɔbr] *nm:* **jeter l'**~ **sur qqn** to cast opprobrium on sb.

opter [ɔpte] [3] *vi:* ~ **pour** to opt for.

opticien, **-ienne** [ɔptisjɛ̃, jɛn] *nm, f* optician.

optimal, **-e**, **-aux** [ɔptimal, o] *adj* optimal.

optimiser [ɔptimize], **optimaliser** [ɔptimalize] [3] *vt* to optimize.

optimisme [ɔptimism] *nm* optimism.

optimiste [ɔptimist] ◇ *nmf* optimist. ◇ *adj* optimistic.

optimum [ɔptimɔm] (*pl* **optimums** OU **optima** [ɔptima]) *nm & adj* optimum.

option [ɔpsjɔ̃] *nf* **-1.** [gén] option; **prendre une ~ sur** FIN to take (out) an option on. **-2.** [accessoire] optional extra.

optionnel, -elle [ɔpsjɔnɛl] *adj* optional.

optique [ɔptik] ◇ *nf* **-1.** [science, technique] optics (*U*). **-2.** [perspective] viewpoint; **dans l'~ de faire qqch** with a mind OU view to doing sthg. ◇ *adj* [nerf] optic; [verre] optical.

opulence [ɔpylɑ̃s] *nf* **-1.** [richesse] opulence; **vivre** OU **nager dans l'~** to live a life of luxury. **-2.** [ampleur] fullness, ampleness.

opulent, -e [ɔpylɑ̃, ɑ̃t] *adj* **-1.** [riche] rich. **-2.** [gros] ample.

OQ (*abr de* **ouvrier qualifié**) *nm* skilled worker.

or[1] [ɔr] *nm* **-1.** [métal, couleur] gold; **en ~** [objet] gold (*avant n*); **une occasion en ~** a golden opportunity; **une affaire en ~** [achat] an excellent bargain; [commerce] a lucrative line of business; **j'ai une femme en ~** I've a wonderful wife; **~ blanc** white gold; **~ massif** solid gold; **~ noir** *fig* black gold; **pour tout l'~ du monde** *fig* for all the tea in China; **rouler sur l'~** *fig* to be rolling in it. **-2.** [dorure] gilding.

or[2] [ɔr] *conj* [au début d'une phrase] now; [pour introduire un contraste] well, but.

oracle [ɔrakl] *nm* oracle.

orage [ɔraʒ] *nm* **-1.** [tempête] storm; **il y a de l'~ dans l'air** *fig* there's a storm brewing. **-2.** *fig* [tumulte, revers] turmoil.

orageux, -euse [ɔraʒø, øz] *adj* stormy.

oraison [ɔrezɔ̃] *nf* prayer; **~ funèbre** funeral oration.

oral, -e, -aux [ɔral, o] *adj* oral.
◆ **oral** *nm* oral (examination); **~ de rattrapage** *oral examination taken after failing written exams.*

oralement [ɔralmɑ̃] *adv* orally.

orange [ɔrɑ̃ʒ] ◇ *nf* orange; **~ pressée** freshly squeezed orange juice. ◇ *nm & adj inv* [couleur] orange.

orangé, -e [ɔrɑ̃ʒe] *adj* orangey.
◆ **orangé** *nm* orangey color *Am* OU colour *Br*.

orangeade [ɔrɑ̃ʒad] *nf* orange squash.

oranger [ɔrɑ̃ʒe] *nm* orange tree.

orangeraie [ɔrɑ̃ʒrɛ] *nf* orange grove.

orang-outan(g) (*pl* **orangs-outan(g)s**) [ɔrɑ̃-utɑ̃] *nm* orangutang.

orateur, -trice [ɔratœr, tris] *nm, f* **-1.** [conférencier] speaker. **-2.** [personne éloquente] orator.

orbital, -e, -aux [ɔrbital, o] *adj* [mouvement] orbital; [station] orbiting.

orbite [ɔrbit] *nf* **-1.** ANAT (eye) socket. **-2.** ASTRON & *fig* orbit; **mettre sur ~** AÉRON to put into orbit; *fig* to launch.

Orcades [ɔrkad] *nfpl* **les ~** the Orkney Islands, the Orkneys.

orchestral, -e, -aux [ɔrkɛstral, o] *adj* orchestral.

orchestration [ɔrkɛstrasjɔ̃] *nf* orchestration.

orchestre [ɔrkɛstr] *nm* **-1.** MUS orchestra. **-2.** CIN & THÉÂTRE orchestra *Am*, stalls (*pl*) *Br*; **fauteuil d' ~** orchestra seat *Am*, seat in the stalls *Br*.

orchestrer [ɔrkɛstre] [3] *vt litt* & *fig* to orchestrate.

orchidée [ɔrkide] *nf* orchid.

ordinaire [ɔrdinɛr] ◇ *adj* **-1.** [usuel, standard] ordinary, normal. **-2.** *péj* [commun] ordinary, common. ◇ *nm* **-1.** [moyenne]: **l'~** the ordinary. **-2.** [alimentation] usual diet.
◆ **d'ordinaire** *loc adv* normally, usually.

ordinal, -e, -aux [ɔrdinal, o] *adj* ordinal.
◆ **ordinal, -aux** *nm* ordinal (number).

ordinateur [ɔrdinatœr] *nm* computer; **~ personnel** personal computer, PC.

ordonnance [ɔrdɔnɑ̃s] ◇ *nf* **-1.** MÉD prescription. **-2.** [de gouvernement, juge] order. ◇ *nm ou nf* MIL orderly.

ordonnateur, -trice [ɔrdɔnatœr, tris] *nm, f* organizer.

ordonné, -e [ɔrdɔne] *adj* [maison, élève] tidy.

ordonner [ɔrdɔne] [3] *vt* **-1.** [ranger] to organize, to put in order. **-2.** [enjoindre] to order, to tell; **~ à qqn de faire qqch** to order sb to do sthg. **-3.** MÉD: **~ qqch à qqn** to prescribe sb sthg. **-4.** RELIG to ordain. **-5.** MATHS to arrange in order.
◆ **s'ordonner** *vp* to be arranged OU put in order.

ordre [ɔrdr] *nm* **-1.** [gén, MIL & RELIG] order; **par ~ alphabétique/chronologique/décroissant** in alphabetical/chronological/descending order; **par ~ d'entrée en scène** in order of appearance; **procéder par ~** to take one thing at a time; **rétablir l'~** to restore order; **rappeler qqn à l'~** to call sb to order; **donner un ~ à qqn** to give sb an order; **être aux ~s de qqn** to be at sb's disposal; **intimer à qqn l'~ de faire qqch** to order sb to do sthg; **jusqu'à nouvel ~** until further notice; **entrer dans les ~s** RELIG to take holy orders; **l'~ établi** the established order; ~ **de mission** MIL orders (*pl*) (*for a particular mission*); **l'~ public** law and order; **troubler l'~ public** to disturb the peace. **-2.** [bonne organisation] tidiness, orderliness; **en ~ orderly**, tidy; **avoir de l'~** to be orderly OU tidy; **mettre en ~** to put in order, to tidy (up); **mettre bon ~ à** to sort out. **-3.** [catégorie]: **de premier/second ~** first-/second-rate; **d'~ privé/pratique** of a private/practical nature; **dans un tout autre ~ d'idées** in a quite different connection; **pouvez-vous me donner un ~ de grandeur?** can you give me some idea of the size/amount *etc*? **-4.** [corporation] professional association; **l'Ordre des médecins** ≃ the American Medical Association *Am*, ≃ the British Medical Association *Br*. **-5.** FIN: **à l'~ de** payable to.

◆ **ordre du jour** *nm* **-1.** [de réunion] agenda; **à l'~ du jour** [de réunion] on the agenda; *fig* topical. **-2.** MIL order of the day.

ordure [ɔrdyr] *nf* **-1.** *fig* [grossièreté] filth (*U*). **-2.** *péj* [personne] scum (*U*), bastard.

◆ **ordures** *nfpl* [déchets] garbage (*U*) *Am*, rubbish (*U*) *Br*.

ordurier, -ière [ɔrdyrje, jɛr] *adj* filthy, obscene.

orée [ɔre] *nf* edge.

oreille [ɔrɛj] *nf* **-1.** ANAT ear. **-2.** [ouïe] hearing; **avoir de l'~** to have a good ear (for music); **être dur d'~** to be hard of hearing. **-3.** [de fauteuil, écrou] wing; [de marmite, tasse] handle. **-4.** *loc*: **se boucher les ~s** to close one's ears; **dormir sur ses deux ~s** to rest easy; **dresser** OU **tendre l'~** to prick up one's ears; **écorcher les ~s** to grate on the ear; **écouter d'une ~ distraite**, **n'écouter que d'une ~** to only half-listen; **il ne l'entend pas de cette ~** he's dead (set) against it; **faire la sourde ~** to turn a deaf ear; **se faire tirer l'~** to need talking round; **prêter l'~ (à qqch)** to lend an ear (to sthg); **rebattre les ~s à qqn** *fam* to go on at sb.

oreiller [ɔreje] *nm* pillow.

oreillette [ɔrɛjɛt] *nf* **-1.** [du cœur] auricle. **-2.** [de casquette] earflap.

oreillons [ɔrɛjɔ̃] *nmpl* mumps (*sg*).

ores [ɔr]

◆ **d'ores et déjà** *loc adv* from now on.

orfèvre [ɔrfɛvr] *nm* goldsmith; [d'argent] silversmith; **être ~ en la matière** *fig* to be (an) expert on the subject.

orfèvrerie [ɔrfɛvrəri] *nf* **-1.** [art] goldsmith's art; [d'argent] silversmith's art. **-2.** [commerce] goldsmith's trade; [d'argent] silversmith's trade.

orfraie [ɔrfrɛ] *nf* sea eagle.

organdi [ɔrgɑ̃di] *nm* organdie.

organe [ɔrgan] *nm* **-1.** ANAT organ. **-2.** [institution] organ, body. **-3.** [mécanisme] mechanism, system; **~s de commande** controls. **-4.** *littéraire* [voix] voice. **-5.** *fig* [porte-parole] representative.

organigramme [ɔrganigram] *nm* **-1.** [hiérarchique] organization chart. **-2.** INFORM flow chart.

organique [ɔrganik] *adj* organic.

organisateur, -trice [ɔrganizatœr, tris] ◇ *adj* organizing (*avant n*). ◇ *nm, f* organizer.

organisation [ɔrganizasjɔ̃] *nf* organization; **avoir le sens de l'~** to be well-organized.

organisé, -e [ɔrganize] *adj* organized; **~ en** **qqch** organized in sthg.

organiser [ɔrganize] [3] *vt* to organize.

◆ **s'organiser** *vp* **-1.** [personne] to be OU get organized. **-2.** [prendre forme] to take shape.

organisme [ɔrganism] *nm* **-1.** BIOL & ZOOL organism. **-2.** [institution] body, organization.

organiste [ɔrganist] *nmf* organist.

orgasme [ɔrgasm] *nm* orgasm.

orge [ɔrʒ] *nf* barley.

orgeat [ɔrʒa] *nm*: **sirop d'~** barley water.

orgelet [ɔrʒəlɛ] *nm* stye.

orgie [ɔrʒi] *nf* orgy.

orgue [ɔrg] *nm* organ.

◆ **orgues** *nfpl* **-1.** MUS organ (*sg*). **-2.** GÉOL columns.

orgueil [ɔrgœj] *nm* pride.

orgueilleux, -euse [ɔrgœjø, øz] ◇ *adj* proud. ◇ *nm, f* proud person.

orient [ɔrjɑ̃] *nm* east.

◆ **Orient** *nm*: **l'Orient** the Orient, the East.

orientable [ɔrjɑ̃tabl] *adj* adjustable.

oriental, -e, -aux [ɔrjɑ̃tal, o] *adj* [région, frontière] eastern; [d'Extrême-Orient] oriental.

◆ **Oriental, -e, -aux** *nm, f* Oriental.

orientation [ɔrjɑ̃tasjɔ̃] *nf* **-1.** [direction] orientation; **avoir le sens de l'~** to have a good sense of direction. **-2.** SCOL career; **~ professionnelle** careers advice, vocational guidance. **-3.** [de maison] aspect. **-4.** *fig* [de politique, recherche] direction, trend.

orienté, -e [ɔrjɑ̃te] *adj* [tendancieux] biased.

orienter [ɔrjɑ̃te] [3] *vt* **-1.** [disposer] to position. **-2.** [voyageur, élève, recherches] to guide, to direct. **-3.** [navire] to steer; [voile] to trim.

◆ **s'orienter** *vp* **-1.** [se repérer] to find OU

get one's bearings. **-2.** *fig* [se diriger]: **s'~ vers** to move toward *Am* OU towards *Br.*

orifice [ɔrifis] *nm* orifice.

oriflamme [ɔriflam] *nf* banner.

origan [ɔrigɑ̃] *nm* oregano.

originaire [ɔriʒinɛr] *adj* **-1.** [natif]: **être ~ de** to originate from; [personne] to be a native of. **-2.** [premier] original.

original, -e, -aux [ɔriʒinal, o] ◇ *adj* **-1.** [premier, inédit] original. **-2.** [singulier] eccentric. ◇ *nm, f* [personne] (outlandish) character.

◆ **original, -aux** *nm* [œuvre, document] original.

originalité [ɔriʒinalite] *nf* **-1.** [nouveauté] originality; [caractéristique] original feature. **-2.** [excentricité] eccentricity.

origine [ɔriʒin] *nf* **-1.** [gén] origin; **d'~** [originel] original; [de départ] of origin; **pays d'~** country of origin; **d'~ anglaise** of English origin; **à l'~** originally. **-2.** [souche] origins (*pl*). **-3.** [provenance] source.

originel, -elle [ɔriʒinɛl] *adj* original.

orignal, -aux [ɔriɲal, o] *nm* moose.

oripeaux [ɔripo] *nmpl* rags.

ORL *nmf* (*abr de* **oto-rhino-laryngologiste**) ENT specialist.

orme [ɔrm] *nm* elm.

ormeau, -x [ɔrmo] *nm* young elm.

ornement [ɔrnəmɑ̃] *nm* **-1.** [gén & MUS] ornament; **d'~** [plante, arbre] ornamental. **-2.** ARCHIT embellishment.

ornemental, -e, -aux [ɔrnəmɑ̃tal, o] *adj* ornamental.

ornementation [ɔrnəmɑ̃tasjɔ̃] *nf* ornamentation.

ornementer [ɔrnəmɑ̃te] [3] *vt* to ornament.

orner [ɔrne] [3] *vt* **-1.** [décorer]: **~ (de)** to decorate (with). **-2.** [agrémenter] to adorn.

ornière [ɔrnjɛr] *nf* rut.

ornithologie [ɔrnitɔlɔʒi] *nf* ornithology.

orphelin, -e [ɔrfəlɛ̃, in] ◇ *adj* orphan (*avant n*), orphaned; **~ de père** fatherless; **~ de mère** motherless. ◇ *nm, f* orphan.

orphelinat [ɔrfəlina] *nm* orphanage.

Orsay [ɔrsɛ] *n*: **le musée d'~** *art museum in Paris.*

MUSÉE D'ORSAY:
This museum, a converted railway station on the banks of the Seine, houses works of art from the second half of the 19th century and the early 20th century

ORSEC, Orsec [ɔrsɛk] (*abr de* **Organisation**

des secours) *adj*: **le plan ~** *disaster contingency plan.*

LE PLAN ORSEC:
This plan is set in motion whenever there is a major disaster in France, such as flooding or forest fires

ORSECRAD, Orsecrad [ɔrsɛkrad] (*abr de* **Orsec en cas d'accident nucléaire**) *adj*: **plan ~** *disaster contingency plan in case of nuclear accident.*

orteil [ɔrtɛj] *nm* toe; **gros ~** big toe.

orthodontiste [ɔrtɔdɔ̃tist] *nmf* orthodontist.

orthodoxe [ɔrtɔdɔks] ◇ *adj* **-1.** RELIG Orthodox. **-2.** [conformiste] orthodox. ◇ *nmf* **-1.** RELIG Orthodox Christian. **-2.** POLIT conformist.

orthodoxie [ɔrtɔdɔksi] *nf* orthodoxy.

orthogonal, -e, -aux [ɔrtɔgɔnal, o] *adj* orthogonal.

orthographe [ɔrtɔgraf] *nf* spelling.

orthographier [ɔrtɔgrafje] [9] *vt* to spell; **mal ~** to misspell.

orthographique [ɔrtɔgrafik] *adj* orthographic.

orthopédique [ɔrtɔpedik] *adj* orthopaedic.

orthopédiste [ɔrtɔpedist] *nmf* orthopaedist.

orthophoniste [ɔrtɔfɔnist] *nmf* speech therapist.

ortie [ɔrti] *nf* nettle.

ortolan [ɔrtɔlɑ̃] *nm* ortolan.

orvet [ɔrvɛ] *nm* slowworm.

os [ɔs, *pl* o] *nm* **-1.** [gén] bone; **~ à moelle** marrowbone; **~ de seiche** cuttlebone. **-2.** *fam fig* [difficulté] snag, hitch.

OS (*abr de* **ouvrier spécialisé**) *nm* semiskilled worker.

oscillation [ɔsilasjɔ̃] *nf* oscillation; [de navire] rocking.

oscillatoire [ɔsilatwar] *adj* swinging, oscillatory.

osciller [ɔsile] [3] *vi* **-1.** [se balancer] to swing; [navire] to rock. **-2.** [vaciller, hésiter] to waver.

osé, -e [oze] *adj* daring, audacious.

oseille [ozɛj] *nf* **-1.** BOT sorrel. **-2.** *fam* [argent] bread.

oser [oze] [3] *vt* to dare; **~ faire qqch** to dare (to) do sthg; **si j'ose dire** if I may say so.

osier [ozje] *nm* **-1.** BOT osier. **-2.** [fibre] wicker.

Oslo [ɔslo] *n* Oslo.

osmose [ɔsmoz] *nf* osmosis; **en ~** by osmosis.

ossature [ɔsatyr] *nf* **-1.** ANAT skeleton. **-2.** *fig* [structure] framework.

osselet [ɔslɛ] *nm* **-1.** ANAT ossicle. **-2.** [élément de jeu] jack; **jouer aux ~s** to play jacks.

ossements [ɔsmɑ̃] *nmpl* bones.

osseux, -euse [ɔsø, øz] *adj* **-1.** ANAT & MÉD bone (*avant n*). **-2.** [maigre] bony.

ossification [ɔsifikasjɔ̃] *nf* ossification.

ossuaire [ɔsɥɛr] *nm* ossuary.

ostensible [ɔstɑ̃sibl] *adj* conspicuous.

ostensiblement [ɔstɑ̃sibləmɑ̃] *adv* conspicuously.

ostensoir [ɔstɑ̃swar] *nm* monstrance.

ostentation [ɔstɑ̃tasjɔ̃] *nf* ostentation.

ostentatoire [ɔstɑ̃tatwar] *adj* ostentatious.

ostéopathe [ɔsteɔpat] *nmf* osteopath.

ostracisme [ɔstrasism] *nm* ostracism.

otage [ɔtaʒ] *nm* hostage; **prendre qqn en ~** to take sb hostage.

OTAN, Otan [ɔtɑ̃] (*abr de* **Organisation du traité de l'Atlantique Nord**) *nf* NATO.

otarie [ɔtari] *nf* sea lion.

OTASE [ɔtaz] (*abr de* **Organisation du traité de l'Asie du sud-est**) *nf* SEATO.

ôter [ote] [3] *vt* **-1.** [enlever] to take off. **-2.** [soustraire] to take away. **-3.** [retirer, prendre]: **~ qqch à qqn** to take sthg away from sb.

◆ **s'ôter** *vp fam*: **ôte-toi de là!** get out of the way!

otite [ɔtit] *nf* ear infection.

oto-rhino-laryngologie [ɔtɔrinɔlarɛ̃gɔlɔʒi] *nf* ear, nose and throat medicine, ENT.

Ottawa [ɔtawa] *n* Ottawa.

ou [u] *conj* **-1.** [indique une alternative, une approximation] or. **-2.** [sinon]: **~ (bien)** or (else).

◆ **ou (bien) ... ou (bien)** *loc corrélative* either ... or; **~** c'est elle, **~** c'est moi! it's either her or me!

où [u] ◇ *pron rel* **-1.** [spatial] where; **le village ~ j'habite** the village where I live, the village I live in; **pose-le là ~ tu l'as trouvé** put it back where you found it; **partout ~ vous irez** wherever you go. **-2.** [temporel] that; **le jour ~ je suis venu** the day (that) I came. ◇ *adv* where; **je vais ~ je veux** I go where I please; **~ que vous alliez** wherever you go. ◇ *adv interrogatif* where?; **~ vas-tu?** where are you going?; **~ est la voiture?** where's the car?; **dites-moi ~ il est allé** tell me where he's gone.

◆ **d'où** *loc adv* [conséquence] hence; **d'~ on conclut que ...** from which it may be concluded that ....

OUA (*abr de* **Organisation de l'unité africaine**) *nf* OAU.

ouailles [waj] *nfpl* flock (*sg*).

ouais [wɛ] *interj fam* yeah!

ouananiche [wananiʃ] *nf Can* ouananiche (*type of freshwater salmon*).

ouaouaron [wawarɔ̃] *nm Can* bullfrog.

ouate [wat] *nf* **-1.** [pansement] cotton *Am*, cotton wool *Br*. **-2.** [rembourrage] (cotton) wadding.

ouaté, -e [wate] *adj* **-1.** [garni d'ouate] cotton *Am* (*avant n*), cotton wool *Br* (*avant n*); [vêtement] quilted. **-2.** *fig* [feutré] muffled.

oubli [ubli] *nm* **-1.** [acte d'oublier] forgetting. **-2.** [négligence] omission; [étourderie] oversight. **-3.** [abnégation]: **~ de soi** self-effacement. **-4.** [général] oblivion; **tomber dans l'~** to sink into oblivion.

oublier [ublije] [10] *vt* to forget; **~ de faire qqch** to forget to do sthg.

◆ **s'oublier** *vp* **-1.** [emploi passif] to be forgotten. **-2.** [emploi réfléchi] to forget o.s. **-3.** *euphémisme* [chat, enfant] to have an accident.

oubliettes [ublijɛt] *nfpl* dungeon (*sg*); **jeter qqch aux ~** *fam fig* to shelve sthg.

oublieux, -ieuse [ublijø, jøz] *adj* forgetful.

ouest [wɛst] ◇ *nm* west; **un vent d'~** a westerly wind; **le vent d'~** the west wind; **à l'~** in the west; **à l'~ (de)** to the west (of). ◇ *adj inv* [gén] west; [province, région] western.

ouest-allemand, -e [wɛstalmɑ̃, ɑ̃d] *adj* West German.

ouf [uf] *interj* phew!

Ouganda [ugɑ̃da] *nm*: **l'~** Uganda.

ougandais, -e [ugɑ̃dɛ, ɛz] *adj* Ugandan.

◆ **Ougandais, -e** *nm, f* Ugandan.

oui [wi] ◇ *adv* yes; **tu viens? - ~** are you coming? - yes (I am); **tu viens, ~ ou non?** are you coming or not?, are you coming or aren't you?; **je crois que ~** I think so; **faire signe que ~** to nod; **mais ~, bien sûr que ~** yes, of course. ◇ *nm inv* yes; **pour un ~ pour un non** for no apparent reason.

ouï-dire [widir] *nm inv*: **par ~** by OU from hearsay.

ouïe [wi] *nf* hearing; **avoir l'~ fine** to have excellent hearing.

◆ **ouïes** *nfpl* [de poisson] gills.

ouistiti [wistiti] *nm* **-1.** ZOOL marmoset. **-2.** *fam* [type] guy, bloke *Br*.

Oulan-Bator [ulanbatɔr] *n* Ulan Bator.

ouragan [uragã] *nm* **-1.** MÉTÉOR hurricane. **-2.** *fig* [tempête] storm.

ourdir [urdir] [32] *vt fig* & *littéraire* [complot] to hatch.

ourler [urle] [3] *vt* **-1.** COUTURE to hem. **-2.** *littéraire* [border] to edge.

ourlet [urlɛ] *nm* **-1.** COUTURE hem; **faire un** ~ **à** to hem. **-2.** [de l'oreille] helix.

ours [urs] *nm* bear; ~ **(en peluche)** teddy (bear); ~ **polaire** polar bear.

ourse [urs] *nf* she-bear.

◆ **Ourse** *nf*: **la Grande/Petite Ourse** the Great/Little Bear.

oursin [ursɛ̃] *nm* sea urchin.

ourson [ursɔ̃] *nm* bear cub.

oust, ouste [ust] *interj fam* [dehors!] clear off!; [vite!] get a move on!

outarde [utard] *nf* bustard.

outil [uti] *nm* tool.

outillage [utijaʒ] *nm* [équipement] tools (*pl*), equipment.

outrage [utraʒ] *nm* **-1.** *sout* [insulte] insult; **faire subir les derniers** ~**s à qqn** *littéraire* to ravish sb. **-2.** JUR: ~ **aux bonnes mœurs** affront to public decency; ~ **à magistrat** contempt of court; ~ **à la pudeur** indecent behavior (*U*) *Am* OU behaviour (*U*) *Br*.

outrageant, -e [utraʒã, ãt] *adj* insulting, offensive.

outrager [utraʒe] [17] *vt* **-1.** [offenser] to insult. **-2.** [contrevenir] to offend.

outrageusement [utraʒøzmã] *adv* outrageously.

outrance [utrãs] *nf* excess; **à** ~ excessively.

outrancier, -ière [utrãsje, jɛr] *adj* extravagant.

outre[1] [utr] *nf* wineskin.

outre[2] [utr] ◇ *prép* besides, as well as. ◇ *adv*: **passer** ~ to go on, to proceed further; **passer** ~ **à qqch** to disregard sthg.

◆ **en outre** *loc adv* moreover, besides.

◆ **outre que** *loc conj* apart from the fact that.

outre-Atlantique [utratlãtik] *loc adv* across the Atlantic.

outrecuidance [utrəkɥidãs] *nf littéraire* presumptuousness.

outrecuidant, -e [utrəkɥidã, ãt] *adj littéraire* presumptuous.

outre-Manche [utrəmãʃ] *loc adv* across the Channel.

outremer [utrəmɛr] ◇ *nm* [pierre] lapis lazuli; [couleur] ultramarine. ◇ *adj inv* ultramarine.

outre-mer [utrəmɛr] *loc adv* overseas; **d'**~ overseas.

outrepasser [utrəpase] [3] *vt* to exceed.

outrer [utre] [3] *vt* [personne] to outrage.

outre-Rhin [utrərɛ̃] *loc adv* across the Rhine.

outsider [awtsajdœr] *nm* outsider.

ouvert, -e [uvɛr, ɛrt] ◇ *pp* → **ouvrir**. ◇ *adj* **-1.** [gén] open; **grand** ~ wide open. **-2.** [robinet] on, running.

ouvertement [uvɛrtəmã] *adv* openly.

ouverture [uvɛrtyr] *nf* **-1.** [gén] opening; [d'hostilités] outbreak; **l'**~ **de la chasse** the start of the hunting season; ~ **d'esprit** open-mindedness. **-2.** MUS overture. **-3.** PHOT aperture.

◆ **ouvertures** *nfpl* [propositions] overtures.

ouvrable [uvrabl] *adj* working; **heures** ~**s** hours of business.

ouvrage [uvraʒ] *nm* **-1.** [travail] work (*U*), task; **se mettre à l'**~ to start work. **-2.** [objet produit] (piece of) work; COUTURE work (*U*). **-3.** [livre, écrit] work; ~ **de référence** reference work.

ouvragé, -e [uvraʒe] *adj* elaborate.

ouvrant, -e [uvrã, ãt] *adj*: **toit** ~ sunroof.

ouvré, -e [uvre] *adj*: **jour** ~ working day.

ouvre-boîtes [uvrəbwat] *nm inv* can opener, tin opener *Br*.

ouvre-bouteilles [uvrəbutɛj] *nm inv* bottle opener.

ouvreuse [uvrøz] *nf* usherette.

ouvrier, -ière [uvrije, jɛr] ◇ *adj* [quartier, enfance] working-class; [conflit] industrial; [questions, statut] labor (*avant n*) *Am*, labour (*avant n*) *Br*; **classe ouvrière** working class. ◇ *nm, f* worker; ~ **agricole** farm worker; ~ **qualifié** skilled worker; ~ **spécialisé** semi-skilled worker.

◆ **ouvrière** *nf* ZOOL worker.

ouvrir [uvrir] [34] ◇ *vt* **-1.** [gén] to open; ~ **qqch à qqn** to open sthg to sb. **-2.** [chemin, voie] to open up. **-3.** [gaz] to turn on. ◇ *vi* to open; ~ **par qqch** to open with sthg; ~ **sur qqch** to open onto sthg.

◆ **s'ouvrir** *vp* **-1.** [porte, fleur] to open. **-2.** [route, perspectives] to open up. **-3.** [personne]: **s'**~ **(à qqn)** to confide (in sb), to open up (to sb). **-4.** [se blesser]: **s'**~ **le genou** to cut one's knee open; **s'**~ **les veines** to slash OU cut one's wrists. **-5.** [se sensibiliser]: **s'**~ **à qqch** to start to take an interest in sthg.

ovaire [ɔvɛr] *nm* ovary.

ovale [ɔval] *adj* & *nm* oval.

ovation [ɔvasjɔ̃] *nf* ovation; **faire une ~ à qqn** to give sb an ovation.

ovationner [ɔvasjɔne] [3] *vt* to give an ovation to.

overdose [ɔvœrdoz] *nf* overdose.

ovin, -e [ɔvɛ̃, in] *adj* ovine.
♦ **ovin** *nm* sheep.

OVNI, Ovni [ɔvni] (*abr de* **objet volant non identifié**) *nm* UFO.

ovoïde [ɔvɔid] *adj* egg-shaped.

ovuler [ɔvyle] [3] *vi* to ovulate.

oxydable [ɔksidabl] *adj* liable to rust.

oxydation [ɔksidasjɔ̃] *nf* oxidation, oxidization.

oxyde [ɔksid] *nm* oxide; **~ de carbone** carbon monoxide.

oxyder [ɔkside] [3] *vt* to oxidize.
♦ **s'oxyder** *vp* to become oxidized.

oxygène [ɔksiʒɛn] *nm* oxygen; **ballon d'~** oxygen cylinder.

oxygéné, -e [ɔksiʒene] *adj* -1. CHIM oxygenated; → **eau**. -2. [cheveux] peroxide-blond, bleached.

oxygéner [ɔksiʒene] [18] *vt* -1. CHIM to oxygenate. -2. [cheveux] to bleach, to peroxide.
♦ **s'oxygéner** *vp fam* to get some fresh air.

ozone [ozon] *nm* ozone.

P

p¹, P [pe] *nm inv* p, P.

p² -1. (*abr de* **pico**) p. -2. (*abr de* **page**) p. -3. (*abr de* **passable**) *fair grade (as assessment of schoolwork),* ≈ C. -4. *abr de* **pièce**.

Pa (*abr de* **pascal**) Pa.

PA (*abr de* **petites annonces**) *nfpl* small ads.

PAC, Pac [pak] (*abr de* **politique agricole commune**) *nf* CAP.

pacage [pakaʒ] *nm* pasture.

pacemaker [pɛsmekœr] *nm* pacemaker.

pacha [paʃa] *nm* pasha; **mener une vie de ~** *fam fig* to live a life of ease.

pachyderme [paʃidɛrm] *nm* pachyderm.

pacificateur, -trice [pasifikatœr, tris] ◇ *adj* pacifying. ◇ *nm, f* peacemaker.

pacification [pasifikasjɔ̃] *nf* pacification.

pacifier [pasifje] [9] *vt* to pacify.

pacifique [pasifik] *adj* peaceful.

Pacifique [pasifik] → **océan**.

pacifiquement [pasifikmɑ̃] *adv* peacefully.

pacifiste [pasifist] *nmf & adj* pacifist.

pack [pak] *nm* pack.

package [pakadʒ] *nm* INFORM package.

packaging [pakadʒiɲ] *nm* packaging.

pacotille [pakɔtij] *nf* shoddy goods (*pl*), rubbish; **de ~** cheap.

pacte [pakt] *nm* pact.

pactiser [paktize] [3] *vi:* **~ avec** [faire un pacte avec] to make a pact with; [transiger avec] to come to terms with.

pactole [paktɔl] *nm* gold mine *fig*.

paddock [padɔk] *nm* **-1.** [d'un hippodrome] paddock. **-2.** *tfam* [lit]: **se mettre au ~** to hit the sack.

paddy [padi] *nm* paddy (rice).

paella [paela] *nf* paella.

paf [paf] ◇ *interj* wham! ◇ *adj inv fam* [ivre] plastered.

PAF [paf] ◇ *nf* (*abr de* **Police de l'air et des frontières**) *police authority responsible for civil aviation etc.* ◇ *nm* (*abr de* **paysage audiovisuel français**) *French radio and television.*

pagaie [pagɛ] *nf* paddle.

pagaille, pagaye, pagaïe [pagaj] *nf fam* mess; **en ~** [en désordre] in a mess; **des fruits en ~** loads of fruit.

paganisme [paganism] *nm* paganism.

pagaye = **pagaille**.

pagayer [pagɛje] [11] *vi* to paddle.

pagayeur, -euse [pagɛjœr, øz] *nm, f* paddler.

page [paʒ] ◇ *nf* **-1.** [feuillet] page; **~ blanche** blank page; **mettre en ~s** TYPO to make up (into pages); **~ d'accueil** INFORM home page; **~ de garde** flyleaf. **-2.** *fig* [passage] passage; [événement] episode, page. **-3.** *loc:* **être à la ~** to be up-to-date; **tourner la ~** to turn the page. ◇ *nm* page (boy).

pagination [paʒinasjɔ̃] *nf* pagination.

pagne [paɲ] *nm* loincloth.

pagode [pagɔd] *nf* pagoda.

paie¹, paies *etc* → **payer**.

paie², paye [pɛ] *nf* pay (*U*), wages (*pl*).

paiement, payement [pɛmɑ̃] *nm* payment; **~ anticipé** advance payment.

païen, -ïenne [pajɛ̃, jɛn] *adj & nm, f* pagan, heathen.

paierai, paieras *etc* → **payer**.

paillard, -e [pajar, ard] ◇ *adj* bawdy. ◇ *nm, f* rake (*f* slut).

paillasse [pajas] ◇ *nf* **-1.** [matelas] straw mattress. **-2.** [d'évier] draining board. ◇ *nm* clown.

paillasson [pajasɔ̃] *nm* **-1.** [tapis] doormat. **-2.** AGRIC (roll of) matting.

paille [paj] *nf* **-1.** BOT straw; **être sur la ~** *fam fig* to be down and out. **-2.** [pour boire] straw.

◆ **paille de fer** *nf* steel wool.

pailleté, -e [pajte] *adj* sequined.

paillette [pajɛt] *nf* (*gén pl*) **-1.** [sur vêtements] sequin, spangle. **-2.** [d'or] grain of gold dust. **-3.** [de lessive, savon] flake; **savon en ~s** soap flakes (*pl*).

pain [pɛ̃] *nm* **-1.** [aliment] bread; **un ~** a loaf; **petit ~** (bread) roll; **~ azyme** unleavened bread; **~ de campagne** farmhouse loaf; **~ au chocolat** *sweet roll with chocolate filling*; **~ complet** wholemeal bread; **~ d'épice** ≃ gingerbread; **~ au lait** sweet roll, bun; **~ de mie** sandwich loaf; **~ perdu** French toast; **~ de seigle** rye bread; **~ au son** wholemeal bread; **avoir du ~ sur la planche** *fam fig* to have a lot on one's plate; **ôter le ~ de la bouche de qqn** *fig* to take the bread out of sb's mouth. **-2.** [de savon, cire] bar. **-3.** *tfam* [coup] punch.

pair, -e [pɛr] *adj* even.

◆ **pair** *nm* peer.

◆ **paire** *nf* pair; **une ~e de** [lunettes, ciseaux, chaussures] a pair of; **c'est une autre ~e de manches** *fig* that's another story.

◆ **au pair** *loc adv* for one's keep; **jeune fille au ~** au pair (girl).

◆ **de pair** *loc adv*: **aller de ~ avec** to go hand in hand with.

◆ **hors pair** *loc adj* unrivaled *Am*, unrivalled *Br*.

paisible [pɛzibl] *adj* peaceful.

paisiblement [pɛziblǝmɑ̃] *adv* peacefully.

paître [pɛtr] [91] ◇ *vi* to graze. ◇ *vt* to feed on.

paix [pɛ] *nf* peace; **en ~** [en harmonie] at peace; [tranquillement] in peace; **avoir la ~** to have peace and quiet; **faire la ~ avec qqn** to make peace with sb; **ficher la ~ à qqn** *fam* to stop hassling sb; **laisser qqn en ~** to leave sb alone OU in peace.

Pakistan [pakistɑ̃] *nm*: **le ~** Pakistan; **au ~** in Pakistan.

pakistanais, -e [pakistanɛ, ɛz] *adj* Pakistani.

◆ **Pakistanais, -e** *nm, f* Pakistani.

PAL, Pal [pal] (*abr de* **Phase Alternation Line**) *adj* PAL.

palabrer [palabre] [3] *vi* to have interminable discussions.

palabres [palabr] *nmpl ou nfpl* interminable discussions.

palace [palas] *nm* luxury hotel.

palais [palɛ] *nm* **-1.** [château] palace. **-2.** [grand édifice] center *Am*, centre *Br*; **~ des expositions** exhibition center *Am* OU centre *Br*; **le ~ Garnier** *the (old) Paris opera house*; **~ de justice** JUR law courts (*pl*); **le ~ du Luxembourg** *palace in Paris where the French Senate is situated*; **~ omnisports** (multipurpose) sports center *Am* OU centre *Br*; **le ~ des Papes** *the Papal Palace in Avignon*. **-3.** ANAT palate.

palan [palɑ̃] *nm* block and tackle, hoist.

pale [pal] *nf* [de rame, d'hélice] blade.

pâle [pal] *adj* pale.

palefrenier [palfrǝnje] *nm* groom.

paléographie [paleografi] *nf* paleography.

paléolithique [paleolitik] ◇ *nm*: **le ~** the Paleolithic (age). ◇ *adj* paleolithic.

paléontologie [paleɔ̃tɔlɔʒi] *nf* paleontology.

Palerme [palɛrm] *n* Palermo.

Palestine [palɛstin] *nf*: **la ~** Palestine.

palestinien, -ienne [palɛstinjɛ̃, jɛn] *adj* Palestinian.

◆ **Palestinien, -ienne** *nm, f* Palestinian.

palet [palɛ] *nm* HOCKEY puck.

paletot [palto] *nm* (short) overcoat.

palette [palɛt] *nf* **-1.** [de peintre] palette. **-2.** CULIN shoulder. **-3.** [de chariot élévateur] pallet.

palétuvier [paletyvje] *nm* mangrove.

pâleur [palœr] *nf* [de visage] pallor.

pâlichon, -onne [paliʃɔ̃, ɔn] *adj fam* pale, sickly-looking.

palier [palje] *nm* **-1.** [d'escalier] landing. **-2.** [étape] level. **-3.** TECHNOL bearing.

pâlir [palir] [32] ◇ *vt* to turn pale. ◇ *vi* [couleur, lumière] to fade; [personne] to turn OU go pale; **~ de** [angoisse] to turn OU go pale with; [jalousie] to turn OU go green with.

palissade [palisad] *nf* [clôture] fence; [de verdure] hedge.

palissandre [palisɑ̃dr] *nm* rosewood.

palliatif, -ive [paljatif, iv] *adj* palliative.

◆ **palliatif** *nm* **-1.** MÉD palliative. **-2.** *fig* stopgap measure.

pallier [palje] [9] *vt* to make up for.

Palma [palma] *n*: **~ (de Majorque)** Palma (de Majorca).

palmarès [palmarɛs] *nm* **-1.** [de lauréats] list of (medal) winners; SCOL list of prizewinners. **-2.** [de succès] record (of achievements).

palme [palm] *nf* **-1.** [de palmier] palm-leaf. **-2.** [de nageur] flipper. **-3.** [décoration, distinction]: **avec** ~ MIL ≃ with bar; **la** ~ **d'or** *award given to best film at the Cannes Film Festival*; ~s **académiques** *decoration awarded for services to education.*

palmé, -e [palme] *adj* **-1.** BOT palmate. **-2.** ZOOL web-footed; [patte] webbed.

palmeraie [palmərɛ] *nf* palm grove.

palmier [palmje] *nm* **-1.** BOT palm tree. **-2.** CULIN *sweet pastry shaped like a palm leaf.*

palmipède [palmipɛd] ◇ *nm* web-footed bird. ◇ *adj* web-footed.

palombe [palɔ̃b] *nf* woodpigeon.

pâlot, -otte [palo, ɔt] *adj* pale, sickly-looking.

palourde [palurd] *nf* clam.

palpable [palpabl] *adj* palpable, tangible.

palper [palpe] [3] *vt* **-1.** [toucher] to feel, to finger; MÉD to palpate. **-2.** *fam* [de l'argent] to get.

palpitant, -e [palpitɑ̃, ɑ̃t] *adj* exciting, thrilling.

palpitation [palpitasjɔ̃] *nf* palpitation.

palpiter [palpite] [3] *vi* **-1.** [paupières] to flutter; [cœur] to pound. **-2.** [personne]: ~ **de** to tremble OU quiver with. **-3.** *littéraire* [flamme] to tremble, to quiver.

palu [paly] *nm fam* malaria.

paludisme [palydism] *nm* malaria.

pâmer [pame] [3]
◆ **se pâmer** *vp* **-1.** *littéraire* [s'évanouir] to swoon (away). **-2.** *fig*: se ~ **de** to be overcome with.

pâmoison [pamwazɔ̃] *nf littéraire* swoon.

pampa [pɑ̃pa] *nf* pampas (*pl*).

pamphlet [pɑ̃flɛ] *nm* satirical tract.

pamplemousse [pɑ̃pləmus] *nm* grapefruit.

pan [pɑ̃] ◇ *nm* **-1.** [de vêtement] tail. **-2.** [d'affiche] piece, bit; ~ **de mur** section of wall. **-3.** [d'écrou] side. ◇ *interj* bang!

panacée [panase] *nf* panacea.

panachage [panaʃaʒ] *nm* **-1.** [mélange] mix. **-2.** POLIT *splitting one's vote.*

panache [panaʃ] *nm* **-1.** [de plumes, fumée] plume. **-2.** [éclat] panache.

panaché, -e [panaʃe] *adj* **-1.** [de plusieurs couleurs] multicolored *Am*, multicoloured *Br*. **-2.** [mélangé] mixed.
◆ **panaché** *nm* shandy.

panacher [panaʃe] [3] *vt* **-1.** [mélanger] to mix. **-2.** POLIT: ~ **une liste électorale** to split one's vote among several candidates.

panafricanisme [panafrikanism] *nm* Pan-Africanism.

panama [panama] *nm* panama (hat).

Panama [panama] *nm* **-1.** [pays]: **le** ~ Panama; **au** ~ in Panama. **-2.** [ville] Panama City.

panaméen, -enne [panameɛ̃, ɛn], **panamien, -ienne** [panamjɛ̃, jɛn] *adj* Panamanian.
◆ **Panaméen, -enne, Panamien, -ienne** *nm, f* Panamanian.

panard [panar] *nm fam* foot.

panaris [panari] *nm* whitlow.

pancarte [pɑ̃kart] *nf* **-1.** [de manifestant] placard. **-2.** [de signalisation] sign.

pancréas [pɑ̃kreas] *nm* pancreas.

panda [pɑ̃da] *nm* panda.

pané, -e [pane] *adj* breaded, in breadcrumbs.

panégyrique [paneʒirik] *nm* panegyric.

panel [panɛl] *nm* [groupe] sample (group); [jury] panel.

paner [pane] [3] *vt* to coat with breadcrumbs.

panier [panje] *nm* basket; ~ **à provisions** shopping basket; **c'est un** ~ **de crabes** *fig* they're always at each other's throats; ~ **à salade** CULIN salad shaker; *fig* police van; **mettre au** ~ *fig* to throw out.

panier-repas [panjerəpa] (*pl* **paniers-repas**) *nm* packed lunch.

panique [panik] ◇ *nf* panic. ◇ *adj* panicky; **être pris d'une peur** ~ to be panic-stricken.

paniquer [panike] [3] *vt & vi* to panic.
◆ **se paniquer** *vp fam* to panic.

panne [pan] *nf* [arrêt] breakdown; **tomber en** ~ to break down; ~ **de courant** OU **d'électricité** power failure; **tomber en** ~ **d'essence** OU **en** ~ **sèche** to run out of gas *Am* OU petrol *Br*; ~ **de secteur** ÉLECTR mains failure.

panneau, -x [pano] *nm* **-1.** [pancarte] sign; ~ **d'affichage** bulletin board *Am*, noticeboard *Br*; [pour publicité] billboard *Am*, (advertising) hoarding *Br*; ~ **indicateur** signpost; ~ **publicitaire** billboard *Am*, (advertising) hoarding *Br*; ~ **de signalisation** road sign. **-2.** [élément] panel; ~ **de commande** INFORM control panel.

panonceau, -x [panɔ̃so] *nm* **-1.** [plaque] plaque. **-2.** [enseigne] sign.

panoplie [panɔpli] *nf* **-1.** [jouet] outfit. **-2.** [d'armes] display. **-3.** *fig* [de mesures] package.

panorama [panɔrama] *nm* [vue] view, panorama; *fig* overview.

panoramique [panɔramik] ◇ *adj* panoramic. ◇ *nm* CIN pan, panning shot.

panse [pɑ̃s] *nf* **-1.** [d'estomac] first stomach, rumen. **-2.** *fam* [gros ventre] belly, paunch; **se remplir** OU **s'en mettre plein la** ~ to stuff o.s. **-3.** [partie arrondie] bulge.

pansement [pɑ̃smɑ̃] *nm* dressing, bandage; ~ **(adhésif)** Bandaid® *Am*, (sticking) plaster *Br*.

panser [pɑ̃se] [3] *vt* **-1.** [plaie] to dress, to bandage; [jambe] to put a dressing on, to bandage; [avec pansement adhésif] to put a Bandaid® *Am* OU plaster *Br* on. **-2.** [cheval] to groom.

pantagruélique [pɑ̃tagryelik] *adj* gargantuan.

pantalon [pɑ̃talɔ̃] *nm* pants (*pl*) *Am*, trousers (*pl*) *Br*, pair of pants *Am* OU trousers *Br*.

pantelant, -e [pɑ̃tlɑ̃, ɑ̃t] *adj* panting, gasping.

panthéisme [pɑ̃teism] *nm* pantheism.

panthéiste [pɑ̃teist] ◇ *nmf* pantheist. ◇ *adj* pantheistic.

panthéon [pɑ̃teɔ̃] *nm*: **le Panthéon** the Pantheon (*where famous Frenchmen and Frenchwomen are buried*).

panthère [pɑ̃tɛr] *nf* panther; ~ **noire** black panther.

pantin [pɑ̃tɛ̃] *nm* **-1.** [jouet] jumping jack. **-2.** *péj* [personne] puppet.

pantois, -e [pɑ̃twa, az] *adj* astounded, dumbstruck; **rester** ~ to be astounded OU dumbstruck.

pantomime [pɑ̃tɔmim] *nf* **-1.** [art, pièce] mime. **-2.** *fig* & *péj* [manège ridicule]: **qu'est-ce que c'est que cette** ~? what are you playing at?

pantouflard, -e [pɑ̃tuflar, ard] *fam adj* & *nm, f* stay-at-home.

pantoufle [pɑ̃tufl] *nf* slipper.

panure [panyr] *nf* breadcrumbs (*pl*), coating of breadcrumbs.

PAO (*abr de* **publication assistée par ordinateur**) *nf* DTP.

paon [pɑ̃] *nm* peacock; **fier comme un** ~ (as) proud as a peacock.

papa [papa] *nm* dad, daddy; ~ **gâteau** indulgent father.

papal, -e, -aux [papal, o] *adj* papal.

papauté [papote] *nf* papacy.

papaye [papaj] *nf* papaya, pawpaw.

pape [pap] *nm* **-1.** RELIG pope; **sérieux comme un** ~ deadly serious. **-2.** *fig* [de mouvement] leading light.

papelard [paplar] *nm fam* [papier] bit of paper.

paperasse [papras] *nf péj* **-1.** [papier sans importance] papers (*pl*), bumf (*U*) *Br*. **-2.** [papiers administratifs] paperwork (*U*).

paperasserie [paprasri] *nf péj* paperwork.

papeterie [papetri] *nf* [magasin] stationer's; [fabrique] paper mill.

papetier, -ière [paptje, jɛr] *nm, f* [commerçant] stationer; [fabricant] paper manufacturer.

papi, papy [papi] *nm* grandpa, grandad.

papier [papje] *nm* **-1.** [matière, écrit] paper; **noircir du** ~ to scribble; ~ **alu** OU **aluminium** aluminum *Am* OU aluminium *Br* foil, tinfoil; ~ **carbone** carbon paper; ~ **continu** continuous stationery; ~ **crépon** crêpe paper; ~ **d'emballage** wrapping paper; ~ **à en-tête** headed notepaper; ~ **glacé** glazed paper; ~ **hygiénique** toilet paper; ~ **journal** newsprint; [vieux journaux] newspaper; ~ **à lettres** writing paper, notepaper; ~ **mâché** papier-mâché; ~ **machine** typing paper; ~ **millimétré** graph paper; ~ **peint** wallpaper; ~ **de soie** tissue paper; ~ **thermique** thermal paper; ~ **tue-mouches** fly paper; ~ **de verre** glasspaper, sandpaper. **-2.** [article de journal] article.

◆ **papiers** *nmpl*: ~**s (d'identité)** (identity) papers.

papier-calque [papjekalk] (*pl* **papiers-calque**) *nm* tracing paper.

papier-filtre [papjefiltr] (*pl* **papiers-filtres**) *nm* filter paper.

papier-monnaie [papjemɔnɛ] (*pl* **papiers-monnaies**) *nm* paper money.

papille [papij] *nf*: ~**s gustatives** taste buds.

papillon [papijɔ̃] *nm* **-1.** ZOOL butterfly; ~ **de nuit** moth. **-2.** [contravention] (parking) ticket. **-3.** [écrou] wing nut. **-4.** [nage] butterfly (stroke).

papillonner [papijɔne] [3] *vi* to flit about OU around.

papillote [papijɔt] *nf* **-1.** [de bonbon] candy paper *Am*, sweet paper OU wrapper *Br*. **-2.** [de cheveux] curl paper. **-3.** CULIN: **en** ~**s** *baked in tinfoil or greaseproof paper*.

papilloter [papijɔte] [3] *vi* [lumière] to twinkle; [yeux] to blink.

papoter [papɔte] [3] *vi fam* to chatter.

papou, -e [papu] *adj* Papuan.

◆ **papou** *nm* [langue] Papuan.

◆ **Papou, -e** *nm, f* Papuan.

Papouasie-Nouvelle-Guinée [papwazi-nyvɛlgine] *nf*: **la** ~ Papua New Guinea.

paprika [paprika] *nm* paprika.

papy = **papi**.

papyrus [papirys] *nm* papyrus.

Pâque [pak] *nf*: **la** ~ Passover; *voir aussi* **Pâques**.

paquebot [pakbo] *nm* liner.

pâquerette [pakrɛt] *nf* daisy.

Pâques [pak] *nfpl* Easter (*sg*); **joyeuses** ~ Happy Easter; **île de** ~ Easter Island.

PÂQUES:
In France, Easter is symbolized not only by eggs but also by bells; according to legend, church bells fly to Rome at Easter

paquet [pakɛ] *nm* **-1.** [colis] parcel. **-2.** [emballage] packet; ~**-cadeau** gift-wrapped parcel. **-3.** *loc*: **mettre le** ~ *fam* to pull out all the stops, to give it all one's got.

paquetage [pakta3] *nm* MIL kit.

par [par] *prép* **-1.** [spatial] through, by (way of); **passer** ~ **la Suède et le Danemark** to go via Sweden and Denmark; **regarder** ~ **la fenêtre** to look out of the window; ~ **endroits** in places; ~ **ici/là** this/that way; **mon cousin habite** ~ **ici** my cousin lives round here. **-2.** [temporel] on; ~ **un beau jour d'été** on a lovely summer's day; ~ **le passé** in the past. **-3.** [moyen, manière, cause] by; ~ **bateau/train/avion** by boat/train/plane; ~ **pitié** out of OU from pity; ~ **accident** by accident, by chance. **-4.** [introduit le complément d'agent] by; **faire faire qqch** ~ **qqn** to have sthg done by sb. **-5.** [sens distributif] per, a; **une heure** ~ **jour** one hour a OU per day; **deux** ~ **deux** two at a time; **marcher deux** ~ **deux** to walk in twos.
◆ **par-ci par-là** *loc adv* here and there.

para [para] (*abr de* **parachutiste**) *nm* para.

parabole [parabɔl] *nf* **-1.** [récit] parable. **-2.** MATHS parabola.

parabolique [parabɔlik] *adj* parabolic; **antenne** ~ **dish** OU parabolic aerial.

parachever [paraʃve] [19] *vt* to put the finishing touches to.

parachutage [paraʃyta3] *nm* parachuting, dropping by parachute.

parachute [paraʃyt] *nm* parachute; ~ **ascensionnel** parachute (*for parascending*); **faire du** ~ **ascensionnel** to go parascending.

parachuter [paraʃyte] [3] *vt* to parachute, to drop by parachute; **ils l'ont parachuté directeur** *fig* he was unexpectedly given the job of manager.

parachutisme [paraʃytism] *nm* parachuting.

parachutiste [paraʃytist] *nmf* parachutist; MIL paratrooper.

parade [parad] *nf* **-1.** [spectacle] parade. **-2.**
[défense] parry; *fig* riposte. **-3.** [étalage] show.

parader [parade] [3] *vi* to show off.

paradis [paradi] *nm* paradise; **le Paradis terrestre** BIBLE the Garden of Eden; *fig* heaven on earth.

paradisiaque [paradizjak] *adj* heavenly.

paradoxal, -e, -aux [paradɔksal, o] *adj* paradoxical.

paradoxalement [paradɔksalmɑ̃] *adv* paradoxically.

paradoxe [paradɔks] *nm* paradox.

parafe, paraphe [paraf] *nm* initials (*pl*).

parafer, parapher [parafe] [3] *vt* to initial.

paraffine [parafin] *nf* kerosene *Am*, paraffin *Br*; [solide] paraffin wax.

parages [para3] *nmpl* NAVIG waters; **être** OU **se trouver dans les** ~ *fig* to be in the area OU vicinity.

paragraphe [paragraf] *nm* paragraph.

Paraguay [paragwɛ] *nm*: **le** ~ Paraguay; **au** ~ in Paraguay.

paraguayen, -enne [paragwejɛ̃, ɛn] *adj* Paraguayan.
◆ **Paraguayen, -enne** *nm, f* Paraguayan.

paraissais, paraissions *etc* → **paraître**.

paraître [parɛtr] [91] ◇ *v attr* to look, to seem, to appear. ◇ *vi* **-1.** [se montrer] to appear. **-2.** [être publié] to come out, to be published. **-3.** [se manifester] to show (through); **laisser** ~ to show; **ne rien laisser** ~ to let nothing show. **-4.** [briller] to be noticed. ◇ *v impers*: **il paraît/paraîtrait que** it appears/would appear that; **paraît-il** apparently, it seems.

parallèle [paralɛl] ◇ *nm* parallel; **mettre en** ~ *fig* to compare; **établir un** ~ **entre** *fig* to draw a parallel between. ◇ *nf* parallel (line). ◇ *adj* **-1.** [action, en maths] parallel. **-2.** [marché] **unofficial**; [médecine, énergie] alternative.

parallèlement [paralɛlmɑ̃] *adv* in parallel; *fig* at the same time.

parallélépipède [paralelepipɛd] *nm* parallelepiped.

parallélisme [paralelism] *nm* parallelism; [de roues] alignment.

parallélogramme [paralelɔgram] *nm* parallelogram.

paralysant, -e [paralizɑ̃, ɑ̃t] *adj* paralysing.

paralyser [paralize] [3] *vt* to paralyse.

paralysie [paralizi] *nf* paralysis.

paralytique [paralitik] *adj & nmf* paralytic.

paramédical, -e, -aux [paramedikal, o] *adj* paramedical.

paramètre [paramɛtr] *nm* parameter.

paramilitaire [paramilitɛr] *adj* paramilitary.

parangon [parɑ̃gɔ̃] *nm littéraire* paragon.

parano [parano] *adj fam* paranoid.

paranoïa [paranɔja] *nf* paranoia.

paranoïaque [paranɔjak] ◇ *adj* paranoid. ◇ *nmf* paranoiac.

paranormal, -e, -aux [paranɔrmal, o] *adj* paranormal.

parapente [parapɑ̃t] *nm* paragliding.

parapet [parapɛ] *nm* parapet.

paraphe = **parafe**.

parapher = **parafer**.

paraphrase [parafraz] *nf* paraphrase.

paraphraser [parafraze] [3] *vt* to paraphrase.

paraplégique [parapleʒik] *nmf* & *adj* paraplegic.

parapluie [paraplɥi] *nm* umbrella; ~ **atomique** OU **nucléaire** nuclear umbrella.

parapsychologie [parapsikɔlɔʒi] *nf* parapsychology.

parascolaire [paraskɔlɛr] *adj* extracurricular.

parasite [parazit] ◇ *nm* parasite. ◇ *adj* parasitic; **bruits ~s** RADIO & TÉLÉ interference (U).
◆ **parasites** *nmpl* RADIO & TÉLÉ interference (U).

parasiter [parazite] [3] *vt* **-1.** [suj: ver, insecte] to live parasitically on, to parasitize. **-2.** [suj: personne] to leech OU live off. **-3.** RADIO & TÉLÉ to cause interference on.

parasol [parasɔl] *nm* parasol, sunshade.

paratonnerre [paratɔnɛr] *nm* lightning rod *Am* OU conductor *Br*.

paravent [paravɑ̃] *nm* screen.

parbleu [parblø] *interj* (but) of course!

parc [park] *nm* **-1.** [jardin] park; [de château] grounds (*pl*); ~ **d'attractions** amusement park; ~ **national** national park. **-2.** [pour l'élevage] pen; ~ **à huîtres** oyster bed. **-3.** [de bébé] playpen. **-4.** [de voitures] fleet; **le ~ automobile** the number of cars on the roads.

parcelle [parsɛl] *nf* **-1.** [petite partie] fragment, particle. **-2.** [terrain] parcel of land.

parce que [parsk(ə)] *loc conj* because.

parchemin [parʃəmɛ̃] *nm* parchment.

parcheminé, -e [parʃəmine] *adj* wrinkled.

parcimonie [parsimɔni] *nf* parsimoniousness; **avec ~** sparingly, parsimoniously.

parcimonieusement [parsimɔnjøzmɑ̃] *adv* parsimoniously.

parcimonieux, -ieuse [parsimɔnjø, jøz] *adj* parsimonious.

parcmètre [parkmɛtr] *nm* parking meter.

parcourir [parkurir] [45] *vt* **-1.** [région, route] to cover. **-2.** [journal, dossier] to skim OU glance through, to scan.

parcourrai, parcourras *etc* → **parcourir**.

parcours¹, parcourt *etc* → **parcourir**.

parcours² [parkur] *nm* **-1.** [trajet, voyage] journey; [itinéraire] route; ~ **du combattant** assault course. **-2.** GOLF [terrain] course; [trajet] round.

parcouru, -e [parkury] *pp* → **parcourir**.

par-delà [pardəla] *prép* beyond.

par-derrière [pardɛrjɛr] *adv* **-1.** [par le côté arrière] round the back. **-2.** [en cachette] behind one's back.

par-dessous [pardəsu] *prép* & *adv* under, underneath.

pardessus [pardəsy] *nm inv* overcoat.

par-dessus [pardəsy] ◇ *prép* over, over the top of; ~ **tout** above all. ◇ *adv* over, over the top.

par-devant [pardəvɑ̃] ◇ *prép* in front of. ◇ *adv* in front.

pardi [pardi] *interj fam* of course!

pardon [pardɔ̃] ◇ *nm* forgiveness; **demander ~** to say (one is) sorry. ◇ *interj* [excuses] (I'm) sorry!; [pour attirer l'attention] excuse me!; ~? **pardon me?** *Am,* (I beg your) pardon? *Br.*

pardonnable [pardɔnabl] *adj* forgiveable.

pardonner [pardɔne] [3] ◇ *vt* to forgive; ~ **qqch à qqn** to forgive sb for sthg; ~ **à qqn d'avoir fait qqch** to forgive sb for doing sthg. ◇ *vi*: **ce genre d'erreur ne pardonne pas** this kind of mistake is fatal.

paré, -e [pare] *adj* [prêt] ready.

pare-balles [parbal] ◇ *nm inv* [gilet] bulletproof vest; [plaque] bullet-proof shield. ◇ *adj inv* bullet-proof.

pare-brise [parbriz] *nm inv* windshield *Am,* windscreen *Br.*

pare-chocs [parʃɔk] *nm inv* bumper.

pare-feu [parfø] *nm inv* [dispositif] fireguard; [en forêt] fire-break.

pareil, -eille [parɛj] ◇ *adj* **-1.** [semblable]: ~ **(à)** similar (to). **-2.** [tel] such; **un ~ film** such a film, a film like this; **de ~s films** such films, films like these. ◇ *nm, f*: **mes ~s** my equals; **sans ~** matchless; **c'est du ~ au même** it comes to much the same thing; **rendre la pareille à qqn** to pay sb back in his/her own coin, to give sb a taste of his/her own medicine.
◆ **pareil** *adv fam* the same (way).

pareillement [parɛjmɑ̃] *adv* [de même] in the same way; [également, aussi] likewise, also.

parement [parmɑ̃] *nm* facing.

parent, -e [parɑ̃, ɑ̃t] ◇ *adj*: ~ **(de)** related (to). ◇ *nm, f* relative, relation; ~ **éloigné** distant relation OU relative.
◆ **parents** *nmpl* **-1.** [père et mère] parents, mother and father. **-2.** *littéraire* [ancêtres] forefathers.

parental, -e, -aux [parɑ̃tal, o] *adj* parental.

parenté [parɑ̃te] *nf* **-1.** [lien, affinité] relationship. **-2.** [famille] relatives (*pl*), relations (*pl*).

parenthèse [parɑ̃tɛz] *nf* **-1.** [digression] digression, parenthesis. **-2.** TYPO bracket, parenthesis; **entre ~s** in brackets; *fig* incidentally, by the way; **mettre entre ~s** to put in brackets, to bracket; *fig* to put to one side; **ouvrir/fermer la** ~ to open/close brackets.

paréo [pareo] *nm* pareo.

parer [pare] [3] ◇ *vt* **-1.** *sout* [orner] to adorn. **-2.** [vêtir]: ~ **qqn de qqch** to dress sb up in sthg, to deck sb out in sthg; *fig* to attribute sthg to sb. **-3.** [contrer] to ward off, to parry. ◇ *vi*: ~ **à** [faire face à] to deal with; [pourvoir à] to prepare for; ~ **au plus pressé** to see to what is most urgent.
◆ **se parer** *vp* to dress up, to put on all one's finery; **se** ~ **de** to adorn o.s. with; *fig* [titre] to assume.

pare-soleil [parsɔlɛj] *nm inv* sun visor.

paresse [parɛs] *nf* **-1.** [fainéantise] laziness, idleness. **-2.** MÉD sluggishness.

paresser [parese] [4] *vi* to laze about OU around.

paresseusement [paresøzmɑ̃] *adv* lazily, idly.

paresseux, -euse [paresø, øz] ◇ *adj* **-1.** [fainéant] lazy. **-2.** MÉD sluggish. ◇ *nm, f* [personne] lazy OU idle person.
◆ **paresseux** *nm* [animal] sloth.

parfaire [parfɛr] [109] *vt* to complete, to perfect.

parfait, -e [parfɛ, ɛt] *adj* perfect.
◆ **parfait** *nm* **-1.** CULIN parfait. **-2.** GRAM perfect (tense).

parfaitement [parfɛtmɑ̃] *adv* **-1.** [admirablement, très] perfectly. **-2.** [marque l'assentiment] absolutely.

parfois [parfwa] *adv* sometimes.

parfum [parfœ̃] *nm* **-1.** [de fleur] scent, fragrance. **-2.** [à base d'essences] perfume, scent. **-3.** [de glace] flavour. **-4.** *loc*: **être/mettre qqn au** ~ to be/put sb in the know.

parfumé, -e [parfyme] *adj* **-1.** [fleur] fragrant. **-2.** [mouchoir] perfumed. **-3.** [femme]: **elle est trop ~e** she's wearing too much perfume.

parfumer [parfyme] [3] *vt* **-1.** [suj: fleurs] to perfume. **-2.** [mouchoir] to perfume, to scent. **-3.** CULIN to flavour.
◆ **se parfumer** *vp* to put perfume on.

parfumerie [parfymri] *nf* perfumery.

parfumeur, -euse [parfymœr, øz] *nm, f* perfumer.

pari [pari] *nm* **-1.** [entre personnes] bet; **faire un** ~ to make OU lay a bet; **gagner/perdre son** ~ to win/lose one's bet. **-2.** [jeu] betting (*U*).

paria [parja] *nm* pariah.

parier [parje] [9] *vt*: ~ **(sur)** to bet (on); **je l'aurais parié!** *fig* I thought as much!

parieur [parjœr] *nm* punter.

parigot, -ote [parigo, ɔt] *adj fam* Parisian.
◆ **Parigot, -ote** *nm, f fam* Parisian.

Paris [pari] *n* Paris.

PARIS:
The name 'Paris' followed by a number or Roman numeral refers to a Paris university: 'Paris VII' (the science faculty at Jussieu), 'Paris IV' (the Sorbonne), 'Paris X' (Nanterre university) etc.
When 'Paris' is followed by an ordinal number, this refers to an 'arrondissement': 'Paris quinzième', 'Paris quatrième', etc

---

paris-brest [paribrɛst] *nm inv choux pastry ring with cream and almonds.*

parisianisme [parizjanism] *nm* [expression] Parisian idiom; [habitude] Parisian custom.

parisien, -ienne [parizjɛ̃, jɛn] *adj* [vie, société] Parisian; [métro, banlieue, région] Paris (*avant n*).
◆ **Parisien, -ienne** *nm, f* Parisian.

paritaire [paritɛr] *adj*: **commission** ~ joint commission (*with both sides equally represented*).

parité [parite] *nf* parity.

parjure [parʒyr] ◇ *nmf* [personne] perjurer. ◇ *nm* [faux serment] perjury.

parjurer [parʒyre] [3]
◆ **se parjurer** *vp* to perjure o.s.

parka [parka] *nm ou nf* parka.

parking [parkiŋ] *nm* [parc] parking lot *Am*, car park *Br*.

parlant, -e [parlɑ̃, ɑ̃t] *adj* **-1.** [qui parle]: **le cinéma** ~ talking pictures; **l'horloge ~e**

TÉLÉCOM the speaking clock. **-2.** *fig* [chiffres, données] eloquent; [portrait] vivid.

parlement [parləmɑ̃] *nm* parliament; **le Parlement européen** the European Parliament.

parlementaire [parləmɑ̃tɛr] ◇ *nmf* [député] member of parliament; [négociateur] negotiator. ◇ *adj* parliamentary.

parlementarisme [parləmɑ̃tarism] *nm* (system of) parliamentary government.

parlementer [parləmɑ̃te] [3] *vi* **-1.** [négocier] to negotiate, to parley. **-2.** [parler longtemps] to talk at length.

parler [parle] [3] ◇ *vi* **-1.** [gén] to talk, to speak; **les faits parlent d'eux-mêmes** the facts speak for themselves; ~ **à/avec qqn** to speak to/with sb, to talk to/with sb; ~ **de qqch à qqn** to speak OU talk to sb about sthg; ~ **de qqn/qqch** to talk about sb/sthg; ~ **de faire qqch** to talk about doing sthg; ~ **en français** to speak in French; ~ **tout seul** to talk to o.s.; **sans** ~ **de** apart from, not to mention; **à proprement** ~ strictly speaking; ~ **pour ne rien dire** to talk for the sake of talking; **tu parles!** *fam* you can say that again!; **n'en parlons plus** we'll say no more about it. **-2.** [avouer] to talk. ◇ *vt* [langue] to speak; ~ **(le) français** to speak French; ~ **politique/affaires** to talk politics/business. ◇ *nm* **-1.** [manière de parler] speech. **-2.** [patois] dialect.
◆ **se parler** *vp*: **ils ne se parlent pas** they're not on speaking terms.

parleur [parlœr] *nm*: **beau** ~ *péj* fine talker.

parloir [parlwar] *nm* parlor *Am*, parlour *Br*.

parlo(t)te [parlɔt] *nf* chat.

parme [parm] *nm & adj inv* violet.

parmesan [parməzɑ̃] *nm* Parmesan (cheese).

parmi [parmi] *prép* among.

parodie [parɔdi] *nf* parody.

parodier [parɔdje] [9] *vt* to parody.

paroi [parwa] *nf* **-1.** [mur] wall; [cloison] partition; ~ **rocheuse** rock face. **-2.** [de récipient] inner side.

paroisse [parwas] *nf* parish.

paroissial, -e, -iaux [parwasjal, jo] *adj* parish (*avant n*).

paroissien, -ienne [parwasjɛ̃, jɛn] *nm, f* parishioner.

parole [parɔl] *nf* **-1.** [faculté de parler]: **la** ~ speech. **-2.** [propos, discours]: **adresser la** ~ **à qqn** to speak to sb; **couper la** ~ **à qqn** to cut sb off; **prendre la** ~ to speak; **donner** OU **passer la** ~ **à qqn** to hand over to sb. **-3.** [promesse, mot] word; **tenir** ~ to keep one's word; **donner sa** ~ **(d'honneur)** to give one's word (of honor *Am* OU honour

Br); **croire qqn sur** ~ to take sb's word for it; **libérer qqn sur** ~ to free sb on parole.
◆ **paroles** *nfpl* MUS words, lyrics.

parolier, -ière [parɔlje, jɛr] *nm, f* [de chanson] lyricist; [d'opéra] librettist.

paroxysme [parɔksism] *nm* height.

parpaing [parpɛ̃] *nm* breeze block.

parquer [parke] [3] *vt* **-1.** [animaux] to pen in OU up. **-2.** [prisonniers] to shut up OU in. **-3.** [voiture] to park.

parquet [parkɛ] *nm* **-1.** [plancher] parquet floor. **-2.** JUR ≃ District Attorney's office *Am*, ≃ Crown Prosecution Service *Br*.

parrain [parɛ̃] *nm* **-1.** [d'enfant] godfather. **-2.** [de festival, sportif] sponsor.

parrainage [parɛnaʒ] *nm* sponsorship.

parrainer [parɛne] [4] *vt* to sponsor, to back.

parricide [parisid] ◇ *nm* [crime] parricide. ◇ *adj* parricidal.

pars, part → **partir**.

parsemer [parsəme] [19] *vt*: ~ **(de)** to strew (with).

part [par] *nf* **-1.** [de tarte, gâteau] portion; [de bonheur, héritage] share; [partie] part; **réclamer sa** ~ to claim one's share; ~ **de marché** ÉCON market share; **se tailler la** ~ **du lion** *fig* to take the lion's share. **-2.** [participation]: **prendre** ~ **à qqch** to take part in sthg. **-3.** *loc*: **c'est de la** ~ **de qui?** [au téléphone] who's speaking OU calling?; **dites-lui de ma** ~ **que ...** tell him from me that ...; **ce serait bien aimable de votre** ~ it would be very kind of you; **pour ma** ~ as far as I'm concerned; **faire** ~ **à qqn de qqch** to inform sb of sthg; **faire la** ~ **des choses** to make allowances.
◆ **à part** ◇ *loc adv* aside, separately. ◇ *loc adj* exceptional. ◇ *loc prép* apart from.
◆ **autre part** *loc adv* someplace *Am* OU somewhere *Br* else.
◆ **d'autre part** *loc adv* besides, moreover.
◆ **de part en part** *loc adv* right through.
◆ **de part et d'autre** *loc adv* on both sides.
◆ **d'une part ..., d'autre part** *loc corrélative* on the one hand ..., on the other hand.
◆ **nulle part** *loc adv* no-place *Am*, nowhere *Br*.
◆ **quelque part** *loc adv* someplace *Am*, somewhere *Br*.

part. *abr de* **particulier**.

partage [partaʒ] *nm* **-1.** [action] sharing (out). **-2.** JUR distribution.

partager [partaʒe] [17] *vt* **-1.** [morceler] to divide (up); **être partagé** *fig* to be divided. **-2.** [mettre en commun]: ~ **qqch avec qqn** to share sthg with sb. **-3.** [prendre part à] to share (in).

◆ **se partager** *vp* **-1.** [se diviser] to be divided. **-2.** [partager son temps] to divide one's time. **-3.** [se répartir]: **se ~ qqch** to share sthg between themselves/ourselves *etc.*

partance [partɑ̃s] *nf*: **en ~** outward bound; **en ~ pour** bound for.

partant, -e [partɑ̃, ɑ̃t] *adj*: **être ~ pour** to be ready for.

◆ **partant** *nm* starter.

partenaire [partənɛr] *nmf* partner; **~s sociaux** labor *Am* OU labour *Br* and management.

partenariat [partənarja] *nm* partnership.

parterre [partɛr] *nm* **-1.** [de fleurs] (flower) bed. **-2.** THÉÂTRE orchestra *Am*, stalls (*pl*) *Br*.

parti, -e [parti] ◇ *pp* → **partir.** ◇ *adj fam* [ivre] tipsy.

◆ **parti** *nm* **-1.** POLIT party; **~ d'opposition** opposition party. **-2.** [choix, décision] course of action; **prendre ~** to make up one's mind; **prendre le ~ de faire qqch** to make up one's mind to do sthg; **en prendre son ~** to be resigned; **être de ~ pris** to be prejudiced OU biased; **tirer ~ de** to make (good) use of. **-3.** [personne à marier] match; **un beau ~** a good match.

◆ **partie** *nf* **-1.** [élément, portion] part; **en grande ~e** largely; **en majeure ~e** for the most part; **faire ~e (intégrante) de qqch** to be (an integral) part of sthg. **-2.** [domaine d'activité] field, subject. **-3.** SPORT game. **-4.** JUR party; **la ~ adverse** the opposing party. **-5.** *loc*: **prendre qqn à ~e** to attack sb.

◆ **parties** *nfpl fam* private parts, privates.

◆ **en partie** *loc adv* partly, in part.

partial, -e, -iaux [parsjal, jo] *adj* biased.

partialement [parsjalmɑ̃] *adv* in a biased way, with bias.

partialité [parsjalite] *nf* partiality, bias.

participant, -e [partisipɑ̃, ɑ̃t] ◇ *adj* participating. ◇ *nm, f* **-1.** [à réunion] participant. **-2.** SPORT competitor. **-3.** [à concours] entrant.

participatif, -ive [partisipatif, iv] *adj*: **prêt ~ participating** capital loan.

participation [partisipasjɔ̃] *nf* **-1.** [collaboration] participation. **-2.** ÉCON interest; **~ aux frais** (financial) contribution; **~ aux bénéfices** profit-sharing; **~ majoritaire/minoritaire** majority/minority interest.

participe [partisip] *nm* participle; **~ passé/présent** past/present participle.

participer [partisipe] [3] *vi*: **~ à** [réunion, concours] to take part in; [frais] to con-

tribute to; [bénéfices] to share in; **~ de** *littéraire* to have some of the characteristics of.

particularisme [partikylarism] *nm* (sense of) identity.

particularité [partikylarite] *nf* distinctive feature.

particule [partikyl] *nf* **-1.** [gén & LING] particle. **-2.** [nobiliaire] nobiliary particle.

particulier, -ière [partikylje, jɛr] *adj* **-1.** [personnel, privé] private. **-2.** [spécial] particular, special; [propre] peculiar, characteristic; **~ à** peculiar to, characteristic of. **-3.** [remarquable] unusual, exceptional; **cas ~** special case. **-4.** [assez bizarre] peculiar.

◆ **particulier** *nm* [personne] private individual.

◆ **en particulier** *loc adv* **-1.** [seul à seul] in private. **-2.** [surtout] in particular, particularly. **-3.** [à part] separately.

particulièrement [partikyljɛrmɑ̃] *adv* particularly; **tout ~** especially.

partie → **parti.**

partiel, -ielle [parsjɛl] *adj* partial.

◆ **partiel** *nm* UNIV ≃ end-of-term exam.

partiellement [parsjɛlmɑ̃] *adv* partially, partly.

partir [partir] [43] *vi* **-1.** [personne] to go, to leave; **~ à** to go to; **~ pour** to leave for; **~ de** [bureau] to leave; [aéroport, gare] to leave from; [hypothèse, route] to start from; [date] to run from. **-2.** [voiture] to start; **c'est bien/mal parti** *fig* it got off on the right/wrong foot. **-3.** [coup de feu] to go off; [bouchon] to pop. **-4.** [tache] to come out.

◆ **à partir de** *loc prép* from.

partisan, -e [partizɑ̃, an] *adj* [partial] partisan; **être ~ de** to be in favor *Am* OU favour *Br* of.

◆ **partisan** *nm* **-1.** [adepte] supporter, advocate. **-2.** MIL partisan.

partitif, -ive [partitif, iv] *adj* partitive.

◆ **partitif** *nm* partitive.

partition [partisjɔ̃] *nf* **-1.** [séparation] partition. **-2.** MUS score.

partout [partu] *adv* everywhere; **~ ailleurs** everywhere else.

paru, -e [pary] *pp* → **paraître.**

parure [paryr] *nf* (matching) set.

parution [parysjɔ̃] *nf* publication.

parvenir [parvənir] [40] *vi*: **~ à** [atteindre] to reach; [obtenir] to achieve; **~ à faire qqch** to manage to do sthg; **faire ~ qqch à qqn** to send sthg to sb.

parvenu, -e [parvəny] ◇ *pp* → **parvenir.** ◇ *nm, f péj* parvenu, upstart.

parviendrai, parviendras *etc* → **parvenir.**

parvis [parvi] *nm* square (*in front of church*).

pas[1] [pa] *nm* **-1.** [gén] step; **allonger le ~** to quicken one's pace; **marquer le ~** to mark time; **revenir sur ses ~** to retrace one's steps; **~ à ~** step by step; **au ~ cadencé** in quick time; **à ~ de loup** *fig* stealthily; **à ~ feutrés** *fig* with muffled footsteps. **-2.** TECH-NOL. thread. **-3.** *loc:* **c'est à deux ~ (d'ici)** it's very near (here); **emboîter le ~ à qqn** to fall into step with sb; **faire les cent ~** to pace up and down; **faire un faux ~** to slip; *fig* to make a faux pas; **faire le premier ~** to make the first move; **franchir** OU **sauter le ~** to take the plunge; **(rouler) au ~** (to move) at a snail's pace; **sur le ~ de la porte** on the doorstep; **tirer qqn d'un mauvais ~** to get sb out of a tight spot.

pas[2] [pa] *adv* **-1.** [avec ne] not; **elle ne vient ~** she's not OU she isn't coming; **elle n'a ~ mangé** she hasn't eaten; **je ne le connais ~** I don't know him; **il n'y a ~ de vin** there's no wine, there isn't any wine; **je préférerais ne ~ le rencontrer** I would prefer not to meet him, I would rather not meet him. **-2.** [sans ne] not; **l'as-tu vu ou ~ ?** have you seen him or not?; **il est très satisfait, moi ~** he's very pleased, but I'm not; **sincère ou ~** (whether) sincere or not; **une histoire ~ drôle** a story which isn't funny; **~ encore** not yet; **~ du tout** not at all. **-3.** [avec pron indéf]: **~ un** [aucun] none, not one; **~ un d'eux n'est venu** none of them OU not one of them came.

pascal, -e [paskal] (*pl* **pascals** OU **pascaux**) *adj* Easter (*avant n*).

◆ **pascal** *nm* **-1.** INFORM. Pascal. **-2.** PHYS. pascal.

pas-de-porte [pɑdpɔrt] *nm inv* key money.

passable [pɑsabl] *adj* passable, fair.

passablement [pɑsabləmɑ̃] *adv* **-1.** [assez bien] fairly well. **-2.** [beaucoup] quite a bit.

passage [pɑsaʒ] *nm* **-1.** [action - de passer] going past; [- de traverser] crossing; **être de ~** to be passing through; **au ~** [en passant] as he/she *etc* goes by; *fig* in passing. **-2.** [endroit] passage, way; **se frayer un ~ à travers** OU **dans** to force a way through; **«~ interdit»** "no entry"; **~ clouté** pedestrian crossing; **~ à niveau** grade crossing *Am*, level crossing *Br*; **~ protégé** *priority given to traffic on the main road*; **~ souterrain** subway *Am*, underpass *Br*. **-3.** [changement d'état]: **~ de qqch à qqch** change OU transition from sthg to sthg; **~ à vide** dizzy spell; *fig* bad patch. **-4.** [extrait] passage.

passager, -ère [pɑsaʒe, ɛr] ◇ *adj* **-1.** [bonheur] fleeting, short-lived. **-2.** [hôte] short-

stay (*avant n*); **oiseau ~** bird of passage. ◇ *nm, f* passenger; **~ clandestin** stowaway.

passant, -e [pɑsɑ̃, ɑ̃t] ◇ *adj* busy. ◇ *nm, f* passer-by.

◆ **passant** *nm* [de ceinture] (belt) loop.

passation [pɑsasjɔ̃] *nf* **-1.** [conclusion] signing. **-2.** [transmission] hand-over; **~ des pouvoirs** transfer of power.

passe [pɑs] ◇ *nm* passkey. ◇ *nf* **-1.** [au sport] pass. **-2.** NAVIG. channel. **-3.** *fam* [prostitution]: **maison de ~** ≃ brothel. **-4.** *loc:* **être en ~ de faire qqch** to be on the way to doing sthg; **être dans une mauvaise ~** to be in a fix.

passé, -e [pɑse] *adj* **-1.** [qui n'est plus] past; [précédent]: **la semaine ~e** last week; **au cours de la semaine ~e** in the last week; **il est trois heures ~es** it's after three, it's gone three *Br*. **-2.** [fané] faded.

◆ **passé** ◇ *nm* past; **~ composé** perfect tense; **~ simple** past historic. ◇ *prép* after.

passe-droit [pɑsdrwa] (*pl* **passe-droits**) *nm* privilege.

passementerie [pɑsmɑ̃tri] *nf* notions (*pl*) *Am*, haberdashery *Br*.

passe-montagne [pɑsmɔ̃taɲ] (*pl* **passe-montagnes**) *nm* Balaclava (helmet).

passe-partout [pɑspartu] *nm inv* **-1.** [clé] passkey. **-2.** (*en apposition*) [tenue] all-purpose; [phrase] stock (*avant n*).

passe-passe [pɑspɑs] *nm inv:* **tour de ~** [prestidigitation] conjuring trick; *fig* [tromperie] trick.

passe-plat [pɑsplɑ] (*pl* **passe-plats**) *nm* serving hatch.

passeport [pɑspɔr] *nm* passport.

passer [pɑse] [3] ◇ *vi* (*aux:* être) **-1.** [se frayer un chemin] to pass, to get past. **-2.** [défiler] to go by OU past. **-3.** [aller] to go; **~ à** OU **au travers** OU **par** to come OU pass through; **~ chez qqn** to call on sb, to drop in on sb; **~ de qqch à qqch** [changer d'état] to go from sthg to sthg; [changer d'activité] to change from sthg to sthg; **~ devant** [bâtiment] to pass; [juge] to come before; **en passant** in passing; **ne faire que ~** to stay only a short while. **-4.** [venir - facteur] to come, to call. **-5.** SCOL. to pass, to be admitted; **~ dans la classe supérieure** to move up, to be moved up (a class). **-6.** [être accepté] to be accepted; **qu'il soit toujours en retard, passe encore, mais ...** it's one thing OU it's all very well to be late all the time but .... **-7.** [fermer les yeux]: **~ sur qqch** to pass over sthg. **-8.** [temps] to pass, to go by. **-9.** [disparaître - souvenir, couleur] to fade; [- douleur] to pass, to go away.

-10. CIN, TÉLÉ & THÉÂTRE to be on; ~ à la **radio/télévision** to be on the radio/television. **-11.** CARTES to pass. **-12.** [devenir]: ~ **président/directeur** to become president/director, to be appointed president/director. **-13.** loc: ~ **inaperçu** to pass OU go unnoticed; **passons ...** let's move on ...; ~ **pour** to be regarded as; **se faire ~ pour qqn** to pass o.s. off as sb; **il y est passé** fam [mort] he kicked the bucket; **tout son argent y passe** fam all his money goes on that.

◇ vt (aux: avoir) **-1.** [franchir - frontière, rivière] to cross; [- douane] to go through. **-2.** [soirée, vacances] to spend. **-3.** [sauter - ligne, tour] to miss. **-4.** [défauts]: ~ **qqch à qqn** to overlook sthg in sb. **-5.** [faire aller - bras] to pass, to put. **-6.** [peinture] to lay on, to spread. **-7.** [filtrer - huile] to strain; [- café] to filter. **-8.** [film, disque] to put on. **-9.** [vêtement] to slip on. **-10.** [vitesses] to change; ~ **la** OU **en troisième** to change into third (gear). **-11.** [donner]: ~ **qqch à qqn** to pass sb sthg; MÉD to give sb sthg. **-12.** [accord]: ~ **un contrat avec qqn** to have an agreement with sb. **-13.** SCOL & UNIV [examen] to sit, to take. **-14.** [au téléphone]: **je vous passe Mme Ledoux** [transmettre] I'll put you through to Mme Ledoux; [donner l'écouteur à] I'll hand you Mme Ledoux.

◆ **se passer** vp **-1.** [événement] to happen, to take place; **comment ça s'est passé?** how did it go?; **ça ne se passera pas comme ça!** I'm not putting up with that! **-2.** [s'enduire - crème] to put on. **-3.** [s'abstenir]: **se ~ de qqch/de faire qqch** to do without sthg/doing sthg.

passereau [pasro] nm sparrow.

passerelle [pasrɛl] nf **-1.** [pont] footbridge. **-2.** [passage mobile] gangway.

passe-temps [pastã] nm inv pastime.

passe-thé [paste] nm inv tea strainer.

passible [pasibl] adj: ~ **de** JUR liable to.

passif, -ive [pasif, iv] adj passive.
◆ **passif** nm **-1.** GRAM passive. **-2.** FIN liabilities (pl).

passion [pasjɔ̃] nf passion; **avoir la ~ de qqch** to have a passion for sthg.
◆ **Passion** nf MUS & RELIG Passion.

passionnant, -e [pasjɔnɑ̃, ɑ̃t] adj exciting, fascinating.

passionné, -e [pasjɔne] ◇ adj **-1.** [personne] passionate. **-2.** [récit, débat] impassioned. ◇ nm, f passionate person; ~ **de ski/d'échecs** etc skiing/chess etc fanatic.

passionnel, -elle [pasjɔnɛl] adj [crime] of passion.

passionnément [pasjɔnemɑ̃] adv passionately.

passionner [pasjɔne] [3] vt [personne] to grip, to fascinate.
◆ **se passionner** vp: **se ~ pour** to have a passion for.

passivement [pasivmɑ̃] adv passively.

passivité [pasivite] nf passivity.

passoire [paswar] nf [à liquide] sieve; [à légumes] colander.

pastel [pastɛl] ◇ nm pastel. ◇ adj inv [couleur] pastel (avant n).

pastèque [pastɛk] nf watermelon.

pasteur [pastœr] nm **-1.** littéraire [berger] shepherd. **-2.** RELIG pastor, minister.

pasteurisation [pastœrizasjɔ̃] nf pasteurization.

pasteuriser [pastœrize] [3] vt to pasteurize.

pastiche [pastiʃ] nm pastiche.

pastille [pastij] nf [bonbon] pastille, lozenge.

pastis [pastis] nm aniseed-flavoured aperitif.

pastoral, -e, -aux [pastɔral, o] adj littéraire pastoral.
◆ **pastorale** nf ART & LITTÉRATURE pastoral; MUS pastorale.

patagon, -one [patagɔ̃, ɔn] adj Patagonian.
◆ **Patagon, -one** nm, f Patagonian.

Patagonie [patagɔni] nf: la ~ Patagonia.

patapouf [patapuf] nm fam fatty.

patate [patat] nf **-1.** fam [pomme de terre] spud. **-2.** fam [imbécile] fathead.
◆ **patate douce** nf sweet potato.

patati [patati] interj: **et ~ et patata** fam and so on and so forth.

patatras [patatra] interj crash!

pataud, -e [pato, od] ◇ adj clumsy. ◇ nm, f clumsy person.

pataugeoire [patoʒwar] nf paddling pool.

patauger [patoʒe] [17] vi **-1.** [barboter] to splash about. **-2.** fam fig [s'embrouiller] to flounder.

patchouli [patʃuli] nm patchouli.

patchwork [patʃwœrk] nm patchwork.

pâte [pat] nf **-1.** [à tarte] pastry; [à pain] dough; ~ **brisée** shortcrust pastry; ~ **feuilletée** puff pastry; ~ **à frire** batter; ~ **à pain** bread dough; ~ **à tarte** pastry. **-2.** [mélange] paste; ~ **d'amandes** almond paste; ~ **de fruits** jelly made from fruit paste; **une ~ de fruits** a fruit jelly (sweet); ~ **à modeler** modelling clay; ~ **à papier** paper pulp. **-3.** loc: **être bonne ~** to be easy-going.
◆ **pâtes** nfpl pasta (sg).

pâté [pate] *nm* **-1.** CULIN pâté; ~ **de campagne** farmhouse pâté; ~ **en croûte** *pâté baked in a pastry case*; ~ **de foie** liver pâté; ~ **impérial** spring roll. **-2.** [tache] ink blot. **-3.** [bloc]: ~ **de maisons** block (of houses).

pâtée [pate] *nf* mash, feed.

patelin [patlɛ̃] *nm fam* village, place.

patène [patɛn] *nf* paten.

patente [patɑ̃t] *nf* licence fee (*for traders and professionals*).

patenté, -e [patɑ̃te] *adj* **-1.** [commerçant] licensed. **-2.** *fam* [voleur, menteur] habitual.

patère [patɛr] *nf* [portemanteau] coat hook.

paternalisme [patɛrnalism] *nm* paternalism.

paternaliste [patɛrnalist] ◇ *nmf* paternalist. ◇ *adj* paternalistic.

paternel, -elle [patɛrnɛl] *adj* [devoir, autorité] paternal; [amour, ton] fatherly.

◆ **paternel** *nm fam* old man.

paternité [patɛrnite] *nf* paternity, fatherhood; *fig* authorship, paternity.

pâteux, -euse [patø, øz] *adj* **-1.** [aliment] doughy; [encre] thick. **-2.** [style] leaden.

pathétique [patetik] ◇ *nm littéraire* pathos. ◇ *adj* moving, pathetic.

pathologie [patɔlɔʒi] *nf* pathology.

pathologique [patɔlɔʒik] *adj* pathological.

pathos [patos] *nm littéraire* & *péj* pathos.

patibulaire [patibylɛr] *adj péj* sinister.

patiemment [pasjamɑ̃] *adv* patiently.

patience [pasjɑ̃s] *nf* **-1.** [gén] patience; **s'armer de** ~ to be patient, to have patience; **perdre** ~ to lose patience. **-2.** [jeu de cartes] solitaire *Am*, patience *Br*.

patient, -e [pasjɑ̃, ɑ̃t] ◇ *adj* patient. ◇ *nm, f* **-1.** [qui a de la patience] patient person. **-2.** MÉD patient.

patienter [pasjɑ̃te] [3] *vi* to wait; «**veuillez patienter**» "please wait".

patin [patɛ̃] *nm* **-1.** SPORT skate; ~ **à glace/à roulettes** ice/roller skate; **faire du** ~ **à glace/à roulettes** to go ice-/roller-skating. **-2.** [de feutre] *cloth pad used under shoes to protect wooden floor*.

patinage [patinaʒ] *nm* SPORT skating; ~ **artistique/de vitesse** figure/speed skating.

patine [patin] *nf* patina.

patiner [patine] [3] ◇ *vi* **-1.** SPORT to skate. **-2.** [véhicule] to skid. ◇ *vt* [objet] to give a patina to; [avec vernis] to varnish.

◆ **se patiner** *vp* to take on a patina.

patineur, -euse [patinœr, øz] *nm, f* skater.

patinoire [patinwar] *nf* ice OU skating rink.

patio [patjo, pasjo] *nm* patio.

pâtir [patir] [32] *vi*: ~ **de** to suffer the consequences of.

pâtisserie [patisri] *nf* **-1.** [gâteau] pastry. **-2.** [art, métier] pastry-making. **-3.** [commerce] ≃ cake shop.

pâtissier, -ière [patisje, jɛr] ◇ *adj*: **crème pâtissière** confectioner's custard. ◇ *nm, f* pastrycook.

patois, -e [patwa, az] *adj* patois (*avant n*).

◆ **patois** *nm* patois.

patraque [patrak] *adj fam* [personne] out of sorts.

patriarcal, -e, -aux [patrijarkal, o] *adj* patriarchal.

patriarcat [patrijarka] *nm* **-1.** RELIG patriarchate. **-2.** SOCIOL patriarchy.

patriarche [patrijarʃ] *nm* patriarch.

patrie [patri] *nf* country, homeland; ~ **d'adoption** country of adoption.

patrimoine [patrimwan] *nm* [familial] inheritance; [collectif] heritage.

patriote [patrijɔt] ◇ *nmf* patriot. ◇ *adj* patriotic.

patriotique [patrijɔtik] *adj* patriotic.

patriotisme [patrijɔtism] *nm* patriotism.

patron, -onne [patrɔ̃, ɔn] *nm, f* **-1.** [d'entreprise] head. **-2.** [chef] boss. **-3.** RELIG patron saint.

◆ **patron** *nm* [modèle] pattern.

patronage [patrɔnaʒ] *nm* **-1.** [protection] patronage; [de saint] protection. **-2.** [organisation] youth club.

patronal, -e, -aux [patrɔnal, o] *adj* [organisation, intérêts] employers' (*avant n*).

patronat [patrɔna] *nm* employers.

patronnesse [patrɔnɛs] *nf*: (**dame**) ~ *iron* patroness.

patronyme [patrɔnim] *nm* patronymic.

patronymique [patrɔnimik] *adj* patronymic.

patrouille [patruj] *nf* patrol.

patrouiller [patruje] [3] *vi* to patrol.

patte [pat] *nf* **-1.** [d'animal] paw; [d'oiseau] foot; **montrer** ~ **blanche** *fig* to give the password; **à quatre** ~**s** four-legged; *fig* on all fours, on one's hands and knees; **retomber sur ses** ~**s** *fig* to land on one's feet. **-2.** *fam* [jambe] leg; [pied] foot; [main] hand, paw; **graisser la** ~ **à qqn** to grease sb's palm. **-3.** [favori] sideburn. **-4.** [de poche, de portefeuille] fastening.

patte-d'oie [patdwa] (*pl* **pattes-d'oie**) *nf* crow's foot.

pattemouille [patmuj] *nf* damping cloth.

pâturage [patyraʒ] *nm* [lieu] pasture land.

pâture [patyr] *nf* [nourriture] food, fodder; *fig* intellectual nourishment; **donner qqn/ qqch en ~ à, offrir qqn/qqch en ~ à** to feed sb/sthg to.

paume [pom] *nf* **-1.** [de main] palm. **-2.** SPORT real tennis.

paumé, -e [pome] *fam* ◇ *adj* lost. ◇ *nm, f* down and out.

paumer [pome] [3] *fam vt* to lose.
◆ **se paumer** *vp* to get lost.

paupérisation [poperizasjɔ̃] *nf* pauperization.

paupière [popjɛr] *nf* eyelid.

paupiette [popjɛt] *nf thin slice of meat or fish stuffed and rolled;* ~**s de veau** ≃ veal olives.

pause [poz] *nf* **-1.** [arrêt] break; ~-**café** coffee-break. **-2.** MUS pause.

pauvre [povr] ◇ *nmf* poor person; **le/la ~!** the poor thing! ◇ *adj* poor; ~ **en** low in; ~ **d'esprit** feeble-minded.

pauvrement [povrəmɑ̃] *adv* poorly.

pauvreté [povrəte] *nf* poverty.

pavage [pavaʒ] *nm* paving.

pavaner [pavane] [3]
◆ **se pavaner** *vp* to strut.

pavé, -e [pave] *adj* cobbled.
◆ **pavé** *nm* **-1.** [chaussée]: **être sur le ~** *fig* to be out on the streets; **battre le ~** *fig* to walk the streets. **-2.** [de pierre] cobblestone, paving stone. **-3.** *fam* [livre] tome. **-4.** [de viande] slab. **-5.** INFORM: ~ **numérique** numeric keypad.

paver [pave] [3] *vt* to pave.

pavillon [pavijɔ̃] *nm* **-1.** [bâtiment] detached house; ~ **de banlieue** ≃ bungalow; ~ **de chasse** hunting lodge. **-2.** [de trompette] bell. **-3.** [d'oreille] pinna, auricle. **-4.** [drapeau] flag.

pavoiser [pavwaze] [3] ◇ *vt* to decorate with flags. ◇ *vi fam* to crow.

pavot [pavo] *nm* poppy.

payable [pejabl] *adj* payable.

payant, -e [pejɑ̃, ɑ̃t] *adj* **-1.** [hôte] paying (*avant n*). **-2.** [spectacle] with an admission charge. **-3.** *fam* [affaire] profitable.

paye = **paie**.

payement = **paiement**.

payer [peje] [11] ◇ *vt* **-1.** [gén] to pay; [achat] to pay for; ~ **qqch à qqn** to buy sthg for sb, to buy sb sthg, to treat sb to sthg; ~ **qqn de qqch** *fig* [efforts, peine] to reward sb for sthg. **-2.** [expier - crime, faute] to pay for; **il me le paiera!** he'll pay for this! ◇ *vi*: ~ **(pour)** to pay (for); ~ **de sa poche** to pay out of one's own pocket; ~ **de sa personne** [s'exposer au danger] to put o.s. on

the line; [se donner du mal] to put in a lot of effort; ~ **d'audace** to risk one's all.
◆ **se payer** *vp* [s'offrir]: **se ~ qqch** to buy o.s. sthg, to treat o.s. to sthg.

payeur, -euse [pɛjœr, øz] *adj* payments (*avant n*).
◆ **payeur** *nm* payer; **mauvais ~** bad debtor.

pays [pei] *nm* **-1.** [gén] country; ~ **d'adoption** country of adoption; ~ **de cocagne** *fig* land of plenty; **les ~ de l'Est** the Eastern bloc (countries); ~ **natal** native land, native country; **comme en ~ conquis** like the lord of the manor. **-2.** [région, province] region; **être du ~** to be a local. **-3.** [village] village.
◆ **pays de Galles** *nm*: **le ~ de Galles** Wales; **au ~ de Galles** in Wales.

paysage [peizaʒ] *nm* **-1.** [site, vue] landscape, scenery. **-2.** [tableau] landscape. **-3.** *fig* [contexte] scene.

paysager, -ère [peizaʒe, ɛr] *adj* landscaped.

paysagiste [peizaʒist] ◇ *nmf* **-1.** [peintre] landscape artist. **-2.** [concepteur de parcs] landscape gardener. ◇ *adj* landscape (*avant n*).

paysan, -anne [peizɑ̃, an] ◇ *adj* [vie, coutume] country (*avant n*), rural; [organisation, revendication] farmers' (*avant n*); *péj* peasant (*avant n*). ◇ *nm, f* **-1.** [agriculteur] (small) farmer. **-2.** *péj* [rustre] peasant.

paysannat [peizana] *nm* peasantry.

paysannerie [peizanri] *nf* peasantry, peasant class.

Pays-Bas [peiba] *nmpl*: **les ~** the Netherlands; **aux ~** in the Netherlands.

PC *nm* **-1.** (*abr de* **Parti communiste**) Communist Party. **-2.** (*abr de* **personal computer**) PC. **-3.** (*abr de* **prêt conventionné**) *special loan for house purchase*. **-4.** (*abr de* **permis de construire**) planning permission. **-5.** (*abr de* **poste de commandement**) HQ. **-6.** (*abr de* **Petite Ceinture**) *bus following the inner ring road in Paris*.

pcc (*abr de* **pour copie conforme**) certified accurate.

PCF (*abr de* **Parti communiste français**) *nm* French Communist Party.

PCV (*abr de* **à percevoir**) *nm* reverse charge call.

P-DG (*abr de* **président-directeur général**) *nm* Chairman and President *Am*, Chairman and Managing Director *Br*.

p.-ê. *abr de* **peut-être**.

PEA (*abr de* **plan d'épargne en actions**) *nm savings scheme*.

péage [peaʒ] *nm* toll.

peau [po] *nf* **-1.** [gén] skin; ~ **de banane** banana skin; ~ **d'orange** orange peel; MÉD ≃ cellulite; **n'avoir que la ~ sur les os** to be just skin and bones; **être bien/mal dans sa ~** [en général] to feel great/terrible; **risquer sa ~** to risk one's neck; **sauver sa ~** to save one's skin. **-2.** [cuir] hide, leather (*U*); ~ **de vache** *fam fig* [homme] bastard; [femme] bitch.

peaufiner [pofine] [3] *vt litt* & *fig* to polish up.

peccadille [pekadij] *nf* peccadillo.

péché [peʃe] *nm* sin; **les sept ~s capitaux** the seven deadly sins; **le ~ originel** original sin; **un ~ mignon** a weakness.

pêche [pɛʃ] *nf* **-1.** [fruit] peach; ~ **Melba** peach Melba. **-2.** [activité] fishing; [poissons] catch; **aller à la ~** to go fishing; ~ **à la dandinette** jigging; ~ **sous la glace** ice fishing; ~ **à la ligne** angling; ~ **sous-marine** underwater fishing. **-3.** *loc:* **avoir la ~** *fam* to feel great.

pécher [peʃe] [18] *vi* to sin; ~ **par omission** *fig* to commit the sin of omission; **cet exposé pèche par manque d'exemples** *fig* this report falls down because it lacks examples.

pêcher[1] [peʃe] [4] *vt* **-1.** [poisson] to catch. **-2.** *fam* [trouver] to dig up.

pêcher[2] [peʃe] *nm* peach tree.

pêcherie [peʃri] *nf* fishery, fishing ground.

pêcheur, -eresse [peʃœr, peʃrɛs] ◇ *adj* sinful. ◇ *nm, f* sinner.

pêcheur, -euse [pɛʃœr, øz] *nm, f* fisherman (*f* fisherwoman).

pecnot = **péquenot**.

pectine [pɛktin] *nf* pectin.

pectoral, -e, -aux [pɛktɔral, o] *adj* **-1.** [muscle] pectoral. **-2.** [sirop] cough (*avant n*).
◆ **pectoraux** *nmpl* pectorals.

pécule [pekyl] *nm* [économies] savings (*pl*).

pécuniaire [pekynjɛr] *adj* financial.

pédagogie [pedagɔʒi] *nf* **-1.** [science] education, pedagogy. **-2.** [qualité] teaching ability.

pédagogique [pedagɔʒik] *adj* educational; [méthode] teaching (*avant n*).

pédagogue [pedagɔg] ◇ *nmf* teacher. ◇ *adj:* **être ~** to be a good teacher.

pédale [pedal] *nf* **-1.** [gén] pedal; **perdre les ~s** *fam fig* to lose one's head. **-2.** *fam inj* [homosexuel] queer.

pédaler [pedale] [3] *vi* [à bicyclette] to pedal; ~ **dans la choucroute** *fam fig* to be all at sea.

pédalier [pedalje] *nm* **-1.** [de vélo] (bicycle) drive. **-2.** [d'orgue] pedals (*pl*).

pédalo [pedalo] *nm* pedal boat.

pédant, -e [pedã, ãt] ◇ *adj* pedantic. ◇ *nm, f* pedant.

pédé [pede] *nm tfam péj* queer.

pédéraste [pederast] *nm* homosexual, pederast.

pédérastie [pederasti] *nf* homosexuality.

pédestre [pedɛstr] *adj:* **randonnée ~** hike, ramble; **chemin ~** footpath.

pédiatre [pedjatr] *nmf* pediatrician.

pédiatrie [pedjatri] *nf* pediatrics (*U*).

pédicule [pedikyl] *nm* BOT peduncle.

pédicure [pedikyr] *nmf* chiropodist.

pedigree [pedigre] *nm* pedigree.

pédophile [pedɔfil] ◇ *nm* pedophile. ◇ *adj* pedophiliac.

peeling [piliŋ] *nm* face scrub.

pègre [pɛgr] *nf* underworld.

peignais, peignions *etc* → **peindre**.

peigne [pɛɲ] *nm* **-1.** [démêloir, barrette] comb; **se donner un coup de ~** to run a comb through one's hair; **passer qqch au ~ fin** *fig* to go through sthg with a fine-tooth comb; **sale comme un ~** *fig* filthy dirty. **-2.** [de tissage] card.

peigner [peɲe] [4] *vt* **-1.** [cheveux] to comb. **-2.** [fibres] to card.
◆ **se peigner** *vp* to comb one's hair.

peignoir [peɲwar] *nm* robe *Am*, bathrobe *Am*, dressing gown *Br*; ~ **de bain** bathrobe.

peinard, -e, pénard, -e [penar, ard] *adj fam* [emploi] cushy; [personne] comfortable.

peindre [pɛ̃dr] [81] *vt* to paint; *fig* [décrire] to depict.
◆ **se peindre** *vp* [émotion] *fig:* **se ~ sur** to be written on.

peine [pɛn] *nf* **-1.** [châtiment] punishment, penalty; JUR sentence; **sous ~ de qqch** on pain of sthg; ~ **capitale** OU **de mort** capital punishment, death sentence; ~ **incompressible** sentence without remission. **-2.** [chagrin] sorrow, sadness (*U*); **avoir de la ~** to be sad; **faire de la ~ à qqn** to upset sb, to distress sb. **-3.** [effort] trouble; **se donner de la ~** to go to a lot of trouble; **c'est ~ perdue** it's a waste of effort; **prendre la ~ de faire qqch** to go to the trouble of doing sthg; **ça ne vaut pas** OU **ce n'est pas la ~** it's not worth it. **-4.** [difficulté] difficulty; **avoir de la ~ à faire qqch** to have difficulty OU trouble doing sthg; **à grand-~** with great difficulty; **sans ~** without difficulty, easily.

◆ **à peine** *loc adv* scarcely, hardly; **à ~ ...
que** hardly ... than; **c'est à ~ si on se parle**
we hardly speak (to each other).

peiner [pene] [4] ◇ *vt* [affliger] to distress,
to sadden. ◇ *vi* -**1.** [travailler] to work hard.
-**2.** [se fatiguer] to struggle, to labor *Am*, to
labour *Br*.

peint, -e [pɛ̃, pɛ̃t] *pp* → **peindre.**

peintre [pɛ̃tr] *nm* painter; **~ en bâtiment**
painter and decorator.

peinture [pɛ̃tyr] *nf* -**1.** [gén] painting. -**2.**
[produit] paint; **«~ fraîche»** "wet paint".

peinturlurer [pɛ̃tyrlyre] [3] *vt péj* to daub.

◆ **se peinturlurer** *vp péj* to plaster one's
face with make-up.

péjoratif, -ive [peʒɔratif, iv] *adj* pejorative.

Pékin [pekɛ̃] *n* Peking, Beijing.

pékinois, -e [pekinwa, az] *adj* of/from Peking.

◆ **pékinois** *nm* -**1.** [langue] Mandarin. -**2.**
[chien] pekinese.

◆ **Pékinois, -e** *nm, f* native OU inhabitant
of Peking; **les Pékinois** the people of Peking.

PEL, Pel [pɛl] *(abr de* **plan d'épargne logement***) nm savings scheme offering low-interest
mortgages.*

pelage [pəlaʒ] *nm* coat, fur.

pelé, -e [pəle] *adj* -**1.** [crâne] bald. -**2.** *fig*
[colline, paysage] bare.

pêle-mêle [pɛlmɛl] *adv* pell-mell.

peler [pəle] [25] *vt & vi* to peel.

pèlerin [pɛlrɛ̃] *nm* pilgrim.

pèlerinage [pɛlrinaʒ] *nm* -**1.** [voyage] pilgrimage; **en ~** on a pilgrimage. -**2.** [lieu]
place of pilgrimage.

pèlerine [pɛlrin] *nf* cape.

pélican [pelikɑ̃] *nm* pelican.

pelisse [pəlis] *nf* pelisse.

pelle [pɛl] *nf* -**1.** [instrument] shovel; **~ à
tarte** pie server; **à la ~** *fam fig* by the bucketful. -**2.** [machine] digger.

pelletée [pɛlte] *nf* shovelful.

pelleter [pɛlte] [27] *vt* to shovel.

pelleteuse [pɛltøz] *nf* mechanical digger.

pellicule [pelikyl] *nf* film.

◆ **pellicules** *nfpl* dandruff (*U*).

pelote [pəlɔt] *nf* -**1.** [de laine, ficelle] ball. -**2.**
COUTURE pin cushion.

◆ **pelote basque** *nf* pelota.

peloter [pləte] [3] *vt fam* to paw.

peloton [plɔtɔ̃] *nm* -**1.** [de ficelle] small ball.
-**2.** [de soldats] squad; **~ d'exécution** firing
squad. -**3.** [de concurrents] pack; **le ~ de tête**
SPORT the leading group; *fig* the top few.

pelotonner [pəlɔtɔne] [3]

◆ **se pelotonner** *vp* to curl up; **se ~
contre** to snuggle up to.

pelouse [pəluz] *nf* -**1.** [de jardin] lawn. -**2.**
[de champ de courses] public enclosure. -**3.**
FOOTBALL & RUGBY field.

peluche [pəlyʃ] *nf* -**1.** [jouet] soft toy. -**2.**
[tissu] plush. -**3.** [d'étoffe] piece of fluff.

pelucheux, -euse [pəlyʃø, øz] *adj* fluffy.

pelure [pəlyr] *nf* -**1.** [fruit] peel. -**2.** *fam péj*
[habit] coat.

pénal, -e, -aux [penal, o] *adj* penal.

pénalisation [penalizasjɔ̃] *nf* penalty.

pénaliser [penalize] [3] *vt* to penalize.

pénalité [penalite] *nf* penalty.

penalty [penalti] (*pl* **penaltys** OU **penalties**)
nm penalty.

pénard = **peinard.**

pénates [penat] *nmpl*: **regagner ses ~** *fam*
to go home.

penaud, -e [pəno, od] *adj* sheepish.

penchant [pɑ̃ʃɑ̃] *nm* -**1.** [inclination] tendency. -**2.** [sympathie]: **~ pour** liking for.

pencher [pɑ̃ʃe] [3] ◇ *vi* to lean; **~ vers** *fig*
to incline toward *Am* OU towards *Br*; **se ~
pour** to incline in favor *Am* OU favour *Br*
of. ◇ *vt* to bend.

◆ **se pencher** *vp* [s'incliner] to lean over;
[se baisser] to bend down; **se ~ sur qqn/
qqch** to lean over sb/sthg; **se ~ sur qqch**
fig [problème, cas] to look into sthg.

pendable [pɑ̃dabl] *adj*: **tour ~** dirty trick;
ce n'est pas un cas ~ it's not a hanging
matter.

pendaison [pɑ̃dɛzɔ̃] *nf* hanging; **~ de crémaillère** house-warming.

pendant¹, -e [pɑ̃dɑ̃, ɑ̃t] *adj* -**1.** [bras] hanging, dangling. -**2.** [question] pending.

◆ **pendant** *nm* -**1.** [bijou]: **~ d'oreilles**
(drop) earring. -**2.** [de paire] counterpart; **se
faire ~** *fig* to make a pair.

pendant² [pɑ̃dɑ̃] *prép* during.

◆ **pendant que** *loc conj* while, whilst; **~
que j'y suis, ...** while I'm at it, ...

pendeloque [pɑ̃dlɔk] *nf* -**1.** [bijou] pendant.
-**2.** [de lustre] crystal.

pendentif [pɑ̃dɑ̃tif] *nm* pendant.

penderie [pɑ̃dri] *nf* wardrobe.

pendouiller [pɑ̃duje] [3] *vi fam* to dangle.

pendre [pɑ̃dr] [73] ◇ *vi* -**1.** [être fixé en
haut]: **~ (à)** to hang (from). -**2.** [descendre
trop bas] to hang down. ◇ *vt* -**1.** [rideaux, ta-
bleau] to hang (up), to put up. -**2.** [personne]
to hang.

◆ **se pendre** *vp* -**1.** [s'accrocher]: **se ~ à** to
hang from. -**2.** [se suicider] to hang o.s.

pendu, -e [pɑ̃dy] ◇ *pp* → **pendre**. ◇ *adj* **-1.** [objet] hung up, hanging up; *fig*: **il est toujours ~ au téléphone** he's never off the phone. **-2.** [personne] hanged. ◇ *nm, f* hanged person.

pendule [pɑ̃dyl] ◇ *nm* pendulum. ◇ *nf* clock.

pendulette [pɑ̃dylɛt] *nf* small clock.

pêne [pɛn] *nm* bolt.

pénétrant, -e [penetrɑ̃, ɑ̃t] *adj* penetrating; [odeur] pervasive.

pénétration [penetrasjɔ̃] *nf* **-1.** [de projectile, d'idée] penetration. **-2.** [sagacité] shrewdness.

pénétré, -e [penetre] *adj* earnest; **elle est ~e de son importance** she's full of her own importance.

pénétrer [penetre] [18] ◇ *vi* to enter. ◇ *vt* **-1.** [mur, vêtement] to penetrate. **-2.** *fig* [mystère, secret] to fathom out.
◆ **se pénétrer** *vp* [s'imprégner]: **se ~ d'une idée** to let an idea sink in.

pénible [penibl] *adj* **-1.** [travail] laborious. **-2.** [nouvelle, maladie] painful. **-3.** *fam* [personne] tiresome.

péniblement [peniblǝmɑ̃] *adv* **-1.** [avec difficulté] with difficulty, laboriously. **-2.** [cruellement] painfully. **-3.** [à peine] just about.

péniche [peniʃ] *nf* barge.

pénicilline [penisilin] *nf* penicillin.

péninsule [penɛ̃syl] *nf* peninsula; **la ~ d'Arabie** the Arabian Peninsula; **la ~ Ibérique** the Iberian peninsula.

pénis [penis] *nm* penis.

pénitence [penitɑ̃s] *nf* **-1.** [repentir] penitence. **-2.** [peine, punition] penance.

pénitencier [penitɑ̃sje] *nm* prison, penitentiary *Am*.

pénitent, -e [penitɑ̃, ɑ̃t] ◇ *adj* penitent. ◇ *nm, f* penitent.

pénitentiaire [penitɑ̃sjɛr] *adj* prison (*avant n*).

penne [pɛn] *nf* ZOOL quill.

pénombre [penɔ̃br] *nf* half-light.

pensable [pɑ̃sabl] *adj*: **ce n'est pas ~** it's unthinkable.

pensant, -e [pɑ̃sɑ̃, ɑ̃t] *adj* thinking.

pense-bête [pɑ̃sbɛt] (*pl* **pense-bêtes**) *nm* reminder.

pensée [pɑ̃se] *nf* **-1.** [idée, faculté] thought. **-2.** [esprit] mind, thoughts (*pl*); **en/par la ~** in one's mind OU thoughts. **-3.** [opinion] thoughts (*pl*), feelings (*pl*). **-4.** [doctrine] thought, thinking. **-5.** BOT pansy.

penser [pɑ̃se] [3] ◇ *vi* to think; **~ à qqn/qqch** [avoir à l'esprit] to think of sb/sthg, to think about sb/sthg; [se rappeler] to remember sb/sthg; **~ à faire qqch** [avoir à l'esprit] to think of doing sthg; [se rappeler] to remember to do sthg; **qu'est-ce que tu en penses?** what do you think (of it)?; **faire ~ à qqn/qqch** to make one think of sb/sthg; **faire ~ à qqn à faire qqch** to remind sb to do sthg; **sans ~ à mal** without meaning any harm; **n'y pensons plus!** let's forget it!; **laisser** OU **donner à ~ (que)** to make one think (that); **même s'il ne dit rien, il n'en pense pas moins** even if he doesn't say anything, he's thinking it nonetheless.
◇ *vt* to think; **~ que ...** to think (that) ...; **je pense que oui** I think so; **je pense que non** I don't think so; **~ faire qqch** to be planning to do sthg; **pensez-vous!** don't be silly!

penseur [pɑ̃sœr] *nm* thinker.

pensif, -ive [pɑ̃sif, iv] *adj* pensive, thoughtful.

pension [pɑ̃sjɔ̃] *nf* **-1.** [allocation] pension; **~ alimentaire** [dans un divorce] alimony. **-2.** [hébergement] board and lodgings; **~ complète** full board; **demi-~** half board. **-3.** [hôtel] guesthouse; **~ de famille** guesthouse, boarding house. **-4.** [prix de l'hébergement] ≃ rent, keep. **-5.** [internat] boarding school.

pensionnaire [pɑ̃sjɔnɛr] *nmf* **-1.** [élève] boarder. **-2.** [hôte payant] lodger.

pensionnat [pɑ̃sjɔna] *nm* **-1.** [internat] boarding school. **-2.** [élèves] boarders (*pl*).

pensivement [pɑ̃sivmɑ̃] *adv* pensively, thoughtfully.

pensum [pɛ̃sɔm] *nm* **-1.** [travail ennuyeux] chore. **-2.** *vieilli* [punition] imposition.

pentagone [pɛ̃tagɔn] *nm* pentagon.
◆ **Pentagone** *nm*: **le Pentagone** the Pentagon.

pentathlon [pɛ̃tatlɔ̃] *nm* pentathlon.

pente [pɑ̃t] *nf* slope; **en ~** sloping, inclined; **être sur une mauvaise ~** *fig* to be on a downward path; **remonter la ~** *fig* to claw one's way back again.

pentecôte [pɑ̃tkot] *nf* [juive] Pentecost; [chrétienne] Whitsun.

pénurie [penyri] *nf* shortage.

PEP, Pep [pɛp] (*abr de* **plan d'épargne populaire**) *nm* personal pension plan.

pépé [pepe] *nm fam* **-1.** [grand-père] grandad, grandpa. **-2.** [homme âgé] old man.

pépère [pepɛr] *fam* ◇ *nm* [grand-père] grandad, grandpa. ◇ *adj* cushy.

pépier [pepje] [9] *vi* to chirp.

pépin [pepɛ̃] *nm* **-1.** [graine] pip. **-2.** *fam* [ennui] hitch. **-3.** *fam* [parapluie] umbrella, brolly *Br*.

pépinière [pepinjɛr] *nf* tree nursery; *fig* [école, établissement] nursery.

pépite [pepit] *nf* nugget.

péquenot [pekno] *nm*, **pecnot** [pekno] *nm*, **péquenaud, -e** [pekno, od] *nm, f fam péj* country bumpkin.

percale [pɛrkal] *nf* percale.

perçant, -e [pɛrsɑ̃, ɑ̃t] *adj* **-1.** [regard, son] piercing. **-2.** [froid] bitter, biting.

percée [pɛrse] *nf* **-1.** [trouée] opening. **-2.** MIL, SPORT & *fig* breakthrough.

percement [pɛrsəmɑ̃] *nm* opening (up); [d'oreilles] piercing.

perce-neige [pɛrsənɛʒ] *nm inv ou nf inv* snowdrop.

perce-oreille [pɛrsɔrɛj] (*pl* perce-oreilles) *nm* earwig.

percepteur [pɛrsɛptœr] *nm* tax collector.

perceptible [pɛrsɛptibl] *adj* perceptible.

perception [pɛrsɛpsjɔ̃] *nf* **-1.** [d'impôts] collection. **-2.** [bureau] tax office. **-3.** [sensation] perception.

percer [pɛrse] [16] ◇ *vt* **-1.** [mur, roche] to make a hole in; [coffre-fort] to crack. **-2.** [trou] to make; [avec perceuse] to drill. **-3.** [silence, oreille] to pierce. **-4.** [foule] to make one's way through. **-5.** *fig* [mystère] to penetrate. ◇ *vi* **-1.** [soleil] to break through. **-2.** [abcès] to burst; **avoir une dent qui perce** to be cutting a tooth. **-3.** [réussir] to make a name for o.s., to break through.

perceuse [pɛrsøz] *nf* drill.

percevoir [pɛrsəvwar] [52] *vt* **-1.** [intention, nuance] to perceive. **-2.** [retraite, indemnité] to receive. **-3.** [impôts] to collect.

perchaude [pɛrʃod] *nf Can* yellow OU lake perch.

perche [pɛrʃ] *nf* **-1.** [poisson] perch. **-2.** [de bois, métal] pole; **tendre la ~ à qqn** *fig* to throw sb a line.

percher [pɛrʃe] [3] ◇ *vi* **-1.** [oiseau] to perch. **-2.** *fam* [personne] to live. ◇ *vt* to perch.
◆ **se percher** *vp* to perch.

perchiste [pɛrʃist] *nmf* **-1.** SPORT pole vaulter. **-2.** CIN & TÉLÉ boom operator.

perchoir [pɛrʃwar] *nm* perch.

perclus, -e [pɛrkly, yz] *adj*: **~ de** [rhumatismes] crippled with.

perçois, perçoit *etc* → percevoir.

percolateur [pɛrkɔlatœr] *nm* percolator.

perçu, -e [pɛrsy] *pp* → percevoir.

percussion [pɛrkysjɔ̃] *nf* percussion.

percussionniste [pɛrkysjɔnist] *nmf* percussionist.

percutant, -e [pɛrkytɑ̃, ɑ̃t] *adj* **-1.** [obus] explosive. **-2.** *fig* [argument] forceful.

percuter [pɛrkyte] [3] ◇ *vt* to strike, to smash into. ◇ *vi* to explode.

perdant, -e [pɛrdɑ̃, ɑ̃t] ◇ *adj* losing. ◇ *nm, f* loser.

perdition [pɛrdisjɔ̃] *nf* **-1.** [ruine morale] perdition. **-2.** [détresse]: **en ~** in distress.

perdre [pɛrdr] [77] ◇ *vt* **-1.** [gén] to lose. **-2.** [temps] to waste; [occasion] to miss, to waste. **-3.** [suj: bonté, propos] to be the ruin of. **-4.** *loc*: **vous ne perdez rien pour attendre!** just wait until I get my hands on you! ◇ *vi* to lose.
◆ **se perdre** *vp* **-1.** [coutume] to die out, to become lost. **-2.** [personne] to get lost, to lose one's way; **se ~ dans les détails** *fig* to get bogged down in details.

perdreau, -x [pɛrdro] *nm* young partridge.

perdrix [pɛrdri] *nf* partridge.

perdu, -e [pɛrdy] ◇ *pp* → **perdre**.
◇ *adj* **-1.** [égaré] lost. **-2.** [endroit] out-of-the-way. **-3.** [balle] stray. **-4.** [emballage] non-returnable. **-5.** [temps, occasion] wasted. **-6.** [malade] dying. **-7.** [récolte, robe] spoilt, ruined.

perdurer [pɛrdyre] [3] *vi littéraire* to endure.

père [pɛr] *nm* **-1.** [gén] father; **mon ~** RELIG Father; **~ de famille** father; **de ~ en fils** from father to son. **-2.** [d'animal] sire. **-3.** *fam* [homme mûr]: **le ~ Martin** old Martin.
◆ **pères** *nmpl* [ancêtres] forefathers, ancestors.
◆ **père Noël** *nm*: **le ~ Noël** Father Christmas, Santa Claus.

pérégrination [peregrinasjɔ̃] *nf* (*gén pl*) wanderings (*pl*).

péremption [perɑ̃psjɔ̃] *nf* time limit; **date de ~** best-before date.

péremptoire [perɑ̃ptwar] *adj* peremptory.

pérennité [perenite] *nf* durability.

péréquation [perekwasjɔ̃] *nf* equalization.

perfectible [pɛrfɛktibl] *adj* perfectible.

perfection [pɛrfɛksjɔ̃] *nf* **-1.** [qualité] perfection; **à la ~** to perfection. **-2.** [chose parfaite] jewel, gem.

perfectionnement [pɛrfɛksjɔnmɑ̃] *nm* improvement.

perfectionner [pɛrfɛksjɔne] [3] *vt* to perfect.
◆ **se perfectionner** *vp* to improve.

perfectionnisme [pɛrfɛksjɔnism] *nm* perfectionism.

perfectionniste [pɛrfɛksjɔnist] *nmf & adj* perfectionist.

perfide [pɛrfid] *adj* perfidious.

perfidement [pɛrfidmɑ̃] *adv* perfidiously.

perfidie [pɛrfidi] *nf* perfidy.

perforateur, -trice [pɛrfɔratœr, tris] *adj* perforating.
◆ **perforateur** *nm* punch card operator.
◆ **perforatrice** *nf* [perceuse] drill; [de bureau] hole punch.

perforation [pɛrfɔrasjɔ̃] *nf* perforation.

perforer [pɛrfɔre] [3] *vt* to perforate.

performance [pɛrfɔrmɑ̃s] *nf* performance; **les ~s d'une voiture** a car's performance.

performant, -e [pɛrfɔrmɑ̃, ɑ̃t] *adj* **-1.** [personne] efficient. **-2.** [machine] high-performance (*avant n*).

perfusion [pɛrfyzjɔ̃] *nf* perfusion.

pergola [pɛrgɔla] *nf* pergola.

péricliter [periklite] [3] *vi* to collapse.

péridural, -e, -aux [peridyral, o] *adj* epidural.
◆ **péridurale** *nf* epidural.

péril [peril] *nm* peril; **au ~ de ma vie** at the risk of my life.

périlleux, -euse [perijø, øz] *adj* perilous.

périmé, -e [perime] *adj* out-of-date; *fig* [idées] outdated.

périmètre [perimɛtr] *nm* **-1.** [contour] perimeter. **-2.** [contenu] area.

périnatal, -e, -aux [perinatal, o] *adj* perinatal.

périnée [perine] *nm* perineum.

période [perjɔd] *nf* period.

périodique [perjɔdik] ◇ *nm* periodical. ◇ *adj* periodic.

périodiquement [perjɔdikmɑ̃] *adv* periodically.

péripatéticienne [peripatetisjɛn] *nf* streetwalker.

péripétie [peripesi] *nf* event.

périphérie [periferi] *nf* **-1.** [de ville] outskirts (*pl*). **-2.** [bord] periphery; [de cercle] circumference.

périphérique [periferik] ◇ *nm* **-1.** [route] beltway *Am*, ring road *Br*. **-2.** INFORM peripheral device. ◇ *adj* peripheral; **boulevard ~** beltway *Am*, ring road *Br*.

périphrase [perifraz] *nf* periphrasis.

périple [peripl] *nm* **-1.** NAVIG voyage. **-2.** [voyage] trip.

périr [perir] [32] *vi* to perish.

périscolaire [periskɔlɛr] *adj* extracurricular.

périscope [periskɔp] *nm* periscope.

périssable [perisabl] *adj* **-1.** [denrée] perishable. **-2.** *littéraire* [sentiment] transient.

péristyle [peristil] *nm* peristyle.

péritonite [peritɔnit] *nf* peritonitis.

perle [pɛrl] *nf* **-1.** [de nacre] pearl. **-2.** [de bois, verre] bead. **-3.** [de sang, d'eau] drop. **-4.** [personne] gem. **-5.** *fam* [erreur] howler.

perlé, -e [pɛrle] *adj* beaded; **grève ~e** slowdown *Am*, go-slow *Br*.

perler [pɛrle] [3] *vi* to form beads.

perlimpinpin [pɛrlɛ̃pɛ̃pɛ̃] *nm*: **poudre de ~** miracle cure.

permanence [pɛrmanɑ̃s] *nf* **-1.** [continuité] permanence; **en ~** constantly. **-2.** [service]: **être de ~** to be on duty. **-3.** SCOL: **(salle de) ~** study room.

permanent, -e [pɛrmanɑ̃, ɑ̃t] ◇ *adj* permanent; [cinéma] with continuous showings; [comité] standing (*avant n*). ◇ *nm, f* official.
◆ **permanente** *nf* perm.

perméable [pɛrmeabl] *adj*: **~ (à)** permeable (to); *fig* open (to), receptive (to).

permets → **permettre**.

permettais, permettions → **permettre**.

permettre [pɛrmɛtr] [84] *vt* to permit, to allow; **vous permettez?** may I?; **~ qqch à qqn** to allow sb sthg; **~ à qqn de faire qqch** to permit OU allow sb to do sthg.
◆ **se permettre** *vp*: **se ~ qqch** to allow o.s sthg; [avoir les moyens de] to be able to afford sthg; **se ~ de faire qqch** to take the liberty of doing sthg.

permis, -e [pɛrmi, iz] *pp* → **permettre**.
◆ **permis** *nm* license *Am*, licence *Br*, permit; **~ de conduire** driver's license *Am*, driving licence *Br*; **~ de construire** building permit *Am*, planning permission *Br*; **~ de séjour** residence permit; **~ de travail** work permit.

permissif, -ive [pɛrmisif, iv] *adj* permissive.

permission [pɛrmisjɔ̃] *nf* **-1.** [autorisation] permission. **-2.** MIL leave.

permutable [pɛrmytabl] *adj* which can be changed round.

permutation [pɛrmytasjɔ̃] *nf* [de mots, figures] transposition; MATHS permutation.

permuter [pɛrmyte] [3] ◇ *vt* to change round; [mots, figures] to transpose. ◇ *vi* to change, to switch.

pernicieux, -ieuse [pɛrnisjø, jøz] *adj* **-1.** MÉD pernicious. **-2.** [conseil, habitude] harmful.

péroné [perɔne] *nm* fibula.

péroraison [perɔrɛzɔ̃] *nf* peroration.

pérorer [perɔre] [3] *vi* *péj* to hold forth.

Pérou [peru] *nm*: **le ~** Peru; **au ~** in Peru.

perpendiculaire [pɛrpɑ̃dikylɛr] ◇ *nf* perpendicular. ◇ *adj*: ~ (à) perpendicular (to).

perpendiculairement [pɛrpɑ̃dikylɛrmɑ̃] *adv* perpendicularly; ~ à perpendicular to.

perpète, perpette [pɛrpɛt]
◆ **à perpète** *loc adv fam* [loin] miles away; [longtemps] for ever.

perpétrer [perpetre] [18] *vt* to perpetrate.

perpette = **perpète**.

perpétuel, -elle [pɛrpetɥɛl] *adj* -1. [fréquent, continu] perpetual. -2. [rente] life (*avant n*); [secrétaire] permanent.

perpétuellement [pɛrpetɥɛlmɑ̃] *adv* perpetually.

perpétuer [perpetɥe] [7] *vt* to perpetuate.
◆ **se perpétuer** *vp* to continue; [espèce] to perpetuate itself.

perpétuité [pɛrpetɥite] *nf* perpetuity; à ~ for life; **être condamné à** ~ to be sentenced to life imprisonment.

perplexe [pɛrplɛks] *adj* perplexed.

perplexité [pɛrplɛksite] *nf* perplexity.

perquisition [pɛrkizisjɔ̃] *nf* search.

perquisitionner [pɛrkizisjɔne] [3] ◇ *vi* to make a search. ◇ *vt* to search, to make a search of.

perron [pɛrɔ̃] *nm* steps (*pl*) (*at entrance to building*).

perroquet [pɛrɔkɛ] *nm* [animal] parrot.

perruche [pɛryʃ] *nf* budgerigar.

perruque [pɛryk] *nf* wig.

pers [pɛr(s)] *adj littéraire* blue-green.

persan, -e [pɛrsɑ̃, an] *adj* Persian.
◆ **persan** *nm* -1. [langue] Persian. -2. [chat] Persian (cat).
◆ **Persan, -e** *nm, f* Persian.

persécuter [pɛrsekyte] [3] *vt* -1. [martyriser] to persecute. -2. [harceler] to harass.

persécuteur, -trice [pɛrsekytœr, tris] ◇ *adj* persecuting. ◇ *nm, f* persecutor.

persécution [pɛrsekysjɔ̃] *nf* persecution.

persévérance [pɛrseverɑ̃s] *nf* perseverance.

persévérant, -e [pɛrseverɑ̃, ɑ̃t] *adj* persevering.

persévérer [persevere] [18] *vi*: ~ (**dans**) to persevere (in).

persienne [pɛrsjɛn] *nf* shutter.

persiflage [pɛrsiflaʒ] *nm* mockery.

persifler [pɛrsifle] [3] *vt littéraire* to mock.

persifleur, -euse [pɛrsiflœr, øz] ◇ *adj* mocking. ◇ *nm, f* mocker.

persil [pɛrsi] *nm* parsley.

persillé, -e [pɛrsije] *adj* -1. [plat] with parsley. -2. [viande] marbled; [fromage] veined, blue-veined.

Persique [pɛrsik] → **golfe**.

persistance [pɛrsistɑ̃s] *nf* persistence.

persistant, -e [pɛrsistɑ̃, ɑ̃t] *adj* persistent; **arbre à feuillage** ~ evergreen (tree).

persister [pɛrsiste] [3] *vi* to persist; ~ à **faire qqch** to persist in doing sthg; ~ **dans qqch** to persist in sthg.

personnage [pɛrsɔnaʒ] *nm* -1. [dignitaire] figure. -2. THÉÂTRE character; ART figure. -3. [personnalité] image. -4. *péj* [individu] character, individual.

personnaliser [pɛrsɔnalize] [3] *vt* to personalize.

personnalité [pɛrsɔnalite] *nf* -1. [gén] personality. -2. JUR status.

personne [pɛrsɔn] ◇ *nf* person; ~**s** people; **en** ~ in person, personally; ~ **âgée** elderly person; ~ **morale** legal entity.
◇ *pron indéf* -1. [quelqu'un] anybody, anyone; **je me demande si** ~ **arrivera un jour à le convaincre** I wonder if anyone will ever convince him. -2. [aucune personne] nobody, no one; ~ **ne viendra** nobody will come; **il n'y a jamais** ~ there's never anybody there, nobody is ever there; ~ **d'autre** nobody OU no one else.

personnel, -elle [pɛrsɔnɛl] *adj* -1. [gén] personal. -2. [égoïste] self-centred.
◆ **personnel** *nm* staff, personnel; ~ **navigant** flight crew.

personnellement [pɛrsɔnɛlmɑ̃] *adv* personally.

personnification [pɛrsɔnifikasjɔ̃] *nf* personification.

personnifier [pɛrsɔnifje] [9] *vt* to personify.

perspective [pɛrspɛktiv] *nf* -1. [ART & point de vue] perspective. -2. [panorama] view. -3. [éventualité] prospect.

perspicace [pɛrspikas] *adj* perspicacious.

perspicacité [pɛrspikasite] *nf* perspicacity.

persuader [pɛrsɥade] [3] *vt*: ~ **qqn de qqch/de faire qqch** to persuade sb of sthg/to do sthg, to convince sb of sthg/to do sthg.
◆ **se persuader** *vp*: **se** ~ **que** to persuade OU convince o.s. (that); **se** ~ **de** to persuade OU convince o.s. of.

persuasif, -ive [pɛrsɥazif, iv] *adj* persuasive.

persuasion [pɛrsɥazjɔ̃] *nf* persuasion.

perte [pɛrt] *nf* -1. [gén] loss; **à** ~ COMM at a loss; ~ **sèche** dead loss. -2. [gaspillage - de temps] waste; **en pure** ~ for absolutely nothing. -3. [ruine, déchéance] ruin; **courir/aller à sa** ~ to be on the road to ruin.
◆ **pertes** *nfpl* [morts] losses.

◆ **à perte de vue** *loc adv* as far as the eye can see.

pertinemment [pɛrtinamɑ̃] *adv* pertinently.

pertinence [pɛrtinɑ̃s] *nf* pertinence, relevance.

pertinent, -e [pɛrtinɑ̃, ɑ̃t] *adj* pertinent, relevant.

perturbateur, -trice [pɛrtyrbatœr, tris] ◇ *adj* disruptive. ◇ *nm, f* troublemaker.

perturbation [pɛrtyrbasjɔ̃] *nf* disruption; ASTRON & MÉTÉOR disturbance.

perturber [pɛrtyrbe] [3] *vt* to disrupt; ~ l'ordre public to disturb the peace.

péruvien, -ienne [peryvjɛ̃, jɛn] *adj* Peruvian.

◆ **Péruvien, -ienne** *nm, f* Peruvian.

pervenche [pɛrvɑ̃ʃ] ◇ *nf* -1. BOT periwinkle. -2. *fam* [contractuelle] meter maid *Am*, traffic warden *Br.* ◇ *adj inv* (periwinkle) blue.

pervers, -e [pɛrvɛr, ɛrs] ◇ *adj* -1. [vicieux] perverted. -2. [effet] unwanted. ◇ *nm, f* pervert.

perversion [pɛrvɛrsjɔ̃] *nf* perversion.

perversité [pɛrvɛrsite] *nf* perversity.

pervertir [pɛrvɛrtir] [32] *vt* to pervert.

◆ **se pervertir** *vp* to become perverted.

pesage [pəzaʒ] *nm* -1. [pesée] weighing. -2. [de jockey] weigh-in.

pesamment [pəzamɑ̃] *adv* heavily.

pesant, -e [pəzɑ̃, ɑ̃t] *adj* -1. [lourd] heavy. -2. [style, architecture] ponderous.

◆ **pesant** *nm*: **valoir son ~ d'or** *fig* to be worth its/one's weight in gold.

pesanteur [pəzɑ̃tœr] *nf* -1. PHYS gravity. -2. [lourdeur] heaviness.

pesée [pəze] *nf* -1. [opération] weighing. -2. [quantité] weight. -3. [pression] pressure, force.

pèse-lettre [pɛzlɛtr] (*pl inv* OU **pèse-lettres**) *nm* letter-scales.

pèse-personne [pɛzpɛrsɔn] (*pl inv* OU **pèse-personnes**) *nm* scales (*pl*).

peser [pəze] [19] ◇ *vt* to weigh; **tout bien pesé** *fig* all things considered. ◇ *vi* -1. [avoir un certain poids] to weigh. -2. [être lourd] to be heavy; ~ **à qqn** *fig* to weigh on sb; ~ **sur** *fig* [accabler] to weigh heavy on; *fig* [influer sur] to influence. -3. [appuyer]: ~ **sur qqch** to press (down) on sthg.

◆ **se peser** *vp* to weigh o.s.

peseta [pezeta] *nf* peseta.

pessimisme [pesimism] *nm* pessimism.

pessimiste [pesimist] ◇ *nmf* pessimist. ◇ *adj* pessimistic.

peste [pɛst] *nf* -1. MÉD plague; **craindre qqn/qqch comme la ~** *fig* to be terrified of sb/sthg; **fuir qqn/qqch comme la ~** *fig* to avoid sb/sthg like the plague. -2. [personne] pest.

pester [pɛste] [3] *vi*: ~ (**contre qqn/qqch**) to curse (sb/sthg).

pesticide [pɛstisid] ◇ *nm* pesticide. ◇ *adj* pesticidal.

pestiféré, -e [pɛstifere] ◇ *adj* plague-stricken. ◇ *nm, f* plague victim.

pestilentiel, -ielle [pɛstilɑ̃sjɛl] *adj* pestilential.

pet [pɛ] *nm fam* fart.

pétale [petal] *nm* petal.

pétanque [petɑ̃k] *nf* ≃ bowls (*U*).

pétant, -e [petɑ̃, ɑ̃t] *adj fam* on the dot.

pétarader [petarade] [3] *vi* to backfire.

pétard [petar] *nm* -1. [petit explosif] firecracker, banger *Br.* -2. *fam* [revolver] gun. -3. *fam* [postérieur] butt *Am*, bum *Br.* -4. *fam* [haschich] joint.

pet-de-nonne [pɛdnɔn] (*pl* **pets-de-nonne**) *nm* very light fritter.

péter [pete] [18] ◇ *vi* -1. *tfam* [personne] to fart. -2. *fam* [câble, élastique] to snap. ◇ *vt* *fam* to bust.

pète-sec [pɛtsɛk] *adj inv fam* bossy.

pétillant, -e [petijɑ̃, ɑ̃t] *adj litt* & *fig* sparkling.

pétiller [petije] [3] *vi* -1. [vin, eau] to sparkle, to bubble. -2. [feu] to crackle. -3. *fig* [yeux] to sparkle; ~ **de** [personne] to bubble with; [yeux] to sparkle with.

petiot, -e [pətjo, ɔt] ◇ *adj* teeny. ◇ *nm, f* little one.

petit, -e [pəti, it] ◇ *adj* -1. [de taille, jeune] small, little; ~ **frère** little OU younger brother; ~ **e sœur** little OU younger sister. -2. [voyage, visite] short, little. -3. [faible, infime - somme d'argent] small; [- bruit] faint, slight; **c'est une ~e nature** he/she is slightly built. -4. [de peu d'importance, de peu de valeur] minor. -5. [médiocre, mesquin] petty. -6. [de rang modeste - commerçant, propriétaire, pays] small; [- fonctionnaire] minor; **les ~es gens** people of modest means. ◇ *nm, f* -1. [personne de petite taille] small man (*f* woman). -2. [enfant] little one, child; **bonjour, mon ~/ma ~e** good morning, my dear; **pauvre ~!** poor little thing!; **la classe des ~s** SCOL the infant class. ◇ *nm* -1. [jeune animal] young (*U*); **faire des ~s** to have puppies/kittens *etc.* -2. (*gén pl*) [personne modeste] little man.

◆ **petit à petit** *loc adv* little by little, gradually.

petit-beurre [p(ə)tibœr] (*pl* **petits-beurre**) *nm small biscuit.*

petit-bourgeois, **petite-bourgeoise** [p(ə)tiburʒwa, p(ə)titburʒwaz] (*mpl* **petits-bourgeois**, *fpl* **petites-bourgeoises**) *péj* ◇ *adj* lower middle-class. ◇ *nm, f* lower middle-class person.

petit déjeuner [p(ə)tideʒøne] (*pl* **petits déjeuners**) *nm* breakfast.

petit-déjeuner [p(ə)tideʒøne] [5] *vi* to have breakfast, to breakfast.

petite-fille [p(ə)titfij] (*pl* **petites-filles**) *nf* granddaughter.

petitement [p(ə)titmɑ̃] *adv* **-1.** [être logé] in cramped conditions. **-2.** [chichement - vivre] poorly. **-3.** [mesquinement] pettily.

petitesse [p(ə)titɛs] *nf* **-1.** [de personne, de revenu] smallness. **-2.** [d'esprit] pettiness.

petit-fils [p(ə)tifis] (*pl* **petits-fils**) *nm* grandson.

petit-four [p(ə)tifur] (*pl* **petits-fours**) *nm* petit-four.

pétition [petisjɔ̃] *nf* petition.

pétitionner [petisjɔne] [3] *vi* to petition.

petit-lait [p(ə)tilɛ] (*pl* **petits-laits**) *nm* whey.

petit-nègre [p(ə)tinɛgr] *nm inv fam* pidgin French.

petits-enfants [p(ə)tizɑ̃fɑ̃] *nmpl* grandchildren.

petit-suisse [p(ə)tisɥis] (*pl* **petits-suisses**) *nm fresh soft cheese, eaten with sugar.*

peton [pətɔ̃] *nm fam* foot.

pétrifier [petrifje] [9] *vt litt & fig* to petrify.
◆ **se pétrifier** *vp* to become petrified.

pétrin [petrɛ̃] *nm* **-1.** [de boulanger] kneading machine. **-2.** *fam* [embarras] pickle; **se fourrer/être dans le ~** to get into/to be in a pickle.

pétrir [petrir] [32] *vt* **-1.** [pâte, muscle] to knead. **-2.** *fig & littéraire* [personne] to mould; **pétri d'orgueil** filled with pride.

pétrochimie [petrɔʃimi] *nf* petrochemistry.

pétrochimique [petrɔʃimik] *adj* petrochemical.

pétrodollar [petrɔdɔlar] *nm* petrodollar.

pétrole [petrɔl] *nm* oil, petroleum; **~ lampant** kerosene *Am*, paraffin (oil) *Br*.

pétrolier, -ière [petrɔlje, jɛr] *adj* oil (*avant n*), petroleum (*avant n*).
◆ **pétrolier** *nm* **-1.** [navire] oil tanker. **-2.** [personne] oil magnate.

pétrolifère [petrɔlifɛr] *adj* oil-bearing.

pétulant, -e [petylɑ̃, ɑ̃t] *adj* exuberant.

pétunia [petynja] *nm* petunia.

peu [pø] ◇ *adv* **-1.** (*avec verbe, adjectif, adverbe*): **il a ~ dormi** he didn't sleep much, he slept little; **c'est un livre ~ intéressant** it's not a very interesting book; **~ souvent** not very often, rarely; **très ~** very little. **-2.** **~ de** (+ *nom sg*) little, not much; (+ *nom pl*) few, not many; **il a ~ de travail** he hasn't got much work, he has little work; **c'est (bien) ~ de chose** it's not much; **il reste ~ de jours** there aren't many days left; **~ d'élèves l'ont compris** few OU not many students understood him; **~ de gens le connaissent** few OU not many know him.
◇ *nm* **-1.** [petite quantité]: **le ~ de** (+ *nom sg*) the little; (+ *nom pl*) the few; **avec mon ~ de moyens** with the little I possess. **-2.** **un ~ a** little, a bit; **je le connais un ~** I know him slightly OU a little; **un (tout) petit ~** a little bit; **elle est un ~ sotte** she's a bit stupid; **tu parles un ~ fort** you're talking a little too loudly; **un ~ de a** little; **un ~ de vin/patience** a little wine/patience.
◆ **avant peu** *loc adv* soon, before long.
◆ **depuis peu** *loc adv* recently.
◆ **peu à peu** *loc adv* gradually, little by little.
◆ **pour peu que** *loc conj* (+ *subjonctif*) if ever, if only.
◆ **pour un peu** *loc adv* nearly, almost.
◆ **si peu que** *loc conj* (+ *subjonctif*) however little.
◆ **sous peu** *loc adv* soon, shortly.

peul, -e [pøl] *adj* Fulani.
◆ **peul** *nm* [langue] Fulani.
◆ **Peul, -e** *nm, f* Fulani.

peuplade [pœplad] *nf* tribe.

peuple [pœpl] *nm* **-1.** [gén] people; **le ~** the (common) people. **-2.** *fam* [multitude]: **quel ~!** what a crowd!

peuplé, -e [pœple] *adj* populated.

peuplement [pœpləmɑ̃] *nm* **-1.** [action] populating. **-2.** [population] population.

peupler [pœple] [5] *vt* **-1.** [pourvoir d'habitants - région] to populate; [- bois, étang] to stock. **-2.** [habiter, occuper] to inhabit. **-3.** *fig* [remplir] to fill.
◆ **se peupler** *vp* **-1.** [région] to become populated. **-2.** [rue, salle] to be filled.

peuplier [pøplije] *nm* poplar.

peur [pœr] *nf* fear; **avoir ~ de qqn/qqch** to be afraid of sb/sthg; **avoir ~ de faire qqch** to be afraid of doing sthg; **avoir ~ que** (+ *subjonctif*) to be afraid that; **j'ai ~ qu'il ne vienne pas** I'm afraid he won't come; **faire ~ à qqn** to frighten sb; **par** OU **de ~ de ~**

de qqch for fear of sthg; **par** OU **de ~ de faire qqch** for fear of doing sthg; **il n'a pas ~ du ridicule** he doesn't mind making a fool of himself; **avoir une ~ bleue de** to be scared stiff of; **avoir plus de ~ que de mal** to be more frightened than hurt; **laid à faire ~** horribly ugly; **mourir de ~** to die of fright; **prendre ~** to take fright.

peureux, -euse [pœrø, øz] ◇ *adj* fearful, timid. ◇ *nm, f* fearful OU timid person.

peut → pouvoir.

peut-être [pøtɛtr] *adv* perhaps, maybe; **~ qu'ils ne viendront pas, ils ne viendront ~ pas** perhaps OU maybe they won't come; **~ pas** perhaps OU maybe not.

peux → pouvoir.

p. ex. (*abr de* **par exemple**) e.g.

pH (*abr de* **potential of hydrogen**) *nm* pH.

phalange [falɑ̃ʒ] *nf* **-1.** ANAT. phalanx. **-2.** POLIT falange.

phallique [falik] *adj* phallic.

phallocrate [falɔkrat] ◇ *nm* male chauvinist. ◇ *adj* male chauvinist (*avant n*); [milieu] male-dominated.

phallus [falys] *nm* phallus.

pharaon [faraɔ̃] *nm* pharaoh.

phare [far] ◇ *nm* **-1.** [tour] lighthouse. **-2.** AUTOM headlight; **~ antibrouillard** fog lamp. ◇ *adj* landmark (*avant n*); **une industrie ~** flagship OU pioneering industry.

pharmaceutique [farmasøtik] *adj* pharmaceutical.

pharmacie [farmasi] *nf* **-1.** [science] pharmacology. **-2.** [magasin] drugstore *Am,* chemist's *Br.* **-3.** [meuble]: **(armoire à) ~** medicine cupboard.

pharmacien, -ienne [farmasjɛ̃, jɛn] *nm, f* druggist *Am,* chemist *Br.*

pharmacologie [farmakɔlɔʒi] *nf* pharmacology.

pharyngite [farɛ̃ʒit] *nf* pharyngitis (*U*).

pharynx [farɛ̃ks] *nm* pharynx.

phase [faz] *nf* phase; **être en ~ avec qqn** to be on the same wavelength as sb.

phénix [feniks] *nm* **-1.** MYTH phoenix. **-2.** [personne] paragon.

phénoménal, -e, -aux [fenɔmenal, o] *adj* phenomenal.

phénomène [fenɔmɛn] *nm* **-1.** [fait] phenomenon. **-2.** [être anormal] freak. **-3.** *fam* [excentrique] character.

philanthropie [filɑ̃trɔpi] *nf* philanthropy.

philanthropique [filɑ̃trɔpik] *adj* philanthropic.

philatélie [filateli] *nf* philately, stamp-collecting.

philatéliste [filatelist] *nmf* philatelist, stamp-collector.

philharmonique [filarmɔnik] *adj* philharmonic.

philippin, -e [filipɛ̃, in] *adj* Filipino.
◆ **Philippin, -e** *nm, f* Filipino.

Philippines [filipin] *nfpl*: **les ~** the Philippines; **aux ~** in the Philippines.

philistin [filistɛ̃] *nm* philistine.

philodendron [filɔdɛ̃drɔ̃] *nm* philodendron.

philologie [filɔlɔʒi] *nf* philology.

philosophe [filɔzɔf] ◇ *nmf* philosopher. ◇ *adj* philosophical.

philosopher [filɔzɔfe] [3] *vi* to philosophize.

philosophie [filɔzɔfi] *nf* philosophy.

philosophique [filɔzɔfik] *adj* philosophical.

philosophiquement [filɔzɔfikmɑ̃] *adv* philosophically.

philtre [filtr] *nm* love potion.

phlébite [flebit] *nf* phlebitis.

Phnom Penh [pnɔmpɛn] *n* Phnom Penh.

phobie [fɔbi] *nf* phobia.

phobique [fɔbik] *nmf & adj* phobic.

phonème [fɔnɛm] *nm* phoneme.

phonétique [fɔnetik] ◇ *nf* phonetics (*U*). ◇ *adj* phonetic.

phonétiquement [fɔnetikmɑ̃] *adv* phonetically.

phono [fɔno] *nm fam vieilli* phonograph *Am,* gramophone *Br.*

phonographe [fɔnɔgraf] *nm vieilli* phonograph *Am,* gramophone *Br.*

phoque [fɔk] *nm* seal.

phosphate [fɔsfat] *nm* phosphate.

phosphaté, -e [fɔsfate] *adj*: **engrais ~** phosphate fertilizer.

phosphore [fɔsfɔr] *nm* phosphorus.

phosphorescent, -e [fɔsfɔresɑ̃, ɑ̃t] *adj* phosphorescent.

photo [fɔto] ◇ *nf* **-1.** [technique] photography. **-2.** [image] photo, picture; **prendre qqn en ~** to take a photo of sb; **~ d'identité** passport photo; **~ noir et blanc** black and white photo; **~ couleur** color *Am* OU color *Br* photo. ◇ *adj inv*: **appareil ~** camera.

photocomposition [fɔtɔkɔ̃pozisjɔ̃] *nf* photocomposition *Am,* filmsetting *Br.*

photocopie [fɔtɔkɔpi] *nf* **-1.** [procédé] photocopying. **-2.** [document] photocopy.

photocopier [fɔtɔkɔpje] [9] *vt* to photocopy.

photocopieur [fɔtɔkɔpjœr] *nm,* **photocopieuse** [fɔtɔkɔpjøz] *nf* photocopier.

photoélectrique [fɔtɔelɛktrik] *adj* photoelectric.

photogénique [fɔtɔʒenik] *adj* photogenic.

photographe [fɔtɔgraf] *nmf* **-1.** [artiste, technicien] photographer. **-2.** [commerçant] camera dealer.

photographie [fɔtɔgrafi] *nf* **-1.** [technique] photography. **-2.** [cliché] photograph.

photographier [fɔtɔgrafje] [9] *vt* to photograph.

photographique [fɔtɔgrafik] *adj* photographic.

Photomaton® [fɔtɔmatɔ̃] *nm* photo booth.

photomontage [fɔtɔmɔ̃taʒ] *nm* photomontage.

photoreportage [fɔtɔrəpɔrtaʒ] *nm* PRESSE report (consisting mainly of photographs).

photosensible [fɔtɔsɑ̃sibl] *adj* photosensitive.

photothèque [fɔtɔtɛk] *nf* photograph library.

phrase [fraz] *nf* **-1.** LING sentence; ~ **toute faite** stock phrase. **-2.** MUS phrase.

phraséologie [frazeɔlɔʒi] *nf* phraseology; *péj* verbiage.

phraseur, -euse [frazœr, øz] *nm, f péj* verbose person.

phréatique [freatik] *adj*: **nappe** ~ water table.

phrygien, -ienne [friʒjɛ̃, jɛn] *adj* Phrygian.
◆ **Phrygien, -ienne** *nm, f* Phrygian.

phtisie [ftizi] *nf vieilli* consumption.

phylloxéra, phylloxera [filɔksera] *nm* phylloxera.

physicien, -ienne [fizisjɛ̃, jɛn] *nm, f* physicist.

physiologie [fizjɔlɔʒi] *nf* physiology.

physiologique [fizjɔlɔʒik] *adj* physiological.

physiologiquement [fizjɔlɔʒikmɑ̃] *adv* physiologically.

physionomie [fizjɔnɔmi] *nf* **-1.** [faciès] face. **-2.** [apparence] physiognomy.

physionomiste [fizjɔnɔmist] ◇ *nmf* person with a good memory for faces. ◇ *adj*: **être** ~ to have a good memory for faces.

physiothérapie [fizjɔterapi] *nf natural medicine based on treatment using water, air, light etc.*

physique [fizik] ◇ *adj* physical. ◇ *nf* SCIENCE physics (*U*). ◇ *nm* **-1.** [constitution] physical well-being. **-2.** [apparence] physique.

physiquement [fizikmɑ̃] *adv* physically.

phytothérapie [fitɔterapi] *nf* herbal medicine.

p.i. *abr de* **par intérim.**

piaf [pjaf] *nm fam* sparrow.

piaffer [pjafe] [3] *vi* **-1.** [cheval] to paw the ground. **-2.** [personne] to fidget.

piaillement [pjajmɑ̃] *nm* **-1.** [d'oiseau] cheeping. **-2.** [d'enfant] squawking.

piailler [pjaje] [3] *vi* **-1.** [oiseaux] to cheep. **-2.** [enfant] to squawk.

pianiste [pjanist] *nmf* pianist.

piano [pjano] ◇ *nm* piano; ~ **demi-queue** baby grand (piano); ~ **droit** upright (piano); ~ **mécanique** player piano; ~ **à queue** grand (piano). ◇ *adv* **-1.** MUS piano. **-2.** [doucement] gently.

pianoter [pjanɔte] [3] *vi* **-1.** [jouer du piano] to plunk away (on the piano). **-2.** [sur table] to drum one's fingers.

piaule [pjol] *nf fam* [hébergement] place; [chambre] room.

piauler [pjole] [3] *vi* **-1.** [oiseau] to cheep. **-2.** [enfant] to whimper.

PIB (*abr de* **produit intérieur brut**) *nm* GDP.

pic [pik] *nm* **-1.** [outil] pick, pickax *Am,* pickaxe *Br.* **-2.** [montagne] peak. **-3.** [oiseau] woodpecker.
◆ **à pic** *loc adv* **-1.** [verticalement] vertically; **couler à** ~ to sink like a stone. **-2.** *fam* fig [à point nommé] just at the right moment.

pichenette [piʃnɛt] *nf* flick (of the finger).

pichet [piʃɛ] *nm* jug.

pickpocket [pikpɔkɛt] *nm* pickpocket.

pick-up [pikœp] *nm inv* **-1.** *vieilli* [tourne-disque] record player. **-2.** [camionnette] pick-up (truck).

picoler [pikɔle] [3] *vi fam* to booze.

picorer [pikɔre] [3] *vi & vt* to peck.

picotement [pikɔtmɑ̃] *nm* prickling (*U*), prickle.

picoter [pikɔte] [3] *vt* **-1.** [yeux] to make sting. **-2.** [pain] to peck (at).

pictogramme [piktɔgram] *nm* pictogram.

pictural, -e, -aux [piktyral, o] *adj* pictorial.

pic-vert = pivert.

pie [pi] ◇ *nf* **-1.** [oiseau] magpie. **-2.** [bavard] chatterbox. ◇ *adj inv* [cheval] piebald.

pièce [pjɛs] *nf* **-1.** [élément] piece; [de moteur] part; **mettre en** ~**s** [vêtement] to tear to pieces; [assiette, tasse] to smash to pieces; **en** ~**s détachées** in little bits OU pieces; ~ **de collection** collector's item; ~ **détachée** spare part; ~ **de musée** museum piece; **créer/inventer qqch de toutes** ~**s** to create/invent sthg from start to finish. **-2.**

[unité]: **quinze francs** ~ fifteen francs each OU apiece; **acheter/vendre qqch à la** ~ to buy/sell sthg singly, to buy/sell sthg separately; **travailler à la** ~ to do piece work. **-3.** [document] document, paper; ~ **à conviction** object produced as evidence, exhibit; ~ **d'identité** identification papers (*pl*); ~ **justificative** written proof (*U*), supporting document. **-4.** [œuvre littéraire ou musicale] piece; ~ **(de théâtre)** play. **-5.** [argent]: ~ **(de monnaie)** coin. **-6.** [de maison] room. **-7.** COUTURE patch.

♦ **pièce d'eau** *nf* large pond, ornamental lake.

♦ **pièce montée** *nf* tiered cake.

piécette [pjesɛt] *nf* small coin.

pied [pje] *nm* **-1.** [gén] foot; **à** ~ on foot; **avoir** ~ to be able to touch the bottom; **perdre** ~ *litt & fig* to be out of one's depth; **à** ~**s joints** to put one's feet together; **être/marcher** ~**s nus** OU **nu-**~**s** to be/to go barefoot; ~ **bot** [handicap] clubfoot. **-2.** CULIN: ~ **de porc** pig's trotter. **-3.** [base - de montagne, table] foot; [- de verre] stem; [- de lampe] base. **-4.** [plant - de tomate] stalk; [- de vigne] stock. **-5.** *loc*: **attendre qqch/qqn de** ~ **ferme** to be ready for sb/sthg; **c'est le** ~ *fam* it's great; **casser les** ~**s à qqn** *fam* to get on sb's nerves; **comme un** ~ [chanter, conduire] *fam* terribly; **être au** ~ **du mur** to have one's back to the wall; **être sur** ~ to be (back) on one's feet, to be up and about; **être sur un** ~ **d'égalité (avec)** to be on an equal footing (with); **faire du** ~ **à** to play footsie with; **faire le** ~ **de grue** to wait about; **faire des** ~**s et des mains** to move heaven and earth, to do one's utmost; **faire un** ~ **de nez à qqn** to thumb one's nose at sb; **ça te fera les** ~**s!** *fam* it'll serve you right!; **fouler qqch aux** ~**s** to ride roughshod over sthg; **se lever du bon** ~/**du** ~ **gauche** to get out of bed on the right/wrong side; **mettre qqch sur** ~ to get sthg on its feet, to get sthg off the ground; **mettre qqn au** ~ **du mur** to drive sb to the wall; **mettre les** ~**s dans le plat** *fam* to put one's foot in it; **je n'ai jamais mis les** ~**s chez lui** I've never set foot in his house; **au** ~ **de la lettre** literally, to the letter; **de** ~ **en cap** from head to toe; **ne pas savoir sur quel** ~ **danser** not to know which way to turn; **ne pas se laisser marcher sur les** ~**s** not to let anyone tread on one's toes; **prendre son** ~ *fam* [sexuellement] to come; *fig* to be in seventh heaven; **retomber sur ses** ~**s** to land on one's feet.

♦ **en pied** *loc adj* [portrait] full-length.

pied-à-terre [pjetatɛr] *nm inv* pied-à-terre.

pied-de-biche [pjedbiʃ] (*pl* **pieds-de-biche**) *nm* **-1.** [outil] nail claw. **-2.** COUTURE presser foot.

pied-de-poule [pjedpul] (*pl* **pieds-de-poule**) ◇ *nm* houndstooth (material). ◇ *adj inv* houndstooth (*avant n*).

piédestal, -aux [pjedestal, o] *nm* pedestal.

piedmont = **piémont**.

pied-noir (*pl* **pieds-noirs**) [pjenwar] *nmf* French settler in Algeria.

piège [pjeʒ] *nm litt & fig* trap; **être pris au** ~ to be trapped; **tendre un** ~ to set a trap.

piéger [pjeʒe] [22] *vt* **-1.** [animal, personne] to trap. **-2.** [colis, véhicule] to boobytrap.

piémont, piedmont [pjemɔ̃] *nm* piedmont glacier/plain.

pierraille [pjɛraj] *nf* loose stones (*pl*).

pierre [pjɛr] *nf* stone; ~ **d'achoppement** *fig* stumbling block; ~ **précieuse** precious stone; **poser la première** ~ CONSTR to lay the foundation stone; *fig* to lay the foundations; **faire d'une** ~ **deux coups** *fig* to kill two birds with one stone.

pierreries [pjɛrri] *nfpl* precious stones, jewels.

piété [pjete] *nf* piety.

piétiner [pjetine] [3] ◇ *vi* **-1.** [trépigner] to stamp (one's feet). **-2.** *fig* [ne pas avancer] to make no progress, to be at a standstill. ◇ *vt* **-1.** [personne, parterre] to trample. **-2.** *fig* [principes] to ride roughshod over.

piéton, -onne [pjetɔ̃, ɔn] *nm, f* pedestrian. ◇ *adj* pedestrian (*avant n*).

piétonnier, -ière [pjetɔnje, jɛr] *adj* pedestrian (*avant n*).

piètre [pjɛtr] *adj* poor.

pieu, -x [pjø] *nm* **-1.** [poteau] post, stake. **-2.** *fam* [lit] sack *Am*, pit *Br*.

pieusement [pjøzmɑ̃] *adv* **-1.** RELIG piously. **-2.** *fig* [conserver] religiously.

pieuter [pjøte] [3]

♦ **se pieuter** *vp fam* to hit the hay.

pieuvre [pjœvr] *nf* octopus; *fig & péj* leech.

pieux, pieuse [pjø, pjøz] *adj* **-1.** [personne, livre] pious. **-2.** [soins] devoted. **-3.** [silence] reverent.

pif [pif] *nm fam* conk, hooter *Br*; **au** ~ *fig* by guesswork.

pige [piʒ] *nf* **-1.** PRESSE: **travailler à la** ~ to work freelance. **-2.** *fam* [an]: **avoir 30** ~**s** to be 30 (years old).

pigeon [piʒɔ̃] *nm* **-1.** [oiseau] pigeon; ~ **voyageur** carrier pigeon, homing pigeon. **-2.** *fam péj* [personne] sucker.

pigeonnant, -e [piʒɔnɑ̃, ɑ̃t] *adj* [soutien-gorge] uplift (*avant n*); [poitrine] prominent.

pigeonner [piʒɔne] [3] *vt fam* to cheat.

pigeonnier [piʒɔnje] *nm* **-1.** [pour pigeons] pigeon loft, dovecote. **-2.** *fig* & *vieilli* [logement] garret.

piger [piʒe] [17] *fam* ◇ *vt* to understand. ◇ *vi* to catch on, to get it.

pigiste [piʒist] *nmf* freelance.

pigment [pigmã] *nm* pigment.

pigmentation [pigmãtasjɔ̃] *nf* pigmentation.

pignon [piɲɔ̃] *nm* **-1.** [de mur] gable; **avoir ~ sur rue** *fig* to be a person of substance. **-2.** [d'engrenage] gearwheel. **-3.** [de pomme de pin] pine kernel.

pilaf [pilaf] → **riz**.

pile [pil] ◇ *nf* **-1.** [de livres, journaux] pile. **-2.** ÉLECTR battery. **-3.** [de pièce]: **~ ou face** heads or tails. ◇ *adv fam* on the dot; **tomber/arriver ~** to come to/to arrive at just the right time.

piler [pile] [3] ◇ *vt* **-1.** [amandes] to crush, to grind. **-2.** *fam fig* [adversaire] to thrash. ◇ *vi fam* AUTOM to jam on the brakes.

pileux, -euse [pilø, øz] *adj* hairy (*avant n*); **système ~** hair.

pilier [pilje] *nm* **-1.** [de construction] pillar. **-2.** *fig* [soutien] mainstay, pillar. **-3.** *fig* & *péj* [habitué]: **c'est un ~ de bar** he's always propping up the bar. **-4.** RUGBY prop (forward).

pillage [pijaʒ] *nm* looting.

pillard, -e [pijar, ard] ◇ *nm, f* looter. ◇ *adj* looting (*avant n*).

piller [pije] [3] *vt* **-1.** [ville, biens] to loot. **-2.** *fig* [ouvrage, auteur] to plagiarize.

pilon [pilɔ̃] *nm* **-1.** [instrument] pestle; **mettre au ~** to pulp. **-2.** [de poulet] drumstick. **-3.** [jambe de bois] wooden leg.

pilonner [pilɔne] [3] *vt* to pound.

pilori [pilɔri] *nm* pillory; **mettre** OU **clouer qqn au ~** *fig* to pillory sb.

pilotage [pilɔtaʒ] *nm* piloting; **~ automatique** automatic piloting.

pilote [pilɔt] ◇ *nm* **-1.** [d'avion] pilot; [de voiture] driver; **~ automatique** autopilot; **~ de chasse** fighter pilot; **~ de course** race *Am* OU racing *Br* driver; **~ d'essai** test pilot; **~ de ligne** airline pilot. **-2.** [poisson] pilot fish. ◇ *adj* pilot (*avant n*), experimental.

piloter [pilɔte] [3] *vt* **-1.** [avion] to pilot; [voiture] to drive. **-2.** [personne] to show around.

pilotis [pilɔti] *nm* pile.

pilule [pilyl] *nf* pill; **prendre la ~** to be on the pill; **dorer la ~ à qqn** *fig* to sugar the pill for sb.

pimbêche [pɛ̃bɛʃ] *péj* ◇ *nf* stuck-up woman, stuck-up girl. ◇ *adj* stuck-up.

piment [pimã] *nm* **-1.** [plante] pepper, capsicum; **~ rouge** chilli pepper, hot red pepper. **-2.** *fig* [piquant] spice; **donner du ~ à qqch** to spice sthg up.

pimenter [pimãte] [3] *vt* **-1.** [plat] to put chillis in. **-2.** *fig* [récit] to spice up.

pimpant, -e [pɛ̃pɑ̃, ɑ̃t] *adj* smart.

pin [pɛ̃] *nm* pine; **~ parasol** umbrella pine; **~ sylvestre** Scots pine.

pinacle [pinakl] *nm* ARCHIT pinnacle; **porter qqn au ~** *fig* to praise sb to the skies.

pinailler [pinaje] [3] *vi fam* to split hairs; **~ sur** to quibble about.

pinard [pinar] *nm fam* jug wine *Am*, plonk *Br*.

pince [pɛ̃s] *nf* **-1.** [grande] pliers (*pl*). **-2.** [petite]: **~ (à épiler)** tweezers (*pl*); **~ à linge** clothespin *Am*, clothes peg *Br*. **-3.** [de crabe] pincer. **-4.** *fam* [main] mitt. **-5.** *fam* [jambe]: **à ~s** on foot. **-6.** COUTURE dart.

pincé, -e [pɛ̃se] *adj* **-1.** [air, sourire] prim. **-2.** [nez] pinched.

pinceau, -x [pɛ̃so] *nm* **-1.** [pour peindre] brush. **-2.** *fam* [pied] foot.

pincée [pɛ̃se] *nf* pinch.

pincement [pɛ̃smã] *nm* pinching; **~ au cœur** *fig* pang of sorrow.

pince-monseigneur [pɛ̃smɔ̃sɛɲœr] (*pl* **pinces-monseigneur**) *nf* jimmy *Am,* jemmy *Br.*

pince-nez [pɛ̃sne] *nm inv* pince-nez.

pincer [pɛ̃se] [16] ◇ *vt* **-1.** [serrer] to pinch; MUS to pluck; [lèvres] to purse. **-2.** *fam fig* [arrêter] to catch, to nick *Br*; **se faire ~** to get caught, to get nicked *Br*. **-3.** [suj: froid] to nip. ◇ *vi fam* **-1.** [faire froid]: **ça pince!** it's a bit nippy! **-2.** *fig* [avoir le béguin]: **en ~ pour qqn** to be crazy about sb.

◆ **se pincer** *vp*: **se ~ le doigt** to jam OU catch one's finger; **se ~ le nez** to hold one's nose.

pince-sans-rire [pɛ̃sɑ̃rir] *nmf inv* person with a deadpan face.

pincettes [pɛ̃sɛt] *nfpl* [ustensile] tongs; **il n'est pas à prendre avec des ~** *fig* he's like a bear with a sore head.

pinçon [pɛ̃sɔ̃] *nm* pinch mark.

pinède [pinɛd], **pineraie** [pinrɛ], **pinière** [pinjɛr] *nf* pine wood.

pingouin [pɛ̃gwɛ̃] *nm* penguin.

ping-pong [piŋpɔ̃g] (*pl* **ping-pongs**) *nm* ping pong, table tennis.

pingre [pɛ̃gr] *péj adj* stingy.

pingrerie [pɛ̃grəri] *nf péj* stinginess.

pinière = pinède.

pinson [pɛ̃sɔ̃] *nm* chaffinch; **gai comme un** ~ *fig* happy as a lark.

pintade [pɛ̃tad] *nf* guinea fowl.

pintadeau, -x [pɛ̃tado] *nm* young guinea fowl.

pinte [pɛ̃t] *nf* **-1.** [mesure anglo-saxonne] pint. **-2.** *vieilli* [mesure française] quart. **-3.** *Helv* [débit de boissons] drinking establishment.

pin-up [pinœp] *nf inv* pinup (girl).

pioche [pjɔʃ] *nf* **-1.** [outil] pick. **-2.** JEU pile.

piocher [pjɔʃe] [3] ◇ *vt* **-1.** [terre] to dig. **-2.** JEU to take. **-3.** *fig* [choisir] to pick at random. ◇ *vi* **-1.** [creuser] to dig. **-2.** JEU to pick up; ~ **dans** [tas] to delve into; [économies] to dip into.

piolet [pjɔlɛ] *nm* ice ax *Am* OU axe *Br*.

pion, pionne [pjɔ̃, pjɔn] *nm, f fam* SCOL *supervisor (often a student who does this as a part-time job)*.
◆ **pion** *nm* [aux échecs] pawn; [aux dames] piece; **damer le** ~ **à qqn** *fig* to get the better of sb; **n'être qu'un** ~ *fig* to be just a pawn in the game.

pionnier, -ière [pjɔnje, jɛr] *nm, f* pioneer.

pipe [pip] *nf* pipe.

pipeline, pipe-line [pajplajn, piplin] (*pl* **pipe-lines**) *nm* pipeline.

piper [pipe] [3] *vt* **-1.** [cartes] to mark; [dés] to load. **-2.** *loc*: **ne pas** ~ **mot** not to breathe a word.

piperade [piperad] *nf eggs cooked with tomatoes, peppers and onions.*

pipette [pipɛt] *nf* pipette.

pipi [pipi] *nm fam* wee; **faire** ~ to have a wee.

piquant, -e [pikɑ̃, ɑ̃t] *adj* **-1.** [barbe, feuille] prickly. **-2.** [sauce] spicy, hot. **-3.** [froid] biting. **-4.** *fig* [détail] spicy, juicy.
◆ **piquant** *nm* **-1.** [d'animal] spine; [de végétal] thorn, prickle. **-2.** *fig* [d'histoire] spice.

pique [pik] ◇ *nf* **-1.** [arme] pike. **-2.** *fig* [mot blessant] barbed comment. ◇ *nm* [aux cartes] spade.

piqué, -e [pike] *adj* **-1.** [vin] sour, vinegary. **-2.** [meuble] worm-eaten. **-3.** [tissu] spotted, flecked. **-4.** *fam* [personne] loony.
◆ **piqué** *nm* **-1.** [tissu] piqué. **-2.** AÉRON dive.

pique-assiette [pikasjɛt] (*pl inv* OU **pique-assiettes**) *nmf péj* sponger.

pique-nique [piknik] (*pl* **pique-niques**) *nm* picnic.

pique-niquer [piknike] [3] *vi* to picnic.

piquer [pike] [3] ◇ *vt* **-1.** [suj: guêpe, méduse] to sting; [suj: serpent, moustique] to bite. **-2.** [avec pointe] to prick; ~ **qqch de** CULIN to stick sth with. **-3.** MÉD to give an injection to; **se faire** ~ **contre** *fam* to have o.s. inoculated OU vaccinated against. **-4.** [animal] to put down. **-5.** [fleur] to stick sth into. **-6.** [suj: tissu, barbe] to prickle. **-7.** [suj: fumée, froid] to sting. **-8.** COUTURE to sew, to machine. **-9.** *fam* [voler] to pinch. **-10.** *fig* [curiosité] to excite, to arouse. **-11.** *fam* [voleur, escroc] to catch, to nick *Br*; **se faire** ~ to get caught, to get nicked *Br*.
◇ *vi* **-1.** [ronce] to prick; [ortie] to sting. **-2.** [guêpe, méduse] to sting; [serpent, moustique] to bite. **-3.** [épice] to burn. **-4.** COUTURE to machine. **-5.** *fam* [voler]: ~ **(dans)** to pinch (from). **-6.** [avion] to dive.
◆ **se piquer** *vp* **-1.** [avec épingle, dans ronces] to prick o.s. **-2.** [dans orties] to sting o.s. **-3.** *fam* [se droguer] to shoot up. **-4.** *littéraire* [se vexer] to become irritated. **-5.** *littéraire* & *péj* [avoir la prétention]: **se** ~ **de qqch/de faire qqch** to pride o.s. on one's knowledge of sthg/on one's ability to do sthg.

piquet [pikɛ] *nm* **-1.** [pieu] peg, stake. **-2.** JEU piquet.
◆ **piquet de grève** *nm* picket.

piqueter [pikte] [27] *vt* to dot, to spot.

piquette [pikɛt] *nf* **-1.** [vin] cheap wine OU plonk *Br*. **-2.** *fam* [défaite]: **prendre une** OU **la** ~ *fig* to get a hammering OU a thrashing.

piqûre [pikyr] *nf* **-1.** [de guêpe, méduse] sting; [de serpent, moustique] bite. **-2.** [d'ortie] sting. **-3.** [injection] shot, jab *Br*. **-4.** COUTURE stitching (*U*).

piranha [piraɲa], **piraya** [piraja] *nm* piranha.

piratage [pirataʒ] *nm* piracy; INFORM hacking.

pirate [pirat] ◇ *nm* **-1.** [corsaire] pirate; ~ **de l'air** hijacker, skyjacker. **-2.** *fig* [escroc] swindler. ◇ *adj* pirate (*avant n*).

pirater [pirate] [3] *vt* to pirate.

piraterie [piratri] *nf* **-1.** [flibuste] piracy (*U*). **-2.** [acte] act of piracy. **-3.** *fig* [escroquerie] swindling.

piraya = piranha.

pire [pir] ◇ *adj* **-1.** [comparatif relatif] worse. **-2.** [superlatif]: **le/la** ~ the worst. ◇ *nm*: **le** ~ **(de)** the worst (of); **s'attendre au** ~ to expect the worst.

Pirée [pire] *nm*: **Le** ~ Piraeus.

pirogue [pirɔg] *nf* dugout canoe.

pirouette [piʀwɛt] *nf* **-1.** [saut] pirouette. **-2.** *fig* [faux-fuyant] prevarication, evasive answer; **répondre par une ~** to answer evasively; **s'en tirer par une ~** to evade the issue.

pis [pi] ◇ *adj littéraire* [pire] worse. ◇ *adv* worse; **de mal en ~** from bad to worse; **de ~ en ~** worse and worse. ◇ *nm* udder.

pis-aller [pizale] *nm inv* last resort.

pisciculture [pisikyltyʀ] *nf* fish farming.

piscine [pisin] *nf* swimming pool; **~ couverte/découverte** indoor/open-air swimming pool.

Pise [piz] *n* Pisa; **la tour de ~** the Leaning Tower of Pisa.

pisse [pis] *nf tfam* pee, piss.

pisse-froid [pisfʀwa] *nm inv fam péj* wet-blanket.

pissenlit [pisɑ̃li] *nm* dandelion; **manger les ~s par la racine** *fig* to be pushing up daisies.

pisser [pise] [3] *fam* ◇ *vt* **-1.** [suj: personne]: **~ du sang** to pass blood. **-2.** [suj: plaie]: **son genou pissait le sang** blood was gushing from his knee. ◇ *vi* to pee, to piss.

pissotière [pisɔtjɛʀ] *nf fam* public urinal.

pistache [pistaʃ] ◇ *nf* [fruit] pistachio (nut). ◇ *adj inv* [couleur] pistachio (green).

piste [pist] *nf* **-1.** [trace] trail; **suivre/perdre une ~** to follow/to lose a trail; **brouiller les ~s** *fig* to cover one's tracks. **-2.** [zone aménagée]: **~ d'atterrissage** runway; **~ cyclable** cycle track; **~ de danse** dance floor; **~ de ski** ski run. **-3.** [chemin] path, track. **-4.** [d'enregistrement] track.

pister [piste] [3] *vt* [gibier] to track; [suspect] to tail.

pisteur [pistœʀ] *nm* ski patrol member.

pistil [pistil] *nm* pistil.

pistolet [pistɔlɛ] *nm* **-1.** [arme] pistol, gun. **-2.** [à peinture] spray gun.

pistolet-mitrailleur [pistɔlɛmitʀajœʀ] (*pl* **pistolets-mitrailleurs**) *nm* submachine gun.

piston [pistɔ̃] *nm* **-1.** [de moteur] piston. **-2.** MUS [d'instrument] valve. **-3.** *fig* [appui] string-pulling; **avoir du ~** to have friends in the right places.

pistonner [pistɔne] [3] *vt* to pull strings for; **se faire ~** to have strings pulled for one.

pistou [pistu] *nm dish of vegetables served with sauce made from basil.*

pitance [pitɑ̃s] *nf péj & vieilli* sustenance.

piteux, -euse [pitø, øz] *adj* piteous.

pitié [pitje] *nf* pity; **avoir ~ de qqn** to have pity on sb, to pity sb; **sans ~** pitiless, ruthless; **par ~** for pity's sake.

piton [pitɔ̃] *nm* **-1.** [clou] piton. **-2.** [pic] peak.

pitoyable [pitwajabl] *adj* pitiful.

pitre [pitʀ] *nm* clown; **faire le ~** to fool about.

pitrerie [pitʀəʀi] *nf* tomfoolery.

pittoresque [pitɔʀɛsk] ◇ *nm*: **le ~** [de description] the vividness; [d'histoire] the amusing part. ◇ *adj* **-1.** [région] picturesque. **-2.** [détail] colorful *Am*, colourful *Br*, vivid.

pivert, pic-vert (*pl* **pic-verts**) [pivɛʀ] *nm* green woodpecker.

pivoine [pivwan] *nf* peony.

pivot [pivo] *nm* **-1.** [de machine, au basket] pivot. **-2.** [de dent] post. **-3.** [centre] *fig* mainspring.

pivotant, -e [pivɔtɑ̃, ɑ̃t] *adj* [fauteuil] swivel (*avant n*).

pivoter [pivɔte] [3] *vi* to pivot; [porte] to revolve; **faire ~ qqch** to swivel sthg around, to pivot sthg.

pizza [pidza] *nf* pizza.

pizzeria [pidzeʀja] *nf* pizzeria.

PJ ◇ *nf* (*abr de* **police judiciaire**) ≃ FBI *Am*, ≃ CID *Br*. ◇ (*abr de* **pièces jointes**) Encl.

Pl., pl. *abr de* **place**.

PL (*abr de* **poids lourd**) HGV.

placage [plakaʒ] *nm* [de bois] veneer.

placard [plakaʀ] *nm* **-1.** [armoire] cupboard; **mettre qqn au ~** *fam fig* to elbow sb out; **mettre qqch au ~** *fam fig* to shelve sthg. **-2.** [affiche] poster, notice. **-3.** TYPO galley (proof).

placarder [plakaʀde] [3] *vt* [affiche] to put up, to stick up; [mur] to placard, to stick a notice on.

place [plas] *nf* **-1.** [espace] space, room; **prendre de la ~** to take up (a lot of) space; **faire ~ à** [amour, haine] to give way to. **-2.** [emplacement, position] position; **changer qqch de ~** to put sthg in a different place, to move sthg; **prendre la ~ de qqn** to take sb's place; **ne pas tenir** OU **rester en ~** to be unable to stay still; **à la ~ de qqn** instead of sb, in sb's place; **à ta ~** if I were you, in your place. **-3.** [siège] seat; **céder sa ~ à qqn** to give up one's seat to sb; **prendre ~** to take a seat; **~ assise** seat. **-4.** [rang] place. **-5.** [de ville] square. **-6.** [emploi] position, job; **perdre sa ~** to lose one's job. **-7.** COMM market. **-8.** MIL [de garnison] garrison (town); **~ forte** fortified town. **-9.** *loc*: **se mettre à la ~ de qqn** to put o.s. in sb's place OU shoes; **remettre qqn à sa ~** to put sb in his/her place.

placebo [plasebo] *nm* placebo.

placement [plasmɑ̃] *nm* **-1.** [d'argent] investment. **-2.** [d'employé] placing.

placenta [plasɛ̃ta] *nm* ANAT placenta.

placer [plase] [16] *vt* **-1.** [gén] to put, to place; [invités, spectateurs] to seat; **être bien/mal placé** to have a good/bad seat; **être bien/mal placé pour faire qqch** *fig* to be in a position/in no position to do sthg; **être haut placé** *fig* to be highly placed. **-2.** [mot, anecdote] to put in, to get in. **-3.** [argent] to invest.
◆ **se placer** *vp* **-1.** [prendre place - debout] to stand; [- assis] to sit (down). **-2.** *fig* [dans situation] to put o.s. **-3.** [se classer] to come, to be.

placide [plasid] *adj* placid.

placidité [plasidite] *nf* placidity.

plafond [plafɔ̃] *nm litt* & *fig* ceiling; **faux ~** false ceiling.

plafonner [plafɔne] [3] ◇ *vt* to put a ceiling in. ◇ *vi* [prix, élève] to peak; [avion] to reach its ceiling.

plafonnier [plafɔnje] *nm* ceiling light.

plage [plaʒ] *nf* **-1.** [de sable] beach. **-2.** [ville balnéaire] resort. **-3.** [d'ombre, de prix] band; *fig* [de temps] slot. **-4.** [de disque] track. **-5.** [dans voiture]: **~ arrière** back shelf.

plagiaire [plaʒjɛr] *nmf* plagiarist.

plagiat [plaʒja] *nm* plagiarism.

plagier [plaʒje] [9] *vt* to plagiarize.

plagiste [plaʒist] *nm* beach attendant.

plaid [plɛd] *nm* car rug.

plaider [plede] [4] JUR ◇ *vt* to plead. ◇ *vi* to plead; **~ contre qqn** to plead against sb; **~ pour qqn** JUR to plead for sb; [justifier] to plead sb's cause.

plaideur, -euse [plɛdœr, øz] *nm, f* litigant.

plaidoirie [plɛdwari] *nf*, **plaidoyer** [plɛdwaje] *nm* JUR speech for the defense *Am* OU defence *Br*; *fig* plea.

plaie [plɛ] *nf* **-1.** *litt* & *fig* wound. **-2.** *fam* [personne] pest.

plaignais, plaignions *etc* → **plaindre**.

plaignant, -e [plɛɲɑ̃, ɑ̃t] JUR ◇ *adj* litigant (avant n). ◇ *nm, f* plaintiff.

plaindre [plɛ̃dr] [80] *vt* to pity; **ne pas être à ~** to be not to be pitied.
◆ **se plaindre** *vp* to complain; **se ~ de** [souffrir de] to complain of; [être mécontent de] to complain about.

plaine [plɛn] *nf* plain.

plain-pied [plɛ̃pje]
◆ **de plain-pied** *loc adv* **-1.** [pièce] on one floor; **de ~ avec** *litt* & *fig* on a level with. **-2.** *fig* [directement] straight.

plaint, -e [plɛ̃, plɛ̃t] *pp* → **plaindre**.

plainte [plɛ̃t] *nf* **-1.** [gémissement] moan, groan; *fig* & *litt* [du vent] moan. **-2.** [doléance & JUR] complaint; **porter ~** to lodge a complaint; **retirer sa ~** JUR to withdraw one's action OU suit; **~ contre X** ≃ complaint against person or persons unknown.

plaintif, -ive [plɛ̃tif, iv] *adj* plaintive.

plaire [plɛr] [110] *vi* to be liked; **il me plaît** I like him; **ça te plairait d'aller au cinéma?** would you like to go to the cinema?; **s'il vous/te plaît** please.
◆ **se plaire** *vp* **-1.** [s'aimer] to get on well together. **-2.** [prendre plaisir]: **se ~ à faire qqch** to take pleasure in doing sthg; **se ~ avec qqn** to enjoy being with sb; **se ~ à Paris** to enjoy being in Paris.

plaisance [plɛzɑ̃s]
◆ **de plaisance** *loc adj* sailing (avant n); **navigation de ~** sailing; **port de ~** marina.

plaisancier, -ière [plɛzɑ̃sje, jɛr] *nm, f* (amateur) sailor.

plaisant, -e [plɛzɑ̃, ɑ̃t] *adj* pleasant.
◆ **mauvais plaisant** *nm péj* hoaxer.

plaisanter [plɛzɑ̃te] [3] ◇ *vi* to joke; **~ avec qqch** to joke about sthg; **ne pas ~ avec** OU **sur qqch** to take sthg seriously; **tu plaisantes?** you must be joking! ◇ *vt sout* [personne] to tease.

plaisanterie [plɛzɑ̃tri] *nf* joke; **c'est une ~?** *iron* you must be joking!; **c'était une ~** *fig* it was child's play.

plaisantin [plɛzɑ̃tɛ̃] *nm* joker.

plaise → **plaire**.

plaisir [plezir] *nm* pleasure; **les ~s de la vie** life's pleasures; **avoir du/prendre ~ à faire qqch** to have/to take pleasure in doing sthg; **faire ~ à qqn** to please sb; **avec ~** with pleasure; **j'ai le ~ de vous annoncer que ...** I have the (great) pleasure of announcing that ...; **pour le** OU **son ~** for pleasure; **prendre un malin ~ à faire qqch** to take a malicious pleasure in doing sthg; **se faire un ~ de faire qqch** to be only too pleased to do sthg.

plan¹, -e [plɑ̃, plan] *adj* level, flat.

plan² [plɑ̃] *nm* **-1.** [dessin - de ville] map; [- de maison] plan. **-2.** [projet] plan; **faire des ~s** to make plans; **avoir son ~** to have something in mind. **-3.** [domaine]: **sur tous les ~s** in all respects; **sur le ~ affectif** emotionally; **sur le ~ familial** as far as the family is concerned. **-4.** [surface]: **~ d'eau** lake; **~ de travail** work surface, worktop. **-5.** GÉOM plane. **-6.** CINÉMA take; **gros ~** close-up.
◆ **à l'arrière-plan** *loc adv* in the background.

◆ **au premier plan** *loc adv* **-1.** [dans l'espace] in the foreground. **-2.** [dans un ordre]: **c'est au premier ~ de nos préoccupations** it's our chief concern, it's uppermost in our minds.

◆ **de tout premier plan** *loc adj* exceptional.

◆ **en plan** *loc adv*: **laisser qqn en ~** to leave sb stranded, to abandon sb; **il a tout laissé en ~** he dropped everything.

◆ **sur le même plan** *loc adj & loc adv* on the same level.

planche [plɑ̃ʃ] *nf* **-1.** [en bois] plank; **~ à dessin** drawing board; **~ à neige** snowboard; **~ à repasser** ironing board; **~ de salut** *fig* mainstay; **~ à voile** [planche] sailboard; [sport] windsurfing; **faire la ~** *fig* to float. **-2.** [d'illustration] plate.

◆ **planches** *nfpl* **-1.** *fig* THÉÂTRE boards; **monter sur les ~s** to go on the stage. **-2.** *fam* [skis] skis.

plancher[1] [plɑ̃ʃe] *nm* **-1.** [de maison, de voiture] floor; **débarrasser le ~** *fam fig* to clear off. **-2.** *fig* [limite] floor, lower limit.

plancher[2] [plɑ̃ʃe] [3] *vi* **-1.** *arg scol* to be given a test. **-2.** *fam fig* [travailler]: **~ (sur)** to work hard (at).

planchiste [plɑ̃ʃist] *nmf* windsurfer.

plancton [plɑ̃ktɔ̃] *nm* plankton.

planer [plane] [3] *vi* **-1.** [avion, oiseau] to glide. **-2.** [nuage, fumée, brouillard] to float. **-3.** *fig* [danger]: **~ sur qqn** to hang over sb. **-4.** *fam fig* [personne] to be out of touch with reality, to have one's head in the clouds; **~ au-dessus de qqch** to be above sthg.

planétaire [planetɛr] *adj* **-1.** ASTRON planetary. **-2.** [mondial] world (*avant n*).

planétarium [planetarjɔm] *nm* planetarium.

planète [planɛt] *nf* planet.

planeur [plancœr] *nm* glider.

planificateur, -trice [planifikatœr, tris] ◇ *adj* planning (*avant n*). ◇ *nm, f* planner.

planification [planifikasjɔ̃] *nf* ÉCON planning.

planifier [planifje] [9] *vt* ÉCON to plan.

planisphère [planisfɛr] *nm* map of the world, planisphere.

planning [planiŋ] *nm* **-1.** [de fabrication] workflow schedule. **-2.** [agenda personnel] schedule; **~ familial** [contrôle] family planning; [organisme] family planning clinic.

planque [plɑ̃k] *nf fam* **-1.** [cachette] hideout. **-2.** *fig* [situation, travail] cushy number.

planquer [plɑ̃ke] [3] *vt fam* to hide.
◆ **se planquer** *vp fam* to hide.

plant [plɑ̃] *nm* **-1.** [plante] seedling. **-2.** [culture] bed, patch.

plantain [plɑ̃tɛ̃] *nm* plantain.

plantaire [plɑ̃tɛr] *adj* plantar.

plantation [plɑ̃tasjɔ̃] *nf* **-1.** [exploitation - d'arbres, de coton, de café] plantation; [- de légumes] patch. **-2.** [action] planting.

plante [plɑ̃t] *nf* **-1.** BOT plant; **~s médicinales** medicinal herbs; **~ verte** OU **d'appartement** OU **d'intérieur** house OU pot plant. **-2.** ANAT sole.

planté, -e [plɑ̃te] *adj fam* **-1.** [personne]: **rester ~** to be rooted to the spot. **-2.** [machine] broken-down.

planter [plɑ̃te] [3] *vt* **-1.** [arbre, terrain] to plant; **~ qqch de qqch** to plant sthg with sthg. **-2.** [clou] to hammer in, to drive in; [pieu] to drive in; [couteau, griffes] to stick in. **-3.** [tente] to pitch. **-4.** *fam fig* [laisser tomber] to dump; **tout ~ là** to drop everything. **-5.** *fig* [chapeau] to stick; [baiser] to plant; **~ son regard dans celui de qqn** to look sb right in the eyes.

◆ **se planter** *vp* **-1.** [se camper] to plant o.s. **-2.** *fam* [tomber] to go flying; [en voiture] to have a prang. **-3.** *fam* [se tromper] to be wrong.

planteur [plɑ̃tœr, øz] *nm* planter.

planton [plɑ̃tɔ̃] *nm* orderly.

plantureux, -euse [plɑ̃tyrø, øz] *adj* **-1.** [repas] lavish. **-2.** [femme] buxom. **-3.** [terre] fertile.

plaque [plak] *nf* **-1.** [de métal, de verre, de verglas] sheet; [de marbre] slab; **~ chauffante** OU **de cuisson** hotplate; **~ de chocolat** bar of chocolate. **-2.** [gravée] plaque; **~ d'immatriculation** OU **minéralogique** license plate *Am*, number plate *Br*. **-3.** [insigne] badge. **-4.** [sur la peau] patch. **-5.** [dentaire] plaque. **-6.** *loc*: **être à côté de la ~** to be wide of the mark.

◆ **plaque tournante** *nf* RAIL turntable; *fig* hub.

plaqué, -e [plake] *adj* **-1.** [métal] plated; **~ or/argent** gold-/silver-plated. **-2.** [bois] veneered.

◆ **plaqué** *nm* **-1.** [métal]: **du ~ or/argent** gold/silver plate. **-2.** [bois] veneered wood.

plaquer [plake] [3] *vt* **-1.** [métal] to plate. **-2.** [bois] to veneer. **-3.** [aplatir] to flatten; **~ qqn contre qqch** to pin sb against sthg; **~ qqch contre qqch** to stick sthg onto sthg. **-4.** RUGBY to tackle. **-5.** MUS [accord] to play. **-6.** *fam* [travail, personne] to chuck.

◆ **se plaquer** *vp*: **se ~ contre qqch** to flatten o.s. against sthg; **se ~ au sol** to lie flat on the ground; **se ~ les cheveux** to flatten (down) one's hair.

plaquette [plakɛt] *nf* **-1.** [de métal] plaque; [de marbre] **tablet. -2.** [de chocolat] bar; [de beurre] pat. **-3.** [de comprimés] packet, strip. **-4.** (*gén pl*) BIOL platelet. **-5.** [petit livre] slim volume. **-6.** AUTOM: **~ de frein** brake pad.

plasma [plasma] *nm* plasma.

plastic [plastik] *nm* plastic explosive.

plasticage [plastikaʒ] *nm* [de coffre] blowing; **un ~ de la banque** a bomb attack on the bank.

plastifier [plastifje] [9] *vt* to coat with plastic, to plastic-coat.

plastique [plastik] ◇ *adj & nm* plastic. ◇ *nf* **-1.** [en sculpture] art of modelling. **-2.** [beauté] form. **-3.** [arts] plastic arts (*pl*).

plastiquer [plastike] [3] *vt* to blow up (*with plastic explosives*).

plastron [plastrɔ̃] *nm* [de chemise] shirt front.

plastronner [plastrɔne] [3] *vi* [parader] to swagger.

plat, -e [pla, plat] *adj* **-1.** [gén] flat. **-2.** [eau] still.
◆ **plat** *nm* **-1.** [partie plate] flat. **-2.** [récipient] dish; **mettre les petits ~s dans les grands** *fig* to go to town. **-3.** [mets] course; **~ cuisiné** ready-cooked meal OU dish; **~ du jour** today's special; **~ de résistance** main course; **en faire tout un ~** *fig* to make a song and dance about it. **-4.** [plongeon] belly-flop.
◆ **à plat** *loc adv* **-1.** [horizontalement, dégonflé] flat. **-2.** *fam* [épuisé] exhausted.

platane [platan] *nm* plane tree.

plateau, -x [plato] *nm* **-1.** [de cuisine] tray; **~ de/à fromages** cheese board. **-2.** [de balance] pan. **-3.** GÉOGR & *fig* plateau. **-4.** THÉÂTRE **stage**; CIN & TÉLÉ set. **-5.** [de vélo] chain wheel.

plateau-repas [platorəpa] (*pl* **plateaux-repas**) *nm* tray (of food).

plate-bande [platbɑ̃d] (*pl* **plates-bandes**) *nf* flower bed.

platée [plate] *nf* dishful, plateful.

plate-forme [platfɔrm] (*pl* **plates-formes**) *nf* **-1.** [gén] platform; **~ de forage** drilling platform. **-2.** GÉOGR shelf.

platement [platmɑ̃] *adv* **-1.** [sans imagination] dully. **-2.** [servilement] humbly.

platine [platin] ◇ *adj inv* platinum. ◇ *nm* [métal] platinum. ◇ *nf* [de tourne-disque] deck; **~ laser** OU **compact-disc** compact disc player.

platiné, -e [platine] *adj* platinum (*avant n*).

platitude [platityd] *nf* **-1.** [médiocrité] banality. **-2.** [propos sans intérêt] platitude; **débiter des ~s** to spout platitudes.

platonique [platɔnik] *adj* **-1.** [amour, amitié] platonic. **-2.** *littéraire* [protestation] ineffective.

plâtras [platra] *nm* [gravats] rubble.

plâtre [platr] *nm* **-1.** CONSTR & MÉD plaster; **essuyer les ~s** *fig* to be the first to suffer. **-2.** [sculpture] plaster cast. **-3.** *péj* [fromage]: **c'est du vrai ~** it's like sawdust.

plâtrer [platre] [3] *vt* **-1.** [mur] to plaster. **-2.** MÉD to put in plaster.

plâtrier [platrije] ◇ *nm* plasterer. ◇ *adj m*: **ouvrier ~** plasterer.

plausible [plozibl] *adj* plausible.

play-back [plɛbak] *nm inv* miming; **chanter en ~** to mime.

play-boy [plɛbɔj] (*pl* **play-boys**) *nm* playboy.

plèbe [plɛb] *nf* **-1.** *péj* [populace]: **la ~** the plebs (*pl*). **-2.** HIST: **la ~** the plebeians (*pl*).

plébéien, -ienne [plebejɛ̃, jɛn] *adj* plebeian.

plébiscite [plebisit] *nm* plebiscite.

plébisciter [plebisite] [3] *vt* **-1.** POLIT to elect by plebiscite. **-2.** [approuver] to endorse overwhelmingly.

pléiade [plejad] *nf* pleiad.

plein, -e [plɛ̃, plɛn] *adj* **-1.** [rempli, complet] full; **c'est la ~e forme** I am/they are *etc* in top form; **en ~e nuit** in the middle of the night; **en ~ air** in the open air; **~ à craquer** *fig* full to bursting. **-2.** [non creux] solid. **-3.** [femelle] pregnant. **-4.** *fam* [saoul] plastered.
◆ **plein** ◇ *adv fam*: **il a de l'encre ~ les doigts** he has ink all over his fingers; **~ de** lots of; **en ~ dans/sur qqch** right in/on sthg. ◇ *nm* **-1.** [de réservoir] full tank; **le ~, s'il vous plaît** fill her up please; **faire le ~** to fill up. **-2.** *loc*: **battre son ~** to be at its height.

pleinement [plɛnmɑ̃] *adv* fully, totally.

plein-temps [plɛ̃tɑ̃] (*pl* **pleins-temps**) *nm* full-time work (*U*).

plénier, -ière [plenje, jɛr] *adj* plenary.

plénipotentiaire [plenipɔtɑ̃sjɛr] *nm & adj* plenipotentiary.

plénitude [plenityd] *nf* fullness.

pléonasme [pleɔnasm] *nm* pleonasm.

pléthorique [pletɔrik] *adj sout* [classe] overfull.

pleurer [plœre] [5] ◇ *vi* **-1.** [larmoyer] to cry; **~ de joie** to weep for joy, to cry with joy. **-2.** *péj* [se plaindre] to whinge. **-3.** [réclamer]: ~ **après** to cry for. **-4.** [se lamenter]: ~ **sur** to lament. ◇ *vt* to mourn.

pleurésie [plœrezi] *nf* pleurisy.

pleureur, -euse [plœrœr, øz] ◇ *adj* whining. ◇ *nm, f* whinger.

◆ **pleureuse** *nf* professional mourner.

pleurnicher [plœrniʃe] [3] *vi* to whine, to whinge.

pleurnicheur, -euse [plœrniʃœr, øz] ◇ *adj* whining, whingeing. ◇ *nm, f* whinger.

pleurs [plœr] *nmpl*: **être en ~s** to be in tears.

pleut → **pleuvoir**.

pleutre [pløtr] *littéraire* ◇ *nm* coward. ◇ *adj* cowardly.

pleuvoir [pløvwar] [68] *v impers litt* & *fig* to rain; **il pleut** it is raining.

Plexiglas® [plɛksiglas] *nm* Plexiglass®.

plexus [plɛksys] *nm* plexus; ~ **solaire** solar plexus.

pli [pli] *nm* **-1.** [de tissu] pleat; [de pantalon] crease; **faux** ~ crease. **-2.** [forme] shape; **prendre le** ~ **(de faire qqch)** *fig* to get into the habit (of doing sthg). **-3.** [du front] line; [du cou] fold. **-4.** [lettre] letter; [enveloppe] envelope; **sous** ~ **séparé** under separate cover. **-5.** CARTES trick. **-6.** GÉOL fold.

pliable [plijabl] *adj* pliable.

pliant, -e [plijã, ãt] *adj* folding (*avant n*).

◆ **pliant** *nm* folding chair.

plier [plije] [10] ◇ *vt* **-1.** [papier, tissu] to fold. **-2.** [vêtement, vélo] to fold (up). **-3.** [branche, bras] to bend. **-4.** *fig* [personne]: ~ **qqn à sa volonté** to bend sb to one's will; ~ **qqn à la discipline** to impose discipline on sb. ◇ *vi* **-1.** [se courber] to bend. **-2.** [céder] to bow.

◆ **se plier** *vp* **-1.** [être pliable] to fold (up). **-2.** *fig* [se soumettre]: **se ~ à qqch** to bow to sthg.

plinthe [plɛ̃t] *nf* plinth.

plissé, -e [plise] *adj* **-1.** [jupe] pleated. **-2.** [peau] wrinkled.

◆ **plissé** *nm* pleats (*pl*), pleating.

plissement [plismã] *nm* **-1.** [de front] creasing; [d'yeux] screwing up. **-2.** GÉOL fold.

plisser [plise] [3] ◇ *vt* **-1.** COUTURE to pleat. **-2.** [front] to crease; [lèvres] to pucker; [yeux] to screw up. ◇ *vi* [étoffe] to crease.

◆ **se plisser** *vp* **-1.** [étoffe] to crease. **-2.** [front] to crease.

pliure [plijyr] *nf* **-1.** [de tissu, de papier] fold. **-2.** [d'articulation] crook.

plomb [plɔ̃] *nm* **-1.** [métal, de vitrail] lead. **-2.** [de chasse] shot; **avoir du ~ dans l'aile** *fig* to be in a bad way. **-3.** ÉLECTR fuse; **les ~s ont sauté** a fuse has blown OU gone. **-4.** [de pêche] sinker.

plombage [plɔ̃baʒ] *nm* **-1.** *fam* [de dent] filling. **-2.** [de ligne] weighting (with lead).

plombé, -e [plɔ̃be] *adj* **-1.** [dent] filled. **-2.** [ligne] weighted (with lead). **-3.** [teinte] leaden.

plomber [plɔ̃be] [3] *vt* **-1.** [ligne] to weight (with lead). **-2.** [dent] to fill.

◆ **se plomber** *vp* [ciel] to become leaden.

plomberie [plɔ̃bri] *nf* plumbing.

plombier [plɔ̃bje] *nm* plumber.

plonge [plɔ̃ʒ] *nf* dishwashing; **faire la** ~ to wash dishes.

plongeant, -e [plɔ̃ʒã, ãt] *adj* **-1.** [vue] from above. **-2.** [décolleté] plunging.

plongée [plɔ̃ʒe] *nf* **-1.** [immersion] diving. **-2.** CIN & PHOT high-angle shot.

plongeoir [plɔ̃ʒwar] *nm* diving board.

plongeon [plɔ̃ʒɔ̃] *nm* [dans l'eau, au football] dive; **faire un** ~ to plunge; **faire le** ~ *fig* to hit rock bottom.

plonger [plɔ̃ʒe] [17] ◇ *vt* **-1.** [immerger, enfoncer] to plunge; ~ **la tête sous l'eau** to put one's head under the water. **-2.** *fig* [précipiter]: ~ **qqn dans qqch** to throw sb into sthg; ~ **une pièce dans l'obscurité** to plunge a room into darkness. ◇ *vi* **-1.** [dans l'eau, gardien de but] to dive. **-2.** [avion, oiseau]: ~ **sur** to dive (down) onto. **-3.** *fig* [se lancer] to dive OU jump in.

◆ **se plonger** *vp* **-1.** [s'immerger] to submerge. **-2.** *fig* [s'absorber]: **se ~ dans qqch** to immerse o.s. in sthg.

plongeur, -euse [plɔ̃ʒœr, øz] *nm, f* **-1.** [dans l'eau] diver. **-2.** [dans restaurant] dishwasher.

plot [plo] *nm* ÉLECTR contact.

plouc [pluk] *nmf* & *adj fam péj* country bumpkin.

plouf [pluf] *interj* splash!

ployer [plwaje] [13] *vt* & *vi litt* & *fig* to bend.

plu [ply] ◇ *pp inv* → **plaire**. ◇ *pp inv* → **pleuvoir**.

pluie [plɥi] *nf* **-1.** [averse] rain (*U*); **sous la** ~ in the rain; **une** ~ **battante** driving rain; **des ~s diluviennes** torrential rain; **il fait la** ~ **et le beau temps** *fig* what he says goes; **ne pas être né de la dernière** ~ *fig* not to be born yesterday. **-2.** *fig* [grande quantité]: **une ~ de** a shower of.

plumage [plymaʒ] *nm* plumage.

plumard [plymar] *nm fam* bed, sack *Am*.

plume [plym] ◇ *nf* **-1.** [d'oiseau] feather; **y laisser/perdre des ~s** *fig* to come off badly.

-2. [pour écrire - d'oiseau] quill pen; [- de stylo] nib; **un homme de ~** *fig* a man of letters. ◇ *nm fam* [plumard] bed, sack *Am*.

plumeau, -x [plymo] *nm* feather duster.

plumer [plyme] [3] *vt* **-1.** [volaille] to pluck. **-2.** *fam fig* & *péj* [personne] to fleece.

plumier [plymje] *nm* pencil box.

plupart [plypar] *nf*: **la ~ de** most of, the majority of; **la ~ du temps** most of the time, mostly; **pour la ~** mostly, for the most part.

pluralisme [plyralism] *nm* pluralism.

pluralité [plyralite] *nf* plurality.

pluridimensionnel, -elle [plyridimɑ̃sjɔnɛl] *adj* multidimensional.

pluridisciplinaire [plyridisiplinɛr] *adj* multidisciplinary.

pluriel, -ielle [plyrjɛl] *adj* **-1.** GRAM plural. **-2.** [société] pluralist.
◆ **pluriel** *nm* plural; **au ~** in the plural.

plus [ply(s)] ◇ *adv* **-1.** [quantité] more; **je ne peux vous en dire ~** I can't tell you anything more; **il a ~ de travail cette année** he has more work this year; **il en veut ~** he wants more (of it/them); **beaucoup ~ de** (+ *n sg*) a lot more, much more; (+ *n pl*) a lot more, many more; **un peu ~ de** (+ *n sg*) a little more; (+ *n pl*) a few more; **il y a (un peu) ~ de 15 ans** (a little) more than 15 years ago; **~ j'y pense, ~ je me dis que ...** the more I think about it, the more I'm sure .... **-2.** [comparaison] more; **c'est ~ court par là** it's shorter that way; **viens ~ souvent** come more often; **c'est un peu ~ loin** it's a (little) bit further; **~ jeune (que)** younger (than); **c'est ~ simple qu'on ne le croit** it's simpler than you think. **-3.** [superlatif]: **le ~** the most; **c'est lui qui travaille le ~** he's the hardest worker, he's the one who works (the) hardest; **un de ses tableaux les ~ connus** one of his best-known paintings; **le ~ souvent** the most often; **le ~ loin** the furthest; **le ~ souvent possible** as often as possible; **le ~ vite possible** as quickly as possible. **-4.** [négation] no more; **~ un mot!** not another word!; **ne ... ~** no longer, no more; **il n'a ~ d'amis** he no longer has any friends, he has no friends any more; **il ne vient ~ me voir** he doesn't come to see me any more, he no longer comes to see me.
◇ *nm* **-1.** [signe] plus (sign). **-2.** *fig* [atout] plus.
◇ *prép* plus; **trois ~ trois font six** three plus three is six, three and three are six.
◆ **au plus** *loc adv* at the most; **tout au ~** at the very most.

◆ **de plus** *loc adv* **-1.** [en supplément, en trop] more; **elle a cinq ans de ~ que moi** she's five years older than me. **-2.** [en outre] furthermore, what's more.
◆ **de plus en plus** *loc adv* more and more.
◆ **de plus en plus de** *loc prép* more and more.
◆ **en plus** *loc adv* **-1.** [en supplément] extra. **-2.** [d'ailleurs] moreover, what's more.
◆ **en plus de** *loc prép* in addition to.
◆ **ni plus ni moins** *loc adv* no more no less.
◆ **on ne peut plus** *loc adv*: **il est on ne peut ~ bête** he's as stupid as can be.
◆ **plus ou moins** *loc adv* more or less.
◆ **sans plus** *loc adv*: **elle est gentille, sans ~** she's nice, but no more than that.

plusieurs [plyzjœr] *adj indéf pl* & *pron indéf mfpl* several.

plus-que-parfait [plyskəparfɛ] *nm* GRAM pluperfect.

plus-value [plyvaly] (*pl* **plus-values**) *nf* **-1.** [d'investissement] appreciation. **-2.** [excédent] surplus. **-3.** [bénéfice] profit.

plutonium [plytɔnjɔm] *nm* plutonium.

plutôt [plyto] *adv* rather; **~ que de faire qqch** instead of doing sthg, rather than doing OU do sthg.

pluvial, -e, -iaux [plyvjal, jo] *adj*: **eau ~e** rainwater.

pluvieux, -ieuse [plyvjø, jøz] *adj* rainy.

pluviométrie [plyvjɔmetri] *nf* rainfall measurement.

pluviosité [plyvjozite] *nf* rainfall.

p.m. (*abr de* **pour mémoire**) p.m.

PM ◇ *nf* **-1.** (*abr de* **préparation militaire**) *training before military service*. **-2.** (*abr de* **police militaire**) MP. ◇ *nm abr de* **petit modèle**.

PMA ◇ *nf* (*abr de* **procréation médicalement assistée**) assisted reproduction. ◇ *nmpl* (*abr de* **pays les moins avancés**) LDCs.

PME (*abr de* **petite et moyenne entreprise**) *nf* SME.

PMI *nf* **-1.** (*abr de* **petite et moyenne industrie**) small industrial firm. **-2.** (*abr de* **protection maternelle et infantile**) *social service concerned with child welfare*.

PMU (*abr de* **Pari mutuel urbain**) *nm system for betting on horses*.

PNB (*abr de* **produit national brut**) *nm* GNP.

pneu, -x [pnø] *nm* **-1.** [de véhicule] tire *Am*, tyre *Br*; **~ avant** front tire *Am* OU tyre *Br*;

~ **arrière** rear tire *Am* OU tyre *Br*; ~ **à clous** studded tire *Am* OU tyre *Br*; ~ **d'hiver** winter tire *Am* OU tyre *Br*; ~ **quatre-saisons** all-season tire *Am* OU tyre *Br*. **-2.** *vieilli* [message] *letter sent by network of pneumatic tubes.*

pneumatique [pnømatik] ◇ *nf* PHYS pneumatics (*U*). ◇ *nm vieilli* **-1.** [d'un véhicule] tire *Am* OU tyre *Br*. **-2.** [message] *letter sent by network of pneumatic tubes.* ◇ *adj* **-1.** [fonctionnant à l'air] pneumatic. **-2.** [gonflé à l'air] inflatable.

pneumonie [pnømɔni] *nf* pneumonia.

PNUD, Pnud [pnyd] (*abr de* **Programme des Nations unies pour le développement**) *nm* UNDP.

PNUE, Pnue [pny] (*abr de* **Programme des Nations unies pour l'environnement**) *nm* UNEP.

PO (*abr de* **petites ondes**) MW.

poche [pɔʃ] *nf* **-1.** [de vêtement, de sac, d'air] pocket; **de** ~ pocket (*avant n*); ~ **revolver** back OU hip pocket; **c'est dans la** ~ *fig* it's in the bag; **faire les** ~**s de qqn** *fig* to go through sb's pockets; **s'en mettre plein se remplir les** ~**s** *fig* to make a packet. **-2.** [sac, sous les yeux] bag.

pocher [pɔʃe] [3] *vt* **-1.** CULIN to poach. **-2.** [blesser]: ~ **l'œil à qqn** to give sb a black eye.

pochette [pɔʃɛt] *nf* **-1.** [enveloppe] envelope; [d'allumettes] book; [de photos] packet. **-2.** [de disque] sleeve. **-3.** [mouchoir] (pocket) handkerchief.

pochette-surprise [pɔʃɛtsyrpriz] (*pl* **pochettes-surprises**) *nf* lucky bag.

pochoir [pɔʃwar] *nm* stencil.

podium [pɔdjɔm] *nm* podium.

podologue [pɔdɔlɔg] *nmf* chiropodist, podiatrist *Am*.

poêle [pwal] ◇ *nf* pan; ~ **à frire** frying pan. ◇ *nm* stove.

poêlée [pwale] *nf* panful.

poêlon [pwalɔ̃] *nm* casserole.

poème [pɔɛm] *nm* poem.

poésie [pɔezi] *nf* **-1.** [genre, émotion] poetry. **-2.** [pièce écrite] poem.

poète [pɔɛt] ◇ *adj* poetic. ◇ *nm* **-1.** [écrivain] poet. **-2.** *fig & hum* [rêveur] dreamer.

poétique [pɔetik] *adj* poetic.

poétiquement [pɔetikmɑ̃] *adv* poetically.

pognon [pɔɲɔ̃] *nm tfam* dosh.

pogrom(e) [pɔgrɔm] *nm* pogrom.

poids [pwa] *nm* **-1.** [gén] weight; **quel** ~ **fait-il?** how heavy is it/he?; **perdre/prendre du** ~ to lose/gain weight; **vendre au** ~ to sell by weight; **avoir du** ~ *fig* to carry a lot of weight; **donner du** ~ **à** *fig* to lend

weight to; ~ **lourd** BOXE heavyweight; [camion] heavy goods vehicle; ~ **plume** BOXE featherweight; **de** ~ [argument] weighty; **il ne fait pas le** ~ *fig* he's not up to it. **-2.** SPORT [lancer] shot.

poignant, -e [pwaɲɑ̃, ɑ̃t] *adj* poignant.

poignard [pwaɲar] *nm* dagger.

poignarder [pwaɲarde] [3] *vt* to stab.

poigne [pwaɲ] *nf* grip; *fig* authority; **avoir de la** ~ to have a strong grip; *fig* to have authority.

poignée [pwaɲe] *nf* **-1.** [quantité, petit nombre] handful. **-2.** [manche] handle.

◆ **poignée de main** *nf* handshake.

poignet [pwaɲɛ] *nm* **-1.** ANAT wrist. **-2.** [de vêtement] cuff.

poil [pwal] *nm* **-1.** [du corps] hair; **à** ~ *fam* [tout nu] starkers. **-2.** [d'animal] hair, coat; **de tout** ~ *fig* of all kinds. **-3.** [de pinceau] bristle; [de tapis] strand. **-4.** *fam* [peu]: **il s'en est fallu d'un** ~ **que je réussisse** I came within a hair's breadth of succeeding. **-5.** *loc*: **être de bon/mauvais** ~ *fam fig* to be in a good/bad mood; **reprendre du** ~ **de la bête** *fig* to regain strength.

poil-de-carotte [pwaldəkarɔt] *adj inv fam* [personne] red-headed; [cheveux] carroty.

poiler [pwale] [3]

◆ **se poiler** *vp fam* to kill o.s. (laughing).

poilu, -e [pwaly] *adj* hairy.

◆ **poilu** *nm fam* French First World War soldier.

poinçon [pwɛ̃sɔ̃] *nm* **-1.** [outil] awl. **-2.** [marque] hallmark.

poinçonner [pwɛ̃sɔne] [3] *vt* **-1.** [bijou] to hallmark. **-2.** [billet, tôle] to punch.

poinçonneuse [pwɛ̃sɔnøz] *nf* punch.

poindre [pwɛ̃dr] [82] *vi littéraire* **-1.** [jour] to break. **-2.** [plante] to come up. **-3.** *fig* [sentiment] to break through.

poing [pwɛ̃] *nm* fist; **dormir à** ~**s fermés** *fig* to sleep like a log.

point [pwɛ̃] ◇ *nm* **-1.** COUTURE & TRICOT stitch; ~**s de suture** MÉD stitches. **-2.** [de ponctuation]: ~ (**final**) period *Am,* full stop *Br*; ~ **d'interrogation/d'exclamation** question/exclamation mark; ~**s de suspension** suspension points; **mettre les** ~**s sur les i** *fig* to get things straight. **-3.** [petite tache] dot; ~ **noir** [sur la peau] blackhead; *fig* [problème] problem. **-4.** [endroit] spot, point; *fig* point; ~ **d'appui** [support] something to lean on; ~ **chaud** POLIT key issue; [zone dangereuse] trouble spot, hot spot; ~ **culminant** [en montagne] summit; *fig* climax; ~ **d'eau** water supply point; ~ **de mire** *fig* focal point; ~ **névralgique** *fig* sensitive spot; ~

de **ralliement** rallying point; ~ **de repère** [temporel] reference point; [spatial] landmark; ~ **de vente** point of sale, sale outlet; ~ **de vue** [panorama] viewpoint; *fig* [opinion, aspect] point of view; **avoir un ~ commun avec qqn** to have something in common with sb. **-5.** [degré] point; **au ~ que, à tel ~ que** to such an extent that; **je ne pensais pas que cela le vexerait à ce ~** I didn't think it would make him so cross; **être ... au ~ de faire qqch** to be so ... as to do sthg. **-6.** *fig* [position] position; **faire le ~** to take stock (of the situation). **-7.** [réglage]: **mettre au ~** [machine] to adjust; [idée, projet] to finalize; **à ~** [cuisson] just right; **à ~ (nommé)** just in time. **-8.** [question, détail] point, detail; **faible ~** weak point. **-9.** [score] point; **marquer un ~** SPORT & *fig* to score a point. **-10.** [douleur] pain; ~ **de côté** stitch. **-11.** [début]: **être sur le ~ de faire qqch** to be on the point of doing sthg, to be about to do sthg; **au ~ du jour** *sout* at daybreak. **-12.** AUTOM: **au ~ mort** in neutral. **-13.** GÉOGR: ~**s cardinaux** points of the compass.
◇ *adv vieilli*: **ne** ~ not (at all); **ne vous en faites** ~ don't worry.

pointage [pwɛtaʒ] *nm* **-1.** [au travail - d'entrée] clocking in; [- de sortie] clocking out. **-2.** [d'arme] aiming.

pointe [pwɛt] *nf* **-1.** [extrémité] point; [de nez] tip; **se hausser sur la ~ des pieds** to stand on tiptoe; **en ~** pointed; **tailler en ~** to taper; **se terminer en ~** to taper; ~ **d'asperge** asparagus tip. **-2.** [clou] tack. **-3.** [sommet] peak, summit; **à la ~ de** *fig* at the peak of; **à la ~ de la technique** at the forefront OU leading edge of technology. **-4.** [accélération]: **faire** OU **pousser une ~ (jusqu'à)** to put on a spurt (and reach). **-5.** *fig* [trait d'esprit] witticism. **-6.** *fig* [petite quantité]: **une ~ de** a touch of.
◆ **pointes** *nfpl* DANSE points; **faire des** OU **les ~s** to dance on one's points.
◆ **de pointe** *loc adj* **-1.** [maximum] maximum, top. **-2.** [novateur] leading-edge.

pointer [pwɛte] [3] ◇ *vt* **-1.** [cocher] to tick (off). **-2.** [employés - à l'entrée] to check in; [- à la sortie] to check out. **-3.** [diriger]: ~ **qqch vers** to point sthg toward *Am* OU towards *Br*; ~ **qqch sur** to point sthg at. ◇ *vi* **-1.** [à l'usine - à l'entrée] to clock in; [- à la sortie] to clock out. **-2.** [à la pétanque] to get as close to the jack as possible. **-3.** [être en pointe] to stick up. **-4.** [jour] to break. **-5.** *fig* [sentiment] to show through.
◆ **se pointer** *vp fam* to turn up.

pointillé [pwɛtije] *nm* **-1.** [ligne] dotted line; **en ~** [ligne] dotted; *fig* [par sous-entendus] obliquely. **-2.** [perforations] perforations (*pl*).

pointilleux, -euse [pwɛtijø, øz] *adj*: ~ **(sur)** particular (about).

pointu, -e [pwɛty] *adj* **-1.** [objet] pointed. **-2.** [voix, ton] sharp; **-3.** [étude, formation] specialized.

pointure [pwɛtyr] *nf* size.

point-virgule [pwɛvirgyl] (*pl* **points-virgules**) *nm* semi-colon.

poire [pwar] ◇ *nf* **-1.** [fruit] pear; ~ **Belle-Hélène** pear OU poire Belle-Hélène; **couper la ~ en deux** *fig* to compromise. **-2.** MÉD: ~ **à injections** syringe. **-3.** *fam* [visage] face. **-4.** *fam* [naïf] dope. ◇ *adj fam*: **être ~** to be a sucker OU a mug *Br*.

poireau, -x [pwaro] *nm* leek; ~**x vinaigrette** leeks with vinaigrette dressing.

poireauter, poiroter [pwarote] [3] *vi fam* to hang around.

poirier [pwarje] *nm* pear tree; **faire le ~** *fig* to do a headstand.

poiroter = **poireauter**.

pois [pwa] *nm* **-1.** BOT pea; ~ **chiche** chickpea; **petits ~** garden peas, petits pois; ~ **de senteur** sweet pea. **-2.** *fig* [motif] dot, spot; **à ~** spotted, polka-dot.

poison [pwazɔ̃] ◇ *nm* [substance] poison. ◇ *nmf fam fig* [personne] drag, pain; [enfant] brat.

poisse [pwas] *nf fam* bad luck; **porter la ~** to be bad luck.

poisseux, -euse [pwasø, øz] *adj* sticky.

poisson [pwasɔ̃] *nm* fish; ~ **d'avril** [farce] April fool; [en papier] *paper fish pinned to someone's back as a prank on April Fools' Day*; ~**-chat** catfish; ~ **rouge** goldfish; **noyer le ~** *fig* to confuse the issue.
◆ **Poissons** *nmpl* ASTROL Pisces (*sg*); **être Poissons** to be (a) Pisces.

poissonnerie [pwasɔnri] *nf* **-1.** [boutique] fish shop, fishmonger's (shop). **-2.** [métier] fish trade.

poissonneux, -euse [pwasɔnø, øz] *adj* full of fish.

poissonnier, -ière [pwasɔnje, jɛr] *nm, f* fishmonger.

poitevin, -e [pwatvɛ̃, in] *adj* [de Poitiers] of/from Poitiers; [du Poitou] of/from Poitou.
◆ **Poitevin, -e** *nm, f* [de Poitiers] person from Poitiers; [du Poitou] person from Poitou.

poitrail [pwatraj] *nm* breast, chest.

poitrinaire [pwatrinɛr] *nmf & adj* consumptive.

poitrine [pwatrin] *nf* **-1.** [thorax] chest; [de femme] chest, bust. **-2.** [viande] breast.

poivre [pwavr] *nm* pepper; ~ **blanc** white pepper; ~ **gris**, ~ **noir** black pepper; ~ **et sel** *fig* pepper-and-salt.

poivrer [pwavre] [3] *vt* to put pepper on.

poivrière [pwavrijɛr] *nf* pepperbox *Am*, pepper pot *Br*.

poivron [pwavrɔ̃] *nm* pepper, capsicum; ~ **rouge/vert** red/green pepper.

poivrot, -e [pwavro, ɔt] *nm, f fam* boozer.

poix [pwa] *nf* pitch.

poker [pɔkɛr] *nm* poker.

polaire [pɔlɛr] *adj* polar.

polar [pɔlar] *nm fam* thriller, whodunnit.

polariser [pɔlarize] [3] *vt* **-1.** TECHNOL to polarize. **-2.** *fig* [attention] to focus.
◆ **se polariser** *vp*: **se** ~ **sur** to be centred OU focussed on.

Polaroïd® [pɔlarɔid] *nm* Polaroid®.

polder [pɔldɛr] *nm* polder.

pôle [pol] *nm* pole; ~ **Nord/Sud** North/South Pole.

polémique [pɔlemik] ◇ *nf* controversy. ◇ *adj* [style, ton] polemical.

polémiquer [pɔlemike] [3] *vi* to engage in controversy.

poli, -e [pɔli] *adj* **-1.** [personne] polite. **-2.** [surface] polished.
◆ **poli** *nm* polish.

police [pɔlis] *nf* **-1.** [force de l'ordre] police; **être de** OU **dans la** ~ to be in the police; ~ **judiciaire** ≃ FBI *Am*, ≃ CID *Br*; ~ **secours** *emergency service provided by the police*; ~ **secrète** secret police. **-2.** [contrat] policy; ~ **d'assurance** insurance policy. **-3.** TYPO: ~ **(de caractères)** font.

policé, -e [pɔlise] *adj littéraire* civilized.

polichinelle [pɔliʃinɛl] *nm* **-1.** [personnage] Punch; **secret de** ~ *fig* open secret. **-2.** *fam fig* [guignol] buffoon.

policier, -ière [pɔlisje, jɛr] *adj* **-1.** [de la police] police (*avant n*). **-2.** [film, roman] detective (*avant n*).
◆ **policier** *nm* police officer.

policlinique [pɔliklinik] *nf* [partie d'hôpital] ≃ outpatients department.

poliment [pɔlimɑ̃] *adv* politely.

polio [pɔljo] *nf* polio.

poliomyélite [pɔljɔmjelit] *nf* poliomyelitis.

polir [pɔlir] [32] *vt* to polish.

polissage [pɔlisaʒ] *nm* polishing.

polisson, -onne [pɔlisɔ̃, ɔn] ◇ *adj* **-1.** [chanson, propos] lewd, suggestive. **-2.** [en-fant] naughty. ◇ *nm, f* [enfant] naughty child.

politesse [pɔlitɛs] *nf* **-1.** [courtoisie] politeness. **-2.** [action] polite action; **se faire des** ~**s** *iron* to exchange favours.

politicard, -e [pɔlitikar, ard] *péj* ◇ *adj* politicking. ◇ *nm, f* (political) schemer, politico.

politicien, -ienne [pɔlitisjɛ̃, jɛn] ◇ *adj péj* politicking, politically unscrupulous. ◇ *nm, f* politician, politico.

politique [pɔlitik] ◇ *nf* **-1.** [de gouvernement, de personne] policy; ~ **étrangère/intérieure** foreign/domestic policy; **pratiquer la** ~ **de l'autruche** *fig* to bury one's head in the sand. **-2.** [affaires publiques] politics (*U*). ◇ *nm* politician. ◇ *adj* **-1.** [pouvoir, théorie] political. **-2.** *littéraire* [choix, réponse] politic.

politiquement [pɔlitikmɑ̃] *adv* politically.

politisation [pɔlitizasjɔ̃] *nf* politicization.

politiser [pɔlitize] [3] *vt* to politicize.

politologue [pɔlitɔlɔg] *nmf* political expert OU analyst.

polka [pɔlka] *nf* polka.

pollen [pɔlɛn] *nm* pollen.

polluant [pɔlɥɑ̃] *nm* pollutant.

polluer [pɔlɥe] [7] *vt* to pollute.

pollution [pɔlysjɔ̃] *nf* pollution.

polo [pɔlo] *nm* **-1.** [sport] polo. **-2.** [chemise] polo shirt.

polochon [pɔlɔʃɔ̃] *nm fam* bolster.

Pologne [pɔlɔɲ] *nf*: **la** ~ Poland.

polonais, -e [pɔlɔnɛ, ɛz] *adj* Polish.
◆ **polonais** *nm* [langue] Polish.
◆ **polonaise** *nf* **-1.** [danse] polonaise. **-2.** [gâteau] *brioche with an almond filling covered in meringue*.
◆ **Polonais, -e** *nm, f* Pole.

poltron, -onne [pɔltrɔ̃, ɔn] ◇ *nm, f* coward. ◇ *adj* cowardly.

polyamide [pɔliamid] *nm* polyamide.

polychrome [pɔlikrom] *adj* polychrome, polychromatic.

polyclinique [pɔliklinik] *nf* general hospital.

polycopie [pɔlikɔpi] *nf* duplicating.

polycopié, -e [pɔlikɔpje] *adj* duplicate (*avant n*).
◆ **polycopié** *nm* duplicated lecture notes.

polycopier [pɔlikɔpje] [9] *vt* to duplicate.

polyculture [pɔlikyltyr] *nf* mixed farming.

polyester [pɔliɛstɛr] *nm* polyester.

polygame [pɔligam] ◇ *nm* polygamist. ◇ *adj* polygamous.

polygamie [pɔligami] *nf* polygamy.

polyglotte [pɔlyglɔt] *nmf & adj* polyglot.

polygone [pɔligɔn] *nm* **-1.** MATHS polygon. **-2.** MIL: ~ **de tir** rifle range.

polymère [pɔlimɛr] ◇ *nm* polymer. ◇ *adj* polymeric.

polymorphe [pɔlimɔrf] *adj* polymorphous.

Polynésie [pɔlinezi] *nf*: **la ~** Polynesia; **la ~ française** French Polynesia.

polynésien, -ienne [pɔlinezjɛ̃, jɛn] *adj* Polynesian.
◆ **polynésien** *nm* [langue] Polynesian.
◆ **Polynésien, -ienne** *nm, f* Polynesian.

polype [pɔlip] *nm* polyp.

polyphonie [pɔlifɔni] *nf* polyphony.

polysémique [pɔlisemik] *adj* polysemous, polysemic.

polystyrène [pɔlistirɛn] *nm* polystyrene.

polytechnicien, -ienne [pɔliteknisjɛ̃, jɛn] *nm, f student or ex-student of the École Polytechnique.*

Polytechnique [pɔliteknik] *n*: **l'École ~** *prestigious grande école for engineers.*

POLYTECHNIQUE:

This prestigious engineering college in Palaiseau near Paris has close connections with the Ministry of Defence. It is popularly known as 'l'X'

polythéisme [pɔliteism] *nm* polytheism.

polythéiste [pɔliteist] ◇ *nmf* polytheist. ◇ *adj* polytheistic.

polyvalent, -e [pɔlivalɑ̃, ɑ̃t] *adj* **-1.** [salle] multi-purpose. **-2.** [professeur] non-specialized. **-3.** CHIM & MÉD polyvalent. **-4.** [personne] versatile.
◆ **polyvalent** *nm tax inspector specializing in company taxation.*

pomélo [pɔmelo] *nm* grapefruit.

pommade [pɔmad] *nf* [médicament] ointment.

pommader [pɔmade] [3] *vt* to pomade.

pomme [pɔm] *nf* **-1.** [fruit] apple; ~ **de pin** pine OU fir cone. **-2.** [pomme de terre]: ~**s allumettes** *very thin chips*; ~**s frites** (French) fries *Am,* chips *Br;* ~**s vapeur** steamed potatoes. **-3.** *loc:* ~ **de discorde** bone of contention; **tomber dans les** ~**s** *fam* to pass out, to faint.
◆ **pomme d'Adam** *nf* Adam's apple.

pommeau, -x [pɔmo] *nm* **-1.** [de parapluie, de canne] knob. **-2.** [de sabre] pommel.

pomme de terre [pɔmdətɛr] *nf* potato; ~**s de terre à l'eau** boiled potatoes; ~**s de terre au four** baked potatoes; ~**s de terre**

frites (French) fries *Am,* chips *Br;* ~**s de terre en robe des champs** jacket potatoes; ~**s de terre sautées** sauté potatoes.

pommelé, -e [pɔmle] *adj* dappled; **gris ~** dapple gray *Am* OU grey *Br.*

pommette [pɔmɛt] *nf* cheekbone.

pommier [pɔmje] *nm* apple tree.

pompe [pɔ̃p] *nf* **-1.** [appareil] pump; ~ **à essence** gas pump *Am,* petrol pump *Br;* ~ **à incendie** fire truck *Am,* fire engine *Br.* **-2.** [magnificence] pomp, ceremony; **en grande ~** with great ceremony. **-3.** *fam* [chaussure] shoe; **être à côté de ses** ~**s** *fam fig* to be completely out of it.
◆ **pompes funèbres** *nfpl* undertaker's (*sg*), mortician's (*sg*) *Am,* funeral director's (*sg*) *Br.*

Pompéi [pɔ̃pei] *n* Pompeii.

pomper [pɔ̃pe] [3] *vt* **-1.** [eau, air] to pump. **-2.** [avec éponge] to soak up. **-3.** *arg scol* [copier]: ~ **qqch (sur qqn)** to crib sthg (from sb).

pompette [pɔ̃pɛt] *adj fam* merry, tipsy.

pompeusement [pɔ̃pøzmɑ̃] *adv* pompously.

pompeux, -euse [pɔ̃pø, øz] *adj* pompous.

pompier, -ière [pɔ̃pje, jɛr] *adj* pretentious.
◆ **pompier** *nm* fire fighter *Am,* fireman *Br.*

pompiste [pɔ̃pist] *nmf* gas *Am* OU petrol *Br* pump attendant.

pompon [pɔ̃pɔ̃] *nm* pompom; **décrocher le ~** *fam fig* to take the cake OU biscuit *Br.*

pomponner [pɔ̃pɔne] [3]
◆ **se pomponner** *vp* to get dressed up.

ponce [pɔ̃s] *adj*: **pierre ~** pumice (stone).

poncer [pɔ̃se] [16] *vt* [bois] to sand (down).

ponceuse [pɔ̃søz] *nf* sander, sanding machine.

poncif [pɔ̃sif] *nm* [banalité] commonplace, cliché.

ponction [pɔ̃ksjɔ̃] *nf* **-1.** [MÉD - lombaire] puncture; [pulmonaire] tapping. **-2.** *fig* [prélèvement] withdrawal.

ponctionner [pɔ̃ksjɔne] [3] *vt* **-1.** [MÉD - région lombaire] to puncture; [poumon] to tap. **-2.** *fig* [contribuable] to take money from; [argent] to withdraw.

ponctualité [pɔ̃ktɥalite] *nf* punctuality.

ponctuation [pɔ̃ktɥasjɔ̃] *nf* punctuation.

ponctuel, -elle [pɔ̃ktɥɛl] *adj* **-1.** [action] specific, selective. **-2.** [personne] punctual.

ponctuellement [pɔ̃ktɥɛlmɑ̃] *adv* punctually.

ponctuer [pɔ̃ktɥe] [7] *vt* to punctuate; ~ **qqch de qqch** *fig* to punctuate sthg with sthg.

pondéral, -e, -aux [pɔ̃deral, o] *adj* weight (*avant n*).

pondération [pɔ̃derasjɔ̃] *nf* **-1.** [de personne] level-headedness. **-2.** ÉCON weighting.

pondéré, -e [pɔ̃dere] *adj* **-1.** [personne] level-headed. **-2.** ÉCON weighted.

Pondichéry [pɔ̃diʃeri] *n* Pondicherry.

pondre [pɔ̃dr] [75] *vt* **-1.** [œufs] to lay. **-2.** *fam fig* [projet, texte] to produce.

pondu, -e [pɔ̃dy] *pp* → **pondre**.

poney [pɔnɛ] *nm* pony.

pongiste [pɔ̃ʒist] *nmf* table-tennis player.

pont [pɔ̃] *nm* **-1.** CONSTR bridge; ~s et chaussées ADMIN ≃ highways department. **-2.** [lien] link, connection; ~ aérien airlift; couper les ~s avec qqn *fig* to break with sb. **-3.** [congé] *day off granted by an employer to fill the gap between a national holiday and a weekend*; faire le ~ to have a long weekend. **-4.** [de navire] deck.

ponte [pɔ̃t] ◇ *nf* [action] laying; [œufs] clutch. ◇ *nm* **-1.** JEU punter. **-2.** *fam* [autorité] big shot.

pontife [pɔ̃tif] *nm* pontiff.

pontifical, -e, -aux [pɔ̃tifikal, o] *adj* papal.

pontificat [pɔ̃tifika] *nm* pontificate.

pontifier [pɔ̃tifje] [9] *vi fam* to pontificate.

pont-levis [pɔ̃ləvi] (*pl* **ponts-levis**) *nm* drawbridge.

ponton [pɔ̃tɔ̃] *nm* **-1.** [plate-forme] pontoon. **-2.** [chaland] lighter, barge.

pool [pul] *nm* pool.

pop [pɔp] ◇ *nm* pop. ◇ *adj* pop (*avant n*).

pop-corn [pɔpkɔrn] *nm inv* popcorn (U).

pope [pɔp] *nm* priest (*in the Orthodox church*).

popeline [pɔplin] *nf* poplin.

popote [pɔpɔt] *fam* ◇ *adj inv* homeloving. ◇ *nf*: faire la ~ to do the cooking; préparer la ~ to prepare the meal.

populace [pɔpylas] *nf péj* mob.

populaire [pɔpylɛr] *adj* **-1.** [du peuple - volonté] popular, of the people; [- quartier] working-class; [- art, chanson] folk. **-2.** [personne] popular.

populariser [pɔpylarize] [3] *vt* to popularize.

popularité [pɔpylarite] *nf* popularity.

population [pɔpylasjɔ̃] *nf* population; ~ active working population.

populiste [pɔpylist] *nmf & adj* populist.

populo [pɔpylo] *nm fam* **-1.** [peuple] hoi polloi. **-2.** [foule] crowd.

porc [pɔr] *nm* **-1.** [animal] pig, hog *Am*. **-2.**

fig & péj [personne] pig, swine. **-3.** [viande] pork. **-4.** [peau] pigskin.

porcelaine [pɔrsəlɛn] *nf* **-1.** [matière] china, porcelain. **-2.** [objet] piece of china OU porcelain. **-3.** [mollusque] cowrie shell.

porcelet [pɔrsəlɛ] *nm* piglet.

porc-épic [pɔrkepik] (*pl* **porcs-épics**) *nm* porcupine.

porche [pɔrʃ] *nm* porch.

porcherie [pɔrʃəri] *nf litt & fig* pigsty.

porcin, -e [pɔrsɛ̃, in] *adj* **-1.** [élevage] pig (*avant n*). **-2.** *fig & péj* [yeux] piggy.
◆ **porcin** *nm* pig.

pore [pɔr] *nm* pore.

poreux, -euse [pɔrø, øz] *adj* porous.

pornographie [pɔrnɔɡrafi] *nf* pornography.

pornographique [pɔrnɔɡrafik] *adj* pornographic.

porridge [pɔridʒ] *nm* porridge.

port [pɔr] *nm* **-1.** [lieu] port; arriver à bon ~ [personne] to arrive safe and sound; [chose] to arrive in good condition; ~ d'attache home port; ~ de commerce/pêche commercial/fishing port. **-2.** [fait de porter sur soi - d'objet] carrying; [- de vêtement, décoration] wearing; ~ d'armes carrying of weapons. **-3.** [transport] carriage; franco de ~ carriage paid. **-4.** [allure] bearing.

portable [pɔrtabl] ◇ *nm* [TV] portable; INFORM laptop, portable. ◇ *adj* **-1.** [vêtement] wearable. **-2.** [ordinateur, machine à écrire] portable, laptop.

portage [pɔrtaʒ] *nm Can* NAUT portage.

portail [pɔrtaj] *nm* portal.

portant, -e [pɔrtɑ̃, ɑ̃t] *adj*: être bien/mal ~ to be in good/poor health.
◆ **portant** *nm* upright.

portatif, -ive [pɔrtatif, iv] *adj* portable.

Port-au-Prince [pɔrɔprɛ̃s] *n* Port-au-Prince.

porte [pɔrt] *nf* **-1.** [de maison, voiture] door; claquer la ~ to slam the door; claquer/fermer la ~ au nez de qqn to slam/shut the door in sb's face; écouter aux ~s to listen at keyholes; être à la ~ to be locked out; ficher OU foutre qqn à la ~ *fam* to throw OU chuck sb out; mettre qqn à la ~ to throw sb out; ~ cochère carriage entrance; ~ de communication communicating door; ~ d'entrée front door; ~ de secours emergency exit; ~ vitrée glass door. **-2.** [AÉRON & SKI & de ville] gate; la ~ de Versailles *site of a large exhibition complex in Paris where major trade fairs take place*.

porte-à-faux [pɔrtafo] *nm inv* [roche] overhang; CONSTR cantilever; en ~ overhanging;

CONSTR cantilevered; *fig* in a delicate situation.

porte-à-porte [pɔrtapɔrt] *nm inv*: **faire du ~** to sell from door to door.

porte-avions [pɔrtavjɔ̃] *nm inv* aircraft carrier.

porte-bagages [pɔrtbagaʒ] *nm inv* luggage rack; [de voiture] roof rack.

porte-bébé [pɔrtbebe] (*pl* **porte-bébés**) *nm* baby sling, papoose.

porte-bonheur [pɔrtbɔnœr] *nm inv* lucky charm.

porte-bouteilles [pɔrtbutɛj] *nm inv* [casier] wine rack.

porte-cartes, **porte-carte** [pɔrtəkart] *nm inv* card holder.

porte-cigarettes [pɔrtsigarɛt] *nm inv* cigarette case.

porte-clefs, **porte-clés** [pɔrtəkle] *nm inv* keyring.

porte-couteau [pɔrtkuto] (*pl* **porte-couteaux**) *nm* knife-rest.

porte-documents [pɔrtdɔkymɑ̃] *nm inv* attaché OU document case.

porte-drapeau [pɔrtdrapo] (*pl* **porte-drapeaux**) *nm* standard-bearer.

portée [pɔrte] *nf* **-1.** [de missile] range; **à ~ de** within range of; **à ~ de main** within reach; **à ~ de voix** within earshot; **à ~ de vue** in sight; **à la ~ de qqn** *fig* within sb's reach; **hors de la ~ de** out of reach of. **-2.** [d'événement] impact, significance. **-3.** MUS stave, staff. **-4.** [de femelle] litter.

porte-fenêtre [pɔrtfənɛtr] (*pl* **portes-fenêtres**) *nf* French window OU door *Am*.

portefeuille [pɔrtəfœj] *nm* **-1.** [pour billets] wallet. **-2.** FIN & POLIT portfolio.

porte-jarretelles [pɔrtʒartɛl] *nm inv* garter belt *Am*, suspender belt *Br*.

porte-malheur [pɔrtmalœr] *nm inv* jinx.

portemanteau, -x [pɔrtmɑ̃to] *nm* [au mur] coat-rack; [sur pied] coat stand.

portemine, **porte-mine** (*pl* **porte-mine** OU **porte-mines**) [pɔrtəmin] *nm* propelling pencil.

porte-monnaie [pɔrtmɔnɛ] *nm inv* purse.

porte-parapluies [pɔrtparaplɥi] *nm inv* umbrella stand.

porte-parole [pɔrtparɔl] *nm inv* spokesman (*f* spokeswoman); **~ officiel du gouvernement** official government spokesman.

porte-plume [pɔrtəplym] *nm inv* penholder.

porter [pɔrte] [3] ◇ *vt* **-1.** [gén] to carry. **-2.** [vêtement, lunettes, montre] to wear; [barbe] to have. **-3.** [nom, date, inscription] to bear. **-4.** [apporter] to take. **-5.** [inciter] **~ qqn à**

faire qqch to lead sb to do sthg. **-6.** [inscrire] to put down, to write down; **porté disparu** reported missing.

◇ *vi* **-1.** [s'appuyer - balcon]: **~ sur** to be supported by. **-2.** [traiter]: **~ sur qqn/qqch** to be about sb/sthg. **-3.** [remarque] to strike home. **-4.** [voix, tir] to carry.

◆ **se porter** ◇ *vp* **-1.** [se sentir]: **se ~ bien/mal** to be well/unwell. **-2.** [se diriger]: **se ~ sur** [choix, regard] to fall on; [conversation] to turn to. **-3.** [se livrer]: **se ~ à** [violences] to carry out; **se ~ à des extrémités** to go to extremes. ◇ *v attr*: **se ~ garant de qqch** to guarantee sthg, to vouch for sthg; **se ~ candidat à** to run for *Am*, to stand for election to *Br*.

porte-savon [pɔrtsavɔ̃] (*pl inv* OU **porte-savons**) *nm* soap dish.

porte-serviettes [pɔrtsɛrvjɛt] *nm inv* towel rail.

porteur, -euse [pɔrtœr, øz] ◇ *adj*: **marché ~** COMM growth market; **mère porteuse** surrogate mother; **mur ~** load-bearing wall. ◇ *nm, f* **-1.** [de message, nouvelle] bringer, bearer. **-2.** [de bagages] porter. **-3.** [détenteur - de papiers, d'actions] holder; [- de chèque] bearer. **-4.** [de maladie] carrier.

porte-voix [pɔrtəvwa] *nm inv* megaphone, loud-hailer, bullhorn *Am*.

portier [pɔrtje] *nm* commissionaire.

portière [pɔrtjer] *nf* [de voiture, train] door.

portillon [pɔrtijɔ̃] *nm* barrier, gate.

portion [pɔrsjɔ̃] *nf* **-1.** [de gâteau] portion, helping. **-2.** [d'héritage] portion, part; **être réduit à la ~ congrue** *fig* to get the smallest share.

portique [pɔrtik] *nm* **-1.** ARCHIT portico. **-2.** SPORT crossbeam (*for hanging apparatus*).

Port-Louis [pɔrlwi] *n* Port Louis.

porto [pɔrto] *nm* port.

Porto-Novo [pɔrtonovo] *n* Porto Novo.

portoricain, -e [pɔrtɔrikɛ̃, ɛn] *adj* Puerto Rican.

◆ **Portoricain, -e** *nm, f* Puerto Rican.

Porto Rico [pɔrtoriko], **Puerto Rico** [pwɛrtoriko] *n* Puerto Rico.

portrait [pɔrtrɛ] *nm* portrait; PHOT photograph; **être tout le ~ de qqn** *fig* to be the spitting OU very image of sb; **faire le ~ de qqn** *fig* to describe sb.

portraitiste [pɔrtretist] *nmf* portrait painter.

portrait-robot [pɔrtrɛrobo] (*pl* **portraits-robots**) *nm* Photofit® picture, Identikit® picture.

portuaire [pɔrtɥɛr] *adj* port (*avant n*), harbor (*avant n*) *Am*, harbour (*avant n*) *Br*.

portugais, -e [pɔrtygɛ, ɛz] *adj* Portuguese.
◆ **portugais** *nm* [langue] Portuguese.
◆ **Portugais, -e** *nm, f* Portuguese (person); **les Portugais** the Portuguese.

Portugal [pɔrtygal] *nm*: **le ~** Portugal; **au ~** in Portugal.

POS, Pos [pɔs] (*abr de* **plan d'occupation des sols**) *nm land use scheme.*

pose [poz] *nf* **-1.** [de pierre, moquette] laying; [de papier peint, rideaux] hanging. **-2.** [position] pose; **prendre la ~** to pose. **-3.** PHOT exposure.

posé, -e [poze] *adj* sober, steady.

posément [pozemɑ̃] *adv* calmly.

poser [poze] [3] ◇ *vt* **-1.** [mettre] to put down; **~ qqch sur qqch** to put sthg on sthg. **-2.** [installer - rideaux, papier peint] to hang; [- étagère] to put up; [- moquette, carrelage] to lay. **-3.** [affirmer] to lay down, to set out. **-4.** [donner à résoudre - problème, difficulté] to pose; **~ une question** to ask a question; **~ sa candidature** to apply; POLIT to stand for election.
◇ *vi* to pose.
◆ **se poser** *vp* **-1.** [oiseau, avion] to land. **-2.** *fig* [choix, regard]: **se ~ sur** to fall on. **-3.** [question, problème] to arise, to come up. **-4.** [personne]: **se ~ en** to pose as.

poseur, -euse [pozœr, øz] *nm, f vieilli* show-off, poser.

positif, -ive [pozitif, iv] *adj* positive.

position [pozisjɔ̃] *nf* position; **prendre ~** *fig* to take up a position, to take a stand.

positionnement [pozisjɔnmɑ̃] *nm* positioning.

positionner [pozisjɔne] [3] *vt* to position.
◆ **se positionner** *vp* to position o.s.

positivement [pozitivmɑ̃] *adv* positively.

posologie [pozɔlɔʒi] *nf* dosage.

possédant, -e [pɔsedɑ̃, ɑ̃t] ◇ *adj* property-owning (*avant n*). ◇ *nm, f person from the property-owning classes.*

possédé, -e [pɔsede] ◇ *adj* possessed. ◇ *nm, f* person possessed.

posséder [pɔsede] [18] *vt* **-1.** [détenir - voiture, maison] to possess, to own; [- diplôme] to have; [- capacités, connaissances] to possess, to have. **-2.** [langue, art] to have mastered. **-3.** *fam* [personne] to have.

possesseur [pɔsesœr] *nm* **-1.** [de bien] possessor, owner. **-2.** [de secret, diplôme] holder.

possessif, -ive [pɔsesif, iv] *adj* possessive.
◆ **possessif** *nm* GRAM possessive.

possession [pɔsesjɔ̃] *nf* **-1.** [gén] possession; **être en ma/ta** *etc* **~** to be in my/your *etc* possession; **prendre ~ de** to take possession of; **être en ~ de** to be in possession of; **~ de soi** self-possession, composure. **-2.** [de langue] knowledge, command.

possibilité [pɔsibilite] *nf* **-1.** [gén] possibility. **-2.** [moyen] chance, opportunity.
◆ **possibilités** *nfpl* [capacités] potential (*sg*).

possible [pɔsibl] ◇ *adj* possible; **c'est/ce n'est pas ~** that's possible/impossible; **dès que** OU **aussitôt que ~** as soon as possible. ◇ *nm*: **faire tout son ~** to do one's utmost, to do everything possible; **dans la mesure du ~** as far as possible.

postal, -e, -aux [pɔstal, o] *adj* postal.

postdater [pɔstdate] [3] *vt* to postdate.

poste [pɔst] ◇ *nf* **-1.** [service] mail *Am*, post *Br*; **envoyer/recevoir qqch par la ~** to send/receive sthg by post; **~ aérienne** airmail. **-2.** [bureau] post office; **~ centrale** central post office; **~ restante** general delivery *Am*, poste restante *Br*. ◇ *nm* **-1.** [emplacement] post; **~ de police** police station; **~ de secours** first-aid post; **être fidèle au ~** *fig* to stay at one's post. **-2.** [emploi] position, post. **-3.** [appareil]: **~ émetteur** transmitter; **~ de radio** radio; **~ de télévision** television (set). **-4.** TÉLÉCOM extension.

poster¹ [pɔstɛr] *nm* poster.

poster² [pɔste] [3] *vt* **-1.** [lettre] to mail *Am*, to post *Br*. **-2.** [sentinelle] to post.
◆ **se poster** *vp* to position o.s., to station o.s.

postérieur, -e [pɔsterjœr] *adj* **-1.** [date] later, subsequent. **-2.** [membre] hind (*avant n*), back (*avant n*).
◆ **postérieur** *nm hum* posterior.

postérieurement [pɔsterjœrmɑ̃] *adv* subsequently.

posteriori [pɔsterjɔri]
◆ **a posteriori** *loc adv* a posteriori.

postérité [pɔsterite] *nf* **-1.** [générations à venir] posterity. **-2.** *littéraire* [descendance] descendants (*pl*).

postface [pɔstfas] *nf* postscript.

posthume [pɔstym] *adj* posthumous.

postiche [pɔstiʃ] ◇ *nm* hairpiece. ◇ *adj* false.

postier, -ière [pɔstje, jɛr] *nm, f* post-office worker.

postillon [pɔstijɔ̃] *nm* [salive] droplet of saliva.

postillonner [pɔstijɔne] [3] *vi* to splutter.

postindustriel, **-ielle** [pɔstɛ̃dystrijɛl] *adj* post-industrial.

postmoderne [pɔstmɔdɛrn] *adj* postmodern.

postnatal, **-e** [pɔstnatal] (*pl* **postnatals** OU **postnataux** [pɔstnato]) *adj* postnatal.

postopératoire [pɔstɔperatwar] *adj* post-operative.

post-scriptum [pɔstskriptɔm] *nm inv* post-script.

postsynchronisation [pɔstsɛ̃krɔnizasjɔ̃] *nf* dubbing.

postulant, **-e** [pɔstylɑ̃, ɑ̃t] *nm, f* **-1.** [pour emploi] applicant. **-2.** RELIG postulant.

postuler [pɔstyle] [3] *vt* **-1.** [emploi] to apply for. **-2.** PHILO to postulate.

posture [pɔstyr] *nf* posture; **être** OU **se trouver en mauvaise ~** *fig* to be in a difficult position.

pot [po] *nm* **-1.** [récipient] pot, jar; [à eau, à lait] jug; **~ de chambre** chamber pot; **~ de fleurs** flowerpot; **découvrir le ~ aux roses** to get to the bottom of something; **tourner autour du ~** *fam* to beat about the bush. **-2.** AUTOM: **~ catalytique** catalytic convertor; **~ d'échappement** exhaust (pipe); [silencieux] muffler *Am*, silencer *Br*. **-3.** *fam* [boisson] drink; **boire** OU **prendre un ~** to have a drink. **-4.** *fam* [chance]: **avoir du/manquer de ~** to be lucky/unlucky.

potable [pɔtabl] *adj* **-1.** [liquide] drinkable; **eau ~** drinking water. **-2.** *fam* [travail] acceptable.

potache [pɔtaʃ] *nm fam* schoolkid.

potage [pɔtaʒ] *nm* soup; **~ aux légumes** vegetable soup.

potager, **-ère** [pɔtaʒe, ɛr] *adj*: **jardin ~** vegetable garden; **plante potagère** vegetable.

◆ **potager** *nm* vegetable garden.

potasse [pɔtas] *nf* potash.

potasser [pɔtase] [3] *vt fam* [cours] to bone up on *Am*, to swot up *Br*; [examen] to bone up for *Am*, to swot up for *Br*.

potassium [pɔtasjɔm] *nm* potassium.

pot-au-feu [pɔtofø] *nm inv* **-1.** [plat] *boiled beef with vegetables*. **-2.** [viande] ≃ piece of stewbeef *Am* OU stewing steak *Br*.

pot-de-vin [podvɛ̃] (*pl* **pots-de-vin**) *nm* bribe.

pote [pɔt] *nm fam* buddy *Am*, mate *Br*.

poteau, **-x** [pɔto] *nm* post; **~ de but** goalpost; **~ indicateur** signpost; **~ télégraphique** telegraph pole; **coiffer qqn au ~** to pip sb at the post.

potée [pɔte] *nf pot-au-feu made with salt pork*.

potelé, **-e** [pɔtle] *adj* plump, chubby.

potence [pɔtɑ̃s] *nf* **-1.** CONSTR bracket. **-2.** [de pendaison] gallows (*sg*).

potentat [pɔtɑ̃ta] *nm* potentate.

potentiel, **-ielle** [pɔtɑ̃sjɛl] *adj* potential.

◆ **potentiel** *nm* potential.

potentiellement [pɔtɑ̃sjɛlmɑ̃] *adv* potentially.

poterie [pɔtri] *nf* **-1.** [art] pottery. **-2.** [objet] piece of pottery.

potiche [pɔtiʃ] *nf* **-1.** [vase] vase. **-2.** *fam* [personne] figurehead.

potier, **-ière** [pɔtje, jɛr] *nm, f* potter.

potin [pɔtɛ̃] *nm fam* [bruit] din.

◆ **potins** *nmpl fam* [ragots] gossip (*U*).

potion [posjɔ̃] *nf* potion.

potiron [pɔtirɔ̃] *nm* pumpkin.

pot-pourri [popuri] (*pl* **pots-pourris**) *nm* potpourri.

pou, **-x** [pu] *nm* louse.

pouah [pwa] *interj* ugh!

poubelle [pubɛl] *nf* trashcan *Am*, dustbin *Br*.

pouce [pus] *nm* **-1.** [de main] thumb; [de pied] big toe; **sucer son ~** to suck one's thumb; **manger sur le ~** to grab something to eat. **-2.** [mesure] inch; **ne pas bouger/céder d'un ~** not to move/give an inch.

poudre [pudr] *nf* powder; **prendre la ~ d'escampette** to make off.

poudrerie [pudrəri] *nf Can* snowdrift.

poudreux, **-euse** [pudrø, øz] *adj* powdery.

◆ **poudreuse** *nf* powder (snow).

poudrier [pudrije] *nm* **-1.** [boîte] powder compact. **-2.** [fabricant] explosives manufacturer.

poudre [pudrwaje] [13] *vi littéraire* to rise (up) in clouds.

pouf [puf] ◇ *nm* pouffe. ◇ *interj* thud!

pouffer [pufe] [3] *vi*: **~ (de rire)** to snigger.

pouilleux, **-euse** [pujø, øz] ◇ *adj* **-1.** [personne, animal] flea-ridden. **-2.** [endroit] squalid. ◇ *nm, f* **-1.** [couvert de poux] person with fleas. **-2.** [misérable] down-and-out.

poulailler [pulaje] *nm* **-1.** [de ferme] henhouse. **-2.** *fam* THÉÂTRE gods (*sg*).

poulain [pulɛ̃] *nm* foal; *fig* protégé.

poulamon [pulamɔ̃] *nm Can* tomcod.

poularde [pulard] *nf* fattened chicken.

poule [pul] *nf* **-1.** ZOOL hen; **la ~ aux œufs d'or** the goose that lays the golden egg; **~ mouillée** wimp, wet. **-2.** *fam péj* [femme] broad *Am*, bird *Br*. **-3.** SPORT [compétition] round robin; RUGBY [groupe] pool.

poulet [pulɛ] *nm* **-1.** ZOOL chicken; ~ **rôti** roast chicken; ~ **de grain** corn-fed chicken. **-2.** *fam* [policier] cop.

poulette [pulɛt] *nf* **-1.** ZOOL pullet. **-2.** *fam péj* [fille] broad *Am,* bird *Br.*

pouliche [puliʃ] *nf* filly.

poulie [puli] *nf* pulley.

poulpe [pulp] *nm* octopus.

pouls [pu] *nm* pulse.

poumon [pumɔ̃] *nm* lung; **à pleins** ~**s** deeply.

poupe [pup] *nf* stern.

poupée [pupe] *nf* **-1.** [jouet] doll. **-2.** [pansement] finger bandage.

poupin, -e [pupɛ̃, in] *adj* chubby.

poupon [pupɔ̃] *nm* **-1.** [bébé] little baby. **-2.** [jouet] baby doll.

pouponner [pupɔne] [3] *vi* to play mother.

pouponnière [pupɔnjɛr] *nf* nursery.

pour [pur] ⬦ *prép* **-1.** [gén] for. **-2.** (+ *infinitif*): ~ **faire** in order to do, (so as) to do; **je suis venu** ~ **vous voir** I've come to see you; ~ **m'avoir aidé** for having helped me, for helping me. **-3.** [indique un rapport] for; **avancé** ~ **son âge** advanced for his/her age; ~ **moi** for my part, as far as I'm concerned; ~ **ce qui est de** as regards, with regard to. ⬦ *adv*: **je suis** ~ I'm (all) for it. ⬦ *nm*: **le** ~ **et le contre** the pros and cons (*pl*). ◆ **pour que** *loc conj* (+ *subjonctif*) so that, in order that.

pourboire [purbwar] *nm* tip.

pourceau, -x [purso] *nm littéraire* swine.

pourcentage [pursɑ̃taʒ] *nm* percentage.

pourfendeur, -euse [purfɑ̃dœr, øz] *nm, f littéraire*: ~ **d'abus** righter of wrongs.

pourparlers [purparle] *nmpl* talks.

pourpre [purpr] ⬦ *nf* **-1.** [colorant] purple (dye). **-2.** [couleur] purple. ⬦ *nm & adj* crimson.

pourquoi [purkwa] ⬦ *adv* why; ~ **pas?** why not?; **c'est** ~ ... that's why .... ⬦ *nm inv*: **le** ~ **(de)** the reason (for); **les** ~ the questions; **le** ~ **et le comment** the whys and wherefores.

pourrai, pourras *etc* → **pouvoir.**

pourri, -e [puri] *adj* **-1.** [fruit] rotten. **-2.** [personne, milieu] corrupt. **-3.** [enfant] spoiled rotten, ruined. ◆ **pourri** *nm* **-1.** [de fruit] rotten part. **-2.** *fam* [personne] creep.

pourrir [purir] [32] ⬦ *vt* **-1.** [matière, aliment] to rot, to spoil. **-2.** [enfant] to ruin, to spoil rotten. ⬦ *vi* [matière] to rot; [fruit, aliment] to go rotten OU bad.

pourriture [purityr] *nf* **-1.** [d'aliment] rot. **-2.** *fig* [de personne, de milieu] corruption. **-3.** *injurieux* [personne] bastard.

poursuis, poursuit *etc* → **poursuivre.**

poursuite [pursɥit] *nf* **-1.** [de personne] chase; **se lancer à la** ~ **de** to set off after. **-2.** [de négociations] continuation. ◆ **poursuites** *nfpl* JUR (legal) proceedings; **engager des** ~**s judiciaires** to take legal action.

poursuivant, -e [pursɥivɑ̃, ɑ̃t] *nm, f* pursuer.

poursuivi, -e [pursɥivi] *pp* → **poursuivre.**

poursuivre [pursɥivr] [89] ⬦ *vt* **-1.** [voleur] to pursue, to chase; [gibier] to hunt. **-2.** [rêve, vengeance] to pursue. **-3.** [enquête, travail] to carry on with, to continue. **-4.** JUR [criminel] to prosecute; [voisin] to sue. ⬦ *vi* to go on, to carry on.

pourtant [purtɑ̃] *adv* nevertheless, even so.

pourtour [purtur] *nm* perimeter.

pourvoi [purvwa] *nm* JUR appeal; **présenter un** ~ **en cassation** to take one's case to the Appeal Court.

pourvoir [purvwar] [64] ⬦ *vt*: ~ **qqn de** to provide sb with; ~ **qqch de** to equip OU fit sthg with. ⬦ *vi*: ~ **à** to provide for. ◆ **se pourvoir** *vp* **-1.** [se munir]: **se** ~ **de** to provide o.s. with. **-2.** JUR to appeal.

pourvoirie [purvwari] *nf Can* outfitter (*for hunting and fishing*).

pourvoyeur, -euse [purvwajœr, øz] *nm, f* supplier.

pourvu, -e [purvy] *pp* → **pourvoir.** ◆ **pourvu que** *loc conj* (+*subjonctif*) **-1.** [condition] providing, provided (that). **-2.** [souhait] let's hope (that).

pousse [pus] *nf* **-1.** [croissance] growth. **-2.** [bourgeon] shoot; ~**s de bambou** bamboo shoots.

poussé, -e [puse] *adj* **-1.** [travail] meticulous. **-2.** [moteur] souped-up.

pousse-café [puskafe] *nm inv fam* liqueur.

poussée [puse] *nf* **-1.** [pression] pressure. **-2.** [coup] push. **-3.** [de fièvre, inflation] rise.

pousse-pousse [puspus] *nm inv* **-1.** [voiture] rickshaw. **-2.** *Helv* [poussette] pushchair.

pousser [puse] [3] ⬦ *vt* **-1.** [personne, objet] to push; ~ **qqn à bout** *fig* to push sb to breaking point. **-2.** [moteur, voiture] to drive hard. **-3.** [recherches, études] to carry on, to continue. **-4.** [cri, soupir] to give. **-5.** [inciter]: ~ **qqn à faire qqch** to urge sb to do sthg. **-6.** [au crime, au suicide]: ~ **qqn à** to drive sb to.

◇ *vi* **-1.** [exercer une pression] to push. **-2.** [croître] to grow. **-3.** [poursuivre son chemin] to push on. **-4.** *fam* [exagérer] to overdo it.
◆ **se pousser** *vp* to move up.

poussette [pusɛt] *nf* pushchair.

poussière [pusjɛr] *nf* **-1.** [gén] dust; **mordre la ~** to bite the dust; **réduire en ~** to reduce to dust; **et des ~s** *fam* and a bit. **-2.** *littéraire* [de mort] ashes (*pl*).

poussiéreux, -euse [pusjɛrø, øz] *adj* **-1.** [meuble] dusty. **-2.** [teint] dull. **-3.** *fig* [organisation] old-fashioned.

poussif, -ive [pusif, iv] *adj fam* wheezy.

poussin [pusɛ̃] *nm* **-1.** ZOOL chick. **-2.** SPORT under-11.

poussoir [puswar] *nm* push button.

poutre [putr] *nf* beam.

poutrelle [putrɛl] *nf* girder.

pouvoir [puvwar] [58] ◇ *nm* **-1.** [gén] power; **~ d'achat** purchasing power; **les ~s publics** the authorities. **-2.** JUR proxy, power of attorney.
◇ *vt* **-1.** [avoir la possibilité de, parvenir à]: **~ faire qqch** to be able to do sthg; **je ne peux pas venir ce soir** I can't come tonight; **pouvez-vous ...?** can you ...?, could you ...?; **je n'en peux plus** [exaspéré] I'm at the end of my tether; [fatigué] I'm exhausted; **je/tu n'y peux rien** there's nothing I/you can do about it; **tu aurais pu me le dire!** you might have OU could have told me!; **il est on ne peut plus bête/gentil** nobody could be stupider/kinder. **-2.** [avoir la permission de]: **je peux prendre la voiture?** can I borrow the car?; **aucun élève ne peut partir** no pupil may leave. **-3.** [indiquant l'éventualité]: **il peut pleuvoir** it may rain; **vous pourriez rater votre train** you could OU might miss your train.
◆ **se pouvoir** *v impers*: **il se peut que je me trompe** I may be mistaken; **cela se peut/pourrait bien** that's quite possible.

pp (*abr de* **pages**) pp.

p.p. (*abr de* **par procuration**) pp.

PQ ◇ *nm* (*abr de* **papier-cul**) *fam* bog paper. ◇ **-1.** (*abr de* **province de Québec**) PQ. **-2.** (*abr de* **premier quartier (de lune)**) first quarter.

Pr (*abr de* **professeur**) Prof.

PR ◇ *nm* (*abr de* **Parti républicain**) *French political party*. ◇ *nf* (*abr de* **poste restante**) PR.

pragmatique [pragmatik] *adj* pragmatic.

pragois, -e, **praguois, -e** [pragwa, az] *adj* of/from Prague.
◆ **Pragois, -e**, **Praguois, -e** *nm, f* native OU inhabitant of Prague.

Prague [prag] *n* Prague.

praguois, -e = **pragois**.

praire [prɛr] *nf* clam.

prairie [preri] *nf* meadow; [aux États-Unis] prairie.

praline [pralin] *nf* **-1.** [amande] sugared almond. **-2.** *Belg* [chocolat] chocolate.

praliné [praline] *nm* almond-flavoured sponge *covered with praline.*

praticable [pratikabl] ◇ *adj* **-1.** [route] passable. **-2.** [plan] feasible, practicable. ◇ *nm* [CIN & THÉÂTRE - plate-forme] **(tray)** dolly; [- élément de décor] prop.

praticien, -ienne [pratisjɛ̃, jɛn] *nm, f* practitioner; MÉD medical practitioner.

pratiquant, -e [pratikɑ̃, ɑ̃t] ◇ *adj* practising. ◇ *nm, f* practising Christian/Jew/Muslim *etc.*

pratique [pratik] ◇ *nf* **-1.** [expérience] practical experience. **-2.** [usage] practice; **mettre qqch en ~** to put sthg into practice. ◇ *adj* [gadget, outil] handy.

pratiquement [pratikmɑ̃] *adv* **-1.** [en fait] in practice. **-2.** [quasiment] practically.

pratiquer [pratike] [3] ◇ *vt* **-1.** [métier] to practice *Am*, to practise *Br*; [méthode] to apply; **~ la pêche/le football** to be a keen fisherman/football player. **-2.** [ouverture] to make. ◇ *vi* RELIG to be a practising Christian/Jew/Muslim *etc.*
◆ **se pratiquer** *vp* **-1.** SPORT to be played. **-2.** [politique, tradition] to be the practice; [prix] to apply.

pré [pre] *nm* meadow.

préado [preado] *nmf fam* preadolescent.

préalable [prealabl] ◇ *adj* prior, previous; **~ à** prior to, preceding; **sans avis ~** without prior warning OU notice. ◇ *nm* precondition.
◆ **au préalable** *loc adv* first, beforehand.

préalablement [prealabləmɑ̃] *adv* first, beforehand; **~ à** prior to.

préambule [preɑ̃byl] *nm* **-1.** [introduction, propos] preamble; **sans ~** immediately. **-2.** [prélude]: **~ de** prelude to.

préau, -x [preo] *nm* **-1.** [d'école] (covered) play area. **-2.** [de prison] (covered) exercise yard.

préavis [preavi] *nm inv* advance notice OU warning.

précaire [prekɛr] *adj* [incertain] precarious.

précancéreux, -euse [prekɑ̃serø, øz] *adj* precancerous.

précarité [prekarite] *nf* [instabilité] precariousness.

précaution [prekosjɔ̃] *nf* **-1.** [prévoyance] precaution; **par** ~ as a precaution; **prendre des** ~s to take precautions. **-2.** [prudence] caution.

précautionneux, -euse [prekosjɔnø, øz] *adj* cautious.

précédemment [presedamɑ̃] *adv* previously, before.

précédent, -e [presedɑ̃, ɑ̃t] *adj* previous.
◆ **précédent** *nm* precedent; **sans** ~ unprecedented.

précéder [presede] [18] *vt* **-1.** [dans le temps - gén] to precede; [- suj: personne] to arrive before. **-2.** [marcher devant] to go in front of. **-3.** *fig* [devancer] to get ahead of.

précepte [presɛpt] *nm* precept.

précepteur, -trice [preseptœr, tris] *nm, f* (private) tutor.

préchauffer [preʃofe] [3] *vt* to preheat.

prêche [prɛʃ] *nm* sermon; *fig* lecture.

prêcher [preʃe] [4] *vt & vi* to preach.

prêcheur, -euse [prɛʃør, øz] ◇ *adj* preaching, moralizing. ◇ *nm, f* **-1.** RELIG preacher. **-2.** *fig* [moralisateur] moralizer.

prêchi-prêcha [preʃipreʃa] *nm inv* preachifying.

précieusement [presjøzmɑ̃] *adv* preciously.

précieux, -ieuse [presjø, jøz] *adj* **-1.** [pierre, métal] precious; [objet] valuable; [collaborateur] invaluable, valued. **-2.** *péj* [style] precious, affected.

préciosité [presjozite] *nf péj* [affectation] preciosity, affectation.

précipice [presipis] *nm* precipice.

précipitamment [presipitamɑ̃] *adv* hastily.

précipitation [presipitasjɔ̃] *nf* **-1.** [hâte] haste. **-2.** CHIM precipitation.
◆ **précipitations** *nfpl* MÉTÉOR precipitation (U).

précipiter [presipite] [3] *vt* **-1.** [objet, personne] to throw, to hurl; ~ **qqn/qqch du haut de** to throw sb/sthg off, to hurl sb/sthg off. **-2.** [départ] to hasten.
◆ **se précipiter** *vp* **-1.** [se jeter] to throw o.s., to hurl o.s. **-2.** [s'élancer]: **se** ~ **(vers qqn)** to rush (towards sb). **-3.** [s'accélérer - gén] to speed up; [- choses, événements] to move faster.

précis, -e [presi, iz] *adj* **-1.** [exact] precise, accurate. **-2.** [fixé] definite, precise.
◆ **précis** *nm* handbook.

précisément [presizemɑ̃] *adv* precisely, exactly.

préciser [presize] [3] *vt* **-1.** [heure, lieu] to specify. **-2.** [pensée] to clarify.
◆ **se préciser** *vp* to become clear.

précision [presizjɔ̃] *nf* **-1.** [de style, d'explication] precision. **-2.** [détail] detail; **apporter** OU **donner des** ~s to give further information.

précité, -e [presite] *adj* above-mentioned.

précoce [prekɔs] *adj* **-1.** [plante, fruit] early. **-2.** [enfant] precocious.

précocité [prekɔsite] *nf* **-1.** [de plante, de saison] earliness. **-2.** [d'enfant] precociousness.

préconçu, -e [prekɔ̃sy] *adj* preconceived.

préconiser [prekɔnize] [3] *vt* to recommend; ~ **de faire qqch** to recommend doing sthg; ~ **que** (+ *subjonctif*) to recommend that.

précuit, -e [prekɥi, it] *adj* precooked.

précurseur [prekyrsœr] ◇ *nm* precursor, forerunner. ◇ *adj* precursory.

prédateur, -trice [predatœr, tris] *adj* predatory.
◆ **prédateur** *nm* predator.

prédécesseur [predesesœr] *nm* predecessor.

prédécoupé, -e [predekupe] *adj* pre-cut.

prédestination [predɛstinasjɔ̃] *nf* predestination.

prédestiner [predɛstine] [3] *vt* to predestine; **être prédestiné à qqch/à faire qqch** to be predestined for sthg/to do sthg.

prédéterminer [predetɛrmine] [3] *vt* to predetermine.

prédicat [predika] *nm* predicate.

prédicateur, -trice [predikatœr, tris] *nm, f* preacher.

prédication [predikasjɔ̃] *nf* preaching; [discours] sermon.

prédiction [prediksjɔ̃] *nf* prediction.

prédilection [predilɛksjɔ̃] *nf* partiality, liking; **avoir une** ~ **pour** to have a partiality OU liking for; **de** ~ favorite (*avant n*) *Am*, favourite (*avant n*) *Br*.

prédire [predir] [103] *vt* to predict.

prédisposer [predispoze] [3] *vt*: ~ **qqn à qqch** to predispose sb to sthg.

prédisposition [predispozisjɔ̃] *nf*: ~ **à** predisposition to.

prédit, -e [predi, it] *pp* → **prédire**.

prédominant, -e [predɔminɑ̃, ɑ̃t] *adj* predominant.

prédominer [predɔmine] [3] *vt* to predominate.

préélectoral, -e, -aux [preelɛktɔral, o] *adj* pre-election (*avant n*).

préemballé, -e [preɑ̃bale] *adj* prepacked.

prééminence [preeminɑ̃s] *nf* preeminence.

préemption [preɑ̃psjɔ̃] *nf* preemption.

préétabli, -e [preetabli] *adj* pre-established.

préexistant, -e [preɛgzistɑ̃, ɑ̃t] *adj* preexisting.

préfabriqué, -e [prefabrike] *adj* **-1.** [maison] prefabricated. **-2.** [accusation, sourire] false.
◆ **préfabriqué** *nm* prefabricated material.

préface [prefas] *nf* preface.

préfectoral, -e, -aux [prefɛktɔral, o] *adj* prefectorial.

préfecture [prefɛktyr] *nf* prefecture.

préférable [preferabl] *adj* preferable.

préféré, -e [prefere] *adj & nm, f* favorite *Am,* favourite *Br.*

préférence [preferɑ̃s] *nf* preference; **de ~** preferably.

préférentiel, -ielle [preferɑ̃sjɛl] *adj* preferential.

préférer [prefere] [18] *vt:* **~ qqn/qqch (à)** to prefer sb/sthg (to); **~ faire qqch** to prefer to do sthg; **je préfère rentrer** I would rather go home, I would prefer to go home; **je préfère ça!** I like that better!, I prefer that!

préfet [prefɛ] *nm* prefect.

préfigurer [prefigyre] [3] *vt* to prefigure.

préfixe [prefiks] *nm* prefix.

préhistoire [preistwar] *nf* prehistory.

préhistorique [preistɔrik] *adj* prehistoric.

préinscription [preɛ̃skripsjɔ̃] *nf* preregistration.

préjudice [preʒydis] · *nm* harm (*U*), detriment (*U*); **porter ~ à qqn** to harm sb.

préjudiciable [preʒydisjabl] *adj:* **~ (à)** harmful (to), detrimental (to).

préjugé [preʒyʒe] *nm* prejudice.

prélasser [prelase] [3]
◆ **se prélasser** *vp* to lounge.

prélat [prela] *nm* prelate.

prélavage [prelavaʒ] *nm* pre-wash.

prélèvement [prelɛvmɑ̃] *nm* **-1.** MÉD removal; [de sang] sample. **-2.** FIN deduction; **~ automatique** direct debit; **~ mensuel** monthly standing order; **~s obligatoires** tax and social security contributions.

prélever [prelave] [19] *vt* **-1.** FIN: **~ de l'argent (sur)** to deduct money (from). **-2.** MÉD to remove; **~ du sang** to take a blood sample.

préliminaire [preliminɛr] *adj* preliminary.
◆ **préliminaires** *nmpl* **-1.** [de paix] preliminary talks. **-2.** [de discours] preliminaries.

prélude [prelyd] *nm:* **~ (à)** prelude (to).

préluder [prelyde] [3] *vi* **-1.** [marquer le début]: **~ à** to be a prelude to. **-2.** MUS to warm up.

prématuré, -e [prematyre] ◇ *adj* premature. ◇ *nm, f* premature baby.

prématurément [prematyremɑ̃] *adv* prematurely.

préméditation [premeditasjɔ̃] *nf* premeditation; **avec ~** [meurtre] premeditated.

préméditer [premedite] [3] *vt* to premeditate; **~ de faire qqch** to plan to do sthg.

prémices [premis] *nfpl sout* beginnings.

premier, -ière [prəmje, jɛr] ◇ *adj* **-1.** [gén] first; [étage] second *Am,* first *Br.* **-2.** [qualité] top. **-3.** [état] original. ◇ *nm, f* first; **être/sortir ~** to be/come first, to be/come top; **jeune ~** CIN leading man.
◆ **premier** *nm* [étage] second floor *Am,* first floor *Br.*
◆ **première** *nf* **-1.** CIN première; THÉÂTRE première, first night. **-2.** [exploit] first. **-3.** [première classe] first class. **-4.** SCOL ≃ eleventh grade *Am,* ≃ lower sixth year OU form *Br.* **-5.** AUTOM first (gear).
◆ **premier de l'an** *nm:* **le ~ de l'an** New Year's Day.
◆ **en premier** *loc adv* first, firstly.

premièrement [prəmjɛrmɑ̃] *adv* first, firstly.

premier-né, première-née [prəmjene, prəmjɛrne] (*mpl* **premiers-nés,** *fpl* **premières-nées**) *nm, f* first-born (child).

prémisse [premis] *nf* premise.

prémolaire [premɔlɛr] *nf* premolar.

prémonition [premɔnisjɔ̃] *nf* premonition.

prémonitoire [premɔnitwar] *adj* premonitory.

prémunir [premynir] [32] *vt:* **~ qqn (contre)** to protect sb (against).
◆ **se prémunir** *vp* to protect o.s.; **se ~ contre qqch** to guard against sthg.

prenais, prenions *etc* → **prendre.**

prenant, -e [prənɑ̃, ɑ̃t] ◇ *vb* → **prendre.** ◇ *adj* **-1.** [film, histoire] absorbing. **-2.** JUR: **partie ~e** payee.

prénatal, -e (*pl* **prénatals** OU **prénataux** [prenato]) *adj* antenatal; [allocation] maternity (*avant n*).

prendre [prɑ̃dr] [79] ◇ *vt* **-1.** [gén] to take. **-2.** [enlever] to take (away); **~ qqch à qqn** to take sthg from sb. **-3.** [aller chercher - objet] to get, to fetch; [- personne] to pick up. **-4.** [repas, boisson] to have; **vous prendrez quelque chose?** would you like something to eat/drink?. **-5.** [voleur] to catch; **se faire ~** to get caught. **-6.** [responsabilité] to take (on); **~ sur soi de faire qqch** to take it upon o.s. to do sthg. **-7.** [aborder - personne] to handle; [- problème] to tackle; **~ qqn par qqch** to win sb over by sthg; **~ qqn par surprise** to take sb by surprise; **à tout ~ on**

the whole, all things considered. **-8.** [réserver] to book; [louer] to rent, to take; [acheter] to buy. **-9.** [poids] to gain, to put on. **-10.** [embaucher] to take on.

◇ *vi* **-1.** [ciment, sauce] to set. **-2.** [plante, greffe] to take; [mode] to catch on. **-3.** [feu] to catch. **-4.** [se diriger]: ~ **à droite** to turn right.

◆ **se prendre** *vp* **-1.** [vêtement]: **se** ~ **à** to catch on. **-2.** [se considérer]: **pour qui se prend-il?** who does he think he is? **-3.** *loc*: **s'en** ~ **à qqn** [physiquement] to set about sb; [verbalement] to take it out on sb; **je sais comment m'y** ~ I know how to do it OU go about it.

preneur, -euse [prənœr, øz] *nm, f* [locataire] lessee; [acheteur] purchaser.

prenne, prennes *etc* → prendre.

prénom [prenɔ̃] *nm* first name.

prénommer [prenɔme] [3] *vt* to name, to call.

◆ **se prénommer** *vp* to be called.

prénuptial, -e, -iaux [prenypsjal, jo] *adj* premarital.

préoccupant, -e [preɔkypɑ̃, ɑ̃t] *adj* preoccupying.

préoccupation [preɔkypasjɔ̃] *nf* preoccupation.

préoccupé, -e [preɔkype] *adj* preoccupied.

préoccuper [preɔkype] [3] *vt* to preoccupy.
◆ **se préoccuper** *vp*: **se** ~ **de qqch** to be worried about sthg.

préparateur, -trice [preparatœr, tris] *nm, f* lab OU laboratory assistant; ~ **en pharmacie** druggist's assistant *Am*, chemist's assistant *Br*.

préparatifs [preparatif] *nmpl* preparations.

préparation [preparasjɔ̃] *nf* preparation.

préparatoire [preparatwar] *adj* preparatory.

préparer [prepare] [3] *vt* **-1.** [gén] to prepare; [plat, repas] to cook, to prepare; ~ **qqn à qqch** to prepare sb for sthg. **-2.** [réserver]: ~ **qqch à qqn** to have sthg in store for sb. **-3.** [congrès] to organize.
◆ **se préparer** *vp* **-1.** [personne]: **se** ~ **à qqch/à faire qqch** to prepare for sthg/to do sthg. **-2.** [tempête] to be brewing.

prépondérance [prepɔ̃derɑ̃s] *nf*: ~ **(sur)** dominance (over), supremacy (over).

prépondérant, -e [prepɔ̃derɑ̃, ɑ̃t] *adj* dominating.

préposé, -e [prepoze] *nm, f* (minor) official; [de vestiaire] attendant; [facteur] mailman (*f* mailwoman) *Am*, postman (*f* postwoman) *Br*; ~ **à qqch** person in charge of sthg.

préposer [prepoze] [3] *vt* to put in charge; **être préposé à qqch/à faire qqch** to be (put) in charge of sthg/of doing sthg.

préposition [prepozisjɔ̃] *nf* preposition.

prépuce [prepys] *nm* foreskin.

préréglé, -e [preregle] *adj* preset, preprogrammed.

préretraite [prerətret] *nf* early retirement; [allocation] early retirement pension.

prérogative [prerɔgativ] *nf* prerogative.

près [prɛ] *adv* near, close.
◆ **de près** *loc adv* closely; **regarder qqch de** ~ to watch sthg closely; **de plus/très** ~ more/very closely.
◆ **près de** *loc prép* **-1.** [dans l'espace] near, close to. **-2.** [dans le temps] close to; **il est** ~ **de partir** he's about to leave. **-3.** [presque] nearly, almost.
◆ **à peu près** *loc adv* more or less, just about; **il est à peu** ~ **cinq heures** it's about five o'clock.
◆ **à peu de chose(s) près** *loc adv* more or less, approximately.
◆ **à ceci près que, à cela près que** *loc conj* except that, apart from the fact that.
◆ **à ... près** *loc adv*: **à dix centimètres** ~ to within ten centimetres; **il n'en est pas à un ou deux jours** ~ a day or two more or less won't make any difference.

présage [preza3] *nm* omen.

présager [preza3e] [17] *vt* **-1.** [annoncer] to portend. **-2.** [prévoir] to predict; **laisser** ~ **de qqch** to hint at sthg.

pré-salé [presale] (*pl* **prés-salés**) *nm lamb reared on salt marshes*.

presbyte [prɛsbit] ◇ *nmf* farsighted person *Am*, longsighted person *Br*. ◇ *adj* farsighted *Am*, longsighted *Br*.

presbytère [prɛsbitɛr] *nm* presbytery.

presbytérien, -ienne [prɛsbiterjɛ̃, jɛn] *nm, f & adj* Presbyterian.

presbytie [prɛsbisi] *nf* farsightedness *Am*, longsightedness *Br*.

prescience [presjɑ̃s] *nf littéraire* foresight.

préscolaire [preskɔlɛr] *adj* preschool (*avant n*).

prescription [prɛskripsjɔ̃] *nf* **-1.** MÉD prescription. **-2.** JUR limitation.

prescrire [prɛskrir] [99] *vt* **-1.** [mesures, conditions] to lay down, to stipulate. **-2.** MÉD to prescribe.
◆ **se prescrire** *vp* MÉD to be prescribed.

prescrit, e [prɛskri, it] *pp* → prescrire.

prescrivais, prescrivions *etc* → prescrire.

préséance [preseɑ̃s] *nf* precedence.

présélection [preselɛksjɔ̃] *nf* preselection; [pour concours] making a list of finalists, short-listing *Br*.

présélectionner [preselɛksjɔne] [3] *vt* to preselect; [candidats] to put on a list of finalists, to short-list *Br*.

présence [prezɑ̃s] *nf* **-1.** [gén] presence; **en ~ face to face; honorer qqn de sa ~** to honour sb with one's presence; **en ~ de** in the presence of; **en sa** *etc* **~** in his/her *etc* presence. **-2.** [compagnie] company (*U*). **-3.** [assiduité] attendance; **feuille de ~** attendance sheet.

◆ **présence d'esprit** *nf* presence of mind.

présent, -e [prezɑ̃, ɑ̃t] *adj* **-1.** [gén] present; **le ~ ouvrage** this work; **la ~e loi** this law; **avoir qqch ~ à l'esprit** to remember sthg. **-2.** [actif] attentive, involved.

◆ **présent** *nm* **-1.** [gén] present; **faire ~ à qqn de qqch** *sout* to make sb a present of sthg; **à ~** at present; **à ~ que** now that; **jusqu'à ~** up to now, so far; **dès à ~** right away. **-2.** GRAM: **le ~** the present tense.

◆ **présente** *nf*: **je vous informe par la ~e que ...** I hereby inform you that ....

présentable [prezɑ̃tabl] *adj* [d'aspect] presentable.

présentateur, -trice [prezɑ̃tatœr, tris] *nm, f* presenter.

présentation [prezɑ̃tasjɔ̃] *nf* **-1.** [de personne]: **faire les ~s** to make the introductions. **-2.** [aspect extérieur] appearance; **avoir une bonne/mauvaise ~** to be of a pleasing/disagreeable appearance. **-3.** [de papiers, de produit, de film] presentation; **sur ~ de** on presentation of. **-4.** [de magazine] layout.

présentement [prezɑ̃tmɑ̃] *adv* at the moment, at present.

présenter [prezɑ̃te] [3] *vt* **-1.** [gén] to present; [projet] to present, to submit. **-2.** [invité] to introduce. **-3.** [condoléances, félicitations, avantages] to offer; [hommages] to pay; **~ qqch à qqn** to offer sb sthg. ◇ *vi fam*: **~ bien/mal** to make a good/bad impression.

◆ **se présenter** *vp* **-1.** [se faire connaître]: **se ~ (à)** to introduce o.s. (to). **-2.** [être candidat]: **se ~ à** [élection] to run in *Am*, to stand in *Br*; [examen] to take, to sit *Br*. **-3.** [paraître] to appear. **-4.** [occasion, situation] to arise, to present itself. **-5.** [affaire, contrat]: **se ~ bien/mal** to look good/bad.

présentoir [prezɑ̃twar] *nm* display stand.

préservatif [prezɛrvatif] *nm* condom.

préservation [prezɛrvasjɔ̃] *nf* preservation.

préserver [prezɛrve] [3] *vt* to preserve.

◆ **se préserver** *vp*: **se ~ de** to protect o.s. from.

présidence [prezidɑ̃s] *nf* **-1.** [de groupe] chairmanship. **-2.** [d'État] presidency. **-3.** [lieu] presidential residence OU palace.

président, -e [prezidɑ̃, ɑ̃t] *nm, f* **-1.** [d'assemblée] chairman (*f* chairwoman); **~ du conseil d'administration** chairman of the board. **-2.** [d'État] president; **Monsieur/ Madame le Président** Mr/Madam President; **~ de la République** President (of the Republic) of France. **-3.** JUR [de tribunal] presiding judge; [de jury] foreman (*f* forewoman).

◆ **présidente** *nf vieilli* president's wife.

◆ **président-directeur général** *nm* (chairman and) managing director.

présidentiel, -ielle [prezidɑ̃sjɛl] *adj* presidential; **régime ~** presidential system.

présider [prezide] [3] ◇ *vt* **-1.** [réunion] to chair. **-2.** [banquet, dîner] to preside over. ◇ *vi*: **~ à** to be in charge of; *fig* to govern, to preside at.

présomptif, -ive [prezɔ̃ptif, iv] *adj*: **héritier ~** heir apparent.

présomption [prezɔ̃psjɔ̃] *nf* **-1.** [hypothèse] presumption. **-2.** JUR presumption. **-3.** *littéraire* [prétention] presumptuousness.

présomptueux, -euse [prezɔ̃ptɥø, øz] ◇ *adj* presumptuous. ◇ *nm, f littéraire* presumptuous person.

presque [prɛsk] *adv* almost, nearly; **~ rien** next to nothing, scarcely anything; **~ jamais** hardly ever.

presqu'île [prɛskil] *nf* peninsula.

pressant, -e [prɛsɑ̃, ɑ̃t] *adj* pressing.

press-book [prɛsbuk] (*pl* **press-books**) *nm* portfolio.

presse [prɛs] *nf* press; **avoir bonne/ mauvaise ~** to have a good/bad press.

pressé, -e [prese] *adj* **-1.** [travail] urgent; **aller au plus ~** to do first things first. **-2.** [personne]: **être ~** to be in a hurry. **-3.** [citron, orange] freshly squeezed.

presse-citron [prɛssitrɔ̃] *nm inv* lemon squeezer.

pressentiment [presɑ̃timɑ̃] *nm* premonition.

pressentir [presɑ̃tir] [37] *vt* **-1.** [événement] to have a premonition of. **-2.** *sout* [personne] to sound out.

presse-papiers [prɛspapje] *nm inv* paperweight.

presse-purée [prɛspyre] *nm inv* potato masher.

presser [prese] [4] *vt* **-1.** [écraser - olives] to press; [- citron, orange] to squeeze. **-2.** [disque] to press. **-3.** [dans ses bras] to squeeze. **-4.** [bouton] to press, to push. **-5.** *sout* [harceler]: ~ **qqn de faire qqch** to press sb to do sthg; ~ **qqn de questions** to bombard sb with questions. **-6.** [accélérer] to speed up; ~ **le pas** to speed up, to walk faster. ◆ **se presser** *vp* **-1.** [se dépêcher] to hurry (up); **sans se** ~ without hurrying OU rushing. **-2.** [s'agglutiner]: **se** ~ **(autour de)** to crowd (around). **-3.** [se serrer] to huddle.

pressing [presiŋ] *nm* steam pressing; [établissement] dry cleaner's.

pression [presjɔ̃] *nf* **-1.** [gén] pressure; **exercer une** ~ **sur qqch** to exert pressure on sthg; **exercer une** ~ **sur qqn, faire** ~ **sur qqn** to put pressure on sb; **sous** ~ [liquide & *fig*] under pressure; [cabine] pressurized; ~ **artérielle** blood pressure; ~ **atmosphérique** atmospheric pressure. **-2.** [sur vêtement] snap fastener *Am*, press stud *Br*, popper *Br*. **-3.** [bière] draft *Am* OU draught beer *Br*.

pressoir [preswar] *nm* **-1.** [machine] press. **-2.** [lieu] press house.

pressurer [presyre] [3] *vt* **-1.** [objet] to press, to squeeze. **-2.** *fig* [contribuable] to squeeze.

pressurisation [presyrizasjɔ̃] *nf* pressurization.

pressuriser [presyrize] [3] *vt* to pressurize.

prestance [prestɑ̃s] *nf* bearing; **avoir de la** ~ to have presence.

prestataire [prestatɛr] *nmf* **-1.** [bénéficiaire] person in receipt of benefit, claimant. **-2.** [fournisseur] provider; ~ **de service** service provider.

prestation [prestasjɔ̃] *nf* **-1.** [allocation] benefit; ~ **en nature** payment in kind; ~**s familiales** ≃ family allowance. **-2.** [de comédien] performance. **-3.** [de serment] taking.

preste [prest] *adj littéraire* nimble.

prestement [prestəmɑ̃] *adv* nimbly.

prestidigitateur, -trice [prestidiʒitatœr, tris] *nm, f* conjurer.

prestidigitation [prestidiʒitasjɔ̃] *nf* conjuring.

prestige [prestiʒ] *nm* prestige.

prestigieux, -ieuse [prestiʒjø, jøz] *adj* **-1.** [magnifique] splendid. **-2.** [réputé] prestigious.

présumé, -e [prezyme] *adj* presumed.

présumer [prezyme] [3] ◇ *vt* to presume, to assume; ~ **que** to presume (that), to assume (that); **être présumé coupable/**

innocent to be presumed guilty/innocent. ◇ *vi*: ~ **de qqch** to overestimate sthg.

présupposé [presypoze] *nm* presupposition.

présupposer [presypoze] [3] *vt* to presuppose.

présure [prezyr] *nf* rennet.

prêt, -e [prɛ, prɛt] *adj* ready; ~ **à qqch/à faire qqch** ready for sthg/to do sthg; ~ **à tout** ready for anything; ~**s? partez!** SPORT get set, go!
◆ **prêt** *nm* [action] lending (*U*); [somme] loan.

prêt-à-porter [prɛtaporte] (*pl* **prêts-à-porter**) *nm* ready-to-wear clothing (*U*).

prétendant, -e [pretɑ̃dɑ̃, ɑ̃t] *nm, f* claimant. ◆ **prétendant** *nm* **-1.** [au trône] pretender. **-2.** [amoureux] suitor.

prétendre [pretɑ̃dr] [73] ◇ *vt* **-1.** [affecter]: ~ **faire qqch** to claim to do sthg. **-2.** [affirmer]: ~ **que** to claim (that), to maintain (that). ◇ *vi* [aspirer]: ~ **à qqch** to aspire to sthg.
◆ **se prétendre** *vp*: **se** ~ **acteur/écrivain** to claim to be an actor/an author.

prétendu, -e [pretɑ̃dy] ◇ *pp* → **prétendre**. ◇ *adj (avant n)* so-called.

prétendument [pretɑ̃dymɑ̃] *adv* supposedly.

prête-nom [prɛtnɔ̃] (*pl* **prête-noms**) *nm* front man.

prétentieux, -ieuse [pretɑ̃sjø, jøz] ◇ *adj* pretentious. ◇ *nm, f* pretentious person.

prétention [pretɑ̃sjɔ̃] *nf* **-1.** [suffisance] pretentiousness. **-2.** [ambition] pretension, ambition; **avoir la** ~ **de faire qqch** to claim OU pretend to do sthg.

prêter [prete] [4] ◇ *vt* **-1.** [fournir]: ~ **qqch (à qqn)** [objet, argent] to lend (sb) sthg; *fig* [concours, appui] to lend (sb) sthg, to give (sb) sthg. **-2.** [attribuer]: ~ **qqch à qqn** to attribute sthg to sb. ◇ *vi*: ~ **à** to lead to, to generate.
◆ **se prêter** *vp*: **se** ~ **à** [participer à] to go along with; [convenir à] to fit, to suit.

prétérit [preterit] *nm* preterite.

prêteur, -euse [prɛtœr, øz] ◇ *adj* generous. ◇ *nm, f*: ~ **sur gages** pawnbroker.

prétexte [pretɛkst] *nm* pretext, excuse; **sous** ~ **de faire qqch/que** on the pretext of doing sthg/that, under the pretext of doing sthg/that; **sous aucun** ~ on no account.

prétexter [pretɛkste] [4] *vt* to give as an excuse.

Pretoria [pretɔrja] *n* Pretoria.

prêtre [prɛtr] *nm* priest.

prêtresse [prɛtrɛs] *nf* priestess.

preuve [prœv] *nf* **-1.** [gén] proof. **-2.** JUR evidence. **-3.** [témoignage] sign, token; **faire ~ de qqch** to show sthg; **faire ses ~s** to prove o.s./itself.

preux [prø] ◇ *nm* knight valiant. ◇ *adj m* valiant.

prévaloir [prevalwar] [61] *vi* [dominer]: **~ (sur)** to prevail (over).
◆ **se prévaloir** *vp*: **se ~ de** to boast about.

prévalu [prevaly] *pp inv* → **prévaloir**.

prévarication [prevarikasjɔ̃] *nf sout* breach of trust.

prévaut → **prévaloir**.

prévenance [prevnɑ̃s] *nf* **-1.** [attitude] thoughtfulness, consideration. **-2.** [action] considerate OU thoughtful act.

prévenant, -e [prevnɑ̃, ɑ̃t] *adj* considerate, attentive.

prévenir [prevnir] [40] *vt* **-1.** [employé, élève]: **~ qqn (de)** to warn sb (about). **-2.** [police] to inform. **-3.** [désirs] to anticipate. **-4.** [maladie] to prevent. **-5.** *littéraire* [prédisposer]: **~ qqn contre qqn** to prejudice sb against sb.

préventif, -ive [prevɑ̃tif, iv] *adj* **-1.** [mesure, médecine] preventive. **-2.** JUR: **être en détention préventive** to be on remand.

prévention [prevɑ̃sjɔ̃] *nf* **-1.** [protection]: **~ (contre)** prevention (of); **~ routière** road safety (measures). **-2.** JUR remand.

prévenu, -e [prevny] ◇ *pp* → **prévenir**. ◇ *nm, f* accused, defendant.

préviendrai, préviendras *etc* → **prévenir**.

prévisible [previzibl] *adj* foreseeable.

prévision [previzjɔ̃] *nf* forecast (*U*), prediction; [de coûts] estimate; ÉCON forecast; **les ~s météorologiques** the weather forecast.
◆ **en prévision de** *loc prép* in anticipation of.

prévisionnel, -elle [previzjɔnɛl] *adj* anticipatory; **budget ~** budget estimate.

prévoir [prevwar] [63] *vt* **-1.** [s'attendre à] to expect. **-2.** [prédire] to predict. **-3.** [anticiper] to foresee, to anticipate. **-4.** [programmer] to plan; **n'être pas prévu** to be unforeseen; **comme prévu** as planned, according to plan.

prévoyais, prévoyions *etc* → **prévoir**.

prévoyance [prevwajɑ̃s] *nf* [de personne] foresight; *voir aussi* **caisse**.

prévoyant, -e [prevwajɑ̃, ɑ̃t] *adj* provident.

prévu, e [prevy] *pp* → **prévoir**.

prie-Dieu [pridjø] *nm inv* prie-dieu.

prier [prije] [10] ◇ *vt* **-1.** RELIG to pray to. **-2.** [implorer] to beg; **(ne pas) se faire ~ (pour faire qqch)** (not) to need to be persuaded (to do sthg); **je vous en prie** [de grâce] please, I beg you; [de rien] don't mention it, not at all. **-3.** *sout* [demander]: **~ qqn de faire qqch** to request sb to do sthg; **~ instamment qqn de faire qqch** to insist that sb does sthg; **vous êtes priés de** you are requested to. **-4.** *littéraire* [convier] to invite. ◇ *vi* RELIG to pray.

prière [prijɛr] *nf* **-1.** [RELIG - recueillement] prayer (*U*), praying (*U*); [- formule] prayer; [- office] prayers (*pl*). **-2.** *littéraire* [demande] entreaty; **~ de frapper avant d'entrer** please knock before entering.

prieuré [prijœre] *nm* priory.

primaire [primɛr] *adj* **-1.** [premier]: **couleur ~** primary color *Am* OU colour *Br*; **élection ~** primary (election); **ère ~** Palaeozoic era; **études ~s** primary education (*U*). **-2.** *péj* [primitif] limited.

primate [primat] *nm* **-1.** ZOOL primate. **-2.** *fam* [brute] gorilla.

primauté [primote] *nf* primacy.

prime [prim] ◇ *nf* **-1.** [d'employé] bonus; **~ d'intéressement** profit-related bonus; **~ d'objectif** incentive bonus. **-2.** [allocation - de déménagement, de transport] allowance; [- à l'exportation] incentive. **-3.** [d'assurance] premium. **-4.** [cadeau] free gift; **en ~** as a free gift; *fig* in addition. ◇ *adj* **-1.** [premier]: **de ~ abord** at first glance; **de ~ jeunesse** in the first flush of youth. **-2.** MATHS prime.

primer [prime] [3] ◇ *vi* to take precedence, to come first. ◇ *vt* **-1.** [être supérieur à] to take precedence over. **-2.** [récompenser] to award a prize to; **le film a été primé au festival** the film won an award at the festival.

primerose [primroz] *nf* hollyhock.

primesautier, -ière [primsotje, jɛr] *adj* impulsive.

primeur [primœr] *nf* immediacy; **avoir la ~ de qqch** to be the first to hear sthg.
◆ **primeurs** *nfpl* early produce (*U*).

primevère [primvɛr] *nf* primrose.

primitif, -ive [primitif, iv] ◇ *adj* **-1.** [gén] primitive. **-2.** [aspect] original. ◇ *nm, f* primitive.

primo [primo] *adv* firstly.

primordial, -e, -iaux [primɔrdjal, jo] *adj* essential.

prince [prɛ̃s] *nm* prince; **~ consort** prince consort.

prince-de-Galles [prɛ̃sdəgal] *nm inv & adj inv* Prince of Wales check.

princesse [prɛsɛs] *nf* princess.

princier, -ière [prɛsje, jɛr] *adj* princely.

principal, -e, -aux [prɛsipal, o] ◇ *adj* **-1.** [gén] main, principal. **-2.** GRAM main. ◇ *nm,* *f* **-1.** [important]: **le ~** the main thing. **-2.** SCOL principal *Am*, headmaster (*f* headmistress) *Br*.

principalement [prɛsipalmã] *adv* mainly, principally.

principauté [prɛsipote] *nf* principality.

principe [prɛsip] *nm* principle; **par ~** on principle.
◆ **en principe** *loc adv* theoretically, in principle.

printanier, -ière [prɛtanje, jɛr] *adj* **-1.** [temps] spring-like. **-2.** *fig* [humeur] bright and cheerful.

printemps [prɛtã] *nm* **-1.** [saison] spring. **-2.** *fig* [de la vie] springtime. **-3.** *fam* [année]: **avoir 20 ~** to be 20.

priori [priɔri]
◆ **a priori** ◇ *loc adv* in principle. ◇ *nm inv* initial reaction. ◇ *adj inv* a priori.

prioritaire [prijɔritɛr] *adj* **-1.** [industrie, mesure] priority (*avant n*). **-2.** AUTOM with right of way.

priorité [prijɔrite] *nf* **-1.** [importance primordiale] priority; **en ~** first. **-2.** AUTOM right of way; **~ à droite** give way to the right.

pris, -e [pri, priz] ◇ *pp* → **prendre**. ◇ *adj* **-1.** [place] taken; [personne] busy; [mains] full. **-2.** [nez] blocked; [gorge] sore. **-3.** [envahi]: **~ de** seized with.
◆ **prise** *nf* **-1.** [sur barre, sur branche] grip, hold; **lâcher ~e** to let go; *fig* to give up; **avoir ~e sur qqch** to have hold of sthg; **avoir ~e sur qqn** *fig* to have a hold over sb; **être aux ~es avec** *fig* to grapple with. **-2.** [action de prendre - de ville] seizure, capture; **~e en charge** [par Sécurité sociale] (guaranteed) reimbursement; **~e d'otages** hostage taking; **~e de sang** blood test; **~e de vue** shot; **~e de vue** OU **vues** [action] filming, shooting. **-3.** [à la pêche] haul. **-4.** ÉLECTR: **~e (de courant)** [mâle] plug; [femelle] socket. **-5.** [de judo] hold; **faire une ~e à qqn** SPORT to get sb in a hold. **-6.** INFORM outlet.

priser [prize] [3] *vt* **-1.** *sout* [apprécier] to appreciate, to value. **-2.** [aspirer]: **~ du tabac** to take snuff.

prisme [prism] *nm* prism.

prison [prizɔ̃] *nf* **-1.** [établissement] prison. **-2.** [réclusion] imprisonment.

prisonnier, -ière [prizɔnje, jɛr] ◇ *nm, f* prisoner; **faire qqn ~** to take sb prisoner, to capture sb. ◇ *adj* imprisoned; *fig*

trapped; **être ~ de** to be the prisoner of; *fig* to be a prisoner of OU a slave to.

privatif, -ive [privatif, iv] *adj* **-1.** JUR private. **-2.** GRAM privative.

privation [privasjɔ̃] *nf* deprivation.
◆ **privations** *nfpl* privations, hardships.

privatisation [privatizasjɔ̃] *nf* privatization.

privatiser [privatize] [3] *vt* to privatize.

privé, -e [prive] *adj* private.
◆ **privé** *nm* **-1.** ÉCON private sector. **-2.** [détective] private eye. **-3.** [intimité]: **en ~** in private; **dans le ~** in private life.

priver [prive] [3] *vt*: **~ qqn (de)** to deprive sb (of).
◆ **se priver** *vp* **-1.** [s'abstenir]: **se ~ de** to go OU do without, to deprive o.s. of; **ne pas se ~ de faire qqch** not to hesitate to do sthg; **ne pas se ~ de qqch** to indulge in sthg. **-2.** (*emploi absolu*) [économiser] to do OU go without.

privilège [privilɛʒ] *nm* privilege.
◆ **privilèges** *nmpl*: **les ~s** *the privileges of the aristocracy, cities, corporations, guilds etc* abolished in 1789.

privilégié, -e [privileʒje] ◇ *adj* **-1.** [personne] privileged. **-2.** [climat, site] favored *Am*, favoured *Br*. ◇ *nm, f* privileged person.

privilégier [privileʒje] [9] *vt* to favor *Am*, to favour *Br*.

prix [pri] *nm* **-1.** [coût] price; **à** OU **au ~ coûtant** at cost (price); **~ d'achat** purchase price; **à aucun ~** on no account; **à ~ fixe** set-price (*avant n*); **au ~ fort** at a very high price; **hors de ~** too expensive; **à moitié ~** at half price; **à tout ~** at all costs; **~ d'ami** reduced price; **~ net** net (price); **~ de revient** cost price; **acheter** OU **payer qqch à ~ d'or** to pay through the nose for sthg; **mettre la tête de qqn à ~** to put a price on sb's head; **y mettre le ~** to pay a lot. **-2.** [importance] value. **-3.** [récompense] prize; **~ Nobel** Nobel prize; [lauréat] Nobel prizewinner.
◆ **Grand Prix** *nm* Grand Prix.

pro [pro] *nmf & adj fam* pro.

probabilité [prɔbabilite] *nf* **-1.** [chance] probability. **-2.** [vraisemblance] probability, likelihood; **selon toute ~** in all probability.

probable [prɔbabl] *adj* probable, likely; **il est ~ que** it is likely OU probable that.

probablement [prɔbabləmã] *adv* probably.

probant, -e [prɔbã, ãt] *adj* convincing, conclusive.

probatoire [prɔbatwar] *adj* [période] trial (*avant n*); [examen] qualifying.

probité [prɔbite] *nf* integrity.

problématique [prɔblematik] ◇ *nf* problems (*pl*). ◇ *adj* problematic.

problème [prɔblɛm] *nm* problem; **poser un ~** to cause OU pose a problem; **(il n'y a) pas de ~!** *fam* no problem!; **faux ~** imaginary problem; **ça ne lui pose aucun ~** *hum* that doesn't worry him/her.

procédé [prɔsede] *nm* -1. [méthode] process. -2. [conduite] behavior (*U*) *Am*, behaviour (*U*) *Br*.

procéder [prɔsede] [18] *vi* -1. [agir] to proceed. -2. [exécuter]: **~ à qqch** to set about sthg; **il sera procédé au démantèlement de l'entreprise** the company will be dismantled. -3. *sout* [provenir]: **~ de** to come from, to originate in.

procédure [prɔsedyr] *nf* procedure; [démarche] proceedings (*pl*).

procédurier, -ière [prɔsedyrje, jɛr]. ◇ *adj* quibbling. ◇ *nm, f* quibbler.

procès [prɔsɛ] *nm* JUR trial; **intenter un ~ à qqn** to sue sb; **faire le ~ de** *fig* to make a case against.

processeur [prɔsesœr] *nm* processor.

procession [prɔsesjɔ̃] *nf* procession; **en ~** in procession.

processus [prɔsesys] *nm* process.

procès-verbal [prɔsɛvɛrbal] (*pl* **procès-verbaux** [prɔsɛvɛrbo]) *nm* -1. [contravention] (parking) ticket. -2. [compte-rendu] minutes.

prochain, -e [prɔʃɛ̃, ɛn] *adj* -1. [suivant] next; **à la ~e!** *fam* see you! -2. [imminent] impending.
◆ **prochain** *nm littéraire* [semblable] fellow man.

prochainement [prɔʃɛnmɑ̃] *adv* soon, shortly.

proche [prɔʃ] *adj* -1. [dans l'espace] near; **~ de** near, close to; [semblable à] very similar to, closely related to; **je me sens très ~ de ce qu'il dit** my feelings are very close OU similar to his. -2. [dans le temps] imminent, near; **dans un ~ avenir** in the immediate future. -3. [ami, parent] close.
◆ **proches** *nmpl*: **les ~s** the close family (*sg*).
◆ **de proche en proche** *loc adv sout* gradually.

Proche-Orient [prɔʃɔrjɑ̃] *nm*: **le ~** the Near East.

proclamation [prɔklamasjɔ̃] *nf* proclamation.

proclamer [prɔklame] [3] *vt* to proclaim, to declare.

procréation [prɔkreasjɔ̃] *nf* procreation; **~ artificielle** artificial reproduction.

procréer [prɔkree] [15] *vt littéraire* to procreate.

procuration [prɔkyrasjɔ̃] *nf* proxy; **par ~** by proxy.

procurer [prɔkyre] [3] *vt*: **~ qqch à qqn** [suj: personne] to obtain sthg for sb; [suj: chose] to give OU bring sb sthg.
◆ **se procurer** *vp*: **se ~ qqch** to obtain sthg.

procureur [prɔkyrœr] *nm*: **~ général** chief prosecutor; **Procureur de la République** ≃ Attorney General.

prodigalité [prɔdigalite] *nf* extravagance (*U*).

prodige [prɔdiʒ] *nm* -1. [miracle] miracle. -2. [tour de force] marvel, wonder; **c'est un ~ d'ingéniosité** it's incredibly ingenious. -3. [génie] prodigy.

prodigieusement [prɔdiʒjøzmɑ̃] *adv* fantastically, incredibly.

prodigieux, -ieuse [prɔdiʒjø, jøz] *adj* fantastic, incredible.

prodigue [prɔdig] *adj* [dépensier] extravagant; **~ de** *fig* lavish with.

prodiguer [prɔdige] [3] *vt littéraire* [soins, amitié]: **~ qqch (à) qqn** to lavish sthg (on).

producteur, -trice [prɔdyktœr, tris] ◇ *nm, f* -1. [gén] producer. -2. AGRIC producer, grower. ◇ *adj*: **~ de pétrole** oil-producing (*avant n*); **~ d'emplois** which creates jobs.

productif, -ive [prɔdyktif, iv] *adj* productive.

production [prɔdyksjɔ̃] *nf* -1. [gén] production; **coût de ~** production cost; **la ~ littéraire d'un pays** the literature of a country. -2. [producteurs] producers (*pl*).

productivité [prɔdyktivite] *nf* productivity.

produire [prɔdɥir] [98] *vt* -1. [gén] to produce. -2. [provoquer] to cause.
◆ **se produire** *vp* -1. [arriver] to occur, to take place. -2. [acteur, chanteur] to appear.

produisais, produisions *etc* → **produire**.

produit, -e [prɔdɥi, ɥit] *pp* → **produire**.
◆ **produit** *nm* -1. [gén] product; **~ de beauté** cosmetic, beauty product; **~s chimiques** chemicals; **~ de consommation** consumer product; **~s d'entretien** cleaning products; **~ de grande consommation** mass consumption product. -2. [d'investissement] profit, income.

proéminent, -e [prɔeminɑ̃, ɑ̃t] *adj* prominent.

prof [prɔf] *nmf fam* teacher.

profanation [prɔfanasjɔ̃] *nf* desecration.

profane [prɔfan] ◇ *nmf* -1. [non religieux]

non-believer. **-2.** [novice] layman. ◇ *adj* **-1.** [laïc] secular. **-2.** [ignorant] ignorant.

profaner [prɔfane] [3] *vt* **-1.** [église] to desecrate. **-2.** *fig* [mémoire] to defile.

proférer [prɔfere] [18] *vt* to utter.

professer [prɔfese] [4] *vt* to profess.

professeur [prɔfesœr] *nm* **-1.** [enseignant] teacher. **-2.** [titre] professor.

profession [prɔfesjɔ̃] *nf* **-1.** [métier] occupation; **de ~** by trade/profession; **sans ~** unemployed; **~ libérale** profession. **-2.** [corps de métier - libéral] profession; [- manuel] trade.
◆ **profession de foi** *nf* **-1.** RELIG profession of faith. **-2.** [manifeste] manifesto.

professionnel, -elle [prɔfesjɔnɛl] ◇ *adj* **-1.** [gén] professional. **-2.** [école] technical. ◇ *nm, f* professional.

professionnellement [prɔfesjɔnɛlmɑ̃] *adv* professionally.

professoral, -e, -aux [prɔfesɔral, o] *adj* [ton, attitude] professorial; [corps] teaching (*avant n*).

professorat [prɔfesɔra] *nm* teaching.

profil [prɔfil] *nm* **-1.** [de personne, d'emploi] profile; [de bâtiment] outline; **de ~** [visage, corps] in profile; [objet] from the side. **-2.** [coupe] section.

profiler [prɔfile] [3] *vt* to shape.
◆ **se profiler** *vp* **-1.** [bâtiment, arbre] to stand out. **-2.** [solution] to emerge.

profit [prɔfi] *nm* **-1.** [avantage] benefit; **au ~ de** in aid of; **tirer ~ de** to profit from, to benefit from. **-2.** [gain] profit.

profitable [prɔfitabl] *adj* profitable; **être ~ à qqn** to benefit sb, to be beneficial to sb.

profiter [prɔfite] [3] *vi* **-1.** [tirer avantage]: **~ de** [vacances] to benefit from; [personne] to take advantage of; **~ de qqch pour faire qqch** to take advantage of sthg to do sthg; **en ~** to make the most of it; **en ~ pour faire qqch** to take the opportunity to do sthg. **-2.** [servir]: **~ à qqn** to be beneficial to sb.

profiteroles [prɔfitrɔl] *nfpl*: **~ au chocolat** chocolate profiteroles.

profiteur, -euse [prɔfitœr, øz] *nm, f péj* profiteer.

profond, -e [prɔfɔ̃, ɔ̃d] *adj* **-1.** [gén] deep. **-2.** [pensée] deep, profound. **-3.** PSYCHOL: **un débile ~** a profoundly subnormal person.
◆ **profond** ◇ *nm*: **au plus ~ de** in the depths of. ◇ *adv* deep.

profondément [prɔfɔ̃demɑ̃] *adv* **-1.** [enfoui] deep. **-2.** [intensément - aimer, intéresser] deeply; [- dormir] soundly; **être ~ endormi**

to be fast asleep. **-3.** [extrêmement - convaincu, ému] deeply, profoundly; [- différent] profoundly.

profondeur [prɔfɔ̃dœr] *nf* depth; **en ~** in depth; **~ de champ** CIN & PHOT depth of field.
◆ **profondeurs** *nfpl* depths.

profusion [prɔfyzjɔ̃] *nf*: **une ~ de** a profusion of; **à ~** in abundance, in profusion.

progéniture [prɔʒenityr] *nf* offspring.

progiciel [prɔʒisjɛl] *nm* software package.

programmable [prɔgramabl] *adj* programmable.

programmateur, -trice [prɔgramatœr, tris] *nm, f* program *Am* OU programme *Br* planner.
◆ **programmateur** *nm* automatic control unit.

programmation [prɔgramasjɔ̃] *nf* **-1.** INFORM programming; **faire de la ~** to program; **~ linéaire** linear programming. **-2.** RADIO & TÉLÉ program *Am* OU programme *Br* planning.

programme [prɔgram] *nm* **-1.** [gén] program *Am,* programme *Br*; **le ~ des réjouissances** *hum* the treats in store; **c'est tout un ~** it's quite an undertaking. **-2.** INFORM program. **-3.** [planning] schedule. **-4.** SCOL syllabus.

programmé, -e [prɔgrame] *adj* programmed.

programmer [prɔgrame] [3] *vt* **-1.** [organiser] to plan. **-2.** RADIO & TÉLÉ to schedule. **-3.** INFORM to program.

programmeur, -euse [prɔgramœr, øz] *nm, f* INFORM (computer) programmer.

progrès [prɔgrɛ] *nm* progress (*U*); **être en ~** to be making (good) progress; **faire des ~** to make progress.

progresser [prɔgrese] [4] *vi* **-1.** [avancer] to progress, to advance. **-2.** [maladie] to spread. **-3.** [élève] to make progress.

progressif, -ive [prɔgresif, iv] *adj* progressive; [difficulté] increasing.

progression [prɔgresjɔ̃] *nf* **-1.** [avancée] advance. **-2.** [de maladie, du nationalisme] spread.

progressiste [prɔgresist] *nmf & adj* progressive.

progressivement [prɔgresivmɑ̃] *adv* progressively.

prohiber [prɔibe] [3] *vt* to ban, to prohibit.

prohibitif, -ive [prɔibitif, iv] *adj* **-1.** [dissuasif] prohibitive. **-2.** JUR prohibitory.

prohibition [prɔibisjɔ̃] *nf* ban, prohibition.
◆ **Prohibition** *nf*: **la Prohibition** HIST Prohibition.

proie [prwa] *nf* prey; être la ~ de qqn *fig* to be the prey OU victim of sb; être la ~ de qqch *fig* to be the victim of sthg; être en ~ à [sentiment] to be prey to.

projecteur [prɔʒɛktœr] *nm* -1. [de lumière] floodlight; THÉÂTRE spotlight. -2. [d'images] projector.

projectile [prɔʒɛktil] *nm* missile.

projection [prɔʒɛksjɔ̃] *nf* -1. [gén] projection. -2. [jet] throwing.

projectionniste [prɔʒɛksjɔnist] *nmf* projectionist.

projet [prɔʒɛ] *nm* -1. [perspective] plan. -2. [étude, ébauche] draft; ~ de loi bill.

projeter [prɔʃte] [27] *vt* -1. [envisager] to plan; ~ de faire qqch to plan to do sthg. -2. [missile, pierre] to throw. -3. [film, diapositives] to show. -4. GÉOM & PSYCHOL to project.

◆ **se projeter** *vp* [ombre] to be cast.

prolétaire [prɔletɛr] *nmf & adj* proletarian.

prolétariat [prɔletarja] *nm* proletariat.

prolétarien, -ienne [prɔletarjɛ̃, jɛn] *adj* proletarian.

prolifération [prɔliferasjɔ̃] *nf* proliferation.

proliférer [prɔlifere] [18] *vi* to proliferate.

prolifique [prɔlifik] *adj* prolific.

prolixe [prɔliks] *adj sout* wordy, verbose.

prolo [prɔlo] *nmf fam* prole, pleb.

prologue [prɔlɔg] *nm* prologue.

prolongation [prɔlɔ̃gasjɔ̃] *nf* [extension] extension, prolongation.

◆ **prolongations** *nfpl* SPORT extra time (U); jouer les ~s to go into extra time.

prolongement [prɔlɔ̃ʒmɑ̃] *nm* [de mur, quai] extension; être dans le ~ de to be a continuation of.

◆ **prolongements** *nmpl* [conséquences] repercussions.

prolonger [prɔlɔ̃ʒe] [17] *vt* -1. [dans le temps]: ~ qqch (de) to prolong sthg (by). -2. [dans l'espace]: ~ qqch (de) to extend sthg (by).

◆ **se prolonger** *vp* -1. [événement] to go on, to last. -2. [route] to go on, to continue.

promenade [prɔmnad] *nf* -1. [balade] walk, stroll; *fig* trip, excursion; ~ en voiture drive; ~ à vélo (bike) ride; faire une ~ to go for a walk. -2. [lieu] promenade.

promener [prɔmne] [19] *vt* -1. [personne] to take out (for a walk); [en voiture] to take for a drive. -2. *littéraire* [chagrin] to carry (about). -3. *fig* [regard, doigts]: ~ qqch sur to run sthg over.

◆ **se promener** *vp* to go for a walk.

promeneur, -euse [prɔmnœr, øz] *nm, f* walker, stroller.

promesse [prɔmɛs] *nf* -1. [serment] promise; manquer à sa ~ to break one's promise; tenir sa ~ to keep one's promise; ~s en l'air empty promises. -2. [engagement] undertaking; ~ d'achat/de vente JUR agreement to purchase/to sell. -3. *fig* [espérance]: être plein de ~s to be very promising.

promets → promettre.

prometteur, -euse [prɔmɛtœr, øz] *adj* promising.

promettre [prɔmɛtr] [84] ◇ *vt* to promise; ~ qqch à qqn to promise sb sthg; ~ de faire qqch to promise to do sthg; ~ à qqn que to promise sb that. ◇ *vi* to be promising; ça promet! *iron* that bodes well!

◆ **se promettre** *vp*: se ~ de faire qqch to resolve to do sthg.

promis, -e [prɔmi, iz] ◇ *pp* → promettre. ◇ *adj* promised; ~ à qqch destined for sthg. ◇ *nm, f hum* intended.

promiscuité [prɔmiskɥite] *nf* overcrowding; ~ sexuelle (sexual) promiscuity.

promontoire [prɔmɔ̃twar] *nm* promontory.

promoteur, -trice [prɔmɔtœr, tris] *nm, f* -1. [novateur] instigator. -2. [constructeur] property developer.

promotion [prɔmɔsjɔ̃] *nf* -1. [gén] promotion; ~ des ventes sales promotion; en ~ [produit] on special offer. -2. MIL & SCOL year.

promotionnel, -elle [prɔmɔsjɔnɛl] *adj* promotional.

promouvoir [prɔmuvwar] [56] *vt* to promote.

prompt, -e [prɔ̃, prɔ̃t] *adj sout*: ~ (à faire qqch) swift (to do sthg).

promptitude [prɔ̃tityd] *nf sout* swiftness.

promu, -e [prɔmy] *pp* → promouvoir.

promulgation [prɔmylgasjɔ̃] *nf* promulgation.

promulguer [prɔmylge] [3] *vt* to promulgate.

prôner [prone] [3] *vt sout* to advocate.

pronom [prɔnɔ̃] *nm* pronoun; ~ personnel/possessif/relatif personal/possessive/relative pronoun.

pronominal, -e, -aux [prɔnɔminal, o] *adj* pronominal.

prononcé, -e [prɔnɔ̃se] *adj* marked.

◆ **prononcé** *nm* [d'arrêt] delivery; [de sentence] passing.

prononcer [prɔnɔ̃se] [16] *vt* -1. JUR & LING to pronounce. -2. [dire] to utter.

◆ **se prononcer** *vp* **-1.** [se dire] to be pronounced; **comme ça se prononce** as it is pronounced. **-2.** [trancher - assemblée] to decide, to reach a decision; [- magistrat] to deliver a verdict; **se ~ sur** to give one's opinion of.

prononciation [prɔnɔ̃sjasjɔ̃] *nf* **-1.** LING pronunciation. **-2.** JUR pronouncement.

pronostic [prɔnɔstik] *nm* **-1.** (*gén pl*) [prévision] forecast. **-2.** MÉD prognosis.

pronostiquer [prɔnɔstike] [3] *vt* **-1.** [annoncer] to forecast. **-2.** MÉD to make a prognosis of.

pronostiqueur, -euse [prɔnɔstikœr, øz] *nm, f* forecaster.

propagande [prɔpagɑ̃d] *nf* **-1.** [endoctrinement] propaganda. **-2.** *fig* & *hum* [publicité]: **faire de la ~ pour qqch** to plug sthg.

propagation [prɔpagasjɔ̃] *nf* **-1.** [de flammes, de maladie & *fig*] spread, spreading. **-2.** BIOL & PHYS propagation.

propager [prɔpaʒe] [17] *vt* to spread.

◆ **se propager** *vp* to spread; BIOL to be propagated; PHYS to propagate.

propane [prɔpan] *nm* propane.

propension [prɔpɑ̃sjɔ̃] *nf*: **~ à qqch/à faire qqch** propensity for sthg/to do sthg.

prophète [prɔfɛt], **prophétesse** [prɔfetɛs] *nm, f* prophet (*f* prophetess).

◆ **Prophète** *nm*: **le Prophète** the Prophet.

prophétie [prɔfesi] *nf* prophecy.

prophétique [prɔfetik] *adj* prophetic.

prophétiser [prɔfetize] [3] *vt* to prophesy.

prophylactique [prɔfilaktik] *adj* prophylactic.

prophylaxie [prɔfilaksi] *nf* prophylaxis.

propice [prɔpis] *adj* favorable *Am*, favourable *Br*; **~ à** [changement] conducive to; [culture, élevage] good for.

proportion [prɔpɔrsjɔ̃] *nf* proportion; **en ~ de** in proportion to; **toutes ~s gardées** relatively speaking.

proportionné, -e [prɔpɔrsjɔne] *adj*: **bien/mal ~** well-/badly-proportioned; **~ à** proportionate to.

proportionnel, -elle [prɔpɔrsjɔnɛl] *adj*: **~ (à)** proportional (to).

◆ **proportionnelle** *nf*: **la ~le** proportional representation.

proportionnellement [prɔpɔrsjɔnɛlmɑ̃] *adv* proportionally.

propos [prɔpo] ◇ *nm* **-1.** [discours] talk. **-2.** [but] intention; **c'est à quel ~?** what is it about?; **de ~ délibéré** deliberately, on purpose; **hors de ~** at the wrong time. ◇ *nmpl* [paroles] talk (*U*), words; **tenir des ~ d'une**

extrême banalité to say extremely banal things.

◆ **à propos** ◇ *loc adv* **-1.** [opportunément] at (just) the right time. **-2.** [au fait] by the way. ◇ *loc adj* [opportun] opportune.

◆ **à propos de** *loc prép* about.

proposer [prɔpoze] [3] *vt* **-1.** [offrir] to offer, to propose; **~ qqch à qqn** to offer sb sthg, to offer sthg to sb; **~ à qqn de faire qqch** to offer to do sthg for sb. **-2.** [suggérer] to suggest, to propose; **~ de faire qqch** to suggest OU propose doing sthg. **-3.** [loi, candidat] to propose.

◆ **se proposer** *vp* **-1.** [offrir ses services] to offer one's services. **-2.** [décider]: **se ~ de faire qqch** to intend OU mean to do sthg.

proposition [prɔpozisjɔ̃] *nf* **-1.** [offre] offer, proposal; **~ malhonnête** improper suggestion; **faire des ~s à qqn** to proposition sb. **-2.** [suggestion] suggestion, proposal. **-3.** GRAM clause.

◆ **proposition de loi** *nf* bill.

propre [prɔpr] ◇ *adj* **-1.** [nettoyé] clean. **-2.** [soigné] neat, tidy. **-3.** [éduqué - enfant] toilet-trained; [- animal] housebroken *Am*, house-trained *Br*. **-4.** [personnel] own. **-5.** [particulier]: **~ à** peculiar to. **-6.** [approprié]: **~ (à)** suitable (for), appropriate (for). **-7.** [de nature]: **~ à faire qqch** capable of doing sthg. **-8.** *fig* [honnête] respectable. **-9.** *loc*: **nous voilà ~s!** *hum* we're in a fine mess! ◇ *nm* **-1.** [propreté] cleanness, cleanliness; **recopier qqch au ~** to make a fair copy of sthg, to copy sthg up. **-2.** [particularité]: **le ~ de** the characteristic feature of; **avoir qqch en ~** JUR to be the sole owner of sthg.

◆ **au propre** *loc adv* LING literally.

propre-à-rien [prɔprarjɛ̃] (*pl* **propres-à-rien**) *nmf* good-for-nothing.

proprement [prɔprəmɑ̃] *adv* **-1.** [convenablement - habillé] neatly, tidily; [- se tenir] correctly. **-2.** [véritablement] completely; **à ~ parler** strictly OU properly speaking; **l'événement ~ dit** the event itself, the actual event. **-3.** [exclusivement] peculiarly.

propret, -ette [prɔprɛ, ɛt] *adj* neat and tidy.

propreté [prɔprəte] *nf* cleanness, cleanliness.

propriétaire [prɔprijetɛr] *nmf* **-1.** [possesseur] owner; **~ foncier** property owner; **~ terrien** landowner. **-2.** [dans l'immobilier] landlord.

propriété [prɔprijete] *nf* **-1.** [gén] property; **~ industrielle** JUR patent rights (*pl*); **~ privée** private property. **-2.** [droit] ownership.

-3. [terres] property (U). -4. [convenance] suitability.

propulser [prɔpylse] [3] vt litt & fig to propel.
◆ **se propulser** vp to move forward, to propel o.s. forward OU along; fig to shoot.

propulsion [prɔpylsjɔ̃] nf propulsion.

prorata [prɔrata]
◆ **au prorata de** loc prép in proportion to.

prorogation [prɔrɔgasjɔ̃] nf -1. JUR extension. -2. POLIT adjournment.

proroger [prɔrɔʒe] [17] vt -1. JUR to extend. -2. POLIT to adjourn.

prosaïque [prozaik] adj prosaic, mundane.

proscription [prɔskripsjɔ̃] nf [interdiction] banning, prohibition.

proscrire [prɔskrir] [99] vt -1. [interdire] to ban, to prohibit. -2. littéraire [chasser]: ~ qqn (de) to exile sb (from), to banish sb (from).

proscrit, -e [prɔskri, it] ◇ pp → proscrire. ◇ adj -1. [interdit] banned, prohibited. -2. littéraire [chassé] exiled. ◇ nm, f littéraire exile.

proscrivais, proscrivions etc → proscrire.

prose [proz] nf prose; en ~ in prose.

prosélyte [prɔzelit] nmf convert.

prosélytisme [prɔzelitism] nm proselytizing.

prospecter [prɔspɛkte] [4] vt -1. [pays, région] to prospect. -2. COMM to canvass.

prospecteur, -trice [prɔspɛktœr, tris] nm, f -1. [de ressources] prospector. -2. COMM canvasser.

prospectif, -ive [prɔspɛktif, iv] adj: analyse prospective COMM forecast.
◆ **prospective** nf futurology.

prospection [prɔspɛksjɔ̃] nf -1. [de ressources] prospecting. -2. COMM canvassing.

prospectus [prɔspɛktys] nm (advertising) leaflet.

prospère [prɔspɛr] adj -1. [commerce] prosperous. -2. [santé] blooming.

prospérer [prɔspere] [18] vi to prosper, to thrive; [plante, insecte] to thrive.

prospérité [prɔsperite] nf -1. [richesse] prosperity. -2. [bien-être] well-being.

prostate [prɔstat] nf prostate (gland).

prosterner [prɔstɛrne] [3]
◆ **se prosterner** vp to bow down; se ~ devant to bow down before; fig to kowtow to.

prostitué [prɔstitɥe] nm male prostitute.

prostituée [prɔstitɥe] nf prostitute.

prostituer [prɔstitɥe] [7] vt to prostitute.
◆ **se prostituer** vp to prostitute o.s.

prostitution [prɔstitysjɔ̃] nf prostitution.

prostration [prɔstrasjɔ̃] nf prostration.

prostré, -e [prɔstre] adj prostrate.

protagoniste [prɔtagɔnist] nmf protagonist, hero (f heroine).

protecteur, -trice [prɔtɛktœr, tris] ◇ adj protective. ◇ nm, f -1. [défenseur] protector. -2. [des arts] patron. -3. [souteneur] pimp. -4. Can POLIT: le Protecteur du citoyen the Ombudsman.

protection [prɔtɛksjɔ̃] nf -1. [défense] protection; ~ contre protection from OU against; se mettre sous la ~ de qqn to put o.s. under sb's protection; prendre qqn sous sa ~ to take sb under one's wing. -2. [des arts] patronage.

protectionnisme [prɔtɛksjɔnism] nm protectionism.

protectionniste [prɔtɛksjɔnist] nmf & adj protectionist.

protectorat [prɔtɛktɔra] nm protectorate.

protégé, -e [prɔteʒe] ◇ adj protected. ◇ nm, f protégé.

protège-cahier [prɔteʒkaje] (pl protège-cahiers) nm exercise book cover.

protéger [prɔteʒe] [22] vt -1. [gén] to protect. -2. [arts] to be a patron of.
◆ **se protéger** vp [mettre un préservatif] to use a condom.

protéine [prɔtein] nf protein.

protestant, -e [prɔtɛstɑ̃, ɑ̃t] adj & nm, f Protestant.

protestantisme [prɔtɛstɑ̃tism] nm Protestantism.

protestataire [prɔtɛstatɛr] ◇ nmf protestor. ◇ adj sout [vote, écrits] protest (avant n); [cri] of protest.

protestation [prɔtɛstasjɔ̃] nf -1. [contestation] protest. -2. littéraire [déclaration] protestation.

protester [prɔtɛste] [3] vi to protest; ~ contre qqch to protest against sthg, to protest sthg Am; ~ de qqch littéraire to protest sthg.

prothèse [prɔtɛz] nf prosthesis; ~ dentaire dentures (pl), false teeth (pl).

protide [prɔtid] nm protein.

protocolaire [prɔtɔkɔlɛr] adj [poli] conforming to etiquette.

protocole [prɔtɔkɔl] nm protocol.

proton [prɔtɔ̃] nm proton.

prototype [prɔtɔtip] nm prototype.

protubérance [prɔtyberɑ̃s] *nf* bulge, protuberance.

protubérant, -e [prɔtyberɑ̃, ɑ̃t] *adj* bulging, protruding.

proue [pru] *nf* bows (*pl*), prow.

prouesse [pruɛs] *nf* feat.

prouver [pruve] [3] *vt* **-1.** [établir] to prove. **-2.** [montrer] to demonstrate, to show.

◆ **se prouver** *vp* to prove to o.s.

provenance [prɔvnɑ̃s] *nf* origin; **en ~ de** from.

provençal, -e, -aux [prɔvɑ̃sal, o] *adj* **-1.** [de Provence] of/from Provence. **-2.** CULIN *with tomatoes, garlic and onions.*

◆ **provençal** *nm* [langue] Provençal.

◆ **Provençal, -e, -aux** *nm, f* native OU inhabitant of Provence.

◆ **à la provençale** *loc adv* CULIN *with tomatoes, garlic and onions.*

Provence [prɔvɑ̃s] *nf*: **la ~** Provence.

provenir [prɔvnir] [40] *vi*: **~ de** to come from; *fig* to be due to, to be caused by.

provenu, -e [prɔvny] *pp* → **provenir**.

proverbe [prɔvɛrb] *nm* proverb.

proverbial, -e, -iaux [prɔvɛrbjal, jo] *adj* proverbial.

providence [prɔvidɑ̃s] *nf* providence; *fig* guardian angel.

◆ **Providence** *nf* Providence.

providentiel, -ielle [prɔvidɑ̃sjɛl] *adj* providential.

proviendrai, proviendras *etc* → **provenir**.

proviens, provient *etc* → **provenir**.

province [prɔvɛ̃s] *nf* **-1.** [gén] province. **-2.** [campagne] provinces (*pl*).

provincial, -e, -iaux [prɔvɛ̃sjal, jo] *adj & nm, f* provincial.

proviseur [prɔvizœr] *nm* ≃ principal *Am,* ≃ head *Br,* ≃ headteacher *Br,* ≃ headmaster (*f* headmistress) *Br.*

provision [prɔvizjɔ̃] *nf* **-1.** [réserve] stock, supply; **faire ~ de qqch** to stock up on OU with sthg. **-2.** FIN retainer; *voir aussi* **chèque**.

◆ **provisions** *nfpl* provisions.

provisionnel, -elle [prɔvizjɔnɛl] *adj* provisional.

provisoire [prɔvizwar] ◇ *adj* temporary; JUR provisional. ◇ *nm*: **ce n'est que du ~** it's only a temporary arrangement.

provisoirement [prɔvizwarmɑ̃] *adv* temporarily.

provocant, -e [prɔvɔkɑ̃, ɑ̃t] *adj* provocative.

provocateur, -trice [prɔvɔkatœr, tris] ◇ *adj* provocative. ◇ *nm, f* agitator, troublemaker.

provocation [prɔvɔkasjɔ̃] *nf* provocation.

provoquer [prɔvɔke] [3] *vt* **-1.** [entraîner] to cause. **-2.** [personne] to provoke.

◆ **se provoquer** *vp* to provoke each other.

proxénète [prɔksenɛt] *nm* pimp.

proxénétisme [prɔksenetism] *nm* pimping, procuring.

proximité [prɔksimite] *nf* **-1.** [de lieu] proximity, nearness; **à ~ de** near. **-2.** [d'événement] closeness.

prude [pryd] ◇ *nf* prude. ◇ *adj* prudish.

prudemment [prydamɑ̃] *adv* cautiously.

prudence [prydɑ̃s] *nf* care, caution.

prudent, -e [prydɑ̃, ɑ̃t] *adj* careful, cautious; **sois ~!** be careful!

prud'homme [prydɔm] *nm* ≃ member of an industrial tribunal; **Conseil de ~s** ≃ industrial tribunal.

prune [pryn] ◇ *nf* plum; **compter pour des ~s** *fam* to count for nothing. ◇ *adj inv* plum-colored *Am,* plum-coloured *Br.*

pruneau, -x [pryno] *nm* **-1.** [fruit] prune. **-2.** *fam* [balle] slug.

prunelle [prynel] *nf* ANAT pupil; **j'y tiens comme à la ~ de mes yeux** it's the apple of my eye.

prunier [prynje] *nm* plum tree; **secouer qqn comme un ~** *fam* to shake sb until his/her teeth rattle.

Prusse [prys] *nf*: **la ~** Prussia.

prussien, -ienne [prysjɛ̃, jɛn] *adj* Prussian.

◆ **Prussien, -ienne** *nm, f* Prussian.

PS¹ (*abr de* **Parti socialiste**) *nm French socialist party.*

PS², P-S (*abr de* **post-scriptum**) *nm* PS.

psalmodie [psalmɔdi] *nf* chanting.

psalmodier [psalmɔdje] [9] ◇ *vt* to chant; *fig & péj* to drone. ◇ *vi* to drone.

psaume [psom] *nm* psalm.

pseudonyme [psødɔnim] *nm* pseudonym.

PS-G (*abr de* **Paris St-Germain**) *nm Paris football team.*

PSIG (*abr de* **Peloton de surveillance et d'intervention de la gendarmerie**) *nm gendarmerie commando squad.*

PSU (*abr de* **Parti socialiste unifié**) *nm socialist party.*

psy [psi] *fam* ◇ *nmf* (*abr de* **psychiatre**) shrink. ◇ *adj*: **elle est très ~** she's really into psychology.

psychanalyse [psikanaliz] *nf* psychoanalysis; **faire la ~ de qqn** to psychoanalyse sb.

psychanalyser [psikanalize] [3] *vt* to psychoanalyse.

psychanalyste [psikanalist] *nmf* psychoanalyst, analyst.

psychanalytique [psikanalitik] *adj* psychoanalytic, psychoanalytical.

psyché [psiʃe] *nf* cheval mirror.

psychédélique [psikedelik] *adj* psychedelic.

psychiatre [psikjatr] *nmf* psychiatrist.

psychiatrie [psikjatri] *nf* psychiatry.

psychiatrique [psikjatrik] *adj* psychiatric.

psychique [psiʃik] *adj* psychic; [maladie] psychosomatic.

psychisme [psiʃism] *nm* psyche, mind.

psychodrame [psikɔdram] *nm* psychodrama; *fig* melodrama.

psychologie [psikɔlɔʒi] *nf* psychology.

psychologique [psikɔlɔʒik] *adj* psychological.

psychologiquement [psikɔlɔʒikmɑ̃] *adv* psychologically.

psychologue [psikɔlɔg] ◇ *nmf* psychologist. ◇ *adj* psychological.

psychopathe [psikɔpat] *nmf* psychopath.

psychose [psikoz] *nf* **-1.** MÉD psychosis. **-2.** [crainte] obsessive fear.

psychosomatique [psikɔsɔmatik] *adj* psychosomatic.

psychothérapeute [psikɔterapøt] *nmf* psychotherapist.

psychothérapie [psikɔterapi] *nf* psychotherapy.

PTA (*abr de* peseta) Pta, P.

Pte -1. *abr de* porte. **-2.** *abr de* pointe.

PTT (*abr de* Postes, télécommunications et télédiffusion) *nfpl former French post office and telecommunications network.*

pu [py] *pp* → **pouvoir**.

puant, -e [pɥɑ̃, ɑ̃t] *adj* **-1.** [fétide] smelly, stinking. **-2.** *fam fig* [personne] bumptious, full of oneself.

puanteur [pɥɑ̃tœr] *nf* stink, stench.

pub[1] [pyb] *nf fam* ad, advert *Br*; [métier] advertising.

pub[2] [pœb] *nm* pub.

pubère [pybɛr] *adj* pubescent.

puberté [pybɛrte] *nf* puberty.

pubis [pybis] *nm* [zone] pubis.

public, -ique [pyblik] *adj* public.
◆ **public** *nm* **-1.** [auditoire] audience; **en ~** in public. **-2.** [population] public; **grand ~** general public.

publication [pyblikasjɔ̃] *nf* publication.

publicitaire [pyblisitɛr] *adj* [campagne] advertising (*avant n*); [film] promotional.

publicité [pyblisite] *nf* **-1.** [domaine] advertising; **~ comparative** comparative advertising; **~ institutionnelle** corporate advertising; **~ mensongère** misleading advertising, deceptive advertising; **~ sur le lieu de vente** point-of-sale advertising, POS advertising. **-2.** [réclame] advertisement, advert. **-3.** [autour d'une affaire] publicity (*U*).

publier [pyblije] [10] *vt* **-1.** [livre] to publish; [communiqué] to issue, to release. **-2.** [nouvelle] to make public.

publiquement [pyblikmɑ̃] *adv* publicly.

publireportage [pyblirəpɔrtaʒ] *nm* reading notice *Am*, free write-up *Br*.

puce [pys] *nf* **-1.** [animal] flea. **-2.** INFORM (silicon) chip. **-3.** *fig* [terme affectueux] pet, love. **-4.** *loc:* **mettre la ~ à l'oreille de qqn** to make sb suspicious; **secouer les ~s à qqn** *fam* to tear sb off a strip.
◆ **puces** *nfpl:* **les ~s** flea market (*sg*).

puceau, -elle, -x [pyso, ɛl, o] *nm, f & adj fam* virgin.

puceron [pysrɔ̃] *nm* aphid.

pudding [pudiŋ] *nm* plum OU Christmas pudding.

pudeur [pydœr] *nf* **-1.** [physique] modesty, decency. **-2.** [morale] restraint.

pudibond, -e [pydibɔ̃, ɔ̃d] *adj* prudish.

pudibonderie [pydibɔ̃dri] *nf littéraire* prudishness, primness.

pudique [pydik] *adj* **-1.** [physiquement] modest, decent. **-2.** [moralement] restrained.

pudiquement [pydikmɑ̃] *adv* modestly.

puer [pɥe] [7] ◇ *vi* to stink; **ça pue ici!** it stinks in here! ◇ *vt* to reek of, to stink of.

puéricultrice [pɥerikyltris] *nf* nursery nurse.

puériculture [pɥerikyltyr] *nf* childcare.

puéril, -e [pɥeril] *adj* childish.

puérilité [pɥerilite] *nf* childishness.

Puerto Rico = Porto Rico.

PUF, Puf [pyf] (*abr de* Presses Universitaires de France) *nfpl French publishing house.*

pugilat [pyʒila] *nm* fight.

pugnace [pygnas] *adj littéraire* pugnacious.

pugnacité [pygnasite] *nf littéraire* pugnacity.

puis [pɥi] *adv* then; **et ~** [d'ailleurs] and moreover OU besides; **et ~ quoi** OU **après?** *fam* so what?

puisard [pɥizar] *nm* cesspool.

puiser [pɥize] [3] *vt* [liquide] to draw; **~ qqch dans qqch** *fig* to draw OU take sthg from sthg.

puisque [pҷiskə] *conj* **-1.** [gén] since. **-2.** [renforce une affirmation]: **mais puisqu'il m'attend!** but he's waiting for me!

puissamment [pҷisamã] *adv* powerfully.

puissance [pҷisãs] *nf* power; **les grandes ~s** the great powers.
◆ **en puissance** *loc adj* potential.

puissant, -e [pҷisã, ãt] *adj* powerful.
◆ **puissant** *nm*: **les ~s** the powerful.

puisse, puisses *etc* → **pouvoir**.

puits [pҷi] *nm* **-1.** [d'eau] well. **-2.** [de gisement] shaft; **~ de mine** mine shaft; **~ de pétrole** oil well; **~ de sciences** *fig* fount of all knowledge.

pull [pyl], **pull-over** [pylɔvɛr] (*pl* **pull-overs**) *nm* sweater, jumper *Br*.

pulluler [pylyle] [3] *vi* to swarm.

pulmonaire [pylmɔnɛr] *adj* lung (*avant n*), pulmonary.

pulpe [pylp] *nf* pulp.

pulpeux, -euse [pylpø, øz] *adj* **-1.** [fruit] pulpy; [jus] containing pulp. **-2.** *fig* [femme] curvaceous.

pulsation [pylsasjɔ̃] *nf* beat, beating (*U*).

pulsion [pylsjɔ̃] *nf* impulse.

pulvérisateur [pylverizatœr] *nm* spray.

pulvérisation [pylverizasjɔ̃] *nf* **-1.** [d'insecticide] spraying. **-2.** MÉD spray; [traitement] spraying.

pulvériser [pylverize] [3] *vt* **-1.** [projeter] to spray. **-2.** [détruire] to pulverize; *fig* to smash.

puma [pyma] *nm* puma.

punaise [pynɛz] ◇ *nf* **-1.** [insecte] bug. **-2.** *fig* [femme] shrew. **-3.** [clou] thumbtack *Am*, drawing pin *Br*. ◇ *interj* good grief!

punch [pɔ̃ʃ] *nm* punch.

punching-ball [pœnʃiŋbol] (*pl* **punching-balls**) *nm* punchball.

puni, -e [pyni] *adj* punished.

punir [pynir] [32] *vt*: **~ qqn (de)** to punish sb (with).

punitif, -ive [pynitif, iv] *adj* punitive.

punition [pynisjɔ̃] *nf* punishment.

punk [pœnk] *nmf & adj inv* punk.

pupille [pypij] ◇ *nf* ANAT pupil. ◇ *nmf* [orphelin] ward; **~ de l'État** ≃ child in care; **~ de la Nation** war orphan (*in care*).

pupitre [pypitr] *nm* **-1.** [d'orateur] lectern; MUS stand. **-2.** TECHNOL console. **-3.** [d'écolier] desk.

pur, -e [pyr] *adj* **-1.** [gén] pure. **-2.** *fig* [absolu] pure, sheer; **~ et simple** pure and sim-

ple. **-3.** *littéraire* [intention] honorable *Am*, honourable *Br*. **-4.** [lignes] pure, clean.

purée [pyre] *nf* purée; **~ de pois** *fig* pea-souper; **~ de pommes de terre** mashed potatoes.

purement [pyrmã] *adv* purely; **~ et simplement** purely and simply.

pureté [pyrte] *nf* **-1.** [gén] purity. **-2.** [de sculpture, de diamant] perfection. **-3.** [d'intention] honourableness.

purgatif, -ive [pyrgatif, iv] *adj* purgative.
◆ **purgatif** *nm* purgative.

purgatoire [pyrgatwar] *nm* purgatory.

purge [pyrʒ] *nf* **-1.** MÉD & POLIT purge. **-2.** [de radiateur] bleeding.

purger [pyrʒe] [17] *vt* **-1.** MÉD & POLIT to purge. **-2.** [radiateur] to bleed. **-3.** [peine] to serve.
◆ **se purger** *vp* to take a purgative.

purificateur, -trice [pyrifikatœr, tris] *adj* purifying, cleansing.
◆ **purificateur** *nm* purifier.

purification [pyrifikasjɔ̃] *nf* purification.

purifier [pyrifje] [9] *vt* to purify.
◆ **se purifier** *vp* to become pure OU clean; *fig* to purify OU cleanse o.s.

purin [pyrɛ̃] *nm* slurry.

puriste [pyrist] *nmf & adj* purist.

puritain, -e [pyritɛ̃, ɛn] ◇ *adj* **-1.** [pudibond] puritanical. **-2.** RELIG Puritan (*avant n*). ◇ *nm, f* **-1.** [prude] puritan. **-2.** RELIG Puritan.

puritanisme [pyritanism] *nm* puritanism; RELIG Puritanism.

pur-sang [pyrsã] *nm inv* thoroughbred.

purulent, -e [pyrylã, ãt] *adj* purulent.

pus [py] *nm* pus.

pusillanime [pyzilanim] *adj* pusillanimous.

pusillanimité [pyzilanimite] *nf* pusillanimity.

pustule [pystyl] *nf* pustule.

putain [pytɛ̃] ◇ *nf vulg* **-1.** *péj* [prostituée] whore. **-2.** *péj* [femme facile] tart, slag. **-3.** *fig* [pour exprimer le mécontentement]: **(ce) ~ de ...** this/that goddam ... *Am*, this/that sodding ... *Br*. ◇ *interj* goddam! *Am*, sod it! *Br*, bugger! *Br*; [exprime l'étonnement] goddam it! *Am*, (well) bugger me! *Br*.

pute [pyt] *nf vulg péj* [prostituée] whore.

putois [pytwa] *nm* polecat.

putréfaction [pytrefaksjɔ̃] *nf* putrefaction; **en ~** rotting, putrefying.

putréfier [pytrefje] [9]
◆ **se putréfier** *vp* to putrefy, to rot.

putrescent, **-e** [pytrɛsã, ãt] *adj* putrescent, rotting.

putride [pytrid] *adj* **-1.** [corps] putrid. **-2.** [odeur, miasme] fetid, foul.

putsch [putʃ] *nm* uprising, coup.

putschiste [putʃist] *nmf* rebel.

puzzle [pœzl] *nm* jigsaw (puzzle).

P-V *nm abr de* **procès-verbal.**

PVC (*abr de* **polyvinyl chloride**) *nm* PVC.

PVD (*abr de* **pays en voie de développement**) *nm* developing country.

px (*abr de* **prix**): ~ **à déb.** offers.

pygmée [pigme] *adj* pygmy.
◆ **Pygmée** *nmf* Pygmy.

pyjama [piʒama] *nm* pyjamas (*pl*).

pylône [pilon] *nm* pylon.

pyramide [piramid] *nf* pyramid.

pyrénéen, **-enne** [pireneẽ, ɛn] *adj* Pyrenean.
◆ **Pyrénéen**, **-enne** *nm, f* Pyrenean.

Pyrénées [pirene] *nfpl*: **les** ~ the Pyrenees.

Pyrex® [pirɛks] *nm* Pyrex®.

pyromane [pirɔman] *nmf* arsonist; MÉD pyromaniac.

pyrotechnique [pirɔtɛknik] *adj* firework (*avant n*), pyrotechnic.

python [pitɔ̃] *nm* python.

q¹, **Q** [ky] *nm inv* [lettre] q, Q.

q² *abr de* **quintal.**

Qatar, Katar [katar] *nm*: **le** ~ Qatar.

QCM (*abr de* **questionnaire à choix multiple**) *nm* multiple choice questionnaire.

QG (*abr de* **quartier général**) *nm* HQ.

QHS (*abr de* **quartier de haute sécurité**) *nm* high-security wing.

QI (*abr de* **quotient intellectuel**) *nm* IQ.

Qom, Qum [kɔm] *n* Qom.

qqch (*abr de* **quelque chose**) sthg.

qqe *abr de* **quelque.**

qqes *abr de* **quelques.**

qqf *abr de* **quelquefois.**

qqn (*abr de* **quelqu'un**) s.o., sb.

quadragénaire [kwadraʒenɛr] ◇ *nmf* forty year old. ◇ *adj*: **être** ~ to be in one's forties.

quadrangulaire [kwadrãgylɛr] *adj* quadrangular.

quadrature [kwadratyr] *nf* quadrature; **c'est la** ~ **du cercle** it's like trying to square the circle.

quadrichromie [kwadrikrɔmi] *nf* four-color *Am* OU four-colour *Br* printing.

quadrilatère [kwadrilatɛr] *nm* quadrilateral.

quadrillage [kadrijaʒ] *nm* **-1.** [de papier, de tissu] criss-cross pattern. **-2.** [policier] combing.

quadrille [kadrij] *nm* quadrille.

quadriller [kadrije] [3] *vt* **-1.** [papier] to mark with squares. **-2.** [ville - suj: rues] to criss-cross; [- suj: police] to comb.

quadrimoteur [kwadrimɔtœr] ◇ *nm* four-engined plane. ◇ *adj* four-engined.

quadriphonie [kwadrifɔni] *nf* quadraphony.

quadrupède [k(w)adrypɛd] *nm & adj* quadruped.

quadruple [k(w)adrypl] *nm & adj* quadruple.

quadruplés, **-ées** [k(w)adryple] *nm, f pl* quadruplets, quads.

quadrupler [k(w)adryple] [3] *vt & vi* to quadruple, to increase fourfold.

quai [kɛ] *nm* **-1.** [de gare] platform. **-2.** [de port] quay, wharf. **-3.** [de rivière] embankment.

QUAI:
Note that the names 'Quai d'Orsay' and 'Quai des Orfèvres' are often used to refer to the government departments situated on the streets of the same name: the foreign office and the police department respectively. 'Le quai de Conti' is sometimes used to refer to the Académie française

qualifiable [kalifjabl] *adj* [conduite, attitude]: **peu** ~ indescribable.

qualificatif, **-ive** [kalifikatif, iv] *adj* qualifying.
◆ **qualificatif** *nm* term.

qualification [kalifikasjɔ̃] *nf* **-1.** [gén] qualification. **-2.** [désignation] designation.

qualifier [kalifje] [9] *vt* **-1.** [gén] to qualify; **être qualifié pour qqch/pour faire qqch** to be qualified for sthg/to do sthg. **-2.** [caractériser]: ~ **qqn/qqch de qqch** to describe sb/sthg as sthg, to call sb/sthg sthg.
◆ **se qualifier** *vp* to qualify.

qualitatif, -ive [kalitatif, iv] *adj* qualitative.

qualitativement [kalitativmɑ̃] *adv* qualitatively.

qualité [kalite] *nf* **-1.** [gén] quality; **de bonne/mauvaise ~** of good/poor quality; **~ de la vie** quality of life. **-2.** [condition] position, capacity; **en ~ de** in my/his *etc* capacity as.

quand [kɑ̃] ◇ *conj* **-1.** [lorsque, alors que] when; **~ tu le verras, demande-lui de me téléphoner** when you see him, ask him to phone me; **pourquoi rester ici ~ on pourrait partir en week-end?** why stay here when we could go away for the weekend? **-2.** *sout* [introduit une hypothèse] even if. ◇ *adv interr* when; **~ arriveras-tu?** when will you arrive?; **je ne sais pas encore ~ je pars** I don't know yet when I'm leaving; **jusqu'à ~ restez-vous?** how long are you staying for?
◆ **quand même** ◇ *loc conj sout* even though, even if. ◇ *loc adv* all the same; **je pense qu'il ne viendra pas, mais je l'inviterai ~ même** I don't think he'll come but I'll invite him all the same; **tu pourrais faire attention ~ même!** you might at least be careful! ◇ *interj:* **~ même, à son âge!** really, at his/her age!
◆ **quand bien même** *loc conj sout* even though, even if.
◆ **n'importe quand** *loc adv* any time.

quant [kɑ̃]
◆ **quant à** *loc prép* as for.

quant-à-soi [kɑ̃taswa] *nm inv* reserve; **rester sur son ~** to remain aloof.

quantième [kɑ̃tjɛm] *nm* date.

quantifiable [kɑ̃tifjabl] *adj* quantifiable.

quantifier [kɑ̃tifje] [9] *vt* to quantify.

quantitatif, -ive [kɑ̃titatif, iv] *adj* quantitative.

quantitativement [kɑ̃titativmɑ̃] *adv* quantitatively.

quantité [kɑ̃tite] *nf* **-1.** [mesure] quantity, amount. **-2.** [abondance]: **(une) ~ de** a great many, a lot of; **en ~** in large numbers; **des exemplaires en ~** a large number of copies. **-3.** LING & SCIENCE quantity.

quarantaine [karɑ̃tɛn] *nf* **-1.** [nombre]: **une ~ de** about forty. **-2.** [âge]: **avoir la ~** to be in one's forties. **-3.** [isolement] quarantine; **mettre qqn en ~** *fig* to send sb to Coventry.

quarante [karɑ̃t] *adj num & nm* forty; *voir aussi* **six.**

quarantième [karɑ̃tjɛm] *adj num, nm & nmf* fortieth; *voir aussi* **sixième.**

quart [kar] *nm* **-1.** [fraction] quarter; **deux heures moins le ~** (a) quarter to two, (a) quarter of two *Am*; **deux heures et ~** (a) quarter past two, (a) quarter after two *Am*; **il est moins le ~** it's (a) quarter to; **démarrer au ~ de tour** to start first time; *fig* to fly off the handle; **un ~ d'heure** a quarter of an hour; **passer un mauvais ~ d'heure** to have a bad time of it. **-2.** NAVIG watch. **-3.** **~ de finale** quarter final.

quart-arrière [kararjɛr] *nmf Can* SPORT quarterback.

quarté [karte] *nm system of betting involving the first four horses in a race.*

quartette [kwartɛt] *nm* jazz quartet.

quartier [kartje] *nm* **-1.** [de ville] area, district; **les beaux ~s** the smart areas; **~ résidentiel** residential area; **restaurant de ~** local restaurant. **-2.** [de fruit] piece; [de viande] quarter. **-3.** [héraldique, de lune] quarter. **-4.** (*gén pl*) MIL quarters (*pl*); **~ général** headquarters (*pl*); **avoir/donner ~ libre** to have/give permission to leave barracks; *fig* to have/give permission to go out.

quartier-maître [kartjemɛtr] (*pl* quartiers-maîtres) *nm* leading seaman.

quartz [kwarts] *nm* quartz; **montre à ~** quartz watch.

quasi [kazi] *adv* almost, nearly.

quasi- [kazi] *préfixe* near.

quasiment [kazimɑ̃] *adv fam* almost, nearly.

quatorze [katɔrz] *adj num & nm* fourteen; *voir aussi* **six.**

quatorzième [katɔrzjɛm] *adj num, nm & nmf* fourteenth; *voir aussi* **sixième.**

quatrain [katrɛ̃] *nm* quatrain.

quatre [katr] ◇ *adj num* four; **monter l'escalier ~ à ~** to take the stairs four at a time; **se mettre en ~ pour qqn** to bend over backwards for sb. ◇ *nm* four; *voir aussi* **six.**

quatre-quarts [katkar] *nm inv* pound cake.

quatre-vingt = **quatre-vingts.**

quatre-vingt-dix [katrəvɛ̃dis] *adj num & nm* ninety; *voir aussi* **six.**

quatre-vingt-dixième [katrəvɛ̃dizjɛm] *adj num, nm & nmf* ninetieth; *voir aussi* **sixième.**

quatre-vingtième [katrəvɛ̃tjɛm] *adj num, nm & nmf* eightieth; *voir aussi* **sixième.**

quatre-vingts, quatre-vingt [katrəvɛ̃] *adj num & nm* eighty; *voir aussi* **six.**

quatrième [katrijɛm] ◇ *adj num, nm & nmf* fourth; *voir aussi* **sixième.** ◇ *nf* **-1.** SCOL ≃ eighth grade *Am*, ≃ third year OU form *Br*. **-2.** [en danse] fourth position.

quatuor [kwatɥɔr] *nm* quartet; *Can* GOLF foursome.

que [k(ə)] ◇ *conj* **-1.** [introduit une subordonnée] that; **je sais ~ tu mens** I know (that) you're lying; **il a dit qu'il viendrait** he said (that) he'd come; **il veut ~ tu viennes** he wants you to come. **-2.** [introduit une hypothèse] whether; **~ vous le vouliez ou non** whether you like it or not. **-3.** [reprend une autre conjonction]: **s'il fait beau et que nous avons le temps ...** if the weather is good and we have time .... **-4.** [indique un ordre, un souhait]: **qu'il entre!** let him come in!; **~ tout le monde sorte!** everybody out! **-5.** [après un présentatif]: **voilà/voici ~ ça recommence!** here we go again! **-6.** [comparatif - après moins, plus] than; [- après autant, aussi, même] as; **plus jeune ~ moi** younger than I (am) OU than me; **elle a la même robe ~ moi** she has the same dress as I do OU as me. **-7.** [seulement]: **ne ... ~** only; **je n'ai qu'une sœur** I've only got one sister.
◇ *pron relatif* [chose, animal] which, that; [personne] whom, that; **la femme ~ j'aime** the woman (whom OU that) I love; **le livre qu'il m'a prêté** the book (which OU that) he lent me.
◇ *pron interr* what; **~ savez-vous au juste?** what exactly do you know?; **~ faire?** what can I/we/one do?; **je me demande ~ faire** I wonder what I should do.
◇ *adv excl*: **qu'elle est belle!** how beautiful she is!; **~ de monde!** what a lot of people!
◆ **c'est que** *loc conj* it's because; **si je vais me coucher, c'est ~ j'ai sommeil** if I'm going to bed, it's because I'm tired.
◆ **qu'est-ce que** *pron interr* what; **qu'est-ce ~ tu veux encore?** what else do you want?
◆ **qu'est-ce qui** *pron interr* what; **qu'est-ce qui se passe?** what's going on?

Québec [kebɛk] *nm* **-1.** [province]: **le ~** Quebec; **la province de** OU **du ~** Quebec State; **au ~** in Quebec. **-2.** [ville] Quebec; **à ~** in (the city of) Quebec.

québécois, -e [kebekwa, az] *adj* Quebec (*avant n*).
◆ **québécois** *nm* [langue] Quebec French.
◆ **Québécois, -e** *nm, f* Quebecker, Québecois.

quel [kɛl] (*f* **quelle**, *mpl* **quels**, *fpl* **quelles**) ◇ *adj interr* [personne] which; [chose] what, which; **~ homme?** which man?; **~ est cet homme?** who is this man?; **~ livre voulez-vous?** what OU which book do you want?; **de ~ côté es-tu?** which OU which side are you on?; **je ne sais ~s sont ses projets** I don't know what his plans are; **quelle heure est-il?** what time is it?, what's the time?

◇ *adj excl*: **~ idiot!** what an idiot!; **quelle honte!** the shame of it!; **~ beau temps!** what lovely weather!
◇ *adj indéf*: **~ que** (+ *subjonctif*) [chose, animal] whatever; [personne] whoever; **il se baigne, ~ que soit le temps** he goes swimming whatever the weather; **il refuse de voir les nouveaux arrivants, ~s qu'ils soient** he refuses to see new arrivals, whoever they may be.
◇ *pron interr* which (one); **de vous trois, ~ est le plus jeune?** which (one) of you three is the youngest?

quelconque [kɛlkɔ̃k] *adj* **-1.** [n'importe lequel] any; **donner un prétexte ~** to give any old excuse; **si pour une raison ~ ...** if for any reason ...; **une ~ observation** some remark or other. **-2.** (*après n*) *péj* [banal] ordinary, mediocre.

quelque [kɛlk(ə)] ◇ *adj indéf* some; **à ~ distance de là** some way away (from there); **j'ai ~s lettres à écrire** I have some OU a few letters to write; **vous n'avez pas ~s livres à me montrer?** don't you have any books to show me?; **les ~s fois où j'étais absent** the few times I wasn't there; **les ~s 200 francs qu'il m'a prêtés** the 200 francs or so (that) he lent me; **~ route que je prenne** whatever route I take; **~ peu** somewhat, rather.
◇ *adv* [environ] about; **200 francs et ~** some OU about 200 francs; **il est midi et ~** *fam* it's just after midday.

quelque chose [kɛlkəʃoz] *pron indéf* something; **~ de différent** something different; **~ d'autre** something else; **tu veux boire ~?** do you want something OU anything to drink?; **apporter un petit ~ à qqn** to give sb a little something; **c'est ~!** [ton admiratif] it's really something!; **cela m'a fait ~** I really felt it.

quelquefois [kɛlkəfwa] *adv* sometimes, occasionally.

quelque part [kɛlkəpar] *adv* someplace *Am*, somewhere *Br*; **l'as-tu vu ~?** did you see him anyplace *Am* OU anywhere *Br*?, have you seen him anyplace *Am* OU anywhere *Br*?

quelques-uns, quelques-unes [kɛlkəzœ̃, yn] *pron indéf* some, a few.

quelqu'un [kɛlkœ̃] *pron indéf m* someone, somebody; **c'est ~ d'ouvert/d'intelligent** he's/she's a frank/an intelligent person.

quémander [kemɑ̃de] [3] *vt* to beg for; **~ qqch à qqn** to beg sb for sthg.

qu'en-dira-t-on [kɑ̃diratɔ̃] *nm inv fam* tittle-tattle.

quenelle [kənɛl] *nf very finely chopped mixture of fish or chicken cooked in stock.*

quenotte [kənɔt] *nf fam* tooth.

querelle [kərɛl] *nf* quarrel; **chercher ~ à qqn** to pick a quarrel with sb.

quereller [kərele] [4] *vt littéraire* to take to task.

◆ **se quereller** *vp*: **se ~ (avec)** to quarrel (with).

querelleur, -euse [kərɛlœr, øz] ◇ *adj* quarrelsome. ◇ *nm, f* quarrelsome person.

quérir [kerir] *vt*: **faire ~ qqn** to summon sb; **aller ~ qqn** to go and fetch sb.

qu'est-ce que [kɛskə] → **que.**

qu'est-ce qui [kɛski] → **que.**

question [kɛstjɔ̃] *nf* question; **y a-t-il des ~s?** (are there) any questions?; **poser une ~ à qqn** to ask sb a question; **il est ~ de faire qqch** it's a question ou matter of doing sthg; **il n'en est pas ~** there is no question of it; **remettre qqn/qqch en ~** to question sb/sthg, to challenge sb/sthg; **~ subsidiaire** tiebreaker.

questionnaire [kɛstjɔnɛr] *nm* questionnaire.

questionner [kɛstjɔne] [3] *vt* to question.

quête [kɛt] *nf* **-1.** *sout* [d'objet, de personne] quest; **se mettre en ~ de** to go in search of. **-2.** [d'aumône]: **faire la ~** to take a collection.

quêter [kete] [4] ◇ *vi* to collect. ◇ *vt fig* to seek, to look for.

quetsche [kwɛtʃ] *nf* **-1.** [fruit] variety of plum. **-2.** [eau-de-vie] *type of plum brandy.*

queue [kø] *nf* **-1.** [d'animal] tail; **faire une ~ de poisson à qqn** *fig & AUTOM* to cut sb up; **histoire sans ~ ni tête** *fig* cock-and-bull story. **-2.** [de fruit] stalk. **-3.** [de poêle] handle. **-4.** [de liste, de classe] bottom; [de file, peloton] rear. **-5.** [file] line *Am,* queue *Br*; **faire la ~** to stand in line *Am,* to queue *Br*; **à la ~ leu leu** in single file. **-6.** *vulg* [sexe masculin] dick.

queue-de-cheval [kødʃəval] (*pl* **queues-de-cheval**) *nf* ponytail.

queue-de-pie [kødpi] (*pl* **queues-de-pie**) *nf fam* tails (*pl*).

qui [ki] ◇ *pron rel* **-1.** (*sujet*) [personne] who; [chose] which, that; **l'homme ~ parle** the man who's talking; **je l'ai vu ~ passait** I saw him pass; **le chien ~ aboie** the barking dog, the dog which ou that is barking; **~ plus est** (and) what's more; **~ mieux est** even better, better still. **-2.** (*complément d'objet direct*) who; **tu vois ~ je veux dire** you see who I mean; **invite ~ tu veux in-** vite whoever ou anyone you like. **-3.** (*après une préposition*) who, whom; **la personne à ~ je parle** the person I'm talking to, the person to whom I'm talking. **-4.** (*indéfini*): **~ que tu sois** whoever you are; **~ que ce soit** whoever it may be.

◇ *pron interr* **-1.** (*sujet*) who; **~ es-tu?** who are you?; **je voudrais savoir ~ est là** I would like to know who's there. **-2.** (*complément d'objet, après une préposition*) who, whom; **~ demandez-vous?** who do you want to see?; **dites-moi ~ vous demandez** tell me who you want to see; **à ~ vas-tu le donner?** who are you going to give it to?, to whom are you going to give it?

◆ **qui est-ce qui** *pron interr* who.

◆ **qui est-ce que** *pron interr* who, whom.

quiche [kiʃ] *nf* quiche.

quiconque [kikɔ̃k] ◇ *pron indéf* anyone, anybody. ◇ *pron rel indéf sout* anyone who, whoever.

Quid [kwid] *n*: **le ~** *annually updated one-volume encyclopedia of facts and figures.*

quidam [kidam] *nm fam* guy *Am,* chap *Br*.

quiétude [kjetyd] *nf* tranquility *Am,* tranquillity *Br*.

quignon [kiɲɔ̃] *nm fam* hunk.

quille [kij] *nf* **-1.** [de bateau] keel. **-2.** *arg mil*: **la ~** discharge, demob *Br*.

◆ **quilles** *nfpl* **-1.** [jeu]: **(jeu de) ~s** skittles (*U*). **-2.** *fam* [jambes] pins.

quincaillerie [kɛ̃kajri] *nf* **-1.** [ustensiles] hardware, ironmongery *Br*. **-2.** [magasin] hardware shop, ironmonger's (shop) *Br*. **-3.** *fam fig* [bijoux] jewellery..

quincaillier, -ière [kɛ̃kaje, jɛr] *nm, f* hardware dealer, ironmonger *Br*.

quinconce [kɛ̃kɔ̃s] *nm*: **en ~** in a staggered arrangement.

quinine [kinin] *nf* quinine.

quinquagénaire [kɛ̃kaʒenɛr] ◇ *nmf* fifty year old. ◇ *adj*: **être ~** to be in one's fifties.

quinquennal, -e, -aux [kɛ̃kenal, o] *adj* [plan] five-year (*avant n*); [élection] five-yearly.

quintal, -aux [kɛ̃tal, o] *nm* quintal.

quinte [kɛ̃t] *nf MUS* fifth.

◆ **quinte de toux** *nf* coughing fit.

quintessence [kɛ̃tesɑ̃s] *nf* quintessence.

quintette [kɛ̃tɛt] *nm* quintet.

quintuple [kɛ̃typl] *nm & adj* quintuple.

quintupler [kɛ̃typle] [3] *vt & vi* to quintuple, to increase fivefold.

quinzaine [kɛ̃zɛn] *nf* **-1.** [nombre] fifteen (or so); **une ~ de** about fifteen. **-2.** [deux se-**

maines] two weeks (*pl*), fortnight *Br*; ~ **publicitaire/commerciale** two-week advertising campaign/sale.

quinze [kɛ̃z] ◇ *adj num* fifteen; **dans ~ jours** in two weeks, in a fortnight *Br*; *voir aussi* **six**. ◇ *nm* **-1.** [chiffre] fifteen. **-2.** RUGBY: **le Quinze de France** the French fifteen.

quinzième [kɛ̃zjɛm] *adj num, nm & nmf* fifteenth; *voir aussi* **sixième**.

quiproquo [kiprɔko] *nm* misunderstanding.

Quito [kito] *n* Quito.

quittance [kitɑ̃s] *nf* receipt.

quitte [kit] *adj* quits; **être ~ de qqch** to be clear of sthg; **en être ~ pour qqch/pour faire qqch** to get off with sthg/doing sthg; **~ à faire qqch** even if it means doing sthg; **~ ou double** double or quits.

quitter [kite] [3] *vt* **-1.** [gén] to leave; **ne quittez pas!** [au téléphone] hold the line, please! **-2.** [fonctions] to give up. **-3.** [vêtement] to take off.
◆ **se quitter** *vp* to part.

quitus [kitys] *nm* discharge.

qui-vive [kiviv] ◇ *interj* who goes there? ◇ *nm inv*: **être sur le ~** to be on the alert.

quoi [kwa] ◇ *pron rel* (*après prép*): **ce à ~ je me suis intéressée** what I was interested in; **c'est en ~ vous avez tort** that's where you're wrong; **après ~** after which; **avoir de ~ vivre** to have enough to live on; **avez-vous de ~ écrire?** have you got something to write with?; **merci — il n'y a pas de ~** thank you — don't mention it.
◇ *pron interr* what; **à ~ penses-tu?** what are you thinking about?; **je ne sais pas ~ dire** I don't know what to say; **à ~ bon?** what's the point OU use?; **~ de neuf?** what's new?; **~ de plus?** what else?; **décide-toi, ~!** *fam* make your mind up, will you?; **tu viens ou ~?** *fam* are you coming or what?
◆ **quoi que** *loc conj* (+ *subjonctif*) whatever; ~ **qu'il arrive** whatever happens; ~ **qu'il dise** whatever he says; ~ **qu'il en soit** be that as it may.

quoique [kwakə] *conj* although, though.

quolibet [kɔlibɛ] *nm sout* jeer, taunt.

quorum [k(w)ɔrɔm] *nm* quorum.

quota [k(w)ɔta] *nm* quota.

quote-part [kɔtpar] (*pl* **quotes-parts**) *nf* share.

quotidien, -ienne [kɔtidjɛ̃, jɛn] *adj* daily.
◆ **quotidien** *nm* **-1.** [routine] daily life; **au ~** on a day-to-day basis. **-2.** [journal] daily (newspaper).

quotidiennement [kɔtidjɛnmɑ̃] *adv* daily, every day.

quotient [kɔsjɑ̃] *nm* quotient; ~ **intellectuel** intelligence quotient.

r¹, R [ɛr] *nm inv* [lettre] r, R.
◆ **R** (*abr de* **rand**) R.

r² *abr de* **rue**.

rab [rab] *nm fam* [portion] seconds (*pl*); [travail] overtime.

rabâchage [rabɑʃaʒ] *nm fam* constant harping on (*U*).

rabâcher [rabɑʃe] [3] ◇ *vi fam* to harp on. ◇ *vt* to go over (and over).

rabais [rabɛ] *nm* reduction, discount; **au ~** *péj* [artiste] third-rate; [travailler] for a pittance.

rabaisser [rabɛse] [4] *vt* **-1.** [réduire] to reduce; [orgueil] to humble. **-2.** [personne] to belittle.
◆ **se rabaisser** *vp* **-1.** [se déprécier] to belittle o.s. **-2.** [s'humilier]: **se ~ à faire qqch** to demean o.s. by doing sthg.

rabat [raba] *nm* **-1.** [partie rabattue] flap. **-2.** [de robe d'avocat] bands (*pl*).

Rabat [raba] *n* Rabat.

rabat-joie [rabaʒwa] ◇ *nm inv* killjoy. ◇ *adj inv*: **être ~** to be a killjoy.

rabatteur, -euse [rabatœr, øz] *nm, f* **-1.** [de gibier] beater. **-2.** *fig & péj* [de clientèle] tout.

rabattre [rabatr] [83] *vt* **-1.** [col] to turn down. **-2.** [siège] to tilt back; [couvercle] to shut. **-3.** [somme] to deduct. **-4.** [gibier] to drive. **-5.** *fam* [clients] to tout for. **-6.** *loc*: **en ~** to climb down.
◆ **se rabattre** *vp* **-1.** [siège] to tilt back; [couvercle] to shut. **-2.** [voiture, coureur] to cut in. **-3.** [se contenter]: **se ~ sur** to fall back on.

rabattu, -e [rabaty] *pp* → **rabattre**.

rabbin [rabɛ̃] *nm* rabbi.

rabibocher [rabibɔʃe] [3] *vt* **-1.** *fam* [époux] to reconcile, to get back together. **-2.** *vieilli* [voiture] to patch up.
◆ **se rabibocher** *vp fam* to make (it) up.

rabiot [rabjo] *nm fam* [portion] seconds (*pl*), more; [travail] overtime.

râble [rabl] *nm* [de lapin] back; CULIN saddle.

râblé, -e [rable] *adj* stocky.

rabot [rabo] *nm* plane.

raboter [rabɔte] [3] *vt* to plane.

raboteux, -euse [rabɔtø, øz] *adj* uneven, rugged.

◆ **raboteuse** *nf* planing machine.

rabougri, -e [rabugri] *adj* **-1.** [plante] stunted. **-2.** [personne] shrivelled, wizened.

rabrouer [rabrue] [3] *vt* to snub.

racaille [rakaj] *nf péj* riffraff.

raccommodage [rakɔmɔdaʒ] *nm* mending.

raccommoder [rakɔmɔde] [3] *vt* **-1.** [vêtement] to mend. **-2.** *fam fig* [personnes] to reconcile, to get back together.

◆ **se raccommoder** *vp fam* to make (it) up.

raccompagner [rakɔ̃paɲe] [3] *vt* to see home, to take home.

raccord [rakɔr] *nm* **-1.** [liaison] join. **-2.** [pièce] connector, coupling. **-3.** CIN link.

raccordement [rakɔrdəmɑ̃] *nm* connection, linking.

raccorder [rakɔrde] [3] *vt*: ~ qqch (à) to connect sthg (to), to join sthg (to).

◆ **se raccorder** *vp*: se ~ par to be connected OU joined by; se ~ à to be connected to; *fig* [faits] to tie in with.

raccourci [rakursi] *nm* shortcut; en ~ in miniature.

raccourcir [rakursir] [32] ◇ *vt* to shorten. ◇ *vi* to grow shorter.

raccroc [rakro]

◆ **par raccroc** *loc adv* by a fluke.

raccrocher [rakrɔʃe] [3] ◇ *vt* to hang back up. ◇ *vi* **-1.** [au téléphone]: ~ (au nez de qqn) to hang up (on sb), to put the phone down (on sb). **-2.** *fam* [coureur] to give up.

◆ **se raccrocher** *vp*: se ~ à to cling to, to hang on to.

race [ras] *nf* [humaine] race; [animale] breed; de ~ pedigree; [cheval] thoroughbred.

racé, -e [rase] *adj* **-1.** [animal] purebred. **-2.** [voiture] of distinction.

rachat [raʃa] *nm* **-1.** [transaction] repurchase. **-2.** *fig* [de péchés] atonement.

racheter [raʃte] [28] *vt* **-1.** [acheter en plus - gén] to buy another; [- pain, lait] to buy some more. **-2.** [acheter d'occasion] to buy. **-3.** [acheter après avoir vendu] to buy back. **-4.** *fig* [péché, faute] to atone for; [défaut, lapsus] to make up for. **-5.** [prisonnier] to ransom. **-6.** [honneur] to redeem. **-7.** COMM [société] to buy out.

◆ **se racheter** *vp fig* to redeem o.s.

rachitique [raʃitik] *adj* suffering from rickets.

rachitisme [raʃitism] *nm* rickets (*U*).

racial, -e, -iaux [rasjal, jo] *adj* racial.

racine [rasin] *nf* root; [de nez] base; ~ carrée/cubique MATHS square/cube root.

racisme [rasism] *nm* racism.

raciste [rasist] *nmf & adj* racist.

racket [rakɛt] *nm* racket.

racketter [rakɛte] [4] *vt*: ~ qqn to subject sb to a protection racket.

racketteur [rakɛtœr] *nm* racketeer.

raclée [rakle] *nf fam* hiding, thrashing.

racler [rakle] [3] *vt* to scrape; ce vin racle le gosier this wine is a bit rough.

◆ **se racler** *vp*: se ~ la gorge to clear one's throat.

raclette [raklɛt] *nf* **-1.** CULIN *melted cheese served with jacket potatoes*. **-2.** [outil] scraper.

racloir [raklwar] *nm* scraper.

racolage [rakɔlaʒ] *nm fam péj* [par commerçant] touting; [par prostituée] soliciting.

racoler [rakɔle] [3] *vt fam péj* [suj: commerçant] to tout for; [suj: prostituée] to solicit.

racoleur, -euse [rakɔlœr, øz] *adj fam péj* [air, sourire] come-hither; [publicité] strident.

◆ **racoleur** *nm fam péj* tout.

◆ **racoleuse** *nf fam péj* streetwalker.

racontar [rakɔ̃tar] *nm fam péj* piece of gossip.

◆ **racontars** *nmpl fam péj* tittle-tattle (*U*).

raconter [rakɔ̃te] [3] *vt* **-1.** [histoire] to tell, to relate; [événement] to relate, to tell about; ~ qqch à qqn to tell sb sthg, to relate sthg to sb. **-2.** [ragot, mensonge] to tell; qu'est-ce que tu racontes? what are you on about?

racornir [rakɔrnir] [32] *vt* to harden.

◆ **se racornir** *vp* to become hard.

radar [radar] *nm* radar; marcher au ~ *fam* to be on automatic pilot.

rade [rad] *nf* (natural) harbor *Am* OU harbour *Br*; rester en ~ *fam fig* to be left stranded.

radeau, -x [rado] *nm* **-1.** [embarcation] raft. **-2.** [train de bois] timber raft.

radial, -e, -iaux [radjal, jo] *adj* radial.

radiateur [radjatœr] *nm* radiator.

radiation [radjasjɔ̃] *nf* **-1.** PHYS radiation. **-2.** [de liste, du barreau] striking off.

radical, -e, -aux [radikal, o] *adj* radical.

◆ **radical** *nm* **-1.** [gén] radical. **-2.** LING stem.

radicalement [radikalmã] *adv* radically.

radier [radje] [9] *vt* to strike off.

radiesthésiste [radjɛstezist] *nmf* diviner (*by radiation*).

radieux, -ieuse [radjø, jøz] *adj* radiant; [soleil] dazzling.

radin, -e [radɛ̃, in] *fam péj* ◇ *adj* stingy. ◇ *nm, f* skinflint.

radiner [radine] [3]
◆ **se radiner** *vp fam* to get one's skates on, to get a move on.

radio [radjo] ◇ *nf* -1. [station, poste] radio; à la ~ on the radio; **allumer** OU **mettre la ~** to switch on the radio; **éteindre la ~** to switch off the radio; **~ pirate** pirate radio. -2. MÉD: **passer une ~** to have an x-ray, to be x-rayed. ◇ *nm* radio operator.

radioactif, -ive [radjoaktif, iv] *adj* radioactive.

radioactivité [radjoaktivite] *nf* radioactivity.

radioamateur [radjoamatœr] *nm* (radio) ham.

radiodiffuser [radjodifyze] [3] *vt* to broadcast.

radiodiffusion [radjodifyzjɔ̃] *nf* broadcasting.

radioélectrique [radjoelɛktrik] *adj* radio (*avant n*).

radiographie [radjografi] *nf* -1. [technique] radiography. -2. [image] x-ray.

radiographier [radjografje] [9] *vt* to x-ray.

radiologie [radjolɔʒi] *nf* radiology.

radiologue [radjolɔg], **radiologiste** [radjolɔʒist] *nmf* radiologist.

radiophonique [radjofɔnik] *adj* radio (*avant n*).

radioréveil (*pl* **radioréveils**), **radio-réveil** (*pl* **radios-réveils**) [radjorevɛj] *nm* radio alarm, clock radio.

radioscopie [radjoskɔpi] *nf* radioscopy.

radio-taxi [radjotaksi] (*pl* **radio-taxis**) *nm* radio taxi, radio-cab.

radiotéléphone [radjotelefɔn] *nm* cordless telephone, portable telephone.

radiotélévisé, -e [radjotelevize] *adj* broadcast on both radio and television.

radiothérapie [radjoterapi] *nf* radiotherapy.

radis [radi] *nm* radish; **n'avoir plus un ~** *fig* not to have a cent *Am* OU penny *Br* (to one's name).

radium [radjɔm] *nm* radium.

radius [radjys] *nm* radius.

radotage [radotaʒ] *nm* rambling.

radoter [radote] [3] *vi* to ramble.

radouber [radube] [3] *vt* to repair.

radoucir [radusir] [32] *vt* to soften.
◆ **se radoucir** *vp* [temps] to become milder; [personne] to calm down.

radoucissement [radusismã] *nm* -1. [d'attitude] softening. -2. [de température] rise; **un ~ du temps** a spell of milder weather.

rafale [rafal] *nf* -1. [de vent] gust; **en ~s** in gusts OU bursts. -2. [de coups de feu, d'applaudissements] burst.

raffermir [rafɛrmir] [32] *vt* -1. [muscle] to firm up. -2. *fig* [pouvoir] to strengthen.
◆ **se raffermir** *vp* -1. [muscle] to firm up. -2. *fig* [prix, autorité] to strengthen.

raffinage [rafinaʒ] *nm* refining.

raffiné, -e [rafine] *adj* refined.

raffinement [rafinmã] *nm* refinement.

raffiner [rafine] [3] ◇ *vt* to refine. ◇ *vi*: **~ sur** to be meticulous about.

raffinerie [rafinri] *nf* refinery.

raffoler [rafole] [3] *vi*: **~ de qqn/qqch** to adore sb/sthg.

raffut [rafy] *nm fam* row, racket.

rafiot, rafiau [rafjo] *nm fam péj* tub (*boat*).

rafistoler [rafistole] [3] *vt fam* to patch up.

rafle [rafl] *nf* raid.

rafler [rafle] [3] *vt* to swipe.

rafraîchir [rafreʃir] [32] ◇ *vt* -1. [nourriture, vin] to chill, to cool; [air] to cool. -2. [vêtement, appartement] to smarten up; *fig* [mémoire, idées] to refresh; [connaissances] to brush up. ◇ *vi* to cool (down).
◆ **se rafraîchir** *vp* -1. [se refroidir] to cool (down). -2. [en buvant] to have a drink.

rafraîchissant, -e [rafreʃisã, ãt] *adj* refreshing.

rafraîchissement [rafreʃismã] *nm* -1. [de climat] cooling. -2. [boisson] cold drink; **prendre un ~** to have a drink. -3. [de vêtement, d'appartement] smartening up.

raft(ing) [raft(iŋ)] *nm* whitewater rafting.

ragaillardir [ragajardir] [32] *vt fam* to buck up, to perk up.

rage [raʒ] *nf* -1. [fureur] rage; **être ivre** OU **fou de ~** to be mad with rage; **la ~ au ventre** OU **cœur** seething with rage; **faire ~** [tempête] to rage. -2. [manie]: **~ de faire qqch** mania for doing sthg. -3. [maladie] rabies (*U*).
◆ **rage de dents** *nf* (raging) toothache.

rageant, -e [raʒã, ãt] *adj fam* infuriating.

rager [raʒe] [17] *vi fam* to fume.

rageur, -euse [raʒœr, øz] *adj* bad-tempered.

rageusement [raʒøzmã] *adv* furiously.

raglan [raglɑ̃] ◇ *nm inv* raglan coat. ◇ *adj inv* raglan (*avant n*).

ragot [rago] *nm* (*gén pl*) *fam* (malicious) rumour *Am* OU rumour *Br*, tittle-tattle (*U*).

ragoût [ragu] *nm* stew.

ragoûtant, -e [ragutɑ̃, ɑ̃t] *adj*: **peu** OU **pas très ~** *péj* [plat] not very appetizing; *fig* [idée] not very inviting.

rai [rɛ] *nm littéraire* [de soleil] ray.

raid [rɛd] *nm* **-1.** AÉRON, BOURSE & MIL raid; **~ aérien** air raid. **-2.** SPORT long-distance rally.

raide [rɛd] ◇ *adj* **-1.** [cheveux] straight. **-2.** [tendu - corde] taut; [- membre] stiff. **-3.** [pente] steep. **-4.** [personne - attitude physique] stiff, starchy; [- caractère] inflexible. **-5.** *fam* [histoire] hard to swallow, far-fetched. **-6.** *fam* [chanson] rude, blue. **-7.** *fam* [sans le sou] broke. ◇ *adv* **-1.** [abruptement] steeply. **-2.** *loc*: **tomber ~ mort** to fall down dead.

raideur [rɛdœr] *nf* **-1.** [de membre] stiffness. **-2.** [de personne - attitude physique] stiffness, starchiness; [- caractère] inflexibility.

raidillon [rɛdijɔ̃] *nm* steep (section of) road.

raidir [rɛdir] [32] *vt* [muscle] to tense; [corde] to tighten, to tauten.
◆ **se raidir** *vp* **-1.** [se contracter] to grow stiff, to stiffen. **-2.** *fig* [résister]: **se ~ contre** to steel o.s. against.

raie [rɛ] *nf* **-1.** [rayure] stripe. **-2.** [dans les cheveux] part *Am*, parting *Br*. **-3.** [des fesses] crack. **-4.** [poisson] skate.

raifort [rɛfɔr] *nm* horseradish.

rail [raj] *nm* rail; **remettre qqn/qqch sur les ~s** to put sb/sthg back on the rails, to get sb/sthg back on the rails.

railler [raje] [3] *vt sout* to mock (at).
◆ **se railler** *vp*: **se ~ de** *sout* to mock (at).

raillerie [rajri] *nf sout* mockery (*U*).

railleur, -euse [rajœr, øz] *sout* ◇ *adj* mocking. ◇ *nm, f* scoffer.

rainette [rɛnɛt] *nf* tree frog.

rainure [rɛnyr] *nf* [longue] groove, channel; [courte] slot.

raisin [rɛzɛ̃] *nm* [fruit] grapes (*pl*); **~ blanc/noir** white/black grapes; **~s de Corinthe** currants; **~s secs** raisins.

raison [rɛzɔ̃] *nf* **-1.** [gén] reason; **perdre la ~** not to be in one's right mind; **recouvrer la ~** to come to one's senses; **à plus forte ~** all the more (so); **se faire une ~** to resign o.s.; **~ de plus pour faire qqch** all the more reason to do sthg. **-2.** [justesse, équité]: **avoir ~** to be right; **avoir ~ de faire qqch** to be right to do sthg; **avoir ~ de**

qqn/qqch to get the better of sb/sthg; **donner ~ à qqn** to prove sb right.
◆ **à raison de** *loc prép* at (the rate of).
◆ **en raison de** *loc prép* owing to, because of.

raisonnable [rɛzɔnabl] *adj* reasonable.

raisonnablement [rɛzɔnabləmɑ̃] *adv* **-1.** [agir, parler] reasonably. **-2.** [manger, boire] in moderation.

raisonnement [rɛzɔnmɑ̃] *nm* **-1.** [faculté] reason, power of reasoning. **-2.** [argumentation] reasoning, argument.

raisonner [rɛzɔne] [3] ◇ *vt* [personne] to reason with. ◇ *vi* **-1.** [penser] to reason. **-2.** [discuter]: **~ avec** to reason with.
◆ **se raisonner** *vp* [personne] to be reasonable.

raisonneur, -euse [rɛzɔnœr, øz] ◇ *adj* reasoning; *péj* argumentative. ◇ *nm, f* argumentative person.

rajeunir [raʒœnir] [32] ◇ *vt* **-1.** [suj: couleur, vêtement]: **~ qqn** to make sb look younger. **-2.** [suj: personne]: **~ qqn de trois ans** to take three years off sb's age. **-3.** [vêtement, canapé] to renovate, to do up; [meubles] to modernize. **-4.** *fig* [parti] to rejuvenate. ◇ *vi* **-1.** [personne] to look younger; [se sentir plus jeune] to feel younger OU rejuvenated. **-2.** [faubourg] to be modernized.
◆ **se rajeunir** *vp* to lie about one's age.

rajeunissement [raʒœnismɑ̃] *nm* [de population] drop in age.

rajout [raʒu] *nm* addition.

rajouter [raʒute] [3] *vt* to add; **en ~** *fam* to exaggerate.

rajuster [raʒyste], **réajuster** [reaʒyste] [3] *vt* to adjust; [cravate] to straighten.
◆ **se rajuster** *vp* to straighten one's clothes.

râle [ral] *nm* moan; [de mort] death rattle.

ralenti, -e [ralɑ̃ti] *adj* slow.
◆ **ralenti** *nm* **-1.** AUTOM idling speed; **tourner au ~** AUTOM to idle; *fig* to tick over *Br*; **vivre au ~** *fig* to take things easy. **-2.** CIN slow motion.

ralentir [ralɑ̃tir] [32] ◇ *vt* **-1.** [allure, expansion] to slow (down). **-2.** [rythme] to slacken. ◇ *vi* to slow down OU up.
◆ **se ralentir** *vp* to slow down OU up.

ralentissement [ralɑ̃tismɑ̃] *nm* **-1.** [d'allure, d'expansion] slowing (down). **-2.** [de rythme] slackening. **-3.** [embouteillage] hold-up. **-4.** PHYS deceleration.

râler [rale] [3] *vi* **-1.** [malade] to breathe with difficulty. **-2.** *fam* [grogner] to moan.

râleur, -euse [ralœr, øz] *fam* ◇ *adj* moaning (*avant n*). ◇ *nm, f* grumbler, moaner.

ralliement [ralimã] *nm* rallying.

rallier [ralje] [9] *vt* **-1.** [poste, parti] to join. **-2.** [suffrages] to win. **-3.** [troupes] to rally.
◆ **se rallier** *vp* to rally; **se ~ à** [parti] to join; [cause] to rally to; [avis] to come round to.

rallonge [ralɔ̃ʒ] *nf* **-1.** [de table] leaf, extension. **-2.** [électrique] extension (lead). **-3.** *fam* [de crédit] extension (of credit).

rallonger [ralɔ̃ʒe] [17] ◇ *vt* to lengthen. ◇ *vi* to lengthen, to get longer.

rallumer [ralyme] [3] *vt* **-1.** [feu, cigarette] to relight; *fig* [querelle] to revive. **-2.** [appareil, lumière électrique] to switch (back) on again.
◆ **se rallumer** *vp* **-1.** [feu, guerre, colère] to flare up again. **-2.** [lumière électrique] to come on again.

rallye [rali] *nm* rally.

RAM, Ram [ram] (*abr de* **Random access memory**) *nf* RAM.

ramadan [ramadã] *nm* Ramadan.

ramage [ramaʒ] *nm littéraire* [d'oiseau] song.
◆ **ramages** *nmpl* leafy design, foliage (*U*).

ramassage [ramasaʒ] *nm* collection; **~ scolaire** [action] pick-up (of school children); [service] school bus.

ramasse-miettes [ramasmjɛt] *nm inv* crumb-brush and tray (set).

ramasser [ramase] [3] *vt* **-1.** [récolter, réunir] to gather, to collect; *fig* [forces] to gather. **-2.** [prendre] to pick up. **-3.** *fig* [pensée] to sum up. **-4.** *fam* [claque, rhume] to get.
◆ **se ramasser** *vp* **-1.** [se replier] to crouch. **-2.** *fam* [tomber, échouer] to come a cropper.

ramassis [ramasi] *nm péj:* **un ~ de** a collection of.

rambarde [rãbard] *nf* (guard) rail.

rame [ram] *nf* **-1.** [aviron] oar. **-2.** RAIL train; **~ de métro** subway *Am* OU underground *Br* train. **-3.** [de papier] ream. **-4.** [tuteur] stake, pole.

rameau, -x [ramo] *nm* branch.
◆ **Rameaux** *nmpl:* **les Rameaux** Palm Sunday.

ramener [ramne] [19] *vt* **-1.** [remmener] to take back. **-2.** [rapporter, restaurer] to bring back. **-3.** [remettre] to put back. **-4.** [réduire]: **~ qqch à qqch** to reduce sthg to sthg, to bring sthg down to sthg. **-5.** *loc:* **il ramène tout à lui** he sees things only in terms of how they affect him; **la ~** *fam* to stick one's oar in.
◆ **se ramener** *vp* **-1.** [problème]: **se ~ à** to come down to. **-2.** *fam* [arriver] to turn up.

ramequin [ramkɛ̃] *nm* ramekin.

ramer [rame] [3] *vi* **-1.** [rameur] to row. **-2.** *fam fig* [peiner] to slog.

rameur, -euse [ramœr, øz] *nm, f* rower.

rameuter [ramøte] [3] *vt* to round up.

ramier [ramje] *nm* wood pigeon.

ramification [ramifikasjɔ̃] *nf* **-1.** [division] branch. **-2.** (*gén pl*) *fig* [de complot] ramification.

ramifier [ramifje] [9]
◆ **se ramifier** *vp* to branch out.

ramolli, -e [ramɔli] ◇ *adj* soft; *fig* soft (in the head). ◇ *nm, f fam fig* thicko, half-wit.

ramollir [ramɔlir] [32] *vt* **-1.** [beurre] to soften. **-2.** *fam fig* [ardeurs] to cool.
◆ **se ramollir** *vp* **-1.** [beurre] to go soft, to soften. **-2.** *fam fig* [courage] to weaken.

ramonage [ramɔnaʒ] *nm* chimney sweeping.

ramoner [ramɔne] [3] *vt* to sweep.

ramoneur [ramɔnœr] *nm* (chimney) sweep.

rampant, -e [rãpã, ãt] *adj* **-1.** [animal] crawling. **-2.** [plante] creeping. **-3.** *fig* [attitude] grovelling.
◆ **rampants** *nmpl arg aéron* ground staff (*U*).

rampe [rãp] *nf* **-1.** [d'escalier] banister, handrail; **lâcher la ~** *fam* to kick the bucket. **-2.** [d'accès] ramp; **~ de lancement** launch pad. **-3.** THÉÂTRE: **la ~** the footlights (*pl*).

ramper [rãpe] [3] *vi* **-1.** [animal, soldat, enfant] to crawl. **-2.** [plante] to creep. **-3.** *fig* [personne]: **~ devant** to grovel to. **-4.** *fig* [inquiétude] to creep.

rancard, rencard [rãkar] *nm fam* [rendez-vous] date, meeting.

rancart, rencart [rãkar] *nm:* **mettre au ~** to chuck out.

rance [rãs] ◇ *nm:* **sentir le ~** to smell rancid. ◇ *adj* **-1.** [beurre] rancid. **-2.** *fig* [idéologie] stale.

ranch [rãtʃ] *nm* ranch.

rancir [rãsir] [32] *vi* to go rancid.

rancœur [rãkœr] *nf* rancor *Am*, rancour *Br*, resentment.

rançon [rãsɔ̃] *nf* ransom; *fig* price.

rancune [rãkyn] *nf* rancor *Am*, rancour *Br*, spite; **garder** OU **tenir ~ à qqn de qqch** to hold a grudge against sb for sthg; **sans ~!** no hard feelings!

rancunier, -ière [rãkynje, jɛr] ◇ *adj* vindictive, spiteful. ◇ *nm, f* vindictive OU spiteful person.

randonnée [rãdɔne] *nf* **-1.** [à pied] walk. **-2.** [à bicyclette] ride; [en voiture] drive. **-3.** [à skis] cross-country ski run.

randonneur, **-euse** [rɑ̃dɔnœr, øz] *nm, f* walker, rambler.

rang [rɑ̃] *nm* **-1.** [d'objets, de personnes] row; **se mettre en ~ par deux** to line up in twos; **en ~ d'oignons** *fig* in a row OU line. **-2.** MIL rank; **de haut ~** high-ranking; **se mettre sur les ~s** to be in the running; **grossir les ~s de** to swell the ranks of. **-3.** [position sociale] station. **-4.** *Can* [peuplement rural] rural district. **-5.** *Can* [chemin] country road.

rangé, **-e** [rɑ̃ʒe] *adj* [sérieux] well-ordered, well-behaved.

rangée [rɑ̃ʒe] *nf* row.

rangement [rɑ̃ʒmɑ̃] *nm* tidying up.

ranger [rɑ̃ʒe] [17] *vt* **-1.** [élèves, soldats] to line up. **-2.** [chambre] to tidy. **-3.** [objets] to arrange. **-4.** [voiture] to park. **-5.** *fig* [livre, auteur]: **~ parmi** to rank among.
◆ **se ranger** *vp* **-1.** [élèves, soldats] to line up. **-2.** [voiture] to pull in. **-3.** [piéton] to step aside. **-4.** [s'assagir] to settle down. **-5.** *fig* [se rallier]: **se ~ à** to go along with; **se ~ à côté de** to side with.

Rangoon [rɑ̃gun] *n* Rangoon.

ranimer [ranime] [3] *vt* **-1.** [personne] to revive, to bring round. **-2.** [feu] to rekindle. **-3.** *fig* [sentiment] to rekindle, to reawaken.
◆ **se ranimer** *vp* **-1.** [personne] to come round, to come to. **-2.** *fig* [haine, ressentiment] to reawaken, to be renewed; [volcan] to become active again.

rapace [rapas] ◇ *nm* bird of prey. ◇ *adj* [cupide] rapacious, grasping.

rapacité [rapasite] *nf* rapaciousness.

rapatrié, **-e** [rapatrije] ◇ *nm, f* repatriated settler. ◇ *adj* repatriated.

rapatriement [rapatrimɑ̃] *nm* repatriation.

rapatrier [rapatrije] [10] *vt* to repatriate.

râpe [rap] *nf* **-1.** [de cuisine] grater; **~ à fromage** cheese grater. **-2.** [de menuisier] rasp. **-3.** *Helv fam* [avare] miser, skinflint.

râpé, **-e** [rape] *adj* **-1.** CULIN grated. **-2.** [manteau] threadbare. **-3.** *fam* [raté]: **c'est ~!** we've had it!
◆ **râpé** *nm* grated Gruyère cheese.

râper [rape] [3] *vt* **-1.** CULIN to grate. **-2.** [bois, métal] to rasp.

rapetasser [raptase] [3] *vt fam péj* to patch up.

râpeux, **-euse** [rapø, øz] *adj* **-1.** [tissu] rough. **-2.** [vin] harsh.

raphia [rafja] *nm* raffia.

rapide [rapid] ◇ *adj* **-1.** [gén] rapid. **-2.** [train, coureur] fast. **-3.** [pente] steep. **-4.** [mu-sique, intelligence] lively, quick. ◇ *nm* **-1.** [train] express (train). **-2.** [de fleuve] rapid.

rapidement [rapidmɑ̃] *adv* rapidly.

rapidité [rapidite] *nf* rapidity.

rapiécer [rapjese] [20] *vt* to patch.

rapière [rapjɛr] *nf* rapier.

rappel [rapɛl] *nm* **-1.** [de réservistes, d'ambas-sadeur] recall. **-2.** [souvenir] reminder; **~ à l'ordre** call to order. **-3.** [de paiement] back pay. **-4.** [de vaccination] booster. **-5.** [au spectacle] curtain call, encore. **-6.** SPORT abseiling; **descendre en ~** to abseil (down). **-7.** TECHNOL: **ressort de ~** return spring.

rappeler [raple] [24] *vt* **-1.** [gén] to call back; **~ qqn à qqch** *fig* to bring sb back to sthg. **-2.** [faire penser à]: **~ qqch à qqn** to re-mind sb of sthg; **ça rappelle les vacances** it reminds me of my holidays.
◆ **se rappeler** *vp* to remember.

rappelle, **rappelles** *etc* → **rappeler**.

rappliquer [raplike] [3] *vi fam* to turn up, to show up.

rapport [rapɔr] *nm* **-1.** [corrélation] link, connection; **~ de causalité** causal link; **je ne vois pas le ~** I don't see the connec-tion. **-2.** [contact]: **se mettre en ~ avec qqn** to get in touch with sb. **-3.** [compte-rendu] report. **-4.** [profit] return, yield. **-5.** MATHS ratio; **un excellent ~ qualité-prix** excellent value for money.
◆ **rapports** *nmpl* **-1.** [relations] relations. **-2.** [sexuels]: **~s (sexuels)** intercourse *(sg)*; **avoir des ~s (sexuels) avec qqn** to have sex with sb.
◆ **par rapport à** *loc prép* in comparison to, compared with.

rapporter [rapɔrte] [3] *vt* to bring back.
◆ **se rapporter** *vp*: **se ~ à** to refer OU re-late to.

rapporteur, **-euse** [rapɔrtœr, øz] ◇ *adj* sneaky, telltale *(avant n)*. ◇ *nm, f* sneak, telltale.
◆ **rapporteur** *nm* **-1.** [de commission] rap-porteur. **-2.** GÉOM protractor.

rapprochement [raprɔʃmɑ̃] *nm* **-1.** [d'objets, de personnes] bringing together. **-2.** *fig* [entre événements] link, connection. **-3.** *fig* [de pays, de parti] rapprochement, coming to-gether.

rapprocher [raprɔʃe] [3] *vt* **-1.** [mettre plus près]: **~ qqn/qqch de qqch** to bring sb/sthg nearer to sthg, to bring sb/sthg closer to sthg. **-2.** *fig* [personnes] to bring together. **-3.** *fig* [idée, texte]: **~ qqch (de)** to compare sthg (with).
◆ **se rapprocher** *vp* **-1.** [approcher]: **se ~ (de qqn/qqch)** to approach (sb/sthg). **-2.** [se

ressembler]: **se ~ de qqch** to be similar to sthg. **-3.** [se réconcilier]: **se ~ de qqn** to become closer to sb.

rapsodie = **rhapsodie**.

rapt [rapt] *nm* abduction.

raquette [rakɛt] *nf* **-1.** [de tennis, de squash] racket; [de ping-pong] bat. **-2.** [à neige] snowshoe.

rare [rar] *adj* **-1.** [peu commun, peu fréquent] rare; **ses ~s amis** his few friends. **-2.** [peu dense] sparse. **-3.** [surprenant] unusual, surprising.

raréfaction [rarefaksjɔ̃] *nf* scarcity; [d'air] rarefaction.

raréfier [rarefje] [9] *vt* to rarefy.
◆ **se raréfier** *vp* to become rarefied.

rarement [rarmɑ̃] *adv* rarely.

rareté [rarte] *nf* **-1.** [de denrées, de nouvelles] scarcity. **-2.** [de visites, de lettres] infrequency. **-3.** [objet précieux] rarity.

rarissime [rarisim] *adj* extremely rare.

ras, -e [ra, raz] *adj* **-1.** [herbe, poil] short. **-2.** [mesure] full.
◆ **ras** *adv* short; **à ~** short; **à ~ de** level with; **en avoir ~ le bol** *fam* to be fed up.
◆ **ras du cou, ras le cou** *loc adj* crewneck, round-neck.

RAS (*abr de* **rien à signaler**) nothing to report.

rasade [razad] *nf* glassful.

rasage [razaʒ] *nm* shaving.

rasant, -e [razɑ̃, ɑ̃t] *adj* **-1.** [lumière] low-angled. **-2.** *fam* [film, discours] boring.

rascasse [raskas] *nf* scorpion fish.

rase-mottes [razmɔt] *nm inv* hedgehopping.

raser [raze] [3] *vt* **-1.** [barbe, cheveux] to shave off. **-2.** [mur, sol] to hug. **-3.** [village] to raze. **-4.** *fam* [personne] to bore.
◆ **se raser** *vp* **-1.** [avec rasoir] to shave. **-2.** *fam* [s'ennuyer] to be bored.

raseur, -euse [razœr, øz] ◇ *adj* boring. ◇ *nm, f* bore.

ras-le-bol [ralbɔl] *nm inv fam* discontent; **~!** *fam* that's enough!

rasoir [razwar] ◇ *nm* razor; **~ électrique** electric shaver; **~ mécanique** safety razor. ◇ *adj inv fam* boring.

rassasier [rasazje] [9] *vt* to satisfy.
◆ **se rassasier** *vp*: **se ~ de** to tire of, to have one's fill of.

rassemblement [rasɑ̃bləmɑ̃] *nm* **-1.** [d'objets] collecting, gathering. **-2.** [foule] crowd, gathering. **-3.** [union, parti] union. **-4.** MIL parade; **~!** fall in!

rassembler [rasɑ̃ble] [3] *vt* **-1.** [personnes, documents] to collect, to gather. **-2.** [courage] to summon up; [idées] to collect.
◆ **se rassembler** *vp* **-1.** [manifestants] to assemble. **-2.** [famille] to get together.

rasseoir [raswar] [65]
◆ **se rasseoir** *vp* to sit down again.

rasséréner [raserene] [18] *vt sout* to calm down.
◆ **se rasséréner** *vp sout* to recover one's serenity.

rassis, -e [rasi, iz] *adj* **-1.** [pain] stale. **-2.** *sout* [esprit] calm, sober.

rassurant, -e [rasyrɑ̃, ɑ̃t] *adj* reassuring.

rassuré, -e [rasyre] *adj* confident, at ease.

rassurer [rasyre] [3] *vt* to reassure.
◆ **se rassurer** *vp* to feel at ease OU reassured; **rassurez-vous** don't worry.

rat [ra] ◇ *nm* rat; **petit ~** *fig* young ballet pupil; **être fait comme un ~** to be cornered. ◇ *adj fam* [avare] mean, stingy.

ratage [rataʒ] *nm* bungling, messing up.

ratatiné, -e [ratatine] *adj* **-1.** [fruit, personne] shrivelled. **-2.** *fam fig* [vélo, bagnole] wrecked.

ratatiner [ratatine] [3] *vt* **-1.** [fruit, personne] to shrivel. **-2.** *fam* [démolir] to wreck.
◆ **se ratatiner** *vp* to shrivel up, to become wrinkled.

ratatouille [ratatuj] *nf* ratatouille.

rate [rat] *nf* **-1.** [animal] female rat. **-2.** [organe] spleen.

raté, -e [rate] *nm, f* [personne] failure.
◆ **raté** *nm* **-1.** (*gén pl*) AUTOM misfiring (*U*); **faire des ~s** to misfire. **-2.** *fig* [difficulté] problem.

râteau, -x [rato] *nm* rake.

râtelier [ratəlje] *nm* **-1.** [à fourrage, à outils] rack; **manger à tous les ~s** *fig* to have a finger in every pie. **-2.** *fam* [dentier] false teeth (*pl*).

rater [rate] [3] ◇ *vt* **-1.** [train, occasion] to miss. **-2.** [plat, affaire] to make a mess of; [examen] to fail. ◇ *vi* to go wrong.

ratification [ratifikasjɔ̃] *nf* ratification.

ratifier [ratifje] [9] *vt* to ratify.

ration [rasjɔ̃] *nf* [quantité] portion; *fig* share; **~ alimentaire** food intake.

rationalisation [rasjɔnalizasjɔ̃] *nf* rationalization.

rationaliser [rasjɔnalize] [3] *vt* to rationalize.

rationnel, -elle [rasjɔnɛl] *adj* rational.

rationnellement [rasjɔnɛlmɑ̃] *adv* rationally.

rationnement [rasjɔnmɑ̃] *nm* rationing; carte de ~ ration card.

rationner [rasjɔne] [3] *vt* to ration.
◆ **se rationner** *vp* to ration o.s.

ratissage [ratisaʒ] *nm* **-1.** [de jardin] raking. **-2.** [de quartier] search.

ratisser [ratise] [3] *vt* **-1.** [jardin] to rake. **-2.** [quartier] to search, to comb; ~ **large** to cast one's net wide. **-3.** *fam fig* [au jeu] to clean out. **-4.** RUGBY to heel.

raton [ratɔ̃] *nm* **-1.** ZOOL young rat. **-2.** *tfam* [Arabe] *racist term used with reference to North African Arabs.*
◆ **raton laveur** *nm* racoon.

raton(n)ade [ratɔnad] *nf tfam racist term used to describe an attack on North African Arab immigrants.*

RATP (*abr de* **Régie autonome des transports parisiens**) *nf Paris transport authority.*

rattachement [rataʃmɑ̃] *nm* uniting, joining.

rattacher [rataʃe] [3] *vt* **-1.** [attacher de nouveau] to do up, to fasten again. **-2.** [relier]: ~ **qqch à** to join sthg to; *fig* to link sthg with. **-3.** [unir]: ~ **qqn à** to bind sb to.
◆ **se rattacher** *vp*: **se ~ à** to be linked to.

rattrapage [ratrapaʒ] *nm* SCOL: **cours de ~** remedial class.

rattraper [ratrape] [3] *vt* **-1.** [animal, prisonnier] to recapture. **-2.** [temps]: ~ **le temps perdu** to make up for lost time. **-3.** [rejoindre] to catch up with. **-4.** [bus] to catch. **-5.** [erreur] to correct. **-6.** [personne qui tombe] to catch.
◆ **se rattraper** *vp* **-1.** [se retenir]: **se ~ à qqn/qqch** to catch hold of sb/sthg. **-2.** [compenser] to catch up. **-3.** [se faire pardonner] to make amends.

rature [ratyr] *nf* alteration.

raturer [ratyre] [3] *vt* to alter.

rauque [rok] *adj* hoarse, husky.

ravagé, -e [ravaʒe] *adj fam* [fou]: **être ~** to be off one's head.

ravager [ravaʒe] [17] *vt* [gén] to devastate, to ravage.

ravages [ravaʒ] *nmpl* [de troupes] ravages, devastation (*sg*); [d'inondation] devastation (*sg*); [du temps] ravages; **faire des ~** *fig* to break hearts.

ravalement [ravalmɑ̃] *nm* cleaning, restoration.

ravaler [ravale] [3] *vt* **-1.** [façade] to clean, to restore. **-2.** [personne]: ~ **qqn au rang de** to lower sb to the level of. **-3.** [salive] to swallow. **-4.** *fig* [larmes, colère] to stifle, to hold back.

◆ **se ravaler** *vp* to debase o.s., to demean o.s.

ravaudage [ravodaʒ] *nm* mending, repairing.

ravauder [ravode] [3] *vt* to mend, to repair.

rave [rav] *nf* **-1.** BOT rape. **-2.** [fête] rave (party).

ravi, -e [ravi] *adj*: ~ **(de)** delighted (with); **je suis ravi de l'avoir trouvé** I'm delighted that I found it, I'm delighted to have found it; **je suis ravi qu'il soit venu** I'm delighted (that) he has come; ~ **de vous connaître** pleased to meet you.

ravier [ravje] *nm* small dish.

ravigotant, -e [ravigɔtɑ̃, ɑ̃t] *adj fam* refreshing, stimulating.

ravigote [ravigɔt] *nf sauce of mustard, gherkins and capers.*

ravigoter [ravigɔte] [3] *vt fam* to perk up, to buck up.

ravin [ravɛ̃] *nm* ravine, gully.

raviné, -e [ravine] *adj* [visage] furrowed.

raviner [ravine] [3] *vt* to gully.

raviolis [ravjɔli] *nmpl* ravioli (*U*).

ravir [ravir] [32] *vt* **-1.** [charmer] to delight; **à** ~ beautifully. **-2.** *littéraire* [arracher]: ~ **qqch à qqn** to rob sb of sthg.

raviser [ravize] [3]
◆ **se raviser** *vp* to change one's mind.

ravissant, -e [ravisɑ̃, ɑ̃t] *adj* delightful, beautiful.

ravissement [ravismɑ̃] *nm* **-1.** [enchantement] delight. **-2.** *littéraire* [rapt] rape, ravishing.

ravisseur, -euse [ravisœr, øz] *nm, f* abductor.

ravitaillement [ravitajmɑ̃] *nm* [en denrées] resupplying; [en carburant] refuelling.

ravitailler [ravitaje] [3] *vt* [en denrées] to resupply; [en carburant] to refuel.
◆ **se ravitailler** *vp* [en denrées] to get fresh supplies; [en carburant] to refuel.

raviver [ravive] [3] *vt* **-1.** [feu] to rekindle. **-2.** [couleurs] to brighten up. **-3.** *fig* [douleur] to revive. **-4.** [plaie] to reopen.

ravoir [ravwar] *vt* **-1.** [jouet, livre] to get back. **-2.** *fam* [linge] to get clean.

rayé, -e [rɛje] *adj* **-1.** [tissu] striped. **-2.** [disque, vitre] scratched. **-3.** [canon] rifled.

rayer [rɛje] [11] *vt* **-1.** [disque, vitre] to scratch. **-2.** [nom, mot] to cross out; ~ **qqn d'une liste** to cross sb's name off a list. **-3.** [canon] to rifle.

rayon [rɛjɔ̃] *nm* **-1.** [de lumière] beam, ray; *fig* [d'espoir] ray. **-2.** (*gén pl*) [radiation] radia-

tion (*U*); ~ **laser** laser beam; ~**s** X X-rays.
-3. [de roue] spoke. **-4.** GÉOM radius; **dans un** ~ **de** *fig* within a radius of; ~ **d'action** range. **-5.** [étagère] shelf. **-6.** [dans un magasin] department.

rayonnage [rɛjɔnaʒ] *nm* shelving.

rayonnant, -e [rɛjɔnɑ̃, ɑ̃t] *adj litt* & *fig* radiant.

rayonne [rɛjɔn] *nf* rayon.

rayonnement [rɛjɔnmɑ̃] *nm* **-1.** [gén] radiance; [des arts] influence. **-2.** PHYS radiation.

rayonner [rɛjɔne] [3] *vi* **-1.** [soleil] to shine; ~ **de joie** *fig* to radiate happiness. **-2.** [culture] to be influential. **-3.** [avenues, lignes, chaleur] to radiate. **-4.** [touriste] to tour around (*from a base*).

rayure [rɛjyr] *nf* **-1.** [sur étoffe] stripe. **-2.** [sur disque, sur meuble] scratch. **-3.** [de fusil] groove.

raz [ra]
◆ **raz de marée** *nm* tidal wave; POLIT & *fig* landslide.

razzia [razja] *nf fam* raid; **faire une** ~ **sur** to raid, to plunder.

razzier [razje] [9] *vt* to raid, to plunder.

RBE (*abr de* **revenu brut d'exploitation**) *nm* gross profit.

RBL (*abr de* **rouble**) R, Rub.

R-C *abr de* **rez-de-chaussée**.

r.d. (*abr de* **rive droite**) *right (north) bank of the Seine*.

R-D (*abr de* **recherche-développement**) *nf* R & D.

RDA (*abr de* **République démocratique allemande**) *nf* GDR.

RDB (*abr de* **revenu disponible brut**) *nm* gross disposable income.

RdC *abr de* **rez-de-chaussée**.

ré [re] *nm inv* MUS D; [dans la gamme] re.

ré- [re] *préfixe* re-.

réabonnement [reabɔnmɑ̃] *nm* subscription renewal.

réabonner [reabɔne] [3] *vt*: ~ **qqn à** to renew sb's subscription to.
◆ **se réabonner** *vp*: **se** ~ **à** to renew one's subscription to.

réac [reak] *nmf* & *adj péj* reactionary.

réaccoutumer [reakutyme] [3] *vt* to reaccustom.
◆ **se réaccoutumer** *vp*: **se** ~ **à** to reaccustom o.s. to.

réacteur [reaktœr] *nm* [d'avion] jet engine; ~ **nucléaire** nuclear reactor.

réactif, -ive [reaktif, iv] *adj* reactive.

◆ **réactif** *nm* reagent.

réaction [reaksjɔ̃] *nf*: ~ (**à/contre**) reaction (to/against); ~ **en chaîne** chain reaction.

réactionnaire [reaksjɔnɛr] *nmf* & *adj péj* reactionary.

réactiver [reaktive] [3] *vt* to reactivate.

réactualisation [reaktɥalizasjɔ̃] *nf* [modernisation] updating, bringing up to date.

réactualiser [reaktɥalize] [3] *vt* [moderniser] to update, to bring up to date.

réadaptation [readaptasjɔ̃] *nf* rehabilitation.

réadapter [readapte] [3] *vt* to readapt; [accidenté] to rehabilitate.
◆ **se réadapter** *vp*: **se** ~ **à** to readapt to.

réaffirmer [reafirme] [3] *vt* to reaffirm.

réagir [reaʒir] [32] *vi*: ~ (**à/contre**) to react (to/against); ~ **sur** to affect.

réajustement [reaʒystəmɑ̃] *nm* adjustment.

réajuster = **rajuster**.

réalisable [realizabl] *adj* **-1.** [projet] feasible. **-2.** FIN realizable.

réalisateur, -trice [realizatœr, tris] *nm, f* CIN & TÉLÉ director.

réalisation [realizasjɔ̃] *nf* **-1.** [de projet] carrying out. **-2.** CIN & TÉLÉ production.

réaliser [realize] [3] *vt* **-1.** [projet] to carry out; [ambitions, rêves] to achieve, to realize. **-2.** CIN & TÉLÉ to produce. **-3.** [s'apercevoir de] to realize.
◆ **se réaliser** *vp* **-1.** [ambition] to be realized; [rêve] to come true. **-2.** [personne] to fulfil o.s.

réalisme [realism] *nm* realism.

réaliste [realist] ◇ *nmf* realist. ◇ *adj* **-1.** [personne, objectif] realistic. **-2.** ART & LITTÉRATURE realist.

réalité [realite] *nf* reality; **en** ~ in reality.

réaménagement [reamenaʒmɑ̃] *nm* **-1.** [de projet] restructuring. **-2.** [de taux d'intérêt] readjustment.

réamorcer [reamɔrse] [16] *vt* to start up again.

réanimation [reanimasjɔ̃] *nf* resuscitation; **en** ~ in intensive care.

réanimer [reanime] [3] *vt* to resuscitate.

réapparaître [reaparɛtr] [91] *vi* to reappear.

réapparition [reaparisjɔ̃] *nf* reappearance.

réapprendre [reaprɑ̃dr] [79] *vt* to relearn.

réarmement [rearməmɑ̃] *nm* rearmament.

réassort [reasɔr] *nm* **-1.** [action] restocking. **-2.** [result] fresh stock.

réassurance [reasyrɑ̃s] *nf* reinsurance.

rébarbatif, -ive [rebarbatif, iv] *adj* **-1.** [personne, visage] forbidding. **-2.** [travail] daunting.

rebâtir [rəbatir] [32] *vt* to rebuild.

rebattre [rəbatr] [83] *vt* [cartes] to reshuffle.

rebattu, -e [rəbaty] ◇ *pp* → **rebattre**. ◇ *adj* overworked, hackneyed.

rebelle [rəbɛl] *adj* **-1.** [personne] rebellious; [troupes] rebel (*avant n*); ~ **à** [discipline] unamenable to. **-2.** [mèche, boucle] unruly.

rebeller [rəbɛle] [4]
◆ **se rebeller** *vp*: **se ~ (contre)** to rebel (against).

rébellion [rebɛljɔ̃] *nf* rebellion.

rebiffer [rəbife] [3]
◆ **se rebiffer** *vp fam*: **se ~ (contre)** to rebel (against).

reblochon [rəblɔʃɔ̃] *nm* cow's-milk cheese *from Haute-Savoie*.

reboiser [rəbwaze] [3] *vt* to reafforest.

rebond [rəbɔ̃] *nm* bounce.

rebondi, -e [rəbɔ̃di] *adj* rounded.

rebondir [rəbɔ̃dir] [32] *vi* **-1.** [objet] to bounce; [contre mur] to rebound. **-2.** *fig* [affaire] to come to life (again).

rebondissement [rəbɔ̃dismɑ̃] *nm* [d'affaire] new development.

rebord [rəbɔr] *nm* [de table] edge; [de fenêtre] sill, ledge.

reboucher [rəbuʃe] [3] *vt* [bouteille] to put the cork back in, to recork; [trou] to fill in.

rebours [rəbur]
◆ **à rebours** *loc adv* the wrong way; *fig* the wrong way round, back to front.

rebouteux, -euse [rəbutø, øz], **rebouteur, -euse** [rəbutœr, øz] *nm, f fam* bonesetter.

reboutonner [rəbutɔne] [3] *vt* to rebutton.

rebrousse-poil [rəbruspwal]
◆ **à rebrousse-poil** *loc adv* the wrong way; **prendre qqn à ~** *fig* to rub sb up the wrong way.

rebrousser [rəbruse] [3] *vt* to brush back; ~ **chemin** *fig* to retrace one's steps.

rebuffade [rəbyfad] *nf* rebuff; **essuyer une ~** to be rebuffed.

rébus [rebys] *nm* rebus.

rebut [rəby] *nm* scrap; **mettre qqch au ~** to get rid of sthg, to scrap sthg.

rebutant, -e [rəbytɑ̃, ɑ̃t] *adj* **-1.** [travail] disheartening. **-2.** [manières] disgusting.

rebuter [rəbyte] [3] *vt* **-1.** [suj: travail] to dishearten. **-2.** [suj: manières] to disgust.

récalcitrant, -e [rekalsitrɑ̃, ɑ̃t] ◇ *adj* recalcitrant, stubborn. ◇ *nm, f* recalcitrant.

recaler [rəkale] [3] *vt fam* to fail.

récapitulatif, -ive [rekapitylatif, iv] *adj* summary (*avant n*).
◆ **récapitulatif** *nm* summary.

récapitulation [rekapitylasjɔ̃] *nf* recapitulation, recap.

récapituler [rekapityle] [3] *vt* to recapitulate, to recap.

recel [rəsɛl] *nm* [action] receiving OU handling stolen goods; [délit] possession of stolen goods.

receler [rəsəle] [25] *vt* **-1.** [objet volé] to receive, to handle. **-2.** *fig* [secret, trésor] to contain.

receleur, -euse [rəsəlœr, øz] *nm, f* receiver (*of stolen goods*).

récemment [resamɑ̃] *adv* recently.

recensement [rəsɑ̃smɑ̃] *nm* **-1.** [de population] census. **-2.** [d'objets] inventory.

recenser [rəsɑ̃se] [3] *vt* **-1.** [population] to take a census of. **-2.** [objets] to take an inventory of.

récent, -e [resɑ̃, ɑ̃t] *adj* recent.

recentrer [rəsɑ̃tre] [3] *vt* to refocus.

récépissé [resepise] *nm* receipt.

réceptacle [reseptakl] *nm* [lieu] gathering place.

récepteur, -trice [reseptœr, tris] *adj* receiving.
◆ **récepteur** *nm* receiver.

réceptif, -ive [reseptif, iv] *adj* receptive.

réception [resepsjɔ̃] *nf* **-1.** [gén] reception; **donner une ~** to hold a reception. **-2.** [de marchandises] receipt. **-3.** [bureau] reception (desk). **-4.** SPORT [de sauteur, skieur] landing; [du ballon - avec la main] catch; [- avec le pied] **bonne ~ de X qui ...** X traps the ball and ....

réceptionnaire [resepsjɔnɛr] *nmf* **-1.** [de marchandises] receiving clerk. **-2.** [à l'hôtel] head of reception.

réceptionner [resepsjɔne] [3] *vt* **-1.** [marchandises] to take delivery of. **-2.** [SPORT - avec la main] to catch; [- avec le pied] to control.

réceptionniste [resepsjɔnist] *nmf* receptionist.

récessif, -ive [resesif, iv] *adj* recessive.

récession [resesjɔ̃] *nf* recession.

recette [rəsɛt] *nf* **-1.** COMM takings (*pl*); **faire ~** *fig* to be a success. **-2.** CULIN recipe; *fig* [méthode] recipe, formula.

recevable [rəsəvabl] *adj* **-1.** [excuse, offre] acceptable. **-2.** JUR admissible.

receveur, -euse [rəsəvœr, øz] *nm, f* **-1.** ADMIN: ~ **des impôts** tax collector; ~ **des postes** postmaster (*f* postmistress). **-2.** [de bus] conductor (*f* conductress). **-3.** [de greffe] recipient.

recevoir [rəsəvwar] [52] *vt* **-1.** [gén] to receive. **-2.** [coup] to get, to receive. **-3.** [invités] to entertain; [client] to see; ~ **qqn à dîner** to have sb to dinner. **-4.** SCOL & UNIV: **être reçu à un examen** to pass an exam.
◆ **se recevoir** *vp* SPORT to land.

rechange [rəʃɑ̃ʒ]
◆ **de rechange** *loc adj* spare; *fig* alternative.

réchapper [reʃape] [3] *vi:* ~ **de** to survive.

recharge [rəʃarʒ] *nf* **-1.** [cartouche] refill. **-2.** [action - de batterie] recharging.

rechargeable [rəʃarʒabl] *adj* [batterie] rechargeable; [briquet] refillable.

recharger [rəʃarʒe] [17] *vt* **-1.** [batterie] to recharge. **-2.** [stylo, briquet] to refill. **-3.** [arme, camion, appareil-photo] to reload.

réchaud [reʃo] *nm* (portable) stove.

réchauffé, -e [reʃofe] *adj* [plat] reheated; *fig* rehashed.

réchauffement [reʃofmɑ̃] *nm* warming (up).

réchauffer [reʃofe] [3] *vt* **-1.** [nourriture] to reheat. **-2.** [personne] to warm up.
◆ **se réchauffer** *vp* to warm up.

rêche [rɛʃ] *adj* rough.

recherche [rəʃɛrʃ] *nf* **-1.** [quête & INFORM] search; **être à la** ~ **de** to be in search of; **se mettre** OU **partir à la** ~ **de** to go in search of; **faire** OU **effectuer des** ~**s** to make inquiries. **-2.** SCIENCE research; **faire de la** ~ to do research. **-3.** [raffinement] elegance.

recherché, -e [rəʃɛrʃe] *adj* **-1.** [ouvrage] sought-after. **-2.** [raffiné - vocabulaire] refined; [- mets] exquisite.

rechercher [rəʃɛrʃe] [3] *vt* **-1.** [objet, personne] to search for, to hunt for. **-2.** [compagnie] to seek out.

rechigner [rəʃiɲe] [3] *vi:* ~ **à** to balk at.

rechute [rəʃyt] *nf* relapse.

rechuter [rəʃyte] [3] *vi* to relapse.

récidive [residiv] *nf* **-1.** JUR repeat offense *Am* OU offence *Br*. **-2.** MÉD recurrence.

récidiver [residive] [3] *vi* **-1.** JUR to commit another offense *Am* OU offence *Br*. **-2.** MÉD to recur.

récidiviste [residivist] *nmf* repeat OU persistent offender.

récif [resif] *nm* reef; ~ **de corail** coral reef.

récipiendaire [resipjɑ̃dɛr] *nmf sout* **-1.** [dans assemblée] newly elected member. **-2.** [de diplôme] recipient.

récipient [resipjɑ̃] *nm* container.

réciproque [resiprɔk] ◇ *adj* reciprocal. ◇ *nf:* **la** ~ the reverse.

réciproquement [resiprɔkmɑ̃] *adv* mutually; **et** ~ and vice versa.

récit [resi] *nm* story.

récital, -als [resital] *nm* recital.

récitatif [resitatif] *nm* recitative.

récitation [resitasjɔ̃] *nf* recitation.

réciter [resite] [3] *vt* to recite.

réclamation [reklamasjɔ̃] *nf* complaint; **faire/déposer une** ~ to make/lodge a complaint.

réclame [reklam] *nf* **-1.** [annonce] advert, advertisement. **-2.** [publicité]: **la** ~ advertising. **-3.** [promotion]: **en** ~ on special offer.

réclamer [reklame] [3] *vt* **-1.** [demander] to ask for, to request; [avec insistance] to demand. **-2.** [nécessiter] to require, to demand.
◆ **se réclamer** *vp:* **se** ~ **de** [mouvement] to identify with.

reclasser [rəklase] [3] *vt* **-1.** [dossiers] to refile. **-2.** [chômeur] to find a new job for. **-3.** ADMIN to regrade.

reclus, -e [rəkly, yz] ◇ *adj sout* reclusive. ◇ *nm, f* recluse.

réclusion [reklyzjɔ̃] *nf* imprisonment; ~ **à perpétuité** life imprisonment.

recoiffer [rəkwafe] [3] *vt:* ~ **qqn** to do sb's hair again.
◆ **se recoiffer** *vp* to do one's hair again.

recoin [rəkwɛ̃] *nm* nook.

reçois, reçoit *etc* → **recevoir**.

recoller [rəkɔle] [3] *vt* to stick back together.

récolte [rekɔlt] *nf* **-1.** [AGRIC - action] harvesting (*U*), gathering (*U*); [- produit] harvest, crop. **-2.** *fig* collection.

récolter [rekɔlte] [3] *vt* to harvest; *fig* to collect.

recommandable [rəkɔmɑ̃dabl] *adj* commendable; **peu** ~ undesirable.

recommandation [rəkɔmɑ̃dasjɔ̃] *nf* recommendation.

recommandé, -e [rəkɔmɑ̃de] *adj* **-1.** [envoi] registered; **envoyer qqch en** ~ to send sthg by registered mail *Am* OU post *Br*. **-2.** [conseillé] advisable; **ce n'est pas très** ~ it's not really a good idea, it's not very advisable.

recommander [rəkɔmɑ̃de] [3] *vt* to recommend; ~ **à qqn de faire qqch** to advise sb to do sthg; ~ **qqn à qqn** to recommend sb to sb.
◆ **se recommander** *vp* **-1.** [se réclamer]: **se** ~ **de qqn** to use sb as a referee. **-2.** [invoquer la protection de]: **se** ~ **à qqn** to commend o.s. to sb. **-3.** *Helv* [insister] to be persistent.

recommencement [rəkɔmãsmã] *nm* new beginning.

recommencer [rəkɔmãse] [16] ◇ *vt* [travail] to start OU begin again; [erreur] to make again; ~ **à faire qqch** to start OU begin doing sthg again. ◇ *vi* to start OU begin again; **ne recommence pas!** don't do that again!

récompense [rekɔ̃pãs] *nf* reward; **en ~ de** as a reward for.

récompenser [rekɔ̃pãse] [3] *vt* to reward.

recompter [rəkɔ̃te] [3] *vt* to recount.

réconciliation [rekɔ̃siljasjɔ̃] *nf* reconciliation.

réconcilier [rekɔ̃silje] [9] *vt* to reconcile.
◆ **se réconcilier** *vp*: **se ~ avec** to make it up with.

reconductible [rəkɔ̃dyktibl] *adj* renewable.

reconduction [rəkɔ̃dyksjɔ̃] *nf* renewal.

reconduire [rəkɔ̃dɥir] [98] *vt* **-1.** [personne] to accompany, to take. **-2.** [politique, bail] to renew.

reconduit, -e [rəkɔ̃dɥi, ɥit] *pp* → **reconduire**.

réconfort [rekɔ̃fɔr] *nm* comfort; **chercher ~ dans** to seek comfort OU solace in.

réconfortant, -e [rekɔ̃fɔrtã, ãt] *adj* comforting.

réconforter [rekɔ̃fɔrte] [3] *vt* to comfort.

reconnaissable [rəkɔnɛsabl] *adj* recognizable.

reconnaissance [rəkɔnɛsãs] *nf* **-1.** [gén] recognition; ~ **vocale** INFORM voice recognition. **-2.** [aveu] acknowledgment, admission; ~ **de dette** acknowledgment of a debt, IOU. **-3.** MIL reconnaissance; **aller/ partir en ~** to go out on reconnaissance. **-4.** [gratitude] gratitude; **exprimer sa ~ à qqn** to show OU express one's gratitude to sb.

reconnaissant, -e [rəkɔnɛsã, ãt] *adj* grateful; **je vous en suis très ~** I am very grateful to you (for it); **je vous serais ~ de m'aider** I would be grateful if you would help me.

reconnaître [rəkɔnɛtr] [91] *vt* **-1.** [gén] to recognize. **-2.** [erreur] to admit, to acknowledge. **-3.** MIL to reconnoitre.
◆ **se reconnaître** *vp* **-1.** [s'identifier] to recognize o.s.; **se ~ dans** OU **en qqn** to see o.s. in sb. **-2.** [s'orienter] to know where one is, to get one's bearings. **-3.** [s'avouer]: **se ~ coupable** to admit one's guilt.

reconnu, -e [rəkɔny] ◇ *pp* → **reconnaître**.
◇ *adj* well-known.

reconquérir [rəkɔ̃kerir] [39] *vt* to reconquer.

reconquête [rəkɔ̃kɛt] *nf* reconquest.

reconquis, -e [rəkɔki, iz] *pp* → **reconquérir**.

reconquiers, reconquiert *etc* → **reconquérir**.

reconsidérer [rəkɔ̃sidere] [18] *vt* to reconsider.

reconstituant, -e [rəkɔ̃stityã, ãt] *adj* invigorating.
◆ **reconstituant** *nm* tonic.

reconstituer [rəkɔ̃stitɥe] [7] *vt* **-1.** [puzzle] to put together. **-2.** [crime, délit] to reconstruct.

reconstitution [rəkɔ̃stitysjɔ̃] *nf* **-1.** [de puzzle] putting together. **-2.** [de crime, délit] reconstruction; ~ **historique** CIN & TÉLÉ dramatic reconstruction.

reconstruction [rəkɔ̃stryksjɔ̃] *nf* reconstruction, rebuilding.

reconstruire [rəkɔ̃strɥir] [98] *vt* to reconstruct, to rebuild.

reconstruit, -e [rəkɔ̃strɥi, ɥit] *pp* → **reconstruire**.

reconversion [rəkɔ̃vɛrsjɔ̃] *nf* **-1.** [d'employé] redeployment. **-2.** [d'usine, de société] conversion; **opérer une ~** to restructure; ~ **économique/technique** economic/technical restructuring.

reconvertir [rəkɔ̃vɛrtir] [32] *vt* **-1.** [employé] to redeploy. **-2.** [économie] to restructure.
◆ **se reconvertir** *vp*: **se ~ dans** to move into.

recopier [rəkɔpje] [9] *vt* to copy out.

record [rəkɔr] ◇ *nm* record; **détenir/ améliorer/battre un ~** to hold/improve/ beat a record. ◇ *adj* record (*avant n*).

recordman [rəkɔrdman] (*pl* **recordmen** [-mɛn]) *nm* recordholder.

recoucher [rəkuʃe] [3] *vt* to put back to bed.
◆ **se recoucher** *vp* to go back to bed.

recoudre [rəkudr] [86] *vt* to sew (up) again.

recoupement [rəkupmã] *nm* cross-check; **par ~** by cross-checking.

recouper [rəkupe] [3] *vt* **-1.** [pain] to cut again. **-2.** COUTURE to recut. **-3.** *fig* [témoignages] to compare, to cross-check.
◆ **se recouper** *vp* **-1.** [lignes] to intersect. **-2.** [témoignages] to match up.

recourber [rəkurbe] [3] *vt* to bend (over).

recourir [rəkurir] [45] *vi*: ~ **à** [médecin, agence] to turn to; [force, mensonge] to resort to.

recours¹, recourt *etc* → **recourir**.

recours² [rəkur] *nm* **-1.** [emploi]: ~ à use of; **avoir** ~ **à** [médecin, agence] to turn to; [force, mensonge] to resort to, to have recourse to. **-2.** [solution] solution, way out; **en dernier** ~ as a last resort. **-3.** JUR action; ~ **en cassation** appeal; ~ **en justice** legal action; **sans** ~ without appeal; *fig* final.

recouru [rəkury] *pp inv* → **recourir**.

recourrai, recourras *etc* → **recourir**.

recouvert, -e [rəkuvɛr, ɛrt] *pp* → **recouvrir**.

recouvrable [rəkuvrabl] *adj* recoverable.

recouvrement [rəkuvrəmã] *nm* **-1.** [de surface] covering. **-2.** [de dettes, d'impôts] collection.

recouvrer [rəkuvre] [3] *vt* **-1.** [vue, liberté] to regain. **-2.** [dettes, impôts] to collect.

recouvrir [rəkuvrir] [34] *vt* **-1.** [gén] to cover; [fauteuil] to re-cover. **-2.** [personne] to cover (up).
◆ **se recouvrir** *vp* **-1.** [tuiles] to overlap. **-2.** [surface]: **se** ~ **(de)** to be covered (with).

recracher [rəkraʃe] [3] *vt* to spit out.

récréatif, -ive [rekreatif, iv] *adj* entertaining.

récréation [rekreasjɔ̃] *nf* **-1.** [détente] relaxation, recreation. **-2.** SCOL break.

recréer [rəkree] [15] *vt* to recreate.

récrier [rekrije] [10]
◆ **se récrier** *vp sout*: **se** ~ **(à)** to exclaim (at).

récrimination [rekriminasjɔ̃] *nf* complaint.

récriminer [rekrimine] [3] *vi* to complain.

récrire [rekrir], **réécrire** [reekrir] [99] *vt* to rewrite.

recroqueviller [rəkrɔkvije] [3]
◆ **se recroqueviller** *vp* to curl up.

recru, -e [rəkry] *adj*: ~ **de fatigue** *littéraire* exhausted.
◆ **recrue** *nf* recruit.

recrudescence [rəkrydesɑ̃s] *nf* renewed outbreak.

recrutement [rəkrytmã] *nm* recruitment.

recruter [rəkryte] [3] *vt* to recruit.

rectal, -e, -aux [rɛktal, o] *adj* rectal.

rectangle [rɛktɑ̃gl] *nm* rectangle.

rectangulaire [rɛktɑ̃gylɛr] *adj* rectangular.

recteur [rɛktœr] *nm* SCOL *chief administrative officer of an education authority*.

rectificatif, -ive [rɛktifikatif, iv] *adj* correcting.
◆ **rectificatif** *nm* correction.

rectification [rɛktifikasjɔ̃] *nf* **-1.** [correction] correction. **-2.** [de tir] adjustment.

rectifier [rɛktifje] [9] *vt* **-1.** [tir] to adjust. **-2.**

[erreur] to rectify, to correct; [calcul] to correct.

rectiligne [rɛktiliɲ] *adj* rectilinear.

recto [rɛkto] *nm* right side; ~ **verso** on both sides.

rectorat [rɛktɔra] *nm* SCOL *offices of the education authority*, ≃ Education Offices *Br*.

rectum [rɛktɔm] *nm* rectum.

reçu, -e [rəsy] *pp* → **recevoir**.
◆ **reçu** *nm* receipt.

recueil [rəkœj] *nm* collection.

recueillement [rəkœjmã] *nm* meditation.

recueillir [rəkœjir] [41] *vt* **-1.** [fonds] to collect. **-2.** [suffrages] to win. **-3.** [enfant] to take in.
◆ **se recueillir** *vp* to meditate.

recul [rəkyl] *nm* **-1.** [mouvement arrière] step backwards; MIL retreat. **-2.** [d'arme à feu] recoil. **-3.** [de civilisation] decline; [d'inflation, de chômage]: ~ **(de)** downturn (in). **-4.** *fig* [retrait]: **prendre du** ~ to stand back; **avec du** ~ with hindsight.

reculade [rəkylad] *nf* retreat.

reculé, -e [rəkyle] *adj* distant.

reculer [rəkyle] [3] ◇ *vt* **-1.** [voiture] to back up. **-2.** [date] to put back, to postpone. ◇ *vi* **-1.** [aller en arrière] to move backwards; [voiture] to reverse; **ne** ~ **devant rien** *fig* to stop at nothing. **-2.** [maladie, pauvreté] to be brought under control.

reculons [rəkylɔ̃]
◆ **à reculons** *adv* backwards.

récupération [rekyperasjɔ̃] *nf* [de déchets] salvage.

récupérer [rekypere] [18] ◇ *vt* **-1.** [objet] to get back. **-2.** [déchets] to salvage. **-3.** [idée] to pick up. **-4.** [journée] to make up. ◇ *vi* to recover, to recuperate.

récurer [rekyre] [3] *vt* to scour.

récurrent, -e [rekyrã, ãt] *adj* recurrent.

récuser [rekyze] [3] *vt* **-1.** JUR to challenge. **-2.** *sout* [refuser] to reject.
◆ **se récuser** *vp sout* to decline to give an opinion.

recyclage [rəsiklaʒ] *nm* **-1.** [d'employé] retraining. **-2.** [de déchets] recycling.

recycler [rəsikle] [3] *vt* **-1.** [employé] to retrain. **-2.** [déchets] to recycle.
◆ **se recycler** *vp* [employé] to retrain.

rédacteur, -trice [redaktœr, tris] *nm, f* [de journal] subeditor; [d'ouvrage de référence] editor; ~ **en chef** editor-in-chief.

rédaction [redaksjɔ̃] *nf* **-1.** [de texte] editing. **-2.** SCOL essay. **-3.** [personnel] editorial staff.

rédactionnel, -elle [redaksjɔnɛl] *adj* editorial.

reddition [redisjɔ̃] *nf* surrender.

redécouvrir [rədekuvrir] [34] *vt* to rediscover.

redéfinir [rədefinir] [32] *vt* to redefine.

redéfinition [rədefinisjɔ̃] *nf* redefinition.

redemander [rədəmɑ̃de] [3] *vt* to ask again for.

redémarrer [rədemare] [3] *vi* to start again; *fig* to get going again.

rédempteur, -trice [redɑ̃ptœr, tris] ◇ *adj* redeeming. ◇ *nm, f* redeemer.

rédemption [redɑ̃psjɔ̃] *nf* redemption.

redéploiement [rədeplwamɑ̃] *nm* redeployment.

redescendre [rədesɑ̃dr] [73] ◇ *vt* (*aux*: *avoir*) **-1.** [escalier] to go/come down again. **-2.** [objet - d'une étagère] to take down again. ◇ *vi* (*aux*: *être*) to go/come down again.

redevable [rədəvabl] *adj*: être ~ de 10 francs à qqn to owe sb 10 francs; être ~ à qqn de qqch [service] to be indebted to sb for sthg.

redevance [rədəvɑ̃s] *nf* [de radio, télévision] licence fee; [téléphonique] rental (fee).

redevenir [rədəvnir] [40] *vi* to become again.

rédhibitoire [redibitwar] *adj* [défaut] crippling; [prix] prohibitive.

rediffuser [rədifyze] [3] *vt* to broadcast again, to repeat.

rediffusion [rədifyzjɔ̃] *nf* repeat.

rédiger [rediʒe] [17] *vt* to write.

redingote [rədɛ̃gɔt] *nf* [de femme] coat; HIST frock coat.

redire [rədir] [102] *vt* to repeat; avoir OU trouver à ~ à qqch *fig* to find fault with sthg.

redistribuer [rədistribɥe] [7] *vt* to redistribute.

redistribution [rədistribysjɔ̃] *nf* redistribution.

redit, -e [rədi, it] *pp* → redire.

redite [rədit] *nf* repetition.

redondance [rədɔ̃dɑ̃s] *nf* redundancy.

redonner [rədɔne] [3] *vt* to give back; [confiance, forces] to restore.

redoublant, -e [rədublɑ̃, ɑ̃t] *nm, f* pupil who is repeating a year.

redoublé, -e [rəduble] *adj*: à coups ~s twice as hard.

redoubler [rəduble] [3] ◇ *vt* **-1.** [syllabe] to reduplicate. **-2.** [efforts] to intensify. **-3.** SCOL to repeat. ◇ *vi* to intensify; ~ d'efforts to redouble one's efforts; le vent redoubla de fureur the wind blew twice as hard.

redoutable [rədutabl] *adj* formidable.

redouter [rədute] [3] *vt* to fear.

redoux [rədu] *nm* thaw.

redressement [rədrɛsmɑ̃] *nm* **-1.** [de pays, d'économie] recovery. **-2.** JUR: ~ fiscal payment of back taxes.

redresser [rədrɛse] [4] ◇ *vt* **-1.** [poteau, arbre] to put OU set upright; ~ la tête to raise one's head; *fig* to hold up one's head. **-2.** [situation] to set right. ◇ *vi* AUTOM to straighten up.

◆ **se redresser** *vp* **-1.** [personne] to stand OU sit straight. **-2.** [pays] to recover.

redresseur [rədrɛsœr] *nm*: ~ de torts righter of wrongs.

réducteur, -trice [redyktœr, tris] *adj* **-1.** [de quantité] reducing. **-2.** [limitatif] simplistic.

◆ **réducteur** *nm* CHIM reducing agent.

réduction [redyksjɔ̃] *nf* **-1.** [gén] reduction; bénéficier d'une ~ to get a reduction. **-2.** MÉD setting.

réduire [redɥir] [98] ◇ *vt* **-1.** [gén] to reduce; ~ en to reduce to; ~ qqn à qqch/à faire qqch to reduce sb to sthg/to doing sthg; être réduit à faire qqch to be reduced to doing sthg. **-2.** MÉD to set. **-3.** *Helv* [ranger] to put away. ◇ *vi* CULIN to reduce.

◆ **se réduire** *vp* **-1.** [se restreindre] to cut down. **-2.** [se ramener]: se ~ à to come OU boil down to. **-3.** [se transformer]: se ~ en to be reduced to.

réduisais, réduisions *etc* → réduire.

réduit, -e [redɥi, ɥit] ◇ *pp* → réduire. ◇ *adj* reduced.

◆ **réduit** *nm* **-1.** [local] small room. **-2.** [renfoncement] recess.

rééchelonner [reeʃlɔne] [3] *vt* to reschedule.

réécrire = récrire.

rééditer [reedite] [3] *vt* **-1.** [œuvre, auteur] to republish. **-2.** *fam* [méfaits] to give a repeat performance of.

réédition [reedisjɔ̃] *nf* new edition.

rééducation [reedykasjɔ̃] *nf* **-1.** [de membre] re-education. **-2.** [de délinquant, malade] rehabilitation.

rééduquer [reedyke] [3] *vt* **-1.** [membre] to re-educate. **-2.** [délinquant, malade] to rehabilitate.

réel, réelle [reɛl] *adj* real.

◆ **réel** *nm*: le ~ reality.

réélection [reelɛksjɔ̃] *nf* re-election.

réélire [reelir] [106] *vt* to re-elect.

réellement [reɛlmɑ̃] *adv* really.

réembaucher [reãboʃe] [3] *vt* to take on again.

réemploi = remploi.

réemployer = remployer.

réengager = rengager.

rééquilibrer [reekilibre] [3] *vt* to balance (again).

réescompte [reɛskɔ̃t] *nm* rediscount.

réessayer [reeseje], **ressayer** [rɛseje] [11] *vt* to try again.

réévaluer [reevalɥe] [7] *vt* to revalue.

réexaminer [reɛgzamine] [3] *vt* to re-examine.

réexpédier [reɛkspedje] [9] *vt* to send back.

réexporter [reɛkspɔrte] [3] *vt* to re-export.

réf. (*abr de* référence) ref.

refaire [rəfɛr] [109] *vt* -1. [faire de nouveau - travail, devoir] to do again; [- voyage] to make again. -2. [mur, toit] to repair. -3. *fam* [personne] to take in.
◆ **se refaire** *vp* -1. [se rétablir]: **se ~ une santé** to recover (one's health). -2. [se réhabituer]: **se ~ à qqch** to get used to sthg again. -3. *fam* [au jeu] to make up OU win back one's losses.

refaisais, refaisions *etc* → refaire.

refait, -e [rəfɛ, ɛt] *pp* → refaire.

refasse, refasses *etc* → refaire.

réfection [refɛksjɔ̃] *nf* repair.

réfectoire [refɛktwar] *nm* refectory.

référé [refere] *nm* [procédure] special hearing; [arrêt] temporary ruling; [ordonnance] temporary injunction.

référence [referãs] *nf* reference; **faire ~ à** to refer to.
◆ **références** *nfpl* references.

référendum [referɛ̃dɔm] *nm* referendum.

référer [refere] [18] *vi*: **en ~ à qqn** to refer the matter to sb.
◆ **se référer** *vp*: **se ~ à** to refer to.

refermer [rəfɛrme] [3] *vt* to close OU shut again.

refiler [rəfile] [3] *vt fam*: **~ qqch à qqn** [objet] to palm sthg off on sb; [maladie] to give sthg to sb.

réfléchi, -e [refleʃi] *adj* -1. [action] considered; **c'est tout ~** I've made up my mind, I've decided. -2. [personne] thoughtful. -3. GRAM reflexive.

réfléchir [refleʃir] [32] ◇ *vt* -1. [refléter] to reflect. -2. [penser]: **~ que** to think OU reflect that. ◇ *vi* to think, to reflect; **~ à** OU **sur qqch** to think about sthg.
◆ **se réfléchir** *vp* to be reflected.

réfléchissant, -e [refleʃisã, ãt] *adj* reflective.

réflecteur [reflɛktœr] *nm* reflector.

reflet [rəflɛ] *nm* -1. [image] reflection. -2. [de lumière] glint.

refléter [rəflete] [18] *vt* to reflect.
◆ **se refléter** *vp* -1. [se réfléchir] to be reflected. -2. [transparaître] to be mirrored.

refleurir [rəflœrir] [32] *vi* -1. [fleurir à nouveau] to flower again. -2. *fig* [art] to flourish again.

reflex [reflɛks] ◇ *nm* reflex camera. ◇ *adj* reflex (*avant n*).

réflexe [reflɛks] ◇ *nm* reflex. ◇ *adj* reflex (*avant n*).

réflexion [reflɛksjɔ̃] *nf* -1. [de lumière, d'ondes] reflection. -2. [pensée] reflection, thought; **à la ~** on second thoughts; **~ faite** on reflection. -3. [remarque] remark.

refluer [rəflɥe] [3] *vi* -1. [liquide] to flow back. -2. [foule] to flow back; [avec violence] to surge back.

reflux [rəfly] *nm* -1. [d'eau] ebb. -2. [de personnes] backward surge.

refondre [rəfɔ̃dr] [75] *vt* -1. [métal] to remelt. -2. [ouvrage] to recast.

refonte [rəfɔ̃t] *nf* -1. [de métal] remelting. -2. [d'ouvrage] recasting. -3. [d'institution, de système] overhaul, reshaping.

reforestation [rəfɔrestasjɔ̃] *nf* reforestation.

réformateur, -trice [refɔrmatœr, tris] ◇ *adj* reforming. ◇ *nm, f* -1. [personne] reformer. -2. RELIG Reformer.

réforme [refɔrm] *nf* reform.

réformé, -e [refɔrme] *adj & nm, f* Protestant.
◆ **réformé** *nm* MIL *soldier who has been invalided out.*

reformer [rəfɔrme] [3] *vt* to reform.
◆ **se reformer** *vp* to reform.

réformer [refɔrme] [3] *vt* -1. [améliorer] to reform, to improve. -2. MIL to invalid out. -3. [matériel] to scrap.

réformisme [refɔrmism] *nm* reformism.

réformiste [refɔrmist] *adj & nmf* reformist.

refoulé, -e [rəfule] ◇ *adj* repressed, frustrated. ◇ *nm, f* repressed person.

refoulement [rəfulmã] *nm* -1. [de personnes] repelling. -2. PSYCHOL repression.

refouler [rəfule] [3] *vt* -1. [personnes] to repel, to repulse. -2. PSYCHOL to repress.

réfractaire [refraktɛr] ◇ *adj* -1. [rebelle] insubordinate; **~ à** resistant to; **être ~ à la loi** to flout the law. -2. HIST [prêtre] nonjuring. -3. [matière] refractory. ◇ *nmf* insubordinate.

refrain [rəfrɛ̃] *nm* MUS refrain, chorus; **c'est toujours le même ~** *fam fig* it's always the same old story.

refréner [rəfrene] [18] *vt* to check, to hold back.

◆ **se refréner** *vp* to control o.s.

réfrigérant, -e [refriʒerɑ̃, ɑ̃t] *adj* **-1.** [liquide] refrigerating, refrigerant. **-2.** *fam* [accueil] icy.

réfrigérateur [refriʒeratœr] *nm* refrigerator.

réfrigération [refriʒerasjɔ̃] *nf* refrigeration.

réfringent, -e [refrɛ̃ʒɑ̃, ɑ̃t] *adj* refractive.

refroidir [rəfrwadir] [32] ◇ *vt* **-1.** [plat] to cool. **-2.** [décourager] to discourage. **-3.** *fam* [tuer] to rub out, to do in. ◇ *vi* to cool.

◆ **se refroidir** *vp* **-1.** [temps] to get OU turn colder. **-2.** [ardeur] to cool.

refroidissement [rəfrwadismɑ̃] *nm* **-1.** [de température] drop, cooling. **-2.** [grippe] chill. **-3.** *fig* [de sentiment] cooling off.

refuge [rəfyʒ] *nm* **-1.** [abri] refuge; **chercher ~ auprès de qqn** to seek refuge with sb. **-2.** [de montagne] hut. **-3.** [sur chaussée] traffic island.

réfugié, -e [refyʒje] ◇ *adj* refugee (*avant n*). ◇ *nm, f* refugee.

réfugier [refyʒje] [9]

◆ **se réfugier** *vp* to take refuge.

refus [rəfy] *nm inv* refusal; **ce n'est pas de ~** *fam* I wouldn't say no; **essuyer un ~** to meet with a refusal.

refuser [rəfyze] [3] *vt* **-1.** [repousser] to refuse; **~ de faire qqch** to refuse to do sthg. **-2.** [contester]: **~ qqch à qqn** to deny sb sthg. **-3.** [clients, spectateurs] to turn away. **-4.** [candidat]: **être refusé** to fail.

◆ **se refuser** *vp*: **se ~ à faire qqch** to refuse to do sthg; **se ~ à tout commentaire** to refuse to make any comment; **ne rien se ~** not to stint o.s.

réfutation [refytasjɔ̃] *nf* refutation.

réfuter [refyte] [3] *vt* to refute.

regagner [rəgaɲe] [3] *vt* **-1.** [reprendre] to regain, to win back. **-2.** [revenir] to get back to.

regain [rəgɛ̃] *nm* **-1.** [herbe] second crop. **-2.** [retour]: **un ~ de** a revival of, a renewal of; **un ~ de vie** a new lease of life.

régal, -als [regal] *nm* treat, delight.

régaler [regale] [3] *vt* to treat; **c'est moi qui régale!** it's my treat!

◆ **se régaler** *vp*: **je me régale** [nourriture] I'm thoroughly enjoying it; [activité] I'm having the time of my life.

regard [rəgar] *nm* look; **soutenir le ~ de qqn** *fig* to be able to look sb straight in the eye; **fusiller** OU **foudroyer qqn du ~** *fig* to glare at sb, to look daggers at sb.

◆ **au regard de** *loc prép* in relation to, with regard to.

◆ **en regard de** *loc prép* compared with.

regardant, -e [rəgardɑ̃, ɑ̃t] *adj* **-1.** *fam* [économe] mean. **-2.** [minutieux]: **être très/peu ~ sur qqch** to be very/not very particular about sthg.

regarder [rəgarde] [3] ◇ *vt* **-1.** [observer, examiner, consulter] to look at; [télévision, spectacle] to watch; **regarder qqn faire qqch** to watch sb doing sthg; **~ les trains passer** to watch the trains go by. **-2.** [considérer] to consider, to regard; **~ qqn/qqch comme** to regard sb/sthg as, to consider sb/sthg as. **-3.** [concerner] to concern; **cela ne te regarde pas** it's none of your business.
◇ *vi* **-1.** [observer, examiner] to look. **-2.** [faire attention]: **sans ~ à la dépense** regardless of the expense; **y ~ à deux fois** to think twice about it.

◆ **se regarder** *vp* **-1.** [emploi réfléchi] to look at o.s. **-2.** [emploi réciproque] to look at one another.

regarnir [rəgarnir] [32] *vt* to refill, to restock.

régate [regat] *nf* (*gén pl*) regatta.

régence [reʒɑ̃s] *nf* regency.

◆ **Régence** *nf* HIST: **la Régence** the Regency.

régénérer [reʒenere] [18] *vt* to regenerate.

◆ **se régénérer** *vp* to regenerate.

régent, -e [reʒɑ̃, ɑ̃t] *adj, nm, f* regent.

régenter [reʒɑ̃te] [3] *vt*: **vouloir tout ~** *péj* to want to be the boss.

reggae [rege] *nm & adj* reggae.

régie [reʒi] *nf* **-1.** [entreprise] state-controlled company. **-2.** RADIO & TÉLÉ [pièce] control room; CIN, THÉÂTRE & TÉLÉ [équipe] production team.

regimber [rəʒɛ̃be] [3] *vi* to balk.

régime [reʒim] *nm* **-1.** [politique] regime; **l'Ancien Régime** the Ancien Regime. **-2.** [administratif] system; **~ carcéral** prison regime; **~ de Sécurité sociale** subdivision of the French social security system applying to certain professional groups. **-3.** [alimentaire] diet; **se mettre au/suivre un ~** to go on/to be on a diet; **~ amincissant** slimming diet. **-4.** [de moteur] speed. **-5.** [de fleuve, des pluies] cycle. **-6.** [de bananes, dattes] bunch.

RÉGIME DE LA SÉCURITÉ SOCIALE:
The French social security system is divided into the following types of 'régime': 1. 'Le régime général des salariés', which provides

social security cover for people in paid employment; 2. 'Les régimes spéciaux', which provide tailor-made cover for certain socio-professional groups (civil servants, miners, students etc); 3. 'Les régimes particuliers', designed for the self-employed; 4. 'Les régimes complémentaires', which provide additional retirement cover for wage-earners

---

régiment [reʒimɑ̃] *nm* **-1.** MIL regiment. **-2.** *fam* [grande quantité]: **un ~ de** masses of, loads of.

région [reʒjɔ̃] *nf* region; ~ **parisienne** Paris area OU region.

régional, -e, -aux [reʒjɔnal, o] *adj* regional.

régionalisation [reʒjɔnalizasjɔ̃] *nf* regionalization.

régionalisme [reʒjɔnalism] *nm* regionalism.

régionaliste [reʒjɔnalist] *nmf & adj* regionalist.

régir [reʒir] [32] *vt* to govern.

régisseur [reʒisœr] *nm* **-1.** [intendant] steward. **-2.** [de théâtre] stage manager.

registre [rəʒistr] *nm* [gén] register; ~ **du commerce** trade register; ~ **de comptabilité** ledger; ~**s publics d'état civil** register (*sg*) of births, marriages and deaths.

réglable [reglabl] *adj* **-1.** [adaptable] adjustable. **-2.** [payable] payable.

réglage [reglaʒ] *nm* adjustment, setting.

règle [rɛgl] *nf* **-1.** [instrument] ruler; ~ **graduée** graduated ruler. **-2.** [principe, loi] rule; **je suis en ~** my papers are in order; **mets-toi en ~** get your papers in order; **être de ~** to be the rule.
◆ **en règle générale** *loc adv* as a general rule.
◆ **règles** *nfpl* [menstruation] period (*sg*).

réglé, -e [regle] *adj* **-1.** [organisé] regular, well-ordered. **-2.** [papier] lined, ruled.

réglée [regle] *adj f*: **être ~** to have periods, to menstruate.

règlement [rɛgləmɑ̃] *nm* **-1.** [résolution] settling; ~ **de comptes** *fig* settling of scores; ~ **judiciaire** liquidation. **-2.** [règle] regulation; **observer le ~** to follow the rules OU regulations. **-3.** [paiement] settlement.

réglementaire [rɛgləmɑ̃tɛr] *adj* **-1.** [régulier] statutory. **-2.** [imposé] regulation (*avant n*).

réglementation [rɛgləmɑ̃tasjɔ̃] *nf* **-1.** [action] regulation. **-2.** [ensemble de règles] regulations (*pl*), rules (*pl*); ~ **du travail/commerce** work/commercial regulations.

réglementer [rɛgləmɑ̃te] [3] *vt* to control, to regulate.

régler [regle] [18] *vt* **-1.** [affaire, conflit] to settle, to sort out. **-2.** [appareil] to adjust. **-3.** [payer - note] to settle, to pay; [commerçant] to pay.
◆ **se régler** *vp* **-1.** [suivre]: **se ~ sur qqn** to model o.s. on sb. **-2.** [affaire, conflit] to be sorted out, to be settled.

réglisse [reglis] *nf* liquorice.

réglo [reglo] *adj inv fam* straight.

régnant, -e [reɲɑ̃, ɑ̃t] *adj* [monarque] reigning.

règne [rɛɲ] *nm* **-1.** [de souverain] reign; **sous le ~ de** in the reign of. **-2.** [pouvoir] rule. **-3.** BIOL kingdom.

régner [reɲe] [18] *vi* **-1.** [souverain] to rule, to reign. **-2.** [silence] to reign.

regonfler [rəgɔ̃fle] [3] *vt* **-1.** [pneu, ballon] to blow up again, to reinflate. **-2.** *fam* [personne] to cheer up.

regorger [rəgɔrʒe] [17] *vi*: ~ **de** to be abundant in.

régresser [regrese] [4] *vi* **-1.** [sentiment, douleur] to diminish. **-2.** [personne] to regress.

régressif, -ive [regresif, iv] *adj* regressive, backward.

régression [regresjɔ̃] *nf* **-1.** [recul] decline. **-2.** PSYCHOL regression.

regret [rəgrɛ] *nm*: ~ **(de)** regret (for); **tous mes ~s** I'm very sorry; **à ~** with regret; **sans ~** with no regrets; **avoir le** OU **être au ~ d'informer qqn de** to be sorry OU to regret to inform sb of.

regrettable [rəgrɛtabl] *adj* regrettable.

regretter [rəgrɛte] [4] ◇ *vt* **-1.** [époque] to miss, to regret; [personne] to miss. **-2.** [faute] to regret; ~ **d'avoir fait qqch** to regret having done sthg. **-3.** [déplorer]: ~ **que** (+ *subjonctif*) to be sorry OU to regret that. ◇ *vi* to be sorry.

regroupement [rəgrupmɑ̃] *nm* **-1.** [action] gathering together. **-2.** [groupe] group, assembly.

regrouper [rəgrupe] [3] *vt* **-1.** [grouper à nouveau] to regroup, to reassemble. **-2.** [réunir] to group together.
◆ **se regrouper** *vp* to gather, to assemble.

régulariser [regylarize] [3] *vt* **-1.** [documents] to sort out, to put in order; [situation] to straighten out. **-2.** [circulation, fonctionnement] to regulate.

régularité [regylarite] *nf* **-1.** [gén] regularity. **-2.** [de travail, résultats] consistency.

régulateur, -trice [regylatœr, tris] *adj* regulating.
◆ **régulateur** *nm* regulator.

régulation [regylasjɔ̃] *nf* [contrôle] control, regulation; ~ **des naissances** birth control.

réguler [regyle] [3] *vt* to regulate.

régulier, -ière [regylje, jɛr] *adj* **-1.** [gén] regular. **-2.** [uniforme, constant] steady, regular. **-3.** [travail, résultats] consistent. **-4.** [légal] legal; **être en situation régulière** to have all the legally required documents. **-5.** *fam* [correct] straight, above board.

régulièrement [regyljɛrmɑ̃] *adv* **-1.** [gén] regularly. **-2.** [uniformément] steadily, regularly; [étalé, façonné] evenly.

réhabilitation [reabilitasjɔ̃] *nf* rehabilitation.

réhabiliter [reabilite] [3] *vt* **-1.** [accusé] to rehabilitate, to clear; *fig* [racheter] to restore to favor *Am* OU favour *Br*. **-2.** [rénover] to restore.

◆ **se réhabiliter** *vp* to redeem o.s.

réhabituer [reabitчe] [7] *vt* to reaccustom.

◆ **se réhabituer** *vp*: **se ~ à qqch** to get used to sthg again.

rehausser [rɔose] [3] *vt* **-1.** [surélever] to heighten. **-2.** [mettre en valeur] to enhance.

réimporter [reɛ̃pɔrte] [3] *vt* to reimport.

réimposer [reɛ̃poze] [3] *vt* to retax.

réimpression [reɛ̃presjɔ̃] *nf* reprinting, reprint.

réimprimer [reɛ̃prime] [3] *vt* to reprint.

rein [rɛ̃] *nm* kidney; ~ **artificiel** dialysis OU kidney machine.

◆ **reins** *nmpl* small of the back (*sg*); **avoir mal aux ~s** to have backache; **avoir les ~s solides** *fam* [être résistant] to have a strong back; [être riche] not to be short of money.

réincarnation [reɛ̃karnasjɔ̃] *nf* reincarnation.

reine [rɛn] *nf* queen.

reine-claude [rɛnklod] (*pl* **reines-claudes**) *nf* greengage.

reinette [rɛnɛt] *nf* variety of apple similar to pippin.

réinscrire [reɛ̃skrir] [99] *vt*: ~ **qqn à** to re-enrol sb for.

◆ **se réinscrire** *vp*: **se ~ à** to re-enrol for.

réinsérer [reɛ̃sere] [18] *vt* to reinsert.

◆ **se réinsérer** *vp* to become reintegrated.

réinsertion [reɛ̃sɛrsjɔ̃] *nf* [de délinquant] rehabilitation; [dans vie professionnelle] reintegration.

réintégrer [reɛ̃tegre] [18] *vt* **-1.** [rejoindre] to return to. **-2.** JUR to reinstate.

réintroduire [reɛ̃trɔdчir] [98] *vt* to reintroduce.

réitérer [reitere] [18] *vt* [promesse, demande] to repeat, to reiterate; [attaque] to repeat.

rejaillir [rɔʒajir] [32] *vi* to splash up; ~ **sur qqn** *fig* to rebound on sb.

rejet [rɔʒɛ] *nm* **-1.** [gén] rejection. **-2.** [pousse] shoot.

rejeter [rɔʒte] [27] *vt* **-1.** [relancer] to throw back. **-2.** [expulser] to bring up, to vomit. **-3.** [offre, personne] to reject. **-4.** [partie du corps]: ~ **la tête/les bras en arrière** to throw back one's head/one's arms. **-5.** [imputer]: ~ **la responsabilité de qqch sur qqn** to lay the responsibility for sthg at sb's door.

◆ **se rejeter** *vp*: **se ~ la faute l'un sur l'autre** to blame one another for sthg; **se ~ la responsabilité (de qqch) l'un sur l'autre** to hold one another responsible (for sthg).

rejeton [rɔʒtɔ̃] *nm* offspring (*U*).

rejette, rejettes *etc* → **rejeter**.

rejoindre [rɔʒwɛ̃dr] [82] *vt* **-1.** [retrouver] to join. **-2.** [regagner] to return to. **-3.** [concorder avec] to agree with. **-4.** [rattraper] to catch up with.

◆ **se rejoindre** *vp* **-1.** [personnes, routes] to meet. **-2.** [opinions] to agree.

rejoignais, rejoignions *etc* → **rejoindre**.

rejoint, -e [rɔʒwɛ̃, ɛ̃t] *pp* → **rejoindre**.

réjoui, -e [reʒwi] *adj* joyful.

réjouir [reʒwir] [32] *vt* to delight.

◆ **se réjouir** *vp* to be delighted; **se ~ de qqch** to be delighted at OU about sthg.

réjouissance [reʒwisɑ̃s] *nf* rejoicing.

◆ **réjouissances** *nfpl* festivities.

réjouissant, -e [reʒwisɑ̃, ɑ̃t] *adj* joyful, cheerful.

relâche [rɔlɑʃ] *nf* **-1.** [pause]: **sans ~** without respite OU a break. **-2.** THÉÂTRE: **demain c'est le jour de ~** we're closed tomorrow; **faire ~** to be closed.

relâché, -e [rɔlɑʃe] *adj* lax, loose.

relâchement [rɔlɑʃmɑ̃] *nm* relaxation.

relâcher [rɔlɑʃe] [3] *vt* **-1.** [étreinte, cordes] to loosen. **-2.** [discipline, effort] to relax, to slacken. **-3.** [prisonnier] to release.

◆ **se relâcher** *vp* **-1.** [se desserrer] to loosen. **-2.** [faiblir - discipline] to become lax; [- attention] to flag. **-3.** [se laisser aller] to slacken off.

relaie, relaies *etc* → **relayer**.

relais [rɔlɛ] *nm* **-1.** [auberge] post house; ~**-restaurant** roadside restaurant. **-2.** SPORT & TÉLÉ: **prendre/passer le ~** to take/hand over.

relance [rɔlɑ̃s] *nf* **-1.** [économique] revival, boost; [de projet] relaunch. **-2.** [au jeu] stake.

relancer [rɔlɑ̃se] [16] *vt* **-1.** [renvoyer] to throw back. **-2.** [faire reprendre - économie] to boost; [- projet] to relaunch; [- moteur, machine] to restart.

relater [rəlate] [3] *vt littéraire* to relate.

relatif, -ive [rəlatif, iv] *adj* relative; ~ à relating to; **tout est** ~ it's all relative.

◆ **relative** *nf* GRAM relative clause.

relation [rəlasjɔ̃] *nf* relationship; **mettre qqn en** ~ **avec qqn** to put sb in touch with sb.

◆ **relations** *nfpl* **-1.** [rapport] relationship (*sg*); ~s **sexuelles** sexual relations, intercourse (*U*). **-2.** [connaissance] acquaintance; **avoir des** ~s to have connections. **-3.** [communication]: ~s **internationales** international relations; ~s **publiques** public relations.

relationnel, -elle [rəlasjɔnɛl] *adj* [problèmes] relationship (*avant n*).

relative → **relatif**.

relativement [rəlativmɑ̃] *adv* relatively.

relativiser [rəlativize] [3] *vt* to relativize.

relativité [rəlativite] *nf* relativity.

relax, relaxe [rəlaks] *adj fam* relaxed.

relaxation [rəlaksasjɔ̃] *nf* relaxation.

relaxe = **relax**.

relaxer [rəlakse] [3] *vt* **-1.** [reposer] to relax. **-2.** JUR to discharge.

◆ **se relaxer** *vp* to relax.

relayer [rəlɛje] [11] *vt* to relieve.

◆ **se relayer** *vp* to take over from one another.

relecture [rələktyr] *nf* second reading, re-reading.

reléguer [rəlege] [18] *vt* to relegate.

relent [rəlɑ̃] *nm* **-1.** [odeur] stink, stench. **-2.** *fig* [trace] whiff.

relevé, -e [rəlve] *adj* **-1.** [style] elevated. **-2.** CULIN spicy.

◆ **relevé** *nm* reading; **faire le** ~ **de qqch** to read sthg; ~ **de compte** bank statement; ~ **d'identité bancaire** bank account number.

relève [rəlɛv] *nf* relief; **prendre la** ~ to take over.

relèvement [rəlɛvmɑ̃] *nm* **-1.** [redressement] rebuilding. **-2.** [hausse] raising. **-3.** [majoration] increase.

relever [rəlve] [19] ◇ *vt* **-1.** [redresser - personne] to help up; *fig* [pays, économie] to rebuild; [moral, niveau] to raise. **-2.** [ramasser] to collect. **-3.** [tête, col, store] to raise; [manches] to push up. **-4.** [CULIN - mettre en valeur] to bring out; [- pimenter] to season; *fig* [récit] to liven up, to spice up. **-5.** [noter] to note down; [compteur] to read. **-6.** [relayer] to take over from, to relieve. **-7.** [erreur] to note.

◇ *vi* **-1.** [se rétablir]: ~ **de** to recover from. **-2.** [être du domaine]: ~ **de** to come under.

◆ **se relever** *vp* **-1.** [se mettre debout] to stand up; [- du lit] to get up. **-2.** [se rétablir]: **se** ~ **de qqch** to recover from sthg, to get over sthg. **-3.** [se rehausser] to lift.

relief [rəljɛf] *nm* relief; **sans aucun** ~ completely flat; **en** ~ in relief, raised; **une carte en** ~ relief map; **mettre en** ~ *fig* to enhance, to bring out.

◆ **reliefs** *nmpl vieilli* remains.

relier [rəlje] [9] *vt* **-1.** [livre] to bind. **-2.** [attacher]: ~ **qqch à qqch** to link sthg to sthg. **-3.** [joindre] to connect. **-4.** *fig* [associer] to link up.

relieur, -ieuse [rəljœr, jøz] *nm, f* binder.

religieuse → **religieux**.

religieusement [rəliʒjøzmɑ̃] *adv* **-1.** [gén] religiously; [solennellement] reverently. **-2.** [se marier] in church.

religieux, -ieuse [rəliʒjø, jøz] *adj* **-1.** [vie, chant] religious; [mariage] religious, church (*avant n*). **-2.** [respectueux] reverent.

◆ **religieux** *nm* monk.

◆ **religieuse** *nf* **-1.** RELIG nun. **-2.** CULIN: ~ **au café**, ~ **au chocolat** choux pastry filled with coffee or chocolate confectioner's custard.

religion [rəliʒjɔ̃] *nf* **-1.** [culte] religion. **-2.** [foi] faith. **-3.** [croyance] religion, faith; **entrer en** ~ to take one's vows.

reliquaire [rəliker] *nm* reliquary.

reliquat [rəlika] *nm* balance, remainder.

relique [rəlik] *nf* relic.

relire [rəlir] [106] *vt* to reread.

◆ **se relire** *vp* to read what one has written.

reliure [rəljyr] *nf* binding.

relogement [rələʒmɑ̃] *nm* rehousing.

reloger [rələʒe] [17] *vt* to rehouse.

relu, -e [rəly] *pp* → **relire**.

reluire [rəlɥir] [97] *vi* to shine, to gleam; **faire** ~ **qqch** to shine OU polish sthg.

reluisant, -e [rəlɥizɑ̃, ɑ̃t] *adj* shining, gleaming; **peu** OU **pas très** ~ *fig* [avenir, situation] not all that brilliant; [personne] shady.

remâcher [rəmaʃe] [3] *vt fig* to brood over.

remailler [rəmaje] [3] *vt* [filet] to mend; [tricot] to darn.

remake [rimɛjk] *nm* CIN remake.

rémanent, -e [remanɑ̃, ɑ̃t] *adj* residual.

remaniement [rəmanimɑ̃] *nm* restructuring; ~ **ministériel** cabinet reshuffle.

remanier [rəmanje] [9] *vt* to restructure; [ministère] to reshuffle.

remarier [rəmarje] [9]

◆ **se remarier** *vp* to remarry.

remarquable [rəmarkabl] *adj* remarkable.

remarquablement [rəmarkabləmã] *adv* remarkably.

remarque [rəmark] *nf* **-1.** [observation] remark; [critique] critical remark. **-2.** [annotation] note.

remarquer [rəmarke] [3] ◇ *vt* **-1.** [apercevoir] to notice; **faire ~ qqch (à qqn)** to point sthg out (to sb); **se faire ~** *péj* to draw attention to o.s. **-2.** [noter] to remark, to comment. ◇ *vi*: **ce n'est pas l'idéal, remarque!** it's not ideal, mind you!

◆ **se remarquer** *vp* to be noticeable.

remballer [rãbale] [3] *vt* [marchandise] to pack up.

rembarquer [rãbarke] [3] *vt* to reembark.

◆ **se rembarquer** *vp* to reembark.

rembarrer [rãbare] [3] *vt fam* to snub.

remblai [rãblɛ] *nm* embankment.

remblayer [rãbleje] [11] *vt* [hausser] to bank up; [combler] to fill in.

rembobiner [rãbɔbine] [3] *vt* to rewind.

rembourrage [rãburaʒ] *nm* stuffing, padding.

rembourrer [rãbure] [3] *vt* to stuff, to pad.

remboursable [rãbursabl] *adj* refundable.

remboursement [rãbursəmã] *nm* refund, repayment.

rembourser [rãburse] [3] *vt* **-1.** [dette] to pay back, to repay. **-2.** [personne] to pay back; **~ qqn de qqch** to reimburse sb for sthg.

rembrunir [rãbrynir] [32]

◆ **se rembrunir** *vp* to cloud over, to become gloomy.

remède [rəmɛd] *nm litt & fig* remedy, cure.

remédier [rəmedje] [9] *vi*: **~ à qqch** to put sthg right, to remedy sthg.

remembrement [rəmãbrəmã] *nm* land regrouping.

remémorer [rəmemɔre] [3]

◆ **se remémorer** *vp* to recollect.

remerciement [rəmɛrsimã] *nm* thanks (*pl*); **une lettre de ~** a thank-you letter; **avec tous mes ~s** with all my thanks, with many thanks.

remercier [rəmɛrsje] [9] *vt* **-1.** [dire merci à] to thank; **~ qqn de** OU **pour qqch** to thank sb for sthg; **non, je vous remercie** no, thank you. **-2.** [congédier] to dismiss.

remets → **remettre**.

remettre [rəmɛtr] [84] *vt* **-1.** [replacer] to put back; **~ en question** to call into question; **~ qqn à sa place** to put sb in his place. **-2.** [enfiler de nouveau] to put back on. **-3.** [réta-

blir - lumière, son] to put back on; **~ qqch en marche** to restart sthg; **~ de l'ordre dans qqch** to tidy sthg up; **~ une montre à l'heure** to put a watch right; **~ qqch en état de marche** to put sthg back in working order. **-4.** [donner]: **~ qqch à qqn** to hand sthg over to sb; [médaille, prix] to present sthg to sb. **-5.** [ajourner]: **~ qqch (à)** to put sthg off (until). **-6.** *fig* [reconnaître] to place. **-7.** MÉD: **~ qqn** to put sb back on his feet.

◆ **se remettre** *vp* **-1.** [recommencer]: **se ~ à qqch** to take up sthg again; **se ~ à fumer** to start smoking again. **-2.** [se rétablir] to get better; **se ~ de qqch** to get over sthg. **-3.** [redevenir]: **se ~ debout** to stand up again; **le temps s'est remis au beau** the weather has cleared up. **-4.** *loc*: **je m'en remets à toi** it's up to you, I'll leave it up to you.

réminiscence [reminisãs] *nf* reminiscence.

remis, -e [rəmi, iz] *pp* → **remettre**.

remise [rəmiz] *nf* **-1.** [action]: **~ en marche** restarting; **~ en place** putting back in place; **~ en jeu** throw-in; **~ en question** OU **en cause** calling into question. **-2.** [de message, colis] handing over; [de médaille, prix] presentation. **-3.** [réduction] discount; **~ de peine** JUR remission. **-4.** [hangar] shed.

remiser [rəmize] [3] *vt* to put away.

rémission [remisjõ] *nf* remission; **sans ~** [punir, juger] without mercy; [pleuvoir] unremittingly.

remmener [rãmne] [19] *vt* to take OU bring back.

remodeler [rəmɔdle] [25] *vt* **-1.** [forme] to remodel. **-2.** [remanier] to restructure.

rémois, -e [remwa, az] *adj* of/from Rheims.

◆ **Rémois, -e** *nm, f* native OU inhabitant of Rheims.

remontant, -e [rəmõtã, ãt] *adj* [tonique] invigorating.

◆ **remontant** *nm* tonic.

remontée [rəmõte] *nf* **-1.** [des eaux] rising. **-2.** [de pente, rivière] ascent. **-3.** SPORT recovery. **-4.** SKI: **~s mécaniques** ski-lifts. **-5.** [des mineurs] bringing to the surface.

remonte-pente [rəmõtpãt] (*pl* **remonte-pentes**) *nm* ski-tow.

remonter [rəmõte] [3] ◇ *vt* (*aux: avoir*) **-1.** [escalier, pente] to go/come back up. **-2.** [assembler] to put together again. **-3.** [manches] to turn up. **-4.** [horloge, montre] to wind up. **-5.** [ragaillardir] to put new life into, to cheer up.

◇ *vi* (*aux: être*) **-1.** [monter à nouveau - personne] to go/come back up; [- baromètre] to rise again; [- prix, température] to go up again, to rise; [- sur vélo] to get back on; ~ **dans une voiture** to get back into a car. **-2.** [dater]: ~ **à** to date OU go back to.

remontoir [rəmɔ̃twar] *nm* winder.

remontrance [rəmɔ̃trɑ̃s] *nf* (*gén pl*) remonstrance, reprimand.

remontrer [rəmɔ̃tre] [3] *vt* to show again; **vouloir en ~ à qqn** to try to show sb up.

remords [rəmɔr] *nm* remorse; **être bourrelé de ~** *fam* to be conscience-stricken.

remorque [rəmɔrk] *nf* trailer; **être en ~ to** be on tow; **être à la ~** *fig* to drag behind.

remorquer [rəmɔrke] [3] *vt* **-1.** [voiture, bateau] to tow. **-2.** *fam* [personne] to drag along.

remorqueur [rəmɔrkœr] *nm* tug, tugboat.

rémoulade [remulad] *nf* remoulade (sauce).

rémouleur [remulœr] *nm* knife grinder.

remous [rəmu] ◇ *nm* [de bateau] wash, backwash; [de rivière] eddy. ◇ *nmpl fig* stir, upheaval.

rempailler [rɑ̃paje] [3] *vt* to re-cane.

rempart [rɑ̃par] *nm* (*gén pl*) rampart.

rempiler [rɑ̃pile] [3] ◇ *vt* to pile up again. ◇ *vi fam* MIL to sign on again.

remplaçable [rɑ̃plasabl] *adj* replaceable.

remplaçant, -e [rɑ̃plasɑ̃, ɑ̃t] *nm, f* [suppléant] stand-in; SPORT substitute.

remplacement [rɑ̃plasmɑ̃] *nm* **-1.** [changement] replacing, replacement. **-2.** [intérim] substitution; **faire des ~s** to stand in; [docteur] to act as a locum.

remplacer [rɑ̃plase] [16] *vt* **-1.** [gén] to replace. **-2.** [prendre la place de] to stand in for; SPORT to substitute.

remplir [rɑ̃plir] [32] *vt* **-1.** [gén] to fill; ~ **de** to fill with; ~ **qqn de joie/d'orgueil** to fill sb with happiness/pride. **-2.** [questionnaire] to fill in OU out. **-3.** [mission, fonction] to complete, to fulfil.

◆ **se remplir** *vp* to fill up.

remplissage [rɑ̃plisaʒ] *nm* **-1.** [de récipient] filling up. **-2.** *fig & péj* [de texte] padding out.

remploi [rɑ̃plwa], **réemploi** [reɑ̃plwa] *nm* re-use.

remployer [rɑ̃plwaje], **réemployer** [reɑ̃plwaje] [13] *vt* to re-use.

remplumer [rɑ̃plyme] [3]

◆ **se remplumer** *vp fam* **-1.** [financièrement] to get o.s. back in funds. **-2.** [se rétablir] to fill out again.

remporter [rɑ̃pɔrte] [3] *vt* **-1.** [repartir avec] to take away again. **-2.** [gagner] to win.

rempoter [rɑ̃pɔte] [3] *vt* to repot.

remuant, -e [rəmɥɑ̃, ɑ̃t] *adj* restless, over-active.

remue-ménage [rəmymenaʒ] *nm inv* commotion, confusion.

remuer [rəmɥe] [7] ◇ *vt* **-1.** [bouger, émouvoir] to move. **-2.** [café, thé] to stir; [salade] to toss. ◇ *vi* to move, to stir; **arrête de ~ comme ça** stop being so restless.

◆ **se remuer** *vp* **-1.** [se mouvoir] to move. **-2.** *fig* [réagir] to make an effort.

rémunérateur, -trice [remyneratœr, tris] *adj* profitable, lucrative.

rémunération [remynerasjɔ̃] *nf* remuneration.

rémunérer [remynere] [18] *vt* **-1.** [personne] to remunerate, to pay. **-2.** [activité] to pay for.

renâcler [rənakle] [3] *vi fam* to make a fuss; ~ **devant** OU **à qqch** to balk at sthg.

renaissance [rənɛsɑ̃s] *nf* rebirth.

◆ **Renaissance** *nf*: **la Renaissance** the Renaissance.

renaître [rənɛtr] [92] *vi* **-1.** [ressusciter] to come back to life, to come to life again; **se sentir ~** to feel like a new person; **faire ~** [passé, tradition] to revive; ~ **à la vie** to take on a new lease of life. **-2.** [revenir - sentiment, printemps] to return; [- économie] to revive, to recover.

rénal, -e, -aux [renal, o] *adj* renal, kidney (*avant n*).

renard [rənar] *nm* fox.

renardeau, -x [rənardo] *nm* fox cub.

rencard = **rancard**.

rencart = **rancart**.

renchérir [rɑ̃ʃerir] [32] *vi* **-1.** [augmenter] to become more expensive; [prix] to go up. **-2.** [surenchérir] ~ **sur** to add to.

renchérissement [rɑ̃ʃerismɑ̃] *nm* increase in price; ~ **des prix** price increase.

rencontre [rɑ̃kɔ̃tr] *nf* **-1.** [gén] meeting; **faire une bonne ~** to meet somebody interesting; **faire une mauvaise ~** to meet an unpleasant person; **aller/venir à la ~ de qqn** to go/come to meet sb. **-2.** [choc, collision] collision.

rencontrer [rɑ̃kɔ̃tre] [3] *vt* **-1.** [gén] to meet. **-2.** [heurter] to strike.

◆ **se rencontrer** *vp* **-1.** [gén] to meet. **-2.** [opinions] to agree.

rendement [rɑ̃dmɑ̃] *nm* [de machine, travailleur] output; [de terre, placement] yield.

rendez-vous [rɑ̃devu] *nm inv* **-1.** [rencontre] appointment; [amoureux] date; **on a tous ~ au café** we're all meeting at the café; **lors de notre dernier ~** at our last meeting;

prendre ~ **avec qqn** to make an appointment with sb; **donner** ~ **à qqn** to arrange to meet sb. **-2.** [lieu] meeting place.

rendormir [rɑ̃dɔrmir] [36] *vt* to put back to sleep.

◆ **se rendormir** *vp* to go back to sleep.

rendre [rɑ̃dr] [73] ◇ *vt* **-1.** [restituer]: ~ **qqch à qqn** to give sthg back to sb, to return sthg to sb. **-2.** [donner en retour - invitation, coup] to return. **-3.** [JUR - jugement] to pronounce. **-4.** [produire - effet] to produce. **-5.** [vomir] to vomit, to cough up. **-6.** MIL [céder] to surrender; ~ **les armes** to lay down one's arms. **-7.** (+ *adj*) [faire devenir] to make; ~ **qqn fou** to drive sb mad. **-8.** [exprimer] to render.
◇ *vi* **-1.** [produire - champ] to yield. **-2.** [vomir] to vomit, to be sick.

◆ **se rendre** *vp* **-1.** [céder, capituler] to give in; **j'ai dû me** ~ **à l'évidence** I had to face facts. **-2.** [aller]: **se** ~ **à** to go to. **-3.** (+ *adj*) [se faire tel]: **se** ~ **utile/malade** to make o.s. useful/ill.

rêne [rɛn] *nf* rein.

renégat, -e [renega, at] *nm, f sout* renegade.

renégocier [renegɔsje] [9] *vt* to renegotiate.

reneiger [reneʒe] [23] *vi* to snow again.

renfermé, -e [rɑ̃fɛrme] *adj* introverted, withdrawn.

◆ **renfermé** *nm*: **ça sent le** ~ it smells stuffy in here.

renfermer [rɑ̃fɛrme] [3] *vt* [contenir] to contain.

◆ **se renfermer** *vp* to withdraw.

renfiler [rɑ̃file] [3] *vt* **-1.** [perles] to restring. **-2.** [aiguille] to rethread. **-3.** [vêtement] to slip on again.

renflé, -e [rɑ̃fle] *adj* bulging.

renflement [rɑ̃fləmɑ̃] *nm* bulge.

renflouer [rɑ̃flue] [3] *vt* **-1.** [bateau] to refloat. **-2.** *fig* [entreprise, personne] to bail out.
◆ **se renflouer** *vp fam fig* to get back on one's feet (financially).

renfoncement [rɑ̃fɔ̃smɑ̃] *nm* recess.

renfoncer [rɑ̃fɔ̃se] [16] *vt* to push (further) down.

renforcer [rɑ̃fɔrse] [16] *vt* to reinforce, to strengthen; **cela me renforce dans mon opinion** that confirms my opinion.

renfort [rɑ̃fɔr] *nm* reinforcement; **envoyer des** ~**s** to send reinforcements; **venir en** ~ to come as reinforcements; **à grand** ~ **de** *fig* with the help of a lot of.

renfrogné, -e [rɑ̃frɔɲe] *adj* scowling.

renfrogner [rɑ̃frɔɲe] [3]

◆ **se renfrogner** *vp* to scowl, to pull a face.

rengager [rɑ̃gaʒe], **réengager** [reɑ̃gaʒe] [17] ◇ *vt* [personnel] to take on again. ◇ *vi* MIL to re-enlist, to join up again.

◆ **se rengager** *vp* MIL to re-enlist, to join up again.

rengaine [rɑ̃gɛn] *nf* **-1.** [formule répétée] (old) story. **-2.** [chanson] (old) song.

rengainer [rɑ̃gene] [4] *vt* **-1.** [épée] to sheathe; [pistolet] to put back in its holster. **-2.** *fam fig* [compliment] to withold.

rengorger [rɑ̃gɔrʒe] [17]
◆ **se rengorger** *vp fig* to puff o.s. up.

reniement [rənimɑ̃] *nm* renunciation.

renier [rənje] [9] *vt* **-1.** [famille, ami] to disown. **-2.** [foi, opinion] to renounce, to repudiate. **-3.** [signature] to refuse to acknowledge.

renifler [rənifle] [3] ◇ *vi* to sniff. ◇ *vt* to sniff; ~ **quelque chose de louche** to smell a rat.

renne [rɛn] *nm* reindeer (*inv*).

renom [rənɔ̃] *nm* renown, fame; **de grand** ~ of great renown, famous.

renommé, -e [rənɔme] *adj* renowned, famous.

◆ **renommée** *nf* renown, fame; **de** ~ **internationale** world-famous, internationally renowned.

renoncement [rənɔ̃smɑ̃] *nm*: ~ **(à)** renunciation (of).

renoncer [rənɔ̃se] [16] *vi*: ~ **à** to give up; ~ **à comprendre qqch** to give up trying to understand sthg; ~ **à voir qqn** to give up OU abandon the idea of seeing sb.

renoncule [rənɔ̃kyl] *nf* buttercup.

renouer [rənwe] [6] ◇ *vt* **-1.** [lacet, corde] to re-tie, to tie up again. **-2.** [contact, conversation] to resume. ◇ *vi*: ~ **avec qqn** to take up with sb again; ~ **avec sa famille** to make it up with one's family again.

renouveau, -x [rənuvo] *nm* **-1.** [transformation] revival. **-2.** [regain]: **un** ~ **de succès** renewed success.

renouvelable [rənuvlabl] *adj* renewable; [expérience] repeatable.

renouveler [rənuvle] [24] *vt* **-1.** [gén] to renew. **-2.** [rajeunir] to revive.

◆ **se renouveler** *vp* **-1.** [être remplacé] to be renewed. **-2.** [changer, innover] to have new ideas. **-3.** [se répéter] to be repeated, to recur.

renouvelle, renouvelles *etc* → **renouveler**.

renouvellement [rənuvɛlmɑ̃] *nm* renewal.

rénovation [renɔvasjɔ̃] *nf* renovation.

rénover [renɔve] [3] *vt* **-1.** [immeuble] to renovate, to restore. **-2.** [système, méthodes] to reform.

renseignement [rɑ̃sɛɲəmɑ̃] *nm* information (*U*); **un** ~ a piece of information; **prendre des** ~**s (sur)** to make enquiries (about).
◆ **renseignements** *nmpl* **-1.** [service d'information] enquiries, information; **appeler les** ~**s** TÉLÉC to call directory enquiries. **-2.** [sécurité] intelligence (*U*); **les** ~**s généraux** *police department responsible for political security.*

renseigner [rɑ̃seɲe] [4] *vt*: ~ **qqn (sur)** to give sb information (about), to inform sb (about).
◆ **se renseigner** *vp* **-1.** [s'enquérir] to make enquiries, to ask for information. **-2.** [s'informer] to find out.

rentabiliser [rɑ̃tabilize] [3] *vt* to make profitable.

rentabilité [rɑ̃tabilite] *nf* profitability; **seuil de** ~ break-even point.

rentable [rɑ̃tabl] *adj* **-1.** COMM profitable. **-2.** *fam* [qui en vaut la peine] worthwhile.

rente [rɑ̃t] *nf* **-1.** [d'un capital] revenue, income; **vivre de ses** ~**s** to have a private income. **-2.** [pension] pension, annuity; ~ **viagère** life annuity. **-3.** [emprunt d'État] government bond.

rentier, -ière [rɑ̃tje, jɛr] *nm, f* person of independent means; **mener une vie de** ~ *fig* to lead a life of leisure.

rentrée [rɑ̃tre] *nf* **-1.** [fait de rentrer] return. **-2.** [reprise des activités]: **la** ~ **parlementaire** the reopening of parliament; **la** ~ **des classes** the start of the new school year. **-3.** CIN & THÉÂTRE comeback; **faire sa** ~ to make one's comeback. **-4.** [recette] income; **avoir une** ~ **d'argent** to come into some money.

LA RENTRÉE:
The time of the year when children go back to school has considerable cultural significance in France; coming after the long summer break or 'grandes vacances', it is the time when academic, political, social and commercial activity begin again in earnest

rentrer [rɑ̃tre] [3] ◇ *vi (aux: être)* **-1.** [entrer de nouveau] to go/come back in. **-2.** [entrer] to go/come in. **-3.** [revenir chez soi] to go/come back, to go/come home. **-4.** [recouvrer, récupérer]: ~ **dans** to recover, to get back; ~ **dans ses frais** to cover one's costs, to break even. **-5.** [se jeter avec violence]: ~

dans to crash into. **-6.** [s'emboîter] to go in, to fit; ~ **les uns dans les autres** to fit together. **-7.** [être compris]: ~ **dans** to be included in. **-8.** [être perçu - fonds] to come in.
◇ *vt (aux: avoir)* **-1.** [mettre ou remettre à l'intérieur] to bring in. **-2.** [ventre] to pull in; [griffes] to retract, to draw in; [chemise] to tuck in. **-3.** *fig* [rage, larmes] to hold back.

renversant, -e [rɑ̃vɛrsɑ̃, ɑ̃t] *adj* staggering, astounding.

renverse [rɑ̃vɛrs] *nf*: **tomber à la** ~ to fall over backwards.

renversé, -e [rɑ̃vɛrse] *adj* **-1.** [à l'envers] upside down. **-2.** [qu'on a fait tomber] overturned. **-3.** [incliné en arrière] tilted back. **-4.** [stupéfait] staggered.

renversement [rɑ̃vɛrsəmɑ̃] *nm* **-1.** [inversion] turning upside down. **-2.** [de situation] reversal. **-3.** [de régime] overthrow. **-4.** [de tête, buste] tilting back.

renverser [rɑ̃vɛrse] [3] *vt* **-1.** [mettre à l'envers] to turn upside down. **-2.** [faire tomber] to knock over; [- piéton] to run over; [- liquide] to spill. **-3.** *fig* [obstacle] to overcome; [régime] to overthrow; [ministre] to throw out of office. **-4.** [tête, buste] to tilt back. **-5.** [étonner] to bowl over.
◆ **se renverser** *vp* **-1.** [incliner le corps en arrière] to lean back. **-2.** [tomber] to overturn.

renvoi [rɑ̃vwa] *nm* **-1.** [licenciement] dismissal; **notifier à qqn son** ~ to give sb his/her notice. **-2.** [de colis, lettre] return, sending back. **-3.** [ajournement] postponement. **-4.** [référence] cross-reference. **-5.** JUR referral. **-6.** [éructation] belch.

renvoie, renvoies *etc* → **renvoyer**.

renvoyer [rɑ̃vwaje] [30] *vt* **-1.** [faire retourner] to send back. **-2.** [congédier] to dismiss. **-3.** [colis, lettre] to send back, to return. **-4.** [balle] to throw back. **-5.** [réfléchir - lumière] to reflect; [- son] to echo. **-6.** [référer]: ~ **qqn à** to refer sb to. **-7.** [différer] to postpone, to put off.

réorganisation [reɔrganizasjɔ̃] *nf* reorganization.

réorganiser [reɔrganize] [3] *vt* to reorganize.

réorienter [reɔrjɑ̃te] [3] *vt* to reorient, to reorientate.

réouverture [reuvɛrtyr] *nf* reopening.

repaire [rəpɛr] *nm* den.

repaître [rəpɛtr] [91] *vt*: ~ **ses yeux (de)** to feast one's eyes (on).
◆ **se repaître** *vp*: **se** ~ **de** [se rassasier] to eat one's fill of; *fig* to revel in.

répandre [repɑ̃dr] [74] *vt* **-1.** [verser, renverser] to spill; [larmes] to shed. **-2.** [diffuser, dégager] to give off. **-3.** *fig* [bienfaits] to pour out; [effroi, terreur, nouvelle] to spread.

◆ **se répandre** *vp* **-1.** [gén] to spread. **-2.** [liquide] to spill. **-3.** [personne]: **se ~ en injures** to let out a stream of insults; **se ~ en remerciements** to give one's heartfelt thanks.

répandu, -e [repɑ̃dy] ◇ *pp* → **répandre.** ◇ *adj* [opinion, maladie] widespread.

réparable [reparabl] *adj* **-1.** [objet] repairable. **-2.** [erreur] that can be put right.

reparaître [rəparɛtr] [91] *vi* to reappear.

réparateur, -trice [reparatœr, tris] ◇ *adj* [sommeil] refreshing. ◇ *nm, f* repairer.

réparation [reparasjɔ̃] *nf* **-1.** [d'objet - action] repairing; [- résultat] repair; **en ~** under repair. **-2.** [de faute]: **~ (de)** atonement (for). **-3.** [indemnité] reparation, compensation.

réparer [repare] [3] *vt* **-1.** [objet] to repair. **-2.** [faute, oubli] to make up for; **~ ses torts** to make amends.

reparler [rəparle] [3] *vi*: **~ de qqn/qqch** to talk about sb/sthg again; **~ à qqn** to speak to sb again.

◆ **se reparler** *vp* to speak to each other again.

repartie [rəparti] *nf* retort; **avoir de la ~** to be good at repartee.

repartir [rəpartir] [43] *vi* **-1.** [retourner] to go back, to return. **-2.** [partir de nouveau] to set off again. **-3.** [recommencer] to start again.

répartir [repartir] [32] *vt* **-1.** [partager] to share out, to divide up. **-2.** [dans l'espace] to spread out, to distribute. **-3.** [échelonner] to spread out. **-4.** [classer] to divide OU split up.

◆ **se répartir** *vp* to divide up.

répartition [repartisjɔ̃] *nf* **-1.** [partage] sharing out; [de tâches] allocation. **-2.** [dans l'espace] distribution.

reparu [rəpary] *pp* → **reparaître.**

repas [rəpa] *nm* meal; **prendre son ~** to eat; **~ d'affaires** business meal, working lunch/dinner.

repassage [rəpasaʒ] *nm* ironing.

repasser [rəpase] [3] ◇ *vi (aux: être)* [passer à nouveau] to go/come back; [film] to be on again. ◇ *vt (aux: avoir)* **-1.** [frontière, montagne] to cross again, to recross. **-2.** [examen] to resit. **-3.** [film] to show again. **-4.** *fam* [transmettre] to pass on. **-5.** [linge] to iron. **-6.** [leçon] to go over.

repasseuse [rəpasøz] *nf* **-1.** [ouvrière] ironer. **-2.** [machine] ironing machine.

repayer [rəpeje] [11] *vt* to pay again.

repêchage [rəpeʃaʒ] *nm* [de noyé, voiture] recovery.

repêcher [rəpeʃe] [4] *vt* **-1.** [noyé, voiture] to fish out. **-2.** *fam* [candidat] to let through.

repeindre [rəpɛ̃dr] [81] *vt* to repaint.

repeint, -e [rəpɛ̃, ɛ̃t] *pp* → **repeindre.**

repenser [rəpɑ̃se] [3] *vt* to rethink.

repentir [rəpɑ̃tir] [37] *nm* repentance.

◆ **se repentir** *vp* to repent; **se ~ de qqch/d'avoir fait qqch** to be sorry for sthg/for having done sthg.

repérable [rəperabl] *adj*: **difficilement ~** difficult to spot.

repérage [rəperaʒ] *nm* location.

répercussion [repɛrkysjɔ̃] *nf* repercussion.

répercuter [repɛrkyte] [3] *vt* **-1.** [lumière] to reflect; [son] to throw back. **-2.** [ordre, augmentation] to pass on.

◆ **se répercuter** *vp* **-1.** [lumière] to be reflected; [son] to echo. **-2.** [influer]: **se ~ sur** to have repercussions on.

repère [rəpɛr] *nm* [marque] mark; [objet concret] landmark; **point de ~** point of reference.

repérer [rəpere] [18] *vt* **-1.** [situer] to locate, to pinpoint. **-2.** *fam* [remarquer] to spot; **se faire ~** to be spotted.

◆ **se repérer** *vp fam* to find one's way around.

répertoire [repertwar] *nm* **-1.** [agenda] thumb-indexed notebook. **-2.** [inventaire] catalog *Am*, catalogue *Br*, list. **-3.** [de théâtre, d'artiste] repertoire. **-4.** INFORM directory.

répertorier [repertɔrje] [9] *vt* to make a list of.

répéter [repete] [18] ◇ *vt* **-1.** [gén] to repeat; **ne pas se le faire ~ deux fois** not to have to be told twice. **-2.** [leçon] to go over, to learn; [rôle] to rehearse. ◇ *vi* to rehearse.

◆ **se répéter** *vp* **-1.** [radoter] to repeat o.s. **-2.** [se reproduire] to be repeated; **que cela ne se répète pas!** don't let it happen again!

répétitif, -ive [repetitif, iv] *adj* repetitive.

répétition [repetisjɔ̃] *nf* **-1.** [réitération] repetition. **-2.** MUS & THÉÂTRE rehearsal.

repeupler [rəpœple] [5] *vt* **-1.** [région, ville] to repopulate. **-2.** [forêt] to replant; [étang] to restock.

repiquage [rəpikaʒ] *nm* **-1.** [plantation] planting out. **-2.** [enregistrement] re-recording.

repiquer [rəpike] [3] ◇ *vt* **-1.** [replanter] to plant out. **-2.** [disque, cassette] to tape. ◇ *vi fam*: **~ à qqch** to take sthg up again; **~ au plat** to have a second helping.

répit [repi] *nm* respite; **sans ~** without respite.

replacer [rəplase] [16] *vt* **-1.** [remettre] to replace, to put back. **-2.** [situer] to place, to put.

◆ **se replacer** *vp* to find new employment.

replanter [rəplɑ̃te] [3] *vt* to replant.

replat [rəpla] *nm* ledge.

replâtrer [rəplatre] [3] *vt* **-1.** [mur, fissure] to replaster. **-2.** *fam fig* to patch up.

replet, -ète [rəplɛ, ɛt] *adj* chubby.

repli [rəpli] *nm* **-1.** [de tissu] fold; [de rivière] bend. **-2.** [de troupes] withdrawal.

replier [rəplije] [10] *vt* **-1.** [plier de nouveau] to fold up again. **-2.** [ramener en pliant] to fold back. **-3.** [armée] to withdraw.

◆ **se replier** *vp* **-1.** [armée] to withdraw. **-2.** [personne]: **se ~ sur soi-même** to withdraw into o.s. **-3.** [journal, carte] to fold.

réplique [replik] *nf* **-1.** [riposte] reply; **sans ~** [argument] irrefutable. **-2.** [d'acteur] line; **donner la ~ à qqn** to play opposite sb. **-3.** [copie] replica; [sosie] double.

répliquer [replike] [3] ◇ *vt:* **~ à qqn que** to reply to sb that. ◇ *vi* **-1.** [répondre] to reply; [avec impertinence] to answer back. **-2.** *fig* [riposter] to retaliate.

replonger [rəplɔ̃ʒe] [17] ◇ *vt* to plunge back. ◇ *vi* to dive back.

◆ **se replonger** *vp:* **se ~ dans qqch** to immerse o.s. in sthg again.

répondant, -e [repɔ̃dɑ̃, ɑ̃t] *nm, f* guarantor.

◆ **répondant** *nm fam:* **avoir du ~** to have money behind one.

répondeur [repɔ̃dœr] *nm:* **~ (téléphonique** OU **automatique** OU **-enregistreur)** answering machine.

répondre [repɔ̃dr] [75] ◇ *vi:* **~ à qqn** [faire connaître sa pensée] to answer sb, to reply to sb; [riposter] to answer sb back; **~ à qqch** [faire une réponse] to reply to sthg, to answer sthg; [en se défendant] to respond to sthg; **~ au téléphone** to answer the telephone. ◇ *vt* to answer, to reply; **~ que** to reply that, to answer that.

◆ **répondre à** *vt* **-1.** [correspondre à - besoin] to answer; [- conditions] to meet. **-2.** [ressembler à - description] to match.

◆ **répondre de** *vt* to answer for.

répondu, -e [repɔ̃dy] *pp* → **répondre.**

réponse [repɔ̃s] *nf* **-1.** [action de répondre] answer, reply; **en ~ à votre lettre ...** in reply OU in answer OU in response to your letter .... **-2.** [solution] answer. **-3.** [réaction] response.

report [rəpɔr] *nm* **-1.** [de réunion, rendez-vous] postponement. **-2.** COMM [d'écritures] carrying forward. **-3.** POLIT [de voix] transfer.

reportage [rəpɔrtaʒ] *nm* **-1.** [article, enquête] report. **-2.** [métier] reporting.

reporter¹ [rəpɔrtɛr] *nm* reporter.

reporter² [rəpɔrte] [3] *vt* **-1.** [rapporter] to take back. **-2.** [différer]: **~ qqch à** to postpone sthg till, to put sthg off till. **-3.** [somme]: **~ (sur)** to carry forward (to). **-4.** [transférer]: **~ sur** to transfer to.

◆ **se reporter** *vp:* **se ~ à** [se référer à] to refer to; [se transporter en pensée à] to cast one's mind back to.

repos [rəpo] *nm* **-1.** [gén] rest; **prendre un jour de ~** to take a day off. **-2.** [tranquillité] peace and quiet; **ce n'est pas de tout ~** it's not exactly restful. **-3.** MIL: **~!** at ease!

reposant, -e [rəpozɑ̃, ɑ̃t] *adj* restful.

reposé, -e [rəpoze] *adj* rested; **à tête ~e** with a clear head.

reposer [rəpoze] [3] ◇ *vt* **-1.** [poser à nouveau] to put down again, to put back down. **-2.** [remettre] to put back. **-3.** [poser de nouveau - question] to ask again. **-4.** [appuyer] to rest. **-5.** [délasser] to rest, to relax. ◇ *vi* **-1.** [pâte] to sit, to stand; [vin] to stand. **-2.** [mort]: **ici repose ...** here lies .... **-3.** [théorie]: **~ sur** to rest on.

◆ **se reposer** *vp* **-1.** [se délasser] to rest. **-2.** [faire confiance]: **se ~ sur qqn** to rely on sb.

repositionner [rəpozisjɔne] [3] *vt* to reposition.

◆ **se repositionner** *vp* to reposition o.s.

repoussant, -e [rəpusɑ̃, ɑ̃t] *adj* repulsive.

repousser [rəpuse] [3] ◇ *vi* to grow again, to grow back. ◇ *vt* **-1.** [écarter] to push away, to push back; [l'ennemi] to repel, to drive back. **-2.** [éconduire] to reject. **-3.** [proposition] to reject, to turn down. **-4.** [différer] to put back, to postpone.

◆ **se repousser** *vp* [aimants] to repel one another.

repoussoir [rəpuswar] *nm:* **servir de ~ à qqn** to be a foil to sb.

répréhensible [repreɑ̃sibl] *adj* reprehensible.

reprenais, reprenions *etc* → **reprendre.**

reprendre [rəprɑ̃dr] [79] ◇ *vt* **-1.** [prendre de nouveau] to take again; **je passe te ~ dans une heure** I'll come by and pick you up again in an hour; **~ la route** to take to the road again; **~ haleine** to get one's breath back. **-2.** [récupérer - objet prêté] to take back; [- prisonnier, ville] to recapture. **-3.** COMM [entreprise, affaire] to take over; **ni re-**

pris ni échangé goods may not be returned or exchanged. **-4.** [se resservir]: ~ **un gâteau/de la viande** to take another cake/some more meat. **-5.** [recommencer] to resume; «**et ainsi**» **reprit-il** ... "and so", he continued .... **-6.** [retoucher] to repair; [jupe] to alter. **-7.** [corriger] to correct.
◇ *vi* **-1.** [affaires, plante] to pick up. **-2.** [recommencer] to start again.
◆ **se reprendre** *vp* **-1.** [rectifier ce qu'on a dit] to correct o.s. **-2.** [recommencer]: **se** ~ **à espérer** to find new hope; **s'y** ~ **à plusieurs fois** to make several attempts. **-3.** [se ressaisir] to pull o.s. together.

repreneur [rəprənœr] *nm person who takes over a company with the aim of revitalizing it.*

représailles [rəprezaj] *nfpl* reprisals; **par** ~ as a reprisal, in reprisal.

représentant, **-e** [rəprezɑ̃tɑ̃, ɑ̃t] *nm, f* representative.

représentatif, **-ive** [rəprezɑ̃tatif, iv] *adj* representative.

représentation [rəprezɑ̃tasjɔ̃] *nf* **-1.** [gén] representation. **-2.** [spectacle] performance. **-3.** [métier] commercial traveling *Am* OU travelling *Br*.

représentativité [rəprezɑ̃tativite] *nf* representativeness.

représenter [rəprezɑ̃te] [3] *vt* to represent.
◆ **se représenter** *vp* **-1.** [s'imaginer]: **se** ~ **qqch** to visualize sthg. **-2.** [se présenter à nouveau]: **se** ~ **à** [élections] to stand again at; [examen] to resit, to represent.

répressif, **-ive** [represif, iv] *adj* repressive.

répression [represjɔ̃] *nf* **-1.** [de révolte] repression. **-2.** [de criminalité, d'injustices] suppression.

réprimande [reprimɑ̃d] *nf* reprimand.

réprimander [reprimɑ̃de] [3] *vt* to reprimand.

réprimer [reprime] [3] *vt* **-1.** [émotion, rire] to repress, to check. **-2.** [révolte, crimes] to put down, to suppress.

repris, **-e** [rəpri, iz] *pp* → **reprendre**.
◆ **repris** *nm*: ~ **de justice** habitual criminal.

reprisage [rəprizaʒ] *nm* mending.

reprise [rəpriz] *nf* **-1.** [recommencement - des hostilités] resumption, renewal; [- des affaires] revival, recovery; [- de pièce] revival; **à plusieurs** ~**s** on several occasions, several times. **-2.** BOXE round. **-3.** [accélération] acceleration. **-4.** [raccommodage] mending. **-5.** COMM trade-in, part exchange; [somme payée à un locataire] *sum paid for fixtures and fittings left by outgoing tenant.*

repriser [rəprize] [3] *vt* to mend.

réprobateur, **-trice** [reprɔbatœr, tris] *adj* reproachful.

réprobation [reprɔbasjɔ̃] *nf* disapproval.

reproche [rəprɔʃ] *nm* reproach; **faire des** ~**s à qqn** to reproach sb; **avec** ~ reproachfully; **sans** ~ blameless.

reprocher [rəprɔʃe] [3] *vt*: ~ **qqch à qqn** to reproach sb for sthg; **je ne vous reproche rien** I don't reproach OU blame you for anything.
◆ **se reprocher** *vp*: **se** ~ **(qqch)** to blame o.s. (for sthg); **ne rien avoir à se** ~ to have nothing to reproach o.s. for.

reproducteur, **-trice** [rəprɔdyktœr, tris] *adj* reproductive.

reproduction [rəprɔdyksjɔ̃] *nf* reproduction; ~ **interdite** all rights (of reproduction) reserved.

reproduire [rəprɔdɥir] [98] *vt* to reproduce.
◆ **se reproduire** *vp* **-1.** BIOL to reproduce, to breed. **-2.** [se répéter] to recur.

reproduisais, **reproduisions** *etc* → **reproduire**.

reproduit, **-e** [rəprɔdɥi, ɥit] *pp* → **reproduire**.

reprogrammer [rəprɔgrame] [3] *vt* to reprogram.

reprographie [rəprɔgrafi] *nf* reproduction.

réprouvé, **-e** [repruve] ◇ *adj* rejected. ◇ *nm, f* outcast.

réprouver [repruve] [3] *vt* [blâmer] to reprove.

reptation [rɛptasjɔ̃] *nf* creeping.

reptile [rɛptil] *nm* reptile.

repu, **-e** [rəpy] ◇ *pp* → **repaître**. ◇ *adj* full, sated.

républicain, **-e** [repyblikɛ̃, ɛn] *adj* & *nm, f* republican.

république [repyblik] *nf* republic; **la République centrafricaine** Central African Republic; **la République populaire de Chine** the People's Republic of China.

répudiation [repydjasjɔ̃] *nf* repudiation.

répudier [repydje] [9] *vt* **-1.** [femme] to repudiate. **-2.** [principes, engagements] to renounce.

répugnance [repyɲɑ̃s] *nf* **-1.** [horreur] repugnance. **-2.** [réticence] reluctance; **avoir** OU **éprouver de la** ~ **à faire qqch** to be reluctant to do sthg; **avec** ~ reluctantly.

répugnant, **-e** [repyɲɑ̃, ɑ̃t] *adj* repugnant.

répugner [repyɲe] [3] *vi*: ~ **à qqn** to disgust sb, to fill sb with repugnance; ~ **à faire qqch** to be reluctant to do sthg, to be loath to do sthg.

répulsion [repylsjɔ̃] *nf* repulsion.

réputation [repytasjɔ̃] *nf* reputation; **avoir une ~ de** to have a reputation for; **avoir la ~ d'être généreux** to have a reputation for being generous; **connaître qqn/qqch de ~** to know sb/sthg by reputation; **avoir bonne/mauvaise ~** to have a good/bad reputation.

réputé, -e [repyte] *adj* famous, well-known; **être ~ pour** to be famous OU well-known for.

requérir [rəkerir] [39] *vt* **-1.** [nécessiter] to require, to call for. **-2.** [solliciter] to solicit. **-3.** JUR [réclamer au nom de la loi] to demand.

requête [rəkɛt] *nf* **-1.** [prière] petition; **à** OU **sur la ~ de** at the request of. **-2.** JUR appeal. **-3.** INFORM query.

requiem [rekɥijɛm] *nm inv* requiem.

requiers, requiert *etc* → **requérir.**

requin [rəkɛ̃] *nm* shark.

requinquer [rəkɛ̃ke] [3] *vt fam* to perk up, to buck up.

◆ **se requinquer** *vp fam* to perk up, to buck up.

requis, -e [rəki, iz] ◇ *pp* → **requérir.** ◇ *adj* required, requisite.

réquisition [rekizisjɔ̃] *nf* **-1.** MIL requisition. **-2.** JUR closing speech for the prosecution.

réquisitionner [rekizisjɔne] [3] *vt* to requisition.

réquisitoire [rekizitwar] *nm* JUR closing speech for the prosecution; **~ (contre)** *fig* indictment (of).

RER (*abr de* **réseau express régional**) *nm* train service linking central Paris with its suburbs and airports.

rescapé, -e [rɛskape] ◇ *adj* rescued. ◇ *nm, f* survivor.

rescousse [rɛskus]

◆ **à la rescousse** *loc adv*: **venir à la ~ de qqn** to come to sb's rescue; **appeler qqn à la ~** to call on sb for help.

réseau, -x [rezo] *nm* network; **~ ferroviaire/routier** rail/road network.

réséda [rezeda] *nm* mignonette.

réservation [rezɛrvasjɔ̃] *nf* reservation.

réserve [rezɛrv] *nf* **-1.** [gén] reserve; **en ~** in reserve; **officier de ~** MIL reserve officer. **-2.** [restriction] reservation; **faire des ~s (sur)** to have reservations (about); **sous toute ~** OU **toutes ~s** subject to confirmation; **sous ~ de** subject to; **sans ~** unreservedly; **éloges sans ~** unreserved praise. **-3.** [territoire] reserve; **~ d'Indiens** reservation; **~ faunique** *Can* wildlife reserve; **~ naturelle** nature reserve. **-4.** [local] storeroom.

réservé, -e [rezɛrve] *adj* reserved.

réserver [rezɛrve] [3] *vt* **-1.** [destiner]: **~ qqch (à qqn)** [chambre, place] to reserve OU book sthg (for sb); *fig* [surprise, désagrément] to have sthg in store (for sb). **-2.** [mettre de côté, garder]: **~ qqch (pour** OU **à)** to put sthg on one side (for), to keep sthg (for).

◆ **se réserver** *vp* **-1.** [s'accorder]: **se ~ qqch** to keep sthg for o.s.; **se ~ de faire qqch** to wait to do sthg; **se ~ le droit de faire qqch** to reserve the right to do sthg. **-2.** [se ménager] to save o.s.

réserviste [rezɛrvist] *nm* reservist.

réservoir [rezɛrvwar] *nm* **-1.** [cuve] tank. **-2.** [bassin] reservoir. **-3.** *fig* [de main-d'œuvre] reserve, pool; [d'idées] source.

résidant, -e [rezidɑ̃, ɑ̃t] *adj* resident.

résidence [rezidɑ̃s] *nf* **-1.** [habitation] residence; **~ principale** main residence OU home; **~ secondaire** second home; **~ universitaire** hall of residence. **-2.** [immeuble] luxury apartment block *Am*, block of luxury flats *Br*.

◆ **résidence surveillée** *nf*: **en ~** surveillée under house arrest.

résident, -e [rezidɑ̃, ɑ̃t] *nm, f* **-1.** [de pays]: **les ~s français en Écosse** French nationals resident in Scotland. **-2.** [habitant d'une résidence] resident.

résidentiel, -ielle [rezidɑ̃sjɛl] *adj* residential.

résider [rezide] [3] *vi* **-1.** [habiter]: **~ à/dans/en** to reside in. **-2.** [consister]: **~ dans** to lie in.

résidu [rezidy] *nm* [reste] residue; [déchet] waste.

résiduel, -elle [rezidɥɛl] *adj* residual.

résignation [rezinasjɔ̃] *nf* resignation.

résigné, -e [rezine] ◇ *adj* resigned. ◇ *nm, f* resigned person.

résigner [rezine] [3]

◆ **se résigner** *vp*: **se ~ (à)** to resign o.s. (to).

résiliation [reziljasjɔ̃] *nf* cancellation, termination.

résilier [rezilje] [9] *vt* to cancel, to terminate.

résille [rezij] *nf* **-1.** [pour cheveux] hairnet. **-2. bas ~** fishnet stockings.

résine [rezin] *nf* resin.

résiné, -e [rezine] *adj* flavoured with resin.

◆ **résiné** *nm* retsina.

résineux, -euse [rezinø, øz] *adj* resinous.

◆ **résineux** *nm* conifer.

résistance [rezistɑ̃s] *nf* **-1.** [gén, ÉLECTR & PHYS] resistance; **manquer de ~** to lack stamina; **opposer une** ~ to put up resistance; ~ **passive** passive resistance. **-2.** [de radiateur, chaudière] element.

◆ **Résistance** *nf*: **la Résistance** HIST the Résistance.

résistant, -e [rezistɑ̃, ɑ̃t] ◇ *adj* [personne] tough; [tissu] hard-wearing, tough; **être** ~ **au froid/aux infections** to be resistant to the cold/to infection. ◇ *nm, f* [gén] resistance fighter; [de la Résistance] member of the Resistance.

résister [reziste] [3] *vi* to resist; ~ **à** [attaque, désir] to resist; [tempête, fatigue] to withstand; [personne] to stand up to, to oppose.

résolu, -e [rezɔly] ◇ *pp* → **résoudre**. ◇ *adj* resolute; **être bien** ~ **à faire qqch** to be determined to do sthg.

résolument [rezɔlymɑ̃] *adv* resolutely.

résolution [rezɔlysjɔ̃] *nf* **-1.** [décision] resolution; **prendre la** ~ **de faire qqch** to make a resolution to do sthg. **-2.** [détermination] resolve, determination. **-3.** [solution] solving.

résolvais, résolvions *etc* → **résoudre**.

résonance [rezɔnɑ̃s] *nf* **-1.** ÉLECTR & PHYS resonance. **-2.** *fig* [écho] echo.

résonner [rezɔne] [3] *vi* [retentir] to resound; [renvoyer le son] to echo; ~ **de** to resound with.

résorber [rezɔrbe] [3] *vt* **-1.** [déficit] to absorb. **-2.** MÉD to resorb.

◆ **se résorber** *vp* **-1.** [déficit] to be absorbed. **-2.** MÉD to be resorbed.

résoudre [rezudr] [88] *vt* **-1.** [problème] to solve, to resolve. **-2.** [décider]: ~ **qqn à faire qqch** to get sb to make up his/her mind to do sthg. **-3.** [décomposer]: ~ **en** to break up OU resolve into.

◆ **se résoudre** *vp*: **se** ~ **à faire qqch** to make up one's mind to do sthg, to decide OU resolve to do sthg.

respect [rɛspɛ] *nm* respect; **manquer de** ~ **à qqn** to be disrespectful to sb, to show disrespect for sb; **sauf votre** ~ with all (due) respect; **avec tout le** ~ **que je vous dois** with all (due) respect, with the greatest of respect; **tenir qqn en** ~ *fig* to keep sb at bay.

◆ **respects** *nmpl* respects, regards.

respectabilité [rɛspɛktabilite] *nf* respectability.

respectable [rɛspɛktabl] *adj* respectable.

respecter [rɛspɛkte] [4] *vt* to respect; **faire** ~ **la loi** to enforce the law.

◆ **se respecter** *vp*: **un professeur qui se respecte ne ferait pas cela** no self-respecting teacher would do that.

respectif, -ive [rɛspɛktif, iv] *adj* respective.

respectivement [rɛspɛktivmɑ̃] *adv* respectively.

respectueusement [rɛspɛktɥøzmɑ̃] *adv* respectfully.

respectueux, -euse [rɛspɛktɥø, øz] *adj* respectful; **être** ~ **de** to have respect for.

respirable [rɛspirabl] *adj*: **l'air n'est plus** ~ the air is no longer breathable.

respiration [rɛspirasjɔ̃] *nf* breathing (*U*); **retenir sa** ~ to hold one's breath; ~ **artificielle** artificial respiration.

respiratoire [rɛspiratwar] *adj* respiratory.

respirer [rɛspire] [3] ◇ *vi* **-1.** [inspirer-expirer] to breathe. **-2.** *fig* [se reposer] to get one's breath; [être soulagé] to be able to breathe again. ◇ *vt* **-1.** [aspirer] to breathe in. **-2.** *fig* [exprimer] to exude.

resplendir [rɛsplɑ̃dir] [32] *vi* **-1.** [lune] to shine. **-2.** *fig* [personne]: ~ **de joie/santé** to be radiant with joy/health.

resplendissant, -e [rɛsplɑ̃disɑ̃, ɑ̃t] *adj* radiant.

responsabilisation [rɛspɔ̃sabilizasjɔ̃] *nf* making sb aware of his/her responsibilities.

responsabiliser [rɛspɔ̃sabilize] [3] *vt*: ~ **qqn** to make sb aware of his/her responsibilities.

responsabilité [rɛspɔ̃sabilite] *nf* **-1.** [morale] responsibility; **décliner toute** ~ to disclaim all responsibility; **avoir la** ~ **de** to be responsible for, to have the responsibility of. **-2.** JUR liability; ~ **civile** civil liability; ~ **collective/pénale** collective/criminal responsibility.

responsable [rɛspɔ̃sabl] ◇ *adj* **-1.** [gén]: ~ **(de)** responsible (for); [légalement] liable (for); [chargé de] in charge (of), responsible (for). **-2.** [sérieux] responsible. ◇ *nmf* **-1.** [auteur, coupable] person responsible. **-2.** [dirigeant] official. **-3.** [personne compétente] person in charge.

resquille [rɛskij] *nf*, **resquillage** [rɛskijaʒ] *nm* **-1.** [au théâtre etc] sneaking in without paying. **-2.** [dans autobus etc] fare-dodging.

resquiller [rɛskije] [3] *vi* **-1.** [au théâtre etc] to sneak in without paying. **-2.** [dans autobus etc] to dodge paying the fare.

resquilleur, -euse [rɛskijœr, øz] *nm, f* **-1.** [au théâtre etc] person who sneaks in without paying. **-2.** [dans autobus etc] fare-dodger.

ressac [rəsak] *nm* undertow.

ressaisir [rəsezir] [32]
◆ **se ressaisir** *vp* to pull o.s. together.

ressasser [rəsase] [3] *vt* **-1.** [répéter] to keep churning out. **-2.** *fig* [mécontentement] to dwell on.

ressayer = **réessayer**.

ressemblance [rəsɑ̃blɑ̃s] *nf* [gén] resemblance, likeness; [trait] resemblance.

ressemblant, -e [rəsɑ̃blɑ̃, ɑ̃t] *adj* life-like.

ressembler [rəsɑ̃ble] [3] *vi*: ~ **à** [physiquement] to resemble, to look like; [moralement] to be like, to resemble; **cela ne lui ressemble pas** that's not like him.
◆ **se ressembler** *vp* to look alike, to resemble each other; **qui se ressemble s'assemble** *proverbe* birds of a feather flock together *proverb*.

ressemeler [rəsəmle] [24] *vt* to resole.

ressentiment [rəsɑ̃timɑ̃] *nm* resentment.

ressentir [rəsɑ̃tir] [37] *vt* to feel.
◆ **se ressentir** *vp*: **se** ~ **de** [suj: travail] to show the effects of; [suj: personne, pays] to feel the effects of.

resserre [rəsɛr] *nf* storeroom.

resserrer [rəsere] [4] *vt* **-1.** [ceinture, boulon] to tighten. **-2.** *fig* [lien] to strengthen.
◆ **se resserrer** *vp* **-1.** [route] to (become) narrow. **-2.** [nœud, étreinte] to tighten. **-3.** *fig* [relations] to grow stronger.

resservir [rəsɛrvir] [38] ◇ *vt* **-1.** [plat] to serve again; *fig* [histoire] to trot out. **-2.** [personne] to give another helping to. ◇ *vi* to be used again.
◆ **se resservir** *vp*: **se** ~ **de qqch** [ustensile] to use sthg again; [plat] to take another helping of sthg.

ressort [rəsɔr] *nm* **-1.** [mécanisme] spring. **-2.** *fig* [énergie] spirit. **-3.** *fig* [force] force. **-4.** *fig* [compétence]: **être du** ~ **de qqn** to be sb's area of responsibility, to come under sb's jurisdiction.
◆ **en dernier ressort** *loc adv* in the last resort, as a last resort.

ressortir¹ [rəsɔrtir] [43] ◇ *vi* (*aux: être*) **-1.** [personne] to go out again. **-2.** *fig* [couleur]: ~ (**sur**) to stand out (against); **faire** ~ to highlight. **-3.** *fig* [résulter de]: ~ **de** to emerge from. ◇ *vt* (*aux: avoir*) to take OU get OU bring out again.

ressortir² [rəsɔrtir] [32] *vi* [relever]: ~ **à** JUR to be in the province of; *sout* [domaine] to pertain to.

ressortissant, -e [rəsɔrtisɑ̃, ɑ̃t] *nm, f* national.

ressouder [rəsude] [3] *vt* to resolder; *fig* to cement.

ressource [rəsurs] *nf* resort; **votre seule** ~ **est de ...** the only course open to you is to ...; **avoir de la** ~ to be resourceful.
◆ **ressources** *nfpl* **-1.** [financières] means; **être sans** ~**s** to be without means. **-2.** [énergétiques, de langue] resources; ~**s naturelles** natural resources. **-3.** [de personne] resourcefulness (*U*).

ressourcer [rəsurse] [16]
◆ **se ressourcer** *vp* to recharge one's batteries.

ressouvenir [rəsuvnir] [40]
◆ **se ressouvenir** *vp* *littéraire*: **se** ~ **de qqn/qqch** to remember sb/sthg.

ressurgir [rəsyrʒir] [32] *vi* to reappear.

ressusciter [resysite] [3] ◇ *vi* to rise (from the dead); *fig* to revive. ◇ *vt* to bring back to life, to raise; *fig* to revive.

restant, -e [rɛstɑ̃, ɑ̃t] *adj* remaining, left.
◆ **restant** *nm* rest, remainder.

restaurant [rɛstɔrɑ̃] *nm* restaurant; **manger au** ~ to eat out; ~ **d'entreprise** staff canteen.

restaurateur, -trice [rɛstɔratœr, tris] *nm, f* **-1.** CULIN restaurant owner. **-2.** ART restorer.

restauration [rɛstɔrasjɔ̃] *nf* **-1.** CULIN restaurant business; ~ **rapide** fast food. **-2.** ART & POLIT restoration.
◆ **Restauration** *nf*: **la Restauration** the Restoration.

restaurer [rɛstɔre] [3] *vt* to restore.
◆ **se restaurer** *vp* to have something to eat.

reste [rɛst] *nm* **-1.** [de lait, temps]: **le** ~ (**de**) the rest (of). **-2.** MATHS remainder; **ne pas être en** ~ (**avec**) not to be outdone (by).
◆ **restes** *nmpl* **-1.** [de repas] leftovers. **-2.** [de mort] remains.
◆ **au reste, du reste** *loc adv* besides.
◆ **pour le reste** *loc adv* as for the rest.

rester [rɛste] [3] ◇ *vi* **-1.** [dans lieu, état] to stay, to remain; **restez calme!** stay OU keep calm!; ~ **sur** to retain. **-2.** [se perpétuer] to endure. **-3.** [subsister] to remain, to be left; **le seul bien qui me reste** the only thing I have left. **-4.** [s'arrêter]: **en** ~ **à qqch** to stop at sthg; **en** ~ **là** to finish there. **-5.** *loc*: **y** ~ *fam* [mourir] to pop one's clogs.
◇ *v impers*: **il en reste un peu** there's still a little left; **il te reste de l'argent?** do you still have some money left?; **il reste beaucoup à faire** there is still a lot to be done; **il reste que ...**, **il n'en reste pas moins que ...** the fact remains that ...; **reste à savoir si ...** it remains to be seen whether ....

restituer [rɛstitɥe] [7] *vt* **-1.** [argent, objet volé] to return, to restore. **-2.** [archives, texte] to reconstruct. **-3.** [énergie] to release. **-4.** [son] to reproduce.

restitution [rɛstitysjɔ̃] *nf* **-1.** [d'argent, objet volé] return. **-2.** [d'archives, de texte] reconstruction. **-3.** [d'énergie] release. **-4.** [de son] reproduction.

resto [rɛsto] *nm fam* restaurant; **les ~s du cœur** *charity food distribution centres*; **~-U** UNIV refectory.

Restoroute® [rɛstorut] *nm* highway restaurant *Am*, motorway cafe *Br*.

restreignais, **restreignions** *etc* → **restreindre**.

restreindre [rɛstrɛ̃dr] [81] *vt* to restrict.
◆ **se restreindre** *vp* **-1.** [domaine, champ] to narrow. **-2.** [personne] to cut back; **se ~ dans qqch** to restrict sthg.

restreint, -e [rɛstrɛ̃, ɛ̃t] *pp* → **restreindre**.

restrictif, -ive [rɛstriktif, iv] *adj* restrictive.

restriction [rɛstriksjɔ̃] *nf* **-1.** [condition] condition; **sans ~** unconditionally. **-2.** [limitation] restriction.
◆ **restrictions** *nfpl* [alimentaires] rationing (*U*).

restructurer [rəstryktyre] [3] *vt* to restructure.

résultant, -e [rezyltɑ̃, ɑ̃t] *adj* resulting.
◆ **résultante** *nf* **-1.** SCIENCE resultant. **-2.** [conséquence] consequence, outcome.

résultat [rezylta] *nm* result; [d'action] outcome.

résulter [rezylte] [3] ◇ *vi*: **~ de** to be the result of, to result from. ◇ *v impers*: **il en résulte que** ... as a result, ...

résumé [rezyme] *nm* summary, résumé; **en ~** [pour conclure] to sum up; [en bref] in brief, summarized.

résumer [rezyme] [3] *vt* to summarize.
◆ **se résumer** *vp* **-1.** [suj: personne] to sum up. **-2.** [se réduire]: **se ~ à qqch/à faire qqch** to come down to sthg/to doing sthg.

résurgence [rezyrʒɑ̃s] *nf* resurgence.

résurrection [rezyrɛksjɔ̃] *nf* resurrection.

rétablir [retablir] [32] *vt* **-1.** [gén] to restore; [malade] to restore (to health). **-2.** [communications, contact] to re-establish. **-3.** [dans emploi]: **~ qqn (dans)** to reinstate sb (in).
◆ **se rétablir** *vp* **-1.** [silence] to return, to be restored. **-2.** [malade] to recover. **-3.** GYM to pull o.s. up.

rétablissement [retablismɑ̃] *nm* **-1.** [d'ordre] restoration. **-2.** [de communications] re-establishment. **-3.** [de malade] recovery. **-4.**

[dans emploi] reinstatement. **-5.** GYM pull-up.

retaper [rətape] [3] *vt* **-1.** [maison, canapé] to do up. **-2.** [lettre] to retype. **-3.** *fam* [personne] to set up.
◆ **se retaper** *vp fam* [personne] to get back on one's feet.

retard [rətar] *nm* **-1.** [délai] delay; **être en ~** [sur heure] to be late; [sur échéance] to be behind; **avoir du ~** to be late OU delayed; **se mettre en ~** to make o.s. late; **rattraper son ~** to make up lost time; **après bien des ~s** after much delay. **-2.** [de pays, peuple, personne] backwardness.

retardataire [rətardatɛr] ◇ *nmf* **-1.** [en retard] latecomer. **-2.** [enfant] backward OU retarded person. ◇ *adj* **-1.** [sur heure] late. **-2.** [idée, enfant] backward.

retardement [rətardəmɑ̃] *nm*: **à ~** belatedly; *voir aussi* **bombe**.

retarder [rətarde] [3] ◇ *vt* **-1.** [personne, train] to delay; [sur échéance] to put back; **~ qqn dans qqch** to delay sb in sthg. **-2.** [ajourner - rendez-vous] to put back OU off; [- départ] to put back OU off, to delay. **-3.** [montre] to put back. ◇ *vi* **-1.** [horloge] to be slow. **-2.** *fam* [ne pas être au courant] to be behind the times. **-3.** [être en décalage]: **~ sur** to be out of step OU tune with.

retendre [rətɑ̃dr] [73] *vt* to retighten.

retenir [rətənir] [40] *vt* **-1.** [physiquement - objet, personne, cri] to hold back; [- souffle] to hold; **~ qqn de faire qqch** to stop OU restrain sb from doing sthg. **-2.** [retarder] to keep, to detain; **~ qqn à dîner** to have sb stay for dinner. **-3.** [montant, impôt] to keep back, to withhold. **-4.** [chambre] to reserve. **-5.** [leçon, cours] to remember. **-6.** [projet] to accept, to adopt. **-7.** [eau, chaleur] to retain. **-8.** MATHS to carry. **-9.** [intérêt, attention] to hold.
◆ **se retenir** *vp* **-1.** [s'accrocher]: **se ~ à** to hold onto. **-2.** [se contenir] to hold on; **se ~ de faire qqch** to refrain from doing sthg.

rétention [retɑ̃sjɔ̃] *nf* MÉD retention.

retentir [rətɑ̃tir] [32] *vi* **-1.** [son] to ring (out). **-2.** [pièce, rue]: **~ de** to resound with. **-3.** *fig* [fatigue, blessure]: **~ sur** to have an effect on.

retentissant, -e [rətɑ̃tisɑ̃, ɑ̃t] *adj* resounding.

retentissement [rətɑ̃tismɑ̃] *nm* **-1.** [de mesure] repercussions (*pl*). **-2.** [de spectacle] effect.

retenu, -e [rətny] *pp* → **retenir**.

retenue [rətəny] *nf* **-1.** [prélèvement] deduction; **~ à la source** deduction at source. **-2.**

MATHS amount carried. **-3.** SCOL detention. **-4.** *fig* [de personne - dans relations] reticence; [- dans comportement] restraint; **sans ~** without restraint.

réticence [retisɑ̃s] *nf* [hésitation] hesitation, reluctance; **avec ~** hesitantly; **sans ~** without hesitation.

réticent, -e [retisɑ̃, ɑ̃t] *adj* hesitant, reluctant.

retiendrai, retiendras *etc* → retenir.

retienne, retiennes *etc* → retenir.

rétif, -ive [retif, iv] *adj* restive.

rétine [retin] *nf* retina.

retiré, -e [rətire] *adj* **-1.** [lieu] remote, isolated; [vie] quiet. **-2.** [personne] retired.

retirer [rətire] [3] *vt* **-1.** [vêtement, emballage] to take off, to remove; [permis, jouet] to take away; **~ qqch à qqn** to take sthg away from sb. **-2.** [plainte] to withdraw, to take back. **-3.** [enfant - personne] to remove, to extricate; [- casserole] to remove. **-4.** [métal] to extract. **-5.** [avantages, bénéfices]: **~ qqch de qqch** to get OU derive sthg from sthg. **-6.** [bagages, billet] to collect; [argent] to withdraw.
◆ **se retirer** *vp* **-1.** [s'isoler] to withdraw, to retreat. **-2.** [des affaires]: **se ~ (de)** to retire (from). **-3.** [refluer] to recede.

retombées [rətɔ̃be] *nfpl* repercussions, fallout (*sg*); **~s radioactives** radioactive fallout.

retomber [rətɔ̃be] [3] *vi* **-1.** [gymnaste, chat] to land. **-2.** [redevenir]: **~ malade** to relapse. **-3.** [pluie] to fall again. **-4.** *fig* [colère] to die away. **-5.** [cheveux] to hang down. **-6.** *fig* [responsabilité]: **~ sur** to fall on.

retordre [rətɔrdr] [76] *vt* [linge] to wring (out) again.

rétorquer [retɔrke] [3] *vt* to retort; **~ à qqn que ...** to retort to sb that ....

retors, -e [rətɔr, ɔrs] *adj* wily.

rétorsion [retɔrsjɔ̃] *nf* retaliation; **mesures de ~** reprisals.

retouche [rətuʃ] *nf* **-1.** [de texte, vêtement] alteration. **-2.** ART & PHOT touching up.

retoucher [rətuʃe] [3] *vt* **-1.** [texte, vêtement] to alter. **-2.** ART & PHOT to touch up.

retour [rətur] *nm* **-1.** [gén] return; **à mon/ton ~** when I/you get back, on my/your return; **au ~ de** [étant arrivé] on my/his *etc* return from; [en cours de route] on the way back; **être de ~ (de)** to be back (from); «**~ à l'expéditeur** OU **l'envoyeur**» "return to sender"; **~ en arrière** flashback; **~ de chariot** carriage return; **~ de flamme** backfire; **~ de manivelle** OU **de bâton** *fam fig* kickback; **en ~** in return; **sans ~** for ever;

(être) sur le ~ *fig* (to be) over the hill. **-2.** [trajet] journey back, return journey.

retournement [rəturnəmɑ̃] *nm* turnaround, turnabout; **~ de situation** reversal.

retourner [rəturne] [3] ◇ *vt (aux: avoir)* **-1.** [carte, matelas] to turn over; [terre] to turn (over). **-2.** [pull, poche] to turn inside out. **-3.** [compliment, objet prêté]: **~ qqch (à qqn)** to return sthg (to sb). **-4.** [lettre, colis] to send back, to return. **-5.** *fam fig* [personne] to shake up; **en être tout retourné** to be shaken up. ◇ *vi (aux: être)* to come/go back; **~ à** [personne] to go back OU return to; [objet] to be returned to; **~ en arrière** OU **sur ses pas** to retrace one's steps.
◆ **se retourner** *vp* **-1.** [basculer] to turn over. **-2.** [pivoter] to turn round. **-3.** *fam fig* [s'adapter] to sort o.s. out. **-4.** [rentrer]: **s'en ~** to go back (home). **-5.** *fig* [s'opposer]: **se ~ contre** to turn against.

retracer [rətrase] [16] *vt* **-1.** [ligne] to redraw. **-2.** [événement] to relate.

rétracter [retrakte] [3] *vt* to retract.
◆ **se rétracter** *vp* **-1.** [se contracter] to retract. **-2.** [se dédire] to back down.

retraduire [rətradɥir] [98] *vt* to translate again.

retrait [rətrɛ] *nm* **-1.** [gén] withdrawal; **~ du permis** disqualification from driving. **-2.** [de bagages] collection. **-3.** [des eaux] ebbing.
◆ **en retrait** *loc adj & loc adv* **-1.** [maison] set back from the road; **rester en ~** *fig* to hang back. **-2.** [texte] indented.

retraite [rətrɛt] *nf* **-1.** [gén] retreat; **battre en ~** to beat a retreat. **-2.** [cessation d'activité] retirement; **être à la ~** to be retired; **prendre sa ~** to retire; **~ anticipée** early retirement. **-3.** [revenu] (retirement) pension.

retraité, -e [rətrete] ◇ *adj* **-1.** [personne] retired. **-2.** TECHNOL reprocessed. ◇ *nm, f* retired person, pensioner.

retranchement [rətrɑ̃ʃmɑ̃] *nm* entrenchment; **poursuivre** OU **forcer qqn dans ses derniers ~s** *fig* to drive sb into a corner.

retrancher [rətrɑ̃ʃe] [3] *vt* **-1.** [passage]: **~ qqch (de)** to cut sthg out (from), to remove sthg (from). **-2.** [montant]: **~ qqch (de)** to take sthg away (from), to deduct sthg (from).
◆ **se retrancher** *vp* to entrench o.s.; **se ~ derrière/dans** *fig* to take refuge behind/in.

retransmettre [rətrɑ̃smɛtr] [84] *vt* to broadcast.

retransmis, -e [rətrɑ̃smi, iz] *pp* → retransmettre.

retransmission [rətrɑ̃smisjɔ̃] *nf* broadcast.

retravailler [rətravaje] [3] ◇ *vt*: ~ **qqch** to work on sthg again. ◇ *vi* to start work again.

rétrécir [retresir] [32] ◇ *vt* [tissu] to take in. ◇ *vi* [tissu] to shrink.

◆ **se rétrécir** *vp* [tissu] to shrink.

rétrécissement [retresismɑ̃] *nm* **-1.** [de vêtement] shrinkage. **-2.** MÉD stricture.

retremper [rətrɑ̃pe] [3] *vt* **-1.** [linge] to re-soak. **-2.** [acier] to requench.

◆ **se retremper** *vp* to go back into the water; *fig* to reimmerse o.s.

rétribuer [retribɥe] [7] *vt* **-1.** [employé] to pay. **-2.** [travail] to pay for.

rétribution [retribysjɔ̃] *nf* remuneration.

rétro [retro] ◇ *nm* **-1.** [style] old style OU fashion. **-2.** *fam* [rétroviseur] rear-view mirror. ◇ *adj inv* old-style.

rétroactif, -ive [retrɔaktif, iv] *adj* retrospective.

rétroactivement [retrɔaktivmɑ̃] *adv* retrospectively.

rétrocéder [retrɔsede] [18] *vt* to retrocede.

rétrocession [retrɔsesjɔ̃] *nf* retrocession.

rétrograde [retrɔgrad] *adj péj* reactionary.

rétrograder [retrɔgrade] [3] ◇ *vt* to demote. ◇ *vi* **-1.** AUTOM to change down. **-2.** [dans hiérarchie] to move down.

rétroprojecteur [retrɔprɔʒektœr] *nm* overhead projector.

rétrospectif, -ive [retrɔspektif, iv] *adj* retrospective.

◆ **rétrospective** *nf* retrospective.

rétrospectivement [retrɔspektivmɑ̃] *adv* retrospectively.

retroussé, -e [rətruse] *adj* **-1.** [manches, pantalon] rolled up. **-2.** [nez] turned up.

retrousser [rətruse] [3] *vt* **-1.** [manches, pantalon] to roll up. **-2.** [lèvres] to curl.

retrouvailles [rətruvaj] *nfpl* reunion (*sg*).

retrouver [rətruve] [3] *vt* **-1.** [gén] to find; [appétit] to recover, to regain. **-2.** [reconnaître] to recognize. **-3.** [ami] to meet, to see.

◆ **se retrouver** *vp* **-1.** [entre amis] to meet (up) again; **on se retrouve au café?** shall we meet up OU see each other at the café? **-2.** [être de nouveau] to find o.s. again. **-3.** [s'orienter] to find one's way; **ne pas s'y** ~ [dans papiers] to be completely lost. **-4.** [erreur, style] to be found, to crop up. **-5.** [financièrement]: **s'y** ~ *fam* to break even.

rétroviseur [retrɔvizœr] *nm* rear-view mirror.

réunification [reynifikasjɔ̃] *nf* reunification.

réunifier [reynifje] [9] *vt* to reunify.

réunion [reynjɔ̃] *nf* **-1.** [séance] meeting. **-2.** [jonction] union, merging. **-3.** [d'amis, de famille] reunion. **-4.** [collection] collection.

Réunion [reynjɔ̃] *nf*: **(l'île de) la** ~ Réunion; **à la** ~ in Réunion.

réunionnais, -e [reynjɔne, ɛz] *adj* of/from Réunion Island.

◆ **Réunionnais, -e** *nm, f* native OU inhabitant of Réunion.

réunir [reynir] [32] *vt* **-1.** [fonds] to collect. **-2.** [extrémités] to put together, to bring together. **-3.** [qualités] to combine. **-4.** [personnes] to bring together; [- après séparation] to reunite.

◆ **se réunir** *vp* **-1.** [personnes] to meet. **-2.** [entreprises] to combine; [états] to unite. **-3.** [fleuves, rues] to converge.

réussi, -e [reysi] *adj* successful; **c'est** ~! *fig* & *iron* congratulations!, well done!

réussir [reysir] [32] ◇ *vi* **-1.** [personne, affaire] to succeed, to be a success; ~ **à faire qqch** to succeed in doing sthg; ~ **un coup fumant** to pull off a master stroke. **-2.** [climat]: ~ **à** to agree with. ◇ *vt* **-1.** [portrait, plat] to make a success of. **-2.** [examen] to pass.

réussite [reysit] *nf* **-1.** [succès] success. **-2.** [jeu de cartes] solitaire *Am*, patience *Br*.

réutiliser [reytilize] [3] *vt* to reuse.

revaloir [rəvalwar] [60] *vt*: ~ **qqch à qqn** [avec reconnaissance] to repay sb for sthg; [avec hostilité] to get even with sb for sthg.

revalorisation [rəvalɔrizasjɔ̃] *nf* [de monnaie] revaluation; [de salaires] raising; *fig* [d'idée] rehabilitation.

revaloriser [rəvalɔrize] [3] *vt* [monnaie] to revalue; [salaires] to raise; *fig* [idée, doctrine] to rehabilitate.

revanchard, -e [rəvɑ̃ʃar, ard] *péj* ◇ *adj* of revenge. ◇ *nm, f* advocate of revenge.

revanche [rəvɑ̃ʃ] *nf* **-1.** [vengeance] revenge; **prendre sa** ~ to take one's revenge. **-2.** SPORT return (match).

◆ **en revanche** *loc adv* **-1.** [par contre] on the other hand. **-2.** [en contrepartie] in return.

rêvasser [rɛvase] [3] *vi* to daydream.

revaudrai, revaudras *etc* → **revaloir**.

rêve [rɛv] *nm* dream; **de** ~ *fig* dream (*avant n*).

rêvé, -e [rɛve] *adj* ideal.

revêche [rəvɛʃ] *adj* surly.

réveil [revej] *nm* **-1.** [de personne] waking (up); *fig* awakening; **au** ~ on waking (up). **-2.** [pendule] alarm clock. **-3.** [de volcan] reawakening.

réveiller [reveje] [4] *vt* **-1.** [personne] to wake up. **-2.** [courage] to revive.

◆ **se réveiller** *vp* **-1.** [personne] to wake (up). **-2.** [ambitions] to reawaken.

réveillon [revɛjɔ̃] *nm* **-1.** [jour - de Noël] Christmas Eve; [- de nouvel an] New Year's Eve. **-2.** [repas - de Noël] Christmas Eve meal; [- de nouvel an] New Year's Eve meal.

réveillonner [revɛjɔne] [3] *vi* to have a Christmas Eve/New Year's Eve meal.

révélateur, -trice [revelatœr, tris] *adj* revealing.

◆ **révélateur** *nm* PHOT developer; *fig* [ce qui révèle] indication.

révélation [revelasjɔ̃] *nf* **-1.** [gén] revelation. **-2.** [artiste] discovery.

révéler [revele] [18] *vt* **-1.** [gén] to reveal. **-2.** [artiste] to discover.

◆ **se révéler** *vp* **-1.** [apparaître] to be revealed. **-2.** [s'avérer] to prove to be.

revenant [rəvnɑ̃] *nm* **-1.** [fantôme] spirit, ghost. **-2.** *fam* [personne] stranger.

revendeur, -euse [rəvɑ̃dœr, øz] *nm, f* retailer.

revendication [rəvɑ̃dikasjɔ̃] *nf* claim, demand.

revendiquer [rəvɑ̃dike] [3] *vt* [dû, responsabilité] to claim; [avec force] to demand.

revendre [rəvɑ̃dr] [73] *vt* **-1.** [après utilisation] to resell. **-2.** [vendre plus de] to sell more of.

revendu, -e [rəvɑ̃dy] *pp* → **revendre**.

revenir [rəvnir] [40] *vi* **-1.** [gén] to come back, to return; ~ **de** to come back from, to return from; ~ **à** to come back to, to return to; ~ **sur** [sujet] to go over again; [décision] to go back on; ~ **à soi** to come to. **-2.** [mot, sujet] to crop up. **-3.** [à l'esprit]: ~ **à** to come back to. **-4.** [impliquer]: **cela revient au même/à dire que ...** it amounts to the same thing/to saying (that) .... **-5.** [coûter]: ~ **à** to come to, to amount to; ~ **cher** to be expensive. **-6.** [honneur, tâche]: ~ **à** to fall to; **c'est à lui qu'il revient de ...** it is up to him to .... **-7.** CULIN: **faire** ~ to brown. **-8.** *loc*: **sa tête ne me revient pas** I don't like the look of him/her; **il n'en revenait pas** he couldn't get over it; ~ **de loin** to have been at death's door.

revente [rəvɑ̃t] *nf* resale.

revenu, -e [rəvny] *pp* → **revenir**.

◆ **revenu** *nm* [de pays] revenue; [de personne] income.

rêver [reve] [4] ◇ *vi* to dream; [rêvasser] to daydream; ~ **de/à** to dream of/about. ◇ *vt* to dream; ~ **que** to dream (that).

réverbération [revɛrberasjɔ̃] *nf* reverberation.

réverbère [revɛrbɛr] *nm* street lamp OU light.

réverbérer [revɛrbere] [18] *vt* to reverberate.

reverdir [rəvɛrdir] [32] *vi* to become green again.

révérence [reverɑ̃s] *nf* **-1.** [salut] bow. **-2.** *littéraire* [déférence] reverence.

révérencieux, -ieuse [reverɑ̃sjø, jøz] *adj* reverent.

révérend, -e [reverɑ̃, ɑ̃d] *adj* reverend.

◆ **révérend** *nm* reverend.

révérer [revere] [18] *vt* to revere.

rêverie [rɛvri] *nf* reverie.

revers [rəvɛr] *nm* **-1.** [de main] back; [de pièce] reverse; **prendre à** ~ to capture from the rear OU from behind; **le** ~ **de la médaille** *fig* the other side of the coin. **-2.** [de veste] lapel; [de pantalon] cuff *Am*, turn-up *Br*. **-3.** TENNIS backhand. **-4.** *fig* [de fortune] reversal.

reverser [rəvɛrse] [3] *vt* **-1.** [liquide] to pour out more of. **-2.** FIN: ~ **qqch sur** to pay sthg into; ~ **qqch dans** to invest sthg in.

réversible [revɛrsibl] *adj* reversible.

revêtement [rəvɛtmɑ̃] *nm* surface.

revêtir [rəvɛtir] [44] *vt* **-1.** [mur, surface]: ~ **(de)** to cover (with). **-2.** [aspect] to take on, to assume. **-3.** [vêtement] to put on; [personne] to dress. **-4.** *sout* [de dignité, de pouvoir]: ~ **qqn de** to invest sb with.

revêts → **revêtir**.

revêtu, -e [rəvɛty] *pp* → **revêtir**.

rêveur, -euse [rɛvœr, øz] ◇ *adj* dreamy. ◇ *nm, f* dreamer.

reviendrai, reviendras *etc* → **revenir**.

revient [rəvjɛ̃] → **prix**.

revigorer [rəvigɔre] [3] *vt* to invigorate.

revirement [rəvirmɑ̃] *nm* change.

révisable [revizabl] *adj* subject to review.

réviser [revize] [3] *vt* **-1.** [réexaminer, modifier] to revise, to review. **-2.** SCOL to revise. **-3.** [machine] to check.

révision [revizjɔ̃] *nf* **-1.** [réexamen, modification] revision, review. **-2.** SCOL revision. **-3.** [de machine] checkup.

révisionnisme [revizjɔnism] *nm* revisionism.

révisionniste [revizjɔnist] *nmf & adj* revisionist.

revisser [rəvise] [3] *vt* to screw back again.

revitaliser [rəvitalize] [3] *vt* to revitalize.

revivre [rəvivr] [90] ◇ *vi* [personne] to come back to life, to revive; *fig* [espoir] to be revived, to revive. ◇ *vt* to relive; **faire ~** to revive; **faire ~ qqch à qqn** to bring sthg back to sb.

révocation [revɔkasjɔ̃] *nf* **-1.** [de loi] revocation. **-2.** [de fonctionnaire] dismissal.

revoici [rəvwasi] *prép*: **me ~!** it's me again!, I'm back!

revoir [rəvwar] [62] *vt* **-1.** [renouer avec] to see again. **-2.** [corriger, étudier] to review *Am*, to revise *Br*.
◆ **se revoir** *vp* [amis] to see each other again; [professionnellement] to meet again.
◆ **au revoir** *interj* & *nm* goodbye.

révoltant, -e [revɔltɑ̃, ɑ̃t] *adj* revolting.

révolte [revɔlt] *nf* revolt; **inciter** OU **pousser qqn à la ~** to incite sb to revolt; **être en ~ contre** to be in revolt against.

révolter [revɔlte] [3] *vt* to disgust.
◆ **se révolter** *vp*: **se ~ (contre)** to revolt (against).

révolu, -e [revɔly] *adj* past; **avoir 15 ans ~s** ADMIN to be over 15.

révolution [revɔlysjɔ̃] *nf* **-1.** [gén] revolution. **-2.** *fam* [effervescence] uproar; **en ~** in an uproar.

révolutionnaire [revɔlysjɔnɛr] *nmf* & *adj* revolutionary.

révolutionner [revɔlysjɔne] [3] *vt* **-1.** [transformer] to revolutionize. **-2.** [mettre en émoi] to stir up.

revolver [revɔlvɛr] *nm* revolver.

révoquer [revɔke] [3] *vt* **-1.** [fonctionnaire] to dismiss. **-2.** [loi] to revoke.

revue [rəvy] *nf* **-1.** [gén] review; **~ de presse** press review; **passer en ~** *fig* to review. **-2.** [défilé] march-past. **-3.** [magazine] magazine. **-4.** [spectacle] revue.

révulser [revylse] [3] *vt* to disgust.
◆ **se révulser** *vp* to contort.

rewriting [rərajtiŋ] *nm* rewriting.

Reykjavik [rɛkjavik] *n* Reykjavik.

rez-de-chaussée [redʃose] *nm inv* first floor *Am*, ground floor *Br*.

rez-de-jardin [redʒardɛ̃] *nm inv* garden level.

RF *abr de* **République française**.

RFA (*abr de* **République fédérale d'Allemagne**) *nf* FRG.

RFI (*abr de* **Radio France Internationale**) *nf* French world service radio station.

RFO (*abr de* **Radio-télévision française d'outre-mer**) *nf* French overseas broadcasting service.

r.g. (*abr de* **rive gauche**) *left (south) bank of the Seine*.

RG (*abr de* **Renseignements généraux**) *nmpl police department responsible for political security*.

Rh (*abr de* **Rhésus**) Rh.

rhabiller [rabije] [3] *vt* to dress again.
◆ **se rhabiller** *vp* to get dressed again; **aller se ~** *fam fig* to throw in the towel.

rhapsodie, rapsodie [rapsɔdi] *nf* rhapsody.

rhénan, -e [renɑ̃, an] *adj* of/from the Rhine, Rhine (*avant n*).

rhéostat [reɔsta] *nm* rheostat.

rhésus [rezys] *nm* rhesus (factor); **~ positif/négatif** rhesus positive/negative.

rhétorique [retɔrik] *nf* rhetoric.

Rhin [rɛ̃] *nm*: **le ~** the Rhine.

rhinite [rinit] *nf* rhinitis (*U*).

rhinocéros [rinɔserɔs] *nm* rhinoceros.

rhino-pharyngite [rinɔfarɛ̃ʒit] (*pl* **rhino-pharyngites**) *nf* throat infection.

Rhodes [rɔd] *n* Rhodes; **le colosse de ~** the Colossus of Rhodes.

rhododendron [rɔdɔdɛ̃drɔ̃] *nm* rhododendron.

Rhône [ron] *nm*: **le ~** the (River) Rhone.

rhubarbe [rybarb] *nf* rhubarb.

rhum [rɔm] *nm* rum.

rhumatisant, -e [rymatizɑ̃, ɑ̃t] *adj* & *nm, f* rheumatic.

rhumatismal, -e, -aux [rymatismal, o] *adj* rheumatic.

rhumatisme [rymatism] *nm* rheumatism.

rhumatologue [rymatɔlɔg] *nmf* rheumatologist.

rhume [rym] *nm* cold; **attraper un ~** to catch a cold; **~ des foins** hay fever.

ri [ri] *pp inv* → **rire**.

RI ◇ *nm* (*abr de* **régiment d'infanterie**) infantry regiment. ◇ *nmpl* (*abr de* **Républicains indépendants**) *right-wing French political party*.

Riad = **Riyad**.

riant, -e [rijɑ̃, ɑ̃t] *adj* smiling; *fig* cheerful.

RIB, Rib [rib] (*abr de* **relevé d'identité bancaire**) *nm bank account identification slip*.

ribambelle [ribɑ̃bɛl] *nf*: **~ de** string of.

ricanement [rikanmɑ̃] *nm* snigger.

ricaner [rikane] [3] *vi* to snigger.

RICE, Rice [ris] (*abr de* **relevé d'identité de caisse d'épargne**) *nm savings bank account identification slip*.

richard, -e [riʃar, ard] *nm, f fam péj* moneybags (*sg*).

riche [riʃ] ◇ *nmf* rich person; **les ~s** the rich; **nouveau ~** nouveau riche. ◇ *adj* **-1.** [gén] rich; [personne, pays] rich, wealthy; **~ en** OU **de** rich in. **-2.** [habit] expensive. **-3.** [idée] great.

richement [riʃmɑ̃] *adv* richly.

richesse [riʃɛs] *nf* **-1.** [de personne, pays] wealth (U). **-2.** [d'appartement] sumptuousness (U). **-3.** [de faune, flore] abundance; **~ en vitamines** high vitamin content.

◆ **richesses** *nfpl* **-1.** [gén] wealth (U). **-2.** [de musée] riches.

richissime [riʃisim] *adj* super-rich.

ricin [risɛ̃] *nm* castor-oil plant; **huile de ~** castor oil.

ricocher [rikɔʃe] [3] *vi litt* & *fig* to rebound; [balle d'arme] to ricochet.

ricochet [rikɔʃɛ] *nm litt* & *fig* rebound; [de balle d'arme] ricochet; **par ~** in an indirect way.

rictus [riktys] *nm* rictus.

ride [rid] *nf* wrinkle; [de surface d'eau] ripple.

ridé, -e [ride] *adj* wrinkled.

rideau, -x [rido] *nm* curtain; **~ de fer** [frontière] Iron Curtain.

rider [ride] [3] *vt* **-1.** [peau] to wrinkle. **-2.** [surface] to ruffle.

◆ **se rider** *vp* to become wrinkled.

ridicule [ridikyl] ◇ *nm*: **le ~** ridicule; **se couvrir de ~** to make o.s. look ridiculous; **tourner qqn/qqch en ~** to ridicule sb/sthg. ◇ *adj* ridiculous.

ridiculement [ridikylmɑ̃] *adv* ridiculously.

ridiculiser [ridikylize] [3] *vt* to ridicule.

◆ **se ridiculiser** *vp* to make o.s. look ridiculous.

ridule [ridyl] *nf* little wrinkle.

rien [rjɛ̃] ◇ *pron indéf* **-1.** [en contexte négatif]: **ne ... rien** nothing, not ... anything; **je n'ai ~ fait** I've done nothing, I haven't done anything; **je n'en sais ~** I don't know (anything about it), I know nothing about it; **~ ne m'intéresse** nothing interests me; **il n'y a plus ~ dans le réfrigérateur** there's nothing left in the fridge. **-2.** [aucune chose] nothing; **que fais-tu? — ~** what are you doing? — nothing; **~ de nouveau** nothing new; **~ d'autre** nothing else; **~ du tout** nothing at all; **~ à faire** it's no good; **de ~!** don't mention it!, not at all!; **pour ~** for nothing. **-3.** [quelque chose] anything; **sans ~ dire** without saying anything.

◇ *nm*: **pour un ~** [se fâcher, pleurer] for nothing, at the slightest thing; **perdre son temps à des ~s** to waste one's time with trivia; **en un ~ de temps** in no time at all.

◆ **rien que** *loc adv* only, just; **la vérité, ~ que la vérité** the truth and nothing but the truth; **~ que l'idée des vacances la comblait** just thinking about the holiday filled her with joy.

◆ **un rien** *loc adv* a bit, a shade; **sa robe est un ~ trop étroite** her dress is a bit too tight.

rieur, rieuse [rijœr, rijøz] *adj* cheerful.

Riga [riga] *n* Riga.

rigide [riʒid] *adj* rigid; [muscle] tense.

rigidité [riʒidite] *nf* rigidity; [de muscle] tenseness; [de principes, mœurs] strictness.

rigolade [rigɔlad] *nf fam* fun (U); **c'est de la ~** *fig* it's a walkover.

rigolard, -e [rigɔlar, ard] *adj fam* jokey, joking.

rigole [rigɔl] *nf* channel.

rigoler [rigɔle] [3] *vi fam* **-1.** [rire] to laugh. **-2.** [plaisanter]: **~ (de)** to joke (about).

rigolo, -ote [rigɔlo, ɔt] *fam* ◇ *adj* funny. ◇ *nm, f péj* phony *Am*, phoney *Br*.

rigoriste [rigɔrist] ◇ *nmf* puritan. ◇ *adj* austere, puritanical.

rigoureusement [rigurøzmɑ̃] *adv* **-1.** [punir] harshly. **-2.** [vrai, ponctuel] absolutely; **c'est ~ exact** it's the honest truth.

rigoureux, -euse [rigurø, øz] *adj* **-1.** [discipline, hiver] harsh. **-2.** [analyse] rigorous.

rigueur [rigœr] *nf* **-1.** [de punition] severity, harshness. **-2.** [de climat] harshness. **-3.** [d'analyse] rigor *Am*, rigour *Br*, exactness. **-4.** *loc*: **être de ~** to be obligatory; **tenir ~ de qqch à qqn** to hold sthg against sb.

◆ **à la rigueur** *loc adv* if necessary, if need be.

rillettes [rijɛt] *nfpl pork cooked in its own fat and preserved*.

rime [rim] *nf* rhyme; **sans ~ ni raison** *fig* without rhyme or reason.

rimer [rime] [3] *vi*: **~ (avec)** to rhyme (with); **ça ne rime à rien** *fig* that doesn't make sense.

Rimmel® [rimɛl] *nm* mascara.

rinçage [rɛ̃saʒ] *nm* rinsing.

rince-doigts [rɛ̃sdwa] *nm inv* finger bowl.

rincer [rɛ̃se] [16] *vt* [bouteille] to rinse out; [cheveux, linge] to rinse; **se faire ~** *fam fig* to get a soaking.

◆ **se rincer** *vp* to rinse o.s.; **se ~ la bouche** to rinse one's mouth.

ring [riŋ] *nm* **-1.** BOXE ring. **-2.** *Belg* [route] bypass.

ringard, -e [rɛ̃gar, ard] *fam* ◇ *adj* **-1.** [chanson] corny. **-2.** [décor] naff. **-3.** [acteur]

second-rate. **-4.** [personne] nerdy. ◇ *nm, f* nerd.

ringuette [rɛ̃gɛt] *nf* ringette (*women's sport similar to ice hockey*).

Rio de Janeiro [rjodedʒanɛro] *n* Rio de Janeiro.

ripaille [ripaj] *nf*: **faire** ~ *fam vieilli* to have a feast.

riposte [ripɔst] *nf* **-1.** [réponse] retort, riposte. **-2.** [contre-attaque] counterattack.

riposter [ripɔste] [3] ◇ *vt*: ~ **que** to retort OU riposte that. ◇ *vi* **-1.** [répondre] to riposte; ~ **à** [personne] to answer back; [insulte] to reply to. **-2.** [contre-attaquer] to counter, to retaliate.

rire [rir] [95] ◇ *nm* laugh; **avoir un fou** ~ to giggle; **éclater de** ~ to burst out laughing. ◇ *vi* **-1.** [gén] to laugh; ~ **de** to laugh at. **-2.** [plaisanter]: **tu veux/vous voulez** ~? you must be joking!; **pour** ~ *fam* as a joke, for a laugh.

◆ **se rire** *vp sout*: **se** ~ **de** to laugh at.

ris [ri] *nm* **-1.** (*gén pl*) CULIN: ~ **de veau** sweetbread. **-2.** NAVIG reef.

risée [rize] *nf* ridicule; **être la** ~ **de** to be the laughing stock of.

risette [rizɛt] *nf*: **faire (une)** ~ **à qqn** [enfant] to give sb a nice OU sweet smile.

risible [rizibl] *adj* [ridicule] ridiculous.

risotto [rizɔto] *nm* risotto.

risque [risk] *nm* risk; **courir un** ~ to run a risk; **prendre des** ~s to take risks; **à tes/vos** ~s **et périls** at your own risk.

risqué, -e [riske] *adj* **-1.** [entreprise] risky, dangerous. **-2.** [plaisanterie] risqué, daring.

risquer [riske] [3] *vt* **-1.** [vie, prison] to risk; ~ **de faire qqch** to be likely to do sthg; **je risque de perdre tout ce que j'ai** I'm running the risk of losing everything I have; ~ **que** (+ *subjonctif*) to take a risk that; **cela ne risque rien** it will be all right; ~ **gros** to take a big risk; ~ **le tout pour le tout** *fig* to put everything on the line. **-2.** [tenter] to venture.

◆ **se risquer** *vp* to venture; **se** ~ **à faire qqch** to dare to do sthg.

rissoler [risɔle] [3] ◇ *vt* to brown. ◇ *vi* to brown; **faire** ~ to brown.

ristourne [risturn] *nf* discount; **faire une** ~ **à qqn** to give sb a discount.

rite [rit] *nm* **-1.** RELIG rite. **-2.** [cérémonial & *fig*] ritual.

ritournelle [riturnɛl] *nf* **-1.** *fam fig* [rabâchage] old story, old song. **-2.** MUS ritornello.

rituel, -elle [rityɛl] *adj* ritual.

◆ **rituel** *nm* ritual.

rituellement [rityɛlmɑ̃] *adv* **-1.** [selon un rite] ritually, religiously. **-2.** *fig* [immuablement] unfailingly.

rivage [rivaʒ] *nm* shore.

rival, -e, -aux [rival, o] ◇ *adj* rival (*avant n*). ◇ *nm, f* rival.

rivaliser [rivalize] [3] *vi*: ~ **avec** to compete with; ~ **de** to vie in.

rivalité [rivalite] *nf* rivalry.

rive [riv] *nf* [de rivière] bank; **la Rive droite/gauche** the Right/Left Bank.

RIVE DROITE, RIVE GAUCHE:

The Right (North) Bank of the Seine is traditionally associated with business and trade, and has a reputation for being more conservative than the Left Bank. The Left (South) Bank includes districts traditionally favoured by artists, students and intellectuals, and has a reputation for being bohemian and unconventional

river [rive] [3] *vt* **-1.** [fixer]: ~ **qqch à qqch** to rivet sthg to sthg. **-2.** [clou] to clinch; **être rivé à** *fig* to be riveted OU glued to.

riverain, -e [rivrɛ̃, ɛn] ◇ *adj* riverside (*avant n*); [de rue] roadside (*avant n*). ◇ *nm, f* resident.

rivet [rivɛ] *nm* rivet.

rivière [rivjɛr] *nf* river.

◆ **rivière de diamants** *nf* diamond necklace (*with largest stone in the middle*).

rixe [riks] *nf* fight, brawl.

Riyad, Riad [rijad] *n* Riyadh.

riz [ri] *nm* rice; ~ **au lait** rice pudding; ~ **pilaf** pilau rice.

riziculture [rizikyltyr] *nf* rice-growing.

rizière [rizjɛr] *nf* paddy (field).

RMC (*abr de* **Radio Monte-Carlo**) *nf independent radio station*.

RMI (*abr de* **revenu minimum d'insertion**) *nm minimum guaranteed income (for people with no other source of income)*.

RMiste [ɛremist] *nmf person receiving the 'RMI'*.

RN (*abr de* **route nationale**) *nf* ≃ State highway *Am*, ≃ A road *Br*.

RNIS (*abr de* **réseau numérique à intégration de services**) *nm* ISDN.

ro *abr de* recto.

robe [rɔb] *nf* **-1.** [de femme] dress; ~ **chasuble** pinafore dress; ~ **de grossesse** maternity dress; ~ **de mariée** wedding dress. **-2.** [peignoir]: ~ **de chambre** dressing gown. **-3.**

[de magistrat] robe. **-4.** [de cheval] coat. **-5.** [de vin] color *Am,* colour *Br.*

robinet [rɔbinɛ] *nm* faucet *Am,* tap *Br.*

robinetterie [rɔbinɛtri] *nf* [installations] faucets *(pl) Am,* taps *(pl) Br.*

roboratif, -ive [rɔbɔratif, iv] *adj sout* bracing, invigorating.

robot [rɔbo] *nm* **-1.** [gén] robot. **-2.** [ménager] food processor.

robotique [rɔbɔtik] *nf* robotics (*U*).

robotisation [rɔbɔtizasjɔ̃] *nf* automation.

robotiser [rɔbɔtize] [3] *vt* to automate.

robuste [rɔbyst] *adj* **-1.** [personne, santé] robust. **-2.** [plante] hardy. **-3.** [voiture] sturdy.

robustesse [rɔbystɛs] *nf* **-1.** [de personne] robustness. **-2.** [de plante] hardiness. **-3.** [de voiture] sturdiness.

roc [rɔk] *nm* rock.

rocade [rɔkad] *nf* bypass.

rocaille [rɔkaj] ◇ *nf* **-1.** [cailloux] loose stones *(pl).* **-2.** [dans jardin] rock garden, rockery. ◇ *adj inv* rocaille.

rocailleux, -euse [rɔkajø, øz] *adj* **-1.** [terrain] rocky. **-2.** *fig* [voix] harsh.

rocambolesque [rɔkãbɔlɛsk] *adj* fantastic.

roche [rɔʃ] *nf* rock.

rocher [rɔʃe] *nm* rock; **le Rocher** *the town of Monaco;* **le ~ de Gibraltar** the Rock of Gibraltar.

◆ **rocher au chocolat** *nm* nut chocolate.

rocheux, -euse [rɔʃø, øz] *adj* rocky.

◆ **Rocheuses** *nfpl:* **les ~** the Rockies.

rock [rɔk] ◇ *nm* rock ('n' roll). ◇ *adj inv* rock.

rockeur, -euse [rɔkœr, øz] *nm, f* **-1.** [chanteur] rock singer. **-2.** [fan] rock fan.

rocking-chair [rɔkiŋtʃɛr] *(pl* **rocking-chairs)** *nm* rocking chair.

rodage [rɔdaʒ] *nm* **-1.** [de véhicule] running-in; **"en ~»** "running in". **-2.** *fig* [de méthode] running-in OU debugging period.

rodéo [rɔdeo] *nm* rodeo; *fig & iron* free-for-all.

roder [rɔde] [3] *vt* **-1.** [véhicule] to run in. **-2.** *fam* [méthode] to run in, to debug; [personne] to break in.

rôder [rode] [3] *vi* to prowl, to wander about.

rôdeur, -euse [rodœr, øz] *nm, f* prowler.

rodomontade [rɔdɔmɔ̃tad] *nf littéraire* boasting (*U*).

rogations [rɔgasjɔ̃] *nfpl* Rogations.

rogne [rɔɲ] *nf fam* bad temper; **être/se mettre en ~** to be in/to get into a bad mood, to be in/to get into a temper.

rogner [rɔɲe] [3] ◇ *vt* **-1.** [ongles] to trim. **-2.** [revenus] to eat into. ◇ *vi:* **~ sur qqch** to cut down on sthg.

rognon [rɔɲɔ̃] *nm* kidney.

rognures [rɔɲyr] *nfpl* clippings, trimmings.

rogue [rɔg] *adj littéraire* arrogant.

roi [rwa] *nm* king; **être plus royaliste que le ~** *fig* to be more Catholic than the Pope; **tirer les ~s** to celebrate Epiphany.

◆ **Rois mages** *nmpl:* **les Rois mages** RELIG the Three Wise Men.

TIRER LES ROIS:
The French traditionally celebrate Epiphany with a round, almond-flavoured pastry ('la galette des rois') containing a small porcelain figurine ('la fève' — originally a dried bean). The pastry is shared out and the person who finds the 'fève' is appointed 'king' or 'queen' and given a cardboard crown to wear

roitelet [rwatlɛ] *nm* **-1.** [oiseau] wren. **-2.** *péj & vieilli* [petit roi] kinglet.

Roland-Garros [rɔlãgaros] *n tennis stadium in Paris where the French Open is held.*

rôle [rol] *nm* role, part; **jouer un ~** to play a role OU part; **avoir le beau ~** *fig* to come off best.

rôle-titre [roltitr] *nm* title role.

rollmops [rɔlmɔps] *nm* rollmop.

ROM, Rom [rɔm] *(abr de read only memory) nf* ROM.

romain, -e [rɔmɛ̃, ɛn] *adj* Roman.

◆ **romain** *nm* TYPO roman.

◆ **romaine** *nf.* [salade] romaine (lettuce) *Am,* cos (lettuce) *Br.*

◆ **Romain, -e** *nm, f* Roman.

roman, -e [rɔmã, an] *adj* **-1.** [langue] Romance. **-2.** ARCHIT Romanesque.

◆ **roman** *nm* **-1.** LITTÉRATURE novel; **~ d'action** adventure novel; **~ d'anticipation** OU **de science fiction** science fiction novel; **~ noir** thriller. **-2.** *fig & iron* [exagération] story; [aventure] saga. **-3.** ARCHIT: **le ~** the Romanesque.

romance [rɔmãs] *nf* [chanson] love song.

romancer [rɔmãse] [16] *vt* to romanticize.

romanche [rɔmãʃ] *nm & adj* Romansh.

romancier, -ière [rɔmãsje, jɛr] *nm, f* novelist.

romand, -e [rɔmã, ãd] *adj* of/from French-speaking Switzerland.

◆ **Romand, -e** *nm, f* French-speaking Swiss.

romanesque [rɔmanɛsk] *adj* **-1.** LITTÉRATURE novelistic. **-2.** [aventure] fabulous, story-book (*avant n*).

roman-feuilleton [rɔmɑ̃fœjtɔ̃] (*pl* **romans-feuilletons**) *nm* serial; *fig* soap opera.

roman-fleuve [rɔmɑ̃flœv] (*pl* **romans-fleuves**) *nm* saga.

romanichel, -elle [rɔmaniʃɛl] *nm, f* gipsy.

romaniste [rɔmanist] *nmf* Romanist.

roman-photo [rɔmɑ̃fɔto] (*pl* **romans-photos**) *nm* story told in photographs.

romantique [rɔmɑ̃tik] *nmf & adj* romantic.

romantisme [rɔmɑ̃tism] *nm* **-1.** ART Romantic movement. **-2.** [sensibilité] romanticism.

romarin [rɔmarɛ̃] *nm* rosemary.

rombière [rɔ̃bjɛr] *nf fam péj* old biddy.

Rome [rɔm] *n* Rome.

rompre [rɔ̃pr] [78] ◇ *vt* **-1.** *sout* [objet] to break. **-2.** [charme, marché] to break; [fiançailles, relations] to break off. **-3.** *sout* [exercer]: ~ **qqn à** to break sb into. ◇ *vi* to break; ~ **avec qqn** *fig* to break up with sb; ~ **avec qqch** *fig* to break with sthg.
◆ **se rompre** *vp* to break; **se ~ le cou/les reins** to break one's neck/back.

rompu, -e [rɔ̃py] ◇ *pp* → **rompre.** ◇ *adj* **-1.** [exténué] exhausted; ~ **de** exhausted by; ~ **de fatigue** exhausted. **-2.** [expérimenté]: ~ **à** experienced in.

romsteck = **rumsteck.**

ronce [rɔ̃s] *nf* [arbuste] bramble.

ronchon, -onne [rɔ̃ʃɔ̃, ɔn] *fam* ◇ *adj* grumpy. ◇ *nm, f* grumbler.

ronchonner [rɔ̃ʃɔne] [3] *vi fam*: ~ **(après)** to grumble (at).

rond, -e [rɔ̃, rɔ̃d] *adj* **-1.** [forme, chiffre] round. **-2.** [joue, ventre] chubby, plump. **-3.** *fam* [ivre] tight.
◆ **rond** ◇ *nm* **-1.** [cercle] circle; **en ~** in a circle OU ring; **tourner en ~** *fig* to go round in circles. **-2.** [anneau] ring; ~ **de serviette** napkin ring. **-3.** *fam* [argent]: **je n'ai pas un ~** I haven't got a penny OU bean. ◇ *adv*: **ça ne tourne pas ~** *fig* there's something up OU fishy.

rond-de-cuir [rɔ̃dkɥir] (*pl* **ronds-de-cuir**) *nm péj & vieilli* pen pusher.

ronde [rɔ̃d] *nf* **-1.** [de surveillance] rounds (*pl*); [de policier] beat. **-2.** [danse] round. **-3.** MUS whole note *Am*, semibreve *Br*.
◆ **à la ronde** *loc adv*: **à des kilomètres à la ~** for miles around.

rondelet, -ette [rɔ̃dlɛ, ɛt] *adj* **-1.** [grassouillet] plump. **-2.** *fig* [somme] goodish, tidy.

rondelle [rɔ̃dɛl] *nf* **-1.** [de saucisson] slice. **-2.** [de métal] washer. **-3.** *Can* HOCKEY puck.

rondement [rɔ̃dmɑ̃] *adv* [efficacement] efficiently, briskly.

rondeur [rɔ̃dœr] *nf* **-1.** [forme] roundness. **-2.** [partie charnue] curve. **-3.** [de caractère] openness.

rondin [rɔ̃dɛ̃] *nm* log.

rondouillard, -e [rɔ̃dujar, ard] *adj fam* tubby.

rond-point [rɔ̃pwɛ̃] (*pl* **ronds-points**) *nm* traffic circle *Am*, roundabout *Br*.

ronflant, -e [rɔ̃flɑ̃, ɑ̃t] *adj péj* grandiose.

ronflement [rɔ̃fləmɑ̃] *nm* **-1.** [de dormeur] snore. **-2.** [de poêle, moteur] hum, purr.

ronfler [rɔ̃fle] [3] *vi* **-1.** [dormeur] to snore. **-2.** [poêle, moteur] to hum, to purr. **-3.** *fam* [dormir] to be in a deep sleep.

ronger [rɔ̃ʒe] [17] *vt* [bois, os] to gnaw; [métal, falaise] to eat away at; *fig* to gnaw at, to eat away at.
◆ **se ronger** *vp* **-1.** [grignoter]: **se ~ les ongles** to bite one's nails. **-2.** *fig* [se tourmenter] to worry, to torture o.s.

rongeur, -euse [rɔ̃ʒœr, øz] *adj* gnawing, rodent (*avant n*).
◆ **rongeur** *nm* rodent.

ronron [rɔ̃rɔ̃] *nm* **-1.** [de chat] purr; [de moteur] purr, hum. **-2.** *fig & péj* [routine] humdrum existence.

ronronnement [rɔ̃rɔnmɑ̃] *nm* [de chat] purring; [de moteur] purring, humming.

ronronner [rɔ̃rɔne] [3] *vi* [chat] to purr; [moteur] to purr, to hum.

roquefort [rɔkfɔr] *nm* Roquefort (*French blue-veined cheese*).

roquer [rɔke] [3] *vi* ÉCHECS to castle.

roquet [rɔkɛ] *nm péj* **-1.** [chien] nasty little dog. **-2.** *fig* [personne] nasty little squirt.

roquette [rɔkɛt] *nf* rocket.

rosace [rozas] *nf* **-1.** [ornement] rose. **-2.** [vitrail] rose window. **-3.** [figure géométrique] rosette.

rosaire [rozɛr] *nm* rosary.

rosâtre [rozatr] *adj* pinkish.

rosbif [rɔzbif] *nm* **-1.** [viande] roast beef. **-2.** [Anglais] *pejorative term for a British person*.

rose [roz] ◇ *nf* rose; ~ **trémière** hollyhock; **frais comme une ~** fresh as a daisy; **envoyer qqn sur les ~s** *fam fig* to send sb packing. ◇ *nm* pink. ◇ *adj* pink; ~ **bonbon** bright pink.
◆ **rose des vents** *nf* compass card.

ROSE:

The symbol of the French socialists is a rose, and so this word is sometimes used to suggest socialist leanings ('ce maire est un peu moins rose que son prédécesseur').

The word 'rose' can also suggest soft pornography ('les messageries roses' and 'le Minitel® rose' refer to erotic call lines available on Minitel®).

'Les villes roses' (Albi, Montauban and Toulouse) are so called because they are largely built of pink stone.

'Le carnet rose' is the list of births and marriages in a newspaper

---

rosé, -e [roze] *adj* **-1.** [vin] rosé. **-2.** [teinte] rosy.
◆ **rosé** *nm* rosé.
◆ **rosée** *nf* dew.

roseau, -x [rozo] *nm* reed.

roseraie [rozre] *nf* rose garden.

rosette [rozɛt] *nf* **-1.** [nœud] bow. **-2.** [insigne] rosette.
◆ **rosette de Lyon** *nf dry pork sausage.*

rosier [rozje] *nm* rose bush.

rosir [rozir] [32] *vt & vi* to turn pink.

rosse [rɔs] *péj* ◇ *nf* **-1.** *vieilli* [cheval] nag. **-2.** *fig* [femme] bitch, cow; [homme] bastard. ◇ *adj* nasty.

rosser [rɔse] [3] *vt* to thrash.

rosserie [rɔsri] *nf fam* nasty remark.

rossignol [rɔsiɲɔl] *nm* **-1.** [oiseau] nightingale. **-2.** *fam fig* [article invendable] piece of rubbish. **-3.** [passe-partout] picklock.

rot [ro] *nm* burp.

rotatif, -ive [rɔtatif, iv] *adj* rotary.
◆ **rotative** *nf* rotary press.

rotation [rɔtasjɔ̃] *nf* rotation.

roter [rote] [3] *vi fam* to burp.

rôti, -e [roti] *adj* roast.
◆ **rôti** *nm* roast, joint; ~ **de veau/porc** roast veal/pork.

rotin [rɔtɛ̃] *nm* rattan.

rôtir [rotir] [32] ◇ *vt* to roast. ◇ *vi* **-1.** CULIN to roast; **faire** ~ to roast. **-2.** *fam fig* [avoir chaud] to be roasting.
◆ **se rôtir** *vp*: **se** ~ **au soleil** *fig* to bask in the sunshine.

rôtisserie [rotisri] *nf* **-1.** [restaurant] ≃ steakhouse. **-2.** [magasin] *shop selling roast meat.*

rôtissoire [rotiswar] *nf* spit.

rotonde [rɔtɔ̃d] *nf* **-1.** [bâtiment] rotunda. **-2.** [d'autobus] back seat.

rotor [rɔtɔr] *nm* rotor.

rotule [rɔtyl] *nf* kneecap.

roturier, -ière [rɔtyrje, jɛr] ◇ *adj* **-1.** [non noble] common. **-2.** *péj* [commun] plebeian. ◇ *nm, f vieilli* commoner.

rouage [rwaʒ] *nm* cog, gearwheel; **les** ~**s de l'État** *fig* the wheels of State.

roublard, -e [rublar, ard] *fam* ◇ *adj* cunning, crafty. ◇ *nm, f* cunning OU crafty devil.

roublardise [rublardiz] *nf* **-1.** [caractère] cunning, craftiness. **-2.** *vieilli* [acte] cunning OU crafty trick.

rouble [rubl] *nm* rouble.

roucoulement [rukulmɑ̃] *nm* cooing; *fig* billing and cooing.

roucouler [rukule] [3] ◇ *vt* to warble; *fig* to coo. ◇ *vi* to coo; *fig* to bill and coo.

roue [ru] *nf* **-1.** [gén] wheel; **descendre en** ~ **libre** to freewheel downhill; ~ **arrière/avant** back/front wheel; ~ **dentée** cogwheel; ~ **de secours** spare wheel; **un deux** ~**s** a two-wheeled vehicle. **-2.** [de paon]: **faire la** ~ to display. **-3.** GYM cartwheel.

rouer [rwe] [6] *vt*: ~ **qqn de coups** to thrash sb, to beat sb.

rouerie [ruri] *nf littéraire* **-1.** [caractère] cunning. **-2.** *vieilli* [action] cunning trick.

rouet [rwɛ] *nm* [à filer] spinning wheel.

rouge [ruʒ] ◇ *nm* **-1.** [couleur] red. **-2.** *fam* [vin] red (wine); **gros** ~ *fam* cheap red wine, plonk. **-3.** [fard] rouge, blusher; ~ **à lèvres** lipstick. **-4.** AUTOM: **passer au** ~ to turn red; [conducteur] to go through a red light. ◇ *nmf* POLIT & *péj* Red. ◇ *adj* **-1.** [gén] red; ~ **de** red with. **-2.** [fer, tison] red-hot. **-3.** POLIT & *péj* Red. ◇ *adv*: **voir** ~ *fig* to see red.

rougeâtre [ruʒatr] *adj* reddish.

rougeaud, -e [ruʒo, od] ◇ *adj* red-faced. ◇ *nm, f* red-faced person.

rouge-gorge [ruʒgɔrʒ] (*pl* **rouges-gorges**) *nm* robin.

rougeoiement [ruʒwamɑ̃] *nm* reddening.

rougeole [ruʒɔl] *nf* measles (*sg*).

rougeoyer [ruʒwaje] [13] *vi* to turn red.

rouget [ruʒɛ] *nm* mullet.

rougeur [ruʒœr] *nf* **-1.** [teinte] redness. **-2.** [de visage, de chaleur, d'effort] flush; [- de gêne] blush. **-3.** [sur peau] red spot OU blotch.

rougir [ruʒir] [32] ◇ *vt* **-1.** [colorer] to turn red. **-2.** [chauffer] to make red-hot. ◇ *vi* **-1.** [devenir rouge] to turn red. **-2.** [d'émotion]: ~ **(de)** [de plaisir, colère] to flush (with); [de gêne] to blush (with). **-3.** *fig* [avoir honte]: ~ **de qqch** to be ashamed of sthg.

rougissant, -e [ruʒisɑ̃, ɑ̃t] *adj* reddening.

rouille [ruj] ◇ *nf* **-1.** [oxyde] rust. **-2.** CULIN *spicy garlic sauce for fish soup.* ◇ *adj inv* rust.

rouiller [ruje] [3] ◇ *vt* to rust, to make rusty. ◇ *vi* to rust.

◆ **se rouiller** *vp* to rust; *fig* to get rusty.

roulade [rulad] *nf* **-1.** [galipette] roll. **-2.** CULIN rolled meat.

roulant, -e [rulɑ̃, ɑ̃t] *adj* **-1.** [meuble] on wheels, on castors. **-2.** RAIL: **personnel** ~ train crew.

roulé, -e [rule] *adj* rolled; **bien** ~**e** *fam fig* curvy, shapely.

◆ **roulé** *nm* CULIN ≃ swiss roll.

rouleau, -x [rulo] *nm* **-1.** [gén & TECHNOL] roller; ~ **compresseur** steamroller; ~ **encreur** ink roller. **-2.** [de papier] roll. **-3.** [à pâtisserie] rolling pin.

roulé-boulé [rulebule] (*pl* roulés-boulés) *nm* roll.

roulement [rulmɑ̃] *nm* **-1.** [gén] rolling. **-2.** [de hanches] swaying. **-3.** [de personnel] rotation; **travailler par** ~ to work to a rota. **-4.** [de tambour, tonnerre] roll. **-5.** TECHNOL rolling bearing; ~ **à billes** ball bearing. **-6.** FIN circulation.

rouler [rule] [3] ◇ *vt* **-1.** [déplacer] to wheel. **-2.** [enrouler - tapis] to roll up; [- cigarette] to roll. **-3.** *fam* [balancer] to sway. **-4.** LING to roll. **-5.** [faire tourner sur soi] to roll. **-6.** *fam fig* [duper] to swindle, to do.
◇ *vi* **-1.** [ballon, bateau] to roll. **-2.** [véhicule] to go, to run; [suj: personne] to drive. **-3.** [tonnerre] to rumble. **-4.** [suj: conversation]: ~ **sur** to turn on. **-5.** *fam* [aller bien]: **ça roule** everything's OK OU going well.

◆ **se rouler** *vp* to roll about; **se** ~ **par terre** to roll on the ground; **se** ~ **en boule** to roll o.s. into a ball.

roulette [rulɛt] *nf* **-1.** [petite roue] castor; **comme sur des** ~**s** *fam fig* like clockwork. **-2.** [de dentiste] drill. **-3.** JEU roulette; ~ **russe** Russian roulette.

roulis [ruli] *nm* roll.

roulotte [rulɔt] *nf* [de gitan] caravan; [de tourisme] trailer *Am*, caravan *Br*.

roulure [rulyr] *nf fam péj* tart, whore.

roumain, -e [rumɛ̃, ɛn] *adj* Romanian.

◆ **roumain** *nm* [langue] Romanian.

◆ **Roumain, -e** *nm, f* Romanian.

Roumanie [rumani] *nf*: **la** ~ Romania.

round [rawnd] *nm* round.

roupiller [rupije] [3] *vi fam* to snooze.

roupillon [rupijɔ̃] *nm fam* snooze.

rouquin, -e [rukɛ̃, in] *fam* ◇ *adj* red-headed. ◇ *nm, f* redhead.

rouspéter [ruspete] [18] *vi fam* to grumble, to moan.

rousse → roux.

rousseur [rusœr] *nf* redness.

◆ **taches de rousseur** *nfpl* freckles.

roussi [rusi] *nm* burning; **ça sent le** ~ *fam fig* trouble's on its way.

roussir [rusir] [32] ◇ *vt* **-1.** [rendre roux] to turn brown; CULIN to brown. **-2.** [brûler légèrement] to singe. ◇ *vi* to turn brown; CULIN to brown.

routage [rutaʒ] *nm* sorting and mailing.

routard, -e [rutar, ard] *nm, f fam* (hippie) traveler *Am* OU traveller *Br*.

route [rut] *nf* **-1.** [gén] road; ~ **à grande circulation** busy road; **faire de la** ~ to do a lot of mileage; **en** ~ on the way; **en** ~! let's go!; **mettre en** ~ [démarrer] to start up; *fig* to get under way; ~ **nationale** ≃ highway *Am*, ≃ A road *Br*; **tenir la** ~ ~ AUTOM to hold the road; *fig* to hold water. **-2.** [itinéraire] route; **montrer la** ~ **à qqn** to show sb the way; **faire fausse** ~ to go the wrong way; *fig* to be on the wrong track. **-3.** *fig* [voie] path.

routier, -ière [rutje, jɛr] *adj* road (*avant n*).

◆ **routier** *nm* **-1.** [chauffeur] long-distance trucker *Am* OU lorry driver *Br*. **-2.** [restaurant] ≃ truck stop *Am*, ≃ transport cafe *Br*.

routine [rutin] *nf* routine.

routinier, -ière [rutinje, jɛr] *adj* routine.

rouvert, -e [ruvɛr, ɛrt] *pp* → rouvrir.

rouvrir [ruvrir] [34] *vt* to reopen, to open again.

◆ **se rouvrir** *vp* to reopen, to open again.

roux, rousse [ru, rus] ◇ *adj* **-1.** [cheveux] red. **-2.** [feuilles] russet, red-brown. **-3.** [sucre] brown. ◇ *nm, f* [personne] redhead.

◆ **roux** *nm* **-1.** [couleur] red, russet. **-2.** CULIN roux.

royal, -e, -aux [rwajal, o] *adj* **-1.** [de roi] royal. **-2.** [magnifique] princely.

royalement [rwajalmɑ̃] *adv* **-1.** [recevoir] royally; [vivre] like royalty. **-2.** *fig* [complètement]: **elle s'en moque** ~ she couldn't care less.

royaliste [rwajalist] *nmf & adj* royalist.

royalties [rwajalti] *nfpl* royalties.

royaume [rwajom] *nm* kingdom.

Royaume-Uni [rwajomyni] *nm*: **le** ~ the United Kingdom.

royauté [rwajote] *nf* **-1.** [fonction] kingship. **-2.** [régime] monarchy.

RP ◇ *nfpl* (*abr de* **relations publiques**) PR (*sg*). ◇ *nf* **-1.** (*abr de* **recette principale**) main post office. **-2.** *abr de* **région parisienne**.

R.P. (*abr de* **révérend père**) Holy Father.

RPR (*abr de* **Rassemblement pour la République**) *nm French political party to the right of the political spectrum.*

RSVP (*abr de* **répondez s'il vous plaît**) RSVP.

RTB (*abr de* **Radio-télévision belge**) *nf Belgian broadcasting company.*

rte *abr de* **route**.

RTL (*abr de* **Radio-télévision Luxembourg**) *nf Luxembourg broadcasting company.*

RU (*abr de* **restaurant universitaire**) *nm* refectory.

ruade [rɥad] *nf* kick.

Ruanda, Rwanda [rɥɑ̃da] *nm*: **le** ~ Rwanda; **au** ~ in Rwanda.

ruandais, -e [rɥɑ̃dɛ, ɛz] *adj* Rwandan.
◆ **ruandais** *nm* [langue] Rwandan.
◆ **Ruandais, -e** *nm, f* Rwandan.

ruban [rybɑ̃] *nm* ribbon; ~ **adhésif** adhesive tape.

rubéole [rybeɔl] *nf* German measles (*sg*), rubella.

rubicond, -e [rybikɔ̃, ɔ̃d] *adj* rubicund.

rubis [rybi] ◇ *nm* **-1.** [pierre précieuse] ruby. **-2.** [de montre] jewel. **-3.** *loc*: **payer** ~ **sur l'ongle** to pay cash on the nail. ◇ *adj inv* [couleur] ruby.

rubrique [rybrik] *nf* **-1.** [chronique] column. **-2.** [dans classement] heading.

ruche [ryʃ] *nf* **-1.** [abeilles] hive. **-2.** [abri] hive, beehive; *fig* hive of activity.

rucher [ryʃe] *nm* apiary.

rude [ryd] *adj* **-1.** [surface] rough. **-2.** [voix] harsh. **-3.** [personne, manières] rough, uncouth. **-4.** [hiver, épreuve] harsh, severe; [tâche, adversaire] tough. **-5.** [appétit] hearty.

rudement [rydmɑ̃] *adv* **-1.** [brutalement - tomber] hard; [- répondre] harshly. **-2.** *fam* [très] damn.

rudesse [rydɛs] *nf* harshness, severity.

rudimentaire [rydimɑ̃tɛr] *adj* rudimentary.

rudiments [rydimɑ̃] *nmpl* rudiments.

rudoie, rudoies *etc* → **rudoyer**.

rudoyer [rydwaje] [13] *vt* to treat harshly.

rue [ry] *nf* street; **descendre dans la** ~ to take to the streets; **jeter/mettre/être à la** ~ *fig* to throw/to put/to be out on the streets; **ne pas courir les** ~**s** *fig* not to grow on trees, to be thin on the ground.

ruée [rɥe] *nf* rush.

ruelle [rɥɛl] *nf* [rue] alley, lane.

ruer [rɥe] [7] *vi* to kick.
◆ **se ruer** *vp*: **se** ~ **sur** to pounce on.

rugby [rygbi] *nm* rugby; ~ **à treize/quinze** Rugby League/Union.

rugir [ryʒir] [32] ◇ *vt* to roar, to bellow. ◇ *vi* to roar; [vent] to howl; [personne]: ~ **de** to roar with.

rugissement [ryʒismɑ̃] *nm* roar, roaring (*U*); [de vent] howling.

rugosité [rygozite] *nf* **-1.** [de surface] roughness. **-2.** [aspérité] rough patch.

rugueux, -euse [rygø, øz] *adj* rough.

ruine [rɥin] *nf* **-1.** [gén] ruin; **tomber en** ~**s** to fall into ruins. **-2.** [effondrement] ruin, downfall. **-3.** [humaine] wreck. **-4.** [acquisition]: **c'est une vraie** ~ it costs me/you *etc* an arm and a leg.

ruiner [rɥine] [3] *vt* to ruin.
◆ **se ruiner** *vp* to ruin o.s., to bankrupt o.s.

ruineux, -euse [rɥinø, øz] *adj* ruinous.

ruisseau, -x [rɥiso] *nm* **-1.** [cours d'eau] stream; **des** ~**x de larmes** floods of tears. **-2.** *fig* & *péj* [caniveau] gutter.

ruisseler [rɥisle] [24] *vi*: ~ **(de)** to stream (with).

ruissellement [rɥisɛlmɑ̃] *nm* streaming.

rumba [rumba] *nf* rumba.

rumeur [rymœr] *nf* **-1.** [bruit] murmur. **-2.** [nouvelle] rumor *Am*, rumour *Br*.

ruminant, -e [ryminɑ̃, ɑ̃t] *adj* ruminant.
◆ **ruminant** *nm* ruminant.

ruminer [rymine] [3] *vi* to ruminate; *fig* to mull over.

rumsteck, romsteck [rɔmstɛk] *nm* rump steak.

rupestre [rypɛstr] *adj* **-1.** ART cave (*avant n*), rock (*avant n*). **-2.** BOT rock (*avant n*).

rupin, -e [rypɛ̃, in] *fam* ◇ *adj* plush. ◇ *nm, f* moneybags (*sg*).

rupture [ryptyr] *nf* **-1.** [cassure] breaking. **-2.** *fig* [changement] abrupt change; **en** ~ **de ban avec** *fig* at odds with. **-3.** [manque]: **être en** ~ **de stock** to be out of stock. **-4.** [de négociations, fiançailles] breaking off; [de contrat] breach. **-5.** [amoureuse] breakup, split.

rural, -e, -aux [ryral, o] ◇ *adj* country (*avant n*), rural. ◇ *nm, f* country-dweller.

ruse [ryz] *nf* **-1.** [habileté] cunning, craftiness. **-2.** [subterfuge] ruse.

rusé, -e [ryze] ◇ *adj* cunning, crafty. ◇ *nm, f* cunning OU crafty person.

ruser [ryze] [3] *vi* to use trickery.

rush [rœʃ] (*pl* **rushes** [rœʃ]) *nm* rush.

russe [rys] ◇ *adj* Russian. ◇ *nm* [langue] Russian.
◆ **Russe** *nmf* Russian.

Russie [rysi] *nf*: **la** ~ Russia.

rustine [rystin] *nf small rubber patch for repairing bicycle tyres.*

rustique [rystik] ◇ *nm* [style] rustic style. ◇ *adj* rustic.

rustre [rystr] *péj* ◇ *nmf* lout. ◇ *adj* loutish.

rut [ryt] *nm*: être en ~ [mâle] to be rutting; [femelle] to be on heat.

rutabaga [rytabaga] *nm* swede, rutabaga *Am.*

rutilant, -e [rytilɑ̃, ɑ̃t] *adj* [brillant] gleaming.

rutiler [rytile] [3] *vi* to gleam.

R-V (*abr de* **rendez-vous**).

Rwanda = **Ruanda**.

rythme [ritm] *nm* -1. MUS rhythm; en ~ in rhythm. -2. [de travail, production] pace, rate; au ~ de at the rate of; ~ cardiaque heart rate.

rythmer [ritme] [3] *vt* to give rhythm to.

rythmique [ritmik] ◇ *nf* rhythmics (*U*). ◇ *adj* rhythmical.

S

s¹, S [ɛs] *nm inv* -1. [lettre] s, S. -2. [forme] zigzag.
◆ **S** (*abr de* **Sud**) S.

s² (*abr de* **seconde**) s.

s' → **se**.

s/ *abr de* **sur**.

sa → **son**.

SA (*abr de* **société anonyme**) *nf* ≃ Inc. *Am*, ≃ Ltd *Br*.

S.A. (*abr de* **Son Altesse**) H.H.

sabayon [sabajɔ̃] *nm* zabaglione.

sabbat [saba] *nm* -1. RELIG Sabbath. -2. [de sorciers] sabbath.

sabbatique [sabatik] *adj* -1. RELIG Sabbath (*avant n*). -2. [congé] sabbatical.

sable [sabl] ◇ *nm* sand; de ~ [plage] sandy; [tempête] sand (*avant n*); ~s mouvants quicksand (*sg*), quicksands. ◇ *adj inv* [couleur] sandy.

sablé, -e [sable] *adj* -1. [route] sandy. -2. CULIN: gâteau ~ ≃ shortbread (*U*).
◆ **sablé** *nm* ≃ shortbread (*U*).

sabler [sable] [3] *vt* -1. [route] to sand. -2. [façade] to sandblast. -3. [boire]: ~ le champagne to crack a bottle of champagne.

sableux, -euse [sablø, øz] *adj* sandy.
◆ **sableuse** *nf* sandblaster.

sablier [sablije] *nm* hourglass.

sablière [sablijɛr] *nf* -1. [carrière] sand quarry. -2. [poutre] stringer.

sablonneux, -euse [sablɔnø, øz] *adj* sandy.

saborder [sabɔrde] [3] *vt* [navire] to scuttle; *fig* [entreprise] to wind up; *fig* [projet] to scupper.
◆ **se saborder** *vp* -1. [navire] to be scuttled. -2. *fig* [entreprise] to wind up.

sabot [sabo] *nm* -1. [chaussure] clog. -2. [de cheval] hoof. -3. AUTOM: ~ de Denver wheel clamp, Denver boot; ~ de frein brake shoe.

sabotage [sabɔtaʒ] *nm* -1. [volontaire] sabotage. -2. [bâclage] bungling.

saboter [sabɔte] [3] *vt* -1. [volontairement] to sabotage. -2. [bâcler] to bungle.

saboteur, -euse [sabɔtœr, øz] *nm, f* MIL & POLIT saboteur.

sabre [sabr] *nm* saber *Am*, sabre *Br*.

sabrer [sabre] [3] *vt* -1. *vieilli* [avec sabre] to cut down. -2. *fam* [biffer] to slash. -3. *fam* [critiquer] to slam. -4. *fam* [candidat] to fail.

sac [sak] *nm* -1. [gén] bag; [pour grains] sack; [contenu] bag, bagful, sack, sackful; ~ de couchage sleeping bag; ~ à dos rucksack; ~ à main handbag; ~ de voyage traveling *Am* OU travelling *Br* bag; vider son ~ *fig* to get it off one's chest. -2. *fam* [10 francs] 10 francs. -3. *littéraire* [pillage] sack; mettre à ~ [ville] to sack; [maison] to ransack.

saccade [sakad] *nf* jerk.

saccadé, -e [sakade] *adj* jerky.

saccage [sakaʒ] *nm* havoc.

saccager [sakaʒe] [17] *vt* -1. [piller] to sack. -2. [dévaster] to destroy.

saccharine [sakarin] *nf* saccharin.

SACEM, Sacem [sasɛm] (*abr de* **Société des auteurs, compositeurs et éditeurs de musique**) *nf society that safeguards the rights of French writers and musicians.*

sacerdoce [sasɛrdɔs] *nm* priesthood; *fig* vocation.

sacerdotal, -e, -aux [sasɛrdɔtal, o] *adj* priestly.

sachant *ppr* → **savoir**.

sache, saches *etc* → **savoir**.

sachet [saʃɛ] *nm* [de bonbons] bag; [de shampooing] sachet; ~ de thé teabag.

sacoche [sakɔʃ] *nf* -1. [de médecin, d'écolier] bag. -2. [de cycliste] saddlebag, pannier.

sac-poubelle [sakpubɛl] (*pl* **sacs-poubelle**) *nm* [petit] dustbin liner; [grand] garbage bag *Am*, rubbish bag *Br*.

sacquer, **saquer** [sake] [3] *vt fam* **-1.** [renvoyer] to fire, to sack *Br*. **-2.** [élève] to fail. **-3.** *loc*: **je ne peux pas le ~** I can't stand OU stomach him.

sacraliser [sakralize] [3] *vt* to hold as sacred.

sacre [sakr] *nm* [de roi] coronation; [d'évêque] consecration.

sacré, **-e** [sakre] *adj* **-1.** [gén] sacred. **-2.** RELIG [ordres, écritures] holy. **-3.** (*avant n*) *fam* [maudit] goddam *Am* (*avant n*), bloody *Br* (*avant n*). **-4.** (*avant n*) [considérable]: **un ~ ...** a hell of a ....

sacrement [sakrəmɑ̃] *nm* sacrament; **les derniers ~s** the last rites.

sacrément [sakremɑ̃] *adv fam vieilli* dashed.

sacrer [sakre] [3] *vt* **-1.** [roi] to crown; [évêque] to consecrate. **-2.** *fig* [déclarer] to hail.

sacrifice [sakrifis] *nm* sacrifice; **faire un ~/des ~s** *fig* to make a sacrifice/sacrifices.

sacrifié, **-e** [sakrifje] *adj* **-1.** [personne] sacrificed. **-2.** [prix] giveaway (*avant n*).

sacrifier [sakrifje] [9] ◇ *vt* [gén] to sacrifice; **~ qqch pour qqn/qqch** to sacrifice sthg for sb/sthg; **~ qqch pour faire qqch** to sacrifice sthg to do sthg; **~ qqn/qqch à** to sacrifice sb/sthg to. ◇ *vi littéraire* [se conformer]: **~ à** to conform to.

◆ **se sacrifier** *vp*: **se ~ à/pour** to sacrifice o.s. to/for.

sacrilège [sakrilɛʒ] ◇ *nm* sacrilege. ◇ *nmf* sacrilegious person. ◇ *adj* sacrilegious.

sacristain [sakristɛ̃] *nm* sacristan.

sacristie [sakristi] *nf* sacristy.

sacro-saint, **-e** [sakrosɛ̃, ɛt] *adj hum* sacrosanct.

sadique [sadik] ◇ *nmf* sadist. ◇ *adj* sadistic.

sadisme [sadism] *nm* sadism.

sadomasochiste [sadɔmazɔʃist] ◇ *nmf* sadomasochist. ◇ *adj* sadomasochistic.

safari [safari] *nm* safari; **~-photo** photographic safari.

SAFER, **Safer** [safɛr] (*abr de* **Société d'aménagement foncier et d'établissement régional**) *nf agency entitled to buy land and earmark it for agricultural use.*

safran [safrɑ̃] ◇ *nm* **-1.** [épice] saffron. **-2.** NAVIG rudder blade. ◇ *adj inv* [couleur] saffron.

saga [saga] *nf* saga.

sagace [sagas] *adj* sagacious.

sagacité [sagasite] *nf* sagacity.

sagaie [sagɛ] *nf* assegai.

sage [saʒ] ◇ *adj* **-1.** [personne, conseil] wise, sensible. **-2.** [enfant, chien] good. **-3.** [goûts] modest; [propos, vêtement] sober. ◇ *nm* wise man, sage.

sage-femme [saʒfam] (*pl* **sages-femmes**) *nf* midwife.

sagement [saʒmɑ̃] *adv* **-1.** [avec bon sens] wisely, sensibly. **-2.** [docilement] like a good girl/boy.

sagesse [saʒɛs] *nf* **-1.** [bon sens] wisdom, good sense. **-2.** [docilité] good behavior *Am* OU behaviour *Br*.

Sagittaire [saʒitɛr] *nm* ASTROL Sagittarius; **être ~** to be (a) Sagittarius.

sagouin, **-e** [sagwɛ̃, in] *nm*, *f fam* slob.

◆ **sagouin** *nm* ZOOL squirrel monkey.

Sahara [saara] *nm*: **le ~** the Sahara; **au ~** in the Sahara.

saharien, **-ienne** [saarjɛ̃, jɛn] *adj* Saharan.

◆ **saharienne** *nf* safari jacket.

◆ **Saharien**, **-ienne** *nm*, *f* Saharan.

saignant, **-e** [sɛɲɑ̃, ɑ̃t] *adj* **-1.** [blessure] bleeding. **-2.** [viande] rare, underdone. **-3.** *fam fig* [critique] hurtful.

saignée [seɲe] *nf* **-1.** *vieilli & MÉD* bloodletting, bleeding. **-2.** [pli du bras] crook of the arm. **-3.** [sillon - dans sol] ditch; [- dans mur] groove.

saignement [sɛɲmɑ̃] *nm* bleeding.

saigner [seɲe] [4] ◇ *vt* **-1.** [malade, animal] to bleed. **-2.** [financièrement]: **~ qqn (à blanc)** to bleed sb (white). ◇ *vi* to bleed; **je saigne du nez** my nose is bleeding, I've got a nosebleed.

◆ **se saigner** *vp*: **se ~ pour qqn** *fig* to bleed o.s. white for sb.

saillant, **-e** [sajɑ̃, ɑ̃t] *adj* **-1.** [proéminent] projecting, protruding; [muscles] bulging; [pommettes] prominent. **-2.** *fig* [événement] salient, outstanding.

sailli, **-e** [saji] *pp* → **saillir¹**, **saillir²**.

saillie [saji] *nf* **-1.** [avancée] projection; **en ~** projecting. **-2.** ZOOL covering.

saillir¹ [sajir] [50] *vi* [balcon] to project, to protrude; [muscles] to bulge.

saillir² [sajir] [32] *vt* ZOOL to cover.

sain, **-e** [sɛ̃, sɛn] *adj* **-1.** [gén] healthy; **~ et sauf** safe and sound. **-2.** [lecture] wholesome. **-3.** [fruit] fit to eat; [mur, gestion] sound.

saindoux [sɛ̃du] *nm* lard.

sainement [sɛnmɑ̃] *adv* **-1.** [vivre] healthily. **-2.** [raisonner] soundly.

saint, **-e** [sɛ̃, sɛ̃t] ◇ *adj* **-1.** [sacré] holy; **le Saint-Esprit** the Holy Spirit; **la Saint-Sylvestre** New Year's Eve; **la Sainte Vierge**

the Blessed Virgin. **-2.** [pieux] saintly. **-3.** [extrême]: **avoir une ~e horreur de qqch** to detest sthg. ◇ *nm, f* saint; **le ~ des ~s** *fig* the holy of holies.

saint-bernard [sɛbɛrnar] *nm inv* **-1.** [chien] St Bernard. **-2.** *fig* [personne] good Samaritan.

saintement [sɛ̃tmɑ̃] *adv*: **vivre ~** to lead a saintly life.

saint-émilion [sɛ̃temiljɔ̃] *nm inv red wine from the Bordeaux region.*

sainte-nitouche [sɛ̃tnituʃ] (*pl* **saintes-nitouches**) *nf péj*: **c'est une ~** butter wouldn't melt in her mouth.

sainteté [sɛ̃te] *nf* holiness.
◆ **Sainteté** *nf*: **Sa Sainteté** His Holiness.

saint-glinglin [sɛ̃glɛ̃glɛ̃]
◆ **à la saint-glinglin** *loc adv fam* till Doomsday.

saint-honoré [sɛ̃tɔnɔre] *nm inv choux pastry ring filled with confectioner's custard.*

Saint-Marin [sɛ̃marɛ̃] *n* San Marino; **à ~ in** San Marino.

saint-marinais, -e [sɛ̃marinɛ, ɛz] *adj* of/from San Marino.
◆ **Saint-Marinais, -e** *nm, f* native OU inhabitant of San Marino.

Saint-Père [sɛ̃pɛr] *nm* Holy Father.

Saint-Pétersbourg [sɛ̃petɛrsbur] *n* Saint Petersburg.

saint-pierre [sɛ̃pjɛr] *nm inv* John Dory.

Saint-Pierre [sɛ̃pjɛr] *n*: **la basilique ~** Saint Peter's Basilica.

Saint-Siège [sɛ̃sjɛʒ] *nm*: **le ~** the Holy See.

sais, sait *etc* → **savoir**.

saisie [sezi] *nf* **-1.** FISC & JUR distraint, seizure. **-2.** INFORM input; **erreur de ~** input error; **~ de données** data capture.

saisir [sezir] [32] *vt* **-1.** [empoigner] to take hold of; [avec force] to seize; **~ qqn à la gorge** to seize OU grab sb by the throat. **-2.** FIN & JUR to seize, to distrain. **-3.** INFORM to capture. **-4.** [comprendre] to grasp. **-5.** [suj: sensation, émotion] to grip, to seize. **-6.** [surprendre]: **être saisi par** to be struck by. **-7.** CULIN to seal.
◆ **se saisir** *vp*: **se ~ de qqn/qqch** to seize sb/sthg, to grab sb/sthg.

saisissant, -e [sezisɑ̃, ɑ̃t] *adj* **-1.** [spectacle] gripping; [ressemblance] striking. **-2.** [froid] biting.

saisissement [sezismɑ̃] *nm* [émotion] emotion.

saison [sɛzɔ̃] *nf* season; **la belle ~** the summer months (*pl*); **c'est la bonne/mauvaise ~ pour** it's the right/wrong time of year for; **la ~ des amours** the mating season; **en/hors ~** in/out of season; **la haute/basse/morte ~** the high/low/off season.

saisonnalité [sɛzɔnalite] *nf* seasonal nature.

saisonnier, -ière [sɛzɔnje, jɛr] ◇ *adj* seasonal. ◇ *nm, f* seasonal worker.

saké [sake] *nm* sake.

salace [salas] *adj* salacious.

salade [salad] *nf* **-1.** [plante] lettuce. **-2.** [plat] (green) salad; **~ de fruits** fruit salad; **~ niçoise** *salad containing anchovies and tuna.* **-3.** *fam fig* [méli-mélo] mess. **-4.** *fam fig* [baratin] story; **raconter des ~s** to tell stories; **vendre sa ~** to lay it on thick.

saladier [saladje] *nm* salad bowl.

salaire [salɛr] *nm* **-1.** [rémunération] salary, wage; **~ brut/net/de base** gross/net/basic salary, gross/net/basic wage. **-2.** *fig* [récompense] reward.

salaison [salɛzɔ̃] *nf* **-1.** [procédé] salting. **-2.** [aliment] salted food.

salamalecs [salamalɛk] *nmpl fam péj* bowing and scraping (*U*).

salamandre [salamɑ̃dr] *nf* [animal] salamander.

salami [salami] *nm* salami.

salant [salɑ̃] → **marais**.

salarial, -e, -iaux [salarjal, jo] *adj* wage (*avant n*).

salariat [salarja] *nm* **-1.** [système] paid employment. **-2.** [salariés] wage-earners (*pl*).

salarié, -e [salarje] ◇ *adj* **-1.** [personne] wage-earning. **-2.** [travail] paid. ◇ *nm, f* salaried employee.

salaud [salo] *vulg* ◇ *nm* bastard. ◇ *adj m* shitty.

sale [sal] *adj* **-1.** [linge, mains] dirty; [couleur] dirty, dingy. **-2.** (*avant n*) [type, gueule, coup] nasty; [tour, histoire] dirty; [bête, temps] filthy.

salé, -e [sale] *adj* **-1.** [eau, saveur] salty; [beurre] salted; [viande, poisson] salt (*avant n*), salted. **-2.** *fig* [histoire] spicy. **-3.** *fam fig* [addition, facture] steep.
◆ **salé** *nm* **-1.** [aliment salé] savory *Am* OU savoury *Br* food. **-2.** [porc] salt pork.

salement [salmɑ̃] *adv* **-1.** [malproprement] dirtily, disgustingly. **-2.** *fam* [très] damn, bloody *Br*.

saler [sale] [3] *vt* **-1.** [gén] to salt. **-2.** *fam fig* [note] to bump up.

saleté [salte] *nf* **-1.** [malpropreté] dirtiness, filthiness. **-2.** [crasse] dirt (*U*), filth (*U*); **faire des ~s** to make a mess. **-3.** *fam* [pacotille] junk (*U*), rubbish (*U*). **-4.** *fam* [maladie] bug. **-5.** [obscénité] dirty thing, obscenity; **il**

m'a dit des ~s he used obscenities to me. **-6.** [action] disgusting thing; **faire une ~ à qqn** to play a dirty trick on sb. **-7.** *fam péj* [personne] nasty piece of work.

salière [saljɛr] *nf* saltcellar; **~-poivrière** cruet.

salin, -e [salɛ̃, in] *adj* saline; [eau] salt (*avant n*).

salir [salir] [32] *vt* **-1.** [linge, mains] to (make) dirty, to soil. **-2.** *fig* [réputation] to sully.
◆ **se salir** *vp* to get dirty.

salissant, -e [salisɑ̃, ɑ̃t] *adj* **-1.** [tissu] easily soiled. **-2.** [travail] dirty, messy.

salissure [salisyr] *nf* stain.

salivaire [salivɛr] *adj* salivary.

salive [saliv] *nf* saliva; **dépenser beaucoup de ~** *fig* to talk nineteen to the dozen; **perdre sa ~** *fig* to waste one's breath.

saliver [salive] [3] *vi* to salivate.

salle [sal] *nf* **-1.** [pièce] room; **~ d'attente** waiting room; **~ de bains** bathroom; **~ de cinéma** cinema; **~ d'eau, ~ de douches** shower room; **~ d'embarquement** departure lounge; **~ des machines** engine room; **~ à manger** dining room; **~ non-fumeur** ≃ no smoking area; **~ d'opération** operating room *Am* OU theatre *Br*; **~ de séjour** living room; **~ de spectacle** theater *Am*, theatre *Br*; **~ des ventes** salesroom *Am*, saleroom *Br*. **-2.** [de spectacle] auditorium. **-3.** [public] audience, house; **jouer à ~ pleine** to play to a full house; **faire ~ comble** to have a full house.

salmigondis [salmigɔ̃di] *nm* hodgepodge *Am*, hotchpotch *Br*.

salmis [salmi] *nm half-roasted game or poultry finished in wine sauce.*

salmonellose [salmɔneloz] *nf* salmonella poisoning.

salon [salɔ̃] *nm* **-1.** [de maison] living room, lounge *Br*. **-2.** [commerce]: **~ de coiffure** hairdressing salon, hairdresser's; **~ de thé** tearoom. **-3.** [foire-exposition] show.

salopard [salɔpar] *nm tfam* bastard.

salope [salɔp] *nf vulg* bitch.

saloper [salɔpe] [3] *vt fam* to mess up.

saloperie [salɔpri] *nf fam* **-1.** [pacotille] rubbish (*U*). **-2.** [maladie] bug. **-3.** [saleté] junk (*U*), rubbish (*U*); **faire des ~s** to make a mess. **-4.** [action] dirty trick; **faire des ~s à qqn** to play dirty tricks on sb. **-5.** [propos] dirty comment.

salopette [salɔpɛt] *nf* [d'ouvrier] overalls (*pl*); [à bretelles] dungarees (*pl*).

salpêtre [salpɛtr] *nm* saltpeter *Am*, saltpetre *Br*.

salsa [salsa] *nf* salsa.

salsifis [salsifi] *nm* salsify.

SALT [salt] (*abr de* **Strategic Arms Limitation Talks**) SALT.

saltimbanque [saltɛ̃bɑ̃k] *nmf* acrobat.

salubre [salybr] *adj* healthy.

salubrité [salybrite] *nf* healthiness; **la ~ publique** public health.

saluer [salɥe] [7] *vt* **-1.** [accueillir] to greet. **-2.** [dire au revoir à] to take one's leave of. **-3.** MIL & *fig* to salute.
◆ **se saluer** *vp* to say hello/goodbye (to one another).

salut [saly] ◇ *nm* **-1.** [de la main] wave; [de la tête] nod; [propos] greeting. **-2.** MIL salute. **-3.** [d'acteur] bow. **-4.** [sauvegarde] safety. **-5.** RELIG salvation. ◇ *interj fam* [bonjour] hi!; [au revoir] bye!, see you!

salutaire [salytɛr] *adj* **-1.** [conseil, expérience] salutary. **-2.** [remède, repos] beneficial.

salutation [salytasjɔ̃] *nf littéraire* salutation, greeting.
◆ **salutations** *nfpl*: **veuillez agréer, Monsieur, mes ~s distinguées** OU **mes sincères ~s** *sout* yours faithfully, yours sincerely.

salutiste [salytist] *nmf & adj* Salvationist.

Salvador [salvadɔr] *nm*: **le ~** El Salvador; **au ~** in El Salvador.

salvadorien, -ienne [salvadɔrjɛ̃, jɛn] *adj* Salvadorian.
◆ **Salvadorien, -ienne** *nm, f* Salvadorian.

salve [salv] *nf* salvo.

Salzbourg [salzbur] *n* Salzburg.

samaritain, -e [samaritɛ̃, ɛn] *adj* Samaritan.
◆ **samaritain** *nm Helv* first-aid worker.

samba [sũba] *nf* samba.

samedi [samdi] *nm* Saturday; **nous sommes partis ~** we left on Saturday; **~ 13 septembre** Saturday 13th September; **~ dernier/prochain** last/next Saturday; **~ matin/midi/après-midi/soir** Saturday morning/lunchtime/afternoon/evening; **de/du ~** Saturday (*avant n*); **le ~ d'avant** the Saturday before; **le ~** on Saturdays; **~ en huit** a week on Saturday, Saturday week; **~ en quinze** two weeks on Saturday; **un ~ sur deux** every other Saturday; **nous sommes** OU **c'est ~** it's Saturday (today); **tous les ~s** every Saturday.

Samoa [samɔa] *n* Samoa; **à ~** in Samoa.

samoan, -e [samɔã, an] *adj* Samoan.
◆ **Samoan, -e** *nm, f* Samoan.

samouraï, samuraï [samuraj] *nm* samurai.

samovar [samɔvar] *nm* samovar.

SAMU, Samu [samy] (*abr de* **Service d'aide médicale d'urgence**) *nm French ambulance* *and emergency service,* ≃ Paramedics *Am,* ≃ Ambulance Brigade *Br.*

samuraï = **samouraï.**

sanatorium [sanatɔrjɔm] *nm* sanatorium.

sanctifier [sɑ̃ktifje] [9] *vt* **-1.** [rendre saint] to sanctify. **-2.** [révérer] to hallow.

sanction [sɑ̃ksjɔ̃] *nf* sanction; *fig* [conséquence] penalty, price; **prendre des ~s contre** to impose sanctions on.

sanctionner [sɑ̃ksjɔne] [3] *vt* to sanction.

sanctuaire [sɑ̃ktɥɛr] *nm* **-1.** [d'église] sanctuary. **-2.** [lieu saint] shrine.

sandale [sɑ̃dal] *nf* sandal.

sandalette [sɑ̃dalɛt] *nf* sandal.

Sandow® [sɑ̃do] *nm* **-1.** [attache] elastic cable *(for securing luggage etc).* **-2.** AÉRON catapult.

sandwich [sɑ̃dwitʃ] *(pl* **sandwiches** OU **sandwichs)** *nm* sandwich; **être pris en ~ entre** *fam* to be sandwiched between.

sang [sɑ̃] *nm* blood; **en ~** bleeding; **pur-~** thoroughbred; **dans le ~** *fig* in the blood; **se faire du mauvais ~** OU **un ~ d'encre** *fig* to get really worried OU upset; **suer ~ et eau** *fig* to sweat blood.

sang-froid [sɑ̃frwa] *nm inv* calm; **de ~** in cold blood; **perdre/garder son ~** to lose/to keep one's head.

sanglant, -e [sɑ̃glɑ̃, ɑ̃t] *adj* bloody.

sangle [sɑ̃gl] *nf* strap; [de selle] girth.
◆ **sangles** *nfpl* webbing (U).

sangler [sɑ̃gle] [3] *vt* [attacher] to strap; [cheval] to girth.

sanglier [sɑ̃glije] *nm* boar.

sanglot [sɑ̃glo] *nm* sob; **éclater en ~s** to burst into sobs.

sangloter [sɑ̃glɔte] [3] *vi* to sob.

sangria [sɑ̃grija] *nf* sangria.

sangsue [sɑ̃sy] *nf* leech; *fig* [personne] bloodsucker.

sanguin, -e [sɑ̃gɛ̃, in] *adj* **-1.** ANAT blood *(avant n).* **-2.** [rouge - visage] ruddy; [- orange] blood *(avant n).* **-3.** [emporté] quicktempered.
◆ **sanguine** *nf* **-1.** [dessin] red chalk drawing. **-2.** [fruit] blood orange.

sanguinaire [sɑ̃ginɛr] *adj* **-1.** [tyran] bloodthirsty. **-2.** [lutte] bloody.

sanguinolent, -e [sɑ̃ginɔlɑ̃, ɑ̃t] *adj* stained with blood.

Sanisette® [sanizɛt] *nf automatic public toilet,* superloo *Br.*

sanitaire [sanitɛr] ◇ *nm* bathroom fittings and plumbing. ◇ *adj* **-1.** [service, mesure] health *(avant n).* **-2.** [installation, appareil] bathroom *(avant n).*
◆ **sanitaires** *nmpl* toilets and showers.

sans [sɑ̃] ◇ *prép* without; **~ argent** without any money; **~ faire un effort** without making an effort. ◇ *adv*: **passe-moi mon manteau, je ne veux pas sortir ~** pass me my coat, I don't want to go out without it.
◆ **sans que** *loc conj*: **~ que vous le sachiez** without your knowing.

sans-abri [sɑ̃zabri] *nmf inv* homeless person.

San Salvador [sɑ̃salvadɔr] *n* San Salvador.

sanscrit [sɑ̃skri] *nm* Sanskrit.

sans-emploi [sɑ̃zɑ̃plwa] *nmf inv* unemployed person.

sans-gêne [sɑ̃ʒɛn] ◇ *nm inv* [qualité] rudeness, lack of consideration. ◇ *nmf inv* [personne] rude OU inconsiderate person. ◇ *adj inv* rude, inconsiderate.

sans-le-sou [sɑ̃lsu] *nmf inv fam* person who is broke OU hard up.

sans-logis [sɑ̃lɔʒi] *nmf inv* homeless person.

sansonnet [sɑ̃sɔnɛ] *nm* starling.

santal [sɑ̃tal] *nm* sandalwood.

santé [sɑ̃te] *nf* health; **recouvrer la ~** to get one's health back; **~ de fer** strong OU iron constitution; **à ta/votre ~!** cheers!, good health!; **boire à la ~ de qqn** to drink sb's health, to toast sb.

santiag [sɑ̃tjag] *nf* cowboy boot.

Santiago [sɑ̃tjago] *n* Santiago.

santon [sɑ̃tɔ̃] *nm figure placed in Christmas crib.*

Santorin [sɑ̃tɔrɛ̃] *n* Santorini.

São Paulo [saopolo] *n* **-1.** [ville] São Paulo. **-2.** [État]: **l'État de ~** São Paulo (State).

saoudien, -ienne [saudjɛ̃, jɛn] *adj* Saudi (Arabian).
◆ **Saoudien, -ienne** *nm, f* Saudi (Arabian).

saoul = **soûl.**

saouler = **soûler.**

saper [sape] [3] *vt* to undermine.
◆ **se saper** *vp fam* to dress o.s. up.

sapeur [sapœr] *nm* sapper.

sapeur-pompier [sapœrpɔ̃pje] *(pl* **sapeurs-pompiers)** *nm* fireman, fire fighter.

saphir [safir] *nm* sapphire.

sapin [sapɛ̃] *nm* **-1.** [arbre] fir, firtree; **~ de Noël** Christmas tree. **-2.** [bois] fir, deal *Br.*

sapinière [sapinjɛr] *nf* fir forest.

sapristi [sapristi] *interj fam* goodness me!, my goodness!

saquer = **sacquer**.

S.A.R. (*abr de* **Son Altesse royale**) H.R.H.

sarabande [sarabɑ̃d] *nf* **-1.** [danse] saraband. **-2.** *fam* [vacarme] din, racket.

Sarajevo [saraʒɛvo] *n* Sarajevo.

sarbacane [sarbakan] *nf* [arme] blowgun *Am*, blowpipe *Br*; [jouet] peashooter.

sarcasme [sarkasm] *nm* sarcasm.

sarcastique [sarkastik] *adj* sarcastic.

sarcler [sarkle] [3] *vt* to weed.

sarcloir [sarklwar] *nm* hoe.

sarcophage [sarkɔfaʒ] *nm* sarcophagus.

Sardaigne [sardɛɲ] *nf*: **la ~** Sardinia.

sarde [sard] *adj* Sardinian.

◆ **Sarde** *nmf* Sardinian.

sardine [sardin] *nf* sardine; **~s à l'huile** sardines in oil; **être serrés comme des ~s** *fig* to be packed like sardines.

sardinerie [sardinri] *nf* sardine cannery.

sardonique [sardɔnik] *adj* sardonic.

SARL, Sarl (*abr de* **société à responsabilité limitée**) *nf* limited liability company; Leduc, **~** ≃ Leduc Ltd.

sarment [sarmɑ̃] *nm* **-1.** [de vigne] shoot. **-2.** [tige] stem.

sarrasin, -e [sarazɛ̃, in] *adj* Saracen.

◆ **sarrasin** *nm* buckwheat.

◆ **Sarrasin, -e** *nm, f* Saracen.

sarrau [saro] (*pl* **-s** OU **-x**) *nm* smock.

sarriette [sarjet] *nf* savory.

sas [sas] *nm* **-1.** AÉRON & NAVIG airlock. **-2.** [d'écluse] lock. **-3.** [tamis] sieve.

S.A.S. (*abr de* **Son Altesse Sérénissime**) H.S.H.

satané, -e [satane] *adj* (*avant n*) *fam* damned.

satanique [satanik] *adj* satanic.

satellisation [satelizasjɔ̃] *nf* **-1.** [de fusée] putting into orbit. **-2.** [de pays] becoming a satellite.

satelliser [satelize] [3] *vt* **-1.** [fusée] to put into orbit. **-2.** [pays] to make a satellite.

satellite [satelit] ◇ *nm* satellite; **par ~** by satellite; **~-relais** telecommunications satellite. ◇ *adj* satellite (*avant n*).

satiété [sasjete] *nf*: **à ~** [boire, manger] one's fill; [répéter] ad nauseam.

satin [satɛ̃] *nm* satin.

satiné, -e [satine] ◇ *adj* satin (*avant n*); [peau] satiny-smooth. ◇ *nm* satin-like quality.

satinette [satinet] *nf* **-1.** [coton et soie] satinet. **-2.** [coton seul] sateen.

satire [satir] *nf* satire.

satirique [satirik] *adj* satirical.

satisfaction [satisfaksjɔ̃] *nf* satisfaction.

satisfaire [satisfer] [109] *vt* to satisfy; **~ à** [condition, revendication] to meet, to satisfy; [engagement] to fulfil.

◆ **se satisfaire** *vp*: **se ~ de** to be satisfied with.

satisfaisait, satisfaisions *etc* → **satisfaire**.

satisfaisant, -e [satisfəzɑ̃, ɑ̃t] *adj* **-1.** [travail] satisfactory. **-2.** [expérience] satisfying.

satisfait, -e [satisfe, ɛt] ◇ *pp* → **satisfaire**. ◇ *adj* satisfied; **être ~ de** to be satisfied with; **«~ ou remboursé»** "satisfaction guaranteed or your money back".

satisfasse, satisfasses *etc* → **satisfaire**.

saturation [satyrasjɔ̃] *nf* saturation.

saturé, -e [satyre] *adj*: **~ (de)** saturated (with).

saturer [satyre] [3] *vt*: **~ qqch (de)** to saturate sthg (with).

saturne [satyrn] *nm vieilli* lead.

◆ **Saturne** *nf* ASTRON Saturn.

satyre [satir] *nm* satyr; *fig* sex maniac.

sauce [sos] *nf* **-1.** CULIN sauce; **en ~** in a sauce; **~ hollandaise** hollandaise sauce; **~ tartare** tartare sauce; **~ tomate/blanche/piquante** tomato/white/spicy sauce. **-2.** *fig* [accompagnement] presentation; **mettre qqn à toutes les ~s** to use sb as a dogsbody.

saucer [sose] [16] *vt* **-1.** [assiette] to wipe. **-2.** *fam* [personne]: **se faire ~** to get soaked.

saucière [sosjer] *nf* sauceboat.

saucisse [sosis] *nf* **-1.** CULIN sausage; **~ de Francfort** frankfurter; **~ sèche** dried sausage. **-2.** *fam* AÉRON & *vieilli* barrage balloon.

saucisson [sosisɔ̃] *nm* slicing sausage.

saucissonner [sosisɔne] [3] ◇ *vi fam* to have a picnic. ◇ *vt* **-1.** [colis] to truss up. **-2.** [baguette] slice up.

sauf¹, sauve [sof, sov] *adj* [personne] safe, unharmed; *fig* [honneur] saved, intact.

sauf² [sof] *prép* **-1.** [à l'exclusion de] except, apart from. **-2.** [sous réserve de] barring; **~ que** except (that).

sauf-conduit [sofkɔ̃dɥi] (*pl* **sauf-conduits**) *nm* safe-conduct.

sauge [soʒ] *nf* **-1.** CULIN sage. **-2.** [plante ornementale] salvia.

saugrenu, -e [sogrəny] *adj* ridiculous, nonsensical.

saule [sol] *nm* willow; **~ pleureur** weeping willow.

saumâtre [somatʀ] *adj* **-1.** [eau] brackish. **-2.** *fig* [plaisanterie] distasteful.

saumon [somɔ̃] ◇ *nm* salmon. ◇ *adj inv* salmon pink.

saumoné, -e [somɔne] *adj* salmon (*avant n*).

saumure [somyʀ] *nf* brine.

sauna [sona] *nm* sauna.

saupoudrer [sopudʀe] [3] *vt*: ~ qqch de to sprinkle sthg with.

saupoudreuse [sopudʀøz] *nf* dredger.

saur [sɔʀ] → **hareng**.

saurai, sauras *etc* → **savoir**.

saurien [soʀjɛ̃] *nm* saurian.

saut [so] *nm* [bond] leap, jump; ~ en hauteur SPORT high jump; ~ en longueur SPORT long jump, broad jump *Am*; ~ de page INFORM page break; faire un ~ chez qqn *fig* to pop in and see sb.

saute [sot] *nf* sudden change; avoir des ~s d'humeur to have mood swings, to be temperamental.

sauté, -e [sote] *adj* sautéed.

◆ **sauté** *nm*: ~ de veau sautéed veal.

saute-mouton [sotmutɔ̃] *nm inv*: jouer à ~ to play leapfrog.

sauter [sote] [3] ◇ *vi* **-1.** [bondir] to jump, to leap; ~ à la corde to skip; ~ d'un sujet à l'autre *fig* to jump from one subject to another; ~ de joie *fig* to jump for joy; ~ au cou de qqn *fig* to throw one's arms around sb. **-2.** [exploser] to blow up; [fusible] to blow. **-3.** [partir - bouchon] to fly out; [- serrure] to burst off; [- bouton] to fly off; [- chaîne de vélo] to come off. **-4.** *fam* [employé] to get the sack. **-5.** [être annulé] to be cancelled. **-6.** CULIN: faire ~ qqch to sauté sthg. **-7.** *loc*: et que ça saute! *fam* and get a move on!

◇ *vt* **-1.** [fossé, obstacle] to jump OU leap over. **-2.** *fig* [page, repas] to skip. **-3.** *vulg* [personne]: ~ qqn to have it off with sb.

sauterelle [sotʀɛl] *nf* **-1.** ZOOL grasshopper. **-2.** *fam fig* [personne] beanpole.

sauterie [sotʀi] *nf vieilli* do, party.

sauternes [sotɛʀn] *nm sweet dessert wine*.

sauteur, -euse [sotœʀ, øz] ◇ *adj* [insecte] jumping (*avant n*). ◇ *nm, f* [athlète] jumper.

◆ **sauteur** *nm* [cheval] jumper.

◆ **sauteuse** *nf* CULIN frying pan.

sautiller [sotije] [3] *vi* to hop.

sautoir [sotwaʀ] *nm* **-1.** [bijou] chain; ~ de perles string of pearls; porter qqch en ~ to wear sthg on a chain round one's neck. **-2.** SPORT jumping area.

sauvage [sovaʒ] ◇ *nmf* **-1.** [solitaire] recluse. **-2.** *péj* [brute, indigène] savage. ◇ *adj* **-1.**

[plante, animal] wild. **-2.** [farouche - animal familier] shy, timid; [- personne] unsociable. **-3.** [conduite, haine] savage.

sauvagement [sovaʒmɑ̃] *adv* savagely.

sauvageon, -onne [sovaʒɔ̃, ɔn] *nm, f* little savage.

sauvagerie [sovaʒʀi] *nf* **-1.** [férocité] brutality, savagery. **-2.** [insociabilité] unsociableness.

sauvagine [sovaʒin] *nf littéraire* wildfowl.

sauve → **sauf**.

sauvegarde [sovgaʀd] *nf* **-1.** [protection] safeguard. **-2.** INFORM saving; [copie] backup.

sauvegarder [sovgaʀde] [3] *vt* **-1.** [protéger] to safeguard. **-2.** INFORM to save; [copier] to back up.

sauve-qui-peut [sovkipø] ◇ *nm inv* [débandade] stampede. ◇ *interj* every man for himself!

sauver [sove] [3] *vt* **-1.** [gén] to save; ~ qqn/qqch de to save sb/sthg from, to rescue sb/sthg from; ~ qqn de MÉD to cure sb of. **-2.** [navire, biens] to salvage.

◆ **se sauver** *vp*: se ~ (de) to run away (from); [prisonnier] to escape (from).

sauvetage [sovtaʒ] *nm* **-1.** [de personne] rescue. **-2.** [de navire, biens] salvage.

sauveteur [sovtœʀ] *nm* rescuer.

sauvette [sovɛt]

◆ **à la sauvette** *loc adv* hurriedly, at great speed.

sauveur [sovœʀ] *nm* savior *Am*, saviour *Br*.

SAV [sav] (*abr de* service après-vente) *nm* after-sales service.

savamment [savamɑ̃] *adv* **-1.** [avec érudition] learnedly. **-2.** [avec habileté] skilfully, cleverly.

savane [savan] *nf* savanna.

savant, -e [savɑ̃, ɑ̃t] *adj* **-1.** [érudit] scholarly. **-2.** [habile] skilful, clever. **-3.** [animal] performing (*avant n*).

◆ **savant** *nm* scientist.

savarin [savaʀɛ̃] *nm ring-shaped cake containing rum*.

savate [savat] *nf* **-1.** [pantoufle] worn-out slipper; [soulier] worn-out shoe. **-2.** SPORT kick boxing. **-3.** *fam* [personne] clumsy oaf.

saveur [savœʀ] *nf* flavor *Am*, flavour *Br*; *fig* savor *Am*, savour *Br*.

savoir [savwaʀ] [59] ◇ *vt* **-1.** [gén] to know; faire ~ qqch à qqn to tell sb sthg, to inform sb of sthg; si j'avais su ... had I but known ..., if I had only known ...; sans le ~ unconsciously, without being aware of it; en ~ long sur qqn/qqch to know a lot

about sb/sthg; **tu (ne) peux pas** ~ *fam* you have no idea; **pas que je sache** not as far as I know; **(ne pas)** ~ **de quoi il retourne** (not) to know what it's all about. **-2.** [être capable de] to know how to; **sais-tu conduire?** can you drive?
◇ *nm* learning.
◆ **à savoir** *loc conj* namely, that is.

savoir-faire [savwarfɛr] *nm inv* know-how, expertise.

savoir-vivre [savwarvivr] *nm inv* good manners *(pl)*.

savon [savɔ̃] *nm* **-1.** [matière] soap; [pain] cake OU bar of soap. **-2.** *fam* [réprimande] telling-off; **passer un** ~ **à qqn** to give sb a telling-off.

savonner [savɔne] [3] *vt* **-1.** [linge] to soap. **-2.** *fam* [enfant] to tell off.
◆ **se savonner** *vp* to soap o.s.

savonnette [savɔnɛt] *nf* guest soap.

savonneux, -euse [savɔnø, øz] *adj* soapy.

savourer [savure] [3] *vt* to savor *Am*, to savour *Br*.

savoureux, -euse [savurø, øz] *adj* **-1.** [mets] tasty. **-2.** *fig* [anecdote] juicy.

savoyard, -e [savwajar, ard] *adj* of/from Savoy.
◆ **Savoyard, -e** *nm, f* native OU inhabitant of Savoy.

saxophone [saksɔfɔn] *nm* saxophone.

saxophoniste [saksɔfɔnist] *nmf* saxophonist, saxophone player.

saynète [sɛnɛt] *nf* playlet.

SBB *(abr de* **Schweizerische Bundesbahn)** *Swiss federal railways.*

sbire [sbir] *nm péj* henchman, minion.

sc. *(abr de* **scène)** sc.

s/c *(abr de* **sous couvert de)** c/o.

scabreux, -euse [skabrø, øz] *adj* **-1.** [propos] shocking, indecent. **-2.** [entreprise] risky.

scalp [skalp] *nm* **-1.** [action] scalping. **-2.** [trophée] scalp.

scalpel [skalpɛl] *nm* scalpel.

scalper [skalpe] [3] *vt* to scalp.

scampi [skãpi] *nmpl* scampi *(U).*

scandale [skãdal] *nm* **-1.** [fait choquant] scandal. **-2.** [indignation] disgust. **-3.** [tapage] scene; **faire du** OU **un** ~ to make a scene.

scandaleusement [skãdaløzmã] *adj* scandalously, outrageously.

scandaleux, -euse [skãdalø, øz] *adj* scandalous, outrageous.

scandaliser [skãdalize] [3] *vt* to shock, to scandalize.

◆ **se scandaliser** *vp* to be shocked, to be scandalized.

scander [skãde] [3] *vt* **-1.** [vers] to scan. **-2.** [slogan] to chant.

scandinave [skãdinav] *adj* Scandinavian.
◆ **Scandinave** *nmf* Scandinavian.

Scandinavie [skãdinavi] *nf*: **la** ~ Scandinavia.

scanner[1] [skane] [4] *vt* to scan.

scanner[2] [skanɛr] *nm* scanner.

scaphandre [skafãdr] *nm* **-1.** [de plongeur] diving suit; ~ **autonome** aqualung. **-2.** [d'astronaute] spacesuit.

scaphandrier [skafãdrije] *nm* deep-sea diver.

scarabée [skarabe] *nm* beetle, scarab.

scarlatine [skarlatin] *nf* scarlet fever.

scarole [skarɔl] *nf* endive.

scatologique [skatɔlɔʒik] *adj* scatological.

sceau, -x [so] *nm* seal; *fig* stamp, hallmark; **sous le** ~ **du secret** *fig* under the seal of secrecy.

scélérat, -e [selera, at] ◇ *adj* wicked. ◇ *nm, f* villain; *péj* rogue, rascal.

sceller [sele] [4] *vt* **-1.** [gén] to seal. **-2.** CONSTR [fixer] to embed.

scellés [sele] *nmpl* seals; **sous** ~ sealed.

scénario [senarjo] *nm* **-1.** [canevas] scenario. **-2.** [découpage, synopsis] screenplay, script. **-3.** *fig* [rituel] pattern.

scénariste [senarist] *nmf* scriptwriter.

scène [sɛn] *nf* **-1.** [gén] scene; ~ **de ménage** domestic row. **-2.** [estrade] stage; **entrée en** ~ THÉÂTRE entrance; *fig* appearance; **mettre en** ~ THÉÂTRE to stage; CIN to direct.

scénique [senik] *adj* theatrical.

scepticisme [sɛptisism] *nm* skepticism *Am*, scepticism *Br*.

sceptique [sɛptik] ◇ *nmf* skeptic *Am*, sceptic *Br*. ◇ *adj* **-1.** [incrédule] skeptical *Am*, sceptical *Br*. **-2.** PHILO skeptic *Am*, sceptic *Br*.

sceptre [sɛptr] *nm* scepter *Am*, sceptre *Br*.

SCH *(abr de* **schilling)** S, Sch.

schah, shah [ʃa] *nm* shah.

schéma [ʃema] *nm* **-1.** [diagramme] diagram. **-2.** [résumé] outline.

schématique [ʃematik] *adj* **-1.** [dessin] diagrammatic. **-2.** [interprétation, exposé] simplified.

schématiquement [ʃematikmã] *adv* **-1.** [par dessin] diagrammatically. **-2.** [en résumé] briefly.

schématisation [ʃematizasjɔ̃] *nf* **-1.** [présentation graphique] diagrammatic representation. **-2.** *péj* [généralisation] oversimplification.

schématiser [ʃematize] [3] *vt* **-1.** [présenter en schéma] to represent diagrammatically. **-2.** *péj* [généraliser] to oversimplify.

schisme [ʃism] *nm* **-1.** RELIG schism. **-2.** [d'opinion] split.

schiste [ʃist] *nm* shale.

schizo [skizo] *adj fam* schizophrenic.

schizoïde [skizɔid] *adj* schizoid.

schizophrène [skizɔfrɛn] *nmf & adj* schizophrenic.

schizophrénie [skizɔfreni] *nf* schizophrenia.

schizophrénique [skizɔfrenik] *adj* schizophrenic.

schlinguer, chlinguer [ʃlɛ̃ge] [3] *vi tfam* to stink.

schnock, chnoque [ʃnɔk] *nm fam*: **du** ~! dummy!, dimwit!

schuss [ʃus] ◇ *nm* schuss. ◇ *adv*: **descendre (tout)** ~ to schuss down.

sciatique [sjatik] ◇ *nf* sciatica. ◇ *adj* sciatic.

scie [si] *nf* **-1.** [outil] saw; ~ **à métaux** hacksaw; ~ **sauteuse** jigsaw. **-2.** [rengaine] catchphrase. **-3.** *fam* [personne] bore.

sciemment [sjamã] *adv* knowingly.

science [sjãs] *nf* **-1.** [connaissances scientifiques] science; ~**s humaines** OU **sociales** UNIV social sciences; ~**s naturelles** SCOL biology (*sg*). **-2.** [érudition] knowledge; **avoir la** ~ **infuse** *fig* to know a lot. **-3.** [art] art.

science-fiction [sjãsfiksjɔ̃] *nf* science fiction.

sciences-po [sjãspo] *nfpl* UNIV political science (*sg*).

◆ **Sciences-Po** *n grande école for political science.*

scientifique [sjãtifik] ◇ *nmf* scientist. ◇ *adj* scientific.

scientifiquement [sjãtifikmã] *adv* scientifically.

scientisme [sjãtism] *nm* Christian Science.

scier [sje] [9] *vt* **-1.** [branche] to saw. **-2.** *fam* [personne] to stagger.

scierie [siri] *nf* sawmill.

scinder [sɛ̃de] [3] *vt*: ~ **(en)** to split (into), to divide (into).

◆ **se scinder** *vp*: **se** ~ **(en)** to split (into), to divide (into).

scintillant, -e [sɛ̃tijã, ãt] *adj* sparkling.

scintillement [sɛ̃tijmã] *nm* sparkle.

scintiller [sɛ̃tije] [3] *vi* to sparkle.

scission [sisjɔ̃] *nf* split.

sciure [sjyr] *nf* sawdust.

sclérose [skleroz] *nf* sclerosis; *fig* ossification; ~ **en plaques** multiple sclerosis.

sclérosé, -e [skleroze] ◇ *adj* sclerotic; *fig* ossified. ◇ *nm, f* person suffering from sclerosis; *fig* person set in his/her ways.

scléroser [skleroze] [3]

◆ **se scléroser** *vp* to become sclerotic; *fig* to become ossified.

scolaire [skɔlɛr] *adj* school (*avant n*); *péj* bookish.

scolarisable [skɔlarizabl] *adj* of school age.

scolarisation [skɔlarizasjɔ̃] *nf* schooling.

scolariser [skɔlarize] [3] *vt* to provide with schooling.

scolarité [skɔlarite] *nf* schooling; **prolonger la** ~ to raise the school-leaving age; **frais de** ~ SCOL school fees; UNIV tuition fees.

scolastique [skɔlastik] ◇ *nf* scholasticism. ◇ *adj* scholastic.

scoliose [skɔljoz] *nf* curvature of the spine.

scoop [skup] *nm* scoop.

scooter [skutœr] *nm* scooter; ~ **des mers** jet ski; ~ **des neiges** snowmobile.

scorbut [skɔrbyt] *nm* scurvy.

score [skɔr] *nm* **-1.** SPORT score. **-2.** POLIT result.

scorie [skɔri] *nf* **-1.** (*gén pl*) GÉOL scoria. **-2.** IND slag (*U*); *fig* dregs (*pl*).

scorpion [skɔrpjɔ̃] *nm* scorpion.

◆ **Scorpion** *nm* ASTROL Scorpio; **être Scorpion** to be (a) Scorpio.

scotch [skɔtʃ] *nm* [alcool] whisky, Scotch.

Scotch® [skɔtʃ] *nm* [adhésif] ≃ Scotch tape® *Am*, ≃ Sellotape® *Br*.

scotcher [skɔtʃe] [3] *vt* to scotch-tape *Am*, to sellotape *Br*.

scout, -e [skut] *adj* scout (*avant n*).

◆ **scout** *nm* scout.

scoutisme [skutism] *nm* scouting.

Scrabble® [skrabl] *nm* Scrabble®.

scribe [skrib] *nm* HIST scribe.

scribouillard, -e [skribujar, ard] *nm, f péj* pen pusher.

script [skript] *nm* **-1.** TYPO printing, print. **-2.** CIN & TÉLÉ script.

scripte [skript] *nmf* CIN & TÉLÉ continuity person.

scriptural, -e, -aux [skriptyral, o] *adj*: **monnaie** ~**e** substitute money.

scrotum [skrɔtɔm] *nm* scrotum.

scrupule [skrypyl] *nm* scruple; **avec** ~ scrupulously; **sans** ~**s** [être] unscrupulous; [agir] unscrupulously.

scrupuleusement [skrypyløzmɑ̃] *adv* scrupulously.

scrupuleux, -euse [skrypylø, øz] *adj* scrupulous.

scrutateur, -trice [skrytatœr, tris] *adj* searching.
◆ **scrutateur** *nm* POLIT ≃ teller *Am*, ≃ scrutineer *Br*.

scruter [skryte] [3] *vt* to scrutinize.

scrutin [skrytɛ̃] *nm* **-1.** [vote] ballot; **dépouiller un** ~ to count the votes. **-2.** [système] voting system; ~ **majoritaire** first-past-the-post system; ~ **proportionnel** proportional representation system.

sculpter [skylte] [3] *vt* to sculpt.

sculpteur [skyltœr] *nm* sculptor.

sculptural, -e, -aux [skyltyral, o] *adj* sculptural; *fig* statuesque.

sculpture [skyltyr] *nf* sculpture.

sdb *abr de* salle de bains.

SDF (*abr de* sans domicile fixe) *nmf*: les ~ the homeless.

SDN (*abr de* Société des Nations) *nf* League of Nations.

se [sə], **s'** (*devant voyelle ou h muet*) *pron pers* **-1.** (*réfléchi*) [personne] oneself, himself (*f* herself), (*pl*) themselves; [chose, animal] itself, (*pl*) themselves; **elle** ~ **regarde dans le miroir** she looks at herself in the mirror. **-2.** (*réciproque*) each other, one another; **elles** ~ **sont parlé** they spoke to each other OU to one another; **ils** ~ **sont rencontrés hier** they met yesterday. **-3.** (*passif*): **ce produit** ~ **vend bien/partout** this product is selling well/is sold everywhere. **-4.** [remplace l'adjectif possessif]: ~ **laver les mains** to wash one's hands; ~ **couper le doigt** to cut one's finger.

S.E. (*abr de* Son Excellence) H.E.

séance [seɑ̃s] *nf* **-1.** [réunion] meeting, sitting, session; **lever la** ~ *fig* to adjourn the meeting OU session; ~ **extraordinaire** special session, extraordinary meeting. **-2.** [période] session; [de pose] sitting. **-3.** CIN & THÉÂTRE performance. **-4.** *fam* [scène] performance. **-5.** *loc*: ~ **tenante** right away.

séant, -e [seɑ̃, ɑ̃t] *adj* fitting, seemly.
◆ **séant** *nm*: **se dresser** OU **se mettre sur son** ~ *littéraire* to sit up.

seau, -x [so] *nm* **-1.** [récipient] bucket; ~ **à glace** ice bucket. **-2.** [contenu] bucketful.

sébile [sebil] *nf* (begging) bowl.

sébum [sebɔm] *nm* sebum.

sec, sèche [sɛk, sɛʃ] *adj* **-1.** [gén] dry. **-2.** [fruits] dried. **-3.** [alcool] neat. **-4.** [personne - maigre] lean; [- austère] austere. **-5.** *fig* [cœur]

hard; [voix, ton] sharp. **-6.** *fam* [étudiant]: **être** ~ **sur un sujet** to have nothing to say on a subject.
◆ **sec** ◇ *adv* **-1.** [beaucoup]: **boire** ~ to drink heavily. **-2.** [frapper] hard. **-3.** [démarrer] sharply. **-4.** *loc*: **aussi** ~ *fam* right away; **être à** ~ [puits] to be dry OU dried up; *fam* [personne] to be broke. ◇ *nm*: **tenir au** ~ to keep in a dry place.

sécable [sekabl] *adj* divisible.

SECAM, Secam [sekam] (*abr de* procédé séquentiel à mémoire) *nm & adj* French TV broadcasting system.

sécateur [sekatœr] *nm* secateurs (*pl*).

sécession [sesesjɔ̃] *nf* secession; **faire** ~ **(de)** to secede (from).

séchage [seʃaʒ] *nm* drying.

sèche [sɛʃ] *nf fam* cigarette, fag *Br*.

sèche-cheveux [sɛʃʃəvø] *nm inv* hairdryer.

sèche-linge [sɛʃlɛ̃ʒ] *nm inv* tumble-dryer.

sécher [seʃe] [18] ◇ *vt* **-1.** [linge] to dry. **-2.** *arg scol* [cours] to skip, to skive off *Br*. ◇ *vi* **-1.** [linge] to dry. **-2.** [peau] to dry out; [rivière] to dry up. **-3.** *arg scol* [ne pas savoir répondre] to dry up.

sécheresse [sɛʃrɛs] *nf* **-1.** [de terre, climat, style] dryness. **-2.** [absence de pluie] drought. **-3.** [de réponse] curtness.

séchoir [seʃwar] *nm* **-1.** [local] drying shed. **-2.** [tringle] airer, clotheshorse. **-3.** [électrique] dryer; ~ **à cheveux** hairdryer.

second, -e [səgɔ̃, ɔ̃d] ◇ *adj num* second; **dans un état** ~ dazed; *voir aussi* **sixième**. ◇ *nm, f* second; *voir aussi* **sixième**.
◆ **second** *nm* [assistant] assistant.
◆ **seconde** *nf* **-1.** [unité de temps & MUS] second; **une** ~**e!** just a second! **-2.** SCOL ≃ tenth grade *Am*, ≃ fifth year OU form *Br*. **-3.** TRANSPORT second class.

secondaire [səgɔ̃dɛr] ◇ *nm*: **le** ~ GÉOL the Mesozoic; SCOL secondary education; ÉCON the secondary sector. ◇ *adj* **-1.** [gén & SCOL] secondary; **effets** ~**s** MÉD side effects. **-2.** GÉOL Mesozoic.

seconder [səgɔ̃de] [3] *vt* to assist.

secouer [səkwe] [6] *vt* **-1.** [gén] to shake. **-2.** *fam* [réprimander] to shake up.
◆ **se secouer** *vp fam* to snap out of it.

secourable [səkurabl] *adj* helpful.

secourir [səkurir] [45] *vt* [blessé, miséreux] to help; [personne en danger] to rescue.

secourisme [səkurism] *nm* first aid.

secouriste [səkurist] *nmf* first-aid worker.

secourrai, secourras *etc* → secourir.

secours¹, secourt *etc* → secourir.

secours² [sǝkur] *nm* **-1.** [aide] help; **appeler au** ~ to call for help; **au** ~! help!; **porter** ~ **à qqn** to help sb; **voler au** ~ **de qqn** *fig* to rush to sb's aid. **-2.** [dons] aid, relief. **-3.** [renfort] relief, reinforcements (*pl*). **-4.** [soins] aid; **les premiers** ~ first aid (*U*).
◆ **de secours** *loc adj* **-1.** [trousse, poste] first-aid (*avant n*). **-2.** [éclairage, issue] emergency (*avant n*). **-3.** [roue] spare.

secouru, -e [sǝkury] *pp* → **secourir**.

secousse [sǝkus] *nf* **-1.** [mouvement] jerk, jolt. **-2.** *fig* [bouleversement] upheaval; [psychologique] shock. **-3.** [tremblement de terre] tremor.

secret, -ète [sǝkrɛ, ɛt] *adj* **-1.** [gén] secret. **-2.** [personne] reticent.
◆ **secret** *nm* **-1.** [gén] secret; **être/mettre qqn dans le** ~ **de** to be/let sb in on the secret of; **... dont il a le** ~ **...** which he alone knows; ~ **d'alcôve** pillow talk (*U*); ~ **d'État** official secret, state secret; ~ **professionnel** confidentiality. **-2.** [discrétion] secrecy; **dans le plus grand** ~ in the utmost secrecy.
◆ **au secret** *loc adv* JUR in solitary confinement.

secrétaire [sǝkretɛr] ◇ *nmf* [personne] secretary; ~ **de direction** executive secretary; ~ **d'État** minister of state; ~ **général** COMM company secretary; ~ **de rédaction** subeditor. ◇ *nm* [meuble] writing desk, secretaire.

secrétariat [sǝkretarja] *nm* **-1.** [bureau] secretary's office; [d'organisation internationale] secretariat. **-2.** [personnel] secretarial staff; **assurer le** ~ **de qqn** to act as sb's secretary. **-3.** [métier] secretarial work.

secrètement [sǝkrɛtmã] *adv* secretly.

sécréter [sekrete] [18] *vt* to secrete; *fig* to exude.

sécrétion [sekresjɔ̃] *nf* secretion.

sectaire [sɛktɛr] *nmf & adj* sectarian.

sectarisme [sɛktarism] *nm* sectarianism.

secte [sɛkt] *nf* sect.

secteur [sɛktœr] *nm* **-1.** [zone] area; **se trouver dans le** ~ *fam* to be someplace *Am* OU somewhere *Br* around. **-2.** ADMIN district. **-3.** ÉCON, GÉOM & MIL sector; ~ **privé/public** private/public sector; ~ **primaire/secondaire/tertiaire** primary/secondary/tertiary sector. **-4.** ÉLECTR mains; **sur** ~ off OU from the mains.

section [sɛksjɔ̃] *nf* **-1.** [gén] section; [de parti] branch. **-2.** [action] cutting. **-3.** MIL platoon.

sectionnement [sɛksjɔnmã] *nm* **-1.** *fig* [division] division into sections. **-2.** [coupure] severing.

sectionner [sɛksjɔne] [3] *vt* **-1.** *fig* [diviser] to divide into sections. **-2.** [trancher] to sever.
◆ **se sectionner** *vp* to split, to be severed.

sectoriel, -ielle [sɛktɔrjɛl] *adj* sector (*avant n*), sector-based.

sectorisation [sɛktɔrizasjɔ̃] *nf* division into sectors.

sectoriser [sɛktɔrize] [3] *vt* to divide into sectors.

Sécu [seky] *fam abr de* **Sécurité sociale**.

séculaire [sekylɛr] *adj* [ancien] age-old.

séculariser [sekylarize] [3] *vt* to secularize.

séculier, -ière [sekylje, jɛr] *adj* secular.

secundo [sǝgɔ̃do] *adv* in the second place, secondly.

sécurisant, -e [sekyrizã, ãt] *adj* [milieu] secure; [attitude] reassuring.

sécuriser [sekyrize] [3] *vt*: ~ **qqn** to make sb feel secure.

sécurité [sekyrite] *nf* **-1.** [d'esprit] security. **-2.** [absence de danger] safety; **la** ~ **routière** road safety; **en toute** ~ safe and sound. **-3.** [dispositif] safety catch. **-4.** [organisme]: **la Sécurité sociale** ≃ the Social Security *Am,* ≃ the DSS *Br*.

SÉCURITÉ SOCIALE:
The 'Sécu', as it is popularly known, created in 1945-46, provides public health benefits, pensions, maternity leave etc. These benefits are paid for by obligatory insurance contributions ('cotisations') made by employers ('cotisations patronales') and employees ('cotisations salariales'). Many French people have complementary health insurance provided by a 'mutuelle', which guarantees payment of all or part of the expenses not covered by the 'Sécurité sociale'

---

sédatif, -ive [sedatif, iv] *adj* sedative.
◆ **sédatif** *nm* sedative.

sédentaire [sedãtɛr] ◇ *nmf* sedentary person; [casanier] stay-at-home. ◇ *adj* [personne, métier] sedentary; [casanier] stay-at-home.

sédentarisation [sedãtarizasjɔ̃] *nf* settlement (process).

sédentariser [sedãtarize] [3]
◆ **se sédentariser** *vp* [tribu] to settle, to become settled.

sédentarité [sedãtarite] *nf* settled state.

sédiment [sedimã] *nm* sediment.

sédimentaire [sedimãtɛr] *adj* sedimentary.

sédimentation [sedimãtasjɔ̃] *nf* sedimentation.

séditieux, -ieuse [sedisjø, jøz] *littéraire* ◇ *adj* seditious. ◇ *nm, f* rebel.

sédition [sedisjɔ̃] *nf* sedition.

séducteur, -trice [sedyktœr, tris] ◇ *adj* seductive. ◇ *nm, f* seducer (*f* seductress).

séduction [sedyksjɔ̃] *nf* **-1.** [action] seduction. **-2.** [attrait] seductive power.

séduire [sedɥir] [98] *vt* **-1.** [plaire à] to attract, to appeal to. **-2.** [abuser de] to seduce.

séduisais, séduisions *etc* → **séduire**.

séduisant, -e [sedɥizɑ̃, ɑ̃t] *adj* attractive.

séduit, -e [sedɥi, ɥit] *pp* → **séduire**.

séfarade [sefarad] ◇ *nmf* Sephardi. ◇ *adj* Sephardic.

segment [sɛgmɑ̃] *nm* **-1.** GÉOM segment. **-2.** TECHNOL: ~ **de frein** brake shoe; ~ **de piston** piston ring. **-3.** COMM: ~ **de marché** market segment.

segmentation [sɛgmɑ̃tasjɔ̃] *nf* segmentation.

segmenter [sɛgmɑ̃te] [3] *vt* to segment.

ségrégation [segregasjɔ̃] *nf* segregation.

ségrégationniste [segregasjɔnist] *nmf & adj* segregationist.

seiche [sɛʃ] *nf* cuttlefish.

seigle [sɛgl] *nm* rye.

seigneur [sɛɲœr] *nm* lord; **faire le grand** ~ *fig* to throw money about; **vivre en grand** ~ *fig* to live like a lord.
◆ **Seigneur** *nm*: **le Seigneur** the Lord.

seigneurial, -e, -iaux [sɛɲœrjal, jo] *adj* lordly; HIST seigneurial.

sein [sɛ̃] *nm* breast; *fig* bosom; **donner le** ~ (**à un bébé**) to breast-feed (a baby).
◆ **au sein de** *loc prép* within.

Seine [sɛn] *nf*: **la** ~ **the** (River) Seine.

séisme [seism] *nm* earthquake.

SEITA, Seita [sejta] (*abr de* **Société nationale d'exploitation des tabacs et allumettes**) *nf French tobacco and match manufacturer.*

seize [sɛz] *adj num & nm* sixteen; *voir aussi* **six**.

seizième [sɛzjɛm] *adj num, nm & nmf* sixteenth; **le** ~ *wealthy district of Paris*; *voir aussi* **sixième**.

LE SEIZIÈME:
This term often refers to an upper-class social background, lifestyle, way of dressing etc

séjour [seʒur] *nm* **-1.** [durée] stay; **interdit de** ~ ≃ **banned**; ~ **linguistique** stay abroad (*to develop language skills*). **-2.** [pièce] living room.

séjourner [seʒurne] [3] *vi* to stay.

sel [sɛl] *nm* salt; *fig* piquancy; **gros** ~ coarse salt.
◆ **sels** *nmpl* smelling salts; ~**s de bain** bath salts.

sélect, -e [selɛkt] *adj fam* select.

sélecteur [selɛktœr] *nm* **-1.** [dispositif] selector; ~ **de température** thermostat. **-2.** [de moto] gear-change lever.

sélectif, -ive [selɛktif, iv] *adj* selective.

sélection [selɛksjɔ̃] *nf* selection.

sélectionné, -e [selɛksjɔne] *adj* selected.

sélectionner [selɛksjɔne] [3] *vt* to select, to pick.

sélectionneur, -euse [selɛksjɔnœr, øz] *nm, f* selector.

sélectivement [selɛktivmɑ̃] *adv* selectively.

self [sɛlf] *nm fam* self-service (cafeteria).

self-control [sɛlfkɔ̃trol] *nm inv* self-control.

self-made-man [sɛlfmɛdman] (*pl* **self-made-men** [sɛlfmɛdmɛn]) *nm* self-made man.

self-service [sɛlfsɛrvis] (*pl* **self-services**) *nm* self-service cafeteria.

selle [sɛl] *nf* **-1.** [gén] saddle; **se mettre en** ~ to mount. **-2.** [toilettes]: **aller à la** ~ to open one's bowels.

seller [sele] [4] *vt* to saddle.

sellerie [sɛlri] *nf* **-1.** [commerce] saddlery. **-2.** [lieu] tack room.

sellette [sɛlɛt] *nf* hot seat; **mettre qqn/être sur la** ~ *fig* to put sb/be in the hot seat.

sellier [selje] *nm* saddler.

selon [səlɔ̃] *prép* **-1.** [conformément à] in accordance with. **-2.** [d'après] according to; **c'est** ~ *fam fig* that (all) depends.
◆ **selon que** *loc conj* depending on whether.

S.Em (*abr de* **Son Eminence**) H.E.

semailles [səmaj] *nfpl* **-1.** [action] sowing (*U*). **-2.** [période] sowing season (*sg*).

semaine [səmɛn] *nf* **-1.** [période] week; **à la** ~ [être payé] by the week; **en** ~ during the week; **la** ~ **sainte** Holy Week; **faire qqch à la petite** ~ *fig* to do sthg on a short-term basis. **-2.** [salaire] weekly wage.

semainier, -ière [səmenje, jɛr] *nm, f* person on duty for the week.
◆ **semainier** *nm* **-1.** [bijou] seven-band bracelet. **-2.** [meuble] *small chest of drawers*. **-3.** [calendrier] desk diary.

sémantique [semɑ̃tik] ◇ *nf* semantics (*U*). ◇ *adj* semantic.

sémaphore [semafɔr] *nm* **-1.** NAVIG semaphore. **-2.** RAIL semaphore, semaphore signals (*pl*).

semblable [sãblabl] ◇ *nm* [prochain] fellow man; **il n'a pas son** ~ there's nobody like him. ◇ *adj* **-1.** [analogue] similar; ~ **à** like, similar to. **-2.** (*avant n*) [tel] such.

semblant [sãblã] *nm*: **un** ~ **de** a semblance of; **faire** ~ **(de faire qqch)** to pretend (to do sthg).

sembler [sãble] [3] ◇ *vi* to seem. ◇ *v impers*: **il (me/te) semble que** it seems (to me/you) that.

semelle [səmɛl] *nf* **-1.** [de chaussure - dessous] sole; [- à l'intérieur] insole; ~**s** compensées platform soles. **-2.** [de ski] underside. **-3.** CONSTR foundation; [de poutre] flange. **-4.** *loc*: **battre la** ~ to stamp one's feet to keep warm; **ne pas quitter qqn d'une** ~ to stick to sb like glue.

semence [səmãs] *nf* **-1.** [graine] seed. **-2.** [sperme] semen (*U*).

semer [səme] [19] *vt* **-1.** [planter & *fig*] to sow. **-2.** [répandre] to scatter; ~ **qqch de** to scatter sthg with, to strew sthg with. **-3.** *fam* [se débarrasser de] to shake off. **-4.** *fam* [perdre] to lose.

semestre [səmɛstr] *nm* half year, six-month period; SCOL semester.

semestriel, -ielle [səmɛstrijɛl] *adj* **-1.** [qui a lieu tous les six mois] half-yearly, six-monthly. **-2.** [qui dure six mois] six months', six-month.

semeur, -euse [səmœr, øz] *nm, f* sower; *fig* disseminator.

semi-automatique [səmiotɔmatik] *adj* semiautomatic.

semi-fini, -e [səmifini] *adj* semi-finished.

semi-liberté [səmilibɛrte] (*pl* **semi-libertés**) *nf* temporary release from prison.

sémillant, -e [semijã, ãt] *adj* vivacious.

séminaire [seminɛr] *nm* **-1.** RELIG seminary. **-2.** [UNIV & colloque] seminar.

séminal, -e, -aux [seminal, o] *adj* seminal.

séminariste [seminarist] *nm* seminarist.

sémiologie [semjɔlɔʒi] *nf* semiology.

semi-public, -ique [səmipyblik] *adj* semi-public.

semi-remorque [səmirəmɔrk] (*pl* **semi-remorques**) *nm* semitrailer *Am*, articulated lorry *Br*.

semis [səmi] *nm* **-1.** [méthode] sowing broadcast. **-2.** [terrain] seedbed. **-3.** [plant] seedling.

sémite [semit] *adj* Semitic.
◆ **Semite** *nmf* Semite.

sémitique [semitik] *adj* Semitic.

semoir [səmwar] *nm* **-1.** [machine] drill. **-2.** [sac] seedbag.

semonce [səmɔ̃s] *nf* **-1.** [réprimande] reprimand. **-2.** MIL: **coup de** ~ warning shot.

semoule [səmul] *nf* semolina.

sempiternel, -elle [sãpitɛrnɛl] *adj* eternal.

sénat [sena] *nm* senate; **le Sénat** the (French) Senate.

LE SÉNAT:

The Senate is the upper house of the French parliament. Its members are elected for a nine-year mandate by the Deputies of the Assemblée nationale and certain other government officials. The President of the Senate may deputize for the President of the Republic. The powers of the Senate are almost as extensive as those of the Assemblée nationale, although the latter is empowered to override the decisions of the Senate when the two houses disagree

---

sénateur [senatœr] *nm* senator.

Sénégal [senegal] *nm*: **le** ~ Senegal; **au** ~ in Senegal.

sénégalais, -e [senegalɛ, ɛz] *adj* Senegalese.
◆ **Sénégalais, -e** *nm, f* Senegalese person.

sénile [senil] *adj* senile.

sénilité [senilite] *nf* senility.

senior [senjɔr] SPORT ◇ *nmf* senior. ◇ *adj* senior.

sens¹, sent [sã] *etc* → **sentir**.

sens² [sãs] ◇ *nm* **-1.** [fonction, instinct, raison] sense; **avoir un sixième** ~ to have sixth sense; **avoir le** ~ **de l'humour** to have a sense of humor *Am* OU humour *Br*; **avoir le** ~ **de l'orientation** to have a (good) sense of direction; **bon** ~ good sense; **tomber sous le** ~ *fig* to be perfectly obvious. **-2.** [opinion, avis]: **abonder dans le** ~ **de qqn** to agree completely with sb; **à mon** ~ to my way of thinking, to my mind. **-3.** [direction] direction; **dans le** ~ **de la longueur** lengthways; **dans le** ~ **de la marche** in the direction of travel; **dans le** ~ **des aiguilles d'une montre** clockwise; **dans le** ~ **contraire des aiguilles d'une montre** counterclockwise *Am*, anticlockwise *Br*; **en** ~ **inverse** in the opposite direction; ~ **dessus dessous** upside down; ~ **giratoire** traffic circle *Am*, roundabout *Br*; ~ **interdit** OU **unique** one-way street. **-4.** [signification] meaning; **cela n'a pas de** ~! it's nonsensical!; **dans** OU **en un** ~ in one sense; **à double** ~ with a double meaning; **au** ~ **strict du terme** strictly speaking; **vide de** ~ meaningless;

en ce ~ que in the sense that; ~ **propre/** **figuré** literal/figurative sense.
◇ *nmpl* senses.

sensation [sɑ̃sasjɔ̃] *nf* **-1.** [perception] sensation, feeling; **à** ~ sensational; **faire** ~ to cause a sensation. **-2.** [impression] feeling.

sensationnel, **-elle** [sɑ̃sasjɔnɛl] *adj* sensational.

sensé, **-e** [sɑ̃se] *adj* sensible.

sensément [sɑ̃semɑ̃] *adv* sensibly.

sensibilisation [sɑ̃sibilizasjɔ̃] *nf* **-1.** MÉD & PHOT sensitization. **-2.** *fig* [du public] consciousness raising.

sensibiliser [sɑ̃sibilize] [3] *vt* **-1.** MÉD & PHOT to sensitize. **-2.** *fig* [public]: ~ **(à)** to make aware (of).

sensibilité [sɑ̃sibilite] *nf*: ~ **(à)** sensitivity (to).

sensible [sɑ̃sibl] *adj* **-1.** [gén]: ~ **(à)** sensitive (to); ~ **à la vue** visible; ~ **à l'ouïe** audible. **-2.** [notable] considerable, appreciable.

sensiblement [sɑ̃sibləmɑ̃] *adv* **-1.** [quasiment] more or less. **-2.** [notablement] appreciably, considerably.

sensiblerie [sɑ̃sibləri] *nf péj* [morale] sentimentality; [physique] squeamishness.

sensoriel, **-ielle** [sɑ̃sɔrjɛl] *adj* sensory.

sensualité [sɑ̃sɥalite] *nf* [lascivité] sensuousness; [charnelle] sensuality.

sensuel, **-elle** [sɑ̃sɥɛl] *adj* **-1.** [charnel] sensual. **-2.** [lascif] sensuous.

sentence [sɑ̃tɑ̃s] *nf* **-1.** [jugement] sentence. **-2.** [maxime] adage.

sentencieux, **-ieuse** [sɑ̃tɑ̃sjø, jøz] *adj péj* sententious.

senteur [sɑ̃tœr] *nf littéraire* perfume.

senti, **-e** [sɑ̃ti] ◇ *pp* → **sentir**. ◇ *adj*: **bien** ~ [mots] well-chosen.

sentier [sɑ̃tje] *nm* path; **sortir des ~s battus** *fig* to go off the beaten track.

sentiment [sɑ̃timɑ̃] *nm* feeling; **j'ai le ~ de l'avoir déjà vu** I have the feeling that I've seen him before; **plein de bons ~s** full of good intentions; **veuillez agréer, Monsieur, l'expression de mes ~s distingués/ cordiaux/les meilleurs** yours faithfully/ sincerely/truly.

sentimental, **-e**, **-aux** [sɑ̃timɑ̃tal, o] ◇ *adj* **-1.** [amoureux] love *(avant n)*. **-2.** [sensible, romanesque] sentimental. ◇ *nm, f* sentimentalist.

sentimentalisme [sɑ̃timɑ̃talism] *nm* sentimentalism.

sentinelle [sɑ̃tinɛl] *nf* sentry.

sentir [sɑ̃tir] [37] ◇ *vt* **-1.** [percevoir - par l'odorat] to smell; [- par le goût] to taste; [- par le toucher] to feel. **-2.** [exhaler - odeur] to smell of. **-3.** [colère, tendresse] to feel. **-4.** [affectation, plagiat] to smack of. **-5.** [danger] to sense, to be aware of; ~ **que** to feel (that). **-6.** [beauté] to feel, to appreciate. **-7.** *loc*: **je ne peux pas le** ~ *fam* I can't stand him; **le/la** ~ **passer** *fam* to really feel it. ◇ *vi*: ~ **bon/mauvais** to smell good/bad.
◆ **se sentir** ◇ *v attr*: **se** ~ **bien/fatigué** to feel well/tired; **se** ~ **la force de faire qqch** to feel strong enough to do sthg. ◇ *vp* [être perceptible]: **ça se sent!** you can really tell!

seoir [swar] [67] ◇ *vi sout* [aller bien]: ~ **à qqn** to become sb. ◇ *v impers*: **comme il sied** as is fitting.

Séoul [seul] *n* Seoul.

séparable [separabl] *adj* separable.

séparation [separasjɔ̃] *nf* separation.

séparatisme [separatism] *nm* separatism.

séparatiste [separatist] *nmf* separatist.

séparé, **-e** [separe] *adj* **-1.** [intérêts] separate. **-2.** [couple] separated.

séparément [separemɑ̃] *adv* separately.

séparer [separe] [3] *vt* **-1.** [gén]: ~ **(de)** to separate (from). **-2.** [suj: divergence] to divide. **-3.** [maison]: ~ **(en)** to divide (into).
◆ **se séparer** *vp* **-1.** [se défaire de]: **se** ~ **de** to part with. **-2.** [conjoints] to separate, to split up; **se** ~ **de** to separate from, to split up with. **-3.** [participants] to disperse. **-4.** [route]: **se** ~ **(en)** to split (into), to divide (into).

sépia [sepja] ◇ *nf* **-1.** [matière] sepia. **-2.** [dessin] sepia (drawing). ◇ *adj inv* sepia.

sept [sɛt] *adj num & nm* seven; *voir aussi* **six**.

septante [sɛptɑ̃t] *adj num & nm Belg & Helv* seventy.

septembre [sɛptɑ̃br] *nm* September; **de** ~ September *(avant n)*; **en** ~, **au mois de** ~ in September; **début** ~, **au début du mois de** ~ at the beginning of September; **fin** ~, **à la fin du mois de** ~ at the end of September; **d'ici** ~ by September; **(à la) mi-**~ (in) mid-September; **le premier/deux/dix** ~ the first/second/tenth of September.

septennat [sɛptena] *nm* seven-year term (of office).

septentrional, **-e**, **-aux** [sɛptɑ̃trijɔnal, o] *adj* northern.

septicémie [sɛptisemi] *nf* septicemia *Am*, septicaemia *Br*, blood poisoning.

septième [sɛtjɛm] ◇ *adj num, nm & nmf*

seventh; *voir aussi* **sixième**. ◇ *nf* SCOL ≃ fifth grade *Am*, third year OU form (*at junior school*) *Br*.

septièmement [sɛtjɛmmɑ̃] *adv* seventhly, in (the) seventh place.

septique [sɛptik] *adj* [infecté] septic.

septuagénaire [sɛptɥaʒenɛr] ◇ *nmf* 70-year-old. ◇ *adj*: être ~ to be in one's seventies.

sépulcral, -e, -aux [sepylkral, o] *adj* sepulchral.

sépulcre [sepylkr] *nm* sepulcher *Am*, sepulchre *Br*.

sépulture [sepyltyr] *nf* **-1.** [lieu] burial place. **-2.** [inhumation] burial.

séquelle [sekɛl] *nf* (*gén pl*) aftermath; MÉD aftereffect.

séquence [sekɑ̃s] *nf* sequence.

séquentiel, -ielle [sekɑ̃sjɛl] *adj* sequential.

séquestration [sekɛstrasjɔ̃] *nf* **-1.** [de personne] confinement. **-2.** [de biens] impoundment.

séquestre [sekɛstr] *nm* JUR pound; mettre OU placer sous ~ to impound.

séquestrer [sekɛstre] [3] *vt* **-1.** [personne] to confine. **-2.** [biens] to impound.

serai, seras *etc* → être.

sérail [seraj] *nm* seraglio.

serbe [sɛrb] *adj* Serbian.

◆ **Serbe** *nmf* Serb.

Serbie [sɛrbi] *nf*: **la** ~ Serbia.

serbo-croate [sɛrbɔkrɔat] (*pl* **serbo-croates**) ◇ *nm* [langue] Serbo-Croat. ◇ *adj* Serbo-Croat, Serbo-Croatian.

◆ **Serbo-Croate** *nmf* Serbo-Croat speaker.

serein, -e [sərɛ̃, ɛn] *adj* **-1.** [calme] serene. **-2.** [impartial] calm, dispassionate.

sereinement [sərɛnmɑ̃] *adv* serenely, calmly.

sérénade [serenad] *nf* **-1.** MUS serenade. **-2.** *fam* [tapage] hullabaloo.

sérénité [serenite] *nf* serenity.

serf, serve [sɛrf, sɛrv] *nm, f* serf.

serge [sɛrʒ] *nf* serge.

sergent [sɛrʒɑ̃] *nm* sergeant.

sergent-chef [sɛrʒɑ̃ʃɛf] (*pl* **sergents-chefs**) *nm* staff sergeant.

sériciculture [serisikyltyr] *nf* silkworm farming.

série [seri] *nf* **-1.** [gén] series (*sg*); ~ **B** CIN & TÉLÉ B movie. **-2.** SPORT rank; [au tennis] seeding. **-3.** COMM & IND: **produire qqch en** ~ to mass-produce sthg; **de** ~ standard; **hors** ~ custom-made.

◆ **série noire** *nf* **-1.** [roman]: **un roman de** ~ **noire** a detective novel; **c'est un vrai**

personnage de ~ **noire** he's like something out of a detective novel. **-2.** [catastrophes] chapter of accidents.

sérier [serje] [9] *vt* to classify.

sérieusement [serjøzmɑ̃] *adv* seriously.

sérieux, -ieuse [serjø, jøz] *adj* **-1.** [grave] serious. **-2.** [digne de confiance] reliable; [client, offre] genuine. **-3.** [consciencieux] responsible; **ce n'est pas** ~ it's irresponsible. **-4.** [considérable] considerable.

◆ **sérieux** *nm* **-1.** [application] sense of responsibility. **-2.** [gravité] seriousness; **garder son** ~ to keep a straight face; **prendre qqn/qqch au** ~ to take sb/sthg seriously; **se prendre au** ~ to take o.s. (too) seriously.

sérigraphie [serigrafi] *nf* silk-screen printing.

serin, -e [sərɛ̃, in] *nm, f* **-1.** [oiseau] canary. **-2.** *fam* [niais] idiot, twit *Br*.

seriner [sərine] [3] *vt fam* [rabâcher]: ~ **qqch à qqn** to drum sthg into sb.

seringue [sərɛ̃g] *nf* syringe.

serment [sɛrmɑ̃] *nm* **-1.** [affirmation solennelle] oath; **prêter** ~ to take an oath; **sous** ~ on OU under oath; ~ **d'Hippocrate** Hippocratic oath. **-2.** [promesse] vow, pledge.

sermon [sɛrmɔ̃] *nm litt* & *fig* sermon.

sermonner [sɛrmɔne] [3] *vt* to lecture.

SERNAM, Sernam [sɛrnam] (*abr de* **Service national de messageries**) *nm* rail delivery service, ≃ Red Star® *Br*.

séronégatif, -ive [serɔnegatif, iv] *adj* HIV-negative.

séropositif, -ive [serɔpozitif, iv] *adj* HIV-positive.

séropositivité [serɔpozitivite] *nf* HIV infection.

serpe [sɛrp] *nf* billhook.

serpent [sɛrpɑ̃] *nm* ZOOL snake; ~ **à sonnette** OU **sonnettes** rattlesnake.

◆ **serpent monétaire** *nm* (currency) snake.

serpenter [sɛrpɑ̃te] [3] *vi* to wind.

serpentin [sɛrpɑ̃tɛ̃] *nm* **-1.** [de papier] streamer. **-2.** [tuyau] coil.

serpillière [sɛrpijɛr] *nf* floor cloth.

serpolet [sɛrpɔlɛ] *nm* wild thyme.

serre [sɛr] *nf* [bâtiment] greenhouse, glasshouse.

◆ **serres** *nfpl* ZOOL talons, claws.

serré, -e [sere] *adj* **-1.** [écriture] cramped; [tissu] closely-woven; [rangs] serried. **-2.** [style] dense, concise. **-3.** [vêtement, chaussure] tight. **-4.** [discussion] closely argued; [match] close-fought. **-5.** [poing, dents] clenched; **la gorge** ~**e** with a lump in one's throat; **j'en avais le cœur** ~ *fig* it was heartbreaking. -**6.** [café] strong.

◆ **serré** *adv*: **jouer** ~ to be cautious.

serrement [sɛrmɑ̃] *nm* -**1.** [de main] handshake. -**2.** [de cœur] anguish. -**3.** [de gorge] tightening.

serrer [sere] [4] ◇ *vt* -**1.** [saisir] to grip, to hold tight; ~ **la main à qqn** to shake sb's hand; ~ **qqn dans ses bras** to hug sb. -**2.** *fig* [rapprocher] to bring together; ~ **les rangs** to close ranks. -**3.** [poing, dents] to clench; [lèvres] to purse; *fig* [cœur] to wring. -**4.** [suj: vêtement, chaussure] to be too tight for. -**5.** [vis, ceinture] to tighten. -**6.** [trottoir, bordure] to hug.
◇ *vi* AUTOM: ~ **à droite/gauche** to keep right/left.

◆ **se serrer** *vp* -**1.** [se blottir]: **se** ~ **contre** to huddle up to OU against; **se** ~ **autour de** to crowd OU press around. -**2.** [se rapprocher] to squeeze up. -**3.** [poing] to tighten.

serre-tête [sɛrtɛt] *nm inv* headband.

serrure [seryr] *nf* lock.

serrurerie [seryrri] *nf* -**1.** [métier] locksmith's trade. -**2.** [ouvrage] metalwork.

serrurier [seryrje] *nm* locksmith.

sers, **sert** *etc* → **servir**.

sertir [sɛrtir] [32] *vt* -**1.** [pierre précieuse] to set. -**2.** TECHNOL [assujettir] to crimp.

sérum [serɔm] *nm* serum.

servage [sɛrvaʒ] *nm* serfdom; *fig* bondage.

servante [sɛrvɑ̃t] *nf* -**1.** [domestique] maid-servant. -**2.** TECHNOL tool rest.

serve → **serf**.

serveur, -**euse** [sɛrvœr, øz] *nm, f* -**1.** [de restaurant] waiter (*f* waitress); [de bar] barman (*f* barmaid). -**2.** CARTES dealer. -**3.** TEN-NIS server.

◆ **serveur** *nm* INFORM server.

servi, -**e** [sɛrvi] *pp* → **servir**.

serviable [sɛrvjabl] *adj* helpful, obliging.

service [sɛrvis] *nm* -**1.** [gén] service; **être en** ~ to be in use, to be set up; **mettre en** ~ to set up; **hors** ~ out of order. -**2.** [travail] duty; **pendant le** ~ while on duty; **être de** ~ to be on duty. -**3.** [département] department; ~ **de réanimation** intensive care (unit); ~ **de renseignements** intelligence service; ~ **d'ordre** police and stewards (*at a demonstration*). -**4.** MIL: ~ (**militaire**) military OU national service. -**5.** [aide, assistance] favor *Am*, favour *Br*; **rendre un** ~ **à qqn** to do sb a favor *Am* OU favour *Br*; **rendre** ~ to be helpful; ~ **après-vente** after-sales service. -**6.** [à table]: **premier/deuxième** ~ first/second sitting. -**7.** [pourboire] service

(charge). -**8.** [assortiment - de porcelaine] service, set; [- de linge] set.

serviette [sɛrvjɛt] *nf* -**1.** [de table] serviette, napkin. -**2.** [de toilette] towel; ~ **de bain** bath towel. -**3.** [porte-documents] briefcase.

◆ **serviette hygiénique** *nf* sanitary napkin *Am*, sanitary towel *Br*.

serviette-éponge [sɛrvjɛtepɔ̃ʒ] (*pl* **serviettes-éponges**) *nf* terry towel.

servile [sɛrvil] *adj* -**1.** [gén] servile. -**2.** [traduction, imitation] slavish.

servir [sɛrvir] [38] ◇ *vt* -**1.** [gén] to serve; ~ **qqch à qqn** to serve sb sthg, to help sb to sthg; **qu'est-ce que je vous sers?** what can I get you? -**2.** [avantager] to serve (well), to help.
◇ *vi* -**1.** [avoir un usage] to be useful OU of use; **ça peut toujours/encore** ~ it may/may still come in useful. -**2.** [être utile]: ~ **à qqch/à faire qqch** to be used for sthg/for doing sthg; **ça ne sert à rien** it's pointless. -**3.** [tenir lieu]: ~ **de** [personne] to act as; [chose] to serve as. -**4.** [domestique] to be in service. -**5.** MIL & SPORT to serve. -**6.** CARTES to deal.

◆ **se servir** *vp* -**1.** [prendre]: **se** ~ (**de**) to help o.s. (to); **servez-vous!** help yourself! -**2.** [utiliser]: **se** ~ **de qqn/qqch** to use sb/sthg.

serviteur [sɛrvitœr] *nm* servant.

servitude [sɛrvityd] *nf* -**1.** [esclavage] servitude. -**2.** (*gén pl*) *littéraire* [contrainte] constraint. -**3.** JUR easement.

ses → **son**.

sésame [sezam] *nm* -**1.** BOT sesame. -**2.** *fig* [formule magique]: ~ **ouvre-toi** open sesame.

session [sesjɔ̃] *nf* -**1.** [d'assemblée] session, sitting. -**2.** UNIV exam session. -**3.** INFORM: **ouvrir une** ~ to log in OU on; **fermer** OU **clore une** ~ to log out OU off.

set [sɛt] *nm* -**1.** TENNIS set. -**2.** [napperon]: ~ (**de table**) set of table OU place mats.

setter [setɛr] *nm* setter.

seuil [sœj] *nm litt* & *fig* threshold; ~ **de rentabilité** COMM breakeven point.

seul, -**e** [sœl] ◇ *adj* -**1.** [isolé] alone; ~ **à** ~ alone (together), privately. -**2.** [sans compagnie] alone, by o.s.; **parler tout** ~ to talk to o.s. -**3.** [sans aide] on one's own, by o.s. -**4.** [unique]: **le** ~ ... the only ...; **un** ~ ... a single ...; **pas un** ~ ... not one ..., not a single .... -**5.** [esseulé] lonely. ◇ *nm, f*: **le** ~ **the** only one; **un** ~ a single one, only one.

seulement [sœlmɑ̃] *adv* -**1.** [gén] only; [exclusivement] only, solely. -**2.** [même] even.

sève [sɛv] *nf* **-1.** BOT sap. **-2.** *fig* [vigueur] vigor *Am*, vigour *Br*.

sévère [sevɛr] *adj* severe.

sévèrement [sevɛrmɑ̃] *adv* severely.

sévérité [severite] *nf* severity.

sévices [sevis] *nmpl sout* ill treatment (*U*).

Séville [sevij] *n* Seville.

sévir [sevir] [32] *vi* **-1.** [gouvernement] to act ruthlessly OU severely. **-2.** [épidémie, guerre] to rage.

sevrage [səvraʒ] *nm* **-1.** [d'enfant] weaning. **-2.** [de toxicomane] withdrawal.

sevrer [səvre] [19] *vt* to wean; ~ **qqn de** *fig* to deprive sb of.

sexagénaire [sɛksaʒenɛr] ◇ *nmf* sixty-year-old. ◇ *adj*: **être** ~ to be in one's sixties.

sex-appeal [sɛksapil] *nm* sex appeal.

S.Exc (*abr de* **Son Excellence**) H.E.

sexe [sɛks] *nm* **-1.** [gén] sex; **le** ~ **fort/faible** *fam fig* the stronger/weaker sex. **-2.** [organe] genitals (*pl*).

sexisme [sɛksism] *nm* sexism.

sexiste [sɛksist] *nmf & adj* sexist.

sexologie [sɛksɔlɔʒi] *nf* sexology.

sexologue [sɛksɔlɔg] *nmf* sexologist.

sex-shop [sɛksʃɔp] (*pl* **sex-shops**) *nm* sex shop.

sextant [sɛkstɑ̃] *nm* sextant.

sextuple [sɛkstypl] ◇ *nm*: **le** ~ **de 3** 6 times 3. ◇ *adj* sixfold.

sexualité [sɛksɥalite] *nf* sexuality.

sexuel, -elle [sɛksɥɛl] *adj* sexual.

sexuellement [sɛksɥɛlmɑ̃] *adv* sexually.

sexy [sɛksi] *adj inv fam* sexy.

seyais, seyait *etc* → **seoir**.

seyant, -e [sejɑ̃, ɑ̃t] *adj* becoming.

Seychelles [seʃɛl] *nfpl*: **les** ~ the Seychelles; **aux** ~ in the Seychelles.

SFIO (*abr de* **Section française de l'internationale ouvrière**) *nf former name of the French socialist party*.

SG *abr de* **secrétaire général**.

SGA *abr de* **secrétaire général adjoint**.

SGEN (*abr de* **Syndicat général de l'éducation nationale**) *nm teachers' trade union*.

shah = **schah**.

shaker [ʃɛkœr] *nm* cocktail shaker.

shampoing = **shampooing**.

shampooiner = **shampouiner**.

shampooineur = **shampouineur**.

shampooing [ʃɑ̃pwɛ̃] *nm* shampoo.

shampouiner, shampooiner [ʃɑ̃pwine] [3] *vt* to shampoo.

shampouineur, -euse, shampooineur, -euse [ʃɑ̃pwinœr, øz] *nm, f* shampooer.

Shanghai [ʃɑ̃gaj] *n* Shanghai.

shérif [ʃerif] *nm* sheriff.

sherry [ʃeri] *nm* sherry.

shetland [ʃɛtlɑ̃d] *nm* **-1.** [laine] Shetland wool. **-2.** [cheval] Shetland pony.

Shetland [ʃɛtlɑ̃d] *nfpl*: **les** ~ the Shetlands.

shooter [ʃute] [3] *vi* to shoot; ~ **dans qqch** *fam* to kick sthg.

◆ **se shooter** *vp fam arg drogue* to shoot up.

shopping [ʃɔpiŋ] *nm* shopping; **faire du** ~ to go (out) shopping.

short [ʃɔrt] *nm* shorts (*pl*), pair of shorts.

show [ʃo] *nm* show.

show-business [ʃobiznɛs] *nm inv* show business.

si¹ [si] *nm inv* MUS B; [dans la gamme] ti.

si² [si] ◇ *adv* **-1.** [tellement] so; **elle est** ~ **belle** she is so beautiful; **il roulait** ~ **vite qu'il a eu un accident** he was driving so fast (that) he had an accident; **ce n'est pas** ~ **facile que ça** it's not as easy as that; ~ **vieux qu'il soit** however old he may be, old as he is. **-2.** [oui] yes; **tu n'aimes pas le café?** — ~ don't you like coffee? — yes, I do.

◇ *conj* **-1.** [gén] if; ~ **tu veux, on y va** we'll go if you want; ~ **tu faisais cela, je te détesterais** I would hate you if you did that; ~ **seulement** if only. **-2.** [dans une question indirecte] if, whether; **dites-moi** ~ **vous venez** tell me if OU whether you're coming.

◇ *nm inv*: **il y a toujours des** ~ **et des mais** there are always ifs and buts.

◆ **si bien que** *loc conj* so that, with the result that.

◆ **si tant est que** *loc conj* (+ *subjonctif*) providing, provided (that).

SI *nm* **-1.** (*abr de* **syndicat d'initiative**) tourist office. **-2.** (*abr de* **système international**) SI.

siamois, -e [sjamwa, az] *adj* Siamese; **frères** ~, **sœurs** ~**es** MÉD Siamese twins; *fig* inseparable companions.

◆ **Siamois, -e** *nm, f vieilli* Siamese person.

Sibérie [siberi] *nf*: **la** ~ Siberia.

sibérien, -ienne [siberjɛ̃, jɛn] *adj* Siberian.

◆ **Sibérien, -ienne** *nm, f* Siberian.

sibyllin, -e [sibilɛ̃, in] *adj* enigmatic.

sic [sik] *adv* sic.

SICAV, Sicav [sikav] (*abr de* **société d'investissement à capital variable**) *nf* **-1.** [société] unit trust, mutual fund. **-2.** [action] share in a unit trust.

Sicile [sisil] *nf*: **la ~** Sicily.

sicilien, -ienne [sisiljɛ̃, jɛn] *adj* Sicilian.

◆ **Sicilien, -ienne** *nm, f* Sicilian.

Sicob [sikɔb] (*abr de* **Salon des industries du commerce et de l'organisation du bureau** *nm*: **le ~** *annual information technology fair in Paris.*

SIDA, Sida [sida] (*abr de* **syndrome immuno-déficitaire acquis**) *nm* AIDS.

side-car [sidkar] (*pl* **side-cars**) *nm* sidecar.

sidéen, -enne [sideɛ̃, ɛn] *nm, f* person with AIDS.

sidéral, -e, -aux [sideral, o] *adj* sidereal.

sidérant, -e [siderã, ãt] *adj fam* staggering.

sidérer [sidere] [18] *vt fam* to stagger.

sidérurgie [sideryrʒi] *nf* -1. [industrie] iron and steel industry. -2. [technique] iron and steel metallurgy.

sidérurgique [sideryrʒik] *adj* steel (*avant n*).

sidérurgiste [sideryrʒist] *nmf* steelworker.

sidologue [sidɔlɔg] *nmf* AIDS specialist.

siècle [sjɛkl] *nm* -1. [cent ans] century; **l'affaire du ~** the bargain of the century. -2. [époque, âge] age; **le ~ des lumières** (Age of) Enlightenment; **le ~ de l'atome** the atomic age. -3. (*gén pl*) *fam* [longue durée] ages (*pl*); **ça fait des ~s que ...** it's ages since ....

sied, siéra *etc →* **seoir**.

siège [sjɛʒ] *nm* -1. [meuble & POLIT] seat; **~ avant/arrière** front/back seat; **~ éjectable** ejector seat. -2. MIL siege; **lever le ~** to lift the siege. -3. [d'organisme] headquarters, head office; **~ social** registered office. -4. MÉD: **se présenter par le ~** to be in the breech position. -5. JUR bench.

siéger [sjeʒe] [22] *vi* -1. [juge, assemblée] to sit. -2. *littéraire* [mal] to have its seat; [maladie] to be located.

sien [sjɛ̃]

◆ **le sien** (*f* **la sienne** [lasjɛn], *mpl* **les siens** [lesjɛ̃], *fpl* **les siennes** [lesjɛn]) *pron poss* [d'homme] his; [de femme] hers; [de chose, d'animal] its; **les ~s** his/her family; **faire des siennes** to be up to one's usual tricks.

sierra [sjera] *nf* sierra.

sieste [sjɛst] *nf* siesta.

sifflant, -e [siflã, ãt] *adj* [son] whistling; [voix] hissing; LING sibilant.

sifflement [sifləmã] *nm* [son] whistling; [de serpent] hissing.

siffler [sifle] [3] ◇ *vi* to whistle; [serpent] to hiss. ◇ *vt* -1. [air de musique] to whistle. -2. [femme] to whistle at. -3. [chien] to whistle (for). -4. [acteur] to boo, to hiss. -5. *fam* [verre] to knock back.

sifflet [siflɛ] *nm* whistle.

◆ **sifflets** *nmpl* hissing (*U*), boos.

sifflotement [siflɔtmã] *nm* whistling.

siffloter [siflɔte] [3] *vi & vt* to whistle.

sigle [sigl] *nm* acronym, (set of) initials.

signal, -aux [siɲal, o] *nm* -1. [geste, son] signal; **~ d'alarme** alarm (signal); **~ de détresse** distress signal; **donner le ~ (de)** to give the signal (for). -2. [panneau] sign.

signalement [siɲalmã] *nm* description.

signaler [siɲale] [3] ◇ *vt* -1. [fait] to point out; **rien à ~** nothing to report. -2. [à la police] to denounce. ◇ *vi* [à train, navire]: **~ à** to signal to.

◆ **se signaler** *vp*: **se ~ par** to become known for, to distinguish o.s. by.

signalétique [siɲaletik] *adj* identifying.

signalisation [siɲalizasjɔ̃] *nf* -1. [action] signposting. -2. [signaux] signs (*pl*); NAVIG signals (*pl*).

signataire [siɲatɛr] *nmf* signatory.

signature [siɲatyr] *nf* -1. [nom, marque] signature. -2. [acte] signing.

signe [siɲ] *nm* -1. [gén] sign; **être ~ de** to be a sign of; **en ~ de** as a sign of; **être né sous le ~ de** to be born under the sign of; **être placé sous le ~ de** *fig* [conférence, transaction] to be marked by; **~ avant-coureur** advance indication; **~ de ralliement** rallying symbol; **~ de reconnaissance** means of recognition; **~s extérieurs de richesse** outward signs of wealth; **c'est bon/mauvais ~** it's a good/ bad sign; **donner ~ de vie** to get in touch. -2. [trait] mark; **~ distinctif** characteristic; **~ particulier** distinguishing mark.

signer [siɲe] [3] *vt* to sign.

◆ **se signer** *vp* to cross o.s.

signet [siɲe] *nm* bookmark (*attached to spine of book*).

significatif, -ive [siɲifikatif, iv] *adj* significant.

signification [siɲifikasjɔ̃] *nf* -1. [sens] meaning. -2. JUR service (of documents).

signifier [siɲifje] [9] *vt* -1. [vouloir dire] to mean. -2. [faire connaître] to make known. -3. JUR to serve notice of.

silence [silãs] *nm* -1. [gén] silence; **garder le ~ (sur)** to remain silent (about); **~ de glace** stony silence; **~ de mort** deathly hush; **passer qqch sous ~** *fig* to avoid mentioning sthg. -2. MUS rest.

silencieusement [silãsjøzmã] *adv* in silence, silently.

silencieux, -ieuse [silãsjø, jøz] *adj* [lieu, appareil] quiet; [personne - taciturne] quiet; [- muet] silent.

◆ **silencieux** *nm* silencer.

silex [silɛks] *nm* flint.

silhouette [silwɛt] *nf* **-1.** [de personne] silhouette; [de femme] figure; [d'objet] outline. **-2.** ART silhouette.

silice [silis] *nf* silica.

siliceux, -euse [siliso, øz] *adj* silicious, siliceous.

silicium [silisjɔm] *nm* silicon.

silicone [silikon] *nf* silicone.

sillage [sijaʒ] *nm* wake.

sillon [sijɔ̃] *nm* **-1.** [tranchée, ride] furrow. **-2.** [de disque] groove.

sillonner [sijɔne] [3] *vt* **-1.** [champ] to furrow. **-2.** [ciel] to crisscross.

silo [silo] *nm* silo.

simagrées [simagre] *nfpl péj*: faire des ~ to make a fuss.

simiesque [simjɛsk] *adj* simian.

similaire [similɛr] *adj* similar.

similarité [similarite] *nf* similarity.

simili [simili] ◇ *nm* **-1.** *fam* [imitation] imitation; en ~ imitation (*avant n*). **-2.** [de photogravure] halftone plate OU block. ◇ *nf fam* halftone illustration.

similicuir [similikɥir] *nm* imitation leather.

similitude [similityd] *nf* similarity.

simple [sɛ̃pl] ◇ *adj* **-1.** [gén] simple; ~ d'esprit simple-minded. **-2.** [ordinaire] ordinary. **-3.** [billet]: un aller ~ a single ticket. ◇ *nm* TENNIS singles (*sg*).

◆ **simples** *nmpl* medicinal plants OU herbs.

simplement [sɛ̃pləmã] *adv* simply.

simplet, -ette [sɛ̃plɛ, ɛt] *adj* **-1.** [personne] simple. **-2.** *péj* [raisonnement] simplistic.

simplicité [sɛ̃plisite] *nf* simplicity; d'une ~ enfantine childishly simple.

simplificateur, -trice [sɛ̃plifikatœr, tris] *adj* simplifying.

simplification [sɛ̃plifikasjɔ̃] *nf* simplification.

simplifier [sɛ̃plifje] [9] *vt* to simplify.

simplisme [sɛ̃plism] *nm péj* oversimplification.

simpliste [sɛ̃plist] *adj péj* simplistic.

simulacre [simylakr] *nm* **-1.** [semblant]: un ~ de a pretence of, a sham. **-2.** [action simulée] enactment.

simulateur, -trice [simylatœr, tris] *nm, f* pretender; [de maladie] malingerer.

◆ **simulateur** *nm* TECHNOL simulator.

simulation [simylasjɔ̃] *nf* **-1.** [gén] simulation. **-2.** [comédie] shamming, feigning; [de maladie] malingering.

simuler [simyle] [3] *vt* **-1.** [gén] to simulate. **-2.** [feindre] to feign, to sham.

simultané, -e [simyltane] *adj* simultaneous.

simultanéité [simyltaneite] *nf* simultaneousness.

simultanément [simyltanemã] *adv* simultaneously.

Sinaï [sinaj] *n*: le ~ Sinai.

sincère [sɛ̃sɛr] *adj* sincere.

sincèrement [sɛ̃sɛrmã] *adv* **-1.** [franchement] honestly, sincerely; ~ vôtre yours sincerely. **-2.** [vraiment] really, truly.

sincérité [sɛ̃serite] *nf* sincerity; en toute ~ in all sincerity.

sinécure [sinekyr] *nf* sinecure; ce n'est pas une ~ *fam fig* it's not exactly a cushy job.

sine qua non [sinekwanɔn] *adj*: condition ~ sine qua non.

Singapour [sɛ̃gapur] *n* Singapore; à ~ in Singapore.

singe [sɛ̃ʒ] *nm* ZOOL monkey; [de grande taille] ape.

singer [sɛ̃ʒe] [17] *vt* **-1.** [personne] to mimic, to ape. **-2.** [sentiment] to feign.

singerie [sɛ̃ʒri] *nf* **-1.** [grimace] face. **-2.** [manières] fuss (*U*).

singulariser [sɛ̃gylarize] [3] *vt* to draw OU call attention to.

◆ **se singulariser** *vp* to draw OU call attention to o.s.

singularité [sɛ̃gylarite] *nf* **-1.** *littéraire* [bizarrerie] strangeness. **-2.** [particularité] peculiarity.

singulier, -ière [sɛ̃gylje, jɛr] *adj* **-1.** *sout* [bizarre] strange; [spécial] uncommon. **-2.** GRAM singular. **-3.** [d'homme à homme]: combat ~ single combat.

◆ **singulier** *nm* GRAM singular.

singulièrement [sɛ̃gyljɛrmã] *adv* **-1.** *littéraire* [bizarrement] strangely. **-2.** [beaucoup, très] particularly.

sinistre [sinistr] ◇ *nm* **-1.** [catastrophe] disaster. **-2.** JUR damage (*U*). ◇ *adj* **-1.** [personne, regard] sinister; [maison, ambiance] gloomy. **-2.** (*avant n*) *péj* [crétin, imbécile] dreadful, terrible.

sinistré, -e [sinistre] ◇ *adj* [région] disaster (*avant n*), disaster-stricken; [famille] disaster-stricken. ◇ *nm, f* disaster victim.

sinistrose [sinistroz] *nf* pessimism.

sinologue [sinɔlɔg] *nmf* Sinologist, Chinawatcher.

sinon [sinɔ̃] *conj* **-1.** [autrement] or else, otherwise. **-2.** [sauf] except, apart from. **-3.** [si ce n'est] if not.

sinueux, -euse [sinɥø, øz] *adj* winding; *fig* tortuous.

sinuosité [sinɥozite] *nf* bend, twist.

sinus [sinys] *nm* **-1.** ANAT sinus. **-2.** MATHS sine.

sinusite [sinyzit] *nf* sinusitis (*U*).

sionisme [sjɔnism] *nm* Zionism.

sioniste [sjɔnist] *nmf & adj* Zionist.

siphon [sifɔ̃] *nm* **-1.** [tube] siphon. **-2.** [bouteille] soda siphon.

siphonné, -e [sifɔne] *adj fam* [fou] batty, crackers.

siphonner [sifɔne] [3] *vt* to siphon.

sire [sir] *nm* **-1.** HIST lord. **-2.** *loc*: **un triste** ~ a sad character.

◆ **Sire** *nm* Sire.

sirène [sirɛn] *nf* siren.

siroc(c)o [sirɔko] *nm* sirocco.

sirop [siro] *nm* syrup; ~ **d'érable** maple syrup; ~ **de grenadine** (syrup of) grenadine; ~ **de menthe** mint cordial; ~ **d'orgeat** barley water; ~ **contre la toux** cough mixture OU syrup.

siroter [sirɔte] [3] *vt fam* to sip.

SIRPA, Sirpa [sirpa] (*abr de* **Service d'information et de renseignement du public de l'armée**) *nm* French army public information service.

sirupeux, -euse [sirypø, øz] *adj* syrupy.

sis, -e [si, siz] *adj* JUR located.

sismique [sismik] *adj* seismic.

sismographe [sismɔgraf] *nm* seismograph.

sismologie [sismɔlɔʒi] *nf* seismology.

site [sit] *nm* **-1.** [emplacement] site; ~ **archéologique/historique** archaeological/historic site; ~ **naturel** unspoiled site. **-2.** [paysage] beauty spot. **-3.** INFORM: ~ **Web** Web site.

sitôt [sito] *adv*: ~ **après** immediately after; **pas de** ~ not for some time, not for a while; ~ **dit,** ~ **fait** no sooner said than done.

◆ **sitôt que** *loc conj* as soon as.

situation [sitɥasjɔ̃] *nf* **-1.** [position, emplacement] position, location. **-2.** [contexte, circonstance] situation; ~ **de famille** marital status; **être en** ~ **de faire qqch** to be in a position to do sthg. **-3.** [emploi] job, position. **-4.** FIN financial statement.

situer [sitɥe] [7] *vt* **-1.** [maison] to site, to situate; **bien/mal situé** well/badly situated. **-2.** [sur carte] to locate. **-3.** *fam* [personne] to size up.

◆ **se situer** *vp* [scène] to be set; [dans classement] to be.

SIVOM, Sivom [sivɔm] (*abr de* **Syndicat intercommunal à vocation multiple**) *nm* group of local authorities pooling public services.

SIVP (*abr de* **stage d'insertion à la vie professionnelle**) *nm* training scheme for unemployed young people.

six [sis *en fin de phrase*, si *devant consonne ou h aspiré*, siz *devant voyelle ou h muet*] ◇ *adj num* six; **il a un** ~ **ans** he is six (years old); **il est** ~ **heures** it's six (o'clock); **le** ~ **janvier** (on) the sixth of January; **daté du** ~ **septembre** dated the sixth of September; **Charles Six** Charles the Sixth; **page** ~ page six. ◇ *nm inv* **-1.** [gén] six; **le** ~ **de pique** six of spades. **-2.** [adresse] (number) six. **-3.** SPORT: **le** ~ number six. ◇ *pron* six; **ils étaient** ~ there were six of them; **ils sont venus à** ~ six (of them) came; **couper/partager en** ~ to cut/divide into six; ~ **par** ~ six at a time; ~ **d'entre eux/nous/vous** six of them/us/you; **cinq sur** ~ five out of six.

sixième [sizjɛm] ◇ *adj num* sixth. ◇ *nmf* sixth; **arriver/se classer** ~ to come (in)/to be placed sixth. ◇ *nf* SCOL ≃ sixth grade *Am*, ≃ first year OU form *Br*; **être en** ~ to be in sixth grade *Am*, to be in the first year OU form *Br*; **entrer en** ~ to go to secondary school. ◇ *nm* **-1.** [part]: **le/un** ~ **de** one/a sixth of; **cinq** ~s five sixths. **-2.** [arrondissement] sixth arrondissement. **-3.** [étage] seventh floor *Am*, sixth floor *Br*.

sixièmement [sizjɛmmɑ̃] *adv* sixthly, in (the) sixth place.

six-quatre-deux [siskatdø]

◆ **à la six-quatre-deux** *loc adv fam* in a slapdash way.

Skaï® [skaj] *nm inv* leatherette.

skateboard [skɛtbɔrd] *nm* skateboard.

sketch [skɛtʃ] (*pl* **sketches**) *nm* sketch (*in a revue etc*).

ski [ski] *nm* **-1.** [objet] ski. **-2.** [sport] skiing; **faire du** ~ to ski; ~ **acrobatique/alpin/de fond** freestyle/alpine/cross-country skiing; ~ **nautique** water-skiing.

skier [skje] [10] *vi* to ski.

skieur, -ieuse [skjœr, jøz] *nm, f* skier.

skipper [skipœr] *nm* **-1.** [capitaine] skipper. **-2.** [barreur] helmsman.

slalom [slalɔm] *nm* **-1.** SKI slalom; ~ **géant/spécial** giant/special slalom. **-2.** [zigzags]: **faire du** ~ to zigzag.

slalomer [slalɔme] [3] *vi* **-1.** SKI to slalom. **-2.** [zigzaguer] to zigzag.

slave [slav] *adj* Slavonic.

◆ **Slave** *nmf* Slav.

slip [slip] *nm* briefs (*pl*); ~ **de bain** [d'homme] swimming trunks (*pl*); [de femme] bikini bottoms (*pl*).

s.l.n.d. (*abr de* **sans lieu ni date**) date and origin unknown.

sloche [slɔʃ] *nf Can* slush.

slogan [slɔgɑ̃] *nm* slogan.

slovaque [slɔvak] ◇ *adj* Slovak. ◇ *nm* [langue] Slovak.
◆ **Slovaque** *nmf* Slovak.

Slovaquie [slɔvaki] *nf*: **la** ~ Slovakia.

slovène [slɔvɛn] ◇ *adj* Slovenian. ◇ *nm* [langue] Slovenian.
◆ **Slovène** *nmf* Slovenian.

Slovénie [slɔveni] *nf*: **la** ~ Slovenia.

slow [slo] *nm* slow dance.

SM, **S-M** (*abr de* **sado-masochisme**) *nm* S & M.

S.M. (*abr de* **Sa Majesté**) H.M.

SMAG, **Smag** [smag] (*abr de* **salaire minimum agricole garanti**) *nm guaranteed minimum wage for agricultural workers*.

smala(h) [smala] *nf* **-1.** [de chef arabe] retinue. **-2.** *fam* [famille] brood.

smasher [smaʃe] [3] *vi* TENNIS to smash.

SME (*abr de* **Système monétaire européen**) *nm* EMS.

SMIC, **Smic** [smik] (*abr de* **salaire minimum interprofessionnel de croissance**) *nm index-linked guaranteed minimum wage*.

smicard, **-e** [smikar, ard] ◇ *adj minimum-wage-earning*. ◇ *nm, f minimum-wage earner*.

smocks [smɔk] *nmpl* smocking (*U*).

smoking [smɔkiŋ] *nm* dinner jacket, tuxedo *Am*.

SMUR, **Smur** [smyr] (*abr de* **Service médical d'urgence et de réanimation**) *nm French ambulance and emergency unit*.

SNC (*abr de* **service non compris**) service not included.

SNCB (*abr de* **Société nationale des chemins de fer belges**) *nf Belgian railways board*, ≃ BR *Br*.

SNCF (*abr de* **Société nationale des chemins de fer français**) *nf French railways board*, ≃ BR *Br*.

SNES, **Snes** [snɛs] (*abr de* **Syndicat national de l'enseignement secondaire**) *nm secondary school teachers' union*.

Snes-sup [snɛsyp] (*abr de* **Syndicat national de l'enseignement supérieur**) *nm university teachers' union*.

SNI (*abr de* **Syndicat national des instituteurs**) *nm primary school teachers' union*.

SNJ (*abr de* **Syndicat national des journalistes**) *nm national union of journalists*.

snob [snɔb] ◇ *nmf* snob. ◇ *adj* snobbish.

snober [snɔbe] [3] *vt* to snub, to cold-shoulder.

snobinard, **-e** [snɔbinar, ard] *fam péj* ◇ *adj* rather snobbish. ◇ *nm, f* a bit of a snob.

snobisme [snɔbism] *nm* snobbery, snobbishness.

SNSM (*abr de* **Société nationale de sauvetage en mer**) *nf national sea-rescue association*.

sobre [sɔbr] *adj* **-1.** [personne] temperate. **-2.** [style] sober; [décor, repas] simple.

sobrement [sɔbrəmɑ̃] *adv* **-1.** [boire] in moderation. **-2.** [se vêtir] soberly.

sobriété [sɔbrijete] *nf* sobriety.

sobriquet [sɔbrike] *nm* nickname.

soc [sɔk] *nm* plowshare *Am*, ploughshare *Br*.

sociabilité [sɔsjabilite] *nf* sociability.

sociable [sɔsjabl] *adj* sociable.

social, **-e**, **-iaux** [sɔsjal, jo] *adj* **-1.** [rapports, classe, service] social. **-2.** COMM: **capital** ~ share capital; **raison** ~e company name.
◆ **social** *nm*: **le** ~ social affairs (*pl*).

social-démocrate, **sociale-démocrate** [sɔsjaldemɔkrat] (*mpl* **sociaux-démocrates** [sɔsjodemɔkrat], *fpl* **sociales-démocrates**) ◇ *nmf* social democrat. ◇ *adj* social democratic.

socialement [sɔsjalmɑ̃] *adv* socially.

socialisation [sɔsjalizasjɔ̃] *nf* **-1.** [développement social] socialization. **-2.** POLIT nationalization.

socialiser [sɔsjalize] [3] *vt* **-1.** [enfant] to socialize. **-2.** POLIT to nationalize.

socialisme [sɔsjalism] *nm* socialism.

socialiste [sɔsjalist] *nmf & adj* socialist.

sociétaire [sɔsjetɛr] *nmf* member.

société [sɔsjete] *nf* **-1.** [communauté, classe sociale, groupe] society; **en** ~ in society; **la haute** ~ high society; ~ **secrète** secret society. **-2.** SPORT club. **-3.** [présence] company, society. **-4.** COMM company, firm; ~ **de bourse** securities house, brokerage firm; ~ **mère** parent company; ~ **en participation** joint-venture company; ~ **de personnes** partnership, joint-stock company *Am*.

socioculturel, **-elle** [sɔsjɔkyltyrɛl] *adj* social and cultural.

socio-économique [sɔsjɔekɔnɔmik] *adj* socioeconomic.

sociologie [sɔsjɔlɔʒi] *nf* sociology.

sociologique [sɔsjɔlɔʒik] *adj* sociological.

sociologue [sɔsjɔlɔg] *nmf* sociologist.

socioprofessionnel, -elle [sɔsjɔprɔfesjɔnɛl] *adj* socioprofessional.

socle [sɔkl] *nm* **-1.** [de statue] plinth, pedestal. **-2.** [de lampe] base. **-3.** GÉOGR: ~ **continental** continental shelf.

socquette [sɔkɛt] *nf* ankle OU short sock.

soda [sɔda] *nm* fizzy drink.

sodium [sɔdjɔm] *nm* sodium.

sodomie [sɔdɔmi] *nf* buggery, sodomy.

sodomiser [sɔdɔmize] [3] *vt* to sodomize.

sœur [sœr] *nf* **-1.** [gén] sister; **grande/petite** ~ big/little sister; ~ **de lait** foster sister. **-2.** RELIG nun, sister.

sofa [sɔfa] *nm* sofa.

Sofia [sɔfja] *n* Sofia.

SOFRES, Sofres [sɔfrɛs] (*abr de* **Société française d'enquête par sondages**) *nf* French opinion poll company.

software [sɔftwɛr] *nm* software.

soi [swa] *pron pers* oneself; **chacun pour** ~ every man for himself; **en** ~ in itself, per se; **cela va de** ~ that goes without saying; **il va de** ~ **que** it goes without saying that.
♦ **chez soi** *loc adv* at home; **se sentir chez** ~ to feel at home.
♦ **soi-même** *pron pers* oneself.

soi-disant [swadizã] ◇ *adj inv (avant n)* socalled. ◇ *adv fam* supposedly.

soie [swa] *nf* **-1.** [textile] silk; **en** ~ silk; ~ **grège** raw silk; ~ **sauvage** wild silk. **-2.** [poil] bristle.

soierie [swari] *nf* **-1.** (*gén pl*) [textile] silk. **-2.** [industrie] silk trade.

soif [swaf] *nf* thirst; ~ (**de**) *fig* thirst (for), craving (for); **avoir** ~ to be thirsty; **jusqu'à plus** ~ to excess; *fig* until one has had one's fill.

soigné, -e [swaɲe] *adj* **-1.** [travail] meticulous. **-2.** [personne] well-groomed; [jardin, mains] well-cared-for. **-3.** *fam fig* [cuite, raclée] awful, massive.

soigner [swaɲe] [3] *vt* **-1.** [suj: médecin] to treat; [suj: infirmière, parent] to nurse. **-2.** [invités, jardin, mains] to look after. **-3.** [travail, présentation] to take care over.
♦ **se soigner** *vp* to take care of o.s., to look after o.s.

soigneur [swaɲœr] *nm* SPORT trainer; BOXE second.

soigneusement [swaɲøzmã] *adv* carefully.

soigneux, -euse [swaɲø, øz] *adj* **-1.** [personne] tidy, neat. **-2.** [travail] careful; ~ **de** careful with.

soin [swɛ̃] *nm* **-1.** [attention] care; **avoir** OU **prendre** ~ **de** to take care of, to look after; **avoir** OU **prendre** ~ **de faire qqch** to be

sure to do sthg; **aux bons** ~s **de** in the care of, in the hands of; **avec** ~ carefully; **sans** ~ [procéder] carelessly; [travail] careless; **être aux petits** ~s **pour qqn** *fig* to wait on sb hand and foot. **-2.** [souci] concern.
♦ **soins** *nmpl* care (*U*); **les premiers** ~s first aid (*sg*).

soir [swar] *nm* evening; **demain** ~ tomorrow evening OU night; **le** ~ in the evening; **à ce** ~! see you tonight!

soirée [sware] *nf* **-1.** [soir] evening; **en** ~ CIN & THÉÂTRE evening (*avant n*). **-2.** [réception] party; **de** ~ evening (*avant n*).

sois → **être**.

soit¹ [swat] *adv* so be it.

soit² [swa] ◇ *vb* → **être**. ◇ *conj* **-1.** [c'est-à-dire] in other words, that is to say. **-2.** MATHS [étant donné]: ~ **une droite AB** given a straight line AB.
♦ **soit ... soit** *loc corrélative* either ... or.
♦ **soit que ... soit que** *loc corrélative* (+ *subjonctif*) whether ... or (whether).

soixantaine [swasãtɛn] *nf* **-1.** [nombre] **une** ~ (**de**) about sixty, sixty-odd. **-2.** [âge]: **avoir la** ~ to be in one's sixties.

soixante [swasãt] ◇ *adj num* sixty; **les années** ~ the Sixties; *voir aussi* **six**. ◇ *nm* sixty; *voir aussi* **six**.

soixante-dix [swasãtdis] ◇ *adj num* seventy; **les années** ~ the Seventies; *voir aussi* **six**. ◇ *nm* seventy; *voir aussi* **six**.

soixante-dixième [swasãtdizjɛm] *adj num, nm & nmf* seventieth; *voir aussi* **sixième**.

soixante-huitard, -e [swasãtɥitar, ard] ◇ *adj* of May 1968. ◇ *nm, f* person who participated in the events of May 1968.

soixantième [swasãtjɛm] *adj num, nm & nmf* sixtieth; *voir aussi* **sixième**.

soja [sɔʒa] *nm* soya.

sol [sɔl] *nm* **-1.** [terre] ground. **-2.** [de maison] floor. **-3.** [territoire] soil. **-4.** MUS G; [chanté] so.

solaire [sɔlɛr] *adj* **-1.** [énergie, four] solar. **-2.** [crème] sun (*avant n*).

solarium [sɔlarjɔm] *nm* solarium.

soldat [sɔlda] *nm* **-1.** MIL soldier; [grade] private; **le** ~ **inconnu** the Unknown Soldier. **-2.** [jouet] (toy) soldier; ~ **de plomb** tin soldier, toy soldier.

solde [sɔld] ◇ *nm* **-1.** [de compte, facture] balance; ~ **créditeur/débiteur** credit/debit balance. **-2.** [rabais]: **en** ~ [acheter] in a sale. ◇ *nf* MIL pay; **à la** ~ **de qqn** *fig* in the pay of sb.
♦ **soldes** *nmpl* sales.

solder [sɔlde] [3] *vt* **-1.** [compte] to close. **-2.** [marchandises] to sell off.

◆ **se solder** *vp*: se ~ par FIN to show; *fig* [aboutir] to end in.

soldeur, -euse [sɔldœr, øz] *nm, f buyer and seller of discount goods.*

sole [sɔl] *nf* sole; ~ **meunière** *sole coated with flour and fried in butter.*

solécisme [sɔlesism] *nm* solecism.

soleil [sɔlɛj] *nm* **-1.** [astre, motif] sun; ~ **couchant/levant** setting/rising sun; **sous un** ~ **de plomb** *fig* in the blazing sun. **-2.** [lumière, chaleur] sun, sunlight; **au** ~ in the sun; **en plein** ~ right in the sun. **-3.** [tournesol] sunflower.

solennel, -elle [sɔlanɛl] *adj* **-1.** [cérémonieux] ceremonial. **-2.** [grave] solemn. **-3.** *péj* [pompeux] pompous.

solennellement [sɔlanɛlmɑ̃] *adv* **-1.** [avec importance] ceremonially. **-2.** [avec sérieux] solemnly.

solennité [sɔlanite] *nf* **-1.** [gravité] solemnity. **-2.** [raideur] stiffness, formality. **-3.** [fête] special occasion.

Solex® [sɔlɛks] *nm* ≃ moped.

solfège [sɔlfɛʒ] *nm*: **apprendre le** ~ to learn the rudiments of music.

solfier [sɔlfje] [9] *vt* to sol-fa.

solidaire [sɔlidɛr] *adj* **-1.** [lié]: **être** ~ **de qqn** to be behind sb, to show solidarity with sb. **-2.** [relié] interdependent, integral.

solidariser [sɔlidarize] [3]

◆ **se solidariser** *vp*: se ~ (avec) to show solidarity (with).

solidarité [sɔlidarite] *nf* [entraide] solidarity; **par** ~ [se mettre en grève] in sympathy.

solide [sɔlid] ◇ *adj* **-1.** [état, corps] solid. **-2.** [construction] solid, sturdy. **-3.** [personne] sturdy, robust; ~ **sur ses jambes** steady on one's feet. **-4.** [argument] solid, sound. **-5.** [relation] stable, strong. ◇ *nm* solid; **il nous faut du** ~ *fig* we need something solid OU concrete.

solidement [sɔlidmɑ̃] *adv* **-1.** [gén] firmly. **-2.** [attaché] firmly, securely.

solidifier [sɔlidifje] [9] *vt* **-1.** [ciment, eau] to solidify. **-2.** [structure] to reinforce.

◆ **se solidifier** *vp* to solidify.

solidité [sɔlidite] *nf* **-1.** [de matière, construction] solidity. **-2.** [de mariage] stability, strength. **-3.** [de raisonnement, d'argument] soundness.

soliloque [sɔlilɔk] *nm sout* soliloquy.

soliste [sɔlist] *nmf* soloist.

solitaire [sɔlitɛr] ◇ *adj* **-1.** [de caractère] solitary. **-2.** [esseulé, retiré] lonely. ◇ *nmf* [personne] loner, recluse. ◇ *nm* [jeu, diamant] solitaire.

solitude [sɔlityd] *nf* **-1.** [isolement] loneliness. **-2.** [retraite] solitude.

solive [sɔliv] *nf* joist.

sollicitation [sɔlisitasjɔ̃] *nf* (*gén pl*) entreaty.

solliciter [sɔlisite] [3] *vt* **-1.** [demander - entretien, audience] to request; [- attention, intérêt] to seek; ~ **qqch de qqn** to ask sb for sthg, to seek sthg from sb. **-2.** [s'intéresser à]: **être sollicité** to be in demand. **-3.** [faire appel à]: ~ **qqn pour faire qqch** to appeal to sb to do sthg.

sollicitude [sɔlisityd] *nf* solicitude, concern.

solo [sɔlo] ◇ *nm* solo; **en** ~ solo. ◇ *adj* solo (*avant n*).

solstice [sɔlstis] *nm*: ~ **d'été/d'hiver** summer/winter solstice.

solubilité [sɔlybilite] *nf* solubility.

soluble [sɔlybl] *adj* **-1.** [matière] soluble; [café] instant. **-2.** *fig* [problème] solvable.

soluté [sɔlyte] *nm* solution.

solution [sɔlysjɔ̃] *nf* **-1.** [résolution] solution, answer; **chercher/trouver la** ~ to seek/to find the solution, to seek/to find the answer; ~ **de facilité** easy answer, easy way out. **-2.** [liquide] solution.

◆ **solution de continuité** *nf* break; **sans** ~ **de continuité** without a break.

solutionner [sɔlysjɔne] [3] *vt* to solve.

solvabilité [sɔlvabilite] *nf* solvency.

solvable [sɔlvabl] *adj* solvent, creditworthy.

solvant [sɔlvɑ̃] *nm* solvent.

somali = **somalien**.

Somalie [sɔmali] *nf*: **la** ~ Somalia.

somalien, -ienne [sɔmaljɛ̃, jɛn], **somali, -e** [sɔmali] *adj* Somali.

◆ **Somalien, -ienne, Somali, -e** *nm, f* Somali.

sombre [sɔ̃br] *adj* **-1.** [couleur, costume, pièce] dark. **-2.** *fig* [pensées, avenir] dark, gloomy. **-3.** *fig* [complot] murky. **-4.** (*avant n*) *fam* [profond]: **c'est un** ~ **crétin** he's a prize idiot.

sombrer [sɔ̃bre] [3] *vi* to sink; ~ **dans** *fig* to sink into.

sommaire [sɔmɛr] ◇ *adj* **-1.** [explication] brief. **-2.** [exécution] summary. **-3.** [installation] basic. ◇ *nm* summary.

sommairement [sɔmɛrmɑ̃] *adv* **-1.** [expliquer] briefly. **-2.** [délibérer] summarily. **-3.** [peu - vêtu] scantily; [- meublé] basically.

sommation [sɔmasjɔ̃] *nf* **-1.** [assignation] summons (*sg*). **-2.** [ordre - de payer] demand; [- de se rendre] warning.

somme [sɔm] ◇ *nf* **-1.** [addition] total, sum; **faire la ~ de plusieurs choses** to add up several things. **-2.** [d'argent] sum, amount. **-3.** [ouvrage] overview. ◇ *nm* nap.

◆ **en somme** *loc adv* in short.

◆ **somme toute** *loc adv* when all's said and done.

sommeil [sɔmɛj] *nm* sleep; **avoir ~** to be sleepy; **tomber de ~** to be asleep on one's feet; **dormir d'un ~ de plomb** *fig* to be in a deep sleep.

sommeiller [sɔmeje] [4] *vi* **-1.** [personne] to doze. **-2.** *fig* [qualité] to be dormant.

sommelier, -ière [sɔməlje, jɛr] *nm, f* wine waiter (*f* wine waitress).

sommer [sɔme] [3] *vt*: **~ qqn de faire qqch** *sout* to charge sb to do sthg.

sommes → être.

sommet [sɔmɛ] *nm* **-1.** [de montagne] summit, top. **-2.** *fig* [de hiérarchie] top; [de perfection] height; **conférence au ~** summit (meeting OU conference). **-3.** GÉOM apex.

sommier [sɔmje] *nm* base, bed base.

sommité [sɔmite] *nf* **-1.** [personne] leading light. **-2.** BOT head.

somnambule [sɔmnɑ̃byl] ◇ *nmf* sleepwalker. ◇ *adj*: **être ~** to be a sleepwalker.

somnifère [sɔmnifɛr] *nm* sleeping pill.

somnolence [sɔmnɔlɑ̃s] *nf* sleepiness, drowsiness.

somnolent, -e [sɔmnɔlɑ̃, ɑ̃t] *adj* [personne] sleepy, drowsy; *fig* [vie] dull; *fig* [économie] sluggish.

somnoler [sɔmnɔle] [3] *vi* to doze.

somptueusement [sɔ̃ptɥøzmɑ̃] *adv* sumptuously, lavishly.

somptueux, -euse [sɔ̃ptɥø, øz] *adj* sumptuous, lavish.

somptuosité [sɔ̃ptɥozite] *nf* lavishness (*U*).

son[1] [sɔ̃] *nm* **-1.** [bruit] sound; **au ~ de** to the sound of; **~ et lumière** son et lumière. **-2.** [céréale] bran.

son[2] [sɔ̃] (*f* **sa** [sa], *pl* **ses** [se]) *adj poss* **-1.** [possesseur défini - homme] his; [- femme] her; [- chose, animal] its; **il aime ~ père** he loves his father; **elle aime ses parents** she loves her parents; **la ville a perdu ~ charme** the town has lost its charm. **-2.** [possesseur indéfini] one's; [- après «chacun», «tout le monde» etc] his/her, their.

sonar [sɔnar] *nm* sonar.

sonate [sɔnat] *nf* sonata.

sondage [sɔ̃daʒ] *nm* **-1.** [enquête] poll, survey; **~ d'opinion** opinion poll. **-2.** TECHNOL drilling. **-3.** MÉD probing.

sonde [sɔ̃d] *nf* **-1.** MÉTÉOR sonde; [spatiale] probe. **-2.** MÉD probe. **-3.** NAVIG sounding line. **-4.** TECHNOL drill.

sondé, -e [sɔ̃de] *nm, f* poll respondent.

sonder [sɔ̃de] [3] *vt* **-1.** MÉD & NAVIG to sound. **-2.** [terrain] to drill. **-3.** *fig* [opinion, personne] to sound out.

sondeur, -euse [sɔ̃dœr, øz] *nm, f* pollster.

◆ **sondeur** *nm* TECHNOL sounder.

songe [sɔ̃ʒ] *nm littéraire* dream; **en ~** in a dream.

songer [sɔ̃ʒe] [17] ◇ *vt*: **~ que** to consider that. ◇ *vi*: **~ à** to think about.

songeur, -euse [sɔ̃ʒœr, øz] *adj* pensive, thoughtful.

sonnant, -e [sɔnɑ̃, ɑ̃t] *adj*: **à six heures ~es** at six o'clock sharp.

sonné, -e [sɔne] *adj* **-1.** [passé]: **il est trois heures ~es** it's gone three o'clock; **il a quarante ans bien ~s** *fam fig* he's the wrong side of forty. **-2.** *fig* [étourdi] groggy. **-3.** *fam fig* [fou] cracked.

sonner [sɔne] [3] ◇ *vt* **-1.** [cloche] to ring. **-2.** [retraite, alarme] to sound. **-3.** [domestique] to ring for. **-4.** *fam fig* [siffler]: **je ne t'ai pas sonné!** who asked you! ◇ *vi* **-1.** [gén] to ring; **~ chez qqn** to ring sb's bell; **~ faux** to be out of tune; *fig* to ring false. **-2.** [jouer]: **~ de** to sound.

sonnerie [sɔnri] *nf* **-1.** [bruit] ringing. **-2.** [mécanisme] striking mechanism. **-3.** [signal] call.

sonnet [sɔnɛ] *nm* sonnet.

sonnette [sɔnɛt] *nf* bell.

sono [sɔno] *nf fam* [de salle] P.A. (system); [de discothèque] sound system.

sonore [sɔnɔr] *adj* **-1.** CIN & PHYS sound (*avant n*). **-2.** [voix, rire] ringing, resonant. **-3.** [salle] resonant.

sonorisation [sɔnɔrizasjɔ̃] *nf* **-1.** [action - de film] addition of the soundtrack; [- de salle] wiring for sound. **-2.** [matériel - de salle] public address system, P.A. (system); [- de discothèque] sound system.

sonoriser [sɔnɔrize] [3] *vt* **-1.** [film] to add the soundtrack to. **-2.** [salle] to wire for sound.

sonorité [sɔnɔrite] *nf* **-1.** [de piano, voix] tone. **-2.** [de salle] acoustics (*pl*).

sont → être.

sophisme [sɔfism] *nm* sophism.

sophistication [sɔfistikasjɔ̃] *nf* sophistication.

sophistiqué, -e [sɔfistike] *adj* sophisticated.

soporifique [sɔpɔrifik] ◇ *adj* soporific. ◇ *nm* sleeping drug, soporific.

soprano [sɔprano] (*pl* **sopranos** OU **soprani** [sɔprani]) *nm & nmf* soprano.

sorbet [sɔrbɛ] *nm* sorbet.

sorbetière [sɔrbətjɛr] *nf* ice-cream maker.

sorbier [sɔrbje] *nm* sorb, service tree.

Sorbonne [sɔrbɔn] *nf*: **la** ~ the Sorbonne.

LA SORBONNE:
The Sorbonne is the oldest university in Paris. It includes the arts and law faculties. It is also known as 'Paris IV'. The term 'la Sorbonne nouvelle' refers to the arts faculty at Censier, also known as 'Paris III'

sorcellerie [sɔrsɛlri] *nf* witchcraft, sorcery.

sorcier, -ière [sɔrsje, jɛr] ◇ *nm, f* sorcerer (*f* witch). ◇ *adj*: **ce n'est pas** ~ *fig* there's no magic involved.

sordide [sɔrdid] *adj* squalid; *fig* sordid.

Sorlingues [sɔrlɛ̃g] *nfpl*: **les (îles)** ~ the Scilly Isles.

sornettes [sɔrnɛt] *nfpl* nonsense (*U*).

sors → sortir.

sort [sɔr] *nm* **-1.** [maléfice] spell; **jeter un** ~ **(à qqn)** to cast a spell (on sb). **-2.** [destinée] fate; **faire un** ~ **à qqch** *fam fig* to polish sthg off. **-3.** [condition] lot. **-4.** [hasard]: **le** ~ fate; **tirer au** ~ to draw lots.

sortable [sɔrtabl] *adj* presentable; **tu n'es pas** ~! I can't take you anywhere!

sortant, -e [sɔrtɑ̃, ɑ̃t] *adj* **-1.** [numéro] winning. **-2.** [président, directeur] outgoing (*avant n*).

sorte [sɔrt] ◇ *nf* sort, kind; **une** ~ **de** a sort of, a kind of; **toutes** ~s **de** all kinds of, all sorts of; **de la** ~ in that way, in that manner; **de telle** ~ **que** so that, in such a way that; **en quelque** ~ in a way, as it were; **faire en** ~ **que** to see to it that. ◇ *vb* → sortir.

sortie [sɔrti] *nf* **-1.** [issue] exit, way out; [d'eau, d'air] outlet; ~ **de secours** emergency exit. **-2.** [départ]: **c'est la** ~ **de l'école** it's home-time; **à la** ~ **du travail** when work finishes, after work. **-3.** [de produit] launch, launching; [de disque] release; [de livre] publication. **-4.** (*gén pl*) [dépense] outgoings (*pl*), expenditure (*U*). **-5.** [excursion] outing. **-6.** MIL sortie. **-7.** [écoulement - de liquide, gaz] escape. **-8.** INFORM: ~ **imprimante** printout; ~ **papier** hard copy.

sortie-de-bain [sɔrtidbɛ̃] (*pl* **sorties-de-bain**) *nf* bathrobe.

sortilège [sɔrtilɛʒ] *nm* spell.

sortir [sɔrtir] [43] ◇ *vi* (*aux*: *être*) **-1.** [de la maison, du bureau etc] to leave, to go/come out; ~ **de** to go/come out of, to leave. **-2.** [pour se distraire] to go out. **-3.** *fig* [quitter]: ~ **de** [réserve, préjugés] to shed. **-4.** *fig* [de maladie]: ~ **de** to get over, to recover from; [coma] to come out of. **-5.** [film, livre, produit] to come out; [disque] to be released. **-6.** [au jeu - carte, numéro] to come up. **-7.** [s'écarter de]: ~ **de** [sujet] to get away from; [légalité, compétence] to be outside. **-8.** *loc*: ~ **de l'ordinaire** to be out of the ordinary; **ça m'est complètement sorti de la tête** it went clean out of my mind; **d'où il sort, celui-là?** where did HE spring from?
◇ *vt* (*aux*: *avoir*) **-1.** [gén]: ~ **qqch (de)** to take sthg out (of). **-2.** [de situation difficile] to get out, to extract. **-3.** [produit] to launch; [disque] to bring out, to release; [livre] to bring out, to publish. **-4.** *fam* [bêtise] to come out with.
◆ **se sortir** *vp fig* [de pétrin] to get out; **s'en** ~ [en réchapper] to come out of it; [y arriver] to get through it.

S.O.S. *nm* S.O.S.; **lancer un** ~ to send out an S.O.S.

sosie [sɔzi] *nm* double.

sot, sotte [so, sɔt] ◇ *adj* silly, foolish. ◇ *nm, f* fool.

sottement [sɔtmɑ̃] *adv* stupidly, foolishly.

sottise [sɔtiz] *nf* stupidity (*U*), foolishness (*U*); **dire/faire une** ~ to say/do something stupid.

sottisier [sɔtizje] *nm collection of howlers*.

sou [su] *nm*: **être sans le** ~ to be penniless; **je n'ai pas le premier** ~ **pour acheter une voiture** I really can't afford a car.
◆ **sous** *nmpl fam* money (*U*); **être près de ses** ~s to be tightfisted.

souahéli = swahili.

soubassement [subasmɑ̃] *nm* base.

soubresaut [subrəso] *nm* **-1.** [de voiture] jolt. **-2.** [de personne] start.

soubrette [subrɛt] *nf* maid.

souche [suʃ] *nf* **-1.** [d'arbre] stump; **dormir comme une** ~ *fig* to sleep like a log. **-2.** [de carnet] counterfoil, stub. **-3.** [de famille] founder; **de vieille** ~ of old stock. **-4.** LING root.

souci [susi] *nm* **-1.** [tracas] worry; **se faire du** ~ to worry. **-2.** [préoccupation] concern; **c'est le dernier** OU **le cadet de mes** ~s that's the least of my worries. **-3.** [fleur] marigold.

soucier [susje] [9]
◆ **se soucier** *vp*: **se** ~ **de** to care about.

soucieux, -ieuse [susjø, jøz] *adj* **-1.** [préoccupé] worried, concerned. **-2.** [concerné]:

être ~ de qqch/de faire qqch to be concerned about sthg/about doing sthg.

soucoupe [sukup] *nf* -1. [assiette] saucer. -2. [vaisseau]: **~ volante** flying saucer.

soudain, -e [sudɛ̃, ɛn] *adj* sudden.

◆ **soudain** *adv* suddenly, all of a sudden.

soudainement [sudɛnmɑ̃] *adv* suddenly.

Soudan [sudɑ̃] *nm*: **le ~ the** Sudan; **au ~** in the Sudan.

soudanais, -e [sudanɛ, ɛz] *adj* Sudanese.

◆ **Soudanais, -e** *nm, f* Sudanese person.

soude [sud] *nf* soda; **~ caustique** caustic soda.

souder [sude] [3] *vt* -1. TECHNOL to weld, to solder. -2. MÉD to knit. -3. *fig* [unir] to bind together.

soudeur, -euse [sudœr, øz] *nm, f* [personne] welder, solderer.

◆ **soudeuse** *nf* [machine] welding machine.

soudoyer [sudwaje] [13] *vt* to bribe.

soudure [sudyr] *nf* -1. TECHNOL welding; [résultat] weld; **faire la ~** *fig* to bridge the gap. -2. MÉD knitting.

souffert, -e [sufɛr, ɛrt] *pp* → **souffrir**.

souffle [sufl] *nm* -1. [respiration] breathing; [expiration] puff, breath; **un ~ d'air** *fig* a breath of air, a puff of wind. -2. *fig* [inspiration] inspiration. -3. [d'explosion] blast. -4. MÉD: **~ au cœur** heart murmur. -5. *loc*: **avoir le ~ coupé** to have one's breath taken away; **retenir son ~** to hold one's breath.

soufflé, -e [sufle] *adj* -1. CULIN soufflé (*avant n*). -2. *fam fig* [étonné] flabbergasted.

◆ **soufflé** *nm* soufflé; **~ au fromage** cheese soufflé.

souffler [sufle] [3] ◇ *vt* -1. [bougie, vitre] to blow out. -2. [verre] to blow. -3. [chuchoter]: **~ qqch à qqn** to whisper sthg to sb. -4. *fam* [prendre]: **~ qqch à qqn** to pinch sthg from sb. ◇ *vi* -1. [gén] to blow. -2. [respirer] to puff, to pant.

soufflerie [sufləri] *nf* -1. [d'orgue] bellows (*sg*). -2. AÉRON wind tunnel.

soufflet [sufle] *nm* -1. [instrument] bellows (*sg*). -2. [de train] connecting corridor, concertina vestibule. -3. COUTURE gusset. -4. *littéraire* [claque] slap.

souffleur, -euse [suflœr, øz] *nm, f* THÉÂTRE prompt.

◆ **souffleur** *nm* [de verre] blower.

◆ **souffleuse** *nf*: **souffleuse (à neige)** snowblower.

souffrance [sufrɑ̃s] *nf* suffering.

souffrant, -e [sufrɑ̃, ɑ̃t] *adj* poorly.

souffre-douleur [sufrədulœr] *nm inv* whipping boy.

souffreteux, -euse [sufrətø, øz] *adj* sickly.

souffrir [sufrir] [34] ◇ *vi* to suffer; **~ de** to suffer from; **~ du dos/cœur** to have back/heart problems. ◇ *vt* -1. [ressentir] to suffer. -2. *littéraire* [supporter] to stand, to bear.

soufi [sufi] *adj inv* Sufic.

◆ **Soufi** *nm* Sufi.

soufisme [sufism] *nm* Sufism.

soufre [sufr] *nm* sulfur *Am*, sulphur *Br*; **sentir le ~** *fig* to smack of heresy.

souhait [swe] *nm* wish; **tous nos ~s de** our best wishes for; **à ~** to perfection; **à tes/vos ~s!** bless you!

souhaitable [swɛtabl] *adj* desirable; **il est ~ que** (+ *subjonctif*) it is desirable that ....

souhaiter [swete] [4] *vt*: **~ qqch** to wish for sthg; **~ faire qqch** to hope to do sthg; **~ qqch à qqn** to wish sb sthg; **~ à qqn de faire qqch** to hope that sb does sthg; **souhaiter que ...** (+ *subjonctif*) to hope that ....

souiller [suje] [3] *vt littéraire* [salir] to soil; *fig* & *sout* to sully.

souillon [sujɔ̃] *nf péj* slut.

souillure [sujyr] *nf littéraire* -1. (*gén pl*) [déchet] waste (*U*). -2. *fig* [morale] stain.

souk [suk] *nm* souk; *fam fig* chaos.

soul [sul] *nf inv* & *adj inv* MUS soul.

soûl, -e, saoul, -e [su, sul] *adj* drunk; **être ~ de** *fig* to be drunk on.

◆ **soûl** *nm*: **tout mon/son ~** *fig* to my/his/her heart's content.

soulagement [sulaʒmɑ̃] *nm* relief.

soulager [sulaʒe] [17] *vt* -1. [gén] to relieve. -2. [véhicule] to lighten.

◆ **se soulager** *vp* -1. [se libérer] to find relief. -2. [satisfaire un besoin naturel] to relieve o.s.

soûler, saouler [sule] [3] *vt* -1. *fam* [enivrer]: **~ qqn** to get sb drunk; *fig* to intoxicate sb. -2. *fig* & *péj* [de plaintes]: **~ qqn** to bore sb silly.

◆ **se soûler** *vp fam* to get drunk.

soûlerie [sulri] *nf* drinking spree.

soulèvement [sulɛvmɑ̃] *nm* uprising.

soulever [sulve] [19] *vt* -1. [fardeau, poids] to lift; [rideau] to raise. -2. *fig* [question] to raise, to bring up. -3. *fig* [enthousiasme] to generate, to arouse; [tollé] to stir up; **~ qqn contre** to stir sb up against. -4. [foule] to stir.

◆ **se soulever** *vp* -1. [s'élever] to raise o.s., to lift o.s. -2. [se révolter] to rise up.

soulier [sulje] *nm* shoe; **être dans ses petits ~s** *fig* to feel awkward.

souligner [suliɲe] [3] *vt* **-1.** [par un trait] to underline. **-2.** *fig* [insister sur] to underline, to emphasize. **-3.** [mettre en valeur] to emphasize.

soumets → soumettre.

soumettre [sumɛtr] [84] *vt* **-1.** [astreindre]: ~ qqn à to subject sb to. **-2.** [ennemi, peuple] to subjugate. **-3.** [projet, problème]: ~ qqch (à) to submit sthg (to).
◆ **se soumettre** *vp*: se ~ (à) to submit (to).

soumis, -e [sumi, iz] ◇ *pp* → soumettre. ◇ *adj* submissive.

soumission [sumisjɔ̃] *nf* submission.

soupape [supap] *nf* valve; ~ de sûreté safety valve.

soupçon [supsɔ̃] *nm* **-1.** [suspicion, intuition] suspicion; être au-dessus/à l'abri de tout ~ to be above/free from all suspicion. **-2.** *fig* [quantité]: un ~ de a hint of.

soupçonner [supsɔne] [3] *vt* [suspecter] to suspect; ~ qqn de qqch/de faire qqch to suspect sb of sthg/of doing sthg; ~ que (+ *subjonctif*) to suspect that.

soupçonneux, -euse [supsɔnø, øz] *adj* suspicious.

soupe [sup] *nf* **-1.** CULIN soup; ~ à l'oignon onion soup; ~ populaire soup kitchen; être ~ au lait *fig* to have a quick temper; cracher dans la ~ *fig* to bite the hand that feeds. **-2.** *fam fig* [neige] slush.

soupente [supɑ̃t] *nf* cupboard under the stairs.

souper [supe] [3] ◇ *nm* supper. ◇ *vi* to have supper; en avoir soupé de qqch/de faire qqch *fam fig* to be sick and tired of sthg/of doing sthg.

soupeser [supəze] [19] *vt* **-1.** [poids] to feel the weight of. **-2.** *fig* [évaluer] to weigh up.

soupière [supjɛr] *nf* tureen.

soupir [supir] *nm* **-1.** [souffle] sigh; pousser un ~ to let out *OU* give a sigh; rendre le dernier ~ to breathe one's last. **-2.** MUS quarter-note rest *Am*, crotchet rest *Br*.

soupirail, -aux [supiraj, o] *nm* barred basement window (*for ventilation purposes*).

soupirant [supirɑ̃] *nm* suitor.

soupirer [supire] [3] ◇ *vt* to sigh. ◇ *vi* **-1.** [souffler] to sigh. **-2.** *fig & littéraire* [rechercher]: ~ après qqch to sigh for sthg, to yearn after sthg.

souple [supl] *adj* **-1.** [gymnaste] supple. **-2.** [pas] lithe. **-3.** [paquet, col] soft. **-4.** [tissu, cheveux] flowing. **-5.** [tuyau, horaire, caractère] flexible.

souplesse [suplɛs] *nf* **-1.** [de gymnaste] suppleness. **-2.** [flexibilité - de tuyau] pliability, flexibility; [- de matière] suppleness. **-3.** [de personne] flexibility.

sourate = surate.

source [surs] *nf* **-1.** [gén] source; tenir de bonne ~ *OU* de ~ sûre to have sthg on good authority *OU* from a reliable source; puiser à la ~ *OU* to go to the source; ça coule de ~ *fig* it's obvious. **-2.** [d'eau] spring; prendre sa ~ à to rise in.

sourcier, -ière [sursje, jɛr] *nm, f* water diviner.

sourcil [sursi] *nm* eyebrow; froncer les ~s to frown.

sourcilière [sursiljɛr] → arcade.

sourciller [sursije] [3] *vi*: sans ~ without batting an eyelid.

sourcilleux, -euse [sursijø, øz] *adj* fussy, finicky.

sourd¹, -e [sur, surd] ◇ *adj* **-1.** [personne] deaf; être/rester ~ à qqch *fig* to be/to remain deaf to sthg. **-2.** [bruit, voix] muffled. **-3.** [douleur] dull. **-4.** [lutte, hostilité] silent. ◇ *nm, f* deaf person.

sourd², sourdait *etc* → sourdre.

sourdement [surdəmɑ̃] *adv* **-1.** [avec un bruit sourd] dully. **-2.** *fig* [secrètement] silently.

sourdine [surdin] *nf* mute; en ~ [sans bruit] softly; [secrètement] in secret; mettre une ~ à qqch to tone sthg down.

sourd-muet, sourde-muette [surmɥɛ, surdmɥɛt] (*mpl* sourds-muets, *fpl* sourdes-muettes) ◇ *adj* deaf-mute, deaf and dumb. ◇ *nm, f* deaf-mute, deaf and dumb person.

sourdre [surdr] [73] *vi* to well up.

souriant, -e [surjɑ̃, ɑ̃t] *adj* smiling, cheerful.

souriceau [suriso] *nm* baby mouse.

souricière [surisjɛr] *nf* mousetrap; *fig* trap.

sourire [surir] [95] ◇ *vi* to smile; ~ à qqn to smile at sb; *fig* [campagne] to appeal to sb; [destin, chance] to smile on sb; ~ de qqn/qqch [être amusé par] to smile at sb/sthg. ◇ *nm* smile; garder le ~ to keep smiling.

souris [suri] *nf* **-1.** INFORM & ZOOL mouse. **-2.** [viande] knuckle. **-3.** *fam fig* [fille] chick *Am*, bird *Br*.

sournois, -e [surnwa, az] ◇ *adj* **-1.** [personne] underhand. **-2.** *fig* [maladie, phénomène] unpredictable. ◇ *nm, f* underhanded person.

sournoisement [surnwazmɑ̃] *adv* in an underhand way.

sous [su] *prép* **-1.** [gén] under; **nager ~ l'eau** to swim underwater; **~ la pluie** in the rain; **~ cet aspect** OU **angle** from that point of view. **-2.** [dans un délai de] within; **~ huit jours** within a week.

sous-alimentation [suzalimãtasjɔ̃] *nf* malnutrition, undernourishment.

sous-alimenté, -e [suzalimãte] *adj* malnourished, underfed.

sous-bois [subwa] *nm inv* undergrowth.

sous-chef [suʃɛf] (*pl* **sous-chefs**) *nm* second-in-command.

souscripteur, -trice [suskriptœr, tris] *nm, f* subscriber.

souscription [suskripsjɔ̃] *nf* subscription.

souscrire [suskrir] [99] ◇ *vt* to sign. ◇ *vi*: **~ à** to subscribe to.

sous-cutané, -e [sukytane] *adj* MÉD subcutaneous.

sous-développé, -e [sudevlɔpe] *adj* ÉCON underdeveloped; *fig & péj* backward.

sous-directeur, -trice [sudirɛktœr, tris] (*mpl* **sous-directeurs**, *fpl* **sous-directrices**) *nm, f* assistant manager (*f* assistant manageress).

sous-employé, -e [suzãplwaje] *adj* underemployed.

sous-ensemble [suzãsãbl] (*pl* **sous-ensembles**) *nm* subset.

sous-entendre [suzãtãdr] [73] *vt* to imply.

sous-entendu [suzãtãdy] (*pl* **sous-entendus**) *nm* insinuation.

sous-équipé, -e [suzekipe] *adj* underequipped.

sous-estimer [suzɛstime] [3] *vt* to underestimate, to underrate.

◆ **se sous-estimer** *vp* to underrate o.s.

sous-évaluer [suzevalye] [7] *vt* to underestimate.

sous-exploiter [suzɛksplwate] [3] *vt* to underexploit.

sous-exposer [suzɛkspoze] [3] *vt* to underexpose.

sous-fifre [sufifr] (*pl* **sous-fifres**) *nm fam* underling.

sous-jacent, -e [suʒasã, ãt] *adj* underlying.

sous-lieutenant [suljøtnã] (*pl* **sous-lieutenants**) *nm* MIL sub-lieutenant.

sous-location [sulɔkasjɔ̃] (*pl* **sous-locations**) *nf* subletting.

sous-louer [sulwe] [6] *vt* to sublet.

sous-main [sumɛ̃] *nm inv* desk blotter.

sous-marin, -e [sumarɛ̃, in] *adj* underwater (*avant n*).

◆ **sous-marin** (*pl* **sous-marins**) *nm* submarine.

sous-œuvre [suzœvr]

◆ **en sous-œuvre** *loc adv*: **reprise en ~** underpinning.

sous-officier [suzɔfisje] (*pl* **sous-officiers**) *nm* non-commissioned officer.

sous-ordre [suzɔrdr] (*pl* **sous-ordres**) *nm* **-1.** [personne] subordinate. **-2.** [espèce] suborder.

sous-payer [supeje] [11] *vt* to underpay.

sous-peuplé, -e [supœple] *adj* underpopulated.

sous-préfecture [suprefɛktyr] (*pl* **sous-préfectures**) *nf* sub-prefecture.

sous-préfet [suprefɛ] (*pl* **sous-préfets**) *nm* sub-prefect.

sous-produit [suprɔdɥi] (*pl* **sous-produits**) *nm* **-1.** [objet] by-product. **-2.** *fig* [imitation] pale imitation.

sous-secrétaire [susəkretɛr] (*pl* **sous-secrétaires**) *nm*: **~ d'État** Under-Secretary of State.

soussigné, -e [susiɲe] ◇ *adj*: **je ~** I the undersigned; **nous ~s** we the undersigned. ◇ *nm, f* undersigned.

sous-sol [susɔl] (*pl* **sous-sols**) *nm* **-1.** [de bâtiment] basement. **-2.** [naturel] subsoil.

sous-tasse [sutas] (*pl* **sous-tasses**) *nf* saucer.

sous-tendre [sutãdr] [73] *vt* to underpin.

sous-titre [sutitr] (*pl* **sous-titres**) *nm* subtitle.

sous-titrer [sutitre] [3] *vt* to subtitle.

soustraction [sustraksjɔ̃] *nf* MATHS subtraction.

soustraire [sustrɛr] [112] *vt* **-1.** [retrancher]: **~ qqch de** to subtract sthg from. **-2.** *sout* [voler]: **~ qqch de qqch** to remove sthg from sthg; **~ qqch à qqn** to take sthg away from sb. **-3.** [faire échapper]: **~ qqn à qqch** to shield sb from sthg.

◆ **se soustraire** *vp*: **se ~ à** to escape from.

sous-traitance [sutrɛtãs] (*pl* **sous-traitances**) *nf* subcontracting; **donner qqch en ~** to subcontract sthg.

sous-traitant, -e [sutrɛtã, ãt] *adj* subcontracting.

◆ **sous-traitant** (*pl* **sous-traitants**) *nm* subcontractor.

sous-traiter [sutrete] [4] *vt* to subcontract.

soustrayais, soustrayions *etc* → **soustraire**.

sous-verre [suvɛr] *nm inv* picture or document

framed between a sheet of glass and a rigid backing.

sous-vêtement [suvɛtmɑ̃] (*pl* **sous-vêtements**) *nm* undergarment; **~s** underwear (*U*), underclothes.

soutane [sutan] *nf* cassock.

soute [sut] *nf* hold.

soutenable [sutnabl] *adj* **-1.** [défendable] tenable. **-2.** [supportable] bearable.

soutenance [sutnɑ̃s] *nf* viva.

souteneur [sutnœr] *nm* procurer.

soutenir [sutnir] [40] *vt* **-1.** [immeuble, personne] to support, to hold up. **-2.** [effort, intérêt] to sustain. **-3.** [encourager] to support; POLIT to back, to support. **-4.** [affirmer]: ~ que to maintain (that). **-5.** [résister à] to withstand; [regard, comparaison] to bear.
◆ **se soutenir** *vp* **-1.** [se maintenir] to hold o.s. up, to support o.s. **-2.** [s'aider] to support each other, to back each other (up).

soutenu, -e [sutny] *adj* **-1.** [style, langage] elevated. **-2.** [attention, rythme] sustained. **-3.** [couleur] vivid.

souterrain, -e [sutɛrɛ̃, ɛn] *adj* underground.
◆ **souterrain** *nm* underground passage.

soutien [sutjɛ̃] *nm* support; **apporter son ~ à** to give one's support to; **~ de famille** breadwinner.

soutien-gorge [sutjɛ̃gɔrʒ] (*pl* **soutiens-gorge**) *nm* bra.

soutirer [sutire] [3] *vt* **-1.** [liquide] to decant. **-2.** *fig* [tirer]: ~ **qqch à qqn** to extract sthg from sb.

souvenance [suvnɑ̃s] *nf littéraire* recollection.

souvenir [suvnir] [40] *nm* **-1.** [réminiscence, mémoire] memory; **en ~ de** in memory of; **rappeler qqn au bon ~ de qqn** to remember sb to sb; **avec mes meilleurs ~s** with kind regards. **-2.** [objet] souvenir.
◆ **se souvenir** *vp* [ne pas oublier]: **se ~ de qqch/de qqn** to remember sthg/sb; **se ~ que** to remember (that).

souvent [suvɑ̃] *adv* often; **le plus ~** more often than not.

souvenu, -e [suvny] *pp* → **souvenir**.

souverain, -e [suvrɛ̃, ɛn] ◇ *adj* **-1.** [remède, état] sovereign. **-2.** [indifférence] supreme. ◇ *nm, f* [monarque] sovereign, monarch.

souverainement [suvrɛnmɑ̃] *adv* **-1.** [extrêmement] intensely. **-2.** [avec autorité] regally. **-3.** [absolument - bon] supremely; [- parfait] absolutely.

souveraineté [suvrɛnte] *nf* sovereignty.

souviendrai, souviendras *etc* → **souvenir**.

souvienne, souviennes *etc* → **souvenir**.

souviens, souvient *etc* → **souvenir**.

soviet [sɔvjɛt] *nm* soviet; **Soviet suprême** Supreme Soviet.

soviétique [sɔvjetik] *adj* Soviet.
◆ **Soviétique** *nmf* Soviet (citizen).

soviétologue [sɔvjetɔlɔg] *nmf* Kremlinologist.

soyeux, -euse [swajø, øz] *adj* silky.

soyez [swaje] → **être**.

SPA (*abr de* **Société protectrice des animaux**) *nf French society for the protection of animals,* ≃ SPCA *Am,* ≃ RSPCA *Br.*

spacieux, -ieuse [spasjø, jøz] *adj* spacious.

spaghettis [spagɛti] *nmpl* spaghetti (*U*).

sparadrap [sparadra] *nm* sticking plaster.

spartiate [sparsjat] *adj* [austère] Spartan; **à la ~** *fig* in a Spartan fashion.
◆ **spartiates** *nfpl* [sandales] Roman sandals.

spasme [spasm] *nm* spasm.

spasmodique [spasmɔdik] *adj* spasmodic.

spasmophilie [spasmɔfili] *nf* spasmophilia.

spatial, -e, -iaux [spasjal, jo] *adj* space (*avant n*).

spatio-temporel, -elle [spasjɔtɑ̃pɔrɛl] *adj* spatio-temporal.

spatule [spatyl] *nf* **-1.** [ustensile] spatula. **-2.** [de ski] tip.

speaker, speakerine [spikœr, spikrin] *nm, f* announcer.

spécial, -e, -iaux [spesjal, jo] *adj* **-1.** [particulier] special; **~ à** special to. **-2.** *fam* [bizarre] peculiar.

spécialement [spesjalmɑ̃] *adv* **-1.** [exprès] specially. **-2.** [particulièrement] particularly, especially; **pas ~** *fam* not particularly, not specially.

spécialisation [spesjalizasjɔ̃] *nf* specialization.

spécialiser [spesjalize] [3] *vt* to specialize.
◆ **se spécialiser** *vp*: **se ~ (dans)** to specialize (in).

spécialiste [spesjalist] *nmf* specialist.

spécialité [spesjalite] *nf* speciality.

spécieux, -ieuse [spesjø, jøz] *adj littéraire* specious.

spécification [spesifikasjɔ̃] *nf* specification.

spécificité [spesifisite] *nf* specificity.

spécifier [spesifje] [9] *vt* to specify.

spécifique [spesifik] *adj* specific.

spécifiquement [spesifikmɑ̃] *adv* specifically.

spécimen [spesimɛn] *nm* **-1.** [représentant] specimen. **-2.** [exemplaire] sample.

spectacle [spɛktakl] *nm* **-1.** [représentation] show. **-2.** [domaine] show business, entertainment. **-3.** [tableau] spectacle, sight; **se donner en** ~ *fig* to make a spectacle OU an exhibition of o.s.

spectaculaire [spɛktakylɛr] *adj* spectacular.

spectateur, -trice [spɛktatœr, tris] *nm, f* **-1.** [témoin] witness. **-2.** [de spectacle] spectator.

spectre [spɛktr] *nm* **-1.** [fantôme] specter *Am*, spectre *Br*. **-2.** PHYS spectrum.

spéculateur, -trice [spekylatœr, tris] *nm, f* speculator.

spéculatif, -ive [spekylatif, iv] *adj* speculative.

spéculation [spekylasjɔ̃] *nf* speculation.

spéculer [spekyle] [3] *vi*: ~ **sur** FIN to speculate in; *fig* [miser] to count on.

speech [spitʃ] (*pl* speeches) *nm* speech.

spéléologie [speleɔlɔʒi] *nf* [exploration] potholing; [science] speleology.

spéléologue [speleɔlɔg] *nmf* [explorateur] potholer; [scientifique] speleologist.

spencer [spɛnsɛr] *nm* short fitted jacket or coat.

spermatozoïde [spɛrmatɔzɔid] *nm* sperm, spermatozoon.

sperme [spɛrm] *nm* sperm, semen.

sphère [sfɛr] *nf* sphere; **les hautes** ~**s de** the higher reaches of; ~ **d'influence** sphere of influence.

sphérique [sferik] *adj* spherical.

sphincter [sfɛ̃ktɛr] *nm* sphincter.

sphinx [sfɛ̃ks] *nm inv* **-1.** MYTH & *fig* sphinx. **-2.** ZOOL hawk moth.

spirale [spiral] *nf* spiral; **en** ~ spiral.

spiritisme [spiritism] *nm* spiritualism.

spiritualité [spiritɥalite] *nf* spirituality.

spirituel, -elle [spiritɥɛl] *adj* **-1.** [de l'âme, moral] spiritual. **-2.** [vivant, drôle] witty.

spirituellement [spiritɥɛlmɑ̃] *adv* **-1.** [moralement] spiritually. **-2.** [avec humour] wittily.

spiritueux [spiritɥø] *nm* spirit.

spleen [splin] *nm littéraire* spleen.

splendeur [splɑ̃dœr] *nf* **-1.** [beauté, prospérité] splendor *Am*, splendour *Br*. **-2.** [merveille]: **c'est une** ~! it's magnificent!

splendide [splɑ̃did] *adj* magnificent, splendid.

spolier [spɔlje] [9] *vt* to despoil.

spongieux, -ieuse [spɔ̃ʒjø, jøz] *adj* spongy.

sponsor [spɔ̃nsɔr] *nm* sponsor.

sponsoring [spɔ̃sɔriŋ] *nm* sponsoring.

sponsorisation [spɔ̃sɔrizasjɔ̃] *nf* sponsoring, sponsorship.

sponsoriser [spɔ̃nsɔrize] [3] *vt* to sponsor.

spontané, -e [spɔ̃tane] *adj* spontaneous.

spontanéité [spɔ̃taneite] *nf* spontaneity.

spontanément [spɔ̃tanemɑ̃] *adv* spontaneously.

sporadique [spɔradik] *adj* sporadic.

sporadiquement [spɔradikmɑ̃] *adv* sporadically.

sport [spɔr] ◇ *nm* sport; **de** ~ sports (*avant n*); ~ **d'équipe/de combat** team/combat sport; ~**s d'hiver** winter sports; **aller aux** ~**s d'hiver** to go on a skiing holiday. ◇ *adj inv* **-1.** [vêtement] sports (*avant n*). **-2.** [fair play] sporting.

sportif, -ive [spɔrtif, iv] ◇ *adj* **-1.** [association, résultats] sports (*avant n*). **-2.** [personne, physique] sporty, athletic. **-3.** [fair play] sportsmanlike, sporting. ◇ *nm, f* sportsman (*f* sportswoman).

spot [spɔt] *nm* **-1.** [lampe] spot, spotlight. **-2.** [publicité]: ~ **(publicitaire)** commercial, advert.

SPOT, Spot [spɔt] (*abr de* satellite pour l'observation de la terre) *nm* earth observation satellite.

sprint [sprint] *nm* [SPORT - accélération] spurt; [- course] sprint; **piquer un** ~ *fam* to put on a spurt.

sprinter[1] [sprinte] [3] *vi* to sprint.

sprinter[2] [sprintœr] *nm* sprinter.

squale [skwal] *nm* dogfish.

square [skwar] *nm* small public garden.

squash [skwaʃ] *nm* squash.

squat [skwat] *nm* squat.

squatter[1] [skwatœr] *nm* squatter.

squatter[2] [skwate] [3] ◇ *vt* to squat in. ◇ *vi* to squat.

squelette [skəlɛt] *nm* skeleton.

squelettique [skəletik] *adj* **-1.** [corps] emaciated. **-2.** [exposé] sketchy, skeletal.

Sri Lanka [ʃrilɑ̃ka] *nm*: **le** ~ Sri Lanka; **au** ~ in Sri Lanka.

sri lankais, -e [ʃrilɑ̃kɛ, ɛz] *adj* Sri Lankan. ◆ **Sri Lankais, -e** *nm, f* Sri Lankan.

SS ◇ *nf* **-1.** (*abr de* Sécurité sociale) ≃ SSA *Am*, ≃ DSS *Br*. **-2.** (*abr de* SchutzStaffel) SS; **un** ~ a member of the SS. ◇ (*abr de* steamship) SS.

S.S. (*abr de* Sa Sainteté) H.H.

SSR (*abr de* Société suisse romande) *nf* *French-language Swiss broadcasting company*.

St (*abr de* saint) St.

stabilisateur, **-trice** [stabilizatœr, tris] *adj* stabilizing.

stabilisation [stabilizasjɔ̃] *nf* stabilization.

stabiliser [stabilize] [3] *vt* **-1.** [gén] to stabilize; [meuble] to steady. **-2.** [terrain] to make firm.

◆ **se stabiliser** *vp* **-1.** [véhicule, prix, situation] to stabilize. **-2.** [personne] to settle down.

stabilité [stabilite] *nf* stability.

stable [stabl] *adj* **-1.** [gén] stable. **-2.** [meuble] steady, stable.

stade [stad] *nm* **-1.** [terrain] stadium. **-2.** [étape & MÉD] stage; **en être au ~ de/où** to reach the stage of/at which.

staff [staf] *nm* staff.

stage [staʒ] *nm* SCOL work placement; [sur le temps de travail] in-service training; **faire un ~** [cours] to go on a training course; [expérience professionnelle] to go on a work placement.

stagiaire [staʒjɛr] ◇ *nmf* trainee. ◇ *adj* trainee (*avant n*).

stagnant, **-e** [stagnɑ̃, ɑ̃t] *adj* stagnant.

stagnation [stagnasjɔ̃] *nf* stagnation.

stagner [stagne] [3] *vi* to stagnate.

stakhanoviste [stakanɔvist] *nmf & adj* Stakhanovite, hard worker.

stalactite [stalaktit] *nf* stalactite.

stalagmite [stalagmit] *nf* stalagmite.

stalle [stal] *nf* stall.

stand [stɑ̃d] *nm* **-1.** [d'exposition] stand. **-2.** [de fête] stall; **~ de tir** shooting range, firing range.

standard [stɑ̃dar] ◇ *adj inv* standard. ◇ *nm* **-1.** [norme] standard. **-2.** [téléphonique] switchboard.

standardisation [stɑ̃dardizasjɔ̃] *nf* standardization.

standardiser [stɑ̃dardize] [3] *vt* to standardize.

standardiste [stɑ̃dardist] *nmf* switchboard operator.

standing [stɑ̃diŋ] *nm* standing; **immeuble de grand ~** prestigious block of flats.

staphylocoque [stafilɔkɔk] *nm* staphylococcus.

star [star] *nf* CIN star.

starlette [starlɛt] *nf* starlet.

starter [startɛr] *nm* AUTOM choke; **mettre le ~** to pull the choke out.

starting-block [startiŋblɔk] (*pl* **starting-blocks**) *nm* starting-block.

station [stasjɔ̃] *nf* **-1.** [arrêt - de bus] stop; [- de métro] station; **à quelle ~ dois-je des-** cendre? which stop do I get off at?; **~ de taxis** taxi stand. **-2.** [installations] station; **~ d'épuration** sewage treatment plant. **-3.** [ville] resort; **~ balnéaire** seaside resort; **~ de ski/de sports d'hiver** ski/winter sports resort; **~ thermale** spa (town). **-4.** [position] position; **~ debout** standing position. **-5.** INFORM: **~ de travail** work station.

stationnaire [stasjɔnɛr] *adj* stationary.

stationnement [stasjɔnmɑ̃] *nm* parking; **«~ interdit»** "no parking"; **~ en épi** angle OU angled parking.

stationner [stasjɔne] [3] *vi* to park.

station-service [stasjɔ̃sɛrvis] (*pl* **stations-service**) *nf* service station, gas station *Am*, petrol station *Br*.

statique [statik] *adj* static.

statisticien, **-ienne** [statistisjɛ̃, jɛn] *nm, f* statistician.

statistique [statistik] ◇ *adj* statistical. ◇ *nf* **-1.** [science] statistics (*U*). **-2.** [donnée] statistic.

statistiquement [statistikmɑ̃] *adv* statistically.

statuaire [statɥɛr] *nf & adj* statuary.

statue [staty] *nf* statue.

statuer [statɥe] [7] *vi*: **~ sur** to give a decision on.

statuette [statɥɛt] *nf* statuette.

statu quo [statykwo] *nm inv* status quo.

stature [statyr] *nf* stature.

statut [staty] *nm* status.

◆ **statuts** *nmpl* statutes.

statutaire [statytɛr] *adj* statutory.

Ste (*abr de* **sainte**) St.

Sté (*abr de* **société**) Co.

steak [stɛk] *nm* steak; **~ frites** steak and chips; **~ haché** mince; **~ tartare** steak tartare.

stèle [stɛl] *nf* stele.

stellaire [stelɛr] *adj* stellar.

stencil [stɛnsil] *nm* stencil.

sténo [steno] ◇ *nmf* stenographer. ◇ *nf* shorthand.

sténodactylo [stenɔdaktilo] *nmf* shorthand typist.

sténodactylographie [stenɔdaktilɔgrafi] *nf* shorthand typing.

sténographe [stenɔgraf] *nmf* stenographer.

sténographie [stenɔgrafi] *nf* shorthand.

sténographier [stenɔgrafje] [9] *vt* to take down in shorthand.

sténographique [stenɔgrafik] *adj* shorthand (*avant n*).

sténotypiste [stenɔtipist] *nmf* stenotypist.

stentor [stãtɔr] → **voix.**

steppe [stɛp] *nf* steppe.

stéréo [stereo] ◇ *adj inv* stereo. ◇ *nf* stereo; **en** ~ in stereo.

stéréotype [stereɔtip] *nm* stereotype.

stéréotypé, -e [stereɔtipe] *adj* stereotyped.

stérile [steril] *adj* **-1.** [personne] sterile, infertile; [terre] barren. **-2.** *fig* [inutile - discussion] sterile; [- efforts] futile. **-3.** MÉD sterile.

stérilet [sterilɛ] *nm* IUD, intra-uterine device.

stérilisateur [sterilizatœr] *nm* sterilizer.

stérilisation [sterilizasjɔ̃] *nf* sterilization.

stériliser [sterilize] [3] *vt* to sterilize.

stérilité [sterilite] *nf litt* & *fig* sterility; [d'efforts] futility.

sternum [stɛrnɔm] *nm* breastbone, sternum.

stéthoscope [stetɔskɔp] *nm* stethoscope.

steward [stiwart] *nm* steward.

stick [stik] *nm* [tube] stick; **de la colle en** ~ a stick of glue; **un déodorant en** ~ a stick deodorant.

stigmate [stigmat] *nm* (*gén pl*) mark, scar.
◆ **stigmates** *nmpl* RELIG stigmata.

stigmatiser [stigmatize] [3] *vt littéraire* [dénoncer] to denounce.

stimulant, -e [stimylã, ãt] *adj* stimulating.
◆ **stimulant** *nm* **-1.** [remontant] stimulant. **-2.** [motivation] incentive, stimulus.

stimulateur [stimylatœr] *nm*: ~ **cardiaque** pacemaker.

stimulation [stimylasjɔ̃] *nf* stimulation.

stimuler [stimyle] [3] *vt* to stimulate.

stipuler [stipyle] [3] *vt*: ~ **que** to stipulate (that).

stock [stɔk] *nm* stock; **en** ~ in stock; **tout un** ~ **de** *fig* & *iron* a whole stock of, plenty of.

stockage [stɔkaʒ] *nm* **-1.** [de marchandises] stocking. **-2.** INFORM storage.

stocker [stɔke] [3] *vt* **-1.** [marchandises] to stock. **-2.** INFORM to store.

Stockholm [stɔkɔlm] *n* Stockholm.

stoïcisme [stɔisism] *nm* **-1.** PHILO Stoicism. **-2.** *fig* [courage] stoicism.

stoïque [stɔik] ◇ *nmf* Stoic. ◇ *adj* stoical.

stoïquement [stɔikmã] *adv* stoically.

stomacal, -e, -aux [stɔmakal, o] *adj* stomach (*avant n*).

stomatologie [stɔmatɔlɔʒi] *nf* stomatology.

stomatologiste [stɔmatɔlɔʒist], **stomatologue** [stɔmatɔlɔg] *nmf* stomatologist.

stop [stɔp] ◇ *interj* stop!; **dis-moi** ~! say when! ◇ *nm* **-1.** [feu] brake-light. **-2.** [panneau] stop sign. **-3.** [auto-stop] hitch-hiking, hitching; **faire du** ~ to hitch, to hitch-hike; **on y est allé en** ~ we hitch-hiked OU hitched there.

stopper [stɔpe] [3] ◇ *vt* **-1.** [arrêter] to stop, to halt. **-2.** COUTURE to repair by invisible mending. ◇ *vi* to stop.

store [stɔr] *nm* **-1.** [de fenêtre] blind. **-2.** [de magasin] awning.

strabisme [strabism] *nm* squint; **être atteint de** ~ to (have a) squint.

strangulation [strãgylasjɔ̃] *nf* strangulation.

strapontin [strapɔ̃tɛ̃] *nm* **-1.** [siège] pull-down seat. **-2.** *fig* [position] minor role.

strass [stras] *nm* paste.

stratagème [strataʒɛm] *nm* stratagem.

strate [strat] *nf* stratum.

stratège [stratɛʒ] *nm* strategist.

stratégie [strateʒi] *nf* strategy.

stratégique [strateʒik] *adj* strategic.

stratifié, -e [stratifje] *adj* **-1.** GÉOL stratified. **-2.** TECHNOL laminated.

stratosphère [stratɔsfɛr] *nf* stratosphere.

stress [strɛs] *nm* stress.

stressant, -e [strɛsã, ãt] *adj* stressful.

stressé, -e [strɛse] *adj* stressed.

stresser [strɛse] [4] ◇ *vt*: ~ **qqn** to cause sb stress, to put sb under stress. ◇ *vi* to be stressed.

Stretch® [strɛtʃ] *nm inv* stretch *material*.

stretching [strɛtʃiŋ] *nm* SPORT stretching, stretching exercises (*pl*).

strict, -e [strikt] *adj* **-1.** [personne, règlement] strict. **-2.** [sobre] plain. **-3.** [absolu - minimum] bare, absolute; [- vérité] absolute; **dans la plus** ~**e intimité** strictly in private; **au sens** ~ **du terme** in the strict sense of the word.

strictement [striktəmã] *adv* **-1.** [rigoureusement] strictly. **-2.** [sobrement] plainly, soberly.

strident, -e [stridã, ãt] *adj* strident, shrill.

stridulation [stridylasjɔ̃] *nf* chirping.

strie [stri] *nf* (*gén pl*) **-1.** [sillon] groove; [en relief] ridge. **-2.** [rayure] streak.

strié, -e [strije] *adj* **-1.** [rayé] striped. **-2.** GÉOL striated.

strier [strije] [10] *vt* to streak.

string [striŋ] *nm* G-string.

strip-tease [striptiz] (*pl* **strip-teases**) *nm* striptease.

strip-teaseuse [striptizøz] (*pl* **strip-teaseuses**) *nf* stripper.

striure [strijyr] *nf* **-1.** [sillons] grooves (*pl*); [en relief] ridges (*pl*). **-2.** [rayures] streaks (*pl*).

strophe [strɔf] *nf* verse.

structural, -e, -aux [stryktyral, o] *adj* structural.

structuralisme [stryktyralism] *nm* structuralism.

structure [stryktyr] *nf* structure; ~ OU ~s d'accueil reception facilities.

structurel, -elle [stryktyrɛl] *adj* structural.

structurer [stryktyre] [3] *vt* to structure.
◆ **se structurer** *vp* to be/become structured.

strychnine [striknin] *nf* strychnine.

stuc [styk] *nm* stucco.

studieusement [stydjøzmã] *adv* studiously.

studieux, -ieuse [stydjø, jøz] *adj* **-1.** [personne] studious. **-2.** [vacances] study (*avant n*).

studio [stydjo] *nm* **-1.** CIN, PHOT & TÉLÉ studio. **-2.** [appartement] studio apartment *Am*, studio flat *Br*.

stupéfaction [stypefaksjõ] *nf* astonishment, stupefaction.

stupéfait, -e [stypefɛ, ɛt] *adj* astounded, stupefied.

stupéfiant, -e [stypefjã, ãt] *adj* astounding, stunning.
◆ **stupéfiant** *nm* narcotic, drug.

stupéfier [stypefje] [9] *vt* to astonish, to stupefy.

stupeur [stypœr] *nf* **-1.** [stupéfaction] astonishment. **-2.** MÉD stupor.

stupide [stypid] *adj* **-1.** *péj* [abruti] stupid. **-2.** [insensé - mort] senseless; [- accident] stupid. **-3.** *littéraire* [interdit] stunned.

stupidement [stypidmã] *adv* stupidly.

stupidité [stypidite] *nf* stupidity; **faire/dire des ~s** to do/say something stupid.

style [stil] *nm* **-1.** [gén] style; **de ~** period (*avant n*); **~ Empire/Louis XIII** Empire/Louis XIII Style; **~ de vie** lifestyle. **-2.** GRAM: **~ direct/indirect** direct/indirect speech.

styliser [stilize] [3] *vt* to stylize.

stylisme [stilism] *nm* COUTURE design, designing.

styliste [stilist] *nmf* COUTURE designer.

stylistique [stilistik] ◇ *adj* stylistic. ◇ *nf* stylistics (*U*).

stylo [stilo] *nm* pen; **~ bille** ballpoint (pen); **~ plume** fountain pen.

stylo-feutre [stiloføtr] (*pl* **stylos-feutres**) *nm* felt-tip pen.

su, -e [sy] *pp* → savoir.
◆ **au su et au vu de** *loc prép* under the eyes of.

suave [sɥav] *adj* [voix] smooth; [parfum] sweet.

suavité [sɥavite] *nf* pleasantness.

subalpin, -e [sybalpɛ̃, in] *adj* subalpine.

subalterne [sybaltɛrn] ◇ *nmf* subordinate, junior. ◇ *adj* [rôle] subordinate; [employé] junior.

subaquatique [sybakwatik] *adj* underwater.

subconscient, -e [sybkõsjã, ãt] *adj* subconscious.
◆ **subconscient** *nm* subconscious.

subdiviser [sybdivize] [3] *vt* to subdivide.
◆ **se subdiviser** *vp* to be subdivided.

subdivision [sybdivizjõ] *nf* subdivision.

subir [sybir] [32] *vt* **-1.** [conséquences, colère] to suffer; [personne] to put up with. **-2.** [opération, épreuve, examen] to undergo. **-3.** [dommages, pertes] to sustain, to suffer; **~ une hausse** to be increased.

subit, -e [sybi, it] *adj* sudden.

subitement [sybitmã] *adv* suddenly.

subjectif, -ive [sybʒɛktif, iv] *adj* **-1.** [personnel, partial] subjective. **-2.** MÉD: **troubles ~s** symptoms.

subjectivité [sybʒɛktivite] *nf* subjectivity.

subjonctif [sybʒõktif] *nm* subjunctive.

subjuguer [sybʒyge] [3] *vt* to captivate.

sublimation [syblimasjõ] *nf* sublimation.

sublime [syblim] *adj* sublime.

sublimer [syblime] [3] *vt* to sublimate.

submerger [sybmɛrʒe] [17] *vt* **-1.** [inonder] to flood. **-2.** [envahir] to overcome, to overwhelm. **-3.** [déborder] to overwhelm; **être submergé de travail** to be swamped with work.

submersible [sybmɛrsibl] *nm* & *adj* submersible.

subodorer [sybɔdɔre] [3] *vt fam* to smell, to scent.

subordination [sybɔrdinasjõ] *nf* subordination.

subordonné, -e [sybɔrdɔne] ◇ *adj* GRAM subordinate, dependent. ◇ *nm, f* subordinate.
◆ **subordonnée** *nf* GRAM subordinate clause.

subordonner [sybɔrdɔne] [3] *vt* **-1.** [chose]: **~ qqch à qqch** to make sthg dependent on sthg. **-2.** [personne]: **~ qqn à qqn** to subordinate sb to sb.

subornation [sybɔrnasjõ] *nf* bribing, subornation.

suborner [sybɔrne] [3] *vt* **-1.** *littéraire* [séduire] to lead astray. **-2.** JUR to bribe, to suborn.

subreptice [sybrɛptis] *adj* surreptitious.

subrepticement [sybrɛptismɑ̃] *adv* surreptitiously.

subroger [sybrɔʒe] [17] *vt* JUR to substitute.

subséquent, -e [sypsekɑ̃, ɑ̃t] *adj sout* subsequent.

subside [sypsid] *nm* (*gén pl*) grant, subsidy.

subsidiaire [sybzidjɛr] *adj* subsidiary.

subsistance [sybzistɑ̃s] *nf* subsistence; **pourvoir à la ~ de sa famille** to support one's family.

subsister [sybziste] [3] *vi* **-1.** [chose] to remain. **-2.** [personne] to live, to subsist.

subsonique [sypsɔnik] *adj* subsonic.

substance [sypstɑ̃s] *nf* **-1.** [matière] substance. **-2.** [essence] gist; **en ~** in substance.

substantiel, -ielle [sypstɑ̃sjɛl] *adj* substantial.

substantif, -ive [sypstɑ̃tif, iv] *adj* noun (*avant n*).

◆ **substantif** *nm* noun.

substituer [sypstitɥe] [7] *vt*: **~ qqch à qqch** to substitute sthg for sthg.

◆ **se substituer** *vp*: **se ~ à** [personne] to stand in for, to substitute for; [chose] to take the place of.

substitut [sypstity] *nm* **-1.** [remplacement] substitute. **-2.** JUR deputy public prosecutor.

substitution [sypstitysjɔ̃] *nf* substitution.

substrat [sypstra] *nm* **-1.** [de récit, réflexion] basis. **-2.** GÉOL & LING substratum. **-3.** CHIM substrate.

subterfuge [sypterfyʒ] *nm* subterfuge.

subtil, -e [syptil] *adj* subtle.

subtilement [syptilmɑ̃] *adv* subtly.

subtiliser [syptilize] [3] *vt* to steal.

subtilité [syptilite] *nf* subtlety.

subtropical, -e, -aux [syptrɔpikal, o] *adj* subtropical.

suburbain, -e [sybyrbɛ̃, ɛn] *adj* suburban.

subvenir [sybvənir] [40] *vi*: **~ à** to meet, to cover; **~ aux besoins de qqn** to meet sb's needs.

subvention [sybvɑ̃sjɔ̃] *nf* grant, subsidy.

subventionner [sybvɑ̃sjɔne] [3] *vt* to give a grant to, to subsidize.

subvenu, -e [sybvəny] *pp* → **subvenir**.

subversif, -ive [sybvɛrsif, iv] *adj* subversive.

subversion [sybvɛrsjɔ̃] *nf* subversion.

subviendrai, subviendras *etc* → **subvenir**.

subviens, subvient *etc* → **subvenir**.

suc [syk] *nm* **-1.** [d'arbre] sap; [de fruit, viande] juice; **~ gastrique** gastric juices (*pl*). **-2.** *littéraire* [quintessence] essence.

succédané [syksedane] *nm* substitute.

succéder [syksede] [18] *vt*: **~ à** [suivre] to follow; [remplacer] to succeed, to take over from.

◆ **se succéder** *vp* to follow one another.

succès [syksɛ] *nm* **-1.** [gén] success; **avoir du ~** to be very successful; **avoir un ~ fou (auprès de)** to be very successful (with); **à ~ hit** (*avant n*); **sans ~** [essai] unsuccessful; [essayer] unsuccessfully; **avec ~** [essai] successful; [essayer] successfully; **se tailler un franc ~** *fig* to be a great OU huge success. **-2.** [chanson, pièce] hit. **-3.** [conquête] conquest.

successeur [syksesœr] *nm* **-1.** [gén] successor. **-2.** JUR successor, heir.

successif, -ive [syksesif, iv] *adj* successive.

succession [syksesjɔ̃] *nf* **-1.** [gén] succession; **une ~ de** a succession of; **prendre la ~ de qqn** to take over from sb, to succeed sb. **-2.** JUR succession, inheritance; **droits de ~** death duties.

successivement [syksesivmɑ̃] *adv* successively.

succinct, -e [syksɛ̃, ɛ̃t] *adj* **-1.** [résumé] succinct. **-2.** [repas] frugal.

succinctement [syksɛ̃tmɑ̃] *adv* **-1.** [résumer] succinctly. **-2.** [manger] frugally.

succion [syksjɔ̃, sysjɔ̃] *nf* suction, sucking.

succomber [sykɔ̃be] [3] *vi*: **~ (à)** to succumb (to).

succulent, -e [sykylɑ̃, ɑ̃t] *adj* delicious.

succursale [sykyrsal] *nf* branch.

sucer [syse] [16] *vt* to suck.

sucette [sysɛt] *nf* [friandise] lollipop, lolly *Br*; **~ au caramel** caramel lollipop.

suçon [sysɔ̃] *nm* lovebite, hickey *Am*.

sucre [sykr] *nm* sugar; **~ cristallisé** granulated sugar; **~ glace** confectioner's sugar *Am*, icing sugar *Br*; **~ en morceaux** lump sugar; **~ d'orge** barley sugar; **~ en poudre, ~ semoule** caster sugar; **casser du ~ sur le dos de qqn** *fam fig* to talk about sb behind his/her back.

sucré, -e [sykre] *adj* [goût] sweet.

sucrer [sykre] [3] *vt* **-1.** [café, thé] to sweeten, to sugar. **-2.** *fam* [permission] to withdraw; [passage, réplique] to cut; **~ qqch à qqn** to take sthg away from sb.

◆ **se sucrer** *vp fam* **-1.** [se servir en sucre] to take some sugar. **-2.** [s'octroyer une part] to line one's pockets.

sucrerie [sykrəri] *nf* **-1.** [usine] sugar refinery. **-2.** [friandise] candy *Am*, sweet *Br*.

sucrette [sykrɛt] *nf* sweetener.

sucrier, -ière [sykrije, jɛr] *adj* sugar (*avant n*).

◆ **sucrier** *nm* sugar bowl.

sud [syd] ◇ *nm* south; **un vent du ~** a southerly wind; **le vent du ~** the south wind; **au ~** in the south; **au ~ (de)** to the south (of). ◇ *adj inv* [gén] south; [province, région] southern.

sud-africain, -e [sydafrikɛ̃, ɛn] (*mpl* **sud-africains**, *fpl* **sud-africaines**) *adj* South African.

◆ **Sud-Africain, -e** *nm, f* South African.

sud-américain, -e [sydamerikɛ̃, ɛn] (*mpl* **sud-américains**, *fpl* **sud-américaines**) *adj* South American.

◆ **Sud-Américain, -e** *nm, f* South American.

sudation [sydasjɔ̃] *nf* sweating.

sud-coréen, -enne [sydkɔreɛ̃, ɛn] (*mpl* **sud-coréens**, *fpl* **sud-coréennes**) *adj* South Ko- rean.

◆ **Sud-Coréen, -enne** *nm, f* South Korean.

sud-est [sydɛst] *nm & adj inv* southeast.

sud-ouest [sydwɛst] *nm & adj inv* southwest.

Suède [sчɛd] *nf*: **la ~** Sweden.

suédois, -e [sчedwa, az] *adj* Swedish.

◆ **suédois** *nm* [langue] Swedish.

◆ **Suédois, -e** *nm, f* Swede.

suée [sчe] *nf fam* sweat.

suer [sчe] [7] ◇ *vi* [personne] to sweat; **faire ~ qqn** *fam fig* to give sb a hard time; **se faire ~** *fam fig* to be bored to tears. ◇ *vt* to exude.

sueur [sчœr] *nf* sweat; **être en ~** to be sweating; **avoir des ~s froides** *fig* to be in a cold sweat.

Suez [sчɛz] *n*: **le canal de ~** the Suez Canal.

suffi [syfi] *pp inv* → **suffire**.

suffire [syfir] [100] ◇ *vi* **-1.** [être assez]: **~ pour qqch/pour faire qqch** to be enough for sthg/to do sthg, to be sufficient for sthg/to do sthg; **ça suffit!** that's enough! **-2.** [satisfaire]: **~ à** to be enough for. ◇ *v impers*: **il suffit de ...** all that is necessary is ..., all that you have to do is ...; **il suffit d'un moment d'inattention pour que ...** it only takes a moment of carelessness

for ...; **il lui suffit de donner sa démission** all he has to do is resign; **il suffit que** (+ *subjonctif*): **il suffit que vous lui écriviez** all (that) you need do is write to him.

◆ **se suffire** *vp*: **se ~ à soi-même** to be self-sufficient.

suffisais → **suffire**.

suffisamment [syfizamɑ̃] *adv* sufficiently.

suffisance [syfizɑ̃s] *nf* [vanité] self-importance.

suffisant, -e [syfizɑ̃, ɑ̃t] *adj* **-1.** [satisfaisant] sufficient. **-2.** [vaniteux] self-important.

suffise → **suffire**.

suffixe [syfiks] *nm* suffix.

suffocant, -e [syfɔkɑ̃, ɑ̃t] *adj* **-1.** [chaleur, fumée] suffocating. **-2.** *fig* [nouvelle, révélation] astonishing, incredible.

suffocation [syfɔkasjɔ̃] *nf* suffocation.

suffoquer [syfɔke] [3] ◇ *vt* **-1.** [suj: chaleur, fumée] to suffocate. **-2.** *fig* [suj: colère] to choke; [suj: nouvelle, révélation] to astonish, to stun. ◇ *vi* to choke; **~ de** *fig* to choke with.

suffrage [syfraʒ] *nm* vote; **rallier tous les ~s** to win all the votes; **recueillir des ~s** to win votes; **~ indirect/restreint/universel** indirect/restricted/universal suffrage.

suffragette [syfraʒɛt] *nf* suffragette.

suggérer [sygʒere] [18] *vt* **-1.** [proposer] to suggest; **~ qqch à qqn** to suggest sthg to sb; **~ à qqn de faire qqch** to suggest that sb (should) do sthg. **-2.** [faire penser à] to evoke.

suggestif, -ive [sygʒɛstif, iv] *adj* **-1.** [musique] evocative. **-2.** [pose, photo] suggestive.

suggestion [sygʒɛstjɔ̃] *nf* suggestion.

suicidaire [sчisidɛr] *adj* suicidal.

suicide [sчisid] ◇ *nm* suicide. ◇ *adj* suicide (*avant n*).

◆ **se suicider** *vp* to commit suicide, to kill o.s.

suie [sчi] *nf* soot.

suif [sчif] *nm* tallow.

suintant, -e [sчɛ̃tɑ̃, ɑ̃t] *adj* [mur] sweating; [plaie] weeping.

suintement [sчɛ̃tmɑ̃] *nm* **-1.** [de mur] sweating; [de plaie] weeping. **-2.** [d'eau] seeping, oozing.

suinter [sчɛ̃te] [3] *vi* **-1.** [eau, sang] to ooze, to seep. **-2.** [surface, mur] to sweat; [plaie] to weep.

suis¹ → **être**.

suis², suit *etc* → **suivre**.

suisse [sɥis] ◇ *adj* Swiss. ◇ *nm* RELIG ver-ger.
◆ **Suisse** ◇ *nf* [pays]: **la ~** Switzerland; **la ~ allemande/italienne/romande** German-/Italian-/French-speaking Switzerland. ◇ *nmf* [personne] Swiss (person); **les Suisses** the Swiss.
◆ **en suisse** *loc adv fam* alone, on one's own.

Suissesse [sɥisɛs] *nf* Swiss woman.

suite [sɥit] *nf* **-1.** [de liste, feuilleton] continuation. **-2.** [série]: **une ~ de** [de maisons, de succès] series; [d'événements] sequence. **-3.** [succession]: **prendre la ~ de** [personne] to succeed, to take over from; [affaire] to take over; **à la ~** one after the other; **à la ~ de** *fig* following. **-4.** [escorte] retinue. **-5.** MUS suite. **-6.** [appartement] suite.
◆ **suites** *nfpl* consequences.
◆ **de suite** *loc adv* **-1.** [l'un après l'autre] in succession. **-2.** [immédiatement] immediately.
◆ **par suite de** *loc prép* owing to, because of.

suivais, suivions *etc* → **suivre**.

suivant, -e [sɥivɑ̃, ɑ̃t] ◇ *adj* next, following. ◇ *nm, f* next OU following one; **au ~!** next!
◆ **suivant** *prép* according to; **~ que** according to whether.

suiveur [sɥivœr] *nm* follower.

suivi, -e [sɥivi] ◇ *pp* → **suivre**. ◇ *adj* **-1.** [visites] regular; [travail] sustained; [qualité] consistent. **-2.** [raisonnement] coherent.
◆ **suivi** *nm* follow-up.

suivre [sɥivr] [89] ◇ *vt* **-1.** [gén] to follow; **«faire ~»** "please forward"; **à ~** to be continued. **-2.** [suj: médecin] to treat. ◇ *vi* **-1.** SCOL to keep up. **-2.** [venir après] to follow.
◆ **se suivre** *vp* to follow one another.

sujet, -ette [sɥʒɛ, ɛt] ◇ *adj*: **être ~ à qqch** to be subject OU prone to sthg; **être ~ à faire qqch** to be apt OU liable to do sthg; **être ~ à caution** *fig* to be unconfirmed. ◇ *nm, f* [de souverain] subject.
◆ **sujet** *nm* **-1.** [gén] subject; **c'est à quel ~?** what is it about?; **~ de conversation** topic of conversation; **au ~ de** about, concerning. **-2.** [motif]: **~ de** cause for, reason for.

sulfate [sylfat] *nm* sulfate Am, sulphate Br.

sulfure [sylfyr] *nm* sulfide Am, sulphide Br.

sulfureux, -euse [sylfyrø, øz] *adj* sulfurous Am, sulphurous Br.

sulfurique [sylfyrik] *adj* sulfuric Am, sulphuric Br.

sulfurisé, -e [sylfyrize] *adj*: **papier ~** greaseproof paper.

sultan, -e [syltɑ̃, an] *nm, f* sultan (*f* sultana).

sultanat [syltana] *nm* sultanate.

Sumatra [symatra] *n* Sumatra; **à ~** in Sumatra.

summum [sɔmɔm] *nm* summit, height.

super [sypɛr] *fam* ◇ *adj inv* super, great. ◇ *nm* premium Am, four star (petrol) Br.

superbe [sypɛrb] ◇ *adj* superb; [enfant, femme] beautiful. ◇ *nf* pride, arrogance.

superbement [sypɛrbəmɑ̃] *adv* superbly.

supercarburant [sypɛrkarbyrɑ̃] *nm* high-octane gasoline Am OU petrol Br.

supercherie [sypɛrʃəri] *nf* deception, trickery.

superfétatoire [sypɛrfetatwar] *adj littéraire* superfluous.

superficie [sypɛrfisi] *nf* **-1.** [surface] area. **-2.** *fig* [aspect superficiel] surface.

superficiel, -ielle [sypɛrfisjɛl] *adj* superficial.

superficiellement [sypɛrfisjɛlmɑ̃] *adv* superficially.

superflu, -e [sypɛrfly] *adj* superfluous.
◆ **superflu** *nm* superfluity.

superforme [sypɛrfɔrm] *nf fam* top form, top shape.

super-huit [sypɛrɥit] *nm inv* super-eight.

supérieur, -e [sypɛrjœr] ◇ *adj* **-1.** [étage] upper. **-2.** [intelligence, qualité] superior; **~ à** superior to; [température] higher than, above. **-3.** [dominant - équipe] superior; [- cadre] senior. **-4.** SCOL [- classe] upper, senior; [- enseignement] higher. **-5.** *péj* [air] superior. ◇ *nm, f* superior.

supériorité [sypɛrjɔrite] *nf* superiority.

superlatif [sypɛrlatif] *nm* superlative.

supermarché [sypɛrmarʃe] *nm* supermarket.

superposable [sypɛrpozabl] *adj* stacking (*avant n*).

superposer [sypɛrpoze] [3] *vt* to stack.
◆ **se superposer** *vp* to be stacked; GÉOL to be superposed.

superposition [sypɛrpozisjɔ̃] *nf* **-1.** [action - d'objets] stacking. **-2.** [état] superposition. **-3.** *fig* [d'influences] combination.

superproduction [sypɛrprɔdyksjɔ̃] *nf* spectacular.

superpuissance [sypɛrpɥisɑ̃s] *nf* superpower.

supersonique [sypɛrsɔnik] *adj* supersonic.

superstar [sypɛrstar] *nf fam* superstar.

superstitieux, -ieuse [sypɛrstisjø, jøz] ◇ *adj* superstitious. ◇ *nm, f* superstitious person.

superstition [sypɛrstisjɔ̃] *nf* **-1.** [croyance] superstition. **-2.** [obsession] obsessive attachment.

superviser [sypɛrvize] [3] *vt* to supervise.

supervision [sypɛrvizjɔ̃] *nf* supervision.

supplanter [syplɑ̃te] [3] *vt* to supplant.

suppléance [svpleɑ̃s] *nf* substitute post *Am*, supply post *Br*.

suppléant, -e [sypleɑ̃, ɑ̃t] ◇ *adj* acting (*avant n*), temporary. ◇ *nm, f* substitute, deputy.

suppléer [syplee] [15] ◇ *vt* **-1.** *littéraire* [carence] to compensate for. **-2.** [personne] to stand in for. ◇ *vi*: ~ à to compensate for, to make up for.

supplément [syplemɑ̃] *nm* **-1.** [surplus]: un ~ de détails additional details, extra details. **-2.** PRESSE supplement. **-3.** [de billet] extra charge; en ~ extra.

supplémentaire [syplemɑ̃tɛr] *adj* extra, additional.

supplication [syplikasjɔ̃] *nf* plea.

supplice [syplis] *nm* torture; *fig* [souffrance] torture, agony; être un ~ to be agony; être au ~ to be in agony OU torment; mettre qqn au ~ to torture sb; ~ de Tantale torture.

supplicié, -e [syplisje] *nm, f* victim of torture.

supplier [syplije] [10] *vt*: ~ qqn de faire qqch to beg OU implore sb to do sthg; je t'en OU vous en supplie I beg OU implore you.

supplique [syplik] *nf* petition.

support [sypɔr] *nm* **-1.** [socle] support, base. **-2.** *fig* [de communication] medium; ~s audiovisuels audiovisual aids; ~ publicitaire advertising medium.

supportable [sypɔrtabl] *adj* **-1.** [douleur] bearable. **-2.** [conduite] tolerable, acceptable.

supporter¹ [sypɔrte] [3] *vt* **-1.** [soutenir, encourager] to support. **-2.** [endurer] to bear, to stand; ~ que (+ *subjonctif*): il ne supporte pas qu'on le contredise he cannot bear being contradicted. **-3.** [résister à] to withstand.

◆ **se supporter** *vp* [se tolérer] to bear OU stand each other.

supporter² [sypɔrtɛr] *nm* supporter.

supposé, -e [sypoze] *adj* [montant] estimated; [criminel] alleged.

supposer [sypoze] [3] *vt* **-1.** [imaginer] to suppose, to assure; en supposant que, à ~ que supposing (that). **-2.** [impliquer] to imply, to presuppose.

supposition [sypozisjɔ̃] *nf* supposition, assumption.

suppositoire [sypozitwar] *nm* suppository.

suppôt [sypo] *nm littéraire* henchman; ~ du diable OU de satan fiend.

suppression [sypresjɔ̃] *nf* **-1.** [de permis de conduire] withdrawal; [de document] suppression. **-2.** [de mot, passage] deletion. **-3.** [de loi, poste] abolition.

supprimer [syprime] [3] *vt* **-1.** [document] to suppress; [obstacle, difficulté] to remove. **-2.** [mot, passage] to delete. **-3.** [loi, poste] to abolish. **-4.** [témoin] to do away with, to eliminate. **-5.** [permis de conduire, revenus]: ~ qqch à qqn to take sthg away from sb. **-6.** [douleur] to take away, to suppress.

suppurer [sypyre] [3] *vi* to suppurate.

supputation [sypytasjɔ̃] *nf* calculation, computation.

supputer [sypyte] [3] *vt littéraire* to calculate, to compute.

supranational, -e, -aux [sypranasjɔnal, o] *adj* supranational.

suprématie [sypremasi] *nf* supremacy.

suprême [syprɛm] ◇ *adj* **-1.** [gén] supreme. **-2.** *sout* [dernier - moment, pensée] last. ◇ *nm fillets in a cream sauce*.

suprêmement [sypremmɑ̃] *adv* supremely.

sur [syr] *prép* **-1.** [position] on; [- au-dessus de] above, over; ~ la table on the table. **-2.** [direction] toward *Am*, towards *Br*; ~ la droite/gauche on the right/left, to the right/left. **-3.** [distance]: travaux ~ 10 kilomètres roadworks for 10 kilometers *Am* OU kilometres *Br*. **-4.** [d'après] by; juger qqn ~ sa mine to judge sb by his/her appearance. **-5.** [grâce à] on; il vit ~ les revenus de ses parents he lives on OU off his parents' income. **-6.** [au sujet de] on, about. **-7.** [proportion] out of; [mesure] by; 9 ~ 10 9 out of 10; un mètre ~ deux one meter *Am* OU metre *Br* by two; un jour ~ deux every other day; une fois ~ deux every other time.

◆ **sur ce** *loc adv* whereupon.

sûr, -e [syr] *adj* **-1.** [sans danger] safe. **-2.** [digne de confiance - personne] reliable, trustworthy; [- goût] reliable, sound; [- investissement] sound. **-3.** [certain] sure, certain; ~ de sure of; ~ et certain absolutely certain; ~ de soi self-confident.

surabondance [syrabɔ̃dɑ̃s] *nf* overabundance.

surabondant, -e [syrabɔ̃dɑ̃, ɑ̃t] *adj* overabundant.

surabonder [syrabɔ̃de] [3] *vi littéraire* to overabound.

suractivité [syraktivite] *nf* hyperactivity.

suraigu, -ë [syregy] *adj* high-pitched, shrill.

surajouter [syraʒute] [3] *vt* to add (on top).
◆ **se surajouter** *vp* to be added (on top).

suralimenter [syralimɑ̃te] [3] *vt* **-1.** [personne] to overfeed. **-2.** [moteur] to supercharge.

suranné, -e [syrane] *adj littéraire* old-fashioned, outdated.

surate [syrat], **sourate** [surat] *nf* sura.

surcharge [syrʃarʒ] *nf* **-1.** [excès de poids] excess load; [- de bagages] excess weight. **-2.** *fig* [surcroît]: **une ~ de travail** extra work. **-3.** [surabondance] surfeit. **-4.** [de document] alteration. **-5.** [de timbre] surcharge.

surcharger [syrʃarʒe] [17] *vt* **-1.** [véhicule, personne]: ~ **(de)** to overload (with). **-2.** [texte] to alter extensively. **-3.** [timbre] to surcharge.

surchauffe [syrʃof] *nf* overheating.

surchauffer [syrʃofe] [3] *vt* to overheat.

surclasser [syrklase] [3] *vt* to outclass.

surconsommation [syrkɔ̃sɔmasjɔ̃] *nf* overconsumption.

surcroît [syrkrwa] *nm*: **un ~ de travail/ d'inquiétude** *etc* additional work/anxiety *etc*; **de** OU **par ~** moreover, what is more.

surdi-mutité [syrdimytite] *nf* deafmuteness.

surdité [syrdite] *nf* deafness.

surdose [syrdoz] *nf* overdose.

surdoué, -e [syrdwe] *adj* exceptionally OU highly gifted.

sureau, -x [syro] *nm* elder.

sureffectif [syrefɛktif] *nm* overmanning, overstaffing.

surélever [syrelve] [19] *vt* to raise, to heighten.

sûrement [syrmɑ̃] *adv* **-1.** [certainement] certainly; ~ **pas!** *fam* no way!, definitely not! **-2.** [sans doute] certainly, surely. **-3.** [sans risque] surely, safely.

surenchère [syrɑ̃ʃɛr] *nf* higher bid; *fig* overstatement, exaggeration; **faire de la ~** *fig* to try to go one better.

surenchérir [syrɑ̃ʃerir] [32] *vi* to bid higher; *fig* to try to go one better.

surendetté, -e [syrɑ̃dɛte] *adj* overindebted.

surendettement [syrɑ̃dɛtmɑ̃] *nm* overindebtedness.

surestimer [syrɛstime] [3] *vt* **-1.** [exagérer] to overestimate. **-2.** [surévaluer] to overvalue.
◆ **se surestimer** *vp* to overestimate o.s.

sûreté [syrte] *nf* **-1.** [sécurité] safety; **en ~** safe; **de ~** safety (*avant n*). **-2.** [fiabilité] reliability. **-3.** JUR surety.
◆ **Sûreté** *nf*: **la Sûreté** ≃ F.B.I. *Am*, ≃ C.I.D. *Br*.

surexcitation [syrɛksitasjɔ̃] *nf* overexcitement.

surexciter [syrɛksite] [3] *vt* to overexcite.

surexposer [syrɛkspoze] [3] *vt* to overexpose.

surf [sœrf] *nm* surfing.

surface [syrfas] *nf* **-1.** [extérieur, apparence] surface; **faire ~** *litt* & *fig* to surface; **en ~** superficially. **-2.** [superficie] surface area.
◆ **grande surface** *nf* hypermarket.
◆ **moyenne surface** *nf* high-street store.

surfait, -e [syrfɛ, ɛt] *adj* overrated.

surfer [sœrfe] [3] *vi* to go surfing.

surfeur, -euse [sœrfœr, øz] *nm, f* surfer.

surfiler [syrfile] [3] *vt* to oversew.

surfin, -e [syrfɛ̃, in] *adj* superfine, extra fine.

surgelé, -e [syrʒəle] *adj* frozen.
◆ **surgelé** *nm* frozen food.

surgeler [syrʒəle] [25] *vt* to freeze.

surgir [syrʒir] [32] *vi* to appear suddenly; *fig* [difficulté] to arise, to come up.

surhomme [syrɔm] *nm* superman.

surhumain, -e [syrymɛ̃, ɛn] *adj* superhuman.

surimposer [syrɛ̃poze] [3] *vt* to overtax (*financially*).

surimpression [syrɛ̃presjɔ̃] *nf* double exposure.

Surinam(e) [syrinam] *nm*: **le ~** Surinam; **au ~** in Surinam.

surinfection [syrɛ̃fɛksjɔ̃] *nf* secondary infection.

surjet [syrʒɛ] *nm* overcasting stitch.

sur-le-champ [syrləʃɑ̃] *loc adv* immediately, straightaway.

surlendemain [syrlɑ̃dmɛ̃] *nm*: **le ~** two days later; **le ~ de mon départ** two days after I left.

surligner [syrliɲe] [3] *vt* to highlight.

surligneur [syrliɲœr] *nm* highlighter (pen).

surmenage [syrmənaʒ] *nm* overwork.

surmener [syrməne] [19] *vt* to overwork.
◆ **se surmener** *vp* to overwork.

surmontable [syrmɔ̃tabl] *adj* surmountable.

surmonter [syrmɔ̃te] [3] *vt* **-1.** [obstacle, peur] to overcome, to surmount. **-2.** [suj: statue, croix] to surmount, to top.

surnager [syrnaʒe] [17] *vi* **-1.** [flotter] to

float (on the surface). **-2.** *fig* [subsister] to remain, to survive.

surnaturel, **-elle** [syrnatyrɛl] *adj* supernatural.

◆ **surnaturel** *nm*: le ~ the supernatural.

surnom [syrnɔ̃] *nm* nickname.

surnombre [syrnɔ̃br]

◆ **en surnombre** *loc adv* too many.

surnommer [syrnɔme] [3] *vt* to nickname.

surpasser [syrpase] [3] *vt* to surpass, to outdo.

◆ **se surpasser** *vp* to surpass OU excel o.s.

surpayer [syrpeje] [11] *vt* [personne] to overpay; [article] to pay too much for.

surpeuplé, **-e** [syrpœple] *adj* overpopulated.

surpeuplement [syrpœpləmɑ̃] *nm* overpopulation.

surplace [syrplas] *nm*: **faire du** ~ [voiture] to be stuck (in traffic).

surplis [syrpli] *nm* surplice.

surplomb [syrplɔ̃]

◆ **en surplomb** *loc adj* overhanging.

surplomber [syrplɔ̃be] [3] ◇ *vt* to overhang. ◇ *vi* to be out of plumb.

surplus [syrply] *nm* **-1.** [excédent] surplus. **-2.** [magasin] army surplus store.

◆ **au surplus** *loc adv* besides, what is more.

surpopulation [syrpɔpylasjɔ̃] *nf* overpopulation.

surprenant, **-e** [syrprənɑ̃, ɑ̃t] *adj* surprising, amazing.

surprendrai, **surprendras** *etc* → surprendre.

surprendre [syrprɑ̃dr] [79] *vt* **-1.** [voleur] to catch (in the act). **-2.** [secret] to overhear. **-3.** [prendre à l'improviste] to surprise, to catch unawares. **-4.** [étonner] to surprise, to amaze.

◆ **se surprendre** *vp*: se ~ à faire qqch to catch o.s. doing sthg.

surpris, **-e** [syrpri, iz] *pp* → surprendre.

surprise [syrpriz] ◇ *nf* surprise; **par** ~ by surprise; **faire une** ~ **à qqn** to give sb a surprise. ◇ *adj* [inattendu] surprise (*avant n*); **grève** ~ lightning strike.

surproduction [syrprɔdyksjɔ̃] *nf* overproduction.

surréalisme [syrrealism] *nm* surrealism.

surréel, **-elle** [syrreɛl] *adj littéraire* surreal.

sursaut [syrso] *nm* **-1.** [de personne] jump, start; **en** ~ with a start. **-2.** [d'énergie] burst, surge.

sursauter [syrsote] [3] *vi* to start, to give a start.

surseoir [syrswar] [66] *vi*: ~ **à qqch** to postpone OU defer sthg.

sursis [syrsi] *nm* JUR & *fig* reprieve; **six mois avec** ~ six months' suspended sentence; **en** ~ in remission.

sursitaire [syrsitɛr] *nmf* MIL *person whose call-up has been deferred.*

surtaxe [syrtaks] *nf* surcharge.

surtension [syrtɑ̃sjɔ̃] *nf* INFORM power surge.

surtout [syrtu] *adv* **-1.** [avant tout] above all. **-2.** [spécialement] especially, particularly; ~ **pas** certainly not.

◆ **surtout que** *loc conj fam* especially as.

survécu [syrveky] *pp* → survivre.

surveillance [syrvejɑ̃s] *nf* supervision; [de la police, de militaire] surveillance; **être sous** ~ to be under surveillance; **Direction de la** ~ **du territoire** counterespionage section.

surveillant, **-e** [syrvejɑ̃, ɑ̃t] *nm, f* supervisor; [de prison] guard, warder *Br*.

surveiller [syrveje] [4] *vt* **-1.** [enfant] to watch, to keep an eye on; [suspect] to keep a watch on. **-2.** [travaux] to supervise; [examen] to invigilate. **-3.** [ligne, langage] to watch.

◆ **se surveiller** *vp* to watch o.s.

survenir [syrvənir] [40] *vi* **-1.** [personne] to arrive unexpectedly. **-2.** [incident] to occur.

survenu, **-e** [syrvəny] *pp* → survenir.

survêtement [syrvɛtmɑ̃] *nm* tracksuit.

survie [syrvi] *nf* [de personne] survival.

surviendrai, **surviendras** *etc* → survenir.

survient → survenir.

survivant, **-e** [syrvivɑ̃, ɑ̃t] *nm, f* survivor.

survivre [syrvivr] [90] *vi* to survive; ~ **à** [personne] to outlive, to survive; [accident, malheur] to survive.

survol [syrvɔl] *nm* **-1.** [de territoire] flying over. **-2.** [de texte] skimming through.

survoler [syrvɔle] [3] *vt* **-1.** [territoire] to fly over. **-2.** [texte] to skim (through).

sus [sy(s)] *interj*: ~ **à l'ennemi!** at the enemy!

◆ **en sus** *loc adv* moreover, in addition; **en** ~ **de** over and above, in addition to.

susceptibilité [syseptibilite] *nf* touchiness, sensitivity.

susceptible [syseptibl] *adj* **-1.** [ombrageux] touchy, sensitive. **-2.** [en mesure de]: ~ **de faire qqch** liable OU likely to do sthg; ~ **d'amélioration**, ~ **d'être amélioré** open to improvement.

susciter [sysite] [3] *vt* **-1.** [admiration, curiosité] to arouse. **-2.** [ennuis, problèmes] to create; ~ **qqch à qqn** *sout* to make OU cause sthg for sb.

susdit, -e [sysdi, it] ◇ *adj* above-mentioned. ◇ *nm, f* above-mentioned (person).

susnommé, -e [sysnɔme] ◇ *adj* above-named. ◇ *nm, f* above-named (person).

suspect, -e [syspɛ, ɛkt] ◇ *adj* **-1.** [personne] suspicious; ~ **de qqch** suspected of sthg. **-2.** [douteux] suspect. ◇ *nm, f* suspect.

suspecter [syspɛkte] [4] *vt* to suspect, to have one's suspicions about; ~ **qqn de qqch/de faire qqch** to suspect sb of sthg/of doing sthg.

suspendre [syspɑ̃dr] [73] *vt* **-1.** [lustre, tableau] to hang (up); ~ **au plafond/au mur** to hang from the ceiling/on the wall. **-2.** [pourparlers] to suspend; [séance] to adjourn; [journal] to suspend publication of. **-3.** [fonctionnaire, constitution] to suspend. **-4.** [jugement] to postpone, to defer.

◆ **se suspendre** *vp*: **se ~ à** to hang from.

suspendu, -e [syspɑ̃dy] ◇ *pp* → **suspendre.** ◇ *adj* **-1.** [fonctionnaire] suspended. **-2.** [séance] adjourned. **-3.** [lustre, tableau]: ~ **au plafond/au mur** hanging from the ceiling/on the wall. **-4.** [véhicule]: **bien/mal** ~ with good/bad suspension.

suspens [syspɑ̃]

◆ **en suspens** *loc adv* in abeyance.

suspense [syspɑ̃s, syspɛns] *nm* suspense.

suspension [syspɑ̃sjɔ̃] *nf* **-1.** [gén] suspension; **en** ~ in suspension, suspended. **-2.** [de combat] halt; [d'audience] adjournment. **-3.** [lustre] light fitting.

suspicieux, -ieuse [syspisjø, jøz] *adj* suspicious.

suspicion [syspisjɔ̃] *nf* suspicion.

sustentation [systɑ̃tasjɔ̃] *nf* AÉRON lift.

sustenter [systɑ̃te] [3]

◆ **se sustenter** *vp hum* & *sout* to take sustenance.

susurrer [sysyre] [3] *vt* & *vi* to murmur.

suture [sytyr] *nf* suture.

suzeraineté [syzrɛnte] *nf* suzerainty.

svastika [zvastika], **swastika** [swastika] *nm* swastika.

svelte [zvɛlt] *adj* slender.

sveltesse [zvɛltɛs] *nf* slenderness.

SVP *abr de* **s'il vous plaît.**

swahili, -e [swaili], **souahéli, -e** [swaeli] *adj* Swahili.

◆ **swahili, souahéli** *nm* [langue] Swahili.

swastika = svastika.

Swaziland [swazilɑ̃d] *nm*: **le ~** Swaziland.

sweat-shirt [switʃœrt] (*pl* **sweat-shirts**) *nm* sweatshirt.

Sydney [sidnɛ] *n* Sydney.

syllabe [silab] *nf* syllable.

sylphide [silfid] *nf* sylph.

sylvestre [silvɛstr] *adj littéraire* forest (*avant n*); → **pin.**

sylviculture [silvikyltyr] *nf* forestry.

symbiose [sɛ̃bjoz] *nf* symbiosis.

symbole [sɛ̃bɔl] *nm* symbol.

symbolique [sɛ̃bɔlik] ◇ *adj* **-1.** [figure] symbolic. **-2.** [geste, contribution] token (*avant n*). **-3.** [rémunération] nominal. ◇ *nf* **-1.** [système] system of symbols. **-2.** [interprétation] interpretation.

symboliquement [sɛ̃bɔlikmɑ̃] *adv* symbolically.

symboliser [sɛ̃bɔlize] [3] *vt* to symbolize.

symbolisme [sɛ̃bɔlism] *nm* symbolism.

symétrie [simetri] *nf* symmetry.

symétrique [simetrik] *adj* symmetrical.

symétriquement [simetrikmɑ̃] *adv* symmetrically.

sympa [sɛ̃pa] *adj fam* [personne] likeable, nice; [soirée, maison] pleasant, nice; [ambiance] friendly.

sympathie [sɛ̃pati] *nf* **-1.** [pour personne, projet] liking; **avoir de la** ~ **pour qqn** to have a liking for sb, to be fond of sb; **accueillir un projet avec** ~ to look sympathetically on a project. **-2.** [condoléances] sympathy.

sympathique [sɛ̃patik] *adj* **-1.** [personne] likeable, nice; [soirée, maison] pleasant, nice; [ambiance] friendly. **-2.** ANAT & MÉD sympathetic.

sympathisant, -e [sɛ̃patizɑ̃, ɑ̃t] ◇ *adj* sympathizing. ◇ *nm, f* sympathizer.

sympathiser [sɛ̃patize] [3] *vi* to get on well; ~ **avec qqn** to get on well with sb.

symphonie [sɛ̃fɔni] *nf* symphony.

symphonique [sɛ̃fɔnik] *adj* [musique] symphonic; [concert, orchestre] symphony (*avant n*).

symposium [sɛ̃pozjɔm] *nm* symposium.

symptomatique [sɛ̃ptɔmatik] *adj* symptomatic.

symptôme [sɛ̃ptom] *nm* symptom.

synagogue [sinagɔg] *nf* synagogue.

synchrone [sɛ̃krɔn] *adj* synchronous.

synchronique [sɛ̃krɔnik] *adj* synchronic.

synchronisation [sɛ̃krɔnizasjɔ̃] *nf* synchronization.

synchroniser [sɛ̃kʀɔnize] [3] *vt* to synchronize.

syncope [sɛ̃kɔp] *nf* **-1.** [évanouissement] blackout; **tomber en** ~ to faint. **-2.** MUS syncopation.

syncopé, -e [sɛ̃kɔpe] *adj* syncopated.

syndic [sɛ̃dik] *nm* [de copropriété] representative.

syndical, -e, -aux [sɛ̃dikal, o] *adj* **-1.** [délégué, revendication] (trade) union (*avant n*). **-2.** [patronal]: **chambre** ~e employers' association.

syndicalisme [sɛ̃dikalism] *nm* **-1.** [mouvement] trade unionism. **-2.** [activité] (trade) union activity.

syndicaliste [sɛ̃dikalist] ◇ *nmf* trade unionist. ◇ *adj* (trade) union (*avant n*).

syndicat [sɛ̃dika] *nm* [d'employés, d'agriculteurs] (trade) union; [d'employeurs, de propriétaires] association.

◆ **syndicat d'initiative** *nm* tourist office.

syndiqué, -e [sɛ̃dike] ◇ *adj* unionized. ◇ *nm, f* (trade) union member, trade unionist.

syndiquer [sɛ̃dike] [3] *vt* to unionize.

◆ **se syndiquer** *vp* **-1.** [personne] to join a (trade) union. **-2.** [groupe] to form a (trade) union.

syndrome [sɛ̃dʀom] *nm* syndrome.

synergie [sinɛʀʒi] *nf* synergy, synergism.

synode [sinɔd] *nm* synod; **le saint-**~ the holy synod.

synonyme [sinɔnim] ◇ *nm* synonym. ◇ *adj* synonymous.

synoptique [sinɔptik] *adj* synoptic.

synovie [sinɔvi] → **épanchement**.

syntagme [sɛ̃tagm] *nm* phrase.

syntaxe [sɛ̃taks] *nf* syntax.

synthé [sɛ̃te] *nm fam* synth.

synthèse [sɛ̃tɛz] *nf* **-1.** [opération & CHIM] synthesis. **-2.** [exposé] overview.

synthétique [sɛ̃tetik] *adj* **-1.** [vue] overall. **-2.** [produit] synthetic. **-3.** [personne]: **avoir l'esprit** ~ to have a gift for summing things up.

synthétiser [sɛ̃tetize] [3] *vt* to synthesize.

synthétiseur [sɛ̃tetizœʀ] *nm* synthesizer.

syphilis [sifilis] *nf* syphilis.

Syrie [siʀi] *nf*: **la** ~ Syria.

syrien, -ienne [siʀjɛ̃, jɛn] *adj* Syrian.

◆ **Syrien, -ienne** *nm, f* Syrian.

systématique [sistematik] *adj* systematic.

systématiquement [sistematikmɑ̃] *adv* systematically.

systématiser [sistematize] [3] *vt* to systematize.

◆ **se systématiser** *vp* to be/become systematic.

système [sistɛm] *nm* system; ~ **expert** IN-FORM expert system; ~ **d'exploitation** IN-FORM operating system; **le** ~ **D** resourcefulness; ~ **nerveux** nervous system; ~ **solaire** solar system.

t, T [te] *nm inv* t, T.

ta → **ton**.

TAA (*abr de* **train autos accompagnées**) *nm* car-sleeper train, ≃ Motorail® *Br*.

tabac [taba] *nm* **-1.** [plante, produit] tobacco; ~ **blond** mild OU Virginia tobacco; ~ **brun** dark tobacco; ~ **gris** shag; ~ **à priser** snuff. **-2.** [magasin] tobacconist's. **-3.** *loc*: **faire un** ~ to be a huge hit; **passer à** ~ *fam* to beat up, to do over.

tabagie [tabaʒi] *nf* **-1.** [pièce] smoke-filled room. **-2.** *Can* [bureau de tabac] tobacconist's.

tabagisme [tabaʒism] *nm* **-1.** [intoxication] nicotine addiction. **-2.** [habitude] smoking.

tabasser [tabase] [3] *vt fam* to beat up, to do over.

tabatière [tabatjɛʀ] *nf* snuffbox.

tabernacle [tabɛʀnakl] *nm* tabernacle.

table [tabl] *nf* **-1.** [meuble] table; **à** ~! lunch/dinner *etc* is ready!; **être à** ~ to be at table, to be having a meal; **se mettre à** ~ to sit down to eat; *fig* to come clean; **dresser** OU **mettre la** ~ to lay the table; **quitter la** ~ to leave the table; ~ **de chevet** OU **de nuit** bedside table; ~ **basse** coffee table; ~ **gigogne** nest of tables; ~ **de jeu** OU **à jouer** gaming table; ~ **d'opération** operating table; ~ **roulante** trolley; ~ **de travail** desk. **-2.** [nourriture]: **les plaisirs de la** ~ good food.

◆ **table des matières** *nf* contents (*pl*), table of contents.

◆ **table de multiplication** *nf* (multiplication) table.

◆ **table ronde** *nf* [conférence] round table.

tableau, -x [tablo] *nm* **-1.** [peinture] painting, picture; *fig* [description] picture; ~ **de**

maître old master; **noircir le** ~ *fig* to paint a gloomy picture. **-2.** THÉÂTRE scene. **-3.** [panneau] board; ~ **d'affichage** bulletin board *Am*, notice board *Br*; ~ **de bord** AÉRON instrument panel; AUTOM dashboard; ~ **noir** blackboard. **-4.** [liste] register; ~ **de chasse** bag; ~ **d'honneur** honours board. **-5.** [de données] table.

tablée [table] *nf* table.

tabler [table] [3] *vi*: ~ **sur** to count OU bank on.

tablette [tablɛt] *nf* **-1.** [planchette] shelf. **-2.** [de chewing-gum] stick; [de chocolat] bar.

tableur [tablœr] *nm* INFORM spreadsheet.

tablier [tablije] *nm* **-1.** [de cuisinière] apron; [d'écolier] smock. **-2.** [de magasin] shutter; [de cheminée] flue-shutter. **-3.** [de pont] roadway, deck.

tabloïd(e) [tablɔid] *nm* tabloid.

tabou, -e [tabu] *adj* taboo.
◆ **tabou** *nm* taboo.

taboulé [tabule] *nm* Lebanese dish of bulgur wheat, onions, tomatoes and herbs.

tabouret [taburɛ] *nm* stool; ~ **de bar/de cuisine/de piano** bar/kitchen/piano stool.

tabulateur [tabylatœr] *nm* tabulator, tab.

tac [tak] *nm*: **du** ~ **au** ~ **tit** for tat.

TAC (*abr de* **train auto-couchettes**) *nm* car-sleeper train, ≃ Motorail® *Br*.

tache [taʃ] *nf* **-1.** [de pelage] marking; [de peau] mark; ~ **de rousseur** OU **de son** freckle. **-2.** [de couleur, lumière] spot, patch. **-3.** [sur nappe, vêtement] stain; **faire** ~ **d'huile** *fig* to gain ground. **-4.** *littéraire* [morale] blemish.

tâche [taʃ] *nf* task; **travailler à la** ~ to do piecework; **faciliter la** ~ **de qqn** to make sb's task easier; **se tuer à la** ~ *fig* to work o.s. to death.

tacher [taʃe] [3] *vt* **-1.** [nappe, vêtement] to stain, to mark. **-2.** *fig* [réputation] to tarnish.
◆ **se tacher** *vp* **-1.** [enfant] to get one's clothes dirty. **-2.** [nappe] to stain, to mark.

tâcher [taʃe] [3] ◇ *vt*: **tâche que ça soit parfait** try to make sure it's perfect. ◇ *vi*: ~ **de faire qqch** to try to do sthg.

tâcheron [taʃrɔ̃] [3] *nm péj* drudge.

tacheter [taʃte] [27] *vt* to spot, to speckle.

tachycardie [takikardi] *nf* tachycardia.

tacite [tasit] *adj* tacit.

tacitement [tasitmɑ̃] *adv* tacitly.

taciturne [tasityrn] *adj* taciturn.

tacot [tako] *nm fam* jalopy, heap.

tact [takt] *nm* [délicatesse] tact; **avoir du** ~ to be tactful; **manquer de** ~ to be tactless.

tacticien, -ienne [taktisjɛ̃, jɛn] *nm, f* tactician.

tactile [taktil] *adj* tactile.

tactique [taktik] ◇ *adj* tactical. ◇ *nf* tactics (*pl*).

tænia = **ténia**.

taffetas [tafta] *nm* **-1.** [tissu] taffeta. **-2.** [sparadrap] plaster.

tag [tag] *nm identifying name written with a spray can on walls, the sides of trains etc*.

tagine = **tajine**.

tagliatelles [taljatɛl] *nfpl* tagliatelle (*U*).

tagueur, -euse [tagœr, øz] *nm, f person who sprays their "tag" on walls, the sides of trains etc*.

Tahiti [taiti] *n* Tahiti; **à** ~ in Tahiti.

tahitien, -ienne [taisjɛ̃, jɛn] *adj* Tahitian.
◆ **tahitien** *nm* [langue] Tahitian.
◆ **Tahitien, -ienne** *nm, f* Tahitian.

taïaut, tayaut [tajo] *interj* tally-ho.

Taibei [tajbɛ], **T'ai-pei** [tajpɛ] *n* Taipei.

taie [tɛ] *nf* **-1.** [enveloppe]: ~ **(d'oreiller)** pillowcase, pillow slip. **-2.** [sur œil] leucoma, opaque spot.

taïga [tajga] *nf* taiga.

taillader [tajade] [3] *vt* to gash.

taille [taj] *nf* **-1.** [action - de pierre, diamant] cutting; [- d'arbre, haie] pruning. **-2.** [stature] height; **être de** ~ **à faire qqch** *fig* to be capable of doing sthg. **-3.** [mesure, dimensions] size; **vous faites quelle** ~¿ what size are you¿, what size do you take¿; **ce n'est pas à ma** ~ it doesn't fit me; **de** ~ sizeable, considerable. **-4.** [milieu du corps] waist; **avoir une** ~ **de guêpe** *fig* to be waspwaisted.

taille-crayon [tajkrɛjɔ̃] (*pl* **taille-crayons**) *nm* pencil sharpener.

tailler [taje] [3] *vt* **-1.** [couper - chair, pierre, diamant] to cut; [- arbre, haie] to prune; [- crayon] to sharpen; [- bois] to carve. **-2.** [vêtement] to cut out.
◆ **se tailler** *vp* **-1.** [obtenir] to achieve. **-2.** *fam* [se sauver] to beat it, to clear off.

tailleur [tajœr] *nm* **-1.** [couturier] tailor. **-2.** [vêtement] (lady's) suit. **-3.** [de diamants, pierre] cutter. **-4.** *loc*: **s'asseoir en** ~ to sit cross-legged.

tailleur-pantalon [tajœrpɑ̃talɔ̃] (*pl* **tailleurs-pantalons**) *nm* pantsuit *Am*, trouser suit *Br*.

taillis [taji] *nm* coppice, copse.

tain [tɛ̃] *nm* silvering; **miroir sans** ~ twoway mirror.

taire [tɛr] [111] *vt* to conceal.

◆ **se taire** *vp* **-1.** [rester silencieux] to be silent OU quiet. **-2.** [cesser de s'exprimer] to fall silent; **faire se ~ qqn** to make sb be quiet; **tais-toi!** shut up! **-3.** [orchestre] to fall silent; [cris] to cease.

taisais, taisions *etc* → **taire**.

taise, taises *etc* → **taire**.

Taiwan [tajwan] *n* Taiwan; **à ~** in Taiwan.

taiwanais, -e [tajwanɛ, ɛz] *adj* Taiwanese.

◆ **Taiwanais, -e** *nm, f* Taiwanese.

tajine, tagine [taʒin] *nm North African stew of mutton steamed with a variety of vegetables.*

talc [talk] *nm* talcum powder.

talent [talã] *nm* talent; **avoir du ~** to be talented, to have talent; **les jeunes ~s** young talent (*U*).

talentueux, -euse [talãtɥø, øz] *adj* talented.

talion [taljɔ̃] *nm*: **la loi du ~** an eye for an eye (and a tooth for a tooth).

talisman [talismã] *nm* talisman.

talkie-walkie [tɔkiwɔki] (*pl* **talkies-walkies**) *nm* walkie-talkie.

taloche [talɔʃ] *nf fam* [gifle] slap.

talon [talɔ̃] *nm* **-1.** [gén] heel; **~s aiguilles/hauts** stiletto/high heels; **~s plats** low OU flat heels; **~ d'Achille** Achilles' heel; **être/marcher sur les ~s de qqn** *fig* to be/to follow hard on sb's heels; **tourner les ~s** *fig* to turn on one's heel. **-2.** [de chèque] counterfoil, stub. **-3.** CARTES stock.

talonner [talɔne] [3] *vt* **-1.** [suj: poursuivant] to be hard on the heels of. **-2.** [suj: créancier] to harry, to hound.

talonnette [talɔnɛt] *nf* **-1.** [de chaussure] heel cushion, heel-pad. **-2.** [de pantalon] binding (*to reinforce trouser bottoms*).

talquer [talke] [3] *vt* to put talcum powder on.

talus [taly] *nm* embankment.

tamarin [tamarɛ̃] *nm* [fruit] tamarind.

tamarinier [tamarinje] *nm* tamarind tree.

tamaris [tamaris], **tamarix** [tamariks] *nm* tamarisk.

tambouille [tãbuj] *nf fam* **-1.** [plat] grub. **-2.** [cuisine] cooking.

tambour [tãbur] *nm* **-1.** [instrument, cylindre] drum; **sans ~ ni trompette** *fig* without any fuss; **~ battant** *fig* briskly. **-2.** [musicien] drummer. **-3.** [porte à tourniquet] revolving door. **-4.** [à broder] embroidery hoop.

tambourin [tãburɛ̃] *nm* **-1.** [à grelots] tambourine. **-2.** [tambour] tambourin.

tambouriner [tãburine] [3] ◇ *vt* to drum. ◇ *vi*: **~ sur** OU **à** to drum on; **~ contre** to drum against.

tamis [tami] *nm* **-1.** [crible] sieve. **-2.** [de raquette] strings (*pl*).

Tamise [tamiz] *nf*: **la ~** the Thames.

tamisé, -e [tamize] *adj* [éclairage] subdued.

tamiser [tamize] [3] *vt* **-1.** [farine] to sieve. **-2.** [lumière] to filter.

tampon [tãpɔ̃] *nm* **-1.** [bouchon] stopper, plug. **-2.** [éponge] pad; **~ à récurer** scourer. **-3.** [de coton, d'ouate] pad; **~ hygiénique** OU **périodique** tampon. **-4.** [cachet] stamp; **~ encreur** inking pad. **-5.** *litt* & *fig* [amortisseur] buffer.

tamponner [tãpɔne] [3] *vt* **-1.** [document] to stamp. **-2.** [plaie] to dab.

◆ **se tamponner** *vp* to crash into each other.

tamponneuse [tãpɔnøz] → **auto**.

tam-tam [tamtam] (*pl* **tam-tams**) *nm* tom-tom.

tancer [tãse] [16] *vt littéraire* to rebuke.

tanche [tãʃ] *nf* tench.

tandem [tãdɛm] *nm* **-1.** [vélo] tandem. **-2.** [duo] pair; **en ~** together, in tandem.

tandis [tãdi]

◆ **tandis que** *loc conj* **-1.** [pendant que] while. **-2.** [alors que] while, whereas.

tangage [tãgaʒ] *nm* pitching, pitch.

tangent, -e [tãʒã, ãt] *adj*: **~ à** MATHS tangent to, tangential to; **c'était ~** *fig* it was close, it was touch and go.

◆ **tangente** *nf* tangent.

tangible [tãʒibl] *adj* tangible.

tango [tãgo] *nm* tango.

tanguer [tãge] [3] *vi* to pitch.

tanière [tanjɛr] *nf* den, lair.

tanin, tannin [tanɛ̃] *nm* tannin.

tank [tãk] *nm* tank.

tannage [tanaʒ] *nm* tanning.

tannant, -e [tanã, ãt] *adj fam* [assommant] irritating, maddening.

tanner [tane] [3] *vt* **-1.** [peau] to tan. **-2.** *fam* [personne] to pester, to annoy.

tannerie [tanri] *nf* **-1.** [usine] tannery. **-2.** [opération] tanning.

tanneur [tanœr] *nm* **-1.** [ouvrier] tanner. **-2.** [commerçant] leather merchant.

tannin = **tanin**.

tant [tã] *adv* **-1.** [quantité]: **~ de** so much; **~ de travail** so much work. **-2.** [nombre]: **~ de** so many; **~ de livres/d'élèves** so many books/pupils. **-3.** [tellement] such a lot, so much; **il l'aime ~** he loves her so much. **-4.** [quantité indéfinie] so much; **ça coûte ~** it costs so much; **à ~ pour cent** at so many per cent. **-5.** [un jour indéfini]: **votre lettre**

du ~ your letter of such-and-such a date.
-6. [comparatif]: ~ **que** as much as. **-7.** [valeur temporelle]: ~ **que** [aussi longtemps que] as long as; [pendant que] while.

◆ **en tant que** *loc conj* as; **en** ~ **que tel** as such.

◆ **tant bien que mal** *loc adv* after a fashion, somehow or other.

◆ **tant mieux** *loc adv* so much the better; ~ **mieux pour lui** good for him.

◆ **tant pis** *loc adv* too bad; ~ **pis pour lui** too bad for him.

◆ **(un) tant soit peu** *loc adv* the slightest bit.

Tantale [tɑ̃tal] → **supplice**.

tante [tɑ̃t] *nf* **-1.** [parente] aunt. **-2.** *tfam péj* [homosexuel] fairy, poof *Br*.

tantinet [tɑ̃tinɛ] *nm*: **un** ~ **exagéré/trop long** a bit exaggerated/too long.

tantôt [tɑ̃to] *adv* **-1.** [parfois] sometimes. **-2.** *vieilli* [après-midi] this afternoon.

Tanzanie [tɑ̃zani] *nf*: **la** ~ Tanzania.

tanzanien, -ienne [tɑ̃zanjɛ̃, jɛn] *adj* Tanzanian.

◆ **Tanzanien, -ienne** *nm, f* Tanzanian.

TAO (*abr de* **traduction assistée par ordinateur**) *nf* CAT.

taoïsme [taɔism] *nm* Taoism.

taon [tɑ̃] *nm* horsefly.

tapage [tapaʒ] *nm* **-1.** [bruit] row; ~ **nocturne** ≃ disturbance of the peace. **-2.** *fig* [battage] fuss (*U*).

tapageur, -euse [tapaʒœr, øz] *adj* **-1.** [hôte, enfant] rowdy. **-2.** [style] flashy. **-3.** [liaison, publicité] blatant.

tapant, -e [tapɑ̃, ɑ̃t] *adj*: **à six heures** ~ OU ~**es** at six sharp OU on the dot.

tape [tap] *nf* slap.

tape-à-l'œil [tapalœj] ◇ *adj inv* flashy. ◇ *nm inv* show.

tapenade [tapɛnad] *nf pounded anchovies with capers, olives and tuna fish*.

taper [tape] [3] ◇ *vt* **-1.** [personne, cuisse] to slap; ~ **(un coup) à la porte** to knock at the door. **-2.** [à la machine] to type. **-3.** *fam* [demander de l'argent à]: ~ **qqn de** to touch sb for.
◇ *vi* **-1.** [frapper] to hit; ~ **du poing sur** to bang one's fist on; ~ **dans ses mains** to clap. **-2.** [à la machine] to type. **-3.** *fam* [soleil] to beat down. **-4.** *fig* [critiquer]: ~ **sur qqn** to knock sb. **-5.** *fam* [puiser]: ~ **dans** to dip into.

◆ **se taper** *vp fam* **-1.** [chocolat, vin] to put away. **-2.** [corvée] to be landed with.

tapette [tapɛt] *nf* **-1.** [à tapis] carpet beater. **-2.** [à mouches] flyswatter. **-3.** *tfam péj* [homosexuel] fairy, poof *Br*.

tapinois [tapinwa]

◆ **en tapinois** *loc adv* furtively.

tapioca [tapjɔka] *nm* tapioca.

tapir¹ [tapir] *nm* ZOOL tapir.

tapir² [tapir] [32]

◆ **se tapir** *vp* **-1.** [se blottir] to crouch; *fig* [sentiment] to be hidden; **une maison tapie au creux de la vallée** *fig* a house hidden away in the valley. **-2.** [se cacher] to retreat.

tapis [tapi] *nm* **-1.** [gén] carpet; [de gymnase] mat; ~ **roulant** [pour bagages] conveyor belt; [pour personnes] travolator; ~ **de sol** groundsheet; **mettre un sujet sur le** ~ *fig* to bring up a subject. **-2.** INFORM: ~ **de souris** mouse mat.

tapis-brosse [tapibrɔs] (*pl* **tapis-brosses**) *nm* doormat.

tapisser [tapise] [3] *vt*: ~ **(de)** to cover (with).

tapisserie [tapisri] *nf* tapestry; **faire** ~ *fig* to be a wallflower.

tapissier, -ière [tapisje, jɛr] *nm, f* **-1.** [artisan] tapestry maker. **-2.** [décorateur] (interior) decorator. **-3.** [commerçant] upholsterer.

tapotement [tapɔtmɑ̃] *nm* tapping.

tapoter [tapɔte] [3] ◇ *vt* to tap; [joue] to pat. ◇ *vi*: ~ **sur** to tap on.

tapuscrit [tapyskri] *nm* typescript.

taquet [takɛ] *nm* **-1.** [butée] stop, catch. **-2.** [loquet] latch.

taquin, -e [takɛ̃, in] ◇ *adj* teasing. ◇ *nm, f* tease.

taquiner [takine] [3] *vt* **-1.** [suj: personne] to tease. **-2.** [suj: douleur] to worry.

taquinerie [takinri] *nf* teasing.

tarabiscoté, -e [tarabiskɔte] *adj* elaborate.

tarabuster [tarabyste] [3] *vt* **-1.** [suj: personne] to badger. **-2.** [suj: idée] to niggle at.

tarama [tarama] *nm* taramasalata.

tarauder [tarode] [3] *vt* to tap; *fig* to torment.

tard [tar] *adv* late; **plus** ~ later; **au plus** ~ at the latest; **sur le** ~ [en fin de journée] late in the day; [dans la vie] late in life.

tarder [tarde] [3] ◇ *vi*: ~ **à faire qqch** [attendre pour] to delay OU put off doing sthg; [être lent à] to take a long time to do sthg; **ne pas** ~ **à faire qqch** not to take long to do sthg; **le feu ne va pas** ~ **à s'éteindre** it won't be long before the fire goes out; **elle ne devrait plus** ~ **maintenant** she should be here any time now.
◇ *v impers*: **il me tarde de te revoir/qu'il**

vienne I am longing to see you again/for him to come.

tardif, -ive [tardif, iv] *adj* **-1.** [heure] late. **-2.** [excuse] belated.

tardivement [tardivmã] *adv* [arriver] late; [s'excuser] belatedly.

tare [tar] *nf* **-1.** [défaut] defect. **-2.** [de balance] tare. **-3.** *fam péj* [personne] cretin.

taré, -e [tare] ◇ *adj* **-1.** [héréditairement] tainted; *fig* flawed. **-2.** *fam péj* [idiot] cracked. ◇ *nm, f* **-1.** [héréditaire] degenerate. **-2.** *fam péj* [idiot] cretin.

tarentule [tarãtyl] *nf* tarantula.

targette [tarʒɛt] *nf* bolt.

targuer [targe] [3]
◆ **se targuer** *vp sout*: **se ~ de qqch/de faire qqch** to boast about sthg/about doing sthg.

tarif [tarif] *nm* **-1.** [prix - de restaurant, café] price; [- de service] rate, price; [douanier] tariff; **~s postaux** postage rates; **demi-~** half rate OU price; **plein ~** full rate OU price; **~ dégressif** decreasing rate; **~ préférentiel** preferential rate. **-2.** [tableau] price list.

tarifaire [tarifɛr] *adj* tariff *(avant n)*.

tarifer [tarife] [3] *vt* to fix the price OU rate for.

tarification [tarifikasjɔ̃] *nf* fixing of the price OU rate.

tarir [tarir] [32] ◇ *vt* to dry up. ◇ *vi* to dry up; **elle ne tarit pas d'éloges sur son professeur** she never stops praising her teacher.
◆ **se tarir** *vp* to dry up.

tarot [taro] *nm* tarot.
◆ **tarots** *nmpl* tarot cards.

tartare [tartar] *adj* Tartar; **sauce ~** tartare sauce; **(steak) ~** steak tartare.
◆ **Tartare** *nmf* Tartar.

tarte [tart] ◇ *nf* **-1.** [gâteau] tart; **~ aux pommes** apple tart; **~ tatin** ≃ upside-down apple cake. **-2.** *fam fig* [gifle] slap. **-3.** *loc*: **c'est pas de la ~ !** *fam* it's no joke OU picnic!; **~ à la crème** CIN custard pie; [sujet, propos] hackneyed. ◇ *adj (avec ou sans accord) fam* [idiot] stupid.

tartelette [tartəlɛt] *nf* tartlet.

tartine [tartin] *nf* **-1.** [de pain] piece of bread and butter; **~ de confiture** piece of bread and jam; **~ grillée** piece of toast. **-2.** *fam fig* [laïus]: **en mettre une ~** OU **des ~s** to write reams.

tartiner [tartine] [3] *vt* **-1.** [pain] to spread; **chocolat/fromage à ~** chocolate/cheese spread. **-2.** *fam fig* [pages] to cover.

tartre [tartr] *nm* **-1.** [de dents, vin] tartar. **-2.** [de chaudière] fur, scale.

tartuf(f)e [tartyf] *nm* hypocrite.

tas [ta] *nm* heap; **un ~ de** a lot of; **apprendre sur le ~** *fig* to learn on the job.

tasse [tas] *nf* cup; **~ à café/à thé** coffee/tea cup; **~ de café/de thé** cup of coffee/tea; **boire la ~** *fig* to get a mouthful of water.

tasseau, -x [taso] *nm* bracket.

tassement [tasmã] *nm* **-1.** [de neige] compression; [de fondations] settling. **-2.** *fig* [diminution] decline.

tasser [tase] [3] *vt* **-1.** [neige] to compress, to pack down. **-2.** [vêtements, personnes]: **~ qqn/qqch dans** to stuff sb/sthg into.
◆ **se tasser** *vp* **-1.** [fondations] to settle. **-2.** *fig* [vieillard] to shrink. **-3.** [personnes] to squeeze up. **-4.** *fam fig* [situation] to settle down.

taste-vin [tastəvɛ̃], **tâte-vin** [tatvɛ̃] *nm inv* tasting cup.

tata [tata] *nf* auntie.

tâter [tate] [3] ◇ *vt* to feel; *fig* to sound out. ◇ *vi*: **~ de** to have a taste of.
◆ **se tâter** *vp fam fig* [hésiter] to be in two minds.

tâte-vin = taste-vin.

tatillon, -onne [tatijɔ̃, ɔn] ◇ *adj* finicky. ◇ *nm, f* finicky person.

tâtonnement [tatɔnmã] *nm* **-1.** [action] groping. **-2.** *(gén pl)* [tentative] trial and error *(U)*.

tâtonner [tatɔne] [3] *vi* to grope around.

tâtons [tatɔ̃]
◆ **à tâtons** *loc adv*: **marcher/procéder à ~** to feel one's way.

tatou [tatu] *nm* armadillo.

tatouage [tatwaʒ] *nm* **-1.** [action] tattooing. **-2.** [dessin] tattoo.

tatouer [tatwe] [6] *vt* to tattoo.

taudis [todi] *nm* slum.

taulard = tôlard.

taule = tôle.

taulier = tôlier.

taupe [top] *nf litt* & *fig* mole; **être myope comme une ~** *fig* to be as blind as a bat.

taupinière [topinjɛr] *nf* molehill.

taureau, -x [tɔro] *nm* [animal] bull; **prendre le ~ par les cornes** to take the bull by the horns.
◆ **Taureau** *nm* ASTROL Taurus; **être Taureau** to be (a) Taurus.

tauromachie [tɔrɔmaʃi] *nf* bullfighting.

taux [to] *nm* rate; [de cholestérol, d'alcool] level; **~ de change** exchange rate; **~**

d'escompte rate of discount; ~ **d'intérêt** interest rate; ~ **de natalité** birth rate.

taverne [tavɛrn] *nf* tavern.

taxation [taksasjɔ̃] *nf* taxation.

taxe [taks] *nf* tax; **hors** ~ COMM exclusive of tax, before tax; [boutique, achat] duty-free; **toutes** ~**s comprises** inclusive of tax; ~ **sur la valeur ajoutée** value added tax.

taxer [takse] [3] *vt* **-1.** [imposer] to tax. **-2.** [fixer]: ~ **le prix de qqch à** to fix the price of sthg at. **-3.** *fam* [traiter]: ~ **qqn de qqch** to call sb sthg. **-4.** [accuser]: ~ **qqn de qqch** to accuse sb of sthg. **-5.** *fam* [prendre]: ~ **qqch à qqn** to cadge sthg off OU from sb.

taxi [taksi] *nm* **-1.** [voiture] taxi. **-2.** [chauffeur] taxi driver.

taxidermiste [taksidɛrmist] *nmf* taxidermist.

taximètre [taksimɛtr] *nm* meter.

taxinomie [taksinɔmi] *nf* taxonomy.

Taxiphone® [taksifɔn] *nm* pay phone.

tayaut = **taïaut**.

TB, **tb** (*abr de* **très bien**) VG.

TBE, **tbe** (*abr de* **très bon état**) vgc.

TCA (*abr de* **taxe sur le chiffre d'affaires**) *nf* tax on turnover.

TCF (*abr de* **Touring Club de France**) *nm* *French motorists' club*, ≃ AAA *Am*, ≃ AA *Br*.

Tchad [tʃad] *nm*: **le** ~ Chad; **au** ~ in Chad.

tchadien, -ienne [tʃadjɛ̃, jɛn] *adj* of/from Chad.

◆ **tchadien** *nm* [langue] Chadic.

◆ **Tchadien, -ienne** *nm, f* person from Chad.

tchador [tʃadɔr] *nm* chador.

tchécoslovaque [tʃekɔslɔvak] *adj* Czechoslovakian.

◆ **Tchécoslovaque** *nmf* Czechoslovak.

Tchécoslovaquie [tʃekɔslɔvaki] *nf*: **la** ~ Czechoslovakia.

tchèque [tʃɛk] ◇ *adj* Czech. ◇ *nm* [langue] Czech.

◆ **Tchèque** *nmf* Czech.

TCS (*abr de* **Touring Club de Suisse**) *nm* *Swiss motorists' club*, ≃ AAA *Am*, ≃ AA *Br*.

TD (*abr de* **travaux dirigés**) *nmpl* supervised practical work.

TdF (*abr de* **Télévision de France**) *nf* French broadcasting authority.

te [tə], **t'** *pron pers* **-1.** [complément d'objet direct] you. **-2.** [complément d'objet indirect] (to) you. **-3.** [réfléchi] yourself. **-4.** [avec un présentatif]: ~ **voici!** here you are!

té [te] *nm* T-square.

technicien, -ienne [tɛknisjɛ̃, jɛn] *nm, f* **-1.** [professionnel] technician. **-2.** [spécialiste]: ~ **(de)** expert (in).

technicité [tɛknisite] *nf* **-1.** [de produit] technical nature. **-2.** [avance technologique] technological sophistication. **-3.** [savoir-faire] skill.

technico-commercial, -e [tɛknikokɔmɛrsjal] (*mpl* **technico-commerciaux**, *fpl* **technico-commerciales**) ◇ *adj* sales engineer (*avant n*). ◇ *nm, f* sales engineer.

Technicolor® [tɛknikɔlɔr] *nm* Technicolor®.

technique [tɛknik] ◇ *adj* technical. ◇ *nf* technique.

techniquement [tɛknikmã] *adv* technically.

technocrate [tɛknɔkrat] *nmf* technocrat.

technologie [tɛknɔlɔʒi] *nf* technology; **de haute** ~ high-tech.

technologique [tɛknɔlɔʒik] *adj* technological.

technologue [tɛknɔlɔg], **technologiste** [tɛknɔlɔʒist] *nmf* technologist.

teck, tek [tɛk] *nm* teak.

teckel [tɛkɛl] *nm* dachshund.

tectonique [tɛktɔnik] ◇ *adj* tectonic. ◇ *nf* tectonics (U); **la** ~ **des plaques** plate tectonics.

TEE (*abr de* **Trans-Europ-Express**) *nm* TEE.

teen-ager [tinedʒœr] (*pl* **teen-agers**) *nmf* teenager.

tee-shirt (*pl* **tee-shirts**), **T-shirt** (*pl* **T-shirts**) [tiʃœrt] *nm* T-shirt.

Téflon® [teflɔ̃] *nm* Teflon®.

TEG (*abr de* **taux effectif garanti**) *nm* APR.

Téhéran [teerã] *n* Tehran.

teignais, teignions *etc* → **teindre**.

teigne [tɛɲ] *nf* **-1.** [mite] moth. **-2.** MÉD ringworm. **-3.** *fam fig* & *péj* [femme] cow; [homme] bastard.

teigneux, -euse [tɛɲø, øz] *fam fig* & *péj* ◇ *adj*: **être teigneuse** [femme] to be a cow; **être** ~ [homme] to be a bastard. ◇ *nm, f* [femme] cow; [homme] bastard.

teindre [tɛ̃dr] [81] *vt* to dye.

◆ **se teindre** *vp*: **se** ~ **les cheveux** to dye one's hair.

teint, -e [tɛ̃, tɛ̃t] ◇ *pp* → **teindre**. ◇ *adj* dyed.

◆ **teint** *nm* **-1.** [carnation] complexion. **-2.** [couleur]: **tissu bon** OU **grand** ~ colorfast *Am* OU colourfast *Br* material; **bon** ~ *fig* staunch, dyed-in-the-wool.

◆ **teinte** *nf* color *Am*, colour *Br*; **une** ~ **de** *fig* a hint of.

teinté, -e [tɛ̃te] *adj* tinted; ~ **de** *fig* tinged with.

teinter [tɛ̃te] [3] *vt* to stain.

◆ **se teinter** *vp*: se ~ **de** to become tinged with.

teinture [tɛ̃tyr] *nf* **-1.** [action] dyeing. **-2.** [produit] dye.

◆ **teinture d'iode** *nf* tincture of iodine.

teinturerie [tɛ̃tyrri] *nf* **-1.** [pressing] dry cleaner's. **-2.** [métier] dyeing.

teinturier, -ière [tɛ̃tyrje, jɛr] *nm, f* **-1.** [de pressing] dry cleaner. **-2.** [technicien] dyer.

tek = **teck**.

tel [tɛl] (*f* **telle**, *mpl* **tels**, *fpl* **telles**) ◇ *adj* **-1.** [valeur indéterminée] such-and-such a; ~ **et** ~ such-and-such a. **-2.** [semblable] such; **un** ~ **homme** such a man; **une telle générosité** such generosity; **de telles gens** such people; **je n'ai rien dit de** ~ I never said anything of the sort. **-3.** [valeur emphatique ou intensive] such; **un** ~ **génie** such a genius; **un** ~ **bonheur** such happiness. **-4.** [introduit un exemple ou une énumération]: ~ **(que)** such as, like. **-5.** [introduit une comparaison] like; **il est** ~ **que je l'avais toujours rêvé** he's just like I always dreamt he would be; ~ **quel** as it is/was *etc.*

◇ *pron indéf:* ~ **veut marcher, tandis que** ~ **autre veut courir** one will want to walk, while another will want to run; **une telle m'a dit qu'il était parti** someone or other told me he'd left.

◆ **à tel point que** *loc conj* to such an extent that.

◆ **de telle manière que** *loc conj* in such a way that.

◆ **de telle sorte que** *loc conj* with the result that, so that.

tél. (*abr de* **téléphone**) tel.

télé [tele] *nf fam* TV, telly *Br.*

téléachat [teleaʃa] *nm* teleshopping.

téléacteur, -trice [teleaktœr, -tris] *nm, f* telesalesperson.

télébenne [telebɛn], **télécabine** [telekabin] *nf* cablecar.

télécarte [telekart] *nf* phonecard.

télécharger [teleʃarʒe] [17] *vt* to download.

télécommande [telekɔmɑ̃d] *nf* remote control.

télécommander [telekɔmɑ̃de] [3] *vt* to operate by remote control; *fig* to mastermind.

télécommunication [telekɔmynikasjɔ̃] *nf* telecommunications (*pl*).

téléconférence [telekɔ̃ferɑ̃s] *nf* teleconference.

télécopie [telekɔpi] *nf* fax.

télécopieur [telekɔpjœr] *nm* fax (machine).

télédiffuser [teledifyze] [3] *vt* to televise.

télédiffusion [teledifyzjɔ̃] *nf* televising.

télédistribution [teledistribysjɔ̃] *nf* cable television.

télé-enseignement [teleɑ̃sɛɲmɑ̃] (*pl* **télé-enseignements**) *nm* distance learning.

téléfilm [telefilm] *nm* film made for television.

télégramme [telegram] *nm* telegram.

télégraphe [telegraf] *nm* telegraph.

télégraphie [telegrafi] *nf* telegraphy.

télégraphier [telegrafje] [9] *vt* to telegraph.

télégraphique [telegrafik] *adj* [fil, poteau] telegraph (*avant n*); **en style** ~ in telegraphic style, in telegraphese.

télégraphiste [telegrafist] *nmf* **-1.** [technicien] telegraphist. **-2.** [employé] telegraph boy (*f* telegraph girl).

téléguidage [telegidaʒ] *nm* remote control.

téléguider [telegide] [3] *vt* to operate by remote control; *fig* to mastermind.

téléinformatique [teleɛ̃fɔrmatik] *nf* INFORM data communication.

téléobjectif [teleɔbʒɛktif] *nm* telephoto lens (*sg*).

télépathie [telepati] *nf* telepathy.

télépathique [telepatik] *adj* telepathic.

téléphérique [teleferik] *nm* cableway.

téléphone [telefɔn] *nm* telephone; ~ **cellulaire** cellular telephone; ~ **sans fil** cordless telephone; ~ **rouge** hotline; ~ **de voiture** carphone.

téléphoner [telefɔne] [3] ◇ *vt* to telephone, to phone. ◇ *vi* to telephone, to phone; ~ **à qqn** to telephone sb, to phone sb (up).

téléphonique [telefɔnik] *adj* telephone (*avant n*), phone (*avant n*).

téléphoniste [telefɔnist] *nmf* (telephone) operator, telephonist *Br.*

téléprospection [teleprɔspɛksjɔ̃] *nf* telemarketing.

télescopage [teleskɔpaʒ] *nm* **-1.** [de véhicules] concertinaing. **-2.** *fig* [d'idées] cross-fertilization.

télescope [teleskɔp] *nm* telescope.

télescoper [teleskɔpe] [3] *vt* [véhicule] to crash into.

◆ **se télescoper** *vp* **-1.** [véhicules] to concertina. **-2.** *fig* [idées] to influence each other.

télescopique [teleskɔpik] *adj* **-1.** [antenne] telescopic. **-2.** [planète] visible only by telescope.

téléscripteur [teleskriptœr] *nm* teletype-writer *Am*, teleprinter *Br*.

télésiège [telesjɛʒ] *nm* chairlift.

téléski [teleski] *nm* ski tow.

téléspectateur, -trice [telespɛktatœr, tris] *nm, f* (television) viewer.

télésurveillance [telesyrvejɑ̃s] *nf* remote surveillance.

Télétex® [teletɛks] *nm* teletex.

Télétype® [teletip] *nm* Teletype®.

téléviser [televize] [3] *vt* to televise.

téléviseur [televizœr] *nm* television (set).

télévision [televizjɔ̃] *nf* television; **à la ~** on television; **~ câblée** cable television.

télévisuel, -elle [televizɥɛl] *adj* television (*avant n*).

télex [telɛks] *nm inv* telex.

télexer [telekse] [4] *vt* to telex.

tellement [tɛlmɑ̃] *adv* **-1.** [si, à ce point] so (+ *comparatif*) so much; **~ plus jeune que** so much younger than; **pas ~** not especially, not particularly; **ce n'est plus ~ frais/populaire** it's no longer all that fresh/popular. **-2.** [autant]: **~ de** [personnes, objets] so many; [gentillesse, travail] so much. **-3.** [tant] so much; **elle a ~ changé** she's changed so much; **je ne comprends rien ~** il parle vite he talks so quickly that I can't understand a word.

téloche [telɔʃ] *nf fam* telly.

téméraire [temerɛr] ◇ *adj* **-1.** [audacieux] bold. **-2.** [imprudent] rash. ◇ *nmf* hothead.

témérité [temerite] *nf* **-1.** [audace] boldness. **-2.** [imprudence] rashness.

témoignage [temwaɲaʒ] *nm* **-1.** JUR testimony, evidence (*U*); **faux ~** perjury. **-2.** [gage] token, expression; **en ~ de** as a token of. **-3.** [récit] account.

témoigner [temwaɲe] [3] ◇ *vt* **-1.** [manifester] to show, to display. **-2.** JUR: **~ que** to testify that. ◇ *vi* **-1.** JUR to testify; **~ contre** to testify against; **~ en faveur de qqn** to testify in sb's favor *Am* OU favour *Br*. **-2.** **~ de** [être le signe de] to show; [certifier] to testify (as) to.

témoin [temwɛ̃] ◇ *nm* **-1.** [gén] witness; **être ~ de qqch** to be a witness to sthg, to witness sthg; **prendre qqn à ~ (de)** to call on sb as a witness (of); **~ à charge** JUR witness for the prosecution; **~ oculaire** eyewitness. **-2.** INFORM indicator. **-3.** [marque]: **~ de** evidence (*U*) of. **-4.** SPORT baton. ◇ *adj* [appartement] show (*avant n*).

tempe [tɑ̃p] *nf* temple.

tempérament [tɑ̃peramɑ̃] *nm* temperament; **avoir du ~** to be hot-blooded.

tempérance [tɑ̃perɑ̃s] *nf* temperance, moderation.

tempérant, -e [tɑ̃perɑ̃, ɑ̃t] *adj* temperate.

température [tɑ̃peratyr] *nf* temperature; **avoir de la ~** to have a temperature; **prendre sa ~** to take one's temperature.

tempéré, -e [tɑ̃pere] *adj* **-1.** [climat] temperate. **-2.** [personne] even-tempered.

tempérer [tɑ̃pere] [18] *vt* **-1.** [adoucir] to temper; *fig* [enthousiasme, ardeur] to moderate. **-2.** *fig & littéraire* [douleur, peine] to attenuate, to soothe.

tempête [tɑ̃pɛt] *nf* storm; **une ~ de** *fig* a storm of; **~ de sable** sandstorm.

tempêter [tɑ̃pɛte] [4] *vi* to rage.

tempétueux, -euse [tɑ̃petɥø, øz] *adj littéraire* stormy; *fig* tempestuous.

temple [tɑ̃pl] *nm* **-1.** HIST temple. **-2.** [protestant] church.

tempo [tɛmpo] *nm* tempo.

temporaire [tɑ̃pɔrɛr] *adj* temporary.

temporairement [tɑ̃pɔrɛrmɑ̃] *adv* temporarily.

temporel, -elle [tɑ̃pɔrɛl] *adj* **-1.** [défini dans le temps] time (*avant n*). **-2.** [terrestre] temporal.

temporisateur, -trice [tɑ̃pɔrizatœr, tris] ◇ *adj* **-1.** [stratégie] delaying (*avant n*). **-2.** [personne] who stalls OU delays. ◇ *nm, f* person who stalls OU delays.

temporiser [tɑ̃pɔrize] [3] *vi* to play for time, to stall.

temps [tɑ̃] *nm* **-1.** [gén] time; **à plein ~** full-time; **à mi-~** half-time; **à ~ partiel** part-time; **en un ~ record** in record time; **au** OU **du ~ où** (in the days) when; **de mon ~** in my day; **sa prend un certain ~** it takes some time; **ces ~-ci, ces derniers ~** these days; **pendant ce ~** meanwhile; **les premiers ~** at the beginning; **en ~ utile** in due course; **en ~ de guerre/paix** in wartime/peacetime; **il est grand ~ que** it is high time that; **il est grand ~ de partir** it is high time that we left; **il était ~!** *iron* and about time too!; **avoir le ~ de faire qqch** to have time to do sthg; **gagner du ~** to save time; **passer le ~** to pass the time; **~ libre** free time; **~ mort** SPORT stoppage time, injury time; *fig* break, pause; **à ~** in time; **de ~ à autre** now and then OU again; **de ~ en ~** from time to time; **en même ~** at the same time; **tout le ~** all the time; **tuer le ~** to kill time; **avoir tout son ~** to have all the time in the world; **ne pas laisser à qqn le ~ de se retourner** not to give sb the time to catch his/her breath; **rattraper le ~ perdu** to make up for lost time; **par**

les ~ **qui courent** in this day and age. **-2.** MUS beat. **-3.** GRAM tense. **-4.** MÉTÉOR weather; **gros** ~ rough weather OU conditions; **un** ~ **de chien** foul weather.

tenable [tənabl] *adj* bearable.

tenace [tənas] *adj* **-1.** [gén] stubborn. **-2.** *fig* [odeur, rhume] lingering. **-3.** [colle] strong.

ténacité [tenasite] *nf* **-1.** [d'odeur] lingering nature. **-2.** [de préjugé, personne] stubbornness.

tenailler [tənaje] [3] *vt* to torment.

tenailles [tənaj] *nfpl* pincers.

tenancier, -ière [tənɑ̃sje, jɛr] *nm, f* manager (*f* manageress).

tenant [tənɑ̃t] *nm* **-1.** (*gén pl*) [d'opinion] supporter. **-2.** SPORT holder. **-3.** *loc*: **d'un seul** ~ in one piece, intact.

tendance [tɑ̃dɑ̃s] *nf* **-1.** [disposition] tendency; **avoir** ~ **à qqch/à faire qqch** to have a tendency to sthg/to do sthg, to be inclined to sthg/to do sthg. **-2.** [économique, de mode] trend.

tendancieusement [tɑ̃dɑ̃sjøzmɑ̃] *adv* tendentiously.

tendancieux, -ieuse [tɑ̃dɑ̃sjø, jøz] *adj* tendentious.

tendeur [tɑ̃dœr] *nm* **-1.** [sangle] elastic strap (*for fastening luggage etc*). **-2.** [appareil] wire-strainer. **-3.** [de bicyclette] chain-adjuster. **-4.** [de tente] runner.

tendinite [tɑ̃dinit] *nf* tendinitis.

tendon [tɑ̃dɔ̃] *nm* tendon; ~ **d'Achille** Achilles' tendon.

tendre¹ [tɑ̃dr] ◇ *adj* **-1.** [gén] tender. **-2.** [matériau] soft. **-3.** [couleur] delicate. ◇ *nmf* tender-hearted person.

tendre² [tɑ̃dr] [73] ◇ *vt* **-1.** [corde] to tighten. **-2.** [muscle] to tense. **-3.** [objet, main]: ~ **qqch à qqn** to hold out sthg to sb. **-4.** [bâche] to hang. **-5.** [piège] to set (up). ◇ *vi*: ~ **à** [évoluer vers] to tend to; ~ **vers** [viser à] to aim at.

◆ **se tendre** *vp* to tighten; *fig* [relations] to become strained.

tendrement [tɑ̃drəmɑ̃] *adv* tenderly.

tendresse [tɑ̃drɛs] *nf* **-1.** [affection] tenderness. **-2.** [indulgence] sympathy.

◆ **tendresses** *nfpl*: **se faire des** ~**s** to be loving with each other.

tendron [tɑ̃drɔ̃] *nm part of veal rib*.

tendu, -e [tɑ̃dy] ◇ *pp* → **tendre**. ◇ *adj* **-1.** [fil, corde] taut. **-2.** [pièce]: ~ **de** [velours] hung with; [papier peint] covered with. **-3.** [personne] tense. **-4.** [atmosphère, rapports] strained. **-5.** [main] outstretched.

ténèbres [tenɛbr] *nfpl* darkness (*sg*), shadows; *fig* depths.

ténébreux, -euse [tenebrø, øz] *adj* **-1.** *littéraire* [forêt] dark, shadowy. **-2.** *fig* [dessein, affaire] mysterious. **-3.** [personne] serious, solemn.

teneur [tənœr] *nf* content; [de traité] terms (*pl*); ~ **en alcool/cuivre** alcohol/copper content.

ténia, tænia [tenja] *nm* tapeworm.

tenir [tənir] [40] ◇ *vt* **-1.** [objet, personne, solution] to hold. **-2.** [garder, conserver, respecter] to keep. **-3.** [gérer - boutique] to keep, to run. **-4.** [apprendre]: ~ **qqch de qqn** to have sthg from sb. **-5.** [considérer]: ~ **qqn pour** to regard sb as.

◇ *vi* **-1.** [être solide] to stay up, to hold together. **-2.** [durer] to last. **-3.** [pouvoir être contenu] to fit. **-4.** [être attaché]: ~ **à** [personne] to care about; [privilèges] to value. **-5.** [vouloir absolument]: ~ **à faire qqch** to insist on doing sthg. **-6.** [ressembler]: ~ **de** to take after. **-7.** [relever de]: ~ **de** to have something of. **-8.** [dépendre de]: **il ne tient qu'à toi de ...** it's entirely up to you to .... **-9.** *loc*: ~ **bon** to stand firm; **qu'à cela ne tienne** it OU that doesn't matter; **tiens!** [en donnant] here!; [surprise] well, well!; [pour attirer attention] look!

◆ **se tenir** *vp* **-1.** [réunion] to be held. **-2.** [personnes] to hold one another; **se** ~ **par la main** to hold hands. **-3.** [être présent] to be. **-4.** [être cohérent] to make sense. **-5.** [se conduire] to behave (o.s.). **-6.** [se retenir]: **se** ~ **(à)** to hold on (to). **-7.** [se borner]: **s'en** ~ **à** to stick to.

tennis [tenis] ◇ *nm* **-1.** [sport] tennis. **-2.** [terrain] tennis court. ◇ *nmpl* tennis shoes.

tennisman [tenisman] (*pl* **tennismen** [tenismen]) *nm* tennis player.

ténor [tenɔr] ◇ *adj* [instrument de musique] tenor (*avant n*). ◇ *nm* **-1.** [chanteur] tenor. **-2.** *fig* [vedette]: **un** ~ **de la politique** a political star performer.

tensioactif, -ive [tɑ̃sjɔaktif, iv] *adj* surface-active.

tension [tɑ̃sjɔ̃] *nf* **-1.** [contraction, désaccord] tension. **-2.** MÉD pressure; **avoir de la** ~ to have high blood pressure; ~ **artérielle** blood pressure. **-3.** ÉLECTR voltage; **haute/basse** ~ high/low voltage.

tentaculaire [tɑ̃takylɛr] *adj fig* sprawling.

tentacule [tɑ̃takyl] *nm* tentacle.

tentant, -e [tɑ̃tɑ̃, ɑ̃t] *adj* tempting.

tentateur, -trice [tɑ̃tatœr, tris] ◇ *adj* tempting. ◇ *nm, f* tempter (*f* temptress).

tentation [tɑ̃tasjɔ̃] *nf* temptation.

tentative [tãtativ] *nf* attempt; ~ **d'homicide** attempted murder; ~ **de suicide** suicide attempt.

tente [tãt] *nf* tent.

◆ **tente à oxygène** *nf* oxygen tent.

tenter [tãte] [3] *vt* **-1.** [entreprendre]: ~ **qqch/de faire qqch** to attempt sthg/to do sthg. **-2.** [plaire] to tempt; **être tenté par qqch/de faire qqch** to be tempted by sthg/ to do sthg.

tenture [tãtyr] *nf* hanging.

tenu, -e [təny] ⋄ *pp* → **tenir.** ⋄ *adj* **-1.** [obligé]: **être ~ à qqch** to be bound by sthg; **être ~ de faire qqch** to be required OU obliged to do sthg. **-2.** [en ordre]: **bien/mal** ~ [maison] well/badly kept.

badly turned out.

ténu, -e [teny] *adj* **-1.** [fil] fine; *fig* [distinction] tenuous. **-2.** [voix] thin.

tenue [təny] *nf* **-1.** [entretien] running; ~ **de la comptabilité** bookkeeping. **-2.** [manières] good manners (*pl*). **-3.** [maintien du corps] posture. **-4.** [costume] dress; ~ **réglementaire** regulation uniform; ~ **de soirée** evening dress; **être en petite ~** to be scantily dressed.

◆ **tenue de route** *nf* roadholding.

tequila [tekila] *nf* tequila.

ter [tɛr] ⋄ *adv* MUS three times. ⋄ *adj*: **12 ~ 12B.**

térébenthine [terebãtin] *nf* turpentine.

Tergal® [tɛrgal] *nm* ≃ Terylene®.

tergiversation [tɛrʒiversasjɔ̃] *nf* shilly-shallying (*U*).

tergiverser [tɛrʒivɛrse] [3] *vi* to shillyshally.

terme [tɛrm] *nm* **-1.** [fin] end; **mettre un ~ à** to put an end OU a stop to. **-2.** [de grossesse] term; **mener une grossesse à ~** to go full term; **avant ~** prematurely. **-3.** [échéance] time limit; [de loyer] rent day; **à ~** FIN forward (*avant n*); **à court/moyen/long ~** [calculer] in the short/medium/long term; [projet] short-/medium-/long-term. **-4.** [mot, élément] term.

◆ **termes** *nmpl* **-1.** [expressions] words; **en d'autres ~s** in other words. **-2.** [de contrat] terms. **-3.** [relations]: **être en bons/mauvais ~s avec qqn** to be on good/bad terms with sb.

terminaison [tɛrminɛzɔ̃] *nf* GRAM ending.

◆ **terminaison nerveuse** *nf* nerve ending.

terminal, -e, -aux [tɛrminal, o] *adj* **-1.** [au bout] final. **-2.** MÉD [phase] terminal.

◆ **terminal, -aux** *nm* terminal.

◆ **terminale** *nf* SCOL ≃ twelfth grade *Am*, ≃ upper sixth year OU form *Br.*

terminer [tɛrmine] [3] *vt* to end, to finish; [travail, repas] to finish; ~ **qqch par** to finish sthg with.

◆ **se terminer** *vp* to end, to finish; **se ~ par** to end OU finish with; **se ~ en** to end in.

terminologie [tɛrminɔlɔʒi] *nf* terminology.

terminus [tɛrminys] *nm* terminus.

termite [tɛrmit] *nm* termite.

ternaire [tɛrnɛr] *adj* CHIM & MATHS ternary; LITTÉRATURE & MUS triple.

terne [tɛrn] *adj* dull.

ternir [tɛrnir] [32] *vt* to dirty; [métal, réputation] to tarnish.

◆ **se ternir** *vp* to get dirty; [métal, réputation] to tarnish.

terrain [tɛrɛ̃] *nm* **-1.** [sol] soil; **tout ~** all-terrain; **vélo tout ~** mountain bike. **-2.** [surface] piece of land; ~ **vague** waste ground (*U*) OU land (*U*). **-3.** [emplacement - de football, rugby] pitch; [- de golf] course; ~ **d'aviation** airfield; ~ **de camping** campsite. **-4.** MIL terrain. **-5.** *fig* [domaine] ground; **en ~ glissant** *fig* on shaky ground. **-6.** *loc*: **céder du ~ à qqn** to give ground to sb; **déblayer le ~** *fig* to clear the ground; **gagner du ~** to gain ground; **gagner du ~ sur qqn** to gain on sb; **sur le ~** in the field.

terrasse [tɛras] *nf* terrace.

terrassement [tɛrasmã] *nm* [action] excavation.

terrasser [tɛrase] [3] *vt* [suj: personne] to bring down; [suj: émotion] to overwhelm; [suj: maladie] to conquer.

terrassier [tɛrasje] *nm* laborer *Am*, labourer *Br.*

terre [tɛr] *nf* **-1.** [monde] world. **-2.** [sol] ground; **par ~** on the ground; **sous ~** underground; ~ **à ~** *fig* down-to-earth. **-3.** [matière] earth, soil; ~ **cuite** terracotta; ~ **glaise** clay. **-4.** [propriété] land (*U*). **-5.** [territoire, continent] land; **sur la ~ ferme** on dry land; ~ **natale** native land. **-6.** ÉLECTR ground *Am*, earth *Br.*

◆ **Terre** *nf*: **la Terre** Earth; **la Terre promise** the Promised Land; **la Terre Sainte** the Holy Land.

terreau [tɛro] *nm* compost.

terre-neuve [tɛrnœv] *nm inv* Newfoundland (dog).

Terre-Neuve [tɛrnœv] *nf* Newfoundland; **à ~** in Newfoundland.

terre-plein [tɛrplɛ̃] (*pl* **terre-pleins**) *nm* platform.

terrer [tɛre] [4]

◆ **se terrer** *vp* to go to earth.

terrestre [tɛrɛstr] *adj* **-1.** [croûte, atmosphère] of the earth. **-2.** [animal, transport] land (*avant n*). **-3.** [plaisir, paradis] earthly. **-4.** [considérations] worldly.

terreur [tɛrœr] *nf* terror.

terreux, -euse [tɛrø, øz] *adj* **-1.** [substance, goût] earthy. **-2.** [mains, teint] muddy.

terri = terril.

terrible [tɛribl] *adj* **-1.** [gén] terrible. **-2.** [appétit, soif] terrific, enormous; **avoir un travail** ~ to have a terrific OU an enormous amount of work. **-3.** *fam* [excellent] brilliant.

terriblement [tɛribləmɑ̃] *adv* terribly.

terrien, -ienne [tɛrjɛ̃, jɛn] ◇ *adj* **-1.** [foncier]: **propriétaire** ~ landowner. **-2.** [vertu] rural. ◇ *nm, f* [habitant de la Terre] earthling.

terrier [tɛrje] *nm* **-1.** [tanière] burrow. **-2.** [chien] terrier.

terrifier [tɛrifje] [9] *vt* to terrify.

terril [tɛril], **terri** [tɛri] *nm* slag heap.

terrine [tɛrin] *nf* terrine.

territoire [tɛritwar] *nm* **-1.** [pays, zone] territory. **-2.** ADMIN area.

◆ **territoire d'outre-mer** *nm* (French) overseas territory.

territorial, -e, -iaux [tɛritɔrjal, jo] *adj* territorial.

terroir [tɛrwar] *nm* **-1.** [sol] soil. **-2.** [région rurale] country; **du** ~ rural.

terroriser [tɛrɔrize] [3] *vt* to terrorize.

terrorisme [tɛrɔrism] *nm* terrorism.

terroriste [tɛrɔrist] ◇ *nmf* terrorist. ◇ *adj* terrorist (*avant n*).

tertiaire [tɛrsjɛr] ◇ *nm* tertiary sector. ◇ *adj* tertiary.

tertio [tɛrsjo] *adv* third, thirdly.

tes → ton.

tesson [tɛsɔ̃] *nm* piece of broken glass.

test [tɛst] *nm* test; ~ **de grossesse** pregnancy test.

testament [tɛstamɑ̃] *nm* will; *fig* legacy.

◆ **Testament** *nm*: **Ancien/Nouveau Testament** Old/New Testament.

testamentaire [tɛstamɑ̃tɛr] *adj* of a will.

tester [tɛste] [3] ◇ *vt* to test. ◇ *vi* to make a will.

testicule [tɛstikyl] *nm* testicle.

tétaniser [tetanize] [3] *vt* to cause to go into spasm; *fig* to paralyze *Am*, to paralyse *Br*.

tétanos [tetanos] *nm* tetanus.

têtard [tɛtar] *nm* tadpole.

tête [tɛt] *nf* **-1.** [gén] head; **de la** ~ **aux pieds** from head to foot OU toe; **la** ~ **en bas** head down; **la** ~ **la première** head first; **calculer qqch de** ~ to calculate sthg in one's head; **50 francs par** ~ 50 francs a head OU each; ~ **chercheuse** homing head; ~ **d'écriture** INFORM write head; ~ **de lecture** INFORM read head; ~ **de liste** POLIT main candidate; ~ **de mort** death's head; **piquer une** ~ *fam* to have OU go for a dip; **se casser la** ~ **pour faire qqch** *fam* *fig* to kill o.s. doing sthg; **se laver la** ~ to wash one's hair; **se payer la** ~ **de qqn** *fam* to make fun of sb, to take the mickey out of sb; **avoir la grosse** ~ *fam* to be big-headed; **être** ~ **en l'air** to have one's head in the clouds; **avoir la** ~ **sur les épaules** to have a good head on one's shoulders; **faire la** ~ to sulk; **garder la** ~ **froide** to keep a cool head; **perdre la** ~ to lose one's head; **tenir** ~ **à qqn** to stand up to sb. **-2.** [visage] face. **-3.** [devant - de cortège, peloton] head, front; **de** ~ [voiture] front (*avant n*); *fig* [personne] high-powered; **en** ~ SPORT in the lead.

tête-à-queue [tɛtakø] *nm inv* spin.

tête-à-tête [tɛtatɛt] *nm inv* tête-à-tête; **en** ~ alone.

tête-bêche [tɛtbɛʃ] *loc adv* head to tail.

tête-de-nègre [tɛtdənɛgr] *adj inv* dark brown.

tétée [tete] *nf* feed.

tétine [tetin] *nf* **-1.** [de biberon, mamelle] teat. **-2.** [sucette] pacifier *Am*, dummy *Br*.

téton [tetɔ̃] *nm* **-1.** *fam* [sein] breast. **-2.** TECHNOL nipple.

tétralogie [tetralɔʒi] *nf* tetralogy.

tétraplégique [tetrapleʒik] *adj* quadriplegic.

têtu, -e [tety] *adj* stubborn.

teuf-teuf [tœftœf] *nm inv* old banger.

teuton, -onne [tøtɔ̃, ɔn] *péj* ◇ *adj* Teutonic. ◇ *nm, f* Teuton.

texte [tɛkst] *nm* **-1.** [écrit] wording; **dans le** ~ in the original; ~ **intégral** unabridged text; ~ **de loi** legal text. **-2.** [imprimé] text. **-3.** [extrait] passage.

textile [tɛkstil] ◇ *adj* textile (*avant n*). ◇ *nm* **-1.** [matière] textile. **-2.** [industrie] **le** ~ textiles (*pl*), the textile industry.

textuel, -elle [tɛkstɥɛl] *adj* **-1.** [analyse] textual; [citation] exact; **il a dit ça,** ~ those were his very OU exact words. **-2.** [traduction] literal.

textuellement [tɛkstɥɛlmɑ̃] *adv* verbatim.

texture [tɛkstyr] *nf* texture.

TF1 (*abr de* **Télévision Française 1**) *nf French independent television company.*

TG (*abr de* **Trésorerie générale**) *nf local finance office.*

TGI *abr de* **tribunal de grande instance**.

TGV (*abr de* **train à grande vitesse**) *nm* *French high-speed train linking major cities.*

thaï [taj] *nm & adj inv* Thai.
◆ **Thaï** *nm, f* Thai.

thaïlandais, -e [tajlɑ̃dɛ, ɛz] *adj* Thai.
◆ **Thaïlandais, -e** *nm, f* Thai.

Thaïlande [tajlɑ̃d] *nf*: **la ~** Thailand.

thalasso(thérapie) [talasɔ(terapi)] *nf* sea-water therapy.

thaumaturge [tomatyrʒ] *nm littéraire* miracle worker.

thé [te] *nm* tea; **~ au citron/lait** tea with lemon/milk; **~ nature** tea without milk, black tea.

théâtral, -e, -aux [teatral, o] *adj* **-1.** [saison] theatre (*avant n*). **-2.** [ton] theatrical.

théâtralement [teatralmɑ̃] *adv* theatrically.

théâtre [teatr] *nm* **-1.** [bâtiment, représentation] theatre. **-2.** [troupe] theatre company. **-3.** [art]: **faire du ~** to be on the stage; **adapté pour le ~** adapted for the stage. **-4.** [œuvre] plays (*pl*). **-5.** [lieu] scene; **~ d'opérations** MIL theatre of operations.

théière [tejɛr] *nf* teapot.

théine [tein] *nf* caffeine.

thématique [tematik] ◇ *adj* thematic. ◇ *nf* themes (*pl*).

thème [tɛm] *nm* **-1.** [sujet & MUS] theme. **-2.** SCOL prose.
◆ **thème astral** *nm* birth chart.

théocratie [teɔkrasi] *nf* theocracy.

théologie [teɔlɔʒi] *nf* theology.

théologien, -ienne [teɔlɔʒjɛ̃, jɛn] *nm, f* theologian.

théologique [teɔlɔʒik] *adj* theological.

théorème [teɔrɛm] *nm* theorem.

théoricien, -ienne [teɔrisjɛ̃, jɛn] *nm, f* theoretician.

théorie [teɔri] *nf* theory; **en ~** in theory.

théorique [teɔrik] *adj* theoretical.

théoriquement [teɔrikmɑ̃] *adv* theoretically.

théoriser [teɔrize] [3] ◇ *vt* to theorize about. ◇ *vi*: **~ (sur)** to theorize (about).

thérapeute [terapøt] *nmf* therapist.

thérapeutique [terapøtik] ◇ *adj* therapeutic. ◇ *nf* therapy.

thérapie [terapi] *nf* therapy.

thermal, -e, -aux [tɛrmal, o] *adj* thermal.

thermalisme [tɛrmalism] *nm* ≃ hydrotherapy.

thermes [tɛrm] *nmpl* thermal baths.

thermique [tɛrmik] *adj* thermal.

thermodynamique [tɛrmɔdinamik] ◇ *adj* thermodynamic. ◇ *nf* thermodynamics (*U*).

thermomètre [tɛrmɔmɛtr] *nm* [instrument] thermometer.

thermonucléaire [tɛrmɔnykleɛr] *adj* thermonuclear.

Thermos® [tɛrmos] *nm ou nf* Thermos® (flask).

thermostat [tɛrmɔsta] *nm* thermostat.

thésard, -e [tezar, ard] *nm, f fam* PhD student.

thésauriser [tezɔrize] [3] ◇ *vt* to hoard. ◇ *vi* to hoard money.

thésaurus, thesaurus [tezɔrys] *nm inv* thesaurus.

thèse [tɛz] *nf* **-1.** [opinion] argument; **pièce/roman à ~** drama/novel of ideas. **-2.** PHILO & UNIV thesis; **~ de doctorat** doctorate. **-3.** [théorie] theory.

thon [tɔ̃] *nm* tuna.

thoracique [tɔrasik] *adj* thoracic; → **cage**.

thorax [tɔraks] *nm* thorax.

thriller [srilœr, trilœr] *nm* thriller.

thrombose [trɔ̃boz] *nf* thrombosis.

thune, tune [tyn] *nf fam* cash (*U*), dough (*U*).

thym [tɛ̃] *nm* thyme.

thyroïde [tiroid] *nf* thyroid (gland).

TI *abr de* **tribunal d'instance**.

Tibet [tibɛ] *nm*: **le ~** Tibet; **au ~** in Tibet.

tibétain, -e [tibetɛ̃, ɛn] *adj* Tibetan.
◆ **Tibétain, -e** *nm, f* Tibetan.

tibia [tibja] *nm* tibia.

tic [tik] *nm* tic.

ticket [tikɛ] *nm* ticket; **~ de caisse** (till) receipt; **~ modérateur** *proportion of medical expenses payable by the patient*; **~ de rationnement** ration coupon; **~-repas** ≃ luncheon voucher; **avoir un ~ avec qqn** *fam fig* to have made a hit with sb.

tic-tac [tiktak] ◇ *interj* tick-tock! ◇ *nm inv* tick-tock.

tiédasse [tjedas] *adj péj* tepid.

tiède [tjɛd] ◇ *adj* **-1.** [boisson, eau] tepid, lukewarm. **-2.** [vent] mild. **-3.** *fig* [accueil] lukewarm. ◇ *adv*: **à boire ~** serve lukewarm.

tièdement [tjɛdmɑ̃] *adv* half-heartedly.

tiédeur [tjedœr] *nf* **-1.** [chaleur modérée] tepidness. **-2.** *fig* [de climat] mildness. **-3.** *fig* [indifférence] half-heartedness.

tiédir [tjedir] [32] ◇ *vt* to warm. ◇ *vi* to become warm; **faire ~ qqch** to warm sthg.

tien [tjɛ̃]

◆ **le tien** (*f* **la tienne** [latjɛn], *mpl* **les tiens** [letjɛ̃], *fpl* **les tiennes** [letjɛn]) *pron poss* yours; **les ~s** your family; **mets-y du ~!** make an effort!; **à la tienne!** cheers!; **tu as encore fais des tiennes!** you've been up to your tricks again!

tiendrai, **tiendras** *etc* → tenir.

tienne ◇ *vb* → tenir. ◇ *pron poss* → **tien**.

tiens, **tient** *etc* → tenir.

tierce [tjɛrs] ◇ *nf* **-1.** MUS third. **-2.** CARTES & ESCRIME tierce. **-3.** TYPO final proof. ◇ *adj* → **tiers**.

tiercé [tjɛrse] *nm system of betting involving the first three horses in a race.*

tiers, **tierce** [tjɛr, tjɛrs] *adj*: **une tierce personne** a third party.
◆ **tiers** *nm* **-1.** [étranger] outsider, stranger. **-2.** [tierce personne] third party; **assurance au ~** third-party insurance. **-3.** [de fraction]: **le ~ de** one-third of; **~ provisionnel** *thrice-yearly income tax payment based on estimated tax due for the previous year.*

tiers-monde [tjɛrmɔ̃d] *nm*: **le ~** the Third World.

tiers-mondisation [tjɛrmɔ̃dizasjɔ̃] *nf*: **la ~ de ce pays** this country's economic degeneration to Third World levels.

tiers-mondiste [tjɛrmɔ̃dist] ◇ *adj* favouring the Third World. ◇ *nmf* champion of the Third World.

tiers-payant [tjɛrpejɑ̃] *nm system by which a proportion of the fee for medical treatment is paid directly to the hospital, doctor or pharmacist by the patient's insurer.*

tifs [tif] *nmpl fam* hair (*U*).

TIG (*abr de* **travail d'intérêt général**) *nm* community service.

tige [tiʒ] *nf* **-1.** [de plante] stem, stalk. **-2.** [de bois, métal] rod.

tignasse [tiɲas] *nf fam* mop (of hair).

tigre [tigr] *nm* tiger; **jaloux comme un ~** *fig* fiercely jealous.

tigré, **-e** [tigre] *adj* **-1.** [rayé] striped; [chat] tabby (*avant n*). **-2.** [tacheté] spotted; [cheval] piebald.

tigresse [tigrɛs] *nf* tigress.

tilleul [tijœl] *nm* lime (tree).

tilt [tilt] *nm*: **faire ~** *fam fig* to ring a bell.

timbale [tɛ̃bal] *nf* **-1.** [gobelet] (metal) cup; **décrocher la ~** *fig* to hit the jackpot. **-2.** CULIN timbale. **-3.** MUS kettledrum.

timbrage [tɛ̃braʒ] *nm* postmarking.

timbre [tɛ̃br] *nm* **-1.** [gén] stamp. **-2.** [de voix] timbre. **-3.** [de bicyclette] bell.

timbré, **-e** [tɛ̃bre] ◇ *adj* **-1.** [papier, enve-

loppe] stamped. **-2.** [voix] resonant. **-3.** *fam* [fou] barmy, doolally. ◇ *nm*, *f fam* loony.

timbrer [tɛ̃bre] [3] *vt* to stamp.

timide [timid] ◇ *adj* **-1.** [personne] shy. **-2.** [protestation, essai] timid. **-3.** [soleil] uncertain. ◇ *nmf* shy person.

timidement [timidmɑ̃] *adv* shyly; [protester] timidly.

timidité [timidite] *nf* **-1.** [de personne] shyness. **-2.** [de protestation] timidness.

timing [tajmiŋ] *nm* **-1.** [emploi du temps] schedule. **-2.** [organisation] timing.

timonier [timɔnje] *nm* helmsman.

timoré, **-e** [timɔre] *adj* fearful, timorous.

tintamarre [tɛ̃tamar] *nm fam* racket.

tintement [tɛ̃tmɑ̃] *nm* [de cloche, d'horloge] chiming; [de pièces] jingling.

tinter [tɛ̃te] [3] *vi* **-1.** [cloche, horloge] to chime. **-2.** [pièces] to jingle.

tintin [tɛ̃tɛ̃] *interj fam* no way!, not a chance!

tintouin [tɛ̃twɛ̃] *nm fam* **-1.** [vacarme] racket. **-2.** [souci] worry.

TIP [tip] (*abr de* **titre interbancaire de paiement**) *nm payment slip for bills,* ≈ bank giro payment slip *Br.*

tique [tik] *nf* tick.

tiquer [tike] [3] *vi fam*: **~ (sur)** to wince (at).

tir [tir] *nm* **-1.** [SPORT - activité] shooting; [- lieu] (**centre de**) **~** shooting range; **~ à l'arc** archery; **~ au pigeon** clay pigeon shooting. **-2.** [trajectoire] shot. **-3.** [salve] fire (*U*). **-4.** [manière, action de tirer] firing.

TIR (*abr de* **transports internationaux routiers**) *international road transport agreement allowing lorries to avoid customs until they reach their destination.*

tirade [tirad] *nf* **-1.** THÉÂTRE soliloquy. **-2.** [laïus] tirade.

tirage [tiraʒ] *nm* **-1.** [de journal] circulation; [de livre] print run; **à grand ~** mass circulation; **~ limité** limited edition. **-2.** [du loto] draw; **~ au sort** drawing lots. **-3.** [de cheminée] draft *Am*, draught *Br*. **-4.** [de vin] drawing off. **-5.** *loc*: **il y a du tirage** *fam fig* there is some friction.

tiraillement [tirajmɑ̃] *nm* (*gén pl*) **-1.** [crampe] cramp. **-2.** *fig* [conflit] conflict.

tirailler [tiraje] [3] ◇ *vt* **-1.** [tirer sur] to tug (at). **-2.** *fig* [écarteler]: **être tiraillé par/entre qqch** to be torn by/between sthg. ◇ *vi* to fire wildly.

tirailleur [tirajœr] *nm* skirmisher.

Tirana [tirana] *n* Tirane.

tire [tir] *nf* **-1.** *fam* [voiture] wheels (*pl*). **-2.** *loc*: **vol à la ~** *fam* pickpocketing; **voleur à la ~** *fam* pickpocket.

tiré, -e [tire] *adj* [fatigué]: **avoir les traits ~s** OU **le visage ~** to look drawn.

tire-au-flanc [tiroflã] *nm inv fam* shirker, skiver *Br*.

tire-botte [tirbɔt] (*pl* **tire-bottes**) *nm* bootjack.

tire-bouchon [tirbuʃɔ̃] (*pl* **tire-bouchons**) *nm* corkscrew.

◆ **en tire-bouchon** *loc adv* corkscrew (*avant n*).

tire-bouchonner [tirbuʃɔne] [3] ◇ *vt* to twiddle. ◇ *vi* to get OU become twisted.

tire-d'aile [tirdɛl]

◆ **à tire-d'aile** *loc adv* as quickly as possible.

tire-fesses [tirfɛs] *nm inv fam* ski-tow.

tire-lait [tirlɛ] *nm inv* breast pump.

tire-larigot [tirlarigo]

◆ **à tire-larigot** *loc adv fam* to one's heart's content.

tirelire [tirlir] *nf* moneybox.

tirer [tire] [3] ◇ *vt* **-1.** [gén] to pull; [rideaux] to draw; [tiroir] to pull open. **-2.** [tracer - trait] to draw. **-3.** [revue, livre] to print. **-4.** [avec arme] to fire. **-5.** [faire sortir - vin] to draw off; **~ qqn de** *litt* & *fig* to help OU get sb out of; **~ un revolver/un mouchoir de sa poche** to pull a gun/a handkerchief out of one's pocket; **~ la langue** to stick out one's tongue. **-6.** [aux cartes, au loto] to draw. **-7.** [plaisir, profit] to derive. **-8.** [déduire - conclusion] to draw; [- leçon] to learn. **-9.** *loc*: **~ qqch au clair** to shed light on sthg. ◇ *vi* **-1.** [tendre]: **~ sur** to pull on OU at. **-2.** [aspirer]: **~ sur** [pipe] to draw OU pull on. **-3.** [couleur]: **bleu tirant sur le vert** greenish blue. **-4.** [cheminée] to draw. **-5.** [avec arme] to fire, to shoot. **-6.** SPORT to shoot.

◆ **se tirer** *vp* **-1.** *fam* [s'en aller] to push off. **-2.** [se sortir]: **se ~ de** to get o.s. out of; **s'en ~** *fam* to escape.

tiret [tirɛ] *nm* dash.

tirette [tirɛt] *nf* **-1.** [planchette] leaf. **-2.** *Belg* [fermeture] zipper *Am*, zip *Br*. **-3.** [commande] lever.

tireur, -euse [tirœr, øz] *nm, f* [avec arme] gunman; **~ d'élite** marksman (*f* markswoman).

◆ **tireur** *nm* [de chèque] drawer.

◆ **tireuse** *nf*: **tireuse de cartes** fortune teller.

tiroir [tirwar] *nm* drawer.

tiroir-caisse [tirwarkɛs] (*pl* **tiroirs-caisses**) *nm* till.

tisane [tizan] *nf* herb tea.

tison [tizɔ̃] *nm* ember.

tisonnier [tizɔnje] *nm* poker.

tissage [tisaʒ] *nm* weaving.

tisser [tise] [3] *vt litt* & *fig* to weave; [suj: araignée] to spin.

tisserand, -e [tisrɑ̃, ɑ̃d] *nm, f* weaver.

tissu [tisy] *nm* **-1.** [étoffe] cloth, material. **-2.** BIOL tissue; **~ adipeux** adipose tissue; **~ conjonctif** connective tissue.

tissu-éponge [tisyepɔ̃ʒ] (*pl* **tissus-éponges**) *nm* toweling (*U*) *Am*, towelling (*U*) *Br*.

titan [titɑ̃] *nm* Titan; **de ~** *fig* titanic.

titiller [titije] [3] *vt* to titillate.

titrage [titraʒ] *nm* **-1.** [d'œuvre, de film] titling. **-2.** [de liquide] titration.

titre [titr] *nm* **-1.** [gén] title. **-2.** [de presse] headline; **gros ~** headline. **-3.** [universitaire] diploma, qualification. **-4.** JUR title; **~ de propriété** title deed. **-5.** FIN security. **-6.** [de monnaie] fineness. **-7.** *loc*: **à ~ gracieux** OU **gratuit** free of charge; **à ~ indicatif** for information; **à aucun ~** on any account, in any way; **à juste ~** with just cause, justifiably so.

◆ **titre de transport** *nm* ticket.

◆ **à titre de** *loc prép*: **à ~ d'exemple** by way of example; **à ~ d'information** for information.

◆ **au même titre que** *loc prép* in the same way that.

◆ **en titre** *loc adj* **-1.** [titulaire] titular. **-2.** [attitré] official.

titrer [titre] [3] *vt* **-1.** [œuvre] to title. **-2.** [liquide] to titrate.

tituber [titybe] [3] *vi* to totter.

titulaire [titylɛr] ◇ *adj* [employé] permanent; UNIV with tenure. ◇ *nmf* [de passeport, permis] holder; [de poste, chaire] occupant.

titulariser [titylarize] [3] *vt* to give tenure to.

TNT (*abr de* **trinitrotoluène**) *nm* TNT.

toast [tost] *nm* **-1.** [pain grillé] toast (*U*). **-2.** [discours] toast; **porter un ~ à** to drink a toast to.

toasteur [tostœr] *nm* toaster.

toboggan [tɔbɔgɑ̃] *nm* **-1.** [traîneau] toboggan. **-2.** [de terrain de jeu] slide; [de piscine] chute. **-3.** AUTOM overpass *Am*, flyover *Br*.

toc [tɔk] ◇ *interj*: **et ~!** so there! ◇ *nm fam*: **c'est du ~** it's fake; **en ~** fake (*avant n*). ◇ *adj inv* rubbishy.

tocsin [tɔksɛ̃] *nm* alarm bell.

Togo [tɔgo] *nm*: **le ~** Togo; **au ~** in Togo.

togolais, -e [tɔgɔlɛ, ɛz] *adj* Togolese.

◆ **Togolais**, **-e** *nm, f* Togolese person; **les Togolais** the Togolese.

tohu-bohu [tɔybɔy] *nm* commotion.

toi [twa] *pron pers* you.

◆ **toi-même** *pron pers* yourself.

toile [twal] *nf* **-1.** [étoffe] cloth; [de lin] linen; ~ **cirée** oilcloth. **-2.** [tableau] canvas, picture. **-3.** NAVIG [voilure] sails (*pl*).

◆ **toile d'araignée** *nf* spider's web.

◆ **toile de fond** *nf* backdrop.

toilettage [twalɛtaʒ] *nm* grooming.

toilette [twalɛt] *nf* **-1.** [de personne, d'animal] washing; **faire sa** ~ to (have a) wash. **-2.** [parure, vêtements] outfit, clothes (*pl*). **-3.** [de monument, voiture] cleaning. **-4.** [de texte] tidying up.

◆ **toilettes** *nfpl* toilet (*sg*), toilets.

toise [twaz] *nf* height gauge.

toiser [twaze] [3] *vt* to eye (up and down).

◆ **se toiser** *vp* to eye each other up and down.

toison [twazɔ̃] *nf* **-1.** [pelage] fleece. **-2.** [chevelure] mop (of hair).

toit [twa] *nm* roof; ~ **ouvrant** sunroof.

toiture [twatyr] *nf* roof, roofing.

Tokyo [tɔkjo] *n* Tokyo.

tôlard, -e, taulard, -e [tolar, ard] *nm, f tfam* jailbird, con.

tôle [tol] *nf* **-1.** [de métal] sheet metal; ~ **ondulée** corrugated iron. **-2.** *tfam* [prison] clink, nick *Br*.

tolérable [tɔlerabl] *adj* **-1.** [comportement] excusable. **-2.** [douleur] bearable, tolerable.

tolérance [tɔlerɑ̃s] *nf* **-1.** [gén] tolerance. **-2.** [liberté] concession.

tolérant, -e [tɔlerɑ̃, ɑ̃t] *adj* **-1.** [large d'esprit] tolerant. **-2.** [indulgent] liberal.

tolérer [tɔlere] [18] *vt* to tolerate.

◆ **se tolérer** *vp* to put up with OU tolerate each other.

tôlier, -ière, taulier, -ière [tolje, ɛr] *nm, f tfam* [propriétaire] hotel owner.

tollé [tɔle] *nm* protest; **soulever un ~ général** *fig* to cause a general outcry.

tomate [tɔmat] *nf* tomato; ~**s à la provençale** *baked or fried tomatoes with herbs, breadcrumbs and garlic*.

tombal, -e, -aux [tɔ̃bal, o] *adj*: **pierre ~e** gravestone.

tombant, -e [tɔ̃bɑ̃, ɑ̃t] *adj* [moustaches] drooping; [épaules] sloping.

tombe [tɔ̃b] *nf* **-1.** [fosse] grave, tomb. **-2.** [pierre] gravestone, tombstone.

tombeau, -x [tɔ̃bo] *nm* tomb; **rouler à ~ ouvert** *fig* to drive at breakneck speed.

tombée [tɔ̃be] *nf* fall; **à la ~ du jour** OU **de la nuit** at nightfall.

tomber [tɔ̃be] [3] ◇ *vi* (*aux:* être) **-1.** [gén] to fall; **faire ~ qqn** to knock sb over OU down; ~ **raide mort** to drop down dead; **je suis tombé de haut** *fig* you could have knocked me down with a feather; ~ **bien** [robe] to hang well; *fig* [visite, personne] to come at a good time. **-2.** [cheveux] to fall out. **-3.** [nouvelle] to break. **-4.** [diminuer - prix] to drop, to fall; [- fièvre, vent] to drop; [- jour] to come to an end; [- colère] to die down. **-5.** [devenir brusquement]: ~ **malade** to fall ill; ~ **amoureux** to fall in love; **être bien/mal tombé** to be lucky/unlucky. **-6.** [trouver]: ~ **sur** to come across. **-7.** [attaquer]: ~ **sur** to set about. **-8.** [se placer]: ~ **sous** [loi, juridiction] to come OU fall under; ~ **sous la main** to come to hand. **-9.** [date, événement] to fall on. ◇ *vt* (*aux: avoir*) *fam* [séduire] to lay.

tombeur [tɔ̃bœr] *nm fam fig* womanizer, Casanova.

tombola [tɔ̃bɔla] *nf* raffle.

tome [tɔm] *nm* volume.

tomme [tɔm] *nf:* ~ **(de Savoie)** *semi-hard cow's milk cheese from Savoy*.

tommette [tɔmɛt] *nf* terracotta floor tile.

ton¹ [tɔ̃] *nm* **-1.** [de voix] tone; **hausser/baisser le** ~ to raise/lower one's voice. **-2.** MUS key; **donner le** ~ to give the chord; *fig* to set the tone.

ton² [tɔ̃] (*f* **ta** [ta], *pl* **tes** [te]) *adj poss* your.

tonalité [tɔnalite] *nf* **-1.** MUS tonality. **-2.** *fig* [impression] tone. **-3.** [au téléphone] dialling tone.

tondeuse [tɔ̃døz] *nf* [à cheveux] clippers (*pl*); ~ **(à gazon)** mower, lawnmower.

tondre [tɔ̃dr] [75] *vt* [gazon] to mow; [mouton] to shear; [caniche, cheveux] to clip; **se laisser** OU **se faire ~ par qqn** *fig* to be fleeced by sb.

tondu, -e [tɔ̃dy] *adj* [caniche, cheveux] clipped; [pelouse] mown.

tonicité [tɔnisite] *nf* [des muscles] tone.

tonifiant, -e [tɔnifjɑ̃, ɑ̃t] *adj* [climat] invigorating, bracing; [lecture] stimulating.

tonifier [tɔnifje] [9] *vt* [peau] to tone; [esprit] to stimulate.

tonique [tɔnik] ◇ *adj* **-1.** [boisson] tonic (*avant n*); [froid] bracing; [lotion] toning. **-2.** LING & MUS tonic. ◇ *nm* MÉD tonic. ◇ *nf* MUS tonic, keynote.

tonitruant, -e [tɔnitryɑ̃, ɑ̃t] *adj* booming.

tonnage [tɔnaʒ] *nm* tonnage.

tonnant, -e [tɔnɑ̃, ɑ̃t] *adj* thundering.

tonne [tɔn] *nf* **-1.** [1000 kg] tonne. **-2.** [grande quantité]: **des** ~**s de tons** OU **loads of. -3.** [tonneau] tun.

tonneau, -x [tɔno] *nm* **-1.** [baril] **barrel, cask. -2.** [de voiture] **roll. -3.** NAVIG **ton.**

tonnelet [tɔnlɛ] *nm* keg, small cask.

tonnelle [tɔnɛl] *nf* bower, arbour.

tonner [tɔne] [3] *vi* to thunder.

tonnerre [tɔnɛr] *nm* thunder; **coup de** ~ thunderclap; *fig* bombshell; **du** ~ *fam fig* terrific, great.

tonsure [tɔ̃syr] *nf* tonsure.

tonte [tɔ̃t] *nf* [de mouton] **shearing;** [de gazon] **mowing;** [de caniche, cheveux] **clipping.**

tonton [tɔ̃tɔ̃] *nm* uncle.

tonus [tɔnys] *nm* **-1.** [dynamisme] **energy. -2.** [de muscle] **tone.**

top [tɔp] ◇ *nm* [signal] **beep.** ◇ *adj*: **être au** ~ **niveau** to be at the top (level).

◆ **top secret** *adj inv* top secret.

topaze [tɔpaz] *nf* topaz.

toper [tɔpe] [3] *vi*: **tope-là!** right, you're on!

topinambour [tɔpinãbur] *nm* Jerusalem artichoke.

topique [tɔpik] ◇ *adj* pertinent. ◇ *nm* topical OU local remedy.

topo [tɔpo] *nm fam* **spiel; c'est toujours le même** ~ *fig* it's always the same old story.

topographie [tɔpɔgrafi] *nf* topography.

topographique [tɔpɔgrafik] *adj* topographical.

toponymie [tɔpɔnimi] *nf* toponymy.

toquade [tɔkad] *nf*: ~ **(pour)** [personne] **crush (on);** [style, mode] **craze (for).**

toque [tɔk] *nf* [de juge, de jockey] **cap;** [de cuisinier] **hat.**

toqué, -e [tɔke] *fam* ◇ *adj*: ~ **(de)** **crazy** (about), nuts (about). ◇ *nm, f* nutter, nutcase.

torche [tɔrʃ] *nf* torch; ~ **électrique** flashlight *Am*, (electric) torch *Br*.

torcher [tɔrʃe] [3] *vt fam* **-1.** [assiette, fesses] to wipe. **-2.** [travail] to dash off. **-3.** [bouteille] to polish off.

◆ **se torcher** *vp fam* to wipe one's bottom.

torchis [tɔrʃi] *nm* daub (*building material*).

torchon [tɔrʃɔ̃] *nm* **-1.** [serviette] **cloth. -2.** *fam* [travail] **mess. -3.** *fam* [journal] **rag.**

tordant, -e [tɔrdã, ãt] *adj fam* hilarious.

tord-boyaux [tɔrbwajo] *nm inv fam* gutrot.

tordre [tɔrdr] [76] *vt* **-1.** [gén] to twist. **-2.** [linge] to wring (out).

◆ **se tordre** *vp*: **se** ~ **la cheville** to twist one's ankle; **se** ~ **de douleur** *fig* to be

racked with pain; **se** ~ **de rire** *fam fig* to double up with laughter.

tordu, -e [tɔrdy] ◇ *pp* → **tordre.** ◇ *adj fam* [bizarre, fou] **crazy;** [esprit] **warped.** ◇ *nm, f fam* nutcase.

toréador [tɔreadɔr], **torero** [tɔrero] *nm* bullfighter.

tornade [tɔrnad] *nf* tornado.

torpeur [tɔrpœr] *nf* torpor.

torpille [tɔrpij] *nf* **-1.** MIL torpedo. **-2.** [poisson] **torpedo, electric ray.**

torpiller [tɔrpije] [3] *vt* to torpedo.

torpilleur [tɔrpijœr] *nm* torpedo boat.

torréfaction [tɔrefaksjɔ̃] *nf* roasting.

torréfier [tɔrefje] [9] *vt* to roast.

torrent [tɔrã] *nm* torrent; **pleuvoir à** ~**s** *fig* to pour down; **un** ~ **de** *fig* [injures] a stream of; [lumière, larmes] a flood of.

torrentiel, -ielle [tɔrãsjel] *adj* torrential.

torride [tɔrid] *adj* torrid.

tors, -e [tɔr, tɔrs] *adj* twisted.

◆ **torse** *nm* chest; **bomber le** ~ to puff OU throw out one's chest; *fig* to puff up (with pride).

torsade [tɔrsad] *nf* **-1.** [de cheveux] **twist, coil. -2.** [de pull] **cable.**

torsader [tɔrsade] [3] *vt* to twist.

torsion [tɔrsjɔ̃] *nf* twisting; PHYS torsion.

tort [tɔr] *nm* **-1.** [erreur] **fault; avoir** ~ to be wrong; **avoir** ~ **de faire qqch** to be wrong to do sthg; **parler à** ~ **et à travers** to talk nonsense; **être dans son** OU **en** ~ to be in the wrong; **reconnaître ses** ~**s** to acknowledge one's faults; **à** ~ **wrongly; à** ~ **ou à raison** rightly or wrongly. **-2.** [préjudice] **wrong; causer** OU **faire du** ~ **à qqn** to wrong sb.

torticolis [tɔrtikɔli] *nm* stiff neck.

tortillement [tɔrtijmã] *nm* wriggling, writhing.

tortiller [tɔrtije] [3] ◇ *vt* [enrouler] to twist; [moustache] to twirl. ◇ *vi*: ~ **des hanches** to swing one's hips; **il n'y a pas à** ~ *fig* there's no getting out of it.

◆ **se tortiller** *vp* to writhe, to wriggle.

tortionnaire [tɔrsjɔnɛr] ◇ *nmf* torturer. ◇ *adj* given to torture.

tortue [tɔrty] *nf* tortoise; *fig* slowpoke *Am*, slowcoach *Br*.

tortueux, -euse [tɔrtɥø, øz] *adj* winding, twisting; *fig* tortuous.

torture [tɔrtyr] *nf* torture.

torturer [tɔrtyre] [3] *vt* to torture.

◆ **se torturer** *vp* to torment o.s.; **se** ~ **pour** to agonize over.

torve [tɔrv] *adj*: œil OU **regard** ~ threatening look.

tôt [to] *adv* **-1.** [de bonne heure] early. **-2.** [vite] soon, early; **ce n'est pas trop** ~! *fam* and about time too!; ~ **ou tard** sooner or later.

◆ **au plus tôt** *loc adv* at the earliest.

total, -e, -aux [tɔtal, o] *adj* total.

◆ **total** *nm* total; **au** ~ in total; *fig* on the whole, all in all.

totalement [tɔtalmɑ̃] *adv* totally.

totaliser [tɔtalize] [3] *vt* **-1.** [additionner] to add up, to total. **-2.** [réunir] to have a total of.

totalitaire [tɔtalitɛr] *adj* totalitarian.

totalitarisme [tɔtalitarism] *nm* totalitarianism.

totalité [tɔtalite] *nf* whole; **la** ~ **de** [inscrits] all (of); [classe] the whole of, the entire; **en** ~ entirely.

totem [tɔtɛm] *nm* totem.

touareg, -ègue [twarɛg] *adj* Tuareg.

◆ **touareg** *nm* [langue] Tuareg.

◆ **Touareg, -ègue** *nm, f* Tuareg.

toubib [tubib] *nmf fam* doc.

toucan [tukɑ̃] *nm* toucan.

touchant, -e [tuʃɑ̃, ɑ̃t] *adj* touching.

touche [tuʃ] *nf* **-1.** [de clavier] key; ~ **alphanumérique** alphanumeric key; ~ **de fonction** function key. **-2.** [de peinture] stroke. **-3.** *fig* [note]: **une** ~ **de** a touch of. **-4.** *fam* [allure] appearance, look. **-5.** PÊCHE bite; **faire une** ~ *fig* to make a hit. **-6.** [FOOTBALL - ligne] touch line; [- remise en jeu] throw-in; [RUGBY - ligne] touch (line); [- remise en jeu] line-out; **être mis/rester sur la** ~ *fig* to be left/to stay on the sidelines. **-7.** ESCRIME hit.

touche-à-tout [tuʃatu] *nmf inv* [adulte] dabbler; [enfant]: **c'est un petit** ~ he's into everything.

toucher [tuʃe] [3] ◇ *nm*: **le** ~ the (sense of) touch; **au** ~ to the touch.

◇ *vt* -1. [palper, émouvoir] to touch. **-2.** [rivage, correspondant] to reach; [cible] to hit. **-3.** [salaire] to get, to be paid; [chèque] to cash; [gros lot] to win. **-4.** [concerner] to affect, to concern.

◇ *vi*: ~ **à** to touch; [problème] to touch on; [inconscience, folie] to border OU verge on; [maison] to adjoin; ~ **à sa fin** to draw to a close.

◆ **se toucher** *vp* [maisons] to be adjacent (to each other), to adjoin (each other).

touffe [tuf] *nf* tuft.

touffu, -e [tufy] *adj* [forêt] dense; [barbe] bushy.

touiller [tuje] [3] *vt fam* [mélanger] to stir; [salade] to toss.

toujours [tuʒur] *adv* **-1.** [continuité, répétition] always; **ils s'aimeront** ~ they will always love one another, they will love one another forever; ~ **plus** more and more; ~ **moins** less and less. **-2.** [encore] still. **-3.** [de toute façon] anyway, anyhow.

◆ **de toujours** *loc adj*: **ce sont des amis de** ~ they are lifelong friends.

◆ **pour toujours** *loc adv* forever, for good.

◆ **toujours est-il que** *loc conj* the fact remains that.

toundra [tundra] *nf* tundra.

toupet [tupɛ] *nm* **-1.** [de cheveux] tuft of hair, quiff *Br*. **-2.** *fam fig* [aplomb] cheek; **avoir du** ~, **ne pas manquer de** ~ *fam* to have a cheek.

toupie [tupi] *nf* (spinning) top.

tour [tur] ◇ *nm* **-1.** [périmètre] circumference; **faire le** ~ **de** to go round; **faire un** ~ to go for a walk/drive *etc*; **faire le** ~ **du propriétaire** to go on a tour of inspection; ~ **d'horizon** survey; ~ **de piste** SPORT lap; ~ **de taille** waist measurement. **-2.** [rotation] turn; **fermer à double** ~ to double-lock; **à** ~ **de bras** *fig* non-stop; **en un** ~ **de main** *fig* in the twinkling of an eye. **-3.** [plaisanterie] trick; **jouer un bon/mauvais** ~ **à qqn** to play a joke/dirty trick on sb; ~ **de force** amazing feat. **-4.** [succession] turn; **j'ai fait la cuisine/la vaisselle** *etc* **plus souvent qu'à mon** ~ I've done more than my fair share of cooking/washing-up *etc*; ~ **de scrutin** ballot, round of voting; **à** ~ **de rôle** in turn; ~ **à** ~ alternately, in turn. **-5.** [d'événements] turn. **-6.** [de potier] wheel.

◇ *nf* **-1.** [monument, de château] tower; [immeuble] high-rise *Am*, tower-block *Br*. **-2.** ÉCHECS rook, castle.

◆ **tour de contrôle** *nf* control tower.

tourbe [turb] *nf* peat.

tourbière [turbjɛr] *nf* peat bog.

tourbillon [turbijɔ̃] *nm* **-1.** [de vent] whirlwind; **un** ~ **de** a whirl of. **-2.** [de poussière, fumée] swirl. **-3.** [d'eau] whirlpool. **-4.** *fig* [agitation] hurly-burly.

tourbillonnant, -e [turbijɔnɑ̃, ɑ̃t] *adj* swirling, whirling.

tourbillonner [turbijɔne] [3] *vi* to whirl, to swirl; *fig* to whirl (round).

tourelle [turɛl] *nf* turret.

tourisme [turism] *nm* tourism.

tourista [turista] *nf* traveler's *Am* OU traveller's *Br* tummy.

touriste [turist] ◇ *nmf* tourist; **en** ~ as a tourist. ◇ *adj* tourist (*avant n*).

touristique [turistik] *adj* tourist (*avant n*).

tourment [turmã] *nm sout* torment.

tourmente [turmãt] *nf* **-1.** *littéraire* [tempête] storm, tempest. **-2.** *fig* turmoil.

tourmenter [turmãte] [3] *vt* to torment.
◆ **se tourmenter** *vp* to worry o.s., to fret.

tournage [turnaʒ] *nm* CIN shooting.

tournailler [turnaje] [3] *vi fam* to prowl about; ~ **autour de qqn/qqch** to hover around sb/sthg.

tournant, -e [turnã, ãt] *adj* [porte] revolving; [fauteuil] swivel (*avant n*); [pont] swing (*avant n*).
◆ **tournant** *nm* bend, *fig* turning point; **je l'attends au** ~ *fam fig* I'll get even with him/her.

tourné, -e [turne] *adj* **-1.** [lait] sour, off. **-2.** *loc*: **bien** ~ [lettre] well-worded; [personne] shapely; **mal** ~ [lettre] badly-worded; [personne] unattractive; [esprit] warped.

tournebroche [turnəbrɔʃ] *nm* spit.

tourne-disque [turnədisk] (*pl* **tourne-disques**) *nm* record player.

tournedos [turnədo] *nm steak taken from the thickest part of the fillet.*

tournée [turne] *nf* **-1.** [voyage] tour. **-2.** *fam* [consommations] round. **-3.** *fam* [correction] thrashing, hiding.

tourner [turne] [3] ◇ *vt* **-1.** [gén] to turn. **-2.** [pas, pensées] to turn, to direct. **-3.** [obstacle, loi] to get round. **-4.** CIN to shoot. **-5.** *fig* [formuler]: **bien** ~ **qqch** to put sthg well. ◇ *vi* **-1.** [gén] to turn; [moteur] to turn over; [planète] to revolve; ~ **autour de qqn** *fig* to hang around sb; ~ **autour du pot** OU **du sujet** *fig* to beat about the bush; «**tournez s'il vous plaît**» "please turn over". **-2.** *fam* [entreprise] to tick over. **-3.** [lait] to go off.
◆ **se tourner** *vp* to turn (right) round; **se** ~ **vers** to turn toward *Am* OU towards *Br*.

tournesol [turnəsɔl] *nm* **-1.** [plante] sunflower. **-2.** [colorant] litmus.

tourneur, -euse [turnœr, øz] *nm, f* turner, lathe operator.

tournevis [turnəvis] *nm* screwdriver.

tournicoter [turnikɔte] [3] *vi fam* to wander up and down.

tourniquet [turnikɛ] *nm* **-1.** [entrée] turnstile. **-2.** MÉD tourniquet.

tournis [turni] *nm fam*: **avoir le** ~ to feel dizzy OU giddy; **donner le** ~ **à qqn** to make sb dizzy OU giddy.

tournoi [turnwa] *nm* tournament.

tournoiement [turnwamã] *nm* wheeling, whirling.

tournoyer [turnwaje] [13] *vi* to wheel, to whirl.

tournure [turnyr] *nf* **-1.** [apparence] turn; **prendre** ~ to take shape. **-2.** [formulation] form; ~ **de phrase** turn of phrase.

tour-opérateur [turɔperatœr] (*pl* **tour-opérateurs**) *nm* tour operator.

tourte [turt] *nf* pie.

tourteau, -x [turto] *nm* **-1.** [crabe] crab. **-2.** [pour bétail] oil cake.

tourtereau [turtəro] *nm* young turtledove.
◆ **tourtereaux** *nmpl fam fig* [amoureux] lovebirds.

tourterelle [turtərɛl] *nf* turtledove.

tourtière [turtjɛr] *nf* pie-dish.

tous → **tout**.

Toussaint [tusɛ̃] *nf*: **la** ~ All Saints' Day.

tousser [tuse] [3] *vi* to cough.

toussotement [tusɔtmã] *nm* coughing.

toussoter [tusɔte] [3] *vi* to cough.

tout [tu] (*f* **toute** [tut], *mpl* **tous** [tus], *fpl* **toutes** [tut]) ◇ *adj qualificatif* **-1.** [avec substantif singulier déterminé] all; ~ **le vin** all the wine; ~ **un gâteau** a whole cake; **toute la journée/la nuit** all day/night, the whole day/night; **toute sa famille** all his family, his whole family. **-2.** [avec pron dém]: ~ **ceci/cela** all this/that; ~ **ce que je sais** all I know.
◇ *adj indéf* **-1.** [exprime la totalité] all; **tous les gâteaux** all the cakes; **toutes les femmes** all the women; **tous les deux** both of us/them *etc*; **tous les trois** all three of us/them *etc*. **-2.** [chaque] every; **tous les jours** every day; **tous les deux ans** every two years. **-3.** [n'importe quel] any; **à toute heure** at any time.
◇ *pron indéf* everything, all; **je t'ai** ~ **dit** I've told you everything; **ils voulaient tous la voir** they all wanted to see her; **c'est** ~ that's all.
◆ **tout** ◇ *adv* **-1.** [entièrement, tout à fait] very, quite; ~ **jeune/près** very young/near; **ils étaient** ~ **seuls** they were all alone; ~ **en haut** right at the top; ~ **à côté de moi** right next to me. **-2.** [avec un gérondif]: ~ **en marchant** while walking.
◇ *nm*: **un** ~ a whole; **le** ~ **est de ...** the main thing is to ...; **risquer le** ~ **pour le** ~ to risk everything.
◆ **du tout au tout** *loc adv* completely, entirely.
◆ **pas du tout** *loc adv* not at all.
◆ **tout à fait** *loc adv* **-1.** [complètement] quite, entirely. **-2.** [exactement] exactly.
◆ **tout à l'heure** *loc adv* **-1.** [futur] in a little while, shortly; **à** ~ **à l'heure!** see you later! **-2.** [passé] a little while ago.

◆ **tout de suite** *loc adv* immediately, at once.

tout-à-l'égout [tutalegu] *nm inv* mains drainage.

toutefois [tutfwa] *adv* however.

toutou [tutu] *nm fam* doggie.

tout-petit [tup(ə)ti] (*pl* **tout-petits**) *nm* toddler, tot.

tout-puissant, **toute-puissante** [tupɥisɑ̃, tutpɥisɑ̃t] (*mpl* **tout-puissants**, *fpl* **toutes-puissantes**) *adj* omnipotent, all-powerful.
◆ **Tout-Puissant** *nm*: **le Tout-Puissant** the Almighty.

tout-venant [tuvnɑ̃] *nm inv*: **le ~** ordinary people (*pl*).

toux [tu] *nf* cough.

toxicité [tɔksisite] *nf* toxicity.

toxicologie [tɔksikɔlɔʒi] *nf* toxicology.

toxicomane [tɔksikɔman] *nmf* drug addict.

toxicomanie [tɔksikɔmani] *nf* drug addiction.

toxine [tɔksin] *nf* toxin.

toxique [tɔksik] *adj* toxic.

TP ◇ *nmpl* (*abr de* **travaux publics**) civil engineering. ◇ *nm* (*abr de* **Trésor public**) *public revenue office*.

TPG (*abr de* **trésorier payeur général**) *nm* paymaster.

tps *abr de* **temps**.

trac [trak] *nm* nerves (*pl*); THÉÂTRE stage fright; **avoir le ~** to get nervous; THÉÂTRE to get stage fright.

tracas [traka] *nm* worry.

tracasser [trakase] [3] *vt* to worry, to bother.
◆ **se tracasser** *vp* to worry.

tracasserie [trakasri] *nf* annoyance.

tracassier, -ière [trakasje, jɛr] *adj* irksome.

trace [tras] *nf* **-1.** [d'animal] track. **-2.** [de brûlure, fatigue] mark. **-3.** (*gén pl*) [vestige] trace. **-4.** [très petite quantité]: **une ~ de a** trace of. **-5.** SKI trail; **~ directe** direct descent.

tracé [trase] *nm* [lignes] plan, drawing; [de parcours] line.

tracer [trase] [16] ◇ *vt* **-1.** [dessiner, dépeindre] to draw. **-2.** [route, piste] to mark out; **~ la voie/le chemin à qqn** *fig* to show sb the way. ◇ *vi fam* to belt along.

traceur [trasœr] *nm* INFORM plotter.

trachée-artère [traʃeartɛr] (*pl* **trachées-artères**) *nf* windpipe, trachea.

trachéite [trakeit] *nf* throat infection.

tract [trakt] *nm* leaflet.

tractations [traktasjɔ̃] *nfpl* negotiations, dealings.

tracter [trakte] [3] *vt* to tow.

tracteur [traktœr] *nm* tractor.

traction [traksjɔ̃] *nf* **-1.** [action de tirer] towing, pulling; **~ avant/arrière** front-/rear-wheel drive. **-2.** TECHNOL tensile stress. **-3.** [SPORT - au sol] push-up *Am*, press-up *Br*; [- à la barre] pull-up.

tradition [tradisjɔ̃] *nf* tradition; **renouer avec la ~** to revive a tradition.

traditionaliste [tradisjɔnalist] *nmf & adj* traditionalist.

traditionnel, -elle [tradisjɔnɛl] *adj* **-1.** [de tradition] traditional. **-2.** [habituel] usual.

traditionnellement [tradisjɔnɛlmɑ̃] *adv* traditionally.

traducteur, -trice [tradyktœr, tris] *nm, f* translator.
◆ **traducteur** *nm* INFORM translator.

traduction [tradyksjɔ̃] *nf* **-1.** [gén] translation. **-2.** *littéraire* [expression] rendering.

traduire [tradɥir] [98] *vt* **-1.** [texte] to translate; **~ qqch en français/anglais** to translate sthg into French/English. **-2.** [révéler - crise] to reveal, to betray; [- sentiments, pensée] to render, to express. **-3.** JUR: **~ qqn en justice** to bring sb before the courts.

traduisible [tradɥizibl] *adj* translatable.

trafic [trafik] *nm* **-1.** [de marchandises] traffic, trafficking. **-2.** [circulation] traffic.
◆ **trafic d'influence** *nm* corruption, taking bribes.

trafiquant, -e [trafikɑ̃, ɑ̃t] *nm, f* trafficker, dealer.

trafiquer [trafike] [3] ◇ *vt* **-1.** [falsifier] to tamper with. **-2.** *fam* [manigancer]: **qu'est-ce que tu trafiques?** what are you up to?. ◇ *vi* to be involved in trafficking; **~ de qqch** to traffic in sthg.

tragédie [traʒedi] *nf* tragedy.

tragédien, -ienne [traʒedjɛ̃, jɛn] *nm, f* tragedian (*f* tragedienne), tragic actor (*f* actress).

tragi-comédie [traʒikɔmedi] (*pl* **tragi-comédies**) *nf* tragicomedy.

tragi-comique [traʒikɔmik] *adj* tragicomic, tragicomical.

tragique [traʒik] ◇ *adj* tragic. ◇ *nm* **-1.** [auteur] tragedian. **-2.** [caractère]: **le ~** tragedy; **prendre qqch au ~** to act as if sthg were a tragedy; **tourner au ~** to take a tragic turn.

tragiquement [traʒikmɑ̃] *adv* tragically.

trahir [trair] [32] *vt* **-1.** [pays, conjoint] to betray. **-2.** [suj: moteur] to let down; [suj: for-

ces] to fail. **-3.** [secret] to betray, to give away. **-4.** [pensée] to misrepresent.
◆ **se trahir** *vp* to give o.s. away.

trahison [traizɔ̃] *nf* **-1.** [gén] betrayal. **-2.** JUR treason.

train [trɛ̃] *nm* **-1.** TRANSPORT train; ~ **corail** express; ~ **(à) grande vitesse** high-speed train. **-2.** AÉRON: ~ **d'atterrissage** landing gear. **-3.** [allure] pace. **-4.** [série]: **un** ~ **de** a series of. **-5.** *fam* [postérieur] backside, butt *Am*. **-6.** *loc*: **être en** ~ **fig** to be on form.
◆ **train de vie** *nm* lifestyle.
◆ **en train de** *loc prép*: **être en** ~ **de lire/ travailler** *etc* to be reading/working *etc*.

traînailler [trɛnaje], **traînasser** [trɛnase] [3] *vi fam* **-1.** [vagabonder] to loaf about. **-2.** [être lent] to dawdle.

traînant, -e [trɛnɑ̃, ɑ̃t] *adj* **-1.** [robe] trailing. **-2.** [voix] drawling; [démarche] dragging.

traînard, -e [trɛnar, ard] *nm, f fam* straggler; *fig* slowpoke *Am*, slowcoach *Br*.

traînasser = **traînailler**.

traîne [trɛn] *nf* **-1.** [de robe] train. **-2.** PÊCHE dragnet. **-3.** *Can*: ~ **sauvage** toboggan. **-4.** *loc*: **être à la** ~ to lag behind.

traîneau, -x [trɛno] *nm* sleigh, sledge.

traînée [trɛne] *nf* **-1.** [trace] trail; **se répandre comme une** ~ **de poudre** *fig* to spread like wildfire. **-2.** *tfam péj* [prostituée] tart, whore.

traîner [trɛne] [4] ◇ *vt* **-1.** [tirer, emmener] to drag. **-2.** [trimbaler] to lug around, to cart around. **-3.** [maladie] to be unable to shake off. ◇ *vi* **-1.** [personne] to dawdle. **-2.** [maladie, affaire] to drag on; ~ **en longueur** to drag. **-3.** [robe] to trail. **-4.** [vêtements, livres] to lie around OU about.
◆ **se traîner** *vp* **-1.** [personne] to drag o.s. along. **-2.** [jour, semaine] to drag.

training [treniŋ] *nm* **-1.** [entraînement] training. **-2.** [survêtement] tracksuit top.

train-train [trɛ̃trɛ̃] *nm fam* routine, daily grind.

traire [trɛr] [112] *vt* **-1.** [vache] to milk. **-2.** [lait] to draw.

trait [trɛ] *nm* **-1.** [ligne] line, stroke; ~ **d'union** hyphen; **tirer un** ~ **sur qqch** *fig* to put sthg behind one. **-2.** (*gén pl*) [de visage] feature; **ressembler à qqn** ~ **pour** ~ to be the spitting image of sb, to be exactly like sb. **-3.** [caractéristique] trait, feature; ~ **de caractère** character trait. **-4.** [acte] act; ~ **de génie** brainwave. **-5.** *loc*: **avoir** ~ **à** to be to do with, to concern.
◆ **d'un trait** *loc adv* [boire, lire] in one go.

traitant, -e [trɛtɑ̃, ɑ̃t] *adj* [shampooing, crème] medicated; → **médecin**.

traite [trɛt] *nf* **-1.** [de vache] milking. **-2.** COMM bill, draft. **-3.** [d'esclaves]: **la** ~ **des noirs** the slave trade; **la** ~ **des blanches** the white slave trade.
◆ **d'une seule traite** *loc adv* without stopping, in one go.

traité [trɛte] *nm* **-1.** [ouvrage] treatise. **-2.** POLIT treaty.

traitement [trɛtmɑ̃] *nm* **-1.** [gén & MÉD] treatment; **mauvais** ~ ill-treatment; ~ **de faveur** special treatment. **-2.** [rémunération] wage. **-3.** IND & INFORM processing; ~ **anti- rouille** rustproofing; ~ **de texte** word processing. **-4.** [de problème] handling.

traiter [trɛte] [4] ◇ *vt* **-1.** [gén & MÉD] to treat; **se faire** ~ MÉD to be treated; **bien/ mal** ~ **qqn** to treat sb well/badly. **-2.** [qualifier]: ~ **qqn d'imbécile/de lâche** *etc* to call sb an imbecile/a coward *etc*. **-3.** [question, thème] to deal with. **-4.** IND & INFORM to process. ◇ *vi* **-1.** [négocier] to negotiate. **-2.** [livre]: ~ **de** to deal with.

traiteur [trɛtœr] *nm* caterer.

traître, -esse [trɛtr, ɛs] *nm, f* traitor.

traîtreusement [trɛtrøzmɑ̃] *adv* treacherously.

traîtrise [trɛtriz] *nf* **-1.** [déloyauté] treachery. **-2.** [acte] act of treachery.

trajectoire [traʒɛktwar] *nf* trajectory, path; *fig* path.

trajet [traʒɛ] *nm* **-1.** [distance] distance. **-2.** [itinéraire] route. **-3.** [voyage] journey.

trame [tram] *nf* weft; *fig* framework.

tramer [trame] [3] *vt sout* to plot.
◆ **se tramer** ◇ *vp* to be plotted. ◇ *v impers*: **il se trame quelque chose** there's something afoot.

trampoline [trɑ̃pɔlin] *nm* trampoline.

tram(way) [tram(wɛ)] *nm* streetcar *Am*, tram *Br*.

tranchant, -e [trɑ̃ʃɑ̃, ɑ̃t] *adj* **-1.** [instrument] sharp. **-2.** [personne] assertive. **-3.** [ton] curt.
◆ **tranchant** *nm* edge; **à double** ~ *fig* two-edged.

tranche [trɑ̃ʃ] *nf* **-1.** [de gâteau, jambon] slice; ~ **d'âge** *fig* age bracket; ~ **de vie** *fig* slice of life. **-2.** [de livre, pièce] edge. **-3.** [période] part, section; ~ **horaire** time-slot. **-4.** [de revenus] portion; [de paiement] installment *Am*, instalment *Br*; [fiscale] bracket.

tranchée [trɑ̃ʃe] *nf* MIL trench.

trancher [trɑ̃ʃe] [3] ◇ *vt* [couper] to cut; [pain, jambon] to slice; *fig*: ~ **la question** to settle the question. ◇ *vi* **-1.** *fig* [décider] to decide. **-2.** [contraster]: ~ **avec** OU **sur** to contrast with.

tranchoir [trɑ̃ʃwar] *nm* **-1.** [couteau] chopper. **-2.** [planche] chopping board.

tranquille [trɑ̃kil] *adj* **-1.** [endroit, vie] quiet; **laisser qqn/qqch ~** to leave sb/sthg alone; **se tenir/rester ~** to keep/remain quiet. **-2.** [rassuré] at ease, easy; **soyez ~** don't worry.

tranquillement [trɑ̃kilmɑ̃] *adv* **-1.** [sans s'agiter] quietly. **-2.** [sans s'inquiéter] calmly.

tranquillisant, -e [trɑ̃kilizɑ̃, ɑ̃t] *adj* **-1.** [nouvelle] reassuring. **-2.** [médicament] tranquilizing *Am*, tranquillizing *Br*.
◆ **tranquillisant** *nm* tranquilizer *Am*, tranquillizer *Br*.

tranquilliser [trɑ̃kilize] [3] *vt* to reassure.
◆ **se tranquilliser** *vp* to set one's mind at rest.

tranquillité [trɑ̃kilite] *nf* **-1.** [calme] peacefulness, quietness. **-2.** [sérénité] peace, tranquility *Am*, tranquillity *Br*; **~ d'esprit** peace of mind.

transaction [trɑ̃zaksjɔ̃] *nf* transaction.

transactionnel, -elle [trɑ̃zaksjɔnɛl] *adj* **-1.** PSYCHOL transactional. **-2.** JUR compromise (*avant n*).

transalpin, -e [trɑ̃zalpɛ̃, in] *adj* transalpine.

transat [trɑ̃zat] ◇ *nm* deckchair. ◇ *nf* transatlantic race.

transatlantique [trɑ̃zatlɑ̃tik] ◇ *adj* transatlantic. ◇ *nm* transatlantic liner. ◇ *nf* transatlantic race.

transbahuter [trɑ̃sbayte] [3] *vt fam* to hump OU lug along.

transbordement [trɑ̃sbɔrdəmɑ̃] *nm* transfer.

transcendant, -e [trɑ̃sɑ̃dɑ̃, ɑ̃t] *adj fam* [extraordinaire] special, great.

transcender [trɑ̃sɑ̃de] [3] *vt* to transcend.
◆ **se transcender** *vp* to surpass o.s.

transcoder [trɑ̃skɔde] [3] *vt* to transcribe.

transcription [trɑ̃skripsjɔ̃] *nf* [de document & MUS] transcription; [dans un autre alphabet] transliteration.

transcrire [trɑ̃skrir] [99] *vt* [document & MUS] to transcribe; [dans un autre alphabet] to transliterate.

transcrit, -e [trɑ̃skri, it] *pp* → **transcrire**.

transe [trɑ̃s] *nf*: **être en ~** *fig* to be beside o.s.
◆ **transes** *nfpl sout* agony (*U*).

transférer [trɑ̃sfere] [18] *vt* to transfer.

transfert [trɑ̃sfɛr] *nm* transfer.

transfigurer [trɑ̃sfigyre] [3] *vt* to transfigure.

transformable [trɑ̃sfɔrmabl] *adj* convertible.

transformateur, -trice [trɑ̃sfɔrmatœr, tris]

adj **-1.** IND processing (*avant n*). **-2.** *fig* [pouvoir, action] for change.
◆ **transformateur** *nm* transformer.

transformation [trɑ̃sfɔrmasjɔ̃] *nf* **-1.** [de pays, personne] transformation. **-2.** IND processing. **-3.** RUGBY conversion.

transformer [trɑ̃sfɔrme] [3] *vt* **-1.** [gén] to transform; [magasin] to convert; **~ qqch en** to turn sthg into. **-2.** IND & RUGBY to convert.
◆ **se transformer** *vp*: **se ~ en monstre/papillon** to turn into a monster/butterfly.

transfuge [trɑ̃sfyʒ] *nmf* renegade.

transfuser [trɑ̃sfyze] [3] *vt* [sang] to transfuse.

transfusion [trɑ̃sfyzjɔ̃] *nf*: **~ (sanguine)** (blood) transfusion.

transgresser [trɑ̃sgrese] [4] *vt* [loi] to infringe; [ordre] to disobey.

transgression [trɑ̃sgresjɔ̃] *nf* infringement, transgression.

transhumance [trɑ̃zymɑ̃s] *nf* transhumance.

transi, -e [trɑ̃zi] *adj*: **être ~ de** to be paralyzed *Am* OU paralysed *Br*, to be transfixed with; **être ~ de froid** to be chilled to the bone.

transiger [trɑ̃ziʒe] [17] *vi*: **~ (sur)** to compromise (on).

transistor [trɑ̃zistɔr] [3] *nm* transistor.

transit [trɑ̃zit] *nm* transit; **en ~** in transit.

transitaire [trɑ̃zitɛr] *nm* forwarding agent.

transiter [trɑ̃zite] [3] ◇ *vt* to forward. ◇ *vi* to pass in transit; **~ par** to pass through.

transitif, -ive [trɑ̃sitif, iv] *adj* transitive.

transition [trɑ̃zisjɔ̃] *nf* transition; **sans ~** with no transition, abruptly.

transitivité [trɑ̃zitivite] *nf* transitivity.

transitoire [trɑ̃zitwar] *adj* [passager] transitory.

translucide [trɑ̃slysid] *adj* translucent.

transmettre [trɑ̃smɛtr] [84] *vt* **-1.** [message, salutations]: **~ qqch (à)** to pass sthg on (to). **-2.** [tradition, propriété]: **~ qqch (à)** to hand sthg down (to). **-3.** [fonction, pouvoir]: **~ qqch (à)** to hand sthg over (to). **-4.** [maladie]: **~ qqch (à)** to transmit sthg (to), to pass sthg on (to). **-5.** [concert, émission] to broadcast.
◆ **se transmettre** *vp* **-1.** [maladie] to be passed on, to be transmitted. **-2.** [nouvelle] to be passed on. **-3.** [courant, onde] to be transmitted. **-4.** [tradition] to be handed down.

transmis, -e [trɑ̃smi, iz] *pp* → **transmettre**.

transmissible [trɑ̃smisibl] *adj* **-1.** [patrimoine] transferable. **-2.** [maladie] transmissible.

transmission [trăsmisjɔ̃] *nf* **-1.** [de biens] transfer. **-2.** [de maladie] transmission. **-3.** [de message] passing on. **-4.** [de tradition] handing down.

transocéanique [trãzɔseanik] *adj* transoceanic.

transparaître [trăsparɛtr] [91] *vi* to show.

transparence [trăsparãs] *nf* transparency; **par** ~ against the light.

transparent, **-e** [trăsparã, ãt] *adj* transparent.

◆ **transparent** *nm* transparency.

transpercer [trăspɛrse] [16] *vt* to pierce; *fig* [suj: froid, pluie] to go right through.

transpiration [trăspirasjɔ̃] *nf* [sueur] perspiration.

transpirer [trăspire] [3] *vi* **-1.** [suer] to perspire. **-2.** *fig* [se divulguer] to leak out.

transplant [trăsplă] *nm* MÉD transplant.

transplantation [trăsplătasjɔ̃] *nf* **-1.** [d'arbre, de population] transplanting. **-2.** MÉD transplant.

transplanter [trăsplăte] [3] *vt* to transplant.

transport [trăspɔr] *nm* transport (*U*); ~ **aérien** air transport; ~ **ferroviaire** rail transport; ~ **maritime** sea transport; ~**s en commun** public transport (*sg*).

transportable [trăspɔrtabl] *adj* [marchandise] transportable; [blessé] fit to be moved.

transporter [trăspɔrte] [3] *vt* **-1.** [marchandises, personnes] to transport. **-2.** *fig* [enthousiasmer] to delight; **être transporté de joie/bonheur** to be beside o.s. with joy/happiness.

transporteur [trăspɔrtœr] *nm* **-1.** [personne] carrier; ~ **routier** road hauler *Am* OU haulier *Br*. **-2.** [machine] conveyor.

transposer [trăspoze] [3] *vt* **-1.** [déplacer] to transpose. **-2.** [adapter]: ~ **qqch (à)** to adapt sthg (for).

transposition [trăspozisjɔ̃] *nf* **-1.** [déplacement] transposition. **-2.** [adaptation]: ~ **(à)** adaptation (for).

transsexuel, **-elle** [trăssɛksyɛl] *adj & nm, f* transsexual.

transvaser [trăsvaze] [3] *vt* to decant.

transversal, **-e**, **-aux** [trăsvɛrsal, o] *adj* **-1.** [coupe] cross (*avant n*). **-2.** [chemin] running at right angles, cross (*avant n*) *Am*. **-3.** [vallée] transverse.

trapèze [trapɛz] *nm* **-1.** GÉOM trapezium. **-2.** GYM trapeze. **-3.** ANAT trapezius.

trapéziste [trapezist] *nmf* trapeze artist.

trappage [trapaʒ] *nm Can* trapping.

trappe [trap] *nf* **-1.** [ouverture] trapdoor. **-2.** [piège] trap.

trappeur [trapœr] *nm* trapper.

trapu, **-e** [trapy] *adj* **-1.** [personne] stocky, solidly built. **-2.** [édifice] squat.

traquenard [traknar] *nm* trap; *fig* pitfall.

traquer [trake] [3] *vt* [animal] to track; [personne, faute] to track OU hunt down.

traumatisant, **-e** [tromatizã, ãt] *adj* traumatizing.

traumatiser [tromatize] [3] *vt* to traumatize.

traumatisme [tromatism] *nm* traumatism.

traumatologie [tromatɔlɔʒi] *nf* ≃ casualty department.

travail [travaj] *nm* **-1.** [gén] work (*U*); **se mettre au** ~ to get down to work; **demander du** ~ [projet] to require some work; **abattre du** ~ *fig* to get through a lot of work; **mâcher le** ~ **à qqn** *fig* to spoon-feed sb. **-2.** [tâche, emploi] job; ~ **intérimaire** temporary work; ~ **au noir** moonlighting; ~ **précaire** casual labor *Am* OU labour *Br*. **-3.** [du métal, du bois] working. **-4.** [de la mémoire] workings (*pl*). **-5.** [phénomène - du bois] warping; [- du temps, fermentation] action. **-6.** MÉD: **être en** ~ to be in labor *Am* OU labour *Br*; **entrer en** ~ to go into labor *Am* OU labour *Br*.

◆ **travaux** *nmpl* **-1.** [d'aménagement] work (*U*); [routiers] roadworks; **travaux publics** civil engineering (*sg*). **-2.** SCOL: **travaux dirigés** class work; **travaux manuels** arts and crafts; **travaux pratiques** practical work (*U*).

◆ **travaux d'approche** *nmpl* preliminary work (*U*).

travaillé, **-e** [travaje] *adj* **-1.** [matériau] wrought, worked. **-2.** [style] labored *Am*, laboured *Br*. **-3.** [tourmenté]: **être** ~ **par** to be tormented by.

travailler [travaje] [3] ◇ *vi* **-1.** [gén] to work; ~ **chez/dans** to work at/in; ~ **à qqch** to work on sthg. **-2.** [métal, bois] to warp. ◇ *vt* **-1.** [étudier] to work at OU on; [piano] to practise. **-2.** [essayer de convaincre] to work on. **-3.** [suj: idée, remords] to torment. **-4.** [matière] to work, to fashion.

travailleur, **-euse** [travajœr, øz] ◇ *adj* hard-working. ◇ *nm, f* worker; ~ **à domicile** homeworker; ~ **émigré** migrant worker; ~ **indépendant** self-employed person.

travailliste [travajist] ◇ *nmf* member of the Labour Party. ◇ *adj* Labour (*avant n*).

travée [trave] *nf* **-1.** [de bâtiment] bay. **-2.** [de sièges] row.

traveller [travlœr] *nm inv* traveler's check *Am*, traveller's cheque *Br*.

travelling [travliŋ] *nm* [mouvement] travelling *Am* OU **travelling** *Br* shot.

travelo [travlo] *nm* *tfam* drag queen.

travers [travɛr] *nm* failing, fault.
◆ **à travers** *loc adv & loc prép* through.
◆ **au travers** *loc adv* through; **passer au** ~ *fig* to escape.
◆ **au travers de** *loc prép* through.
◆ **de travers** *loc adv* **-1.** [irrégulièrement - écrire] unevenly; **marcher de** ~ to stagger. **-2.** [nez, escalier] crooked. **-3.** [obliquement] sideways; **regarder qqn de** ~ *fig* to look askance at sb. **-4.** [mal] wrong; **aller de** ~ to go wrong; **comprendre qqch de** ~ to misunderstand sthg; **prendre qqch de** ~ to take sthg the wrong way.
◆ **en travers** *loc adv* crosswise.
◆ **en travers de** *loc prép* across.

traverse [travɛrs] *nf* **-1.** [de chemin de fer] sleeper, tie *Am.* **-2.** [chemin] short cut.

traversée [travɛrse] *nf* crossing.

traverser [travɛrse] [3] *vt* **-1.** [rue, mer, montagne] to cross; [ville] to go through. **-2.** [peau, mur] to go through, to pierce. **-3.** [crise, période] to go through.

traversin [travɛrsɛ̃] *nm* bolster.

travestir [travɛstir] [32] *vt* **-1.** [déguiser] to dress up. **-2.** *fig* [vérité, idée] to distort.
◆ **se travestir** *vp* **-1.** [pour bal] to wear fancy dress. **-2.** [en femme] to put on drag.

travestissement [travɛstismɑ̃] *nm* **-1.** [pour bal] wearing fancy dress. **-2.** [en femme] putting on drag. **-3.** *fig* [de vérité] distortion.

trayeuse [trɛjøz] *nf* milking machine.

trébucher [trebyʃe] [3] *vi*: ~ **(sur/contre)** to stumble (over/against).

trèfle [trɛfl] *nm* **-1.** [plante] clover; ~ **à quatre feuilles** four-leaved clover. **-2.** [carte] club; [famille] clubs (*pl*).

tréfonds [trefɔ̃] *nm* *littéraire* depths (*pl*).

treillage [trejaʒ] *nm* [clôture] trellis (fencing).

treille [trej] *nf* **-1.** [vigne] climbing vine. **-2.** [tonnelle] trellised vines (*pl*), vine arbour.

treillis [treji] *nm* **-1.** [clôture] trellis (fencing). **-2.** [toile] canvas. **-3.** MIL combat uniform.

treize [trɛz] *adj num & nm* thirteen; *voir aussi* **six.**

treizième [trɛzjɛm] *adj num, nm & nmf* thirteenth; *voir aussi* **sixième;** ~ **mois** *bonus corresponding to an extra month's salary which is paid annually.*

trekking [trekiŋ] *nm* trek.

tréma [trema] *nm* dieresis *Am*, diaeresis *Br*.

tremblant, -e [trɑ̃blɑ̃, ɑ̃t] *adj* **-1.** [personne - de froid] shivering; [- d'émotion] trembling, shaking; **être tout** ~ to be trembling OU shaking. **-2.** [voix] quavering. **-3.** [lumière] flickering.

tremble [trɑ̃bl] *nm* aspen.

tremblement [trɑ̃bləmɑ̃] *nm* **-1.** [de corps] trembling. **-2.** [de voix] quavering. **-3.** [de feuilles] fluttering.
◆ **tremblement de terre** *nm* earthquake.

trembler [trɑ̃ble] [3] *vi* **-1.** [personne - de froid] to shiver; [- d'émotion] to tremble, to shake. **-2.** *fig & sout* [avoir peur] to fear; ~ **que** (+ *subjonctif*) to fear (that); ~ **de faire qqch** to be scared to do sthg. **-3.** [voix] to quaver. **-4.** [lumière] to flicker. **-5.** [terre] to shake.

tremblotant, -e [trɑ̃blɔtɑ̃, ɑ̃t] *adj* **-1.** [personne] trembling. **-2.** [voix] quavering. **-3.** [lumière] flickering.

trembloter [trɑ̃blɔte] [3] *vi* **-1.** [personne] to tremble. **-2.** [voix] to quaver. **-3.** [lumière] to flicker.

trémière [tremjɛr] → **rose.**

trémolo [tremolo] *nm* tremolo; **avoir des ~s dans la voix** *hum* to have a quaver in one's voice.

trémousser [tremuse] [3]
◆ **se trémousser** *vp* to jig up and down.

trempe [trɑ̃p] *nf* **-1.** [envergure] calibre; **de sa** ~ of his/her calibre. **-2.** *fam* [coups] thrashing.

tremper [trɑ̃pe] [3] ◇ *vt* **-1.** [mouiller] to soak; **faire** ~ to soak. **-2.** [plonger]: ~ **qqch dans** to dip sthg into. **-3.** [métal] to harden, to quench. ◇ *vi* **-1.** [linge] to soak. **-2.** [se compromettre]: ~ **dans** to be involved in.
◆ **se tremper** *vp* **-1.** [se mouiller] to get soaking wet. **-2.** [se plonger] to have a quick dip.

trempette [trɑ̃pɛt] *nf*: **faire** ~ [se baigner] to go for a dip; [avec biscuit] to dunk.

tremplin [trɑ̃plɛ̃] *nm* *litt & fig* springboard; SKI ski jump.

trench-coat [trɛnʃkot] (*pl* **trench-coats**) *nm* trench coat.

trentaine [trɑ̃tɛn] *nf* **-1.** [nombre]: **une** ~ **de** about thirty. **-2.** [âge]: **avoir la** ~ to be in one's thirties.

trente [trɑ̃t] ◇ *adj num* thirty; ~**-trois tours** LP, long-playing record. ◇ *nm* thirty; **être/se mettre sur son** ~ **et un** *fig* to be in/to put on one's Sunday best; *voir aussi* **six.**

trentième [trɑ̃tjɛm] *adj num, nm & nmf* thirtieth; *voir aussi* **sixième.**

trépaner [trepane] [3] *vt* MÉD to trepan.

trépas [trepa] *nm littéraire* demise.

trépasser [trepase] [3] *vi littéraire* to pass away.

trépidant, -e [trepidɑ̃, ɑ̃t] *adj* [vie] hectic.

trépidation [trepidasjɔ̃] *nf* [vibration] vibration.

trépied [trepje] *nm* **-1.** [support] tripod. **-2.** [meuble] three-legged stool/table.

trépignement [trepiɲmɑ̃] *nm* stamping.

trépigner [trepiɲe] [3] *vi* to stamp one's feet.

très [trɛ] *adv* very; ~ **malade** very ill; ~ **bien** very well; **être** ~ **aimé** to be much OU greatly liked; **avoir** ~ **peur/faim** to be very frightened/hungry; **j'ai** ~ **envie de ...** I'd very much like to ....

trésor [trezɔr] *nm* treasure; **mon** ~ *fig* my precious.

◆ **Trésor** *nm*: **le Trésor public** the public revenue department.

◆ **trésors** *nmpl* riches, treasures; **des** ~s **de** *fig* a wealth (*sg*) of.

trésorerie [trezɔrri] *nf* **-1.** [service] accounts department. **-2.** [gestion] accounts (*pl*). **-3.** [fonds] finances (*pl*), funds (*pl*).

trésorier, -ière [trezɔrje, jɛr] *nm, f* treasurer.

tressaillement [tresajmɑ̃] *nm* [de joie] thrill; [de douleur] wince.

tressaillir [tresajir] [47] *vi* **-1.** [de joie] to thrill; [de douleur] to wince. **-2.** [sursauter] to start, to jump.

tressauter [tresote] [3] *vi* [sursauter] to jump, to start; [dans véhicule] to be tossed about; **faire** ~ to toss OU jolt about.

tresse [trɛs] *nf* **-1.** [de cheveux] plait. **-2.** [de rubans] braid.

tresser [trese] [4] *vt* **-1.** [cheveux] to plait. **-2.** [osier] to braid. **-3.** [panier, guirlande] to weave.

tréteau, -x [treto] *nm* trestle.

treuil [trœj] *nm* winch, windlass.

trêve [trɛv] *nf* **-1.** [cessez-le-feu] truce. **-2.** *fig* [répit] rest, respite; ~ **de plaisanteries/de sottises** that's enough joking/nonsense.

◆ **sans trêve** *loc adv* relentlessly.

tri [tri] *nm* [de lettres] sorting; [de candidats] selection; **faire le** ~ **dans qqch** *fig* to sort sthg out.

triage [trijaʒ] *nm* [de lettres] sorting; [de candidats] selection.

triangle [trijɑ̃gl] *nm* triangle; ~ **isocèle** isosceles triangle; ~ **rectangle** right-angled triangle.

triangulaire [trijɑ̃gylɛr] *adj* triangular.

triathlon [trijatlɔ̃] *nm* triathlon.

tribal, -e, -aux [tribal, o] *adj* tribal.

tribord [tribɔr] *nm* starboard; **à** ~ on the starboard side, to starboard.

tribu [triby] *nf* tribe.

tribulations [tribylasjɔ̃] *nfpl* tribulations, trials.

tribun [tribœ̃] *nm* **-1.** HIST tribune. **-2.** [orateur] popular orator.

tribunal, -aux [tribynal, o] *nm* **-1.** JUR court; ~ **correctionnel** ≃ County court *Am*, ≃ Magistrates' Court *Br*; ~ **pour enfants** juvenile court; ~ **d'exception** special court; ~ **de grande instance** ≃ Circuit court *Am*, ≃ Crown Court *Br*; ~ **d'instance** ≃ County court *Am*, ≃ Magistrates' Court *Br*; ~ **de police** police court. **-2.** *fig* & *littéraire* [jugement] judgment.

tribune [tribyn] *nf* **-1.** [d'orateur] platform. **-2.** (*gén pl*) [de stade] stand. **-3.** *fig* [lieu d'expression] forum; ~ **libre** PRESSE opinion column.

tribut [triby] *nm littéraire* tribute.

tributaire [tribytɛr] *adj*: **être** ~ **de** to depend on OU be dependent on.

tricentenaire [trisɑ̃tnɛr] *nm* tricentennial.

triceps [trisɛps] *nm* triceps.

triche [triʃ] *nf fam* cheating.

tricher [triʃe] [3] *vi* **-1.** [au jeu, à examen] to cheat. **-2.** [mentir]: ~ **sur** to lie about.

tricherie [triʃri] *nf* cheating.

tricheur, -euse [triʃœr, øz] *nm, f* cheat.

tricolore [trikɔlɔr] *adj* **-1.** [à trois couleurs] three-colored *Am*, three-coloured *Br*. **-2.** [français] French.

tricot [triko] *nm* **-1.** [vêtement] sweater, jumper *Br*; ~ **de corps** undershirt *Am*, vest *Br*. **-2.** [ouvrage] knitting; **faire du** ~ to knit. **-3.** [étoffe] knitted fabric, jersey.

tricoter [trikɔte] [3] *vi* & *vt* to knit.

tricycle [trisikl] *nm* tricycle.

trident [tridɑ̃] *nm* **-1.** MYTH trident. **-2.** [fourche] pitchfork.

tridimensionnel, -elle [tridimɑ̃sjɔnɛl] *adj* three-dimensional.

triennal, -e, -aux [trienal, o] *adj* **-1.** [mandat] three-year. **-2.** [élection] three-yearly.

trier [trije] [10] *vt* **-1.** [classer] to sort out. **-2.** [sélectionner] to select.

trifouiller [trifuje] [3] *vi fam* to rummage around.

trigonométrie [trigɔnɔmetri] *nf* trigonometry.

trilingue [trilɛ̃g] ◇ *nmf* person who is trilingual. ◇ *adj* trilingual.

trille [trij] *nm* trill.

trilogie [trilɔʒi] *nf* trilogy.

trim. -1. (*abr de* **trimestre**) quarter. **-2.** (*abr de* **trimestriel**) quarterly.

trimaran [trimarɑ̃] *nm* trimaran.

trimbaler [trɛ̃bale] [3] *vt fam* [personne] to trail around; [chose] to cart around.
◆ **se trimbaler** *vp fam* to trail around.

trimer [trime] [3] *vi fam* to slave away.

trimestre [trimɛstr] *nm* **-1.** [période] term. **-2.** [loyer] quarter's rent; [rente] quarter's income.

trimestriel, -ielle [trimɛstrijɛl] *adj* [loyer, magazine] quarterly; SCOL end-of-term (*avant n*).

trimoteur [trimɔtœr] ◇ *nm* three-engined plane. ◇ *adj* three-engined.

tringle [trɛ̃gl] *nf* rod; ~ **à rideaux** curtain rod.

trinité [trinite] *nf littéraire* trinity.
◆ **Trinité** *nf*: **la Trinité** the Trinity.

trinquer [trɛ̃ke] [3] *vi* **-1.** [boire] to toast, to clink glasses; ~ **à** to drink to. **-2.** *fam* [personne] to get the worst of it; [voiture] to be damaged.

trio [trijo] *nm* trio.

triomphal, -e, -aux [trijɔ̃fal, o] *adj* [succès] triumphal; [accueil] triumphant.

triomphalement [trijɔ̃falmɑ̃] *adv* **-1.** [en triomphe] in triumph. **-2.** [fièrement] triumphantly.

triomphalisme [trijɔ̃falism] *nm* triumphalism.

triomphant, -e [trijɔ̃fɑ̃, ɑ̃t] *adj* [équipe] winning; [air] triumphant.

triomphateur, -trice [trijɔ̃fatœr, tris] ◇ *adj* triumphant. ◇ *nm, f* victor.

triomphe [trijɔ̃f] *nm* triumph.

triompher [trijɔ̃fe] [3] *vi* **-1.** [gén] to triumph; ~ **de** to triumph over; **faire** ~ **qqch** to ensure the success of sthg. **-2.** [crier victoire] to rejoice.

trip [trip] *nm arg drogue* trip.

triparti, -e [triparti], **tripartite** [tripartit] *adj* tripartite.

tripatouiller [tripatuje] [3] *vt fam* **-1.** [fruits] to paw. **-2.** [texte, compte] to fiddle with.

tripes [trip] *nfpl* **-1.** [d'animal, de personne] guts; **prendre qqn aux** ~ *fam fig* to get sb in the guts. **-2.** CULIN tripe (*sg*).

triperie [tripri] *nf* **-1.** [commerce] tripe trade. **-2.** [boutique] tripe shop. **-3.** [aliments] tripe.

tripier, -ière [tripje, jɛr] *nm, f* tripe butcher.

triple [tripl] ◇ *adj* triple. ◇ *nm*: **le** ~ **(de)** three times as much (as).

triplé [triple] *nm* [au turf] bet on three horses winning in three different races.

◆ **triplés, -ées** *nm, f pl* triplets.

triplement [triplǝmɑ̃] ◇ *adv* trebly. ◇ *nm* threefold increase, tripling.

tripler [triple] [3] *vt & vi* to triple.

triporteur [tripɔrtœr] *nm* tricycle (*used for deliveries*).

tripot [tripo] *nm péj* gambling-den.

tripotage [tripɔtaʒ] *nm* (*gén pl*) *fam* [manigances] fiddling (*U*).

tripoter [tripɔte] [3] ◇ *vt* **-1.** *fam* [stylo, montre] to play with. **-2.** *vulg* [femme] to feel up. ◇ *vi fam*: ~ **dans** [fouiller dans] to rummage about in; [trafiquer] to dabble in.

tripous, tripoux [tripu] *nmpl stuffed tripe.*

triptyque [triptik] *nm* triptych.

trique [trik] *nf* cudgel.

triste [trist] *adj* **-1.** [personne, nouvelle] sad; **être** ~ **de qqch/de faire qqch** to be sad about sthg/about doing sthg. **-2.** [paysage, temps] gloomy; [couleur] dull. **-3.** (*avant n*) [lamentable] sorry.

tristement [tristǝmɑ̃] *adv* **-1.** [d'un air triste] sadly. **-2.** [lugubrement] gloomily. **-3.** [de façon regrettable] sadly, regrettably; ~ **célèbre** notorious.

tristesse [tristɛs] *nf* **-1.** [de personne, nouvelle] sadness. **-2.** [de paysage, temps] gloominess.

tristounet, -ette [tristunɛ, ɛt] *adj fam* **-1.** [personne] sad. **-2.** *péj* [humeur] gloomy.

triton [tritɔ̃] *nm* triton.

triturer [trityre] [3] *vt* **-1.** [sel] to grind. **-2.** *fam* [mouchoir] to knead.
◆ **se triturer** *vp fam*: **se** ~ **l'esprit** OU **les méninges** to rack one's brains.

trivial, -e, -iaux [trivjal, jo] *adj* **-1.** [banal] trivial. **-2.** *péj* [vulgaire] crude, coarse.

trivialité [trivjalite] *nf* **-1.** [banalité] triviality. **-2.** *péj* [vulgarité] vulgar OU coarse expression.

tr/mn, tr/min (*abr de* **tour par minute**) r/min, rpm.

troc [trɔk] *nm* **-1.** [échange] exchange. **-2.** [système économique] barter.

troène [trɔɛn] *nm* privet.

troglodyte [trɔglɔdit] *nm* cave dweller, troglodyte.

trogne [trɔɲ] *nf fam* [visage] mug.

trognon [trɔɲɔ̃] *nm* [de fruit] core.

troïka [trɔika] *nf* troika.

trois [trwa] ◇ *nm* three; *voir aussi* **six**. ◇ *adj num* three; **les** ~**-huit** shift work; ~ **fois rien** *fig* nothing at all; **les** ~ **jours** MIL *induction course preceding military service (now lasting one day)*; *voir aussi* **six**.

trois-étoiles [trwazetwal] ◇ *adj* three-star (*avant n*). ◇ *nm* three-star hotel/restaurant.

troisième [trwazjɛm] ◇ *adj num & nmf* third. ◇ *nm* third; [étage] fourth floor *Am*, third floor *Br*. ◇ *nf* **-1.** SCOL ≃ ninth grade *Am*, ≃ fourth year OU form *Br*. **-2.** [vitesse] third (gear); *voir aussi* **sixième**.

troisièmement [trwazjɛmmɑ̃] *adv* thirdly.

trois-mâts [trwama] *nm inv* three-master.

trois-quarts [trwakar] *nm inv* RUGBY three-quarter.

trolley(bus) [trɔlɛ(bys)] *nm* trolleybus.

trombe [trɔ̃b] *nf* water spout; **passer en ~** *fig* to zoom past, to speed past; **des ~s d'eau** torrential rain (*U*).

trombone [trɔ̃bɔn] *nm* **-1.** [agrafe] paper clip. **-2.** [instrument] trombone; **~ à coulisse** slide trombone. **-3.** [joueur] trombone player, trombonist.

trompe [trɔ̃p] *nf* **-1.** [instrument] trumpet. **-2.** [d'éléphant] trunk. **-3.** [d'insecte] proboscis. **-4.** ANAT tube.

trompe-l'œil [trɔ̃plœj] *nm inv* **-1.** [peinture] trompe-l'oeil; **en ~** done in trompe-l'oeil. **-2.** [apparence] deception.

tromper [trɔ̃pe] [3] *vt* **-1.** [personne] to deceive; [époux] to be unfaithful to. **-2.** [vigilance] to elude. **-3.** *littéraire* [espoirs] to fall short of. **-4.** [faim] to stave off.

◆ **se tromper** *vp* to make a mistake, to be mistaken; **se ~ de jour/maison** to get the wrong day/house.

tromperie [trɔ̃pri] *nf* deception.

trompette [trɔ̃pet] *nf* trumpet.

trompettiste [trɔ̃petist] *nmf* trumpeter.

trompeur, -euse [trɔ̃pœr, øz] ◇ *adj* **-1.** [personne] deceitful. **-2.** [calme, apparence] deceptive. ◇ *nm, f* deceitful person.

trompeusement [trɔ̃pøzmɑ̃] *adv* **-1.** [hypocritement] deceitfully. **-2.** [apparemment] deceptively.

tronc [trɔ̃] *nm* **-1.** [d'arbre, de personne] trunk. **-2.** [d'église] collection box. **-3.** [de veine, nerf] stem.

◆ **tronc commun** *nm* [de programmes] common element OU feature; SCOL core syllabus.

tronche [trɔ̃ʃ] *nf fam péj* [visage] mug.

tronçon [trɔ̃sɔ̃] *nm* **-1.** [morceau] piece, length. **-2.** [de route, de chemin de fer] section.

tronçonner [trɔ̃sɔne] [3] *vt* to cut into pieces.

tronçonneuse [trɔ̃sɔnøz] *nf* chain saw.

trône [tron] *nm* throne.

trôner [trone] [3] *vi* **-1.** [personne] to sit enthroned; [objet] to have pride of place. **-2.** *hum* [faire l'important] to lord it.

tronquer [trɔ̃ke] [3] *vt* to truncate.

trop [tro] *adv* **-1.** (*devant adj, adv*) too; **~ vieux/loin** too old/far; **nous étions ~ nombreux** there were too many of us; **avoir ~ chaud/froid/peur** to be too hot/cold/frightened. **-2.** (*avec verbe*) too much; **il mange ~** he eats too much; **nous étions ~** there were too many of us; **je n'aime pas ~ le chocolat** I don't like chocolate very much; **on ne se voit plus ~** we don't really see each other any more; **sans ~ savoir pourquoi** without really knowing why. **-3.** (*avec complément*): **~ de** (*quantité*) too much; (*nombre*) too many.

◆ **en trop, de trop** *loc adv* too much/many; **10 francs de** OU **en ~** 10 francs too much; **une personne de** OU **en ~** one person too many; **être de ~** [personne] to be in the way, to be unwelcome.

trophée [trɔfe] *nm* trophy.

tropical, -e, -aux [trɔpikal, o] *adj* tropical.

tropique [trɔpik] *nm* tropic; **~ du Cancer/du Capricorne** Tropic of Cancer/Capricorn.

◆ **tropiques** *nmpl* tropics.

trop-perçu [trɔpɛrsy] (*pl* **trop-perçus**) *nm* excess payment.

trop-plein [trɔplɛ̃] (*pl* **trop-pleins**) *nm* **-1.** [excès] excess; *fig* excess, surplus. **-2.** [déversoir] overflow.

troquer [trɔke] [3] *vt*: **~ qqch (contre)** to barter sthg (for); *fig* to swap sthg (for).

troquet [trɔkɛ] *nm fam* (small) café.

trot [tro] *nm* trot; **au ~** at a trot; **au ~!** *fam fig* at the double!

trotter [trɔte] [3] *vi* **-1.** [cheval] to trot. **-2.** [personne] to run around.

trotteur, -euse [trɔtœr, øz] *nm, f* trotter.

◆ **trotteuse** *nf* second hand.

trottiner [trɔtine] [3] *vi* to trot.

trottinette [trɔtinɛt] *nf* child's scooter.

trottoir [trɔtwar] *nm* sidewalk *Am*, pavement *Br*; **faire le ~** *fam fig* to walk the streets.

trou [tru] *nm* **-1.** [gén] hole; **~ d'aération** air vent; **~ d'air** air pocket; **~ de serrure** keyhole. **-2.** [manque, espace vide] gap; **~ de mémoire** memory lapse. **-3.** *fam* [prison] clink, nick *Br*.

troublant, -e [trublɑ̃, ɑ̃t] *adj* disturbing.

trouble [trubl] ◇ *adj* **-1.** [eau] cloudy. **-2.** [image, vue] blurred. **-3.** [affaire] shady. ◇ *nm* **-1.** [désordre] trouble, discord. **-2.** [gêne]

tubulaire

confusion; [émoi] agitation. **-3.** (*gén pl*) [dérèglement] disorder; ~s **moteurs** motor disorders; ~s **respiratoires** respiratory disorders.

◆ **troubles** *nmpl* [sociaux] unrest (*U*).

trouble-fête [trubləfɛt] *nmf inv* spoilsport.

troubler [truble] [3] *vt* **-1.** [eau] to cloud, to make cloudy. **-2.** [image, vue] to blur. **-3.** [sommeil, événement] to disrupt, to disturb. **-4.** [esprit, raison] to cloud. **-5.** [inquiéter, émouvoir] to disturb. **-6.** [rendre perplexe] to trouble.

◆ **se troubler** *vp* **-1.** [eau] to become cloudy. **-2.** [personne] to become flustered.

trouée [true] *nf* gap; MIL breach.

trouer [true] [3] *vt* **-1.** [chaussette] to make a hole in. **-2.** *fig* [silence] to disturb.

troufion [trufjɔ̃] *nm fam* soldier.

trouillard, -e [trujar, ard] *fam* ◇ *adj* yellow, chicken. ◇ *nm, f* chicken.

trouille [truj] *nf fam* fear, terror.

troupe [trup] *nf* **-1.** MIL troop. **-2.** [d'amis] group, band; [- de singes] troop. **-3.** THÉÂTRE theatre group.

troupeau, -x [trupo] *nm* [de vaches, d'éléphants] herd; [de moutons, d'oies] flock; *péj* [de personnes] herd.

trousse [trus] *nf* case, bag; ~ **de secours** first-aid kit; ~ **de toilette** toilet bag.

◆ **trousses** *nfpl*: **avoir qqn à ses** ~s *fig* to have sb hot on one's heels; **être aux** ~s **de qqn** *fig* to be hot on the heels of sb.

trousseau, -x [truso] *nm* **-1.** [de mariée] trousseau. **-2.** [de clefs] bunch.

trousser [truse] [3] *vt* **-1.** [manches] to roll up; [jupe] to hitch up. **-2.** CULIN to truss.

trouvaille [truvaj] *nf* **-1.** [découverte] find, discovery. **-2.** [invention] new idea.

trouver [truve] [3] ◇ *vt* to find; ~ **que** to feel (that); ~ **qqch à qqn** to think sb has sthg; ~ **bon/mauvais que ...** to think (that) it is right/wrong that ...; ~ **qqch à faire/à dire** *etc* to find sthg to do/say *etc*; ~ **à s'occuper** to find something to do. ◇ *v impers*: **il se trouve que ...** the fact is that ....

◆ **se trouver** *vp* **-1.** [dans un endroit] to be. **-2.** [dans un état] to find o.s. **-3.** [se sentir] to feel; **se** ~ **mal** [s'évanouir] to faint.

truand [tryɑ̃] *nm* crook.

truander [tryɑ̃de] [3] *vt fam* to rip off.

trublion [tryblijɔ̃] *nm* troublemaker.

truc [tryk] *nm* **-1.** [combine] trick. **-2.** *fam* [chose] thing, thingamajig; **ce n'est pas son** ~ it's not his thing.

trucage = **truquage**.

truchement [tryʃmɑ̃] *nm*: **par le** ~ **de qqn** through sb.

trucider [tryside] [3] *vt fam* to bump off.

truculence [trykylɑ̃s] *nf* vividness, colorfulness *Am*, colourfulness *Br*.

truculent, -e [trykylɑ̃, ɑ̃t] *adj* colorful *Am*, colourful *Br*.

truelle [tryɛl] *nf* trowel.

truffe [tryf] *nf* **-1.** [champignon] truffle; ~ **en chocolat** chocolate truffle. **-2.** [museau] muzzle.

truffer [tryfe] [3] *vt* **-1.** [volaille] to garnish with truffles. **-2.** *fig* [discours]: ~ **de** to stuff with.

truie [trɥi] *nf* sow.

truite [trɥit] *nf* trout.

truquage, trucage [trykaʒ] *nm* **-1.** [d'élections] rigging; [de dés] loading. **-2.** CIN (special) effect.

truquer [tryke] [3] *vt* **-1.** [élections] to rig; [dés] to load. **-2.** CIN to use special effects in.

trust [trœst] *nm* **-1.** [groupement] trust. **-2.** [entreprise] corporation.

ts *abr de* **tous.**

tsar, tzar [tzar] *nm* tsar.

tsé-tsé [tsetse] → **mouche.**

tsigane = **tzigane.**

TSVP (*abr de* **tournez s'il vous plaît**) PTO.

tt *abr de* **tout.**

TT, TTA (*abr de* **transit temporaire (autorisé)**) *registration for vehicles bought in France for tax-free export by non-residents.*

tt conf. *abr de* **tout confort.**

ttes *abr de* **toutes.**

TTX (*abr de* **traitement de texte**) WP.

tu¹, -e [ty] *pp* → **taire.**

tu² [ty] *pron pers* you; **dire** ~ **à qqn** to use the "tu" form to sb.

TU (*abr de* **temps universel**) *nm* UT, GMT.

tuant, -e [tɥɑ̃, ɑ̃t] *adj* **-1.** [épuisant] exhausting. **-2.** [énervant] tiresome.

tuba [tyba] *nm* **-1.** MUS tuba. **-2.** [de plongée] snorkel.

tube [tyb] *nm* **-1.** [gén] tube; ~ **cathodique** cathode ray tube; **à pleins** ~s *fig* [chanter, crier] at the top of one's voice; [mettre la musique] at full blast. **-2.** *fam* [chanson] hit.

◆ **tube digestif** *nm* digestive tract.

tubercule [tybɛrkyl] *nm* **-1.** BOT tuber. **-2.** ANAT tubercle.

tuberculeux, -euse [tybɛrkylø, øz] ◇ *adj* tubercular. ◇ *nm, f* tuberculosis sufferer.

tuberculose [tybɛrkyloz] *nf* tuberculosis.

tubulaire [tybylɛr] *adj* tubular.

TUC, Tuc [tyk] (*abr de* **travail d'utilité collective**) *nm community work scheme for unemployed young people.*

tue-mouches [tymuʃ] → **papier**.

tuer [tɥe] [7] *vt* to kill.

◆ **se tuer** *vp* **-1.** [se suicider] to kill o.s. **-2.** [par accident] to die. **-3.** *fig* [s'épuiser]: **se ~ à faire qqch** to wear o.s. out doing sthg.

tuerie [tyri] *nf* slaughter.

tue-tête [tytɛt]

◆ **à tue-tête** *loc adv* at the top of one's voice.

tueur, -euse [tɥœr, øz] *nm, f* **-1.** [meurtrier] killer; **~ à gages** hit man. **-2.** [dans abattoir] slaughterer.

tuile [tɥil] *nf* **-1.** [de toit] tile. **-2.** *fam* [désagrément] blow.

tulipe [tylip] *nf* tulip.

tulle [tyl] *nm* tulle.

tuméfié, -e [tymefje] *adj* swollen.

tumeur [tymœr] *nf* tumor *Am*, tumour *Br*.

tumoral, -e, -aux [tymɔral, o] *adj* tumorous.

tumulte [tymylt] *nm* [désordre] hubbub.

tumultueux, -euse [tymyltɥø, øz] *adj* stormy.

tune = **thune**.

tuner [tynɛr] *nm* tuner.

tungstène [tœ̃kstɛn] *nm* tungsten.

tunique [tynik] *nf* tunic.

Tunis [tynis] *n* Tunis.

Tunisie [tynizi] *nf*: **la ~** Tunisia.

tunisien, -ienne [tynizjɛ̃, jɛn] *adj* Tunisian.
◆ **Tunisien, -ienne** *nm, f* Tunisian.

tunnel [tynɛl] *nm* tunnel.

TUP [typ] (*abr de* **titre universel de paiement**) *nm payment slip formerly used to settle bills.*

tuque [tyk] *nf Can* wool hat, tuque *Can*.

turban [tyrbɑ̃] *nm* turban.

turbin [tyrbɛ̃] *nm fam*: **aller au ~** to go to work.

turbine [tyrbin] *nf* turbine.

turbo [tyrbo] *nm & nf* turbo.

turboréacteur [tyrbɔreaktœr] *nm* turbojet.

turbot [tyrbo] *nm* turbot.

turbotrain [tyrbɔtrɛ̃] *nm* turbotrain.

turbulence [tyrbylɑ̃s] *nf* **-1.** [de personne] boisterousness. **-2.** MÉTÉOR turbulence.

turbulent, -e [tyrbylɑ̃, ɑ̃t] *adj* boisterous.

turc, turque [tyrk] *adj* Turkish.
◆ **turc** *nm* [langue] Turkish.
◆ **Turc, Turque** *nm, f* Turk.

turf [tœrf] *nm* [activité]: **le ~** racing.

turfiste [tœrfist] *nmf* racegoer.

turkmène [tyrkmɛn] ◇ *adj* Turkmen. ◇ *nm* [langue] Turkmen.
◆ **Turkmène** *nmf* Turkoman.

turlupiner [tyrlypine] [3] *vt fam* to nag.

turnover [tœrnɔvœr] *nm* turnover.

turpitude [tyrpityd] *nf littéraire* turpitude.

turque → **turc**.

Turquie [tyrki] *nf*: **la ~** Turkey.

turquoise [tyrkwaz] *nf & adj inv* turquoise.

tutelle [tytɛl] *nf* **-1.** JUR guardianship. **-2.** [dépendance] supervision; **sous la ~ des Nations unies** under United Nations supervision. **-3.** [protection] protection.

tuteur, -trice [tytœr, tris] *nm, f* guardian.
◆ **tuteur** *nm* [pour plante] stake.

tutoiement [tytwamɑ̃] *nm* use of "tu".

tutoyer [tytwaje] [13] *vt*: **~ qqn** to use the "tu" form to sb.

tutu [tyty] *nm* tutu.

tuyau, -x [tɥijo] *nm* **-1.** [conduit] pipe; **~ d'arrosage** hosepipe. **-2.** *fam* [renseignement] tip.

tuyauter [tɥijote] [3] *vt fam* to give a tip to.

tuyauterie [tɥijotri] *nf* piping (*U*), pipes (*pl*).

TV (*abr de* **télévision**) *nf* TV.

TVA (*abr de* **taxe à la valeur ajoutée**) *nf* ≃ VAT.

TVHD (*abr de* **télévision haute définition**) *nf* HDTV.

tweed [twid] *nm* tweed.

twin-set [twinsɛt] (*pl* **twin-sets**) *nm* sweater set *Am*, twin set *Br*.

tympan [tɛ̃pɑ̃] *nm* **-1.** ANAT eardrum. **-2.** ARCHIT tympanum.

type [tip] ◇ *nm* **-1.** [exemple caractéristique] perfect example; **il est le ~ parfait du professeur** he's the classic example of a teacher. **-2.** [genre] type; **avoir le ~ nordique/méditerranéen** to have Nordic/Mediterranean features. **-3.** *fam* [individu] guy, bloke. ◇ *adj inv* [caractéristique] typical.

typé, -e [tipe] *adj*: **il est bien** OU **très ~** he has all the characteristic features.

typhoïde [tifɔid] ◇ *nf* typhoid. ◇ *adj*: **fièvre ~** typhoid fever.

typhon [tifɔ̃] *nm* typhoon.

typhus [tifys] *nm* typhus.

typique [tipik] *adj* typical.

typiquement [tipikmɑ̃] *adv* typically.

typographe [tipɔgraf] *nmf* typographer.

typographie [tipɔgrafi] *nf* typography.

typographique [tipɔgrafik] *adj* typographical.

typologie [tipɔlɔʒi] *nf* typology.

tyran [tirɑ̃] *nm* tyrant.

tyrannie [tirani] *nf* tyranny.

tyrannique [tiranik] *adj* tyrannical.

tyranniser [tiranize] [3] *vt* to tyrannize.

tyrolien, -ienne [tirɔljɛ̃, jɛn] *adj* Tyrolean.

◆ **tyrolienne** *nf* [air] Tyrolienne.

◆ **Tyrolien, -ienne** *nm, f* Tyrolean.

tzar = tsar.

tzigane, tsigane [tsigan] ◇ *nmf* gipsy. ◇ *adj* gipsy (*avant n*).

u, U [y] *nm inv* u, U.

ubiquité [ybikɥite] *nf* ubiquity; **je n'ai pas le don d'~** I can't be everywhere (at once).

UDF (*abr de* **Union pour la démocratie française**) *nf French political party to the right of the political spectrum.*

UEFA (*abr de* **Union of European Football Associations**) *nf* UEFA.

UEO (*abr de* **Union de l'Europe occidentale**) *nf* WEU.

UER *nf* **-1.** (*abr de* **unité d'enseignement et de recherche**) *former name for a university department.* **-2.** (*abr de* **Union européenne de radiodiffusion**) EBU.

UFC (*abr de* **Union fédérale des consommateurs**) *nf French consumers' association.*

UFR (*abr de* **unité de formation et de recherche**) *nf* university department.

UHF (*abr de* **ultra-haute fréquence**) *nf* UHF.

UHT (*abr de* **ultra-haute température**) *nf* UHT.

Ukraine [ykrɛn] *nf*: **l'~** the Ukraine.

ukrainien, -ienne [ykrɛnjɛ̃, jɛn] *adj* Ukrainian.

◆ **ukrainien** *nm* [langue] Ukrainian.

◆ **Ukrainien, -ienne** *nm, f* Ukrainian.

ulcère [ylsɛr] *nm* ulcer.

ulcérer [ylsere] [18] *vt* **-1.** MÉD to ulcerate. **-2.** *sout* [mettre en colère] to enrage.

◆ **s'ulcérer** *vp* to ulcerate, to fester.

ulcéreux, -euse [ylserø, øz] *adj* [plaie] ulcerous; [organe] ulcerated.

ULM (*abr de* **ultra léger motorisé**) *nm* microlight.

Ulster [ylstɛr] *nm*: **l'~** Ulster.

ultérieur, -ieure [ylterjœr] *adj* later, subsequent.

ultérieurement [ylterjœrmɑ̃] *adv* later, subsequently.

ultimatum [yltimatɔm] *nm* ultimatum.

ultime [yltim] *adj* ultimate, final.

ultramoderne [yltramɔdɛrn] *adj* ultra-modern.

ultrasensible [yltrasɑ̃sibl] *adj* [personne] ultra-sensitive; [pellicule] high-speed.

ultrason [yltrasɔ̃] *nm* ultrasound (*U*).

ultraviolet, -ette [yltravjɔlɛ, ɛt] *adj* ultraviolet.

◆ **ultraviolet** *nm* ultraviolet.

ululement, hululement [ylylmɑ̃] *nm* hoot, hooting (*U*).

ululer, hululer [ylyle] [3] *vi* to hoot.

un [œ̃] (*f* **une** [yn]) ◇ *art indéf* a, an (*devant voyelle*); **~ homme** a man; **~ livre** a book; **une femme** a woman; **une pomme** an apple.

◇ *pron indéf* one; **l'~** de mes amis one of my friends; **l'~ l'autre** each other; **les ~s les autres** one another; **l'~ ..., l'autre** one ..., the other; **les ~s ..., les autres** some ..., others; **l'~ et l'autre** both (of them); **l'~ ou l'autre** either (of them); **ni l'~ ni l'autre** neither one nor the other, neither (of them).

◇ *adj num* one; **une personne à la fois** one person at a time.

◇ *nm* one; *voir aussi* **six.**

◆ **une** *nf*: **faire la/être à la une** PRESSE to make the/to be on the front page; **ne faire ni une ni deux** not to think twice.

unanime [ynanim] *adj* unanimous.

unanimement [ynanimmɑ̃] *adv* unanimously.

unanimité [ynanimite] *nf* unanimity; **faire l'~** to be unanimously approved; **à l'~** unanimously.

underground [œndœrgraɔnd] ◇ *nm inv* underground. ◇ *adj inv* underground (*avant n*).

UNEF, Unef [ynɛf] (*abr de* **Union nationale des étudiants de France**) *nf students' union,* ≈ NUS *Br.*

UNESCO, Unesco [ynɛsko] (*abr de* **United Nations Educational, Scientific and Cultural Organization**) *nf* UNESCO.

uni, -e [yni] *adj* **-1.** [joint, réuni] united. **-2.** [famille, couple] close. **-3.** [surface, mer] smooth; [route] even. **-4.** [étoffe, robe] self-colored *Am,* self-coloured *Br.*

UNICEF, Unicef [ynisɛf] (*abr de* **United**

Nations International Children's Emergency Fund) *nm* UNICEF.

unicité [ynisite] *nf littéraire* uniqueness.

unième [ynjɛm] *adj num*: **cinquante et ~** fifty-first.

unificateur, -trice [ynifikatœr, tris] *adj* unifying.

unification [ynifikasjɔ̃] *nf* unification.

unifier [ynifje] [9] *vt* **-1.** [régions, parti] to unify. **-2.** [programmes] to standardize.
◆ **s'unifier** *vp* to unite, to unify.

uniforme [ynifɔrm] ◇ *adj* uniform; [régulier] regular. ◇ *nm* uniform.

uniformément [ynifɔrmemɑ̃] *adv* uniformly.

uniformisation [ynifɔrmizasjɔ̃] *nf* standardization.

uniformiser [ynifɔrmize] [3] *vt* **-1.** [couleur] to make uniform. **-2.** [programmes, lois] to standardize.

uniformité [ynifɔrmite] *nf* **-1.** [gén] uniformity; [de mouvement] regularity. **-2.** [monotonie] monotony.

unijambiste [yniʒãbist] ◇ *adj* one-legged. ◇ *nmf* one-legged person.

unilatéral, -e, -aux [ynilateral, o] *adj* unilateral; **stationnement ~** parking on only one side of the street.

unilatéralement [ynilateralmɑ̃] *adv* unilaterally.

union [ynjɔ̃] *nf* **-1.** [de couleurs] blending. **-2.** [mariage] union; **~ conjugale** marriage; **~ libre** cohabitation. **-3.** [de pays] union; [de syndicats] confederation; **~ douanière** customs union. **-4.** [entente] unity.
◆ **Union soviétique** *nf*: **l'(ex-)Union soviétique** the (former) Soviet Union.

unique [ynik] *adj* **-1.** [seul - enfant, veston] only; [- préoccupation] sole. **-2.** [principe, prix] single. **-3.** [exceptionnel] unique; **tu es vraiment ~!** *iron* you're priceless!

uniquement [ynikmɑ̃] *adv* **-1.** [exclusivement] only, solely. **-2.** [seulement] only, just.

unir [ynir] [32] *vt* **-1.** [assembler - mots, qualités] to put together, to combine; [- pays] to unite; **~ qqch à** [pays] to unite sthg with; [mot, qualité] to combine sthg with. **-2.** [réunir - partis, familles] to unite. **-3.** [marier] to unite, to join in marriage.
◆ **s'unir** *vp* **-1.** [s'associer] to unite, to join together. **-2.** [se joindre - rivières] to merge; [- couleurs] to go together. **-3.** [se marier] to be joined in marriage.

unisexe [ynisɛks] *adj* unisex.

unisson [ynisɔ̃] *nm* unison; **à l'~** in unison.

unitaire [yniter] *adj* **-1.** [à l'unité]: **prix ~** unit price. **-2.** [manifestation, politique] joint *(avant n)*.

unité [ynite] *nf* **-1.** [cohésion] unity. **-2.** COMM, MATHS & MIL unit; **à l'~** COMM unit *(avant n)*.
◆ **unité centrale** *nf* INFORM central processing unit.
◆ **unité de valeur** *nf* university course unit, ≃ credit.

univers [yniver] *nm* universe; *fig* world.

universaliser [yniversalize] [3] *vt* to universalize, to make universal.
◆ **s'universaliser** *vp* to become universal.

universalité [yniversalite] *nf* universality.

universel, -elle [yniversɛl] *adj* universal.

universellement [yniverselmɑ̃] *adv* universally.

universitaire [yniversiter] ◇ *adj* university *(avant n)*. ◇ *nmf* academic.

université [yniversite] *nf* university.

univoque [ynivɔk] *adj* **-1.** [mot, tournure] unambiguous. **-2.** [relation] one-on-one *Am*, one-to-one *Br*.

uppercut [ypɛrkyt] *nm* uppercut.

uranium [yranjɔm] *nm* uranium.

urbain, -e [yrbɛ̃, ɛn] *adj* **-1.** [de la ville] urban. **-2.** *littéraire* [affable] urbane.

urbanisation [yrbanizasjɔ̃] *nf* urbanization.

urbaniser [yrbanize] [3] *vt* to urbanize.
◆ **s'urbaniser** *vp* to become urbanized.

urbanisme [yrbanism] *nm* town planning.

urbanité [yrbanite] *nf* urbanity.

urée [yre] *nf* urea.

urgence [yrʒɑ̃s] *nf* **-1.** [de mission] urgency. **-2.** MÉD emergency; **les ~s** the casualty department *(sg)*.
◆ **d'urgence** *loc adv* immediately.

urgent, -e [yrʒɑ̃, ɑ̃t] *adj* urgent.

urinaire [yriner] *adj* urinary.

urine [yrin] *nf* urine.

uriner [yrine] [3] *vi* to urinate.

urinoir [yrinwar] *nm* urinal.

urne [yrn] *nf* **-1.** [vase] urn. **-2.** [de vote] ballot box; **aller aux ~s** to go to the polls.

urologie [yrɔlɔʒi] *nf* urology.

URSS *(abr de Union des républiques socialistes soviétiques) nf*: **l'(ex-)~** the (former) USSR.

URSSAF, Urssaf [yrsaf] *(abr de Union pour le recouvrement des cotisations de la sécurité sociale et des allocations familiales) nf administrative body responsible for collecting social security funds.*

urticaire [yrtiker] *nf* urticaria, hives.

Uruguay [yrygwɛ] *nm*: **l'~** Uruguay.

uruguayen, -enne [yrygwejɛ̃, ɛn] *adj* Uruguayan.

◆ **Uruguayen, -enne** *nm, f* Uruguayan.

us [ys] *nmpl*: **les ~ et coutumes** the ways and customs.

USA (*abr de* **United States of America**) *nmpl* USA.

usage [yzaʒ] *nm* **-1.** [gén] use; **faire ~ de qqch** to use sthg; **en ~** in use; **à l'~** [à l'emploi] with use; [vêtement] with wear; **à l'~ de qqn** for (the use of) sb; **à ~ externe/interne** for external/internal use; **hors d'~** out of action. **-2.** [coutume] custom; **d'~** customary. **-3.** LING usage.

usagé, -e [yzaʒe] *adj* worn, old.

usager [yzaʒe] *nm* user; **les ~s de la route** road-users.

usé, -e [yze] *adj* **-1.** [détérioré] worn; **eaux ~es** waste water (*sg*). **-2.** [personne] worn-out. **-3.** [plaisanterie] hackneyed, well-worn.

user [yze] [3] ◇ *vt* **-1.** [consommer] to use. **-2.** [vêtement] to wear out. **-3.** [forces] to use up; [santé] to ruin; [personne] to wear out. ◇ *vi* **-1.** [se servir]: **~ de** [charme] to use; [droit, privilège] to exercise. **-2.** [traiter]: **en ~ bien avec qqn** *littéraire* to treat sb well.

◆ **s'user** *vp* **-1.** [chaussure] to wear out. **-2.** [personne] to wear o.s. out. **-3.** [amour] to burn itself out.

usinage [yzinaʒ] *nm* **-1.** [façonnage] machining. **-2.** [fabrication] manufacturing.

usine [yzin] *nf* factory.

usiner [yzine] [3] *vt* **-1.** [façonner] to machine. **-2.** [fabriquer] to manufacture.

usité, -e [yzite] *adj* in common use; **très/peu ~** commonly/rarely used.

ustensile [ystãsil] *nm* implement, tool; **~s de cuisine** kitchen utensils.

usuel, -elle [yzɥɛl] *adj* common, usual.

usuellement [yzɥɛlmã] *adv* usually, ordinarily.

usufruit [yzyfrɥi] *nm* usufruct.

usuraire [yzyrɛr] *adj* usurious.

usure [yzyr] *nf* **-1.** [de vêtement, meuble] wear; [de forces] wearing down; **avoir qqn à l'~** *fam* to wear sb down; **obtenir qqch à l'~** to get sthg through sheer persistence. **-2.** [intérêt] usury.

usurier, -ière [yzyrje, jɛr] *nm, f* usurer.

usurpateur, -trice [yzyrpatœr, tris] ◇ *adj* usurping (*avant n*). ◇ *nm, f* usurper.

usurpation [yzyrpasjɔ̃] [3] *nf* usurpation.

usurper [yzyrpe] [3] *vt* to usurp.

ut [yt] *nm inv* C.

UTA (*abr de* **Union des transporteurs aériens**) *nf* French airline company.

utérin, -ine [yterɛ̃, in] *adj* uterine.

utérus [yterys] *nm* uterus, womb.

utile [ytil] *adj* useful; **être ~ à qqn** to be useful OU of help to sb, to help sb.

utilement [ytilmã] *adv* usefully, profitably.

utilisable [ytilizabl] *adj* usable.

utilisateur, -trice [ytilizatœr, tris] *nm, f* user; **~ étranger** INFORM unauthorized user.

utilisation [ytilizasjɔ̃] *nf* use.

utiliser [ytilize] [3] *vt* to use.

utilitaire [ytilitɛr] ◇ *adj* **-1.** [pratique] utilitarian; [véhicule] commercial. **-2.** *péj* [préoccupations] material; [caractère] materialistic. ◇ *nm* INFORM utility (program).

utilité [ytilite] *nf* **-1.** [usage] usefulness. **-2.** JUR: **entreprise d'~ publique** public utility; **organisme d'~ publique** registered charity. **-3.** *loc*: **jouer les ~s** THÉÂTRE to play bit parts; *fig* to play second fiddle.

utopie [ytɔpi] *nf* **-1.** [idéal] utopia. **-2.** [projet irréalisable] unrealistic idea.

utopique [ytɔpik] *adj* utopian.

utopiste [ytɔpist] *nmf* utopian.

UV ◇ *nf* (*abr de* **unité de valeur**) *university course unit*, ≈ credit. ◇ (*abr de* **ultra-violet**) UV.

v, V [ve] *nm inv* v, V; **pull en v** V-neck sweater.

v.¹ -1. (*abr de* **vers**) LITTÉRATURE v. **-2.** (*abr de* **verset**) v. **-3.** (*abr de* **vers**) [environ] approx.

v.², V. *abr de* **voir**.

va [va] *interj*: **courage, ~!** come on, cheer up!; **~ donc!** come on!; **~ pour 50 francs/demain** OK, let's say 50 francs/tomorrow.

VA (*abr de* **voltampère**) VA.

vacance [vakãs] *nf* vacancy; **~ du pouvoir** power vacuum.

◆ **vacances** *nfpl* vacation *Am* (*sg*), holiday *Br* (*sg*); **bonnes ~s!** have a good holiday!; **les grandes ~s** the summer holidays.

vacancier, -ière [vakãsje, jɛr] *nm, f* vacationer *Am*, holiday-maker *Br*.

vacant, -e [vakɑ̃, ɑ̃t] *adj* [poste] vacant; [logement] vacant, unoccupied.

vacarme [vakarm] *nm* racket, din.

vacataire [vakatɛr] ◇ *adj* [employé] temporary. ◇ *nmf* temporary worker.

vacation [vakasjɔ̃] *nf* [d'expert] session.

vaccin [vaksɛ̃] *nm* vaccine; ~ **antirabique** rabies vaccine.

vaccination [vaksinasjɔ̃] *nf* vaccination.

vacciner [vaksine] [3] *vt*: ~ **qqn (contre)** MÉD to vaccinate sb (against); *fam fig* to make sb immune (to).

vache [vaʃ] ◇ *nf* **-1.** ZOOL cow. **-2.** [cuir] cowhide. **-3.** *fam péj* [femme] cow; [homme] pig. **-4.** *loc*: **la** ~! hell! ◇ *adj fam* rotten.

vachement [vaʃmɑ̃] *adv fam* real *Am*, bloody *Br*, dead *Br*.

vacherie [vaʃri] *nf fam* nastiness; **faire/dire une** ~ to do/say something nasty.

vacherin [vaʃrɛ̃] *nm* [dessert] *meringue filled with ice-cream and fruit.*

vachette [vaʃɛt] *nf* **-1.** [jeune vache] calf. **-2.** [cuir] calfskin.

vacillant, -e [vasijɑ̃, ɑ̃t] *adj* **-1.** [jambes, fondations] unsteady; [lumière] flickering. **-2.** [mémoire, santé] failing; [caractère] wavering, indecisive.

vaciller [vasije] [3] *vi* **-1.** [jambes, fondations] to shake; [lumière] to flicker; ~ **sur ses jambes** to be unsteady on one's legs. **-2.** [mémoire, santé] to fail.

vacuité [vakɥite] *nf sout* [de propos] emptiness, vacuousness.

vade-mecum [vademekɔm] *nm inv* vade mecum.

vadrouille [vadruj] *nf fam*: **être/partir en** ~ to be/to go off gallivanting.

va-et-vient [vaevjɛ̃] *nm inv* **-1.** [de personnes] comings and goings (*pl*), toing and froing. **-2.** [de balancier] to-and-fro movement. **-3.** (porte) ~ swing door. **-4.** ÉLECTR two way switch.

vagabond, -e [vagabɔ̃, ɔ̃d] ◇ *adj* **-1.** [chien] stray; [vie] vagabond (*avant n*). **-2.** [humeur] restless. ◇ *nm, f* [rôdeur] vagrant, tramp; *littéraire* [voyageur] wanderer.

vagabondage [vagabɔ̃daʒ] *nm* [délit] vagrancy; [errance] wandering, roaming.

vagabonder [vagabɔ̃de] [3] *vi* **-1.** [personne] to wander, to roam. **-2.** [esprit, imagination] to wander.

vagin [vaʒɛ̃] *nm* vagina.

vaginal, -e, -aux [vaʒinal, o] *adj* vaginal.

vaginite [vaʒinit] *nf* vaginitis.

vagir [vaʒir] [32] *vi* to cry, to wail.

vagissement [vaʒismɑ̃] *nm* cry, wail.

vague [vag] ◇ *adj* **-1.** [idée, promesse] vague. **-2.** [vêtement] loose-fitting. **-3.** (*avant n*) [quelconque]: **il a un** ~ **travail dans un bureau** he has some job or other in an office. ◇ *nf* wave; **une** ~ **de** [touristes, immigrants] a wave of; [d'enthousiasme] a surge of; **une** ~ **de froid** a cold spell; **la nouvelle** ~ the new wave; ~ **de chaleur** heatwave. ◇ *nm*: **rester dans le** ~ *fig* to remain vague; **avoir du** ~ **à l'âme** *fig* to be wistful.

vaguelette [vaglɛt] *nf* ripple, wave.

vaguement [vagmɑ̃] *adv* vaguely.

vahiné [vaine] *nf* Tahitian woman.

vaillamment [vajamɑ̃] *adv* bravely, valiantly.

vaillance [vajɑ̃s] *nf littéraire* bravery, courage; MIL valor *Am*, valour *Br*.

vaillant, -e [vajɑ̃, ɑ̃t] *adj* **-1.** [enfant, vieillard] hale and hearty. **-2.** *littéraire* [héros] valiant.

vain, -e [vɛ̃, vɛn] *adj* **-1.** [inutile] vain, useless; **en** ~ in vain, to no avail. **-2.** *littéraire* [vaniteux] vain.

vaincre [vɛ̃kr] [114] *vt* **-1.** [ennemi] to defeat. **-2.** [obstacle, peur] to overcome.

vaincu, -e [vɛ̃ky] ◇ *pp* → **vaincre**. ◇ *adj* defeated; **s'avouer** ~ to admit defeat. ◇ *nm, f* defeated person.

vainement [vɛnmɑ̃] *adv* vainly.

vainqueur [vɛ̃kœr] ◇ *nm* **-1.** [de combat] conqueror, victor. **-2.** SPORT winner. ◇ *adj m* victorious, conquering.

vairon [vɛrɔ̃] ◇ *adj m* **-1.** [yeux] of different colours. **-2.** [cheval] wall-eyed. ◇ *nm* minnow.

vais → **aller**.

vaisseau, -x [vɛso] *nm* **-1.** NAVIG vessel, ship; ~ **spatial** AÉRON spaceship. **-2.** ANAT vessel. **-3.** ARCHIT nave.

vaisselier [vɛsəlje] *nm* dresser.

vaisselle [vɛsɛl] *nf* crockery; **faire** OU **laver la** ~ to do the dishes, to wash up.

val [val] (*pl* **vals** OU **vaux** [vo]) *nm* valley.

valable [valabl] *adj* **-1.** [passeport] valid. **-2.** [raison, excuse] valid, legitimate. **-3.** [œuvre] good, worthwhile.

valériane [valerjan] *nf* valerian.

valet [valɛ] *nm* **-1.** [serviteur] servant; ~ **de chambre** manservant, valet; ~ **de pied** footman. **-2.** *fig* & *péj* [homme servile] lackey. **-3.** CARTES jack, knave.

valeur [valœr] *nf* **-1.** [gén & MUS] value; **avoir de la** ~ to be valuable; **prendre de la** ~ to increase in value; **perdre de sa** ~ to lose its value; **mettre en** ~ [talents] to bring out; [terre] to exploit; ~ **absolue** absolute value; ~ **ajoutée** ÉCON added value; **de (grande)** ~ [chose] **(very)** valuable; [personne] of (great) worth OU merit. **-2.** (*gén pl*) BOURSE stocks and shares (*pl*), securities (*pl*). **-3.** [mérite] worth, merit. **-4.** *fig* [importance] value, importance. **-5.** [équivalent]: **la** ~ **de** the equivalent of.

◆ **valeurs** *nfpl* [critères de référence] values.

valeureusement [valœrøzmɑ̃] *adv* valorously.

valeureux, -euse [valœrø, øz] *adj* valorous.

validation [validasjɔ̃] *nf* validation, authentication.

valide [valid] *adj* **-1.** [personne] spry. **-2.** [contrat] valid.

valider [valide] [3] *vt* to validate, to authenticate.

validité [validite] *nf* validity.

valise [valiz] *nf* case, suitcase; **faire sa** ~/**ses** ~**s** to pack one's case/cases; *fam fig* [partir] to pack one's bags; ~ **diplomatique** diplomatic bag.

vallée [vale] *nf* valley.

vallon [valɔ̃] *nm* small valley.

vallonné, -e [valɔne] *adj* undulating.

valoir [valwar] [60] ◇ *vi* **-1.** [gén] to be worth; **que vaut ce film?** is this film any good?; **ne rien** ~ not to be any good, to be worthless; **ça vaut mieux** *fam* that's best; **ça ne vaut pas la peine** it's not worth it; **faire** ~ [vues] to assert; [talent] to show. **-2.** [règle]: ~ **pour** to apply to, to hold good for.
◇ *vt* [médaille, gloire] to bring, to earn.
◇ *v impers*: **il vaudrait mieux que nous partions** it would be better if we left, we'd better leave.

◆ **se valoir** *vp* to be equally good/bad.

valorisant, -e [valɔrizɑ̃, ɑ̃t] *adj* good for one's image.

valorisation [valɔrizasjɔ̃] *nf* [d'immeuble, de région] development; ~ **de soi** good self-image.

valoriser [valɔrize] [3] *vt* [immeuble, région] to develop; [individu, société] to improve the image of.

valse [vals] *nf* waltz; *fam fig* [de personnel] reshuffle.

valser [valse] [3] *vi* to waltz; **envoyer** ~ **qqch** *fam fig* to send sthg flying; **envoyer** ~ **qqn** *fam fig* [employé] to give sb the elbow.

valseur, -euse [valsœr, øz] *nm, f* [danseur] waltzer.

valu [valy] *pp inv* → **valoir**.

valve [valv] *nf* valve.

vamp [vɑ̃p] *nf* vamp.

vamper [vɑ̃pe] [3] *vt fam* to vamp.

vampire [vɑ̃pir] *nm* **-1.** [fantôme] vampire. **-2.** *fig* [personne avide] vulture. **-3.** ZOOL vampire bat.

vampiriser [vɑ̃pirize] [3] *vt fig* to control.

van [vɑ̃] *nm* [fourgon] horsecar *Am*, horsebox *Br*.

vandale [vɑ̃dal] *nmf* vandal.

vandalisme [vɑ̃dalism] *nm* vandalism.

vanille [vanij] *nf* vanilla.

vanillé, -e [vanije] *adj* vanilla (*avant n*).

vanité [vanite] *nf* vanity.

vaniteux, -euse [vanitø, øz] ◇ *adj* vain, conceited. ◇ *nm, f* vain OU conceited person.

vanity-case [vanitikez] (*pl* **vanity-cases**) *nm* vanity case.

vanne [van] *nf* **-1.** [d'écluse] lockgate. **-2.** *fam* [remarque] gibe.

vanné, -e [vane] *adj fam* [personne] dead beat.

vanner [vane] [3] *vt* **-1.** [grain] to winnow. **-2.** *fam* [fatiguer] to wear out. **-3.** *fam* [se moquer de] to have a go at.

vannerie [vanri] *nf* basketwork, wickerwork.

vannier [vanje] *nm* basket maker.

vantail, -aux [vɑ̃taj, o] *nm* [de porte] leaf; [d'armoire] door.

vantard, -e [vɑ̃tar, ard] ◇ *adj* bragging, boastful. ◇ *nm, f* boaster.

vantardise [vɑ̃tardiz] *nf* boasting (*U*), bragging (*U*).

vanter [vɑ̃te] [3] *vt* to vaunt.

◆ **se vanter** *vp* to boast, to brag; **se** ~ **de qqch** to boast OU brag about sthg; **se** ~ **de faire qqch** to boast OU brag about doing sthg.

Vanuatu [vanwaty] *nm* Vanuatu.

va-nu-pieds [vanypje] *nmf inv fam* beggar.

vapes [vap] *nfpl fam*: **être dans les** ~ to have one's head in the clouds; **tomber dans les** ~ to pass out.

vapeur [vapœr] ◇ *nf* **-1.** [d'eau] steam; **à la** ~ steamed; **renverser la** ~ NAVIG to reverse engines; *fig* to backpedal. **-2.** [émanation] vapor *Am*, vapour *Br*. ◇ *nm* steamer.

◆ **vapeurs** *nfpl* **-1.** [malaise]: **avoir ses** ~**s** to have the vapors *Am* OU vapours *Br*. **-2.** [émanations] fumes.

vapocuiseur [vapokɥizœr] *nm* pressure cooker.

vaporeux, -euse [vapɔrø, øz] *adj* **-1.** *littéraire* [ciel, lumière] hazy. **-2.** [tissu] filmy.

vaporisateur [vapɔrizatœr] *nm* **-1.** [atomiseur] spray, atomizer. **-2.** IND vaporizer.

vaporisation [vapɔrizasjɔ̃] *nf* **-1.** [de parfum, déodorant] spraying. **-2.** PHYS vaporization.

vaporiser [vapɔrize] [3] *vt* **-1.** [parfum, déodorant] to spray. **-2.** PHYS to vaporize.
◆ **se vaporiser** *vp* to vaporize.

vaquer [vake] [3] *vi*: ~ à to see to, to attend to.

varappe [varap] *nf* rock climbing.

varappeur, -euse [varapœr, øz] *nm, f* (rock) climber.

varech [varɛk] *nm* kelp.

vareuse [varøz] *nf* **-1.** [veste] loose-fitting jacket. **-2.** [de marin] pea jacket. **-3.** [d'uniforme] tunic.

variable [varjabl] ◇ *adj* **-1.** [temps] changeable. **-2.** [distance, résultats] varied, varying. **-3.** [température] variable. ◇ *nf* variable.

variante [varjɑ̃t] *nf* variant.

variateur [varjatœr] *nm* ÉLECTR dimmer switch.

variation [varjasjɔ̃] *nf* variation.

varice [varis] *nf* varicose vein.

varicelle [varisɛl] *nf* chickenpox.

varié, -e [varje] *adj* **-1.** [divers] various. **-2.** [non monotone] varied, varying.

varier [varje] [9] *vt & vi* to vary.

variété [varjete] *nf* variety.
◆ **variétés** *nfpl* variety show (*sg*).

variole [varjɔl] *nf* smallpox.

variqueux, -euse [varikø, øz] *adj* varicose.

Varsovie [varsɔvi] *n* Warsaw; **le pacte de ~** the Warsaw Pact.

vasculaire [vaskylɛr] *adj* vascular.

vase [vaz] ◇ *nm* vase; **en ~ clos** *fig* in a vacuum. ◇ *nf* mud, silt.

vasectomie [vazɛktɔmi] *nf* vasectomy.

vaseline [vazlin] *nf* Vaseline®, petroleum jelly.

vaseux, -euse [vazø, øz] *adj* **-1.** [fond] muddy, silty. **-2.** *fam* [personne] under the weather. **-3.** *fam* [raisonnement, article] woolly.

vasistas [vazistas] *nm* fanlight.

vasque [vask] *nf* **-1.** [de fontaine] basin. **-2.** [coupe] bowl.

vassal, -e, -aux [vasal, o] *nm, f* vassal.

vaste [vast] *adj* vast, immense.

Vatican [vatikɑ̃] *nm*: **le ~** the Vatican; **l'État de la cité du ~** Vatican City; **au ~** in Vatican City.

va-tout [vatu] *nm inv*: **jouer son ~** *fig* to stake one's all.

vaudeville [vodvil] *nm* vaudeville.

vaudevillesque [vodvilɛsk] *adj* ludicrous.

vaudou [vodu] *nm* voodoo.

vaudrait → **valoir**.

vau-l'eau [volo]
◆ **à vau-l'eau** *loc adv littéraire* with the flow; **aller à** ~ *fig* to go down the drain.

vaurien, -ienne [vorjɛ̃, jɛn] *nm, f* good-for-nothing.

vaut → **valoir**.

vautour [votur] *nm* vulture.

vautrer [votre] [3]
◆ **se vautrer** *vp* [dans boue, dans débauche] to wallow; [sur l'herbe, dans fauteuil] to sprawl.

va-vite [vavit]
◆ **à la va-vite** *loc adv fam* in a rush.

vd *abr de* **vend**.

VDQS (*abr de* **vin délimité de qualité supérieure**) *nm label indicating quality of wine.*

vds *abr de* **vends**.

veau [vo] *nm* **-1.** [animal] calf; **le Veau d'or** the golden calf. **-2.** [viande] veal. **-3.** [peau] calfskin. **-4.** *péj* [personne] lump.

vecteur [vɛktœr] *nm* **-1.** GÉOM vector. **-2.** [intermédiaire] vehicle; MÉD carrier.

vécu, -e [veky] ◇ *pp* → **vivre**. ◇ *adj* real.

vedettariat [vədɛtarja] *nm* stardom.

vedette [vədɛt] *nf* **-1.** NAVIG patrol boat. **-2.** [star] star; **mettre en** ~ *fig* to turn the spotlight on.

végétal, -e, -aux [veʒetal, o] *adj* [huile] vegetable (*avant n*); [cellule, fibre] plant (*avant n*).

végétalien, -ienne [veʒetaljɛ̃, jɛn] *adj & nm, f* vegan.

végétarien, -ienne [veʒetarjɛ̃, jɛn] *adj & nm, f* vegetarian.

végétarisme [veʒetarism] *nm* vegetarianism.

végétatif, -tive [veʒetatif, iv] *adj* vegetative; *fig & péj* vegetable-like.

végétation [veʒetasjɔ̃] *nf* vegetation.
◆ **végétations** *nfpl* adenoids.

végéter [veʒete] [18] *vi* to vegetate.

véhémence [veemɑ̃s] *nf* vehemence.

véhément, -e [veemɑ̃, ɑ̃t] *adj* vehement.

véhicule [veikyl] *nm* vehicle; ~ **banalisé** unmarked vehicle.

véhiculer [veikyle] [3] *vt* to transport; *fig* to convey.

veille [vɛj] *nf* **-1.** [jour précédent] day before, eve; **la ~ au soir** the previous evening, the evening before; **la ~ de mon anniversaire** the day before my birthday; **à la ~ de** *fig* on the eve of. **-2.** [éveil] wakefulness; [privation de sommeil] **sleeplessness. -3.** [garde]: **être de** ~ to be on night duty.

veillée [veje] *nf* **-1.** [soirée] evening. **-2.** [de mort] watch.

veiller [veje] [4] ◇ *vi* **-1.** [rester éveillé] to stay up. **-2.** [rester vigilant]: ~ **à qqch** to look after sthg; ~ **à faire qqch** to see that sthg is done; ~ **sur** to watch over. ◇ *vt* to sit up with.

veilleur [vejœr] *nm*: ~ **de nuit** night watchman.

veilleuse [vejøz] *nf* **-1.** [lampe] nightlight. **-2.** AUTOM sidelight. **-3.** [de chauffe-eau] pilot light.

veinard, -e [vɛnar, ard] *fam* ◇ *adj* lucky. ◇ *nm, f* lucky devil.

veine [vɛn] *nf* **-1.** [gén] vein; **en** ~ **de** in the mood for; **s'ouvrir les** ~**s** to slash one's wrists; **se saigner aux quatre** ~**s** *fig* to bleed o.s. white. **-2.** [de marbre] vein; [de bois] grain. **-3.** [filon] seam, vein. **-4.** *fam* [chance] luck; **avoir de la** ~ to be lucky; **avoir une** ~ **de cocu** *fig* to have the luck of the devil.

veiné, -e [vene] *adj* [marbre] veined; [bois] grained.

veineux, -euse [venø, øz] *adj* **-1.** ANAT venous. **-2.** [marbre] veined; [bois] grainy.

veinule [venyl] *nf* venule.

Velcro® [vɛlkro] *nm* Velcro®.

vêler [vele] [4] *vi* to calve.

vélin [velɛ̃] *nm* vellum.

véliplanchiste [veliplɑ̃ʃist] *nmf* windsurfer.

velléitaire [veleitɛr] ◇ *nmf* indecisive person. ◇ *adj* indecisive.

velléité [veleite] *nf* whim.

vélo [velo] *nm fam* bike; **faire du** ~ to go cycling.

véloce [velɔs] *adj* swift.

vélocité [velɔsite] *nf* swiftness, speed.

vélodrome [velɔdrom] *nm* velodrome.

vélomoteur [velɔmɔtœr] *nm* light motorcycle.

velours [vəlur] *nm* velvet.

velouté, -e [vəlute] *adj* velvety.

◆ **velouté** *nm* **-1.** [de peau] velvetiness. **-2.** [potage] cream soup; ~ **d'asperges** cream of asparagus soup.

velu, -e [vəly] *adj* hairy.

venaison [vənɛzɔ̃] *nf* venison.

vénal, -e, -aux [venal, o] *adj* venal.

vénalité [venalite] *nf* venality.

venant [vənɑ̃]

◆ **à tout venant** *loc adv* to all comers.

vendange [vɑ̃dɑ̃ʒ] *nf* **-1.** [récolte] grape harvest, wine harvest. **-2.** [raisins] grape crop. **-3.** [période]: **les** ~**s** (grape) harvest time (*sg*).

vendanger [vɑ̃dɑ̃ʒe] [17] ◇ *vt* to harvest grapes from. ◇ *vi* to harvest the grapes.

vendangeur, -euse [vɑ̃dɑ̃ʒœr, øz] *nm, f* grape-picker.

vendetta [vɑ̃deta] *nf* vendetta.

vendeur, -euse [vɑ̃dœr, øz] *nm, f* salesman (*f* saleswoman).

vendre [vɑ̃dr] [73] *vt* to sell; «**à** ~» "for sale".

◆ **se vendre** *vp* **-1.** [maison, produit] to be sold. **-2.** *péj* [se laisser corrompre] to sell o.s. **-3.** [se trahir] to give o.s. away.

vendredi [vɑ̃drədi] *nm* Friday; **Vendredi Saint** Good Friday; *voir aussi* **samedi**.

vendu, -e [vɑ̃dy] ◇ *pp* → **vendre**. ◇ *adj* **-1.** [cédé] sold. **-2.** [corrompu] corrupt. ◇ *nm, f* traitor.

venelle [vənɛl] *nf* alley.

vénéneux, -euse [venenø, øz] *adj* poisonous.

vénérable [venerabl] *adj* venerable.

vénération [venerasjɔ̃] *nf* veneration, reverence.

vénérer [venere] [18] *vt* to venerate, to revere.

vénerie [vɛnri] *nf* hunting.

vénérien, -ienne [venerjɛ̃, jɛn] *adj* venereal.

Venezuela [venezɥela] *nm*: **le** ~ Venezuela; **au** ~ in Venezuela.

vénézuélien, -ienne [venezɥeljɛ̃, jɛn] *adj* Venezuelan.

◆ **Vénézuélien, -ienne** *nm, f* Venezuelan.

vengeance [vɑ̃ʒɑ̃s] *nf* vengeance.

venger [vɑ̃ʒe] [17] *vt* to avenge.

◆ **se venger** *vp* to get one's revenge; **se** ~ **de qqn** to take revenge on sb; **se** ~ **de qqch** to take revenge for sthg; **se** ~ **sur** to take it out on.

vengeur, vengeresse [vɑ̃ʒœr, vɑ̃ʒrɛs] ◇ *adj* vengeful. ◇ *nm, f* avenger.

véniel, -ielle [venjɛl] *adj* venial.

venimeux, -euse [vənimø, øz] *adj* venomous.

venin [vənɛ̃] *nm* venom.

venir [vənir] [40] *vi* to come; [plante, arbre] to come on; ~ **de** [personne, mot] to come from; [échec] to be due to; ~ **à** [maturité] to reach; [question, sujet] to come to; **il lui vient à l'épaule** he comes up to his/her shoulder; ~ **de faire qqch** to have just done sthg; **je viens de la voir** I've just seen her; **s'il venait à mourir ...** if he was to die

...; **où veux-tu en** ~? what are you getting at?.

◆ **s'en venir** *vp littéraire* to come (along).

Venise [vəniz] *n* Venice.

vénitien, -ienne [venisjɛ̃, jɛn] *adj* Venetian.

◆ **Vénitien, -ienne** *nm, f* Venetian.

vent [vɑ̃] *nm* wind; ~ **contraire** headwind; **dans le** ~ trendy; **avoir** ~ **de** *fig* to get wind of; **bon** ~! *fig* good riddance!; **contre** ~s **et marées** *fig* come hell or high water.

vente [vɑ̃t] *nf* -1. [cession, transaction] sale; **en** ~ on sale; **en** ~ **libre** available over the counter; ~ **de charité** (charity) bazaar; ~ **par correspondance** mail order; ~ **à la criée** sale by auction; ~ **en demi-gros** cash-and-carry; ~ **au détail** retail sales; ~ **directe** direct selling; ~ **aux enchères** auction; ~ **en gros** wholesale sales. -2. [service] sales (department). -3. [technique] selling.

venteux, -euse [vɑ̃tø, øz] *adj* windy.

ventilateur [vɑ̃tilatœr] *nm* fan.

ventilation [vɑ̃tilasjɔ̃] *nf* -1. [de pièce] ventilation. -2. FIN breakdown.

ventiler [vɑ̃tile] [3] *vt* -1. [pièce] to ventilate. -2. FIN to break down.

ventouse [vɑ̃tuz] *nf* -1. [de caoutchouc] suction pad; [d'animal] sucker. -2. MÉD cupping glass. -3. TECHNOL air vent.

ventral, -e, -aux [vɑ̃tral, o] *adj* ventral.

ventre [vɑ̃tr] *nm* [de personne] stomach; **avoir/prendre du** ~ to have/be getting a bit of) a paunch; **avoir mal au** ~ to have (a) stomach ache; **avoir le** ~ **ballonné** to have a bloated stomach; **à plat** ~ flat on one's stomach; ~ **à terre** *fig* flat out; **avoir quelque chose dans le** ~ *fig* to have guts.

ventricule [vɑ̃trikyl] *nm* ventricle.

ventriloque [vɑ̃trilɔk] *nmf* ventriloquist.

ventripotent, -e [vɑ̃tripɔtɑ̃, ɑ̃t] *adj fam* pot-bellied.

ventru, -e [vɑ̃try] *adj* -1. *fam* [personne] pot-bellied. -2. [cruche] round; [commode] bow-fronted.

venu, -e [vəny] ◇ *pp* → **venir**. ◇ *adj*: **bien** ~ welcome; **mal** ~ unwelcome; **il serait mal** ~ **de faire cela** it would be improper to do that. ◇ *nm, f*: **nouveau** ~ newcomer.

◆ **venue** *nf* coming, arrival.

vêpres [vɛpr] *nfpl* vespers.

ver [vɛr] *nm* worm; ~ **luisant** glow-worm; ~ **à soie** silkworm; ~ **solitaire** tapeworm; ~ **de terre** earthworm; **nu comme un** ~ *fig* stark naked; **tirer les** ~s **du nez à qqn** *fig* to worm information out of sb.

véracité [verasite] *nf* truthfulness.

véranda [verɑ̃da] *nf* veranda.

verbal, -e, -aux [vɛrbal, o] *adj* -1. [promesse, violence] verbal. -2. GRAM verb (*avant n*).

verbalement [vɛrbalmɑ̃] *adv* verbally.

verbaliser [vɛrbalize] [3] ◇ *vt* to verbalize. ◇ *vi* to make out a report.

verbe [vɛrb] *nm* -1. GRAM verb; ~ **impersonnel** impersonal verb. -2. *littéraire* [langage] words (*pl*), language.

verbeux, -euse [vɛrbø, øz] *adj* wordy, verbose.

verbiage [vɛrbjaʒ] *nm* verbiage.

verdâtre [vɛrdatr] *adj* greenish.

verdeur [vɛrdœr] *nf* -1. [de personne] vigor *Am*, vigour *Br*, vitality. -2. [de langage] crudeness. -3. [de fruit] tartness; [de vin] acidity. -4. [de bois] greenness.

verdict [vɛrdikt] *nm* verdict.

verdir [vɛrdir] [32] *vt & vi* to turn green.

verdoyant, -e [vɛrdwajɑ̃, ɑ̃t] *adj* green.

verdoyer [vɛrdwaje] [13] *vi* to turn green.

verdure [vɛrdyr] *nf* -1. [végétation] greenery. -2. [couleur] greenness. -3. [légumes verts] green vegetables (*pl*), greens (*pl*).

véreux, -euse [verø, øz] *adj* worm-eaten, maggoty; *fig* shady.

verge [vɛrʒ] *nf* -1. ANAT penis. -2. *littéraire* [baguette] rod, stick.

verger [vɛrʒe] *nm* orchard.

vergeture [vɛrʒətyr] *nf* stretchmark.

verglacé, -e [vɛrglase] *adj* icy.

verglas [vɛrgla] *nm* (black) ice.

vergogne [vɛrgɔɲ]

◆ **sans vergogne** *loc adv* shamelessly.

vergue [vɛrg] *nf* yard.

véridique [veridik] *adj* truthful.

vérifiable [verifjabl] *adj* verifiable.

vérificateur, -trice [verifikatœr, tris] ◇ *adj*: **comptable** ~ auditor. ◇ *nm, f* inspector.

vérification [verifikasjɔ̃] *nf* -1. [contrôle] check, checking. -2. [confirmation] proof, confirmation.

vérifier [verifje] [9] *vt* -1. [contrôler] to check. -2. [confirmer] to prove, to confirm.

◆ **se vérifier** *vp* to prove accurate.

vérin [verɛ̃] *nm* jack.

véritable [veritabl] *adj* real; [ami] true; **du cuir/de l'or** ~ real leather/gold.

véritablement [veritabləmɑ̃] *adv* really.

vérité [verite] *nf* -1. [chose vraie, réalité, principe] truth (*U*); **dire ses quatre** ~s **à qqn** *fam* to tell sb a few home truths. -2. [sincérité] sincerity. -3. [ressemblance - de reproduction] accuracy; [- de personnage, portrait] trueness to life.

◆ **en vérité** *loc adv* actually, really.

verlan [vɛrlɑ̃] *nm* back slang.

vermeil, -eille [vɛrmɛj] *adj* scarlet.

◆ **vermeil** *nm* silver-gilt.

vermicelle [vɛrmisɛl] *nm* vermicelli (U).

vermifuge [vɛrmifyʒ] *nm* [pour chat, chien] worm tablet.

vermillon [vɛrmijɔ̃] *nm & adj inv* vermilion.

vermine [vɛrmin] *nf* **-1.** [parasites] vermin. **-2.** *fig* [canaille] rat.

vermisseau, -x [vɛrmiso] *nm* **-1.** [ver] small worm. **-2.** *fig* [être chétif] runt.

vermoulu, -e [vɛrmuly] *adj* riddled with woodworm; *fig* moth-eaten.

vermouth [vɛrmut] *nm* vermouth.

vernaculaire [vɛrnakylɛr] *adj* vernacular.

verni, -e [vɛrni] *adj* **-1.** [souliers]: **chaussures ~es** patent-leather shoes. **-2.** [chanceux] *fam* lucky.

vernir [vɛrnir] [32] *vt* to varnish.

vernis [vɛrni] *nm* varnish; *fig* veneer; **~ à ongles** nail polish OU varnish.

vernissage [vɛrnisaʒ] *nm* **-1.** [de meuble] varnishing. **-2.** [d'exposition] private viewing.

vérole [vɛrɔl] *nf* MÉD: **petite ~** smallpox.

verrat [vera] *nm* boar.

verre [vɛr] *nm* **-1.** [matière, récipient] glass; [quantité] glassful, glass; **~ dépoli** frosted glass; **~ ballon** brandy glass; **~ à dents** tooth mug OU glass; **~ à moutarde** mustard jar; **~ à pied** long-stemmed glass; **~ à vin** wine glass. **-2.** [optique] lens; **porter des ~s** to wear glasses; **~s antireflet** anti-glare coated lenses; **~s de contact** contact lenses; **~ grossissant** magnifying glass. **-3.** [boisson] drink; **boire un ~** to have a drink.

verrerie [vɛrri] *nf* **-1.** [fabrication] glassmaking. **-2.** [usine] glassworks (sg). **-3.** [objets] glassware.

verrier [vɛrje] *nm* glass-maker.

verrière [vɛrjɛr] *nf* **-1.** [pièce] conservatory. **-2.** [toit] glass roof.

verroterie [vɛrɔtri] *nf* (colored Am OU coloured Br) glass beads (pl).

verrou [vɛru] *nm* bolt; **mettre qqn/être sous les ~s** to put sb/to be behind bars.

verrouillage [vɛrujaʒ] *nm* AUTOM: **~ central** central locking.

verrouiller [vɛruje] [3] *vt* **-1.** [porte] to bolt. **-2.** [personne] to lock up.

◆ **se verrouiller** *vp* to lock o.s. in.

verrue [vɛry] *nf* wart; **~ plantaire** verruca.

vers¹ [vɛr] ◇ *nm* line. ◇ *nmpl*: **en ~** in verse; **faire des ~** to write poetry.

vers² [vɛr] *prép* **-1.** [dans la direction de] toward Am, towards Br. **-2.** [aux environs de - temporel] around, about; [- spatial] near; **~ la fin du mois** toward Am OU towards Br the end of the month.

Versailles [vɛrsaj] *n* Versailles; **le château de ~** (the Palace of) Versailles.

versant [vɛrsɑ̃] *nm* side.

versatile [vɛrsatil] *adj* changeable, fickle.

verse [vɛrs]

◆ **à verse** *loc adv*: **pleuvoir à ~** to pour down.

versé, -e [vɛrse] *adj*: **être ~ dans** to be versed OU well-versed in.

Verseau [vɛrso] *nm* ASTROL Aquarius; **être ~** to be (an) Aquarius.

versement [vɛrsəmɑ̃] *nm* payment.

verser [vɛrse] [3] ◇ *vt* **-1.** [eau] to pour; [larmes, sang] to shed. **-2.** [argent] to pay. ◇ *vi* to overturn, to tip over; **~ dans** *fig* to lapse into.

verset [vɛrsɛ] *nm* verse.

verseur, -euse [vɛrsœr, øz] *adj* pouring (avant n).

◆ **verseur** *nm* pourer.

◆ **verseuse** *nf* pot, jug (for coffee maker).

versification [vɛrsifikasjɔ̃] *nf* versification.

version [vɛrsjɔ̃] *nf* **-1.** [gén] version; **~ française/originale** French/original version. **-2.** [traduction] translation (into mother tongue).

verso [vɛrso] *nm* back.

versus [vɛrsys] *prép* versus.

vert, -e [vɛr, vɛrt] *adj* **-1.** [couleur, fruit, bois] green. **-2.** *fig* [vieillard] spry, sprightly. **-3.** [réprimande] sharp. **-4.** *fam* [histoire] smutty; **(en entendre) des ~es et des pas mûres** (to hear) all sorts of awful things.

◆ **vert** *nm* **-1.** [couleur] green; **~ bouteille/d'eau/pomme/tendre** bottle/sea/apple/soft green. **-2.** [verdure]: **se mettre au ~** to take a break in the country.

◆ **Verts** *nmpl*: **les Verts** POLIT the Greens.

vert-de-gris [vɛrdəgri] ◇ *nm* verdigris. ◇ *adj* gray-green Am, grey-green Br.

vertébral, -e, -aux [vɛrtebral, o] *adj* vertebral.

vertèbre [vɛrtɛbr] *nf* vertebra.

vertébré, -e [vɛrtebre] *adj & nm* vertebrate.

vertement [vɛrtəmɑ̃] *adv* sharply.

vertical, -e, -aux [vɛrtikal, o] *adj* vertical.

◆ **verticale** *nf* vertical; **à la ~** [descente] vertical; [descendre] vertically.

verticalement [vɛrtikalmɑ̃] *adv* vertically.

vertige [vɛrtiʒ] *nm* **-1.** [peur du vide] vertigo; **donner le ~ à qqn** to make sb dizzy. **-2.** [étourdissement] dizziness; *fig* intoxication; **avoir des ~s** to suffer from OU have dizzy spells.

vertigineux, -euse [vɛrtiʒinø, øz] *adj* **-1.** *fig* [vue, vitesse] breathtaking. **-2.** [hauteur] dizzy.

vertu [vɛrty] *nf* **-1.** [morale, chasteté] virtue; **de petite ~** of easy virtue. **-2.** *littéraire* [pouvoir] properties (*pl*), power.
◆ **en vertu de** *loc prép* in accordance with.

vertueusement [vɛrtɥøzmɑ̃] *adv* virtuously.

vertueux, -euse [vɛrtɥø, øz] *adj* virtuous.

verve [vɛrv] *nf* eloquence; **être en ~** to be particularly eloquent.

verveine [vɛrvɛn] *nf* **-1.** [plante] verbena. **-2.** [infusion] verbena tea.

vésicule [vezikyl] *nf* vesicle; **~ biliaire** gall bladder.

Vespa® [vɛspa] *nf* scooter.

vespasienne [vɛspazjɛn] *nf* public urinal.

vespéral, -e, -aux [vɛsperal, o] *adj littéraire* evening (*avant n*).

vessie [vesi] *nf* bladder.

veste [vɛst] *nf* **-1.** [vêtement] jacket; **~ croisée/droite** double-/single-breasted jacket; **retourner sa ~** *fam fig* to change one's colours. **-2.** *fam* [échec]: **ramasser** OU **prendre une ~** to come a cropper.

vestiaire [vɛstjɛr] *nm* **-1.** [au théâtre] cloakroom. **-2.** (*gén pl*) SPORT changing-room, locker-room.

vestibule [vɛstibyl] *nm* [pièce] hall, vestibule.

vestige [vɛstiʒ] *nm* (*gén pl*) [de ville] remains (*pl*); *fig* [de civilisation, grandeur] vestiges, relic.

vestimentaire [vɛstimɑ̃tɛr] *adj* [industrie] clothing (*avant n*); [dépense] on clothes; **détail ~** accessory.

veston [vɛstɔ̃] *nm* jacket.

vêtement [vɛtmɑ̃] *nm* garment, article of clothing; **~s** clothing (*U*), clothes.

vétéran [veterɑ̃] *nm* veteran.

vétérinaire [veterinɛr] ◇ *adj* veterinary (*avant n*). ◇ *nmf* vet, veterinary surgeon.

vétille [vetij] *nf* triviality.

vêtir [vetir] (44) *vt* to dress.
◆ **se vêtir** *vp* to dress, to get dressed.

vétiver [vetivɛr] *nm* vetiver.

veto [veto] *nm inv* veto; **mettre son ~ à qqch** to veto sthg.

vêtu, -e [vɛty] ◇ *pp* → **vêtir**. ◇ *adj*: **~ (de)** dressed (in); **à demi-~** half-dressed.

vétuste [vetyst] *adj* dilapidated.

vétusté [vetyste] *nf* dilapidation.

veuf, veuve [vœf, vœv] ◇ *adj* widowed. ◇ *nm, f* widower (*f* widow).

veuille *etc* → **vouloir**.

veule [vøl] *adj* spineless.

veulerie [vølri] *nf* spinelessness.

veuvage [vœvaʒ] *nm* [de femme] widowhood; [d'homme] widowerhood.

veuve → **veuf**.

vexant, -e [vɛksɑ̃, ɑ̃t] *adj* **-1.** [contrariant] annoying, vexing. **-2.** [blessant] hurtful.

vexation [vɛksasjɔ̃] *nf* [humiliation] insult.

vexatoire [vɛksatwar] *adj* offensive.

vexer [vɛkse] (4) *vt* to offend.
◆ **se vexer** *vp* to take offense *Am* OU offence *Br*.

VF (*abr de* **version française**) *nf indicates that a film has been dubbed into French.*

VHF (*abr de* **very high frequency**) *nf* VHF.

via [vja] *prép* via.

viabiliser [vjabilize] (3) *vt* to service.

viabilité [vjabilite] *nf* **-1.** [de route] passable state. **-2.** [d'entreprise, organisme] viability.

viable [vjabl] *adj* viable.

viaduc [vjadyk] *nm* viaduct.

viager, -ère [vjaʒe, ɛr] *adj* life (*avant n*).
◆ **viager** *nm* life annuity; **mettre qqch en ~** to sell sthg in return for a life annuity.

viande [vjɑ̃d] *nf* meat; **~ blanche** white meat; **~ froide** cold meat; **~ rouge** red meat.

viatique [vjatik] *nm* **-1.** RELIG: **recevoir le ~** to receive the last rites (*pl*). **-2.** *littéraire* [soutien] lifeline.

vibrant, -e [vibrɑ̃, ɑ̃t] *adj* **-1.** [corde] vibrating. **-2.** *fig* [discours] stirring.

vibraphone [vibrafɔn] *nm* vibraphone.

vibration [vibrasjɔ̃] *nf* vibration.

vibratoire [vibratwar] *adj* vibratory.

vibrer [vibre] (3) *vi* **-1.** [trembler] to vibrate. **-2.** [être ému]: **~ (de)** to be stirred (with).

vibromasseur [vibromasœr] *nm* vibrator.

vicaire [vikɛr] *nm* curate.

vice [vis] *nm* **-1.** [de personne] vice. **-2.** [d'objet] fault, defect; **~ caché** hidden flaw; **~ de forme** JUR flaw.

vice-consul [viskɔ̃syl] (*pl* **vice-consuls**) *nm* vice-consul.

vice-présidence [visprezidɑ̃s] (*pl* **vice-présidences**) *nf* POLIT vice-presidency; [de société] vice-chairmanship.

vice-président, **-e** [visprezidɑ̃, ɑ̃t] (*mpl* **vice-présidents**, *fpl* **vice-présidentes**) *nm, f* POLIT vice-president; [de société] vice-chairman (*f* vice-chairwoman).

vice versa [visvɛrsa] *loc adv* vice versa.

vichy [viʃi] *nm* **-1.** [étoffe] gingham. **-2.** [eau] vichy (water).

vicié, **-e** [visje] *adj* [air] polluted, tainted.

vicier [visje] [9] *vt* **-1.** [air] to pollute, to taint. **-2.** JUR to invalidate.

vicieux, **-ieuse** [visjø, jøz] *adj* **-1.** [personne, conduite] perverted, depraved. **-2.** [animal] restive. **-3.** [attaque] underhand. **-4.** *sout* [prononciation, locution] incorrect.

vicinal, **-e**, **-aux** [visinal, o] → chemin.

vicissitudes [visisityd] *nfpl* vicissitudes.

vicomte, **vicomtesse** [vikɔ̃t, vikɔ̃tɛs] *nm, f* viscount (*f* viscountess).

victime [viktim] *nf* victim; [blessé] casualty.

victoire [viktwar] *nf* MIL victory; POLIT & SPORT win, victory; **chanter** OU **crier** ~ to boast of one's success.

victorieux, **-ieuse** [viktɔrjø, jøz] *adj* **-1.** MIL victorious; POLIT & SPORT winning (*avant n*), victorious. **-2.** [air] triumphant.

victuailles [viktɥaj] *nfpl* provisions.

vidange [vidɑ̃ʒ] *nf* **-1.** [action] emptying, draining. **-2.** AUTOM oil change. **-3.** [mécanisme] waste outlet.

◆ **vidanges** *nfpl* sewage (*U*).

vidanger [vidɑ̃ʒe] [17] *vt* to empty, to drain.

vide [vid] ◇ *nm* **-1.** [espace] void; *fig* [néant, manque] emptiness. **-2.** [absence d'air] vacuum; **conditionné sous** ~ vacuum-packed. **-3.** [ouverture] gap, space. **-4.** *loc*: **faire le** ~ [se détendre] to have some time on one's own; **parler dans le** ~ [sans objet] to talk aimlessly; [sans auditeur] to talk to a brick wall OU to o.s.; **regarder dans le** ~ to stare into space. ◇ *adj* empty; ~ **de** *fig* devoid of.

◆ **à vide** *loc adj & loc adv* empty.

vidéo [video] ◇ *nf* video. ◇ *adj inv* video (*avant n*).

vidéocassette [videokasɛt] *nf* video cassette.

vidéodisque [videodisk] *nm* videodisc.

vide-ordures [vidɔrdyr] *nm inv* rubbish chute.

vidéothèque [videotɛk] *nf* video library.

vidéotransmission [videotrɑ̃smisjɔ̃] *nf* video transmission.

vide-poches [vidpɔʃ] *nm inv* **-1.** [chez soi] tidy. **-2.** [de voiture] glove compartment.

vide-pomme [vidpɔm] (*pl inv* OU **vide-pommes**) *nm* apple corer.

vider [vide] [3] *vt* **-1.** [rendre vide] to empty. **-2.** [évacuer]: ~ **les lieux** to vacate the premises. **-3.** [poulet] to clean. **-4.** *fam* [personne - épuiser] to drain; [- expulser] to chuck out.

◆ **se vider** *vp* **-1.** [eaux]: **se** ~ **dans** to empty into, to drain into. **-2.** [baignoire, salle] to empty.

videur [vidœr] *nm* bouncer.

vie [vi] *nf* **-1.** [gén] life; **attenter à la** ~ **de qqn** to make an attempt on sb's life; **coûter la** ~ **à qqn** to cost sb his/her life; **sauver la** ~ **à qqn** to save sb's life; **être en** ~ to be alive; **être entre la** ~ **et la mort** to be at death's door; **sa** ~ **durant** for one's entire life; **à** ~ for life; **une** ~ **de chien** *fam* a dog's life; **mener la** ~ **dure à qqn** to make sb's life hell; **prendre la** ~ **du bon côté** to look on the bright side of life; **voir la** ~ **en rose** to see life through rose-colored *Am* OU rose-coloured *Br* spectacles; **enterrer sa** ~ **de garçon** to have a stag party OU night. **-2.** [subsistance] cost of living; **gagner sa** ~ to earn one's living.

vieil → vieux.

vieillard [vjɛjar] *nm* old man.

vieille → vieux.

vieillerie [vjɛjri] *nf* [objet] old thing.

vieillesse [vjɛjɛs] *nf* **-1.** [fin de la vie] old age. **-2.** [vieillards]: **la** ~ old people (*pl*).

vieilli, **-e** [vjeji] *adj* [mode, attitude] dated.

vieillir [vjejir] [32] ◇ *vi* **-1.** [personne] to grow old, to age; ~ **bien/mal** to age well/badly. **-2.** CULIN to mature, to age. **-3.** [tradition, idée] to become dated OU outdated. ◇ *vt* **-1.** [suj: coiffure, vêtement]: ~ **qqn** to make sb look older. **-2.** [suj: personne]: **ils m'ont vieilli de cinq ans** they said I was five years older than I actually am.

◆ **se vieillir** *vp* [d'apparence] to make o.s. look older; [dans les propos] to say one is older than one really is.

vieillissement [vjejismɑ̃] *nm* **-1.** [de personne] ageing. **-2.** [de mot, d'idée] obsolescence. **-3.** [de vin, fromage] maturing, ageing.

vieillot, **-otte** [vjejo, ɔt] *adj* old-fashioned.

vielle [vjɛl] *nf* hurdy-gurdy.

Vienne [vjɛn] *n* **-1.** [en France] Vienne. **-2.** [en Autriche] Vienna.

viennois, **-e** [vjɛnwa, az] *adj* Viennese; **pain** ~ Vienna loaf.

◆ **Viennois**, **-e** *nm, f* Viennese.

vierge [vjɛrʒ] ◇ *nf* virgin; **la (Sainte) Vierge** the Virgin (Mary). ◇ *adj* **-1.** [personne] virgin. **-2.** [terre] virgin; [page] blank; [casier judiciaire] clean; ~ **de** unsullied by.

◆ **Vierge** *nf* ASTROL Virgo; **être Vierge** to be (a) Virgo.

Viêt-Nam [vjɛtnam] *nm*: **le** ~ Vietnam; **au** ~ in Vietnam; **le Nord** ~ North Vietnam; **le Sud** ~ South Vietnam.

vietnamien, -ienne [vjɛtnamjɛ̃, jɛn] *adj* Vietnamese.

◆ **vietnamien** *nm* [langue] Vietnamese.

◆ **Vietnamien, -ienne** *nm, f* Vietnamese person.

vieux, vieille [vjø, vjɛj] ◇ *adj* (**vieil** *devant voyelle ou h muet*) old; **se faire** ~ to get old; ~ **jeu** old-fashioned. ◇ *nm, f* **-1.** [personne âgée] old man (*f* woman); **les** ~ the old; **un petit** ~ a little old man. **-2.** *fam* [ami]: **mon** ~ old buddy *Am*, old chap OU boy *Br*; **ma vieille** old girl. **-3.** *tfam* [parent] old man (*f* woman); **ses** ~ his folks. ◇ *nm* [meubles] antique furniture.

vif, vive [vif, viv] *adj* **-1.** [preste - enfant] lively; [- imagination] vivid. **-2.** [couleur, œil] bright; **rouge/jaune** ~ bright red/yellow. **-3.** [reproche] sharp; [discussion] bitter. **-4.** *sout* [vivant] alive. **-5.** [douleur, déception] acute; [intérêt] keen; [amour, haine] intense, deep.

◆ **vif** *nm* **-1.** JUR living person. **-2.** PÊCHE live bait. **-3.** *loc*: **entrer dans le** ~ **du sujet** to get to the heart of the matter; **piquer au** ~ to touch a raw nerve; **prendre qqn sur le** ~ to catch sb red-handed; **une photo prise sur le** ~ an action photograph.

◆ **à vif** *loc adj* [plaie] open; **j'ai les nerfs à** ~ *fig* my nerves are frayed.

vif-argent [vifarʒɑ̃] *nm inv* quicksilver; *fig* [personne] live wire.

vigie [viʒi] *nf* **-1.** [NAVIG - personne] lookout; [- poste] crow's nest. **-2.** RAIL observation box.

vigilance [viʒilɑ̃s] *nf* vigilance.

vigilant, -e [viʒilɑ̃, ɑ̃t] *adj* vigilant, watchful.

vigile [viʒil] *nm* watchman.

vigne [viɲ] *nf* **-1.** [plante] vine, grapevine. **-2.** [plantation] vineyard.

◆ **vigne vierge** *nf* Virginia creeper.

vigneron, -onne [viɲrɔ̃, ɔn] *nm, f* wine grower.

vignette [viɲɛt] *nf* **-1.** [timbre] label; [de médicament] price sticker (*for reimbursement by the social security services*); AUTOM license sticker *Am*, tax disc *Br*. **-2.** [motif] vignette.

vignoble [viɲɔbl] *nm* **-1.** [plantation] vineyard. **-2.** [vignes] vineyards (*pl*).

vigoureusement [vigurøzmɑ̃] *adv* vigorously.

vigoureux, -euse [vigurø, øz] *adj* [corps, personne] vigorous; [bras, sentiment] strong.

vigueur [vigœr] *nf* vigor *Am*, vigour *Br*.

◆ **en vigueur** *loc adj* in force.

vil, -e [vil] *adj* vile, base.

vilain, -e [vilɛ̃, ɛn] *adj* **-1.** [gén] nasty. **-2.** [laid] ugly.

◆ **vilain** *nm* **-1.** HIST villein. **-2.** *fam* [grabuge]: **il y aura du** ~ there's going to be trouble.

vilebrequin [vilbrəkɛ̃] *nm* **-1.** [outil] brace and bit. **-2.** AUTOM crankshaft.

vilenie [vileni] *nf* **-1.** [caractère] vileness, baseness. **-2.** [action] vile deed; [parole] vile comment.

vilipender [vilipɑ̃de] [3] *vt littéraire* to vilify.

villa [vila] *nf* villa.

village [vilaʒ] *nm* village; ~ **de vacances** vacation village *Am*, holiday village *Br*.

villageois, -e [vilaʒwa, az] ◇ *adj* rustic. ◇ *nm, f* villager.

ville [vil] *nf* [petite, moyenne] town; [importante] city; **aller en** ~ to go into town; **habiter en** ~ to live in town; ~ **champignon** town which has mushroomed; ~ **dortoir/nouvelle** dormitory/new town.

villégiature [vileʒjatyr] *nf* holiday.

Villette [vilɛt] *n*: **la** ~ *cultural complex in north Paris (science museum, theatre and park)*.

Vilnious [vilnjus] *n* Vilnius.

vin [vɛ̃] *nm* wine; ~ **blanc/rosé/rouge** white/rosé/red wine; ~ **champagnisé** champagne-style wine; ~ **résiné** retsina; ~ **de table** table wine.

◆ **vin d'honneur** *nm* reception.

vinaigre [vinɛgr] *nm* vinegar; ~ **de framboise/de vin** raspberry/wine vinegar; ~ **balsamique** balsamic vinegar; **tourner au** ~ *fig* to turn sour.

vinaigrer [vinegre] [4] *vt* to put vinegar on.

vinaigrette [vinɛgrɛt] *nf* oil and vinegar dressing.

vinasse [vinas] *nf péj* plonk.

vindicatif, -ive [vɛ̃dikatif, iv] *adj* vindictive.

vindicte [vɛ̃dikt] *nf*: ~ **publique** JUR justice.

vingt [vɛ̃] *adj num & nm* twenty; *voir aussi* **six**.

vingtaine [vɛ̃tɛn] *nf*: **une** ~ **de** about twenty.

vingtième [vɛ̃tjɛm] *adj num, nm & nmf* twentieth; *voir aussi* **sixième**.

vinicole [vinikɔl] *adj* wine-growing, wine-producing.

vinification [vinifikasjɔ̃] *nf* wine-making.

viol [vjɔl] *nm* **-1.** [de femme] rape; **au ~!** rape! **-2.** [de sépulture] desecration; [de sanctuaire] violation.

violacé, -e [vjɔlase] *adj* purplish.

violation [vjɔlasjɔ̃] *nf* violation, breach; **~ de domicile** unauthorized entry.

viole [vjɔl] *nf* viol.

violemment [vjɔlamɑ̃] *adv* **-1.** [frapper] violently. **-2.** [rétorquer] sharply.

violence [vjɔlɑ̃s] *nf* violence; **se faire ~** to force o.s.

violent, -e [vjɔlɑ̃, ɑ̃t] *adj* **-1.** [personne, tempête] violent. **-2.** *fig* [douleur, angoisse, chagrin] acute; [haine, passion] violent. **-3.** *fam* [excessif] annoying.

violenter [vjɔlɑ̃te] [3] *vt* to assault sexually.

violer [vjɔle] [3] *vt* **-1.** [femme] to rape. **-2.** [loi, traité] to break. **-3.** [sépulture] to desecrate; [sanctuaire] to violate.

violet, -ette [vjɔlɛ, ɛt] *adj* purple; [pâle] violet.
◆ **violet** *nm* purple; [pâle] violet.

violette [vjɔlɛt] *nf* violet.

violeur [vjɔlœr] *nm* rapist.

violon [vjɔlɔ̃] *nm* **-1.** [instrument] violin; **accorder ses ~s** *fig* to come to an agreement. **-2.** [musicien] violin (player). **-3.** *fam* [prison] clink, nick *Br*.
◆ **violon d'Ingres** *nm* hobby.

violoncelle [vjɔlɔ̃sɛl] *nm* **-1.** [instrument] cello. **-2.** [musicien] cello (player).

violoncelliste [vjɔlɔ̃selist] *nmf* cellist.

violoneux [vjɔlɔnø] *nm* fiddler.

violoniste [vjɔlɔnist] *nmf* violinist.

VIP (*abr de* **very important person**) *nm* VIP.

vipère [viper] *nf* viper.

virage [viraʒ] *nm* **-1.** [sur route] bend; **négocier un ~** to negotiate a bend; **prendre un ~** to take a bend; **~ sans visibilité** blind corner; **~ en épingle à cheveux** hairpin bend. **-2.** [changement] turn. **-3.** CHIM color *Am* OU colour *Br* change. **-4.** MÉD positive reaction.

viral, -e, -aux [viral, o] *adj* viral.

virée [vire] *nf fam*: **faire une ~** [en voiture] to go for a spin; [dans bars] ≃ to go on a pub crawl.

virement [virmɑ̃] *nm* **-1.** FIN transfer; **~ bancaire/postal** bank/giro transfer. **-2.** NAVIG: **~ (de bord)** tacking.

virer [vire] [3] ◇ *vi* **-1.** [tourner]: **~ à droite/à gauche** to turn right/left. **-2.** [étoffe] to change color *Am* OU colour *Br*; **~ au blanc/jaune** to go white/yellow. **-3.** PHOT to tone. **-4.** MÉD to react positively. ◇

vt **-1.** FIN to transfer. **-2.** *fam* [renvoyer] to kick out.

virevolte [virvɔlt] *nf* **-1.** [mouvement] twirl. **-2.** *fig* [volte-face] about-turn, U-turn.

virevolter [virvɔlte] [3] *vi* **-1.** [tourner] to twirl OU spin round. **-2.** *fig* [changer de sujet] to flit from one subject to another.

virginal, -e, -aux [virʒinal, o] *adj* virginal.

virginité [virʒinite] *nf* **-1.** [de personne] virginity. **-2.** [de sentiment] purity.

virgule [virgyl] *nf* [entre mots] comma; [entre chiffres] (decimal) point.

viril, -e [viril] *adj* virile.

virilité [virilite] *nf* virility.

virtuel, -elle [virtɥɛl] *adj* potential.

virtuellement [virtɥɛlmɑ̃] *adv* **-1.** [potentiellement] potentially. **-2.** [pratiquement] virtually.

virtuose [virtɥoz] *nmf* virtuoso.

virtuosité [virtɥozite] *nf* virtuosity.

virulence [virylɑ̃s] *nf* virulence.

virulent, -e [virylɑ̃, ɑ̃t] *adj* virulent.

virus [virys] *nm* INFORM & MÉD virus; *fig* bug.

vis [vis] *nf* screw; **serrer la ~ à qqn** *fig* to put the screws on sb.

visa [viza] *nm* visa; **~ de censure** censor's certificate.

visage [vizaʒ] *nm* face; **à ~ découvert** *fig* openly.

visagiste [vizaʒist] *nmf* beautician.

vis-à-vis [vizavi] *nm* **-1.** [personne] person sitting opposite. **-2.** [tête-à-tête] encounter. **-3.** [immeuble]: **avoir un ~** to have a building opposite.
◆ **vis-à-vis de** *loc prép* **-1.** [en face de] opposite. **-2.** [en comparaison de] beside, compared with. **-3.** [à l'égard de] toward *Am*, towards *Br*.

viscéral, -e, -aux [viseral, o] *adj* **-1.** ANAT visceral. **-2.** *fam* [réaction] gut (*avant n*); [haine, peur] deep-seated.

viscère [visɛr] *nm* (*gén pl*) innards (*pl*).

viscose [viskoz] *nf* viscose.

viscosité [viskozite] *nf* **-1.** [de liquide] viscosity. **-2.** [de surface] stickiness.

visé, -e [vize] *adj* **-1.** [concerné] concerned. **-2.** [vérifié] stamped.

visée [vize] *nf* **-1.** [avec arme] aiming. **-2.** (*gén pl*) *fig* [intention, dessein] aim.

viser [vize] [3] ◇ *vt* **-1.** [cible] to aim at. **-2.** *fig* [poste] to aspire to, to aim for; [personne] to be directed OU aimed at. **-3.** *fam* [fille, voiture] to get a load of. **-4.** [document] to check, to stamp. ◇ *vi* to aim, to take aim; **~ à** to aim at; **~ à faire qqch** to aim to do sthg, to be intended to do sthg; ~ **haut** *fig* to aim high; **ne pas** ~ **juste** not to aim accurately, to aim wide.

viseur [vizœr] *nm* **-1.** [d'arme] sights (*pl*). **-2.** PHOT viewfinder.

visibilité [vizibilite] *nf* visibility.

visible [vizibl] *adj* **-1.** [gén] visible. **-2.** [personne]: **il n'est pas** ~ he's not seeing visitors.

visiblement [vizibləmɑ̃] *adv* visibly.

visière [vizjɛr] *nf* **-1.** [de casque] visor. **-2.** [de casquette] peak. **-3.** [de protection] eyeshade.

vision [vizjɔ̃] *nf* **-1.** [faculté] eyesight, vision. **-2.** [représentation] view, vision. **-3.** [mirage] vision.

visionnaire [vizjɔnɛr] *nmf & adj* visionary.

visionner [vizjɔne] [3] *vt* to view.

visionneuse [vizjɔnøz] *nf* viewer.

visite [vizit] *nf* **-1.** [chez ami, officielle] visit; **avoir de la** ~ OU **une** ~ to have visitors; **rendre** ~ **à qqn** to pay sb a visit. **-2.** [MÉD - à l'extérieur] call, visit; [- dans hôpital] rounds (*pl*); **passer une** ~ **médicale** to have a medical. **-3.** [de monument] tour. **-4.** [d'expert] inspection.

visiter [vizite] [3] *vt* **-1.** [en touriste] to tour. **-2.** [malade, prisonnier] to visit.

visiteur, -euse [vizitœr, øz] *nm, f* visitor.

vison [vizɔ̃] *nm* mink.

visqueux, -euse [viskø, øz] *adj* **-1.** [liquide] viscous. **-2.** [surface] sticky. **-3.** *péj* [personne, manières] slimy, smarmy.

visser [vise] [3] *vt* **-1.** [planches] to screw together. **-2.** [couvercle] to screw down. **-3.** [bouchon] to screw in; [écrou] to screw on. **-4.** *fam fig* [enfant] to keep a tight rein on.

visualisation [vizɥalizasjɔ̃] *nf* INFORM display mode.

visualiser [vizɥalize] [3] *vt* **-1.** [gén] to visualize. **-2.** INFORM to display; TECHNOL to make visible.

visuel, -elle [vizɥɛl] *adj* visual.

visuellement [vizɥɛlmɑ̃] *adv* visually.

vital, -e, -aux [vital, o] *adj* vital.

vitalité [vitalite] *nf* vitality.

vitamine [vitamin] *nf* vitamin.

vitaminé, -e [vitamine] *adj* with added vitamins, vitamin-enriched.

vite [vit] *adv* **-1.** [rapidement] quickly, fast; **fais** ~! hurry up!; **avoir** ~ **fait de faire qqch** to have been quick to do sthg. **-2.** [tôt] soon.

vitesse [vitɛs] *nf* **-1.** [gén] speed; **prendre de la** ~ to pick up OU gather speed; **pren-**

dre qqn de ~ *fig* to outstrip sb; **à toute** ~ at top speed; ~ **de croisière** cruising speed. **-2.** AUTOM gear; **changer de** ~ to change gear; **en quatrième** ~ *fam fig* at the double.

viticole [vitikɔl] *adj* wine-growing.

viticulteur, -trice [vitikyltœr, tris] *nm, f* wine-grower.

viticulture [vitikyltyr] *nf* wine-growing.

vitrage [vitraʒ] *nm* **-1.** [vitres] windows (*pl*). **-2.** [toit] glass roof.

vitrail, -aux [vitraj, o] *nm* stained-glass window.

vitre [vitr] *nf* **-1.** [de fenêtre] pane of glass, window pane. **-2.** [de voiture, train] window.

vitré, -e [vitre] *adj* glass (*avant n*).

vitrer [vitre] [3] *vt* to glaze.

vitreux, -euse [vitrø, øz] *adj* **-1.** [roche] vitreous. **-2.** [œil, regard] glassy, glazed.

vitrier [vitrije] *nm* glazier.

vitrification [vitrifikasjɔ̃] *nf* **-1.** [de parquet] sealing and varnishing. **-2.** [d'émail] vitrification.

vitrifier [vitrifje] [9] *vt* **-1.** [parquet] to seal and varnish. **-2.** [émail] to vitrify.

vitrine [vitrin] *nf* **-1.** [de boutique] (shop) window; *fig* showcase; **lécher les** ~**s** to go window-shopping. **-2.** [meuble] display cabinet.

vitriol [vitrijɔl] *nm* vitriol.

vitupération [vityperasjɔ̃] *nf* vituperation.

vitupérer [vitypere] [18] *vt* to rail against.

vivable [vivabl] *adj* [appartement] livable-in; [situation] bearable, tolerable; [personne]: **il n'est pas** ~ he's impossible to live with.

vivace [vivas] *adj* **-1.** [plante] perennial; [arbre] hardy. **-2.** *fig* [haine, ressentiment] deep-rooted, entrenched; [souvenir] enduring.

vivacité [vivasite] *nf* **-1.** [promptitude - de personne] liveliness, vivacity; ~ **d'esprit** quick-wittedness. **-2.** [de coloris, teint] intensity, brightness. **-3.** [de propos] sharpness.

vivant, -e [vivɑ̃, ɑ̃t] *adj* **-1.** [en vie] alive, living. **-2.** [enfant, quartier] lively. **-3.** [souvenir] still fresh. **-4.** *fig* [preuve] living.
◆ **vivant** *nm* **-1.** [vie]: **du** ~ **de qqn** in sb's lifetime. **-2.** [personne]: **les** ~**s** the living; **un bon** ~ *fig* a person who enjoys (the good things in) life.

vivarium [vivarjɔm] *nm* vivarium.

vivats [viva] *nmpl* cheers, cheering (*sg*).

vive¹ [viv] *nf* [poisson] weever.

vive² [viv] *interj* three cheers for; ~ **le roi!** long live the King!

vivement [vivmɑ̃] ◇ *adv* **-1.** [agir] quickly. **-2.** [répondre] sharply. **-3.** [affecter] deeply. ◇ *interj*: ~ **les vacances!** roll on the holidays!; ~ **que l'été arrive** I'll be glad when summer comes, summer can't come quick enough.

vivier [vivje] *nm* **-1.** [de poissons] fish pond; [dans restaurant] fish tank. **-2.** *fig* [concentration] breeding-ground.

vivifiant, -e [vivifjɑ̃, ɑ̃t] *adj* invigorating, bracing.

vivifier [vivifje] [9] *vt* to invigorate.

vivipare [vivipar] *adj* viviparous.

vivisection [viviseksjɔ̃] *nf* vivisection.

vivoter [vivɔte] [3] *vi* **-1.** [personne] to live from hand to mouth. **-2.** [affaire, commerce] to struggle to survive.

vivre [vivr] [90] ◇ *vi* to live; [être en vie] to be alive; ~ **de** to live on; **faire** ~ **sa famille** to support one's family; **être difficile/facile à** ~ to be hard/easy to get on with; **avoir vécu** to have seen life. ◇ *vt* **-1.** [passer] to spend. **-2.** [éprouver] to experience. ◇ *nm*: **le** ~ **et le couvert** board and lodging.
◆ **vivres** *nmpl* provisions; **couper les** ~**s à qqn** *fig* to cut off sb's livelihood.

vivrier, -ière [vivrije, jɛr] *adj*: **culture vivrière food crops** (*pl*).

vizir [vizir] *nm* vizier.

VL (*abr de* **véhicule lourd**) *nm* HGV.

vlan [vlɑ̃] *interj* wham!, bang!

vo *abr de* **verso**.

VO (*abr de* **version originale**) *nf* indicates that a film has not been dubbed.

vocable [vɔkabl] *nm* term.

vocabulaire [vɔkabylɛr] *nm* **-1.** [gén] vocabulary. **-2.** [livre] lexicon, glossary.

vocal, -e, -aux [vɔkal, o] *adj*: **ensemble** ~ choir; → **corde**.

vocalise [vɔkaliz] *nf*: **faire des** ~**s** to do singing exercises.

vocaliser [vɔkalize] [3] *vi* to do singing exercises.

vocatif [vɔkatif] *nm* vocative (case).

vocation [vɔkasjɔ̃] *nf* **-1.** [gén] vocation. **-2.** [d'organisation] mission.

vocifération [vɔsiferasjɔ̃] *nf* shout, scream.

vociférer [vɔsifere] [18] *vt* to shout, to scream.

vodka [vɔdka] *nf* vodka.

vœu, -x [vø] *nm* **-1.** [RELIG & résolution] vow; **faire le** ~ **de faire qqch** to vow to do sthg; **faire** ~ **de silence** to take a vow of silence. **-2.** [souhait, requête] wish.
◆ **vœux** *nmpl* greetings; **meilleurs** ~**x** best

wishes; **tous nos** ~**x de bonheur** our best wishes for your future happiness.

vogue [vɔg] *nf* vogue, fashion; **en** ~ fashionable, in vogue.

voguer [vɔge] [3] *vi littéraire* to sail.

voici [vwasi] *prép* **-1.** [pour désigner, introduire] here is/are; **le** ~ here he/it is; **les** ~ here they are; **vous cherchiez des allumettes?** — **en** ~ were you looking for matches? — there are some here; **l'homme que** ~ this man (here); ~ **ce qui s'est passé** this is what happened. **-2.** [il y a]: ~ **trois mois** three months ago; ~ **quelques années que je ne l'ai pas vu** I haven't seen him for some years (now), it's been some years since I last saw him.

voie [vwa] *nf* **-1.** [route] road; **route à deux** ~**s** two-lane road; **la** ~ **publique** the public highway; ~ **navigable** waterway. **-2.** RAIL track, line; ~ **ferrée** railroad line *Am*, railway line *Br*; ~ **de garage** siding; *fig* dead-end job. **-3.** [mode de transport] route; **par la** ~ **maritime/aérienne** by sea/air. **-4.** ANAT passage, tract; **par** ~ **buccale** OU **orale** orally, by mouth; **par** ~ **rectale** by rectum; ~ **respiratoire** respiratory tract. **-5.** *fig* [chemin] way; **être en bonne** ~ to be going well; **être sur la bonne/mauvaise** ~ to be on the right/wrong track; **mettre qqn sur la** ~ to put sb on the right track; **ouvrir la** ~ to pave the way; **la** ~ **royale** *fig* the high road (to success); **trouver sa** ~ to find one's feet. **-6.** [filière, moyen] means (*pl*); **suivre la** ~ **hiérarchique** to go through the official channels (*pl*).
◆ **voie de fait** *nf* assault.
◆ **Voie lactée** *nf*: **la Voie lactée** the Milky Way.
◆ **en voie de** *loc prép* on the way OU road to; **en** ~ **de développement** developing.

voilà [vwala] *prép* **-1.** [pour désigner] there is/are; **le** ~ there he/it is; **les** ~ there they are; **me** ~ that's me, there I am; **le** ~ **qui arrive** (look) he's here; **vous cherchiez de l'encre** — **en** ~ you were looking for ink — there is some (over) there; **la maison que** ~ that house (there); **nous** ~ **arrivés** we've arrived. **-2.** [reprend ce dont on a parlé] that is; [introduit ce dont on va parler] this is; ~ **ce que j'en pense** this is/that is what I think; ~ **tout** that's all; **et** ~**!** there we are! **-3.** [il y a]: ~ **dix jours** ten days ago; ~ **dix ans que je le connais** I've known him for ten years (now).

voilage [vwalaʒ] *nm* **-1.** [rideau] net curtain. **-2.** [garniture] veil.

voile [vwal] ◇ *nf* **-1.** [de bateau] sail; **mettre les** ~**s** *fam fig* to do a bunk, to scarper. **-2.**

[activité] sailing. ◇ *nm* **-1.** [textile] voile. **-2.** [coiffure] veil; **lever le ~ sur** *fig* to lift the veil on. **-3.** [de brume] mist. **-4.** PHOT fogging (*U*). **-5.** MÉD shadow.

voilé, -e [vwale] *adj* **-1.** [visage, allusion] veiled. **-2.** [ciel, regard] dull. **-3.** [roue] buckled. **-4.** PHOT fogged. **-5.** [son, voix] muffled.

voiler [vwale] [3] *vt* **-1.** [visage] to veil. **-2.** [vérité, sentiment] to hide. **-3.** [suj: brouillard, nuages] to cover. **-4.** [roue] to buckle.

◆ **se voiler** *vp* **-1.** [femme] to wear a veil. **-2.** [ciel] to cloud over; [yeux] to mist over. **-3.** [roue] to buckle.

voilette [vwalɛt] *nf* veil.

voilier [vwalje] *nm* [bateau] sailing boat, sailboat *Am*.

voilure [vwalyr] *nf* **-1.** [de bateau] sails (*pl*). **-2.** [d'avion] wings (*pl*). **-3.** [de parachute] canopy.

voir [vwar] [62] ◇ *vt* **-1.** [gén] to see; **je l'ai vu tomber** I saw him fall; **faire ~ qqch à qqn** to show sb sthg; **avoir assez vu qqn** *fam* to be fed up with sb; **ne rien avoir à ~ avec** *fig* to have nothing to do with; **je te vois bien papa!** I can just see you as a father!; **essaie un peu, pour ~!** go on, just try it!; **voyons, ...** [en réfléchissant] let's see, ...; **ni vu ni connu** *fam* without anyone being any the wiser. **-2.** [dossier, affaire] to look at OU into, to go over.

◇ *vi* to see.

◆ **se voir** *vp* **-1.** [se regarder] to see o.s., to watch o.s. **-2.** [se rencontrer] to see one another OU each other. **-3.** [se remarquer] to be obvious, to show; **ça se voit!** you can tell!

voire [vwar] *adv* even.

voirie [vwari] *nf* **-1.** ADMIN ≃ Department of Transport. **-2.** [décharge] garbage dump *Am*, rubbish dump *Br*.

voisin, -e [vwazɛ̃, in] ◇ *adj* **-1.** [pays, ville] neighboring *Am*, neighbouring *Br*; [maison] next-door. **-2.** [idée] similar. ◇ *nm, f* neighbor *Am*, neighbour *Br*; **~ de palier** next-door neighbor *Am* OU neighbour *Br* (*in a flat*).

voisinage [vwazinaʒ] *nm* **-1.** [quartier] neighborhood *Am*, neighbourhood *Br*. **-2.** [relations] neighborliness *Am*, neighbourliness *Br*. **-3.** [environs] vicinity.

voisiner [vwazine] [3] *vi*: **~ avec** to be next to.

voiture [vwatyr] *nf* **-1.** [automobile] car; **~ de fonction** company car; **~ de location** hire car; **~ d'occasion/de sport** second-hand/sports car. **-2.** [de train] carriage.

◆ **voiture d'enfant** *nf* baby carriage *Am*, pram *Br*.

voix [vwa] *nf* **-1.** [gén] voice; **~ caverneuse** hollow voice; **~ de fausset** falsetto voice; **~ de stentor** stentorian voice; **~ de ténor** tenor voice; **~ off** voice-over; **à mi-~** in an undertone; **à ~ basse** in a low voice, quietly; **à ~ haute** [parler] in a loud voice; [lire] aloud; **de vive ~** in person; **avoir ~ au chapitre** to have a say in the matter. **-2.** [suffrage] vote; **recueillir des ~** to win votes.

Vojvodine [vojvodin] *nf*: **la ~** Vojvodina.

vol [vɔl] *nm* **-1.** [d'oiseau, avion] flight; **attraper qqch au ~** to catch sthg in mid-air; **~ à voile** gliding; **à ~ d'oiseau** as the crow flies; **en plein ~** in flight. **-2.** [groupe d'oiseaux] flight, flock. **-3.** [délit] theft; **~ avec effraction** breaking and entering; **~ à l'étalage** shoplifting.

vol. (*abr de* volume) vol.

volage [vɔlaʒ] *adj littéraire* fickle.

volaille [vɔlaj] *nf*: **la ~** poultry, (domestic) fowl.

volant, -e [vɔlɑ̃, ɑ̃t] *adj* **-1.** [qui vole] flying; **personnel ~** aircrew. **-2.** [mobile]: **feuille ~e** loose sheet.

◆ **volant** *nm* **-1.** [de voiture] steering wheel. **-2.** [de robe] flounce. **-3.** [de badminton] shuttlecock.

volatil, -e [vɔlatil] *adj* volatile.

◆ **volatile** *nm* (domestic) fowl.

volatiliser [vɔlatilize] [3]

◆ **se volatiliser** *vp* to volatilize; *fig* to vanish into thin air.

vol-au-vent [vɔlovɑ̃] *nm inv* vol-au-vent.

volcan [vɔlkɑ̃] *nm* volcano; *fig* spitfire; **être assis sur un ~** *fig* to be sitting on the edge of a volcano.

volcanique [vɔlkanik] *adj* volcanic; *fig* [tempérament] fiery.

volcanologue = vulcanologue.

volée [vɔle] *nf* **-1.** [d'oiseau] flight. **-2.** [de flèches] volley; **une ~ de coups** a hail of blows. **-3.** FOOTBALL & TENNIS volley. **-4.** *fam* [gifle] thrashing, hiding.

voler [vɔle] [3] ◇ *vi* to fly. ◇ *vt* [personne] to rob; [chose] to steal; **~ qqch à qqn** to steal sthg from sb.

volet [vɔlɛ] *nm* **-1.** [de maison] shutter. **-2.** [de dépliant] leaf; [d'émission] part. **-3.** INFORM drive door.

voleter [vɔlte] [27] *vi* **-1.** [papillon] to flit OU flutter about. **-2.** [robe] to flutter.

voleur, -euse [vɔlœr, øz] ◇ *adj* thieving. ◇ *nm, f* thief; **au ~!** stop thief!

volière [vɔljɛr] *nf* aviary.

volley-ball [vɔlɛbol] (*pl* **volley-balls**) *nm* volleyball.

volleyeur, -euse [vɔlɛjœr, øz] *nm, f* volley-ball player.

volontaire [vɔlɔ̃tɛr] ◇ *nmf* volunteer. ◇ *adj* **-1.** [omission] deliberate; [activité] voluntary. **-2.** [enfant] strong-willed.

volontairement [vɔlɔ̃tɛrmã] *adv* deliberately; [offrir] voluntarily.

volontariat [vɔlɔ̃tarja] *nm* voluntary service (*in armed forces*).

volontariste [vɔlɔ̃tarist] *nmf & adj* voluntarist.

volonté [vɔlɔ̃te] *nf* **-1.** [vouloir] will; **à ~** unlimited, as much as you like; **les dernières ~s** last wishes; **faire les quatre ~s de qqn** *fam fig* to obey sb's every whim. **-2.** [disposition]: **bonne ~** willingness, good will; **mauvaise ~** unwillingness. **-3.** [détermination] willpower.

volontiers [vɔlɔ̃tje] *adv* **-1.** [avec plaisir] with pleasure, gladly, willingly. **-2.** [affable, bavard] naturally.

volt [vɔlt] *nm* volt.

voltage [vɔltaʒ] *nm* voltage.

volte [vɔlt] *nf* **-1.** [de cheval] volt, volte. **-2.** *littéraire* [pirouette] pirouette.

volte-face [vɔltəfas] *nf inv* about-face *Am*, about-turn *Br*; *fig* U-turn, about-face *Am*, about-turn *Br*.

voltige [vɔltiʒ] *nf* **-1.** [au trapèze] trapeze work; **haute ~** flying trapeze act; *fam fig* mental gymnastics (*U*). **-2.** [à cheval] circus riding. **-3.** [en avion] aerobatics (*U*).

voltiger [vɔltiʒe] [17] *vi* **-1.** [acrobate] to perform on a flying trapeze. **-2.** [insecte, oiseau] to flit OU flutter about. **-3.** [feuilles] to flutter about.

voltigeur [vɔltiʒœr] *nm* **-1.** [acrobate] trapeze artist. **-2.** MIL light infantryman. **-3.** *Can* BASE-BALL: **~ gauche/droit** left/right fielder; **~ du centre** centre fielder.

volubile [vɔlybil] *adj* voluble.

volubilis [vɔlybilis] *nm* morning glory.

volubilité [vɔlybilite] *nf* volubility.

volume [vɔlym] *nm* volume.

volumineux, -euse [vɔlyminø, øz] *adj* voluminous, bulky.

volupté [vɔlypte] *nf* [sensuelle] sensual OU voluptuous pleasure; [morale, esthétique] delight.

voluptueusement [vɔlyptɥøzmã] *adv* voluptuously.

voluptueux, -euse [vɔlyptɥø, øz] *adj* voluptuous.

volute [vɔlyt] *nf* **-1.** [de fumée] wreath. **-2.** ARCHIT volute, helix.

vomi [vɔmi] *nm fam* vomit.

vomir [vɔmir] [32] *vt* **-1.** [aliments] to bring up. **-2.** [fumées] to belch, to spew (out); [injures] to spit out.

vomissement [vɔmismã] *nm* **-1.** [action] vomiting. **-2.** [vomissure] vomit.

vomitif, -ive [vɔmitif, iv] *adj* emetic; *fam fig* revolting, sickening.
◆ **vomitif** *nm* emetic.

vorace [vɔras] *adj* voracious.

voracement [vɔrasmã] *adv* voraciously.

voracité [vɔrasite] *nf* voracity.

vos → **votre**.

votant, -e [vɔtã, ãt] *nm, f* voter.

vote [vɔt] *nm* vote; **~ à main levée** (ballot by) show of hands; **~ secret, ~ à bulletins secrets** secret ballot.

voter [vɔte] [3] ◇ *vi* to vote. ◇ *vt* POLIT to vote for; [crédits] to vote; [loi] to pass.

votre [vɔtr] (*pl* **vos** [vo]) *adj poss* your.

vôtre [votr]
◆ **le vôtre** (*f* **la vôtre**, *pl* **les vôtres**) *pron poss* yours; **les ~s** your family; **vous et les ~s** people like you; **je suis des ~s** I'm on your side; **vous devriez y mettre du ~** you ought to pull your weight; **à la ~!** your good health!

vouer [vwe] [6] *vt* **-1.** [promettre, jurer]: **~ qqch à qqn** to swear OU vow sthg to sb. **-2.** [consacrer] to devote. **-3.** [condamner]: **être voué à** to be doomed to.
◆ **se vouer** *vp*: **se ~ à** to dedicate OU devote o.s. to.

vouloir [vulwar] [57] ◇ *vt* **-1.** [gén] to want; **voulez-vous boire quelque chose?** would you like something to drink?; **veux-tu te taire!** will you be quiet!; **je voudrais savoir** I would like to know; **~ que** (+ *subjonctif*): **je veux qu'il parte** I want him to leave; **~ qqch de qqn/qqch** to want sthg from sb/sthg; **combien en voulez-vous?** how much do you want for it?; **ne pas ~ de qqn/qqch** not to want sb/sthg; **je veux bien** I don't mind; **si tu veux** if you like, if you want; **comme tu veux!** as you like!; **veuillez vous asseoir** please take a seat; **sans le ~** without meaning OU wishing to, unintentionally. **-2.** [suj: coutume] to demand. **-3.** [s'attendre à] to expect; **que voulez-vous que j'y fasse?** what do you want me to do about it? **-4.** *loc*: **~ dire** to mean; **si on veut** more or less, if you like; **en ~ à** to be a real go-getter; **en ~ à qqn** to have a grudge against sb; **tu l'auras voulu!** on your own head (be it)!
◇ *nm*: **le bon ~ de qqn** sb's good will.

◆ **se vouloir** *vp*: **elle se veut différente** she thinks she's different; **s'en ~ de faire qqch** to be cross with o.s. for doing sthg.

voulu, -e [vuly] ◇ *pp* → **vouloir**. ◇ *adj* **-1.** [requis] requisite. **-2.** [délibéré] intentional.

vous [vu] *pron pers* **-1.** [sujet, objet direct] you; **dire ~ à qqn** to use the "vous" form to sb. **-2.** [objet indirect] (to) you. **-3.** [après préposition, comparatif] you. **-4.** [réfléchi] yourself, (*pl*) yourselves.
◆ **vous-même** *pron pers* yourself.
◆ **vous-mêmes** *pron pers* yourselves.

voûte [vut] *nf* **-1.** ARCHIT vault; *fig* arch; **la ~ céleste** the sky. **-2.** ANAT: **~ du palais** roof of the mouth; **~ plantaire** arch (of the foot).

voûter [vute] [3] *vt* to arch over, to vault.
◆ **se voûter** *vp* to be OU become stooped.

vouvoiement [vuvwamã] *nm* use of the "vous" form.

vouvoyer [vuvwaje] [13] *vt*: **~ qqn** to use the "vous" form to sb.

voyage [vwajaʒ] *nm* journey, trip; **les ~s** travel (*sg*), traveling (*U*) *Am*, travelling (*U*) *Br*; **bon ~!** have a good OU safe journey!; **partir en ~** to go away, to go on a trip; **~ d'affaires** business trip; **~ organisé** package tour; **~ de noces** honeymoon.

voyager [vwajaʒe] [17] *vi* to travel.

voyageur, -euse [vwajaʒœr, øz] *nm, f* traveler *Am* OU traveller *Br*; **~ de commerce** commercial traveler *Am* OU traveller *Br*.

voyagiste [vwajaʒist] *nm* tour operator.

voyance [vwajãs] *nf* clairvoyance.

voyant, -e [vwajã, ãt] ◇ *adj* loud, gaudy. ◇ *nm, f* [devin] seer; **~e extralucide** clairvoyant.
◆ **voyant** *nm* [lampe] light; AUTOM indicator (light); **~ d'essence/d'huile** petrol/oil warning light.

voyelle [vwajɛl] *nf* vowel.

voyeur, -euse [vwajœr, øz] *nm, f* voyeur, Peeping Tom.

voyeurisme [vwajœrism] *nm* voyeurism.

voyou [vwaju] *nm* **-1.** [garnement] urchin. **-2.** [loubard] lout.

VPC (*abr de* **vente par correspondance**) *nf* mail order sales.

vrac [vrak]
◆ **en vrac** *loc adv* **-1.** [sans emballage] loose. **-2.** [en désordre] higgledy-piggledy. **-3.** [au poids] in bulk.

vrai, -e [vrɛ] *adj* **-1.** [histoire] true; **c'est** OU **il est ~ que ...** it's true that ...; **c'est pas ~!** *fam* never!, I don't believe it! **-2.** [or, perle, nom] real. **-3.** [personne] natural. **-4.** [ami, raison] real, true.
◆ **vrai** *nm*: **le ~** truth; **être dans le ~** to be right; **à ~ dire, à dire ~** to tell the truth.

vraiment [vremã] *adv* really.

vraisemblable [vrɛsãblabl] *adj* likely, probable; [excuse] plausible.

vraisemblablement [vrɛsãblabləmã] *adv* probably, in all probability.

vraisemblance [vrɛsãblãs] *nf* likelihood, probability; [d'excuse] plausibility; **contre toute ~** implausibly; **selon toute ~** in all probability.

V/Réf (*abr de* **Votre référence**) your ref.

vrille [vrij] *nf* **-1.** BOT tendril. **-2.** [outil] gimlet. **-3.** [spirale] spiral.

vriller [vrije] [3] ◇ *vi* **-1.** [avion] to spin. **-2.** [parachute] to twist. ◇ *vt* to bore into.

vrombir [vrɔbir] [32] *vi* to hum.

vrombissement [vrɔbismã] *nm* humming (*U*).

VRP (*abr de* **voyageur, représentant, placier**) *nm* rep.

VTT (*abr de* **vélo tout terrain**) *nm* mountain bike.

vu, -e [vy] ◇ *pp* → **voir**. ◇ *adj* **-1.** [perçu]: **être bien/mal ~** to be acceptable/unacceptable. **-2.** [compris] clear.
◆ **vu** *prép* given, in view of.
◆ **vue** *nf* **-1.** [sens, vision] sight, eyesight. **-2.** [regard] gaze; **à première ~e** at first sight; **à ~e on** sight; **de ~e** by sight; **en ~e** [vedette] in the public eye; **à ~e de nez** at a rough guess; **à ~e d'œil** visibly; **en mettre plein la ~e à qqn** *fam fig* to dazzle sb; **perdre qqn de ~e** to lose touch with sb. **-3.** [panorama, idée] view; **~e d'ensemble** *fig* overview; **avoir qqn/qqch en ~e** to have sb/sthg in mind; **~e panoramique** panoramic view. **-4.** CIN → **prise**.
◆ **vues** *nfpl* plans; **avoir des ~es sur** to have designs on, to have one's eye on.
◆ **en vue de** *loc prép* with a view to.
◆ **vu que** *loc conj* given that, seeing that.

vulcaniser [vylkanize] [3] *vt* to vulcanize.

vulcanologue [vylkanɔlɔg], **volcanologue** [vɔlkanɔlɔg] *nmf* vulcanologist, volcanologist.

vulgaire [vylgɛr] *adj* **-1.** [grossier] vulgar, coarse. **-2.** (*avant n*) *péj* [quelconque] common. **-3.** [courant] common, popular.

vulgairement [vylgɛrmã] *adv* **-1.** [grossièrement] vulgarly, coarsely. **-2.** [couramment] commonly, popularly.

vulgarisation [vylgarizasjɔ̃] *nf* popularization.

vulgariser [vylgarize] [3] *vt* to popularize.

vulgarité [vylgarite] *nf* vulgarity, coarseness.

vulnérabilité [vylnerabilite] *nf* vulnerability.

vulnérable [vylnerabl] *adj* vulnerable.

vulve [vylv] *nf* vulva.

VVF (*abr de* **village vacances famille**) *nm* state-subsidized holiday village.

vx *abr de* **vieux**.

western [wɛstɛrn] *nm* western.

Wh (*abr de* **wattheure**) Wh.

whisky [wiski] (*pl* **whiskies**) *nm* whisky; ~ **sec** straight OU neat whisky.

whist [wist] *nm* whist.

white-spirit [wajtspirit] (*pl* **white-spirits**) *nm* white spirit.

WYSIWYG [wiziwig] (*abr de* **what you see is what you get**) WYSIWYG.

w, **W** [dubləve] *nm inv* w, W.

wagon [vagɔ̃] *nm* carriage; ~ **fumeurs** smoking carriage; ~ **de marchandises** goods wagon OU truck; ~ **non-fumeurs** non-smoking carriage; ~ **de première/ seconde classe** first-class/second-class carriage.

wagon-citerne [vagɔ̃sitɛrn] (*pl* **wagons-citernes**) *nm* tank wagon.

wagon-lit [vagɔ̃li] (*pl* **wagons-lits**) *nm* sleeping car, sleeper.

wagonnet [vagɔnɛ] *nm* small truck.

wagon-restaurant [vagɔ̃rɛstɔrɑ̃] (*pl* **wagons-restaurants**) *nm* restaurant OU dining car.

Walkman® [wɔkman] *nm* personal stereo, Walkman®.

wallon, -onne [walɔ̃, ɔn] *adj* Walloon.
◆ **wallon** *nm* [langue] Walloon.
◆ **Wallon, -onne** *nm, f* Walloon.

Wallonie [walɔni] *nf:* **la** ~ Southern Belgium (*where French and Walloon are spoken*).

wapiti [wapiti] *nm* wapiti.

Washington [waʃiŋtɔn] *n* **-1.** [ville] Washington D.C. **-2.** [État] Washington State.

water-polo [watɛrpɔlo] *nm* water polo.

watt [wat] *nm* watt.

Wb *abr de* **weber**.

W.-C. [vese] (*abr de* **water closet**) *nmpl* WC (*sg*), toilets.

week-end [wikɛnd] (*pl* **week-ends**) *nm* weekend; **bon** ~! have a good OU nice weekend!; **partir en** ~ to go away for the weekend.

Wellington [wɛliŋtɔn] *n* Wellington.

x, **X** [iks] *nm inv* x, X; **l'X** *prestigious engineering college in Paris*.

xénophobe [gzenɔfɔb] ◇ *nmf* xenophobe.
◇ *adj* xenophobic.

xénophobie [gzenɔfɔbi] *nf* xenophobia.

xérès [gzerɛs, kserɛs] *nm* sherry.

xylophone [ksilɔfɔn] *nm* xylophone.

y¹, **Y** [igrɛk] *nm inv* y, Y.

y² [i] ◇ *adv* [lieu] there; **j'y vais demain** I'm going there tomorrow; **mets-y du sel** put some salt in it; **va voir sur la table si les clefs y sont** go and see if the keys are on the table; **on ne peut pas couper cet arbre, des oiseaux y ont fait leur nid** you can't cut down that tree, some birds have built their nest there OU in it; **ils ont ramené des vases anciens et y ont fait pousser des fleurs exotiques** they brought back some antique vases and grew exotic flowers in them.
◇ *pron* (*la traduction varie selon la préposition utilisée avec le verbe en question*): **pensez-y** think about it; **n'y comptez pas** don't count on it; **j'y suis!** I've got it!; *voir aussi* **aller, avoir** *etc*.

yacht [jot] *nm* yacht.

yacht-club [jotklœb] (*pl* **yacht-clubs**) *nm* yacht club.

Yaoundé [jaunde] *n* Yaoundé.

yaourt [jaurt], **yogourt**, **yoghourt** [jɔgurt] *nm* yoghurt; ~ **aux fruits/nature** fruit/plain yoghurt.

yaourtière [jaurtjɛr] *nf* yoghurt maker.

Yémen [jemɛn] *nm*: **le** ~ Yemen; **au** ~ in Yemen; **le** ~ **du Nord** North Yemen; **le** ~ **du Sud** South Yemen.

yéménite [jemenit] *adj* Yemeni.
◆ **Yéménite** *nmf* Yemeni.

yen [jɛn] *nm* yen.

yeux → **œil.**

yé-yé [jeje] *vieilli* ◇ *nmf inv* pop fan. ◇ *adj inv* pop (*avant n*).

yiddish [jidiʃ] *nm inv & adj inv* Yiddish.

yoga [jɔga] *nm* yoga.

yoghourt = **yaourt.**

yogi [jɔgi] *nm* yogi.

yogourt = **yaourt.**

yougoslave [jugɔslav] *adj* Yugoslav, Yugoslavian.
◆ **Yougoslave** *nmf* Yugoslav, Yugoslavian.

Yougoslavie [jugɔslavi] *nf*: **la** ~ Yugoslavia.

youpi [jupi] *interj* yippee!

youyou [juju] *nm* dinghy.

Yo-yo® [jɔjɔ] *nm inv* yo-yo.

yucca [juka] *nm* yucca.

Z

z, **Z** [zɛd] *nm inv* z, Z.

ZAC, **Zac** [zak] (*abr de* **zone d'aménagement concerté**) *nf* area earmarked for local government planning project.

ZAD, **Zad** [zad] (*abr de* **zone d'aménagement différé**) *nf* area earmarked for future development.

Zagreb [zagrɛb] *n* Zagreb.

Zaïre [zair] *nm*: **le** ~ Zaïre; **au** ~ in Zaïre.

zaïrois, **-e** [zairwa, az] *adj* Zairian.
◆ **Zaïrois**, **-e** *nm, f* Zairian.

zakouski [zakuski] *nmpl* zakuski, zakouski.

Zambie [zãbi] *nf*: **la** ~ Zambia.

zambien, **-ienne** [zãbjɛ̃, jɛn] *adj* Zambian.
◆ **Zambien**, **-ienne** *nm, f* Zambian.

zapper [zape] [3] *vi* to zap, to channel-hop.

zappeur, **-euse** *nm, f* channel hopper, zapper.

zapping [zapiŋ] *nm* zapping, channel-hopping.

zèbre [zɛbr] *nm* zebra; **un drôle de** ~ *fam fig* an oddball.

zébrer [zebre] [18] *vt* to streak, to stripe.

zébrure [zebryr] *nf* **-1.** [de pelage] stripe. **-2.** [marque] weal.

zébu [zeby] *nm* zebu.

ZEC [zɛk] (*abr de* **zone d'exploitation contrôlée**) *nf Can* controlled harvesting zone.

zèle [zɛl] *nm* zeal; **faire du** ~ *péj* to be over-zealous.

zélé, **-e** [zele] *adj* zealous.

zen [zɛn] *adj inv & nm* Zen.

zénith [zenit] *nm* zenith; **être au** ~ **de** *fig* to be at the height OU peak of.

ZEP, **Zep** [zep] (*abr de* **zone d'éducation prioritaire**) *nf* designated area with special educational needs.

zéro [zero] ◇ *nm* **-1.** [chiffre] zero, nought; [dans numéro de téléphone] zero *Am*, O *Br*. **-2.** [nombre] nought, nothing; **deux buts à** ~ two goals to nil. **-3.** [de graduation] freezing point, zero; **au-dessus/au-dessous de** ~ above/below (zero); **avoir le moral à** ~ *fig* to be OU feel down; **repartir à** OU **de** ~ to start again from scratch. **-4.** *fam* [personne] dead loss. ◇ *adj*: ~ **faute** no mistakes.

zeste [zɛst] *nm* peel, zest; ~ **de citron** lemon peel OU zest.

zézaiement [zezɛmã] *nm* lisp.

zézayer [zezeje] [11] *vi* to lisp.

ZI *abr de* **zone industrielle.**

zibeline [ziblin] *nf* sable.

zieuter, **zyeuter** [zjøte] [3] *vt fam* to get an eyeful of.

ZIF, **Zif** [zif] (*abr de* **zone d'intervention foncière**) *nf* area earmarked for local government planning project.

zigoto [zigɔto] *nm fam*: **un drôle de** ~ an oddball.

zigouiller [ziguje] [3] *vt fam* to bump off.

zigzag [zigzag] *nm* zigzag; **en** ~ winding.

zigzaguer [zigzage] [3] *vi* to zigzag (along).

Zimbabwe [zimbabwe] *nm*: **le** ~ Zimbabwe; **au** ~ in Zimbabwe.

zimbabwéen, **-enne** [zimbabweɛ̃, ɛn] *adj* Zimbabwean.

◆ **Zimbabwéen**, **-enne** *nm, f* Zimbabwean.

zinc [zɛ̃g] *nm* **-1.** [matière] zinc. **-2.** *fam* [comptoir] bar. **-3.** *fam* [avion] crate.

zinzin [zɛ̃zɛ̃] *adj fam* cracked.

Zip® [zip] *nm* zipper *Am*, zip *Br*.

zipper [zipe] [3] *vt* to zip up.

zizanie [zizani] *nf*: **semer la ~** *fig* to sow discord.

zizi [zizi] *nm fam* peter *Am*, willy *Br*.

zodiacal, **-e**, **-aux** [zɔdjakal, o] *adj* [signe] of the zodiac; [position] in the zodiac.

zodiaque [zɔdjak] *nm* zodiac.

zombi [zɔ̃bi] *nm fam* zombie.

zona [zona] *nm* shingles (*U*).

zone [zon] *nf* **-1.** [région] zone, area; **~ d'action** area of operations; **~ bleue** restricted parking zone; **~ érogène** erogenous zone; **~ franche** free zone; **~ industrielle** industrial park *Am* OU estate *Br*. **-2.** *fam* [faubourg]: **la ~** the slum belt.

zoner [zone] [3] *vi* to hang about, to hang around.

zoo [zo(o)] *nm* zoo.

zoologie [zɔɔlɔʒi] *nf* zoology.

zoologiste [zɔɔlɔʒist] *nmf* zoologist.

zoom [zum] *nm* **-1.** [objectif] zoom (lens). **-2.** [gros plan] zoom.

zoophile [zɔɔfil] ◇ *nmf* person who practises bestiality. ◇ *adj* of OU relating to bestiality.

zoulou, **-e** [zulu] *adj* Zulu.

◆ **Zoulou**, **-e** *nm, f*: **les Zoulous** the Zulus.

zozo [zozo] *nm fam* mug.

zozoter [zɔzɔte] [3] *vi* to lisp.

ZUP, **Zup** [zyp] (*abr de* **zone à urbaniser en priorité**) *nf* area earmarked for urgent urban development.

Zurich [zyrik] *n* Zürich.

zut [zyt] *interj fam* damn!

zyeuter = **zieuter**.

zygomatique [zigɔmatik] *adj* zygomatic.

LIVING IN FRANCE, BELGIUM, SWITZERLAND AND QUEBEC

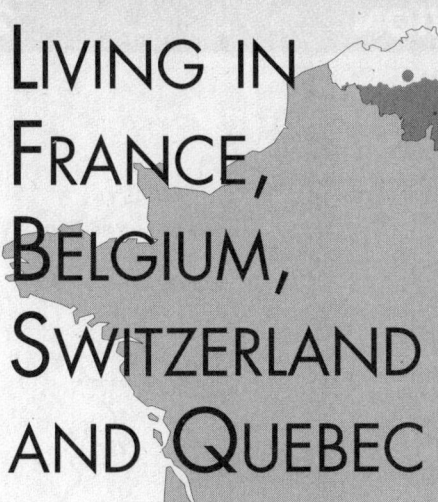

CONTENTS

FRANCE

Lille
NORD-PAS-
DE-CALAIS
HAUTE-
NORMANDIE
Amiens
PICARDIE
Caen
Rouen
Châlons-
sur-Marne
Metz
BASSE-
NORMANDIE
Paris
ÎLE-DE-
FRANCE
LORRAINE
Strasbourg
Rennes
CHAMPAGNE-
ARDENNE
ALSACE
BRETAGNE
Orléans
PAYS DE
LA LOIRE
FRANCHE-
COMTÉ
CENTRE
Dijon
Nantes
Besançon
BOURGOGNE
Poitiers
POITOU-
CHARENTES
Clermont-
Ferrand
Lyon
Limoges
LIMOUSIN
RHÔNE-ALPES
AUVERGNE
Bordeaux
AQUITAINE
MIDI-PYRÉNÉES
PROVENCE-
ALPES-
CÔTE D'AZUR
200 km
Toulouse
Montpellier
Marseille
LANGUEDOC-
ROUSSILLON
CORSE
Ajaccio

BELGIQUE

Bruges
FLANDRE-
ORIENTALE
Anvers
ANVERS
FLANDRE-
OCCIDENTALE
Gand
LIMBOURG
BRABANT-FLAMAND
Hasselt
Bruxelles
Louvain
Wavre
Liège
BRABANT-WALLON
HAINAUT
LIÈGE
Mons
Namur
NAMUR
50 km
LUXEMBOURG
Arlon

FRANCE France has a surface area of 549 000 square kilometres and a population of 59 million. This includes not only metropolitan France, i.e. the mainland plus Corsica, but also the overseas territories called the *départements et territoires d'outre-mer* (*DOM-TOM*). France shares borders with Belgium, Luxembourg, Germany, Switzerland, Italy and Spain and its coasts are washed by the English Channel, the Atlantic Ocean and the Mediterranean Sea. With the *DOM-TOM* it also has a presence in the Pacific and the Indian Oceans.

Administration is centralized in the capital, Paris. Although a law was passed in 1983 to increase power at local and regional level, there remains a clear divide between Paris and the rest of France. With 11 million people living in Paris and its suburbs, the capital dwarfs the next-largest cities, Marseilles (801 000) and Lyons (415 000).

In 1958 the current Constitution established the Fifth Republic, under which the independence of the executive, legislature and judiciary is guaranteed. France belongs to the United Nations, the Council of Europe and the European Union.

Division of Power French administrative structures form a hierarchy made up of (in descending order of size) *régions, départements, communes* and *arrondissements*.

▶ **Régions** are administered by a regional council (*conseil régional*), headed by a president (*président*). There are 22 regions in metropolitan France. They are responsible for the economic, social, health, cultural and scientific affairs of the region, and may also draw up development plans.

▶ **Départements** are assigned a number according to alphabetical order; this number is used in postcodes (*Am*: zip codes) and on vehicle numberplates (*Am*: license plates). There are 100 *départements* (96 in metropolitan France and 4 overseas). Responsibility for running the *département* is shared between the President of the General Council (*président du conseil général*), the body managing the *département*'s affairs, and the Prefect (*préfet*), who is appointed by the Cabinet to be the Government's representative within the *département*. The town where administrative power is centred is known as the *chef-lieu*. The mandate of the *conseil général* ranges from the upkeep of museums and monuments, managing schools, keeping up the artistic life of the *département* and providing social security, to maintaining the road network.

▶ **Communes** form the basic administrative unit. There are 36 000 in all, and they vary greatly in size. Each is administered by a mayor, his or her staff and town councillors elected by local residents for a period of six years. They are responsible for the upkeep of the museums and monuments of the *commune*, issue building permits and oversee nursery and primary schools. Paris, Lyons and Marseilles, which are *communes* in their own right, are subdivided into *arrondissements*.

The Executive

▶ **The President of the Republic (*président de la République*)** is the French head of state and is elected by the people for a period of seven years. He appoints the Prime Minister (*Premier ministre*) and chairs cabinet meetings every Wednesday in the Élysée Palace. He is head of the armed forces and has the power to call a referendum and dissolve the National Assembly (*see below*).

▶ **The French Government** (*Am*: Cabinet) is made up of the Prime Minister, with his or her ministers and Secretaries of State. The Prime Minister may give certain members of the Government the title of *ministre d'État,* which means that they take precedence over the other ministers, even though they are not in charge of any specific department.

▶ **The Prime Minister** is appointed by the President of the Republic and is always a member of the majority party in the National Assembly. As well as having overall responsibility for government affairs, he is in charge of defence and has the power to propose new laws.

The Legislature

The French Parliament is made up of a lower house, the National Assembly (*Assemblée nationale*), and an upper house, the Senate (*Sénat*).

French Institutions and their Locations	
residence of the President of the Republic	palais de l'Élysée
residence of the Prime Minister	hôtel Matignon
Ministry of the Interior	place Beauvau
Ministry of Foreign Affairs	quai d'Orsay
Justice Ministry	place Vendôme
National Assembly	palais Bourbon
Senate	palais du Luxembourg

▶ **The National Assembly** has 577 members, known as *députés*, who are elected by universal suffrage for a period of five years. They sit every Wednesday during the parliamentary session, which runs from October to June.

▶ **The Senate** has 319 members, known as *sénateurs*, who are elected by an electoral college of *députés* and members of the *conseil général* of each *département*. They are elected for a period of nine years; every three years, however, one-third of the *sénateurs* come up for re-election. The President of the Senate (*président du Sénat*) stands in for the President of the Republic if he is unable to fulfil his duties.

▶ **The role of Parliament** is to pass laws and vote on the national budget. Members debate the performance of the Government and, like the Prime Minister, may propose new laws.

▶ **The Constitutional Council (*Conseil constitutionnel*)** consists of nine members who serve for a period of nine years. It is responsible for ensuring that the Constitution is respected.

Elections

To be eligible to vote in France, and thus receive a voter's card (*carte d'électeur*), you must be a French national, be over 18 years of age, and not have a criminal record.

Main Political Parties	
Parti communiste (Communist party)	PC
Parti socialiste (left of centre)	PS
Génération écologie (green party)	
Les Verts (green party)	
Union pour la démocratie française (right of centre)	UDF
Rassemblement pour la République (right of centre)	RPR
Front national (far right)	FN

▶ **The first-past-the-post system** usually involves two rounds of voting. If a candidate does not achieve an absolute majority in the first round, i.e. more than 50% of the votes, then a second round is held. In this second round, the candidate who gains the most votes wins. This form of ballot is used in presidential and general elections.

▶ **Proportional representation** means that seats are allocated in proportion to the number of votes obtained. This form of ballot is used in particular in regional and European elections.

▶ **Local elections** use different systems depending on the size of the commune: first-past-the-post in small *communes*, and proportional representation in larger ones.

The Judiciary The Justice Minister (*ministre de la Justice*) also has the title Guardian of the Seals (*garde des Sceaux*). The French Constitution guarantees the independence of a public and free legal system in which every defendant has the right to a lawyer, irrespective of his or her means. Any case can go to appeal and be retried in the Appeal Court (*Cour d'appel*). If there is any legal irregularity, the case can go to the *Cour de cassation* (the highest court of appeal), which may order a retrial.

▶ **Civil courts** hear disputes between private individuals. Cases are dealt with by a *tribunal d'instance* or, if they are more complicated, by a *tribunal de grande instance*. There are also special courts such as the *tribunaux de commerce* which deal with industrial disputes, *tribunaux des baux ruraux* which rule on agricultural disputes, *tribunaux des affaires de la Sécurité sociale* for social security matters, and *conseils de prud'hommes*, which are local industrial tribunals.

▶ **Criminal courts** differ according to the offence being tried. The French legal system distinguishes between *crimes* (crimes such as treason, murder, manslaughter, sexual abuse and robbery with violence) and *délits* (offences such as fraud, resisting arrest, forgery and petty theft). *Délits* are ruled on by *tribunaux de police* or *tribunaux correctionnels*, which can impose fines and prison sentences. *Crimes* are dealt with by *Cours d'assises*, which sit in the main town of each *département*. They have the power to acquit defendants or to impose punishments ranging from fines to life imprisonment. (The death penalty was abolished in 1981.) There are special courts for defendants under the age of 18.

▶ **The High Court (*Haute cour de justice*)** sits in cases where the President of the Republic or members of the Government (*Am*: Cabinet) are impeached.

▶ **Tribunaux administratifs** are bodies to which individuals may appeal if they feel aggrieved by a decision of the French civil service, or if they believe the law has been violated. There are 30 of these courts. Appeals against rulings made here may be taken to the *Conseil d'État*.

▶ **A criminal record (*casier judiciaire*)** disqualifies you from working in the civil service, banking or insurance. To qualify to vote you must have no record.

BELGIUM Belgium has a surface area of 30 518 square kilometres and a population of approximately 10 million. Its capital, Brussels, houses the headquarters of the European Parliament. The Belgian Constitution states that the country is made up of three linguistic and cultural communities (French, Flemish and German) and three regions (Flanders in the north, Wallonia in the south, and the area around Brussels). Belgium has a complex institutional structure in which the Government devolves a lot of power to federal bodies. It is a constitutional and parliamentary monarchy.

The Executive The executive consists of the King and the Government (*Am*: Cabinet), headed by a Prime Minister appointed by the monarch. The Government must have majority support in both chambers of the Belgian Parliament. To ensure equality, there are equal numbers of French-speaking and Dutch-speaking ministers.

The Legislature The Belgian Parliament consists of an upper and a lower chamber, the Senate (*Sénat*) and the House of Representatives (*Chambre des représentants*), which together with the King have the power to pass laws.

The Judiciary The Belgian legal system is quite similar to that of France. Magistrates are appointed by the King.

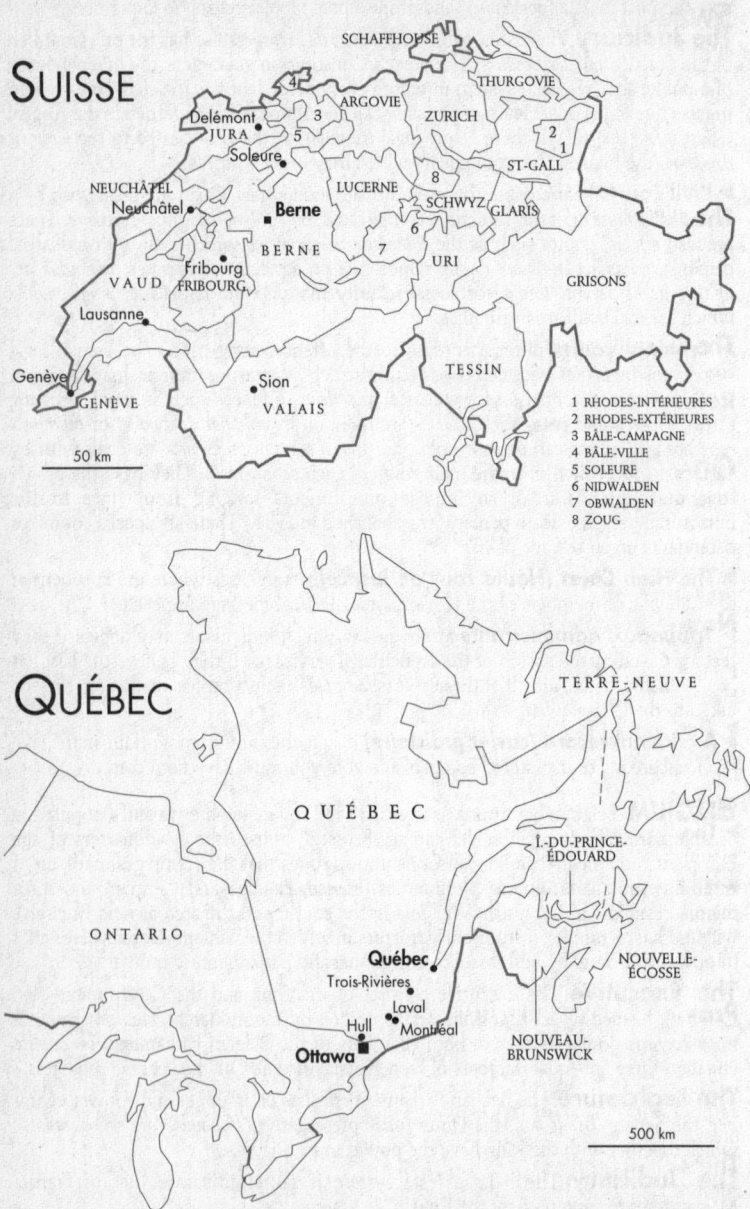

SUISSE

SCHAFFHOUSE

THURGOVIE

ARGOVIE

ZURICH

Delémont
JURA

Soleure

NEUCHÂTEL

Neuchâtel

Berne

LUCERNE

ST-GALL

SCHWYZ

GLARIS

BERNE

URI

Fribourg
FRIBOURG

VAUD

GRISONS

Lausanne

Genève

GENÈVE

Sion

VALAIS

TESSIN

50 km

1 RHODES-INTÉRIEURES
2 RHODES-EXTÉRIEURES
3 BÂLE-CAMPAGNE
4 BÂLE-VILLE
5 SOLEURE
6 NIDWALDEN
7 OBWALDEN
8 ZOUG

QUÉBEC

TERRE-NEUVE

QUÉBEC

Î.-DU-PRINCE-
ÉDOUARD

ONTARIO

Québec

Trois-Rivières

NOUVELLE-
ÉCOSSE

Laval

Hull

Montréal

Ottawa

NOUVEAU-
BRUNSWICK

500 km

SWITZERLAND The Swiss Confederation, as it is officially known, has a surface area of 41 293 square kilometres and a population of 7 million. It can be divided into a German-speaking part including the capital Bern; a French-speaking part; and the canton of Ticino, where Italian is spoken. Romansch is the official language in the canton of Graubünden (Grisons). Switzerland is a parliamentary republic divided into 23 self-governing districts known as *cantons*, three of which are themselves divided into *demi-cantons*. It is a neutral country, and some important international bodies are based in Geneva.

The Executive Executive power is exercised by the Federal Council (*Conseil fédéral*), made up of seven members elected by the representatives of the two chambers of the Swiss Parliament. From within its ranks a President is elected for a period of one year to represent Switzerland at home and abroad. He or she has no more power than any other member, however.

The Legislature The Swiss Parliament, the Federal Assembly (*Assemblée fédérale*), consists of two chambers: the *Conseil des États* and the *Conseil national*.

Referenda In Switzerland referenda are widely used to amend laws and even the Constitution itself.

QUEBEC Quebec is the largest of the ten Canadian provinces, occupying 1 540 680 square kilometres. The population is just under 7 million but only 2.5% of the land is inhabited. The official language is French. Although the capital, Quebec City, is the administrative centre, the business and cultural heart of the province beats in Montreal. In 1995 the pro-independence movement lost a referendum on independence from Canada by a tiny margin.

National Administration The head of state is the British Queen, represented by the Governor-General, a Canadian appointed by the monarch on the advice of the Canadian Prime Minister. Parliament consists of the Queen, the Senate (*Sénat*) and the House of Commons (*Chambre des communes*).

▶ **The Senate** has 104 members, 24 from Quebec. Senators are appointed by the Prime Minister and the Cabinet. The Senate can introduce, amend or reject a law as long as it does not relate to the budget. It also holds enquiries on questions of public interest.

▶ **The House of Commons** has 282 members, 75 from Quebec. They are elected by universal suffrage in a one-round first-past-the-post system (*see p4*).

▶ **The Prime Minister** chooses his or her ministers and has the power to dismiss them. Usually an MP, he is the leader of the party with the most seats and, together with his Cabinet, is responsible for drawing up laws. His Government (*Am*: administration) is responsible to the House of Commons and must resign if a vote of no confidence is passed or if his party loses its majority.

Provincial Administration Quebec is ruled by a Legislative Assembly which operates like the national House of Commons and has its own Constitution. All bills receive sanction by the Lieutenant Governor, who represents the Queen, before becoming law. The Assembly devolves power to city, town, village and district authorities. Executive power lies with the *Conseil exécutif*, or Council of Ministers, presided over by the Prime Minister of Quebec.

The Legal System The Canadian legal system is independent. Almost all the courts are administered by the individual provinces, but judges are appointed by the national Government.

FRANCE Since 1991 *France Télécom* and the French postal service (*La Poste*) have been private companies whose operations are monitored by the Ministry for Information Technology and the Postal Service (*ministère des Technologies de l'information et de la poste*) and by Parliament. Their employees are civil servants.

The Postal Service *La Poste* has a monopoly on the issuing of stamps and on the delivery of letters, but there is no monopoly on the delivery of parcels or the distribution of newspapers.

▶ **Stamps** are sold in post offices and newsagents' (*bureaux de tabac*). The basic postal rate is the same for all mail within the European Union but prices vary according to weight and whether you are sending a letter, postcard etc. If you want a guarantee of delivery or proof of posting, then you should send your letter or parcel by *recommandé* with or without *accusé de réception* (acknowledgment of receipt).

▶ **Post office branches**, mail vans and letterboxes (*Am*: mailboxes) are instantly recognizable by their distinctive yellow colour. There is an average of one post office for every 3300 people.

▶ **Other services** are offered by *La Poste*, as well as the day-to-day delivery of mail. For example, *Chronopost* guarantees delivery of letters and parcels under 25 kg within 24 hours inside France and within 72 hours otherwise. There is also a fax service called *Postéclair*. In addition, *La Poste* offers financial services similar to banks (savings accounts, chequebooks and a variety of investment opportunities).

▶ **Postcodes** (*Am*: zip codes) consist of five figures. The first two show the code of the *département* and the last three the sorting office code. Codes ending in 000 are reserved for *chefs-lieux*. The word *Cedex* may appear after the postcode and the name of the town in business addresses.

Telecommunications

▶ **Telephones** are usually rented from *France Télécom* but if they are bought they must be approved by a *France Télécom* engineer. About 90% of French households have a telephone, and charges vary depending on when calls are made: days and weeks are divided into red, white, blue and *bleu nuit* periods with different rates (*see right*).

Telephone Rates		
Period	**Length of unit**	**Time**
red	standard	office hours
white	40% longer than standard	lunchtime and evening
blue	100% longer than standard	weekends
bleu nuit	180% longer than standard	nighttime

Public telephones are common in towns and villages, but card-operated telephones are gradually replacing coin-operated ones. Vandalism is rife, with 35% of public phones in towns being vandalized every two months.

▶ **Telephone directories** for each *département* are updated annually. They consist of white pages for private individuals and yellow pages for companies and services. If you do not want your number to be listed you can pay a small charge and it will be added to the *liste rouge*. Customers can also make use of a directory enquiry service (*Am*: directory assistance) by dialling 12. The same service can be accessed via *Minitel (see below)* by dialling 11. The international dialling code for France is 33.

▶ **Numéros verts** are freefone (*Am*: 800) numbers, mostly used to advertise products and services but also to provide information, in particular on health matters.

▶ **New services** for mobile phones, attempting to keep France at the forefront of the telecommunications market, have been introduced by *France Télécom*: they are *Itineris*, which is a nationwide network; and *Be-Bop*, which serves the Paris region.

Emergency Numbers	
directory enquiries	12
line and equipment problems	13
police	17
fire brigade	18

Minitel is the name of a computer terminal which allows users to access an electronic telephone directory free of charge via the telephone lines and to send E-mail messages by using *Télétel*, the French Videotex network which also gives access to a wide range of other services. The E-mail service is not free. Other *Minitel* services include carrying out bank transactions, buying train or concert tickets (dial the code 3614), and consulting train timetables and doing mail order shopping (dial code 3615). This code also gives access to the *Minitel rose*, which carries erotic chat lines and soft porn advertising. Other frequently used codes include 3616 and 3617, used mostly by companies and professionals. *Minitel* has become extremely popular in recent years and there are currently about 6 million terminals in use.

BELGIUM The dialling code for Belgium is 32. Post offices are open from 9 a.m. to 5 p.m., Monday to Friday, and some branches are also open on Saturday mornings. They are run by the state-owned postal and telecommunications company *Belgacom*.

SWITZERLAND The dialling code for Switzerland is 41. As well as offering the usual postal services, the state-owned postal system deals with radio and television licences (a fee must be paid annually for the use of these).

QUEBEC

The Postal System In Canada the postal system is state-run, but 70% of services are contracted out to private companies. As well as delivering letters and parcels, the postal service distributes advertising, samples and catalogues. Other services, such as the fax service *Intelpost* and the goods shipping service *Telepost*, are also state-owned.

Telephones The number of households with a telephone in Quebec is lower than the national average. There are 16 regional telephone authorities in the province which own the lines and telephones, and are overseen by the *Régie des services publics du Québec* (the Quebec public utilities authority). *Québec Téléphone* and *Télébel Limitée* have large market shares, but the largest company remains the nationwide state-owned *Bell Canada*. Within larger districts rates are not calculated on the length of calls as elsewhere; instead subscribers pay a monthly sum which allows them to make an unlimited number of local calls.

FRANCE The French transport network spreads out like a spider's web centred on Paris. Travelling east–west or west–east in France is difficult, as there are few cross-country road, rail or air links.

Roads French roads are classified as *routes départementales* (minor roads marked in yellow on maps and mileposts), *routes nationales* (major roads marked in red) and *autoroutes* (motorways, *Am*: freeways). Tolls are charged for use of the motorway network but as the motorways are run by private companies, amounts differ. The amount to be paid always depends on distance travelled.

▶ **The périphérique** most commonly refers to the Paris ring road (*Am*: beltway), although the word can be used to refer to any major road bypassing a large town. Access from the ring road to the city centre is via points corresponding broadly to the gates *(portes)* in the city walls built in 1870, e.g. porte d'Italie, porte d'Orléans, porte de Vincennes.

▶ **Traffic management** is carefully worked out in an attempt to prevent traffic congestion during peak periods. For that reason school holidays

French Motorways		
Number	**Known as**	**Linking**
A1	Autoroute du Nord	Paris–Lille
A4	Autoroute de l'Est	Paris–Strasbourg
A6–A7	Autoroute du Sud	Paris–Marseilles
A8	la Provençale	Aix–Nice
A9	la Languedocienne	Orange–le Perthus
A10	l'Aquitaine	Paris–Bordeaux
A11	l'Océane	Paris–Nantes
A13	Autoroute de Normandie	Paris–Caen
A40	la Blanche	Switzerland–le Fayet
A62	Autoroute des Deux-Mers	Bordeaux–Narbonne

(*Am*: vacations) in France are taken at different times (*see* **EDUCATION**) depending on which of three areas you live in. An organization called *Bison futé* ('crafty bison'), set up by the Ministry of Transport and run in conjunction with the police and radio and television companies, also provides information on traffic conditions and suggests alternative routes (known as *itinéraires bis*) avoiding major roads.

▶ **Road safety** has been targeted by the French Government, which has implemented strict measures to reduce the number of road accidents caused by speeding and by drinking and driving. Breatha-

Speed Limits in France	
built-up areas	50 kilometres per hour (km/h)
open road	90 km/h
motorway	130 km/h

lyser tests (the maximum blood/alcohol level is 0.5 grams per litre) and speed cameras have been introduced, and if drivers fail the test or are caught speeding they are liable to a fine. They may also have points deducted from their licence, and for a serious offence the licence may be withdrawn altogether. Safety regulations state that seat belts must be worn by both drivers and passengers. Vehicles more than five years old have to undergo a check (the *contrôle technique*) every three years for roadworthiness. If they pass, a sticker is placed on the windscreen (*Am*: windshield).

▶ **Driving licences** can only be held by people aged 18 or over. The test is in two parts: candidates must pass the theoretical part, known as *le code*, before taking the practical part, *la conduite*. From the age of 16, people who are learning to drive may practise either with a driving school or with a relative or friend who has the appropriate qualifications. This is known as *conduite accompagnée*. Learners then take the driving test itself at 18.

▶ **Public transport in towns** is, as a rule, managed by the local authority. As well as buses, some towns, such as Strasbourg, also have trams (streetcars). In Paris the bus and metro networks are run by the *RATP* (*Régie autonome de transports parisiens*). Tickets are valid for both bus and metro, and books (*carnets*) of ten tickets are available at a reduced price. Further savings can be made by buying a weekly or monthly season ticket (*Am*: travel pass) known as a *carte orange*. Paris and its suburbs are divided into eight zones for travel purposes. The *carte orange* is valid for the number of zones you pay for and also allows the holder to use trains serving the suburbs (both the slow stopping services and the high-speed *RER* – *réseau express régional* – trains).

Main *SNCF* Discount Railcards	
carte jeune	for 12- to 26-year-olds
carte Kiwi	for those 16 and under, with up to three accompanying adults
Inter-Rail card	for those 26 and under (valid for France and certain foreign countries)
carte Vermeil	for those over 60

Rail

▶ **The SNCF** (*Société nationale des chemins de fer français*) is the state-owned company which owns and runs the entire French rail network and all rolling stock. It sets fares, and employs 200 000 people. Its current policy is to close down smaller branch lines gradually in favour of the more profitable main lines.

▶ **Tickets** are normally valid for two months and must be validated by inserting them in an automatic stamping machine before boarding the train. Various reduced-price tickets and railcards are available (*see above*). Prices vary according to when you travel: the *SNCF*'s blue periods are for off-peak travel, white are peak periods, and red a few high-peak periods when no concessions are allowed.

Main Paris Railway Stations and Regions Served by them	
gare du Nord	North
gare de l'Est	East
gare d'Austerlitz	Southwest
gare de Lyon	Southeast
gare Montparnasse	West
gare Saint-Lazare	western suburbs and Normandy

▶ **Trains** may be divided into: *trains de banlieue* (slow stopping trains serving the suburbs), those run by the *TER* or *transports express régionaux* (linking a city or town with smaller towns within a given region), main-line trains sometimes called *trains Corail*, and *TGV* or *trains à grande vitesse* (reaching speeds of 270 to 300 kilometres per hour, which run on main lines such as Paris–Lyons–Marseilles, Paris–Bordeaux, Paris–Nantes and Paris–Lille). Paris and London are now also linked by rail via the Channel Tunnel. The journey (*Am*: trip) takes just three hours on the Eurostar train.

Air The biggest airlines are Air France, which flies to all the large international airports, and Air Inter, which specializes in domestic flights. There are also several regional airlines operating mostly within France. The main airports are Orly and Roissy-Charles-de-Gaulle serving Paris. Several cities such as Lyons, Marseilles, Nice, Toulouse and Strasbourg also have international airports.

BELGIUM The Belgian motorway (*Am*: freeway) network is modern and expanding; it links up with other motorways serving Amsterdam, Cologne and Paris. Similarly, the Belgian rail network, run by the state-owned *SNCB* (*Société nationale des chemins de fer belges*), links Belgium with the rest of Europe. The main airline, *Sabena*, is state-owned. There are two airports in the French-speaking part of Belgium: Liège and Brussels South Charleroi, which relieve the congestion on Brussels National airport.

SWITZERLAND Switzerland has an extensive motorway (*Am*: freeway) network on which a toll system operates. Users pay an annual charge and display a sticker on their windscreen (*Am*: windshield). Foreigners who wish to use Swiss motorways must buy the sticker when they cross the border. As Switzerland is a mountainous country there are many tunnels, including the Saint-Gothard, at 17 kilometres the longest tunnel in the world. To reduce the volume of traffic on the roads and to prevent pollution, the Swiss authorities have endeavoured to ensure that goods are transported as often as possible by train rather than by road. There are three international airports in Switzerland: Zürich, Basel and Geneva. The national airline is *Swissair*.

Speed Limits in French-speaking Countries			
	Belgium	Switzerland	Quebec
built-up areas	60 km/h	50 km/h	50 km/h
open road	90 km/h	80 km/h	90 km/h
motorway	120 km/h	120 km/h	100 km/h

QUEBEC In Quebec road travel is by far the most common means of transport. While the national Government is responsible for international travel and travel between provinces, the Quebec Government builds and maintains the province's road system, finances public transport and supervises car insurance. Individual town councils are responsible for the road system within towns and cities.

Roads The road network in Quebec is 58 000 km long. The majority of goods transported by road are manufactured goods and timber.

Rail The Quebec rail network is 9000 km long and is operated almost exclusively by two companies, *Canadien National* (60%) and *Canadien Pacifique* (30%). There has been a marked decrease in the number of rail users and hundreds of kilometres of track have been closed down.

Air Air travel and air transport are becoming increasingly popular and now rival the train. The main airports are Dorval and Mirabel (which both serve Montreal and together account for 86% of all air traffic), and Quebec City airport. The most popular international destinations are the USA and Europe, 82% of all passengers to Europe flying from Montreal to Paris.

FRANCE France is the fourth largest economic power in the world and thus belongs to the G7 (the group of the seven most industrialized countries). It was one of the founders of the European Union. Its annual gross national product (GNP) is approximately $18 000 per person.

The Economic System Economic policy is decided by the Economy and Finance Ministry (*ministère de l'Économie et des Finances*) and the *Commissariat général au Plan* (the administrative organization which draws up and executes the five-year economic plan and reports to the Prime Minister).

French society is based on an open economy promoting competition and private enterprise. Private companies may be owned and managed by the same person (usually in the craft industry, the hotel trade and small businesses). They may also be formed into limited companies, and they then have the initials *SA* (*société anonyme*) or *SARL* (*société anonyme à responsabilité limitée*) placed after their

The Six Largest French Companies	
Renault	cars
Peugeot	cars
Elf Aquitaine	oil
EDF–GDF	electricity/gas
CGE (Alcatel Alsthom Compagnie Générale d'Électricité)	electrical supplies
Usinor–Sacilor	steel

name. The French economy is heavily dependent on small and medium-sized businesses which are the biggest exporters and employ the most people. Nevertheless, there are also many large French companies and multinationals established throughout the world.

▶ **State control** regulates this market economy. For example, the French Government fixes the prices of certain products (bread, petrol (*Am*: gas) etc.) and controls rent increases. It also owns companies, including some with monopolies like *SEITA* (tobacco), *RATP* (Paris transport network), and *EDF–GDF* (electricity and gas). It has a supervisory role in the case of the so-called *sociétés d'économie mixte* such as Air France, which are owned jointly by the State and private individuals. The Government has the power to appoint and dismiss managers in companies under their control, and audits their accounts. If necessary, the Government may intervene to make good a loss.

The System in Action The working population of France represents 43% of all inhabitants.

▶ **The primary sector** consists mostly of agriculture, and employs only 6% of the working population. The average farm covers 28 hectares; overall, though, the size and prosperity of French farms vary greatly. Cereals are grown mostly in the Paris Basin and Picardy, and the biggest wine-producing areas are the region around Bordeaux, the Rhône valley and Burgundy. There seems to be no end in sight to the continuing depopulation of the countryside, in spite of grants from the French Government and the European Union, such as the one given to farmers obliged to leave some of their land fallow (the so-called 'setaside' policy).

▶ **The secondary sector**, which includes industry and construction, and employs about 30% of the labour force, has been hit particularly hard by the current economic slump. It has been affected by technological developments and competition from developing countries. Parts of the energy industry are in decline, notably coalmining in the north and east. France imports oil, but has concentrated on developing nuclear power, which now accounts for 74% of electricity production. Most successful are the telecommunications, railway rolling stock and aerospace industries.

▶ **The tertiary sector** covers banks, commerce, transport, administration and service industries. Although it is continually expanding, the tertiary sector is still unable to absorb the job losses in the other two sectors.

▶ **International trade** is mainly with the European Union, Japan and the USA. France is the fourth largest exporter in the world; its main exports are machinery, cars, foodstuffs and, to a lesser degree, clothing and luxury goods. Its main imports are oil, gas, machinery, cars, motorcycles, hi-fi equipment and optical instruments.

The World of Work

Employment law in France is determined by the Constitution, the *code du travail* and international agreements and treaties.

▶ **Working hours** are fixed by law at 39 hours per week, with a daily maximum of 10 hours. Employees may work an extra 130 hours per year, paid at a higher rate. Part-time work is also possible, of course. Time off must by law total at least 24 hours per week (usually Sunday) but two days per week is the norm. Paid annual holiday is 30 working days. Additional days off are allowed for by law in some special cases, e.g. 16 weeks' maternity leave and 12 days per year for training.

Public Holidays	
1 January	
Easter Monday	
1 May	Labour Day
8 May	Armistice Day 1945
Ascension Day	
Whit Monday	
14 July	Bastille Day
15 August	the Assumption
1 November	All Saints' Day
11 November	Armistice Day 1918
25 December	Christmas

▶ **Salaries** are paid monthly. Many companies offer an annual bonus, known as the *treizième mois* as it is equal to an extra month's salary, and a holiday (*Am*: vacation) bonus. There is a minimum wage, the *SMIC* (*salaire minimum interprofessionnel de croissance*), which is adjusted annually on 1 July.

▶ **Workers who are made redundant** (*Am*: laid off) are entitled to claim benefit (*Am*: unemployment) for six months; this is provided jointly by the employer, the Government and the *ASSEDIC* (*Association pour l'emploi dans l'industrie et le commerce* – an association providing insurance against unemployment). Employees must be given prior notice of any decision to dismiss them. The *ANPE* (*Agence nationale pour l'emploi*) is the government agency charged with providing an information service for job seekers and trying to place them in work. The *ANPE* has offices in the regions and *départements* and many local branches. People no longer able to claim unemployment benefit from the *ASSEDIC* are entitled to the *RMI* (*revenu minimum d'insertion*), an allowance from the State providing claimants with a guaranteed minimum income.

▶ **Strikes** are legal in France for all employees, including civil servants.

However, 'lockouts' (temporary closure of a company by an employer to impose certain working conditions or salary levels) are illegal.

▶ **Unions** representing workers in allied sectors may be grouped into a federation. All employees, both French and foreign nationals, may belong to the union of their choice.

Taxes

▶ **Income tax** increases in proportion to taxable income. Everyone liable to pay tax must register with the *fisc* (the government department responsible for collecting taxes) and complete a tax return. Income tax is payable either monthly or in three instalments (in February, May and September).

▶ **VAT** (called *TVA – taxe à la valeur ajoutée*) is an indirect tax imposed on consumer products and services. The standard rate is 20.6% on manufactured products and services, but books and food are taxed at the lower rate of 5.5% and there is a special rate of 2.1% for drugs and the press.

Banking The French banking system and stock market are based in Paris, as is the *ministère de l'Économie et des Finances* which draws up and implements monetary policy.

▶ **The *Banque de France*** is nationalized. It has charge of the country's gold reserves, is the sole issuer of money, and monitors the performance of other banks, fixing the interest rates of loans granted to them. It is also banker to the Treasury, i.e. the Government.

▶ **Banks** in France are as a rule open from 9 a.m. to 5 p.m., with a break from noon to 2 p.m. They close during long weekends. A total of 98% of people over the age of 18 have a bank account, which allows salaries, pensions and social security benefits to be deposited directly.

Main French Banks
■ Crédit Agricole
■ BNP (Banque Nationale de Paris)
■ Crédit Lyonnais
■ Société Générale
■ Caisse d'Épargne Écureuil

▶ **Means of payment** are mainly cheques and credit cards. Even though shopkeepers may refuse it, a cheque drawn on a current (*Am*: checking) account is still the most common means of payment in France. In the last 20 years credit cards have become increasingly popular with the growth of the *Carte bleue* network, the French equivalent of Visa. It allows holders to pay immediately or to defer payment by having all purchases debited from their account at the end of the month. These cards can also be used to withdraw cash from a large number of cash dispensers. To prevent fraud, a growing number of banks distribute smart cards equipped with a microchip.

▶ **Savings** in France are high, people investing about 13% of their incomes. The best-known savings bank is the *Caisse d'Épargne Écureuil*.

The French Stock Market *La Bourse*, the French stock market, is based in Paris in the palais Brongniart and is open for trading between 10 a.m. and 4 or 5 p.m. Stockbrokers work on the trading floor, *la corbeille*. There are two markets, an official market of large French and foreign companies, and a second market of medium-sized companies, almost all French.

Currency The French unit of currency is the franc (F). One franc equals 100 centimes (c). There are coins to the value of 5c, 10c, 20c, 50c, 1F, 2F, 5F, 10F and 20F, and notes to the value of 20F, 50F, 100F, 200F and 500F.

BELGIUM Although a small country with a small population, Belgium is rich. Its annual GNP is $15 000 per person.

Agriculture In Belgium agriculture consists mainly of pig- and cattle-breeding. Belgian farmers are making a net loss.

Industry The coal industry in Belgium, previously the mainstay of the economy, is currently in decline. A total of 63% of the country's energy comes from nuclear power. One of the most buoyant sectors is the automobile industry, as many multinationals have set up in the country.

Banking Banks are as a rule open between 9 a.m. and 3 or 3.30 p.m., Monday to Friday, although some branches also open on Saturday mornings. Paying by cheque is still the most common means of payment.

Currency The unit of currency is the Belgian franc (FB). One Belgian franc equals 100 centimes (c).

SWITZERLAND With an annual GNP of $36 000 per person, this tiny country is one of the richest in the world. Its wealth comes from industry and, in particular, the many banks established there.

Agriculture Four times more land is used for cattle-breeding than for growing crops, with dairy farming predominating, but Swiss farmers still make a net loss.

Industry Industry in Switzerland is concentrated in the specialist fields of chemicals, precision instruments and watchmaking. Switzerland exports mostly to Germany, France and Italy.

Banking Zürich, in the German-speaking part of Switzerland, is considered one of the biggest financial centres in the world. Switzerland owes its wealth to its stable currency, its highly developed banking infrastructure and the discretion for which its banks are famous.

> **Main Swiss Banks**
>
> - Union des Banques suisses
> - Société de Banque suisse
> - Crédit suisse
> - Banque populaire suisse
> - Banque cantonale de Zürich

Currency The unit of currency is the Swiss franc (FS). One Swiss franc equals 100 centimes (c).

QUEBEC Quebec is twentieth in the list of world economies, and eleventh in terms of standard of living. Although it has 63.5% of its population in employment, this is still lower than the national average.

Agriculture Just 4% of the working population is employed in agriculture, but farming is very productive and technologically advanced. Quebec meets 65% of its food requirements and also exports a lot, in particular cereals.

Industry Industry accounts for 19.3% of the working population. The most dynamic sectors are electrical and electronic goods, timber, paper-making, metal processing and plastics.

Banking The province's financial centre and stock market are based in Montreal. Banks are open from 10 a.m. to 3 p.m., Monday to Wednesday; from 10 a.m. to 6 p.m., Thursdays and Fridays; and are closed at weekends.

Currency The unit of currency is the Canadian dollar ($). One Canadian dollar equals 100 cents (c).

FRANCE The French enjoy freedom of the press. However, this is balanced by the public's right to reply if they have been implicated by a news story and by certain restrictions on reporting aimed at protecting children and ethnic minorities. Most of the news which appears in the French media is gathered by the news agency *Agence France-Presse (AF-P)*.

The Press The average French household spends about 750 francs a year on newspapers. These are sold in kiosks, newsagents' (both *tabacs* and *maisons de la presse*) and some bookshops. It is also possible to subscribe. In Paris there are still a few street vendors left selling evening papers.

▶ **The national press** is distributed throughout the country but the majority of its readership is in Paris. The main daily papers contain both international and national news. Some newspapers like *Le Monde* appear in the evening, and others like *Le Figaro* or *Libération* (commonly referred to as *Libé*) in the morning. They each have their own political leanings. *Le Monde* also publishes monthly supplements on

Circulation of the Main Newspapers			
National		**Regional**	
Le Figaro	502 000	Ouest-France	875 000
Le Monde	485 000	Sud-Ouest	349 000
France-Soir	320 000	La Voix du Nord	400 000
Libération	250 000	Le Progrès (Lyons)	519 000

specific subject areas such as education, music and diplomacy. French newspapers carry classified advertisements and announcements (jobs, property, births and deaths) which partially finance them, the bulk of their income coming from advertising. Some papers devote pages to specific subjects (e.g. the arts, housing, economy, literature) on a given day of the week.

▶ **The regional press** devotes many of its pages to local news, as well as covering national and international events. They also contain classified advertisements and weekend supplements.

▶ **Magazines** covering current affairs, such as the weeklies *Le Point*, *L'Express* and *Le Nouvel Observateur*, are particularly favoured by the French. Other well-known magazines such as *Paris Match* specialize in stories about celebrities. On Saturdays *Le Figaro* publishes three colour supplements (a current affairs magazine, a women's magazine and a TV magazine). Women's magazines, both weekly like *Elle* and monthly like *Marie-Claire*, also have large circulations. There is a growing number of specialist magazines on a wide range of subjects such as cars (e.g. *L'Action automoto*), sport (e.g. *France-Football, Tennis Magazine*), food (e.g. *Gault-Millau Magazine*), interior decoration (e.g. *Art et Décoration, Maisons Côté Sud*), travel (e.g. *Géo, Grands Reportages*), animals (e.g. *30 Millions d'amis*), photography (e.g. *Photo Magazine*), cinema (e.g. *Première*) and science (e.g. *Science et Vie*).

▶ **Press consortiums** now own many French newspapers. Some of the biggest groups are *Hachette–Filipacchi, Hersant, Prisma Presse* and *Bayard Presse*. Many do not restrict themselves to newspapers but are also involved in distribution, publishing, radio and advertising.

Radio and Television French radio and television are financed by a licence fee (paid annually by all users to the State), advertising revenue and a sponsorship system. Although radio and TV are state monopolies, there are many independent channels existing alongside the publicly owned ones. Following recent reform of the broadcasting industry, involving privatization and the creation of independent radio stations, the term *paysage audiovisuel français (PAF)*, coined by the late President François Mitterrand, has come to be used to refer to all French radio and television.

▶ **State-owned radio stations** are part of *Radio France*. Although it has its headquarters in Paris at *la Maison de la Radio*, some of its stations broadcast from studios outside the capital. The national station with the most listeners is *France-Inter*, which broadcasts a mix of light entertainment and news. Other stations include *France Info*, a round-the-clock news station; *France-Musique*, which plays mostly classical music and jazz; *France-Culture*, which specializes in documentaries and arts programmes; *Radio Bleue*, which caters for older listeners and broadcasts French popular songs; and *FIP*, which broadcasts uninterrupted music and short news bulletins from its 47 regional studios. *Radio France Internationale (RFI)*, which broadcasts worldwide in French and foreign languages, and *RFO*, which serves the *DOM-TOM*, are both state-owned but independent from *Radio France*.

Frequencies (Long Wave) of Main Radio Stations	
France-Inter	162 kHz
Europe 1	183 kHz
RTL	216 kHz
RMC	234 kHz

▶ **Radios périphériques** are independent stations broadcasting programmes in French from outside the country, e.g. from Germany or Luxembourg. The most popular are *Europe 1*, *RTL* and *Radio Monte-Carlo (RMC)*. With a mixture of game shows, light entertainment and news, they have acquired a large share of the French audience.

▶ **Independent radio stations** have been increasing their share of the French market since 1981. They include music stations like *Europe 2*, *NRJ* and *Fun Radio* targeted at teenagers, and stations catering for specific communities such as *Radio Beur* (for North Africans living in France) and *Radio Shalom* (for the Jewish community).

▶ **Public television** is run by two channels in France: *France 2* and *France 3*. *France 2* broadcasts mostly news and drama, while *France 3* specializes in arts programmes relayed from regional studios. In addition to its normal programming, it also carries regional news and magazine programmes.

▶ **Arte and La Cinquième** share a television frequency. *Arte* is a Franco-German arts channel. Its programmes (mostly documentaries, discussion shows, theme evenings and art-house films) start at 7 p.m. When *Arte* is off the air, an educational channel called *La Cinquième* broadcasts instead.

French Television Channels
■ *TF1*
■ *France 2*
■ *France 3*
■ *M6*
■ *Canal +*
■ *La Cinquième/Arte*

▶ **Independent channels** are headed in popularity by *TF1*, formerly publicly owned but privatized in 1987, which broadcasts news, sport, films and light entertainment. Other channels include *M6*, which shows American series, soap operas and music videos, and *Canal +* (pronounced *Canal Plus*). *Canal +* is the only pay television channel in France. In order to receive it, viewers must pay a subscription, in return for which they are given a decoder which unscrambles the signal. Subscribers benefit from almost round-the-clock programming and a high number of recently released feature films (including some pornographic ones). Some programmes can be viewed without a decoder, notably the popular satirical show *Les Guignols de l'info*.

▶ **Cable television** is available in some regions of France and some large towns. The network allows viewers to watch a greater variety of channels, in particular foreign channels or ones specializing in music videos, documentaries or sport, etc.

▶ **The *Conseil supérieur de l'audiovisuel* (CSA)** is an independent body whose function is to guarantee the independence of the public sector, to encourage competition and to ensure programme quality. It has particular responsibility for ensuring that children are protected in broadcasting. The promotion of the French language and French culture is another of its duties.

BELGIUM

There are about 20 French-language daily newspapers in Belgium, including *Le Soir*, *La Lanterne* and *La Gazette de Liège*, plus a large number of weeklies and magazines.

The public French-language broadcasting body is *Radio Télévision belge de la Communauté française (RTBF)*, which gets 80% of its funding from the State but also receives advertising revenue. It has two channels. Belgians may subscribe to the Belgian version of *Canal +*, *Canal + Belgique*, and there are also cable television networks.

SWITZERLAND

The multilingual nature of Switzerland is reflected in its media. Of the 103 daily newspapers available in the country, 80 are in German, 18 in French and 5 in Italian. The most widely read papers in Geneva are *La Suisse*, *La Tribune de Genève* and *Le Journal de Genève*, while in Lausanne *Le Matin* is the most popular. Newspapers can be bought from coin-operated machines on the pavements, from kiosks and from newsagents'.

The Swiss national broadcasting company has three German channels, three French and one Italian.

QUEBEC

The Press Of the 559 magazines and newspapers available in Quebec, 72.6% are in French, 13.4% are in English and 10.3% are bilingual. The most popular French-language daily papers in Montreal are *La Presse*, *Le Devoir* and *Le Journal de Montréal*, and in Quebec City *Le Soleil* and *Le Journal de Québec*. Papers can be bought from kiosks, groceries and chemists' (*Am*: pharmacies).

Radio There are 116 radio stations in Quebec, 104 of which broadcast in French. Most of them are privately owned.

Television Of the 35 channels in Quebec, 17 are private companies and 18 are state-owned. *Radio Québec*, the main French-language network, has three channels, *les Téléviseurs Associés (TVA)* has ten, and Radio Canada nine. Montreal and much of Quebec City have a cable network, via which viewers have access to a number of foreign programmes, in particular from the United States, as well as round-the-clock information services (on, for example, traffic conditions and the weather).

FRANCE France has a centralized education system, controlled by the *ministère de l'Éducation nationale* (Ministry for National Education), which has the highest budget of all the ministries. A department of the Ministry called the *secrétariat d'État aux Universités* is responsible for higher education. Five different levels of education can be identified: *école maternelle* (nursery school), *école primaire* or *élémentaire* (primary school), *collège* (between the ages of 11 and 15), *lycée* (between 15 and 18), and *le supérieur* (higher education).

Centralization The curriculum is drawn up by the Government and is handed down to schools in an official publication called *le Bulletin officiel de l'Éducation nationale*. The country is divided into 28 educational areas known as *académies*, each presided over by a *recteur*. The dates of school terms are set by the Ministry. Christmas holidays (*Am*: vacations) and the two months of summer holidays are the same throughout the country. There are also breaks in February, in spring and around 1 November (*la Toussaint* or All Saints' Day). The exact dates of these holidays depend on which part of France you live in: for these purposes the country is split into three zones, and the order in which each zone takes its holidays changes every year.

School Year	
term one	September to December
term two	January to March
term three	April to June

Public and Private Education Education in France is public, non-denominational and free from *maternelle* to *lycée*. Attendance is obligatory between the ages of 6 and 16. Nursery and primary schools are run by a head teacher known as a *maître-directeur*, and are managed by the local town councils. The head teacher of a *collège* is known as a *principal* and his or her school is the responsibility of the *département*. In *lycées* the head teacher is called a *proviseur* and these schools receive their funding from the region. All teachers and administrative staff are civil servants paid by the State.

Running in parallel to the state system there are private schools, which are said to be *sous contrat* ('under contract'). This means that the teachers are paid by the State and teach the national curriculum. Some private schools are denominational and are owned by religious orders. A small number of private schools are *hors contrat*. These establishments own their premises, recruit and pay staff themselves and are not obliged to teach the national curriculum.

▶ **The *carte scolaire*** is a list of state schools divided by region. Students are assigned a school depending on where they live.

▶ **Grants** are awarded to students for all types of school if their parents have low incomes.

The Recruitment of Teachers Teachers are recruited after graduating from university (three years' study) and studying for two years at a teacher training college called an *IUFM* (*institut universitaire de formation des maîtres*). All prospective teachers follow a core curriculum and then sit an exam depending on their intended career. The different types of teacher are:

❏ *professeurs d'écoles* (at nursery and primary school level)

❏ *professeurs de collège* and *professeurs de lycée* (at secondary school level), who have to pass the *CAPES* teaching diploma or hold an *agrégation*, the highest qualification of all, and specialize in one subject

❏ *maîtres auxiliaires* (supply (*Am*: substitute) teachers), who are not government employees and have less strict training requirements.

From Nursery to *Lycée*

▶ **Nursery school (2–6)** is optional, but almost all children attend.

▶ **Primary school (6–11)** is structured in five levels: *le cours préparatoire* (*CP*), *cours élémentaires 1* and *2* (*CE1* and *CE2*), and *cours moyens 1* and *2* (*CM1* and *CM2*). Here pupils acquire reading, writing and arithmetic skills.

▶ **Collège (11–15)** involves four years' study culminating in the first national exam taken by students, the *brevet national des collèges*. After the exam, students choose which subject area they want to specialize in and hence which type of *lycée* they attend.

▶ **Lycée (15–18)** leads after three years' study to the school-leaving certificate (*Am*: high-school diploma), the *baccalauréat* (or *bac*, as it is commonly known), whatever type of *lycée* students opt for. A *lycée professionnel* prepares students for specific vocational

Grades at *Baccalauréat*	
mention passable	10–12 out of 20
mention assez bien	12–14 out of 20
mention bien	14–16 out of 20
mention très bien	more than 16 out of 20

bac courses, a *lycée général* offers general and vocational courses, and a *lycée technologique* specializes in technical subjects. There are two parts to the exam: the first, which consists of written and oral French tests, is taken at the end of the second year of *lycée*; and in the second part, taken at the end of the final year (called *la terminale*), students take oral and written exams in their other subjects. Successful completion of the *bac* qualifies students to enter university. There are 12 types of *bac*: three general (literature, *série L*; science, *série S*; and economics and social studies, *série ES*) and nine technical. *Lycées professionnels* offer other courses leading to vocational diplomas called the *CAP* (*certificat d'aptitude professionnelle*) and the *BEP* (*brevet d'études professionnelles*), which are completed earlier than the *bac.*

Higher Education

▶ **BTS (brevets de technicien supérieur)** are vocational diplomas awarded after two years' study at a *lycée* or a private school.

▶ **Universities and IUTs (instituts universitaires de technologie)** are open to all holders of a general or technical *baccalauréat*. Students pay no course fees (*Am*: tuition), and degrees are nationally recognized. After two years students take an exam, and if they pass they receive the *DEUG* (*diplôme d'études universitaires générales*) and may go on to take a *licence* (one year's study) or a *maîtrise* (two years' study). Those students who are interested in going on to do research, and possibly a doctorate, may then take one of two courses, the *DEA* (*diplôme d'études approfondies*) or the *DESS* (*diplôme d'études supérieures spécialisées*). The final qualification from an *IUT* is known as the *DUT* (*diplôme universitaire de technologie*). Establishments called *IUPs* (*instituts universitaires professionnels*) have been set up in an attempt to forge closer links between higher education and local businesses. The most illustrious French university remains the Sorbonne in Paris.

▶ **Classes préparatoires** are two years of study available in some lycées after the *bac* which prepare students to take entrance exams for the *grandes* *écoles* (*see below*). The first year of the literature course is known as the *lettres supérieures*, or more colloquially the *hypokhâgne*, and the second as the *première supérieure* or *khâgne*. There are also science classes and mathematics courses, *mathématiques supérieures* and *mathématiques spéciales*.

▶ **The *grandes écoles*** are prestigious establishments whose students are selected by competitive examination after the *classes préparatoires*. Graduates

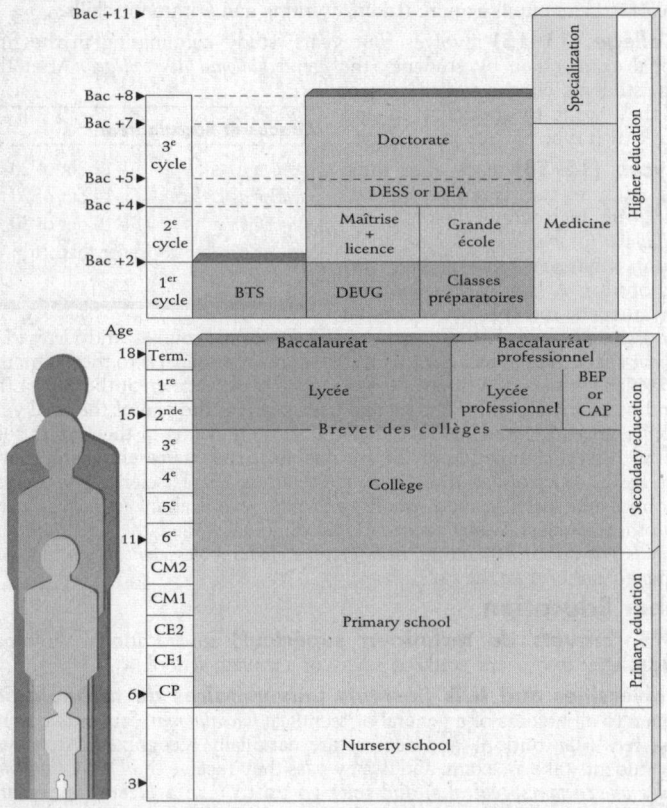

become senior civil servants, politicians, directors of large companies, engineers and academics. The most famous schools are the *Polytechnique*, the *Centrale*, the *Mines* and the *Arts et Métiers*, which all specialize in engineering; the *ENA* (*École nationale d'administration*), which trains senior civil servants; and the *ENS* (*École normale supérieure*), which trains high-ranking teachers and researchers. They are public and free, and students are in some cases paid a salary.

▶ **The *CNED* (*Centre national d'enseignement à distance*)** administers distance-learning, running correspondence courses at all levels.

BELGIUM Each linguistic community organizes and funds its own education system.

Full-time and Part-time Learning School attendance is obligatory between the ages of 6 and 18. During the last two years of this period students can study part-time while they complete an apprenticeship. Those students who want to go on to higher education, however, must study full-time in an *athénée*, the Belgian equivalent of a *lycée*, from the ages of 16 to 18 and take the university entrance exam, the *DAES (diplôme d'aptitude à accéder à l'enseignement supérieur)*.

Higher Education There are three universities in the French-speaking part of Belgium, plus one with courses in a limited number of subjects. In addition to the universities, there are seven other types of establishment running specialized vocational courses, e.g. in agriculture, nursing etc.

SWITZERLAND Each Swiss *canton* is responsible for its own education system.

Compulsory Schooling This lasts for nine years. The length of time spent in primary schools varies from four to six years depending on the *canton*. Students then go on to enter the *degré secondaire I*. German classes are compulsory from primary school.

Further Education Depending on their ability, students may choose either to follow a vocational course or to enter the *degré secondaire II*. The latter option is more popular in the French-speaking part of the country. Vocational courses all involve work placements in addition to studies at college. The *degré secondaire II* is followed either at secondary schools called *gymnases*, which prepare students to take the *maturité*, the Swiss equivalent of the *baccalauréat*, or at *écoles de degré diplôme (EDD)* where students follow a two- or three-year vocational course.

Higher Education As well as the universities, *écoles supérieures* offer courses in technical subjects, tourism or art, and *hautes écoles* run courses with a high research component.

QUEBEC In Canada each province is responsible for its own education system. As 80% of the population of Quebec is French-speaking, most classes are in French.

Compulsory Schooling At primary level school is compulsory for six years, and at secondary level for five years.

Pre-university Education After these 11 years, students may leave school or enter a *collège d'enseignement général et professionnel (cégep)* where they take either a two-year general course leading to university entrance, or a three-year vocational course leading to the job market.

Universities In Quebec universities enjoy a high degree of independence and award their own degrees. There are four French-speaking universities and three English-speaking ones. Successful students receive a qualification called a *baccalauréat* after three years. They may then study for a further two years, leading to a specialized master's degree (*maîtrise*), and continue for three years more to gain a doctorate.

FRANCE In France medical research, hospitals and chemists' (*Am*: pharmacies), as well as all staff working in these fields, are the responsibility of the Ministry of Health (*ministère de la Santé*). There is a national health service run by a public body called *la Sécurité sociale*, or *la Sécu* for short, which provides free treatment for all employees and their families, and for senior citizens. Individuals are free to take out additional private health insurance from companies known as *mutuelles* (*see below*).

Paying for Health

▶ **La Sécurité sociale** consists of a *Caisse nationale*, *caisses régionales* (governing bodies at national and regional level respectively) and *caisses primaires d'assurance maladie* (offices handling medical insurance). As well as ensuring a free health service, *la Sécu* provides maternity benefit, old age pensions (*Am*: social security) and bereavement payments. Funded by compulsory contributions from employers, employees and the self-employed, and from various taxes, it has a huge budget and has been running a deficit for many years. The body charged with collecting contributions is

Government Expenditure on Health	
hospitals and clinics	44%
doctors and dentists	25%
drugs	15%
sickness benefit	6%
transport	5.5%
prevention	2.5%
spectacles and dentures	2%

called the *URSSAF* (*Union pour le recouvrement des cotisations de Sécurité sociale et d'Allocations familiales*). *La Sécu* refunds the cost of medical treatment, including drugs, tests and X-rays, as well as dental treatment, dentures and spa cures. Usually 70% of the costs are repaid but in the case of maternity expenses, certain long-term illnesses and occupational accidents, *la Sécu* pays in full. As a rule patients pay for their treatment and then send a *feuille de maladie* (a document listing medical treatment received and drugs purchased) to their *caisse primaire d'assurance maladie* to claim a refund, though for some years a system known as *tiers payant* has been in force, whereby the hospital, doctor or chemist (pharmacy) is paid directly by the insurance company.

▶ **Mutuelles** are becoming increasingly popular. Non-profitmaking co-operative companies, they make up the difference (the *ticket modérateur*) between what is paid by *la Sécu* and the rest of the cost of the treatment.

Health Professionals

▶ **Doctors** can be chosen by the patient in France. At night, weekends and on bank holidays, though, you have to telephone the doctor on call or *SOS-Médecins*, the emergency medical service available in the larger towns. The charge for consultation by a doctor is fixed by the *Sécurité sociale*. If a doctor applies this rate, he or she is termed *conventionné*, which means that the entire cost of the consultation is refunded. If, however, you visit a *médecin conventionné à honoraires libres*, he will charge more than the rate set by *la Sécu* and you will have to pay the difference. In the case of those few doctors who are *non conventionné*, patients will receive only a small refund. Specialists charge higher fees. Only doctors and dentists are entitled to write prescriptions.

▶ **Chemists'** (*Am*: pharmacies) number 1 shop per 2000 people in the countryside; in towns the average is 1 per 3000. Chemists' issue prescription drugs and sell other drugs for which the cost is not reimbursed by *la Sécu*, as well as cosmetics, health foods and baby food. Just as there are duty doctors on call, there are duty chemists (pharmacists). Chemists' are marked by a green neon sign in the shape of a cross.

▶ **Hospitals** are managed by an authority called the *Assistance publique*. All hospital treatment is free of charge. Each hospital runs a round-the-clock emergency service of ambulances and teams of paramedics, the *SAMU* (*Service d'aide médicale d'urgence*). As well as doctors and nurses, care is provided by housemen (*Am*: interns), medical students who have completed their studies and passed their final exams known as *l'internat*. Each hospital department is run by a senior consultant known as a *patron*. Clinics are all privately run and may or may not be subsidized by the *Sécurité sociale*.

Life Expectancy in France	
life expectancy for men	72.4
life expectancy for women	80.9
death rate	10.7%
most common causes of death	
– circulatory disorders	
– cancer	
– major accidents and poisoning	

▶ **The *Institut Pasteur*** develops and distributes vaccines (for rabies, polio, hepatitis B, AIDS etc.). It has research centres throughout France and indeed the whole world.

BELGIUM There is no public body in charge of social security in Belgium and so all employees pay into a *mutuelle* insurance scheme of their choice, either one managed by an independent insurance company or one set up by a political party. In Belgium all doctors are *conventionné*; patients are free to choose their own doctor. A smaller proportion of the cost of drugs is refunded than in France, but refunds are made directly as patients only pay the costs which are not met by the *mutuelle*. Only a small proportion of the cost of dental treatment is refunded.

SWITZERLAND In Switzerland life expectancy is 74 for men and 81 for women. As there is no social security system, 98% of Swiss people take out insurance, either with private health insurance companies that have been recognized by the State, or with publicly owned insurance companies run by *cantons* or *communes*. There is considerable disparity between the level of social security cover provided in the different *cantons*.

QUEBEC The health and social security system of the province is overseen by the Ministry of Health and Social Services (*ministère de la Santé et des Services sociaux – MSSS*).

Hospitals and Clinics There are 224 hospitals in Quebec: 182 are public, 41 are privately run but receive some state funding, and 1 is owned by the Canadian Government. Doctors and surgeons are either paid depending on how many patients they see or are salaried.

La Régie de l'assurance maladie du Québec (RAMQ) This is the body which oversees health programmes, scholarships and research, and attempts to make up for the shortage of doctors in the more remote areas. All residents are eligible for *RAMQ* aid.

Life Expectancy Life expectancy is lower than in the rest of Canada (72 for men and 79 for women).

FRANCE The average French family spends over half its income on housing, food, and car and other transport costs.

Everyday Purchases Although there is a growing number of supermarkets and hypermarkets in France, people still do most of their shopping at smaller food stores and at markets. It is illegal for shops to open on Sundays, with the exception of small grocers' and florists'. In small towns most shops are also closed on Monday. There are no fixed opening times and these vary from region to region and from shop to shop. Shops may open any time between 8.30 and 10 a.m. and close anywhere between 6.30 and 8 p.m.; some supermarkets stay open until 10 p.m.

Household Expenditure	
housing	19%
food	18.5%
transport	17%
other goods and services	16%
health	9.5%
leisure	7.5%
clothes	7%
furniture	2.5%
electrical appliances	1.5%
cigarettes and tobacco	1.5%

▶ **Markets** can be found everywhere: almost every French village, however small, will organize a market once or twice a week. Markets sell fruit and vegetables, clothes and all kinds of everyday consumer goods. Once a year larger towns hold a *foire*, an exhibition of household electrical appliances, furniture, gardening equipment or local food products.

▶ **Antiques** are a flourishing business in France. As well as in antique shops, antiques are sold at weekend flea markets (*marchés aux puces*) held in the large towns. The best-known markets in Paris are those in the suburbs of Saint-Ouen and Vanves. Sales of bric-a-brac where anyone can set up stalls, sometimes called *foires à tout*, are a common sight in villages.

▶ **Department stores** like *Printemps*, *Galeries Lafayette* and *Bazar de l'Hôtel de Ville* (sometimes abbreviated to *BHV*) have branches throughout the country, but the oldest and most prestigious stores are concentrated in Paris. Chains such as *Bon Marché* and *Samaritaine* only have stores in the capital.

▶ **Mail order shopping** is extremely popular in France, especially among people living in the countryside. The biggest companies that publish catalogues are *La Redoute* and *Les Trois Suisses*, specializing in clothing. Advertisements by mail order firms are also carried on *Minitel* and shoppers can make purchases via *Télétel* (*see* **POST AND TELECOMMUNICATIONS**).

Luxury Goods

▶ **Fashion** in France may be divided into *haute couture*, exclusive ready-to-wear clothes and ready-to-wear clothes for the mass market. Collections are shown twice a year (autumn–winter/spring–summer) at Parisian fashion shows. The big names in the French *haute couture* industry are Chanel, Saint Laurent, Dior, Lanvin and Givenchy, whose shops are grouped on the north bank of the Seine around the avenue Montaigne, or in the Saint-Honoré district. These couturiers also market exclusive ready-to-wear lines.

▶ **Accessories and perfumes** generate a lot of income for the big names in fashion, with items such as leather goods, scarves, jewellery and cosmetics. A lot of perfume is sold in France, as 9 out of 10 French women wear it regularly. Big players in this field are Hermès and Guerlain.

▶ **Jewellery** shops are concentrated around the place Vendôme in Paris. Some of the big names are Boucheron, Chaumet, Van Cleef and Arpels, Mauboussin and Cartier. Two-thirds of their products are exported.

▶ **Tableware** is another part of the luxury goods industry: porcelain (that made in Limoges is particularly famous); hand-blown glassware (Baccarat, Daum, Saint-Louis), produced in Lorraine; and silverware (the most famous brands being Christofle, Ercuis and Puiforcat).

▶ **Gourmet food** is closely associated with France. Two of the biggest names in the specialist food business are Fauchon and Hédiard, who sell fine foods in delicatessens throughout the country and in Paris.

Shopping Trends

▶ **Bread** is an essential element of every French meal. The basic French loaf is a long stick known as a *baguette*, but there are also other varieties, such as a *ficelle* (long and thin) or a *bâtard* (short). Other types of bread found in bakers' are wholemeal loaves (*pains complets*), farm-house loaves (*pains de campagne*) and bread with added grains (*pains aux céréales*).

▶ **Cakes and pastries** include *croissants*, *brioches* and *pains au chocolat* (usually eaten with coffee at breakfast), éclairs, *religieuses* (choux pastry buns filled with cream), *mille-feuilles* (layered slices of puff pastry and cream), rum babas and fruit tarts (all usually eaten for dessert). These traditional pastries are found in all pâtisseries, but there are also regional specialities like *far breton* (custard tart with prunes) in Brittany, and *kouglof* (a dome-shaped cake made with raisins and almonds) in Alsace.

Food Consumption per Person per Year in France	
milk	66 litres
vegetables	60 kilograms
fruit	57 kilograms
meat	51 kilograms
bread	46 kilograms
wine	31 litres
cheese	15 kilograms
fish	6.4 kilograms

▶ **Meat**, most commonly beef and veal, is usually fried or grilled. Game is popular too during the hunting season.

▶ **Wine** is almost synonymous with France, one of the biggest producers and consumers of wine in the world. The most famous wine-producing regions are Bordeaux, Burgundy and Champagne. A total of 80% of Bordeaux wines are red (such as those grown in the Graves, Pomerol, Médoc and Saint-Émilion districts) and may be called *vins de garde* as they are made to be aged. However, Bordeaux also produces dry white wines and dessert wines, like

Classification of Wines	
Region	**Classification in order of quality**
Bordeaux	*appellation d'origine contrôlée*
	cru bourgeois
	premier cru
	premier grand cru classé
Burgundy	*vin de qualité supérieure*
	appellation d'origine contrôlée
	premier cru
	grand cru
Champagne	*autre cru*
	premier cru
	grand cru

Sauternes. The words *château* and *côtes* on Bordeaux labels refer to the vineyard and region where the wine was made. In Burgundy too, mostly red wine is made in the côte de Nuits and côte de Beaune regions south of Dijon (where some of the best-known vintages include Chambertin, Pommard and Clos-de-Vougeot), although high-quality whites and rosés are also produced. In the Burgundy area, the word *clos* sometimes appears on labels before the name of the vineyard. The Champagne region in northeast France has given its name to the sparkling white wine produced there. Other large wine-producing areas are Languedoc–Roussillon, Provence, the Loire and Rhône valleys, and Alsace.

▶ **Cheese** comes in about 340 types, and is made from cow's, goat's or sheep's milk. Cheeses can be categorized as soft, like Camembert and Brie; hard, like Comté and Cantal; and blue, like Roquefort.

Consumer Advice and Support The *Institut national de la consommation* (*INC*) is a state-funded organization that publishes the results of tests on products in its magazine *50 Millions de consommateurs*. It also deals with customer complaints and provides legal advice in disputes.

BELGIUM Shops in Belgium are usually open between 9 a.m. and 6 p.m., Monday to Saturday. They often close between noon and 2 p.m. The biggest shops are concentrated in the capital, Brussels. There are still some specialized markets selling, for example, flowers, books or poultry.

SWITZERLAND Although Switzerland has a very high standard of living, wealth is concentrated in large cities like Geneva and Lausanne with their cosmopolitan populations, and people living in some *cantons* like Jura have much less purchasing power. Shop opening hours are fixed by the individual *cantons*, but as a rule shops are open from 8.30 to 6.30, Monday to Friday, and close early on Saturdays at 4 p.m.

QUEBEC

▶ **Household spending** patterns differ in Quebec from the rest of Canada. People in the province tend to spend more on food, clothing, cosmetics, cigarettes and tobacco and alcohol, and less on housing, transport, entertainment and education.

▶ **Shops** are mostly privately run. A total of 72% of retail sales are made in these shops, which employ 15% of the working population. The growth in the number of shops of this type has been to the detriment of larger shops and chain stores, a trend unique to Quebec and not repeated in the rest of Canada. Indeed, some Canadian chain stores do not have branches in Quebec.

▶ **Opening hours** are from 9 a.m. to 6 p.m., Monday to Wednesday, with late-night opening on Thursday and Friday. On Saturdays shops close at 5 p.m. On Sundays the only shops which stay open are a few large food stores and chemists' (*Am*: pharmacies).

▶ **Typical products** from Quebec centre on arts and crafts (woven blankets, sealskin shoes, furs and wickerwork).

▶ **The sale of alcohol** is regulated by the *Société des alcools du Québec* (*SAQ*), which has a monopoly on the distribution of alcohol in Quebec and sets the prices in the shops it owns.

FRANCE The French spend about 10.5% of their income on entertainment.

Sport Just 10% of French people play sport on a regular basis, although this percentage is higher among teenagers, who enjoy football (*Am*: soccer), tennis and judo. French women prefer to go to gyms and exercise classes and these are becoming increasingly popular, especially in towns and cities.

▶ **Motor racing** is watched by a large number of French people, both on television and live at circuits like Le Mans, where the famous 24-hour endurance race takes place.

▶ **Cycling** too is popular. The best-known cycle race, perhaps in the world, is the Tour de France, which takes place every year in July. There are about 20 stages which differ from year to year, but the race always finishes on the Champs-Élysées with the President of the Republic in attendance. The leader always wears a yellow cycling jersey (the *maillot jaune*).

▶ **Football** (*Am*: soccer), the most popular sport in the world, enjoys a high standing in France, where almost every town and village have their own team. The national league has two divisions. The best-supported French teams are Paris-Saint-Germain, also known as PSG, Nantes, Monaco and Olympique de Marseille, usually referred to as OM. International games and the finals of national competitions are often hosted at the Parc des Princes in Paris.

▶ **Horse racing** and betting on horse races are very popular in France. As well as taking part in on-course betting, people can place bets in betting offices (sometimes counters in bars) run by a national authority known as the *PMU*. The most famous race courses are at Saint-Cloud, Maisons-Laffitte, Longchamp and Chantilly.

▶ **Rugby**'s heartland is the southwest, where Toulouse, Agen and Lourdes all have successful teams. The highlight of the international season is the Five Nations Championship, which France contests with England, Scotland, Wales and Ireland.

▶ **Skiing** is enjoyed by 9.5% of French people, who make use of the excellent opportunities for winter sports offered in the Alps and the Pyrenees.

▶ **Tennis** is a well-established sport in France, with over 10 000 clubs. The French Open, *les Internationaux de France*, is held every year in June at the Roland Garros stadium in Paris and is one of the major world tournaments.

▶ **Yachting** has been made popular by famous French sailors such as Éric Tabarly, Olivier de Kersauson and Florence Arthaud. There is now a lot of interest in transatlantic and single-handed round-the-world races.

▶ **Regional sports** like *pétanque*, which originated in the South of France, and pelota (*pelote basque*) from the Basque Country are minority sports, but have become a part of French culture. *Pétanque* is played with metal bowls and a small wooden ball called a *cochonnet* (the jack); the object is to throw the bowls as close to the jack as possible. The most common version of pelota is played with a ball called a *pelote* which is thrown against a wall.

Arts

▶ **Music** is particularly enjoyed by French teenagers, 50% of whom play a musical instrument, the piano and guitar being the most popular. Paris is home to large concert halls such as Pleyel and Gaveau, and music hall theatres such as Olympia, which also hosts pop concerts. Jazz festivals are usually held in the South of France in places like Antibes and Juan-les-Pins. Most French cities have an opera house; indeed, Paris has two, the Palais Garnier and the Bastille. The latter was opened in 1990, its stated objective to popularize opera. Some towns in the South of France, like Aix-en-Provence and Orange, hold opera festivals in summer. During the *fête de la Musique*, which takes place every year on 21 June, both amateur and professional musicians take to the streets to give free concerts.

▶ **The largest ballet school in France** is also housed in the Palais Garnier. Students of this school are commonly referred to as *les petits rats de l'Opéra*. Ballets from the repertory are performed every year.

▶ **Theatre** companies like the independent *Comédie-Française* (the national theatre company), *Théâtre de l'Europe* (also known as *l'Odéon*), *Chaillot* and *TEP* (*Théâtre de l'Est parisien*) are based in Paris. Strasbourg, however, is also home to a national theatre company, the *TNS* (*Théâtre national de Strasbourg*). Members of the *Comédie-Française* are known as *sociétaires* or *pensionnaires* and are often former students of the Paris music school, the *Conservatoire de Paris*. Two of the highlights of the theatrical year are the *Festival d'Avignon* in July and the *Festival d'automne* held in Paris. There is an annual awards ceremony, *les Molières*, at which the best plays and actors of the year are rewarded.

▶ **Cinema** is highly regarded in France. The most famous film festival takes place every year in Cannes, where the *palme d'or* (golden palm) is given to the best film. The *festival d'Avoriaz*, held in a ski resort in the Alps, is dedicated to science fiction; the *festival de Cognac* to detective films; and the *festival de Deauville* to American films. There is a French equivalent of the American Oscars ceremony, *les Césars*, and the *prix Louis-Delluc* is awarded every December to the best French film of the year. The *fête du cinéma* has become an annual event and aims to promote cinema attendance. On this day you can see an unlimited number of films with a single ticket. Cinema tickets are normally cheaper on Mondays or Wednesdays, depending on the cinema.

▶ **Architecture** was a particular concern of the late President Mitterrand. A major programme was initiated 15 years ago to erect modern public buildings in Paris and the rest of France. The most notable results have been the futuristic office block *l'Arche de la Défense*, the opera house *l'Opéra de la Bastille*, the pyramid outside the Louvre, the *Institut du monde arabe*, the science park *la Cité des sciences de la Villette*, the offices of the Finance Ministry in the Paris suburb of Bercy, and the *Très Grande Bibliothèque*, the new national library.

▶ **Museums** number 1400, 34 of which are national. These are closed on Tuesdays and some have no admission charge on Sundays. As well as permanent collections, they also house temporary exhibitions. Some museums, like the Grand Palais, are devoted entirely to special exhibitions.

▶ **The price of books** in France is regulated by the Government in an

Main Parisian Museums	
Louvre	antiques, sculpture, paintings
Musée d'Orsay	Impressionist paintings
Musée Rodin	sculptures by Rodin
Musée Picasso	works by Picasso
Musée national d'art moderne	modern art
Centre Georges-Pompidou	modern art

attempt to encourage people to buy them. The most famous literary publishers are Gallimard, Le Seuil and Grasset, who all have large lists. The most prestigious annual literary prize is the *prix Goncourt*, judged by a jury of ten authors. The *Académie française* is the body responsible for setting models for use of the French language and for producing the definitive reference work, *le Dictionnaire de l'Académie française*. When the *Académie* meets, its members have to wear green ceremonial dress and cocked hats, and carry a sword.

Main Literary Prizes
■ Goncourt
■ Médicis
■ Fémina
■ Interallié
■ Renaudot

Tourism

▶ **Annual holidays** (*Am*: vacations) are taken by two-thirds of French people, usually in summer, although there is a growing trend towards taking a skiing holiday. French seaside resorts are still the favourite holiday destination but more and more people are choosing to take holidays abroad.

▶ **The theme parks** *Euro Disneyland* and *Parc Astérix* outside Paris have had huge amounts of money poured into them, but investment has not paid off as well as had been hoped. *Futuroscope* near Poitiers draws large numbers to its more educationally orientated attractions.

Most Popular Tourist Attractions
■ Pompidou Centre
■ Eiffel Tower
■ Louvre
■ Cité des sciences de la Villette
■ Versailles

▶ **Hotels** in France are assessed by the Ministry of Tourism (*ministère du Tourisme*) and awarded a number of stars from 1 to 4, depending on the level of comfort they afford. The best hotels are classified as four-star *luxe*. There is a growing trend towards hotel chains aimed at a specific clientele: businessmen, holidaymakers (*Am*: vacationers) or those on a low budget. Times are hard for small, traditional, family-run hotels which are facing stiff competition from inexpensive alternatives like *chambres d'hôtes* (bed and breakfast accommodation in someone's house) and *gîtes ruraux* (converted farmhouses or outbuildings which can be rented).

Most Popular Types of Accommodation	
staying with relatives or friends	40%
camping	18%
rented	18%
second home	10%
hotel	7.5%
holiday camp	3.5%
youth hostel	3%

▶ **Restaurants** must display their menu and prices always include a service charge. Different systems (stars, forks, chefs' hats) are used to categorize restaurants by different specialist guides, the most illustrious and authoritative of which is the *Guide Michelin*.

▶ **France's gastronomic reputation** rests on its wide range of products, on the variety to be found in its regional cuisine, and on the skills of its chefs (such as Paul Bocuse, Joël Robuchon and the Troisgros brothers). The high reputation of traditional French cuisine today lies in the hands of Parisian establishments like La Tour d'Argent, Lasserre and Maxim's.

BELGIUM Cycling is the biggest sport in Belgium and is popular at both professional and amateur level. The use of bicycles is encouraged by the large number of cycle lanes and paths. Hiking on the 4500 kilometres of way-marked (*Am*: marked) paths throughout the country, and skiing in winter in the Ardennes are also popular. Many of the cartoons (*bandes dessinées*) enjoyed around the world are of Belgian origin, e.g. Tintin, Lucky Luke and Gaston Lagaffe. Tourist attractions in Belgium include carnivals, in particular the one held in the town of Binche, and the many traditional celebrations, often with a historical or religious theme, that take place between March and September. Belgium is renowned throughout the world for its chocolates but it also exports beer, notably that brewed by Trappist monks and *gueuze* (a strong beer that has been brewed twice), Spa mineral water and fruit cordials. The archetypal Belgian dish is *moules-frites* (mussels and chips, *Am*: fries).

SWITZERLAND The most popular sports in Switzerland are mountaineering and winter sports. The big ski resorts are in the German-speaking part of the country. Lakeland regions have, however, done much to develop water sports and have succeeded in attracting a large number of tourists. In the arts, one of the highlights of the year is the jazz festival in Montreux which draws top musicians from all over the world. The most famous Swiss foods are cheeses such as Emmental and Vacherin, and chocolate.

QUEBEC

Sport Most sports clubs in Quebec belong to the *Regroupement Loisir Québec*. Winter sports predominate, and include Alpine skiing (there are 1170 runs in the province); cross-country skiing in the national parks or at special centres; and snowmobiling, which is particularly popular and accessible as there are 30 000 kilometres of marked tracks. In summer, water sports like canoeing, whitewater rafting, sailing and jet-skiing are widely practised on the many lakes and rivers. Cycling is gaining in popularity year by year, helped by a network of 1600 kilometres of cycle lanes and paths.

Parks and Nature Reserves There are 19 nature reserves (three of which are managed by the Canadian Government) where hunting is banned, and 18 wildlife reserves where fishing is permitted and hunting is regulated. Camping is allowed and there are chalets which can be rented.

Arts Many music and drama festivals are held in the province, such as the classical music festival in Lanaudière and the famous *Festival du Théâtre des Amériques*. 'Barn theater' (plays put on in villages) is also popular. Montreal has an internationally renowned symphony orchestra, and mention should also be made of the many singer-songwriters who sing in French. Quebec has a lively film industry but suffers from small audiences and is in constant need of government aid. Film dubbing is a growth sector. Although not widely read in Europe, 1500 books by writers from Quebec are published every year.

Tourism Hotels in Quebec are classified according to a star system by a national body called Canada Select. Staying in a *gîte du passant* (bed and breakfast accommodation at somebody's house) is also popular.

Cuisine The Québécois use different words from the French to talk about mealtimes: *déjeuner* for breakfast, *dîner* for lunch and *souper* for dinner. Maple syrup is probably the most typical food product and is widely used.

ENGLISH–FRENCH
ANGLAIS–FRANÇAIS

a¹ (*pl* **as** OR **a's**), **A** (*pl* **As** OR **A's**) [eɪ] *n* [letter] a *m inv*, A *m inv*; **to get from A to B** aller d'un point à un autre; **from A to Z** de A à Z, depuis A jusqu'à Z.
◆ **A** *n* -**1.** MUS la *m inv*. -**2.** SCH [mark] A *m inv*.

a² [stressed eɪ, unstressed ə] (*before vowel or silent 'h'* **an** [stressed æn, unstressed ən]) *indef art* -**1.** [gen] un (une); **a boy** un garçon; **a table** une table; **an orange** une orange. -**2.** [referring to occupation]: **to be a doctor/lawyer/ plumber** être médecin/avocat/plombier. -**3.** [instead of the number one] un (une); **a hundred/thousand pounds** cent/mille livres. -**4.** [to express prices, ratios etc]: **20p a kilo** 20p le kilo; **£10 a person** 10 livres par personne; **twice a week/month** deux fois par semaine/mois; **50 km an hour** 50 km à l'heure. -**5.** [preceding person's name] un certain (une certaine); **a Mr Jones** un certain M. Jones.

a. *abbr of* **acre.**

A-1 *adj inf* excellent(e).

A4 *n Br* format *m* A4.

AA ◇ *adj abbr of* **anti-aircraft.** ◇ *n* -**1.** (*abbr of* **Automobile Association**) *automobile club britannique,* ≃ ACF *m,* ≃ TCF *m.* -**2.** (*abbr of* **Associate in Arts**) *diplôme universitaire américain de lettres.* -**3.** (*abbr of* **Alcoholics Anonymous**) Alcooliques Anonymes *mpl.*

AAA *n* -**1.** (*abbr of* **Amateur Athletics Association**) *fédération britannique d'athlétisme.* -**2.** (*abbr of* **American Automobile Association**) *automobile club américain,* ≃ ACF *m,* ≃ TCF *m.*

AAUP (*abbr of* **American Association of University Professors**) *n syndicat universitaire américain des professeurs d'université.*

AB ◇ *n Am abbr of* **Bachelor of Arts.** ◇ *abbr of* **Alberta.**

aback [ə'bæk] *adv*: **to be taken** ~ être décontenancé(e).

abacus ['æbəkəs] (*pl* **-cuses** OR **-ci** ['æbəsaɪ]) *n* boulier *m,* abaque *m.*

abandon [ə'bændən] ◇ *vt* abandonner. ◇ *n*: **with** ~ avec abandon.

abandoned [ə'bændənd] *adj* abandonné(e).

abashed [ə'bæʃt] *adj* confus(e).

abate [ə'beɪt] *vi* [storm, fear] se calmer; [noise] faiblir.

abattoir ['æbətwɑːr] *n* abattoir *m.*

abbess ['æbes] *n* abbesse *f.*

abbey ['æbɪ] *n* abbaye *f.*

abbot ['æbət] *n* abbé *m.*

abbreviate [ə'briːvɪeɪt] *vt* abréger.

abbreviation [ə,briːvɪ'eɪʃn] *n* abréviation *f.*

ABC *n* -**1.** [alphabet] alphabet *m.* -**2.** *fig* [basics] B.A.-Ba *m,* abc *m.* -**3.** (*abbr of* **American Broadcasting Company**) *chaîne de télévision américaine.*

abdicate ['æbdɪkeɪt] *vt & vi* abdiquer.

abdication [,æbdɪ'keɪʃn] *n* abdication *f.*

abdomen ['æbdəmen] *n* abdomen *m.*

abdominal [æb'dɒmɪnl] *adj* abdominal(e).

abduct [əb'dʌkt] *vt* enlever.

abduction [æb'dʌkʃn] *n* enlèvement *m.*

aberration [,æbə'reɪʃn] *n* aberration *f.*

abet [ə'bet] (*pt & pp* **-ted,** *cont* **-ting**) *vt* → **aid.**

abeyance [ə'beɪəns] *n*: **in** ~ en attente.

abhor [əb'hɔːr] (*pt & pp* **-red,** *cont* **-ring**) *vt* exécrer, abhorrer.

abhorrent [əb'hɒrənt] *adj* répugnant(e).

abide [ə'baɪd] *vt* supporter, souffrir.

◆ **abide by** *vt fus* respecter, se soumettre à.

abiding [ə'baɪdɪŋ] *adj* [lasting - feeling, interest] constant(e); [memory] éternel(elle), impérissable.

ability [ə'bɪlətɪ] (*pl* -ies) *n* -1. [capacity, capability] aptitude *f*; **to do sthg to the best of one's** ~ faire qqch de son mieux. -2. [skill] talent *m*.

abject ['æbdʒekt] *adj* -1. [poverty] noir(e). -2. [person] pitoyable; [apology] servile.

ablaze [ə'bleɪz] *adj* -1. [on fire] en feu. -2. *fig* [bright]: **to be** ~ **with** être resplendissant(e) de.

able ['eɪbl] *adj* -1. [capable]: **to be** ~ **to do sthg** pouvoir faire qqch. -2. [accomplished] compétent(e).

able-bodied [-ˌbɒdɪd] *adj* en bonne santé, valide.

ablutions [ə'bluːʃnz] *npl fml* ablutions *fpl*.

ably ['eɪblɪ] *adv* avec compétence, habilement.

ABM (*abbr of* **anti-ballistic missile**) *n* ABM *m*.

abnormal [æb'nɔːml] *adj* anormal(e).

abnormality [ˌæbnɔː'mælətɪ] (*pl* -ies) *n* -1. [gen] anomalie *f*. -2. MED malformation *f*.

abnormally [æb'nɔːməlɪ] *adv* anormalement.

aboard [ə'bɔːd] ◇ *adv* à bord. ◇ *prep* [ship, plane] à bord; [bus, train] dans.

abode [ə'bəʊd] *n fml*: **of no fixed** ~ sans domicile fixe.

abolish [ə'bɒlɪʃ] *vt* abolir.

abolition [ˌæbə'lɪʃn] *n* abolition *f*.

A-bomb (*abbr of* **atom bomb**) *n* bombe *f* atomique.

abominable [ə'bɒmɪnəbl] *adj* abominable.

abominable snowman *n*: **the** ~ l'abominable homme *m* des neiges.

abominably [ə'bɒmɪnəblɪ] *adv* abominablement.

aborigine [ˌæbə'rɪdʒənɪ] *n* aborigène *mf* d'Australie.

abort [ə'bɔːt] ◇ *vt* -1. [pregnancy] interrompre. -2. *fig* [plan, project] abandonner, faire avorter. -3. COMPUT abandonner. ◇ *vi* COMPUT abandonner.

abortion [ə'bɔːʃn] *n* avortement *m*, interruption *f* (volontaire) de grossesse; **to have an** ~ se faire avorter.

abortive [ə'bɔːtɪv] *adj* manqué(e).

abound [ə'baʊnd] *vi* -1. [be plentiful] abon-

der. -2. [be full]: **to** ~ **with** OR **in** abonder en.

about [ə'baʊt] ◇ *adv* -1. [approximately] environ, à peu près; ~ **fifty/a hundred/a thousand** environ cinquante/cent/mille; **at** ~ **five o'clock** vers cinq heures; **I'm just** ~ **ready** je suis presque prêt. -2. [referring to place]: **to run** ~ courir çà et là; **to leave things lying** ~ laisser traîner des affaires; **to walk** ~ aller et venir, se promener. -3. [on the point of]: **to be** ~ **to do sthg** être sur le point de faire qqch.
◇ *prep* -1. [relating to, concerning] au sujet de; **a film** ~ **Paris** un film sur Paris; **what is it** ~? de quoi s'agit-il?; **to talk** ~ **sthg** parler de qqch. -2. [referring to place]: **his belongings were scattered** ~ **the room** ses affaires étaient éparpillées dans toute la pièce; **to wander** ~ **the streets** errer de par les rues.

about-turn, about-face *n* MIL demi-tour *m*; *fig* volte-face *f inv*.

above [ə'bʌv] ◇ *adv* -1. [on top, higher up] au-dessus. -2. [in text] ci-dessus, plus haut. -3. [more, over] plus; **children aged 5 and** ~ les enfants âgés de 5 ans et plus OR de plus de 5 ans. ◇ *prep* -1. [on top of, higher up than] au-dessus de. -2. [more than] plus de. -3. [too good for]: **to be** ~ **doing sthg** ne pas s'abaisser à faire qqch.

◆ **above all** *adv* avant tout.

aboveboard [ˌə,bʌv'bɔːd] *adj* honnête.

abracadabra [ˌæbrəkə'dæbrə] *excl* abracadabra!

abrasion [ə'breɪʒn] *n fml* [on skin] écorchure *f*, égratignure *f*.

abrasive [ə'breɪsɪv] ◇ *adj* [substance] abrasif(ive); *fig* caustique, acerbe. ◇ *n* abrasif *m*.

abreast [ə'brest] *adv* de front, côte à côte.

◆ **abreast of** *prep*: **to keep** ~ **of** se tenir au courant de.

abridged [ə'brɪdʒd] *adj* abrégé(e).

abroad [ə'brɔːd] *adv* à l'étranger.

abrupt [ə'brʌpt] *adj* -1. [sudden] soudain(e), brusque. -2. [brusque] abrupt(e).

abruptly [ə'brʌptlɪ] *adv* -1. [suddenly] brusquement. -2. [brusquely] abruptement.

ABS (*abbr of* **Antiblockiersystem**) *n* ABS *m*.

abscess ['æbsɪs] *n* abcès *m*.

abscond [əb'skɒnd] *vi* s'enfuir.

abseil ['æbseɪl] *vi* descendre en rappel.

absence ['æbsəns] *n* absence *f*; **in the** ~ **of** [thing] faute de; [person] en l'absence de.

absent ['æbsənt] *adj*: ~ **(from)** absent(e)

(de); **to be ~ without leave** MIL être en absence irrégulière.

absentee [ˌæbsən'tiː] *n* absent *m*, -e *f*.

absenteeism [ˌæbsən'tiːɪzm] *n* absentéisme *m*.

absent-minded [-'maɪndɪd] *adj* distrait(e).

absent-mindedly [-'maɪndɪdlɪ] *adv* distraitement.

absinth(e) ['æbsɪnθ] *n* absinthe *f*.

absolute ['æbsəluːt] *adj* **-1.** [complete - fool, disgrace] complet(ète). **-2.** [totalitarian - ruler, power] absolu(e).

absolutely ['æbsəluːtlɪ] *adv* absolument.

absolute majority *n* majorité *f* absolue.

absolution [ˌæbsə'luːʃn] *n* absolution *f*.

absolve [əb'zɒlv] *vt*: **to ~ sb (from)** absoudre qqn (de).

absorb [əb'sɔːb] *vt* absorber; [information] retenir, assimiler; **to be ~ed in sthg** être absorbé dans qqch.

absorbent [əb'sɔːbənt] *adj* absorbant(e).

absorbing [əb'sɔːbɪŋ] *adj* captivant(e).

absorption [əb'sɔːpʃn] *n* absorption *f*.

abstain [əb'steɪn] *vi*: **to ~ (from)** s'abstenir (de).

abstemious [æb'stiːmjəs] *adj fml* frugal(e), sobre.

abstention [əb'stenʃn] *n* abstention *f*.

abstinence ['æbstɪnəns] *n* abstinence *f*.

abstract [*adj & n* 'æbstrækt, *vb* æb'strækt] ◇ *adj* abstrait(e). ◇ *n* [summary] résumé *m*, abrégé *m*. ◇ *vt* [summarize] résumer.

abstraction [æb'strækʃn] *n* **-1.** [distractedness] distraction *f*. **-2.** [abstract idea] abstraction *f*.

abstruse [æb'struːs] *adj* abstrus(e).

absurd [əb'sɜːd] *adj* absurde.

absurdity [əb'sɜːdətɪ] (*pl* **-ies**) *n* absurdité *f*.

absurdly [əb'sɜːdlɪ] *adv* absurdement.

ABTA ['æbtə] (*abbr of* **Association of British Travel Agents**) *n* association des agences de voyage britanniques.

Abu Dhabi [ˌæbuː'dɑːbɪ] *n* Abou Dhabi.

abundance [ə'bʌndəns] *n* abondance *f*; **in ~** en abondance.

abundant [ə'bʌndənt] *adj* abondant(e).

abundantly [ə'bʌndəntlɪ] *adv* **-1.** [clear, obvious] parfaitement, tout à fait. **-2.** [exist, grow] en abondance.

abuse [*n* ə'bjuːs, *vb* ə'bjuːz] ◇ *n* (*U*) **-1.** [offensive remarks] insultes *fpl*, injures *fpl*. **-2.** [maltreatment] mauvais traitement *m*; **child ~** mauvais traitements infligés aux enfants; **physical ~** sévices *mpl* corporels; **sexual ~** abus *mpl* sexuels. **-3.** [of power, drugs etc]

abus *m.* ◇ *vt* **-1.** [insult] insulter, injurier. **-2.** [maltreat] maltraiter. **-3.** [power, drugs etc] abuser de.

abusive [ə'bjuːsɪv] *adj* grossier(ière), injurieux(ieuse).

abut [ə'bʌt] (*pt & pp* **-ted**, *cont* **-ting**) *vi* [adjoin]: **to ~ on to** être contigu(ë) à.

abysmal [ə'bɪzml] *adj* épouvantable, abominable.

abysmally [ə'bɪzməlɪ] *adv* abominablement.

abyss [ə'bɪs] *n* abîme *m*, gouffre *m*.

Abyssinia [ˌæbɪ'sɪnjə] *n* Abyssinie *f*; **in ~** en Abyssinie.

Abyssinian [ˌæbɪ'sɪnɪən] ◇ *adj* abyssinien(ienne). ◇ *n* Abyssinien *m*, -ienne *f*.

a/c (*abbr of* **account (current)**) cc.

AC *n* **-1.** (*abbr of* **athletics club**) *club britannique d'athlétisme.* **-2.** (*abbr of* **alternating current**) courant *m* alternatif.

acacia [ə'keɪʃə] *n* acacia *m*.

academic [ˌækə'demɪk] ◇ *adj* **-1.** [of college, university] universitaire. **-2.** [person] intellectuel(elle). **-3.** [question, discussion] théorique. ◇ *n* universitaire *mf*.

academic year *n* année *f* scolaire OR universitaire.

academy [ə'kædəmɪ] (*pl* **-ies**) *n* **-1.** [school, college] école *f*; **~ of music** conservatoire *m*. **-2.** [institution, society] académie *f*.

ACAS ['eɪkæs] (*abbr of* **Advisory Conciliation and Arbitration Service**) *n organisme britannique de conciliation des conflits du travail.*

accede [æk'siːd] *vi* **-1.** [agree]: **to ~ to** agréer, donner suite à. **-2.** [monarch]: **to ~ to the throne** monter sur le trône.

accelerate [ək'seləreɪt] *vi* **-1.** [car, driver] accélérer. **-2.** [inflation, growth] s'accélérer.

acceleration [ək,selə'reɪʃn] *n* accélération *f*.

accelerator [ək'seləreɪtə'] *n* accélérateur *m*.

accelerator board, accelerator card *n* COMPUT carte *f* accélérateur OR accélératrice.

accent ['æksent] *n* accent *m*.

accentuate [æk'sentjʊeɪt] *vt* accentuer.

accept [ək'sept] *vt* **-1.** [gen] accepter; [for job, as member of club] recevoir, admettre. **-2.** [agree]: **to ~ that ...** admettre que ....

acceptable [ək'septəbl] *adj* acceptable.

acceptably [ək'septəblɪ] *adv* convenablement.

acceptance [ək'septəns] *n* **-1.** [gen] acceptation *f*. **-2.** [for job, as member of club] admission *f*.

accepted [ək'septɪd] *adj* [ideas, fact] reconnu(e).

access ['ækses] ◇ *n* **-1.** [entry, way in] accès *m*; **to gain ~ to** avoir accès à. **-2.** [opportunity to use, see]: **to have ~ to sthg** avoir qqch à sa disposition, disposer de qqch. ◇ *vt* COMPUT avoir accès à.

accessibility [ək,sesə'bɪlətɪ] *n* **-1.** [of place] accessibilité *f*. **-2.** [availability] accès *m*.

accessible [ək'sesəbl] *adj* **-1.** [reachable - place] accessible. **-2.** [available] disponible.

accession [æk'seʃn] *n* [of monarch] accession *f*.

accessory [ək'sesərɪ] (*pl* **-ies**) *n* **-1.** [of car, vacuum cleaner] accessoire *m*. **-2.** JUR complice *mf*.

◆ **accessories** *npl* accessoires *mpl*.

access road *n Br* [to motorway] bretelle *f* de raccordement OR d'accès.

access time *n* COMPUT temps *m* d'accès.

accident ['æksɪdənt] *n* accident *m*; **by ~** par hasard, par accident.

accidental [,æksɪ'dentl] *adj* accidentel(elle).

accidentally [,æksɪ'dentəlɪ] *adv* **-1.** [drop, break] par mégarde. **-2.** [meet] par hasard.

accident-prone *adj* prédisposé(e) aux accidents.

acclaim [ə'kleɪm] ◇ *n* (*U*) éloges *mpl*. ◇ *vt* louer.

acclamation [,æklə'meɪʃn] *n* (*U*) acclamation *f*.

acclimatize, -ise [ə'klaɪmətaɪz], **acclimate** *Am* ['ækləmeɪt] *vi*: **to ~ (to)** s'acclimater (à).

accolade ['ækəleɪd] *n* accolade *f*; **the ultimate ~** la consécration suprême.

accommodate [ə'kɒmədeɪt] *vt* **-1.** [provide room for] loger. **-2.** [oblige - person, wishes] satisfaire.

accommodating [ə'kɒmədeɪtɪŋ] *adj* obligeant(e).

accommodation *Br* [ə,kɒmə'deɪʃn] *n*, **accommodations** *Am* [ə,kɒmə'deɪʃnz] *npl* logement *m*; **office ~** bureaux *mpl*.

accompaniment [ə'kʌmpənɪmənt] *n* MUS accompagnement *m*.

accompanist [ə'kʌmpənɪst] *n* MUS accompagnateur *m*, -trice *f*.

accompany [ə'kʌmpənɪ] (*pt* & *pp* **-ied**) *vt* **-1.** [gen] accompagner. **-2.** MUS: **to ~ sb (on)** accompagner qqn (à).

accomplice [ə'kʌmplɪs] *n* complice *mf*.

accomplish [ə'kʌmplɪʃ] *vt* accomplir.

accomplished [ə'kʌmplɪʃt] *adj* accompli(e).

accomplishment [ə'kʌmplɪʃmənt] *n* **-1.** [action] accomplissement *m*. **-2.** [achievement] réussite *f*.

◆ **accomplishments** *npl* talents *mpl*.

accord [ə'kɔːd] *n*: **to do sthg of one's own ~** faire qqch de son propre chef OR de soi-même; **to be in ~ with** être d'accord avec; **with one ~** d'un commun accord.

accordance [ə'kɔːdəns] *n*: **in ~ with** conformément à.

according [ə'kɔːdɪŋ]

◆ **according to** *prep* **-1.** [as stated or shown by] d'après; **to go ~ to plan** se passer comme prévu. **-2.** [with regard to] suivant, en fonction de.

accordingly [ə'kɔːdɪŋlɪ] *adv* **-1.** [appropriately] en conséquence. **-2.** [consequently] par conséquent.

accordion [ə'kɔːdjən] *n* accordéon *m*.

accordionist [ə'kɔːdjənɪst] *n* accordéoniste *mf*.

accost [ə'kɒst] *vt* accoster.

account [ə'kaunt] *n* **-1.** [with bank, shop, company] compte *m*. **-2.** [report] compterendu *m*. **-3.** *phr*: **to call sb to ~** demander des comptes à qqn; **to give a good ~ of o.s.** faire bonne impression; **to take ~ of sthg, to take sthg into ~** prendre qqch en compte; **to be of no ~** n'avoir aucune importance; **on no ~** sous aucun prétexte, en aucun cas.

◆ **accounts** *npl* [of business] comptabilité *f*, comptes *mpl*; **to do the ~s** faire les comptes.

◆ **by all accounts** *adv* d'après ce que l'on dit, au dire de tous.

◆ **on account of** *prep* à cause de.

◆ **account for** *vt fus* **-1.** [explain] justifier, expliquer; **has everyone been ~ed for?** personne n'a été oublié? **-2.** [represent] représenter.

accountability [ə,kauntə'bɪlətɪ] *n* (*U*) responsabilité *f*.

accountable [ə'kauntəbl] *adj* **-1.** [responsible]: **~ (for)** responsable (de). **-2.** [answerable]: **to be ~ to** rendre compte à, rendre des comptes à.

accountancy [ə'kauntənsɪ] *n* comptabilité *f*.

accountant [ə'kauntənt] *n* comptable *mf*.

accounting [ə'kauntɪŋ] *n* comptabilité *f*.

accoutrements *Br* [ə'kuːtrəmənts], **accouterments** *Am* [ə'kuːtərmənts] *npl fml* attirail *m*.

accredited [ə'kredɪtɪd] *adj* attitré(e).

accrue [ə'kruː] *vi* [money] fructifier; [interest] courir.

accumulate [ə'kjuːmjʊleɪt] ◇ *vt* accumuler, amasser. ◇ *vi* s'accumuler.

accumulation [ə,kjuːmjʊ'leɪʃn] *n* **-1.** (*U*)

[act of accumulating] **accumulation** f. **-2.** [things accumulated] amas m.

accuracy ['ækjʊrəsɪ] n **-1.** [of description, report] **exactitude** f. **-2.** [of weapon, typist, figures] précision f.

accurate ['ækjʊrət] adj **-1.** [description, report] **exact(e).** **-2.** [weapon, typist, figures] précis(e).

accurately ['ækjʊrətlɪ] adv **-1.** [truthfully - describe, report] **fidèlement.** **-2.** [precisely - aim] avec précision; [- type] sans faute.

accusation [ˌækjuːˈzeɪʃn] n accusation f.

accuse [əˈkjuːz] vt: **to ~ sb of sthg/of doing sthg** accuser qqn de qqch/de faire qqch.

accused [əˈkjuːzd] (pl inv) n JUR: **the ~** l'accusé m, -e f.

accusing [əˈkjuːzɪŋ] adj accusateur(trice).

accusingly [əˈkjuːzɪŋlɪ] adv d'une manière accusatrice.

accustomed [əˈkʌstəmd] adj: **to be ~ to sthg/to doing sthg** avoir l'habitude de qqch/de faire qqch.

ace [eɪs] ◇ n as m; **to be within an ~ of** fig être à deux doigts de. ◇ adj [top-class] de haut niveau.

acerbic [əˈsɜːbɪk] adj acerbe.

acetate ['æsɪteɪt] n acétate m.

acetic acid [əˈsiːtɪk] n acide m acétique.

acetone ['æsɪtəʊn] n acétone f.

acetylene [əˈsetɪliːn] n acétylène m.

ACGB (abbr of **Arts Council of Great Britain**) n organisme public britannique d'aide à la création artistique.

ache [eɪk] ◇ n douleur f. ◇ vi **-1.** [back, limb] faire mal; **my head ~s** j'ai mal à la tête. **-2.** fig [want]: **to be aching for sthg/to do sthg** mourir d'envie de qqch/de faire qqch.

achieve [əˈtʃiːv] vt [success, victory] obtenir, remporter; [goal] atteindre; [ambition] réaliser; [fame] parvenir à.

achievement [əˈtʃiːvmənt] n **-1.** [success] réussite f. **-2.** [of goal, objective] réalisation f.

Achilles' heel [əˈkɪliːz-] n talon m d'Achille.

Achilles' tendon [əˈkɪliːz-] n tendon m d'Achille.

acid ['æsɪd] ◇ adj lit & fig acide. ◇ n acide m.

acidic [əˈsɪdɪk] adj acide.

acidity [əˈsɪdətɪ] n acidité f.

acid rain n (U) pluies fpl acides.

acid test n fig épreuve f décisive.

acknowledge [əkˈnɒlɪdʒ] vt **-1.** [fact, situation, person] reconnaître. **-2.** [of letter]: **to ~**

(receipt of) accuser réception de. **-3.** [greet] saluer.

acknowledg(e)ment [əkˈnɒlɪdʒmənt] n **-1.** [gen] reconnaissance f. **-2.** [letter] accusé m de réception.
◆ **acknowledg(e)ments** npl [in book] remerciements mpl.

ACLU (abbr of **American Civil Liberties Union**) n ligue américaine des droits du citoyen.

acme ['ækmɪ] n apogée m.

acne ['æknɪ] n acné f.

acorn ['eɪkɔːn] n gland m.

acoustic [əˈkuːstɪk] adj acoustique.
◆ **acoustics** npl [of room] acoustique f.

acoustic guitar n guitare f sèche.

ACPO ['ækpəʊ] (abbr of **Association of Chief Police Officers**) n syndicat d'officiers supérieurs de la police britannique.

acquaint [əˈkweɪnt] vt: **to ~ sb with sthg** mettre qqn au courant de qqch; **to be ~ed with sb** connaître qqn.

acquaintance [əˈkweɪntəns] n **-1.** [person] connaissance f. **-2.** [with person]: **to make sb's ~** faire la connaissance de qqn.

acquiesce [ˌækwɪˈes] vi: **to ~ (to OR in sthg)** donner son accord (à qqch).

acquiescence [ˌækwɪˈesns] n consentement m.

acquire [əˈkwaɪəʳ] vt acquérir.

acquired taste [əˈkwaɪəd-] n: **it's an ~** on finit par aimer ça.

acquisition [ˌækwɪˈzɪʃn] n acquisition f.

acquisitive [əˈkwɪzɪtɪv] adj avide de possessions.

acquit [əˈkwɪt] (pt & pp **-ted**, cont **-ting**) vt **-1.** JUR acquitter. **-2.** [perform]: **to ~ o.s. well/badly** bien/mal se comporter.

acquittal [əˈkwɪtl] n acquittement m.

acre ['eɪkəʳ] n = 4046,9 m², ≈ demi-hectare m.

acreage ['eɪkərɪdʒ] n superficie f, aire f.

acrid ['ækrɪd] adj [taste, smell] âcre; fig acerbe.

acrimonious [ˌækrɪˈməʊnjəs] adj acrimonieux(ieuse).

acrobat ['ækrəbæt] n acrobate mf.

acrobatic [ˌækrəˈbætɪk] adj acrobatique.
◆ **acrobatics** npl acrobatie f.

acronym ['ækrənɪm] n acronyme m.

across [əˈkrɒs] ◇ adv **-1.** [from one side to the other] en travers; **to run ~** traverser en courant. **-2.** [in measurements]: **the river is 2 km ~** la rivière mesure 2 km de large. **-3.** [in crossword]: **21 ~** 21 horizontalement. **-4.** phr: **to get sthg ~ (to sb)** faire comprendre qqch (à qqn).

◇ *prep* **-1.** [from one side to the other] d'un côté à l'autre de, en travers de; **to walk ~ the road** traverser la route; **to run ~ the road** traverser la route en courant; **there's a bridge ~ the river** il y a un pont sur la rivière. **-2.** [on the other side of] de l'autre côté de; **the house ~ the road** la maison d'en face.
◆ **across from** *prep* en face de.

across-the-board *adj* général(e).

acrylic [ə'krɪlɪk] ◇ *adj* acrylique. ◇ *n* acrylique *m*.

act [ækt] ◇ *n* **-1.** [action, deed] acte *m*; **to catch sb in the ~** prendre qqn sur le fait; **to catch sb in the ~ of doing sthg** surprendre qqn en train de faire qqch. **-2.** JUR loi *f*. **-3.** [of play, opera] acte *m*; [in cabaret etc] numéro *m*; *fig* [pretence]: **to put on an ~** jouer la comédie. **-4.** *phr*: **to get in on the ~** s'y mettre; **to get one's ~ together** se reprendre en main.
◇ *vi* **-1.** [gen] agir. **-2.** [behave] se comporter; **to ~ as if** se conduire comme si, se comporter comme si; **to ~ like** se conduire comme, se comporter comme. **-3.** [in play, film] jouer; *fig* [pretend] jouer la comédie. **-4.** [function]: **to ~ as** [person] être; [object] servir de; **to ~ for sb, to ~ on behalf of sb** représenter qqn.
◇ *vt* [part] jouer; **to ~ the fool** faire l'imbécile; **~ your age!** ce n'est plus de ton âge!
◆ **act out** *vt sep* **-1.** [feelings, thoughts] exprimer. **-2.** [event] mimer.
◆ **act up** *vi* fam faire des siennes.

ACT (*abbr of* **American College Test**) *n* examen américain de fin d'études secondaires.

acting ['æktɪŋ] ◇ *adj* par intérim, provisoire. ◇ *n* [in play, film] interprétation *f*.

action ['ækʃn] *n* **-1.** [gen] action *f*; **to take ~** agir, prendre des mesures; **to put sthg into ~** mettre qqch à exécution; **in ~** [person] en action; [machine] en marche; **out of ~** [person] hors de combat; [machine] hors service, hors d'usage; **to be killed in ~** mourir au combat. **-2.** JUR procès *m*, action *f*; **to bring an ~ against sb** intenter un procès à OR contre qqn, intenter une action contre qqn.

action group *n* groupe *m* de pression.

action replay *n* répétition *f* immédiate (au ralenti).

activate ['æktɪveɪt] *vt* mettre en marche.

active ['æktɪv] *adj* **-1.** [gen] actif(ive); [encouragement] vif (vive). **-2.** [volcano] en activité.

actively ['æktɪvlɪ] *adv* activement.

active service *n*: **to be killed on ~** mourir au champ d'honneur.

activist ['æktɪvɪst] *n* activiste *mf*.

activity [æk'tɪvətɪ] (*pl* **-ies**) *n* activité *f*.

act of God *n* catastrophe *f* naturelle.

actor ['æktər] *n* acteur *m*.

actress ['æktrɪs] *n* actrice *f*.

actual ['æktʃuəl] *adj* réel(elle); **the ~ ceremony starts at ten am** la cérémonie proprement dite commence à dix heures.

actuality [,æktʃʊ'ælətɪ] *n*: **in ~** en fait.

actually ['æktʃuəlɪ] *adv* **-1.** [really, in truth] vraiment. **-2.** [by the way] au fait.

actuary ['æktjuərɪ] (*pl* **-ies**) *n* actuaire *mf*.

actuate ['æktjueɪt] *vt* mettre en marche.

acuity [ə'kjuːətɪ] *n* acuité *f*.

acumen ['ækjumen] *n* flair *m*; **business ~** le sens des affaires.

acupuncture ['ækjupʌŋktʃər] *n* acuponcture *f*.

acute [ə'kjuːt] *adj* **-1.** [severe - pain, illness] aigu(ë); [- danger] sérieux(ieuse), grave. **-2.** [perceptive - person, mind] perspicace. **-3.** [keen - eyesight] perçant(e); [- hearing] fin(e); [- sense of smell] développé(e). **-4.** MATH: **~ angle** angle *m* aigu. **-5.** LING: **e ~** e accent aigu.

acute accent *n* accent *m* aigu.

acutely [ə'kjuːtlɪ] *adv* [extremely] extrêmement.

ad [æd] (*abbr of* **advertisement**) *n* inf [in newspaper] annonce *f*; [on TV] pub *f*.

AD (*abbr of* **Anno Domini**) ap. J.-C.

adage ['ædɪdʒ] *n* adage *m*.

adamant ['ædəmənt] *adj*: **to be ~** être inflexible.

Adam's apple ['ædəmz-] *n* pomme *f* d'Adam.

adapt [ə'dæpt] ◇ *vt* adapter. ◇ *vi*: **to ~ (to)** s'adapter (à).

adaptability [ə,dæptə'bɪlətɪ] *n* souplesse *f*.

adaptable [ə'dæptəbl] *adj* [person] souple.

adaptation [,ædæp'teɪʃn] *n* [of book, play] adaptation *f*.

adapter, adaptor [ə'dæptər] *n* [ELEC - for several devices] prise *f* multiple; [- for foreign plug] adaptateur *m*.

ADC *n* **-1.** *abbr of* **aide-de-camp**. **-2.** (*abbr of* **Aid to Dependent Children**) *aux États-Unis, aide pour enfants assistés*. **-3.** (*abbr of* **analogue-digital converter**) CAN *m*.

add [æd] *vt* **-1.** [gen]: **to ~ sthg (to)** ajouter qqch (à). **-2.** [numbers] additionner.
◆ **add in** *vt sep* ajouter.

◆ **add on** *vt sep*: **to ~ sthg on (to)** ajouter qqch (à); [charge, tax] rajouter qqch (à).

◆ **add to** *vt fus* ajouter à, augmenter.

◆ **add up** ◇ *vt sep* additionner. ◇ *vi inf* [make sense]: **it doesn't ~ up** c'est pas logique.

◆ **add up to** *vt fus* se monter à, s'élever à.

addendum [ə'dendəm] (*pl* **-da** [-də]) *n* addenda *m inv*.

adder ['ædə'] *n* vipère *f*.

addict [æ'dıkt] *n lit* & *fig* drogué *m*, -e *f*; **drug ~** drogué.

addicted [ə'dıktıd] *adj*: **~ (to)** drogué(e) (à); *fig* passionné(e) (de).

addiction [ə'dıkʃn] *n*: **~ (to)** dépendance *f* (à); *fig* penchant *m* (pour).

addictive [ə'dıktıv] *adj* qui rend dépendant(e).

Addis Ababa ['ædıs 'æbəbə] *n* Addis-Ababa, Addis-Abeba.

addition [ə'dıʃn] *n* addition *f*; **in ~ (to)** en plus (de).

additional [ə'dıʃənl] *adj* supplémentaire.

additive ['ædıtıv] *n* additif *m*.

addled ['ædld] *adj* **-1.** [egg] pourri(e). **-2.** [brain] embrouillé(e).

add-on COMPUT ◇ *adj* supplémentaire. ◇ *n* dispositif *m* supplémentaire.

address [ə'dres] ◇ *n* **-1.** [place] adresse *f*. **-2.** [speech] discours *m*. ◇ *vt* **-1.** [gen] adresser. **-2.** [meeting, conference] prendre la parole à. **-3.** [problem, issue] aborder, examiner; **to ~ o.s. to** s'attaquer à.

address book *n* carnet *m* d'adresses.

addressee [,ædre'si:] *n* destinataire *mf*.

Aden ['eıdn] *n* Aden.

adenoids ['ædınɔıdz] *npl* végétations *fpl*.

adept ['ædept] *adj*: **~ (at)** doué(e) (pour).

adequacy ['ædıkwəsı] *n* **-1.** [of amount] quantité *f* nécessaire. **-2.** [of person] compétence *f*.

adequate ['ædıkwət] *adj* adéquat(e).

adequately ['ædıkwətlı] *adv* **-1.** [sufficiently] suffisamment. **-2.** [well enough] de façon satisfaisante OR adéquate.

adhere [əd'hıə'] *vi* **-1.** [stick]: **to ~ (to)** adhérer (à). **-2.** [observe]: **to ~ to** obéir à. **-3.** [keep]: **to ~ to** adhérer à.

adherence [əd'hıərəns] *n*: **~ to** adhésion *f* à.

adhesive [əd'hi:sıv] ◇ *adj* adhésif(ive). ◇ *n* adhésif *m*.

adhesive tape *n* ruban *m* adhésif.

ad hoc [,æd'hɒk] *adj* ad hoc.

ad infinitum [,ædınfı'naıtəm] *adv* à l'infini.

adjacent [ə'dʒeısənt] *adj*: **~ (to)** adjacent(e) (à), contigu(ë) (à).

adjective ['ædʒıktıv] *n* adjectif *m*.

adjoin [ə'dʒɔın] *vt* être contigu(ë) à, toucher.

adjoining [ə'dʒɔınıŋ] ◇ *adj* voisin(e). ◇ *prep* attenant à.

adjourn [ə'dʒɜːn] ◇ *vt* ajourner. ◇ *vi* suspendre la séance.

adjournment [ə'dʒɜːnmənt] *n* ajournement *m*.

Adjt (*abbr of* **adjutant**) adjt.

adjudge [ə'dʒʌdʒ] *vt* déclarer.

adjudicate [ə'dʒuːdıkeıt] ◇ *vt* juger, décider. ◇ *vi*: **to ~ (on OR upon)** se prononcer (sur).

adjudication [ə,dʒuːdı'keıʃn] *n* jugement *m*.

adjunct ['ædʒʌŋkt] *n* complément *m*.

adjust [ə'dʒʌst] ◇ *vt* ajuster, régler. ◇ *vi*: **to ~ (to)** s'adapter (à).

adjustable [ə'dʒʌstəbl] *adj* réglable.

adjustable spanner *n* clé *f* universelle.

adjusted [ə'dʒʌstıd] *adj*: **to be well ~** être (bien) équilibré(e).

adjustment [ə'dʒʌstmənt] *n* **-1.** [modification] ajustement *m*; TECH réglage *m*; **to make an ~ to** apporter une modification à; TECH faire (un) réglage à. **-2.** [change in attitude]: **~ (to)** adaptation *f* (à).

adjutant ['ædʒʊtənt] *n* adjudant *m*.

ad lib [,æd'lıb] (*pt* & *pp* **ad-libbed**, *cont* **ad-libbing**) ◇ *adj* improvisé(e). ◇ *adv* à volonté. ◇ *n* improvisation *f*.

◆ **ad-lib** *vi* improviser.

adman ['ædmæn] (*pl* **-men** [-men]) *n* publicitaire *m*.

admin ['ædmın] (*abbr of* **administration**) *n Br inf* administration *f*.

administer [əd'mınıstə'] *vt* **-1.** [company, business] administrer, gérer. **-2.** [justice, punishment] dispenser. **-3.** [drug, medication] administrer.

administration [əd,mını'streıʃn] *n* administration *f*.

◆ **Administration** *n Am*: **the Administration** le gouvernement.

administrative [əd'mınıstrətıv] *adj* administratif(ive).

administrator [əd'mınıstreıtə'] *n* administrateur *m*, -trice *f*.

admirable ['ædmərəbl] *adj* admirable.

admirably ['ædmərəblı] *adv* admirablement.

admiral ['ædmərəl] *n* amiral *m*.

Admiralty [ˈædmərəltɪ] *n Br*: the ~ le ministère de la Marine.

admiration [ˌædməˈreɪʃn] *n* admiration *f*.

admire [ədˈmaɪəʳ] *vt* admirer.

admirer [ədˈmaɪərəʳ] *n* admirateur *m*, -trice *f*.

admiring [ədˈmaɪərɪŋ] *adj* admiratif(ive).

admiringly [ədˈmaɪərɪŋlɪ] *adv* avec admiration.

admissible [ədˈmɪsəbl] *adj* JUR recevable.

admission [ədˈmɪʃn] *n* -1. [permission to enter] admission *f*. -2. [to museum etc] entrée *f*. -3. [confession] confession *f*, aveu *m*; by his/her *etc* own ~ de son propre aveu.

admit [ədˈmɪt] (*pt & pp* -ted, *cont* -ting) ◇ *vt* -1. [confess] reconnaître; to ~ (that) ... reconnaître que ...; to ~ doing sthg reconnaître avoir fait qqch; to ~ defeat *fig* s'avouer vaincu(e). -2. [allow to enter, join] admettre; ~s two [on ticket] valable pour deux personnes; to be admitted to hospital *Br* OR to the hospital *Am* être admis(e) à l'hôpital. ◇ *vi*: to ~ to admettre, reconnaître.

admittance [ədˈmɪtəns] *n* admission *f*; to gain ~ to parvenir à, entrer dans; "no ~" «entrée interdite».

admittedly [ədˈmɪtɪdlɪ] *adv* de l'aveu général.

admixture [ædˈmɪkstʃəʳ] *n* mélange *m*.

admonish [ədˈmɒnɪʃ] *vt* réprimander.

ad nauseam [ˌædˈnɔːzɪæm] *adv* [talk] à n'en plus finir.

ado [əˈduː] *n*: without further OR more ~ sans plus de cérémonie.

adolescence [ˌædəˈlesns] *n* adolescence *f*.

adolescent [ˌædəˈlesnt] ◇ *adj* adolescent(e); *pej* puéril(e). ◇ *n* adolescent *m*, -e *f*.

adopt [əˈdɒpt] *vt* adopter.

adoption [əˈdɒpʃn] *n* adoption *f*.

adoptive [əˈdɒptɪv] *adj* adoptif(ive).

adorable [əˈdɔːrəbl] *adj* adorable.

adoration [ˌædəˈreɪʃn] *n* adoration *f*.

adore [əˈdɔːʳ] *vt* adorer.

adoring [əˈdɔːrɪŋ] *adj* [person] adorateur(trice); [look] d'adoration.

adorn [əˈdɔːn] *vt* orner.

adornment [əˈdɔːnmənt] *n* décoration *f*.

ADP (*abbr of* **automatic data processing**) *n* traitement automatique de données.

adrenalin [əˈdrenəlɪn] *n* adrénaline *f*.

Adriatic [eɪdrɪˈætɪk] *n*: the ~ (Sea) l'Adriatique *f*, la mer Adriatique.

adrift [əˈdrɪft] ◇ *adj* à la dérive. ◇ *adv*: to go ~ *fig* aller à la dérive.

adroit [əˈdrɔɪt] *adj* adroit(e).

ADT (*abbr of* **Atlantic Daylight Time**) *n* heure d'été de la côte est des États-Unis.

adulation [ˌædjuˈleɪʃn] *n* adulation *f*.

adult [ˈædʌlt] ◇ *adj* -1. [gen] adulte. -2. [films, literature] pour adultes. ◇ *n* adulte *mf*.

adult education *n* enseignement *m* pour adultes.

adulterate [əˈdʌltəreɪt] *vt* frelater.

adulteration [əˌdʌltəˈreɪʃn] *n* frelatage *m*.

adulterer [əˈdʌltərəʳ] *n* personne *f* adultère.

adultery [əˈdʌltərɪ] *n* adultère *m*.

adulthood [ˈædʌlthʊd] *n* âge *m* adulte.

advance [ədˈvɑːns] ◇ *n* -1. [gen] avance *f*. -2. [progress] progrès *m*. ◇ *comp* à l'avance. ◇ *vt* -1. [gen] avancer. -2. [improve] faire progresser OR avancer. ◇ *vi* -1. [gen] avancer. -2. [improve] progresser. ◆ **advances** *npl*: to make ~s to sb [sexual] faire des avances à qqn; [business] faire des propositions à qqn. ◆ **in advance** *adv* à l'avance. ◆ **in advance of** *prep* -1. [in front of] en avance sur. -2. [prior to] en avance de, avant.

advanced [ədˈvɑːnst] *adj* avancé(e); ~ in years *euphemism* d'un âge avancé.

advancement [ədˈvɑːnsmənt] *n* -1. [promotion] avancement *m*. -2. [progress] progrès *m*.

advantage [ədˈvɑːntɪdʒ] *n*: ~ (over) avantage *m* (sur); to be to one's ~ être à son avantage; to take ~ of sthg profiter de qqch; to take ~ of sb exploiter qqn.

advantageous [ˌædvənˈteɪdʒəs] *adj* avantageux(euse).

advent [ˈædvənt] *n* avènement *m*. ◆ **Advent** *n* RELIG Avent *m*.

Advent calendar *n* calendrier *m* de l'Avent.

adventure [ədˈventʃəʳ] *n* aventure *f*.

adventure holiday *n* vacances organisées avec des activités sportives.

adventure playground *n* terrain *m* d'aventures.

adventurer [ədˈventʃərəʳ] *n* aventurier *m*, -ière *f*.

adventurous [ədˈventʃərəs] *adj* aventureux(euse).

adverb [ˈædvɜːb] *n* adverbe *m*.

adversary [ˈædvəsərɪ] (*pl* -ies) *n* adversaire *mf*.

adverse [ˈædvɜːs] *adj* défavorable.

adversely [ˈædvɜːslɪ] *adv* de façon défavorable.

adversity [əd'vɜːsəti] *n* adversité *f*.

advert [əd'vɜːt] *Br* = **advertisement**.

advertise ['ædvətaɪz] ◇ *vt* COMM faire de la publicité pour; [event] annoncer. ◇ *vi* faire de la publicité; **to ~ for sb/sthg** chercher qqn/qqch par voie d'annonce.

advertisement [əd'vɜːtɪsmənt] *n* [in newspaper] annonce *f*; COMM & *fig* publicité *f*.

advertiser ['ædvətaɪzər] *n* annonceur *m*.

advertising ['ædvətaɪzɪŋ] *n* (*U*) publicité *f*.

advertising agency *n* agence *f* de publicité.

advertising campaign *n* campagne *f* de publicité.

advice [əd'vaɪs] *n* (*U*) conseils *mpl*; **a piece of ~** un conseil; **to give sb ~** donner des conseils à qqn; **to take sb's ~** suivre les conseils de qqn.

advice note *n* avis *m*.

advisability [əd,vaɪzə'bɪləti] *n* bien-fondé *m*.

advisable [əd'vaɪzəbl] *adj* conseillé(e), recommandé(e).

advise [əd'vaɪz] ◇ *vt* **-1.** [give advice to]: **to ~ sb to do sthg** conseiller à qqn de faire qqch; **to ~ sb against sthg** déconseiller qqch à qqn; **to ~ sb against doing sthg** déconseiller à qqn de faire qqch. **-2.** [professionally]: **to ~ sb on sthg** conseiller qqn sur qqch. **-3.** [inform]: **to ~ sb (of sthg)** aviser qqn (de qqch). ◇ *vi* **-1.** [give advice]: **to ~ against sthg/against doing sthg** déconseiller qqch/de faire qqch. **-2.** [professionally]: **to ~ on sthg** conseiller sur qqch.

advisedly [əd'vaɪzɪdlɪ] *adv* en connaissance de cause, délibérément.

adviser *Br*, **advisor** *Am* [əd'vaɪzər] *n* conseiller *m*, -ère *f*.

advisory [əd'vaɪzəri] *adj* consultatif(ive); **in an ~ capacity** OR **role** à titre consultatif.

advocacy ['ædvəkəsi] *n* plaidoyer *m*.

advocate [*n* 'ædvəkət, *vb* 'ædvəkeɪt] ◇ *n* **-1.** JUR avocat *m*, -e *f*. **-2.** [supporter] partisan *m*. ◇ *vt* préconiser, recommander.

advt. *abbr of* **advertisement**.

AEA (*abbr of* **Atomic Energy Authority**) *n* *commission britannique à l'énergie nucléaire*, ≃ CEA *f*.

AEC (*abbr of* **Atomic Energy Commission**) *n* *commission américaine à l'énergie nucléaire*, ≃ CEA *f*.

AEEU (*abbr of* **Amalgamated Engineering and Electrical Union**) *n* *syndicat britannique d'ingénieurs et d'électriciens*.

Aegean [iː'dʒiːən] *n*: **the ~ (Sea)** la mer Égée.

aegis ['iːdʒɪs] *n*: **under the ~ of** sous l'égide de.

Aeolian Islands [iː'əʊljən-] *npl*: **the ~** les îles *fpl* Éoliennes.

aeon *Br*, **eon** *Am* ['iːən] *n* *fig* éternité *f*.

aerial ['eəriəl] ◇ *adj* aérien(ienne). ◇ *n* *Br* antenne *f*.

aerobatics [,eərəʊ'bætɪks] *n* (*U*) acrobatie *f* aérienne.

aerobics [eə'rəʊbɪks] *n* (*U*) aérobic *m*.

aerodrome ['eərədrəʊm] *n* aérodrome *m*.

aerodynamic [,eərəʊdaɪ'næmɪk] *adj* aérodynamique.

◆ **aerodynamics** ◇ *n* (*U*) aérodynamique *f*. ◇ *npl* [aerodynamic qualities] aérodynamisme *m*.

aerogramme ['eərəgræm] *n* aérogramme *m*.

aeronautics [,eərə'nɔːtɪks] *n* (*U*) aéronautique *f*.

aeroplane ['eərəpleɪn] *n* *Br* avion *m*.

aerosol ['eərəsɒl] *n* aérosol *m*.

aerospace ['eərəʊspeɪs] *n*: **the ~ industry** l'industrie *f* aérospatiale.

aesthete, **esthete** *Am* ['iːsθiːt] *n* esthète *mf*.

aesthetic, **esthetic** *Am* [iːs'θetɪk] *adj* esthétique.

aesthetically, **esthetically** *Am* [iːs'θetɪklɪ] *adv* esthétiquement.

aesthetics, **esthetics** *Am* [iːs'θetɪks] *n* (*U*) esthétique *f*.

afar [ə'fɑːr] *adv*: **from ~** de loin.

AFB (*abbr of* **Air Force Base**) *n* *Am* base de l'armée de l'air.

AFDC (*abbr of* **Aid to Families with Dependent Children**) *n* *aux États-Unis, aide pour les familles d'enfants assistés*.

affable ['æfəbl] *adj* affable.

affair [ə'feər] *n* **-1.** [gen] affaire *f*. **-2.** [extramarital relationship] liaison *f*.

◆ **affairs** *npl* affaires *fpl*.

affect [ə'fekt] *vt* **-1.** [influence] avoir un effet OR des conséquences sur. **-2.** [emotionally] affecter, émouvoir. **-3.** [put on] affecter.

affectation [,æfek'teɪʃn] *n* affectation *f*.

affected [ə'fektɪd] *adj* affecté(e).

affection [ə'fekʃn] *n* affection *f*.

affectionate [ə'fekʃnət] *adj* affectueux(euse).

affectionately [ə'fekʃnətlɪ] *adv* affectueusement.

affidavit [,æfɪ'deɪvɪt] *n* déclaration écrite sous serment.

affiliate [n ə'fɪlɪət, vb ə'fɪlɪeɪt] ◇ n affilié m, -e f. ◇ vt: **to be ~d to** OR **with** être affilié(e) à.

affiliation [ə‚fɪlɪ'eɪʃn] n affiliation f.

affinity [ə'fɪnətɪ] (pl **-ies**) n affinité f; **to have an ~ with sb** avoir des affinités avec qqn.

affirm [ə'fɜːm] vt **-1.** [declare] affirmer. **-2.** [confirm] confirmer.

affirmation [‚æfə'meɪʃn] n **-1.** [declaration] affirmation f. **-2.** [confirmation] confirmation f.

affirmative [ə'fɜːmətɪv] ◇ adj affirmatif(ive). ◇ n: **in the ~** par l'affirmative.

affix [ə'fɪks] vt [stamp] coller.

afflict [ə'flɪkt] vt affliger; **to be ~ed with** souffrir de.

affliction [ə'flɪkʃn] n affliction f.

affluence ['æfluəns] n prospérité f.

affluent ['æfluənt] adj riche.

affluent society n société f d'abondance.

afford [ə'fɔːd] vt **-1.** [buy, pay for]: **to be able to ~ sthg** avoir les moyens d'acheter qqch. **-2.** [spare]: **to be able to ~ the time (to do sthg)** avoir le temps (de faire qqch). **-3.** [harmful, embarrassing thing]: **to be able to ~ sthg** pouvoir se permettre qqch. **-4.** [provide, give] procurer.

affordable [ə'fɔːdəbl] adj que l'on peut se permettre.

afforestation [æ‚fɒrɪ'steɪʃn] n boisement m.

affray [ə'freɪ] n Br bagarre f.

affront [ə'frʌnt] ◇ n affront m, insulte f. ◇ vt insulter, faire un affront à.

Afghan ['æfgæn], **Afghani** [æf'gænɪ] ◇ adj afghan(e). ◇ n Afghan m, -e f.

Afghan hound n lévrier m afghan.

Afghani = **Afghan**.

Afghanistan [æf'gænɪstæn] n Afghanistan m; **in ~** en Afghanistan.

afield [ə'fiːld] adv: **far ~** loin.

AFL-CIO (abbr of **American Federation of Labor and Congress of Industrial Organizations**) n confédération syndicale américaine.

afloat [ə'fləʊt] adj lit & fig à flot.

afoot [ə'fʊt] adj en préparation.

aforementioned [ə‚fɔː'menʃənd], **aforesaid** [ə'fɔːsed] adj susmentionné(e).

afraid [ə'freɪd] adj **-1.** [frightened]: **to be ~ (of)** avoir peur (de); **to be ~ of doing** OR **to do sthg** avoir peur de faire qqch. **-2.** [reluctant, apprehensive]: **to be ~ of** craindre. **-3.** [in apologies]: **to be ~ (that)** ... regretter que ...; **I'm ~ so/not** j'ai bien peur que oui/non.

afresh [ə'freʃ] adv de nouveau.

Africa ['æfrɪkə] n Afrique f; **in ~** en Afrique.

African ['æfrɪkən] ◇ adj africain(e). ◇ n Africain m, -e f.

African American n Noir américain m, Noire américaine f.

Afrikaans [‚æfrɪ'kɑːns] n afrikaans m.

Afrikaner [‚æfrɪ'kɑːnəʳ] n Afrikaner mf.

aft [ɑːft] adv sur OR à l'arrière.

AFT (abbr of **American Federation of Teachers**) n syndicat américain d'enseignants.

after ['ɑːftəʳ] ◇ prep **-1.** [gen] après; **~ you!** après vous!; **to shout ~ sb** crier à qqn; **to be ~ sb/sthg** inf [in search of] chercher qqn/qqch; **to name sb ~ sb** Br donner à qqn le nom de qqn. **-2.** Am [telling the time]: **it's twenty ~ three** il est trois heures vingt. ◇ adv après. ◇ conj après que.
♦ **afters** npl Br inf dessert m.
♦ **after all** adv après tout.

afterbirth ['ɑːftəbɜːθ] n placenta m.

aftercare ['ɑːftəkeəʳ] n postcure f.

aftereffects ['ɑːftərɪ‚fekts] npl suites fpl, répercussions fpl.

afterlife ['ɑːftəlaɪf] (pl **-lives** [-laɪvz]) n vie f future.

aftermath ['ɑːftəmæθ] n conséquences fpl, suites fpl.

afternoon [‚ɑːftə'nuːn] n après-midi m inv; **in the ~** l'après-midi; **good ~** bonjour.
♦ **afternoons** adv l'après-midi.

aftershave ['ɑːftəʃeɪv] n après-rasage m.

aftershock ['ɑːftəʃɒk] n réplique f.

aftertaste ['ɑːftəteɪst] n lit & fig arrière-goût m.

afterthought ['ɑːftəθɔːt] n pensée f OR réflexion f après coup.

afterward(s) ['ɑːftəwəd(z)] adv après.

again [ə'gen] adv encore une fois, de nouveau; **to do ~** refaire; **to say ~** répéter; **to start ~** recommencer; **~ and ~** à plusieurs reprises; **all over ~** une fois de plus; **time and ~** maintes et maintes fois; **half as much ~** à moitié autant; **(twice) as much ~** deux fois autant; **come ~?** inf comment?, pardon?; **then** OR **there ~** d'autre part.

against [ə'genst] prep & adv contre; **(as) ~** contre.

age [eɪdʒ] (cont **ageing** OR **aging**) ◇ n **-1.** [gen] âge m; **she's 20 years of ~** elle a 20 ans; **what ~ are you?** quel âge avez-vous?; **to be of ~** Am avoir l'âge légal pour consommer de l'alcool dans un lieu public; **to be under ~** être mineur; **to come of ~** atteindre sa majorité. **-2.** [old age] vieillesse f. **-3.** [in history] époque f. ◇ vt & vi vieillir.

◆ **ages** *npl*: ~**s ago** il y a une éternité; **I haven't seen him for** ~**s** je ne l'ai pas vu depuis une éternité.

aged [*adj sense 1* eɪdʒd, *adj sense 2 & npl* 'eɪdʒɪd] ◇ *adj* **-1.** [of stated age]: ~ **15** âgé(e) de 15 ans. **-2.** [very old] âgé(e), vieux (vieille). ◇ *npl*: **the** ~ les personnes *fpl* âgées.

age group *n* tranche *f* d'âge.

ageing ['eɪdʒɪŋ] ◇ *adj* vieillissant(e). ◇ *n* vieillissement *m*.

ageless ['eɪdʒlɪs] *adj* sans âge.

agency ['eɪdʒənsɪ] (*pl* **-ies**) *n* **-1.** [business] agence *f*; **employment** ~ agence OR bureau *m* de placement; **travel** ~ agence de voyages. **-2.** [organization] organisme *m*.

agenda [ə'dʒendə] (*pl* **-s**) *n* ordre *m* du jour.

agent ['eɪdʒənt] *n* agent *m*.

age-old *adj* antique.

aggravate ['ægrəveɪt] *vt* **-1.** [make worse] aggraver. **-2.** [annoy] agacer.

aggravating ['ægrəveɪtɪŋ] *adj* [annoying] agaçant(e).

aggravation [,ægrə'veɪʃn] *n* **-1.** (*U*) [trouble] agacements *mpl*. **-2.** [annoying thing] agacement *m*.

aggregate ['ægrɪgət] ◇ *adj* total(e). ◇ *n* **-1.** [total] total *m*. **-2.** [material] agrégat *m*.

aggression [ə'greʃn] *n* agression *f*.

aggressive [ə'gresɪv] *adj* agressif(ive).

aggressively [ə'gresɪvlɪ] *adv* d'une manière agressive.

aggressor [ə'gresər] *n* agresseur *m*.

aggrieved [ə'griːvd] *adj* blessé(e), froissé(e).

aggro ['ægrəʊ] *n Br inf* enquiquinement *m*.

aghast [ə'gɑːst] *adj*: ~ **(at sthg)** atterré(e) (par qqch).

agile [*Br* 'ædʒaɪl, *Am* 'ædʒəl] *adj* agile.

agility [ə'dʒɪlətɪ] *n* agilité *f*.

aging ['eɪdʒɪŋ] = **ageing**.

agitate ['ædʒɪteɪt] ◇ *vt* **-1.** [disturb] inquiéter. **-2.** [shake] agiter. ◇ *vi*: **to** ~ **for/against** faire campagne pour/contre.

agitated ['ædʒɪteɪtɪd] *adj* agité(e).

agitation [,ædʒɪ'teɪʃn] *n* **-1.** [anxiety] agitation *f*. **-2.** POL campagne *f*.

agitator ['ædʒɪteɪtər] *n* agitateur *m*, -trice *f*.

AGM (*abbr of* **annual general meeting**) *n Br* AGA *f*.

agnostic [æg'nɒstɪk] ◇ *adj* agnostique. ◇ *n* agnostique *mf*.

ago [ə'gəʊ] *adv*: **a long time** ~ il y a longtemps; **three days** ~ il y a trois jours.

agog [ə'gɒg] *adj*: **to be** ~ **(with)** être en ébullition (à propos de).

agonize, -ise ['ægənaɪz] *vi*: **to** ~ **over** OR **about sthg** se tourmenter au sujet de qqch.

agonized ['ægənaɪzd] *adj* atroce.

agonizing ['ægənaɪzɪŋ] *adj* déchirant(e).

agonizingly ['ægənaɪzɪŋlɪ] *adv* [difficult etc] extrêmement.

agony ['ægənɪ] (*pl* **-ies**) *n* **-1.** [physical pain] douleur *f* atroce; **to be in** ~ souffrir le martyre. **-2.** [mental pain] angoisse *f*; **to be in** ~ être angoissé, être rempli d'angoisse.

agony aunt *n Br inf* personne qui tient la rubrique du courrier du cœur.

agony column *n Br inf* courrier *m* du cœur.

agoraphobia [,ægərə'fəʊbjə] *n* agoraphobie *f*.

agree [ə'griː] ◇ *vi* **-1.** [concur]: **to** ~ **(with/about)** être d'accord (avec/au sujet de); **to** ~ **on** [price, terms] convenir de. **-2.** [consent]: **to** ~ **(to sthg)** donner son consentement (à qqch). **-3.** [be consistent] concorder. **-4.** [food]: **to** ~ **with** être bon (bonne) pour, réussir à. **-5.** GRAMM: **to** ~ **(with)** s'accorder (avec). ◇ *vt* **-1.** [price, conditions] accepter, convenir de. **-2.** [concur, concede]: **to** ~ **(that)** ... admettre que .... **-3.** [arrange]: **to** ~ **to do sthg** se mettre d'accord pour faire qqch.

agreeable [ə'grɪəbl] *adj* **-1.** [pleasant] agréable. **-2.** [willing]: **to be** ~ **to** consentir à.

agreeably [ə'grɪəblɪ] *adv* agréablement.

agreed [ə'griːd] *adj*: **to be** ~ **(on sthg)** être d'accord (à propos de qqch).

agreement [ə'griːmənt] *n* **-1.** [gen] accord *m*; **to be in** ~ **(with)** être d'accord (avec); **to reach an** ~ parvenir à un accord. **-2.** [consistency] concordance *f*.

agricultural [,ægrɪ'kʌltʃərəl] *adj* agricole.

agriculture ['ægrɪkʌltʃər] *n* agriculture *f*.

aground [ə'graʊnd] *adv*: **to run** ~ s'échouer.

ah [ɑː] *excl* ah!

aha [ɑː'hɑː] *excl* ah, ah!

ahead [ə'hed] *adv* **-1.** [in front] devant, en avant; **to go/be sent on** ~ partir/être envoyé en avant; **right** ~, **straight** ~ droit devant. **-2.** [in better position] en avance; **Scotland are** ~ **by two goals to one** l'Écosse mène par deux à un; **to get** ~ [be successful] réussir. **-3.** [in time] à l'avance; **the months** ~ les mois à venir.

◆ **ahead of** *prep* **-1.** [in front of] devant. **-2.** [in time] avant; ~ **of schedule** [work] en avance sur le planning; ~ **of time** en avance.

ahoy [ə'hɔɪ] *excl* NAUT ohé!; **ship** ~! ohé du bateau!

AI *n* **-1.** (*abbr of* **Amnesty International**) AI *m.* **-2.** (*abbr of* **artificial intelligence**) IA *f.* **-3.** *abbr of* **artificial insemination**.

AIB (*abbr of* **Accident Investigation Bureau**) *n* commission d'enquête sur les accidents en Grande-Bretagne.

aid [eɪd] ◇ *n* aide *f*; **with the** ~ **of** [person] avec l'aide de; [thing] à l'aide de; **to go to sb's** ~ aller à l'aide de qqn; **in** ~ **of** au profit de. ◇ *vt* **-1.** [help] aider. **-2.** JUR: **to** ~ **and abet** être complice de.

AID *n* **-1.** (*abbr of* **artificial insemination by donor**) IAD *f.* **-2.** (*abbr of* **Agency for International Development**) AID *f.*

aide [eɪd] *n* POL aide *mf*.

aide-de-camp [ˌeɪddə'kɑ̃ː] (*pl* **aides-de-camp** [ˌeɪdz-]) *n* aide *m* de camp.

AIDS, Aids [eɪdz] (*abbr of* **acquired immune deficiency syndrome**) ◇ *n* SIDA *m,* Sida *m.* ◇ *comp*: ~ **specialist** sidologue *mf*; ~ **patient** sidéen *m,* -enne *f.*

AIH (*abbr of* **artificial insemination by husband**) *n* IAC *f.*

ail [eɪl] *vi* souffrir.

ailing ['eɪlɪŋ] *adj* **-1.** [ill] souffrant(e). **-2.** *fig* [economy, industry] dans une mauvaise passe.

ailment ['eɪlmənt] *n* maladie *f.*

aim [eɪm] ◇ *n* **-1.** [objective] but *m,* objectif *m.* **-2.** [in firing gun, arrow]: **to take** ~ **at** viser. ◇ *vt* **-1.** [gun, camera]: **to** ~ **sthg at** braquer qqch sur. **-2.** *fig*: **to be** ~**ed at** [plan, campaign etc] être destiné(e) à, viser; [criticism] être dirigé(e) contre. ◇ *vi*: **to** ~ **(at)** viser; **to** ~ **at** OR **for** *fig* viser; **to** ~ **to do sthg** viser à faire qqch.

aimless ['eɪmlɪs] *adj* [person] désœuvré(e); [life] sans but.

aimlessly ['eɪmlɪslɪ] *adv* sans but.

ain't [eɪnt] *inf* = **am not, are not, is not, have not, has not**.

air [eər] ◇ *n* **-1.** [gen] air *m*; **to throw sthg into the** ~ jeter qqch en l'air; **by** ~ [travel] par avion; **to be (up) in the** ~ *fig* [plans] être vague; **to clear the** ~ *fig* dissiper les malentendus. **-2.** RADIO & TV: **on the** ~ à l'antenne. ◇ *comp* [transport] aérien(ienne). ◇ *vt* **-1.** [gen] aérer. **-2.** [make publicly known] faire connaître OR communiquer. **-3.** [broadcast] diffuser. ◇ *vi* sécher.

◆ **airs** *npl*: ~**s and graces** manières *fpl*; **to give o.s.** ~**s**, **to put on** ~**s** prendre de grands airs.

airbag ['eəbæg] *n* AUT coussin *m* pneumatique (de sécurité).

airbase ['eəbeɪs] *n* base *f* aérienne.

airbed ['eəbed] *n* Br matelas *m* pneumatique.

airborne ['eəbɔːn] *adj* **-1.** [troops etc] aéroporté(e); [seeds] emporté(e) par le vent. **-2.** [plane] qui a décollé.

airbrake ['eəbreɪk] *n* frein *m* à air comprimé.

airbus ['eəbʌs] *n* airbus *m.*

air-conditioned [-kən'dɪʃnd] *adj* climatisé(e), à air conditionné.

air-conditioning [-kən'dɪʃnɪŋ] *n* climatisation *f.*

aircraft ['eəkrɑːft] (*pl inv*) *n* avion *m.*

aircraft carrier *n* porte-avions *m inv.*

air cushion *n* coussin *m* pneumatique OR gonflable.

airfield ['eəfiːld] *n* terrain *m* d'aviation.

airforce ['eəfɔːs] ◇ *n* armée *f* de l'air. ◇ *comp* aérien(ienne).

air freight *n* fret *m* aérien.

airgun ['eəgʌn] *n* carabine *f* OR fusil *m* à air comprimé.

airhostess ['eəˌhəʊstɪs] *n* hôtesse *f* de l'air.

airily ['eərəlɪ] *adv* à la légère.

airing ['eərɪŋ] *n*: **to give sthg an** ~ aérer qqch; *fig* [opinions] exposer qqch.

airing cupboard *n* Br placard *m* séchoir.

airkiss ['eəkɪs] *vi* se faire la bise sans se toucher.

airlane ['eəleɪn] *n* couloir *m* aérien.

airless ['eəlɪs] *adj* [room] qui sent le renfermé.

airletter ['eəletər] *n* lettre *f* par avion.

airlift ['eəlɪft] ◇ *n* pont *m* aérien. ◇ *vt* transporter par pont aérien.

airline ['eəlaɪn] *n* compagnie *f* aérienne.

airliner ['eəlaɪnər] *n* [short-distance] (avion *m*) moyen-courrier *m*; [long-distance] (avion) long-courrier *m.*

airlock ['eəlɒk] *n* **-1.** [in tube, pipe] poche *f* d'air. **-2.** [airtight chamber] sas *m.*

airmail ['eəmeɪl] *n* poste *f* aérienne; **by** ~ par avion.

airman ['eəmən] (*pl* **-men** [-mən]) *n* [aviator] aviateur *m.*

air mattress *n* matelas *m* pneumatique.

airplane ['eəpleɪn] *n* Am avion *m.*

airplay ['eəpleɪ] *n* RADIO: **to get a lot of** ~ passer beaucoup à la radio.

airpocket ['eəpɒkɪt] *n* trou *m* d'air.

airport ['eəpɔːt] ◇ *n* aéroport *m.* ◇ *comp* de l'aéroport.

air raid n raid m aérien, attaque f aérienne.

air-raid shelter n abri m antiaérien.

air rifle n carabine f à air comprimé.

airship ['eəʃɪp] n (ballon m) dirigeable m.

airsick ['eəsɪk] adj: **to be ~** avoir le mal de l'air.

airspace ['eəspeɪs] n espace m aérien.

airspeed ['eəspiːd] n vitesse f vraie (d'un avion).

air steward n steward m.

air stewardess n hôtesse f de l'air.

airstrip ['eəstrɪp] n piste f.

air terminal n aérogare f.

airtight ['eətaɪt] adj hermétique.

airtime ['eətaɪm] n temps m d'antenne.

air-to-air adj [missile, rocket] air-air (inv).

air-traffic control n contrôle m du trafic (aérien).

air-traffic controller n aiguilleur m (du ciel).

air travel n déplacement m OR voyage m par avion.

airwaves ['eəweɪvz] npl ondes fpl (hertziennes).

airy ['eərɪ] (compar **-ier**, superl **-iest**) adj **-1.** [room] aéré(e). **-2.** [notions, promises] chimérique. **-3.** [nonchalant] nonchalant(e).

aisle [aɪl] n allée f; [in plane] couloir m.

ajar [ə'dʒɑːr] adj entrouvert(e).

AK abbr of **Alaska**.

aka (abbr of **also known as**) alias.

akin [ə'kɪn] adj: **to be ~ to** être semblable à.

AL abbr of **Alabama**.

Alabama [,ælə'bæmə] n Alabama m; **in ~** dans l'Alabama.

alabaster [,ælə'bɑːstər] n albâtre m.

alacrity [ə'lækrətɪ] n empressement m.

alarm [ə'lɑːm] ◇ n **-1.** [fear] alarme f, inquiétude f. **-2.** [device] alarme f; **fire ~** sirène f d'incendie; **to raise** OR **sound the ~** donner OR sonner l'alarme. ◇ vt alarmer, alerter.

alarm clock n réveil m, réveille-matin m inv.

alarming [ə'lɑːmɪŋ] adj alarmant(e), inquiétant(e).

alarmingly [ə'lɑːmɪŋlɪ] adv d'une manière alarmante OR inquiétante.

alarmist [ə'lɑːmɪst] adj alarmiste.

alas [ə'læs] excl hélas!

Alaska [ə'læskə] n Alaska m; **in ~** en Alaska.

Albania [æl'beɪnjə] n Albanie f; **in ~** en Albanie.

Albanian [æl'beɪnjən] ◇ adj albanais(e). ◇ n **-1.** [person] Albanais m, -e f. **-2.** [language] albanais m.

albatross ['ælbətrɒs] (pl inv OR **-es**) n albatros m.

albeit [ɔːl'biːɪt] conj bien que (+ subjunctive).

Alberta [æl'bɜːtə] n Alberta f.

Albert Hall ['ælbət-] n: **the ~** salle de concert à Londres.

THE ALBERT HALL:
Grande salle londonienne accueillant concerts et manifestations diverses, y compris sportives; elle a été nommée en l'honneur du prince Albert, époux de la reine Victoria

---

albino [æl'biːnəʊ] (pl **-s**) ◇ n albinos mf. ◇ comp albinos (inv).

album ['ælbəm] n album m.

albumen ['ælbjʊmɪn] n [of egg] albumen m.

alchemy ['ælkəmɪ] n alchimie f.

alcohol ['ælkəhɒl] n alcool m.

alcoholic [,ælkə'hɒlɪk] ◇ adj [person] alcoolique; [drink] alcoolisé(e). ◇ n alcoolique mf.

alcoholism ['ælkəhɒlɪzm] n alcoolisme m.

alcopop ['ælkəʊpɒp] n boisson gazeuse faiblement alcoolisée.

alcove ['ælkəʊv] n alcôve f.

alderman ['ɔːldəmən] (pl **-men** [-mən]) n conseiller m municipal.

ale [eɪl] n bière f.

alert [ə'lɜːt] ◇ adj **-1.** [vigilant] vigilant(e). **-2.** [perceptive] vif (vive), éveillé(e). **-3.** [aware]: **to be ~ to** être conscient(e) de. ◇ n [warning] alerte f; **on the ~** [watchful] sur le qui-vive; MIL en état d'alerte. ◇ vt alerter; **to ~ sb to sthg** avertir qqn de qqch.

Aleutian Islands [ə'luːʃən-] npl: **the ~** les îles fpl Aléoutiennes.

A-level (abbr of **Advanced level**) n examen de fin d'études secondaires en Grande-Bretagne.

A-LEVEL:
Cet examen, qui ouvre l'accès aux études supérieures en Grande-Bretagne, est beaucoup plus spécialisé que le baccalauréat français; il ne comprend que deux ou trois matières (exceptionnellement quatre). D'autre part, les mentions sont très importantes pour pouvoir choisir l'université où l'on souhaite faire ses études

Alexandria [ˌælɪg'zɑːndrɪə] *n* Alexandrie.

alfalfa [æl'fælfə] *n* luzerne *f*.

alfresco [æl'freskəʊ] *adj & adv* en plein air.

algae ['ældʒiː] *npl* algues *fpl*.

Algarve [æl'gɑːv] *n*: the ~ l'Algarve *f*.

algebra ['ældʒɪbrə] *n* algèbre *f*.

Algeria [æl'dʒɪərɪə] *n* Algérie *f*; **in** ~ en Algérie.

Algerian [æl'dʒɪərɪən] ◇ *adj* algérien(ienne). ◇ *n* Algérien *m*, -ienne *f*.

Algiers [æl'dʒɪəz] *n* Alger.

algorithm ['ælgərɪðm] *n* algorithme *m*.

alias ['eɪlɪəs] (*pl* **-es**) ◇ *adv* alias. ◇ *n* faux nom *m*, nom d'emprunt.

alibi ['ælɪbaɪ] *n* alibi *m*.

alien ['eɪljən] ◇ *adj* **-1.** [gen] étranger(ère). **-2.** [from outer space] extraterrestre. ◇ *n* **-1.** [from outer space] extraterrestre *mf*. **-2.** JUR [foreigner] étranger *m*, -ère *f*.

alienate ['eɪljəneɪt] *vt* aliéner.

alienation [ˌeɪljə'neɪʃn] *n* PSYCH aliénation *f*.

alight [ə'laɪt] (*pt & pp* **-ed** OR **alit**) ◇ *adj* allumé(e), en feu. ◇ *vi* **-1.** [bird etc] se poser. **-2.** [from bus, train]: **to** ~ **from** descendre de.

align [ə'laɪn] *vt* **-1.** [line up] aligner. **-2.** [ally]: **to** ~ **o.s. with sb** s'aligner sur qqn.

alignment [ə'laɪnmənt] *n* alignement *m*.

alike [ə'laɪk] ◇ *adj* semblable. ◇ *adv* de la même façon; **to look** ~ se ressembler.

alimentary canal [ˌælɪ'mentərɪ-] *n* tube *m* digestif.

alimony ['ælɪmənɪ] *n* pension *f* alimentaire.

A-line *adj* trapèze (*inv*).

alit [ə'lɪt] *pt & pp* → **alight**.

alive [ə'laɪv] *adj* **-1.** [living] vivant(e), en vie. **-2.** [practice, tradition] vivace; **to keep** ~ préserver. **-3.** [lively] plein(e) de vitalité; **to come** ~ [story, description] prendre vie; [person, place] s'animer. **-4.** [aware]: **to be** ~ **to sthg** être conscient(e) de qqch. **-5.** [full of]: **to be** ~ **with sthg** grouiller de, pulluler de.

alkali ['ælkəlaɪ] (*pl* **-s** OR **-es**) *n* alcali *m*.

alkaline ['ælkəlaɪn] *adj* alcalin(e).

all [ɔːl] ◇ *adj* **-1.** (*with sg noun*) tout (toute); ~ **day/night/evening** toute la journée/la nuit/la soirée; ~ **the drink** toute la boisson; ~ **the time** tout le temps. **-2.** (*with pl noun*) tous (toutes); ~ **the boxes** toutes les boîtes; ~ **men** tous les hommes; ~ **three died** ils sont morts tous les trois, tous les trois sont morts.

◇ *pron* **-1.** (*sg*) [the whole amount] tout *m*; **she drank it** ~, **she drank** ~ **of it** elle a tout bu. **-2.** (*pl*) [everybody, everything] tous (toutes); ~ **of them came, they** ~ **came** ils sont tous venus. **-3.** (*with superl*): ... **of** ~ ... de tous (toutes); **I like this one best of** ~ je préfère celui-ci entre tous; **hers was the best/worst essay of** ~ sa dissertation était la meilleure/la pire de toutes. **-4. above** ~ → **above**; **after** ~ → **after**; **at** ~ → **at**.

◇ *adv* **-1.** [entirely] complètement; **I'd forgotten** ~ **about that** j'avais complètement oublié cela; ~ **alone** tout seul (toute seule); **that's** ~ **very well, but** ... tout cela est bien beau, mais .... **-2.** [in sport, competitions]: **the score is five** ~ le score est cinq partout. **-3.** (*with compar*): **to run** ~ **the faster** courir d'autant plus vite; ~ **the better** d'autant mieux.

◆ **all but** *adv* presque, pratiquement.

◆ **all in all** *adv* dans l'ensemble.

◆ **all that** *adv* **si** ... **que ça**; **it's not** ~ **that interesting** ce n'est pas si intéressant que ça.

◆ **for all** ◇ *prep* malgré; **for** ~ **his money** ... malgré tout son argent .... ◇ *conj*: **for** ~ **I know** pour autant que je sache.

◆ **in all** *adv* en tout.

Allah ['ælə] *n* Allah *m*.

all-around *Am* = **all-round**.

allay [ə'leɪ] *vt* [fears, anger] apaiser, calmer; [doubts] dissiper.

all clear *n* signal *m* de fin d'alerte; *fig* feu *m* vert.

allegation [ˌælɪ'geɪʃn] *n* allégation *f*; **to make** ~**s (about)** faire des allégations (sur).

allege [ə'ledʒ] *vt* prétendre, alléguer; **to** ~ **(that)** ... prétendre que ..., alléguer que ...; **she is** ~**d to have done it** on prétend qu'elle l'a fait.

alleged [ə'ledʒd] *adj* prétendu(e).

allegedly [ə'ledʒɪdlɪ] *adv* prétendument.

allegiance [ə'liːdʒəns] *n* allégeance *f*.

allegorical [ˌælɪ'gɒrɪkl] *adj* allégorique.

allegory ['ælɪgərɪ] (*pl* **-ies**) *n* allégorie *f*.

alleluia [ˌælɪ'luːjə] *excl* alléluia!

allergic [ə'lɜːdʒɪk] *adj*: ~ **(to)** allergique (à); **to be** ~ **to hard work** *hum* être allergique au travail.

allergy ['ælədʒɪ] (*pl* **-ies**) *n* allergie *f*; **to have an** ~ **to sthg** être allergique à qqch.

alleviate [ə'liːvɪeɪt] *vt* apaiser, soulager.

alley(way) ['ælɪ(weɪ)] *n* [street] ruelle *f*; [in garden] allée *f*.

alliance [ə'laɪəns] *n* alliance *f*.

allied ['ælaɪd] *adj* **-1.** MIL allié(e). **-2.** [related] connexe.

alligator ['ælɪgeɪtər] (*pl inv* OR **-s**) *n* alligator *m*.

all-important *adj* capital(e), crucial(e).

all-in *adj* Br [price] global(e).
◆ **all in** ◇ *adv* [inclusive] tout compris. ◇ *adj inf* [tired] crevé(e).

all-in wrestling *n* lutte *f* libre.

alliteration [ə,lɪtə'reɪʃn] *n* allitération *f*.

all-night *adj* [party etc] qui dure toute la nuit; [bar etc] ouvert(e) toute la nuit.

allocate ['æləkeɪt] *vt* [money, resources]: **to ~ sthg (to sb)** attribuer qqch (à qqn).

allocation [,ælə'keɪʃn] *n* **-1.** [gen] attribution *f*. **-2.** [share of money] somme *f* allouée.

allot [ə'lɒt] (*pt & pp* **-ted**, *cont* **-ting**) *vt* [job] assigner; [money, resources] attribuer; [time] allouer.

allotment [ə'lɒtmənt] *n* **-1.** Br [garden] jardin *m* ouvrier (*loué par la commune*). **-2.** [sharing out] attribution *f*. **-3.** [share] part *f*.

all-out *adj* [effort] maximum (*inv*); [war] total(e).

allow [ə'laʊ] *vt* **-1.** [permit - activity, behaviour] autoriser, permettre; **to ~ sb to do sthg** permettre à qqn de faire qqch, autoriser qqn à faire qqch; **~ me** permettez-moi. **-2.** [set aside - money, time] prévoir. **-3.** [officially accept] accepter. **-4.** [concede]: **to ~ that ...** admettre que ....
◆ **allow for** *vt fus* tenir compte de.

allowable [ə'laʊəbl] *adj* admissible.

allowance [ə'laʊəns] *n* **-1.** [money received] indemnité *f*; **maternity ~** allocation *f* de maternité. **-2.** Am [pocket money] argent *m* de poche. **-3.** FIN: **tax ~** ≃ abattement *m* fiscal. **-4.** [excuse]: **to make ~s for sb** faire preuve d'indulgence envers qqn; **to make ~s for sthg** prendre qqch en considération.

alloy ['ælɔɪ] *n* alliage *m*.

all-powerful *adj* tout-puissant (toute-puissante).

all right ◇ *adv* bien; [in answer - yes] d'accord; **~, let's go!** bon, on y va¿ ◇ *adj* **-1.** [healthy] en bonne santé; [unharmed] sain et sauf (saine et sauve). **-2.** *inf* [acceptable, satisfactory]: **it was ~** c'était pas mal; **that's ~** [never mind] ce n'est pas grave. **-3.** [allowable]: **is it ~ if ...¿** ça ne vous dérange pas si ...¿

all-round Br, **all-around** Am *adj* **-1.** [multi-skilled] doué(e) dans tous les domaines. **-2.** [comprehensive] complet(ète).

all-rounder [-'raʊndər] *n* **-1.** [versatile person]: **to be an ~** être bon (bonne) en tout.

-2. SPORT sportif complet *m*, sportive complète *f*.

all-time *adj* [record] sans précédent.

allude [ə'luːd] *vi*: **to ~ to** faire allusion à.

allure [ə'ljʊər] *n* charme *m*.

alluring [ə'ljʊərɪŋ] *adj* séduisant(e).

allusion [ə'luːʒn] *n* allusion *f*.

ally [*n* 'ælaɪ, *vb* ə'laɪ] (*pl* **-ies**, *pt & pp* **-ied**) ◇ *n* allié *m*, -e *f*. ◇ *vt*: **to ~ o.s. with** s'allier à.

almanac ['ɔːlmənæk] *n* almanach *m*.

almighty [ɔːl'maɪtɪ] *adj inf* [noise] terrible.
◆ **Almighty** *n*: **the Almighty** le Tout-Puissant.

almond ['ɑːmənd] *n* [nut] amande *f*; **~ (tree)** amandier *m*.

almond paste *n* pâte *f* d'amande.

almost ['ɔːlməʊst] *adv* presque; **I ~ missed the bus** j'ai failli rater le bus.

alms [ɑːmz] *npl dated* aumône *f*.

aloft [ə'lɒft] *adv* **-1.** [in the air] en l'air. **-2.** NAUT dans la mâture.

alone [ə'ləʊn] ◇ *adj* seul(e); **all ~** tout seul (toute seule). ◇ *adv* seul; **to leave sthg ~** ne pas toucher à qqch; **leave me ~!** laisse-moi tranquille!; **to go it ~** faire cavalier seul.
◆ **let alone** *conj* encore moins.

along [ə'lɒŋ] ◇ *adv*: **to walk ~** se promener; **to move ~** avancer; **can I come ~ (with you)¿** est-ce que je peux venir (avec vous)¿ ◇ *prep* le long de; **to run/walk ~ the street** courir/marcher le long de la rue.
◆ **all along** *adv* depuis le début.
◆ **along with** *prep* ainsi que.

alongside [ə,lɒŋ'saɪd] ◇ *prep* le long de, à côté de; [person] à côté de. ◇ *adv* bord à bord.

aloof [ə'luːf] ◇ *adj* distant(e). ◇ *adv*: **to remain ~ (from)** garder ses distances (vis-à-vis de).

aloud [ə'laʊd] *adv* à voix haute, tout haut.

alpaca [æl'pækə] *n* alpaga *m*.

alphabet ['ælfəbet] *n* alphabet *m*.

alphabetical [,ælfə'betɪkl] *adj* alphabétique; **in ~ order** par ordre alphabétique.

alphabetically [,ælfə'betɪklɪ] *adv* par ordre alphabétique.

alphabetize, **-ise** ['ælfəbətaɪz] *vt* classer par ordre alphabétique.

alphanumeric [,ælfənjuː'merɪk] *adj* alphanumérique.

alphanumeric key *n* COMPUT touche *f* alphanumérique.

alpine ['ælpaɪn] *adj* alpin(e).

Alps [ælps] *npl*: **the** ~ les Alpes *fpl*.

already [ɔːlˈredɪ] *adv* déjà.

alright [ˌɔːlˈraɪt] = **all right**.

Alsace [ælˈsæs] *n* Alsace *f*; **in** ~ en Alsace.

Alsatian [ælˈseɪʃn] ◇ *adj* alsacien(ienne). ◇ *n* **-1.** [person] Alsacien *m*, -ienne *f*. **-2.** [dog] berger *m* allemand.

also [ˈɔːlsəʊ] *adv* aussi.

also-ran *n* [person] perdant *m*, -e *f*.

Alta. *abbr of* **Alberta**.

altar [ˈɔːltər] *n* autel *m*.

alter [ˈɔːltər] ◇ *vt* changer, modifier; **to have a dress/suit** ~**ed** faire retoucher une robe/un costume. ◇ *vi* changer.

alteration [ˌɔːltəˈreɪʃn] *n* modification *f*, changement *m*; **to make an** ~ OR ~**s to sthg** changer OR modifier qqch.

altercation [ˌɔːltəˈkeɪʃn] *n* altercation *f*.

alter ego [ˈɔːltər-] *(pl* **-s**) *n* alter ego *m*.

alternate [*adj Br* ɔːlˈtɜːnət, *Am* ˈɒltərnət, *vb* ˈɔːltərneɪt] ◇ *adj* alterné(e), alternatif(ive); ~ **days** tous les deux jours, un jour sur deux. ◇ *vt* faire alterner. ◇ *vi*: **to** ~ **(with)** alterner (avec); **to** ~ **between sthg and sthg** passer de qqch à qqch.

alternately [ɔːlˈtɜːnətlɪ] *adv* alternativement.

alternating current [ˈɔːltəneɪtɪŋ-] *n* courant *m* alternatif.

alternation [ˌɔːltəˈneɪʃn] *n* alternance *f*.

alternative [ɔːlˈtɜːnətɪv] ◇ *adj* **-1.** [different] autre. **-2.** [non-traditional - society] parallèle; [- art, energy] alternatif(ive). ◇ *n* **-1.** [between two solutions] alternative *f*. **-2.** [other possibility]: ~ **(to)** solution *f* de remplacement (à); **to have no** ~ ne pas avoir le choix; **to have no** ~ **but to do sthg** ne pas avoir d'autre choix que de faire qqch.

alternatively [ɔːlˈtɜːnətɪvlɪ] *adv* ou bien.

alternative medicine *n* médecine *f* parallèle OR douce.

alternator [ˈɔːltəneɪtər] *n* ELEC alternateur *m*.

although [ɔːlˈðəʊ] *conj* bien que (+ *subjunctive*).

altitude [ˈæltɪtjuːd] *n* altitude *f*.

alto [ˈæltəʊ] *(pl* **-s**) ◇ *n* **-1.** [male voice] haute-contre *f*. **-2.** [female voice] contralto *m*. ◇ *comp* alto.

altogether [ˌɔːltəˈgeðər] *adv* **-1.** [completely] entièrement, tout à fait. **-2.** [considering all things] tout compte fait. **-3.** [in all] en tout.

altruism [ˈæltruɪzm] *n* altruisme *m*.

altruistic [ˌæltruˈɪstɪk] *adj* altruiste.

aluminium *Br* [ˌæljʊˈmɪnɪəm], **aluminum**

Am [əˈluːmɪnəm] ◇ *n* aluminium *m*. ◇ *comp* en aluminium; ~ **foil** papier *m* aluminium.

alumnus [əˈlʌmnəs] *(pl* **-ni** [-naɪ]) *n* ancien étudiant *m*, ancienne étudiante *f* (*d'une université*).

always [ˈɔːlweɪz] *adv* toujours.

am [æm] → **be**.

a.m. (*abbr of* **ante meridiem**): **at 3** ~ à 3h (du matin).

AM (*abbr of* **amplitude modulation**) *n* AM *f*.

AMA (*abbr of* **American Medical Association**) *n* ordre américain des médecins.

amalgam [əˈmælgəm] *n* amalgame *m*.

amalgamate [əˈmælgəmeɪt] *vt & vi* [unite] fusionner.

amalgamation [ə,mælgəˈmeɪʃn] *n* [of companies] fusion *f*.

amass [əˈmæs] *vt* amasser.

amateur [ˈæmətər] ◇ *adj* amateur (*inv*); *pej* d'amateur. ◇ *n* amateur *m*.

amateurish [ˌæməˈtɜːrɪʃ] *adj* d'amateur.

amaze [əˈmeɪz] *vt* étonner, stupéfier.

amazed [əˈmeɪzd] *adj* stupéfait(e).

amazement [əˈmeɪzmənt] *n* stupéfaction *f*.

amazing [əˈmeɪzɪŋ] *adj* **-1.** [surprising] étonnant(e), ahurissant(e). **-2.** [wonderful] excellent(e).

amazingly [əˈmeɪzɪŋlɪ] *adv* étonnamment.

Amazon [ˈæməzn] *n* **-1.** [river]: **the** ~ l'Amazone *f*. **-2.** [region]: **the** ~ **(Basin)** l'Amazonie *f*; **in the** ~ en Amazonie; **the** ~ **rainforest** la forêt amazonienne.

Amazonian [ˌæməˈzəʊnjən] *adj* amazonien(ienne).

ambassador [æmˈbæsədər] *n* ambassadeur *m*, -drice *f*.

amber [ˈæmbər] ◇ *adj* **-1.** [amber-coloured] ambré(e). **-2.** *Br* [traffic light] orange (*inv*). ◇ *n* **-1.** [substance] ambre *m*. **-2.** [colour - of traffic light] orange *m*. ◇ *comp* [made of amber] d'ambre.

ambiance [ˈæmbɪəns] = **ambience**.

ambidextrous [ˌæmbɪˈdekstrəs] *adj* ambidextre.

ambience [ˈæmbɪəns] *n* ambiance *f*.

ambiguity [ˌæmbɪˈgjuːətɪ] *(pl* **-ies**) *n* ambiguïté *f*.

ambiguous [æmˈbɪgjʊəs] *adj* ambigu(ë).

ambiguously [æmˈbɪgjʊəslɪ] *adv* de façon ambiguë.

ambition [æmˈbɪʃn] *n* ambition *f*.

ambitious [æmˈbɪʃəs] *adj* ambitieux(ieuse).

ambivalence [æmˈbɪvələns] *n* ambivalence *f*.

ambivalent [æm'bɪvələnt] *adj* ambivalent(e).

amble ['æmbl] *vi* déambuler.

ambulance ['æmbjʊləns] ◇ *n* ambulance *f.* ◇ *comp:* ~ **man** ambulancier *m;* ~ **woman** ambulancière *f.*

ambush ['æmbʊʃ] ◇ *n* embuscade *f.* ◇ *vt* tendre une embuscade à.

ameba *Am* = amoeba.

ameliorate [ə'miːljəreɪt] *fml* ◇ *vt* améliorer. ◇ *vi* s'améliorer.

amen [ˌɑːˈmen] *excl* amen!

amenable [ə'miːnəbl] *adj:* ~ **(to)** ouvert(e) (à).

amend [ə'mend] *vt* modifier; [law] amender. ◆ **amends** *npl:* **to make ~s (for)** se racheter (pour).

amendment [ə'mendmənt] *n* modification *f;* [to law] amendement *m.*

amenities [ə'miːnətɪz] *npl* aménagements *mpl,* équipements *mpl.*

America [ə'merɪkə] *n* Amérique *f;* **in** ~ en Amérique. ◆ **Americas** *npl:* **the** ~**s** les Amériques.

American [ə'merɪkn] ◇ *adj* américain(e). ◇ *n* Américain *m,* -e *f.*

American Indian *n* Indien *m,* -ienne *f* d'Amérique, Amérindien *m,* -ienne *f.*

Americanism [ə'merɪkənɪzm] *n* américanisme *m.*

americanize, -ise [ə'merɪkənaɪz] *vt* américaniser.

amethyst ['æmɪθɪst] *n* améthyste *f.*

Amex ['æmeks] *n* **-1.** *(abbr of* **American Stock Exchange)** *deuxième place boursière des États-Unis.* **-2.** *abbr of* **American Express.**

amiable ['eɪmjəbl] *adj* aimable.

amiably ['eɪmjəblɪ] *adv* aimablement.

amicable ['æmɪkəbl] *adj* amical(e).

amicably ['æmɪkəblɪ] *adv* amicalement.

amid(st) [ə'mɪd(st)] *prep* au milieu de, parmi.

amino acid [ə'miːnəʊ-] *n* acide *m* aminé.

amiss [ə'mɪs] ◇ *adj:* **is there anything ~?** y a-t-il quelque chose qui ne va pas? ◇ *adv:* **to take sthg ~** prendre qqch de travers.

Amman [ə'mɑːn] *n* Amman.

ammo ['æməʊ] *n (U) inf* munitions *fpl.*

ammonia [ə'məʊnjə] *n* [liquid] ammoniaque *f.*

ammunition [ˌæmjʊ'nɪʃn] *n (U)* **-1.** MIL munitions *fpl.* **-2.** *fig* [argument] argument *m.*

ammunition dump *n* dépôt *m* de munitions.

amnesia [æm'niːzjə] *n* amnésie *f.*

amnesty ['æmnəstɪ] *(pl* **-ies)** *n* amnistie *f.*

Amnesty International *n* Amnesty International *f.*

amoeba [ə'miːbə] *(pl* **-bas** OR **-bae** [-biː]), **ameba** *Am (pl* **-bas** OR **-bae** [-biː]) amibe *f.*

amok [ə'mɒk] *adv:* **to run** ~ être pris(e) d'une crise de folie furieuse.

among(st) [ə'mʌŋ(st)] *prep* parmi, entre; ~ **other things** entre autres (choses).

amoral [ˌeɪ'mɒrəl] *adj* amoral(e).

amorous ['æmərəs] *adj* amoureux(euse).

amorphous [ə'mɔːfəs] *adj* informe.

amortize [ə'mɔːtaɪz] *vt* FIN amortir.

amount [ə'maʊnt] *n* **-1.** [quantity] quantité *f;* **a great** ~ **of** beaucoup de. **-2.** [sum of money] somme *f,* montant *m.* ◆ **amount to** *vt fus* **-1.** [total] se monter à, s'élever à. **-2.** [be equivalent to] revenir à, équivaloir à.

amp [æmp] *n* **-1.** *abbr of* **ampere. -2.** *inf (abbr of* **amplifier)** ampli *m.*

amperage ['æmpərɪdʒ] *n* intensité *f* de courant.

ampere ['æmpeə*] *n* ampère *m.*

ampersand ['æmpəsænd] *n* esperluette *f.*

amphetamine [æm'fetəmiːn] *n* amphétamine *f.*

amphibian [æm'fɪbɪən] *n* batracien *m.*

amphibious [æm'fɪbɪəs] *adj* amphibie.

amphitheatre *Br,* **amphitheater** *Am* ['æmfɪˌθɪətə*] *n* amphithéâtre *m.*

ample ['æmpl] *adj* **-1.** [enough] suffisamment de, assez de. **-2.** [large] ample.

amplification [ˌæmplɪfɪ'keɪʃn] *n* **-1.** [of sound] amplification *f.* **-2.** [of idea, statement] développement *m.*

amplifier ['æmplɪfaɪə*] *n* amplificateur *m.*

amplify ['æmplɪfaɪ] *(pt & pp* **-ied)** ◇ *vt* **-1.** [sound] amplifier. **-2.** [idea, statement] développer. ◇ *vi:* **to** ~ **on sthg** développer qqch.

amply ['æmplɪ] *adv* **-1.** [sufficiently] amplement. **-2.** [considerably] largement.

ampoule *Br,* **ampule** *Am* ['æmpuːl] *n* ampoule *f.*

amputate ['æmpjuteɪt] *vt & vi* amputer.

amputation [ˌæmpjʊ'teɪʃn] *n* amputation *f.*

Amsterdam [ˌæmstə'dæm] *n* Amsterdam.

amt *abbr of* **amount.**

Amtrak ['æmtræk] *n société nationale de chemins de fer aux États-Unis.*

amuck [ə'mʌk] = amok.

amulet ['æmjʊlɪt] *n* amulette *f.*

amuse [ə'mjuːz] *vt* **-1.** [make laugh] amuser, faire rire. **-2.** [entertain] divertir, distraire; **to**

~ **o.s. (by doing sthg)** s'occuper (à faire qqch).

amused [ə'mjuːzd] *adj* **-1.** [laughing] amusé(e); **to be** ~ **at** OR **by sthg** trouver qqch amusant. **-2.** [entertained]: **to keep o.s.** ~ s'occuper.

amusement [ə'mjuːzmənt] *n* **-1.** [laughter] amusement *m*. **-2.** [diversion, game] distraction *f*.

amusement arcade *n* galerie *f* de jeux.

amusement park *n* parc *m* d'attractions.

amusing [ə'mjuːzɪŋ] *adj* amusant(e).

an [*stressed* æn, *unstressed* ən] → **a**.

ANA *n* **-1.** (*abbr of* **American Newspaper Association**) *syndicat américain de la presse écrite*. **-2.** (*abbr of* **American Nurses Association**) *syndicat américain d'infirmiers*.

anabolic steroid [,ænə'bɒlɪk-] *n* (stéroïde *m*) anabolisant *m*.

anachronism [ə'nækrənɪzm] *n* anachronisme *m*.

anachronistic [ə,nækrə'nɪstɪk] *adj* anachronique.

anaemia *Br*, **anemia** *Am* [ə'niːmjə] *n* anémie *f*.

anaemic *Br*, **anemic** *Am* [ə'niːmɪk] *adj* anémique; *fig* & *pej* fade, plat(e).

anaesthesia *Br*, **anesthesia** *Am* [,ænɪs'θiːzjə] *n* anesthésie *f*.

anaesthetic *Br*, **anesthetic** *Am* [,ænɪs'θetɪk] *n* anesthésique *m*; **under** ~ sous anesthésie; **local/general** ~ anesthésie *f* locale/générale.

anaesthetist *Br*, **anesthetist** *Am* [æ'niːsθətɪst] *n* anesthésiste *mf*.

anaesthetize *Br*, **-ise** *Br*, **anesthetize** *Am* [æ'niːsθətaɪz] *vt* anesthésier.

anagram ['ænəgræm] *n* anagramme *f*.

anal ['eɪnl] *adj* anal(e).

analgesic [,ænæl'dʒiːsɪk] ◇ *adj* analgésique. ◇ *n* analgésique *m*.

analog *Am* = **analogue**.

analogous [ə'næləgəs] *adj*: ~ **(to)** analogue (à).

analogue *Br*, **analog** *Am* ['ænəlɒg] ◇ *adj* [watch, clock] analogique. ◇ *n* analogue *m*.

analogy [ə'nælədʒɪ] (*pl* **-ies**) *n* analogie *f*; **to draw an** ~ **with/between** faire une comparaison avec/entre; **by** ~ par analogie.

analyse *Br*, **analyze** *Am* ['ænəlaɪz] *vt* analyser.

analysis [ə'næləsɪs] (*pl* **analyses** [ə'næləsiːz]) *n* analyse *f*; **in the final** OR **last** ~ en dernière analyse.

analyst ['ænəlɪst] *n* analyste *mf*.

analytic(al) [,ænə'lɪtɪk(l)] *adj* analytique.

analyze *Am* = **analyse**.

anarchic [æ'nɑːkɪk] *adj* anarchique.

anarchist ['ænəkɪst] *n* anarchiste *mf*.

anarchy ['ænəkɪ] *n* anarchie *f*.

anathema [ə'næθəmə] *n* anathème *m*.

anatomical [,ænə'tɒmɪkl] *adj* anatomique.

anatomy [ə'nætəmɪ] (*pl* **-ies**) *n* anatomie *f*.

ANC (*abbr of* **African National Congress**) *n* ANC *m*.

ancestor ['ænsestər] *n* lit & fig ancêtre *m*.

ancestral home [æn'sestrəl-] *n* demeure *f* ancestrale.

ancestry ['ænsestrɪ] (*pl* **-ies**) *n* **-1.** [past] ascendance *f*. **-2.** (*U*) [ancestors] ancêtres *mpl*.

anchor ['æŋkər] ◇ *n* ancre *f*; **to drop/weigh** ~ jeter/lever l'ancre. ◇ *vt* **-1.** [secure] ancrer. **-2.** TV présenter. ◇ *vi* NAUT jeter l'ancre.

anchorage ['æŋkərɪdʒ] *n*. **-1.** NAUT mouillage *m*. **-2.** [means of securing] ancrage *m*.

anchorman ['æŋkəmæn] (*pl* **-men** [-men]) *n* TV présentateur *m*.

anchorwoman ['æŋkə,wʊmən] (*pl* **-women** [-,wɪmɪn]) *n* TV présentatrice *f*.

anchovy ['æntʃəvɪ] (*pl inv* OR **-ies**) *n* anchois *m*.

ancient ['eɪnʃənt] *adj* **-1.** [monument etc] historique; [custom] ancien(ienne). **-2.** *hum* [car etc] antique; [person] vieux (vieille).

ancillary [æn'sɪlərɪ] *adj* auxiliaire.

and [*strong form* ænd, *weak form* ənd, ən] *conj* **-1.** [as well as, plus] et. **-2.** [in numbers]: **one hundred** ~ **eighty** cent quatre-vingts; **six** ~ **a half** six et demi. **-3.** [to]: **come** ~ **see!** venez voir!; **try** ~ **come** essayez de venir; **wait** ~ **see** vous verrez bien.

◆ **and so on, and so forth** *adv* et ainsi de suite.

Andes ['ændiːz] *npl*: **the** ~ les Andes *fpl*.

Andorra [æn'dɔːrə] *n* Andorre *f*; **in** ~ en Andorre.

androgynous [æn'drɒdʒɪnəs] *adj* androgyne.

android ['ændrɔɪd] *n* androïde *m*.

anecdote ['ænɪkdəʊt] *n* anecdote *f*.

anemia *Am* = **anaemia**.

anemic *Am* = **anaemic**.

anemone [ə'nemənɪ] *n* anémone *f*.

anesthesia *etc Am* = **anaesthesia** *etc*.

anew [ə'njuː] *adv*: **to start** ~ recommencer (à zéro).

angel ['eɪndʒəl] *n* ange *m*.

Angeleno [,ændʒə'liːnəʊ] *n habitant de Los Angeles*.

angelic [æn'dʒelɪk] *adj* angélique.

anger ['æŋgər] ◇ n colère f. ◇ vt fâcher, irriter.

angina [æn'dʒaɪnə] n angine f de poitrine.

angle ['æŋgl] ◇ n -1. [gen] angle m; **at an** ~ de travers, en biais. -2. [point of view] point m de vue, angle m. ◇ vi pêcher (à la ligne); **to** ~ **for** fig [invitation, compliments] chercher à obtenir, quêter.

angler ['æŋglər] n pêcheur m (à la ligne).

Anglican ['æŋglɪkən] ◇ adj anglican(e). ◇ n anglican m, -e f.

anglicism ['æŋglɪsɪzm] n anglicisme m.

angling ['æŋglɪŋ] n pêche f à la ligne.

Anglo- ['æŋgləʊ] prefix anglo-.

Anglo-Saxon ◇ adj anglo-saxon(onne). ◇ n -1. [person] Anglo-saxon m, -onne f. -2. [language] anglo-saxon m.

Angola [æŋ'gəʊlə] n Angola m; **in** ~ en Angola.

Angolan [æŋ'gəʊlən] ◇ adj angolais(e). ◇ n Angolais m, -e f.

angora [æŋ'gɔːrə] n angora m.

angrily ['æŋgrəlɪ] adv avec colère.

angry ['æŋgrɪ] (compar **-ier**, superl **-iest**) adj [person] en colère, fâché(e); [words, quarrel] violent(e); **to be** ~ **with** OR **at sb** être en colère OR fâché contre qqn; **to get** ~ se mettre en colère, se fâcher.

angst [æŋst] n anxiété f.

anguish ['æŋgwɪʃ] n angoisse f.

anguished ['æŋgwɪʃt] adj angoissé(e).

angular ['æŋgjʊlər] adj anguleux(euse).

animal ['ænɪml] ◇ n animal m; pej brute f. ◇ adj animal(e).

animate ['ænɪmət] adj animé(e), vivant(e).

animated ['ænɪmeɪtɪd] adj animé(e).

animated cartoon n dessin m animé.

animation [ˌænɪ'meɪʃn] n animation f.

animosity [ˌænɪ'mɒsətɪ] (pl **-ies**) n animosité f.

aniseed ['ænɪsiːd] n anis m.

ankle ['æŋkl] ◇ n cheville f. ◇ comp: ~ **socks** socquettes fpl; ~ **boots** bottines fpl.

annals ['ænlz] npl annales fpl.

annex(e) ['æneks] ◇ n [building] annexe f. ◇ vt annexer.

annexation [ˌænek'seɪʃn] n annexion f.

annihilate [ə'naɪəleɪt] vt anéantir, annihiler.

annihilation [əˌnaɪə'leɪʃn] n anéantissement m.

anniversary [ˌænɪ'vɜːsərɪ] (pl **-ies**) n anniversaire m.

annotate ['ænəteɪt] vt annoter.

announce [ə'naʊns] vt annoncer.

announcement [ə'naʊnsmənt] n -1. [statement] déclaration f; [in newspaper] avis m. -2. (U) [act of stating] annonce f.

announcer [ə'naʊnsər] n RADIO & TV speaker m, speakerine f.

annoy [ə'nɔɪ] vt agacer, contrarier.

annoyance [ə'nɔɪəns] n contrariété f.

annoyed [ə'nɔɪd] adj mécontent(e), agacé(e); **to get** ~ se fâcher; **to be** ~ **at sthg** être contrarié par qqch; **to be** ~ **with sb** être fâché contre qqn.

annoying [ə'nɔɪɪŋ] adj agaçant(e), énervant(e).

annual ['ænjʊəl] ◇ adj annuel(elle). ◇ n -1. [plant] plante f annuelle. -2. [book - gen] publication f annuelle; [- for children] album m.

annual general meeting n assemblée f générale annuelle.

annually ['ænjʊəlɪ] adv annuellement.

annuity [ə'njuːɪtɪ] (pl **-ies**) n rente f.

annul [ə'nʌl] (pt & pp **-led**, cont **-ling**) vt annuler; [law] abroger.

annulment [ə'nʌlmənt] n annulation f; [of law] abrogation f.

annum ['ænəm] n: **per** ~ par an.

Annunciation [əˌnʌnsɪ'eɪʃn] n: **the** ~ l'Annonciation f.

anode ['ænəʊd] n anode f.

anoint [ə'nɔɪnt] vt oindre.

anomalous [ə'nɒmələs] adj anormal(e).

anomaly [ə'nɒməlɪ] (pl **-ies**) n anomalie f.

anon. [ə'nɒn] (abbr of **anonymous**) anon.

anonymity [ˌænə'nɪmətɪ] n anonymat m.

anonymous [ə'nɒnɪməs] adj anonyme.

anonymously [ə'nɒnɪməslɪ] adv anonymement.

anorak ['ænəræk] n anorak m.

anorexia (nervosa) [ˌænə'reksɪə(nɜː'vəʊsə)] n anorexie f mentale.

anorexic [ˌænə'reksɪk] ◇ adj anorexique. ◇ n anorexique mf.

another [ə'nʌðər] ◇ adj -1. [additional]: ~ **apple** encore une pomme, une pomme de plus, une autre pomme; **in** ~ **few minutes** dans quelques minutes; **(would you like)** ~ **drink?** encore un verre? -2. [different]: ~ **job** un autre travail.

◇ pron -1. [additional one] un autre (une autre), encore un (encore une); **one after** ~ l'un après l'autre (l'une après l'autre). -2. [different one] un autre (une autre); **one** ~ l'un l'autre (l'une l'autre).

ANSI (abbr of **American National Standards Institute**) n association américaine de normalisation.

answer ['ɑːnsəʳ] ◇ n **-1.** [gen] réponse f; in ~ to en réponse à. **-2.** [to problem] solution f. ◇ vt répondre à; to ~ **the door** aller ouvrir la porte; **to ~ the phone** répondre au téléphone. ◇ vi [reply] répondre.
◆ **answer back** ◇ vt sep répondre à. ◇ vi répondre.
◆ **answer for** vt fus être responsable de, répondre de.

answerable ['ɑːnsərəbl] adj: ~ **to sb/for sthg** responsable devant qqn/de qqch.

answering machine ['ɑːnsərɪŋ-] n répondeur m.

ant [ænt] n fourmi f.

antacid [,ænt'æsɪd] n (médicament m) alcalin m.

antagonism [æn'tægənɪzm] n antagonisme m, hostilité f.

antagonist [æn'tægənɪst] n antagoniste mf, adversaire mf.

antagonistic [æn,tægə'nɪstɪk] adj [hostile] hostile.

antagonize, **-ise** [æn'tægənaɪz] vt éveiller l'hostilité de.

Antarctic [æn'tɑːktɪk] ◇ n: the ~ l'Antarctique m; **in the ~** dans l'Antarctique. ◇ adj antarctique.

Antarctica [æn'tɑːktɪkə] n Antarctique m, le continent m antarctique.

Antarctic Circle n: the ~ le cercle polaire antarctique.

Antarctic Ocean n: the ~ l'océan m Antarctique, l'océan Austral.

ante ['æntɪ] n inf fig: **to up** OR **raise the ~** faire monter les enchères.

anteater ['ænt,iːtəʳ] n tamanoir m, fourmilier m.

antecedent [,æntɪ'siːdənt] n antécédent m.

antediluvian [,æntɪdɪ'luːvjən] adj antédiluvien(ienne).

antelope ['æntɪləʊp] (pl inv OR **-s**) n antilope f.

antenatal [,æntɪ'neɪtl] adj prénatal(e).

antenatal clinic n service m de consultation prénatale.

antenna [æn'tenə] (pl sense 1 **-nae** [-niː], pl sense 2 **-s**) n **-1.** [of insect] antenne f. **-2.** Am [for TV, radio] antenne f.

anteroom ['æntɪrʊm] n antichambre f.

anthem ['ænθəm] n hymne m.

anthill ['ænthɪl] n fourmilière f.

anthology [æn'θɒlədʒɪ] (pl **-ies**) n anthologie f.

anthrax ['ænθræks] n charbon m.

anthropologist [,ænθrə'pɒlədʒɪst] n anthropologue mf.

anthropology [,ænθrə'pɒlədʒɪ] n anthropologie f.

anti- ['æntɪ] prefix anti-.

antiaircraft [,æntɪ'eəkrɑːft] adj antiaérien(ienne).

antiapartheid [,æntɪə'pɑːtheɪt] adj antiapartheid (inv).

antiballistic missile [,æntɪbə'lɪstɪk-] n missile m antibalistique.

antibiotic [,æntɪbaɪ'ɒtɪk] n antibiotique m.

antibody ['æntɪ,bɒdɪ] (pl **-ies**) n anticorps m.

anticipate [æn'tɪsɪpeɪt] vt **-1.** [expect] s'attendre à, prévoir. **-2.** [request, movement] anticiper; [competitor] prendre de l'avance sur. **-3.** [look forward to] savourer à l'avance.

anticipation [æn,tɪsɪ'peɪʃn] n [expectation] attente f; [eagerness] impatience f; **in ~** avec impatience; **in ~ of** en prévision de; **thanking you in ~** en vous remerciant d'avance.

anticlimax [,æntɪ'klaɪmæks] n déception f.

anticlockwise [,æntɪ'klɒkwaɪz] adj & adv Br dans le sens inverse des aiguilles d'une montre.

antics ['æntɪks] npl **-1.** [of children, animals] gambades fpl. **-2.** pej [of politicians etc] bouffonneries fpl.

anticyclone [,æntɪ'saɪkləʊn] n anticyclone m.

antidepressant [,æntɪdə'presnt] n antidépresseur m.

antidote ['æntɪdəʊt] n lit & fig: ~ **(to)** antidote m (contre).

antifreeze ['æntɪfriːz] n antigel m.

Antigua [æn'tiːgə] n Antigua.

antihero ['æntɪ,hɪərəʊ] (pl **-es**) n antihéros m.

antihistamine [,æntɪ'hɪstəmɪn] n antihistaminique m.

antinuclear [,æntɪ'njuːklɪəʳ] adj antinucléaire.

antipathy [æn'tɪpəθɪ] n: ~ **(to** OR **towards)** antipathie f (pour).

antipersonnel ['æntɪ,pɜːsə'nel] adj MIL antipersonnel (inv).

antiperspirant [,æntɪ'pɜːspərənt] n déodorant m.

Antipodes [æn'tɪpədiːz] npl: the ~ l'Australie f et la Nouvelle-Zélande.

antiquarian [,æntɪ'kweərɪən] ◇ adj: ~ **bookshop** librairie f spécialisée dans les

vieilles éditions. ◇ *n* amateur *m* d'antiquités.

antiquated ['æntɪkweɪtɪd] *adj* dépassé(e).

antique [æn'tiːk] ◇ *adj* ancien(ienne). ◇ *n*
[object] objet *m* ancien; [piece of furniture]
meuble *m* ancien.

antique dealer *n* antiquaire *mf*.

antique shop *n* magasin *m* d'antiquités.

antiquity [æn'tɪkwətɪ] (*pl* **-ies**) *n* antiquité *f*.

anti-Semitic [-sɪ'mɪtɪk] *adj* antisémite.

anti-Semitism [-'semɪtɪzəm] *n* antisémitisme *m*.

antiseptic [ˌæntɪ'septɪk] ◇ *adj* antiseptique.
◇ *n* désinfectant *m*.

antisocial [ˌæntɪ'səʊʃl] *adj* **-1.** [against soci-
ety] antisocial(e). **-2.** [unsociable] peu sociable, sauvage.

antistatic [ˌæntɪ'stætɪk] *adj* antistatique.

antitank [ˌæntɪ'tæŋk] *adj* antichar (*inv*).

antithesis [æn'tɪθɪsɪs] (*pl* **-theses** [-θɪsiːz]) *n*
opposé *m*, antithèse *f*.

antlers ['æntləz] *npl* bois *mpl*.

antonym ['æntənɪm] *n* antonyme *m*.

Antwerp ['æntwɜːp] *n* Anvers.

anus ['eɪnəs] *n* anus *m*.

anvil ['ænvɪl] *n* enclume *f*.

anxiety [æŋ'zaɪətɪ] (*pl* **-ies**) *n* **-1.** [worry]
anxiété *f*. **-2.** [cause of worry] souci *m*. **-3.**
[keenness] désir *m* farouche.

anxious ['æŋkʃəs] *adj* **-1.** [worried]
anxieux(ieuse), très inquiet(iète); **to be ~
about** se faire du souci au sujet de. **-2.**
[keen]: **to be ~ to do sthg** tenir à faire
qqch; **to be ~ that** tenir à ce que (+ *subjunctive*).

anxiously ['æŋkʃəslɪ] *adv* avec anxiété.

any ['enɪ] ◇ *adj* **-1.** (*with negative*) de, d'; **I
haven't got ~ money/tickets** je n'ai pas
d'argent/de billets; **he never does ~ work**
il ne travaille jamais. **-2.** [some - *with sg
noun*] du, de l', de la; [- *with pl noun*] des;
have you got ~ money/milk/cousins? est-
ce que vous avez de l'argent/du lait/des
cousins? **-3.** [no matter which] n'importe
quel (n'importe quelle); **~ box will do**
n'importe quelle boîte fera l'affaire; *see also*
case, day, moment, rate.
◇ *pron* **-1.** (*with negative*) en; **I didn't buy ~**
(of them) je n'en ai pas acheté; **I didn't
know ~ of the guests** je ne connaissais aucun des invités. **-2.** [some] en; **do you have
~?** est-ce que vous en avez?; **can ~ of you
change a tyre?** est-ce que l'un d'entre vous
sait changer un pneu?; **if ~** si tant est qu'il
y en ait; **few, if ~, are likely to be successful** il y en a très peu, si tant est qu'il y en

ait, qui ont une chance de réussir. **-3.** [no
matter which one or ones] n'importe lequel
(n'importe laquelle); **take ~ you like** prenez n'importe lequel/laquelle, prenez
celui/celle que vous voulez.
◇ *adv* **-1.** (*with negative*): **I can't see it ~
more** je ne le vois plus; **I can't stand it ~
longer** je ne peux plus le supporter. **-2.**
[some, a little] un peu; **do you want ~ more
potatoes?** voulez-vous encore des pommes
de terre?; **are you finding the course ~
easier now?** est-ce que tu trouves le cours
un peu plus facile maintenant?; **is that ~
better/different?** est-ce que c'est mieux/
différent comme ça?

anybody ['enɪ,bɒdɪ] = **anyone**.

anyhow ['enɪhaʊ] *adv* **-1.** [in spite of that]
quand même, néanmoins. **-2.** [carelessly]
n'importe comment. **-3.** [in any case] de
toute façon.

anyone ['enɪwʌn] *pron* **-1.** (*in negative sentences*): **I didn't see ~** je n'ai vu personne.
-2. (*in questions*) quelqu'un. **-3.** [any person]
n'importe qui.

anyplace *Am* = **anywhere**.

anything ['enɪθɪŋ] *pron* **-1.** (*in negative sentences*): **I didn't see ~** je n'ai rien vu. **-2.** (*in
questions*) quelque chose. **-3.** [any object,
event] n'importe quoi; **if ~ happens ...** s'il
arrive quoi que ce soit ....
◆ **anything but** *adv* pas du tout.

anyway ['enɪweɪ] *adv* [in any case] de toute
façon.

anywhere ['enɪweəʳ], **anyplace** *Am*
['enɪpleɪs] *adv* **-1.** (*in negative sentences*): **I
haven't seen him ~** je ne l'ai vu nulle part.
-2. (*in questions*) quelque part. **-3.** [any place]
n'importe où. **-4.** [any amount, number]: **~
between 5,000 and 10,000** quelque chose
entre 5 000 et 10 000.

Anzac ['ænzæk] (*abbr of* **Australia-New
Zealand Army Corps**) *n* soldat *australien ou
néo-zélandais*.

AOB, a.o.b. (*abbr of* **any other business**)
divers.

Apache [ə'pætʃɪ] *n* Apache *mf*.

apart [ə'pɑːt] *adv* **-1.** [separated] séparé(e),
éloigné(e); **to keep ~** séparer; **we're living
~** nous sommes séparés. **-2.** [to one side] à
l'écart. **-3.** [in several parts]: **to take sthg ~**
démonter qqch; **to fall ~** tomber en morceaux. **-4.** [aside]: **joking ~** sans plaisanter,
plaisanterie à part.
◆ **apart from** *prep* **-1.** [except for] à part,
sauf. **-2.** [as well as] en plus de, outre.

apartheid [ə'pɑːtheɪt] *n* apartheid *m*.

apartment [ə'pɑːtmənt] *n* appartement *m*.

apartment building *n Am* immeuble *m* d'habitation.

apathetic [,æpə'θetɪk] *adj* apathique.

apathy ['æpəθɪ] *n* apathie *f.*

APB (*abbr of* **all points bulletin**) *n* message radio diffusé par la police concernant une personne recherchée.

ape [eɪp] ◇ *n* singe *m.* ◇ *vt* singer.

Apennines ['æpɪnaɪnz] *npl*: **the ~** l'Apennin *m,* les Apennins *mpl.*

aperitif [əperə'tiːf] *n* apéritif *m.*

aperture ['æpə,tjʊəʳ] *n* **-1.** [hole, opening] orifice *m,* ouverture *f.* **-2.** PHOT ouverture *f.*

apex ['eɪpeks] (*pl* **-es** OR **apices**) *n* sommet *m.*

APEX ['eɪpeks] (*abbr of* **advance purchase excursion**) *n Br*: **~ ticket** billet *m* APEX.

aphid ['eɪfɪd] *n* puceron *m.*

aphorism ['æfərɪzm] *n* aphorisme *m.*

aphrodisiac [,æfrə'dɪzɪæk] *n* aphrodisiaque *m..*

apices ['eɪpɪsiːz] *pl* → **apex.**

apiece [ə'piːs] *adv* [for each person] chacun(e), par personne; [for each thing] chacun(e), pièce (*inv*).

aplomb [ə'plɒm] *n* aplomb *m,* assurance *f.*

APO (*abbr of* **Army Post Office**) *n* service postal de l'armée.

apocalypse [ə'pɒkəlɪps] *n* apocalypse *f.*

apocalyptic [ə,pɒkə'lɪptɪk] *adj* apocalyptique.

apogee ['æpədʒiː] *n* apogée *m.*

apolitical [,eɪpə'lɪtɪkəl] *adj* apolitique.

apologetic [ə,pɒlə'dʒetɪk] *adj* [letter etc] d'excuse; **to be ~ about sthg** s'excuser de qqch.

apologetically [ə,pɒlə'dʒetɪklɪ] *adv* en s'excusant, pour s'excuser.

apologize, -ise [ə'pɒlədʒaɪz] *vi* s'excuser; **to ~ to sb (for sthg)** faire des excuses à qqn (pour qqch).

apology [ə'pɒlədʒɪ] (*pl* **-ies**) *n* excuses *fpl.*

apoplectic [,æpə'plektɪk] *adj* **-1.** MED apoplectique. **-2.** *inf* [very angry] hors de soi.

apoplexy ['æpəpleksɪ] *n* apoplexie *f.*

apostle [ə'pɒsl] *n* RELIG apôtre *m.*

apostrophe [ə'pɒstrəfɪ] *n* apostrophe *f.*

appal *Br* (*pt* & *pp* **-led**, *cont* **-ling**), **appall** *Am* [ə'pɔːl] *vt* horrifier.

Appalachian [,æpə'leɪtʃən] *n*: **the ~s, the ~ Mountains** (les monts) Appalaches *mpl.*

appall *Am* = **appal.**

appalled [ə'pɔːld] *adj* horrifié(e).

appalling [ə'pɔːlɪŋ] *adj* épouvantable.

appallingly [ə'pɔːlɪŋlɪ] *adv* épouvantablement.

apparatus [,æpə'reɪtəs] (*pl inv* OR **-es**) *n* **-1.** [device] appareil *m,* dispositif *m.* **-2.** (*U*) [in gym] agrès *mpl.* **-3.** [system, organization] appareil *m.*

apparel [ə'pærəl] *n Am* habillement *m.*

apparent [ə'pærənt] *adj* **-1.** [evident] évident(e); **for no ~ reason** sans raison particulière. **-2.** [seeming] apparent(e).

apparently [ə'pærəntlɪ] *adv* **-1.** [it seems] à ce qu'il paraît. **-2.** [seemingly] apparemment, en apparence.

apparition [,æpə'rɪʃn] *n* apparition *f.*

appeal [ə'piːl] ◇ *vi* **-1.** [request]: **to ~ (to sb for sthg)** lancer un appel (à qqn pour obtenir qqch). **-2.** [make a plea]: **to ~ to** faire appel à. **-3.** JUR: **to ~ (against)** faire appel (de). **-4.** [attract, interest]: **to ~ to sb** plaire à qqn; **it ~s to me** ça me plaît. ◇ *n* **-1.** [request] appel *m.* **-2.** JUR appel *m.* **-3.** [charm, interest] intérêt *m,* attrait *m.*

appealing [ə'piːlɪŋ] *adj* **-1.** [attractive] attirant(e), sympathique. **-2.** [pleading] suppliant(e).

appear [ə'pɪəʳ] *vi* **-1.** [gen] apparaître; [book] sortir, paraître. **-2.** [seem] sembler, paraître; **to ~ to be/do** sembler être/faire; **it would ~ (that)** ... il semblerait que .... **-3.** [in play, film etc] jouer. **-4.** JUR comparaître.

appearance [ə'pɪərəns] *n* **-1.** [gen] apparition *f;* **to make an ~** se montrer; **to put in an ~** faire acte de présence. **-2.** [look] apparence *f,* aspect *m;* **by** OR **to all ~s** selon toute apparence; **to keep up ~s** sauver les apparences.

appease [ə'piːz] *vt* apaiser.

appeasement [ə'piːzmənt] *n* apaisement *m.*

append [ə'pend] *vt* ajouter; [signature] apposer.

appendage [ə'pendɪdʒ] *n* appendice *m.*

appendices [ə'pendɪsiːz] *pl* → **appendix.**

appendicitis [ə,pendɪ'saɪtɪs] *n* (*U*) appendicite *f.*

appendix [ə'pendɪks] (*pl* **-dixes** OR **-dices**) *n* appendice *m;* **to have one's ~ out** OR **removed** se faire opérer de l'appendicite.

appertain [,æpə'teɪn] *vi fml*: **to ~ to** se rapporter à.

appetite ['æpɪtaɪt] *n* **-1.** [for food]: **~ (for)** appétit *m* (pour). **-2.** *fig* [enthusiasm]: **~ (for)** goût *m* (de OR pour).

appetizer, -iser ['æpɪtaɪzəʳ] *n* [food] amuse-gueule *m inv;* [drink] apéritif *m.*

appetizing, -ising ['æpɪtaɪzɪŋ] *adj* [food] appétissant(e).

applaud [ə'plɔːd] ◇ vt **-1.** [clap] applaudir. **-2.** [approve] approuver, applaudir à. ◇ vi applaudir.

applause [ə'plɔːz] n (U) applaudissements mpl.

apple ['æpl] n pomme f; she's the ~ of her father's eye inf son père tient à elle comme à la prunelle de ses yeux.

apple pie n tourte f aux pommes.

appliance [ə'plaɪəns] n [device] appareil m; domestic ~ appareil ménager.

applicable [ə'plɪkəbl] adj: ~ (to) applicable (à).

applicant ['æplɪkənt] n: ~ (for) [job] candidat m, -e f (à); [state benefit] demandeur m, -euse f (de).

application [,æplɪ'keɪʃn] n **-1.** [gen] application f. **-2.** [for job etc]: ~ (for) demande f (de). **-3.** COMPUT: ~ (program) programme m d'application.

application form n formulaire m de demande.

applicator ['æplɪkeɪtə'] n [for lotion, glue etc] applicateur m.

applied [ə'plaɪd] adj [science] appliqué(e).

appliqué [ə'pliːkeɪ] n application f.

apply [ə'plaɪ] (pt & pp -ied) ◇ vt appliquer; to ~ o.s. (to sthg) s'appliquer (à qqch); to ~ one's mind (to sthg) s'appliquer (à qqch); to ~ the brakes freiner. ◇ vi **-1.** [for work, grant]: to ~ (for) faire une demande (de); to ~ for a job faire une demande d'emploi; to ~ to sb (for sthg) s'adresser à qqn (pour obtenir qqch). **-2.** [be relevant]: to ~ (to) s'appliquer (à), concerner.

appoint [ə'pɔɪnt] vt **-1.** [to job, position]: to ~ sb (as sthg) nommer qqn (qqch); to ~ sb to sthg nommer qqn à qqch. **-2.** [time, place] fixer.

appointment [ə'pɔɪntmənt] n **-1.** [to job, position] nomination f, désignation f; "by ~ to Her Majesty the Queen" «fournisseur de sa Majesté la Reine». **-2.** [job, position] poste m, emploi m. **-3.** [arrangement to meet] rendez-vous m; to make an ~ prendre un rendez-vous; by ~ sur rendez-vous.

apportion [ə'pɔːʃn] vt répartir.

apposite ['æpəzɪt] adj pertinent(e), approprié(e).

appraisal [ə'preɪzl] n évaluation f.

appraise [ə'preɪz] vt évaluer.

appreciable [ə'priːʃəbl] adj [difference] sensible; [amount] appréciable.

appreciably [ə'priːʃəblɪ] adv sensiblement.

appreciate [ə'priːʃɪeɪt] ◇ vt **-1.** [value, like] apprécier, aimer. **-2.** [recognize, understand] comprendre, se rendre compte de. **-3.** [be grateful for] être reconnaissant(e) de. ◇ vi FIN prendre de la valeur.

appreciation [ə,priːʃɪ'eɪʃn] n **-1.** [liking] contentement m. **-2.** [understanding] compréhension f. **-3.** [gratitude] reconnaissance f. **-4.** FIN augmentation f de valeur. **-5.** [of novel, play etc] critique f.

appreciative [ə'priːʃjətɪv] adj [person] reconnaissant(e); [remark] élogieux(ieuse).

apprehend [,æprɪ'hend] vt fml [arrest] appréhender, arrêter.

apprehension [,æprɪ'henʃn] n [anxiety] appréhension f, crainte f.

apprehensive [,æprɪ'hensɪv] adj inquiet(iète); to be ~ about sthg appréhender OR craindre qqch.

apprehensively [,æprɪ'hensɪvlɪ] adv avec appréhension.

apprentice [ə'prentɪs] ◇ n apprenti m, -e f. ◇ vt: to be ~d to sb être apprenti(e) chez qqn.

apprenticeship [ə'prentɪʃɪp] n apprentissage m.

appro. ['æprəu] (abbr of approval) n inf: on ~ à condition, à l'essai.

approach [ə'prəutʃ] ◇ n **-1.** [gen] approche f. **-2.** [method] démarche f, approche f. **-3.** [to person]: to make an ~ to sb faire une proposition à qqn. ◇ vt **-1.** [come near to - place, person, thing] s'approcher de. **-2.** [ask]: to ~ sb about sthg aborder qqch avec qqn; COMM entrer en contact avec qqn au sujet de qqch. **-3.** [tackle - problem] aborder. ◇ vi s'approcher.

approachable [ə'prəutʃəbl] adj accessible.

approaching [ə'prəutʃɪŋ] adj qui approche.

approbation [,æprə'beɪʃn] n approbation f.

appropriate [adj ə'prəupriət, vb ə'prəuprieɪt] ◇ adj [clothing] convenable; [action] approprié(e); [moment] opportun(e). ◇ vt **-1.** JUR s'approprier. **-2.** [allocate] affecter.

appropriately [ə'prəupriətlɪ] adv [dress] convenablement; [behave] de manière appropriée.

appropriation [ə,prəuprɪ'eɪʃn] n **-1.** [taking] appropriation f. **-2.** [allocation] affectation f.

approval [ə'pruːvl] n approbation f; on ~ COMM à condition, à l'essai.

approve [ə'pruːv] ◇ vi: to ~ (of sthg) approuver (qqch); I don't ~ of him il me déplaît. ◇ vt [ratify] approuver, ratifier.

approved [ə'pruːvd] adj approuvé(e), agréé(e).

approving [ə'pruːvɪŋ] adj approbateur(trice).

approx. [ə'prɒks] (*abbr of* **approximately**)
approx., env.

approximate [*adj* ə'prɒksɪmət, *vb* ə'prɒksɪmeɪt] ◇ *adj* approximatif(ive). ◇ *vi*: **to ~ to** se rapprocher de.

approximately [ə'prɒksɪmətlɪ] *adv* à peu près, environ.

approximation [ə,prɒksɪ'meɪʃn] *n*: **~ (to)** approximation *f* (de).

Apr. (*abbr of* **April**) avr.

APR *n* **-1.** (*abbr of* **annualized percentage rate**) TEG *m*. **-2.** (*abbr of* **annual purchase rate**) taux *m* annuel.

après-ski [,æpreɪ'skiː] *n* (U) activités *fpl* après-ski.

apricot ['eɪprɪkɒt] ◇ *n* abricot *m*. ◇ *comp* à l'abricot.

April ['eɪprəl] *n* avril *m; see also* **September**.
April Fools' Day *n* le premier avril.

APRIL FOOLS' DAY:
En Grande-Bretagne, le premier avril est l'occasion de canulars en tous genres; par contre, la tradition du poisson en papier n'existe pas

apron ['eɪprən] *n* **-1.** [clothing] tablier *m*; **to be tied to sb's ~ strings** *inf* être toujours dans les jupes de qqn. **-2.** AERON aire *f* de stationnement.

apropos ['æprəpəʊ] ◇ *adj* pertinent(e), à propos. ◇ *prep*: **~ (of)** à propos (de).

apt [æpt] *adj* **-1.** [pertinent] pertinent(e), approprié(e). **-2.** [likely]: **to be ~ to do sthg** avoir tendance à faire qqch.

Apt. (*abbr of* **apartment**) appt.

APT (*abbr of* **advanced passenger train**) *n* ≃ TGV *m*.

aptitude ['æptɪtjuːd] *n* aptitude *f*, disposition *f*; **to have an ~ for** avoir des dispositions pour.

aptitude test *n* test *m* d'aptitude.

aptly ['æptlɪ] *adv* avec justesse, à propos.

aqualung ['ækwəlʌŋ] *n* scaphandre *m* autonome.

aquamarine [,ækwəmə'riːn] *n* [colour] bleu vert *m*.

aquaplane ['ækwəpleɪn] *vi Br* AUT faire de l'aquaplaning.

aquarium [ə'kweərɪəm] (*pl* **-riums** OR **-ria** [-rɪə]) *n* aquarium *m*.

Aquarius [ə'kweərɪəs] *n* Verseau *m*; **to be (an) ~** être Verseau.

aquatic [ə'kwætɪk] *adj* **-1.** [animal, plant] aquatique. **-2.** [sport] nautique.

aqueduct ['ækwɪdʌkt] *n* aqueduc *m*.

AR *abbr of* **Arkansas**.

ARA (*abbr of* **Associate of the Royal Academy**) *n* membre associé de la RA.

Arab ['ærəb] ◇ *adj* arabe. ◇ *n* **-1.** [person] Arabe *mf*. **-2.** [horse] pur-sang *m* arabe.

Arabia [ə'reɪbjə] *n* Arabie *f*.

Arabian [ə'reɪbjən] *adj* d'Arabie, arabe.

Arabian desert *n*: **the ~** le désert d'Arabie.

Arabian Peninsula *n*: **the ~** la péninsule d'Arabie.

Arabian Sea *n*: **the ~** la mer d'Arabie, la mer d'Oman.

Arabic ['ærəbɪk] ◇ *adj* arabe. ◇ *n* arabe *m*.

Arabic numeral *n* chiffre *m* arabe.

arable ['ærəbl] *adj* arable.

ARAM (*abbr of* **Associate of the Royal Academy of Music**) *n* membre associé de l'académie britannique de musique.

arbiter ['ɑːbɪtər] *n fml* arbitre *m*.

arbitrary ['ɑːbɪtrərɪ] *adj* arbitraire.

arbitrate ['ɑːbɪtreɪt] *vi* arbitrer.

arbitration [,ɑːbɪ'treɪʃn] *n* arbitrage *m*; **to go to ~** recourir à l'arbitrage.

arc [ɑːk] *n* arc *m*.

ARC (*abbr of* **AIDS-related complex**) *n* ARC *m*.

arcade [ɑː'keɪd] *n* **-1.** [for shopping] galerie *f* marchande. **-2.** [covered passage] arcades *fpl*.

arch [ɑːtʃ] ◇ *adj* malicieux(ieuse), espiègle. ◇ *n* **-1.** ARCHIT arc *m*, voûte *f*. **-2.** [of foot] voûte *f* plantaire, cambrure *f*. ◇ *vt* cambrer, arquer. ◇ *vi* former une voûte.

arch- [ɑːtʃ] *prefix* grand(e), principal(e).

archaeological [,ɑːkɪə'lɒdʒɪkl] *adj* archéologique.

archaeologist [,ɑːkɪ'ɒlədʒɪst] *n* archéologue *mf*.

archaeology [,ɑːkɪ'ɒlədʒɪ] *n* archéologie *f*.

archaic [ɑː'keɪɪk] *adj* archaïque.

archangel ['ɑːk,eɪndʒəl] *n* archange *m*.

archbishop [,ɑːtʃ'bɪʃəp] *n* archevêque *m*.

archduchess [,ɑːtʃ'dʌtʃɪs] *n* archiduchesse *f*.

archduke [,ɑːtʃ'djuːk] *n* archiduc *m*.

arched [ɑːtʃt] *adj* **-1.** ARCHIT cintré(e), courbé(e). **-2.** [curved] arqué(e), cambré(e).

archenemy [,ɑːtʃ'enɪmɪ] (*pl* **-ies**) *n* ennemi *m* numéro un.

archeology [,ɑːkɪ'ɒlədʒɪ] *etc* = **archaeology** *etc*.

archer ['ɑːtʃər] *n* archer *m*.

archery ['ɑːtʃərɪ] *n* tir *m* à l'arc.

archetypal [,ɑːkɪ'taɪpl] *adj* typique.

archetype ['ɑːkɪtaɪp] *n* archétype *m*.

archipelago [,ɑːkɪ'peligəʊ] (*pl* **-es** OR **-s**) *n* archipel *m*.

architect ['ɑːkɪtekt] *n lit* & *fig* architecte *m*.

architectural [,ɑːkɪ'tektʃərəl] *adj* architectural(e).

architecture ['ɑːkɪtektʃəˈ] *n* [gen & COMPUT] architecture *f*.

archive file ['ɑːkaɪv-] *n* COMPUT fichier *m* archives.

archives ['ɑːkaɪvz] *npl* archives *fpl*.

archivist ['ɑːkɪvɪst] *n* archiviste *mf*.

archway ['ɑːtʃweɪ] *n* passage *m* voûté.

ARCM (*abbr of* **Associate of the Royal College of Music**) *n* membre associé du conservatoire de musique britannique.

Arctic ['ɑːktɪk] ◇ *adj* **-1.** GEOGR arctique. **-2.** *inf* [very cold] glacial(e). ◇ *n*: **the ~** l'Arctique *m*; **in the ~** dans l'Arctique. ◇ *adj* arctique.

Arctic Circle *n*: **the ~** le cercle arctique.

Arctic Ocean *n*: **the ~** l'océan *m* Arctique.

ardent ['ɑːdənt] *adj* fervent(e), passionné(e).

ardour *Br*, **ardor** *Am* ['ɑːdəˈ] *n* ardeur *f*, ferveur *f*.

arduous ['ɑːdjʊəs] *adj* ardu(e).

are [*weak form* əˈ, *strong form* ɑːʳ] → **be**.

area ['eərɪə] *n* **-1.** [region] région *f*; **landing ~** aire *f* d'atterrissage; **parking ~** aire de stationnement; **in the ~** dans la région; **in the ~ of** [approximately] environ, à peu près. **-2.** [surface size] aire *f*, superficie *f*. **-3.** [of knowledge, interest etc] domaine *m*.

area code *n* indicatif *m* de zone.

arena [ə'riːnə] *n lit* & *fig* arène *f*.

aren't ['ɑːnt] = **are not**.

Argentina [,ɑːdʒən'tiːnə] *n* Argentine *f*; **in ~** en Argentine.

Argentine ['ɑːdʒəntaɪn], **Argentinian** [,ɑːdʒən'tɪnɪən] ◇ *adj* argentin(ine). ◇ *n* Argentin *m*, **-ine** *f*.

arguable ['ɑːgjʊəbl] *adj* discutable, contestable.

arguably ['ɑːgjʊəblɪ] *adv*: **she's ~ the best** on peut soutenir qu'elle est la meilleure.

argue ['ɑːgjuː] ◇ *vi* **-1.** [quarrel]: **to ~ (with sb about sthg)** se disputer (avec qqn à propos de qqch). **-2.** [reason]: **to ~ (for/against)** argumenter (pour/contre). ◇ *vt* débattre de, discuter de; **to ~ that** soutenir OR maintenir que.

argument ['ɑːgjʊmənt] *n* **-1.** [quarrel] dispute *f*; **to have an ~ (with sb)** se disputer

(avec qqn). **-2.** [reason] argument *m*. **-3.** (*U*) [reasoning] discussion *f*, débat *m*.

argumentative [,ɑːgjʊ'mentətɪv] *adj* querelleur(euse), batailleur(euse).

aria ['ɑːrɪə] *n* aria *f*.

arid ['ærɪd] *adj lit* & *fig* aride.

Aries ['eəriːz] *n* Bélier *m*; **to be (an) ~** être Bélier.

arise [ə'raɪz] (*pt* **arose**, *pp* **arisen** [ə'rɪzn]) *vi* [appear] surgir, survenir; **to ~ from** résulter de, provenir de; **if the need ~s** si le besoin se fait sentir.

aristocracy [,ærɪ'stɒkrəsɪ] (*pl* **-ies**) *n* aristocratie *f*.

aristocrat [*Br* 'ærɪstəkræt, *Am* ə'rɪstəkræt] *n* aristocrate *mf*.

aristocratic [*Br* ,ærɪstə'krætɪk, *Am* ə,rɪstə'krætɪk] *adj* aristocratique.

arithmetic [ə'rɪθmətɪk] *n* arithmétique *f*.

Arizona [,ærɪ'zəʊnə] *n* Arizona *m*; **in ~** dans l'Arizona.

ark [ɑːk] *n* arche *f*.

Arkansas ['ɑːkənsɔː] *n* Arkansas *m*; **in ~** dans l'Arkansas.

arm [ɑːm] ◇ *n* **-1.** [of person, chair] bras *m*; **~ in ~** bras dessus bras dessous; **to chance one's ~** *fig* tenter le coup; **to keep sb at ~'s length** *fig* tenir qqn à distance; **to twist sb's ~** *fig* forcer la main à qqn. **-2.** [of garment] manche *f*. **-3.** [of organization] section *f*, aile *f*. ◇ *vt* armer.
  ◆ **arms** *npl* armes *fpl*; **to take up ~s** prendre les armes; **to be up in ~s about sthg** s'élever contre qqch.

armada [ɑː'mɑːdə] *n* armada *f*.

armadillo [,ɑːmə'dɪləʊ] (*pl* **-s**) *n* tatou *m*.

Armageddon [,ɑːmə'gedn] *n* Armageddon *m*.

armaments ['ɑːməmənts] *npl* [weapons] matériel *m* de guerre, armements *mpl*.

armchair ['ɑːmtʃeəˈ] *n* fauteuil *m*.

armed [ɑːmd] *adj lit* & *fig*: **~ (with)** armé(e) (de).

armed forces *npl* forces *fpl* armées.

Armenia [ɑː'miːnjə] *n* Arménie *f*; **in ~** en Arménie.

Armenian [ɑː'miːnjən] ◇ *adj* arménien(ienne). ◇ *n* **-1.** [person] Arménien *m*, **-ienne** *f*. **-2.** [language] arménien *m*.

armhole ['ɑːmhəʊl] *n* emmanchure *f*.

armistice ['ɑːmɪstɪs] *n* armistice *m*.

armour *Br*, **armor** *Am* ['ɑːməˈ] *n* **-1.** [for person] armure *f*. **-2.** [for military vehicle] blindage *m*.

armoured *Br*, **armored** *Am* ['ɑːməd] *adj*
MIL blindé(e).

armoured car *n* voiture *f* blindée.

armour-plated [-pleɪtɪd] *adj* blindé(e).

armoury *Br* (*pl* -ies), **armory** *Am* (*pl* -ies)
['ɑːmərɪ] arsenal *m*.

armpit ['ɑːmpɪt] *n* aisselle *f*.

armrest ['ɑːmrəst] *n* accoudoir *m*.

arms control ['ɑːmz-] *n* contrôle *m* des armements.

army ['ɑːmɪ] (*pl* -ies) *n* lit & fig armée *f*.
A road *n Br* route *f* nationale.

aroma [ə'rəʊmə] *n* arôme *m*.

aromatherapy [ərəʊmə'θerəpɪ] *n* aromathé-
rapie *f*.

aromatic [,ærə'mætɪk] *adj* aromatique.

arose [ə'rəʊz] *pt* → arise.

around [ə'raʊnd] ◇ *adv* **-1.** [about, round]:
to walk ~ marcher par-ci par-là, errer; **to
lie ~** [clothes etc] traîner. **-2.** [on all sides]
(tout) autour. **-3.** [near] dans les parages.
-4. [in circular movement]: **to turn ~** se retourner. **-5.** *phr*: **he has been ~** *inf* il n'est
pas né d'hier, il a de l'expérience.
◇ *prep* **-1.** [gen] autour de; **to walk ~** a
garden/town faire le tour d'un jardin/d'une
ville; **all ~ the country** dans tout le pays.
-2. [near]: **~ here** ici. **-3.** [approximately]
environ, à peu près.

arousal [ə'raʊzl] *n* éveil *m*.

arouse [ə'raʊz] *vt* **-1.** [excite - feeling] éveiller, susciter; [- person] exciter. **-2.** [wake] réveiller.

arrange [ə'reɪndʒ] *vt* **-1.** [flowers, books, fur-
niture] arranger, disposer. **-2.** [event, meeting
etc] organiser, fixer; **to ~ to do sthg** convenir de faire qqch; **she ~d for him to come
to Edinburgh** elle a fait le nécessaire pour
qu'il vienne à Édimbourg. **-3.** MUS arranger.

arranged marriage [ə'reɪndʒd-] *n* mariage
m arrangé.

arrangement [ə'reɪndʒmənt] *n* **-1.** [agree-
ment] accord *m*, arrangement *m*; **to come to
an ~** s'entendre, s'arranger. **-2.** [of furniture,
books] arrangement *m*; **flower ~** composition *f* florale. **-3.** MUS arrangement *m*.
◆ **arrangements** *npl* dispositions *fpl*, préparatifs *mpl*; **to make ~s** prendre des mesures OR dispositions.

array [ə'reɪ] ◇ *n* **-1.** [of objects] étalage *m*.
-2. COMPUT tableau *m*. ◇ *vt* [ornaments etc]
disposer.

arrears [ə'rɪəz] *npl* [money owed] arriéré *m*;
to be in ~ [late] être en retard; [owing
money] avoir des arriérés.

arrest [ə'rest] ◇ *n* [by police] arrestation *f*;
under ~ en état d'arrestation. ◇ *vt* **-1.**
[gen] arrêter. **-2.** *fml* [sb's attention] attirer,
retenir.

arresting [ə'restɪŋ] *adj* [striking] frappant(e),
saisissant(e).

arrival [ə'raɪvl] *n* **-1.** [gen] arrivée *f*; **late ~**
[of train etc] retard *m*. **-2.** [person - at airport,
hotel] arrivant *m*, -e *f*; **new ~** [person] nouveau venu *m*, nouvelle venue *f*; [baby]
nouveau-né *m*, nouveau-née *f*.

arrive [ə'raɪv] *vi* arriver; [baby] être né(e);
to ~ at [conclusion, decision] arriver à.

arrogance ['ærəgəns] *n* arrogance *f*.

arrogant ['ærəgənt] *adj* arrogant(e).

arrogantly ['ærəgəntlɪ] *adv* avec arrogance.

arrow ['ærəʊ] *n* flèche *f*.

arrowroot ['ærəʊruːt] *n* arrow-root *m*.

arse *Br* [ɑːs], **ass** *Am* [æs] *n v inf* cul *m*.

arsenal ['ɑːsənl] *n* arsenal *m*.

arsenic ['ɑːsnɪk] *n* arsenic *m*.

arson ['ɑːsn] *n* incendie *m* criminel OR volontaire.

arsonist ['ɑːsənɪst] *n* incendiaire *mf*.

art [ɑːt] ◇ *n* art *m*. ◇ *comp* [exhibition] d'art;
[college] des beaux-arts; **~ student** étudiant
m, -e *f* d'une école des beaux-arts.
◆ **arts** ◇ *npl* **-1.** SCH & UNIV lettres *fpl*. **-2.**
[fine arts]: **the ~s** les arts *mpl*. ◇ *comp* SCH &
UNIV de lettres; **~s student** étudiant *m*, -e *f*
en lettres.

art deco [-'dekəʊ] *n* art *m* déco.

artefact ['ɑːtɪfækt] = artifact.

arterial [ɑː'tɪərɪəl] *adj* **-1.** [blood] arté-
riel(ielle). **-2.** [road] à grande circulation.

arteriosclerosis [ɑː,tɪərɪəʊsklɪ'rəʊsɪs] *n* artériosclérose *f*.

artery ['ɑːtərɪ] (*pl* -ies) *n* artère *f*.

artful ['ɑːtfʊl] *adj* rusé(e), malin(igne).

art gallery *n* [public] musée *m* d'art; [for
selling paintings] galerie *f* d'art.

arthritic [ɑː'θrɪtɪk] *adj* arthritique.

arthritis [ɑː'θraɪtɪs] *n* arthrite *f*.

artic [ɑː'tɪk] (*abbr of* articulated lorry) *n Br
inf* semi-remorque *m*.

artichoke ['ɑːtɪtʃəʊk] *n* artichaut *m*.

article ['ɑːtɪkl] *n* article *m*; **~ of clothing**
vêtement *m*.

articled clerk ['ɑːtɪkld-] *n Br* avocat *m* stagiaire.

articles of association ['ɑːtɪklz-] *npl* statuts *mpl* d'une société.

articulate [*adj* ɑː'tɪkjʊlət, *vb* ɑː'tɪkjʊleɪt] ◇
adj [person] qui sait s'exprimer; [speech] net

(nette), distinct(e). ◇ *vt* [thought, wish] formuler.

articulated lorry [ɑːˈtɪkjʊleɪtɪd-] *n Br* semi-remorque *m*.

articulation [ɑːˌtɪkjʊˈleɪʃn] *n* articulation *f*.

artifact [ˈɑːtɪfækt] *n* objet *m* fabriqué.

artifice [ˈɑːtɪfɪs] *n* **-1.** [trick] artifice *m*, ruse *f*. **-2.** [trickery] ingéniosité *f*, habileté *f*.

artificial [ˌɑːtɪˈfɪʃl] *adj* **-1.** [not natural] artificiel(ielle). **-2.** [insincere] affecté(e).

artificial insemination *n* insémination *f* artificielle.

artificial intelligence *n* intelligence *f* artificielle.

artificially [ˌɑːtɪˈfɪʃəlɪ] *adv* artificiellement.

artificial respiration *n* respiration *f* artificielle.

artillery [ɑːˈtɪlərɪ] *n* artillerie *f*.

artisan [ˌɑːtɪˈzæn] *n* artisan *m*.

artist [ˈɑːtɪst] *n* artiste *mf*.

artiste [ɑːˈtiːst] *n* artiste *mf*.

artistic [ɑːˈtɪstɪk] *adj* [person] artiste; [style etc] artistique.

artistically [ɑːˈtɪstɪklɪ] *adv* avec art, de façon artistique.

artistry [ˈɑːtɪstrɪ] *n* art *m*, talent *m* artistique.

artless [ˈɑːtlɪs] *adj* naturel(elle), ingénu(e).

art nouveau [ˌɑːnuːˈvəʊ] *n* art *m* nouveau.

ARV (*abbr of* **American Revised Version**) *n* traduction américaine de la Bible.

as [unstressed əz, stressed æz] ◇ *conj* **-1.** [referring to time] comme, alors que; **she rang (just) ~ I was leaving** elle m'a téléphoné au moment même où OR juste comme je partais; **~ time goes by** à mesure que le temps passe, avec le temps. **-2.** [referring to manner, way] comme; **do ~ I say** fais ce que je (te) dis; **~ it is déjà**; **she's working too hard ~ it is** elle travaille déjà assez dur comme ça; **~ it turns out** finalement, en fin de compte; **~ things stand** les choses étant ce qu'elles sont. **-3.** [introducing a statement] comme; **~ you see, ...** comme tu le vois, ...; **~ you know, ...** comme tu le sais, ... **-4.** [because] comme.

◇ *prep* **-1.** [referring to function, characteristic] en, comme, en tant que; **I'm speaking ~ your friend** je te parle en ami; **he made a name ~ an actor** il s'est fait un nom comme acteur; **she works ~ a nurse** elle est infirmière. **-2.** [referring to attitude, reaction]: **it came ~ a shock** cela nous a fait un choc; **she treats it ~ a game** elle prend ça à la rigolade.

◇ *adv* (*in comparisons*): **~ rich ~** aussi riche que; **~ red ~ a tomato** rouge comme une tomate; **he's ~ tall ~ I am** il est aussi grand que moi; **twice ~ big ~** deux fois plus gros que; **~ much/many ~** autant que; **~ much wine/many chocolates ~** autant de vin/de chocolats que.

◆ **as it were** *adv* pour ainsi dire.

◆ **as for** *prep* quant à.

◆ **as from, as of** *prep* dès, à partir de.

◆ **as if, as though** *conj* comme si; **it looks ~ if** OR **~ though it will rain** on dirait qu'il va pleuvoir.

◆ **as to** *prep* **-1.** [concerning] en ce qui concerne, au sujet de. **-2.** = **as for**.

AS ◇ *n* (*abbr of* **Associate in/of Science**) *diplômé en sciences*. ◇ *abbr of* **American Samoa**.

ASA (*abbr of* **American Standards Association**) *n association américaine de normalisation*, ≃ AFNOR *f*.

a.s.a.p. (*abbr of* **as soon as possible**) d'urgence, dans les meilleurs délais.

asbestos [æsˈbestəs] *n* asbeste *m*, amiante *m*.

asbestosis [ˌæsbesˈtəʊsɪs] *n* asbestose *f*.

ascend [əˈsend] *vt & vi* monter; **to ~ the throne** monter sur le trône.

ascendancy [əˈsendənsɪ] *n* ascendant *m*.

ascendant [əˈsendənt] *n*: **to be in the ~** avoir le dessus.

ascendency [əˈsendənsɪ] = **ascendancy**.

ascending [əˈsendɪŋ] *adj* croissant(e); **in ~ order** en ordre croissant.

ascension [əˈsenʃn] *n* ascension *f*.

◆ **Ascension** *n* RELIG l'Ascension *f*.

Ascension Island *n* île *f* de l'Ascension.

ascent [əˈsent] *n lit & fig* ascension *f*.

ascertain [ˌæsəˈteɪn] *vt* établir.

ascetic [əˈsetɪk] ◇ *adj* ascétique. ◇ *n* ascète *mf*.

ASCII [ˈæskɪ] (*abbr of* **American Standard Code for Information**) *n* ASCII *m*.

ascorbic acid [əˈskɔːbɪk-] *n* acide *m* ascorbique.

ascribe [əˈskraɪb] *vt*: **to ~ sthg to** attribuer qqch à; [blame] imputer qqch à.

ASCU (*abbr of* **Association of State Colleges and Universities**) *n association des établissements universitaires d'État aux États-Unis*.

ASE (*abbr of* **American Stock Exchange**) *n la Bourse américaine*.

aseptic [ˌeɪˈseptɪk] *adj* aseptique.

asexual [ˌeɪˈseksjʊəl] *adj* asexué(e).

ash [æʃ] *n* **-1.** [from cigarette, fire] cendre *f*. **-2.** [tree] frêne *m*.

◆ **ashes** *npl* cendres *fpl*.

ASH [æʃ] (*abbr of* **Action on Smoking and Health**) *n* ligue antitabac britannique.

ashamed [əˈʃeɪmd] *adj* honteux(euse), confus(e); **to be ~ of** avoir honte de; **to be ~ to do sthg** avoir honte de faire qqch.

ashcan [ˈæʃkæn] *n Am* poubelle *f*.

ashen-faced [ˈæʃn,feɪst] *adj* blême.

ashore [əˈʃɔːr] *adv* à terre.

ashtray [ˈæʃtreɪ] *n* cendrier *m*.

Ash Wednesday *n* le mercredi des Cendres.

Asia [*Br* ˈeɪʃə, *Am* ˈeɪʒə] *n* Asie *f*; **in ~** en Asie.

Asia Minor *n* Asie *f* Mineure.

Asian [*Br* ˈeɪʃn, *Am* ˈeɪʒn] ◇ *adj* asiatique. ◇ *n* [person] Asiatique *mf*.

Asiatic [*Br* ,eɪʃɪˈætɪk, *Am* ,eɪʒɪˈætɪk] *adj* asiatique.

aside [əˈsaɪd] ◇ *adv* -1. [to one side] de côté; **to move ~** s'écarter; **to take sb ~** prendre qqn à part; **to brush** OR **sweep sthg ~** balayer OR repousser qqch. -2. [apart] à part; **~ from** hormis à l'exception de. ◇ *n* -1. [in play] aparté *m*. -2. [remark] réflexion *f*, commentaire *m*.

ask [ɑːsk] ◇ *vt* -1. [gen] demander; **to ~ sb sthg** demander qqch à qqn; **he ~ed me my name** il m'a demandé mon nom; **to ~ sb for sthg** demander qqch à qqn; **to ~ sb to do sthg** demander à qqn de faire qqch; **if you ~ me ...** si tu veux mon avis .... -2. [put - question] poser. -3. [invite] inviter. ◇ *vi* demander.

◆ **ask after** *vt fus* demander des nouvelles de.

◆ **ask for** *vt fus* -1. [person] demander à voir. -2. [thing] demander.

askance [əˈskæns] *adv*: **to look ~ at sb** regarder qqn d'un air désapprobateur.

askew [əˈskjuː] *adj* [not straight] de travers.

asking price [ˈɑːskɪŋ-] *n* prix *m* demandé.

asleep [əˈsliːp] *adj* endormi(e); **to fall ~** s'endormir; **to be fast** OR **sound ~** dormir profondément OR à poings fermés.

ASLEF [ˈæzlef] (*abbr of* **Associated Society of Locomotive Engineers and Firemen**) *n* syndicat des cheminots en Grande-Bretagne.

ASM (*abbr of* **air-to-surface missile**) *n* ASM *m*.

asparagus [əˈspærəgəs] *n* (*U*) asperges *fpl*.

aspartame [*Br* əˈspɑːteɪm, *Am* ˈæspərteɪm] *n* aspartame *m*.

ASPCA (*abbr of* **American Society for the Prevention of Cruelty to Animals**) *n* société américaine protectrice des animaux.

aspect [ˈæspekt] *n* -1. [gen] aspect *m*. -2. [of building] orientation *f*.

aspen [ˈæspən] *n* tremble *m*.

aspersions [əˈspɜːʃnz] *npl*: **to cast ~ on** jeter le discrédit sur.

asphalt [ˈæsfælt] *n* asphalte *m*.

asphyxiate [əsˈfɪksɪeɪt] *vt* asphyxier.

aspic [ˈæspɪk] *n* aspic *m*.

aspirate [ˈæspərət] *adj* LING aspiré(e).

aspiration [,æspəˈreɪʃn] *n* aspiration *f*.

aspire [əˈspaɪər] *vi*: **to ~ to sthg/to do sthg** aspirer à qqch/à faire qqch.

aspirin [ˈæsprɪn] *n* aspirine *f*.

aspiring [əˈspaɪərɪŋ] *adj*: **she was an ~ writer** elle avait pour ambition de devenir écrivain.

ass [æs] *n* -1. [donkey] âne *m*. -2. *Br inf* [idiot] imbécile *mf*, idiot *m*, -e *f*. -3. *Am v inf* = **arse**.

assail [əˈseɪl] *vt* assaillir.

assailant [əˈseɪlənt] *n* assaillant *m*, -e *f*.

assassin [əˈsæsɪn] *n* assassin *m*.

assassinate [əˈsæsɪneɪt] *vt* assassiner.

assassination [ə,sæsɪˈneɪʃn] *n* assassinat *m*.

assault [əˈsɔːlt] ◇ *n* -1. MIL: **~ (on)** assaut *m* (de), attaque *f* (de). -2. [physical attack]: **~ (on sb)** agression *f* (contre qqn); **~ and battery** JUR coups *mpl* et blessures. ◇ *vt* [attack - physically] agresser; [- sexually] violenter.

assault course *n* parcours *m* du combattant.

assemble [əˈsembl] ◇ *vt* -1. [gather] réunir. -2. [fit together] assembler, monter. ◇ *vi* se réunir, s'assembler.

assembly [əˈsemblɪ] (*pl* **-ies**) *n* -1. [gen] assemblée *f*. -2. [fitting together] assemblage *m*.

assembly language *n* COMPUT langage *m* d'assemblage.

assembly line *n* chaîne *f* de montage.

assent [əˈsent] ◇ *n* consentement *m*, assentiment *m*. ◇ *vi*: **to ~ (to)** donner son consentement OR assentiment (à).

assert [əˈsɜːt] *vt* -1. [fact, belief] affirmer, soutenir. -2. [authority] imposer; **to ~ o.s.** s'imposer.

assertion [əˈsɜːʃn] *n* [claim] assertion *f*, affirmation *f*.

assertive [əˈsɜːtɪv] *adj* assuré(e).

assess [əˈses] *vt* évaluer, estimer.

assessment [əˈsesmənt] *n* -1. [opinion] opinion *f*. -2. [calculation] évaluation *f*, estimation *f*.

assessor [əˈsesər] *n* [of tax] contrôleur *m* (des impôts).

asset ['æset] *n* avantage *m,* atout *m;* **she will be an ~ to the company** sa compétence sera un atout pour la société.
◆ **assets** *npl* COMM actif *m.*

asset-stripping [-ˌstrɪpɪŋ] *n* rachat d'une société pour en récupérer l'actif.

assiduous [ə'sɪdjʊəs] *adj* assidu(e).

assiduously [ə'sɪdjʊəslɪ] *adv* assidûment.

assign [ə'saɪn] *vt* **-1.** [allot]: **to ~ sthg (to)** assigner qqch (à). **-2.** [give task to]: **to ~ sb (to sthg/to do sthg)** nommer qqn (à qqch/ pour faire qqch).

assignation [ˌæsɪg'neɪʃn] *n* rendez-vous *m* (amoureux).

assignment [ə'saɪnmənt] *n* **-1.** [task] mission *f;* SCH devoir *m.* **-2.** [act of assigning] attribution *f.*

assimilate [ə'sɪmɪleɪt] *vt* assimiler.

assimilation [əˌsɪmɪ'leɪʃn] *n* assimilation *f.*

assist [ə'sɪst] *vt*: **to ~ sb (with sthg/in doing sthg)** aider qqn (dans qqch/à faire qqch); [professionally] assister qqn (dans qqch/pour faire qqch).

assistance [ə'sɪstəns] *n* aide *f;* **to be of ~ (to)** être utile (à).

assistant [ə'sɪstənt] ◇ *n* assistant *m,* -e *f;* (shop) ~ vendeur *m,* -euse *f.* ◇ *comp*: ~ **editor** rédacteur en chef adjoint *m,* rédactrice en chef adjointe *f;* ~ **manager** sous-directeur *m,* -trice *f.*

associate [*adj & n* ə'səʊʃɪət, *vb* ə'səʊʃɪeɪt] ◇ *adj* associé(e). ◇ *n* associé *m,* -e *f.* ◇ *vt*: **to ~ sb/sthg (with)** associer qqn/qqch (à); **to be ~d with** être associé(e) à. ◇ *vi*: **to ~ with sb** fréquenter qqn.

association [əˌsəʊsɪ'eɪʃn] *n* association *f;* **in ~ with** avec la collaboration de.

assonance ['æsənəns] *n* assonance *f.*

assorted [ə'sɔːtɪd] *adj* varié(e).

assortment [ə'sɔːtmənt] *n* mélange *m.*

Asst. *abbr of* **assistant.**

assuage [ə'sweɪdʒ] *vt* [thirst, hunger] assouvir; [grief] soulager.

assume [ə'sjuːm] *vt* **-1.** [suppose] supposer, présumer. **-2.** [power, responsibility] assumer. **-3.** [appearance, attitude] adopter.

assumed name [ə'sjuːmd-] *n* nom *m* d'emprunt.

assuming [ə'sjuːmɪŋ] *conj* en supposant que.

assumption [ə'sʌmpʃn] *n* **-1.** [supposition] supposition *f.* **-2.** [of power] prise *f.*
◆ **Assumption** *n* RELIG: **the Assumption** l'Assomption *f.*

assurance [ə'ʃɔːrəns] *n* **-1.** [gen] assurance *f.* **-2.** [promise] garantie *f,* promesse *f.*

assure [ə'ʃɔːr] *vt*: **to ~ sb (of)** assurer qqn (de).

assured [ə'ʃɔːd] *adj* assuré(e).

AST (*abbr of* **Atlantic Standard Time**) *n* heure d'hiver de la côte est des États-Unis.

asterisk ['æstərɪsk] *n* astérisque *m.*

astern [ə'stɜːn] *adv* NAUT en poupe.

asteroid ['æstərɔɪd] *n* astéroïde *m.*

asthma ['æsmə] *n* asthme *m.*

asthmatic [æs'mætɪk] ◇ *adj* asthmatique. ◇ *n* asthmatique *mf.*

astigmatism [ə'stɪgmətɪzm] *n* astigmatisme *m.*

astonish [ə'stɒnɪʃ] *vt* étonner.

astonishing [ə'stɒnɪʃɪŋ] *adj* étonnant(e).

astonishment [ə'stɒnɪʃmənt] *n* étonnement *m.*

astound [ə'staʊnd] *vt* stupéfier.

astounding [ə'staʊndɪŋ] *adj* stupéfiant(e).

astrakhan [ˌæstrə'kæn] *n* astrakan *m.*

astray [ə'streɪ] *adv*: **to go ~** [become lost] s'égarer; **to lead sb ~** détourner qqn du droit chemin.

astride [ə'straɪd] ◇ *adv* à cheval, à califourchon. ◇ *prep* à cheval OR califourchon sur.

astringent [ə'strɪndʒənt] ◇ *adj* astringent(e). ◇ *n* astringent *m.*

astrologer [ə'strɒlədʒər] *n* astrologue *mf.*

astrological [ˌæstrə'lɒdʒɪkl] *adj* astrologique.

astrologist [ə'strɒlədʒɪst] = **astrologer.**

astrology [ə'strɒlədʒɪ] *n* astrologie *f.*

astronaut ['æstrənɔːt] *n* astronaute *mf.*

astronomer [ə'strɒnəmər] *n* astronome *mf.*

astronomical [ˌæstrə'nɒmɪkl] *adj* astronomique.

astronomy [ə'strɒnəmɪ] *n* astronomie *f.*

astrophysics [ˌæstrəʊ'fɪzɪks] *n* astrophysique *f.*

astute [ə'stjuːt] *adj* malin(igne).

asunder [ə'sʌndər] *adv* literary: **to tear ~** déchirer en deux.

ASV (*abbr of* **American Standard Version**) *n* traduction américaine de la Bible.

asylum [ə'saɪləm] *n* asile *m.*

asymmetrical [ˌeɪsɪ'metrɪkl] *adj* asymétrique.

at [*unstressed* ət, *stressed* æt] *prep* **-1.** [indicating place, position] à; **they arrived ~ the airport** ils sont arrivés à l'aéroport; ~ **my father's** chez mon père; ~ **home** à la maison, chez soi; ~ **school** à l'école; ~ **work** au travail. **-2.** [indicating direction] vers; **to look ~ sb** regarder qqn; **to smile ~ sb** sourire à qqn; **to shoot ~ sb** tirer sur qqn. **-3.**

[indicating a particular time] à; ~ **midnight/ noon/eleven o'clock** à minuit/midi/onze heures; ~ **night** la nuit; ~ **Christmas/Easter** à Noël/Pâques. **-4.** [indicating age, speed, rate] à; ~ **52 (years of age)** à 52 ans; ~ **100 mph** à 160 km/h. **-5.** [indicating price]: ~ **£50 a pair** 50 livres la paire. **-6.** [indicating particular state, condition] en; ~ **peace/war** en paix/guerre; **to be** ~ **lunch/dinner** être en train de déjeuner/dîner. **-7.** [indicating tentativeness, noncompletion]: **to snatch** ~ **sthg** essayer de saisir qqch; **to nibble** ~ **sthg** grignoter qqch. **-8.** (after adjectives): **amused/ appalled/puzzled** ~ **sthg** diverti/effaré/ intrigué par qqch; **delighted** ~ **sthg** ravi de qqch; **to be bad/good** ~ **sthg** être mauvais/bon en qqch.
◆ **at all** adv ◇ **-1.** (with negative): **not** ~ **all** [when thanked] je vous en prie; [when answering a question] pas du tout; **she's not** ~ **all happy** elle n'est pas du tout contente. **-2.** [in the slightest]: **anything** ~ **all will do** n'importe quoi fera l'affaire; **do you know her** ~ **all?** est-ce que vous la connaissez?

ATC (abbr of **Air Training Corps**) n unité de formation de l'armée de l'air britannique.

ate [Br et, Am ɪt] pt → **eat.**

atheism ['eɪθɪɪzm] n athéisme m.

atheist ['eɪθɪɪst] n athée mf.

Athenian [ə'θiːnjən] ◇ adj athénien(ienne). ◇ n Athénien m, -ienne f.

Athens ['æθɪnz] n Athènes.

athlete ['æθliːt] n athlète mf.

athlete's foot n (U) mycose f.

athletic [æθ'letɪk] adj athlétique.
◆ **athletics** npl athlétisme m.

Atlantic [ət'læntɪk] ◇ adj atlantique. ◇ n: **the** ~ **(ocean)** l'océan m Atlantique, l'Atlantique m.

Atlantis [ət'læntɪs] n Atlantide f.

atlas ['ætləs] n atlas m.

Atlas ['ætləs] n: **the** ~ **Mountains** l'Atlas m.

atm. (abbr of **atmosphere**) atm.

ATM (abbr of **automatic teller machine**) n Am GAB m.

atmosphere ['ætmə,sfɪəʳ] n atmosphère f.

atmospheric [,ætməs'ferɪk] adj **-1.** [pressure, pollution etc] atmosphérique. **-2.** [film, music etc] d'ambiance.

atoll ['ætɒl] n atoll m.

atom ['ætəm] n **-1.** TECH atome m. **-2.** fig [tiny amount] grain m, parcelle f.

atom bomb n bombe f atomique.

atomic [ə'tɒmɪk] adj atomique.

atomic bomb = **atom bomb**.

atomic energy n énergie f atomique.

atomic number n nombre m OR numéro m atomique.

atomizer, -iser ['ætəmaɪzəʳ] n atomiseur m, vaporisateur m.

atone [ə'təʊn] vi: **to** ~ **for** racheter.

atonement [ə'təʊnmənt] n: ~ **(for)** réparation f (de).

A to Z n plan m de ville.

ATP (abbr of **Association of Tennis Professionals**) n ATP f.

atrocious [ə'trəʊʃəs] adj [very bad] atroce, affreux(euse).

atrocity [ə'trɒsətɪ] (pl **-ies**) n [terrible act] atrocité f.

attach [ə'tætʃ] vt **-1.** [gen]: **to** ~ **sthg (to)** attacher qqch (à). **-2.** [letter etc] joindre.

attaché [ə'tæʃeɪ] n attaché m, -e f.

attaché case n attaché-case m.

attached [ə'tætʃt] adj **-1.** [fastened on] attaché(e). **-2.** [letter etc] joint(e). **-3.** [for work, job]: ~ **to** rattaché(e) à. **-4.** [fond]: **to** ~ **to** attaché(e) à.

attachment [ə'tætʃmənt] n **-1.** [device] accessoire m. **-2.** [fondness]: ~ **(to)** attachement m (à).

attack [ə'tæk] ◇ n **-1.** [physical, verbal]: ~ **(on)** attaque f (contre). **-2.** [of illness] crise f. ◇ vt **-1.** [gen] attaquer. **-2.** [job, problem] s'attaquer à. ◇ vi attaquer.

attacker [ə'tækəʳ] n **-1.** [assailant] agresseur m. **-2.** SPORT attaquant m, -e f.

attain [ə'teɪn] vt atteindre, parvenir à.

attainment [ə'teɪnmənt] n **-1.** [of success, aims etc] réalisation f. **-2.** [skill] talent m.

attempt [ə'tempt] ◇ n: ~ **(at)** tentative f (de); ~ **on sb's life** tentative d'assassinat. ◇ vt tenter, essayer; **to** ~ **to do sthg** essayer OR tenter de faire qqch.

attend [ə'tend] ◇ vt **-1.** [meeting, party] assister à. **-2.** [school, church] aller à. ◇ vi **-1.** [be present] être présent(e). **-2.** [pay attention]: **to** ~ **(to)** prêter attention (à).
◆ **attend to** vt fus **-1.** [deal with] s'occuper de, régler. **-2.** [look after - customer] s'occuper de; [- patient] soigner.

attendance [ə'tendəns] n **-1.** [number present] assistance f, public m. **-2.** [presence] présence f.

attendant [ə'tendənt] ◇ adj [problems] qui en découle. ◇ n [at museum, car park] gardien m, -ienne f; [at petrol station] pompiste mf; **swimming-pool** ~ maître-nageur m, -euse f.

attention [ə'tenʃn] ◇ n (U) **-1.** [gen] attention f; **to bring sthg to sb's** ~, **to draw sb's** ~ **to sthg** attirer l'attention de qqn sur qqch; **to attract** OR **catch sb's** ~ attirer l'attention de qqn; **to pay** ~ **to** prêter attention à; **for the** ~ **of** COMM à l'attention de. **-2.** [care] soins *mpl*, attentions *fpl*. **-3.** MIL: **to stand to** ~ se mettre au garde-à-vous. ◇ *excl* MIL garde-à-vous!

attentive [ə'tentɪv] *adj* attentif(ive).

attentively [ə'tentɪvlɪ] *adv* attentivement.

attenuate [ə'tenjʊeɪt] ◇ *vt* atténuer. ◇ *vi* s'atténuer.

attest [ə'test] ◇ *vt* attester, certifier. ◇ *vi*: **to** ~ **to** témoigner de.

attic ['ætɪk] *n* grenier *m*.

attire [ə'taɪəʳ] *n* (*U*) *fml* tenue *f*.

attitude ['ætɪtjuːd] *n* **-1.** [gen]: ~ **(to** OR **towards)** attitude *f* (envers). **-2.** [posture] pose *f*.

attn. (*abbr of* **for the attention of**) à l'attention de.

attorney [ə'tɜːnɪ] *n Am* avocat *m*, -e *f*.

attorney general (*pl* **attorneys general**) *n* ministre *m* de la Justice.

attract [ə'trækt] *vt* attirer; **to be** ~**ed to** être attiré par.

attraction [ə'trækʃn] *n* **-1.** [gen] attraction *f*; ~ **to sb** attirance *f* envers qqn. **-2.** [of thing] attrait *m*.

attractive [ə'træktɪv] *adj* [person] attirant(e), séduisant(e); [thing, idea] attrayant(e), séduisant; [investment] intéressant(e).

attractively [ə'træktɪvlɪ] *adv* [decorated, arranged] de manière attrayante; [smile, dressed] de manière séduisante.

attributable [ə'trɪbjutəbl] *adj*: ~ **to** dû (due) à, attribuable à.

attribute [*vb* ə'trɪbjuːt, *n* 'ætrɪbjuːt] ◇ *vt*: **to** ~ **sthg to** attribuer qqch à. ◇ *n* attribut *m*.

attribution [ˌætrɪ'bjuːʃn] *n*: ~ **(to)** attribution *f* (à).

attrition [ə'trɪʃn] *n* usure *f*; **war of** ~ guerre *f* d'usure.

attuned [ə'tjuːnd] *adj*: ~ **to** accoutumé(e) à; [ears] habitué(e) à.

Atty. Gen. *abbr of* **Attorney General**.

ATV *n* **-1.** (*abbr of* **Associated Television**) *société britannique de télévision*. **-2.** (*abbr of* **all terrain vehicle**) *véhicule tout-terrain*.

atypical [ˌeɪ'tɪpɪkl] *adj* atypique.

atypically [ˌeɪ'tɪpɪklɪ] *adv* pas typiquement.

aubergine ['əʊbəʒiːn] *n Br* aubergine *f*.

auburn ['ɔːbən] *adj* auburn (*inv*).

auction ['ɔːkʃn] ◇ *n* vente *f* aux enchères; **at** OR **by** ~ aux enchères; **to put sthg up for** ~ mettre qqch (dans une vente) aux enchères. ◇ *vt* vendre aux enchères.

◆ **auction off** *vt sep* vendre aux enchères.

auctioneer [ˌɔːkʃə'nɪəʳ] *n* commissaire-priseur *m*.

audacious [ɔː'deɪʃəs] *adj* audacieux(ieuse).

audacity [ɔː'dæsətɪ] *n* audace *f*.

audible ['ɔːdəbl] *adj* audible.

audience ['ɔːdjəns] *n* **-1.** [of play, film] public *m*, spectateurs *mpl*; [of TV programme] téléspectateurs *mpl*. **-2.** [formal meeting] audience *f*.

audio ['ɔːdɪəʊ] *adj* audio (*inv*).

audio frequency *n* audiofréquence *f*.

audiotyping ['ɔːdɪəʊˌtaɪpɪŋ] *n* audiotypie *f*.

audiotypist ['ɔːdɪəʊˌtaɪpɪst] *n* audiotypiste *mf*.

audio-visual *adj* audiovisuel(elle).

audit ['ɔːdɪt] ◇ *n* audit *m*, vérification *f* des comptes. ◇ *vt* vérifier, apurer.

audition [ɔː'dɪʃn] ◇ *n* THEATRE audition *f*; CINEMA bout *m* d'essai. ◇ *vi*: **to** ~ **for** passer une audition pour.

auditor ['ɔːdɪtəʳ] *n* auditeur *m*, -trice *f*.

auditorium [ˌɔːdɪ'tɔːrɪəm] (*pl* **-riums** OR **-ria** [-rɪə]) *n* salle *f*.

au fait [ˌəʊ'feɪ] *adj*: **to be** ~ **with sthg** être au fait de qqch, connaître qqch.

Aug. *abbr of* **August**.

augment [ɔːg'ment] *vt* augmenter, accroître.

augur ['ɔːgəʳ] *vi*: **to** ~ **well/badly** être de bon/mauvais augure.

august [ɔː'gʌst] *adj* auguste, noble.

August ['ɔːgəst] *n* août *m*; *see also* **September**.

Auld Lang Syne [ˌɔːldlæŋ'saɪn] *n chant traditionnel britannique correspondant à «ce n'est qu'un au revoir, mes frères».*

aunt [ɑːnt] *n* tante *f*.

auntie, aunty ['ɑːntɪ] (*pl* **-ies**) *n inf* tata *f*, tantine *f*.

au pair [ˌəʊ'peəʳ] *n* jeune fille *f* au pair.

aura ['ɔːrə] *n* atmosphère *f*.

aural ['ɔːrəl] *adj* auditif(ive).

aurally ['ɔːrəlɪ] *adv*: ~ **handicapped** mal entendant(e).

auspices ['ɔːspɪsɪz] *npl*: **under the** ~ **of** sous les auspices de.

auspicious [ɔː'spɪʃəs] *adj* prometteur(euse).

Aussie ['ɒzɪ] *inf* ◇ *adj* australien(ienne). ◇ *n* Australien *m*, -ienne *f*.

austere [ɒ'stɪəʳ] *adj* austère.

austerity [ɒ'sterətɪ] *n* austérité *f*.

austerity measures *npl* restrictions *fpl*.

Australasia [ˌɒstrə'leɪʒə] *n* Australasie *f*.

Australia [ɒ'streɪljə] *n* Australie *f*; **in** ~ en Australie.

Australian [ɒ'streɪljən] ◇ *adj* australien(ienne). ◇ *n* Australien *m*, -ienne *f*.

Austria ['ɒstrɪə] *n* Autriche *f*; **in** ~ en Autriche.

Austrian ['ɒstrɪən] ◇ *adj* autrichien(ienne). ◇ *n* Autrichien *m*, -ienne *f*.

AUT (*abbr of* **Association of University Teachers**) *n syndicat britannique d'enseignants universitaires.*

authentic [ɔ:'θentɪk] *adj* authentique.

authenticate [ɔ:'θentɪkeɪt] *vt* établir l'authenticité de.

authentication [ɔ:,θentɪ'keɪʃn] *n* authentification *f*.

authenticity [,ɔ:θen'tɪsətɪ] *n* authenticité *f*.

author ['ɔ:θəʳ] *n* auteur *m*.

authoritarian [ɔ:,θɒrɪ'teərɪən] *adj* autoritaire.

authoritative [ɔ:'θɒrɪtətɪv] *adj* -1. [person, voice] autoritaire. -2. [study] qui fait autorité.

authority [ɔ:'θɒrətɪ] (*pl* -ies) *n* -1. [organization, power] autorité *f*; **to be in** ~ être le/la responsable. -2. [permission] autorisation *f*. -3. [expert]: ~ **(on sthg)** expert *m*, -e *f* (en qqch). -4. *phr*: **to have it on good** ~ OR source sûre. ◆ **authorities** *npl*: **the authorities** les autorités *fpl*.

authorize, -ise ['ɔ:θəraɪz] *vt*: **to** ~ **sb (to do sthg)** autoriser qqn (à faire qqch).

Authorized Version ['ɔ:θəraɪzd-] *n*: **the** ~ la Bible de 1611.

authorship ['ɔ:θəʃɪp] *n* paternité *f*.

autistic [ɔ:'tɪstɪk] *adj* [child] autiste; [behaviour] autistique.

auto ['ɔ:təʊ] (*pl* -s) *n Am* auto *f*, voiture *f*.

autobiographical ['ɔ:tə,baɪə'græfɪkl] *adj* autobiographique.

autobiography [,ɔ:təbaɪ'ɒgrəfɪ] (*pl* -ies) *n* autobiographie *f*.

autocrat ['ɔ:təkræt] *n* autocrate *m*.

autocratic [,ɔ:tə'krætɪk] *adj* autocratique.

autocross ['ɔ:təʊkrɒs] *n Br* auto-cross *m*.

Autocue® ['ɔ:təʊkju:] *n Br* téléprompteur *m*.

autograph ['ɔ:təgrɑ:f] ◇ *n* autographe *m*. ◇ *vt* signer.

Automat® ['ɔ:təmæt] *n Am restaurant où les plats sont vendus dans des distributeurs automatiques.*

automata [ɔ:'tɒmətə] *pl* → **automaton**.

automate ['ɔ:təmeɪt] *vt* automatiser.

automatic [,ɔ:tə'mætɪk] ◇ *adj* -1. [gen] automatique. -2. [gesture] machinal(e). ◇ *n* -1. [car] voiture *f* à transmission automatique. -2. [gun] automatique *m*. -3. [washing machine] lave-linge *m* automatique.

automatically [,ɔ:tə'mætɪklɪ] *adv* -1. [gen] automatiquement. -2. [move, reply] machinalement.

automatic pilot *n lit & fig* pilote *m* automatique.

automation [,ɔ:tə'meɪʃn] *n* automatisation *f*, automation *f*.

automaton [ɔ:'tɒmətən] (*pl* -**tons** OR -**ta**) *n lit & fig* automate *m*.

automobile ['ɔ:təməbi:l] *n Am* automobile *f*.

automotive [,ɔ:tə'məʊtɪv] *adj* automobile.

autonomous [ɔ:'tɒnəməs] *adj* autonome.

autonomy [ɔ:'tɒnəmɪ] *n* autonomie *f*.

autopilot ['ɔ:təʊpaɪlət] = **automatic pilot**.

autopsy ['ɔ:tɒpsɪ] (*pl* -**ies**) *n* autopsie *f*.

autumn ['ɔ:təm] ◇ *n* automne *m*; **in** ~ en automne. ◇ *comp* d'automne.

autumnal [ɔ:'tʌmnəl] *adj* automnal(e).

auxiliary [ɔ:g'zɪljərɪ] (*pl* -**ies**) ◇ *adj* auxiliaire. ◇ *n* auxiliaire *mf*.

Av. (*abbr of* **avenue**) av.

AV ◇ *n abbr of* **Authorized Version**. ◇ *abbr of* **audiovisual**.

avail [ə'veɪl] ◇ *n*: **to no** ~ en vain, sans résultat. ◇ *vt*: **to** ~ **o.s. of** profiter de.

availability [ə,veɪlə'bɪlətɪ] *n* disponibilité *f*.

available [ə'veɪləbl] *adj* disponible.

avalanche ['ævəlɑ:nʃ] *n lit & fig* avalanche *f*.

avant-garde [,ævɒŋ'gɑ:d] *adj* d'avant-garde.

avarice ['ævərɪs] *n* avarice *f*.

avaricious [,ævə'rɪʃəs] *adj* avare.

avdp. (*abbr of* **avoirdupois**) *système avoirdupois.*

Ave. (*abbr of* **avenue**) av.

avenge [ə'vendʒ] *vt* venger.

avenue ['ævənju:] *n* avenue *f*.

average ['ævərɪdʒ] ◇ *adj* moyen(enne). ◇ *n* moyenne *f*; **on** ~ en moyenne. ◇ *vt*: **the cars were averaging 90 mph** les voitures roulaient en moyenne à 150 km/h. ◆ **average out** ◇ *vt sep* établir la moyenne de. ◇ *vi*: **to** ~ **out at** donner la moyenne de.

averse [ə'vɜ:s] *adj*: **I'm not** ~ **to the occasional drink** *hum* je ne dis pas non à un verre de temps en temps.

aversion [ə'vɜːʃn] n: ~ **(to)** aversion f (pour).

avert [ə'vɜːt] vt **-1.** [avoid] écarter; [accident] empêcher. **-2.** [eyes, glance] détourner.

aviary ['eɪvjəri] (pl **-ies**) n volière f.

aviation [,eɪvɪ'eɪʃn] n aviation f.

aviator ['eɪvɪeɪtər] n dated aviateur m, -trice f.

avid ['ævɪd] adj: ~ **(for)** avide (de).

avocado [,ævə'kɑːdəʊ] (pl **-s** OR **-es**) n: ~ **(pear)** avocat m.

avoid [ə'vɔɪd] vt éviter; **to ~ doing sthg** éviter de faire qqch.

avoidable [ə'vɔɪdəbl] adj qui peut être évité(e).

avoidance [ə'vɔɪdəns] n → tax avoidance.

avowed [ə'vaʊd] adj **-1.** [supporter, opponent] déclaré(e). **-2.** [aim, belief] avoué(e).

AVP (abbr of **assistant vice-president**) n vice-président adjoint.

AWACS ['eɪwæks] (abbr of **airborne warning and control system**) n AWACS m.

await [ə'weɪt] vt attendre.

awake [ə'weɪk] (pt **awoke** OR **awaked**, pp **awoken**) ◇ adj **-1.** [not sleeping] réveillé(e); **are you ~?** tu dors?; **to be wide ~** être complètement réveillé. **-2.** fig [aware]: ~ **to** conscient(e) de. ◇ vt **-1.** [wake up] réveiller. **-2.** fig [feeling] éveiller. ◇ vi **-1.** [wake up] se réveiller. **-2.** fig [feeling] s'éveiller.

awakening [ə'weɪknɪŋ] n **-1.** [from sleep] réveil m; **a rude ~** un réveil brutal. **-2.** fig [of feeling] éveil m.

award [ə'wɔːd] ◇ n **-1.** [prize] prix m. **-2.** [compensation] dommages-intérêts mpl. ◇ vt: **to ~ sb sthg, to ~ sthg to sb** [prize] décerner qqch à qqn; [compensation, free kick] accorder qqch à qqn.

aware [ə'weər] adj: **to be ~ of sthg** se rendre compte de qqch, être conscient(e) de qqch; **to be ~ that** se rendre compte que, être conscient que; **politically ~** politisé(e).

awareness [ə'weənɪs] n (U) conscience f.

awash [ə'wɒʃ] adj lit & fig: ~ **(with)** inondé(e) (de).

away [ə'weɪ] ◇ adv **-1.** [in opposite direction]: **to move** OR **walk ~ (from)** s'éloigner (de); **to look ~** détourner le regard; **to turn ~ se détourner. -2.** [in distance]: **we live 4 miles ~ (from here)** nous habitons à 6 kilomètres (d'ici); **to keep sb ~** empêcher qqn de s'approcher. **-3.** [in time]: **the elections are a month ~** les élections se dérouleront dans un mois. **-4.** [absent] absent(e); **she's ~ on holiday** elle est partie en vacances. **-5.** [in safe place]: **to put sthg ~** ranger

qqch. **-6.** [so as to be gone or used up]: **to fade ~** disparaître; **to give sthg ~** donner qqch, faire don de qqch; **to take sthg ~** emporter qqch. **-7.** [continuously]: **to be working ~** travailler sans arrêt.
◇ adj SPORT [team, fans] de l'équipe des visiteurs; ~ **game** match m à l'extérieur.

awe [ɔː] n respect m mêlé de crainte; **to be in ~ of sb** être impressionné par qqn.

awesome ['ɔːsəm] adj impressionnant(e).

awestruck ['ɔːstrʌk] adj impressionné(e).

awful ['ɔːfʊl] adj **-1.** [terrible] affreux(euse). **-2.** inf [very great]: **an ~ lot (of)** énormément (de).

awfully ['ɔːflɪ] adv inf [bad, difficult] affreusement; [nice, good] extrêmement.

awhile [ə'waɪl] adv un moment.

awkward ['ɔːkwəd] adj **-1.** [clumsy] gauche, maladroit(e). **-2.** [embarrassed] mal à l'aise, gêné(e). **-3.** [difficult - person, problem, task] difficile. **-4.** [inconvenient] incommode. **-5.** [embarrassing] embarrassant(e), gênant(e).

awkwardly ['ɔːkwədlɪ] adv **-1.** [move etc] gauchement, maladroitement. **-2.** [with embarrassment] avec gêne OR embarras.

awkwardness ['ɔːkwədnɪs] n **-1.** [of person, movement] gaucherie f, maladresse f. **-2.** [embarrassment] gêne f, embarras m.

awl [ɔːl] n poinçon m, alêne f.

awning ['ɔːnɪŋ] n **-1.** [of tent] auvent m. **-2.** [of shop] banne f.

awoke [ə'wəʊk] pt → awake.

awoken [ə'wəʊkn] pp → awake.

AWOL ['eɪwɒl] (abbr of **absent without leave**): **to be/go ~** MIL être/partir en absence irrégulière.

awry [ə'raɪ] ◇ adj de travers. ◇ adv: **to go ~** aller de travers, mal tourner.

axe Br, **ax** Am [æks] ◇ n hache f; **to have an ~ to grind** prêcher pour sa paroisse. ◇ vt [project] abandonner; [jobs] supprimer.

axes ['æksiːz] pl → axis.

axiom ['æksɪəm] n axiome m.

axis ['æksɪs] (pl **axes**) n axe m.

axle ['æksl] n essieu m.

ayatollah [,aɪə'tɒlə] n ayatollah m.

aye [aɪ] ◇ adv oui. ◇ n voix f pour.

AYH (abbr of **American Youth Hostels**) n association américaine des auberges de jeunesse.

AZ abbr of **Arizona**.

azalea [ə'zeɪljə] n azalée f.

Azerbaijan [,æzəbaɪ'dʒɑːn] n Azerbaïdjan m.

Azerbaijani [,æzəbaɪ'dʒɑːnɪ] ◇ adj azerbaïdjanais(e). ◇ n Azerbaïdjanais m, -e f.

Azeri [ə'zeri] ◇ *adj* azéri(e). ◇ *n* Azeri *mf*.

Azores [ə'zɔ:z] *npl*: **the ~** les Açores *fpl*; **in the ~** aux Açores.

AZT (*abbr of* **azidothymidine**) *n* AZT *f*.

Aztec ['æztek] ◇ *adj* aztèque. ◇ *n* Aztèque *mf*.

azure ['æʒər] *adj* azuré(e), bleu(e) d'azur.

B

b (*pl* **b's** OR **bs**), **B** (*pl* **B's** OR **Bs**) [bi:] *n* [letter] b *m inv*, B *m inv*.
◆ **B** *n* **-1.** MUS si *m*. **-2.** SCH [mark] B *m inv*.

b. *abbr of* **born**.

BA *n* **-1.** *abbr of* **Bachelor of Arts. -2.** (*abbr of* **British Academy**) *organisme public d'aide à la recherche dans le domaine des lettres.* **-3.** (*abbr of* **British Airways**) *compagnie aérienne britannique.*

BAA (*abbr of* **British Airports' Authority**) *n organisme autonome responsable des aéroports en Grande-Bretagne.*

babble ['bæbl] ◇ *n* [of voices] murmure *m*, rumeur *f*. ◇ *vi* [person] babiller.

babe [beɪb] *n* **-1.** *literary* [baby] bébé *m*. **-2.** *Am inf* [term of affection] chéri *m*, -e *f*.

baboon [bə'bu:n] *n* babouin *m*.

baby ['beɪbɪ] (*pl* **-ies**) *n* **-1.** [child] bébé *m*. **-2.** *inf* [darling] chéri *m*, -e *f*.

baby boomer [-,bu:mər] *n Am personne née lors du baby boom d'après-guerre.*

baby buggy *n* **-1.** *Br* [foldable pushchair] poussette *f*. **-2.** *Am* = **baby carriage.**

baby carriage *n Am* landau *m*.

babyish ['beɪbɪɪʃ] *adj* puéril(e), enfantin(e).

baby-minder *n Br* nourrice *f*.

baby-sit *vi* faire du baby-sitting.

baby-sitter *n* baby-sitter *mf*.

bachelor ['bætʃələr] *n* célibataire *m*.

Bachelor of Arts *n* licencié *m*, -e *f* en OR ès Lettres.

Bachelor of Science *n* licencié *m*, -e *f* en OR ès Sciences.

bachelor's degree *n* ≃ licence *f*.

back [bæk] ◇ *adv* **-1.** [backwards] en arrière; **to step/move ~** reculer; **to push ~** repousser; **to tie one's hair ~** attacher ses cheveux en arrière. **-2.** [to former position or state]: **I'll be ~ at five** je rentrerai OR serai de retour à dix-sept heures; **I'd like my money ~** [in shop] je voudrais me faire rembourser; **to go ~** retourner; **to come ~** revenir, rentrer; **to go ~ to sleep** se rendormir; **to go ~ and forth** [person] faire des allées et venues; **to be ~ (in fashion)** revenir à la mode. **-3.** [in time]: **to think ~ (to)** se souvenir (de). **-4.** [in return]: **to phone** OR **call ~** rappeler; **to write ~** répondre; **to pay sb ~** rembourser qqn.

◇ *n* **-1.** [of person, animal] dos *m*; **to break the ~ of a job** faire le plus gros d'un travail; **behind sb's ~** *fig* derrière le dos de qqn; **to stab sb in the ~** *fig* poignarder qqn dans le dos; **to put sb's ~ up** casser les pieds de qqn; **to turn one's ~ on sb/sthg** ignorer qqn/qqch. **-2.** [of door, book, hand] dos *m*; [of head] derrière *m*; [of envelope, cheque] revers *m*; [of page] verso *m*; [of chair] dossier *m*; **to know somewhere like the ~ of one's hand** connaître un endroit comme sa poche. **-3.** [of room, fridge] fond *m*; [of car] arrière *m*; **it's the ~ of beyond** *Br* c'est un trou perdu. **-4.** SPORT arrière *m*.

◇ *adj* (*in compounds*) **-1.** [at the back] de derrière; [seat, wheel] arrière (*inv*); [page] dernier(ière). **-2.** [overdue]: **~ rent** arriéré *m* de loyer.

◇ *vt* **-1.** [reverse] reculer. **-2.** [support] appuyer, soutenir. **-3.** [bet on] parier sur, miser sur.

◇ *vi* reculer.

◆ **back to back** *adv* **-1.** [stand] dos à dos. **-2.** [happen] l'un après l'autre.

◆ **back to front** *adv* à l'envers.

◆ **back away** *vi* reculer.

◆ **back down** *vi* céder.

◆ **back off** *vi* reculer.

◆ **back onto** *vt Br*: **the house ~s onto the park** la maison donne sur le parc par derrière.

◆ **back out** *vi* [of promise etc] se dédire.

◆ **back up** ◇ *vt sep* **-1.** [support - claim] appuyer, soutenir; [- person] épauler, soutenir. **-2.** [reverse] reculer. **-3.** COMPUT sauvegarder, faire une copie de sauvegarde de. ◇ *vi* [reverse] reculer.

backache ['bækeɪk] *n*: **to have ~** avoir mal aux reins OR au dos.

backbencher [,bæk'bentʃər] *n Br* POL *député qui n'a aucune position officielle au gouvernement ni dans aucun parti.*

backbenches [,bæk'bentʃiz] *npl Br* POL bancs *mpl* des députés sans portefeuille.

backbiting ['bækbaɪtɪŋ] *n* médisance *f*.

backbone ['bækbəʊn] *n* épine *f* dorsale, colonne *f* vertébrale; *fig* [main support] pivot *m*.

backbreaking ['bæk,breɪkɪŋ] *adj* éreintant(e).

back burner *n*: to put sthg on the ~ mettre qqch en veilleuse.

backchat *Br* ['bæktʃæt], **backtalk** *Am* ['bæktɔːk] *n inf* insolence *f*.

backcloth ['bækklɒθ] *Br* = backdrop.

backcomb ['bækkəʊm] *vt Br* crêper.

back copy *n* vieux numéro *m*.

backdate [,bæk'deɪt] *vt* antidater.

back door *n* porte *f* de derrière; to get a job through OR by the ~ *fig* obtenir un emploi par relations.

backdrop ['bækdrɒp] *n lit* & *fig* toile *f* de fond.

backer ['bækər] *n* commanditaire *m*, bailleur *m* de fonds.

backfire [,bæk'faɪər] *vi* -1. AUT pétarader. -2. [plan]: to ~ (on sb) se retourner (contre qqn).

backgammon ['bæk,gæmən] *n* backgammon *m*, ≃ jacquet *m*.

background ['bækgraʊnd] ◇ *n* -1. [in picture, view] arrière-plan *m*; in the ~ dans le fond, à l'arrière-plan; *fig* au second plan. -2. [of event, situation] contexte *m*. -3. [upbringing] milieu *m*. ◇ *comp* [music, noise] de fond; ~ **reading/information** lectures/informations générales (*pour un certain sujet*).

backhand ['bækhænd] *n* revers *m*.

backhanded ['bækhændɪd] *adj fig* ambigu(ë), équivoque.

backhander ['bækhændər] *n Br inf* pot-de-vin *m*.

backing ['bækɪŋ] *n* -1. [support] soutien *m*. -2. [lining] doublage *m*. -3. MUS accompagnement *m*.

back issue = back number.

backlash ['bæklæʃ] *n* contrecoup *m*, choc *m* en retour.

backless ['bæklɪs] *adj* [dress etc] décolleté(e) dans le dos.

backlog ['bæklɒg] *n*: ~ **(of work)** arriéré *m* de travail, travail *m* en retard.

back number *n* vieux numéro *m*.

backpack ['bækpæk] *n* sac *m* à dos.

backpacker ['bækpækər] *n* randonneur *m*, -euse *f* (*avec sac à dos*).

backpacking ['bækpækɪŋ] *n*: to go ~ faire de la randonnée (*avec sac à dos*).

back passage *n euphemism* rectum *m*.

back pay *n* rappel *m* de salaire.

backpedal [,bæk'pedl] (*Br pt* & *pp* **-led**, *cont* **-ling**, *Am pt* & *pp* **-ed**, *cont* **-ing**) *vi fig*: to ~ **(on)** faire marche OR machine arrière (sur).

back seat *n* [in car] siège *m* OR banquette *f* arrière; to take a ~ *fig* jouer un rôle secondaire.

back-seat driver *n personne qui n'arrête pas de donner des conseils au conducteur.*

backside [,bæk'saɪd] *n inf* postérieur *m*, derrière *m*.

backslash ['bækslæʃ] *n* COMPUT barre *f* oblique inversée.

backslide [,bæk'slaɪd] (*pt* & *pp* **-slid** [-'slɪd]) *vi* rechuter, récidiver.

backspace ['bækspeɪs] ◇ *n* [key] touche *f* de retour en arrière. ◇ *vi* [in typing] reculer d'un espace.

backstage [,bæk'steɪdʒ] *adv* dans les coulisses.

back street *n* petite rue *f*.

back-street abortion *n* avortement *m* clandestin.

backstroke ['bækstrəʊk] *n* dos *m* crawlé.

backtalk *Am* = backchat.

backtrack ['bæktræk] = backpedal.

backup ['bækʌp] ◇ *adj* -1. [plan, team] de secours, de remplacement. -2. COMPUT de sauvegarde. ◇ *n* -1. [gen] aide *f*, soutien *m*. -2. COMPUT (copie *f* de) sauvegarde *f*.

backward ['bækwəd] ◇ *adj* -1. [movement, look] en arrière. -2. [country] arriéré(e); [person] arriéré, attardé(e). ◇ *adv Am* = backwards.

backward-looking [-,lʊkɪŋ] *adj pej* rétrograde.

backwards ['bækwədz], **backward** *Am* ['bækwəd] *adv* [move, go] en arrière, à reculons; [read list] à rebours, à l'envers; ~ **and forwards** [movement] de va-et-vient, d'avant en arrière et d'arrière en avant; to **walk ~ and forwards** aller et venir.

backwash ['bækwɒʃ] *n* remous *m*.

backwater ['bæk,wɔːtər] *n fig* désert *m*.

backwoods ['bækwʊdz] *npl fig*: to live in the ~ of France habiter la France profonde.

backyard [,bæk'jɑːd] *n* -1. *Br* [yard] arrière-cour *f*. -2. *Am* [garden] jardin *m* de derrière.

bacon ['beɪkən] *n* bacon *m*.

bacteria [bæk'tɪərɪə] *npl* bactéries *fpl*.

bacteriology [bæk,tɪər'ɒlədʒɪ] *n* bactériologie *f*.

bad [bæd] (*compar* **worse**, *superl* **worst**) ◇ *adj* -1. [not good] mauvais(e); to be ~ **at** sthg être mauvais en qqch; to go ~ **from** ~ **to worse** aller de mal en pis, empirer; too ~! dommage!; **not** ~ pas mal. -2. [un-

healthy] malade; **smoking is** ~ **for you** fumer est mauvais pour la santé; **I'm feeling** ~ je ne suis pas dans mon assiette. **-3.** [serious]: **a** ~ **cold** un gros rhume. **-4.** [rotten] pourri(e), gâté(e); **to go** ~ se gâter, s'avarier. **-5.** [guilty]: **to feel** ~ **about sthg** se sentir coupable de qqch. **-6.** [naughty] méchant(e).
◇ *adv Am* = **badly.**

bad blood *n* ressentiment *m*, rancune *f*.

bad cheque *n* chèque *m* sans provision.

bad debt *n* créance *f* irrécouvrable.

bade [bæd] *pt* → **bid.**

bad feeling *n* (*U*) rancœur *f*.

badge [bædʒ] *n* **-1.** [metal, plastic] badge *m*. **-2.** [sewn-on] écusson *m*.

badger ['bædʒəʳ] ◇ *n* blaireau *m*. ◇ *vt*: **to** ~ **sb (to do sthg)** harceler qqn (pour qu'il fasse qqch).

badly ['bædlɪ] (*compar* **worse,** *superl* **worst**) *adv* **-1.** [not well] mal; **to think** ~ **of sb** penser du mal de qqn. **-2.** [seriously - wounded] grièvement; [- affected] gravement, sérieusement; **to be** ~ **in need of sthg** avoir vraiment OR absolument besoin de qqch.

badly-off *adj* **-1.** [poor] pauvre, dans le besoin. **-2.** [lacking]: **to be** ~ **for sthg** manquer de qqch.

bad-mannered [-'mænəd] *adj* [child] mal élevé(e); [shop assistant] impoli(e).

badminton ['bædmɪntən] *n* badminton *m*.

bad-mouth *vt inf* casser du sucre sur le dos de.

badness ['bædnɪs] *n* [of behaviour] méchanceté *f*.

bad-tempered *adj* **-1.** [by nature] qui a mauvais caractère. **-2.** [in a bad mood] de mauvaise humeur.

baffle ['bæfl] *vt* déconcerter, confondre.

baffling ['bæflɪŋ] *adj* déconcertant(e).

bag [bæg] (*pt* & *pp* **-ged,** *cont* **-ging**) ◇ *n* **-1.** [gen] sac *m*; **she's a** ~ **of bones** elle n'a que la peau sur les os; **it's in the** ~ *inf* c'est dans la poche, l'affaire est dans le sac; **to pack one's** ~**s** *fig* plier bagage. **-2.** [handbag] sac *m* à main. ◇ *vt* **-1.** [put into bags] mettre en sac, ensacher. **-2.** *Br inf* [reserve] garder.
◆ **bags** *npl* **-1.** [under eyes] poches *fpl*. **-2.** *inf* [lots]: ~**s of** plein OR beaucoup de.

bagel ['beɪgəl] *n petit pain en couronne.*

baggage ['bægɪdʒ] *n* (*U*) bagages *mpl*.

baggage car *n Am* fourgon *m* (*d'un train*).

baggage reclaim *n* retrait *m* des bagages.

baggage room *n Am* consigne *f*.

baggy ['bægɪ] (*compar* **-ier,** *superl* **-iest**) *adj* ample.

Baghdad [bæg'dæd] *n* Bagdad.

bag lady *n inf* clocharde *f*.

bagpipes ['bægpaɪps] *npl* cornemuse *f*.

bagsnatcher ['bægsnætʃəʳ] *n* voleur *m*, -euse *f* à la tire.

bah [bɑː] *excl* bah!

Bahamas [bə'hɑːməz] *npl*: **the** ~ les Bahamas *fpl*; **in the** ~ aux Bahamas.

Bahrain, Bahrein [bɑː'reɪn] *n* Bahreïn *m*, Bahrayn *m*; **in** ~ au Bahreïn.

Bahraini, Bahreini [bɑː'reɪnɪ] ◇ *adj* bahreïni(e). ◇ *n* Bahreïni *m*, -e *f*.

Bahrein = **Bahrain.**

bail [beɪl] *n* (*U*) caution *f*; **on** ~ sous caution.
◆ **bail out** ◇ *vt sep* **-1.** [pay bail for] se porter garant de. **-2.** *fig* [rescue] tirer d'affaire. ◇ *vi* [from plane] sauter (en parachute).

bailiff ['beɪlɪf] *n* huissier *m*.

bait [beɪt] ◇ *n* appât *m*; **to rise to** OR **take the** ~ *fig* mordre à l'hameçon. ◇ *vt* **-1.** [put bait on] appâter. **-2.** [tease] tourmenter, tarabuster.

baize [beɪz] *n* feutrine *f*.

bake [beɪk] ◇ *vt* **-1.** CULIN faire cuire au four. **-2.** [clay, bricks] cuire. ◇ *vi* [food] cuire au four.

baked beans [beɪkt-] *npl* haricots *mpl* blancs à la tomate.

baked potato [beɪkt-] *n* pomme *f* de terre en robe de chambre.

Bakelite® ['beɪkəlaɪt] *n* Bakélite® *f*.

baker ['beɪkəʳ] *n* boulanger *m*, -ère *f*; ~**'s (shop)** boulangerie *f*.

bakery ['beɪkərɪ] (*pl* **-ies**) *n* boulangerie *f*.

baking ['beɪkɪŋ] ◇ *adj inf*: **it's a** ~ **hot day!** on cuit aujourd'hui! ◇ *n* cuisson *f*.

baking powder *n* levure *f* (chimique).

baking tin *n* [for cakes] moule *m* à gâteau; [for meat] plat *m* à rôtir.

balaclava (helmet) [bælə'klɑːvə-] *n Br* passe-montagne *m*.

balance ['bæləns] ◇ *n* **-1.** [equilibrium] équilibre *m*; **to keep/lose one's** ~ garder/perdre l'équilibre; **off** ~ déséquilibré(e). **-2.** *fig* [counterweight] contrepoids *m*; [of evidence] poids *m*, force *f*. **-3.** [scales] balance *f*; **to be** OR **hang in the** ~ *fig* être en balance. **-4.** FIN solde *m*.
◇ *vt* **-1.** [keep in balance] maintenir en équilibre. **-2.** [compare]: **to** ~ **sthg against sthg** mettre qqch et qqch en balance. **-3.** [in accounting]: **to** ~ **a budget** équilibrer un bud-

get; **to ~ the books** clôturer les comptes, dresser le bilan.
◇ *vi* **-1.** [maintain equilibrium] se tenir en équilibre. **-2.** [budget, accounts] s'équilibrer.
◆ **on balance** *adv* tout bien considéré.
balanced ['bælənst] *adj* [fair] juste, impartial(e).
balanced diet *n* alimentation *f* équilibrée.
balance of payments *n* balance *f* des paiements.
balance of power *n* équilibre *m* OR balance *f* des forces.
balance of trade *n* balance *f* commerciale.
balance sheet *n* bilan *m*.
balancing act ['bælənsıŋ-] *n* fig acrobaties *fpl*.
balcony ['bælkənı] (*pl* **-ies**) *n* balcon *m*.
bald [bɔːld] *adj* **-1.** [head, man] chauve. **-2.** [tyre] lisse. **-3.** fig [blunt] direct(e).
bald eagle *n* aigle *m* à tête blanche (*cet oiseau est le symbole des États-Unis*).
balding ['bɔːldıŋ] *adj* qui devient chauve.
baldness ['bɔːldnıs] *n* calvitie *f*.
bale [beıl] *n* balle *f*.
◆ **bale out** *Br* ◇ *vt sep* [boat] écoper, vider. ◇ *vi* [from plane] sauter en parachute.
Balearic Islands [,bælı'ærık-], **Balearics** [,bælı'ærıks] *npl*: **the ~** les Baléares *fpl*; **in the ~** aux Baléares.
baleful ['beılfυl] *adj* sinistre.
Bali ['bɑːlı] *n* Bali *m*; **in ~** à Bali.
balk [bɔːk] *vi*: **to ~ (at)** hésiter OR reculer (devant).
Balkan ['bɔːlkən] *adj* balkanique.
Balkans ['bɔːlkənz], **Balkan States** *npl*: **the ~** les Balkans *mpl*, les États *mpl* balkaniques; **in the ~** dans les Balkans.
ball [bɔːl] *n* **-1.** [round shape] boule *f*; [in game] balle *f*; [football] ballon *m*; **to be on the ~** fig connaître son affaire, s'y connaître; **to play ~ with sb** fig coopérer avec qqn; **to start the ~ rolling** fig lancer la discussion. **-2.** [of foot] plante *f*. **-3.** [dance] bal *m*; **to have a ~** fig bien s'amuser.
◆ **balls** *v* inf ◇ *npl* [testicles] couilles *fpl*. ◇ *n* (*U*) [nonsense] conneries *fpl*.
ballad ['bæləd] *n* ballade *f*.
ball-and-socket joint *n* TECH rotule *f*.
ballast ['bæləst] *n* lest *m*.
ball bearing *n* roulement *m* à billes.
ball boy *n* ramasseur *m* de balles.
ballcock ['bɔːlkɒk] *n* (robinet *m* à) flotteur *m*.
ballerina [,bælə'riːnə] *n* ballerine *f*.
ballet ['bæleı] *n* **-1.** (*U*) [art of dance] danse *f*. **-2.** [work] ballet *m*.

ballet dancer *n* danseur *m*, **-euse** *f* de ballet.
ball game *n* **-1.** *Am* [baseball match] match *m* de base-ball. **-2.** *inf* [situation]: **it's a whole new ~** c'est une autre paire de manches.
ball girl *n* ramasseuse *f* de balles.
ballistic missile [bə'lıstık-] *n* missile *m* balistique.
ballistics [bə'lıstıks] *n* (*U*) balistique *f*.
ballocks ['bɒləks] = **bollocks**.
balloon [bə'luːn] ◇ *n* **-1.** [gen] ballon *m*. **-2.** [in cartoon] bulle *f*. ◇ *vi* [swell] gonfler.
ballooning [bə'luːnıŋ] *n*: **to go ~** monter en ballon.
ballot ['bælət] ◇ *n* **-1.** [voting paper] bulletin *m* de vote. **-2.** [voting process] scrutin *m*. ◇ *vt* appeler à voter. ◇ *vi*: **to ~ for sthg** voter pour qqch.
ballot box *n* **-1.** [container] urne *f*. **-2.** [voting process] scrutin *m*.
ballot paper *n* bulletin *m* de vote.
ball park *n Am* terrain *m* de base-ball.
ball-park figure *n* inf chiffre *m* approximatif.
ballpoint (pen) ['bɔːlpɔınt-] *n* stylo *m* à bille.
ballroom ['bɔːlrυm] *n* salle *f* de bal.
ballroom dancing *n* (*U*) danse *f* de salon.
balls-up *Br*, **ball-up** *Am n v* inf: **to make a ~ of sthg** saloper qqch.
balm [bɑːm] *n* baume *m*.
balmy ['bɑːmı] (*compar* **-ier**, *superl* **-iest**) *adj* doux (douce).
baloney [bə'ləυnı] *n* (*U*) inf foutaises *fpl*, bêtises *fpl*.
balsa(wood) ['bɒlsə(wυd)] *n* balsa *m*.
balsam ['bɔːlsəm] *n* baume *m*.
balsamic vinegar [bɔːl'sæmık-] *n* vinaigre *m* balsamique.
balti ['bɔːltı] *n* [pan] *récipient métallique utilisé dans la cuisine indienne*; [food] *plat épicé préparé dans un 'balti'*.
Baltic ['bɔːltık] ◇ *adj* [port, coast] de la Baltique. ◇ *n*: **the ~ (Sea)** la Baltique.
Baltic Republic *n*: **the ~s** les républiques *fpl* baltes.
Baltic State *n*: **the ~s** les pays *mpl* baltes.
balustrade [,bæləs'treıd] *n* balustrade *f*.
bamboo [bæm'buː] *n* bambou *m*.
bamboozle [bæm'buːzl] *vt* inf embobiner.
ban [bæn] (*pt* & *pp* **-ned**, *cont* **-ning**) ◇ *n* interdiction *f*; **there is a ~ on smoking** il est interdit de fumer. ◇ *vt* interdire; **to ~ sb**

from doing sthg interdire à qqn de faire qqch.

banal [bə'nɑːl] *adj pej* banal(e), ordinaire.

banana [bə'nɑːnə] *n* banane *f.*

banana republic *n* république *f* bananière.

banana split *n* banana split *m.*

band [bænd] *n* **-1.** [MUS - rock] groupe *m*; [- military] fanfare *f*; [- jazz] orchestre *m.* **-2.** [group, strip] bande *f.* **-3.** [stripe] rayure *f.* **-4.** [range] tranche *f.*
◆ **band together** *vi* se grouper, s'unir.

bandage ['bændɪdʒ] ◇ *n* bandage *m,* bande *f.* ◇ *vt* mettre un pansement OR un bandage sur.

Band-Aid® *n* pansement *m* adhésif.

bandan(n)a [bæn'dænə] *n* bandana *m.*

b and b, B and B *n abbr of* bed and breakfast.

bandeau ['bændəʊ] (*pl* **-x** [-z]) *n* bandeau *m.*

bandit ['bændit] *n* bandit *m.*

bandmaster ['bænd,mɑːstər] *n* chef *m* d'orchestre.

band saw *n* scie *f* à ruban.

bandsman ['bændzmən] (*pl* **-men** [-mən]) *n* musicien *m* (d'orchestre).

bandstand ['bændstænd] *n* kiosque *m* à musique.

bandwagon ['bændwægən] *n*: **to jump on the ~** suivre le mouvement.

bandy ['bændi] (*compar* **-ier**, *superl* **-iest**, *pt* & *pp* **-ied**) *adj* qui a les jambes arquées.
◆ **bandy about, bandy around** *vt sep* répandre, faire circuler.

bandy-legged [-'legɪd] *adj* = bandy.

bane [beɪn] *n*: **he's the ~ of my life** c'est le fléau de ma vie.

bang [bæŋ] ◇ *adv* **-1.** [exactly]: **~ in the middle** en plein milieu; **to be ~ on time** être pile à l'heure. **-2.** *inf* [away]: **~ goes my holiday!** mes vacances sont tombées dans le lac OR à l'eau! ◇ *n* **-1.** [blow] coup *m* violent. **-2.** [of gun etc] détonation *f*; [of door] claquement *m*; **to go with a ~** *inf fig* être du tonnerre. ◇ *vt* frapper violemment; [door] claquer; **to ~ one's head/knee** se cogner la tête/le genou. ◇ *vi* **-1.** [knock]: **to ~ on** frapper à. **-2.** [make a loud noise - gun etc] détoner; [- door] claquer. **-3.** [crash]: **to ~ into** se cogner contre. ◇ *excl* boum!
◆ **bangs** *npl Am* frange *f.*
◆ **bang down** *vt sep* poser violemment.

banger ['bæŋər] *n Br* **-1.** *inf* [sausage] sau-

cisse *f.* **-2.** *inf* [old car] vieille guimbarde *f,* vieux tacot *m.* **-3.** [firework] pétard *m.*

Bangkok [,bæŋ'kɒk] *n* Bangkok.

Bangladesh [,bæŋglə'deʃ] *n* Bangladesh *m*; **in ~** au Bangladesh.

Bangladeshi [,bæŋglə'deʃɪ] ◇ *adj* bangladais(e), bangladeshi. ◇ *n* Bangladais *m,* -e *f,* Bangladeshi *mf.*

bangle ['bæŋgl] *n* bracelet *m.*

banish ['bænɪʃ] *vt* bannir.

banister ['bænɪstər] *n,* **banisters** ['bænɪstəz] *npl* rampe *f.*

banjo ['bændʒəʊ] (*pl* **-s** OR **-es**) *n* banjo *m.*

bank [bæŋk] ◇ *n* **-1.** FIN & *fig* banque *f.* **-2.** [of river, lake] rive *f,* bord *m.* **-3.** [of earth] talus *m.* **-4.** [of clouds] masse *f*; [of fog] nappe *f.* ◇ *vt* FIN mettre OR déposer à la banque. ◇ *vi* **-1.** FIN: **to ~ with** avoir un compte à. **-2.** [plane] tourner.
◆ **bank on** *vt fus* compter sur.

bank account *n* compte *m* en banque.

bank balance *n* solde *m* bancaire.

bankbook ['bæŋkbʊk] *n* livret *m* de banque.

bank card = banker's card.

bank charges *npl* frais *mpl* bancaires.

bank draft *n* traite *f* bancaire.

banker ['bæŋkər] *n* banquier *m.*

banker's card *n Br* carte *f* d'identité bancaire.

banker's order *n Br* prélèvement *m* automatique.

bank holiday *n Br* jour *m* férié.

banking ['bæŋkɪŋ] *n*: **to go into ~** travailler dans la banque.

banking house *n* banque *f,* établissement *m* bancaire.

bank loan *n* emprunt *m* (bancaire).

bank manager *n* directeur *m* de banque.

bank note *n* billet *m* de banque.

bank rate *n* taux *m* d'escompte.

bankrupt ['bæŋkrʌpt] ◇ *adj* failli(e); **to go ~** faire faillite. ◇ *n* failli *m,* -e *f.* ◇ *vt* mettre en faillite.

bankruptcy ['bæŋkrʌptsɪ] (*pl* **-ies**) *n* **-1.** [gen] faillite *f.* **-2.** *fig* [lack]: **moral ~** manque *m* de crédibilité.

bank statement *n* relevé *m* de compte.

banner ['bænər] *n* banderole *f.*

bannister(s) ['bænɪstə(z)] = banister(s).

banns [bænz] *npl*: **to publish the ~** publier les bans.

banquet ['bæŋkwɪt] *n* banquet *m.*

bantam ['bæntəm] *n* poule *f* naine.

bantamweight ['bæntəmweɪt] *n* poids *m* coq.

banter ['bæntər] ⋄ *n* (U) plaisanterie *f*, badinage *m*. ⋄ *vi* plaisanter, badiner.

BAOR (*abbr of* **British Army of the Rhine**) *n* forces britanniques en Allemagne.

bap [bæp] *n Br* petit pain *m*.

baptism ['bæptɪzm] *n* baptême *m*; ~ **of fire** baptême du feu.

Baptist ['bæptɪst] *n* baptiste *mf*.

baptize, -ise [*Br* bæp'taɪz, *Am* 'bæptaɪz] *vt* baptiser.

bar [baː] (*pt & pp* **-red**, *cont* **-ring**) ⋄ *n* **-1.** [piece - of gold] lingot *m*; [- of chocolate] tablette *f*; **a ~ of soap** une savonnette. **-2.** [length of wood, metal] barre *f*; **to be behind ~s** être derrière les barreaux OR sous les verrous. **-3.** *fig* [obstacle] obstacle *m*. **-4.** [pub] bar *m*. **-5.** [counter of pub] comptoir *m*, zinc *m*. **-6.** MUS mesure *f*.
⋄ *vt* **-1.** [door, road] barrer; [window] mettre des barreaux à; **to ~ sb's way** barrer la route OR le passage à qqn. **-2.** [ban] interdire, défendre; **to ~ sb (from)** interdire à qqn (de).
⋄ *prep* sauf, excepté; ~ **none** sans exception.
◆ **Bar** *n* JUR: **the Bar** *Br* le barreau; *Am* les avocats *mpl*.

Barbados [baː'beɪdɒs] *n* Barbade *f*; **in ~** à la Barbade.

barbarian [baː'beərɪən] *n* barbare *mf*.

barbaric [baː'bærɪk] *adj* barbare.

barbarous ['baːbərəs] *adj* barbare.

barbecue ['baːbɪkjuː] ⋄ *n* barbecue *m*. ⋄ *vt* griller sur un barbecue.

barbed ['baːbd] *adj* barbelé(e); *fig* [comment] acerbe, acide.

barbed wire *n* (U) fil *m* de fer barbelé.

barber ['baːbər] *n* coiffeur *m* (pour hommes); ~**'s (shop)** salon *m* de coiffure (pour hommes); **to go to the ~'s** aller chez le coiffeur.

barbiturate [baː'bɪtjʊrət] *n* barbiturique *m*.

Barcelona [,baːsɪ'leʊnə] *n* Barcelone *f*.

bar chart, **bar graph** *Am n* diagramme *m* en bâtons.

bar code *n* code *m* (à) barres.

bare [beər] ⋄ *adj* **-1.** [feet, arms etc] nu(e); [trees, hills etc] dénudé(e). **-2.** [absolute, minimum]: **the ~ facts** les simples faits; **the ~ minimum** le strict minimum; **the ~ essentials** le strict nécessaire. **-3.** [empty] vide. **-4.** [mere]: **it cost us a ~ £10** cela nous a coûté simplement 10 livres. ⋄ *vt* découvrir; **to ~ one's teeth** montrer les dents.

bareback ['beəbæk] ⋄ *adj* qui monte à cru OR à nu. ⋄ *adv* à cru, à nu.

barefaced ['beəfeɪst] *adj* éhonté(e).

barefoot(ed) [,beə'fut(ɪd)] ⋄ *adj* aux pieds nus. ⋄ *adv* nu-pieds, pieds nus.

bareheaded [,beə'hedɪd] ⋄ *adj* nu-tête (*inv*). ⋄ *adv* nu-tête.

barelegged [,beə'legd] ⋄ *adj* aux jambes nues. ⋄ *adv* les jambes nues.

barely ['beəlɪ] *adv* [scarcely] à peine, tout juste.

Barents Sea ['bærənts-] *n*: **the ~** la mer de Barents.

bargain ['baːgɪn] ⋄ *n* **-1.** [agreement] marché *m*; **into the ~** en plus, par-dessus le marché. **-2.** [good buy] affaire *f*, occasion *f*.
⋄ *vi* négocier; **to ~ with sb for sthg** négocier qqch avec qqn.
◆ **bargain for**, **bargain on** *vt fus* compter sur, prévoir.

bargaining ['baːgɪnɪŋ] *n* (U) négociations *fpl*.

bargaining power *n* influence *f* sur les négociations.

barge [baːdʒ] ⋄ *n* péniche *f*. ⋄ *vi inf*: **to ~ past sb** bousculer qqn; **to ~ into sb** rentrer dans qqn.
◆ **barge in** *vi inf*: **to ~ in (on)** interrompre.

barge pole *n*: **I wouldn't touch it with a ~** *inf* je ne m'y frotterais pas.

bar graph *Am* = **bar chart**.

baritone ['bærɪtəʊn] *n* baryton *m*.

barium meal ['beərɪəm-] *n Br* baryte *f*.

bark [baːk] ⋄ *n* **-1.** [of dog] aboiement *m*; **his ~ is worse than his bite** *inf* il n'est pas si terrible qu'il en a l'air. **-2.** [on tree] écorce *f*. ⋄ *vt* [subj: person] aboyer. ⋄ *vi* [dog]: **to ~ (at)** aboyer (après).

barking ['baːkɪŋ] *n* (U) aboiement *m*.

barley ['baːlɪ] *n* orge *f*.

barley sugar *n Br* sucre *m* d'orge.

barley water *n Br* orgeat *m*.

barmaid ['baːmeɪd] *n* barmaid *f*, serveuse *f* de bar.

barman ['baːmən] (*pl* **-men** [-mən]) *n* barman *m*, serveur *m* de bar.

barmy ['baːmɪ] (*compar* **-ier**, *superl* **-iest**) *adj Br inf* toqué(e), timbré(e).

barn [baːn] *n* grange *f*.

barnacle ['baːnəkl] *n* anatife *m*, bernache *f*.

barn dance *n* **-1.** [occasion] soirée *f* de danse campagnarde. **-2.** *Br* [type of dance] danse *f* campagnarde.

barn owl *n* chouette *f*.

barometer [bə'rɒmɪtə'] n lit & fig baromètre m.

baron ['bærən] n baron m; **press/oil** ~ fig baron m de la presse/du pétrole, magnat m de la presse/du pétrole.

baroness ['bærənɪs] n baronne f.

baronet ['bærənɪt] n baronnet m.

baroque [bə'rɒk] adj baroque.

barrack ['bærək] vt Br huer, conspuer.

◆ **barracks** npl caserne f.

barracking ['bærəkɪŋ] n Br chahut m, huée f.

barracuda [,bærə'ku:də] n barracuda m.

barrage ['bærɑ:ʒ] n -1. [of firing] barrage m. -2. [of questions etc] avalanche f, déluge m. -3. Br [dam] barrage m.

barred [bɑ:d] adj [window] à barreaux.

barrel ['bærəl] n -1. [for beer, wine] tonneau m, fût m. -2. [for oil] baril m. -3. [of gun] canon m.

barrel organ n orgue m de Barbarie.

barren ['bærən] adj stérile.

barrette [bə'ret] n Am barrette f.

barricade [,bærɪ'keɪd] ◇ n barricade f. ◇ vt barricader; **to** ~ **o.s.** in se barricader.

barrier ['bærɪə'] n lit & fig barrière f.

barrier cream n Br crème f protectrice.

barring ['bɑ:rɪŋ] prep sauf.

barrister ['bærɪstə'] n Br avocat m, -e f.

barroom ['bɑ:rʊm] n Am bar m.

barrow ['bærəʊ] n brouette f.

bar stool n tabouret m de bar.

Bart. abbr of **baronet**.

bartender ['bɑ:tendə'] n Am barman m.

barter ['bɑ:tə'] ◇ n troc m. ◇ vt: **to** ~ **sthg (for)** troquer OR échanger qqch (contre). ◇ vi faire du troc.

base [beɪs] ◇ n base f. ◇ vt baser; **to** ~ **sthg on** OR **upon** baser OR fonder qqch sur. ◇ adj indigne, ignoble.

baseball ['beɪsbɔ:l] n base-ball m.

baseball cap n casquette f de base-ball.

base camp n camp m de base.

Basel ['bɑ:zl] n Bâle.

baseless ['beɪslɪs] adj sans fondement.

baseline ['beɪslaɪn] n ligne f de fond.

basement ['beɪsmənt] n sous-sol m.

base metal n dated métal m vil.

base rate n taux m de base.

bases ['beɪsi:z] pl → **basis**.

bash [bæʃ] inf ◇ n -1. [painful blow] coup m. -2. [attempt]: **to have a** ~ tenter le coup. -3. [party] fête f, boum f. ◇ vt -1. [hit - gen] frapper, cogner; [- car] percuter. -2. [criticize] critiquer, attaquer.

bashful ['bæʃfʊl] adj timide.

basic ['beɪsɪk] adj fondamental(e); [vocabulary, salary] de base.

◆ **basics** npl -1. [rudiments] éléments mpl, bases fpl. -2. [essential foodstuffs] aliments mpl de première nécessité.

BASIC ['beɪsɪk] (abbr of **Beginner's All-purpose Symbolic Instruction Code**) n basic m.

basically ['beɪsɪklɪ] adv -1. [essentially] au fond, fondamentalement. -2. [really] en fait.

basic rate n Br taux m de base.

basic wage n salaire m de base.

basil ['bæzl] n basilic m.

basin ['beɪsn] n -1. Br [bowl - for cooking] terrine f; [- for washing] cuvette f. -2. [in bathroom] lavabo m. -3. GEOGR bassin m.

basis ['beɪsɪs] (pl **-ses**) n base f; **on the** ~ **of** sur la base de; **on a regular** ~ de façon régulière; **to be paid on a weekly/monthly** ~ toucher un salaire hebdomadaire/mensuel.

bask [bɑ:sk] vi: **to** ~ **in the sun** se chauffer au soleil; **to** ~ **in sb's approval** fig jouir de la faveur de qqn.

basket [bɑ:skɪt] n corbeille f; [with handle] panier m.

basketball ['bɑ:skɪtbɔ:l] ◇ n basket-ball m, basket m. ◇ comp de basket.

basketwork ['bɑ:skɪtwɜ:k] n vannerie f.

basking shark ['bɑ:skɪŋ-] n requin m pèlerin.

Basle [bɑ:l] = **Basel**.

Basque [bɑ:sk] ◇ adj basque. ◇ n -1. [person] Basque mf. -2. [language] basque m.

bass¹ [beɪs] ◇ adj bas (basse). ◇ n -1. [singer] basse f. -2. [double bass] contrebasse f. -3. = **bass guitar**.

bass² [bæs] (pl inv OR **-es**) n [fish] perche f.

bass clef [beɪs-] n clef f de fa.

bass drum [beɪs-] n grosse caisse f.

basset (hound) ['bæsɪt-] n basset m.

bass guitar [beɪs-] n basse f.

bassoon [bə'su:n] n basson m.

bastard ['bɑ:stəd] n -1. [illegitimate child] bâtard m, -e f, enfant naturel m, enfant naturelle f. -2. v inf [unpleasant person] salaud m, saligaud m.

baste [beɪst] vt arroser.

bastion ['bæstɪən] n bastion m.

BASW (abbr of **British Association of Social Workers**) n syndicat britannique des travailleurs sociaux.

bat [bæt] (*pt* & *pp* **-ted**, *cont* **-ting**) ◇ *n* **-1.** [animal] chauve-souris *f.* **-2.** [for cricket, baseball] batte *f*; [for table-tennis] raquette *f.* **-3.** *phr*: **to do sthg off one's own ~** faire qqch de son propre chef. ◇ *vt* [ball] frapper (avec la batte). ◇ *vi* manier la batte.

batch [bætʃ] *n* **-1.** [of papers] tas *m,* liasse *f*; [of letters, applicants] série *f.* **-2.** [of products] lot *m.*

batch file *n* COMPUT fichier *m* de commandes.

batch processing *n* COMPUT traitement *m* par lots.

bated ['beɪtɪd] *adj*: **with ~ breath** en retenant son souffle.

bath [bɑːθ] ◇ *n* **-1.** [bathtub] baignoire *f.* **-2.** [act of washing] bain *m*; **to have** OR **take a bath** prendre un bain. ◇ *vt* baigner, donner un bain à.
◆ **baths** *npl Br* piscine *f.*

bath chair *n* fauteuil *m* roulant.

bath cube *n* sels *mpl* de bain (en forme de cube).

bathe [beɪð] ◇ *vt* **-1.** [wound] laver. **-2.** [subj: light, sunshine]: **to be ~d in** OR **with** être baigné(e) de. ◇ *vi* **-1.** [swim] se baigner. **-2.** *Am* [take a bath] prendre un bain.

bather ['beɪðər] *n* baigneur *m*, -euse *f.*

bathing ['beɪðɪŋ] *n* (*U*) baignade *f.*

bathing cap *n* bonnet *m* de bain.

bathing costume, **bathing suit** *n* maillot *m* de bain.

bathing trunks *npl* slip *m* OR caleçon *m* de bain.

bath mat *n* tapis *m* de bain.

bath oil *n* huile *f* de bain.

bathrobe ['bɑːθrəʊb] *n* [made of towelling] sortie *f* de bain; [dressing gown] peignoir *m.*

bathroom ['bɑːθrʊm] *n* **-1.** *Br* [room with bath] salle *f* de bains. **-2.** *Am* [toilet] toilettes *fpl.*

bath salts *npl* sels *mpl* de bain.

bath towel *n* serviette *f* de bain.

bathtub ['bɑːθtʌb] *n* baignoire *f.*

batik [bə'tiːk] *n* batik *m.*

baton ['bætən] *n* **-1.** [of conductor] baguette *f.* **-2.** [in relay race] témoin *m.* **-3.** *Br* [of policeman] bâton *m,* matraque *f.*

baton charge *n Br* [by police] charge *f* à la matraque.

batsman ['bætsmən] (*pl* **-men** [-mən]) *n* batteur *m.*

battalion [bə'tæljən] *n* bataillon *m.*

batten ['bætn] *n* planche *f,* latte *f.*

◆ **batten down** *vt fus*: **to ~ down the hatches** fermer les écoutilles.

batter ['bætər] ◇ *n* (*U*) pâte *f.* ◇ *vt* battre.
◆ **batter down** *vt sep* [door] abattre.

battered ['bætəd] *adj* **-1.** [child, woman] battu(e). **-2.** [car, hat] cabossé(e).

battering ['bætərɪŋ] *n*: **to take a ~** *fig* être ébranlé(e).

battering ram *n* bélier *m.*

battery ['bætəri] (*pl* **-ies**) *n* batterie *f*; [of calculator, toy] pile *f.*

battery charger *n* chargeur *m.*

battery hen *n* poulet *m* de batterie.

battle ['bætl] ◇ *n* **-1.** [in war] bataille *f.* **-2.** [struggle]: **~ (for/against/with)** lutte *f* (pour/contre/avec), combat *m* (pour/contre/avec); **~ of wits** joute *f* d'esprit; **that's half the ~** le plus dur est fait; **to be fighting a losing ~** mener un combat perdu d'avance. ◇ *vi*: **to ~ (for/against/with)** se battre (pour/contre/avec), lutter (pour/contre/avec).

battledress ['bætldres] *n Br* tenue *f* de combat.

battlefield ['bætlfiːld], **battleground** ['bætlgraʊnd] *n* **-1.** MIL champ *m* de bataille. **-2.** *fig* [controversial subject] polémique *f.*

battlements ['bætlmənts] *npl* remparts *mpl.*

battleship ['bætlʃɪp] *n* cuirassé *m.*

bauble ['bɔːbl] *n* babiole *f,* colifichet *m.*

baud [bɔːd] *n* COMPUT baud *m.*

baud rate *n* COMPUT vitesse *f* de transmission.

baulk [bɔːk] = **balk.**

Bavaria [bə'veərɪə] *n* Bavière *f*; **in ~** en Bavière.

Bavarian [bə'veərɪən] ◇ *adj* bavarois(e). ◇ *n* Bavarois *m*, -e *f.*

bawdy ['bɔːdɪ] (*compar* **-ier**, *superl* **-iest**) *adj* grivois(e), salé(e).

bawl [bɔːl] *vt* & *vi* brailler.

bay [beɪ] ◇ *n* **-1.** GEOGR baie *f.* **-2.** [for loading] aire *f* (de chargement). **-3.** [for parking] place *f* (de stationnement). **-4.** [horse] cheval *m* bai. **-5.** *phr*: **to keep sb/sthg at ~** tenir qqn/qqch à distance, tenir qqn/qqch en échec. ◇ *vi* hurler.

bay leaf *n* feuille *f* de laurier.

bayonet ['beɪənɪt] *n* baïonnette *f.*

bay tree *n* laurier *m.*

bay window *n* fenêtre *f* en saillie.

bazaar [bə'zɑːr] *n* **-1.** [market] bazar *m.* **-2.** *Br* [charity sale] vente *f* de charité.

bazooka [bə'zuːkə] *n* bazooka *m.*

BB (*abbr of* **Boys' Brigade**) *n mouvement chrétien de jeunesse en Grande-Bretagne*.

B & B *n abbr of* **bed and breakfast**.

BBB (*abbr of* **Better Business Bureau**) *n organisme de défense de la déontologie professionnelle dans le secteur tertiaire*.

BBC (*abbr of* **British Broadcasting Corporation**) *n office national britannique de radiodiffusion*.

BC -1. (*abbr of* **before Christ**) av. J.-C. **-2.** *abbr of* **British Columbia**.

BCG (*abbr of* **Bacillus Calmette-Guérin**) *n* BCG *m*.

BD (*abbr of* **Bachelor of Divinity**) *n (titulaire d'une) licence de théologie*.

BDS (*abbr of* **Bachelor of Dental Science**) *n (titulaire d'une) licence de chirurgie dentaire*.

be [bi:] (*pt* **was** OR **were**, *pp* **been**) ◇ *aux vb* **-1.** (*in combination with ppr: to form cont tense*): **what is he doing?** qu'est-ce qu'il fait?; **it's snowing** il neige; **they've been promising reform for years** ça fait des années qu'ils nous promettent des réformes. **-2.** (*in combination with pp: to form passive*) être; **to ~ loved** être aimé(e); **there was no one to ~ seen** il n'y avait personne. **-3.** (*in question tags*): **she's pretty, isn't she?** elle est jolie, n'est-ce pas?; **the meal was delicious, wasn't it?** le repas était délicieux, non? OR vous n'avez pas trouvé? **-4.** (*followed by "to" + infin*): **to ~ sold** on va vendre la société; **I'm to ~ promoted** je vais avoir de l'avancement; **you're not to tell anyone** ne le dis à personne.

◇ *copulative vb* **-1.** (*with adj, n*) être; **to ~ a doctor/lawyer/plumber** être médecin/avocat/plombier; **she's intelligent/attractive** elle est intelligente/jolie; **I'm hot/cold** j'ai chaud/froid; **~ quiet!** tais-toi!; **1 and 1 are 2** 1 et 1 font 2. **-2.** (*referring to health*) aller, se porter; **to ~ seriously ill** être gravement malade; **she's better now** elle va mieux maintenant; **how are you?** comment allez-vous? **-3.** (*referring to age*): **how old are you?** quel âge avez-vous?; **I'm 20 (years old)** j'ai 20 ans. **-4.** (*cost*) coûter, faire; **how much was it?** combien cela a-t-il coûté?, combien ça faisait?; **that will ~ £10, please** cela fait 10 livres, s'il vous plaît.

◇ *vi* **-1.** [exist] être, exister; **~ that as it may** quoi qu'il en soit. **-2.** [referring to place] être; **Toulouse is in France** Toulouse se trouve OR est en France; **he will ~ here tomorrow** il sera là demain. **-3.** [referring to movement] aller, être; **I've been to the cinema** j'ai été OR je suis allé au cinéma.

◇ *v impers* **-1.** [referring to time, dates, distance] être; **it's two o'clock** il est deux heu-res; **it's 3 km to the next town** la ville voisine est à 3 km. **-2.** [referring to the weather] faire; **it's hot/cold** il fait chaud/froid; **it's windy** il fait du vent, il y a du vent. **-3.** [for emphasis]: **it's me/Paul/the milkman** c'est moi/Paul/le laitier.

B/E *abbr of* **bill of exchange**.

beach [bi:tʃ] ◇ *n* plage *f*. ◇ *vt* échouer.

beach ball *n* ballon *m* de plage.

beach buggy *n* buggy *m*.

beachcomber ['bi:tʃ,kəʊmər] *n ramasseur d'objets trouvés sur la plage*.

beachhead ['bi:tʃhed] *n* MIL tête *f* de pont.

beachwear ['bi:tʃweər] *n* (*U*) tenue *f* de plage.

beacon ['bi:kən] *n* **-1.** [warning fire] feu *m*, fanal *m*. **-2.** [lighthouse] phare *m*. **-3.** [radio beacon] radiophare *m*.

bead [bi:d] *n* **-1.** [of wood, glass] perle *f*. **-2.** [of sweat] goutte *f*.

beaded ['bi:dɪd] *adj* orné(e) de perles.

beading ['bi:dɪŋ] *n* (*U*) baguette *f* de recouvrement.

beady ['bi:dɪ] (*compar* **-ier**, *superl* **-iest**) *adj*: **~ eyes** petits yeux perçants.

beagle ['bi:gl] *n* beagle *m*.

beak [bi:k] *n* bec *m*.

beaker ['bi:kər] *n* gobelet *m*.

be-all *n*: **the ~ and end-all** la seule chose qui compte.

beam [bi:m] ◇ *n* **-1.** [of wood, concrete] poutre *f*. **-2.** [of light] rayon *m*. ◇ *vt* [signal, news] transmettre. ◇ *vi* **-1.** [smile] faire un sourire radieux. **-2.** [shine] rayonner.

beaming ['bi:mɪŋ] *adj* **-1.** [smiling] radieux(ieuse). **-2.** [shining] rayonnant(e).

bean [bi:n] *n* [gen] haricot *m*; [of coffee] grain *m*; **to be full of ~s** *inf* péter le feu; **to spill the ~s** *inf* manger le morceau.

beanbag ['bi:nbæg] *n* [chair] sacco *m*.

beanshoot ['bi:nʃu:t], **beansprout** ['bi:nspraʊt] *n* germe *m* OR pousse *f* de soja.

bear [beər] (*pt* **bore**, *pp* **borne**) ◇ *n* **-1.** [animal] ours *m*. **-2.** ST EX baissier *m*.

◇ *vt* **-1.** [carry] porter. **-2.** [support, tolerate] supporter; **I can't ~ Christmas** je n'aime pas Noël; **to ~ responsibility (for)** assumer OR prendre la responsabilité (de). **-3.** [child] donner naissance à. **-4.** [feeling]: **to ~ sb a grudge** garder rancune à qqn. **-5.** FIN [interest] rapporter.

◇ *vi*: **to ~ left/right** se diriger vers la gauche/la droite; **to bring pressure/influence to ~ on sb** exercer une pression/une influence sur qqn.

◆ **bear down** *vi*: to ~ down on sb/sthg s'approcher de qqn/qqch de façon menaçante.

◆ **bear out** *vt sep* confirmer, corroborer.

◆ **bear up** *vi* tenir le coup.

◆ **bear with** *vt fus* être patient(e) avec.

bearable ['beərəbl] *adj* [tolerable] supportable.

beard [bɪəd] *n* barbe *f*.

bearded ['bɪədɪd] *adj* barbu(e).

bearer ['beərə'] *n* -1. [gen] porteur *m*, -euse *f*. -2. [of passport] titulaire *mf*.

bear hug *n inf*: to give sb a ~ serrer qqn très fort.

bearing ['beərɪŋ] *n* -1. [connection]: ~ **(on)** rapport *m* (avec). -2. [deportment] allure *f*, maintien *m*. -3. TECH [for shaft] palier *m*; **rolling** ~ roulement *m*. -4. [on compass] orientation *f*; **to get one's ~s** s'orienter, se repérer.

bear market *n* ST EX marché *m* à la baisse.

bearskin ['beəskɪn] *n* -1. [fur] peau *f* d'ours. -2. [hat] bonnet *m* à poil.

beast [biːst] *n* -1. [animal] bête *f*. -2. *inf pej* [person] brute *f*.

beastly ['biːstlɪ] (*compar* **-ier**, *superl* **-iest**) *adj dated* [person] malveillant(e), cruel(elle); [headache, weather] épouvantable.

beat [biːt] (*pt* **beat**, *pp* **beaten**) ◇ *n* -1. [of heart, drum, wings] battement *m*. -2. MUS [rhythm] mesure *f*, temps *m*. -3. [of policeman] ronde *f*. ◇ *adj inf* crevé(e).
◇ *vt* -1. [gen] battre; **it ~s me** *inf* ça me dépasse. -2. [reach ahead of]: **they ~ us to it** ils nous ont devancés, ils sont arrivés avant nous. -3. [be better than] être bien mieux que, valoir mieux que. -4. *phr*: ~ **it!** *inf* décampe!, fiche le camp!
◇ *vi* battre.

◆ **beat down** ◇ *vi* -1. [sun] taper, cogner. -2. [rain] s'abattre. ◇ *vt sep* [seller] faire baisser son prix à.

◆ **beat off** *vt sep* [resist] repousser.

◆ **beat up** *vt sep inf* tabasser, passer à tabac.

beaten ['biːtn] *adj* battu(e).

beater ['biːtə'] *n* -1. [for eggs] batteur *m*, fouet *m*. -2. [for carpet] tapette *f*. -3. [of wife, child] bourreau *m*.

beating ['biːtɪŋ] *n* -1. [blows] raclée *f*, rossée *f*. -2. [defeat] défaite *f*; **that will take some ~!** *inf* on ne pourra sans doute jamais faire mieux.

beating up (*pl* **beatings up**) *n inf* passage *m* à tabac.

beatnik ['biːtnɪk] *n* beatnik *mf*.

beat-up *adj inf* déglingué(e).

beautician [bjuː'tɪʃn] *n* esthéticien *m*, -ienne *f*.

beautiful ['bjuːtɪful] *adj* -1. [gen] beau (belle). -2. *inf* [very good] joli(e).

beautifully ['bjuːtəflɪ] *adv* -1. [attractively - dressed] élégamment; [- decorated] avec goût. -2. *inf* [very well] parfaitement, à la perfection.

beauty ['bjuːtɪ] (*pl* **-ies**) ◇ *n* -1. [gen] beauté *f*. -2. *inf* [very good thing] merveille *f*. ◇ *comp* [products etc] de beauté.

beauty contest *n* concours *m* de beauté.

beauty parlour *n* institut *m* de beauté.

beauty queen *n* reine *f* de beauté.

beauty salon = **beauty parlour**.

beauty spot *n* -1. [picturesque place] site *m* pittoresque. -2. [on skin] grain *m* de beauté.

beaver ['biːvə'] *n* castor *m*.

◆ **beaver away** *vi* travailler d'arrache-pied.

becalmed [bɪ'kɑːmd] *adj* [ship] encalminé(e).

became [bɪ'keɪm] *pt* → **become**.

because [bɪ'kɒz] *conj* parce que.

◆ **because of** *prep* à cause de.

béchamel sauce [ˌbeɪʃə'mel-] *n* sauce *f* béchamel, béchamel *f*.

beck [bek] *n*: **to be at sb's ~ and call** être aux ordres OR à la disposition de qqn.

beckon ['bekən] ◇ *vt* -1. [signal to] faire signe à. -2. *fig* [draw, attract] séduire. ◇ *vi* [signal]: **to ~ to sb** faire signe à qqn.

become [bɪ'kʌm] (*pt* **became**, *pp* **become**) *vi* devenir; **to ~ quieter** se calmer; **to ~ irritated** s'énerver; **what has ~ of them?** que sont-ils devenus?

becoming [bɪ'kʌmɪŋ] *adj* -1. [attractive] seyant(e), qui va bien. -2. [appropriate] convenable.

BECTU ['bektu] (*abbr of* **Broadcasting, Entertainment, Cinematograph and Theatre Union**) *n syndicat britannique des techniciens des médias audiovisuels.*

bed [bed] (*pt & pp* **-ded**, *cont* **-ding**) *n* -1. [to sleep on] lit *m*; **to go to ~** se coucher; **to go to ~ with sb** *euphemism* coucher avec qqn; **to make the ~** faire le lit. -2. [flowerbed] parterre *m*; **it's not a ~ of roses** *fig* ce n'est pas tout rose. -3. [of sea, river] lit *m*, fond *m*.

◆ **bed down** *vi* coucher, se coucher.

BEd [ˌbiː'ed] (*abbr of* **Bachelor of Education**) *n (titulaire d'une) licence de sciences de l'éducation.*

bed and breakfast *n* ≃ chambre *f* d'hôte.

bed-bath *n* toilette *f* d'un malade.

bedbug ['bedbʌg] *n* punaise *f.*

bedclothes ['bedkləʊðz] *npl* draps *mpl* et couvertures *fpl.*

bedcover ['bed,kʌvər] *n* couvre-lit *m,* dessus-de-lit *m.*

bedding ['bedɪŋ] *n* (*U*) = bedclothes.

bedding plant *n* plant *m* à repiquer.

bedeck [bɪ'dek] *vt*: **to ~ sthg with** parer OR orner qqch de.

bedevil [bɪ'devl] (*Br pt* & *pp* **-led,** *cont* **-ling,** *Am pt* & *pp* **-ed,** *cont* **-ing**) *vt*: **to be bedevilled with** être surchargé(e) de.

bedfellow ['bed,feləʊ] *n fig* partenaire *mf.*

bedlam ['bedləm] *n* pagaille *f.*

bed linen *n* (*U*) draps *mpl* et taies *fpl.*

Bedouin, Beduin ['beduɪn] ◇ *adj* bédouin(e). ◇ *n* Bédouin *m,* -e *f.*

bedpan ['bedpæn] *n* bassin *m.*

bedraggled [bɪ'drægld] *adj* [person] débraillé(e); [hair] embroussaillé(e).

bedridden ['bed,rɪdn] *adj* grabataire.

bedrock ['bedrɒk] *n* (*U*) **-1.** GEOL soubassement *m.* **-2.** *fig* [basis] base *f,* fondement *m.*

bedroom ['bedrʊm] *n* chambre *f* (à coucher).

Beds [bedz] (*abbr of* **Bedfordshire**) *comté anglais.*

bedside ['bedsaɪd] *n* chevet *m.*

bedside manner *n* [of doctor] comportement *m* envers les malades.

bed-sit(ter) *n Br* chambre *f* meublée.

bedsore ['bedsɔːr] *n* escarre *f.*

bedspread ['bedspred] *n* couvre-lit *m,* dessus-de-lit *m.*

bedtime ['bedtaɪm] *n* heure *f* du coucher.

Beduin = Bedouin.

bed-wetting [-wetɪŋ] *n* énurésie *f,* incontinence *f* nocturne.

bee [biː] *n* abeille *f*; **to have a ~ in one's bonnet (about)** avoir une idée fixe (à propos de).

Beeb [biːb] *n Br inf*: **the ~** la BBC.

beech [biːtʃ] *n* hêtre *m.*

beef [biːf] *n* bœuf *m.*

◆ **beef up** *vt sep inf* [strengthen] renforcer; [story] corser.

beefburger ['biːf,bɜːgər] *n* hamburger *m.*

Beefeater ['biːf,iːtə] *n* hallebardier *m* (de la Tour de Londres).

beefsteak [,biːf'steɪk] *n* bifteck *m.*

beehive ['biːhaɪv] *n* **-1.** [for bees] ruche *f.* **-2.** [hairstyle] coiffure *f* en forme de dôme.

beekeeper ['biː,kiːpər] *n* apiculteur *m,* -trice *f.*

beeline ['biːlaɪn] *n*: **to make a ~ for** *inf* aller tout droit OR directement vers.

been [biːn] *pp* → **be.**

beep [biːp] *inf* ◇ *n* bip *m.* ◇ *vi* faire bip.

beer [bɪər] *n* bière *f.*

beer garden *n* terrasse *f,* jardin *m* (*à l'arrière*).

beeswax ['biːzwæks] *n* cire *f* d'abeille.

beet [biːt] *n* betterave *f.*

beetle ['biːtl] *n* scarabée *m.*

beetroot ['biːtruːt] *n* betterave *f.*

befall [bɪ'fɔːl] (*pt* **befell** [-'fel],* *pp* **befallen** [-fɔːlən]) *literary* ◇ *vt* advenir à. ◇ *vi* arriver, survenir.

befit [bɪ'fɪt] (*pt* & *pp* **-ted,** *cont* **-ting**) *vt* seoir à.

before [bɪ'fɔːr] ◇ *adv* auparavant, avant; **I've never been there ~** je n'y suis jamais allé; **I've seen it ~** je l'ai déjà vu; **the year ~** l'année d'avant OR précédente. ◇ *prep* **-1.** [in time] avant. **-2.** [in space] devant. ◇ *conj* avant de (+ *infin*), avant que (+ *subjunctive*); **~ leaving** avant de partir; **~ you leave** avant que vous ne partiez.

beforehand [bɪ'fɔːhænd] *adv* à l'avance.

befriend [bɪ'frend] *vt* prendre en amitié.

befuddled [bɪ'fʌdld] *adj* [confused] embrouillé(e).

beg [beg] (*pt* & *pp* **-ged,** *cont* **-ging**) ◇ *vt* **-1.** [money, food] mendier. **-2.** [favour] solliciter, quémander; [forgiveness] demander; **to ~ sb to do sthg** prier OR supplier qqn de faire qqch; **to ~ sb for sthg** implorer qqch de qqn. ◇ *vi* **-1.** [for money, food]: **to ~ (for sthg)** mendier (qqch). **-2.** [plead] supplier; **to ~ for** [forgiveness etc] demander.

began [bɪ'gæn] *pt* → **begin.**

beggar ['begər] *n* mendiant *m,* -e *f.*

begin [bɪ'gɪn] (*pt* **began,** *pp* **begun,** *cont* **-ning**) ◇ *vt* commencer; **to ~ doing** OR **to do sthg** commencer OR se mettre à faire qqch. ◇ *vi* commencer; **to ~ with** pour commencer, premièrement.

beginner [bɪ'gɪnər] *n* débutant *m,* -e *f.*

beginning [bɪ'gɪnɪŋ] *n* début *m,* commencement *m.*

begonia [bɪ'gəʊnjə] *n* bégonia *m.*

begrudge [bɪ'grʌdʒ] *vt* **-1.** [envy]: **to ~ sb sthg** envier qqch à qqn. **-2.** [do unwillingly]: **to ~ doing sthg** rechigner à faire qqch.

beguile [bɪ'gaɪl] *vt* [charm] séduire.

beguiling [bɪ'gaɪlɪŋ] *adj* [charming] séduisant(e).

begun [bɪ'gʌn] *pp* → **begin.**

behalf [bɪ'hɑːf] *n*: **on ~ of** *Br*, **in ~ of** *Am* de la part de, au nom de.

behave [bɪ'heɪv] ◇ *vt*: **to ~ o.s.** se conduire OR se comporter bien. ◇ *vi* **-1.** [in a particular way] se conduire, se comporter. **-2.** [acceptably] se tenir bien.

behaviour *Br*, **behavior** *Am* [bɪ'heɪvjə'] *n* conduite *f*, comportement *m*.

behaviourism *Br*, **behaviorism** *Am* [bɪ'heɪvjərɪzm] *n* béhaviorisme *m*.

behead [bɪ'hed] *vt* décapiter.

beheld [bɪ'held] *pt & pp* → behold.

behind [bɪ'haɪnd] ◇ *prep* **-1.** [gen] derrière. **-2.** [in time] en retard sur; **they arrived two hours ~ us** ils sont arrivés deux heures après nous. ◇ *adv* **-1.** [gen] derrière. **-2.** [in time] en retard; **to leave sthg ~** oublier qqch; **to stay ~** rester; **to be ~ with sthg** être en retard dans qqch. ◇ *n inf* derrière *m*, postérieur *m*.

behold [bɪ'həʊld] (*pt & pp* **beheld**) *vt literary* voir, regarder.

beige [beɪʒ] ◇ *adj* beige. ◇ *n* beige *m*; **in ~** en beige.

Beijing [,beɪ'dʒɪŋ] *n* Beijing.

being ['biːɪŋ] *n* **-1.** [creature] être *m*. **-2.** [existence]: **in ~** existant(e); **to come into ~** voir le jour, prendre naissance.

Beirut [,beɪ'ruːt] *n* Beyrouth; **East ~** Beyrouth-Est; **West ~** Beyrouth-Ouest.

belated [bɪ'leɪtɪd] *adj* tardif(ive).

belatedly [bɪ'leɪtɪdlɪ] *adv* tardivement.

belch [beltʃ] ◇ *n* renvoi *m*, rot *m*. ◇ *vt* [smoke, fire] vomir, cracher. ◇ *vi* **-1.** [person] éructer, roter. **-2.** [smoke, fire] cracher, vomir.

beleaguered [bɪ'liːgəd] *adj* assiégé(e); *fig* harcelé(e), tracassé(e).

belfry ['belfrɪ] (*pl* **-ies**) *n* beffroi *m*, clocher *m*.

Belgian ['beldʒən] ◇ *adj* belge. ◇ *n* Belge *mf*.

Belgium ['beldʒəm] *n* Belgique *f*; **in ~** en Belgique.

Belgrade [,bel'greɪd] *n* Belgrade.

belie [bɪ'laɪ] (*cont* **belying**) *vt* **-1.** [disprove] démentir. **-2.** [give false idea of] donner une fausse idée de.

belief [bɪ'liːf] *n* **-1.** [faith, certainty]: **~ (in)** croyance *f* (en); **beyond ~** incroyable. **-2.** [principle, opinion] opinion *f*, conviction *f*; **in the ~ that** persuadé OR convaincu que.

believable [bɪ'liːvəbl] *adj* croyable.

believe [bɪ'liːv] ◇ *vt* croire; **~ it or not** tu ne me croiras peut-être pas. ◇ *vi* croire; **to**

~ in sb croire en qqn; **to ~ in sthg** croire à qqch.

believer [bɪ'liːvə'] *n* **-1.** RELIG croyant *m*, -e *f*. **-2.** [in idea, action]: **~ in** partisan *m*, -e *f* de.

Belisha beacon [bɪ'liːʃə-] *n Br* globe lumineux indiquant un passage clouté.

belittle [bɪ'lɪtl] *vt* dénigrer, rabaisser.

Belize [be'liːz] *n* Belize *m*; **in ~** au Belize.

bell [bel] *n* [of church] cloche *f*; [handbell] clochette *f*; [on door] sonnette *f*; [on bike] timbre *m*; **the name rings a ~** ce nom me dit quelque chose.

bell-bottoms *npl* pantalon *m* à pattes d'éléphant.

bellhop ['belhɒp] *n Am* groum *m*, chasseur *m*.

belligerence [bɪ'lɪdʒərəns] *n* belligérance *f*.

belligerent [bɪ'lɪdʒərənt] *adj* **-1.** [at war] belligérant(e). **-2.** [aggressive] belliqueux(euse).

bellow ['beləʊ] ◇ *vt* [order] hurler, brailler. ◇ *vi* **-1.** [person] brailler, beugler. **-2.** [bull] beugler.

bellows ['beləʊz] *npl* soufflet *m*.

bell push *n Br* bouton *m* de sonnette.

bell-ringer *n* carillonneur *m*, -euse *f*.

belly ['belɪ] (*pl* **-ies**) *n* [of person] ventre *m*; [of animal] panse *f*.

bellyache ['belɪeɪk] ◇ *n* mal *m* de ventre. ◇ *vi inf* râler, rouspéter.

belly button *n inf* nombril *m*.

belly dancer *n* danseuse *f* orientale.

belong [bɪ'lɒŋ] *vi* **-1.** [be property]: **to ~ to sb** appartenir OR être à qqn. **-2.** [be member]: **to ~ to sthg** être membre de qqch. **-3.** [be in right place] être à sa place; **that chair ~s here** ce fauteuil va ici.

belongings [bɪ'lɒŋɪŋz] *npl* affaires *fpl*.

Belorussia [,beləʊ'rʌʃə] *n* Biélorussie *f*; **in ~** en Biélorussie.

beloved [bɪ'lʌvd] ◇ *adj* bien-aimé(e). ◇ *n* bien-aimé *m*, -e *f*.

below [bɪ'ləʊ] ◇ *adv* **-1.** [lower] en dessous, en bas. **-2.** [in text] ci-dessous. **-3.** NAUT en bas. ◇ *prep* sous, au-dessous de; **to be ~ sb in rank** occuper un rang inférieur à qqn.

belt [belt] ◇ *n* **-1.** [for clothing] ceinture *f*; **that was below the ~** *inf* c'était un coup bas; **to tighten one's ~** *fig* se serrer la ceinture; **under one's ~** *fig* à son actif. **-2.** TECH courroie *f*. **-3.** [of land, sea] région *f*. ◇ *vt inf* flanquer une raclée à. ◇ *vi Br inf* [car] rouler à toute allure OR à pleins gaz; [person] foncer.

◆ **belt out** *vt sep inf* [song] beugler.

◆ **belt up** *vi Br inf* la fermer, la boucler.

beltway ['belt,weɪ] *n Am* route *f* périphérique.

bemused [bɪ'mjuːzd] *adj* perplexe.

bench [bentʃ] *n* **-1.** [gen & POL] banc *m*. **-2.** [in lab, workshop] établi *m*.

bend [bend] (*pt* & *pp* **bent**) ◇ *n* **-1.** [in road] courbe *f*, virage *m*. **-2.** [in pipe, river] coude *m*. **-3.** *phr*: **round the** ~ *inf* dingue, fou (folle). ◇ *vt* **-1.** [arm, leg] plier. **-2.** [wire, fork etc] tordre, courber. ◇ *vi* [person] se baisser, se courber; [tree, rod] plier; **to** ~ **over backwards for sb** se mettre en quatre pour qqn.
◆ **bends** *npl*: **the** ~**s** la maladie des caissons.

bendy ['bendɪ] (*compar* **-ier**, *superl* **-iest**) *adj Br* flexible.

beneath [bɪ'niːθ] ◇ *adv* dessous, en bas. ◇ *prep* **-1.** [under] sous. **-2.** [unworthy of] indigne de.

benediction [,benɪ'dɪkʃn] *n* bénédiction *f*.

benefactor ['benɪfæktər] *n* bienfaiteur *m*.

benefactress ['benɪfæktrɪs] *n* bienfaitrice *f*.

beneficial [,benɪ'fɪʃl] *adj*: ~ **(to sb)** salutaire (à qqn); ~ **(to sthg)** utile (à qqch).

beneficiary [,benɪ'fɪʃərɪ] (*pl* **-ies**) *n* bénéficiaire *mf*.

benefit ['benɪfɪt] ◇ *n* **-1.** [advantage] avantage *m*; **for the** ~ **of** dans l'intérêt de; **to be to sb's** ~, **to be of** ~ **to sb** être dans l'intérêt de qqn. **-2.** ADMIN [allowance of money] allocation *f*, prestation *f*. ◇ *comp*: ~ **performance** représentation *f* de bienfaisance. ◇ *vt* profiter à, être avantageux pour. ◇ *vi*: **to** ~ **from** tirer avantage de, profiter de.

Benelux ['benɪlʌks] *n* Bénélux *m*; **the** ~ **countries** les pays du Bénélux.

benevolent [bɪ'nevələnt] *adj* bienveillant(e).

BEng [,biː'endʒ] (*abbr of* **Bachelor of Engineering**) *n* (*titulaire d'une*) *licence de mécanique.*

Bengal [,beŋ'gɔːl] *n* Bengale *m*; **in** ~ au Bengale; **the Bay of** ~ le golfe du Bengale.

benign [bɪ'naɪn] *adj* **-1.** [person] gentil(ille), bienveillant(e). **-2.** MED bénin(igne).

Benin [be'nɪn] *n* Bénin *m*; **in** ~ au Bénin.

bent [bent] ◇ *pt* & *pp* → **bend**. ◇ *adj* **-1.** [wire, bar] tordu(e). **-2.** [person, body] courbé(e), voûté(e). **-3.** *Br inf* [dishonest] véreux(euse). **-4.** [determined]: **to be** ~ **on doing sthg** être décidé(e) à faire qqch. ◇ *n*: ~ **(for)** penchant *m* (pour).

bequeath [bɪ'kwiːð] *vt lit* & *fig* léguer.

bequest [bɪ'kwest] *n* legs *m*.

berate [bɪ'reɪt] *vt* réprimander.

Berber ['bɜːbər] ◇ *adj* berbère. ◇ *n* **-1.** [person] Berbère *mf*. **-2.** [language] berbère *m*.

bereaved [bɪ'riːvd] (*pl inv*) ◇ *adj* endeuillé(e), affligé(e). ◇ *n*: **the** ~ la famille du défunt.

bereavement [bɪ'riːvmənt] *n* deuil *m*.

bereft [bɪ'reft] *adj literary*: ~ **of** privé(e) de.

beret ['bereɪ] *n* béret *m*.

Bering Sea ['berɪŋ-] *n*: **the** ~ la mer de Béring.

Bering Strait ['berɪŋ-] *n*: **the** ~ le détroit de Béring.

berk [bɜːk] *n Br inf* idiot *m*, -e *f*, andouille *f*.

Berks [bɑːks] (*abbr of* **Berkshire**) *comté anglais.*

Berlin [bɜː'lɪn] *n* Berlin; **East** ~ Berlin-Est; **West** ~ Berlin-Ouest; **the** ~ **Wall** le mur de Berlin.

Berliner [bɜː'lɪnə] *n* Berlinois *m*, -e *f*.

berm [bɜːm] *n Am* bas-côté *m*.

Bermuda [bə'mjuːdə] *n* Bermudes *fpl*; **in** ~ aux Bermudes.

Bermuda shorts *npl* bermuda *m*.

Bern [bɜːn] *n* Berne.

berry ['berɪ] (*pl* **-ies**) *n* baie *f*.

berserk [bə'zɜːk] *adj*: **to go** ~ devenir fou furieux (folle furieuse).

berth [bɜːθ] ◇ *n* **-1.** [in harbour] poste *m* d'amarrage, mouillage *m*. **-2.** [in ship, train] couchette *f*. **-3.** *phr*: **to give sb a wide** ~ éviter qqn. ◇ *vi* [ship] amener à quai. ◇ *vi* [ship] accoster, se ranger à quai.

beseech [bɪ'siːtʃ] (*pt* & *pp* **besought** OR **beseeched**) *vt literary*: **to** ~ **sb (to do sthg)** implorer OR supplier qqn (de faire qqch).

beset [bɪ'set] (*pt* & *pp* **beset**, *cont* **-ting**) ◇ *adj*: ~ **with** OR **by** [doubts etc] assailli(e) de; **the plan is** ~ **with risks** le plan comporte une multitude de risques. ◇ *vt* assaillir.

beside [bɪ'saɪd] *prep* **-1.** [next to] à côté de, auprès de. **-2.** [compared with] comparé(e) à, à côté de. **-3.** *phr*: **to be** ~ **o.s. with anger** être hors de soi; **to be** ~ **o.s. with joy** être fou (folle) de joie.

besides [bɪ'saɪdz] ◇ *adv* en outre, en plus. ◇ *prep* en plus de.

besiege [bɪ'siːdʒ] *vt* **-1.** [town, fortress] assiéger. **-2.** *fig* [trouble, annoy] assaillir, harceler; **to be** ~**d with** être assailli OR harcelé de.

besotted [bɪ'sɒtɪd] *adj*: ~ **(with sb)** entiché(e) (de qqn).

besought [bɪ'sɔːt] *pt* & *pp* → **beseech**.

bespectacled [bɪ'spektəkld] *adj* qui porte des lunettes, à lunettes.

bespoke [bɪ'spəʊk] *adj Br* [clothes] fait(e) sur mesure; [tailor] à façon.

best [best] ◇ *adj* le meilleur (la meilleure). ◇ *adv* le mieux. ◇ *n* le mieux; **to do one's** ~ faire de son mieux; **all the** ~! meilleurs souhaits!; **to be for the** ~ être pour le mieux; **to make the** ~ **of sthg** s'accommoder de qqch, prendre son parti de qqch; **he wants the** ~ **of both worlds** il veut le beurre et l'argent du beurre.
◆ **at best** *adv* au mieux.

bestial ['bestjəl] *adj* bestial(e).

best man *n* garçon *m* d'honneur.

BEST MAN:
Dans les pays anglo-saxons, le garçon d'honneur présente l'alliance au marié et prononce un discours lors de la réception de mariage

bestow [bɪ'stəʊ] *vt fml*: **to** ~ **sthg on sb** conférer qqch à qqn.

best-seller *n* [book] best-seller *m*.

best-selling *adj* à succès.

bet [bet] (*pt & pp* **bet** OR **-ted**, *cont* **-ting**) ◇ *n* pari *m*; **it's a safe** ~ **that ...** *fig* il est certain que ...; **to hedge one's** ~**s** se couvrir. ◇ *vt* parier. ◇ *vi* parier; **I wouldn't** ~ **on it** *fig* je n'en suis pas si sûr; **you** ~! *inf* un peu!, et comment!

beta-blocker ['biːtə,blɒkər] *n* bêtabloquant *m*.

Bethlehem ['beθlɪhem] *n* Bethléem.

betray [bɪ'treɪ] *vt* trahir.

betrayal [bɪ'treɪəl] *n* **-1.** [of person] trahison *f*. **-2.** ~ **of trust** abus *m* de confiance. **-3.** [of secret] révélation *f*.

betrothed [bɪ'trəʊðd] *adj dated*: ~ **(to)** fiancé(e) (à).

better ['betər] ◇ *adj (compar of good)* meilleur(e); **to get** ~ s'améliorer; [after illness] se remettre, se rétablir. ◇ *adv (compar of well)* mieux; **I'd** ~ **leave** il faut que je parte, je dois partir; **you'd** ~ **let your mother know** tu ferais mieux de le dire à ta mère. ◇ *n* meilleur *m*, -e *f*; **to get the** ~ **of sb** avoir raison de qqn. ◇ *vt* améliorer; **to** ~ **o.s.** s'élever.

better half *n inf* moitié *f*.

better off *adj* **-1.** [financially] plus à son aise. **-2.** [in better situation] mieux.
◆ **better-off** *npl*: **the** ~ les gens riches OR aisés.

betting ['betɪŋ] *n (U)* paris *mpl*.

betting shop *n Br* ≃ bureau *m* de P.M.U.

between [bɪ'twiːn] ◇ *prep* entre; **he sat (in)** ~ **Paul and Anne** il s'est assis entre Paul et Anne. ◇ *adv*: **(in)** ~ [in space] au milieu; [in time] dans l'intervalle.

bevelled *Br*, **beveled** *Am* ['bevld] *adj* biseauté(e).

beverage ['bevərɪdʒ] *n fml* boisson *f*.

bevy ['bevɪ] (*pl* **-ies**) *n* bande *f*, troupe *f*.

beware [bɪ'weər] *vi*: **to** ~ **(of)** prendre garde (à), se méfier (de); ~ **of ...** attention à ....

bewildered [bɪ'wɪldəd] *adj* déconcerté(e), perplexe.

bewildering [bɪ'wɪldərɪŋ] *adj* déconcertant(e), déroutant(e).

bewitched [bɪ'wɪtʃt] *adj* ensorcelé(e), enchanté(e).

bewitching [bɪ'wɪtʃɪŋ] *adj* charmeur(euse), ensorcelant(e).

beyond [bɪ'jɒnd] ◇ *prep* **-1.** [in space] au-delà de. **-2.** [in time] après, plus tard que. **-3.** [exceeding] au-dessus de; **it's** ~ **my control** je n'y peux rien; **it's** ~ **my responsibility** cela n'entre pas dans le cadre de mes responsabilités. ◇ *adv* au-delà.

b/f *abbr of* **brought forward**.

bhp *abbr of* **brake horsepower**.

bi- [baɪ] *prefix* bi-.

biannual [baɪ'ænjʊəl] *adj* semestriel(ielle).

bias ['baɪəs] *n* **-1.** [prejudice] préjugé *m*, parti *m* pris. **-2.** [tendency] tendance *f*.

biased ['baɪəst] *adj* partial(e); **to be** ~ **towards sb/sthg** favoriser qqn/qqch; **to be** ~ **against sb/sthg** défavoriser qqn/qqch.

bib [bɪb] *n* [for baby] bavoir *m*, bavette *f*.

Bible ['baɪbl] *n*: **the** ~ la Bible.
◆ **bible** *n* bible *f*.

biblical ['bɪblɪkl] *adj* biblique.

bibliography [,bɪblɪ'ɒgrəfɪ] (*pl* **-ies**) *n* bibliographie *f*.

bicarbonate of soda [baɪ'kɑːbənət-] *n* bicarbonate *m* de soude.

bicentenary *Br* [,baɪsen'tiːnərɪ] (*pl* **-ies**), **bicentennial** *Am* [,baɪsen'tenjəl] *n* bicentenaire *m*.

biceps ['baɪseps] (*pl inv*) *n* biceps *m*.

bicker ['bɪkər] *vi* se chamailler.

bickering ['bɪkərɪŋ] *n (U)* chamailleries *fpl*.

bicycle ['baɪsɪkl] ◇ *n* bicyclette *f*, vélo *m*. ◇ *vi* aller en bicyclette OR vélo.

bicycle path *n* piste *f* cyclable.

bicycle pump *n* pompe *f* à vélo.

bid [bɪd] (*pt & pp vt sense 1 & vi* **bid**, *cont* **bidding**, *pt vt senses 2 & 3* **bid** OR **bade**, *pp vt senses 2 & 3* **bid** OR **bidden** ['bɪdn], *cont* **bidding**) ◇ *n* **-1.** [attempt] tentative *f*. **-2.** [at auction] enchère *f*. **-3.** COMM offre *f*. ◇ *vt* **-1.**

[at auction] faire une enchère de. **-2.** *literary* [request]: **to ~ sb do sthg** prier qqn de faire qqch. **-3.** *fml* [say]: **to ~ sb good morning** souhaiter le bonjour à qqn. ◇ *vi* **-1.** [at auction]: **to ~ (for)** faire une enchère (pour). **-2.** [attempt]: **to ~ for sthg** briguer.

bidder ['bɪdə*] *n* enchérisseur *m*, -euse *f*.

bidding ['bɪdɪŋ] *n* (*U*) enchères *fpl*.

bide [baɪd] *vt*: **to ~ one's time** attendre son heure OR le bon moment.

bidet ['biːdeɪ] *n* bidet *m*.

biennial [baɪ'enɪəl] ◇ *adj* biennal(e). ◇ *n* plante *f* bisannuelle.

bier [bɪə*] *n* bière *f*.

bifocals [,baɪ'fəʊklz] *npl* lunettes *fpl* bifocales.

BIFU ['bɪfuː] (*abbr of* **The Banking, Insurance and Finance Union**) *n syndicat britannique des employés du secteur financier.*

big [bɪg] (*compar* **-ger**, *superl* **-gest**) *adj* **-1.** [gen] grand(e). **-2.** [in amount, bulk - box, problem, book] gros (grosse). **-3.** *phr*: **to do things in a ~ way** faire les choses en grand.

bigamist ['bɪgəmɪst] *n* bigame *mf*.

bigamy ['bɪgəmɪ] *n* bigamie *f*.

Big Apple *n*: **the ~** surnom de New York.

Big Ben [-'ben] *n* Big Ben.

big business *n* (*U*) les grandes entreprises *fpl*.

big cat *n* fauve *m*.

big deal *inf* ◇ *n*: **it's no ~** ce n'est pas dramatique; **what's the ~?** où est le problème? ◇ *excl* tu parles!, et alors?

Big Dipper [-'dɪpə*] *n* **-1.** *Br* [rollercoaster] montagnes *fpl* russes. **-2.** *Am* ASTRON: **the ~** la Grande Ourse.

big end *n* tête *f* de bielle.

big fish *n inf fig* huile *f*, gros bonnet *m*.

big game *n* gros gibier *m*.

big hand *n* **-1.** [on clock] grande aiguille *f*. **-2.** *inf* [applause]: **let's give him a ~** applaudissons-le bien fort.

bighead ['bɪghed] *n inf* crâneur *m*, -euse *f*.

bigheaded [,bɪg'hedɪd] *adj inf* crâneur(euse).

big-hearted [-'hɑːtɪd] *adj* qui a du cœur.

big money *n inf*: **to make ~** se faire du pognon.

big mouth *n inf* grande gueule *f*; **she's got a ~** elle ne sait pas tenir sa langue.

big name *n inf* personne *f* connue, célébrité *f*.

bigot ['bɪgət] *n* sectaire *mf*.

bigoted ['bɪgətɪd] *adj* sectaire.

bigotry ['bɪgətrɪ] *n* sectarisme *m*.

big shot *n inf* huile *f*, grosse légume *f*.

big time *n inf*: **to make the ~** réussir, arriver en haut de l'échelle.

big toe *n* gros orteil *m*.

big top *n* chapiteau *m*.

big wheel *n* **-1.** *Br* [at fairground] grande roue *f*. **-2.** *inf* [big shot] huile *f*, grosse légume *f*.

bigwig ['bɪgwɪg] *n inf* huile *f*, gros bonnet *m*.

bike [baɪk] *n inf* **-1.** [bicycle] vélo *m*, bécane *f*. **-2.** [motorcycle] bécane *f*, moto *f*.

bikeway ['baɪkweɪ] *n Am* piste *f* cyclable.

bikini [bɪ'kiːnɪ] *n* bikini *m*.

bilateral [,baɪ'lætərəl] *adj* bilatéral(e).

bilberry ['bɪlbərɪ] (*pl* **-ies**) *n* myrtille *f*.

bile [baɪl] *n* **-1.** [fluid] bile *f*. **-2.** [anger] mauvaise humeur *f*.

bilingual [baɪ'lɪŋgwəl] *adj* bilingue.

bilious ['bɪlɪəs] *adj* **-1.** [sickening] écœurant(e). **-2.** [nauseous] qui a envie de vomir.

bill [bɪl] ◇ *n* **-1.** [statement of cost]: **~ (for)** note *f* OR facture *f* (de); [in restaurant] addition *f* (de). **-2.** [in parliament] projet *m* de loi. **-3.** [of show, concert] programme *m*. **-4.** *Am* [banknote] billet *m* de banque. **-5.** [poster]: **"post** OR **stick no ~s"** «défense d'afficher». **-6.** [beak] bec *m*. **-7.** *phr*: **to be given a clean ~ of health** être déclaré en parfait état de santé. ◇ *vt* [invoice]: **to ~ sb (for)** envoyer une facture à qqn (pour).

billboard ['bɪlbɔːd] *n* panneau *m* d'affichage.

billet ['bɪlɪt] ◇ *n* logement *m* (chez l'habitant). ◇ *vt* loger, cantonner.

billfold ['bɪlfəʊld] *n Am* portefeuille *m*.

billiards ['bɪljədz] *n* billard *m*.

billion ['bɪljən] *num* **-1.** *Am* [thousand million] milliard *m*. **-2.** *Br* [million million] billion *m*.

billionaire [,bɪljə'neə*] *n* milliardaire *mf*.

bill of exchange *n* effet *m* OR lettre *f* de change.

bill of lading [-'leɪdɪŋ] *n* connaissement *m*.

Bill of Rights *n*: **the ~** les dix premiers amendements à la Constitution américaine.

BILL OF RIGHTS:
Ces amendements garantissent, entre autres droits, la liberté d'expression, de religion, et de réunion

bill of sale *n* acte *m* de vente.

billow ['bɪləʊ] ◇ *n* nuage *m*, volute *f*. ◇ *vi* [smoke, steam] **tournoyer**; [skirt, sail] **se gonfler**.

billycan ['bɪlɪkæn] *n* gamelle *f*.

billy goat ['bɪlɪ-] *n* bouc *m*.

bimbo ['bɪmbəʊ] (*pl* -s OR -es) *n* inf *pej*: **she's a bit of a ~** c'est le genre 'pin-up'.

bimonthly [,baɪ'mʌnθlɪ] ◇ *adj* **-1.** [every two months] bimestriel(ielle). **-2.** [twice a month] bimensuel(elle). ◇ *adv* **-1.** [every two months] tous les deux mois. **-2.** [twice a month] deux fois par mois.

bin [bɪn] ◇ *n* **-1.** Br [for rubbish] poubelle *f*. **-2.** [for grain, coal] coffre *m*. **-3.** [for bread] huche *f*, boîte *f*. ◇ *vt* inf balancer.

binary ['baɪnərɪ] *adj* binaire.

bind [baɪnd] (*pt* & *pp* **bound**) ◇ *vt* **-1.** [tie up] attacher, lier. **-2.** [unite - people] lier. **-3.** [bandage] panser. **-4.** [book] relier. **-5.** [constrain] contraindre, forcer. ◇ *n* inf **-1.** Br [nuisance] corvée *f*. **-2.** [difficult situation]: **to be in a bit of a ~** être dans le pétrin.
◆ **bind over** *vt sep*: **to be bound over** être sommé(e) d'observer une bonne conduite.

binder ['baɪndər] *n* **-1.** [machine] lieuse *f*. **-2.** [person] relieur *m*, -ieuse *f*. **-3.** [cover] classeur *m*.

binding ['baɪndɪŋ] ◇ *adj* qui lie OR engage; [agreement] irrévocable. ◇ *n* **-1.** [on book] reliure *f*. **-2.** [on dress, tablecloth] liséré *m*.

binge [bɪndʒ] inf ◇ *n*: **to go on a ~** prendre une cuite. ◇ *vi*: **to ~ on sthg** se gaver OR se bourrer de qqch.

bingo ['bɪŋgəʊ] *n* bingo *m*, ≃ loto *m*.

BINGO:
Ce jeu d'argent très populaire en Grande-Bretagne consiste à cocher des chiffres sur une carte jusqu'à ce qu'elle soit remplie; il est souvent pratiqué dans d'anciens cinémas ou des salles municipales

bin-liner *n* Br sac *m* (à) poubelle.

binoculars [bɪ'nɒkjʊləz] *npl* jumelles *fpl*.

biochemistry [,baɪəʊ'kemɪstrɪ] *n* biochimie *f*.

biodegradable [,baɪəʊdɪ'greɪdəbl] *adj* biodégradable.

biodiversity [,baɪəʊdaɪ'vɜːsətɪ] *n* biodiversité *f*.

biographer [baɪ'ɒgrəfər] *n* biographe *mf*.

biographic(al) [,baɪə'græfɪk(l)] *adj* biographique.

biography [baɪ'ɒgrəfɪ] (*pl* -ies) *n* biographie *f*.

biological [,baɪə'lɒdʒɪkl] *adj* biologique; [washing powder] aux enzymes.

biological weapon *n* arme *f* biologique.

biologist [baɪ'ɒlədʒɪst] *n* biologiste *mf*.

biology [baɪ'ɒlədʒɪ] *n* biologie *f*.

biopic ['baɪəʊpɪk] *n* inf film *m* biographique.

biopsy ['baɪɒpsɪ] (*pl* -ies) *n* biopsie *f*.

bipartite [,baɪ'pɑːtaɪt] *adj* bipartite.

biplane ['baɪpleɪn] *n* biplan *m*.

birch [bɜːtʃ] *n* **-1.** [tree] bouleau *m*. **-2.** [stick]: **the ~** la verge, le fouet.

bird [bɜːd] *n* **-1.** [creature] oiseau *m*; **to kill two ~s with one stone** faire d'une pierre deux coups. **-2.** inf [woman] gonzesse *f*.

birdcage ['bɜːdkeɪdʒ] *n* cage *f* à oiseaux.

birdie ['bɜːdɪ] *n* **-1.** [bird] petit oiseau *m*. **-2.** GOLF birdie *m*.

bird of paradise *n* paradisier *m*, oiseau *m* de paradis.

bird of prey *n* oiseau *m* de proie.

birdseed ['bɜːdsiːd] *n* graine *f* pour oiseaux.

bird's-eye view *n* vue *f* aérienne.

bird-watcher [-,wɒtʃər] *n* observateur *m*, -trice *f* d'oiseaux.

Biro® ['baɪərəʊ] *n* stylo *m* à bille.

birth [bɜːθ] *n* lit & fig naissance *f*; **to give ~ (to)** donner naissance (à).

birth certificate *n* acte *m* OR extrait *m* de naissance.

birth control *n* (U) régulation *f* OR contrôle *m* des naissances.

birthday ['bɜːθdeɪ] ◇ *n* anniversaire *m*. ◇ *comp* [party, present etc] d'anniversaire.

birthmark ['bɜːθmɑːk] *n* tache *f* de vin.

birthplace ['bɜːθpleɪs] *n* lieu *m* de naissance.

birthrate ['bɜːθreɪt] *n* (taux *m* de) natalité *f*.

birthright ['bɜːθraɪt] *n* droit *m* de naissance OR du sang.

Biscay ['bɪskeɪ] *n*: **the Bay of ~** le golfe de Gascogne.

biscuit ['bɪskɪt] *n* Br gâteau *m* sec, biscuit *m*; Am scone *m*.

bisect [baɪ'sekt] *vt* couper OR diviser en deux.

bisexual [,baɪ'sekʃjʊəl] ◇ *adj* bisexuel(elle). ◇ *n* bisexuel *m*, -elle *f*.

bishop ['bɪʃəp] *n* **-1.** RELIG évêque *m*. **-2.** [in chess] fou *m*.

bison ['baɪsn] (*pl* inv OR -s) *n* bison *m*.

bistro ['biːstrəʊ] (*pl* -s) *n* bistro *m*.

bit [bɪt] ◇ *pt* → **bite**.

◇ *n* **-1.** [small piece - of paper, cheese etc] morceau *m*, bout *m*; [- of book, film] passage *m*; **I just want a** ~ je ne veux qu'un petit peu; **~s and pieces** *Br* petites affaires *fpl* OR choses *fpl*; **to fall to ~s** tomber en morceaux; **to take sthg to ~s** démonter qqch. **-2.** [amount]: **a ~ of** un peu de; **a ~ of shopping** quelques courses; **it's a ~ of a nuisance** c'est un peu embêtant; **a ~ of trouble** un petit problème; **quite a ~ of** pas mal de, beaucoup de. **-3.** [short time]: **for a ~** pendant quelque temps. **-4.** [of drill] mèche *f*. **-5.** [of bridle] mors *m*. **-6.** COMPUT bit *m*. **-7.** *phr*: **to do one's ~** *Br* faire sa part; **every ~ as ... as** tout aussi ... que; **it's all a ~ much** [overwhelming] c'en est trop; **it's a ~ much** c'est un peu fort; **not a ~** [not at all] pas du tout.
◆ **a bit** *adv* un peu; **I'm a ~ tired** je suis un peu fatigué.
◆ **bit by bit** *adv* petit à petit, peu à peu.

bitch [bɪtʃ] ◇ *n* **-1.** [female dog] chienne *f*. **-2.** *v inf pej* [woman] salope *f*, garce *f*. ◇ *vi inf* rouspéter, râler; **to ~ about sb** casser du sucre sur le dos de qqn.

bitchy ['bɪtʃɪ] (*compar* **-ier**, *superl* **-iest**) *adj inf* vache, rosse.

bite [baɪt] (*pt* bit, *pp* bitten) ◇ *n* **-1.** [act of biting] morsure *f*, coup *m* de dent. **-2.** *inf* [food]: **to have a ~ (to eat)** manger un morceau. **-3.** [wound] piqûre *f*. **-4.** *Br* [sharp flavour] piquant *m*.
◇ *vt* **-1.** [subj: person, animal] mordre. **-2.** [subj: insect, snake] piquer, mordre.
◇ *vi* **-1.** [animal, person]: **to ~ (into)** mordre (dans); **to ~ off sthg** arracher qqch d'un coup de dents; **to ~ off more than one can chew** *fig* avoir les yeux plus gros que le ventre. **-2.** [insect, snake] mordre, piquer. **-3.** [grip] adhérer, mordre. **-4.** *fig* [take effect] se faire sentir.

biting ['baɪtɪŋ] *adj* **-1.** [very cold] cinglant(e), piquant(e). **-2.** [humour, comment] mordant(e), caustique.

bit part *n* petit rôle *m*, utilités *fpl*.

bitten ['bɪtn] *pp* → **bite**.

bitter ['bɪtər] ◇ *adj* **-1.** [gen] amer(ère); **to the ~ end** jusqu'au bout. **-2.** [icy] glacial(e). **-3.** [argument] violent(e). ◇ *n Br* bière relativement amère, à forte teneur en houblon.

bitter lemon *n* Schweppes® *m* au citron.

bitterly ['bɪtəlɪ] *adv* **-1.** [of weather]: **it's ~ cold** il fait un froid de canard. **-2.** [disappointed] cruellement; [cry, complain] amèrement; [criticize] âprement, violemment.

bitterness ['bɪtənɪs] *n* **-1.** [gen] amertume *f*. **-2.** [of wind, weather] âpreté *f*.

bittersweet ['bɪtəswiːt] *adj* [taste] aigredoux (-douce); [memory] doux-amer (-amère).

bitty ['bɪtɪ] (*compar* **-ier**, *superl* **-iest**) *adj Br inf* décousu(e).

bitumen ['bɪtjʊmɪn] *n* bitume *m*.

bivouac ['bɪvuæk] (*pt* & *pp* **-ked**, *cont* **-king**) ◇ *n* bivouac *m*. ◇ *vi* bivouaquer.

biweekly [ˌbaɪ'wiːklɪ] ◇ *adj* **-1.** [every two weeks] bimensuel(elle). **-2.** [twice a week] bihebdomadaire. ◇ *adv* **-1.** [every two weeks] tous les quinze jours. **-2.** [twice a week] deux fois par semaine.

bizarre [bɪ'zɑːr] *adj* bizarre.

bk -1. *abbr of* **bank**. **-2.** *abbr of* **book**.

bl *abbr of* **bill of lading**.

BL *n* **-1.** (*abbr of* **Bachelor of Law(s)**) (*titulaire d'une*) *licence de droit*. **-2.** (*abbr of* **Bachelor of Letters**) (*titulaire d'une*) *licence de lettres*. **-3.** (*abbr of* **Bachelor of Literature**) (*titulaire d'une*) *licence de littérature*.

blab [blæb] (*pt* & *pp* **-bed**, *cont* **-bing**) *vi inf* lâcher le morceau.

black [blæk] ◇ *adj* noir(e); **~ and blue** [person, body] couvert de bleus; **~ and white** [films, photos] noir et blanc. ◇ *n* **-1.** [colour] noir *m*. **-2.** [person] noir *m*, -e *f*. **-3.** *phr*: **in ~ and white** [in writing] noir sur blanc, par écrit; **in the ~** [financially solvent] solvable, sans dettes. ◇ *vt Br* [boycott] boycotter.
◆ **black out** ◇ *vt sep* **-1.** [city etc] faire le black-out dans. **-2.** [TV programme] faire le black-out sur. ◇ *vi* [faint] s'évanouir.

blackball ['blækbɔːl] *vt* blackbouler.

black belt *n* ceinture *f* noire.

blackberry ['blækbərɪ] (*pl* **-ies**) *n* mûre *f*.

blackbird ['blækbɜːd] *n* merle *m*.

blackboard ['blækbɔːd] *n* tableau *m* (noir).

black box *n* [flight recorder] boîte *f* noire.

black comedy *n* comédie *f* d'humour noir.

blackcurrant [ˌblæk'kʌrənt] *n* cassis *m*.

black economy *n* économie *f* parallèle.

blacken ['blækn] ◇ *vt* **-1.** [make dark] noircir. **-2.** *fig* [reputation] ternir. ◇ *vi* s'assombrir.

black eye *n* oeil *m* poché OR au beurre noir.

blackhead ['blækhed] *n* point *m* noir.

black hole *n* trou *m* noir.

black ice *n* verglas *m*.

blackjack ['blækdʒæk] *n* **-1.** [card game] vingt-et-un *m*. **-2.** *Am* [weapon] matraque *f*.

blackleg ['blækleg] *n pej* jaune *m*.

blacklist ['blæklɪst] ⬦ *n* liste *f* noire. ⬦ *vt* mettre sur la liste noire.

black magic *n* magie *f* noire.

blackmail ['blækmeɪl] ⬦ *n lit* & *fig* chantage *m*. ⬦ *vt* **-1.** [for money] faire chanter. **-2.** *fig* [emotionally] faire du chantage à.

blackmailer ['blækmeɪlə'] *n* maître-chanteur *m*.

Black Maria [-mə'raɪə] *n inf* panier *m* à salade.

black mark *n fig* mauvais point *m*.

black market *n* marché *m* noir.

blackout ['blækaʊt] *n* **-1.** MIL & PRESS blackout *m*. **-2.** [power cut] panne *f* d'électricité. **-3.** [fainting fit] évanouissement *m*.

Black Power *n* mouvement séparatiste noir né dans les années 60 aux États-Unis.

black pudding *n Br* boudin *m*.

Black Sea *n*: the ~ la mer Noire.

black sheep *n* brebis *f* galeuse.

blacksmith ['blæksmɪθ] *n* forgeron *m*; [for horses] maréchal-ferrant *m*.

black spot *n* AUT point *m* noir.

black-tie *adj* [dinner] habillé(e), en smoking.

bladder ['blædə'] *n* vessie *f*.

blade [bleɪd] *n* **-1.** [of knife, saw] lame *f*. **-2.** [of propeller] pale *f*. **-3.** [of grass] brin *m*.

blame [bleɪm] ⬦ *n* responsabilité *f*, faute *f*; to take the ~ for sthg endosser la responsabilité de qqch. ⬦ *vt* blâmer, condamner; to ~ sthg on rejeter la responsabilité de qqch sur, imputer qqch à; to ~ sb/sthg for sthg reprocher qqch à qqn/qqch; to be to ~ for sthg être responsable de qqch.

blameless ['bleɪmlɪs] *adj* [person] innocent(e); [life] irréprochable.

blanch [blɑːntʃ] ⬦ *vt* blanchir. ⬦ *vi* blêmir, pâlir.

blancmange [blə'mɒndʒ] *n* blanc-manger *m*.

bland [blænd] *adj* **-1.** [person] terne. **-2.** [food] fade, insipide. **-3.** [music, style] insipide.

blank [blæŋk] ⬦ *adj* **-1.** [sheet of paper] blanc (blanche); [wall] nu(e). **-2.** *fig* [look] vide, sans expression. ⬦ *n* **-1.** [empty space] blanc *m*. **-2.** [cartridge] cartouche *f* à blanc. **-3.** *phr*: to draw a ~ faire chou blanc.

blank cheque *n* chèque *m* en blanc; *fig* carte *f* blanche.

blanket ['blæŋkɪt] ⬦ *adj* global(e), général(e). ⬦ *n* **-1.** [for bed] couverture *f*. **-2.** [of snow] couche *f*, manteau *m*; [of fog] nappe *f*. ⬦ *vt* recouvrir.

blanket bath *n Br* toilette *f* d'un malade.

blankly ['blæŋklɪ] *adv* [stare] avec les yeux vides.

blank verse *n* (*U*) vers *mpl* blancs OR non rimés.

blare [bleə'] *vi* hurler; [radio] beugler.

◆ **blare out** *vi* hurler, beugler.

blasé [*Br* 'blɑːzeɪ, *Am* ,blɑː'zeɪ] *adj* blasé(e).

blasphemous ['blæsfəməs] *adj* [words] blasphématoire; [person] blasphémateur(trice).

blasphemy ['blæsfəmɪ] (*pl* **-ies**) *n* blasphème *m*.

blast [blɑːst] ⬦ *n* **-1.** [explosion] explosion *f*. **-2.** [of air, from bomb] souffle *m*. ⬦ *vt* [hole, tunnel] creuser à la dynamite. ⬦ *excl Br inf* zut!, mince!

◆ **(at) full blast** *adv* [play music etc] à pleins gaz OR tubes; [work] d'arrache-pied.

◆ **blast off** *vi* SPACE être mis à feu, décoller.

blasted ['blɑːstɪd] *adj inf* fichu(e), maudit(e).

blast furnace *n* haut fourneau *m*.

blast-off *n* SPACE mise *f* à feu, lancement *m*.

blatant ['bleɪtənt] *adj* criant(e), flagrant(e).

blatantly ['bleɪtəntlɪ] *adv* d'une manière flagrante.

blaze [bleɪz] ⬦ *n* **-1.** [fire] incendie *m*. **-2.** *fig* [of colour, light] éclat *m*, flamboiement *m*; in a ~ of publicity à grand renfort de publicité. ⬦ *vi* **-1.** [fire] flamber. **-2.** *fig* [with colour] flamboyer.

blazer ['bleɪzə'] *n* blazer *m*.

blazing ['bleɪzɪŋ] *adj* **-1.** [sun, heat] ardent(e); ~ **hot** torride, brûlant. **-2.** [row] violent(e).

bleach [bliːtʃ] ⬦ *n* eau *f* de Javel. ⬦ *vt* [hair] décolorer; [clothes] blanchir.

bleached [bliːtʃt] *adj* décoloré(e).

bleachers ['bliːtʃəz] *npl Am* SPORT gradins *mpl*.

bleak [bliːk] *adj* **-1.** [future] sombre. **-2.** [place, weather, face] lugubre, triste.

bleary ['blɪərɪ] (*compar* **-ier**, *superl* **-iest**) *adj* [eyes] trouble, voilé(e).

bleary-eyed [-'aɪd] *adj* aux yeux troubles OR voilés.

bleat [bliːt] ⬦ *n* bêlement *m*. ⬦ *vi* bêler; *fig* [person] se plaindre, geindre.

bleed [bliːd] (*pt* & *pp* **bled** [bled]) ⬦ *vt* [radiator etc] purger. ⬦ *vi* saigner.

bleep [bliːp] ⬦ *n* bip *m*, bip-bip *m*. ⬦ *vt* appeler avec un bip, biper. ⬦ *vi* faire bip-bip.

bleeper ['bliːpə'] *n* bip *m*, bip-bip *m*.

blemish ['blemɪʃ] ◇ *n lit & fig* défaut *m.* ◇ *vt* [reputation] souiller, tacher.

blend [blend] ◇ *n* mélange *m.* ◇ *vt*: **to ~ sthg (with)** mélanger qqch (avec OR à). ◇ *vi*: **to ~ (with)** se mêler (à OR avec).

◆ **blend in** *vi* se fondre.

◆ **blend into** *vt fus* se fondre dans.

blender ['blendər] *n* mixer *m.*

bless [bles] (*pt & pp* **-ed** OR **blest**) *vt* bénir; **to be ~ed with** [talent etc] être doué de; [children] avoir la chance OR le bonheur d'avoir; **~ you!** [after sneezing] à vos souhaits!; [thank you] merci mille fois.

blessed ['blesɪd] *adj* **-1.** RELIG saint(e), béni(e). **-2.** [relief, silence] merveilleux(euse). **-3.** *inf* [blasted] fichu(e), maudit(e).

blessing ['blesɪŋ] *n lit & fig* bénédiction *f*; **a ~ in disguise** une bonne chose en fin de compte; **to count one's ~s** s'estimer heureux de ce que l'on a; **a mixed ~** quelque chose qui a du bon et du mauvais.

blest [blest] *pt & pp* → **bless.**

blew [bluː] *pt* → **blow.**

blight [blaɪt] ◇ *n* **-1.** [plant disease] rouille *f*, charbon *m.* **-2.** *fig* [scourge] fléau *m*, calamité *f.* ◇ *vt* gâcher, briser.

blimey ['blaɪmɪ] *excl Br inf* zut alors!, mince alors!

blind [blaɪnd] ◇ *adj* **-1.** *lit & fig* aveugle; **to be ~ to sthg** ne pas voir qqch. **-2.** *Br inf* [for emphasis]: **it doesn't make a ~ bit of difference to me** cela m'est complètement égal. ◇ *adv*: **~ drunk** complètement rond(e), bourré(e). ◇ *n* [for window] store *m.* ◇ *npl*: **the ~** les aveugles *mpl.* ◇ *vt* aveugler; **to ~ sb to sthg** *fig* cacher qqch à qqn.

blind alley *n lit & fig* impasse *f.*

blind corner *n* virage *m* sans visibilité.

blind date *n* rendez-vous *avec quelqu'un qu'on ne connaît pas.*

blinders ['blaɪndəz] *npl Am* œillères *fpl.*

blindfold ['blaɪndfəʊld] ◇ *adv* les yeux bandés. ◇ *n* bandeau *m.* ◇ *vt* bander les yeux à.

blinding ['blaɪndɪŋ] *adj* **-1.** [light] aveuglant(e). **-2.** [obvious] évident(e), manifeste.

blindly ['blaɪndlɪ] *adv lit & fig* à l'aveuglette, aveuglément.

blindness ['blaɪndnɪs] *n* cécité *f*; **~ (to)** *fig* aveuglement *m* (devant).

blind spot *n* **-1.** AUT angle *m* mort. **-2.** *fig* [inability to understand] blocage *m.*

blink [blɪŋk] ◇ *n* **-1.** [of eyes] clignement *m.* **-2.** [of light] clignotement *m.* **-3.** *phr*: **on the ~** [machine] détraqué(e). ◇ *vt* **-1.** [eyes] cli-

gner. **-2.** *Am* AUT: **to ~ one's lights** faire un appel de phares. ◇ *vi* **-1.** [person] cligner des yeux. **-2.** [light] clignoter.

blinkered ['blɪŋkəd] *adj*: **to be ~** *lit & fig* avoir des œillères.

blinkers ['blɪŋkəz] *npl Br* œillères *fpl.*

blinking ['blɪŋkɪŋ] *adj Br inf* sacré(e), fichu(e).

blip [blɪp] *n* **-1.** [sound] bip *m.* **-2.** [on radar] spot *m.* **-3.** *fig* [temporary problem] problème *m* passager.

bliss [blɪs] *n* bonheur *m* suprême, félicité *f.*

blissful ['blɪsfʊl] *adj* [day, silence] merveilleux(euse), divin(e); [ignorance] total(e).

blissfully ['blɪsfʊlɪ] *adv* [smile] d'un air heureux; [happy, unaware] parfaitement.

blister ['blɪstər] ◇ *n* [on skin] ampoule *f*, cloque *f.* ◇ *vi* **-1.** [skin] se couvrir d'ampoules. **-2.** [paint] cloquer, se boursoufler.

blistering ['blɪstərɪŋ] *adj* [sun] brûlant(e), ardent(e); [attack] caustique, cinglant(e).

blister pack *n* blister *m.*

blithe [blaɪð] *adj* **-1.** [unworried] insouciant(e). **-2.** *dated* [cheerful] joyeux(euse), gai(e).

blithely ['blaɪðlɪ] *adv* gaiement, joyeusement.

BLitt [ˌbiːˈlɪt] (*abbr of* **Bachelor of Letters (Baccalaureus Litterarum)**) *n* (titulaire d'une) licence de lettres.

blitz [blɪts] *n* **-1.** MIL bombardement *m* aérien. **-2.** *Br fig*: **to have a ~ on sthg** s'attaquer à qqch.

blizzard ['blɪzəd] *n* tempête *f* de neige.

BLM (*abbr of* **Bureau of Land Management**) *n* service de l'aménagement du territoire aux États-Unis.

bloated ['bləʊtɪd] *adj* **-1.** [face] bouffi(e), boursouflé(e). **-2.** [with food] ballonné(e).

blob [blɒb] *n* **-1.** [drop] goutte *f.* **-2.** [indistinct shape] forme *f*; **a ~ of colour** une tache de couleur.

bloc [blɒk] *n* bloc *m.*

block [blɒk] ◇ *n* **-1.** [building]: **office ~** immeuble *m* de bureaux; **~ of flats** *Br* immeuble *m.* **-2.** *Am* [of buildings] pâté *m* de maisons; **it's five ~s from here** c'est cinq rues plus loin. **-3.** [of stone, ice] bloc *m.* **-4.** [obstruction] blocage *m.* **-5.** **~ and tackle** palan *m*, moufle *f.* ◇ *vt* **-1.** [road, pipe, view] boucher. **-2.** [prevent] bloquer, empêcher.

◆ **block off** *vt sep* [road] barrer; [pipe, entrance] boucher.

◆ **block out** *vt sep* **-1.** [from mind] chasser. **-2.** [light] empêcher d'entrer.

◆ **block up** ◇ *vt sep* boucher. ◇ *vi* se boucher.

blockade [blɒ'keɪd] ◇ *n* blocus *m*. ◇ *vt* faire le blocus de.

blockage ['blɒkɪdʒ] *n* obstruction *f*.

block booking *n* location *f* en bloc.

blockbuster ['blɒk,bʌstəʳ] *n* inf [book] best-seller *m*; [film] film *m* à succès, superproduction *f*.

block capitals *npl* majuscules *fpl* d'imprimerie.

blockhead ['blɒkhed] *n* inf crétin *m*, -e *f*, imbécile *mf*.

block letters *npl* majuscules *fpl* d'imprimerie.

block release *n* Br stage de formation de plusieurs semaines.

block vote *n* Br vote *m* groupé.

bloke [bləʊk] *n* Br inf type *m*.

blond [blɒnd] *adj* blond(e).

blonde [blɒnd] ◇ *adj* blond(e). ◇ *n* [woman] blonde *f*.

blood [blʌd] *n* sang *m*; **in cold** ~ de sang-froid; **it made my** ~ **boil** cela m'a mis dans une colère noire; **it made my** ~ **run cold** cela m'a glacé le sang; **it's in his** ~ fig il a cela dans le sang; **new** OR **fresh** ~ fig sang frais.

blood bank *n* banque *f* de sang.

bloodbath ['blʌdbɑːθ, *pl* -bɑːðz] *n* bain *m* de sang, massacre *m*.

blood brother *n* frère *m* de sang.

blood cell *n* cellule *f* sanguine.

blood count *n* numération *f* globulaire.

bloodcurdling ['blʌd,kɜːdlɪŋ] *adj* à vous glacer le sang.

blood donor *n* donneur *m*, -euse *f* de sang.

blood group *n* groupe *m* sanguin.

bloodhound ['blʌdhaʊnd] *n* limier *m*.

bloodless ['blʌdlɪs] *adj* -**1.** [face, lips] exsangue, pâle. -**2.** [coup, victory] sans effusion de sang.

bloodletting ['blʌd,letɪŋ] *n* [killing] tuerie *f*.

blood money *n* prix *m* du sang.

blood orange *n* orange *f* sanguine.

blood poisoning *n* septicémie *f*.

blood pressure *n* tension *f* artérielle; **to have high** ~ faire de l'hypertension.

blood relation, blood relative *n* parent *m*, -e *f* par le sang.

bloodshed ['blʌdʃed] *n* carnage *m*.

bloodshot ['blʌdʃɒt] *adj* [eyes] injecté(e) de sang.

blood sports *npl* la chasse.

bloodstained ['blʌdsteɪnd] *adj* taché(e) de sang, ensanglanté(e).

bloodstream ['blʌdstriːm] *n* sang *m*.

blood test *n* prise *f* de sang, examen *m* du sang.

bloodthirsty ['blʌd,θɜːstɪ] *adj* sanguinaire.

blood transfusion *n* transfusion *f* sanguine.

blood type *n* groupe *m* sanguin.

blood vessel *n* vaisseau *m* sanguin.

bloody ['blʌdɪ] (*compar* -ier, *superl* -iest) ◇ *adj* -**1.** [gen] sanglant(e). -**2.** Br v inf foutu(e); **you** ~ **idiot!** espèce de con! ◇ *adv* Br v inf vachement.

bloody-minded [-'maɪndɪd] *adj* Br inf contrariant(e).

bloom [bluːm] ◇ *n* fleur *f*. ◇ *vi* fleurir.

blooming ['bluːmɪŋ] ◇ *adj* -**1.** Br inf [to show annoyance] sacré(e), fichu(e). -**2.** [person] éclatant(e), resplendissant(e). ◇ *adv* Br inf sacrément.

blossom ['blɒsəm] ◇ *n* [of tree] fleurs *fpl*; **in** ~ en fleur OR fleurs. ◇ *vi* -**1.** [tree] fleurir. -**2.** fig [person] s'épanouir.

blot [blɒt] (*pt* & *pp* -ted, *cont* -ting) ◇ *n* lit & fig tache *f*. ◇ *vt* -**1.** [paper] faire des pâtés sur. -**2.** [ink] sécher.

◆ **blot out** *vt sep* voiler, cacher; [memories] effacer.

blotchy ['blɒtʃɪ] (*compar* -ier, *superl* -iest) *adj* couvert(e) de marbrures OR taches.

blotting paper ['blɒtɪŋ-] *n* (papier *m*) buvard *m*.

blouse [blaʊz] *n* chemisier *m*.

blouson ['bluːzɒn] *n* Br blouson *m*.

blow [bləʊ] (*pt* blew, *pp* blown) ◇ *vi* -**1.** [gen] souffler. -**2.** [in wind]: **to** ~ **off** s'envoler; **the door blew open** la porte s'ouvrit à la volée; **the door blew shut** la porte a claqué. -**3.** [fuse] sauter. ◇ *vt* -**1.** [subj: wind] faire voler, chasser. -**2.** [clear]: **to** ~ **one's nose** se moucher. -**3.** [trumpet] jouer de, souffler dans; **to** ~ **a whistle** donner un coup de sifflet, siffler. -**4.** [bubbles] faire. -**5.** inf [money] claquer. ◇ *n* [hit] coup *m*; **to come to** ~**s** en venir aux mains; **to soften the** ~ fig adoucir le coup; **to strike a** ~ **for** fig servir la cause de.

◆ **blow out** ◇ *vt sep* souffler. ◇ *vi* -**1.** [candle] s'éteindre. -**2.** [tyre] éclater.

◆ **blow over** *vi* se calmer.

◆ **blow up** ◇ *vt sep* -**1.** [inflate] gonfler. -**2.** [with bomb] faire sauter. -**3.** [photograph] agrandir. ◇ *vi* exploser.

blow-by-blow *adj* fig détaillé(e).

blow-dry ◇ *n* brushing *m.* ◇ *vt* faire un brushing à.

blowfly ['bləʊflaɪ] (*pl* **-flies**) *n* mouche *f* bleue, mouche de la viande.

blowgun *Am* = blowpipe.

blowlamp *Br* ['bləʊlæmp], **blowtorch** ['bləʊtɔːtʃ] *n* chalumeau *m,* lampe *f* à souder.

blown [bləʊn] *pp* → blow.

blowout ['bləʊaʊt] *n* **-1.** [of tyre] éclatement *m.* **-2.** *inf* [big meal] grande bouffe *f,* gueuleton *m.*

blowpipe *Br* ['bləʊpaɪp], **blowgun** *Am* ['bləʊgʌn] *n* sarbacane *f.*

blowtorch = blowlamp.

blowzy ['blaʊzɪ] *adj Br* négligé(e).

BLS (*abbr of* **Bureau of Labor Statistics**) *n* institut de statistiques du travail aux États-Unis.

blubber ['blʌbər] ◇ *n* graisse *f* de baleine. ◇ *vi pej* chialer, pleurer comme un veau.

bludgeon ['blʌdʒən] *vt* matraquer.

blue [bluː] ◇ *adj* **-1.** [colour] bleu(e). **-2.** *inf* [sad] triste, cafardeux(euse). **-3.** [pornographic] porno (*inv*). ◇ *n* bleu *m;* **in ~** en bleu; **out of the ~** [happen] subitement; [arrive] à l'improviste.

◆ **blues** *npl:* **the ~s** MUS le blues; *inf* [sad feeling] le blues, le cafard.

blue baby *n* enfant *m* bleu.

bluebell ['bluːbel] *n* jacinthe *f* des bois.

blueberry ['bluːbərɪ] *n* myrtille *f.*

bluebird ['bluːbɜːd] *n* oiseau *m* bleu.

blue-black *adj* bleu noir (*inv*).

blue-blooded [-'blʌdɪd] *adj* de sang noble, qui a du sang bleu.

bluebottle ['bluːˌbɒtl] *n* mouche *f* bleue, mouche de la viande.

blue cheese *n* (fromage *m*) bleu *m.*

blue chip *n* ST EX valeur *f* sûre, titre *m* de premier ordre.

◆ **blue-chip** *comp* de premier ordre.

blue-collar *adj* manuel(elle).

blue-eyed boy [-aɪd-] *n inf* chouchou *m.*

blue jeans *npl Am* blue-jean *m,* jean *m.*

blue moon *n:* once in a ~ tous les trente-six du mois.

blueprint ['bluːprɪnt] *n* photocalque *m; fig* plan *m,* projet *m.*

bluestocking ['bluːˌstɒkɪŋ] *n pej* bas-bleu *m.*

blue tit *n Br* mésange *f* bleue.

bluff [blʌf] ◇ *adj* franc (franche). ◇ *n* **-1.** [deception] bluff *m;* **to call sb's ~** prendre qqn au mot. **-2.** [cliff] falaise *f* à pic. ◇ *vt*

bluffer, donner le change à. ◇ *vi* faire du bluff, bluffer.

blunder ['blʌndər] ◇ *n* gaffe *f,* bévue *f.* ◇ *vi* **-1.** [make mistake] faire une gaffe, commettre une bévue. **-2.** [move clumsily] avancer d'un pas maladroit.

blundering ['blʌndərɪŋ] *adj* maladroit(e).

blunt [blʌnt] ◇ *adj* **-1.** [knife] émoussé(e); [pencil] épointé(e); [object, instrument] contondant(e). **-2.** [person, manner] direct(e), carré(e). ◇ *vt lit* & *fig* émousser.

bluntly ['blʌntlɪ] *adv* carrément, brutalement.

bluntness ['blʌntnɪs] *n* brusquerie *f.*

blur [blɜːr] (*pt* & *pp* **-red,** *cont* **-ring**) ◇ *n* forme *f* confuse, tache *f* floue. ◇ *vt* **-1.** [vision] troubler, brouiller. **-2.** [distinction] rendre moins net (nette).

blurb [blɜːb] *n* texte *m* publicitaire.

blurred [blɜːd] *adj* **-1.** [photograph] flou(e). **-2.** [vision] trouble. **-3.** [distinction] peu net (nette), vague.

blurt [blɜːt]

◆ **blurt out** *vt sep* laisser échapper.

blush [blʌʃ] ◇ *n* rougeur *f.* ◇ *vi* rougir.

blusher ['blʌʃər] *n* fard *m* à joues, blush *m.*

bluster ['blʌstər] ◇ *n* (*U*) propos *mpl* coléreux. ◇ *vi* tempêter.

blustery ['blʌstərɪ] *adj* venteux(euse).

Blvd (*abbr of* **Boulevard**) bd, boul.

BM *n* **-1.** (*abbr of* **Bachelor of Medicine**) (*titulaire d'une*) *licence de médecine.* **-2.** (*abbr of* **British Museum**) *grand musée et bibliothèque célèbre, situés à Londres.*

BMA (*abbr of* **British Medical Association**) *n ordre britannique des médecins.*

BMJ (*abbr of* **British Medical Journal**) *n organe de la BMA.*

BMus (*abbr of* **Bachelor of Music**) *n* (*titulaire d'une*) *licence de musique.*

BMX (*abbr of* **bicycle motorcross**) *n* bicross *m.*

BO *abbr of* **body odour.**

boa constrictor ['bəʊəkənˈstrɪktər] *n* boa *m* constricteur.

boar [bɔːr] *n* **-1.** [male pig] verrat *m.* **-2.** [wild pig] sanglier *m.*

board [bɔːd] ◇ *n* **-1.** [plank] planche *f.* **-2.** [for notices] panneau *m* d'affichage. **-3.** [for games - gen] tableau *m;* [- for chess] échiquier *m.* **-4.** [blackboard] tableau *m* (noir). **-5.** [of company]: ~ (**of directors**) conseil *m* d'administration. **-6.** [committee] comité *m,* conseil *m.* **-7.** *Br* [at hotel, guesthouse] pension *f;* ~ **and lodging** pension; **full ~** pension complète; **half ~** demi-pension *f.* **-8.**

on ~ [on ship, plane, bus, train] à bord. **-9.** *phr*: **to take sthg on** ~ [knowledge] assimiler qqch; [advice] accepter qqch; **above** ~ régulier(ière), dans les règles; **across the** ~ [agreement etc] général(e); [apply] de façon générale; **to go by the** ~ aller à vau-l'eau, être abandonné(e); **to sweep the** ~ tout rafler OR gagner.
◇ *vt* [ship, aeroplane] monter à bord de; [train, bus] monter dans.

boarder ['bɔːdəʳ] *n* **-1.** [lodger] pensionnaire *mf*. **-2.** [at school] interne *mf*, pensionnaire *mf*.

board game *n* jeu *m* de société.

boarding card ['bɔːdɪŋ-] *n* carte *f* d'embarquement.

boardinghouse ['bɔːdɪŋhaʊs, *pl* -haʊzɪz] *n* pension *f* de famille.

boarding school ['bɔːdɪŋ-] *n* pensionnat *m*, internat *m*.

board meeting *n* réunion *f* du conseil d'administration.

Board of Trade *n Br*: **the** ~ ≃ le ministère *m* du Commerce.

boardroom ['bɔːdrʊm] *n* salle *f* du conseil (d'administration).

boardwalk ['bɔːdwɔːk] *n Am* trottoir *m* en planches.

boast [bəʊst] ◇ *n* vantardise *f*, fanfaronnade *f*. ◇ *vt* [special feature] s'enorgueillir de. ◇ *vi*: **to** ~ **(about)** se vanter (de).

boastful ['bəʊstfʊl] *adj* vantard(e), fanfaron(onne).

boat [bəʊt] *n* [large] bateau *m*; [small] canot *m*, embarcation *f*; **by** ~ en bateau; **to rock the** ~ semer le trouble; **to be in the same** ~ être logé à la même enseigne.

boater ['bəʊtəʳ] *n* [hat] canotier *m*.

boating ['bəʊtɪŋ] *n* canotage *m*.

boatswain ['bəʊsn] *n* maître *m* d'équipage.

boat train *n* train qui assure la correspondance avec le bateau.

bob [bɒb] (*pt* & *pp* -**bed**, *cont* -**bing**) ◇ *n* **-1.** [hairstyle] coupe *f* au carré. **-2.** *Br inf dated* [shilling] shilling *m*. **-3.** = **bobsleigh**. ◇ *vi* [boat, ship] tanguer.

bobbin ['bɒbɪn] *n* bobine *f*.

bobble [bɒbl] *n* pompon *m*.

bobby ['bɒbɪ] (*pl* -**ies**) *n Br inf* agent *m* de police.

bobby pin *n Am* pince *f* à cheveux.

bobby socks, bobby sox *npl Am* socquettes *fpl* (de fille).

bobsleigh ['bɒbsleɪ] *n* bobsleigh *m*.

bode [bəʊd] *vi literary*: **to** ~ **ill/well (for)** être de mauvais/bon augure (pour).

bodice ['bɒdɪs] *n* corsage *m*.

bodily ['bɒdɪlɪ] ◇ *adj* [needs] matériel(ielle); [pain] physique. ◇ *adv* [lift, move] à bras-le-corps.

body ['bɒdɪ] (*pl* -**ies**) *n* **-1.** [of person] corps *m*; **to keep** ~ **and soul together** subsister. **-2.** [corpse] corps *m*, cadavre *m*; **over my dead** ~! il faudra d'abord me passer sur le corps! **-3.** [organization] organisme *m*, organisation *f*. **-4.** [of car] carrosserie *f*; [of plane] fuselage *m*. **-5.** (*U*) [of wine] corps *m*. **-6.** (*U*) [of hair] volume *m*. **-7.** [garment] body *m*.

body building *n* culturisme *m*.

bodyguard ['bɒdɪɡɑːd] *n* garde *m* du corps.

body odour *n* odeur *f* corporelle.

body search *n* fouille *f* corporelle.

body shop *n* **-1.** [garage] atelier *m*. **-2.** *Am inf* [gym] club *m* de gym.

body stocking *n* justaucorps *m*.

bodywork ['bɒdɪwɜːk] *n* carrosserie *f*.

boffin ['bɒfɪn] *n Br inf* savant *m*.

bog [bɒɡ] *n* **-1.** [marsh] marécage *m*. **-2.** *Br v inf* [toilet] chiottes *fpl*.

bogey ['bəʊɡɪ] *n* GOLF bogey *m*.

bogged down [bɒɡd-] *adj* **-1.** *fig* [in work]: ~ **(in)** submergé(e) (de). **-2.** [car etc]: ~ **(in)** enlisé(e) (dans).

boggle ['bɒɡl] *vi*: **the mind** ~**s!** ce n'est pas croyable!, on croit rêver!

boggy ['bɒɡɪ] *adj* marécageux(euse).

bogie ['bəʊɡɪ] *n* RAIL bogie *m*.

Bogotá [,bɒɡəˈtɑː] *n* Bogotá.

bogus ['bəʊɡəs] *adj* faux (fausse), bidon (*inv*).

Bohemia [bəʊˈhiːmjə] *n* Bohême *f*; **in** ~ en Bohême.

bohemian [bəʊˈhiːmɪən] ◇ *adj* [person] bohème; [lifestyle] de bohème. ◇ *n* bohème *mf*.

◆ **Bohemian** ◇ *adj* bohémien(ienne). ◇ *n* Bohémien *m*, -ienne *f*.

boil [bɔɪl] ◇ *n* **-1.** MED furoncle *m*. **-2.** [boiling point]: **to bring sthg to the** ~ porter qqch à ébullition; **to come to the** ~ venir à ébullition. ◇ *vt* **-1.** [water, food] faire bouillir. **-2.** [kettle] mettre sur le feu. ◇ *vi* [water] bouillir.

◆ **boil away** *vi* [evaporate] s'évaporer.

◆ **boil down to** *vt fus fig* revenir à, se résumer à.

◆ **boil over** *vi* **-1.** [liquid] déborder. **-2.** *fig* [feelings] exploser.

boiled ['bɔɪld] *adj* bouilli(e); ~ **egg** œuf *m* à la coque; ~ **sweet** *Br* bonbon *m* (dur).

boiler ['bɔɪləʳ] *n* chaudière *f*.

boiler suit *n* Br bleu *m* de travail.

boiling ['bɔɪlɪŋ] *adj* -1. [liquid] bouillant(e). -2. *inf* [weather] très chaud(e), torride; [person]: I'm ~ (hot)! je crève de chaleur! -3. [angry]: ~ with rage en rage, écumant(e) de rage.

boiling point *n* point *m* d'ébullition.

boisterous ['bɔɪstərəs] *adj* turbulent(e), remuant(e).

bold [bəʊld] *adj* -1. [confident] hardi(e), audacieux(ieuse). -2. [lines, design] hardi(e); [colour] vif (vive), éclatant(e). -3. TYPO: ~ type OR print caractères *mpl* gras.

boldly ['bəʊldlɪ] *adv* hardiment, avec audace.

Bolivia [bə'lɪvɪə] *n* Bolivie *f*; in ~ en Bolivie.

Bolivian [bə'lɪvɪən] ◇ *adj* bolivien(ienne). ◇ *n* Bolivien *m*, -ienne *f*.

bollard ['bɒlɑːd] *n* [on road] borne *f*.

bollocks ['bɒləks] Br *v inf* ◇ *npl* couilles *fpl*. ◇ *excl* quelles conneries!

Bolshevik ['bɒlʃɪvɪk] ◇ *adj* bolchevique. ◇ *n* bolchevique *mf*.

bolster ['bəʊlstər] ◇ *n* [pillow] traversin *m*. ◇ *vt* renforcer, affirmer.

◆ **bolster up** *vt fus* soutenir, appuyer.

bolt [bəʊlt] ◇ *n* -1. [on door, window] verrou *m*. -2. [type of screw] boulon *m*. ◇ *adv*: ~ upright droit(e) comme un piquet. ◇ *vt* -1. [fasten together] boulonner. -2. [close - door, window] verrouiller, fermer au verrou. -3. [food] engouffrer, engloutir. ◇ *vi* [run] détaler.

bomb [bɒm] ◇ *n* bombe *f*. ◇ *vt* bombarder.

bombard [bɒm'bɑːd] *vt* MIL & *fig*: to ~ (with) bombarder (de).

bombardment [bɒm'bɑːdmənt] *n* bombardement *m*.

bombastic [bɒm'bæstɪk] *adj* pompeux(euse).

bomb disposal squad *n* équipe *f* de déminage.

bomber ['bɒmər] *n* -1. [plane] bombardier *m*. -2. [person] plastiqueur *m*.

bomber jacket *n* blouson *m* d'aviateur.

bombing ['bɒmɪŋ] *n* bombardement *m*.

bombproof ['bɒmpruːf] *adj* à l'épreuve des bombes.

bombshell ['bɒmʃel] *n fig* bombe *f*.

bombsite ['bɒmsaɪt] *n* lieu *m* bombardé.

bona fide ['bəʊnə'faɪdɪ] *adj* véritable, authentique; [offer] sérieux(ieuse).

bonanza [bə'nænzə] *n* aubaine *f*, filon *m*.

bond [bɒnd] ◇ *n* -1. [between people] lien *m*. -2. [promise] engagement *m*. -3. FIN bon *m*, titre *m*. ◇ *vt* -1. [glue]: to ~ sthg to sthg coller qqch sur qqch. -2. *fig* [people] unir. ◇ *vi* -1. [stick together]: to ~ (together) être collé(e) (ensemble). -2. *fig* [people] établir des liens.

bondage ['bɒndɪdʒ] *n* servitude *f*, esclavage *m*.

bonded warehouse ['bɒndɪd-] *n* entrepôt *m* de douane.

bone [bəʊn] ◇ *n* os *m*; [of fish] arête *f*; ~ of contention pomme *f* de discorde; to feel OR know sthg in one's ~s avoir le pressentiment de qqch; to make no ~s about sthg ne pas cacher qqch. ◇ *vt* [meat] désosser; [fish] enlever les arêtes de.

bone china *n* porcelaine *f* tendre.

bone-dry *adj* tout à fait sec (sèche).

bone-idle *adj* paresseux(euse) comme une couleuvre OR un lézard.

boneless ['bəʊnlɪs] *adj* [meat] sans os; [fish] sans arêtes.

bone marrow *n* moelle *f* osseuse.

bonfire ['bɒn,faɪər] *n* [for fun] feu *m* de joie; [to burn rubbish] feu.

bonfire night *n* Br le 5 novembre (commémoration de la tentative de Guy Fawkes de faire sauter le Parlement en 1605).

bongo ['bɒŋgəʊ] (*pl* -s OR -es) *n*: ~ (drum) bongo *m*.

Bonn [bɒn] *n* Bonn.

bonnet ['bɒnɪt] *n* -1. Br [of car] capot *m*. -2. [hat] bonnet *m*.

bonny ['bɒnɪ] (*compar* -ier, *superl* -iest) *adj* Scot beau (belle), joli(e).

bonus ['bəʊnəs] (*pl* -es) *n* -1. [extra money] prime *f*, gratification *f*. -2. *fig* [added advantage] plus *m*.

bonus issue *n* Br FIN émission *f* d'actions gratuites.

bony ['bəʊnɪ] (*compar* -ier, *superl* -iest) *adj* -1. [person, hand, face] maigre, osseux(euse). -2. [meat] plein(e) d'os; [fish] plein d'arêtes.

boo [buː] (*pl* -s) ◇ *excl* hou! ◇ *n* huée *f*. ◇ *vt & vi* huer.

boob [buːb] *n inf* [mistake] gaffe *f*, bourde *f*.

◆ **boobs** *npl* Br *v inf* nichons *mpl*.

boob tube *n* -1. Br [garment] bustier *m*. -2. Am *inf* télé *f*.

booby prize ['buːbɪ-] *n* prix *m* de consolation.

booby trap ['buːbɪ-] *n* -1. [bomb] objet *m* piégé. -2. [practical joke] farce *f*.

◆ **booby-trap** *vt* piéger.

boogie ['buːgɪ] *inf* ◇ *n*: to have a ~ danser. ◇ *vi* danser.

book [bʊk] ◇ *n* -1. [for reading] livre *m*; to do sthg by the ~ faire qqch selon les règles; to throw the ~ at sb passer un savon à qqn. -2. [of stamps, tickets, cheques] carnet *m*; [of matches] pochette *f*. ◇ *vt* -1. [reserve - gen] réserver; [- performer] engager; to be fully ~ed être complet. -2. *inf* [subj: police] coller un PV à. -3. *Br* FTBL prendre le nom de. ◇ *vi* réserver.

◆ **books** *npl* COMM livres *mpl* de comptes; to do the ~s tenir les livres; to be in sb's bad ~s être mal vu de qqn; to be in sb's good ~s être dans les petits papiers de qqn.

◆ **book in** ◇ *vt sep* réserver une chambre à. ◇ *vi* [at hotel] prendre une chambre.

◆ **book up** *vt sep* réserver, retenir.

bookable ['bʊkəbl] *adj Br* -1. [seats, tickets] qu'on peut réserver OR louer. -2. FTBL [offence] pour laquelle l'arbitre donne un carton jaune.

bookbinding ['bʊk,baɪndɪŋ] *n* reliure *f*.

bookcase ['bʊkkeɪs] *n* bibliothèque *f*.

book club *n* club *m* de livres.

bookends ['bʊkendz] *npl* serre-livres *m inv*, presse-livres *m inv*.

bookie ['bʊkɪ] *n inf* bookmaker *m*, book *m*.

booking ['bʊkɪŋ] *n* -1. [reservation] réservation *f*. -2. *Br* FTBL: to get a ~ recevoir un carton jaune.

booking clerk *n* préposé *m*, -e *f* à la location OR la vente des billets.

booking office *n* bureau *m* de réservation OR location.

bookish ['bʊkɪʃ] *adj* toujours plongé(e) dans ses livres.

bookkeeper ['bʊk,kiːpə'] *n* comptable *mf*.

bookkeeping ['bʊk,kiːpɪŋ] *n* comptabilité *f*.

booklet ['bʊklɪt] *n* brochure *f*.

bookmaker ['bʊk,meɪkə'] *n* bookmaker *m*.

bookmark ['bʊkmɑːk] *n* signet *m*.

bookseller ['bʊk,selə'] *n* libraire *mf*.

bookshelf ['bʊkʃelf] (*pl* -shelves) *n* rayon *m* OR étagère *f* à livres.

bookshop *Br* ['bʊkʃɒp], **bookstore** *Am* ['bʊkstɔːr] *n* librairie *f*.

bookstall ['bʊkstɔːl] *n Br* kiosque *m* (à journaux).

bookstore = bookshop.

book token *n* chèque-livre *m*.

bookworm ['bʊkwɜːm] *n* rat *m* de bibliothèque.

boom [buːm] ◇ *n* -1. [loud noise] grondement *m*. -2. [in business, trade] boom *m*. -3.

NAUT bôme *f*. -4. [for TV camera, microphone] girafe *f*, perche *f*. ◇ *vi* -1. [make noise] gronder. -2. [business, trade] être en plein essor OR en hausse.

boomerang ['buːməræŋ] *n* boomerang *m*.

boon [buːn] *n* avantage *m*, bénédiction *f*.

boor [bʊə'] *n* butor *m*, rustre *m*.

boorish ['bʊərɪʃ] *adj* rustre, grossier(ière).

boost [buːst] ◇ *n* [to production, sales] augmentation *f*; [to economy] croissance *f*; to give a ~ to stimuler. ◇ *vt* -1. [production, sales] accroître, stimuler. -2. [popularity] accroître, renforcer; to ~ sb's spirits OR morale remonter le moral à qqn.

booster ['buːstə'] *n* MED rappel *m*.

booster seat *n* AUT (siège *m*) rehausseur *m*.

boot [buːt] ◇ *n* -1. [for walking, sport] chaussure *f*. -2. [fashion item] botte *f*. -3. *Br* [of car] coffre *m*. ◇ *vt inf* flanquer des coups de pied à.

◆ **to boot** *adv* par-dessus le marché, en plus.

◆ **boot out** *vt sep inf* flanquer à la porte.

booth [buːð] *n* -1. [at fair] baraque *f* foraine. -2. [telephone booth] cabine *f*. -3. [voting booth] isoloir *m*.

bootleg ['buːtleg] *adj inf* [recording] pirate; [whisky etc] de contrebande.

bootlegger ['buːt,legə'] *n inf* contrebandier *m* d'alcool.

booty ['buːtɪ] *n* butin *m*.

booze [buːz] *inf* ◇ *n* (U) alcool *m*, boisson *f* alcoolisée. ◇ *vi* picoler, lever le coude.

boozer ['buːzə'] *n inf* -1. [person] picoleur *m*, -euse *f*. -2. *Br* [pub] pub *m*.

bop [bɒp] (*pt & pp* -ped, *cont* -ping) *inf* ◇ *n* -1. [hit] coup *m*. -2. [disco, dance] boum *f*. ◇ *vt* [hit] taper, donner un coup à. ◇ *vi* [dance] danser.

border ['bɔːdə'] ◇ *n* -1. [between countries] frontière *f*. -2. [edge] bord *m*. -3. [in garden] bordure *f*. ◇ *vt* -1. [country] toucher à, être limitrophe de. -2. [edge] border.

◆ **border on** *vt fus* friser, être voisin(e) de.

borderline ['bɔːdəlaɪn] ◇ *adj*: ~ case cas *m* limite. ◇ *n fig* limite *f*, ligne *f* de démarcation.

bore [bɔːr] ◇ *pt* → bear. ◇ *n* -1. [person] raseur *m*, -euse *f*; [situation, event] corvée *f*. -2. [of gun] calibre *m*. ◇ *vt* -1. [not interest] ennuyer, raser; to ~ sb stiff OR to tears OR to death ennuyer qqn à mourir. -2. [drill] forer, percer.

bored [bɔːd] *adj* [person] qui s'ennuie; [look] d'ennui; to be ~ with en avoir assez de; I'm ~ with this book ce livre m'ennuie.

boredom ['bɔːdəm] n (U) ennui m.

boring ['bɔːrɪŋ] adj ennuyeux(euse), assommant(e).

born [bɔːn] adj né(e); **to be ~** naître; **I was ~ in 1965** je suis né en 1965; **when were you ~?** quelle est ta date de naissance?; **~ and bred** né et élevé.

born-again adj [Christian] régénéré(e).

borne [bɔːn] pp → bear.

Borneo ['bɔːnɪəʊ] n Bornéo m; **in ~** à Bornéo.

borough ['bʌrə] n municipalité f.

borrow ['bɒrəʊ] vt emprunter; **to ~ sthg (from sb)** emprunter qqch (à qqn).

borrower ['bɒrəʊər] n emprunteur m, -euse f.

borrowing ['bɒrəʊɪŋ] n (U) emprunt m.

borstal ['bɔːstl] n Br maison f de redressement.

Bosnia ['bɒznɪə] n Bosnie f; **in ~** en Bosnie.

Bosnia-Herzegovina [-,hɜːtsəgə'viːnə] n Bosnie-Herzégovine f.

Bosnian ['bɒznɪən] ◇ adj bosnien(ienne). ◇ n Bosnien m, -ienne f.

bosom ['bʊzəm] n poitrine f, seins mpl; fig sein m; **~ friend** ami m intime.

Bosporus ['bɒspərəs], **Bosphorus** ['bɒsfərəs] n: **the ~** le Bosphore.

boss [bɒs] ◇ n patron m, -onne f, chef m; **to be one's own ~** travailler à son compte. ◇ vt pej donner des ordres à, régenter.

◆ **boss about, boss around** vt sep pej donner des ordres à, régenter.

bossy ['bɒsɪ] (compar -ier, superl -iest) adj autoritaire.

bosun ['bəʊsn] = boatswain.

botanic(al) [bə'tænɪk(l)] adj botanique.

botanical garden n jardin m botanique.

botanist ['bɒtənɪst] n botaniste mf.

botany ['bɒtənɪ] n botanique f.

botch [bɒtʃ]

◆ **botch up** vt sep inf bousiller, saboter.

both [bəʊθ] ◇ adj les deux. ◇ pron: **~ (of them) (tous) les deux ((toutes) les deux); ~ of us are coming** on vient tous les deux. ◇ adv: **she is ~ intelligent and amusing** elle est à la fois intelligente et drôle.

bother ['bɒðər] ◇ vt **-1.** [worry] ennuyer, inquiéter; **to ~ o.s. (about)** se tracasser (au sujet de); **I can't be ~ed to do it** je n'ai vraiment pas envie de le faire. **-2.** [pester, annoy] embêter; **I'm sorry to ~ you** excusez-moi de vous déranger.

◇ vi: **to ~ about sthg** s'inquiéter de qqch; **don't ~ (to do it)** ce n'est pas la peine (de le faire); **don't ~ getting up** ne vous donnez pas la peine de vous lever.

◇ n (U) embêtement m; **I hope I'm not putting you to any ~** j'espère que je ne vous cause pas trop de dérangement; **it's no ~ at all** cela ne me dérange OR m'ennuie pas du tout.

bothered ['bɒðəd] adj inquiet(iète).

Botswana [bɒ'tswɑːnə] n Botswana m; **in ~** au Botswana.

bottle ['bɒtl] ◇ n **-1.** [gen] bouteille f; [for medicine, perfume] flacon m; [for baby] biberon m. **-2.** (U) Br inf [courage] cran m, culot m. ◇ vt [wine etc] mettre en bouteilles; [fruit] mettre en bocal.

◆ **bottle out** vi Br inf se dégonfler.

◆ **bottle up** vt sep [feelings] refouler, contenir.

bottle bank n container m pour verre usagé.

bottled ['bɒtld] adj en bouteille.

bottle-feed vt nourrir au biberon.

bottleneck ['bɒtlnek] n **-1.** [in traffic] bouchon m, embouteillage m. **-2.** [in production] goulet m d'étranglement.

bottle-opener n ouvre-bouteilles m, décapsuleur m.

bottle party n soirée f (où chacun apporte quelque chose à boire).

bottom ['bɒtəm] ◇ adj **-1.** [lowest] du bas. **-2.** [in class] dernier(ière). ◇ n **-1.** [of bottle, lake, garden] fond m; [of page, ladder, street] bas m; [of hill] pied m. **-2.** [of scale] bas m; [of class] dernier m, -ière f. **-3.** [buttocks] derrière m. **-4.** [cause]: **what's at the ~ of it?** qu'est-ce qui en est la cause?; **to get to the ~ of sthg** aller au fond de qqch, découvrir la cause de qqch.

◆ **bottom out** vi atteindre son niveau le plus bas.

bottomless ['bɒtəmlɪs] adj **-1.** [very deep] sans fond. **-2.** [endless] inépuisable.

bottom line n fig: **the ~** l'essentiel m.

botulism ['bɒtjʊlɪzm] n botulisme m.

bough [baʊ] n branche f.

bought [bɔːt] pt & pp → buy.

boulder ['bəʊldər] n rocher m.

boulevard ['buːləvɑːd] n boulevard m.

bounce [baʊns] ◇ vi **-1.** [ball] rebondir; [person] sauter. **-2.** [light] être réfléchi(e); [sound] être renvoyé(e). **-3.** inf [cheque] être sans provision. ◇ vt [ball] faire rebondir. ◇ n rebond m.

◆ **bounce back** vi fig se remettre vite.

bouncer ['baʊnsəʳ] n inf videur m.

bouncy ['baʊnsɪ] (compar **-ier**, superl **-iest**) adj **-1.** [lively] dynamique. **-2.** [ball] qui rebondit; [bed] élastique, souple.

bound [baʊnd] ◇ pt & pp → **bind**.
◇ adj **-1.** [certain]: **he's ~ to win** il va sûrement gagner; **she's ~ to see it** elle ne peut pas manquer de le voir. **-2.** [obliged]: **to be ~ to do sthg** être obligé(e) OR tenu(e) de faire qqch; **I'm ~ to say/admit** je dois dire/ reconnaître. **-3.** [for place]: **to be ~ for** [subj: person] être en route pour; [subj: plane, train] être à destination de.
◇ n [leap] bond m, saut m.
◇ vt: **to be ~ed by** [subj: field] être limité(e) OR délimité(e) par; [subj: country] être limitrophe de.
◇ vi [leap] bondir, sauter.
◆ **bounds** npl limites fpl; **out of ~s** interdit, défendu.

boundary ['baʊndərɪ] (pl **-ies**) n [gen] frontière f; [of property] limite f, borne f.

boundless ['baʊndlɪs] adj illimité(e), sans bornes.

bountiful ['baʊntɪfʊl] adj literary [ample] abondant(e).

bounty ['baʊntɪ] n literary [generosity] générosité f, libéralité f.

bouquet [bʊ'keɪ] n bouquet m.

bourbon ['bɜːbən] n bourbon m.

bourgeois ['bɔːʒwɑː] adj pej bourgeois(e).

bout [baʊt] n **-1.** [of illness] accès m; **a ~ of flu** une grippe. **-2.** [session] période f; **a ~ of drinking** une beuverie. **-3.** [boxing match] combat m.

boutique [buː'tiːk] n boutique f.

bow¹ [baʊ] ◇ n **-1.** [in greeting] révérence f. **-2.** [of ship] proue f, avant m. ◇ vt [head] baisser, incliner. ◇ vi **-1.** [make a bow] saluer. **-2.** [defer]: **to ~ to** s'incliner devant.
◆ **bow down** vi s'incliner.
◆ **bow out** vi tirer sa révérence.

bow² [bəʊ] n **-1.** [weapon] arc m. **-2.** MUS archet m. **-3.** [knot] nœud m.

bowels ['baʊəlz] npl intestins mpl; fig entrailles fpl.

bowl [bəʊl] ◇ n **-1.** [container - gen] jatte f, saladier m; [- small] bol m; [- for washing up] cuvette f; **sugar ~** sucrier m. **-2.** [of toilet, sink] cuvette f; [of pipe] fourneau m. ◇ vt CRICKET lancer. ◇ vi CRICKET lancer la balle.
◆ **bowls** n (U) boules fpl (sur herbe).
◆ **bowl over** vt sep lit & fig renverser.

bow-legged [,bəʊ'legɪd] adj aux jambes arquées.

bowler ['bəʊləʳ] n **-1.** CRICKET lanceur m. **-2.** **~ (hat)** chapeau m melon.

bowling ['bəʊlɪŋ] n (U) bowling m.

bowling alley n [building] bowling m; [alley] piste f de bowling.

bowling green n terrain m de boules (sur herbe).

bow tie [bəʊ-] n nœud m papillon.

bow window [bəʊ-] n fenêtre f en saillie.

box [bɒks] ◇ n **-1.** [gen] boîte f. **-2.** THEATRE loge f. **-3.** Br inf [television]: **the ~** la télé. ◇ vi boxer, faire de la boxe.
◆ **box in** vt sep **-1.** [trap] coincer. **-2.** [enclose - pipes etc] encastrer.

boxed [bɒkst] adj en boîte, en coffret.

boxer ['bɒksəʳ] n **-1.** [fighter] boxeur m. **-2.** [dog] boxer m.

boxer shorts npl caleçon m.

boxing ['bɒksɪŋ] n boxe f.

Boxing Day n jour des étrennes en Grande-Bretagne (le 26 décembre).

boxing glove n gant m de boxe.

boxing ring n ring m.

box junction n Br carrefour m à l'accès réglementé.

box number n numéro m d'annonce, référence f.

box office n bureau m de location.

boxroom ['bɒksrʊm] n Br débarras m.

boy [bɔɪ] ◇ n **-1.** [male child] garçon m. **-2.** inf [male friend]: **I'm going out with the ~s tonight** je sors avec mes potes ce soir. ◇ excl inf: **(oh) ~!** ben, mon vieux!, ben, dis-donc!

boycott ['bɔɪkɒt] ◇ n boycott m, boycottage m. ◇ vt boycotter.

boyfriend ['bɔɪfrend] n copain m, petit ami m.

boyish ['bɔɪɪʃ] adj [appearance - of man] gamin(e); [- of woman] de garçon; [behaviour] garçonnier(ière).

boy scout n scout m, éclaireur m.

Bp (abbr of **Bishop**) Mgr.

Br (abbr of **brother**) RELIG F.

BR (abbr of **British Rail**) n ≃ SNCF f.

bra [brɑː] n soutien-gorge m.

brace [breɪs] ◇ n **-1.** [on teeth] appareil m (dentaire). **-2.** [on leg] appareil m orthopédique. **-3.** [pair] paire f, couple m. ◇ vt **-1.** [steady] soutenir, consolider; **to ~ o.s.** s'accrocher, se cramponner. **-2.** fig [prepare]: **to ~ o.s. (for sthg)** se préparer (à qqch).
◆ **braces** npl Br bretelles fpl.

bracelet ['breɪslɪt] n bracelet m.

bracing ['breɪsɪŋ] adj vivifiant(e).

bracken ['brækn] *n* fougère *f*.

bracket ['brækɪt] ◇ *n* **-1.** [support] support *m*. **-2.** [parenthesis - round] parenthèse *f*; [- square] crochet *m*; **in** ~**s** entre parenthèses/crochets. **-3.** [group]: **age/income** ~ tranche *f* d'âge/de revenus. ◇ *vt* **-1.** [enclose in brackets] mettre entre parenthèses/crochets. **-2.** [group]: **to** ~ **sb/sthg (together) with** mettre qqn/qqch dans le même groupe que.

brackish ['brækɪʃ] *adj* saumâtre.

brag [bræg] (*pt* & *pp* **-ged**, *cont* **-ging**) *vi* se vanter.

braid [breɪd] ◇ *n* **-1.** [on uniform] galon *m*. **-2.** [of hair] tresse *f*, natte *f*. ◇ *vt* [hair] tresser, natter.

braille [breɪl] *n* braille *m*.

brain [breɪn] *n* cerveau *m*; **he's got money on the** ~ il ne pense qu'à l'argent.
◆ **brains** *npl* [intelligence] intelligence *f*; **to pick sb's** ~**s** faire appel aux lumières de qqn; **to rack** *Br* **OR cudgel** *Am* **one's** ~**s** se creuser la tête OR la cervelle.

brainchild ['breɪntʃaɪld] *n inf* idée *f* personnelle, invention *f* personnelle.

brain death *n* mort *f* cérébrale, coma *m* dépassé.

brain drain *n* fuite *f* OR exode *m* des cerveaux.

brainless ['breɪnlɪs] *adj* stupide.

brainstorm ['breɪnstɔ:m] *n* **-1.** *Br* [mental aberration] moment *m* d'aberration. **-2.** *Am* [brilliant idea] idée *f* géniale OR de génie.

brainstorming ['breɪn,stɔ:mɪŋ] *n* brainstorming *m*.

brainteaser ['breɪn,ti:zər] *n* colle *f*.

brainwash ['breɪnwɒʃ] *vt* faire un lavage de cerveau à.

brainwave ['breɪnweɪv] *n* idée *f* géniale OR de génie.

brainy ['breɪnɪ] (*compar* **-ier**, *superl* **-iest**) *adj inf* intelligent(e).

braise [breɪz] *vt* braiser.

brake [breɪk] ◇ *n lit* & *fig* frein *m*. ◇ *vi* freiner.

brake horsepower *n* puissance *f* de freinage.

brake light *n* stop *m*, feu *m* arrière.

brake lining *n* garniture *f* de frein.

brake pedal *n* (pédale *f* de) frein *m*.

brake shoe *n* sabot *m* OR patin *m* de frein.

bramble ['bræmbl] *n* [bush] ronce *f*; [fruit] mûre *f*.

bran [bræn] *n* son *m*.

branch [brɑ:ntʃ] ◇ *n* **-1.** [of tree, subject] branche *f*. **-2.** [of railway] bifurcation *f*, embranchement *m*. **-3.** [of company] filiale *f*, succursale *f*; [of bank] agence *f*. ◇ *vi* bifurquer.
◆ **branch off** *vi* bifurquer.
◆ **branch out** *vi* [person, company] étendre ses activités, se diversifier.

branch line *n* RAIL ligne *f* secondaire.

brand [brænd] ◇ *n* **-1.** COMM marque *f*. **-2.** *fig* [type, style] type *m*, genre *m*. ◇ *vt* **-1.** [cattle] marquer au fer rouge. **-2.** *fig* [classify]: **to** ~ **sb (as) sthg** étiqueter qqn comme qqch, coller à qqn l'étiquette de qqch.

brandish ['brændɪʃ] *vt* brandir.

brand leader *n* marque *f* dominante.

brand name *n* marque *f*.

brand-new *adj* flambant neuf (flambant neuve), tout neuf (toute neuve).

brandy ['brændɪ] (*pl* **-ies**) *n* cognac *m*.

brash [bræʃ] *adj* effronté(e).

Brasilia [brə'zɪljə] *n* Brasilia.

brass [brɑ:s] *n* **-1.** [metal] laiton *m*, cuivre *m* jaune. **-2.** MUS: **the** ~ les cuivres *mpl*.

brass band *n* fanfare *f*.

brasserie ['bræsərɪ] *n* brasserie *f*.

brassiere [*Br* 'bræsɪər, *Am* brə'zɪr] *n* soutien-gorge *m*.

brass knuckles *npl Am* coup-de-poing *m* américain.

brass tacks *npl inf*: **to get down to** ~ en venir aux choses sérieuses.

brat [bræt] *n inf pej* sale gosse *m*.

bravado [brə'vɑ:dəʊ] *n* bravade *f*.

brave [breɪv] ◇ *adj* courageux(euse), brave. ◇ *n* guerrier *m* indien, brave *m*. ◇ *vt* braver, affronter.

bravely ['breɪvlɪ] *adv* courageusement, vaillamment.

bravery ['breɪvərɪ] *n* courage *m*, bravoure *f*.

bravo [,brɑ:'vəʊ] *excl* bravo!

brawl [brɔ:l] *n* bagarre *f*, rixe *f*.

brawn [brɔ:n] *n* (*U*) **-1.** [muscle] muscle *m*. **-2.** *Br* [meat] fromage *m* de tête.

brawny ['brɔ:nɪ] (*compar* **-ier**, *superl* **-iest**) *adj* musclé(e).

bray [breɪ] *vi* [donkey] braire.

brazen ['breɪzn] *adj* [person] effronté(e), impudent(e); [lie] éhonté(e).
◆ **brazen out** *vt sep*: **to** ~ **it out** crâner.

brazier ['breɪzjər] *n* brasero *m*.

Brazil [brə'zɪl] *n* Brésil *m*; **in** ~ au Brésil.

Brazilian [brə'zɪljən] ◇ *adj* brésilien(ienne). ◇ *n* Brésilien *m*, -ienne *f*.

brazil nut *n* noix *f* du Brésil.

breach [briːtʃ] ◇ *n* -1. [of law, agreement] infraction *f*, violation *f*; [of promise] rupture *f*; **to be in ~ of sthg** enfreindre OR violer qqch; **~ of confidence** abus *m* de confiance; **~ of contract** rupture *f* de contrat. -2. [opening, gap] trou *m*, brèche *f*; **to step into the ~** remplacer quelqu'un au pied levé. -3. [in friendship, marriage] brouille *f*. ◇ *vt* -1. [agreement, contract] rompre. -2. [make hole in] faire une brèche dans.

breach of the peace *n* atteinte *f* à l'ordre public.

bread [bred] *n* pain *m*; **~ and butter** tartine *f* beurrée, pain beurré; *fig* gagne-pain *m*.

bread bin *Br*, **bread box** *Am n* boîte *f* à pain.

breadboard ['bredbɔːd] *n* planche *f* à pain.

bread box *Am* = **bread bin**.

breadcrumbs ['bredkrʌmz] *npl* chapelure *f*.

breaded ['bredɪd] *adj* pané(e).

breadline ['bredlaɪn] *n*: **to be on the ~** être sans ressources OR sans le sou.

breadth [bretθ] *n* -1. [width] largeur *f*. -2. *fig* [scope] ampleur *f*, étendue *f*.

breadwinner ['bred,wɪnəʳ] *n* soutien *m* de famille.

break [breɪk] (*pt* **broke**, *pp* **broken**) ◇ *n* -1. [gap]: **~ (in)** trouée *f* (dans). -2. [fracture] fracture *f*. -3. [change]: **a ~ with tradition** une rupture d'avec les traditions. -4. [pause - gen] pause *f*; [- at school] récréation *f*; **to take a ~** [short] faire une pause; [longer] prendre des jours de congé; **without a ~** sans interruption; **to have a ~ from doing sthg** arrêter de faire qqch. -5. *inf* [luck]: **(lucky) ~** chance *f*, veine *f*. -6. *literary* [of day]: **at ~ of day** au point du jour, à l'aube. -7. COMPUT [key] **break** *m*.
◇ *vt* -1. [gen] casser, briser; **to ~ one's arm/leg** se casser le bras/la jambe; **the river broke its banks** la rivière est sortie de son lit; **to ~ a habit** se défaire d'une (mauvaise) habitude; **to ~ sb's hold** se dégager de l'étreinte de qqn; **to ~ a record** battre un record; **to ~ a strike** briser une grève. -2. [interrupt - journey] interrompre; [- contact, silence] rompre. -3. [not keep - law, rule] enfreindre, violer; [- promise] manquer à. -4. [tell]: **to ~ the news (of sthg to sb)** annoncer la nouvelle (de qqch à qqn). -5. TENNIS: **to ~ sb's serve** prendre le service de qqn.
◇ *vi* -1. [gen] se casser, se briser; **to ~ loose** OR **free** se dégager, s'échapper. -2. [pause] s'arrêter, faire une pause. -3. [day] poindre, se lever. -4. [weather] se gâter. -5. [wave] se briser. -6. [voice - with emotion] se briser; [- at puberty] muer. -7. [news] se ré-

pandre, éclater. -8. *phr*: **to ~ even** rentrer dans ses frais.

◆ **break away** *vi* -1. [escape] s'échapper. -2. [end relationship]: **to ~ away (from sb)** abandonner (qqn), quitter (qqn).

◆ **break down** ◇ *vt sep* -1. [destroy - barrier] démolir; [- door] enfoncer. -2. [analyse] analyser. -3. [substance] décomposer. ◇ *vi* -1. [car, machine] tomber en panne; [resistance] céder; [negotiations] échouer. -2. [emotionally] fondre en larmes, éclater en sanglots. -3. [decompose] se décomposer.

◆ **break in** ◇ *vi* -1. [burglar] entrer par effraction. -2. [interrupt]: **to ~ in (on sb/sthg)** interrompre (qqn/qqch). ◇ *vt sep* -1. [horse] dresser; [person] rompre, accoutumer. -2. [shoes] faire.

◆ **break into** *vt fus* -1. [subj: burglar] entrer par effraction dans. -2. [begin]: **to ~ into song/applause** se mettre à chanter/applaudir. -3. [become involved in]: **to ~ into a market** pénétrer un marché; **to ~ into the music business** percer dans la chanson.

◆ **break off** ◇ *vt sep* -1. [detach] détacher. -2. [talks, relationship] rompre; [holiday] interrompre. ◇ *vi* -1. [become detached] se casser, se détacher. -2. [stop talking] s'interrompre, se taire. -3. [stop working] faire une pause, s'arrêter de travailler.

◆ **break out** *vi* -1. [begin - fire] se déclarer; [- fighting] éclater. -2. [skin, person]: **to ~ out in spots** se couvrir de boutons. -3. [escape]: **to ~ out (of)** s'échapper (de), s'évader (de).

◆ **break through** *vt fus* [subj: sun] percer; **she broke through the crowd** elle se fraya un chemin à travers la foule. ◇ *vi* [sun] percer.

◆ **break up** ◇ *vt sep* -1. [into smaller pieces] mettre en morceaux. -2. [end - marriage, relationship] détruire; [- fight, party] mettre fin à. ◇ *vi* -1. [into smaller pieces - gen] se casser en morceaux; [- ship] se briser. -2. [end - marriage, relationship] se briser; [- talks, party] prendre fin; [- school] finir, fermer; **to ~ up (with sb)** rompre (avec qqn). -3. [crowd] se disperser.

◆ **break with** *vt fus* rompre avec.

breakable ['breɪkəbl] *adj* cassable, fragile.

breakage ['breɪkɪdʒ] *n* bris *m*.

breakaway ['breɪkəweɪ] *adj* [faction etc] dissident(e).

break dancing *n* smurf *m*.

breakdown ['breɪkdaʊn] *n* -1. [of vehicle, machine] panne *f*; [of negotiations] échec *m*; [in communications] rupture *f*; **nervous ~** dépression *f* nerveuse. -2. [analysis] analyse *f*.

breaker ['breɪkəʳ] n [wave] brisant m.

breakeven [,breɪk'iːvn] n seuil m de rentabilité.

breakfast ['brekfəst] ◇ n petit déjeuner m. ◇ vi: **to ~ (on)** déjeuner (de).

breakfast cereal n céréales fpl.

breakfast television n Br télévision f du matin.

break-in n cambriolage m.

breaking ['breɪkɪŋ] n: **~ and entering** JUR entrée f par effraction.

breaking point n limite f.

breakneck ['breɪknek] adj: **at ~ speed** à fond de train.

breakthrough ['breɪkθruː] n percée f.

breakup ['breɪkʌp] n [of marriage, relationship] rupture f.

breakup value n COMM valeur f liquidative.

bream [briːm] (pl inv OR **-s**) n brème f.

breast [brest] n **-1.** [of woman] sein m; [of man] poitrine f. **-2.** [meat of bird] blanc m. **-3.** phr: **to make a clean ~ of it** tout avouer.

breast-feed vt & vi allaiter.

breast pocket n poche f de poitrine.

breaststroke ['breststrəʊk] n brasse f.

breath [breθ] n souffle m, haleine f; **to take a deep ~** inspirer profondément; **to go out for a ~ of (fresh) air** sortir prendre l'air; **she/it was a ~ of fresh air** elle représentait/c'était une véritable bouffée d'oxygène; **out of ~** hors d'haleine, à bout de souffle; **to get one's ~ back** reprendre haleine OR son souffle; **to hold one's ~** lit & fig retenir son souffle; **it took my ~ away** cela m'a coupé le souffle.

breathable ['briːðəbl] adj respirable.

breathalyse Br, **-yze** Am ['breθəlaɪz] vt faire subir l'Alcootest® à.

Breathalyser® Br, **-yzer®** Am ['breθəlaɪzəʳ] n Alcootest® m.

breathe [briːð] ◇ vi respirer; **I can ~ more easily now** fig je respire maintenant. ◇ vt **-1.** [inhale] respirer. **-2.** [exhale - smell] souffler des relents de.
◆ **breathe in** ◇ vi inspirer. ◇ vt sep aspirer.
◆ **breathe out** vi expirer.

breather ['briːðəʳ] n inf moment m de repos OR répit.

breathing ['briːðɪŋ] n respiration f, souffle m.

breathing space n fig répit m.

breathless ['breθlɪs] adj **-1.** [out of breath] hors d'haleine, essoufflé(e). **-2.** [with excitement] fébrile, fiévreux(euse).

breathtaking ['breθ,teɪkɪŋ] adj à vous couper le souffle.

breath test n Alcootest® m.

breed [briːd] (pt & pp **bred** [bred]) ◇ n lit & fig race f, espèce f. ◇ vt **-1.** [animals, plants] élever. **-2.** fig [suspicion, contempt] faire naître, engendrer. ◇ vi se reproduire.

breeder ['briːdəʳ] n éleveur m, -euse f.

breeder reactor n surgénérateur m.

breeding ['briːdɪŋ] n (U) **-1.** [of animals, plants] élevage m. **-2.** [manners] bonnes manières fpl, savoir-vivre m.

breeding-ground n fig terrain m propice.

breeze [briːz] ◇ n brise f. ◇ vi: **to ~ in/out** [quickly] entrer/sortir en coup de vent; [casually] entrer/sortir d'un air désinvolte.

breezeblock ['briːzblɒk] n Br parpaing m.

breezy ['briːzɪ] (compar **-ier**, superl **-iest**) adj **-1.** [windy] venteux(euse). **-2.** [cheerful] jovial(e), enjoué(e).

Breton ['bretn] ◇ adj breton(onne). ◇ n **-1.** [person] Breton m, -onne f. **-2.** [language] breton m.

brevity ['brevɪtɪ] n brièveté f.

brew [bruː] ◇ vt [beer] brasser; [tea] faire infuser; [coffee] préparer, faire. ◇ vi **-1.** [tea] infuser; [coffee] se faire. **-2.** fig [trouble, storm] se préparer, couver.

brewer ['bruːəʳ] n brasseur m.

brewery ['bruːərɪ] (pl **-ies**) n brasserie f.

briar ['braɪəʳ] n églantier m.

bribe [braɪb] ◇ n pot-de-vin m. ◇ vt: **to ~ sb (to do sthg)** soudoyer qqn (pour qu'il fasse qqch).

bribery ['braɪbərɪ] n corruption f.

bric-a-brac ['brɪkəbræk] n bric-à-brac m.

brick [brɪk] n brique f.
◆ **brick up** vt sep murer.

bricklayer ['brɪk,leɪəʳ] n maçon m.

brickwork ['brɪkwɜːk] n briquetage m.

bridal ['braɪdl] adj [dress] de mariée; [suite etc] nuptial(e).

bride [braɪd] n mariée f.

bridegroom ['braɪdgrʊm] n marié m.

bridesmaid ['braɪdzmeɪd] n demoiselle f d'honneur.

bridge [brɪdʒ] ◇ n **-1.** [gen] pont m; **I'll cross that ~ when I come to it** chaque chose en son temps. **-2.** [on ship] passerelle f. **-3.** [of nose] arête f. **-4.** [card game, for teeth] bridge m. ◇ vt fig [gap] réduire.

bridging loan ['brɪdʒɪŋ-] *n Br* crédit-relais *m*.

bridle ['braɪdl] ◇ *n* bride *f*. ◇ *vt* mettre la bride à, brider. ◇ *vi*: **to ~ (at sthg)** se rebiffer (contre qqch).

bridle path *n* piste *f* cavalière.

brief [briːf] ◇ *adj* **-1.** [short] bref (brève), court(e); **in ~** en bref, en deux mots. **-2.** [revealing] très court(e). ◇ *n* **-1.** JUR affaire *f*, dossier *m*. **-2.** *Br* [instructions] instructions *fpl*. ◇ *vt*: **to ~ sb (on)** [bring up to date] mettre qqn au courant (de); [instruct] briefer qqn (sur).
◆ **briefs** *npl* slip *m*.

briefcase ['briːfkeɪs] *n* serviette *f*.

briefing ['briːfɪŋ] *n* instructions *fpl*, briefing *m*.

briefly ['briːflɪ] *adv* **-1.** [for a short time] un instant. **-2.** [concisely] brièvement.

Brig. *abbr of* **brigadier**.

brigade [brɪ'geɪd] *n* brigade *f*; **fire ~** pompiers *mpl*.

brigadier [,brɪgə'dɪəʳ] *n* général *m* de brigade.

bright [braɪt] *adj* **-1.** [room] clair(e); [light, colour] vif (vive); [sunlight] éclatant(e); [eyes, future] brillant(e). **-2.** [intelligent] intelligent(e).
◆ **brights** *npl Am inf* feux *mpl* de route, phares *mpl*.
◆ **bright and early** *adv* de bon matin.

brighten ['braɪtn] *vi* **-1.** [become lighter] s'éclaircir. **-2.** [face, mood] s'éclairer.
◆ **brighten up** ◇ *vt sep* égayer. ◇ *vi* **-1.** [person] s'égayer, s'animer. **-2.** [weather] se dégager, s'éclaircir.

brightly ['braɪtlɪ] *adv* **-1.** [shine] avec éclat. **-2.** [coloured] vivement. **-3.** [cheerfully] gaiement.

brightness ['braɪtnɪs] *n* [of light, colour] éclat *m*; [of TV] intensité *f*.

brilliance ['brɪljəns] *n* **-1.** [cleverness] intelligence *f*. **-2.** [of colour, light] éclat *m*.

brilliant ['brɪljənt] *adj* **-1.** [gen] brillant(e). **-2.** [colour] éclatant(e). **-3.** *inf* [wonderful] super (*inv*), génial(e).

brilliantly ['brɪljəntlɪ] *adv* **-1.** [cleverly] brillamment. **-2.** [coloured] vivement. **-3.** [shine] avec éclat.

Brillo pad® ['brɪləʊ-] *n* ≃ tampon *m* Jex®.

brim [brɪm] (*pt* & *pp* **-med**, *cont* **-ming**) ◇ *n* bord *m*. ◇ *vi*: **to ~ with** *lit* & *fig* être plein(e) de.
◆ **brim over** *vi*: **to ~ over (with)** *lit* & *fig* déborder (de).

brine [braɪn] *n* saumure *f*.

bring [brɪŋ] (*pt* & *pp* **brought**) *vt* **-1.** [person] amener; [object] apporter. **-2.** [cause - happiness, shame] entraîner, causer; **to ~ sthg to an end** mettre fin à qqch. **-3.** JUR: **to ~ charges against sb** porter plainte contre qqn; **to be brought to trial** comparaître en justice. **-4.** *phr*: **I couldn't ~ myself to do it** je ne pouvais me résoudre à le faire.
◆ **bring about** *vt sep* causer, provoquer.
◆ **bring along** *vt sep* [person] amener; [object] apporter.
◆ **bring around** *vt sep* [make conscious] ranimer.
◆ **bring back** *vt sep* **-1.** [object] rapporter; [person] ramener. **-2.** [memories] rappeler. **-3.** [reinstate] rétablir.
◆ **bring down** *vt sep* **-1.** [plane] abattre; [government] renverser. **-2.** [prices] faire baisser.
◆ **bring forward** *vt sep* **-1.** [gen] avancer. **-2.** [in bookkeeping] reporter.
◆ **bring in** *vt sep* **-1.** [law] introduire. **-2.** [money - subj: person] gagner; [- subj: deal] rapporter. **-3.** JUR [verdict] rendre.
◆ **bring off** *vt sep* [plan] réaliser, réussir; [deal] conclure, mener à bien.
◆ **bring on** *vt sep* [cause] provoquer, causer; **you've brought it on yourself** tu l'as cherché.
◆ **bring out** *vt sep* **-1.** [product] lancer; [book] publier, faire paraître. **-2.** [cause to appear] faire ressortir.
◆ **bring round, bring to** = **bring around**.
◆ **bring up** *vt sep* **-1.** [raise - children] élever. **-2.** [mention] mentionner. **-3.** [vomit] rendre, vomir.

brink [brɪŋk] *n*: **on the ~ of** au bord de, à la veille de.

brisk [brɪsk] *adj* **-1.** [quick] vif (vive), rapide. **-2.** [busy]: **business is ~** les affaires marchent bien. **-3.** [manner, tone] déterminé(e). **-4.** [wind] frais (fraîche).

brisket ['brɪskɪt] *n* poitrine *f* de bœuf.

briskly ['brɪsklɪ] *adv* **-1.** [quickly] d'un bon pas. **-2.** [efficiently, confidently] avec détermination.

bristle ['brɪsl] ◇ *n* poil *m*. ◇ *vi lit* & *fig* se hérisser.
◆ **bristle with** *vt fus* grouiller de.

bristly ['brɪslɪ] (*compar* **-ier**, *superl* **-iest**) *adj* aux poils raides.

Brit [brɪt] (*abbr of* **Briton**) *n inf* Britannique *mf*.

Britain ['brɪtn] *n* Grande-Bretagne *f*; **in ~** en Grande-Bretagne.

British ['brɪtɪʃ] *adj* britannique.

British Columbia *n* Colombie-Britannique *f*; **in** ~ en Colombie-Britannique.

British Council *n*: **the** ~ *organisme culturel public*.

BRITISH COUNCIL:
Le British Council est chargé de promouvoir la langue et la culture anglaises, et de renforcer les liens culturels avec les autres pays

Britisher ['brɪtɪʃə'] *n Am* Anglais *m*, -e *f*, Britannique *mf*.

British Isles *npl*: **the** ~ les îles *fpl* Britanniques.

British Rail *n société des chemins de fer britanniques*, ≃ SNCF *f*.

British Summer Time *n* heure *f* d'été (*en Grande-Bretagne*).

British Telecom [-'telɪkɒm] *n société britannique de télécommunications*.

Briton ['brɪtn] *n* Britannique *mf*.

Brittany ['brɪtənɪ] *n* Bretagne *f*; **in** ~ en Bretagne.

brittle ['brɪtl] *adj* fragile.

Bro = **Br**.

broach [brəʊtʃ] *vt* [subject] aborder.

B road ['biːrəʊd] *n Br* route *f* départementale.

broad [brɔːd] *adj* -1. [wide] large; [- range, interests] divers(e), varié(e). -2. [description] général(e). -3. [hint] transparent(e); [accent] prononcé(e).
◆ **in broad daylight** *adv* en plein jour.

broad bean *n* fève *f*.

broadcast ['brɔːdkɑːst] (*pt* & *pp* **broadcast**) ◇ *n* RADIO & TV émission *f*. ◇ *vt* RADIO radiodiffuser, diffuser; TV téléviser.

broadcaster ['brɔːdkɑːstə'] *n* personnalité *f* de la télévision/de la radio.

broadcasting ['brɔːdkɑːstɪŋ] *n* (*U*) RADIO radiodiffusion *f*; TV télévision *f*.

broaden ['brɔːdn] ◇ *vt* élargir. ◇ *vi* s'élargir.
◆ **broaden out** ◇ *vt sep* élargir. ◇ *vi* s'élargir, s'étendre.

broadly ['brɔːdlɪ] *adv* -1. [generally] généralement; ~ **speaking** généralement parlant. -2. [smile] jusqu'aux oreilles.

broadly-based [-beɪst] *adj* varié(e), divers(e).

broadminded [ˌbrɔːd'maɪndɪd] *adj* large d'esprit.

broadsheet ['brɔːdʃiːt] *n* journal *m* de qualité.

BROADSHEET:
Les principaux journaux nationaux de qualité en Grande-Bretagne sont les suivants:
The Guardian (tendance centre-gauche)
The Independent
The Daily Telegraph (tendance conservatrice)
The Times (tendance centre-droite)
The Financial Times

brocade [brə'keɪd] *n* brocart *m*.

broccoli ['brɒkəlɪ] *n* brocoli *m*.

brochure ['brəʊʃə'] *n* brochure *f*, prospectus *m*.

brogues [brəʊgz] *npl chaussures lourdes souvent ornées de petits trous*.

broil [brɔɪl] *vt Am* griller, faire cuire au gril.

broiler ['brɔɪlə'] *n* -1. [young chicken] poulet *m* (à rôtir). -2. *Am* [pan] gril *m*.

broke [brəʊk] ◇ *pt* → **break**. ◇ *adj inf* fauché(e); **to go** ~ [company] faire faillite; **to go for** ~ risquer le tout pour le tout.

broken ['brəʊkn] ◇ *pp* → **break**. ◇ *adj* -1. cassé(e); **to have a** ~ **leg** avoir la jambe cassée. -2. [interrupted - journey, sleep] interrompu(e); [- line] brisé(e). -3. [promise] non respecté(e). -4. [marriage] brisé(e), détruit(e); [home] désuni(e). -5. [hesitant]: **to speak in** ~ **English** parler un anglais hésitant.

broken-down *adj* -1. [not working] en panne. -2. [dilapidated] délabré(e).

broker ['brəʊkə'] *n* courtier *m*; (**insurance**) ~ assureur *m*, courtier *m* d'assurances.

brokerage ['brəʊkərɪdʒ] *n* courtage *m*.

brolly ['brɒlɪ] (*pl* -**ies**) *n Br inf* pépin *m*.

bronchitis [brɒŋ'kaɪtɪs] *n* (*U*) bronchite *f*.

bronze [brɒnz] ◇ *adj* [colour] (couleur) bronze (*inv*). ◇ *n* -1. [gen] bronze *m*. -2. = **bronze medal**. ◇ *comp* en bronze.

bronzed [brɒnzd] *adj* bronzé(e).

bronze medal *n* médaille *f* de bronze.

brooch [brəʊtʃ] *n* broche *f*.

brood [bruːd] ◇ *n* -1. [of animals] couvée *f*. -2. *fig* [of children] nichée *f*, marmaille *f*. ◇ *vi*: **to** ~ (**over** OR **about sthg**) ressasser (qqch), remâcher (qqch).

broody ['bruːdɪ] (*compar* -**ier**, *superl* -**iest**) *adj* -1. [sad] triste, cafardeux(euse). -2. [hen] couveuse.

brook [brʊk] ◇ *n* ruisseau *m*. ◇ *vt fml* tolérer, souffrir.

broom [bruːm] *n* balai *m*.

broomstick ['bruːmstɪk] *n* manche *m* à balai.

Bros, bros (*abbr of* **brothers**) Frères.

broth [brɒθ] *n* bouillon *m*.

brothel ['brɒθl] *n* bordel *m*.

brother ['brʌðər] ◇ *n* frère *m*. ◇ *excl Am inf* ben, dis-donc!

brotherhood ['brʌðəhʊd] *n* **-1.** [companionship] fraternité *f*. **-2.** [organization] confrérie *f*, société *f*.

brother-in-law (*pl* **brothers-in-law**) *n* beau-frère *m*.

brotherly ['brʌðəlɪ] *adj* fraternel(elle).

brought [brɔːt] *pt & pp* → **bring**.

brow [braʊ] *n* **-1.** [forehead] front *m*. **-2.** [eyebrow] sourcil *m*; **to knit one's ~s** froncer les sourcils. **-3.** [of hill] sommet *m*.

browbeat ['braʊbiːt] (*pt* **browbeat**, *pp* **-en**) *vt* rudoyer, brutaliser.

browbeaten ['braʊbiːtn] *adj* opprimé(e), tyrannisé(e).

brown [braʊn] ◇ *adj* **-1.** [colour] brun(e), marron (*inv*); **~ bread** pain *m* bis. **-2.** [tanned] bronzé(e), hâlé(e). ◇ *n* [colour] marron *m*, brun *m*; **in ~** en marron. ◇ *vt* [food] faire dorer.

Brownie (Guide) ['braʊnɪ-] *n* ≈ jeannette *f*.

Brownie point *n fig* bon point *m*.

brown point *n* bon point *m*.

brown paper *n* papier *m* d'emballage, papier kraft.

brown rice *n* riz *m* complet.

brown sugar *n* sucre *m* roux.

browse [braʊz] *vi* **-1.** [look]: **I'm just browsing** [in shop] je ne fais que regarder; **to ~ through** [magazines etc] feuilleter. **-2.** [animal] brouter.

bruise [bruːz] ◇ *n* bleu *m*. ◇ *vt* **-1.** [skin, arm] se faire un bleu à; [fruit] taler. **-2.** *fig* [pride] meurtrir, blesser. ◇ *vi* [person] se faire un bleu; [fruit] se taler.

bruised [bruːzd] *adj* **-1.** [skin, arm] qui a des bleus; [fruit] talé(e). **-2.** *fig* [pride] meurtri(e), blessé(e).

Brum [brʌm] *n Br inf* (*abbr of* **Birmingham**) ville anglaise.

Brummie, Brummy ['brʌmɪ] *n Br inf* habitant de Birmingham.

brunch [brʌntʃ] *n* brunch *m*.

Brunei ['bruːnaɪ] *n* Brunei *m*; **in ~** au Brunei.

brunette [bruː'net] *n* brunette *f*.

brunt [brʌnt] *n*: **to bear** OR **take the ~ of** subir le plus gros de.

brush [brʌʃ] ◇ *n* **-1.** [gen] brosse *f*; [of painter] pinceau *m*. **-2.** [encounter]: **to have a ~ with the police** avoir des ennuis avec la

police. ◇ *vt* **-1.** [clean with brush] brosser. **-2.** [move with hand]: **he ~ed away some crumbs** il a enlevé quelques miettes (avec sa main). **-3.** [touch lightly] effleurer.

◆ **brush aside** *vt sep fig* écarter, repousser.

◆ **brush off** *vt sep* [dismiss] envoyer promener.

◆ **brush up** ◇ *vt sep* [revise] réviser. ◇ *vi*: **to ~ up on sthg** réviser qqch.

brushed [brʌʃt] *adj* [metal] poli(e); [cotton, nylon] peigné(e).

brush-off *n inf*: **to give sb the ~** envoyer promener qqn.

brush-up *n inf*: **to have a wash and ~** se donner un coup de peigne.

brushwood ['brʌʃwʊd] *n* (*U*) brindilles *fpl*.

brushwork ['brʌʃwɜːk] *n* facture *f*.

brusque [bruːsk] *adj* brusque.

Brussels ['brʌslz] *n* Bruxelles.

brussels sprout *n* chou *m* de Bruxelles.

brutal ['bruːtl] *adj* brutal(e).

brutality [bruː'tælətɪ] (*pl* **-ies**) *n* brutalité *f*.

brutalize, -ise ['bruːtəlaɪz] *vt* brutaliser.

brute [bruːt] ◇ *adj* [force] brutal(e). ◇ *n* brute *f*.

bs *abbr of* **bill of sale**.

BS (*abbr of* **Bachelor of Science**) *n* (*titulaire d'une*) *licence de sciences*.

BSA (*abbr of* **Boy Scouts of America**) *n* *association américaine de scouts*.

BSc (*abbr of* **Bachelor of Science**) *n* (*titulaire d'une*) *licence de sciences*.

BSE (*abbr of* **bovine spongiform encephalopathy**) *n* EBS *f*.

BSI (*abbr of* **British Standards Institution**) *n* *association britannique de normalisation*, ≈ AFNOR *f*.

B-side *n* face *f* B.

BST -1. (*abbr of* **British Summer Time**) *heure d'été britannique*. **-2.** (*abbr of* **British Standard Time**) *heure officielle britannique*.

Bt. *abbr of* **baronet**.

BT (*abbr of* **British Telecom**) *n* *société britannique de télécommunications*.

btu (*abbr of* **British thermal unit**) *n* *unité de chaleur (1054,2 joules)*.

bubble ['bʌbl] ◇ *n* bulle *f*. ◇ *vi* **-1.** [liquid] faire des bulles, bouillonner. **-2.** *fig* [person]: **to ~ with** déborder de.

bubble bath *n* bain *m* moussant.

bubble gum *n* bubble-gum *m*.

bubblejet printer ['bʌbl,dʒet-] *n* imprimante *f* à bulle d'encre.

bubbly ['bʌblɪ] (*compar* **-ier**, *superl* **-iest**) ◇ *adj* **-1.** [water] pétillant(e). **-2.** *fig* [lively] plein(e) de vie. ◇ *n inf* champagne *m*.

Bucharest [,bu:kə'rest] *n* Bucarest.

buck [bʌk] (*pl inv* OR **-s**) ◇ *n* **-1.** [male animal] mâle *m*. **-2.** *inf* [dollar] dollar *m*; **to make a fast ~** gagner facilement du fric. **-3.** *inf* [responsibility]: **the ~ stops here** maintenant, j'en prends la responsabilité; **to pass the ~** refiler la responsabilité. ◇ *vt* **-1.** [subj: horse] désarçonner d'une ruade. **-2.** *inf* [trend]: **to ~ the trend** aller à contre-courant. ◇ *vi* [horse] ruer.
◆ **buck up** *inf* ◇ *vt sep* **-1.** [improve]: **~ your ideas up!** reprenez-vous! **-2.** [cheer up] remonter le moral à qqn. ◇ *vi* **-1.** [hurry up] se remuer, se dépêcher. **-2.** [cheer up] ne pas se laisser abattre.

bucket ['bʌkɪt] *n* **-1.** [gen] seau *m*. **-2.** *inf fig* [lots]: **~s of rain** des trombes d'eau; **he has ~s of charm** il a énormément de charme; **she has ~s of money** elle est pleine aux as.

Buckingham Palace ['bʌkɪŋəm-] *n* le palais de Buckingham (*résidence officielle du souverain britannique*).

buckle ['bʌkl] ◇ *n* boucle *f*. ◇ *vt* **-1.** [fasten] boucler. **-2.** [bend] voiler. ◇ *vi* [wheel] se voiler; [knees, legs] se plier.
◆ **buckle down** *vi*: **to ~ down (to)** s'atteler (à).

Bucks [bʌks] (*abbr of* **Buckinghamshire**) *comté anglais*.

buckshot ['bʌkʃɒt] *n* chevrotine *f*.

buckskin ['bʌkskɪn] *n* (*U*) peau *f* de daim.

buckteeth [bʌk'ti:θ] *npl* dents *fpl* en avant.

buckwheat ['bʌkwi:t] *n* blé *m* noir.

bud [bʌd] (*pt* & *pp* **-ded**, *cont* **-ding**) ◇ *n* bourgeon *m*; **to nip sthg in the ~** *fig* écraser OR étouffer qqch dans l'œuf. ◇ *vi* bourgeonner.

Budapest [,bju:də'pest] *n* Budapest.

Buddha ['bʊdə] *n* Bouddha *m*.

Buddhism ['bʊdɪzm] *n* bouddhisme *m*.

Buddhist ['bʊdɪst] ◇ *adj* bouddhiste. ◇ *n* bouddhiste *mf*.

budding ['bʌdɪŋ] *adj* [writer, artist] en herbe.

buddy ['bʌdɪ] (*pl* **-ies**) *n inf* pote *m*.

budge [bʌdʒ] ◇ *vt* faire bouger. ◇ *vi* bouger.

budgerigar ['bʌdʒərɪgɑ:] *n* perruche *f*.

budget ['bʌdʒɪt] ◇ *adj* [holiday, price] pour petits budgets. ◇ *n* budget *m*; **the Budget** *Br* le budget. ◇ *vt* budgétiser. ◇ *vi* préparer un budget.
◆ **budget for** *vt fus* prévoir.

budget account *n Br* compte-crédit *m*.

budgetary ['bʌdʒɪtrɪ] *adj* budgétaire.

budgie ['bʌdʒɪ] *n inf* perruche *f*.

Buenos Aires [,bwenəs'aɪrɪz] *n* Buenos Aires.

buff [bʌf] ◇ *adj* [brown] chamois (*inv*). ◇ *n inf* [expert] mordu *m*, -e *f*.

buffalo ['bʌfələʊ] (*pl inv* OR **-es** OR **-s**) *n* buffle *m*.

buffer ['bʌfə] *n* **-1.** [gen] tampon *m*. **-2.** COMPUT mémoire *f* tampon.

buffer state *n* État *m* tampon.

buffet¹ [*Br* 'bʊfeɪ, *Am* bə'feɪ] *n* [food, cafeteria] buffet *m*.

buffet² ['bʌfɪt] *vt* [physically] frapper.

buffet car ['bʊfeɪ-] *n* wagon-restaurant *m*.

buffoon [bə'fu:n] *n* bouffon *m*.

bug [bʌg] (*pt* & *pp* **-ged**, *cont* **-ging**) ◇ *n* **-1.** [insect] punaise *f*. **-2.** *inf* [germ] microbe *m*. **-3.** *inf* [listening device] micro *m*. **-4.** COMPUT défaut *m*, bug *m*. **-5.** [enthusiasm]: **the travel ~** le virus des voyages. ◇ *vt* **-1.** *inf* [telephone] mettre sur table d'écoute; [room] cacher les micros dans. **-2.** *inf* [annoy] embêter.

bugbear ['bʌgbeə] *n* cauchemar *m*.

bugger ['bʌgə] *Br v inf* ◇ *n* **-1.** [person] con *m*, conne *f*. **-2.** [job]: **this job's a real ~!** ce travail est vraiment chiant! ◇ *excl* merde! ◇ *vt*: **~ it!** merde alors!
◆ **bugger off** *vi*: **~ off!** fous le camp!

buggy ['bʌgɪ] (*pl* **-ies**) *n* **-1.** [carriage] boghei *m*. **-2.** [pushchair] poussette *f*; *Am* [pram] landau *m*.

bugle ['bju:gl] *n* clairon *m*.

build [bɪld] (*pt* & *pp* **built**) ◇ *vt lit* & *fig* construire, bâtir. ◇ *n* carrure *f*.
◆ **build into** *vt sep* **-1.** CONSTR encastrer. **-2.** [include in] inclure dans.
◆ **build on**, **build upon** ◇ *vt fus* [success] tirer avantage de. ◇ *vt sep* [base on] baser sur.
◆ **build up** ◇ *vt sep* [business] développer; [reputation] bâtir; **to ~ up one's strength** reprendre des forces. ◇ *vi* [clouds] s'amonceler; [traffic] augmenter.

builder ['bɪldə] *n* entrepreneur *m*.

building ['bɪldɪŋ] *n* bâtiment *m*.

building and loan association *n Am* ≃ société *f* d'épargne et de financement immobilier.

building block *n* **-1.** [toy] cube *m*. **-2.** *fig* [element] élément *m*, composante *f*.

building contractor *n* entrepreneur *m*.

building site *n* chantier *m*.

building society *n Br* ≃ société *f* d'épargne et de financement immobilier.

BUILDING SOCIETY:
Les 'building societies' fonctionnent comme des banques, mais n'ont pas de système de compensation. Établissements consentant des prêts immobiliers aux particuliers, elles jouent un rôle important dans la vie en Grande-Bretagne

buildup ['bɪldʌp] *n* [increase] accroissement *m*.

built [bɪlt] ◇ *pt & pp* → **build**. ◇ *adj* [person] bâti(e).

built-in *adj* **-1.** CONSTR encastré(e). **-2.** [inherent] inné(e).

built-up *adj*: ~ **area** agglomération *f*.

bulb [bʌlb] *n* **-1.** ELEC ampoule *f*. **-2.** BOT oignon *m*. **-3.** [of thermometer] cuvette *f*.

bulbous ['bʌlbəs] *adj* bulbeux(euse).

Bulgaria [bʌl'geərɪə] *n* Bulgarie *f*; **in** ~ en Bulgarie.

Bulgarian [bʌl'geərɪən] ◇ *adj* bulgare. ◇ *n* **-1.** [person] Bulgare *mf*. **-2.** [language] bulgare *m*.

bulge [bʌldʒ] ◇ *n* **-1.** [lump] bosse *f*. **-2.** [in sales etc] croissance *f* soudaine. ◇ *vi*: **to** ~ **(with)** être gonflé (de).

bulging ['bʌldʒɪŋ] *adj* [pocket, bag] bourré(e), plein(e) à craquer; [muscles] gonflé(e).

bulimia (nervosa) [bjʊ'lɪmɪə-] *n* boulimie *f*.

bulk [bʌlk] ◇ *n* **-1.** [mass] volume *m*. **-2.** [of person] corpulence *f*. **-3.** COMM: **in** ~ en gros. **-4.** [majority]: **the** ~ **of** le plus gros de. ◇ *adj* en gros.

bulk buying [-'baɪɪŋ] *n* (U) achat *m* en gros.

bulkhead ['bʌlkhed] *n* cloison *f*.

bulky ['bʌlkɪ] (*compar* **-ier**, *superl* **-iest**) *adj* volumineux(euse).

bull [bʊl] *n* **-1.** [male cow] taureau *m*; [male elephant, seal] mâle *m*. **-2.** ST EX haussier *m*. **-3.** (U) *v inf* [nonsense] conneries *fpl*.

bulldog ['bʊldɒg] *n* bouledogue *m*.

bulldog clip *n* pince *f* à dessin.

bulldoze ['bʊldəʊz] *vt* **-1.** CONSTR passer au bulldozer. **-2.** *fig* [force]: **to** ~ **one's way** forcer son chemin; **to** ~ **sb into doing sthg** contraindre OR forcer qqn à faire qqch.

bulldozer ['bʊldəʊzəʳ] *n* bulldozer *m*.

bullet ['bʊlɪt] *n* [for gun] balle *f*.

bulletin ['bʊlətɪn] *n* bulletin *m*.

bulletin board *n* tableau *m* d'affichage.

bullet-proof *adj* pare-balles (*inv*).

bullfight ['bʊlfaɪt] *n* corrida *f*.

bullfighter ['bʊlfaɪtəʳ] *n* toréador *m*.

bullfighting ['bʊlfaɪtɪŋ] *n* (U) courses *fpl* de taureaux; [art] tauromachie *f*.

bullfinch ['bʊlfɪntʃ] *n* bouvreuil *m*.

bullion ['bʊljən] *n* (U): **gold** ~ **or** *m* en barres.

bullish ['bʊlɪʃ] *adj* ST EX à la hausse.

bull market *n* ST EX marché *m* à la hausse.

bullock ['bʊlək] *n* bœuf *m*.

bullring ['bʊlrɪŋ] *n* arène *f*.

bullrush ['bʊlrʌʃ] = **bulrush**.

bull's-eye *n* centre *m*.

bullshit ['bʊlʃɪt] (*pt & pp* **-ted**, *cont* **-ting**) *vulg* ◇ *n* (U) conneries *fpl*. ◇ *vi* dire des conneries.

bull terrier *n* bull-terrier *m*.

bully ['bʊlɪ] (*pl* **-ies**, *pt & pp* **-ied**) ◇ *n* tyran *m*. ◇ *vt* tyranniser, brutaliser; **to** ~ **sb into doing sthg** forcer OR obliger qqn à faire qqch.

bullying ['bʊlɪŋ] *n* (U) brimades *fpl*.

bulrush ['bʊlrʌʃ] *n* jonc *m*.

bum [bʌm] (*pt & pp* **-med**, *cont* **-ming**) *n* **-1.** *v inf* [bottom] derrière *m*. **-2.** *inf pej* [tramp] clochard *m*. **-3.** *inf* [idler] bon à rien *m*.

◆ **bum around** *vi inf* **-1.** [waste time] perdre son temps. **-2.** [travel aimlessly] se balader.

bumblebee ['bʌmblbiː] *n* bourdon *m*.

bumbling ['bʌmblɪŋ] *adj inf* empoté(e).

bumf [bʌmf] *n* (U) *Br inf* paperasses *fpl*.

bump [bʌmp] ◇ *n* **-1.** [lump] bosse *f*. **-2.** [knock, blow] choc *m*. **-3.** [noise] bruit *m* sourd. ◇ *vt* [head etc] cogner; [car] heurter. ◇ *vi* [car]: **to** ~ **along** cahoter.

◆ **bump into** *vt fus* [meet by chance] rencontrer par hasard.

◆ **bump off** *vt sep inf* liquider.

◆ **bump up** *vt sep inf* faire grimper.

bumper ['bʌmpəʳ] ◇ *adj* [harvest, edition] exceptionnel(elle). ◇ *n* **-1.** AUT pare-chocs *m*. **-2.** *Am* RAIL tampon *m*.

bumper-to-bumper *adj* pare-chocs contre pare-chocs.

bumph [bʌmf] = **bumf**.

bumptious ['bʌmpʃəs] *adj* suffisant(e).

bumpy ['bʌmpɪ] (*compar* **-ier**, *superl* **-iest**) *adj* **-1.** [surface] défoncé(e). **-2.** [ride] cahoteux(euse); [sea crossing] agité(e).

bun [bʌn] *n* **-1.** [cake] petit pain *m* aux raisins; [bread roll] petit pain au lait. **-2.** [hairstyle] chignon *m*.

bunch [bʌntʃ] ◇ *n* [of people] groupe *m*; [of flowers] bouquet *m*; [of grapes] grappe *f*; [of bananas] régime *m*; [of keys] trousseau *m*. ◇ *vt* grouper. ◇ *vi* se grouper.

◆ **bunches** [hairstyle] couettes *fpl*.

bundle ['bʌndl] ◇ *n* [of clothes] paquet *m*; [of notes, newspapers] liasse *f*; [of wood] fagot *m*. ◇ *vt* [put roughly - person] entasser; [- clothes] fourrer, entasser.

◆ **bundle off** *vt sep* [person] envoyer en hâte.

◆ **bundle up** *vt sep* [clothes] mettre en tas; [newspapers] mettre en liasse; [wood] mettre en fagot.

bundled software ['bʌndld-] *n* (U) COMPUT logiciel *m* inclus à l'achat d'un ordinateur.

bung [bʌŋ] ◇ *n* bonde *f*. ◇ *vt* Br *inf* envoyer.

bungalow ['bʌŋgələʊ] *n* bungalow *m*.

bunged up [bʌŋd-] *adj* bouché(e).

bungee-jumping ['bʌndʒi:-] *n* saut *m* à l'élastique.

bungle ['bʌŋgl] *vt* gâcher, bâcler.

bunion ['bʌnjən] *n* oignon *m*.

bunk [bʌŋk] *n* -1. [bed] couchette *f*. -2. (U) *inf* [nonsense] foutaises *fpl*. -3. *phr*: to do a ~ *inf* mettre les voiles.

bunk bed *n* lit *m* superposé.

bunker ['bʌŋkə*r*] *n* -1. GOLF & MIL bunker *m*. -2. [for coal] coffre *m*.

bunkhouse ['bʌŋkhaʊs, *pl* -haʊzɪz] *n* dortoir *m*.

bunny ['bʌnɪ] (*pl* -ies) *n*: ~ (**rabbit**) lapin *m*.

bunny hill *n* Am SKI piste *f* pour débutants.

Bunsen burner ['bʌnsn-] *n* bec *m* Bunsen.

bunting ['bʌntɪŋ] *n* (U) guirlandes *fpl* (de drapeaux).

buoy [Br bɔɪ, Am 'bu:ɪ] *n* bouée *f*.

◆ **buoy up** *vt sep* [encourage] soutenir.

buoyancy ['bɔɪənsɪ] *n* -1. [ability to float] flottabilité *f*. -2. *fig* [optimism] entrain *m*.

buoyant ['bɔɪənt] *adj* -1. [able to float] qui flotte. -2. *fig* [person] enjoué(e); [economy] florissant(e); [market] ferme.

burden ['bɜːdn] ◇ *n* lit & fig: ~ (**on**) charge *f* (pour), fardeau *m* (pour). ◇ *vt*: to ~ sb with [responsibilities, worries] accabler qqn de.

bureau ['bjʊərəʊ] (*pl* -x) *n* -1. Br [desk] bureau *m*; Am [chest of drawers] commode *f*. -2. [office] bureau *m*. -3. Am POL service *m* (gouvernemental).

bureaucracy [bjʊə'rɒkrəsɪ] (*pl* -ies) *n* bureaucratie *f*.

bureaucrat ['bjʊərəkræt] *n* bureaucrate *mf*.

bureaucratic [,bjʊərə'krætɪk] *adj* bureaucratique.

bureaux ['bjʊərəʊz] *pl* → **bureau**.

burger ['bɜːgə*r*] *n* hamburger *m*.

burglar ['bɜːglə*r*] *n* cambrioleur *m*, -euse *f*.

burglar alarm *n* système *m* d'alarme.

burglarize Am = **burgle**.

burglary ['bɜːglərɪ] (*pl* -ies) *n* cambriolage *m*.

burgle ['bɜːgl], **burglarize** Am ['bɜːgləraɪz] *vt* cambrioler.

Burgundy ['bɜːgəndɪ] *n* Bourgogne *f*; **in** ~ en Bourgogne.

burial ['berɪəl] *n* enterrement *m*.

burial ground *n* cimetière *m*.

burk [bɜːk] *n* Br *inf* idiot *m*, -e *f*.

Burkina Faso [bɜː,kiːnə'fæsəʊ] *n* Burkina *m*; **in** ~ au Burkina.

burly ['bɜːlɪ] (*compar* -ier, *superl* -iest) *adj* bien charpenté(e).

Burma ['bɜːmə] *n* Birmanie *f*.

Burmese [,bɜːmiːz] ◇ *adj* birman(e). ◇ *n* -1. [person] Birman *m*, -e *f*. -2. [language] birman *m*.

burn [bɜːn] (*pt* & *pp* **burnt** OR **-ed**) ◇ *vt* brûler; to ~ o.s. se brûler; I've ~ed my hand je me suis brûlé la main. ◇ *vi* brûler; my skin ~s easily j'attrape facilement des coups de soleil; to ~ with *fig* brûler de. ◇ *n* brûlure *f*.

◆ **burn down** ◇ *vt sep* [building, town] incendier. ◇ *vi* -1. [building] brûler complètement. -2. [fire] baisser d'intensité.

◆ **burn out** ◇ *vt sep* [exhaust]: to ~ o.s. out s'user. ◇ *vi* [fire] s'éteindre.

◆ **burn up** ◇ *vt sep* [fuel] brûler. ◇ *vi* [satellite] se désintégrer (sous l'effet de la chaleur).

burner ['bɜːnə*r*] *n* brûleur *m*.

burning ['bɜːnɪŋ] *adj* -1. [on fire] en flammes. -2. [very hot] brûlant(e); [cheeks, face] en feu. -3. [passion, desire] ardent(e); [interest] passionné(e); ~ **question** question *f* brûlante.

burnish ['bɜːnɪʃ] *vt* astiquer, polir.

Burns' Night *n* fête célébrée en l'honneur du poète écossais Robert Burns, le 25 janvier.

burnt [bɜːnt] *pt* & *pp* → **burn**.

burnt-out *adj* -1. [building, car etc] détruit(e) (par le feu). -2. *fig* [person] usé(e).

burp [bɜːp] *inf* ◇ *n* rot *m*. ◇ *vi* roter.

burrow ['bʌrəʊ] ◇ *n* terrier *m*. ◇ *vi* -1. [dig] creuser un terrier. -2. *fig* [search] fouiller.

bursar ['bɜːsə*r*] *n* intendant *m*, -e *f*.

bursary ['bɜːsərɪ] (*pl* -ies) *n* Br [scholarship, grant] bourse *f*.

burst [bɜːst] (*pt* & *pp* **burst**) ◇ *vi* -1. [gen] éclater. -2. [door, lid]: to ~ open ouvrir violemment. ◇ *vt* faire éclater. ◇ *n* [of gunfire] rafale *f*; [of enthusiasm] **élan** *m*; **a ~ of applause** un tonnerre d'applaudissements.

◆ **burst into** *vt fus* **-1.** [room] faire irruption dans. **-2.** [begin suddenly]: **to ~ into tears** fondre en larmes; **to ~ into song** se mettre tout d'un coup à chanter; **to ~ into flames** prendre feu.

◆ **burst out** *vt fus* [say suddenly] s'exclamer; **to ~ out laughing** éclater de rire; **to ~ out crying** fondre en larmes.

bursting ['bɜːstɪŋ] *adj* **-1.** [full] plein(e), bourré(e). **-2.** [with emotion]: **~ with** débordé(e) de. **-3.** [eager]: **to be ~ to do sthg** mourir d'envie de faire qqch.

Burundi [bʊ'rʊndɪ] *n* Burundi *m*; **in ~** au Burundi.

bury ['berɪ] (*pt & pp* **-ied**) *vt* **-1.** [in ground] enterrer; **to ~ o.s. in sthg** *fig* se plonger dans qqch. **-2.** [hide] cacher, enfouir.

bus [bʌs] *n* autobus *m*, bus *m*; [long-distance] car *m*; **by ~** en autobus/car.

bus conductor *n* receveur *m*, -euse *f* d'autobus.

bus driver *n* conducteur *m*, -trice *f* d'autobus.

bush [bʊʃ] *n* **-1.** [plant] buisson *m*. **-2.** [open country]: **the ~** la brousse. **-3.** *phr*: **she doesn't beat about the ~** elle n'y va pas par quatre chemins.

bushel ['bʊʃl] *n* boisseau *m*.

bushy ['bʊʃɪ] (*compar* **-ier**, *superl* **-iest**) *adj* touffu(e).

business ['bɪznɪs] ◇ *n* **-1.** (*U*) [commerce] affaires *fpl*; **we do a lot of ~ with them** nous travaillons beaucoup avec eux; **she's in the publishing ~** elle est dans l'édition; **on ~** pour affaires; **to mean ~** *inf* ne pas plaisanter; **to go out of ~** fermer, faire faillite. **-2.** [company, duty] affaire *f*; **he had no ~ to tell you that** ce n'était pas à lui de vous le dire; **mind your own ~!** *inf* occupe-toi de tes oignons! **-3.** [affair, matter] histoire *f*, affaire *f*. ◇ *comp* [meeting] d'affaires; **~ hours** heures *fpl* ouvrables.

business address *n* adresse *f* de travail.

business card *n* carte *f* de visite.

business class *n* classe *f* affaires.

businesslike ['bɪznɪslaɪk] *adj* efficace.

businessman ['bɪznɪsmæn] (*pl* **-men** [-men]) *n* homme *m* d'affaires.

business school *n* école *f* de commerce.

business trip *n* voyage *m* d'affaires.

businesswoman ['bɪznɪs,wʊmən] (*pl* **-women** [-,wɪmɪn]) *n* femme *f* d'affaires.

busker ['bʌskər] *n Br* chanteur *m*, -euse *f* des rues.

bus lane *n* voie *f* des bus.

bus-shelter *n* abri-bus *m*.

bus station *n* gare *f* routière.

bus stop *n* arrêt *m* de bus.

bust [bʌst] (*pt & pp* **bust** OR **-ed**) ◇ *adj inf* **-1.** [broken] foutu(e). **-2.** [bankrupt]: **to go ~** faire faillite. ◇ *n* **-1.** [bosom] poitrine *f*. **-2.** [statue] buste *m*. **-3.** *police sl* [raid] descente *f*. ◇ *vt* **-1.** [break] péter. **-2.** *police sl* [arrest] arrêter; [raid] faire une descente à.

bustle ['bʌsl] ◇ *n* (*U*) [activity] remueménage *m*. ◇ *vi* s'affairer.

bustling ['bʌslɪŋ] *adj* [place] qui bourdonne d'activité.

bust-up *n inf* **-1.** [quarrel] engueulade *f*. **-2.** [of marriage, relationship] rupture *f*.

busy ['bɪzɪ] (*compar* **-ier**, *superl* **-iest**) ◇ *adj* **-1.** [gen] occupé(e); **to be ~ doing sthg** être occupé à faire qqch. **-2.** [life, week] chargé(e); [town, office] animé(e). **-3.** TELEC [engaged] occupé(e). ◇ *vt*: **to ~ o.s. (doing sthg)** s'occuper (à faire qqch).

busybody ['bɪzɪ,bɒdɪ] (*pl* **-ies**) *n pej* mouche *f* du coche.

busy signal *n Am* TELEC tonalité *f* «occupé».

but [bʌt] ◇ *conj* mais; **I'm sorry, ~ I don't agree** je suis désolé, mais je ne suis pas d'accord; **~ now let's talk about you** mais parlons plutôt de toi.
◇ *prep* sauf, excepté; **everyone was at the party ~ Jane** tout le monde était à la soirée sauf Jane; **he has no one ~ himself to blame** il ne peut s'en prendre qu'à lui-même.
◇ *adv fml* seulement, ne ... que; **had I known!** si j'avais su!; **we can ~ try** on peut toujours essayer; **she has ~ recently joined the firm** elle n'est entrée dans la société que depuis peu.

◆ **but for** *prep* sans; **~ for her** sans elle.

◆ **but then** *adv* mais; **... ~ then I've known him for years** ... mais il faut dire OR il est vrai que je le connais depuis des années.

butane ['bjuːteɪn] *n* butane *m*.

butch [bʊtʃ] *adj inf* [woman] hommasse.

butcher ['bʊtʃər] ◇ *n* boucher *m*; **~'s (shop)** boucherie *f*. ◇ *vt* **-1.** [animal] abattre. **-2.** *fig* [massacre] massacrer.

butchery ['bʊtʃərɪ] *n lit & fig* boucherie *f*.

butler ['bʌtlər] *n* maître *m* d'hôtel (*chez un particulier*).

butt [bʌt] ◇ *n* **-1.** [of cigarette, cigar] mégot *m*. **-2.** [of rifle] crosse *f*. **-3.** [for water] tonneau *m.* **-4.** [of joke, criticism] cible *f.* ◇ *vt* donner un coup de tête à.

◆ **butt in** *vi* [interrupt]: **to ~ in on sb** interrompre qqn; **to ~ in on sthg** s'immiscer OR s'imposer dans qqch.

butter ['bʌtər] ◇ *n* beurre *m*; **~ wouldn't melt in her mouth** *inf* on lui donnerait le bon Dieu sans confession. ◇ *vt* beurrer.

◆ **butter up** *vt sep inf* passer de la pommade à.

butter bean *n* haricot *m* beurre.

buttercup ['bʌtəkʌp] *n* bouton *m* d'or.

butter dish *n* beurrier *m*.

buttered ['bʌtəd] *adj* [bread] beurré(e).

butterfingers ['bʌtə,fiŋgəz] (*pl inv*) *n inf* maladroit *m*, -e *f*.

butterfly ['bʌtəflaɪ] (*pl* **-ies**) *n* SWIMMING & ZOOL papillon *m*; **to have butterflies in one's stomach** avoir le trac.

buttermilk ['bʌtəmɪlk] *n* babeurre *m*.

butterscotch ['bʌtəskɒtʃ] *n* caramel *m* dur.

buttocks ['bʌtəks] *npl* fesses *fpl*.

button ['bʌtn] ◇ *n* **-1.** [gen] bouton *m*. **-2.** *Am* [badge] badge *m*. ◇ *vt* = **button up**.

◆ **button up** *vt sep* boutonner.

buttonhole ['bʌtnhəʊl] ◇ *n* **-1.** [hole] boutonnière *f*. **-2.** *Br* [flower] fleur *f* à la boutonnière. ◇ *vt inf* coincer.

button mushroom *n* champignon *m* de Paris.

buttress ['bʌtrɪs] ◇ *n* contrefort *m*. ◇ *vt* [wall] soutenir, étayer.

buxom ['bʌksəm] *adj* bien en chair.

buy [baɪ] (*pt & pp* **bought**) ◇ *vt* acheter. ◇ *n*: **a good ~** une bonne affaire.

◆ **buy in** *vt sep Br* stocker.

◆ **buy into** *vt fus* acquérir des parts dans.

◆ **buy off** *vt sep*: **to ~ sb off** acheter le silence de qqn.

◆ **buy out** *vt sep* **-1.** COMM racheter la part de. **-2.** [from army]: **to ~ o.s. out** se racheter.

◆ **buy up** *vt sep* acheter en masse.

buyer ['baɪər] *n* acheteur *m*, -euse *f*.

buyer's market *n* marché *m* acheteur.

buyout ['baɪaʊt] *n* rachat *m*.

buzz [bʌz] ◇ *n* **-1.** [of insect] bourdonnement *m*. **-2.** *inf* [telephone call]: **to give sb a ~** passer un coup de fil à qqn. ◇ *vi*: **to ~ (with)** bourdonner (de). ◇ *vt* [on intercom] appeler.

◆ **buzz off** *vi Br inf*: **~ off!** file!, fous le camp!

buzzard ['bʌzəd] *n* **-1.** *Br* [hawk] buse *f*. **-2.** *Am* [vulture] urubu *m*.

buzzer ['bʌzər] *n* sonnerie *f*.

buzzing ['bʌzɪŋ] *n* [of insect] bourdonnement *m*; [of machine] ronronnement *m*.

buzzword ['bʌzwɜːd] *n inf* mot *m* à la mode.

by [baɪ] ◇ *prep* **-1.** [indicating cause, agent] par; **caused/written/killed ~** causé/écrit/tué par. **-2.** [indicating means, method, manner]: **to dine ~ candlelight** dîner aux chandelles; **to pay ~ cheque** payer par chèque; **to travel ~ bus/train/plane/ship** voyager en bus/par le train/en avion/en bateau; **he's a lawyer ~ profession** il est avocat de son métier; **~ doing sthg** en faisant qqch; **~ nature** de nature, de tempérament. **-3.** [to explain a word or expression] par; **what do you mean ~ "all right"?** qu'est-ce que tu veux dire par «très bien»? **-4.** [beside, close to] près de; **~ the sea** au bord de la mer; **I sat ~ her bed** j'étais assis à son chevet. **-5.** [past]: **to pass ~ sb/sthg** passer devant qqn/qqch; **to drive by sb/sthg** passer en voiture devant qqn/qqch. **-6.** [via, through] par; **come in ~ the back door** entrez par la porte de derrière. **-7.** [at or before a particular time] avant, pas plus tard que; **I'll be there ~ eight** j'y serai avant huit heures; **~ 1914 it was all over** en 1914 c'était fini; **~ now** déjà. **-8.** [during]: **~ day** le OR de jour; **~ night** la OR de nuit. **-9.** [according to] selon, suivant; **~ law** conformément à la loi. **-10.** [in arithmetic] par; **divide/multiply 20 ~ 2** divisez/multipliez 20 par 2. **-11.** [in measurements]: **2 metres ~ 4** 2 mètres sur 4. **-12.** [in quantities, amounts] à; **~ the yard** au mètre; **~ the thousands** par milliers; **paid ~ the day/week/month** payé à la journée/à la semaine/au mois; **to cut prices ~ 50%** réduire les prix de 50%. **-13.** [indicating gradual change]: **week ~ week** de semaine en semaine; **day ~ day** jour après jour, de jour en jour; **one ~ one** un à un, un par un. **-14.** *phr*: **(all) ~ oneself** (tout) seul ((toute) seule); **I'm all ~ myself today** je suis tout seul aujourd'hui.

◇ *adv* → **go, pass, walk** *etc.*

bye(-bye) [baɪ(-baɪ)] *excl inf* au revoir!, salut!

bye-election = **by-election**.

byelaw ['baɪlɔː] = **bylaw**.

by-election *n* élection *f* partielle.

Byelorussia [bɪ,eləʊ'rʌʃə] = **Belorussia**.

bygone ['baɪgɒn] *adj* d'autrefois.

◆ **bygones** *npl*: **to let ~s be ~s** oublier le passé.

bylaw ['baɪlɔː] *n* arrêté *m*.

by-line *n* PRESS signature *f*.

bypass ['baɪpɑːs] ◇ n -**1.** [road] route f de contournement. -**2.** MED: ~ **(operation)** pontage m. ◇ vt [town, difficulty] contourner; [subject] éviter.

by-product n -**1.** [product] dérivé m. -**2.** fig [consequence] conséquence f.

bystander ['baɪˌstændə'] n spectateur m, -trice f.

byte [baɪt] n COMPUT octet m.

byword ['baɪwɜːd] n [symbol]: **to be a ~ for** être synonyme de.

C

c¹ (pl **c's** OR **cs**), **C** (pl **C's** OR **Cs**) [siː] n [letter] c m inv, C m inv.

◆ **C** n -**1.** MUS do m. -**2.** SCH [mark] C m inv. -**3.** (abbr of **celsius, centigrade**) C.

c² [siː] -**1.** (abbr of **century**) s. -**2.** (abbr of **cent(s)**) ct.

c., ca. abbr of **circa**.

c/a -**1.** abbr of **credit account**. -**2.** abbr of **current account**.

CA ◇ n -**1.** abbr of **chartered accountant**. -**2.** (abbr of **Consumers' Association**) union de défense des consommateurs. ◇ -**1.** abbr of **Central America**. -**2.** abbr of **California**.

CAA n -**1.** (abbr of **Civil Aviation Authority**) direction britannique de l'aviation civile. -**2.** (abbr of **Civil Aeronautics Authority**) direction américaine de l'aviation civile.

cab [kæb] n -**1.** [taxi] taxi m. -**2.** [of lorry] cabine f.

CAB (abbr of **Citizens' Advice Bureau**) n service britannique d'information et d'aide au consommateur.

cabaret ['kæbəreɪ] n cabaret m.

cabbage ['kæbɪdʒ] n [vegetable] chou m.

cabbie, cabby ['kæbɪ] n inf chauffeur m de taxi.

caber ['keɪbə'] n Scot: **tossing the ~** le lancement du tronc (épreuve des 'Highland Games').

cabin ['kæbɪn] n -**1.** [on ship, plane] cabine f. -**2.** [house] cabane f.

cabin class n seconde classe f.

cabin cruiser n bateau m de croisière.

cabinet ['kæbɪnɪt] n -**1.** [cupboard] meuble m. -**2.** POL cabinet m.

cabinet-maker n ébéniste m.

cabinet minister n ministre m.

cable ['keɪbl] ◇ n câble m. ◇ vt [news] câbler; [person] câbler à.

cable car n téléphérique m.

cablegram ['keɪblgræm] n câblogramme m.

cable railway n funiculaire m.

cable television, cable TV n télévision f par câble.

caboodle [kə'buːdl] n inf: **the whole ~** et tout le tremblement.

cache [kæʃ] ◇ n -**1.** [store] cache f. -**2.** COMPUT mémoire-cache f, antémémoire f. ◇ vt COMPUT stocker dans la mémoire-cache.

cachet ['kæʃeɪ] n cachet m.

cackle ['kækl] ◇ n -**1.** [of hen] caquet m. -**2.** [of person] jacassement m. ◇ vi -**1.** [hen] caqueter. -**2.** [person] jacasser.

cacophony [kæ'kɒfənɪ] n cacophonie f.

cactus ['kæktəs] (pl -**tuses** OR -**ti** ['kæktaɪ]) n cactus m.

CAD (abbr of **computer-aided design**) n CAO f.

caddie ['kædɪ] ◇ n caddie m. ◇ vi: **to ~ for sb** servir de caddie à qqn.

caddy ['kædɪ] (pl -**ies**) n boîte f à thé.

cadence ['keɪdəns] n [of voice] intonation f.

cadet [kə'det] n élève m officier.

cadge [kædʒ] Br inf ◇ vt: **to ~ sthg off** OR **from sb** taper qqn de qqch. ◇ vi: **to ~ off** OR **from sb** taper qqn.

Cadiz [kə'dɪz] n Cadix.

Caesar ['siːzə'] n César m.

caesarean (section) Br, **cesarean (section)** Am [sɪ'zeərɪən-] n césarienne f.

CAF (abbr of **cost and freight**) C et F.

cafe, café ['kæfeɪ] n café m.

cafeteria [ˌkæfɪ'tɪərɪə] n cafétéria f.

caffeine ['kæfiːn] n caféine f.

cage [keɪdʒ] n [for animal] cage f.

caged [keɪdʒd] adj en cage.

cagey ['keɪdʒɪ] (compar -**ier**, superl -**iest**) adj inf discret(ète).

cagoule [kə'guːl] n Br K-way® m inv.

cahoots [kə'huːts] n inf: **to be in ~ (with)** être de mèche (avec).

CAI (abbr of **computer-aided instruction**) n EAO m.

cairn [keən] n [pile of rocks] cairn m.

Cairo ['kaɪrəʊ] n Le Caire.

cajole [kə'dʒəʊl] vt: **to ~ sb (into doing sthg)** enjôler qqn (pour qu'il fasse qqch).

cake ['keɪk] n -1. CULIN gâteau m; [of fish, potato] croquette f; **it's a piece of** ~ inf fig c'est du gâteau; **to sell like hot** ~**s** se vendre comme des petits pains; **you can't have your** ~ **and eat it** on ne peut pas avoir le beurre et l'argent du beurre. -2. [of soap] pain m.

caked ['keɪkt] adj: ~ **with mud** recouvert(e) de boue séchée.

cake tin Br, **cake pan** Am n moule m à gâteau.

cal [kæl] (abbr of **calorie**) n cal.

calamine lotion ['kæləmaɪn-] n (U) lotion f à la calamine.

calamitous [kə'læmɪtəs] adj catastrophique.

calamity [kə'læmətɪ] (pl -ies) n calamité f.

calcium ['kælsɪəm] n calcium m.

calculate ['kælkjuleɪt] vt -1. [result, number] calculer; [consequences] évaluer. -2. [plan]: **to be** ~**d to do sthg** être calculé(e) pour faire qqch.

◆ **calculate on** vi: **to** ~ **on sthg** compter sur qqch; **to** ~ **on doing sthg** compter faire qqch.

calculated ['kælkjuleɪtɪd] adj calculé(e).

calculating ['kælkjuleɪtɪŋ] adj pej calculateur(trice).

calculation [,kælkju'leɪʃn] n calcul m.

calculator ['kælkjuleɪtə'] n calculatrice f.

calculus ['kælkjuləs] n calcul m.

calendar ['kælɪndə'] n calendrier m.

calendar month n mois m (de calendrier).

calendar year n année f civile.

calf [kɑːf] (pl **calves**) n -1. [of cow, leather] veau m; [of elephant] éléphanteau m; [of seal] bébé m phoque. -2. ANAT mollet m.

caliber Am = **calibre**.

calibrate ['kælɪbreɪt] vt [scale] étalonner; [gun] calibrer.

calibre, caliber Am ['kælɪbə'] n calibre m.

calico ['kælɪkəu] n calicot m.

California [,kælɪ'fɔːnjə] n Californie f; **in** ~ en Californie.

Californian [,kælɪ'fɔːnjən] ◇ adj californien(ienne). ◇ n Californien m, -ienne f.

calipers Am = **callipers**.

call [kɔːl] ◇ n -1. [cry] appel m, cri m. -2. TELEC appel m (téléphonique); **I'll give you a** ~ je t'appellerai. -3. [summons, invitation] appel m; **to be on** ~ [doctor etc] être de garde. -4. [visit] visite f; **to pay a** ~ **on sb** rendre visite à qqn. -5. [demand]: ~ **(for)** demande f (de). ◇ vt -1. [name, summon, phone] appeler; **what's this thing** ~**ed**? comment ça s'appelle ce truc?; **she's** ~**ed** Joan elle s'appelle Joan; **let's** ~ **it £10** disons 10 livres. -2. [label]: **he** ~**ed me a liar** il m'a traité de menteur. -3. [shout] appeler, crier. -4. [announce - meeting] convoquer; [- strike] lancer; [- flight] appeler; [- election] annoncer. ◇ vi -1. [shout - person] crier; [- animal, bird] pousser un cri/des cris. -2. TELEC appeler; **who's** ~**ing**? qui est à l'appareil? -3. [visit] passer.

◆ **call back** ◇ vt sep rappeler. ◇ vi -1. TELEC rappeler. -2. [visit again] repasser.

◆ **call by** vi inf passer.

◆ **call for** vt fus -1. [collect - person] passer prendre; [- package, goods] passer chercher. -2. [demand] demander.

◆ **call in** ◇ vt sep -1. [expert, police etc] faire venir. -2. COMM [goods] rappeler; FIN [loan] exiger le remboursement de. ◇ vi passer.

◆ **call off** vt sep -1. [cancel] annuler; **to** ~ **off a strike** rapporter un ordre de grève. -2. [dog] rappeler.

◆ **call on** vt fus -1. [visit] passer voir. -2. [ask]: **to** ~ **on sb to do sthg** demander à qqn de faire qqch.

◆ **call out** ◇ vt sep -1. [police, doctor] appeler. -2. [order to strike]: **they** ~**ed the workers out** ils ont donné la consigne de grève aux ouvriers. -3. [cry out] crier. ◇ vi [cry out] crier.

◆ **call round** vi passer.

◆ **call up** vt sep -1. MIL & TELEC appeler. -2. COMPUT rappeler.

call box n Br cabine f (téléphonique).

caller ['kɔːlə'] n -1. [visitor] visiteur m, -euse f. -2. TELEC demandeur m.

call girl n call-girl f.

calligraphy [kə'lɪgrəfɪ] n calligraphie f.

call-in n Am RADIO & TV programme m à ligne ouverte.

calling ['kɔːlɪŋ] n -1. [profession] métier m. -2. [vocation] vocation f.

calling card n Am carte f de visite.

callipers Br, **calipers** Am ['kælɪpəz] npl -1. MATH compas m. -2. MED appareil m orthopédique.

callous ['kæləs] adj dur(e).

callously ['kæləslɪ] adv durement.

callousness ['kæləsnɪs] n dureté f.

call-up n Br ordre m de mobilisation.

callus ['kæləs] (pl -es) n cal m, durillon m.

calm [kɑːm] ◇ adj calme. ◇ n calme m. ◇ vt calmer.

◆ **calm down** ◇ vt sep calmer. ◇ vi se calmer.

calmly ['kɑːmlɪ] adv calmement.

calmness ['kɑːmnɪs] n calme m.

Calor gas® ['kælə-] *n Br* butane *m*.

calorie ['kælərɪ] *n* calorie *f*.

calorific [,kælə'rɪfɪk] *adj* calorifique.

calve [kɑ:v] *vi* vêler.

calves [kɑ:vz] *pl* → **calf**.

cam [kæm] *n* came *f*.

CAM (*abbr of* **computer-aided manufactur-ing**) *n* FAO *f*.

camaraderie [,kæmə'rɑ:dərɪ] *n* camaraderie *f*.

camber ['kæmbə-] *n* [of road] bombement *m*.

Cambodia [kæm'bəʊdjə] *n* Cambodge *m*; **in ~** au Cambodge.

Cambodian [kæm'bəʊdjən] ◇ *adj* cambod-gien(ienne). ◇ *n* Cambodgien *m*, -ienne *f*.

Cambs (*abbr of* **Cambridgeshire**) *comté an-glais*.

camcorder ['kæm,kɔːdə-] *n* Caméscope® *m*.

came [keɪm] *pt* → **come**.

camel ['kæml] ◇ *adj* ocre (*inv*). ◇ *n* cha-meau *m*.

camellia [kə'mi:ljə] *n* camélia *m*.

cameo ['kæmɪəʊ] (*pl* -s) *n* **-1.** [jewellery] ca-mée *m*. **-2.** CINEMA & THEATRE courte appari-tion *f* (d'une grande vedette).

camera ['kæmərə] *n* PHOT appareil-photo *m*; CINEMA & TV caméra *f*; **video ~** caméra vi-déo.
◆ **in camera** *adv* à huis clos.

cameraman ['kæmərəmæn] (*pl* -**men** [-men]) *n* caméraman *m*.

Cameroon [,kæmə'ru:n] *n* Cameroun *m*; **in ~** au Cameroun.

Cameroonian [,kæmə'ru:nɪən] ◇ *adj* came-rounais(e). ◇ *n* Camerounais *m*, -e *f*.

camisole ['kæmɪsəʊl] *n* camisole *f*.

camomile ['kæməmaɪl] ◇ *n* camomille *f*. ◇ *comp*: **~ tea** infusion *f* de camomille.

camouflage ['kæmflɑ:ʒ] ◇ *n* camouflage *m*. ◇ *vt* camoufler.

camp [kæmp] ◇ *n* camp *m*. ◇ *vi* camper.
◆ **camp out** *vi* camper.

campaign [kæm'peɪn] ◇ *n* campagne *f*. ◇ *vi*: **to ~ (for/against)** mener une cam-pagne (pour/contre).

campaigner [kæm'peɪnə-] *n* militant *m*, -e *f*.

camp bed *n* lit *m* de camp.

camper ['kæmpə-] *n* **-1.** [person] campeur *m*, -euse *f*. **-2.** [vehicle]: **~ (van)** camping-car *m*.

campground ['kæmpgraʊnd] *n Am* terrain *m* de camping.

camphor ['kæmfə-] *n* camphre *m*.

camping ['kæmpɪŋ] *n* camping *m*; **to go ~** faire du camping.

camping site, **campsite** ['kæmpsaɪt] *n* (ter-rain *m* de) camping *m*.

campus ['kæmpəs] (*pl* -es) *n* campus *m*.

camshaft ['kæmʃɑːft] *n* arbre *m* à cames.

can¹ [kæn] (*pt* & *pp* -**ned**, *cont* -**ning**) ◇ *n* [of drink, food] boîte *f*; [of oil] bidon *m*; [of paint] pot *m*. ◇ *vt* mettre en boîte.

can² [*weak form* kən , *strong form* kæn] (*pt* & *conditional* **could**, *negative* **cannot** OR **can't**) *modal vb* **-1.** [be able to] pouvoir; **~ you come to lunch?** tu peux venir déjeuner?; **she couldn't come elle** n'a pas pu venir; **I ~'t** OR **cannot afford it** je ne peux pas me le payer; **~ you see/hear/smell/something?** tu vois/entends/sens quelque chose? **-2.** [know how to] savoir; **I ~ play the piano** je sais jouer du piano; **~ you drive/cook?** tu sais conduire/cuisiner?; **I ~ speak French** je parle le français. **-3.** [indicating permission, in polite requests] pouvoir; **you ~ use my car if you like** tu peux prendre ma voiture si tu veux; **we ~'t wear jeans to work** on ne peut pas aller au travail en jeans; **~ I speak to John, please** est-ce que je pourrais parler à John, s'il vous plaît? **-4.** [indicating disbelief, puzzlement] pouvoir; **what ~ she have done with it?** qu'est-ce qu'elle a bien pu en faire?; **we ~'t just leave him here ou** ne peut pas tout de même pas le laisser ici; **you ~'t be serious!** tu ne parles pas sérieu-sement! **-5.** [indicating possibility]: **I could see you tomorrow** je pourrais vous voir demain; **the train could have been can-celled** peut-être que le train a été annulé. **-6.** [indicating usual state or behaviour]: **she ~ be a bit difficult sometimes** elle peut par-fois être (un peu) difficile; **Edinburgh ~ be very chilly** il peut faire très froid à Édim-bourg, il arrive qu'il fasse très froid à Édimbourg.

Canada ['kænədə] *n* Canada *m*; **in ~** au Ca-nada.

Canadian [kə'neɪdjən] ◇ *adj* cana-dien(ienne). ◇ *n* Canadien *m*, -ienne *f*.

canal [kə'næl] *n* canal *m*.

Canaries [kə'neərɪz] *npl*: **the ~** les Canaries *fpl*.

canary [kə'neərɪ] (*pl* -ies) *n* canari *m*.

Canary Islands *npl*: **the ~** les îles *fpl* Ca-naries; **in the ~** aux Canaries.

cancan ['kænkæn] *n* cancan *m*.

cancel ['kænsl] (*Br pt* & *pp* -**led**, *cont* -**ling**, *Am pt* & *pp* -**ed**, *cont* -**ing**) *vt* **-1.** [gen] annu-ler; [appointment, delivery] décommander. **-2.** [stamp] oblitérer; [cheque] faire opposi-tion à.

◆ **cancel out** *vt sep* annuler; **to ~ each other out** s'annuler.

cancellation [,kænsə'leɪʃn] *n* annulation *f.*

cancer ['kænsər] ◇ *n* cancer *m.* ◇ *comp*: ~ **patient** cancéreux *m*, -euse *f*; ~ **research** lutte *f* contre le cancer; ~ **ward** service *m* de cancérologie.

◆ **Cancer** *n* Cancer *m*; **to be (a) Cancer** être Cancer.

cancerous ['kænsərəs] *adj* cancéreux(euse).

candelabra [,kændɪ'lɑːbrə] *n* candélabre *m.*

C and F, C & F (*abbr of* **cost and freight**) C et F.

candid ['kændɪd] *adj* franc (franche).

candidacy ['kændɪdəsɪ] *n* candidature *f.*

candidate ['kændɪdət] *n*: ~ **(for)** candidat *m*, -e *f* (pour).

candidature ['kændɪdətʃər] *n* candidature *f.*

candidly ['kændɪdlɪ] *adv* franchement.

candidness ['kændɪdnɪs] = **candour.**

candied ['kændɪd] *adj* confit(e).

candle ['kændl] *n* bougie *f*, chandelle *f*; **to burn the ~ at both ends** *inf* brûler la chandelle par les deux bouts.

candlelight ['kændllaɪt] *n* lueur *f* d'une bougie OR d'une chandelle.

candlelit ['kændlɪt] *adj* aux chandelles.

candlestick ['kændlstɪk] *n* bougeoir *m.*

candour *Br*, **candor** *Am* ['kændər] *n* franchise *f.*

candy ['kændɪ] (*pl* **-ies**) *n* **-1.** (*U*) [confectionery] confiserie *f.* **-2.** [sweet] bonbon *m.*

candyfloss *Br* ['kændɪflɒs] *n* barbe *f* à papa.

cane [keɪn] ◇ *n* **-1.** (*U*) [for furniture] rotin *m.* **-2.** [walking stick] canne *f.* **-3.** [for punishment]: **the ~** la verge. **-4.** [for supporting plant] tuteur *m.* ◇ *comp* en rotin. ◇ *vt* fouetter.

cane sugar *n* sucre *m* de canne.

canine ['keɪnaɪn] ◇ *adj* canin(e). ◇ *n*: ~ **(tooth)** canine *f.*

canister ['kænɪstər] *n* [for film, tea] boîte *f*; [for gas, smoke] bombe *f.*

cannabis ['kænəbɪs] *n* cannabis *m.*

canned [kænd] *adj* **-1.** [food, drink] en boîte. **-2.** *inf fig* [music] enregistré(e); [laughter] préenregistré(e).

cannelloni [,kænɪ'ləʊnɪ] *n* cannelloni *m.*

cannery ['kænərɪ] (*pl* **-ies**) *n* conserverie *f.*

cannibal ['kænɪbl] *n* cannibale *mf.*

cannibalize, -ise ['kænɪbəlaɪz] *vt* cannibaliser.

cannon ['kænən] (*pl inv* OR **-s**) *n* canon *m.*
◆ **cannon into** *vt fus Br* percuter.

cannonball ['kænənbɔːl] *n* boulet *m* de canon.

cannot ['kænɒt] *fml* → **can.**

canny ['kænɪ] (*compar* **-ier**, *superl* **-iest**) *adj* [shrewd] adroit(e).

canoe [kə'nuː] (*pt* & *pp* **-d**, *cont* **canoeing**) ◇ *n* canoë *m*, kayak *m.* ◇ *vi* faire du canoë.

canoeing [kə'nuːɪŋ] *n* (*U*) canoë-kayak *m.*

canon ['kænən] *n* canon *m.*

canonize, -ise ['kænənaɪz] *vt* canoniser.

canoodle [kə'nuːdl] *vi Br inf* se faire des mamours.

can opener *n* ouvre-boîtes *m inv.*

canopy ['kænəpɪ] (*pl* **-ies**) *n* **-1.** [over bed] ciel *m* de lit, baldaquin *m*; [over seat] dais *m.* **-2.** [of trees, branches] voûte *f.*

cant [kænt] *n* (*U*) paroles *fpl* hypocrites.

can't [kɑːnt] = **cannot.**

Cantab. [kæn'tæb] (*abbr of* **cantabrigiensis**) *de l'université de Cambridge.*

Cantabrian Mountains [kæn'teɪbrɪən-] *npl*: **the ~** les monts *mpl* Cantabriques.

cantaloup *Br*, **cantaloupe** *Am* ['kæntəluːp] *n* cantaloup *m.*

cantankerous [kæn'tæŋkərəs] *adj* hargneux(euse).

canteen [kæn'tiːn] *n* **-1.** [restaurant] cantine *f.* **-2.** [box of cutlery] ménagère *f.*

canter ['kæntər] ◇ *n* petit galop *m.* ◇ *vi* aller au petit galop.

Canterbury ['kæntəbrɪ] *n* Cantorbéry.

cantilever ['kæntɪliːvər] *n* cantilever *m.*

Canton [kæn'tɒn] *n* Canton.

Cantonese [,kæntə'niːz] ◇ *adj* cantonais(e). ◇ *n* [language] cantonais *m.*

canvas ['kænvəs] *n* toile *f*; **under ~** [in a tent] sous la tente.

canvass ['kænvəs] ◇ *vt* **-1.** POL [person] solliciter la voix de. **-2.** [opinion] sonder. ◇ *vi* POL solliciter des voix.

canvasser ['kænvəsər] *n* **-1.** POL agent *m* électoral. **-2.** [for opinion poll] sondeur *m*, -euse *f.*

canvassing ['kænvəsɪŋ] *n* **-1.** POL démarchage *m* électoral. **-2.** [for opinion poll] sondage *m.*

canyon ['kænjən] *n* cañon *m.*

cap [kæp] (*pt* & *pp* **-ped**, *cont* **-ping**) ◇ *n* **-1.** [hat - gen] casquette *f*; [swimming ~] bonnet *m* de bain; **to go ~ in hand to sb** se présenter humblement devant qqn. **-2.** [of pen] capuchon *m*; [of bottle] capsule *f*; [of lipstick] bouchon *m.* **-3.** *Br* [contraceptive device] diaphragme *m.* ◇ *vt* **-1.** [top]: **to be capped**

with être coiffé(e) de. **-2.** [outdo]: **to ~ it all** pour couronner le tout.

CAP [kæp, siːeɪ'piː] (abbr of **Common Agricultural Policy**) n PAC f.

capability [ˌkeɪpə'bɪlətɪ] (pl **-ies**) n capacité f.

capable ['keɪpəbl] adj: ~ **(of)** capable (de).

capably ['keɪpəblɪ] adv avec compétence.

capacious [kə'peɪʃəs] adj fml vaste.

capacitor [kə'pæsɪtəʳ] n condensateur m.

capacity [kə'pæsɪtɪ] (pl **-ies**) ◇ n **-1.** (U) [limit] capacité f; contenance f; **full to ~** plein, comble; **to work at full ~** [factory] travailler à plein rendement; **seating ~** nombre m de places (assises). **-2.** [ability]: ~ **(for)** aptitude f (à). **-3.** [role] qualité f; **in my ~ as ...** en ma qualité de ...; **in an advisory ~** en tant que conseiller. ◇ comp: ~ **audience** salle f comble.

cape [keɪp] n **-1.** GEOGR cap m. **-2.** [cloak] cape f.

Cape Canaveral [-kə'nævərəl] n le cap Canaveral.

Cape Cod n le cap Cod.

Cape Horn n le cap Horn.

Cape of Good Hope n: **the ~** le cap de Bonne-Espérance.

caper ['keɪpəʳ] ◇ n **-1.** CULIN câpre f. **-2.** inf [dishonest activity] coup m, combine f. ◇ vi gambader.

Cape Town n Le Cap.

Cape Verde [-'vɜːd] n: **the ~ Islands** les îles fpl du Cap-Vert; **in ~** au Cap-Vert.

capillary [kə'pɪlərɪ] (pl **-ies**) n capillaire m.

capita → **per capita**.

capital ['kæpɪtl] ◇ adj **-1.** [letter] majuscule. **-2.** [offence] capital(e). ◇ n **-1.** [of country]: ~ **(city)** capitale f. **-2.** TYPO: ~ **(letter)** majuscule f; **in ~s** en lettres majuscules. **-3.** (U) [money] capital m; **to make ~ (out) of** fig tirer profit de.

capital allowance n amortissement m fiscal pour investissement.

capital assets npl actif m immobilisé, immobilisations fpl.

capital expenditure n (U) dépenses fpl d'investissement.

capital gains tax n impôt m sur les plus-values.

capital goods npl biens mpl d'équipement.

capital-intensive adj à fort coefficient de capitaux.

capitalism ['kæpɪtəlɪzm] n capitalisme m.

capitalist ['kæpɪtəlɪst] ◇ adj capitaliste. ◇ n capitaliste mf.

capitalize, -ise ['kæpɪtəlaɪz] vi: **to ~ on** tirer parti de.

capital punishment n peine f capitale OR de mort.

capital stock n capital m social.

capital transfer tax n droits mpl de mutation.

Capitol ['kæpɪtl] n: **the ~** le Capitole.

Capitol Hill n siège du Congrès à Washington.

capitulate [kə'pɪtjʊleɪt] vi capituler.

capitulation [kəˌpɪtjʊ'leɪʃn] n capitulation f.

cappuccino [ˌkæpʊ'tʃiːnəʊ] (pl **-s**) n cappuccino m.

capricious [kə'prɪʃəs] adj capricieux(ieuse).

Capricorn ['kæprɪkɔːn] n Capricorne m; **to be (a) ~** être Capricorne.

caps [kæps] (abbr of **capital letters**) npl cap.

capsicum ['kæpsɪkəm] n poivron m.

capsize [kæp'saɪz] ◇ vt faire chavirer. ◇ vi chavirer.

capsule ['kæpsjuːl] n **-1.** [gen] capsule f. **-2.** MED gélule f.

Capt. (abbr of **captain**) cap.

captain ['kæptɪn] ◇ n capitaine m. ◇ vt **-1.** [ship] commander. **-2.** [sports team] être le capitaine de.

caption ['kæpʃn] n légende f.

captivate ['kæptɪveɪt] vt captiver.

captivating ['kæptɪveɪtɪŋ] adj captivant(e).

captive ['kæptɪv] ◇ adj captif(ive). ◇ n captif m, -ive f.

captivity [kæp'tɪvətɪ] n (U): **in ~** en captivité f.

captor ['kæptəʳ] n ravisseur m, -euse f.

capture ['kæptʃəʳ] ◇ vt **-1.** [person, animal] capturer; [city] prendre; [market] conquérir. **-2.** [attention, imagination] captiver. **-3.** [subj: painting, photo] rendre. **-4.** COMPUT saisir. ◇ n [of person, animal] capture f; [of city] prise f.

car [kɑːʳ] ◇ n **-1.** AUT voiture f. **-2.** RAIL wagon m, voiture f. ◇ comp [door, accident] de voiture; [industry] automobile.

Caracas [kə'rækəs] n Caracas.

carafe [kə'ræf] n carafe f.

caramel ['kærəmel] n caramel m.

caramelize, -ise ['kærəməlaɪz] vi se caraméliser.

carat ['kærət] n Br carat m; **24-~ gold** or à 24 carats.

caravan ['kærəvæn] ◇ n [gen] caravane f; [towed by horse] roulotte f. ◇ comp [holiday] en caravane.

caravanning ['kærəvænɪŋ] *n Br* caravaning *m*.

caravan site *n Br* camping *m* pour caravanes.

caraway seed ['kærəweɪ-] *n* graine *f* de carvi.

carbohydrate [,kɑːbəʊ'haɪdreɪt] *n* CHEM hydrate *m* de carbone.

◆ **carbohydrates** *npl* [foods] féculents *mpl*.

carbon ['kɑːbən] *n* **-1.** [element] carbone *m*. **-2.** = carbon copy. **-3.** = carbon paper.

carbonated ['kɑːbəneɪtɪd] *adj* [mineral water] gazeux(euse).

carbon copy *n* **-1.** [document] carbone *m*. **-2.** *fig* [exact copy] réplique *f*.

carbon dating [-'deɪtɪŋ] *n* datation *f* au carbone 14.

carbon dioxide [-daɪ'ɒksaɪd] *n* gaz *m* carbonique.

carbon fibre *n* fibre *f* de carbone.

carbon monoxide *n* oxyde *m* de carbone.

carbon paper *n* (U) (papier *m*) carbone *m*.

car-boot sale *n Br* brocante en plein air où les coffres des voitures servent d'étal.

carburettor *Br*, **carburetor** *Am* [,kɑːbə'retər] *n* carburateur *m*.

carcass ['kɑːkəs] *n* [of animal] carcasse *f*.

carcinogenic [,kɑː'sɪnə'dʒenɪk] *adj* carcinogène.

card [kɑːd] *n* **-1.** [gen] carte *f*; **to play one's ~s right** *fig* bien jouer son jeu; **to put** OR **lay one's ~s on the table** *fig* jouer cartes sur table. **-2.** (U) [cardboard] carton *m*.

◆ **cards** *npl*: **to play ~s** jouer aux cartes.

◆ **on the cards** *Br*, **in the cards** *Am adv inf*: **it's on the ~s that ...** il y a de grandes chances pour que ....

cardamom ['kɑːdəməm] *n* cardamome *f*.

cardboard ['kɑːdbɔːd] ◇ *n* (U) carton *m*. ◇ *comp* en carton.

cardboard box *n* boîte *f* en carton.

card-carrying [-'kærɪŋ] *adj*: **~ member** membre *m*.

card catalog *n Am* fichier *m*.

cardiac ['kɑːdɪæk] *adj* cardiaque.

cardiac arrest *n* arrêt *m* du cœur.

cardigan ['kɑːdɪgən] *n* cardigan *m*.

cardinal ['kɑːdɪnl] ◇ *adj* cardinal(e). ◇ *n* RELIG cardinal *m*.

cardinal number, **cardinal numeral** *n* nombre *m* cardinal.

card index *n Br* fichier *m*.

cardiograph ['kɑːdɪəgrɑːf] *n* cardiographe *m*.

cardiology [,kɑːdɪ'ɒlədʒɪ] *n* cardiologie *f*.

cardiovascular [,kɑːdɪəʊ'væskjʊlər] *adj* cardiovasculaire.

cardsharp ['kɑːd,ʃɑːp] *n* tricheur professionnel *m*, tricheuse professionnelle *f*.

card table *n* table *f* de jeu.

card vote *n Br* vote *m* par carte (*chaque carte comptant pour le nombre de voix d'adhérents représentés*).

care [keər] ◇ *n* **-1.** (U) [protection, attention] soin *m*, attention *f*; **to be in ~** *Br* être à l'Assistance publique; **to take ~ of** [look after] s'occuper de; **to take ~ (to do sthg)** prendre soin (de faire qqch); **take ~!** faites bien attention à vous! **-2.** [cause of worry] souci *m*.

◇ *vi* **-1.** [be concerned] se sentir concerné(e); **to ~ about** se soucier de. **-2.** [mind]: **I don't ~** ça m'est égal; **who ~s?** qu'est-ce que ça peut faire?; **I couldn't ~ less** *inf* je m'en moque pas mal.

◆ **care of** *prep* chez.

◆ **care for** *vt fus dated* [like] aimer.

CARE [keər] (*abbr of* **Cooperative for American Relief Everywhere**) *n* organisation humanitaire américaine.

career [kə'rɪər] ◇ *n* carrière *f*. ◇ *comp* de carrière. ◇ *vi* aller à toute vitesse.

careerist [kə'rɪərɪst] *n pej* carriériste *mf*.

careers [kə'rɪəz] *comp* [office, teacher] d'orientation.

careers adviser *n* conseiller *m*, -ère *f* d'orientation.

career woman *n* femme *f* que suit une carrière.

carefree ['keəfriː] *adj* insouciant(e).

careful ['keəfʊl] *adj* **-1.** [cautious] prudent(e); **to be ~ to do sthg** prendre soin de faire qqch, faire attention à faire qqch; **be ~!** fais attention!; **to be ~ with one's money** regarder à la dépense. **-2.** [work] soigné(e); [worker] consciencieux(ieuse).

carefully ['keəflɪ] *adv* **-1.** [cautiously] prudemment. **-2.** [thoroughly] soigneusement.

careless ['keəlɪs] *adj* **-1.** [work] peu soigné(e); [driver] négligent(e). **-2.** [unconcerned] insouciant(e).

carelessly ['keəlɪslɪ] **-1.** [inattentively] sans faire attention. **-2.** [unconcernedly] avec insouciance.

carelessness ['keəlɪsnɪs] *n* **-1.** [inattention] manque *f* d'attention. **-2.** [lack of concern] insouciance *f*.

carer ['keərə] *n personne qui s'occupe d'un parent malade ou handicapé*.

caress [kə'res] ◇ *n* caresse *f*. ◇ *vt* caresser.

caretaker *Br* ['keə,teɪkə'] *n* gardien *m*, -ienne *f*.

caretaker government *n* gouvernement *m* intérimaire.

car ferry *n* ferry *m*.

cargo ['kɑːgəʊ] (*pl* -es OR -s) ◇ *n* cargaison *m*. ◇ *comp*: ~ **ship** cargo *m*.

car hire *n Br* location *f* de voitures.

Carib ['kærɪb] *n* Caraïbe *mf*.

Caribbean [*Br* kærɪ'biːən, *Am* kə'rɪbɪən] ◇ *adj* caraïbe. ◇ *n*: **the ~ (Sea)** la mer des Caraïbes OR des Antilles; **in the ~** dans les Caraïbes.

caribou ['kærɪbuː] (*pl inv* OR -s) *n* caribou *m*.

caricature ['kærɪkə,tjʊə'] ◇ *n* **-1.** [cartoon] caricature *f*. **-2.** [travesty] parodie *f*. ◇ *vt* caricaturer.

caries ['keəriːz] *n* carie *f*.

caring ['keərɪŋ] *adj* bienveillant(e).

caring professions *npl*: **the ~** les professions *mpl* à but social.

carnage ['kɑːnɪdʒ] *n* carnage *m*.

carnal ['kɑːnl] *adj literary* charnel(elle).

carnation [kɑː'neɪʃn] *n* œillet *m*.

carnival ['kɑːnɪvl] *n* carnaval *m*.

carnivore ['kɑːnɪvɔː'] *n* carnivore *mf*.

carnivorous [kɑː'nɪvərəs] *adj* carnivore.

carol ['kærəl] *n*: **(Christmas) ~** chant *m* de Noël.

carouse [kə'rauz] *vi* faire la fête.

carousel [,kærə'sel] *n* **-1.** [at fair] manège *m*. **-2.** [at airport] carrousel *m*.

carp [kɑːp] (*pl inv* OR -s) ◇ *n* carpe *f*. ◇ *vi*: **to ~ (about sthg)** critiquer (qqch).

Carpathians [kɑː'peɪθɪənz] *npl*: **the ~** les Carpates *fpl*; **in the ~** dans les Carpates.

carpenter ['kɑːpəntə'] *n* [on building site, in shipyard] charpentier *m*; [furniture-maker] menuisier *m*.

carpentry ['kɑːpəntrɪ] *n* [on building site, in shipyard] charpenterie *f*; [furniture-making] menuiserie *f*.

carpet ['kɑːpɪt] ◇ *n* lit & *fig* tapis *m*; **(fitted) ~** moquette *f*; **to sweep sthg under the ~** *fig* tirer le rideau sur qqch. ◇ *vt* [floor] recouvrir d'un tapis; [with fitted carpet] recouvrir de moquette, moquetter; **~ed with snow** *fig* recouvert d'un tapis de neige.

carpet slipper *n* pantoufle *f*.

carpet sweeper *n* balai *m* mécanique.

car phone *n* téléphone *m* pour automobile.

car pool *n Br* [fleet of cars] parc *m* de voitures.

carport ['kɑː,pɔːt] *n* appentis *m* (pour voitures).

car rental *n Am* location *f* de voitures.

carriage ['kærɪdʒ] *n* **-1.** [of train, horsedrawn] voiture *f*. **-2.** (*U*) [transport of goods] transport *m*; **~ paid** OR **free** *Br* franco de port; **~ forward** *Br* en port dû. **-3.** [on typewriter] chariot *m*. **-4.** (*U*) *literary* [bearing] port *m*.

carriage clock *n petite horloge décorative munie d'une anse sur le dessus.*

carriage return *n* retour *m* chariot.

carriageway ['kærɪdʒweɪ] *n Br* chaussée *f*.

carrier ['kærɪə'] *n* **-1.** COMM transporteur *m*. **-2.** [of disease] porteur *m*, -euse *f*. **-3.** MIL: **(aircraft) ~** porte-avions *m inv*. **-4.** [on bicycle] porte-bagages *m inv*. **-5.** = **carrier bag**.

carrier bag *n* sac *m* (en plastique).

carrier pigeon *n* pigeon *m* voyageur.

carrion ['kærɪən] *n* (*U*) charogne *f*.

carrot ['kærət] *n* carotte *f*.

carry ['kærɪ] (*pt* & *pp* -ied) ◇ *vt* **-1.** [subj: person, wind, water] porter; [- subj: vehicle] transporter. **-2.** [disease] transmettre. **-3.** [responsibility] impliquer; [consequences] entraîner; **this offence carries a fine of £50 ce délit entraînera une amende de 50 livres. -4.** [motion, proposal] voter. **-5.** [baby] attendre. **-6.** MATH retenir. ◇ *vi* [sound] porter.

◆ **carry away** *vt fus*: **to get carried away** s'enthousiasmer.

◆ **carry forward** *vt sep* FIN reporter.

◆ **carry off** *vt sep* **-1.** [plan] mener à bien. **-2.** [prize] remporter.

◆ **carry on** ◇ *vt fus* continuer; **to ~ on doing sthg** continuer à OR de faire qqch. ◇ *vi* **-1.** [continue] continuer; **to ~ on with sthg** continuer qqch. **-2.** *inf* [make a fuss] faire des histoires. **-3.** *inf* [have a love affair]: **to ~ on with sb** avoir une liaison avec qqn.

◆ **carry out** *vt fus* [task] remplir; [plan, order] exécuter; [experiment] effectuer; [investigation] mener.

◆ **carry through** *vt sep* [accomplish] réaliser.

carryall ['kærɪɔːl] *n Am* fourre-tout *m inv*.

carrycot ['kærɪkɒt] *n* couffin *m*.

carry-on *n Br inf*: **what a ~!** quelle histoire!

carry-out *n* plat *m* à emporter.

carsick ['kɑː,sɪk] *adj*: **to be ~** être malade en voiture.

cart [kɑːt] ◇ *n* charrette *f*. ◇ *vt inf* traîner.

carte blanche [ˌkɑːtˈblɑ̃ʃ] n carte f blanche.

cartel [kɑːˈtel] n cartel m.

cartilage [ˈkɑːtɪlɪdʒ] n cartilage m.

carton [ˈkɑːtn] n **-1.** [box] boîte f en carton. **-2.** [of cream, yoghurt] pot m; [of milk] carton m.

cartoon [kɑːˈtuːn] n **-1.** [satirical drawing] dessin m humoristique. **-2.** [comic strip] bande f dessinée. **-3.** [film] dessin m animé.

cartoonist [kɑːˈtuːnɪst] n **-1.** [of satirical drawings] dessinateur m, -trice f humoristique. **-2.** [of comic strips] dessinateur m, -trice f de bandes dessinées.

cartridge [ˈkɑːtrɪdʒ] n **-1.** [for gun, pen] cartouche f. **-2.** [for camera] chargeur m. **-3.** [for record player] tête f de lecture.

cartridge paper n papier-cartouche m.

cartwheel [ˈkɑːtwiːl] n [movement] roue f.

carve [kɑːv] ◇ vt **-1.** [wood, stone] sculpter; [design, name] graver. **-2.** [slice - meat] découper. ◇ vi découper.

◆ **carve out** vt sep fig se tailler.

◆ **carve up** vt sep fig diviser.

carving [ˈkɑːvɪŋ] n [of wood] sculpture f; [of stone] ciselure f.

carving knife n couteau m à découper.

car wash n [process] lavage m de voitures; [place] station f de lavage de voitures.

Casablanca [ˌkæsəˈblæŋkə] n Casablanca.

cascade [kæˈskeɪd] ◇ n [waterfall] cascade f. ◇ vi [water] tomber en cascade.

case [keɪs] n **-1.** [gen] cas m; **to be the ~** être le cas; **in ~ of** en cas de; **in that ~** dans ce cas; **in which ~** auquel cas; **as** OR **whatever the ~ may be** selon le cas; **a ~ in point** un bon exemple. **-2.** [argument]: **~ (for/against)** arguments mpl (pour/contre). **-3.** JUR affaire f, procès m. **-4.** [container - gen] caisse f; [- for glasses etc] étui m. **-5.** Br [suitcase] valise f.

◆ **in any case** adv quoi qu'il en soit, de toute façon.

◆ **in case** ◇ conj au cas où. ◇ adv: **(just) in ~** à tout hasard.

case-hardened [-ˈhɑːdnd] adj [person] endurci(e).

case history n MED antécédents mpl.

case study n étude f de cas.

cash [kæʃ] ◇ n (U) **-1.** [notes and coins] liquide m; **to pay (in) ~** payer comptant OR en espèces. **-2.** inf [money] sous mpl, fric m. **-3.** [payment]: **~ in advance** paiement m à l'avance; **~ on delivery** paiement à la livraison. ◇ vt encaisser.

◆ **cash in** vi inf: **to ~ in on** tirer profit de.

cash and carry n libre-service m de gros, cash-and-carry m.

cashbook [ˈkæʃbuk] n livre m de caisse.

cash box n caisse f.

cash card n carte f de retrait.

cash crop n culture f de rapport.

cash desk n Br caisse f.

cash discount n remise f OR rabais m au comptant.

cash dispenser n distributeur m automatique de billets.

cashew (nut) [ˈkæʃuː-] n noix f de cajou.

cash flow n marge f d'auto-financement, cash-flow m.

cashier [kæˈʃɪər] n caissier m, -ière f.

cash machine n distributeur m de billets.

cashmere [kæʃˈmɪər] ◇ n cachemire m. ◇ comp en OR de cachemire.

cash payment n paiement m comptant, versement m en espèces.

cash price n prix m comptant.

cash register n caisse f enregistreuse.

cash sale n vente f au comptant.

casing [ˈkeɪsɪŋ] n revêtement m; TECH boîtier m.

casino [kəˈsiːnəu] (pl -s) n casino m.

cask [kɑːsk] n tonneau m.

casket [ˈkɑːskɪt] n **-1.** [for jewels] coffret m. **-2.** Am [coffin] cercueil m.

Caspian Sea [ˈkæspɪən-] n: **the ~** la (mer) Caspienne.

casserole [ˈkæsərəul] n **-1.** [stew] ragoût m. **-2.** [pan] cocotte f.

cassette [kæˈset] n [of magnetic tape] cassette f; PHOT recharge f.

cassette deck n platine f à cassettes.

cassette player n lecteur m de cassettes.

cassette recorder n magnétophone m à cassettes.

cassock [ˈkæsək] n soutane f.

cast [kɑːst] (pt & pp cast) ◇ n **-1.** [CINEMA & THEATRE - actors] acteurs mpl; [- list of actors] distribution f. ◇ vt **-1.** [throw] jeter; **to ~ doubt on sthg** jeter le doute sur qqch; **to ~ a spell (on)** jeter un sort (à). **-2.** CINEMA & THEATRE donner un rôle à. **-3.** [vote]: **to ~ one's vote** voter. **-4.** [metal] couler; [statue] mouler.

◆ **cast about, cast around** vi: **to ~ about for sthg** chercher qqch.

◆ **cast aside** vt sep fig écarter, rejeter.

◆ **cast off** ◇ vt sep [old practices] se défaire de. ◇ vi NAUT larguer les amarres.

castanets [ˌkæstəˈnets] npl castagnettes fpl.

castaway [ˈkɑːstəweɪ] n naufragé m, -e f.

caste [kɑːst] *n* caste *f*.

caster ['kɑːstər] *n* [wheel] roulette *f*.

caster sugar *n Br* sucre *m* en poudre.

castigate ['kæstɪgeɪt] *vt fml* châtier, punir.

casting ['kɑːstɪŋ] *n* [for film, play] distribution *f*.

casting vote *n* voix *f* prépondérante.

cast iron *n* fonte *f*.

◆ **cast-iron** *adj* **-1.** [made of cast iron] en OR de fonte. **-2.** [will] de fer; [alibi] de béton.

castle ['kɑːsl] *n* **-1.** [building] château *m*. **-2.** CHESS tour *f*.

castoffs ['kɑːstɒfs] *npl* vieilles frusques *fpl*.

castor ['kɑːstər] = **caster**.

castor oil *n* huile *f* de ricin.

castor sugar = **caster sugar**.

castrate [kæ'streɪt] *vt* châtrer.

castration [kæ'streɪʃn] *n* castration *f*.

casual ['kæʒʊəl] *adj* **-1.** [relaxed, indifferent] désinvolte. **-2.** [offhand] sans-gêne. **-3.** [chance] fortuit(e). **-4.** [clothes] décontracté(e), sport (*inv*). **-5.** [work, worker] temporaire.

casually ['kæʒʊəlɪ] *adv* [in a relaxed manner] avec désinvolture; ~ dressed habillé simplement.

casualty ['kæʒjʊəltɪ] (*pl* -ies) *n* **-1.** [dead person] mort *m*, -e *f*; [injured person] blessé *m*, -e *f*; [of road accident] accidenté *m*, -e *f*. **-2.** = **casualty department**.

casualty department *n* service *m* des urgences.

cat [kæt] *n* **-1.** [domestic] chat *m*; **to be like a ~ on hot bricks** *Br* OR **on a hot tin roof** *Am* être sur des charbons ardents; **to let the ~ out of the bag** vendre la mèche; **to put the ~ among the pigeons** *Br* jeter un pavé dans la mare; **to rain ~s and dogs** pleuvoir des cordes; **the ~'s whiskers** *Br* le nombril du monde. **-2.** [wild] fauve *m*.

cataclysmic [ˌkætə'klɪzmɪk] *adj* catastrophique.

catacombs ['kætəkuːmz] *npl* catacombes *fpl*.

Catalan ['kætəˌlæn] ◇ *adj* catalan(e). ◇ *n* **-1.** [person] Catalan *m*, -e *f*. **-2.** [language] catalan *m*.

catalogue *Br*, **catalog** *Am* ['kætəlɒg] ◇ *n* [gen] catalogue *m*; [in library] fichier *m*. ◇ *vt* cataloguer.

Catalonia [ˌkætə'ləʊnɪə] *n* Catalogne *f*; **in ~** en Catalogne.

Catalonian [ˌkætə'ləʊnɪən] ◇ *adj* catalan(e). ◇ *n* [person] Catalan *m*, -e *f*.

catalyst ['kætəlɪst] *n lit* & *fig* catalyseur *m*.

catalytic convertor [ˌkætə'lɪtɪk-] *n* pot *m* catalytique.

catamaran [ˌkætəmə'ræn] *n* catamaran *m*.

catapult ['kætəpʌlt] *Br* ◇ *n* **-1.** [hand-held] lance-pierres *m inv*. **-2.** HISTORY [machine] catapulte *f*. ◇ *vt lit* & *fig* catapulter.

cataract ['kætərækt] *n* cataracte *f*.

catarrh [kə'tɑːr] *n* catarrhe *m*.

catastrophe [kə'tæstrəfɪ] *n* catastrophe *f*.

catastrophic [ˌkætə'strɒfɪk] *adj* catastrophique.

cat burglar *n Br* monte-en-l'air *m inv*.

catcall ['kætkɔːl] *n* sifflet *m*.

catch [kætʃ] (*pt* & *pp* **caught**) ◇ *vt* **-1.** [gen] attraper; **to ~ sight** OR **a glimpse of** apercevoir; **to ~ sb's attention** attirer l'attention de qqn; **to ~ sb's imagination** séduire qqn; **to ~ the post** *Br* arriver à temps pour la levée. **-2.** [discover, surprise] prendre, surprendre; **to ~ sb doing sthg** surprendre qqn à faire qqch. **-3.** [hear clearly] saisir, comprendre. **-4.** [trap]: **I caught my finger in the door** je me suis pris le doigt dans la porte. **-5.** [strike] frapper.
◇ *vi* **-1.** [become hooked, get stuck] se prendre. **-2.** [fire] prendre, partir.
◇ *n* **-1.** [of ball, thing caught] prise *f*. **-2.** [fastener - of box] fermoir *m*; [- of window] loqueteau *m*; [- of door] loquet *m*. **-3.** [snag] hic *m*, entourloupette *f*.

◆ **catch at** *vt fus* attraper, essayer d'attraper.

◆ **catch on** *vi* **-1.** [become popular] prendre. **-2.** *inf* [understand]: **to ~ on (to sthg)** piger (qqch).

◆ **catch out** *vt sep* [trick] prendre en défaut, coincer.

◆ **catch up** ◇ *vt sep* rattraper. ◇ *vi*: **to ~ up on sthg** rattraper qqch.

◆ **catch up with** *vt fus* rattraper.

catch-22 [-twentɪ'tuː] *n*: **it's a ~ situation** on ne peut pas s'en sortir.

catch-all *adj* fourre-tout (*inv*).

catching ['kætʃɪŋ] *adj* contagieux(ieuse).

catchment area ['kætʃmənt-] *n Br* [of school] secteur *m* de recrutement scolaire; [of hospital] circonscription *f* hospitalière.

catchphrase ['kætʃfreɪz] *n* rengaine *f*, scie *f*.

catchword ['kætʃwɜːd] *n* slogan *m*.

catchy ['kætʃɪ] (*compar* -ier, *superl* -iest) *adj* facile à retenir, entraînant(e).

catechism ['kætəkɪzm] *n* catéchisme *m*.

categorical [ˌkætə'gɒrɪkl] *adj* catégorique.

categorically [ˌkætɪ'gɒrɪklɪ] *adv* catégoriquement.

categorize, -ise ['kætəgəraɪz] *vt* [classify]: **to ~ sb (as sthg)** cataloguer qqn (en tant que OR comme).

category ['kætəgərɪ] (*pl* **-ies**) *n* catégorie *f*.

cater ['keɪtər] *vi* [provide food] s'occuper de la nourriture, prévoir les repas.

◆ **cater for** *vt fus Br* **-1.** [tastes, needs] pourvoir à, satisfaire; [customers] s'adresser à. **-2.** [anticipate] prévoir.

◆ **cater to** *vt fus* satisfaire.

caterer ['keɪtərər] *n* traiteur *m*.

catering ['keɪtərɪŋ] *n* [trade] restauration *f*.

caterpillar ['kætəpɪlər] *n* chenille *f*.

caterpillar tracks *npl* chenille *f*.

cat flap *n Br* chatière *f*.

cathedral [kə'θiːdrəl] *n* cathédrale *f*.

catheter ['kæθɪtər] *n* cathéter *m*.

cathode ray tube ['kæθəʊd-] *n* tube *m* cathodique.

Catholic ['kæθlɪk] ◇ *adj* catholique. ◇ *n* catholique *mf*.

◆ **catholic** *adj* [tastes] éclectique.

Catholicism [kə'θɒlɪsɪzm] *n* catholicisme *m*.

catkin ['kætkɪn] *n* chaton *m*.

Catseyes® ['kætsaɪz] *npl Br* catadioptres *mpl*.

catsuit ['kætsuːt] *n Br* combinaison-pantalon *f*.

catsup ['kætsəp] *n Am* ketchup *m*.

cattle ['kætl] *npl* bétail *m*.

cattle grid *n Br* grille incluse dans le sol empêchant le bétail mais non les véhicules de passer.

catty ['kætɪ] (*compar* **-ier**, *superl* **-iest**) *adj inf pej* [spiteful] rosse, vache.

catwalk ['kætwɔːk] *n* passerelle *f*.

Caucasian [kɔː'keɪzjən] ◇ *adj* caucasien(ienne). ◇ *n* **-1.** GEOGR Caucasien *m*, -ienne *f*. **-2.** [white person] Blanc *m*, Blanche *f*.

Caucasus ['kɔːkəsəs] *n*: **the ~** le Caucase.

caucus ['kɔːkəs] *n* **-1.** *Am* POL comité *m* électoral (*d'un parti*). **-2.** *Br* POL comité *m* (*d'un parti*).

CAUCUS:
Les Caucuses aux États-Unis sont d'immenses rassemblements politiques, au cours desquels les deux partis nationaux américains choisissent leurs candidats et définissent leurs objectifs

caught [kɔːt] *pt & pp* → **catch**.

cauliflower ['kɒlɪˌflaʊər] *n* chou-fleur *m*.

causal ['kɔːzl] *adj* causal(e).

cause [kɔːz] ◇ *n* cause *f*; **I have no ~ for complaint** je n'ai pas à me plaindre, je n'ai pas lieu de me plaindre; **to have ~ to do sthg** avoir lieu OR des raisons de faire qqch. ◇ *vt* causer; **to ~ sb to do sthg** faire faire qqch à qqn; **to ~ sthg to be done** faire faire qqch; **to ~ a sensation** faire sensation.

causeway ['kɔːzweɪ] *n* chaussée *f*.

caustic ['kɔːstɪk] *adj* caustique.

caustic soda *n* soude *f* caustique.

cauterize, -ise ['kɔːtəraɪz] *vt* MED cautériser.

caution ['kɔːʃn] ◇ *n* **-1.** (*U*) [care] précaution *f*, prudence *f*. **-2.** [warning] avertissement *m*. **-3.** *Br* JUR réprimande *f*. ◇ *vt* **-1.** [warn]: **to ~ sb against doing sthg** déconseiller à qqn de faire qqch. **-2.** *Br* [subj: policeman] *informer un suspect que tout ce qu'il dira peut être retenu contre lui*; **to ~ sb for sthg** réprimander qqn pour qqch.

cautionary ['kɔːʃənərɪ] *adj* [tale] édifiant(e).

cautious ['kɔːʃəs] *adj* prudent(e).

cautiously ['kɔːʃəslɪ] *adv* avec prudence, prudemment.

cautiousness ['kɔːʃəsnɪs] *n* prudence *f*, circonspection *f*.

cavalier [ˌkævə'lɪər] *adj* [offhand] cavalier(ière).

cavalry ['kævlrɪ] *n* cavalerie *f*.

cave [keɪv] *n* caverne *f*, grotte *f*.

◆ **cave in** *vi* **-1.** [roof, ceiling] s'affaisser. **-2.** [yield]: **to ~ in (to sthg)** capituler OR céder (devant qqch).

caveman ['keɪvmæn] (*pl* **-men** [-men]) *n* homme *m* des cavernes.

cavern ['kævən] *n* caverne *f*.

cavernous ['kævənəs] *adj* [room, building] immense.

caviar(e) ['kævɪɑːr] *n* caviar *m*.

caving ['keɪvɪŋ] *n Br* spéléologie *f*; **to go ~** faire de la spéléologie.

cavity ['kævətɪ] (*pl* **-ies**) *n* cavité *f*.

cavity wall insulation *n Br* isolation *f* des murs creux.

cavort [kə'vɔːt] *vi* gambader.

cayenne (pepper) [keɪ'en-] *n* poivre *m* de cayenne.

CB *n* **-1.** (*abbr of* **citizens' band**) CB *f*. **-2.** (*abbr of* **Companion of (the Order of) the Bath**) *distinction honorifique britannique*.

CBC (*abbr of* **Canadian Broadcasting Cor-**

poration) *n office national canadien de radiodiffusion.*

CBE (*abbr of* **Companion of (the Order of) the British Empire**) *n distinction honorifique britannique.*

CBI *n abbr of* **Confederation of British Industry**.

CBS (*abbr of* **Columbia Broadcasting System**) *n chaîne de télévision américaine.*

cc ◇ *n* (*abbr of* **cubic centimetre**) cm³. ◇ (*abbr of* **carbon copy**) pcc.

CC *n abbr of* **county council**.

CCTV *n abbr of* **closed-circuit television**.

CD ◇ *n* (*abbr of* **compact disc**) CD *m.* ◇ **-1.** *abbr of* **civil defence**. **-2.** (*abbr of* **Corps Diplomatique**) CD.

CDI (*abbr of* **compact disc interactive**) *n* CDI *m.*

CD player *n* lecteur *m* de CD.

Cdr. *abbr of* **commander**.

CD-ROM [ˌsiːdiːˈrɒm] (*abbr of* **compact disc read only memory**) *n* CD-ROM *m,* CD-Rom *m.*

CDT (*abbr of* **Central Daylight Time**) *n heure d'été du centre des États-Unis.*

CDV (*abbr of* **compact disc video**) *n* CD vidéo *m.*

CDW *abbr of* **collision damage waiver**.

CE *abbr of* **Church of England**.

cease [siːs] *fml* ◇ *vt* cesser; **to ~ doing** OR **to do sthg** cesser de faire qqch. ◇ *vi* cesser.

cease-fire *n* cessez-le-feu *m inv.*

ceaseless [ˈsiːslɪs] *adj fml* incessant(e), continuel(elle).

ceaselessly [ˈsiːslɪslɪ] *adv fml* sans arrêt OR cesse, continuellement.

cedar (tree) [ˈsiːdər-] *n* cèdre *m.*

cede [siːd] *vt* céder.

cedilla [sɪˈdɪlə] *n* cédille *f.*

CEEB (*abbr of* **College Entry Examination Board**) *n commission d'admission dans l'enseignement supérieur aux États-Unis.*

Ceefax® [ˈsiːfæks] *n Br* télétexte *m* de la BBC.

ceilidh [ˈkeɪlɪ] *n manifestations informelles avec chants, contes et danses en Écosse et en Irlande.*

ceiling [ˈsiːlɪŋ] *n lit & fig* plafond *m.*

celebrate [ˈselɪbreɪt] ◇ *vt* **-1.** [gen] célébrer, fêter. **-2.** RELIG célébrer. ◇ *vi* faire la fête.

celebrated [ˈselɪbreɪtɪd] *adj* célèbre.

celebration [ˌselɪˈbreɪʃn] *n* **-1.** (*U*) [activity, feeling] fête *f,* festivités *fpl.* **-2.** [event] festivités *fpl.*

celebrity [sɪˈlebrətɪ] (*pl* **-ies**) *n* célébrité *f.*

celeriac [sɪˈlerɪæk] *n* céleri-rave *m.*

celery [ˈselərɪ] *n* céleri *m* (en branches).

celestial [sɪˈlestjəl] *adj* céleste.

celibacy [ˈselɪbəsɪ] *n* célibat *m.*

celibate [ˈselɪbət] *adj* célibataire.

cell [sel] *n* [gen & COMPUT] cellule *f.*

cellar [ˈselər] *n* cave *f.*

cellist [ˈtʃelɪst] *n* violoncelliste *mf.*

cello [ˈtʃeləʊ] (*pl* **-s**) *n* violoncelle *m.*

Cellophane® [ˈseləfeɪn] *n* cellophane® *f.*

cellphone [selfəʊn], **cellular phone** [ˈseljʊlər-] *n* téléphone *m* cellulaire.

cellulite [ˈseljʊlaɪt] *n* cellulite *f.*

Celluloid® [ˈseljʊlɔɪd] *n* celluloïd® *m.*

cellulose [ˈseljʊləʊs] *n* cellulose *f.*

Celsius [ˈselsɪəs] *adj* Celsius (*inv*).

Celt [kelt] *n* Celte *mf.*

Celtic [ˈkeltɪk] ◇ *adj* celte. ◇ *n* [language] celte *m.*

cement [sɪˈment] ◇ *n* ciment *m.* ◇ *vt lit & fig* cimenter.

cement mixer *n* bétonnière *f.*

cemetery [ˈsemɪtrɪ] (*pl* **-ies**) *n* cimetière *m.*

cenotaph [ˈsenətɑːf] *n* cénotaphe *m.*

censor [ˈsensər] ◇ *n* censeur *m.* ◇ *vt* censurer.

censorship [ˈsensəʃɪp] *n* censure *f.*

censure [ˈsenʃər] ◇ *n* blâme *m,* critique *f.* ◇ *vt* blâmer, critiquer.

census [ˈsensəs] (*pl* **censuses**) *n* recensement *m.*

cent [sent] *n* cent *m.*

centenary [senˈtiːnərɪ] *Br* (*pl* **-ies**), **centennial** *Am* [senˈtenjəl] *n* centenaire *m.*

center *Am* = **centre**.

centigrade [ˈsentɪgreɪd] *adj* centigrade.

centigram(me) [ˈsentɪgræm] *n* centigramme *m.*

centilitre *Br,* **centiliter** *Am* [ˈsentɪˌliːtər] *n* centilitre *m.*

centimetre *Br,* **centimeter** *Am* [ˈsentɪˌmiːtər] *n* centimètre *m.*

centipede [ˈsentɪpiːd] *n* mille-pattes *m inv.*

central [ˈsentrəl] *adj* central(e); **~ to essentiel(ielle) à**; **Central Europe** Europe *f* centrale.

Central African ◇ *adj* centrafricain(e). ◇ *n* Centrafricain *m,* -e *f.*

Central African Republic *n*: **the ~** la République centrafricaine; **in the ~** en République centrafricaine.

Central America *n* Amérique *f* centrale; **in ~** en Amérique centrale.

Central American ◇ *adj* centraméricain(e). ◇ *n* Centraméricain *m*, -e *f*.

Central Asia *n* Asie *f* centrale; **in ~** en Asie centrale.

central government *n* gouvernement *m* central.

central heating *n* chauffage *m* central.

centralization [ˌsentrəlaɪˈzeɪʃn] *n* centralisation *f*.

centralize, -ise [ˈsentrəlaɪz] *vt* centraliser.

centralized [ˈsentrəlaɪzd] *adj* centralisé(e).

central locking [-ˈlɒkɪŋ] *n* AUT verrouillage *m* centralisé.

centrally [ˈsentrəlɪ] *adv* centralement.

centrally heated *adj* équipé(e) du chauffage central.

central nervous system *n* système *m* nerveux central.

central processing unit *n* COMPUT unité *f* centrale (de traitement).

central reservation *n* Br AUT terre-plein *m* central.

centre Br, **center** Am [ˈsentər] ◇ *n* centre *m*; **~ of attention** centre d'attraction, point *m* de mire; **~ of gravity** centre de gravité. ◇ *adj* **-1.** [middle] central(e); **a ~ parting** une raie au milieu. **-2.** POL du centre, centriste. ◇ *vt* centrer.

◆ **centre around, centre on** *vt fus* se concentrer sur.

centre back *n* FTBL arrière *m* central.

centre-fold *n* [poster] photo *f* de pin-up.

centre forward *n* FTBL avant-centre *m inv*.

centre half *n* FTBL arrière *m* central.

centrepiece Br, **centerpiece** Am [ˈsentəpiːs] *n* **-1.** [decoration] centre *m* de table. **-2.** *fig* [principal element] élément *m* principal.

centre-spread *n* double page *f* centrale.

centrifugal force [sentrɪˈfjuːgl-] *n* force *f* centrifuge.

century [ˈsentʃurɪ] (*pl* **-ies**) *n* siècle *m*.

CEO (*abbr of* **chief executive officer**) *n* Am directeur-général.

ceramic [sɪˈræmɪk] *adj* en céramique.

◆ **ceramics** *npl* [objects] objets *mpl* en céramique.

cereal [ˈsɪərɪəl] *n* céréale *f*.

cerebral [ˈserɪbrəl] *adj* cérébral(e).

cerebral palsy [ˈserɪbrəl-] *n* paralysie *f* cérébrale.

ceremonial [ˌserɪˈməunjəl] ◇ *adj* [dress] de cérémonie; [duties] honorifique. ◇ *n* cérémonial *m*.

ceremonious [ˌserɪˈməunjəs] *adj* solennel(elle).

ceremony [ˈserɪmənɪ] (*pl* **-ies**) *n* **-1.** [event] cérémonie *f*. **-2.** (*U*) [pomp, formality] cérémonies *fpl*; **without ~** sans cérémonie; **to stand on ~** faire des cérémonies.

cert [sɜːt] *n* Br inf: **it's a (dead) ~** c'est tout ce qu'il y a de sûr, c'est couru.

cert. *abbr of* **certificate**.

certain [ˈsɜːtn] *adj* **-1.** [gen] certain(e); **he is ~ to be late** il est certain qu'il sera en retard, il sera certainement en retard; **to be ~ of sthg/of doing sthg** être assuré de qqch/de faire qqch, être sûr de qqch/de faire qqch; **to make ~** vérifier; **to make ~ of s'**assurer de; **I know for ~ that ...** je suis sûr OR certain que ...; **to a ~ extent** jusqu'à un certain point, dans une certaine mesure. **-2.** [named person]: **a ~ ...** un certain (une certaine) ....

certainly [ˈsɜːtnlɪ] *adv* certainement.

certainty [ˈsɜːtntɪ] (*pl* **-ies**) *n* certitude *f*.

CertEd [sɜːtˈed] (*abbr of* **Certificate in Education**) *n* diplôme universitaire en sciences de l'éducation.

certifiable [ˌsɜːtɪˈfaɪəbl] *adj* [mad] bon (bonne) à enfermer.

certificate [səˈtɪfɪkət] *n* certificat *m*.

certification [ˌsɜːtɪfɪˈkeɪʃn] *n* certification *f*.

certified [ˈsɜːtɪfaɪd] *adj* [teacher] diplômé(e); [document] certifié(e).

certified mail *n* Am envoi *m* recommandé.

certified public accountant *n* Am expert-comptable *m*.

certify [ˈsɜːtɪfaɪ] (*pt* & *pp* **-ied**) *vt* **-1.** [declare true]: **to ~ (that)** certifier OR attester que. **-2.** [give certificate to] diplômer. **-3.** [declare insane] déclarer mentalement aliéné(e); **you should be certified!** on devrait t'enfermer!

cervical [səˈvaɪkl] *adj* [cancer] du col de l'utérus.

cervical smear *n* frottis *m* vaginal.

cervix [ˈsɜːvɪks] (*pl* **-ices** [-ɪsiːz]) *n* col *m* de l'utérus.

cesarean (section) = **caesarean (section)**.

cessation [seˈseɪʃn] *n* cessation *f*.

cesspit [ˈsespɪt], **cesspool** [ˈsespuːl] *n* fosse *f* d'aisance.

CET (*abbr of* **Central European Time**) *n* heure d'Europe centrale.

cf. (*abbr of* **confer**) cf.

c/f *abbr of* **carried forward**.

CFC (*abbr of* **chlorofluorocarbon**) *n* CFC *m*.

cg (*abbr of* **centigram**) cg.

CG *n abbr of* **coastguard**.

C & G (*abbr of* **City and Guilds**) *n* diplôme britannique d'enseignement technique.

CGA (*abbr of* **colour graphics adapter**) *n* adapteur *m* graphique couleur CGA.

CGT *n abbr of* **capital gains tax**.

ch (*abbr of* **central heating**) ch. cent.

ch. (*abbr of* **chapter**) chap.

CH (*abbr of* **Companion of Honour**) *n* distinction honorifique britannique.

Chad [tʃæd] *n* Tchad *m*; **in** ~ au Tchad.

chafe [tʃeɪf] ◇ *vt* [rub] irriter. ◇ *vi* **-1.** [skin] être irrité(e). **-2.** [person]: **to** ~ **at** s'irriter OR s'énerver de.

chaff [tʃɑːf] *n* (*U*) balle *f*.

chaffinch ['tʃæfɪntʃ] *n* pinson *m*.

chain [tʃeɪn] ◇ *n* chaîne *f*; ~ **of events** suite *f* OR série *f* d'événements; ~ **of office** chaîne *f* (*insigne de la fonction de maire*). ◇ *vt* [person, animal] **enchaîner**; [object] **attacher avec une chaîne**.

chain letter *n* chaîne *f*.

chain reaction *n* réaction *f* en chaîne.

chain saw *n* tronçonneuse *f*.

chain-smoke *vi* fumer cigarette sur cigarette.

chain-smoker *n* grand fumeur *m*, grande fumeuse *f*.

chain store *n* grand magasin *m* (*à succursales multiples*).

chair [tʃeəʳ] ◇ *n* **-1.** [gen] chaise *f*; [armchair] fauteuil *m*. **-2.** [university post] chaire *f*. **-3.** [of meeting] présidence *f*; **to take the** ~ présider. ◇ *vt* [meeting] **présider**; [discussion] **diriger**.

chair lift *n* télésiège *m*.

chairman ['tʃeəmən] (*pl* **-men** [-mən]) *n* président *m*.

chairmanship ['tʃeəmənʃɪp] *n* présidence *f*.

chairperson ['tʃeə,pɜːsn] (*pl* **-s**) *n* président *m*, -e *f*.

chairwoman ['tʃeə,wumən] (*pl* **-women** [,wɪmɪn]) *n* présidente *f*.

chaise longue [ʃeɪz'lɒŋ] (*pl* **chaises longues**) *n* méridienne *f*.

chalet ['ʃæleɪ] *n* chalet *m*.

chalice ['tʃælɪs] *n* calice *m*.

chalk [tʃɔːk] *n* craie *f*.
◆ **by a long chalk** *adv* de loin.
◆ **not by a long chalk** *adv* loin s'en faut, loin de là.
◆ **chalk up** *vt sep* [victory, success] remporter.

chalkboard ['tʃɔːkbɔːd] *n* Am tableau *m* (noir).

challenge ['tʃælɪndʒ] ◇ *n* défi *m*. ◇ *vt* **-1.** [to fight, competition]: **she** ~**d me to a race/a game of chess** elle m'a défié à la course/ aux échecs; **to** ~ **sb to do sthg** défier qqn de faire qqch. **-2.** [question] mettre en question OR en doute.

challenger ['tʃælɪndʒəʳ] *n* challenger *m*.

challenging ['tʃælɪndʒɪŋ] *adj* **-1.** [task, job] stimulant(e). **-2.** [look, tone of voice] provocateur(trice).

chamber ['tʃeɪmbəʳ] *n* [gen] chambre *f*.
◆ **chambers** *npl* [of barrister, judge] cabinet *m*.

chambermaid ['tʃeɪmbəmeɪd] *n* femme *f* de chambre.

chamber music *n* musique *f* de chambre.

chamber of commerce *n* chambre *f* de commerce.

chamber orchestra *n* orchestre *m* de chambre.

chameleon [kə'miːljən] *n* caméléon *m*.

chamois¹ ['ʃæmwɑː] (*pl inv*) *n* [animal] chamois *m*.

chamois² ['ʃæmɪ] *n*: ~ **(leather)** peau *f* de chamois.

champ [tʃæmp] ◇ *n inf* champion *m*, -ionne *f*. ◇ *vi* [horse] ronger, mâchonner.

champagne [,ʃæm'peɪn] *n* champagne *m*.

champion ['tʃæmpjən] *n* champion *m*, -ionne *f*.

championship ['tʃæmpjənʃɪp] *n* championnat *m*.

chance [tʃɑːns] ◇ *n* **-1.** (*U*) [luck] hasard *m*; **by** ~ par hasard; **if by any** ~ si par hasard. **-2.** [likelihood] chance *f*; **she didn't stand a** ~ **(of doing sthg)** elle n'avait aucune chance (de faire qqch); **on the off** ~ à tout hasard. **-3.** [opportunity] occasion *f*. **-4.** [risk] risque *m*; **to take a** ~ risquer le coup; **to take a** ~ **on doing sthg** se risquer à faire qqch.
◇ *adj* fortuit(e), accidentel(elle).
◇ *vt* **-1.** [risk] risquer; **to** ~ **it** tenter sa chance. **-2.** *literary* [happen]: **to** ~ **to do sthg** faire qqch par hasard.

chancellor ['tʃɑːnsələʳ] *n* **-1.** [chief minister] chancelier *m*. **-2.** UNIV président *m*, -e *f* honoraire.

Chancellor of the Exchequer *n Br* Chancelier *m* de l'Échiquier, ≃ ministre *m* des finances.

chancy ['tʃɑːnsɪ] (*compar* **-ier**, *superl* **-iest**) *adj inf* [risky] risqué(e).

chandelier [,ʃændə'lɪəʳ] *n* lustre *m*.

change [tʃeɪndʒ] ◇ *n* **-1.** [gen]: ~ **(in sb/in sthg)** changement *m* (en qqn/de qqch); ~

of clothes vêtements *mpl* de rechange; **to make a ~** changer un peu; **for a ~** pour changer (un peu). **-2.** [money] monnaie *f*. ◇ *vt* **-1.** [gen] changer; **to ~ sthg into sthg** changer OR transformer qqch en qqch; **to ~ one's mind** changer d'avis. **-2.** [jobs, trains, sides] changer de; **to ~ hands** COMM changer de main. **-3.** [money - into smaller units] faire la monnaie de; [- into different currency] changer. ◇ *vi* **-1.** [gen] changer. **-2.** [change clothes] se changer; **to ~ into another pair of trousers** changer de pantalon. **-3.** [be transformed]: **to ~ into** se changer en.
◆ **change over** *vi* [convert] passer.

changeable ['tʃeɪndʒəbəl] *adj* [mood] changeable; [weather] variable.

changed [tʃeɪndʒd] *adj* changé(e).

change machine *n* distributeur *m* de monnaie.

change of life *n*: **the ~** le retour *m* d'âge.

changeover ['tʃeɪndʒˌəʊvəʳ] *n*: **~ (to)** passage *m* (à), changement *m* (pour).

change purse *n* Am porte-monnaie *m* inv.

changing ['tʃeɪndʒɪŋ] *adj* changeant(e).

changing room *n* SPORT vestiaire *m*; [in shop] cabine *f* d'essayage.

channel ['tʃænl] (*Br pt & pp* **-led**, *cont* **-ling**, *Am pt & pp* **-ed**, *cont* **-ing**) ◇ *n* **-1.** TV chaîne *f*; RADIO station *f*. **-2.** [for irrigation] canal *m*; [duct] conduit *m*. **-3.** [on river, sea] chenal *m*. ◇ *vt lit & fig* canaliser.
◆ **Channel** *n*: **the (English) Channel** la Manche.
◆ **channels** *npl*: **to go through the proper ~s** suivre OR passer la filière.

Channel Islands *npl*: **the ~** les îles *fpl* Anglo-Normandes; **in the ~** dans les îles Anglo-Normandes.

Channel tunnel *n*: **the ~** le tunnel sous la Manche.

chant [tʃɑːnt] ◇ *n* chant *m*. ◇ *vt* **-1.** RELIG chanter. **-2.** [words, slogan] scander. ◇ *vi* **-1.** RELIG chanter. **-2.** [repeat words] scander des mots/des slogans.

chaos ['keɪɒs] *n* chaos *m*.

chaotic [keɪ'ɒtɪk] *adj* chaotique.

chap [tʃæp] *n* Br inf [man] type *m*.

chapat(t)i [tʃə'pætɪ] *n* galette *f* de pain indienne.

chapel ['tʃæpl] *n* chapelle *f*.

chaperon(e) ['ʃæpərəʊn] ◇ *n* chaperon *m*. ◇ *vt* chaperonner.

chaplain ['tʃæplɪn] *n* aumônier *m*.

chapped [tʃæpt] *adj* [skin, lips] gercé(e).

chapter ['tʃæptəʳ] *n* chapitre *m*.

char [tʃɑːʳ] (*pt & pp* **-red**, *cont* **-ring**) ◇ *n* Br [cleaner] femme *f* de ménage. ◇ *vt* [burn] calciner. ◇ *vi* [work as cleaner] faire des ménages.

character ['kærəktəʳ] *n* **-1.** [gen] caractère *m*; **her behaviour is out of ~** ce comportement ne lui ressemble pas. **-2.** [in film, book, play] personnage *m*. **-3.** *inf* [eccentric] phénomène *m*, original *m*.

character code *n* COMPUT code *m* de caractère.

characteristic [ˌkærəktə'rɪstɪk] ◇ *adj* caractéristique. ◇ *n* caractéristique *f*.

characteristically [ˌkærəktə'rɪstɪklɪ] *adv* de façon caractéristique.

characterization [ˌkærəktəraɪ'zeɪʃn] *n* caractérisation *f*.

characterize, -ise ['kærəktəraɪz] *vt* caractériser.

charade [ʃə'rɑːd] *n* farce *f*.
◆ **charades** *n* charades *fpl*.

charcoal ['tʃɑːkəʊl] *n* [for drawing] charbon *m*; [for burning] charbon de bois.

chard [tʃɑːd] *n* bette *f*, blette *f*.

charge [tʃɑːdʒ] ◇ *n* **-1.** [cost] prix *m*; **free of ~** gratuit; **admission ~** prix d'entrée; **delivery ~** frais *mpl* de port. **-2.** JUR accusation *f*, inculpation *f*. **-3.** [responsibility]: **to take ~ of** se charger de; **to be in ~ of**, **to have ~ of** être responsable de, s'occuper de; **in ~** responsable. **-4.** ELEC & MIL charge *f*.
◇ *vt* **-1.** [customer, sum] faire payer; **they ~ £5 for admission** le prix d'entrée est 5 livres; **how much do you ~?** vous prenez combien?; **to ~ sthg to sb** mettre qqch sur le compte de qqn. **-2.** [suspect, criminal]: **to ~ sb (with)** accuser qqn (de). **-3.** ELEC & MIL charger.
◇ *vi* **-1.** [ask in payment]: **they don't ~ for delivery** ils livrent gratuitement. **-2.** [rush] se précipiter, foncer.

chargeable ['tʃɑːdʒəbl] *adj* **-1.** [costs]: **~ to** à la charge de. **-2.** [offence] qui entraîne une inculpation.

charge account *n* compte *m* crédit.

charge card *n* carte *f* de compte crédit (*auprès d'un magasin*).

charged [tʃɑːdʒd] *adj* [emotional] chargé(e).

charge hand *n* Br chef *m* d'équipe.

charge nurse *n* Br infirmier *m* en chef.

charger ['tʃɑːdʒəʳ] *n* **-1.** [for batteries] chargeur *m*. **-2.** *literary* [soldier's horse] cheval *m* de bataille.

charge sheet *n* Br procès-verbal *m*.

chariot ['tʃærɪət] *n* char *m*.

charisma [kə'rızmə] *n* charisme *m*.

charismatic [ˌkærız'mætık] *adj* charismatique.

charitable ['tʃærətəbl] *adj* **-1.** [person, remark] charitable. **-2.** [organization] de charité.

charity ['tʃærətɪ] (*pl* **-ies**) *n* charité *f*.

charlatan ['ʃɑːlətən] *n* charlatan *m*.

charm [tʃɑːm] ◇ *n* charme *m*. ◇ *vt* charmer.

charm bracelet *n* bracelet *m* à breloques.

charmer ['tʃɑːmə'] *n* charmeur *m*, -euse *f*.

charming ['tʃɑːmɪŋ] *adj* charmant(e).

charmingly ['tʃɑːmɪŋlɪ] *adv* [attractive etc] de façon charmante; [smile, dressed] avec charme.

charred [tʃɑːd] *adj* calciné(e).

chart [tʃɑːt] ◇ *n* **-1.** [diagram] graphique *m*, diagramme *m*. **-2.** [map] carte *f*; **weather ~** carte *f* météorologique. ◇ *vt* **-1.** [plot, map] porter sur une carte. **-2.** *fig* [record] retracer.
◆ **charts** *npl*: **the ~s** le hit-parade.

charter ['tʃɑːtə'] ◇ *n* [document] charte *f*. ◇ *vt* [plane, boat] affréter.

chartered accountant ['tʃɑːtəd-] *n* *Br* expert-comptable *m*.

charter flight *n* vol *m* charter.

chart-topping *adj* *Br* qui est en tête du hit-parade.

chary ['tʃeərɪ] (*compar* **-ier**, *superl* **-iest**) *adj*: **to be ~ of doing sthg** hésiter à faire qqch.

chase [tʃeɪs] ◇ *n* [pursuit] poursuite *f*, chasse *f*; **to give ~** poursuivre. ◇ *vt* **-1.** [pursue] poursuivre. **-2.** [drive away] chasser. **-3.** *fig* [money, jobs] faire la chasse à. ◇ *vi*: **to ~ after sb/sthg** courir après qqn/qqch.
◆ **chase up** *vt sep* *Br* [person, information] rechercher, faire la chasse à.

chaser ['tʃeɪsə'] *n* [drink] verre d'alcool qu'on prend après une bière.

chasm ['kæzm] *n* lit & *fig* abîme *m*.

chassis ['ʃæsɪ] (*pl inv*) *n* châssis *m*.

chaste [tʃeɪst] *adj* chaste.

chasten ['tʃeɪsn] *vt* châtier.

chastise [tʃæ'staɪz] *vt* *fml* [scold] punir, châtier.

chastity ['tʃæstətɪ] *n* chasteté *f*.

chat [tʃæt] (*pt* & *pp* **-ted**, *cont* **-ting**) ◇ *n* causerie *f*, bavardage *m*; **to have a ~** causer, bavarder. ◇ *vi* causer, bavarder.
◆ **chat up** *vt sep* *Br* *inf* baratiner.

chat show *n* *Br* talk-show *m*.

chatter ['tʃætə'] ◇ *n* **-1.** [of person] bavardage *m*. **-2.** [of animal, bird] caquetage *m*. ◇

vi **-1.** [person] bavarder. **-2.** [animal, bird] jacasser, caqueter. **-3.** [teeth]: **his teeth were ~ing** il claquait des dents.

chatterbox ['tʃætəbɒks] *n* *inf* moulin *m* à paroles.

chatty ['tʃætɪ] (*compar* **-ier**, *superl* **-iest**) *adj* [person] bavard(e); [letter] plein(e) de bavardages.

chauffeur ['ʃəʊfə'] ◇ *n* chauffeur *m*. ◇ *vt* conduire.

chauvinist ['ʃəʊvɪnɪst] *n* **-1.** [sexist] macho *m*. **-2.** [nationalist] chauvin *m*, -e *f*.

chauvinistic ['ʃəʊvɪ'nɪstɪk] *adj* **-1.** [sexist] macho, machiste. **-2.** [nationalistic] chauvin(e).

cheap [tʃiːp] ◇ *adj* **-1.** [inexpensive] pas cher (chère), bon marché (*inv*). **-2.** [at a reduced price - fare, rate] réduit(e); [- ticket] à prix réduit. **-3.** [low-quality] de mauvaise qualité. **-4.** [joke, comment] facile. ◇ *adv* (à) bon marché. ◇ *n*: **on the ~** pour pas cher.

cheapen ['tʃiːpn] *vt* [degrade] rabaisser.

cheaply ['tʃiːplɪ] *adv* à bon marché, pour pas cher.

cheapness ['tʃiːpnɪs] *n* **-1.** [low cost] bas prix *m*. **-2.** [low quality] mauvaise qualité *f*. **-3.** [of joke, comment] facilité *f*.

cheapskate ['tʃiːpskeɪt] *n* *inf* grigou *m*.

cheat [tʃiːt] ◇ *n* tricheur *m*, -euse *f*. ◇ *vt* tromper; **to ~ sb out of sthg** escroquer qqch à qqn; **to feel ~ed** se sentir lésé OR frustré. ◇ *vi* **-1.** [in game, exam] tricher. **-2.** *inf* [be unfaithful]: **to ~ on sb** tromper qqn.

cheating ['tʃiːtɪŋ] *n* tricherie *f*.

check [tʃek] ◇ *n* **-1.** [inspection, test]: **~ (on)** contrôle *m* (de). **-2.** [restraint]: **~ (on)** frein *m* (à), restriction *f* (sur); **to put a ~ on sthg** freiner qqch; **to keep** OR **hold sthg in ~** [emotions] maîtriser qqch. **-3.** *Am* [bill] note *f*. **-4.** [pattern] carreaux *mpl*. **-5.** *Am* = **cheque**.
◇ *vt* **-1.** [test, verify] vérifier; [passport, ticket] contrôler. **-2.** [restrain, stop] enrayer, arrêter.
◇ *vi*: **to ~ (for sthg)** vérifier (qqch); **to ~ on sthg** vérifier OR contrôler qqch.
◆ **check in** ◇ *vt sep* [luggage, coat] enregistrer. ◇ *vi* **-1.** [at hotel] signer le registre. **-2.** [at airport] se présenter à l'enregistrement.
◆ **check off** *vt sep* pointer, cocher.
◆ **check out** ◇ *vt sep* **-1.** [luggage, coat] retirer. **-2.** [investigate] vérifier. ◇ *vi* [from hotel] régler sa note.
◆ **check up** *vi*: **to ~ up on sb** prendre des renseignements sur qqn; **to ~ up (on sthg)** vérifier (qqch).

checkbook *Am* = **chequebook**.

checked [tʃekt] *adj* à carreaux.

checkered *Am* = chequered.

checkers ['tʃekəz] *n* (U) *Am* jeu *m* de dames.

check guarantee card *n Am* carte *f* bancaire.

check-in *n* enregistrement *m*.

checking account ['tʃekɪŋ-] *n Am* compte *m* courant.

checklist ['tʃeklɪst] *n* liste *f* de contrôle.

checkmate ['tʃekmeɪt] *n* échec et mat *m*.

checkout ['tʃekaʊt] *n* [in supermarket] caisse *f*.

checkpoint ['tʃekpɔɪnt] *n* [place] (poste *m* de) contrôle *m*.

checkup ['tʃekʌp] *n* MED bilan *m* de santé, check-up *m*.

Cheddar (cheese) ['tʃedər-] *n* (fromage *m* de) cheddar *m*.

cheek [tʃiːk] ◇ *n* -1. [of face] joue *f*. -2. *inf* [impudence] culot *m*. ◇ *vt inf* être insolent(e) avec.

cheekbone ['tʃiːkbəʊn] *n* pommette *f*.

cheekily ['tʃiːkɪlɪ] *adv* avec insolence.

cheekiness ['tʃiːkɪnɪs] *n* insolence *f*.

cheeky ['tʃiːkɪ] (*compar* -ier, *superl* -iest) *adj* insolent(e), effronté(e).

cheer [tʃɪə*] ◇ *n* [shout] acclamation *f*. ◇ *vt* -1. [shout for] acclamer. -2. [gladden] réjouir. ◇ *vi* applaudir.

◆ **cheers** *excl* -1. [said before drinking] santé! -2. *inf* [goodbye] salut!, ciao!, tchao! -3. *inf* [thank you] merci.

◆ **cheer on** *vt sep* encourager.

◆ **cheer up** ◇ *vt sep* remonter le moral à. ◇ *vi* s'égayer.

cheerful ['tʃɪəfʊl] *adj* joyeux(euse), gai(e).

cheerfully ['tʃɪəfʊlɪ] *adv* -1. [joyfully] joyeusement, gaiement. -2. [willingly] de bon gré OR cœur.

cheerfulness ['tʃɪəfʊlnɪs] *n* gaieté *f*.

cheering ['tʃɪərɪŋ] ◇ *adj* [news, story] réconfortant(e). ◇ *n* (U) acclamations *fpl*.

cheerio [,tʃɪərɪ'əʊ] *excl inf* au revoir!, salut!

cheerleader ['tʃɪə,liːdə*] *n* meneur *m*, -euse *f*.

cheerless ['tʃɪəlɪs] *adj* morne, triste.

cheery ['tʃɪərɪ] (*compar* -ier, *superl* -iest) *adj* joyeux(euse).

cheese [tʃiːz] *n* fromage *m*.

cheeseboard ['tʃiːzbɔːd] *n* plateau *m* à fromage.

cheeseburger ['tʃiːz,bɜːgə*] *n* cheeseburger *m*, hamburger *m* au fromage.

cheesecake ['tʃiːzkeɪk] *n* CULIN gâteau *m* au fromage blanc, cheesecake *m*.

cheesy ['tʃiːzɪ] (*compar* -ier, *superl* -iest) *adj* [tasting of cheese] au goût de fromage.

cheetah ['tʃiːtə] *n* guépard *m*.

chef [ʃef] *n* chef *m*.

chemical ['kemɪkl] ◇ *adj* chimique. ◇ *n* produit *m* chimique.

chemically ['kemɪklɪ] *adv* chimiquement.

chemical weapons *npl* armes *fpl* chimiques.

chemist ['kemɪst] *n* -1. *Br* [pharmacist] pharmacien *m*, -ienne *f*; ~'s **(shop)** pharmacie *f*. -2. [scientist] chimiste *mf*.

chemistry ['kemɪstrɪ] *n* chimie *f*.

chemotherapy [,kiːməʊ'θerəpɪ] *n* chimiothérapie *f*.

cheque *Br*, **check** *Am* [tʃek] *n* chèque *m*; to pay by ~ payer par chèque.

cheque account *n* compte *m* chèques.

chequebook *Br*, **checkbook** *Am* ['tʃekbʊk] *n* chéquier *m*, carnet *m* de chèques.

cheque card *n Br* carte *f* bancaire.

chequered *Br* ['tʃekəd], **checkered** *Am* ['tʃekərd] *adj* -1. [patterned] à carreaux. -2. *fig* [career, life] mouvementé(e).

Chequers ['tʃekəz] *n* résidence secondaire officielle du Premier ministre britannique.

cherish ['tʃerɪʃ] *vt* chérir; [hope] nourrir, caresser.

cherished ['tʃerɪʃt] *adj* cher (chère).

cherry ['tʃerɪ] (*pl* -ies) *n* [fruit] cerise *f*; ~ **(tree)** cerisier *m*.

cherub ['tʃerəb] (*pl* -s OR -im [-ɪm]) *n* chérubin *m*.

chervil ['tʃɜːvɪl] *n* cerfeuil *m*.

Ches. (*abbr of* Cheshire) *comté anglais*.

chess [tʃes] *n* échecs *mpl*.

chessboard ['tʃesbɔːd] *n* échiquier *m*.

chessman ['tʃesmæn] (*pl* -men [-men]) *n* pièce *f*.

chest [tʃest] *n* -1. ANAT poitrine *f*; to get sthg off one's ~ *inf* déballer ce qu'on a sur le cœur. -2. [box] coffre *m*.

chesterfield ['tʃestəfiːld] *n* canapé *m*.

chestnut ['tʃesnʌt] ◇ *adj* [colour] châtain (*inv*). ◇ *n* [nut] châtaigne *f*; ~ **(tree)** châtaignier *m*.

chest of drawers (*pl* chests of drawers) *n* commode *f*.

chesty ['tʃestɪ] (*compar* -ier, *superl* -iest) *adj* [cough] de poitrine.

chevron ['ʃevrən] *n* chevron *m*.

chew [tʃuː] ◇ *n* [sweet] bonbon *m* (à mâcher). ◇ *vt* mâcher.

◆ **chew over** *vt sep fig* [think over] ruminer, remâcher.

◆ **chew up** *vt sep* mâchouiller.

chewing gum ['tʃuːɪŋ-] *n* chewing-gum *m*.

chewy [tʃuːɪ] (*compar* -ier, *superl* -iest) *adj* [food] difficile à mâcher.

chic [ʃiːk] ◇ *adj* chic (*inv*). ◇ *n* chic *m*.

chicanery [ʃɪ'keɪnərɪ] *n* (*U*) chicane *f*.

chick [tʃɪk] *n* [baby bird] oisillon *m*.

chicken ['tʃɪkɪn] ◇ *adj inf* [cowardly] froussard(e). ◇ *n* -1. [bird, food] poulet *m*; **it's a ~ and egg situation** c'est l'histoire de la poule et de l'œuf. -2. *inf* [coward] froussard *m*, -e *f*.

◆ **chicken out** *vi inf* se dégonfler.

chickenfeed ['tʃɪkɪnfiːd] *n* (*U*) *fig* bagatelle *f*.

chickenpox ['tʃɪkɪnpɒks] *n* (*U*) varicelle *f*.

chicken wire *n* grillage *m*.

chickpea ['tʃɪkpiː] *n* pois *m* chiche.

chicory ['tʃɪkərɪ] *n* [vegetable] endive *f*.

chide [tʃaɪd] (*pt* chided OR chid [tʃɪd], *pp* chid OR chidden ['tʃɪdn]) *vt literary*: **to ~ sb (for sthg)** réprimander qqn (à propos de qqch).

chief [tʃiːf] ◇ *adj* -1. [main - aim, problem] principal(e). -2. [head] en chef. ◇ *n* chef *m*.

chief constable *n* Br commissaire *m* de police divisionnaire.

chief executive *n* directeur général *m*, directrice générale *f*.

◆ **Chief Executive** *n* Am: **the Chief Executive** le président des États-Unis.

chief justice *n* président *m* de la Cour Suprême (des États-Unis).

chiefly ['tʃiːflɪ] *adv* -1. [mainly] principalement. -2. [above all] surtout.

chief of staff *n* chef *m* d'état-major.

chief superintendent *n* Br commissaire *m* de police principal.

chieftain ['tʃiːftən] *n* chef *m*.

chiffon ['ʃɪfɒn] *n* mousseline *f*.

chihuahua [tʃɪ'wɑːwə] *n* chihuahua *m*.

chilblain ['tʃɪlbleɪn] *n* engelure *f*.

child [tʃaɪld] (*pl* children) *n* enfant *mf*.

childbearing ['tʃaɪld,beərɪŋ] *n* maternité *f*.

child benefit *n* (*U*) Br ≃ allocations *fpl* familiales.

childbirth ['tʃaɪldbɜːθ] *n* (*U*) accouchement *m*.

childhood ['tʃaɪldhʊd] *n* enfance *f*.

childish ['tʃaɪldɪʃ] *adj pej* puéril(e), enfantin(e).

childishly ['tʃaɪldɪʃlɪ] *adv pej* de façon puérile.

childless ['tʃaɪldlɪs] *adj* sans enfants.

childlike ['tʃaɪldlaɪk] *adj* enfantin(e), d'enfant.

childminder ['tʃaɪld,maɪndər] *n* Br gardienne *f* d'enfants, nourrice *f*.

child prodigy *n* enfant *mf* prodige.

childproof ['tʃaɪldpruːf] *adj* [container] *qui ne peut pas être ouvert par les enfants*; **~ lock** verrouillage *m* de sécurité pour enfants.

children ['tʃɪldrən] *pl* → child.

children's home *n* maison *f* d'enfants.

Chile ['tʃɪlɪ] *n* Chili *m*; **in ~** au Chili.

Chilean ['tʃɪlɪən] ◇ *adj* chilien(ienne). ◇ *n* Chilien *m*, -ienne *f*.

chili ['tʃɪlɪ] = **chilli**.

chill [tʃɪl] ◇ *adj* frais (fraîche). ◇ *n* -1. [illness] coup *m* de froid. -2. [in temperature]: **there's a ~ in the air** le fond de l'air est frais. -3. [feeling of fear] frisson *m*. ◇ *vt* -1. [drink, food] mettre au frais. -2. [person] faire frissonner. ◇ *vi* [drink, food] rafraîchir.

chilli ['tʃɪlɪ] (*pl* -ies) *n* [vegetable] piment *m*.

chilling ['tʃɪlɪŋ] *adj* -1. [very cold] glacial(e). -2. [frightening] qui glace le sang.

chilli powder *n* poudre *f* de piment.

chilly ['tʃɪlɪ] (*compar* -ier, *superl* -iest) *adj* froid(e); **to feel ~** avoir froid; **it's ~** il fait froid.

chime [tʃaɪm] ◇ *n* [of bell, clock] carillon *m*. ◇ *vt* [time] sonner. ◇ *vi* [bell, clock] carillonner.

chimney ['tʃɪmnɪ] *n* cheminée *f*.

chimneypot ['rʃɪmnɪpɒt] *n* mitre *f* de cheminée.

chimneysweep ['tʃɪmnɪswiːp] *n* ramoneur *m*.

chimp(anzee) ['tʃɪmp(ən'ziː)] *n* chimpanzé *m*.

chin [tʃɪn] *n* menton *m*.

china ['tʃaɪnə] ◇ *n* porcelaine *f*. ◇ *comp* en porcelaine.

China ['tʃaɪnə] *n* Chine *f*; **in ~** en Chine; **the People's Republic of ~** la République populaire de Chine.

china clay *n* kaolin *m*.

China Sea *n*: **the ~** la mer de Chine.

Chinatown ['tʃaɪnətaʊn] *n* quartier *m* chinois.

chinchilla [tʃɪn'tʃɪlə] *n* chinchilla *m*.

Chinese [,tʃaɪ'niːz] ◇ *adj* chinois(e). ◇ *n* [language] chinois *m*. ◇ *npl*: **the ~** les Chinois *mpl*.

Chinese cabbage *n* chou *m* chinois.

Chinese lantern *n* lanterne *f* vénitienne.

Chinese leaves *npl* Br = **Chinese cabbage**.

chink [tʃɪŋk] ◇ *n* -1. [narrow opening] fente *f*. -2. [sound] tintement *m*. ◇ *vi* tinter.

chinos ['tʃiːnəʊz] *npl* pantalon de grosse toile beige porté à l'origine par les militaires de l'armée de l'air américaine.

chintz [tʃɪnts] ◇ *n* chintz *m*. ◇ *comp* de chintz.

chinwag ['tʃɪnwæg] *n inf*: **to have a ~** tailler une bavette.

chip [tʃɪp] (*pt* & *pp* **-ped**, *cont* **-ping**) ◇ *n* -1. *Br* [fried potato] frite *f*; *Am* [potato crisp] chip *m*. -2. [of glass, metal] éclat *m*; [of wood] copeau *m*. -3. [flaw] ébréchure *f*. -4. [microchip] puce *f*. -5. [for gambling] jeton *m*. -6. *phr*: **when the ~s are down** en cas de coup dur; **to have a ~ on one's shoulder** en avoir gros sur le cœur. ◇ *vt* [cup, glass] ébrécher.

◆ **chip in** *inf* ◇ *vt fus* [contribute] contribuer. ◇ *vi* -1. [contribute] contribuer. -2. [interrupt] mettre son grain de sel.

◆ **chip off** *vt sep* enlever petit morceau par petit morceau.

chip-based *adj* COMPUT à puce.

chipboard ['tʃɪpbɔːd] *n* aggloméré *m*.

chipmunk ['tʃɪpmʌŋk] *n* tamia *m*.

chipolata [ˌtʃɪpə'lɑːtə] *n* chipolata *f*.

chipped *adj* [flawed] ébréché(e).

chippings ['tʃɪpɪŋz] *npl* [on road] gravillons *mpl*; [of wood] copeaux *mpl*; "**loose ~**" «attention, gravillons».

chip shop *n Br* friterie *f*.

chiropodist [kɪ'rɒpədɪst] *n* pédicure *mf*.

chiropody [kɪ'rɒpədɪ] *n* podologie *f*.

chirp [tʃɜːp] *vi* [bird] pépier; [cricket] chanter.

chirpy ['tʃɜːpɪ] (*compar* **-ier**, *superl* **-iest**) *adj* gai(e).

chisel ['tʃɪzl] (*Br pt* & *pp* **-led**, *cont* **-ling**, *Am pt* & *pp* **-ed**, *cont* **-ing**) ◇ *n* [for wood] ciseau *m*; [for metal, rock] burin *m*. ◇ *vt* ciseler.

chit [tʃɪt] *n* [note] note *f*, reçu *m*.

chitchat ['tʃɪttʃæt] *n* (*U*) *inf* bavardage *m*.

chivalrous ['ʃɪvlrəs] *adj* chevaleresque.

chivalry ['ʃɪvlrɪ] *n* (*U*) -1. *literary* [of knights] chevalerie *f*. -2. [good manners] galanterie *f*.

chives [tʃaɪvz] *npl* ciboulette *f*.

chivy (*pt* & *pp* **-ied**), **chivvy** (*pt* & *pp* **-ied**) ['tʃɪvɪ] *vt inf* harceler; **to ~ sb along** faire se dépêcher qqn.

chloride ['klɔːraɪd] *n* chlorure *m*.

chlorinated ['klɔːrɪneɪtɪd] *adj* chloré(e).

chlorine ['klɔːriːn] *n* chlore *m*.

chlorofluorocarbon ['klɔrə,flʊərəʊ'kɑːbən] *n* chlorofluorocarbone *m*.

chloroform ['klɒrəfɔːm] *n* chloroforme *m*.

choc-ice ['tʃɒkaɪs] *n Br* esquimau® *m*.

chock [tʃɒk] *n* cale *f*.

chock-a-block, chock-full *adj inf*: **~ (with)** plein(e) à craquer (de).

chocolate ['tʃɒkələt] ◇ *n* chocolat *m*. ◇ *comp* au chocolat.

choice [tʃɔɪs] ◇ *n* choix *m*; **we had no ~ but to accept** nous ne pouvions pas faire autrement que d'accepter; **by** OR **from ~** par choix. ◇ *adj* de choix.

choir ['kwaɪəʳ] *n* chœur *m*.

choirboy ['kwaɪəbɔɪ] *n* jeune choriste *m*.

choke [tʃəʊk] ◇ *n* AUT starter *m*. ◇ *vt* -1. [strangle] étrangler, étouffer. -2. [block] obstruer, boucher. ◇ *vi* s'étrangler.

◆ **choke back** *vt fus* [anger] étouffer; [tears] refouler.

cholera ['kɒlərə] *n* choléra *m*.

cholesterol [kə'lestərɒl] *n* cholestérol *m*.

choose [tʃuːz] (*pt* **chose**, *pp* **chosen**) ◇ *vt* -1. [select] choisir; **there's little** OR **not much to ~ between them** ils se valent. -2. [decide]: **to ~ to do sthg** décider OR choisir de faire qqch. ◇ *vi* [select]: **to ~ (from)** choisir (parmi OR entre).

choos(e)y ['tʃuːzɪ] (*compar* **-ier**, *superl* **-iest**) *adj* difficile.

chop [tʃɒp] (*pt* & *pp* **-ped**, *cont* **-ping**) ◇ *n* -1. CULIN côtelette *f*. -2. [blow] coup *m* (de hache *etc*); **he's for the ~** *fig* il va sûrement se faire saquer. ◇ *vt* -1. [wood] couper; [vegetables] hacher. -2. *inf fig* [funding, budget] réduire. -3. *phr*: **to ~ and change** changer sans cesse d'avis.

◆ **chops** *npl inf* babines *fpl*.

◆ **chop down** *vt sep* [tree] abattre.

◆ **chop up** *vt sep* couper en morceaux.

chopper ['tʃɒpəʳ] *n* -1. [axe] couperet *m*. -2. *inf* [helicopter] hélico *m*.

chopping board ['tʃɒpɪŋ-] *n* hachoir *m*.

choppy ['tʃɒpɪ] (*compar* **-ier**, *superl* **-iest**) *adj* [sea] agité(e).

chopsticks ['tʃɒpstɪks] *npl* baguettes *fpl*.

choral ['kɔːrəl] *adj* choral(e).

chord [kɔːd] *n* MUS accord *m*; **to strike a ~ with sb** toucher qqn.

chore [tʃɔːʳ] *n* corvée *f*; **household ~s** travaux *mpl* ménagers.

choreographer [ˌkɒrɪ'ɒgrəfəʳ] *n* chorégraphe *mf*.

choreography [ˌkɒrɪ'ɒgrəfɪ] *n* chorégraphie *f*.

chortle ['tʃɔːtl] *vi* glousser.

chorus ['kɔːrəs] ◇ n -1. [part of song] refrain m. -2. [singers] chœur m. -3. fig [of praise, complaints] concert m. ◇ vt répondre en chœur.

chose [tʃəuz] pt → choose.

chosen ['tʃəuzn] pp → choose.

choux pastry [ʃuː-] n pâte f à choux.

chow [tʃau] n [dog] chow-chow m.

chowder ['tʃaudər] n [of fish] soupe f aux poissons; [of seafood] soupe aux fruits de mer.

Christ [kraist] ◇ n Christ m. ◇ excl Seigneur!, bon Dieu!

christen ['krisn] vt -1. [baby] baptiser. -2. [name] nommer.

christening ['krisniŋ] ◇ n baptême m. ◇ comp de baptême.

Christian ['kristʃən] ◇ adj -1. RELIG chrétien(ienne). -2. [kind] charitable. ◇ n chrétien m, -ienne f.

Christianity [,kristi'ænəti]. n christianisme m.

Christian name n prénom m.

Christmas ['krisməs] ◇ n Noël m; **happy** OR **merry ~**! joyeux Noël! ◇ comp de Noël.

Christmas cake n Br gâteau m de Noël.

Christmas card n carte f de Noël.

Christmas cracker n Br diablotin m.

Christmas Day n jour m de Noël.

Christmas Eve n veille f de Noël.

Christmas Island n l'île f Christmas; **on ~** à l'île Christmas.

Christmas pudding n Br pudding m (de Noël).

Christmas stocking n ≃ soulier m de Noël.

Christmastime ['krisməstaim] n: **at ~** à Noël.

Christmas tree n arbre m de Noël.

chrome [krəum], **chromium** ['krəumiəm] ◇ n chrome m. ◇ comp chromé(e).

chromosome ['krəuməsəum] n chromosome m.

chronic ['krɒnik] adj [illness, unemployment] chronique; [liar, alcoholic] invétéré(e).

chronically ['krɒnikli] adv de façon chronique.

chronicle ['krɒnikl] ◇ n chronique f. ◇ vt faire la chronique de.

chronological [,krɒnə'lɒdʒikl] adj chronologique.

chronologically [,krɒnə'lɒdʒikli] adv chronologiquement.

chronology [krə'nɒlədʒi] n chronologie f.

chrysalis ['krisəlis] (pl **-lises** [-lisiːz]) n chrysalide f.

chrysanthemum [kri'sænθəməm] (pl **-s**) n chrysanthème m.

chubbiness ['tʃʌbinis] n rondeur f.

chubby ['tʃʌbi] (compar **-bier**, superl **-biest**) adj [cheeks, face] joufflu(e); [person, hands] potelé(e).

chuck [tʃʌk] vt inf -1. [throw] lancer, envoyer. -2. [job, boyfriend] laisser tomber.
◆ **chuck away**, **chuck out** vt sep inf jeter, balancer.

chuckle ['tʃʌkl] ◇ n petit rire m. ◇ vi glousser.

chuffed [tʃʌft] adj Br inf: **~ (with sthg/to do sthg)** ravi(e) (de qqch/de faire qqch).

chug [tʃʌg] (pt & pp **-ged**, cont **-ging**) vi [train] faire teuf-teuf.

chum [tʃʌm] n inf copain m, copine f.

chummy ['tʃʌmi] (compar **-mier**, superl **-miest**) adj inf: **to be ~ with sb** être copain (copine) avec qqn.

chump [tʃʌmp] n inf imbécile mf.

chunk [tʃʌŋk] n gros morceau m.

chunky ['tʃʌŋki] (compar **-ier**, superl **-iest**) adj [person, furniture] trapu(e); [sweater, jewellery] gros (grosse).

church [tʃɜːtʃ] n -1. [building] église f; **to go to ~** aller à l'église; [Catholics] aller à la messe. -2. [organization] Église f.

churchgoer ['tʃɜːtʃ,gəuər] n pratiquant m, -e f.

Church of England n: **the ~** l'Église f d'Angleterre.

THE CHURCH OF ENGLAND:
L'Église d'Angleterre (de confession anglicane) est l'Église officielle de la Grande-Bretagne; son chef laïc est le souverain, son chef spirituel l'archevêque de Cantorbéry

---

Church of Scotland n: **the ~** l'Église f d'Écosse.

churchman ['tʃɜːtʃmən] (pl **-men** [-mən]) n membre m du clergé, ecclésiastique m.

churchyard ['tʃɜːtʃjɑːd] n cimetière m.

churlish ['tʃɜːliʃ] adj grossier(ière).

churn [tʃɜːn] ◇ n -1. [for making butter] baratte f. -2. [for milk] bidon m. ◇ vt [stir up] battre. ◇ vi: **my stomach was ~ing** j'avais l'estomac tout retourné.
◆ **churn out** vt sep inf produire en série.
◆ **churn up** vt sep battre.

chute [ʃuːt] n glissière f; **rubbish ~** vide-ordures m inv.

chutney ['tʃʌtni] n chutney m.

CI *abbr of* **Channel Islands.**

CIA (*abbr of* **Central Intelligence Agency**) *n* CIA *f.*

CIB (*abbr of* **Criminal Investigation Branch**) *n la police judiciaire américaine.*

cicada [sɪ'kɑːdə] *n* cigale *f.*

CID (*abbr of* **Criminal Investigation Department**) *n la police judiciaire britannique.*

cider ['saɪdər] *n* cidre *m.*

CIF (*abbr of* **cost, insurance and freight**) CAF, caf.

cigar [sɪ'gɑːr] *n* cigare *m.*

cigarette [ˌsɪgə'ret] *n* cigarette *f.*

cigarette butt *n* mégot *m.*

cigarette end *Br* = **cigarette butt.**

cigarette holder *n* fume-cigarette *m inv.*

cigarette lighter *n* briquet *m.*

cigarette paper *n* papier *m* à cigarettes.

C-in-C *n abbr of* **commander-in-chief.**

cinch [sɪntʃ] *n inf*: **it's a ~** c'est un jeu d'enfants.

cinder ['sɪndər] *n* cendre *f.*

cinderblock ['sɪndəblɒk] *n Am* parpaing *m.*

Cinderella [ˌsɪndə'relə] *n* Cendrillon *f.*

cine-camera ['sɪnɪˌkæmərə] *n* caméra *f.*

cine-film ['sɪnɪ-] *n* film *m.*

cinema ['sɪnəmə] *n* cinéma *m.*

cinematic [ˌsɪnɪ'mætɪk] *adj* cinématographique.

cinnamon ['sɪnəmən] *n* cannelle *f.*

cipher ['saɪfər] *n* [secret writing] code *m.*

circa ['sɜːkə] *prep* environ.

circle ['sɜːkl] ◇ *n* **-1.** [gen] cercle *m*; **to come full ~** revenir à son point de départ; **to go round in ~s** *fig* tourner en rond. **-2.** [in theatre, cinema] balcon *m.* ◇ *vt* **-1.** [draw a circle round] entourer (d'un cercle). **-2.** [move round] faire le tour de. ◇ *vi* [plane] tourner en rond.

circuit ['sɜːkɪt] *n* **-1.** [gen & ELEC] circuit *m.* **-2.** [lap] tour *m*; [movement round] révolution *f.*

circuit board *n* plaquette *f* (de circuits imprimés).

circuit breaker *n* disjoncteur *m.*

circuitous [sə'kjuːɪtəs] *adj* indirect(e).

circular ['sɜːkjʊlər] ◇ *adj* **-1.** [gen] circulaire. **-2.** [argument] qui tourne en rond. ◇ *n* [letter] circulaire *f*; [advertisement] prospectus *m.*

circulate ['sɜːkjʊleɪt] ◇ *vi* **-1.** [gen] circuler. **-2.** [socialize] se mêler aux invités. ◇ *vt* [rumour] propager; [document] faire circuler.

circulation [ˌsɜːkjʊ'leɪʃn] *n* **-1.** [gen] circulation *f.* **-2.** PRESS tirage *m.*

circumcise ['sɜːkəmsaɪz] *vt* circoncire.

circumcision [ˌsɜːkəm'sɪʒn] *n* circoncision *f.*

circumference [sə'kʌmfərəns] *n* circonférence *f.*

circumflex ['sɜːkəmfleks] *n*: **~ (accent)** accent *m* circonflexe.

circumnavigate [ˌsɜːkəm'nævɪgeɪt] *vt*: **to ~ the world** faire le tour du monde en bateau.

circumscribe ['sɜːkəmskraɪb] *vt fml* [restrict] limiter.

circumspect ['sɜːkəmspekt] *adj* circonspect(e).

circumstances ['sɜːkəmstənsɪz] *npl* circonstances *fpl*; **under** OR **in no ~** en aucun cas; **under** OR **in the ~** en de telles circonstances.

circumstantial [ˌsɜːkəm'stænʃl] *adj fml*: **~ evidence** preuve *f* indirecte.

circumvent [ˌsɜːkəm'vent] *vt fml* [law, rule] tourner.

circus ['sɜːkəs] *n* cirque *m.*

cirrhosis [sɪ'rəʊsɪs] *n* cirrhose *f.*

CIS (*abbr of* **Commonwealth of Independent States**) *n* CEI *f.*

cissy ['sɪsɪ] (*pl* **-ies**) *n Br inf* femmelette *f.*

cistern ['sɪstən] *n* **-1.** *Br* [inside roof] réservoir *m* d'eau. **-2.** [in toilet] réservoir *m* de chasse d'eau.

citation [saɪ'teɪʃn] *n* citation *f.*

cite [saɪt] *vt* citer.

citizen ['sɪtɪzn] *n* **-1.** [of country] citoyen *m*, -enne *f.* **-2.** [of town] habitant *m*, -e *f.*

Citizens' Band *n fréquence radio réservée au public,* citizen band *f.*

citizenship ['sɪtɪznʃɪp] *n* citoyenneté *f.*

citric acid ['sɪtrɪk-] *n* acide *m* citrique.

citrus fruit ['sɪtrəs-] *n* agrume *m.*

city ['sɪtɪ] (*pl* **-ies**) *n* ville *f,* cité *f.*
◆ **City** *n Br*: **the City** la City.

THE CITY:

La City, quartier financier de la capitale, est une circonscription administrative autonome de Londres ayant sa propre police. Le terme 'the City' est souvent employé pour désigner le monde britannique de la finance

city centre *n* centre *m* ville.

city hall *n Am* ≃ mairie *f,* ≃ hôtel *m* de ville.

city technology college n Br établissement d'enseignement technique du secondaire subventionné par les entreprises.

civic ['sɪvɪk] adj [leader, event] municipal(e); [duty, pride] civique.

civic centre n Br centre m administratif municipal.

civil ['sɪvl] adj **-1.** [public] civil(e). **-2.** [polite] courtois(e), poli(e).

civil defence n protection f civile.

civil disobedience n résistance f passive à la loi.

civil engineer n ingénieur m des travaux publics.

civil engineering n génie m civil.

civilian [sɪ'vɪljən] ◇ n civil m, -e f. ◇ comp civil(e).

civility [sɪ'vɪlətɪ] n politesse f.

civilization [ˌsɪvɪlaɪ'zeɪʃn] n civilisation f.

civilize, -ise ['sɪvɪlaɪz] vt civiliser.

civilized ['sɪvɪlaɪzd] adj civilisé(e).

civil law n droit m civil.

civil liberties npl libertés fpl civiques.

civil list n Br liste f civile (allouée à la famille royale par le Parlement britannique).

civil rights npl droits mpl civils.

civil servant n fonctionnaire mf.

civil service n fonction f publique.

civil war n guerre f civile.

cl (abbr of **centilitre**) cl.

clad [klæd] adj literary [dressed]: ~ **in** vêtu(e) de.

cladding ['klædɪŋ] n Br revêtement m.

claim [kleɪm] ◇ n **-1.** [for pay etc] revendication f; [for expenses, insurance] demande f. **-2.** [right] droit m; **to lay ~ to sthg** revendiquer qqch. **-3.** [assertion] affirmation f. ◇ vt **-1.** [ask for] réclamer. **-2.** [responsibility, credit] revendiquer. **-3.** [maintain] prétendre. ◇ vi: **to ~ for sthg** faire une demande d'indemnité pour qqch; **to ~ (on one's insurance)** faire une déclaration de sinistre.

claimant ['kleɪmənt] n [to throne] prétendant m, -e f; [of state benefit] demandeur m, -eresse f, requérant m, -e f.

claim form n [for expenses] note f de frais; [for insurance] formulaire m de déclaration de sinistre.

clairvoyant [kleə'vɔɪənt] ◇ adj [person] qui a des dons de double vue. ◇ n voyant m, -e f.

clam [klæm] (pt & pp **-med**, cont **-ming**) n palourde f.

◆ **clam up** vi inf la boucler.

clamber ['klæmbər] vi grimper.

clammy ['klæmɪ] (compar **-mier**, superl **-miest**) adj [skin] moite; [weather] lourd et humide.

clamor Am = **clamour**.

clamorous ['klæmərəs] adj bruyant(e).

clamour Br, **clamor** Am ['klæmər] ◇ n (U) **-1.** [noise] cris mpl. **-2.** [demand] revendication f bruyante. ◇ vi: **to ~ for sthg** demander qqch à cor et à cri.

clamp [klæmp] ◇ n [gen] pince f, agrafe f; [for carpentry] serre-joint m; MED clamp m. ◇ vt **-1.** [gen] serrer. **-2.** AUT poser un sabot de Denver à.

◆ **clamp down** vi: **to ~ down (on)** sévir (contre).

clampdown ['klæmpdaʊn] n: ~ **(on)** répression f (contre).

clan [klæn] n clan m.

clandestine [klæn'destɪn] adj clandestin(e).

clang [klæŋ] ◇ n bruit m métallique. ◇ vi émettre un bruit métallique.

clanger ['klæŋər] n Br inf gaffe f.

clank [klæŋk] ◇ n cliquetis m. ◇ vi cliqueter.

clap [klæp] (pt & pp **-ped**, cont **-ping**) ◇ n **-1.** [of hands] applaudissement m, battement m (de main). **-2.** [of thunder] coup m. ◇ vt **-1.** [hands]: **to ~ one's hands** applaudir, taper des mains. **-2.** inf [place] mettre; **to ~ eyes on sb** apercevoir qqn. ◇ vi applaudir, taper des mains.

clapboard ['klæpbɔːd] n Am bardeau m.

clapped-out [klæpt-] adj Br inf déglingué(e).

clapperboard ['klæpəbɔːd] n claquette f.

clapping ['klæpɪŋ] n (U) applaudissements mpl.

claptrap ['klæptræp] n (U) inf sottises fpl.

claret ['klærət] n **-1.** [wine] bordeaux m rouge. **-2.** [colour] bordeaux m inv.

clarification [ˌklærɪfɪ'keɪʃn] n [explanation] éclaircissement m, clarification f.

clarify ['klærɪfaɪ] (pt & pp **-ied**) vt [explain] éclaircir, clarifier.

clarinet [ˌklærə'net] n clarinette f.

clarity ['klærətɪ] n clarté f.

clash [klæʃ] ◇ n **-1.** [of interests, personalities] conflit m. **-2.** [fight, disagreement] heurt m, affrontement m. **-3.** [noise] fracas m. ◇ vi **-1.** [fight, disagree] se heurter. **-2.** [differ, conflict] entrer en conflit. **-3.** [coincide]: **to ~ (with sthg)** tomber en même temps (que qqch). **-4.** [colours] jurer. **-5.** [cymbals etc] résonner.

clasp [klɑːsp] ◇ n [on necklace etc] fermoir

m; [on belt] **boucle** *f.* ◇ *vt* [hold tight] serrer; **to ~ hands** se serrer la main.

class [klɑːs] ◇ *n* **-1.** [gen] classe *f.* **-2.** [lesson] cours *m*, classe *f.* **-3.** [category] catégorie *f*; **to be in a ~ of one's own** être d'une tout autre classe. ◇ *comp* de classe. ◇ *vt* classer.

class-conscious *adj pej* snob (*inv*).

classic ['klæsɪk] ◇ *adj* classique. ◇ *n* classique *m*.

◆ **classics** *npl* humanités *fpl*.

classical ['klæsɪkl] *adj* classique.

classical music *n* musique *f* classique.

classification [ˌklæsɪfɪ'keɪʃn] *n* classification *f*.

classified ['klæsɪfaɪd] *adj* [information, document] classé secret (classée secrète).

classified ad *n* petite annonce *f*.

classify ['klæsɪfaɪ] (*pt* & *pp* **-ied**) *vt* classifier, classer.

classless ['klɑːslɪs] *adj* sans distinctions sociales.

classmate ['klɑːsmeɪt] *n* camarade *mf* de classe.

classroom ['klɑːsrʊm] *n* (salle *f* de) classe *f*.

classy ['klɑːsɪ] (*compar* **-ier**, *superl* **-iest**) *adj inf* chic (*inv*).

clatter ['klætə*r*] ◇ *n* cliquetis *m*; [louder] fracas *m.* ◇ *vi* [metal object] cliqueter.

clause [klɔːz] *n* **-1.** [in document] clause *f.* **-2.** GRAMM proposition *f*.

claustrophobia [ˌklɔːstrə'fəʊbjə] *n* claustrophobie *f*.

claustrophobic [ˌklɔːstrə'fəʊbɪk] *adj* **-1.** [atmosphere] qui rend claustrophobe. **-2.** [person] claustrophobe.

claw [klɔː] ◇ *n* **-1.** [of cat, bird] griffe *f.* **-2.** [of crab, lobster] pince *f.* ◇ *vt* griffer. ◇ *vi* [person]: **to ~ at** s'agripper à.

◆ **claw back** *vt sep Br* [money] récupérer.

clay [kleɪ] *n* argile *f*.

clay pigeon shooting *n* ball-trap *m*.

clean [kliːn] ◇ *adj* **-1.** [not dirty] propre. **-2.** [sheet of paper, driving licence] vierge; [reputation] sans tache; **to come ~ about sthg** *inf* confesser qqch. **-3.** [joke] de bon goût. **-4.** [smooth] net (nette).

◇ *adv*: **I ~ forgot** j'ai complètement oublié.

◇ *vt* nettoyer; **to ~ one's teeth** se brosser OR laver les dents.

◇ *vi* faire le ménage.

◇ *n*: **to give sthg a ~** nettoyer qqch.

◆ **clean out** *vt sep* **-1.** [room, drawer] nettoyer à fond. **-2.** *inf fig* [person] nettoyer.

◆ **clean up** ◇ *vt sep* [clear up] nettoyer. ◇ *vi inf* [make a profit] ramasser de l'argent.

cleaner ['kliːnə*r*] *n* **-1.** [person] personne *f* qui fait le ménage; **window ~** laveur *m*, -euse *f* de vitres. **-2.** [substance] produit *m* d'entretien. **-3.** [machine] appareil *m* de nettoyage. **-4.** [shop]: **~'s** pressing *m*.

cleaning ['kliːnɪŋ] *n* nettoyage *m*.

cleaning lady *n* femme *f* de ménage.

cleanliness ['klenlɪnɪs] *n* propreté *f*.

cleanly ['kliːnlɪ] *adv* [cut] nettement.

cleanness ['kliːnnɪs] *n* propreté *f*.

cleanse [klenz] *vt* **-1.** [skin, wound] nettoyer. **-2.** *fig* [make pure] purifier; **to ~ sb/sthg of** délivrer qqn/qqch de.

cleanser ['klenzə*r*] *n* [detergent] détergent *m*; [for skin] démaquillant *m*.

clean-shaven *adj* rasé(e) de près.

cleanup ['kliːnʌp] *n* nettoyage *m*.

clear [klɪə*r*] ◇ *adj* **-1.** [gen] clair(e); [glass, plastic] transparent(e); [difference] net (nette); **to make sthg ~ (to sb)** expliquer qqch clairement (à qqn); **to make it ~ that** préciser que; **to make o.s. ~** bien se faire comprendre. **-2.** [voice, sound] qui s'entend nettement. **-3.** [road, space] libre, dégagé(e); **we have two ~ days to get there** on a deux jours entiers pour y aller. **-4.** [not guilty]: **to have a ~ conscience** avoir la conscience tranquille.

◇ *adv*: **to stand ~** s'écarter; **to stay ~ of sb/sthg**, **to steer ~ of sb/sthg** éviter qqn/qqch.

◇ *n*: **in the ~** [out of danger] hors de danger; [free from suspicion] au-dessus de tout soupçon.

◇ *vt* **-1.** [road, path] dégager; [table] débarrasser; **to ~ one's throat** s'éclaircir la voix. **-2.** [obstacle, fallen tree] enlever. **-3.** [jump] sauter, franchir. **-4.** [debt] s'acquitter de. **-5.** [authorize] donner le feu vert à. **-6.** JUR innocenter. **-7.** [cheque] compenser.

◇ *vi* [fog, smoke] se dissiper; [weather, sky] s'éclaircir.

◆ **clear away** *vt sep* [plates] débarrasser; [books] enlever.

◆ **clear off** *vi Br inf* dégager.

◆ **clear out** ◇ *vt sep* [cupboard] vider; [room] ranger. ◇ *vi inf* [leave] dégager.

◆ **clear up** ◇ *vt sep* **-1.** [tidy] ranger. **-2.** [mystery, misunderstanding] éclaircir. ◇ *vi* **-1.** [weather] s'éclaircir. **-2.** [tidy up] tout ranger.

clearance ['klɪərəns] *n* **-1.** [of rubbish] enlèvement *m*; [of land] déblaiement *m*. **-2.** [permission] autorisation *f*. **-3.** [free space] dégagement *m*.

clearance sale *n* soldes *mpl*.

clear-cut *adj* net (nette).

clear-headed [-'hedɪd] *adj* lucide.

clearing ['klɪərɪŋ] *n* [in wood] clairière *f*.

clearing bank *n* Br banque *f* de clearing.

clearing house *n* **-1.** [organization] bureau *m* central. **-2.** [bank] chambre *f* de compensation.

clearing up *n* rangement *m*.

clearly ['klɪəlɪ] *adv* **-1.** [distinctly, lucidly] clairement. **-2.** [obviously] manifestement.

clearout ['klɪəraʊt] *n inf* (grand) nettoyage *m*.

clear-sighted [-'saɪtɪd] *adj* qui voit juste.

clearway ['klɪəweɪ] *n Br* route où le stationnement n'est autorisé qu'en cas d'urgence.

cleavage ['kliːvɪdʒ] *n* **-1.** [between breasts] décolleté *m*. **-2.** [division] division *f*.

cleaver ['kliːvər] *n* couperet *m*.

clef [klef] *n* clef *f*.

cleft [kleft] *n* fente *f*.

cleft palate *n* fente *f* de la voûte du palais.

clematis ['klemətɪs] *n* clématite *f*.

clemency ['klemənsɪ] *n* clémence *f*.

clementine ['kleməntaɪn] *n* clémentine *f*.

clench [klentʃ] *vt* serrer.

clergy ['klɜːdʒɪ] *npl*: **the** ~ le clergé.

clergyman ['klɜːdʒɪmən] (*pl* **-men** [-mən]) *n* membre *m* du clergé.

cleric ['klerɪk] *n* membre *m* du clergé.

clerical ['klerɪkl] *adj* **-1.** ADMIN de bureau. **-2.** RELIG clérical(e).

clerk [*Br* klɑːk, *Am* klɜːrk] *n* **-1.** [in office] employé *m*, -e *f* de bureau. **-2.** JUR clerc *m*. **-3.** *Am* [shop assistant] vendeur *m*, -euse *f*.

clever ['klevər] *adj* **-1.** [intelligent - person] intelligent(e); [- idea] ingénieux(ieuse). **-2.** [skilful] habile, adroit(e).

cleverly ['klevəlɪ] *adv* **-1.** [intelligently] intelligemment. **-2.** [skilfully] habilement.

cleverness ['klevənɪs] *n* **-1.** [intelligence] intelligence *f*. **-2.** [skill] habileté *f*.

cliché ['kliːʃeɪ] *n* cliché *m*.

click [klɪk] ◇ *n* [of lock] déclic *m*; [of tongue, heels] claquement *m*. ◇ *vt* faire claquer. ◇ *vi* **-1.** [heels] claquer; [camera] faire un déclic. **-2.** *inf fig* [become clear]: **it** ~**ed** cela a fait tilt. **-3.** COMPUT cliquer.

client ['klaɪənt] *n* client *m*, -e *f*.

clientele [,kliːɒn'tel] *n* clientèle *f*.

cliff [klɪf] *n* falaise *f*.

cliffhanger ['klɪf,hæŋər] *n inf* épisode *m* à suspense.

climactic [klaɪ'mæktɪk] *adj* [point] culminant(e).

climate ['klaɪmɪt] *n* climat *m*.

climatic [klaɪ'mætɪk] *adj* climatique.

climax ['klaɪmæks] *n* [culmination] apogée *m*.

climb [klaɪm] ◇ *n* ascension *f*, montée *f*. ◇ *vt* [tree, rope] monter à; [stairs] monter; [wall, hill] escalader. ◇ *vi* **-1.** [person] monter, grimper; **they** ~**ed over the fence** ils passèrent par-dessus la barrière. **-2.** [plant] grimper; [road] monter; [plane] prendre de l'altitude. **-3.** [increase] augmenter.

◆ **climb down** *vi fig* reconnaître qu'on a tort.

climb-down *n* reculade *f*.

climber ['klaɪmər] *n* **-1.** [person] alpiniste *mf*, grimpeur *m*, -euse *f*. **-2.** [plant] plante *f* grimpante.

climbing ['klaɪmɪŋ] *n* [rock climbing] varappe *f*; [mountain climbing] alpinisme *m*.

climbing frame *n Br* cage *f* à poules.

climes [klaɪmz] *npl*: **in sunnier** ~ sous des cieux plus cléments.

clinch [klɪntʃ] *vt* [deal] conclure.

cling [klɪŋ] (*pt* & *pp* **clung**) *vi* **-1.** [hold tightly]: **to** ~ **(to)** s'accrocher (à), se cramponner (à). **-2.** [clothes]: **to** ~ **(to)** coller (à).

clingfilm ['klɪŋfɪlm] *n Br* film *m* alimentaire transparent.

clinging ['klɪŋɪŋ] *adj lit* & *fig* collant(e).

clinic ['klɪnɪk] *n* [building] centre *m* médical, clinique *f*.

clinical ['klɪnɪkl] *adj* **-1.** MED clinique. **-2.** *fig* [attitude] froid(e).

clinically ['klɪnɪklɪ] *adv* MED cliniquement.

clink [klɪŋk] ◇ *n* cliquetis *m*. ◇ *vi* tinter.

clip [klɪp] (*pt* & *pp* **-ped**, *cont* **-ping**) ◇ *n* **-1.** [for paper] trombone *m*; [for hair] pince *f*; [of earring] clip *m*; TECH collier *m*. **-2.** [excerpt] extrait *m*. ◇ *vt* **-1.** [fasten] attacher. **-2.** [nails] couper; [hedge] tailler; [newspaper cutting] découper. **-3.** *inf* [hit]: **to** ~ **sb round the ear** flanquer une gifle à qqn.

clipboard ['klɪpbɔːd] *n* écritoire *f* à pince, clipboard *m*.

clip-on *adj* [badge etc] à pince; ~ **earrings** clips *mpl*.

clipped [klɪpt] *adj* [voice] saccadé(e).

clippers ['klɪpəz] *npl* [for hair] tondeuse *f*; [for nails] pince *f* à ongles; [for hedge] cisaille *f* à haie; [for pruning] sécateur *m*.

clipping ['klɪpɪŋ] *n* [from newspaper] coupure *f*.

clique [kliːk] *n* clique *f*.

cloak [kləʊk] ◇ *n* **-1.** [garment] cape *f*. **-2.** *fig* [for secret] couverture *f*. ◇ *vt*: **to be** ~**ed in** être entouré(e) de.

cloak-and-dagger *adj* [story] de cape et d'épée.

cloakroom ['kləʊkrʊm] *n* **-1.** [for clothes] vestiaire *m.* **-2.** *Br* [toilets] toilettes *fpl.*

clobber ['klɒbə'] *inf* ◇ *n* (*U*) *Br* **-1.** [belongings] affaires *fpl.* **-2.** [clothes] vêtements *mpl.* ◇ *vt* [hit] frapper, tabasser.

clock [klɒk] *n* **-1.** [large] horloge *f;* [small] pendule *f;* **round the ~** [work, be open] 24 heures sur 24; **to put the ~ back** retarder l'horloge; *fig* revenir en arrière; **to put the ~ forward** avancer l'horloge. **-2.** AUT [mileometer] compteur *m.*
◆ **clock in, clock on** *vi Br* [at work] pointer (à l'arrivée).
◆ **clock off, clock out** *vi Br* [at work] pointer (à la sortie).
◆ **clock on** = clock in.
◆ **clock up** *vt fus* [miles] faire, avaler.

clockwise ['klɒkwaɪz] *adj & adv* dans le sens des aiguilles d'une montre.

clockwork ['klɒkwɜːk] ◇ *n:* **to go like ~** *fig* aller OR marcher comme sur des roulettes. ◇ *comp* [toy] mécanique.

clod [klɒd] *n* [of earth] motte *f.*

clog [klɒg] (*pt & pp* **-ged**, *cont* **-ging**) *vt* boucher.
◆ **clogs** *npl* sabots *mpl.*
◆ **clog up** ◇ *vt sep* boucher. ◇ *vi* se boucher.

clogged [klɒgd] *adj* bouché(e).

cloister ['klɔɪstə'] *n* [passage] cloître *m.*

cloistered ['klɔɪstəd] *adj* cloîtré(e).

clone [kləʊn] ◇ *n* [gen & COMPUT] clone *m.* ◇ *vt* cloner.

close[1] [kləʊs] ◇ *adj* **-1.** [near]: **~ (to)** proche (de), près (de); **a ~ friend** un ami intime (une amie intime); **~ to tears** au bord des larmes; **~ up**, **~ to** de près; **~ by**, **~ at hand** tout près; **that was a ~ shave** OR **thing** OR **call** on l'a échappé belle. **-2.** [link, resemblance] fort(e); [cooperation, connection] étroit(e). **-3.** [questioning] serré(e); [examination] minutieux(ieuse); **to keep a ~ watch on sb/sthg** surveiller qqn/qqch de près; **to pay ~ attention** faire très attention; **to have a ~ look at sb/sthg** regarder qqn/qqch de près. **-4.** [weather] lourd(e); [air in room] renfermé(e). **-5.** [result, contest, race] serré(e).
◇ *adv:* **~ (to)** près (de); **to come ~r (together)** se rapprocher.
◇ *n* [street] cul-de-sac *m.*
◆ **close on, close to** *prep* [almost] près de.

close[2] [kləʊz] ◇ *vt* **-1.** [gen] fermer; **to ~ one's eyes** fermer les yeux. **-2.** [end] clore. ◇ *vi* **-1.** [shop, bank] fermer; [door, lid] (se) fermer. **-2.** [end] se terminer, finir. ◇ *n* fin *f;* **to bring sthg to a ~** mettre fin à qqch.

◆ **close down** *vt sep & vi* fermer.
◆ **close in** *vi* [night, fog] descendre; [person]: **to ~ in (on)** approcher OR se rapprocher (de).
◆ **close off** *vt fus* [road] barrer.

close-cropped [kləʊs-] *adj* ras(e).

closed [kləʊzd] *adj* fermé(e).

closed circuit television *n* télévision *f* en circuit fermé.

closedown ['kləʊzdaʊn] *n* **-1.** *Br* RADIO & TV fin *f* (des émissions). **-2.** [of factory] fermeture *f.*

closed shop *n* atelier qui n'embauche que du personnel syndiqué.

close-fitting [kləʊs-] *adj* près du corps.

close-knit [kləʊs-] *adj* (très) uni(e).

closely ['kləʊslɪ] *adv* [listen, examine, watch] de près; [resemble] beaucoup; **to be ~ related to** OR **with** être proche parent de; **to work ~ with sb** travailler en étroite collaboration avec qqn.

closeness ['kləʊsnɪs] *n* **-1.** [nearness] proximité *f.* **-2.** [intimacy] intimité *f.*

closeout ['kləʊzaʊt] *n Am* liquidation *f.*

close quarters [kləʊs-] *npl:* **at ~** de près.

close season [kləʊs-] *n Br* fermeture *f* de la chasse OR de la pêche.

closet ['klɒzɪt] ◇ *n Am* [cupboard] placard *m.* ◇ *adj inf* non avoué(e). ◇ *vt:* **to be ~ed with sb** être enfermé(e) avec qqn.

close-up [kləʊs-] *n* gros plan *m.*

closing ['kləʊzɪŋ] *adj* [stages, remarks] final(e); [speech] de clôture.

closing price *n* prix *m* de clôture.

closing time *n* heure *f* de fermeture.

closure ['kləʊʒə'] *n* fermeture *f.*

clot [klɒt] (*pt & pp* **-ted**, *cont* **-ting**) ◇ *n* **-1.** [of blood, milk] caillot *m.* **-2.** *Br inf* [fool] empoté *m*, **-e** *f.* ◇ *vi* [blood] coaguler.

cloth [klɒθ] *n* **-1.** (*U*) [fabric] tissu *m.* **-2.** [duster] chiffon *m;* [for drying] torchon *m.*

clothe [kləʊð] *vt fml* [dress] habiller; **~d in** habillé(e) de.

clothes [kləʊðz] *npl* vêtements *mpl*, habits *mpl;* **to put one's ~ on** s'habiller; **to take one's ~ off** se déshabiller.

clothes basket *n* panier *m* à linge.

clothes brush *n* brosse *f* à habits.

clotheshorse ['kləʊðzhɔːs] *n* séchoir *m* à linge.

clothesline ['kləʊðzlaɪn] *n* corde *f* à linge.

clothes peg *Br*, **clothespin** *Am* ['kləʊðzpɪn] *n* pince *f* à linge.

clothing ['kləʊðɪŋ] *n* (*U*) vêtements *mpl*, habits *mpl.*

clotted cream ['klɒtɪd-] n Br crème épaisse, spécialité de la Cornouailles.

cloud [klaʊd] ◇ n nuage m; **to be under a ~** être mal vu. ◇ vt **-1.** [mirror] embuer. **-2.** fig [memory, happiness] gâcher; **to ~ the issue** brouiller les cartes.
◆ **cloud over** vi **-1.** [sky] se couvrir. **-2.** [face] s'assombrir.

cloudburst ['klaʊdbɜːst] n trombe f d'eau.

cloudless ['klaʊdlɪs] adj sans nuages.

cloudy ['klaʊdɪ] (compar **-ier**, superl **-iest**) adj **-1.** [sky, day] nuageux(euse). **-2.** [liquid] trouble.

clout [klaʊt] inf ◇ n **-1.** [blow] coup m. **-2.** (U) [influence] poids m, influence f. ◇ vt donner un coup à.

clove [kləʊv] n: **a ~ of garlic** une gousse d'ail.
◆ **cloves** npl [spice] clous mpl de girofle.

clover ['kləʊvər] n trèfle m.

cloverleaf ['kləʊvəliːf] (pl **-leaves** [-liːvz]) n [plant] feuille f de trèfle.

clown [klaʊn] ◇ n **-1.** [performer] clown m. **-2.** [fool] pitre m. ◇ vi faire le pitre.

cloying ['klɔɪɪŋ] adj **-1.** [smell] écœurant(e). **-2.** [sentimentality] à l'eau de rose.

club [klʌb] (pt & pp **-bed**, cont **-bing**) ◇ n **-1.** [organization, place] club m. **-2.** [weapon] massue f. **-3.** (golf) ~ club m. **-4.** [playing card] trèfle m. ◇ comp [member, fees] du club. ◇ vt matraquer.
◆ **clubs** npl CARDS trèfle m; **the six of ~s** le six de trèfle.
◆ **club together** vi se cotiser.

club car n Am RAIL wagon-restaurant m.

clubhouse ['klʌbhaʊs, pl **-hauziz**] n club m, pavillon m.

cluck [klʌk] vi glousser.

clue [kluː] n **-1.** [in crime] indice m; **I haven't (got) a ~ (about)** je n'ai aucune idée (sur). **-2.** [answer]: **the ~ to sthg** la solution de qqch. **-3.** [in crossword] définition f.

clued-up [kluːd-] adj Br inf calé(e).

clueless ['kluːlɪs] adj Br inf qui n'a aucune idée.

clump [klʌmp] ◇ n **-1.** [of trees, bushes] massif m, bouquet m. **-2.** [sound] bruit m sourd. ◇ vi: **to ~ about** marcher d'un pas lourd.

clumsily ['klʌmzɪlɪ] adv **-1.** [ungracefully] gauchement, maladroitement. **-2.** [tactlessly] sans tact.

clumsy ['klʌmzɪ] (compar **-ier**, superl **-iest**) adj **-1.** [ungraceful] gauche, maladroit(e). **-2.**

[tool, object] peu pratique. **-3.** [tactless] sans tact.

clung [klʌŋ] pt & pp → **cling**.

cluster ['klʌstər] ◇ n [group] groupe m. ◇ vi [people] se rassembler; [buildings etc] être regroupé(e).

clutch [klʌtʃ] ◇ n AUT embrayage m. ◇ vt agripper. ◇ vi: **to ~ at** s'agripper à.
◆ **clutches** npl: **in the ~es of** dans les griffes de.

clutch bag n pochette f.

clutter ['klʌtər] ◇ n désordre m; **in a ~** en désordre. ◇ vt mettre en désordre.

cm (abbr of **centimetre**) n cm.

CNAA (abbr of **Council for National Academic Awards**) n organisme non universitaire délivrant des diplômes en Grande-Bretagne.

CND (abbr of **Campaign for Nuclear Disarmament**) n mouvement pour le désarmement nucléaire.

c/o (abbr of **care of**) a/s.

co- [kəʊ] prefix co-.

Co. -1. (abbr of **Company**) Cie. **-2.** abbr of **County**.

CO ◇ n **-1.** abbr of **commanding officer**. **-2.** (abbr of **Commonwealth Office**) secrétariat d'État au Commonwealth. **-3.** abbr of **conscientious objector**. ◇ abbr of **Colorado**.

coach [kəʊtʃ] ◇ n **-1.** [bus] car m, autocar m. **-2.** RAIL voiture f. **-3.** [horsedrawn] carrosse m. **-4.** SPORT entraîneur m. **-5.** [tutor] répétiteur m, -trice f. ◇ vt **-1.** SPORT entraîner. **-2.** [tutor] donner des leçons (particulières) à.

coaching ['kəʊtʃɪŋ] n (U) **-1.** SPORT entraînement m. **-2.** [tutoring] leçons fpl particulières.

coach trip n Br excursion f en autocar.

coagulate [kəʊ'æɡjʊleɪt] vi coaguler.

coal [kəʊl] n charbon m.

coalesce [ˌkəʊə'les] vi s'unir.

coalface ['kəʊlfeɪs] n front m de taille.

coalfield ['kəʊlfiːld] n bassin m houiller.

coal gas n gaz m.

coalition [ˌkəʊə'lɪʃn] n coalition f.

coalman ['kəʊlmæn] (pl **-men** [-men]) n Br charbonnier m.

coalmine ['kəʊlmaɪn] n mine f de charbon.

coalminer ['kəʊlˌmaɪnər] n mineur m.

coalmining ['kəʊlˌmaɪnɪŋ] n charbonnage m.

coarse [kɔːs] adj **-1.** [rough - cloth] grossier(ière); [- hair] épais(aisse); [- skin] granuleux(euse). **-2.** [vulgar] grossier(ière).

coarse fishing *n* Br pêche *f* en eau douce (*à l'exclusion du saumon*).

coarsen ['kɔːsn] ◇ *vt* rendre grossier(ière). ◇ *vi* devenir grossier(ière).

coast [kəust] ◇ *n* côte *f.* ◇ *vi* [in car, on bike] avancer en roue libre.

coastal [kəustl] *adj* côtier(ière).

coaster ['kəustə'] *n* [small mat] dessous *m* de verre.

coastguard ['kəustgɑːd] *n* -1. [person] garde-côte *m.* -2. [organization]: **the ~** la gendarmerie maritime.

coastline ['kəustlaɪn] *n* côte *f.*

coat [kəut] ◇ *n* -1. [garment] manteau *m.* -2. [of animal] pelage *m.* -3. [layer] couche *f.* ◇ *vt*: **to ~ sthg (with)** recouvrir qqch (de); [with paint etc] enduire qqch (de).

coat hanger *n* cintre *m.*

coating ['kəutɪŋ] *n* couche *f,* CULIN glaçage *m.*

coat of arms (*pl* **coats of arms**) *n* blason *m.*

coauthor [kəu'ɔːθə'] *n* co-auteur *m.*

coax [kəuks] *vt*: **to ~ sb (to do OR into doing sthg)** persuader qqn (de faire qqch) à force de cajoleries.

co-axial cable [,kəu'aksɪəl-] *n* COMPUT câble *m* co-axial.

cob [kɒb] *n* → **corn.**

cobalt [kəu'bɔːlt] *n* cobalt *m.*

cobble ['kɒbl]
♦ **cobble together** *vt sep* [agreement, book] bricoler; [speech] improviser.

cobbled ['kɒbld] *adj* pavé(e).

cobbler ['kɒblə'] *n* cordonnier *m.*

cobbles ['kɒblz], **cobblestones** ['kɒblstəunz] *npl* pavés *mpl.*

Cobol ['kəubɒl] (*abbr of* **Common Business Oriented Language**) *n* COBOL *m.*

cobra ['kəubrə] *n* cobra *m.*

cobweb ['kɒbweb] *n* toile *f* d'araignée.

Coca-Cola® [,kəukə'kəulə] *n* Coca-Cola® *m.*

cocaine [kəu'keɪn] *n* cocaïne *f.*

cock [kɒk] ◇ *n* -1. [male chicken] coq *m.* -2. [male bird] mâle *m.* ◇ *vt* -1. [gun] armer. -2. [head] incliner.
♦ **cock up** *vt sep* Br v inf faire merder.

cock-a-hoop *adj inf* ravi(e).

cockatoo [,kɒkə'tuː] (*pl* -s) *n* cacatoès *m.*

cockerel ['kɒkrəl] *n* jeune coq *m.*

cocker spaniel [,kɒkə'spænjəl] *n* cocker *m.*

cockeyed ['kɒkaɪd] *adj inf* -1. [lopsided] de travers. -2. [foolish] complètement fou (folle).

cockfight ['kɒkfaɪt] *n* combat *m* de coqs.

cockle ['kɒkl] *n* [shellfish] coque *f.*

Cockney ['kɒknɪ] (*pl* **Cockneys**) ◇ *n* -1. [person] Cockney *mf* (*personne issue des quartiers populaires de l'est de Londres*). -2. [dialect, accent] cockney *m.* ◇ *comp* cockney (*inv*).

cockpit ['kɒkpɪt] *n* [in plane] cockpit *m.*

cockroach ['kɒkrəutʃ] *n* cafard *m.*

cocksure [,kɒk'ʃɔː'] *adj* trop sûr(e) de soi.

cocktail ['kɒkteɪl] *n* cocktail *m.*

cocktail dress *n* robe *f* de soirée.

cocktail shaker [-,ʃeɪkə'] *n* shaker *m.*

cocktail stick *n* bâtonnet *m* à apéritif.

cock-up *n v inf*: **to make a ~** se planter.

cocky ['kɒkɪ] (*compar* -ier, *superl* -iest) *adj inf* suffisant(e).

cocoa ['kəukəu] *n* cacao *m.*

coconut ['kəukənʌt] *n* noix *f* de coco.

cocoon [kə'kuːn] ◇ *n* lit & *fig* cocon *m.* ◇ *vt fig* [person] couver.

cod [kɒd] (*pl inv*) *n* morue *f.*

COD -1. *abbr of* **cash on delivery.** -2. *abbr of* **collect on delivery.**

code [kəud] ◇ *n* code *m.* ◇ *vt* coder.

coded ['kəudɪd] *adj* codé(e).

codeine ['kəudiːn] *n* codéine *f.*

code name *n* nom *m* de code.

code of practice *n* déontologie *f.*

cod-liver oil *n* huile *f* de foie de morue.

codswallop ['kɒdz,wɒləp] *n* (U) Br inf bêtises *fpl.*

co-ed [kəu'ed] ◇ *adj abbr of* **coeducational.** ◇ *n* -1. (*abbr of* **coeducational student**) *étudiante d'une université mixte américaine.* -2. (*abbr of* **coeducational school**) *école mixte britannique.*

coeducational [,kəuedjuː'keɪʃənl] *adj* mixte.

coefficient [,kəu'fɪʃnt] *n* coefficient *m.*

coerce [kəu'ɜːs] *vt*: **to ~ sb (into doing sthg)** contraindre qqn (à faire qqch).

coercion [kəu'ɜːʃn] *n* coercition *f.*

coexist [,kəuɪg'zɪst] *vi* coexister.

coexistence [,kəuɪg'zɪstəns] *n* coexistence *f.*

C. of C. (*abbr of* **chamber of commerce**) *n* CC *f.*

C of E *abbr of* **Church of England.**

coffee ['kɒfɪ] *n* café *m.*

coffee bar *n* Br café *m.*

coffee beans *npl* grains *mpl* de café.

coffee break *n* pause-café *f.*

coffee cup *n* tasse *f* à café.

coffee mill *n* moulin *m* à café.

coffee morning *n* Br réunion matinale pour prendre le café.

coffeepot ['kɒfɪpɒt] *n* cafetière *f*.
coffee shop *n* **-1.** *Br* [shop] café *m*. **-2.** *Am* [restaurant] ≃ café-restaurant *m*.
coffee table *n* table *f* basse.
coffee-table book *n* beau livre *m*.
coffers ['kɒfəz] *npl* coffres *mpl*.
coffin ['kɒfɪn] *n* cercueil *m*.
cog [kɒg] *n* [tooth on wheel] dent *f*; [wheel] roue *f* dentée; **a ~ in the machine** *fig* un simple rouage.
cogent ['kəʊdʒənt] *adj* convaincant(e).
cogitate ['kɒdʒɪteɪt] *vi fml* réfléchir.
cognac ['kɒnjæk] *n* cognac *m*.
cognitive ['kɒgnɪtɪv] *adj* cognitif(ive).
cogwheel ['kɒgwiːl] *n* roue *f* dentée.
cohabit [,kəʊ'hæbɪt] *vi fml* cohabiter.
coherent [kəʊ'hɪərənt] *adj* cohérent(e).
coherently [kəʊ'hɪərəntlɪ] *adv* de façon cohérente.
cohesion [kəʊ'hiːʒn] *n* cohésion *f*.
cohesive [kəʊ'hiːsɪv] *adj* cohésif(ive).
cohort ['kəʊhɔːt] *n* cohorte *f*.
COHSE ['kəʊzɪ] (*abbr of* **Confederation of Health Service Employees**) *n* ancien syndicat britannique des employés des services de santé.
COI (*abbr of* **Central Office of Information**) *n* service public britannique d'information en Grande-Bretagne.
coil [kɔɪl] ◇ *n* **-1.** [of rope etc] rouleau *m*; [one loop] boucle *f*. **-2.** ELEC bobine *f*. **-3.** *Br* [contraceptive device] stérilet *m*. ◇ *vt* enrouler. ◇ *vi* s'enrouler.
◆ **coil up** *vt sep* enrouler.
coiled [kɔɪld] *adj* enroulé(e).
coin [kɔɪn] ◇ *n* pièce *f* (de monnaie). ◇ *vt* [word] inventer; **to ~ a phrase** pour employer un lieu commun.
coinage ['kɔɪnɪdʒ] *n* **-1.** (U) [currency] monnaie *f*. **-2.** [new word] néologisme *m*.
coin-box *n Br* cabine *f* (publique) à pièces.
coincide [,kəʊɪn'saɪd] *vi* coïncider.
coincidence [kəʊ'ɪnsɪdəns] *n* coïncidence *f*.
coincidental [kəʊ,ɪnsɪ'dentl] *adj* de coïncidence.
coincidentally [kəʊ,ɪnsɪ'dentəlɪ] *adv* par hasard.
coin-operated ['ɒpə,reɪtɪd] *adj* automatique.
coitus ['kəʊɪtəs] *n* coït *m*.
coke [kəʊk] *n* **-1.** [fuel] coke *m*. **-2.** *drugs sl* coco *f*.
Coke® *n* Coca® *m*.
Col. (*abbr of* **colonel**) Col.
cola ['kəʊlə] *n* cola *m*.

COLA (*abbr of* **cost-of-living adjustment**) *n* actualisation des salaires, indemnités etc en fonction du coût de la vie.
colander ['kʌləndəʳ] *n* passoire *f*.
cold [kəʊld] ◇ *adj* froid(e); **it's ~** il fait froid; **to be ~** avoir froid; **to get ~** [person] avoir froid; [hot food] refroidir. ◇ *n* **-1.** [illness] rhume *m*; **to catch (a) ~** attraper un rhume, s'enrhumer. **-2.** [low temperature] froid *m*.
cold-blooded [-'blʌdɪd] *adj* **-1.** [animal] à sang-froid. **-2.** *fig* [killer] sans pitié; [murder] de sang-froid.
cold cream *n* cold-cream *m*.
cold cuts *npl* assiette *f* anglaise.
cold feet *npl*: **to have** OR **get ~** *inf* avoir la trouille.
cold-hearted [-'hɑːtɪd] *adj* insensible.
coldly ['kəʊldlɪ] *adv* froidement.
coldness ['kəʊldnɪs] *n* froideur *f*.
cold shoulder *n*: **to give sb the ~** *inf* être froid(e) avec qqn.
cold sore *n* bouton *m* de fièvre.
cold storage *n*: **to put sthg into ~** [food] mettre qqch en chambre froide.
cold sweat *n* sueur *f* froide.
cold war *n*: **the ~** la guerre froide.
coleslaw ['kəʊlslɔː] *n* chou *m* cru mayonnaise.
colic ['kɒlɪk] *n* colique *f*.
collaborate [kə'læbəreɪt] *vi* collaborer.
collaboration [kə,læbə'reɪʃn] *n* collaboration *f*.
collaborative [kə'læbərətɪv] *adj* fait(e) en collaboration OR en commun.
collaborator [kə'læbəreɪtəʳ] *n* collaborateur *m*, -trice *f*.
collage ['kɒlɑːʒ] *n* collage *m*.
collagen ['kɒlədʒən] *n* collagène *m*.
collapse [kə'læps] ◇ *n* [gen] écroulement *m*, effondrement *m*; [of marriage] échec *m*. ◇ *vi* **-1.** [building, person] s'effondrer, s'écrouler; [marriage] échouer. **-2.** [fold up] être pliant(e).
collapsible [kə'læpsəbl] *adj* pliant(e).
collar ['kɒləʳ] ◇ *n* **-1.** [on clothes] col *m*. **-2.** [for dog] collier *m*. **-3.** TECH collier *m*, bague *f*. ◇ *vt inf* [detain] coincer.
collarbone ['kɒləbəʊn] *n* clavicule *f*.
collate [kə'leɪt] *vt* collationner.
collateral [kɒ'lætərəl] *n* (U) nantissement *m*.
collation [kə'leɪʃn] *n* collation *f*.
colleague ['kɒliːg] *n* collègue *mf*.

collect [kə'lekt] ◇ vt -1. [gather together - gen] rassembler, recueillir; [- wood etc] ramasser; **to ~ o.s.** se reprendre. -2. [as a hobby] collectionner. -3. [go to get] aller chercher, passer prendre. -4. [money] recueillir; [taxes] percevoir; **~ on delivery** Am paiement à la livraison.
◇ vi -1. [crowd, people] se rassembler. -2. [dust, leaves, dirt] s'amasser, s'accumuler. -3. [for charity, gift] faire la quête.
◇ adv Am TELEC: **to call (sb) ~** téléphoner (à qqn) en PCV.
◆ **collect up** vt sep ramasser.

collectable [kə'lektəbl] ◇ adj prisé(e) (par les collectionneurs). ◇ n objet m prisé par les collectionneurs.

collected [kə'lektɪd] adj -1. [calm] posé(e), maître de soi. -2. LITERATURE: **~ works** œuvres fpl complètes.

collecting [kə'lektɪŋ] n (U) [hobby] fait m de collectionner.

collection [kə'lekʃn] n -1. [of objects] collection f. -2. LITERATURE recueil m. -3. [of rubbish] ramassage m; [of taxes] perception f. -4. [of money] quête f. -5. [of mail] levée f.

collective [kə'lektɪv] ◇ adj collectif(ive). ◇ n coopérative f.

collective bargaining n (U) négociations de convention collective.

collectively [kə'lektɪvlɪ] adv collectivement.

collective ownership n propriété f collective.

collector [kə'lektər] n -1. [as a hobby] collectionneur m, -euse f. -2. [of debts, rent] encaisseur m; **~ of taxes** percepteur m.

collector's item n pièce f de collection.

college ['kɒlɪdʒ] n -1. [gen] ≃ école f d'enseignement (technique) supérieur. -2. [of university] maison communautaire d'étudiants sur un campus universitaire.

college of education n ≃ institut m de formation de maîtres.

collide [kə'laɪd] vi: **to ~ (with)** entrer en collision (avec).

collie ['kɒlɪ] n colley m.

colliery ['kɒljərɪ] (pl -ies) n mine f.

collision [kə'lɪʒn] n -1. [crash]: **~ (with/between)** collision f (avec/entre); **to be on a ~ course (with)** fig aller au-devant de l'affrontement (avec). -2. fig [conflict] conflit m.

collision damage waiver n rachat m de franchise.

colloquial [kə'ləʊkwɪəl] adj familier(ière).

collude [kə'luːd] vi: **to ~ with sb** comploter avec qqn.

collusion [kə'luːʒn] n: **in ~ with** de connivence f avec.

cologne [kə'ləʊn] n eau f de cologne.

Colombia [kə'lʌmbɪə] n Colombie f; **in ~** en Colombie.

Colombian [kə'lʌmbɪən] ◇ adj colombien(ienne). ◇ n Colombien m, -ienne f.

Colombo [kə'lʌmbəʊ] n Colombo.

colon ['kəʊlən] n -1. ANAT côlon m. -2. [punctuation mark] deux-points m inv.

colonel ['kɜːnl] n colonel m.

colonial [kə'ləʊnjəl] adj colonial(e).

colonialism [kə'ləʊnjəlɪzm] n colonialisme m.

colonist ['kɒlənɪst] n colon m.

colonize, -ise ['kɒlənaɪz] vt coloniser.

colonnade [,kɒlə'neɪd] n colonnade f.

colony ['kɒlənɪ] (pl -ies) n colonie f.

color etc Am = **colour** etc.

Colorado [,kɒlə'rɑːdəʊ] n Colorado m; **in ~** dans le Colorado.

colorado beetle n doryphore m.

colossal [kə'lɒsl] adj colossal(e).

colostomy [kə'lɒstəmɪ] (pl -ies) n colostomie f.

colour Br, **color** Am ['kʌlər] ◇ n couleur f; **in ~** en couleur. ◇ adj en couleur. ◇ vt -1. [food, liquid etc] · colorer; [with pen, crayon] colorier. -2. [dye] teindre. -3. fig [judgment] fausser. ◇ vi rougir.
◆ **colours** npl [flag, of team] couleurs fpl.
◆ **colour in** vt sep colorier.

colour bar n discrimination f raciale.

colour-blind adj daltonien(ienne).

colour-coded adj codé(e) par couleur.

coloured Br, **colored** Am ['kʌləd] adj de couleur; **brightly ~** de couleur vive.

colourfast Br, **colorfast** Am ['kʌləfɑːst] adj grand teint (inv).

colourful Br, **colorful** Am ['kʌləful] adj -1. [gen] coloré(e). -2. [person, area] haut en couleur (inv).

colouring Br, **coloring** Am ['kʌlərɪŋ] n -1. [dye] colorant m. -2. (U) [complexion] teint m.

colourless Br, **colorless** Am ['kʌləlɪs] adj -1. [not coloured] sans couleur, incolore. -2. fig [uninteresting] terne.

colour scheme n combinaison f de couleurs.

colour supplement n Br supplément m illustré.

colt [kəʊlt] n [young horse] poulain m.

column ['kɒləm] n -1. [gen] colonne f. -2. PRESS [article] rubrique f.

columnist ['kɒləmnɪst] *n* chroniqueur *m*.

coma ['kəumə] *n* coma *m*.

comatose ['kəumətəus] *adj* comateux(euse).

comb [kəum] ◇ *n* [for hair] peigne *m*. ◇ *vt* **-1.** [hair] peigner. **-2.** [search] ratisser.

combat ['kɒmbæt] ◇ *n* combat *m*. ◇ *vt* combattre.

combative ['kɒmbətɪv] *adj* combatif(ive).

combination [ˌkɒmbɪ'neɪʃn] *n* combinaison *f*.

combination lock *n* serrure *f* à combinaison.

combine [*vb* kəm'baɪn *n* 'kɒmbaɪn] ◇ *vt* [gen] rassembler; [pieces] combiner; **to ~ sthg with sthg** [two substances] mélanger qqch. avec OR à qqch; *fig* allier qqch à qqch. ◇ *vi* COMM & POL: **to ~ (with)** fusionner (avec). ◇ *n* **-1.** [group] cartel *m*. **-2.** = **combine harvester**.

combine **harvester** [-'hɑːvɪstər] *n* moissonneuse-batteuse *f*.

combustible [kəm'bʌstəbl] *adj* combustible.

combustion [kəm'bʌstʃn] *n* combustion *f*.

come [kʌm] (*pt* **came**, *pp* **come**) *vi* **-1.** [move] venir; [arrive] arriver, venir; **the news came as a shock** la nouvelle m'a/lui a *etc* fait un choc; **coming!** j'arrive!; **the time has ~** le moment est venu; **he doesn't know whether he's coming or going** *fig* il ne sait plus où il en est. **-2.** [reach]: **to ~ up to arriver à, monter jusqu'à; the water came up to my knees** l'eau m'arrivait aux genoux; **to ~ down to** descendre OR tomber jusqu'à. **-3.** [happen] arriver, se produire; **~ what may** quoi qu'il arrive; **how did you ~ to fail your exam?** comment as-tu fait pour échouer à ton examen? **-4.** [become]: **to ~ true** se réaliser; **to ~ undone** se défaire; **to ~ unstuck** se décoller. **-5.** [begin gradually]: **to ~ to do sthg** en arriver à OR en venir à faire qqch. **-6.** [be placed in order] venir, être placé(e); **P ~s before Q** P vient avant Q, P précède Q; **who came first?** qui a été placé premier?; **she came second in the exam** elle était deuxième à l'examen. **-7.** *v inf* [sexually] jouir. **-8.** *phr*: **~ to think of it** maintenant que j'y pense, réflexion faite.

◆ **to come** *adv* à venir; **in (the) days/years to ~** dans les jours/années à venir.

◆ **come about** *vi* [happen] arriver, se produire.

◆ **come across** ◇ *vt fus* tomber sur, trouver par hasard. ◇ *vi* [speaker, message] faire de l'effet; **you don't ~ across very well** tu présentes mal; **to ~ across as being sincere** donner l'impression d'être sincère.

◆ **come along** *vi* **-1.** [arrive by chance] arriver. **-2.** [improve - work] avancer; [- student] faire des progrès; **the project is coming along nicely** le projet avance bien. **-3.** *phr*: **~ along!** [expressing encouragement] allez!; [hurry up] allez, dépêche-toi!

◆ **come apart** *vi* **-1.** [fall to pieces] tomber en morceaux. **-2.** [come off] se détacher.

◆ **come at** *vt fus* [attack] attaquer.

◆ **come back** *vi* **-1.** [in talk, writing]: **to ~ back to sthg** revenir à qqch. **-2.** [memory]: **to ~ back (to sb)** revenir (à qqn). **-3.** [become fashionable again] redevenir à la mode.

◆ **come by** *vt fus* **-1.** [get, obtain] trouver, dénicher. **-2.** *Am* [visit, drop in on]: **they came by the house** ils sont passés à la maison.

◆ **come down** *vi* **-1.** [decrease] baisser. **-2.** [descend] descendre.

◆ **come down to** *vt fus* se résumer à, se réduire à.

◆ **come down with** *vt fus* se résumer à, se réduire à; [cold, flu] attraper.

◆ **come forward** *vi* se présenter.

◆ **come from** *vt fus* venir de.

◆ **come in** *vi* **-1.** [enter] entrer. **-2.** [arrive, be received] arriver. **-3.** [be involved] jouer un rôle; **I don't see where I ~ in** je ne vois pas quel rôle je vais jouer.

◆ **come in for** *vt fus* [criticism] être l'objet de.

◆ **come into** *vt fus* **-1.** [inherit] hériter de. **-2.** [begin to be]: **to ~ into being** prendre naissance, voir le jour; **to ~ into sight** apparaître.

◆ **come of** *vt fus* [result from] résulter de.

◆ **come off** *vi* **-1.** [button, label] se détacher; [stain] s'enlever. **-2.** [joke, attempt] réussir. **-3.** [person]: **to ~ off well/badly** bien/mal s'en tirer. **-4.** *phr*: **~ off it!** *inf* et puis quoi encore!, non mais sans blague!

◆ **come on** *vi* **-1.** [start] commencer, apparaître. **-2.** [start working - light, heating] s'allumer. **-3.** [progress, improve] avancer, faire des progrès. **-4.** *phr*: **~ on!** [expressing encouragement] allez!; [hurry up] allez, dépêche-toi!; [expressing disbelief] allons donc!

◆ **come out** *vi* **-1.** [become known] être découvert(e). **-2.** [appear - product, book, film] sortir, paraître; [- sun, moon, stars] paraître. **-3.** [in exam, race etc] finir, se classer. **-4.** [go on strike] faire grève. **-5.** [declare publicly]: **to ~ out for/against sthg** se déclarer pour/contre qqch. **-6.** [photograph] réussir.

◆ **come out in** *vt fus*: **to ~ out in spots** avoir une éruption.

◆ **come over** *vt fus* [subj: sensation, emotion] envahir; **I don't know what's ~ over**

her je ne sais pas ce qui lui a pris.
◆ **come round** *vi* **-1.** [change opinion] changer d'avis. **-2.** [regain consciousness] reprendre connaissance, revenir à soi. **-3.** [happen] venir, revenir.
◆ **come through** *vt fus* survivre à. ◇ *vi* **-1.** [arrive] arriver. **-2.** [survive] s'en tirer.
◆ **come to** ◇ *vt fus* **-1.** [reach]: **to ~ to an end** se terminer, prendre fin; **to ~ to power** arriver au pouvoir; **to ~ to a decision** arriver à OR prendre une décision. **-2.** [amount to] s'élever à. ◇ *vi* [regain consciousness] revenir à soi, reprendre connaissance.
◆ **come under** *vt fus* **-1.** [be governed by] être soumis(e) à. **-2.** [heading] se trouver sous. **-3.** [suffer]: **to ~ under attack (from)** être en butte aux attaques (de).
◆ **come up** *vi* **-1.** [be mentioned] survenir. **-2.** [be imminent] approcher. **-3.** [happen unexpectedly] se présenter. **-4.** [sun, moon] se lever.
◆ **come up against** *vt fus* se heurter à.
◆ **come upon** *vt fus* [find] tomber sur.
◆ **come up to** *vt fus* **-1.** [approach - in space] s'approcher de; [- in time] approcher. **-2.** [equal] répondre à.
◆ **come up with** *vt fus* [answer, idea] proposer.
comeback ['kʌmbæk] *n* come-back *m*; **to make a ~** [fashion] revenir à la mode; [actor etc] revenir à la scène.
Comecon ['kɒmɪkɒn] (*abbr of* **Council for Mutual Economic Aid**) *n* Comecon *m*.
comedian [kə'miːdjən] *n* [comic] comique *m*; THEATRE comédien *m*.
comedienne [kə,miːdɪ'en] *n* [comic] actrice *f* comique; THEATRE comédienne *f*.
comedown ['kʌmdaʊn] *n inf*: **it was a ~ for her** elle est tombée bien bas pour faire ça.
comedy ['kɒmədɪ] (*pl* **-ies**) *n* comédie *f*.
comely ['kʌmlɪ] *adj literary* attrayant(e).
come-on *n*: **to give sb the ~** *inf* essayer d'aguicher qqn.
comet ['kɒmɪt] *n* comète *f*.
come-uppance [,kʌm'ʌpəns] *n*: **to get one's ~** *inf* recevoir ce qu'on mérite.
comfort ['kʌmfət] ◇ *n* **-1.** (U) [ease] confort *m*; **that was too close for ~** c'était moins cinq. **-2.** [luxury] commodité *f*. **-3.** [solace] réconfort *m*, consolation *f*. ◇ *vt* réconforter, consoler.
comfortable ['kʌmftəbl] *adj* **-1.** [gen] confortable. **-2.** *fig* [person at ease, financially] à l'aise. **-3.** [after operation, accident]: **he's ~** son état est stationnaire.
comfortably ['kʌmftəblɪ] *adv* **-1.** [sit, sleep] confortablement. **-2.** [without financial diffi-

culty] à l'aise; **~ off** à l'aise. **-3.** [win] aisément.
comforter ['kʌmfətər] *n* **-1.** [person] soutien *m* moral. **-2.** *Am* [quilt] édredon *m*.
comforting ['kʌmfətɪŋ] *adj* [thought, words] réconfortant(e).
comfort station *n Am* toilettes *fpl* publiques.
comfy ['kʌmfɪ] (*compar* **-ier**, *superl* **-iest**) *adj inf* confortable.
comic ['kɒmɪk] ◇ *adj* comique, amusant(e). ◇ *n* **-1.** [comedian] comique *m*, actrice *f* comique. **-2.** [magazine] bande *f* dessinée.
◆ **comics** *npl Am* [in newspaper] bandes *fpl* dessinées.
comical ['kɒmɪkl] *adj* comique, drôle.
comic strip *n* bande *f* dessinée.
coming ['kʌmɪŋ] ◇ *adj* [future] à venir, futur(e). ◇ *n*: **~s and goings** allées et venues *fpl*.
comma ['kɒmə] *n* virgule *f*.
command [kə'mɑːnd] ◇ *n* **-1.** [order] ordre *m*. **-2.** (U) [control] commandement *m*; **in ~ of** à la tête de; *fig* en possession de. **-3.** [of language, subject] maîtrise *f*; **to have at one's ~** [language] maîtriser; [resources] avoir à sa disposition. **-4.** COMPUT commande *f*. ◇ *vt* **-1.** [order]: **to ~ sb to do sthg** ordonner OR commander à qqn de faire qqch. **-2.** MIL [control] commander. **-3.** [deserve - respect] inspirer; [- attention, high price] mériter.
commandant [,kɒmən'dænt] *n* commandant *m*.
commandeer [,kɒmən'dɪər] *vt* réquisitionner.
commander [kə'mɑːndər] *n* **-1.** [in army] commandant *m*. **-2.** [in navy] capitaine *m* de frégate.
commander in chief (*pl* **commanders in chief**) *n* commandant *m* en chef.
commanding [kə'mɑːndɪŋ] *adj* **-1.** [lead, position] dominant(e). **-2.** [voice, manner] impérieux(ieuse).
commanding officer *n* commandant *m*.
commandment [kə'mɑːndmənt] *n* RELIG commandement *m*.
command module *n* module *m* de commande.
commando [kə'mɑːndəʊ] (*pl* **-s** OR **-es**) *n* commando *m*.
command performance *n* représentation de gala organisée à la demande d'un chef d'État.
commemorate [kə'memərɪt] *vt* commémorer.

commemoration [kə,memə'reɪʃn] *n* commémoration *f*.

commemorative [kə'memərətɪv] *adj* commémoratif(ive).

commence [kə'mens] *fml* ◇ *vt* commencer, entamer; **to ~ doing sthg** commencer à faire qqch. ◇ *vi* commencer.

commencement [kə'mensmənt] *n fml* commencement *m*, début *m*.

commend [kə'mend] *vt* **-1.** [praise]: **to ~ sb (on** OR **for)** féliciter qqn (de). **-2.** [recommend]: **to ~ sthg (to sb)** recommander qqch (à qqn).

commendable [kə'mendəbl] *adj* louable.

commendation [,kɒmen'deɪʃn] *n*: **to get a ~ for sthg** être récompensé(e) pour qqch.

commensurate [kə'menʃərət] *adj fml*: **~ with** correspondant(e) à.

comment ['kɒment] ◇ *n* commentaire *m*, remarque *f*; **no ~!** sans commentaire! ◇ *vt*: **to ~ that** remarquer que. ◇ *vi*: **to ~ (on)** faire des commentaires OR remarques (sur).

commentary ['kɒməntrɪ] (*pl* **-ies**) *n* commentaire *m*.

commentate ['kɒmənteɪt] *vi* RADIO & TV: **to ~ (on)** faire un reportage (sur).

commentator ['kɒmənteɪtə'] *n* commentateur *m*, -trice *f*.

commerce ['kɒmɜːs] *n* (*U*) commerce *m*, affaires *fpl*.

commercial [kə'mɜːʃl] ◇ *adj* commercial(e). ◇ *n* publicité *f*, spot *m* publicitaire.

commercial bank *n* banque *f* commerciale OR de commerce.

commercial break *n* publicités *fpl*.

commercial college *n* école *f* de secrétariat.

commercialism [kə'mɜːʃəlɪzm] *n* mercantilisme *m*.

commercialize, -ise [kə'mɜːʃəlaɪz] *vt* commercialiser.

commercialized [kə'mɜːʃəlaɪzd] *adj* commercial(e).

commercially [kə'mɜːʃəlɪ] *adv* commercialement.

commercial television *n Br* chaînes *fpl* (de télévision) privées OR commerciales.

commercial traveller *n Br dated* voyageur *m* OR représentant *m* de commerce.

commercial vehicle *n Br* véhicule *m* utilitaire.

commie ['kɒmɪ] *inf pej* ◇ *adj* coco. ◇ *n* coco *mf*.

commiserate [kə'mɪzəreɪt] *vi*: **to ~ with sb** témoigner de la compassion pour qqn.

commiseration [kə,mɪzə'reɪʃn] *n* compassion *f*.

commission [kə'mɪʃn] ◇ *n* **-1.** [money, investigative body] commission *f*. **-2.** [order for work] commande *f*. ◇ *vt* [work] commander; **to ~ sb to do sthg** charger qqn de faire qqch.

commissionaire [kə,mɪʃə'neə'] *n Br* chasseur *m*.

commissioned officer [kə'mɪʃənd-] *n* officier *m*.

commissioner [kə'mɪʃnə'] *n* **-1.** [in police] commissaire *m*. **-2.** [commission member] membre *m* d'une commission.

commit [kə'mɪt] (*pt* & *pp* **-ted**, *cont* **-ting**) *vt* **-1.** [crime, sin etc] commettre; **to ~ suicide** se suicider. **-2.** [promise - money, resources] allouer; **to ~ o.s. (to sthg/to doing sthg)** s'engager (à qqch/à faire qqch). **-3.** [consign]: **to ~ sb to prison** faire incarcérer qqn; **to ~ sthg to memory** apprendre qqch par cœur.

commitment [kə'mɪtmənt] *n* **-1.** (*U*) [dedication] engagement *m*. **-2.** [responsibility] obligation *f*.

committed [kə'mɪtɪd] *adj* [writer, politician] engagé(e); [Christian] convaincu(e); **he's ~ to his work** il fait preuve d'engagement dans son travail.

committee [kə'mɪtɪ] *n* commission *f*, comité *m*.

commode [kə'məʊd] *n* [with chamber pot] chaise *f* percée.

commodity [kə'mɒdətɪ] (*pl* **-ies**) *n* marchandise *f*.

commodity exchange *n* bourse *f* des matières premières.

common ['kɒmən] ◇ *adj* **-1.** [frequent] courant(e). **-2.** [shared]: **~ (to)** commun(e) (à). **-3.** [ordinary] banal(e); **the ~ man** Monsieur *m* tout-le-monde. **-4.** *Br pej* [vulgar] vulgaire. ◇ *n* [land] terrain *m* communal.

◆ **in common** *adv* en commun.

commoner ['kɒmənə'] *n* roturier *m*, -ière *f*.

common good *n*: **for the ~** dans l'intérêt général.

common ground *n fig* terrain *m* d'entente.

common knowledge *n*: **it is ~ that ...** il est de notoriété publique que ....

common land *n* (*U*) terrain *m* communal.

common law *n* droit *m* coutumier.

◆ **common-law** *adj*: **common-law wife** concubine *f*.

commonly ['kɒmənlɪ] *adv* [generally] d'une manière générale, généralement.

Common Market *n*: **the ~** le Marché commun.

commonplace ['kɒmənpleɪs] *adj* banal(e), ordinaire.

common room *n* [staffroom] salle *f* des professeurs; [for students] salle commune.

Commons ['kɒmənz] *npl Br*: **the ~** les Communes *fpl*, la Chambre des Communes.

common sense *n* (*U*) bon sens *m*.

Commonwealth ['kɒmənwelθ] *n*: **the ~** le Commonwealth.

Commonwealth of Independent States *n*: **the ~** la Communauté des États Indépendants.

commotion [kə'məʊʃn] *n* remue-ménage *m*.

communal ['kɒmjunl] *adj* [kitchen, garden] commun(e); [life etc] communautaire, collectif(ive).

commune [*n* 'kɒmjuːn, *vb* kə'mjuːn] ◇ *n* communauté *f*. ◇ *vi*: **to ~ with** communier avec.

communicate [kə'mjuːnɪkeɪt] *vt & vi* communiquer.

communicating [kə'mjuːnɪkeɪtɪŋ] *adj* [rooms] communicant(e); **~ door** porte *f* de communication.

communication [kə,mjuːnɪ'keɪʃn] *n* contact *m*; TELEC communication *f*.
◆ **communications** *npl* moyens *mpl* de communication.

communication cord *n Br* sonnette *f* d'alarme.

communications satellite *n* satellite *m* de communication.

communicative [kə'mjuːnɪkətɪv] *adj* [talkative] communicatif(ive).

communicator [kə'mjuːnɪkeɪtəʳ] *n*: **to be a good ~** avoir le don de la communication; **to be a bad ~** avoir des difficultés de communication.

communion [kə'mjuːnjən] *n* communion *f*.
◆ **Communion** *n* (*U*) RELIG communion *f*.

communiqué [kə'mjuːnɪkeɪ] *n* communiqué *m*.

Communism ['kɒmjunɪzm] *n* communisme *m*.

Communist ['kɒmjunɪst] ◇ *adj* communiste. ◇ *n* communiste *mf*.

community [kə'mjuːnətɪ] (*pl* **-ies**) *n* communauté *f*.

community centre *n* foyer *m* municipal.

community charge *n Br* ≈ impôts *mpl* locaux.

community home *n Br* centre *m* d'éducation surveillée.

community policing *n* ≈ îlotage *m*.

community service *n* (*U*) travail *m* d'intérêt général.

community spirit *n* esprit *m* de communauté.

commutable [kə'mjuːtəbl] *adj* JUR commuable.

commutation ticket [,kɒmjuː'teɪʃn-] *n Am* carte *f* de transport.

commute [kə'mjuːt] ◇ *vt* JUR commuer. ◇ *vi* [to work] faire la navette pour se rendre à son travail.

commuter [kə'mjuːtəʳ] *n* personne qui fait tous les jours la navette de banlieue en ville pour se rendre à son travail.

commy ['kɒmɪ] (*pl* **-ies**) = **commie**.

Comoro Islands ['kɒmərəʊ-] *npl*: **the ~** les îles *fpl* Comores; **in the ~** aux îles Comores.

compact [*adj & vb* kəm'pækt, *n* 'kɒmpækt] ◇ *adj* compact(e). ◇ *n* **-1.** [for face powder] poudrier *m*. **-2.** *Am* AUT: **~ (car)** petite voiture *f*. ◇ *vt* tasser, rendre compact.

compact disc *n* compact *m* (disc *m*), disque *m* compact.

compact disc player *n* lecteur *m* de disques compacts.

companion [kəm'pænjən] *n* [person] camarade *mf*; **travelling ~** compagnon *m*, compagne *f* de voyage.

companionable [kəm'pænjənəbl] *adj* sociable.

companionship [kəm'pænjənʃɪp] *n* compagnie *f*.

company ['kʌmpənɪ] (*pl* **-ies**) *n* **-1.** [COMM - gen] société *f*; [- insurance, airline, shipping company] compagnie *f*. **-2.** [companionship] compagnie *f*; **to keep sb ~** tenir compagnie à qqn; **to part ~ (with)** se séparer (de). **-3.** [of actors] troupe *f*.

company car *n* voiture *f* de fonction.

company director *n* directeur *m*, -trice *f*.

company secretary *n* secrétaire géneral *m*, secrétaire générale *f*.

comparable ['kɒmprəbl] *adj*: **~ (to OR with)** comparable (à).

comparative [kəm'pærətɪv] *adj* **-1.** [relative] relatif(ive). **-2.** [study, in grammar] comparatif(ive).

comparatively [kəm'pærətɪvlɪ] *adv* [relatively] relativement.

compare [kəm'peəʳ] ◇ *vt*: **to ~ sb/sthg (with), to ~ sb/sthg (to)** comparer qqn/qqch (avec), comparer qqn/qqch (à); **~d**

with OR **to** par rapport à. ◇ *vi*: **to ~ (with)** être comparable (à); **to ~ favourably/ unfavourably with** supporter/ne pas supporter la comparaison avec.

comparison [kəm'pærɪsn] *n* comparaison *f*; **in ~ with** OR **to** en comparaison de, par rapport à.

compartment [kəm'pɑːtmənt] *n* compartiment *m*.

compartmentalize, **-ise** [,kɒmpɑːt 'mentəlaɪz] *vt* compartimenter.

compass ['kʌmpəs] *n* **-1.** [magnetic] boussole *f*. **-2.** *fml* [scope - of person] compétences *fpl*; [- of report] limites *fpl*.
◆ **compasses** *npl*: **(a pair of) ~es** un compas.

compassion [kəm'pæʃn] *n* compassion *f*.

compassionate [kəm'pæʃənət] *adj* compatissant(e).

compatibility [kəm,pætə'bɪlətɪ] *n* [gen & COMPUT]: **~ (with)** compatibilité *f* (avec).

compatible [kəm'pætəbl] *adj* [gen & COMPUT]: **~ (with)** compatible (avec).

compatriot [kəm'pætrɪət] *n* compatriote *mf*.

compel [kəm'pel] (*pt* & *pp* **-led**, *cont* **-ling**) *vt* **-1.** [force]: **to ~ sb (to do sthg)** contraindre OR obliger qqn (à faire qqch). **-2.** [cause - sympathy, attention etc] susciter.

compelling [kəm'pelɪŋ] *adj* [forceful] irrésistible.

compendium [kəm'pendɪəm] (*pl* **-diums** OR **-dia** [-dɪə]) *n* [book] abrégé *m*.

compensate ['kɒmpenseɪt] ◇ *vt*: **to ~ sb for sthg** [financially] dédommager OR indemniser qqn de qqch. ◇ *vi*: **to ~ for sthg** compenser qqch.

compensation [,kɒmpen'seɪʃn] *n* **-1.** [money]: **~ (for)** dédommagement *m* (pour). **-2.** [way of compensating]: **~ (for)** compensation *f* (pour).

compere ['kɒmpeəʳ] *Br* ◇ *n* animateur *m*, -trice *f*. ◇ *vt* présenter, animer.

compete [kəm'piːt] *vi* **-1.** [vie - people]: **to ~ with sb for sthg** disputer qqch à qqn; **to ~ for sthg** se disputer qqch. **-2.** COMM: **to ~ (with)** être en concurrence (avec); **to ~ for sthg** se faire concurrence pour qqch. **-3.** [take part] être en compétition.

competence ['kɒmpɪtəns] *n* (*U*) [proficiency] compétence *f*, capacité *f*.

competent ['kɒmpɪtənt] *adj* compétent(e).

competently ['kɒmpɪtəntlɪ] *adv* avec compétence.

competing [kəm'piːtɪŋ] *adj* [theories etc] opposé(e).

competition [,kɒmpɪ'tɪʃn] *n* **-1.** (*U*) [rivalry] rivalité *f*, concurrence *f*. **-2.** (*U*) COMM concurrence *f*. **-3.** [race, contest] concours *m*, compétition *f*.

competitive [kəm'petətɪv] *adj* **-1.** [person] qui a l'esprit de compétition; [match, sport] de compétition; **~ examination** concours *m*. **-2.** [COMM - goods] compétitif(ive); [- manufacturer] concurrentiel(ielle).

competitively [kəm'petətɪvlɪ] *adv* **-1.** [play] dans un esprit de compétition. **-2.** COMM: **~ priced** à un prix compétitif.

competitor [kəm'petɪtəʳ] *n* concurrent *m*, -e *f*.

compilation [,kɒmpɪ'leɪʃn] *n* compilation *f*.

compile [kəm'paɪl] *vt* rédiger.

complacency [kəm'pleɪsnsɪ] *n* autosatisfaction *f*.

complacent [kəm'pleɪsnt] *adj* content(e) de soi.

complacently [kəm'pleɪsntlɪ] *adv* d'une manière hautaine; [say] d'un ton hautain.

complain [kəm'pleɪn] *vi* **-1.** [moan]: **to ~ (about)** se plaindre (de). **-2.** MED: **to ~ of** se plaindre de.

complaining [kəm'pleɪnɪŋ] *adj* [customer] mécontent(e).

complaint [kəm'pleɪnt] *n* **-1.** [gen] plainte *f*; [in shop] réclamation *f*. **-2.** MED affection *f*, maladie *f*.

complement [*n* 'kɒmplɪmənt, *vb* 'kɒmplɪ ,ment] ◇ *n* **-1.** [accompaniment] accompagnement *m*. **-2.** [number] effectif *m*; **full ~** effectif complet. **-3.** GRAMM complément *m*. ◇ *vt* aller bien avec.

complementary [,kɒmplɪ'mentərɪ] *adj* complémentaire.

complete [kəm'pliːt] ◇ *adj* **-1.** [gen] complet(ète); **~ with** doté(e) de, muni(e) de. **-2.** [finished] achevé(e). ◇ *vt* **-1.** [make whole] compléter. **-2.** [finish] achever, terminer. **-3.** [questionnaire, form] remplir.

completely [kəm'pliːtlɪ] *adv* complètement.

completion [kəm'pliːʃn] *n* achèvement *m*.

complex ['kɒmpleks] ◇ *adj* complexe. ◇ *n* [mental, of buildings] complexe *m*.

complexion [kəm'plekʃn] *n* teint *m*; **of all ~s** *fig* de tous bords.

complexity [kəm'pleksətɪ] (*pl* **-ies**) *n* complexité *f*.

compliance [kəm'plaɪəns] *n*: **~ (with)** conformité *f* (à).

compliant [kəm'plaɪənt] *adj* docile.

complicate ['kɒmplɪkeɪt] *vt* compliquer.

complicated ['kɒmplɪkeɪtɪd] *adj* compliqué(e).

complication [ˌkɒmplɪˈkeɪʃn] *n* complication *f*.

complicity [kəmˈplɪsətɪ] *n*: ~ **(in)** complicité *f* (dans).

compliment [*n* 'kɒmplɪmənt, *vb* 'kɒmplɪˌment] ◇ *n* compliment *m*. ◇ *vt*: **to ~ sb (on)** féliciter qqn (de).

◆ **compliments** *npl fml* compliments *mpl*.

complimentary [ˌkɒmplɪˈmentərɪ] *adj* -**1.** [admiring] flatteur(euse). -**2.** [free] gratuit(e).

complimentary ticket *n* billet *m* de faveur.

compliments slip *n* papillon *m* (*joint à un envoi etc*).

comply [kəmˈplaɪ] (*pt & pp* -**ied**) *vi*: **to ~ with** se conformer à.

component [kəmˈpəʊnənt] *n* composant *m*.

compose [kəmˈpəʊz] *vt* -**1.** [gen] composer; **to be ~d of** se composer de, être composé de. -**2.** [calm]: **to ~ o.s.** se calmer.

composed [kəmˈpəʊzd] *adj* [calm] calme.

composer [kəmˈpəʊzər] *n* compositeur *m*, -trice *f*.

composite ['kɒmpəzɪt] ◇ *adj* composite. ◇ *n* composite *m*.

composition [ˌkɒmpəˈzɪʃn] *n* composition *f*.

compost [*Br* 'kɒmpɒst, *Am* 'kɒmpəʊst] *n* compost *m*.

composure [kəmˈpəʊʒər] *n* sang-froid *m*, calme *m*.

compound [*adj & n* 'kɒmpaʊnd, *vb* kəmˈpaʊnd] ◇ *adj* composé(e). ◇ *n* -**1.** CHEM & LING composé *m*. -**2.** [enclosed area] enceinte *f*. ◇ *vt* -**1.** [mixture, substance]: **to be ~ed of** se composer de, être composé(e) de. -**2.** [difficulties] aggraver.

compound fracture *n* fracture *f* compliquée.

compound interest *n* intérêt *m* composé.

comprehend [ˌkɒmprɪˈhend] *vt* [understand] comprendre.

comprehension [ˌkɒmprɪˈhenʃn] *n* compréhension *f*.

comprehensive [ˌkɒmprɪˈhensɪv] ◇ *adj* -**1.** [account, report] exhaustif(ive), détaillé(e). -**2.** [insurance] tous-risques (*inv*). ◇ *n Br* lycée *m* polyvalent.

comprehensively [ˌkɒmprɪˈhensɪvlɪ] *adv* [study, cover] exhaustivement.

comprehensive school *n établissement secondaire britannique d'enseignement général*.

compress [kəmˈpres] *vt* -**1.** [squeeze, press] comprimer. -**2.** [shorten - text] condenser.

compression [kəmˈpreʃn] *n* -**1.** [of air] compression *f*. -**2.** [of text] condensation *f*.

comprise [kəmˈpraɪz] *vt* comprendre; **to be ~d of** consister en, comprendre.

compromise ['kɒmprəmaɪz] ◇ *n* compromis *m*. ◇ *vt* compromettre; **to ~ o.s.** se compromettre. ◇ *vi* transiger.

compromising ['kɒmprəmaɪzɪŋ] *adj* compromettant(e).

compulsion [kəmˈpʌlʃn] *n* -**1.** [strong desire]: **to have a ~ to do sthg** ne pas pouvoir s'empêcher de faire qqch. -**2.** (*U*) [obligation] obligation *f*.

compulsive [kəmˈpʌlsɪv] *adj* -**1.** [smoker, liar etc] invétéré(e). -**2.** [book, TV programme] captivant(e).

compulsory [kəmˈpʌlsərɪ] *adj* obligatoire.

compulsory purchase *n Br* expropriation *f* (*pour cause d'utilité publique*).

compunction [kəmˈpʌŋkʃn] *n* (*U*) scrupule *m*, remords *m*.

computation [ˌkɒmpjuːˈteɪʃn] *n* calcul *m*.

compute [kəmˈpjuːt] *vt* calculer.

computer [kəmˈpjuːtər] ◇ *n* ordinateur *m*. ◇ *comp*: ~ **graphics** infographie *f*; ~ **program** programme *m* informatique.

computer dating [-'deɪtɪŋ] *n* (*U*) ≈ rencontres *fpl* par minitel.

computer game *n* jeu *m* électronique.

computerization [kəmˌpjuːtəraɪˈzeɪʃn] *n* informatisation *f*.

computerize, -ise [kəmˈpjuːtəraɪz] *vt* informatiser.

computerized [kəmˈpjuːtəraɪzd] *adj* informatisé(e).

computer language *n* langage *m* de programmation.

computer-literate *adj* qui a des connaissances en informatique.

computing [kəmˈpjuːtɪŋ], **computer science** *n* informatique *f*.

comrade ['kɒmreɪd] *n* camarade *mf*.

comradeship ['kɒmreɪdʃɪp] *n* camaraderie *f*.

comsat ['kɒmsæt] *abbr of* **communications satellite**.

con [kɒn] (*pt & pp* -**ned**, *cont* -**ning**) *inf* ◇ *n* -**1.** [trick] escroquerie *f*. -**2.** *prison sl* taulard *m*. ◇ *vt* [trick]: **to ~ sb (out of)** escroquer qqn (de); **to ~ sb into doing sthg** persuader qqn de faire qqch (en lui mentant).

concave [ˌkɒnˈkeɪv] *adj* concave.

conceal [kənˈsiːl] *vt* cacher, dissimuler; **to ~ sthg from sb** cacher qqch à qqn.

concede [kənˈsiːd] ◇ *vt* concéder. ◇ *vi* céder.

conceit [kənˈsiːt] *n* [arrogance] vanité *f*.

conceited [kən'siːtɪd] *adj* vaniteux(euse).

conceivable [kən'siːvəbl] *adj* concevable.

conceivably [ken'siːvəblɪ] *adv*: **they might ~ win** il se peut qu'ils gagnent; **I can't ~ do that** il n'est pas question que je fasse ça.

conceive [kən'siːv] ◇ *vt* concevoir. ◇ *vi* **-1.** MED concevoir. **-2.** [imagine]: **to ~ of** concevoir.

concentrate ['kɒnsəntreɪt] ◇ *vt* concentrer. ◇ *vi*: **to ~ (on)** se concentrer (sur).

concentrated ['kɒnsəntreɪtɪd] *adj* concentré(e); [effort] intense.

concentration [,kɒnsən'treɪʃn] *n* concentration *f*.

concentration camp *n* camp *m* de concentration.

concentric [kən'sentrɪk] *adj* concentrique.

concept ['kɒnsept] *n* concept *m*.

conception [kən'sepʃn] *n* [gen & MED] conception *f*.

conceptualize, **-ise** [kən'septʃuəlaɪz] *vt* conceptualiser.

concern [kən'sɜːn] ◇ *n* **-1.** [worry, anxiety] souci *m*, inquiétude *f*; **to show ~ for** s'inquiéter de. **-2.** [matter of interest]: **it's no ~ of mine** cela ne me regarde pas. **-3.** COMM [company] affaire *f*.
◇ *vt* **-1.** [worry] inquiéter; **to be ~ed (about)** s'inquiéter (de). **-2.** [involve] concerner, intéresser; **as far as I'm ~ed** en ce qui me concerne; **to be ~ed with** [subj: person] s'intéresser à; **to ~ o.s. with sthg** s'intéresser à, s'occuper de. **-3.** [subj: book, film] traiter de.

concerning [kən'sɜːnɪŋ] *prep* en ce qui concerne.

concert ['kɒnsət] *n* concert *m*.
◆ **in concert** *adv* **-1.** MUS à l'unisson. **-2.** *fml* [acting as one] de concert.

concerted [kən'sɜːtɪd] *adj* [effort] concerté(e).

concertgoer ['kɒnsət,gəuə[r]] *n* amateur *m* de concerts.

concert hall *n* salle *f* de concert.

concertina [,kɒnsə'tiːnə] (*pt* & *pp* **-ed**, *cont* **-ing**) ◇ *n* concertina *m*. ◇ *vi* [cars] s'écraser en accordéon.

concerto [kən'tʃeətəu] (*pl* **-s**) *n* concerto *m*.

concession [kən'seʃn] *n* **-1.** [gen] concession *f*. **-2.** [special price] réduction *f*.

concessionaire [kən,seʃə'neə[r]] *n* concessionnaire *mf*.

concessionary [kən'seʃnərɪ] *adj* [fare] à prix réduit.

conciliation [kən,sɪlɪ'eɪʃn] *n* conciliation *f*.

conciliatory [kən'sɪlɪətrɪ] *adj* conciliant(e).

concise [kən'saɪs] *adj* concis(e).

concisely [kən'saɪslɪ] *adv* de façon concise, avec concision.

conclave ['kɒŋkleɪv] *n* conclave *m*.

conclude [kən'kluːd] ◇ *vt* conclure. ◇ *vi* [meeting] prendre fin; [speaker] conclure.

conclusion [kən'kluːʒn] *n* conclusion *f*; **it was a foregone ~** c'était à prévoir; **to jump to the wrong ~** tirer des conclusions trop hâtives.

conclusive [kən'kluːsɪv] *adj* concluant(e).

concoct [kən'kɒkt] *vt* préparer; *fig* concocter.

concoction [kən'kɒkʃn] *n* préparation *f*.

concord ['kɒŋkɔːd] *n* [harmony] concorde *f*.

concourse ['kɒŋkɔːs] *n* [hall] hall *m*.

concrete ['kɒŋkriːt] ◇ *adj* [definite] concret(ète). ◇ *n* (*U*) béton *m*. ◇ *comp* [made of concrete] en béton. ◇ *vt* bétonner.

concrete mixer *n* bétonnière *f*.

concubine ['kɒŋkjubaɪn] *n* maîtresse *f*.

concur [kən'kɜː[r]] (*pt* & *pp* **-red**, *cont* **-ring**) *vi* [agree]: **to ~ (with)** être d'accord (avec).

concurrently [kən'kʌrəntlɪ] *adv* simultanément.

concussed [kən'kʌst] *adj* commotionné(e).

concussion [kən'kʌʃn] *n* commotion *f*.

condemn [kən'dem] *vt* condamner.

condemnation [,kɒndem'neɪʃn] *n* condamnation *f*.

condemned [kən'demd] *adj* condamné(e).

condensation [,kɒnden'seɪʃn] *n* condensation *f*.

condense [kən'dens] ◇ *vt* condenser. ◇ *vi* se condenser.

condensed milk [kən'denst-] *n* lait *m* condensé.

condescend [,kɒndɪ'send] *vi* **-1.** [talk down]: **to ~ to sb** se montrer condescendant(e) envers qqn. **-2.** [deign]: **to ~ to do sthg** daigner faire qqch, condescendre à faire qqch.

condescending [,kɒndɪ'sendɪŋ] *adj* condescendant(e).

condiment ['kɒndɪmənt] *n* condiment *m*.

condition [kən'dɪʃn] ◇ *n* **-1.** [gen] condition *f*; **in (a) good/bad ~** en bon/mauvais état; **out of ~** pas en forme. **-2.** MED maladie *f*. ◇ *vt* **-1.** [gen] conditionner. **-2.** [hair]: **to ~ one's hair** mettre de l'après-shampooing.
◆ **conditions** *npl* conditions *fpl*.

conditional [kən'dɪʃənl] *adj* conditionnel(elle); **to be ~ on** OR **upon** dépendre de.

conditionally [kən'dɪʃnəlɪ] *adv* condition-nellement.

conditioner [kən'dɪʃnəʳ] **-1.** [for hair] après-shampooing *m.* **-2.** [for clothes] assou-plissant *m.*

conditioning [kən'dɪʃnɪŋ] *n* PSYCH condi-tionnement *m.*

condo ['kɒndəʊ] *n inf abbr of* **condominium.**

condolences [kən'dəʊlənsɪz] *npl* condo-léances *fpl.*

condom ['kɒndəm] *n* préservatif *m.*

condominium [,kɒndə'mɪnɪəm] *n Am* **-1.** [apartment] appartement *m* dans un immeu-ble en copropriété. **-2.** [apartment block] im-meuble *m* en copropriété.

condone [kən'dəʊn] *vt* pardonner.

condor ['kɒndɔːʳ] *n* condor *m.*

conducive [kən'djuːsɪv] *adj*: **to be ~ to sthg/to doing sthg** inciter à qqch/à faire qqch.

conduct [*n* 'kɒndʌkt, *vb* kən'dʌkt] ◇ *n* conduite *f.* ◇ *vt* **-1.** [carry out, transmit] conduire. **-2.** [behave]: **to ~ o.s. well/badly** se conduire bien/mal. **-3.** MUS diriger. ◇ *vi* MUS diriger.

conducted tour [kən'dʌktɪd-] *n* visite *f* gui-dée.

conductor [kən'dʌktəʳ] *n* **-1.** MUS chef *m* d'orchestre. **-2.** [on bus] receveur *m.* **-3.** *Am* [on train] chef *m* de train.

conductress [kən'dʌktrɪs] *n* [on bus] rece-veuse *f.*

conduit ['kɒndɪt] *n* conduit *m.*

cone [kəʊn] *n* **-1.** [shape] cône *m.* **-2.** [for ice cream] cornet *m.* **-3.** [from tree] pomme *f* de pin.

◆ **cone off** *vt sep Br* [road, lane] fermer à la circulation.

confectioner [kən'fekʃnəʳ] *n* confiseur *m*; **~'s (shop)** confiserie *f.*

confectionery [kən'fekʃnərɪ] *n* confiserie *f.*

confederation [kən,fedə'reɪʃn] *n* confédéra-tion *f.*

Confederation of British Industry *n*: **the ~** ≃ le conseil du patronnat.

confer [kən'fɜːʳ] (*pt & pp* **-red**, *cont* **-ring**) ◇ *vt*: **to ~ sthg (on sb)** conférer qqch (à qqn). ◇ *vi*: **to ~ (with sb on OR about sthg)** s'en-tretenir (avec qqn de qqch).

conference ['kɒnfərəns] *n* conférence *f*; **in ~** en conférence.

conference call *n* audioconférence *f.*

conference centre *n* centre *m* de confé-rences.

conference hall *n* salle *f* de conférence.

conferencing ['kɒnfərənsɪŋ] *n* (*U*) audio-conférence *f.*

confess [kən'fes] ◇ *vt* **-1.** [admit] avouer, confesser. **-2.** RELIG confesser. ◇ *vi*: **to ~ (to sthg)** avouer (qqch).

confession [kən'feʃn] *n* confession *f*; **I've a ~ to make** j'ai un aveu à vous faire.

confessional [kən'feʃənl] *n* confessionnal *m.*

confetti [kən'fetɪ] *n* (*U*) confettis *mpl.*

confidant [,kɒnfɪ'dænt] *n* confident *m.*

confidante [,kɒnfɪ'dænt] *n* confidente *f.*

confide [kən'faɪd] ◇ *vt* confier. ◇ *vi*: **to ~ in sb** se confier à qqn.

confidence ['kɒnfɪdəns] *n* **-1.** [self-assurance] confiance *f* en soi, assurance *f.* **-2.** [trust] confiance *f*; **to have ~ in** avoir confiance en. **-3.** [secrecy]: **in ~** en confidence. **-4.** [se-cret] confidence *f.*

confidence trick *n* abus *m* de confiance.

confident ['kɒnfɪdənt] *adj* **-1.** [self-assured]: **to be ~** avoir confiance en soi. **-2.** [sure] sûr(e).

confidential [,kɒnfɪ'denʃl] *adj* confiden-tiel(ielle).

confidentiality ['kɒnfɪ,denʃɪ'ælətɪ] *n* confi-dentialité *f.*

confidentially [,kɒnfɪ'denʃəlɪ] *adv* confiden-tiellement.

confidently ['kɒnfɪdəntlɪ] *adv* [speak, predict] avec assurance.

configuration [kən,fɪgə'reɪʃn] *n* [gen & COM-PUT] configuration *f.*

confine [kən'faɪn] *vt* **-1.** [limit] limiter; **to ~ o.s. to** se limiter à. **-2.** [shut up] enfermer, confiner.

◆ **confines** *npl* confins *mpl.*

confined [kən'faɪnd] *adj* [space, area] res-treint(e).

confinement [kən'faɪnmənt] *n* **-1.** [imprison-ment] emprisonnement *m.* **-2.** *dated* MED couches *fpl.*

confirm [kən'fɜːm] *vt* confirmer.

confirmation [,kɒnfə'meɪʃn] *n* confirmation *f.*

confirmed [kən'fɜːmd] *adj* [habitual] invété-ré(e); [bachelor, spinster] endurci(e).

confiscate ['kɒnfɪskeɪt] *vt* confisquer.

confiscation [,kɒnfɪ'skeɪʃn] *n* confiscation *f.*

conflagration [,kɒnflə'greɪʃn] *n* conflagra-tion *f.*

conflict [*n* 'kɒnflɪkt, *vb* kən'flɪkt] ◇ *n* conflit *m.* ◇ *vi*: **to ~ (with)** s'opposer (à), être en conflit (avec).

conflicting [kən'flɪktɪŋ] *adj* contradictoire.

conform [kən'fɔːm] *vi*: **to ~ (to** OR **with)** se conformer (à).

conformist [kən'fɔːmɪst] ◇ *adj* conformiste. ◇ *n* conformiste *mf*.

conformity [kən'fɔːmətɪ] *n*: **~ (to** OR **with)** conformité *f* (à).

confound [kən'faʊnd] *vt* [confuse, defeat] déconcerter.

confounded [kən'faʊndɪd] *adj inf* sacré(e).

confront [kən'frʌnt] *vt* **-1.** [problem, enemy] affronter. **-2.** [challenge]: **to ~ sb (with)** confronter qqn (avec).

confrontation [ˌkɒnfrʌn'teɪʃn] *n* affrontement *m*.

confuse [kən'fjuːz] *vt* **-1.** [disconcert] troubler; **to ~ the issue** brouiller les cartes. **-2.** [mix up] confondre.

confused [kən'fjuːzd] *adj* **-1.** [not clear] compliqué(e). **-2.** [disconcerted] troublé(e), désorienté(e); **I'm ~** je n'y comprends rien.

confusing [kən'fjuːzɪŋ] *adj* pas clair(e).

confusion [kən'fjuːʒn] *n* confusion *f*.

conga ['kɒŋgə] *n*: **the ~** la conga.

congeal [kən'dʒiːl] *vi* [blood] se coaguler.

congenial [kən'dʒiːnjəl] *adj* sympathique, agréable.

congenital [kən'dʒenɪtl] *adj* MED congénital(e).

conger eel ['kɒŋgə-] *n* congre *m*.

congested [kən'dʒestɪd] *adj* **-1.** [street, area] encombré(e). **-2.** MED congestionné(e).

congestion [kən'dʒestʃn] *n* **-1.** [of traffic] encombrement *m*. **-2.** MED congestion *f*.

conglomerate [kən'glɒmərət] *n* COMM conglomérat *m*.

conglomeration [kənˌglɒmə'reɪʃn] *n* conglomération *f*.

Congo ['kɒŋgəʊ] *n* **-1.** [country]: **the ~** le Congo; **in the ~** au Congo. **-2.** [river]: **the ~** le fleuve Zaïre.

Congolese [ˌkɒŋgə'liːz] ◇ *adj* congolais(e). ◇ *n* Congolais *m*, -e *f*.

congratulate [kən'grætʃʊleɪt] *vt*: **to ~ sb (on sthg/on doing sthg)** féliciter qqn (de qqch/d'avoir fait qqch).

congratulations [kənˌgrætʃʊ'leɪʃənz] *npl* félicitations *fpl*.

congratulatory [kən'grætʃʊlətrɪ] *adj* de félicitations.

congregate ['kɒŋgrɪgeɪt] *vi* se rassembler.

congregation [ˌkɒŋgrɪ'geɪʃn] *n* assemblée *f* des fidèles.

congress ['kɒŋgres] *n* [meeting] congrès *m*.

◆ **Congress** *n Am* POL le Congrès.

CONGRESS:

Le Congrès, organe législatif américain, est constitué du Sénat et de la Chambre des Représentants; une proposition de loi doit obligatoirement être approuvée séparément par ces deux chambres

congressional [kəŋ'greʃənl] *adj Am* POL du Congrès.

congressman ['kɒŋgresmən] (*pl* **-men** [-mən]) *n Am* POL membre *m* du Congrès.

congresswoman ['kɒŋgres,wʊmən] (*pl* **-women** [-,wɪmɪn]) *n Am* POL membre *m* (féminin) du Congrès.

conical ['kɒnɪkl] *adj* conique.

conifer ['kɒnɪfə-] *n* conifère *m*.

coniferous [kə'nɪfərəs] *adj* [tree] conifère; [forest] de conifères.

conjecture [kən'dʒektʃə-] ◇ *n* conjecture *f*. ◇ *vt & vi* conjecturer.

conjugal ['kɒndʒʊgl] *adj* conjugal(e).

conjugation [ˌkɒndʒʊ'geɪʃn] *n* GRAMM conjugaison *f*.

conjunction [kən'dʒʌŋkʃn] *n* **-1.** GRAMM conjonction *f*. **-2.** [combination] combinaison *f*, mélange *m*; **in ~ with** conjointement avec.

conjunctivitis [kənˌdʒʌŋktɪ'vaɪtɪs] *n* conjonctivite *f*.

conjure ['kʌndʒə-, *vt* kən'dʒʊə-] ◇ *vt fml* supplier. ◇ *vi* [by magic] faire des tours de prestidigitation.

◆ **conjure up** *vt sep* évoquer.

conjurer ['kʌndʒərə-] *n* prestidigitateur *m*, -trice *f*.

conjuring trick ['kʌndʒərɪŋ-] *n* tour *m* de prestidigitation.

conjuror ['kʌndʒərə-] = **conjurer**.

conk [kɒŋk] *n inf* pif *m*.

◆ **conk out** *vi inf* tomber en panne.

conker ['kɒŋkə-] *n Br* marron *m*.

conman ['kɒnmæn] (*pl* **-men** [-men]) *n* escroc *m*.

connect [kə'nekt] ◇ *vt* **-1.** [join]: **to ~ sthg (to)** relier qqch (à). **-2.** [on telephone] mettre en communication. **-3.** [associate] associer; **to ~ sb/sthg to, to ~ sb/sthg with** associer qqn/qqch à. **-4.** ELEC [to power supply]: **to ~ sthg to** brancher qqch à. ◇ *vi* [train, plane, bus]: **to ~ (with)** assurer la correspondance (avec).

connected [kə'nektɪd] *adj* [related]: **to be ~ with** avoir un rapport avec; **they are not ~** il n'y a aucun rapport entre eux.

Connecticut [kə'netıkət] *n* Connecticut *m*; **in** ~ dans le Connecticut.

connecting [kə'nektıŋ] *adj*: ~ **flight/train** correspondance *f*.

connection [kə'nekʃn] *n* **-1.** [relationship]: ~ **(between/with)** rapport *m* (entre/avec); **in** ~ **with** à propos de. **-2.** ELEC branchement *m*, connexion *f*. **-3.** [on telephone] communication *f*; **it's a bad** ~ la ligne est mauvaise. **-4.** [plane, train, bus] correspondance *f*. **-5.** [professional acquaintance] relation *f*.

connective tissue [kə'nektıv-] *n* tissu *m* conjonctif.

connexion [kə'nekʃn] *Br* = **connection**.

connive [kə'naıv] *vi* **-1.** [plot] comploter; **to** ~ **with sb** être de connivence avec qqn. **-2.** [allow to happen]: **to** ~ **at sthg** fermer les yeux sur qqch.

conniving [kə'naıvıŋ] *adj*: **you** ~ **wretch!** espèce de sale comploteur!

connoisseur [ˌkɒnə'sɜːr] *n* connaisseur *m*, -euse *f*.

connotation [ˌkɒnə'teıʃn] *n* connotation *f*.

conquer ['kɒŋkər] *vt* **-1.** [country, people etc] conquérir. **-2.** [fears, inflation etc] vaincre.

conqueror ['kɒŋkərər] *n* conquérant *m*, -e *f*.

conquest ['kɒŋkwest] *n* conquête *f*.

cons [kɒnz] *npl* **-1.** *Br inf*: **all mod** ~ tout confort. **-2.** → **pro**.

Cons. *abbr of* **Conservative**.

conscience ['kɒnʃəns] *n* conscience *f*; **to have a guilty** ~ avoir mauvaise conscience; **in all** ~ en mon/votre *etc* âme et conscience.

conscientious [ˌkɒnʃı'enʃəs] *adj* consciencieux(ieuse).

conscientiously [ˌkɒnʃı'enʃəslı] *adv* consciencieusement.

conscientiousness [ˌkɒnʃı'enʃəsnıs] *n* conscience *f*.

conscientious objector *n* objecteur *m* de conscience.

conscious ['kɒnʃəs] *adj* **-1.** [not unconscious] conscient(e). **-2.** [aware]: ~ **of sthg** conscient(e) de qqch; **fashion-**~ qui suit la mode; **money-**~ qui fait attention à ses dépenses. **-3.** [intentional - insult] délibéré(e), intentionnel(elle); [- effort] conscient(e).

consciously ['kɒnʃəslı] *adv* intentionnellement.

consciousness ['kɒnʃəsnıs] *n* conscience *f*.

conscript [*n* 'kɒnskrıpt, *vb* kən'skrıpt] MIL ◇ *n* conscrit *m*. ◇ *vt* appeler sous les drapeaux.

conscription [kən'skrıpʃn] *n* conscription *f*.

consecrate ['kɒnsıkreıt] *vt* consacrer.

consecration [ˌkɒnsı'kreıʃn] *n* consécration *f*.

consecutive [kən'sekjutıv] *adj* consécutif(ive).

consecutively [kən'sekjutıvlı] *adv* consécutivement.

consensus [kən'sensəs] *n* consensus *m*.

consent [kən'sent] ◇ *n* (U) **-1.** [permission] consentement *m*. **-2.** [agreement] accord *m*. ◇ *vi*: **to** ~ **(to)** consentir (à).

consenting [kən'sentıŋ] *adj*: ~ **adults** adultes consentants.

consequence ['kɒnsıkwəns] *n* **-1.** [result] conséquence *f*; **in** ~ par conséquent. **-2.** [importance] importance *f*.

consequent ['kɒnsıkwənt] *adj fml* consécutif(ive); [resulting] résultant(e).

consequently ['kɒnsıkwəntlı] *adv* par conséquent.

conservation [ˌkɒnsə'veıʃn] *n* [of nature] protection *f*; [of buildings] conservation *f*; [of energy, water] économie *f*.

conservation area *n* secteur *m* sauvegardé.

conservationist [ˌkɒnsə'veıʃənıst] *n* écologiste *mf*.

conservatism [kən'sɜːvətızm] *n* conservatisme *m*.

◆ **Conservatism** *n* POL conservatisme *m*.

conservative [kən'sɜːvətıv] ◇ *adj* **-1.** [not modern] traditionnel(elle). **-2.** [cautious] prudent(e). ◇ *n* traditionaliste *mf*.

◆ **Conservative** POL ◇ *adj* conservateur(trice). ◇ *n* conservateur *m*, -trice *f*.

Conservative Party *n*: **the** ~ le parti conservateur.

conservatory [kən'sɜːvətrı] (*pl* **-ies**) *n* [of house] véranda *f*.

conserve [*n* 'kɒnsɜːv, *vb* kən'sɜːv] ◇ *n* confiture *f*. ◇ *vt* [energy, supplies] économiser; [nature, wildlife] protéger.

consider [kən'sıdər] *vt* **-1.** [think about] examiner. **-2.** [take into account] prendre en compte; **all things** ~**ed** tout compte fait. **-3.** [judge] considérer.

considerable [kən'sıdrəbl] *adj* considérable.

considerably [kən'sıdrəblı] *adv* considérablement.

considerate [kən'sıdərət] *adj* prévenant(e); **that's very** ~ **of you** c'est très gentil à vous OR de votre part.

consideration [kənˌsıdə'reıʃn] *n* **-1.** (U) [careful thought] réflexion *f*; **to take sthg into** ~ tenir compte de qqch, prendre qqch en considération; **under** ~ à l'étude. **-2.** (U) [care] attention *f*. **-3.** [factor] facteur *m*.

considered [kən'sɪdəd] *adj*: **it's my ~ opin-**
ion that ... après mûre réflexion je pense
que ....

considering [kən'sɪdərɪŋ] ◇ *prep* étant
donné. ◇ *conj* étant donné que.

consign [kən'saɪn] *vt*: **to ~ sb/sthg to** reléguer qqn/qqch à.

consignee [ˌkɒnsaɪ'niː] *n* destinataire *mf*.

consignment [ˌkən'saɪnmənt] *n* [load] expédition *f*.

consignment note *n* bordereau *m* d'expédition.

consignor [kən'saɪnər] *n* expéditeur *m*,
-trice *f*.

consist [kən'sɪst]

♦ **consist in** *vt fus*: **to ~ in sthg** consister
dans qqch; **to ~ in doing sthg** consister à
faire qqch.

♦ **consist of** *vt fus* consister en.

consistency [kən'sɪstənsɪ] (*pl* **-ies**) *n* **-1.** [co-
herence] cohérence *f*. **-2.** [texture] consistance *f*.

consistent [kən'sɪstənt] *adj* **-1.** [regular - be-
haviour] conséquent(e); [- improvement] ré-
gulier(ière); [- supporter] constant(e). **-2.** [co-
herent] cohérent(e); **to be ~ with** [with one's
position] être compatible avec; [with the
facts] correspondre avec.

consistently [kən'sɪstəntlɪ] *adv* **-1.** [without
exception] invariablement. **-2.** [argue, reason]
de manière cohérente.

consolation [ˌkɒnsə'leɪʃn] *n* réconfort *m*.

consolation prize *n* prix *m* de consolation.

console [*n* 'kɒnsəʊl, *vt* kən'səʊl] ◇ *n* tableau
m de commande; MUS console *f*. ◇ *vt*
consoler; **he had to ~ himself with** second
place il a dû se contenter de la deuxième
place.

consolidate [kən'sɒlɪdeɪt] ◇ *vt* **-1.** [strength-
en] consolider. **-2.** [merge] fusionner. ◇ *vi*
fusionner.

consolidation [kənˌsɒlɪ'deɪʃn] *n* (*U*) **-1.**
[strengthening] affermissement *m*. **-2.** [merg-
ing] fusion *f*.

consols ['kɒnsəlz] *npl Br* fonds *mpl* consoli-
dés.

consommé [*Br* kən'sɒmeɪ, *Am* ˌkɒnsə'meɪ] *n*
consommé *m*.

consonant ['kɒnsənənt] *n* consonne *f*.

consort [*vb* kən'sɔːt, *n* 'kɒnsɔːt] ◇ *vi fml*: **to**
~ with sb fréquenter qqn. ◇ *n*: **prince ~**
prince *m* consort.

consortium [kən'sɔːtjəm] (*pl* **-tiums** OR **-tia**
[-tjə]) *n* consortium *m*.

conspicuous [kən'spɪkjʊəs] *adj* voyant(e),
qui se remarque.

conspicuously [kən'spɪkjʊəslɪ] *adv* [dressed]
de manière voyante; [wealthy] ostensiblement.

conspiracy [kən'spɪrəsɪ] (*pl* **-ies**) *n* conspiration *f*, complot *m*.

conspirator [kən'spɪrətər] *n* conspirateur *m*,
-trice *f*.

conspiratorial [kənˌspɪrə'tɔːrɪəl] *adj* de
conspirateur.

conspire [kən'spaɪər] ◇ *vt*: **to ~ to do sthg**
comploter de faire qqch; [subj: events]
contribuer à faire qqch. ◇ *vi*: **to ~**
against/with sb conspirer contre/avec qqn.

constable ['kʌnstəbl] *n Br* [policeman] agent
m de police.

constabulary [kən'stæbjʊlərɪ] (*pl* **-ies**) *n* police *f*.

constancy ['kɒnstənsɪ] *n* constance *f*.

constant ['kɒnstənt] *adj* **-1.** [unvarying]
constant(e). **-2.** [recurring] continuel(elle).
-3. *literary* [faithful] fidèle.

constantly ['kɒnstəntlɪ] *adv* constamment.

constellation [ˌkɒnstə'leɪʃn] *n* constellation
f.

consternation [ˌkɒnstə'neɪʃn] *n* consternation *f*.

constipated ['kɒnstɪpeɪtɪd] *adj* constipé(e).

constipation [ˌkɒnstɪ'peɪʃn] *n* constipation
f.

constituency [kən'stɪtjʊənsɪ] (*pl* **-ies**) *n* [area]
circonscription *f* électorale.

constituency party *n Br* section *f* locale
du parti.

constituent [kən'stɪtjʊənt] ◇ *adj* consti-
tuant(e). ◇ *n* **-1.** [voter] électeur *m*, -trice *f*.
-2. [element] composant *m*.

constitute ['kɒnstɪtjuːt] *vt* **-1.** [form, repre-
sent] représenter, constituer. **-2.** [establish,
set up] constituer.

constitution [ˌkɒnstɪ'tjuːʃn] *n* constitution
f.

♦ **Constitution** *n*: **the (United States)**
Constitution la Constitution américaine.

CONSTITUTION:

Il est à noter que la Constitution britannique, à la différence de la Constitution américaine (texte écrit et définitif), n'est pas un
document en soi, mais le résultat virtuel de
la succession des lois dans le temps, fonc-
tionnant sur le principe de la jurisprudence

---

constitutional [ˌkɒnstɪ'tjuːʃənl] *adj* consti-
tutionnel(elle).

constrain [kən'streɪn] *vt* **-1.** [coerce] forcer, contraindre; **to ~ sb to do sthg** forcer qqn à faire qqch. **-2.** [restrict] limiter.

constrained [kən'streɪnd] *adj* [inhibited] contraint(e).

constraint [kən'streɪnt] *n* **-1.** [restriction]: ~ **(on)** limitation *f* (à). **-2.** (U) [self-control] retenue *f*, réserve *f*. **-3.** [coercion] contrainte *f*.

constrict [kən'strɪkt] *vt* **-1.** [compress] serrer. **-2.** [limit] limiter.

constricting [kən'strɪktɪŋ] *adj* **-1.** [clothes] qui entrave les mouvements. **-2.** [circumstances, lifestyle] contraignant(e).

construct [*vb* kən'strʌkt, *n* 'kɒnstrʌkt] ◇ *vt* construire. ◇ *n fml* [concept] concept *m*.

construction [kən'strʌkʃn] ◇ *n* construction *f*; **under ~** en construction. ◇ *comp* [worker] du bâtiment; ~ **site** chantier *m*.

construction industry *n* industrie *f* du bâtiment.

constructive [kən'strʌktɪv] *adj* constructif(ive).

constructively [kən'strʌktɪvlɪ] *adv* d'une manière constructive.

construe [kən'struː] *vt fml* [interpret]: **to ~ sthg as** interpréter qqch comme.

consul ['kɒnsəl] *n* consul *m*.

consular ['kɒnsjʊlər] *adj* consulaire.

consulate ['kɒnsjʊlət] *n* consulat *m*.

consult [kən'sʌlt] ◇ *vt* consulter. ◇ *vi*: **to ~ with sb** s'entretenir avec qqn.

consultancy [kən'sʌltənsɪ] (*pl* -ies) *n* [company] cabinet *m* d'expert-conseil.

consultancy fee *n* honoraires *mpl* d'expert.

consultant [kən'sʌltənt] *n* **-1.** [expert] expert-conseil *m*. **-2.** *Br* [hospital doctor] spécialiste *mf*.

consultation [,kɒnsəl'teɪʃn] *n* **-1.** [meeting, discussion] entretien *m*. **-2.** [reference] consultation *f*.

consulting room [kən'sʌltɪŋ-] *n* cabinet *m* de consultation.

consume [kən'sjuːm] *vt* **-1.** [food, fuel etc] consommer. **-2.** *literary* [fill]: **to be ~d by hatred/passion** être consumé(e) par la haine/la passion.

consumer [kən'sjuːmər] ◇ *n* consommateur *m*, -trice *f*. ◇ *comp* du consommateur.

consumer credit *n* (U) crédit *m* à la consommation.

consumer durables *npl* biens *mpl* de consommation durables.

consumer goods *npl* biens *mpl* de consommation.

consumerism [kən'sjuːmərɪzm] *n* (U) **-1.** [buying] (règne *m* de la) société *f* de consommation. **-2.** [protection of rights] consumérisme *m*.

consumer society *n* société *f* de consommation.

consumer spending *n* (U) dépenses *fpl* de consommation.

consummate [*adj* kən'sʌmət, *vb* 'kɒnsəmeɪt] ◇ *adj* consommé(e); [liar] fieffé(e). ◇ *vt* consommer.

consummation [,kɒnsə'meɪʃn] *n* **-1.** [of marriage] consommation *f*. **-2.** [culmination] apogée *m*.

consumption [kən'sʌmpʃn] *n* **-1.** [use] consommation *f*. **-2.** *dated* [tuberculosis] phtisie *f*.

cont. *abbr of* **continued**.

contact ['kɒntækt] ◇ *n* **-1.** (U) [touch, communication] contact *m*; **in ~ (with sb)** en rapport OR contact (avec qqn); **to lose ~ with sb** perdre le contact avec qqn; **to make ~ with sb** prendre contact OR entrer en contact avec qqn. **-2.** [person] relation *f*, contact *m*. ◇ *vt* contacter, prendre contact avec; [by phone] joindre, contacter.

contact lens *n* verre *m* de contact, lentille *f* (cornéenne).

contact number *n*: **do you have a ~?** tu as un numéro où on peut te joindre?

contagious [kən'teɪdʒəs] *adj* contagieux(ieuse).

contain [kən'teɪn] *vt* **-1.** [hold, include] contenir, renfermer. **-2.** *fml* [control] contenir; [epidemic] circonscrire.

contained [kən'teɪnd] *adj* [person] maître (maîtresse) de soi.

container [kən'teɪnər] *n* **-1.** [box, bottle etc] récipient *m*. **-2.** [for transporting goods] conteneur *m*, container *m*.

containerize, -ise [kən'teɪnəraɪz] *vt* COMM [goods] conteneuriser; [port] convertir à la conteneurisation.

container ship *n* porte-conteneurs *m*.

containment [kən'teɪnmənt] *n* (U) **-1.** [limitation]: **our efforts at the ~ of this violence** nos efforts pour contenir cette violence. **-2.** POL: **policy of ~** politique *f* d'endiguement.

contaminate [kən'tæmɪneɪt] *vt* contaminer.

contaminated [kən'tæmɪneɪtɪd] *adj* contaminé(e).

contamination [kən,tæmɪ'neɪʃn] *n* contamination *f*.

cont'd *abbr of* **continued**.

contemplate ['kɒntempleɪt] ◇ *vt* **-1.** [consider] envisager; **to ~ doing sthg** envisager de faire qqch. **-2.** *fml* [look at] contempler. ◇ *vi* [consider] méditer.

contemplation [ˌkɒntem'pleɪʃn] *n* contemplation *f*.

contemplative [kən'templətɪv] *adj* contemplatif(ive).

contemporary [kən'tempərərɪ] (*pl* **-ies**) ◇ *adj* contemporain(e). ◇ *n* contemporain *m*, -e *f*.

contempt [kən'tempt] *n* **-1.** [scorn]: **~ (for)** mépris *m* (pour); **to hold sb in ~** mépriser qqn. **-2.** JUR: **~ (of court)** outrage *m* à la cour.

contemptible [kən'temptəbl] *adj* méprisable.

contemptuous [kən'temptʃʊəs] *adj* méprisant(e); **~ of sthg** dédaigneux(euse) de qqch.

contend [kən'tend] ◇ *vi* **-1.** [deal]: **to ~ with sthg** faire face à qqch; **I've got enough to ~ with** j'ai assez de problèmes comme ça. **-2.** [compete]: **to ~ for** [subj: several people] se disputer; [subj: one person] se battre pour; **to ~ against** lutter contre. ◇ *vt fml* [claim]: **to ~ that ...** soutenir OR prétendre que ....

contender [kən'tendər] *n* [in election] candidat *m*, -e *f*; [in competition] concurrent *m*, -e *f*; [in boxing etc] prétendant *m*, -e *f*.

content [*n* 'kɒntent, *adj & vb* kən'tent] ◇ *adj*: **~ (with)** satisfait(e) (de), content(e) (de); **to be ~ to do sthg** ne pas demander mieux que de faire qqch. ◇ *n* **-1.** [amount] teneur *f*; **it has a high fibre ~** c'est riche en fibres. **-2.** [subject matter] contenu *m*. ◇ *vt*: **to ~ o.s. with sthg/with doing sthg** se contenter de qqch/de faire qqch.
◆ **contents** *npl* **-1.** [of container, document] contenu *m*. **-2.** [at front of book] table *f* des matières.

contented [kən'tentɪd] *adj* satisfait(e).

contentedly [kən'tentɪdlɪ] *adv* avec contentement.

contention [kən'tenʃn] *n fml* **-1.** [argument, assertion] assertion *f*, affirmation *f*. **-2.** (*U*) [disagreement] dispute *f*, contestation *f*. **-3.** [competition]: **to be in ~** être en lice.

contentious [kən'tenʃəs] *adj* contentieux(ieuse), contesté(e).

contentment [kən'tentmənt] *n* contentement *m*.

contest [*n* 'kɒntest, *vb* kən'test] ◇ *n* **-1.** [competition] concours *m*. **-2.** [for power, control] combat *m*, lutte *f*. ◇ *vt* **-1.** [compete for] disputer. **-2.** [dispute] contester.

contestant [kən'testənt] *n* concurrent *m*, -e *f*.

context ['kɒntekst] *n* contexte *m*; **out of ~** [word] hors contexte; [remark] hors de son contexte.

continent ['kɒntɪnənt] *n* continent *m*.
◆ **Continent** *n Br*: **the Continent** l'Europe *f* continentale.

continental [ˌkɒntɪ'nentl] ◇ *adj* **-1.** GEOGR continental(e). **-2.** *Br* [European - food] d'Europe continentale; [- holidays] en Europe continentale. ◇ *n Br* Européen continental *m*, Européenne continentale *f*.

continental breakfast *n* petit déjeuner *m* continental.

CONTINENTAL BREAKFAST:
Ce terme désigne un petit déjeuner léger, par opposition au breakfast anglais, beaucoup plus copieux et comportant parfois un plat chaud

---

continental climate *n* climat *m* continental.

continental quilt *n Br* couette *f*.

contingency [kən'tɪndʒənsɪ] (*pl* **-ies**) *n* éventualité *f*.

contingency plan *n* plan *m* d'urgence.

contingent [kən'tɪndʒənt] ◇ *adj fml*: **to be ~ on** OR **upon** dépendre de. ◇ *n* contingent *m*.

continual [kən'tɪnjʊəl] *adj* continuel(elle).

continually [kən'tɪnjʊəlɪ] *adv* continuellement.

continuation [kənˌtɪnjʊ'eɪʃn] *n* **-1.** (*U*) [act] continuation *f*. **-2.** [sequel] suite *f*.

continue [kən'tɪnjuː] ◇ *vt* **-1.** [carry on] continuer, poursuivre; **to ~ doing** OR **to do sthg** continuer à OR de faire qqch. **-2.** [after an interruption] reprendre. ◇ *vi* **-1.** [carry on] continuer; **to ~ with sthg** poursuivre qqch, continuer qqch. **-2.** [after an interruption] reprendre, se poursuivre.

continuity [ˌkɒntɪ'njuːətɪ] ◇ *n* continuité *f*.

continuous [kən'tɪnjʊəs] *adj* continu(e).

continuous assessment *n* contrôle *m* continu des connaissances.

continuously [kən'tɪnjʊəslɪ] *adv* sans arrêt, continuellement.

contort [kən'tɔːt] ◇ *vt* tordre. ◇ *vi* se tordre.

contortion [kən'tɔːʃn] *n* **-1.** (*U*) [twisting] torsion *f*. **-2.** [position] contorsion *f*.

contour ['kɒnˌtʊər] ◇ *n* **-1.** [outline] contour *m*. **-2.** [on map] courbe *f* de niveau. ◇ *comp*

[map] avec courbes de niveau; ~ **line** courbe *f* de niveau.

contraband ['kɒntrəbænd] ◇ *adj* de contrebande. ◇ *n* contrebande *f.*

contraception [,kɒntrə'sepʃn] *n* contraception *f.*

contraceptive [,kɒntrə'septɪv] ◇ *adj* [method, device] anticonceptionnel(elle), contraceptif(ive); [advice] sur la contraception. ◇ *n* contraceptif *m.*

contraceptive pill *n* pilule *f* anticonceptionnelle OR contraceptive.

contract [*n* 'kɒntrækt, *vb* kən'trækt] ◇ *n* contrat *m.* ◇ *vt* **-1.** [gen] contracter. **-2.** COMM: **to ~ sb (to do sthg)** passer un contrat avec qqn (pour faire qqch); **to ~ to do sthg** s'engager par contrat à faire qqch. ◇ *vi* [decrease in size, length] se contracter.
◆ **contract in** *vi* s'engager par contrat.
◆ **contract out** ◇ *vt sep* donner en sous-traitance à. ◇ *vi*: **to ~ out (of)** se dégager (de).

contraction [kən'trækʃn] *n* contraction *f.*

contractor [kən'træktər] *n* entrepreneur *m.*

contractual [kən'træktʃʊəl] *adj* contractuel(elle).

contradict [,kɒntrə'dɪkt] *vt* contredire.

contradiction [,kɒntrə'dɪkʃn] *n* contradiction *f;* ~ **in terms** contradiction dans les termes.

contradictory [,kɒntrə'dɪktəri] *adj* contradictoire; [behaviour] incohérent(e).

contraflow ['kɒntrəfləʊ] *n* circulation *f* à contre-sens.

contralto [kən'træltəʊ] (*pl* **-s**) *n* contralto *m.*

contraption [kən'træpʃn] *n* machin *m,* truc *m.*

contrary ['kɒntrəri, *adj sense 2* kən'treəri] ◇ *adj* **-1.** [opposite]: ~ **(to)** contraire (à), opposé(e) (à). **-2.** [awkward] contrariant(e). ◇ *n* contraire *m;* **on the ~** au contraire; **evidence to the ~** preuves tendant à démontrer le contraire; **his statements to the ~** ses propos soutenant le contraire.
◆ **contrary to** *prep* contrairement à.

contrast [*n* 'kɒntrɑːst, *vb* kən'trɑːst] ◇ *n* contraste *m;* **by** OR **in ~** par contraste; **in ~ with** OR **to sthg** par contraste avec qqch. ◇ *vt* contraster. ◇ *vi*: **to ~ (with)** faire contraste (avec).

contrasting [kən'trɑːstɪŋ] *adj* [colours] contrasté(e); [personalities, views] opposé(e), contraire.

contravene [,kɒntrə'viːn] *vt* enfreindre, transgresser.

contravention ['kɒntrə'venʃn] *n* infraction *f,* contravention *f.*

contribute [kən'trɪbjuːt] ◇ *vt* **-1.** [money] contribuer, cotiser; [help, advice, ideas] donner, apporter. **-2.** [write]: **to ~ an article to a magazine** écrire un article pour un magazine. ◇ *vi* **-1.** [gen]: **to ~ (to)** contribuer (à). **-2.** [write material]: **to ~ to** collaborer à.

contributing [kən'trɪbjuːtɪŋ] *adj*: **to be a ~ factor in** contribuer à.

contribution [,kɒntrɪ'bjuːʃn] *n* **-1.** [of money]: ~ **(to)** cotisation *f* (à), contribution *f* (à). **-2.** [to debate]: **his ~ to the discussion** ce qu'il a apporté à la discussion. **-3.** [article] article *m.*

contributor [kən'trɪbjʊtər] *n* **-1.** [of money] donateur *m,* -trice *f.* **-2.** [to magazine, newspaper] collaborateur *m,* -trice *f.*

contributory [kən'trɪbjʊtəri] *adj*: **to be a ~ factor in** contribuer à.

contributory pension scheme *n* système *m* de retraite par répartition.

contrite ['kɒntraɪt] *adj literary* contrit(e), pénitent(e).

contrition [kən'trɪʃn] *n literary* contrition *f,* pénitence *f.*

contrivance [kən'traɪvns] *n* [contraption] machine *f,* appareil *m.*

contrive [kən'traɪv] *vt fml* **-1.** [engineer] combiner. **-2.** [manage]: **to ~ to do sthg** se débrouiller pour faire qqch, trouver moyen de faire qqch.

contrived [kən'traɪvd] *adj* tiré(e) par les cheveux.

control [kən'trəʊl] (*pt* & *pp* **-led**, *cont* **-ling**) ◇ *n* **-1.** [gen] contrôle *m;* [of traffic] régulation *f;* **to gain** OR **take ~ (of)** prendre le contrôle (de); **beyond** OR **outside sb's ~** indépendant de la volonté de qqn; **to get sb/sthg under ~** maîtriser qqn/qqch; **to be in ~ of sthg** [subj: boss, government] diriger qqch; [subj: army] avoir le contrôle de qqch; [of emotions, situation] maîtriser qqch; **to get out of ~** [subj: crowd] devenir impossible à contrôler; **his car went out of ~** il a perdu le contrôle de sa voiture; **to lose ~** [of emotions] perdre le contrôle. **-2.** [in experiment] témoin *m.*
◇ *vt* **-1.** [company, country] être à la tête de, diriger. **-2.** [operate] commander, faire fonctionner. **-3.** [restrict, restrain - disease] enrayer, juguler; [- inflation] mettre un frein à, contenir; [- children] tenir; [- crowd] contenir; [- traffic] régler; [- emotions] maîtriser, contenir; **to ~ o.s.** se maîtriser, se contrôler.
◇ *comp* de commande.

◆ **controls** *npl* [of machine, vehicle] commandes *fpl*.

control code *n* COMPUT code *m* de commande.

control group *n* groupe *m* témoin.

control key *n* COMPUT touche *f* «control».

controlled [kən'trəʊld] *adj* **-1.** [person] maître (maîtresse) de soi. **-2.** ECON dirigé(e).

controller [kən'trəʊləʳ] *n* [person] contrôleur *m*.

controlling [kən'trəʊlɪŋ] *adj* [factor] déterminant(e).

controlling interest *n* participation *f* majoritaire.

control panel *n* tableau *m* de bord.

control tower *n* tour *f* de contrôle.

controversial [,kɒntrə'vɜːʃl] *adj* [writer, theory etc] controversé(e); **to be ~** donner matière à controverse.

controversy ['kɒntrəvɜːsɪ, *Br* kən'trɒvəsɪ] (*pl* -ies) *n* controverse *f*, polémique *f*.

conundrum [kə'nʌndrəm] (*pl* -s) *n* énigme *f*.

conurbation [,kɒnɜː'beɪʃn] *n* conurbation *f*.

convalesce [,kɒnvə'les] *vi* se remettre d'une maladie, relever de maladie.

convalescence [,kɒnvə'lesns] *n* convalescence *f*.

convalescent [,kɒnvə'lesnt] ◇ *adj* de convalescence. ◇ *n* convalescent *m*, -e *f*.

convection [kən'vekʃn] *n* convection *f*.

convector [kən'vektəʳ] *n* radiateur *m* à convection.

convene [kən'viːn] ◇ *vt* convoquer, réunir. ◇ *vi* se réunir, s'assembler.

convener [kən'viːnəʳ] *n* *Br* président *m*, -e *f* (*d'une commission*).

convenience [kən'viːnjəns] *n* **-1.** [usefulness] commodité *f*. **-2.** [personal comfort, advantage] agrément *m*, confort *m*; **at your earliest ~** *fml* dès que possible. **-3.** [facility] confort *m*.

convenience food *n* aliment *m* tout préparé.

convenience store *n* *Am* petit supermarché de quartier.

convenient [kən'viːnjənt] *adj* **-1.** [suitable] qui convient. **-2.** [handy] pratique, commode.

conveniently [kən'viːnjəntlɪ] *adv* d'une manière commode; **~ situated** bien situé.

convent ['kɒnvənt] *n* couvent *m*.

convention [kən'venʃn] *n* **-1.** [agreement, assembly] convention *f*. **-2.** [practice] usage *m*, convention *f*.

conventional [kən'venʃənl] *adj* conventionnel(elle); **it's ~ to ...** l'usage veut que ....

conventionally [kən'venʃnəlɪ] *adv* d'une manière conventionnelle.

convent school *n* couvent *m*.

converge [kən'vɜːdʒ] *vi*: **to ~ (on)** converger (sur).

conversant [kən'vɜːsənt] *adj* *fml*: **~ with sthg** familiarisé(e) avec qqch, qui connaît bien qqch.

conversation [,kɒnvə'seɪʃn] *n* conversation *f*; **to make ~** faire la conversation.

conversational [,kɒnvə'seɪʃənl] *adj* de la conversation.

conversationalist [,kɒnvə'seɪʃnəlɪst] *n* causeur *m*, -euse *f*.

converse [*adj* & *n* 'kɒnvɜːs, *vb* kən'vɜːs] ◇ *adj* *fml* opposé(e), contraire. ◇ *n* [opposite]: **the ~** le contraire, l'inverse *m*. ◇ *vi* *fml* converser.

conversely [kən'vɜːslɪ] *adv* *fml* inversement.

conversion [kən'vɜːʃn] *n* **-1.** [changing, in religious beliefs] conversion *f*. **-2.** [in building] aménagement *m*, transformation *f*. **-3.** RUGBY transformation *f*.

conversion table *n* table *f* de conversion.

convert [*vb* kən'vɜːt, *n* 'kɒnvɜːt] ◇ *vt* **-1.** [change]: **to ~ sthg to** OR **into** convertir qqch en; **to ~ sb (to)** RELIG convertir qqn (à). **-2.** [building, ship]: **to ~ sthg to** OR **into** transformer qqch en, aménager qqch en. **-3.** RUGBY transformer. ◇ *vi*: **to ~ from sthg to sthg** passer de qqch à qqch. ◇ *n* converti *m*, -e *f*.

converted [kən'vɜːtɪd] *adj* **-1.** [building, ship] aménagé(e). **-2.** RELIG converti(e).

convertible [kən'vɜːtəbl] ◇ *adj* **-1.** [bed, sofa] transformable, convertible. **-2.** [currency] convertible. **-3.** [car] décapotable. ◇ *n* (voiture) décapotable *f*.

convex [kɒn'veks] *adj* convexe.

convey [kən'veɪ] *vt* **-1.** *fml* [transport] transporter. **-2.** [express]: **to ~ sthg (to sb)** communiquer qqch (à qqn).

conveyancing [kən'veɪənsɪŋ] *n* (*U*) procédure *f* translative de propriété.

conveyer belt [kən'veɪəʳ-] *n* convoyeur *m*, tapis *m* roulant.

convict [*n* 'kɒnvɪkt, *vb* kən'vɪkt] ◇ *n* détenu *m*. ◇ *vt*: **to ~ sb of sthg** reconnaître qqn coupable de qqch.

convicted [kən'vɪktɪd] *adj*: **he's a ~ murderer** il a été reconnu coupable d'un meurtre.

conviction [kən'vɪkʃn] n **-1.** [belief, fervour] conviction f. **-2.** JUR [of criminal] condamnation f.

convince [kən'vɪns] vt convaincre, persuader; **to ~ sb of sthg/to do sthg** convaincre qqn de qqch/de faire qqch, persuader qqn de qqch/de faire qqch.

convinced [kən'vɪnst] adj; **(of)** persuadé(e) (de), convaincu(e) (de).

convincing [kən'vɪnsɪŋ] adj **-1.** [persuasive] convaincant(e). **-2.** [resounding - victory] retentissant(e), éclatant(e).

convivial [kən'vɪvɪəl] adj convivial(e), joyeux(euse).

convoluted ['kɒnvəluːtɪd] adj [tortuous] compliqué(e).

convoy ['kɒnvɔɪ] n convoi m; **in ~** en convoi.

convulse [kən'vʌls] vt [person]: **to be ~d with** se tordre de.

convulsion [kən'vʌlʃn] n MED convulsion f.

convulsive [kən'vʌlsɪv] adj convulsif(ive).

coo [kuː] vi roucouler.

cook [kʊk] ◇ n cuisinier m, -ière f; **she's a good ~** elle fait bien la cuisine. ◇ vt **-1.** [food] faire cuire; [meal] préparer. **-2.** inf [falsify] maquiller. ◇ vi [person] cuisiner, faire la cuisine; [food] cuire.
◆ **cook up** vt sep [plan] combiner; [excuse] inventer.

cookbook ['kʊk,bʊk] = **cookery book**.

cooked [kʊkt] adj cuit(e).

cooker ['kʊkə'] n [stove] cuisinière f.

cookery ['kʊkərɪ] n cuisine f.

cookery book n livre m de cuisine.

cookie ['kʊkɪ] n Am [biscuit] biscuit m, gâteau m sec.

cooking ['kʊkɪŋ] ◇ n cuisine f; **do you like ~?** tu aimes faire la cuisine? ◇ comp de cuisine; [chocolate] à cuire; **~ oil** huile f de friture.

cooking apple n pomme f à cuire.

cookout ['kʊkaʊt] n Am barbecue m.

cool [kuːl] ◇ adj **-1.** [not warm] frais (fraîche); [dress] léger(ère). **-2.** [calm] calme. **-3.** [unfriendly] froid(e). **-4.** inf [excellent] génial(e); [trendy] branché(e). ◇ vt faire refroidir. ◇ vi **-1.** [become less warm] refroidir. **-2.** [abate] se calmer. ◇ n [calm]: **to keep/lose one's ~** garder/perdre son sang-froid, garder/perdre son calme.
◆ **cool down** ◇ vt sep **-1.** [make less warm - food etc] faire refroidir; [- person] rafraîchir. **-2.** [make less angry] calmer, apaiser. ◇ vi **-1.** [become less warm - food, engine] re-

froidir; [- person] se rafraîchir. **-2.** [become less angry] se calmer.
◆ **cool off** vi **-1.** [become less warm] refroidir; [person] se rafraîchir. **-2.** [become less angry] se calmer.

coolant ['kuːlənt] n agent m de refroidissement.

cool box n glacière f.

cool-headed [-'hedɪd] adj calme.

cooling-off period ['kuːlɪŋ-] n délai m de réflexion.

cooling tower ['kuːlɪŋ-] n refroidisseur m.

coolly ['kuːlɪ] adv **-1.** [calmly] calmement. **-2.** [in unfriendly way] froidement.

coolness ['kuːlnɪs] n **-1.** [in temperature] fraîcheur f. **-2.** [unfriendliness] froideur f.

coop [kuːp] n poulailler m.
◆ **coop up** vt sep inf confiner.

Co-op ['kəʊɒp] (abbr of **co-operative society**) n Coop f.

cooperate [kəʊ'ɒpəreɪt] vi: **to ~ (with sb/sthg)** coopérer (avec qqn/à qqch), collaborer (avec qqn/à qqch).

cooperation [kəʊ,ɒpə'reɪʃn] n (U) **-1.** [collaboration] coopération f, collaboration f. **-2.** [assistance] aide f, concours m.

cooperative [kəʊ'ɒpərətɪv] ◇ adj coopératif(ive). ◇ n coopérative f.

co-opt vt: **to ~ sb (into** OR **onto)** coopter qqn (à).

coordinate [n kəʊ'ɔːdɪnət, vt kəʊ'ɔːdɪneɪt] ◇ n [on map, graph] coordonnée f. ◇ vt coordonner.
◆ **coordinates** npl [clothes] coordonnés mpl.

coordination [kəʊ,ɔːdɪ'neɪʃn] n coordination f.

co-ownership n copropriété f.

cop [kɒp] (pt & pp **-ped**, cont **-ping**) n inf flic m.
◆ **cop out** vi inf: **to ~ out (of sthg)** se défiler OR se dérober (à qqch).

cope [kəʊp] vi se débrouiller; **to ~ with** faire face à.

Copenhagen [,kəʊpən'heɪgən] n Copenhague.

copier ['kɒpɪə'] n copieur m, photocopieur m.

copilot ['kəʊ,paɪlət] n copilote mf.

copious ['kəʊpjəs] adj [notes] copieux(ieuse); [supply] abondant(e).

cop-out n inf dérobade f, échappatoire f.

copper ['kɒpə'] n **-1.** [metal] cuivre m. **-2.** Br inf [policeman] flic m.

coppice ['kɒpɪs], **copse** [kɒps] n taillis m, hallier m.

copulate ['kɒpjʊleɪt] vi: **to ~ (with)** s'accoupler (à OR avec).

copulation [,kɒpjʊ'leɪʃn] n copulation f.

copy ['kɒpɪ] (pt & pp -ied) ◇ n -1. [imitation] copie f, reproduction f. -2. [duplicate] copie f. -3. [of book] exemplaire m; [of magazine] numéro m. ◇ vt -1. [imitate] copier, imiter. -2. [photocopy] photocopier. ◇ vi copier.
◆ **copy down** vt sep prendre des notes de.
◆ **copy out** vt sep recopier.

copycat ['kɒpɪkæt] ◇ n inf copieur m, -ieuse f. ◇ comp inspiré(e) par un autre (une autre).

copy protect vt protéger contre la copie.

copyright ['kɒpɪraɪt] n copyright m, droit m d'auteur.

copy typist n Br dactylo f, dactylographe f.

copywriter ['kɒpɪ,raɪtər] n concepteur-rédacteur publicitaire m, conceptrice-rédactrice publicitaire f.

coral ['kɒrəl] ◇ n corail m. ◇ comp de corail.

coral reef n récif m de corail.

Coral Sea n: **the ~** la mer de Corail.

cord [kɔːd] ◇ n -1. [string] ficelle f; [rope] corde f. -2. [electric] fil m, cordon m. -3. [fabric] velours m côtelé. ◇ comp en velours côtelé.
◆ **cords** npl pantalon m en velours côtelé.

cordial ['kɔːdjəl] ◇ adj cordial(e), chaleureux(euse). ◇ n cordial m.

cordially ['kɔːdɪəlɪ] adv cordialement.

cordless ['kɔːdlɪs] adj [telephone] sans fil; [shaver] à piles.

Cordoba ['kɔːdəbə] n Cordoue.

cordon ['kɔːdn] n cordon m.
◆ **cordon off** vt sep barrer (par un cordon de police).

cordon bleu [-blɜː] adj cordon bleu.

corduroy ['kɔːdərɔɪ] ◇ n velours m côtelé. ◇ comp en velours côtelé.

core [kɔːr] ◇ n -1. [of apple etc] trognon m, cœur m. -2. [of cable, Earth] noyau m; [of nuclear reactor] cœur m. -3. fig [of people] noyau m; [of problem, policy] essentiel m. ◇ vt enlever le cœur de.

CORE [kɔːr] (abbr of **Congress on Racial Equality**) n ligue américaine contre le racisme.

corer ['kɔːrər] n vide-pomme m inv.

corespondent [,kəʊrɪ'spɒndənt] n JUR codéfendeur m, -eresse f.

core time n Br plage f fixe.

Corfu [kɔː'fuː] n Corfou; **in ~** à Corfou.

corgi ['kɔːgɪ] (pl -s) n corgi m.

coriander [,kɒrɪ'ændər] n coriandre f.

cork [kɔːk] n -1. [material] liège m. -2. [stopper] bouchon m.

corkage ['kɔːkɪdʒ] n droit de débouchage sur un vin apporté par le consommateur.

corked [kɔːkt] adj [wine] qui a le goût de bouchon.

corkscrew ['kɔːkskruː] n tire-bouchon m.

cormorant ['kɔːmərənt] n cormoran m.

corn [kɔːn] ◇ n -1. Br [wheat] grain m; Am [maize] maïs m; **~ on the cob** épi m de maïs cuit. -2. [on foot] cor m. ◇ comp: **~ bread** pain m de farine de maïs; **~ oil** huile f de maïs.

Corn (abbr of **Cornwall**) comté anglais.

cornea ['kɔːnɪə] (pl -s) n cornée f.

corned beef [kɔːnd-] n corned-beef m inv.

corner ['kɔːnər] ◇ n -1. [angle] coin m, angle m; **to cut ~s** fig brûler les étapes. -2. [bend in road] virage m, tournant m. -3. FTBL corner m. ◇ vt -1. [person, animal] acculer. -2. [market] accaparer.

corner flag n piquet m de coin.

corner kick n FTBL = **corner**.

corner shop n magasin m du coin OR du quartier.

cornerstone ['kɔːnəstəʊn] n fig pierre f angulaire.

cornet ['kɔːnɪt] n -1. [instrument] cornet m à pistons. -2. Br [ice-cream cone] cornet m de glace.

cornfield ['kɔːnfiːld] n -1. Br [of wheat] champ m de blé. -2. Am [of maize] champ m de maïs.

cornflakes ['kɔːnfleɪks] npl corn-flakes mpl.

cornflour Br ['kɔːnflaʊər], **cornstarch** Am ['kɔːnstɑːtʃ] n maïzena f, farine f de maïs.

cornice ['kɔːnɪs] n corniche f.

Cornish ['kɔːnɪʃ] ◇ adj de Cornouailles, cornouaillais(e). ◇ npl: **the ~** les Cornouaillais mpl.

Cornishman ['kɔːnɪʃmən] (pl -men [-mən]) n Cornouaillais m.

Cornishwoman ['kɔːnɪʃ,wumən] (pl -women [-wɪmɪn]) n Cornouaillaise f.

cornstarch Am = **cornflour**.

cornucopia [,kɔːnjʊ'kəʊpjə] n literary corne f d'abondance.

Cornwall ['kɔːnwɔːl] n Cornouailles f; **in ~** en Cornouailles.

corny ['kɔːnɪ] (compar -ier, superl -iest) adj inf [joke] peu original(e); [story, film] à l'eau de rose.

corollary [kə'rɒlərɪ] (*pl* **-ies**) *n* corollaire *m*.

coronary ['kɒrənrɪ] (*pl* **-ies**), **coronary thrombosis** (*pl* **coronary thromboses**) *n* infarctus *m* du myocarde.

coronation [,kɒrə'neɪʃn] *n* couronnement *m*.

coroner ['kɒrənə] *n* coroner *m*.

Corp. (*abbr of* **corporation**) Cie.

corpora ['kɔːpərə] *pl* → **corpus**.

corporal ['kɔːpərəl] *n* [gen] caporal *m*; [in artillery] brigadier *m*.

corporal punishment *n* châtiment *m* corporel.

corporate ['kɔːpərət] *adj* **-1.** [business] corporatif(ive), de société. **-2.** [collective] collectif(ive).

corporate hospitality *n* (U) *réceptions données par une société pour ses clients*.

corporate identity, **corporate image** *n* image *f* de marque de la société.

corporation [,kɔːpə'reɪʃn] *n* **-1.** [town council] conseil *m* municipal. **-2.** [large company] compagnie *f*, société *f* enregistrée.

corporation tax *n Br* impôt *m* sur les sociétés.

corps [kɔːr] (*pl inv*) *n* corps *m*; **the press ~** la presse.

corpse [kɔːps] *n* cadavre *m*.

corpulent ['kɔːpjʊlənt] *adj* corpulent(e).

corpus ['kɔːpəs] (*pl* **-pora** OR **-puses**) *n* corpus *m*, recueil *m*.

corpuscle ['kɔːpʌsl] *n* globule *m*.

corral [kɒ'rɑːl] *n* corral *m*.

correct [kə'rekt] ◇ *adj* **-1.** [accurate] correct(e), exact(e); **you're quite ~** tu as parfaitement raison. **-2.** [proper, socially acceptable] correct(e), convenable. ◇ *vt* corriger.

correction [kə'rekʃn] *n* correction *f*.

correctly [kə'rektlɪ] *adv* **-1.** [accurately] correctement, exactement. **-2.** [properly, acceptably] correctement, comme il faut.

correlate ['kɒrəleɪt] ◇ *vt* mettre en corrélation, corréler. ◇ *vi*: **to ~ (with)** correspondre (à), être en corrélation (avec).

correlation [,kɒrə'leɪʃn] *n* corrélation *f*.

correspond [,kɒrɪ'spɒnd] *vi* **-1.** [gen]: **to ~ (with OR to)** correspondre (à). **-2.** [write letters]: **to ~ (with sb)** correspondre (avec qqn).

correspondence [,kɒrɪ'spɒndəns] *n*: **~ (with)** correspondance *f* (avec).

correspondence course *n* cours *m* par correspondance.

correspondent [,kɒrɪ'spɒndənt] *n* correspondant *m*, -e *f*.

corresponding [,kɒrɪ'spɒndɪŋ] *adj* correspondant(e).

corridor ['kɒrɪdɔːr] *n* [in building] couloir *m*, corridor *m*.

corroborate [kə'rɒbəreɪt] *vt* corroborer, confirmer.

corroboration [kə,rɒbə'reɪʃən] *n* corroboration *f*, confirmation *f*.

corrode [kə'rəʊd] ◇ *vt* corroder, attaquer. ◇ *vi* se corroder.

corrosion [kə'rəʊʒn] *n* corrosion *f*.

corrosive [kə'rəʊsɪv] *adj* corrosif(ive).

corrugated ['kɒrəgeɪtɪd] *adj* ondulé(e).

corrugated iron *n* tôle *f* ondulée.

corrupt [kə'rʌpt] ◇ *adj* [gen & COMPUT] corrompu(e). ◇ *vt* corrompre, dépraver.

corruption [kə'rʌpʃn] *n* corruption *f*.

corsage [kɔː'sɑːʒ] *n* petit bouquet *m* de fleurs (*porté au corsage*).

corset ['kɔːsɪt] *n* corset *m*.

Corsica ['kɔːsɪkə] *n* Corse *f*; **in ~** en Corse.

Corsican ['kɔːsɪkən] ◇ *adj* corse. ◇ *n* **-1.** [person] Corse *mf*. **-2.** [language] corse *m*.

cortege, cortège [kɔː'teɪʒ] *n* cortège *m*.

cortisone ['kɔːtɪzəʊn] *n* cortisone *f*.

cos¹ [kɒz] *Br inf* = **because**.

cos² [kɒs] = **cos lettuce**.

c.o.s. (*abbr of* **cash on shipment**) paiement à l'expédition.

cosh [kɒʃ] ◇ *n* matraque *f*, gourdin *m*. ◇ *vt* frapper, matraquer.

cosignatory [,kəʊ'sɪgnətrɪ] (*pl* **-ies**) *n* cosignataire *mf*.

cosine ['kəʊsaɪn] *n* cosinus *m*.

cos lettuce [kɒs-] *n Br* romaine *f*.

cosmetic [kɒz'metɪk] ◇ *n* cosmétique *m*, produit *m* de beauté. ◇ *adj fig* superficiel(ielle).

cosmetic surgery *n* chirurgie *f* plastique OR esthétique.

cosmic ['kɒzmɪk] *adj* cosmique.

cosmonaut ['kɒzmənɔːt] *n* cosmonaute *mf*.

cosmopolitan [kɒzmə'pɒlɪtn] *adj* cosmopolite.

cosmos ['kɒzmɒs] *n*: **the ~** le cosmos.

Cossack ['kɒsæk] *n* cosaque *m*.

cosset ['kɒsɪt] *vt* dorloter, choyer.

cost [kɒst] (*pt & pp* **cost** OR **-ed**) ◇ *n lit & fig* coût *m*; **at all ~s** à tout prix, coûte que coûte. ◇ *vt* **-1.** *lit & fig* coûter; **it ~ me £10** ça m'a coûté 10 livres; **it ~ us a lot of time and effort** ça nous a demandé beaucoup de temps et de travail. **-2.** COMM [estimate] évaluer le coût de. ◇ *vi* coûter; **how much**

does it ~? combien ça coûte?, combien cela coûte-t-il?

◆ **costs** *npl* JUR dépens *mpl*, frais *mpl* judiciaires.

cost accountant *n* responsable *m* de la comptabilité analytique.

co-star ◇ *n* partenaire *mf*. ◇ *vt* [subj: film] avoir comme vedettes. ◇ *vi*: **to ~ with** partager la vedette avec.

Costa Rica [ˌkɒstəˈriːkə] *n* Costa Rica *m*; **in ~** au Costa Rica.

Costa Rican [ˌkɒstəˈriːkən] ◇ *adj* costaricien(ienne). ◇ *n* Costaricien *m*, -ienne *f*.

cost-benefit analysis *n* analyse *f* coûts-bénéfices.

cost-effective *adj* rentable.

cost-effectiveness *n* rentabilité *f*.

costing [ˈkɒstɪŋ] *n* évaluation *f* du coût.

costly [ˈkɒstlɪ] (*compar* **-ier**, *superl* **-iest**) *adj* *lit* & *fig* coûteux(euse).

cost of living *n*: **the ~** le coût de la vie.

cost-of-living index *n* indice *m* du coût de la vie.

cost price *n* prix *m* coûtant.

costume [ˈkɒstjuːm] *n* **-1.** [gen] costume *m*. **-2.** [swimming costume] maillot *m* (de bain).

costume jewellery *n* (*U*) bijoux *mpl* fantaisie.

cosy (*Br compar* **-ier**, *superl* **-iest**, *pl* **-ies**), **cozy** (*Am compar* **-ier**, *superl* **-iest**, *pl* **-ies**) [ˈkəʊzɪ] ◇ *adj* **-1.** [house, room] douillet(ette); [atmosphere] chaleureux(euse); **to feel ~** se sentir bien au chaud. **-2.** [intimate] intime. ◇ *n* cosy *m*.

cot [kɒt] *n* **-1.** *Br* [for child] lit *m* d'enfant, petit lit. **-2.** *Am* [folding bed] lit *m* de camp.

cot death *n* mort *f* subite du nourrisson.

cottage [ˈkɒtɪdʒ] *n* cottage *m*, petite maison *f* (de campagne).

cottage cheese *n* fromage *m* blanc.

cottage hospital *n Br* petit hôpital *m* (en zone rurale).

cottage industry *n* industrie *f* artisanale.

cottage pie *n Br* ≃ hachis *m* parmentier.

cotton [ˈkɒtn] ◇ *n* **-1.** [gen] coton *m*. **-2.** [thread] fil *m* de coton. ◇ *comp* de coton.

◆ **cotton on** *vi inf*: **to ~ on (to sthg)** piger (qqch), comprendre (qqch).

cotton bud *Br*, **cotton swab** *Am n* coton-tige *m*.

cotton candy *n Am* barbe *f* à papa.

cotton swab *Am* = **cotton bud**.

cotton wool *n* ouate *f*, coton *m* hydrophile.

couch [kaʊtʃ] ◇ *n* **-1.** [sofa] canapé *m*. **-2.** [in doctor's surgery] lit *m*. ◇ *vt* exprimer, formuler.

couchette [kuːˈʃet] *n Br* couchette *f*.

couch potato *n inf* flemmard *m*, -e *f* (*qui passe son temps devant la télé*).

cougar [ˈkuːgər] (*pl inv* OR **-s**) *n* cougouar *m*, couguar *m*.

cough [kɒf] ◇ *n* toux *f*; **I've got a ~** je tousse. ◇ *vi* tousser. ◇ *vt* [blood] cracher (en toussant).

◆ **cough up** *vt sep* **-1.** [bring up] cracher (en toussant). **-2.** *v inf* [pay up] casquer, cracher.

cough mixture *n Br* sirop *m* pour la toux.

cough sweet *n Br* pastille *f* pour la toux.

cough syrup = **cough mixture**.

coughing [ˈkɒfɪŋ] *n* (*U*) toux *fpl*.

could [kʊd] *pt* → **can**.

couldn't [ˈkʊdnt] = **could not**.

could've [ˈkʊdəv] = **could have**.

council [ˈkaʊnsl] ◇ *n* conseil *m* municipal. ◇ *comp* du conseil.

council estate *n* quartier *m* de logements sociaux.

council house *n Br* maison *f* qui appartient à la municipalité, ≃ H.L.M. *m or f*.

councillor [ˈkaʊnsələr] *n* conseiller municipal *m*, conseillère municipale *f*.

Council of Europe *n* conseil *m* de l'Europe.

council of war *n* conseil *m* de guerre.

council tax *n Br* ≃ impôts *mpl* locaux.

counsel [ˈkaʊnsəl] (*Br pt* & *pp* **-led**, *cont* **-ling**, *Am pt* & *pp* **-ed**, *cont* **-ing**) ◇ *n* **-1.** (*U*) *fml* [advice] conseil *m*. **-2.** [lawyer] avocat *m*, -e *f*. ◇ *vt*: **to ~ sb to do sthg** *fml* conseiller à qqn de faire qqch.

counselling *Br*, **counseling** *Am* [ˈkaʊnsəlɪŋ] *n* (*U*) conseils *mpl*.

counsellor *Br*, **counselor** *Am* [ˈkaʊnsələr] *n* **-1.** [gen] conseiller *m*, -ère *f*. **-2.** *Am* [lawyer] avocat *m*.

count [kaʊnt] ◇ *n* **-1.** [total] total *m*; **to keep ~ of** tenir le compte de; **to lose ~ of sthg** ne plus savoir qqch, ne pas se rappeler qqch. **-2.** [point]: **I disagree with him on two ~s** je ne suis pas d'accord avec lui sur deux points. **-3.** JUR [charge] chef *m* d'accusation. **-4.** [aristocrat] comte *m*.
◇ *vt* **-1.** [gen] compter; **there are five people, not ~ing me** sans moi, on est cinq. **-2.** [consider]: **to ~ sb as sthg** considérer qqn comme qqch.
◇ *vi* **-1.** [gen] compter; **to ~ (up) to** comp-

ter jusqu'à. **-2.** [be considered]: **to ~ as** être considéré(e) comme.

◆ **count against** vt fus jouer contre.

◆ **count in** vt sep inf: **~ me in!** je suis de la partie!

◆ **count (up)on** vt fus **-1.** [rely on] compter sur. **-2.** [expect] s'attendre à, prévoir.

◆ **count out** vt sep **-1.** [money] compter. **-2.** inf [leave out]: **~ me out!** ne comptez pas sur moi!

◆ **count up** vt fus compter.

countdown ['kaʊntdaʊn] n compte m à rebours.

countenance ['kaʊntənəns] ◇ n literary [face] visage m. ◇ vt approuver, admettre.

counter ['kaʊntər] ◇ n **-1.** [in shop, bank] comptoir m. **-2.** [in board game] pion m. ◇ vt: **to ~ sthg (with)** [criticism etc] riposter à qqch (par); **to ~ sthg by doing sthg** s'opposer à qqch en faisant qqch. ◇ vi: **to ~ with sthg/by doing sthg** riposter par qqch/en faisant qqch.

◆ **counter to** ◇ adv contrairement à; **to run ~ to** aller à l'encontre de.

counteract [,kaʊntə'rækt] vt contrebalancer, compenser.

counterattack [,kaʊntərə'tæk] ◇ n contre-attaque f. ◇ vt & vi contre-attaquer.

counterbalance [,kaʊntə'bæləns] vt fig contrebalancer, compenser.

counterclaim ['kaʊntəkleɪm] n demande f reconventionnelle.

counterclockwise [,kaʊntə'klɒkwaɪz] adj & adv Am dans le sens inverse des aiguilles d'une montre.

counterespionage [,kaʊntər'espɪənɑːʒ] n contre-espionnage m.

counterfeit ['kaʊntəfɪt] ◇ adj faux (fausse). ◇ vt contrefaire.

counterfoil ['kaʊntəfɔɪl] n talon m, souche f.

counterintelligence [,kaʊntərɪn'telɪdʒəns] n contre-espionnage m.

countermand [,kaʊtə'mɑːnd] vt annuler.

countermeasure [,kaʊtə'meʒər] n contre-mesure f.

counteroffensive [,kaʊntərə'fensɪv] n contre-offensive f.

counterpane ['kaʊntəpeɪn] n couvre-lit m, dessus-de-lit m.

counterpart ['kaʊntəpɑːt] n [person] homologue mf; [thing] équivalent m, -e f.

counterpoint ['kaʊntəpɔɪnt] n MUS contrepoint m.

counterproductive [,kaʊntəprə'dʌktɪv] adj qui a l'effet inverse.

counter-revolution n contre-révolution f.

countersank ['kaʊntəsæŋk] pt → **countersink**.

countersign ['kantəsaɪn] vt contresigner.

countersink ['kaʊntəsɪŋk] (pt **-sank**, pp **-sunk** [-sʌŋk]) vt [hole] fraiser; [screw] noyer.

countess ['kaʊntɪs] n comtesse f.

countless ['kaʊntlɪs] adj innombrable.

countrified ['kʌntrɪfaɪd] adj pej campagnard(e), rustique.

country ['kʌntrɪ] (pl **-ies**) ◇ n **-1.** [nation] pays m. **-2.** [countryside]: **the ~** la campagne; **in the ~** à la campagne. **-3.** [region] région f; [terrain] terrain m. ◇ comp de la campagne, campagnard(e).

country and western ◇ n country m. ◇ comp country (inv).

country club n club m de loisirs (à la campagne).

country dancing n (U) danse f folklorique.

country house n manoir m.

countryman ['kʌntrɪmən] (pl **-men** [-mən]) n [from same country] compatriote m.

country music n = **country and western**.

country park n Br parc m naturel.

countryside ['kʌntrɪsaɪd] n campagne f.

countrywoman ['kʌntrɪ,wʊmən] (pl **-women** [-,wɪmɪn]) n [from same country] compatriote f.

county ['kaʊntɪ] (pl **-ies**) n comté m.

county council n Br conseil m général.

county court n Br ≃ tribunal m de grande instance.

county town Br, **county seat** Am n chef-lieu m.

coup [kuː] n **-1.** [rebellion]: **~ (d'état)** coup m d'état. **-2.** [success] coup m (de maître), beau coup m.

coupé ['kuːpeɪ] n coupé m.

couple ['kʌpl] ◇ n **-1.** [in relationship] couple m. **-2.** [small number]: **a ~ (of)** [two] deux; [a few] quelques, deux ou trois. ◇ vt **-1.** [join]: **to ~ sthg (to)** atteler qqch (à). **-2.** fig [associate]: **to ~ sthg with** associer qqch à; **~d with** ajouté OR joint à.

couplet ['kʌplɪt] n couplet m.

coupling ['kʌplɪŋ] n RAIL attelage m.

coupon ['kuːpɒn] n **-1.** [voucher] bon m. **-2.** [form] coupon m.

courage ['kʌrɪdʒ] n courage m; **to take ~ (from sthg)** être encouragé (par qqch); **to have the ~ of one's convictions** avoir le courage de ses opinions.

courageous [kə'reɪdʒəs] *adj* coura-geux(euse).

courageously [kə'reɪdʒəslɪ] *adv* courageu-sement, avec courage.

courgette [kuː'ʒet] *n Br* courgette *f*.

courier ['kurɪə] *n* **-1.** [on holiday] guide *m*, accompagnateur *m*, -trice *f*. **-2.** [to deliver letters, packages] courrier *m*, messager *m*.

course [kɔːs] ◇ *n* **-1.** [gen & SCH] cours *m*; **to take a ~ (in)** suivre un cours (de); **~ of action** ligne *f* de conduite; **in the ~ of** au cours de; **to run** OR **take its ~** [illness, event] suivre son cours. **-2.** MED [of injections] série *f*; **~ of treatment** traitement *m*. **-3.** [of ship, plane] route *f*; **to be on ~** suivre le cap fixé; *fig* [on target] être dans la bonne voie; **to be off ~** faire fausse route. **-4.** [of meal] plat *m*. **-5.** SPORT terrain *m*. ◇ *vi literary* [flow] couler.
◆ **of course** *adv* **-1.** [inevitably, not surpris-ingly] évidemment, naturellement. **-2.** [certainly] bien sûr; **of ~ not** bien sûr que non.

coursebook ['kɔːsbuk] *n* livre *m* de cours.

coursework ['kɔːswɜːk] *n* (*U*) travail *m* personnel.

court [kɔːt] ◇ *n* **-1.** [JUR - building, room] cour *f*, tribunal *m*; [- judge, jury etc]: **the ~** la justice; **to appear in ~** comparaître devant un tribunal; **to go to ~** aller en justice; **to take sb to ~** faire un procès à qqn. **-2.** [SPORT - gen] court *m*; [- for basketball, volley-ball] terrain *m*; **on ~** sur le court. **-3.** [court-yard, of monarch] cour *f*. ◇ *vt* [danger, disaster] braver, aller au-devant de; [favour] rechercher. ◇ *vi dated* sortir ensemble, se fréquenter.

court circular *n Br* bulletin *m* quotidien de la cour.

courteous ['kɜːtjəs] *adj* courtois(e), poli(e).

courtesan [ˌkɔːtɪ'zæn] *n* courtisane *f*.

courtesy ['kɜːtɪsɪ] *n* courtoisie *f*, politesse *f*.
◆ **(by) courtesy of** *prep* avec la permis-sion de.

courtesy car *n* voiture *f* mise gratuite-ment à la disposition du client.

courtesy coach *n* car *m* servant au trans-port des clients.

courthouse ['kɔːthaus, *pl* -hauzɪz] *n Am* pa-lais *m* de justice, tribunal *m*.

courtier ['kɔːtjər] *n* courtisan *m*.

court-martial (*pl* **court-martials** OR **courts-martial**, *Br pt* & *pp* **-led**, *cont* **-ling**, *Am pt* & *pp* **-ed**, *cont* **-ing**) ◇ *n* cour *f* mar-tiale. ◇ *vt* traduire en cour *f* martiale.

court of appeal *Br*, **court of appeals** *Am n* cour *f* d'appel.

court of inquiry *n* commission *f* d'en-quête.

court of law *n* tribunal *m*, cour *f* de jus-tice.

courtroom ['kɔːtrum] *n* salle *f* de tribunal.

courtship ['kɔːtʃɪp] *n* **-1.** [of people] cour *f*. **-2.** [of animals] parade *f*.

court shoe *n* escarpin *m*.

courtyard ['kɔːtjɑːd] *n* cour *f*.

cousin ['kʌzn] *n* cousin *m*, -e *f*.

couture [kuː'tuər] *n* haute couture *f*.

cove [kəuv] *n* [bay] crique *f*.

coven ['kʌvən] *n* réunion *f* de sorcières.

covenant ['kʌvənənt] *n* **-1.** [of money] enga-gement *m* contractuel. **-2.** [agreement] convention *f*, contrat *m*.

Covent Garden ['kɒvənt-] *n* Covent Gar-den.

COVENT GARDEN:
'Covent Garden', jadis le marché aux fruits, légumes et fleurs du centre de Londres, est aujourd'hui une importante galerie mar-chande; ce nom désigne également la 'Royal Opera House', située près de l'ancien mar-ché

Coventry ['kɒvəntrɪ] *n*: **to send sb to ~** mettre qqn en quarantaine.

cover ['kʌvər] ◇ *n* **-1.** [covering - of furniture] housse *f*; [- of pan] couvercle *m*; [- of book, magazine] couverture *f*. **-2.** [blanket] couver-ture *f*; **bed ~** couvre-lit *m*. **-3.** [protection, shelter] abri *m*; **to take ~** s'abriter, se mettre à l'abri; **under ~** à l'abri, à couvert; **under ~ of darkness** à la faveur de la nuit; **to break ~** [person] sortir à découvert OR de sa cachette. **-4.** [concealment] couverture *f*. **-5.** [insurance] couverture *f*, garantie *f*. ◇ *vt* **-1.** [gen]: **to ~ sthg (with)** couvrir qqch (de). **-2.** [insure]: **to ~ sb against** cou-vrir qqn en cas de. **-3.** [include] englober, comprendre.
◆ **cover up** *vt sep* **-1.** [person, object, face] couvrir. **-2.** *fig* [scandal etc] dissimuler, ca-cher.

coverage ['kʌvərɪdʒ] *n* [of news] reportage *m*.

coveralls ['kʌvərɔːlz] *npl Am* bleu *m* de tra-vail.

cover charge *n* couvert *m*.

cover girl *n* cover-girl *f*.

covering ['kʌvərɪŋ] *n* [of floor etc] revête-ment *m*; [of snow, dust] couche *f*.

covering letter *Br*, **cover letter** *Am n* let-tre *f* explicative OR d'accompagnement.

cover note n Br lettre f de couverture, attestation f provisoire d'assurance.

cover price n [of magazine etc] prix m.

covert ['kʌvət] adj [activity] clandestin(e); [look, glance] furtif(ive).

cover-up n étouffement m, dissimulation f.

cover version n reprise f.

covet ['kʌvɪt] vt convoiter.

cow [kaʊ] ◇ n -1. [female type of cattle] vache f. -2. [female elephant etc] femelle f. -3. Br inf pej [woman] vache f, chameau m. ◇ vt intimider, effrayer.

coward ['kaʊəd] n lâche mf, poltron m, -onne f.

cowardice ['kaʊədɪs] n lâcheté f.

cowardly ['kaʊədlɪ] adj lâche.

cowboy ['kaʊbɔɪ] ◇ n -1. [cattlehand] cowboy m. -2. Br inf [dishonest workman] fumiste m. ◇ comp de cow-boys.

cower ['kaʊə'] vi se recroqueviller.

cowhide ['kaʊhaɪd] n peau f de vache.

cowl neck [kaʊl-] n col m capuche.

cowpat ['kaʊpæt] n bouse f de vache.

cowshed ['kaʊʃed] n étable f.

cox [kɒks], **coxswain** ['kɒksən] n barreur m.

coy [kɔɪ] adj qui fait le/la timide.

coyly ['kɔɪlɪ] adv en faisant le/la timide.

coyote [kɔɪ'əʊtɪ] n coyote m.

cozy Am = cosy.

cp. (abbr of **compare**) cf.

c/p (abbr of **carriage paid**) pp.

CP (abbr of **Communist Party**) n PC m.

CPA n abbr of **certified public accountant**.

CPI (abbr of **Consumer Price Index**) n IPC m.

Cpl. (abbr of **corporal**) C.

CP/M (abbr of **control program for microcomputers**) n CP/M m.

c.p.s. (abbr of **characters per second**) cps.

CPS (abbr of **Crown Prosecution Service**) n ≃ ministère m publique.

CPSA (abbr of **Civil and Public Services Association**) n syndicat britannique de la fonction publique.

CPU n abbr of **central processing unit**.

cr. -1. abbr of **credit**. -2. abbr of **creditor**.

crab [kræb] n crabe m.

crab apple n pomme f sauvage.

crack [kræk] ◇ n -1. [in glass, pottery] fêlure f; [in wall, wood, ground] fissure f; [in skin] gerçure f. -2. [gap - in door] entrebâillement m; [- in curtains] interstice m; **at the ~ of dawn** au point du jour. -3. [noise - of whip]

claquement m; [- of twigs] craquement m. -4. [joke] plaisanterie f. -5. inf [attempt]: **to have a ~ at sthg** tenter qqch, essayer de faire qqch. -6. drugs sl crack m. ◇ adj [troops etc] de première classe; **~ shot** tireur m, -euse f d'élite. ◇ vt -1. [glass, plate] fêler; [wood, wall] fissurer. -2. [egg, nut] casser. -3. [whip] faire claquer. -4. [bang, hit sharply]: **to ~ one's head** se cogner la tête. -5. inf [bottle]: **to ~ (open) a bottle** ouvrir une bouteille. -6. [solve - problem] résoudre; [- code] déchiffrer. -7. inf [make - joke] faire. ◇ vi -1. [glass, pottery] se fêler; [ground, wood, wall] se fissurer; [skin] se crevasser, se gercer. -2. [whip] claquer; [twigs] craquer. -3. [break down - person] craquer, s'effondrer; [- system, empire] s'écrouler; [- resistance] se briser. -4. Br inf [act quickly]: **to get ~ing** s'y mettre.
♦ **crack down** vi: **to ~ down (on)** sévir (contre).
♦ **crack up** vi craquer.

crackdown ['krækdaʊn] n: **~ (on)** mesures fpl énergiques (contre).

cracked [krækt] adj -1. [vase, glass] fêlé(e); [wall] fissuré(e); [paint, varnish] craquelé(e). -2. [voice] fêlé(e). -3. inf [mad] cinglé(e), toqué(e).

cracker ['krækə'] n -1. [biscuit] cracker m, craquelin m. -2. Br [for Christmas] diablotin m.

crackers ['krækəz] adj Br inf dingue, cinglé(e).

cracking ['krækɪŋ] adj inf: **to walk at a ~ pace** marcher à toute allure.

crackle ['krækl] ◇ n [of fire] crépitement m; [of cooking] grésillement m; [on phone, radio] friture f. ◇ vi [frying food] grésiller; [fire] crépiter; [radio etc] crachoter.

crackling ['kræklɪŋ] n (U) -1. [on phone, radio] friture f; [of fire] crépitement m; [of cooking] grésillement m. -2. [pork skin] couenne f rissolée.

crackpot ['krækpɒt] inf ◇ adj fou (folle). ◇ n cinglé m, -e f, tordu m, -e f.

cradle ['kreɪdl] ◇ n berceau m; TECH nacelle f. ◇ vt [baby] bercer; [object] tenir délicatement.

craft [krɑːft] (pl sense 2 inv) n -1. [trade, skill] métier m. -2. [boat] embarcation f.

craftsman ['krɑːftsmən] (pl -men [-mən]) n artisan m, homme m de métier.

craftsmanship ['krɑːftsmənʃɪp] n (U) -1. [skill] dextérité f, art m. -2. [skilled work] travail m, exécution f.

craftsmen pl → **craftsman**.

crafty ['krɑːftɪ] (*compar* **-ier,** *superl* **-iest**) *adj* rusé(e).

crag [kræg] *n* rocher *m* escarpé.

craggy ['krægɪ] (*compar* **-ier,** *superl* **-iest**) *adj* **-1.** [rock] escarpé(e). **-2.** [face] anguleux(euse).

Crakow ['krækau] *n* Cracovie.

cram [kræm] (*pt* & *pp* **-med,** *cont* **-ming**) ◇ *vt* **-1.** [stuff] fourrer. **-2.** [overfill]: **to** ~ **sthg with** bourrer qqch de. ◇ *vi* bachoter.

cramming ['kræmɪŋ] *n* bachotage *m*.

cramp [kræmp] ◇ *n* crampe *f*. ◇ *vt* gêner, entraver.

cramped [kræmpt] *adj* [room] exigu(ë); **it's a bit ~ in here** on est un peu à l'étroit ici.

crampon ['kræmpən] *n* crampon *m*.

cranberry ['krænbərɪ] (*pl* **-ies**) *n* canneberge *f*.

crane [kreɪn] ◇ *n* grue *f*. ◇ *vt*: **to ~ one's neck** tendre le cou. ◇ *vi* tendre le cou.

crane fly *n* tipule *f*.

cranium ['kreɪnjəm] (*pl* **-niums** OR **-nia** [-njə]) *n* crâne *m*.

crank [kræŋk] ◇ *n* **-1.** TECH manivelle *f*. **-2.** *inf* [person] excentrique *mf*. ◇ *vt* **-1.** [windhandle] tourner; [- mechanism] remonter (à la manivelle). **-2.** AUT faire démarrer à la manivelle.

crankshaft ['kræŋkʃɑːft] *n* vilebrequin *m*.

cranky ['kræŋkɪ] (*compar* **-ier,** *superl* **-iest**) *adj inf* **-1.** [odd] excentrique. **-2.** *Am* [bad-tempered] grognon(onne).

cranny ['krænɪ] (*pl* **-ies**) *n* faille *f*.

crap [kræp] *n* (*U*) *v inf* merde *f*; **it's a load of ~** tout ça, c'est des conneries.

crappy ['kræpɪ] (*compar* **-ier,** *superl* **-iest**) *adj v inf* merdique.

crash [kræʃ] ◇ *n* **-1.** [accident] accident *m*. **-2.** [noise] fracas *m*. **-3.** FIN krach *m*. ◇ *vt*: **I ~ed the car** j'ai eu un accident avec la voiture. ◇ *vi* **-1.** [cars, trains] se percuter, se rentrer dedans; [car, train] avoir un accident; [plane] s'écraser; **to ~ into** [wall] rentrer dans, emboutir. **-2.** [plate] se fracasser. **-3.** [FIN - business, company] faire faillite; [- stockmarket] s'effondrer. **-4.** COMPUT tomber en panne.

crash barrier *n* glissière *f* de sécurité.

crash course *n* cours *m* intensif.

crash diet *n* régime *m* intensif.

crash-dive *vi* faire une plongée rapide.

crash helmet *n* casque *m* de protection.

crash-land ◇ *vt* faire atterrir en catastrophe. ◇ *vi* atterrir en catastrophe.

crash landing *n* atterrissage *m* en catastrophe.

crass [kræs] *adj* grossier(ière).

crate [kreɪt] *n* cageot *m,* caisse *f*.

crater ['kreɪtə˞] *n* cratère *m*.

cravat [krə'væt] *n* cravate *f*.

crave [kreɪv] ◇ *vt* [affection, luxury] avoir soif de; [cigarette, chocolat] avoir un besoin fou OR maladif de. ◇ *vi*: **to ~ for** [affection, luxury] avoir soif de; [cigarette, chocolate] avoir un besoin fou OR maladif de.

craving ['kreɪvɪŋ] *n*: ~ **for** [affection, luxury] soif *f* de; [cigarette, chocolate] besoin *m* fou OR maladif de.

crawl [krɔːl] ◇ *vi* **-1.** [baby] marcher à quatre pattes; [person] se traîner. **-2.** [insect] ramper. **-3.** [vehicle, traffic] avancer au pas. **-4.** *inf* [place, floor]: **to be ~ing with** grouiller de. **-5.** *inf* [grovel]: **to ~ (to sb)** ramper (devant qqn). ◇ *n* **-1.** [slow pace]: **at a ~** au pas, au ralenti. **-2.** [swimming stroke]: **the ~** le crawl.

crawler lane ['krɔːlə˞-] *n Br* voie *f* pour véhicules lents.

crayfish ['kreɪfɪʃ] (*pl inv* OR **-es**) *n* écrevisse *f*.

crayon ['kreɪɒn] *n* crayon *m* de couleur.

craze [kreɪz] *n* engouement *m*.

crazed [kreɪzd] *adj*: ~ **(with)** rendu fou (rendue folle) (de).

crazy ['kreɪzɪ] (*compar* **-ier,** *superl* **-iest**) *adj inf* **-1.** [mad] fou (folle). **-2.** [enthusiastic]: **to be ~ about sb/sthg** être fou (folle) de qqn/qqch.

crazy paving *n Br* dallage *m* irrégulier.

creak [kriːk] ◇ *n* [of door, handle] craquement *m*. ◇ *vi* [door, handle] craquer; [floorboard, bed] grincer.

creaky ['kriːkɪ] (*compar* **-ier,** *superl* **-iest**) *adj* [door, handle] qui craque; [floorboard, bed] qui grince.

cream [kriːm] ◇ *adj* [in colour] crème (*inv*). ◇ *n* **-1.** [gen] crème *f*. **-2.** [colour] crème *m*. ◇ *vt* [potatoes] mettre en purée.

◆ **cream off** *vt sep fig* écrémer.

cream cake *n Br* gâteau *m* à la crème.

cream cheese *n* fromage *m* frais.

cream cracker *n Br* biscuit *m* salé (*souvent mangé avec du fromage*).

cream of tartar *n* crème *f* de tartre.

cream tea *n Br* goûter se composant de thé et de scones servis avec de la crème et de la confiture.

creamy ['kriːmɪ] (*compar* **-ier,** *superl* **-iest**) *adj* **-1.** [taste, texture] crémeux(euse). **-2.** [colour] crème (*inv*).

crease [kriːs] ◇ *n* [in fabric - deliberate] pli *m*; [- accidental] (faux) pli. ◇ *vt* froisser. ◇ *vi* **-1.** [fabric] se froisser. **-2.** [face, forehead] se plisser.

creased [kriːst] *adj* **-1.** [fabric] froissé(e). **-2.** [face] plissé(e).

crease-resistant *adj* infroissable.

create [kriːˈeɪt] *vt* créer.

creation [kriːˈeɪʃən] *n* création *f*.

creative [kriːˈeɪtɪv] *adj* créatif(ive).

creativity [ˌkriːeɪˈtɪvətɪ] *n* créativité *f*.

creator [kriːˈeɪtəʳ] *n* créateur *m*, -trice *f*.

creature [ˈkriːtʃəʳ] *n* créature *f*.

crèche [kreʃ] *n* Br crèche *f*.

credence [ˈkriːdns] *n*: **to give** OR **lend ~ to sthg** ajouter foi à qqch.

credentials [krɪˈdenʃlz] *npl* **-1.** [papers] pièce *f* d'identité; *fig* [qualifications] capacités *fpl*. **-2.** [references] références *fpl*.

credibility [ˌkredəˈbɪlətɪ] *n* crédibilité *f*.

credible [ˈkredəbl] *adj* crédible.

credit [ˈkredɪt] ◇ *n* **-1.** FIN crédit *m*; **to be in ~** [person] avoir un compte approvisionné; [account] être approvisionné; **on ~** à crédit. **-2.** (*U*) [praise] honneur *m*, mérite *m*; **to be to sb's ~** [successfully completed] être à l'actif de qqn; [in sb's favour] être à l'honneur de qqn; **to do sb ~** faire honneur à qqn; **to give sb ~ for sthg** reconnaître que qqn a fait qqch. **-3.** SCH & UNIV unité *f* de valeur. ◇ *vt* **-1.** FIN: **to ~ £10 to an account**, **to ~ an account with £10** créditer un compte de 10 livres. **-2.** *inf* [believe] croire. **-3.** [give the credit to]: **to ~ sb with sthg** accorder OR attribuer qqch à qqn; **he's ~ed with inventing ... il a, dit-on, inventé ....**

◆ **credits** *npl* CINEMA générique *m*.

creditable [ˈkredɪtəbl] *adj* honorable.

credit account *n* Br compte *m* créditeur.

credit broker *n* courtier *m* en crédits OR en prêts.

credit card *n* carte *f* de crédit.

credit control *n* [on spending] encadrement *m* du crédit; [debt recovery] recouvrement *m* de créances.

credit facilities *npl* facilités *fpl* de paiement OR de crédit.

credit limit Br, **credit line** Am *n* limite *f* de crédit.

credit note *n* avoir *m*; FIN note *f* de crédit.

creditor [ˈkredɪtəʳ] *n* créancier *m*, -ière *f*.

credit rating *n* degré *m* de solvabilité.

credit squeeze *n* restriction *f* de crédit.

credit transfer *n* virement *m* de crédits.

creditworthy [ˈkredɪtˌwɜːðɪ] *adj* solvable.

credulity [krɪˈdjuːlətɪ] *n* crédulité *f*.

credulous [ˈkredjʊləs] *adj* crédule.

creed [kriːd] *n* **-1.** [belief] principes *mpl*. **-2.** RELIG croyance *f*.

creek [kriːk] *n* **-1.** [inlet] crique *f*. **-2.** Am [stream] ruisseau *m*.

creep [kriːp] (*pt* & *pp* **crept**) ◇ *vi* **-1.** [insect] ramper; [traffic] avancer au pas. **-2.** [move stealthily] se glisser. **-3.** *inf* [grovel]: **to ~ (to sb)** ramper (devant qqn). ◇ *n inf* [nasty person] sale type *m*.

◆ **creeps** *npl*: **to give sb the ~s** *inf* donner la chair de poule à qqn.

◆ **creep in** *vi* [appear] apparaître.

◆ **creep up on** *vt* surprendre.

creeper [ˈkriːpəʳ] *n* [plant] plante *f* grimpante.

◆ **creepers** *npl* chaussures *fpl* à semelles de crêpe.

creepy [ˈkriːpɪ] (*compar* **-ier**, *superl* **-iest**) *adj inf* qui donne la chair de poule.

creepy-crawly [-ˈkrɔːlɪ] (*pl* **creepy-crawlies**) *n inf* bestiole *f* qui rampe.

cremate [krɪˈmeɪt] *vt* incinérer.

cremation [krɪˈmeɪʃn] *n* incinération *f*.

crematorium [ˌkreməˈtɔːrɪəm] Br (*pl* **-riums** OR **-ria** [-rɪə]), **crematory** Am [ˈkremətrɪ] (*pl* **-ies**) *n* crématorium *m*.

creosote [ˈkrɪəsəʊt] ◇ *n* créosote *f*. ◇ *vt* créosoter.

crepe [kreɪp] *n* **-1.** [cloth, rubber] crêpe *m*. **-2.** [pancake] crêpe *f*.

crepe bandage *n* Br bande *f* Velpeau®.

crepe paper *n* papier *m* crépon.

crepe-soled shoes [-səʊld-] *npl* Br chaussures *fpl* à semelles de crêpe.

crept [krept] *pt* & *pp* → **creep**.

Cres. *abbr of* **Crescent**.

crescendo [krɪˈʃendəʊ] (*pl* **-s**) *n* crescendo *m*.

crescent [ˈkresnt] ◇ *adj* en forme de croissant; **~ moon** croissant *m* de lune. ◇ *n* **-1.** [shape] croissant *m*. **-2.** [street] rue *f* en demi-cercle.

cress [kres] *n* cresson *m*.

crest [krest] *n* **-1.** [of bird, hill] crête *f*. **-2.** [on coat of arms] timbre *m*.

crestfallen [ˈkrestˌfɔːln] *adj* découragé(e).

Crete [kriːt] *n* Crète *f*; **in ~** en Crète.

cretin [ˈkretɪn] *n inf* [idiot] crétin *m*, -e *f*.

crevasse [krɪˈvæs] *n* crevasse *f*.

crevice [ˈkrevɪs] *n* fissure *f*.

crew [kruː] *n* **-1.** [of ship, plane] équipage *m*. **-2.** [team] équipe *f*; **ambulance ~** ambulanciers *mpl*.

crew cut *n* coupe *f* en brosse.

crewman ['kru:mæn] (*pl* **-men** [-men]) *n* membre *m* d'équipage.

crew-neck(ed) [-nek(t)] *adj* ras du cou.

crib [krɪb] (*pt* & *pp* **-bed**, *cont* **-bing**) ◇ *n* [cot] berceau *m*. ◇ *vt inf* [copy]: **to ~ sthg off** OR **from sb** copier qqch sur qqn.

cribbage ['krɪbɪdʒ] *n* jeu de cartes dans lequel les points sont comptabilisés sur une tablette.

crick [krɪk] ◇ *n* [in neck] torticolis *m*. ◇ *vt*: **to ~ one's neck** attraper un torticolis; **to ~ one's back** se faire un tour de reins.

cricket ['krɪkɪt] ◇ *n* **-1.** [game] cricket *m*. **-2.** [insect] grillon *m*. ◇ *comp* de cricket.

cricketer ['krɪkɪtə'] *n* joueur *m* de cricket.

crikey ['kraɪkɪ] *excl Br inf dated* zut alors!

crime [kraɪm] ◇ *n* crime *m*. ◇ *comp*: **~ novel** policier *m*; **~ prevention** lutte *f* contre le crime.

Crimea [kraɪ'mɪə] *n*: **the ~** la Crimée; **in the ~** en Crimée.

crime wave *n* vague *f* de criminalité.

criminal ['krɪmɪnl] ◇ *adj* criminel(elle); **~ lawyer** avocat *m* pénaliste. ◇ *n* criminel *m*, -elle *f*.

criminal law *n* droit *m* pénal.

criminalize, -ise ['krɪmɪnəlaɪz] *vt* criminaliser.

criminology [,krɪmɪ'nɒlədʒɪ] *n* criminologie *f*.

crimp [krɪmp] *vt* [hair] crêper.

crimson ['krɪmzn] ◇ *adj* [in colour] rouge foncé (*inv*); [with embarrassment] cramoisi(e). ◇ *n* cramoisi *m*.

cringe [krɪndʒ] *vi* **-1.** [in fear] avoir un mouvement de recul (par peur). **-2.** *inf* [with embarrassment]: **to ~ (at sthg)** ne plus savoir où se mettre (devant qqch).

crinkle ['krɪŋkl] ◇ *n* [in paper] pli *m*; [in cloth] (**faux**) pli. ◇ *vt* [clothes] froisser. ◇ *vi* [clothes] se froisser.

cripple ['krɪpl] ◇ *n dated & offensive* infirme *mf*. ◇ *vt* **-1.** MED [disable] estropier. **-2.** [country] paralyser; [ship, plane] endommager.

crippling ['krɪplɪŋ] *adj* **-1.** MED [disease] qui rend infirme. **-2.** [taxes, debts] écrasant(e).

crisis ['kraɪsɪs] (*pl* **crises** ['kraɪsi:z]) *n* crise *f*.

crisp [krɪsp] *adj* **-1.** [pastry] croustillant(e); [apple, vegetables] croquant(e); [snow] craquant(e). **-2.** [weather, manner] vif (vive).
◆ **crisps** *npl Br* chips *fpl*.

crispbread ['krɪspbred] *n* pain *m* suédois.

crispy ['krɪspɪ] (*compar* **-ier**, *superl* **-iest**) *adj*

[pastry] **croustillant(e)**; [apple, vegetables] **croquant(e)**.

crisscross ['krɪskrɒs] ◇ *adj* entrecroisé(e). ◇ *vt* entrecroiser. ◇ *vi* s'entrecroiser.

criterion [kraɪ'tɪərɪən] (*pl* **-rions** OR **-ria** [-rɪə]) *n* critère *m*.

critic ['krɪtɪk] *n* **-1.** [reviewer] critique *m*. **-2.** [detractor] détracteur *m*, -trice *f*.

critical ['krɪtɪkl] *adj* critique; **to be ~ of sb/sthg** critiquer qqn/qqch.

critically ['krɪtɪklɪ] *adv* **-1.** [ill] gravement; **~ important** d'une importance capitale. **-2.** [analytically] de façon critique.

criticism ['krɪtɪsɪzm] *n* critique *f*.

criticize, -ise ['krɪtɪsaɪz] *vt* & *vi* critiquer.

critique [krɪ'ti:k] *n* critique *f*.

croak [krəʊk] ◇ *n* **-1.** [of frog] coassement *m*; [of raven] croassement *m*. **-2.** [hoarse voice] voix *f* rauque. ◇ *vi* **-1.** [frog] coasser; [raven] croasser. **-2.** [person] parler d'une voix rauque.

Croat ['krəʊæt], **Croatian** [krəʊ'eɪʃn] ◇ *adj* croate. ◇ *n* **-1.** [person] Croate *mf*. **-2.** [language] croate *m*.

Croatia [krəʊ'eɪʃə] *n* Croatie *f*; **in ~** en Croatie.

Croatian = **Croat**.

crochet ['krəʊʃeɪ] ◇ *n* crochet *m*. ◇ *vt* faire au crochet.

crockery ['krɒkərɪ] *n* vaisselle *f*.

crocodile ['krɒkədaɪl] (*pl inv* OR **-s**) *n* crocodile *m*.

crocus ['krəʊkəs] (*pl* **-cuses**) *n* crocus *m*.

croft [krɒft] *n Br* petite ferme *f* (*particulièrement en Écosse*).

croissant ['krwæsã] *n* croissant *m*.

crony ['krəʊnɪ] (*pl* **-ies**) *n inf* copain *m*, copine *f*.

crook [krʊk] ◇ *n* **-1.** [criminal] escroc *m*. **-2.** [of arm, elbow] pliure *f*. **-3.** [shepherd's staff] houlette *f*. ◇ *vt* [finger, arm] plier.

crooked ['krʊkɪd] *adj* **-1.** [bent] courbé(e). **-2.** [teeth, tie] de travers. **-3.** *inf* [dishonest] malhonnête.

croon [kru:n] *vt* & *vi* chantonner.

crop [krɒp] (*pt* & *pp* **-ped**, *cont* **-ping**) ◇ *n* **-1.** [kind of plant] culture *f*. **-2.** [harvested produce] récolte *f*. **-3.** [whip] cravache *f*. ◇ *vt* **-1.** [hair] couper très court. **-2.** [subj: cows, sheep] brouter.
◆ **crop up** *vi* survenir.

cropper ['krɒpə'] *n inf*: **to come a ~** [fall over] se casser la figure; [make mistake] se planter.

crop spraying [-,spreɪɪŋ] *n* pulvérisation *f* des cultures.

croquet ['krəʊkeɪ] *n* croquet *m*.

croquette [krɒ'ket] *n* croquette *f*.

cross [krɒs] ◇ *adj* [person] fâché(e); [look] méchant(e); **to get ~ (with sb)** se fâcher (contre qqn). ◇ *n* **-1.** [gen] croix *f*. **-2.** [hybrid] croisement *m*. ◇ *vt* **-1.** [gen] traverser. **-2.** [arms, legs] croiser. **-3.** RELIG: **to ~ o.s.** faire le signe de croix, se signer. **-4.** *Br* [cheque] barrer. ◇ *vi* **-1.** [intersect] se croiser. **-2.** [traverse - boat] faire la traversée.

◆ **cross off, cross out** *vt sep* rayer.

crossbar ['krɒsbɑːʳ] *n* **-1.** SPORT barre *f* transversale. **-2.** [on bicycle] barre *f*.

crossbow ['krɒsbəʊ] *n* arbalète *f*.

crossbreed ['krɒsbriːd] *n* hybride *m*.

cross-Channel *adj* transManche.

cross-check *n* contre-vérification *f*.

◆ **crosscheck** *vt* faire une contre-vérification de.

cross-country ◇ *adj*: **~ running** cross *m*; **~ skiing** ski *m* de fond. ◇ *adv* à travers champs. ◇ *n* cross-country *m*, cross *m*.

cross-cultural *adj* interculturel(elle).

cross-dressing *n* travestisme *m*.

crossed line [krɒst-] *n* TELEC: **we've got a ~** il y a des interférences.

cross-examination *n* JUR contre-interrogatoire *m*.

cross-examine *vt* JUR faire subir un contre-interrogatoire à; *fig* questionner de près.

cross-eyed ['krɒsaɪd] *adj* qui louche.

cross-fertilize *vt* [plants] croiser.

crossfire ['krɒs,faɪəʳ] *n* (*U*) feu *m* croisé.

crosshead ['krɒs,hed] *adj*: **~ screw** vis *m* cruciforme; **~ screwdriver** tournevis *m* cruciforme.

crossing ['krɒsɪŋ] *n* **-1.** [on road] passage *m* clouté; [on railway line] passage à niveau. **-2.** [sea journey] traversée *f*.

cross-legged ['krɒslegd] *adv* en tailleur.

crossly ['krɒslɪ] *adv* [say] d'un air fâché.

crossply ['krɒsplaɪ] (*pl* -ies) ◇ *adj* [tyre] à carcasse diagonale. ◇ *n* pneu *m* à carcasse diagonale.

cross-purposes *npl*: **to talk at ~** ne pas parler de la même chose; **to be at ~** ne pas être sur la même longueur d'ondes.

cross-question *vt* faire subir un contre-interrogatoire à.

cross-refer *vt & vi* renvoyer.

cross-reference *n* renvoi *m*.

crossroads ['krɒsrəʊdz] (*pl inv*) *n* croisement *m*; **to be at a ~** *fig* se trouver à un point critique.

cross-section *n* **-1.** [drawing] coupe *f* transversale. **-2.** [sample] échantillon *m*.

crosswalk ['krɒswɔːk] *n Am* passage *m* clouté, passage pour piétons.

crossways ['krɒsweɪz] = **crosswise**.

crosswind ['krɒswɪnd] *n* vent *m* de travers.

crosswise ['krɒswaɪz] *adv* en travers.

crossword (puzzle) ['krɒswɜːd-] *n* mots croisés *mpl*.

crotch [krɒtʃ] *n* entrejambe *m*.

crotchet ['krɒtʃɪt] *n* noire *f*.

crotchety ['krɒtʃɪtɪ] *adj Br inf* grognon(onne).

crouch [kraʊtʃ] *vi* s'accroupir.

croup [kruːp] *n* **-1.** [illness] croup *m*. **-2.** [of horse] croupe *f*.

croupier ['kruːpɪəʳ] *n* croupier *m*.

crouton ['kruːtɒn] *n* croûton *m*.

crow [krəʊ] ◇ *n* corbeau *m*; **as the ~ flies** à vol d'oiseau. ◇ *vi* **-1.** [cock] chanter. **-2.** *inf* [person] frimer.

crowbar ['krəʊbɑːʳ] *n* pied-de-biche *m*.

crowd [kraʊd] ◇ *n* **-1.** [mass of people] foule *f*. **-2.** [particular group] bande *f*, groupe *m*. ◇ *vi* s'amasser. ◇ *vt* **-1.** [streets, town] remplir. **-2.** [force into small space] entasser.

crowded ['kraʊdɪd] *adj*: **~ (with)** bondé(e) (de), plein(e) (de).

crown [kraʊn] ◇ *n* **-1.** [of king, on tooth] couronne *f*. **-2.** [of head, hill] sommet *m*; [of hat] fond *m*. ◇ *vt* couronner.

◆ **Crown** ◇ *n*: **the Crown** [monarchy] la Couronne. ◇ *comp* de la Couronne.

crown court *n* tribunal *m* de grande instance.

crowning ['kraʊnɪŋ] *adj fig* suprême; **the ~ glory of her career** le plus grand triomphe de sa carrière.

crown jewels *npl* joyaux *mpl* de la Couronne.

crown prince *n* prince *m* héritier.

crow's feet *npl* pattes *fpl* d'oie.

crow's nest *n* nid *m* de pie.

crucial ['kruːʃl] *adj* crucial(e).

crucially ['kruːʃlɪ] *adv* de façon cruciale; **~ important** d'une importance cruciale.

crucible ['kruːsɪbl] *n* creuset *m*.

crucifix ['kruːsɪfɪks] *n* crucifix *m*.

Crucifixion [,kruːsɪ'fɪkʃn] *n*: **the ~** la Crucifixion.

crucify ['kruːsɪfaɪ] (*pt & pp* -ied) *vt* crucifier.

curiously ['kjʊərɪəslɪ] *adv* -**1.** [inquisitively] avec curiosité. -**2.** [strangely] curieusement; ~ **enough** curieusement, chose curieuse.

curl [kɜːl] ◇ *n* -**1.** [of hair] boucle *f.* -**2.** [of smoke] **volute** *f.* ◇ *vt* -**1.** [hair] boucler. -**2.** [roll up] **enrouler.** ◇ *vi* -**1.** [hair] boucler. -**2.** [roll up] s'enrouler; **to ~ into a ball** se mettre en boule.

◆ **curl up** *vi* [person, animal] se mettre en boule, se pelotonner.

curler ['kɜːlə'] *n* bigoudi *m.*

curling ['kɜːlɪŋ] *n* curling *m.*

curling tongs *npl* fer *m* à friser.

curly ['kɜːlɪ] (*compar* -**ier**, *superl* -**iest**) *adj* [hair] bouclé(e).

currant ['kʌrənt] *n* [dried grape] raisin *m* de Corinthe, raisin sec.

currency ['kʌrənsɪ] (*pl* -**ies**) *n* -**1.** [type of money] **monnaie** *f.* -**2.** (*U*) [money] **devise** *f.* -**3.** *fml* [acceptability]: **to gain ~** s'accréditer.

current ['kʌrənt] ◇ *adj* [price, method] actuel(elle); [year, week] **en cours;** [boyfriend, girlfriend] **du moment;** ~ **issue** dernier numéro. ◇ *n* -**1.** [of water, air, electricity] courant *m.* -**2.** [trend] tendance *f.*

current account *n Br* compte *m* courant.

current affairs *npl* actualité *f,* questions *fpl* d'actualité.

current assets *npl* actif *m* circulant.

current liabilities *npl* passif *m* exigible à court terme.

currently ['kʌrəntlɪ] *adv* actuellement.

curricular [kə'rɪkjələ'] *adj* au programme.

curriculum [kə'rɪkjələm] (*pl* -**lums** OR -**la** [-lə]) *n* programme *m* d'études.

curriculum vitae [-'viːtaɪ] (*pl* **curricula vitae**) *n* curriculum vitae *m.*

curried ['kʌrɪd] *adj* au curry.

curry ['kʌrɪ] (*pl* -**ies**) *n* curry *m.*

curry powder *n* poudre *f* de curry.

curse [kɜːs] ◇ *n* -**1.** [evil spell] malédiction *f; fig* fléau *m.* -**2.** [swearword] juron *m.* ◇ *vt* maudire. ◇ *vi* jurer.

cursor ['kɜːsə'] *n* COMPUT curseur *m.*

cursory ['kɜːsərɪ] *adj* superficiel(ielle).

curt [kɜːt] *adj* brusque.

curtail [kɜː'teɪl] *vt* -**1.** [visit] écourter. -**2.** [rights, expenditure] **réduire.**

curtailment [kɜː'teɪlmənt] *n* [of rights, expenditure] réduction *f.*

curtain ['kɜːtn] *n* rideau *m.*

◆ **curtain off** *vt sep* [bed] cacher derrière un rideau; [room] diviser par un rideau.

curtain call *n* rappel *m.*

curtain raiser *n fig* lever *m* de rideau.

curts(e)y ['kɜːtsɪ] (*pt & pp* **curtsied**) ◇ *n* révérence *f.* ◇ *vi* faire une révérence.

curvaceous [kɜː'veɪʃəs] *adj inf* bien roulé(e).

curvature ['kɜːvətjə'] *n* courbure *f;* MED [of spine] déviation *f.*

curve [kɜːv] ◇ *n* courbe *f.* ◇ *vi* faire une courbe.

curved [kɜːvd] *adj* courbe.

curvy ['kɜːvɪ] (*compar* -**ier**, *superl* -**iest**) *adj* [line] courbé(e); [woman] bien roulée.

cushion ['kʊʃn] ◇ *n* coussin *m.* ◇ *vt* [fall, blow, effects] amortir; **to be ~ed against** [inflation, reality] être paré contre.

cushy ['kʊʃɪ] (*compar* -**ier**, *superl* -**iest**) *adj inf* pépère, peinard(e).

custard ['kʌstəd] *n* crème *f* anglaise.

custard pie *n* tarte *f* à la crème.

custard powder *n* crème *f* anglaise instantanée en poudre.

custodian [kʌ'stəʊdjən] *n* [of building] gardien *m,* -**ienne** *f;* [of museum] conservateur *m.*

custody ['kʌstədɪ] *n* -**1.** [of child] **garde** *f.* -**2.** JUR: **in ~** en garde à vue.

custom ['kʌstəm] *n* -**1.** [tradition, habit] coutume *f.* -**2.** COMM clientèle *f;* **thank you for your ~** merci de nous avoir honorés de votre commande.

◆ **customs** *n* [place] douane *f;* **to go through ~s** passer (à) la douane.

customary ['kʌstəmrɪ] *adj* [behaviour] coutumier(ière); [way, time] habituel(elle).

custom-built *adj* fait(e) sur commande OR mesure.

customer ['kʌstəmə'] *n* -**1.** [client] client *m,* -**e** *f.* -**2.** *inf* [person] type *m.*

customer services *npl* service *m* (à la) clientèle.

customize, -ise ['kʌstəmaɪz] *vt* [make] fabriquer OR assembler sur commande; [modify] modifier sur commande.

custom-made *adj* fait(e) sur mesure.

Customs and Excise *n Br* ≈ service *m* des contributions indirectes.

customs duty *n* droit *m* de douane.

customs officer *n* douanier *m,* -**ière** *f.*

cut [kʌt] (*pt & pp* **cut**, *cont* -**ting**) ◇ *n* -**1.** [in wood etc] entaille *f;* [in skin] coupure *f.* -**2.** [of meat] morceau *m.* -**3.** [reduction]: ~ **(in)** [taxes, salary, personnel] réduction *f* (de); [film, article] coupure *f* (dans). -**4.** *inf* [share] part *f.* -**5.** [of suit, hair] coupe *f.* -**6.** *phr:* **a ~ above (the rest)** *inf* supérieur(e) aux autres. ◇ *vt* -**1.** [gen] couper; [taxes, costs, workforce] réduire; **to ~ one's finger** se couper le doigt. **-2.** [subj: baby]: **he's cutting a tooth** il fait ses dents. **-3.** *inf* [lecture, class] sécher. ◇ *vi* **-1.** [gen] couper. **-2.** [intersect] se couper.

◆ **cut across** *vt fus* **-1.** [as short cut] couper à travers. **-2.** [transcend] ne pas tenir compte de.

◆ **cut back** ◇ *vt sep* **-1.** [prune] tailler. **-2.** [reduce] réduire. ◇ *vi*: **to ~ back on** réduire, diminuer.

◆ **cut down** ◇ *vt sep* **-1.** [chop down] couper. **-2.** [reduce] réduire, diminuer. ◇ *vi*: **to ~ down on smoking/eating/spending** fumer/manger/dépenser moins.

◆ **cut in** *vi* **-1.** [interrupt]: **to ~ in (on sb)** interrompre (qqn). **-2.** AUT & SPORT se rabattre.

◆ **cut off** *vt sep* **-1.** [piece, crust] couper; [finger, leg - subj: surgeon] amputer. **-2.** [power, telephone, funding] couper. **-3.** [separate]: **to be ~ off (from)** [person] être coupé(e) (de); [village] être isolé(e) (de).

◆ **cut out** ◇ *vt sep* **-1.** [photo, article] découper; [sewing pattern] couper; [dress] tailler; **to be ~ out for sthg** *fig* [person] être fait pour qqch. **-2.** [stop]: **to ~ out smoking/chocolates** arrêter de fumer/de manger des chocolats; **~ it out!** *inf* ça suffit! **-3.** [exclude] exclure. ◇ *vi* [stall] caler.

◆ **cut up** *vt sep* [chop up] couper, hacher.

cut-and-dried *adj* tout fait (toute faite).

cut and paste *vt & vi* COMPUT couper-coller.

cutback ['kʌtbæk] *n*: **~ (in)** réduction *f* (de).

cute [kjuːt] *adj* [appealing] mignon(onne).

cut glass ◇ *n* cristal *m* taillé. ◇ *comp* en cristal taillé.

cuticle ['kjuːtɪkl] *n* envie *f*.

cutlery ['kʌtlərɪ] *n* (U) couverts *mpl*.

cutlet ['kʌtlɪt] *n* côtelette *f*.

cutoff (point) ['kʌtɒf-] *n* [limit] point *m* de limite.

cutout ['kʌtaʊt] *n* **-1.** [on machine] disjoncteur *m*. **-2.** [shape] découpage *m*.

cut-price, cut-rate *Am adj* à prix réduit.

cutter ['kʌtə¹] *n* [tool] coupoir *m*.

cutthroat ['kʌtθrəʊt] *adj* [ruthless] acharné(e).

cutting ['kʌtɪŋ] ◇ *adj* [sarcastic - remark] cinglant(e); [- wit] acerbe. ◇ *n* **-1.** [of plant] bouture *f*. **-2.** [from newspaper] coupure *f*. **-3.** *Br* [for road, railway] tranchée *f*.

cuttlefish ['kʌtlfɪʃ] (*pl inv*) *n* seiche *f*.

cut up *adj Br inf* [upset] affligé(e).

CV (*abbr of* **curriculum vitae**) *n* CV *m*.

C & W *abbr of* **country and western.**

cwo (*abbr of* **cash with order**) *payable à la commande.*

cwt. *abbr of* **hundredweight.**

cyanide ['saɪənaɪd] *n* cyanure *m*.

cybernetics [,saɪbə'netɪks] *n* (U) cybernétique *f*.

cyclamen ['sɪkləmən] (*pl inv*) *n* cyclamen *m*.

cycle ['saɪkl] ◇ *n* **-1.** [of events, songs] cycle *m*. **-2.** [bicycle] bicyclette *f*. ◇ *comp* [path, track] cyclable; [race] cycliste; [shop] de cycles. ◇ *vi* faire de la bicyclette.

cyclic(al) ['saɪklɪk(l)] *adj* cyclique.

cycling ['saɪklɪŋ] *n* cyclisme *m*.

cyclist ['saɪklɪst] *n* cycliste *mf*.

cyclone ['saɪkləʊn] *n* cyclone *m*.

cygnet ['sɪgnɪt] *n* jeune cygne *m*.

cylinder ['sɪlɪndə¹] *n* cylindre *m*.

cylinder block *n* bloc-cylindres *m*.

cylinder head *n* culasse *f*.

cylinder-head gasket *n* joint *m* de culasse.

cylindrical [sɪ'lɪndrɪkl] *adj* cylindrique.

cymbals ['sɪmblz] *npl* cymbales *fpl*.

cynic ['sɪnɪk] *n* cynique *mf*.

cynical ['sɪnɪkl] *adj* cynique.

cynically ['sɪnɪklɪ] *adv* cyniquement.

cynicism ['sɪnɪsɪzm] *n* cynisme *m*.

CYO (*abbr of* **Catholic Youth Association**) *n aux États-Unis, association de jeunes catholiques.*

cypher ['saɪfə¹] = **cipher.**

cypress ['saɪprəs] *n* cyprès *m*.

Cypriot ['sɪprɪət] ◇ *adj* chypriote. ◇ *n* Chypriote *mf*; **Greek/Turkish ~** Chypriote grec (grecque)/turc (turque).

Cyprus ['saɪprəs] *n* Chypre *f*; **in ~** à Chypre.

cyst [sɪst] *n* kyste *m*.

cystitis [sɪs'taɪtɪs] *n* cystite *f*.

cystic fibrosis [,sɪstɪkfaɪ'brəʊsɪs] *n* mucoviscidose *f*.

cytology [saɪ'tɒlədʒɪ] *n* cytologie *f*.

CZ (*abbr of* **canal zone**) *zone du canal de Panama.*

czar [zɑː¹] *n* tsar *m*.

Czech [tʃek] ◇ *adj* tchèque. ◇ *n* **-1.** [person] Tchèque *mf*. **-2.** [language] tchèque *m*.

Czechoslovak [,tʃekə'sləʊvæk] = **Czechoslovakian.**

Czechoslovakia [,tʃekəslə'vækɪə] *n* Tchécoslovaquie *f*; **in ~** en Tchécoslovaquie.

Czechoslovakian [,tʃekəslə'vækɪən] ◇ *adj* tchécoslovaque. ◇ *n* Tchécoslovaque *mf*.

D

d¹ (*pl* **d's** OR **ds**), **D** (*pl* **D's** OR **Ds**) [diː] *n* [letter] d *m inv*, D *m inv*.
◆ **D** ◇ *n* **-1.** MUS ré *m*. **-2.** SCH [mark] D *m inv*. ◇ *Am abbr of* **Democrat(ic)**.

d² [diː] (*abbr of* **penny**) *symbole du penny anglais jusqu'en 1971*.

d. (*abbr of* **died**): ~ 1913 mort en 1913.

DA *abbr of* **district attorney**.

dab [dæb] (*pt & pp* **-bed**, *cont* **-bing**) ◇ *n* [of cream, powder, ointment] petit peu *m*; [of paint] touche *f*. ◇ *vt* **-1.** [skin, wound] tamponner. **-2.** [apply - cream, ointment] **to ~ sthg on** OR **onto** appliquer qqch sur. ◇ *vi*: **to ~ at** sthg tamponner qqch.

dabble ['dæbl] ◇ *vt* tremper dans l'eau. ◇ *vi*: **to ~ in** toucher un peu à.

dab hand *n Br* **to be a ~ (at** sthg**)** être doué(e) (pour qqch).

Dacca ['dækə] *n* Dacca.

dachshund ['dækshʊnd] *n* teckel *m*.

dad [dæd], **daddy** ['dædɪ] (*pl* **-ies**) *n inf* papa *m*.

daddy longlegs [-'lɒŋlegz] (*pl inv*) *n* faucheur *m*.

daffodil ['dæfədɪl] *n* jonquille *f*.

daft [dɑːft] *adj inf* stupide, idiot(e).

dagger ['dægə'] *n* poignard *m*.

dahlia ['deɪljə] *n* dahlia *m*.

daily ['deɪlɪ] (*pl* **-ies**) ◇ *adj* **-1.** [newspaper, occurrence] quotidien(ienne). **-2.** [rate, output] journalier(ière). ◇ *adv* [happen, write] quotidiennement; **twice ~** deux fois par jour. ◇ *n* **-1.** [newspaper] quotidien *m*. **-2.** [cleaning woman] femme *f* de ménage.

daintily ['deɪntɪlɪ] *adv* [made, eat, walk] délicatement; [dressed] coquettement.

dainty ['deɪntɪ] (*compar* **-ier**, *superl* **-iest**) *adj* délicat(e).

dairy ['deərɪ] (*pl* **-ies**) *n* **-1.** [on farm] laiterie *f*. **-2.** [shop] crèmerie *f*.

dairy cattle *npl* vaches *fpl* laitières.

dairy farm *n* ferme *f* laitière.

dairy products *npl* produits *mpl* laitiers.

dais ['deɪɪs] *n* estrade *f*.

daisy ['deɪzɪ] (*pl* **-ies**) *n* [weed] pâquerette *f*; [cultivated] marguerite *f*.

daisy wheel *n* marguerite *f*.

daisy-wheel printer *n* imprimante *f* à marguerite.

Dakar ['dækɑː] *n* Dakar.

Dakota [də'kəʊtə] *n* Dakota *m*; **in ~** dans le Dakota.

dal [dɑːl] = **dhal**.

dale [deɪl] *n* vallée *f*.

dalmatian [dæl'meɪʃn] *n* [dog] dalmatien *m*.

dam [dæm] (*pt & pp* **-med**, *cont* **-ming**) ◇ *n* [across river] barrage *m*. ◇ *vt* construire un barrage sur.
◆ **dam up** *vt sep* endiguer.

damage ['dæmɪdʒ] ◇ *n* **-1.** [physical harm] dommage *m*, dégât *m*. **-2.** [harmful effect] tort *m*. ◇ *vt* **-1.** [harm physically] endommager, abîmer. **-2.** [have harmful effect on] nuire à.
◆ **damages** *npl* JUR dommages et intérêts *mpl*.

damaging ['dæmɪdʒɪŋ] *adj*: ~ **(to)** préjudiciable (à).

Damascus [də'mæskəs] *n* Damas.

Dame [deɪm] *n Br titre accordé aux femmes titulaires de certaines décorations*.

damn [dæm] ◇ *adj inf* fichu(e), sacré(e). ◇ *adv inf* sacrément. ◇ *n inf*: **not to give** OR **care a ~ (about** sthg**)** se ficher pas mal (de qqch). ◇ *vt* **-1.** RELIG [condemn] damner. **-2.** *inf* [curse]: ~ **you!** va au diable!; ~ **it!** zut! ◇ *excl inf* zut!

damnable ['dæmnəbl] *adj dated* [appalling] détestable.

damnation [dæm'neɪʃn] *n* RELIG damnation *f*.

damned [dæmd] *inf* ◇ *adj* fichu(e), sacré(e); **I'm ~ if** ... si tu crois que ...; **well I'll be** OR **I'm ~!** c'est trop fort!, elle est bien bonne celle-là! ◇ *adv* sacrément.

damning ['dæmɪŋ] *adj* accablant(e).

damp [dæmp] ◇ *adj* humide. ◇ *n* humidité *f*. ◇ *vt* [make wet] humecter.
◆ **damp down** *vt sep* [restrain - unrest, violence] contenir, maîtriser; [- enthusiasm] refroidir.

damp course *n Br* couche *f* d'isolation.

dampen ['dæmpən] *vt* **-1.** [make wet] humecter. **-2.** *fig* [emotion] abattre.

damper ['dæmpə'] *n* **-1.** MUS étouffoir *m*. **-2.** [for fire] registre *m*. **-3.** *phr*: **to put a ~ on** sthg jeter un froid sur qqch.

dampness ['dæmpnɪs] *n* humidité *f*.

damson ['dæmzn] *n* prune *f* de Damas.

dance [dɑːns] ◇ n -1. [gen] danse f. -2. [social event] bal m. ◇ vi danser.

dance floor n piste f de danse.

dancer ['dɑːnsəʳ] n danseur m, -euse f.

dancing ['dɑːnsɪŋ] n (U) danse f.

D and C (abbr of dilation and curettage) n dilation et curetage.

dandelion ['dændɪlaɪən] n pissenlit m.

dandruff ['dændrʌf] n (U) pellicules fpl.

dandy ['dændɪ] (pl -ies) n dandy m.

Dane [deɪn] n Danois m, -e f.

danger ['deɪndʒəʳ] n -1. (U) [possibility of harm] danger m; in ~ en danger; out of ~ hors de danger. -2. [hazard, risk]: ~ (to) risque m (pour); to be in ~ of doing sthg risquer de faire qqch.

danger list n Br: to be on the ~ être dans un état critique.

danger money n (U) Br prime f de risque.

dangerous ['deɪndʒərəs] adj dangereux(euse).

dangerous driving n JUR conduite f dangereuse.

dangerously ['deɪndʒərəslɪ] adv dangereusement; ~ ill gravement malade.

danger zone n zone f dangereuse.

dangle ['dæŋgl] ◇ vt laisser pendre. ◇ vi pendre.

Danish ['deɪnɪʃ] ◇ adj danois(e). ◇ n -1. [language] danois m. -2. Am = **Danish pastry**. ◇ npl: the ~ les Danois mpl.

Danish blue n bleu m danois.

Danish pastry n gâteau feuilleté fourré aux fruits.

dank [dæŋk] adj humide et froid(e).

Danube ['dænjuːb] n: the ~ le Danube.

dapper ['dæpəʳ] adj pimpant(e).

dappled ['dæpld] adj -1. [light] tacheté(e). -2. [horse] pommelé(e).

Dardanelles [,dɑːdə'nelz] npl: the ~ les Dardanelles fpl.

dare [deəʳ] ◇ vt -1. [be brave enough]: to ~ to do sthg oser faire qqch. -2. [challenge]: to ~ sb to do sthg défier qqn de faire qqch. -3. phr: I ~ say je suppose, sans doute. ◇ vi oser; how ~ you! comment osez-vous! ◇ n défi m; to do sthg for a ~ faire qqch par défi.

daredevil ['deə,devl] n casse-cou m inv.

daren't [deənt] = **dare not**.

Dar es-Salaam [,dɑːressə'lɑːm] n Dar es-Salaam.

daring ['deərɪŋ] ◇ adj audacieux(ieuse). ◇ n audace f.

dark [dɑːk] ◇ adj -1. [room, night] sombre; it's getting ~ il commence à faire nuit. -2. [in colour] foncé(e). -3. [dark-haired] brun(e); [dark-skinned] basané(e). -4. fig [days, thoughts] sombre, triste; [look] noir(e). ◇ n -1. [darkness]: the ~ l'obscurité f; to be afraid of the ~ avoir peur du noir; to be in the ~ about sthg ignorer tout de qqch. -2. [night]: before/after ~ avant/après la tombée de la nuit.

Dark Ages npl: the ~ le haut Moyen Âge.

darken ['dɑːkn] ◇ vt assombrir. ◇ vi s'assombrir.

dark glasses npl lunettes fpl noires.

dark horse n fig quantité f inconnue.

darkness ['dɑːknɪs] n obscurité f.

darkroom ['dɑːkrum] n chambre f noire.

darling ['dɑːlɪŋ] ◇ adj -1. [dear] chéri(e). -2. inf [cute] adorable. ◇ n -1. [loved person, term of address] chéri m, -e f. -2. [idol] chouchou m, idole f.

darn [dɑːn] ◇ n reprise f. ◇ vt repriser. ◇ adj inf sacré(e), satané(e). ◇ adv inf sacrément. ◇ excl inf zut!

darning ['dɑːnɪŋ] n [work] reprisage m.

darning needle n aiguille f à repriser.

dart [dɑːt] ◇ n -1. [arrow] fléchette f. -2. SEWING pince f. ◇ vt darder. ◇ vi se précipiter.
◆ **darts** n [game] jeu m de fléchettes.

dartboard ['dɑːtbɔːd] n cible f de jeu de fléchettes.

dash [dæʃ] ◇ n -1. [of milk, wine] goutte f; [of cream] soupçon m; [of salt] pincée f; [of colour, paint] touche f. -2. [in punctuation] tiret m. -3. AUT tableau m de bord. -4. [rush]: to make a ~ for se ruer vers. ◇ vt -1. [throw] jeter avec violence. -2. [hopes] anéantir. ◇ vi se précipiter; I must ~! je dois me sauver!
◆ **dash off** vt sep [write quickly] écrire en vitesse.

dashboard ['dæʃbɔːd] n tableau m de bord.

dashing ['dæʃɪŋ] adj fringant(e).

dastardly ['dæstədlɪ] adj dated lâche.

DAT [dæt] (abbr of digital audio tape) n DAT m.

data ['deɪtə] n (U) données fpl.

databank ['deɪtəbæŋk] n banque f de données.

database ['deɪtəbeɪs] n base f de données.

data capture n saisie f de données.

data processing n traitement m de données.

data transmission n transmission f de données.

date [deɪt] ◇ n **-1.** [in time] date f; **to ~ à** ce jour. **-2.** [appointment] rendez-vous m. **-3.** [person] petit ami m, petite amie f. **-4.** [fruit] datte f. ◇ vt **-1.** [gen] dater. **-2.** [go out with] sortir avec. ◇ vi [go out of fashion] dater.

◆ **date back to, date from** vt fus dater de.

dated ['deɪtɪd] adj qui date.

date line n ligne f de changement de date.

date of birth n date f de naissance.

date stamp n cachet m.

daub [dɔːb] vt: **to ~ sthg with sthg** barbouiller qqch de qqch.

daughter ['dɔːtər] n fille f.

daughter-in-law (pl **daughters-in-law**) n belle-fille f.

daunt [dɔːnt] vt intimider.

daunting ['dɔːntɪŋ] adj intimidant(e).

dawdle ['dɔːdl] vi flâner.

dawn [dɔːn] ◇ n lit & fig aube f; **at ~ à** l'aube; **from ~ to dusk** du matin au soir. ◇ vi **-1.** [day] poindre. **-2.** [era, period] naître.

◆ **dawn (up)on** vt fus venir à l'esprit de.

dawn chorus n concert m des oiseaux à l'aube.

day [deɪ] n jour m; [duration] journée f; **the ~ before** la veille; **the ~ after** le lendemain; **the ~ before yesterday** l'avant-veille f; **the ~ after tomorrow** le surlendemain; **any ~ now** d'un jour à l'autre; **one ~, some ~, one of these ~s** un jour (ou l'autre), un de ces jours; **~ and night** jour et nuit; **in my ~** de mon temps; **in this ~ and age** de nos jours; **to call it a ~** laisser tomber; **to make sb's ~** réchauffer le cœur de qqn; **his ~s are numbered** ses jours sont comptés; **to save sthg for a rainy ~** garder qqch pour les longues soirées d'hiver; **to save money for a rainy ~** mettre de l'argent de côté en cas de besoin; **it's early ~s yet** ce n'est que le début.

◆ **days** adv le jour.

dayboy ['deɪbɔɪ] n Br SCH externe m.

daybreak ['deɪbreɪk] n aube f; **at ~ à** l'aube.

day-care centre n garderie f.

daycentre ['deɪsentər] n Br [for children] garderie f; [for elderly people] centre de jour pour les personnes du troisième âge.

daydream ['deɪdriːm] ◇ n rêverie f. ◇ vi rêvasser.

daygirl ['deɪgɜːl] n Br SCH externe f.

Day-Glo® ['deɪgləʊ] adj fluorescent(e).

daylight ['deɪlaɪt] n **-1.** [light] lumière f du jour. **-2.** [dawn] aube f. **-3.** phr: **to scare the (living) ~s out of sb** inf faire une peur bleue à qqn.

daylight robbery n: **that's ~** inf c'est du vol manifeste.

daylight saving time n heure f d'été.

day nursery n garderie f, crèche f.

day off (pl **days off**) n jour m de congé.

day pupil n Br SCH externe mf.

day release n Br jour de formation.

day return n Br billet aller et retour valable pour une journée.

dayroom ['deɪruːm] n salle f de détente.

day school n externat m.

day shift n équipe f de jour.

daytime ['deɪtaɪm] ◇ n jour m, journée f. ◇ comp [television] pendant la journée; [job, flight] de jour.

day-to-day adj [routine, life] journalier(ière); **on a ~ basis** au jour le jour.

day trip n excursion f d'une journée.

day-tripper n Br excursionniste mf.

daze [deɪz] ◇ n: **in a ~** hébété(e), ahuri(e). ◇ vt **-1.** [subj: blow] étourdir. **-2.** fig [subj: shock, event] abasourdir, sidérer.

dazed [deɪzd] adj **-1.** [by blow] étourdi(e). **-2.** fig [by shock, event] abasourdi(e), sidéré(e).

dazzle ['dæzl] ◇ n (U) éblouissement m. ◇ vt éblouir.

dazzling ['dæzlɪŋ] adj éblouissant(e).

DBE (abbr of **Dame Commander of the Order of the British Empire**) n distinction honorifique britannique pour les femmes.

DBS (abbr of **direct broadcasting by satellite**) n téléfusion directe par satellite.

DC ◇ n (abbr of **direct current**) courant m continu. ◇ abbr of **District of Columbia**.

dd. abbr of **delivered**.

DD (abbr of **Doctor of Divinity**) n docteur en théologie.

D/D abbr of **direct debit**.

D-day ['diːdeɪ] n le jour J.

DDS (abbr of **Doctor of Dental Science**) n docteur en dentisterie.

DDT (abbr of **dichlorodiphenyltrichloroethane**) n DDT m.

DE abbr of **Delaware**.

DEA (abbr of **Drug Enforcement Administration**) n agence américaine de lutte contre la drogue.

deacon ['diːkn] n diacre m.

deaconess [,diːkə'nes] n diaconesse f.

deactivate [,diː'æktɪvet] vt désamorcer.

dead [ded] ◇ *adj* **-1.** [not alive, not lively] mort(e); **to shoot sb ~** abattre qqn; **he wouldn't be seen ~ doing that** il ne ferait cela pour rien au monde. **-2.** [numb] engourdi(e). **-3.** [not operating - battery] à plat; **the telephone's ~** il n'y a pas de tonalité. **-4.** [complete - silence] de mort; **to come to a ~ stop** s'arrêter pile. ◇ *adv* **-1.** [directly, precisely]: **~ ahead** droit devant soi; **~ on time** pile à l'heure. **-2.** *inf* [completely] tout à fait; **to be ~ set against sthg** être tout à fait opposé à qqch; **to be ~ set on sthg** vouloir faire qqch à tout prix. **-3.** [suddenly]: **to stop ~** s'arrêter net. ◇ *n*: **in the ~ of night/winter** au cœur de la nuit/de l'hiver. ◇ *npl*: **the ~** les morts *mpl*.

deadbeat ['dedbi:t] *n Am inf* flemmard *m*, -e *f*.

dead centre *n* plein milieu *m*.

dead duck *n*: **it's a ~** *inf* c'est foutu, c'est fichu.

deaden ['dedn] *vt* [sound] assourdir; [pain] calmer.

dead end *n* impasse *f*.

dead-end job *n* travail *m* sans débouchés.

deadhead ['dedhed] *vt* enlever les fleurs fanées de.

dead heat *n* arrivée *f* ex-aequo.

dead letter *n fig* [rule, law] lettre *f* morte.

deadline ['dedlaɪn] *n* dernière limite *f*.

deadlock ['dedlɒk] *n* impasse *f*.

deadlocked ['dedlɒkt] *adj* dans une impasse.

dead loss *n inf*: **to be a ~** [person] être bon (bonne) à rien; [object] ne rien valoir.

deadly ['dedlɪ] (*compar* **-ier**, *superl* **-iest**) ◇ *adj* **-1.** [poison, enemy] mortel(elle). **-2.** [accuracy] imparable. ◇ *adv* [boring, serious] tout à fait; **~ pale** d'une pâleur mortelle.

deadly nightshade [-'naɪtʃeɪd] *n* belladone *f*.

deadpan ['dedpæn] ◇ *adj* pince-sans-rire (*inv*). ◇ *adv* impassiblement.

Dead Sea *n*: **the ~** la mer Morte.

dead wood *Br*, **deadwood** *Am* ['dedwud] *n* (*U*) *fig* [people] personnes *fpl* improductives; [things, material] choses *fpl* inutiles.

deaf [def] ◇ *adj* sourd(e); **to be ~ to sthg** être sourd à qqch. ◇ *npl*: **the ~** les sourds *mpl*.

deaf-aid *n Br* appareil *m* acoustique.

deaf-and-dumb *adj* sourd-muet (sourde-muette).

deafen ['defn] *vt* assourdir.

deafening ['defnɪŋ] *adj* assourdissant(e).

deaf-mute ◇ *adj* sourd-muet (sourde-muette). ◇ *n* sourd-muet *m*, sourde-muette *f*.

deafness ['defnɪs] *n* surdité *f*.

deal [di:l] (*pt* & *pp* **dealt**) ◇ *n* **-1.** [quantity]: **a good** OR **great ~** beaucoup; **a good** OR **great ~ of** beaucoup de, bien de/des. **-2.** [business agreement] marché *m*, affaire *f*; **to do** OR **strike a ~ with sb** conclure un marché avec qqn. **-3.** *inf* [treatment]: **to get a bad ~** ne pas faire une affaire; **big ~!** et alors!, tu parles! ◇ *vt* **-1.** [strike]: **to ~ sb/sthg a blow, to ~ a blow to sb/sthg** porter un coup à qqn/qqch. **-2.** [cards] donner, distribuer. ◇ *vi* **-1.** [at cards] donner, distribuer. **-2.** [in drugs] faire le trafic (de drogues).

◆ **deal in** *vt fus* COMM faire le commerce de.

◆ **deal out** *vt sep* distribuer.

◆ **deal with** *vt fus* **-1.** [handle] s'occuper de. **-2.** [be about] traiter de. **-3.** [be faced with] avoir affaire à.

dealer ['di:lə˞] *n* **-1.** [trader] négociant *m*; [in drugs] trafiquant *m*. **-2.** [cards] donneur *m*.

dealership ['di:ləʃɪp] *n* concession *f*.

dealing ['di:lɪŋ] *n* commerce *m*.

◆ **dealings** *npl* relations *fpl*, rapports *mpl*.

dealt [delt] *pt* & *pp* → **deal**.

dean [di:n] *n* doyen *m*.

dear [dɪə˞] ◇ *adj*: **~ (to)** cher (chère) (à); **Dear Sir** [in letter] Cher Monsieur; **Dear Madam** Chère Madame. ◇ *n* chéri *m*, -e *f*. ◇ *excl*: **oh ~!** mon Dieu!

dearly ['dɪəlɪ] *adv* [love, wish] de tout son cœur.

dearth [dɜ:θ] *n* pénurie *f*.

death [deθ] *n* mort *f*; **to be put to ~** être mis à mort, être exécuté; **to frighten sb to ~** faire une peur bleue à qqn; **to worry sb to ~** rendre qqn fou d'inquiétude; **to be sick to ~ of sthg/of doing sthg** en avoir marre de qqch/de faire qqch; **to be at ~'s door** être à l'article de la mort.

deathbed ['deθbed] *n* lit *m* de mort.

death certificate *n* acte *m* de décès.

death duty *Br*, **death tax** *Am n* droits *mpl* de succession.

death knell *n* glas *m*.

deathly ['deθlɪ] (*compar* **-ier**, *superl* **-iest**) ◇ *adj* de mort. ◇ *adv* comme la mort.

death penalty *n* peine *f* de mort.

death rate *n* taux *m* de mortalité.

death row *n Am* quartier *m* des condamnés à mort.

death sentence *n* condamnation *f* à mort.

death squad *n* escadron *m* de la mort.

death tax *Am* = **death duty**.

death toll *n* nombre *m* de morts.

death trap *n* *inf* véhicule *m*/bâtiment *m* dangereux.

Death Valley *n* la Vallée de la Mort.

deathwatch beetle ['deθwɒtʃ-] *n* vrillette *f*.

death wish *n* désir *m* de mort.

deb [deb] *n* *Br* *inf* débutante *f*.

débâcle [de'bɑːkl] *n* débâcle *f*.

debar [diː'bɑː] (*pt & pp* -**red**, *cont* -**ring**) *vt*: **to ~ sb (from)** [place] exclure qqn (de); **to ~ sb from doing sthg** interdire à qqn de faire qqch.

debase [di'beis] *vt* dégrader; **to ~ o.s.** s'avilir.

debasement [di'beismənt] *n* dégradation *f*; [of person] avilissement *m*.

debatable [di'beitəbl] *adj* discutable, contestable.

debate [di'beit] ◇ *n* débat *m*; **open to ~** discutable. ◇ *vt* débattre, discuter; **to ~ whether** s'interroger pour savoir si. ◇ *vi* débattre.

debating society [di'beitiŋ-] *n* club *m* de débats.

debauched [di'bɔːtʃt] *adj* débauché(e).

debauchery [di'bɔːtʃəri] *n* débauche *f*.

debenture [di'bentʃər] *n* obligation *f* (sans garantie).

debenture stock *n* *Br* capital *m* obligations.

debilitate [di'biliteit] *vt* débiliter, affaiblir.

debilitating [di'biliteitiŋ] *adj* débilitant(e).

debility [di'biləti] *n* débilité *f*, faiblesse *f*.

debit ['debit] ◇ *n* débit *m*. ◇ *vt* débiter.

debit note *n* note *f* de débit.

debonair [,debə'neər] *adj* fringant(e).

debrief [,diː'briːf] *vt* faire faire un compte-rendu de mission à.

debriefing [,diː'briːfiŋ] *n* compte-rendu *m* (de mission).

debris ['deibriː] *n* (*U*) débris *mpl*.

debt [det] *n* dette *f*; **to be in ~** avoir des dettes, être endetté(e); **to be in sb's ~** être redevable à qqn.

debt collector *n* agent *m* de recouvrements.

debtor ['detər] *n* débiteur *m*, -trice *f*.

debug [,diː'bʌg] (*pt & pp* -**ged**, *cont* -**ging**) *vt* -**1.** [room] enlever les micros cachés dans. -**2.** COMPUT [program] mettre au point, déboguer.

debunk [,diː'bʌŋk] *vt* démentir.

debut ['deibjuː] *n* débuts *mpl*.

debutante ['debjutɑːnt] *n* débutante *f*.

Dec. (*abbr of* **December**) déc.

decade ['dekeid] *n* décennie *f*.

decadence ['dekədəns] *n* décadence *f*.

decadent ['dekədənt] *adj* décadent(e).

decaff ['diːkæf] *n* *inf* déca *m*.

decaffeinated [di'kæfineitid] *adj* décaféiné(e).

decal ['diːkæl] *n* *Am* décalcomanie *f*.

decamp [di'kæmp] *vi* *inf* décamper, filer.

decant [di'kænt] *vt* décanter.

decanter [di'kæntər] *n* carafe *f*.

decapitate [di'kæpiteit] *vt* décapiter.

decathlete [di'kæθliːt] *n* décathlonien *m*.

decathlon [di'kæθlɒn] *n* décathlon *m*.

decay [di'kei] ◇ *n* -**1.** [of body, plant] pourriture *f*, putréfaction *f*; [of tooth] carie *f*. -**2.** *fig* [of building] délabrement *m*; [of society] décadence *f*. ◇ *vi* -**1.** [rot] pourrir; [tooth] se carier. -**2.** *fig* [building] se délabrer, tomber en ruines; [society] tomber en décadence.

deceased [di'siːst] (*pl inv*) ◇ *adj* décédé(e). ◇ *n*: **the ~** le défunt, la défunte.

deceit [di'siːt] *n* tromperie *f*, supercherie *f*.

deceitful [di'siːtful] *adj* trompeur(euse), fourbe.

deceive [di'siːv] *vt* [person] tromper, duper; [subj: memory, eyes] jouer des tours à; **to ~ o.s.** se leurrer, s'abuser.

decelerate [,diː'seləreit] *vi* ralentir.

December [di'sembər] *n* décembre *m*; *see also* **September**.

decency ['diːsnsi] *n* décence *f*, bienséance *f*; **to have the ~ to do sthg** avoir la décence de faire qqch.

decent ['diːsnt] *adj* -**1.** [behaviour, dress] décent(e). -**2.** [wage, meal] correct(e), décent(e). -**3.** [person] gentil(ille), brave.

decently ['diːsntli] *adv* -**1.** [properly] décemment, convenablement. -**2.** [adequately] correctement.

decentralization [diː,sentrəlai'zeiʃn] *n* décentralisation *f*.

decentralize, -ise [,diː'sentrəlaiz] *vt* décentraliser.

deception [di'sepʃn] *n* -**1.** [lie, pretence] tromperie *f*, duperie *f*. -**2.** (*U*) [act of lying] supercherie *f*.

deceptive [di'septiv] *adj* trompeur(euse).

deceptively [di'septivli] *adv* en apparence.

decibel ['desibel] *n* décibel *m*.

decide [di'said] ◇ *vt* décider; **to ~ to do sthg** décider de faire qqch. ◇ *vi* se décider.

◆ **decide (up)on** vt fus se décider pour, choisir.

decided [dɪ'saɪdɪd] adj **-1.** [definite] certain(e), incontestable. **-2.** [resolute] décidé(e), résolu(e).

decidedly [dɪ'saɪdɪdlɪ] adv **-1.** [clearly] manifestement, incontestablement. **-2.** [resolutely] résolument.

deciding [dɪ'saɪdɪŋ] adj: ~ **vote** vote m décisif.

deciduous [dɪ'sɪdjʊəs] adj à feuilles caduques.

decimal ['desɪml] ◇ adj décimal(e). ◇ n décimale f.

decimal currency n monnaie f décimale.

decimalize, -ise ['desɪmǝlaɪz] vt Br décimaliser.

decimal place n décimale f.

decimal point n virgule f.

decimate ['desɪmeɪt] vt décimer.

decimation [,desɪ'meɪʃn] n décimation f.

decipher [dɪ'saɪfǝ] vt déchiffrer.

decision [dɪ'sɪʒn] n décision f; **to make a ~** prendre une décision.

decision-making n prise f de décisions.

decisive [dɪ'saɪsɪv] adj **-1.** [person] déterminé(e), résolu(e). **-2.** [factor, event] décisif(ive).

decisively [dɪ'saɪsɪvlɪ] adv **-1.** [speak] d'un ton décidé; [act] avec décision. **-2.** [considerably, definitely] nettement, bien.

decisiveness [dɪ'saɪsɪvnɪs] n fermeté f, résolution f.

deck [dek] ◇ n **-1.** [of ship] pont m. **-2.** [of bus] impériale f. **-3.** [of cards] jeu m. **-4.** Am [of house] véranda f. ◇ vt [decorate]: **to ~ sthg with** parer OR orner qqch de.

◆ **deck out** vt sep agrémenter, parer.

deckchair ['dektʃeǝ] n chaise longue f, transat m.

deckhand ['dekhænd] n matelot m.

declaration [,deklǝ'reɪʃn] n déclaration f.

Declaration of Independence n: **the ~** la Déclaration d'Indépendance des États-Unis d'Amérique (1776).

declare [dɪ'kleǝ] vt déclarer.

declared [dɪ'kleǝd] adj [intention, supporter] avoué(e), déclaré(e).

declassify [,di:'klæsɪfaɪ] (pt & pp -ied) vt rayer de la liste des documents secrets.

decline [dɪ'klaɪn] ◇ n déclin m; **to be in ~** être en déclin; **on the ~** en baisse. ◇ vt décliner; **to ~ to do sthg** refuser de faire qqch. ◇ vi **-1.** [deteriorate] décliner. **-2.** [refuse] refuser.

declutch [dɪ'klʌtʃ] vi débrayer.

decode [,di:'kǝʊd] vt décoder.

decoder [,di:'kǝʊdǝ] n décodeur m.

decommission [,di:kǝ'mɪʃn] vt mettre hors service.

decompose [,di:kǝm'pǝʊz] vi se décomposer.

decomposition [,di:kɒmpǝ'zɪʃn] n décomposition f.

decompression chamber [,di:kǝm'preʃn-] n caisson m de décompression.

decompression sickness [,di:kǝm'preʃn-] n maladie f des caissons.

decongestant [,di:kǝn'dʒestǝnt] n décongestionnant m.

decontaminate [,di:kǝn'tæmɪneɪt] vt décontaminer.

décor ['deɪkɔ:] n décor m.

decorate ['dekǝreɪt] vt décorer.

decoration [,dekǝ'reɪʃn] n décoration f.

decorative ['dekǝrǝtɪv] adj décoratif(ive).

decorator ['dekǝreɪtǝ] n décorateur m, -trice f.

decorous ['dekǝrǝs] adj bienséant(e), convenable.

decorum [dɪ'kɔ:rǝm] n décorum m.

decoy [n 'di:kɔɪ, vt dɪ'kɔɪ] ◇ n [for hunting] appât m, leurre m; [person] compère m. ◇ vt attirer dans un piège.

decrease [di:'kri:s] ◇ n: ~ **(in)** diminution f (de), baisse f (de). ◇ vt diminuer, réduire. ◇ vi diminuer, décroître.

decreasing [di:'kri:sɪŋ] adj qui diminue, décroissant(e).

decree [dɪ'kri:] ◇ n **-1.** [order, decision] décret m. **-2.** Am JUR arrêt m, jugement m. ◇ vt décréter, ordonner.

decree absolute (pl **decrees absolute**) n Br jugement m définitif.

decree nisi [-'naɪsaɪ] (pl **decrees nisi**) n Br jugement m provisoire.

decrepit [dɪ'krepɪt] adj [person] décrépit(e); [house] délabré(e).

decry [dɪ'kraɪ] (pt & pp -ied) vt décrier, dénigrer.

dedicate ['dedɪkeɪt] vt **-1.** [book etc] dédier. **-2.** [life, career] consacrer; **to ~ o.s. to sthg** se consacrer à qqch.

dedicated ['dedɪkrɪtɪd] adj **-1.** [person] dévoué(e). **-2.** COMPUT spécialisé(e).

dedication [,dedɪ'keɪʃn] n **-1.** [commitment] dévouement m. **-2.** [in book] dédicace f.

deduce [dɪ'dju:s] vt déduire, conclure.

deduct [dɪ'dʌkt] vt déduire, retrancher.

deduction [dɪ'dʌkʃn] n déduction f.

deed [diːd] *n* **-1.** [action] action *f*, acte *m*. **-2.** JUR acte *m* notarié.

deed poll (*pl* **deed polls** OR **deeds poll**) *n* *Br*: **to change one's name by ~** changer de nom légalement OR officiellement.

deem [diːm] *vt* juger, considérer; **to ~ it wise to do sthg** juger prudent de faire qqch.

deep [diːp] ◇ *adj* profond(e); **to be thrown in at the ~ end** *fig* recevoir le baptême du feu. ◇ *adv* profondément; **feelings were running ~** les sentiments se sont exacerbés; **~ down** [fundamentally] au fond; **to be ~ in thought** être perdu(e) dans ses pensées.

deepen ['diːpn] ◇ *vt* [hole, channel] creuser. ◇ *vi* **-1.** [river, sea] devenir profond(e). **-2.** [crisis, recession, feeling] s'aggraver. **-3.** [darkness] augmenter.

deepening ['diːpnɪŋ] *adj* [crisis, recession] qui s'aggrave.

deep freeze *n* congélateur *m*.
◆ **deep-freeze** *vt* congeler.

deep fry *vt* faire frire.

deeply ['diːplɪ] *adv* profondément.

deep-rooted *adj* [prejudice] ancré(e), enraciné(e); [hatred] vivace, tenace; [affection] profond(e).

deep-sea *adj*: **~ diving** plongée *f* sous-marine; **~ fishing** pêche *f* hauturière.

deep-seated *adj* [belief, fear] profond(e), enraciné(e).

deep-set *adj* [eyes] enfoncé(e).

deer [dɪər] (*pl inv*) *n* cerf *m*.

deerstalker ['dɪəˌstɔːkər] *n* [hat] casquette *f* de chasse.

de-escalate [ˌdiːˈeskəleɪt] ◇ *vt* faire diminuer. ◇ *vi* diminuer.

deface [dɪˈfeɪs] *vt* barbouiller.

defamation [ˌdefəˈmeɪʃn] *n* diffamation *f*.

defamatory [dɪˈfæmətrɪ] *adj* diffamatoire, diffamant(e).

default [dɪˈfɔːlt] ◇ *n* **-1.** [failure] défaillance *f*; **by ~** par défaut. **-2.** COMPUT valeur *f* par défaut. ◇ *comp* COMPUT implicite, par défaut. ◇ *vi* manquer à ses engagements; **to ~ on** manquer à.

defaulter [dɪˈfɔːltər] *n* partie *f* défaillante.

default value *n* COMPUT valeur *f* par défaut.

defeat [dɪˈfiːt] ◇ *n* défaite *f*; **to admit ~** s'avouer battu(e) OR vaincu(e). ◇ *vt* **-1.** [team, opponent] vaincre, battre. **-2.** [motion, proposal] rejeter. **-3.** [plans] faire échouer.

defeatism [dɪˈfiːtɪzm] *n* défaitisme *m*.

defeatist [dɪˈfiːtɪst] ◇ *adj* défaitiste. ◇ *n* défaitiste *mf*.

defecate ['defəkeɪt] *vi* déféquer.

defect [*n* 'diːfekt, *vi* dɪˈfekt] ◇ *n* défaut *m*. ◇ *vi*: **to ~ to** passer à.

defection [dɪˈfekʃn] *n* défection *f*.

defective [dɪˈfektɪv] *adj* défectueux(euse).

defector [dɪˈfektər] *n* transfuge *mf*.

defence *Br*, **defense** *Am* [dɪˈfens] *n* **-1.** [gen] défense *f*. **-2.** [protective device, system] protection *f*. **-3.** JUR: **the ~** la défense; **he said in ~ that ...** il a répondu pour sa défense que ...
◆ **defences** *npl* [of country] moyens *mpl* de défense.

defenceless *Br*, **defenseless** *Am* [dɪˈfenslɪs] *adj* sans défense.

defend [dɪˈfend] ◇ *vt* défendre; **to ~ o.s.** se défendre. ◇ *vi* SPORT défendre.

defendant [dɪˈfendənt] *n* défendeur *m*, -eresse *f*.

defender [dɪˈfendər] *n* défenseur *m*.

defense *Am* = defence.

defensive [dɪˈfensɪv] ◇ *adj* défensif(ive). ◇ *n*: **on the ~** sur la défensive.

defer [dɪˈfɜːr] (*pt* & *pp* **-red**, *cont* **-ring**) ◇ *vt* différer. ◇ *vi*: **to ~ to sb** s'en remettre à (l'opinion de) qqn.

deference ['defərəns] *n* déférence *f*.

deferential [ˌdefəˈrenʃl] *adj* respectueux(euse).

defiance [dɪˈfaɪəns] *n* défi *m*; **in ~ of** au mépris de.

defiant [dɪˈfaɪənt] *adj* [person] intraitable, intransigeant(e); [action] de défi.

defiantly [dɪˈfaɪəntlɪ] *adv* [say] d'un ton de défi.

deficiency [dɪˈfɪʃnsɪ] (*pl* **-ies**) *n* **-1.** [lack] manque *m*; [of vitamins etc] carence *f*. **-2.** [inadequacy] imperfection *f*, défaut *m*.

deficient [dɪˈfɪʃnt] *adj* **-1.** [lacking]: **to be ~ in** manquer de. **-2.** [inadequate] insuffisant(e), médiocre.

deficit ['defɪsɪt] *n* déficit *m*.

defile [dɪˈfaɪl] *vt* souiller, salir.

define [dɪˈfaɪn] *vt* définir.

definite ['defɪnɪt] *adj* **-1.** [plan] bien déterminé(e); [date] certain(e). **-2.** [improvement, difference] net (nette), marqué(e). **-3.** [answer] précis(e), catégorique. **-4.** [confident - person] assuré(e).

definitely ['defɪnɪtlɪ] *adv* **-1.** [without doubt] sans aucun doute, certainement. **-2.** [for emphasis] catégoriquement.

definition [defɪ'nɪʃn] *n* **-1.** [gen] définition *f.* **-2.** [clarity] clarté *f,* précision *f.*

definitive [dɪ'fɪnɪtɪv] *adj* définitif(ive).

deflate [dɪ'fleɪt] ⬦ *vt* **-1.** [balloon, tyre] dégonfler. **-2.** *fig* [person] rabaisser, humilier. **-3.** ECON provoquer la déflation de. ⬦ *vi* [balloon, tyre] se dégonfler.

deflation [dɪ'fleɪʃn] *n* ECON déflation *f.*

deflationary [dɪ'fleɪʃnərɪ] *adj* [policy] de déflation; [measure] déflationniste.

deflect [dɪ'flekt] *vt* [ball, bullet] dévier; [stream] détourner, dériver; [criticism] détourner.

deflection [dɪ'flekʃn] *n* [of ball, bullet] déviation *f;* [of stream] dérivation *f,* détournement *m.*

defog [,diː'fɒg] *vt Am* AUT désembuer.

defogger [,diː'fɒgər] *n Am* AUT dispositif *m* anti-buée (*inv*).

deforest [,diː'fɒrɪst] *vt* déboiser.

deforestation [diː,fɒrɪ'streɪʃn] *n* déforestation *f,* déboisement *m.*

deform [diː'fɔːm] *vt* déformer.

deformed [dɪ'fɔːmd] *adj* difforme.

deformity [dɪ'fɔːmətɪ] · (*pl* **-ies**) *n* difformité *f,* malformation *f.*

defraud [dɪ'frɔːd] *vt* [person] escroquer; [Inland Revenue etc] frauder.

defray [dɪ'freɪ] *vt* [costs] couvrir; [expenses] rembourser.

defrost [,diː'frɒst] ⬦ *vt* **-1.** [fridge] dégivrer; [frozen food] décongeler. **-2.** *Am* [AUT - de-ice] dégivrer; [- demist] désembuer. ⬦ *vi* [fridge] dégivrer; [frozen food] se décongeler.

deft [deft] *adj* adroit(e).

deftly ['deftlɪ] *adv* adroitement.

defunct [dɪ'fʌŋkt] *adj* qui n'existe plus; [person] défunt(e).

defuse [,diː'fjuːz] *vt Br* désamorcer.

defy [dɪ'faɪ] (*pt* & *pp* **-ied**) *vt* **-1.** [gen] défier; to ~ sb to do sthg mettre qqn au défi de faire qqch. **-2.** [efforts] résister à, faire échouer.

degenerate [*adj* & *n* dɪ'dʒenərət, *vb* dɪ'dʒenəreɪt] ⬦ *adj* dégénéré(e). ⬦ *n* dégénéré *m,* -e *f.* ⬦ *vi:* to ~ (into) dégénérer (en).

degradation [,degrə'deɪʃn] *n* [of person] déchéance *f;* [of place] dégradation *f.*

degrade [dɪ'greɪd] *vt* [person] avilir.

degrading [dɪ'greɪdɪŋ] *adj* dégradant(e), avilissant(e).

degree [dɪ'griː] *n* **-1.** [measurement] degré *m.* **-2.** UNIV diplôme *m* universitaire; to have/take a ~ (in) avoir/faire une licence (de).

-3. [amount]: to a certain ~ jusqu'à un certain point, dans une certaine mesure; a ~ of risk un certain risque; a ~ of truth une certaine part de vérité; by ~s progressivement, petit à petit.

dehumanize, -ise [diː'hjuːmənaɪz] *vt* déshumaniser.

dehydrated [,diːhaɪ'dreɪtɪd] *adj* déshydraté(e).

dehydration [,diːhaɪ'dreɪʃn] *n* déshydratation *f.*

de-ice *vt* dégivrer.

de-icer [diː'aɪsər] *n* dégivreur *m.*

deign [deɪn] *vt:* to ~ to do sthg daigner faire qqch.

deity ['diːɪtɪ] (*pl* **-ies**) *n* dieu *m,* déesse *f,* divinité *f.*

déjà vu [,deʒɑː'vjuː] *n* déjà vu *m.*

dejected [dɪ'dʒektɪd] *adj* abattu(e), découragé(e).

dejection [dɪ'dʒekʃn] *n* abattement *m,* découragement *m.*

del. (*abbr of* **delete**) [on keyboard] suppr.

Del. *abbr of* **Delaware**.

Delaware ['deləweər] *n* Delaware *m;* **in** ~ dans le Delaware.

delay [dɪ'leɪ] ⬦ *n* retard *m,* délai *m;* **without** ~ sans délai. ⬦ *vt* **-1.** [cause to be late] retarder. **-2.** [defer] différer; to ~ doing sthg tarder à faire qqch. ⬦ *vi:* to ~ (in doing sthg) tarder (à faire qqch).

delayed-action [dɪ'leɪd-] *adj* [response] après coup; ~ **shutter** PHOT dispositif *m* à retardement.

delectable [dɪ'lektəbl] *adj* délicieux(ieuse).

delegate [*n* 'delɪgət, *vb* 'delɪgeɪt] ⬦ *n* délégué *m,* -e *f.* ⬦ *vt* déléguer; to ~ sb to do sthg déléguer qqn pour faire qqch; to ~ sthg to sb déléguer qqch à qqn. ⬦ *vi* déléguer.

delegation [,delɪ'geɪʃn] *n* délégation *f.*

delete [dɪ'liːt] *vt* supprimer, effacer.

deletion [dɪ'liːʃn] *n* suppression *f,* effacement *m.*

Delhi ['delɪ] *n* Delhi.

deli ['delɪ] *n inf abbr of* **delicatessen**.

deliberate [*adj* dɪ'lɪbərət, *vb* dɪ'lɪbəreɪt] ⬦ *adj* **-1.** [intentional] voulu(e), délibéré(e). **-2.** [slow] lent(e), sans hâte. ⬦ *vi* délibérer.

deliberately [dɪ'lɪbərətlɪ] *adv* **-1.** [on purpose] exprès, à dessein. **-2.** [slowly] posément, sans se presser.

deliberation [dɪ,lɪbə'reɪʃn] *n* **-1.** [consideration] délibération *f.* **-2.** [slowness] mesure *f.*

◆ **deliberations** *npl* délibérations *fpl*, discussions *fpl*.

delicacy ['delɪkəsɪ] (*pl* **-ies**) *n* -1. [gen] délicatesse *f*. -2. [food] mets *m* délicat.

delicate ['delɪkət] *adj* délicat(e); [movement] gracieux(ieuse).

delicately ['delɪkətlɪ] *adv* -1. [gen] délicatement; [move] gracieusement, avec grâce. -2. [tactfully] avec délicatesse, subtilement.

delicatessen [,delɪkə'tesn] *n* épicerie *f* fine.

delicious [dɪ'lɪʃəs] *adj* délicieux(ieuse).

delight [dɪ'laɪt] ◇ *n* -1. [great pleasure] délice *m*; to take ~ in doing sthg prendre grand plaisir à faire qqch. -2. [wonderful thing, person]: she's a ~ to work with c'est un plaisir de travailler avec elle; a ~ to the eyes un régal pour les yeux. ◇ *vt* enchanter, charmer. ◇ *vi*: to ~ in sthg/in doing sthg prendre grand plaisir à qqch/à faire qqch.

delighted [dɪ'laɪtɪd] *adj*: ~ (by OR with) enchanté(e) (de), ravi(e) (de); to be ~ that être enchanté OR ravi que; to be ~ to do sthg être enchanté OR ravi de faire qqch.

delightful [dɪ'laɪtful] *adj* ravissant(e), charmant(e); [meal] délicieux(ieuse).

delightfully [dɪ'laɪtfulɪ] *adv* d'une façon charmante.

delimit [diː'lɪmɪt] *vt* délimiter.

delineate [dɪ'lɪnɪeɪt] *vt* exposer, énoncer.

delinquency [dɪ'lɪŋkwənsɪ] *n* délinquance *f*.

delinquent [dɪ'lɪŋkwənt] ◇ *adj* délinquant(e). ◇ *n* délinquant *m*, -e *f*.

delirious [dɪ'lɪrɪəs] *adj lit* & *fig* délirant(e).

delirium [dɪ'lɪrɪəm] *n* délire *m*.

deliver [dɪ'lɪvər] ◇ *vt* -1. [distribute]: to ~ sthg (to sb) [mail, newspaper] distribuer qqch (à qqn); COMM livrer qqch (à qqn). -2. [speech] faire; [warning] donner; [message] remettre; [blow, kick] donner, porter. -3. [baby] mettre au monde. -4. [free] délivrer. -5. *Am* POL [votes] obtenir. ◇ *vi* -1. COMM livrer. -2. [fulfil promise] tenir sa promesse.

deliverance [dɪ'lɪvərəns] *n* délivrance *f*.

delivery [dɪ'lɪvərɪ] (*pl* **-ies**) *n* -1. COMM livraison *f*. -2. [way of speaking] élocution *f*. -3. [birth] accouchement *m*.

delivery note *n* bulletin *m* de livraison.

delivery van *Br*, **delivery truck** *Am* *n* camionnette *f* de livraison.

delphinium [del'fɪnɪəm] (*pl* **-s**) *n* delphinium *m*, pied-d'alouette *m*.

delta ['deltə] (*pl* **-s**) *n* delta *m*.

delude [dɪ'luːd] *vt* tromper, induire en erreur; to ~ o.s. se faire des illusions.

deluge ['deljuːdʒ] ◇ *n* déluge *m*; *fig* avalanche *f*. ◇ *vt*: to be ~d with être débordé(e) OR submergé(e) de.

delusion [dɪ'luːʒn] *n* illusion *f*; ~s of grandeur folie *f* des grandeurs.

de luxe [də'lʌks] *adj* de luxe.

delve [delv] *vi*: to ~ into [past] fouiller; [bag etc] fouiller dans.

Dem. *abbr of* **Democrat(ic)**.

demagogue ['deməgɒg] *n* démagogue *m*.

demand [dɪ'mɑːnd] ◇ *n* -1. [claim, firm request] revendication *f*, exigence *f*; wage ~ revendication salariale; on ~ sur demande. -2. [need]: ~ (for) demande *f* (de); in ~ demandé(e), recherché(e). ◇ *vt* -1. [ask for - justice, money] réclamer; [- explanation, apology] exiger; to ~ to do sthg exiger de faire qqch. -2. [require] demander, exiger.

demanding [dɪ'mɑːndɪŋ] *adj* -1. [exhausting] astreignant(e). -2. [not easily satisfied] exigeant(e).

demarcation [,diːmɑː'keɪʃn] *n* démarcation *f*.

demarcation dispute *n* conflit *m* de compétence.

dematerialize, -ise [diːmə'tɪərɪəlaɪz] *vi* se volatiliser.

demean [dɪ'miːn] *vt* avilir, déshonorer; to ~ o.s. s'abaisser.

demeaning [dɪ'miːnɪŋ] *adj* avilissant(e), dégradant(e).

demeanour *Br*, **demeanor** *Am* [dɪ'miːnər] *n* (*U*) *fml* comportement *m*.

demented [dɪ'mentɪd] *adj* fou (folle), dément(e).

dementia [dɪ'menʃə] *n* démence *f*.

demerara sugar [,demə'reərə-] *n Br* cassonade *f*.

demigod ['demɪgɒd] *n* demi-dieu *m*.

demijohn ['demɪdʒɒn] *n* dame-jeanne *f*, bonbonne *f*.

demilitarized zone, demilitarised zone [,diː'mɪlɪtəraɪzd-] *n* zone *f* démilitarisée.

demise [dɪ'maɪz] *n* (*U*) décès *m*; *fig* mort *f*, fin *f*.

demist [,diː'mɪst] *vt Br* désembuer.

demister [,diː'mɪstər] *n Br* dispositif *m* antibuée (*inv*).

demo ['deməu] (*abbr of* **demonstration**) *n inf* manif *f*.

demobilize, -ise [,diː'məubɪlaɪz] *vt* démobiliser.

democracy [dɪ'mɒkrəsɪ] (*pl* **-ies**) *n* démocratie *f*.

democrat ['deməkræt] *n* démocrate *mf*.

◆ **Democrat** n Am démocrate mf.

democratic [demə'krætɪk] adj démocratique.

◆ **Democratic** adj Am: démocrate.

democratically [,demə'krætɪklɪ] adv démocratiquement.

Democratic Party n Am: the ~ le Parti démocrate.

democratize, -ise [dɪ'mɒkrətaɪz] vt démocratiser.

demographic [,demə'græfɪk] adj démographique.

demolish [dɪ'mɒlɪʃ] vt -1. [destroy] démolir. -2. inf [eat] engloutir, engouffrer.

demolition [,demə'lɪʃn] n démolition f.

demon ['diːmən] ◇ n [evil spirit] démon m. ◇ comp inf: ~ **driver/chess player** as du volant/des échecs.

demonstrable [dɪ'mɒnstrəbl] adj démontrable.

demonstrably [dɪ'mɒnstrəblɪ] adv manifestement.

demonstrate ['demənstreɪt] ◇ vt -1. [prove] démontrer, prouver. -2. [machine, computer] faire une démonstration de. ◇ vi: **to ~ (for/against)** manifester (pour/contre).

demonstration [demən'streɪʃn] n -1. [of machine, emotions] démonstration f. -2. [public meeting] manifestation f.

demonstrative [dɪ'mɒnstrətɪv] adj expansif(ive), démonstratif(ive).

demonstrator [demənstreɪtə'] n -1. [in march] manifestant m, -e f. -2. [of machine, product] démonstrateur m, -trice f.

demoralize, -ise [dɪ'mɒrəlaɪz] vt démoraliser.

demoralized [dɪ'mɒrəlaɪzd] adj démoralisé(e).

demote [,diː'məʊt] vt rétrograder.

demotion [,diː'məʊʃn] n rétrogradation f.

demotivate [,diː'məʊtɪveɪt] vt démotiver.

demure [dɪ'mjʊə'] adj modeste, réservé(e).

demystify [,diː'mɪstɪfaɪ] (pt & pp **-ied**) vt démystifier.

den [den] n [of animal] antre m, tanière f.

denationalization ['diː,næʃnəlaɪ'zeɪʃn] n dénationalisation f.

denationalize, -ise [,diː'næʃnəlaɪz] vt dénationaliser.

denial [dɪ'naɪəl] n [of rights, facts, truth] dénégation f; [of accusation] démenti m.

denier ['denɪə] n denier m.

denigrate ['denɪɡreɪt] vt dénigrer.

denim [denɪm] n jean m.

◆ **denims** npl: **a pair of ~s** un jean.

denim jacket n veste f en jean.

denizen ['denɪzn] n literary or hum habitant m, -e f.

Denmark ['denmɑːk] n Danemark m; **in ~** au Danemark.

denomination [dɪ,nɒmɪ'neɪʃn] n -1. RELIG confession f. -2. [money] valeur f.

denominator [dɪ'nɒmɪneɪtə'] n dénominateur m.

denote [dɪ'nəʊt] vt dénoter.

denounce [dɪ'naʊns] vt dénoncer.

dense [dens] adj -1. [crowd, forest] dense; [fog] dense, épais(aisse). -2. inf [stupid] bouché(e).

densely ['denslɪ] adv: ~ **packed** [hall etc] complètement bondé(e); ~ **populated** très peuplé(e); ~ **wooded** couvert(e) de forêts épaisses.

density ['densətɪ] (pl **-ies**) n densité f.

dent [dent] ◇ n bosse f. ◇ vt cabosser.

dental ['dentl] adj dentaire; ~ **appointment** rendez-vous m chez le dentiste.

dental floss n fil m dentaire.

dental plate n prothèse f dentaire.

dental surgeon n chirurgien-dentiste m.

dental treatment n traitement m dentaire.

dented ['dentɪd] adj cabossé(e).

dentist ['dentɪst] n dentiste mf.

dentistry ['dentɪstrɪ] n dentisterie f.

dentures ['dentʃəz] npl dentier m.

denude [dɪ'njuːd] vt fml: **to ~ sthg (of)** dépouiller qqch (de).

denunciation [dɪ,nʌnsɪ'eɪʃn] n dénonciation f.

deny [dɪ'naɪ] (pt & pp **-ied**) vt -1. [refute] nier. -2. fml [refuse] nier, refuser; **to ~ sb sthg** refuser qqch à qqn.

deodorant [diː'əʊdərənt] n déodorant m.

depart [dɪ'pɑːt] vi fml -1. [leave]: **to ~ (from)** partir de. -2. [differ]: **to ~ from sthg** s'écarter de qqch.

department [dɪ'pɑːtmənt] n -1. [in organization] service m. -2. [in shop] rayon m. -3. SCH & UNIV département m. -4. [in government] département m, ministère m.

departmental [,diːpɑːt'mentl] adj de service.

department store n grand magasin m.

departure [dɪ'pɑːtʃə'] n -1. [leaving] départ m. -2. [change] nouveau départ m; **a ~ from tradition** un écart par rapport à la tradition.

departure lounge n salle f d'embarquement.

depend [dɪ'pend] vi: **to ~ on** [be dependent on] dépendre de; [rely on] compter sur; [emotionally] se reposer sur; **it ~s on you/the weather** cela dépend de vous/du temps; **it ~s** cela dépend; **~ing on** selon.

dependable [dɪ'pendəbl] adj [person] sur qui on peut compter; [source of income] sûr(e); [car] fiable.

dependant [dɪ'pendənt] n personne f à charge.

dependence [dɪ'pendəns] n: **~ (on)** dépendance f (de).

dependent [dɪ'pendənt] adj **-1.** [reliant]: **~ (on)** dépendant(e) (de); **to be ~ on sb/sthg** dépendre de qqn/qqch; **the economy is ~ on oil** l'économie repose sur le pétrole. **-2.** [addicted] dépendant(e), accro. **-3.** [contingent]: **to be ~ on** dépendre de.

depict [dɪ'pɪkt] vt **-1.** [show in picture] représenter. **-2.** [describe]: **to ~ sb/sthg as** dépeindre qqn/qqch comme.

depilatory [dɪ'pɪlətrɪ] adj dépilatoire.

deplete [dɪ'pliːt] vt épuiser.

depletion [dɪ'pliːʃn] n épuisement m.

deplorable [dɪ'plɔːrəbl] adj déplorable.

deplore [dɪ'plɔː] vt déplorer.

deploy [dɪ'plɔɪ] vt déployer.

deployment [dɪ'plɔɪmənt] n déploiement m.

depopulated [,diː'pɒpjʊleɪtɪd] adj dépeuplé(e).

depopulation [diː,pɒpjʊ'leɪʃn] n dépeuplement m.

deport [dɪ'pɔːt] vt expulser.

deportation [,diːpɔː'teɪʃn] n expulsion f.

deportation order n arrêt m d'expulsion.

depose [dɪ'pəʊz] vt déposer.

deposit [dɪ'pɒzɪt] ◇ n **-1.** [gen] dépôt m; **to make a ~** [into bank account] déposer de l'argent. **-2.** [payment - as guarantee] caution f; [- as instalment] acompte m; [- on bottle] consigne f. ◇ vt déposer.

deposit account n Br compte m sur livret.

depositor [də'pɒzɪtə'] n déposant m, -e f.

depot ['depəʊ] n **-1.** [gen] dépôt m. **-2.** Am [station] gare f.

depraved [dɪ'preɪvd] adj dépravé(e).

depravity [dɪ'prævətɪ] n dépravation f.

deprecate ['deprɪkeɪt] vt fml désapprouver.

deprecating ['deprɪkeɪtɪŋ] adj désapprobateur(trice).

depreciate [dɪ'priːʃɪeɪt] vi se déprécier.

depreciation [dɪ,priːʃɪ'eɪʃn] n dépréciation f.

depress [dɪ'pres] vt **-1.** [sadden, discourage] déprimer. **-2.** [weaken - economy] affaiblir; [- prices] faire baisser.

depressant [dɪ'presənt] n dépresseur m.

depressed [dɪ'prest] adj **-1.** [sad] déprimé(e). **-2.** [run-down - area] en déclin.

depressing [dɪ'presɪŋ] adj déprimant(e).

depression [dɪ'preʃn] n **-1.** [gen] dépression f. **-2.** [sadness] tristesse f.
◆ **Depression** n ECON: **the (Great) Depression** la Grande Dépression.

depressive [dɪ'presɪv] adj dépressif(ive).

deprivation [,deprɪ'veɪʃn] n privation f.

deprive [dɪ'praɪv] vt: **to ~ sb of sthg** priver qqn de qqch.

deprived [dɪ'praɪvd] adj défavorisé(e).

dept. abbr of **department**.

depth [depθ] n profondeur f; **in ~** [study, analyse] en profondeur; **to be out of one's ~** [in water] ne pas avoir pied; fig avoir perdu pied, être dépassé.
◆ **depths** npl: **the ~s** [of seas] les profondeurs fpl; [of memory, archives] le fin fond; **in the ~s of winter** au cœur de l'hiver; **to be in the ~s of despair** toucher le fond du désespoir.

depth charge n grenade f sous-marine.

deputation [,depjʊ'teɪʃn] n délégation f.

deputize, -ise ['depjʊtaɪz] vi: **to ~ for sb** assurer les fonctions de qqn, remplacer qqn.

deputy ['depjʊtɪ] (pl **-ies**) ◇ adj adjoint(e); **~ chairman** vice-président m; **~ head** SCH directeur m adjoint; **~ leader** POL vice-président m. ◇ n **-1.** [second-in-command] adjoint m, -e f. **-2.** Am [deputy sheriff] shérif m adjoint.

derail [dɪ'reɪl] vt [train] faire dérailler.

derailment [dɪ'reɪlmənt] n déraillement m.

deranged [dɪ'reɪndʒd] adj dérangé(e).

derby [Br 'dɑːbɪ, Am 'dɜːbɪ] (pl **-ies**) n **-1.** SPORT derby m. **-2.** Am [hat] chapeau m melon.

deregulate [,diː'regjʊleɪt] vt déréglementer.

deregulation [,diːregjʊ'leɪʃn] n déréglementation f.

derelict ['derəlɪkt] adj en ruines.

deride [dɪ'raɪd] vt railler.

derision [dɪ'rɪʒn] n dérision f.

derisive [dɪ'raɪsɪv] adj moqueur(euse).

derisory [də'raɪzərɪ] adj **-1.** [puny, trivial] dérisoire. **-2.** [derisive] moqueur(euse).

derivation [,derɪ'veɪʃn] n [of word] dérivation f.

derivative [dɪˈrɪvətɪv] ◇ *adj pej* pas origi-nal(e). ◇ *n* dérivé *m*.

derive [dɪˈraɪv] ◇ *vt* -1. [draw, gain]: **to ~ sthg from sthg** tirer qqch de qqch. -2. [origi-nate]: **to be ~d from** venir de. ◇ *vi*: **to ~ from** venir de.

dermatitis [ˌdɜːməˈtaɪtɪs] *n* dermatite *f*.

dermatologist [ˌdɜːməˈtɒlədʒɪst] *n* derma-tologue *mf*.

dermatology [ˌdɜːməˈtɒlədʒɪ] *n* dermatolo-gie *f*.

derogatory [dɪˈrɒgətrɪ] *adj* désobligeant(e).

derrick [ˈderɪk] *n* -1. [crane] mât *m* de charge. -2. [over oil well] derrick *m*.

derv [dɜːv] *n Br* gas-oil *m*.

desalination [diːˌsælɪˈneɪʃn] *n* dessalement *m*, dessalaison *f*.

descant [ˈdeskænt] *n* [tune] déchant *m*.

descend [dɪˈsend] ◇ *vt fml* [go down] des-cendre. ◇ *vi* -1. *fml* [go down] descendre. -2. [fall]: **to ~ (on)** [enemy] s'abattre (sur); [subj: silence, gloom] tomber (sur). -3. [ar-rive]: **to ~ on** [a town] arriver en nombre dans, envahir; [subj: in-laws etc] arriver à l'improviste chez. -4. [stoop]: **to ~ to sthg/to doing sthg** s'abaisser à qqch/à faire qqch.

descendant [dɪˈsendənt] *n* descendant *m*, -e *f*.

descended [dɪˈsendɪd] *adj*: **to be ~ from sb** descendre de qqn.

descending [dɪˈsendɪŋ] *adj*: **in ~ order** en ordre décroissant.

descent [dɪˈsent] *n* -1. [downwards move-ment] descente *f*. -2. (U) [origin] origine *f*.

describe [dɪˈskraɪb] *vt* décrire.

description [dɪˈskrɪpʃn] *n* -1. [account] des-cription *f*. -2. [type] sorte *f*, genre *m*.

descriptive [dɪˈskrɪptɪv] *adj* descriptif(ive).

desecrate [ˈdesɪkreɪt] *vt* profaner.

desecration [ˌdesɪˈkreɪʃn] *n* profanation *f*.

desegregate [ˌdiːˈsegrɪgeɪt] *vt* pratiquer la déségrégation dans.

deselect [ˌdiːsɪˈlekt] *vt Br* ne pas resélec-tionner pour une réélection.

desert [*n* ˈdezət, *vb & npl* dɪˈzɜːt] ◇ *n* dé-sert *m*. ◇ *vt* -1. [place] déserter. -2. [person, group] déserter, abandonner. ◇ *vi* MIL dé-serter.

◆ **deserts** *npl*: **to get one's just ~s** rece-voir ce que l'on mérite.

deserted [dɪˈzɜːtɪd] *adj* désert(e).

deserter [dɪˈzɜːtə*r*] *n* déserteur *m*.

desertion [dɪˈzɜːʃn] *n* -1. MIL désertion *f*. -2. [of person] abandon *m*.

desert island [ˈdezət-] *n* île *f* déserte.

deserve [dɪˈzɜːv] *vt* mériter; **to ~ to do sthg** mériter de faire qqch.

deserved [dɪˈzɜːvd] *adj* mérité(e).

deservedly [dɪˈzɜːvɪdlɪ] *adv* à juste titre.

deserving [dɪˈzɜːvɪŋ] *adj* [person] méri-tant(e); [cause, charity] méritoire; **to be ~ of sthg** *fml* mériter qqch.

desiccated [ˈdesɪkeɪtɪd] *adj* séché(e).

design [dɪˈzaɪn] ◇ *n* -1. [plan, drawing] plan *m*, étude *f*. -2. (U) [art] design *m*. -3. [pat-tern] motif *m*, dessin *m*. -4. [shape] ligne *f*; [of dress] style *m*. -5. *fml* [intention] dessein *m*; **by ~** à dessein; **to have ~s on sb/sthg** avoir des desseins sur qqn/qqch.
◇ *vt* -1. [draw plans for - building, car] faire les plans de, dessiner; [- dress] créer. -2. [plan] concevoir, mettre au point; **to be ~ed for sthg/to do sthg** être conçu pour qqch/pour faire qqch.

designate [*adj* ˈdezɪgnət, *vb* ˈdezɪgneɪt] ◇ *adj* désigné(e). ◇ *vt* désigner; **to ~ sb as sthg/to do sthg** désigner qqn à qqch/pour faire qqch.

designation [ˌdezɪgˈneɪʃn] *n fml* [name] ap-pellation *f*.

designer [dɪˈzaɪnə*r*] ◇ *adj* de marque. ◇ *n* INDUSTRY concepteur *m*, -trice *f*; ARCHIT des-sinateur *m*, -trice *f*; [of dresses etc] styliste *mf*; THEATRE décorateur *m*, -trice *f*.

desirable [dɪˈzaɪərəbl] *adj* -1. [enviable, at-tractive] désirable. -2. *fml* [appropriate] dé-sirable, souhaitable.

desire [dɪˈzaɪə*r*] ◇ *n* désir *m*; **~ for sthg/to do sthg** désir de qqch/de faire qqch. ◇ *vt* désirer; **it leaves a lot to be ~d** ça laisse beaucoup à désirer.

desirous [dɪˈzaɪərəs] *adj fml*: **~ of sthg/of doing sthg** désireux(euse) de qqch/de faire qqch.

desist [dɪˈzɪst] *vi fml*: **to ~ (from doing sthg)** cesser (de faire qqch).

desk [desk] *n* bureau *m*; **reception ~** récep-tion *f*; **information ~** bureau *m* de rensei-gnements.

desk clerk *n Am* réceptionniste *mf*.

desk lamp *n* lampe *f* de bureau.

desktop [ˈdeskˌtɒp] *adj* [computer] de bu-reau.

desktop publishing *n* publication *f* assis-tée par ordinateur, PAO *f*.

desolate [ˈdesələt] *adj* -1. [place] abandon-né(e). -2. [person] désespéré(e), désolé(e).

desolation [ˌdesəˈleɪʃn] *n* désolation *f*.

despair [dɪˈspeə*r*] ◇ *n* (U) désespoir *m*; **to be in ~** être au désespoir. ◇ *vi* désespérer;

to ~ of désespérer de; to ~ of doing sthg désespérer de faire qqch.

despairing [dı'speərıŋ] *adj* de désespoir.

despairingly [dı'speərıŋlı] *adv* avec désespoir.

despatch [dı'spætʃ] = dispatch.

desperate ['desprət] *adj* désespéré(e); to be ~ for sthg avoir absolument besoin de qqch.

desperately ['desprətlı] *adv* désespérément; ~ ill gravement malade.

desperation [,despə'reıʃn] *n* désespoir *m*; in ~ de désespoir.

despicable [dı'spıkəbl] *adj* ignoble.

despise [dı'spaız] *vt* [person] mépriser; [racism] exécrer.

despite [dı'spaıt] *prep* malgré.

despondent [dı'spɒndənt] *adj* découragé(e).

despot ['despɒt] *n* despote *m*.

despotic [de'spɒtık] *adj* despotique.

dessert [dı'zɜːt] *n* dessert *m*.

dessertspoon [dı'zɜːtspuːn] *n* **-1.** [spoon] cuillère *f* à dessert. **-2.** [spoonful] cuillerée *f* à dessert.

dessert wine *n* vin *m* doux.

destabilize, **-ise** [,diː'steıbılaız] *vt* déstabiliser.

destination [,destı'neıʃn] *n* destination *f*.

destined ['destınd] *adj* **-1.** [intended]: ~ for destiné(e) à; ~ to do sthg destiné à faire qqch. **-2.** [bound]: ~ for à destination de.

destiny ['destını] (*pl* -ies) *n* destinée *f*.

destitute ['destıtjuːt] *adj* indigent(e).

destroy [dı'strɔı] *vt* **-1.** [ruin] détruire. **-2.** [put down - animal] faire piquer.

destroyer [dı'strɔıəʳ] *n* **-1.** [ship] destroyer *m*. **-2.** [person, thing] destructeur *m*, -trice *f*.

destruction [dı'strʌkʃn] *n* destruction *f*.

destructive [dı'strʌktıv] *adj* [harmful] destructeur(trice).

destructively [dı'strʌktıvlı] *adv* de façon destructrice.

desultory ['desəltrı] *adj fml* [conversation] décousu(e); [attempt] peu enthousiaste.

Det. *abbr of* **Detective**.

detach [dı'tætʃ] *vt* **-1.** [pull off] détacher; to ~ sthg from sthg détacher qqch de qqch. **-2.** [dissociate]: to ~ o.s. from sthg [from reality] se détacher de qqch; [from proceedings, discussions] s'écarter de qqch.

detachable [dı'tætʃəbl] *adj* détachable, amovible.

detached [dı'tætʃt] *adj* [unemotional] détaché(e).

detached house *n* maison *f* individuelle.

detachment [dı'tætʃmənt] *n* détachement *m*.

detail ['diːteıl] ◇ *n* **-1.** [small point] détail *m*; to go into ~ entrer dans les détails; in ~ en détail. **-2.** MIL détachement *m*. ◇ *vt* [list] détailler.

◆ **details** *npl* [personal information] coordonnées *fpl*.

detailed ['diːteıld] *adj* détaillé(e).

detain [dı'teın] *vt* **-1.** [in police station] détenir; [in hospital] garder. **-2.** [delay] retenir.

detainee [,diːteı'niː] *n* détenu *m*, -e *f*.

detect [dı'tekt] *vt* **-1.** [subj: person] déceler. **-2.** [subj: machine] détecter.

detection [dı'tekʃn] *n* (*U*) **-1.** [of crime] dépistage *m*. **-2.** [of aircraft, submarine] détection *f*.

detective [dı'tektıv] *n* détective *m*.

detective novel *n* roman *m* policier.

detector [dı'tektəʳ] *n* détecteur *m*.

détente [deı'tɒnt] *n* POL détente *f*.

detention [dı'tenʃn] *n* **-1.** [of suspect, criminal] détention *f*; in ~ en détention. **-2.** SCH retenue *f*; in ~ en retenue.

detention centre *n* Br centre *m* de détention.

deter [dı'tɜːʳ] (*pt & pp* -red, *cont* -ring) *vt* dissuader; to ~ sb from doing sthg dissuader qqn de faire qqch.

detergent [dı'tɜːdʒənt] *n* détergent *m*.

deteriorate [dı'tıərıəreıt] *vi* se détériorer.

deterioration [dı,tıərıə'reıʃn] *n* détérioration *f*.

determination [dı,tɜːmı'neıʃn] *n* détermination *f*.

determine [dı'tɜːmın] *vt* **-1.** [establish, control] déterminer. **-2.** *fml* [decide]: to ~ to do sthg décider de faire qqch.

determined [dı'tɜːmınd] *adj* **-1.** [person] déterminé(e); ~ to do sthg déterminé à faire qqch. **-2.** [effort] obstiné(e).

deterrent [dı'terənt] ◇ *adj* de dissuasion, dissuasif(ive). ◇ *n* moyen *m* de dissuasion.

detest [dı'test] *vt* détester.

detestable [dı'testəbl] *adj* détestable.

dethrone [dı'θrəun] *vt* détrôner.

detonate ['detəneıt] ◇ *vt* faire détoner. ◇ *vi* détoner.

detonator ['detəneıtəʳ] *n* détonateur *m*.

detour ['diː,tuəʳ] *n* détour *m*.

detract [dı'trækt] *vi*: to ~ from diminuer.

detractor [dı'træktəʳ] *n* détracteur *m*, -trice *f*.

detriment ['detrımənt] *n*: to the ~ of au détriment de.

detrimental [,detrɪ'mentl] *adj* préjudiciable.

detritus [dɪ'traɪtəs] *n* (*U*) détritus *m*.

deuce [dju:s] *n* TENNIS égalité *f*.

Deutschmark ['dɔɪtʃ,mɑːk] *n* mark *m* allemand.

devaluation [,diːvælju'eɪʃn] *n* dévaluation *f*.

devalue [,diː'vælju:] *vt* dévaluer.

devastate ['devəsteɪt] *vt* **-1.** [destroy - area, city] dévaster. **-2.** *fig* [person] anéantir.

devastated ['devəsteɪtɪd] *adj* **-1.** [area, city] dévasté(e). **-2.** *fig* [person] accablé(e).

devastating ['devəsteɪtɪŋ] *adj* **-1.** [hurricane, remark] dévastateur(trice). **-2.** [upsetting] accablant(e). **-3.** [attractive] irrésistible.

devastation [,devə'steɪʃn] *n* dévastation *f*.

develop [dɪ'veləp] ◇ *vt* **-1.** [gen] développer. **-2.** [land, area] aménager, développer. **-3.** [illness, fault, habit] contracter. **-4.** [resources] développer, exploiter. ◇ *vi* **-1.** [grow, advance] se développer. **-2.** [appear - problem, trouble] se déclarer.

developer [dɪ'veləpəʳ] *n* **-1.** [of land] promoteur *m* immobilier. **-2.** [person]: **to be an early/a late ~** être en avance/en retard sur son âge. **-3.** PHOT [chemical] développateur *m*, révélateur *m*.

developing country [dɪ'veləpɪŋ-] *n* pays *m* en voie de développement.

development [dɪ'veləpmənt] *n* **-1.** [gen] développement *m*. **-2.** (*U*) [of land, area] exploitation *f*. **-3.** [land being developed] zone *f* d'aménagement; [developed area] zone aménagée. **-4.** (*U*) [of illness, fault] évolution *f*.

development area *n Br* zone *f* d'aménagement.

deviant ['diːvjənt] ◇ *adj* déviant(e). ◇ *n* déviant *m*, -e *f*.

deviate ['diːvɪeɪt] *vi*: **to ~ (from)** dévier (de), s'écarter (de).

deviation [,diːvɪ'eɪʃn] *n* **-1.** [abnormality] déviance *f*. **-2.** [departure - from rule, plan] écart *m*; *pej* déviation *f*.

device [dɪ'vaɪs] *n* **-1.** [apparatus] appareil *m*, dispositif *m*. **-2.** [plan, method] moyen *m*; **to leave sb to their own ~s** laisser qqn se débrouiller tout seul.

devil ['devl] *n* **-1.** [evil spirit] diable *m*. **-2.** *inf* [person] type *m*; **poor ~!** pauvre diable! **-3.** [for emphasis]: **who/where/why the ~ ...?** qui/où/pourquoi diable ...? ◆ **Devil** *n* [Satan]: **the Devil** le Diable.

devilish ['devlɪʃ] *adj* diabolique.

devil-may-care *adj* insouciant(e).

devil's advocate *n* avocat *m* du diable.

devious ['diːvjəs] *adj* **-1.** [dishonest - person] retors(e), à l'esprit tortueux; [- scheme, means] détourné(e). **-2.** [tortuous] tortueux(euse).

deviousness ['diːvjəsnɪs] *n* [dishonesty] sournoiserie *f*.

devise [dɪ'vaɪz] *vt* concevoir.

devoid [dɪ'vɔɪd] *adj fml*: **~ of** dépourvu(e) de, dénué(e) de.

devolution [,diːvə'luːʃn] *n* POL décentralisation *f*.

devolve [dɪ'vɒlv] *vi fml*: **to ~ on** OR **upon sb** incomber à qqn.

devote [dɪ'vəʊt] *vt*: **to ~ sthg to sthg** consacrer qqch à qqch; **to ~ o.s. to sthg** se vouer OR se consacrer à qqch.

devoted [dɪ'vəʊtɪd] *adj* dévoué(e); **a ~ mother** une mère dévouée à ses enfants.

devotee [,devə'tiː] *n* [fan] passionné *m*, -e *f*.

devotion [dɪ'vəʊʃn] *n* **-1.** [commitment]: **~ (to)** dévouement *m* (à). **-2.** RELIG dévotion *f*.

devour [dɪ'vaʊəʳ] *vt lit* & *fig* dévorer.

devout [dɪ'vaʊt] *adj* dévot(e).

dew [dju:] *n* rosée *f*.

dexterity [dek'sterətɪ] *n* dextérité *f*.

dextrose ['dekstrəʊs] *n* dextrose *m*.

dext(e)rous ['dekstrəs] *adj* habile.

DFE (*abbr of* **Department for Education**) *n* ministère britannique de l'éducation nationale.

dhal [dɑːl] *n* dal *m*.

DHSS (*abbr of* **Department of Health and Social Security**) *n* ancien nom du ministère britannique de la santé et de la sécurité sociale.

diabetes [,daɪə'biːtiːz] *n* diabète *m*.

diabetic [,daɪə'betɪk] ◇ *adj* **-1.** [person] diabétique. **-2.** [jam, chocolate] pour diabétiques. ◇ *n* diabétique *mf*.

diabolic(al) [,daɪə'bɒlɪk(l)] *adj* **-1.** [evil] diabolique. **-2.** *inf* [very bad] atroce.

diaeresis *Br* (*pl* **-eses** [-iːsiːz]), **dieresis** *Am* (*pl* **-eses**) [daɪ'erɪsɪs] *n* tréma *m*.

diagnose ['daɪəgnəʊz] *vt* diagnostiquer.

diagnosis [,daɪəg'nəʊsɪs] (*pl* **-oses** [-əʊsiːz]) *n* diagnostic *m*.

diagnostic [,daɪəg'nɒstɪk] *adj* diagnostique.

diagonal [daɪ'ægənl] ◇ *adj* [line] diagonal(e). ◇ *n* diagonale *f*.

diagonally [daɪ'ægənəlɪ] *adv* en diagonale.

diagram ['daɪəgræm] *n* diagramme *m*.

diagrammatic [,daɪəgrə'mætɪk] *adj* en forme de diagramme.

dial ['daɪəl] (*Br pt* & *pp* **-led**, *cont* **-ling**, *Am pt* & *pp* **-ed**, *cont* **-ing**) ◇ *n* cadran *m*; [of radio] cadran de fréquences. ◇ *vt* [number] composer.

dialect ['daɪəlekt] *n* dialecte *m*.

dialling code ['daɪəlɪŋ-] *n Br* indicatif *m*.

dialling tone ['daɪəlɪŋ-] *Br*, **dial tone** *Am n* tonalité *f*.

dialogue *Br*, **dialog** *Am* ['daɪəlɒg] *n* dialogue *m*.

dial tone *Am* = **dialling tone**.

dialysis [daɪ'ælɪsɪs] *n* dialyse *f*.

diamanté [dɪə'mɒnteɪ] *adj* diamanté(e).

diameter [daɪ'æmɪtəʳ] *n* diamètre *m*.

diametrically [ˌdaɪə'metrɪklɪ] *adv*: ~ **opposed** diamétralement opposé(e).

diamond ['daɪəmənd] *n* **-1.** [gem] diamant *m*. **-2.** [shape] losange *m*. **-3.** [playing card] carreau *m*.
◆ **diamonds** *npl* carreau *m*; **the six of ~s** le six de carreau.

diamond wedding *n* noces *fpl* de diamant.

diaper ['daɪəpəʳ] *n Am* couche *f*.

diaphanous [daɪ'æfənəs] *adj* diaphane.

diaphragm ['daɪəfræm] *n* diaphragme *m*.

diarrh(o)ea [ˌdaɪə'rɪə] *n* diarrhée *f*.

diary ['daɪərɪ] (*pl* **-ies**) *n* **-1.** [appointment book] agenda *m*. **-2.** [journal] journal *m*.

diatribe ['daɪətraɪb] *n* diatribe *f*.

dice [daɪs] (*pl inv*) ◇ *n* [for games] dé *m*; **no ~** *Am inf* pas question. ◇ *vt* couper en dés.

dicey ['daɪsɪ] (*compar* **-ier**, *superl* **-iest**) *adj inf* risqué(e).

dichotomy [daɪ'kɒtəmɪ] (*pl* **-ies**) *n* dichotomie *f*.

dickens ['dɪkɪnz] *n Br inf dated*: **who/what/where the ~ ...?** qui/que/où diable ...?

Dictaphone® ['dɪktəfəʊn] *n* Dictaphone® *m*.

dictate [*vb* dɪk'teɪt, *n* 'dɪkteɪt] ◇ *vt* dicter; **to ~ sthg to sb** dicter qqch à qqn. ◇ *vi* **-1.** [read aloud]: **to ~ to sb** dicter à qqn. **-2.** [give orders]: **to ~ to sb** commander à qqn, donner des ordres à qqn. ◇ *n* ordre *m*.

dictation [dɪk'teɪʃn] *n* dictée *f*.

dictator [dɪk'teɪtəʳ] *n* dictateur *m*.

dictatorship [dɪk'teɪtəʃɪp] *n* dictature *f*.

diction ['dɪkʃn] *n* diction *f*.

dictionary ['dɪkʃənrɪ] (*pl* **-ies**) *n* dictionnaire *m*.

did [dɪd] *pt* → **do**.

didactic [dɪ'dæktɪk] *adj* didactique.

diddle ['dɪdl] *vt inf* escroquer, rouler.

didn't ['dɪdnt] = **did not**.

die [daɪ] (*pl sense 2 only* **dice**, *pt & pp* **died**, *cont* **dying**) ◇ *vi* mourir; **to be dying** se mourir; **to be dying to do sthg** mourir d'envie de faire qqch; **to be dying for a drink/cigarette** mourir d'envie de boire un

verre/de fumer une cigarette. ◇ *n* **-1.** [for shaping metal] matrice *f*. **-2.** [dice] dé *m*.
◆ **die away** *vi* [sound] s'éteindre; [wind] tomber.
◆ **die down** *vi* [sound] s'affaiblir; [wind] tomber; [fire] baisser.
◆ **die out** *vi* s'éteindre, disparaître.

diehard ['daɪhɑːd] *n*: **to be a ~** être coriace; [reactionary] être réactionnaire.

dieresis *Am* = **diaeresis**.

diesel ['diːzl] *n* diesel *m*.

diesel engine *n* AUT moteur *m* diesel; RAIL locomotive *f* diesel.

diesel fuel, **diesel oil** *n* diesel *m*.

diet ['daɪət] ◇ *n* **-1.** [eating pattern] alimentation *f*. **-2.** [to lose weight] régime *m*; **to be on a ~** être au régime, faire un régime. ◇ *comp* [low-calorie] de régime. ◇ *vi* suivre un régime.

dietary ['daɪətrɪ] *adj* diététique.

dietary fibre *n* (*U*) fibres *fpl* alimentaires.

dieter ['daɪətəʳ] *n* personne *f* qui suit un régime.

dietician [ˌdaɪə'tɪʃn] *n* diététicien *m*, **-ienne** *f*.

differ ['dɪfəʳ] *vi* **-1.** [be different] être différent(e), différer; [people] être différent; **to ~ from** être différent de. **-2.** [disagree]: **to ~ with sb (about sthg)** ne pas être d'accord avec qqn (à propos de qqch).

difference ['dɪfrəns] *n* différence *f*; **it doesn't make any ~** cela ne change rien; **to make all the ~** faire toute la différence.

different ['dɪfrənt] *adj*: **~ (from)** différent(e) (de).

differential [ˌdɪfə'renʃl] ◇ *adj* différentiel(ielle). ◇ *n* **-1.** [between pay scales] écart *m*. **-2.** TECH différentielle *f*.

differentiate [ˌdɪfə'renʃɪeɪt] ◇ *vt*: **to ~ sthg from sthg** différencier qqch de qqch, faire la différence entre qqch et qqch. ◇ *vi*: **to ~ (between)** faire la différence (entre).

differently ['dɪfrəntlɪ] *adv* différemment, autrement; **to think ~** ne pas être d'accord.

difficult ['dɪfɪkəlt] *adj* difficile.

difficulty ['dɪfɪkəltɪ] (*pl* **-ies**) *n* difficulté *f*; **to have ~ in doing sthg** avoir de la difficulté OR du mal à faire qqch.

diffidence ['dɪfɪdəns] *n* manque *m* d'assurance.

diffident ['dɪfɪdənt] *adj* [person] qui manque d'assurance; [manner, voice, approach] hésitant(e).

diffuse [*adj* dɪ'fjuːs, *vb* dɪ'fjuːz] ◇ *adj* **-1.** [vague] diffus(e). **-2.** [spread out - city] étendu(e); [- company] éparpillé(e). ◇ *vt* diffuser, répandre. ◇ *vi* **-1.** [light] se diffuser, se répandre. **-2.** [information] se répandre.

diffusion [dɪ'fjuːʒn] *n* diffusion *f*.

dig [dɪg] (*pt* & *pp* dug, *cont* digging) ◇ *vi* **-1.** [in ground] creuser. **-2.** [subj: belt, strap]: his elbow was digging into my side son coude me rentrait dans les côtes; to ~ into sb couper qqn. ◇ *n* **-1.** *fig* [unkind remark] pique *f*. **-2.** ARCHEOL fouilles *fpl.* ◇ *vt* **-1.** [hole] creuser. **-2.** [garden] bêcher. **-3.** [press]: to ~ sthg into sthg enfoncer qqch dans qqch.
◆ **dig out** *vt sep* **-1.** [rescue] dégager. **-2.** *inf* [find] dénicher.
◆ **dig up** *vt sep* **-1.** [from ground] déterrer; [potatoes] arracher. **-2.** *inf* [information] dénicher.

digest [*n* 'daɪdʒest, *vb* dɪ'dʒest] ◇ *n* résumé *m*, digest *m*. ◇ *vt lit* & *fig* digérer.

digestible [dɪ'dʒestəbl] *adj* digeste.

digestion [dɪ'dʒestʃn] *n* digestion *f*.

digestive [dɪ'dʒestɪv] *adj* digestif(ive).

digestive biscuit *n Br* ≃ sablé *m* (à la farine complète).

digit ['dɪdʒɪt] *n* **-1.** [figure] chiffre *m*. **-2.** [finger] doigt *m*; [toe] orteil *m*.

digital ['dɪdʒɪtl] *adj* numérique, digital(e).

digital recording *n* enregistrement *m* numérique.

digital watch *n* montre *f* à affichage digital.

digitize, -ise ['dɪdʒɪtaɪz] digitaliser.

dignified ['dɪgnɪfaɪd] *adj* digne, plein(e) de dignité.

dignify ['dɪgnɪfaɪ] (*pt* & *pp* -ied) *vt* [place, appearance] donner de la grandeur à.

dignitary ['dɪgnɪtrɪ] (*pl* -ies) *n* dignitaire *m*.

dignity ['dɪgnətɪ] *n* dignité *f*.

digress [daɪ'gres] *vi*: to ~ (from) s'écarter (de).

digression [daɪ'greʃn] *n* digression *f*.

digs [dɪgz] *npl Br inf* piaule *f*.

dike [daɪk] *n* **-1.** [wall, bank] digue *f*. **-2.** *inf pej* [lesbian] gouine *f*.

diktat ['dɪktaːt] *n* diktat *m*.

dilapidated [dɪ'læpɪdeɪtɪd] *adj* délabré(e).

dilate [daɪ'leɪt] ◇ *vt* dilater. ◇ *vi* se dilater.

dilated [daɪ'leɪtɪd] *adj* dilaté(e).

dilemma [dɪ'lemə] *n* dilemme *m*.

dilettante [ˌdɪlɪ'tæntɪ] (*pl* -tes OR -ti [-tɪ]) *n* dilettante *mf*.

diligence ['dɪlɪdʒəns] *n* application *f*.

diligent ['dɪlɪdʒənt] *adj* appliqué(e).

dill [dɪl] *n* aneth *m*.

dillydally ['dɪlɪdælɪ] (*pt* & *pp* -ied) *vi inf* lambiner.

dilute [daɪ'ljuːt] ◇ *adj* dilué(e). ◇ *vt*: to ~ sthg (with) diluer qqch (avec).

dilution [daɪ'luːʃn] *n* dilution *f*.

dim [dɪm] (*compar* -mer, *superl* -mest, *pt* & *pp* -med, *cont* -ming) ◇ *adj* **-1.** [dark - light] faible; [- room] sombre. **-2.** [indistinct - memory, outline] vague. **-3.** [weak - eyesight] faible. **-4.** *inf* [stupid] borné(e). ◇ *vt* & *vi* baisser.

dime [daɪm] *n Am* (pièce de) dix cents *mpl*; they're a ~ a dozen [common] il y en a à la pelle.

dimension [dɪ'menʃn] *n* dimension *f*.

-dimensional [dɪ'menʃənl] *suffix* -dimensionnel(elle).

diminish [dɪ'mɪnɪʃ] *vt* & *vi* diminuer.

diminished [dɪ'mɪnɪʃt] *adj* réduit(e).

diminished responsibility *n* JUR responsabilité *f* atténuée.

diminishing returns [dɪ'mɪnɪʃɪŋ-] *npl* rendements *mpl* décroissants.

diminutive [dɪ'mɪnjutɪv] *fml* ◇ *adj* minuscule. ◇ *n* GRAMM diminutif *m*.

dimly ['dɪmlɪ] *adv* [lit] faiblement; [remember] vaguement.

dimmers ['dɪməz] *npl Am* [dipped headlights] phares *mpl* code *inv*; [parking lights] feux *mpl* de position.

dimmer (switch) ['dɪmə-] *n* variateur *m* de lumière.

dimple ['dɪmpl] *n* fossette *f*.

dimwit ['dɪmwɪt] *n inf* crétin *m*, -e *f*.

dim-witted [-'wɪtɪd] *adj inf* crétin(e).

din [dɪn] *n inf* barouf *m*.

dine [daɪn] *vi fml* dîner.
◆ **dine out** *vi* dîner dehors.

diner ['daɪnə-] *n* **-1.** [person] dîneur *m*, -euse *f*. **-2.** *Am* [café] ≃ resto *m* routier.

dingdong [ˌdɪŋ'dɒŋ] ◇ *adj inf* [battle, argument] acharné(e). ◇ *n* [of bell] ding dong *m*.

dinghy ['dɪŋgɪ] (*pl* -ies) *n* [for sailing] dériveur *m*; [for rowing] (petit) canot *m*.

dingo ['dɪŋgəu] (*pl* -es) *n* dingo *m*, chien *m* sauvage.

dingy ['dɪndʒɪ] (*compar* -ier, *superl* -iest) *adj* miteux(euse), crasseux(euse).

dining car [daɪnɪŋ-] *n* wagon-restaurant *m*.

dining room [daɪnɪŋ-] *n* **-1.** [in house] salle *f* à manger. **-2.** [in hotel] restaurant *m*.

dining table [daɪnɪŋ-] *n* table *f* (*de salle à manger*).

dinner ['dɪnə-] *n* dîner *m*.

dinner dance *n* dîner *m* dansant.

dinner jacket *n* smoking *m*.

dinner party *n* dîner *m*.

dinner service *n* service *m* de table.

dinner table *n* table *f* (de salle à manger).

dinnertime ['dɪnətaɪm] *n* heure *f* du dîner.

dinosaur ['daɪnəsɔːr] *n* dinosaure *m*.

dint [dɪnt] *n fml:* **by ~ of** à force de.

diocese ['daɪəsɪs] *n* diocèse *m*.

diode ['daɪəʊd] *n* diode *f*.

dip [dɪp] (*pt* & *pp* **-ped**, *cont* **-ping**) ◇ *n* **-1.** [in road, ground] déclivité *f*. **-2.** [sauce] sauce *f*, dip *m*. **-3.** [swim] baignade *f* (rapide); **to go for a ~** aller se baigner en vitesse, aller faire trempette. ◇ *vt* **-1.** [into liquid]: **to ~ sthg in** OR **into** tremper OR plonger qqch dans. **-2.** *Br* AUT: **to ~ one's headlights** se mettre en code. ◇ *vi* **-1.** [sun] baisser, descendre à l'horizon; [wing] plonger. **-2.** [road, ground] descendre.

Dip. *Br abbr of* **diploma**.

diphtheria [dɪf'θɪərɪə] *n* diphtérie *f*.

diphthong ['dɪfθɒŋ] *n* diphtongue *f*.

diploma [dɪ'pləʊmə] (*pl* **-s**) *n* diplôme *m*.

diplomacy [dɪ'pləʊməsɪ] *n* diplomatie *f*.

diplomat ['dɪpləmæt] *n* diplomate *m*.

diplomatic [,dɪplə'mætɪk] *adj* **-1.** [service, corps] diplomatique. **-2.** [tactful] diplomate.

diplomatic bag *n* valise *f* diplomatique.

diplomatic corps *n* corps *m* diplomatique.

diplomatic immunity *n* immunité *f* diplomatique.

diplomatic relations *npl* relations *fpl* diplomatiques.

dipsomaniac [,dɪpsə'meɪnɪæk] *n* dipsomane *mf*.

dipstick ['dɪpstɪk] *n* AUT jauge *f* (*de niveau d'huile*).

dipswitch ['dɪpswɪtʃ] *n Br* AUT manette *f* des codes.

dire ['daɪər] *adj* [need, consequences] extrême; [warning] funeste.

direct [dɪ'rekt] ◇ *adj* direct(e); [challenge] manifeste. ◇ *vt* **-1.** [gen] diriger. **-2.** [aim]: **to ~ sthg at sb** [question, remark] adresser qqch à qqn; **the campaign is ~ed at teenagers** cette campagne vise les adolescents. **-3.** [order]: **to ~ sb to do sthg** ordonner à qqn de faire qqch. ◇ *adv* directement.

direct action *n* action *f* directe.

direct current *n* courant *m* continu.

direct debit *n Br* prélèvement *m* automatique.

direct dialling [-'daɪəlɪŋ] *n* automatique *m*.

direct hit *n* coup *m* au but OR de plein fouet.

direction [dɪ'rekʃn] *n* direction *f*; **under the ~ of** sous la direction de.

◆ **directions** *npl* **-1.** [to find a place] indications *fpl*. **-2.** [for use] instructions *fpl*.

directive [dɪ'rektɪv] *n* directive *f*.

directly [dɪ'rektlɪ] *adv* **-1.** [in straight line] directement. **-2.** [honestly, clearly] sans détours. **-3.** [exactly - behind, above] exactement. **-4.** [immediately] immédiatement. **-5.** [very soon] tout de suite.

direct mail *n* publipostage *m*.

director [dɪ'rektər] *n* **-1.** [of company] directeur *m*, -trice *f*. **-2.** THEATRE metteur *m* en scène; CINEMA & TV réalisateur *m*, -trice *f*.

directorate [dɪ'rektərət] *n* conseil *m* d'administration.

director-general (*pl* **directors-general** OR **director-generals**) *n* directeur général *m*.

Director of Public Prosecutions *n Br* ≃ procureur *m* général.

directorship [dɪ'rektəʃɪp] *n* **-1.** [position] poste *m* de directeur. **-2.** [period] direction *f*.

directory [dɪ'rektərɪ] (*pl* **-ies**) *n* **-1.** [annual publication] annuaire *m*. **-2.** COMPUT répertoire *m*.

directory enquiries *n Br* renseignements *mpl* (téléphoniques).

direct rule *n* centralisation *f* de pouvoir.

direct selling *n* (*U*) vente *f* directe.

direct speech *n* discours *m* direct.

direct taxation *n* imposition *f* directe.

dire straits *npl:* **in ~** dans une situation désespérée.

dirge [dɜːdʒ] *n* chant *m* funèbre.

dirt [dɜːt] *n* (*U*) **-1.** [mud, dust] saleté *f*. **-2.** [earth] terre *f*.

dirt cheap *inf* ◇ *adj* très bon marché, donné(e). ◇ *adv* pour trois fois rien.

dirt track *n* chemin *m* de terre.

dirty ['dɜːtɪ] (*compar* **-ier**, *superl* **-iest**, *pt* & *pp* **-ied**) ◇ *adj* **-1.** [not clean, not fair] sale. **-2.** [smutty - language, person] grossier(ière); [- book, joke] cochon(onne). ◇ *vt* salir.

disability [,dɪsə'bɪlətɪ] (*pl* **-ies**) *n* infirmité *f*.

disable [dɪs'eɪbl] *vt* **-1.** [injure] rendre infirme. **-2.** [put out of action - guns, vehicle] mettre hors d'action.

disabled [dɪs'eɪbld] ◇ *adj* [person] handicapé(e), infirme. ◇ *npl:* **the ~** les handicapés, les infirmes.

disablement [dɪs'eɪblmənt] *n* invalidité *f*.

disabuse [,dɪsə'bjuːz] *vt fml:* **to ~ sb (of)** détromper qqn (sur).

disadvantage [‚dɪsəd'vɑːntɪdʒ] *n* désavantage *m,* inconvénient *m*; **to be at a ~** être désavantagé; **to be to sb's ~** être au désavantage de qqn.

disadvantaged [‚dɪsəd'vɑːntɪdʒd] *adj* défavorisé(e).

disadvantageous [‚dɪsædvɑːn'teɪdʒəs] *adj* désavantageux(euse).

disaffected [‚dɪsə'fektɪd] *adj* mécontent(e).

disaffection [‚dɪsə'fekʃn] *n* mécontentement *m.*

disagree [‚dɪsə'griː] *vi* **-1.** [have different opinions]: **to ~ (with)** ne pas être d'accord (avec). **-2.** [differ] ne pas concorder. **-3.** [subj: food, drink]: **to ~ with sb** ne pas réussir à qqn.

disagreeable [‚dɪsə'griːəbl] *adj* désagréable.

disagreement [‚dɪsə'griːmənt] *n* **-1.** [in opinion] désaccord *m.* **-2.** [argument] différend *m.* **-3.** [dissimilarity] différence *f.*

disallow [‚dɪsə'laʊ] *vt* **-1.** *fml* [appeal, claim] rejeter. **-2.** [goal] refuser.

disappear [‚dɪsə'pɪəʳ] *vi* disparaître.

disappearance [‚dɪsə'pɪərəns] *n* disparition *f.*

disappoint [‚dɪsə'pɔɪnt] *vt* décevoir.

disappointed [‚dɪsə'pɔɪntɪd] *adj*: **~ (in** OR **with)** déçu(e) (par).

disappointing [‚dɪsə'pɔɪntɪŋ] *adj* décevant(e).

disappointment [‚dɪsə'pɔɪntmənt] *n* déception *f.*

disapproval [‚dɪsə'pruːvl] *n* désapprobation *f.*

disapprove [‚dɪsə'pruːv] *vi*: **to ~ of sb/sthg** désapprouver qqn/qqch; **do you ~?** est-ce que tu as quelque chose contre?

disapproving [‚dɪsə'pruːvɪŋ] *adj* désapprobateur(trice).

disarm [dɪs'ɑːm] *vt & vi lit & fig* désarmer.

disarmament [dɪs'ɑːməmənt] *n* désarmement *m.*

disarming [dɪs'ɑːmɪŋ] *adj* désarmant(e).

disarray [‚dɪsə'reɪ] *n*: **in ~** en désordre; [government] en pleine confusion.

disassociate [‚dɪsə'səʊʃɪeɪt] *vt*: **to ~ o.s. from** se dissocier de.

disaster [dɪ'zɑːstəʳ] *n* **-1.** [damaging event] catastrophe *f.* **-2.** (*U*) [misfortune] échec *m,* désastre *m.* **-3.** *inf* [failure] désastre *m.*

disaster area *n* [after natural disaster] zone *f* sinistrée.

disastrous [dɪ'zɑːstrəs] *adj* désastreux(euse).

disastrously [dɪ'zɑːstrəslɪ] *adv* de façon désastreuse.

disband [dɪs'bænd] ◇ *vt* dissoudre. ◇ *vi* se dissoudre.

disbelief [‚dɪsbɪ'liːf] *n*: **in** OR **with ~** avec incrédulité.

disbelieve [‚dɪsbɪ'liːv] *vt* ne pas croire.

disc *Br,* **disk** *Am* [dɪsk] *n* disque *m.*

disc. *abbr of* **discount.**

discard [dɪ'skɑːd] *vt* mettre au rebut.

discarded [dɪ'skɑːdɪd] *adj* mis(e) au rebut.

disc brake *n* frein *m* à disque.

discern [dɪ'sɜːn] *vt* discerner, distinguer.

discernible [dɪ'sɜːnəbl] *adj* **-1.** [visible] visible. **-2.** [noticeable] sensible.

discerning [dɪ'sɜːnɪŋ] *adj* judicieux(ieuse).

discharge [*n* 'dɪstʃɑːdʒ, *vt* dɪs'tʃɑːdʒ] ◇ *n* **-1.** [of patient] autorisation *f* de sortie, décharge *f*; JUR relaxe *f*; **to get one's ~** MIL être rendu à la vie civile. **-2.** *fml* [fulfilment - of duties] accomplissement *m.* **-3.** [emission - of smoke] émission *f*; [- of sewage] déversement *m*; MED écoulement *m.* **-4.** [payment] acquittement *m.*
◇ *vt* **-1.** [allow to leave - patient] signer la décharge de; [- prisoner, defendant] relaxer; [- soldier] rendre à la vie civile. **-2.** *fml* [fulfil] assumer. **-3.** [emit - smoke] émettre; [- sewage, chemicals] déverser. **-4.** [pay] acquitter, régler.

discharged bankrupt [dɪs'tʃɑːdʒd-] *n* failli *m* réhabilité.

disciple [dɪ'saɪpl] *n* disciple *m.*

disciplinarian [‚dɪsɪplɪ'neərɪən] *n* personne *impitoyable en matière de discipline.*

disciplinary ['dɪsɪplɪnərɪ] *adj* disciplinaire; **to take ~ action against sb** prendre des mesures disciplinaires contre qqn.

discipline ['dɪsɪplɪn] ◇ *n* discipline *f.* ◇ *vt* **-1.** [control] discipliner. **-2.** [punish] punir.

disciplined ['dɪsɪplɪnd] *adj* discipliné(e).

disc jockey *n* disc-jockey *m.*

disclaim [dɪs'kleɪm] *vt fml* nier.

disclaimer [dɪs'kleɪməʳ] *n* dénégation *f,* désaveu *m.*

disclose [dɪs'kləʊz] *vt* révéler, divulguer.

disclosure [dɪs'kləʊʒəʳ] *n* révélation *f,* divulgation *f.*

disco ['dɪskəʊ] (*pl* **-s**) (*abbr of* **discotheque**) *n* discothèque *f.*

discoloration [dɪs‚kʌlə'reɪʃn] *n* décoloration *f.*

discolour *Br,* **discolor** *Am* [dɪs'kʌləʳ] ◇ *vt* décolorer; [teeth] jaunir. ◇ *vi* se décolorer; [teeth] jaunir.

discoloured *Br*, **discolored** *Am* [dɪs'kʌləd] *adj* décoloré(e); [teeth] jauni(e).

discomfort [dɪs'kʌmfət] *n* **-1.** (*U*) [physical pain] douleur *f*; **to be in some ~** ne pas se sentir très bien; **to cause sb ~** gêner qqn. **-2.** (*U*) [anxiety, embarrassment] malaise *m*. **-3.** [uncomfortable condition] inconfort *m*.

disconcert [,dɪskən'sɜːt] *vt* déconcerter.

disconcerting [,dɪskən'sɜːtɪŋ] *adj* déconcertant(e).

disconnect [,dɪskə'nekt] *vt* **-1.** [detach] détacher. **-2.** [from gas, electricity - appliance] débrancher; [- house] couper. **-3.** TELEC couper.

disconnected [,dɪskə'nektɪd] *adj* [thoughts] sans suite; [events] sans rapport.

disconsolate [dɪs'kɒnsələt] *adj* inconsolable.

discontent [,dɪskən'tent] *n*: **~ (with)** mécontentement *m* (à propos de).

discontented [,dɪskən'tentɪd] *adj* mécontent(e).

discontentment [,dɪskən'tentmənt] *n*: **~ (with)** mécontentement *m* (à propos de).

discontinue [,dɪskən'tɪnjuː] *vt* cesser, interrompre.

discontinued line [,dɪskən'tɪnjuːd-] *n* COMM fin *f* de série.

discord ['dɪskɔːd] *n* **-1.** (*U*) [disagreement] discorde *f*, désaccord *m*. **-2.** MUS dissonance *f*.

discordant [dɪ'skɔːdənt] *adj* **-1.** [conflicting] discordant(e); [relationship] plein(e) de discordance. **-2.** MUS dissonant(e).

discotheque ['dɪskəʊtek] *n* discothèque *f*.

discount [*n* 'dɪskaʊnt, *vb Br* dɪs'kaʊnt, *Am* 'dɪskaʊnt] ◇ *n* remise *f*. ◇ *vt* [report, claim] ne pas tenir compte de.

discount house *n* **-1.** FIN maison *f* d'escompte. **-2.** [store] magasin *m* de vente au rabais.

discount rate *n* taux *m* d'escompte.

discount store *n* COMM magasin *m* de vente au rabais.

discourage [dɪ'skʌrɪdʒ] *vt* décourager; **to ~ sb from doing sthg** dissuader qqn de faire qqch.

discouraging [dɪ'skʌrɪdʒɪŋ] *adj* décourageant(e).

discourse ['dɪskɔːs] *n fml*: **~ (on)** discours *m* (sur).

discourteous [dɪs'kɜːtjəs] *adj* discourtois(e).

discourtesy [dɪs'kɜːtɪsɪ] *n* manque *m* de courtoisie.

discover [dɪ'skʌvəʳ] *vt* découvrir.

discoverer [dɪ'skʌvərəʳ] *n*: **the ~ of sthg** la personne qui a découvert qqch.

discovery [dɪ'skʌvərɪ] (*pl* **-ies**) *n* découverte *f*.

discredit [dɪs'kredɪt] ◇ *n* discrédit *m*. ◇ *vt* discréditer.

discredited [dɪs'kredɪtɪd] *adj* discrédité(e).

discreet [dɪ'skriːt] *adj* discret(ète).

discreetly [dɪ'skriːtlɪ] *adv* discrètement.

discrepancy [dɪ'skrepənsɪ] (*pl* **-ies**) *n*: **~ (in/between)** divergence *f* (entre).

discrete [dɪs'kriːt] *adj fml* séparé(e), bien distinct(e).

discretion [dɪ'skreʃn] *n* (*U*) **-1.** [tact] discrétion *f*. **-2.** [judgment] jugement *m*, discernement *m*; **use your own ~** à vous de juger; **at the ~ of** avec l'autorisation de.

discretionary [dɪ'skreʃnərɪ] *adj* discrétionnaire.

discriminate [dɪ'skrɪmɪneɪt] *vi* **-1.** [distinguish] différencier, distinguer; **to ~ between** faire la distinction entre. **-2.** [be prejudiced]: **to ~ against sb** faire de la discrimination envers qqn.

discriminating [dɪ'skrɪmɪneɪtɪŋ] *adj* avisé(e).

discrimination [dɪ,skrɪmɪ'neɪʃn] *n* **-1.** [prejudice] discrimination *f*. **-2.** [judgment] discernement *m*, jugement *m*.

discus ['dɪskəs] (*pl* **-es**) *n* disque *m*.

discuss [dɪ'skʌs] *vt* discuter (de); **to ~ sthg with sb** discuter de qqch avec qqn.

discussion [dɪ'skʌʃn] *n* discussion *f*; **under ~** en discussion.

disdain [dɪs'deɪn] ◇ *n*: **~ (for)** dédain *m* (pour). ◇ *vt* dédaigner; **to ~ to do sthg** dédaigner de faire qqch.

disdainful [dɪs'deɪnful] *adj* dédaigneux(euse).

disease [dɪ'ziːz] *n* **-1.** [illness] maladie *f*. **-2.** *fig* [unhealthy attitude, habit] mal *m*.

diseased [dɪ'ziːzd] *adj* [plant, body] malade.

disembark [,dɪsɪm'bɑːk] *vi* débarquer.

disembarkation [,dɪsembɑː'keɪʃn] *n* débarquement *m*.

disembodied [,dɪsɪm'bɒdɪd] *adj* désincarné(e).

disembowel [,dɪsɪm'baʊəl] (*Br pt* & *pp* **-led**, *cont* **-ling**, *Am pt* & *pp* **-ed**, *cont* **-ing**) *vt* éviscérer.

disenchanted [,dɪsɪn'tʃɑːntɪd] *adj*: **~ (with)** désenchanté(e) (de).

disenchantment [,dɪsɪn'tʃɑːntmənt] *n* désillusion *f*, désenchantement *m*.

disenfranchise [ˌdɪsɪnˈfræntʃaɪz] = **disfranchise**.

disengage [ˌdɪsɪnˈgeɪdʒ] vt **-1.** [release]: to ~ sthg (from) libérer OR dégager qqch (de); to ~ o.s. from se libérer OR se dégager de. **-2.** TECH déclencher; to ~ the gears débrayer.

disengagement [ˌdɪsɪnˈgeɪdʒmənt] n désengagement m.

disentangle [ˌdɪsɪnˈtæŋgl] vt: to ~ sthg from enlever qqch de; to ~ o.s. from se dégager de.

disfavour Br, **disfavor** Am [ˌdɪsˈfeɪvəʳ] n **-1.** [dislike, disapproval] désapprobation f. **-2.** [state of disapproval]: to be in ~ with sb être mal vu de qqn.

disfigure [dɪsˈfɪgəʳ] vt défigurer.

disfranchise [ˌdɪsˈfræntʃaɪz] vt priver du droit électoral.

disgorge [dɪsˈgɔːdʒ] vt **-1.** [from stomach] vomir. **-2.** [emit] déverser.

disgrace [dɪsˈgreɪs] ⬦ n **-1.** [shame] honte f; to bring ~ on sb jeter la honte sur qqn; in ~ en défaveur. **-2.** [cause of shame - thing] honte f, scandale m; [- person] honte f. ⬦ vt faire honte à; to ~ o.s. se couvrir de honte.

disgraceful [dɪsˈgreɪsful] adj honteux(euse), scandaleux(euse).

disgruntled [dɪsˈgrʌntld] adj mécontent(e).

disguise [dɪsˈgaɪz] ⬦ n déguisement m; in ~ déguisé(e). ⬦ vt **-1.** [person, voice] déguiser; to ~ o.s. as se déguiser en. **-2.** [hide - fact, feelings] dissimuler.

disgust [dɪsˈgʌst] ⬦ n: ~ **(at)** [behaviour, violence etc] dégoût m (pour); [decision] dégoût (devant); in ~ dégoûté(e), écœuré(e). ⬦ vt dégoûter, écœurer.

disgusting [dɪsˈgʌstɪŋ] adj dégoûtant(e).

dish [dɪʃ] n plat m; Am [plate] assiette f.
◆ **dishes** npl vaisselle f; to do OR wash the ~es faire la vaisselle.
◆ **dish out** vt sep inf distribuer.
◆ **dish up** vt sep inf servir.

dish aerial Br, **dish antenna** Am n antenne f parabolique.

disharmony [ˌdɪsˈhɑːmənɪ] n désaccord m, mésentente f.

dishcloth [ˈdɪʃklɒθ] n lavette f.

disheartened [dɪsˈhɑːtnd] adj découragé(e).

disheartening [dɪsˈhɑːtnɪŋ] adj décourageant(e).

dishevelled Br, **disheveled** Am [diˈʃevəld] adj [person] échevelé(e); [hair] en désordre.

dishonest [dɪsˈɒnɪst] adj malhonnête.

dishonesty [dɪsˈɒnɪstɪ] n malhonnêteté f.

dishonorable Am = dishonourable.

dishonour Br, **dishonor** Am [dɪsˈɒnəʳ] ⬦ n déshonneur m. ⬦ vt déshonorer.

dishonourable Br, **dishonorable** Am [dɪsˈɒnərəbl] adj [person] peu honorable; [behaviour] déshonorant(e).

dish soap n Am liquide m pour la vaisselle.

dish towel n Am torchon m.

dishwasher [ˈdɪʃˌwɒʃəʳ] n [machine] lave-vaisselle m inv.

dishy [ˈdɪʃɪ] (compar **-ier**, superl **-iest**) adj Br inf mignon(onne), sexy (inv).

disillusioned [ˌdɪsɪˈluːʒnd] adj désillusionné(e), désenchanté(e); to become ~ perdre ses illusions; to be ~ with ne plus avoir d'illusions sur.

disillusionment [ˌdɪsɪˈluːʒnmənt] n: ~ **(with)** désillusion f OR désenchantement m (en ce qui concerne).

disincentive [ˌdɪsɪnˈsentɪv] n: to be a ~ avoir un effet dissuasif; [in work context] être démotivant(e).

disinclined [ˌdɪsɪnˈklaɪnd] adj: to be ~ to do sthg être peu disposé(e) à faire qqch.

disinfect [ˌdɪsɪnˈfekt] vt désinfecter.

disinfectant [ˌdɪsɪnˈfektənt] n désinfectant m.

disinformation [ˌdɪsɪnfəˈmeɪʃn] n désinformation f.

disingenuous [ˌdɪsɪnˈdʒenjuəs] adj peu sincère.

disinherit [ˌdɪsɪnˈherɪt] vt déshériter.

disintegrate [dɪsˈɪntɪgreɪt] vi **-1.** [object] se désintégrer, se désagréger. **-2.** fig [project] s'écrouler; [marriage] se désagréger.

disintegration [dɪsˌɪntɪˈgreɪʃn] n **-1.** [of object] désintégration f, désagrégation f. **-2.** fig [of project, marriage] effondrement m.

disinterested [ˌdɪsˈɪntrəstɪd] adj **-1.** [objective] désintéressé(e). **-2.** inf [uninterested]: ~ **(in)** indifférent(e) (à).

disinvestment [ˌdɪsɪnˈvestmənt] n désinvestissement m.

disjointed [dɪsˈdʒɔɪntɪd] adj décousu(e).

disk [dɪsk] n **-1.** COMPUT disque m, disquette f. **-2.** Am = **disc**.

disk drive Br, **diskette drive** Am n COMPUT lecteur m de disques OR de disquettes.

diskette [dɪskˈet] n COMPUT disquette f.

diskette drive n Am = disk drive.

disk operating system [-ˌɒpəreɪtɪŋ-] n COMPUT système m d'exploitation (à disques).

dislike [dɪsˈlaɪk] ⬦ n: ~ **(of)** aversion f (pour); her likes and ~s ce qu'elle aime et ce qu'elle n'aime pas; to take a ~ to sb/

sthg prendre qqn/qqch en grippe. ◇ *vt* ne pas aimer.

dislocate ['dısləkeıt] *vt* **-1.** MED se démettre. **-2.** [disrupt] désorganiser.

dislodge [dıs'lodʒ] *vt*: **to ~ sthg (from)** déplacer qqch (de); [free] décoincer qqch (de); **to ~ sb from a position** déloger qqn d'un poste.

disloyal [,dıs'lɔıəl] *adj*: **~ (to)** déloyal(e) (envers).

dismal ['dızml] *adj* **-1.** [gloomy, depressing] lugubre. **-2.** [unsuccessful - attempt] infructueux(euse); [- failure] lamentable.

dismantle [dıs'mæntl] *vt* démanteler.

dismay [dıs'meı] ◇ *n* consternation *f*; **to sb's ~** à la consternation de qqn. ◇ *vt* consterner.

dismember [dıs'membər] *vt* démembrer.

dismiss [dıs'mıs] *vt* **-1.** [from job]: **to ~ sb (from)** congédier qqn (de). **-2.** [refuse to take seriously - idea, person] écarter; [- plan, challenge] rejeter. **-3.** [allow to leave - class] laisser sortir; [- troops] faire rompre les rangs à.

dismissal [dıs'mısl] *n* **-1.** [from job] licenciement *m*, renvoi *m*. **-2.** [refusal to take seriously] rejet *m*.

dismissive [dıs'mısıv] *adj* méprisant(e); **to be ~ of** ne faire aucun cas de.

dismount [,dıs'maʊnt] *vi*: **to ~ (from)** descendre (de).

disobedience [,dısə'biːdjəns] *n* désobéissance *f*.

disobedient [,dısə'biːdjənt] *adj* désobéissant(e).

disobey [,dısə'beı] ◇ *vt* désobéir à. ◇ *vi* désobéir.

disorder [dıs'ɔːdər] *n* **-1.** [disarray]: **in ~** en désordre. **-2.** (*U*) [rioting] troubles *mpl*. **-3.** MED trouble *m*.

disordered [dıs'ɔːdəd] *adj* **-1.** [in disarray] en désordre. **-2.** MED: **mentally ~** déséquilibré(e).

disorderly [dıs'ɔːdəlı] *adj* **-1.** [untidy - room] en désordre; [- appearance] désordonné(e). **-2.** [unruly] indiscipliné(e).

disorderly conduct *n* JUR trouble *m* de l'ordre public.

disorganized, **-ised** [dıs'ɔːgənaızd] *adj* [person] désordonné(e), brouillon(onne); [system] mal conçu(e).

disorientated [dıs'ɔːrıənteıtıd] *Br*, **disoriented** [dıs'ɔːrıəntıd] *Am adj* désorienté(e).

disown [dıs'əʊn] *vt* désavouer.

disparage [dı'spærıdʒ] *vt* dénigrer.

disparaging [dı'spærıdʒıŋ] *adj* désobligeant(e).

disparate ['dıspərət] *adj* disparate.

disparity [dı'spærətı] (*pl* **-ies**) *n*: **~ (between** OR **in)** disparité *f* (entre).

dispassionate [dı'spæʃnət] *adj* impartial(e).

dispatch [dı'spætʃ] ◇ *n* [message] dépêche *f*. ◇ *vt* [send] envoyer, expédier.

dispatch box *n Br* POL [box] valise *f* officielle; [in House of Commons] *tribune d'où parlent les membres du gouvernement et leurs homologues du cabinet fantôme.*

dispatch rider *n* MIL estafette *f*; [courier] coursier *m*.

dispel [dı'spel] (*pt* & *pp* **-led**, *cont* **-ling**) *vt* [feeling] dissiper, chasser.

dispensable [dı'spensəbl] *adj* [person] dont on peut se passer; [expenses, luxury] superflu(e).

dispensary [dı'spensərı] (*pl* **-ies**) *n* officine *f*.

dispensation [,dıspen'seıʃn] *n* [permission] dispense *f*.

dispense [dı'spens] *vt* [justice, medicine] administrer.

◆ **dispense with** *vt fus* **-1.** [do without] se passer de. **-2.** [make unnecessary] rendre superflu(e); **to ~ with the need for sthg** rendre qqch superflu.

dispenser [dı'spensər] *n* distributeur *m*.

dispensing chemist *Br*, **dispensing pharmacist** *Am* [dı'spensıŋ-] *n* pharmacien *m*, -ienne *f*.

dispersal [dı'spɜːsl] *n* dispersion *f*.

disperse [dı'spɜːs] ◇ *vt* **-1.** [crowd] disperser. **-2.** [knowledge, news] répandre, propager. ◇ *vi* se disperser.

dispirited [dı'spırıtıd] *adj* découragé(e), abattu(e).

dispiriting [dı'spırıtıŋ] *adj* décourageant(e).

displace [dıs'pleıs] *vt* **-1.** [cause to move] déplacer. **-2.** [supplant] supplanter.

displaced person [dıs'pleıst-] *n* personne *f* déplacée.

displacement [dıs'pleısmənt] *n* déplacement *m*.

display [dı'spleı] ◇ *n* **-1.** [arrangement] exposition *f*; **on ~** exposé. **-2.** [demonstration] manifestation *f*. **-3.** [public event] spectacle *m*. **-4.** [COMPUT - device] écran *m*; [- information displayed] affichage *m*, visualisation *f*. ◇ *vt* **-1.** [arrange] exposer. **-2.** [show] faire preuve de, montrer.

display advertising *n* (*U*) placards *mpl* publicitaires.

displease [dɪs'pliːz] *vt* déplaire à, mécontenter; **to be ~d with** être mécontent(e) de.

displeasure [dɪs'pleʒəʳ] *n* mécontentement *m*.

disposable [dɪ'spəʊzəbl] *adj* **-1.** [throwaway] jetable. **-2.** [income] disponible.

disposal [dɪ'spəʊzl] *n* **-1.** [removal] enlèvement *m*. **-2.** [availability]: **at sb's ~** à la disposition de qqn.

dispose [dɪ'spəʊz]
◆ **dispose of** *vt fus* [get rid of] se débarrasser de; [problem] résoudre.

disposed [dɪ'spəʊzd] *adj* **-1.** [willing]: **to be ~ to do sthg** être disposé(e) à faire qqch. **-2.** [friendly]: **to be well ~ to** OR **towards sb** être bien disposé(e) envers qqn.

disposition [,dɪspə'zɪʃn] *n* **-1.** [temperament] caractère *m*, tempérament *m*. **-2.** [tendency]: **~ to do sthg** tendance *f* à faire qqch.

dispossess [,dɪspə'zes] *vt fml*: **to ~ sb of sthg** déposséder qqn de qqch.

disproportion [,dɪsprə'pɔːʃn] *n* disproportion *f*.

disproportionate [,dɪsprə'pɔːʃnət] *adj*: **~ (to)** disproportionné(e) (à).

disprove [,dɪs'pruːv] *vt* réfuter.

dispute [dɪ'spjuːt] ◇ *n* **-1.** [quarrel] dispute *f*. **-2.** (U) [disagreement] désaccord *m*; **in ~** [people] en désaccord; [matter] en discussion. **-3.** INDUSTRY conflit *m*. ◇ *vt* contester.

disqualification [dɪs,kwɒlɪfɪ'keɪʃn] *n* disqualification *f*.

disqualify [,dɪs'kwɒlɪfaɪ] (*pt* & *pp* **-ied**) *vt* **-1.** [subj: authority]: **to ~ sb (from doing sthg)** interdire à qqn (de faire qqch); **to ~ sb from driving** *Br* retirer le permis de conduire à qqn. **-2.** [subj: illness, criminal record]: **to ~ sb (from doing sthg)** rendre qqn incapable (de faire qqch). **-3.** SPORT disqualifier.

disquiet [dɪs'kwaɪət] *n* inquiétude *f*.

disregard [,dɪsrɪ'gɑːd] ◇ *n* (U): **~ (for)** [money, danger] mépris *m* (pour); [feelings] indifférence *f* (à). ◇ *vt* [fact] ignorer; [danger] mépriser; [warning] ne pas tenir compte de.

disrepair [,dɪsrɪ'peəʳ] *n* délabrement *m*; **to fall into ~** tomber en ruines.

disreputable [dɪs'repjʊtəbl] *adj* peu respectable.

disrepute [,dɪsrɪ'pjuːt] *n*: **to bring sthg into ~** discréditer qqch; **to fall into ~** acquérir une mauvaise réputation.

disrespectful [,dɪsrɪ'spektfʊl] *adj* irrespectueux(euse).

disrupt [dɪs'rʌpt] *vt* perturber.

disruption [dɪs'rʌpʃn] *n* perturbation *f*.

disruptive [dɪs'rʌptɪv] *adj* perturbateur(trice).

dissatisfaction ['dɪs,sætɪs'fækʃn] *n* mécontentement *m*.

dissatisfied [,dɪs'sætɪsfaɪd] *adj*: **~ (with)** mécontent(e) (de), pas satisfait(e) (de).

dissect [dɪ'sekt] *vt lit* & *fig* disséquer.

dissection [dɪ'sekʃn] *n lit* & *fig* dissection *f*.

disseminate [dɪ'semɪneɪt] *vt* disséminer.

dissemination [dɪ,semɪ'neɪʃn] *n* dissémination *f*.

dissension [dɪ'senʃn] *n* discorde *f*, dissension *f*.

dissent [dɪ'sent] ◇ *n* dissentiment *m*. ◇ *vi*: **to ~ (from)** être en désaccord (avec).

dissenter [dɪ'sentəʳ] *n* dissident *m*, -e *f*.

dissenting [dɪ'sentɪŋ] *adj*: **~ voice** opinion *f* contraire.

dissertation [,dɪsə'teɪʃn] *n* dissertation *f*.

disservice [,dɪs'sɜːvɪs] *n*: **to do sb a ~** rendre un mauvais service à qqn.

dissident ['dɪsɪdənt] *n* dissident *m*, -e *f*.

dissimilar [,dɪ'sɪmɪləʳ] *adj*: **~ (to)** différent(e) (de).

dissipate ['dɪsɪpeɪt] ◇ *vt* **-1.** [heat] dissiper. **-2.** [efforts, money] gaspiller. ◇ *vi* se dissiper.

dissipated ['dɪsɪpeɪtɪd] *adj* [person, life] dissolu(e).

dissociate [dɪ'səʊʃɪeɪt] *vt* dissocier; **to ~ o.s. from** se désolidariser de.

dissolute ['dɪsəluːt] *adj* dissolu(e).

dissolution [,dɪsə'luːʃn] *n* dissolution *f*.

dissolve [dɪ'zɒlv] ◇ *vt* dissoudre. ◇ *vi* **-1.** [substance] se dissoudre. **-2.** *fig* [disappear] disparaître.
◆ **dissolve in(to)** *vt fus*: **to ~ into tears** fondre en larmes.

dissuade [dɪ'sweɪd] *vt*: **to ~ sb (from)** dissuader qqn (de).

distance ['dɪstəns] ◇ *n* distance *f*; **at a ~** assez loin; **from a ~** de loin; **in the ~** au loin. ◇ *vt*: **to ~ o.s. from** se distancier de.

distant ['dɪstənt] *adj* **-1.** [gen]: **~ (from)** éloigné(e) (de). **-2.** [reserved - person, manner] distant(e).

distaste [dɪs'teɪst] *n*: **~ (for)** dégoût *m* (pour).

distasteful [dɪs'teɪstfʊl] *adj* répugnant(e), déplaisant(e).

Dist. Atty *abbr of* **district attorney**.

distemper [dɪ'stempəʳ] *n* (U) **-1.** [paint] détrempe *f*. **-2.** [disease] maladie *f* de Carré.

distended [dɪ'stendɪd] *adj* [stomach] distendu(e).

distil *Br* (*pt* & *pp* **-led**, *cont* **-ling**), **distill** *Am* [dɪ'stɪl] *vt* **-1.** [liquid] distiller. **-2.** *fig* [information] tirer.

distiller [dɪ'stɪlə'] *n* distillateur *m*.

distillery [dɪ'stɪlərɪ] (*pl* **-ies**) *n* distillerie *f*.

distinct [dɪ'stɪŋkt] *adj* **-1.** [different]: ~ (**from**) distinct(e) (de), différent(e) (de); **as** ~ **from** par opposition à. **-2.** [definite - improvement] net (nette); **a** ~ **possibility** une forte chance.

distinction [dɪ'stɪŋʃn] *n* **-1.** [difference] distinction *f*, différence *f*; **to draw** OR **make a** ~ **between** faire une distinction entre. **-2.** (*U*) [excellence] distinction *f*. **-3.** [exam result] mention *f* très bien.

distinctive [dɪ'stɪŋktɪv] *adj* caractéristique.

distinctly [dɪ'stɪŋklɪ] *adv* [see, remember] clairement.

distinguish [dɪ'stɪŋgwɪʃ] *vt* **-1.** [tell apart]: **to** ~ **sthg from sthg** distinguer qqch de qqch, faire la différence entre qqch et qqch. **-2.** [perceive] distinguer. **-3.** [characterize] caractériser. **-4.** [excel]: **to** ~ **o.s.** se distinguer.

distinguished [dɪ'stɪŋgwɪʃt] *adj* distingué(e).

distinguishing [dɪ'stɪŋgwɪʃɪŋ] *adj* [feature, mark] caractéristique.

distort [dɪ'stɔːt] *vt* déformer.

distorted [dɪ'stɔːtɪd] *adj* déformé(e).

distortion [dɪ'stɔːʃn] *n* déformation *f*.

distract [dɪ'strækt] *vt*: **to** ~ **sb (from)** distraire qqn (de).

distracted [dɪ'stræktɪd] *adj* [preoccupied] soucieux(ieuse).

distraction [dɪ'strækʃn] *n* **-1.** [interruption, diversion] distraction *f*. **-2.** [state of mind] confusion *f*; **to drive sb to** ~ rendre qqn fou.

distraught [dɪ'strɔːt] *adj* éperdu(e).

distress [dɪ'stres] ◇ *n* [anxiety] détresse *f*; [pain] douleur *f*, souffrance *f*. ◇ *vt* affliger.

distressed [dɪ'strest] *adj* [anxious, upset] affligé(e).

distressing [dɪ'stresɪŋ] *adj* [news, image] pénible.

distress signal *n* signal *m* de détresse.

distribute [dɪ'strɪbjuːt] *vt* **-1.** [gen] distribuer. **-2.** [spread out] répartir.

distribution [ˌdɪstrɪ'bjuːʃn] *n* **-1.** [gen] distribution *f*. **-2.** [spreading out] répartition *f*.

distributor [dɪ'strɪbjuːtə'] *n* AUT & COMM distributeur *m*.

district ['dɪstrɪkt] *n* **-1.** [region, area] région *f*. **-2.** ADMIN district *m*.

district attorney *n Am* ≃ procureur *m* de la République.

district council *n Br* ≃ conseil *m* général.

district nurse *n Br* infirmière *f* visiteuse OR à domicile.

District of Columbia *n* district *m* de Columbia; **in the** ~ dans le district de Columbia.

distrust [dɪs'trʌst] ◇ *n* méfiance *f*. ◇ *vt* se méfier de.

distrustful [dɪs'trʌstful] *adj* méfiant(e).

disturb [dɪ'stɜːb] *vt* **-1.** [interrupt] déranger. **-2.** [upset, worry] inquiéter. **-3.** [sleep, surface] troubler.

disturbance [dɪ'stɜːbəns] *n* **-1.** POL troubles *mpl*; [fight] tapage *m*; ~ **of the peace** JUR trouble *m* de l'ordre public. **-2.** [interruption] dérangement *m*. **-3.** [of mind, emotions] trouble *m*.

disturbed [dɪ'stɜːbd] *adj* **-1.** [emotionally, mentally] perturbé(e). **-2.** [worried] inquiet(iète).

disturbing [dɪ'stɜːbɪŋ] *adj* [image] bouleversant(e); [news] inquiétant(e).

disunity [ˌdɪs'juːnətɪ] *n* désunion *f*.

disuse [ˌdɪs'juːs] *n*: **to fall into** ~ [factory] être à l'abandon; [regulation] tomber en désuétude.

disused [ˌdɪs'juːzd] *adj* désaffecté(e).

ditch [dɪtʃ] ◇ *n* fossé *m*. ◇ *vt inf* [boyfriend, girlfriend] plaquer; [old car, clothes] se débarrasser de; [plan] abandonner.

dither ['dɪðə'] *vi* hésiter.

ditto ['dɪtəʊ] *adv* idem.

diuretic [ˌdaɪjʊ'retɪk] *n* diurétique *m*.

diva ['diːvə] (*pl* **-s**) *n* diva *f*.

divan [dɪ'væn] *n* divan *m*.

divan bed *n* divan-lit *m*.

dive [daɪv] (*Br pt* & *pp* **-d**, *Am pt* & *pp* **-d** OR **dove**) ◇ *vi* plonger; [bird, plane] piquer; **she** ~**d into the crowd** elle se jeta dans la foule. ◇ *n* **-1.** [gen] plongeon *m*. **-2.** [of plane] piqué *m*. **-3.** *inf pej* [bar, restaurant] bouge *m*.

dive-bomb *vt* bombarder en piqué.

diver ['daɪvə'] *n* plongeur *m*, -euse *f*.

diverge [daɪ'vɜːdʒ] *vi*: **to** ~ **(from)** diverger (de).

divergence [daɪ'vɜːdʒəns] *n* divergence *f*.

divergent [daɪ'vɜːdʒənt] *adj* divergent(e).

diverse [daɪ'vɜːs] *adj* divers(e).

diversification [daɪˌvɜːsɪfɪ'keɪʃn] *n* diversification *f*.

diversify [daɪ'vɜːsɪfaɪ] (*pt* & *pp* **-ied**) ◇ *vt* diversifier. ◇ *vi* se diversifier.

diversion [daɪ'vɜːʃn] *n* **-1.** [amusement] distraction *f*; [tactical] diversion *f*. **-2.** [of traffic] déviation *f*. **-3.** [of river, funds] détournement *m*.

diversionary [daɪ'vɜːʃnrɪ] *adj* [tactics] de diversion.

diversity [daɪ'vɜːsətɪ] *n* diversité *f*.

divert [daɪ'vɜːt] *vt* **-1.** [traffic] dévier. **-2.** [river, funds] détourner. **-3.** [person - amuse] distraire; [- tactically] détourner.

divest [daɪ'vest] *vt fml*: **to ~ sb of** dépouiller qqn de; **to ~ o.s. of** se défaire de.

divide [dɪ'vaɪd] ◇ *vt* **-1.** [separate] séparer. **-2.** [share out] diviser, partager; **to ~ sthg between** OR **among** partager qqch entre. **-3.** [split up]: **to ~ sthg (into)** diviser qqch (en). **-4.** MATH: **89 ~d by 3** 89 divisé par 3. **-5.** [people - in disagreement] diviser. ◇ *vi* se diviser. ◇ *n* [difference] division *f*.
◆ **divide up** *vt sep* **-1.** [split up] diviser. **-2.** [share out] partager.

divided [dɪ'vaɪdɪd] *adj* [nation] divisé(e); [opinions, loyalties] partagé(e).

dividend ['dɪvɪdend] *n* dividende *m*; **to pay ~s** *fig* porter ses fruits.

dividers [dɪ'vaɪdəz] *npl* compas *m* à pointes sèches.

dividing line [dɪ'vaɪdɪŋ-] *n* ligne *f* de démarcation.

divine [dɪ'vaɪn] ◇ *adj* divin(e). ◇ *vt* **-1.** [truth, meaning] deviner; [future] prédire. **-2.** [water] découvrir, détecter.

diving ['daɪvɪŋ] *n* (*U*) plongeon *m*; [with breathing apparatus] plongée *f* (sous-marine).

divingboard ['daɪvɪŋbɔːd] *n* plongeoir *m*.

diving suit *n* combinaison *f* de plongée.

divinity [dɪ'vɪnətɪ] (*pl* **-ies**) *n* **-1.** [godliness, god] divinité *f*. **-2.** [study] théologie *f*.

divisible [dɪ'vɪzəbl] *adj*: **~ (by)** divisible (par).

division [dɪ'vɪʒn] *n* **-1.** [gen] division *f*. **-2.** [separation] séparation *f*.

division sign *n* signe *m* de division.

divisive [dɪ'vaɪsɪv] *adj* qui sème la division OR la discorde.

divorce [dɪ'vɔːs] ◇ *n* divorce *m*. ◇ *vt* **-1.** [husband, wife] divorcer. **-2.** [separate]: **to ~ sthg from** séparer qqch de.

divorced [dɪ'vɔːst] *adj* divorcé(e).

divorcee [dɪvɔː'siː] *n* divorcé *m*, -e *f*.

divulge [daɪ'vʌldʒ] *vt* divulguer.

DIY (*abbr of* **do-it-yourself**) *n Br* bricolage *m*.

dizziness ['dɪzɪnɪs] *n* vertige *m*.

dizzy ['dɪzɪ] (*compar* **-ier**, *superl* **-iest**) *adj* **-1.** [giddy]: **to feel ~** avoir la tête qui tourne. **-2.** *fig* [height] vertigineux(euse).

DJ *n* **-1.** (*abbr of* **disc jockey**) disc-jockey *m*. **-2.** (*abbr of* **dinner jacket**) smoking *m*.

Djakarta [dʒə'kɑːtə] → **Jakarta**.

DJIA (*abbr of* **Dow Jones Industrial Average**) *n Am indice* Dow Jones.

Djibouti [dʒɪ'buːtɪ] *n* Djibouti *m*; **in ~** au Djibouti.

dl (*abbr of* **decilitre**) dl.

DLit(t) ['diː'lɪt] (*abbr of* **Doctor of Letters**) *n docteur ès lettres*.

DLO (*abbr of* **dead-letter office**) *n centre de recherche du courrier*.

dm (*abbr of* **decimetre**) dm.

DM (*abbr of* **Deutsche Mark**) DM.

DMA (*abbr of* **direct memory access**) *n accès direct à la mémoire*.

DMus ['diː'mʌz] (*abbr of* **Doctor of Music**) *n docteur en musique*.

DMZ (*abbr of* **demilitarized zone**) *n zone démilitarisée*.

DNA (*abbr of* **deoxyribonucleic acid**) *n* ADN *m*.

D-notice *n Br* censure imposée à la presse pour sécurité d'État.

do¹ [duː] (*pt* **did**, *pp* **done**, *pl* **dos** OR **do's**) ◇ *aux vb* **-1.** (*in negatives*): **don't leave it there** ne le laisse pas là; **I didn't want to see him** je ne voulais pas le voir. **-2.** (*in questions*): **what did he want?** qu'est-ce qu'il voulait?; **~ you think she'll come?** tu crois qu'elle viendra? **-3.** (*referring back to previous verb*): **she reads more than I ~** elle lit plus que moi; **I like reading — so ~ I** j'aime lire — moi aussi. **-4.** (*in question tags*): **you know her, don't you?** tu la connais, n'est-ce pas?; **I upset you, didn't I?** je t'ai fait de la peine, n'est-ce pas?; **so you think you can dance, ~ you?** alors tu t'imagines que tu sais danser, c'est ça? **-5.** [for emphasis]: **I did tell you but you've forgotten** je te l'avais bien dit, mais tu l'as oublié; **~ come in** entrez donc.
◇ *vt* **-1.** [perform an activity, a service] faire; **to ~ aerobics/gymnastics** faire de l'aérobic/de la gymnastique; **they ~ gourmet dinners** ils font OR préparent des repas gastronomiques; **to ~ the cooking/housework** faire la cuisine/le ménage; **to ~ one's hair** se coiffer; **to ~ one's teeth** se laver OR se brosser les dents. **-2.** [take action] faire; **to ~ something about sthg** trouver une solution pour qqch; **I don't know what to ~ with him!** je ne sais vraiment

pas que faire de lui! **-3.** [have particular effect] faire; **to ~ more harm than good** faire plus de mal que de bien. **-4.** [referring to job]: **what do you ~?** qu'est-ce que vous faites dans la vie? **-5.** [study] faire; **I did physics at school** j'ai fait de la physique à l'école. **-6.** [travel at a particular speed] faire, rouler; **the car can ~ 110 mph** ≃ la voiture peut faire du 180 à l'heure. **-7.** [be good enough for]: **that'll ~ me nicely** cela m'ira très bien, cela fera très bien mon affaire.
◇ *vi* **-1.** [act] faire; **~ as I tell you** fais comme je te dis; **you would ~ well to reconsider** tu ferais bien de reconsidérer la question. **-2.** [perform in a particular way]: **they're ~ing really well** leurs affaires marchent bien; **he could ~ better** il pourrait mieux faire; **how did you ~ in the exam?** comment ça a marché à l'examen? **-3.** [be good enough, be sufficient] suffire, aller; **will £6 ~?** est-ce que 6 livres suffiront?, 6 livres, ça ira?; **that will ~** ça suffit.
◇ *n* [party] fête *f*, soirée *f*.
◆ **dos** *npl*: **~s and don'ts** ce qu'il faut faire et ne pas faire.
◆ **do away with** *vt fus* supprimer.
◆ **do down** *vt sep inf* dire du mal de.
◆ **do for** *vt fus inf*: **these kids will ~ for me** ces gosses vont me tuer; **I'm done for** je suis fichu OR foutu.
◆ **do in** *vt sep inf* supprimer, assassiner.
◆ **do out of** *vt sep inf*: **to ~ sb out of sthg** escroquer OR carotter qqch à qqn.
◆ **do up** *vt sep* **-1.** [fasten - shoelaces, shoes] attacher; [- buttons, coat] boutonner; **your shirt's not done up** ta chemise est déboutonnée. **-2.** [decorate - room, house] refaire. **-3.** [wrap up] emballer.
◆ **do with** *vt fus* **-1.** [need] avoir besoin de. **-2.** [have connection with]: **that has nothing to ~ with it** ça n'a rien à voir, ça n'a aucun rapport; **what's that got to ~ with it?** et alors, quel rapport?, qu'est-ce que ça a à voir?; **I had nothing to ~ with it** je n'y étais pour rien.
◆ **do without** ◇ *vt fus* se passer de. ◇ *vi* s'en passer.

do[2] (*abbr of* ditto) do.

DOA (*abbr of* dead on arrival) *adj* mort(e) pendant son transport à l'hôpital.

doable ['duːəbl] *adj inf* faisable.

dob *abbr of* date of birth.

Doberman ['dəubəmən] (*pl* **-s**) *n*: **~ (pinscher)** doberman *m*.

docile [*Br* 'dəusaɪl, *Am* 'dɒsəl] *adj* docile.

dock [dɒk] ◇ *n* **-1.** [in harbour] docks *mpl*. **-2.** JUR banc *m* des accusés. ◇ *vt* [wages] faire une retenue sur. ◇ *vi* [ship] arriver à quai.

docker ['dɒkər] *n* docker *m*.

docket ['dɒkɪt] *n Br* fiche *f* (descriptive).

docklands ['dɒkləndz] *npl Br* docks *mpl*.

dockworker ['dɒkwɜːkər] = **docker**.

dockyard ['dɒkjɑːd] *n* chantier *m* naval.

doctor ['dɒktər] ◇ *n* **-1.** MED docteur *m*, médecin *m*; **to go to the ~'s** aller chez le docteur. **-2.** UNIV docteur *m*. ◇ *vt* **-1.** [results, report] falsifier; [text, food] altérer. **-2.** *Br* [cat] châtrer.

doctorate ['dɒktərət], **doctor's degree** *n* doctorat *m*.

doctrinaire [,dɒktrɪ'neər] *adj* doctrinaire.

doctrine ['dɒktrɪn] *n* doctrine *f*.

docudrama [,dɒkju'drɑːmə] (*pl* **-s**) *n* docudrame *m*.

document [*n* 'dɒkjumənt, *vt* 'dɒkjument] ◇ *n* document *m*. ◇ *vt* documenter.

documentary [,dɒkju'mentərɪ] (*pl* **-ies**) ◇ *adj* documentaire. ◇ *n* documentaire *m*.

documentation [,dɒkjumen'teɪʃn] *n* documentation *f*.

DOD (*abbr of* Department of Defense) *n* ministère américain de la défense.

doddering ['dɒdərɪŋ], **doddery** ['dɒdərɪ] *adj inf* branlant(e).

doddle ['dɒdl] *n Br inf*: **it was a ~** c'était du gâteau.

Dodecanese [,dəudɪkə'niːz] *npl*: **the ~** le Dodécanèse; **in the ~** dans le Dodécanèse.

dodge [dɒdʒ] ◇ *n inf* combine *f*. ◇ *vt* éviter, esquiver. ◇ *vi* s'esquiver.

dodgems ['dɒdʒəmz] *npl Br* autos *fpl* tamponneuses.

dodgy ['dɒdʒɪ] *adj Br inf* [plan, deal] douteux(euse).

doe [dəu] *n* **-1.** [deer] biche *f*. **-2.** [rabbit] lapine *f*.

DOE *n* **-1.** (*abbr of* Department of the Environment) *ministère britannique de l'environnement*. **-2.** (*abbr of* Department of Energy) *ministère américain de l'énergie*.

doer ['duːər] *n inf* personne *f* dynamique.

does [weak form dəz, strong form dʌz] → **do**.

doesn't ['dʌznt] = **does not**.

dog [dɒg] (*pt* & *pp* **-ged**, *cont* **-ging**) ◇ *n* **-1.** [animal] chien *m*, chienne *f*; **it's a ~'s life** c'est une vie de chien; **this country is going to the ~s** *inf* ce pays va à vau-l'eau. **-2.** *Am* [hot dog] hot dog *m*. ◇ *vt* **-1.** [subj: person - follow] suivre de près. **-2.** [subj: problems, bad luck] poursuivre.

dog biscuit *n* biscuit *m* pour chien.

dog collar n **-1.** [of dog] collier m de chien.
-2. [of priest] col m d'ecclésiastique.

dog-eared [-ɪəd] adj écorné(e).

dog-eat-dog adj: it's ~ c'est la loi de la jungle.

dog-end n inf [of cigarette] mégot m.

dogfight ['dɒgfaɪt] n **-1.** [between dogs] combat m de chiens. **-2.** [between aircraft] combat m aérien.

dog food n nourriture f pour chiens.

dogged ['dɒgɪd] adj opiniâtre.

doggone ['dɒgɒn], **doggoned** ['dɒgɒnd] adj Am inf fichu(e).

doggy ['dɒgɪ] (pl **-ies**) n toutou m.

doggy bag n sac en plastique pour emporter les restes d'un repas.

dogma ['dɒgmə] n dogme m.

dogmatic [dɒg'mætɪk] adj dogmatique.

do-gooder [-'gudər] n pej bonne âme f.

dog paddle n nage f du chien.

dogsbody ['dɒgz,bɒdɪ] (pl **-ies**) n Br inf [woman] bonne f à tout faire; [man] factotum m.

dog tag n plaque f d'identification.

doing ['duːɪŋ] n: is this your ~? c'est toi qui est cause de cela?
◆ **doings** npl actions fpl.

do-it-yourself n (U) bricolage m.

doldrums ['dɒldrəmz] npl: to be in the ~ fig être dans le marasme.

dole [dəul] n Br [unemployment benefit] allocation f de chômage; to be on the ~ être au chômage.
◆ **dole out** vt sep [food, money] distribuer au compte-gouttes.

doleful ['dəulful] adj morne.

doll [dɒl] n poupée f.

dollar ['dɒlər] n dollar m.

dolled up [dɒld-] adj inf pomponné(e).

dollhouse Am = **doll's house**.

dollop ['dɒləp] n inf bonne cuillerée f.

doll's house Br, **dollhouse** [dɒlhaus] Am n maison f de poupée.

dolly ['dɒlɪ] (pl **-ies**) n **-1.** [doll] poupée f. **-2.** [for TV or film camera] travelling m.

dolly bird n Br inf dated poupée f.

Dolomites ['dɒləmaɪts] npl: the ~ les Dolomites fpl.

dolphin ['dɒlfɪn] n dauphin m.

domain [də'meɪn] n lit & fig domaine m.

dome [dəum] n dôme m.

domestic [də'mestɪk] ◇ adj **-1.** [policy, politics, flight] intérieur(e). **-2.** [chores, animal] domestique. **-3.** [home-loving] casanier(ière).
◇ n domestique mf.

domestic appliance n appareil m ménager.

domesticated [də'mestɪkeɪtɪd] adj **-1.** [animal] domestiqué(e). **-2.** hum [person] popote (inv).

domesticity [,dəume'stɪsətɪ] n (U) vie f de famille.

domicile ['dɒmɪsaɪl] n domicile m.

dominance ['dɒmɪnəns] n prédominance f; [of person] supériorité f.

dominant ['dɒmɪnənt] adj dominant(e); [personality, group] dominateur(trice).

dominate ['dɒmɪneɪt] vt dominer.

dominating ['dɒmɪneɪtɪŋ] adj [person] dominateur(trice).

domination [,dɒmɪ'neɪʃn] n domination f.

domineering [,dɒmɪ'nɪərɪŋ] adj autoritaire.

Dominica [də'mɪnɪkə] n la Dominique; in ~ à la Dominique.

Dominican Republic [də'mɪnɪkən-] n: the ~ la République Dominicaine; in the ~ en République Dominicaine.

dominion [də'mɪnjən] n **-1.** (U) [power] domination f. **-2.** [land] territoire m.

domino [dɒ'mɪnəu] (pl **-es**) n domino m.
◆ **dominoes** npl dominos mpl.

domino effect n réaction f en chaîne.

don [dɒn] (pt & pp **-ned**, cont **-ning**) ◇ n Br UNIV professeur m d'université. ◇ vt [clothing] revêtir.

donate [də'neɪt] vt faire don de.

donation [də'neɪʃn] n don m.

done [dʌn] ◇ pp → **do**. ◇ adj **-1.** [job, work] achevé(e); I'm nearly ~ j'ai presque fini. **-2.** [cooked] cuit(e). **-3.** [socially acceptable]: that's not the ~ thing ça ne se fait pas. ◇ excl [to conclude deal] tope!

donkey ['dɒŋkɪ] (pl **donkeys**) n âne m, ânesse f.

donkey jacket n Br grosse veste f.

donkeywork ['dɒŋkɪwɜːk] n Br inf: to do the ~ faire le sale boulot.

donor ['dəunər] n **-1.** MED donneur m, -euse f. **-2.** [to charity] donateur m, -trice f.

donor card n carte f de donneur.

don't [dəunt] = **do not**.

doodle ['duːdl] ◇ n griffonnage m. ◇ vi griffonner.

doom [duːm] n [fate] destin m.

doomed [duːmd] adj condamné(e); they were ~ to die ils étaient condamnés à mourir; the plan was ~ to failure le plan était voué à l'échec.

door [dɔːr] n porte f; [of vehicle] portière f;

to open the ~ to sthg *fig* ouvrir la voie à qqch.

doorbell ['dɔːbel] *n* sonnette *f*.

doorhandle ['dɔːhændl] *n* poignée *f* de porte.

doorknob ['dɔːnɒb] *n* bouton *m* de porte.

doorknocker ['dɔːˌnɒkəʳ] *n* heurtoir *m*.

doorman ['dɔːmən] (*pl* -**men** [-mən]) *n* portier *m*.

doormat ['dɔːmæt] *n lit* & *fig* paillasson *m*.

doorstep ['dɔːstep] *n* pas *m* de la porte.

doorstop ['dɔːstɒp] *n* butoir *m* de porte.

door-to-door *adj* [salesman, selling] à domicile.

doorway ['dɔːweɪ] *n* embrasure *f* de la porte.

dope [dəʊp] ◇ *n inf* -**1.** *drugs sl* dope *f*. -**2.** [for athlete, horse] dopant *m*. -**3.** *inf* [fool] imbécile *mf*. ◇ *vt* [horse] doper.

dope test *n* contrôle *m* anti-dopage.

dopey ['dəʊpɪ] (*compar* -**ier**, *superl* -**iest**) *adj inf* abruti(e).

dormant ['dɔːmənt] *adj* -**1.** [volcano] endormi(e). -**2.** [law] inappliqué(e).

dormer (window) ['dɔːməʳ-] *n* lucarne *f*.

dormice ['dɔːmaɪs] *pl* → **dormouse**.

dormitory ['dɔːmətrɪ] (*pl* -**ies**) *n* -**1.** [gen] dortoir *m*. -**2.** *Am* [in university] ≈ cité *f* universitaire.

Dormobile® ['dɔːməˌbiːl] *n Br* camping-car *m*.

dormouse ['dɔːmaʊs] (*pl* -**mice**) *n* loir *m*.

Dors (*abbr of* **Dorset**) *comté anglais*.

DOS [dɒs] (*abbr of* **disk operating system**) *n* DOS *m*.

dosage ['dəʊsɪdʒ] *n* dosage *m*.

dose [dəʊs] ◇ *n* -**1.** MED dose *f*. -**2.** *fig* [amount]: **a ~ of the measles** la rougeole. ◇ *vt*: **to ~ sb with sthg** administrer qqch à qqn.

doss [dɒs]

◆ **doss down** *vi Br inf* crécher.

dosser ['dɒsəʳ] *n Br inf* clochard *m*, -e *f*.

dosshouse ['dɒshaʊs] *n Br inf* asile *m* de nuit.

dossier ['dɒsɪeɪ] *n* dossier *m*.

dot [dɒt] (*pt* & *pp* -**ted**, *cont* -**ting**) ◇ *n* point *m*; **on the ~** à l'heure pile. ◇ *vt*: **dotted with** parsemé(e) de.

DOT (*abbr of* **Department of Transportation**) *n ministère américain du transport*.

dotage ['dəʊtɪdʒ] *n*: **to be in one's ~** être gâteux(euse).

dote [dəʊt]

◆ **dote (up)on** *vt fus* adorer.

doting ['dəʊtɪŋ] *adj*: **she has a ~ grandfather** elle a un grand-père qui l'adore.

dot-matrix printer *n* imprimante *f* matricielle.

dotted line ['dɒtɪd-] *n* ligne *f* pointillée; **to sign on the ~** *fig* donner formellement son accord.

dotty ['dɒtɪ] (*compar* -**ier**, *superl* -**iest**) *adj inf* toqué(e).

double ['dʌbl] ◇ *adj* double; **~ doors** porte *f* à deux battants; **"ally" is spelt "a", ~ "l", "y"** «ally» s'écrit «a», deux «l», «y». ◇ *adv* -**1.** [twice]: **~ the amount** deux fois plus; **to see ~** voir double. -**2.** [in two] en deux; **to bend ~** se plier en deux. ◇ *n* -**1.** [twice as much]: **I earn ~ what I used to** je gagne le double de ce que je gagnais auparavant. -**2.** [drink, look-alike] double *m*. -**3.** CINEMA doublure *f*. ◇ *vt* doubler. ◇ *vi* -**1.** [increase twofold] doubler. -**2.** [have second purpose]: **to ~ as** faire office de.

◆ **doubles** *npl* TENNIS double *m*.

◆ **double up** ◇ *vt sep*: **to be ~d up** être plié(e) en deux. ◇ *vi* [bend over] se plier en deux.

double act *n* duo *m*.

double agent *n* agent *m* double.

double-barrelled *Br*, **double-barreled** *Am* [-'bærəld] *adj* -**1.** [shotgun] à deux coups. -**2.** [name] à rallonge.

double bass [-beɪs] *n* contrebasse *f*.

double bed *n* lit *m* pour deux personnes, grand lit.

double-breasted [-'brestɪd] *adj* [jacket] croisé(e).

double-check *vt* & *vi* revérifier.

double chin *n* double menton *m*.

double cream *n Br* crème *f* fraîche épaisse.

double-cross *vt* trahir.

double-dealer *n*: **to be a ~** jouer double jeu.

double-decker [-dekəʳ] *n* [bus] autobus *m* à impériale.

double-declutch [-diː'klʌtʃ] *vi Br* AUT faire un double débrayage.

double-density *adj* COMPUT [disk] double-densité (*inv*).

double-dutch *n Br* charabia *m*.

double-edged [-'edʒd] *adj lit* & *fig* à double tranchant.

double entendre [ˌduːblɑ̃'tɑ̃dr] *n* allusion *f* grivoise.

double figures *npl*: **to be in ~** être au-dessus de dix.

double-glazing [-'gleɪzɪŋ] *n* double vitrage *m*.

double-jointed [-'dʒɔɪntɪd] *adj* désarticulé(e).

double-park *vi* se garer en double file.

double-quick *adj & adv inf* en deux temps trois mouvements.

double room *n* chambre *f* pour deux personnes.

double-sided *adj* COMPUT [disk] double-face.

double standards *npl*: to have ~ avoir deux poids, deux mesures.

double take *n*: to do a ~ marquer un temps d'arrêt.

double-talk *n* (*U*) propos *mpl* ambigus.

double time *n* tarif *m* double.

double vision *n* vue *f* double.

double whammy [-'wæmɪ] *n* double malédiction *f*.

doubly ['dʌblɪ] *adv* doublement.

doubt [daʊt] ◇ *n* doute *m*; there is no ~ that il n'y a aucun doute que; without (a) ~ sans aucun doute; beyond all ~ indubitablement; to be in ~ [person] ne pas être sûr(e); [outcome] être incertain(e); to cast ~ on sthg mettre qqch en doute; no ~ sans aucun doute. ◇ *vt* douter; to ~ whether OR if douter que.

doubtful ['daʊtfʊl] *adj* -1. [decision, future] incertain(e). -2. [unsure]: to be ~ about OR of douter de. -3. [person, value] douteux(euse).

doubtless ['daʊtlɪs] *adv* sans aucun doute.

dough [dəʊ] *n* (*U*) -1. CULIN pâte *f*. -2. *v inf* [money] fric *m*.

doughnut ['dəʊnʌt] *n* beignet *m*.

dour [dʊə˞] *adj* austère.

douse [daʊs] *vt* -1. [fire, flames] éteindre. -2. [drench] tremper.

dove[1] [dʌv] *n* [bird] colombe *f*.

dove[2] [dəʊv] *Am pt* → dive.

dovecot(e) ['dʌvkɒt] *n* colombier *m*.

Dover ['dəʊvə˞] *n* Douvres.

dovetail ['dʌvteɪl] *fig* ◇ *vt* faire coïncider. ◇ *vi* coïncider.

dovetail joint *n* assemblage *m* à queue d'aronde.

dowager ['daʊədʒə˞] *n* douairière *f*.

dowdy ['daʊdɪ] (*compar* -ier, *superl* -iest) *adj* sans chic.

Dow-Jones average [,daʊ'dʒəʊnz-] *n*: the ~ le Dow-Jones, l'indice *m* Dow-Jones.

down [daʊn] ◇ *adv* -1. [downwards] en bas, vers le bas; to bend ~ se pencher; to climb ~ descendre; to fall ~ tomber (par terre); to pull ~ tirer vers le bas. -2. [along]: we went ~ to have a look on est allé jeter un coup d'œil; I'm going ~ to the shop je vais au magasin. -3. [southwards]: we travelled ~ to London on est descendu à Londres. -4. [lower in amount]: prices are coming ~ les prix baissent; ~ to the last detail jusqu'au moindre détail. -5. [in written form]: to write sthg ~ noter qqch. ◇ *prep* -1. [downwards]: they ran ~ the hill/stairs ils ont descendu la colline/l'escalier en courant. -2. [along]: to walk ~ the street descendre la rue. ◇ *adj* -1. *inf* [depressed]: to feel ~ avoir le cafard. -2. [behind]: they're two goals ~ ils perdent de deux buts. -3. [lower in amount]: prices are ~ again les prix ont encore baissé. -4. [computer, telephones] en panne. ◇ *n* (*U*) duvet *m*. ◇ *vt* -1. [knock over] abattre. -2. [drink] avaler d'un trait.

◆ **downs** *npl Br* collines *fpl*.

down-and-out ◇ *adj* indigent(e). ◇ *n* personne dans le besoin.

down-at-heel *adj* déguenillé(e).

downbeat ['daʊnbiːt] *adj inf* pessimiste.

downcast ['daʊnkɑːst] *adj* -1. [sad] démoralisé(e). -2. [eyes] baissé(e).

downer ['daʊnə˞] *n inf* -1. [drug] tranquillisant *m*. -2. [depressing event or person]: he's/it's a real ~ il est/c'est flippant.

downfall ['daʊnfɔːl] *n* (*U*) ruine *f*.

downgrade ['daʊngreɪd] *vt* [job] déclasser; [employee] rétrograder.

downhearted [,daʊn'hɑːtɪd] *adj* découragé(e).

downhill [,daʊn'hɪl] ◇ *adj* -1. [downward] en pente; it's ~ all the way now *fig* ça va être du gâteau maintenant. -2. SKIING: ~ skier descendeur *m*, -euse *f*. ◇ *n* SKIING [race] descente *f*. ◇ *adv*: to walk ~ descendre la côte; her career is going ~ *fig* sa carrière est sur le déclin.

Downing Street ['daʊnɪŋ-] *n* rue du centre de Londres.

DOWNING STREET:
C'est à Downing Street que se trouvent les résidences officielles du Premier ministre, au n° 10, et du ministre des Finances, au n° 11. Le terme 'Downing Street' est souvent employé pour désigner le gouvernement

download [,daʊn'ləʊd] *vt* COMPUT transférer.

down-market *adj* [area] populaire, pas très chic (*inv*); [product] bas de gamme (*inv*).

down payment *n* acompte *m*.

downplay ['daʊnpleɪ] *vt* minimiser.

downpour ['daʊnpɔːr] *n* pluie *f* torrentielle.

downright ['daʊnraɪt] ◇ *adj* franc (franche); [lie] effronté(e). ◇ *adv* franchement.

downside ['daʊnsaɪd] *n* désavantage *m*.

Down's syndrome *n* trisomie *f* 21.

downstairs [,daʊn'steəz] ◇ *adj* du bas; [on floor below] à l'étage en-dessous. ◇ *adv* en bas; [on floor below] à l'étage en-dessous; **to come** OR **go** ~ descendre.

downstream [,daʊn'striːm] *adv* en aval.

downtime ['daʊntaɪm] *n* temps *m* improductif.

down-to-earth *adj* pragmatique, terre-à-terre (*inv*).

downtown [,daʊn'taʊn] ◇ *adj*: ~ **New York** le centre de New York. ◇ *adv* en ville.

downtrodden ['daʊn,trɒdn] *adj* opprimé(e).

downturn ['daʊntɜːn] *n*: ~ **(in)** baisse *f* (de).

down under *adv* en Australie/Nouvelle-Zélande.

downward ['daʊnwəd] ◇ *adj* **-1.** [towards ground] vers le bas. **-2.** [trend] à la baisse. ◇ *adv* Am = **downwards**.

downwards ['daʊnwədz] *adv* **-1.** [look, move] vers le bas. **-2.** [in hierarchy]: **from the president** ~ du président jusqu'au bas de la hiérarchie.

downwind [,daʊn'wɪnd] *adv* dans le sens du vent.

dowry ['daʊərɪ] (*pl* **-ies**) *n* dot *f*.

doz. (*abbr of* **dozen**) douz.

doze [dəʊz] ◇ *n* somme *m*. ◇ *vi* sommeiller.

◆ **doze off** *vi* s'assoupir.

dozen ['dʌzn] ◇ *num adj*: **a** ~ **eggs** une douzaine d'œufs. ◇ *n* douzaine *f*; **50p a** ~ 50p la douzaine; **~s of** *inf* des centaines de.

dozy ['dəʊzɪ] (*compar* **-ier**, *superl* **-iest**) *adj* **-1.** [sleepy] somnolent(e). **-2.** Br *inf* [stupid] lent(e).

DP (*abbr of* **data processing**) *n* informatique *f*.

DPh, DPhil [,diː'fɪl] (*abbr of* **Doctor of Philosophy**) *n* docteur *en philosophie*.

DPP *abbr of* **Director of Public Prosecutions**.

DPT (*abbr of* **diphtheria, pertussis, tetanus**) *n* DCT *m*.

DPW (*abbr of* **Department of Public Works**) *n* ministère de l'équipement.

dr *abbr of* **debtor**.

Dr. -1. (*abbr of* **Drive**) av. **-2.** (*abbr of* **Doctor**) Dr.

drab [dræb] (*compar* **-ber**, *superl* **-best**) *adj* terne.

draconian [drə'kəʊnjən] *adj* draconien(ienne).

draft [drɑːft] ◇ *n* **-1.** [early version] premier jet *m*, ébauche *f*; [of letter] brouillon *m*. **-2.** [money order] traite *f*. **-3.** Am MIL: **the** ~ la conscription *f*. **-4.** Am = **draught**. ◇ *vt* **-1.** [speech] ébaucher, faire le plan de; [letter] faire le brouillon de. **-2.** Am MIL appeler. **-3.** [staff] muter.

draft dodger [-dɒdʒər] *n* Am insoumis *m*.

draftee [,drɑːf'tiː] *n* Am appelé *m*.

draftsman Am = **draughtsman**.

draftsmanship Am = **draughtsmanship**.

drafty Am = **draughty**.

drag [dræg] (*pt* & *pp* **-ged**, *cont* **-ging**) ◇ *vt* **-1.** [gen] traîner. **-2.** [lake, river] draguer. ◇ *vi* **-1.** [dress, coat] traîner. **-2.** *fig* [time, action] traîner en longueur. ◇ *n* **-1.** *inf* [bore] plaie *f*. **-2.** *inf* [on cigarette] bouffée *f*. **-3.** [wind resistance] coefficient *m* de pénétration (dans l'air). **-4.** [cross-dressing]: **in** ~ en travesti.

◆ **drag down** *vt sep fig*: **they dragged him down with them** ils l'ont entraîné dans leur chute.

◆ **drag in** *vt sep* [include - person] mêler; [- subject] faire allusion à.

◆ **drag on** *vi* [meeting, time] s'éterniser, traîner en longueur.

◆ **drag out** *vt sep* **-1.** [protract] prolonger, faire traîner. **-2.** [facts] tirer, arracher; **to** ~ **sthg out of sb** soutirer qqch à qqn.

dragnet ['drægnet] *n* **-1.** [net] drège *f*. **-2.** *fig* [to catch criminal] piège *m*.

dragon ['drægən] *n lit* & *fig* dragon *m*.

dragonfly ['drægənflaɪ] (*pl* **-ies**) *n* libellule *f*.

dragoon [drə'guːn] ◇ *n* dragon *m*. ◇ *vt*: **to** ~ **sb into doing sthg** contraindre qqn à faire qqch.

drag racing *n* course *f* de dragster.

dragster ['drægstər] *n* dragster *m*.

drain [dreɪn] ◇ *n* **-1.** [pipe] égout *m*; **down the** ~ [money] jeté par les fenêtres. **-2.** [depletion - of resources, funds] ~ **on** épuisement *m* de. ◇ *vt* **-1.** [vegetables] égoutter; [land] assécher, drainer. **-2.** [strength, resources] épuiser; **to feel ~ed** être vidé(e). **-3.** [drink, glass] boire. ◇ *vi* [dishes] égoutter; **the blood ~ed from his face** il blêmit.

drainage ['dreɪnɪdʒ] *n* **-1.** [pipes, ditches] (système *m* du) tout-à-l'égout *m*. **-2.** [draining - of land] drainage *m*.

draining board ['dreɪnɪŋ-] *Br*, **drainboard** ['dreɪnbɔːrd] *Am n* égouttoir *m*.

drainpipe ['dreɪnpaɪp] *n* tuyau *m* d'écoulement.

drainpipes, drainpipe trousers *npl Br* pantalon-cigarette *m*.

drake [dreɪk] *n* canard *m*.

dram [dræm] *n* goutte *f* (de whisky).

drama ['drɑːmə] ◇ *n* **-1.** [play, excitement] drame *m*. **-2.** (U) [art] théâtre *m*. ◇ *comp* [school] d'art dramatique; [critic] dramatique.

dramatic [drə'mætɪk] *adj* **-1.** [gen] dramatique. **-2.** [sudden, noticeable] spectaculaire.

dramatically [drə'mætɪklɪ] *adv* **-1.** [noticeably] de façon spectaculaire. **-2.** [theatrically] de façon théâtrale.

dramatist ['dræmətɪst] *n* dramaturge *mf*.

dramatization [ˌdræmətaɪ'zeɪʃn] *n* adaptation *f* pour la télévision/la scène/l'écran.

dramatize, -ise ['dræmətaɪz] *vt* **-1.** [rewrite as play, film] adapter pour la télévision/la scène/l'écran. **-2.** *pej* [make exciting] dramatiser.

drank [dræŋk] *pt* → **drink**.

drape [dreɪp] *vt* draper; **to be ~d with** OR **in** être drapé(e) de.
◆ **drapes** *npl Am* rideaux *mpl*.

draper ['dreɪpər] *n* marchand *m*, -e *f* de tissus.

drastic ['dræstɪk] *adj* **-1.** [measures] drastique, radical(e). **-2.** [improvement, decline] spectaculaire.

drastically ['dræstɪklɪ] *adv* [change, decline] de façon spectaculaire.

draught *Br*, **draft** *Am* [drɑːft] *n* **-1.** [air current] courant *m* d'air. **-2.** *literary* [gulp] gorgée *f*. **-3.** [from barrel]: **on ~** [beer] à la pression.
◆ **draughts** *n Br* jeu *m* de dames.

draught beer *n Br* bière *f* à la pression.

draughtboard ['drɑːftbɔːd] *n Br* damier *m*.

draughtsman *Br* (*pl* **-men** [-mən]), **draftsman** *Am* (*pl* **-men** [-mən]) ['drɑːftsmən] *n* dessinateur *m*, -trice *f*.

draughtsmanship *Br*, **draftsmanship** *Am* ['drɑːftsmənʃɪp] *n* [skill] talent *m* de dessinateur.

draughty *Br* (*compar* **-ier**, *superl* **-iest**), **drafty** *Am* (*compar* **-ier**, *superl* **-iest**) ['drɑːftɪ] *adj* plein(e) de courants d'air.

draw [drɔː] (*pt* **drew**, *pp* **drawn**) ◇ *vt* **-1.** [gen] tirer; **to ~ breath** *fig* souffler. **-2.** [sketch] dessiner. **-3.** [comparison, distinction] établir, faire. **-4.** [attract] attirer, entraîner; **to ~ sb's attention to** attirer l'attention de

qqn sur; **to be** OR **feel drawn to** être OR se sentir attiré(e) par.
◇ *vi* **-1.** [sketch] dessiner. **-2.** [move]: **to ~ near** [person] s'approcher; [time] approcher; **to ~ away** reculer; **to ~ to an end** OR **a close** tirer à sa fin. **-3.** SPORT faire match nul; **to be ~ing** être à égalité.
◇ *n* **-1.** SPORT [result] match *m* nul. **-2.** [lottery] tirage *m*. **-3.** [attraction] attraction *f*.
◆ **draw in** *vi* [days] raccourcir.
◆ **draw into** *vt sep*: **to ~ sb into sthg** mêler qqn à qqch.
◆ **draw on** *vt fus* **-1.** = **draw upon**. **-2.** [cigarette] tirer sur.
◆ **draw out** *vt sep* **-1.** [encourage - person] faire sortir de sa coquille. **-2.** [prolong] prolonger. **-3.** [money] faire un retrait de, retirer.
◆ **draw up** ◇ *vt sep* [contract, plan] établir, dresser. ◇ *vi* [vehicle] s'arrêter.
◆ **draw upon** *vt fus* [information] utiliser, se servir de; [reserves, resources] puiser dans.

drawback ['drɔːbæk] *n* inconvénient *m*, désavantage *m*.

drawbridge ['drɔːbrɪdʒ] *n* pont-levis *m*.

drawer [drɔːr] *n* [in desk, chest] tiroir *m*.

drawing ['drɔːɪŋ] *n* dessin *m*.

drawing board *n* planche *f* à dessin; **back to the ~** *inf* retour à la case départ.

drawing pin *n Br* punaise *f*.

drawing room *n* salon *m*.

drawl [drɔːl] ◇ *n* voix *f* traînante. ◇ *vt* dire d'une voix traînante.

drawn [drɔːn] ◇ *pp* → **draw**. ◇ *adj* **-1.** [curtains] tiré(e). **-2.** [face] fatigué(e), tiré(e).

drawn-out *adj* prolongé(e).

drawstring ['drɔːstrɪŋ] *n* cordon *m*.

dread [dred] ◇ *n* (U) épouvante *f*. ◇ *vt* appréhender; **to ~ doing sthg** appréhender de faire qqch; **I ~ to think** je n'ose pas imaginer.

dreaded ['dredɪd] *adj* redouté(e).

dreadful ['dredfʊl] *adj* affreux(euse), épouvantable.

dreadfully ['dredfʊlɪ] *adv* **-1.** [badly] terriblement. **-2.** [extremely] extrêmement; **I'm ~ sorry** je regrette infiniment.

dreadlocks ['dredlɒks] *npl* coiffure *f* rasta.

dream [driːm] (*pt & pp* **-ed** OR **dreamt**) ◇ *n* rêve *m*. ◇ *adj* de rêve. ◇ *vt*: **to ~ (that)** ... rêver que ...; **I never ~ed this would happen** je n'aurais jamais pensé que cela puisse arriver. ◇ *vi*: **to ~ (of** OR **about)** rêver (de); **I wouldn't ~ of it** cela ne me viendrait même pas à l'idée.
◆ **dream up** *vt sep* inventer.

dreamer ['dri:mər] *n* [unrealistic person] utopiste *mf*.

dreamily ['dri:mɪlɪ] *adv* rêveusement.

dreamlike ['dri:mlaɪk] *adj* comme dans un rêve.

dreamt [dremt] *pp* → **dream**.

dream world *n* monde *m* imaginaire.

dreamy ['dri:mɪ] (*compar* **-ier**, *superl* **-iest**) *adj* **-1.** [distracted] rêveur(euse). **-2.** [dreamlike] de rêve.

dreary ['drɪərɪ] (*compar* **-ier**, *superl* **-iest**) *adj* **-1.** [weather] morne. **-2.** [dull, boring] ennuyeux(euse).

dredge [dredʒ] *vt* draguer.
◆ **dredge up** *vt sep* **-1.** [with dredger] draguer. **-2.** *fig* [from past] déterrer.

dredger ['dredʒər] *n* [ship] dragueur *m*; [machine] drague *f*.

dregs [dregz] *npl lit* & *fig* lie *f*.

drench [drentʃ] *vt* tremper; **to be ~ed in** OR **with** être inondé(e) de.

Dresden ['drezdən] *n* Dresde.

dress [dres] ◇ *n* **-1.** [woman's garment] robe *f*. **-2.** (*U*) [clothing] costume *m*, tenue *f*. ◇ *vt* **-1.** [clothe] habiller; **to be ~ed** être habillé(e); **to be ~ed in** être vêtu(e) de; **to get ~ed** s'habiller. **-2.** [bandage] panser. **-3.** CULIN [salad] assaisonner. ◇ *vi* s'habiller.
◆ **dress up** ◇ *vt sep* [facts] maquiller. ◇ *vi* **-1.** [in costume] se déguiser. **-2.** [in best clothes] s'habiller (élégamment).

dressage ['dresɑːʒ] *n* dressage *m*.

dress circle *n* premier balcon *m*.

dresser ['dresər] *n* **-1.** [for dishes] vaisselier *m*. **-2.** *Am* [chest of drawers] commode *f*. **-3.** [person]: **a smart ~** une personne qui s'habille avec chic.

dressing ['dresɪŋ] *n* **-1.** [bandage] pansement *m*. **-2.** [for salad] assaisonnement *m*. **-3.** *Am* [for turkey etc] farce *f*.

dressing gown *n* robe *f* de chambre.

dressing room *n* **-1.** THEATRE loge *f*. **-2.** SPORT vestiaire *m*.

dressing table *n* coiffeuse *f*.

dressmaker ['dres,meɪkər] *n* couturier *m*, -ière *f*.

dressmaking ['dres,meɪkɪŋ] *n* couture *f*.

dress rehearsal *n* générale *f*.

dress shirt *n* chemise *f* de soirée.

dressy ['dresɪ] (*compar* **-ier**, *superl* **-iest**) *adj* habillé(e).

drew [druː] *pt* → **draw**.

dribble ['drɪbl] ◇ *n* **-1.** [saliva] bave *f*. **-2.** [trickle] traînée *f*. ◇ *vt* SPORT dribbler. ◇ *vi*

-1. [drool] baver. **-2.** [liquid] tomber goutte à goutte, couler.

dribs [drɪbz] *npl*: **in ~ and drabs** peu à peu, petit à petit.

dried [draɪd] ◇ *pp* → **dry**. ◇ *adj* [milk, eggs] en poudre; [fruit] sec (sèche); [flowers] séché(e).

dried fruit *n* (*U*) fruits *mpl* secs.

dried-up *adj* asséché(e).

drier ['draɪər] = **dryer**.

drift [drɪft] ◇ *n* **-1.** [movement] mouvement *m*; [direction] direction *f*, sens *m*. **-2.** [meaning] sens *m* général; **I get your ~** je vois ce que vous voulez dire. **-3.** [of snow] congère *f*; [of sand, leaves] amoncellement *m*, entassement *m*.
◇ *vi* **-1.** [boat] dériver. **-2.** [snow, sand, leaves] s'amasser, s'amonceler. **-3.** [person] errer; **to ~ into sthg** se retrouver dans qqch; **to ~ apart** se détacher l'un de l'autre.
◆ **drift off** *vi* [person] s'assoupir.

drifter ['drɪftər] *n* [person] personne *f* sans but dans la vie.

driftwood ['drɪftwʊd] *n* bois *m* flottant.

drill [drɪl] ◇ *n* **-1.** [tool] perceuse *f*; [dentist's] fraise *f*; [in mine etc] perforatrice *f*. **-2.** [exercise, training] exercice *m*. ◇ *vt* **-1.** [wood, hole] percer; [tooth] fraiser; [well] forer. **-2.** [soldiers] entraîner; **to ~ sthg into sb** faire rentrer qqch dans la tête de qqn. ◇ *vi* **-1.** [bore]: **to ~ into** [wood] percer dans; [tooth] fraiser dans. **-2.** [excavate]: **to ~ for oil** forer à la recherche de pétrole.

drilling platform ['drɪlɪŋ-] *n* plate-forme *f* pétrolière OR de forage.

drily ['draɪlɪ] = **dryly**.

drink [drɪŋk] (*pt* **drank**, *pp* **drunk**) ◇ *n* **-1.** [gen] boisson *f*; **to have a ~** boire un verre. **-2.** (*U*) [alcohol] alcool *m*. ◇ *vt* boire. ◇ *vi* boire; **to ~ to sb/to sb's success** boire à qqn/à la réussite de qqn.

drinkable ['drɪŋkəbl] *adj* **-1.** [water] potable. **-2.** [palatable] buvable.

drink-driving *Br*, **drunk-driving** *Am* *n* conduite *f* en état d'ivresse.

drinker ['drɪŋkər] *n* buveur *m*, -euse *f*.

drinking ['drɪŋkɪŋ] ◇ *adj*: **I'm not a ~ man** je ne bois pas. ◇ *n* (*U*) boisson *f*.

drinking fountain *n* fontaine *f* d'eau potable.

drinking-up time *n Br* période pendant laquelle les clients d'un pub doivent terminer leur verre avant la fermeture.

drinking water *n* eau *f* potable.

drip [drɪp] (*pt* & *pp* **-ped**, *cont* **-ping**) ◇ *n* **-1.** [drop] goutte *f*. **-2.** MED goutte-à-goutte *m inv*. **-3.** *inf* [wimp] femmelette *f*. ◇ *vt* laisser tomber goutte à goutte. ◇ *vi* **-1.** [gen] goutter, tomber goutte à goutte. **-2.** [person]: **to be dripping with** *lit* & *fig* être ruisselant(e) de.

drip-dry *adj* qui ne se repasse pas.

drip-feed ◇ *n* goutte-à-goutte *m inv*. ◇ *vt* alimenter par perfusion.

dripping ['drɪpɪŋ] ◇ *adj*: ~ **(wet)** dégoulinant(e). ◇ *n* (*U*) graisse *f*.

drive [draɪv] (*pt* **drove**, *pp* **driven**) ◇ *n* **-1.** [in car] trajet *m* (en voiture); **to go for a** ~ faire une promenade (en voiture). **-2.** [urge] désir *m*, besoin *m*. **-3.** [campaign] campagne *f*. **-4.** (*U*) [energy] dynamisme *m*, énergie *f*. **-5.** [road to house] allée *f*. **-6.** SPORT drive *m*. ◇ *vt* **-1.** [vehicle, passenger] conduire. **-2.** TECH entraîner, actionner. **-3.** [animals, people] pousser. **-4.** [motivate] pousser. **-5.** [force]: **to** ~ **sb to sthg/to do sthg** pousser qqn à qqch, faire qqch, conduire qqn à qqch/à faire qqch; **to** ~ **sb mad** OR **crazy** rendre qqn fou. **-6.** [nail, stake] enfoncer. **-7.** SPORT driver. ◇ *vi* [driver] conduire; [travel by car] aller en voiture.

◆ **drive at** *vt fus*: **what are you driving at?** où voulez-vous en venir?

drive-in ◇ *n* drive-in *m*. ◇ *adj* drive-in (*inv*).

drivel ['drɪvl] *n* (*U*) *inf* foutaises *fpl*, idioties *fpl*.

driven ['drɪvn] *pp* → **drive**.

driver ['draɪvə'] *n* **-1.** [of vehicle - gen] conducteur *m*, -trice *f*; [- of taxi] chauffeur *m*. **-2.** COMPUT logiciel *m* de commande de périphérique.

driver's license *Am* = **driving licence**.

drive shaft *n* arbre *m* de transmission.

driveway ['draɪvweɪ] *n* allée *f*.

driving ['draɪvɪŋ] ◇ *adj* [rain] battant(e); [wind] cinglant(e). ◇ *n* (*U*) conduite *f*.

driving force *n* force *f* motrice.

driving instructor *n* moniteur *m*, -trice *f* d'auto-école.

driving lesson *n* leçon *f* de conduite.

driving licence *Br*, **driver's license** *Am n* permis *m* de conduire.

driving mirror *n* rétroviseur *m*.

driving school *n* auto-école *f*.

driving test *n* (examen *m* du) permis *m* de conduire.

drizzle ['drɪzl] ◇ *n* bruine *f*. ◇ *v impers* bruiner.

drizzly ['drɪzlɪ] (*compar* **-ier**, *superl* **-iest**) *adj* bruineux(euse).

droll [drəʊl] *adj* drôle.

dromedary ['drɒmədrɪ] (*pl* **-ies**) *n* dromadaire *m*.

drone [drəʊn] ◇ *n* **-1.** [of traffic, voices] ronronnement *m*; [of insect] bourdonnement *m*. **-2.** [male bee] abeille *f* mâle, faux-bourdon *m*. ◇ *vi* [engine] ronronner; [insect] bourdonner.

◆ **drone on** *vi* parler d'une voix monotone; **to** ~ **on about sthg** rabâcher qqch.

drool [druːl] *vi* baver; **to** ~ **over** *fig* baver (d'admiration) devant.

droop [druːp] *vi* **-1.** [head] pencher; [shoulders, eyelids] tomber. **-2.** *fig* [spirits] faiblir.

drop [drɒp] (*pt* & *pp* **-ped**, *cont* **-ping**) ◇ *n* **-1.** [of liquid] goutte *f*. **-2.** [sweet] pastille *f*. **-3.** [decrease]: ~ **(in)** baisse *f* (de). **-4.** [distance down] dénivellation *f*; **sheer** ~ à-pic *m inv*. ◇ *vt* **-1.** [let fall] laisser tomber. **-2.** [voice, speed, price] baisser. **-3.** [abandon] abandonner; [player] exclure. **-4.** [let out of car] déposer. **-5.** [utter]: **to** ~ **a hint that** laisser entendre que. **-6.** TENNIS [game, set] perdre. **-7.** [write]: **to** ~ **sb a note** OR **line** écrire un petit mot à qqn. ◇ *vi* **-1.** [fall] tomber. **-2.** [temperature, demand] baisser; [voice, wind] tomber.

◆ **drops** *npl* MED gouttes *fpl*.

◆ **drop by** *vi inf* passer.

◆ **drop in** *vi inf*: **to** ~ **in (on sb)** passer (chez qqn).

◆ **drop off** ◇ *vt sep* déposer. ◇ *vi* **-1.** [fall asleep] s'endormir. **-2.** [interest, sales] baisser.

◆ **drop out** *vi*: **to** ~ **out (of** OR **from sthg)** abandonner (qqch); **to** ~ **out of society** vivre en marge de la société.

drop-in centre *n* centre d'assistance sociale permanente.

droplet ['drɒplɪt] *n* gouttelette *f*.

dropout ['drɒpaʊt] *n* [from society] marginal *m*, -e *f*; [from college] étudiant *m*, -e *f* qui abandonne ses études.

dropper ['drɒpə'] *n* compte-gouttes *m inv*.

droppings ['drɒpɪŋz] *npl* [of bird] fiente *f*; [of animal] crottes *fpl*.

drop shot *n* amorti *m*.

dross [drɒs] *n* (*U*) déchets *mpl*; *fig* rebut *m*.

drought [draʊt] *n* sécheresse *f*.

drove [drəʊv] ◇ *pt* → **drive**. ◇ *n* [of people] foule *f*.

drown [draʊn] ◇ *vt* **-1.** [in water] noyer. **-2.** [sound]: **to** ~ **(out)** couvrir. ◇ *vi* se noyer.

drowsy ['drauzı] (*compar* -ier, *superl* -iest) *adj* assoupi(e), somnolent(e).

drudge [drʌdʒ] *n* homme *m* de peine, femme *f* de peine.

drudgery ['drʌdʒərı] *n* (*U*) corvée *f*.

drug [drʌg] (*pt* & *pp* -ged, *cont* -ging) ◇ *n* -1. [medicine] médicament *m*. -2. [narcotic] drogue *f*. ◇ *vt* droguer.

drug abuse *n* usage *m* de stupéfiants.

drug addict *n* drogué *m*, -e *f*.

drug addiction *n* toxicomanie *f*.

druggist ['drʌgɪst] *n* Am pharmacien *m*, -ienne *f*.

drug pedlar *n* revendeur *m*, -euse *f* de drogue.

drugstore ['drʌgstɔːr] *n* Am drugstore *m*.

druid ['druːɪd] *n* druide *m*.

drum [drʌm] (*pt* & *pp* -med, *cont* -ming) ◇ *n* -1. MUS tambour *m*. -2. [container] bidon *m*. ◇ *vt* & *vi* tambouriner.

◆ **drums** *npl* batterie *f*.

◆ **drum into** *vt sep*: to ~ sthg into sb enfoncer qqch dans la tête de qqn.

◆ **drum up** *vt sep* [support, business] rechercher, solliciter.

drumbeat ['drʌmbiːt] *n* roulement *m* de tambour.

drum brake *n* frein *m* à tambour.

drummer ['drʌmər] *n* [gen] (joueur *m*, -euse *f* de) tambour *m*; [in pop group] batteur *m*, -euse *f*.

drumming ['drʌmɪŋ] *n* [of rain, fingers] tambourinage *m*.

drum roll *n* roulement *m* de tambour.

drumstick ['drʌmstɪk] *n* -1. [for drum] baguette *f* de tambour. -2. [of chicken] pilon *m*.

drunk [drʌŋk] ◇ *pp* → drink. ◇ *adj* -1. [on alcohol] ivre, soûl(e); to get ~ se soûler, s'enivrer; ~ and disorderly en état d'ivresse sur la voie publique. -2. *fig* [excited, carried away]: to be ~ with OR on être enivré(e) OR grisé(e) par. ◇ *n* soûlard *m*, -e *f*.

drunkard ['drʌŋkəd] *n* alcoolique *mf*.

drunk-driving Am = drink-driving.

drunken ['drʌŋkn] *adj* [person] ivre; [quarrel] d'ivrognes.

drunken driving = drink-driving.

drunkenness ['drʌŋkənıs] *n* ivresse *f*.

dry [draɪ] (*compar* -ier, *superl* -iest, *pt* & *pp* dried) ◇ *adj* -1. [gen] sec (sèche); [day] sans pluie. -2. [river, earth] asséché(e). -3. [wry] pince-sans-rire (*inv*). -4. [dull] aride. ◇ *vt* [gen] sécher; [with cloth] essuyer. ◇ *vi* sécher.

◆ **dry out** *vt sep* & *vi* sécher.

◆ **dry up** ◇ *vt sep* [dishes] essuyer. ◇ *vi* -1. [river, lake] s'assécher. -2. [supply] se tarir. -3. [actor, speaker] avoir un trou, sécher. -4. [dry dishes] essuyer.

dry battery *n* batterie *f* sèche.

dry-clean *vt* nettoyer à sec.

dry cleaner *n*: ~'s pressing *m*.

dry-cleaning *n* nettoyage *m* à sec.

dry dock *n* cale *f* sèche.

dryer ['draɪər] *n* [for clothes] séchoir *m*.

dry ginger *n* boisson gazeuse au gingembre.

dry goods *npl* mercerie *f*.

dry ice *n* neige *f* carbonique.

dry land *n* terre *f* ferme.

dryly ['draɪlı] *adv* [wryly] sèchement.

dryness ['draɪnıs] *n* (*U*) -1. [of ground] sécheresse *f*; [of humour] causticité *f*. -2. [dullness] aridité *f*.

dry rot *n* pourriture *f* sèche.

dry run *n* répétition *f*.

dry ski slope *n* piste *f* de ski artificielle.

dry-stone wall *n* mur *m* de pierres sèches.

DSc (*abbr of* Doctor of Science) *n* docteur ès sciences.

DSS (*abbr of* Department of Social Security) *n* ministère britannique de la sécurité sociale.

DST (*abbr of* daylight saving time) *heure d'été aux États-Unis*.

DT *abbr of* data transmission.

DTI (*abbr of* Department of Trade and Industry) *n* ministère britannique du commerce et de l'industrie.

DTP (*abbr of* desktop publishing) *n* PAO *f*.

DT's [ˌdiːˈtiːz] (*abbr of* delirium tremens) *npl inf*: to have the ~ avoir une crise de délirium tremens.

dual ['djuːəl] *adj* double.

dual carriageway *n* Br route *f* à quatre voies.

dual control *n* double commande *f*.

dual nationality *n* double nationalité *f*.

dual-purpose *adj* à double emploi.

Dubai [ˌduːˈbaɪ] *n* Dubayy.

dubbed [dʌbd] *adj* -1. CINEMA doublé(e). -2. [nicknamed] surnommé(e).

dubious ['djuːbjəs] *adj* -1. [suspect] douteux(euse). -2. [uncertain] hésitant(e), incertain(e); to be ~ about doing sthg hésiter à faire qqch.

Dublin ['dʌblın] *n* Dublin.

Dubliner ['dʌblınər] *n* Dublinois *m*, -e *f*.

duchess ['dʌtʃıs] *n* duchesse *f*.

duchy ['dʌtʃı] (*pl* -ies) *n* duché *m*.

duck [dʌk] ◇ n canard m; **she took to it like a ~ to water** elle était comme un poisson dans l'eau. ◇ vt -1. [head] baisser. -2. [responsibility] esquiver, se dérober à. -3. [submerge]: **to ~ sb** mettre la tête de qqn sous l'eau. ◇ vi -1. [lower head] se baisser. -2. [dive]: **he ~ed behind the wall** il se cacha derrière le mur.

◆ **duck out** vi: **to ~ out (of sthg)** se soustraire (à qqch).

duckling ['dʌklɪŋ] n caneton m.

duct [dʌkt] n -1. [pipe] canalisation f. -2. ANAT canal m.

dud [dʌd] ◇ adj [bomb] non éclaté(e); [cheque] sans provision, en bois. ◇ n obus m non éclaté.

dude [dju:d] n Am inf [man] gars m, type m.

dude ranch n aux États-Unis, ranch qui propose des activités touristiques.

due [dju:] ◇ adj -1. [expected]: **the book is ~ out in May** le livre doit sortir en mai; **she's ~ back shortly** elle devrait rentrer sous peu; **when is the train ~?** à quelle heure le train doit-il arriver? -2. [appropriate] dû (due), qui convient; **in ~ course** [at the appropriate time] en temps voulu; [eventually] à la longue. -3. [owed, owing] dû (due); **she's ~ a pay rise** elle devrait recevoir une augmentation. ◇ adv: **~ west** droit vers l'ouest. ◇ n dû m; **to give him his ~** il faut lui rendre cette justice.

◆ **dues** npl cotisation f.

◆ **due to** prep [owing to] dû à; [because of] provoqué par, à cause de.

due date n jour m de l'échéance.

duel ['dju:əl] (Br pt & pp **-led**, cont **-ling**, Am pt & pp **-ed**, cont **-ing**) ◇ n duel m. ◇ vi se battre en duel.

duet [dju:'et] n duo m.

duff [dʌf] adj Br inf [useless] nul (nulle).

◆ **duff up** vt sep Br inf tabasser.

duffel bag ['dʌfl-] n sac m marin.

duffel coat ['dʌfl-] n duffel-coat m.

duffle bag = duffel bag.

duffle coat = duffel coat.

dug [dʌg] pt & pp → dig.

dugout ['dʌgaʊt] n -1. [canoe] pirogue f. -2. SPORT abri m de touche.

duke [dju:k] n duc m.

dull [dʌl] ◇ adj -1. [boring - book, conversation] ennuyeux(euse); [- person] terne. -2. [colour, light] terne. -3. [weather] maussade. -4. [sound, ache] sourd(e). ◇ vt -1. [pain] atténuer; [senses] émousser. -2. [make less bright] ternir.

duly ['dju:lɪ] adv -1. [properly] dûment. -2. [as expected] comme prévu.

dumb [dʌm] adj -1. [unable to speak] muet(ette). -2. inf [stupid] idiot(e).

dumbbell ['dʌmbel] n [weight] haltère m.

dumbfound [dʌm'faʊnd] vt stupéfier, abasourdir; **to be ~ed** ne pas en revenir.

dumbstruck ['dʌmstrʌk] adj muet(ette) de stupeur.

dumbwaiter [,dʌm'weɪtər] n [lift] monte-plats m inv.

dumdum (bullet) ['dʌmdʌm-] n dum-dum f.

dummy ['dʌmɪ] (pl **-ies**) ◇ adj faux (fausse). ◇ n -1. [of tailor] mannequin m. -2. [copy] maquette f. -3. Br [for baby] sucette f, tétine f. -4. SPORT feinte f. ◇ vt & vi SPORT feinter.

dummy run n essai m.

dump [dʌmp] ◇ n -1. [for rubbish] décharge f. -2. MIL dépôt m. -3. inf [ugly place] taudis m. ◇ vt -1. [put down] déposer. -2. [dispose of] jeter. -3. COMPUT vider. -4. inf [boyfriend, girlfriend] laisser tomber, plaquer.

◆ **dumps** npl: **to be (down) in the ~s** avoir le cafard.

dumper (truck) ['dʌmpər-] Br, **dump truck** Am n tombereau m, dumper m.

dumping ['dʌmpɪŋ] n décharge f; **"no ~"** «décharge interdite».

dumping ground n décharge f.

dumpling ['dʌmplɪŋ] n boulette f de pâte.

dump truck Am = dumper (truck).

dumpy ['dʌmpɪ] (compar **-ier**, superl **-iest**) adj inf boulot(otte).

dunce [dʌns] n cancre m.

dune [dju:n] n dune f.

dung [dʌŋ] n fumier m.

dungarees [,dʌŋgə'ri:z] npl -1. Br [for work] bleu m de travail; [fashion garment] salopette f. -2. Am [heavy jeans] jean m épais.

dungeon ['dʌndʒən] n cachot m.

dunk [dʌŋk] vt inf tremper.

Dunkirk [dʌn'kɜ:k] n Dunkerque f.

duo ['dju:əʊ] n duo m.

duodenal ulcer [,dju:əʊ'di:nl-] n ulcère m duodénal.

dupe [dju:p] ◇ n dupe f. ◇ vt [trick] duper; **to ~ sb into doing sthg** amener qqn à faire qqch en le dupant.

duplex ['dju:pleks] n Am -1. [apartment] duplex m. -2. [house] maison f jumelée.

duplicate [adj & n 'dju:plɪkət, vb 'dju:plɪkeɪt] ◇ adj [key, document] en double. ◇ n double m; **in ~** en double. ◇ vt -1. [copy - gen] faire un double de; [- on photocopier] photocopier. **-2.** [repeat]: **to ~ work** faire double emploi.

duplication [ˌdjuːplɪ'keɪʃn] n (U) **-1.** [copying] copie f. **-2.** [repetition] répétition f.

duplicity [djuː'plɪsətɪ] n duplicité f.

Dur (abbr of **Durham**) comté anglais.

durability [ˌdjʊərə'bɪlətɪ] n [of product] solidité f.

durable ['djʊərəbl] adj solide, résistant(e).

duration [djʊ'reɪʃn] n durée f; **for the ~ of** jusqu'à la fin de.

duress [djʊ'res] n: **under ~** sous la contrainte.

Durex® ['djʊəreks] n préservatif m Durex®.

during ['djʊərɪŋ] prep pendant, au cours de.

dusk [dʌsk] n crépuscule m.

dusky ['dʌskɪ] (compar **-ier**, superl **-iest**) adj literary mordoré(e).

dust [dʌst] ◇ n (U) poussière f; **to gather ~** [get dusty] se couvrir de poussière; fig tomber dans l'oubli. ◇ vt **-1.** [clean] épousseter. **-2.** [cover with powder]: **to ~ sthg (with)** saupoudrer qqch (de). ◇ vi faire la poussière.
◆ **dust off** vt sep épousseter; fig dépoussiérer.

dustbin ['dʌstbɪn] n Br poubelle f.

dustbowl [dʌstbəʊl] n désert m de poussière.

dustcart ['dʌstkɑːt] n Br camion m des boueux.

dust cover n [on book] jaquette f.

duster ['dʌstə*] n **-1.** [cloth] chiffon m (à poussière). **-2.** Am [overall] blouse f, tablier m.

dust jacket n [on book] jaquette f.

dustman ['dʌstmən] (pl **-men** [-mən]) n Br éboueur m.

dustpan ['dʌstpæn] n pelle f à poussière.

dustsheet [dʌstʃiːt] n Br housse f.

dust storm n tempête f de poussière.

dustup [dʌstʌp] n inf bagarre f.

dusty ['dʌstɪ] (compar **-ier**, superl **-iest**) adj poussiéreux(euse).

Dutch [dʌtʃ] ◇ adj néerlandais(e), hollandais(e). ◇ n [language] néerlandais m, hollandais m. ◇ npl: **the ~** les Néerlandais, les Hollandais. ◇ adv: **to go ~** partager les frais.

Dutch auction n Br enchères fpl au rabais.

Dutch barn n Br hangar m à récoltes.

Dutch cap n Br diaphragme m.

Dutch courage n: **he had a drink to give himself some ~** il but un verre pour se donner du courage.

Dutch elm disease n maladie f des ormes.

Dutchman ['dʌtʃmən] (pl **-men** [-mən]) n Néerlandais m, Hollandais m.

Dutchwoman ['dʌtʃˌwʊmən] (pl **-women** [-ˌwɪmɪn]) n Néerlandaise f, Hollandaise f.

dutiable ['djuːtjəbl] adj [goods] taxable.

dutiful ['djuːtɪfʊl] adj obéissant(e).

duty ['djuːtɪ] (pl **-ies**) n **-1.** (U) [responsibility] devoir m; **to do one's ~** faire son devoir. **-2.** [work]: **to be on/off ~** être/ne pas être de service. **-3.** [tax] droit m.
◆ **duties** npl fonctions fpl.

duty bound adj: **to be ~ (to do sthg)** être tenu(e) (de faire qqch).

duty-free adj hors taxe.

duty-free shop n boutique f hors taxe.

duty officer n préposé m, -e f de service.

duvet ['duːveɪ] n Br couette f.

duvet cover n Br housse f de couette.

DVLC (abbr of **Driver and Vehicle Licensing Centre**) n service des immatriculations et des permis de conduire en Grande-Bretagne.

DVM (abbr of **Doctor of Veterinary Medicine**) n docteur vétérinaire.

dwarf [dwɔːf] (pl **-s** OR **dwarves** [dwɔːvz]) ◇ adj [plant, animal] nain(e). ◇ n nain m, -e f. ◇ vt [tower over] écraser.

dwell [dwel] (pt & pp **dwelt** OR **-ed**) vi literary habiter.
◆ **dwell on** vt fus s'étendre sur.

-dweller ['dwelə*] suffix: **city~** habitant m, -e f de la ville.

dwelling ['dwelɪŋ] n literary habitation f.

dwelt [dwelt] pt & pp → **dwell**.

dwindle ['dwɪndl] vi diminuer.

dwindling ['dwɪndlɪŋ] adj en diminution.

dye [daɪ] ◇ n teinture f. ◇ vt teindre.

dyed [daɪd] adj teint(e).

dying ['daɪɪŋ] ◇ cont → **die**. ◇ adj [person] mourant(e), moribond(e); [plant, language, industry] moribond. ◇ npl: **the ~** les mourants mpl.

dyke [daɪk] = **dike**.

dynamic [daɪ'næmɪk] adj dynamique.
◆ **dynamics** npl dynamique f.

dynamism ['daɪnəmɪzm] n dynamisme m.

dynamite ['daɪnəmaɪt] ◇ n (U) lit & fig dynamite f. ◇ vt dynamiter, faire sauter.

dynamo ['daɪnəməʊ] (pl **-s**) n dynamo f.

dynasty [Br dɪnəstɪ, Am 'daɪnəstɪ] (pl **-ies**) n dynastie f.

dysentery ['dɪsntrɪ] n dysenterie f.

dyslexia [dɪs'leksɪə] n dyslexie f.

dyslexic [dɪs'leksɪk] adj dyslexique.

dyspepsia [dɪs'pepsɪə] *n* dyspepsie *f.*

dystrophy ['dɪstrəfɪ] *n* → **muscular dystrophy**.

E

e (*pl* **e's** OR **es**), **E** (*pl* **E's** OR **Es**) [iː] *n* [letter] e *m inv*, E *m inv*.

◆ **E** *n* **-1.** MUS mi *m.* **-2.** (*abbr of* **east**) E.

ea. (*abbr of* **each**): £3.00 ~ 3 livres pièce.

each [iːtʃ] ◇ *adj* chaque. ◇ *pron* chacun(e); **the books cost £10.99** ~ les livres coûtent 10,99 livres (la) pièce; ~ **other** l'un l'autre (l'une l'autre), les uns les autres (les unes les autres); **they love** ~ **other** ils s'aiment; **we've known** ~ **other for years** nous nous connaissons depuis des années.

eager ['iːgəʳ] *adj* passionné(e), avide; **to be** ~ **for** être avide de; **to be** ~ **to do sthg** être impatient de faire qqch.

eagerly ['iːgəlɪ] *adv* [talk, plan] avec passion, avidement; [wait] avec impatience.

eagle ['iːgl] *n* [bird] aigle *m.*

eagle-eyed [-aɪd] *adj* qui a des yeux d'aigle.

eaglet ['iːglɪt] *n* aiglon *m,* -onne *f.*

E and OE (*abbr of* **errors and omissions excepted**) s. e & o.

ear [ɪəʳ] *n* **-1.** [gen] oreille *f;* **by** ~ MUS à l'oreille; **to have an** ~ **for** [music, languages] avoir (de) l'oreille pour; **to go in one** ~ **and out the other** *inf* entrer par une oreille et ressortir par l'autre; **to have** OR **keep one's** ~ **to the ground** *inf* être aux écoutes; **to play it by** ~ *fig* improviser, voir sur le moment. **-2.** [of corn] épi *m.*

earache ['ɪəreɪk] *n*: **to have** ~ avoir mal à l'oreille.

eardrum ['ɪədrʌm] *n* tympan *m.*

earl [ɜːl] *n* comte *m.*

earlier ['ɜːlɪʳ] ◇ *adj* [previous] précédent(e); [more early] plus tôt. ◇ *adv* plus tôt; **as I mentioned** ~ comme je l'ai signalé tout à l'heure; ~ **on** plus tôt.

earliest ['ɜːlɪəst] ◇ *adj* [first] premier(ière); [most early] le plus tôt. ◇ *n*: **at the** ~ au plus tôt.

earlobe ['ɪələub] *n* lobe *m* de l'oreille.

early ['ɜːlɪ] (*compar* **-ier**, *superl* **-iest**) ◇ *adj* **-1.** [before expected time] en avance. **-2.** [in day] de bonne heure; **the** ~ **train** le premier train; **to make an** ~ **start** partir de bonne heure. **-3.** [at beginning]: **in the** ~ **sixties** au début des années soixante; **the** ~ **chapters** les premiers chapitres.

◇ *adv* **-1.** [before expected time] en avance; **I was ten minutes** ~ j'étais en avance de dix minutes. **-2.** [in day] tôt, de bonne heure; **as** ~ **as** dès; ~ **on** tôt. **-3.** [at beginning]: ~ **in her life** dans sa jeunesse.

early retirement *n* retraite *f* anticipée.

early warning system *n* système *m* de première alerte.

earmark ['ɪəmɑːk] *vt*: **to be** ~**ed for** être réservé(e) à.

earn [ɜːn] *vt* **-1.** [as salary] gagner. **-2.** COMM rapporter. **-3.** *fig* [respect, praise] gagner, mériter.

earned income [ɜːnd-] *n* revenus *mpl* salariaux.

earner ['ɜːnəʳ] *n* **-1.** [person] salarié *m,* -e *f.* **-2.** *Br inf* [deal]: **a nice little** ~ une affaire juteuse.

earnest ['ɜːnɪst] *adj* sérieux(ieuse).

◆ **in earnest** ◇ *adj* sérieux(ieuse). ◇ *adv* pour de bon, sérieusement.

earnestly ['ɜːnɪstlɪ] *adv* sérieusement.

earnings ['ɜːnɪŋz] *npl* [of person] salaire *m,* gains *mpl;* [of company] bénéfices *mpl.*

earnings-related *adj* [pension, payment] proportionnel(elle) au salaire.

ear, nose and throat specialist *n* otorhino-laryngologiste *mf,* oto-rhino *mf.*

earphones ['ɪəfəunz] *npl* casque *m.*

earplugs ['ɪəplʌgz] *npl* boules *fpl* Quiès®.

earring ['ɪərɪŋ] *n* boucle *f* d'oreille.

earshot ['ɪəʃɒt] *n*: **within** ~ à portée de voix; **out of** ~ hors de portée de voix.

ear-splitting *adj* assourdissant(e).

earth [ɜːθ] ◇ *n* [gen & ELEC] terre *f;* **how/what/where/why on** ~ ...? mais comment/que/où/pourquoi donc ...?; **to cost the** ~ *Br* coûter les yeux de la tête. ◇ *vt Br*: **to be** ~**ed** être à la masse.

earthenware ['ɜːθnweəʳ] ◇ *adj* en terre cuite. ◇ *n* (*U*) poteries *fpl.*

earthling ['ɜːθlɪŋ] *n* terrien *m,* -ienne *f.*

earthly ['ɜːθlɪ] *adj* terrestre; **what** ~ **reason could she have for doing that?** *inf* pourquoi diable a-t-elle fait ça?

earthquake ['ɜːθkweɪk] *n* tremblement *m* de terre.

earthshattering ['ɜːθ,ʃætərɪŋ] *adj Br inf* [news] renversant(e).

earth tremor *n* secousse *f* sismique.

earthward(s) ['ɜːθwəd(z)] *adv* vers la terre.

earthworks ['ɜːθwɜːks] *npl* ARCHEOL fortifications *fpl* en terre.

earthworm ['ɜːθwɜːm] *n* ver *m* de terre.

earthy ['ɜːθɪ] (*compar* **-ier**, *superl* **-iest**) *adj* **-1.** *fig* [humour, person] truculent(e). **-2.** [taste, smell] de terre, terreux(euse).

earwax ['ɪəwæks] *n* cérumen *m*.

earwig ['ɪəwɪg] *n* perce-oreille *m*.

ease [iːz] ◇ *n* (U) **-1.** [lack of difficulty] facilité *f*; **to do sthg with** ~ faire qqch sans difficulté OR facilement. **-2.** [comfort]: **a life of** ~ une vie facile; **at** ~ à l'aise; **ill at** ~ mal à l'aise. ◇ *vt* **-1.** [pain] calmer; [restrictions] modérer. **-2.** [move carefully]: **to** ~ **sthg in/out** faire entrer/sortir qqch délicatement. ◇ *vi* [problem] s'arranger; [pain] s'atténuer; [rain] diminuer.
  ◆ **ease off** *vi* [pain] s'atténuer; [rain] diminuer.
  ◆ **ease up** *vi* **-1.** [rain] diminuer. **-2.** [relax] se détendre.

easel ['iːzl] *n* chevalet *m*.

easily ['iːzɪlɪ] *adv* **-1.** [without difficulty] facilement. **-2.** [without doubt] de loin. **-3.** [in a relaxed manner] tranquillement.

easiness ['iːzɪnɪs] *n* [lack of difficulty] facilité *f*.

east [iːst] ◇ *n* **-1.** [direction] est *m*. **-2.** [region]: **the** ~ l'est. ◇ *adj* est (*inv*); [wind] d'est. ◇ *adv* à l'est, vers l'est; ~ **of** à l'est de.
  ◆ **East** *n*: **the East** [gen & POL] l'Est *m*; [Asia] l'Orient *m*.

eastbound ['iːstbaʊnd] *adj* en direction de l'est.

East End *n*: **the** ~ *les quartiers est de Londres*.

Easter ['iːstə'] *n* Pâques *m*.

Easter egg *n* œuf *m* de Pâques.

Easter Island *n* l'île *f* de Pâques; **in** OR **on** ~ à l'île de Pâques.

easterly ['iːstəlɪ] *adj* à l'est, de l'est; [wind] de l'est; **in an** ~ **direction** vers l'est.

eastern ['iːstən] *adj* de l'est.
  ◆ **Eastern** *adj* [gen & POL] de l'Est; [from Asia] oriental(e).

Eastern bloc [-blɒk] *n*: **the** ~ le bloc de l'Est.

Easterner ['iːstənə'] *n* personne qui vient de l'est.

Easter Sunday *n* dimanche *m* de Pâques.

East German ◇ *adj* d'Allemagne de l'Est. ◇ *n* Allemand *m*, -e *f* de l'Est.

East Germany *n*: (former) ~ (l'ex-) Allemagne *f* de l'Est; **in** ~ en Allemagne de l'Est.

eastward ['iːstwəd] ◇ *adj* à l'est, vers l'est. ◇ *adv* = **eastwards**.

eastwards ['iːstwədz] *adv* vers l'est.

easy ['iːzɪ] (*compar* **-ier**, *superl* **-iest**) ◇ *adj* **-1.** [not difficult, comfortable] facile. **-2.** [relaxed - manner] naturel(elle). ◇ *adv*: **to go** ~ **on** *inf* y aller doucement avec; **to take it** OR **things** ~ *inf* ne pas se fatiguer.

easy-care *adj Br* [garment] d'entretien facile.

easy chair *n* fauteuil *m*.

easygoing ['iːzɪ'gəʊɪŋ] *adj* [person] facile à vivre; [manner] complaisant(e).

eat [iːt] (*pt* **ate**, *pp* **eaten**) *vt* & *vi* manger.
  ◆ **eat away, eat into** *vt fus* **-1.** [subj: acid, rust] ronger. **-2.** [deplete] grignoter.
  ◆ **eat out** *vi* manger au restaurant.
  ◆ **eat up** *vt sep* **-1.** [food] manger. **-2.** *fig* [use up]: **to** ~ **up money** revenir très cher; **to** ~ **up time** demander beaucoup de temps.

eatable ['iːtəbl] *adj* [palatable] mangeable.

eaten ['iːtn] *pp* → **eat**.

eater ['iːtə'] *n* mangeur *m*, -euse *f*.

eatery ['iːtərɪ] *n Am* restaurant *m*.

eating apple ['iːtɪŋ-] *n* pomme *f* à couteau.

eau de cologne [,əʊdəkə'ləʊn] *n* eau *f* de Cologne.

eaves ['iːvz] *npl* avant-toit *m*.

eavesdrop ['iːvzdrɒp] (*pt* & *pp* **-ped**, *cont* **-ping**) *vi*: **to** ~ **(on sb)** écouter (qqn) de façon indiscrète.

ebb [eb] ◇ *n* reflux *m*; **the** ~ **and flow** *fig* les hauts et les bas; **to be at a low** ~ *fig* aller mal. ◇ *vi* **-1.** [tide, sea] se retirer, refluer. **-2.** *literary* [strength]: **to** ~ **(away)** décliner.

ebb tide *n* marée *f* descendante.

ebony ['ebənɪ] ◇ *adj* [colour] noir(e) d'ébène. ◇ *n* ébène *f*.

ebullient [ɪ'bʊljənt] *adj* exubérant(e).

EC (*abbr of* **European Community**) *n* CE *f*.

eccentric [ɪk'sentrɪk] ◇ *adj* [odd] excentrique, bizarre. ◇ *n* [person] excentrique *mf*.

eccentricity [,eksen'trɪsətɪ] (*pl* **-ies**) *n* [oddity] excentricité *f*, bizarrerie *f*.

ecclesiastic(al) [ɪ,kliːzɪ'æstɪk(l)] *adj* ecclésiastique.

ECG *n* **-1.** (*abbr of* **electrocardiogram**) ECG *m*. **-2.** (*abbr of* **electrocardiograph**) ECG *m*.

ECGD (*abbr of* **Export Credits Guarantee Department**) *n* organisme d'assurance pour le commerce extérieur, ≃ COFACE *f*.

ECH Br (abbr of **electric central heating**) chauffage central électrique.

echelon ['eʃəlɒn] n échelon m.

echo ['ekəu] (pl -es, pt & pp -ed, cont -ing) ◇ n lit & fig écho m. ◇ vt [words] répéter; [opinion] faire écho à. ◇ vi retentir, résonner.

éclair [eɪ'kleər] n [cake] éclair m.

eclectic [e'klektɪk] adj éclectique.

eclipse [ɪ'klɪps] ◇ n lit & fig éclipse f. ◇ vt fig éclipser.

ECM Am (abbr of **European Common Market**) n Marché commun européen.

ecological [ˌiːkə'lɒdʒɪkl] adj écologique.

ecologically [ˌiːkə'lɒdʒɪklɪ] adv du point de vue écologique.

ecologist [ɪ'kɒlədʒɪst] n écologiste mf.

ecology [ɪ'kɒlədʒɪ] n écologie f.

economic [ˌiːkə'nɒmɪk] adj **-1.** ECON économique. **-2.** [profitable] rentable.

economical [ˌiːkə'nɒmɪkl] adj **-1.** [cheap] économique. **-2.** [person] économe.

economics [ˌiːkə'nɒmɪks] ◇ n (U) économie f politique, économique f. ◇ npl [of plan, business] aspect m financier.

economist [ɪ'kɒnəmɪst] n économiste mf.

economize, -ise [ɪ'kɒnəmaɪz] vi économiser.

economy [ɪ'kɒnəmɪ] (pl -ies) n économie f; **economies of scale** économies d'échelle.

economy class n classe f touriste.

economy drive n campagne f de restrictions.

economy-size(d) adj [pack, jar] taille économique (inv).

ecosystem ['iːkəu,sɪstəm] n écosystème m.

ECSC (abbr of **European Coal & Steel Community**) n CECA f.

ecstasy ['ekstəsɪ] (pl -ies) n extase f, ravissement m; **to go into ecstasies about sthg** s'extasier sur qqch.

ecstatic [ek'stætɪk] adj [person] en extase; [feeling] extatique.

ecstatically [ek'stætɪklɪ] adv [say, shout] d'un air extasié; **to be ~ happy** être au comble du bonheur.

ECT (abbr of **electroconvulsive therapy**) n électrochocs mpl.

ectoplasm ['ektəplæzm] n ectoplasme m.

ECU, Ecu ['ekjuː] (abbr of **European Currency Unit**) n ECU m, écu m.

Ecuador ['ekwədɔːr] n Équateur m; **in ~** en Équateur.

Ecuadoran [ˌekwə'dɔːrən], **Ecuadorian** [ˌekwə'dɔːrɪən] ◇ adj équatorien(ienne). ◇ n Équatorien m, -ienne f.

ecumenical [ˌiːkjuˈmenɪkl] adj œcuménique.

eczema ['eksɪmə] n eczéma m.

ed. -1. (abbr of **edited**) sous la dir. de, coll. **-2.** abbr of **edition**. **-3.** abbr of **editor**.

eddy ['edɪ] (pl -ies, pt & pp -ied) ◇ n tourbillon m. ◇ vi tourbillonner.

Eden ['iːdn] n: **(the Garden of) ~** le jardin m d'Éden, l'Éden m.

edge [edʒ] ◇ n **-1.** [gen] bord m; [of coin, book] tranche f; [of knife] tranchant m; **to be on the ~ of** fig être à deux doigts de. **-2.** [advantage]: **to have an ~ over** OR **the ~ on** avoir un léger avantage sur. **-3.** fig [in voice] note f tranchante. ◇ vi: **to ~ forward** avancer tout doucement.
♦ **on edge** adj contracté(e), tendu(e).

edged [edʒd] adj: **~ with** bordé(e) de.

edgeways ['edʒweɪz], **edgewise** ['edʒwaɪz] adv latéralement, de côté.

edging ['edʒɪŋ] n [of cloth] liseré m; [of paper] bordure f.

edgy ['edʒɪ] (compar -ier, superl -iest) adj contracté(e), tendu(e).

edible ['edɪbl] adj [safe to eat] comestible.

edict ['iːdɪkt] n décret m.

edifice ['edɪfɪs] n édifice m.

edify ['edɪfaɪ] (pt & pp -ied) vt édifier (intellectuellement).

edifying ['edɪfaɪɪŋ] adj édifiant(e).

Edinburgh ['edɪnbrə] n Édimbourg.

Edinburgh Festival n: **the ~** le Festival d'Édimbourg.

EDINBURGH FESTIVAL:
Le Festival international d'Édimbourg, créé en 1947, est aujourd'hui un des plus grands festivals de théâtre, de musique et de cinéma au monde; il se tient chaque année en août et en septembre. Le festival "off" (the Fringe) est une grande rencontre de théâtre expérimental

edit ['edɪt] vt **-1.** [correct - text] corriger. **-2.** CINEMA monter; RADIO & TV réaliser. **-3.** [magazine] diriger; [newspaper] être le rédacteur en chef de.
♦ **edit out** vt sep couper.

edition [ɪ'dɪʃn] n édition f.

editor ['edɪtər] n **-1.** [of magazine] directeur m, -trice f; [of newspaper] rédacteur m, -trice f en chef. **-2.** [of text] correcteur m, -trice f. **-3.** CINEMA monteur m, -euse f; RADIO & TV réalisateur m, -trice f.

editorial [,edɪ'tɔːrɪəl] ◇ *adj* [department, staff] de la rédaction; [style, policy] éditorial(e). ◇ *n* éditorial *m*.

EDP (*abbr of* **electronic data processing**) *n* traitement électronique de données.

EDT (*abbr of* **Eastern Daylight Time**) *n* heure d'été de l'Est des États-Unis.

educate ['edʒʊkeɪt] *vt* **-1.** SCH & UNIV instruire. **-2.** [inform] informer, éduquer.

educated ['edʒʊkeɪtɪd] *adj* [cultured] cultivé(e).

education [,edʒʊ'keɪʃn] *n* **-1.** [gen] éducation *f*. **-2.** [teaching] enseignement *m*, instruction *f*.

educational [,edʒʊ'keɪʃənl] *adj* **-1.** [establishment, policy] pédagogique. **-2.** [toy, experience] éducatif(ive).

educationalist [,edʒʊ'keɪʃnəlɪst] *n* pédagogue *mf*.

educative ['edʒʊkətɪv] *adj* éducatif(ive).

educator ['edʒʊkeɪtəʳ] *n* éducateur *m*, -trice *f*.

Edwardian [ed'wɔːdɪən] *adj* de l'époque 1900.

EEC (*abbr of* **European Economic Community**) *n* ancien nom de la Communauté Européenne.

EEG *n* **-1.** (*abbr of* **electroencephalogram**) EEG *m*. **-2.** (*abbr of* **electroencephalograph**) EEG *m*.

eel [iːl] *n* anguille *f*.

EENT (*abbr of* **eye, ear, nose and throat**) *n* ophtalmologie *f* et ORL *f*.

EEOC (*abbr of* **Equal Employment Opportunity Commission**) *n* commission britannique pour la non-discrimination dans l'emploi.

eerie ['ɪərɪ] *adj* inquiétant(e), sinistre.

EET (*abbr of* **Eastern European Time**) *n* heure d'Europe orientale.

efface [ɪ'feɪs] *vt* effacer.

effect [ɪ'fekt] ◇ *n* **-1.** [gen] effet *m*; **to have an ~ on** avoir OR produire un effet sur; **for ~** pour attirer l'attention, pour se faire remarquer; **to take ~** [law] prendre effet, entrer en vigueur; **to put sthg into ~** [policy, law] mettre qqch en application. **-2.** [meaning]: **a statement to the ~ that ...** une déclaration selon laquelle ...; **or words to that ~** ou quelque chose de ce genre. ◇ *vt* [repairs, change] effectuer; [reconciliation] amener.

◆ **effects** *npl*: (**special**) **~s** effets *mpl* spéciaux.

effective [ɪ'fektɪv] *adj* **-1.** [successful] efficace. **-2.** [actual, real] effectif(ive).

effectively [ɪ'fektɪvlɪ] *adv* **-1.** [successfully] efficacement. **-2.** [in fact] effectivement.

effectiveness [ɪ'fektɪvnɪs] *n* efficacité *f*.

effeminate [ɪ'femɪnət] *adj* efféminé(e).

effervesce [,efə'ves] *vi* pétiller.

effervescent [,efə'vesənt] *adj* [liquid] effervescent(e); [drink] gazeux(euse).

effete [ɪ'fiːt] *adj* [person, gesture] veule.

efficacious [efɪ'keɪʃəs] *adj fml* efficace.

efficacy ['efɪkəsɪ] *n* efficacité *f*.

efficiency [ɪ'fɪʃənsɪ] *n* [of person, method] efficacité *f*; [of factory, system] rendement *m*.

efficient [ɪ'fɪʃənt] *adj* efficace.

efficiently [ɪ'fɪʃəntlɪ] *adv* efficacement.

effigy ['efɪdʒɪ] (*pl* -**ies**) *n* effigie *f*.

effluent ['efluənt] *n* effluent *m*.

effort ['efət] *n* effort *m*; **to be worth the ~** valoir la peine; **with ~** avec peine; **to make the ~ to do sthg** s'efforcer de faire qqch; **to make an/no ~ to do sthg** faire un effort/ne faire aucun effort pour faire qqch.

effortless ['efətlɪs] *adj* [easy] facile; [natural] aisé(e).

effortlessly ['efətlɪslɪ] *adv* sans effort, facilement.

effrontery [ɪ'frʌntərɪ] *n* effronterie *f*.

effusive [ɪ'fjuːsɪv] *adj* [person] démonstratif(ive); [welcome] plein(e) d'effusions.

effusively [ɪ'fjuːsɪvlɪ] *adv* avec effusion.

EFL ['efəl] (*abbr of* **English as a foreign language**) *n* anglais langue étrangère.

EFTA ['eftə] (*abbr of* **European Free Trade Association**) *n* AELE *f*, AEL-E *f*.

EFTS [efts] (*abbr of* **electronic funds transfer system**) *n* système électronique de transferts de fonds.

e.g. (*abbr of* **exempli gratia**) *adv* par exemple.

EGA (*abbr of* **enhanced graphics adapter**) *n* adapteur *m* graphique couleur EGA.

egalitarian [ɪ,gælɪ'teərɪən] *adj* égalitaire.

egg [eg] *n* œuf *m*.

◆ **egg on** *vt sep* pousser, inciter.

eggcup ['egkʌp] *n* coquetier *m*.

eggplant ['egplɑːnt] *n Am* aubergine *f*.

eggshell ['egʃel] *n* coquille *f* d'œuf.

egg timer *n* [with sand] sablier *m*; [mechanical] minuteur *m*.

egg whisk *n* fouet *m*.

egg white *n* blanc *m* d'œuf.

egg yolk *n* jaune *m* d'œuf.

ego ['iːgəʊ] (*pl* -s) *n* moi *m*.

egocentric [,iːgəʊ'sentrɪk] *adj* égocentrique.

egoism ['iːgəʊɪzm] *n* égoïsme *m*.

egoist ['i:gəʊɪst] *n* égoïste *mf*.

egoistic [,i:gəʊ'ɪstɪk] *adj* égoïste.

egotism ['i:gətɪzm] *n* égotisme *m*.

egotist ['i:gətɪst] *n* égotiste *mf*.

egotistic(al) [,i:gə'tɪstɪk(l)] *adj* égotiste.

ego trip *n inf*: **she's just on an ~** c'est par vanité qu'elle le fait.

Egypt ['i:dʒɪpt] *n* Égypte *f*; **in ~** en Égypte.

Egyptian [ɪ'dʒɪpʃn] ◇ *adj* égyptien(ienne). ◇ *n* Égyptien *m*, -ienne *f*.

eh [eɪ] *excl Br inf* hein?

eiderdown ['aɪdədaʊn] *n* [bed cover] édredon *m*.

eight [eɪt] *num* huit; *see also* **six**.

eighteen [,eɪ'ti:n] *num* dix-huit; *see also* **six**.

eighteenth [,eɪ'ti:nθ] *num* dix-huitième; *see also* **sixth**.

eighth [eɪtθ] *num* huitième; *see also* **sixth**.

eightieth ['eɪtɪɪθ] *num* quatre-vingtième; *see also* **sixth**.

eighty ['eɪtɪ] (*pl* **-ies**) *num* quatre-vingts; *see also* **sixty**.

Eire ['eərə] *n* République *f* d'Irlande.

EIS (*abbr of* **Educational Institute of Scotland**) *n* syndicat écossais d'enseignants.

either ['aɪðəʳ, 'i:ðəʳ] ◇ *adj* **-1.** [one or the other] l'un ou l'autre (l'une ou l'autre) (des deux); **she couldn't find ~ jumper** elle ne trouva ni l'un ni l'autre des pulls; **~ way** de toute façon. **-2.** [each] chaque; **on ~ side** de chaque côté.
◇ *pron*: **~ (of them)** l'un ou l'autre *m*, l'une ou l'autre *f*; **I don't like ~ (of them)** je n'aime aucun des deux, je n'aime ni l'un ni l'autre.
◇ *adv* (*in negatives*) non plus; **I don't ~** moi non plus.
◇ *conj*: **~ ... or** soit ... soit, ou ... ou; **I'm not fond of ~ him or his wife** je ne les aime ni lui ni sa femme.

ejaculate [ɪ'dʒækjʊleɪt] ◇ *vt* [exclaim] s'écrier. ◇ *vi* [have orgasm] éjaculer.

eject [ɪ'dʒekt] *vt* **-1.** [object] éjecter, émettre. **-2.** [person] éjecter, expulser.

ejector seat *Br* [ɪ'dʒektəʳ-], **ejection seat** *Am* [ɪ'dʒekʃn-] *n* siège *m* éjectable.

eke [i:k]
◆ **eke out** ◇ *vt sep* [money, food] économiser, faire durer. ◇ *vt fus*: **to ~ out a living** subsister.

EKG (*abbr of* **electrocardiogram**) *n Am* ECG *m*.

el [el] (*abbr of* **elevated railroad**) *n Am inf* chemin *m* de fer aérien.

elaborate [*adj* ɪ'læbrət, *vb* ɪ'læbəreɪt] ◇ *adj* [ceremony, procedure] complexe; [explanation, plan] détaillé(e), minutieux(ieuse). ◇ *vi*: **to ~ (on)** donner des précisions (sur).

elaborately [ɪ'læbərətlɪ] *adv* [planned] minutieusement; [decorated] avec recherche.

elapse [ɪ'læps] *vi* s'écouler.

elastic [ɪ'læstɪk] ◇ *adj lit* & *fig* élastique. ◇ *n* (*U*) élastique *m*.

elasticated [ɪ'læstɪkeɪtɪd] *adj* élastique.

elastic band *n Br* élastique *m*, caoutchouc *m*.

elasticity [,elæ'stɪsətɪ] *n* élasticité *f*.

elated [ɪ'leɪtɪd] *adj* transporté(e) (de joie).

elation [ɪ'leɪʃn] *n* exultation *f*, joie *f*.

elbow ['elbəʊ] ◇ *n* coude *m*. ◇ *vt*: **to ~ sb aside** écarter qqn du coude.

elbow grease *n inf* huile *f* de coude.

elbowroom ['elbəʊrʊm] *n inf*: **to have some ~** avoir ses coudées franches.

elder ['eldəʳ] ◇ *adj* aîné(e). ◇ *n* **-1.** [older person] aîné *m*, -e *f*. **-2.** [of tribe, church] ancien *m*. **-3. ~ (tree)** sureau *m*.

elder statesman *n* vétéran *m* de la politique.

elderberry ['eldə,berɪ] (*pl* **-ies**) *n* [fruit] baie *f* de sureau; [tree] sureau *m*.

elderly ['eldəlɪ] ◇ *adj* âgé(e). ◇ *npl*: **the ~** les personnes *fpl* âgées.

eldest ['eldɪst] *adj* aîné(e).

Eldorado [,eldɔ'rɑ:dəʊ] *n* Eldorado *m*.

elect [ɪ'lekt] ◇ *adj* élu(e). ◇ *vt* **-1.** [by voting] élire. **-2.** *fml* [choose]: **to ~ to do sthg** choisir de faire qqch.

elected [ɪ'lektɪd] *adj* élu(e).

election [ɪ'lekʃn] *n* élection *f*; **to have** OR **hold an ~** procéder à une élection; **local ~s** élections locales.

election campaign *n* campagne *f* électorale.

electioneering [ɪ,lekʃə'nɪərɪŋ] *n* (*U*) *usu pej* propagande *f* électorale.

elective [ɪ'lektɪv] *n Am* SCH cours *m* facultatif.

elector [ɪ'lektəʳ] *n* électeur *m*, -trice *f*.

electoral [ɪ'lektərəl] *adj* électoral(e).

electoral college *n* collège *m* électoral.

electoral register, electoral roll *n*: **the ~** la liste électorale.

electorate [ɪ'lektərət] *n*: **the ~** l'électorat *m*.

electric [ɪ'lektrɪk] *adj lit* & *fig* électrique.
◆ **electrics** *npl Br inf* [in car, machine] installation *f* électrique.

electrical [ɪ'lektrɪkl] *adj* électrique.

electrical engineer *n* ingénieur *m* électricien.

electrical engineering *n* électrotechnique *f*.

electrically [ɪ'lektrɪklɪ] *adv* [heated] à l'électricité; [charged, powered] électriquement.

electrical shock *Am* = electric shock.

electric blanket *n* couverture *f* chauffante.

electric chair *n*: the ~ la chaise électrique.

electric cooker *n* cuisinière *f* électrique.

electric current *n* courant *m* électrique.

electric fire *n* radiateur *m* électrique.

electric guitar *n* guitare *f* électrique.

electrician [,ɪlek'trɪʃn] *n* électricien *m*, -ienne *f*.

electricity [,ɪlek'trɪsətɪ] *n* électricité *f*.

electric light *n* lumière *f* électrique.

electric shock *Br*, **electrical shock** *Am n* décharge *f* électrique.

electric shock therapy *n* (*U*) électrochocs *mpl*.

electric storm *n* orage *m* magnétique.

electrify [ɪ'lektrɪfaɪ] (*pt* & *pp* **-ied**) *vt* **-1.** TECH électrifier. **-2.** *fig* [excite] galvaniser, électriser.

electrifying [ɪ'lektrɪfaɪŋ] *adj* [exciting] galvanisant(e), électrisant(e).

electro- [ɪ'lektrəʊ] *prefix* électro-.

electrocardiograph [ɪ,lektrəʊ'kɑːdɪəgrɑːf] *n* électrocardiographe *m*.

electrocute [ɪ'lektrəkjuːt] *vt* électrocuter.

electrode [ɪ'lektrəʊd] *n* électrode *f*.

electroencephalograph [ɪ,lektrəʊen-'sefələgrɑːf] *n* électroencéphalographie *f*.

electrolysis [,ɪlek'trɒləsɪs] *n* électrolyse *f*.

electromagnet [ɪ,lektrəʊ'mægnɪt] *n* électro-aimant *m*.

electromagnetic [ɪ,lektrəʊmæg'netɪk] *adj* électromagnétique.

electron [ɪ'lektrɒn] *n* électron *m*.

electronic [,ɪlek'trɒnɪk] *adj* électronique.

electronic data processing *n* traitement *m* électronique de données.

electronic mail *n* courrier *m* électronique.

electronics [ɪlek'trɒnɪks] ◇ *n* (*U*) [technology, science] électronique *f*. ◇ *npl* [equipment] (équipement *m*) électronique *f*.

electron microscope *n* microscope *m* électronique.

electroplated [ɪ'lektrəʊpleɪtɪd] *adj* métallisé(e) par galvanoplastie.

elegance ['elɪgəns] *n* élégance *f*.

elegant ['elɪgənt] *adj* élégant(e).

elegantly ['elɪgəntlɪ] *adv* élégamment.

elegy ['elɪdʒɪ] (*pl* **-ies**) *n* élégie *f*.

element ['elɪmənt] ◇ *n* **-1.** [gen] élément *m*; **an ~ of truth** une part de vérité. **-2.** [in heater, kettle] résistance *f*. **-3.** *phr*: **to be in one's** ~ être dans son élément. ◆ **elements** *npl* **-1.** [basics] rudiments *mpl*. **-2.** [weather]: **the** ~**s** les éléments *mpl*.

elementary [,elɪ'mentərɪ] *adj* élémentaire.

elementary school *n Am* école *f* primaire.

elephant ['elɪfənt] (*pl inv* OR **-s**) *n* éléphant *m*.

elevate ['elɪveɪt] *vt* **-1.** [give importance to]: **to** ~ **sb/sthg (to)** élever qqn/qqch (à). **-2.** [raise] soulever.

elevated ['elɪveɪtɪd] *adj* **-1.** [important] important(e). **-2.** [lofty] élevé(e). **-3.** [raised] surélevé(e).

elevation [,elɪ'veɪʃn] *n* **-1.** [promotion] élévation *f*. **-2.** [height] hauteur *f*.

elevator ['elɪveɪtə'] *n Am* ascenseur *m*.

eleven [ɪ'levn] *num* onze; *see also* **six**.

elevenses [ɪ'levnzɪz] *n* (*U*) *Br* ≃ pause-café *f*.

eleventh [ɪ'levnθ] *num* onzième; *see also* **sixth**.

eleventh hour *n fig*: **the** ~ la onzième heure, la dernière minute.

elf [elf] (*pl* **elves**) *n* elfe *m*, lutin *m*.

elicit [ɪ'lɪsɪt] *vt fml*: **to** ~ **sthg (from sb)** arracher qqch (à qqn).

eligibility [,elɪdʒə'bɪlətɪ] *n* **-1.** [suitability] admissibilité *f*. **-2.** *dated* [of bachelor] acceptabilité *f*.

eligible ['elɪdʒəbl] *adj* **-1.** [suitable, qualified] admissible; **to be** ~ **for sthg** avoir droit à qqch; **to be** ~ **to do sthg** avoir le droit de faire qqch. **-2.** *dated* [bachelor]: **to be** ~ être un bon parti.

eliminate [ɪ'lɪmɪneɪt] *vt*: **to** ~ **sb/sthg (from)** éliminer qqn/qqch (de).

elimination [ɪ,lɪmɪ'neɪʃn] *n* élimination *f*.

elite [ɪ'liːt] ◇ *adj* d'élite. ◇ *n* élite *f*.

elitism [eɪ'liːtɪzm] *n* élitisme *m*.

elitist [eɪ'liːtɪst] ◇ *adj* élitiste. ◇ *n* élitiste *mf*.

elixir [ɪ'lɪksə'] *n* **-1.** [magic drink] élixir *m*. **-2.** *fig* [magic cure] panacée *f*.

Elizabethan [ɪ,lɪzə'biːθn] ◇ *adj* élisabéthain(e). ◇ *n* Élisabéthain *m*, -e *f*.

elk [elk] (*pl inv* OR **-s**) *n* élan *m*.

ellipse [ɪ'lɪps] *n* ellipse *f*.

elliptical *adj* **-1.** [in shape] en ellipse. **-2.** *fml* [indirect, cryptic] elliptique.

elm [elm] *n*: ~ **(tree)** orme *m*.

elocution [ˌeləˈkjuːʃn] *n* élocution *f*, diction *f*.

elongated [ˈiːlɒŋgeɪtɪd] *adj* allongé(e); [fingers] long (longue).

elope [ɪˈləʊp] *vi*: to ~ (with) s'enfuir (avec).

elopement [ɪˈləʊpmənt] *n* fugue *f* (amoureuse).

eloquence [ˈeləkwəns] *n* éloquence *f*.

eloquent [ˈeləkwənt] *adj* éloquent(e).

eloquently [ˈeləkwəntlɪ] *adv* avec éloquence.

El Salvador [ˌelˈsælvədɔːr] *n* Salvador *m*; in ~ au Salvador.

else [els] *adv*: **anything** ~ n'importe quoi d'autre; **anything** ~? quelque chose d'autre?; **he doesn't need anything** ~ il n'a besoin de rien d'autre; **everyone** ~ tous les autres; **nothing** ~ rien d'autre; **someone** ~ quelqu'un d'autre; **something** ~ quelque chose d'autre; **somewhere** ~ autre part; **who/what** ~? qui/quoi d'autre?; **where** ~? (à) quel autre endroit?
◆ **or else** *conj* **-1.** [or if not] sinon, sans quoi. **-2.** [as threat] ou alors ...!, sinon ...!

elsewhere [elsˈweər] *adv* ailleurs, autre part.

ELT (*abbr of* **English language teaching**) *n* enseignement de l'anglais.

elucidate [ɪˈluːsɪdeɪt] *fml* ◇ *vt* élucider. ◇ *vi* s'éclaircir.

elude [ɪˈluːd] *vt* échapper à.

elusive [ɪˈluːsɪv] *adj* insaisissable; [success] qui échappe.

elves [elvz] *pl* → elf.

'em [əm] *pron inf* = them.

emaciated [ɪˈmeɪʃɪeɪtɪd] *adj* [face] émacié(e); [person, limb] décharné(e).

E-mail (*abbr of* **electronic mail**) *n* BAL *f*.

emanate [ˈeməneɪt] *fml* ◇ *vt* dégager. ◇ *vi*: to ~ from émaner de.

emancipate [ɪˈmænsɪpeɪt] *vt*: to ~ sb (from) affranchir OR émanciper qqn (de).

emancipation [ɪˌmænsɪˈpeɪʃn] *n* affranchissement *m*, émancipation *f*.

emasculate [ɪˈmæskjʊleɪt] *vt* [weaken] émasculer.

emasculation [ɪˌmæskjʊˈleɪʃn] *n* [weakening] émasculation *f*.

embalm [ɪmˈbɑːm] *vt* embaumer.

embankment [ɪmˈbæŋkmənt] *n* [of river] berge *f*; [of railway] remblai *m*; [of road] banquette *f*.

embargo [emˈbɑːgəʊ] (*pl* **-es**, *pt* & *pp* **-ed**, *cont* **-ing**) ◇ *n*: ~ (on) embargo *m* (sur). ◇ *vt* mettre l'embargo sur.

embark [ɪmˈbɑːk] *vi* **-1.** [board ship]: to ~ (on) embarquer (sur). **-2.** [start]: to ~ on OR upon sthg s'embarquer dans qqch.

embarkation [ˌembɑːˈkeɪʃn] *n* embarquement *m*.

embarkation card *n* Br carte *f* d'embarquement.

embarrass [ɪmˈbærəs] *vt* embarrasser.

embarrassed [ɪmˈbærəst] *adj* embarrassé(e).

embarrassing [ɪmˈbærəsɪŋ] *adj* embarrassant(e).

embarrassment [ɪmˈbærəsmənt] *n* embarras *m*; to be an ~ [person] causer de l'embarras; [thing] être embarrassant.

embassy [ˈembəsɪ] (*pl* **-ies**) *n* ambassade *f*.

embattled [ɪmˈbætld] *adj* [troubled] en difficulté.

embedded [ɪmˈbedɪd] *adj* **-1.** [buried]: ~ in [in rock, wood] incrusté(e) dans; [in mud] noyé(e) dans. **-2.** [ingrained] enraciné(e).

embellish [ɪmˈbelɪʃ] *vt* **-1.** [decorate]: to ~ sthg (with) [room, house] décorer qqch (de); [dress] orner qqch (de). **-2.** [story] enjoliver.

embers [ˈembəz] *npl* braises *fpl*.

embezzle [ɪmˈbezl] *vt* détourner.

embezzlement [ɪmˈbezlmənt] *n* détournement *m* de fonds.

embezzler [ɪmˈbezlər] *n* escroc *m*.

embittered [ɪmˈbɪtəd] *adj* aigri(e).

emblazoned [ɪmˈbleɪznd] *adj* **-1.** [design, emblem]: ~ (on) blasonné(e) (sur). **-2.** [flag, garment]: ~ with arborant l'insigne OR le blason de.

emblem [ˈembləm] *n* emblème *m*.

embodiment [ɪmˈbɒdɪmənt] *n* incarnation *f*.

embody [ɪmˈbɒdɪ] (*pt* & *pp* **-ied**) *vt* incarner; to be embodied in sthg être exprimé dans qqch.

embolism [ˈembəlɪzm] *n* embolie *f*.

embossed [ɪmˈbɒst] *adj* **-1.** [heading, design]: ~ (on) inscrit(e) (sur), gravé(e) en relief (sur). **-2.** [wallpaper] gaufré(e); [leather] frappé(e).

embrace [ɪmˈbreɪs] ◇ *n* étreinte *f*. ◇ *vt* embrasser. ◇ *vi* s'embrasser, s'étreindre.

embrocation [ˌembrəˈkeɪʃn] *n* embrocation *f*.

embroider [ɪmˈbrɔɪdər] ◇ *vt* **-1.** SEWING broder. **-2.** *pej* [embellish] enjoliver. ◇ *vi* SEWING broder.

embroidered [ɪmˈbrɔɪdəd] *adj* SEWING brodé(e).

embroidery [ɪmˈbrɔɪdərɪ] *n* (U) broderie *f*.

embroil [ɪm'brɔɪl] *vt*: **to be ~ed (in)** être mêlé(e) (à).

embryo ['embrɪəʊ] (*pl* **-s**) *n* embryon *m*; **in ~** *fig* à l'état embryonnaire.

embryonic [ˌembrɪ'ɒnɪk] *adj* embryonnaire.

emcee [ˌem'siː] *Am abbr of* **master of ceremonies**.

emend [ɪ'mend] *vt* corriger.

emerald ['emərəld] ◇ *adj* [colour] émeraude (*inv*). ◇ *n* [stone] émeraude *f*.

emerge [ɪ'mɜːdʒ] ◇ *vi* **-1.** [come out]: **to ~ (from)** émerger (de). **-2.** [from experience, situation]: **to ~ from** sortir de. **-3.** [become known] apparaître. **-4.** [come into existence - poet, artist] percer; [- movement, organization] émerger. ◇ *vt*: **it ~s that ...** il ressort OR il apparaît que ....

emergence [ɪ'mɜːdʒəns] *n* émergence *f*.

emergency [ɪ'mɜːdʒənsɪ] (*pl* **-ies**) ◇ *adj* d'urgence. ◇ *n* urgence *f*; **in an ~, in emergencies** en cas d'urgence.

emergency exit *n* sortie *f* de secours.

emergency landing *n* atterrissage *m* forcé.

emergency services *npl* ≃ police-secours *f*.

emergency stop *n* arrêt *m* d'urgence.

emergent [ɪ'mɜːdʒənt] *adj* qui émerge.

emery board ['emərɪ-] *n* lime *f* à ongles.

emetic [ɪ'metɪk] ◇ *adj* émétique. ◇ *n* émétique *m*.

emigrant ['emɪɡrənt] *n* émigré *m*, -e *f*.

emigrate ['emɪɡreɪt] *vi*: **to ~ (to)** émigrer (en/à).

emigration [ˌemɪ'ɡreɪʃn] *n* émigration *f*.

émigré ['emɪɡreɪ] *n* émigré *m*, -e *f*.

eminence ['emɪnəns] *n* (*U*) [prominence] renom *m*.

eminent ['emɪnənt] *adj* éminent(e).

eminently ['emɪnəntlɪ] *adv fml* éminemment.

emir [e'mɪəʳ] *n* émir *m*.

emirate ['emərət] *n* émirat *m*.

emissary ['emɪsərɪ] (*pl* **-ies**) *n* émissaire *m*.

emission [ɪ'mɪʃn] *n* émission *f*.

emit [ɪ'mɪt] (*pt* & *pp* **-ted**, *cont* **-ting**) *vt* émettre.

emollient [ɪ'mɒlɪənt] *n fml* émollient *m*.

emolument [ɪ'mɒljʊmənt] *n fml* émoluments *mpl*.

emotion [ɪ'məʊʃn] *n* **-1.** (*U*) [strength of feeling] émotion *f*. **-2.** [particular feeling] sentiment *m*.

emotional [ɪ'məʊʃənl] *adj* **-1.** [sensitive, de-

monstrative] émotif(ive). **-2.** [moving] émouvant(e). **-3.** [psychological] émotionnel(elle).

emotionally [ɪ'məʊʃnəlɪ] *adv* **-1.** [with strong feeling] avec émotion. **-2.** [psychologically] émotionnellement.

emotionless [ɪ'məʊʃnlɪs] *adj* impassible.

emotive [ɪ'məʊtɪv] *adj* qui enflamme l'esprit.

empathy ['empəθɪ] *n* (*U*): **~ (with)** empathie *f* (avec), communion *f* de sentiments (avec).

emperor ['empərəʳ] *n* empereur *m*.

emphasis ['emfəsɪs] (*pl* **-ases** [-əsiːz]) *n*: **~ (on)** accent *m* (sur); **with great ~** avec insistance; **to lay** OR **place ~ on sthg** insister sur OR souligner qqch.

emphasize, -ise ['emfəsaɪz] *vt* insister sur.

emphatic [ɪm'fætɪk] *adj* [forceful] catégorique.

emphatically [ɪm'fætɪklɪ] *adv* **-1.** [with emphasis] catégoriquement. **-2.** [certainly] absolument.

emphysema [ˌemfɪ'siːmə] *n* emphysème *m*.

empire ['empaɪəʳ] *n* empire *m*.

empire building *n* édification *f* d'empires.

empirical [ɪm'pɪrɪkl] *adj* empirique.

empiricism [ɪm'pɪrɪsɪzm] *n* empirisme *m*.

employ [ɪm'plɔɪ] *vt* employer; **to be ~ed as** être employé comme; **to ~ sthg as sthg/to do sthg** employer qqch comme qqch/pour faire qqch.

employable [ɪm'plɔɪəbl] *adj* qui peut être employé(e).

employee [ɪm'plɔɪiː] *n* employé *m*, -e *f*.

employer [ɪm'plɔɪəʳ] *n* employeur *m*, -euse *f*.

employment [ɪm'plɔɪmənt] *n* emploi *m*, travail *m*.

employment agency *n* bureau *m* OR agence *f* de placement.

employment office *n* ≃ Agence *f* Nationale pour l'Emploi.

emporium [em'pɔːrɪəm] *n* [shop] grand magasin *m*.

empower [ɪm'paʊəʳ] *vt fml*: **to be ~ed to do sthg** être habilité(e) à faire qqch.

empress ['emprɪs] *n* impératrice *f*.

emptiness ['emptɪnɪs] *n* (*U*) vide *m*.

empty ['emptɪ] (*compar* **-ier**, *superl* **-iest**, *pt* & *pp* **-ied**, *pl* **-ies**) ◇ *adj* **-1.** [containing nothing] vide. **-2.** *pej* [meaningless] vain(e). **-3.** *literary* [tedious] morne. ◇ *vt* vider; **to ~ sthg into/out of** vider qqch dans/de. ◇ *vi* se vider. ◇ *n inf* bouteille *f* vide.

empty-handed [-'hændɪd] *adv* les mains vides.

empty-headed [-'hedɪd] *adj* sans cervelle.

EMS (*abbr of* **European Monetary System**) *n* SME *m*.

EMT (*abbr of* **emergency medical technician**) *n* technicien médical des services d'urgence.

emu ['iːmjuː] (*pl inv* OR **-s**) *n* émeu *m*.

emulate ['emjʊleɪt] *vt* imiter.

emulsion [ɪ'mʌlʃn] ◇ *n* **-1.** ~ (**paint**) peinture *f* mate OR à émulsion. **-2.** PHOT émulsion *f*. ◇ *vt Br* peindre.

enable [ɪ'neɪbl] *vt*: **to ~ sb to do sthg** permettre à qqn de faire qqch.

enact [ɪ'nækt] *vt* **-1.** JUR promulguer. **-2.** THEATRE jouer.

enactment [ɪ'næktmənt] *n* JUR promulgation *f*.

enamel [ɪ'næml] *n* **-1.** [material] émail *m*. **-2.** [paint] peinture *f* laquée.

enamelled *Br*, **enameled** *Am* [ɪ'næmld] *adj* en émail.

enamel paint *n* peinture *f* laquée.

enamoured *Br*, **enamored** *Am* [ɪ'næməd] *adj*: ~ **of** amoureux(euse) de.

en bloc [ɑ̃'blɒk] *adv* en bloc.

enc. -1. *abbr of* **enclosure. -2.** *abbr of* **enclosed.**

encamp [ɪn'kæmp] *vi* camper.

encampment [ɪn'kæmpmənt] *n* campement *m*.

encapsulate [ɪn'kæpsjʊleɪt] *vt*: **to ~ sthg (in)** résumer qqch (en).

encase [ɪn'keɪs] *vt*: **to be ~d in** [armour] être enfermé(e) dans; [leather] être bardé(e) de.

encash [ɪn'kæʃ] *vt Br* encaisser.

enchanted [ɪn'tʃɑːntɪd] *adj*: ~ (**by/with**) enchanté(e) (par/de).

enchanting [ɪn'tʃɑːntɪŋ] *adj* enchanteur(eresse).

encircle [ɪn'sɜːkl] *vt* entourer; [subj: troops] encercler.

enclave ['enkleɪv] *n* enclave *f*.

enclose [ɪn'kləʊz] *vt* **-1.** [surround, contain] entourer. **-2.** [put in envelope] joindre; **please find ~d ...** veuillez trouver ci-joint ....

enclosure [ɪn'kləʊʒər] *n* **-1.** [place] enceinte *f*. **-2.** [in letter] pièce *f* jointe.

encompass [ɪn'kʌmpəs] *vt fml* **-1.** [include] contenir. **-2.** [surround] entourer; [subj: troops] encercler.

encore ['ɒŋkɔːr] ◇ *n* rappel *m*. ◇ *excl* bis!

encounter [ɪn'kaʊntər] ◇ *n* rencontre *f.* ◇ *vt fml* rencontrer.

encourage [ɪn'kʌrɪdʒ] *vt* **-1.** [give confidence to]: **to ~ sb (to do sthg)** encourager qqn (à faire qqch). **-2.** [promote] encourager, favoriser.

encouragement [ɪn'kʌrɪdʒmənt] *n* encouragement *m*.

encouraging [ɪn'kʌrɪdʒɪŋ] *adj* encourageant(e).

encroach [ɪn'krəʊtʃ] *vi*: **to ~ on** OR **upon** empiéter sur.

encrusted [ɪn'krʌstɪd] *adj*: ~ **with** incrusté(e) de; [with mud] encroûté(e) de.

encumber [ɪn'kʌmbər] *vt fml*: **to be ~ed with** être encombré(e) de; [with debts] être grevé(e) de.

encyclop(a)edia [ɪn,saɪklə'piːdjə] *n* encyclopédie *f.*

encyclop(a)edic [ɪn,saɪkləʊ'piːdɪk] *adj* encyclopédique.

end [end] ◇ *n* **-1.** [gen] fin *f*; **at an ~** terminé, fini; **to come to an ~** se terminer, s'arrêter; **to put an ~ to sthg** mettre fin à qqch; **at the ~ of the day** *fig* en fin de compte; **in the ~** [finally] finalement; **an ~ in itself** une fin en soi. **-2.** [of rope, path, garden, table etc] bout *m*, extrémité *f*; [of box] côté *m*; ~ **to ~** bout à bout. **-3.** [leftover part - of cigarette] mégot *m*; [- of pencil] bout *m*. ◇ *vt* mettre fin à; [day] finir; **to ~ sthg with** terminer OR finir qqch par. ◇ *vi* se terminer; **to ~ in** se terminer par; **to ~ with** se terminer par OR avec.

◆ **on end** *adv* **-1.** [upright] debout. **-2.** [continuously] d'affilée.

◆ **no end** *adv inf* [pleased, worried] vachement.

◆ **no end of** *prep inf* énormément de.

◆ **end up** *vi* finir; **to ~ up doing sthg** finir par faire qqch.

endanger [ɪn'deɪndʒər] *vt* mettre en danger.

endangered species [ɪn'deɪndʒəd-] *n* espèce *f* en voie de disparition.

endear [ɪn'dɪər] *vt*: **to ~ sb to sb** faire aimer OR apprécier qqn de qqn; **to ~ o.s. to sb** se faire aimer de qqn, plaire à qqn.

endearing [ɪn'dɪərɪŋ] *adj* engageant(e).

endearment [ɪn'dɪəmənt] *n* paroles *fpl* affectueuses.

endeavour *Br*, **endeavor** *Am* [ɪn'devər] *fml* ◇ *n* effort *m*, tentative *f.* ◇ *vt*: **to ~ to do sthg** s'efforcer OR tenter de faire qqch.

endemic [en'demɪk] *adj* endémique.

ending ['endɪŋ] *n* fin *f*, dénouement *m*.

endive ['endaɪv] *n* -1. [salad vegetable] endive *f*. -2. [chicory] chicorée *f*.

endless ['endlɪs] *adj* -1. [unending] interminable; [patience, possibilities] infini(e); [resources] inépuisable. -2. [vast] infini(e).

endlessly ['endlɪslɪ] *adv* sans arrêt, continuellement; [stretch] à perte de vue; ~ patient/kind d'une patience/gentillesse infinie.

endorse [ɪn'dɔːs] *vt* -1. [approve] approuver. -2. [cheque] endosser. -3. *Br* [driving licence] porter une contravention à.

endorsement [ɪn'dɔːsmənt] *n* -1. [approval] approbation *f*. -2. [of cheque] endossement *m*. -3. *Br* [on driving licence] *contravention portée au permis de conduire.*

endow [ɪn'daʊ] *vt* -1. [equip]: **to be ~ed with sthg** être doté(e) de qqch. -2. [donate money to] faire des dons à.

endowment [ɪn'daʊmənt] *n* -1. *fml* [ability] capacité *f*, qualité *f*. -2. [donation] don *m*.

endowment insurance *n* assurance *f* à capital différé.

endowment mortgage *n* *prêt-logement lié à une assurance-vie.*

end product *n* produit *m* fini.

end result *n* résultat *m* final.

endurable [ɪn'djʊərəbl] *adj* supportable.

endurance [ɪn'djʊərəns] *n* endurance *f*.

endurance test *n* épreuve *f* d'endurance.

endure [ɪn'djʊə[r]] ◇ *vt* supporter, endurer. ◇ *vi* perdurer.

enduring [ɪn'djʊərɪŋ] *adj* durable.

end user *n* utilisateur final *m*, utilisatrice finale *f*.

endways *Br* ['endweɪz], **endwise** *Am* ['endwaɪz] *adv* -1. [not sideways] en long. -2. [with ends touching] bout à bout.

enema ['enɪmə] *n* lavement *m*.

enemy ['enɪmɪ] (*pl* -ies) ◇ *n* ennemi *m*, -e *f*. ◇ *comp* ennemi(e).

energetic [ˌenə'dʒetɪk] *adj* énergique; [person] plein(e) d'entrain.

energy ['enədʒɪ] (*pl* -ies) *n* énergie *f*.

energy-saving *adj* d'économie d'énergie.

enervate ['enɜːveɪt] *vt* *fml* affaiblir.

enervating ['enɜːveɪtɪŋ] *adj* *fml* débilitant(e).

enfold [ɪn'fəʊld] *vt* *literary* -1. [embrace]: **to ~ sb/sthg (in)** envelopper qqn/qqch (dans); **to ~ sb in one's arms** étreindre qqn. -2. [engulf] envelopper.

enforce [ɪn'fɔːs] *vt* appliquer, faire respecter.

enforceable [ɪn'fɔːsəbl] *adj* applicable.

enforced [ɪn'fɔːst] *adj* forcé(e).

enforcement [ɪn'fɔːsmənt] *n* application *f*.

enfranchise [ɪn'fræntʃaɪz] *vt* -1. [give vote to] accorder le droit de vote à. -2. [set free] affranchir.

engage [ɪn'geɪdʒ] ◇ *vt* -1. [attention, interest] susciter, éveiller; **to ~ sb in conversation** engager la conversation avec qqn. -2. TECH engager. -3. *fml* [employ] engager; **to be ~d in OR on sthg** prendre part à qqch. ◇ *vi* [be involved]: **to ~ in** s'occuper de.

engaged [ɪn'geɪdʒd] *adj* -1. [to be married]: ~ **(to sb)** fiancé(e) (à qqn); **to get ~** se fiancer. -2. [busy] occupé(e); ~ **in sthg** engagé dans qqch. -3. [telephone, toilet] occupé(e).

engaged tone *n* *Br* tonalité *f* «occupé».

engagement [ɪn'geɪdʒmənt] *n* -1. [to be married] fiançailles *fpl*. -2. [appointment] rendez-vous *m* *inv*.

engagement ring *n* bague *f* de fiançailles.

engaging [ɪn'geɪdʒɪŋ] *adj* engageant(e); [personality] attirant(e).

engender [ɪn'dʒendə[r]] *vt* *fml* engendrer, susciter.

engine ['endʒɪn] *n* -1. [of vehicle] moteur *m*. -2. RAIL locomotive *f*.

engine driver *n* *Br* mécanicien *m*.

engineer [ˌendʒɪ'nɪə[r]] ◇ *n* -1. [of roads] ingénieur *m*; [of machinery, on ship] mécanicien *m*; [of electrical equipment] technicien *m*. -2. *Am* [engine driver] mécanicien *m*. ◇ *vt* -1. [construct] construire. -2. [contrive] manigancer.

engineering [ˌendʒɪ'nɪərɪŋ] *n* ingénierie *f*.

England ['ɪŋglənd] *n* Angleterre *f*; **in ~** en Angleterre.

English ['ɪŋglɪʃ] ◇ *adj* anglais(e). ◇ *n* [language] anglais *m*. ◇ *npl*: **the ~** les Anglais.

English breakfast *n* petit déjeuner *m* anglais.

ENGLISH BREAKFAST:
Le petit déjeuner traditionnel anglais se compose d'un plat chaud (des œufs au bacon, par exemple), de céréales ou de porridge, et de toasts à la marmelade d'oranges, le tout accompagné de café ou de thé; aujourd'hui il est souvent remplacé par une collation plus légère

English Channel *n*: **the ~** la Manche.

Englishman ['ɪŋglɪʃmən] (*pl* -men [-mən]) *n* Anglais *m*.

English muffin *n* *Am* sorte de gaufre.

Englishwoman ['ɪŋglɪʃ,wumən] (*pl* -**women** [-wimin]) *n* Anglaise *f*.

engrave [ɪn'greɪv] *vt*: **to ~ sthg (on stone/in one's memory)** graver qqch (sur la pierre/ dans sa mémoire).

engraver [ɪn'greɪvər] *n* graveur *m*.

engraving [ɪn'greɪvɪŋ] *n* gravure *f*.

engrossed [ɪn'grəust] *adj*: **to be ~ (in sthg)** être absorbé(e) (par qqch).

engrossing [ɪn'grəusɪŋ] *adj* captivant(e).

engulf [ɪn'gʌlf] *vt* engloutir.

enhance [ɪn'hɑːns] *vt* accroître.

enhancement [ɪn'hɑːnsmənt] *n* amélioration *f*.

enigma [ɪ'nɪgmə] *n* énigme *f*.

enigmatic [,enɪg'mætɪk] *adj* énigmatique.

enjoy [ɪn'dʒɔɪ] ◇ *vt* **-1.** [like] aimer; **to ~ doing sthg** avoir plaisir à OR aimer faire qqch; **to ~ o.s.** s'amuser. **-2.** *fml* [possess] jouir de. ◇ *vi Am*: ~! [enjoy yourself] amuse-toi bien!; [before meal] bon appétit!

enjoyable [ɪn'dʒɔɪəbl] *adj* agréable.

enjoyment [ɪn'dʒɔɪmənt] *n* **-1.** [gen] plaisir *m*. **-2.** *fml* [possession] jouissance *f*.

enlarge [ɪn'lɑːdʒ] *vt* agrandir.

◆ **enlarge (up)on** *vt fus* développer.

enlargement [ɪn'lɑːdʒmənt] *n* **-1.** [expansion] extension *f*. **-2.** PHOT agrandissement *m*.

enlighten [ɪn'laɪtn] *vt* éclairer.

enlightened [ɪn'laɪtnd] *adj* éclairé(e).

enlightening [ɪn'laɪtnɪŋ] *adj* édifiant(e).

enlightenment [ɪn'laɪtnmənt] *n* (*U*) éclaircissement *m*.

◆ **Enlightenment** *n*: **the Enlightenment** le siècle des Lumières.

enlist [ɪn'lɪst] ◇ *vt* **-1.** MIL enrôler. **-2.** [recruit] recruter. **-3.** [obtain] s'assurer. ◇ *vi* MIL: **to ~ (in)** s'enrôler (dans).

enlisted man [ɪn'lɪstɪd-] *n Am* simple soldat *m*.

enliven [ɪn'laɪvn] *vt* animer; [book, film] égayer.

en masse [ɑ̃ː'mæs] *adv* en masse, massivement.

enmeshed [ɪn'meʃt] *adj*: ~ **in** empêtré(e) dans.

enmity ['enmətɪ] (*pl* -**ies**) *n* hostilité *f*.

ennoble [ɪ'nəubl] *vt* **-1.** [elevate to nobility] anoblir. **-2.** [dignify] ennoblir.

enormity [ɪ'nɔːmətɪ] *n* [extent] étendue *f*.

enormous [ɪ'nɔːməs] *adj* énorme; [patience, success] immense.

enormously [ɪ'nɔːməslɪ] *adv* énormément; [long, pleased] immensément.

enough [ɪ'nʌf] ◇ *adj* assez.

◇ *pron* assez; ~ **money/time** assez d'argent/de temps; **more than ~** largement, bien assez; ~ **is ~** trop c'est trop; **that's ~ (of that)!** ça suffit maintenant!; **to have had ~ (of sthg)** en avoir assez (de qqch).

◇ *adv* **-1.** [sufficiently] assez; **to be good ~ to do sthg** *fml* être assez gentil pour OR de faire qqch, être assez aimable pour OR de faire qqch. **-2.** [rather] plutôt; **strangely ~** bizarrement, c'est bizarre.

enquire [ɪn'kwaɪər] ◇ *vt*: **to ~ when/ whether/how ...** demander quand/si/ comment .... ◇ *vi*: **to ~ (about)** se renseigner (sur).

enquiry [ɪn'kwaɪərɪ] (*pl* -**ies**) *n* **-1.** [question] demande *f* de renseignements; "**Enquiries**" «renseignements». **-2.** [investigation] enquête *f*.

enraged [ɪn'reɪdʒd] *adj* déchaîné(e); [animal] enragé(e).

enrich [ɪn'rɪtʃ] *vt* enrichir.

enrol (*pt* & *pp* **-led**, *cont* **-ling**), **enroll** *Am* [ɪn'rəul] ◇ *vt* inscrire. ◇ *vi*: **to ~ (in)** s'inscrire (à).

enrolment *Br*, **enrollment** *Am* [ɪn'rəulmənt] *n* **-1.** (*U*) [registration] inscription *f*. **-2.** [person enrolled] inscrit *m*.

en route [ɑ̃ːn'ruːt] *adv*: ~ **(to)** en route (vers); ~ **from** en provenance de.

ensconced [ɪn'skɒnst] *adj hum*: ~ **(in)** bien installé(e) (dans).

enshrine [ɪn'ʃraɪn] *vt*: **to be ~d in** être garanti(e) par.

ensign ['ensaɪn] *n* **-1.** [flag] pavillon *m*. **-2.** *Am* [sailor] enseigne *m*.

enslave [ɪn'sleɪv] *vt* asservir.

ensue [ɪn'sjuː] *vi* s'ensuivre.

ensuing [ɪn'sjuːɪŋ] *adj* qui s'ensuit.

ensure [ɪn'ʃɔːr] *vt* assurer; **to ~ (that) ...** s'assurer que ....

ENT (*abbr of* **Ear, Nose & Throat**) *n* ORL *f*.

entail [ɪn'teɪl] *vt* entraîner; **what does the work ~?** en quoi consiste le travail?

entangled [ɪn'tæŋgld] *adj* **-1.** [caught]: **to be ~ in** être emmêlé(e) OR enchevêtré(e) dans. **-2.** [in problem, difficult situation]: **to be ~ in** être empêtré(e) dans. **-3.** *fig* [with person]: **to be ~ with** avoir une liaison avec.

entanglement [ɪn'tæŋglmənt] *n* liaison *f* (amoureuse).

enter ['entər] ◇ *vt* **-1.** [room, vehicle] entrer dans. **-2.** [university, army] entrer à; [school] s'inscrire à, s'inscrire dans. **-3.** [competition, race] s'inscrire à; [politics] se lancer dans.

-4. [register]: to ~ **sb/sthg for sthg** inscrire qqn/qqch à qqch. **-5.** [write down] inscrire. **-6.** COMPUT entrer. ◇ *vi* **-1.** [come or go in] entrer. **-2.** [register]: to ~ **(for)** s'inscrire (à). ◆ **enter into** *vt fus* [negotiations, correspondence] entamer.

enteritis [ˌentəˈraɪtɪs] *n* entérite *f.*

enter key *n* COMPUT (touche *f*) entrée *f.*

enterprise [ˈentəpraɪz] *n* entreprise *f.*

enterprise culture *n* culture *f* d'entreprise.

enterprise zone *n* zone dans une région défavorisée qui bénéficie de subsides de l'État.

enterprising [ˈentəpraɪzɪŋ] *adj* qui fait preuve d'initiative.

entertain [ˌentəˈteɪn] ◇ *vt* **-1.** [amuse] divertir. **-2.** [invite - guests] recevoir. **-3.** *fml* [thought, proposal] considérer. **-4.** *fml* [hopes] nourrir. ◇ *vi* **-1.** [amuse] se divertir. **-2.** [have guests] recevoir.

entertainer [ˌentəˈteɪnər] *n* fantaisiste *mf.*

entertaining [ˌentəˈteɪnɪŋ] ◇ *adj* divertissant(e). ◇ *n*: **to do a lot of** ~ recevoir beaucoup.

entertainment [ˌentəˈteɪnmənt] ◇ *n* **-1.** (*U*) [amusement] divertissement *m.* **-2.** [show] spectacle *m.* ◇ *comp* du spectacle.

entertainment allowance *n* frais *mpl* de représentation.

enthral (*pt* & *pp* **-led**, *cont* **-ling**), **enthrall** *Am* [ɪnˈθrɔːl] *vt* captiver.

enthralling [ɪnˈθrɔːlɪŋ] *adj* captivant(e).

enthuse [ɪnˈθjuːz] *vi*: to ~ **(about)** s'enthousiasmer (pour).

enthusiasm [ɪnˈθjuːzɪæzm] *n* **-1.** [passion, eagerness]: ~ **(for)** enthousiasme *m* (pour). **-2.** [interest] passion *f.*

enthusiast [ɪnˈθjuːzɪæst] *n* amateur *m*, -trice *f.*

enthusiastic [ɪnˌθjuːzɪˈæstɪk] *adj* enthousiaste.

enthusiastically [ɪnˌθjuːzɪˈæstɪklɪ] *adv* avec enthousiasme.

entice [ɪnˈtaɪs] *vt* entraîner.

enticing [ɪnˈtaɪsɪŋ] *adj* alléchant(e); [smile] séduisant(e).

entire [ɪnˈtaɪər] *adj* entier(ière).

entirely [ɪnˈtaɪəlɪ] *adv* totalement.

entirety [ɪnˈtaɪrətɪ] *n*: **in its** ~ en entier.

entitle [ɪnˈtaɪtl] *vt* [allow]: to ~ **sb to sthg** donner droit à qqch à qqn; to ~ **sb to do sthg** autoriser qqn à faire qqch.

entitled [ɪnˈtaɪtld] *adj* **-1.** [allowed] autorisé(e); to be ~ **to sthg** avoir droit à qqch; to

be ~ **to do sthg** avoir le droit de faire qqch. **-2.** [called] intitulé(e).

entitlement [ɪnˈtaɪtlmənt] *n* droit *m.*

entity [ˈentətɪ] (*pl* **-ies**) *n* entité *f.*

entomology [ˌentəˈmɒlədʒɪ] *n* entomologie *f.*

entourage [ˌɒntuˈrɑːʒ] *n* entourage *m.*

entrails [ˈentreɪlz] *npl* entrailles *fpl.*

entrance [*n* ˈentrəns, *vt* ɪnˈtrɑːns] ◇ *n* **-1.** [way in]: ~ **(to)** entrée *f* (de). **-2.** [arrival] entrée *f.* **-3.** [entry]: **to gain** ~ **to** [building] obtenir l'accès à; [society, university] être admis(e) dans. ◇ *vt* ravir, enivrer.

entrance examination *n* examen *m* d'entrée.

entrance fee *n* **-1.** [to cinema, museum] droit *m* d'entrée. **-2.** [for club] droit *m* d'inscription.

entrancing [ɪnˈtrɑːnsɪŋ] *adj* épatant(e).

entrant [ˈentrənt] *n* [in race, competition] concurrent *m*, -e *f.*

entreat [ɪnˈtriːt] *vt*: to ~ **sb (to do sthg)** supplier qqn (de faire qqch).

entreaty [ɪnˈtriːtɪ] (*pl* **-ies**) *n* prière *f*, supplication *f.*

entrenched [ɪnˈtrentʃt] *adj* ancré(e).

entrepreneur [ˌɒntrəprəˈnɜːr] *n* entrepreneur *m.*

entrepreneurial [ˌɒntrəprəˈnɜːrɪəl] *adj* [person] qui a l'esprit d'entreprise; [skill] d'entrepreneur.

entrust [ɪnˈtrʌst] *vt*: to ~ **sthg to sb**, to ~ **sb with sthg** confier qqch à qqn.

entry [ˈentrɪ] (*pl* **-ies**) *n* **-1.** [gen] entrée *f*; to gain ~ to avoir accès à; "no ~" «défense d'entrer»; AUT «sens interdit». **-2.** [in competition] inscription *f.* **-3.** [in dictionary] entrée *f*; [in diary, ledger] inscription *f.*

entry fee *n* entrée *f.*

entry form *n* formulaire *m* OR feuille *f* d'inscription.

entry phone *n* portier *m* électronique.

entryway [ˈentrɪˌweɪ] *n* Am entrée *f.*

entwine [ɪnˈtwaɪn] ◇ *vt* entrelacer. ◇ *vi* s'entrelacer.

E number *n* additif *m* E.

enumerate [ɪˈnjuːməreɪt] *vt* énumérer.

enunciate [ɪˈnʌnsɪeɪt] ◇ *vt* **-1.** [word] articuler. **-2.** [idea, plan] énoncer, exposer. ◇ *vi* articuler.

envelop [ɪnˈveləp] *vt* envelopper.

envelope [ˈenvələup] *n* enveloppe *f.*

enviable [ˈenvɪəbl] *adj* enviable.

envious [ˈenvɪəs] *adj* envieux(ieuse).

enviously [ˈenvɪəslɪ] *adv* avec envie.

environment [ɪn'vaɪərənmənt] n -1. [surroundings] milieu m, cadre m. -2. [natural world]: the ~ l'environnement m; Department of the Environment Br ≃ ministère m de l'Environnement. -3. COMPUT environnement m.

environmental [ɪn,vaɪərən'mentl] adj [pollution, awareness] de l'environnement; [impact] sur l'environnement.

environmentalist [ɪn,vaɪərən'mentəlɪst] n écologiste mf.

environmentally [ɪn,vaɪərən'mentəlɪ] adv [damaging] pour l'environnement; to be ~ aware être sensible aux problèmes de l'environnement; ~ friendly qui préserve l'environnement.

Environmental Protection Agency n Am ≃ ministère m de l'Environnement.

environs [ɪn'vaɪərənz] npl environs mpl.

envisage [ɪn'vɪzɪdʒ], **envision** Am [ɪn'vɪʒn] vt envisager.

envoy ['envɔɪ] n émissaire m.

envy ['envɪ] (pt & pp -ied) ◇ n envie f, jalousie f; to be the ~ of faire envie à; to be green with ~ être malade de jalousie. ◇ vt envier; to ~ sb sthg envier qqch à qqn.

enzyme ['enzaɪm] n enzyme f.

EOC abbr of **Equal Opportunities Commission**.

eon Am = aeon.

EPA (abbr of **Environmental Protection Agency**) n agence américaine pour la protection de l'environnement.

epaulet(te) ['epəlet] n épaulette f.

ephemeral [ɪ'femərəl] adj éphémère.

epic ['epɪk] ◇ adj épique. ◇ n épopée f.

epicentre Br, **epicenter** Am ['episentər] n épicentre m.

epidemic [,epɪ'demɪk] n épidémie f.

epidural [,epɪ'djʊərəl] n péridurale f.

epigram ['epɪgræm] n épigramme f.

epilepsy ['epɪlepsɪ] n épilepsie f.

epileptic [,epɪ'leptɪk] ◇ adj épileptique. ◇ n épileptique mf.

epilogue Br, **epilog** Am ['epɪlɒg] n épilogue m.

Epiphany [ɪ'pɪfənɪ] n Épiphanie f.

episcopal [ɪ'pɪskəpl] adj épiscopal(e).

episode ['episəʊd] n épisode m.

episodic [,epɪ'sɒdɪk] adj [story, play] en épisodes.

epistle [ɪ'pɪsl] n épître f.

epitaph ['epɪtɑːf] n épitaphe f.

epithet ['epɪθet] n épithète f.

epitome [ɪ'pɪtəmɪ] n: the ~ of le modèle de.

epitomize, -ise [ɪ'pɪtəmaɪz] vt incarner.

epoch ['iːpɒk] n époque f.

epoch-making [-'meɪkɪŋ] adj qui fait date.

eponymous [ɪ'pɒnɪməs] adj éponyme.

EPOS ['iːpɒs] (abbr of **electronic point of sale**) n point de vente électronique.

equable ['ekwəbl] adj égal(e), constant(e).

equal ['iːkwəl] (Br pt & pp -led, cont -ling, Am pt & pp -ed, cont -ing) ◇ adj -1. [gen]: (to) égal(e) (à); on ~ terms d'égal à égal. -2. [capable]: ~ to sthg à la hauteur de qqch. ◇ n égal m, -e f. ◇ vt égaler.

equality [iː'kwɒlətɪ] n égalité f.

equalize, -ise ['iːkwəlaɪz] ◇ vt niveler. ◇ vi SPORT égaliser.

equalizer ['iːkwəlaɪzər] n SPORT but m égalisateur.

equally ['iːkwəlɪ] adv -1. [important, stupid etc] tout aussi; I like them ~ je les apprécie de la même façon. -2. [in amount] en parts égales. -3. [also] en même temps.

equal opportunities npl égalité f des chances.

Equal Opportunities Commission n commission britannique pour l'égalité des chances dans le travail.

equal(s) sign n le signe m d'égalité.

equanimity [,ekwə'nɪmətɪ] n sérénité f, égalité f d'âme.

equate [ɪ'kweɪt] vt: to ~ sthg with assimiler qqch à.

equation [ɪ'kweɪʒn] n équation f.

equator ['ɪkweɪtər] n: the ~ l'équateur m.

equatorial [,ekwə'tɔːrɪəl] adj équatorial(e).

Equatorial Guinea n Guinée f équatoriale.

equestrian [ɪ'kwestrɪən] adj équestre.

equidistant [,iːkwɪ'dɪstənt] adj: ~ (from) équidistant(e) (de).

equilateral triangle [,iːkwɪ'lætərəl-] n triangle m équilatéral.

equilibrium [,iːkwɪ'lɪbrɪəm] n équilibre m.

equine ['ekwaɪn] adj chevalin(e).

equinox ['iːkwɪnɒks] n équinoxe m.

equip [ɪ'kwɪp] (pt & pp -ped, cont -ping) vt équiper; to ~ sb/sthg with équiper qqn/qqch de, munir qqn/qqch de; he's well equipped for the job il est bien préparé pour ce travail.

equipment [ɪ'kwɪpmənt] n (U) équipement m, matériel m.

equitable ['ekwɪtəbl] adj équitable.

equities ['ekwətız] *npl* ST EX actions *fpl* ordinaires.

equivalent [ı'kwıvələnt] ◇ *adj* équivalent(e); **to be ~ to** être équivalent à, équivaloir à. ◇ *n* équivalent *m*.

equivocal [ı'kwıvəkl] *adj* équivoque.

equivocate [ı'kwıvəkeıt] *vi* parler de façon équivoque.

er [ɜːr] *excl* euh!

ER (*abbr of* **Elizabeth Regina**) *emblème de la reine Elizabeth.*

era ['ıərə] (*pl* **-s**) *n* ère *f*, période *f*.

ERA ['ıərə] (*abbr of* **Equal Rights Amendment**) *n* loi américaine sur l'égalité des droits des femmes.

eradicate [ı'rædıkeıt] *vt* éradiquer.

eradication [ı,rædı'keıʃn] *n* éradication *f*.

erase [ı'reız] *vt* **-1.** [rub out] gommer. **-2.** *fig* [memory] effacer; [hunger, poverty] éliminer.

eraser [ı'reızər] *n* gomme *f*.

erect [ı'rekt] ◇ *adj* **-1.** [person, posture] droit(e). **-2.** [penis] en érection. ◇ *vt* **-1.** [statue] ériger; [building] construire. **-2.** [tent] dresser.

erection [ı'rekʃn] *n* **-1.** (*U*) [of statue] érection *f*; [of building] construction *f*. **-2.** [erect penis] érection *f*.

ergonomics [,ɜːgə'nɒmıks] *n* ergonomie *f*.

ERISA [ə'riːsə] (*abbr of* **Employee Retirement Income Security Act**) *n* loi américaine sur les pensions de retraite.

Eritrea [,erı'treıə] *n* Érythrée *f*; **in ~** en Érythrée.

Eritrean [,erı'treıən] ◇ *adj* érythréen(enne). ◇ *n* Érythréen *m*, -enne *f*.

ERM (*abbr of* **Exchange Rate Mechanism**) *n* mécanisme *m* des changes (du SME).

ermine ['ɜːmın] *n* [fur] hermine *f*.

ERNIE ['ɜːnı] (*abbr of* **Electronic Random Number Indicator Equipment**) *n* dispositif de tirage des numéros gagnants des 'Premium Bonds'.

erode [ı'rəʊd] ◇ *vt* **-1.** [rock, soil] éroder. **-2.** *fig* [confidence, rights] réduire. ◇ *vi* **-1.** [rock, soil] s'éroder. **-2.** *fig* [confidence] diminuer; [rights] se réduire.

erogenous zone [ı'rɒdʒınəs-] *n* zone *f* érogène.

erosion [ı'rəʊʒn] *n* **-1.** [of rock, soil] érosion *f*. **-2.** *fig* [of confidence] baisse *f*; [of rights] diminution *f*.

erotic [ı'rɒtık] *adj* érotique.

eroticism [ı'rɒtısızm] *n* érotisme *m*.

err [ɜːr] *vi* se tromper; **to ~ is human** l'er-

reur est humaine; **to ~ on the side of** pécher par excès de.

errand ['erənd] *n* course *f*, commission *f*; **to go on** OR **run an ~** faire une course.

errand boy *n* garçon *m* de courses.

erratic [ı'rætık] *adj* irrégulier(ière).

erroneous [ı'rəʊnjəs] *adj fml* erroné(e).

error ['erər] *n* erreur *f*; **a spelling/typing ~** une faute d'orthographe/de frappe; **an ~ of judgment** une erreur de jugement; **in ~** par erreur.

error message *n* COMPUT message *m* d'erreur.

erstwhile ['ɜːstwaıl] *adj literary* d'autrefois.

erudite ['eruːdaıt] *adj* savant(e).

erupt [ı'rʌpt] *vi* **-1.** [volcano] entrer en éruption. **-2.** *fig* [violence, war] éclater.

eruption [ı'rʌpʃn] *n* **-1.** [of volcano] éruption *f*. **-2.** [of violence] explosion *f*; [of war] déclenchement *m*.

ESA (*abbr of* **European Space Agency**) *n* ESA *f*, ASE *f*.

escalate ['eskəleıt] *vi* **-1.** [conflict] s'intensifier. **-2.** [costs] monter en flèche.

escalation [,eskə'leıʃn] *n* **-1.** [of conflict, violence] intensification *f*. **-2.** [of costs] montée *f* en flèche.

escalator ['eskəleıtər] *n* escalier *m* roulant.

escalator clause *n* clause *f* d'indexation.

escapade [,eskə'peıd] *n* aventure *f*, exploit *m*.

escape [ı'skeıp] ◇ *n* **-1.** [gen] fuite *f*, évasion *f*; **to make one's ~** s'échapper; **to have a lucky ~** l'échapper belle. **-2.** [leakage - of gas, water] fuite *f*. ◇ *vt* échapper à; **to ~ notice** échapper à l'attention. ◇ *vi* **-1.** [gen] s'échapper, fuir; [from prison] s'évader; **to ~ from** [place] s'échapper de; [danger, person] échapper à. **-2.** [survive] s'en tirer.

escape clause *n* clause *f* échappatoire.

escape key *n* COMPUT touche *f* d'échappement.

escape route *n* **-1.** [from prison] moyen *m* d'évasion. **-2.** [from fire] itinéraire d'évacuation en cas d'incendie.

escapism [ı'skeıpızm] *n* (*U*) évasion *f* (de la réalité).

escapist [ı'skeıpıst] *adj* [literature, film] d'évasion.

escapologist [,eskə'pɒlədʒıst] *n* virtuose *mf* de l'évasion.

escarpment [ı'skɑːpmənt] *n* escarpement *m*.

eschew [ıs'tʃuː] *vt fml* s'abstenir de.

escort [*n* 'eskɔːt, *vb* ɪ'skɔːt] ◇ *n* **-1.** [guard] escorte *f*; **under ~** sous escorte. **-2.** [companion - male] cavalier *m*; [- female] hôtesse *f*. ◇ *vt* escorter, accompagner.

escort agency *n* agence *f* d'hôtesses.

Eskimo ['eskɪməʊ] (*pl* **-s**) ◇ *adj* esquimau(aude). ◇ *n* **-1.** [person] Esquimau *m*, -aude *f*. **-2.** [language] esquimau *m*.

ESL (*abbr of* **English as a Second Language**) *n* anglais deuxième langue.

esophagus *Am* = **oesophagus**.

esoteric [ˌesə'terɪk] *adj* ésotérique.

esp. *abbr of* **especially**.

ESP *n* **-1.** (*abbr of* **extrasensory perception**) perception *f* extrasensorielle. **-2.** (*abbr of* **English for special purposes**) anglais à usage professionnel.

espadrille [ˌespə'drɪl] *n* espadrille *f*.

especial [ɪ'speʃl] *adj* spécial(e), particulier(ère).

especially [ɪ'speʃəlɪ] *adv* **-1.** [in particular] surtout. **-2.** [more than usually] particulièrement. **-3.** [specifically] spécialement.

Esperanto [ˌespə'ræntəʊ] *n* espéranto *m*.

espionage ['espɪə,nɑːʒ] *n* espionnage *m*.

esplanade [ˌesplə'neɪd] *n* esplanade *f*.

espouse [ɪ'spaʊz] *vt* épouser.

espresso [e'spresəʊ] (*pl* **-s**) *n* express *m inv*.

Esq. *abbr of* **Esquire**.

Esquire [ɪ'skwaɪəʳ] *n*: **G. Curry ~** Monsieur G. Curry.

essay ['eseɪ] *n* **-1.** SCH & UNIV dissertation *f*. **-2.** LITERATURE essai *m*.

essayist ['eseɪɪst] *n* essayiste *mf*.

essence ['esns] *n* **-1.** [nature] essence *f*, nature *f*; **in ~** par essence. **-2.** CULIN extrait *m*.

essential [ɪ'senʃl] *adj* **-1.** [absolutely necessary]: **~ (to** OR **for)** indispensable (à). **-2.** [basic] essentiel(ielle), de base.
◆ **essentials** *npl* **-1.** [basic commodities] produits *mpl* de première nécessité. **-2.** [most important elements] essentiel *m*.

essentially [ɪ'senʃəlɪ] *adv* fondamentalement, avant tout.

est. -1. *abbr of* **established**. **-2.** *abbr of* **estimated**.

EST (*abbr of* **Eastern Standard Time**) *n* heure d'été de la côte est des États-Unis.

establish [ɪ'stæblɪʃ] *vt* **-1.** [gen] établir; **to ~ contact with** établir le contact avec. **-2.** [organization, business] fonder, créer.

established [ɪ'stæblɪʃt] *adj* **-1.** [custom] établi(e). **-2.** [business, company] fondé(e).

establishment [ɪ'stæblɪʃmənt] *n* **-1.** [gen]

établissement *m*. **-2.** [of organization, business] fondation *f*, création *f*.
◆ **Establishment** *n* [status quo]: **the Establishment** l'ordre *m* établi, l'Establishment *m*.

estate [ɪ'steɪt] *n* **-1.** [land, property] propriété *f*, domaine *m*. **-2.** (**housing**) ~ lotissement *m*. **-3.** (**industrial**) ~ zone *f* industrielle. **-4.** JUR [inheritance] biens *mpl*.

estate agency *n Br* agence *f* immobilière.

estate agent *n Br* agent *m* immobilier.

estate car *n Br* break *m*.

estd., est'd. *abbr of* **established**.

esteem [ɪ'stiːm] ◇ *n* estime *f*; **to hold sb/ sthg in high ~** tenir qqn/qqch en haute estime. ◇ *vt* estimer.

esthete *etc Am* = **aesthete** *etc*.

estimate [*n* 'estɪmət, *vb* 'estɪmeɪt] ◇ *n* **-1.** [calculation, judgment] estimation *f*, évaluation *f*. **-2.** COMM devis *m*. ◇ *vt* estimer, évaluer. ◇ *vi* COMM: **to ~ for** faire OR établir un devis pour.

estimated ['estɪmeɪtɪd] *adj* estimé(e).

estimation [ˌestɪ'meɪʃn] *n* **-1.** [opinion] opinion *f*. **-2.** [calculation] estimation *f*, évaluation *f*.

Estonia [e'stəʊnɪə] *n* Estonie *f*; **in ~** en Estonie.

Estonian [e'stəʊnɪən] ◇ *adj* estonien(ienne). ◇ *n* **-1.** [person] Estonien *m*, -ienne *f*. **-2.** [language] estonien *m*.

estranged [ɪ'streɪndʒd] *adj* [couple] séparé(e); [husband, wife] dont on s'est séparé.

estrogen *Am* = **oestrogen**.

estuary ['estjʊərɪ] (*pl* **-ies**) *n* estuaire *m*.

ETA (*abbr of* **estimated time of arrival**) *n* HPA *f*.

et al. ['etæl] (*abbr of* **et alii**) et coll., et al.

etc. (*abbr of* **et caetera**) etc.

etcetera [ɪt'setərə] *adv* et cetera.

etch [etʃ] *vt* graver à l'eau forte; **to be ~ed on sb's memory** être gravé dans la mémoire de qqn.

etching ['etʃɪŋ] *n* gravure *f* à l'eau forte.

ETD (*abbr of* **estimated time of departure**) *n* HPD *f*.

eternal [iː'tɜːnl] *adj* **-1.** [life] éternel(elle). **-2.** *fig* [complaints, whining] sempiternel(elle). **-3.** [truth, value] immuable.

eternally [iː'tɜːnəlɪ] *adv* éternellement.

eternity [iː'tɜːnətɪ] *n* éternité *f*.

eternity ring *n Br* bague *f* de fidélité.

ether ['iːθəʳ] *n* éther *m*.

ethereal [iː'θɪərɪəl] *adj* éthéré(e).

ethic ['eθɪk] *n* éthique *f*, morale *f*.

◆ **ethics** ◇ *n* (U) [study] éthique *f*, morale *f*. ◇ *npl* [morals] morale *f*.

ethical ['eθɪkl] *adj* moral(e).

Ethiopia [,i:θɪ'əʊpɪə] *n* Éthiopie *f*; **in ~** en Éthiopie.

Ethiopian [,i:θɪ'əʊpɪən] ◇ *adj* éthiopien(ienne). ◇ *n* Éthiopien *m*, -ienne *f*.

ethnic ['eθnɪk] *adj* **-1.** [traditions, groups] ethnique. **-2.** [clothes] folklorique.

ethnic cleansing [-'klenzɪŋ] *n* purification *f* ethnique.

ethnic minority *n* minorité *f* ethnique.

ethnology [eθ'nɒlədʒɪ] *n* ethnologie *f*.

ethos ['i:θɒs] *n* génie *m* (d'un peuple/d'une civilisation).

etiquette ['etɪket] *n* convenances *fpl*, étiquette *f*.

ETU (*abbr of* **Electrical Trades Union**) *n* syndicat d'électriciens.

ETV (*abbr of* **educational television**) *n* télévision scolaire.

etymology [,etɪ'mɒlədʒɪ] (*pl* **-ies**) *n* étymologie *f*.

eucalyptus [,ju:kə'lɪptəs] *n* eucalyptus *m*.

eulogize, -ise ['ju:lədʒaɪz] *vt* faire le panégyrique de.

eulogy ['ju:lədʒɪ] (*pl* **-ies**) *n* panégyrique *m*.

eunuch ['ju:nək] *n* eunuque *m*.

euphemism ['ju:fəmɪzm] *n* euphémisme *m*.

euphemistic [,ju:fə'mɪstɪk] *adj* euphémique.

euphoria [ju:'fɔ:rɪə] *n* euphorie *f*.

euphoric [ju:'fɒrɪk] *adj* euphorique.

Eurasia [jʊə'reɪʒə] *n* Eurasie *f*.

Eurasian [jʊə'reɪʒən] ◇ *adj* eurasien(ienne). ◇ *n* Eurasien *m*, -ienne *f*.

eureka [jʊə'ri:kə] *excl* eurêka!

Euro- ['jʊərəʊ] *prefix* euro-.

Eurocheque ['jʊərəʊ,tʃek] *n* eurochèque *m*.

Eurocrat ['jʊərə,kræt] *n* eurocrate *mf*.

Eurocurrency ['ju:rəʊ,kʌrənsɪ] (*pl* **-ies**) *n* eurodevise *f*.

Eurodollar ['jʊərəʊ,dɒlə`] *n* eurodollar *m*.

Euro MP *n* député *m* européen.

Europe ['jʊərəp] *n* Europe *f*.

European [,jʊərə'pɪən] ◇ *adj* européen(enne). ◇ *n* Européen *m*, -enne *f*.

European Community *n*: **the ~** la Communauté européenne.

European Court of Human Rights *n*: **the ~** la Cour européenne des droits de l'homme.

European Court of Justice *n*: **the ~** la Cour européenne de justice.

European Currency Unit *n* Unité *f* monétaire européenne.

Europeanism [,jʊərə'pi:ənɪzm] *n* européanisme *m*.

Europeanize, -ise [,jʊərə'pi:ənaɪz] *vt* européaniser.

European Monetary System *n*: **the ~** le Système monétaire européen.

European Parliament *n*: **the ~** le Parlement européen.

euthanasia [,ju:θə'neɪzjə] *n* euthanasie *f*.

evacuate [ɪ'vækjʊeɪt] *vt* évacuer.

evacuation [ɪ,vækjʊ'eɪʃn] *n* évacuation *f*.

evacuee [ɪ,vækjʊ'i:] *n* évacué *m*, -e *f*.

evade [ɪ'veɪd] *vt* **-1.** [gen] échapper à. **-2.** [issue, question] esquiver, éluder.

evaluate [ɪ'væljʊeɪt] *vt* évaluer.

evaluation [ɪ,væljʊ'eɪʃn] *n* évaluation *f*.

evangelical [,i:væn'dʒelɪkl] *adj* évangélique.

evangelism [ɪ'vændʒəlɪzm] *n* évangélisation *f*.

evangelist [ɪ'vændʒəlɪst] *n* évangéliste *mf*.

evangelize, -ise [ɪ'vændʒəlaɪz] *vt* évangéliser.

evaporate [ɪ'væpəreɪt] *vi* **-1.** [liquid] s'évaporer. **-2.** *fig* [hopes, fears] s'envoler; [confidence] disparaître.

evaporated milk [ɪ'væpəreɪtɪd-] *n* lait *m* condensé (non sucré).

evaporation [ɪ,væpə'reɪʃn] *n* évaporation *f*.

evasion [ɪ'veɪʒn] *n* **-1.** [of responsibility] dérobade *f*; **tax ~** évasion *f* fiscale. **-2.** [lie] faux-fuyant *m*.

evasive [ɪ'veɪsɪv] *adj* évasif(ive); **to take ~ action** faire une manœuvre d'évitement.

evasiveness [ɪ'veɪsɪvnɪs] *n* caractère *m* évasif.

eve [i:v] *n* veille *f*.

even ['i:vn] ◇ *adj* **-1.** [speed, rate] régulier(ière); [temperature, temperament] égal(e). **-2.** [flat, level] plat(e), régulier(ière). **-3.** [equal - contest] équilibré(e); [- teams, players] de la même force; [- scores] à égalité; **to get ~ with sb** se venger de qqn. **-4.** [not odd - number] pair(e).

◇ *adv* **-1.** [gen] même; **~ now** encore maintenant; **~ then** même alors. **-2.** [in comparisons]: **~ bigger/better/more stupid** encore plus grand/mieux/plus bête.

◆ **even as** *conj* au moment même où.

◆ **even if** *conj* même si.

◆ **even so** *adv* quand même.

◆ **even though** *conj* bien que (+ *subjunctive*).

◆ **even out** ◇ *vt sep* égaliser. ◇ *vi* s'égaliser.

even-handed [-'hændɪd] *adj* impartial(e).

evening ['iːvnɪŋ] *n* soir *m*; [duration, entertainment] soirée *f*; **in the ~** le soir.

◆ **evenings** *adv Am* le soir.

evening class *n* cours *m* du soir.

evening dress *n* [worn by man] habit *m* de soirée; [worn by woman] robe *f* du soir.

evening star *n*: **the ~** l'étoile *f* du berger.

evenly ['iːvnlɪ] *adv* **-1.** [breathe, distributed] régulièrement. **-2.** [equally - divided] également; **to be ~ matched** être de la même force. **-3.** [calmly] calmement, sur un ton égal.

evenness ['iːvnnɪs] *n* **-1.** [of breathing] régularité *f*. **-2.** [equality] bon équilibre *m*.

evensong ['iːvnsɒŋ] *n* vêpres *fpl*.

event [ɪ'vent] *n* **-1.** [happening] événement *m*. **-2.** SPORT épreuve *f*. **-3.** [case]: **in the ~ of** en cas de; **in the ~ that** au cas où.

◆ **in any event** *adv* en tout cas, de toute façon.

◆ **in the event** *adv Br* en l'occurrence, en réalité.

even-tempered [-'tempəd] *adj* d'humeur égale.

eventful [ɪ'ventful] *adj* mouvementé(e).

eventide home ['iːvntaɪd-] *n Br euphemism* hospice *m* de vieillards.

eventing [ɪ'ventɪŋ] *n Br* SPORT: **(three-day) ~** concours *m* complet.

eventual [ɪ'ventʃuəl] *adj* final(e); **the ~ winner was X** finalement, le vainqueur a été X.

eventuality [ɪ,ventʃu'ælətɪ] *(pl* -**ies)** *n* éventualité *f*.

eventually [ɪ'ventʃuəlɪ] *adv* finalement, en fin de compte.

ever ['evəʳ] *adv* **-1.** [at any time] jamais; **have you ~ been to Paris?** êtes-vous déjà allé à Paris?; **I hardly ~ see him** je ne le vois presque jamais; **if ~** si jamais. **-2.** [all the time] toujours; **as ~** comme toujours; **for ~** pour toujours. **-3.** [for emphasis]: **~ so** tellement; **~ such** vraiment; **why/how ~?** pourquoi/comment donc?

◆ **ever since** ◇ *adv* depuis (ce moment-là). ◇ *conj* depuis que. ◇ *prep* depuis.

Everest ['evərɪst] *n* l'Everest *m*.

Everglades ['evə,gleɪdz] *n*: **the ~** les Everglades *mpl*.

evergreen ['evəgriːn] ◇ *adj* à feuilles persistantes. ◇ *n* arbre *m* à feuilles persistantes.

everlasting [,evə'laːstɪŋ] *adj* éternel(elle).

every ['evrɪ] *adj* chaque; **~ morning** chaque matin, tous les matins; **there's ~ chance**

she'll pass the exam elle a toutes les chances de réussir à son examen.

◆ **every now and then**, **every so often** *adv* de temps en temps, de temps à autre.

◆ **every other** *adj*: **~ day** tous les deux jours, un jour sur deux; **~ other street** une rue sur deux.

◆ **every which way** *adv Am* partout, de tous côtés.

everybody ['evrɪ,bɒdɪ] = **everyone**.

everyday ['evrɪdeɪ] *adj* quotidien(ienne).

everyone ['evrɪwʌn] *pron* chacun, tout le monde.

everyplace *Am* = **everywhere**.

everything ['evrɪθɪŋ] *pron* tout.

everywhere ['evrɪweəʳ], **everyplace** *Am* ['evrɪ,pleɪs] *adv* partout.

evict [ɪ'vɪkt] *vt* expulser.

eviction [ɪ'vɪkʃn] *n* expulsion *f*.

eviction notice *n* avis *m* d'expulsion.

evidence ['evɪdəns] *n (U)* **-1.** [proof] preuve *f*. **-2.** JUR [of witness] témoignage *m*; **to give ~** témoigner.

◆ **in evidence** [noticeable] en évidence.

evident ['evɪdənt] *adj* évident(e), manifeste.

evidently ['evɪdəntlɪ] *adv* **-1.** [seemingly] apparemment. **-2.** [obviously] de toute évidence, manifestement.

evil ['iːvl] ◇ *adj* [person] mauvais(e), malveillant(e). ◇ *n* mal *m*.

evil-minded [-'maɪndɪd] *adj* malveillant(e), malintentionné(e).

evince [ɪ'vɪns] *vt fml* faire montre de.

evocation [,evəʊ'keɪʃn] *n* évocation *f*.

evocative [ɪ'vɒkətɪv] *adj* évocateur(trice).

evoke [ɪ'vəʊk] *vt* [memory] évoquer; [emotion, response] susciter.

evolution [,iːvə'luːʃn] *n* évolution *f*.

evolve [ɪ'vɒlv] ◇ *vt* développer. ◇ *vi*: **to ~ (into/from)** se développer (en/à partir de).

ewe [juː] *n* brebis *f*.

ex- [eks] *prefix* ex-.

exacerbate [ɪg'zæsəbeɪt] *vt* [feeling] exacerber; [problems] aggraver.

exact [ɪg'zækt] ◇ *adj* exact(e), précis(e); **to be ~** pour être exact OR précis, exactement. ◇ *vt*: **to ~ sthg (from)** exiger qqch (de).

exacting [ɪg'zæktɪŋ] *adj* [job, standards] astreignant(e); [person] exigeant(e).

exactitude [ɪg'zæktɪtjuːd] *n* exactitude *f*.

exactly [ɪg'zæktlɪ] ◇ *adv* exactement; **it's not ~ what I expected** ce n'est pas tout à fait ce que j'attendais. ◇ *excl* exactement!, parfaitement!

exaggerate [ɪgˈzædʒəreɪt] *vt & vi* exagérer.

exaggerated [ɪgˈzædʒəreɪtɪd] *adj* [sigh, smile] forcé(e).

exaggeration [ɪgˌzædʒəˈreɪʃn] *n* exagération *f.*

exalted [ɪgˈzɔːltɪd] *adj* haut placé(e).

exam [ɪgˈzæm] *n* examen *m*; **to take** OR **sit an** ~ passer un examen.

examination [ɪgˌzæmɪˈneɪʃn] *n* examen *m.*

examination board *n* comité *m* d'examen.

examination paper *n Br* [test] sujet *m* (d'examen); [answers] copie *f.*

examine [ɪgˈzæmɪn] *vt* **-1.** [gen] examiner; [passport] contrôler. **-2.** JUR, SCH & UNIV interroger.

examiner [ɪgˈzæmɪnəʳ] *n* examinateur *m*, -trice *f*; **internal/external** ~ UNIV examinateur *m* de l'établissement/de l'extérieur.

example [ɪgˈzɑːmpl] *n* exemple *m*; **for** ~ par exemple; **to follow sb's** ~ suivre l'exemple de qqn; **to make an** ~ **of sb** punir qqn pour l'exemple.

exasperate [ɪgˈzæspəreɪt] *vt* exaspérer.

exasperating [ɪgˈzæspəreɪtɪŋ] *adj* énervant(e), exaspérant(e).

exasperation [ɪgˌzæspəˈreɪʃn] *n* exaspération *f.*

excavate [ˈekskəveɪt] *vt* **-1.** [land] creuser. **-2.** [object] déterrer.

excavation [ˌekskəˈveɪʃn] *n* **-1.** [gen] excavation *f.* **-2.** ARCHEOL fouilles *fpl.*

excavator [ˌekskəˈveɪtəʳ] *n Br* [machine] pelleteuse *f.*

exceed [ɪkˈsiːd] *vt* **-1.** [amount, number] excéder. **-2.** [limit, expectations] dépasser.

exceedingly [ɪkˈsiːdɪŋlɪ] *adv* extrêmement.

excel [ɪkˈsel] (*pt & pp* **-led**, *cont* **-ling**) *vi*: **to** ~ **(in** OR **at)** exceller (dans); **to** ~ **o.s.** *Br* se surpasser.

excellence [ˈeksələns] *n* excellence *f*, supériorité *f.*

Excellency [ˈeksələnsɪ] (*pl* **-ies**) *n* Excellence *f.*

excellent [ˈeksələnt] *adj* excellent(e).

except [ɪkˈsept] ◇ *prep & conj*: ~ **(for)** à part, sauf. ◇ *vt*: **to** ~ **sb (from)** exclure qqn (de).

excepted [ɪkˈseptɪd] *adj* à part, excepté(e).

excepting [ɪkˈseptɪŋ] = **except**.

exception [ɪkˈsepʃn] *n* **-1.** [exclusion]: ~ **(to)** exception *f* (à); **with the** ~ **of** à l'exception de; **without** ~ sans exception. **-2.** [offence]: **to take** ~ **to** s'offenser de, se froisser de.

exceptional [ɪkˈsepʃənl] *adj* exceptionnel(elle).

exceptionally [ɪkˈsepʃnəlɪ] *adv* exceptionnellement.

excerpt [ˈeksɜːpt] *n*: ~ **(from)** extrait *m* (de), passage *m* (de).

excess [ɪkˈses, *before nouns* ˈekses] ◇ *adj* excédentaire. ◇ *n* excès *m*; **to be in** ~ **of** dépasser; **to** ~ à l'excès.

excess baggage *n* excédent *m* de bagages.

excess fare *n Br* supplément *m.*

excessive [ɪkˈsesɪv] *adj* excessif(ive).

excess luggage = **excess baggage**.

exchange [ɪksˈtʃeɪndʒ] ◇ *n* **-1.** [gen] échange *m*; **in** ~ **(for)** en échange (de). **-2.** TELEC (**telephone**) ~ **central** *m* (téléphonique). ◇ *vt* [swap] échanger; **to** ~ **sthg for sthg** échanger qqch contre qqch; **to** ~ **sthg with sb** échanger qqch avec qqn.

exchange rate *n* FIN taux *m* de change.

Exchequer [ɪksˈtʃekəʳ] *n Br*: **the** ~ ≃ le ministère des Finances.

excise [ˈeksaɪz] ◇ *n* (U) contributions *fpl* indirectes. ◇ *vt fml* [tumour] exciser; [passage from book] supprimer.

excise duties *npl* droits *mpl* de régie.

excitable [ɪkˈsaɪtəbl] *adj* excitable.

excite [ɪkˈsaɪt] *vt* exciter.

excited [ɪkˈsaɪtɪd] *adj* excité(e).

excitement [ɪkˈsaɪtmənt] *n* **-1.** [state] excitation *f.* **-2.** [exciting thing] sensation *f*, émotion *f.*

exciting [ɪkˈsaɪtɪŋ] *adj* passionnant(e); [prospect] excitant(e).

excl. (*abbr of* **excluding**): ~ **taxes** HT.

exclaim [ɪkˈskleɪm] ◇ *vt* s'écrier. ◇ *vi* s'exclamer.

exclamation [ˌekskləˈmeɪʃən] *n* exclamation *f.*

exclamation mark *Br*, **exclamation point** *Am n* point *m* d'exclamation.

exclude [ɪkˈskluːd] *vt*: **to** ~ **sb/sthg (from)** exclure qqn/qqch (de).

excluding [ɪkˈskluːdɪŋ] *prep* sans compter, à l'exclusion de.

exclusion [ɪkˈskluːʒn] *n*: ~ **(from)** exclusion *f* (de); **to the** ~ **of** à l'exclusion de.

exclusion clause *n* clause *f* d'exclusion.

exclusive [ɪkˈskluːsɪv] ◇ *adj* **-1.** [high-class] fermé(e). **-2.** [unique - use, news story] exclusif(ive). ◇ *n* PRESS exclusivité *f.*

◆ **exclusive of** *prep*: ~ **of interest** intérêts non compris.

exclusively [ɪkˈskluːsɪvlɪ] *adv* exclusivement.

excommunicate [,ekskə'mju:nɪkeɪt] *vt* ex-communier.

excommunication ['ekskə,mju:nɪ'keɪʃn] *n* excommunication *f*.

excrement ['ekskrɪmənt] *n* excrément *m*.

excrete [ɪk'skri:t] *vt* excréter.

excruciating [ɪk'skru:ʃɪeɪtɪŋ] *adj* atroce.

excursion [ɪk'skɜ:ʃn] *n* [trip] excursion *f*.

excusable [ɪk'skju:zəbl] *adj* excusable.

excuse [*n* ɪk'skju:s, *vb* ɪk'skju:z] ◇ *n* excuse *f*. ◇ *vt* **-1.** [gen] excuser; **to ~ sb for sthg/ for doing sthg** excuser qqn de qqch/de faire qqch; **to ~ o.s. (for doing sthg)** s'excuser (de faire qqch); **~ me** [to attract attention] excusez-moi; [forgive me] pardon, excusez-moi; *Am* [sorry] pardon. **-2.** [let off]: **to ~ sb (from)** dispenser qqn (de).

ex-directory *adj Br* qui est sur la liste rouge.

exec [ɪg'zek] *abbr of* **executive**.

execrable ['eksɪkrəbl] *adj* exécrable.

execute ['eksɪkju:t] *vt* exécuter.

execution [,eksɪ'kju:ʃn] *n* exécution *f*.

executioner [,eksɪ'kju:ʃnər] *n* bourreau *m*.

executive [ɪg'zekjʊtɪv] ◇ *adj* **-1.** [power, board] exécutif(ive). **-2.** [desk, chair] de cadre, spécial(e) cadre; [washroom] de la direction. ◇ *n* **-1.** COMM cadre *m*. **-2.** [of government] exécutif *m*; [of political party] comité *m* central, bureau *m*.

executive director *n* cadre *m* supérieur.

executive toy *n* gadget *m* pour cadres.

executor [ɪg'zekʊtər] *n* exécuteur *m* testamentaire.

exemplary [ɪg'zemplərɪ] *adj* exemplaire.

exemplify [ɪg'zemplɪfaɪ] (*pt & pp* **-ied**) *vt* **-1.** [typify] exemplifier. **-2.** [give example of] exemplifier, illustrer.

exempt [ɪg'zempt] ◇ *adj*: **~ (from)** exempt(e) (de). ◇ *vt*: **to ~ sb (from)** exempter qqn (de).

exemption [ɪg'zemptʃn] *n* exemption *f*.

exercise ['eksəsaɪz] ◇ *n* exercice *m*; **to take ~** prendre de l'exercice. ◇ *vt* **-1.** [gen] exercer. **-2.** [trouble]: **to ~ sb's mind** préoccuper qqn. ◇ *vi* prendre de l'exercice.

exercise bike *n* vélo *m* d'appartement.

exercise book *n* [notebook] cahier *m* d'exercices; [published book] livre *m* d'exercices.

exert [ɪg'zɜ:t] *vt* exercer; [strength] employer; **to ~ o.s.** se donner du mal.

exertion [ɪg'zɜ:ʃn] *n* effort *m*.

ex gratia [eks'greɪʃə] *adj Br* [payment] à titre gracieux.

exhale [eks'heɪl] ◇ *vt* exhaler. ◇ *vi* expirer.

exhaust [ɪg'zɔ:st] ◇ *n* **-1.** (*U*) [fumes] gaz *mpl* d'échappement. **-2.** **~ (pipe)** pot *m* d'échappement. ◇ *vt* épuiser.

exhausted [ɪg'zɔ:stɪd] *adj* épuisé(e).

exhausting [ɪg'zɔ:stɪŋ] *adj* épuisant(e).

exhaustion [ɪg'zɔ:stʃn] *n* épuisement *m*.

exhaustive [ɪg'zɔ:stɪv] *adj* complet(ète), exhaustif(ive).

exhibit [ɪg'zɪbɪt] ◇ *n* **-1.** ART objet *m* exposé. **-2.** JUR pièce *f* à conviction. ◇ *vt* **-1.** [demonstrate - feeling] montrer; [- skill] faire preuve de. **-2.** ART exposer. ◇ *vi* ART exposer.

exhibition [,egsɪ'bɪʃn] *n* **-1.** ART exposition *f*. **-2.** [of feeling] démonstration *f*. **-3.** *phr*: **to make an ~ of o.s.** *Br* se donner en spectacle.

exhibitionist [,eksɪ'bɪʃnɪst] *n* exhibitionniste *mf*.

exhibitor [ɪg'zɪbɪtər] *n* exposant *m*, -e *f*.

exhilarating [ɪg'zɪləreɪtɪŋ] *adj* [experience] grisant(e); [walk] vivifiant(e).

exhort [ɪg'zɔ:t] *vt*: **to ~ sb to do sthg** exhorter qqn à faire qqch.

exhume [eks'hju:m] *vt* exhumer.

exile ['eksaɪl] ◇ *n* **-1.** [condition] exil *m*; **in ~** en exil. **-2.** [person] exilé *m*, -e *f*. ◇ *vt*: **to ~ sb (from/to)** exiler qqn (de/vers).

exiled ['eksaɪld] *adj* exilé(e).

exist [ɪg'zɪst] *vi* exister.

existence [ɪg'zɪstəns] *n* existence *f*; **in ~** qui existe, existant(e); **to come into ~** naître.

existentialism [,egzɪ'stenʃəlɪzm] *n* existentialisme *m*.

existentialist [,egzɪ'stenʃəlɪst] ◇ *adj* existentialiste. ◇ *n* existentialiste *mf*.

existing [ɪg'zɪstɪŋ] *adj* existant(e).

exit ['eksɪt] ◇ *n* sortie *f*; **to make one's ~** sortir; THEATRE faire sa sortie. ◇ *vi* sortir.

exit poll *n Br* sondage *effectué après que les électeurs aient voté*.

exit visa *n* visa *m* de sortie.

exodus ['eksədəs] *n* exode *m*.

ex officio [eksə'fɪʃɪəʊ] *adj & adv* ex officio.

exonerate [ɪg'zɒnəreɪt] *vt*: **to ~ sb (from)** disculper qqn (de).

exorbitant [ɪg'zɔ:bɪtənt] *adj* exorbitant(e).

exorcist ['eksɔ:sɪst] *n* exorciste *mf*.

exorcize, -ise ['eksɔ:saɪz] *vt* exorciser.

exotic [ɪg'zɒtɪk] *adj* exotique.

expand [ɪk'spænd] ◇ *vt* [production, influence] accroître; [business, department, area] développer. ◇ *vi* [population, influence] s'ac-

croître; [business, department, market] **se développer**; [metal] **se dilater**.
◆ **expand (up)on** *vt fus* développer.

expanse [ɪk'spæns] *n* étendue *f*.

expansion [ɪk'spænʃn] *n* [of production,
population] accroissement *m*; [of business,
department, area] développement *m*; [of me-
tal] dilatation *f*.

expansion card *n* COMPUT carte *f* d'extension.

expansionism [ɪk'spænʃənɪzm] *n* expan-
sionnisme *m*.

expansionist [ɪk'spænʃənɪst] *adj* expansionniste.

expansion slot *n* COMPUT créneau *m* pour
carte d'extension.

expansive [ɪk'spænsɪv] *adj* expansif(ive).

expatriate [eks'pætrɪət] ◇ *adj* expatrié(e).
◇ *n* expatrié *m*, -e *f*.

expect [ɪk'spekt] ◇ *vt* **-1.** [anticipate] s'attendre à; [event, letter, baby] attendre; **when
do you ~ it to be ready?** quand pensez-
vous que cela sera prêt?; **to ~ sb to do
sthg** s'attendre à ce que qqn fasse qqch.
-2. [count on] compter sur. **-3.** [demand] exiger, demander; **to ~ sb to do sthg** attendre
de qqn qu'il fasse qqch; **to ~ sthg from sb**
exiger qqch de qqn. **-4.** [suppose] supposer;
I ~ so je crois que oui.
◇ *vi* **-1.** [anticipate]: **to ~ to do sthg** compter faire qqch. **-2.** [be pregnant]: **to be ~ing**
être enceinte, attendre un bébé.

expectancy → **life expectancy**.

expectant [ɪk'spektənt] *adj* qui est dans
l'expectative.

expectantly [ɪk'spektəntlɪ] *adv* dans l'expectative.

expectant mother *n* femme *f* enceinte.

expectation [,ekspek'teɪʃn] *n* **-1.** [hope] espoir *m*, attente *f*. **-2.** [belief]: **it's my ~ that
... à mon avis, ...; **against all ~** OR **~s**, contrary to all **~** OR **~s** contre toute attente.

expectorant [ɪk'spektərənt] *n* expectorant
m.

expedient [ɪk'spiːdjənt] *fml* ◇ *adj* indi-
qué(e). ◇ *n* expédient *m*.

expedite ['ekspɪdaɪt] *vt fml* accélérer; [arri-
val, departure] hâter.

expedition [,ekspɪ'dɪʃn] *n* expédition *f*.

expeditionary force ['ekspɪ'dɪʃnərɪ-] *n*
corps *m* expéditionnaire.

expel [ɪk'spel] (*pt* & *pp* **-led**, *cont* **-ling**) *vt*
-1. [gen] expulser. **-2.** SCH renvoyer.

expend [ɪk'spend] *vt*: **to ~ time/money (on)**
consacrer du temps/de l'argent (à).

expendable [ɪk'spendəbl] *adj* dont on peut
se passer, qui n'est pas indispensable.

expenditure [ɪk'spendɪtʃər] *n* (U) dépense
f.

expense [ɪk'spens] *n* **-1.** [amount spent] dépense *f*. **-2.** (U) [cost] frais *mpl*; **to go to
great ~ (to do sthg)** faire beaucoup de frais
(pour faire qqch); **at the ~ of** au prix de; **at
sb's ~** [financial] aux frais de qqn; *fig* aux
dépens de qqn.
◆ **expenses** *npl* COMM frais *mpl*; **on ~s** sur
la note de frais.

expense account *n* frais *mpl* de représentation.

expensive [ɪk'spensɪv] *adj* **-1.** [financially -
gen] cher (chère), coûteux(euse); [- tastes]
dispendieux(ieuse). **-2.** [mistake] qui coûte
cher.

experience [ɪk'spɪərɪəns] ◇ *n* expérience *f*.
◇ *vt* [difficulty] connaître; [disappointment]
éprouver, ressentir; [loss, change] subir.

experienced [ɪk'spɪərɪənst] *adj* expérimen-
té(e); **to be ~ at** OR **in sthg** avoir de l'expérience en OR en matière de qqch.

experiment [ɪk'sperɪmənt] ◇ *n* expérience
f; **to carry out an ~** faire une expérience.
◇ *vi*: **to ~ (with sthg)** expérimenter (qqch);
to ~ on faire une expérience sur.

experimental [ɪk,sperɪ'mentl] *adj* expéri-
mental(e).

expert ['ekspɜːt] ◇ *adj* expert(e); [advice]
d'expert; **~ at sthg/at doing sthg** expert en
qqch/à faire qqch. ◇ *n* expert *m*, -e *f*.

expertise [,ekspɜː'tiːz] *n* (U) compétence *f*.

expert system *n* COMPUT système *m* expert.

expiate ['ekspɪeɪt] *vt* expier.

expire [ɪk'spaɪər] *vi* expirer.

expiry [ɪk'spaɪərɪ] *n* expiration *f*.

expiry date *n* date *f* de péremption.

explain [ɪk'spleɪn] ◇ *vt* expliquer; **to ~
sthg to sb** expliquer qqch à qqn. ◇ *vi*
s'expliquer; **to ~ to sb (about sthg)** expliquer (qqch) à qqn.
◆ **explain away** *vt sep* justifier.

explanation [,eksplən'eɪʃn] *n*: **~ (for)** explication *f* (de).

explanatory [ɪk'splænətrɪ] *adj* explica-
tif(ive).

expletive [ɪk'spliːtɪv] *n fml* juron *m*.

explicit [ɪk'splɪsɪt] *adj* explicite; **sexually ~**
à teneur sexuelle explicite.

explode [ɪk'spləʊd] ◇ *vt* **-1.** [bomb] faire
exploser. **-2.** *fig* [theory] discréditer. ◇ *vi lit*
& *fig* exploser.

exploit [*n* 'eksplɔɪt, *vb* ɪk'splɔɪt] ◇ *n* exploit *m*. ◇ *vt* exploiter.

exploitation [,eksplɔɪ'teɪʃn] *n* (U) exploitation *f*.

exploration [,eksplə'reɪʃn] *n* exploration *f*.

exploratory [ɪk'splɒrətrɪ] *adj* exploratoire.

explore [ɪk'splɔːr] *vt* & *vi* explorer.

explorer [ɪk'splɔːrəʳ] *n* explorateur *m*, -trice *f*.

explosion [ɪk'spləʊʒn] *n* explosion *f*; [of interest] débordement *m*.

explosive [ɪk'spləʊsɪv] ◇ *adj lit* & *fig* explosif(ive). ◇ *n* explosif *m*.

explosive device *n* engin *m* explosif.

exponent [ɪk'spəʊnənt] *n* [of theory] défenseur *m*.

exponential [,ekspə'nenʃl] *adj* exponentiel(ielle).

export [*n* & *comp* 'ekspɔːt, *vb* ɪk'spɔːt] ◇ *n* exportation *f*. ◇ *comp* d'exportation. ◇ *vt* exporter.

◆ **exports** *npl* exportations *fpl*.

exportable [ɪk'spɔːtəbl] *adj* exportable.

exportation [,ekspɔː'teɪʃn] *n* exportation *f*.

exporter [ek'spɔːtəʳ] *n* exportateur *m*, -trice *f*.

export licence *n Br* permis *m* d'exportation.

expose [ɪk'spəʊz] *vt* **-1.** [uncover] exposer, découvrir; **to be ~d to sthg** être exposé à qqch. **-2.** [unmask - corruption] révéler; [- person] démasquer.

exposé [eks'pəʊzeɪ] *n* exposé *m*.

exposed [ɪk'spəʊzd] *adj* [land, house, position] exposé(e).

exposition [,ekspə'zɪʃn] *n* **-1.** *fml* [explanation] exposé *m*. **-2.** [exhibition] exposition *f*.

exposure [ɪk'spəʊʒəʳ] *n* **-1.** [to light, radiation] exposition *f*. **-2.** MED: **to die of ~** mourir de froid. **-3.** [unmasking - of corruption] révélation *f*; [- of person] dénonciation *f*. **-4.** [PHOT - time] temps *m* de pose; [- photograph] pose *f*. **-5.** (U) [publicity] publicité *f*; [coverage] couverture *f*.

exposure meter *n* posemètre *m*.

expound [ɪk'spaʊnd] *fml* ◇ *vt* exposer. ◇ *vi*: **to ~ on** faire un exposé sur.

express [ɪk'spres] ◇ *adj* **-1.** *Br* [letter, delivery] exprès (*inv*). **-2.** [train, coach] express (*inv*). **-3.** *fml* [specific] exprès(esse). ◇ *adv* exprès. ◇ *n* [train] rapide *m*, express *m*. ◇ *vt* exprimer; **to ~ o.s.** s'exprimer.

expression [ɪk'spreʃn] *n* expression *f*.

expressionism [ɪk'spreʃənɪzm] *n* expressionnisme *m*.

expressionist [ɪk'spreʃənɪst] ◇ *adj* expressionniste. ◇ *n* expressionniste *mf*.

expressionless [ɪk'spreʃənlɪs] *adj* [voice] sans expression; [face] impassible.

expressive [ɪk'spresɪv] *adj* expressif(ive).

expressively [ɪk'spresɪvlɪ] *adv* de façon expressive.

expressly [ɪk'spreslɪ] *adv* expressément.

expressway [ɪk'spresweɪ] *n Am* voie *f* express.

expropriate [eks'prəʊprɪeɪt] *vt* exproprier.

expropriation [eks,prəʊprɪ'eɪʃn] *n* expropriation *f*.

expulsion [ɪk'spʌlʃn] *n* **-1.** [gen] expulsion *f*. **-2.** SCH renvoi *m*.

exquisite [ɪk'skwɪzɪt] *adj* exquis(e).

exquisitely [ɪk'skwɪzɪtlɪ] *adv* de façon exquise.

ex-serviceman *n Br* ancien combattant *m*.

ex-servicewoman *n Br* ancienne combattante *f*.

ext., extn. (*abbr of* extension): **~ 4174** p. 4174.

extant [ek'stænt] *adj* qui existe encore.

extemporize, -ise [ɪk'stempəraɪz] *vi fml* improviser.

extend [ɪk'stend] ◇ *vt* **-1.** [enlarge - building] agrandir. **-2.** [make longer - gen] prolonger; [- visa] proroger; [- deadline] repousser. **-3.** [expand - rules, law] étendre (la portée de); [- power] accroître. **-4.** [stretch out - arm, hand] étendre. **-5.** [offer - help] apporter, offrir; [- credit] accorder; **to ~ a welcome to sb** souhaiter la bienvenue à qqn. ◇ *vi* **-1.** [stretch - in space] s'étendre; [- in time] continuer. **-2.** [rule, law]: **to ~ to sb/sthg** inclure qqn/qqch.

extendable [ɪk'stendəbl] *adj* [contract] qui peut être prolongé(e).

extended-play [ɪk'stendɪd-] *adj* [record] double-durée.

extension [ɪk'stenʃn] *n* **-1.** [to building] agrandissement *m*. **-2.** [lengthening - gen] prolongement *m*; [- of visit] prolongation *f*; [- of visa] prorogation *f*; [- of deadline] report *m*. **-3.** [of power] accroissement *m*; [of law] élargissement *m*. **-4.** TELEC poste *m*. **-5.** ELEC prolongateur *m*. **-6.** COMPUT: **filename ~** extension *m* de nom de fichier.

extension cable *n* rallonge *f*.

extensive [ɪk'stensɪv] *adj* **-1.** [in amount] considérable. **-2.** [in area] vaste. **-3.** [in range - discussions] approfondi(e); [- changes, use] considérable.

extensively [ɪk'stensɪvlɪ] *adv* **-1.** [in amount]

considérablement. **-2.** [in range] abondamment, largement.

extent [ik'stent] *n* **-1.** [of land, area] étendue *f*, superficie *f*; [of problem, damage] étendue. **-2.** [degree]: **to what ~ ...?** dans quelle mesure ...?; **to the ~ that** [in so far as] dans la mesure où; [to the point where] au point que; **to a certain ~** jusqu'à un certain point; **to a large** OR **great ~** en grande partie; **to some ~** en partie.

extenuating circumstances [ik'stenjʊeitiŋ-] *npl* circonstances *fpl* atténuantes.

exterior [ik'stiəriər] ◇ *adj* extérieur(e). ◇ *n* **-1.** [of house, car] extérieur *m*. **-2.** [of person] dehors *m*, extérieur *m*.

exterminate [ik'stɜːmineit] *vt* exterminer.

extermination [ik,stɜːmi'neiʃn] *n* extermination *f*.

external [ik'stɜːnl] *adj* externe.
♦ **externals** *npl* apparences *fpl*.

externally [ik'stɜːnəli] *adv* extérieurement.

extinct [ik'stiŋkt] *adj* **-1.** [species] disparu(e). **-2.** [volcano] éteint(e).

extinction [ik'stiŋkʃn] *n* [of species] extinction *f*, disparition *f*.

extinguish [ik'stiŋgwiʃ] *vt* **-1.** [fire, cigarette] éteindre. **-2.** *fig* [memory, feeling] anéantir.

extinguisher [ik'stiŋgwiʃər] *n* extincteur *m*.

extn. = **ext**.

extol (*pt* & *pp* **-led**, *cont* **-ling**), **extoll** *Am* [ik'stəʊl] *vt* louer.

extort [ik'stɔːt] *vt*: **to ~ sthg from sb** extorquer qqch à qqn.

extortion [ik'stɔːʃn] *n* extorsion *f*.

extortionate [ik'stɔːʃnət] *adj* exorbitant(e).

extra ['ekstrə] ◇ *adj* supplémentaire. ◇ *n* **-1.** [addition] supplément *m*; **optional ~** option *f*. **-2.** CINEMA & THEATRE figurant *m*, -e *f*. ◇ *adv* [hard, big etc] extra; [pay, charge etc] en plus.

extra- ['ekstrə] *prefix* extra-.

extract [*n* 'ekstrækt, *vb* ik'strækt] ◇ *n* extrait *m*. ◇ *vt* **-1.** [take out - tooth] arracher; **to ~ sthg from** tirer qqch de. **-2.** [confession, information]: **to ~ sthg (from sb)** arracher qqch (à qqn), tirer qqch (de qqn). **-3.** [coal, oil] extraire.

extraction [ik'strækʃn] *n* (*U*) **-1.** [origin] origine *f*. **-2.** [of coal, tooth] extraction *f*.

extractor (fan) [ik'stræktər-] *n Br* ventilateur *m*.

extracurricular [,ekstrəkə'rikjʊlər] *adj* en dehors du programme.

extradite ['ekstrədait] *vt*: **to ~ sb (from/to)** extrader qqn (de/vers).

extradition [,ekstrə'diʃn] ◇ *n* extradition *f*. ◇ *comp* d'extradition.

extramarital [,ekstrə'mæritl] *adj* extra-conjugal(e).

extramural [,ekstrə'mjʊərəl] *adj* UNIV hors faculté.

extraneous [ik'streinjəs] *adj* **-1.** [irrelevant] superflu(e). **-2.** [outside] extérieur(e).

extraordinary [ik'strɔːdnri] *adj* extraordinaire.

extraordinary general meeting *n* assemblée *f* générale extraordinaire.

extrapolate [ik'stræpəleit] *vt* & *vi* extrapoler.

extrasensory perception [,ekstrə'sensəri-] *n* perception *f* extrasensorielle.

extraterrestrial [,ekstrətə'restriəl] *adj* extra-terrestre.

extra time *n Br* SPORT prolongation *f*.

extravagance [ik'strævəgəns] *n* **-1.** (*U*) [excessive spending] gaspillage *m*, prodigalités *fpl*. **-2.** [luxury] extravagance *f*, folie *f*.

extravagant [ik'strævəgənt] *adj* **-1.** [wasteful - person] dépensier(ière); [- use, tastes] dispendieux(ieuse). **-2.** [elaborate, exaggerated] extravagant(e).

extravaganza [ik,strævə'gænza] *n* folie *f*, fantaisie *f*.

extreme [ik'striːm] ◇ *adj* extrême. ◇ *n* extrême *m*; **to ~s** à l'extrême; **to take sthg to ~s** mener qqch à l'extrême; **in the ~** à l'extrême.

extremely [ik'striːmli] *adv* extrêmement.

extremism [ik'striːmizm] *n* extrémisme *m*.

extremist [ik'striːmist] ◇ *adj* extrémiste. ◇ *n* extrémiste *mf*.

extremity [ik'streməti] (*pl* **-ies**) *n* extrémité *f*.

extricate ['ekstrikeit] *vt*: **to ~ sthg (from)** dégager qqch (de); **to ~ o.s. (from)** [from seat belt etc] s'extirper (de); [from difficult situation] se tirer (de).

extrovert ['ekstrəvɜːt] ◇ *adj* extraverti(e). ◇ *n* extraverti *m*, -e *f*.

extruded [ik'struːdid] *adj* extrudé(e).

exuberance [ig'zjuːbərəns] *n* exubérance *f*.

exuberant [ig'zjuːbərənt] *adj* exubérant(e).

exude [ig'zjuːd] *vt* **-1.** [liquid, smell] exsuder. **-2.** *fig* [confidence] respirer; [charm] déborder de.

exult [ig'zʌlt] *vi* exulter; **to ~ at** OR **in** se réjouir de.

exultant [ig'zʌltənt] *adj* triomphant(e).

eye [ai] (*cont* **eyeing** OR **eying**) ◇ *n* **-1.** [gen] œil *m*; **before my** *etc* **(very) ~s** juste sous

mes *etc* yeux; **to cast** OR **run one's ~ over sthg** jeter un coup d'œil sur qqch; **to catch one's ~** attirer le regard; **to catch sb's ~** attirer l'attention de qqn; **to clap** OR **lay** OR **set ~s on sb** poser les yeux sur qqn; **to cry one's ~s out** pleurer toutes les larmes de son corps; **to feast one's ~s on sthg** se délecter à regarder qqch; **to have an ~ for sthg** avoir le coup d'œil pour qqch, s'y connaître en qqch; **to have one's ~ on sb** avoir qqn à l'œil; **to have one's ~ on sthg** avoir repéré qqch; **in my** *etc* **~s** à mes *etc* yeux; **to keep one's ~s open** avoir l'œil; **to keep one's ~s open for sthg** [try to find] essayer de repérer qqch; **to keep an ~ on sthg** surveiller qqch, garder l'œil sur qqch; **there is more to this than meets the ~** ce n'est pas aussi simple que cela OR qu'il y paraît; **to open sb's ~s (to sthg)** ouvrir les yeux de qqn (sur qqch); **not to see ~ to ~ with sb** ne pas partager la même opinion que qqn; **to close** OR **shut one's ~s to sthg** fermer les yeux sur qqch; **to turn a blind ~ to sthg** ignorer qqch; **I'm up to my ~s in work** *Br* j'ai du travail jusque par-dessus la tête. **-2.** [of needle] chas *m*.
◇ *vt* regarder, reluquer.
◆ **eye up** *vt sep Br* reluquer.

eyeball ['aɪbɔːl] ◇ *n* globe *m* oculaire. ◇ *vt Am inf* fixer.

eyebath ['aɪbɑːθ] *n* œillère *f* (*pour bains d'œil*).

eyebrow ['aɪbrau] *n* sourcil *m*; **to raise one's ~s** tiquer, sourciller.

eyebrow pencil *n* crayon *m* à sourcils.

eye-catching *adj* voyant(e).

eye contact *n*: **to make ~ with sb** regarder qqn dans les yeux; **to avoid ~ with sb** éviter le regard de qqn.

eyelash ['aɪlæʃ] *n* cil *m*.

eyelet ['aɪlɪt] *n* œillet *m*.

eye-level *adj* qui est au niveau OR à la hauteur de l'œil.

eyelid ['aɪlɪd] *n* paupière *f*; **she didn't bat an ~** *inf* elle n'a pas sourcillé OR bronché.

eyeliner ['aɪˌlaɪnə'] *n* eye-liner *m*.

eye-opener *n inf* révélation *f*.

eyepatch ['aɪpætʃ] *n* cache *m*.

eye shadow *n* fard *m* à paupières.

eyesight ['aɪsaɪt] *n* vue *f*.

eyesore ['aɪsɔːʳ] *n* horreur *f*.

eyestrain ['aɪstreɪn] *n* fatigue *f* des yeux.

eyetooth ['aɪtuːθ] (*pl* **-teeth**) *n*: **to give one's eyeteeth for sthg/to do sthg** donner n'importe quoi pour qqch/pour faire qqch.

eyewash ['aɪwɒʃ] *n* (*U*) *inf* [nonsense] fadaises *fpl*.

eyewitness [ˌaɪ'wɪtnɪs] *n* témoin *m* oculaire.

eyrie ['aɪərɪ] *n* aire *f* (*d'un aigle*).

F

f (*pl* **f's** OR **fs**), **F** (*pl* **F's** OR **Fs**) [ef] *n* [letter] f *m inv*, F *m inv*.
◆ **F** *n* **-1.** MUS fa *m*. **-2.** (*abbr of* **Fahrenheit**) F.

FA (*abbr of* **Football Association**) *n* fédération britannique de football.

FAA (*abbr of* **Federal Aviation Administration**) *n* direction fédérale de l'aviation civile américaine.

fable ['feɪbl] *n* fable *f*.

fabled ['feɪbld] *adj* fabuleux(euse), légendaire.

fabric ['fæbrɪk] *n* **-1.** [cloth] tissu *m*. **-2.** [of building, society] structure *f*.

fabricate ['fæbrɪkeɪt] *vt* fabriquer.

fabrication [ˌfæbrɪ'keɪʃn] *n* **-1.** [lie, lying] fabrication *f*, invention *f*. **-2.** [manufacture] fabrication *f*.

fabulous ['fæbjʊləs] *adj* **-1.** [gen] fabuleux(euse). **-2.** *inf* [excellent] sensationnel(elle), fabuleux(euse).

fabulously ['fæbjʊləslɪ] *adv* fabuleusement.

facade [fə'sɑːd] *n* façade *f*.

face [feɪs] ◇ *n* **-1.** [of person] visage *m*, figure *f*; **~ to ~** face à face; **to look sb in the ~** regarder qqn dans les yeux; **to say sthg to sb's ~** dire qqch à qqn en face; **to show one's ~** se montrer. **-2.** [expression] visage *m*, mine *f*; **to make** OR **pull a ~** faire la grimace; **her ~ fell** son visage s'est assombri. **-3.** [of cliff, mountain] face *f*, paroi *f*; [of building] façade *f*; [of clock, watch] cadran *m*; [of coin, shape] face *f*. **-4.** [surface - of planet] surface *f*; **on the ~ of it** à première vue. **-5.** [respect]: **to save/lose ~** sauver/perdre la face. **-6.** *phr*: **to fly in the ~ of sthg** être en contradiction avec qqch; **it flies in the ~ of logic** ce n'est pas logique.
◇ *vt* **-1.** [look towards - subj: person] faire face à; **the house ~s the sea/south** la mai-

son donne sur la mer/est orientée vers le sud. **-2.** [decision, crisis] être confronté(e) à; [problem, danger] faire face à. **-3.** [facts, truth] faire face à, admettre. **-4.** *inf* [cope with] affronter.

◆ **face down** *adv* [person] face contre terre; [object] à l'envers; [card] face en dessous.

◆ **face up** *adv* [person] sur le dos; [object] à l'endroit; [card] face en dessus.

◆ **in the face of** *prep* devant.

◆ **face up to** *vt fus* faire face à.

facecloth ['feɪsklɒθ] *n Br* gant *m* de toilette.

face cream *n* crème *f* pour le visage.

faceless ['feɪslɪs] *adj* anonyme.

face-lift *n* lifting *m*; *fig* restauration *f*, rénovation *f*.

face pack *n* masque *m* de beauté.

face powder *n* poudre *f* de riz, poudre pour le visage.

face-saving [-'seɪvɪŋ] *adj* qui sauve la face.

facet ['fæsɪt] *n* facette *f*.

facetious [fə'si:ʃəs] *adj* facétieux(ieuse).

facetiously [fə'si:ʃəslɪ] *adv* facétieusement.

face-to-face *adj* face à face.

face value *n* [of coin, stamp] valeur *f* nominale; **to take sthg at** ~ prendre qqch au pied de la lettre.

facial ['feɪʃl] ◇ *adj* facial(e). ◇ *n* nettoyage *m* de peau.

facile [*Br* 'fæsaɪl, *Am* fæsl] *adj pej* facile.

facilitate [fə'sɪlɪteɪt] *vt* faciliter.

facility [fə'sɪlətɪ] (*pl* **-ies**) *n* **-1.** [ability]: **to have a** ~ **for sthg** avoir de la facilité OR de l'aptitude pour qqch. **-2.** [feature] fonction *f*.

◆ **facilities** *npl* [amenities] équipement *m*, aménagement *m*.

facing ['feɪsɪŋ] *adj* d'en face; [sides] opposé(e).

facsimile [fæk'sɪmɪlɪ] *n* **-1.** [fax] télécopie *f*, fax *m*. **-2.** [copy] fac-similé *m*.

facsimile machine *fml* = **fax machine**.

fact [fækt] *n* **-1.** [true piece of information] fait *m*; **the** ~ **is** le fait est; **the** ~ **remains that** ... toujours est-il que ...; **to know sthg for a** ~ savoir pertinemment qqch. **-2.** (*U*) [truth] faits *mpl*, réalité *f*.

◆ **in fact** ◇ *adv* de fait, effectivement. ◇ *conj* en fait.

fact-finding [-'faɪndɪŋ] *adj* d'enquête.

faction ['fækʃn] *n* faction *f*.

factional ['fækʃənl] *adj* [dispute] de factions.

fact of life *n* fait *m*, réalité *f*; **the facts of life** *euphemism* les choses *fpl* de la vie.

factor ['fæktə*r*] *n* facteur *m*.

factory ['fæktərɪ] (*pl* **-ies**) *n* fabrique *f*, usine *f*.

factory farming *n* élevage *m* industriel.

factory ship *n* navire-usine *m*.

factotum [fæk'təʊtəm] (*pl* **-s**) *n* factotum *m*, intendant *m*, -e *f*.

fact sheet *n Br* résumé *m*, brochure *f*.

factual ['fæktʃʊəl] *adj* factuel(elle), basé(e) sur les faits.

faculty ['fækltɪ] (*pl* **-ies**) *n* **-1.** [gen] faculté *f*. **-2.** *Am* [in college]: **the** ~ le corps enseignant.

FA Cup *n* en Angleterre, championnat de football dont la finale se joue à Wembley.

fad [fæd] *n* engouement *m*, mode *f*; [personal] marotte *f*.

faddy ['fædɪ] (*compar* **-ier**, *superl* **-iest**) *adj inf pej* capricieux(ieuse).

fade [feɪd] ◇ *vt* [jeans, curtains, paint] décolorer. ◇ *vi* **-1.** [jeans, curtains, paint] se décolorer; [colour] passer; [flower] se flétrir, faner. **-2.** [light] baisser, diminuer. **-3.** [sound] diminuer, s'affaiblir. **-4.** [memory] s'effacer; [feeling, interest] diminuer. **-5.** [smile] s'effacer, s'évanouir.

◆ **fade away**, **fade out** *vi* [sound, anger] diminuer; [image] s'effacer.

faded ['feɪdɪd] *adj* passé(e).

faeces *Br*, **feces** *Am* ['fi:si:z] *npl* fèces *fpl*.

Faeroe, **Faroe** ['feərəʊ] *n*: **the** ~ **Islands**, **the** ~**s** les îles *fpl* Féroé; **in the** ~ **Islands** aux îles Féroé.

faff [fæf]

◆ **faff about**, **faff around** *vi Br inf* glander.

fag [fæg] *n inf* **-1.** *Br* [cigarette] clope *m*. **-2.** *Br* [chore] corvée *f*. **-3.** *Am pej* [homosexual] pédé *m*.

fag end *n Br inf* mégot *m*.

fagged out [fægd-] *adj Br inf* crevé(e).

faggot, **fagot** *Am* ['fægət] *n* **-1.** *Br* CULIN crépinette *f*. **-2.** *Am inf pej* [homosexual] pédé *m*.

Fahrenheit ['færənhaɪt] *adj* Fahrenheit (*inv*).

fail [feɪl] ◇ *vt* **-1.** [exam, test] rater, échouer à. **-2.** [not succeed]: **to** ~ **to do sthg** ne pas arriver à faire qqch. **-3.** [neglect]: **to** ~ **to do sthg** manquer OR omettre de faire qqch. **-4.** [candidate] refuser. **-5.** [subj: courage] manquer à; [subj: friend, memory] lâcher.

◇ *vi* **-1.** [not succeed] ne pas réussir OR y arriver. **-2.** [not pass exam] échouer. **-3.** [stop functioning] lâcher. **-4.** [weaken - health, daylight] décliner; [- eyesight] baisser.

failed [feɪld] *adj* [singer, writer etc] raté(e).

failing ['feɪlɪŋ] ◇ n [weakness] défaut m, point m faible. ◇ prep à moins de; ~ that à défaut.

fail-safe adj [device etc] à sûreté intégrée.

failure ['feɪljər] n -1. [lack of success, unsuccessful thing] échec m; **her** ~ **to attend** le fait qu'elle ne soit pas venue. -2. [person] raté m, -e f. -3. [of engine, brake etc] défaillance f; [of crop] perte f; **heart** ~ arrêt m cardiaque.

faint [feɪnt] ◇ adj -1. [smell] léger(ère); [memory] **vague**; [sound, hope] **faible**. -2. [slight - chance] **petit(e)**, faible. -3. [dizzy]: **I'm feeling a bit** ~ je ne me sens pas bien. ◇ vi s'évanouir.

faint-hearted [-'hɑːtɪd] adj timoré(e), timide.

faintly ['feɪntlɪ] adv -1. [recall] **vaguement**; [shine] **faiblement**; [smile - indifferently] **vaguement**; [- sadly] **faiblement**. -2. [rather, slightly] **légèrement**.

faintness ['feɪntnɪs] n -1. [dizziness] étourdissement m, étourdissements mpl. -2. [of image] flou m. -3. [of smell, sound, hope] faiblesse f; [of memory] imprécision f.

fair [feər] ◇ adj -1. [just] **juste**, équitable; **it's not** ~! ce n'est pas juste!; **to be** ~ ... il faut dire que .... -2. [quite large] **grand(e)**, important(e). -3. [quite good] assez bon (assez bonne); **to have a** ~ **idea of sthg** avoir sa petite idée sur qqch. -4. [hair] **blond(e)**. -5. [skin, complexion] **clair(e)**. -6. [weather] **beau (belle)**. ◇ n -1. Br [funfair] **fête f foraine**. -2. [trade fair] **foire f**. ◇ adv [fairly] **loyalement**.

◆ **fair enough** adv Br inf OK, d'accord.

fair copy n copie f au propre.

fair game n proie f rêvée.

fairground ['feəgraʊnd] n champ m de foire.

fair-haired [-'heəd] adj [person] blond(e).

fairly ['feəlɪ] adv -1. [rather] **assez**; ~ **certain** presque sûr. -2. [justly] **équitablement**; [describe] **avec impartialité**; [fight, play] **loyalement**.

fair-minded [-'maɪndɪd] adj impartial(e), équitable.

fairness ['feənɪs] n [justness] **équité f**; **in** ~ **(to sb)** pour être juste (envers qqn).

fair play n fair-play m.

fairway ['feəweɪ] n fairway m.

fairy ['feərɪ] (pl -ies) n [imaginary creature] fée f.

fairy lights npl Br guirlande f électrique.

fairy tale n conte m de fées.

fait accompli [,feɪtə'kɒmpliː] (pl **faits accomplis**) n fait m accompli.

faith [feɪθ] n -1. [belief] **foi f**, confiance f; ~ **in sb/sthg** confiance en qqn/qqch; **in bad** ~ de mauvaise foi; **in good** ~ en toute bonne foi. -2. RELIG **foi f**.

faithful ['feɪθful] ◇ adj **fidèle**. ◇ npl RELIG: **the** ~ les fidèles mpl.

faithfully ['feɪθfulɪ] adv [loyally] **fidèlement**; **to promise** ~ **that** ... donner sa parole que ...; **Yours** ~ Br [in letter] je vous prie d'agréer mes salutations distinguées.

faithfulness ['feɪθfulnɪs] n -1. [loyalty] **fidélité f**. -2. [truth - of account, translation] **exactitude f**.

faith healer n guérisseur m, -euse f.

faithless ['feɪθlɪs] adj déloyal(e).

fake [feɪk] ◇ adj **faux (fausse)**. ◇ n -1. [object, painting] **faux m**. -2. [person] **imposteur m**. ◇ vt -1. [results] **falsifier**; [signature] **imiter**. -2. [illness, emotions] **simuler**. ◇ vi [pretend] simuler, faire semblant.

falcon ['fɔːlkən] n faucon m.

Falkland Islands ['fɔːklənd-], **Falklands** ['fɔːkləndz] npl: **the** ~ les îles fpl Falkland, les Malouines fpl; **in the** ~ aux îles Falkland, aux Malouines.

fall [fɔːl] (pt **fell**, pp **fallen**) ◇ vi -1. [gen] tomber; **to** ~ **flat** [joke] tomber à plat. -2. [decrease] **baisser**. -3. [become]: **to** ~ **asleep** s'endormir; **to** ~ **ill** tomber malade; **to** ~ **in love** tomber amoureux(euse); **to** ~ **open** s'ouvrir; **to** ~ **silent** se taire; **to** ~ **vacant** se libérer. -4. [belong, be classed]: **to** ~ **into two groups** se diviser en deux groupes; **the matter** ~s **under our jurisdiction** cette question relève de notre juridiction. -5. [disintegrate]: **to** ~ **to bits** OR **pieces** tomber en morceaux. -6. [be captured - city] **to** ~ **(to sb)** tomber (aux mains de qqn). -7. Br POL [constituency]: **to** ~ **to sb** passer à qqn. ◇ n -1. [gen]: ~ **(in)** chute f (de). -2. Am [autumn] automne m.

◆ **falls** npl chutes fpl.

◆ **fall about** vi Br inf: **to** ~ **about (laughing)** se tordre (de rire).

◆ **fall apart** vi -1. [disintegrate - book, chair] tomber en morceaux. -2. fig [country] tomber en ruine; [person] s'effondrer.

◆ **fall away** vi [land] descendre, s'abaisser.

◆ **fall back** vi [person, crowd] reculer.

◆ **fall back on** vt fus [resort to] se rabattre sur.

◆ **fall behind** vi -1. [in race] se faire distancer. -2. [with rent] être en retard; **to** ~ **behind with one's work** avoir du retard dans son travail.

◆ **fall down** *vi* [fail] échouer; **the plan ~s down on three points** ce plan pèche sur trois points.

◆ **fall for** *vt fus* **-1.** *inf* [fall in love with] tomber amoureux(euse) de. **-2.** [trick, lie] se laisser prendre à; **to ~ for it** tomber dans le panneau.

◆ **fall in** *vi* **-1.** [roof, ceiling] s'écrouler, s'affaisser. **-2.** MIL former les rangs.

◆ **fall in with** *vt fus* [go along with] accepter.

◆ **fall off** *vi* **-1.** [branch, handle] se détacher, tomber. **-2.** [demand, numbers] baisser, diminuer.

◆ **fall on** *vt fus* **-1.** [subj: eyes, gaze] tomber sur. **-2.** [attack] se jeter sur.

◆ **fall out** *vi* **-1.** [hair, tooth] tomber. **-2.** [friends] se brouiller. **-3.** MIL rompre les rangs.

◆ **fall over** ◇ *vt fus*: **to ~ over sthg** trébucher sur qqch et tomber; **to be ~ing over o.s. to do sthg** *inf* se mettre en quatre pour faire qqch. ◇ *vi* [person, chair etc] tomber.

◆ **fall through** *vi* [plan, deal] échouer.

◆ **fall to** *vt fus* [subj: duty] incomber à, revenir à; **it ~s to me to ...** c'est à moi de ....

fallacious [fə'leɪʃəs] *adj fml* fallacieux(ieuse).

fallacy ['fæləsɪ] (*pl* **-ies**) *n* erreur *f*, idée *f* fausse.

fallen ['fɔːln] *pp* → **fall**.

fall guy *n* *Am* *inf* [scapegoat] bouc *m* émissaire.

fallible ['fæləbl] *adj* faillible.

falling ['fɔːlɪŋ] *adj* [decreasing] en baisse.

fallopian tube [fə'ləʊpɪən-] *n* trompe *f* de Fallope.

fallout ['fɔːlaʊt] *n* (*U*) [radiation] retombées *fpl*.

fallout shelter *n* abri *m* antiatomique.

fallow ['fæləʊ] *adj*: **to lie ~** être en jachère.

false [fɔːls] *adj* faux (fausse).

false alarm *n* fausse alerte *f*.

falsehood ['fɔːlshʊd] *n* *fml* **-1.** [lie] mensonge *m*. **-2.** (*U*) [lack of truth] fausseté *f*.

falsely ['fɔːlslɪ] *adv* à tort; [smile, laugh] faussement.

false start *n* *lit* & *fig* faux départ *m*.

false teeth *npl* dentier *m*.

falsetto [fɔːl'setəʊ] (*pl* **-s**) ◇ *n* [singer] fausset *m*. ◇ *adv* [sing] en fausset.

falsify ['fɔːlsɪfaɪ] (*pt* & *pp* **-ied**) *vt* falsifier.

falter ['fɔːltə] *vi* **-1.** [move unsteadily] chanceler. **-2.** [steps, voice] devenir hésitant(e). **-3.** [hesitate, lose confidence] hésiter.

faltering ['fɔːltərɪŋ] *adj* [steps, voice] hésitant(e).

fame [feɪm] *n* gloire *f*, renommée *f*.

familiar [fə'mɪljə] *adj* familier(ière); **~ to sb** connu de qqn; **~ with sthg** familiarisé(e) avec qqch; **to be on ~ terms with sb** être en termes familiers avec qqn.

familiarity [fə,mɪlɪ'ærətɪ] *n* (*U*) **-1.** [knowledge]: **~ with sthg** connaissance *f* de qqch, familiarité *f* avec qqch. **-2.** [normality] caractère *m* familier. **-3.** *pej* [excessive informality] familiarité *f*.

familiarize, -ise [fə'mɪljəraɪz] *vt*: **to ~ o.s. with sthg** se familiariser avec qqch; **to ~ sb with sthg** familiariser qqn avec qqch.

family ['fæmlɪ] (*pl* **-ies**) ◇ *n* famille *f*. ◇ *comp* **-1.** [belonging to family] de famille. **-2.** [suitable for all ages] familial(e).

family business *n* entreprise *f* familiale.

family credit *n* (*U*) *Br* ≃ complément *m* familial.

family doctor *n* médecin *m* de famille.

family life *n* vie *f* de famille.

family planning *n* planning *m* familial; **~ clinic** centre *m* de planning familial.

family tree *n* arbre *m* généalogique.

famine ['fæmɪn] *n* famine *f*.

famished ['fæmɪʃt] *adj* *inf* [very hungry] affamé(e); **I'm ~!** je meurs de faim!

famous ['feɪməs] *adj*: **~ (for)** célèbre (pour).

famously ['feɪməslɪ] *adv* *dated*: **to get on** OR **along ~** s'entendre comme larrons en foire.

fan [fæn] (*pt* & *pp* **-ned**, *cont* **-ning**) ◇ *n* **-1.** [of paper, silk] éventail *m*. **-2.** [electric or mechanical] ventilateur *m*. **-3.** [enthusiast] fan *mf*. ◇ *vt* **-1.** [face] éventer; **to ~ o.s.** s'éventer. **-2.** [fire, feelings] attiser.

◆ **fan out** *vi* se déployer.

fanatic [fə'nætɪk] *n* fanatique *mf*.

fanatical [fə'nætɪkl] *adj* fanatique.

fanaticism [fə'nætɪsɪzm] *n* fanatisme *m*.

fan belt *n* courroie *f* de ventilateur.

fanciful ['fænsɪfʊl] *adj* **-1.** [odd] bizarre, fantasque. **-2.** [elaborate] extravagant(e).

fan club *n* fan-club *m*.

fancy ['fænsɪ] (*compar* **-ier**, *superl* **-iest**, *pl* **-ies**, *pt* & *pp* **-ied**) ◇ *adj* **-1.** [elaborate - hat, clothes] extravagant(e); [- food, cakes] raffiné(e). **-2.** [expensive - restaurant, hotel] de luxe; [- prices] fantaisiste.

◇ *n* **-1.** [desire, liking] envie *f*, lubie *f*; **to take a ~ to sb** se prendre d'affection pour qqn; **to take a ~ to sthg** se mettre à aimer qqch; **to take sb's ~** faire envie à qqn, plaire à qqn. **-2.** [fantasy] rêve *m*.

◇ *vt* **-1.** *inf* [want] avoir envie de; **to ~ doing sthg** avoir envie de faire qqch. **-2.** *inf* [like]: **I ~ her** elle me plaît; **to ~ o.s.** ne pas se prendre pour rien OR n'importe qui; **to ~ o.s. as sthg** se prendre pour qqch. **-3.** [imagine]: **~ meeting you here!** tiens, c'est toi! Je n'aurais jamais pensé te rencontrer ici!; **~ that!** ça alors! **-4.** *dated* [think] penser.

fancy dress *n* (U) déguisement *m*.

fancy-dress party *n* bal *m* costumé.

fancy goods *npl* articles *mpl* fantaisie.

fanfare ['fænfeə'] *n* fanfare *f*.

fang [fæŋ] *n* [of wolf] croc *m*; [of snake] crochet *m*.

fan heater *n* radiateur *m* soufflant.

fanlight ['fænlaɪt] *n Br* imposte *f*.

fan mail *n* courrier *m* de fans.

fanny ['fænɪ] *n Am inf* [buttocks] fesses *fpl*.

fanny pack *n Am* banane *f* (sac).

fantasize, -ise ['fæntəsaɪz] *vi*: **to ~ (about sthg/about doing sthg)** fantasmer (sur qqch/sur le fait de faire qqch).

fantastic [fæn'tæstɪk] *adj* **-1.** *inf* [wonderful] fantastique, formidable. **-2.** [incredible] extraordinaire, incroyable. **-3.** [exotic] fabuleux(euse).

fantastically [fæn'tæstɪklɪ] *adv* **-1.** [extremely] extrêmement. **-2.** [exotically] fabuleusement, extraordinairement.

fantasy ['fæntəsɪ] (pl **-ies**) ◇ *n* **-1.** [dream, imaginary event] rêve *m*, fantasme *m*. **-2.** (U) [fiction] fiction *f*. **-3.** [imagination] fantaisie *f*. ◇ *comp* imaginaire.

fanzine ['fænziːn] *n* fanzine *m*.

fao (abbr of **for the attention of**) à l'attention de.

FAO (abbr of **Food and Agriculture Organization**) *n* FAO *f*.

FAQ (abbr of **free alongside quay**) FLQ.

far [fɑːʳ] (compar **farther** OR **further**, superl **farthest** OR **furthest**) ◇ *adv* **-1.** [in distance] loin; **how ~ is it?** à quelle distance est-ce?; **have you come ~?** vous venez de loin?; **~ away** OR **off** loin; **~ and wide** partout; **as ~ as** jusqu'à. **-2.** [in time]: **~ away** OR **off** loin; **as ~ back as** [be founded etc] dès; [remember, go etc] jusqu'à; **so ~** jusqu'à maintenant, jusqu'ici. **-3.** [in degree or extent] bien; **I wouldn't trust him very ~** je ne lui ferais pas tellement confiance; **he's not ~ wrong** OR **out** OR **off** il n'est pas loin; **as ~ as** autant que; **as ~ as I'm concerned** en ce qui me concerne; **as ~ as possible** autant que possible, dans la mesure du possible; **it's all right as ~ as it goes** pour ce qui est de

ça, pas de problème; **~ and away, by ~** de loin; **~ from it** loin de là, au contraire; **so ~ so good** jusqu'ici tout va bien; **to go so ~ as to do sthg** aller jusqu'à faire qqch; **to go too ~** aller trop loin. ◇ *adj* **-1.** [extreme]: **the ~ end of the street** l'autre bout de la rue; **the ~ right of the party** l'extrême droite du parti; **the door on the ~ left** la porte la plus à gauche. **-2.** *literary* [remote] lointain(e).

faraway ['fɑːrəweɪ] *adj* lointain(e).

farce [fɑːs] *n* **-1.** THEATRE farce *f*. **-2.** *fig* [disaster] pagaille *f*, vaste rigolade *f*.

farcical ['fɑːsɪkl] *adj* grotesque.

fare [feəʳ] ◇ *n* **-1.** [payment] prix *m*, tarif *m*. **-2.** *dated* [food] nourriture *f*. ◇ *vi* [manage]: **to ~ well/badly** bien/mal se débrouiller.

Far East *n*: **the ~** l'Extrême-Orient *m*.

fare stage *n Br* section *f*.

farewell [,feə'wel] ◇ *n* adieu *m*. ◇ *excl literary* adieu!

farfetched [,fɑː'fetʃt] *adj* tiré(e) par les cheveux.

farm [fɑːm] ◇ *n* ferme *f*. ◇ *vt* cultiver. ◇ *vi* être cultivateur.

◆ **farm out** *vt sep* confier en sous-traitance.

farmer ['fɑːməʳ] *n* fermier *m*.

farmhand ['fɑːmhænd] *n* ouvrier *m*, -ière *f* agricole.

farmhouse ['fɑːmhaus, pl -hauzɪz] *n* ferme *f*.

farming ['fɑːmɪŋ] *n* (U) agriculture *f*; [of animals] élevage *m*.

farm labourer = **farmhand**.

farmland ['fɑːmlænd] *n* (U) terres *fpl* cultivées OR arables.

farmstead ['fɑːmsted] *n Am* ferme *f*.

farm worker = **farmhand**.

farmyard ['fɑːmjɑːd] *n* cour *f* de ferme.

Faroe = **Faeroe**.

far-off *adj* **-1.** [days] lointain(e); [time] reculé(e). **-2.** [in distance] lointain(e).

far-reaching [-'riːtʃɪŋ] *adj* d'une grande portée.

farrier ['færɪəʳ] *n* maréchal *m* ferrant.

farsighted [,fɑː'saɪtɪd] *adj* **-1.** [person] prévoyant(e); [plan] élaboré(e) avec clairvoyance. **-2.** *Am* [longsighted] hypermétrope.

fart [fɑːt] *v inf* ◇ *n* **-1.** [air] pet *m*. **-2.** [person] con *m*, conne *f*. ◇ *vi* péter.

farther ['fɑːðəʳ] *compar* → **far**.

farthest ['fɑːðəst] *superl* → **far**.

FAS (abbr of **free alongside ship**) FLB.

fascia ['feɪʃə] *n* [on shop] enseigne *f*; [in car] tableau *m* de bord.

fascinate ['fæsɪneɪt] *vt* fasciner.

fascinating ['fæsɪneɪtɪŋ] *adj* [person, country] fascinant(e); [job] passionnant(e); [idea, thought] très intéressant(e).

fascination [,fæsɪ'neɪʃn] *n* fascination *f*.

fascism ['fæʃɪzm] *n* fascisme *m*.

fascist ['fæʃɪst] ◇ *adj* fasciste. ◇ *n* fasciste *mf*.

fashion ['fæʃn] ◇ *n* -1. [clothing, style] mode *f*; **to be in/out of ~** être/ne plus être à la mode; **~ model** mannequin *m* (de mode). -2. [manner] manière *f*. ◇ *vt fml* façonner, fabriquer.

fashionable ['fæʃnəbl] *adj* à la mode.

fashion-conscious *adj* qui suit la mode.

fashion designer *n* styliste *mf*.

fashion show *n* défilé *m* de mode.

fast [fɑːst] ◇ *adj* -1. [rapid] rapide. -2. [clock, watch] qui avance. ◇ *adv* -1. [rapidly] vite; **how ~ does this car go?** à quelle vitesse va cette voiture? -2. [firmly] solidement; **to hold ~ to sthg** *lit* & *fig* s'accrocher à qqch; **~ asleep** profondément endormi. ◇ *n* jeûne *m*. ◇ *vi* jeûner.

fast breeder reactor *n* surrégénérateur *m*.

fasten ['fɑːsn] ◇ *vt* [jacket, bag] fermer; [seat belt] attacher; **to ~ sthg to sthg** attacher qqch à qqch. ◇ *vi*: **to ~ on to sb/sthg** se cramponner à qqn/qqch.

fastener ['fɑːsnə'] *n* [of bag, necklace] fermoir *m*; [of dress] fermeture *f*.

fastening ['fɑːsnɪŋ] *n* fermeture *f*.

fast food *n* fast food *m*.

fast-forward ◇ *n* avance *f* rapide. ◇ *vt* mettre en avance rapide. ◇ *vi* mettre la bande en avance rapide.

fastidious [fə'stɪdɪəs] *adj* [fussy] méticuleux(euse).

fast lane *n* [on motorway] voie *f* rapide; **life in the ~** *fig* la vie à cent à l'heure.

fat [fæt] (*compar* **-ter**, *superl* **-test**) ◇ *adj* -1. [overweight] gros (grosse), gras (grasse); **to get ~** grossir. -2. [not lean - meat] gras (grasse). -3. [thick - file, wallet] gros (grosse), épais(aisse). -4. [large - profit, cheque] gros (grosse). -5. *iro* [small]: **a ~ lot of good that did you!** ça t'a bien avancé! ◇ *n* -1. [flesh, on meat, in food] graisse *f*. -2. (*U*) [for cooking] matière *f* grasse; **pork ~** saindoux *m*.

fatal ['feɪtl] *adj* -1. [serious - mistake] fatal(e); [- decision, words] fatidique. -2. [accident, illness] mortel(elle).

fatalism ['feɪtəlɪzm] *n* fatalisme *m*.

fatalistic [,feɪtə'lɪstɪk] *adj* fataliste.

fatality [fə'tælətɪ] (*pl* **-ies**) *n* -1. [accident victim] mort *m*. -2. = **fatalism**.

fatally ['feɪtəlɪ] *adv* -1. [seriously] sérieusement, gravement. -2. [wounded] mortellement; **~ ill** dans un état désespéré.

fate [feɪt] *n* -1. [destiny] destin *m*; **to tempt ~** tenter le diable. -2. [result, end] sort *m*.

fated ['feɪtɪd] *adj* fatal(e), marqué(e) par le destin; **to be ~ to do sthg** être voué OR destiné à faire qqch.

fateful ['feɪtful] *adj* fatidique.

fathead ['fæthed] *n inf* imbécile *mf*, patate *f*.

father ['fɑːðə'] *n* père *m*. ◇ *vt* engendrer.

◆ **Father** *n* -1. [priest] Père *m*. -2. [God] Dieu le Père *m*; **Our Father** notre Père.

Father Christmas *n Br* Père Noël *m*.

fatherhood ['fɑːðəhud] *n* (*U*) paternité *f*.

father-in-law (*pl* **father-in-laws** OR **fathers-in-law**) *n* beau-père *m*.

fatherly ['fɑːðəlɪ] *adj* paternel(elle).

Father's Day *n* fête *f* des Pères.

fathom ['fæðəm] ◇ *n* brasse *f*. ◇ *vt*: **to ~ sb/sthg (out)** comprendre qqn/qqch.

fatigue [fə'tiːg] ◇ *n* -1. [exhaustion] épuisement *m*. -2. [in metal] fatigue *f*. ◇ *vt* épuiser.

◆ **fatigues** *npl* tenue *f* de corvée, treillis *m*.

fatless ['fætlɪs] *adj* sans matières grasses.

fatness ['fætnɪs] *n* [of person] embonpoint *m*.

fatten ['fætn] *vt* engraisser.

◆ **fatten up** *vt sep* engraisser.

fattening ['fætnɪŋ] *adj* qui fait grossir.

fatty ['fætɪ] (*compar* **-ier**, *superl* **-iest**, *pl* **-ies**) ◇ *adj* gras (grasse). ◇ *n inf pej* gros *m*, grosse *f*.

fatuous ['fætjuəs] *adj* stupide, niais(e).

fatuously ['fætjuəslɪ] *adv* stupidement, niaisement.

faucet ['fɔːsɪt] *n Am* robinet *m*.

fault ['fɔːlt] ◇ *n* -1. [responsibility, in tennis] faute *f*; **it's my ~** c'est de ma faute. -2. [mistake, imperfection] défaut *m*; **to find ~ with sb/sthg** critiquer qqn/qqch; **at ~** fautif(ive). -3. GEOL faille *f*. ◇ *vt*: **to ~ sb (on sthg)** prendre qqn en défaut (sur qqch).

faultless ['fɔːltlɪs] *adj* impeccable.

faulty ['fɔːltɪ] (*compar* **-ier**, *superl* **-iest**) *adj* défectueux(euse).

fauna ['fɔːnə] *n* faune *f*.

faux pas [,fəu'pɑː] (*pl inv*) *n* faux-pas *m*.

favour *Br*, **favor** *Am* ['feɪvə'] ◇ *n* -1. [approval] faveur *f*, approbation *f*; **to look with ~ on sb** considérer qqn favorablement; **in**

sb's ~ en faveur de qqn; **to be in/out of ~ with sb** avoir/ne pas avoir les faveurs de qqn, avoir/ne pas avoir la cote avec qqn; **to curry ~ with sb** chercher à gagner la faveur de qqn. **-2.** [kind act] service *m*; **to do sb a ~** rendre (un) service à qqn. **-3.** [favouritism] favoritisme *m*. **-4.** [advantage]: **to rule in sb's ~** décider OR statuer en faveur de qqn. ◇ *vt* **-1.** [prefer] préférer, privilégier. **-2.** [treat better, help] favoriser. **-3.** *iro* [honour]: **to ~ sb with sthg** faire à qqn l'honneur de qqch.
◆ **in favour** *adv* [in agreement] pour, d'accord.
◆ **in favour of** *prep* **-1.** [in preference to] au profit de. **-2.** [in agreement with]: **to be in ~ of sthg/of doing sthg** être partisan(e) de qqch/de faire qqch.

favourable *Br*, **favorable** *Am* ['feɪvrəbl] *adj* [positive] favorable.

favourably *Br*, **favorably** *Am* ['feɪvrəblɪ] *adv* favorablement; [placed] bien.

favoured *Br*, **favored** *Am* ['feɪvəd] *adj* favorisé(e).

favourite *Br*, **favorite** *Am* ['feɪvrɪt] ◇ *adj* favori(ite). ◇ *n* favori *m*, -ite *f*.

favouritism *Br*, **favoritism** *Am* ['feɪvrɪtɪzm] *n* favoritisme *m*.

fawn [fɔːn] ◇ *adj* fauve (*inv*). ◇ *n* [animal] faon *m*. ◇ *vi*: **to ~ on sb** flatter qqn servilement.

fax [fæks] ◇ *n* fax *m*, télécopie *f*. ◇ *vt* **-1.** [person] envoyer un fax à. **-2.** [document] envoyer en fax.

fax machine *n* fax *m*, télécopieur *m*.

fax number *n* numéro *m* de fax.

faze [feɪz] *vt inf* démonter, déconcerter.

FBI (*abbr of* **Federal Bureau of Investigation**) *n* FBI *m*.

FCC (*abbr of* **Federal Communications Commission**) *n* conseil fédéral de l'audiovisuel aux États-Unis, ≃ CSA *m*.

FCO (*abbr of* **Foreign and Commonwealth Office**) *n* ministère britannique des affaires étrangères et du Commonwealth.

FD (*abbr of* **Fire Department**) *n* sapeurs-pompiers.

FDA *n* **-1.** (*abbr of* **Food and Drug Administration**) *administration délivrant l'autorisation de mise sur le marché des médicaments et des produits alimentaires aux États-Unis. **-2.** (*abbr of* **Association of First Division Civil Servants**) *syndicat britannique des hauts fonctionnaires.

FE *n abbr of* **Further Education.**

fear [fɪər] ◇ *n* **-1.** (*U*) [feeling] peur *f*. **-2.** [object of fear] crainte *f*. **-3.** [risk] risque *m*; **for ~ of** de peur de (+ *infin*), de peur que (+ *subjunctive*). ◇ *vt* **-1.** [be afraid of] craindre, avoir peur de. **-2.** [anticipate] craindre; **to ~ (that)** ... craindre que ..., avoir peur que .... ◇ *vi* [be afraid]: **to ~ for sb/sthg** avoir peur pour qqn/qqch, craindre pour qqn/qqch.

fearful ['fɪəful] *adj* **-1.** *fml* [frightened] peureux(euse); **to be ~ of sthg** avoir peur de qqch. **-2.** [frightening] effrayant(e).

fearless ['fɪəlɪs] *adj* intrépide.

fearlessly ['fɪəlɪslɪ] *adv* courageusement.

fearsome ['fɪəsəm] *adj* [temper] effroyable.

feasibility [,fiːzə'bɪlətɪ] *n* (*U*) possibilité *f*.

feasibility study *n* étude *f* de faisabilité.

feasible ['fiːzəbl] *adj* faisable, possible.

feast [fiːst] ◇ *n* [meal] festin *m*, banquet *m*. ◇ *vi*: **to ~ on** OR **off sthg** se régaler de qqch.

feat [fiːt] *n* exploit *m*, prouesse *f*.

feather ['feðər] *n* plume *f*.

feather bed *n* lit *m* de plume.

featherbrained ['feðəbreɪnd] *adj* [person] écervelé(e); [idea, scheme] **inconsidéré(e)**.

featherweight ['feðəweɪt] *n* [boxer] poids *m* plume.

feature [,fiːtʃər] ◇ *n* **-1.** [characteristic] caractéristique *f*. **-2.** GEOGR particularité *f*. **-3.** [article] article *m* de fond. **-4.** RADIO & TV émission *f* spéciale, spécial *m*. **-5.** CINEMA long métrage *m*. ◇ *vt* **-1.** [subj: film, exhibition] mettre en vedette; **featuring James Dean** avec, dans le rôle principal, James Dean. **-2.** [comprise] présenter, comporter. ◇ *vi* [be] **(in)** figurer en vedette (dans).
◆ **features** *npl* [of face] traits *mpl*.

feature film *n* long métrage *m*.

featureless ['fiːtʃəlɪs] *adj* sans trait distinctif.

Feb. [feb] (*abbr of* **February**) févr.

February ['februərɪ] *n* février *m*; *see also* **September**.

feces *Am* = **faeces**.

feckless ['feklɪs] *adj* inepte.

fed [fed] *pt & pp* → **feed**.

Fed [fed] ◇ *n inf* (*abbr of* **Federal Reserve Board**) *organe de contrôle de la Banque centrale américaine*. ◇ **-1.** *abbr of* **federal. -2.** *abbr of* **federation.**

federal ['fedrəl] *adj* fédéral(e).

Federal Bureau of Investigation *n* FBI *m*, ≃ police *f* judiciaire.

federalism ['fedrəlɪzm] *n* fédéralisme *m*.

federation [ˌfedəˈreɪʃn] *n* fédération *f*.

fed up *adj*: to be ~ (with) en avoir marre (de).

fee [fiː] *n* [of school] frais *mpl*; [of doctor] honoraires *mpl*; [for membership] cotisation *f*; [for entrance] tarif *m*, prix *m*.

feeble [ˈfiːbl] *adj* faible.

feebleminded [ˈfiːblˈmaɪndɪd] *adj* débile.

feebleness [ˈfiːblnɪs] *n* faiblesse *f*.

feebly [ˈfiːblɪ] *adv* faiblement.

feed [fiːd] (*pt* & *pp* fed) ◇ *vt* -1. [give food to] nourrir. -2. [fire, fears etc] alimenter. -3. [put, insert]: to ~ sthg into sthg mettre OR insérer qqch dans qqch. ◇ *vi* -1. [take food]: to ~ (on OR off) se nourrir (de). -2. [be strengthened]: to ~ on OR off s'appuyer sur. ◇ *n* -1. [for baby] repas *m*. -2. [animal food] nourriture *f*.

feedback [ˈfiːdbæk] *n* (*U*) -1. [reaction] réactions *fpl*. -2. ELEC réaction *f*, rétroaction *f*.

feedbag [ˈfiːdbæg] *n Am* musette *f* (mangeoire).

feeder [ˈfiːdər] ◇ *n* [eater] mangeur *m*, -euse *f*. ◇ *comp* [road, railway line] secondaire.

feeding bottle [ˈfiːdɪŋ-] *n Br* biberon *m*.

feel [fiːl] (*pt* & *pp* felt) ◇ *vt* -1. [touch] toucher. -2. [sense, experience, notice] sentir; [emotion] ressentir; to ~ o.s. doing sthg se sentir faire qqch. -3. [believe]: to ~ (that) ... croire que ..., penser que ... -4. *phr*: I'm not ~ing myself today je ne suis pas dans mon assiette aujourd'hui.
◇ *vi* -1. [have sensation]: to ~ cold/hot/sleepy avoir froid/chaud/sommeil; to ~ safe se sentir en sécurité; to ~ like sthg/like doing sthg [be in mood for] avoir envie de qqch/de faire qqch. -2. [have emotion] se sentir; to ~ angry être en colère. -3. [seem] sembler; it ~s strange ça fait drôle; it ~s like leather on dirait du cuir. -4. [by touch]: to ~ for sthg chercher qqch.
◇ *n* -1. [sensation, touch] toucher *m*, sensation *f*. -2. [atmosphere] atmosphère *f*. -3. *phr*: to have a ~ for sthg avoir l'instinct pour qqch.

feeler [ˈfiːlər] *n* antenne *f*.

feeling [ˈfiːlɪŋ] *n* -1. [emotion] sentiment *m*; I know the ~ je sais ce que c'est; bad ~ animosité *f*, hostilité *f*. -2. [physical sensation] sensation *f*. -3. [intuition, sense] sentiment *m*, impression *f*. -4. [understanding] sensibilité *f*; to have a ~ for sthg comprendre OR apprécier qqch.
◆ **feelings** *npl* sentiments *mpl*; to hurt sb's ~s blesser (la sensibilité de) qqn; no hard ~s! sans rancune!

fee-paying [-ˈpeɪɪŋ] *adj Br* [pupil] d'un établissement privé; [school] privé(e).

feet [fiːt] *pl* → foot.

feign [feɪn] *vt fml* feindre.

feint [feɪnt] ◇ *n* feinte *f*. ◇ *vi* feinter.

feisty [ˈfeɪstɪ] (*compar* -ier, *superl* -iest) *adj inf* [lively] plein(e) d'entrain; [combative] qui a du cran.

felicitous [fɪˈlɪsɪtəs] *adj fml* heureux(euse).

feline [ˈfiːlaɪn] ◇ *adj* félin(e). ◇ *n* félin *m*.

fell [fel] ◇ *pt* → fall. ◇ *vt* [tree, person] abattre.
◆ **fells** *npl* GEOGR lande *f*.

fellow [ˈfeləʊ] ◇ *n* -1. *dated* [man] homme *m*. -2. [comrade, peer] camarade *m*, compagnon *m*. -3. [of society, college] membre *m*, associé *m*. ◇ *adj*: one's ~ men ses semblables; ~ feeling sympathie *f*; ~ passenger compagnon *m*, compagne *f* (de voyage); ~ student camarade *mf* (d'études).

fellowship [ˈfeləʊʃɪp] *n* -1. [comradeship] amitié *f*, camaraderie *f*. -2. [society] association *f*, corporation *f*. -3. [of society, college] titre *m* de membre OR d'associé.

felony [ˈfelənɪ] (*pl* -ies) *n* JUR crime *m*, forfait *m*.

felt [felt] ◇ *pt* & *pp* → feel. ◇ *n* (*U*) feutre *m*.

felt-tip pen *n* stylo-feutre *m*.

female [ˈfiːmeɪl] ◇ *adj* [person] de sexe féminin; [animal, plant] femelle; [sex, figure] féminin(e); ~ student étudiante *f*; ~ worker travailleuse *f*, ouvrière *f*. ◇ *n* femelle *f*.

feminine [ˈfemɪnɪn] ◇ *adj* féminin(e). ◇ *n* GRAMM féminin *m*.

femininity [femɪˈnɪnətɪ] *n* (*U*) féminité *f*.

feminism [ˈfemɪnɪzm] *n* féminisme *m*.

feminist [ˈfemɪnɪst] *n* féministe *mf*.

fence [fens] ◇ *n* [barrier] clôture *f*; to sit on the ~ *fig* ménager la chèvre et le chou. ◇ *vt* clôturer, entourer d'une clôture.
◆ **fence off** *vt sep* séparer par une clôture.

fencing [ˈfensɪŋ] *n* -1. SPORT escrime *f*. -2. [material] clôture *f*.

fend [fend] *vi*: to ~ for o.s. se débrouiller tout seul.
◆ **fend off** *vt sep* [blows] parer; [questions, reporters] écarter.

fender [ˈfendər] *n* -1. [round fireplace] pare-feu *m inv*. -2. [on boat] pare-battage *m inv*. -3. *Am* [on car] aile *f*.

fennel [ˈfenl] *n* fenouil *m*.

fens [fenz] *npl Br* marais *mpl*.

feral [ˈfɪərəl] *adj* sauvage.

ferment [n 'fɜːment, vb fə'ment] ◇ n (U) [unrest] **agitation** f, **effervescence** f; **in ~ en** effervescence. ◇ vi [wine, beer] fermenter.

fermentation [,fɜːmən'teɪʃn] n fermentation f.

fermented [fə'mentɪd] adj fermenté(e).

fern [fɜːn] n fougère f.

ferocious [fə'rəʊʃəs] adj féroce.

ferociously [fə'rəʊʃəslɪ] adv férocement, avec férocité.

ferocity [fə'rɒsətɪ] n férocité f.

ferret ['ferɪt] n furet m.
◆ **ferret about, ferret around** vi inf fureter un peu partout.
◆ **ferret out** vt sep inf dénicher.

ferris wheel ['ferɪs-] n grande roue f.

ferry ['ferɪ] ◇ n ferry m, ferry-boat m; [smaller] bac m. ◇ vt transporter.

ferryboat ['ferɪbəʊt] n = ferry.

ferryman ['ferɪmən] (pl -men [-mən]) n passeur m.

fertile ['fɜːtaɪl] adj -1. [land, imagination] fertile, fécond(e). -2. [woman] féconde.

fertility [fɜː'tɪlətɪ] n -1. [of land, imagination] fertilité f. -2. [of woman] fécondité f.

fertility drug n traitement m contre la stérilité.

fertilization [,fɜːtɪlaɪ'zeɪʃn] n -1. [of soil] fertilisation f. -2. [of egg] fécondation f.

fertilize, -ise ['fɜːtɪlaɪz] vt -1. [soil] fertiliser, amender. -2. [egg] féconder.

fertilizer ['fɜːtɪlaɪzə'] n engrais m.

fervent ['fɜːvənt] adj fervent(e).

fervour Br, **fervor** Am ['fɜːvə'] n ferveur f.

fester ['festə'] vi -1. [wound, sore] suppurer. -2. [emotion, quarrel] s'aigrir.

festival ['festəvl] n -1. [event, celebration] festival m. -2. [holiday] fête f.

festive ['festɪv] adj de fête.

festive season n: **the ~ la période des fêtes.**

festivities [fes'tɪvətɪz] npl réjouissances fpl.

festoon [fe'stuːn] vt décorer de guirlandes; **to be ~ed with** être décoré de.

fetal ['fiːtl] = **foetal**.

fetch [fetʃ] vt -1. [go and get] aller chercher. -2. [raise - money] rapporter.

fetching ['fetʃɪŋ] adj séduisant(e).

fete, fête [feɪt] ◇ n fête f, kermesse f. ◇ vt fêter, faire fête à.

fetid ['fetɪd] adj fétide.

fetish ['fetɪʃ] n -1. [sexual obsession] objet m de fétichisme. -2. [mania] manie f, obsession f.

fetishism ['fetɪʃɪzm] n fétichisme m.

fetlock ['fetlɒk] n boulet m.

fetter ['fetə'] vt [person] enchaîner; [movements] entraver.
◆ **fetters** npl fers mpl, chaînes fpl.

fettle ['fetl] n: **in fine ~ en pleine forme.**

fetus ['fiːtəs] = **foetus**.

feud [fjuːd] ◇ n querelle f. ◇ vi se quereller.

feudal ['fjuːdl] adj féodal(e).

fever ['fiːvə'] n fièvre f.

fevered ['fiːvəd] adj fiévreux(euse).

feverish ['fiːvərɪʃ] adj fiévreux(euse).

fever pitch n comble m.

few [fjuː] ◇ adj peu de; **the first ~ pages** les toutes premières pages; **quite a ~, a good ~ pas mal de, un bon nombre de; ~ and far between** rares. ◇ pron peu; **a ~** quelques-uns mpl, quelques-unes fpl.

fewer ['fjuːə] ◇ adj moins (de); **no ~ than** pas moins de. ◇ pron moins.

fewest ['fjuːəst] adj le moins (de).

FH Br abbr of **fire hydrant**.

FHA (abbr of **Federal Housing Administration**) n organisme de gestion des logements sociaux aux États-Unis.

fiancé [fɪ'ɒnseɪ] n fiancé m.

fiancée [fɪ'ɒnseɪ] n fiancée f.

fiasco [fɪ'æskəʊ] (Br pl -s, Am pl -es) n fiasco m.

fib [fɪb] (pt & pp -bed, cont -bing) inf ◇ n bobard m, blague f. ◇ vi raconter des bobards OR des blagues.

fibber ['fɪbə] n inf menteur m, -euse f.

fibre Br, **fiber** Am ['faɪbə'] n fibre f.

fibreboard Br, **fiberboard** Am ['faɪbəbɔːd] n (U) panneau m fibreux.

fibreglass Br, **fiberglass** Am ['faɪbəglɑːs] ◇ n (U) fibre f de verre. ◇ comp en fibre de verre.

fibre optics n (U) fibre f optique.

fibroid ['faɪbrɔɪd] n fibrome m.

fibrositis [,faɪbrə'saɪtɪs] n fibrosite f.

FICA (abbr of **Federal Insurance Contributions Act**) n loi américaine régissant les cotisations sociales.

fickle ['fɪkl] adj versatile.

fiction ['fɪkʃn] *n* fiction *f.*

fictional ['fɪkʃənl] *adj* fictif(ive).

fictionalize, -ise ['fɪkʃənəlaɪz] *vt* romancer.

fictitious [fɪk'tɪʃəs] *adj* [false] fictif(ive).

fiddle ['fɪdəl] ◇ *vi* [play around]: **to ~ with sthg** tripoter qqch. ◇ *vt Br inf* truquer. ◇ *n* **-1.** [violin] violon *m*; **to be (as) fit as a ~** se porter comme un charme; **to play second ~ (to sb)** jouer un rôle secondaire (auprès de qqn), passer au second plan (auprès de qqn). **-2.** *Br inf* [fraud] combine *f*, escroquerie *f.*

◆ **fiddle about, fiddle around** *vi* **-1.** [fidget] ne pas se tenir tranquille, s'agiter; **to ~ about with sthg** tripoter qqch. **-2.** [waste time] perdre son temps.

fiddler ['fɪdlər] *n* joueur *m*, -euse *f* de violon.

fiddly ['fɪdlɪ] (*compar* -ier, *superl* -iest) *adj Br inf* délicat(e).

fidelity [fɪ'delətɪ] *n* **-1.** [loyalty] fidélité *f.* **-2.** [accuracy - of report] fidélité *f.*

fidget ['fɪdʒɪt] *vi* remuer.

fidgety ['fɪdʒɪtɪ] *adj inf* remuant(e).

fiduciary [fɪ'duːʃjərɪ] (*pl* -ies) ◇ *adj* fiduciaire. ◇ *n* fiduciaire *mf.*

field [fiːld] ◇ *n* **-1.** [gen & COMPUT] champ *m*; **~ of vision** champ de vision. **-2.** [for sports] terrain *m.* **-3.** [of knowledge] domaine *m.* **-4.** [real environment]: **in the ~** sur le terrain. ◇ *vi* tenir le champ.

field day *n*: **to have a ~** s'en donner à cœur joie.

fielder ['fiːldər] *n* joueur *m* qui tient le champ.

field event *n* compétition *f* d'athlétisme (*hormis la course*).

field glasses *npl* jumelles *fpl.*

field marshal *n* ≃ maréchal *m* (de France).

field mouse *n* mulot *m.*

field trip *n* voyage *m* d'étude.

fieldwork ['fiːldwɜːk] *n* (*U*) recherches *fpl* sur le terrain.

fieldworker ['fiːldwɜːkər] *n* chercheur *m*, -euse *f* OR enquêteur *m*, -trice *f* sur le terrain.

fiend [fiːnd] *n* **-1.** [cruel person] monstre *m.* **-2.** *inf* [fanatic] fou *m*, folle *f*, mordu *m*, -e *f.*

fiendish ['fiːndɪʃ] *adj* **-1.** [evil] abominable. **-2.** *inf* [very difficult, complex] compliqué(e), complexe.

fierce [fɪəs] *adj* féroce; [heat] torride; [storm, temper] violent(e).

fiercely ['fɪəslɪ] *adv* férocement; [attack] violemment; [defend] avec acharnement.

fiery ['faɪərɪ] (*compar* -ier, *superl* -iest) *adj* **-1.** [burning] ardent(e). **-2.** [spicy] très piquant(e). **-3.** [volatile - speech] enflammé(e); [- temper, person] fougueux(euse). **-4.** [bright red] flamboyant(e).

FIFA ['fiːfə] (*abbr of* **Fédération Internationale de Football Association**) *n* FIFA *f.*

fifteen [fɪf'tiːn] *num* quinze; *see also* **six.**

fifteenth [ˌfɪf'tiːnθ] *num* quinzième; *see also* **sixth.**

fifth [fɪfθ] *num* cinquième; *see also* **sixth.**

Fifth Amendment *n*: **the ~** le Cinquième Amendement (*qui garantit les droits des inculpés, aux États-Unis*).

fifth column *n* cinquième colonne *f.*

fiftieth ['fɪftɪəθ] *num* cinquantième; *see also* **sixth.**

fifty ['fɪftɪ] *num* cinquante; *see also* **sixty.**

fifty-fifty ◇ *adj* moitié-moitié, fifty-fifty; **to have a ~ chance** avoir cinquante pour cent de chances. ◇ *adv* moitié-moitié, fifty-fifty.

fig [fɪg] *n* figue *f.*

fight [faɪt] (*pt* & *pp* **fought**) ◇ *n* **-1.** [physical] bagarre *f*; **to have a ~ (with sb)** se battre (avec qqn), se bagarrer (avec qqn); **to put up a ~** se battre, se défendre. **-2.** *fig* [battle, struggle] lutte *f*, combat *m.* **-3.** [argument] dispute *f*; **to have a ~ (with sb)** se disputer (avec qqn).

◇ *vt* **-1.** [conduct - war] mener. **-2.** [enemy, racism] combattre.

◇ *vi* **-1.** [in war, punch-up] se battre. **-2.** *fig* [struggle]: **to ~ for/against sthg** lutter pour/contre qqch. **-3.** [argue]: **to ~ (about** OR **over)** se battre OR se disputer (à propos de).

◆ **fight back** ◇ *vt fus* refouler. ◇ *vi* riposter.

◆ **fight off** *vt sep* **-1.** [attacker] repousser. **-2.** [illness, desire] venir à bout de.

◆ **fight out** *vt sep*: **leave them to ~ it out** laisse-les se bagarrer et régler cela entre eux.

fighter ['faɪtər] *n* **-1.** [plane] avion *m* de chasse, chasseur *m.* **-2.** [soldier] combattant *m.* **-3.** [combative person] battant *m*, -e *f.*

fighting ['faɪtɪŋ] *n* (*U*) [punch-up] bagarres *fpl*; [in war] conflits *mpl.*

fighting chance *n*: **to have a ~** avoir une petite chance.

figment ['fɪgmənt] *n*: **a ~ of sb's imagination** le fruit de l'imagination de qqn.

figurative ['fɪgərətɪv] *adj* figuratif(ive).

figuratively ['fɪgərətɪvlɪ] *adv* au figuré.

figure 196

figure [*Br* 'fɪgə', *Am* 'fɪgjər] ◇ *n* **-1.** [statistic, number] chiffre *m*; **to put a ~ on sthg** chiffrer qqch. **-2.** [human shape, outline] silhouette *f*, forme *f*. **-3.** [personality, diagram] figure *f*. **-4.** [shape of body] ligne *f*. ◇ *vt* [suppose] penser, supposer. ◇ *vi* [feature] figurer, apparaître.

◆ **figure out** *vt sep* [understand] comprendre; [find] trouver.

figurehead ['fɪgəhed] *n* **-1.** [on ship] figure *f* de proue. **-2.** *fig & pej* [leader] homme *m* de paille.

figure of eight *Br*, **figure eight** *Am n* huit *m inv*.

figure of speech *n* figure *f* de rhétorique.

figure skating *n* patinage *m* artistique.

figurine [*Br* 'fɪgəriːn, *Am* ˌfɪgjə'riːn] *n* figurine *f*.

Fiji ['fiːdʒiː] *n* Fidji *fpl*; **in ~** à Fidji.

Fijian [ˌfiːdʒiːən] ◇ *adj* fidjien(ienne). ◇ *n* Fidjien *m*, -ienne *f*.

filament ['fɪləmənt] *n* [in light bulb] filament *m*.

filch [fɪltʃ] *vt inf* chiper.

file [faɪl] ◇ *n* **-1.** [folder, report] dossier *m*; **on ~, on the ~s** répertorié dans les dossiers. **-2.** COMPUT fichier *m*. **-3.** [tool] lime *f*. **-4.** [line]: **in single ~** en file indienne. ◇ *vt* **-1.** [document] classer. **-2.** JUR - accusation, complaint] porter, déposer; [- lawsuit] intenter. **-3.** [fingernails, wood] limer. ◇ *vi* **-1.** [walk in single file] marcher en file indienne. **-2.** JUR: **to ~ for divorce** demander le divorce.

file clerk *Am* = **filing clerk**.

filename ['faɪlˌneɪm] *n* COMPUT nom *m* de fichier.

filet *Am* = **fillet**.

filibuster ['fɪlɪbʌstə'] *vi* POL faire de l'obstruction parlementaire.

filigree ['fɪlɪgriː] ◇ *adj* en filigrane. ◇ *n* filigrane *m*.

filing cabinet ['faɪlɪŋ-] *n* classeur *m*, fichier *m*.

filing clerk ['faɪlɪŋ-] *n Br* documentaliste *mf*.

Filipino [ˌfɪlɪ'piːnəʊ] (*pl* -s) ◇ *adj* philippin(e). ◇ *n* Philippin *m*, -e *f*.

fill [fɪl] ◇ *vt* **-1.** [gen] remplir; **to ~ sthg with sthg** remplir qqch de qqch. **-2.** [gap, hole] boucher. **-3.** [vacancy - subj: employer] pourvoir à; [- subj: employee] prendre. ◇ *n*: **to eat one's ~** manger à sa faim; **to have had one's ~ of sthg** en avoir assez de qqch.

◆ **fill in** *vt sep* **-1.** [form] remplir. **-2.** [inform]: **to ~ sb in (on)** mettre qqn au courant (de). ◇ *vt fus*: **I'm just ~ing in time** je fais ça en attendant. ◇ *vi* [substitute]: **to ~ in for sb** remplacer qqn.

◆ **fill out** *vt sep* [form] remplir. ◇ *vi* [get fatter] prendre de l'embonpoint.

◆ **fill up** *vt sep* remplir. ◇ *vi* se remplir.

filled [fɪld] *adj* **-1.** [roll] garni(e). **-2.** [with emotion]: **~ (with)** plein(e) (de).

filler ['fɪlə'] *n* [for cracks] mastic *m*.

filler cap *n Br* bouchon *m* du réservoir d'essence.

fillet *Br*, **filet** *Am* ['fɪlɪt] *n* filet *m*.

fillet steak *n* filet *m* de bœuf.

fill-in *n inf* pis-aller *m inv*.

filling ['fɪlɪŋ] ◇ *adj* substantiel(ielle), qui rassasie. ◇ *n* **-1.** [in tooth] plombage *m*. **-2.** [in cake, sandwich] garniture *f*.

filling station *n* station-service *f*.

fillip ['fɪlɪp] *n* coup *m* de fouet.

filly ['fɪlɪ] (*pl* -ies) *n* pouliche *f*.

film [fɪlm] ◇ *n* **-1.** [movie] film *m*. **-2.** [layer, for camera] pellicule *f*. **-3.** [footage] images *fpl*. ◇ *vt & vi* filmer.

filming ['fɪlmɪŋ] *n* (*U*) tournage *m*.

film star *n* vedette *f* de cinéma.

filmstrip ['fɪlmstrɪp] *n* film *m* fixe.

film studio *n* studio *m* (de cinéma).

Filofax® ['faɪləʊfæks] *n* Filofax® *m*.

filter ['fɪltə'] ◇ *n* filtre *m*. ◇ *vt* [coffee] passer; [water, oil, air] filtrer. ◇ *vi* [people]: **to ~ in** entrer par petits groupes.

◆ **filter out** *vt sep* filtrer.

◆ **filter through** *vi* filtrer.

filter coffee *n* café *m* filtre.

filter lane *n Br* ≃ voie *f* de droite.

filter paper *n* papier *m* filtre.

filter-tipped [-tɪpt] *adj* à bout filtre.

filth [fɪlθ] *n* (*U*) **-1.** [dirt] saleté *f*, crasse *f*. **-2.** [obscenity] obscénités *fpl*.

filthy ['fɪlθɪ] (*compar* -ier, *superl* -iest) *adj* **-1.** [very dirty] dégoûtant(e), répugnant(e). **-2.** [obscene] obscène.

filtration plant [fɪl'treɪʃn-] *n* station *f* d'épuration.

Fimbra ['fɪmbrə] (*abbr of* **Financial Intermediaries, Managers and Brokers Regulatory Association**) *n* organisme britannique contrôlant les activités des courtiers d'assurances.

fin [fɪn] *n* **-1.** [of fish] nageoire *f*. **-2.** *Am* [for swimmer] palme *f*.

final ['faɪnl] ◇ *adj* **-1.** [last] dernier(ière). **-2.** [at end] final(e). **-3.** [definitive] définitif(ive). ◇ *n* finale *f*.

◆ **finals** *npl* UNIV examens *mpl* de dernière année.

final demand *n* dernier avertissement *m*.

finale [fɪˈnɑːlɪ] *n* finale *m*.

finalist [ˈfaɪnəlɪst] *n* finaliste *mf*.

finalize, -ise [ˈfaɪnəlaɪz] *vt* mettre au point.

finally [ˈfaɪnəlɪ] *adv* enfin.

finance [ˈfaɪnæns, faɪˈnæns] ◇ *n* (U) finance *f*. ◇ *vt* financer.

◆ **finances** *npl* finances *fpl*.

financial [fɪˈnænʃl] *adj* financier(ière).

financial adviser *n* conseiller financier *m*, conseillère financière *f*.

financially [fɪˈnænʃəlɪ] *adv* financièrement.

financial services *npl* services *mpl* financiers.

financial year *Br*, **fiscal year** *Am n* exercice *m*.

financier [fɪˈnænsɪəʳ] *n Br* financier *m*.

finch [fɪntʃ] *n* fringillidé *m*.

find [faɪnd] (*pt* & *pp* **found**) ◇ *vt* **-1.** [gen] trouver; **to ~ one's way** trouver son chemin. **-2.** [realize]: **to ~ (that)** ... s'apercevoir que .... **-3.** JUR: **to be found guilty/not guilty (of)** être déclaré(e) coupable/non coupable (de). ◇ *n* trouvaille *f*.

◆ **find out** ◇ *vt fus* découvrir, apprendre. ◇ *vt sep* démasquer.

findings [ˈfaɪndɪŋz] *npl* conclusions *fpl*.

fine [faɪn] ◇ *adj* **-1.** [good - work] excellent(e); [- building, weather] beau (belle). **-2.** [perfectly satisfactory] très bien; **I'm ~** ça va bien. **-3.** [thin, smooth] fin(e). **-4.** [minute - detail, distinction] subtil(e); [- adjustment, tuning] délicat(e). ◇ *adv* [very well] très bien. ◇ *n* amende *f*. ◇ *vt* condamner à une amende.

fine arts *npl* beaux-arts *mpl*.

finely [ˈfaɪnlɪ] *adv* **-1.** [chopped, ground] fin. **-2.** [tuned, balanced] délicatement.

finery [ˈfaɪnərɪ] *n* (U) parure *f*.

finesse [fɪˈnes] *n* finesse *f*.

fine-tooth comb *n*: **to go over sthg with a ~** passer qqch au peigne fin.

fine-tune *vt* [mechanism] régler au quart de tour; *fig* régler minutieusement.

finger [ˈfɪŋgəʳ] ◇ *n* doigt *m*; **to keep one's ~s crossed** croiser les doigts; **she didn't lay a ~ on him** elle n'a pas touché un cheveu de sa tête; **he didn't lift a ~ to help** il n'a pas levé le petit doigt; **to point a** OR **the ~ at sb** [accuse] accuser qqn; **to put one's ~ on sthg** mettre le doigt sur qqch; **to twist sb round one's little ~** faire ce qu'on veut de qqn. ◇ *vt* [feel] palper.

fingermark [ˈfɪŋgəmɑːk] *n* trace *f* de doigt.

fingernail [ˈfɪŋgəneɪl] *n* ongle *m* (*de la main*).

fingerprint [ˈfɪŋgəprɪnt] *n* empreinte *f* (digitale); **to take sb's ~s** prendre les empreintes de qqn.

fingertip [ˈfɪŋgətɪp] *n* bout *m* du doigt; **at one's ~s** sur le bout des doigts.

finicky [ˈfɪnɪkɪ] *adj pej* [eater, task] difficile; [person] tatillon(onne).

finish [ˈfɪnɪʃ] ◇ *n* **-1.** [end] fin *f*; [of race] arrivée *f*. **-2.** [texture] finition *f*. ◇ *vt* finir, terminer; **to ~ doing sthg** finir OR terminer de faire qqch. ◇ *vi* finir, terminer; [school, film] se terminer.

◆ **finish off** *vt sep* finir, terminer.

◆ **finish up** *vi* finir.

◆ **finish with** *vt fus* [friend] en finir avec; [boyfriend, girlfrien d] rompre avec.

finished [ˈfɪnɪʃt] *adj* **-1.** [ready, done, over] fini(e), terminé(e). **-2.** [no longer interested]: **to be ~ with sthg** en avoir fini avec qqch. **-3.** *inf* [done for] fichu(e).

finishing line [ˈfɪnɪʃɪŋ-] *n* ligne *f* d'arrivée.

finishing school [ˈfɪnɪʃɪŋ-] *n* école privée pour jeunes filles surtout axée sur l'enseignement de bonnes manières.

finite [ˈfaɪnaɪt] *adj* fini(e).

Finland [ˈfɪnlənd] *n* Finlande *f*; **in ~** en Finlande.

Finn [fɪn] *n* Finlandais *m*, -e *f*.

Finnish [ˈfɪnɪʃ] ◇ *adj* finlandais(e), finnois(e). ◇ *n* [language] finnois *m*.

fiord [fjɔːd] = **fjord**.

fir [fɜːʳ] *n* sapin *m*.

fire [ˈfaɪəʳ] ◇ *n* **-1.** [gen] feu *m*; **on ~** en feu; **to catch ~** prendre feu; **to set ~ to sthg** mettre le feu à qqch. **-2.** [out of control] incendie *m*. **-3.** *Br* [heater] appareil *m* de chauffage. **-4.** (U) [shooting] coups *mpl* de feu; **to open ~ (on)** ouvrir le feu (sur). ◇ *vt* **-1.** [shoot] tirer. **-2.** *fig* [questions, accusations] lancer. **-3.** [dismiss] renvoyer. ◇ *vi*: **to ~ (on** OR **at)** faire feu (sur), tirer (sur).

fire alarm *n* avertisseur *m* d'incendie.

firearm [ˈfaɪərɑːm] *n* arme *f* à feu.

fireball [ˈfaɪəbɔːl] *n* boule *f* de feu.

firebomb [ˈfaɪəbɒm] ◇ *n* bombe *f* incendiaire. ◇ *vt* lancer des bombes incendiaires à.

firebreak [ˈfaɪəbreɪk] *n* pare-feu *m inv*.

fire brigade *Br*, **fire department** *Am n* sapeurs-pompiers *mpl*.

fire chief *Am* = **fire master**.

firecracker [ˈfaɪəˌkrækəʳ] *n* pétard *m*.

fire-damaged *adj* endommagé(e) par le feu.

fire department *Am* = **fire brigade**.

fire door *n* porte *f* coupe-feu.

fire drill *n* exercice *m* d'évacuation en cas d'incendie.

fire-eater *n* [performer] avaleur *m* de feu.

fire engine *n* voiture *f* de pompiers.

fire escape *n* escalier *m* de secours.

fire extinguisher *n* extincteur *m* d'incendie.

fire fighter *n* pompier *m*.

fireguard ['faɪəgɑːd] *n* garde-feu *m inv*.

fire hazard *n*: **to be a** ~ présenter un risque d'incendie.

fire hydrant [-'haɪdrənt], **fireplug** *Am* ['faɪəplʌg] *n* bouche *f* d'incendie.

firelight ['faɪəlaɪt] *n* (*U*) lueur *f* du feu.

firelighter ['faɪəlaɪtər] *n* allume-feu *m inv*.

fireman ['faɪəmən] (*pl* **-men** [-mən]) *n* pompier *m*.

fire master *Br*, **fire chief** *Am* *n* capitaine *m* des pompiers.

fireplace ['faɪəpleɪs] *n* cheminée *f*.

fireplug *Am* = **fire hydrant**.

firepower ['faɪə,paʊər] *n* puissance *f* de feu.

fireproof ['faɪəpruːf] *adj* ignifugé(e).

fire-raiser [-,reɪzər] *n Br* pyromane *mf*.

fire regulations *npl* consignes *fpl* en cas d'incendie.

fire service *n Br* sapeurs-pompiers *mpl*.

fireside ['faɪəsaɪd] *n*: **by the** ~ au coin du feu.

fire station *n* caserne *f* des pompiers.

firewood ['faɪəwud] *n* bois *m* de chauffage.

firework ['faɪəwɜːk] *n* fusée *f* de feu d'artifice.
◆ **fireworks** *npl* [outburst of anger] étincelles *fpl*.

firework display *n* feu *m* d'artifice.

firing ['faɪərɪŋ] *n* (*U*) MIL tir *m*, fusillade *f*.

firing squad *n* peloton *m* d'exécution.

firm [fɜːm] ◇ *adj* **-1.** [gen] ferme; **to stand** ~ tenir bon. **-2.** [support, structure] solide. **-3.** [evidence, news] certain(e). ◇ *n* firme *f*, société *f*.
◆ **firm up** ◇ *vt sep* **-1.** [prices, trade] renforcer. **-2.** [agreement] rendre définitif(ive). ◇ *vi* [prices, trade] se renforcer.

firmly ['fɜːmlɪ] *adv* fermement.

firmness ['fɜːmnɪs] *n* **-1.** [gen] fermeté *f*. **-2.** [discipline] rigueur *f*. **-3.** [of beliefs] force *f*.

first [fɜːst] ◇ *adj* premier(ière); **for the** ~ **time** pour la première fois; ~ **thing in the morning** tôt le matin; ~ **things** ~ commençons par le plus important; **I don't know the** ~ **thing about it** je ne sais absolument rien là-dessus, je n'y connais rien du tout. ◇ *adv* **-1.** [before anyone else] en premier. **-2.** [before anything else] d'abord; ~ **of all** tout d'abord. **-3.** [for the first time] (pour) la première fois. ◇ *n* **-1.** [person] premier *m*, -ière *f*. **-2.** [unprecedented event] première *f*. **-3.** *Br* UNIV diplôme universitaire avec mention très bien.
◆ **at first** *adv* d'abord.
◆ **at first hand** *adv* de première main.

first aid *n* (*U*) premiers secours *mpl*.

first-aider [-'eɪdər] *n* secouriste *mf*.

first-aid kit *n* trousse *f* de premiers secours.

first-class *adj* **-1.** [excellent] excellent(e). **-2.** *Br* UNIV avec mention très bien. **-3.** [ticket, compartment] de première classe; [stamp, letter] tarif normal.

first-class mail *n* courrier *m* tarif normal.

first cousin *n* cousin germain *m*, cousine germaine *f*.

first day cover *n* émission *f* du premier jour.

first-degree *adj* **-1.** MED: ~ **burn** brûlure *f* au premier degré. **-2.** *Am* JUR: ~ **murder** ≃ homicide *m* volontaire.

first floor *n Br* premier étage *m*; *Am* rez-de-chaussée *m inv*.

firsthand [fɜːst'hænd] *adj* & *adv* de première main.

first lady *n* première dame *f* du pays, femme *f* du Président.

first language *n* langue *f* maternelle.

first lieutenant *n* lieutenant *m*.

firstly ['fɜːstlɪ] *adv* premièrement.

first mate *n* second *m*.

first name *n* prénom *m*.
◆ **first-name** *adj*: **to be on first-name terms with sb** appeler qqn par son prénom.

first night *n* première *f*.

first offender *n* délinquant *m* primaire.

first officer = **first mate**.

first-past-the-post system *n Br* système *m* majoritaire simple.

first-rate *adj* excellent(e).

first refusal *n* priorité *f*.

First World War *n*: **the** ~ la Première Guerre Mondiale.

firtree ['fɜːtriː] = **fir**.

FIS (*abbr of* **Family Income Supplement**) *n complément familial en Grande-Bretagne*.

fiscal ['fıskl] *adj* fiscal(e).

fiscal year *Am* = **financial year**.

fish [fıʃ] (*pl inv*) ◇ *n* poisson *m*. ◇ *vt* [river, sea] pêcher dans. ◇ *vi* **-1.** [fisherman]: **to ~ (for sthg)** pêcher (qqch). **-2.** [try to obtain]: **to ~ for** [compliments] essayer de s'attirer; [information] essayer d'obtenir.

◆ **fish out** *vt sep inf* sortir, extirper.

fish and chips *npl Br* poisson *m* frit avec frites.

fish and chip shop *n Br* endroit où l'on vend du poisson frit et des frites.

fishbowl ['fıʃbəul] *n* bocal *m* (à poissons).

fishcake ['fıʃkeık] *n* croquette *f* de poisson.

fisherman ['fıʃəmən] (*pl* **-men** [-mən]) *n* pêcheur *m*.

fishery ['fıʃərı] (*pl* **-ies**) *n* pêcherie *f*.

fish-eye lens *n* objectif *m* ultra-grand angle.

fish factory *n* usine *f* piscicole.

fish farm *n* centre *m* de pisciculture.

fish fingers *Br*, **fish sticks** *Am npl* bâtonnets *mpl* de poisson panés.

fishhook ['fıʃhuk] *n* hameçon *m*.

fishing ['fıʃıŋ] *n* pêche *f*; **to go ~** aller à la pêche.

fishing boat *n* bateau *m* de pêche.

fishing line *n* ligne *f*.

fishing rod *n* canne *f* à pêche.

fishmonger ['fıʃ,mʌŋgəʳ] *n* poissonnier *m*, -ière *f*; **~'s (shop)** poissonnerie *f*.

fishnet ['fıʃnet] *n* **-1.** [for fishing] filet *m*. **-2.** [material]: **~ stockings/tights** bas *mpl*/collant *m* résille.

fish slice *n Br* pelle *f* à poisson.

fish sticks *Am* = **fish fingers**.

fishwife ['fıʃwaıf] (*pl* **-wives** [-waıvz]) *n pej* mégère *f*.

fishy ['fıʃı] (*compar* **-ier**, *superl* **-iest**) *adj* **-1.** [smell, taste] de poisson. **-2.** [suspicious] louche.

fission ['fıʃn] *n* fission *f*.

fissure ['fıʃəʳ] *n* fissure *f*.

fist [fıst] *n* poignet *m*.

fit [fıt] (*pt & pp* **-ted**, *cont* **-ting**) ◇ *adj* **-1.** [suitable] convenable; **to be ~ for sthg** être bon (bonne) à qqch; **to be ~ to do sthg** être apte à faire qqch; **to see** OR **think ~ (to do sthg)** juger bon (de faire qqch). **-2.** [healthy] en forme; **to keep ~** se maintenir en forme.

◇ *n* **-1.** [of clothes, shoes etc] ajustement *m*; **it's a tight ~** c'est un peu juste; **it's a good ~** c'est la bonne taille. **-2.** [epileptic seizure] crise *f*; **to have a ~** avoir une crise; *fig* pi-

quer une crise. **-3.** [bout - of crying] crise *f*; [- of rage] accès *m*; [- of sneezing] suite *f*; **in ~s and starts** par à-coups.

◇ *vt* **-1.** [be correct size for] aller à. **-2.** [place]: **to ~ sthg into sthg** insérer qqch dans qqch. **-3.** [provide]: **to ~ sthg with sthg** équiper OR munir qqch de qqch. **-4.** [be suitable for] correspondre à. **-5.** [for clothes]: **to be fitted for** essayer.

◇ *vi* [be correct size, go] aller; [into container] entrer.

◆ **fit in** ◇ *vt sep* [accommodate] prendre. ◇ *vi* s'intégrer; **to ~ in with sthg** correspondre à qqch; **to ~ in with sb** s'accorder à qqn.

fitful ['fıtful] *adj* [sleep] agité(e); [wind, showers] intermittent(e).

fitment ['fıtmənt] *n* meuble *m* encastré.

fitness ['fıtnıs] *n* (*U*) **-1.** [health] forme *f*. **-2.** [suitability]: **~ (for)** aptitude *f* (pour).

fitted ['fıtəd] *adj* **-1.** [suited]: **~ for** OR **to** apte à; **to be ~ to do sthg** être apte à faire qqch. **-2.** [tailored - shirt, jacket] ajusté(e); **~ carpet** moquette *f*; **~ sheet** drap-housse *m*. **-3.** *Br* [built-in] encastré(e).

fitted kitchen *n Br* cuisine *f* intégrée.

fitter ['fıtəʳ] *n* [mechanic] monteur *m*.

fitting ['fıtıŋ] ◇ *adj fml* approprié(e). ◇ *n* **-1.** [part] appareil *m*. **-2.** [for clothing] essayage *m*.

◆ **fittings** *npl* installations *fpl*.

fitting room *n* cabine *f* d'essayage.

five [faıv] *num* cinq; *see also* **six**.

five-day week *n* semaine *f* de cinq jours.

fiver ['faıvəʳ] *n inf* **-1.** *Br* [amount] cinq livres *fpl*; [note] billet *m* de cinq livres. **-2.** *Am* [amount] cinq dollars *mpl*; [note] billet *m* de cinq dollars.

five-star *adj* [hotel] cinq étoiles; [treatment] exceptionnel(elle).

fix [fıks] ◇ *vt* **-1.** [gen] fixer; **to ~ sthg to sthg** fixer qqch à qqch. **-2.** [in memory] graver. **-3.** [repair] réparer. **-4.** *inf* [rig] truquer. **-5.** [food, drink] préparer. ◇ *n* **-1.** *inf* [difficult situation]: **to be in a ~** être dans le pétrin. **-2.** *drugs sl* piqûre *f*.

◆ **fix up** *vt sep* **-1.** [provide]: **to ~ sb up with sthg** obtenir qqch pour qqn. **-2.** [arrange] arranger.

fixation [fık'seıʃn] *n*: **~ (on** OR **about)** obsession *f* (de).

fixed [fıkst] *adj* **-1.** [attached] fixé(e). **-2.** [set, unchanging] fixe; [smile] figé(e).

fixed assets *npl* immobilisations *fpl*.

fixture ['fıkstʃəʳ] *n* **-1.** [furniture] installation *f.* -2. [permanent feature] tradition *f* bien établie. -3. SPORT rencontre *f* (sportive).

fizz [fɪz] ◇ *vi* [lemonade, champagne] pétiller; [fireworks] crépiter. ◇ *n* [sound] pétillement *m*.

fizzle ['fɪzl]
◆ **fizzle out** *vi* [fire] s'éteindre; [firework] se terminer; [interest, enthusiasm] se dissiper.

fizzy ['fɪzɪ] (*compar* -**ier**, *superl* -**iest**) *adj* pétillant(e).

fjord [fjɔːd] *n* fjord *m*.

FL *abbr of* **Florida**.

flab [flæb] *n* graisse *f*.

flabbergasted ['flæbəɡɑːstɪd] *adj* sidéré(e).

flabby ['flæbɪ] (*compar* -**ier**, *superl* -**iest**) *adj* mou (molle).

flaccid ['flæsɪd] *adj* flasque.

flag [flæɡ] (*pt & pp* -**ged**, *cont* -**ging**) ◇ *n* drapeau *m*. ◇ *vi* [person, enthusiasm, energy] faiblir; [conversation] traîner.
◆ **flag down** *vt sep* [taxi] héler; **to ~ sb down** faire signe à qqn de s'arrêter.

Flag Day *n* [in US] *le 14 juin, jour férié qui commémore la création du drapeau américain.*

flag of convenience *n* pavillon *m* de complaisance.

flagon ['flæɡən] *n* -1. [bottle] bonbonne *f*. -2. [jug] cruche *f*.

flagpole ['flæɡpəʊl] *n* mât *m*.

flagrant ['fleɪɡrənt] *adj* flagrant(e).

flagship ['flæɡʃɪp] *n* -1. [ship] vaisseau *m* amiral. -2. *fig* [product] produit *m* vedette; [company] fleuron *m*.

flagstone ['flæɡstəʊn] *n* dalle *f*.

flail [fleɪl] *vi* battre l'air.

flair [fleə] *n* -1. [talent] don; **to have a ~ for sthg** avoir un don pour qqch. -2. (*U*) [stylishness] style *m*.

flak [flæk] *n* (*U*) -1. [gunfire] tir *m* antiaérien. -2. *inf* [criticism] critiques *fpl* sévères.

flake [fleɪk] ◇ *n* [of paint, plaster] écaille *f*; [of snow] flocon *m*; [of skin] petit lambeau *m*. ◇ *vi* [paint, plaster] s'écailler; [skin] peler.
◆ **flake out** *vi inf* s'écrouler de fatigue.

flaky ['fleɪkɪ] (*compar* -**ier**, *superl* -**iest**) *adj* -1. [flaking - skin] qui pèle; [- paintwork] écaillé(e); [- texture] floconneux(euse). -2. *Am inf* [person] barjo.

flaky pastry *n* (*U*) pâte *f* feuilletée.

flambé ['flãbe] (*pt & pp* -**ed**, *cont* -**ing**) ◇ *adj* flambé(e). ◇ *vt* flamber.

flamboyant [flæm'bɔɪənt] -1. [showy, confident] extravagant(e). -2. [brightly coloured] flamboyant(e).

flame [fleɪm] ◇ *n* flamme *f*; **in ~s** en flammes; **to burst into ~s** s'enflammer; **old ~** ancien béguin *m*. ◇ *vi* -1. [be on fire] flamber. -2. [redden] s'empourprer.

flameproof ['fleɪmpruːf] *adj* [dish] allant au feu.

flame-retardant [-rɪ'tɑːdənt] *adj* qui ralentit la propagation des flammes.

flame-thrower [-,θrəʊə] *n* lance-flammes *m inv*.

flaming ['fleɪmɪŋ] *adj* -1. [fire-coloured] flamboyant(e). -2. *Br* [very angry] furibond(e). -3. *Br inf* [expressing annoyance] foutu(e), fichu(e).

flamingo [flə'mɪŋɡəʊ] (*pl* -**s** OR -**es**) *n* flamant *m* rose.

flammable ['flæməbl] *adj* inflammable.

flan [flæn] *n* tarte *f*.

Flanders ['flɑːndəz] *n* Flandre *f*, Flandres *fpl*.

flange [flændʒ] *n* bride *f*.

flank [flæŋk] ◇ *n* flanc *m*. ◇ *vt*: **to be ~ed by** être flanqué(e) de.

flannel ['flænl] *n* -1. [fabric] flanelle *f*. -2. *Br* [facecloth] gant *m* de toilette.
◆ **flannels** *npl* pantalon *m* de flanelle.

flannelette [flænə'let] *n* pilou *m*.

flap [flæp] (*pt & pp* -**ped**, *cont* -**ping**) ◇ *n* -1. [of envelope, pocket] rabat *m*; [of skin] lambeau *m*. -2. *inf* [panic]: **in a ~** paniqué(e). ◇ *vt & vi* battre.

flapjack ['flæpdʒæk] *n* -1. *Br* [biscuit] biscuit *m* à l'avoine. -2. *Am* [pancake] crêpe *f* épaisse.

flare [fleə] ◇ *n* [distress signal] fusée *f* éclairante. ◇ *vi* -1. [burn brightly]: **to ~ (up)** s'embraser. -2. [intensify]: **to ~ (up)** [war, revolution] s'intensifier soudainement; [person] s'emporter. -3. [widen - trousers, skirt] s'évaser; [- nostrils] se dilater.
◆ **flares** *npl Br* pantalon *m* à pattes d'éléphant.

flared [fleəd] *adj* [trousers] à pattes d'éléphant; [skirt] évasé(e).

flash [flæʃ] ◇ *adj* -1. PHOT au flash. -2. *inf* [expensive-looking] tape-à-l'œil (*inv*).
◇ *n* -1. [of light, colour] éclat *m*; **~ of lightning** éclair *m*. -2. PHOT flash *m*. -3. [sudden moment] éclair *m*; **in a ~** en un rien de temps; **quick as a ~** rapide comme l'éclair.
◇ *vt* -1. [shine] projeter; **to ~ one's headlights** faire un appel de phares. -2. [send out - signal, smile] envoyer; [- look] jeter. -3. [show] montrer.
◇ *vi* -1. [torch] briller. -2. [light - on and off] clignoter; [eyes] jeter des éclairs. -3. [rush]:

to ~ **by** OR **past** passer comme un éclair. **-4.** [thought]: to ~ **into one's mind** venir soudainement à l'esprit. **-5.** [appear] surgir.

flashback ['flæʃbæk] n flashback m, retour m en arrière.

flashbulb ['flæʃbʌlb] n ampoule f de flash.

flash card n carte portant un mot, une image etc utilisée comme aide à l'apprentissage.

flashcube ['flæʃkjuːb] n flash m en forme de cube.

flasher ['flæʃər] n **-1.** Br [light] clignotant m. **-2.** Br inf [man] exhibitionniste m.

flash flood n crue f subite.

flashgun ['flæʃgʌn] n flash m.

flashlight ['flæʃlaɪt] n [torch] lampe f électrique.

flash point n **-1.** [moment] moment m critique. **-2.** [place] point m chaud.

flashy ['flæʃɪ] (compar **-ier**, superl **-iest**) adj inf tape-à-l'œil (inv).

flask [flɑːsk] n **-1.** [thermos flask] thermos® m or f. **-2.** CHEM ballon m. **-3.** [hip flask] flasque f.

flat [flæt] (compar **-ter**, superl **-test**) ◇ adj **-1.** [gen] plat(e). **-2.** [tyre] crevé(e). **-3.** [refusal, denial] catégorique. **-4.** [business, trade] calme. **-5.** [dull - voice, tone] monotone; [- performance, writing] terne. **-6.** [MUS - person] qui chante faux; [- note] bémol. **-7.** [fare, price] fixe. **-8.** [beer, lemonade] éventé(e). **-9.** [battery] à plat.
◇ adv **-1.** [level] à plat. **-2.** [absolutely]: ~ **broke** complètement fauché(e). **-3.** [exactly]: **two hours** ~ deux heures pile. **-4.** MUS faux.
◇ n **-1.** Br [apartment] appartement m. **-2.** MUS bémol m.
◆ **flat out** adv [work] d'arrache-pied; [travel - subj: vehicle] le plus vite possible.

flat cap n Br casquette f.

flat-chested [-'tʃestɪd] adj plate comme une limande.

flatfish ['flætfɪʃ] (pl inv) n poisson m plat.

flat-footed [-'futɪd] adj aux pieds plats.

flatlet ['flætlɪt] n Br studio m.

flatly ['flætlɪ] adv **-1.** [absolutely] catégoriquement. **-2.** [dully - say] avec monotonie; [- perform] de façon terne.

flatmate ['flætmeɪt] n Br personne f avec laquelle on partage le même appartement.

flat racing n (U) courses fpl de plat.

flat rate n tarif m forfaitaire.

flatten ['flætn] vt **-1.** [make flat - steel, paper] aplatir; [- wrinkles, bumps] aplanir; to ~ **o.s. against sthg** s'aplatir contre qqch. **-2.** [destroy] raser. **-3.** inf [knock out] assommer.

◆ **flatten out** ◇ vi s'aplanir. ◇ vt sep aplanir.

flatter ['flætər] vt flatter; to ~ **o.s. (that)** se flatter (de + infin).

flatterer ['flætərər] n flatteur m, -euse f.

flattering ['flætərɪŋ] adj **-1.** [complimentary] flatteur(euse). **-2.** [clothes] seyant(e).

flattery ['flætərɪ] n flatterie f.

flatulence ['flætjuləns] n flatulence f.

flatware ['flætweər] n (U) Am couverts mpl.

flaunt [flɔːnt] vt faire étalage de.

flautist Br ['flɔːtɪst], **flutist** Am ['fluːtɪst] n flûtiste mf.

flavour Br, **flavor** Am ['fleɪvər] ◇ n **-1.** [of food] goût m; [of ice cream, yoghurt] parfum m. **-2.** fig [atmosphere] atmosphère f. ◇ vt parfumer.

flavouring Br, **flavoring** Am ['fleɪvərɪŋ] n (U) parfum m.

flaw [flɔː] n [in material, character] défaut m; [in plan, argument] faille f.

flawed [flɔːd] adj [material, character] qui présente des défauts; [plan, argument] qui présente des failles.

flawless ['flɔːlɪs] adj parfait(e).

flax [flæks] n lin m.

flay [fleɪ] vt [skin] écorcher.

flea [fliː] n puce f; to send sb away with a ~ **in his/her ear** envoyer promener qqn.

flea market n marché m aux puces.

fleck [flek] ◇ n moucheture f, petite tache f. ◇ vt: ~**ed with** moucheté(e) de.

fled [fled] pt & pp → flee.

fledg(e)ling ['fledʒlɪŋ] ◇ adj [industry] nouveau(elle); [doctor, democracy] jeune. ◇ n oisillon m.

flee [fliː] (pt & pp fled) vt & vi fuir.

fleece [fliːs] ◇ n toison f. ◇ vt inf escroquer.

fleet [fliːt] n **-1.** [of ships] flotte f. **-2.** [of cars, buses] parc m.

fleeting ['fliːtɪŋ] adj [moment] bref (brève); [look] fugitif(ive); [visit] éclair (inv).

Fleet Street n rue de Londres.

FLEET STREET:
Cette rue de la City est traditionnellement celle des journaux. Aujourd'hui, beaucoup de journaux ont établi leur siège dans d'autres quartiers, notamment les Docklands. Cependant, le terme 'Fleet Street' est encore employé pour désigner la presse et le monde du journalisme

---

Fleming ['flemɪŋ] n Flamand m, -e f.

Flemish ['flemɪʃ] ◇ adj flamand(e). ◇ n [language] flamand m. ◇ npl: **the ~** les Flamands mpl.

flesh [fleʃ] n chair f; **his/her ~ and blood** [family] les siens; **in the ~** en chair et en os.
◆ **flesh out** vt sep étoffer.

flesh wound n blessure f superficielle.

fleshy ['fleʃɪ] (compar -ier, superl -iest) adj [arms] charnu(e); [person] bien en chair; [cheeks] joufflu(e).

flew [fluː] pt → **fly**.

flex [fleks] ◇ n ELEC fil m. ◇ vt [bend] fléchir.

flexibility ['fleksə'bɪlətɪ] n flexibilité f.

flexible ['fleksəbl] adj flexible.

flexitime ['fleksɪtaɪm] n (U) horaire m à la carte OR flexible.

flick [flɪk] ◇ n **-1.** [of whip, towel] petit coup m. **-2.** [with finger] chiquenaude f. ◇ vt **-1.** [whip, towel] donner un petit coup de. **-2.** [with finger - remove] enlever d'une chiquenaude; [- throw] envoyer d'une chiquenaude. **-3.** [switch] appuyer sur.
◆ **flicks** npl inf: **the ~s** le ciné.
◆ **flick through** vt fus feuilleter.

flicker ['flɪkər] ◇ n **-1.** [of light, candle] vacillement m. **-2.** [of hope, interest] lueur f. ◇ vi **-1.** [candle, light] vaciller. **-2.** [shadow] trembler; [eyelids] ciller.

flick knife n Br couteau m à cran d'arrêt.

flier ['flaɪər] n **-1.** [pilot] aviateur m, -trice f. **-2.** [advertising leaflet] prospectus m.

flight [flaɪt] n **-1.** [gen] vol m; **~ of fancy** OR **of the imagination** envolée f de l'imagination. **-2.** [of steps, stairs] volée f. **-3.** [escape] fuite f.

flight attendant n steward m, hôtesse f de l'air.

flight crew n équipage m.

flight deck n **-1.** [of aircraft carrier] pont m d'envol. **-2.** [of plane] cabine f de pilotage.

flight path n trajectoire f.

flight recorder n enregistreur m de vol.

flighty ['flaɪtɪ] (compar -ier, superl -iest) adj frivole.

flimsy ['flɪmzɪ] (compar -ier, superl -iest) adj [dress, material] léger(ère); [building, bookcase] peu solide; [excuse] piètre.

flinch [flɪntʃ] vi tressaillir; **to ~ from sthg/ from doing sthg** reculer devant qqch/à l'idée de faire qqch.

fling [flɪŋ] (pt & pp **flung**) ◇ n [affair] aventure f, affaire f. ◇ vt lancer; **to ~ o.s. into an armchair/onto the ground** se jeter dans un fauteuil/par terre.

flint [flɪnt] n **-1.** [rock] silex m. **-2.** [in lighter] pierre f.

flip [flɪp] (pt & pp **-ped**, cont **-ping**) ◇ vt **-1.** [turn - pancake] faire sauter; [- record] tourner. **-2.** [switch] appuyer sur. **-3.** [flick] envoyer d'une chiquenaude; **to ~ a coin** jouer à pile ou face. ◇ vi inf [become angry] piquer une colère. ◇ n **-1.** [flick] chiquenaude f. **-2.** [somersault] saut m périlleux.
◆ **flip through** vt fus feuilleter.

flip-flop n [shoe] tong f.

flippant ['flɪpənt] adj désinvolte.

flippantly ['flɪpəntlɪ] adv avec désinvolture.

flipper ['flɪpər] n **-1.** [of animal] nageoire f. **-2.** [for swimmer, diver] palme f.

flipping ['flɪpɪŋ] Br inf ◇ adj fichu(e). ◇ adv sacrément.

flip side n [of record] face f B.

flirt [flɜːt] ◇ n flirt m. ◇ vi **-1.** [with person]: **to ~ (with sb)** flirter (avec qqn). **-2.** [with idea]: **to ~ with sthg** caresser qqch.

flirtation [flɜː'teɪʃn] n **-1.** [gen] flirt m. **-2.** [brief interest]: **to have a ~ with sthg** caresser qqch.

flirtatious [flɜː'teɪʃəs] adj flirteur(euse).

flit [flɪt] (pt & pp **-ted**, cont **-ting**) vi **-1.** [bird] voleter. **-2.** [expression, idea]: **to ~ across** traverser.

float [fləʊt] ◇ n **-1.** [for buoyancy] flotteur m. **-2.** [in procession] char m. **-3.** [money] petite caisse f. ◇ vt **-1.** [on water] faire flotter. **-2.** [idea, project] lancer. ◇ vi [on water] flotter; [through air] glisser.

floating ['fləʊtɪŋ] adj **-1.** [on water] flottant(e). **-2.** [transitory] instable.

floating voter n Br électeur indécis m, électrice indécise f.

flock [flɒk] ◇ n **-1.** [of birds] vol m; [of sheep] troupeau m. **-2.** fig [of people] foule f. ◇ vi: **to ~ to** aller en masse à.

floe [fləʊ] n banquise f.

flog [flɒg] (pt & pp **-ged**, cont **-ging**) vt **-1.** [whip] flageller. **-2.** Br inf [sell] refiler.

flood [flʌd] ◇ n **-1.** [of water] inondation f. **-2.** [great amount] déluge m, avalanche f. ◇ vt **-1.** [with water, light] inonder. **-2.** [overwhelm]: **to ~ sthg (with)** inonder qqch (de); **to ~ the market** inonder le marché. ◇ vi **-1.** [river] déborder. **-2.** [street, land] être inondé(e). **-3.** [arrive in great amounts]: **applications have ~ed in** on a été inondé de demandes; **to ~ back** revenir en foule.
◆ **floods** npl **-1.** [of water] inondations fpl. **-2.** fig [of tears] torrents mpl.

floodgates ['flʌdgeɪts] npl: **to open the ~** ouvrir les vannes.

flooding ['flʌdɪŋ] n (U) inondations fpl.

floodlight ['flʌdlaɪt] n projecteur m.

floodlit ['flʌdlɪt] adj [match, ground] éclairé(e) (avec des projecteurs); [building] illuminé(e).

flood tide n marée f haute.

floor [flɔːʳ] ◇ n -1. [of room] sol m; [of club, disco] piste f. -2. [of valley, sea, forest] fond m. -3. [storey] étage m. -4. [at meeting, debate] auditoire m. -5. ST EX corbeille f. ◇ vt -1. [knock down] terrasser. -2. [baffle] dérouter.

floorboard ['flɔːbɔːd] n plancher m.

floor cloth n Br serpillière f.

flooring ['flɔːrɪŋ] n planchéiage m.

floor lamp n Am lampadaire m.

floor show n spectacle m de cabaret.

floorwalker ['flɔːˌwɔːkəʳ] n surveillant m, -e f de magasin.

floozy ['fluːzɪ] (pl -ies) n dated & pej pouffiasse f.

flop [flɒp] (pt & pp -ped, cont -ping) inf ◇ n [failure] fiasco m. ◇ vi -1. [fail] être un fiasco. -2. [fall - subj: person] s'affaler.

floppy ['flɒpɪ] (compar -ier, superl -iest) adj [flower] flasque; [collar] lâche.

floppy (disk) n disquette f, disque m souple.

flora ['flɔːrə] n flore f; ~ and fauna la flore et la faune.

floral ['flɔːrəl] adj floral(e); [pattern, dress] à fleurs.

Florence ['flɒrəns] n Florence.

floret ['flɒrɪt] n [of cauliflower, broccoli] bouquet m.

florid ['flɒrɪd] adj -1. [red] rougeaud(e). -2. [extravagant] fleuri(e).

Florida ['flɒrɪdə] n Floride f; in ~ en Floride.

florist ['flɒrɪst] n fleuriste mf; ~'s (shop) magasin m de fleuriste.

floss [flɒs] ◇ n (U) -1. [silk] bourre f de soie. -2. [dental floss] fil m dentaire. ◇ vt: to ~ one's teeth se nettoyer les dents au fil dentaire.

flotation [fləʊ'teɪʃn] n COMM lancement m.

flotilla [flə'tɪlə] n flottille f.

flotsam ['flɒtsəm] n (U): ~ and jetsam débris mpl; fig épaves fpl.

flounce [flaʊns] ◇ n volant m. ◇ vi: to ~ out/off sortir/partir dans un mouvement d'humeur.

flounder ['flaʊndəʳ] (pl inv OR -s) ◇ n flet m. ◇ vi -1. [in water, mud, snow] patauger. -2. [in conversation] bredouiller.

flour ['flaʊəʳ] n farine f.

flourish ['flʌrɪʃ] ◇ vi [plant, flower] bien pousser; [children] être en pleine santé; [company, business] prospérer; [arts] s'épanouir. ◇ vt brandir. ◇ n grand geste m.

flourishing ['flʌrɪʃɪŋ] adj [plant, garden] florissant(e); [children] resplendissant(e), de santé; [company, arts] prospère.

flout [flaʊt] vt bafouer.

flow [fləʊ] ◇ n -1. [movement - of water, information] circulation f; [- of funds] mouvement m; [- of words] flot m. -2. [of tide] flux m. ◇ vi -1. [gen] couler. -2. [traffic, days, weeks] s'écouler. -3. [tide] monter. -4. [hair, clothes] flotter. -5. [result]: to ~ from découler de.

flow chart, flow diagram n organigramme m.

flower ['flaʊəʳ] ◇ n fleur f. ◇ comp [arrangement, pattern] floral(e). ◇ vi -1. [bloom] fleurir. -2. fig [flourish] s'épanouir.

flowerbed ['flaʊəbed] n parterre m.

flowered ['flaʊəd] adj à fleurs.

flowering ['flaʊərɪŋ] ◇ adj à fleurs. ◇ n épanouissement m.

flowerpot ['flaʊəpɒt] n pot m de fleurs.

flowery ['flaʊərɪ] (compar -ier, superl -iest) adj -1. [dress, material] à fleurs. -2. pej [style] fleuri(e).

flowing ['fləʊɪŋ] adj [water, writing] coulant(e); [hair, robes] flottant(e).

flown [fləʊn] pp → fly.

fl. oz. abbr of fluid ounce.

flu [fluː] n (U) grippe f; to have ~ avoir la grippe.

fluctuate ['flʌktʃʊeɪt] vi fluctuer.

fluctuation [ˌflʌktʃʊ'eɪʃn] n fluctuation f.

flue [fluː] n conduit m, tuyau m.

fluency ['fluːənsɪ] n aisance f; ~ in French aisance à s'exprimer en français.

fluent ['fluːənt] adj -1. [in foreign language]: to speak ~ French parler couramment le français; to be ~ (in French) parler couramment (le français). -2. [writing, style] coulant(e), aisé(e).

fluently ['fluːəntlɪ] adv -1. [speak - in foreign language] couramment. -2. [read, speak, write] avec aisance.

fluff [flʌf] ◇ n (U) -1. [down] duvet m. -2. [dust] moutons mpl. ◇ vt -1. [puff up] faire bouffer. -2. inf [do badly] rater.

fluffy ['flʌfɪ] (compar -ier, superl -iest) adj duveteux(euse); [toy] en peluche.

fluid ['fluːɪd] ◇ n fluide m; [in diet, for cleaning] liquide m. ◇ adj -1. [flowing] fluide. -2. [unfixed] changeant(e).

fluid ounce n = 0,03 litre.

fluke [fluːk] n inf [chance] coup m de bol.

flummox ['flʌməks] vt inf désarçonner.

flung [flʌŋ] pt & pp → **fling**.

flunk [flʌŋk] inf ◇ vt -1. [exam, test] rater. -2. [student] recaler. ◇ vi se faire recaler.

fluorescent [flɔː'resənt] adj fluorescent(e).

fluorescent light n lumière f fluorescente.

fluoridate ['flɔːrɪdeɪt] vt fluorurer.

fluoride ['flɔːraɪd] n fluorure m.

fluorine ['flɔːriːn] n fluor m.

flurry ['flʌrɪ] (pl -ies) n -1. [of rain, snow] rafale f. -2. fig [of objections] concert m; [of activity, excitement] débordement m.

flush [flʌʃ] ◇ adj -1. [level]: ~ **with** de niveau avec. -2. inf [rich] plein(e) aux as.
◇ n -1. [in lavatory] chasse f d'eau. -2. [blush] rougeur f. -3. [sudden feeling] accès m; **in the first** ~ **of** sthg literary dans la première ivresse de qqch.
◇ vt -1. [toilet]: **to** ~ **the toilet** tirer la chasse d'eau; **to** ~ **sthg down the toilet** faire partir qqch en tirant la chasse d'eau. -2. [force out of hiding]: **to** ~ **sb out** déloger qqn.
◇ vi [blush] rougir.

flushed [flʌʃt] adj -1. [red-faced] rouge. -2. [excited]: ~ **with** exalté(e) par.

fluster ['flʌstər] ◇ n trouble m. ◇ vt troubler.

flustered ['flʌstəd] adj troublé(e).

flute [fluːt] n MUS flûte f.

fluted ['fluːtɪd] adj cannelé(e).

flutist Am = flautist.

flutter ['flʌtər] ◇ n -1. [of wings] battement m. -2. [of heart] palpitation f. -3. inf [of excitement] émoi m. ◇ vt battre. ◇ vi -1. [bird, insect] voleter; [wings] battre. -2. [flag, dress] flotter. -3. [heart] palpiter.

flux [flʌks] n [change]: **to be in a state of** ~ être en proie à des changements permanents.

fly [flaɪ] (pt **flew**, pp **flown**, pl **flies**) ◇ n -1. [insect] mouche f; **a** ~ **in the ointment** fig un ennui, un hic. -2. [of trousers] braguette f.
◇ vt -1. [kite, plane] faire voler. -2. [passengers, supplies] transporter par avion. -3. [flag] faire flotter.
◇ vi -1. [bird, insect, plane] voler. -2. [pilot] faire voler un avion. -3. [passenger] voyager en avion. -4. [move fast, pass quickly] filer; **time flies** comme le temps passe. -5. [rumours, stories] se répandre comme une traînée de poudre. -6. [attack]: **to** ~ **at sb** sauter sur qqn. -7. [flag] flotter.

◆ **fly away** vi s'envoler.

◆ **fly in** ◇ vt sep envoyer par avion. ◇ vi [plane] arriver; [person] arriver par avion.

◆ **fly into** vt fus: **to** ~ **into a rage/temper** s'emporter.

◆ **fly out** ◇ vt sep envoyer par avion. ◇ vi [plane] partir; [person] partir en avion.

flyby ['flaɪ,baɪ] Am = flypast.

fly-fishing n pêche f à la mouche.

fly half n Br demi m d'ouverture.

flying ['flaɪɪŋ] ◇ adj volant(e). ◇ n aviation f; **to like** ~ aimer prendre l'avion.

flying colours npl: **to pass (sthg) with** ~ réussir (qqch) haut la main.

flying doctor n médecin m volant.

flying officer n Br lieutenant m de l'armée de l'air.

flying picket n piquet m de grève volant.

flying saucer n soucoupe f volante.

flying squad n Br force d'intervention rapide de la police.

flying start n: **to get off to a** ~ prendre un départ sur les chapeaux de roue.

flying visit n visite f éclair.

flyleaf ['flaɪliːf] (pl **-leaves**) n page f de garde.

flyover ['flaɪ,əʊvər] n Br autopont m.

flypast ['flaɪ,pɑːst] n Br défilé m aérien.

flysheet ['flaɪʃiːt] n auvent m.

fly spray n insecticide m.

flyweight ['flaɪweɪt] n poids m mouche.

flywheel ['flaɪwiːl] n volant m.

FM -1. (abbr of **frequency modulation**) FM f. **-2.** abbr of **field marshal**.

FMB (abbr of **Federal Maritime Board**) n conseil supérieur de la marine marchande américaine.

FMCS (abbr of **Federal Mediation and Conciliation Services**) n organisme américain de conciliation des conflits du travail.

FO (abbr of **Foreign Office**) n ministère britannique des affaires étrangères.

foal [fəʊl] n poulain m.

foam [fəʊm] ◇ n (U) -1. [bubbles] mousse f. -2. ~ (**rubber**) caoutchouc m mousse. ◇ vi [water, champagne] mousser.

foamy ['fəʊmɪ] (compar **-ier**, superl **-iest**) adj [with bubbles] mousseux(euse).

fob [fɒb] (pt & pp **-bed**, cont **-bing**)

◆ **fob off** vt sep repousser; **to** ~ **sthg off on sb** refiler qqch à qqn; **to** ~ **sb off with sthg** se débarrasser de qqn à l'aide de qqch.

FOB, f.o.b. (abbr of **free on board**) FOB.

fob watch n montre f de gousset.

foc (*abbr of* **free of charge**) Fco.

focal ['fəukl] *adj lit* & *fig* focal(e).

focal point *n* foyer *m*; *fig* point *m* central.

focus ['fəukəs] (*pl* **-cuses** OR **-ci** [-kaɪ]) ◇ *n* **-1.** PHOT mise *f* au point; **in ~** net; **out of ~** flou. **-2.** [centre - of rays] foyer *m*; [- of earthquake] centre *m*; **~ of attention** centre d'attention.
◇ *vt* [lens, camera] mettre au point; **to ~ sthg on** [lens, camera, eyes] ajuster qqch sur; [attention] concentrer qqch sur.
◇ *vi* **-1.** [with camera, lens] se fixer; [eyes] accommoder; **to ~ on sthg** [with camera, lens] se fixer sur qqch; [with eyes] fixer qqch. **-2.** [attention]: **to ~ on sthg** se concentrer sur qqch.

fodder ['fɒdə'] *n* (*U*) fourrage *m*.

foe [fəu] *n literary* ennemi *m*.

FOE *n* **-1.** (*abbr of* **Friends of the Earth**) AT *mpl*. **-2.** (*abbr of* **Fraternal Order of Eagles**) *organisation caritative américaine*.

foetal ['fiːtl] *adj* [position] fœtal(e); [death] du fœtus.

foetus ['fiːtəs] *n* fœtus *m*.

fog [fɒg] *n* (*U*) brouillard *m*.

fogbound ['fɒgbaund] *adj* bloqué(e) par le brouillard.

fogey ['fəugɪ] = **fogy**.

foggiest ['fɒgɪəst] *n inf*: **I haven't the ~** je n'en ai pas la moindre idée.

foggy ['fɒgɪ] (*compar* **-ier**, *superl* **-iest**) *adj* [misty] brumeux(euse).

foghorn ['fɒghɔːn] *n* sirène *f* de brume.

fog lamp *n* feu *m* de brouillard.

fogy ['fəugɪ] (*pl* **-ies**) *n inf*: **old ~** vieux machin *m*.

foible ['fɔɪbl] *n* marotte *f*.

foil [fɔɪl] ◇ *n* **-1.** (*U*) [metal sheet - of tin, silver] feuille *f*; [- CULIN] papier *m* d'aluminium. **-2.** [contrast]: **to be a ~ to** OR **for** servir de repoussoir *m* à. ◇ *vt* déjouer.

foist [fɔɪst] *vt*: **to ~ sthg on sb** imposer qqch à qqn.

fold [fəuld] ◇ *vt* **-1.** [bend, close up] plier; **to ~ one's arms** croiser les bras. **-2.** [wrap] envelopper. ◇ *vi* **-1.** [close up - table, chair] se plier; [- petals, leaves] se refermer. **-2.** *inf* [company, project] échouer; THEATRE quitter l'affiche. ◇ *n* **-1.** [in material, paper] pli *m*. **-2.** [for animals] parc *m*. **-3.** *fig* [spiritual home]: **the ~** le bercail.
◆ **fold up** ◇ *vt sep* plier. ◇ *vi* **-1.** [close up - table, map] se plier; [- petals, leaves] se refermer. **-2.** [company, project] échouer.

foldaway ['fəuldə,weɪ] *adj* pliant(e).

folder ['fəuldə'] *n* **-1.** [for papers - wallet] chemise *f*; [- binder] classeur *m*. **-2.** COMPUT classeur *m*.

folding ['fəuldɪŋ] *adj* [table, umbrella] pliant(e); [doors] en accordéon.

foliage ['fəulɪdʒ] *n* feuillage *m*.

folk [fəuk] ◇ *adj* [art, dancing] folklorique; [medicine] populaire. ◇ *n* **-1.** [people] gens *mpl*. **-2.** [music] musique *f* folk.
◆ **folks** *npl inf* **-1.** [relatives] famille *f*. **-2.** [everyone]: **hi there ~s!** bonjour tout le monde!

folklore ['fəuklɔːʳ] *n* folklore *m*.

folk music *n* musique *f* folk.

folk singer *n* chanteur *m*, -euse *f* folk.

folk song *n* chanson *f* folk.

folksy ['fəuksɪ] (*compar* **-ier**, *superl* **-iest**) *adj Am inf* sympa (*inv*), décontract (*inv*).

follicle ['fɒlɪkl] *n* follicule *m*.

follow ['fɒləu] ◇ *vt* suivre; **(to be) ~ed by sthg** (être) suivi de qqch. ◇ *vi* **-1.** [gen] suivre; **as ~s** comme suit. **-2.** [be logical] tenir debout; **it ~s that ...** il s'ensuit que ....
◆ **follow up** *vt sep* **-1.** [pursue - idea, suggestion] prendre en considération; [- advertisement] donner suite à. **-2.** [complete]: **to ~ sthg up with** faire suivre qqch de.

follower ['fɒləuə'] *n* [believer] disciple *mf*.

following ['fɒləuɪŋ] ◇ *adj* suivant(e). ◇ *n* groupe *m* d'admirateurs. ◇ *prep* après.

follow-up ◇ *adj* complémentaire. ◇ *n* suite *f*.

folly ['fɒlɪ] *n* (*U*) [foolishness] folie *f*.

foment [fəu'ment] *vt fml* fomenter.

fond [fɒnd] *adj* **-1.** [affectionate] affectueux(euse); **to be ~ of** aimer beaucoup. **-2.** *literary* [hope, wish] naïf (naïve).

fondle ['fɒndl] *vt* caresser.

fondly ['fɒndlɪ] *adv* **-1.** [affectionately - gaze, smile] affectueusement; [- remember] avec tendresse. **-2.** *literary* [believe, wish] naïvement.

fondness ['fɒndnɪs] *n* [for person] affection *f*; [for thing] penchant *m*.

fondue ['fɒndjuː] *n* fondue *f*.

font [fɒnt] *n* **-1.** [in church] fonts *mpl* baptismaux. **-2.** COMPUT & TYPO police *f* (de caractères).

food [fuːd] *n* nourriture *f*; **that's ~ for thought** cela donne à réfléchir.

food chain *n* chaîne *f* alimentaire.

food mixer *n* mixer *m*.

food poisoning [-'pɔɪznɪŋ] *n* intoxication *f* alimentaire.

food processor *n* robot *m* ménager.

food stamp n Am bon m alimentaire (accordé aux personnes sans ressources).

foodstuffs ['fu:dstʌfs] npl denrées fpl alimentaires.

fool [fu:l] ◇ n **-1.** [idiot] idiot m, -e f; **to make a ~ of sb** tourner qqn en ridicule; **to make a ~ of o.s.** se rendre ridicule; **to act** OR **play the ~** faire l'imbécile. **-2.** Br [dessert] ≃ mousse f. ◇ vt duper; **to ~ sb into doing sthg** amener qqn à faire qqch en le dupant. ◇ vi faire l'imbécile.
◆ **fool about, fool around** vi **-1.** [behave foolishly] faire l'imbécile. **-2.** [be unfaithful] être infidèle.

foolhardy ['fu:l,hɑ:dɪ] adj téméraire.

foolish ['fu:lɪʃ] adj idiot(e), stupide.

foolishly ['fu:lɪʃlɪ] adv stupidement, bêtement.

foolishness ['fu:lɪʃnɪs] n (U) bêtise f.

foolproof ['fu:lpru:f] adj infaillible.

foolscap ['fu:lzkæp] n (U) papier m ministre.

foot [fut] (pl sense 1 feet, pl sense 2 inv OR feet) ◇ n **-1.** [gen] pied m; [of animal] patte f; [of page, stairs] bas m; **to be on one's feet** être debout; **to get to one's feet** se mettre debout, se lever; **on ~** à pied; **to be back on one's feet** être remis (d'une maladie); **to have itchy feet** avoir la bougeotte; **to put one's ~ down** mettre le holà; **to put one's ~ in it** mettre les pieds dans le plat; **to put one's feet up** se reposer; **to be rushed off one's feet** ne pas avoir le temps de souffler; **to set ~ in** mettre le pied en; **to stand on one's own two feet** se débrouiller (par soi-même). **-2.** [unit of measurement] = 30,48cm, ≃ pied m.
◇ vt inf: **to ~ the bill** payer la note.

footage ['fudɪdʒ] n (U) séquences fpl.

foot-and-mouth disease n fièvre f aphteuse.

football ['futbɔ:l] n **-1.** [game - soccer] football m, foot m; [- American football] football américain. **-2.** [ball] ballon m de football OR foot.

football club n Br club m de football.

footballer ['futbɔ:lə'] n Br joueur m, -euse f de football, footballeur m, -euse f.

football field n Am terrain m de football américain.

football game n Am match m de football américain.

football ground n Br terrain m de football.

football match n Br match m de football.

football player = footballer.

football pools npl Br ≃ loto m sportif.

football supporter n supporter m (de football).

footbrake ['futbreɪk] n frein m (à pied).

footbridge ['futbrɪdʒ] n passerelle f.

foot fault n faute f de pied.

foothills ['futhɪlz] npl contreforts mpl.

foothold ['futhəuld] n prise f (de pied); **to get a ~** trouver une prise; fig prendre pied, s'imposer.

footing ['futɪŋ] n **-1.** [foothold] prise f; **to lose one's ~** trébucher. **-2.** fig [basis] position f; **on an equal ~ (with)** sur un pied d'égalité (avec).

footlights ['futlaɪts] npl rampe f.

footling ['fu:tlɪŋ] adj dated & pej futile.

footman ['futmən] (pl -men [-mən]) n valet m de pied.

footmark ['futmɑ:k] = footprint.

footnote ['futnəut] n note f en bas de page.

footpath ['futpɑ:θ] n sentier m.

footprint ['futprɪnt] n empreinte f (de pied), trace f (de pas).

footsore ['futsɔ:'] adj: **to be ~** avoir mal aux pieds.

footstep ['futstep] n **-1.** [sound] bruit m de pas. **-2.** [footprint] empreinte f (de pied); **to follow in sb's ~s** marcher sur OR suivre les traces de qqn.

footwear ['futweə'] n (U) chaussures fpl.

footwork ['futwɜ:k] n (U) SPORT jeu m de jambes.

for [fɔ:'] prep **-1.** [referring to intention, destination, purpose] pour; **this is ~ you** c'est pour vous; **the plane ~ Paris** l'avion à destination de Paris; **I'm going ~ the papers** je vais prendre OR acheter les journaux; **let's meet ~ a drink** retrouvons-nous pour prendre un verre; **we did it ~ a laugh** OR **~ fun** on l'a fait pour rire; **what's it ~?** ça sert à quoi? **-2.** [representing, on behalf of] pour; **the MP ~ Barnsley** le député de Barnsley; **let me do that ~ you** laissez-moi faire, je vais vous le faire. **-3.** [because of] pour, en raison de; **~ various reasons** pour plusieurs raisons; **the town is famous ~ its cathedral** la ville est célèbre pour sa cathédrale; **a prize ~ swimming** un prix de natation; **~ fear of being ridiculed** de OR par peur d'être ridiculisé. **-4.** [with regard to] pour; **to be ready ~ sthg** être prêt à OR pour qqch; **it's not ~ me to say** ce n'est pas à moi à le dire; **to be young ~ one's age** être jeune pour son âge; **to feel sorry ~ sb** plaindre qqn. **-5.** [indicating amount of time, space]: **there's no time ~ that now** on

n'a pas le temps de faire cela OR de s'occuper de cela maintenant; there's room ~ another person il y a de la place pour encore une personne. **-6.** [indicating period of time]: **she'll be away ~ a month** elle sera absente (pendant) un mois; **we talked ~ hours** on a parlé pendant des heures; **I've lived here ~ 3 years** j'habite ici depuis 3 ans, cela fait 3 ans que j'habite ici; **I can do it for you ~ tomorrow** je peux vous le faire pour demain. **-7.** [indicating distance] pendant, sur; ~ **50 kilometres** pendant OR sur 50 kilomètres; **I walked ~ miles** j'ai marché (pendant) des kilomètres. **-8.** [indicating particular occasion] pour; ~ **Christmas** pour Noël; **the meeting scheduled ~ the 30th** la réunion prévue pour le 30. **-9.** [indicating amount of money, price]: **they're 50p ~ ten** cela coûte 50p les dix; **I bought/sold it ~ £10** je l'ai acheté/vendu 10 livres. **-10.** [in favour of, in support of] pour; **to vote ~ sthg** voter pour qqch; **to be all ~ sthg** être tout à fait pour OR en faveur de qqch. **-11.** [in ratios] pour. **-12.** [indicating meaning]: **P ~ Peter** P comme Peter; **what's the Greek ~ "mother"** comment dit-on «mère» en grec?
◆ **for all** ◇ *prep* malgré. ◇ *conj* bien que (+ *subjunctive*); ~ **all I know** pour ce que j'en sais; ~ **all I care** pour ce que cela me fait.

FOR (*abbr of* **free on rail**) franco wagon.

forage ['fɒrɪdʒ] *vi*: **to ~ (for)** fouiller (pour trouver).

foray ['fɒreɪ] *n*: ~ **(into)** *lit* & *fig* incursion *f* (dans).

forbad [fə'bæd], **forbade** [fə'beɪd] *pt* → **forbid**.

forbearing [fɔː'beərɪŋ] *adj* tolérant(e).

forbid [fə'bɪd] (*pt* **-bade** OR **-bad**, *pp* **forbid** OR **-bidden**, *cont* **-bidding**) *vt* interdire, défendre; **to ~ sb to do sthg** interdire OR défendre à qqn de faire qqch; **God** OR **Heaven ~!** pourvu que non!

forbidden [fə'bɪdn] ◇ *pp* → **forbid**. ◇ *adj* interdit(e), défendu(e).

forbidding [fə'bɪdɪŋ] *adj* [severe, unfriendly] austère; [threatening] sinistre.

force [fɔːs] ◇ *n* **-1.** [gen] force *f*; ~ **of habit** force de l'habitude; **by ~** de force. **-2.** [group]: **sales ~** représentants *mpl* de commerce; **security ~s** forces *fpl* de sécurité; **in ~** en force. **-3.** [effect]: **to be in/to come into ~** être/entrer en vigueur.
◇ *vt* **-1.** [gen] forcer; **to ~ sb to do sthg** forcer qqn à faire qqch; **to ~ sthg open** forcer qqch (pour l'ouvrir); **to ~ one's way**

through se frayer un chemin à travers; **to ~ one's way into** entrer de force dans. **-2.** [press]: **to ~ sthg on sb** imposer qqch à qqn.
◆ **forces** *npl*: **the ~s** les forces *fpl* armées; **to join ~s** joindre ses efforts.
◆ **by force of** *prep* à force de.
◆ **force back** *vt sep* [crowd etc] repousser; [emotion, tears] refouler.
◆ **force down** *vt sep* **-1.** [food] se forcer à manger. **-2.** [aeroplane] forcer à atterrir.

forced [fɔːst] *adj* forcé(e).

forced landing *n* atterrissage *m* forcé.

force-feed *vt* nourrir de force.

forceful ['fɔːsfʊl] *adj* [person] énergique; [speech] vigoureux(euse).

forcefully ['fɔːsfʊlɪ] *adv* avec force.

forcemeat ['fɔːsmiːt] *n* farce *f*.

forceps ['fɔːseps] *npl* forceps *m*.

forcible ['fɔːsəbl] *adj* **-1.** [using physical force] par (la) force. **-2.** [powerful] fort(e).

forcibly ['fɔːsəblɪ] *adv* **-1.** [using physical force] de force. **-2.** [powerfully] avec vigueur.

ford [fɔːd] ◇ *n* gué *m*. ◇ *vt* traverser à gué.

fore [fɔːr] ◇ *adj* NAUT à l'avant. ◇ *n*: **to come to the ~** s'imposer.

forearm ['fɔːrɑːm] *n* avant-bras *m inv*.

forebears ['fɔːbeəz] *npl* aïeux *mpl*.

foreboding [fɔː'bəʊdɪŋ] *n* pressentiment *m*.

forecast ['fɔːkɑːst] (*pt* & *pp* **forecast** OR **-ed**) ◇ *n* prévision *f*; **(weather) ~** prévisions météorologiques. ◇ *vt* prévoir.

forecaster ['fɔːkɑːstər] *n* **-1.** [analyst] prévisionniste *mf*. **-2.** [of weather] présentateur *m*, **-trice** *f* de la météo.

foreclose [fɔː'kləʊz] ◇ *vt* saisir. ◇ *vi*: **to ~ on sb** saisir qqn.

foreclosure [fɔː'kləʊʒər] *n* saisie *f*.

forecourt ['fɔːkɔːt] *n* [of petrol station] devant *m*; [of building] avant-cour *f*.

forefathers ['fɔːˌfɑːðəz] = **forebears**.

forefinger ['fɔːˌfɪŋgər] *n* index *m*.

forefront ['fɔːfrʌnt] *n*: **in** OR **at the ~** au premier plan de.

forego [fɔː'gəʊ] = **forgo**.

foregoing [fɔː'gəʊɪŋ] ◇ *adj* précédent(e). ◇ *n fml*: **the ~** ce qui précède.

foregone conclusion ['fɔːgɒn-] *n*: **it's a ~** c'est couru.

foreground ['fɔːgraʊnd] *n* premier plan *m*; **in the ~** au premier plan.

forehand ['fɔːhænd] *n* TENNIS coup *m* droit.

forehead ['fɔːhed] *n* front *m*.

foreign ['fɒrən] *adj* **-1.** [gen] étranger(ère);

[correspondent] à l'étranger. **-2.** [policy, trade] extérieur(e).

foreign affairs *npl* affaires *fpl* étrangères.

foreign aid *n* aide *f* extérieure.

foreign body *n* corps *m* étranger.

foreign competition *n* concurrence *f* étrangère.

foreign currency *n* (*U*) devises *fpl* étrangères.

foreigner ['fɒrənə'] *n* étranger *m*, -ère *f*.

foreign exchange *n* change *m*; ~ **markets** marchés *mpl* des devises; ~ **rates** taux *mpl* de change.

foreign investment *n* (*U*) investissement *m* étranger.

foreign minister *n* ministre *m* des Affaires étrangères.

Foreign Office *n Br*: the ~ ≃ le ministère des Affaires étrangères.

Foreign Secretary *n Br* ≃ ministre *m* des Affaires étrangères.

foreleg ['fɔːleg] *n* [of horse] membre *m* antérieur; [of other animals] patte *f* de devant.

foreman ['fɔːmən] (*pl* **-men** [-mən]) *n* **-1.** [of workers] contremaître *m*. **-2.** JUR président *m* du jury.

foremost ['fɔːməʊst] ◇ *adj* principal(e). ◇ *adv*: **first and** ~ tout d'abord.

forename ['fɔːneɪm] *n* prénom *m*.

forensic [fə'rensɪk] *adj* [department, investigation] médico-légal(e).

forensic medicine, forensic science *n* médecine *f* légale.

forerunner ['fɔːˌrʌnə'] *n* précurseur *m*.

foresee [fɔː'siː] (*pt* **-saw** [-'sɔː], *pp* **-seen**) *vt* prévoir.

foreseeable [fɔː'siːəbl] *adj* prévisible; **for the** ~ **future** pour tous les jours/mois *etc* à venir; **in the** ~ **future** dans un futur proche.

foreseen [fɔː'siːn] *pp* → **foresee**.

foreshadow [fɔː'ʃædəʊ] *vt* présager.

foreshortened [fɔː'ʃɔːtnd] *adj* réduit(e).

foresight ['fɔːsaɪt] *n* (*U*) prévoyance *f*.

foreskin ['fɔːskɪn] *n* prépuce *m*.

forest ['fɒrɪst] *n* forêt *f*.

forestall [fɔː'stɔːl] *vt* [attempt, discussion] prévenir; [person] devancer.

forestry ['fɒrɪstrɪ] *n* sylviculture *f*.

Forestry Commission *n Br*: the ~ ≃ les Eaux *fpl* et Forêts.

foretaste ['fɔːteɪst] *n* avant-goût *m*.

foretell [fɔː'tel] (*pt & pp* **-told**) *vt* prédire.

forethought ['fɔːθɔːt] *n* prévoyance *f*.

foretold [fɔː'təʊld] *pt & pp* → **foretell**.

forever [fə'revə'] *adv* **-1.** [eternally] (pour) toujours. **-2.** *inf* [long time]: **don't take** ~ **about it!** et ne mets pas des heures!

forewarn [fɔː'wɔːn] *vt* avertir.

foreword ['fɔːwɜːd] *n* avant-propos *m inv*.

forfeit ['fɔːfɪt] ◇ *n* amende *f*; [in game] gage *m*. ◇ *vt* perdre.

forgave [fə'geɪv] *pt* → **forgive**.

forge [fɔːdʒ] ◇ *n* forge *f*. ◇ *vt* **-1.** INDUSTRY & *fig* forger. **-2.** [signature, money] contrefaire; [passport] falsifier.

◆ **forge ahead** *vi* prendre de l'avance.

forger ['fɔːdʒə'] *n* faussaire *mf*.

forgery ['fɔːdʒərɪ] (*pl* **-ies**) *n* **-1.** (*U*) [crime] contrefaçon *f*. **-2.** [forged article] faux *m*.

forget [fə'get] (*pt* **-got**, *pp* **-gotten**, *cont* **-getting**) ◇ *vt* oublier; **let's** ~ **the whole business** n'en parlons plus; **to** ~ **to do sthg** oublier de faire qqch; ~ **it!** laisse tomber!; **to** ~ **o.s.** perdre le contrôle de soi. ◇ *vi*: **to** ~ **(about sthg)** oublier (qqch).

forgetful [fə'getfʊl] *adj* distrait(e), étourdi(e).

forgetfulness [fə'getfʊlnɪs] *n* étourderie *f*.

forget-me-not *n* myosotis *m*.

forgive [fə'gɪv] (*pt* **-gave**, *pp* **-given**) *vt* pardonner; **to** ~ **sb for sthg/for doing sthg** pardonner qqch à qqn/à qqn d'avoir fait qqch.

forgiveness [fə'gɪvnɪs] *n* (*U*) pardon *m*.

forgiving [fə'gɪvɪŋ] *adj* indulgent(e).

forgo [fɔː'gəʊ] (*pt* **-went**, *pp* **-gone** [-'gɒn]) *vt* renoncer à.

forgot [fə'gɒt] *pt* → **forget**.

forgotten [fə'gɒtn] *pp* → **forget**.

fork [fɔːk] ◇ *n* **-1.** [for eating] fourchette *f*. **-2.** [for gardening] fourche *f*. **-3.** [in road] bifurcation *f*; [of river] embranchement *m*. ◇ *vi* bifurquer.

◆ **fork out** *inf* ◇ *vt fus* allonger, débourser; **to** ~ **out money on** OR **for** allonger OR débourser de l'argent pour. ◇ *vi*: **to** ~ **out (for)** casquer (pour).

forklift truck ['fɔːklɪft-] *n* chariot *m* élévateur.

forlorn [fə'lɔːn] *adj* **-1.** [person, face] malheureux(euse), triste. **-2.** [place, landscape] désolé(e). **-3.** [hope, attempt] désespéré(e).

form [fɔːm] ◇ *n* **-1.** [shape, fitness, type] forme *f*; **on** ~ *Br*, **in** ~ *Am* en forme; **off** ~ pas en forme; **in the** ~ **of** sous forme de; **to take the** ~ **of** prendre la forme de. **-2.** [questionnaire] formulaire *m*. **-3.** *Br* SCH classe *f*. **-4.** [usual behaviour]: **true to** ~ typiquement. ◇ *vt* former. ◇ *vi* se former.

formal ['fɔːml] *adj* **-1.** [person] formaliste; [language] soutenu(e). **-2.** [dinner party, announcement] officiel(ielle); [dress] de cérémonie.

formality [fɔː'mælətɪ] (*pl* **-ies**) *n* formalité *f.*

formalize, -ise ['fɔːməlaɪz] *vt* organiser de façon formelle.

formally ['fɔːməlɪ] *adv* **-1.** [correctly, seriously] de façon correcte. **-2.** [not casually]: **to be ~ dressed** être en tenue de cérémonie. **-3.** [officially] officiellement.

format ['fɔːmæt] (*pt* & *pp* **-ted**, *cont* **-ting**) ◇ *n* [gen & COMPUT] format *m.* ◇ *vt* COMPUT formater.

formation [fɔː'meɪʃn] *n* **-1.** [gen] formation *f.* **-2.** [of idea, plan] élaboration *f.*

formative ['fɔːmətɪv] *adj* formateur(trice).

former ['fɔːmər] ◇ *adj* **-1.** [previous] ancien(ienne); **~ husband** ex-mari *m;* **~ pupil** ancien élève *m,* ancienne élève *f.* **-2.** [first of two] premier(ière). ◇ *n:* **the ~** le premier (la première), celui-ci (celle-ci).

formerly ['fɔːməlɪ] *adv* autrefois.

form feed *n* changement *m* de page.

Formica® [fɔː'maɪkə] *n* Formica® *m.*

formidable ['fɔːmɪdəbl] *adj* impressionnant(e).

formless ['fɔːmlɪs] *adj* informe.

Formosa [fɔː'məʊsə] *n* Formose; **in ~** à Formose.

formula ['fɔːmjʊlə] (*pl* **-as** OR **-ae** [-liː]) *n* formule *f.*

formulate ['fɔːmjʊleɪt] *vt* formuler.

formulation [,fɔːmjʊ'leɪʃn] *n* formulation *f.*

fornicate ['fɔːnɪkeɪt] *vi* *fml* forniquer.

forsake [fə'seɪk] (*pt* forsook, *pp* forsaken) *vt* *literary* [person] abandonner; [habit] renoncer à.

forsaken [fə'seɪkn] *adj* abandonné(e).

forsook [fə'sʊk] *pt* → **forsake**.

forsythia [fɔː'saɪθɪə] *n* forsythia *m.*

fort [fɔːt] *n* fort *m;* **to hold the ~** [at office, shop] garder la boutique.

forte ['fɔːtɪ] *n* point *m* fort.

forth [fɔːθ] *adv* *literary* en avant; **from that day ~** dorénavant.

forthcoming [fɔːθ'kʌmɪŋ] *adj* **-1.** [imminent] à venir. **-2.** [available]: **no answer was ~** on n'a pas eu de réponse. **-3.** [helpful] communicatif(ive).

forthright ['fɔːθraɪt] *adj* franc (franche), direct(e).

forthwith [,fɔːθ'wɪθ] *adv* *fml* aussitôt.

fortieth ['fɔːtɪɪθ] *num* quarantième; *see also* **sixth**.

fortification [,fɔːtɪfɪ'keɪʃn] *n* fortification *f.*

fortified wine ['fɔːtɪfaɪd-] *n* vin *m* de liqueur.

fortify ['fɔːtɪfaɪ] (*pt* & *pp* **-ied**) *vt* **-1.** MIL fortifier. **-2.** *fig* [resolve etc] renforcer.

fortitude ['fɔːtɪtjuːd] *n* courage *m.*

fortnight ['fɔːtnaɪt] *n* quinze jours *mpl,* quinzaine *f.*

fortnightly ['fɔːt,naɪtlɪ] ◇ *adj* bimensuel(elle). ◇ *adv* tous les quinze jours.

fortress ['fɔːtrɪs] *n* forteresse *f.*

fortuitous [fɔː'tjuːɪtəs] *adj* fortuit(e).

fortunate ['fɔːtʃnət] *adj* heureux(euse); **to be ~** avoir de la chance.

fortunately ['fɔːtʃnətlɪ] *adv* heureusement.

fortune ['fɔːtʃuːn] *n* **-1.** [wealth] fortune *f.* **-2.** [luck] fortune *f,* chance *f.* **-3.** [future]: **to tell sb's ~** dire la bonne aventure à qqn. ◆ **fortunes** *npl* fortune *f.*

fortune-teller *n* diseuse *f* de bonne aventure.

forty ['fɔːtɪ] *num* quarante; *see also* **sixty**.

forum ['fɔːrəm] (*pl* **-s**) *n* forum *m,* tribune *f.*

forward ['fɔːwəd] ◇ *adj* **-1.** [movement] en avant. **-2.** [planning] à long terme. **-3.** [impudent] effronté(e). ◇ *adv* **-1.** [ahead] en avant; **to go** OR **move ~** avancer. **-2.** [in time]: **to bring a meeting ~** avancer la date d'une réunion; **to put a watch ~** avancer une montre. ◇ *n* SPORT avant *m.* ◇ *vt* **-1.** [letter] faire suivre; [goods] expédier. **-2.** [career] faire avancer.

forwarding address ['fɔːwədɪŋ-] *n* adresse *f* où faire suivre le courrier.

forward-looking [-'lʊkɪŋ] *adj* tourné(e) vers le futur.

forwardness ['fɔːwədnɪs] *n* [boldness] effronterie *f.*

forwards ['fɔːwədz] *adv* = **forward**.

forwent [fɔː'went] *pt* → **forgo**.

fossil ['fɒsl] *n* fossile *m.*

fossil fuel *n* combustible *m* fossile.

fossilized, -ised ['fɒsɪlaɪzd] *adj* fossilisé(e).

foster ['fɒstər] ◇ *adj* [family] d'accueil. ◇ *vt* **-1.** [child] accueillir. **-2.** *fig* [nurture] nourrir, entretenir.

foster child *n* enfant *m* placé en famille d'accueil.

foster parent *n* parent *m* nourricier.

fought [fɔːt] *pt* & *pp* → **fight**.

foul [faʊl] ◇ *adj* **-1.** [gen] infect(e); [water] croupi(e); **to fall ~ of sb** se mettre qqn à dos. **-2.** [language] ordurier(ière). ◇ *n* SPORT faute *f.* ◇ *vt* **-1.** [make dirty] souiller, salir.

-2. SPORT commettre une faute contre. **-3.** [mechanism, propeller] entraver.
♦ **foul up** vt sep inf gâcher.

foul-mouthed [-'maʊðd] adj au langage grossier.

foul play n (U) **-1.** SPORT antijeu m. **-2.** [crime] acte m malveillant.

found [faʊnd] ◇ pt & pp → **find**. ◇ vt **-1.** [hospital, town] fonder. **-2.** [base]: **to ~ sthg on** fonder OR baser sur.

foundation [faʊn'deɪʃn] n **-1.** [creation, organization] fondation f. **-2.** [basis] fondement m, base f. **-3.** ~ **(cream)** fond m de teint.
♦ **foundations** npl CONSTR fondations fpl.

foundation stone n première pierre f.

founder ['faʊndər] ◇ n fondateur m, -trice f. ◇ vi **-1.** [ship] sombrer. **-2.** fig [plan, hopes] s'effondrer, s'écrouler.

founder member n membre m fondateur.

founding ['faʊndɪŋ] n [of hospital etc] fondation f, création f.

founding father n père m fondateur.

foundry ['faʊndrɪ] (pl -ies) n fonderie f.

fount [faʊnt] n [origin] source f.

fountain ['faʊntɪn] n fontaine f.

fountain pen n stylo m à encre.

four [fɔːr] num quatre; **on all ~s** à quatre pattes; see also **six**.

four-leaved clover [-liːvd-] n trèfle m à quatre feuilles.

four-letter word n mot m grossier.

four-poster (bed) n lit m à baldaquin.

foursome ['fɔːsəm] n groupe m de quatre.

four-star adj [hotel] quatre étoiles.

fourteen [ˌfɔː'tiːn] num quatorze; see also **six**.

fourteenth [ˌfɔː'tiːnθ] num quatorzième; see also **sixth**.

fourth [fɔːθ] num quatrième; see also **sixth**.

Fourth of July n: **the ~** Fête de l'Indépendance américaine.

four-way stop n Am carrefour m à quatre stops.

four-wheel drive n: **with ~** à quatre roues motrices.

fowl [faʊl] (pl inv OR -s) n volaille f.

fox [fɒks] ◇ n renard m. ◇ vt laisser perplexe.

foxglove ['fɒksglʌv] n digitale f.

foxhole ['fɒkshəʊl] n terrier m de renard.

foxhound ['fɒkshaʊnd] n fox-hound m.

foxhunt ['fɒkshʌnt] n chasse f au renard.

foxhunting ['fɒks,hʌntɪŋ] n (U) chasse f au renard.

foxy ['fɒksɪ] adj inf [sexy] sexy (inv).

foyer ['fɔɪeɪ] n **-1.** [of hotel, theatre] foyer m. **-2.** Am [of house] hall m d'entrée.

FP n **-1.** abbr of **former pupil**. **-2.** abbr of **fireplug**.

FPA (abbr of **Family Planning Association**) n association britannique pour le planning familial.

fr. (abbr of **franc**) F.

Fr. (abbr of **father**) P.

fracas ['frækɑː, Am 'freɪkəs] (Br pl inv, Am pl -cases) n bagarre f.

fraction ['frækʃn] n fraction f; **a ~ too big** légèrement OR un petit peu trop grand.

fractionally ['frækʃnəlɪ] adv un tout petit peu.

fractious ['frækʃəs] adj grincheux(euse).

fracture ['fræktʃər] ◇ n fracture f. ◇ vt fracturer.

fragile ['frædʒaɪl] adj fragile.

fragility [frə'dʒɪlətɪ] n fragilité f.

fragment [n 'frægmənt, vb fræg'ment] ◇ n fragment m. ◇ vi se fragmenter.

fragmentary ['frægməntrɪ] adj fragmentaire.

fragmented [fræg'mentɪd] adj fragmenté(e).

fragrance ['freɪgrəns] n parfum m.

fragrant ['freɪgrənt] adj parfumé(e).

frail [freɪl] adj fragile.

frailty ['freɪltɪ] (pl -ies) n **-1.** [gen] fragilité f. **-2.** [moral weakness] faiblesse f.

frame [freɪm] ◇ n **-1.** [gen] cadre m; [of glasses] monture f; [of door, window] encadrement m; [of boat] carcasse m. **-2.** [physique] charpente f. ◇ vt **-1.** [gen] encadrer. **-2.** [express] formuler. **-3.** inf [set up] monter un coup contre.

frame of mind n état m d'esprit.

framework ['freɪmwɜːk] n **-1.** [structure] armature f, carcasse f. **-2.** fig [basis] structure f, cadre m.

France [frɑːns] n France f; **in ~** en France.

franchise ['fræntʃaɪz] n **-1.** POL droit m de vote. **-2.** COMM franchise f.

franchisee [ˌfræntʃaɪ'ziː] n franchisé m.

franchisor n franchiseur m.

frank [fræŋk] ◇ adj franc (franche). ◇ vt affranchir.

Frankfurt ['fræŋkfət] n: **~ (am Main)** Francfort(-sur-le-Main).

frankfurter ['fræŋkfɜːtər] n saucisse f de Francfort.

frankincense ['fræŋkɪnsens] n encens m.

franking machine ['fræŋkɪŋ-] n machine f à affranchir.

frankly ['fræŋklɪ] *adv* franchement.

frankness ['fræŋknɪs] *n* franchise *f*.

frantic ['fræntɪk] *adj* frénétique; **to be ~ (with worry)** être fou (folle) d'inquiétude.

frantically ['fræntɪklɪ] *adv* frénétiquement, avec frénésie.

fraternal [frə'tɜːnl] *adj* fraternel(elle).

fraternity [frə'tɜːnətɪ] (*pl* **-ies**) *n* **-1.** [community] confrérie *f*. **-2.** (*U*) [friendship] fraternité *f*. **-3.** *Am* [of students] club *m* d'étudiants.

fraternize, -ise ['frætənaɪz] *vi* fraterniser.

fraud [frɔːd] *n* **-1.** (*U*) [crime] fraude *f*. **-2.** *pej* [impostor] imposteur *m*.

fraudulent ['frɔːdjʊlənt] *adj* frauduleux(euse).

fraught [frɔːt] *adj* **-1.** [full]: **~ with** plein(e) de. **-2.** *Br* [person] tendu(e); [time, situation] difficile.

fray [freɪ] ◇ *vt fig*: **my nerves were ~ed** j'étais extrêment tendu(e), j'étais à bout de nerfs. ◇ *vi* [material, sleeves] s'user; **tempers ~ed** *fig* l'atmosphère était tendue OR électrique. ◇ *n literary* bagarre *f*.

frayed [freɪd] *adj* [jeans, collar] élimé(e).

frazzled ['fræzld] *adj inf* éreinté(e).

FRB (*abbr of* **Federal Reserve Board**) *n organe de contrôle de la Banque centrale américaine.*

FRCP (*abbr of* **Fellow of the Royal College of Physicians**) *membre de l'académie de médecine britannique.*

FRCS (*abbr of* **Fellow of the Royal College of Surgeons**) *membre de l'académie de chirurgie britannique.*

freak [friːk] ◇ *adj* bizarre, insolite. ◇ *n* **-1.** [strange creature] monstre *m*, phénomène *m*. **-2.** [unusual event] accident *m* bizarre. **-3.** *inf* [fanatic] fana *mf*.

◆ **freak out** *inf* ◇ *vi* [get angry] exploser (de colère); [panic] paniquer. ◇ *vt sep*: **to ~ sb out** faire sauter qqn au plafond.

freakish ['friːkɪʃ] *adj* bizarre, insolite.

freckle ['frekl] *n* tache *f* de rousseur.

free [friː] (*compar* **freer**, *superl* **freest**, *pt* & *pp* **freed**) ◇ *adj* **-1.** [gen] libre; **to be ~ to do sthg** être libre de faire qqch; **feel ~!** je t'en prie!; **to set ~** libérer; **~ from** OR **of worry** sans souci. **-2.** [not paid for] gratuit(e); **~ of charge** gratuitement. **-3.** [generous]: **to be ~ with money** dépenser sans compter.

◇ *adv* **-1.** [without payment] gratuitement; **for ~** gratuitement. **-2.** [run, live] librement. ◇ *vt* **-1.** [gen] libérer. **-2.** [trapped person, object] dégager.

-free [friː] *suffix* sans.

freebie ['friːbɪ] *n inf* faveur *f*.

freedom ['friːdəm] *n* **-1.** [gen] liberté *f*; **~ of speech** liberté d'expresssion. **-2.** [exception]: **~ (from)** exemption *f* (de).

freedom fighter *n* partisan *m*, -e *f*.

free enterprise *n* (*U*) libre entreprise *f*.

free-fall *n* (*U*) chute *f* libre.

freefone ['friːfəʊn] *n Br* (*U*) ≃ numéro *m* vert.

free-for-all *n* mêlée *f* générale.

free gift *n* prime *f*.

freehand [,friː'hænd] *adj & adv* à main levée.

freehold ['friːhəʊld] ◇ *adv* en propriété inaliénable. ◇ *n* propriété *f* foncière inaliénable.

freeholder ['friːhəʊldər] *n* propriétaire foncier *m*, propriétaire foncière *f*.

free house *n* pub *m* en gérance libre.

free kick *n* coup *m* franc.

freelance ['friːlɑːns] ◇ *adj* indépendant(e), free-lance (*inv*). ◇ *adv* en free-lance. ◇ *n* indépendant *m*, -e *f*, free-lance *mf*. ◇ *vi* travailler en indépendant OR en free-lance.

freeloader ['friːləʊdər] *n inf* parasite *m*.

freely ['friːlɪ] *adv* **-1.** [gen] librement. **-2.** [generously] sans compter.

freeman ['friːmən] (*pl* **-men**) *n* citoyen *m*, -enne *f* d'honneur.

free-market economy *n* économie *f* de marché libre.

Freemason ['friː,meɪsn] *n* franc-maçon *m*.

Freemasonry ['friː,meɪsnrɪ] *n* franc-maçonnerie *f*.

freemen ['friːmən] *pl* → **freeman**.

freephone ['friːfəʊn] = **freefone**.

freepost ['friːpəʊst] *n* port *m* payé.

free-range *adj* de ferme.

free sample *n* échantillon *m* gratuit.

freesia ['friːzjə] *n* freesia *m*.

free speech *n* liberté *f* d'expression.

freestanding [,friː'stændɪŋ] *adj* [furniture] non-encastré(e).

freestyle ['friːstaɪl] *n* SWIMMING nage *f* libre.

freethinker [friː'θɪŋkər] *n* libre-penseur *m*, -euse *f*.

Freetown ['friːtaʊn] *n* Freetown.

free trade *n* (*U*) libre-échange *m*.

freeway ['friːweɪ] *n Am* autoroute *f*.

freewheel [,friː'wiːl] *vi* [on bicycle] rouler en roue libre; [in car] rouler au point mort.

freewheeling [,friː'wiːlɪŋ] *adj inf* sans contrainte.

free will n (U) libre arbitre m; **to do sthg of one's own ~** faire qqch de son propre gré.

free world n: **the ~** les pays mpl non-communistes.

freeze [friːz] (pt **froze**, pp **frozen**) ◇ vt **-1.** [gen] geler; [food] congeler. **-2.** [wages, prices] bloquer. ◇ vi **-1.** [gen] geler. **-2.** [stop moving] s'arrêter. ◇ n **-1.** [cold weather] gel m. **-2.** [of wages, prices] blocage m.
◆ **freeze over** vi geler.
◆ **freeze up** vi geler.

freeze-dried [-'draɪd] adj lyophilisé(e).

freeze frame n [on video] arrêt m sur image.

freezer ['friːzə'] n congélateur m.

freezing ['friːzɪŋ] ◇ adj glacé(e); **I'm ~** je gèle. ◇ n = **freezing point**.

freezing point n point m de congélation.

freight [freɪt] n [goods] fret m.

freight train n train m de marchandises.

French [frentʃ] ◇ adj français(e). ◇ n [language] français m. ◇ npl: **the ~** les Français mpl.

French bean n haricot m vert.

French bread n (U) baguette f.

French Canadian ◇ adj canadien français (canadienne française). ◇ n Canadien français m, Canadienne française f.

French chalk n (U) craie f de tailleur.

French doors = **French windows**.

French dressing n [in UK] vinaigrette f; [in US] sauce-salade à base de mayonnaise et de ketchup.

French fries npl frites fpl.

Frenchman ['frentʃmən] (pl **-men** [-mən]) n Français m.

French polish n (U) vernis m à l'alcool.

French Riviera n: **the ~** la Côte d'Azur.

French stick n Br baguette f.

French toast n pain m perdu.

French windows npl porte-fenêtre f.

Frenchwoman ['frentʃ,wumən] (pl **-women** [-,wɪmɪn]) n Française f.

frenetic [frə'netɪk] adj frénétique.

frenzied ['frenzɪd] adj [haste, activity] frénétique; [attack] déchaîné(e); [mob] en délire.

frenzy ['frenzɪ] (pl **-ies**) n frénésie f.

frequency ['friːkwənsɪ] (pl **-ies**) n fréquence f.

frequency modulation n modulation f de fréquence.

frequent [adj 'friːkwənt, vb frɪ'kwent] ◇ adj fréquent(e). ◇ vt fréquenter.

frequently ['friːkwəntlɪ] adv fréquemment.

fresco ['freskəʊ] (pl **-es** OR **-s**) n fresque f.

fresh [freʃ] ◇ adj **-1.** [gen] frais (fraîche); **~ from** [the oven] qui sort de; [university] frais émoulu (fraîche émoulue) de. **-2.** [not salty] doux (douce). **-3.** [new - drink, piece of paper] autre; [- look, approach] nouvel(elle); **to make a ~ start** repartir à zéro. **-4.** inf dated [cheeky] familier(ière); **to get ~ with sb** se montrer osé avec qqn.
◇ adv: **~-ground/made** qui vient juste d'être moulu/fait; **to be ~ out of sthg** inf ne plus avoir de qqch.

freshen ['freʃn] ◇ vt rafraîchir. ◇ vi [wind] devenir plus fort.
◆ **freshen up** ◇ vt sep **-1.** [wash]: **to ~ o.s. up** faire un brin de toilette. **-2.** [smarten up] rafraîchir. ◇ vi faire un brin de toilette.

fresher ['freʃə'] n Br inf bleu m, -e f.

freshly ['freʃlɪ] adv [squeezed, ironed] fraîchement.

freshman ['freʃmən] (pl **-men** [-mən]) n étudiant m, -e f de première année.

freshness ['freʃnɪs] n (U) **-1.** [gen] fraîcheur f. **-2.** [originality] nouveauté f.

freshwater ['freʃ,wɔːtə'] adj d'eau douce.

fret [fret] (pt & pp **-ted**, cont **-ting**) vi [worry] s'inquiéter.

fretful ['fretful] adj [baby] grognon(onne); [night, sleep] agité(e).

fretsaw ['fretsɔː] n scie f à découper.

Freudian slip ['frɔɪdɪən-] n lapsus m.

FRG (abbr of **Federal Republic of Germany**) n RFA f.

Fri. (abbr of **Friday**) ven.

friar ['fraɪə'] n frère m.

friction ['frɪkʃn] n (U) friction f.

Friday ['fraɪdɪ] n vendredi m; see also **Saturday**.

fridge [frɪdʒ] n frigo m.

fridge-freezer n Br réfrigérateur-congélateur m.

fried [fraɪd] adj frit(e); **~ egg** œuf m au plat.

friend [frend] n ami m, -e f; **to be ~s** être amis; **to be ~s with sb** être ami avec qqn; **to make ~s (with sb)** se lier d'amitié (avec qqn).

friendless ['frendlɪs] adj sans amis.

friendly ['frendlɪ] (compar **-ier**, superl **-iest**, pl **-ies**) ◇ adj [person, manner, match] amical(e); [nation] ami(e); [argument] sans conséquence; **to be ~ with sb** être ami avec qqn. ◇ n match m amical.

friendly society n Br mutuelle f.

friendship ['frendʃɪp] n amitié f.

fries [fraɪz] = **French fries**.

Friesian (cow) ['friːzjən-] *n* (vache *f*) frisonne *f*.

frieze [friːz] *n* frise *f*.

frigate ['frɪgət] *n* frégate *f*.

fright [fraɪt] *n* peur *f*; **to give sb a ~** faire peur à qqn; **to take ~** prendre peur.

frighten ['fraɪtn] *vt* faire peur à, effrayer; **to ~ sb into doing sthg** forcer qqn à faire qqch sous la menace.

◆ **frighten away** *vt sep* chasser en faisant peur à.

◆ **frighten off** *vt sep* chasser en faisant peur à.

frightened ['fraɪtnd] *adj* apeuré(e); **to be ~ of sthg/of doing sthg** avoir peur de qqch/ de faire qqch.

frightening ['fraɪtnɪŋ] *adj* effrayant(e).

frightful ['fraɪtful] *adj dated* effroyable.

frigid ['frɪdʒɪd] *adj* [sexually] frigide.

frill [frɪl] *n* **-1.** [decoration] volant *m*. **-2.** *inf* [extra] supplément *m*.

frilly ['frɪlɪ] (*compar* **-ier**, *superl* **-iest**) *adj* à fanfreluches.

fringe ['frɪndʒ] ◇ *n* **-1.** [gen] frange *f*. **-2.** [edge - of village] bordure *f*; [- of wood, forest] lisière *f*. ◇ *vt* [edge] border.

fringe benefit *n* avantage *m* extrasalarial.

fringe group *n* groupe *m* marginal.

fringe theatre *n Br* théâtre *m* d'avant-garde.

Frisbee® ['frɪzbɪ] *n* Frisbee *m inv*.

Frisian Islands ['frɪzjən-] *npl*: **the ~** l'archipel *m* frison.

frisk [frɪsk] ◇ *vt* fouiller. ◇ *vi* gambader.

frisky ['frɪskɪ] (*compar* **-ier**, *superl* **-iest**) *adj inf* vif (vive).

fritter ['frɪtər] *n* beignet *m*.

◆ **fritter away** *vt sep* gaspiller; **to ~ money/time on sthg** gaspiller son argent/son temps en qqch.

frivolity [frɪ'vɒlətɪ] (*pl* **-ies**) *n* frivolité *f*.

frivolous ['frɪvələs] *adj* frivole.

frizzy ['frɪzɪ] (*compar* **-ier**, *superl* **-iest**) *adj* crépu(e).

fro [frəʊ] *adv*: **to and ~** de-ci de-là.

frock [frɒk] *n dated* robe *f*.

frog [frɒg] *n* [animal] grenouille *f*; **to have a ~ in one's throat** avoir un chat dans la gorge.

frogman ['frɒgmən] (*pl* **-men**) *n* homme-grenouille *m*.

frogmarch ['frɒgmɑːtʃ] *vt* emmener quelqu'un de force en lui tenant les bras dans le dos.

frogmen ['frɒgmən] *pl* → **frogman**.

frogspawn ['frɒgspɔːn] *n* (U) œufs *mpl* de grenouille.

frolic ['frɒlɪk] (*pt* & *pp* **-ked**, *cont* **-king**) ◇ *n* ébats *mpl*. ◇ *vi* folâtrer.

from [weak form frəm, strong form frɒm] *prep* **-1.** [indicating source, origin, removal] **de**; **where are you ~?** d'où venez-vous?, d'où êtes-vous?; **I got a letter ~ her today** j'ai reçu une lettre d'elle aujourd'hui; **a flight ~ Paris** un vol en provenance de Paris; **to translate ~ Spanish into English** traduire d'espagnol en anglais; **to drink ~ a glass** boire dans un verre; **he's not back ~ work yet** il n'est pas encore rentré de son travail; **he took a notebook ~ his pocket** il a sorti un carnet de sa poche; **to take sthg (away) ~ sb** prendre qqch à qqn. **-2.** [indicating a deduction] **de**; **to deduct sthg ~ sthg** retrancher qqch de qqch. **-3.** [indicating escape, separation] **de**; **he ran away ~ home** il a fait une fugue, il s'est sauvé de chez lui. **-4.** [indicating position] **de**; **seen ~ above/ below** vu d'en haut/d'en bas. **-5.** [indicating distance] **de**; **it's 60 km ~ here** c'est à 60 km d'ici; **how far is it ~ Paris to Lyons?** combien y a-t-il de Paris à Lyon? **-6.** [indicating material object is made out of] **en**; **it's made ~ wood/plastic** c'est en bois/ plastique. **-7.** [starting at a particular time] **de**; **~ 2 pm to** OR **till 6 pm** de 14 h à 18 h; **~ birth** de naissance; **~ the moment I saw him** dès que OR dès l'instant où je l'ai vu. **-8.** [indicating difference] **de**; **to be different ~ sb/sthg** être différent de qqn/qqch. **-9.** [indicating change] **...** **to ~ ... de ... à**; **the price went up ~ £100 to £150** le prix est passé OR monté de 100 livres à 150 livres. **-10.** [because of, as a result of] **de**; **to suffer ~ cold/hunger** souffrir du froid/de la faim. **-11.** [on the evidence of] **d'après, à**; **to speak ~ personal experience** parler par expérience OR d'après son expérience personnelle; **~ what you're saying ...** d'après ce que vous dites .... **-12.** [indicating lowest amount] **depuis, à partir de**; **prices start ~ £50** le premier prix est de 50 livres.

frond [frɒnd] *n* fronde *f*.

front [frʌnt] ◇ *n* **-1.** [most forward part - gen] avant *m*; [- of dress, envelope, house] devant *m*; [- of class] premier rang *m*. **-2.** METEOR & MIL front *m*. **-3.** [issue, area] plan *m*; **on the domestic/employment ~** sur le plan intérieur/du travail. **-4. (sea) ~** front *m* de mer. **-5.** [outward appearance - of person] contenance *f*; *pej* [- of business] façade *f*. ◇ *adj* [tooth, garden] de devant; [row, page] premier(ière); **~ cover** couverture *f*.

◇ *vt* **-1.** [be opposite] être en face de. **-2.** [TV programme] présenter. ◇ *vi*: **to ~ onto sthg** donner sur qqch.

◆ **in front** *adv* **-1.** [further forward - walk, push] devant; [- people] à l'avant. **-2.** [winning]: **to be in ~** mener.

◆ **in front of** *prep* devant.

frontage ['frʌntɪdʒ] *n* [of house] façade *f*; [of shop] devanture *f*.

frontal ['frʌntl] *adj* **-1.** [attack] de front. **-2.** [view] de face.

frontbench ['frʌntbentʃ] *n* à la chambre des Communes, bancs occupés respectivement par les ministres du gouvernement en exercice et ceux du gouvernement fantôme.

front desk *n* réception *f*.

front door *n* porte *f* d'entrée.

frontier ['frʌn,tɪər, *Am* frʌn'tɪr] *n* [border] frontière *f*; *fig* limite *f*.

frontispiece ['frʌntɪspiːs] *n* frontispice *m*.

front line *n*: **the ~** le front.

front man *n* **-1.** [of company, organization] porte-parole *m*. **-2.** TV présentateur *m*.

front-page *adj* [article] de première page.

front room *n* salon *m*.

front-runner *n* favori *m*, -ite *f*.

front-wheel drive *n* traction *f* avant.

frost [frɒst] ◇ *n* gel *m*. ◇ *vi*: **to ~ over** OR **up** geler.

frostbite ['frɒstbaɪt] *n* (U) gelure *f*.

frostbitten ['frɒst,bɪtn] *adj* [toe, finger] gelé(e).

frosted ['frɒstɪd] *adj* **-1.** [glass] dépoli(e). **-2.** *Am* CULIN glacé(e).

frosting ['frɒstɪŋ] *n Am* (U) glaçage *m*.

frosty ['frɒstɪ] (*compar* **-ier**, *superl* **-iest**) *adj* **-1.** [weather, welcome] glacial(e). **-2.** [field, window] gelé(e).

froth [frɒθ] ◇ *n* [on beer] mousse *f*; [on sea] écume *f*. ◇ *vi* [beer] mousser; [sea] écumer.

frothy ['frɒθɪ] (*compar* **-ier**, *superl* **-iest**) *adj* [beer] mousseux(euse); [sea] écumeux(euse).

frown [fraun] ◇ *n* froncement *m* de sourcils. ◇ *vi* froncer les sourcils.

◆ **frown (up)on** *vt fus* désapprouver.

froze [frəuz] *pt* → **freeze**.

frozen [frəuzn] ◇ *pp* → **freeze**. ◇ *adj* gelé(e); [food] congelé(e); **~ with fear** *fig* mort(e) de peur.

FRS *n* **-1.** (*abbr of* **Fellow of the Royal Society**) membre de l'académie des sciences britannique. **-2.** (*abbr of* **Federal Reserve System**) banque centrale américaine.

frugal ['fruːgl] *adj* **-1.** [meal] frugal(e). **-2.** [person, life] économe.

fruit [fruːt] (*pl inv* OR **fruits**) ◇ *n* fruit *m*; **to bear ~** *fig* porter ses fruits. ◇ *comp* [flan] aux fruits; **~ tree** arbre *m* fruitier. ◇ *vi* donner des fruits.

fruitcake ['fruːtkeɪk] *n* cake *m*.

fruiterer ['fruːtərər] *n Br* fruitier *m*.

fruitful ['fruːtful] *adj* [successful] fructueux(euse).

fruition [fruː'ɪʃn] *n*: **to come to ~** se réaliser.

fruit juice *n* jus *m* de fruits.

fruitless ['fruːtlɪs] *adj* vain(e).

fruit machine *n Br* machine *f* à sous.

fruit salad *n* salade *f* de fruits.

frumpy ['frʌmpɪ] (*compar* **-ier**, *superl* **-iest**) *adj* mal attifé(e), mal fagoté(e).

frustrate [frʌ'streɪt] *vt* **-1.** [annoy, disappoint] frustrer. **-2.** [prevent] faire échouer.

frustrated [frʌ'streɪtɪd] *adj* **-1.** [person, artist] frustré(e). **-2.** [effort, love] vain(e).

frustrating [frʌ'streɪtɪŋ] *adj* frustrant(e).

frustration *n* frustration *f*.

fry [fraɪ] (*pt* & *pp* **-ied**) *vt* & *vi* frire.

frying pan ['fraɪɪŋ-] *n* poêle *f* à frire; **to jump out of the ~ into the fire** tomber de Charybde en Scylla.

ft. *abbr of* **foot, feet**.

FT (*abbr of* **Financial Times**) *n* quotidien britannique d'information financière; **the ~ index** l'indice *m* boursier du FT, ≃ le Cac 40.

FTC (*abbr of* **Federal Trade Commission**) *n* organisme américain chargé de faire respecter les lois anti-trust.

fuchsia ['fjuːʃə] *n* fuchsia *m*.

fuck [fʌk] *vulg* ◇ *vt* & *vi* baiser. ◇ *excl* putain de merde!

◆ **fuck off** *vi vulg* foutre le camp; **~ off!** fous le camp!

fucking ['fʌkɪŋ] *adj vulg* putain de.

fuddled ['fʌdld] *adj* confus(e).

fuddy-duddy ['fʌdɪ,dʌdɪ] (*pl* **-ies**) *n inf* personne *f* vieux jeu.

fudge [fʌdʒ] ◇ *n* (U) [sweet] caramel *m* (mou). ◇ *vt inf* [figures] truquer; [issue] esquiver.

fuel [fjuəl] (*Br pt* & *pp* **-led**, *cont* **-ling**, *Am pt* & *pp* **-ed**, *cont* **-ing**) ◇ *n* combustible *m*; [for engine] carburant *m*; **to add ~ to** *fig* alimenter. ◇ *vt* **-1.** [supply with fuel] alimenter (en combustible/carburant). **-2.** *fig* [speculation] nourrir.

fuel pump *n* pompe *f* d'alimentation.

fuel tank *n* réservoir *m* à carburant.

fugitive ['fjuːdʒətɪv] *n* fugitif *m*, -ive *f*.

fugue [fjuːg] *n* fugue *f*.

fulcrum ['fʊlkrəm] (*pl* **-crums** OR **-cra** [-krə]) *n* pivot *m*.

fulfil (*pt* & *pp* **-led**, *cont* **-ling**), **fulfill** *Am* [fʊl'fɪl] *vt* **-1.** [duty, role] remplir; [hope] répondre à; [ambition, prophecy] réaliser. **-2.** [satisfy - need] satisfaire; **to ~ o.s.** s'épanouir.

fulfilling [fʊl'fɪlɪŋ] *adj* épanouissant(e).

fulfilment, **fulfillment** *Am* [fʊl'fɪlmənt] *n* (*U*) **-1.** [satisfaction] grande satisfaction *f*. **-2.** [of ambition, dream] réalisation *f*; [of role, promise] exécution *f*; [of need] satisfaction *f*.

full [fʊl] ◇ *adj* **-1.** [gen] plein(e); [bus, car park] complet(ète); [with food] gavé(e), repu(e). **-2.** [complete - recovery, control] total(e); [- explanation, day] entier(ière); [- volume] maximum. **-3.** [busy - life] rempli(e); [- timetable, day] chargé(e). **-4.** [flavour] riche. **-5.** [plump - figure] rondelet(ette); [- mouth] charnu(e). **-6.** [skirt, sleeve] ample. ◇ *adv* **-1.** [directly]: **~ in the face** en plein (dans le) visage. **-2.** [very]: **you know ~ well that ...** tu sais très bien que .... **-3.** [at maximum] au maximum.
◇ *n*: **in ~** complètement, entièrement; **to the ~** pleinement.

fullback ['fʊlbæk] *n* arrière *m*.

full-blooded [-'blʌdɪd] *adj* **-1.** [pure-blooded] de race pure. **-2.** [strong, complete] robuste.

full-blown [-'bləʊn] *adj* général(e); **to have ~ AIDS** avoir le sida avéré.

full board *n* pension *f* complète.

full-bodied [-'bɒdɪd] *adj* qui a du corps.

full dress *n* (*U*) tenue *f* de cérémonie.

full-face *adj* de face.

full-fashioned *Am* = **fully-fashioned**.

full-fledged *Am* = **fully-fledged**.

full-frontal *adj* de face.

full-grown [-'grəʊn] *adj* adulte.

full house *n* [at show, event] représentation *f* à bureaux fermés.

full-length ◇ *adj* **-1.** [portrait, mirror] en pied. **-2.** [dress, novel] long (longue); **~ film** long métrage. ◇ *adv* de tout son long.

full moon *n* pleine lune *f*.

fullness ['fʊlnɪs] *n* [of voice] ampleur *f*; [of life] richesse *f*; **in the ~ of time** avec le temps.

full-page *adj* sur toute une page.

full-scale *adj* **-1.** [life-size] grandeur nature (*inv*). **-2.** [complete] de grande envergure.

full-size(d) *adj* **-1.** [life-size] grandeur nature (*inv*). **-2.** [adult] adulte. **-3.** *Am* AUT: **~ car** grande berline *f*.

full stop ◇ *n* point *m*. ◇ *adv* *Br* un point c'est tout.

full time *n* *Br* SPORT fin *f* de match.

◆ **full-time** ◇ *adj* & *adv* [work, worker] à temps plein.

full up *adj* [bus, train] complet (complète); [with food] gavé(e), repu(e).

fully ['fʊlɪ] *adv* [understand, satisfy] tout à fait; [trained, describe] entièrement.

fully-fashioned *Br*, **full-fashioned** *Am* [-'fæʃnd] *adj* moulant(e).

fully-fledged *Br*, **full-fledged** *Am* [-'fledʒd] *adj* diplômé(e).

fulness ['fʊlnɪs] = **fullness**.

fulsome ['fʊlsəm] *adj* excessif(ive).

fumble ['fʌmbl] ◇ *vt* [catch] mal attraper. ◇ *vi* fouiller, tâtonner; **to ~ for** fouiller pour trouver.

fume [fjuːm] *vi* [with anger] rager.

◆ **fumes** *npl* [from paint] émanations *fpl*; [from smoke] fumées *fpl*; [from car] gaz *mpl* d'échappement.

fumigate ['fjuːmɪɡeɪt] *vt* fumiger.

fun [fʌn] ◇ *n* (*U*) **-1.** [pleasure, amusement]: **the game is great ~** ce jeu est très amusant; **to have ~** s'amuser; **for ~**, **for the ~ of it** pour s'amuser. **-2.** [playfulness]: **to be full of ~** être très amusant(e). **-3.** [ridicule]: **to make ~ of** OR **poke ~ at sb** se moquer de qqn. ◇ *adj* amusant(e).

function ['fʌŋkʃn] ◇ *n* **-1.** [gen] fonction *f*. **-2.** [formal social event] réception *f* officielle. ◇ *vi* fonctionner; **to ~ as** servir de.

functional ['fʌŋkʃnəl] *adj* **-1.** [practical] fonctionnel(elle). **-2.** [operational] en état de marche.

functionary ['fʌŋkʃnərɪ] (*pl* **-ies**) *n* fonctionnaire *mf*.

function key *n* COMPUT touche *f* de fonction.

fund [fʌnd] ◇ *n* fonds *m*; *fig* [of knowledge] puits *m*. ◇ *vt* financer.

◆ **funds** *npl* fonds *mpl*.

fundamental [ˌfʌndə'mentl] *adj*: **~ (to)** fondamental(e) (à).

◆ **fundamentals** *npl* principes *mpl* de base.

fundamentalism [ˌfʌndə'mentəlɪzm] *n* fondamentalisme *m*.

fundamentally [ˌfʌndə'mentəlɪ] *adv* fondamentalement.

funding ['fʌndɪŋ] *n* (*U*) financement *m*.

fund-raising [-ˌreɪzɪŋ] ◇ *n* (*U*) collecte *f* de fonds. ◇ *comp* [event, campaign] organisé(e) pour collecter des fonds.

funeral ['fjuːnərəl] *n* obsèques *fpl*.

funeral director n entrepreneur m de pompes funèbres.

funeral parlour n entreprise f de pompes funèbres.

funeral service n service m funèbre.

funereal [fjuːˈnɪərɪəl] adj funèbre.

funfair [ˈfʌnfeəʳ] n fête f foraine.

fungus [ˈfʌŋgəs] (pl -gi [-gaɪ] OR -guses) n champignon m.

funk [fʌŋk] n (U) -1. MUS funk m. -2. dated [fear] frayeur f.

funky [ˈfʌŋkɪ] (compar -ier, superl -iest) adj MUS funky (inv).

funnel [ˈfʌnl] (Br pt & pp -led, cont -ling, Am pt & pp -ed, cont -ing) ◇ n -1. [tube] entonnoir m. -2. [of ship] cheminée f. ◇ vt [crowd] canaliser; [money, food] diriger. ◇ vi se diriger.

funnily [ˈfʌnɪlɪ] adv [strangely] bizarrement; ~ **enough** chose curieuse.

funny [ˈfʌnɪ] (compar -ier, superl -iest) adj -1. [amusing, odd] drôle. -2. [ill] tout drôle (toute drôle).

funny bone n petit juif m.

funny farm n inf hum maison f de fous.

fun run n course à pied organisée pour collecter des fonds.

fur [fɜːʳ] n fourrure f.

fur coat n (manteau m de) fourrure f.

furious [ˈfjʊərɪəs] adj -1. [very angry] furieux(ieuse). -2. [wild - effort, battle] acharné(e); [- temper] déchaîné(e).

furiously [ˈfjʊərɪəslɪ] adv -1. [angrily] furieusement. -2. [wildly - fight, try] avec acharnement; [- run] à une allure folle.

furled [fɜːld] adj [umbrella, flag] roulé(e); [sail] serré(e).

furlong [ˈfɜːlɒŋ] n = 201,17 mètres.

furnace [ˈfɜːnɪs] n [fire] fournaise f.

furnish [ˈfɜːnɪʃ] vt -1. [fit out] meubler. -2. fml [provide] fournir; **to** ~ **sb with sthg** fournir qqch à qqn.

furnished [ˈfɜːnɪʃt] adj meublé(e).

furnishings [ˈfɜːnɪʃɪŋz] npl mobilier m.

furniture [ˈfɜːnɪtʃəʳ] n (U) meubles mpl; a piece of ~ un meuble.

furniture polish n encaustique m, produit m d'entretien des meubles.

furore Br [ˈfjʊərɔːrɪ], **furor** Am [ˈfjʊrɔːr] n scandale m.

furrier [ˈfʌrɪəʳ] n fourreur m.

furrow [ˈfʌrəʊ] n -1. [in field] sillon m. -2. [on forehead] ride f.

furrowed [ˈfʌrəʊd] adj -1. [field, land] labouré(e). -2. [brow] ridé(e).

furry [ˈfɜːrɪ] (compar -ier, superl -iest) adj -1. [animal] à fourrure. -2. [material] recouvert(e) de fourrure.

further [ˈfɜːðəʳ] ◇ compar → far.
◇ adv -1. [gen] plus loin; **how much** ~ **is it?** combien de kilomètres y a-t-il?; ~ **on** plus loin; **this mustn't go any** ~ ceci doit rester entre nous. -2. [more - complicate, develop] davantage; [- enquire] plus avant. -3. [in addition] de plus.
◇ adj nouveau(elle), supplémentaire; **until** ~ **notice** jusqu'à nouvel ordre.
◇ vt [career, aims] faire avancer; [cause] encourager.
◆ **further to** prep fml suite à.

further education n Br éducation f postscolaire.

furthermore [ˌfɜːðəˈmɔː] adv de plus.

furthermost [ˈfɜːðəməʊst] adj le plus éloigné (la plus éloignée).

furthest [ˈfɜːðɪst] ◇ superl → far. ◇ adj le plus éloigné (la plus éloignée). ◇ adv le plus loin.

furtive [ˈfɜːtɪv] adj [person] sournois(e); [glance] furtif(ive).

furtively [ˈfɜːtɪvlɪ] adv furtivement.

fury [ˈfjʊərɪ] n fureur f; **in a** ~ en fureur.

fuse esp Br, **fuze** Am [fjuːz] ◇ n -1. ELEC fusible m, plomb m. -2. [of bomb] détonateur m; [of firework] amorce f. ◇ vt -1. [join by heat] réunir par la fusion. -2. [combine] fusionner. ◇ vi -1. ELEC: **the lights have** ~**d** les plombs ont sauté. -2. [join by heat] fondre. -3. [combine] fusionner.

fuse-box n boîte f à fusibles.

fused [fjuːzd] adj [plug] avec fusible incorporé.

fuselage [ˈfjuːzəlɑːʒ] n fuselage m.

fuse wire n fusible m.

fusillade [ˌfjuːzəˈleɪd] n fusillade f.

fusion [ˈfjuːʒn] n fusion f.

fuss [fʌs] ◇ n -1. [excitement, anxiety] agitation f; **to make a** ~ faire des histoires. -2. (U) [complaints] protestations fpl. -3. phr: **to make a** ~ **of sb** Br être aux petits soins pour qqn. ◇ vi faire des histoires.
◆ **fuss over** vt fus être aux petits soins pour.

fusspot [ˈfʌspɒt] n inf tatillon m, -onne f.

fussy [ˈfʌsɪ] (compar -ier, superl -iest) adj -1. [fastidious - person] tatillon(onne); [- eater] difficile. -2. [over-decorated] tarabiscoté(e).

fusty [ˈfʌstɪ] (compar -ier, superl -iest) adj -1. [not fresh] qui sent le renfermé. -2. [old-fashioned] vieillot(otte).

futile [ˈfjuːtaɪl] adj vain(e).

gallon

futility [fjuːˈtɪlətɪ] *n* futilité *f.*
futon [ˈfjuːtɒn] *n* futon *m.*
future [ˈfjuːtʃə'] ◇ *n* **-1.** [gen] avenir *m*; **in**
~ à l'avenir; **in the** ~ dans le futur, à l'avenir. **-2.** GRAMM: ~ **(tense)** futur *m.* ◇ *adj*
futur(e).
◆ **futures** *npl* FIN transactions *fpl* à terme.
futuristic [,fjuːtʃə'rɪstɪk] *adj* futuriste.
fuze *Am* = **fuse.**
fuzz [fʌz] *n* **-1.** [hair] cheveux *mpl* crépus.
-2. *inf* [police]: **the** ~ les flics *mpl.*
fuzzy [ˈfʌzɪ] *(compar* **-ier,** *superl* **-iest)** *adj* **-1.**
[hair] crépu(e). **-2.** [photo, image] flou(e). **-3.**
[thoughts, mind] confus(e).
fwd. *abbr of* **forward.**
fwy *abbr of* **freeway.**
FY *n abbr of* **fiscal year.**
FYI *abbr of* **for your information.**

G

g¹ *(pl* **g's** OR **gs),** **G** *(pl* **G's** OR **Gs)** [dʒiː] *n*
[letter] g *m inv,* G *m inv.*
◆ **G** ◇ *n* MUS sol *m.* ◇ **-1.** *(abbr of* **good)** B.
-2. *(abbr of* **general (audience))** *tous publics.*
g² **-1.** *(abbr of* **gram)** g. **-2.** *(abbr of* **gravity)**
g.
GA *abbr of* **Georgia.**
gab [gæb] → **gift.**
gabardine [,gæbə'diːn] *n* gabardine *f.*
gabble [ˈgæbl] ◇ *vt & vi* baragouiner. ◇ *n*
charabia *m.*
gable [ˈgeɪbl] *n* pignon *m.*
Gabon [gæ'bɒn] *n* Gabon *m*; **in** ~ au Gabon.
Gabonese [,gæbɒ'niːz] ◇ *adj* gabonais(e).
◇ *npl*: **the** ~ les Gabonais.
gad [gæd] *(pt & pp* **-ded,** *cont* **-ding)**
◆ **gad about** *vi inf* partir en vadrouille.
gadget [ˈgædʒɪt] *n* gadget *m.*
gadgetry [ˈgædʒɪtrɪ] *n (U)* gadgets *mpl.*
Gaelic [ˈgeɪlɪk] ◇ *adj* gaélique. ◇ *n* gaélique *m.*
gaffe [gæf] *n* gaffe *f.*
gaffer [ˈgæfə'] *n Br inf* [boss] patron *m.*
gag [gæg] *(pt & pp* **-ged,** *cont* **-ging)** ◇ *n* **-1.**
[for mouth] bâillon *m.* **-2.** *inf* [joke] blague *f,*

gag *m.* ◇ *vt* [put gag on] bâillonner. ◇ *vi*
[choke] s'étrangler.
gage *Am* = **gauge.**
gaiety [ˈgeɪətɪ] *n* gaieté *f.*
gaily [ˈgeɪlɪ] *adv* **-1.** [cheerfully] gaiement.
-2. [thoughtlessly] allègrement.
gain [geɪn] ◇ *n* **-1.** [gen] profit *m.* **-2.** [improvement] augmentation *f.* ◇ *vt* **-1.** [acquire] gagner. **-2.** [increase in - speed, weight]
prendre; [- confidence] gagner en. **-3.** [subj:
watch, clock]: **to** ~ **10 minutes** avancer de
10 minutes. ◇ *vi* **-1.** [advance]: **to** ~ **in sthg**
gagner en qqch. **-2.** [benefit]: **to** ~ **from** OR
by sthg tirer un avantage de qqch. **-3.**
[watch, clock] avancer.
◆ **gain on** *vt fus* rattraper.
gainful [ˈgeɪnful] *adj fml* lucratif(ive).
gainfully [ˈgeɪnfulɪ] *adv fml* lucrativement.
gainsay [,geɪn'seɪ] *(pt & pp* **-said)** *vt fml*
contredire.
gait [geɪt] *n* démarche *f.*
gaiters [ˈgeɪtəz] *npl* guêtres *fpl.*
gal. *abbr of* **gallon.**
gala [ˈgɑːlə] ◇ *n* [celebration] gala *m.* ◇ *comp*
de gala.
Galapagos Islands [gə'læpəgəs-] *npl*: **the** ~
les (îles *fpl*) Galapagos; **in the** ~ aux (îles)
Galapagos.
galaxy [ˈgæləksɪ] *(pl* **-ies)** *n* galaxie *f.*
gale [geɪl] *n* [wind] grand vent *m.*
Galicia [gə'lɪʃɪə] *n* **-1.** [in Central Europe] Galicie *f*; **in** ~ en Galicie. **-2.** [in Spain] Galice
f; **in** ~ en Galice.
gall [gɔːl] ◇ *n* [nerve]: **to have the** ~ **to do**
sthg avoir le toupet de faire qqch. ◇ *vt*
contrarier.
gall. *abbr of* **gallon.**
gallant [*sense 1* 'gælənt, *sense 2* gə'lænt,
'gælənt] *adj* **-1.** [courageous] courageux(euse). **-2.** [polite to women] galant.
gallantry [ˈgæləntrɪ] *n* **-1.** [courage] bravoure *f.* **-2.** [politeness to women] galanterie
f.
gall bladder *n* vésicule *f* biliaire.
galleon [ˈgælɪən] *n* galion *m.*
gallery [ˈgælərɪ] *(pl* **-ies)** *n* **-1.** [gen] galerie *f.*
-2. [for displaying art] musée *m.* **-3.** [in
theatre] paradis *m.*
galley [ˈgælɪ] *(pl* **galleys)** *n* **-1.** [ship] galère
f. **-2.** [kitchen] coquerie *f.*
Gallic [ˈgælɪk] *adj* français(e).
galling [ˈgɔːlɪŋ] *adj* humiliant(e).
gallivant [,gælɪ'vænt] *vi inf* mener une vie
de patachon.
gallon [ˈgælən] *n* = 4,546 litres, gallon *m.*

gallop ['gæləp] ◇ *n* galop *m*. ◇ *vi* galoper.

galloping ['gæləpɪŋ] *adj* [inflation] galopant(e).

gallows ['gæləuz] (*pl inv*) *n* gibet *m*.

gallstone ['gɔːlstəun] *n* calcul *m* biliaire.

Gallup poll ['gæləp-] *n Br* sondage *m* d'opinion.

galore [gə'lɔːr] *adj* en abondance.

galoshes [gə'lɒʃɪz] *npl* caoutchoucs *mpl*.

galvanize, -ise ['gælvənaɪz] *vt* **-1.** TECH galvaniser. **-2.** [impel]: **to ~ sb into action** pousser qqn à agir.

Gambia ['gæmbɪə] *n*: **(the) ~** Gambie *f*; **in (the) ~** en Gambie.

Gambian ['gæmbɪən] ◇ *adj* gambien(ienne). ◇ *n* Gambien *m*, -ienne *f*.

gambit ['gæmbɪt] *n* entrée *f* en matière.

gamble ['gæmbl] ◇ *n* [calculated risk] risque *m*; **to take a.~** prendre un risque. ◇ *vi* **-1.** [bet] jouer; **to ~ on** jouer de l'argent sur. **-2.** [take risk]: **to ~ on** miser sur.

gambler ['gæmblər] *n* joueur *m*, -euse *f*.

gambling ['gæmblɪŋ] *n* (*U*) jeu *m*.

gambol ['gæmbl] (*Br pt* & *pp* **-led**, *cont* **-ling**, *Am pt* & *pp* **-ed**, *cont* **-ing**) *vi* gambader.

game [geɪm] ◇ *n* **-1.** [gen] jeu *m*; **what's your ~?** *inf* à quoi joues-tu? **-2.** [match] match *m*. **-3.** (*U*) [hunted animals] gibier *m*. **-4.** *phr*: **to beat sb at their own ~** battre qqn sur son propre terrain; **the ~'s up** tout est vendre la mèche. ◇ *adj* **-1.** [brave] courageux(euse). **-2.** [willing]: **~ (for sthg/to do sthg)** partant(e) pour qqch/pour faire qqch.
◆ **games** ◇ *n* SCH éducation *f* physique. ◇ *npl* [sporting contest] jeux *mpl*.

gamekeeper ['geɪm,kiːpər] *n* garde-chasse *m*.

gamely ['geɪmlɪ] *adj* **-1.** [bravely] courageusement. **-2.** [willingly] volontairement.

game reserve *n* réserve *f* (de chasse).

gamesmanship ['geɪmzmənʃɪp] *n* art de gagner habilement.

gamma rays ['gæmə-] *npl* rayons *mpl* gamma.

gammon ['gæmən] *n* jambon *m* fumé.

gammy ['gæmɪ] (*compar* **-ier**, *superl* **-iest**) *adj Br inf* boiteux(euse).

gamut ['gæmət] *n* gamme *f*; **to run the ~ of** passer par toute la gamme de.

gander ['gændər] *n* [male goose] jars *m*.

gang [gæŋ] *n* **-1.** [of criminals] gang *m*. **-2.** [of young people] bande *f*.

◆ **gang up** *vi inf*: **to ~ up (on)** se liguer (contre).

Ganges ['gændʒiːz] *n*: **the (River) ~** le Gange.

gangland ['gæŋlænd] *n* (*U*) milieu *m*.

gangling ['gæŋglɪŋ], **gangly** ['gæŋglɪ] (*compar* **-ier**, *superl* **-iest**) *adj* dégingandé(e).

gangplank ['gæŋplæŋk] *n* passerelle *f*.

gangrene ['gæŋgriːn] *n* gangrène *f*.

gangrenous ['gæŋgrɪnəs] *adj* gangreneux(euse).

gangster ['gæŋstər] *n* gangster *m*.

gangway ['gæŋweɪ] *n* **-1.** *Br* [aisle] allée *f*. **-2.** [gangplank] passerelle *f*.

gannet ['gænɪt] (*pl inv* OR **-s**) *n* [bird] fou *m* (de Bassan).

gantry ['gæntrɪ] (*pl* **-ies**) *n* portique *m*.

GAO (*abbr of* **General Accounting Office**) *n* Cour des comptes américaine.

gaol [dʒeɪl] *Br* = **jail**.

gap [gæp] *n* **-1.** [empty space] trou *m*; [in text] blanc *m*; *fig* [in knowledge, report] lacune *f*. **-2.** [interval of time] période *f*. **-3.** *fig* [great difference] fossé *m*.

gape [geɪp] *vi* **-1.** [person] rester bouche bée. **-2.** [hole, shirt] bâiller.

gaping ['geɪpɪŋ] *adj* **-1.** [open-mouthed] bouche bée (*inv*). **-2.** [wide-open] béant(e); [shirt] grand ouvert (grande ouverte).

garage [*Br* 'gærɑːʒ, 'gærɪdʒ, *Am* gə'rɑːʒ] *n* **-1.** [gen] garage *m*. **-2.** *Br* [for fuel] station-service *f*.

garb [gɑːb] *n* (*U*) *fml* tenue *f*.

garbage ['gɑːbɪdʒ] *n* (*U*) **-1.** [refuse] détritus *mpl*. **-2.** *inf* [nonsense] idioties *fpl*.

garbage can *n Am* poubelle *f*.

garbage collector *n Am* éboueur *m*.

garbage truck *n Am* camion-poubelle *m*.

garbled ['gɑːbld] *adj* confus(e).

garden ['gɑːdn] ◇ *n* jardin *m*. ◇ *comp* de jardin. ◇ *vi* jardiner.
◆ **gardens** *npl* jardins *mpl* (publics).

garden centre *n* jardinerie *f*, garden centre *m*.

garden city *n Br* cité-jardin *f*.

gardener ['gɑːdnər] *n* [professional] jardinier *m*, -ière *f*; [amateur] personne *f* qui aime jardiner, amateur *m* de jardinage.

gardenia [gɑː'diːnjə] *n* gardénia *m*.

gardening ['gɑːdnɪŋ] ◇ *n* jardinage *m*. ◇ *comp* [gloves, equipment, book] de jardinage; [expert] en jardinage.

garden party *n* garden-party *f*.

gargantuan [gɑː'gæntjuən] *adj* gargantuesque.

gargle ['gɑːgl] *vi* se gargariser.

gargoyle ['gɑːgɔɪl] *n* gargouille *f*.

garish ['geərɪʃ] *adj* criard(e).

garland ['gɑːlənd] *n* guirlande *f* de fleurs.

garlic ['gɑːlɪk] *n* ail *m*.

garlic bread *n* pain *m* à l'ail.

garlicky ['gɑːlɪkɪ] *adj inf* qui sent l'ail.

garment ['gɑːmənt] *n* vêtement *m*.

garner ['gɑːnə'] *vt fml* recueillir.

garnet ['gɑːnɪt] *n* [red stone] grenat *m*.

garnish ['gɑːnɪʃ] ◇ *n* garniture *f*. ◇ *vt* garnir.

garret ['gærət] *n* mansarde *f*.

garrison ['gærɪsn] ◇ *n* [soldiers] garnison *f*. ◇ *vt* tenir en garnison.

garrulous ['gærələs] *adj* volubile.

garter ['gɑːtə'] *n* **-1.** [for socks] support-chaussette *m*; [for stockings] jarretière *f*. **-2.** *Am* [suspender] jarretelle *f*.

gas [gæs] (*pl* **-es** OR **-ses**, *pt* & *pp* **-sed**, *cont* **-sing**) ◇ *n* **-1.** [gen] gaz *m inv*. **-2.** *Am* [for vehicle] essence *f*. ◇ *vt* gazer.

gas chamber *n* chambre *f* à gaz.

Gascony ['gæskənɪ] *n* Gascogne *f*; **in ~** en Gascogne.

gas cooker *n Br* cuisinière *f* à gaz.

gas cylinder *n* bouteille *f* de gaz.

gaseous ['gæsjəs] *adj* gazeux(euse).

gas fire *n Br* appareil *m* de chauffage à gaz.

gas fitter *n* ajusteur *m* gazier.

gas gauge *n Am* jauge *f* d'essence.

gash [gæʃ] ◇ *n* entaille *f*. ◇ *vt* entailler.

gasket ['gæskɪt] *n* joint *m* d'étanchéité.

gasman ['gæsmæn] (*pl* **-men** [-men]) *n* [who reads meter] employé *m* du gaz; [for repairs] installateur *m* de gaz.

gas mask *n* masque *m* à gaz.

gas meter *n* compteur *m* à gaz.

gasoline ['gæsəliːn] *n Am* essence *f*.

gasometer [gæ'sɒmɪtə'] *n* réservoir *m* collecteur de gaz.

gas oven *n* **-1.** [for cooking] four *m* à gaz. **-2.** [gas chamber] chambre *f* à gaz.

gasp [gɑːsp] ◇ *n* halètement *m*. ◇ *vi* **-1.** [breathe quickly] haleter. **-2.** [in shock, surprise] avoir le souffle coupé.

gas pedal *n Am* accélérateur *m*.

gasping ['gɑːspɪŋ] *adj Br inf* mort(e) de soif.

gas station *n Am* station-service *f*.

gas stove = **gas cooker**.

gassy ['gæsɪ] (*compar* **-ier**, *superl* **-iest**) *adj pej* gazeux(euse).

gas tank *n Am* réservoir *m*.

gas tap *n* [for mains supply] robinet *m* de gaz; [on gas fire] prise *f* de gaz.

gastric ['gæstrɪk] *adj* gastrique.

gastric ulcer *n* ulcère *m* gastrique.

gastritis [gæs'traɪtɪs] *n* gastrite *f*.

gastroenteritis ['gæstrəʊˌentə'raɪtɪs] *n* gastro-entérite *f*.

gastronomic [ˌgæstrə'nɒmɪk] *adj* gastronomique.

gastronomy [gæs'trɒnəmɪ] *n* gastronomie *f*.

gasworks ['gæswɜːks] (*pl inv*) *n* usine *f* à gaz.

gate [geɪt] *n* [of garden, farm] barrière *f*; [of town, at airport] porte *f*; [of park] grille *f*.

gâteau ['gætəʊ] (*pl* **-x** [-z]) *n Br* gâteau *m*.

gatecrash ['geɪtkræʃ] *inf vt* & *vi* prendre part à une réunion, une réception sans y avoir été convié.

gatecrasher ['geɪtˌkræʃə'] *n inf* intrus *m*, -e *f*.

gatehouse ['geɪthaʊs] *n* loge *f* du gardien.

gatekeeper ['geɪtˌkiːpə'] *n* gardien *m*, -ienne *f*.

gatepost ['geɪtpəʊst] *n* montant *m* de barrière.

gateway ['geɪtweɪ] *n* **-1.** [entrance] entrée *f*. **-2.** [means of access]: **~ to** porte *f* de; *fig* clé *f* de.

gather ['gæðə'] ◇ *vt* **-1.** [collect] ramasser; [flowers] cueillir; [information] recueillir; [courage, strength] rassembler; **to ~ together** rassembler. **-2.** [increase - speed, force] prendre. **-3.** [understand]: **to ~ (that)** ... croire comprendre que .... **-4.** [cloth - into folds] plisser. ◇ *vi* [come together] se rassembler; [clouds] s'amonceler.

♦ **gather up** *vt sep* rassembler.

gathering ['gæðərɪŋ] *n* [meeting] rassemblement *m*.

GATT [gæt] (*abbr of* **General Agreement on Tariffs and Trade**) *n* GATT *m*.

gauche [gəʊʃ] *adj* gauche.

gaudy ['gɔːdɪ] (*compar* **-ier**, *superl* **-iest**) *adj* voyant(e).

gauge, gage *Am* [geɪdʒ] ◇ *n* **-1.** [for rain] pluviomètre *m*; [for fuel] jauge *f* (d'essence); [for tyre pressure] manomètre *m*. **-2.** [of gun, wire] calibre *m*. **-3.** RAIL écartement *m*. ◇ *vt* **-1.** [measure] mesurer. **-2.** [evaluate] jauger.

Gaul [gɔːl] *n* **-1.** [country] Gaule *f*. **-2.** [person] Gaulois *m*, -e *f*.

gaunt [gɔːnt] *adj* **-1.** [thin] hâve. **-2.** [bare, grim] désolé(e).

gauntlet ['gɔːntlɪt] *n* gant *m* (de protection); **to run the ~ of** sthg endurer qqch;

to throw down the ~ (to sb) jeter le gant (à qqn).

gauze [gɔːz] n gaze f.

gave [geɪv] pt → **give**.

gawky ['gɔːkɪ] (compar **-ier**, superl **-iest**) adj [person] dégingandé(e); [movement] désordonné(e).

gawp [gɔːp] vi: to ~ (at) rester bouche bée (devant).

gay [geɪ] ◇ adj **-1.** [gen] gai(e). **-2.** [homosexual] homo (inv), gay (inv). ◇ n homo mf, gay mf.

Gaza Strip ['gɑːzə-] n: the ~ la bande de Gaza.

gaze [geɪz] ◇ n regard m (fixe). ◇ vi: to ~ at sb/sthg regarder qqn/qqch (fixement).

gazebo [gə'ziːbəʊ] (pl inv OR **-s**) n belvédère m.

gazelle [gə'zel] (pl inv OR **-s**) n gazelle f.

gazette [gə'zet] n [newspaper] gazette f.

gazetteer [ˌgæzɪ'tɪər] n index m géographique.

gazump [gə'zʌmp] vt Br inf: to be ~ed être victime d'une suroffre.

GB (abbr of **Great Britain**) n G-B f.

GBH (abbr of **grievous bodily harm**) n coups mpl et blessures.

GC (abbr of **George Cross**) n distinction honorifique britannique.

GCE (abbr of **General Certificate of Education**) n certificat de fin d'études secondaires en Grande-Bretagne.

GCH Br (abbr of **gas central heating**) chauffage central à gaz.

GCHQ (abbr of **Government Communications Headquarters**) n en Grande-Bretagne, centre d'interception des télécommunications étrangères.

GCSE (abbr of **General Certificate of Secondary Education**) n examen de fin d'études secondaires en Grande-Bretagne.

Gdns abbr of **Gardens**.

GDP (abbr of **gross domestic product**) n PIB m.

GDR (abbr of **German Democratic Republic**) n RDA f.

gear [gɪər] ◇ n **-1.** TECH [mechanism] embrayage m. **-2.** [speed - of car, bicycle] vitesse f; to be in/out of ~ être en prise/au point mort. **-3.** (U) [equipment, clothes] équipement m. ◇ vt: to ~ sthg to sb/sthg destiner qqch à qqn/qqch.
◆ **gear up** vi: to ~ up for sthg/to do sthg se préparer pour qqch/à faire qqch.

gearbox ['gɪəbɒks] n boîte f de vitesses.

gearing ['gɪərɪŋ] n TECH engrenage m.

gear lever, **gear stick** Br, **gear shift** Am n levier m de changement de vitesse.

gear wheel n pignon m, roue f d'engrenage.

gee [dʒiː] excl **-1.** [to horse]: ~ **up!** hue! **-2.** Am inf [expressing surprise, excitement]: ~ **(whiz)!** ça alors!

geese [giːs] pl → **goose**.

Geiger counter ['gaɪgər-] n compteur m Geiger.

geisha (girl) ['geɪʃə-] n geisha f.

gel [dʒel] (pt & pp **-led**, cont **-ling**) ◇ n [for hair] gel m. ◇ vi **-1.** [thicken] prendre. **-2.** fig [take shape] prendre tournure.

gelatin ['dʒelətɪn], **gelatine** [ˌdʒelə'tiːn] n gélatine f.

gelding ['geldɪŋ] n hongre m.

gelignite ['dʒelɪgnaɪt] n gélignite f.

gem [dʒem] n **-1.** [jewel] pierre f précieuse, gemme f. **-2.** fig [person, thing] perle f.

Gemini ['dʒemɪnaɪ] n Gémeaux mpl; to be (a) ~ être Gémeaux.

gemstone ['dʒemstəʊn] n pierre f précieuse.

gen [dʒen] (pt & pp **-ned**, cont **-ning**) Br inf n (U) info f.
◆ **gen up** vi: to ~ up (on sthg) se rancarder (sur qqch).

gen. (abbr of **general, generally**) gén.

Gen. (abbr of **General**) Gal.

gender ['dʒendər] n **-1.** [sex] sexe m. **-2.** GRAMM genre m.

gene [dʒiːn] n gène m.

genealogist [ˌdʒiːnɪ'ælədʒɪst] n généalogiste mf.

genealogy [ˌdʒiːnɪ'ælədʒɪ] (pl **-ies**) n généalogie f.

genera ['dʒenərə] pl → **genus**.

general ['dʒenərəl] ◇ adj général(e). ◇ n général m.
◆ **in general** adv en général.

general anaesthetic n anesthésie f générale.

general delivery n Am poste f restante.

general election n élection f générale.

generality [ˌdʒenə'rælətɪ] (pl **-ies**) n généralité f.

generalization [ˌdʒenərəlaɪ'zeɪʃn] n généralisation f.

generalize, **-ise** ['dʒenərəlaɪz] vi: to ~ (about) généraliser (au sujet de OR sur).

general knowledge n culture f générale.

generally ['dʒenərəlɪ] adv **-1.** [usually, in most cases] généralement. **-2.** [unspecifically] en général; [describe] en gros.

general manager n directeur général m, directrice générale f.

general practice n -1. [work] médecine f générale. -2. [place] cabinet m de généraliste.

general practitioner n (médecin m) généraliste m.

general public n: **the ~** le grand public.

general-purpose adj polyvalent(e).

general strike n grève f générale.

generate ['dʒenəreɪt] vt [energy, jobs] générer; [electricity, heat] **produire**; [interest, excitement] susciter.

generation [,dʒenə'reɪʃn] n -1. [gen] génération f; **first/second ~** première/deuxième génération. -2. [creation - of jobs] création f; [- of interest, excitement] induction f; [- of electricity] production f.

generation gap n fossé m des générations.

generator ['dʒenəreɪtə'] n générateur m; ELEC génératrice f, générateur.

generic [dʒɪ'nerɪk] adj générique.

generosity [,dʒenə'rɒsətɪ] n générosité f.

generous ['dʒenərəs] adj généreux(euse).

generously ['dʒenərəslɪ] adv généreusement.

genesis ['dʒenəsɪs] (pl **-eses** [-əsiːz]) n [origin] genèse f.

genetic [dʒɪ'netɪk] adj génétique.

genetic engineering n (U) manipulation f génétique.

genetic fingerprinting [-'fɪŋɡəprɪntɪŋ] n identification génétique à l'aide des empreintes digitales.

genetics [dʒɪ'netɪks] n (U) génétique f.

Geneva [dʒɪ'niːvə] n Genève.

Geneva convention n: **the ~** la Convention de Genève.

genial ['dʒiːnjəl] adj affable.

genie ['dʒiːnɪ] (pl **genies** OR **genii** ['dʒiːnɪaɪ]) n génie m.

genitals ['dʒenɪtlz] npl organes mpl génitaux.

genius ['dʒiːnjəs] (pl **-es**) n génie m; **~ for sthg/for doing sthg** génie de qqch/pour faire qqch.

Genoa ['dʒenəʊə] n Gênes.

genocide ['dʒenəsaɪd] n génocide m.

genre ['ʒɑ̃rə] n genre m.

gent [dʒent] n Br inf gentleman m.
◆ **gents** n Br [toilets] toilettes fpl pour hommes; [sign on door] messieurs.

genteel [dʒen'tiːl] adj raffiné(e).

gentile ['dʒentaɪl] ◇ adj gentil(ille). ◇ n gentil m, -ille f.

gentle ['dʒentl] adj doux (douce); [hint] discret(ète); [telling-off] léger(ère).

gentleman ['dʒentlmən] (pl **-men** [-mən]) n -1. [well-behaved man] gentleman m; **~'s agreement** accord m qui repose sur l'honneur. -2. [man] monsieur m.

gentlemanly ['dʒentlmənlɪ] adj courtois(e).

gentleness ['dʒentlnɪs] n douceur f.

gently ['dʒentlɪ] adv [gen] doucement; [speak, smile] avec douceur.

gentry ['dʒentrɪ] n petite noblesse.

genuflect ['dʒenjuːflekt] vi fml faire une génuflexion.

genuine ['dʒenjʊɪn] adj authentique; [interest, customer] sérieux(ieuse); [person, concern] sincère.

genuinely ['dʒenjʊɪnlɪ] adv réellement.

genus ['dʒiːnəs] (pl **genera** ['dʒenərə]) n genre m.

geographer [dʒɪ'ɒɡrəfə'] n géographe mf.

geographical [dʒɪə'ɡræfɪkl] adj géographique.

geography [dʒɪ'ɒɡrəfɪ] n géographie f.

geological [,dʒɪə'lɒdʒɪkl] adj géologique.

geologist [dʒɪ'ɒlədʒɪst] n géologue mf.

geology [dʒɪ'ɒlədʒɪ] n géologie f.

geometric(al) [,dʒɪə'metrɪk(l)] adj géométrique.

geometry [dʒɪ'ɒmətrɪ] n géométrie f.

geophysics [,dʒiːəʊ'fɪzɪks] n géophysique f.

Geordie ['dʒɔːdɪ] n personne originaire de Tyneside.

George Cross ['dʒɔːdʒ-] n Br décoration décernée pour actes de bravoure.

Georgia ['dʒɔːdʒə] n [in US, in CIS] Géorgie f; **in ~** en Géorgie.

Georgian ['dʒɔːdʒən] ◇ adj -1. Br [house, furniture] ≈ style XVIIIᵉ (siècle). -2. GEOGR géorgien(ienne). ◇ n Géorgien m, -ienne f.

geranium [dʒɪ'reɪnjəm] (pl **-s**) n géranium m.

gerbil ['dʒɜːbɪl] n gerbille f.

geriatric [,dʒerɪ'ætrɪk] adj -1. MED gériatrique. -2. pej [person] décrépit(e); [object] vétuste.

germ [dʒɜːm] n -1. [bacterium] germe m. -2. fig [of idea, plan] embryon m.

German ['dʒɜːmən] ◇ adj allemand(e). ◇ n -1. [person] Allemand m, -e f. -2. [language] allemand m.

Germanic [dʒɜː'mænɪk] adj germanique.

German measles n (U) rubéole f.

German shepherd (dog) *n* berger *m* allemand.

Germany ['dʒɜːmənɪ] (*pl* -ies) *n* Allemagne *f*; **in** ~ en Allemagne.

germicide ['dʒɜːmɪsaɪd] *n* germicide *m*.

germinate ['dʒɜːmɪneɪt] ◇ *vt* -1. [seed] faire germer. -2. *fig* [idea, feeling] faire naître. ◇ *vi lit* & *fig* germer.

germination [,dʒɜːmɪ'neɪʃn] *n* -1. [of seed] germination *f*. -2. *fig* [of idea, feeling] développement *m*.

germ warfare *n* (*U*) guerre *f* bactériologique.

gerrymandering ['dʒerɪmændərɪŋ] *n* (*U*) charcutage *m* électoral.

gerund ['dʒerənd] *n* gérondif *m*.

gestation [dʒe'steɪʃn] *n* gestation *f*.

gestation period *n lit* & *fig* période *f* de gestation.

gesticulate [dʒes'tɪkjʊleɪt] *vi* gesticuler.

gesticulation [dʒe,stɪkjʊ'leɪʃn] *n* gesticulation *f*.

gesture ['dʒestʃəʳ] ◇ *n* geste *m*. ◇ *vi*: **to ~ to OR towards sb** faire signe à qqn.

get [get] (*Br pt* & *pp* got, *cont* -ting, *Am pt* got, *pp* gotten, *cont* -ting) ◇ *vt* -1. [cause to do]: **to ~ sb to do sthg** faire faire qqch à qqn; **I'll ~ my sister to help** je vais demander à ma sœur de nous aider. -2. [cause to be done]: **to ~ sthg done** faire faire qqch; **I got the car fixed** j'ai fait réparer la voiture. -3. [cause to become]: **to ~ sb pregnant** rendre qqn enceinte; **I can't ~ the car started** je n'arrive pas à mettre la voiture en marche; **to ~ things going** faire avancer les choses. -4. [cause to move]: **to ~ sb/sthg through sthg** faire passer qqn/qqch par qqch; **to ~ sb/sthg out of sthg** faire sortir qqn/qqch de qqch. -5. [bring, fetch] aller chercher; **can I ~ you something to eat/drink?** est-ce que je peux vous offrir quelque chose à manger/boire?; **I'll ~ my coat** je vais chercher mon manteau. -6. [obtain - gen] obtenir; [- job, house] trouver. -7. [receive] recevoir, avoir; **what did you ~ for your birthday?** qu'est-ce que tu as eu pour ton anniversaire?; **she ~s a good salary** elle touche un bon traitement; **when did you ~ the news?** quand as-tu reçu la nouvelle? -8. [experience a sensation] avoir; **do you ~ the feeling he doesn't like us?** tu n'as pas l'impression qu'il ne nous aime pas?; **I ~ a real thrill out of driving fast** cela me donne des sensations fortes de conduire vite. -9. [be infected with, suffer from] avoir, attraper; **to ~ a cold** attraper un rhume. -10. [understand] comprendre, saisir; **I don't ~ it** *inf* je

ne comprends pas, je ne saisis pas; **he didn't seem to ~ the point** il ne semblait pas comprendre OR piger. -11. [catch - bus, train, plane] prendre. -12. [capture] prendre, attraper. -13. *inf* [annoy]: **what really ~s me is his smugness** c'est sa suffisance qui m'agace OR qui m'énerve. -14. [find]: **you ~ a lot of artists here** on trouve OR il y a beaucoup d'artistes ici; *see also* **have**.
◇ *vi* -1. [become] devenir; **to ~ suspicious** devenir méfiant; **I'm getting cold/bored** je commence à avoir froid/à m'ennuyer; **it's getting late** il se fait tard. -2. [arrive] arriver; **he never got there** il n'est jamais arrivé; **I only got back yesterday** je suis rentré hier seulement. -3. [eventually succeed in]: **to ~ to do sthg** parvenir à OR finir par faire qqch; **did you ~ to see him?** est-ce que tu as réussi à le voir?; **she got to enjoy the classes** elle a fini par aimer les cours; **I never got to visit Beijing** je n'ai jamais pu aller à Beijing. -4. [progress]: **how far have you got?** où en es-tu?; **we got as far as buying the paint** on est allé jusqu'à acheter la peinture; **I got to the point where I didn't care any more** j'en suis arrivé à m'en ficher complètement; **now we're getting somewhere** enfin on avance; **we're getting nowhere** on n'arrive à rien.
◇ *aux vb*: **to ~ excited** s'exciter; **to ~ hurt** se faire mal; **to ~ beaten up** se faire tabasser; **let's ~ going OR moving** allons-y; *see also* **have**.

◆ **get about, get around** *vi* -1. [move from place to place] se déplacer. -2. [circulate - news, rumour] circuler, se répandre; *see also* **get around**.

◆ **get across** *vt sep* [idea, policy] communiquer; **to ~ one's message across** se faire comprendre.

◆ **get ahead** *vi* avancer.

◆ **get along** *vi* -1. [manage] se débrouiller. -2. [progress] avancer, faire des progrès. -3. [have a good relationship] s'entendre.

◆ **get around, get round** ◇ *vt fus* [overcome] venir à bout de, surmonter. ◇ *vi* -1. [circulate] circuler, se répandre. -2. [eventually do]: **to ~ around to (doing) sthg** trouver le temps de faire qqch; *see also* **get about**.

◆ **get at** *vt fus* -1. [reach] parvenir à. -2. [imply] vouloir dire; **what are you getting at?** où veux-tu en venir? -3. *inf* [criticize] critiquer, dénigrer.

◆ **get away** *vi* -1. [leave] partir, s'en aller. -2. [go on holiday] partir en vacances; **to ~ away from it all** partir se détendre loin de tout. -3. [escape] s'échapper, s'évader.

◆ **get away with** *vt fus*: **to let sb ~ away**

with sthg passer qqch à qqn; **she just lets him ~ away with it** elle le laisse tout faire, elle lui passe tout.

◆ **get back** ◇ *vt sep* [recover, regain] retrouver, récupérer. ◇ *vi* [move away] s'écarter.

◆ **get back to** ◇ *vt fus* **-1.** [return to previous state, activity] revenir à; **to ~ back to sleep** se rendormir; **things are getting back to normal** la situation redevient normale; **to ~ back to work** [after pause] se remettre au travail; [after illness] reprendre son travail. **-2.** *inf* [phone back] rappeler; **I'll ~ back to you on that** je te reparlerai de ça plus tard.

◆ **get by** *vi* se débrouiller, s'en sortir.

◆ **get down** *vt sep* **-1.** [depress] déprimer. **-2.** [fetch from higher level] descendre.

◆ **get down to** *vt fus* s'attaquer à; **to ~ down to doing sthg** se mettre à faire qqch; **to ~ down to work** se mettre au travail.

◆ **get in** ◇ *vi* **-1.** [enter] entrer. **-2.** [arrive] arriver; [arrive home] rentrer. **-3.** [be elected] être élu(e). ◇ *vt sep* **-1.** [bring in] rentrer. **-2.** [interject]: **to ~ a word in** placer un mot.

◆ **get in on** *vi* se mêler de, participer à.

◆ **get into** *vt fus* **-1.** [car] monter dans. **-2.** [become involved in] se lancer dans; **to ~ into an argument with sb** se disputer avec qqn. **-3.** [enter into a particular situation, state]: **to ~ into a panic** s'affoler; **to ~ into trouble** s'attirer des ennuis; **to ~ into the habit of doing sthg** prendre l'habitude de faire qqch. **-4.** [be accepted as a student at] être admis(e) OR accepté(e) à. **-5.** *inf* [affect]: **what's got into you?** qu'est-ce qui te prend?

◆ **get off** ◇ *vt sep* [remove] enlever. ◇ *vt fus* **-1.** [go away from] partir de. **-2.** [train, bus etc] descendre de. ◇ *vi* **-1.** [leave bus, train] descendre. **-2.** [escape punishment] s'en tirer; **he got off lightly** il s'en est tiré à bon compte. **-3.** [depart] partir.

◆ **get off with** ◇ *vt fus Br inf* avoir la touche avec.

◆ **get on** ◇ *vt sep* [put on] mettre. ◇ *vt fus* **-1.** [bus, train, plane] monter dans. **-2.** [horse] monter sur. ◇ *vi* **-1.** [enter bus, train] monter. **-2.** [have good relationship] s'entendre, s'accorder. **-3.** [progress] avancer, progresser. **-4.** [proceed]: **to ~ on (with sthg)** continuer (qqch), poursuivre (qqch). **-5.** [be successful professionally] réussir. **-6.** [grow old]: **to be getting on** se faire vieux (vieille).

◆ **get on for** *vt fus inf* [be approximately]: **to be getting on for** approcher de; **there were getting on for 5,000 people at the concert** il y avait près de 5000 personnes au concert.

◆ **get on to** *vt fus* **-1.** [begin talking about] se mettre à parler de. **-2.** [contact] contac-

ter.

◆ **get out** ◇ *vt sep* **-1.** [take out] sortir. **-2.** [remove] enlever. ◇ *vi* **-1.** [from car, bus, train] descendre. **-2.** [news] s'ébruiter.

◆ **get out of** ◇ *vt fus* **-1.** [car etc] descendre de. **-2.** [escape from] s'évader de, s'échapper de. **-3.** [avoid] éviter, se dérober à; **to ~ out of doing sthg** se dispenser de faire qqch. ◇ *vt sep* [cause to escape from]: **to ~ sb out of jail** faire sortir qqn de prison.

◆ **get over** *vt fus* **-1.** [recover from] se remettre de. **-2.** [overcome] surmonter, venir à bout de. **-3.** [communicate] communiquer.

◆ **get over with** *vt sep*: **to ~ sthg over with** en finir avec qqch.

◆ **get round** = get around.

◆ **get through** ◇ *vt fus* **-1.** [job, task] arriver au bout de. **-2.** [exam] réussir à. **-3.** [food, drink] consommer. **-4.** [unpleasant situation] endurer, supporter. ◇ *vi* **-1.** [make o.s. understood]: **to ~ through (to sb)** se faire comprendre (de qqn). **-2.** TELEC obtenir la communication.

◆ **get to** *vt fus inf* [annoy] taper sur les nerfs à.

◆ **get together** ◇ *vt sep* [organize - team, belongings] rassembler; [- project, report] préparer. ◇ *vi* se réunir.

◆ **get up** ◇ *vi* se lever. ◇ *vt fus* [petition, demonstration] organiser.

◆ **get up to** *vt fus inf* faire; **I wonder what they're getting up to** je me demande ce qu'ils fabriquent OR ce qu'ils sont en train de faire encore.

getaway ['getəweı] *n* fuite *f*.

getaway car *n* voiture qui sert à la fuite des gangsters.

get-together *n inf* réunion *f*.

getup ['getʌp] *n inf* accoutrement *m*.

get-up-and-go *n* (U) *inf* tonus *m*.

get-well card *n* carte *f* de vœux de prompt rétablissement.

geyser ['giːzər] *n* **-1.** [hot spring] geyser *m*. **-2.** *Br* [water heater] chauffe-eau *m inv*.

Ghana ['gɑːnə] *n* Ghana *m*; **in ~** au Ghana.

Ghan(a)ian [gɑːˈneıən] ◇ *adj* ghanéen(enne). ◇ *n* Ghanéen *m*, -enne *f*.

ghastly ['gɑːstlı] (*compar* -**ier**, *superl* -**iest**) *adj* **-1.** *inf* [very bad, unpleasant] épouvantable; **to feel/look ~** être dans un état/avoir une mine épouvantable. **-2.** [horrifying, macabre] effroyable.

gherkin ['gɜːkın] *n* cornichon *m*.

ghetto ['getəʊ] (*pl* -**s** OR -**es**) *n* ghetto *m*.

ghetto blaster [-ˈblɑːstər] *n inf* grand radiocassette *m* portatif.

ghost [gəʊst] ◇ *n* [spirit] spectre *m*; **he doesn't have a ~ of a chance** il n'a pas l'ombre d'une chance. ◇ *vt* = **ghostwrite**.

ghostly ['gəʊstlɪ] (*compar* **-ier**, *superl* **-iest**) *adj* spectral(e).

ghost town *n* ville *f* fantôme.

ghostwrite ['gəʊstraɪt] (*pt* **-wrote**, *pp* **-written**) *vt* écrire à la place de l'auteur.

ghostwriter ['gəʊst,raɪtə'] *n* nègre *m*.

ghostwritten ['gəʊst,rɪtn] *pp* → **ghostwrite**.

ghostwrote ['gəʊstrəʊt] *pt* → **ghostwrite**.

ghoul [guːl] *n* **-1.** [spirit] goule *f*. **-2.** *pej* [ghoulish person] personne *f* macabre.

ghoulish ['guːlɪʃ] *adj* macabre.

GHQ (*abbr of* **general headquarters**) *n* GQG *m*.

GI (*abbr of* **government issue**) *n* GI *m*.

giant ['dʒaɪənt] ◇ *adj* géant(e). ◇ *n* géant *m*.

giant-size(d) *adj* géant(e).

gibber ['dʒɪbə'] *vi* bredouiller.

gibberish ['dʒɪbərɪʃ] *n* (*U*) charabia *m*, inepties *fpl*.

gibbon ['gɪbən] *n* gibbon *m*.

gibe [dʒaɪb] ◇ *n* insulte *f*. ◇ *vi*: **to ~ at sb/sthg** insulter qqn/qqch.

giblets ['dʒɪblɪts] *npl* abats *mpl*.

Gibraltar [dʒɪ'brɔːltə'] *n* Gibraltar *m*; **in ~** à Gibraltar; **the Rock of ~** le rocher de Gibraltar.

giddy ['gɪdɪ] (*compar* **-ier**, *superl* **-iest**) *adj* [dizzy]: **to feel ~** avoir la tête qui tourne.

gift [gɪft] *n* **-1.** [present] cadeau *m*. **-2.** [talent] don *m*; **to have a ~ for sthg/for doing sthg** avoir un don pour qqch/pour faire qqch; **the ~ of the gab** le bagou.

GIFT [gɪft] (*abbr of* **gamete in fallopian transfer**) *n* fivete *f*.

gift certificate *Am* = **gift token**.

gifted ['gɪftɪd] *adj* doué(e).

gift token, **gift voucher** *n Br* chèque-cadeau *m*.

gift-wrapped [-ræpt] *adj* sous emballage-cadeau.

gig [gɪg] *n inf* [concert] concert *m*.

gigabyte ['gaɪgəbaɪt] *n* COMPUT giga-octet *m*.

gigantic [dʒaɪ'gæntɪk] *adj* énorme, gigantesque.

giggle ['gɪgl] ◇ *n* **-1.** [laugh] gloussement *m*. **-2.** *Br inf* [fun]: **to be a ~** être marrant(e) OR tordant(e); **to have a ~** bien s'amuser. ◇ *vi* [laugh] glousser.

giggly ['gɪglɪ] (*compar* **-ier**, *superl* **-iest**) *adj* qui pouffe.

GIGO ['gaɪgəʊ] (*abbr of* **garbage in, garbage out**) COMPUT qualité à l'entrée = qualité à la sortie.

gigolo ['ʒɪgələʊ] (*pl* **-s**) *n pej* gigolo *m*.

gigot ['ʒiːgəʊ] *n* gigot *m*.

gilded ['gɪldɪd] *adj* = **gilt**.

gill [dʒɪl] *n* [unit of measurement] = 0,142 litre, quart *m* de pinte.

gills [gɪlz] *npl* [of fish] branchies *fpl*.

gilt [gɪlt] ◇ *adj* [covered in gold] doré(e). ◇ *n* (*U*) [gold layer] dorure *f*.

◆ **gilts** *npl* FIN valeurs *fpl* de père de famille.

gilt-edged [-edʒd] *adj* FIN de père de famille.

gimme ['gɪmɪ] *inf* = **give me**.

gimmick ['gɪmɪk] *n pej* artifice *m*.

gin [dʒɪn] *n* gin *m*; **~ and tonic** gin tonic.

ginger ['dʒɪndʒə'] ◇ *n* **-1.** [root] gingembre *m*. **-2.** [powder] gingembre *m* en poudre. ◇ *adj Br* [colour] roux (rousse).

ginger ale *n* boisson gazeuse au gingembre.

ginger beer *n* boisson non-alcoolisée au gingembre.

gingerbread ['dʒɪndʒəbred] *n* pain *m* d'épice.

ginger group *n Br* groupe *m* de pression.

ginger-haired [-heəd] *adj* roux (rousse).

gingerly ['dʒɪndʒəlɪ] *adv* avec précaution.

gingham ['gɪŋəm] *n* [cloth] vichy *m*.

gingivitis [,dʒɪndʒɪ'vaɪtɪs] *n* gingivite *f*.

ginseng ['dʒɪnseŋ] *n* ginseng *m*.

gipsy ['dʒɪpsɪ] (*pl* **-ies**) ◇ *adj* gitan(e). ◇ *n* gitan *m*, -e *f*; *Br pej* bohémien *m*, -ienne *f*.

giraffe [dʒɪ'rɑːf] (*pl inv* OR **-s**) *n* girafe *f*.

gird [gɜːd] (*pt & pp* **-ed** OR **girt**) *vt* → **loin**.

girder ['gɜːdə'] *n* poutrelle *f*.

girdle ['gɜːdl] *n* [corset] gaine *f*.

girl [gɜːl] *n* **-1.** [gen] fille *f*. **-2.** [girlfriend] petite amie *f*.

girl Friday *n* aide *f*.

girlfriend ['gɜːlfrend] *n* **-1.** [female lover] petite amie *f*. **-2.** [female friend] amie *f*.

girl guide *Br*, **girl scout** *Am n* éclaireuse *f*, guide *f*.

◆ **Girl Guides** *n*: **the Girl Guides** les Guides *fpl*.

girlie magazine ['gɜːlɪ-] *n inf* magazine *m* érotique OR déshabillé.

girlish ['gɜːlɪʃ] *adj* de petite fille.

girl scout *Am* = **girl guide**.

giro ['dʒaɪrəʊ] *n Br* **-1.** (*U*) [system] virement *m* postal. **-2.** **~ (cheque)** chèque *m* d'indemnisation *f* (chômage OR maladie).

girt [gɜ:t] *pt & pp* → **gird**.

girth [gɜ:θ] *n* **-1.** [circumference - of tree] circonférence *f*; [- of person] tour *m* de taille. **-2.** [of horse] sangle *f*.

gist [dʒɪst] *n* substance *f*; **to get the ~ of sthg** comprendre OR saisir l'essentiel de qqch.

give [gɪv] (*pt* gave, *pp* given) ◇ *vt* **-1.** [gen] donner; [message] transmettre; [attention, time] consacrer; **to ~ sb/sthg sthg** donner qqch à qqn/qqch; **to ~ sb pleasure/a fright/a smile** faire plaisir/peur/un sourire à qqn; **to ~ sb a look** jeter un regard à qqn; **to ~ a shrug** hausser les épaules; **to ~ a sigh** pousser un soupir; **to ~ a speech** faire un discours. **-2.** [as present]: **to ~ sb sthg, to ~ sthg to sb** donner qqch à qqn, offrir qqch à qqn. **-3.** [pay]: **how much did you ~ for it?** combien l'avez-vous payé? **-4.** *phr*: **I was given to believe OR understand that ...** *fml* on m'a fait comprendre que ...; **I'd ~ anything OR my right arm to do that** je donnerais n'importe quoi OR très cher pour faire ça. ◇ *vi* [collapse, break] céder, s'affaisser. ◇ *n* [elasticity] élasticité *f*, souplesse *f*.

◆ **give or take** *prep*: **~ or take a day/£10** à un jour/10 livres près.

◆ **give away** *vt sep* **-1.** [get rid of] donner. **-2.** [reveal] révéler.

◆ **give back** *vt sep* [return] rendre.

◆ **give in** *vi* **-1.** [admit defeat] abandonner, se rendre. **-2.** [agree unwillingly]: **to ~ in to sthg** céder à qqch.

◆ **give off** *vt fus* [smell] exhaler; [smoke] faire; [heat] produire.

◆ **give out** ◇ *vt sep* [distribute] distribuer. ◇ *vi* [supplies] s'épuiser; [car] lâcher.

◆ **give over** ◇ *vt sep* [dedicate]: **to be given over to** [subj: time] être consacré(e) à; [subj: building] être réservé(e) à. ◇ *vi Br inf* [stop]: **~ over!** arrête!

◆ **give up** ◇ *vt sep* **-1.** [stop] renoncer à; **to ~ up drinking/smoking** arrêter de boire/de fumer. **-2.** [surrender]: **to ~ o.s. up (to sb)** se rendre (à qqn). ◇ *vi* abandonner, se rendre.

◆ **give up on** *vt fus* [abandon] laisser tomber.

give-and-take *n* (*U*) [compromise] concessions *fpl* de part et d'autre.

giveaway ['gɪvə,weɪ] ◇ *adj* **-1.** [tell-tale] révélateur(trice). **-2.** [very cheap] dérisoire. ◇ *n* [tell-tale sign] signe *m* révélateur.

given ['gɪvn] ◇ *pp* → **give**. ◇ *adj* **-1.** [set, fixed] convenu(e), fixé(e); **at any ~ time** à un moment donné. **-2.** [prone]: **to be ~ to sthg/to doing sthg** être enclin(e) à qqch/à faire qqch. ◇ *prep* étant donné; **~ that** étant donné que.

given name *n Am* prénom *m*.

giver ['gɪvər] *n* donneur *m*, -euse *f*.

glacé cherry ['glæseɪ-] *n* cerise *f* confite.

glacial ['gleɪsjəl] *adj* **-1.** [of glacier] glaciaire. **-2.** [unfriendly] glacial(e).

glacier ['glæsjər] *n* glacier *m*.

glad [glæd] (*compar* **-der**, *superl* **-dest**) *adj* **-1.** [happy, pleased] content(e); **to be ~about sthg** être content de qqch; **to be ~ that** être content que. **-2.** [willing]: **to be ~ to do sthg** faire qqch volontiers OR avec plaisir. **-3.** [grateful]: **to be ~ of sthg** être content(e) de qqch.

gladden ['glædn] *vt literary* réjouir.

glade [gleɪd] *n literary* clairière *f*.

gladiator ['glædɪeɪtər] *n* gladiateur *m*.

gladioli [,glædɪ'əʊlaɪ] *npl* glaïeuls *mpl*.

gladly ['glædlɪ] *adv* **-1.** [happily, eagerly] avec joie. **-2.** [willingly] avec plaisir.

glamor *Am* = **glamour**.

glamorize, -ise ['glæməraɪz] *vt* faire apparaître sous un jour séduisant.

glamorous ['glæmərəs] *adj* [person] séduisant(e); [appearance] élégant(e); [job, place] prestigieux(ieuse).

glamour *Br*, **glamor** *Am* ['glæmər] *n* [of person] charme *m*; [of appearance] élégance *f*, chic *m*; [of job, place] prestige *m*.

glance [glɑ:ns] ◇ *n* [quick look] regard *m*, coup d'œil *m*; **to cast OR take a ~ at sthg** jeter un coup d'œil à qqch; **at a ~** d'un coup d'œil; **at first ~** au premier coup d'œil. ◇ *vi* [look quickly]: **to ~ at sb/sthg** jeter un coup d'œil à qqn/qqch; **to ~ at OR through sthg** jeter un coup d'œil à OR sur qqch.

◆ **glance off** *vt fus* [subj: ball, bullet] ricocher sur.

glancing ['glɑ:nsɪŋ] *adj* de côté, oblique.

gland [glænd] *n* glande *f*.

glandular fever ['glændjʊlər-] *n* mononucléose *f* infectieuse.

glare [gleər] ◇ *n* **-1.** [scowl] regard *m* mauvais. **-2.** (*U*) [of headlights, publicity] lumière *f* aveuglante. ◇ *vi* **-1.** [scowl] jeter un regard mauvais; **to ~ at sb/sthg** regarder qqn/qqch d'un œil mauvais. **-2.** [sun, lamp] briller d'une lumière éblouissante.

glaring ['gleərɪŋ] *adj* **-1.** [very obvious] flagrant(e). **-2.** [blazing, dazzling] aveuglant(e).

glasnost ['glæznɒst] *n* glasnost *f*, transparence *f*.

glass [glɑ:s] ◇ *n* **-1.** [gen] verre *m*. **-2.** (*U*) [glassware] **verrerie** f. ◇ comp [bottle, jar] en OR de verre; [door, partition] vitré(e).

◆ **glasses** npl [spectacles] **lunettes** fpl.

glassblowing ['glɑːs,bləʊɪŋ] n **soufflage** m du verre.

glass fibre n (U) Br **fibre** f de verre.

glasshouse ['glɑːshaʊs, pl -haʊzɪz] n Br **serre** f.

glassware ['glɑːsweəʳ] n (U) **verrerie** f.

glassy ['glɑːsɪ] (compar -ier, superl -iest) adj -1. [smooth, shiny] **lisse comme un miroir**. -2. [blank, lifeless] **vitreux(euse)**.

Glaswegian [glæz'wiːdʒən] ◇ adj de Glasgow. ◇ n -1. **habitant** m, -e f de Glasgow. -2. [dialect] **dialecte** m de Glasgow.

glaucoma [glɔː'kəʊmə] n **glaucome** m.

glaze [gleɪz] ◇ n [on pottery] **vernis** m; [on pastry, flan] **glaçage** m. ◇ vt [pottery, tiles, bricks] **vernisser**; [pastry, flan] **glacer**.

◆ **glaze over** vi **devenir terne** OR **vitreux(euse)**.

glazed [gleɪzd] adj -1. [dull, bored] **terne, vitreux(euse)**. -2. [covered with shiny layer - pottery] **vernissé(e)**; [- pastry, flan] **glacé(e)**. -3. [with glass] **vitré(e)**.

glazier ['gleɪzjəʳ] n **vitrier** m.

GLC (abbr of **Greater London Council**) n ancien organe administratif du grand Londres.

gleam [gliːm] ◇ n [of gold] **reflet** m; [of fire, sunset, disapproval] **lueur** f. ◇ vi -1. [surface, object] **luire**. -2. [light, eyes] **briller**.

gleaming ['gliːmɪŋ] adj **brillant(e)**.

glean [gliːn] vt [gather] **glaner**.

glee [gliː] n (U) [joy] **joie** f, **jubilation** f.

gleeful ['gliːfʊl] adj **joyeux(euse)**.

glen [glen] n Scot **vallée** f.

glib [glɪb] (compar -ber, superl -best) adj pej [salesman, politician] **qui a du bagout**; [promise, excuse] **facile**.

glibly ['glɪblɪ] adv pej **trop facilement**.

glide [glaɪd] vi -1. [move smoothly - dancer, boat] **glisser sans effort**; [- person] **se mouvoir sans effort**. -2. [fly] **planer**.

glider ['glaɪdəʳ] n [plane] **planeur** m.

gliding ['glaɪdɪŋ] n [sport] **vol** m à voile.

glimmer ['glɪməʳ] ◇ n [faint light] **faible lueur** f; fig **signe** m, **lueur**; **a ~ of hope** une **lueur d'espoir**. ◇ vi **luire** OR **briller faiblement**.

glimpse [glɪmps] ◇ n -1. [look, sight] **aperçu** m; **to catch a ~ of sb/sthg** **apercevoir qqn/qqch, entrevoir qqn/qqch**. -2. [idea, perception] **idée** f. ◇ vt -1. [catch sight of] **apercevoir, entrevoir**. -2. [perceive] **pressentir**.

glint [glɪnt] ◇ n -1. [flash] **reflet** m. -2. [in eyes] **éclair** m. ◇ vi **étinceler**.

glisten ['glɪsn] vi **briller**.

glitch [glɪtʃ] n Am inf [in plan] **pépin** m.

glitter ['glɪtəʳ] ◇ n (U) **scintillement** m. ◇ vi -1. [object, light] **scintiller**. -2. [eyes] **briller**.

glittering ['glɪtərɪŋ] adj **brillant(e)**.

glitzy ['glɪtsɪ] (compar -ier, superl -iest) adj inf [glamorous] **chic**.

gloat [gləʊt] vi: **to ~ (over sthg)** **se réjouir (de qqch)**.

global ['gləʊbl] adj [worldwide] **mondial(e)**.

globally ['gləʊbəlɪ] adv **à l'échelle mondiale, mondialement**.

global warming [-'wɔːmɪŋ] n **réchauffement** m de la planète.

globe [gləʊb] n -1. [Earth]: **the ~** **la terre**. -2. [spherical map] **globe** m **terrestre**. -3. [spherical object] **globe** m.

globetrotter ['gləʊb,trɒtəʳ] n inf **globetrotter** m.

globule ['glɒbjuːl] n **gouttelette** f.

gloom [gluːm] n (U) -1. [darkness] **obscurité** f. -2. [unhappiness] **tristesse** f.

gloomy ['gluːmɪ] (compar -ier, superl -iest) adj -1. [room, sky, prospects] **sombre**. -2. [person, atmosphere, mood] **triste, lugubre**.

glorification [,glɔːrɪfɪ'keɪʃn] n **glorification** f.

glorified ['glɔːrɪfaɪd] adj pej: **it's just a ~ swimming pool** il ne s'agit que d'une vulgaire piscine.

glorify ['glɔːrɪfaɪ] (pt & pp -ied) vt **exalter**.

glorious ['glɔːrɪəs] adj -1. [beautiful, splendid] **splendide**. -2. [very enjoyable] **formidable**. -3. [successful, impressive] **magnifique**.

glory ['glɔːrɪ] (pl -ies) n -1. (U) [fame, admiration] **gloire** f. -2. (U) [beauty] **splendeur** f. -3. [best feature] **merveille** f.

◆ **glories** npl [triumphs] **triomphes** mpl.

◆ **glory in** vt fus [relish] **savourer**.

Glos (abbr of **Gloucestershire**) comté anglais.

gloss [glɒs] n -1. (U) [shine] **brillant** m, **lustre** m. -2. **~ (paint)** **peinture** f **brillante**.

◆ **gloss over** vt fus **passer sur**.

glossary ['glɒsərɪ] (pl -ies) n **glossaire** m.

glossy ['glɒsɪ] (compar -ier, superl -iest) adj -1. [hair, surface] **brillant(e)**. -2. [book, photo] **sur papier glacé**.

glossy magazine n **magazine** m de luxe.

glove [glʌv] n **gant** m.

glove compartment n **boîte** f à gants.

glove puppet n Br **marionnette** f.

glow [gləʊ] ◇ n (U) -1. [of fire, light, sunset] lueur f. -2. [of skin - because of heat, exercise] rougeur f; [- because of health] teint m rose et frais. -3. [feeling - of pride] sensation f; [- of anger] élan m; [- of shame, pleasure] sentiment m. ◇ vi -1. [shine out - fire] rougeoyer; [light, stars, eyes] flamboyer. -2. [shine in light] briller. -3. [with colour] flamboyer. -4. [flush]: to ~ (with) [heat] être rouge (de); [pleasure, health] rayonner (de).

glower ['glaʊəʳ] vi: to ~ (at) lancer des regards noirs (à).

glowing ['gləʊɪŋ] adj [very favourable] dithyrambique.

glow-worm n ver m luisant.

glucose ['glu:kəʊs] n glucose m.

glue [glu:] (cont glueing OR gluing) ◇ n (U) colle f. ◇ vt [stick with glue] coller; to ~ sthg to sthg coller qqch à OR avec qqch; to be ~d to the TV fig être rivé à la télé.

glue-sniffing [-ˌsnɪfɪŋ] n intoxication f à la colle.

glum [glʌm] (compar -mer, superl -mest) adj [unhappy] morne.

glut [glʌt] n surplus m.

gluten ['glu:tən] n gluten m.

glutinous ['glu:tɪnəs] adj glutineux(euse).

glutton ['glʌtn] n [greedy person] glouton m, -onne f; to be a ~ for punishment être maso, être masochiste.

gluttony ['glʌtənɪ] n gloutonnerie f.

glycerin ['glɪsərɪn], **glycerine** ['glɪsəri:n] n glycérine f.

gm (abbr of gram) g.

GMAT (abbr of Graduate Management Admissions Test) n test d'admission dans le 2e cycle de l'enseignement supérieur aux États-Unis.

GMB n important syndicat ouvrier britannique.

GMT (abbr of Greenwich Mean Time) n GMT m.

gnarled [nɑ:ld] adj [tree, hands] noueux(euse).

gnash [næʃ] vt: to ~ one's teeth grincer des dents.

gnat [næt] n moucheron m.

gnaw [nɔ:] ◇ vt [chew] ronger. ◇ vi [worry]: to ~ (away) at sb ronger qqn.

gnome [nəʊm] n gnome m, lutin m.

GNP (abbr of gross national product) n PNB m.

gnu [nu:] (pl inv OR -s) n gnou m.

go [gəʊ] (pt went, pp gone, pl goes) ◇ vi -1. [move, travel] aller; where are you ~ing? où vas-tu?; he's gone to Portugal il est allé au Portugal; we went by bus/train nous sommes allés en bus/par le train; where does this path ~? où mène ce chemin?; to ~ and do sthg aller faire qqch; to ~ swimming/shopping/jogging aller nager/faire les courses/faire du jogging; to ~ for a walk aller se promener, faire une promenade; to ~ to church/school/university aller à l'église/l'école/l'université; to ~ to work aller travailler OR à son travail; where do we ~ from here? fig qu'est-ce qu'on fait maintenant? -2. [depart] partir, s'en aller; I must ~, I have to ~ il faut que je m'en aille; what time does the bus ~? à quelle heure part le bus?; let's ~! allons-y! -3. [be or remain in a particular state]: to ~ hungry souffrir de la faim; we went in fear of our lives nous craignions pour notre vie; to ~ unpunished rester impuni. -4. [become] devenir; to ~ grey grisonner, devenir gris; to ~ mad devenir fou. -5. [pass - time] passer; the time went slowly/quickly le temps a passé lentement/a vite passé. -6. [progress] marcher, se dérouler; the conference went very smoothly la conférence s'est déroulée sans problème OR s'est très bien passée; to ~ well/badly aller bien/mal; how's it ~ing? inf comment ça va? -7. [function, work] marcher; the clock's stopped ~ing la pendule s'est arrêtée; the car won't ~ la voiture ne veut pas démarrer. -8. [indicating intention, expectation]: to be ~ing to do sthg aller faire qqch; what are you ~ing to do now? qu'est-ce que tu vas faire maintenant?; he said he was ~ing to be late il a prévenu qu'il allait arriver en retard; we're ~ing (to ~) to America in June on va (aller) en Amérique en juin; it's ~ing to rain/snow il va pleuvoir/neiger; she's ~ing to have a baby elle attend un bébé; it's not ~ing to be easy cela ne va pas être facile. -9. [bell, alarm] sonner. -10. [be spent] passer, partir; all my money goes on food and rent tout mon argent est passé OR parti en nourriture et en loyer. -11. [be given]: to ~ to aller à, être donné(e) à. -12. [be disposed of]: he'll have to ~ il va falloir le congédier OR le mettre à la porte; everything must ~ tout doit disparaître. -13. [stop working, break - light bulb, fuse] sauter; [- rope] céder. -14. [deteriorate - hearing, sight etc] baisser. -15. [match, be compatible]: to ~ (with) aller (avec); this blouse goes well with the skirt ce chemisier va bien avec la jupe; those colours don't really ~ ces couleurs ne vont pas bien ensemble; red wine goes well with meat le vin rouge se marie bien avec la viande. -16. [fit] aller; that goes at the bottom ça va au fond. -17. [belong] aller, se mettre; the plates ~ **in the cupboard** les assiettes vont OR se mettent dans le placard. **-18.** [in division]: **three into two won't** ~ deux divisé par trois n'y va pas. **-19.** [when referring to saying, story or song]: **how does that tune/song** ~? c'est quoi déjà l'air/la chanson ?; **as the saying goes** comme on dit, comme dit le proverbe. **-20.** *inf* [with negative - in giving advice] **now, don't** ~ **catching cold** ne va pas attraper froid surtout. **-21.** *inf* [expressing irritation, surprise]: **now what's he gone and done?** qu'est-ce qu'il a fait encore?; **she's gone and bought a new car!** elle a été s'acheter une nouvelle voiture!; **you've gone and done it now!** eh bien cette fois-ci, on peut dire que tu en as fait une belle! **-22.** *phr*: **it just goes to show** c'est bien vrai, vous voyez bien; **it just goes to show that none of us is perfect** cela prouve bien que personne n'est parfait.

◇ *vt* [make noise of] faire; **the dog went "woof"** le chien a fait «oua-oua».

◇ *n* **-1.** [turn] tour *m*; **it's my** ~ c'est à moi (de jouer). **-2.** *inf* [attempt]: **to have a** ~ **(at sthg)** essayer (de faire qqch); **have a** ~! tente le coup!, vas-y! **-3.** *inf* [success]: **to make a** ~ **of sthg** réussir qqch. **-4.** *phr*: **to have a** ~ **at sb** *inf* s'en prendre à qqn, engueuler qqn; **to be on the** ~ *inf* être sur la brèche.

◆ **to go** *adv* **-1.** [remaining]: **there are only three days to** ~ il ne reste que trois jours. **-2.** *Am* [to take away] à emporter.

◆ **go about** ◇ *vt fus* **-1.** [perform]: **to** ~ **about one's business** vaquer à ses occupations. **-2.** [tackle] s'y prendre; **how do you intend** ~**ing about it?** comment comptes-tu faire OR t'y prendre? ◇ *vi* = **go around.**

◆ **go after** *vt fus* [person] courir après; [prize] viser; [job] essayer d'obtenir.

◆ **go against** *vt fus* **-1.** [conflict with] heurter, aller à l'encontre de. **-2.** [act contrary to] contrarier, s'opposer à. **-3.** [decision, public opinion] être défavorable à.

◆ **go ahead** *vi* **-1.** [proceed]: **to** ~ **ahead with sthg** mettre qqch à exécution; ~ **ahead!** allez-y! **-2.** [take place] avoir lieu.

◆ **go along** *vi* [proceed] avancer; **as you** ~ **along** au fur et à mesure; **he makes it up as he goes along** il invente au fur et à mesure.

◆ **go along with** *vt fus* [suggestion, idea] appuyer, soutenir; [person] suivre.

◆ **go around** *vi* **-1.** [behave in a certain way]: **she goes around putting everyone's back up** elle n'arrête pas de prendre les gens à rebrousse-poil; **there's no need to** ~ **around telling everyone** tu n'as pas besoin d'aller le crier sur les toits. **-2.** [frequent]: **to** ~ **around with sb** fréquenter qqn. **-3.** [spread] circuler, courir; **there's a rumour** ~**ing around about her** il court un bruit sur elle.

◆ **go back on** *vt fus* [one's word, promise] revenir sur.

◆ **go back to** *vt fus* **-1.** [return to activity] reprendre, se remettre à; **to** ~ **back to sleep** se rendormir. **-2.** [return to previous topic] revenir à. **-3.** [date from] remonter à, dater de.

◆ **go before** *vi*: **her new paintings were unlike anything that had gone before** ses nouveaux tableaux étaient complètement différents de ses précédents; **we wanted to forget what had gone before** nous voulions oublier ce qui s'était passé avant.

◆ **go by** ◇ *vi* [time] s'écouler, passer. ◇ *vt fus* **-1.** [be guided by] suivre. **-2.** [judge from] juger d'après.

◆ **go down** ◇ *vi* **-1.** [get lower - prices etc] baisser. **-2.** [be accepted] être accepté(e); **to** ~ **down well /badly** être bien/mal accueilli. **-3.** [sun] se coucher. **-4.** [tyre, balloon] se dégonfler. ◇ *vt fus* descendre.

◆ **go down with** *vt fus* [illness] attraper.

◆ **go for** *vt fus* **-1.** [choose] choisir. **-2.** [be attracted to] être attiré(e) par. **-3.** [attack] tomber sur, attaquer. **-4.** [try to obtain - job, record] essayer d'obtenir. **-5.** [be valid] s'appliquer à; **does that** ~ **for me too?** est-ce que cela vaut pour OR s'applique à moi aussi?

◆ **go in** *vi* entrer.

◆ **go in for** *vt fus* **-1.** [competition] prendre part à; [exam] se présenter à. **-2.** [take up as a profession] entrer dans. **-3.** [activity - enjoy] aimer; [- participate in] faire, s'adonner à.

◆ **go into** *vt fus* **-1.** [discuss, describe in detail]: **I'd rather not** ~ **into that now** je préférerais ne pas en parler pour le moment; **to** ~ **into detail** OR **details** entrer dans le détail OR les détails. **-2.** [investigate] étudier, examiner. **-3.** [take up as a profession] entrer dans. **-4.** [be put into]: **a lot of hard work went into that book** ce livre a demandé OR nécessité beaucoup de travail. **-5.** [begin]: **to** ~ **into a rage** se mettre en rage; **to** ~ **into a spin** [plane] tomber en vrille.

◆ **go off** ◇ *vi* **-1.** [explode] exploser. **-2.** [alarm] sonner. **-3.** [go bad - food] se gâter. **-4.** [lights, heating] s'éteindre. **-5.** [happen] se passer, se dérouler. ◇ *vt fus* [lose interest in] ne plus aimer.

◆ **go off with** ◇ *vt fus* prendre.

◆ **go on** ◇ *vi* **-1.** [take place, happen] se passer. **-2.** [heating etc] se mettre en marche. **-3.** [continue]: **to** ~ **on (doing)** continuer (à faire); **I can't ~ on!** je n'en peux plus!; **~ on** [continue talking] allez-y. **-4.** [proceed to further activity]: **to ~ on to sthg** passer à qqch; **to ~ on to do sthg** faire qqch après. **-5.** [proceed to another place]: **are you ~ing on to Richard's?** vous allez chez Richard après? **-6.** [go in advance] partir devant. **-7.** [talk for too long] parler à n'en plus finir; **to ~ on about sthg** ne pas arrêter de parler de qqch. **-8.** [pass - time] passer. ◇ *vt fus* [be guided by] se fonder sur. ◇ *excl* allez; **~ on, treat yourself** allez, fais-toi plaisir.

◆ **go on at** *vt fus* [nag] harceler.

◆ **go out** *vi* **-1.** [leave] sortir. **-2.** [for amusement]: **to ~ out (with sb)** sortir (avec qqn). **-3.** [light, fire, cigarette] s'éteindre. **-4.** [stop being fashionable] passer de mode.

◆ **go over** *vt fus* **-1.** [examine] examiner, vérifier. **-2.** [repeat, review] repasser.

◆ **go over to** *vt fus* **-1.** [change to] adopter, passer à. **-2.** [change sides to] passer à; **to ~ over to the other side** changer de parti. **-3.** RADIO & TV passer l'antenne à.

◆ **go round** *vi* **-1.** [be enough for everyone] suffire; **there's just enough to ~ round** il y en a juste assez pour tout le monde. **-2.** [revolve] tourner; *see also* **go around.**

◆ **go through** ◇ *vt fus* **-1.** [experience] subir, souffrir. **-2.** [spend] dépenser. **-3.** [study, search through] examiner; **she went through his pockets** elle lui a fait les poches, elle a fouillé dans ses poches. **-4.** [a list - reading] lire; [- speaking] lire à haute voix. ◇ *vi* [be approved] passer, être accepté(e).

◆ **go through with** *vt fus* [action, threat] aller jusqu'au bout de.

◆ **go towards** *vt fus* contribuer à.

◆ **go under** *vi lit* & *fig* couler.

◆ **go up** ◇ *vi* **-1.** [gen] monter. **-2.** [prices] augmenter. **-3.** [be built] se construire. **-4.** [explode] exploser, sauter. **-5.** [burst into flames]: **to ~ up (in flames)** prendre feu, s'enflammer. **-6.** [be uttered]: **a cheer went up** on a applaudi. ◇ *vt fus* monter.

◆ **go with** *vt fus* aller avec.

◆ **go without** ◇ *vt fus* se passer de. ◇ *vi* s'en passer.

goad [gəʊd] *vt* [provoke] talonner; **to ~ sb into doing sthg** talonner qqn jusqu'à ce qu'il fasse qqch.

go-ahead ◇ *adj* [dynamic] dynamique. ◇ *n* (U) [permission] feu *m* vert; **to give sb the ~ (for sthg)** donner à qqn le feu vert (pour qqch).

goal [gəʊl] *n* but *m*; **to score a ~** SPORT marquer un but.

goalie ['gəʊlı] *n inf* gardien *m* (de but).

goalkeeper ['gəʊl,kiːpər] *n* gardien *m* de but.

goalless ['gəʊllıs] *adj*: **~ draw** match *m* sans but marqué.

goalmouth ['gəʊlmaʊθ *pl* -maʊðz] *n* but *m*.

goalpost ['gəʊlpəʊst] *n* poteau *m* de but.

goat [gəʊt] *n* chèvre *f*; **to act the ~** Br inf faire l'imbécile.

gob [gɒb] (*pt* & *pp* **-bed**, *cont* **-bing**) *v inf* ◇ *n Br* [mouth] gueule *f*. ◇ *vi* [spit] mollarder.

gobble ['gɒbl] *vt* engloutir.

◆ **gobble down, gobble up** *vt sep* engloutir.

gobbledygook ['gɒbldıguːk] *n* **-1.** [pompous official language] jargon *m*. **-2.** *inf* [nonsense] charabia *m*.

go-between *n* intermédiaire *mf*.

Gobi ['gəʊbı] *n*: **the ~ Desert** le désert de Gobi.

goblet ['gɒblıt] *n* verre *m* à pied.

goblin ['gɒblın] *n* lutin *m*, farfadet *m*.

gobsmacked ['gɒbsmækt] *adj Br inf* bouche bée (*inv*).

go-cart = **go-kart**.

god [gɒd] *n* dieu *m*, divinité *f*.

◆ **God** ◇ *n* Dieu *m*; **God knows** Dieu seul le sait; **for God's sake** pour l'amour de Dieu; **thank God** Dieu merci. ◇ *excl*: **(my) God!** mon Dieu!

◆ **gods** *npl Br inf* [in theatre]: **the ~s** le poulailler.

godchild ['gɒdtʃaɪld] (*pl* **-children** [-,tʃɪldrən]) *n* filleul *m*, -e *f*.

goddam(n) ['gɒdæm] *inf* ◇ *adj* foutu(e). ◇ *excl* bordel!

goddaughter ['gɒd,dɔːtər] *n* filleule *f*.

goddess ['gɒdıs] *n* déesse *f*.

godfather ['gɒd,fɑːðər] *n* parrain *m*.

godforsaken ['gɒdfə,seɪkn] *adj* morne, désolé(e).

godmother ['gɒd,mʌðər] *n* marraine *f*.

godparents ['gɒd,peərənts] *npl* parrain et marraine *mpl*.

godsend ['gɒdsend] *n* aubaine *f*.

godson ['gɒdsʌn] *n* filleul *m*.

goes [gəʊz] → **go**.

gofer ['gəʊfər] *n Am inf* larbin *m*.

go-getter [-'getər] *n* battant *m*, -e *f*.

goggle ['gɒgl] *vi*: **to ~ (at sb/sthg)** regarder (qqn/qqch) avec des yeux ronds.

◆ **goggles** *npl* lunettes *fpl*.

go-go dancer *n* danseuse *f* de cabaret.

going ['gəʊıŋ] ◇ *n* (U) **-1.** [rate of advance] allure *f*; **that was good ~** ça a été vite. **-2.** [travel conditions] conditions *fpl*. ◇ *adj* **-1.** *Br* [available] disponible; **you've got a lot ~ for you** vous avez beaucoup d'atouts. **-2.** [rate, salary] en vigueur.

going concern *n* affaire *f* qui marche.

goings-on *npl* événements *mpl*, histoires *fpl*.

go-kart [-kɑːt] *n* kart *m*.

Golan Heights ['gəʊ,læn-] *npl*: **the ~** le plateau du Golan.

gold [gəʊld] ◇ *n* **-1.** (*U*) [metal, jewellery] or *m*; **to be as good as ~** être sage comme une image, être mignon tout plein. **-2.** [medal] médaille *f* d'or. ◇ *comp* [made of gold] en or. ◇ *adj* [gold-coloured] doré(e).

golden ['gəʊldən] *adj* **-1.** [made of gold] en or. **-2.** [gold-coloured] doré(e).

golden age *n* âge *m* d'or.

golden eagle *n* aigle *m* royal.

golden handshake *n* prime *f* de départ.

golden opportunity *n* occasion *f* en or.

golden retriever *n* (golden) retriever *m*.

golden rule *n* règle *f* d'or.

golden wedding *n* noces *fpl* d'or.

goldfish ['gəʊldfɪʃ] (*pl inv*) *n* poisson *m* rouge.

goldfish bowl *n* bocal *m* (à poissons).

gold leaf *n* (*U*) feuille *f* d'or.

gold medal *n* médaille *f* d'or.

goldmine ['gəʊldmaɪn] *n* lit & fig mine *f* d'or.

gold-plated [-'pleɪtɪd] *adj* plaqué(e) or.

goldsmith ['gəʊldsmɪθ] *n* orfèvre *m*.

gold standard *n*: **the ~** l'étalon-or *m*.

golf [gɒlf] *n* golf *m*.

golf ball *n* **-1.** [for golf] balle *f* de golf. **-2.** [for typewriter] boule *f*.

golf club *n* [stick, place] club *m* de golf.

golf course *n* terrain *m* de golf.

golfer ['gɒlfə^r] *n* golfeur *m*, -euse *f*.

golly ['gɒlɪ] *excl inf dated* mince!

gondola ['gɒndələ] *n* [boat] gondole *f*.

gondolier [,gɒndə'lɪə^r] *n* gondolier *m*.

gone [gɒn] ◇ *pp* → **go**. ◇ *adj* [no longer here] parti(e). ◇ *prep*: **it's ~ ten (o'clock)** il est dix heures passées.

gong [gɒŋ] *n* gong *m*.

gonna ['gɒnə] *inf* = **going to**.

gonorrh(o)ea [,gɒnə'rɪə] *n* blennorragie *f*.

goo [guː] *n* (*U*) *inf* truc *m* poisseux.

good [gʊd] (*compar* **better**, *superl* **best**) ◇ *adj* **-1.** [gen] bon (bonne); **it's ~ to see you again** ça fait plaisir de te revoir; **it feels ~ to be outside** ça fait du bien d'être dehors; **to be ~ at sthg** être bon en qqch; **to be ~**

with [animals, children] savoir y faire avec; [one's hands] être habile de; **it's ~ for you** c'est bon pour toi OR pour la santé; **to feel ~** [person] se sentir bien; **it's ~ that ...** c'est bien que ...; ~! très bien! **-2.** [kind - person] gentil(ille); **to be ~ to sb** être très attentionné envers qqn; **to be ~ enough to do sthg** avoir l'amabilité de faire qqch. **-3.** [well-behaved - child] sage; [- behaviour] correct(e); **be ~!** sois sage, tiens-toi tranquille. **-4.** [attractive - legs, figure] joli(e). **-5.** *phr*: **it's a ~ job** OR **thing (that) ...** c'est très bien que ..., c'est une bonne chose que ...; **~ for you!** très bien!; **to give as ~ as one gets** rendre la pareille; **to make sthg ~** réparer qqch.

◇ *n* **-1.** (*U*) [benefit] bien *m*; **for the ~ of** pour le bien de; **for your own ~** pour ton/votre bien; **it will do him ~** ça lui fera du bien. **-2.** [use] utilité *f*; **what's the ~ of doing that?** à quoi bon faire ça?; **it's no ~** ça ne sert à rien; **it's no ~ crying/worrying** ça ne sert à rien de pleurer/de s'en faire; **will this be any ~?** cela peut-il faire l'affaire? **-3.** (*U*) [morally correct behaviour] bien *m*; **to be up to no ~** préparer un sale coup.

◆ **goods** *npl* [merchandise] marchandises *fpl*, articles *mpl*; **to come up with** OR **deliver the ~s** *Br inf* tenir ses promesses.

◆ **as good as** *adv* pratiquement, pour ainsi dire.

◆ **for good** *adv* [forever] pour de bon, définitivement.

◆ **good afternoon** *excl* bonjour!

◆ **good day** *excl* bonjour!

◆ **good evening** *excl* bonsoir!

◆ **good morning** *excl* bonjour!

◆ **good night** *excl* bonsoir!; [at bedtime] bonne nuit!

goodbye [,gʊd'baɪ] ◇ *excl* au revoir! ◇ *n* au revoir *m*.

good-for-nothing ◇ *adj* bon (bonne) à rien. ◇ *n* bon *m*, bonne *f* à rien.

Good Friday *n* vendredi *m* saint.

good-humoured [-'hjuːməd] *adj* [person] de bonne humeur; [smile, rivalry] bon enfant.

good-looking [-'lʊkɪŋ] *adj* [person] beau (belle).

good-natured [-'neɪtʃəd] *adj* [person] d'un naturel aimable; [rivalry, argument] bon enfant.

goodness ['gʊdnɪs] ◇ *n* (*U*) **-1.** [kindness] bonté *f*. **-2.** [nutritive quality] valeur *f* nutritive. ◇ *excl*: **(my) ~!** mon Dieu!, Seigneur!; **for ~ sake!** par pitié!, pour l'amour de Dieu!; **thank ~!** grâce à Dieu!

goods train *n Br* train *m* de marchandises.

good-tempered [-'tempəd] *adj* [meeting, discussion] agréable; [person] qui a bon caractère.

good turn *n*: to do sb a ~ rendre un service à qqn.

goodwill [,gʊd'wɪl] *n* bienveillance *f*.

goody ['gʊdɪ] (*pl* -ies) *inf* ◇ *n* [person] bon *m*. ◇ *excl* chouette!
◆ **goodies** *npl inf* -1. [delicious food] friandises *fpl*. -2. [desirable objects] merveilles *fpl*, trésors *mpl*.

gooey ['guːɪ] (*compar* gooier, *superl* gooiest) *adj inf* [sticky] qui colle; *pej* poisseux(euse).

goof [guːf] *Am inf* ◇ *n* [mistake] gaffe *f*. ◇ *vi* faire une gaffe.
◆ **goof off** *vi Am inf* tirer au flanc.

goofy ['guːfɪ] (*compar* -ier, *superl* -iest) *adj inf* [silly] dingue.

goose [guːs] (*pl* geese) *n* [bird] oie *f*.

gooseberry ['gʊzbərɪ] (*pl* -ies) *n* -1. [fruit] groseille *f* à maquereau. -2. *Br inf* [third person]: to play ~ tenir la chandelle.

gooseflesh ['guːsfleʃ] *n*, **goose pimples** *Br*, **goosebumps** *Am* ['guːsbʌmps] *npl* chair *f* de poule.

goosestep ['guːstep] (*pt* & *pp* -ped, *cont* -ping) ◇ *n* pas *m* de l'oie. ◇ *vi* faire le pas de l'oie.

GOP (*abbr of* **Grand Old Party**) *n* le parti républicain aux États-Unis.

gopher ['gəʊfər] *n* geomys *m*.

gore [gɔːr] ◇ *n* (U) *literary* [blood] sang *m*. ◇ *vt* encorner.

gorge [gɔːdʒ] ◇ *n* gorge *f*, défilé *m*. ◇ *vt*: to ~ o.s. on OR with sthg se bourrer OR se goinfrer de qqch. ◇ *vi* se goinfrer.

gorgeous ['gɔːdʒəs] *adj* divin(e); *inf* [good-looking] magnifique, splendide.

gorilla [gə'rɪlə] *n* gorille *m*.

gormless ['gɔːmlɪs] *adj Br inf* bêta (bêtasse).

gorse [gɔːs] *n* (U) ajonc *m*.

gory ['gɔːrɪ] (*compar* -ier, *superl* -iest) *adj* sanglant(e).

gosh [gɒʃ] *excl inf* ça alors!

go-slow *n Br* grève *f* du zèle.

gospel ['gɒspl] ◇ *n* [doctrine] évangile *m*; ~ (truth) parole *f* d'évangile. ◇ *comp* [singer] de gospel; ~ song OR music gospel *m*.
◆ **Gospel** *n* Évangile *m*.

gossamer ['gɒsəmər] *n* (U) -1. [spider's thread] fils *mpl* de la Vierge. -2. [material] étoffe *f* légère.

gossip ['gɒsɪp] ◇ *n* -1. [conversation] bavardage *m*; *pej* commérage *m*. -2. [person] commère *f*. ◇ *vi* [talk] bavarder, papoter; *pej* cancaner.

gossip column *n* échos *mpl*.

got [gɒt] *pt* & *pp* → get.

Gothic ['gɒθɪk] *adj* gothique.

gotta ['gɒtə] *inf* = got to.

gotten ['gɒtn] *Am pp* → get.

gouge [gaʊdʒ]
◆ **gouge out** *vt sep* [hole] creuser; [eyes] arracher.

goulash ['guːlæʃ] *n* goulache *m*, goulasch *m*.

gourd [gʊəd] *n* gourde *f*.

gourmet ['gʊəmeɪ] ◇ *n* gourmet *m*. ◇ *comp* [food, restaurant] gastronomique; [cook] gastronome.

gout [gaʊt] *n* (U) goutte *f*.

govern ['gʌvən] ◇ *vt* -1. [gen] gouverner. -2. [control] régir. ◇ *vi* POL gouverner.

governable ['gʌvnəbl] *adj* gouvernable.

governess ['gʌvnɪs] *n* gouvernante *f*.

governing ['gʌvnɪŋ] *adj* gouvernant(e).

governing body *n* conseil *m* d'administration.

government ['gʌvnmənt] ◇ *n* gouvernement *m*; the art of ~ l'art de gouverner. ◇ *comp* du gouvernement.

governmental [,gʌvn'mentl] *adj* gouvernemental(e).

government stock *n* (U) fonds *mpl* publics OR d'État.

governor ['gʌvənər] *n* -1. POL gouverneur *m*. -2. [of school] ≃ membre *m* du conseil d'établissement; [of bank] gouverneur *m*. -3. [of prison] directeur *m*.

governor-general (*pl* **governor-generals** OR **governors-general**) *n* gouverneur *m* général.

govt (*abbr of* **government**) gvt.

gown [gaʊn] *n* -1. [for woman] robe *f*. -2. [for surgeon] blouse *f*; [for judge, academic] robe *f*, toge *f*.

GP *n abbr of* **general practitioner**.

GPMU (*abbr of* **Graphical, Paper and Media Union**) *n* syndicat britannique des ouvriers du livre.

GPO (*abbr of* **General Post Office**) *n* -1. [in UK] ancien nom des services postaux britanniques. -2. [in US] les services postaux américains.

gr. *abbr of* **gross**.

grab [græb] (*pt* & *pp* -bed, *cont* -bing) ◇ *vt* -1. [seize] saisir. -2. *inf* [sandwich] avaler en vitesse; to ~ a few hours' sleep dormir quelques heures. -3. *inf* [appeal to] emballer. ◇ *vi*: to ~ at sthg faire un geste pour attraper qqch. ◇ *n*: to make a ~ at OR for sthg faire un geste pour attraper qqch.

grace [greɪs] ◇ *n* **-1.** [elegance] grâce *f.* **-2.** [graciousness]: **to do sthg with good ~** faire qqch de bonne grâce; **to have the ~ to do sthg** avoir la bonne grâce de faire qqch. **-3.** (U) [extra time] répit *m.* **-4.** [prayer] grâces *fpl.* ◇ *vt fml* **-1.** [honour] honorer de sa présence. **-2.** [decorate] orner, décorer.

graceful ['greɪsful] *adj* gracieux(ieuse), élégant(e).

graceless ['greɪslɪs] *adj* **-1.** [ugly] sans attrait. **-2.** [ill-mannered] grossier(ière), peu élégant(e).

gracious ['greɪʃəs] ◇ *adj* **-1.** [polite] courtois(e). **-2.** [elegant] élégant(e). ◇ *excl*: **(good) ~!** juste ciel!

graciously ['greɪʃəslɪ] *adv* [politely] poliment.

gradation [grə'deɪʃn] *n* gradation *f.*

grade [greɪd] ◇ *n* **-1.** [quality of worker] catégorie *f*; [of wool, paper] qualité *f*; [of petrol] type *m*; [of eggs] calibre *m*; **to make the ~** y arriver, être à la hauteur. **-2.** *Am* [class] classe *f.* **-3.** [mark] note *f.* ◇ *vt* **-1.** [classify] classer. **-2.** [mark, assess] noter.

grade crossing *n Am* passage *m* à niveau.

grade school *n Am* école *f* primaire.

gradient ['greɪdjənt] *n* pente *f*, inclinaison *f.*

gradual ['grædʒʊəl] *adj* graduel(elle), progressif(ive).

gradually ['grædʒʊəlɪ] *adv* graduellement, petit à petit.

graduate [*n* 'grædʒʊət, *vb* 'grædjʊeɪt] ◇ *n* **-1.** [from university] diplômé *m*, -e *f.* **-2.** *Am* [of high school] ≃ titulaire *mf* du baccalauréat. ◇ *comp Am* [postgraduate] de troisième cycle. ◇ *vi* **-1.** [from university]: **to ~ (from)** ≃ obtenir son diplôme (à). **-2.** *Am* [from high school]: **to ~ (from)** ≃ obtenir son baccalauréat (à). **-3.** [progress]: **to ~ from sthg (to sthg)** passer de qqch (à qqch).

graduated ['grædjʊeɪtɪd] *adj* [ruler etc] gradué(e); [tax] progressif(ive); **~ pension scheme** régime *m* de retraite proportionnelle.

graduate school *n Am* troisième cycle *m* d'université.

graduation [,grædʒʊ'eɪʃn] *n* (U) **-1.** [ceremony] remise *f* des diplômes. **-2.** [completion of course] obtention *f* de son diplôme.

graffiti [grə'fiːtɪ] *n* (U) graffiti *mpl.*

graft [grɑːft] ◇ *n* **-1.** [from plant] greffe *f*, greffon *m.* **-2.** MED greffe *f.* **-3.** *Br* [hard work] boulot *m.* **-4.** *Am inf* [corruption] graissage *m* de patte. ◇ *vt* **-1.** [plant, skin] greffer; **to ~ sthg onto sthg** greffer qqch sur qqch. **-2.** *fig* [idea, system] incorporer, inté-

grer; **to ~ sthg onto sthg** incorporer qqch à qqch, intégrer qqch dans qqch.

grain [greɪn] *n* **-1.** [gen] grain *m.* **-2.** (U) [crops] céréales *fpl*, grain *m*, grains *mpl.* **-3.** (U) [pattern - in wood] fil *m*; [- in material] grain *m*; [- in stone, marble] veines *fpl*; **it goes against the ~ (for me)** cela va à l'encontre de mes principes.

gram [græm] *n* gramme *m.*

grammar ['græmə'] *n* grammaire *f.*

grammar school *n* [in UK] ≃ lycée *m*; [in US] école *f* primaire.

GRAMMAR SCHOOL:
En Grande-Bretagne, le terme 'grammar school' désigne une école secondaire recevant une aide de l'État mais pouvant être privée, réputée dispenser un enseignement de qualité de type traditionnel et préparant aux études supérieures. L'admission se fait sur concours ou sur dossier. Moins de cinq pour cent des élèves du pays fréquentent ce type d'école

grammatical [grə'mætɪkl] *adj* grammatical(e).

gramme [græm] *Br* = **gram.**

gramophone ['græməfəun] *n dated* gramophone *m*, phonographe *m.*

gran [græn] *n Br inf* mamie *f*, mémé *f.*

Granada [grə'nɑːdə] *n* Grenade.

granary ['grænərɪ] (*pl* **-ies**) *n* grenier *m* (à grain).

grand [grænd] ◇ *adj* **-1.** [impressive] grandiose, imposant(e). **-2.** [ambitious] grand(e). **-3.** [important] important(e); [socially] distingué(e). **-4.** *inf dated* [excellent] sensationnel(elle), formidable. ◇ *n inf* [thousand pounds] mille livres *fpl*; [thousand dollars] mille dollars *mpl.*

grand(d)ad ['grændæd] *n inf* papi *m*, pépé *m.*

Grand Canyon *n*: **the ~** le Grand Canyon.

grandchild ['græntʃaɪld] (*pl* **-children** [-,tʃɪldrən]) *n* [boy] petit-fils *m*; [girl] petite-fille *f.*

◆ **grandchildren** *npl* petits-enfants *mpl.*

granddaughter ['græn,dɔːtə'] *n* petite-fille *f.*

grand duke *n* grand duc *m.*

grandeur ['grændʒə'] *n* **-1.** [splendour] splendeur *f*, magnificence *f.* **-2.** [status] éminence *f.*

grandfather ['grænd,fɑːðə'] *n* grand-père *m.*

grandfather clock *n* horloge *f*, pendule *f* de parquet.

grandiose ['grændɪəʊz] *adj pej* [building] prétentieux(ieuse); [plan] extravagant(e).

grand jury *n Am* tribunal *m* d'accusation.

grandma ['grænmɑː] *n inf* mamie *f*, mémé *f*.

grand master *n* grand maître *m*.

grandmother ['græn,mʌðə'] *n* grand-mère *f*.

Grand National *n*: the ~ *la plus importante course d'obstacles de Grande-Bretagne, se déroulant à Aintree dans la banlieue de Liverpool.*

grandpa ['grænpɑː] *n inf* papi *m*, pépé *m*.

grandparents ['græn,peərnts] *npl* grands-parents *mpl*.

grand piano *n* piano *m* à queue.

grand prix [,grɒn'priː] (*pl* **grands prix** [,grɒn'priː]) *n* grand prix *m*.

grand slam *n* SPORT grand chelem *m*.

grandson ['grænsʌn] *n* petit-fils *m*.

grandstand ['grændstænd] *n* tribune *f*.

grand total *n* somme *f* globale, total *m* général.

granite ['grænɪt] *n* granit *m*.

granny ['grænɪ] (*pl* **-ies**) *n inf* mamie *f*, mémé *f*.

granny flat *n Br appartement indépendant dans une maison, pour y loger un parent âgé.*

granola [grə'nəʊlə] *n Am* müesli *m*.

grant [grɑːnt] ◇ *n* subvention *f*; [for study] bourse *f*.

◇ *vt* **-1.** [wish, appeal] accorder; [request] accéder à. **-2.** [admit] admettre, reconnaître; **I ~ (that) ...** je reconnais OR j'admets que .... **-3.** [give] accorder; **to take sb for ~ed** [not appreciate sb's help] penser que tout ce que qqn fait va de soi; [not value sb's presence] penser que qqn fait partie des meubles; **to take sthg for ~ed** [result, sb's agreement] considérer qqch comme acquis; **it is taken for ~ed that ...** cela semble aller de soi que ..., cela paraît normal OR tout naturel que ....

granulated sugar ['grænjʊleɪtɪd-] *n* sucre *m* cristallisé.

granule ['grænjuːl] *n* granule *m*; [of sugar] grain *m*.

grape [greɪp] *n* (grain *m* de) raisin *m*; **some ~s** du raisin; **a bunch of ~s** une grappe de raisin.

grapefruit ['greɪpfruːt] (*pl inv* OR **-s**) *n* pamplemousse *m*.

grape picking [-'pɪkɪŋ] *n* (U) vendange *f*, vendanges *fpl*.

grapevine ['greɪpvaɪn] *n* vigne *f*; **on the ~** *fig* par le téléphone arabe.

graph [grɑːf] *n* graphique *m*.

graphic ['græfɪk] *adj* **-1.** [vivid] vivant(e). **-2.** ART graphique.
◆ **graphics** *npl* graphique *f*; **computer ~s** infographie *f*.

graphic design *n* design *m* graphique.

graphic designer *n* graphiste *mf*.

graphic equalizer *n* égaliseur *m* graphique.

graphics card *n* COMPUT carte *f* graphique.

graphite ['græfaɪt] *n* (U) graphite *m*, mine *f* de plomb.

graphology [græ'fɒlədʒɪ] *n* graphologie *f*.

graph paper *n* (U) papier *m* millimétré.

grapple ['græpl]
◆ **grapple with** *vt fus* **-1.** [person, animal] lutter avec. **-2.** [problem] se débattre avec, se colleter avec.

grappling iron ['græplɪŋ-] *n* grappin *m*.

grasp [grɑːsp] ◇ *n* **-1.** [grip] prise *f*; **in** OR **within one's ~** *fig* à portée de la main. **-2.** [understanding] compréhension *f*; **to have a good ~ of sthg** avoir une bonne connaissance de qqch. ◇ *vt* **-1.** [grip, seize] saisir, empoigner. **-2.** [understand] saisir, comprendre. **-3.** [opportunity] saisir.

grasping ['grɑːspɪŋ] *adj pej* avide, cupide.

grass [grɑːs] ◇ *n* BOT & *drugs sl* herbe *f*. ◇ *vi Br crime sl* moucharder; **to ~ on sb** dénoncer qqn.

grasshopper ['grɑːs,hɒpə'] *n* sauterelle *f*.

grassland ['grɑːslænd] *n* prairie *f*.

grass roots ◇ *npl fig* base *f*. ◇ *comp* du peuple.

grass snake *n* couleuvre *f*.

grassy ['grɑːsɪ] (*compar* **-ier**, *superl* **-iest**) *adj* herbeux(euse), herbu(e).

grate [greɪt] ◇ *n* grille *f* de foyer. ◇ *vt* râper. ◇ *vi* grincer, crisser; **to ~ on sb's nerves** taper sur les nerfs de qqn.

grateful ['greɪtfʊl] *adj*: **to be ~ to sb (for sthg)** être reconnaissant(e) à qqn (de qqch).

gratefully ['greɪtfʊlɪ] *adv* avec reconnaissance.

grater ['greɪtə'] *n* râpe *f*.

gratification [,grætɪfɪ'keɪʃn] *n* **-1.** [pleasure] plaisir *m*, satisfaction *f*. **-2.** [satisfaction - of wish] assouvissement *m*, satisfaction *f*.

gratify ['grætɪfaɪ] (*pt* & *pp* **-ied**) *vt* **-1.** [please - person]: **to be gratified** être content(e), être satisfait(e). **-2.** [satisfy - wish] satisfaire, assouvir.

gratifying ['grætıfaıŋ] *adj* gratifiant(e).

grating ['greıtıŋ] ◇ *adj* grinçant(e); [voix] de crécelle. ◇ *n* [grille] grille *f*.

gratitude ['grætıtjuːd] *n* (*U*): ~ **(to sb for sthg)** gratitude *f* OR reconnaissance *f* (envers qqn de qqch).

gratuitous [grə'tjuːıtəs] *adj fml* gratuit(e).

gratuity [grə'tjuːıtı] (*pl* -**ies**) *n fml* [tip] pourboire *m*, gratification *f*.

grave[1] [greıv] ◇ *adj* grave; [concern] sérieux(ieuse). ◇ *n* tombe *f*; **to turn in one's** ~ se retourner dans sa tombe.

grave[2] [grɑːv] *adj* LING: **e** ~ **e** *m* accent grave.

grave accent [grɑːv-] *n* accent *m* grave.

gravedigger ['greıv,dıgə'] *n* fossoyeur *m*.

gravel ['grævl] ◇ *n* (*U*) gravier *m*. ◇ *comp* de gravier.

gravelled *Br*, **graveled** *Am* ['grævld] *adj* couvert(e) de gravier.

gravestone ['greıvstəʊn] *n* pierre *f* tombale.

graveyard ['greıvjɑːd] *n* cimetière *m*.

gravitate ['grævıteıt] *vi*: **to** ~ **towards** être attiré(e) par.

gravity ['grævətı] *n* -**1.** [force] gravité *f*, pesanteur *f*. -**2.** [seriousness] gravité *f*.

gravy ['greıvı] *n* -**1.** (*U*) [meat juice] jus *m* de viande. -**2.** *Am v inf* [easy money] bénef *m*.

gravy boat *n* saucière *f*.

gravy train *n inf*: **the** ~ le fromage, l'assiette *f* au beurre.

gray *Am* = **grey**.

grayscale *Am* = **greyscale**.

graze [greız] ◇ *vt* -**1.** [subj: cows, sheep] brouter, paître. -**2.** [subj: farmer] faire paître. -**3.** [skin] écorcher, égratigner. -**4.** [touch lightly] frôler, effleurer. ◇ *vi* brouter, paître. ◇ *n* écorchure *f*, égratignure *f*.

grease [griːs] ◇ *n* graisse *f*; ~ **stains** des traces de gras. ◇ *vt* graisser.

grease gun *n* pistolet *m* graisseur.

greasepaint ['griːspeınt] *n* fard *m* gras.

greaseproof paper ['griːspruːf-] *n* (*U*) *Br* papier *m* sulfurisé.

greasy ['griːzı] (*compar* -**ier**, *superl* -**iest**) *adj* -**1.** [covered in grease] graisseux(euse); [clothes] taché(e) de graisse. -**2.** [food, skin, hair] gras (grasse).

great [greıt] ◇ *adj* -**1.** [gen] grand(e); ~ **big** énorme; **a** ~ **big coward/layabout** un gros lâche/fainéant. -**2.** *inf* [splendid] génial(e), formidable; **to feel** ~ se sentir en pleine forme; ~! super!, génial! ◇ *n* grand *m*, -e *f*.

Great Barrier Reef *n*: **the** ~ la Grande Barrière.

Great Bear *n*: **the** ~ la Grande Ourse.

Great Britain *n* Grande-Bretagne *f*; **in** ~ en Grande-Bretagne.

greatcoat ['greıtkəʊt] *n* pardessus *m*.

Great Dane *n* danois *m*.

Greater ['greıtə'] *adj*: ~ **Manchester/New York** l'agglomération *f* de Manchester/New York.

great-grandchild *n* [boy] arrière-petit-fils *m*; [girl] arrière-petite-fille *f*.

◆ **great-grandchildren** *npl* arrière-petits-enfants *mpl*.

great-grandfather *n* arrière-grand-père *m*.

great-grandmother *n* arrière-grand-mère *f*.

Great Lakes *npl*: **the** ~ les Grands Lacs *mpl*.

greatly ['greıtlı] *adv* beaucoup; [different] très.

greatness ['greıtnıs] *n* grandeur *f*.

Great Wall of China *n*: **the** ~ la Grande Muraille (de Chine).

Great War *n*: **the** ~ la Grande Guerre, la guerre de 1914-18.

Grecian ['griːʃn] *adj* grec (grecque).

Greece [griːs] *n* Grèce *f*; **in** ~ en Grèce.

greed [griːd] *n* (*U*) -**1.** [for food] gloutonnerie *f*. -**2.** *fig* [for money, power]: ~ **(for)** avidité *f* (de).

greedily ['griːdılı] *adv* gloutonnement; [look at food] avec gourmandise.

greedy ['griːdı] (*compar* -**ier**, *superl* -**iest**) *adj* -**1.** [for food] glouton(onne). -**2.** [for money, power]: ~ **for sthg** avide de qqch.

Greek [griːk] ◇ *adj* grec (grecque); **the** ~ **Islands** les îles *fpl* grecques. ◇ *n* -**1.** [person] Grec *m*, Grecque *f*. -**2.** [language] grec *m*.

green [griːn] ◇ *adj* -**1.** [in colour, unripe] vert(e). -**2.** [ecological - issue, politics] écologique; [- person] vert(e). -**3.** *inf* [inexperienced] inexpérimenté(e), jeune. -**4.** *inf* [jealous]: ~ **(with envy)** malade de jalousie. ◇ *n* -**1.** [colour] vert *m*; **in** ~ en vert. -**2.** GOLF vert *m*. -**3.** **village** ~ pelouse *f* communale.

◆ **Green** *n* POL vert *m*, -e *f*, écologiste *mf*; **the Greens** les Verts, les Écologistes.

◆ **greens** *npl* [vegetables] légumes *mpl* verts.

greenback ['griːnbæk] *n Am inf* billet *m* vert.

green bean *n* haricot *m* vert.

green belt *n Br* ceinture *f* verte.

Green Beret n Am inf: **the ~s** les bérets mpl verts.

green card n **-1.** Br [for vehicle] carte f verte. **-2.** Am [residence permit] carte f de séjour.

Green Cross Code n Br code de sécurité routière destiné aux enfants.

greenery ['griːnəri] n verdure f.

greenfinch ['griːnfɪntʃ] n verdier m.

green fingers npl Br: **to have ~** avoir la main verte.

greenfly ['griːnflaɪ] (pl inv OR **-ies**) n puceron m.

greengage ['griːngeɪdʒ] n reine-claude f.

greengrocer ['griːn,grəʊsər] n marchand m, -e f de légumes; **~'s (shop)** magasin m de fruits et légumes.

greenhorn ['griːnhɔːn] n Am **-1.** [newcomer] immigrant m, -e f. **-2.** [novice] novice mf.

greenhouse ['griːnhaʊs, pl -haʊzɪz] n serre f.

greenhouse effect n: **the ~** l'effet m de serre.

greenish ['griːnɪʃ] adj verdâtre, qui tire sur le vert.

greenkeeper ['griːn,kiːpər] n personne chargée de l'entretien d'un terrain de golf ou de bowling.

Greenland ['griːnlənd] n Groenland m; **in ~** au Groenland.

Greenlander ['griːnləndər] n Groenlandais m, -e f.

green light n fig: **to give sb/sthg the ~** donner le feu vert à qqn/qqch.

green paper n POL ≃ livre m blanc.

Green Party n: **the ~** le Parti écologiste.

green salad n salade f verte.

green thumb n Am: **to have a ~** avoir la main verte.

greet [griːt] vt **-1.** [say hello to] saluer. **-2.** [receive] accueillir. **-3.** [subj: sight, smell] s'offrir à.

greeting ['griːtɪŋ] n salutation f, salut m.
♦ **greetings** npl: **Christmas/birthday ~s** vœux mpl de Noël/d'anniversaire.

greetings card Br, **greeting card** Am n carte f de vœux.

gregarious [grɪ'geərɪəs] adj sociable.

gremlin ['gremlɪn] n inf lutin m.

Grenada [grə'neɪdə] n Grenade f; **in ~** à la Grenade.

grenade [grə'neɪd] n: **(hand) ~** grenade f (à main).

Grenadian [grə'neɪdɪən] ◇ adj grenadin(ine). ◇ n Grenadin m, -ine f.

grenadier [,grenə'dɪər] n grenadier m.

grenadine ['grenədiːn] n grenadine f.

grew [gruː] pt → **grow**.

grey Br, **gray** Am [greɪ] ◇ adj **-1.** [in colour] gris(e). **-2.** [grey-haired]: **to go ~** grisonner. **-3.** [unhealthily pale] blême. **-4.** [dull, gloomy] morne, triste. ◇ n gris m; **in ~** en gris.

grey area n zone f d'ombre.

grey-haired [-'heəd] adj aux cheveux gris.

greyhound ['greɪhaʊnd] n lévrier m.

greying Br, **graying** Am ['greɪɪŋ] adj grisonnant(e).

grey matter n matière f grise.

greyscale Br, **grayscale** Am ['greɪskeɪl] n COMPUT échelle f de gris.

grey squirrel n écureuil m gris.

grid [grɪd] n **-1.** [grating] grille f. **-2.** [system of squares] quadrillage m.

griddle ['grɪdl] n plaque f à cuire.

gridiron ['grɪd,aɪən] n **-1.** [in cooking] gril m. **-2.** Am [game] football m américain; [field] terrain m de football américain.

gridlock ['grɪdlɒk] n Am embouteillage m.

grief [griːf] n (U) **-1.** [sorrow] chagrin m, peine f. **-2.** inf [trouble] ennuis mpl. **-3.** phr: **to come to ~** avoir de gros problèmes; **good ~!** Dieu du ciel!, mon Dieu!

grief-stricken adj accablé(e) de douleur.

grievance ['griːvns] n grief m, doléance f.

grieve [griːv] ◇ vt fml: **it ~s me to ...** cela me peine OR me consterne de .... ◇ vi [at death] être en deuil; **to ~ for sb/sthg** pleurer qqn/qqch.

grieving ['griːvɪŋ] n deuil m.

grievous ['griːvəs] adj fml grave; [shock] cruel(elle).

grievous bodily harm n (U) coups mpl et blessures fpl.

grievously ['griːvəslɪ] adv fml gravement; [wounded] grièvement.

grill [grɪl] ◇ n **-1.** [on cooker, fire] gril m. **-2.** [food] grillade f. ◇ vt **-1.** [cook on grill] griller, faire griller. **-2.** inf [interrogate] cuisiner.

grille [grɪl] n grille f.

grim [grɪm] (compar **-mer**, superl **-mest**) adj **-1.** [stern - face, expression] sévère; [- determination] inflexible. **-2.** [cheerless - truth, news] sinistre; [- room, walls] lugubre; [- day] morne, triste.

grimace [grɪ'meɪs] ◇ n grimace f. ◇ vi grimacer, faire la grimace.

grime [graɪm] n (U) crasse f, saleté f.

grimly ['grɪmlɪ] adv sévèrement.

grimy ['graɪmɪ] (compar **-ier**, superl **-iest**) adj sale, encrassé(e).

grin [grɪn] (*pt & pp* -**ned**, *cont* -**ning**) ◇ *n* (large) sourire *m*. ◇ *vi*: **to ~ (at sb/sthg)** adresser un large sourire (à qqn/qqch); **to ~ and bear it** en prendre son parti.

grind [graɪnd] (*pt & pp* **ground**) ◇ *vt* -**1.** [crush] moudre. -**2.** [press]: **to ~ sthg into sthg** enfoncer qqch dans qqch; [ash, cigarette] écraser qqch dans qqch. ◇ *vi* [scrape] grincer. ◇ *n* -**1.** [hard, boring work] corvée *f*; **the daily ~** le train-train quotidien. -**2.** *Am inf* [hard worker] bûcheur *m*, -euse *f*, bosseur *m*, -euse *f*.
◆ **grind down** *vt sep* [oppress] opprimer.
◆ **grind up** *vt sep* pulvériser.

grinder ['graɪndə'] *n* moulin *m*.

grinding ['graɪndɪŋ] *adj* écrasant(e); **~ poverty** misère *f* noire.

grinning ['grɪnɪŋ] *adj* souriant(e).

grip [grɪp] (*pt & pp* -**ped**, *cont* -**ping**) ◇ *n* -**1.** [grasp, hold] prise *f*; **to release one's ~ on sb/sthg** lâcher qqn/qqch; **to have a good ~ on sb/sthg** bien tenir qqn/qqch. -**2.** [control] contrôle *m*; **he's got a good ~ on the situation** il a la situation bien en main; **in the ~ of sthg** en proie à qqch; **to get to ~s with sthg** s'attaquer à qqch; **to get a ~ on o.s.** se ressaisir; **to lose one's ~** *fig* perdre les pédales. -**3.** [adhesion] adhérence *f*. -**4.** [handle] poignée *f*. -**5.** [bag] sac *m* (de voyage).
◇ *vt* -**1.** [grasp] saisir; [subj: tyres] adhérer à. -**2.** *fig* [imagination, country] captiver.

gripe [graɪp] *inf* ◇ *n* [complaint] plainte *f*. ◇ *vi*: **to ~ (about sthg)** râler OR rouspéter (contre qqch).

gripping ['grɪpɪŋ] *adj* passionnant(e).

grisly ['grɪzlɪ] (*compar* -**ier**, *superl* -**iest**) *adj* [horrible, macabre] macabre.

grist [grɪst] *n*: **it's all ~ to the mill for him** cela apporte de l'eau à son moulin.

gristle ['grɪsl] *n* (*U*) nerfs *mpl*.

gristly ['grɪslɪ] (*compar* -**ier**, *superl* -**iest**) *adj* nerveux(euse).

grit [grɪt] (*pt & pp* -**ted**, *cont* -**ting**) ◇ *n* (*U*) -**1.** [stones] gravillon *m*; [in eye] poussière *f*. -**2.** *inf* [courage] cran *m*. ◇ *vt* sabler.
◆ **grits** *npl Am* gruau *m* de maïs.

gritter ['grɪtə'] *n* camion *m* de sablage.

gritty ['grɪtɪ] (*compar* -**ier**, *superl* -**iest**) *adj* -**1.** [stony] couvert(e) de gravillon. -**2.** *inf* [brave - person] qui a du cran; [- performance, determination] courageux(euse).

grizzled ['grɪzld] *adj* grisonnant(e).

grizzly ['grɪzlɪ] (*pl* -**ies**) *n*: **~ (bear)** ours *m* gris, grizzli *m*.

groan [grəʊn] ◇ *n* gémissement *m*. ◇ *vi* -**1.** [moan] gémir. -**2.** [creak] grincer, gémir.

grocer ['grəʊsə'] *n* épicier *m*, -ière *f*; **~'s (shop)** épicerie *f*.

groceries ['grəʊsərɪz] *npl* [foods] provisions *fpl*.

grocery ['grəʊsərɪ] (*pl* -**ies**) *n* [shop] épicerie *f*.

groggy ['grɒgɪ] (*compar* -**ier**, *superl* -**iest**) *adj* groggy (*inv*).

groin [grɔɪn] *n* aine *f*.

groom [gru:m] ◇ *n* -**1.** [of horses] palefrenier *m*, garçon *m* d'écurie. -**2.** [bridegroom] marié *m*. ◇ *vt* -**1.** [brush] panser. -**2.** *fig* [prepare]: **to ~ sb (for sthg)** préparer OR former qqn (pour qqch).

groove [gru:v] *n* [in metal, wood] rainure *f*; [in record] sillon *m*.

grope [grəʊp] ◇ *vt* -**1.** [woman] peloter. -**2.** [try to find]: **to ~ one's way** avancer à tâtons. ◇ *vi*: **to ~ (about) for sthg** chercher qqch à tâtons.

gross [grəʊs] (*pl inv* OR -**es**) ◇ *adj* -**1.** [total] brut(e). -**2.** *fml* [serious - negligence] coupable; [- misconduct] choquant(e); [- inequality] flagrant(e). -**3.** [coarse, vulgar] grossier(ière). -**4.** *inf* [obese] obèse, énorme. ◇ *n* grosse *f*, douze douzaines *fpl*. ◇ *vt* gagner brut, faire une recette brute de.

gross domestic product *n* produit *m* intérieur brut.

grossly ['grəʊslɪ] *adv* [seriously] extrêmement, énormément; **~ overweight** obèse; **~ unjust** d'une injustice criante.

gross national product *n* produit *m* national brut.

gross profit *n* bénéfice *m* brut.

grotesque [grəʊ'tesk] *adj* grotesque.

grotto ['grɒtəʊ] (*pl* -**es** OR -**s**) *n* grotte *f*.

grotty ['grɒtɪ] (*compar* -**ier**, *superl* -**iest**) *adj Br inf* minable.

grouchy ['graʊtʃɪ] (*compar* -**ier**, *superl* -**iest**) *adj inf* grognon(onne), maussade.

ground [graʊnd] ◇ *pt & pp* → **grind**.
◇ *n* -**1.** (*U*) [surface of earth] sol *m*, terre *f*; **above ~** en surface; **below ~** sous terre; **on the ~** par terre, au sol; **to be thin on the ~** être rare; **to get sthg off the ~** *fig* faire démarrer qqch; **to break fresh** OR **new ~** innover, faire œuvre de pionnier. -**2.** (*U*) [area of land] terrain *m*. -**3.** [for sport etc] terrain *m*. -**4.** [advantage]: **to gain/lose ~** gagner/perdre du terrain. -**5.** *phr*: **to cut the ~ from under sb's feet** couper l'herbe sous les pieds de qqn; **to go to ~** se terrer; **to run sb/sthg to ~** traquer qqn/qqch; **to**

stand one's ~ tenir bon, rester sur ses positions.
◇ vt -1. [base]: **to be** ~**ed on** OR **in sthg** être fondé(e) sur qqch. -2. [aircraft, pilot] interdire de vol. -3. inf [child] priver de sortie. -4. Am ELEC: **to be** ~**ed** être à la masse.
◆ **grounds** npl -1. [reason] motif m, raison f; **on the** ~**s of** pour raison de; **on the** ~**s that** en raison du fait que; ~**s for sthg** motifs de qqch; ~**s for doing sthg** raisons de faire qqch. -2. [land round building] parc m. -3. [area]: **hunting** ~**s** terrain m de chasse; **fishing** ~**s** lieux mpl de pêche.

ground control n contrôle m au sol.

ground cover n (U) sous-bois mpl.

ground crew n personnel m au sol.

ground floor n rez-de-chaussée m.

ground-in adj [dirt] incrusté(e).

grounding ['graʊndɪŋ] n: ~ **(in)** connaissance f de base (de).

groundless ['graʊndlɪs] adj sans fondement.

ground level n: **at** ~ au rez-de-chaussée, au niveau du sol.

groundnut ['graʊndnʌt] n arachide f.

ground plan n [of building] plan m horizontal.

ground rent n redevance f foncière.

ground rules npl règles fpl de base.

groundsheet ['graʊndʃiːt] n tapis m de sol.

groundsman ['graʊndzmən] (pl **-men** [-mən]) n Br personne chargée de l'entretien d'un terrain de sport.

ground staff n -1. [at sports ground] personnel m d'entretien (d'un terrain de sport). -2. Br = **ground crew**.

groundswell ['graʊndswel] n vague f de fond.

groundwork ['graʊndwɜːk] n (U) travail m préparatoire.

group [gruːp] ◇ n groupe m. ◇ vt grouper, réunir. ◇ vi: **to** ~ **(together)** se grouper.

group captain n Br colonel m de l'armée de l'air.

groupie ['gruːpɪ] n inf groupie f.

group practice n cabinet m de groupe.

group therapy n thérapie f de groupe.

grouse [graʊs] ◇ n -1. [bird] grouse f, coq m de bruyère. -2. inf [complaint] plainte f. ◇ vi inf râler, rouspéter.

grove [graʊv] n [group of trees] bosquet m; **orange** ~ orangerie f.

grovel ['grɒvl] (Br pt & pp **-led**, cont **-ling**, Am pt & pp **-ed**, cont **-ing**) vi: **to** ~ **(to sb)** ramper (devant qqn).

grow [graʊ] (pt **grew**, pp **grown**) ◇ vi -1. [gen] pousser; [person, animal] grandir; [company, city] s'agrandir; [fears, influence, traffic] augmenter, s'accroître; [problem, idea, plan] prendre de l'ampleur; [enonomy] se développer. -2. [become] devenir; **to** ~ **old** vieillir; **to** ~ **tired of sthg** se fatiguer de qqch. -3. [do eventually]: **to** ~ **to like sb/sthg** finir par aimer qqn/qqch; **to** ~ **to hate sb/sthg** finir par détester qqn/qqch.
◇ vt -1. [plants] faire pousser. -2. [hair, beard] laisser pousser.
◆ **grow apart** vi [friends] s'éloigner; [family] se défaire.
◆ **grow into** vt fus [clothes, shoes] devenir assez grand pour mettre.
◆ **grow on** vt fus inf plaire de plus en plus à; **it'll** ~ **on you** cela finira par te plaire.
◆ **grow out** vi [perm, dye] disparaître.
◆ **grow out of** vt fus -1. [clothes, shoes] devenir trop grand pour. -2. [habit] perdre.
◆ **grow up** vi -1. [become adult] grandir, devenir adulte; ~ **up!** ne fais pas l'enfant! -2. [develop] se développer.

grower ['graʊə'] n cultivateur m, -trice f.

growl [graʊl] ◇ n [of animal, engine] grondement m; [of person] grognement m. ◇ vi [animal] grogner, gronder; [engine] vrombir, gronder; [person] grogner.

grown [graʊn] ◇ pp → **grow**. ◇ adj adulte.

grown-up ◇ adj -1. [fully grown] adulte, grand(e). -2. [mature] mûr(e). ◇ n adulte mf, grande personne f.

growth [graʊθ] n -1. [increase - gen] croissance f; [- of opposition, company] développement m; [- of population] augmentation f, accroissement m. -2. MED [lump] tumeur f, excroissance f.

growth rate n taux m de croissance.

GRSM (abbr of **Graduate of the Royal Schools of Music**) n diplômé du conservatoire de musique britannique.

grub [grʌb] n -1. [insect] larve f. -2. [food] bouffe f.

grubby ['grʌbɪ] (compar **-ier**, superl **-iest**) adj sale, malpropre.

grudge [grʌdʒ] ◇ n rancune f; **to bear sb a** ~, **to bear a** ~ **against sb** garder rancune à qqn. ◇ vt: **to** ~ **sb sthg** donner qqch à qqn à contrecœur; [success] en vouloir à qqn à cause de qqch; **to** ~ **doing sthg** faire qqch à contrecœur.

grudging ['grʌdʒɪŋ] adj peu enthousiaste.

grudgingly ['grʌdʒɪŋlɪ] adv à contrecœur, de mauvaise grâce.

gruelling Br, **grueling** Am ['gruəlɪŋ] adj épuisant(e), exténuant(e).

gruesome ['gruːsəm] *adj* horrible, effroyable.

gruff [grʌf] *adj* **-1.** [hoarse] gros (grosse). **-2.** [rough, unfriendly] brusque, bourru(e).

grumble ['grʌmbl] ◇ *n* **-1.** [complaint] ronchonnement *m*, grognement *m*. **-2.** [rumble - of thunder, train] grondement *m*; [- of stomach] gargouillement *m*. ◇ *vi* **-1.** [complain]: **to ~ about sthg** rouspéter OR grommeler contre qqch. **-2.** [rumble - thunder, train] gronder; [- stomach] gargouiller.

grumbling ['grʌmblɪŋ] *n* **-1.** [complaining] rouspétance *f*. **-2.** [rumbling] grondement *m*.

grumpy ['grʌmpɪ] (*compar* -ier, *superl* -iest) *adj inf* renfrogné(e).

grunt [grʌnt] ◇ *n* grognement *m*. ◇ *vi* grogner.

G-string *n* cache-sexe *m inv*.

GU *abbr of* **Guam**.

Guadeloupe [ˌgwɑːdə'luːp] *n* la Guadeloupe *f*; **in ~** à la Guadeloupe.

Guam [gwɑːm] *n* Guam *f*.

guarantee [ˌgærən'tiː] ◇ *n* garantie *f*; **there's no ~ that he'll arrive on time** ce n'est pas sûr OR certain qu'il arrivera à l'heure; **under ~** sous garantie. ◇ *vt* garantir.

guarantor [ˌgærən'tɔːr] *n* garant *m*, -e *f*, caution *f*.

guard [gɑːd] ◇ *n* **-1.** [person] garde *m*; [in prison] gardien *m*. **-2.** [group of guards] garde *f*. **-3.** [defensive operation] garde *f*; **to stand ~** monter la garde; **to be on ~** être de garde OR de faction; **to be on (one's) ~ (against)** se tenir OR être sur ses gardes (contre); **to catch sb off ~** prendre qqn au dépourvu. **-4.** *Br* RAIL chef *m* de train. **-5.** [protective device - for body] **protection** *f*; [- for fire] garde-feu *m inv*. ◇ *vt* **-1.** [protect - building] protéger, garder; [- person] protéger. **-2.** [prisoner] garder, surveiller. **-3.** [hide - secret] garder. ◆ **guard against** *vt fus* se protéger contre.

guard dog *n* chien *m* de garde.

guarded ['gɑːdɪd] *adj* prudent(e); **he's always very ~** il surveille toujours ses paroles.

guardian ['gɑːdjən] *n* **-1.** [of child] tuteur *m*, -trice *f*. **-2.** [protector] gardien *m*, -ienne *f*, protecteur *m*, -trice *f*.

guardian angel *n* ange *m* gardien.

guardianship ['gɑːdjənʃɪp] *n* tutelle *f*.

guardrail ['gɑːdreɪl] *n Am* [on road] barrière *f* de sécurité.

guardsman ['gɑːdzmən] (*pl* -men [-mən]) *n* soldat *m* de la garde royale.

guard's van *n Br* wagon *m* du chef de train.

Guatemala [ˌgwɑːtə'mɑːlə] *n* Guatemala *m*; **in ~** au Guatemala.

Guatemalan [ˌgwɑːtə'mɑːlən] ◇ *adj* guatémaltèque. ◇ *n* Guatémaltèque *mf*.

guava ['gwɑːvə] [fruit] goyave *f*; [tree] goyavier *m*.

guerilla [gə'rɪlə] = **guerrilla**.

Guernsey ['gɜːnzɪ] *n* **-1.** [place] Guernesey *f*; **in ~** à Guernesey. **-2.** [sweater] jersey *m*. **-3.** [cow] vache *f* de Guernesey.

guerrilla [gə'rɪlə] *n* guérillero *m*; **urban ~** guérilléro *m* des villes.

guerrilla warfare *n* (*U*) guérilla *f*.

guess [ges] ◇ *n* conjecture *f*; **to take a ~** essayer de deviner; **it's anybody's ~** Dieu seul le sait, qui sait? ◇ *vt* deviner; **~ what?** tu sais quoi? ◇ *vi* **-1.** [conjecture] deviner; **to ~ at sthg** deviner qqch; **to keep sb ~ing** laisser qqn dans l'ignorance. **-2.** [suppose]: **I ~ (so)** je suppose (que oui).

guesstimate ['gestɪmət] *n inf* calcul *m* au pif.

guesswork ['geswɜːk] *n* (*U*) conjectures *fpl*, hypothèses *fpl*.

guest [gest] *n* **-1.** [gen] invité *m*, -e *f*. **-2.** [at hotel] client *m*, -e *f*. **-3.** *phr*: **be my ~!** je t'en prie!

guesthouse ['gesthaus, *pl* -hauzɪz] *n* pension *f* de famille.

guest of honour *n* invité *m*, -e *f* d'honneur.

guestroom ['gestrum] *n* chambre *f* d'amis.

guest star *n* invité-vedette *m*, invitée-vedette *f*.

guffaw [gʌ'fɔː] ◇ *n* gros rire *m*. ◇ *vi* rire bruyamment.

Guiana [gaɪ'ænə] *n* Guyane *f*.

guidance ['gaɪdəns] *n* (*U*) **-1.** [help] conseils *mpl*. **-2.** [leadership] direction *f*; **under the ~ of** sous la houlette de.

guide [gaɪd] ◇ *n* **-1.** [person, book] guide *m*. **-2.** [indication] indication *f*. ◇ *vt* **-1.** [show by leading] guider. **-2.** [control] diriger. **-3.** [influence]: **to be ~d by sb/sthg** se laisser guider par qqn/qqch. ◆ **Guide** *n* = **Girl Guide**.

guide book *n* guide *m*.

guided missile ['gaɪdɪd-] *n* missile *m* guidé.

guide dog *n* chien *m* d'aveugle.

guidelines ['gaɪdlaɪnz] *npl* directives *fpl*, lignes *fpl* directrices.

guiding ['gaɪdɪŋ] *adj* qui sert de guide; [principle] directeur(trice).

guild [gɪld] *n* **-1.** HISTORY corporation *f*, guilde *f*. **-2.** [association] association *f*.

guildhall ['gɪldhɔːl] *n* salle *f* de réunion d'une corporation.

guile [gaɪl] *n* (*U*) *literary* ruse *f*, astuce *f*.

guileless ['gaɪllɪs] *adj literary* franc (franche).

guillemot ['gɪlɪmɒt] *n* guillemot *m*.

guillotine ['gɪlə,tiːn] ◇ *n* **-1.** [for executions] guillotine *f*. **-2.** [for paper] massicot *m*. **-3.** *Br* POL limite de temps fixée pour le vote d'une loi au Parlement. ◇ *vt* [execute] guillotiner.

guilt [gɪlt] *n* culpabilité *f*.

guiltily ['gɪltɪlɪ] *adv* d'un air coupable; [behave] d'une façon coupable.

guilty ['gɪltɪ] (*compar* **-ier**, *superl* **-iest**) *adj* coupable; **to be** ~ **of** sthg être coupable de qqch; **to be found** ~/**not** ~ JUR être reconnu coupable/non coupable; **to have a** ~ **con-science** avoir mauvaise conscience.

guinea ['gɪnɪ] *n* guinée *f*.

Guinea ['gɪnɪ] *n* Guinée *f*; **in** ~ en Guinée.

Guinea-Bissau [-bɪ'saʊ] *n* Guinée-Bissau *f*.

guinea fowl *n* pintade *f*.

guinea pig *n* cobaye *m*.

guise [gaɪz] *n fml* apparence *f*, aspect *m*.

guitar [gɪ'taːr] *n* guitare *f*.

guitarist [gɪ'taːrɪst] *n* guitariste *mf*.

gulch [gʌltʃ] *n Am* ravin *m*.

gulf [gʌlf] *n* **-1.** [sea] golfe *m*. **-2.** [breach, chasm]: ~ **(between)** abîme *m* (entre).

◆ **Gulf** *n*: **the Gulf** le Golfe.

Gulf States *npl*: **the** ~ [in US] les États du golfe du Mexique; [around Persian Gulf] les États du Golfe.

Gulf Stream *n*: **the** ~ le Gulf Stream.

gull [gʌl] *n* mouette *f*.

gullet ['gʌlɪt] *n* œsophage *m*; [of bird] gosier *m*.

gullible ['gʌləbl] *adj* crédule.

gully ['gʌlɪ] (*pl* **-ies**) *n* **-1.** [valley] ravine *f*. **-2.** [ditch] rigole *f*.

gulp [gʌlp] ◇ *n* [of drink] grande gorgée *f*; [of food] grosse bouchée *f*. ◇ *vt* avaler. ◇ *vi* avoir la gorge nouée.

◆ **gulp down** *vt sep* avaler.

gum [gʌm] (*pt* & *pp* **-med**, *cont* **-ming**) ◇ *n* **-1.** [chewing gum] chewing-gum *m*. **-2.** [adhesive] colle *f*, gomme *f*. **-3.** ANAT gencive *f*. ◇ *vt* coller.

gumboil ['gʌmbɔɪl] *n* abcès *m* à la gencive.

gumboots ['gʌmbuːts] *npl Br* bottes *fpl* de caoutchouc.

gumption ['gʌmpʃn] *n inf* **-1.** [common sense] jugeote *f*. **-2.** [determination] cran *m*.

gumshoe ['gʌmʃuː] *n Am crime sl* privé *m*.

gun [gʌn] (*pt* & *pp* **-ned**, *cont* **-ning**) *n* **-1.** [weapon] fusil *m*; **to stick to one's** ~**s** tenir bon, ne pas en démordre. **-2.** [starting pistol] pistolet *m*; **to jump the** ~ agir prématurément. **-3.** [tool] pistolet *m*; [for staples] agrafeuse *f*.

◆ **gun down** *vt sep* abattre.

gunboat ['gʌnbəʊt] *n* canonnière *f*.

gundog ['gʌndɒg] *n* chien *m* de chasse.

gunfire ['gʌnfaɪər] *n* (*U*) coups *mpl* de feu.

gunge [gʌndʒ] *n* (*U*) *Br inf* matière *f* poisseuse.

gung-ho [,gʌŋ'həʊ] *adj inf* trop enthousiaste.

gunk [gʌŋk] *n inf* matière *f* poisseuse.

gunman ['gʌnmən] (*pl* **-men** [-mən]) *n* personne *f* armée.

gunner ['gʌnər] *n* artilleur *m*.

gunpoint ['gʌnpɔɪnt] *n*: **at** ~ sous la menace d'un fusil OR pistolet.

gunpowder ['gʌn,paʊdər] *n* poudre *f* à canon.

gunrunning ['gʌn,rʌnɪŋ] *n* trafic *m* d'armes.

gunshot ['gʌnʃɒt] *n* [firing of gun] coup *m* de feu.

gunsmith ['gʌnsmɪθ] *n* armurier *m*.

gurgle ['gɜːgl] ◇ *vi* **-1.** [water] glouglouter. **-2.** [baby] gazouiller. ◇ *n* **-1.** [of water] glouglou *m*. **-2.** [of baby] gazouillis *m*.

guru ['guːruː] *n* gourou *m*, guru *m*.

gush [gʌʃ] ◇ *n* jaillissement *m*. ◇ *vt* [blood] pisser; [oil] cracher. ◇ *vi* **-1.** [flow out] jaillir. **-2.** *pej* [enthuse] s'exprimer de façon exubérante.

gushing ['gʌʃɪŋ] *adj pej* trop exubérant(e).

gusset ['gʌsɪt] *n* gousset *m*.

gust ['gʌst] ◇ *n* rafale *f*, coup *m* de vent. ◇ *vi* souffler par rafales.

gusto ['gʌstəʊ] *n*: **with** ~ avec enthousiasme.

gusty ['gʌstɪ] (*compar* **-ier**, *superl* **-iest**) *adj* venteux(euse), de grand vent; [wind] qui souffle par rafales.

gut [gʌt] (*pt* & *pp* **-ted**, *cont* **-ting**) ◇ *n* MED intestin *m*. ◇ *vt* **-1.** [remove organs from] vider. **-2.** [destroy] réduire à rien.

◆ **guts** *npl inf* **-1.** [intestines] intestins *mpl*; **to hate sb's** ~**s** ne pas pouvoir piffer qqn, ne pas pouvoir voir qqn en peinture. **-2.** [courage] cran *m*; **to have** ~**s** avoir du cran.

gut reaction *n* réaction *f* viscérale.

gutter ['gʌtər] *n* **-1.** [ditch] rigole *f*. **-2.** [on roof] gouttière *f*.

guttering ['gʌtərɪŋ] *n* (*U*) gouttières *fpl*.

gutter press *n* presse *f* à sensation.

guttural ['gʌtərəl] *adj* guttural(e).

guv [gʌv] *n Br inf* chef *m*.

guy [gaɪ] *n* -1. *inf* [man] type *m*. -2. [person] copain *m*, copine *f*. -3. *Br* [dummy] *effigie de Guy Fawkes*.

Guyana [gaɪ'ænə] *n* Guyana *m*; **in ~** au Guyana.

Guy Fawkes' Night [-'fɔːks-] *n fête célébrée le 5 novembre en commémoration de la Conspiration des Poudres*.

GUY FAWKES' NIGHT:
Cette fête familiale se déroule en plein air autour d'un grand feu de joie sur lequel on brûle une effigie ('the Guy') censée représenter Guy Fawkes, l'instigateur de la Conspiration des Poudres. C'est également l'occasion d'un feu d'artifice

guy rope *n* corde *f* de tente.

guzzle ['gʌzl] ◇ *vt* bâfrer; [drink] lamper. ◇ *vi* s'empiffrer.

gym [dʒɪm] *n inf* -1. [gymnasium] gymnase *m*. -2. [exercises] gym *f*.

gymkhana [dʒɪm'kɑːnə] *n* gymkhana *m*.

gymnasium [dʒɪm'neɪzjəm] (*pl* **-iums** OR **-ia** [-zjə]) *n* gymnase *m*.

gymnast ['dʒɪmnæst] *n* gymnaste *mf*.

gymnastics [dʒɪm'næstɪks] *n* (*U*) gymnastique *f*.

gym shoes *npl* (chaussures *fpl* de) tennis *mpl*.

gymslip ['dʒɪm,slɪp] *n Br* tunique *f*.

gynaecological *Br*, **gynecological** *Am* [,gaɪnəkə'lɒdʒɪkl] *adj* gynécologique.

gynaecologist *Br*, **gynecologist** *Am* [,gaɪnə'kɒlədʒɪst] *n* gynécologue *mf*.

gynaecology *Br*, **gynecology** *Am* [,gaɪnə'kɒlədʒɪ] *n* gynécologie *f*.

gyp [dʒɪp] *Am* ◇ *vt* escroquer. ◇ *n* escroc.

gypsy ['dʒɪpsɪ] (*pl* **-ies**) = **gipsy**.

gyrate [dʒaɪ'reɪt] *vi* tournoyer.

gyration [dʒaɪ'reɪʃn] *n* mouvement *m* giratoire.

gyroscope ['dʒaɪrəskəʊp] *n* gyroscope *m*.

h (*pl* **h's** OR **hs**), **H** (*pl* **H's** OR **Hs**) [eɪtʃ] *n* [letter] h *m inv*, H *m inv*.

ha [hɑː] *excl* ha!

habeas corpus [,heɪbjə'skɔːpəs] *n* habeas corpus *m*.

haberdashery ['hæbədæʃərɪ] (*pl* **-ies**) *n* mercerie *f*.

habit ['hæbɪt] *n* -1. [customary practice] habitude *f*; **out of ~** par habitude; **to be in/get into the ~ of doing sthg** avoir/prendre l'habitude de faire qqch; **to make a ~ of doing sthg** avoir l'habitude de faire qqch. -2. [garment] habit *m*.

habitable ['hæbɪtəbl] *adj* habitable.

habitat ['hæbɪtæt] *n* habitat *m*.

habitation [hæbɪ'teɪʃn] *n* habitation *f*.

habit-forming [-,fɔːmɪŋ] *adj* qui crée une accoutumance.

habitual [hə'bɪtʃʊəl] *adj* -1. [usual, characteristic] habituel(elle). -2. [regular] invétéré(e).

habitually [hə'bɪtʃʊəlɪ] *adv* habituellement.

hack [hæk] ◇ *n* [writer] écrivailleur *m*, -euse *f*. ◇ *vt* -1. [cut] tailler. -2. COMPUT pirater. -3. *Am inf* [taxi] taxi *m*. ◇ *vi* [cut] taillader.
◆ **hack into** *vt fus* COMPUT pirater.
◆ **hack through** *vt fus* [jungle etc]: **to ~ through sthg** se frayer un chemin dans qqch à coups de hache.

hacker ['hækər] *n*: **(computer) ~** pirate *m* informatique.

hackie ['hækɪ] *n Am inf* chauffeur *m* de taxi.

hacking ['hækɪŋ] *n* COMPUT piratage *f* informatique.

hacking cough *n* toux *f* sèche et douloureuse.

hackles ['hæklz] *npl* [on animal] plumes *fpl* du cou; **to make sb's ~ rise** hérisser qqn.

hackney cab, hackney carriage ['hæknɪ-] *n fml* [taxi] taxi *m*.

hackneyed ['hæknɪd] *adj* rebattu(e).

hacksaw ['hæksɔː] *n* scie *f* à métaux.

had [*weak form* həd, *strong form* hæd] *pt & pp* → **have**.

haddock ['hædək] (*pl inv*) *n* églefin *m*, aiglefin *m*.

hadn't ['hædnt] = **had not**.

haematology [,hi:mə'tɒlədʒɪ] = **hematology**.

haemoglobin [,hi:mə'gləʊbɪn] = **hemoglobin**.

haemophilia [,hi:mə'fɪlɪə] = **hemophilia**.

haemophiliac [,hi:mə'fɪlɪˌæk] = **hemophiliac**.

haemorrhage ['hemərɪdʒ] = **hemorrhage**.

haemorrhoids ['hemərɔɪdʒ] = **hemorrhoids**.

hag [hæg] *n* vieille sorcière *f*.

haggard ['hægəd] *adj* [face] défait(e); [person] abattu(e).

haggis ['hægɪs] *n* plat typique écossais fait d'une panse de brebis farcie, le plus souvent servie avec des navets et des pommes de terre.

haggle ['hægl] *vi* marchander; **to ~ over** OR **about sthg** marchander qqch; **to ~ with sb** marchander avec qqn.

haggling ['hæglɪŋ] *n* marchandage *m*.

Hague [heɪg] *n*: **The ~** La Haye.

hail [heɪl] ◇ *n* grêle *f*; *fig* pluie *f*. ◇ *vt* -1. [call] héler. -2. [acclaim]: **to ~ sb/sthg as sthg** acclamer qqn/qqch comme qqch. ◇ *v impers* grêler.

hailstone ['heɪlstəʊn] *n* grêlon *m*.

hair [heəʳ] ◇ *n* -1. (U) [on human head] cheveux *mpl*; **to do one's ~** se coiffer; **to let one's ~ down** se défouler; **to make sb's ~ stand on end** faire dresser les cheveux sur la tête à qqn. -2. (U) [on animal, human skin] poils *mpl*. -3. [individual hair - on head] cheveu *m*; [- on skin] poil *m*; **to split ~s** couper les cheveux en quatre. ◇ *comp* capillaire.

hairbrush ['heəbrʌʃ] *n* brosse *f* à cheveux.

haircut ['heəkʌt] *n* coupe *f* de cheveux.

hairdo ['heəduː] (*pl* -s) *n inf* coiffure *f*.

hairdresser ['heə,dresəʳ] *n* coiffeur *m*, -euse *f*; **~'s (salon)** salon *m* de coiffure.

hairdressing ['heə,dresɪŋ] ◇ *n* coiffure *f*. ◇ *comp* de coiffure.

hairdryer ['heə,draɪəʳ] *n* [handheld] sèche-cheveux *m*; [with hood] casque *m*.

hair gel *n* gel *m* coiffant.

hairgrip ['heəgrɪp] *n Br* pince *f* à cheveux.

hairline ['heəlaɪn] naissance *f* des cheveux.

hairline fracture *n* fêlure *f*.

hairnet ['heənet] *n* filet *m* à cheveux.

hairpiece ['heəpiːs] *n* postiche *m*.

hairpin ['heəpɪn] *n* épingle *f* à cheveux.

hairpin bend *n* virage *m* en épingle à cheveux.

hair-raising [-,reɪzɪŋ] *adj* à faire dresser les cheveux sur la tête; [journey] effrayant(e).

hair remover *n* (crème *f*) dépilatoire *m*.

hair-restorer *n* lotion *f* capillaire régénératrice.

hair's breadth *n*: **by a ~** d'un cheveu, de justesse.

hair slide *n Br* barrette *f*.

hair-splitting *n* ergotage *m*.

hairspray ['heəspreɪ] *n* laque *f*.

hairstyle ['heəstaɪl] *n* coiffure *f*.

hairstylist ['heə,staɪlɪst] *n* coiffeur *m*, -euse *f*.

hairy ['heərɪ] (*compar* -ier, *superl* -iest) *adj* -1. [covered in hair] velu(e), poilu(e). -2. *inf* [dangerous] à faire dresser les cheveux sur la tête.

Haiti ['heɪtɪ] *n* Haïti *m*; **in ~** à Haïti.

Haitian ['heɪʃn] ◇ *adj* haïtien(ienne). ◇ *n* Haïtien *m*, -ienne *f*.

hake [heɪk] (*pl inv* OR -s) *n* colin *m*, merluche *f*.

halal [hə'lɑːl] ◇ *adj* hallal (*inv*). ◇ *n* viande *f* hallal.

halcyon ['hælsɪən] *adj* paradisiaque.

hale [heɪl] *adj*: **~ and hearty** en pleine forme.

half [*Br* hɑːf, *Am* hæf] (*pl senses 1 and 2* **halves**, *pl senses 3, 4 and 5* **halves** OR **halfs**) ◇ *adj* demi(e); **~ a dozen** une demi-douzaine; **~ an hour** une demi-heure; **~ a pound** une demi-livre; **~ English** à moitié Anglais; **~ my life** la moitié de ma vie. ◇ *adv* -1. [gen] à moitié; **~-and-~** moitié-moitié; **not ~!** *Br inf* tu parles! -2. [by half] de moitié. -3. [in telling the time]: **~ past ten** *Br*, **~ after ten** *Am* dix heures et demie; **it's ~ past** il est la demie. ◇ *n* -1. [gen] moitié *f*; **by ~** de moitié; **in ~** en deux; **to be too clever by ~** être un peu trop malin; **he doesn't do things by halves** il ne fait pas les choses à moitié; **to go halves (with sb)** partager (avec qqn). -2. SPORT [of match] mi-temps *f*. -3. SPORT [half-back] demi *m*. -4. [of beer] demi *m*. -5. [child's ticket] demi-tarif *m*, tarif *m* enfant. ◇ *pron* la moitié; **~ of them** la moitié d'entre eux; **I wrote ~ of it** j'en ai écrit la moitié.

halfback ['hɑːfbæk] *n* demi *m*.

half-baked [-'beɪkt] *adj* à la noix.

half board *n* demi-pension *f*.

half-breed ◇ *adj* métis(isse). ◇ *n* métis *m*,

-isse *f* (*attention*: *le terme 'half-breed' est considéré raciste*).

half-brother *n* demi-frère *m*.

half-caste ◇ *adj* métis(isse). ◇ *n* métis *m*, -isse *f* (*attention*: *le terme 'half-caste' est considéré raciste*).

half cock *n*: **to go off (at)** ~ mal partir.

half-day *n* demi-journée *f*.

half-hearted [-'hɑːtɪd] *adj* sans enthousiasme.

half-heartedly [-'hɑːtɪdlɪ] *adv* sans enthousiasme.

half hour *n* demi-heure *f*.
◆ **half-hour** *adj* = **half-hourly**.

half-hourly *adj* (de) toutes les demi-heures.

half-length *adj* [coat, jacket] court(e).

half-light *n* pénombre *f*.

half-mast *n*: **at** ~ [flag] en berne.

half measure *n* demi-mesure *f*.

half moon *n* demi-lune *f*.

half note *n Am* MUS blanche *f*.

halfpenny ['heɪpnɪ] (*pl* **-pennies** OR **-pence**) *n* demi-penny *m*.

half-price *adj* à moitié prix.
◆ **half price** *adv* moitié prix.

half-sister *n* demi-sœur *f*.

half step *n Am* MUS demi-ton *m*.

half term *n Br* congé *m* de mi-trimestre.

half time *n* (*U*) mi-temps *f*.

half tone *n Am* MUS demi-ton *m*.

half-truth *n* demi-vérité *f*.

halfway [hɑːf'weɪ] ◇ *adj* à mi-chemin. ◇ *adv* **-1.** [in space] à mi-chemin. **-2.** [in time] à la moitié. **-3.** *phr*: **to meet sb** ~ arriver à un compromis avec qqn.

half-wit *n* faible *mf* d'esprit.

half-yearly *adj* semestriel(ielle).
◆ **half yearly** *adv* tous les six mois.

halibut ['hælɪbət] (*pl inv* OR **-s**) *n* flétan *m*.

halitosis [,hælɪ'təʊsɪs] *n* mauvaise haleine *f*.

hall [hɔːl] *n* **-1.** [in house] vestibule *m*, entrée *f*. **-2.** [meeting room, building] salle *f*. **-3.** *Br* UNIV [hall of residence] résidence *f* universitaire; **to live in** ~ loger en cité universitaire. **-4.** [country house] manoir *m*.

halleluja [,hælɪ'luːjə] *excl* alléluia!

hallmark ['hɔːlmɑːk] *n* **-1.** [typical feature] marque *f*. **-2.** [on metal] poinçon *m*.

hallo [hə'ləʊ] = **hello**.

hall of residence (*pl* **halls of residence**) *n Br* UNIV résidence *f* universitaire.

hallowed ['hæləʊd] *adj* [respected] consacré(e).

Hallowe'en [,hæləʊ'iːn] *n* veille *f* de la Toussaint.

HALLOWE'EN:

Fête célébrée le 31 octobre au cours de laquelle les enfants déguisés présentent des paniers pour qu'on y dépose des friandises

hallucinate [hə'luːsɪneɪt] *vi* avoir des hallucinations.

hallucination [,həluːsɪ'neɪʃn] *n* hallucination *f*.

hallucinogenic [hə,luːsɪnə'dʒenɪk] *adj* hallucinogène.

hallway ['hɔːlweɪ] *n* vestibule *m*.

halo ['heɪləʊ] (*pl* **-es** OR **-s**) *n* nimbe *m*; ASTRON halo *m*.

halogen ['hælədʒen] ◇ *n* halogène *m*. ◇ *comp* halogène.

halt [hɔːlt] ◇ *n* [stop]: **to come to a** ~ [vehicle] s'arrêter, s'immobiliser; [activity] s'interrompre; **to grind to a** ~ [stop moving] s'arrêter; [stop working] péricliter; **to call a** ~ **to sthg** mettre fin à qqch. ◇ *vt* arrêter. ◇ *vi* s'arrêter.

halter ['hɔːltər] *n* [for horse] licou *m*.

halterneck ['hɔːltənek] *adj* dos nu (*inv*).

halting ['hɔːltɪŋ] *adj* hésitant(e).

halve [*Br* hɑːv, *Am* hæv] *vt* **-1.** [reduce by half] réduire de moitié. **-2.** [divide] couper en deux.

halves [*Br* hɑːvz, *Am* hævz] *pl* → **half**.

ham [hæm] (*pt & pp* **-med**, *cont* **-ming**) ◇ *n* **-1.** [meat] jambon *m*. **-2.** *pej* [actor] cabotin *m*. **-3.** [radio fanatic]: **(radio)** ~ radioamateur *m*. ◇ *comp* au jambon. ◇ *vt*: **to** ~ **it up** caboter.

Hamburg ['hæmbɜːg] *n* Hambourg.

hamburger ['hæmbɜːgər] *n* **-1.** [burger] hamburger *m*. **-2.** (*U*) *Am* [mince] viande *f* hachée.

ham-fisted [-'fɪstɪd] *adj* maladroit(e).

hamlet ['hæmlɪt] *n* hameau *m*.

hammer ['hæmər] ◇ *n* marteau *m*. ◇ *vt* **-1.** [with tool] marteler; [nail] enfoncer à coups de marteau. **-2.** [with fist] marteler du poing. **-3.** [fig]: **to** ~ **sthg into sb** faire entrer qqch dans la tête de qqn. **-4.** *inf* [defeat] battre à plates coutures. ◇ *vi* **-1.** [with tool] frapper au marteau. **-2.** [with fist]: **to** ~ **(on)** cogner du poing (à). **-3.** *fig*: **to** ~ **away at** [task] s'acharner à.
◆ **hammer in** *vt sep*: **to** ~ **sthg into sb** faire entrer qqch dans la tête de qqn.
◆ **hammer out** ◇ *vt fus* [agreement, solu-

tion] **parvenir finalement à.** ◇ *vt sep* [dent]
enlever à coups de marteau.

hammock ['hæmək] *n* hamac *m*.

hammy ['hæmɪ] (*compar* **-ier,** *superl* **-iest**) *adj*
inf cabotin(e).

hamper ['hæmpəʳ] ◇ *n* **-1.** [for food] panier
m d'osier. **-2.** *Am* [for laundry] coffre *m* à
linge. ◇ *vt* gêner.

hamster ['hæmstəʳ] *n* hamster *m*.

hamstring ['hæmstrɪŋ] ◇ *n* tendon *m* du
jarret. ◇ *vt* paralyser.

hand [hænd] ◇ *n* **-1.** [part of body] main *f*;
to hold ~s se tenir la main; **~ in ~** [people]
main dans la main; **~s up!** haut les mains!;
by ~ à la main; **at the ~s of** aux mains de;
with one's bare ~s à mains nues; **to
change ~s** [car, house etc] changer de propriétaire; **to force sb's ~** forcer la main à
qqn; **to get** OR **lay one's ~s on** mettre la
main sur; **to get out of ~** échapper à tout
contrôle; **to give sb a free ~** donner carte
blanche à qqn; **to go ~ in ~** [things] aller
de pair; **to have a ~ in sthg** être impliqué
dans qqch; **to have a ~ in doing sthg**
contribuer à faire qqch; **to have a situation
in ~** avoir une situation en main; **to have
one's ~s full** avoir du pain sur la planche;
to have time in ~ avoir du temps libre; **to
take sb in ~** prendre qqn en main; **to try
one's ~ at sthg** s'essayer à qqch; **to wait
on sb ~ and foot** être aux petits soins pour
qqn; **to wash one's ~s of sthg** se laver les
mains de qqch. **-2.** [help] coup *m* de main;
to give OR **lend sb a ~ (with sthg)** donner
un coup de main à qqn (pour faire qqch).
-3. [worker] ouvrier *m*, -ière *f*. **-4.** [of clock,
watch] aiguille *f*. **-5.** [handwriting] écriture *f*.
-6. [of cards] jeu *m*, main *f*; **to overplay
one's ~** *fig* trop présumer de ses capacités.
◇ *vt*: **to ~ sthg to sb, to ~ sb sthg** passer
qqch à qqn.
◆ **(close) at hand** *adv* proche.
◆ **on hand** *adv* disponible.
◆ **on the other hand** *conj* d'autre part.
◆ **out of hand** *adv* [completely] d'emblée.
◆ **to hand** *adv* à portée de la main, sous
la main.
◆ **hand down** *vt sep* transmettre.
◆ **hand in** *vt sep* remettre.
◆ **hand on** *vt sep* transmettre.
◆ **hand out** *vt sep* distribuer.
◆ **hand over** ◇ *vt sep* **-1.** [baton, money]
remettre. **-2.** [responsibility, power] transmettre. ◇ *vi*: **to ~ over (to)** passer le relais
(à).

handbag ['hændbæg] *n* sac *m* à main.

handball ['hændbɔːl] *n* [game] handball *m*.

handbill ['hændbɪl] *n* prospectus *m*.

handbook ['hændbʊk] *n* manuel *m*; [for
tourist] guide *m*.

handbrake ['hændbreɪk] *n* frein *m* à main.

handclap ['hændklæp] *n*: **to give the slow
~** taper des mains lentement pour manifester sa
désapprobation.

handcrafted ['hændkrɑːftɪd] *adj* fait(e) (à la)
main.

handcuff ['hændkʌf] *vt* mettre OR passer
les menottes à.
◆ **handcuffs** *npl* menottes *fpl*.

handful ['hændful] *n* **-1.** [of sand, grass,
people] poignée *f*. **-2.** *inf* [person]: **to be a ~**
être difficile.

handgun ['hændgʌn] *n* revolver *m*, pistolet
m.

handicap ['hændɪkæp] (*pt* & *pp* **-ped,** *cont*
-ping) ◇ *n* handicap *m*. ◇ *vt* handicaper;
[progress, work] entraver.

handicapped ['hændɪkæpt] ◇ *adj* handica-
pé(e). ◇ *npl*: **the ~** les handicapés *mpl*.

handicraft ['hændɪkrɑːft] *n* activité *f* artisanale.

handiwork ['hændɪwɜːk] *n* (*U*) ouvrage *m*.

handkerchief ['hæŋkətʃɪf] (*pl* **-chiefs** OR
-chieves [-tʃiːvz]) *n* mouchoir *m*.

handle ['hændl] ◇ *n* poignée *f*; [of jug, cup]
anse *f*; [of knife, pan] manche *m*; **to fly off
the ~** sortir de ses gonds. ◇ *vt* **-1.** [with
hands] manipuler; [without permission] toucher à. **-2.** [deal with, be responsible for] s'occuper de; [difficult situation] faire face à. **-3.**
[treat] traiter, s'y prendre avec. ◇ *vi* [car]: **to
~ well/badly** être maniable/peu maniable.

handlebars ['hændlbɑːz] *npl* guidon *m*.

handler ['hændləʳ] *n* **-1.** [of dog] maître-
chien *m*. **-2.** [at airport]: **(baggage) ~** bagagiste *m*.

handling charges ['hændlɪŋ-] *npl* [at bank]
frais *mpl* de gestion.

hand lotion *n* lotion *f* pour les mains.

hand luggage *n* (*U*) *Br* bagages *mpl* à
main.

handmade [ˌhænd'meɪd] *adj* fait(e) (à la)
main.

hand-me-down *n* *inf* vêtement *m* usagé.

handout ['hændaʊt] *n* **-1.** [gift] don *m*. **-2.**
[leaflet] prospectus *m*.

handover ['hændəʊvəʳ] *n* remise *f*; [of
power] passation *f*; [in relay race] passage *m*.

handpicked [ˌhænd'pɪkt] *adj* trié(e) sur le
volet.

handrail ['hændreɪl] *n* rampe *f*.

handset ['hændset] *n* combiné *m*.

handshake ['hændʃeɪk] *n* serrement *m* OR poignée *f* de main.

hands-off *adj* non-interventionniste.

handsome ['hænsəm] *adj* **-1.** [good-looking] beau (belle). **-2.** [reward, profit] beau (belle); [gift] généreux(euse).

handsomely ['hænsəmlɪ] *adv* généreusement.

hands-on *adj* [training] pratique; [manager] qui s'implique.

handstand ['hændstænd] *n* équilibre *m* (*sur les mains*).

hand-to-mouth *adj* précaire.

◆ **hand to mouth** *adv* au jour le jour.

handwriting ['hænd,raɪtɪŋ] *n* écriture *f*.

handwritten ['hænd,rɪtn] *adj* écrit(e) à la main, manuscrit(e).

handy ['hændɪ] (*compar* **-ier**, *superl* **-iest**) *adj inf* **-1.** [useful] pratique; **to come in** ~ être utile. **-2.** [skilful] adroit(e). **-3.** [near] tout près, à deux pas; **to keep sthg** ~ garder qqch à portée de la main.

handyman ['hændɪmæn] (*pl* **-men** [-mən]) *n* bricoleur *m*.

hang [hæŋ] (*pt* & *pp sense 1* **hung**, *pt* & *pp sense 2* **hung** OR **hanged**) ◇ *vt* **-1.** [fasten] suspendre. **-2.** [execute] pendre. ◇ *vi* **-1.** [be fastened] pendre, être accroché(e). **-2.** [be executed] être pendu(e). ◇ *n*: **to get the** ~ **of sthg** *inf* saisir le truc OR attraper le coup pour faire qqch.

◆ **hang about, hang around** *vi* traîner.

◆ **hang on** ◇ *vt fus* [depend on] dépendre de. ◇ *vi* **-1.** [keep hold]: **to** ~ **on (to)** s'accrocher OR se cramponner (à). **-2.** *inf* [continue waiting] attendre. **-3.** [persevere] tenir bon.

◆ **hang onto** *vt fus* **-1.** [keep hold of] se cramponner à, s'accrocher à. **-2.** [keep] garder.

◆ **hang out** ◇ *vt sep* [washing] étendre. ◇ *vi inf* [spend time] traîner.

◆ **hang round** = **hang about**.

◆ **hang together** *vi* [alibi, argument] se tenir.

◆ **hang up** ◇ *vt sep* pendre. ◇ *vi* **-1.** [on telephone] raccrocher. **-2.** [hang] être accroché(e), pendre.

◆ **hang up on** *vt fus* TELEC raccrocher au nez de.

hangar ['hæŋər] *n* hangar *m*.

hangdog ['hæŋdɒg] *adj* de chien battu.

hanger ['hæŋər] *n* cintre *m*.

hanger-on (*pl* **hangers-on**) *n* parasite *m*.

hang glider *n* [apparatus] deltaplane *m*.

hang gliding *n* deltaplane *m*, vol *m* libre.

hanging ['hæŋɪŋ] *n* **-1.** [execution] pendaison *f*. **-2.** [drapery] tenture *f*.

hangman ['hæŋmən] (*pl* **-men** [-mən]) *n* bourreau *m*.

hangover ['hæŋ,əʊvər] *n* **-1.** [from drinking] gueule *f* de bois. **-2.** [from past]: ~ **(from)** reliquat *m* (de).

hang-up *n inf* complexe *m*.

hank [hæŋk] *n* écheveau *m*.

hanker ['hæŋkər]

◆ **hanker after, hanker for** *vt fus* convoiter.

hankering ['hæŋkərɪŋ] *n*: ~ **after** OR **for** envie *f* de.

hankie, hanky ['hæŋkɪ] (*pl* **-ies**) (*abbr of* **handkerchief**) *n inf* mouchoir *m*.

Hanoi [hæ'nɔɪ] *n* Hanoi.

Hansard ['hænsɑːd] *n* compte-rendu officiel des débats parlementaires en Grande-Bretagne.

Hants [hænts] (*abbr of* **Hampshire**) comté anglais.

haphazard [,hæp'hæzəd] *adj* fait(e) au hasard.

haphazardly [,hæp'hæzədlɪ] *adv* au hasard.

hapless ['hæplɪs] *adj literary* infortuné(e).

happen ['hæpən] *vi* **-1.** [occur] arriver, se passer; **to** ~ **to sb** arriver à qqn. **-2.** [chance]: **I just** ~ed **to meet him** je l'ai rencontré par hasard; **it** ~s **to be right** il se trouve que c'est juste; **as it** ~s en fait.

happening ['hæpənɪŋ] *n* événement *m*.

happily ['hæpɪlɪ] *adv* **-1.** [with pleasure] de bon cœur. **-2.** [contentedly]: **to be** ~ **doing sthg** être bien tranquillement en train de faire qqch. **-3.** [fortunately] heureusement.

happiness ['hæpɪnɪs] *n* bonheur *m*.

happy ['hæpɪ] (*compar* **-ier**, *superl* **-iest**) *adj* **-1.** [gen] heureux(euse); **to be** ~ **to do sthg** être heureux de faire qqch; ~ **Christmas/birthday!** joyeux Noël/anniversaire!; ~ **New Year!** bonne année! **-2.** [satisfied] heureux(euse), content(e); **to be** ~ **with** OR **about sthg** être heureux de qqch.

happy event *n* heureux événement *m*.

happy-go-lucky *adj* décontracté(e).

happy hour *n inf moment dans la journée où les boissons sont vendues moins cher dans les bars.*

happy medium *n* juste milieu *m*.

harangue [hə'ræŋ] ◇ *n* harangue *f*. ◇ *vt* haranguer.

Harare [hə'rɑːrɪ] *n* Harare.

harass ['hærəs] *vt* harceler.

harassed ['hærəst] *adj* harcelé(e), tourmenté(e).

harassment ['hærəsmənt] *n* harcèlement *m*.
harbinger ['hɑːbɪndʒər] *n literary* signe *m*
avant-coureur.
harbour *Br*, **harbor** *Am* ['hɑːbər] ◇ *n* port
m. ◇ *vt* **-1.** [feeling] entretenir; [doubt,
grudge] garder. **-2.** [person] héberger.
harbour master *n* capitaine *m* de port.
hard [hɑːd] ◇ *adj* **-1.** [gen] dur(e); **to be ~
on sb/sthg** être dur avec qqn/pour qqch.
-2. [winter, frost] rude. **-3.** [water] calcaire.
-4. [fact] concret(ète); [news] sûr(e), véri-
fié(e). **-5.** *Br* POL: **~ left/right** extrême
gauche/droite.
◇ *adv* **-1.** [strenuously - work] dur; [- listen,
concentrate] avec effort; **to try ~ (to do
sthg)** faire de son mieux (pour faire qqch).
-2. [forcefully] fort. **-3.** [heavily - rain] à
verse; [- snow] dru. **-4.** *phr*: **to be ~ pushed**
OR **put** OR **pressed to do** avoir bien de la
peine à faire; **to feel ~ done by** avoir l'impression d'avoir été traité injustement.
hard-and-fast *adj* [rule] absolu(e).
hardback ['hɑːdbæk] ◇ *adj* relié(e). ◇ *n*
livre *m* relié.
hard-bitten *adj* dur(e) à cuire.
hardboard ['hɑːdbɔːd] *n* contreplaqué *m*.
hard-boiled *adj* **-1.** CULIN: **~ egg** œuf *m*
dur. **-2.** [person] dur(e) à cuire.
hard cash *n* (*U*) espèces *fpl*.
hard cider *n Am* cidre *m*.
hard copy *n* COMPUT sortie *f* papier.
hard-core *adj* **-1.** [criminal] endurci(e). **-2.**
[pornography] hard (*inv*).
◆ **hard core** *n* [of group] noyau *m* (dur).
hard court *n* court *m* en dur.
hard currency *n* devise *f* forte.
hard disk *n* COMPUT disque *m* dur.
hard drugs *npl* drogues *fpl* dures.
harden ['hɑːdn] ◇ *vt* durcir; [steel] tremper.
◇ *vi* **-1.** [glue, concrete] durcir. **-2.** [person]
s'endurcir. **-3.** [attitude, opposition] se durcir.
hardened ['hɑːdnd] *adj* [criminal] endurci(e).
hardening ['hɑːdnɪŋ] *n* durcissement *m*.
hard hat *n* casque *m*.
hard-headed [-'hedɪd] *adj* [decision] pragmatique; **to be ~** [person] avoir la tête
froide.
hard-hearted [-'hɑːtɪd] *adj* insensible, impitoyable.
hard-hitting [-'hɪtɪŋ] *adj* [report] sans indulgence.
hard labour *n* (*U*) travaux *mpl* forcés.
hard line *n*: **to take a ~ on sthg** adopter
une position ferme vis-à-vis de qqch.
◆ **hard-line** *adj* convaincu(e).

◆ **hard lines** *npl Br inf*: **~s!** pas de
chance!
hard-liner *n* partisan *m* de la manière
forte.
hardly ['hɑːdlɪ] *adv* **-1.** [scarcely] à peine, ne
... guère; **this is ~ the time for complaints**
ce n'est guère le moment de se plaindre; **~
ever/anything** presque jamais/rien; **I can ~
move/wait** je peux à peine bouger/
attendre. **-2.** [only just] à peine.
hardness ['hɑːdnɪs] *n* **-1.** [firmness] dureté *f*.
-2. [difficulty] difficulté *f*.
hard-nosed [-nəʊzd] *adj* [businessman] à la
tête froide; [approach] pragmatique.
hard sell *n* vente *f* agressive; **to give sb
the ~** y aller à la vente agressive avec qqn.
hardship ['hɑːdʃɪp] *n* **-1.** (*U*) [difficult condi-
tions] épreuves *fpl*. **-2.** [difficult circumstance]
épreuve *f*.
hard shoulder *n Br* AUT bande *f* d'arrêt
d'urgence.
hard up *adj inf* fauché(e).
hardware ['hɑːdweər] *n* (*U*) **-1.** [tools,
equipment] quincaillerie *f*. **-2.** COMPUT hardware *m*, matériel *m*.
hardware shop *n* quincaillerie *f*.
hardwearing [ˌhɑːd'weərɪŋ] *adj Br* résis-
tant(e).
hardwood ['hɑːdwʊd] *n* bois *m* dur.
hardworking [ˌhɑːd'wɜːkɪŋ] *adj* travail-
leur(euse).
hardy ['hɑːdɪ] (*compar* **-ier**, *superl* **-iest**) *adj*
-1. [person, animal] vigoureux(euse), ro-
buste. **-2.** [plant] résistant(e), vivace.
hare [heər] ◇ *n* lièvre *m*. ◇ *vi Br inf*: **to ~
off** partir à fond de train.
harebrained ['heəˌbreɪnd] *adj inf* [person]
écervelé(e); [scheme, idea] insensé(e).
harelip [ˌheə'lɪp] *n* bec-de-lièvre *m*.
harem [*Br* hɑː'riːm, *Am* 'hærəm] *n* harem *m*.
haricot (bean) ['hærɪkəʊ] *n* haricot *m*
blanc.
hark [hɑːk]
◆ **hark back** *vi*: **to ~ back to** revenir à.
harlequin ['hɑːlɪkwɪn] *n* arlequin *m*.
Harley Street ['hɑːlɪ-] *n* rue du centre de
Londres célèbre pour ses spécialistes en médecine.
harm [hɑːm] ◇ *n* **-1.** [injury] mal *m*. **-2.**
[damage - to clothes, plant] dommage *m*; [- to
reputation] tort *m*; **to do ~ to sb, to do sb ~**
faire du tort à qqn; **to do ~ to sthg, to do
sthg ~** endommager qqch; **to mean no ~
by sthg** ne pas faire qqch méchamment;
there's no ~ in it il n'y a pas de mal à cela;
to be out of ~'s way [person] être en sûreté

OR lieu sûr; [thing] être en lieu sûr; **she/it came to no ~** il ne lui est rien arrivé.
◇ *vt* **-1.** [injure] faire du mal à. **-2.** [damage - clothes, plant] endommager; [- reputation] faire du tort à.

harmful ['hɑːmfʊl] *adj* nuisible, nocif(ive).

harmless ['hɑːmlɪs] *adj* **-1.** [not dangerous] inoffensif(ive). **-2.** [inoffensive] innocent(e).

harmlessly ['hɑːmlɪslɪ] *adv* sans faire de mal; [explode] sans faire de dégâts.

harmonic [hɑː'mɒnɪk] *adj* harmonique.

harmonica [hɑː'mɒnɪkə] *n* harmonica *m*.

harmonious [hɑː'məʊnjəs] *adj* harmonieux(ieuse).

harmonium [hɑː'məʊnjəm] (*pl* **-s**) *n* harmonium *m*.

harmonize, -ise ['hɑːmə,naɪz] ◇ *vt* harmoniser. ◇ *vi* s'harmoniser.

harmony ['hɑːmənɪ] (*pl* **-ies**) *n* harmonie *f*; **in ~ with** [in agreement] en harmonie OR en accord avec.

harness ['hɑːnɪs] ◇ *n* [for horse, child] harnais *m*. ◇ *vt* **-1.** [horse] harnacher. **-2.** [energy, resources] exploiter.

harp [hɑːp] *n* harpe *f*.
◆ **harp on** *vi*: **to ~ on (about sthg)** rabâcher (qqch).

harpist ['hɑːpɪst] *n* harpiste *mf*.

harpoon [hɑː'puːn] ◇ *n* harpon *m*. ◇ *vt* harponner.

harpsichord ['hɑːpsɪkɔːd] *n* clavecin *m*.

harrowing ['hærəʊɪŋ] *adj* [experience] éprouvant(e); [report, film] déchirant(e).

harry ['hærɪ] (*pt* & *pp* **-ied**) *vt*: **to ~ sb (for sthg)** harceler qqn (pour obtenir qqch).

harsh [hɑːʃ] *adj* **-1.** [life, conditions] rude; [criticism, treatment] sévère. **-2.** [to senses - sound] discordant(e); [- light, voice] criard(e); [- surface] rugueux(euse), rêche; [- taste] âpre.

harshly ['hɑːʃlɪ] *adv* **-1.** [punish, treat, criticize] sévèrement; [speak] durement. **-2.** [to senses - shine] de façon criarde.

harshness ['hɑːʃnɪs] *n* **-1.** [of life, conditions] rigueur *f*; [of criticism, treatment] sévérité *f*, dureté *f*. **-2.** [to senses - of sound] discordance *f*; [- of texture] rugosité *f*, dureté *f*; [- of light, colour] aspect *m* criard.

harvest ['hɑːvɪst] ◇ *n* [of cereal crops] moisson *f*; [of fruit] récolte *f*; [of grapes] vendange *f*, vendanges *fpl*. ◇ *vt* [cereals] moissonner; [fruit] récolter; [grapes] vendanger.

harvest festival *n* fête *f* de la moisson.

has [*weak form* həz, *strong form* hæz] → **have**.

has-been *n inf pej* ringard *m*, -e *f*.

hash [hæʃ] *n* **-1.** [meat] hachis *m*. **-2.** *inf* [mess]: **to make a ~ of sthg** faire un beau gâchis de qqch. **-3.** *drugs sl* hasch *m*.
◆ **hash up** *vt sep Br inf* faire un beau gâchis de.

hash browns *npl Am* pommes de terre *fpl* sautées.

hashish ['hæʃiːʃ] *n* haschich *m*.

hasn't ['hæznt] = **has not**.

hassle ['hæsl] *inf* ◇ *n* [annoyance] tracas *m*, embêtement *m*; **it can be a real ~** ça peut être vraiment l'horreur. ◇ *vt* tracasser.

haste [heɪst] *n* hâte *f*; **to do sthg in ~** faire qqch à la hâte; **to make ~** *dated* se hâter.

hasten ['heɪsn] *fml* ◇ *vt* hâter, accélérer. ◇ *vi* se hâter, se dépêcher; **to ~ to do sthg** s'empresser de faire qqch.

hastily ['heɪstɪlɪ] *adv* **-1.** [quickly] à la hâte. **-2.** [rashly] sans réfléchir.

hasty ['heɪstɪ] (*compar* **-ier**, *superl* **-iest**) *adj* **-1.** [quick] hâtif(ive). **-2.** [rash] irréfléchi(e).

hat [hæt] *n* chapeau *m*; **keep it under your ~** gardez-le pour vous; **to be talking through one's ~** dire n'importe quoi; **old ~** vieux jeu, dépassé.

hatbox ['hætbɒks] *n* carton *m* à chapeau.

hatch [hætʃ] ◇ *vt* **-1.** [chick] faire éclore; [egg] couver. **-2.** *fig* [scheme, plot] tramer. ◇ *vi* [chick, egg] éclore. ◇ *n* [for serving food] passe-plats *m inv*.

hatchback ['hætʃ,bæk] *n* voiture *f* avec hayon.

hatchet ['hætʃɪt] *n* hachette *f*; **to bury the ~** enterrer la hache de guerre.

hatchet job *n inf*: **to do a ~ on sb** démolir qqn.

hatchway ['hætʃ,weɪ] *n* passe-plats *m inv*, guichet *m*.

hate [heɪt] ◇ *n* (*U*) haine *f*. ◇ *vt* **-1.** [detest] haïr. **-2.** [dislike] détester; **I ~ to bother you, but ...** je suis désolé de vous déranger, mais ...; **to ~ doing sthg** avoir horreur de faire qqch.

hateful ['heɪtfʊl] *adj* odieux(ieuse).

hatred ['heɪtrɪd] *n* (*U*) haine *f*.

hat trick *n* SPORT: **to score a ~** marquer trois buts.

haughty ['hɔːtɪ] (*compar* **-ier**, *superl* **-iest**) *adj* hautain(e).

haul [hɔːl] ◇ *n* **-1.** [of drugs, stolen goods] prise *f*, butin *m*. **-2.** [distance]: **long ~** long voyage *m* OR trajet *m*. ◇ *vt* **-1.** [pull] traîner, tirer. **-2.** [transport by lorry] camionner.

haulage ['hɔːlɪdʒ] *n* transport *m* routier, camionnage *m*.

haulage contractor *n* entrepreneur *m* de transports routiers.

haulier *Br* ['hɔːlɪər], **hauler** *Am* ['hɔːlər] *n* entrepreneur *m* de transports routiers.

haunch [hɔːntʃ] *n* [of person] hanche *f*; [of animal] derrière *m*, arrière-train *m*; **a ~ of venison** un cuissot de chevreuil.

haunt [hɔːnt] ◇ *n* repaire *m*. ◇ *vt* hanter.

haunted ['hɔːntɪd] *adj* **-1.** [house, castle] hanté(e). **-2.** [look] égaré(e).

haunting ['hɔːntɪŋ] *adj* obsédant(e).

Havana [hə'vænə] *n* La Havane.

have [hæv] (*pt & pp* had) ◇ *aux vb* (*to form perfect tenses - gen*) avoir; (- *with many intransitive verbs*) être; **to ~ eaten** avoir mangé; **to ~ left** être parti(e); **I've been on holiday** j'étais en vacances; **she hasn't gone yet, has she?** elle n'est pas encore partie, si?; **no, she hasn't** non; **yes, she has** oui; **I was out of breath, having run all the way** j'étais essoufflé d'avoir couru tout le long du chemin.
◇ *vt* **-1.** [possess, receive]: **to ~ (got)** avoir; **I ~ no money, I haven't got any money** je n'ai pas d'argent; **she's got loads of imagination** elle a plein d'imagination; **I've got things to do** j'ai (des choses) à faire. **-2.** [experience illness] avoir; **to ~ flu** avoir la grippe. **-3.** [referring to an action, instead of another verb]: **to ~ a read** lire; **to ~ a swim** nager; **to ~ a bath/shower** prendre un bain/une douche; **to ~ a cigarette** fumer une cigarette; **to ~ a meeting** tenir une réunion; **to ~ a bad day** passer une mauvaise journée. **-4.** [give birth to] avoir; **to ~ a baby** avoir un bébé. **-5.** [cause to be done]: **to ~ sb do sthg** faire faire qqch à qqn; **to ~ sthg done** faire faire qqch; **I'm having the house decorated** je fais décorer la maison; **to ~ one's hair cut** se faire couper les cheveux. **-6.** [be treated in a certain way]: **I had my car stolen** je me suis fait voler ma voiture, on m'a volé ma voiture. **-7.** *inf* [cheat]: **to be had** se faire avoir. **-8.** *phr*: **to ~ it in for sb** en avoir après qqn, en vouloir à qqn; **to ~ had it** [car, machine, clothes] avoir fait son temps; **I've had it!** je n'en peux plus!
◇ *modal vb* [be obliged]: **to ~ (got) to do sthg** devoir faire qqch, être obligé(e) de faire qqch; **do you ~ to go?**, **~ you got to go?** est-ce que tu dois partir?, est-ce que tu es obligé de partir?; **I've got to go to work** il faut que j'aille travailler.
◆ **haves** *npl*: **the ~s and the ~ nots** les riches et les pauvres.
◆ **have on** *vt sep* **-1.** [be wearing] porter; **to ~ nothing on** être tout nu. **-2.** [tease] faire

marcher. **-3.** [have to do]: **to ~ (got) a lot on** être très pris(e).
◆ **have out** *vt sep* **-1.** [have removed]: **to have one's appendix/tonsils out** se faire opérer de l'appendicite/des amygdales; **to ~ a tooth out** se faire arracher une dent. **-2.** [discuss frankly]: **to ~ it out with sb** s'expliquer avec qqn.
◆ **have up** *vt sep Br inf*: **to ~ sb up for sthg** traduire qqn en justice pour qqch.

haven ['heɪvn] *n* havre *m*.

haven't ['hævnt] = **have not**.

haversack ['hævəsæk] *n* sac *m* à dos.

havoc ['hævək] *n* (*U*) dégâts *mpl*; **to play ~ with** [gen] abîmer; [with health] détraquer; [with plans] ruiner.

Hawaii [hə'waɪiː] *n* Hawaii *m*; **in ~** à Hawaii.

Hawaiian [hə'waɪjən] ◇ *adj* hawaiien(ienne). ◇ *n* Hawaiien *m*, -ienne *f*.

hawk [hɔːk] ◇ *n* faucon *m*; **to watch sb like a ~** ne pas lâcher qqn des yeux. ◇ *vt* colporter.

hawker ['hɔːkər] *n* colporteur *m*.

hawthorn ['hɔːθɔːn] *n* aubépine *f*.

hay [heɪ] *n* foin *m*.

hay fever *n* (*U*) rhume *m* des foins.

haymaking ['heɪˌmeɪkɪŋ] *n* fenaison *f*.

haystack ['heɪˌstæk] *n* meule *f* de foin.

haywire ['heɪˌwaɪər] *adj inf*: **to go ~** [person] perdre la tête; [machine] se détraquer.

hazard ['hæzəd] ◇ *n* hasard *m*. ◇ *vt* hasarder.

hazardous ['hæzədəs] *adj* hasardeux(euse).

hazard warning lights *npl Br* AUT feux *mpl* de détresse.

haze ['heɪz] *n* brume *f*.

hazel ['heɪzl] ◇ *adj* noisette (*inv*). ◇ *n* [tree] noisetier *m*.

hazelnut ['heɪzlˌnʌt] *n* noisette *f*.

hazy ['heɪzɪ] (*compar* -ier, *superl* -iest) *adj* **-1.** [misty] brumeux(euse). **-2.** [memory, ideas] flou(e), vague.

H-bomb *n* bombe *f* H.

h & c *abbr of* **hot and cold (water)**.

he [hiː] ◇ *pers pron* **-1.** (*unstressed*) il; **~'s tall** il est grand; **~ who** *fml* (celui) qui; **there ~ is** le voilà. **-2.** (*stressed*) lui; **HE can't do it** lui ne peut pas le faire. ◇ *n inf* [referring to animal, baby]: **it's a ~** [animal] c'est un mâle; [baby] c'est un garçon. ◇ *comp* mâle; **~-goat** bouc *m*.

HE -1. *abbr of* **high explosive**. **-2.** (*abbr of* **His (or Her) Excellency**) S.Exc., S.E.

head [hed] ◇ *n* **-1.** [of person, animal] tête *f*; a OR per ~ par tête, par personne; **off the top of my ~**, I'd say ... comme ça je dirais ...; **I couldn't make ~ nor tail of it** je n'y comprenais rien; **on your own ~ be it** à vos risques et périls; **I'm banging my ~ against a brick wall** je me tape la tête contre les murs; **to bite** OR **snap sb's ~ off** rembarrer qqn; **to laugh one's ~ off** rire à gorge déployée; **to sing/shout one's ~ off** chanter/crier à tue-tête; **to be off one's ~** *Br*, **to be out of one's ~** *Am* être dingue; **to be soft in the ~** être débile; **to go to one's ~** [alcohol, praise] monter à la tête; **to keep one's ~** garder son sang-froid; **to lose one's ~** perdre la tête; **we put our ~s together** nous avons conjugué nos efforts. **-2.** [of table, bed, hammer] tête *f*; [of stairs, page] haut *m*. **-3.** [of flower] tête *f*; [of cabbage] pomme *f*. **-4.** [leader] chef *m*. **-5.** [head teacher] directeur *m*, -trice *f*. **-6.** *phr*: **to come to a ~** atteindre un point critique. ◇ *vt* **-1.** [procession, list] être en tête de. **-2.** [be in charge of] être à la tête de. **-3.** FTBL: **to ~ the ball** faire une tête. ◇ *vi*: **where are you ~ing**? où allez-vous? ◆ **heads** *npl* [on coin] face *f*; **~s or tails**? pile ou face? ◆ **head for** *vt fus* **-1.** [place] se diriger vers. **-2.** *fig* [trouble, disaster] aller au devant de. ◆ **head off** *vt sep* **-1.** [intercept] intercepter. **-2.** *fig* [threat, disaster] parer à.

headache ['hedeɪk] *n* mal *m* de tête; **to have a ~** avoir mal à la tête.

headband ['hedbænd] *n* bandeau *m*.

headboard ['hedbɔːd] *n* dosseret *m*.

head boy *n Br* élève *chargé de la discipline et qui siège aux conseils de son école.*

head cold *n* rhume *m* de cerveau.

head count *n* compte *m*.

headdress ['hed,dres] *n* coiffe *f*.

header ['hedə'] *n* FTBL tête *f*.

headfirst [,hed'fɜːst] *adv* (la) tête la première.

headgear ['hed,gɪə'] *n* (*U*) couvre-chef *m*.

head girl *n Br* élève *chargée de la discipline et qui siège aux conseils de son école.*

headhunt ['hedhʌnt] *vt* recruter (chez la concurrence).

headhunter ['hed,hʌntə'] *n* chasseur *m* de têtes.

heading ['hedɪŋ] *n* titre *m*, intitulé *m*.

headlamp ['hedlæmp] *n Br* phare *m*.

headland ['hedlənd] *n* cap *m*.

headlight ['hedlaɪt] *n* phare *m*.

headline ['hedlaɪn] *n* [in newspaper] gros titre *m*; TV & RADIO grand titre *m*.

headlong ['hedlɒŋ] ◇ *adv* **-1.** [quickly] à toute allure. **-2.** [unthinkingly] tête baissée. **-3.** [headfirst] (la) tête la première. ◇ *adj* [unthinking] irréfléchi(e).

headmaster [,hed'mɑːstə'] *n* directeur *m* (d'une école).

headmistress [,hed'mɪstrɪs] *n* directrice *f* (d'une école).

head office *n* siège *m* social.

head-on ◇ *adj* [collision] de plein fouet; [confrontation] de front. ◇ *adv* de plein fouet.

headphones ['hedfəʊnz] *npl* casque *m*.

headquarters [,hed'kwɔːtəz] *npl* [of business, organization] siège *m*; [of armed forces] quartier *m* général.

headrest ['hedrest] *n* appui-tête *m*.

headroom ['hedrʊm] *n* (*U*) hauteur *f*.

headscarf ['hedskɑːf] (*pl* **-scarves** [-skɑːvz] OR **-scarfs**) *n* foulard *m*.

headset ['hedset] *n* casque *m*.

headship ['hedʃɪp] *n* direction *f* (d'une école).

headstand ['hedstænd] *n* poirier *m*.

head start *n* avantage *m* au départ; **~ on** OR **over** avantage sur.

headstone ['hedstəʊn] *n* pierre *f* tombale.

headstrong ['hedstrɒŋ] *adj* volontaire, têtu(e).

head teacher *n* directeur *m*, -trice *f* (d'une école).

head waiter *n* maître *m* d'hôtel.

headway ['hedweɪ] *n*: **to make ~** faire des progrès.

headwind ['hedwɪnd] *n* vent *m* contraire.

heady ['hedɪ] (*compar* **-ier**, *superl* **-iest**) *adj* **-1.** [exciting] grisant(e). **-2.** [causing giddiness] capiteux(euse).

heal [hiːl] ◇ *vt* **-1.** [cure] guérir. **-2.** *fig* [troubles, discord] apaiser. ◇ *vi* se guérir. ◆ **heal up** *vi* se cicatriser, se refermer.

healing ['hiːlɪŋ] ◇ *adj* curatif(ive). ◇ *n* (*U*) guérison *f*.

health [helθ] *n* santé *f*; **to be in good/poor ~** être en bonne/mauvaise santé; **to drink (to) sb's ~** boire à la santé de qqn.

health centre *n* ≃ centre *m* médico-social.

health-conscious *adj* soucieux(ieuse) de sa santé.

health farm *n* établissement *m* de cure.

health food *n* produits *mpl* diététiques OR naturels.

health food shop n magasin m de produits diététiques.

health hazard n danger m OR risque m pour la santé.

health service n ≃ Sécurité f Sociale.

health visitor n Br infirmière f visiteuse.

healthy ['helθɪ] (compar -ier, superl -iest) adj -1. [gen] sain(e). -2. [well] en bonne santé, bien portant(e). -3. fig [economy, company] qui se porte bien. -4. [profit] bon (bonne).

heap [hi:p] ◇ n tas m; **in a ~** en tas. ◇ vt -1. [pile up] entasser. -2. fig [give]: **to ~ gifts on sb** couvrir qqn de cadeaux; **to ~ praise on sb** combler qqn d'éloges; **to ~ scorn on sb** accabler qqn de mépris.

◆ **heaps** npl inf: **~s of** [people, objects] des tas de; [time, money] énormément de.

hear [hɪəʳ] (pt & pp **heard** [hɜ:d]) ◇ vt -1. [gen & JUR] entendre. -2. [learn of] apprendre; **to ~ (that) ...** apprendre que ....
◇ vi -1. [perceive sound] entendre. -2. [know]: **to ~ about** entendre parler de; **did you ~ about her husband?** tu es au courant, pour son mari? -3. [receive news]: **to ~ about** avoir des nouvelles de; **have you heard about your blood test yet?** as-tu déjà reçu des nouvelles à propos de ta prise de sang?; **to ~ from sb** recevoir des nouvelles de qqn. -4. phr: **to have heard of** avoir entendu parler de; **I won't ~ of it!** je ne veux pas en entendre parler!

◆ **hear out** vt sep écouter jusqu'au bout.

hearing ['hɪərɪŋ] n -1. [sense] ouïe f; **Joe was in** OR **within Jim's ~** Jim était à portée de voix de Joe; **hard of ~** dur(e) d'oreille. -2. [trial] audience f; **to get a fair ~** pouvoir défendre sa cause; JUR être jugé équitablement.

hearing aid n audiophone m.

hearsay ['hɪəseɪ] n ouï-dire m.

hearse [hɜ:s] n corbillard m.

heart [hɑ:t] n lit & fig cœur m; **from the ~** du fond du cœur; **to lose ~** perdre courage; **my ~ leapt** j'ai bondi de joie; **my ~ sank** je me suis senti abattu; **it's a subject close to my ~** c'est un sujet qui me tient à cœur; **from the bottom of my ~** du fond du cœur; **his ~ isn't in it** il n'a pas le cœur à cela; **in one's ~ of ~s** au plus profond de son cœur; **to do sthg to one's ~'s content** faire qqch à souhait; **to break sb's ~** briser le cœur à qqn; **to set one's ~ on sthg/on doing sthg** désirer absolument qqch/faire qqch, vouloir à tout prix qqch/faire qqch; **to take sthg to ~** prendre qqch à cœur; **to have a ~ of gold** avoir un cœur d'or.

◆ **hearts** npl cœur m; **the six of ~s** le six de cœur.

◆ **at heart** adv au fond (de soi).

◆ **by heart** adv par cœur.

heartache ['hɑ:teɪk] n peine f de cœur.

heart attack n crise f cardiaque.

heartbeat ['hɑ:tbi:t] n battement m de cœur.

heartbreaking ['hɑ:t,breɪkɪŋ] adj à fendre le cœur.

heartbroken ['hɑ:t,brəʊkn] adj qui a le cœur brisé.

heartburn ['hɑ:tbɜ:n] n (U) brûlures fpl d'estomac.

heart disease n maladie f de cœur.

heartening ['hɑ:tnɪŋ] adj encourageant(e).

heart failure n arrêt m cardiaque.

heartfelt ['hɑ:tfelt] adj sincère.

hearth [hɑ:θ] n foyer m.

heartland ['hɑ:tlænd] n centre m, cœur m.

heartless ['hɑ:tlɪs] adj sans cœur.

heartrending ['hɑ:t,rendɪŋ] adj déchirant(e), qui fend le cœur.

heart-searching n: **after a lot of ~** après s'être beaucoup interrogé.

heartthrob ['hɑ:tθrɒb] n inf idole f, coqueluche f.

heart-to-heart ◇ adj à cœur ouvert. ◇ n conversation f à cœur ouvert.

heart transplant n greffe f du cœur.

heartwarming ['hɑ:t,wɔ:mɪŋ] adj réconfortant(e).

hearty ['hɑ:tɪ] (compar -ier, superl -iest) adj -1. [greeting, person] cordial(e). -2. [substantial - meal] copieux(ieuse); [- appetite] gros (grosse).

heat [hi:t] ◇ n -1. (U) [warmth] chaleur f. -2. (U) fig [pressure] pression f. -3. [eliminating round] éliminatoire f. -4. ZOOL: **on** Br OR **in ~** en chaleur. ◇ vt chauffer.

◆ **heat up** ◇ vt sep réchauffer. ◇ vi chauffer.

heated ['hi:tɪd] adj [argument, discussion, person] animé(e); [issue] chaud(e).

heater ['hi:təʳ] n appareil m de chauffage.

heath [hi:θ] n lande f.

heathen ['hi:ðn] ◇ adj païen(enne). ◇ n païen m, -enne f.

heather ['heðəʳ] n bruyère f.

heating ['hi:tɪŋ] n chauffage m.

heat rash n boutons mpl de chaleur.

heat-resistant adj résistant(e) à la chaleur.

heat-seeking [-,si:kɪŋ] adj guidé(e) par la chaleur.

heatstroke ['hi:tstrəʊk] *n* (*U*) coup *m* de chaleur.

heat wave *n* canicule *f,* vague *f* de chaleur.

heave [hi:v] ◇ *vt* **-1.** [pull] tirer (avec effort); [push] pousser (avec effort). **-2.** *inf* [throw] lancer. ◇ *vi* **-1.** [pull] tirer. **-2.** [rise and fall] se soulever. **-3.** [retch] avoir des haut-le-cœur. ◇ *n*: **to give sthg a ~** [pull/push] tirer/pousser qqch (avec effort).

heaven ['hevn] *n* paradis *m*; **it was ~** *fig* c'était divin OR merveilleux; **~ (alone) knows!** Dieu seul le sait!
◆ **heavens** ◇ *npl*: **the ~s** *literary* les cieux *mpl.* ◇ *excl*: **(good) ~s!** juste ciel!

heavenly ['hevnlɪ] *adj* **-1.** *inf* [delightful] délicieux(ieuse), merveilleux(euse). **-2.** *literary* [of the skies] céleste.

heavily ['hevɪlɪ] *adv* **-1.** [booked, in debt] lourdement; [rain, smoke, drink] énormément. **-2.** [solidly - built] solidement. **-3.** [breathe, sigh] péniblement, bruyamment. **-4.** [fall, sit down] lourdement.

heaviness ['hevɪnɪs] *n* **-1.** [gen] lourdeur *f.* **-2.** [intensity] intensité *f.*

heavy ['hevɪ] (*compar* **-ier,** *superl* **-iest**) *adj* **-1.** [gen] lourd(e); **how ~ is it?** ça pèse combien?; **with a ~ heart** [sad] le cœur gros. **-2.** [traffic] dense; [rain] battant(e); [fighting] acharné(e); [casualties, corrections] nombreux(euses); [smoker, drinker] gros (grosse); **to be ~ on petrol** consommer beaucoup (d'essence). **-3.** [noisy - breathing] bruyant(e). **-4.** [schedule] chargé(e). **-5.** [physically exacting - work, job] pénible.

heavy cream *n Am* crème *f* fraîche épaisse.

heavy-duty *adj* solide, robuste.

heavy goods vehicle *n Br* poids lourd *m.*

heavy-handed [-'hændɪd] *adj* maladroit(e).

heavy industry *n* industrie *f* lourde.

heavy metal *n* MUS heavy metal *m.*

heavyweight ['hevɪweɪt] SPORT ◇ *adj* poids lourd. ◇ *n* poids lourd *m.*

Hebrew ['hi:bru:] ◇ *adj* hébreu, hébraïque. ◇ *n* **-1.** [person] Hébreu *m,* Israélite *mf.* **-2.** [language] hébreu *m.*

Hebrides ['hebrɪdi:z] *npl*: **the ~** les (îles *fpl*) Hébrides; **in the ~** aux Hébrides.

heck [hek] *excl inf*: **what/where/why the ~ ...?** que/où/pourquoi diable ...?; **a ~ of a nice guy** un type vachement sympa; **a ~ of a lot of people** un tas de gens.

heckle ['hekl] ◇ *vt* interpeller, interrompre. ◇ *vi* interrompre bruyamment.

heckler ['heklər] *n* perturbateur *m,* -trice *f.*

hectare ['hekteər] *n* hectare *m.*

hectic ['hektɪk] *adj* [meeting, day] agité(e), mouvementé(e).

hector ['hektər] ◇ *vt* rudoyer. ◇ *vi* agir de façon autoritaire.

he'd [hi:d] = **he had, he would.**

hedge [hedʒ] ◇ *n* haie *f.* ◇ *vi* [prevaricate] répondre de façon détournée.

hedgehog ['hedʒhɒg] *n* hérisson *m.*

hedgerow ['hedʒrəʊ] *n* bordure *f* d'arbres.

hedonism ['hi:dənɪzm] *n* hédonisme *m.*

hedonist ['hi:dənɪst] *n* hédoniste *mf.*

heed [hi:d] ◇ *n*: **to pay ~ to sb** prêter attention à qqn; **to take ~ of sthg** tenir compte de qqch. ◇ *vt fml* tenir compte de.

heedless ['hi:dlɪs] *adj*: **~ of sthg** qui ne tient pas compte de qqch.

heel [hi:l] *n* talon *m*; **to dig one's ~s in** *fig* se buter; **to follow hard on the ~s of sb** être sur les talons de qqn; **to follow hard on the ~s of sthg** arriver immédiatement après qqch; **to take to one's ~s** prendre ses jambes à son cou; **to turn on one's ~** tourner les talons.

hefty ['heftɪ] (*compar* **-ier,** *superl* **-iest**) *adj* **-1.** [well-built] costaud(e). **-2.** [large] gros (grosse).

heifer ['hefər] *n* génisse *f.*

height [haɪt] *n* **-1.** [of building, mountain] hauteur *f*; [of person] taille *f*; **5 metres in ~** 5 mètres de haut; **what ~ is it?** combien cela mesure-t-il?; **what ~ are you?** combien mesurez-vous? **-2.** [above ground - of aircraft] altitude *f*; **to gain/lose ~** gagner/perdre de l'altitude; **at shoulder ~** à hauteur de l'épaule. **-3.** [zenith]: **at the ~ of the summer/season** au cœur de l'été/de la saison; **at the ~ of his fame** au sommet de sa gloire.
◆ **heights** *npl* [high places] hauteurs *fpl*; **to be afraid of ~s** avoir le vertige.

heighten ['heɪtn] *vt & vi* augmenter.

heinous ['heɪnəs] *adj fml* odieux(ieuse).

heir [eər] *n* héritier *m.*

heir apparent (*pl* **heirs apparent**) *n* héritier *m* présomptif.

heiress ['eərɪs] *n* héritière *f.*

heirloom ['eəlu:m] *n* meuble *m*/bijou *m* de famille.

heist [haɪst] *n inf* casse *m.*

held [held] *pt & pp* → **hold.**

helices ['helɪsi:z] *pl* → **helix.**

helicopter ['helɪkɒptər] *n* hélicoptère *m.*

heliport ['helɪpɔ:t] *n* héliport *m.*

helium ['hi:lɪəm] *n* hélium *m.*

helix ['hi:lɪks] (*pl* **-es** OR **helices**) *n* hélice *f*.

hell [hel] ◇ *n* **-1.** *lit* & *fig* enfer *m*. **-2.** *inf* [for emphasis]: **he's a ~ of a nice guy** c'est un type vachement sympa; **what/where/ why the ~ ...?** que/où/pourquoi ..., bon sang?; **a ~ of a mess** un sacré bazar; **to hurt like ~** faire vachement mal; **like ~ you will!** il n'y a pas de danger!; **to get the ~ out (of)** foutre le camp (de). **-3.** *phr*: **all ~ broke loose** *inf* il y a eu de l'orage; **to do sthg for the ~ of it** *inf* faire qqch pour le plaisir, faire qqch juste comme ça; **to give sb ~** *inf* [verbally] engueuler qqn; **go to ~!** *v inf* va te faire foutre!; **to play ~ with sthg** *inf* foutre qqch en l'air; **to ~ with him!** *inf* il peut aller se faire voir!; **to ~ with the expense!** *inf* au diable l'avarice! ◇ *excl inf* merde!, zut!

he'll [hi:l] = **he will**.

hell-bent *adj*: **to be ~ on sthg/on doing sthg** vouloir à tout prix qqch/faire qqch.

hellish ['helɪʃ] *adj inf* infernal(e).

hello [hə'ləʊ] *excl* **-1.** [as greeting] bonjour!; [on phone] allô! **-2.** [to attract attention] hé!

helm [helm] *n lit* & *fig* barre *f*; **at the ~** à la barre.

helmet ['helmɪt] *n* casque *m*.

helmsman ['helmzmən] (*pl* **-men**) *n* NAUT timonier *m*.

help [help] ◇ *n* **-1.** (*U*) [assistance] aide *f*; **he gave me a lot of ~** il m'a beaucoup aidé; **with the ~ of sthg** à l'aide de qqch; **with sb's ~** avec l'aide de qqn; **to be of ~** rendre service. **-2.** (*U*) [emergency aid] secours *m*. **-3.** [useful person or object]: **to be a ~** aider, rendre service.
◇ *vi* aider.
◇ *vt* **-1.** [assist] aider; **to ~ sb (to) do sthg** aider qqn à faire qqch; **to ~ sb with sthg** aider qqn à faire qqch; **can I ~ you?** que désirez-vous? **-2.** [avoid]: **I can't ~ it** je n'y peux rien; **I can't ~ feeling sad about it** je n'y peux rien, cela me rend triste; **I couldn't ~ laughing** je ne pouvais pas m'empêcher de rire. **-3.** *phr*: **to ~ o.s. (to sthg)** se servir (de qqch).
◇ *excl* au secours!, à l'aide!
◆ **help out** *vt sep* & *vi* aider.

helper ['helpə˞] *n* **-1.** [gen] aide *mf*. **-2.** *Am* [to do housework] femme *f* de ménage.

helpful ['helpfʊl] *adj* **-1.** [person] serviable; **you've been very ~** vous (nous) avez bien rendu service. **-2.** [advice, suggestion] utile.

helping ['helpɪŋ] *n* portion *f*; [of cake, tart] part *f*.

helping hand *n* coup *m* de main.

helpless ['helplɪs] *adj* impuissant(e); [look, gesture] d'impuissance.

helplessly ['helplɪslɪ] *adv* **-1.** [stand by, watch] sans rien pouvoir faire. **-2.** [uncontrollably]: **to laugh ~** avoir le fou rire.

helpline ['helplaɪn] *n* ligne *f* d'assistance téléphonique.

Helsinki ['helsɪŋkɪ] *n* Helsinki.

helter-skelter ['heltə'skeltə˞] *Br* ◇ *n* toboggan *m*. ◇ *adv* pêle-mêle.

hem [hem] (*pt* & *pp* **-med**, *cont* **-ming**) ◇ *n* ourlet *m*. ◇ *vt* ourler.
◆ **hem in** *vt sep* encercler.

he-man *n inf hum* vrai mâle *m*.

hematology [,hi:mə'tɒlədʒɪ] *n* hématologie *f*.

hemisphere ['hemɪ,sfɪə˞] *n* hémisphère *m*.

hemline ['hemlaɪn] *n* ourlet *m*.

hemoglobin [,hi:mə'gləʊbɪn] *n* hémoglobine *f*.

hemophilia [,hi:mə'fɪlɪə] *n* hémophilie *f*.

hemophiliac [,hi:mə'fɪlɪæk] *n* hémophile *mf*.

hemorrhage ['hemərɪdʒ] ◇ *n* hémorragie *f*. ◇ *vi* faire une hémorragie.

hemorrhoids ['hemərɔɪdz] *npl* hémorroïdes *fpl*.

hemp [hemp] *n* [plant, fibre] chanvre *m*.

hen [hen] *n* **-1.** [female chicken] poule *f*. **-2.** [female bird] femelle *f*.

hence [hens] *adv fml* **-1.** [therefore] d'où. **-2.** [from now] d'ici.

henceforth [,hens'fɔ:θ] *adv fml* dorénavant.

henchman ['hentʃmən] (*pl* **-men** [-mən]) *n pej* acolyte *m*.

henna ['henə] ◇ *n* henné *m*. ◇ *vt* [hair] appliquer du henné sur.

hen party *n* soirée *f* entre femmes; [before wedding] *soirée où une future mariée enterre sa vie de célibataire avec ses amies*.

henpecked ['henpekt] *adj pej* dominé par sa femme.

hepatitis [,hepə'taɪtɪs] *n* hépatite *f*.

her [hɜ:r] ◇ *pers pron* **-1.** (*direct - unstressed*) la, l' (+ *vowel or silent 'h'*); (- *stressed*) elle; **I know/like ~** je la connais/l'aime; **it's ~** c'est elle; **if I were** OR **was ~** si j'étais elle, à sa place; **you can't expect** HER **to do it** tu ne peux pas exiger que ce soit elle qui le fasse. **-2.** (*referring to animal, car, ship etc*) *follow the gender of your translation*. **-3.** (*indirect*) lui; **we spoke to ~** nous lui avons parlé; **he sent ~ a letter** il lui a envoyé une lettre. **-4.** (*after prep, in comparisons etc*) elle; **I'm shorter than ~** je suis plus petit qu'elle.

◇ *poss adj* son (sa), ses (*pl*); ~ **coat** son manteau; ~ **bedroom** sa chambre; ~ **children** ses enfants; ~ **name is Sarah** elle s'appelle Sarah; **it was** HER **fault** c'était de sa faute à elle.

herald ['herəld] ◇ *vt fml* annoncer. ◇ *n* -1. [messenger] héraut *m*. -2. [sign] signe *m*.

heraldry ['herəldrɪ] *n* héraldique *f*.

herb [hɜ:b] *n* herbe *f*.

herbaceous [hɜ:'beɪʃəs] *adj* herbacé(e).

herbal ['hɜ:bl] *adj* à base de plantes.

herbicide ['hɜ:bɪsaɪd] *n* herbicide *m*.

herbivore ['hɜ:bɪvɔ:ʳ] *n* herbivore *m*.

herb tea *n* tisane *f*.

herd [hɜ:d] ◇ *n* troupeau *m*. ◇ *vt* -1. [cattle, sheep] mener. -2. *fig* [people] conduire, mener; [into confined space] parquer.

herdsman ['hɜ:dzmən] (*pl* -men [-mən]) *n* gardien *m* de troupeau.

here [hɪəʳ] *adv* -1. [in this place] ici; ~ **he is/they are** le/les voici; ~ **it is** le/la voici; ~ **is/are** voici; ~ **and there** ça et là. -2. [present] là; **he's not** ~ **today** il n'est pas là aujourd'hui. -3. [in toasts]: ~**'s to** à la santé de.

hereabouts *Br* [,hɪərə'baʊts], **hereabout** *Am* [,hɪərə'baʊt] *adv* par ici.

hereafter [,hɪər'ɑ:ftəʳ] ◇ *adv fml* ci-après. ◇ *n*: **the** ~ l'au-delà *m*.

hereby [,hɪə'baɪ] *adv fml* par la présente.

hereditary [hɪ'redɪtrɪ] *adj* héréditaire.

heredity [hɪ'redətɪ] *n* hérédité *f*.

heresy ['herəsɪ] (*pl* -ies) *n* hérésie *f*.

heretic ['herətɪk] *n* hérétique *mf*.

herewith [,hɪə'wɪð] *adv fml* [with letter] ci-joint, ci-inclus.

heritage ['herɪtɪdʒ] *n* héritage *m*, patrimoine *m*.

heritage centre *n* musée *m*.

hermaphrodite [hɜ:'mæfrədaɪt] ◇ *adj* hermaphrodite. ◇ *n* hermaphrodite *m*.

hermetic [hɜ:'metɪk] *adj* hermétique.

hermetically [hɜ:'metɪkəlɪ] *adv*: ~ **sealed** fermé(e) hermétiquement.

hermit ['hɜ:mɪt] *n* ermite *m*.

hernia ['hɜ:njə] *n* hernie *f*.

hero ['hɪərəʊ] (*pl* -es) *n* héros *m*.

heroic [hɪ'rəʊɪk] *adj* héroïque.

heroin ['herəʊɪn] *n* héroïne *f*.

heroine ['herəʊɪn] *n* héroïne *f*.

heroism ['herəʊɪzm] *n* héroïsme *m*.

heron ['herən] (*pl inv* OR -s) *n* héron *m*.

hero worship *n* culte *m* du héros.

herpes ['hɜ:pi:z] *n* herpès *m*.

herring ['herɪŋ] (*pl inv* OR -s) *n* hareng *m*.

herringbone ['herɪŋbəʊn] *n* [pattern] chevrons *mpl*.

hers [hɜ:z] *poss pron* le sien (la sienne), les siens (les siennes) (*pl*); **that money is** ~ cet argent est à elle OR est le sien; **it wasn't his fault, it was** HERS ce n'était pas de sa faute à lui, c'était de sa faute à elle; **a friend of** ~ un ami à elle, un de ses amis.

herself [hɜ:'self] *pron* -1. (*reflexive*) se; (*after prep*) elle. -2. (*for emphasis*) elle-même; **she did it** ~ elle l'a fait toute seule.

Herts [hɑ:ts] (*abbr of* **Hertfordshire**) *comté anglais*.

he's [hi:z] = **he is, he has**.

hesitant ['hezɪtənt] *adj* hésitant(e); **to be** ~ **about doing sthg** hésiter à faire qqch.

hesitate ['hezɪteɪt] *vi* hésiter; **to** ~ **to do sthg** hésiter à faire qqch.

hesitation [,hezɪ'teɪʃn] *n* hésitation *f*; **to have no** ~ **in doing sthg** ne pas hésiter à faire qqch.

hessian ['hesɪən] *n* Br jute *m*.

heterogeneous [,hetərə'dʒi:njəs] *adj fml* hétérogène.

heterosexual [,hetərəʊ'sekʃʊəl] ◇ *adj* hétérosexuel(elle). ◇ *n* hétérosexuel *m*, -elle *f*.

het up [het-] *adj inf* excité(e), énervé(e).

hew [hju:] (*pt* -ed, *pp* -ed OR **hewn** [hju:n]) *vt literary* [stone] tailler; [wood] couper.

HEW (*abbr of* (**Department of**) **Health, Education and Welfare**) *n ministère américain de l'éducation et de la santé publique.*

hex [heks] *n* [curse] sort *m*.

hexagon ['heksəgən] *n* hexagone *m*.

hexagonal [hek'sægənl] *adj* hexagonal(e).

hey [heɪ] *excl* hé!

heyday ['heɪdeɪ] *n* âge *m* d'or.

hey presto [-'prestəʊ] *excl* passez muscade!

hi [haɪ] *excl inf* salut!

HF (*abbr of* **high frequency**) HF.

HGV (*abbr of* **heavy goods vehicle**) *n* PL *m*; **an** ~ **licence** un permis PL.

HI *abbr of* **Hawaii**.

hiatus [haɪ'eɪtəs] (*pl* -es) *n fml* pause *f*.

hiatus hernia *n* hernie *f* hiatale.

hibernate ['haɪbəneɪt] *vi* hiberner.

hibernation [,haɪbə'neɪʃn] *n* hibernation *f*.

hiccough, hiccup ['hɪkʌp] (*pt* & *pp* -ped, *cont* -ping) ◇ *n* hoquet *m*; *fig* [difficulty] accroc *m*; **to have** ~**s** avoir le hoquet. ◇ *vi* hoqueter.

hick [hɪk] *n inf pej* péquenaud *m*, -e *f*.

hid [hɪd] *pt* → **hide**.

hidden ['hɪdn] ◇ *pp* → **hide**. ◇ *adj* caché(e).

hide [haɪd] (*pt* **hid**, *pp* **hidden**) ◇ *vt*: **to ~ sthg (from sb)** cacher qqch (à qqn); [information] taire qqch (à qqn). ◇ *vi* se cacher. ◇ *n* **-1.** [animal skin] **peau** *f*. **-2.** [for watching birds, animals] **cachette** *f*.

hide-and-seek *n* cache-cache *m*.

hideaway ['haɪdəweɪ] *n* cachette *f*.

hidebound ['haɪdbaʊnd] *adj pej* [person] borné(e); [institution] rigide.

hideous ['hɪdɪəs] *adj* hideux(euse); [error, conditions] abominable.

hideout ['haɪdaʊt] *n* cachette *f*.

hiding ['haɪdɪŋ] *n* **-1.** [concealment]: **to be in ~** se tenir caché(e). **-2.** *inf* [beating]: **to give sb a (good) ~** donner une (bonne) raclée OR correction à qqn.

hiding place *n* cachette *f*.

hierarchical [,haɪə'rɑːkɪkl] *adj* hiérarchique.

hierarchy ['haɪərɑːkɪ] (*pl* **-ies**) *n* hiérarchie *f*.

hieroglyphics [,haɪərə'glɪfɪks] *npl* hiéroglyphes *mpl*.

hi-fi ['haɪfaɪ] *n* hi-fi *f*.

higgledy-piggledy [,hɪɡldɪ'pɪɡldɪ] *inf* ◇ *adj* pêle-mêle (*inv*). ◇ *adv* pêle-mêle.

high [haɪ] ◇ *adj* **-1.** [gen] haut(e); **it's 3 feet/6 metres ~** cela fait 3 pieds/6 mètres de haut; **how ~ is it?** cela fait combien de haut?; **to have a ~ opinion of sb/sthg** avoir une haute opinion de qqn/qqch. **-2.** [speed, figure, altitude, office] élevé(e). **-3.** [high-pitched] aigu(uë). **-4.** *drugs sl* qui plane, défoncé(e). **-5.** *inf* [drunk] bourré(e). ◇ *adv* haut. ◇ *n* [highest point] maximum *m*; **to reach a new ~** atteindre un nouveau record OR maximum.

highball ['haɪbɔːl] *n Am* whisky *m* à l'eau avec de la glace.

highbrow ['haɪbraʊ] *adj* intellectuel(elle).

high chair *n* chaise *f* haute (*d'enfant*).

high-class *adj* de premier ordre; [hotel, restaurant] de grande classe.

high command *n* haut commandement *m*.

high commissioner *n* haut commissaire *m*.

High Court *n Br* JUR Cour *f* Suprême.

high-density *adj* COMPUT haute densité (*inv*).

higher ['haɪə'] *adj* [exam, qualification] supérieur(e).

◆ **Higher** *n*: **Higher (Grade)** SCH *examen de fin d'études secondaires en Écosse*.

higher education *n* (*U*) études *fpl* supérieures.

high explosive *n* explosif *m* puissant.

high-fidelity *adj* haute-fidélité (*inv*).

high-flier *n* ambitieux *m*, -ieuse *f*.

high-flying *adj* [ambitious] ambitieux(ieuse).

high-handed [-'hændɪd] *adj* despotique.

high-heeled [-'hiːld] *adj* à talons hauts.

high horse *n inf*: **to get on one's ~** monter sur ses grands chevaux.

high jump *n* saut *m* en hauteur; **to be for the ~** *Br inf* être bon pour une engueulade.

Highland Games ['haɪlənd-] *npl* jeux *mpl* écossais.

HIGHLAND GAMES:
En Écosse, sorte de kermesse locale en plein air où se déroulent simultanément toutes sortes de concours (danse, cornemuse) et d'épreuves sportives (courses, lancer du marteau, mais aussi 'tossing the caber', 'tug of war' etc). Certaines épreuves sont ouvertes à tous, d'autres sont réservées à la population locale

Highlands ['haɪləndz] *npl*: **the ~** [of Scotland] les Highlands *fpl* (*région montagneuse du nord de l'Écosse*).

high-level *adj* [talks, discussions] à haut niveau; [diplomats, officials] de haut niveau.

high life *n*: **the ~** la grande vie.

highlight ['haɪlaɪt] ◇ *n* [of event, occasion] moment *m* OR point *m* fort. ◇ *vt* souligner; [with highlighter] surligner.

◆ **highlights** *npl* [in hair] reflets *mpl*, mèches *fpl*.

highlighter (pen) ['haɪlaɪtə'] *n* surligneur *m*.

highly ['haɪlɪ] *adv* **-1.** [very] extrêmement, très. **-2.** [in important position]: **~ placed** haut placé(e). **-3.** [favourably]: **to think ~ of sb/sthg** penser du bien de qqn/qqch; **to speak ~ of sb/sthg** dire du bien de qqn/qqch.

highly-strung *adj* nerveux(euse).

high mass *n* grand-messe *f*.

high-minded [-'maɪndɪd] *adj* au caractère noble.

Highness ['haɪnɪs] *n*: **His/Her/Your (Royal) ~** Son/Votre Altesse (Royale); **their (Royal) ~es** leurs Altesses (Royales).

high-octane *adj* à indice d'octane élevé.

high-pitched *adj* aigu(uë).

high point *n* [of occasion] point *m* fort.

high-powered [-'pauəd] *adj* **-1.** [powerful] de forte puissance. **-2.** [prestigious - activity, place] de haut niveau; [- job] important(e); [- person] plein(e) de dynamisme.

high-pressure *adj* **-1.** [air, gas] à haute pression; ~ **area** METEOR zone *f* de hautes pressions. **-2.** [selling] agressif(ive).

high priest *n* RELIG grand prêtre *m*.

high-ranking *adj* de haut rang.

high resolution *n* COMPUT haute résolution *f*.

high-rise *adj*: ~ **block of flats** tour *f*.

high-risk *adj* à haut risque.

high school *n* Br lycée *m*; Am établissement *m* d'enseignement supérieur.

high seas *npl*: **the** ~ la haute mer *f*.

high season *n* haute saison *f*.

high-speed *adj* **-1.** [train] à grande vitesse. **-2.** PHOT à obturation rapide.

high-spirited *adj* [person] plein(e) d'entrain.

high spot *n* point *m* fort.

high street *n* Br rue *f* principale.

hightail ['haɪteɪl] *vt inf*: **to** ~ **it** filer.

high tea *n* Br repas tenant lieu de goûter et de dîner, pris en fin d'après-midi.

high-tech [-tek] *adj* [method, industry] de pointe.

high technology *n* technologie *f* de pointe.

high-tension *adj* à haute tension.

high tide *n* marée *f* haute.

high treason *n* haute trahison *f*.

high water *n* (U) marée *f* haute.

highway ['haɪweɪ] *n* **-1.** Am [motorway] autoroute *f*. **-2.** [main road] grande route *f*.

Highway Code *n* Br: **the** ~ le code de la route.

high wire *n* corde *f* raide.

hijack ['haɪdʒæk] ◇ *n* détournement *m*. ◇ *vt* détourner.

hijacker ['haɪdʒækə'] *n* [of aircraft] pirate *m* de l'air; [of vehicle] pirate *m* de la route.

hike [haɪk] ◇ *n* [long walk] randonnée *f*. ◇ *vi* faire une randonnée.

hiker ['haɪkə'] *n* randonneur *m*, -euse *f*.

hiking ['haɪkɪŋ] *n* marche *f*.

hilarious [hɪ'leərɪəs] *adj* hilarant(e).

hilarity [hɪ'lærətɪ] *n* hilarité *f*.

hill [hɪl] *n* **-1.** [mound] colline *f*. **-2.** [slope] côte *f*.

hillbilly ['hɪl,bɪlɪ] (*pl* **-ies**) *n* Am inf pej péquenaud *m*, -e *f*.

hillock ['hɪlək] *n* petite colline *f*; [smaller] petite élévation *f*.

hillside ['hɪlsaɪd] *n* coteau *m*.

hill start *n* démarrage *m* en côte.

hilltop ['hɪltɒp] ◇ *adj* au sommet de la colline. ◇ *n* sommet *m*.

hilly ['hɪlɪ] (*compar* **-ier**, *superl* **-iest**) *adj* vallonné(e).

hilt [hɪlt] *n* garde *f*; **to the** ~ jusqu'au cou; **to support/defend sb to the** ~ soutenir/défendre qqn à fond.

him [hɪm] *pers pron* **-1.** (*direct - unstressed*) le, l' (+ *vowel or silent 'h'*); (- *stressed*) lui; **I know/like** ~ je le connais/l'aime; **it's** ~ c'est lui; **if I were** OR **was** ~ si j'étais lui, à sa place; **you can't expect** HIM **to do it** tu ne peux pas exiger que ce soit lui qui le fasse. **-2.** (*indirect*) lui; **we spoke to** ~ nous lui avons parlé; **she sent** ~ **a letter** elle lui a envoyé une lettre. **-3.** (*after prep, in comparisons etc*) lui; **I'm shorter than** ~ je suis plus petit que lui.

Himalayan [,hɪmə'leɪən] *adj* himalayen(enne).

Himalayas [,hɪmə'leɪəz] *npl*: **the** ~ l'Himalaya *m*; **in the** ~ dans l'Himalaya.

himself [hɪm'self] *pron* **-1.** (*reflexive*) se; (*after prep*) lui. **-2.** (*for emphasis*) lui-même; **he did it** ~ il l'a fait tout seul.

hind [haɪnd] (*pl inv* OR **-s**) ◇ *adj* de derrière. ◇ *n* biche *f*.

hinder ['hɪndə'] *vt* gêner, entraver.

Hindi ['hɪndɪ] *n* hindi *m*.

hindmost ['haɪndməʊst] *adj* arrière.

hindquarters ['haɪndkwɔːtəz] *npl* arrière-train *m*.

hindrance ['hɪndrəns] *n* obstacle *m*.

hindsight ['haɪndsaɪt] *n*: **with the benefit of** ~ avec du recul.

Hindu ['hɪnduː] (*pl* **-s**) ◇ *adj* hindou(e). ◇ *n* Hindou *m*, -e *f*.

Hinduism ['hɪnduːɪzm] *n* hindouisme *m*.

hinge [hɪndʒ] (*cont* **hingeing**) *n* [whole fitting] charnière *f*; [pin] gond *m*.
◆ **hinge (up)on** *vt fus* [depend on] dépendre de.

hint [hɪnt] ◇ *n* **-1.** [indication] allusion *f*; **to drop a** ~ faire une allusion; **to take the** ~ saisir l'allusion. **-2.** [piece of advice] conseil *m*, indication *f*. **-3.** [small amount] soupçon *m*. ◇ *vi*: **to** ~ **at sthg** faire allusion à qqch. ◇ *vt*: **to** ~ **that ...** insinuer que ....

hinterland ['hɪntəlænd] *n* arrière-pays *m*.

hip [hɪp] *n* hanche *f*.

hipbath ['hɪpbɑːθ] *n* bain *m* de siège.

hipbone ['hɪpbəʊn] *n* os *m* de la hanche, os *m* iliaque.

hip flask *n* flasque *f*.

hip-hop *n* [music] hip-hop *m*.

hippie ['hɪpɪ] = **hippy**.

hippo ['hɪpəʊ] (*pl* -s) *n* hippopotame *m*.

hippopotamus ['hɪpə'pɒtəməs] (*pl* -muses OR -mi [-maɪ]) *n* hippopotame *m*.

hippy ['hɪpɪ] (*pl* -ies) *n* hippie *mf*.

hire ['haɪər] ◇ *n* (U) [of car, equipment] location *f*; **for** ~ [bicycles etc] à louer; [taxi] libre; **on** ~ en location. ◇ *vt* -1. [rent] louer. -2. [employ] employer les services de.
◆ **hire out** *vt sep* louer.

hire car *n* Br voiture *f* de location.

hire purchase *n* (U) Br achat *m* à crédit OR à tempérament; **to buy sthg on** ~ acheter qqch à crédit OR à tempérament.

his [hɪz] ◇ *poss adj* son (sa), ses (*pl*); ~ **house** sa maison; ~ **money** son argent; ~ **children** ses enfants; ~ **name is Joe** il s'appelle Joe; **it wasn't** HIS **fault** ce n'était pas de sa faute à lui.
◇ *poss pron* le sien (la sienne), les siens (les siennes) (*pl*); **that money is** ~ cet argent est à lui OR est le sien; **it wasn't her fault, it was** HIS ce n'était pas de sa faute à elle, c'était de sa faute à lui; **a friend of** ~ un ami à lui, un de ses amis.

Hispanic [hɪ'spænɪk] ◇ *adj* hispanique. ◇ *n* Hispano-américain *m*, -e *f*.

hiss [hɪs] ◇ *n* [of animal, gas etc] sifflement *m*; [of crowd] sifflet *m*. ◇ *vt* [speaker, speech] siffler. ◇ *vi* [animal, gas etc] siffler.

histogram ['hɪstəgræm] *n* histogramme *m*.

historian [hɪ'stɔːrɪən] *n* historien *m*, -ienne *f*.

historic [hɪ'stɒrɪk] *adj* historique.

historical [hɪ'stɒrɪkəl] *adj* historique.

history ['hɪstərɪ] (*pl* -ies) *n* -1. [gen] histoire *f*; **to go down in** ~ entrer dans l'histoire; **to make** ~ faire l'histoire. -2. [past record] antécédents *mpl*; **medical** ~ passé *m* médical.

histrionics [hɪstrɪ'ɒnɪks] *npl pej* drame *m*.

hit [hɪt] (*pt* & *pp* hit, *cont* -ting) ◇ *n* -1. [blow] coup *m*. -2. [successful strike] coup *m* OR tir *m* réussi; [in fencing] touche *f*; **to score a** ~ **on sthg** toucher qqch. -3. [success] succès *m*; **to be a** ~ **with** plaire à. ◇ *comp* à succès.
◇ *vt* -1. [strike] frapper; [nail] taper sur. -2. [crash into] heurter, percuter. -3. [reach] atteindre. -4. [affect badly] toucher, affecter. -5. *phr*: **to** ~ **it off (with sb)** bien s'entendre (avec qqn).
◆ **hit back** *vi*: **to** ~ **back (at)** répondre (à).

◆ **hit on** *vt fus* -1. = **hit upon**. -2. *Am inf* [chat up] draguer.

◆ **hit out** *vt fus*: **to** ~ **out at** [physically] envoyer un coup à; [criticize] attaquer.

◆ **hit upon** *vt fus* [think of] trouver.

hit-and-miss = **hit-or-miss**.

hit-and-run *adj* [accident] avec délit de fuite; ~ **driver** chauffard *m* (*qui a commis un délit de fuite*).

hitch [hɪtʃ] ◇ *n* [problem, snag] ennui *m*. ◇ *vt* -1. [catch]: **to** ~ **a lift** faire du stop. -2. [fasten]: **to** ~ **sthg on** OR **onto** accrocher OR attacher qqch à. ◇ *vi* [hitchhike] faire du stop.
◆ **hitch up** *vt sep* [pull up] remonter.

hitchhike ['hɪtʃhaɪk] *vi* faire de l'auto-stop.

hitchhiker ['hɪtʃhaɪkər] *n* auto-stoppeur *m*, -euse *f*.

hi-tech ['haɪˌtek] = **high-tech**.

hither ['hɪðər] *adv literary* ici; ~ **and thither** çà et là.

hitherto [ˌhɪðə'tuː] *adv fml* jusqu'ici.

hit list *n* liste *f* noire.

hit man *n* tueur *m* (*à gages*).

hit-or-miss *adj* aléatoire.

hit parade *n dated* hit-parade *m*.

HIV (*abbr of* **human immunodeficiency virus**) *n* VIH *m*, HIV *m*; **to be** ~**-positive** être séropositif.

hive [haɪv] *n* ruche *f*; **a** ~ **of activity** une véritable ruche.
◆ **hive off** *vt sep* [assets] séparer.

hl (*abbr of* **hectolitre**) hl.

HM (*abbr of* **His (or Her) Majesty**) SM.

HMG (*abbr of* **His (or Her) Majesty's Government**) *expression utilisée sur des documents officiels en Grande-Bretagne*.

HMI (*abbr of* **His (or Her) Majesty's Inspector**) *n inspecteur de l'éducation nationale en Grande-Bretagne*.

HMO (*abbr of* **health maintenance organization**) *n organisme américain pour la santé publique*.

HMS (*abbr of* **His (or Her) Majesty's Ship**) *expression précédant le nom d'un bâtiment de la marine britannique*.

HMSO (*abbr of* **His (or Her) Majesty's Stationery Office**) *n service officiel des publications en Grande-Bretagne*, ≃ Imprimerie *f* nationale.

HNC (*abbr of* **Higher National Certificate**) *n brevet de technicien en Grande-Bretagne*.

HND (*abbr of* **Higher National Diploma**) *n brevet de technicien supérieur en Grande-Bretagne*.

hoard [hɔːd] ◇ n [store] réserves fpl; [of useless items] tas m. ◇ vt amasser; [food, petrol] faire des provisions de.

hoarding ['hɔːdɪŋ] n Br [for advertisements] panneau m d'affichage publicitaire.

hoarfrost [,hɔː'frɒst] n gelée f blanche.

hoarse [hɔːs] adj [person, voice] enroué(e); [shout, whisper] rauque.

hoax [həʊks] n canular m.

hoaxer ['həʊksər] n mauvais plaisant m.

hob [hɒb] n Br [on cooker] rond m, plaque f.

hobble ['hɒbl] vi [limp] boitiller.

hobby ['hɒbɪ] (pl -ies) n passe-temps m inv, hobby m.

hobbyhorse ['hɒbɪhɔːs] n -1. [toy] cheval m à bascule. -2. fig [favourite topic] dada m.

hobnob ['hɒbnɒb] (pt & pp -bed, cont -bing) vi: to ~ with sb frayer avec qqn.

hobo ['həʊbəʊ] (pl -es OR -s) n Am clochard m, -e f.

Ho Chi Minh City ['həʊ,tʃiː'mɪn-] n Hô Chi Minh-Ville.

hock [hɒk] n [wine] vin m du Rhin.

hockey ['hɒkɪ] n -1. [on grass] hockey m. -2. Am [ice hockey] hockey m sur glace.

hocus-pocus ['həʊkəs'pəʊkəs] n [trickery] supercherie f, tromperie f.

hod [hɒd] n hotte f.

hodgepodge = hotchpotch.

hoe [həʊ] ◇ n houe f. ◇ vt biner.

hog [hɒg] (pt & pp -ged, cont -ging) ◇ n -1. Am [pig] cochon m. -2. inf [greedy person] goinfre m. -3. phr: to go the whole ~ aller jusqu'au bout. ◇ vt inf [monopolize] accaparer, monopoliser.

Hogmanay ['hɒgməneɪ] n la Saint-Sylvestre en Écosse.

hoist [hɔɪst] ◇ n [device] treuil m. ◇ vt hisser.

hokum ['həʊkəm] n (U) Am inf niaiseries fpl.

hold [həʊld] (pt & pp held) ◇ vt -1. [gen] tenir. -2. [keep in position] maintenir. -3. [as prisoner] détenir; to ~ sb prisoner/hostage détenir qqn prisonnier/comme otage. -4. [have, possess] avoir. -5. fml [consider] considérer, estimer; to ~ (that) ... considérer que ..., estimer que ...; to ~ sb responsible for sthg rendre qqn responsable de qqch, tenir qqn pour responsable de qqch; to ~ sthg dear tenir à qqch. -6. [on telephone]: please ~ the line ne quittez pas, je vous prie. -7. [keep, maintain] retenir. -8. [sustain, support] supporter. -9. [contain] contenir; the main hall ~s 500 on peut tenir à 500 dans la grande salle; what does the future

~ for him? que lui réserve l'avenir? -10. phr: ~ it!, ~ everything! attendez!, arrêtez!; to ~ one's own se défendre.
◇ vi -1. [remain unchanged - gen] tenir; [- luck] persister; [- weather] se maintenir; to ~ still OR steady ne pas bouger, rester tranquille. -2. [on phone] attendre.
◇ n -1. [grasp, grip] prise f, étreinte f; to take OR lay ~ of sthg saisir qqch; to get ~ of sthg [obtain] se procurer qqch; to get ~ of sb [find] joindre. -2. [of ship, aircraft] cale f. -3. [control, influence] prise f; to take ~ [fire] prendre.

◆ **hold against** vt sep: to ~ sthg against sb fig en vouloir à qqn de qqch.

◆ **hold back** ◇ vi [hesitate] se retenir; to ~ back from doing sthg se retenir de faire qqch. ◇ vt sep -1. [restrain, prevent] retenir; [anger] réprimer; to ~ sb back from doing sthg retenir qqn de faire qqch. -2. [keep secret] cacher.

◆ **hold down** vt sep [job] garder.

◆ **hold off** ◇ vt sep [fend off] tenir à distance. ◇ vi: the rain held off il n'a pas plu.

◆ **hold on** vi -1. [wait] attendre; [on phone] ne pas quitter. -2. [grip]: to ~ on (to sthg) se tenir (à qqch).

◆ **hold onto** vt fus [power, job] garder.

◆ **hold out** ◇ vt sep [hand, arms] tendre. ◇ vi -1. [last] durer. -2. [resist]: to ~ out (against sb/sthg) résister (à qqn/qqch).

◆ **hold out for** vt fus continuer à réclamer.

◆ **hold up** vt sep -1. [raise] lever. -2. [delay] retarder. -3. inf [rob] faire un hold-up dans.

◆ **hold with** vt fus [approve of] approuver.

holdall ['həʊldɔːl] n Br fourre-tout m.

holder ['həʊldər] n -1. [for cigarette] porte-cigarettes m. -2. [owner] détenteur m, -trice f; [of position, title] titulaire mf.

holding ['həʊldɪŋ] ◇ n -1. [investment] effets mpl en portefeuille. -2. [farm] ferme f. ◇ adj [action, operation] mené en vue de maintenir le statu quo.

holding company n holding m.

holdup ['həʊldʌp] n -1. [robbery] hold-up m. -2. [delay] retard m.

hole [həʊl] n -1. [gen] trou m; GOLF: ~ in one trou réussi en un coup; to pick ~s in sthg [criticize] trouver à redire à qqch. -2. inf [predicament] pétrin m.

◆ **hole up** vi [hide, take shelter] se terrer.

holiday ['hɒlɪdeɪ] n -1. [vacation] vacances fpl; to be/go on ~ être/partir en vacances. -2. [public holiday] jour m férié.

holiday camp n Br camp m de vacances.

holidaymaker ['hɒlɪdɪ,meɪkəʳ] *n Br* vacancier *m*, -ière *f*.

holiday pay *n Br salaire payé pendant les vacances.*

holiday resort *n Br* lieu *m* de vacances.

holiday season *n Br* période *f* des vacances.

holiness ['həʊlɪnɪs] *n* [holy quality] sainteté *f*.

◆ **Holiness** *n* [in titles]: **His/Your Holiness** Sa/Votre Sainteté.

holistic [həʊ'lɪstɪk] *adj* holistique.

Holland ['hɒlənd] *n* Hollande *f*; **in ~** en Hollande.

hollandaise sauce [,hɒlən'deɪz-] *n* sauce *f* hollandaise.

holler ['hɒləʳ] *vi & vt inf* gueuler, brailler.

hollow ['hɒləʊ] ◇ *adj* creux (creuse); [eyes] cave; [promise, victory] **faux (fausse)**; [laugh] qui sonne faux. ◇ *n* creux *m*.

◆ **hollow out** *vt sep* creuser, évider.

holly ['hɒlɪ] *n* houx *m*.

Hollywood ['hɒlɪwʊd] ◇ *n* [film industry] Hollywood. ◇ *comp* hollywoodien(ienne).

holocaust ['hɒləkɔːst] *n* [destruction] destruction *f*, holocauste *m*.

◆ **Holocaust** *n*: **the Holocaust** l'holocauste *m*.

hologram ['hɒləgræm] *n* hologramme *m*.

hols [hɒlz] *npl Br inf* vacances *fpl*.

holster ['həʊlstəʳ] *n* étui *m*.

holy ['həʊlɪ] (*compar* **-ier**, *superl* **-iest**) *adj* saint(e); [ground] sacré(e).

Holy Communion *n* Sainte Communion *f*.

Holy Ghost *n*: **the ~** le Saint-Esprit.

Holy Grail [-greɪl] *n*: **the ~** le Saint-Graal.

Holy Land *n*: **the ~** la Terre Sainte.

holy orders *npl* ordres *mpl* sacrés.

Holy Spirit *n*: **the ~** le Saint-Esprit.

homage ['hɒmɪdʒ] *n* (U) *fml* hommage *m*; **to pay ~ to sb/sthg** rendre hommage à qqn/qqch.

home [həʊm] ◇ *n* **-1.** [house, institution] maison *f*; **to make one's ~** s'établir, s'installer; **it's a ~ from ~** *Br* OR **~ away from ~** *Am* on est ici comme chez soi. **-2.** [own country] patrie *f*; [city] ville *f* natale. **-3.** [one's family] foyer *m*; **to leave ~** quitter la maison. **-4.** *fig* [place of origin] berceau *m*. ◇ *adj* **-1.** [not foreign] intérieur(e); [- product] national(e). **-2.** [in one's own home - cooking] familial(e); [- life] de famille; [- improvements] domestique. **-3.** [SPORT - game] sur son propre terrain; [- team] qui reçoit.

◇ *adv* **-1.** [to or at one's house] chez soi, à la maison. **-2.** *phr*: **to bring sthg ~ (to sb)** faire prendre conscience de qqch (à qqn); **to drive** OR **hammer sthg ~ to sb** enfoncer OR faire rentrer qqch dans la tête de qqn.

◆ **at home** *adv* **-1.** [in one's house, flat] chez soi, à la maison. **-2.** [comfortable] à l'aise; **at ~ with sthg** à l'aise dans qqch; **to make o.s. at ~** faire comme chez soi. **-3.** [in one's own country] chez nous. **-4.** SPORT: **to play at ~** jouer sur son propre terrain.

◆ **home in** *vi*: **to ~ in on sthg** viser qqch, se diriger vers qqch; *fig* pointer sur qqch.

home address *n* adresse *f* du domicile.

home banking *n opérations bancaires effectuées à domicile par ordinateur.*

home brew *n* (U) [beer] bière *f* faite à la maison.

homecoming ['həʊm,kʌmɪŋ] *n* **-1.** [return] retour *m* au foyer OR à la maison. **-2.** *Am* SCH & UNIV *fête donnée en l'honneur de l'équipe de football et à laquelle sont invités les anciens élèves.*

home computer *n* ordinateur *m* domestique.

Home Counties *n*: **the ~** *les comtés entourant Londres.*

home economics *n* (U) économie *f* domestique.

home fries *npl Am* pommes de terre *fpl* sautées.

home ground *n* **-1.** [familiar territory]: **to be on ~** *lit* & *fig* être sur son terrain. **-2.** SPORT terrain *m* du club.

homegrown [,həʊm'grəʊn] *adj* du jardin.

home help *n Br* aide *f* ménagère.

homeland ['həʊmlænd] *n* **-1.** [country of birth] patrie *f*. **-2.** [in South Africa] homeland *m*, bantoustan *m*.

homeless ['həʊmlɪs] ◇ *adj* sans abri. ◇ *npl*: **the ~** les sans-abri *mpl*.

homelessness ['həʊmləsnəs] *n fait d'être sans abri.*

home loan *n* prêt *m* d'accession à la propriété.

homely ['həʊmlɪ] *adj* **-1.** [simple] simple. **-2.** [unattractive] ordinaire.

homemade [,həʊm'meɪd] *adj* fait(e) (à la) maison.

home movie *n* film *m* amateur.

Home Office *n Br*: **the ~** ≃ le ministère de l'Intérieur.

homeopathic [,həʊmɪəʊ'pæθɪk] *adj* homéopathique.

homeopathy [,həʊmɪ'ɒpəθɪ] *n* homéopathie *f*.

homeowner ['həum,əunə'] *n* propriétaire *mf* (d'une maison/d'un appartement).

home rule *n* autonomie *f*.

home run *n Am inf* coup *m* de circuit.

Home Secretary *n Br* ≃ ministre *m* de l'Intérieur.

homesick ['həumsɪk] *adj* qui a le mal du pays.

homesickness ['həum,sɪknɪs] *n* mal *m* du pays.

homespun ['həumspʌn] *adj fig* simple.

homestead ['həumsted] *n Am* ferme *f* (avec dépendances).

home straight *n*: **the ~** [of race] la dernière ligne droite; [of task] le dernier stade.

hometown ['həumtaun] *n* ville *f* natale.

home truth *n*: **to tell sb a few ~s** dire ses quatre vérités à qqn.

homeward ['həumwəd] ◇ *adj* de retour. ◇ *adv* = **homewards**.

homewards ['həumwədz] *adv* vers la maison.

homework ['həumwɜːk] *n* (*U*) **-1.** SCH devoirs *mpl*. **-2.** *inf* [preparation] boulot *m*.

homey, homy ['həumɪ] *adj Am* confortable, agréable.

homicidal ['hɒmɪsaɪdl] *adj* homicide.

homicide ['hɒmɪsaɪd] *n* homicide *m*.

homily ['hɒmɪlɪ] (*pl* **-ies**) *n* [lecture] homélie *f*.

homing ['həumɪŋ] *adj* de retour au gîte; MIL: **~ device** tête *f* chercheuse.

homing pigeon *n* pigeon *m* voyageur.

homoeopathy *etc* [,həumɪ'ɒpəθɪ] = **homeopathy** *etc*.

homogeneous [,hɒmə'dʒiːnjəs] *adj* homogène.

homogenize, -ise [hə'mɒdʒənaɪz] *vt Br* homogénéiser.

homosexual [,hɒmə'seksjuəl] ◇ *adj* homosexuel(elle). ◇ *n* homosexuel *m*, -elle *f*.

homosexuality [,hɒmə,seksju'ælətɪ] *n* homosexualité *f*.

homy = **homey**.

Hon. -1. *abbr of* **Honourable. -2.** *abbr of* **Honorary.**

Honduran [hɒn'djuərən] ◇ *adj* hondurien(ienne). ◇ *n* Hondurien *m*, -ienne *f*.

Honduras [hɒn'djuərəs] *n* Honduras *m*; **in ~** au Honduras.

hone [həun] *vt* aiguiser.

honest ['ɒnɪst] ◇ *adj* **-1.** [trustworthy] honnête, probe. **-2.** [frank] franc (franche), sincère; **to be ~ ...** pour dire la vérité, à dire

vrai. **-3.** [legal] légitime. ◇ *adv inf* = **honestly 2.**

honestly ['ɒnɪstlɪ] ◇ *adv* **-1.** [truthfully] honnêtement. **-2.** [expressing sincerity] je vous assure. ◇ *excl* [expressing impatience, disapproval] franchement!

honesty ['ɒnɪstɪ] *n* honnêteté *f*, probité *f*.

honey ['hʌnɪ] *n* **-1.** [food] miel *m*. **-2.** [dear] chéri *m*, -e *f*.

honeybee ['hʌnɪbiː] *n* abeille *f*.

honeycomb ['hʌnɪkəum] *n* gâteau *m* de miel.

honeymoon ['hʌnɪmuːn] ◇ *n lit* & *fig* lune *f* de miel. ◇ *vi* aller en voyage de noces, passer sa lune de miel.

honeysuckle ['hʌnɪ,sʌkl] *n* chèvrefeuille *m*.

Hong Kong [,hɒŋ'kɒŋ] *n* Hong Kong, Hongkong; **in ~** à Hongkong.

honk [hɒŋk] ◇ *vi* **-1.** [motorist] klaxonner. **-2.** [goose] cacarder. ◇ *vt*: **to ~ the horn** klaxonner. ◇ *n* **-1.** [of horn] coup *m* de klaxon. **-2.** [of goose] cri *m*.

honky ['hɒŋkɪ] (*pl* **-ies**) *n Am v inf* terme injurieux désignant un Blanc.

Honolulu [,hɒnə'luːluː] *n* Honolulu.

honor *etc Am* = **honour** *etc*.

honorary [*Br* 'ɒnərərɪ, *Am* ɒnə'reərɪ] *adj* honoraire.

honor roll *n Am* tableau *m* d'honneur.

honour *Br*, **honor** *Am* ['ɒnə'] ◇ *n* honneur *m*; **in ~ of sb/sthg** en l'honneur de qqn/qqch. ◇ *vt* honorer.

◆ **Honour** *n*: **His/Your Honour** Son/Votre Honneur.

◆ **honours** *npl* **-1.** [tokens of respect] honneurs *mpl*. **-2.** [of university degree] ≃ licence *f*. **-3.** *phr*: **to do the ~s** [serve food] servir; [introduce people] faire les présentations.

honourable *Br*, **honorable** *Am* ['ɒnrəbl] *adj* honorable.

◆ **Honourable** *adj* [in titles]: **the Honourable ...** l'honorable ....

honourably *Br*, **honorably** *Am* ['ɒnərəblɪ] *adv* honorablement.

honour bound *adj*: **to be ~ to do sthg** être tenu(e) par l'honneur de faire qqch.

honours list *n Br* liste des personnes qui doivent recevoir des titres honorifiques (conférés par la reine).

Hons. (*abbr of* **honours degree**) licence.

hooch [huːtʃ] *n inf* [drink] gnôle *f*.

hood [hud] *n* **-1.** [on cloak, jacket] capuchon *m*. **-2.** [of cooker] hotte *f*. **-3.** [of pram, convertible car] capote *f*. **-4.** *Am* [car bonnet] capot *m*.

hooded ['hʊdɪd] *adj* -1. [wearing a hood] encapuchonné(e). -2. [eyes] aux paupières tombantes.

hoodlum ['huːdləm] *n Am inf* gangster *m*, truand *m*.

hoodwink ['hʊdwɪŋk] *vt* tromper, berner.

hooey ['huːɪ] *n* (U) *Am inf* salades *fpl*.

hoof [huːf, hʊf] (*pl* -s OR **hooves**) *n* sabot *m*.

hook [hʊk] ◇ *n* -1. [for hanging things on] crochet *m*. -2. [for catching fish] hameçon *m*. -3. [fastener] agrafe *f*. -4. [of telephone]: **off the ~** décroché. -5. *phr*: **to get sb off the ~** tirer qqn d'affaire. ◇ *vt* -1. [attach with hook] accrocher. -2. [catch with hook] prendre. -3. [arm, leg]: **to ~ one's arm round sthg** passer son bras autour de qqch.

◆ **hook up** *vt sep*: **to ~ sthg up to sthg** connecter qqch à qqch.

hook and eye (*pl* **hooks and eyes**) *n* agrafe *f*.

hooked [hʊkt] *adj* -1. [shaped like a hook] crochu(e). -2. *inf* [addicted]: **to be ~ (on)** être accro (à); [music, art] être mordu(e) (de).

hooker ['hʊkə'] *n Am inf* putain *f*.

hook(e)y ['hʊkɪ] *n Am inf*: **to play ~** faire l'école buissonnière.

hooligan ['huːlɪgən] *n* hooligan *m*, vandale *m*.

hooliganism ['huːlɪgənɪzm] *n* hooliganisme *m*, vandalisme *m*.

hoop [huːp] *n* -1. [circular band] cercle *m*. -2. [toy] cerceau *m*.

hoop-la ['huːplɑː] *n* (U) [game] jeu *m* d'anneaux.

hooray [hʊ'reɪ] = **hurray**.

hoot [huːt] ◇ *n* -1. [of owl] hululement *m*. -2. [of horn] coup *m* de klaxon. -3. [of person]: **a ~ of laughter** un hurlement de rire. -4. *Br inf* [something amusing]: **to be a ~** être tordant(e). ◇ *vi* -1. [owl] hululer. -2. [horn] klaxonner. -3. *inf* [person]: **to ~ with laughter** hurler de rire, rire aux éclats. ◇ *vt*: **to ~ the horn** klaxonner.

hooter ['huːtə'] *n* -1. [horn] klaxon *m*. -2. *Br inf* [nose] pif *m*.

Hoover® *Br* ['huːvə'] *n* aspirateur *m*.

◆ **hoover** ◇ *vt* [room] passer l'aspirateur dans; [carpet] passer à l'aspirateur. ◇ *vi* passer l'aspirateur.

hooves [huːvz] *pl* → **hoof**.

hop [hɒp] (*pt* & *pp* -**ped**, *cont* -**ping**) ◇ *n* saut *m*. -2. [on one leg] saut à cloche-pied. ◇ *vi* sauter; [on one leg] sauter à cloche-pied; [bird] sautiller. ◇ *vt Am inf* [bus, train] sauter dans.

◆ **hops** *npl* houblon *m*.

hope [həʊp] ◇ *vi* espérer; **to ~ for sthg** espérer qqch; **I ~ so** j'espère bien; **I ~ not** j'espère bien que non; **to ~ for the best** espérer que tout aille pour le mieux.
◇ *vt*: **to ~ (that)** espérer (que); **to ~ to do sthg** espérer faire qqch.
◇ *n* espoir *m*; **in the ~ of** dans l'espoir de; **I don't hold out much ~** je n'ai pas beaucoup d'espoir, je n'y compte pas trop; **to pin one's ~s on sthg** mettre tous ses espoirs dans qqch; **to raise sb's ~s** donner de l'espoir à qqn.

hope chest *n Am* trousseau *m*.

hopeful ['həʊpfʊl] ◇ *adj* -1. [optimistic] plein(e) d'espoir; **to be ~ of doing sthg** avoir l'espoir de faire qqch; **to be ~ of sthg** espérer qqch. -2. [promising] encourageant(e), qui promet. ◇ *n* espoir *m*.

hopefully ['həʊpfəlɪ] *adv* -1. [in a hopeful way] avec bon espoir, avec optimisme. -2. [with luck]: **~, ...** espérons que ....

hopeless ['həʊplɪs] *adj* -1. [gen] désespéré(e); [tears] de désespoir. -2. *inf* [useless] nul (nulle).

hopelessly ['həʊplɪslɪ] *adv* -1. [despairingly] avec désespoir. -2. [completely] complètement.

hopper ['hɒpə'] *n* [funnel] trémie *f*.

hopping ['hɒpɪŋ] *adv*: **to be ~ mad** être fou (folle) de colère.

hopscotch ['hɒpskɒtʃ] *n* marelle *f*.

horde [hɔːd] *n* horde *f*, foule *f*.

◆ **hordes** *npl*: **~s of** une foule de.

horizon [hə'raɪzn] *n* horizon *m*; **on the ~** *lit* & *fig* à l'horizon.

◆ **horizons** *npl* horizons *mpl*.

horizontal [ˌhɒrɪ'zɒntl] ◇ *adj* horizontal(e). ◇ *n*: **the ~** l'horizontale *f*.

hormone ['hɔːməʊn] *n* hormone *f*.

hormone replacement therapy *n* traitement *m* hormonal substitutif.

horn [hɔːn] *n* -1. [of animal] corne *f*. -2. MUS [instrument] cor *m*. -3. [on car] klaxon *m*; [on ship] sirène *f*.

hornet ['hɔːnɪt] *n* frelon *m*.

horn-rimmed [-rɪmd] *adj* à monture d'écaille.

horny ['hɔːnɪ] (*compar* -**ier**, *superl* -**iest**) *adj* -1. [hard] corné(e); [hand] calleux(euse). -2. *v inf* [sexually excited] excité(e) (sexuellement).

horoscope ['hɒrəskəʊp] *n* horoscope *m*.

horrendous [hɒ'rendəs] *adj* horrible.

horrible ['hɒrəbl] *adj* horrible.

horribly ['hɒrəblɪ] *adv* horriblement.

horrid ['hɒrɪd] *adj* [unpleasant] horrible.

horrific [hɒ'rɪfɪk] *adj* horrible.

horrify ['hɒrɪfaɪ] (*pt & pp* **-ied**) *vt* horrifier.

horrifying ['hɒrɪfaɪɪŋ] *adj* horrifiant(e).

horror ['hɒrər] *n* horreur *f*; **to have a ~ of sthg** avoir horreur de qqch; **to my/his ~ à** ma/sa grande horreur.

horror film *n* film *m* d'épouvante.

horror-struck *adj* frappé(e) d'horreur.

hors d'oeuvre [ɔː'dɜːvr] (*pl* **hors d'oeuvres**) *n* hors-d'œuvre *m inv*.

horse [hɔːs] *n* [animal] cheval *m*.

horseback ['hɔːsbæk] ◇ *adj* à cheval; **~ riding** *Am* équitation *f*. ◇ *n*: **on ~** à cheval.

horsebox *Br* ['hɔːsbɒks], **horsecar** *Am* ['hɔːskɑːr] *n* van *m*.

horse chestnut *n* [nut] marron *m* d'Inde; **~ (tree)** marronnier *m* d'Inde.

horse-drawn *adj* tiré(e) par des chevaux.

horsefly ['hɔːsflaɪ] (*pl* **-flies**) *n* taon *m*.

horsehair ['hɔːsheər] *n* crin *m*.

horseman ['hɔːsmən] (*pl* **-men** [-mən]) *n* cavalier *m*.

horse opera *n Am hum* western *m*.

horseplay ['hɔːspleɪ] *n* chahut *m*.

horsepower ['hɔːs,pauər] *n* puissance *f* en chevaux.

horse racing *n* (*U*) courses *fpl* de chevaux.

horseradish ['hɔːs,rædɪʃ] *n* [plant] raifort *m*.

horse riding *n* équitation *f*.

horseshoe ['hɔːsʃuː] *n* fer *m* à cheval.

horse show *n* concours *m* hippique.

horse-trading *n fig & pej* maquignonnage *m*.

horse trials *npl* concours *m* hippique.

horsewhip ['hɔːswɪp] (*pt & pp* **-ped**, *cont* **-ping**) *vt* cravacher.

horsewoman ['hɔːs,wʊmən] (*pl* **-women** [-,wɪmɪn]) *n* cavalière *f*.

horticultural [,hɔːtɪ'kʌltʃərəl] *adj* d'horticulture.

horticulture ['hɔːtɪkʌltʃər] *n* horticulture *f*.

hose [həʊz] ◇ *n* [hosepipe] tuyau *m*. ◇ *vt* arroser au jet.

◆ **hose down** *vt sep* laver au jet.

hosepipe ['həʊzpaɪp] *n* = hose.

hosiery ['həʊzɪərɪ] *n* bonneterie *f*.

hospice ['hɒspɪs] *n* hospice *m*.

hospitable [hɒ'spɪtəbl] *adj* hospitalier(ière), accueillant(e).

hospital ['hɒspɪtl] *n* hôpital *m*.

hospitality [,hɒspɪ'tælətɪ] *n* hospitalité *f*.

hospitality suite *n salon privé où sont offerts des rafraîchissements (lors d'une conférence etc).*

hospitalize, -ise ['hɒspɪtəlaɪz] *vt* hospitaliser.

host [həʊst] ◇ *n* **-1.** [gen] hôte *m*; **~ city/ country** ville *f*/pays *m* d'accueil. **-2.** [compere] animateur *m*, -trice *f*. **-3.** [large number]: **a ~ of** une foule de. ◇ *vt* présenter, animer.

hostage ['hɒstɪdʒ] *n* otage *m*; **to be taken ~** être pris en otage; **to be held ~** être détenu comme otage.

hostel ['hɒstl] *n* **-1.** [basic accommodation] foyer *m*. **-2.** [youth hostel] auberge *f* de jeunesse.

hostelry ['hɒstəlrɪ] (*pl* **-ries**) *n hum* hostellerie *f*.

hostess ['həʊstes] *n* hôtesse *f*.

hostile [*Br* 'hɒstaɪl, *Am* 'hɒstl] *adj*: **~ (to)** hostile (à).

hostility [hɒs'tɪlətɪ] *n* [antagonism, unfriendliness] hostilité *f*.

◆ **hostilities** *npl* hostilités *fpl*.

hot [hɒt] (*compar* **-ter**, *superl* **-test**, *pt & pp* **-ted**, *cont* **-ting**) *adj* **-1.** [gen] chaud(e); **I'm ~** j'ai chaud; **it's ~** il fait chaud. **-2.** [spicy] épicé(e). **-3.** *inf* [expert] fort(e), calé(e); **to be ~ on** OR **at sthg** être fort OR calé en qqch. **-4.** [recent] de dernière heure OR minute. **-5.** [temper] colérique.

◆ **hot up** *vi inf* chauffer.

hot-air balloon *n* montgolfière *f*.

hotbed ['hɒtbed] *n* foyer *m*.

hotchpotch *Br* ['hɒtʃpɒtʃ], **hodgepodge** *Am* ['hɒdʒpɒdʒ] *n inf* fouillis *m,* méli-mélo *m*.

hot-cross bun *n petit pain sucré que l'on mange le Vendredi saint.*

hot dog *n* hot dog *m*.

hotel [həʊ'tel] ◇ *n* hôtel *m*. ◇ *comp* d'hôtel.

hotelier [həʊ'telɪər] *n* hôtelier *m*, -ière *f*.

hot flush *Br*, **hot flash** *Am n* bouffée *f* de chaleur.

hotfoot ['hɒt,fʊt] *adv* à toute vitesse.

hotheaded [,hɒt'hedɪd] *adj* impulsif(ive).

hothouse ['hɒthaʊs, *pl* -haʊzɪz] ◇ *n* [greenhouse] serre *f*. ◇ *comp* de serre.

hot line *n* **-1.** [between government heads] téléphone *m* rouge. **-2.** [special line] *ligne ouverte 24 heures sur 24.*

hotly ['hɒtlɪ] *adv* **-1.** [passionately] avec véhémence. **-2.** [closely] de près.

hotplate ['hɒtpleɪt] *n* plaque *f* chauffante.

hotpot ['hɒtpɒt] *n Br type de ragoût.*

hot potato n inf fig affaire f brûlante.

hot rod n voiture f gonflée.

hot seat n inf: **to be in the ~** être sur la sellette.

hot spot n -1. [exciting place] endroit m à la mode. -2. [politically unsettled area] point m chaud.

hot-tempered adj colérique.

hot water n fig: **to get into ~** s'attirer des ennuis; **to be in ~** être dans le pétrin.

hot-water bottle n bouillotte f.

hot-wire vt inf faire démarrer en court-circuitant l'allumage.

hound [haund] ◇ n [dog] chien m. ◇ vt -1. [persecute] poursuivre, pourchasser. -2. [drive]: **to ~ sb out (of)** chasser qqn (de).

hour ['auə'] n heure f; **half an ~** une demi-heure; **70 miles per** OR **an ~** 110km à l'heure; **on the ~** à l'heure juste; **in the small ~s** au petit matin OR jour.
◆ **hours** npl -1. [of business] heures fpl d'ouverture; **after ~s** après l'heure de fermeture, après la fermeture. -2. [routine]: **to keep late ~s** se coucher très tard; **to keep regular ~s** avoir une vie réglée.

hourly ['auəlɪ] adj -1. [happening every hour] toutes les heures. -2. [per hour] à l'heure ◇ adv -1. [every hour] toutes les heures. -2. [per hour] à l'heure. -3. fig [constantly] sans cesse, constamment.

house [n haus, pl 'hauzɪz, vb hauz] ◇ n -1. [gen] maison f; **on the ~** aux frais de la maison; **to put** OR **set one's ~ in order** balayer devant sa porte. -2. POL chambre f. -3. [in debates] assistance f. -4. THEATRE [audience] auditoire m, salle f; **to bring the ~ down** inf faire crouler la salle sous les applaudissements.
◇ vt [accommodate] loger, héberger; [department, store] abriter.
◇ adj -1. [within business] d'entreprise; [style] de la maison. -2. [wine] maison (inv).

house arrest n: **under ~** en résidence surveillée.

houseboat ['hausbəut] n péniche f aménagée.

housebound ['hausbaund] adj confiné(e) chez soi.

housebreaking ['haus,breɪkɪŋ] n (U) cambriolage m.

housebroken ['haus,brəukn] adj Am [pet] propre.

housecoat ['hauskəut] n peignoir m.

household ['haushəuld] ◇ adj -1. [domestic] ménager(ère). -2. [word, name] connu(e) de tous. ◇ n maison f, ménage m.

householder ['haus,həuldə'] n propriétaire mf (d'une maison).

househunting ['haus,hʌntɪŋ] n recherche f d'une maison (à acheter OR louer).

house husband n homme m au foyer.

housekeeper ['haus,kiːpə'] n gouvernante f.

housekeeping ['haus,kiːpɪŋ] n (U) -1. [work] ménage m. -2. **~ (money)** argent m du ménage.

houseman ['hausmən] (pl **-men**) n Br ≃ interne m.

housemen ['hausmən] pl → **houseman**.

house music n house music f.

House of Commons n Br: **the ~** la Chambre des communes.

HOUSE OF COMMONS:
La Chambre des communes est composée de 650 députés ('MPs') élus pour 5 ans et qui siègent environ 175 jours par an

House of Lords n Br: **the ~** la Chambre des lords.

HOUSE OF LORDS:
La Chambre des lords est composée de pairs et d'hommes d'Église. Il s'agit de la plus haute cour au Royaume-Uni (en excluant l'Écosse). Elle a le pouvoir d'amender certains projets de loi qui ont été votés par la Chambre des communes

House of Representatives n Am: **the ~** la Chambre des représentants.

HOUSE OF REPRESENTATIVES:
La Chambre des représentants constitue, avec le Sénat, l'organe législatif américain; ses membres sont élus par le peuple en proportion de la population de chaque État

house-owner n propriétaire mf d'une maison.

houseplant ['hausplɑːnt] n plante f d'appartement.

house-proud adj qui a la manie d'astiquer.

Houses of Parliament npl: **the ~** le Parlement britannique (où se réunissent la Chambre des communes et la Chambre des lords).

house-to-house adj de porte en porte, maison par maison.

house-train vt Br [animal] dresser à être propre.

housewarming (party) ['haus,wɔːmɪŋ] n pendaison f de crémaillère.

housewife ['hauswaɪf] (*pl* **-wives** [-waɪvz]) *n* femme *f* au foyer.

housework ['hauswɜːk] *n* (*U*) ménage *m*.

housing ['hauzɪŋ] ◇ *n* **-1.** (*U*) [accommodation] logement *m*. **-2.** [TECH - gen] boîtier *m*; [- of engine] coquille *f*. ◇ *comp* [policy] du logement; [conditions] de logement; [shortage] de logements.

housing association *n* Br association *f* d'aide au logement.

housing benefit *n* Br (*U*) allocation *f* logement.

housing development *n* ensemble *m* immobilier.

housing estate Br, **housing project** Am *n* cité *f*.

hovel ['hɒvl] *n* masure *f*, taudis *m*.

hover ['hɒvər] *vi* **-1.** [fly] planer. **-2.** [person]: to ~ **round sb** tourner OR rôder autour de qqn. **-3.** [hesitate] hésiter.

hovercraft ['hɒvəkrɑːft] (*pl inv* OR **-s**) *n* aéroglisseur *m*, hovercraft *m*.

hoverport ['hɒvəpɔːt] *n* hoverport *m*.

how [hau] *adv* **-1.** [gen] comment; ~ **do you do it?** comment fait-on?; ~ **are you?** comment allez-vous?; ~ **do you do?** enchanté(e) (de faire votre connaissance). **-2.** [referring to degree, amount]: ~ **high is it?** combien cela fait-il de haut?, quelle en est la hauteur?; ~ **long have you been waiting?** cela fait combien de temps que vous attendez?; ~ **many people came?** combien de personnes sont venues?; ~ **old are you?** quel âge as-tu? **-3.** [in exclamations]: ~ **nice!** que c'est bien!; ~ **awful!** quelle horreur!; ~ **pretty you look!** que tu es jolie! **-4.** [expressing surprise]: ~ **can you be so rude?** comment peux-tu être aussi grossier?

◆ **how about** *adv*: ~ **about a drink?** si on prenait un verre?; ~ **about you?** et toi?

◆ **how much** ◇ *pron* combien; ~ **much does it cost?** combien ça coûte? ◇ *adj* combien de; ~ **much bread?** combien de pain?

howdy ['haudɪ] *excl* Am *inf* salut!

however [hau'evər] ◇ *adv* **-1.** [nevertheless] cependant, toutefois. **-2.** [no matter how] quelque ... que (+ *subjunctive*), si ... que (+ *subjunctive*); ~ **many/much** peu importe la quantité de. **-3.** [how] comment. ◇ *conj* [in whatever way] de quelque manière que (+ *subjunctive*).

howl [haul] ◇ *n* hurlement *m*; [of laughter] éclat *m*. ◇ *vi* hurler; [with laughter] rire aux éclats.

howler ['haulər] *n inf* bourde *f*, gaffe *f*.

howling ['haulɪŋ] *adj inf* [success] fou (folle).

hp (*abbr of* **horsepower**) *n* CV *m*.

HP *n* **-1.** (*abbr of* **hire purchase**) Br: **to buy sthg on** ~ acheter qqch à crédit. **-2.** = **hp**.

HQ (*abbr of* **headquarters**) *n* QG *m*.

hr (*abbr of* **hour**) h.

HRH (*abbr of* **His (or Her) Royal Highness**) SAR.

HS *abbr of* **high school**.

HST (*abbr of* **Hawaiian Standard Time**) *heure de Hawaii*.

ht (*abbr of* **height**) haut.

HT (*abbr of* **high tension**) HT.

hub [hʌb] *n* **-1.** [of wheel] moyeu *m*. **-2.** [of activity] centre *m*.

hub airport *n* Am aéroport *m* important.

hubbub ['hʌbʌb] *n* vacarme *m*, brouhaha *m*.

hubcap ['hʌbkæp] *n* enjoliveur *m*.

HUD (*abbr of* **Department of Housing and Urban Development**) *n ancien ministère américain de l'urbanisme et du logement*.

huddle ['hʌdl] ◇ *vi* se blottir. ◇ *n* petit groupe *m*.

hue [hjuː] *n* [colour] teinte *f*, nuance *f*.

huff [hʌf] ◇ *n*: in a ~ froissé(e). ◇ *vi*: to ~ **and puff** souffler et haleter.

huffy ['hʌfɪ] (*compar* **-ier**, *superl* **-iest**) *adj inf* **-1.** [offended] froissé(e). **-2.** [touchy] susceptible.

hug [hʌg] (*pt* & *pp* **-ged**, *cont* **-ging**) ◇ *n* étreinte *f*; to give sb a ~ serrer qqn dans ses bras. ◇ *vt* **-1.** [embrace] étreindre, serrer dans ses bras. **-2.** [hold] tenir; to ~ **sthg to o.s.** serrer qqch contre soi. **-3.** [stay close to] serrer.

huge [hjuːdʒ] *adj* énorme; [subject] vaste; [success] fou (folle).

huh [hʌ] *excl* **-1.** [gen] hein? **-2.** [expressing scorn] berk!

hulk [hʌlk] *n* **-1.** [of ship] carcasse *f*. **-2.** [person] malabar *m*, mastodonte *m*.

hulking ['hʌlkɪŋ] *adj* énorme.

hull [hʌl] *n* coque *f*.

hullabaloo [ˌhʌləbə'luː] *n inf* tintamarre *m*, raffut *m*.

hullo [hə'ləu] *excl* = **hello**.

hum [hʌm] (*pt* & *pp* **-med**, *cont* **-ming**) ◇ *vi* **-1.** [buzz] bourdonner; [machine] vrombir, ronfler. **-2.** [sing] fredonner, chantonner. **-3.** [be busy] être en pleine activité. **-4.** *phr*: to ~ **and haw** bredouiller, bafouiller. ◇ *vt* fredonner, chantonner. ◇ *n* (*U*) bourdonnement *m*; [of machine] vrombissement *m*, ronflement *m*; [of conversation] brouhaha *m*.

human ['hju:mən] ◇ *adj* humain(e). ◇ *n*: ~ **(being)** être *m* humain.

humane [hju:'meɪn] *adj* humain(e).

humanely [hju:'meɪnlɪ] *adv* humainement.

human error *n* erreur *f* humaine.

humanist ['hju:mənɪst] *n* humaniste *mf*.

humanitarian [hju:,mænɪ'teərɪən] ◇ *adj* humanitaire. ◇ *n* humanitaire *mf*.

humanity [hju:'mænətɪ] *n* humanité *f*.
◆ **humanities** *npl*: **the ~** les humanités *fpl*, les sciences *fpl* humaines.

humanly ['hju:mənlɪ] *adv*: **~ possible** humainement possible.

human nature *n* nature *f* humaine.

human race *n*: **the ~** la race humaine.

human resources *npl* ressources *fpl* humaines.

human rights *npl* droits *mpl* de l'homme.

humble ['hʌmbl] ◇ *adj* humble; [origins, employee] modeste. ◇ *vt* humilier; **to ~ o.s.** s'abaisser, s'humilier.

humbly ['hʌmblɪ] *adv* **-1.** [not proudly] humblement. **-2.** [live, begin] modestement.

humbug ['hʌmbʌg] *n* **-1.** *dated* [hypocrisy] hypocrisie *f*. **-2.** *Br* [sweet] *type de bonbon dur*.

humdrum ['hʌmdrʌm] *adj* monotone.

humid ['hju:mɪd] *adj* humide.

humidity [hju:'mɪdətɪ] *n* humidité *f*.

humiliate [hju:'mɪlɪeɪt] *vt* humilier.

humiliating [hju:'mɪlɪeɪtɪŋ] *adj* humiliant(e).

humiliation [hju:,mɪlɪ'eɪʃn] *n* humiliation *f*.

humility [hju:'mɪlətɪ] *n* humilité *f*.

hummingbird ['hʌmɪŋbɜ:d] *n* colibri *m*, oiseau-mouche *m*.

humor *Am* = **humour**.

humorist ['hju:mərɪst] *n* humoriste *mf*.

humorous ['hju:mərəs] *adj* humoristique; [person] plein(e) d'humour.

humour *Br*, **humor** *Am* ['hju:mər] ◇ *n* **-1.** [sense of fun] humour *m*. **-2.** [of situation, remark] côté *m* comique. **-3.** *dated* [mood] humeur *f*. ◇ *vt* se montrer conciliant(e) envers.

hump [hʌmp] ◇ *n* bosse *f*. ◇ *vt* *inf* [carry] porter, coltiner.

humpbacked bridge ['hʌmpbækt-] *n* pont *m* en dos d'âne.

humus ['hju:məs] *n* humus *m*.

hunch [hʌntʃ] ◇ *n* *inf* pressentiment *m*, intuition *f*. ◇ *vt* voûter. ◇ *vi* se pencher.

hunchback ['hʌntʃbæk] *n* bossu *m*, -e *f*.

hunched [hʌntʃt] *adj* voûté(e).

hundred ['hʌndrəd] *num* cent; **a** OR **one ~** cent; **about a ~ pupils** une centaine d'élèves; *see also* **six**.
◆ **hundreds** *npl* des centaines.

hundredth ['hʌndrətθ] *num* centième; *see also* **sixth**.

hundredweight ['hʌndrədweɪt] *n* [in UK] poids *m* de 112 livres, = *50,8 kg*; [in US] poids *m* de 100 livres, = *45,3 kg*.

hung [hʌŋ] ◇ *pt & pp* → **hang**. ◇ *adj* [parliament, jury] sans majorité.

Hungarian [hʌŋ'geərɪən] ◇ *adj* hongrois(e). ◇ *n* **-1.** [person] Hongrois *m*, -e *f*. **-2.** [language] hongrois *m*.

Hungary ['hʌŋgərɪ] *n* Hongrie *f*; **in ~** en Hongrie.

hunger ['hʌŋgər] *n* **-1.** [gen] faim *f*. **-2.** [strong desire] soif *f*.
◆ **hunger after**, **hunger for** *vt fus* avoir faim de, avoir soif de.

hunger strike *n* grève *f* de la faim.

hung over *adj* *inf*: **to be ~** avoir la gueule de bois.

hungry ['hʌŋgrɪ] (*compar* -ier, *superl* -iest) *adj* **-1.** [for food]: **to be ~** avoir faim; [starving] être affamé(e); **to go ~** souffrir de la faim. **-2.** [eager]: **to be ~ for** être avide de.

hung up *adj* *inf*: **to be ~ (on** OR **about)** être obsédé(e) (par).

hunk [hʌŋk] *n* **-1.** [large piece] gros morceau *m*. **-2.** *inf* [man] beau mec *m*.

hunky-dory [,hʌŋkɪ'dɔ:rɪ] *adj* *inf* au poil.

hunt [hʌnt] ◇ *n* chasse *f*; [for missing person] recherches *fpl*. ◇ *vi* **-1.** [chase animals, birds] chasser. **-2.** *Br* [chase foxes] chasser le renard. **-3.** [search]: **to ~ (for sthg)** chercher partout (qqch). ◇ *vt* **-1.** [animals, birds] chasser. **-2.** [person] poursuivre, pourchasser.
◆ **hunt down** *vt sep* traquer.

hunter ['hʌntər] *n* **-1.** [of animals, birds] chasseur *m*. **-2.** [of things]: **bargain ~** dénicheur *m*, -euse *f* d'occasions; **autograph ~** collectionneur *m*, -euse *f* d'autographes.

hunting ['hʌntɪŋ] *n* **-1.** [of animals] chasse *f*. **-2.** *Br* [of foxes] chasse *f* au renard. ◇ *comp* de chasse.

huntsman ['hʌntsmən] (*pl* -men [-mən]) *n* chasseur *m*.

hurdle ['hɜ:dl] ◇ *n* **-1.** [in race] haie *f*. **-2.** [obstacle] obstacle *m*. ◇ *vt* [jump over] sauter.

hurl [hɜ:l] *vt* **-1.** [throw] lancer avec violence. **-2.** [shout] lancer.

hurrah [hʊ'rɑ:] *excl* *dated* hourra!

hurray [hʊ'reɪ] *excl* hourra!

hurricane ['hʌrɪkən] *n* ouragan *m*.

hurried ['hʌrɪd] *adj* [hasty] précipité(e).

hurriedly ['hʌrɪdlɪ] *adv* précipitamment; [eat, write] vite, en toute hâte.

hurry ['hʌrɪ] (*pt* & *pp* **-ied**) ◇ *vt* [person] faire se dépêcher; [process] hâter; **to ~ to do sthg** se dépêcher OR se presser de faire qqch. ◇ *vi* se dépêcher, se presser. ◇ *n* hâte *f*, précipitation *f*; **to be in a ~** être pressé; **to do sthg in a ~** faire qqch à la hâte; **to be in no ~ to do sthg** [unwilling] ne pas être pressé de faire qqch.

◆ **hurry up** ◇ *vi* se dépêcher. ◇ *vt sep* faire se dépêcher.

hurt [hɜːt] (*pt* & *pp* **hurt**) ◇ *vt* **-1.** [physically, emotionally] blesser; [one's leg, arm] se faire mal à; **to ~ o.s.** se faire mal. **-2.** *fig* [harm] faire du mal à. ◇ *vi* **-1.** [gen] faire mal; **my leg ~s** ma jambe me fait mal. **-2.** *fig* [do harm] faire du mal. ◇ *adj* blessé(e); [voice] offensé(e). ◇ *n* (U) [emotional pain] peine *f*.

hurtful ['hɜːtful] *adj* blessant(e).

hurtle ['hɜːtl] *vi* aller à toute allure.

husband ['hʌzbənd] *n* mari *m*.

husbandry ['hʌzbəndrɪ] *n fml* agriculture *f*.

hush [hʌʃ] ◇ *n* silence *m*. ◇ *excl* silence!, chut!

hush money *n* (U) *inf* pot-de-vin *m* (*pour acheter le silence de qqn*).

husk [hʌsk] *n* [of seed, grain] enveloppe *f*.

husky ['hʌskɪ] (*compar* **-ier**, *superl* **-iest**) ◇ *adj* [hoarse] rauque. ◇ *n* chien *m* esquimau.

hustings ['hʌstɪŋz] *npl Br* plate-forme *f* électorale.

hustle ['hʌsl] ◇ *vt* **-1.** [hurry] pousser, bousculer. **-2.** *Am* [persuade]: **to ~ sb into doing sthg** forcer la main à qqn pour qu'il fasse qqch. ◇ *n* agitation *f*.

hut [hʌt] *n* **-1.** [rough house] hutte *f*. **-2.** [shed] cabane *f*.

hutch [hʌtʃ] *n* clapier *m*.

hyacinth ['haɪəsɪnθ] *n* jacinthe *f*.

hybrid ['haɪbrɪd] ◇ *adj* hybride. ◇ *n* **-1.** [plant, animal] hybride *m*. **-2.** [mixture] entité *f* hybride.

hydrangea [haɪ'dreɪndʒə] *n* hortensia *m*.

hydrant ['haɪdrənt] *n* bouche *f* d'incendie.

hydraulic [haɪ'drɔːlɪk] *adj* hydraulique.

◆ **hydraulics** *n* hydraulique *f*.

hydrocarbon [,haɪdrə'kɑːbən] *n* hydrocarbure *m*.

hydrochloric acid [,haɪdrə'klɔːrɪk-] *n* acide *m* chlorhydrique.

hydroelectric [,haɪdrəʊɪ'lektrɪk] *adj* hydro-électrique.

hydroelectricity [,haɪdrəʊɪlek'trɪsətɪ] *n* hydro-électricité *f*.

hydrofoil ['haɪdrəfɔɪl] *n* hydrofoil *m*.

hydrogen ['haɪdrədʒən] *n* hydrogène *m*.

hydrogen bomb *n* bombe *f* à hydrogène.

hydrophobia [,haɪdrə'fəʊbjə] *n* hydrophobie *f*.

hydroplane ['haɪdrəpleɪn] *n* **-1.** [speedboat] hydro-glisseur *m*. **-2.** [hydrofoil] hydrofoil *m*.

hyena [haɪ'iːnə] *n* hyène *f*.

hygiene ['haɪdʒiːn] *n* hygiène *f*.

hygienic [haɪ'dʒiːnɪk] *adj* hygiénique.

hygienist [haɪ'dʒiːnɪst] *n* personne qui se charge du détartrage des dents.

hymn [hɪm] *n* hymne *m*, cantique *m*.

hymn book *n* livre *m* de cantiques.

hype [haɪp] *inf* ◇ *n* (U) battage *m* publicitaire. ◇ *vt* faire un battage publicitaire autour de.

hyped up [haɪpd-] *adj inf* [person] excité(e).

hyper ['haɪpər] *adj inf* qui a la bougeotte.

hyperactive [,haɪpər'æktɪv] *adj* hyperactif(ive).

hyperbole [haɪ'pɜːbəlɪ] *n* hyperbole *f*.

hyperinflation [,haɪpərɪn'fleɪʃn] *n* hyperinflation *f*.

hypermarket ['haɪpə,mɑːkɪt] *n* hypermarché *m*.

hypersensitive [,haɪpə'sensɪtɪv] *adj* hypersensible.

hypertension [,haɪpə'tenʃn] *n* hypertension *f*.

hypertext ['haɪpətekst] *n* COMPUT hypertexte *m*.

hyperventilate [,haɪpə'ventɪleɪt] *vi* faire de l'hyperventilation.

hyphen ['haɪfn] *n* trait *m* d'union.

hyphenate ['haɪfəneɪt] *vt* mettre un trait d'union à.

hypnosis [hɪp'nəʊsɪs] *n* hypnose *f*; **under ~** sous hypnose, en état d'hypnose.

hypnotic [hɪp'nɒtɪk] *adj* hypnotique.

hypnotism ['hɪpnətɪzm] *n* hypnotisme *m*.

hypnotist ['hɪpnətɪst] *n* hypnotiseur *m*.

hypnotize, -ise ['hɪpnətaɪz] *vt* hypnotiser.

hypoallergenic ['haɪpəʊ,ælə'dʒenɪk] *adj* hypo-allergique.

hypochondriac [,haɪpə'kɒndriæk] *n* hypochondriaque *mf*.

hypocrisy [hɪ'pɒkrəsɪ] *n* hypocrisie *f*.

hypocrite ['hɪpəkrɪt] *n* hypocrite *mf*.

hypocritical [,hɪpə'krɪtɪkl] *adj* hypocrite.

hypodermic needle [ˌhaɪpə'dɜːmɪk-] *n* aiguille *f* hypodermique.

hypodermic syringe [ˌhaɪpə'dɜːmɪk-] *n* seringue *f* hypodermique.

hypothermia [ˌhaɪpəʊ'θɜːmɪə] *n* hypothermie *f.*

hypothesis [haɪ'pɒθɪsɪs] (*pl* **-theses** [-θɪsiːz]) *n* hypothèse *f.*

hypothesize, -ise [haɪ'pɒθɪsaɪz] ◇ *vt* émettre une hypothèse OR des hypothèses sur. ◇ *vi* émettre une hypothèse OR des hypothèses.

hypothetical [ˌhaɪpə'θetɪkl] *adj* hypothétique.

hysterectomy [ˌhɪstə'rektəmɪ] (*pl* **-ies**) *n* hystérectomie *f.*

hysteria [hɪs'tɪərɪə] *n* hystérie *f.*

hysterical [hɪs'terɪkl] *adj* **-1.** [gen] hystérique. **-2.** *inf* [very funny] désopilant(e).

hysterics [hɪs'terɪks] *npl* **-1.** [panic, excitement] crise *f* de nerfs. **-2.** *inf* [laughter] fou rire *m.*

HZ (*abbr of* **hertz**) Hz.

I

i (*pl* **i's** OR **is**), **I** (*pl* **I's** OR **Is**) [aɪ] *n* [letter] i *m inv*, I *m inv.*

I¹ [aɪ] *pers pron* **-1.** (*unstressed*) je, j' (*before vowel or silent 'h'*); **he and I are leaving for Paris** lui et moi (nous) partons pour Paris; **it is I** *fml* c'est moi. **-2.** (*stressed*) moi; **I can't do it** moi je ne peux pas le faire.

I² *abbr of* **Island, Isle.**

IA *abbr of* **Iowa.**

IAEA (*abbr of* **International Atomic Energy Agency**) *n* AIEA *f.*

IBA (*abbr of* **Independent Broadcasting Authority**) *n organisme d'agrément et de coordination des stations de radio et chaînes de télévision du secteur privé en Grande-Bretagne.*

Iberian [aɪ'bɪərɪən] ◇ *adj* ibérique. ◇ *n* Ibère *mf.*

Iberian peninsula *n*: **the ~** la péninsule ibérique.

ibid (*abbr of* **ibidem**) ibid.

i/c *abbr of* **in charge.**

ICA (*abbr of* **Institute of Contemporary Art**) *n centre d'art moderne à Londres.*

ICBM (*abbr of* **intercontinental ballistic missile**) *n* ICBM *m.*

ICC *n* **-1.** (*abbr of* **International Chamber of Commerce**) CCI *f.* **-2.** (*abbr of* **Interstate Commerce Commission**) *commission fédérale américaine réglementant le commerce entre les États.*

ice [aɪs] ◇ *n* **-1.** [frozen water, ice cream] glace *f*; **to break the ~** *fig* rompre OR briser la glace. **-2.** (*U*) [ice cubes] glaçons *mpl.* ◇ *vt Br* glacer.

◆ **ice over, ice up** *vi* [lake, pond] geler; [window, windscreen] givrer; [road] se couvrir de verglas.

ice age *n* période *f* glaciaire.

iceberg ['aɪsbɜːg] *n* iceberg *m.*

iceberg lettuce *n* laitue *f* iceberg.

icebox ['aɪsbɒks] *n* **-1.** *Br* [in refrigerator] freezer *m.* **-2.** *Am* [refrigerator] réfrigérateur *m.*

icebreaker ['aɪsˌbreɪkəʳ] *n* [ship] brise-glace *m,* brise-glaces *m.*

ice bucket *n* seau *m* à glace.

ice cap *n* calotte *f* glaciaire.

ice-cold *adj* glacé(e).

ice cream *n* glace *f.*

ice cream van *n Br* camionnette *f* de vendeur de glaces.

ICE CREAM VAN:
La petite camionnette du vendeur de glaces est très caractéristique; elle se reconnaît au carillon qui annonce son arrivée dans un quartier

---

ice cube *n* glaçon *m.*

iced [aɪst] *adj* glacé(e).

ice floe *n* banquise *f.*

ice hockey *n* hockey *m* sur glace.

Iceland ['aɪslənd] *n* Islande *f*; **in ~** en Islande.

Icelander ['aɪsləndəʳ] *n* Islandais *m,* -e *f.*

Icelandic [aɪs'lændɪk] ◇ *adj* islandais(e). ◇ *n* [language] islandais *m.*

ice lolly *n Br* sucette *f* glacée.

ice pick *n* pic *m* à glace.

ice rink *n* patinoire *f.*

ice skate *n* patin *m* à glace.

◆ **ice-skate** *vi* faire du patin (à glace).

ice-skater *n* patineur *m,* -euse *f.*

ice-skating *n* patinage *m* (sur glace).

icicle ['aɪsɪkl] *n* glaçon *m* (naturel).

icily ['aɪsɪlɪ] *adv* [in unfriendly way] d'une manière glaciale; [say, reply] d'un ton glacial.

icing ['aɪsɪŋ] *n* (*U*) glaçage *m*, glace *f*; **the ~ on the cake** *fig* un plus, la cerise sur le gâteau.

icing sugar *n Br* sucre *m* glace.

ICJ (*abbr of* **International Court of Justice**) *n* CIJ *f*.

icon ['aɪkɒn] *n* [gen & COMPUT] icône *f*.

iconoclast [aɪ'kɒnəklæst] *n* iconoclaste *mf*.

ICR (*abbr of* **Institute for Cancer Research**) *n* institut de recherche contre le cancer.

ICU (*abbr of* **intensive care unit**) *n* unité de réanimation.

icy ['aɪsɪ] (*compar* **-ier**, *superl* **-iest**) *adj* **-1.** [weather, manner] glacial(e). **-2.** [covered in ice] verglacé(e).

id [ɪd] *n* ça *m*.

I'd [aɪd] = **I would, I had**.

ID ◇ *n* (*abbr of* **identification**) (*U*) papiers *mpl*. ◇ *abbr of* **Idaho**.

Idaho ['aɪdə,həʊ] *n* Idaho *m*; **in ~** dans l'Idaho.

ID card = **identity card**.

IDD (*abbr of* **international direct dialling**) *n* automatique *m* international.

idea [aɪ'dɪə] *n* idée *f*; [intention] intention *f*; **to have an ~ of** avoir une idée de; **to have an ~ (that)** ... avoir idée que ...; **to have no ~** n'avoir aucune idée; **to get the ~** *inf* piger; **don't get the ~ (that)** ... ne va pas croire OR t'imaginer que ...; **the ~ is to** ... l'idée est de ..., l'intention est de ....

ideal [aɪ'dɪəl] ◇ *adj* idéal(e); **to be ~ for** être idéal OR parfait pour. ◇ *n* idéal *m*.

idealism [aɪ'dɪəlɪzm] *n* idéalisme *m*.

idealist [aɪ'dɪəlɪst] *n* idéaliste *mf*.

idealize, -ise [aɪ'dɪəlaɪz] *vt* idéaliser.

ideally [aɪ'dɪəlɪ] *adv* idéalement; [suited] parfaitement.

identical [aɪ'dentɪkl] *adj* identique.

identical twins *npl* vrais jumeaux *mpl*, vraies jumelles *fpl*.

identifiable [aɪ'dentɪfaɪəbl] *adj* identifiable, reconnaissable.

identification [aɪ,dentɪfɪ'keɪʃn] *n* (*U*) **-1.** [gen]: ~ **(with)** identification *f* (à). **-2.** [documentation] pièce *f* d'identité.

identify [aɪ'dentɪfaɪ] (*pt* & *pp* **-ied**) ◇ *vt* **-1.** [recognize] identifier. **-2.** [subj: document, card] permettre de reconnaître. **-3.** [associate]: **to ~ sb with sthg** associer qqn à qqch. ◇ *vi* [empathize]: **to ~ with** s'identifier à.

Identikit picture® [aɪ'dentɪkɪt-] *n* portrait-robot *m*.

identity [aɪ'dentətɪ] (*pl* **-ies**) *n* identité *f*.

identity card *n* carte *f* d'identité.

identity parade *n* séance d'identification d'un suspect dans un échantillon de plusieurs personnes.

ideological [,aɪdɪə'lɒdʒɪkl] *adj* idéologique.

ideology [,aɪdɪ'ɒlədʒɪ] (*pl* **-ies**) *n* idéologie *f*.

idiom ['ɪdɪəm] *n* **-1.** [phrase] expression *f* idiomatique. **-2.** *fml* [style] langue *f*.

idiomatic [,ɪdɪə'mætɪk] *adj* idiomatique.

idiosyncrasy [,ɪdɪə'sɪŋkrəsɪ] (*pl* **-ies**) *n* particularité *f*, caractéristique *f*.

idiot ['ɪdɪət] *n* idiot *m*, -e *f*, imbécile *mf*.

idiotic [,ɪdɪ'ɒtɪk] *adj* idiot(e).

idle ['aɪdl] ◇ *adj* **-1.** [lazy] oisif(ive), désœuvré(e). **-2.** [not working - machine, factory] arrêté(e); [- worker] qui chôme, en chômage. **-3.** [threat] vain(e). **-4.** [curiosity] simple, pur(e). ◇ *vi* tourner au ralenti.
 ◆ **idle away** *vt sep* [time] perdre à ne rien faire.

idleness ['aɪdlnɪs] *n* oisiveté *f*, désœuvrement *m*.

idler ['aɪdlər] *n* paresseux *m*, -euse *f*.

idly ['aɪdlɪ] *adv* **-1.** [lazily] paresseusement. **-2.** [without purpose] négligemment.

idol ['aɪdl] *n* idole *f*.

idolize, -ise ['aɪdəlaɪz] *vt* idolâtrer, adorer.

idyl(l) ['ɪdɪl] *n* idylle *f*.

idyllic [ɪ'dɪlɪk] *adj* idyllique.

i.e. (*abbr of* **id est**) c-à-d.

if [ɪf] ◇ *conj* **-1.** [gen] si; ~ **I were you** à ta place, si j'étais toi. **-2.** [though] bien que. **-3.** [that] que. ◇ *n*: ~**s and buts** les si et les mais *mpl*.
 ◆ **if not** *conj* sinon.
 ◆ **if only** ◇ *conj* **-1.** [naming a reason] ne serait-ce que. **-2.** [expressing regret] si seulement. ◇ *excl* si seulement!

iffy ['ɪfɪ] (*compar* **-ier**, *superl* **-iest**) *adj inf* incertain(e).

igloo ['ɪgluː] (*pl* **-s**) *n* igloo *m*, iglou *m*.

ignite [ɪg'naɪt] ◇ *vt* mettre le feu à, enflammer; [firework] tirer. ◇ *vi* prendre feu, s'enflammer.

ignition [ɪg'nɪʃn] *n* **-1.** [act of igniting] ignition *f*. **-2.** AUT allumage *m*.

ignition key *n* clef *f* de contact.

ignoble [ɪg'nəʊbl] *adj fml* infâme.

ignominious [,ɪgnə'mɪnɪəs] *adj* ignominieux(ieuse).

ignominy ['ɪgnəmɪnɪ] *n* ignominie *f*.

ignoramus [ˌɪgnəˈreɪməs] (*pl* **-es**) *n* ignare *mf*.

ignorance [ˈɪgnərəns] *n* ignorance *f*.

ignorant [ˈɪgnərənt] *adj* **-1.** [uneducated, unaware] ignorant(e); **to be ~ of sthg** être ignorant de qqch. **-2.** [rude] mal élevé(e).

ignore [ɪgˈnɔːr] *vt* [advice, facts] ne pas tenir compte de; [person] faire semblant de ne pas voir.

iguana [ɪˈgwɑːnə] (*pl inv* OR **-s**) *n* iguane *m*.

ikon [ˈaɪkɒn] = **icon**.

IL *abbr of* **Illinois**.

ILEA [ˈɪlɪə] (*abbr of* **Inner London Education Authority**) *n anciens services londoniens de l'enseignement*.

ileum [ˈɪlɪəm] (*pl* **ilea** [ˈɪlɪə]) *n* iléon *m*.

ilk [ɪlk] *n*: **of that ~** [of that sort] de cet acabit, de ce genre.

ill [ɪl] ◇ *adj* **-1.** [unwell] malade; **to feel ~** se sentir malade OR souffrant; **to be taken ~**, **to fall ~** tomber malade. **-2.** [bad] mauvais(e); **~ luck** malchance *f*. ◇ *adv* mal; **to speak/think ~ of sb** dire/penser du mal de qqn.
♦ **ills** *npl* maux *mpl*, malheurs *mpl*.

ill. (*abbr of* **illustration**) ill.

I'll [aɪl] = **I will, I shall**.

ill-advised [-ədˈvaɪzd] *adj* [remark, action] peu judicieux(ieuse); [person] malavisé(e); **to be ~ to do sthg** être malavisé de faire qqch.

ill at ease *adj* mal à l'aise.

ill-bred *adj* mal élevé(e).

ill-considered *adj* irréfléchi(e).

ill-disposed *adj*: **to be ~ towards sb** être mal disposé(e) OR malintentionné(e) envers qqn.

illegal [ɪˈliːgl] *adj* illégal(e); [immigrant] en situation irrégulière.

illegally [ɪˈliːgəlɪ] *adv* illégalement, d'une manière illégale.

illegible [ɪˈledʒəbl] *adj* illisible.

illegitimate [ˌɪlɪˈdʒɪtɪmət] *adj* illégitime.

ill-equipped *adj*: **to be ~ to do sthg** être mal placé(e) pour faire qqch.

ill-fated *adj* fatal(e), funeste.

ill feeling *n* animosité *f*.

ill-founded [-ˈfaʊndɪd] *adj* [confidence, trust] mal fondé(e); [doubts] sans fondement.

ill-gotten gains [-ˈgɒtən-] *npl hum* biens *mpl* mal acquis.

ill health *n* mauvaise santé *f*.

illicit [ɪˈlɪsɪt] *adj* illicite.

illicitly [ɪˈlɪsɪtlɪ] *adv* illicitement.

ill-informed *adj* mal renseigné(e).

Illinois [ˌɪlɪˈnɔɪ] *n* Illinois *m*; **in ~** dans l'Illinois.

illiteracy [ɪˈlɪtərəsɪ] *n* analphabétisme *m*, illettrisme *m*.

illiterate [ɪˈlɪtərət] ◇ *adj* analphabète, illettré(e). ◇ *n* analphabète *mf*, illettré *m*, -e *f*.

ill-mannered *adj* mal élevé(e); [behaviour] grossier(ière).

illness [ˈɪlnɪs] *n* maladie *f*.

illogical [ɪˈlɒdʒɪkl] *adj* illogique.

ill-suited *adj* mal assorti(e); **to be ~ for sthg** être inapte à qqch.

ill-tempered *adj* qui a mauvais caractère.

ill-timed [-ˈtaɪmd] *adj* déplacé(e), mal à propos.

ill-treat *vt* maltraiter.

ill-treatment *n* mauvais traitement *m*.

illuminate [ɪˈluːmɪneɪt] *vt* éclairer.

illuminated [ɪˈluːmɪneɪtɪd] *adj* **-1.** [lit up] lumineux(euse). **-2.** [book, manuscript] enluminé(e).

illuminating [ɪˈluːmɪneɪtɪŋ] *adj* éclairant(e).

illumination [ɪˌluːmɪˈneɪʃn] *n* [lighting] éclairage *m*.
♦ **illuminations** *npl Br* illuminations *fpl*.

illusion [ɪˈluːʒn] *n* illusion *f*; **to have no ~s about** ne se faire OR n'avoir aucune illusion sur; **to be under the ~ that** croire OR s'imaginer que, avoir l'illusion que.

illusionist [ɪˈluːʒənɪst] *n* prestidigitateur *m*, -euse *f*, illusionniste *mf*.

illusory [ɪˈluːsərɪ] *adj* illusoire.

illustrate [ˈɪləstreɪt] *vt* illustrer.

illustration [ˌɪləˈstreɪʃn] *n* illustration *f*.

illustrator [ˈɪləstreɪtər] *n* illustrateur *m*, -trice *f*.

illustrious [ɪˈlʌstrɪəs] *adj* illustre, célèbre.

ill will *n* animosité *f*.

ill wind *n*: **it's an ~ (that blows nobody any good)** *proverb* à quelque chose malheur est bon.

ILO (*abbr of* **International Labour Organization**) *n* OIT *f*.

ILWU (*abbr of* **International Longshoremen's and Warehousemen's Union**) *n syndicat international de dockers et de magasiniers*.

I'm [aɪm] = **I am**.

image [ˈɪmɪdʒ] *n* **-1.** [gen] image *f*; **to be the ~ of sb** *fig* être tout le portrait de qqn, être qqn tout craché. **-2.** [of company, politician] image *f* de marque.

imagery [ˈɪmɪdʒrɪ] *n* (U) images *fpl*.

imaginable [ɪˈmædʒɪnəbl] *adj* imaginable.

imaginary [ɪˈmædʒɪnrɪ] *adj* imaginaire.

imagination [ɪˌmædʒɪ'neɪʃn] *n* **-1.** [ability] imagination *f.* **-2.** [fantasy] invention *f.*

imaginative [ɪ'mædʒɪnətɪv] *adj* imaginatif(ive); [solution] plein(e) d'imagination.

imagine [ɪ'mædʒɪn] *vt* imaginer; **to ~ doing sthg** s'imaginer OR se voir faisant qqch; **~ (that)!** tu t'imagines!

imaginings [ɪ'mædʒɪnɪŋz] *npl* imaginations *fpl.*

imbalance [ˌɪm'bæləns] *n* déséquilibre *m.*

imbecile ['ɪmbɪsiːl] *n* imbécile *mf,* idiot *m,* -e *f.*

imbue [ɪm'bjuː] *vt*: **to be ~d with** être imbu(e) de.

IMF (*abbr of* **International Monetary Fund**) *n* FMI *m.*

imitate ['ɪmɪteɪt] *vt* imiter.

imitation [ˌɪmɪ'teɪʃn] ◇ *n* imitation *f.* ◇ *adj* [leather] imitation (*before n*); [jewellery] en toc.

imitator ['ɪmɪteɪtər] *n* imitateur *m,* -trice *f.*

immaculate [ɪ'mækjulət] *adj* impeccable.

immaculately [ɪ'mækjulətlɪ] *adv* impeccablement.

immaterial [ˌɪmə'tɪərɪəl] *adj* [unimportant] sans importance.

immature [ˌɪmə'tjuər] *adj* **-1.** [lacking judgment] qui manque de maturité. **-2.** [not fully grown] jeune, immature.

immaturity [ˌɪmə'tjuərətɪ] *n* immaturité *f.*

immeasurable [ɪ'meʒrəbl] *adj* incommensurable.

immediacy [ɪ'miːdjəsɪ] *n* caractère *m* immédiat.

immediate [ɪ'miːdjət] *adj* **-1.** [urgent] immédiat(e); [problem, meeting] urgent(e). **-2.** [very near] immédiat(e); [family] le plus proche.

immediately [ɪ'miːdjətlɪ] ◇ *adv* **-1.** [at once] immédiatement. **-2.** [directly] directement. ◇ *conj* dès que.

immemorial [ˌɪmɪ'mɔːrɪəl] *adj* immémorial(e); **from time ~** de temps immémorial.

immense [ɪ'mens] *adj* immense; [improvement, change] énorme.

immensely [ɪ'menslɪ] *adv* extrêmement, immensément.

immensity [ɪ'mensətɪ] *n* immensité *f.*

immerse [ɪ'mɜːs] *vt*: **to ~ sthg in sthg** immerger OR plonger qqch dans qqch; **to ~ o.s. in sthg** *fig* se plonger dans qqch.

immersion heater [ɪ'mɜːʃn] *n* chauffe-eau *m* électrique.

immigrant ['ɪmɪɡrənt] ◇ *n* immigré *m,* -e *f.* ◇ *comp* d'immigrés.

immigration [ˌɪmɪ'ɡreɪʃn] ◇ *n* immigration *f.* ◇ *comp* de l'immigration.

imminence ['ɪmɪnəns] *n* imminence *f.*

imminent ['ɪmɪnənt] *adj* imminent(e).

immobile [ɪ'məubaɪl] *adj* immobile.

immobilization [ɪˌməubɪlaɪ'zeɪʃn] *n* immobilisation *f.*

immobilize, -ise [ɪ'məubɪlaɪz] *vt* immobiliser.

immodest [ɪ'mɒdɪst] *adj* **-1.** [vain] vaniteux(euse), présomptueux(euse). **-2.** [indecent] impudique.

immoral [ɪ'mɒrəl] *adj* immoral(e).

immorality [ˌɪmə'rælətɪ] *n* immoralité *f.*

immortal [ɪ'mɔːtl] ◇ *adj* immortel(elle). ◇ *n* immortel *m,* -elle *f.*

immortality [ˌɪmɔː'tælətɪ] *n* immortalité *f.*

immortalize, -ise [ɪ'mɔːtəlaɪz] *vt* immortaliser.

immovable [ɪ'muːvəbl] *adj* **-1.** [fixed] fixe. **-2.** [determined] inébranlable.

immune [ɪ'mjuːn] *adj* **-1.** MED: **~ (to)** immunisé(e) (contre). **-2.** *fig* [protected]: **to be ~ to** OR **from** être à l'abri de.

immune system *n* système *m* immunitaire.

immunity [ɪ'mjuːnətɪ] *n* **-1.** MED: **~ (to)** immunité *f* (contre). **-2.** *fig* [protection]: **~ to** OR **from** immunité *f* contre.

immunization [ˌɪmjuːnaɪ'zeɪʃn] *n* immunisation *f.*

immunize, -ise ['ɪmjuːnaɪz] *vt*: **to ~ sb (against)** immuniser qqn (contre).

immunodeficiency [ˌɪmjuːnəudɪ'fɪʃənsɪ] *n* immunodéficience *f.*

immunology [ˌɪmjuːn'ɒlədʒɪ] *n* immunologie *f.*

immutable [ɪ'mjuːtəbl] *adj* immuable.

imp [ɪmp] *n* **-1.** [creature] lutin *m.* **-2.** [naughty child] petit diable *m,* coquin *m,* -e *f.*

impact [*n* 'ɪmpækt, *vb* ɪm'pækt] ◇ *n* impact *m*; **to make an ~ on** OR **upon sb** faire une forte impression sur qqn; **to make an ~ on** OR **upon sthg** avoir un impact sur qqch; **on ~** au moment de l'impact. ◇ *vt* **-1.** [collide with] entrer en collision avec. **-2.** [influence] avoir un impact sur.

impair [ɪm'peər] *vt* affaiblir, abîmer; [efficiency] réduire.

impaired [ɪm'peəd] *adj* affaibli(e); [efficiency] réduit(e).

impale [ɪm'peɪl] *vt*: **to ~ sb/sthg (on)** empaler qqn/qqch (sur).

impart [ɪm'pɑːt] *vt* *fml* **-1.** [information]: **to ~ sthg (to sb)** communiquer OR transmettre qqch (à qqn). **-2.** [feeling, quality]: **to ~ sthg (to)** donner qqch (à).

impartial [ɪmˈpɑːʃl] *adj* impartial(e).

impartiality [ɪmˌpɑːʃɪˈælətɪ] *n* impartialité *f*.

impassable [ɪmˈpɑːsəbl] *adj* impraticable.

impasse [æmˈpɑːs] *n* impasse *f*; **to reach an ~** aboutir à une impasse.

impassioned [ɪmˈpæʃnd] *adj* passionné(e).

impassive [ɪmˈpæsɪv] *adj* impassible.

impatience [ɪmˈpeɪʃns] *n* **-1.** [gen] impatience *f*. **-2.** [irritability] irritation *f*.

impatient [ɪmˈpeɪʃnt] *adj* **-1.** [gen] impatient(e); **to be ~ to do sthg** être impatient de faire qqch; **to be ~ for sthg** attendre qqch avec impatience. **-2.** [irritable]: **to become** OR **get ~** s'impatienter.

impatiently [ɪmˈpeɪʃntlɪ] *adv* avec impatience.

impeach [ɪmˈpiːtʃ] *vt* [official] mettre en accusation; [president] entamer la procédure d'impeachment contre.

impeachment [ɪmˈpiːtʃmənt] *n* [of president] procédure *f* d'impeachment.

impeccable [ɪmˈpekəbl] *adj* impeccable.

impeccably [ɪmˈpekəblɪ] *adv* impeccablement.

impecunious [ˌɪmpɪˈkjuːnjəs] *adj* impécunieux(ieuse).

impede [ɪmˈpiːd] *vt* entraver, empêcher; [person] gêner.

impediment [ɪmˈpedɪmənt] *n* **-1.** [obstacle] obstacle *m*. **-2.** [disability] défaut *m*.

impel [ɪmˈpel] (*pt* & *pp* **-led**, *cont* **-ling**) *vt*: **to ~ sb to do sthg** inciter qqn à faire qqch.

impending [ɪmˈpendɪŋ] *adj* imminent(e).

impenetrable [ɪmˈpenɪtrəbl] *adj* impénétrable.

imperative [ɪmˈperətɪv] ◇ *adj* [essential] impératif(ive), essentiel(ielle). ◇ *n* impératif *m*.

imperceptible [ˌɪmpəˈseptəbl] *adj* imperceptible.

imperfect [ɪmˈpɜːfɪkt] ◇ *adj* imparfait(e). ◇ *n* GRAMM: **~ (tense)** imparfait *m*.

imperfection [ˌɪmpəˈfekʃn] *n* **-1.** [gen] imperfection *f*. **-2.** [failing] défaut *m*.

imperial [ɪmˈpɪərɪəl] *adj* **-1.** [of empire] impérial(e). **-2.** [system of measurement] *qui a cours légal dans le Royaume-Uni.*

imperialism [ɪmˈpɪərɪəlɪzm] *n* impérialisme *m*.

imperialist [ɪmˈpɪərɪəlɪst] ◇ *adj* impérialiste. ◇ *n* impérialiste *mf*.

imperil [ɪmˈperɪl] (*Br pt* & *pp* **-led**, *cont* **-ling**, *Am pt* & *pp* **-ed**, *cont* **-ing**) *vt* mettre en péril OR en danger; [project] compromettre.

imperious [ɪmˈpɪərɪəs] *adj* impérieux(ieuse).

impersonal [ɪmˈpɜːsnl] *adj* impersonnel(elle).

impersonate [ɪmˈpɜːsəneɪt] *vt* se faire passer pour.

impersonation [ɪmˌpɜːsəˈneɪʃn] *n* usurpation *f* d'identité; [by mimic] imitation *f*.

impersonator [ɪmˈpɜːsəneɪtər] *n* imitateur *m*, -trice *f*.

impertinence [ɪmˈpɜːtɪnəns] *n* impertinence *f*.

impertinent [ɪmˈpɜːtɪnənt] *adj* impertinent(e).

imperturbable [ˌɪmpəˈtɜːbəbl] *adj* imperturbable.

impervious [ɪmˈpɜːvjəs] *adj* [not influenced]: **~ to** indifférent(e) à.

impetuous [ɪmˈpetʃʊəs] *adj* impétueux(euse).

impetus [ˈɪmpɪtəs] *n* (*U*) **-1.** [momentum] élan *m*. **-2.** [stimulus] impulsion *f*.

impinge [ɪmˈpɪndʒ] *vi*: **to ~ on sb/sthg** affecter qqn/qqch.

impish [ˈɪmpɪʃ] *adj* espiègle.

implacable [ɪmˈplækəbl] *adj* implacable.

implant [*n* ˈɪmplɑːnt, *vb* ɪmˈplɑːnt] ◇ *n* implant *m*. ◇ *vt*: **to ~ sthg in** OR **into sb** implanter qqch dans qqn.

implausible [ɪmˈplɔːzəbl] *adj* peu plausible.

implement [*n* ˈɪmplɪmənt, *vt* ˈɪmplɪment] ◇ *n* outil *m*, instrument *m*. ◇ *vt* exécuter, appliquer.

implementation [ˌɪmplɪmenˈteɪʃn] *n* application *f*, exécution *f*.

implicate [ˈɪmplɪkeɪt] *vt*: **to ~ sb in sthg** impliquer qqn dans qqch.

implication [ˌɪmplɪˈkeɪʃn] *n* implication *f*; **by ~** implicitement.

implicit [ɪmˈplɪsɪt] *adj* **-1.** [inferred] implicite. **-2.** [belief, faith] absolu(e).

implicitly [ɪmˈplɪsɪtlɪ] *adv* **-1.** [by inference] implicitement. **-2.** [believe] absolument.

implied [ɪmˈplaɪd] *adj* implicite.

implode [ɪmˈpləʊd] *vi* imploser.

implore [ɪmˈplɔːr] *vt*: **to ~ sb (to do sthg)** implorer qqn (de faire qqch).

imply [ɪmˈplaɪ] (*pt* & *pp* **-ied**) *vt* **-1.** [suggest] sous-entendre, laisser supposer OR entendre. **-2.** [involve] impliquer.

impolite [ˌɪmpəˈlaɪt] *adj* impoli(e).

imponderable [ɪm'pɒndrəbl] *adj* impondérable.

◆ **imponderables** *npl* impondérables *mpl*.

import [*n* 'ɪmpɔːt, *vt* ɪm'pɔːt] ◇ *n* **-1.** [product, action] importation *f*. **-2.** *fml* [meaning] teneur *f*. **-3.** *fml* [importance] importance *f*. ◇ *vt* [gen & COMPUT] importer.

importance [ɪm'pɔːtns] *n* importance *f*.

important [ɪm'pɔːtnt] *adj* important(e); **to be ~ to sb** importer à qqn.

importantly [ɪm'pɔːtntlɪ] *adv*: **more ~** ce qui est plus important.

importation [,ɪmpɔː'teɪʃn] *n* importation *f*.

imported [ɪm'pɔːtɪd] *adj* importé(e).

importer [ɪm'pɔːtəʳ] *n* importateur *m*, -trice *f*.

impose [ɪm'pəʊz] ◇ *vt* [force]: **to ~ sthg (on)** imposer qqch (à). ◇ *vi* [cause trouble]: **to ~ (on sb)** abuser (de la gentillesse de qqn).

imposing [ɪm'pəʊzɪŋ] *adj* imposant(e).

imposition [,ɪmpə'zɪʃn] *n* **-1.** [of tax, limitations etc] imposition *f*. **-2.** [cause of trouble]: **it's an ~** c'est abuser de ma/notre gentillesse.

impossibility [ɪm,pɒsə'bɪlətɪ] (*pl* **-ies**) *n* impossibilité *f*.

impossible [ɪm'pɒsəbl] ◇ *adj* impossible. ◇ *n*: **to do the ~** faire l'impossible.

impostor, imposter *Am* [ɪm'pɒstəʳ] *n* imposteur *m*.

impotence ['ɪmpətəns] *n* impuissance *f*.

impotent ['ɪmpətənt] *adj* impuissant(e).

impound [ɪm'paʊnd] *vt* confisquer.

impoverished [ɪm'pɒvərɪʃt] *adj* appauvri(e).

impracticable [ɪm'præktɪkəbl] *adj* irréalisable.

impractical [ɪm'præktɪkl] *adj* pas pratique.

imprecation [,ɪmprɪ'keɪʃn] *n* imprécation *f*.

imprecise [ɪmprɪ'saɪs] *adj* imprécis(e).

impregnable [ɪm'pregnəbl] *adj* **-1.** [fortress, defences] imprenable. **-2.** *fig* [person] inattaquable.

impregnate ['ɪmpregneɪt] *vt* **-1.** [introduce substance into]: **to ~ sthg with** imprégner qqch de. **-2.** *fml* [fertilize] féconder.

impresario [,ɪmprɪ'sɑːrɪəʊ] (*pl* **-s**) *n* impresario *m*.

impress [ɪm'pres] *vt* **-1.** [person] impressionner. **-2.** [stress]: **to ~ sthg on sb** faire bien comprendre qqch à qqn.

impression [ɪm'preʃn] *n* **-1.** [gen] impression *f*; **to be under the ~ (that)** ... avoir l'impression que ...; **to make an ~** faire impression. **-2.** [by mimic] imitation *f*. **-3.** [of stamp, book] impression *f*, empreinte *f*.

impressionable [ɪm'preʃnəbl] *adj* impressionnable.

Impressionism [ɪm'preʃənɪzm] *n* impressionnisme *m*.

impressionist [ɪm'preʃənɪst] *n* imitateur *m*, -trice *f*.

◆ **Impressionist** ◇ *adj* impressionniste. ◇ *n* impressionniste *mf*.

impressive [ɪm'presɪv] *adj* impressionnant(e).

imprint [*n* 'ɪmprɪnt, *vt* ɪm'prɪnt] *n* **-1.** [mark] empreinte *f*. **-2.** [publisher's name] nom *m* de l'éditeur.

imprinted [ɪm'prɪntɪd] *adj* imprimé(e).

imprison [ɪm'prɪzn] *vt* emprisonner.

imprisonment [ɪm'prɪznmənt] *n* emprisonnement *m*.

improbable [ɪm'prɒbəbl] *adj* **-1.** [story, excuse] improbable. **-2.** [hat, contraption] bizarre.

impromptu [ɪm'prɒmptjuː] *adj* impromptu(e).

improper [ɪm'prɒpəʳ] *adj* **-1.** [unsuitable] impropre. **-2.** [incorrect, illegal] incorrect(e). **-3.** [rude] indécent(e).

impropriety [ɪmprə'praɪətɪ] *n* inconvenance *f*.

improve [ɪm'pruːv] ◇ *vi* s'améliorer; [patient] aller mieux; **to ~ on** OR **upon sthg** améliorer qqch. ◇ *vt* améliorer.

improved [ɪm'pruːvd] *adj* amélioré(e).

improvement [ɪm'pruːvmənt] *n*: **~ (in/on)** amélioration *f* (de/par rapport à).

improvisation [,ɪmprəvaɪ'zeɪʃn] *n* improvisation *f*.

improvise ['ɪmprəvaɪz] *vt* & *vi* improviser.

imprudent [ɪm'pruːdənt] *adj* imprudent(e).

impudent ['ɪmpjʊdənt] *adj* impudent(e).

impugn [ɪm'pjuːn] *vt* *fml* contester.

impulse ['ɪmpʌls] *n* impulsion *f*; **on ~** par impulsion.

impulse buying [-'baɪɪŋ] *n* (*U*) achats *mpl* impulsifs.

impulsive [ɪm'pʌlsɪv] *adj* impulsif(ive).

impunity [ɪm'pjuːnətɪ] *n*: **with ~** avec impunité.

impure [ɪm'pjʊəʳ] *adj* impur(e).

impurity [ɪm'pjʊərətɪ] (*pl* **-ies**) *n* impureté *f*.

IMRO ['ɪmrəʊ] (*abbr of* **Investment Management Regulatory Organization**) *organisme britannique contrôlant les activités de banques d'affaires et de gestionnaires de fonds de retraite.*

in [ɪn] ◇ *prep* **-1.** [indicating place, position] dans; ~ **a box/bag/drawer** dans une boîte/un sac/un tiroir; ~ **the room/garden/lake** dans la pièce/le jardin/le lac; ~ **Paris** à Paris; ~ **Belgium** en Belgique; ~ **Canada** au Canada; ~ **the United States** aux États-Unis; ~ **the country** à la campagne; **to be** ~ **hospital/prison** être à l'hôpital/en prison; ~ **here** ici; ~ **there** là. **-2.** [wearing] en; **she was still** ~ **her nightclothes** elle était encore en chemise de nuit; **dressed** ~ **a suit** vêtu d'un costume. **-3.** [appearing in, included in] dans; **there's a mistake** ~ **this paragraph** il y a une erreur dans ce paragraphe; ~ **chapter six** au sixième chapitre. **-4.** [at a particular time, season]: ~ **1994** en 1994; ~ **April** en avril; ~ **(the) spring** au printemps; ~ **(the) winter** en hiver; **at two o'clock** ~ **the afternoon** à deux heures de l'après-midi. **-5.** [period of time - within] en; [- after] dans; **he learned to type** ~ **two weeks** il a appris à taper à la machine en deux semaines; **I'll be ready** ~ **five minutes** je serai prêt dans 5 minutes. **-6.** [during]: **it's my first decent meal** ~ **weeks** c'est mon premier repas correct depuis des semaines. **-7.** [indicating situation, circumstances]: ~ **the sun** au soleil; ~ **the rain** sous la pluie; ~ **these circumstances** dans ces circonstances, en de telles circonstances; **a rise** ~ **prices** une augmentation des prix; **to live/die** ~ **poverty** vivre/mourir dans la misère; ~ **danger/difficulty** en danger/difficulté. **-8.** [indicating manner, condition]: ~ **a loud/soft voice** d'une voix forte/douce; **to write** ~ **pencil/ink** écrire au crayon/à l'encre; **to speak** ~ **English/French** parler (en) anglais/français. **-9.** [indicating emotional state]: ~ **anger** sous le coup de la colère; ~ **joy/delight** avec joie/plaisir; **he looked at me** ~ **amazement/horror** il me regarda stupéfait/horrifié. **-10.** [specifying area of activity] dans; **he's** ~ **computers** il est dans l'informatique; **advances** ~ **science** des progrès en science. **-11.** [referring to quantity, numbers, age]: ~ **large/small quantities** en grande/petite quantité; ~ **(their) thousands** par milliers; **she's** ~ **her sixties** elle a la soixantaine. **-12.** [describing arrangement]: ~ **twos** par deux; ~ **a line/row/circle** en ligne/rang/cercle. **-13.** [as regards]: **to be three metres** ~ **length/width** faire trois mètres de long/large; **a change** ~ **direction** un changement de direction. **-14.** [in ratios]: **5 pence** ~ **the pound** 5 pence par livre sterling; **one** ~ **ten** un sur dix. **-15.** (*after superl*) de; **the longest river** ~ **the world** le fleuve le plus long du monde. **-16.** (+ *present participle*): ~ **doing sthg** en faisant qqch.

◇ *adv* **-1.** [inside] dedans, à l'intérieur; **put the clothes** ~ mets les vêtements dedans; **do come** ~! entrez donc! **-2.** [at home, work] là; **I'm staying** ~ **tonight** je reste à la maison OR chez moi ce soir; **is Judith** ~? est-ce que Judith est là? **-3.** [of train, boat, plane]: **to be** ~ être arrivé(e). **-4.** [of tide]: **the tide's** ~ c'est la marée haute. **-5.** *phr*: **we're** ~ **for some bad weather** nous allons avoir du mauvais temps; **you're** ~ **for a shock** tu vas avoir un choc; **to be** ~ **on sthg** être au courant de qqch.

◇ *adj inf* à la mode; **short skirts are** ~ **this year** les jupes courtes sont à la mode cette année.

◆ **ins** *npl*: **the** ~**s and outs** les tenants et les aboutissants *mpl*.

◆ **in that** *conj* étant donné que.

in. *abbr of* **inch.**

IN *abbr of* **Indiana.**

inability [ˌɪnəˈbɪlətɪ] *n*: ~ **(to do sthg)** incapacité *f* (à faire qqch).

inaccessible [ˌɪnəkˈsesəbl] *adj* inaccessible.

inaccuracy [ɪnˈækjʊrəsɪ] (*pl* **-ies**) *n* inexactitude *f*.

inaccurate [ɪnˈækjʊrət] *adj* inexact(e).

inaction [ɪnˈækʃn] *n* inaction *f*.

inactive [ɪnˈæktɪv] *adj* inactif(ive).

inactivity [ˌɪnækˈtɪvətɪ] *n* inactivité *f*.

inadequacy [ɪnˈædɪkwəsɪ] (*pl* **-ies**) *n* insuffisance *f*.

inadequate [ɪnˈædɪkwət] *adj* insuffisant(e).

inadmissible [ˌɪnədˈmɪsəbl] *adj* inadmissible; [evidence] irrecevable.

inadvertent [ˌɪnədˈvɜːtnt] *adj* commis(e) par inadvertance.

inadvertently [ˌɪnədˈvɜːtəntlɪ] *adv* par inadvertance.

inadvisable [ˌɪnədˈvaɪzəbl] *adj* déconseillé(e).

inalienable [ɪnˈeɪljənəbl] *adj* inaliénable.

inane [ɪˈneɪn] *adj* inepte; [person] stupide.

inanely [ɪˈneɪnlɪ] *adv* stupidement.

inanimate [ɪnˈænɪmət] *adj* inanimé(e).

inanity [ɪˈnænətɪ] *n* ineptie *f*; [of person] stupidité *f*.

inapplicable [ɪnˈæplɪkəbl] *adj* inapplicable.

inappropriate [ˌɪnəˈprəʊprɪət] *adj* inopportun(e); [expression, word] impropre; [clothing] peu approprié(e).

inarticulate [ˌɪnɑːˈtɪkjʊlət] *adj* inarticulé(e), indistinct(e); [person] qui s'exprime avec difficulté; [explanation] mal exprimé(e).

inasmuch [ˌɪnəzˈmʌtʃ]

◆ **inasmuch as** *conj fml* attendu que.

inattention [ˌɪnə'tenʃn] *n*: ~ **(to)** inattention *f* (à).

inattentive [ˌɪnə'tentɪv] *adj*: ~ **(to)** inattentif(ive) (à).

inaudible [ɪ'nɔːdɪbl] *adj* inaudible.

inaugural [ɪ'nɔːgjʊrəl] *adj* inaugural(e).

inaugurate [ɪ'nɔːgjʊreɪt] *vt* [leader, president] investir; [building, system] inaugurer.

inauguration [ɪˌnɔːgjʊ'reɪʃn] *n* [of leader, president] investiture *f*; [of building, system] inauguration *f*.

inauspicious [ˌɪnɔː'spɪʃəs] *adj* peu propice.

in-between *adj* intermédiaire.

inboard ['ɪnbɔːd] *adj* in-bord (*inv*).

inborn [ˌɪn'bɔːn] *adj* inné(e).

inbound ['ɪnbaʊnd] *adj Am* qui arrive.

inbred [ˌɪn'bred] *adj* **-1.** [closely related] consanguin(e); [animal] croisé(e). **-2.** [inborn] inné(e).

inbreeding ['ɪnˌbriːdɪŋ] *n* consanguinité *f*; [of animals] croisement *m*.

inbuilt ['ɪnbɪlt] *adj* [inborn] inné(e).

inc. (*abbr of* **inclusive**): **12-15 April** ~ du 12 au 15 avril inclus.

Inc. [ɪŋk] (*abbr of* **incorporated**) ≃ SARL.

Inca ['ɪŋkə] *n* Inca *mf*.

incalculable [ɪn'kælkjʊləbl] *adj* incalculable.

incandescent [ˌɪnkæn'desnt] *adj* incandescent(e).

incantation [ˌɪnkæn'teɪʃn] *n* incantation *f*.

incapable [ɪn'keɪpəbl] *adj* incapable; **to be** ~ **of sthg/of doing sthg** être incapable de qqch/de faire qqch.

incapacitate [ˌɪnkə'pæsɪteɪt] *vt* rendre inapte physiquement.

incapacitated [ˌɪnkə'pæsɪteɪtɪd] *adj* inapte physiquement; ~ **for work** mis(e) dans l'incapacité de travailler.

incapacity [ˌɪnkə'pæsətɪ] *n*: ~ **(for)** incapacité *f* (eu égard à).

incarcerate [ɪn'kɑːsəreɪt] *vt* incarcérer.

incarceration [ɪnˌkɑːsə'reɪʃn] *n* incarcération *f*.

incarnate [ɪn'kɑːneɪt] *adj* incarné(e).

incarnation [ˌɪnkɑː'neɪʃn] *n* incarnation *f*.

incendiary device [ɪn'sendjərɪ-] *n* dispositif *m* incendiaire.

incense [*n* 'ɪnsens, *vt* ɪn'sens] ◇ *n* encens *m*. ◇ *vt* [anger] mettre en colère.

incentive [ɪn'sentɪv] *n* **-1.** [encouragement] motivation *f*. **-2.** COMM récompense *f*, prime *f*.

incentive scheme *n* programme *m* d'encouragement.

inception [ɪn'sepʃn] *n fml* commencement *m*.

incessant [ɪn'sesnt] *adj* incessant(e).

incessantly [ɪn'sesntlɪ] *adv* sans cesse.

incest ['ɪnsest] *n* inceste *m*.

incestuous [ɪn'sestjʊəs] *adj* **-1.** [sexual] incestueux(euse). **-2.** *fig* [too close] très fermé(e); [relationship] en vase clos.

inch [ɪntʃ] ◇ *n* = 2.5 cm, ≃ pouce *m*. ◇ *vi*: **to** ~ **forward** avancer petit à petit.

incidence ['ɪnsɪdəns] *n* [of disease, theft] fréquence *f*.

incident ['ɪnsɪdənt] *n* incident *m*.

incidental [ˌɪnsɪ'dentl] *adj* accessoire.

incidentally [ˌɪnsɪ'dentəlɪ] *adv* à propos.

incidental music *n* musique *f* de fond.

incinerate [ɪn'sɪnəreɪt] *vt* incinérer.

incinerator [ɪn'sɪnəreɪtəʳ] *n* incinérateur *m*.

incipient [ɪn'sɪpɪənt] *adj fml* naissant(e).

incision [ɪn'sɪʒn] *n* incision *f*.

incisive [ɪn'saɪsɪv] *adj* incisif(ive).

incisor [ɪn'saɪzəʳ] *n* incisive *f*.

incite [ɪn'saɪt] *vt* inciter; **to** ~ **sb to do sthg** inciter qqn à faire qqch.

incitement [ɪn'saɪtmənt] *n* (*U*): ~ **(to sthg/to do sthg)** incitation *f* (à qqch/à faire qqch).

incl. *abbr of* **including, inclusive**.

inclement [ɪn'klemənt] *adj* inclément(e).

inclination [ˌɪnklɪ'neɪʃn] *n* **-1.** (*U*) [liking, preference] inclination *f*, goût *m*. **-2.** [tendency]: ~ **to do sthg** inclination *f* à faire qqch.

incline [*n* 'ɪnklaɪn, *vt* ɪn'klaɪn] ◇ *n* inclinaison *f*. ◇ *vt* [head] incliner.

inclined [ɪn'klaɪnd] *adj* **-1.** [tending]: **to be** ~ **to sthg/to do sthg** avoir tendance à qqch/à faire qqch. **-2.** [wanting]: **to be** ~ **to do sthg** être enclin(e) à faire qqch. **-3.** [sloping] incliné(e).

include [ɪn'kluːd] *vt* inclure.

included [ɪn'kluːdɪd] *adj* inclus(e).

including [ɪn'kluːdɪŋ] *prep* y compris.

inclusion [ɪn'kluːʒn] *n* inclusion *f*.

inclusive [ɪn'kluːsɪv] *adj* inclus(e); [including all costs] tout compris; ~ **of VAT** TVA incluse OR comprise.

incognito [ˌɪnkɒg'niːtəʊ] *adv* incognito.

incoherent [ˌɪnkəʊ'hɪərənt] *adj* incohérent(e).

income ['ɪŋkʌm] *n* revenu *m*.

incomes policy *n Br* politique *f* des revenus OR salariale.

income support *n* Br *allocations supplémentaires accordées aux personnes ayant un faible revenu.*

income tax *n* impôt *m* sur le revenu.

incoming ['ɪn,kʌmɪŋ] *adj* **-1.** [tide, wave] montant(e). **-2.** [plane, passengers, mail] qui arrive; [phone call] de l'extérieur. **-3.** [government, official] nouveau (nouvelle).

incommunicado [,ɪnkəmjuːnɪ'kɑːdəʊ] *adv*: to be held ~ être tenu(e) au secret.

incomparable [ɪn'kɒmpərəbl] *adj* incomparable.

incompatible [,ɪnkəm'pætɪbl] *adj*: ~ **(with)** incompatible (avec).

incompetence [ɪn'kɒmpɪtəns] *n* incompétence *f.*

incompetent [ɪn'kɒmpɪtənt] *adj* incompétent(e).

incomplete [,ɪnkəm'pliːt] *adj* incomplet(ète).

incomprehensible [ɪn,kɒmprɪ'hensəbl] *adj* incompréhensible.

inconceivable [,ɪnkən'siːvəbl] *adj* inconcevable.

inconclusive [,ɪnkən'kluːsɪv] *adj* peu concluant(e).

incongruous [ɪn'kɒŋgrʊəs] *adj* incongru(e).

inconsequential [,ɪnkɒnsɪ'kwenʃl] *adj* sans importance.

inconsiderable [,ɪnkən'sɪdərəbl] *adj*: not ~ non négligeable.

inconsiderate [,ɪnkən'sɪdərət] *adj* inconsidéré(e); [person] qui manque de considération.

inconsistency [,ɪnkən'sɪstənsɪ] (*pl* **-ies**) *n* inconsistance *f.*

inconsistent [,ɪnkən'sɪstənt] *adj* **-1.** [not agreeing, contradictory] contradictoire; [person] inconséquent(e); ~ **with sthg** en contradiction avec qqch. **-2.** [erratic] inconsistant(e).

inconsolable [,ɪnkən'səʊləbl] *adj* inconsolable.

inconspicuous [,ɪnkən'spɪkjʊəs] *adj* qui passe inaperçu(e).

incontinence [ɪn'kɒntɪnəns] *n* incontinence *f.*

incontinent [ɪn'kɒntɪnənt] *adj* incontinent(e).

incontrovertible [,ɪnkɒntrə'vɜːtəbl] *adj* indéniable, irréfutable.

inconvenience [,ɪnkən'viːnjəns] ◇ *n* désagrément *m.* ◇ *vt* déranger.

inconvenient [,ɪnkən'viːnjənt] *adj* inopportun(e).

incorporate [ɪn'kɔːpəreɪt] *vt* **-1.** [integrate]: to ~ **sb/sthg (into)** incorporer qqn/qqch (dans). **-2.** [comprise] contenir, comprendre.

incorporated [ɪn'kɔːpəreɪtɪd] *adj* COMM constitué(e) en société commerciale.

incorporation [ɪn,kɔːpə'reɪʃn] *n* **-1.** [integration] incorporation *f.* **-2.** COMM [of company] constitution *f* en société commerciale.

incorrect [,ɪnkə'rekt] *adj* incorrect(e).

incorrigible [ɪn'kɒrɪdʒəbl] *adj* incorrigible.

incorruptible [,ɪnkə'rʌptəbl] *adj* incorruptible.

increase [*n* 'ɪnkriːs, *vb* ɪn'kriːs] ◇ *n*: ~ **(in)** augmentation *f* (de); to be on the ~ aller en augmentant. ◇ *vt* & *vi* augmenter.

increased [ɪn'kriːst] *adj* accru(e).

increasing [ɪn'kriːsɪŋ] *adj* croissant(e).

increasingly [ɪn'kriːsɪŋlɪ] *adv* de plus en plus.

incredible [ɪn'kredəbl] *adj* incroyable.

incredulous [ɪn'kredjʊləs] *adj* incrédule.

increment ['ɪnkrɪmənt] *n* augmentation *f.*

incriminate [ɪn'krɪmɪneɪt] *vt* incriminer; to ~ **o.s.** se compromettre.

incriminating [ɪn'krɪmɪneɪtɪŋ] *adj* compromettant(e).

incrust [ɪn'krʌst] = **encrust**.

incubate ['ɪnkjʊbeɪt] ◇ *vt* incuber. ◇ *vi* être en incubation.

incubation [,ɪnkjʊ'beɪʃn] *n* incubation *f.*

incubator ['ɪnkjʊbeɪtə'] *n* [for baby] incubateur *m,* couveuse *f.*

inculcate ['ɪnkʌlkeɪt] *vt*: to ~ **sthg in** OR **into sb** inculquer qqch à qqn.

incumbent [ɪn'kʌmbənt] *fml* ◇ *adj*: to be ~ on OR upon sb to do sthg incomber à qqn de faire qqch. ◇ *n* [of post] titulaire *m.*

incur [ɪn'kɜːʳ] (*pt* & *pp* **-red**, *cont* **-ring**) *vt* encourir.

incurable [ɪn'kjʊərəbl] *adj* [disease] incurable.

incursion [Br ɪn'kɜːʃn, Am ɪn'kɜːʒn] *n* incursion *f.*

indebted [ɪn'detɪd] *adj* [grateful]: ~ **to sb** redevable à qqn.

indecency [ɪn'diːsnsɪ] *n* indécence *f.*

indecent [ɪn'diːsnt] *adj* **-1.** [improper] indécent(e). **-2.** [unreasonable] malséant(e).

indecent assault *n* attentat *m* à la pudeur.

indecent exposure *n* outrage *m* public à la pudeur.

indecipherable [,ɪndɪ'saɪfərəbl] *adj* indéchiffrable.

indecision [,ɪndɪ'sɪʒn] *n* indécision *f.*

indecisive [,ɪndɪ'saɪsɪv] *adj* indécis(e).

indeed [ɪn'diːd] *adv* **-1.** [certainly, to express surprise] vraiment; ~ **I am, yes** ~ certainement. **-2.** [in fact] en effet. **-3.** [for emphasis]: **very big/bad** ~ extrêmement grand/mauvais, vraiment grand/mauvais.

indefatigable [ˌɪndɪ'fætɪgəbl] *adj* infatigable.

indefensible [ˌɪndɪ'fensəbl] *adj* indéfendable.

indefinable [ˌɪndɪ'faɪnəbl] *adj* indéfinissable.

indefinite [ɪn'defɪnɪt] *adj* **-1.** [not fixed] indéfini(e). **-2.** [imprecise] vague.

indefinitely [ɪn'defɪnətlɪ] *adv* **-1.** [for unfixed period] indéfiniment. **-2.** [imprecisely] vaguement.

indelible [ɪn'deləbl] *adj* indélébile.

indelicate [ɪn'delɪkət] *adj* indélicat(e).

indemnify [ɪn'demnɪfaɪ] (*pt & pp* **-ied**) *vt*: to ~ **sb for** OR **against sthg** indemniser qqn de qqch.

indemnity [ɪn'demnətɪ] *n* indemnité *f*.

indent [ɪn'dent] *vt* **-1.** [dent] entailler. **-2.** [text] mettre en retrait.

indentation [ˌɪnden'teɪʃn] *n* **-1.** [dent] découpure *f*, entaille *f*. **-2.** [in text] alinéa *m*.

indenture [ɪn'dentʃəʳ] *n* contrat *m* d'apprentissage.

independence [ˌɪndɪ'pendəns] *n* indépendance *f*.

Independence Day *n* fête de l'indépendance américaine, le 4 juillet.

independent [ˌɪndɪ'pendənt] *adj*: ~ **(of)** indépendant(e) (de).

independently [ˌɪndɪ'pendəntlɪ] *adv* de façon indépendante; ~ **of sb/sthg** indépendamment de qqn/qqch.

independent school *n* Br école *f* privée.

in-depth *adj* approfondi(e).

indescribable [ˌɪndɪ'skraɪbəbl] *adj* indescriptible.

indestructible [ˌɪndɪ'strʌktəbl] *adj* indestructible.

indeterminate [ˌɪndɪ'tɜːmɪnət] *adj* indéterminé(e).

index ['ɪndeks] (*pl senses 1 and 2* **-es**, *sense 3* **-es** OR **indices**) ◇ *n* **-1.** [of book] index *m*. **-2.** [in library] répertoire *m*, fichier *m*. **-3.** ECON indice *m*. ◇ *vt* [book] faire l'index de.

index card *n* fiche *f*.

index finger *n* index *m*.

index-linked *adj* indexé(e).

India ['ɪndjə] *n* Inde *f*; **in** ~ en Inde.

India ink *Am* = **Indian ink**.

Indian ['ɪndjən] ◇ *adj* indien(ienne). ◇ *n* Indien *m*, -ienne *f*.

Indiana [ˌɪndɪ'ænə] *n* Indiana *m*; **in** ~ dans l'Indiana.

Indian ink *Br*, **India ink** *Am* *n* encre *f* de Chine.

Indian Ocean *n*: **the** ~ l'océan *m* Indien.

Indian summer *n* été *m* indien.

india rubber *n* caoutchouc *m*.

indicate ['ɪndɪkeɪt] ◇ *vt* indiquer. ◇ *vi* AUT mettre son clignotant.

indication [ˌɪndɪ'keɪʃn] *n* **-1.** [suggestion] indication *f*. **-2.** [sign] signe *m*.

indicative [ɪn'dɪkətɪv] ◇ *adj*: ~ **of indicatif(ive) de.** ◇ *n* GRAMM indicatif *m*.

indicator ['ɪndɪkeɪtəʳ] *n* **-1.** [sign] indicateur *m*. **-2.** AUT clignotant *m*.

indices ['ɪndɪsiːz] *pl* → **index**.

indict [ɪn'daɪt] *vt*: **to** ~ **sb (for)** accuser qqn (de).

indictable [ɪn'daɪtəbl] *adj* [person] qui peut être traduit(e) en justice; [offence] punissable.

indictment [ɪn'daɪtmənt] *n* **-1.** JUR acte *m* d'accusation. **-2.** [criticism] mise *f* en accusation.

indie ['ɪndɪ] *adj* Br *inf* indépendant(e).

indifference [ɪn'dɪfrəns] *n* indifférence *f*.

indifferent [ɪn'dɪfrənt] *adj* **-1.** [uninterested]: ~ **(to)** indifférent(e) (à). **-2.** [mediocre] médiocre.

indigenous [ɪn'dɪdʒɪnəs] *adj* indigène.

indigestible [ˌɪndɪ'dʒestəbl] *adj* indigeste.

indigestion [ˌɪndɪ'dʒestʃn] *n* (*U*) indigestion *f*.

indignant [ɪn'dɪgnənt] *adj*: ~ **(at)** indigné(e) (de).

indignantly [ɪn'dɪgnəntlɪ] *adv* avec indignation.

indignation [ˌɪndɪg'neɪʃn] *n* indignation *f*.

indignity [ɪn'dɪgnətɪ] (*pl* **-ies**) *n* indignité *f*.

indigo ['ɪndɪgəʊ] ◇ *adj* indigo (*inv*). ◇ *n* indigo *m*.

indirect [ˌɪndɪ'rekt] *adj* indirect(e).

indirect costs *npl* frais *mpl* généraux.

indirect lighting *n* éclairage *m* indirect.

indirectly [ˌɪndɪ'rektlɪ] *adv* indirectement.

indirect speech *n* discours *m* indirect.

indirect taxation *n* (*U*) contributions *fpl* indirectes, impôts *mpl* indirects.

indiscreet [ˌɪndɪ'skriːt] *adj* indiscret(ète).

indiscretion [ˌɪndɪ'skreʃn] *n* indiscrétion *f*.

indiscriminate [ˌɪndɪ'skrɪmɪnət] *adj* [person]

qui manque de discernement; [treatment] sans distinction; [killing] commis au hasard.

indiscriminately [,ɪndɪˈskrɪmɪnətlɪ] *adv* [admire] aveuglément; [treat] sans faire de distinction; [kill] au hasard.

indispensable [,ɪndɪˈspensəbl] *adj* indispensable.

indisposed [,ɪndɪˈspəuzd] *adj fml* [unwell] indisposé(e).

indisputable [,ɪndɪˈspjuːtəbl] *adj* indiscutable.

indistinct [,ɪndɪˈstɪŋkt] *adj* indistinct(e); [memory] vague.

indistinguishable [,ɪndɪˈstɪŋgwɪʃəbl] *adj*: ~ (from) que l'on ne peut distinguer (de).

individual [,ɪndɪˈvɪdʒuəl] ◇ *adj* **-1.** [separate, for one person] individuel(elle). **-2.** [distinctive] personnel(elle). ◇ *n* individu *m*.

individualist [,ɪndɪˈvɪdʒuəlɪst] *n* individualiste *mf*.

individualistic [ˈɪndɪˌvɪdʒuəˈlɪstɪk] *adj* individualiste.

individuality [ˈɪndɪˌvɪdʒuˈælətɪ] *n* individualité *f*.

individually [,ɪndɪˈvɪdʒuəlɪ] *adv* individuellement.

indivisible [,ɪndɪˈvɪzəbl] *adj* indivisible.

Indochina [,ɪndəʊˈtʃaɪnə] *n* Indochine *f*; in ~ en Indochine.

indoctrinate [ɪnˈdɒktrɪneɪt] *vt* endoctriner.

indoctrination [ɪn,dɒktrɪˈneɪʃn] *n* endoctrinement *m*.

indolent [ˈɪndələnt] *adj* indolent(e).

indomitable [ɪnˈdɒmɪtəbl] *adj* indomptable.

Indonesia [,ɪndəˈniːzjə] *n* Indonésie *f*; in ~ en Indonésie.

Indonesian [,ɪndəˈniːzjən] ◇ *adj* indonésien(ienne). ◇ *n* **-1.** [person] Indonésien *m*, -ienne *f*. **-2.** [language] indonésien *m*.

indoor [ˈɪndɔːr] *adj* d'intérieur; [swimming pool] couvert(e); [sports] en salle.

indoors [,ɪnˈdɔːz] *adv* à l'intérieur.

indubitably [ɪnˈdjuːbɪtəblɪ] *adv* indubitablement.

induce [ɪnˈdjuːs] *vt* **-1.** [persuade]: to ~ sb to do sthg inciter OR pousser qqn à faire qqch. **-2.** MED [labour] provoquer; [woman] provoquer l'accouchement de. **-3.** [bring about] provoquer.

inducement [ɪnˈdjuːsmənt] *n* [incentive] incitation *f*, encouragement *m*.

induction [ɪnˈdʌkʃn] *n* **-1.** [into official position]: ~ (into) installation *f* (à). **-2.** [introduction to job] introduction *f*. **-3.** ELEC induction *f*.

induction course *n* cours *m* préparatoire.

indulge [ɪnˈdʌldʒ] ◇ *vt* **-1.** [whim, passion] céder à. **-2.** [child, person] gâter; to ~ o.s. se faire plaisir. ◇ *vi*: to ~ in sthg se permettre qqch.

indulgence [ɪnˈdʌldʒəns] *n* **-1.** [act of indulging] indulgence *f*. **-2.** [special treat] gâterie *f*.

indulgent [ɪnˈdʌldʒənt] *adj* indulgent(e).

Indus [ˈɪndəs] *n*: the (River) ~ l'Indus *m*.

industrial [ɪnˈdʌstrɪəl] *adj* industriel(ielle).

industrial action *n*: to take ~ se mettre en grève.

industrial estate *Br*, **industrial park** *Am* *n* zone *f* industrielle.

industrial injury *n* accident *m* du travail.

industrialist [ɪnˈdʌstrɪəlɪst] *n* industriel *m*.

industrialization [ɪn,dʌstrɪəlaɪˈzeɪʃn] *n* industrialisation *f*.

industrialize, -ise [ɪnˈdʌstrɪəlaɪz] ◇ *vt* industrialiser. ◇ *vi* s'industrialiser.

industrial park *Am* = **industrial estate**.

industrial relations *npl* relations *fpl* patronat-syndicats.

industrial revolution *n*: the ~ révolution *f* industrielle.

industrial tribunal *n* ≃ conseil *m* de prud'hommes.

industrious [ɪnˈdʌstrɪəs] *adj* industrieux(ieuse).

industry [ˈɪndəstrɪ] (*pl* **-ies**) *n* **-1.** [gen] industrie *f*. **-2.** (*U*) [hard work] assiduité *f*, application *f*.

inebriated [ɪˈniːbrɪeɪtɪd] *adj fml* ivre.

inedible [ɪnˈedɪbl] *adj* **-1.** [meal, food] immangeable. **-2.** [plant, mushroom] non comestible.

ineffective [,ɪnɪˈfektɪv] *adj* inefficace.

ineffectual [,ɪnɪˈfektʃuəl] *adj* inefficace; [person] incapable, incompétent(e).

inefficiency [,ɪnɪˈfɪʃnsɪ] *n* inefficacité *f*; [of person] incapacité *f*, incompétence *f*.

inefficient [,ɪnɪˈfɪʃnt] *adj* inefficace; [person] incapable, incompétent(e).

inelegant [ɪnˈelɪgənt] *adj* inélégant(e), sans élégance.

ineligible [ɪnˈelɪdʒəbl] *adj* inéligible; to be ~ for sthg ne pas avoir droit à qqch.

inept [ɪˈnept] *adj* inepte; [person] stupide.

ineptitude [ɪˈneptɪtjuːd] *n* ineptie *f*; [of person] stupidité *f*.

inequality [,ɪnɪˈkwɒlətɪ] (*pl* **-ies**) *n* inégalité *f*.

inequitable [ɪnˈekwɪtəbl] *adj fml* inéquitable.

ineradicable [ˌɪnɪˈrædɪkəbl] *adj fml* tenace, dont on ne peut se débarrasser.

inert [ɪˈnɜːt] *adj* inerte.

inertia [ɪˈnɜːʃə] *n* inertie *f*.

inertia-reel seat belt *n* ceinture *f* de sécurité à enrouleur.

inescapable [ˌɪnɪˈskeɪpəbl] *adj* inéluctable.

inessential [ˌɪnɪˈsenʃl] *adj* superflu(e).

inestimable [ɪnˈestɪməbl] *adj* inestimable.

inevitable [ɪnˈevɪtəbl] ◇ *adj* inévitable. ◇ *n*: **the** ~ l'inévitable *m*.

inevitably [ɪnˈevɪtəblɪ] *adv* inévitablement.

inexact [ˌɪnɪgˈzækt] *adj* inexact(e).

inexcusable [ˌɪnɪkˈskjuːzəbl] *adj* inexcusable, impardonnable.

inexhaustible [ˌɪnɪgˈzɔːstəbl] *adj* inépuisable.

inexorable [ɪnˈeksərəbl] *adj* inexorable.

inexorably [ɪnˈeksərəblɪ] *adv* inexorablement.

inexpensive [ˌɪnɪkˈspensɪv] *adj* bon marché (*inv*), pas cher (chère).

inexperience [ˌɪnɪkˈspɪərɪəns] *n* inexpérience *f*.

inexperienced [ˌɪnɪkˈspɪərɪənst] *adj* inexpérimenté(e), qui manque d'expérience.

inexpert [ɪnˈekspɜːt] *adj* inexpert(e).

inexplicable [ˌɪnɪkˈsplɪkəbl] *adj* inexplicable.

inexplicably [ˌɪnɪkˈsplɪkəblɪ] *adv* inexplicablement.

inextricably [ɪnˈekstrɪkəblɪ] *adv* inextricablement.

infallible [ɪnˈfæləbl] *adj* infaillible.

infamous [ˈɪnfəməs] *adj* infâme.

infamy [ˈɪnfəmɪ] *n* infamie *f*.

infancy [ˈɪnfənsɪ] *n* petite enfance *f*; **in its** ~ *fig* à ses débuts.

infant [ˈɪnfənt] *n* **-1.** [baby] nouveau-né *m*, nouveau-née *f*, nourrisson *m*. **-2.** [young child] enfant *mf* en bas âge.

infantile [ˈɪnfəntaɪl] *adj lit* & *pej* infantile.

infant mortality *n* mortalité *f* infantile.

infantry [ˈɪnfəntrɪ] *n* infanterie *f*.

infantryman [ˈɪnfəntrɪmən] (*pl* **-men** [-mən]) *n* fantassin *m*.

infant school *n* *Br* école *f* maternelle (*de 5 à 7 ans*).

infatuated [ɪnˈfætjʊeɪtɪd] *adj*: ~ **(with)** entiché(e) (de).

infatuation [ɪnˌfætjʊˈeɪʃn] *n*: ~ **(with)** béguin *m* (pour).

infect [ɪnˈfekt] *vt* **-1.** MED infecter. **-2.** *fig* [subj: enthusiasm etc] se propager à.

infected [ɪnˈfektɪd] *adj*: ~ **(with)** infecté(e) (par).

infection [ɪnˈfekʃn] *n* infection *f*.

infectious [ɪnˈfekʃəs] *adj* **-1.** [disease] infectieux(euse). **-2.** *fig* [feeling, laugh] contagieux(euse).

infer [ɪnˈfɜːr] (*pt* & *pp* **-red**, *cont* **-ring**) *vt* [deduce]: **to** ~ **sthg (from)** déduire qqch (de).

inference [ˈɪnfrəns] *n* **-1.** [conclusion] conclusion *f*. **-2.** [process of deduction]: **by** ~ par déduction.

inferior [ɪnˈfɪərɪər] ◇ *adj* **-1.** [in status] inférieur(e). **-2.** [product] de qualité inférieure; [work] médiocre. ◇ *n* [in status] subalterne *mf*.

inferiority [ɪnˌfɪərɪˈɒrətɪ] *n* infériorité *f*.

inferiority complex *n* complexe *m* d'infériorité.

infernal [ɪnˈfɜːnl] *adj inf dated* infernal(e).

inferno [ɪnˈfɜːnəʊ] (*pl* **-s**) *n* brasier *m*.

infertile [ɪnˈfɜːtaɪl] *adj* **-1.** [woman] stérile. **-2.** [soil] infertile.

infertility [ˌɪnfəˈtɪlətɪ] *n* **-1.** [of woman] stérilité *f*. **-2.** [of soil] infertilité *f*.

infestation [ˌɪnfeˈsteɪʃn] *n* infestation *f*.

infested [ɪnˈfestɪd] *adj*: ~ **with** infesté(e) de.

infidelity [ˌɪnfɪˈdelətɪ] *n* infidélité *f*.

infighting [ˈɪnˌfaɪtɪŋ] *n* (*U*) querelles *fpl* intestines.

infiltrate [ˈɪnfɪltreɪt] ◇ *vt* infiltrer. ◇ *vi*: **to** ~ **into** s'infiltrer dans.

infinite [ˈɪnfɪnət] *adj* infini(e).

infinitely [ˈɪnfɪnətlɪ] *adv* infiniment.

infinitesimal [ˌɪnfɪnɪˈtesɪml] *adj* infinitésimal(e).

infinitive [ɪnˈfɪnɪtɪv] *n* infinitif *m*.

infinity [ɪnˈfɪnətɪ] *n* infini *m*.

infirm [ɪnˈfɜːm] ◇ *adj* infirme. ◇ *npl*: **the** ~ les infirmes *mpl*.

infirmary [ɪnˈfɜːmərɪ] (*pl* **-ies**) *n* [hospital] hôpital *m*.

infirmity [ɪnˈfɜːmətɪ] (*pl* **-ies**) *n* infirmité *f*.

inflamed [ɪnˈfleɪmd] *adj* MED enflammé(e).

inflammable [ɪnˈflæməbl] *adj* inflammable.

inflammation [ˌɪnfləˈmeɪʃn] *n* MED inflammation *f*.

inflammatory [ɪnˈflæmətrɪ] *adj* inflammatoire.

inflatable [ɪnˈfleɪtəbl] *adj* gonflable.

inflate [ɪnˈfleɪt] *vt* **-1.** [tyre, life jacket etc] gonfler. **-2.** ECON [prices, salaries] hausser, gonfler.

inflated [ɪnˈfleɪtɪd] *adj* **-1.** [tyre, life jacket etc] gonflé(e). **-2.** *pej* [exaggerated]: **he has an**

~ **opinion of himself** il a une haute opinion de lui-même. **-3.** ECON [salary, prices] exagéré(e), gonflé(e).

inflation [ɪn'fleɪʃn] n ECON inflation f.

inflationary [ɪn'fleɪʃnrɪ] adj ECON inflationniste.

inflationary spiral n spirale f inflationniste.

inflation-proof adj protégé(e), contre les effets de l'inflation.

inflexible [ɪn'fleksəbl] adj **-1.** [material] rigide. **-2.** [person, arrangement] inflexible.

inflict [ɪn'flɪkt] vt: **to ~ sthg on sb** infliger qqch à qqn.

in-flight adj en vol (inv).

inflow ['ɪnfləʊ] n afflux m.

influence ['ɪnflʊəns] ◇ n influence f; **under the ~ of** [person, group] sous l'influence de; [alcohol, drugs] sous l'effet OR l'empire de. ◇ vt influencer.

influential [,ɪnflʊ'enʃl] adj influent(e).

influenza [,ɪnflʊ'enzə] n (U) grippe f.

influx ['ɪnflʌks] n afflux m.

info ['ɪnfəʊ] n (U) inf info f.

inform [ɪn'fɔːm] vt: **to ~ sb (of)** informer qqn (de); **to ~ sb about** renseigner qqn sur.

◆ **inform on** vt fus dénoncer.

informal [ɪn'fɔːml] adj **-1.** [party, person] simple; [clothes] de tous les jours. **-2.** [negotiations, visit] officieux(ieuse); [meeting] informel(elle).

informally [ɪn'fɔːməlɪ] adv **-1.** [talk, dress] simplement. **-2.** [meet, agree] officieusement.

informant [ɪn'fɔːmənt] n informateur m, -trice f.

information [,ɪnfə'meɪʃn] n (U): ~ **(on** OR **about)** renseignements mpl OR informations fpl (sur); **a piece of ~** un renseignement; **for your ~** fml à titre d'information.

information desk n bureau m de renseignements.

information office n bureau m de renseignements.

information retrieval n recherche f documentaire sur ordinateur.

information technology n informatique f.

informative [ɪn'fɔːmətɪv] adj informatif(ive).

informed [ɪn'fɔːmd] adj: **well/badly ~** bien/mal renseigné(e); **he made an ~ guess** il a essayé de deviner en s'aidant de ce qu'il savait.

informer [ɪn'fɔːmər] n indicateur m, -trice f.

infra dig [,ɪnfrə-] adj dégradant(e).

infrared [,ɪnfrə'red] adj infrarouge.

infrastructure ['ɪnfrə,strʌktʃər] n infrastructure f.

infrequent [ɪn'friːkwənt] adj peu fréquent(e).

infringe [ɪn'frɪndʒ] (cont **infringeing**) ◇ vt **-1.** [right] empiéter sur. **-2.** [law, agreement] enfreindre. ◇ vi **-1.** [on right]: **to ~ on** empiéter sur. **-2.** [on law, agreement]: **to ~ on** enfreindre.

infringement [ɪn'frɪndʒmənt] n **-1.** [of right]: ~ **(of)** atteinte f (à). **-2.** [of law, agreement] transgression f.

infuriate [ɪn'fjʊərɪeɪt] vt rendre furieux(ieuse).

infuriating [ɪn'fjʊərɪeɪtɪŋ] adj exaspérant(e).

infuse [ɪn'fjuːz] ◇ vt: **to ~ sb with sthg** fig insuffler qqch à qqn. ◇ vi [tea] infuser.

infusion [ɪn'fjuːʒn] n **-1.** [of enthusiasm, ideas] fait m d'insuffler; [of money] injection f. **-2.** [of tea, herbs] infusion f.

ingenious [ɪn'dʒiːnjəs] adj ingénieux(ieuse).

ingenuity [,ɪndʒɪ'njuːətɪ] n ingéniosité f.

ingenuous [ɪn'dʒenjʊəs] adj ingénu(e), naïf (naïve).

ingest [ɪn'dʒest] vt ingérer.

ingot ['ɪŋgət] n lingot m.

ingrained [ɪn'greɪnd] adj **-1.** [dirt] incrusté(e). **-2.** fig [belief, hatred] enraciné(e).

ingratiate [ɪn'greɪʃɪeɪt] vt: **to ~ o.s. with sb** se faire bien voir de qqn.

ingratiating [ɪn'greɪʃɪeɪtɪŋ] adj doucereux(euse), mielleux(euse).

ingratitude [ɪn'grætɪtjuːd] n ingratitude f.

ingredient [ɪn'griːdjənt] n ingrédient m; fig élément m.

ingrowing ['ɪn,grəʊɪŋ], **ingrown** ['ɪn,grəʊn] adj: ~ **toenail** ongle m incarné.

inhabit [ɪn'hæbɪt] vt habiter.

inhabitant [ɪn'hæbɪtənt] n habitant m, -e f.

inhalation [,ɪnhə'leɪʃn] n inhalation f.

inhale [ɪn'heɪl] ◇ vt inhaler, respirer. ◇ vi [breathe in] respirer.

inhaler [ɪn'heɪlər] n MED inhalateur m.

inherent [ɪn'hɪərənt, ɪn'herənt] adj: ~ **(in)** inhérent(e) (à).

inherently [ɪn'hɪərəntlɪ, ɪn'herəntlɪ] adv fondamentalement, en soi.

inherit [ɪn'herɪt] ◇ vt: **to ~ sthg (from sb)** hériter qqch (de qqn). ◇ vi hériter.

inheritance [ɪn'herɪtəns] n héritage m.

inheritor [ɪn'herɪtər] n héritier m, -ière f.

inhibit [ɪn'hɪbɪt] vt **-1.** [prevent] empêcher. **-2.** PSYCH inhiber.

inhibited [ɪn'hɪbɪtɪd] adj [person] inhibé(e).

inhibition [ˌɪnhɪ'bɪʃn] n inhibition f.

inhospitable [ˌɪnhɒ'spɪtəbl] adj inhospitalier(ière).

in-house ◇ adj interne; [staff] de la maison. ◇ adv [produce, work] sur place.

inhuman [ɪn'hjuːmən] adj inhumain(e).

inhumane [ˌɪnhjuː'meɪn] adj inhumain(e).

inimitable [ɪ'nɪmɪtəbl] adj inimitable.

iniquitous [ɪ'nɪkwɪtəs] adj inique.

iniquity [ɪ'nɪkwətɪ] (pl -ies) n iniquité f.

initial [ɪ'nɪʃl] (Br pt & pp -led, cont -ling, Am pt & pp -ed, cont -ing) ◇ adj initial(e), premier(ière); ~ letter initiale f. ◇ vt parapher.

◆ **initials** npl initiales fpl.

initialize, -ise [ɪ'nɪʃəlaɪz] vt COMPUT initialiser.

initially [ɪ'nɪʃəlɪ] adv initialement, au début.

initiate [ɪ'nɪʃɪeɪt] ◇ vt **-1.** [talks] engager; [scheme] ébaucher, inaugurer. **-2.** [teach]: to ~ sb into sth initier qqn à qqch. ◇ n initié m, -e f.

initiation [ɪˌnɪʃɪ'eɪʃn] n **-1.** [of talks] commencement m, début m; [of scheme] ébauche f, inauguration f. **-2.** [teaching] initiation f.

initiative [ɪ'nɪʃətɪv] n **-1.** [gen] initiative f; on one's own ~ de sa propre initiative; to take the ~ prendre l'initiative; to use one's ~ faire preuve d'initiative. **-2.** [advantage]: to have the ~ avoir l'avantage m.

inject [ɪn'dʒekt] vt **-1.** MED: to ~ sb with sthg, to ~ sthg into sb injecter qqch à qqn. **-2.** fig [excitement] insuffler; [money] injecter.

injection [ɪn'dʒekʃn] n lit & fig injection f.

injudicious [ˌɪndʒuː'dɪʃəs] adj peu judicieux(ieuse).

injunction [ɪn'dʒʌŋkʃn] n JUR injonction f.

injure [ˈɪndʒər] vt **-1.** [limb, person] blesser; to ~ o.s. se blesser; to ~ one's arm se blesser au bras. **-2.** fig [reputation, chances] compromettre.

injured [ɪn'dʒəd] ◇ adj **-1.** [limb, person] blessé(e). **-2.** fig [reputation] compromis(e); [pride] froissé(e). ◇ npl: the ~ les blessés mpl.

injurious [ɪn'dʒʊərɪəs] adj fml: ~ (to) nuisible (à), néfaste (à).

injury [ˈɪndʒərɪ] (pl -ies) n **-1.** [to limb, person] blessure f; to do o.s. an ~ se blesser. **-2.** fig [to reputation] coup m, atteinte f.

injury time n (U) arrêts mpl de jeu.

injustice [ɪn'dʒʌstɪs] n injustice f; to do sb an ~ se montrer injuste envers qqn.

ink [ɪŋk] ◇ n encre f. ◇ comp [pen] à encre; [stain, blot] d'encre.

◆ **ink in** vt sep repasser à l'encre.

ink-jet printer n COMPUT imprimante f à jet d'encre.

inkling [ˈɪŋklɪŋ] n: to have an ~ of avoir une petite idée de.

inkpad [ˈɪŋkpæd] n tampon m encreur.

inkwell [ˈɪŋkwel] n encrier m.

inlaid [ˌɪn'leɪd] adj: ~ (with) incrusté(e) (de).

inland [adj 'ɪnlənd, adv ɪn'lænd] ◇ adj intérieur(e). ◇ adv à l'intérieur.

Inland Revenue n Br: the ~ ≃ le fisc.

in-laws npl inf beaux-parents mpl.

inlet [ˈɪnlet] n **-1.** [of lake, sea] avancée f. **-2.** TECH arrivée f.

inmate [ˈɪnmeɪt] n [of prison] détenu m, -e f; [of mental hospital] interné m, -e f.

inmost [ˈɪnməʊst] adj literary [secrets, thoughts] le plus profond (la plus profonde), le plus secret (la plus secrète).

inn [ɪn] n auberge f.

innards [ˈɪnədz] npl entrailles fpl.

innate [ˌɪ'neɪt] adj inné(e).

inner [ˈɪnər] adj **-1.** [on inside] interne, intérieur(e). **-2.** [feelings] intime.

inner city ◇ n: the ~ les quartiers mpl pauvres. ◇ comp des quartiers pauvres.

innermost [ˈɪnəməʊst] adj = inmost.

inner tube n chambre f à air.

innings [ˈɪnɪŋz] (pl inv) n Br CRICKET tour m de batte; to have had a good ~ fig avoir bien profité de l'existence.

innocence [ˈɪnəsəns] n innocence f.

innocent [ˈɪnəsənt] ◇ adj innocent(e); ~ of [crime] non coupable de. ◇ n innocent m, -e f.

innocuous [ɪ'nɒkjuəs] adj inoffensif(ive).

innovation [ˌɪnə'veɪʃn] n innovation f.

innovative [ˈɪnəvətɪv] adj **-1.** [idea, design] innovateur(trice). **-2.** [person, company] novateur(trice).

innovator [ˈɪnəveɪtər] n innovateur m, -trice f.

innuendo [ˌɪnjuː'endəʊ] (pl -es OR -s) n insinuation f.

innumerable [ɪ'njuːmərəbl] adj innombrable.

inoculate [ɪ'nɒkjuleɪt] vt: to ~ sb (with sthg) inoculer (qqch à) qqn; to ~ sb (against) vacciner qqn (contre).

inoculation [ɪ,nɒkjʊ'leɪʃn] *n* inoculation *f*.

inoffensive [,ɪnə'fensɪv] *adj* inoffensif(ive).

inoperable [ɪn'ɒprəbl] *adj* **-1.** MED inopérable. **-2.** [method] impossible à mettre en œuvre.

inoperative [ɪn'ɒprətɪv] *adj* **-1.** [rule, tax] inopérant(e). **-2.** [machine] qui ne marche pas.

inopportune [ɪn'ɒpətjuːn] *adj* inopportun(e).

inordinate [ɪ'nɔːdɪnət] *adj* excessif(ive), démesuré(e).

inordinately [ɪ'nɔːdɪnətlɪ] *adv* excessivement.

inorganic [,ɪnɔː'gænɪk] *adj* inorganique.

in-patient *n* malade hospitalisé *m*, malade hospitalisée *f*.

input ['ɪnpʊt] (*pt* & *pp* input OR **-ted**, *cont* **-ting**) ⋄ *n* **-1.** [contribution] contribution *f*, concours *m*. **-2.** COMPUT & ELEC entrée *f*. ⋄ *vt* COMPUT entrer.

input/output *n* COMPUT entrée-sortie *f*.

inquest ['ɪnkwest] *n* enquête *f*.

inquire [ɪn'kwaɪə'] ⋄ *vt*: **to ~ when/ whether/how** ... demander quand/si/ comment .... ⋄ *vi*: **to ~ (about)** se renseigner (sur).
◆ **inquire after** *vt fus* s'enquérir de.
◆ **inquire into** *vt fus* enquêter sur.

inquiring [ɪn'kwaɪərɪŋ] *adj* **-1.** [person, mind] curieux(ieuse). **-2.** [look, tone] interrogateur(trice).

inquiry [*Br* ɪn'kwaɪərɪ, *Am* 'ɪnkwərɪ] (*pl* **-ies**) *n* **-1.** [question] demande *f* de renseignements; **"Inquiries"** «renseignements». **-2.** [investigation] enquête *f*.

inquiry desk *n* bureau *m* de renseignements.

inquisition [,ɪnkwɪ'zɪʃn] *n* inquisition *f*.
◆ **Inquisition** *n*: **the Inquisition** l'Inquisition *f*.

inquisitive [ɪn'kwɪzətɪv] *adj* inquisiteur(trice).

inroads ['ɪnrəʊdz] *npl*: **to make ~ into** [savings] entamer.

insane [ɪn'seɪn] ⋄ *adj* fou (folle). ⋄ *npl*: **the ~ les malades** *mpl* mentaux.

insanitary [ɪn'sænɪtrɪ] *adj* insalubre.

insanity [ɪn'sænətɪ] *n* folie *f*.

insatiable [ɪn'seɪʃəbl] *adj* insatiable.

inscribe [ɪn'skraɪb] *vt* **-1.** [engrave] graver. **-2.** [write] inscrire.

inscription [ɪn'skrɪpʃn] *n* **-1.** [engraved] inscription *f*. **-2.** [written] dédicace *f*.

inscrutable [ɪn'skruːtəbl] *adj* impénétrable.

insect ['ɪnsekt] *n* insecte *m*.

insect bite *n* piqûre *f* d'insecte.

insecticide [ɪn'sektɪsaɪd] *n* insecticide *m*.

insect repellent *n* crème *f* anti-insectes.

insecure [,ɪnsɪ'kjʊə'] *adj* **-1.** [person] anxieux(euse). **-2.** [job, investment] incertain(e).

insecurity [,ɪnsɪ'kjʊərətɪ] *n* insécurité *f*.

insensible [ɪn'sensəbl] *adj* **-1.** [unconscious] inconscient(e). **-2.** [unaware, not feeling]: **~ of/to** insensible à.

insensitive [ɪn'sensətɪv] *adj*: **~ (to)** insensible (à).

insensitivity [ɪn,sensə'tɪvətɪ] *n* insensibilité *f*.

inseparable [ɪn'seprəbl] *adj* inséparable.

insert [*vb* ɪn'sɜːt, *n* 'ɪnsɜːt] ⋄ *vt*: **to ~ sthg (in** OR **into)** insérer qqch (dans). ⋄ *n* [in newspaper] encart *m*.

insertion [ɪn'sɜːʃn] *n* insertion *f*.

in-service training *n Br* formation *f* en cours d'emploi.

inset ['ɪnset] *n* encadré *m*.

inshore [*adj* 'ɪnʃɔːʳ, *adv* ɪn'ʃɔːʳ] ⋄ *adj* côtier(ière). ⋄ *adv* [be situated] près de la côte; [move] vers la côte.

inside [ɪn'saɪd] ⋄ *prep* **-1.** [building, object] à l'intérieur de, dans; [group, organization] au sein de. **-2.** [time]: **~ three weeks** en moins de trois semaines.
⋄ *adv* **-1.** [gen] dedans, à l'intérieur; **to go ~** entrer; **come ~!** entrez! **-2.** *prison sl* en taule.
⋄ *adj* intérieur(e).
⋄ *n* **-1.** [interior]: **the ~** l'intérieur *m*; **~ out** [clothes] à l'envers; **to know sthg ~ out** connaître qqch à fond. **-2.** AUT: **the ~** [in UK] la gauche; [in Europe, US etc] la droite.
◆ **insides** *npl inf* tripes *fpl*.
◆ **inside of** *prep Am* [building, object] à l'intérieur de, dans.

inside information *n* (*U*) renseignements *mpl* obtenus à la source.

inside job *n inf* coup *m* monté de l'intérieur.

inside lane *n* AUT [in UK] voie *f* de gauche; [in Europe, US etc] voie de droite.

insider [,ɪn'saɪdə'] *n* initié *m*, -e *f*.

insider dealing, insider trading *n* (*U*) délits *mpl* d'initiés.

inside story *n*: **I got the ~ from his wife** j'ai appris la vérité sur cette affaire par sa femme.

insidious [ɪn'sɪdɪəs] *adj* insidieux(ieuse).

insight ['ɪnsaɪt] *n* **-1.** [wisdom] sagacité *f*,

perspicacité f. **-2.** [glimpse]: ~ **(into)** aperçu m (de).

insignia [ɪn'sɪɡnɪə] (pl inv) n insigne m.

insignificance [ˌɪnsɪɡ'nɪfɪkəns] n insignifiance f.

insignificant [ˌɪnsɪɡ'nɪfɪkənt] adj insignifiant(e).

insincere [ˌɪnsɪn'sɪəʳ] adj pas sincère.

insincerity [ˌɪnsɪn'serətɪ] n manque m de sincérité.

insinuate [ɪn'sɪnjʊeɪt] vt insinuer, laisser entendre.

insinuation [ɪnˌsɪnjʊ'eɪʃn] n insinuation f.

insipid [ɪn'sɪpɪd] adj insipide.

insist [ɪn'sɪst] ◇ vt **-1.** [claim]: **to** ~ **(that)** ... insister sur le fait que .... **-2.** [demand]: **to** ~ **(that)** ... insister pour que (+ subjunctive) .... ◇ vi: **to** ~ **(on sth)** exiger (qqch); **to** ~ **on doing sth** tenir à faire qqch, vouloir absolument faire qqch.

insistence [ɪn'sɪstəns] n: ~ **(on)** insistance f (à).

insistent [ɪn'sɪstənt] adj **-1.** [determined] insistant(e); **to be** ~ **on** insister sur. **-2.** [continual] incessant(e).

in situ [ˌɪn'sɪtjuː] adv in situ.

insofar [ˌɪnsəʊ'fɑːʳ]

◆ **insofar as** conj dans la mesure où.

insole ['ɪnsəʊl] n semelle f intérieure.

insolence ['ɪnsələns] n insolence f.

insolent ['ɪnsələnt] adj insolent(e).

insoluble Br [ɪn'sɒljʊbl], **insolvable** Am [ɪn'sɒlvəbl] adj insoluble.

insolvency [ɪn'sɒlvənsɪ] n insolvabilité f.

insolvent [ɪn'sɒlvənt] adj insolvable.

insomnia [ɪn'sɒmnɪə] n insomnie f.

insomniac [ɪn'sɒmnɪæk] n insomniaque mf.

insomuch [ˌɪnsəʊ'mʌtʃ]

◆ **insomuch as** conj d'autant que.

inspect [ɪn'spekt] vt **-1.** [letter, person] examiner. **-2.** [factory, troops etc] inspecter.

inspection [ɪn'spekʃn] n **-1.** [investigation] examen m. **-2.** [official check] inspection f.

inspector [ɪn'spektəʳ] n inspecteur m, -trice f.

inspector of taxes n inspecteur m, -trice f des impôts.

inspiration [ˌɪnspə'reɪʃn] n inspiration f.

inspire [ɪn'spaɪəʳ] vt: **to** ~ **sb to do sth** pousser OR encourager qqn à faire qqch; **to** ~ **sb with sth, to** ~ **sth in sb** inspirer qqch à qqn.

inspired [ɪn'spaɪəd] adj **-1.** [artist, performance] inspiré(e). **-2.** [guess, idea] brillant(e).

inspiring [ɪn'spaɪərɪŋ] adj qui inspire.

inst. (abbr of **instant**): **on the 4th** ~ le 4 courant.

instability [ˌɪnstə'bɪlətɪ] n instabilité f.

install Br, **instal** Am [ɪn'stɔːl] vt **-1.** [fit] installer. **-2.** [appoint]: **to** ~ **sb (as sthg)** nommer qqn (qqch). **-3.** [settle]: **to** ~ **o.s.** s'installer.

installation [ˌɪnstə'leɪʃn] n installation f.

installment plan n Am achat m à crédit.

instalment Br, **installment** Am [ɪn'stɔːlmənt] n **-1.** [payment] acompte m; **in** ~**s** par acomptes. **-2.** [episode] épisode m.

instance ['ɪnstəns] n exemple m; **for** ~ par exemple; **in the first** ~ en premier lieu.

instant ['ɪnstənt] ◇ adj **-1.** [immediate] instantané(e), immédiat(e). **-2.** [coffee] soluble; [food] à préparation rapide. ◇ n instant m; **the** ~ **(that)** ... dès OR aussitôt que ...; **this** ~ tout de suite, immédiatement.

instantaneous [ˌɪnstən'teɪnjəs] adj instantané(e).

instantly ['ɪnstəntlɪ] adv immédiatement.

instead [ɪn'sted] adv au lieu de cela.

◆ **instead of** prep au lieu de; ~ **of him** à sa place.

instep ['ɪnstep] n cou-de-pied m.

instigate ['ɪnstɪɡeɪt] vt être à l'origine de, entreprendre.

instigation [ˌɪnstɪ'ɡeɪʃn] n: **at the** ~ **of** à l'instigation f de.

instigator ['ɪnstɪɡeɪtəʳ] n instigateur m, -trice f.

instil Br (pt & pp **-led**, cont **-ling**), **instill** Am (pt & pp **-ed**, cont **-ing**) [ɪn'stɪl] vt: **to** ~ **sthg in** OR **into sb** instiller qqch à qqn.

instinct ['ɪnstɪŋkt] n **-1.** [intuition] instinct m. **-2.** [impulse] réaction f, mouvement m.

instinctive [ɪn'stɪŋktɪv] adj instinctif(ive).

instinctively [ɪn'stɪŋktɪvlɪ] adv instinctivement.

institute ['ɪnstɪtjuːt] ◇ n institut m. ◇ vt instituer.

institution [ˌɪnstɪ'tjuːʃn] n institution f.

institutional [ˌɪnstɪ'tjuːʃənl] adj institutionnel(elle); pej [food] d'internat.

institutionalized, -ised [ˌɪnstɪ'tjuːʃnəˌlaɪzd] adj **-1.** pej [person] influencé(e) par la vie en collectivité. **-2.** [established] institutionnalisé(e).

instruct [ɪn'strʌkt] vt **-1.** [tell, order]: **to** ~ **sb to do sth** charger qqn de faire qqch. **-2.** [teach] instruire; **to** ~ **sb in sthg** enseigner qqch à qqn.

instruction [ɪn'strʌkʃn] n instruction f.

◆ **instructions** npl mode m d'emploi, instructions fpl.

instruction manual *n* manuel *m*.

instructive [ɪn'strʌktɪv] *adj* instructif(ive).

instructor [ɪn'strʌktə'] *n* **-1.** [gen] instructeur *m*, -trice *f*, moniteur *m*, -trice *f*. **-2.** *Am* SCH enseignant *m*, -e *f*.

instructress [ɪn'strʌktrɪs] *n* instructrice *f*, monitrice *f*.

instrument ['ɪnstrʊmənt] *n* lit & fig instrument *m*.

instrumental [,ɪnstrʊ'mentl] ◇ *adj* **-1.** [important, helpful]: **to be ~ in** contribuer à. **-2.** [music] instrumental(e). ◇ *n* morceau *m* instrumental.

instrumentalist [,ɪnstrʊ'mentəlɪst] *n* instrumentiste *mf*.

instrument panel *n* tableau *m* de bord.

insubordinate [,ɪnsə'bɔːdɪnət] *adj* insubordonné(e).

insubordination ['ɪnsə,bɔːdɪ'neɪʃn] *n* insubordination *f*.

insubstantial [,ɪnsəb'stænʃl] *adj* [structure] peu solide; [meal] peu substantiel(ielle).

insufferable [ɪn'sʌfərəbl] *adj fml* insupportable.

insufficient [,ɪnsə'fɪʃnt] *adj fml* insuffisant(e).

insular ['ɪnsjʊlə'] *adj* [outlook] borné(e); [person] à l'esprit étroit.

insulate ['ɪnsjʊleɪt] *vt* **-1.** [loft, cable] isoler; [hot water tank] calorifuger. **-2.** [protect]: **to ~ sb against** OR **from sthg** protéger qqn de qqch.

insulating tape ['ɪnsjʊleɪtɪŋ-] *n Br* chatterton *m*.

insulation [,ɪnsjʊ'leɪʃn] *n* isolation *f*.

insulin ['ɪnsjʊlɪn] *n* insuline *f*.

insult [*vt* ɪn'sʌlt, *n* 'ɪnsʌlt] ◇ *vt* insulter, injurier. ◇ *n* insulte *f*, injure *f*; **to add ~ to injury** aggraver les choses.

insulting [ɪn'sʌltɪŋ] *adj* insultant(e), injurieux(ieuse).

insuperable [ɪn'suːprəbl] *adj fml* insurmontable.

insurance [ɪn'ʃɔːrəns] ◇ *n* **-1.** [against fire, accident, theft] assurance *f*. **-2.** *fig* [safeguard, protection] protection *f*, garantie *f*. ◇ *comp* [company, agent] d'assurances; [certificate] d'assurance.

insurance broker *n* courtier *m* d'assurances.

insurance policy *n* police *f* d'assurance.

insurance premium *n* prime *f* d'assurance.

insure [ɪn'ʃɔː'] ◇ *vt* **-1.** [against fire, accident, theft]: **to ~ sb/sthg against sthg** assurer

insured [ɪn'ʃɔːd] ◇ *adj* **-1.** [against fire, accident, theft]: **~ (against** OR **for sthg)** assuré(e) (contre qqch). **-2.** *Am* [certain] certain(e), sûr(e). ◇ *n*: **the ~** l'assuré.

insurer [ɪn'ʃɔːrə'] *n* assureur *m*.

insurgent [ɪn'sɜːdʒənt] *n* insurgé *m*, -e *f*.

insurmountable [,ɪnsə'maʊntəbl] *adj fml* insurmontable.

insurrection [,ɪnsə'rekʃn] *n* insurrection *f*.

intact [ɪn'tækt] *adj* intact(e).

intake ['ɪnteɪk] *n* **-1.** [amount consumed] consommation *f*. **-2.** [people recruited] admission *f*. **-3.** [inlet] prise *f*, arrivée *f*.

intangible [ɪn'tændʒəbl] *adj* intangible, impalpable; [proof] non tangible.

integral ['ɪntɪgrəl] *adj* intégral(e); **to be ~ to sthg** faire partie intégrante de qqch.

integrate ['ɪntɪgreɪt] ◇ *vi* s'intégrer; **to ~ with** OR **into sthg** s'intégrer dans qqch. ◇ *vt* intégrer; **to ~ sb/sthg with sthg, to ~ sb/sthg into sthg** intégrer qqn/qqch dans qqch.

integrated ['ɪntɪgreɪtɪd] *adj* intégré(e).

integrated circuit *n* circuit *m* intégré.

integration [,ɪntɪ'greɪʃn] *n*: **~ (with/into)** intégration *f* (à/dans).

integrity [ɪn'tegrɪtɪ] *n* **-1.** [honour] intégrité *f*, honnêteté *f*. **-2.** *fml* [wholeness] intégrité *f*, totalité *f*.

intellect ['ɪntəlekt] *n* **-1.** [ability to think] intellect *m*. **-2.** [cleverness] intelligence *f*.

intellectual [,ɪntə'lektjʊəl] ◇ *adj* intellectuel(elle). ◇ *n* intellectuel *m*, -elle *f*.

intellectualize, -ise [,ɪntə'lektjʊəlaɪz] *vt* intellectualiser.

intelligence [ɪn'telɪdʒəns] *n* (*U*) **-1.** [ability to think] intelligence *f*. **-2.** [information service] service *m* de renseignements. **-3.** [information] informations *fpl*, renseignements *mpl*.

intelligence quotient *n* quotient *m* intellectuel.

intelligence test *n* test *m* d'aptitude intellectuelle.

intelligent [ɪn'telɪdʒənt] *adj* intelligent(e).

intelligent card *n* carte *f* à puce OR à mémoire.

intelligently [ɪn'telɪdʒəntlɪ] *adv* intelligemment, avec intelligence.

intelligentsia [ɪn,telɪ'dʒentsɪə] *n*: **the ~** l'intelligentsia *f*.

intelligible [ɪn'telɪdʒəbl] *adj* intelligible.

intemperate [ɪn'tempərət] *adj fml* immodéré(e).

intend [ɪn'tend] *vt* [mean] avoir l'intention de; **it was ~ed as advice** je voulais/il voulait juste donner des conseils; **it wasn't ~ed as criticism** je n'ai pas/il n'a pas dit pour critiquer; **to be ~ed for** être destiné à; **to be ~ed to do sthg** être destiné à faire qqch, viser à faire qqch; **to ~ doing** OR **to do sthg** avoir l'intention de faire qqch.

intended [ɪn'tendɪd] *adj* [result] voulu(e); [victim] visé(e).

intense [ɪn'tens] *adj* **-1.** [gen] intense. **-2.** [serious - person] sérieux(ieuse).

intensely [ɪn'tenslɪ] *adv* **-1.** [irritating, boring] extrêmement; [suffer] énormément. **-2.** [look] intensément.

intensify [ɪn'tensɪfaɪ] (*pt* & *pp* **-ied**) ◇ *vt* intensifier, augmenter. ◇ *vi* s'intensifier.

intensity [ɪn'tensətɪ] *n* intensité *f*.

intensive [ɪn'tensɪv] *adj* intensif(ive).

intensive care *n* réanimation *f*.

intensive care unit *n* service *m* de réanimation.

intent [ɪn'tent] ◇ *adj* **-1.** [absorbed] absorbé(e). **-2.** [determined]: **to be ~ on** OR **upon doing sthg** être résolu(e) OR décidé(e) à faire qqch. ◇ *n fml* intention *f*, dessein *m*; **to all ~s and purposes** pratiquement, virtuellement.

intention [ɪn'tenʃn] *n* intention *f*.

intentional [ɪn'tenʃənl] *adj* intentionnel(elle), voulu(e).

intentionally [ɪn'tenʃənəlɪ] *adv* intentionnellement; **I didn't do it ~** je ne l'ai pas fait exprès.

intently [ɪn'tentlɪ] *adv* avec attention, attentivement.

inter [ɪn't3ːr] (*pt* & *pp* **-red**, *cont* **-ring**) *vt fml* enterrer.

interact [,ɪntər'ækt] *vi* **-1.** [communicate, work together]: **to ~ (with sb)** communiquer (avec qqn). **-2.** [react]: **to ~ (with sthg)** interagir (avec qqch).

interaction [,ɪntər'ækʃn] *n* interaction *f*.

interactive [,ɪntər'æktɪv] *adj* COMPUT interactif(ive).

intercede [,ɪntə'siːd] *vi fml*: **to ~ (with sb)** intercéder (auprès de qqn).

intercept [,ɪntə'sept] *vt* intercepter.

interception [,ɪntə'sepʃn] *n* interception *f*.

interchange [*n* 'ɪntətʃeɪndʒ, *vb* ,ɪntə'tʃeɪndʒ] ◇ *n* **-1.** [exchange] échange *m*. **-2.** [road junction] échangeur *m*. ◇ *vt* échanger.

interchangeable [,ɪntə'tʃeɪndʒəbl] *adj*: **(with)** interchangeable (avec).

intercity [,ɪntə'sɪtɪ] ◇ *adj Br* interurbain(e). ◇ *n* système de trains rapides reliant les grandes villes en Grande-Bretagne; **Intercity 125®** *train rapide pouvant rouler à 125 miles (200 kms) à l'heure.*

intercom ['ɪntəkɒm] *n* interphone *m*; **on** OR **over the ~** à l'interphone.

interconnect [,ɪntəkə'nekt] *vi*: **to ~ (with)** être relié(e) (à), être connecté(e) (à).

intercontinental ['ɪntə,kɒntɪ'nentl] *adj* intercontinental(e).

intercontinental ballistic missile *n* missile *m* balistique intercontinental.

intercourse ['ɪntəkɔːs] *n* (*U*) [sexual] rapports *mpl* (sexuels).

interdenominational ['ɪntədɪ,nɒmɪ'neɪʃənl] *adj* interconfessionnel(elle).

interdepartmental ['ɪntə,diːpɑːt'mentl] *adj* entre services; [in government] entre départements.

interdependent [,ɪntədɪ'pendənt] *adj* interdépendant(e).

interdict ['ɪntədɪkt] *n* **-1.** JUR interdiction *f*. **-2.** RELIG interdit *m*.

interest ['ɪntrəst] ◇ *n* **-1.** [gen] intérêt *m*; **to have an ~ in** s'intéresser à; **to lose ~** se désintéresser; **in the ~s of** dans l'intérêt de. **-2.** [hobby] centre *m* d'intérêt. **-3.** (*U*) FIN intérêt *m*, intérêts *mpl*. ◇ *vt* intéresser; **to ~ sb in sthg** [arouse interest] intéresser qqn à qqch; **can I ~ you in a drink?** je peux vous offrir un verre?

interested ['ɪntrəstɪd] *adj* intéressé(e); **to be ~ in** s'intéresser à; **I'm not ~ in that** cela ne m'intéresse pas; **to be ~ in doing sthg** avoir envie de faire qqch.

interest-free *adj* sans intérêt, gratuit(e).

interesting ['ɪntrəstɪŋ] *adj* intéressant(e).

interest rate *n* taux *m* d'intérêt.

interface [*n* 'ɪntəfeɪs, *vb* ,ɪntə'feɪs] ◇ *n* **-1.** COMPUT interface *f*. **-2.** *fig* [junction] rapports *mpl*, relations *fpl*. ◇ *vt* COMPUT interfacer.

interfere [,ɪntə'fɪər] *vi* **-1.** [meddle]: **to ~ in sthg** s'immiscer dans qqch, se mêler de qqch; **don't ~!** ne t'en mêle pas! **-2.** [damage]: **to ~ with sthg** gêner OR contrarier qqch; [routine] déranger qqch.

interference [,ɪntə'fɪərəns] *n* (*U*) **-1.** [meddling]: **~ (with** OR **in)** ingérence *f* (dans), intrusion *f* (dans). **-2.** TELEC parasites *mpl*.

interfering [,ɪntə'fɪərɪŋ] *adj pej* qui se mêle de tout.

intergalactic [,ɪntəgə'læktɪk] *adj* intergalactique.

interim ['ɪntərɪm] ◇ *adj* provisoire. ◇ *n*: **in the ~** dans l'intérim, entre-temps.

interior [ɪn'tɪərɪəʳ] ◇ *adj* **-1.** [inner] intérieur(e). **-2.** POL de l'Intérieur. ◇ *n* intérieur *m*.

interior decorator *n* décorateur *m*, -trice *f*.

interior designer *n* architecte *mf* d'intérieur.

interject [ˌɪntə'dʒekt] ◇ *vt* **-1.** [add] lancer. **-2.** [interrupt] interrompre. ◇ *vi* interrompre, lancer une remarque.

interjection [ˌɪntə'dʒekʃn] *n* **-1.** [remark] interruption *f*. **-2.** GRAMM interjection *f*.

interleave [ˌɪntə'liːv] *vt*: **to ~ sthg with sthg** interfolier qqch avec qqch.

interlock [ˌɪntə'lɒk] ◇ *vi* [gears] s'enclencher, s'engrener; [fingers] s'entrelacer. ◇ *vt* [gears] enclencher, engrener; [fingers] entrelacer.

interloper ['ɪntələʊpəʳ] *n* intrus *m*, -e *f*.

interlude ['ɪntəluːd] *n* **-1.** [pause] intervalle *m*. **-2.** [interval] interlude *m*.

intermarry [ˌɪntə'mærɪ] (*pt* & *pp* **-ied**) *vi*: **to ~ (with)** se marier (avec).

intermediary [ˌɪntə'miːdjərɪ] (*pl* **-ies**) *n* intermédiaire *mf*.

intermediate [ˌɪntə'miːdjət] *adj* **-1.** [transitional] intermédiaire. **-2.** [post-beginner - level] moyen(enne); [- student, group] de niveau moyen.

interminable [ɪn'tɜːmɪnəbl] *adj* interminable, sans fin.

intermingle [ˌɪntə'mɪŋgl] *vi*: **to ~ with sb** se mêler à qqn; **to ~ with sthg** se mélanger avec qqch.

intermission [ˌɪntə'mɪʃn] *n* entracte *m*.

intermittent [ˌɪntə'mɪtənt] *adj* intermittent(e).

intern [*vb* ɪn'tɜːn, *n* 'ɪntɜːn] ◇ *vt* interner. ◇ *n Am* [gen] stagiaire *mf*; MED interne *mf*.

internal [ɪn'tɜːnl] *adj* **-1.** [gen] interne. **-2.** [within country] intérieur(e).

internal-combustion engine *n* moteur *m* à combustion interne.

internally [ɪn'tɜːnəlɪ] *adv* **-1.** [within the body]: **to bleed ~** faire une hémorragie interne. **-2.** [within country] à l'intérieur. **-3.** [within organization] intérieurement.

Internal Revenue *n Am*: **the ~ ≃** le fisc.

international [ˌɪntə'næʃənl] ◇ *adj* international(e). ◇ *n Br* SPORT **-1.** [match] match *m* international. **-2.** [player] international *m*, -e *f*.

international date line *n*: **the ~** la ligne de changement de date.

internationally [ˌɪntə'næʃnəlɪ] *adv* dans le monde entier.

International Monetary Fund *n*: **the ~** le Fonds monétaire international.

international relations *npl* relations *fpl* internationales.

internecine [*Br* ˌɪntə'niːsaɪn, *Am* ɪntər'niːsn] *adj fml* intestin(e).

internee [ˌɪntɜː'niː] *n* interné *m*, -e *f* politique.

internment [ɪn'tɜːnmənt] *n* internement *m* politique.

interpersonal [ˌɪntə'pɜːsənl] *adj* de personne à personne, entre personnes; [skills] de communication.

interplay ['ɪntəpleɪ] *n*: **~ (of/between)** interaction *f* (de/entre).

Interpol ['ɪntəpɒl] *n* Interpol *m*.

interpolate [ɪn'tɜːpəleɪt] *vt fml* **-1.** [add]: **to ~ sthg (into)** ajouter qqch (à). **-2.** [interrupt] interrompre.

interpose [ˌɪntə'pəʊz] *vt fml* **-1.** [add] ajouter. **-2.** [interrupt] interrompre.

interpret [ɪn'tɜːprɪt] ◇ *vt*: **to ~ sthg (as)** interpréter qqch (comme). ◇ *vi* [translate] faire l'interprète.

interpretation [ɪnˌtɜːprɪ'teɪʃn] *n* interprétation *f*.

interpreter [ɪn'tɜːprɪtəʳ] *n* interprète *mf*.

interpreting [ɪn'tɜːprɪtɪŋ] *n* [occupation] interprétariat *m*.

interracial [ˌɪntə'reɪʃl] *adj* entre des races différentes, racial(e).

interrelate [ˌɪntərɪ'leɪt] ◇ *vt* mettre en corrélation. ◇ *vi*: **to ~ (with)** être lié(e) (à), être en corrélation (avec).

interrogate [ɪn'terəgeɪt] *vt* interroger.

interrogation [ɪnˌterə'geɪʃn] *n* interrogatoire *m*.

interrogation mark *n Am* point *m* d'interrogation.

interrogative [ˌɪntə'rɒgətɪv] GRAMM ◇ *adj* interrogatif(ive). ◇ *n* interrogatif *m*.

interrogator [ɪn'terəgeɪtəʳ] *n* interrogateur *m*, -trice *f*.

interrupt [ˌɪntə'rʌpt] ◇ *vt* interrompre; [calm] rompre. ◇ *vi* interrompre.

interruption [ˌɪntə'rʌpʃn] *n* interruption *f*.

intersect [ˌɪntə'sekt] ◇ *vi* s'entrecroiser, s'entrecouper. ◇ *vt* croiser, couper.

intersection [ˌɪntə'sekʃn] *n* [in road] croisement *m*, carrefour *m*.

intersperse [ˌɪntə'spɜːs] *vt*: **to be ~d with** être émaillé(e) de, être entremêlé(e) de.

interstate (highway) ['ɪntərsteɪt-] *n Am* autoroute *f*.

interval ['ɪntəvl] *n* -1. [gen] intervalle *m*; at ~s par intervalles; at monthly/yearly ~s tous les mois/ans. -2. *Br* [at play, concert] entracte *m*.

intervene [,ɪntə'viːn] *vi* -1. [person, police]: to ~ (in) intervenir (dans), s'interposer (dans). -2. [event, war, strike] survenir. -3. [time] s'écouler.

intervening [,ɪntə'viːnɪŋ] *adj* [period] qui s'est écoulé(e).

intervention [,ɪntə'venʃn] *n* intervention *f*.

interventionist [,ɪntə'venʃənɪst] ◇ *adj* interventionniste. ◇ *n* interventionniste *mf*.

interview ['ɪntəvjuː] ◇ *n* -1. [for job] entrevue *f*, entretien *m*. -2. PRESS interview *f*. ◇ *vt* -1. [for job] faire passer une entrevue OR un entretien à. -2. PRESS interviewer.

interviewee [,ɪntəvjuː'iː] *n* -1. [for job] candidat *m*, -e *f*. -2. PRESS interviewé *m*, -e *f*.

interviewer ['ɪntəvjuːə'] *n* -1. [for job] personne *f* qui fait passer une entrevue. -2. PRESS interviewer *m*.

interweave [,ɪntə'wiːv] (*pt* -wove, *pp* -woven) *fig* ◇ *vt* entremêler. ◇ *vi* s'entremêler.

intestate [ɪn'testeɪt] *adj*: to die ~ mourir intestat.

intestine [ɪn'testɪn] *n* intestin *m*.
◆ **intestines** *npl* intestins *mpl*.

intimacy ['ɪntɪməsɪ] (*pl* -ies) *n* -1. [closeness]: ~ (between/with) intimité *f* (entre/avec). -2. [intimate remark] familiarité *f*.

intimate [*adj & n* 'ɪntɪmət, *vb* 'ɪntɪmeɪt] ◇ *adj* -1. [gen] intime. -2. *fml* [sexually]: to be ~ with sb avoir des rapports intimes avec qqn. -3. [detailed - knowledge] approfondi(e). ◇ *n fml* intime *mf*. ◇ *vt fml* faire savoir, faire connaître.

intimately ['ɪntɪmətlɪ] *adv* -1. [very closely] étroitement. -2. [as close friends] intimement. -3. [in detail] à fond.

intimation [,ɪntɪ'meɪʃn] *n fml* signe *m*, indication *f*.

intimidate [ɪn'tɪmɪdeɪt] *vt* intimider.

intimidation [ɪn,tɪmɪ'deɪʃn] *n* intimidation *f*.

into ['ɪntʊ] *prep* -1. [inside] dans. -2. [against] to bump ~ sthg se cogner contre qqch; to crash ~ rentrer dans. -3. [referring to change in state] en; to translate sthg ~ Spanish traduire qqch en espagnol. -4. [concerning]: research/investigation ~ recherche *f*/enquête *f* sur. -5. MATH: 3 ~ 2 2 divisé par 3. -6. *inf* [interested in]: to be ~ sthg être passionné(e) par qqch.

intolerable [ɪn'tɒlrəbl] *adj* intolérable, insupportable.

intolerance [ɪn'tɒlərəns] *n* intolérance *f*.

intolerant [ɪn'tɒlərənt] *adj* intolérant(e); to be ~ of faire preuve d'intolérance à l'égard de.

intonation [,ɪntə'neɪʃn] *n* intonation *f*.

intone [ɪn'təʊn] *vt* psalmodier.

intoxicated [ɪn'tɒksɪkeɪtɪd] *adj* -1. [drunk] ivre. -2. *fig* [excited]: to be ~ by OR with sthg être grisé(e) OR enivré(e) par qqch.

intoxicating [ɪn'tɒksɪkeɪtɪŋ] *adj* -1. [alcoholic] alcoolisé(e). -2. *fig* [exciting] grisant(e), enivrant(e).

intoxication [ɪn,tɒksɪ'keɪʃn] *n* -1. [drunkenness] ivresse *f*. -2. [excitement] griserie *f*, ivresse *f*.

intractable [ɪn'træktəbl] *adj* -1. [stubborn] intraitable. -2. [insoluble] insoluble.

intransigent [ɪn'trænzɪdʒənt] *adj* intransigeant(e).

intransitive [ɪn'trænzətɪv] *adj* intransitif(ive).

intrauterine device [,ɪntrə'juːtəraɪn] *n* stérilet *m*, dispositif *m* anticonceptionnel intra-utérin.

intravenous [,ɪntrə'viːnəs] *adj* intraveineux(euse).

in-tray *n* casier *m* des affaires à traiter.

intrepid [ɪn'trepɪd] *adj* intrépide.

intricacy ['ɪntrɪkəsɪ] (*pl* -ies) *n* complexité *f*.

intricate ['ɪntrɪkət] *adj* compliqué(e).

intrigue [ɪn'triːg] ◇ *n* intrigue *f*. ◇ *vt* intriguer, exciter la curiosité de. ◇ *vi*: to ~ against intriguer OR comploter contre.

intriguing [ɪn'triːgɪŋ] *adj* fascinant(e).

intrinsic [ɪn'trɪnsɪk] *adj* intrinsèque.

intro ['ɪntrəʊ] (*pl* -s) *n inf* introduction *f*.

introduce [,ɪntrə'djuːs] *vt* -1. [present] présenter; to ~ sb to sb présenter qqn à qqn. -2. [bring in]: to ~ sthg (to OR into) introduire qqch (dans). -3. [allow to experience]: to ~ sb to sthg initier qqn à qqch, faire découvrir qqch à qqn. -4. [signal beginning of] annoncer.

introduction [,ɪntrə'dʌkʃn] *n* -1. [in book, of new method etc] introduction *f*. -2. [first experience]: ~ to sthg premier contact *m* avec qqch. -3. [of people]: ~ (to sb) présentation *f* (à qqn).

introductory [,ɪntrə'dʌktrɪ] *adj* d'introduction, préliminaire.

introspective [,ɪntrə'spektɪv] *adj* introspectif(ive).

introvert ['ɪntrəvɜːt] *n* introverti *m*, -e *f*.

introverted [ˌɪntrə'vɜːtɪd] *adj* introverti(e).

intrude [ɪn'truːd] *vi* faire intrusion; **to ~ on sb** déranger qqn.

intruder [ɪn'truːdə'] *n* intrus *m*, -e *f*.

intrusion [ɪn'truːʒn] *n* intrusion *f*.

intrusive [ɪn'truːsɪv] *adj* gênant(e), importun(e).

intuition [ˌɪntjuː'ɪʃn] *n* intuition *f*.

intuitive [ɪn'tjuːɪtɪv] *adj* intuitif(ive).

Inuit ['ɪnʊɪt] ◇ *adj* inuit (*inv*). ◇ *n* Inuit *mf inv*.

inundate ['ɪnʌndeɪt] *vt* **-1.** *fml* [flood] inonder. **-2.** [overwhelm]: **to be ~d with** être submergé(e) de.

inured [ɪ'njʊəd] *adj fml*: **to be ~ to sthg** être aguerri(e) à qqch, être endurci(e) à qqch; **to become ~ to sthg** s'aguerrir à qqch, s'endurcir à qqch.

invade [ɪn'veɪd] *vt* **-1.** MIL & *fig* envahir. **-2.** [disturb - privacy etc] **violer**.

invader [ɪn'veɪdə'] *n* envahisseur *m*, -euse *f*.

invading [ɪn'veɪdɪŋ] *adj* [troops] d'invasion.

invalid [*adj* ɪn'vælɪd, *n* & *vb* 'ɪnvəlɪd] ◇ *adj* **-1.** [illegal, unacceptable] **non valide, non valable**. **-2.** [not reasonable] **non valable**. ◇ *n* invalide *mf*.

◆ **invalid out** *vt sep*: **to be ~ed out of the army** être réformé(e) pour raisons de santé.

invalidate [ɪn'vælɪdeɪt] *vt* invalider, annuler.

invalid chair ['ɪnvəlɪd-] *n* fauteuil *m* roulant.

invaluable [ɪn'væljʊəbl] *adj*: **~ (to)** [help, advice, person] **précieux(ieuse) (pour)**; [experience, information] **inestimable (pour)**.

invariable [ɪn'veərɪəbl] *adj* invariable.

invariably [ɪn'veərɪəblɪ] *adv* invariablement, toujours.

invasion [ɪn'veɪʒn] *n lit* & *fig* invasion *f*.

invective [ɪn'vektɪv] *n* (*U*) invectives *fpl*.

inveigle [ɪn'veɪgl] *vt*: **to ~ sb into sthg** attirer qqn dans qqch par la ruse; **to ~ sb into doing sthg** amener qqn à faire qqch (par la ruse), persuader qqn de faire qqch (par la ruse).

invent [ɪn'vent] *vt* inventer.

invention [ɪn'venʃn] *n* invention *f*.

inventive [ɪn'ventɪv] *adj* inventif(ive).

inventor [ɪn'ventə'] *n* inventeur *m*, -trice *f*.

inventory [ɪn'ventrɪ] (*pl* -ies) *n* **-1.** [list] inventaire *m*. **-2.** *Am* [goods] stock *m*.

inventory control *n* gestion *f* du stock.

inverse [ɪn'vɜːs] ◇ *adj* inverse. ◇ *n* inverse *m*, contraire *m*.

invert [ɪn'vɜːt] *vt* retourner.

invertebrate [ɪn'vɜːtɪbreɪt] *n* invertébré *m*.

inverted commas [ɪn'vɜːtɪd-] *npl Br* guillemets *mpl*.

inverted snob [ɪn'vɜːtɪd-] *n* snob *mf* à l'envers, personne *f* qui fait du snobisme à l'envers.

invest [ɪn'vest] ◇ *vt* **-1.** [money]: **to ~ sthg (in)** investir qqch (dans). **-2.** [time, energy]: **to ~ sthg in sthg/in doing sthg** consacrer qqch à qqch/à faire qqch, employer qqch à qqch/à faire qqch. **-3.** *fml* [endow]: **to ~ sb with sthg** investir qqn de qqch. ◇ *vi* **-1.** FIN: **to ~ (in sthg)** investir (dans qqch). **-2.** *fig* [buy]: **to ~ in sthg** se payer qqch, s'acheter qqch.

investigate [ɪn'vestɪgeɪt] ◇ *vt* enquêter sur, faire une enquête sur; [subj: scientist] faire des recherches sur. ◇ *vi* faire une enquête.

investigation [ɪnˌvestɪ'geɪʃn] *n* **-1.** [enquiry]: **~ (into)** enquête *f* (sur); [scientific] recherches *fpl* (sur). **-2.** (*U*) [investigating] investigation *f*.

investigative [ɪn'vestɪgətɪv] *adj* d'investigation; [journalist] qui fait des enquêtes-reportages; **~ journalism** enquêtes-reportages *fpl*.

investigator [ɪn'vestɪgeɪtə'] *n* investigateur *m*, -trice *f*.

investiture [ɪn'vestɪtʃə'] *n* investiture *f*.

investment [ɪn'vestmənt] *n* **-1.** FIN investissement *m*, placement *m*. **-2.** [of energy] dépense *f*.

investment analyst *n* analyste *mf* en placements.

investment trust *n* société *f* d'investissement.

investor [ɪn'vestə'] *n* investisseur *m*.

inveterate [ɪn'vetərət] *adj* invétéré(e).

invidious [ɪn'vɪdɪəs] *adj* [task] ingrat(e); [comparison] injuste.

invigilate [ɪn'vɪdʒɪleɪt] *Br* ◇ *vi* surveiller les candidats (à un examen). ◇ *vt* surveiller.

invigilator [ɪn'vɪdʒɪleɪtə'] *n Br* surveillant *m*, -e *f*.

invigorating [ɪn'vɪgəreɪtɪŋ] *adj* tonifiant(e), vivifiant(e).

invincible [ɪn'vɪnsɪbl] *adj* [army, champion] invincible; [record] imbattable.

inviolate [ɪn'vaɪələt] *adj literary* inviolé(e).

invisible [ɪn'vɪzɪbl] *adj* invisible.

invisible assets *npl* biens *mpl* incorporels.

invisible earnings *npl* revenus *mpl* invisibles.

invisible ink *n* encre *f* sympathique.

invitation [,ɪnvɪ'teɪʃn] *n* -1. [request] invitation *f*. -2. [encouragement]: **an ~ to sthg/to do sthg** une incitation à qqch/à faire qqch, une invite à qqch/à faire qqch.

invite [ɪn'vaɪt] *vt* -1. [ask to come]: **to ~ sb (to)** inviter qqn (à). -2. [ask politely]: **to ~ sb to do sthg** inviter qqn à faire qqch. -3. [ask for]: **the chairman ~d questions** le président a invité l'assistance à poser des questions. -4. [encourage]: **to ~ trouble** aller au devant des ennuis; **to ~ gossip** faire causer.

inviting [ɪn'vaɪtɪŋ] *adj* attrayant(e), agréable; [food] appétissant(e).

in vitro fertilization [,ɪn'viːtrəʊ-] *n* fécondation *f* in vitro.

invoice ['ɪnvɔɪs] ◇ *n* facture *f*. ◇ *vt* -1. [client] envoyer la facture à. -2. [goods] facturer.

invoke [ɪn'vəʊk] *vt* -1. *fml* [law, act] invoquer. -2. [feelings] susciter, faire naître; [help] demander, implorer.

involuntary [ɪn'vɒləntrɪ] *adj* involontaire.

involve [ɪn'vɒlv] *vt* -1. [entail] nécessiter; **what's ~d?** de quoi s'agit-il?; **to ~ doing sthg** nécessiter de faire qqch. -2. [concern, affect] toucher; **to be ~d in an accident** avoir un accident. -3. [person]: **to ~ sb in sthg** impliquer qqn dans qqch; **to ~ o.s. in sthg** s'impliquer dans qqch, prendre part à qqch.

involved [ɪn'vɒlvd] *adj* -1. [complex] complexe, compliqué(e). -2. [participating]: **to be ~ in sthg** participer OR prendre part à qqch. -3. [in relationship]: **to be ~ with sb** avoir des relations intimes avec qqn; **he doesn't want to get ~** il ne veut pas s'attacher.

involvement [ɪn'vɒlvmənt] *n* -1. [participation]: **~ (in)** participation *f* (à). -2. [concern, enthusiasm]: **~ (in)** engagement *m* (dans).

invulnerable [ɪn'vʌlnərəbl] *adj*: **~ (to)** invulnérable (à).

inward ['ɪnwəd] ◇ *adj* -1. [inner] intérieur(e). -2. [towards the inside] vers l'intérieur. ◇ *adv Am* = **inwards**.

inwardly ['ɪnwədlɪ] *adv* intérieurement.

inwards ['ɪnwədz] *adv* vers l'intérieur.

I/O (*abbr of* **input/output**) E/S.

IOC (*abbr of* **International Olympic Committee**) *n* CIO *m*.

iodine [*Br* 'aɪədiːn, *Am* 'aɪədaɪn] *n* iode *m*.

IOM *abbr of* **Isle of Man**.

ion ['aɪən] *n* ion *m*.

Ionian Sea [aɪ'əʊnjən-] *n*: **the ~** la mer Ionienne.

iota [aɪ'əʊtə] *n* brin *m*, grain *m*.

IOU (*abbr of* **I owe you**) *n* reconnaissance *f* de dette.

IOW *abbr of* **Isle of Wight**.

Iowa ['aɪəʊə] *n* Iowa *m*; **in ~** dans l'Iowa.

IPA (*abbr of* **International Phonetic Alphabet**) *n* API *m*.

IQ (*abbr of* **intelligence quotient**) *n* QI *m*.

IRA *n* -1. (*abbr of* **Irish Republican Army**) IRA *f*. -2. (*abbr of* **individual retirement account**) *aux États-Unis, compte d'épargne retraite (à avantages fiscaux)*.

Iran [ɪ'rɑːn] *n* Iran *m*; **in ~** en Iran.

Iranian [ɪ'reɪnjən] ◇ *adj* iranien(ienne). ◇ *n* Iranien *m*, -ienne *f*.

Iraq [ɪ'rɑːk] *n* Iraq *m*, Irak *m*; **in ~** en Iraq.

Iraqi [ɪ'rɑːkɪ] ◇ *adj* iraquien(ienne), irakien(ienne). ◇ *n* Iraquien *m*, -ienne *f*, Irakien *m*, -ienne *f*.

irascible [ɪ'ræsəbl] *adj* irascible, coléreux(euse).

irate [aɪ'reɪt] *adj* furieux(ieuse).

Ireland ['aɪələnd] *n* Irlande *f*; **in ~** en Irlande; **the Republic of ~** la République d'Irlande.

iridescent [,ɪrɪ'desənt] *adj literary* irisé(e); [silk] chatoyant(e).

iris ['aɪərɪs] (*pl* **-es**) *n* iris *m*.

Irish ['aɪrɪʃ] ◇ *adj* irlandais(e). ◇ *n* [language] irlandais *m*. ◇ *npl*: **the ~** les Irlandais.

Irish coffee *n* Irish coffee *m*.

Irishman ['aɪrɪʃmən] (*pl* **-men** [-mən]) *n* Irlandais *m*.

Irish Sea *n*: **the ~** la mer d'Irlande.

Irish stew *n* ragoût *m* de viande à l'irlandaise.

Irishwoman ['aɪrɪʃ,wʊmən] (*pl* **-women** [-,wɪmɪn]) *n* Irlandaise *f*.

irk [ɜːk] *vt* ennuyer, contrarier.

irksome ['ɜːksəm] *adj* ennuyeux(euse), assommant(e).

IRN (*abbr of* **Independent Radio News**) *n* agence de presse radiophonique.

IRO (*abbr of* **International Refugee Organization**) *n* organisation humanitaire américaine pour les réfugiés.

iron ['aɪən] ◇ *adj* -1. [made of iron] de OR en fer. -2. *fig* [very strict] de fer. ◇ *n* -1. [metal, golf club] fer *m*. -2. [for clothes] fer *m* à repasser. ◇ *vt* repasser.
◆ **iron out** *vt sep fig* [difficulties] aplanir; [problems] résoudre.

Iron Age ◇ *n*: **the ~** l'âge de fer. ◇ *comp* de l'âge de fer.

Iron Curtain *n*: the ~ le rideau de fer.

ironic(al) [aɪ'rɒnɪk(l)] *adj* ironique.

ironically [aɪ'rɒnɪklɪ] *adv* ironiquement.

ironing ['aɪənɪŋ] *n* repassage *m*; to do the ~ faire le repassage.

ironing board *n* planche *f* OR table *f* à repasser.

iron lung *n* poumon *m* d'acier.

ironmonger ['aɪən,mʌŋgə'] *n* Br quincaillier *m*; ~'s (shop) quincaillerie *f*.

ironworks ['aɪənwɜːks] (*pl inv*) *n* usine *f* sidérurgique.

irony ['aɪrənɪ] (*pl -ies*) *n* ironie *f*.

irradiate [ɪ'reɪdɪeɪt] *vt* irradier.

irrational [ɪ'ræʃənl] *adj* irrationnel(elle), déraisonnable; [person] non rationnel(elle).

irreconcilable [ɪ'rekənsaɪləbl] *adj* inconciliable.

irredeemable [,ɪrɪ'diːməbl] *adj fml* **-1.** [irreplaceable] irréparable. **-2.** [hopeless] irrémédiable.

irrefutable [ɪ'refjʊtəbl] *adj* irréfutable.

irregular [ɪ'regjʊlə'] *adj* irrégulier(ière).

irregularity [ɪ,regjʊ'lærətɪ] (*pl -ies*) *n* irrégularité *f*.

irregularly [ɪ'regjʊləlɪ] *adv* irrégulièrement.

irrelevance [ɪ'reləvəns], **irrelevancy** [ɪ'reləvənsɪ] (*pl -ies*) *n* manque *m* de pertinence.

irrelevant [ɪ'reləvənt] *adj* sans rapport.

irreligious [,ɪrɪ'lɪdʒəs] *adj* irréligieux(ieuse).

irremediable [,ɪrɪ'miːdjəbl] *adj fml* irrémédiable.

irreparable [ɪ'repərəbl] *adj* irréparable.

irreplaceable [,ɪrɪ'pleɪsəbl] *adj* irremplaçable.

irrepressible [,ɪrɪ'presəbl] *adj* [enthusiasm] que rien ne peut entamer; he's ~ il est d'une bonne humeur à toute épreuve.

irreproachable [,ɪrɪ'prəʊtʃəbl] *adj* irréprochable.

irresistible [,ɪrɪ'zɪstəbl] *adj* irrésistible.

irresolute [ɪ'rezəluːt] *adj* irrésolu(e), indécis(e).

irrespective [,ɪrɪ'spektɪv]
♦ **irrespective of** *prep* sans tenir compte de.

irresponsible [,ɪrɪ'spɒnsəbl] *adj* irresponsable.

irretrievable [,ɪrɪ'triːvəbl] *adj* irréparable, irrémédiable.

irreverent [ɪ'revərənt] *adj* irrévérencieux(ieuse).

irreversible [,ɪrɪ'vɜːsəbl] *adj* [judgement, decision] irrévocable; [change, damage] irréversible.

irrevocable [ɪ'revəkəbl] *adj* irrévocable.

irrigate ['ɪrɪgeɪt] *vt* irriguer.

irrigation [,ɪrɪ'geɪʃn] ◇ *n* irrigation *f*. ◇ *comp* d'irrigation.

irritable ['ɪrɪtəbl] *adj* irritable.

irritant ['ɪrɪtənt] ◇ *adj* irritant(e). ◇ *n* **-1.** [irritating situation] source *f* d'irritation. **-2.** [substance] irritant *m*.

irritate ['ɪrɪteɪt] *vt* irriter.

irritating ['ɪrɪteɪtɪŋ] *adj* irritant(e).

irritation [ɪrɪ'teɪʃn] *n* **-1.** [anger, soreness] irritation *f*. **-2.** [cause of anger] source *f* d'irritation.

IRS (*abbr of* **Internal Revenue Service**) *n* Am: the ~ ≃ le fisc.

is [ɪz] → **be**.

ISBN (*abbr of* **International Standard Book Number**) *n* ISBN *m*.

Islam ['ɪzlɑːm] *n* islam *m*.

Islamabad [ɪz'lɑːməbæd] *n* Islamabad.

Islamic [ɪz'læmɪk] *adj* islamique.

island ['aɪlənd] *n* **-1.** [isle] île *f*. **-2.** AUT refuge *m* pour piétons.

islander ['aɪləndə'] *n* habitant *m*, -e *f* d'une île.

isle [aɪl] *n* île *f*.

Isle of Man *n*: the ~ l'île *f* de Man; in OR on the ~ à l'île de Man.

Isle of Wight [-waɪt] *n*: the ~ l'île *f* de Wight; on the ~ à l'île de Wight.

isn't ['ɪznt] = **is not**.

isobar ['aɪsəbɑː'] *n* isobare *f*.

isolate ['aɪsəleɪt] *vt*: to ~ sb/sthg (from) isoler qqn/qqch (de).

isolated ['aɪsəleɪtɪd] *adj* isolé(e).

isolation [aɪsə'leɪʃn] *n* isolement *m*; in ~ [alone] dans l'isolement; [separately] isolément.

isolationism [,aɪsə'leɪʃənɪzm] *n* isolationnisme *m*.

isosceles triangle [aɪ'sɒsɪliːz-] *n* triangle *m* isocèle.

isotope ['aɪsətəʊp] *n* isotope *m*.

Israel ['ɪzreɪəl] *n* Israël *m*; in ~ en Israël.

Israeli [ɪz'reɪlɪ] ◇ *adj* israélien(ienne). ◇ *n* Israélien *m*, -ienne *f*.

Israelite ['ɪz,rɪəlaɪt] ◇ *adj* israélite. ◇ *n* Israélite *mf*.

issue ['ɪʃuː] ◇ *n* **-1.** [important subject] question *f*, problème *m*; to make an ~ of sthg faire tout un plat OR toute une affaire de qqch; at ~ en question, en cause. **-2.** [edition] numéro *m*. **-3.** [bringing out - of bank-

tion] **numéro** *m.* **-3.** [bringing out - of banknotes, shares] **émission** *f.*
◇ *vt* **-1.** [make public - decree, statement] **faire**; [- warning] **lancer.** **-2.** [bring out - banknotes, shares] **émettre**; [- book] **publier.** **-3.** [passport *etc*] **délivrer**; **to ~ sthg to sb, to ~ sb with sthg fournir** qqch à qqn.
◇ *vi* **-1.** [smoke, steam]: **to ~ from** sortir de, s'échapper de. **-2.** [problems]: **to ~ from** découler de.

Istanbul [ˌɪstænˈbʊl] *n* Istanbul.

ISTC (*abbr of* **Iron and Steels Confederation**) *n syndicat britannique des ouvriers de la sidérurgie.*

isthmus [ˈɪsməs] *n* isthme *m.*

it [ɪt] *pron* **-1.** [referring to specific person or thing - subj] **il** (elle); [- direct object] **le** (la), **l'** (+ *vowel or silent* 'h'); [- indirect object] **lui**; **did you find ~¿** tu l'as trouvé(e)¿; **give ~ to me at once** donne-le-moi (donne-la-moi) tout de suite; **give ~ a shake** secoue-le. **-2.** [with prepositions]: **in/to/at ~** y; **put the vegetables in ~** mettez-y les légumes; **on ~** dessus; **about ~** en; **under ~** dessous; **beside ~** à côté; **from/of ~** en; **he's very proud of ~** il en est très fier. **-3.** [impersonal use] **il, ce**; **~ is cold today** il fait froid aujourd'hui; **~'s two o'clock** il est deux heures; **who is ~¿ — it's Mary/me** qui est-ce¿ — c'est Mary/moi; **~'s the children who worry me most** ce sont les enfants qui m'inquiètent le plus.

IT *n abbr of* **information technology.**

Italian [ɪˈtæljən] ◇ *adj* italien(ienne). ◇ *n* **-1.** [person] **Italien** *m*, **-ienne** *f.* **-2.** [language] **italien** *m.*

italic [ɪˈtælɪk] *adj* italique.
◆ **italics** *npl* italiques *fpl.*

Italy [ˈɪtəlɪ] *n* Italie *f*; **in ~** en Italie.

itch [ɪtʃ] ◇ *n* démangeaison *f.* ◇ *vi* **-1.** [be itchy]: **my arm ~es** mon bras me démange. **-2.** *fig* [be impatient]: **to be ~ing to do sthg** mourir d'envie de faire qqch.

itchy [ˈɪtʃɪ] (*compar* **-ier**, *superl* **-iest**) *adj* qui démange.

it'd [ˈɪtəd] = **it would, it had.**

item [ˈaɪtəm] *n* **-1.** [gen] **chose** *f*, **article** *m*; [on agenda] **question** *f*, **point** *m.* **-2.** PRESS **article** *m.*

itemize, -ise [ˈaɪtəmaɪz] *vt* détailler.

itemized bill [ˈaɪtəmaɪzd-] *n* facture *f* détaillée.

itinerant [ɪˈtɪnərənt] *adj* [salesperson] **ambulant(e)**; [preacher] **itinérant(e)**.

itinerary [aɪˈtɪnərərɪ] (*pl* **-ies**) *n* itinéraire *m.*

it'll [ɪtl] = **it will.**

ITN (*abbr of* **Independent Television News**) *n service britannique d'actualités télévisées pour les chaînes relevant de l'IBA.*

it's [ɪts] = **it is, it has.**

its [ɪts] *poss adj* son (sa), ses (*pl*).

itself [ɪtˈself] *pron* **-1.** (*reflexive*) **se**; (*after prep*) **soi. -2.** (*for emphasis*) **lui-même** (elle-même); **in ~** en soi.

ITV (*abbr of* **Independent Television**) *n sigle désignant les programmes diffusés par les chaînes relevant de l'IBA.*

IUCD (*abbr of* **intrauterine contraceptive device**) *n* stérilet *m.*

IUD (*abbr of* **intrauterine device**) *n* stérilet *m.*

I've [aɪv] = **I have.**

IVF *n* (*abbr of* **in vitro fertilization**) FVI *f.*

ivory [ˈaɪvərɪ] ◇ *adj* [ivory-coloured] **ivoire** (*inv*). ◇ *n* **ivoire** *m.* ◇ *comp* [made of ivory] **en ivoire, d'ivoire.**

Ivory Coast *n*: **the ~ la Côte-d'Ivoire**; **in the ~** en Côte-d'Ivoire.

ivory tower *n fig* tour *f* d'ivoire.

ivy [ˈaɪvɪ] *n* lierre *m.*

Ivy League *n Am* les huit grandes universités de l'est des États-Unis.

j (*pl* **j's** OR **js**), **J** (*pl* **J's** OR **Js**) [dʒeɪ] *n* [letter] **j** *m inv*, **J** *m inv.*

J/A *abbr of* **joint account.**

jab [dʒæb] (*pt & pp* **-bed**, *cont* **-bing**) ◇ *n* **-1.** *Br inf* [injection] **piqûre** *f.* **-2.** BOXING **direct** *m.* ◇ *vt*: **to ~ sthg into** planter OR enfoncer qqch dans. ◇ *vi*: **to ~ at** BOXING envoyer un direct à.

jabber [ˈdʒæbər] *vt & vi* baragouiner.

jack [dʒæk] *n* **-1.** [device] **cric** *m.* **-2.** [playing card] **valet** *m.*
◆ **jack in** *vt sep Br inf* laisser tomber, plaquer.
◆ **jack up** *vt sep* **-1.** [car] **soulever avec un cric. -2.** *fig* [prices] **faire grimper.**

jackal [ˈdʒækəl] *n* chacal *m.*

jacket [ˈdʒækɪt] *n* **-1.** [garment] **veste** *f.* **-2.**

[of potato] peau *f*, pelure *f*. **-3.** [of book] jaquette *f*. **-4.** *Am* [of record] pochette *f*.

jacket potato *n* pomme de terre *f* en robe de chambre.

jackhammer ['dʒækhæməʳ] *n Am* marteau-piqueur *m*.

jack-in-the-box *n* diable *m* qui sort de sa boîte.

jack knife *n* canif *m*.

◆ **jack-knife** *vi* [lorry] se mettre en travers de la route.

jack-of-all-trades (*pl* **jacks-of-all-trades**) *n* touche-à-tout *m*.

jack plug *n* fiche *f* de jack.

jackpot ['dʒækpɒt] *n* gros lot *m*.

Jacobean [,dʒækə'bɪən] *adj* de l'époque de Jacques Ier.

Jacobite ['dʒækəbaɪt] ◇ *adj* jacobite. ◇ *n* jacobite *mf*.

Jacuzzi® [dʒə'kuːzɪ] *n* Jacuzzi® *m*.

jade [dʒeɪd] ◇ *adj* [jade-coloured] vert (de) jade (*inv*). ◇ *n* **-1.** [stone] jade *m*. **-2.** [colour] vert *m* jade. ◇ *comp* [made of jade] de jade (*inv*).

jaded ['dʒeɪdɪd] *adj* blasé(e).

jagged ['dʒægɪd] *adj* déchiqueté(e), dentelé(e).

jaguar ['dʒægjʊəʳ] *n* jaguar *m*.

jail [dʒeɪl] ◇ *n* prison *f*. ◇ *vt* emprisonner, mettre en prison.

jailbird ['dʒeɪlbɜːd] *n inf* taulard *m*, -e *f*.

jailbreak ['dʒeɪlbreɪk] *n* évasion *f* de prison.

jailer ['dʒeɪləʳ] *n* geôlier *m*, -ière *f*.

Jakarta [dʒə'kɑːtə] *n* Djakarta, Jakarta.

jam [dʒæm] (*pt* & *pp* **-med**, *cont* **-ming**) ◇ *n* **-1.** [preserve] confiture *f*. **-2.** [of traffic] embouteillage *m*, bouchon *m*. **-3.** *inf* [difficult situation]: **to get into/be in a ~** se mettre/être dans le pétrin.
◇ *vt* **-1.** [mechanism, door] bloquer, coincer. **-2.** [push tightly]: **to ~ sthg into** entasser qqch dans: **to ~ sthg onto** enfoncer qqch sur. **-3.** [block - streets] embouteiller; [- switchboard] surcharger. **-4.** RADIO brouiller.
◇ *vi* [lever, door] se coincer; [brakes] se bloquer.

Jamaica [dʒə'meɪkə] *n* la Jamaïque *f*; **in ~** à la Jamaïque.

Jamaican [dʒə'meɪkn] ◇ *adj* jamaïcain(e), jamaïquain(e). ◇ *n* Jamaïcain *m*, -e *f*, Jamaïquain *m*, -e *f*.

jamb [dʒæm] *n* chambranle *m*, montant *m*.

jamboree [,dʒæmbə'riː] *n* **-1.** [celebration] fête *f*, festivités *fpl*. **-2.** [gathering of scouts] jamboree *m*.

jamming ['dʒæmɪŋ] *n* RADIO brouillage *m*.

jam-packed [-'pækt] *adj inf* plein(e) à craquer.

jam session *n* jam-session *f*.

Jan. ['dʒæn] (*abbr of* **January**) janv.

jangle ['dʒæŋgl] ◇ *n* [of keys] cliquetis *m*; [of bells] tintamarre *m*. ◇ *vt* [keys] faire cliqueter; [bells] faire retentir. ◇ *vi* [keys] cliqueter; [bells] retentir.

janitor ['dʒænɪtəʳ] *n Am* & *Scot* concierge *mf*.

January ['dʒænjʊərɪ] *n* janvier *m*; *see also* **September**.

Japan [dʒə'pæn] *n* Japon *m*; **in ~** au Japon.

Japanese [,dʒæpə'niːz] (*pl inv*) ◇ *adj* japonais(e). ◇ *n* [language] japonais *m*. ◇ *npl* [people]: **the ~** les Japonais *mpl*.

jape [dʒeɪp] *n dated* tour *m*, farce *f*.

jar [dʒɑːʳ] (*pt* & *pp* **-red**, *cont* **-ring**) ◇ *n* pot *m*. ◇ *vt* [shake] secouer. ◇ *vi* **-1.** [noise, voice]: **to ~ (on sb)** irriter (qqn), agacer (qqn). **-2.** [colours] jurer.

jargon ['dʒɑːgən] *n* jargon *m*.

jarring ['dʒɑːrɪŋ] *adj* [noise, colours] discordant(e).

Jas. (*abbr of* **James**) *Jacques*.

jasmine ['dʒæzmɪn] *n* jasmin *m*.

jaundice ['dʒɔːndɪs] *n* jaunisse *f*.

jaundiced [dʒɔːndɪst] *adj fig* [attitude, view] aigri(e).

jaunt [dʒɔːnt] *n* balade *f*.

jaunty ['dʒɔːntɪ] (*compar* **-ier**, *superl* **-iest**) *adj* désinvolte, insouciant(e).

Java ['dʒɑːvə] *n* Java; **in ~** à Java.

javelin ['dʒævlɪn] *n* javelot *m*.

jaw [dʒɔː] ◇ *n* mâchoire *f*. ◇ *vi inf* tailler une bavette.

jawbone ['dʒɔːbəʊn] *n* (os *m*) maxillaire *m*.

jay [dʒeɪ] *n* geai *m*.

jaywalk ['dʒeɪwɔːk] *vi* traverser en dehors des clous.

jaywalker ['dʒeɪwɔːkəʳ] *n* piéton *m* qui traverse en dehors des clous.

jazz [dʒæz] *n* **-1.** MUS jazz *m*. **-2.** *Am inf* [insincere talk] baratin *m*.

◆ **jazz up** *vt sep inf* égayer.

jazz band *n* orchestre *m* de jazz.

jazz singer *n* chanteur *m*, -euse *f* de jazz.

jazzy ['dʒæzɪ] (*compar* **-ier**, *superl* **-iest**) *adj* [bright] voyant(e).

JCR (*abbr of* **junior common room**) *n salle des étudiants*.

JCS *n abbr of* **Joint Chiefs of Staff**.

JD (*abbr of* **Justice Department**) *n ministère américain de la Justice*.

jealous ['dʒeləs] *adj* jaloux(ouse).

jealously ['dʒeləslı] *adv* jalousement.

jealousy ['dʒeləsı] *n* jalousie *f*.

jeans [dʒiːnz] *npl* jean *m*, blue-jean *m*.

Jedda ['dʒedə] *n* Djedda.

jeep [dʒiːp] *n* jeep *f*.

jeer [dʒɪəʳ] ◇ *vt* huer, conspuer. ◇ *vi*: **to ~ (at sb)** huer (qqn), conspuer (qqn).
✦ **jeers** *npl* huées *fpl*.

jeering ['dʒɪərɪŋ] *adj* moqueur(euse), railleur(euse).

Jehovah's Witness [dʒɪ'həʊvəz-] *n* témoin *m* de Jéhovah.

Jello® ['dʒeləʊ] *n Am* gelée *f*.

jelly ['dʒelı] (*pl* -ies) *n* gelée *f*.

jelly baby *n Br* bonbon à la gélatine en forme de bébé.

jelly bean *n* bonbon à la gélatine couvert de sucre.

jellyfish ['dʒelıfıʃ] (*pl inv* OR -es) *n* méduse *f*.

jelly roll *n Am* gâteau *m* roulé.

jemmy *Br* ['dʒemı], **jimmy** *Am* ['dʒımı] (*pl* -ies) *n* pince-monseigneur *f*.

jeopardize, -ise ['dʒepədaız] *vt* compromettre, mettre en danger.

jeopardy ['dʒepədı] *n*: **in ~** en péril OR danger, menacé(e).

jerk [dʒɜːk] ◇ *n* -1. [movement] secousse *f*, saccade *f*. -2. *v inf* [fool] abruti *m*, -e *f*. ◇ *vt*: **he ~ed his head round** il tourna la tête brusquement; **he ~ed the door open** il ouvrit la porte d'un coup sec. ◇ *vi* [person] sursauter; [vehicle] cahoter.

jerkily ['dʒɜːkılı] *adv* par à-coups, par saccades.

jerkin ['dʒɜːkın] *n* blouson *m*.

jerky ['dʒɜːkı] (*compar* -ier, *superl* -iest) *adj* saccadé(e).

jerry-built ['dʒerı-] *adj* construit(e) à la va-vite.

jersey ['dʒɜːzı] (*pl* jerseys) *n* -1. [sweater] pull *m*. -2. [cloth] jersey *m*.

Jersey ['dʒɜːzı] *n* Jersey *f*; **in ~** à Jersey.

Jerusalem [dʒə'ruːsələm] *n* Jérusalem.

jest [dʒest] *n* plaisanterie *f*; **in ~** pour rire.

jester ['dʒestəʳ] *n* bouffon *m*.

Jesuit ['dʒezjʊıt] ◇ *adj* jésuite. ◇ *n* jésuite *m*.

Jesus (Christ) ['dʒiːzəs-] *n* Jésus *m*, Jésus-Christ *m*.

jet [dʒet] (*pt* & *pp* -ted, *cont* -ting) ◇ *n* -1. [plane] jet *m*, avion *m* à réaction. -2. [of fluid] jet *m*. -3. [nozzle, outlet] ajutage *m*. ◇ *vi* [travel by jet] voyager en jet OR en avion.

jet-black *adj* noir(e) comme (du) jais.

jet engine *n* moteur *m* à réaction.

jetfoil ['dʒetfɔıl] *n* hydro-glisseur *m*.

jet lag *n* fatigue *f* due au décalage horaire.

jet-propelled [-prə'peld] *adj* à réaction.

jetsam ['dʒetsəm] → **flotsam**.

jet set *n*: **the ~** la jet-set.

jettison ['dʒetısən] *vt* -1. [cargo] jeter, larguer. -2. *fig* [ideas] abandonner, renoncer à.

jetty ['dʒetı] (*pl* -ies) *n* jetée *f*.

Jew [dʒuː] *n* Juif *m*, -ive *f*.

jewel ['dʒuːəl] ◇ *n* bijou *m*; [in watch] rubis *m*. ◇ *comp* [box, chest] à bijoux.

jeweller *Br*, **jeweler** *Am* ['dʒuːələʳ] *n* bijoutier *m*; **~'s (shop)** bijouterie *f*.

jewellery *Br*, **jewelry** *Am* ['dʒuːəlrı] *n* (*U*) bijoux *mpl*.

Jewess ['dʒuːıs] *n* juive *f*.

Jewish ['dʒuːıʃ] *adj* juif(ive).

JFK (*abbr of* **John Fitzgerald Kennedy International Airport**) *n* aéroport de New York.

jib [dʒıb] (*pt* & *pp* -bed, *cont* -bing) ◇ *n* -1. [of crane] flèche *f*. -2. [sail] foc *m*. ◇ *vi*: **to ~ at rechigner à**.

jibe [dʒaıb] *n* sarcasme *m*, moquerie *f*.

Jidda ['dʒıdə] = **Jedda**.

jiffy ['dʒıfı] *n inf*: **in a ~** en un clin d'œil.

Jiffy bag® *n* enveloppe *f* matelassée.

jig [dʒıg] (*pt* & *pp* -ged, *cont* -ging) ◇ *n* gigue *f*. ◇ *vi* danser la gigue; **to ~ about** se trémousser.

jiggle ['dʒıgl] *vt* secouer.

jigsaw (puzzle) ['dʒıgsɔː-] *n* puzzle *m*.

jihad [dʒı'hɑːd] *n* djihad *m*.

jilt [dʒılt] *vt* laisser tomber.

jimmy *Am* = **jemmy**.

jingle ['dʒıŋgl] ◇ *n* -1. [sound] cliquetis *m*. -2. [song] jingle *m*, indicatif *m*. ◇ *vi* [bell] tinter; [coins, bracelets] cliqueter.

jingoism ['dʒıŋgəʊızm] *n* chauvinisme *m*.

jinx [dʒıŋks] *n* poisse *f*.

jinxed [dʒıŋkst] *adj* qui a la poisse.

jitters ['dʒıtəz] *npl inf*: **the ~** le trac.

jittery ['dʒıtərı] *adj inf* nerveux(euse).

jive [dʒaıv] ◇ *n* -1. [dance] rock *m*. -2. *Am inf* [glib talk] baratin *m*. ◇ *vi* danser le rock.

job [dʒɒb] *n* -1. [employment] emploi *m*, boulot *m inf*. -2. [task] travail *m*, tâche *f*; **to do a good ~** faire du bon travail; **to make a good ~ of sthg** faire bien OR réussir qqch; **it's not my ~ to ...** ce n'est pas à moi de .... -3. [difficult task]: **to have a ~ doing sthg** avoir du mal à faire qqch. -4. *inf* [plastic surgery]: **to have a nose ~** se faire refaire le nez. **-5.** *phr*: **that's just the** ~ *Br inf* c'est exactement OR tout à fait ce qu'il faut.

jobbing ['dʒɒbɪŋ] *adj Br* qui travaille à la tâche.

job centre *n Br* agence *f* pour l'emploi.

job creation scheme *n* plan *m* de création d'emplois.

job description *n* profil *m* du poste.

jobless ['dʒɒblɪs] ◇ *adj* au chômage. ◇ *npl*: **the** ~ les chômeurs *mpl*.

job lot *n* lot *m* de marchandises.

job satisfaction *n* satisfaction *f* dans le travail.

job security *n* sécurité *f* de l'emploi.

jobsharing ['dʒɒbʃeərɪŋ] *n* partage *m* de l'emploi.

Joburg, Jo'burg ['dʒəʊbɜːg] *n inf* Johannesburg.

jockey ['dʒɒkɪ] (*pl* **jockeys**) ◇ *n* jockey *m*. ◇ *vi*: **to** ~ **for position** manœuvrer pour devancer ses concurrents.

jockstrap ['dʒɒkstræp] *n* suspensoir *m*.

jocular ['dʒɒkjʊlər] *adj* **-1.** [cheerful] enjoué(e), jovial(e). **-2.** [funny] amusant(e).

jodhpurs ['dʒɒdpəz] *npl* jodhpurs *mpl*, culotte *f* de cheval.

Joe Public [dʒəʊ-] *n* l'homme *m* de la rue.

jog [dʒɒg] (*pt* & *pp* **-ged**, *cont* **-ging**) ◇ *n*: **to go for a** ~ faire du jogging. ◇ *vt* pousser; **to** ~ **sb's memory** rafraîchir la mémoire de qqn. ◇ *vi* faire du jogging, jogger.

jogger ['dʒɒgər] *n* joggeur *m*, -euse *f*.

jogging ['dʒɒgɪŋ] *n* jogging *m*.

joggle ['dʒɒgl] *vt* secouer.

Johannesburg [dʒə'hænɪsbɜːg] *n* Johannesburg.

john [dʒɒn] *n Am inf* petit coin *m*, cabinets *mpl*.

John Hancock [-'hænkɒk] *n Am inf* signature *f*.

join [dʒɔɪn] ◇ *n* raccord *m*, joint *m*. ◇ *vt* **-1.** [connect - gen] unir, joindre; [- towns etc] relier. **-2.** [get together with] rejoindre, retrouver. **-3.** [political party] devenir membre de; [club] s'inscrire à; [army] s'engager dans; **to** ~ **a queue** *Br*, **to** ~ **a line** *Am* prendre la queue. ◇ *vi* **-1.** [connect] se joindre. **-2.** [become a member - gen] devenir membre; [- of club] s'inscrire.
◆ **join in** ◇ *vt fus* prendre part à, participer à. ◇ *vi* participer.
◆ **join up** *vi* MIL s'engager dans l'armée.

joiner ['dʒɔɪnər] *n* menuisier *m*.

joinery ['dʒɔɪnərɪ] *n* menuiserie *f*.

joint [dʒɔɪnt] ◇ *adj* [effort] conjugué(e); [responsibility] collectif(ive). ◇ *n* **-1.** [gen & TECH] joint *m*. **-2.** ANAT articulation *f*. **-3.** *Br* [of meat] rôti *m*. **-4.** *inf* [place] bouge *m*. **-5.** *drugs sl* joint *m*.

joint account *n* compte *m* joint.

Joint Chiefs of Staff *npl*: **the** ~ l'organe consultatif du ministère américain de la Défense, composé des chefs d'état-major des trois armées.

jointed ['dʒɔɪntɪd] *adj* articulé(e).

jointly ['dʒɔɪntlɪ] *adv* conjointement.

joint ownership *n* copropriété *f*.

joint-stock company *n* société *f* anonyme par actions.

joint venture *n* joint-venture *m*.

joist [dʒɔɪst] *n* poutre *f*, solive *f*.

jojoba [hə'həʊbə] *n* jojoba *m*.

joke [dʒəʊk] ◇ *n* blague *f*, plaisanterie *f*; **he's just a** ~ il est un objet de risée; **to play a** ~ **on sb** faire une blague à qqn, jouer un tour à qqn; **it's gone beyond a** ~ ça commence à bien faire; **it's no** ~ *inf* [not easy] ce n'est pas de la tarte. ◇ *vi* plaisanter, blaguer; **to** ~ **about sthg** plaisanter sur qqch, se moquer de qqch.

joker ['dʒəʊkər] *n* **-1.** [person] blagueur *m*, blagueuse *f*. **-2.** [playing card] joker *m*.

jollity ['dʒɒlətɪ] *n* jovialité *f*, gaieté *f*.

jolly ['dʒɒlɪ] (*compar* **-ier**, *superl* **-iest**) ◇ *adj* [person] jovial(e), enjoué(e); [time, party] agréable. ◇ *adv Br inf* drôlement, rudement.

jolt [dʒəʊlt] ◇ *n* **-1.** [jerk] secousse *f*, soubresaut *m*. **-2.** [shock] choc *m*. ◇ *vt* secouer; **to** ~ **sb into doing sthg** inciter fortement qqn à faire qqch. ◇ *vi* cahoter.

Joneses ['dʒəʊnzɪz] *npl*: **to keep up with the** ~ essayer d'avoir le même standing que ses voisins.

Jordan ['dʒɔːdn] *n* Jordanie *f*; **in** ~ en Jordanie; **the (River)** ~ le Jourdain.

Jordanian [dʒɔː'deɪnjən] ◇ *adj* jordanien(ienne). ◇ *n* Jordanien *m*, -ienne *f*.

joss stick [dʒɒs-] *n* bâton *m* d'encens.

jostle ['dʒɒsl] ◇ *vt* bousculer. ◇ *vi* se bousculer.

jot [dʒɒt] (*pt* & *pp* **-ted**, *cont* **-ting**) *n* [of truth] grain *m*, brin *m*.
◆ **jot down** *vt sep* noter, prendre note de.

jotter ['dʒɒtər] *n* [notepad] bloc-notes *m*.

jottings ['dʒɒtɪŋz] *npl* notes *fpl*.

journal ['dʒɜːnl] *n* **-1.** [magazine] revue *f*. **-2.** [diary] journal *m*.

journalese [,dʒɜːnə'liːz] *n pej* jargon *m* journalistique.

journalism ['dʒɜːnəlɪzm] *n* journalisme *m*.

journalist ['dʒɜːnəlɪst] *n* journaliste *mf*.

journey ['dʒɜːnɪ] (*pl* **journeys**) *n* voyage *m*.

joust [dʒaʊst] *vi* jouter.

jovial ['dʒəʊvjəl] *adj* jovial(e).

jowls [dʒaʊlz] *npl* bajoues *fpl*.

joy [dʒɔɪ] *n* joie *f*.

joyful ['dʒɔɪfʊl] *adj* joyeux(euse).

joyfully ['dʒɔɪfʊlɪ] *adv* joyeusement, avec joie.

joyous ['dʒɔɪəs] *adj* joyeux(euse).

joyously ['dʒɔɪəslɪ] *adv* avec joie, joyeusement.

joyride ['dʒɔɪraɪd] (*pt* **-rode**, *pp* **-ridden**) *vi* faire une virée dans une voiture volée.

joyrider ['dʒɔɪraɪdə^r] *n personne qui vole une voiture pour aller faire une virée.*

joyrode ['dʒɔɪrəʊd] *pt* → **joyride**.

joystick ['dʒɔɪstɪk] *n* AERON manche *m* (à balai); COMPUT manette *f*.

JP *n abbr of* **Justice of the Peace**.

Jr. (*abbr of* **Junior**) Jr.

JTPA (*abbr of* **Job Training Partnership Act**) *n programme gouvernemental américain de formation.*

jubilant ['dʒuːbɪlənt] *adj* [person] débordant(e) de joie, qui jubile; [shout] de joie.

jubilation [,dʒuːbɪ'leɪʃn] *n* joie *f*, jubilation *f*.

jubilee ['dʒuːbɪliː] *n* jubilé *m*.

Judaism [dʒuː'deɪɪzm] *n* judaïsme *m*.

judder ['dʒʌdə^r] *vi Br* trembler violemment.

judge [dʒʌdʒ] ◇ *n* juge *m*. ◇ *vt* **-1.** [gen] juger. **-2.** [estimate] évaluer, juger. ◇ *vi* juger; **to ~ from** OR **by, judging from** OR **by** à en juger par.

judg(e)ment ['dʒʌdʒmənt] *n* jugement *m*; **to pass ~ (on)** JUR prononcer OR rendre un jugement (sur); *fig* [on person, situation] porter un jugement (sur); **to reserve ~** s'abstenir de donner son avis OR de porter un jugement; **against my better ~** sachant pertinemment que j'avais tort.

judg(e)mental [dʒʌdʒ'mentl] *adj pej* qui critique, qui porte des jugements.

judicial [dʒuː'dɪʃl] *adj* judiciaire.

judiciary [dʒuː'dɪʃərɪ] *n*: **the ~** la magistrature.

judicious [dʒuː'dɪʃəs] *adj* judicieux(ieuse).

judo ['dʒuːdəʊ] *n* judo *m*.

jug [dʒʌg] *n* pot *m*, pichet *m*.

juggernaut ['dʒʌgənɔːt] *n* poids *m* lourd.

juggle ['dʒʌgl] ◇ *vt lit* & *fig* jongler avec. ◇ *vi* jongler.

juggler ['dʒʌglə^r] *n* jongleur *m*, -euse *f*.

jugular (vein) ['dʒʌgjʊlə^r-] *n* (veine *f*) jugulaire *f*.

juice [dʒuːs] *n* jus *m*.
◆ **juices** *npl* [in stomach] sucs *mpl*.

juicy ['dʒuːsɪ] (*compar* **-ier**, *superl* **-iest**) *adj* **-1.** [fruit] juteux(euse). **-2.** *inf* [story] croustillant(e). **-3.** [role] séduisant(e), tentant(e).

jujitsu [dʒuː'dʒɪtsuː] *n* jiu-jitsu *m*.

jukebox ['dʒuːkbɒks] *n* juke-box *m*.

Jul. (*abbr of* **July**) juill.

July [dʒuː'laɪ] *n* juillet *m*; *see also* **September**.

jumble ['dʒʌmbl] ◇ *n* [mixture] mélange *m*, fatras *m*. ◇ *vt*: **to ~ (up)** mélanger, embrouiller.

jumble sale *n Br* vente *f* de charité (*où sont vendus des articles d'occasion*).

jumbo jet ['dʒʌmbəʊ-] *n* jumbo-jet *m*.

jumbo-sized *adj* géant(e), énorme.

jump [dʒʌmp] ◇ *n* **-1.** [leap] saut *m*, bond *m*. **-2.** [fence] obstacle *m*. **-3.** [rapid increase] flambée *f*, hausse *f* brutale. **-4.** *phr*: **to keep one ~ ahead of sb** avoir une longueur d'avance sur qqn.
◇ *vt* **-1.** [fence, stream etc] sauter, franchir d'un bond. **-2.** *inf* [attack] sauter sur, tomber sur. **-3.** *Am* [train, bus] prendre sans payer.
◇ *vi* **-1.** [gen] sauter, bondir; [in surprise] sursauter; **to ~ across sthg** traverser qqch d'un bond. **-2.** [increase rapidly] grimper en flèche, faire un bond.
◆ **jump at** *vt fus fig* sauter sur.

jumped-up ['dʒʌmpt-] *adj Br inf pej* prétentieux(ieuse).

jumper ['dʒʌmpə^r] *n* **-1.** *Br* [pullover] pull *m*. **-2.** *Am* [dress] robe *f* chasuble.

jump jet *n* avion *m* à décollage vertical.

jump leads *npl* câbles *mpl* de démarrage.

jump-start *vt*: **to ~ a car** faire démarrer une voiture en la poussant.

jumpsuit ['dʒʌmpsuːt] *n* combinaison-pantalon *f*.

jumpy ['dʒʌmpɪ] (*compar* **-ier**, *superl* **-iest**) *adj* nerveux(euse).

junction ['dʒʌŋkʃn] *n* [of roads] carrefour *m*; RAIL embranchement *m*.

junction box *n* ELEC boîte *f* d'accouplement.

juncture ['dʒʌŋktʃə^r] *n fml*: **at this ~** à ce moment même.

Jun. -1. *abbr of* **June. -2.** = **Junr.**

June [dʒuːn] *n* juin *m*; *see also* **September**.

jungle ['dʒʌŋgl] *n lit* & *fig* jungle *f*.

jungle gym *n* *Am* cage *f* d'écureuil.

junior ['dʒuːnjə⁻] ◇ *adj* **-1.** [gen] jeune. **-2.** *Am* [after name] junior. ◇ *n* **-1.** [in rank] subalterne *mf*. **-2.** [in age] cadet *m*, -ette *f*. **-3.** *Am* SCH ≃ élève *mf* de première; UNIV ≃ étudiant *m*, -e *f* de deuxième année.

junior college *n* *Am* établissement d'enseignement supérieur où l'on obtient un diplôme en deux ans.

junior doctor *n* interne *mf*.

junior high school *n* *Am* ≃ collège *m* d'enseignement secondaire.

junior minister *n* *Br* secrétaire *mf* d'État.

junior school *n* *Br* école *f* primaire.

juniper ['dʒuːnɪpə⁻] *n* genièvre *m*.

junk [dʒʌŋk] ◇ *n* [unwanted objects] bric-à-brac *m*. ◇ *vt* balancer, se débarrasser de.

junket ['dʒʌŋkɪt] *n* **-1.** [pudding] lait *m* caillé. **-2.** *inf pej* [trip] voyage *m* aux frais de la princesse.

junk food *n* (U) *pej* cochonneries *fpl*.

junkie ['dʒʌŋkɪ] *n* *drugs sl* drogué *m*, -e *f*.

junk mail *n* (U) *pej* prospectus *mpl* publicitaires envoyés par la poste.

junk shop *n* boutique *f* de brocanteur.

Junr (*abbr of Junior*) Jr.

junta [*Br* 'dʒʌntə, *Am* 'hʊntə] *n* junte *f*.

Jupiter ['dʒuːpɪtə⁻] *n* [planet] Jupiter *f*.

jurisdiction [,dʒʊərɪs'dɪkʃn] *n* juridiction *f*.

jurisprudence [,dʒʊərɪs'pruːdəns] *n* jurisprudence *f*.

juror ['dʒʊərə⁻] *n* juré *m*, -e *f*.

jury ['dʒʊərɪ] (*pl* **-ies**) *n* jury *m*.

jury box *n* banc *m* des jurés.

jury service *n* participation *f* à un jury.

just [dʒʌst] ◇ *adv* **-1.** [recently]: **he's** ~ **left** il vient de partir. **-2.** [at that moment]: **I was** ~ **about to go** j'allais juste partir, j'étais sur le point de partir; **I'm** ~ **going to do it now** je vais le faire tout de suite OR à l'instant; **she arrived** ~ **as I was leaving** elle est arrivée au moment même où je partais OR juste comme je partais. **-3.** [only, simply]: **it's** ~ **a rumour** ce n'est qu'une rumeur; ~ **add water** vous n'avez plus qu'à ajouter de l'eau; ~ **a minute** OR **moment** OR **second!** un (petit) instant! **-4.** [almost not] tout juste, à peine; **I only** ~ **missed the train** j'ai manqué le train de peu; **we have** ~ **enough time** on a juste assez de temps. **-5.** [for emphasis]: **the coast is** ~ **marvellous** la côte est vraiment magnifique; ~ **look at this mess!** non, mais regarde un peu ce désordre! **-6.** [exactly, precisely] tout à fait, exactement; **it's** ~ **what I need** c'est tout à fait ce qu'il me faut. **-7.** [in requests]: **could you**

~ **move over please?** pourriez-vous vous pousser un peu s'il vous plaît? ◇ *adj* juste, équitable.

◆ **just about** *adv* à peu près, plus ou moins.

◆ **just as** *adv* [in comparison] tout aussi; **you're** ~ **as clever as he is** tu es tout aussi intelligent que lui.

◆ **just now** *adv* **-1.** [a short time ago] il y a un moment, tout à l'heure. **-2.** [at this moment] en ce moment.

justice ['dʒʌstɪs] *n* **-1.** [gen] justice *f*. **-2.** [of claim, cause] bien-fondé *m*. **-3.** *phr*: **to do** ~ **to sthg** [job] faire bien qqch, faire qqch comme il faut; **to do** ~ **to a meal** faire honneur à un repas.

Justice of the Peace (*pl* **Justices of the Peace**) *n* juge *m* de paix.

justifiable ['dʒʌstɪfaɪəbl] *adj* justifiable, défendable.

justifiable homicide *n* homicide *m* par légitime défense.

justifiably ['dʒʌstɪfaɪəblɪ] *adv* à juste titre.

justification [,dʒʌstɪfɪ'keɪʃn] *n* justification *f*.

justify ['dʒʌstɪfaɪ] (*pt* & *pp* **-ied**) *vt* [give reasons for] justifier.

justly ['dʒʌstlɪ] *adv* [act] avec justice; [deserved] à juste titre.

justness ['dʒʌstnɪs] *n* bien-fondé *m*.

jut [dʒʌt] (*pt* & *pp* **-ted**, *cont* **-ting**) *vi*: **to** ~ (**out**) faire saillie, avancer.

jute [dʒuːt] *n* jute *m*.

juvenile ['dʒuːvənaɪl] ◇ *adj* **-1.** JUR mineur(e), juvénile. **-2.** [childish] puéril(e). ◇ *n* JUR mineur *m*, -e *f*.

juvenile court *n* tribunal *m* pour enfants.

juvenile delinquent *n* jeune délinquant *m*, -e *f*.

juxtapose [,dʒʌkstə'pəʊz] *vt* juxtaposer.

juxtaposition [,dʒʌkstəpə'zɪʃn] *n* juxtaposition *f*.

K

k (*pl* **k's** OR **ks**), **K** (*pl* **K's** OR **Ks**) [keɪ] *n* [letter] k *m inv*, K *m inv*.

◆ **K** **-1.** (*abbr of* **kilobyte**) Ko. **-2.** *abbr of* **Knight. -3.** (*abbr of* **thousand**) K.

Kabul ['kɑːbl] *n* Kaboul.

kaftan ['kæftæn] *n* cafetan *m*.

Kalahari Desert [ˌkælə'hɑːrɪ] *n*: **the ~** le (désert du) Kalahari.

kale [keɪl] *n* chou *m* frisé.

kaleidoscope [kə'laɪdəskəʊp] *n* kaléidoscope *m*.

kamikaze [ˌkæmɪ'kɑːzɪ] *n* kamikaze *m*.

Kampala [kæm'pɑːlə] *n* Kampala.

Kampuchea [ˌkæmpuː'tʃɪə] *n* Kampuchéa *m*; **in ~** au Kampuchéa.

Kampuchean [ˌkæmpuː'tʃɪən] ◇ *adj* cambodgien(ienne). ◇ *n* Cambodgien *m*, -ienne *f*.

kangaroo [ˌkæŋgə'ruː] *n* kangourou *m*.

Kansas ['kænzəs] *n* Kansas *m*; **in ~** dans le Kansas.

kaolin ['keɪəlɪn] *n* kaolin *m*.

kaput [kə'pʊt] *adj inf* fichu(e), foutu(e).

karat ['kærət] *n Am* carat *m*.

karate [kə'rɑːtɪ] *n* karaté *m*.

Kashmir [kæʃ'mɪəʳ] *n* Cachemire *m*; **in ~** au Cachemire.

Katar [kæ'tɑːʳ] = **Qatar**.

Katmandu [ˌkætmæn'duː] *n* Katmandou, Katmandu.

kayak ['kaɪæk] *n* kayak *m*.

Kazakhstan [ˌkæzæk'stɑːn] *n* Kazakhstan *m*; **in ~** au Kazakhstan.

KB (*abbr of* **kilobyte(s)**) *n* COMPUT ko *m*, Ko *m*.

KC (*abbr of* **King's Counsel**) *n* ≃ bâtonnier *m* de l'ordre.

kcal (*abbr of* **kilocalorie**) Kcal.

kd (*abbr of* **knocked down**) *livré en kit, à monter soi-même*.

kebab [kɪ'bæb] *n* brochette *f*.

kedgeree [ˌkedʒə'riː] *n Br plat de riz, poisson et œufs durs mélangés*.

keel [kiːl] *n* quille *f*; **on an even ~** stable.

◆ **keel over** *vi* [ship] chavirer; [person] tomber dans les pommes.

keen [kiːn] *adj* **-1.** [enthusiastic] enthousiaste, passionné(e); **to be ~ on sthg** avoir la passion de qqch; **he's ~ on her** elle lui plaît; **to be ~ to do** OR **on doing sthg** tenir à faire qqch. **-2.** [interest, desire, mind] vif (vive); [competition] âpre, acharné(e). **-3.** [sense of smell] fin(e); [eyesight] perçant(e).

keenly ['kiːnlɪ] *adv* **-1.** [contested, interested] vivement. **-2.** [listen, watch] attentivement.

keenness ['kiːnnɪs] *n* **-1.** [enthusiasm] enthousiasme *m*. **-2.** [of competition] intensité *f*. **-3.** [of eyesight] acuité *f*; [of hearing] finesse *f*.

keep [kiːp] (*pt* & *pp* **kept**) ◇ *vt* **-1.** [retain, store] garder; **~ the change!** gardez la monnaie!; **to ~ sthg warm** garder OR tenir qqch au chaud. **-2.** [prevent]: **to keep sb/sthg from doing sthg** empêcher qqn/qqch de faire qqch. **-3.** [detain] retenir; [prisoner] détenir; **I don't want to ~ you** je ne voudrais pas vous retenir; **what kept you?** qu'est-ce qui t'a retardé?; **to ~ sb waiting** faire attendre qqn. **-4.** [promise] tenir; [appointment] aller à; [vow] être fidèle à. **-5.** [not disclose]: **to ~ sthg from sb** cacher qqch à qqn; **to ~ sthg to o.s.** garder qqch pour soi. **-6.** [diary, record, notes] tenir. **-7.** [own - sheep, pigs etc] élever; [- shop] tenir; [- car] avoir, posséder. **-8.** *phr*: **they ~ themselves to themselves** ils restent entre eux, ils se tiennent à l'écart.
◇ *vi* **-1.** [remain]: **to ~ warm** se tenir au chaud; **to ~ quiet** garder le silence; **~ quiet!** taisez-vous! **-2.** [continue]: **he ~s interrupting me** il n'arrête pas de m'interrompre; **to ~ talking/walking** continuer à parler/à marcher. **-3.** [continue moving]: **to ~ left/right** garder sa gauche/sa droite; **to ~ north/south** continuer vers le nord/le sud. **-4.** [food] se conserver. **-5.** *Br* [in health]: **how are you ~ing?** comment allez-vous?; **she's ~ing well** elle va bien.
◇ *n*: **to earn one's ~** gagner sa vie.

◆ **keeps** *n*: **for ~s** pour toujours.

◆ **keep at** *vt fus*: **to ~ at it** [work hard] travailler d'arrache-pied.

◆ **keep back** *vt sep* [information] cacher, ne pas divulguer; [money] retenir.

◆ **keep down** *vt sep* [prices] empêcher de monter; [numbers, costs] restreindre, limiter.

◆ **keep off** *vt fus*: "**~ off the grass**" «(il est) interdit de marcher sur la pelouse».

◆ **keep on** *vi* **-1.** [continue]: **to ~ on (doing sthg)** [without stopping] continuer (de OR à faire qqch); [repeatedly] ne pas arrêter (de faire qqch). **-2.** [talk incessantly]: **to ~ on** (about sthg) ne pas arrêter de parler (de qqch).

◆ **keep on at** *vt fus Br* harceler.

◆ **keep out** ◇ *vt sep* empêcher d'entrer. ◇ *vi:* "~ out» «défense d'entrer».

◆ **keep to** ◇ *vt fus* [rules, deadline] respecter, observer. ◇ *vt sep* [limit]: **we must ~ spending to a minimum** il faut limiter les dépenses au minimum.

◆ **keep up** ◇ *vt sep* [continue to do] continuer; [maintain] maintenir; **to ~ up appearances** sauver les apparences. ◇ *vi* **-1.** [maintain pace, level etc]: **to ~ up (with sb)** aller aussi vite (que qqn); **to ~ up with the news** suivre l'actualité. **-2.** [remain in contact]: **to ~ up with sb** rester en contact avec qqn.

keeper ['ki:pə'] *n* gardien *m*, -ienne *f*.

keep-fit *Br* ◇ *n* (*U*) gymnastique *f*. ◇ *comp* de gymnastique.

keeping ['ki:pɪŋ] *n* **-1.** [care] garde *f*. **-2.** [conformity, harmony]: **to be in/out of ~ with** [rules etc] être/ne pas être conforme à; [subj: clothes, furniture] aller/ne pas aller avec.

keepsake ['ki:pseɪk] *n* souvenir *m*.

keg [keg] *n* tonnelet *m*, baril *m*.

kelp [kelp] *n* varech *m*.

ken [ken] *n*: **it's beyond my ~** ça dépasse mes compétences.

kennel ['kenl] *n* **-1.** [shelter for dog] niche *f*. **-2.** *Am* = **kennels**.

◆ **kennels** *npl Br* chenil *m*.

Kentucky [ken'tʌkɪ] *n* Kentucky *m*; **in ~** dans le Kentucky.

Kenya ['kenjə] *n* Kenya *m*; **in ~** au Kenya.

Kenyan ['kenjən] ◇ *adj* kenyan(e). ◇ *n* Kenyan *m*, -e *f*.

kept [kept] *pt & pp* → **keep**.

kerb [kɜ:b] *n Br* bordure *f* du trottoir.

kerb crawler [-ˌkrɔ:lə'] *n Br* homme en voiture qui accoste les prostituées.

kerbstone ['kɜ:bstəʊn] *n Br* pierre *f* de bordure de trottoir.

kerfuffle [kə'fʌfl] *n Br inf*: **what a ~!** quelle histoire!

kernel ['kɜ:nl] *n* amande *f*.

kerosene ['kerəsi:n] *n* kérosène *m*.

kestrel ['kestrəl] *n* crécerelle *f*.

ketch [ketʃ] *n* ketch *m*.

ketchup ['ketʃəp] *n* ketchup *m*.

kettle ['ketl] *n* bouilloire *f*.

kettledrum ['ketldrʌm] *n* timbale *f*.

key [ki:] ◇ *n* **-1.** [gen & MUS] clef *f*, clé *f*; **the ~ (to sthg)** *fig* la clé (de qqch). **-2.** [of typewriter, computer, piano] touche *f*. **-3.** [of map] légende *f*. ◇ *adj* clé (*after n*).

◆ **key in** *vt sep* [data] saisir.

keyboard ['ki:bɔ:d] ◇ *n* [gen & COMPUT] clavier *m*. ◇ *vt* COMPUT [text, data] saisir.

keyboarder ['ki:bɔ:də'] *n* COMPUT claviste *mf*.

keyed up [ki:d-] *adj* tendu(e), énervé(e).

keyhole ['ki:həʊl] *n* trou *m* de serrure.

keynote ['ki:nəʊt] ◇ *n* note *f* dominante. ◇ *comp*: **~ speech** discours-programme *m*.

keypad ['ki:pæd] *n* COMPUT pavé *m* numérique.

keypunch ['ki:pʌntʃ] *n Am* perforatrice *f* à clavier.

key ring *n* porte-clés *m inv*.

keystone ['ki:stəʊn] *n lit & fig* clef *f* de voûte.

keystroke ['ki:strəʊk] *n* COMPUT frappe *f* d'une touche.

kg (*abbr of* **kilogram**) kg.

KGB *n* KGB *m*.

khaki ['kɑ:kɪ] ◇ *adj* kaki (*inv*). ◇ *n* **-1.** [colour] kaki *m*. **-2.** [cloth] toile *f* kaki.

Khmer [kmeə'] ◇ *adj* khmer (khmère). ◇ *n* **-1.** [person] Khmer *m*, -ère *f*; **~ Rouge** Khmer rouge. **-2.** [language] khmer *m*.

kibbutz [kɪ'buts] (*pl* **kibbutzim** [kɪbu'tsi:m] OR **-es**) *n* kibboutz *m*.

kick [kɪk] ◇ *n* **-1.** [with foot] coup *m* de pied. **-2.** *inf* [excitement]: **to get a ~ from sthg** trouver qqch excitant; **to do sthg for ~s** faire qqch pour le plaisir.

◇ *vt* **-1.** [with foot] donner un coup de pied à; **to ~ o.s.** *fig* se donner des gifles OR des claques. **-2.** *inf* [give up]: **to ~ the habit** arrêter.

◇ *vi* [person - repeatedly] donner des coups de pied; [- once] donner un coup de pied; [baby] gigoter; [animal] ruer.

◆ **kick about**, **kick around** *vi Br inf* traîner.

◆ **kick off** *vi* **-1.** FTBL donner le coup d'envoi. **-2.** *inf fig* [start] démarrer.

◆ **kick out** *vt sep inf* vider, jeter dehors.

◆ **kick up** *vt fus inf*: **to ~ up a fuss/row** faire toute une histoire.

kickoff ['kɪkɒf] *n* engagement *m*.

kick-start *vt* faire démarrer à l'aide du pied OR au kick.

kid [kɪd] (*pt & pp* **-ded**, *cont* **-ding**) ◇ *n* **-1.** *inf* [child] gosse *mf*, gamin *m*, -e *f*. **-2.** *inf* [young person] petit jeune *m*, petite jeune *f*. **-3.** [goat, leather] chevreau *m*. ◇ *comp inf* [brother, sister] petit(e). ◇ *vt inf* **-1.** [tease] faire marcher. **-2.** [delude]: **to ~ o.s.** se faire des illusions. ◇ *vi inf*: **to be kidding** plaisanter; **no kidding!** sans blague!

kiddie, kiddy ['kɪdɪ] (*pl* **-ies**) *n inf* gosse *mf*, gamin *m*, -e *f*.

kid gloves *npl*: **to treat** OR **handle sb with ~** prendre des gants avec qqn.

kidnap ['kɪdnæp] (*Br pt* & *pp* **-ped**, *cont* **-ping**, *Am pt* & *pp* **-ed**, *cont* **-ing**) *vt* kidnapper, enlever.

kidnapper *Br*, **kidnaper** *Am* ['kɪdnæpər] *n* kidnappeur *m*, -euse *f*, ravisseur *m*, -euse *f*.

kidnapping *Br*, **kidnaping** *Am* ['kɪdnæpɪŋ] *n* enlèvement *m*.

kidney ['kɪdnɪ] (*pl* **kidneys**) *n* **-1.** ANAT rein *m*. **-2.** CULIN rognon *m*.

kidney bean *n* haricot *m* rouge.

kidney machine *n* rein *m* artificiel.

Kilimanjaro [ˌkɪlɪmən'dʒɑːrəʊ] *n* Kilimandjaro *m*.

kill [kɪl] ◇ *vt* **-1.** [cause death of] tuer; **my feet are killing me** *fig* j'ai horriblement mal aux pieds; **to ~ time** tuer le temps. **-2.** *fig* [hope, chances] mettre fin à; [pain] supprimer. ◇ *vi* tuer. ◇ *n* mise *f* à mort.

◆ **kill off** *vt sep* **-1.** [species, animal] exterminer. **-2.** *fig* [hope, chances] mettre fin à.

killer ['kɪlər] *n* [person] meurtrier *m*, -ière *f*; [animal] tueur *m*, -euse *f*.

killer whale *n* épaulard *m*, orque *f*.

killing ['kɪlɪŋ] ◇ *adj inf* [very funny] tordant(e). ◇ *n* meurtre *m*; **to make a ~** *inf* faire une bonne affaire, réussir un beau coup.

killjoy ['kɪldʒɔɪ] *n* rabat-joie *m inv*.

kiln [kɪln] *n* four *m*.

kilo ['kiːləʊ] (*pl* **-s**) (*abbr of* **kilogram**) *n* kilo *m*.

kilo- ['kɪlə] *prefix* kilo-.

kilobyte ['kɪləbaɪt] *n* COMPUT kilo-octet *m*.

kilocalorie ['kɪləˌkælərɪ] *n* kilocalorie *f*.

kilogram(me) ['kɪləgræm] *n* kilogramme *m*.

kilohertz ['kɪləhɜːtz] (*pl inv*) *n* kilohertz *m*.

kilojoule ['kɪlədʒuːl] *n* kilojoule *m*.

kilometre *Br* ['kɪləˌmiːtər], **kilometer** *Am* [kɪ'lɒmɪtər] *n* kilomètre *m*.

kilowatt ['kɪləwɒt] *n* kilowatt *m*.

kilt [kɪlt] *n* kilt *m*.

kimono [kɪ'məʊnəʊ] (*pl* **-s**) *n* kimono *m*.

kin [kɪn] *n* → **kith**.

kind [kaɪnd] ◇ *adj* gentil(ille), aimable; **would you be so ~ as to ...?** voulez-vous avoir la gentillesse OR l'amabilité de ...? ◇ *n* genre *m*, sorte *f*; **an agreement of a ~** une sorte d'accord; **they're two of a ~** ils se ressemblent; **in ~** [payment] en nature; **a**

~ of une espèce de, une sorte de; **~ of** *Am inf* un peu.

kindergarten ['kɪndəˌgɑːtn] *n* jardin *m* d'enfants.

kind-hearted [-'hɑːtɪd] *adj* qui a bon cœur, bon (bonne).

kindle ['kɪndl] *vt* **-1.** [fire] allumer. **-2.** *fig* [feeling] susciter.

kindling ['kɪndlɪŋ] *n* (*U*) petit bois *m*.

kindly ['kaɪndlɪ] (*compar* **-ier**, *superl* **-iest**) ◇ *adj* **-1.** [person] plein(e) de bonté, bienveillant(e). **-2.** [gesture] plein(e) de gentillesse. ◇ *adv* **-1.** [speak, smile etc] avec gentillesse; **to look ~ on** *fig* être favorable à. **-2.** [please]: **~ leave the room!** veuillez sortir, s'il vous plaît!; **will you ~ ...?** veuillez ..., je vous prie de .... **-3.** *phr*: **not to take ~ to sthg** mal prendre qqch.

kindness ['kaɪndnɪs] *n* gentillesse *f*.

kindred ['kɪndrɪd] *adj* [similar] semblable, similaire; **~ spirit** âme *f* sœur.

kinetic [kɪ'netɪk] *adj* cinétique.

kinfolk(s) ['kɪnfəʊk(s)] *Am* = **kinsfolk**.

king [kɪŋ] *n* roi *m*.

kingdom ['kɪŋdəm] *n* **-1.** [country] royaume *m*. **-2.** [of animals, plants] règne *m*.

kingfisher ['kɪŋˌfɪʃər] *n* martin-pêcheur *m*.

kingpin ['kɪŋpɪn] *n* **-1.** AUT pivot *m* de l'essieu avant. **-2.** *fig* [person] pilier *m*, cheville *f* ouvrière.

king-size(d) *adj* [cigarette] long (longue); [pack] géant(e); **a ~ bed** un grand lit (*de 195cm*).

kink [kɪŋk] *n* [in rope] entortillement *m*.

kinky ['kɪŋkɪ] (*compar* **-ier**, *superl* **-iest**) *adj inf* vicieux(ieuse).

kinsfolk ['kɪnzfəʊk] *npl* famille *f*.

kinship ['kɪnʃɪp] *n* (*U*) **-1.** [family relationship] parenté *f*. **-2.** [closeness] affinités *fpl*.

kiosk ['kiːɒsk] *n* **-1.** [small shop] kiosque *m*. **-2.** *Br* [telephone box] cabine *f* (téléphonique).

kip [kɪp] (*pt* & *pp* **-ped**, *cont* **-ping**) *Br inf*. ◇ *n* somme *m*, roupillon *m*. ◇ *vi* faire OR piquer un petit somme.

kipper ['kɪpər] *n* hareng *m* fumé OR saur.

Kirk [kɜːk] *n* *Scot*: **the ~** l'Église *f* (presbytérienne) d'Écosse.

kirsch [kɪəʃ] *n* kirsch *m*.

kiss [kɪs] ◇ *n* baiser *m*; **to give sb a ~** embrasser qqn, donner un baiser à qqn. ◇ *vt* embrasser; **to ~ sb's cheek** embrasser qqn sur la joue; **to ~ sb goodbye** dire au revoir à qqn en l'embrassant. ◇ *vi* s'embrasser.

kissagram ['kɪsəgræm] *n* service de «télégramme parlé» comprenant un baiser, à l'occasion d'un anniversaire, par exemple.

kiss curl *n Br* accroche-cœur *m*.

kiss of life *n*: the ~ le bouche-à-bouche.

kit [kɪt] (*pt* & *pp* **-ted**, *cont* **-ting**) *n* **-1.** [set] trousse *f*. **-2.** *Br* (*U*) SPORT affaires *fpl*, équipement *m*. **-3.** [to be assembled] kit *m*.
◆ **kit out** *vt sep Br* équiper.

kit bag *n* sac *m* de marin.

kitchen ['kɪtʃɪn] *n* cuisine *f*.

kitchenette [ˌkɪtʃɪ'net] *n* kitchenette *f*.

kitchen garden *n* (jardin *m*) potager *m*.

kitchen sink *n* évier *m*.

kitchen unit *n* élément *m* de cuisine.

kitchenware ['kɪtʃɪnweəʳ] *n* (*U*) ustensiles *mpl* de cuisine.

kite [kaɪt] *n* **-1.** [toy] cerf-volant *m*. **-2.** [bird] milan *m*.

Kite mark *n Br* ≃ NF (*conforme aux normes françaises de sécurité*).

kith [kɪθ] *n*: ~ and kin parents et amis *mpl*.

kitsch [kɪtʃ] *n* kitsch *m inv*.

kitten ['kɪtn] *n* chaton *m*.

kitty ['kɪtɪ] (*pl* **-ies**) *n* [shared fund] cagnotte *f*.

kiwi ['kiːwiː] *n* **-1.** [bird] kiwi *m*, aptéryx *m*. **-2.** *inf* [New Zealander] Néo-Zélandais *m*, -e *f*.

kiwi fruit *n* kiwi *m*.

KKK *abbr of* **Ku Klux Klan**.

klaxon ['klæksn] *n* sirène *f*.

Kleenex® ['kliːneks] *n* Kleenex® *m*.

kleptomaniac [ˌkleptə'meɪnɪæk] *n* kleptomane *mf*.

km (*abbr of* **kilometre**) km.

km/h (*abbr of* **kilometres per hour**) km/h.

knack [næk] *n*: to have a OR the ~ (for doing sthg) avoir le coup (pour faire qqch).

knacker ['nækəʳ] *Br* ◇ *n* [horse slaughterer] équarrisseur *m*. ◇ *vt v inf* épuiser.

knackered ['nækəd] *adj Br v inf* crevé(e), claqué(e).

knapsack ['næpsæk] *n* sac *m* à dos.

knave [neɪv] *n* [in cards] valet *m*.

knead [niːd] *vt* pétrir.

knee [niː] *n* genou *m*; to be on one's ~s être à genoux; *fig* être sur les genoux; to bring sb to their ~s *fig* faire capituler qqn.

kneecap ['niːkæp] *n* rotule *f*.

knee-deep *adj*: we were ~ in snow/water la neige/l'eau nous arrivait jusqu'aux genoux.

knee-high *adj* à hauteur de genou.

kneel [niːl] (*Br pt* & *pp* **knelt**, *Am pt* & *pp* **knelt** OR **-ed**) se mettre à genoux, s'agenouiller.
◆ **kneel down** *vi* se mettre à genoux, s'agenouiller.

knee-length *adj* [skirt] qui arrive aux genoux; [boots] qui montent jusqu'aux genoux.

knees-up *n Br inf* fête *f*.

knell [nel] *n* glas *m*.

knelt [nelt] *pt* & *pp* → **kneel**.

knew [njuː] *pt* → **know**.

knickers ['nɪkəz] *npl* **-1.** *Br* [underwear] culotte *f*. **-2.** *Am* [knickerbockers] pantalon *m* de golf.

knick-knack ['nɪknæk] *n* babiole *f*, bibelot *m*.

knife [naɪf] (*pl* **knives**) ◇ *n* couteau *m*. ◇ *vt* donner un coup de couteau à, poignarder.

knifing ['naɪfɪŋ] *n* bagarre *f* au couteau.

knight [naɪt] ◇ *n* **-1.** [in history, member of nobility] chevalier *m*. **-2.** [in chess] cavalier *m*. ◇ *vt* faire chevalier.

knighthood ['naɪthʊd] *n* titre *m* de chevalier.

knit [nɪt] (*pt* & *pp* **knit** OR **-ted**, *cont* **-ting**) ◇ *adj*: **closely** OR **tightly** ~ *fig* très uni(e). ◇ *vt* tricoter. ◇ *vi* **-1.** [with wool] tricoter. **-2.** [broken bones] se souder.

knitted ['nɪtɪd] *adj* tricoté(e).

knitting ['nɪtɪŋ] *n* (*U*) tricot *m*.

knitting machine *n* machine *f* à tricoter.

knitting needle *n* aiguille *f* à tricoter.

knitting pattern *n* modèle *m* (de tricot).

knitwear ['nɪtweəʳ] *n* (*U*) tricots *mpl*.

knives [naɪvz] *pl* → **knife**.

knob [nɒb] *n* **-1.** [on door] poignée *f*, bouton *m*; [on drawer] poignée; [on bedstead] pomme *f*. **-2.** [on TV, radio etc] bouton *m*.

knobbly *Br* ['nɒblɪ] (*compar* **-ier**, *superl* **-iest**), **knobby** *Am* ['nɒbɪ] (*compar* **-ier**, *superl* **-iest**) *adj* noueux(euse).

knock [nɒk] ◇ *n* **-1.** [hit] coup *m*. **-2.** *inf* [piece of bad luck] coup *m* dur. ◇ *vt* **-1.** [hit] frapper, cogner; to ~ a hole in a wall faire un trou dans un mur; to ~ a nail into a wall enfoncer un clou dans un mur; to ~ sb/sthg over renverser qqn/qqch. **-2.** *inf* [criticize] critiquer, dire du mal de. ◇ *vi* **-1.** [on door]: to ~ (at OR on) frapper (à). **-2.** [car engine] cogner, avoir des ratés.
◆ **knock about**, **knock around** *inf* ◇ *vt sep* tabasser. ◇ *vi* **-1.** [travel] bourlinguer. **-2.** [spend time]: to ~ about with sb fréquenter qqn.
◆ **knock back** *vt sep inf* [drink] s'enfiler.

◆ **knock down** *vt sep* **-1.** [subj: car, driver] renverser. **-2.** [building] démolir. **-3.** [price] (faire) baisser.

◆ **knock off** ◇ *vt sep* **-1.** [money]: to ~ £5 off faire un rabais de 5 livres. **-2.** *Br inf* [steal] chiper, piquer. ◇ *vi inf* [stop working] finir son travail OR sa journée.

◆ **knock out** *vt sep* **-1.** [make unconscious] assommer. **-2.** [from competition] éliminer.

◆ **knock up** ◇ *vt sep* [meal, report] préparer OR faire en vitesse; [structure] construire à la va-vite. ◇ *vi* TENNIS faire des balles.

knocker ['nɒkəʳ] *n* [on door] heurtoir *m*.

knocking ['nɒkɪŋ] *n* (*U*) **-1.** [on door etc] coups *mpl*. **-2.** *inf* [criticism] critique *f*, critiques *fpl*.

knock-kneed [-niːd] *adj* cagneux(euse), qui a les genoux cagneux.

knock-on effect *n Br* réaction *f* en chaîne.

knockout ['nɒkaʊt] *n* knock-out *m*, K.-O. *m*.

knockout competition *n Br* compétition *f* avec éliminatoires.

knock-up *n* TENNIS: to have a ~ faire des balles.

knot [nɒt] (*pt & pp* -ted, *cont* -ting) ◇ *n* **-1.** [gen] nœud *m*; to tie/untie a ~ faire/défaire un nœud. **-2.** [of people] petit attroupement *m*. ◇ *vt* nouer, faire un nœud à.

knotted ['nɒtɪd] *adj* noué(e).

knotty ['nɒtɪ] (*compar* -ier, *superl* -iest) *adj fig* épineux(euse).

know [nəʊ] (*pt* knew, *pp* known) ◇ *vt* **-1.** [gen] savoir; [language] savoir parler; to ~ (that) ... savoir que ...; to let sb ~ (about sthg) faire savoir (qqch) à qqn, informer qqn (de qqch); to ~ how to do sthg savoir faire qqch; to get to ~ sthg apprendre qqch. **-2.** [person, place] connaître; to get to ~ sb apprendre à mieux connaître qqn. ◇ *vi* savoir; to ~ of sthg connaître qqch; to ~ about [be aware of] être au courant de; [be expert in] s'y connaître en; God OR Heaven ~s! Dieu seul le sait!; he ought to have known better il aurait dû réfléchir. ◇ *n*: to be in the ~ être au courant.

know-all *n Br* (monsieur) je-sais-tout *m*, (madame) je-sais-tout *f*.

know-how *n* savoir-faire *m*, technique *f*.

knowing ['nəʊɪŋ] *adj* [smile, look] entendu(e).

knowingly ['nəʊɪŋlɪ] *adv* **-1.** [smile, look] d'un air entendu. **-2.** [intentionally] sciemment.

know-it-all = **know-all**.

knowledge ['nɒlɪdʒ] *n* (*U*) **-1.** [gen] connaissance *f*; it's common ~ that ... tout le monde sait que ...; without my ~ à mon insu; to my ~ à ma connaissance; to the best of my ~ à ma connaissance, autant que je sache. **-2.** [learning, understanding] savoir *m*, connaissances *fpl*.

knowledgeable ['nɒlɪdʒəbl] *adj* bien informé(e).

known [nəʊn] ◇ *pp* → **know**. ◇ *adj* connu(e).

knuckle ['nʌkl] *n* **-1.** ANAT articulation *f* OR jointure *f* du doigt. **-2.** [of meat] jarret *m*.

◆ **knuckle down** *vi* s'y mettre, se mettre au travail; to ~ down to sthg/to doing sthg se mettre sérieusement à qqch/a faire qqch.

◆ **knuckle under** *vi* céder, capituler.

knuckle-duster *n* coup-de-poing *m* américain.

KO (*abbr of* knock-out) *n* K.-O. *m*.

koala (bear) [kəʊ'ɑːlə-] *n* koala *m*.

kook [kuːk] *n Am inf* fou *m*, folle *f*, dingue *mf*.

kooky ['kuːkɪ] (*compar* -ier, *superl* -iest) *adj Am inf* fêlé(e), dingue.

Koran [kɒ'rɑːn] *n*: the ~ le Coran.

Korea [kə'rɪə] *n* Corée *f*; in ~ en Corée.

Korean [kə'rɪən] ◇ *adj* coréen(enne). ◇ *n* **-1.** [person] Coréen *m*, -enne *f*. **-2.** [language] coréen *m*.

kosher ['kəʊʃəʳ] *adj* **-1.** [meat] kasher (*inv*). **-2.** *inf* [reputable] O.K. (*inv*), réglo (*inv*).

Koweit = **Kuwait**.

kowtow [ˌkaʊ'taʊ] *vi*: to ~ (to sb) faire des courbettes (à OR devant qqn).

Krakow = **Cracow**.

Kremlin ['kremlɪn] *n*: the ~ le Kremlin.

KS *abbr of* **Kansas**.

KT *abbr of* **Knight**.

Kuala Lumpur [ˌkwɑːlə'lʊmˌpʊəʳ] *n* Kuala Lumpur.

kudos ['kjuːdɒs] *n* prestige *m*, gloire *f*.

Ku Klux Klan [ˌkuːklʌks'klæn] *n*: the ~ le Ku Klux Klan.

kumquat ['kʌmkwɒt] *n* kumquat *m*.

kung fu [ˌkʌŋ'fuː] *n* kung-fu *m*.

Kurd [kɜːd] *n* Kurde *mf*.

Kurdish ['kɜːdɪʃ] *adj* kurde.

Kurdistan [ˌkɜːdɪ'stɑːn] *n* Kurdistan *m*; in ~ au Kurdistan.

Kuwait [kʊ'weɪt], **Koweit** [kəʊ'weɪt] *n* **-1.** [country] Koweït *m*; in ~ au Koweït. **-2.** [city] Koweït City.

Kuwaiti [kʊ'weɪtɪ] ◇ *adj* koweïtien(ienne). ◇ *n* Koweïtien *m*, -ienne *f*.

kW (*abbr of* **kilowatt**) kW.

KY *abbr of* **Kentucky**.

l¹ (*pl* **l's** OR **ls**), **L** (*pl* **L's** OR **Ls**) [el] *n* [letter] l *m inv*, L *m inv*.

◆ **L -1.** *abbr of* **lake. -2.** *abbr of* **large. -3.** (*abbr of* **left**) g. **-4.** *abbr of* **learner.**

L:
En Grande-Bretagne, la lettre 'L' apposée sur l'arrière d'un véhicule indique que le conducteur n'a pas encore son permis mais qu'il est en conduite accompagnée

---

l² (*abbr of* **litre**) l.

la [lɑː] *n* MUS la *m*.

La *abbr of* **Louisiana.**

LA -1. *abbr of* **Los Angeles. -2.** *abbr of* **Louisiana.**

L.A. (*abbr of* **Los Angeles**) *n* Los Angeles.

lab [læb] *n inf* labo *m*.

label ['leɪbl] (*Br pt* & *pp* **-led**, *cont* **-ling**, *Am pt* & *pp* **-ed**, *cont* **-ing**) ◇ *n* **-1.** [identification] étiquette *f*. **-2.** [of record] label *m*, maison *f* de disques. ◇ *vt* **-1.** [fix label to] étiqueter. **-2.** [describe]: **to ~ sb (as)** cataloguer OR étiqueter qqn (comme).

labor *etc Am* = **labour** *etc*.

laboratory [*Br* lə'bɒrətrɪ, *Am* 'læbrə,tɔːrɪ] (*pl* **-ies**) ◇ *n* laboratoire *m*. ◇ *comp* de laboratoire.

Labor Day *n* fête du travail américaine (*premier lundi de septembre*).

laborious [lə'bɔːrɪəs] *adj* laborieux(ieuse).

labor union *n Am* syndicat *m*.

labour *Br*, **labor** *Am* ['leɪbər] ◇ *n* **-1.** [gen. & MED] travail *m*; **she went into ~** MED le travail a commencé. **-2.** [workers, work carried out] main d'œuvre *f*. ◇ *vt*: **there's no need to ~ the point** pas besoin de s'appesantir là-dessus. ◇ *vi* travailler dur; **to ~ at** OR **over** peiner sur; **to ~ under a delusion** se faire des illusions OR des idées; **to ~ under a misapprehension** être dans l'erreur.

◆ **Labour** POL ◇ *adj* travailliste. ◇ *n* (*U*) *Br* les travaillistes *mpl*.

labour camp *n* camp *m* de travaux forcés.

labour costs *npl* coûts *mpl* de la main-d'œuvre.

laboured *Br*, **labored** *Am* ['leɪbəd] *adj* [breathing] pénible; [style] lourd(e), laborieux(ieuse).

labourer *Br*, **laborer** *Am* ['leɪbərər] *n* travailleur manuel *m*, travailleuse manuelle *f*; [agricultural] ouvrier agricole *m*, ouvrière agricole *f*.

labour force *n* main-d'œuvre *f*.

labour-intensive *adj* à forte main d'œuvre.

labour market *n* marché *m* du travail.

labour of love *n* tâche *f* effectuée par plaisir.

labour pains *npl* douleurs *fpl* de l'accouchement.

Labour Party *n Br*: **the ~** le parti travailliste.

labour relations *npl* relations *fpl* entre employeurs et employés.

laboursaving *Br*, **laborsaving** *Am* ['leɪbə,seɪvɪŋ] *adj*: **~ device** appareil *m* ménager.

Labrador ['læbrədɔːr] *n* **-1.** [dog] labrador *m*. **-2.** GEOGR Labrador *m*.

labyrinth ['læbərɪnθ] *n* labyrinthe *m*.

lace [leɪs] ◇ *n* **-1.** [fabric] dentelle *f*. **-2.** [of shoe etc] lacet *m*. ◇ *comp* en OR de dentelle. ◇ *vt* **-1.** [shoe etc] lacer. **-2.** [drink] verser de l'alcool dans.

◆ **lace up** *vt sep* lacer.

lacemaking ['leɪs,meɪkɪŋ] *n* fabrication *f* de (la) dentelle.

laceration [,læsə'reɪʃn] *n* lacération *f*.

lace-up ◇ *adj* [shoes] à lacets. ◇ *n Br* chaussure *f* à lacets.

lack [læk] ◇ *n* manque *f*; **for** OR **through ~ of** par manque de; **no ~ of** bien assez de. ◇ *vt* manquer de. ◇ *vi*: **to be ~ing in sthg** manquer de qqch; **to be ~ing** manquer, faire défaut.

lackadaisical [,lækə'deɪzɪkl] *adj pej* nonchalant(e).

lackey ['lækɪ] (*pl* **lackeys**) *n pej* larbin *m*.

lacklustre *Br*, **lackluster** *Am* ['læk,lʌstər] *adj* terne.

laconic [lə'kɒnɪk] *adj* laconique.

lacquer ['lækər] ◇ *n* [for wood] vernis *m*, laque *f*; [for hair] laque *f*. ◇ *vt* laquer.

lacrosse [lə'krɒs] *n* crosse *f*.

lactic acid ['læktɪk-] *n* acide *m* lactique.

lacy ['leɪsɪ] (*compar* **-ier**, *superl* **-iest**) *adj* de OR en dentelle.

lad [læd] *n* **-1.** *inf* [boy] garçon *m*, gars *m*. **-2.** *Br* [stable boy] lad *m*.

ladder ['lædər] ◇ *n* **-1.** [for climbing] échelle *f*. **-2.** *Br* [in tights] maille *f* filée, estafilade *f*. ◇ *vt & vi Br* [tights] filer.

laden ['leɪdn] *adj*: ~ **(with)** chargé(e) (de).

la-di-da [,lɑːdɪ'dɑː] *adj inf pej* maniéré(e).

ladies *Br* ['leɪdɪz], **ladies' room** *Am n* toilettes *fpl* (pour dames).

lading ['leɪdɪŋ] → **bill of lading**.

ladle ['leɪdl] ◇ *n* louche *f*. ◇ *vt* servir (à la louche).

lady ['leɪdɪ] (*pl* **-ies**) ◇ *n* **-1.** [gen] dame *f*. **-2.** *Am inf* [to address woman] ma petite dame. ◇ *comp*: **a** ~ **doctor** une femme docteur.
◆ **Lady** *n* Lady *f*; **Our Lady** Notre-Dame *f*.

ladybird *Br* ['leɪdɪbɜːd], **ladybug** *Am* ['leɪdɪbʌg] *n* coccinelle *f*.

lady-in-waiting [-'weɪtɪŋ] (*pl* **ladies-in-waiting**) *n* dame *f* d'honneur.

lady-killer *n inf* bourreau *m* des cœurs, don Juan *m*.

ladylike ['leɪdɪlaɪk] *adj* distingué(e).

Ladyship ['leɪdɪʃɪp] *n*: **her/your** ~ Madame la baronne/la duchesse *etc*.

lag [læg] (*pt & pp* **-ged**, *cont* **-ging**) ◇ *vi*: **to** ~ **(behind)** [person, runner] traîner; [economy, development] être en retard, avoir du retard. ◇ *vt* [roof, pipe] calorifuger. ◇ *n* [timelag] décalage *m*.

lager ['lɑːgər] *n* (bière *f*) blonde *f*.

lager lout *n Br* jeune qui, sous l'influence de l'alcool, cherche la bagarre ou commet des actes de vandalisme.

lagging ['lægɪŋ] *n* calorifuge *m*.

lagoon [lə'guːn] *n* lagune *f*.

Lagos ['leɪgɒs] *n* Lagos.

lah-di-dah = **la-di-da**.

laid [leɪd] *pt & pp* → **lay**.

laid-back *adj inf* relaxe, décontracté(e).

lain [leɪn] *pp* → **lie**.

lair [leər] *n* repaire *m*, antre *m*.

laissez-faire ['leɪseɪ'feər] ◇ *adj* non-interventionniste. ◇ *n* non-interventionnisme *m*.

laity ['leɪətɪ] *n* RELIG: **the** ~ les laïcs *mpl*.

lake [leɪk] *n* lac *m*.

Lake District *n*: **the** ~ la région des lacs (*au nord-ouest de l'Angleterre*).

Lake Geneva *n* le lac Léman OR de Genève.

lakeside ['leɪksaɪd] *adj* au bord de l'eau.

lama ['lɑːmə] (*pl* **-s**) *n* lama *m*.

lamb [læm] *n* agneau *m*.

lambast [læm'bæst], **lambaste** [læm'beɪst] *vt* démolir.

lamb chop *n* côtelette *f* d'agneau.

lambing ['læmɪŋ] *n* agnelage *m*.

lambskin ['læmskɪn] *n* agneau *m*, peau *f* d'agneau.

lambswool ['læmzwʊl] ◇ *n* lambswool *m*. ◇ *comp* en lambswool, en laine d'agneau.

lame [leɪm] *adj lit & fig* boiteux(euse).

lamé ['lɑːmeɪ] *n* lamé *m*.

lame duck *n* **-1.** *fig* [person, business] canard *m* boiteux. **-2.** *Am* [President] *président non réélu, pendant la période séparant l'élection de l'investiture de son successeur.*

lamely ['leɪmlɪ] *adv* [argue, lie etc] maladroitement.

lament [lə'ment] ◇ *n* lamentation *f*. ◇ *vt* se lamenter sur.

lamentable ['læməntəbl] *adj* lamentable.

laminated ['læmɪneɪtɪd] *adj* [wood] stratifié(e); [glass] feuilleté(e); [steel] laminé(e).

lamp [læmp] *n* lampe *f*.

lamplight ['læmplaɪt] *n* lumière *f* de la lampe.

lampoon [læm'puːn] ◇ *n* satire *f*. ◇ *vt* faire la satire de.

lamppost ['læmppəʊst] *n* réverbère *m*.

lampshade ['læmpʃeɪd] *n* abat-jour *m*.

lance [lɑːns] ◇ *n* lance *f*. ◇ *vt* [boil] percer.

lance corporal *n* caporal *m*.

lancet ['lɑːnsɪt] *n* bistouri *m*, lancette *f*.

Lancs [læŋks] (*abbr of* **Lancashire**) *comté anglais.*

land [lænd] ◇ *n* **-1.** [solid ground] terre *f* (ferme); [farming ground] terre, terrain *m*. **-2.** [property] terres *fpl*, propriété *f*. **-3.** [nation] pays *m*. ◇ *vt* **-1.** [from ship, plane] débarquer. **-2.** [catch - fish] prendre. **-3.** [plane] atterrir. **-4.** *inf* [obtain] décrocher. **-5.** *inf* [place]: **to** ~ **sb in trouble** attirer des ennuis à qqn; **to be** ~**ed with sthg** se coltiner qqch. ◇ *vi* **-1.** [plane] atterrir. **-2.** [fall] tomber. **-3.** [from ship] débarquer.
◆ **land up** *vi inf* atterrir.

landed gentry ['lændɪd-] *npl* noblesse *f* de province.

landing ['lændɪŋ] *n* **-1.** [of stairs] palier *m*. **-2.** AERON atterrissage *m*. **-3.** [of goods from ship] débarquement *m*.

landing card *n* carte *f* de débarquement.

landing craft *n* péniche *f* de débarquement.

landing gear *n* (*U*) train *m* d'atterrissage.

landing stage *n* débarcadère *m*.

landing strip *n* piste *f* d'atterrissage.

landlady ['lænd,leɪdɪ] (*pl* **-ies**) *n* [living in] logeuse *f*; [owner] propriétaire *f*.

landlocked ['lændlɒkt] *adj* sans accès à la mer.

landlord ['lændlɔːd] *n* **-1.** [of rented property] propriétaire *m*. **-2.** [of pub] patron *m*.

landmark ['lændmɑːk] *n* point *m* de repère; *fig* événement *m* marquant.

landmine ['lændmaɪn] *n* mine *f* (terrestre).

landowner ['lænd,əʊnəʳ] *n* propriétaire foncier *m*, propriétaire foncière *f*.

Land Rover® [-rəʊvəʳ] *n* Land Rover® *f*.

landscape ['lændskeɪp] ◇ *n* paysage *m*. ◇ *vt* concevoir les plans de, aménager.

landscape gardener *n* (jardinier *m*) paysagiste *mf*.

landslide ['lændslaɪd] ◇ *n* **-1.** [of earth] glissement *m* de terrain; [of rocks] éboulement *m*. **-2.** *fig* [election victory] victoire *f* écrasante.

landslip ['lændslɪp] *n* glissement *m* de terrain.

lane [leɪn] *n* **-1.** [in country] petite route *f*, chemin *m*. **-2.** [in town] ruelle *f*. **-3.** [for traffic] voie *f*; "keep in ~" «ne changez pas de file». **-4.** AERON & SPORT couloir *m*. **-5.** [for shipping] route *f* de navigation.

language ['læŋgwɪdʒ] *n* **-1.** [of people, country] langue *f*. **-2.** [terminology, ability to speak] langage *m*.

language laboratory *n* laboratoire *m* de langues.

languid ['læŋgwɪd] *adj* indolent(e).

languish ['læŋgwɪʃ] *vi* languir.

languorous ['læŋgərəs] *adj literary* langoureux(euse).

lank [læŋk] *adj* terne.

lanky ['læŋkɪ] (*compar* **-ier**, *superl* **-iest**) *adj* dégingandé(e).

lanolin(e) ['lænəlɪn] *n* lanoline *f*.

lantern ['læntən] *n* lanterne *f*.

Laos [laʊs] *n* Laos *m*; **in** ~ au Laos.

Laotian ['laʊʃn] ◇ *adj* laotien(ienne). ◇ *n* **-1.** [person] Laotien *m*, -ienne *f*. **-2.** [language] laotien *m*.

lap [læp] (*pt* & *pp* **-ped**, *cont* **-ping**) ◇ *n* **-1.** [of person]: **on sb's** ~ sur les genoux de qqn. **-2.** [of race] tour *m* de piste. ◇ *vt* **-1.** [subj: animal] laper. **-2.** [in race] prendre un tour d'avance sur. ◇ *vi* [water, waves] clapoter.

◆ **lap up** *vt sep* **-1.** [drink] laper. **-2.** *fig* [compliments] se gargariser de; [lies] gober, avaler.

laparoscopy [,læpə'rɒskəpɪ] (*pl* **-ies**) *n* laparoscopie *f*.

La Paz [læ'pæz] *n* La Paz.

lapdog ['læpdɒg] *n* petit chien *m* d'appartement; *fig* [person] toutou *m*, caniche *m*.

lapel [lə'pel] *n* revers *m*.

Lapland ['læplænd] *n* Laponie *f*; **in** ~ en Laponie.

Lapp [læp] ◇ *adj* lapon(e). ◇ *n* **-1.** [person] Lapon *m*, -e *f*. **-2.** [language] lapon *m*.

lapse [læps] ◇ *n* **-1.** [failing] défaillance *f*. **-2.** [in behaviour] écart *m* de conduite. **-3.** [of time] intervalle *m*, laps *m* de temps. ◇ *vi* **-1.** [passport] être périmé(e); [membership] prendre fin; [tradition] se perdre. **-2.** [person]: **to** ~ **into bad habits** prendre de mauvaises habitudes; **to** ~ **into silence** se taire.

lapsed [læpst] *adj* [Catholic etc] qui ne pratique plus.

lap-top (computer) *n* (ordinateur *m*) portable *m*.

larceny ['lɑːsənɪ] *n* (*U*) vol *m* (simple).

larch [lɑːtʃ] *n* mélèze *m*.

lard [lɑːd] *n* saindoux *m*.

larder ['lɑːdəʳ] *n* garde-manger *m*.

large [lɑːdʒ] *adj* grand(e); [person, animal, book] gros (grosse).

◆ **at large** *adv* **-1.** [as a whole] dans son ensemble. **-2.** [prisoner, animal] en liberté.

◆ **by and large** *adv* dans l'ensemble.

largely ['lɑːdʒlɪ] *adv* en grande partie.

larger-than-life ['lɑːdʒəʳ-] *adj* exagéré(e).

large-scale *adj* à grande échelle.

largesse, largess *Am* [lɑː'dʒes] *n* (*U*) largesses *fpl*.

lark [lɑːk] *n* **-1.** [bird] alouette *f*. **-2.** *inf* [joke] blague *f*; **for a** ~ pour rigoler.

◆ **lark about** *vi* s'amuser.

larva ['lɑːvə] (*pl* **-vae** [-viː]) *n* larve *f*.

laryngitis [,lærɪn'dʒaɪtɪs] *n* (*U*) laryngite *f*.

larynx ['lærɪŋks] (*pl* **larynges** OR **larynxes**) *n* larynx *m*.

lasagna, lasagne [lə'zænjə] *n* (*U*) lasagnes *fpl*.

lascivious [lə'sɪvɪəs] *adj* lascif(ive).

laser ['leɪzəʳ] *n* laser *m*.

laser beam *n* rayon *m* laser.

laser printer *n* imprimante *f* (à) laser.

laser show *n* spectacle *m* laser.

lash [læʃ] ◇ *n* **-1.** [eyelash] cil *m*. **-2.** [with whip] coup *m* de fouet. ◇ *vt* **-1.** [gen] fouetter. **-2.** [tie] attacher.

◆ **lash out** *vi* **-1.** [physically]: **to ~ out (at** OR **against)** envoyer un coup (à). **-2.** *Br inf* [spend money]: **to ~ out (on sthg)** faire une folie (en s'achetant qqch).

lass [læs] *n* jeune fille *f.*

lasso [læ'suː] (*pl* **-s**, *pt* & *pp* **-ed**, *cont* **-ing**) ◇ *n* lasso *m.* ◇ *vt* attraper au lasso.

last [lɑːst] ◇ *adj* dernier(ière); **~ week/year** la semaine/l'année dernière, la semaine/ l'année passée; **~ night** hier soir; **~ but one** avant-dernier (avant-dernière); **down to the ~ detail/penny** jusqu'au moindre détail/dernier sou.
◇ *adv* **-1.** [most recently] la dernière fois. **-2.** [finally] en dernier, le dernier (la dernière).
◇ *pron*: **the day before ~** avant-hier; **the year before ~** il y a deux ans; **the ~ but one** l'avant-dernier *m*, l'avant-dernière *f*; **to leave sthg till ~** faire qqch en dernier.
◇ *n*: **the ~ I saw of him** la dernière fois que je l'ai vu.
◇ *vi* durer; [food] se garder, se conserver; [feeling] persister.

◆ **at (long) last** *adv* enfin.

last-ditch *adj* ultime, désespéré(e).

lasting ['lɑːstɪŋ] *adj* durable.

lastly ['lɑːstlɪ] *adv* pour terminer, finalement.

last-minute *adj* de dernière minute.

last name *n* nom *m* de famille.

last post *n Br* **-1.** [postal collection] dernière levée *f.* **-2.** MIL extinction *f* des feux.

last rites *npl* derniers sacrements *mpl.*

last straw *n*: **it was the ~** cela a été la goutte (d'eau) qui fait déborder le vase.

Last Supper *n*: **the ~** la Cène.

last word *n*: **to have the ~** avoir le dernier mot.

Las Vegas [,læs'veɪgəs] *n* Las Vegas.

latch [lætʃ] ◇ *n* loquet *m*; **on the ~** qui n'est pas fermé à clef. ◇ *vt* fermer au loquet.

◆ **latch onto** *vt fus inf* s'accrocher à.

latchkey ['lætʃkiː] (*pl* **latchkeys**) *n* clef *f* de la porte d'entrée.

late [leɪt] ◇ *adj* **-1.** [not on time]: **to be ~ (for sthg)** être en retard (pour qqch). **-2.** [near end of]: **in ~ December** vers la fin décembre. **-3.** [later than normal] tardif(ive). **-4.** [former] ancien(ienne). **-5.** [dead] feu(e). ◇ *adv* **-1.** [not on time] en retard; **to arrive 20 minutes ~** arriver avec 20 minutes de retard. **-2.** [later than normal] tard; **to work/go to bed ~** travailler/se coucher tard.

◆ **of late** *adv* récemment, dernièrement.

latecomer ['leɪt,kʌmər] *n* retardataire *mf.*

lately ['leɪtlɪ] *adv* ces derniers temps, dernièrement.

lateness ['leɪtnɪs] *n* (*U*) **-1.** [of person, train] retard *m.* **-2.** [of meeting, event] heure *f* tardive.

late-night *adj* [TV programme] programmé(e) à une heure tardive; [shop] ouvert(e) en nocturne.

latent ['leɪtənt] *adj* latent(e).

later ['leɪtər] ◇ *adj* [date] ultérieur(e); [edition] postérieur(e); **in ~ life** plus tard (dans la vie). ◇ *adv* plus tard.

lateral ['lætərəl] *adj* latéral(e).

latest ['leɪtɪst] ◇ *adj* dernier(ière). ◇ *n*: **at the ~** au plus tard.

latex ['leɪteks] ◇ *n* latex *m.* ◇ *comp* en latex.

lath [lɑːθ] *n* latte *f.*

lathe [leɪð] *n* tour *m.*

lather ['lɑːðər] ◇ *n* mousse *f* (de savon). ◇ *vt* savonner. ◇ *vi* mousser.

Latin ['lætɪn] ◇ *adj* latin(e). ◇ *n* [language] latin *m.*

Latin America *n* Amérique *f* latine; **in ~** en Amérique latine.

Latin American ◇ *adj* latino-américain(e). ◇ *n* [person] Latino-Américain *m*, -e *f.*

latitude ['lætɪtjuːd] *n* latitude *f.*

latrine [lə'triːn] *n* latrines *fpl.*

latter ['lætər] ◇ *adj* **-1.** [later] dernier(ière). **-2.** [second] deuxième. ◇ *n*: **the ~** ce dernier (cette dernière).

latter-day *adj* moderne.

latterly ['lætəlɪ] *adv* récemment.

lattice ['lætɪs] *n* treillis *m*, treillage *m.*

lattice window *n* fenêtre *f* treillagée.

Latvia ['lætvɪə] *n* Lettonie *f*; **in ~** en Lettonie.

Latvian ['lætvɪən] ◇ *adj* letton(onne). ◇ *n* **-1.** [person] Letton *m*, -onne *f.* **-2.** [language] letton *m.*

laudable ['lɔːdəbl] *adj* louable.

laugh [lɑːf] ◇ *n* rire *m*; **we had a good ~** *inf* on a bien rigolé, on s'est bien amusé; **to do sthg for ~s** OR **a ~** *inf* faire qqch pour rire OR rigoler; **they had the last ~** finalement, ce sont eux qui ont bien ri. ◇ *vi* rire.

◆ **laugh at** *vt fus* [mock] se moquer de, rire de.

◆ **laugh off** *vt sep* tourner en plaisanterie.

laughable ['lɑːfəbl] *adj* ridicule, risible.

laughing gas ['lɑːfɪŋ-] *n* gaz *m* hilarant.

laughingstock ['lɑːfɪŋstɒk] *n* risée *f.*

laughter ['lɑːftər] *n* (*U*) rire *m*, rires *mpl.*

launch [lɔːntʃ] ◇ n **-1.** [gen] lancement m. **-2.** [boat] chaloupe f. ◇ vt lancer.
◆ **launch into** vt fus se lancer dans.

launching ['lɔːntʃɪŋ] n lancement m.

launch(ing) pad n pas m de tir.

launder ['lɔːndə'] vt lit & fig blanchir.

laund(e)rette [lɔːn'dret], **Laundromat**® Am ['lɔːndrəmæt] n laverie f automatique.

laundry ['lɔːndrɪ] (pl **-ies**) n **-1.** (U) [clothes] lessive f. **-2.** [business] blanchisserie f. **-3.** [room] buanderie f.

laundry basket n panier m à linge.

laureate ['lɔːrɪət] → **poet laureate**.

laurels ['lɒrəlz] npl: **to rest on one's ~** se reposer sur ses lauriers.

Lautro ['lautrəu] (abbr of **Life Assurance and Unit Trust Regulatory Organization**) n organisme britannique contrôlant les activités de compagnies d'assurance-vie et de SICAV.

lava ['lɑːvə] n lave f.

lavatory ['lævətrɪ] (pl **-ies**) n toilettes fpl.

lavatory paper n Br papier m hygiénique.

lavender ['lævəndə'] ◇ adj [colour] (bleu) lavande (inv). ◇ n [plant] lavande f.

lavish ['lævɪʃ] ◇ adj **-1.** [generous] généreux(euse); **to be ~ with** être prodigue de. **-2.** [sumptuous] somptueux(euse). ◇ vt: **to ~ sthg on sb** prodiguer qqch à qqn.

lavishly ['lævɪʃlɪ] adv **-1.** [generously] généreusement. **-2.** [sumptuously] somptueusement.

law [lɔː] ◇ n **-1.** [gen] loi f; **against the ~** contraire à la loi, illégal(e); **to break the ~** enfreindre OR transgresser la loi; **~ and order** ordre m public; **to lay down the ~** pej faire la loi; **the ~ of the jungle** la loi de la jungle. **-2.** JUR droit m. **-3.** inf [police]: **the ~** les flics mpl. ◇ comp [student, degree] en droit.

law-abiding adj respectueux(euse) des lois.

law-breaker n personne f qui enfreint OR transgresse les lois.

law court n tribunal m, cour f de justice.

lawful ['lɔːful] adj légal(e).

lawfully ['lɔːfulɪ] adv légalement.

lawless ['lɔːlɪs] adj **-1.** [illegal] contraire à la loi, illégal(e). **-2.** [without laws] sans loi.

Law Lords npl Br JUR: **the ~** les juges mpl de la Chambre des Lords.

lawmaker ['lɔːˌmeɪkə'] n législateur m, -trice f.

lawn [lɔːn] n pelouse f, gazon m.

lawnmower ['lɔːnˌməuə'] n tondeuse f à gazon.

lawn party n Am garden-party f.

lawn tennis n tennis m.

law school n faculté f de droit.

lawsuit ['lɔːsuːt] n procès m.

lawyer ['lɔːjə'] n [in court] avocat m; [of company] conseiller m juridique; [for wills, sales] notaire m.

lax [læks] adj relâché(e).

laxative ['læksətɪv] n laxatif m.

laxity ['læksətɪ], **laxness** ['læksnɪs] n relâchement m.

lay [leɪ] (pt & pp **laid**) ◇ pt → **lie**. ◇ vt **-1.** [gen] poser, mettre; fig: **to ~ the blame for sthg on sb** rejeter la responsabilité de qqch sur qqn. **-2.** [trap, snare] tendre, dresser; [plans] faire; **to ~ the table** mettre la table OR le couvert. **-3.** [egg] pondre. ◇ adj **-1.** RELIG laïque. **-2.** [untrained] profane.
◆ **lay aside** vt sep mettre de côté.
◆ **lay before** vt sep: **to ~ sthg before sb** [proposal] présenter OR soumettre qqch à qqn.
◆ **lay down** vt sep **-1.** [guidelines, rules] imposer, stipuler. **-2.** [put down] déposer.
◆ **lay into** vt fus inf attaquer.
◆ **lay off** ◇ vt sep [make redundant] licencier. ◇ vt fus inf **-1.** [leave alone] ficher la paix à. **-2.** [give up] arrêter.
◆ **lay on** vt sep Br [provide, supply] organiser.
◆ **lay out** vt sep **-1.** [arrange] arranger, disposer. **-2.** [design] concevoir.
◆ **lay over** vi Am faire escale.

layabout ['leɪəbaut] n Br inf fainéant m, -e f.

lay-by (pl **lay-bys**) n Br aire f de stationnement.

lay days npl starie f, jours mpl de planche.

layer ['leɪə'] n couche f; fig [level] niveau m.

layette [leɪ'et] n layette f.

layman ['leɪmən] (pl **-men** [-mən]) n **-1.** [untrained person] profane m. **-2.** RELIG laïc m.

lay-off n licenciement m.

layout ['leɪaut] n [of office, building] agencement m; [of garden] plan m; [of page] mise f en page.

layover ['leɪəuvə'] n Am escale f.

laze [leɪz] vi: **to ~ (about OR around)** paresser.

lazily ['leɪzɪlɪ] adv paresseusement, avec nonchalance.

laziness ['leɪzɪnɪs] n paresse f.

lazy ['leɪzɪ] (compar **-ier**, superl **-iest**) adj [person] paresseux(euse), fainéant(e); [action] nonchalant(e).

lazybones ['leɪzɪbəunz] (pl inv) n paresseux m, -euse f, fainéant m, -e f.

lb (*abbr of* **pound**) *livre (unité de poids)*.

LB *abbr of* **Labrador**.

lbw (*abbr of* **leg before wicket**) *au cricket, faute d'un joueur qui met une jambe devant le guichet.*

lc (*abbr of* **lower case**) bdc.

L/C *abbr of* **letter of credit**.

LCD (*abbr of* **liquid crystal display**) *n* affichage à cristaux liquides.

Ld *abbr of* **Lord**.

L-driver *n* Br conducteur *m* débutant, conductrice débutante *f* (*qui n'a pas encore son permis*).

LDS *n* (*abbr of* **Licentiate in Dental Surgery**) *diplômé en chirurgie dentaire.*

LEA (*abbr of* **local education authority**) *n services régionaux de l'enseignement en Grande-Bretagne.*

lead[1] [li:d] (*pt & pp* **led**) ◇ *n* **-1.** [winning position]: **to be in** OR **have the ~** mener, être en tête. **-2.** [amount ahead]: **to have a ~ of ...** devancer de .... **-3.** [initiative, example] initiative *f*, exemple *m*; **to take the ~** montrer l'exemple. **-4.** THEATRE: **the ~** le rôle principal. **-5.** [clue] indice *m*. **-6.** [for dog] laisse *f*. **-7.** [wire, cable] câble *m*, fil *m*. ◇ *adj* [role etc] principal(e); **~ singer** chanteur *m*; -euse *f*. ◇ *vt* **-1.** [be at front of] mener, être à la tête de. **-2.** [guide] guider, conduire. **-3.** [be in charge of] être à la tête de, diriger. **-4.** [organize - protest etc] mener, organiser; **to ~ the way** *lit & fig* ouvrir la marche. **-5.** [life] mener. **-6.** [cause]: **to ~ sb to do sthg** inciter OR pousser qqn à faire qqch. ◇ *vi* **-1.** [path, cable etc] mener, conduire. **-2.** [give access]: **to ~ to/into** donner sur, donner accès à. **-3.** [in race, match] mener. **-4.** [result in]: **to ~ to sthg** aboutir à qqch, causer qqch.
◆ **lead off** ◇ *vt fus* [subj: door, room] donner sur. ◇ *vi* **-1.** [road, corridor]: **to ~ off (from)** partir (de). **-2.** [begin] commencer.
◆ **lead up to** *vt fus* **-1.** [precede] conduire à, aboutir à. **-2.** [build up to] amener.

lead[2] [led] ◇ *n* plomb *m*; [in pencil] mine *f*. ◇ *comp* en OR de plomb.

leaded ['ledɪd] *adj* [petrol] au plomb; [window] à petits carreaux.

leaden ['ledn] *adj* **-1.** *literary* [sky] de plomb. **-2.** *fig* [very dull] mortellement ennuyeux(euse).

leader ['li:dər] *n* **-1.** [head, chief] chef *m*; POL leader *m*. **-2.** [in race, competition] premier *m*, -ière *f*. **-3.** Br PRESS éditorial *m*.

leadership ['li:dəʃɪp] *n* **-1.** [people in charge]: **the ~** les dirigeants *mpl*. **-2.** [position of leader] direction *f*. **-3.** [qualities of leader] qualités *fpl* de chef.

lead-free [led-] *adj* sans plomb.

leading ['li:dɪŋ] *adj* **-1.** [most important] principal(e). **-2.** [main]: **~ part** OR **role** THEATRE rôle *m* principal; *fig* rôle prépondérant. **-3.** [at front] de tête.

leading article *n* Br éditorial *m*.

leading lady *n* vedette *f*, premier rôle *m* féminin.

leading light *n* personnage *m* très important OR influent.

leading man *n* premier rôle *m* masculin.

leading question *n* question *f* insidieuse.

lead pencil [led-] *n* crayon *m* à mine de plomb OR à papier.

lead poisoning [led-] *n* saturnisme *m*.

lead time [li:d-] *n* COMM délai *m* de livraison.

leaf [li:f] (*pl* **leaves**) *n* **-1.** [of tree, plant] feuille *f*. **-2.** [of table - hinged] abattant *m*; [- pull-out] rallonge *f*. **-3.** [of book] feuille *f*, page *f*.
◆ **leaf through** *vt fus* [magazine etc] parcourir, feuilleter.

leaflet ['li:flɪt] ◇ *n* prospectus *m*. ◇ *vt* [area] distribuer des prospectus dans.

leafy ['li:fɪ] (*compar* **-ier**, *superl* **-iest**) *adj* feuillu(e); [suburb, lane] planté(e) d'arbres.

league [li:g] *n* ligue *f*; SPORT championnat *m*; **to be in ~ with** être de connivence avec.

league table *n* classement *m* du championnat.

leak [li:k] ◇ *n* *lit & fig* fuite *f*. ◇ *vt* *fig* [secret, information] divulguer. ◇ *vi* fuir.
◆ **leak out** *vi* **-1.** [liquid] fuir. **-2.** *fig* [secret, information] transpirer, être divulgué(e).

leakage ['li:kɪdʒ] *n* fuite *f*.

leaky ['li:kɪ] (*compar* **-ier**, *superl* **-iest**) *adj* qui fuit.

lean [li:n] (*pt & pp* **leant** OR **-ed**) ◇ *adj* **-1.** [slim] mince. **-2.** [meat] maigre. **-3.** *fig* [month, time] mauvais(e). ◇ *vt* [rest]: **to ~ sthg against** appuyer qqch contre, adosser qqch à. ◇ *vi* **-1.** [bend, slope] se pencher. **-2.** [rest]: **to ~ on/against** s'appuyer sur/contre.

leaning ['li:nɪŋ] *n*: **~ (towards)** penchant *m* (pour).

leant [lent] *pt & pp* → **lean**.

lean-to (*pl* **lean-tos**) *n* appentis *m*.

leap [li:p] (*pt & pp* **leapt** OR **-ed**) ◇ *n* *lit & fig* bond *m*. ◇ *vi* **-1.** [gen] bondir. **-2.** *fig* [increase] faire un bond.
◆ **leap at** *vt fus* *fig* [opportunity] sauter sur.

leapfrog ['liːpfrɒg] (*pt & pp* -**ged**, *cont* -**ging**) ◇ *n* saute-mouton *m*. ◇ *vt* dépasser (d'un bond). ◇ *vi*: **to ~ over** sauter par-dessus.

leapt [lept] *pt & pp* → **leap**.

leap year *n* année *f* bissextile.

learn [lɜːn] (*pt & pp* -**ed** OR **learnt**) ◇ *vt*: **to ~ (that)** ... apprendre que ...; **to ~ (how) to do sthg** apprendre à faire qqch. ◇ *vi*: **to ~ (of** OR **about sthg)** apprendre (qqch).

learned ['lɜːnɪd] *adj* savant(e).

learner ['lɜːnər] *n* débutant *m*, -e *f*.

learner (driver) *n* conducteur *m* débutant, conductrice débutante *f* (*qui n'a pas encore son permis*).

learning ['lɜːnɪŋ] *n* savoir *m*, érudition *f*.

learning curve *n* courbe *f* d'apprentissage.

learnt [lɜːnt] *pt & pp* → **learn**.

lease [liːs] ◇ *n* bail *m*; **a new ~ of life** *Br*, **a new ~ on life** *Am* une seconde jeunesse. ◇ *vt* louer; **to ~ sthg from sb** louer qqch à qqn; **to ~ sthg to sb** louer qqch à qqn.

leaseback ['liːsbæk] *n* cession *f* de bail, cession-bail *f*.

leasehold ['liːshəʊld] ◇ *adj* loué(e) à bail, tenu(e) à bail. ◇ *adv* à bail.

leaseholder ['liːs,həʊldər] *n* locataire *mf*.

leash [liːʃ] *n* laisse *f*.

least [liːst] (*superl of* **little**) ◇ *adj*: **the ~** le moindre (la moindre), le plus petit (la plus petite); **he earns the ~ money of any of us** de nous tous, c'est lui qui gagne le moins. ◇ *pron* [smallest amount]: **the ~** le moins; **it's the ~ (that) he can do** c'est la moindre des choses qu'il puisse faire; **not in the ~** pas du tout, pas le moins du monde; **to say the ~** c'est le moins qu'on puisse dire. ◇ *adv*: **(the) ~** le moins (la moins).

◆ **at least** *adv* au moins; [to correct] du moins.

◆ **least of all** *adv* surtout pas, encore moins.

◆ **not least** *adv fml* notamment.

leather ['leðər] ◇ *n* cuir *m*. ◇ *comp* en cuir.

leatherette [,leðə'ret] *n* similicuir *m*.

leave [liːv] (*pt & pp* **left**) ◇ *vt* -**1.** [gen] laisser. -**2.** [go away from] quitter; **to ~ sb alone** laisser qqn tranquille; **it ~s me cold** ça me laisse froid. -**3.** [bequeath]: **to ~ sb sthg**, **to ~ sthg to sb** léguer OR laisser qqch à qqn; *see also* **left**. ◇ *vi* partir. ◇ *n* congé *m*; **to be on ~** [from work] être en congé; [from army] être en permission.

◆ **leave behind** *vt sep* -**1.** [abandon] abandonner, laisser. -**2.** [forget] oublier, laisser.

◆ **leave off** ◇ *vt sep* -**1.** [omit]: **to ~ sthg off (sthg)** omettre qqch (de qqch). -**2.**

[stop]: **to ~ off doing sthg** s'arrêter de faire qqch. ◇ *vi* s'arrêter.

◆ **leave out** *vt sep* omettre, exclure; **to feel left out** se sentir de trop, se sentir exclu.

leave of absence *n* congé *m*.

leaves [liːvz] *pl* → **leaf**.

Lebanese [,lebə'niːz] (*pl inv*) ◇ *adj* libanais(e). ◇ *n* [person] Libanais *m*, -e *f*.

Lebanon ['lebənən] *n* Liban *m*; **in (the) ~** au Liban.

lecherous ['letʃərəs] *adj* lubrique, libidineux(euse).

lechery ['letʃərɪ] *n* lubricité *f*.

lectern ['lektən] *n* lutrin *m*.

lecture ['lektʃər] ◇ *n* -**1.** [talk - gen] conférence *f*; [- UNIV] cours *m* magistral; **to give a ~ (on sthg)** faire une conférence (sur qqch); UNIV faire un cours (sur qqch). -**2.** [scolding]: **to give sb a ~** réprimander qqn, sermonner qqn. ◇ *vt* [scold] réprimander, sermonner. ◇ *vi*: **to ~ on sthg** faire un cours sur qqch; **to ~ in sthg** être professeur de qqch.

lecture hall *n* amphithéâtre *m*.

lecturer ['lektʃərər] *n* [speaker] conférencier *m*, -ière *f*; UNIV maître *m* assistant.

lecture theatre *n* amphithéâtre *m*.

led [led] *pt & pp* → **lead¹**.

LED (*abbr of* **light-emitting diode**) *n* LED *f*.

ledge [ledʒ] *n* -**1.** [of window] rebord *m*. -**2.** [of mountain] corniche *f*.

ledger ['ledʒər] *n* grand livre *m*.

lee [liː] *n*: **in the ~ of** à l'abri de.

leech [liːtʃ] *n lit & fig* sangsue *f*.

leek [liːk] *n* poireau *m*.

leer [lɪər] ◇ *n* regard *m* libidineux. ◇ *vi*: **to ~ at** reluquer.

Leeward Islands ['liːwəd-] *npl*: **the ~** les îles *fpl* Sous-le-Vent.

leeway ['liːweɪ] *n* -**1.** [room to manoeuvre] marge *f* de manœuvre. -**2.** [time lost]: **to make up ~** rattraper son retard.

left [left] ◇ *pt & pp* → **leave**. ◇ *adj* -**1.** [remaining]: **to be ~** rester; **have you any money ~?** il te reste de l'argent? -**2.** [not right] gauche. ◇ *adv* à gauche. ◇ *n*: **on** OR **to the ~** à gauche; **keep to the ~** gardez votre gauche.

◆ **Left** *n* POL: **the Left** la Gauche.

left-hand *adj* de gauche; **~ side** gauche *f*, côté *m* gauche.

left-hand drive ◇ *adj* [car] avec la conduite à gauche. ◇ *n* conduite *f* à gauche.

left-handed [-'hændɪd] ◇ *adj* **-1.** [person] gaucher(ère). **-2.** [implement] pour gaucher. **-3.** *Am* [compliment] faux (fausse). ◇ *adv* de la main gauche.

left-hander [-'hændəʳ] *n* gaucher *m*, -ère *f*.

Leftist ['leftɪst] POL ◇ *adj* de gauche, gauchiste. ◇ *n* gauchiste *mf*.

left luggage (office) *n Br* consigne *f*.

leftover ['leftəʊvəʳ] *adj* qui reste, en surplus.

◆ **leftovers** *npl* restes *mpl*.

left wing POL *n* gauche *f*.

◆ **left-wing** *adj* de gauche.

left-winger *n* POL homme *m*, femme *f* de gauche.

lefty ['leftɪ] (*pl* -**ies**) *n* **-1.** *Br inf* POL gauchiste *mf*, gaucho *m*. **-2.** *Am* [left-handed person] gaucher *m*, -ère *f*.

leg [leg] *n* **-1.** [of person, trousers] jambe *f*; [of animal] patte *f*; **to be on one's last ~s** être à bout de souffle; **you don't have a ~ to stand on!** ça ne tient pas debout!; **to pull sb's ~** faire marcher qqn. **-2.** CULIN [of lamb] gigot *m*; [of pork, chicken] cuisse *f*. **-3.** [of furniture] pied *m*. **-4.** [of journey, match] étape *f*; **away ~** FTBL match *m* à l'extérieur OR sur terrain adverse.

legacy ['legəsɪ] (*pl* -**ies**) *n lit* & *fig* legs *m*, héritage *m*.

legal ['liːgl] *adj* **-1.** [concerning the law] juridique. **-2.** [lawful] légal(e).

legal action *n*: **to take ~ against sb** intenter un procès à qqn, engager des poursuites contre qqn.

legal aid *n* assistance *f* judiciaire.

legality [liː'gælətɪ] *n* légalité *f*.

legalize, -ise ['liːgəlaɪz] *vt* légaliser, rendre légal.

legally ['liːgəlɪ] *adv* légalement; **~ binding** qui oblige en droit.

legal tender *n* monnaie *f* légale.

legation [lɪ'geɪʃn] *n* légation *f*.

legend ['ledʒənd] *n lit* & *fig* légende *f*.

legendary ['ledʒəndrɪ] *adj lit* & *fig* légendaire.

leggings ['legɪŋz] *npl* jambières *fpl*, leggings *mpl* or *fpl*.

leggy ['legɪ] (*compar* -**ier**, *superl* -**iest**) *adj* [woman] qui a des jambes interminables.

legible ['ledʒəbl] *adj* lisible.

legibly ['ledʒəblɪ] *adv* lisiblement.

legion ['liːdʒən] ◇ *n lit* & *fig* légion *f*. ◇ *adj fml*: **to be ~** être légion (*inv*).

legionnaire's disease [ˌliːdʒə'neəʳz-] *n* maladie *f* du légionnaire.

legislate ['ledʒɪsleɪt] *vi*: **to ~ (for/against)** faire des lois (pour/contre).

legislation [ˌledʒɪs'leɪʃn] *n* législation *f*.

legislative ['ledʒɪslətɪv] *adj* législatif(ive).

legislator ['ledʒɪsleɪtəʳ] *n* législateur *m*, -trice *f*.

legislature ['ledʒɪsleɪtʃəʳ] *n* corps *m* législatif.

legitimacy [lɪ'dʒɪtɪməsɪ] *n* légitimité *f*.

legitimate [lɪ'dʒɪtɪmət] *adj* légitime.

legitimately [lɪ'dʒɪtɪmətlɪ] *adv* légitimement.

legitimize, -ise [lɪ'dʒɪtəmaɪz] *vt* légitimer.

legless ['legləs] *adj Br inf* [drunk] bourré(e), rond(e).

legroom ['legrʊm] *n* (*U*) place *f* pour les jambes.

leg-warmers [-wɔːməz] *npl* jambières *fpl*.

legwork ['legwɜːk] *n*: **I had to do the ~** *inf* j'ai dû beaucoup me déplacer.

Leics (*abbr of* **Leicestershire**) *comté anglais*.

leisure [*Br* 'leʒəʳ, *Am* 'liːʒər] *n* loisir *m*, temps *m* libre; **at (one's) ~** à loisir, tout à loisir.

leisure centre *n* centre *m* de loisirs.

leisurely [*Br* 'leʒəlɪ, *Am* 'liːʒərlɪ] ◇ *adj* [pace] lent(e), tranquille. ◇ *adv* [walk] sans se presser.

leisure time *n* (*U*) temps *m* libre, loisirs *mpl*.

lemming ['lemɪŋ] *n* lemming *m*; **like ~s** *fig* comme les moutons de Panurge.

lemon ['lemən] *n* [fruit] citron *m*.

lemonade [ˌlemə'neɪd] *n* **-1.** *Br* [fizzy] limonade *f*. **-2.** [still] citronnade *f*.

lemon curd *n Br* crème *f* au citron.

lemon juice *n* jus *m* de citron.

lemon sole *n* limande-sole *f*.

lemon squash *n Br* citronnade *f*.

lemon squeezer *n* presse-citron *m inv*.

lemon tea *n* thé *m* (au) citron.

lend [lend] (*pt* & *pp* **lent**) *vt* **-1.** [loan] prêter; **to ~ sb sthg, to ~ sthg to sb** prêter qqch à qqn. **-2.** [offer]: **to ~ support (to sb)** offrir son soutien (à qqn); **to ~ assistance (to sb)** prêter assistance (à qqn). **-3.** [add]: **to ~ sthg to sthg** [quality etc] ajouter qqch à qqch.

lender ['lendəʳ] *n* prêteur *m*, -euse *f*.

lending library ['lendɪŋ-] *n* bibliothèque *f* de prêt.

lending rate ['lendɪŋ-] *n* taux *m* de crédit.

length [leŋθ] *n* **-1.** [gen] longueur *f*; **what ~ is it?** ça mesure combien?; **it's five metres in ~** cela fait cinq mètres de long; **the ~**

and breadth of partout dans, dans tout. **-2.** [piece - of string, wood] morceau *m*, bout *m*; [- of cloth] coupon *m*. **-3.** [duration] durée *f*. **-4.** *phr*: **to go to great ~s to do sthg** tout faire pour faire qqch.

♦ **at length** *adv* **-1.** [eventually] enfin. **-2.** [in detail] à fond.

lengthen ['leŋθən] ◇ *vt* [dress etc] rallonger; [life] prolonger. ◇ *vi* allonger.

lengthways ['leŋθweiz] *adv* dans le sens de la longueur.

lengthy ['leŋθi] (*compar* -ier, *superl* -iest) *adj* très long (longue).

leniency ['li:njənsi] *n* clémence *f*, indulgence *f*.

lenient ['li:njənt] *adj* [person] indulgent(e); [laws] clément(e).

lens [lenz] *n* **-1.** [of camera] objectif *m*; [of glasses] verre *m*. **-2.** [contact lens] verre *m* de contact, lentille *f* (cornéenne).

lent [lent] *pt & pp* → **lend**.

Lent [lent] *n* Carême *m*.

lentil ['lentil] *n* lentille *f*.

Leo ['li:əʊ] *n* le Lion; **to be (a) ~** être Lion.

leopard ['lepəd] *n* léopard *m*.

leopardess ['lepədis] *n* léopard *m* femelle.

leotard ['li:ətɑ:d] *n* collant *m*.

leper ['lepər] *n* lépreux *m*, -euse *f*.

leprechaun ['leprəkɔ:n] *n* lutin *m* (*irlandais*).

leprosy ['leprəsi] *n* lèpre *f*.

lesbian ['lezbiən] ◇ *adj* lesbien(ienne). ◇ *n* lesbienne *f*.

lesbianism ['lezbiənizm] *n* lesbianisme *m*.

lesion ['li:ʒn] *n* lésion *f*.

Lesotho [lə'su:tu:] *n* Lesotho *m*.

less [les] (*compar of* **little**) ◇ *adj* moins de; **~ money/time** moins d'argent/de temps que moi. ◇ *pron* moins; **it costs ~ than you think** ça coûte moins cher que tu ne le crois; **no ~ than £50** pas moins de 50 livres; **the ~ ... the ~ ...** moins ... moins .... ◇ *adv* moins; **~ than five** moins de cinq; **~ and ~** de moins en moins. ◇ *prep* [minus] moins.

lessee [le'si:] *n* preneur *m*, -euse *f*, locataire *mf*.

lessen ['lesn] ◇ *vt* [risk, chance] diminuer, réduire; [pain] atténuer. ◇ *vi* [gen] diminuer; [pain] s'atténuer.

lesser ['lesər] *adj* moindre; **to a ~ extent** OR **degree** à un degré moindre.

lesson ['lesn] *n* leçon *f*, cours *m*; **to give/take ~s (in)** donner/prendre des leçons (de); **to teach sb a ~** *fig* donner une (bonne) leçon à qqn.

lessor [le'sɔ:r] *n* bailleur *m*, -eresse *f*.

lest [lest] *conj fml* de crainte que.

let [let] (*pt & pp* **let**, *cont* -**ting**) *vt* **-1.** [allow]: **to ~ sb do sthg** laisser qqn faire qqch; **she ~ her hair grow** elle s'est laissé pousser les cheveux; **we can't ~ this happen** on ne peut pas laisser faire ça; **to ~ sb know sthg** dire qqch à qqn; **to ~ go of sb/sthg** lâcher qqn/qqch; **to ~ sb go** [gen] laisser (partir) qqn; [prisoner] libérer qqn. **-2.** [in verb forms]: **~ them wait** qu'ils attendent; **~'s go!** allons-y!; **~'s see** voyons. **-3.** [rent out] louer; **"to ~"** «à louer».

♦ **let alone** *adv* encore moins, sans parler de.

♦ **let down** *vt sep* **-1.** [deflate] dégonfler. **-2.** [disappoint] décevoir.

♦ **let in** *vt sep* [admit] laisser OR faire entrer.

♦ **let in for** *vt sep*: **you don't know what you're letting yourself in for** tu ne sais pas à quoi tu t'engages.

♦ **let in on** *vt sep*: **to ~ sb in on sthg** mettre qqn au courant de qqch.

♦ **let off** *vt sep* **-1.** [excuse]: **to ~ sb off sthg** dispenser qqn de qqch. **-2.** [not punish] ne pas punir. **-3.** [bomb] faire éclater; [gun, firework] faire partir.

♦ **let on** *vi*: **don't ~ on!** ne dis rien (à personne)!

♦ **let out** *vt sep* **-1.** [allow to go out] laisser sortir; **to ~ air out of sthg** dégonfler qqch. **-2.** [laugh, scream] laisser échapper.

♦ **let up** *vi* **-1.** [rain] diminuer. **-2.** [person] s'arrêter.

letdown ['letdaʊn] *n inf* déception *f*.

lethal ['li:θl] *adj* mortel(elle), fatal(e).

lethargic [lə'θɑ:dʒik] *adj* léthargique.

lethargy ['leθədʒi] *n* léthargie *f*.

Letraset® ['letrəset] *n* Letraset®.

let's [lets] = **let us**.

letter ['letər] *n* lettre *f*.

letter bomb *n* lettre *f* piégée.

letterbox ['letəbɒks] *n Br* boîte *f* aux OR à lettres.

letterhead ['letəhed] *n* en-tête *m*.

lettering ['letəriŋ] *n* (*U*) caractères *mpl*.

letter of credit *n* lettre *f* de crédit.

letter opener *n* coupe-papier *m inv*.

letter-perfect *adj Am* absolument parfait(e).

letter quality *n* COMPUT qualité *f* courrier.

letters patent *npl* lettres *fpl* patentes.

lettuce ['letis] *n* laitue *f*, salade *f*.

letup ['letʌp] *n* [in fighting] répit *m*; [in work] relâchement *m*.

leuk(a)emia [luːˈkiːmɪə] n leucémie f.

levee [ˈlevɪ] n Am [embankment] digue f.

level [ˈlevl] (Br pt & pp -led, cont -ling, Am pt & pp -ed, cont -ing) ◇ adj -1. [equal in height] à la même hauteur; [horizontal] horizontal(e); to be ~ with être au niveau de. -2. [equal in standard] à égalité. -3. [flat] plat(e), plan(e). ◇ adv: to draw ~ with sb arriver à la même hauteur que qqn, rejoindre qqn. ◇ n -1. [gen] niveau m; to be on a ~ (with) être du même niveau (que); to be on the ~ inf être réglo. -2. Am [spirit level] niveau m à bulle. ◇ vt -1. [make flat] niveler, aplanir. -2. [demolish] raser. -3. [aim]: to ~ a gun at pointer OR braquer un fusil sur; to ~ an accusation at OR against sb lancer une accusation contre qqn.
◆ **level off, level out** vi -1. [inflation etc] se stabiliser. -2. [aeroplane] se mettre en palier.
◆ **level with** vt fus inf être franc (franche) OR honnête avec.

level crossing n Br passage m à niveau.

level-headed [-ˈhedɪd] adj raisonnable.

level pegging [-ˈpegɪŋ] adj Br: to be ~ être à égalité.

lever [Br ˈliːvəʳ, Am ˈlevəʳ] n levier m.

leverage [Br ˈliːvərɪdʒ, Am ˈlevərɪdʒ] n (U) -1. [force]: to get ~ on sthg avoir une prise sur qqch. -2. fig [influence] influence f.

leviathan [lɪˈvaɪəθn] n fig colosse m.

levitation [ˌlevɪˈteɪʃn] n lévitation f.

levity [ˈlevətɪ] n légèreté f.

levy [ˈlevɪ] (pt & pp -ied) ◇ n prélèvement m, impôt m. ◇ vt prélever, percevoir.

lewd [ljuːd] adj obscène.

lexical [ˈleksɪkl] adj lexical(e).

LI abbr of Long Island.

liability [ˌlaɪəˈbɪlətɪ] (pl -ies) n responsabilité f; fig [person] danger m public.
◆ **liabilities** npl FIN dettes fpl, passif m.

liable [ˈlaɪəbl] adj -1. [likely]: to be ~ to do sthg risquer de faire qqch, être susceptible de faire qqch. -2. [prone]: to be ~ to sthg être sujet(ette) à qqch. -3. JUR: to be ~ (for) être responsable (de); to be ~ to être passible de.

liaise [lɪˈeɪz] vi: to ~ with assurer la liaison avec.

liaison [lɪˈeɪzɒn] n liaison f.

liar [ˈlaɪəʳ] n menteur m, -euse f.

Lib. [lɪb] abbr of Liberal.

libel [ˈlaɪbl] (Br pt & pp -led, cont -ling, Am pt & pp -ed, cont -ing) ◇ n diffamation f. ◇ vt diffamer.

libellous Br, **libelous** Am [ˈlaɪbələs] adj diffamatoire.

liberal [ˈlɪbərəl] ◇ adj -1. [tolerant] libéral(e). -2. [generous] généreux(euse). ◇ n libéral m, -e f.
◆ **Liberal** POL ◇ adj libéral(e). ◇ n libéral m, -e f.

liberal arts npl arts mpl libéraux.

Liberal Democrat n adhérent du principal parti centriste britannique.

liberalize, -ise [ˈlɪbərəlaɪz] vt libéraliser.

liberal-minded [-ˈmaɪndɪd] adj large d'esprit.

Liberal Party n: the ~ le parti libéral.

liberate [ˈlɪbəreɪt] vt libérer.

liberation [ˌlɪbəˈreɪʃn] n libération f.

liberator [ˈlɪbəreɪtəʳ] n libérateur m, -trice f.

Liberia [laɪˈbɪərɪə] n Liberia m; in ~ au Liberia.

Liberian [laɪˈbɪərɪən] ◇ adj libérien(ienne). ◇ n Libérien m, -ienne f.

libertine [ˈlɪbətiːn] n libertin m.

liberty [ˈlɪbətɪ] (pl -ies) n liberté f; at ~ en liberté; to be at ~ to do sthg être libre de faire qqch; to take liberties (with sb) prendre des libertés (avec qqn).

libido [lɪˈbiːdəʊ] (pl -s) n libido f.

Libra [ˈliːbrə] n Balance f; to be (a) ~ être Balance.

librarian [laɪˈbreərɪən] n bibliothécaire mf.

librarianship [laɪˈbreərɪənʃɪp] n: diploma in ~ diplôme de bibliothécaire.

library [ˈlaɪbrərɪ] (pl -ies) n bibliothèque f.

library book n livre m de bibliothèque.

libretto [lɪˈbretəʊ] (pl -s) n livret m.

Libya [ˈlɪbɪə] n Libye f; in ~ en Libye.

Libyan [ˈlɪbɪən] ◇ adj libyen(enne). ◇ n Libyen m, -enne f.

lice [laɪs] pl → louse.

licence [ˈlaɪsəns] ◇ n -1. [gen] permis m, autorisation f; driving ~ permis m de conduire; TV ~ redevance f télé. -2. COMM licence f; under ~ sous licence. ◇ vt Am = license.

license [ˈlaɪsəns] ◇ vt autoriser. ◇ n Am = licence.

licensed [ˈlaɪsənst] adj -1. [person]: to be ~ to do sthg avoir un permis pour OR l'autorisation de faire qqch. -2. Br [premises] qui détient une licence de débit de boissons.

licensee [ˌlaɪsənˈsiː] n [of pub] gérant m, -e f.

license plate *n Am* plaque *f* d'immatriculation.

licensing hours ['laɪsənsɪŋ-] *npl Br* heures d'ouverture des débits de boissons.

LICENSING HOURS:
Traditionnellement, les heures d'ouverture des pubs répondent à une réglementation très stricte (liée à la législation sur la vente des boissons alcoolisées), mais celle-ci a été assouplie en 1988. Au lieu d'ouvrir uniquement de 11h 30 à 14h 30 et de 18h à 23h, les pubs peuvent désormais rester ouverts de 11h à 23h, sauf le dimanche (de 11h à 15h et de 19h à 22h 30)

---

licensing laws ['laɪsɪnsɪŋ-] *npl Br* lois réglementant la vente d'alcool.

licentious [laɪ'senʃəs] *adj* licencieux(ieuse).

lichen ['laɪkən] *n* lichen *m*.

lick [lɪk] ◇ *n* **-1.** [act of licking]: **to give sthg a ~** lécher qqch. **-2.** *inf* [small amount]: **a ~ of paint** un petit coup de peinture. ◇ *vt* **-1.** [gen] lécher; **to ~ one's lips** se lécher les lèvres; *fig* se frotter les mains. **-2.** *inf* [defeat] écraser, battre à plates coutures.

licorice ['lɪkərɪs] = **liquorice**.

lid [lɪd] *n* **-1.** [cover] couvercle *m*. **-2.** [eyelid] paupière *f*.

lido ['liːdəʊ] (*pl* **-es**) *n* **-1.** *Br* [swimming pool] piscine *f* en plein air. **-2.** [beach] plage *f*.

lie [laɪ] (*pt sense 1* **lied**, *pt senses 2-5* **lay**, *pp sense 1* **lied**, *pp senses 2-5* **lain**, *cont all senses* **lying**) ◇ *n* mensonge *m*; **to tell ~s** mentir, dire des mensonges. ◇ *vi* **-1.** [tell lie]: **to ~ (to sb)** mentir (à qqn). **-2.** [be horizontal] être allongé(e), être couché(e). **-3.** [be situated] se trouver, être. **-4.** [difficulty, solution etc] résider. **-5.** *phr*: **to ~ low** se planquer, se tapir.

◆ **lie about**, **lie around** *vi* traîner.

◆ **lie down** *vi* s'allonger, se coucher; **he won't take it lying down** il ne va pas accepter ça sans rien dire.

◆ **lie in** *vi Br* rester au lit, faire la grasse matinée.

Liechtenstein ['lɪktənstaɪn] *n* Liechtenstein *m*; **in ~** au Liechtenstein.

lie detector *n* détecteur *m* de mensonges.

lie-down *n Br*: **to have a ~** faire une sieste OR un (petit) somme.

lie-in *n Br*: **to have a ~** faire la grasse matinée.

lieu [ljuː, luː]

◆ **in lieu** *adv* à la place; **in ~ of** au lieu de, à la place de.

Lieut. (*abbr of* **lieutenant**) lieut.

lieutenant [*Br* lef'tenənt, *Am* luː'tenənt] *n* lieutenant *m*.

lieutenant colonel *n* lieutenant-colonel *m*.

life [laɪf] (*pl* **lives**) ◇ *n* **-1.** [gen] vie *f*; **that's ~!** c'est la vie!; **for ~** à vie; **I can't for the ~ of me remember ...** j'ai beau me creuser, je n'arrive pas à me rappeler ...; **to breathe ~ into** donner vie à; **to come to ~** s'éveiller, s'animer; **to lay down one's ~** donner sa vie; **to risk ~ and limb** risquer sa peau; **to scare the ~ out of sb** faire une peur bleue à qqn; **to take sb's ~** tuer qqn; **to take one's own ~** se donner la mort. **-2.** (*U*) *inf* [life imprisonment] emprisonnement *m* perpétuel.

◇ *comp* [member etc] à vie.

life-and-death *adj* extrêmement grave OR critique.

life annuity *n* rente *f* viagère.

life assurance = **life insurance**.

life belt *n* bouée *f* de sauvetage.

lifeblood ['laɪfblʌd] *n fig* élément *m* vital, âme *f*.

lifeboat ['laɪfbəʊt] *n* canot *m* de sauvetage.

lifeboatman ['laɪfbəʊtmən] (*pl* **-men** [-mən]) *n* sauveteur *m* en mer.

life buoy *n* bouée *f* de sauvetage.

life expectancy [-ɪk'spektənsɪ] *n* espérance *f* de vie.

lifeguard ['laɪfgɑːd] *n* [at swimming pool] maître-nageur sauveteur *m*; [at beach] gardien *m* de plage.

life imprisonment *n* emprisonnement *m* perpétuel.

life insurance *n* assurance-vie *f*.

life jacket *n* gilet *m* de sauvetage.

lifeless ['laɪflɪs] *adj* **-1.** [dead] sans vie, inanimé(e). **-2.** [listless - performance] qui manque de vie; [- voice] monotone.

lifelike ['laɪflaɪk] *adj* [statue, portrait] qui semble vivant(e).

lifeline ['laɪflaɪn] *n* corde *f* (de sauvetage); *fig* lien *m* vital (avec l'extérieur).

lifelong ['laɪflɒŋ] *adj* de toujours.

life peer *n Br* pair *m* à vie.

life preserver [-prɪ,zɜːvəʳ] *n Am* [life belt] bouée *f* de sauvetage; [life jacket] gilet *m* de sauvetage.

life raft *n* canot *m* pneumatique (de sauvetage).

lifesaver ['laɪf,seɪvəʳ] *n* [person] maître-nageur sauveteur *m*.

life sentence *n* condamnation *f* à perpétuité.

life-size(d) *adj* grandeur nature (*inv*).

lifespan ['laɪfspæn] *n* -1. [of person, animal] espérance *f* de vie. -2. [of product, machine] durée *f* de vie.

lifestyle ['laɪfstaɪl] *n* style *m* de vie.

life-support system *n* respirateur *m* artificiel.

lifetime ['laɪftaɪm] *n* vie *f*; **in my ~** de mon vivant.

lift [lɪft] ◇ *n* -1. [in car]: **to give sb a ~** emmener OR prendre qqn en voiture. -2. *Br* [elevator] ascenseur *m*. ◇ *vt* -1. [gen] lever; [weight] soulever. -2. [plagiarize] plagier. -3. *inf* [steal] voler. ◇ *vi* -1. [lid etc] s'ouvrir. -2. [fog etc] se lever.

lift-off *n* décollage *m*.

ligament ['lɪgəmənt] *n* ligament *m*.

light [laɪt] (*pt* & *pp* **lit** OR **-ed**) ◇ *adj* -1. [not dark] clair(e); **~ blue/green** bleu/vert clair (*inv*). -2. [not heavy] léger(ère); **to be a ~ sleeper** avoir le sommeil léger. -3. [traffic] fluide; [corrections] peu nombreux(euses). -4. [work] facile.
◇ *n* -1. (*U*) [brightness] lumière *f*. -2. [device] lampe *f*; [AUT - gen] feu *m*; [- headlamp] phare *m*. -3. [for cigarette etc] feu *m*; **have you got a ~?** vous avez du feu?; **to set ~ to sthg** mettre le feu à qqch. -4. [perspective]: **in the ~ of** *Br*, **in ~ of** *Am* à la lumière de; **to see sb/sthg in a different ~** voir qqn/qqch sous un jour nouveau. -5. *phr*: **to come to ~** être découvert(e) OR dévoilé(e); **to see the ~** [understand] comprendre; **to throw** OR **cast** OR **shed ~ on sthg** clarifier qqch.
◇ *vt* -1. [fire, cigarette] allumer. -2. [room, stage] éclairer. ◇ *adv*: **to travel ~** voyager léger.
◆ **light out** *vi Am inf* se tirer.
◆ **light up** ◇ *vt sep* -1. [illuminate] éclairer. -2. [cigarette etc] allumer. ◇ *vi* -1. [face] s'éclairer. -2. *inf* [start smoking] allumer une cigarette.

light aircraft *n* avion *m* léger.

light ale *n Br bière blonde légère*.

light bulb *n* ampoule *f*.

light cream *n Am* crème *f* liquide.

lighted ['laɪtɪd] *adj* [room] éclairé(e).

light-emitting diode [-ɪ'mɪtɪŋ-] *n* diode *f* électroluminescente.

lighten ['laɪtn] ◇ *vt* -1. [give light to] éclairer; [make less dark] éclaircir. -2. [make less heavy] alléger. ◇ *vi* [brighten] s'éclaircir.
◆ **lighten up** *vi inf* se dérider.

lighter ['laɪtər] *n* [cigarette lighter] briquet *m*.

light-fingered [-'fɪŋgəd] *adj inf* chapardeur(euse).

light-headed [-'hedɪd] *adj*: **to feel ~** avoir la tête qui tourne.

light-hearted [-'hɑːtɪd] *adj* -1. [cheerful] joyeux(euse), gai(e). -2. [amusing] amusant(e).

lighthouse ['laɪthaʊs, *pl* -haʊzɪz] *n* phare *m*.

light industry *n* industrie *f* légère.

lighting ['laɪtɪŋ] *n* éclairage *m*.

lighting-up time *n heure où les véhicules doivent allumer leurs phares*.

lightly ['laɪtlɪ] *adv* -1. [gen] légèrement. -2. [frivolously] à la légère.

light meter *n* posemètre *m*, cellule *f* photoélectrique.

lightning ['laɪtnɪŋ] *n* (*U*) éclair *m*, foudre *f*.

lightning conductor *Br*, **lightning rod** *Am n* paratonnerre *m*.

lightning strike *n Br* grève *f* surprise.

light opera *n* opérette *f*.

light pen *n* crayon *m* optique, photostyle *m*.

lightship ['laɪtʃɪp] *n* bateau-feu *m*, bateau-phare *m*.

lights-out *n* extinction *f* des feux.

lightweight ['laɪtweɪt] ◇ *adj* -1. [object] léger(ère). -2. *fig* & *pej* [person] insignifiant(e). ◇ *n* -1. [boxer] poids *m* léger. -2. *fig* & *pej* [person] personne *f* insignifiante.

light year *n* année-lumière *f*.

likable ['laɪkəbl] *adj* sympathique.

like [laɪk] ◇ *prep* -1. [gen] comme; **to look ~ sb/sthg** ressembler à qqn/qqch; **to taste ~ sthg** avoir un goût de qqch; **~ this/that** comme ci/ça. -2. [typical of]: **that's just ~ him!** c'est bien de lui!, ça lui ressemble! -3. [such as] tel que, comme.
◇ *vt* -1. [gen] aimer; **I ~ her** elle me plaît; **to ~ doing** OR **to do sthg** aimer faire qqch. -2. [expressing a wish]: **would you ~ some more cake?** vous prendrez encore du gâteau?; **I'd ~ to go** je voudrais bien OR j'aimerais y aller; **I'd ~ you to come** je voudrais bien OR j'aimerais que vous veniez; **if you ~** si vous voulez.
◇ *adj*: **people of ~ mind** des gens qui pensent comme lui/moi *etc*.
◇ *n*: **the ~** une chose pareille; **and the ~** et d'autres choses du même genre.
◆ **likes** *npl*: **~s and dislikes** goûts *mpl*.

likeable ['laɪkəbl] = **likable**.

likelihood ['laɪklɪhʊd] *n* (*U*) chances *fpl*, probabilité *f*; **in all ~** selon toute probabilité.

likely ['laɪklɪ] *adj* **-1.** [probable] probable; he's ~ to get angry il risque de se fâcher; they're ~ to win ils vont sûrement gagner; a ~ story! *iro* à d'autres! **-2.** [candidate] prometteur(euse).

like-minded [-'maɪndɪd] *adj* de même opinion.

liken ['laɪkn] *vt*: to ~ sb/sthg to assimiler qqn/qqch à.

likeness ['laɪknɪs] *n* **-1.** [resemblance]: ~ (to) ressemblance *f* (avec). **-2.** [portrait] portrait *m*.

likewise ['laɪkwaɪz] *adv* [similarly] de même; to do ~ faire pareil OR de même.

liking ['laɪkɪŋ] *n* [for person] affection *f*, sympathie *f*; [for food, music] goût *m*, penchant *m*; to have a ~ for sthg avoir le goût de qqch; to be to sb's ~ être du goût de qqn, plaire à qqn.

lilac ['laɪlək] ◇ *adj* [colour] lilas (*inv*). ◇ *n* lilas *m*.

Lilo® ['laɪləʊ] (*pl* -s) *n Br* matelas *m* pneumatique.

lilt [lɪlt] *n* rythme *m*, cadence *f*.

lilting ['lɪltɪŋ] *adj* [voice] mélodieux(ieuse), chantant(e).

lily ['lɪlɪ] (*pl* -ies) *n* lis *m*.

lily of the valley (*pl* lilies of the valley) *n* muguet *m*.

Lima ['liːmə] *n* Lima.

limb [lɪm] *n* **-1.** [of body] membre *m*. **-2.** [of tree] branche *f*. **-3.** *phr*: to be out on a ~ être en mauvaise posture.

limber ['lɪmbər]
◆ **limber up** *vi* s'échauffer.

limbo ['lɪmbəʊ] (*pl* -s) *n* **-1.** (*U*) [uncertain state]: to be in ~ être dans les limbes. **-2.** [dance]: the ~ le limbo.

lime [laɪm] *n* **-1.** [fruit] citron *m* vert. **-2.** [drink]: ~ (juice) jus *m* de citron vert. **-3.** [linden tree] tilleul *m*. **-4.** [substance] chaux *f*.

lime cordial *n* sirop *m* de citron vert.

lime-green *adj* vert jaune (*inv*).

limelight ['laɪmlaɪt] *n*: to be in the ~ être au premier plan.

limerick ['lɪmərɪk] *n* poème humoristique en cinq vers.

limestone ['laɪmstəʊn] *n* (*U*) pierre *f* à chaux, calcaire *m*.

limey ['laɪmɪ] (*pl* limeys) *n Am inf* terme péjoratif désignant un Anglais.

limit ['lɪmɪt] ◇ *n* limite *f*; he's/she's the ~! *inf* il/elle dépasse les bornes!; off ~s d'accès interdit; within ~s [to an extent] dans une certaine mesure. ◇ *vt* limiter, restreindre; to ~ o.s. to sthg se limiter à qqch.

limitation [ˌlɪmɪ'teɪʃn] *n* limitation *f*, restriction *f*; to know one's ~s connaître ses limites.

limited ['lɪmɪtɪd] *adj* limité(e), restreint(e).

limited edition *n* [of book] édition *f* à tirage limité.

limited (liability) company *n* société *f* anonyme.

limitless ['lɪmɪtlɪs] *adj* illimité(e).

limo ['lɪməʊ] *n inf abbr of* **limousine**.

limousine ['lɪməziːn] *n* limousine *f*.

limp [lɪmp] ◇ *adj* mou (molle). ◇ *n*: to have a ~ boiter. ◇ *vi* boiter.

limpet ['lɪmpɪt] *n* patelle *f*, bernique *f*.

limpid ['lɪmpɪd] *adj literary* limpide.

limply ['lɪmplɪ] *adv* mollement.

linchpin ['lɪntʃpɪn] *n fig* cheville *f* ouvrière.

Lincs. [lɪŋks] (*abbr of* **Lincolnshire**) *comté anglais*.

linctus ['lɪŋktəs] *n Br* sirop *m* pour la toux.

line [laɪn] ◇ *n* **-1.** [gen] ligne *f*; to walk in a straight ~ marcher en ligne droite. **-2.** [row] rangée *f*. **-3.** [queue] file *f*, queue *f*; to stand OR wait in ~ faire la queue; he's in ~ for promotion il devrait être promu bientôt. **-4.** RAIL voie *f*; [route] ligne *f*. **-5.** NAUT: shipping ~ compagnie *f* de navigation. **-6.** [of poem, song] vers *m*. **-7.** [wrinkle] ride *f*. **-8.** [string, wire etc] corde *f*; a fishing ~ une ligne. **-9.** TELEC ligne *f*; hold the ~! ne quittez pas! **-10.** *inf* [short letter]: to drop sb a ~ écrire un (petit) mot à qqn. **-11.** [course of action]: what ~ did you take? quelle stratégie as-tu adoptée?; to think along the same ~s partager la même opinion; ~ of argument raisonnement *m*. **-12.** *inf* [work]: ~ of business branche *f*. **-13.** [borderline] frontière *f*. **-14.** [lineage] lignée *f*. **-15.** COMM gamme *f*. **-16.** *phr*: to be on the right ~s être sur la bonne voie; to read between the ~s lire entre les lignes; to draw the ~ at sthg refuser de faire OR d'aller jusqu'à faire qqch; to step out of ~ faire cavalier seul.
◇ *vt* **-1.** [form rows along]: trees ~d the streets les rues étaient bordées d'arbres. **-2.** [drawer, box] tapisser; [clothes] doubler.
◆ **lines** *npl* **-1.** SCH: to be given 100 ~s avoir 100 lignes à faire. **-2.** THEATRE texte *m*.
◆ **on the line** *adv*: to put sthg/to be on the ~ mettre qqch/être en jeu.
◆ **out of line** *adj* [remark, behaviour] déplacé(e).
◆ **line up** ◇ *vt sep* **-1.** [in rows] aligner. **-2.** [organize] prévoir. ◇ *vi* [in row] s'aligner; [in queue] faire la queue.

lineage ['lɪnɪɪdʒ] *n* lignée *f*.

linear ['lɪnɪə'] *adj* linéaire.

lined [laɪnd] *adj* -1. [paper] réglé(e). -2. [wrinkled] ridé(e).

line drawing *n* dessin *m* au trait.

line feed *n* saut *m* de ligne.

linen ['lɪnɪn] ◇ *n* (U) -1. [cloth] lin *m*. -2. [tablecloths, sheets] linge *m* (de maison). ◇ *comp* -1. [suit etc] de OR en lin. -2. [cupboard] à linge.

linen basket *n* panier *m* à linge.

line printer *n* imprimante *f* ligne par ligne.

liner ['laɪnə'] *n* [ship] paquebot *m*.

linesman ['laɪnzmən] (*pl* **-men** [-mən]) *n* TENNIS juge *m* de ligne; FTBL juge de touche.

lineup ['laɪnʌp] *n* -1. SPORT équipe *f*. -2. Am [identification parade] rangée *f* de suspects (*pour identification par un témoin*).

linger ['lɪŋgə'] *vi* -1. [person] s'attarder. -2. [doubt, pain] persister.

lingerie ['lænʒərɪ] *n* (U) lingerie *f*.

lingering ['lɪŋgrɪŋ] *adj* [doubt] persistant(e); [hope] faible; [illness] long (longue).

lingo ['lɪŋgəʊ] (*pl* **-es**) *n inf* jargon *m*.

linguist ['lɪŋgwɪst] *n* linguiste *mf*.

linguistic [lɪŋ'gwɪstɪk] *adj* linguistique.

linguistics [lɪŋ'gwɪstɪks] *n* (U) linguistique *f*.

liniment ['lɪnɪmənt] *n* liniment *m*.

lining ['laɪnɪŋ] *n* -1. [of coat, curtains, box] doublure *f*. -2. [of stomach] muqueuse *f*. -3. AUT [of brakes] garniture *f*.

link [lɪŋk] ◇ *n* -1. [of chain] maillon *m*. -2. [connection]: ~ **(between/with)** lien *m* (entre/avec); **a rail/telephone** ~ une liaison ferroviaire/téléphonique. ◇ *vt* [cities, parts] relier; [events etc] lier; **to** ~ **arms** se donner le bras.
◆ **link up** *vt sep* relier; **to** ~ **sthg up with sthg** relier qqch avec OR à qqch.

linkage ['lɪŋkɪdʒ] *n* (U) [relationship] lien *m*, relation *f*.

linked [lɪŋkt] *adj* lié(e).

links [lɪŋks] (*pl inv*) *n* terrain *m* de golf (*au bord de la mer*).

linkup ['lɪŋkʌp] *n* liaison *f*.

lino ['laɪnəʊ], **linoleum** [lɪ'nəʊlɪəm] *n* lino *m*, linoléum *m*.

linseed oil ['lɪnsiːd-] *n* huile *f* de lin.

lint [lɪnt] *n* (U) -1. [dressing] compresse *f*. -2. Am [fluff] peluches *fpl*.

lintel ['lɪntl] *n* linteau *m*.

lion ['laɪən] *n* lion *m*.

lion cub *n* lionceau *m*.

lioness ['laɪənes] *n* lionne *f*.

lionize, -ise ['laɪənaɪz] *vt* porter aux nues.

lip [lɪp] *n* -1. [of mouth] lèvre *f*; **my ~s are sealed** je ne dirai rien. -2. [of container] bord *m*.

lip-read *vi* lire sur les lèvres.

lip-reading *n* lecture *f* sur les lèvres.

lip salve *n Br* pommade *f* pour les lèvres.

lip service *n*: **to pay** ~ **to sthg** approuver qqch pour la forme.

lipstick ['lɪpstɪk] *n* rouge *m* à lèvres.

liquefy ['lɪkwɪfaɪ] (*pt & pp* **-ied**) ◇ *vt* liquéfier. ◇ *vi* se liquéfier.

liqueur [lɪ'kjʊə'] *n* liqueur *f*.

liquid ['lɪkwɪd] ◇ *adj* liquide. ◇ *n* liquide *m*.

liquid assets *npl* liquidités *fpl*.

liquidate ['lɪkwɪdeɪt] *vt* liquider.

liquidation [,lɪkwɪ'deɪʃn] *n* liquidation *f*.

liquidator ['lɪkwɪdeɪtə'] *n* liquidateur *m*, -trice *f*.

liquid crystal display *n* affichage *m* à cristaux liquides.

liquidity [lɪ'kwɪdətɪ] *n* liquidité *f*.

liquidize, -ise ['lɪkwɪdaɪz] *vt Br* CULIN passer au mixer.

liquidizer ['lɪkwɪdaɪzə'] *n Br* mixer *m*.

liquor ['lɪkə'] *n* (U) alcool *m*, spiritueux *mpl*.

liquorice ['lɪkərɪs] *n* réglisse *f*.

liquor store *n Am* magasin *m* de vins et d'alcools.

lira ['lɪərə] *n* lire *f*.

Lisbon ['lɪzbən] *n* Lisbonne.

lisp [lɪsp] ◇ *n* zézaiement *m*. ◇ *vi* zézayer.

lissom(e) ['lɪsəm] *adj* gracile.

list [lɪst] ◇ *n* liste *f*. ◇ *vt* [in writing] faire la liste de; [in speech] énumérer. ◇ *vi* NAUT donner de la bande, gîter.

listed building ['lɪstɪd-] *n Br* monument *m* classé.

listed company ['lɪstɪd-] *n Br* société *f* cotée en Bourse.

listen ['lɪsn] *vi*: **to** ~ **to (sb/sthg)** écouter (qqn/qqch); **to** ~ **for sthg** guetter qqch.
◆ **listen in** *vi* -1. RADIO être à l'écoute, écouter. -2. [eavesdrop]: **to** ~ **in (on sthg)** écouter (qqch).
◆ **listen up** *vi Am inf* écouter.

listener ['lɪsnə'] *n* auditeur *m*, -trice *f*.

listing ['lɪstɪŋ] *n* [COMPUT - action] listage *m*; [- result] listing *m*.
◆ **listings** *npl*: **the** ~**s** le calendrier des spectacles.

listless ['lɪstlɪs] *adj* apathique, mou (molle).

list price *n* prix *m* de catalogue.

lit [lɪt] *pt & pp* → **light**.

litany ['lɪtənɪ] (*pl* -ies) *n* litanie *f*.

liter *Am* = **litre**.

literacy ['lɪtərəsɪ] *n* fait *m* de savoir lire et écrire.

literal ['lɪtərəl] *adj* littéral(e).

literally ['lɪtərəlɪ] *adv* littéralement; **to take sthg** ~ prendre qqch au pied de la lettre.

literary ['lɪtərərɪ] *adj* littéraire.

literate ['lɪtərət] *adj* -1. [able to read and write] qui sait lire et écrire. -2. [well-read] cultivé(e).

literature ['lɪtrətʃər] ◇ *n* littérature *f*; [printed information] documentation *f*.

lithe [laɪð] *adj* souple, agile.

lithograph ['lɪθəgrɑːf] *n* lithographie *f*.

lithography [lɪ'θɒgrəfɪ] *n* lithographie *f*.

Lithuania [ˌlɪθjʊ'eɪnjə] *n* Lituanie *f*; **in** ~ en Lituanie.

Lithuanian [ˌlɪθjʊ'eɪnjən] ◇ *adj* lituanien(ienne). ◇ *n* -1. [person] Lituanien *m*, -ienne *f*. -2. [language] lituanien *m*.

litigant ['lɪtɪgənt] *n* plaideur *m*, -euse *f*.

litigate ['lɪtɪgeɪt] *vi* plaider.

litigation [ˌlɪtɪ'geɪʃn] *n* litige *m*; **to go to** ~ aller en justice.

litmus paper ['lɪtməs-] *n* papier *m* de tournesol.

litre *Br*, **liter** *Am* ['liːtər] *n* litre *m*.

litter ['lɪtər] ◇ *n* -1. (*U*) [rubbish] ordures *fpl*, détritus *mpl*. -2. [of animals] portée *f*. ◇ *vt*: **to be ~ed with** être couvert(e) de.

litterbin ['lɪtəbɪn] *n Br* boîte *f* à ordures.

litterlout *Br* ['lɪtəlaʊt], **litterbug** ['lɪtəbʌg] *n* personne qui jette des ordures n'importe où.

litter tray *n* caisse *f* (pour litière).

little ['lɪtl] (*compar sense 2* **less**, *superl sense 2* **least**) ◇ *adj* -1. [not big] petit(e); **a** ~ **chat** un brin de causette; **a** ~ **while** un petit moment. -2. [not much] peu de; ~ **money** peu d'argent; **a** ~ **money** un peu d'argent. ◇ *pron*: ~ **of the money was left** il ne restait pas beaucoup d'argent, il restait peu d'argent; **I understood** ~ **of what was said** je n'ai pas compris grand-chose à ce qu'ils ont dit; **I see very** ~ **of him now** je ne le vois plus beaucoup, je ne le vois guère; **a** ~ un peu. ◇ *adv* peu, pas beaucoup; ~ **by** ~ peu à peu.

little finger *n* petit doigt *m*, auriculaire *m*.

little-known *adj* peu connu(e).

liturgy ['lɪtədʒɪ] (*pl* -ies) *n* liturgie *f*.

live[1] [lɪv] ◇ *vi* -1. [gen] vivre; **long** ~ **the Queen!** vive la reine! -2. [have one's home] habiter, vivre; **to** ~ **in Paris** habiter (à) Paris. ◇ *vt*: **to** ~ **a quiet life** mener une vie tranquille; **to** ~ **it up** *inf* faire la noce.

◆ **live down** *vt sep* faire oublier.

◆ **live for** *vt fus* vivre pour.

◆ **live in** *vi* [student] être interne.

◆ **live off** *vt fus* [savings, the land] vivre de; [family] vivre aux dépens de.

◆ **live on** ◇ *vt fus* vivre de. ◇ *vi* [memory, feeling] rester, survivre.

◆ **live out** ◇ *vt fus* passer. ◇ *vi* [student] être externe.

◆ **live together** *vi* vivre ensemble.

◆ **live up to** *vt fus*: **to** ~ **up to sb's expectations** répondre à l'attente de qqn; **to** ~ **up to one's reputation** faire honneur à sa réputation.

◆ **live with** *vt fus* -1. [cohabit with] vivre avec. -2. *inf* [accept] se faire à, accepter.

live[2] [laɪv] ◇ *adj* -1. [living] vivant(e). -2. [coal] ardent(e). -3. [bullet, bomb] non explosé(e); ~ **ammunition** munitions *fpl* de combat. -4. ELEC sous tension. -5. RADIO & TV en direct; [performance] en public. ◇ *adv* RADIO & TV en direct; [perform] en public.

live-in [lɪv-] *adj* [housekeeper] logé(e) et nourri(e); **a** ~ **boyfriend/girlfriend** un petit ami/une petite amie avec qui on vit.

livelihood ['laɪvlɪhʊd] *n* gagne-pain *m*.

liveliness ['laɪvlɪnɪs] *n* vivacité *f*.

lively ['laɪvlɪ] (*compar* -ier, *superl* -iest) *adj* -1. [person] plein(e) d'entrain. -2. [debate, meeting] animé(e). -3. [mind] vif (vive).

liven ['laɪvn]

◆ **liven up** ◇ *vt sep* [person] égayer; [place] animer. ◇ *vi* s'animer.

liver ['lɪvər] *n* foie *m*.

Liverpudlian ◇ *adj* de Liverpool. ◇ *n* habitant *m*, -e *f* de Liverpool.

liver sausage *Br*, **liverwurst** *Am* ['lɪvəwɜːst] *n* saucisse *f* (au pâté) de foie.

livery ['lɪvərɪ] (*pl* -ies) *n* livrée *f*.

lives [laɪvz] *pl* → **life**.

livestock ['laɪvstɒk] *n* (*U*) bétail *m*.

live wire [laɪv-] *n* fil *m* sous tension; *inf fig* boute-en-train *m inv*.

livid ['lɪvɪd] *adj* -1. [angry] furieux(ieuse). -2. [bruise] violacé(e).

living ['lɪvɪŋ] ◇ *adj* vivant(e), en vie. ◇ *n*: **to earn** OR **make a** ~ gagner sa vie; **what do you do for a** ~? qu'est-ce que vous faites dans la vie?

living conditions *npl* conditions *fpl* de vie.

living expenses *npl* frais *mpl* de subsistance.

living room *n* salle *f* de séjour, living *m*.

living standards *npl* niveau *m* de vie.

living wage *n* minimum *m* vital.

lizard ['lɪzəd] *n* lézard *m*.

llama ['lɑːmə] (*pl inv* OR **-s**) *n* lama *m*.

LLB (*abbr of* **Bachelor of Laws**) *n* (*titulaire d'une*) *licence de droit.*

LLD (*abbr of* **Doctor of Laws**) *n docteur en droit.*

LMT (*abbr of* **Local Mean Time**) *n heure locale aux États-Unis.*

lo [ləʊ] *excl*: ~ **and behold** et comme par miracle.

load [ləʊd] ◇ *n* **-1.** [something carried] chargement *m*, charge *f*. **-2.** [large amount]: ~**s of, a** ~ **of** *inf* des tas de, plein de; **a** ~ **of rubbish** *inf* de la foutaise. ◇ *vt* [gen & COMPUT] charger; [video recorder] mettre une vidéo-cassette dans; **to** ~ **sb/sthg with** charger qqn/qqch de; **to** ~ **a gun/camera (with)** charger un fusil/un appareil (avec).
◆ **load up** *vt sep & vi* charger.

loaded ['ləʊdɪd] *adj* **-1.** [question] insidieux(ieuse). **-2.** *inf* [rich] plein(e) aux as.

loading bay ['ləʊdɪŋ-] *n* aire *f* de chargement.

loaf [ləʊf] (*pl* **loaves**) *n*: **a** ~ **(of bread)** un pain.

loafer ['ləʊfər] *n* [shoe] mocassin *m*.

loam [ləʊm] *n* terreau *m*.

loan [ləʊn] ◇ *n* prêt *m*; **on** ~ prêté(e). ◇ *vt* prêter; **to** ~ **sthg to sb, to** ~ **sb sthg** prêter qqch à qqn.

loan account *n* compte *m* d'avances.

loan capital *n* capital-obligations *m*.

loan shark *n inf pej* usurier *m*.

loath [ləʊθ] *adj*: **to be** ~ **to do sthg** ne pas vouloir faire qqch, hésiter à faire qqch.

loathe [ləʊð] *vt* détester; **to** ~ **doing sthg** avoir horreur de OR détester faire qqch.

loathing ['ləʊðɪŋ] *n* dégoût *m*, répugnance *f*.

loathsome ['ləʊðsəm] *adj* dégoûtant(e), répugnant(e).

loaves [ləʊvz] *pl* → **loaf**.

lob [lɒb] (*pt & pp* **-bed**, *cont* **-bing**) ◇ *n* TENNIS lob *m*. ◇ *vt* **-1.** [throw] lancer. **-2.** TENNIS: **to** ~ **a ball** lober, faire un lob.

lobby ['lɒbɪ] (*pl* **-ies**, *pt & pp* **-ied**) ◇ *n* **-1.** [of hotel] hall *m*. **-2.** [pressure group] lobby *m*, group *m* de pression. ◇ *vt* faire pression sur.

lobbyist ['lɒbɪɪst] *n* membre *m* d'un groupe de pression.

lobe [ləʊb] *n* lobe *m*.

lobelia [lə'biːljə] *n* lobélie *f*.

lobotomy [lə'bɒtəmɪ] (*pl* **-ies**) *n* lobotomie *f*.

lobster ['lɒbstər] *n* homard *m*.

local ['ləʊkl] ◇ *adj* local(e). ◇ *n inf* **-1.** [person]: **the** ~**s** les gens *mpl* du coin OR du pays. **-2.** *Br* [pub] café *m* OR bistro *m* du coin. **-3.** *Am* [bus, train] omnibus *m*.

local anaesthetic *n* anesthésie *f* locale.

local area network *n* COMPUT réseau *m* local.

local authority *n Br* autorités *fpl* locales.

local call *n* communication *f* urbaine.

local colour *n* couleur *f* locale.

local derby *n Br* derby *m*.

locale [ləʊ'kɑːl] *n fml* lieu *m*, endroit *m*.

local government *n* administration *f* municipale.

locality [lə'kælətɪ] (*pl* **-ies**) *n* endroit *m*.

localized, -ised ['ləʊkəlaɪzd] *adj* localisé(e).

locally ['ləʊkəlɪ] *adv* **-1.** [on local basis] localement. **-2.** [nearby] dans les environs, à proximité.

local time *n* heure *f* locale.

locate [*Br* ləʊ'keɪt, *Am* 'ləʊkeɪt] ◇ *vt* **-1.** [find - position] trouver, repérer; [- source, problem] localiser. **-2.** [situate - business, factory] implanter, établir; **to be** ~**d** être situé. ◇ *vi Am* [settle] s'installer.

location [ləʊ'keɪʃn] *n* **-1.** [place] emplacement *m*. **-2.** CINEMA: **on** ~ en extérieur.

loc. cit. (*abbr of* **loco citato**) loc. cit.

loch [lɒk, lɒx] *n Scot* loch *m*, lac *m*.

lock [lɒk] ◇ *n* **-1.** [of door etc] serrure *f*; **under** ~ **and key** [object] sous clef; [person] sous les verrous. **-2.** [on canal] écluse *f*. **-3.** AUT [steering lock] angle *m* de braquage. **-4.** [of hair] mèche *f*. **-5.** *phr*: ~, **stock and barrel** en bloc.
◇ *vt* **-1.** [door, car, drawer] fermer à clef; [bicycle] cadenasser. **-2.** [immobilize] bloquer. **-3.** [hold firmly]: **to be** ~**ed in an embrace** être étroitement enlacés.
◇ *vi* **-1.** [door, suitcase] fermer à clef. **-2.** [become immobilized] se bloquer.
◆ **locks** *npl literary* chevelure *f*, cheveux *mpl*.
◆ **lock in** *vt sep* enfermer (à clef).
◆ **lock out** *vt sep* **-1.** [accidentally] enfermer dehors, laisser dehors; **to** ~ **o.s. out** s'enfermer dehors. **-2.** [deliberately] empêcher d'entrer, mettre à la porte.

◆ **lock up** ◇ *vt sep* [person - in prison] mettre en prison OR sous les verrous; [- in asylum] enfermer; [house] fermer à clef; [valuables] enfermer, mettre sous clef. ◇ *vi* fermer (à clef).

lockable ['lɒkəbl] *adj* qu'on peut fermer à clef.

locker ['lɒkə'] *n* casier *m*.

locker room *n Am* vestiaire *m*.

locket ['lɒkɪt] *n* médaillon *m*.

lockjaw ['lɒkdʒɔ:] *n* tétanos *m*.

lockout ['lɒkaʊt] *n* lock-out *m inv*.

locksmith ['lɒksmɪθ] *n* serrurier *m*.

lockup ['lɒkʌp] *n* -1. [prison] prison *f*. -2. *Br* [garage] garage *m*, box *m*.

loco ['ləʊkəʊ] (*pl* -s) *inf* ◇ *adj Am* timbré(e). ◇ *n Br* locomotive.

locomotive ['ləʊkə,məʊtɪv] *n* locomotive *f*.

locum ['ləʊkəm] (*pl* -s) *n* remplaçant *m*, -e *f*.

locust ['ləʊkəst] *n* sauterelle *f*, locuste *f*.

lodge [lɒdʒ] ◇ *n* -1. [of caretaker, freemasons] loge *f*. -2. [of manor house] pavillon *m* (de gardien). -3. [for hunting] pavillon *m* de chasse. ◇ *vi* -1. [stay]: **to ~ with sb** loger chez qqn. -2. [become stuck] se loger, se coincer. -3. *fig* [in mind] s'enraciner, s'ancrer. ◇ *vt* [complaint] déposer; **to ~ an appeal** interjeter OR faire appel.

lodger ['lɒdʒə'] *n* locataire *mf*.

lodging ['lɒdʒɪŋ] *n* → **board**.

◆ **lodgings** *npl* chambre *f* meublée.

loft [lɒft] *n* grenier *m*.

lofty ['lɒftɪ] (*compar* -ier, *superl* -iest) *adj* -1. [noble] noble. -2. *pej* [haughty] hautain(e), arrogant(e). -3. *literary* [high] haut(e), élevé(e).

log [lɒg] (*pt & pp* -ged, *cont* -ging) ◇ *n* -1. [of wood] bûche *f*. -2. [of ship] journal *m* de bord; [of plane] carnet *m* de vol. ◇ *vt* consigner, enregistrer.

◆ **log in** *vi* COMPUT ouvrir une session.

◆ **log out** *vi* COMPUT fermer une session.

loganberry ['ləʊgənbərɪ] (*pl* -ies) *n* sorte de framboise.

logarithm ['lɒgərɪθm] *n* logarithme *m*.

logbook ['lɒgbʊk] *n* -1. [of ship] journal *m* de bord; [of plane] carnet *m* de vol. -2. [of car] ≃ carte *f* grise.

log cabin *n* cabane *f* en rondins.

log fire *n* feu *m* de bois.

loggerheads ['lɒgəhedz] *n*: **at ~** en désaccord.

logic ['lɒdʒɪk] *n* logique *f*.

logical ['lɒdʒɪkl] *adj* logique.

logically ['lɒdʒɪklɪ] *adv* logiquement.

logistical [lə'dʒɪstɪkl] *adj* logistique.

logistics [lə'dʒɪstɪks] ◇ *n* (U) MIL logistique *f*. ◇ *npl fig* organisation *f*.

logjam ['lɒgdʒæm] *n* impasse *f*.

logo ['ləʊgəʊ] (*pl* -s) *n* logo *m*.

logrolling ['lɒgrəʊlɪŋ] *n* (U) *Am* échange *m* de faveurs.

logy ['ləʊgɪ] *adj Am inf* patraque.

loin [lɔɪn] *n* filet *m*.

◆ **loins** *npl* reins *mpl*; **to gird one's ~s** prendre son courage à deux mains.

loincloth ['lɔɪnklɒθ] *n* pagne *m*.

loiter ['lɔɪtə'] *vi* traîner.

loll [lɒl] *vi* -1. [sit, lie about] se prélasser. -2. [hang down - head, tongue] pendre.

lollipop ['lɒlɪpɒp] *n* sucette *f*.

lollipop lady *n Br* dame qui fait traverser la rue aux enfants à la sortie des écoles.

lollipop man *n Br* monsieur qui fait traverser la rue aux enfants à la sortie des écoles.

lolly ['lɒlɪ] (*pl* -ies) *n inf* -1. [lollipop] sucette *f*. -2. *Br* [ice cream] esquimau *m*. -3. *Br* [money] fric *m*, blé *m*.

London ['lʌndən] *n* Londres.

Londoner ['lʌndənə'] *n* Londonien *m*, -ienne *f*.

lone [ləʊn] *adj* solitaire.

loneliness ['ləʊnlɪnɪs] *n* [of person] solitude *f*; [of place] isolement *m*.

lonely ['ləʊnlɪ] (*compar* -ier, *superl* -iest) *adj* -1. [person] solitaire, seul(e); **to feel ~** se sentir seul. -2. [childhood] solitaire. -3. [place] isolé(e).

lone parent *n Br* père *m*/mère *f* célibataire.

loner ['ləʊnə'] *n* solitaire *mf*.

lonesome ['ləʊnsəm] *adj Am inf* -1. [person] solitaire, seul(e). -2. [place] isolé(e).

long [lɒŋ] ◇ *adj* long (longue); **two days/ years ~** de deux jours/ans, qui dure deux jours/ans; **10 metres/miles ~** long de 10 mètres/milles, de 10 mètres/milles (de long); **a ~ memory** une bonne mémoire.

◇ *adv* longtemps; **how ~ will it take?** combien de temps cela va-t-il prendre?; **how ~ will you be?** tu en as pour combien de temps?; **how ~ is the book?** quelle est la longueur du livre?; **I no ~er like him** je ne l'aime plus; **I can't wait any ~er** je ne peux pas attendre plus longtemps; **so ~!** *inf* au revoir!, salut!; **before ~** sous peu; **for ~** pour longtemps.

◇ *n*: **the ~ and the short of it is that ...** le fin mot de l'histoire, c'est que ..., enfin bref ....

◇ *vt*: **to ~ to do sthg** avoir très envie de faire qqch.

◆ **as long as**, **so long as** *conj* tant que.

◆ **long for** *vt fus* [peace and quiet] désirer ardemment; [holidays] attendre avec impatience.

long. (*abbr of* **longitude**) long.

long-awaited [-ə'weɪtɪd] *adj* tant attendu(e).

long-distance *adj* [runner, race] de fond; ~ **lorry driver** routier *m*.

long-distance call *n* communication *f* interurbaine.

long division *n* division *f* par écrit.

long-drawn-out *adj* interminable, qui n'en finit pas.

long drink *n* long drink *m*.

longevity [lɒn'dʒevətɪ] *n* longévité *f*.

longhaired [‚lɒŋ'heəd] *adj* [person] aux cheveux longs; [animal] à longs poils.

longhand ['lɒŋhænd] *n* écriture *f* normale.

long-haul *adj* long-courrier.

longing ['lɒŋɪŋ] ◇ *adj* plein(e) de convoitise. ◇ *n* **-1.** [desire] envie *f*, convoitise *f*; a ~ **for** un grand désir OR une grande envie de. **-2.** [nostalgia] nostalgie *f*, regret *m*.

longingly ['lɒŋɪŋlɪ] *adv* [with desire] avec envie; [nostalgically] avec nostalgie.

Long Island *n* Long Island; **in** ~ à Long Island.

longitude ['lɒndʒɪtjuːd] *n* longitude *f*.

long johns *npl* caleçon *m* long.

long jump *n* saut *m* en longueur.

long-lasting *adj* qui dure longtemps, durable.

long-life *adj* [milk] longue conservation (*inv*); [battery] longue durée (*inv*).

long-lost *adj* [artefact] perdu(e) depuis longtemps; [relative] perdu(e) de vue depuis longtemps.

long-playing record [-'pleɪɪŋ-] *n* 33 tours *m*.

long-range *adj* **-1.** [missile, bomber] à longue portée. **-2.** [plan, forecast] à long terme.

long-running *adj* [TV programme] diffusé(e) depuis de nombreuses années; [play] qui tient depuis longtemps l'affiche; [dispute] qui dure depuis longtemps.

longshoreman ['lɒŋʃɔːmən] (*pl* -men [-mən]) *n Am* docker *m*.

long shot *n* [guess] coup *m* à tenter (*sans grand espoir de succès*).

longsighted [‚lɒŋ'saɪtɪd] *adj* hypermétrope, presbyte.

long-standing *adj* de longue date.

longsuffering [‚lɒŋ'sʌfərɪŋ] *adj* [person] à la patience infinie.

long term *n*: **in the** ~ à long terme.

◆ **long-term** *adj* à long terme.

long vacation *n Br* grandes vacances *fpl*.

long wave *n* (*U*) grandes ondes *fpl*.

longways ['lɒŋweɪz] *adv* dans le sens de la longueur.

longwearing [‚lɒŋ'weərɪŋ] *adj Am* solide, résistant(e).

long weekend *n* long week-end *m*.

longwinded [‚lɒŋ'wɪndɪd] *adj* [person] prolixe, verbeux(euse); [speech] interminable, qui n'en finit pas.

loo [luː] (*pl* -s) *n Br inf* cabinets *mpl*, petit coin *m*.

loofa(h) ['luːfə] *n* luffa *m*, éponge *f*.

look [lʊk] ◇ *n* **-1.** [with eyes] regard *m*; **to take** OR **have a** ~ **(at sthg)** regarder (qqch), jeter un coup d'œil (à qqch); **to give sb a** ~ jeter un regard à qqn, regarder qqn de travers. **-2.** [search]: **to have a** ~ **(for sthg)** chercher (qqch). **-3.** [appearance] aspect *m*, air *m*; **by the** ~ OR **~s of it**, **by the** ~ OR **~s of things** vraisemblablement, selon toute probabilité.
◇ *vi* **-1.** [with eyes] regarder. **-2.** [search] chercher. **-3.** [building, window]: **to** ~ **(out) onto** donner sur. **-4.** [seem] avoir l'air, sembler; **he** ~**s as if he hasn't slept** il a l'air d'avoir mal dormi; **it** ~**s like rain** OR **as if it will rain** on dirait qu'il va pleuvoir; **she** ~**s like her mother** elle ressemble à sa mère.
◇ *vt* **-1.** [look at]: ~ **what you've done!** regarde ce que tu as fait! **-2.** [appear]: **to** ~ **one's age** faire OR porter son âge; **to** ~ **one's best** être OR paraître à son avantage.
◇ *excl*: ~!, ~ **here!** dites donc!

◆ **looks** *npl* [attractiveness] beauté *f*.

◆ **look after** *vt fus* s'occuper de.

◆ **look at** *vt fus* **-1.** [see, glance at] regarder; [examine] examiner. **-2.** [judge] considérer.

◆ **look back** *vi* [reminisce] penser au passé, évoquer le passé; **she's never** ~**ed back** depuis, elle a accumulé les succès.

◆ **look down on** *vt fus* [condescend to] mépriser.

◆ **look for** *vt fus* chercher.

◆ **look forward to** *vt fus* attendre avec impatience.

◆ **look into** *vt fus* examiner, étudier.

◆ **look on** ◇ *vt fus* = **look upon**. ◇ *vi* regarder.

◆ **look out** *vi* prendre garde, faire attention; ~ **out!** attention!

◆ **look out for** *vt fus* [person] guetter; [new book] être à l'affût de, essayer de repérer.

◆ **look round** ◇ *vt fus* [house, shop, town] faire le tour de. ◇ *vi* regarder.

◆ **look through** vt fus [gen] examiner; [newspaper] parcourir.

◆ **look to** vt fus **-1.** [depend on] compter sur. **-2.** [future] songer à.

◆ **look up** ◇ vt sep **-1.** [in book] chercher. **-2.** [visit - person] aller OR passer voir. ◇ vi [improve - business] reprendre; **things are ~ing up** ça va mieux, la situation s'améliore.

◆ **look upon** vt fus: **to ~ upon sb/sthg as** considérer qqn/qqch comme.

◆ **look up to** vt fus admirer.

look-alike n sosie m.

look-in n Br inf: **to get a ~** avoir une chance (de faire qqch).

lookout ['lukaut] n **-1.** [place] poste m de guet. **-2.** [person] guetteur m. **-3.** [search]: **to be on the ~ for** être à la recherche de.

look-up table n COMPUT table f de recherche.

loom [lu:m] ◇ n métier m à tisser. ◇ vi [building, person] se dresser; fig [date, threat] être imminent(e); **to ~ large** être un sujet d'inquiétude OR de préoccupation.

◆ **loom up** vi surgir.

LOOM (abbr of **Loyal Order of the Moose**) n association caritative américaine.

looming ['lu:mɪŋ] adj imminent(e).

loony ['lu:nɪ] (compar **-ier**, superl **-iest**, pl **-ies**) inf ◇ adj cinglé(e), timbré(e). ◇ n cinglé m, -e f, fou m, folle f.

loop [lu:p] ◇ n **-1.** [gen & COMPUT] boucle f. **-2.** [contraceptive] stérilet m. ◇ vt faire une boucle à. ◇ vi faire une boucle.

loophole ['lu:phəul] n faille f, échappatoire f.

loo roll n Br inf rouleau m de papier hygiénique.

loose [lu:s] ◇ adj **-1.** [not firm - joint] desserré(e); [- handle, post] branlant(e); [- tooth] qui bouge OR branle; [- knot] défait(e). **-2.** [unpackaged - sweets, nails] en vrac, au poids. **-3.** [clothes] ample, large. **-4.** [not restrained - hair] dénoué(e); [- animal] en liberté, détaché(e). **-5.** pej & dated [woman] facile; [living] dissolu(e). **-6.** [inexact - translation] approximatif(ive). **-7.** Am inf [relaxed]: **to stay ~** rester cool. ◇ n: **on the ~** en liberté.

loose change n petite OR menue monnaie f.

loose end n détail m inexpliqué; **to be at a ~** Br, **to be at ~s** Am être désœuvré, n'avoir rien à faire.

loose-fitting adj ample.

loose-leaf binder n classeur m.

loosely ['lu:slɪ] adv **-1.** [not firmly] sans serrer. **-2.** [inexactly] approximativement.

loosen ['lu:sn] ◇ vt desserrer, défaire. ◇ vi se desserrer.

◆ **loosen up** vi **-1.** [before game, race] s'échauffer. **-2.** inf [relax] se détendre.

loot [lu:t] ◇ n butin m. ◇ vt piller.

looter ['lu:tər] n pillard m, -e f.

looting ['lu:tɪŋ] n pillage m.

lop [lop] (pt & pp **-ped**, cont **-ping**) vt élaguer, émonder.

◆ **lop off** vt sep couper.

lope [ləup] vi courir en faisant des bonds.

lop-sided [-'saɪdɪd] adj **-1.** [table] bancal(e), boiteux(euse); [picture] de travers. **-2.** fig [biased] tendancieux(ieuse).

lord [lɔ:d] n Br seigneur m.

◆ **Lord** n **-1.** RELIG: **the Lord** [God] le Seigneur; **good Lord!** Br Seigneur!, mon Dieu! **-2.** [in titles] Lord m; [as form of address]: **my Lord** Monsieur le duc/comte etc.

◆ **Lords** npl Br POL: **the (House of) Lords** la Chambre des Lords.

Lord Chancellor n Br Lord Chancelier m.

lordly ['lɔ:dlɪ] (compar **-ier**, superl **-iest**) adj **-1.** [noble] noble. **-2.** pej [arrogant] arrogant(e), hautain(e).

Lord Mayor n Br Lord-Maire m.

Lordship ['lɔ:dʃɪp] n: **your/his ~** Monsieur le duc/comte etc.

Lord's Prayer n: **the ~** le Notre Père.

lore [lɔ:r] n (U) traditions fpl.

lorry ['lɒrɪ] (pl **-ies**) n Br camion m.

lorry driver n Br camionneur m, conducteur m de poids lourd.

lose [lu:z] (pt & pp **lost**) ◇ vt **-1.** [gen] perdre; **to ~ sight of** lit & fig perdre de vue; **to ~ one's way** se perdre, perdre son chemin; fig être un peu perdu. **-2.** [subj: clock, watch] retarder de; **to ~ time** retarder. **-3.** [pursuers] semer. ◇ vi perdre.

◆ **lose out** vi être perdant(e); **to ~ out on a deal** être perdant dans une affaire.

loser ['lu:zər] n **-1.** [gen] perdant m, -e f; **a good/bad ~** un bon/mauvais joueur m, une bonne/mauvaise joueuse f. **-2.** inf pej [unsuccessful person] raté m, -e f.

losing ['lu:zɪŋ] adj perdant(e).

loss [lɒs] n **-1.** [gen] perte f. **-2.** COMM: **to make a ~** perdre de l'argent. **-3.** phr: **to be at a ~** être perplexe, être embarrassé(e); **I'm at a ~ to explain what happened** je n'arrive pas à expliquer comment cela a pu se produire; **to cut one's ~es** faire la part du feu.

loss adjuster [-ə'dʒʌstər] *n* responsable *m* de l'évaluation des sinistres.

loss leader *n* COMM *article vendu à perte dans le but d'attirer la clientèle.*

lost [lɒst] ◇ *pt & pp* → **lose**. ◇ *adj* -1. [gen] perdu(e); **get ~!** *inf* fous/foutez le camp! -2. [ineffective]: **to be ~ on sb** [advice, warning] être sans effet sur qqn, n'avoir aucun effet sur qqn. -3. [opportunity] perdu(e), manqué(e).

lost-and-found office *n Am* bureau *m* des objets trouvés.

lost cause *n* cause *f* perdue.

lost property *n* (*U*) objets *mpl* trouvés.

lost property office *n Br* bureau *m* des objets trouvés.

lot [lɒt] *n* -1. [large amount]: **a ~ (of), ~s (of)** beaucoup (de); [entire amount]: **the ~** le tout. -2. [at auction] lot *m*. -3. *inf* [group of people]: **they're a strange ~** ce sont des gens bizarres. -4. [destiny] sort *m*. -5. *Am* [of land] terrain *m*; [car park] parking *m*. -6. *phr*: **to draw ~s** tirer au sort.
◆ **a lot** *adv* beaucoup.

loth [ləʊθ] = **loath**.

lotion ['ləʊʃn] *n* lotion *f*.

lottery ['lɒtərɪ] (*pl* -ies) *n lit & fig* loterie *f*.

lotus position ['ləʊtəs-] *n* position *f* du lotus.

loud [laʊd] ◇ *adj* -1. [not quiet, noisy - gen] fort(e); [- person] bruyant(e). -2. [colour, clothes] voyant(e). ◇ *adv* fort; **~ and clear** clairement; **out ~** tout haut.

loudhailer [,laʊd'heɪlər] *n Br* mégaphone *m*, porte-voix *m*.

loudly ['laʊdlɪ] *adv* -1. [noisily] fort. -2. [gaudily] de façon voyante.

loudmouth ['laʊdmaʊθ, *pl* -maʊðz] *n inf* grande gueule *f*.

loudness ['laʊdnɪs] *n* force *f*, intensité *f*; [of TV, radio] bruit *m*.

loudspeaker [,laʊd'spiːkər] *n* haut-parleur *m*.

Louisiana [luː,iːzɪ'ænə] *n* Louisiane *f*; **in ~** en Louisiane.

lounge [laʊndʒ] (*cont* **lounging**) ◇ *n* -1. [in house] salon *m*. -2. [in airport] hall *m*, salle *f*. -3. *Br* = **lounge bar**. ◇ *vi* se prélasser.
◆ **lounge about, lounge around** *vi* flemmarder, traîner.

lounge bar *n Br* *l'une des deux salles d'un bar, la plus confortable.*

lounge suit *n Br* complet *m*, complet-veston *m*.

louse [laʊs] (*pl sense 1* **lice**, *pl sense 2* -s) *n* -1. [insect] pou *m*. -2. *inf pej* [person] salaud *m*.
◆ **louse up** *vt sep Am v inf* foutre en l'air.

lousy ['laʊzɪ] (*compar* -ier, *superl* -iest) *adj inf* minable, nul(le); [weather] pourri(e); **to feel ~** être mal fichu.

lout [laʊt] *n* rustre *m*.

louvre *Br*, **louver** *Am* ['luːvər] *n* persienne *f*.

lovable ['lʌvəbl] *adj* adorable.

love [lʌv] ◇ *n* -1. [gen] amour *m*; **a ~ of** OR **for football** une passion pour le football; **to be in ~** être amoureux(euse); **to fall in ~** tomber amoureux(euse); **to make ~** faire l'amour; **give her my ~** embrasse-la pour moi; **~ from** [at end of letter] affectueusement, grosses bises; **a ~-hate relationship** des rapports *mpl* d'attraction-répulsion. -2. *inf* [form of address] mon chéri (ma chérie). -3. TENNIS zéro *m*.
◇ *vt* aimer; **to ~ to do sthg** OR **doing sthg** aimer OR adorer faire qqch.

love affair *n* liaison *f*.

lovebite ['lʌvbaɪt] *n* suçon *m*.

loveless ['lʌvlɪs] *adj* sans amour.

love letter *n* lettre *f* d'amour.

love life *n* vie *f* amoureuse.

lovely ['lʌvlɪ] (*compar* -ier, *superl* -iest) *adj* -1. [beautiful] très joli(e). -2. [pleasant] très agréable, excellent(e).

lovemaking ['lʌv,meɪkɪŋ] *n* (*U*) amour *m*, rapports *mpl*.

lover ['lʌvər] *n* -1. [sexual partner] amant *m*, -e *f*. -2. [enthusiast] passionné *m*, -e *f*, amoureux *m*, -euse *f*.

lovesick ['lʌvsɪk] *adj* qui languit d'amour.

love song *n* chanson *f* d'amour.

love story *n* histoire *f* d'amour.

loving ['lʌvɪŋ] *adj* [person, relationship] affectueux(euse); [care] tendre.

lovingly ['lʌvɪŋlɪ] *adv* avec amour.

low [ləʊ] ◇ *adj* -1. [not high - gen] bas (basse); [- wall, building] peu élevé(e); [- standard, quality] mauvais(e); [- intelligence] faible; [- neckline] décolleté(e); **to have a ~ opinion of sb** avoir mauvaise opinion de qqn; **to cook sthg over a ~ heat** faire cuire qqch à petit feu. -2. [little remaining] presque épuisé(e); **to be ~ on sthg** manquer de qqch. -3. [not loud - voice] bas (basse); [- whisper, moan] faible. -4. [depressed] déprimé(e). -5. [not respectable] bas (basse).
◇ *adv* -1. [not high] bas; **to fly ~** [plane] voler à basse altitude. -2. [not loudly - speak] à voix basse; [- whisper] faiblement.

◇ n -1. [low point] niveau m OR point m bas. -2. METEOR dépression f.

low-alcohol adj à faible teneur en alcool.

lowbrow ['ləʊbraʊ] adj peu intellectuel(elle).

low-calorie adj à basses calories.

Low Church n Basse Église f.

Low Countries npl: the ~ les Pays-Bas mpl.

low-cut adj décolleté(e).

low-down inf ◇ adj méprisable. ◇ n: to give sb the ~ (on sthg) mettre qqn au parfum (de qqch).

lower[1] ['ləʊə'] ◇ adj inférieur(e). ◇ vt -1. [gen] baisser; [flag] abaisser. -2. [reduce - price, level] baisser; [- age of consent] abaisser; [resistance] diminuer.

lower[2] ['laʊə'] vi -1. [sky] se faire menaçant(e). -2. [person]: to ~ at sb regarder qqn d'un air menaçant.

Lower Chamber ['ləʊə'-] n POL Chambre f basse OR des communes.

lower class ['ləʊə'-] n: the ~ OR ~es les classes populaires fpl.

Lower House ['ləʊə'-] n = Lower Chamber.

lowest common denominator ['ləʊɪst-] n: the ~ le plus petit dénominateur commun.

low-fat adj [yoghurt, crisps] allégé(e); [milk] demi-écrémé(e).

low-flying adj volant à basse altitude.

low frequency n basse fréquence f.

low gear n Am première (vitesse) f.

low-key adj discret(ète).

Lowlands ['ləʊləndz] npl: the ~ [of Scotland] les Basses Terres fpl (d'Écosse).

low-level language n COMPUT langage m de bas niveau.

low-loader [-'ləʊdə'] n Br -1. AUT semi-remorque m à plateforme surbaissée. -2. RAIL wagon m à plateforme surbaissée.

lowly ['ləʊlɪ] (compar -ier, superl -iest) adj modeste, humble.

low-lying adj bas (basse).

Low Mass n messe f basse.

low-necked [-'nekt] adj décolleté(e).

low-paid adj mal payé(e).

low-rise adj bas (basse).

low season n basse saison f.

low tide n marée f basse.

loyal ['lɔɪəl] adj loyal(e).

loyalist ['lɔɪəlɪst] n loyaliste mf.

loyalty ['lɔɪəltɪ] (pl -ies) n loyauté f.

lozenge ['lɒzɪndʒ] n -1. [tablet] pastille f. -2. [shape] losange m.

LP (abbr of long-playing record) n 33 tours m.

L-plate n Br plaque signalant que le conducteur du véhicule est en conduite accompagnée.

LPN (abbr of licensed practical nurse) n aide infirmière diplômée.

LRAM (abbr of Licentiate of the Royal Academy of Music) n membre de l'Académie de musique britannique.

LSAT (abbr of Law School Admissions Test) n aux États-Unis, test d'admission aux études de droit.

LSD (abbr of lysergic acid diethylamide) n LSD m.

LSD, L.S.D., £.s.d., l.s.d. (abbr of pounds, shillings and pence - librae, solidi, denarii) système monétaire en usage en Grande-Bretagne jusqu'en 1971.

LSE (abbr of London School of Economics) n grande école de sciences économiques et politiques à Londres.

LSO (abbr of London Symphony Orchestra) n orchestre symphonique de Londres.

Lt. (abbr of lieutenant) Lieut.

LT (abbr of low tension) n BT.

Ltd, ltd (abbr of limited) ≃ SARL; Smith and Sons, ~ ≃ Smith & Fils, SARL.

lubricant ['lu:brɪkənt] n lubrifiant m.

lubricate ['lu:brɪkeɪt] vt lubrifier.

lubrication [,lu:brɪ'keɪʃn] n lubrification f.

lucid ['lu:sɪd] adj lucide.

lucidly ['lu:sɪdlɪ] adv lucidement.

luck [lʌk] n chance f; good ~ chance f; good ~! bonne chance!; bad ~ malchance f; bad OR hard ~! pas de chance!; to be in ~ avoir de la chance; to try one's ~ at sthg tenter sa chance à qqch; with (any) ~ avec un peu de chance.

♦ **luck out** vi Am inf avoir un coup de pot.

luckily ['lʌkɪlɪ] adv heureusement.

luckless ['lʌklɪs] adj malchanceux(euse).

lucky ['lʌkɪ] (compar -ier, superl -iest) adj -1. [fortunate - person] qui a de la chance; [- event] heureux(euse); to have a ~ escape l'échapper belle. -2. [bringing good luck] porte-bonheur (inv).

lucky dip n Br sac rempli de cadeaux que l'on pioche sans regarder.

lucrative ['lu:krətɪv] adj lucratif(ive).

ludicrous ['lu:dɪkrəs] adj ridicule.

ludo ['lu:dəʊ] n Br jeu m des petits chevaux.

lug [lʌg] (pt & pp **-ged**, cont **-ging**) vt inf traîner.

luggage ['lʌgɪdʒ] n (U) Br bagages mpl.

luggage rack n Br porte-bagages m inv.

luggage van n Br fourgon m.

lugubrious [luːˈguːbrɪəs] adj lugubre.

lukewarm ['luːkwɔːm] adj lit & fig tiède.

lull [lʌl] ◇ n: ~ (**in**) [storm] accalmie f (de); [fighting, conversation] arrêt m (de); **the ~ before the storm** fig le calme avant la tempête. ◇ vt: **to ~ sb to sleep** endormir qqn en le berçant; **to ~ sb into a false sense of security** endormir les soupçons de qqn.

lullaby ['lʌləbaɪ] (pl **-ies**) n berceuse f.

lumbago [lʌmˈbeɪgəʊ] n (U) lumbago m.

lumber ['lʌmbər] ◇ n (U) **-1.** Am [timber] bois m de charpente. **-2.** Br [bric-a-brac] bric-à-brac m inv. ◇ vi se traîner d'un pas lourd.

◆ **lumber with** vt sep Br inf: **to ~ sb with sthg** coller qqch à qqn.

lumbering ['lʌmbərɪŋ] adj lourd(e), pesant(e).

lumberjack ['lʌmbədʒæk] n bûcheron m, -onne f.

lumbermill ['lʌmbə̩mɪl] n Am scierie f.

lumber-room n Br débarras m.

lumberyard ['lʌmbəjɑːd] n chantier m de bois.

luminous ['luːmɪnəs] adj [dial] lumineux(euse); [paint, armband] phosphorescent(e).

lump [lʌmp] ◇ n **-1.** [gen] morceau m; [of earth, clay] motte f; [in sauce] grumeau m. **-2.** [on body] grosseur f. ◇ vt: **to ~ sthg together** réunir qqch; **to ~ it** inf faire avec, s'en accommoder.

lumpectomy [ˌlʌmpˈektəmɪ] (pl **-ies**) n ablation f d'une tumeur au sein.

lump sum n somme f globale.

lumpy ['lʌmpɪ] (compar **-ier**, superl **-iest**) adj [sauce] plein(e) de grumeaux; [mattress] défoncé(e).

lunacy ['luːnəsɪ] n folie f.

lunar ['luːnər] adj lunaire.

lunatic ['luːnətɪk] ◇ adj pej dément(e), démentiel(ielle). ◇ n **-1.** pej [fool] fou m, folle f. **-2.** [insane person] fou m, folle f, aliéné m, -e f.

lunatic asylum n asile m d'aliénés.

lunatic fringe n éléments mpl extrémistes.

lunch [lʌnʃ] ◇ n déjeuner m. ◇ vi déjeuner.

luncheon ['lʌnʃən] n fml déjeuner m.

luncheonette [ˌlʌnʃəˈnet] n Am ≃ cafétéria f.

luncheon meat n sorte f de saucisson.

luncheon voucher n Br ticket-restaurant m.

lunch hour n pause f de midi.

lunchtime ['lʌnʃtaɪm] n heure f du déjeuner.

lung [lʌŋ] n poumon m.

lung cancer n cancer m du poumon.

lunge [lʌndʒ] (cont **lungeing**) vi faire un brusque mouvement (du bras) en avant; **to ~ at sb** s'élancer sur qqn.

lupin Br ['luːpɪn], **lupine** Am ['luːpaɪn] n lupin m.

lurch [lɜːtʃ] ◇ n [of person] écart m brusque; [of car] embardée f; **to leave sb in the ~** laisser qqn dans le pétrin. ◇ vi [person] tituber; [car] faire une embardée.

lure [ljʊər] ◇ n charme m trompeur. ◇ vt attirer OR persuader par la ruse.

lurid ['ljʊərɪd] adj **-1.** [outfit] aux couleurs criardes. **-2.** [story, details] affreux(euse).

lurk [lɜːk] vi **-1.** [person] se cacher, se dissimuler. **-2.** [memory, danger, fear] subsister.

lurking ['lɜːkɪŋ] adj [doubts, fear] vague.

Lusaka [luːˈsɑːkə] n Lusaka.

luscious ['lʌʃəs] adj **-1.** [delicious] succulent(e). **-2.** fig [woman] appétissant(e).

lush [lʌʃ] ◇ adj **-1.** [luxuriant] luxuriant(e). **-2.** [rich] luxueux(euse). ◇ n Am inf [drunkard] alcolo mf.

lust [lʌst] n **-1.** [sexual desire] désir m. **-2.** fig: ~ **for sthg** soif de qqch; ~ **for life** fureur de vivre.

◆ **lust after**, **lust for** vt fus **-1.** [wealth, power etc] être assoiffé(e) de. **-2.** [person] désirer.

luster Am = **lustre**.

lustful ['lʌstful] adj lubrique.

lustre Br, **luster** Am ['lʌstər] n lustre m.

lusty ['lʌstɪ] (compar **-ier**, superl **-iest**) adj vigoureux(euse).

lute [luːt] n luth m.

luv [lʌv] n Br inf chéri m, -e f.

Luxembourg ['lʌksəmbɜːg] n **-1.** [country] Luxembourg m; **in ~** au Luxembourg. **-2.** [city] Luxembourg.

luxuriant [lʌgˈʒʊərɪənt] adj luxuriant(e).

luxuriate [lʌgˈʒʊərɪeɪt] vi: **to ~ in** s'abandonner aux plaisirs de.

luxurious [lʌgˈʒʊərɪəs] adj **-1.** [expensive] luxueux(euse). **-2.** [pleasurable] voluptueux(euse).

luxury ['lʌkʃərɪ] (*pl* **-ies**) ◇ *n* luxe *m.* ◇ *comp* de luxe.

luxury goods *npl* produits *mpl* de luxe.

LV *abbr of* **luncheon voucher**.

LW (*abbr of* **long wave**) GO.

lychee [,laɪ'tʃiː] *n* litchi *m.*

Lycra® ['laɪkrə] ◇ *n* Lycra® *m.* ◇ *comp* en Lycra®.

lying ['laɪɪŋ] ◇ *adj* [person] menteur(euse). ◇ *n* (*U*) mensonges *mpl.*

lymph gland [lɪmf-] *n* ganglion *m* lymphatique.

lynch [lɪntʃ] *vt* lyncher.

lynx [lɪŋks] (*pl inv* OR **-es**) *n* lynx *m inv.*

Lyons ['laɪənz] *n* Lyon.

lyre ['laɪə'] *n* lyre *f.*

lyric ['lɪrɪk] *adj* lyrique.

lyrical ['lɪrɪkl] *adj* lyrique.

lyrics ['lɪrɪks] *npl* paroles *fpl.*

m¹ (*pl* **m's** OR **ms**), **M** (*pl* **M's** OR **Ms**) [em] *n* [letter] m *m inv,* M *m inv.*
◆ **M -1.** *Br abbr of* **motorway. -2.** (*abbr of* **medium**) M.

m² -1. (*abbr of* **metre**) m. **-2.** (*abbr of* **million**) M. **-3.** *abbr of* **mile.**

ma [mɑː] *n inf* maman *f.*

MA ◇ *n abbr of* **Master of Arts.** ◇ *abbr of* **Massachusetts.**

ma'am [mæm] *n* madame *f.*

mac [mæk] (*abbr of* **macintosh**) *n Br inf* [coat] imper *m.*

macabre [mə'kɑːbrə] *adj* macabre.

Macao [mə'kaʊ] *n* Macao *m;* **in** ~ à Macao.

macaroni [,mækə'rəʊnɪ] *n* (*U*) macaronis *mpl.*

macaroni cheese *n* macaronis *mpl* au gratin.

macaroon [,mækə'ruːn] *n* macaron *m.*

mace [meɪs] *n* **-1.** [ornamental rod] masse *f.* **-2.** [spice] macis *m.*

Macedonia [,mæsɪ'dəʊnjə] *n* Macédoine *f;* **in** ~ en Macédoine.

Macedonian ['mæsɪ'dəʊnjən] ◇ *adj* macédonien(ienne). ◇ *n* Macédonien *m,* -ienne *f.*

machete [mə'ʃetɪ] *n* machette *f.*

Machiavellian [,mækɪə'velɪən] *adj* machiavélique.

machinations [,mækɪ'neɪʃnz] *npl* machinations *fpl.*

machine [mə'ʃiːn] ◇ *n lit* & *fig* machine *f.* ◇ *vt* **-1.** SEWING coudre à la machine. **-2.** TECH fabriquer, usiner.

machine code *n* COMPUT code *m* machine.

machinegun [mə'ʃiːngʌn] (*pt* & *pp* **-ned,** *cont* **-ning**) ◇ *n* mitrailleuse *f.* ◇ *vt* mitrailler.

machine language *n* COMPUT langage *m* machine.

machine-readable *adj* COMPUT en langage machine.

machinery [mə'ʃiːnərɪ] *n* (*U*) machines *fpl; fig* mécanisme *m.*

machine shop *n* atelier *m* d'usinage.

machine tool *n* machine-outil *f.*

machine-washable *adj* lavable en machine.

machinist [mə'ʃiːnɪst] *n* **-1.** SEWING mécanicienne *f.* **-2.** TECH machiniste *mf,* opérateur *m,* -trice *f.*

machismo [mə'tʃɪzməʊ] *n* machisme *m.*

macho ['mætʃəʊ] *adj* macho (*inv*).

mackerel ['mækrəl] (*pl inv* OR **-s**) *n* maquereau *m.*

mackintosh ['mækɪntɒʃ] *n Br* imperméable *m.*

macramé [mə'krɑːmɪ] *n* macramé *m.*

macro ['mækrəʊ] (*abbr of* **macroinstruction**) *n* COMPUT macro-instruction *f.*

macrobiotic [,mækrəʊbaɪ'ɒtɪk] *adj* macrobiotique.

macrocosm ['mækrəʊkɒzm] *n* macrocosme *m.*

macroeconomics ['mækrəʊ,iːkə'nɒmɪks] *n* (*U*) macroéconomie *f.*

mad [mæd] (*compar* **-der,** *superl* **-dest**) *adj* **-1.** [insane] fou (folle); **to go** ~ devenir fou. **-2.** [foolish] insensé(e). **-3.** [furious] furieux(ieuse). **-4.** [hectic - rush, pace] fou (folle); **like** ~ *inf* comme un fou. **-5.** [very enthusiastic]: **to be** ~ **about sb/sthg** être fou (folle) de qqn/qqch.

Madagascan [,mædə'gæskn] ◇ *adj* malgache. ◇ *n* **-1.** [person] Malgache *mf.* **-2.** [language] malgache *m.*

Madagascar [,mædə'gæskə'] *n* Madagascar *m;* **in** ~ à Madagascar.

madam ['mædəm] *n* madame *f*.

madcap ['mædkæp] *adj* risqué(e), insensé(e).

madden ['mædn] *vt* exaspérer.

maddening ['mædnɪŋ] *adj* exaspérant(e).

made [meɪd] *pt & pp* → **make**.

-made [meɪd] *suffix* fait(e); **factory** ~ fait OR fabriqué en usine; **French** ~ de fabrication française.

Madeira [mə'dɪərə] *n* **-1.** [wine] madère *m*. **-2.** GEOGR Madère *f*; **in** ~ à Madère.

made-to-measure *adj* fait(e) sur mesure.

made-up *adj* **-1.** [with make-up] maquillé(e). **-2.** [prepared] préparé(e). **-3.** [invented] fabriqué(e).

madhouse ['mædhaus] *n fig* maison *f* de fous.

madly ['mædlɪ] *adv* [frantically] comme un fou; ~ **in love** follement amoureux.

madman ['mædmən] (*pl* **-men** [-mən]) *n* fou *m*.

madness ['mædnɪs] *n lit & fig* folie *f*, démence *f*.

Madonna [mə'dɒnə] *n* Madone *f*.

Madrid [mə'drɪd] *n* Madrid.

madrigal ['mædrɪgl] *n* madrigal *m*.

madwoman ['mæd,wumən] (*pl* **-women** [-,wɪmɪn]) *n* folle *f*.

maestro ['maɪstrəu] (*pl* **-tros** OR **-tri** [-trɪ]) *n* maestro *m*.

Mafia ['mæfɪə] *n*: **the** ~ la Mafia.

mag [mæg] (*abbr of* **magazine**) *n inf* revue *f*, magazine *m*.

magazine [,mægə'ziːn] *n* **-1.** PRESS revue *f*, magazine *m*; RADIO & TV magazine *m*. **-2.** [of gun] magasin *m*.

magenta [mə'dʒentə] ◇ *adj* magenta (*inv*). ◇ *n* magenta *m*.

maggot ['mægət] *n* ver *m*, asticot *m*.

Maghreb ['mɑːgrəb] *n*: **the** ~ le Maghreb.

magic ['mædʒɪk] ◇ *adj* magique. ◇ *n* magie *f*.

magical ['mædʒɪkl] *adj* magique.

magic carpet *n* tapis *m* volant.

magic eye *n Br* cellule *f* photo-électrique, œil *m* électrique.

magician [mə'dʒɪʃn] *n* magicien *m*.

magic wand *n* baguette *f* magique.

magisterial [,mædʒɪ'stɪərɪəl] *adj* **-1.** [behaviour, manner] magistral(e). **-2.** JUR de magistrat.

magistrate ['mædʒɪstreɪt] *n* magistrat *m*, juge *m*.

magistrates' court *n Br* ≃ tribunal *m* d'instance.

Magna Carta ['mægnə'kɑːtə] *n*: **the** ~ La Grande Charte d'Angleterre.

magnanimous [mæg'nænɪməs] *adj* magnanime.

magnate ['mægneɪt] *n* magnat *m*.

magnesium [mæg'niːzɪəm] *n* magnésium *m*.

magnet ['mægnɪt] *n* aimant *m*.

magnetic [mæg'netɪk] *adj lit & fig* magnétique.

magnetic disk *n* disque *m* magnétique.

magnetic field *n* champ *m* magnétique.

magnetic tape *n* bande *f* magnétique.

magnetism ['mægnɪtɪzm] *n lit & fig* magnétisme *m*.

magnification [,mægnɪfɪ'keɪʃn] *n* grossissement *m*.

magnificence [mæg'nɪfɪsəns] *n* splendeur *f*.

magnificent [mæg'nɪfɪsənt] *adj* magnifique, superbe.

magnify ['mægnɪfaɪ] (*pt & pp* **-ied**) *vt* [in vision] grossir; [sound] amplifier; *fig* exagérer.

magnifying glass ['mægnɪfaɪɪŋ-] *n* loupe *f*.

magnitude ['mægnɪtjuːd] *n* envergure *f*, ampleur *f*.

magnolia [mæg'nəuljə] *n* **-1.** [tree] magnolia *m*. **-2.** [flower] fleur *f* de magnolia.

magnum ['mægnəm] (*pl* **-s**) *n* magnum *m*.

magpie ['mægpaɪ] *n* pie *f*.

maharaja(h) [,mɑːhə'rɑːdʒə] *n* maharaja *m*, maharajah *m*.

mahogany [mə'hɒgənɪ] *n* acajou *m*.

maid [meɪd] *n* [servant] domestique *f*.

maiden ['meɪdn] ◇ *adj* [flight, voyage] premier(ière). ◇ *n literary* jeune fille *f*.

maiden aunt *n* tante *f* célibataire.

maiden name *n* nom *m* de jeune fille.

maiden speech *n* POL premier discours *m*.

mail [meɪl] ◇ *n* **-1.** [letters, parcels] courrier *m*. **-2.** [system] poste *f*. ◇ *vt* poster.

mailbag ['meɪlbæg] *n* sac *m* postal.

mailbox ['meɪlbɒks] *n Am* boîte *f* à OR aux lettres.

mailing list ['meɪlɪŋ-] *n* liste *f* d'adresses.

mailman ['meɪlmən] (*pl* **-men** [-mən]) *n Am* facteur *m*.

mail order *n* vente *f* par correspondance.

mailshot ['meɪlʃɒt] *n* publipostage *m*.

mail train *n* train *m* postal.

mail truck *n Am* fourgonnette *f* des postes.

mail van *n Br* **-1.** AUT fourgonnette *f* des postes. **-2.** RAIL wagon-poste *m*.

maim [meɪm] *vt* estropier.

main [meɪn] ◇ *adj* principal(e). ◇ *n* [pipe] conduite *f*.
◆ **mains** *npl*: **the ~s** le secteur.
◆ **in the main** *adj* dans l'ensemble.

main course *n* plat *m* principal.

Maine [meɪn] *n* le Maine; **in ~** dans le Maine.

mainframe (computer) ['meɪnfreɪm-] *n* ordinateur *m* central.

mainland ['meɪnlənd] ◇ *adj* continental(e). ◇ *n*: **the ~** le continent.

main line *n* RAIL grande ligne *f*.
◆ **mainline** ◇ *adj* RAIL de grande ligne. ◇ *vt drugs sl* shooter. ◇ *vi drugs sl* se shooter.

mainly ['meɪnlɪ] *adv* principalement.

main road *n* route *f* à grande circulation.

mainsail ['meɪnseɪl, 'meɪnsəl] *n* grand-voile *f*.

mainstay ['meɪnsteɪ] *n* pilier *m*, élément *m* principal.

mainstream ['meɪnstriːm] ◇ *adj* dominant(e). ◇ *n*: **the ~** la tendance générale.

maintain [meɪn'teɪn] *vt* **-1.** [preserve, keep constant] maintenir. **-2.** [provide for, look after] entretenir. **-3.** [assert]: **to ~ (that)** ... maintenir que ..., soutenir que ....

maintenance ['meɪntənəns] *n* **-1.** [of public order] maintien *m*. **-2.** [care] entretien *m*, maintenance *f*. **-3.** JUR pension *f* alimentaire.

maintenance order *n Br* JUR obligation *f* alimentaire.

maisonette [,meɪzə'net] *n* duplex *m*.

maize [meɪz] *n* maïs *m*.

Maj. (*abbr of* **Major**) ≃ Cdt.

majestic [mə'dʒestɪk] *adj* majestueux(euse).

majestically [mə'dʒestɪklɪ] *adv* majestueusement.

majesty ['mædʒəstɪ] (*pl* **-ies**) *n* [grandeur] majesté *f*.
◆ **Majesty** *n*: **his/her Majesty** sa Majesté le roi/la reine.

major ['meɪdʒəʳ] ◇ *adj* **-1.** [important] majeur(e). **-2.** [main] principal(e). **-3.** MUS majeur(e). ◇ *n* **-1.** [in army] ≃ chef *m* de bataillon; [in air force] commandant *m*. **-2.** UNIV [subject] matière *f*. ◇ *vi*: **to ~ in** se spécialiser en.

Majorca [mə'dʒɔːkə, mə'jɔːkə] *n* Majorque *f*; **in ~** à Majorque.

Majorcan [mə'dʒɔːkn, mə'jɔːkn] ◇ *adj* majorquin(e). ◇ *n* Majorquin *m*, -e *f*.

majorette [,meɪdʒə'ret] *n* majorette *f*.

major general *n* général *m* de division.

majority [mə'dʒɒrətɪ] (*pl* **-ies**) *n* majorité *f*; **in a** OR **the ~** dans la majorité.

majority shareholder *n* actionnaire *mf* majoritaire.

make [meɪk] (*pt & pp* **made**) ◇ *vt* **-1.** [gen - produce] faire; [- manufacture] faire, fabriquer; **to ~ a meal** préparer un repas; **to ~ a film** tourner OR réaliser un film. **-2.** [perform an action] faire; **to ~ a decision** prendre une décision; **to ~ a mistake** faire une erreur, se tromper. **-3.** [cause to be] rendre; **to ~ sb happy/sad** rendre qqn heureux/triste; **he made her a manager** il l'a nommée directrice; **to ~ o.s. heard** se faire entendre. **-4.** [force, cause to do]: **to ~ sb do sthg** faire faire qqch à qqn, obliger qqn à faire qqch; **you made me jump** tu m'as fait sursauter; **we were made to wait in the hall** on nous a fait attendre dans le vestibule; **to ~ sb laugh/cry** faire rire/pleurer qqn. **-5.** [be constructed]: **to be made of** être en; **it's made of wood/metal/wool** c'est en bois/métal/laine; **what's it made of?** c'est en quoi? **-6.** [add up to] faire; **2 and 2 ~ 4** 2 et 2 font 4. **-7.** [calculate]: **I ~ it 50** d'après moi il y en a 50, j'en ai compté 50; **what time do you ~ it?** quelle heure as-tu?; **I ~ it 6 o'clock** il est 6 heures (à ma montre). **-8.** [earn] gagner, se faire; **she ~s £30,000 a year** elle se fait OR elle gagne 30 000 livres par an; **to ~ a profit** faire des bénéfices; **to ~ a loss** essuyer des pertes. **-9.** [have the right qualities for]: **she'd ~ a good dancer** elle ferait une bonne danseuse; **books ~ excellent presents** les livres constituent de très beaux cadeaux. **-10.** [reach] arriver à. **-11.** [cause to be a success] assurer OR faire le succès de; **she really ~s the play/film** c'est elle qui fait le succès de la pièce/du film. **-12.** [gain - friend, enemy] se faire; **to ~ friends (with sb)** se lier d'amitié (avec qqn). **-13.** *phr*: **to ~ it** [reach in time] arriver à temps; [be a success] réussir, arriver; [be able to attend] se libérer, pouvoir venir; **to have it made** avoir trouvé le filon; **to ~ do with** se contenter de.
◇ *n* **-1.** [brand] marque *f*; **what ~ is your car?** de quelle marque est votre voiture? **-2.** *inf pej*: **to be on the ~** [act dishonestly, selfishly] être intéressé(e).
◆ **make for** *vt fus* **-1.** [move towards] se diriger vers. **-2.** [contribute to, be conducive to] rendre probable, favoriser.
◆ **make of** *vt sep* **-1.** [understand] comprendre. **-2.** [have opinion of] penser de.
◆ **make off** *vi* filer.
◆ **make off with** *vt fus* filer avec.

◆ **make out** ◇ *vt sep* **-1.** [see, hear] discerner; [understand] **comprendre. -2.** [fill out - cheque] **libeller**; [- bill, receipt] **faire**; [- form] **remplir**. ◇ *vt fus* [pretend, claim]: **to ~ out (that) ... prétendre que ....**

◆ **make up** ◇ *vt sep* **-1.** [compose, constitute] **composer, constituer. -2.** [story, excuse] **inventer. -3.** [apply cosmetics to] **maquiller**; **to ~ o.s. up se maquiller. -4.** [prepare - gen] **faire**; [- prescription] **préparer, exécuter. -5.** [make complete] **compléter. -6.** [resolve - quarrel] **to ~ it up (with sb)** se réconcilier (avec qqn). ◇ *vi* **-1.** [become friends again] **se réconcilier.**

◆ **make up for** *vt fus* **compenser**; **to ~ up for lost time rattraper le temps perdu.**

◆ **make up to** *vt sep*: **to ~ it up to sb (for sthg)** se racheter auprès de qqn pour qqch.

make-believe *n*: **it's all ~** c'est (de la) pure fantaisie.

maker ['meɪkər] *n* [of product] **fabricant** *m*, -e *f*; [of film] **réalisateur** *m*, -trice *f*.

makeshift ['meɪkʃɪft] *adj* **de fortune.**

make-up *n* **-1.** [cosmetics] **maquillage** *m*; ~ **bag trousse** *f* **de maquillage**; ~ **remover démaquillant** *m*. **-2.** [person's character] **caractère** *m*. **-3.** [of team, group, object] **constitution** *f*.

makeweight ['meɪkweɪt] *n* **complément** *m* **de poids.**

making ['meɪkɪŋ] *n* **fabrication** *f*; **to be the ~ of sb/sthg** être l'origine de la réussite de qqn/qqch; **his problems are of his own ~** ses problèmes sont de sa faute; **in the ~** en formation; **history in the ~** l'histoire en train de se faire; **to have the ~s of** avoir l'étoffe de.

maladjusted [,mælə'dʒʌstɪd] *adj* **inadapté(e).**

malaise [mə'leɪz] *n fml* **malaise** *m*.

malaria [mə'leərɪə] *n* **malaria** *f*.

Malawi [mə'lɑːwɪ] *n* **Malawi** *m*; **in ~** au **Malawi.**

Malawian [mə'lɑːwɪən] ◇ *adj* **malawite.** ◇ *n* **Malawite** *mf*.

Malay [mə'leɪ] ◇ *adj* **malais(e).** ◇ *n* **-1.** [person] **Malais** *m*, -e *f*. **-2.** [language] **malais** *m*.

Malaya [mə'leɪə] *n* **Malaisie** *f*, **Malaysia** *f* **Occidentale**; **in ~** en **Malaisie.**

Malayan [mə'leɪən] ◇ *adj* **malais(e).** ◇ *n* **Malais** *m*, -e *f*.

Malaysia [mə'leɪzɪə] *n* **Malaysia** *f*; **in ~** en **Malaysia.**

Malaysian [mə'leɪzɪən] ◇ *adj* **malaysien(ienne).** ◇ *n* **Malaysien** *m*, -ienne *f*.

malcontent ['mælkən,tent] *n fml* **mécontent** *m*, -e *f*.

Maldives ['mɔːldaɪvz] *npl*: **the ~** les (îles *fpl*) **Maldives**; **in the ~** aux **Maldives.**

male [meɪl] ◇ *adj* [gen] **mâle**; [sex] **masculin(e).** ◇ *n* **mâle** *m*.

male chauvinist (pig) *n pej* **phallocrate** *m*.

male nurse *n* **infirmier** *m*.

malevolent [mə'levələnt] *adj* **malveillant(e).**

malformed [mæl'fɔːmd] *adj* **difforme.**

malfunction [mæl'fʌŋkʃn] ◇ *n* **mauvais fonctionnement** *m*. ◇ *vi* **mal fonctionner.**

Mali ['mɑːlɪ] *n* **Mali** *m*; **in ~** au **Mali.**

malice ['mælɪs] *n* **méchanceté** *f*.

malicious [mə'lɪʃəs] *adj* **malveillant(e).**

malign [mə'laɪn] ◇ *adj* **pernicieux(ieuse).** ◇ *vt* **calomnier.**

malignant [mə'lɪgnənt] *adj* MED **malin(igne).**

malinger [mə'lɪŋgər] *vi pej* **simuler une maladie.**

malingerer [mə'lɪŋgərər] *n pej* **simulateur** *m*, -trice *f*.

mall [mɔːl] *n*: **(shopping) ~ centre** *m* **commercial.**

malleable ['mælɪəbl] *adj lit & fig* **malléable.**

mallet ['mælɪt] *n* **maillet** *m*.

malnourished [,mæl'nʌrɪʃt] *adj* **sous-alimenté(e).**

malnutrition [,mælnjuː'trɪʃn] *n* **malnutrition** *f*.

malpractice [,mæl'præktɪs] *n* (U) JUR **faute** *f* **professionnelle.**

malt [mɔːlt] *n* **malt** *m*.

Malta ['mɔːltə] *n* **Malte** *f*; **in ~** à **Malte.**

Maltese [,mɔːl'tiːz] (*pl inv*) ◇ *adj* **maltais(e).** ◇ *n* **-1.** [person] **Maltais** *m*, -e *f*. **-2.** [language] **maltais** *m*.

maltreat [,mæl'triːt] *vt* **maltraiter.**

maltreatment [,mæl'triːtmənt] *n* **mauvais traitement** *m*.

malt whisky *n* **whisky** *m* **pur, malt** *m inv*.

mammal ['mæml] *n* **mammifère** *m*.

Mammon ['mæmən] *n* **le Veau d'or.**

mammoth ['mæməθ] ◇ *adj* **gigantesque.** ◇ *n* **mammouth** *m*.

man [mæn] (*pl* **men** [men], *pt* & *pp* **-ned**, *cont* **-ning**) ◇ *n* **-1.** **homme** *m*; **the ~ in the street** l'homme de la rue; **to talk ~ to ~** parler d'homme à homme; **to be ~ enough to do sthg** avoir le courage de faire qqch. **-2.** [as form of address] **mon vieux.** ◇ *vt* [ship, spaceship] **fournir du personnel pour**; [telephone] **répondre au**; [switchboard] **assurer le service de.**

manacles ['mænəklz] *npl* [round wrists] me-nottes *fpl*; [round legs] chaînes *fpl*.

manage ['mænɪdʒ] ◇ *vi* **-1.** [cope] se débrouiller, y arriver. **-2.** [survive, get by] s'en sortir. ◇ *vt* **-1.** [succeed]: **to ~ to do sthg** arriver à faire qqch. **-2.** [be responsible for, control] gérer.

manageable ['mænɪdʒəbl] *adj* maniable.

management ['mænɪdʒmənt] *n* **-1.** [control, running] gestion *f*. **-2.** [people in control] direction *f*.

management consultant *n* conseiller *m*, -ère *f* en gestion.

manager ['mænɪdʒəʳ] *n* [of organization] directeur *m*, -trice *f*; [of shop, restaurant, hotel] gérant *m*, -e *f*; [of football team, pop star] manager *m*.

manageress [,mænɪdʒə'res] *n Br* [of organization] directrice *f*; [of shop, restaurant, hotel] gérante *f*.

managerial [,mænɪ'dʒɪərɪəl] *adj* directorial(e).

managing director ['mænɪdʒɪŋ-] *n* directeur général *m*, directrice générale *f*.

Managua [mə'nægwə] *n* Managua.

Mancunian [mæŋ'kjuːnjən] ◇ *adj* de Manchester. ◇ *n* [person] habitant *m*, -e *f* de Manchester.

mandarin ['mændərɪn] *n* **-1.** [fruit] mandarine *f*. **-2.** [civil servant] mandarin *m*.

mandate ['mændeɪt] *n* mandat *m*.

mandatory ['mændətrɪ] *adj* obligatoire.

mandolin [mændə'lɪn] *n* mandoline *f*.

mane [meɪn] *n* crinière *f*.

man-eating [-,iːtɪŋ] *adj* mangeur d'hommes.

maneuver *Am* = manoeuvre.

manfully ['mænfʊlɪ] *adv* courageusement, vaillamment.

manganese ['mæŋgəniːz] *n* manganèse *m*.

mange [meɪndʒ] *n* gale *f*.

manger ['meɪndʒəʳ] *n* mangeoire *f*.

mangetout (pea) [,mɑ̃ʒ'tuː(-)] *n Br* mangetout *m inv*.

mangle ['mæŋgl] *vt* mutiler, déchirer.

mango ['mæŋgəʊ] (*pl* **-es** OR **-s**) *n* mangue *f*.

mangrove ['mæŋgrəʊv] *n* palétuvier *m*.

mangy ['meɪndʒɪ] (*compar* **-ier**, *superl* **-iest**) *adj* galeux(euse).

manhandle ['mæn,hændl] *vt* malmener.

manhole ['mænhəʊl] *n* regard *m*, trou *m* d'homme.

manhood ['mænhʊd] *n*: **to reach ~** devenir un homme.

manhour ['mæn'aʊəʳ] *n* heure-homme *f*.

manhunt ['mænhʌnt] *n* chasse *f* à l'homme.

mania ['meɪnjə] *n*: **~ (for)** manie *f* (de).

maniac ['meɪnɪæk] *n* fou *m*, folle *f*; **a sex ~** un obsédé sexuel (une obsédée sexuelle).

manic ['mænɪk] *adj fig* [person] surexcité(e); [behaviour] de fou.

manic-depressive ◇ *adj* maniaco-dépressif (maniaco-dépressive). ◇ *n* maniaco-dépressif *m*, maniaco-dépressive *f*.

manicure ['mænɪ,kjʊəʳ] ◇ *n* manucure *f*. ◇ *vt* [person] faire une manucure à; **to ~ one's nails** se faire les ongles.

manifest ['mænɪfest] *fml* ◇ *adj* manifeste, évident(e). ◇ *vt* manifester.

manifestation [,mænɪfes'teɪʃn] *n fml* manifestation *f*.

manifestly ['mænɪfestlɪ] *adv fml* manifestement.

manifesto [,mænɪ'festəʊ] (*pl* **-s** OR **-es**) *n* manifeste *m*.

manifold ['mænɪfəʊld] ◇ *adj literary* nombreux(euse), multiple. ◇ *n* AUT tubulure *f*, collecteur *m*.

Manila [mə'nɪlə] *n* Manille.

manil(l)a [mə'nɪlə] *adj* en papier kraft.

manipulate [mə'nɪpjʊleɪt] *vt lit & fig* manipuler.

manipulation [mə,nɪpjʊ'leɪʃn] *n lit & fig* manipulation *f*.

manipulative [mə'nɪpjʊlətɪv] *adj* [person] rusé(e); [behaviour] habile, subtil(e).

Manitoba [,mænɪ'təʊbə] *n* Manitoba *m*; **in ~** dans le Manitoba.

mankind [mæn'kaɪnd] *n* humanité *f*, genre *m* humain.

manly ['mænlɪ] (*compar* **-ier**, *superl* **-iest**) *adj* viril(e).

man-made *adj* [fabric, fibre] synthétique; [environment] artificiel(ielle); [problem] causé (causée) par l'homme.

manna ['mænə] *n* manne *f*.

manned [mænd] *adj* [vehicle] doté(e) d'un équipage; [flight] habité(e).

mannequin ['mænɪkɪn] *n* mannequin *m*.

manner ['mænəʳ] *n* **-1.** [method] manière *f*, façon *f*; **in a ~ of speaking** pour ainsi dire. **-2.** [attitude] attitude *f*, comportement *m*. **-3.** [type, sort]: **all ~ of** toutes sortes de. ◆ **manners** *npl* manières *fpl*.

mannered ['mænəd] *adj fml* maniéré(e), affecté(e).

mannerism ['mænərɪzm] *n* tic *m*, manie *f*.

mannish ['mænɪʃ] *adj* masculin(e).

manoeuvrable *Br*, **maneuverable** *Am* [mə'nuːvrəbl] *adj* facile à manœuvrer, maniable.

manoeuvre *Br*, **maneuver** *Am* [mə'nuːvəʳ] ◇ *n* manœuvre *f.* ◇ *vt & vi* manœuvrer.

◆ **manoeuvres** *npl* MIL manœuvres *fpl.*

manor ['mænəʳ] *n* manoir *m.*

manpower ['mæn,pauəʳ] *n* main-d'œuvre *f.*

manservant ['mænsɜːvənt] (*pl* **menservants**) *n* dated valet *m* de chambre.

mansion ['mænʃn] *n* château *m.*

man-size(d) *adj* grand(e), de grande personne.

manslaughter ['mæn,slɔːtəʳ] *n* homicide *m* involontaire.

mantelpiece ['mæntlpiːs] *n* (dessus *m* de) cheminée *f.*

mantle ['mæntl] *n* -1. *literary* [of snow] manteau *m.* -2. [of leadership, high office] responsabilité *f.*

man-to-man *adj* d'homme à homme.

manual ['mænjuəl] ◇ *adj* manuel(elle). ◇ *n* manuel *m.*

manually ['mænjuəli] *adv* à la main, manuellement.

manual worker *n* travailleur manuel *m*, travailleuse manuelle *f.*

manufacture [,mænjuˈfæktʃəʳ] ◇ *n* fabrication *f*; [of cars] construction *f.* ◇ *vt* fabriquer; [cars] construire.

manufacturer [,mænjuˈfæktʃərəʳ] *n* fabricant *m*; [of cars] constructeur *m.*

manufacturing [,mænjuˈfæktʃərɪŋ] *n* fabrication *f.*

manufacturing industries *npl* industries *fpl* de fabrication.

manure [məˈnjuəʳ] *n* fumier *m.*

manuscript ['mænjuskrɪpt] *n* manuscrit *m.*

Manx [mæŋks] ◇ *adj* de l'île de Man, manxois(e). ◇ *n* [language] manx *m.*

many ['meni] (*compar* **more**, *superl* **most**) ◇ *adj* beaucoup de; **how ~ ...?** combien de ...?; **too ~** trop de; **as ~ ... as** autant de ... que; **so ~** autant de; **a good** OR **great ~** un grand nombre de. ◇ *pron* [a lot, plenty] beaucoup.

Maori ['maurɪ] ◇ *adj* maori(e). ◇ *n* Maori *m*, -e *f.*

map [mæp] (*pt & pp* **-ped**, *cont* **-ping**) *n* carte *f.*

◆ **map out** *vt sep* [plan] élaborer; [timetable] établir; [task] définir.

maple ['meɪpl] *n* érable *m.*

maple leaf *n* feuille *f* d'érable.

maple syrup *n* sirop *m* d'érable.

Maputo [məˈpuːtəu] *n* Maputo.

mar [maːʳ] (*pt & pp* **-red**, *cont* **-ring**) *vt* gâter, gâcher.

Mar. *abbr of* **March**.

marathon ['mærəθn] ◇ *adj* marathon (*inv*). ◇ *n* marathon *m.*

marathon runner *n* marathonien *m*, -ienne *f.*

marauder [məˈrɔːdəʳ] *n* maraudeur *m*, -euse *f.*

marauding [məˈrɔːdɪŋ] *adj* maraudeur(euse).

marble ['maːbl] *n* -1. [stone] marbre *m.* -2. [for game] bille *f.*

◆ **marbles** *n* (*U*) [game] billes *fpl.*

march [maːtʃ] ◇ *n* marche *f.* ◇ *vi* -1. [soldiers etc] marcher au pas. -2. [demonstrators] manifester, faire une marche de protestation. -3. [quickly]: **to ~ up to sb** s'approcher de qqn d'un pas décidé. ◇ *vt*: **to ~ sb out the door** faire sortir qqn.

March [maːtʃ] *n* mars *m; see also* **September**.

marcher ['maːtʃəʳ] *n* [protester] marcheur *m*, -euse *f.*

marching orders ['maːtʃɪŋ-] *npl*: **to get one's ~** se faire mettre à la porte.

marchioness ['maːʃənes] *n* marquise *f.*

march-past *n* défilé *m.*

Mardi Gras [,maːdɪˈgraː] *n* mardi *m* gras, carnaval *m.*

mare [meəʳ] *n* jument *f.*

marg. [maːdʒ] *n inf abbr of* **margarine**.

margarine [,maːdʒəˈriːn, ,maːgəˈriːn] *n* margarine *f.*

marge [maːdʒ] *n inf* margarine *f.*

margin ['maːdʒɪn] *n* -1. [gen] marge *f*; **to win by a narrow ~** gagner de peu OR de justesse. -2. [edge - of an area] bord *m.*

marginal ['maːdʒɪnl] *adj* -1. [unimportant] marginal(e), secondaire. -2. *Br* POL: **~ seat** siège *m* disputé.

marginally ['maːdʒɪnəlɪ] *adv* très peu.

marigold ['mærɪgəuld] *n* souci *m.*

marihuana, **marijuana** [,mærɪˈwaːnə] *n* marihuana *f.*

marina [məˈriːnə] *n* marina *f.*

marinade [,mærɪˈneɪd] ◇ *n* marinade *f.* ◇ *vt & vi* mariner.

marinate ['mærɪneɪt] ◇ *vt & vi* mariner.

marine [məˈriːn] ◇ *adj* marin(e). ◇ *n* marine *m.*

marionette [,mærɪəˈnet] *n* marionnette *f.*

marital ['mærɪtl] *adj* [sex, happiness] conjugal(e); [problems] matrimonial(e).

marital status *n* situation *f* de famille.

maritime ['mærɪtaɪm] *adj* maritime.

Maritime Provinces, Maritimes *npl*: the ~ les Provinces *fpl* Maritimes.

marjoram ['mɑːdʒərəm] *n* marjolaine *f*.

mark [mɑːk] ◇ *n* **-1.** [stain] tache *f*, marque *f*. **-2.** [sign, written symbol] marque *f*. **-3.** [in exam] note *f*, point *m*. **-4.** [stage, level] barre *f*. **-5.** [currency] mark *m*. **-6.** *phr*: **to make one's ~** se faire un nom, réussir; **to be quick off the ~ in doing sthg** faire qqch sans perdre de temps; **wide of the ~** à côté de la question. ◇ *vt* **-1.** [gen] marquer. **-2.** [stain] marquer, tacher. **-3.** [exam, essay] noter, corriger.

◆ **mark down** *vt sep* **-1.** [COMM - prices] baisser; [- goods] baisser le prix de, démarquer. **-2.** [downgrade] baisser la note de.

◆ **mark off** *vt sep* [cross off] cocher.

◆ **mark up** *vt sep* [COMM - prices] augmenter; [- goods] augmenter le prix de.

marked [mɑːkt] *adj* [change, difference] marqué(e); [improvement, deterioration] sensible.

markedly ['mɑːkɪdlɪ] *adv* [different] d'une façon marquée; [worse, better] sensiblement, manifestement.

marker ['mɑːkər] *n* [sign] repère *m*.

marker pen *n* marqueur *m*.

market ['mɑːkɪt] ◇ *n* marché *m*; **to be on the ~** être sur le marché OR en vente. ◇ *vt* commercialiser. ◇ *vi Am* [shop]: **to go ~ing** aller faire ses courses.

marketable ['mɑːkɪtəbl] *adj* commercialisable.

market analysis *n* analyse *f* de marché.

market day *n* jour *m* de marché.

market forces *npl* forces *fpl* OR tendances *fpl* du marché.

market garden *n* jardin *m* maraîcher.

marketing ['mɑːkɪtɪŋ] *n* marketing *m*.

marketplace ['mɑːkɪtpleɪs] *n* **-1.** [in a town] place *f* du marché. **-2.** COMM marché *m*.

market price *n* prix *m* du marché.

market research *n* étude *f* de marché.

market town *n* marché *m*.

market value *n* valeur *f* marchande.

marking ['mɑːkɪŋ] *n* SCH correction *f*.

◆ **markings** *npl* [on animal, flower] taches *fpl*, marques *fpl*; [on road] signalisation *f* horizontale.

marksman ['mɑːksmən] (*pl* **-men** [-mən]) *n* tireur *m* d'élite.

marksmanship ['mɑːksmənʃɪp] *n* adresse *f* au tir.

markup ['mɑːkʌp] *n* majoration *f*.

marmalade ['mɑːməleɪd] *n* confiture *f* d'oranges amères.

maroon [mə'ruːn] *adj* bordeaux (*inv*).

marooned [mə'ruːnd] *adj* abandonné(e).

marquee [mɑː'kiː] *n* grande tente *f*.

marquess ['mɑːkwɪs] = **marquis**.

marquetry ['mɑːkɪtrɪ] *n* marqueterie *f*.

marquis ['mɑːkwɪs] *n* marquis *m*.

marriage ['mærɪdʒ] *n* mariage *m*.

marriage bureau *n Br* agence *f* matrimoniale.

marriage certificate *n* acte *m* de mariage.

marriage guidance *n* conseil *m* conjugal.

marriage guidance counsellor *n* conseiller conjugal *m*, conseillère conjugale *f*.

married ['mærɪd] *adj* **-1.** [person] marié(e); **to get ~** se marier. **-2.** [life] conjugal(e).

marrow ['mærəʊ] *n* **-1.** *Br* [vegetable] courge *f*. **-2.** [in bones] moelle *f*.

marry ['mærɪ] (*pt* & *pp* **-ied**) ◇ *vt* **-1.** [become spouse of] épouser, se marier avec. **-2.** [subj: priest, registrar] marier. ◇ *vi* se marier.

Mars [mɑːz] *n* [planet] Mars *f*.

Marseilles [mɑː'seɪlz] *n* Marseille.

marsh [mɑːʃ] *n* marais *m*, marécage *m*.

marshal ['mɑːʃl] (*Br pt* & *pp* **-led**, *cont* **-ling**, *Am pt* & *pp* **-ed**, *cont* **-ing**) ◇ *n* **-1.** MIL maréchal *m*. **-2.** [steward] membre *m* du service d'ordre. **-3.** *Am* [law officer] officier *m* de police fédérale. ◇ *vt lit* & *fig* rassembler.

marshalling yard ['mɑːʃlɪŋ-] *n* gare *f* de triage.

marshland ['mɑːʃlænd] *n* terrain *m* marécageux.

marshmallow [*Br* ˌmɑːʃ'mæləʊ, *Am* 'mɑːrʃˌmeləʊ] *n* guimauve *f*.

marshy ['mɑːʃɪ] (*compar* **-ier**, *superl* **-iest**) *adj* marécageux(euse).

marsupial [mɑː'suːpjəl] *n* marsupial *m*.

martial ['mɑːʃl] *adj* martial(e).

martial arts *npl* arts *mpl* martiaux.

martial law *n* loi *f* martiale.

Martian ['mɑːʃn] ◇ *adj* martien(ienne). ◇ *n* Martien *m*, -ienne *f*.

martin ['mɑːtɪn] *n* martinet *m*.

martini [mɑː'tiːnɪ] *n* [cocktail] martini *m*.

Martinique [ˌmɑːtɪ'niːk] *n* la Martinique *f*; **in ~** à la Martinique.

martyr ['mɑːtər] *n* martyr *m*, -e *f*.

martyrdom ['mɑːtədəm] *n* martyre *m*.

martyred ['mɑːtəd] *adj* de martyr.

marvel ['mɑːvl] (*Br pt* & *pp* **-led**, *cont* **-ling**, *Am pt* & *pp* **-ed**, *cont* **-ing**) ◇ *n* merveille *f*; **it's a ~ that ...** c'est un miracle que ... (+

subjunctive). ◇ *vt*: **to ~ that** s'étonner de ce que. ◇ *vi*: **to ~ (at)** s'émerveiller (de), s'étonner (de).

marvellous *Br*, **marvelous** *Am* ['mɑːvələs] *adj* merveilleux(euse).

Marxism ['mɑːksɪzm] *n* marxisme *m*.

Marxist ['mɑːksɪst] ◇ *adj* marxiste. ◇ *n* marxiste *mf*.

Maryland ['meərɪlænd] *n* Maryland *m*; **in ~** dans le Maryland.

marzipan ['mɑːzɪpæn] *n* (U) pâte *f* d'amandes.

mascara [mæs'kɑːrə] *n* mascara *m*.

mascot ['mæskət] *n* mascotte *f*.

masculine ['mæskjʊlɪn] *adj* masculin(e).

masculinity [,mæskjʊ'lɪnətɪ] *n* masculinité *f*.

mash [mæʃ] *vt* faire une purée de.

MASH [mæʃ] (*abbr of* **mobile army surgical hospital**) *n* hôpital militaire de campagne.

mashed potatoes [mæʃt-] *npl* purée *f* de pommes de terre.

mask [mɑːsk] *lit* & *fig* ◇ *n* masque *m*. ◇ *vt* masquer.

masked [mɑːskt] *adj* masqué(e).

masking tape ['mɑːskɪŋ-] *n* papier *m* cache.

masochism ['mæsəkɪzm] *n* masochisme *m*.

masochist ['mæsəkɪst] *n* masochiste *mf*.

masochistic [,mæsə'kɪstɪk] *adj* masochiste.

mason ['meɪsn] *n* **-1.** [stonemason] maçon *m*. **-2.** [freemason] franc-maçon *m*.

masonic [mə'sɒnɪk] *adj* maçonnique.

masonry ['meɪsnrɪ] *n* [stones] maçonnerie *f*.

masquerade [,mæskə'reɪd] *vi*: **to ~ as** se faire passer pour; **to ~ under an assumed name** se cacher sous un faux nom.

mass [mæs] ◇ *n* [gen & PHYSICS] masse *f*. ◇ *adj* [protest, meeting] en masse, en nombre; [unemployment, support] massif(ive). ◇ *vt* masser. ◇ *vi* se masser.
◆ **Mass** *n* RELIG messe *f*.
◆ **masses** *npl* **-1.** *inf* [lots]: **~es (of)** des masses (de); [food] des tonnes (de). **-2.** [workers]: **the ~es** les masses *fpl*.

Massachusetts [,mæsə'tʃuːsɪts] *n* Massachusetts *m*; **in ~** dans le Massachusetts.

massacre ['mæsəkər] ◇ *n* massacre *m*. ◇ *vt* massacrer.

massage [*Br* 'mæsɑːz, *Am* mə'sɑːʒ] ◇ *n* massage *m*. ◇ *vt* masser.

massage parlour *n* institut *m* de massage.

masseur [mæ'sɜːr] *n* masseur *m*.

masseuse [mæ'sɜːz] *n* masseuse *f*.

massive ['mæsɪv] *adj* massif(ive), énorme.

massively ['mæsɪvlɪ] *adv* massivement.

mass-market *adj* grand public (*inv*).

mass media *n*: **the ~** les (mass) media *mpl*.

mass-produce *vt* fabriquer en série.

mass production *n* fabrication *f* OR production *f* en série.

mast [mɑːst] *n* **-1.** [on boat] mât *m*. **-2.** RADIO & TV pylône *m*.

mastectomy [mæs'tektəmɪ] (*pl* **-ies**) *n* mastectomie *f*.

master ['mɑːstər] ◇ *n* **-1.** [gen] maître *m*. **-2.** *Br* [SCH - in primary school] instituteur *m*, maître *m*; [- in secondary school] professeur *m*. ◇ *adj* maître. ◇ *vt* maîtriser; [difficulty] surmonter, vaincre; [situation] se rendre maître de.

master bedroom *n* chambre *f* principale.

master disk *n* COMPUT disque *m* d'exploitation.

masterful ['mɑːstəfʊl] *adj* autoritaire.

master key *n* passe *m*, passe-partout *m*.

masterly ['mɑːstəlɪ] *adj* magistral(e).

mastermind ['mɑːstəmaɪnd] ◇ *n* cerveau *m*. ◇ *vt* organiser, diriger.

Master of Arts (*pl* **Masters of Arts**) *n* **-1.** [degree] maîtrise *f* ès lettres. **-2.** [person] titulaire *mf* d'une maîtrise ès lettres.

master of ceremonies (*pl* **masters of ceremonies**) *n* maître *m* de cérémonie.

Master of Science (*pl* **Masters of Science**) *n* **-1.** [degree] maîtrise *f* ès sciences. **-2.** [person] titulaire *mf* d'une maîtrise ès sciences.

masterpiece ['mɑːstəpiːs] *n* chef-d'œuvre *m*.

master plan *n* stratégie *f* globale.

master's degree *n* ≃ maîtrise *f*.

masterstroke ['mɑːstəstrəʊk] *n* coup *m* magistral OR de maître.

master switch *n* interrupteur *m* général OR principal.

masterwork ['mɑːstəwɜːk] *n* chef-d'œuvre *m*.

mastery ['mɑːstərɪ] *n* maîtrise *f*.

mastic ['mæstɪk] *n* mastic *m*.

masticate ['mæstɪkeɪt] *vt* & *vi* *fml* mastiquer, mâcher.

mastiff ['mæstɪf] *n* mastiff *m*.

masturbate ['mæstəbeɪt] *vi* se masturber.

masturbation [,mæstə'beɪʃn] *n* masturbation *f*.

mat [mæt] *n* **-1.** [on floor] petit tapis *m*; [at door] paillasson *m*. **-2.** [on table] set *m* de table; [coaster] dessous *m* de verre.

match [mætʃ] ◇ *n* **-1.** [game] match *m*. **-2.** [for lighting] allumette *f*. **-3.** [equal]: **to be no**

~ **for sb** ne pas être de taille à lutter contre qqn. ◇ *vt* **-1.** [be the same as] correspondre à, s'accorder avec. **-2.** [pair off] faire correspondre. **-3.** [be equal with] égaler, rivaliser avec. ◇ *vi* **-1.** [be the same] correspondre. **-2.** [go together well] être assorti(e).

matchbox ['mætʃbɒks] *n* boîte *f* à allumettes.

matched [mætʃt] *adj*: **to be well ~** [well suited] être bien assorti(e)s; [equal in strength] être de force égale.

matching ['mætʃɪŋ] *adj* assorti(e).

matchless ['mætʃlɪs] *adj* sans pareil, incomparable.

matchmaker ['mætʃ,meɪkər] *n* marieur *m*, -ieuse *f*.

match play *n* GOLF match-play *m*.

match point *n* TENNIS balle *f* de match.

matchstick ['mætʃstɪk] *n* allumette *f*.

mate [meɪt] ◇ *n* **-1.** *inf* [friend] copain *m*, copine *f*, pote *m*. **-2.** *Br inf* [term of address] mon vieux. **-3.** [of female animal] mâle *m*; [of male animal] femelle *f*. **-4.** NAUT: **(first) ~** second *m*. ◇ *vi* s'accoupler.

material [mə'tɪərɪəl] ◇ *adj* **-1.** [goods, benefits, world] matériel(ielle). **-2.** [important] important(e), essentiel(ielle). ◇ *n* **-1.** [substance] matière *f*, substance *f*; [type of substance] matériau *m*, matière *f*. **-2.** [fabric] tissu *m*, étoffe *f*; [type of fabric] tissu. **-3.** (U) [information - for book, article etc] matériaux *mpl*.

◆ **materials** *npl* matériaux *mpl*.

materialism [mə'tɪərɪəlɪzm] *n* matérialisme *m*.

materialist [mə'tɪərɪəlɪst] *n* matérialiste *mf*.

materialistic [mə,tɪərɪə'lɪstɪk] *adj* matérialiste.

materialize, -ise [mə'tɪərɪəlaɪz] *vi* **-1.** [offer, threat] se concrétiser, se réaliser. **-2.** [person, object] apparaître.

materially [mə'tɪərɪəlɪ] *adv* **-1.** [benefit, suffer] matériellement. **-2.** [different] essentiellement.

maternal [mə'tɜːnl] *adj* maternel(elle).

maternity [mə'tɜːnətɪ] *n* maternité *f*.

maternity benefit *n* (U) allocations *fpl* (de) maternité.

maternity dress *n* robe *f* de grossesse.

maternity hospital *n* maternité *f*.

math *Am* = **maths**.

mathematical [,mæθə'mætɪkl] *adj* mathématique.

mathematician [,mæθəmə'tɪʃn] *n* mathématicien *m*, -ienne *f*.

mathematics [,mæθə'mætɪks] *n* (U) mathématiques *fpl*.

maths *Br* [mæθs], **math** *Am* [mæθ] (*abbr of* **mathematics**) *inf* ◇ *n* (U) maths *fpl*. ◇ *comp* de maths.

maths coprocessor [-,kəʊ'prəʊsesər] *n* COMPUT coprocesseur *m* mathématique.

matinée ['mætɪneɪ] *n* matinée *f*.

matinée jacket *n Br* veste *f* de bébé.

mating call ['meɪtɪŋ-] *n* appel *m* du mâle.

mating season ['meɪtɪŋ-] *n* saison *f* des amours.

matriarch ['meɪtrɪɑːk] *n* **-1.** [of society] *femme ayant une autorité matriarcale.* **-2.** *literary* [of family] aïeule *f*, doyenne *f*.

matrices ['meɪtrɪsiːz] *pl* → **matrix**.

matriculate [mə'trɪkjʊleɪt] *vi* s'inscrire.

matriculation [me,trɪkjʊ'leɪʃn] *n* inscription *f*.

matrimonial [,mætrɪ'məʊnjəl] *adj* matrimonial(e), conjugal(e).

matrimony ['mætrɪmənɪ] *n* (U) mariage *m*.

matrix ['meɪtrɪks] (*pl* **matrices** OR **-es**) *n* **-1.** [context, framework] contexte *m*, structure *f*. **-2.** MATH & TECH matrice *f*.

matron ['meɪtrən] *n* **-1.** *Br* [in hospital] infirmière *f* en chef. **-2.** [in school] infirmière *f*. **-3.** *Am* [in prison] gardienne *f*.

matronly ['meɪtrənlɪ] *adj euphemism* [woman] qui a l'allure d'une matrone; [figure] de matrone.

matt *Br*, **matte** *Am* [mæt] *adj* mat(e).

matted ['mætɪd] *adj* emmêlé(e).

matter ['mætər] ◇ *n* **-1.** [question, situation] question *f*, affaire *f*; **a ~ of life and death** une question de vie ou de mort; **the fact** OR **truth of the ~ is ...** la vérité c'est que ..., le fait est que ...; **that's another** OR **a different ~** c'est tout autre chose, c'est une autre histoire; **as a ~ of course** automatiquement; **to make ~s worse** aggraver la situation; **and to make ~s worse ...** pour tout arranger ...; **as a ~ of principle** par principe; **within a ~ of hours** en l'affaire de quelques heures; **that's a ~ of opinion** c'est (une) affaire OR question d'opinion; **a ~ of time** une question de temps. **-2.** [trouble, cause of pain]: **there's something the ~ with my radio** il y a quelque chose qui cloche OR ne va pas dans ma radio; **what's the ~?** qu'est-ce qu'il y a?; **what's the ~ with him?** qu'est-ce qu'il a? **-3.** PHYSICS matière *f*. **-4.** (U) [material] matière *f*; **reading ~** choses *fpl* à lire; **printed ~** imprimés *mpl*.

◇ *vi* [be important] importer, avoir de l'importance; **it doesn't** ~ cela n'a pas d'importance.

◆ **no matter** *adv*: **no** ~ **what** coûte que coûte, à tout prix; **no** ~ **how hard I try to explain ...** j'ai beau essayer de lui expliquer ....

◆ **as a matter of fact** *adv* en fait, à vrai dire.

◆ **for that matter** *adv* d'ailleurs.

Matterhorn ['mætəhɔːn] *n*: **the** ~ le mont Cervin.

matter-of-fact *adj* terre-à-terre, neutre.

matting ['mætɪŋ] *n* natte *f*.

mattress ['mætrɪs] *n* matelas *m*.

mature [mə'tjʊəʳ] ◇ *adj* -**1.** [person, attitude] mûr(e). -**2.** [cheese] fait(e); [wine] arrivé(e) à maturité. ◇ *vi* -**1.** [person] mûrir. -**2.** [cheese, wine] se faire.

mature student *n* Br UNIV étudiant qui a commencé ses études sur le tard.

maturity [mə'tjʊərətɪ] *n* maturité *f*.

maudlin ['mɔːdlɪn] *adj* larmoyant(e).

maul [mɔːl] *vt* mutiler.

Mauritania [,mɒrɪ'teɪnjə] *n* Mauritanie *f*; **in** ~ en Mauritanie.

Mauritanian [,mɒrɪ'teɪnjən] ◇ *adj* mauritanien(ienne). ◇ *n* Mauritanien *m*, -ienne *f*.

Mauritian [mə'rɪʃn] ◇ *adj* mauricien(ienne). ◇ *n* Mauricien *m*, -ienne *f*.

Mauritius [mə'rɪʃəs] *n* l'île *f* Maurice; **in** ~ à l'île Maurice.

mausoleum [,mɔːsə'lɪəm] (*pl* -**s**) *n* mausolée *m*.

mauve [məʊv] ◇ *adj* mauve. ◇ *n* mauve *m*.

maverick ['mævərɪk] *n* non-conformiste *mf*.

mawkish ['mɔːkɪʃ] *adj* d'une sentimentalité excessive.

max. ['mæks] (*abbr of* **maximum**) max.

maxim ['mæksɪm] (*pl* -**s**) *n* maxime *f*.

maxima ['mæksɪmə] *pl* → **maximum**.

maximize, -ise ['mæksɪmaɪz] *vt* maximiser, porter au maximum.

maximum ['mæksɪməm] (*pl* **maxima** OR -**s**) ◇ *adj* maximum (*inv*). ◇ *n* maximum *m*.

may [meɪ] *modal vb* -**1.** [expressing possibility]: **it** ~ **rain** il se peut qu'il pleuve, il va peut-être pleuvoir; **be that as it** ~ quoi qu'il en soit. -**2.** [can] pouvoir; **on a clear day the coast** ~ **be seen** on peut voir la côte par temps clair. -**3.** [asking permission]: ~ **I come in?** puis-je entrer? -**4.** [as contrast]: **it** ~ **be expensive but ...** c'est peut-être cher, mais .... -**5.** *fml* [expressing wish,

hope]: ~ **they be happy!** qu'ils soient heureux!; *see also* **might**.

May [meɪ] *n* mai *m*; *see also* **September**.

Maya ['maɪə] *n*: **the** ~ les Mayas *mpl*.

Mayan ['maɪən] *adj* maya.

maybe ['meɪbiː] *adv* peut-être; ~ **I'll come** je viendrai peut-être.

mayday ['meɪdeɪ] *n* S.O.S. *m*.

May Day *n* le Premier mai.

mayfly ['meɪflaɪ] (*pl* -**flies**) *n* éphémère *m*.

mayhem ['meɪhem] *n* pagaille *f*.

mayn't [meɪnt] = **may not**.

mayonnaise [,meɪə'neɪz] *n* mayonnaise *f*.

mayor [meəʳ] *n* maire *m*.

mayoress ['meərɪs] *n* -**1.** [female mayor] femme *f* maire. -**2.** [mayor's wife] femme *f* du maire.

maypole ['meɪpəʊl] *n* ≃ mai *m*.

may've ['meɪəv] = **may have**.

maze [meɪz] *n* *lit* & *fig* labyrinthe *m*, dédale *m*.

MB -**1.** (*abbr of* **megabyte**) Mo. -**2.** *abbr of* **Manitoba**.

MBA (*abbr of* **Master of Business Administration**) *n* (*titulaire d'une*) maîtrise de gestion.

MBBS (*abbr of* **Bachelor of Medicine and Surgery**) *n* (*titulaire d'une*) licence de médecine et de chirurgie.

MBE (*abbr of* **Member of the Order of the British Empire**) *n* distinction honorifique britannique.

MC *abbr of* **master of ceremonies**.

MCAT (*abbr of* **Medical College Admissions Test**) *n* test d'admission aux études de médecine.

MCC (*abbr of* **Marylebone Cricket Club**) *n* célèbre club de cricket de Londres.

McCarthyism [mə'kɑːθɪɪzm] *n* Maccarthisme *m*, Maccarthysme *m*.

McCoy [mə'kɔɪ] *n* *inf*: **the real** ~ de l'authentique, du vrai de vrai.

MCP (*abbr of* **male chauvinist pig**) *n* *inf* phallo *m*.

MD ◇ *n* -**1.** *abbr of* **Doctor of Medicine**. -**2.** *abbr of* **managing director**. ◇ *abbr of* **Maryland**.

MDT (*abbr of* **Mountain Daylight Time**) *n* heure d'été des montagnes Rocheuses.

me [miː] *pers pron* -**1.** [direct, indirect] me, m' (+ *vowel or silent "h"*); **can you see/hear** ~? tu me vois/m'entends?; **it's** ~ c'est moi; **they spoke to** ~ ils m'ont parlé; **she gave it to** ~ elle me l'a donné. -**2.** [stressed, after prep, in comparisons etc] moi; **you can't expect ME to do it** tu ne peux pas exiger que ce soit moi qui le fasse; **she's shorter than** ~ elle est plus petite que moi.

ME ◇ *n* (*abbr of* **myalgic encephalomyelitis**) myélo-encéphalite *f.* ◇ *abbr of* **Maine**.

meadow ['medəʊ] *n* prairie *f,* pré *m.*

meagre *Br,* **meager** *Am* ['miːgəʳ] *adj* maigre.

meal [miːl] *n* repas *m;* **to make a** ~ **of sthg** *Br fig & pej* faire toute une histoire OR tout un plat de qqch.

meals on wheels *npl Br* repas *mpl* à domicile (*pour personnes âgées ou handicapées*).

mealtime ['miːltaɪm] *n* heure *f* du repas; **at** ~**s** aux heures des repas.

mealy-mouthed [,miːlɪ'maʊðd] *adj pej* mielleux(euse), patelin(e).

mean [miːn] (*pt & pp* **meant**) ◇ *vt* **-1.** [signify] signifier, vouloir dire; **money** ~**s nothing to him** l'argent ne compte pas pour lui. **-2.** [intend]: **to** ~ **to do sthg** vouloir faire qqch, avoir l'intention de faire qqch; **I didn't** ~ **to drop it** je n'ai pas fait exprès de le laisser tomber; **to be meant for sb/ sthg** être destiné(e) à qqn/qqch; **to be meant to do sthg** être censé(e) faire qqch; **to** ~ **well** agir dans une bonne intention. **-3.** [be serious about]: **I** ~ **it** je suis sérieux(ieuse). **-4.** [entail] occasionner, entraîner. **-5.** *phr:* **I** ~ [as explanation] c'est vrai; [as correction] je **veux dire**.
◇ *adj* **-1.** [miserly] radin(e), chiche; **to be** ~. **with sthg** être avare de qqch. **-2.** [unkind] mesquin(e), méchant(e); **to be** ~ **to sb** être mesquin envers qqn. **-3.** [average] moyen(enne). **-4.** *iro:* **she's no** ~ **singer** elle a de la voix; **that's no** ~ **feat** c'est un véritable exploit.
◇ *n* [average] moyenne *f; see also* **means.**

meander [mɪ'ændəʳ] *vi* [river, road] serpenter; [person] errer.

meaning ['miːnɪŋ] *n* sens *m,* signification *f.*

meaningful ['miːnɪŋfʊl] *adj* [look] significatif(ive); [relationship, discussion] **important(e).**

meaningless ['miːnɪŋlɪs] *adj* [gesture, word] dénué(e) OR vide de sens; [proposal, discussion] sans importance.

meanness ['miːnnɪs] *n* **-1.** [stinginess] avarice *f.* **-2.** [unkindness] mesquinerie *f,* méchanceté *f.*

means [miːnz] ◇ *n* [method, way] moyen *m;* **a** ~ **to an end** un moyen d'arriver à ses fins; **by** ~ **of** au moyen de. ◇ *npl* [money] moyens *mpl,* ressources *fpl.*
◆ **by all means** *adv* mais certainement, bien sûr.
◆ **by no means** *adv fml* nullement, en aucune façon.

means test *n* enquête sur les ressources d'une personne (*qui demande une aide financière à l'État*).

meant [ment] *pt & pp* → **mean.**

meantime ['miːn,taɪm] *n:* **in the** ~ en attendant.

meanwhile ['miːn,waɪl] *adv* **-1.** [at the same time] pendant ce temps. **-2.** [between two events] en attendant.

measles ['miːzlz] *n:* **(the)** ~ la rougeole.

measly ['miːzlɪ] (*compar* **-ier**, *superl* **-iest**) *adj inf* misérable, minable.

measurable ['meʒərəbl] *adj* [improvement, deterioration] sensible.

measurably ['meʒərəblɪ] *adv* sensiblement.

measure ['meʒəʳ] ◇ *n* **-1.** [gen] mesure *f.* **-2.** [amount]: **to achieve a** ~ **of independence** parvenir à une certaine indépendance; **for good** ~ pour faire bonne mesure. **-3.** [indication]: **it is a** ~ **of her success that ...** la preuve de son succès, c'est que .... ◇ *vt & vi* mesurer.
◆ **measure up** *vi:* **to** ~ **up (to)** être à la hauteur (de).

measured ['meʒəd] *adj* [steps, tone] mesuré(e).

measurement ['meʒəmənt] *n* mesure *f.*

measuring tape ['meʒərɪŋ-] *n* mètre *m* (à ruban); [in dressmaking] centimètre *m.*

meat [miːt] *n* viande *f.*

meatball ['miːtbɔːl] *n* boulette *f* de viande.

meat pie *n Br* tourte *f* à la viande.

meaty ['miːtɪ] (*compar* **-ier**, *superl* **-iest**) *adj fig* important(e).

Mecca ['mekə] *n* La Mecque; *fig:* **a** ~ **for** la Mecque de.

mechanic [mɪ'kænɪk] *n* mécanicien *m,* -ienne *f.*
◆ **mechanics** ◇ *n* (*U*) [study] mécanique *f.* ◇ *npl fig* mécanisme *m.*

mechanical [mɪ'kænɪkl] *adj* **-1.** [device] mécanique. **-2.** [person, mind] fort(e) en mécanique. **-3.** [routine, automatic] machinal(e).

mechanical engineering *n* génie *m* mécanique.

mechanism ['mekənɪzm] *n lit & fig* mécanisme *m.*

mechanization [,mekənaɪ'zeɪʃn] *n* mécanisation *f.*

mechanize, -ise ['mekənaɪz] *vt & vi* mécaniser.

MEd [,em'ed] (*abbr of* **Master of Education**) *n* (titulaire d'une) maîtrise en sciences de l'éducation.

medal ['medl] *n* médaille *f.*

medallion [mɪˈdæljən] *n* médaillon *m*.

medallist *Br*, **medalist** *Am* [ˈmedəlɪst] *n* médaillé *m*, -e *f*.

meddle [ˈmedl] *vi*: **to ~ in** se mêler de.

meddlesome [ˈmedlsəm] *adj* [person] qui met son nez partout.

media [ˈmiːdjə] ⋄ *pl* → **medium**. ⋄ *n or npl*: **the ~** les médias *mpl*.

mediaeval [ˌmedɪˈiːvl] = **medieval**.

media event *n* événement *m* médiatique.

median [ˈmiːdjən] ⋄ *adj* MATH médian(e). ⋄ *n Am* [of road] bande *f* médiane (*qui sépare les deux côtés d'une grande route*).

mediate [ˈmiːdɪeɪt] ⋄ *vt* négocier. ⋄ *vi*: **to ~ (for/between)** servir de médiateur (pour/entre).

mediation [ˌmiːdɪˈeɪʃn] *n* médiation *f*.

mediator [ˈmiːdɪeɪtə] *n* médiateur *m*, -trice *f*.

medic [ˈmedɪk] *n inf* **-1.** [medical student] carabin *m*. **-2.** [doctor] toubib *m*.

Medicaid [ˈmedɪkeɪd] *n Am assistance médicale aux personnes sans ressources*.

medical [ˈmedɪkl] ⋄ *adj* médical(e). ⋄ *n* examen *m* médical.

medical certificate *n* certificat *m* médical.

medical insurance *n* assurance *f* maladie.

medical student *n* étudiant *m*, -e *f* en médecine.

medicament [ˈmedɪkəment] *n* médicament *m*.

Medicare [ˈmedɪkeə] *n Am programme fédéral d'assistance médicale pour personnes âgées*.

medicated [ˈmedɪkeɪtɪd] *adj* traitant(e).

medication [ˌmedɪˈkeɪʃn] *n* **-1.** [use of medicines] médication *f*. **-2.** [medicine] médicament *m*.

medicinal [meˈdɪsɪnl] *adj* médicinal(e).

medicine [ˈmedsɪn] *n* **-1.** [subject, treatment] médecine *f*; **Doctor of Medicine** UNIV docteur *m* en médecine. **-2.** [substance] médicament *m*.

medicine man *n* sorcier *m*.

medieval [ˌmedɪˈiːvl] *adj* médiéval(e).

mediocre [ˌmiːdɪˈəʊkə] *adj* médiocre.

mediocrity [ˌmiːdɪˈɒkrətɪ] *n* médiocrité *f*.

meditate [ˈmedɪteɪt] *vi*: **to ~ (on OR upon)** méditer (sur).

meditation [ˌmedɪˈteɪʃn] *n* méditation *f*.

Mediterranean [ˌmedɪtəˈreɪnjən] ⋄ *n* **-1.** [sea]: **the ~ (Sea)** la (mer) Méditerranée. **-2.** [person] Méditerranéen *m*, -enne *f*. ⋄ *adj* méditerranéen(enne).

medium [ˈmiːdjəm] (*pl sense 1* **media**, *pl sense 2* **mediums**) ⋄ *adj* moyen(enne). ⋄ *n*

-1. [way of communicating] **moyen** *m*. **-2.** [spiritualist] médium *m*.

medium-dry *adj* demi-sec.

medium-size(d) *adj* de taille moyenne.

medium wave *n* onde *f* moyenne.

medley [ˈmedlɪ] (*pl* **medleys**) *n* **-1.** [mixture] mélange *m*. **-2.** MUS pot-pourri *m*.

meek [miːk] *adj* docile.

meekly [ˈmiːklɪ] *adv* docilement.

meet [miːt] (*pt & pp* **met**) ⋄ *vt* **-1.** [gen] rencontrer; [by arrangement] retrouver. **-2.** [go to meet - person] aller/venir attendre, aller/venir chercher; [- train, plane] aller attendre. **-3.** [need, requirement] satisfaire, répondre à. **-4.** [problem] résoudre; [challenge] répondre à. **-5.** [costs] payer. **-6.** [join] rejoindre. ⋄ *vi* **-1.** [gen] se rencontrer; [by arrangement] se retrouver; [for a purpose] se réunir. **-2.** [join] se joindre. ⋄ *n Am* [meeting] meeting *m*.
◆ **meet up** *vi* se retrouver; **to ~ up with sb** rencontrer qqn, retrouver qqn.
◆ **meet with** *vt fus* **-1.** [encounter - disapproval] être accueilli(e) par; [- success] remporter; [- failure] essuyer. **-2.** *Am* [by arrangement] retrouver.

meeting [ˈmiːtɪŋ] *n* **-1.** [for discussions, business] réunion *f*. **-2.** [by chance] rencontre *f*; [by arrangement] entrevue *f*. **-3.** [people at meeting]: **the ~** l'assemblée *f*.

meeting place *n* lieu *m* de réunion.

mega- [ˈmegə] *prefix* méga-.

megabit [ˈmegəbɪt] *n* COMPUT méga-bit *m*.

megabyte [ˈmegəbaɪt] *n* COMPUT méga-octet *m*.

megahertz [ˈmegəhɜːts] *n* mégahertz *m*.

megalomania [ˌmegələˈmeɪnjə] *n* mégalomanie *f*.

megalomaniac [ˌmegələˈmeɪnɪæk] *n* mégalomane *mf*.

megaphone [ˈmegəfəʊn] *n* mégaphone *m*, porte-voix *m*.

megaton [ˈmegətʌn] *n* mégatonne *f*.

megawatt [ˈmegəwɒt] *n* mégawatt *m*.

melamine [ˈmeləmiːn] *n* mélamine *f*.

melancholy [ˈmelənkəlɪ] ⋄ *adj* [person] mélancolique; [news, facts] triste. ⋄ *n* mélancolie *f*.

mellow [ˈmeləʊ] ⋄ *adj* [light, voice] doux (douce); [taste, wine] moelleux(euse). ⋄ *vt*: **to be ~ed by age** s'assagir avec l'âge. ⋄ *vi* s'adoucir.

melodic [mɪˈlɒdɪk] *adj* mélodique.

melodious [mɪˈləʊdjəs] *adj* mélodieux(ieuse).

melodrama [ˈmelədrɑːmə] *n* mélodrame *m*.

melodramatic [ˌmelədrə'mætɪk] *adj* mélo-dramatique.

melody ['melədɪ] (*pl* **-ies**) *n* mélodie *f*.

melon ['melən] *n* melon *m*.

melt [melt] ◇ *vt* faire fondre. ◇ *vi* **-1.** [become liquid] fondre. **-2.** *fig*: **his heart ~ed at the sight** il fut tout attendri devant ce spectacle. **-3.** [disappear]: **to ~ (away)** fondre; **to ~ into the background** s'effacer.

◆ **melt down** *vt sep* fondre.

meltdown ['meltdaʊn] *n* fusion *f* du cœur (du réacteur).

melting point ['meltɪŋ-] *n* point *m* de fusion.

melting pot ['meltɪŋ-] *n fig* creuset *m*.

member ['membər] ◇ *n* membre *m*; [of club] adhérent *m*, -e *f*. ◇ *comp* membre.

Member of Congress (*pl* **Members of Congress**) *n Am* membre *m* du Congrès.

Member of Parliament (*pl* **Members of Parliament**) *n Br* ≃ député *m*.

membership ['membəʃɪp] *n* **-1.** [of organization] adhésion *f*. **-2.** [number of members] nombre *m* d'adhérents. **-3.** [members]: **the ~** les membres *mpl*.

membership card *n* carte *f* d'adhésion.

membrane ['membreɪn] *n* membrane *f*.

memento [mɪ'mentəʊ] (*pl* **-s**) *n* souvenir *m*.

memo ['meməʊ] (*pl* **-s**) *n* note *f* de service.

memoirs ['memwɑːz] *npl* mémoires *mpl*.

memo pad *n* bloc-notes *m*.

memorabilia [ˌmemərə'bɪlɪə] *npl* souvenirs *mpl*.

memorable ['memərəbl] *adj* mémorable.

memorandum [ˌmemə'rændəm] (*pl* **-da** [-də] OR **-dums**) *n* note *f* de service.

memorial [mɪ'mɔːrɪəl] ◇ *adj* commémoratif(ive). ◇ *n* monument *m*.

memorize, -ise ['meməraɪz] *vt* [phone number, list] retenir; [poem] apprendre par cœur.

memory ['memərɪ] (*pl* **-ies**) *n* **-1.** [gen & COMPUT] mémoire *f*; **from ~** de mémoire; **to lose one's ~** perdre la mémoire; **within living ~** de mémoire d'homme. **-2.** [event, experience] souvenir *m*; **I have no ~ of it** je n'en ai aucun souvenir; **in ~ of** en souvenir de.

memory card *n* COMPUT carte *f* d'extension mémoire.

men [men] *pl* → **man**.

menace ['menəs] ◇ *n* **-1.** [gen] menace *f*. **-2.** *inf* [nuisance] plaie *f*. ◇ *vt* menacer.

menacing ['menəsɪŋ] *adj* menaçant(e).

menacingly ['menəsɪŋlɪ] *adv* [speak] d'un ton menaçant; [look] d'un air menaçant.

menagerie [mɪ'nædʒərɪ] *n* ménagerie *f*.

mend [mend] ◇ *n inf*: **to be on the ~** aller mieux. ◇ *vt* réparer; [clothes] raccommoder; [sock, pullover] repriser; **to ~ one's ways** s'amender.

mending ['mendɪŋ] *n*: **to do the ~** faire le raccommodage.

menfolk ['menfəʊk] *npl* hommes *mpl*.

menial ['miːnjəl] *adj* avilissant(e).

meningitis [ˌmenɪn'dʒaɪtɪs] *n* (*U*) méningite *f*.

menopause ['menəpɔːz] *n*: **the ~** la ménopause.

menservants ['mensɜːvənts] *pl* → **manservant**.

men's room *n Am*: **the ~** les toilettes *fpl* pour hommes.

menstrual ['menstrʊəl] *adj* menstruel(elle).

menstruate ['menstrʊeɪt] *vi* avoir ses règles.

menstruation [ˌmenstrʊ'eɪʃn] *n* menstruation *f*.

menswear ['menzweər] *n* (*U*) vêtements *mpl* pour hommes.

mental ['mentl] *adj* mental(e); [image, picture] dans la tête.

mental age *n* âge *m* mental.

mental block *n*: **to have a ~ about sthg** ne pas arriver à comprendre qqch.

mental hospital *n* hôpital *m* psychiatrique.

mentality [men'tælətɪ] *n* mentalité *f*.

mentally ['mentəlɪ] *adv* mentalement; **to be ~ ill** être malade mental; **to be ~ retarded** être arriéré mental.

mentally handicapped *npl*: **the ~** les handicapés *mpl* mentaux.

◆ **mentally-handicapped** *adj*: **to be mentally-handicapped** être handicapé mental (handicapée mentale).

mental note *n*: **to make a ~ to do sthg** prendre note mentalement de faire qqch.

menthol ['menθɒl] *n* menthol *m*.

mentholated ['menθəleɪtɪd] *adj* mentholé(e).

mention ['menʃn] ◇ *vt* mentionner, signaler; **not to ~** sans parler de; **don't ~ it!** je vous en prie. ◇ *n* mention *f*.

mentor ['mentɔːr] *n* mentor *m*.

menu ['menjuː] *n* [gen & COMPUT] menu *m*.

menu-driven *adj* COMPUT dirigé(e) par menu.

meow *Am* = **miaow**.

MEP (*abbr of* **Member of the European Parliament**) *n* parlementaire *m* européen.

mercantile ['mɜːkəntaɪl] *adj* commercial(e).

mercenary ['mɜːsɪnrɪ] (*pl* **-ies**) ◇ *adj* mercenaire. ◇ *n* mercenaire *m*.

merchandise ['mɜːtʃəndaɪz] *n* (*U*) marchandises *fpl*.

merchant ['mɜːtʃənt] ◇ *adj* marchand(e). ◇ *n* marchand *m*, -e *f*, commerçant *m*, -e *f*.

merchant bank *n Br* banque *f* d'affaires.

merchant navy *Br*, **merchant marine** *Am n* marine *f* marchande.

merciful ['mɜːsɪfʊl] *adj* **-1.** [person] clément(e). **-2.** [death, release] qui est une délivrance.

mercifully ['mɜːsɪfʊlɪ] *adv* [fortunately] par bonheur, heureusement.

merciless ['mɜːsɪlɪs] *adj* impitoyable.

mercilessly ['mɜːsɪlɪslɪ] *adv* impitoyablement.

mercurial [mɜːˈkjʊərɪəl] *adj literary* [temperament] changeant(e), inégal(e); [person] d'humeur changeante.

mercury ['mɜːkjʊrɪ] *n* mercure *m*.

Mercury ['mɜːkjʊrɪ] *n* [planet] Mercure *f*.

mercy ['mɜːsɪ] (*pl* **-ies**) *n* **-1.** [kindness, pity] pitié *f*; **at the ~ of** *fig* à la merci de. **-2.** [blessing]: **what a ~ (that ...)** quelle chance (que ...).

mercy killing *n* euthanasie *f*.

mere [mɪəˈ] *adj* seul(e); **she's a ~ child** ce n'est qu'une enfant; **it cost a ~ £10** cela n'a coûté que 10 livres.

merely ['mɪəlɪ] *adv* seulement, simplement.

meretricious [ˌmerɪˈtrɪʃəs] *adj* factice.

merge [mɜːdʒ] ◇ *vt* COMM & COMPUT fusionner. ◇ *vi* **-1.** COMM: **to ~ (with)** fusionner (avec). **-2.** [roads, lines]: **to ~ (with)** ce joindre (à). **-3.** [colours] se fondre. ◇ *n* COMPUT fusion *f*.

merger ['mɜːdʒəˈ] *n* fusion *f*.

meridian [məˈrɪdɪən] *n* méridien *m*.

meringue [məˈræŋ] *n* meringue *f*.

merino [məˈriːnəʊ] *adj* de mérinos.

merit ['merɪt] ◇ *n* [value] mérite *m*, valeur *f*. ◇ *vt* mériter.

◆ **merits** *npl* [advantages] qualités *fpl*; **to judge sthg on its ~s** juger qqch selon ses qualités.

meritocracy [ˌmerɪˈtɒkrəsɪ] (*pl* **-ies**) *n* méritocratie *f*.

mermaid ['mɜːmeɪd] *n* sirène *f*.

merrily ['merɪlɪ] *adv* joyeusement; *iro* allègrement.

merriment ['merɪmənt] *n* hilarité *f*.

merry ['merɪ] (*compar* **-ier**, *superl* **-iest**) *adj* **-1.** *literary* [happy] joyeux(euse); **Merry Christmas!** joyeux Noël! **-2.** *inf* [tipsy] gai(e), éméché(e).

merry-go-round *n* manège *m*.

merrymaking ['merɪˌmeɪkɪŋ] *n* (*U*) réjouissances *fpl*.

mesh [meʃ] ◇ *n* maille *f* (du filet); **wire ~** grillage *m*. ◇ *vi* [gears] s'engrener.

mesmerize, -ise ['mezməraɪz] *vt*: **to be ~d by** être fasciné(e) par.

mess [mes] *n* **-1.** [untidy state] désordre *m*; *fig* gâchis *m*; **to be (in) a ~** [room] être en désordre; [hair] être ébouriffé; *fig* [life] être sens dessus dessous. **-2.** MIL mess *m*.

◆ **mess about, mess around** *inf* ◇ *vt sep*: **to ~ sb about** traiter qqn par-dessus OR par-dessous la jambe. ◇ *vi* **-1.** [fool around] perdre OR gaspiller son temps. **-2.** [interfere]: **to ~ about with sthg** s'immiscer dans qqch.

◆ **mess up** *vt sep inf* **-1.** [room] mettre en désordre; [clothes] salir. **-2.** *fig* [spoil] gâcher.

◆ **mess with** *vt fus inf*: **don't ~ with them** tiens-toi à l'écart.

message ['mesɪdʒ] *n* message *m*; **to get the ~** *inf* piger.

messenger ['mesɪndʒəˈ] *n* messager *m*, -ère *f*; **by ~** par porteur.

Messiah [mɪˈsaɪə] *n*: **the ~** le Messie.

Messrs, Messrs. ['mesəz] (*abbr of* **messieurs**) MM.

messy ['mesɪ] (*compar* **-ier**, *superl* **-iest**) *adj* **-1.** [dirty] sale; [untidy] désordonné(e); **a ~ job** un travail salissant. **-2.** *inf* [divorce] difficile; [situation] embrouillé(e).

met [met] *pt & pp* → **meet**.

Met [met] (*abbr of* **Metropolitan Opera**) *n*: **the ~** l'opéra *m* de New-York.

metabolism [meˈtæbəlɪzm] *n* métabolisme *m*.

metal ['metl] ◇ *n* métal *m*. ◇ *comp* en OR de métal.

metallic [mɪˈtælɪk] *adj* **-1.** [sound, ore] métallique. **-2.** [paint, finish] métallisé(e).

metallurgist [meˈtælədʒɪst] *n* métallurgiste *m*.

metallurgy [meˈtælədʒɪ] *n* métallurgie *f*.

metalwork ['metlwɜːk] *n* [craft] ferronnerie *f*.

metalworker ['metlˌwɜːkəˈ] *n* [craftsman] ferronnier *m*; [in industry] métallurgiste *m*.

metamorphose [ˌmetəˈmɔːfəʊz] *vi*: **to ~ (into)** se métamorphoser (en).

metamorphosis [ˌmetəˈmɔːfəsɪs, ˌmetəmɔːˈfəʊsɪs] (*pl* **-phoses** [-ˈfəʊsiːz]) *n* métamorphose *f*.

metaphor ['metəfəˈ] *n* métaphore *f*.

metaphorical [ˌmetə'fɒrɪkl] *adj* métaphorique.

metaphysical [ˌmetə'fɪzɪkl] *adj* métaphysique.

metaphysics [ˌmetə'fɪzɪks] *n* métaphysique *f*.

mete [miːt]
◆ **mete out** *vt sep* [punishment] infliger.

meteor ['miːtɪəʳ] *n* météore *m*.

meteoric [miːtɪ'ɒrɪk] *adj* météorique.

meteorite ['miːtjəraɪt] *n* météorite *m or f*.

meteorological [ˌmiːtjərə'lɒdʒɪkl] *adj* météorologique.

meteorologist [miːtjə'rɒlədʒɪst] *n* météorologue *mf*, météorologiste *mf*.

meteorology [miːtjə'rɒlədʒɪ] *n* météorologie *f*.

meter ['miːtəʳ] ◇ *n* **-1.** [device] compteur *m*; parking ~ parcmètre *m*. **-2.** *Am* = **metre**. ◇ *vt* [gas, electricity] établir la consommation de.

methadone ['meθədəʊn] *n* méthadone *f*.

methane ['miːθeɪn] *n* méthane *m*.

method ['meθəd] *n* méthode *f*.

methodical [mɪ'θɒdɪkl] *adj* méthodique.

methodically [mɪ'θɒdɪklɪ] *adv* méthodiquement.

Methodist ['meθədɪst] ◇ *adj* méthodiste. ◇ *n* méthodiste *mf*.

methodology [ˌmeθə'dɒlədʒɪ] (*pl* **-ies**) *n* méthodologie *f*.

meths [meθs] *n Br inf* alcool *m* à brûler.

methylated spirits ['meθɪleɪtɪd-] *n* alcool *m* à brûler.

meticulous [mɪ'tɪkjʊləs] *adj* méticuleux(euse).

meticulously [mɪ'tɪkjʊləslɪ] *adv* méticuleusement.

Met Office (*abbr of* **Meteorological Office**) *n la météo britannique.*

metre *Br*, **meter** *Am* ['miːtəʳ] *n* mètre *m*.

metric ['metrɪk] *adj* métrique.

metrication [ˌmetrɪ'keɪʃn] *n Br* adoption *f* du système métrique.

metric system *n*: the ~ le système métrique.

metric ton *n* tonne *f*.

metro ['metrəʊ] (*pl* **-s**) *n* métro *m*.

metronome ['metrənəʊm] *n* métronome *m*.

metropolis [mɪ'trɒpəlɪs] (*pl* **-es**) *n* métropole *f*.

metropolitan [ˌmetrə'pɒlɪtn] *adj* métropolitain(e).

Metropolitan Police *npl*: the ~ la police de Londres.

mettle ['metl] *n*: to be on one's ~ être d'attaque; to show OR prove one's ~ montrer ce dont on est capable.

mew [mjuː] = **miaow**.

mews [mjuːz] (*pl inv*) *n Br* ruelle *f*.

Mexican ['meksɪkn] ◇ *adj* mexicain(e). ◇ *n* Mexicain *m*, -e *f*.

Mexico ['meksɪkəʊ] *n* Mexique *m*; in ~ au Mexique.

Mexico City *n* Mexico.

mezzanine ['metsəniːn] *n* **-1.** [floor] mezzanine *f*. **-2.** *Am* [in theatre] corbeille *f*.

MFA (*abbr of* **Master of Fine Arts**) *n (titulaire d'une) maîtrise en beaux-arts.*

mfr *abbr of* **manufacturer.**

mg (*abbr of* **milligram**) mg.

Mgr -1. (*abbr of* **Monseigneur, Monsignor**) Mgr. **-2.** *abbr of* **manager.**

MHR *abbr of* **Member of the House of Representatives.**

MHz (*abbr of* **megahertz**) MHz.

MI *abbr of* **Michigan.**

MI5 (*abbr of* **Military Intelligence 5**) *n service de contre-espionnage britannique.*

MI6 (*abbr of* **Military Intelligence 6**) *n service de renseignements britannique.*

MIA (*abbr of* **missing in action**) *expression indiquant qu'une personne a disparu lors d'un combat.*

miaow *Br* [miː'aʊ], **meow** *Am* [mɪ'aʊ] ◇ *n* miaulement *m*, miaou *m*. ◇ *vi* miauler.

mice [maɪs] *pl* → **mouse.**

Mich. *abbr of* **Michigan.**

Michigan ['mɪʃɪgən] *n* Michigan *m*; in ~ dans le Michigan.

mickey ['mɪkɪ] *n*: to take the ~ out of sb *Br inf* se payer la tête de qqn, faire marcher qqn.

MICR (*abbr of* **magnetic ink character recognition**) *n reconnaissance magnétique de caractères.*

micro ['maɪkrəʊ] (*pl* **-s**) *n* micro *m*.

micro- ['maɪkrəʊ] *prefix* micro-.

microbe ['maɪkrəʊb] *n* microbe *m*.

microbiologist [ˌmaɪkrəʊbaɪ'ɒlədʒɪst] *n* microbiologiste *mf*.

microbiology [ˌmaɪkrəʊbaɪ'ɒlədʒɪ] *n* microbiologie *f*.

microchip ['maɪkrəʊtʃɪp] *n* COMPUT puce *f*.

microcircuit ['maɪkrəʊˌsɜːkɪt] *n* microcircuit *m*.

microcomputer [ˌmaɪkrəʊkəm'pjuːtəʳ] *n* micro-ordinateur *m*.

microcosm ['maɪkrəkɒzm] *n* microcosme *m*.

microfiche ['maɪkrəʊfiːʃ] (*pl inv* OR **-s**) *n* microfiche *f*.

microfilm ['maɪkrəʊfɪlm] *n* microfilm *m*.

microlight ['maɪkrəlaɪt] *n* ULM *m*.

micromesh ['maɪkrəʊmeʃ] *n* maille *f* super-fine.

micron ['maɪkrɒn] *n* micron *m*.

microorganism [,maɪkrəʊˈɔːgənɪzm] *n* micro-organisme *m*.

microphone ['mɪkrəfəʊn] *n* microphone *m*, micro *m*.

microprocessor ['maɪkrəʊ,prəʊsesər] *n* COMPUT microprocesseur *m*.

microscope ['maɪkrəskəʊp] *n* microscope *m*.

microscopic [,maɪkrəˈskɒpɪk] *adj* microscopique.

microsecond ['maɪkrəʊ,sekənd] *n* microseconde *m*.

microsurgery [,maɪkrəˈsɜːdʒərɪ] *n* microchirurgie *f*.

microwave (oven) ['maɪkrəweɪv-] *n* (four *m* à) micro-ondes *m*.

mid- [mɪd] *prefix*: ~**height** mi-hauteur; ~**morning** milieu de la matinée; ~**winter** plein hiver.

midair [mɪdˈeər] ◇ *adj* en plein ciel. ◇ *n*: **in** ~ en plein ciel.

midday ['mɪddeɪ] *n* midi *m*.

middle ['mɪdl] ◇ *adj* **-1.** [centre] du milieu, du centre. **-2.** [in time]: **she was in her** ~ **twenties** elle avait dans les 25 ans. ◇ *n* **-1.** [centre] milieu *m*, centre *m*; **in the** ~ **(of)** au milieu (de); **in the** ~ **of nowhere** en pleine cambrousse. **-2.** [in time] milieu *m*; **to be in the** ~ **of doing sthg** être en train de faire qqch; **to be in the** ~ **of a meeting** être en pleine réunion; **in the** ~ **of the night** au milieu de la nuit, en pleine nuit. **-3.** [waist] taille *f*.

middle age *n* âge *m* mûr.

middle-aged *adj* d'une cinquantaine d'années.

Middle Ages *npl*: **the** ~ le Moyen Âge.

middle-class *adj* bourgeois(e).

middle classes *npl*: **the** ~ la bourgeoisie.

middle distance *n*: **in the** ~ au second plan.

Middle East *n*: **the** ~ le Moyen-Orient.

Middle Eastern *adj* du Moyen-Orient.

middleman ['mɪdlmæn] (*pl* **-men** [-mən]) *n* intermédiaire *mf*.

middle management *n* (*U*) cadres *mpl* moyens.

middle name *n* second prénom *m*.

middle-of-the-road *adj* modéré(e).

middle school *n* *Br* ≃ premier cycle *m* du secondaire.

middleweight ['mɪdlweɪt] *n* poids *m* moyen.

middling ['mɪdlɪŋ] *adj* moyen(enne).

Middx (*abbr of* **Middlesex**) ancien comté anglais.

Mideast [,mɪdˈiːst] *n* *Am*: **the** ~ le Moyen-Orient.

midfield [,mɪdˈfiːld] *n* FTBL milieu *m* de terrain.

midge ['mɪdʒ] *n* moucheron *m*.

midget ['mɪdʒɪt] *n* nain *m*, -e *f*.

midi system ['mɪdɪ-] *n* chaîne *f* midi.

Midlands ['mɪdləndz] *npl*: **the** ~ *les comtés du centre de l'Angleterre.*

midnight ['mɪdnaɪt] ◇ *n* minuit *m*. ◇ *comp* de minuit.

midriff ['mɪdrɪf] *n* diaphragme *m*.

midst [mɪdst] *n* **-1.** [in space]: **in the** ~ **of** au milieu de; **in our** ~ parmi nous. **-2.** [in time]: **to be in the** ~ **of doing sthg** être en train de faire qqch.

midstream [mɪdˈstriːm] *n*: **in** ~ [in river] au milieu du courant; *fig* [when talking] en plein milieu.

midsummer ['mɪd,sʌmər] *n* cœur *m* de l'été.

Midsummer Day *n* la Saint-Jean.

midway [,mɪdˈweɪ] *adv* **-1.** [in space]: ~ **(between)** à mi-chemin (entre). **-2.** [in time]: ~ **through the meeting** en pleine réunion.

midweek [*adj* mɪdˈwiːk, *adv* 'mɪdwiːk] ◇ *adj* du milieu de la semaine. ◇ *adv* en milieu de semaine.

Midwest [,mɪdˈwest] *n*: **the** ~ le Midwest.

Midwestern [,mɪdˈwestən] *adj* du Midwest.

midwife ['mɪdwaɪf] (*pl* **-wives** [-waɪvz]) *n* sage-femme *f*.

midwifery ['mɪdwɪfərɪ] *n* obstétrique *f*.

miffed [mɪft] *adj inf* vexé(e).

might [maɪt] ◇ *modal vb* **-1.** [expressing possibility]: **the criminal** ~ **be armed** il est possible que le criminel soit armé. **-2.** [expressing suggestion]: **it** ~ **be better to wait** il vaut peut-être mieux attendre. **-3.** *fml* [asking permission]: **he asked if he** ~ **leave the room** il demanda s'il pouvait sortir de la pièce. **-4.** [expressing concession]: **you** ~ **well be right** vous avez peut-être raison. **-5.** *phr*: **I** ~ **have known** OR **guessed** j'aurais dû m'en douter.
◇ *n* (*U*) force *f*.

mightn't ['maɪtənt] = **might not**.

might've ['maɪtəv] = **might have**.

mighty ['maɪtɪ] (*compar* -ier, *superl* -iest) ◇ *adj* -1. [powerful] puissant(e). -2. [very large] imposant(e). ◇ *adv Am inf* drôlement, vachement.

migraine ['miːgreɪn, 'maɪgreɪn] *n* migraine *f*.

migrant ['maɪgrənt] ◇ *adj* -1. [bird, animal] migrateur(trice). -2. [workers] émigré(e). ◇ *n* -1. [bird, animal] migrateur *m*. -2. [person] émigré *m*, -e *f*.

migrate [*Br* maɪ'greɪt, *Am* 'maɪgreɪt] *vi* -1. [bird, animal] migrer. -2. [person] émigrer.

migration [maɪ'greɪʃn] *n* migration *f*.

migratory ['maɪgrətrɪ] *adj* [bird] migrateur(trice); [journey] migratoire.

mike [maɪk] (*abbr of* **microphone**) *n inf* micro *m*.

mild [maɪld] ◇ *adj* -1. [disinfectant, reproach] léger(ère). -2. [tone, weather] doux (douce). -3. [illness] bénin(igne). ◇ *n* bière anglaise légère.

mildew ['mɪldjuː] *n* (*U*) moississure *f*.

mildly ['maɪldlɪ] *adv* -1. [gently] doucement; **to put it** ~ le moins qu'on puisse dire. -2. [not strongly] légèrement. -3. [slightly] un peu.

mild-mannered *adj* mesuré(e), calme.

mildness ['maɪldnɪs] *n* (*U*) douceur *f*.

mile [maɪl] *n* mille *m*; **to see for** ~s voir sur des kilomètres; **to walk for** ~s marcher pendant des kilomètres; **this is** ~s **better** c'est cent fois mieux; **to be** ~s **away** *fig* être très loin.

mileage ['maɪlɪdʒ] *n* distance *f* en milles, ≃ kilométrage *m*.

mileage allowance *n* ≃ indemnité *f* kilométrique.

mileometer [maɪ'lɒmɪtər] *n* compteur *m* de milles, ≃ compteur kilométrique.

milestone ['maɪlstəʊn] *n* [marker stone] borne *f*; *fig* événement *m* marquant OR important.

milieu [*Br* 'miːljə, *Am* miːl'juː] (*pl* -s OR -x) *n* milieu *m*.

militant ['mɪlɪtənt] ◇ *adj* militant(e). ◇ *n* militant *m*, -e *f*.

militarism ['mɪlɪtərɪzm] *n* militarisme *m*.

militarist ['mɪlɪtərɪst] *n* militariste *mf*.

militarized zone, **militarised zone** ['mɪlɪtəraɪzd-] *n* zone *f* militarisée.

military ['mɪlɪtrɪ] ◇ *adj* militaire. ◇ *n*: **the** ~ les militaires *mpl*, l'armée *f*.

military police *n* police *f* militaire.

militate ['mɪlɪteɪt] *vi*: **to** ~ **against** militer contre.

militia [mɪ'lɪʃə] *n* milice *f*.

milk [mɪlk] ◇ *n* lait *m*. ◇ *vt* -1. [cow] traire. -2. *fig* [use to own ends] exploiter.

milk chocolate ◇ *n* chocolat *m* au lait. ◇ *comp* au chocolat au lait.

milk float *Br*, **milk truck** *Am n* voiture *f* de laitier.

milking ['mɪlkɪŋ] *n* traite *f*.

milkman ['mɪlkmən] (*pl* -men [-mən]) *n* laitier *m*.

milk round *n Br* [by milkman] tournée *f* du laitier.

milk shake *n* milk-shake *m*.

milk tooth *n* dent *m* de lait.

milk truck *Am* = **milk float**.

milky ['mɪlkɪ] (*compar* -ier, *superl* -iest) *adj* -1. *Br* [coffee] avec beaucoup de lait. -2. [pale white] laiteux(euse).

Milky Way *n*: **the** ~ la Voie lactée.

mill [mɪl] ◇ *n* -1. [flour-mill, grinder] moulin *m*. -2. [factory] usine *f*. ◇ *vt* moudre.

♦ **mill about**, **mill around** *vi* grouiller.

millennium [mɪ'lenɪəm] (*pl* -nnia [-nɪə]) *n* millénaire *m*.

miller ['mɪlər] *n* meunier *m*.

millet ['mɪlɪt] *n* millet *m*.

milli- ['mɪlɪ] *prefix* milli-.

millibar ['mɪlɪbɑːr] *n* millibar *m*.

milligram(me) ['mɪlɪgræm] *n* milligramme *m*.

millilitre *Br*, **milliliter** *Am* ['mɪlɪ,liːtər] *n* millilitre *m*.

millimetre *Br*, **millimeter** *Am* ['mɪlɪ,miːtər] *n* millimètre *m*.

millinery ['mɪlɪnrɪ] *n* chapellerie *f* féminine.

million ['mɪljən] *n* million *m*; **a** ~, ~**s of** *fig* des milliers de, un million de.

millionaire [,mɪljə'neər] *n* millionnaire *mf*.

millionairess [,mɪljə'neərɪs] *n* millionnaire *f*.

millipede ['mɪlɪpiːd] *n* mille-pattes *m inv*.

millisecond ['mɪlɪ,sekənd] *n* millième *m* de seconde.

millstone ['mɪlstəʊn] *n* meule *f*; **he's like a** ~ **round my neck** c'est un boulet que je traîne.

millwheel ['mɪlwiːl] *n* roue *f* de moulin.

milometer [maɪ'lɒmɪtər] = **mileometer**.

mime [maɪm] ◇ *n* mime *m*. ◇ *vt & vi* mimer.

mimic ['mɪmɪk] (*pt* & *pp* **-ked**, *cont* **-king**) ◇ *n* imitateur *m*, -trice *f*. ◇ *vt* imiter.

mimicry ['mɪmɪkrɪ] *n* imitation *f*.

mimosa [mɪ'məuzə] *n* mimosa *m*.

min. [mɪn] **-1.** (*abbr of* **minute**) mn, min. **-2.** (*abbr of* **minimum**) min.

Min. *abbr of* **ministry**.

mince [mɪns] ◇ *n* Br viande *f* hachée. ◇ *vt* [meat] hacher. ◇ *vi* marcher à petits pas maniérés.

mincemeat ['mɪnsmiːt] *n* **-1.** [fruit] *mélange de pommes, raisins secs et épices utilisé en pâtisserie.* **-2.** Am [meat] viande *f* hachée.

mince pie *n* tartelette *f* de Noël.

mincer ['mɪnsəʳ] *n* hachoir *m*.

mind [maɪnd] ◇ *n* **-1.** [gen] esprit *m*; **state of ~** état d'esprit; **to bear sthg in ~** ne pas oublier qqch; **to call sthg to ~** se rappeler qqch; **to cast one's ~ back to sthg** repenser à qqch; **to come into/cross sb's ~** venir à/ traverser l'esprit de qqn; **to have sthg on one's ~** avoir l'esprit préoccupé, être préoccupé par qqch; **to keep an open ~** réserver son jugement; **the trip took her ~ off her worries** ce petit voyage lui a changé les idées; **that's a load** OR **weight off my ~!** je me sens soulagé, quel soulagement!; **to have a ~ to do sthg** avoir bien envie de faire qqch; **to have sthg in ~** avoir qqch dans l'idée; **to broaden one's ~** enrichir l'esprit; **to make one's ~ up** se décider; **to put** OR **set sb's ~ at rest** rassurer qqn. **-2.** [attention]: **to put one's ~ to sthg** s'appliquer à qqch; **to keep one's ~ on sthg** se concentrer sur qqch; **to slip one's ~** sortir de l'esprit. **-3.** [opinion]: **to change one's ~** changer d'avis; **to my ~** à mon avis; **to speak one's ~** parler franchement; **to be in two ~s (about sthg)** se tâter OR être indécis (à propos de qqch). **-4.** [person] cerveau *m*; **great ~s think alike** les grands esprits se rencontrent.

◇ *vi* **-1.** [be bothered]: **I don't ~** ça m'est égal; **I hope you don't ~** j'espère que vous n'y voyez pas d'inconvénient; **never ~** [don't worry] ne t'en fais pas; [it's not important] ça ne fait rien. **-2.** [be careful]: **~ out!** *Br* attention!

◇ *vt* **-1.** [be bothered about, dislike]: **I don't ~ waiting** ça ne me dérange pas d'attendre; **do you ~ if ...?** cela ne vous ennuie pas si ...?; **I wouldn't ~ a beer** je prendrais bien une bière. **-2.** [pay attention to] faire attention à, prendre garde à. **-3.** [take care of - luggage] garder, surveiller; [- shop] tenir.

◆ **mind you** *adv* remarquez.

mind-bending [-,bendɪŋ] *adj inf* hallucinant(e).

minder ['maɪndəʳ] *n* Br inf [bodyguard] ange *m* gardien.

mindful ['maɪndful] *adj*: **~ of** [risks] attentif(ive) à; [responsibility] soucieux(ieuse) de.

mindless ['maɪndlɪs] *adj* stupide, idiot(e).

mind reader *n*: **I'm not a ~** *hum* je ne suis pas devin.

mindset ['maɪndset] *n* façon *f* de voir les choses.

mind's eye *n*: **in my ~** dans mon imagination.

mine[1] [maɪn] *poss pron* le mien (la mienne), les miens (les miennes) (*pl*); **that money is ~** cet argent est à moi OR est le mien; **it wasn't your fault, it was MINE** ce n'était pas de votre faute, c'était de la mienne OR de ma faute à moi; **a friend of ~** un ami à moi, un de mes amis.

mine[2] [maɪn] ◇ *n* mine *f*; **a ~ of information** *fig* une mine de renseignements. ◇ *vt* **-1.** [coal, gold] extraire. **-2.** [road, beach, sea] miner.

mine detector *n* détecteur *m* de mines.

minefield ['maɪnfiːld] *n* champ *m* de mines; *fig* situation *f* explosive.

minelayer ['maɪn,leɪəʳ] *n* mouilleur *m* de mines.

miner ['maɪnəʳ] *n* mineur *m*.

mineral ['mɪnərəl] ◇ *adj* minéral(e). ◇ *n* minéral *m*.

mineralogy [,mɪnə'rælədʒɪ] *n* minéralogie *f*.

mineral water *n* eau *f* minérale.

minestrone [,mɪnɪ'strəunɪ] *n* minestrone *m*.

minesweeper ['maɪn,swiːpəʳ] *n* dragueur *m* de mines.

mingle ['mɪŋgl] ◇ *vt*: **to ~ sthg with sthg** mélanger qqch à qqch. ◇ *vi*: **to ~ (with)** [sounds, fragrances] se mélanger (à); [people] se mêler (à).

mini ['mɪnɪ] *n* [skirt] minijupe *f*.

miniature ['mɪnətʃəʳ] ◇ *adj* miniature. ◇ *n* **-1.** [painting] miniature *f*. **-2.** [of alcohol] bouteille *f* miniature. **-3.** [small scale]: **in ~** en miniature.

minibus ['mɪnɪbʌs] (*pl* **-es**) *n* minibus *m*.

minicab ['mɪnɪkæb] *n* Br radiotaxi *m*.

minicomputer [,mɪnɪkəm'pjuːtəʳ] *n* mini-ordinateur *m*.

minim ['mɪnɪm] *n* MUS blanche *f*.

minima ['mɪnɪmə] *pl* → **minimum**.

minimal ['mɪnɪml] *adj* [cost] insignifiant(e); [damage] minime.

minimize, -ise ['mɪnɪ,maɪz] *vt* minimiser.

minimum ['mɪnɪməm] (*pl* **-mums** OR **-ma**) ◇ *adj* minimum (*inv*). ◇ *n* minimum *m*.

minimum lending rate [-'lendɪŋ-] *n* taux *m* de crédit minimum.

minimum wage *n* salaire *m* minimum.

mining ['maɪnɪŋ] ◇ *n* exploitation *f* minière. ◇ *adj* minier(ière); ~ **engineer** ingénieur *m* des mines.

minion ['mɪnjən] *n* larbin *m*, laquais *m*.

miniseries ['mɪnɪsɪərɪz] (*pl inv*) *n* mini-série *f* télévisée.

miniskirt ['mɪnɪskɜːt] *n* minijupe *f*.

minister ['mɪnɪstər] *n* **-1.** POL ministre *m*. **-2.** RELIG pasteur *m*.
◆ **minister to** *vt fus* [person] donner OR prodiguer ses soins à; [needs] pourvoir à.

ministerial [,mɪnɪ'stɪərɪəl] *adj* ministériel(ielle).

minister of state *n* secrétaire *mf* d'État.

ministry ['mɪnɪstrɪ] (*pl* **-ies**) *n* **-1.** POL ministère *m*; **Ministry of Defence** ministère *m* de la Défense. **-2.** RELIG: **the** ~ le saint ministère.

mink [mɪŋk] (*pl inv*) *n* vison *m*.

mink coat *n* manteau *m* de vison.

Minnesota [,mɪnɪ'səʊtə] *n* Minnesota *m*; **in** ~ dans le Minnesota.

minnow ['mɪnəʊ] *n* vairon *m*.

minor ['maɪnər] ◇ *adj* [gen & MUS] mineur(e); [detail] petit(e); [role] secondaire. ◇ *n* mineur *m*, -e *f*.

minority [maɪ'nɒrətɪ] (*pl* **-ies**) *n* minorité *f*; **to be in a** OR **the** ~ être en minorité.

minority government *n* gouvernement *m* minoritaire.

minster ['mɪnstər] *n* cathédrale *f*.

minstrel ['mɪnstrəl] *n* ménestrel *m*.

mint [mɪnt] ◇ *n* **-1.** [herb] menthe *f*. **-2.** [sweet] bonbon *m* à la menthe. **-3.** [for coins]: **the Mint** l'hôtel de la Monnaie; **in ~ condition** en parfait état. ◇ *vt* [coins] battre.

mint sauce *n* sauce *f* à la menthe.

minuet [,mɪnjʊ'et] *n* menuet *m*.

minus ['maɪnəs] (*pl* **-es**) ◇ *prep* moins. ◇ *adj* [answer, quantity] négatif(ive). ◇ *n* **-1.** MATH signe *m* moins. **-2.** [disadvantage] handicap *m*.

minus sign *n* signe *m* moins.

minute¹ ['mɪnɪt] *n* minute *f*; **at any** ~ à tout moment, d'une minute à l'autre; **at the last** ~ au dernier moment, à la dernière minute; **stop that this** ~! arrête tout de suite OR immédiatement!; **up to the** ~

[news] de dernière heure; [design] dernier cri (*inv*); **wait a** ~! attendez une minute OR un instant!
◆ **minutes** *npl* procès-verbal *m*, compterendu *m*.

minute² [maɪ'njuːt] *adj* minuscule; **in** ~ **detail** par le menu.

minutiae [maɪ'njuːʃiː] *npl* menus détails *mpl*.

miracle ['mɪrəkl] *n* miracle *m*.

miraculous [mɪ'rækjʊləs] *adj* miraculeux(euse).

miraculously [mɪ'rækjʊləslɪ] *adv* miraculeusement, par miracle.

mirage [mɪ'rɑːʒ] *n lit* & *fig* mirage *m*.

mire [maɪər] *n* fange *f*, boue *f*.

mirror ['mɪrər] ◇ *n* miroir *m*, glace *f*. ◇ *vt* refléter.

mirror image *n* image *f* inversée.

mirth [mɜːθ] *n* hilarité *f*, gaieté *f*.

misadventure [,mɪsəd'ventʃər] *n*: **death by** ~ JUR mort *f* accidentelle.

misanthropist [mɪ'sænθrəpɪst] *n* misanthrope *mf*.

misapplication ['mɪs,æplɪ'keɪʃn] *n* mauvaise application *f*, application erronée.

misapprehension ['mɪs,æprɪ'henʃn] *n* idée *f* fausse.

misappropriate [,mɪsə'prəʊprɪeɪt] *vt* détourner.

misappropriation ['mɪsə,prəʊprɪ'eɪʃn] *n* détournement *m*.

misbehave [,mɪsbɪ'heɪv] *vi* se conduire mal.

misbehaviour *Br*, **misbehavior** *Am* [,mɪsbɪ'heɪvjər] *n* mauvaise conduite *f*.

misc [mɪsk] *abbr of* **miscellaneous**.

miscalculate [,mɪs'kælkjʊleɪt] ◇ *vt* mal calculer. ◇ *vi* se tromper.

miscalculation [,mɪskælkjʊ'leɪʃn] *n* mauvais calcul *m*, erreur *f* de calcul.

miscarriage [,mɪs'kærɪdʒ] *n* MED fausse couche *f*; **to have a** ~ faire une fausse couche.

miscarriage of justice *n* erreur *f* judiciaire.

miscarry [,mɪs'kærɪ] (*pt* & *pp* **-ied**) *vi* **-1.** [woman] faire une fausse couche. **-2.** [plan] échouer.

miscellaneous [,mɪsə'leɪnjəs] *adj* varié(e), divers(e).

miscellany [*Br* mɪ'selənɪ *Am* 'mɪsəleɪnɪ] (*pl* **-ies**) *n* recueil *m*.

mischance [,mɪs'tʃɑːns] *n* malchance *f*; **by** ~ par malheur.

mischief ['mɪstʃɪf] *n* (U) **-1.** [playfulness] malice *f*, espièglerie *f*. **-2.** [naughty behaviour] sottises *fpl*, bêtises *fpl*. **-3.** [harm] dégât *m*.

mischievous ['mɪstʃɪvəs] *adj* **-1.** [playful] malicieux(ieuse). **-2.** [naughty] espiègle, coquin(e).

misconceived [,mɪskən'siːvd] *adj* [idea] mal conçu(e).

misconception [,mɪskən'sepʃn] *n* idée *f* fausse.

misconduct [,mɪskən'strʌkʃn] *n* inconduite *f*.

misconstrue [,mɪskən'struː] *vt fml* mal interpréter.

miscount [,mɪs'kaʊnt] *vt & vi* mal compter.

misdeed [,mɪs'diːd] *n* méfait *m*.

misdemeanour *Br*, **misdemeanor** *Am* [,mɪsdɪ'miːnər] *n* JUR délit *m*.

misdirected [,mɪsdɪ'rektɪd] *adj* [letter] mal adressé(e); [efforts, energy] mal dirigé(e).

miser ['maɪzər] *n* avare *mf*.

miserable ['mɪzrəbl] *adj* **-1.** [person] malheureux(euse), triste. **-2.** [conditions, life] misérable; [pay] dérisoire; [weather] maussade. **-3.** [failure] pitoyable, lamentable.

miserably ['mɪzrəblɪ] *adv* **-1.** [reply, cry] pitoyablement. **-2.** [live] misérablement. **-3.** [fail] pitoyablement, lamentablement.

miserly ['maɪzəlɪ] *adj* avare.

misery ['mɪzərɪ] (*pl* **-ies**) *n* **-1.** [of person] tristesse *f*. **-2.** [of conditions, life] misère *f*.

misfire [,mɪs'faɪər] *vi* **-1.** [gun, plan] rater. **-2.** [car engine] avoir des ratés.

misfit ['mɪsfɪt] *n* inadapté *m*, -e *f*.

misfortune [mɪs'fɔːtʃuːn] *n* **-1.** [bad luck] malchance *f*. **-2.** [piece of bad luck] malheur *m*.

misgivings [mɪs'gɪvɪŋz] *npl* craintes *fpl*, doutes *mpl*.

misguided [,mɪs'gaɪdəd] *adj* [person] malavisé(e); [attempt] malencontreux(euse); [opinion] peu judicieux(ieuse).

mishandle [,mɪs'hændl] *vt* **-1.** [person, animal] manier sans précaution. **-2.** [negotiations] mal mener; [business] mal gérer.

mishap ['mɪshæp] *n* mésaventure *f*; **without** ~ sans encombre OR incident.

mishear [,mɪs'hɪər] (*pt & pp* **-heard** [-'hɜːd]) *vt & vi* mal entendre.

mishmash ['mɪʃmæʃ] *n inf* méli-mélo *m*.

misinform [,mɪsɪn'fɔːm] *vt* mal renseigner, mal informer.

misinformation [,mɪsɪnfə'meɪʃn] *n* POL désinformation *f*.

misinterpret [,mɪsɪn'tɜːprɪt] *vt* mal interpréter.

misjudge [,mɪs'dʒʌdʒ] *vt* **-1.** [distance, time] mal évaluer. **-2.** [person, mood] méjuger, se méprendre sur.

misjudg(e)ment [,mɪs'dʒʌdʒmənt] *n*: **to make a** ~ faire une erreur de jugement.

mislay [,mɪs'leɪ] (*pt & pp* **-laid** [-'leɪd]) *vt* égarer.

mislead [,mɪs'liːd] (*pt & pp* **-led**) *vt* induire en erreur.

misleading [,mɪs'liːdɪŋ] *adj* trompeur(euse).

misled [,mɪs'led] *pt & pp* → **mislead**.

mismanage [,mɪs'mænɪdʒ] *vt* mal gérer, mal administrer.

mismanagement [,mɪs'mænɪdʒmənt] *n* mauvaise gestion *f* OR administration *f*.

mismatch [,mɪs'mætʃ] *vt*: **to be** ~**ed** être mal assorti(e).

misnomer [,mɪs'nəʊmər] *n* nom *m* mal approprié.

misogynist [mɪ'sɒdʒɪnɪst] *n* misogyne *mf*.

misplace [,mɪs'pleɪs] *vt* égarer.

misplaced [,mɪs'pleɪst] *adj* mal placé(e), déplacé(e).

misprint ['mɪsprɪnt] *n* faute *f* d'impression.

mispronounce [,mɪsprə'naʊns] *vt* mal prononcer.

misquote [,mɪs'kwəʊt] *vt* citer de façon inexacte.

misread [,mɪs'riːd] (*pt & pp* **-read** [-'red]) *vt* **-1.** [read wrongly] mal lire. **-2.** [misinterpret] mal interpréter.

misrepresent ['mɪs,reprɪ'zent] *vt* dénaturer.

misrepresentation ['mɪs,reprɪzen'teɪʃn] *n* **-1.** (U) [wrong interpretation] mauvaise interprétation *f*. **-2.** [false account] déformation *f*.

misrule [,mɪs'ruːl] *n* mauvais gouvernement *m*, mauvaise administration *f*.

miss [mɪs] ◇ *vt* **-1.** [gen] rater, manquer. **-2.** [home, person]: **I** ~ **my family/her** ma famille/elle me manque. **-3.** [avoid, escape] échapper à; **I just** ~**ed being run over** j'ai failli me faire écraser. ◇ *vi* rater. ◇ *n*: **to give sthg a** ~ *inf* ne pas aller à qqch.
♦ **miss out** ◇ *vt sep* [omit - by accident] oublier; [- deliberately] omettre. ◇ *vi*: **to** ~ **out (on sthg)** laisser passer (qqch).

Miss [mɪs] *n* Mademoiselle *f*.

misshapen [,mɪs'ʃeɪpn] *adj* difforme.

missile [*Br* 'mɪsaɪl, *Am* 'mɪsəl] *n* **-1.** [weapon] missile *m*. **-2.** [thrown object] projectile *m*.

missile launcher [-,lɔːntʃər] *n* lance-missiles *m inv*.

missing ['mɪsɪŋ] *adj* **-1.** [lost] perdu(e), égaré(e). **-2.** [not present] manquant(e), qui manque.

missing link *n* maillon *m* qui manque à la chaîne.

missing person *n* personne *f* disparue.

mission ['mɪʃn] *n* mission *f*.

missionary ['mɪʃənrɪ] (*pl* **-ies**) *n* missionnaire *mf*.

Mississippi [,mɪsɪ'sɪpɪ] **-1.** [river]: **the ~ (River)** le Mississippi. **-2.** [state] Mississippi *m*; **in ~** dans le Mississippi.

missive ['mɪsɪv] *n* missive *f*.

Missouri [mɪ'zuərɪ] *n* Missouri *m*; **in ~** dans le Missouri.

misspell [,mɪs'spel] (*pt* & *pp* **-spelt** OR **-spelled**) *vt* mal orthographier.

misspelling [,mɪs'spelɪŋ] *n* faute *f* d'orthographe.

misspelt [,mɪs'spelt] *pt* & *pp* → **misspell**.

misspend [,mɪs'spend] (*pt* & *pp* **-spent** [-'spent]) *vt* gaspiller.

mist [mɪst] *n* brume *f*.
◆ **mist over, mist up** *vi* s'embuer.

mistake [mɪ'steɪk] (*pt* **-took**, *pp* **-taken**) ◇ *n* erreur *f*; **by ~** par erreur; **to make a ~** faire une erreur, se tromper. ◇ *vt* **-1.** [misunderstand - meaning] mal comprendre; [- intention] se méprendre sur. **-2.** [fail to recognize]: **to ~ sb/sthg for** prendre qqn/qqch pour, confondre qqn/qqch avec; **there's no mistaking ...** il est impossible de ne pas reconnaître ....

mistaken [mɪ'steɪkn] ◇ *pp* → **mistake** ◇ *adj* **-1.** [person]: **to be ~ (about)** se tromper (en ce qui concerne OR sur). **-2.** [belief, idea] erroné(e), faux (fausse).

mistaken identity *n*: **a case of ~** une erreur sur la personne.

mistakenly [mɪ'steɪknlɪ] *adv* par erreur.

mister ['mɪstər] *n* *inf* monsieur *m*.
◆ **Mister** *n* Monsieur *m*.

mistime [,mɪs'taɪm] *vt* [tackle, shot] mal calculer; [announcement] faire au mauvais moment.

mistletoe ['mɪsltəu] *n* gui *m*.

mistook [mɪ'stuk] *pt* → **mistake**.

mistranslation [,mɪstræns'leɪʃn] *n* erreur *f* de traduction.

mistreat [,mɪs'triːt] *vt* maltraiter.

mistreatment [,mɪs'triːtmənt] *n* mauvais traitement *m*.

mistress ['mɪstrɪs] *n* maîtresse *f*.

mistrial ['mɪstraɪəl] *n* [in UK] erreur *f* judiciaire; [in US] procès annulé par manque d'unanimité parmi les jurés.

mistrust [,mɪs'trʌst] ◇ *n* méfiance *f*. ◇ *vt* se méfier de.

mistrustful [,mɪs'trʌstful] *adj*: **~ (of)** méfiant(e) (à l'égard de).

misty ['mɪstɪ] (*compar* **-ier**, *superl* **-iest**) *adj* brumeux(euse).

misunderstand [,mɪsʌndə'stænd] (*pt* & *pp* **-stood**) *vt* & *vi* mal comprendre.

misunderstanding [,mɪsʌndə'stændɪŋ] *n* malentendu *m*.

misunderstood [,mɪsʌndə'stud] *pt* & *pp* → **misunderstand**.

misuse [*n* ,mɪs'juːs, *vb* ,mɪs'juːz] ◇ *n* **-1.** [of one's time, resources] mauvais emploi *m*. **-2.** [of power] abus *m*; [of funds] détournement *m*. ◇ *vt* **-1.** [one's time, resources] mal employer. **-2.** [power] abuser de; [funds] détourner.

MIT (*abbr of* **Massachusetts Institute of Technology**) *n* l'institut de technologie du Massachusetts.

mite [maɪt] *n* **-1.** [insect] mite *f*. **-2.** *inf* [small amount]: **a ~** un brin, un tantinet. **-3.** [small child] petit *m*, -e *f*.

miter *Am* = **mitre**.

mitigate ['mɪtɪgeɪt] *vt* atténuer, mitiger.

mitigating ['mɪtɪgeɪtɪŋ] *adj*: **~ circumstances** circonstances *fpl* atténuantes.

mitigation [,mɪtɪ'geɪʃn] *n* atténuation *f*.

mitre *Br*, **miter** *Am* ['maɪtər] *n* **-1.** [hat] mitre *f*. **-2.** [joint] onglet *m*.

mitt [mɪt] *n* **-1.** = **mitten**. **-2.** [in baseball] gant *m*.

mitten ['mɪtn] *n* moufle *f*.

mix [mɪks] ◇ *vt* **-1.** [gen] mélanger. **-2.** [activities]: **to ~ sthg with sthg** combiner OR associer qqch et qqch. **-3.** [drink] préparer; [cement] malaxer. ◇ *vi* **-1.** [gen] se mélanger. **-2.** [socially]: **to ~ with** fréquenter. ◇ *n* **-1.** [gen] mélange *m*. **-2.** MUS mixage *m*.
◆ **mix up** *vt sep* **-1.** [confuse] confondre. **-2.** [disorganize] mélanger.

mixed [mɪkst] *adj* **-1.** [assorted] assortis(es); **to have ~ feelings** être partagé. **-2.** [education] mixte.

mixed-ability *adj Br* [class] tous niveaux confondus.

mixed blessing *n* quelque chose qui a du bon et du mauvais.

mixed doubles *n* double *m* mixte.

mixed economy *n* économie *f* mixte.

mixed grill *n* assortiment *m* de grillades.

mixed marriage *n* mariage *m* mixte.

mixed up *adj* **-1.** [confused - person] qui ne sait plus où il en est, paumé(e); [- mind] embrouillé(e). **-2.** [involved]: **to be ~ in sthg** être mêlé(e) à qqch.

mixer ['mɪksər] *n* [for food] mixer *m*.

mixer tap *n Br* (robinet *m*) mélangeur *m*.

mixing bowl ['mɪksɪŋ-] *n* grand bol *m* de cuisine.

mixture ['mɪkstʃər] *n* **-1.** [gen] mélange *m*. **-2.** MED préparation *f*.

mix-up *n inf* confusion *f*.

mk, MK *abbr of* **mark**.

mkt *abbr of* **market**.

MLitt [em'lɪt] (*abbr of* **Master of Literature, Master of Letters**) *n* (titulaire d'une) maîtrise de lettres.

MLR *abbr of* **minimum lending rate**.

mm (*abbr of* **millimetre**) mm.

MN ◇ *n abbr of* **Merchant Navy**. ◇ *abbr of* **Minnesota**.

mnemonic [nɪ'mɒnɪk] *n* mnémotechnique *f*.

m.o. *abbr of* **money order**.

MO ◇ *n abbr of* **medical officer**. ◇ *abbr of* **Missouri**.

moan [məʊn] ◇ *n* **-1.** [of pain, sadness] gémissement *m*. **-2.** *inf* [complaint] plainte *f*. ◇ *vi* **-1.** [in pain, sadness] gémir. **-2.** *inf* [complain]: **to ~ (about)** rouspéter OR râler (à propos de).

moaning ['məʊnɪŋ] *n* (*U*) [complaining] plaintes *fpl*, jérémiades *fpl*.

moat [məʊt] *n* douves *fpl*.

mob [mɒb] (*pt & pp* **-bed**, *cont* **-bing**) ◇ *n* foule *f*. ◇ *vt* assaillir.

mobile ['məʊbaɪl] ◇ *adj* **-1.** [gen] mobile. **-2.** [able to travel] motorisé(e). ◇ *n* mobile *m*.

mobile home *n* auto-caravane *f*.

mobile library *n* bibliobus *m*.

mobile phone *n* téléphone *m* portatif.

mobile shop *n* marchand *m* ambulant.

mobility [mə'bɪlətɪ] *n* mobilité *f*.

mobility allowance *n Br* allocation *f* de transport.

mobilization [,məʊbɪlaɪ'zeɪʃn] *n* mobilisation *f*.

mobilize, -ise ['məʊbɪlaɪz] *vt & vi* mobiliser.

moccasin ['mɒkəsɪn] *n* mocassin *m*.

mock [mɒk] ◇ *adj* faux (fausse); **~ exam** examen blanc. ◇ *vt* se moquer de. ◇ *vi* se moquer.

mockery ['mɒkərɪ] *n* moquerie *f*; **to make a ~ of sthg** tourner qqch en dérision.

mocking ['mɒkɪŋ] *adj* moqueur(euse).

mockingbird ['mɒkɪŋbɜːd] *n* moqueur *m*.

mock-up *n* maquette *f*.

mod [mɒd] *n en Angleterre, membre d'un groupe de jeunes des années 60 qui s'opposaient aux rockers.*

MoD *n abbr of* **Ministry of Defence**.

mod cons (*abbr of* **modern conveniences**) *npl Br inf*: **all ~** tout confort, tt. conf.

mode [məʊd] *n* mode *m*.

model ['mɒdl] (*Br pt & pp* **-led**, *cont* **-ling**, *Am pt & pp* **-ed**, *cont* **-ing**) ◇ *n* **-1.** [gen] modèle *m*. **-2.** [fashion model] mannequin *m*. ◇ *adj* **-1.** [perfect] modèle. **-2.** [reduced-scale] (en) modèle réduit. ◇ *vt* **-1.** [clay] modeler. **-2.** [clothes]: **to ~ a dress** présenter un modèle de robe. **-3.** [copy]: **to ~ o.s. on sb** prendre modèle OR exemple sur qqn, se modeler sur qqn. ◇ *vi* être mannequin.

modem ['məʊdem] *n* COMPUT modem *m*.

moderate [*adj & n* 'mɒdərət, *vb* 'mɒdəreɪt] ◇ *adj* modéré(e). ◇ *n* POL modéré *m*, -e *f*. ◇ *vt* modérer. ◇ *vi* se modérer.

moderately ['mɒdərətlɪ] *adv* [not very] pas très, plus ou moins.

moderation [,mɒdə'reɪʃn] *n* modération *f*; **in ~** avec modération.

moderator ['mɒdəreɪtər] *n* [of exam] examinateur *m*, -trice *f*.

modern ['mɒdən] *adj* moderne.

modern-day *adj* moderne, d'aujourd'hui.

modernism ['mɒdənɪzm] *n* modernisme *m*.

modernization [,mɒdənaɪ'zeɪʃn] *n* modernisation *f*.

modernize, -ise ['mɒdənaɪz] ◇ *vt* moderniser. ◇ *vi* se moderniser.

modern languages *npl* langues *fpl* vivantes.

modest ['mɒdɪst] *adj* modeste.

modestly ['mɒdɪstlɪ] *adv* modestement.

modesty ['mɒdɪstɪ] *n* modestie *f*.

modicum ['mɒdɪkəm] *n* minimum *m*.

modification [,mɒdɪfɪ'keɪʃn] *n* modification *f*.

modify ['mɒdɪfaɪ] (*pt & pp* **-ied**) *vt* modifier.

modular ['mɒdjʊlər] *adj* modulaire.

modulated ['mɒdjʊleɪtɪd] *adj* modulé(e).

modulation [,mɒdjʊ'leɪʃn] *n* modulation *f*.

module ['mɒdjuːl] *n* module *m*.

Mogadishu [,mɒgə'dɪʃuː] *n* Mogadishu.

moggy ['mɒgɪ] (*pl* **-ies**) *n Br inf* minou *m*.

mogul ['məʊgl] *n fig* magnat *m*.

MOH (*abbr of* **Medical Officer of Health**) *n en Grande-Bretagne, direction de la santé publique.*

mohair ['məʊheəʳ] ◇ *n* mohair *m*. ◇ *comp* en mohair.

Mohammedan [mə'hæmɪdn] ◇ *adj* mahométan(e), musulman(e). ◇ *n* Mahométan *m*, -e *f*.

Mohican [məʊ'hiːkən,'məʊɪkən] *n* Mohican *m*.

moist [mɔɪst] *adj* [soil, climate] humide; [cake] moelleux(euse).

moisten ['mɔɪsn] *vt* humecter.

moisture ['mɔɪstʃəʳ] *n* humidité *f*.

moisturize, -ise ['mɔɪstʃəraɪz] *vt* hydrater.

moisturizer ['mɔɪstʃəraɪzəʳ] *n* crème *f* hydratante, lait *m* hydratant.

molar ['məʊləʳ] *n* molaire *f*.

molasses [mə'læsɪz] *n* (*U*) mélasse *f*.

mold *etc Am* = **mould**.

Moldavia [mɒl'deɪvjə] *n* Moldavie *f*; **in ~** en Moldavie.

mole [məʊl] *n* **-1.** [animal, spy] taupe *f*. **-2.** [on skin] grain *m* de beauté.

molecular [mə'lekjʊləʳ] *adj* moléculaire.

molecule ['mɒlɪkjuːl] *n* molécule *f*.

molehill ['məʊlhɪl] *n* taupinière *f*.

molest [mə'lest] *vt* **-1.** [attack sexually] attenter à la pudeur de. **-2.** [attack] molester.

molester [mə'lestəʳ] *n*: **child ~** *personne qui est coupable d'attentat à la pudeur sur des enfants*.

mollify ['mɒlɪfaɪ] (*pt & pp* **-ied**) *vt* apaiser, calmer.

mollusc, mollusk *Am* ['mɒləsk] *n* mollusque *m*.

mollycoddle ['mɒlɪ,kɒdl] *vt inf* chouchouter.

Molotov cocktail ['mɒlətɒf-] *n* cocktail *m* Molotov.

molt *Am* = **moult**.

molten ['məʊltn] *adj* en fusion.

mom [mɒm] *n Am inf* maman *f*.

moment ['məʊmənt] *n* moment *m*, instant *m*; **to choose the right ~** choisir son moment; **~ of truth** minute *f* de vérité; **at any ~** d'un moment à l'autre; **at the ~** en ce moment; **at the last ~** au dernier moment; **for the ~** pour le moment; **for one ~** pendant un instant.

momentarily ['məʊməntərɪlɪ] *adv* **-1.** [for a short time] momentanément. **-2.** *Am* [soon] très bientôt.

momentary ['məʊməntrɪ] *adj* momentané(e), passager(ère).

momentous [mə'mentəs] *adj* capital(e), très important(e).

momentum [mə'mentəm] *n* (*U*) **-1.** PHYSICS moment *m*. **-2.** *fig* [speed, force] vitesse *f*; **to gather ~** prendre de la vitesse.

momma ['mɒmə], **mommy** ['mɒmɪ] *n Am* maman *f*.

Mon. (*abbr of* **Monday**) lun.

Monaco ['mɒnəkəʊ] *n* Monaco.

monarch ['mɒnək] *n* monarque *m*.

monarchist ['mɒnəkɪst] *n* monarchiste *mf*.

monarchy ['mɒnəkɪ] (*pl* **-ies**) *n* monarchie *f*.

monastery ['mɒnəstrɪ] (*pl* **-ies**) *n* monastère *m*.

monastic [mə'næstɪk] *adj* monastique.

Monday ['mʌndɪ] *n* lundi *m*; *see also* **Saturday**.

monetarism ['mʌnɪtərɪzm] *n* monétarisme *m*.

monetarist ['mʌnɪtərɪst] *n* monétariste *mf*.

monetary ['mʌnɪtrɪ] *adj* monétaire.

money ['mʌnɪ] *n* argent *m*; **to make ~** gagner de l'argent; **to get one's ~'s worth** en avoir pour son argent.

moneybox ['mʌnɪbɒks] *n* tirelire *f*.

moneyed ['mʌnɪd] *adj* riche, cossu(e).

moneylender ['mʌnɪ,lendəʳ] *n* prêteur *m*, -euse *f* sur gages.

moneymaker ['mʌnɪ,meɪkəʳ] *n* affaire *f* lucrative.

moneymaking ['mʌnɪ,meɪkɪŋ] *adj* lucratif(ive).

money market *n* marché *m* monétaire.

money order *n* mandat *m* postal.

money-spinner *n inf* mine *f* d'or.

money supply *n* masse *f* monétaire.

mongol ['mɒŋgəl] *dated & offensive* ◇ *adj* mongolien(ienne). ◇ *n* mongolien *m*, -ienne *f*.

◆ **Mongol** = **Mongolian**.

Mongolia [mɒŋ'gəʊlɪə] *n* Mongolie *f*; **in ~** en Mongolie.

Mongolian [mɒŋ'gəʊlɪən] ◇ *adj* mongol(e). ◇ *n* **-1.** [person] Mongol *m*, -e *f*. **-2.** [language] mongol *m*.

mongoose ['mɒŋguːs] (*pl* **-s**) *n* mangouste *f*.

mongrel ['mʌŋgrəl] *n* [dog] bâtard *m*.

monitor ['mɒnɪtəʳ] ◇ *n* COMPUT, MED & TV moniteur *m*. ◇ *vt* **-1.** [check] contrôler, suivre de près. **-2.** [broadcasts, messages] être à l'écoute de.

monk [mʌŋk] *n* moine *m*.

monkey ['mʌŋkɪ] (*pl* **monkeys**) *n* singe *m*.

monkey nut *n* cacahuète *f*.

monkey wrench *n* clef *f* à molette.

mono ['mɒnəʊ] ◇ *adj* mono (*inv*). ◇ *n* **-1.** [sound] monophonie *f*. **-2.** *Am inf* [glandular fever] mononucléose *f* (infectieuse).

monochrome ['mɒnəkrəʊm] *adj* monochrome.

monocle ['mɒnəkl] *n* monocle *m*.

monogamous [mɒ'nɒgəməs] *adj* monogame.

monogamy [mɒ'nɒgəmɪ] *n* monogamie *f*.

monogrammed ['mɒnəgræmd] *adj* marqué(é) d'un monogramme.

monolingual [,mɒnə'lɪŋgwəl] *adj* monolingue.

monolithic [,mɒnə'lɪθɪk] *adj* monolithique.

monologue, monolog *Am* ['mɒnəlɒg] *n* monologue *m*.

mononucleosis ['mɒnəʊ,njuːklɪ'əʊsɪs] *n Am* mononucléose *f* (infectieuse).

monoplane ['mɒnəpleɪn] *n* monoplan *m*.

monopolize, -ise [mə'nɒpəlaɪz] *vt* monopoliser.

monopoly [mə'nɒpəlɪ] (*pl* **-ies**) *n*: ~ **(on** OR **of)** monopole *m* (de); **the Monopolies and Mergers Commission** *Br* organisme chargé de contrôler le fusionnement des entreprises.

monorail ['mɒnəreɪl] *n* monorail *m*.

monosodium glutamate [,mɒnə'səʊdjəm-'gluːtəmeɪt] *n* glutamate *m* (de sodium).

monosyllabic ['mɒnəsɪ'læbɪk] *adj* monosyllabique.

monosyllable ['mɒnə,sɪləbl] *n* monosyllabe *m*.

monotone ['mɒnətəʊn] *n* ton *m* monocorde.

monotonous [mə'nɒtənəs] *adj* monotone.

monotonously [mə'nɒtənəslɪ] *adv* de façon monotone.

monotony [mə'nɒtənɪ] *n* monotonie *f*.

monoxide [mɒ'nɒksaɪd] *n* monoxyde *m*.

Monrovia [mən'rəʊvɪə] *n* Monrovia.

Monsignor [,mɒn'siːnjəʳ] *n* monsignor *m*.

monsoon [mɒn'suːn] *n* mousson *f*.

monster ['mɒnstəʳ] ◇ *n* **-1.** [creature, cruel person] monstre *m*. **-2.** [huge thing, person] colosse *m*. ◇ *adj* géant(e), monstre.

monstrosity [mɒn'strɒsətɪ] (*pl* **-ies**) *n* monstruosité *f*.

monstrous ['mɒnstrəs] *adj* monstrueux-(euse).

montage ['mɒntɑːʒ] *n* montage *m*.

Montana [mɒn'tænə] *n* Montana *m*; **in** ~ dans le Montana.

Mont Blanc [,mɔ̃'blɑ̃] *n* le mont Blanc.

Montenegro [,mɒntɪ'niːgrəʊ] *n* Monténégro *m*.

Montevideo [,mɒntɪvɪ'deɪəʊ] *n* Montevideo.

month [mʌnθ] *n* mois *m*.

monthly ['mʌnθlɪ] (*pl* **-ies**) ◇ *adj* mensuel(elle). ◇ *adv* mensuellement. ◇ *n* [publication] mensuel *m*.

Montreal [,mɒntrɪ'ɔːl] *n* Montréal.

monument ['mɒnjʊmənt] *n* monument *m*.

monumental [,mɒnjʊ'mentl] *adj* monumental(e).

moo [muː] (*pl* **-s**) ◇ *n* meuglement *m*, beuglement *m*. ◇ *vi* meugler, beugler.

mooch [muːtʃ]
◆ **mooch about, mooch around** *vi inf* traîner.

mood [muːd] *n* humeur *f*; **in a (bad)** ~ de mauvaise humeur; **in a good** ~ de bonne humeur.

moody ['muːdɪ] (*compar* **-ier**, *superl* **-iest**) *adj pej* **-1.** [changeable] lunatique. **-2.** [bad-tempered] de mauvaise humeur, mal luné(e).

moon [muːn] *n* lune *f*; **to be over the** ~ *inf* être aux anges.

moonbeam ['muːnbiːm] *n* rayon *m* de lune.

moonlight ['muːnlaɪt] (*pt* & *pp* **-ed**) ◇ *n* clair *m* de lune. ◇ *vi* travailler au noir.

moonlighting ['muːnlaɪtɪŋ] *n* (*U*) travail *m* (au) noir.

moonlit ['muːnlɪt] *adj* [countryside] éclairé(e) par la lune; [night] de lune.

moonscape ['muːnskeɪp] *n* paysage *m* lunaire.

moon shot *n* tir *m* lunaire.

moonstone ['muːnstəʊn] *n* pierre *f* de lune.

moonstruck ['muːnstrʌk] *adj inf* fêlé(e).

moony ['muːnɪ] (*compar* **-ier**, *superl* **-iest**) *adj Br inf* rêveur(euse).

moor [mɔːʳ] ◇ *n* lande *f*. ◇ *vt* amarrer. ◇ *vi* mouiller.

Moor [mɔːʳ] *n* Maure *m*, Mauresque *f*.

moorings ['mɔːrɪŋz] *npl* [ropes, chains] amarres *fpl*; [place] mouillage *m*.

Moorish ['mɔːrɪʃ] *adj* mauresque.

moorland ['mɔːlənd] *n* lande *f*.

moose [muːs] (*pl inv*) *n* [North American] orignal *m*.

moot [muːt] *vt* [question] soulever.

moot point *n* point *m* discutable.

mop [mɒp] (*pt* & *pp* **-ped**, *cont* **-ping**) ◇ *n* **-1.** [for cleaning] balai *m* à laver. **-2.** *inf* [hair] tignasse *f*. ◇ *vt* **-1.** [floor] laver. **-2.** [sweat] essuyer; **to** ~ **one's face** s'essuyer le visage.
◆ **mop up** *vt sep* [clean up] éponger.

mope [məʊp] *vi* broyer du noir.

◆ **mope about**, **mope around** *vi* traîner.

moped ['məʊped] *n* vélomoteur *m*.

moral ['mɒrəl] ◇ *adj* moral(e); ~ **support** soutien *m* moral. ◇ *n* [lesson] morale *f*.

◆ **morals** *npl* moralité *f*.

morale [mə'rɑːl] *n* (*U*) moral *m*.

moralistic [ˌmɒrə'lɪstɪk] *adj pej* moralisateur(trice).

morality [mə'rælətɪ] (*pl* **-ies**) *n* moralité *f*.

moralize, **-ise** ['mɒrəlaɪz] *vi pej*: **to ~ (about** OR **on)** moraliser (sur).

morally ['mɒrəlɪ] *adv* moralement.

Moral Majority *n* groupe de pression américain ultra-conservateur lié aux églises fondamentalistes.

morass [mə'ræs] *n fig* [of detail, paperwork] fatras *m*.

moratorium [ˌmɒrə'tɔːrɪəm] (*pl* **-ria** [-rɪə]) *n* moratoire *m*.

morbid ['mɔːbɪd] *adj* morbide.

more [mɔːʳ] ◇ *adv* **-1.** (with adjectives and adverbs) plus; ~ **important (than)** plus important (que); ~ **often/quickly (than)** plus souvent/rapidement (que). **-2.** [to a greater degree] plus, davantage; **she's ~ like a mother to me than a sister** elle est davantage une mère qu'une sœur pour moi; **we were ~ hurt than angry** nous étions plus offensés que fâchés, nous étions offensés plutôt que fâchés. **-3.** [another time]: **once/twice ~** une fois/deux fois de plus, encore une fois/deux fois.

◇ *adj* **-1.** [larger number, amount of] plus (de), davantage; **there are ~ trains in the morning** il y a plus de trains le matin; ~ **than 70 people died** plus de 70 personnes ont péri. **-2.** [an extra amount of] encore (de); **have some ~ tea** prends encore du thé; **I finished two ~ chapters today** j'ai fini deux autres OR encore deux chapitres aujourd'hui; **we need ~ money/time** il nous faut plus d'argent/de temps, il nous faut davantage d'argent/de temps.

◇ *pron* plus, davantage; ~ **than five** plus de cinq; **he's got ~ than I have** il en a plus que moi; **there's ~ if you want it** il y en a encore si vous en voulez; **there's no ~ (left)** il n'y en a plus, il n'en reste plus; **what ~ do you want?** qu'est-ce que tu veux de plus?; **(and) what's ~** de plus, qui plus est.

◆ **any more** *adv*: **not ... any ~ ne ... plus.**

◆ **more and more** ◇ *adv & pron* de plus en plus; ~ **and ~ depressed** de plus en plus déprimé. ◇ *adj* de plus en plus de;

there are ~ **and ~ cars on the roads** il y a de plus en plus de voitures sur les routes.

◆ **more or less** *adv* **-1.** [almost] plus ou moins. **-2.** [approximately] environ, à peu près.

moreover [mɔː'rəʊvəʳ] *adv* de plus.

morgue [mɔːg] *n* morgue *f*.

MORI ['mɒrɪ] (*abbr of* **Market & Opinion Research Institute**) *n* institut de sondage.

moribund ['mɒrɪbʌnd] *adj* moribond(e).

Mormon ['mɔːmən] *n* mormon *m*, -e *f*.

morning ['mɔːnɪŋ] *n* matin *m*; [duration] matinée *f*; **I work in the ~** je travaille le matin; **I'll do it tomorrow ~** OR **in the ~** je le ferai demain.

◆ **mornings** *adv Am* le matin.

morning-after pill *n* pilule *f* du lendemain.

morning dress *n* habit *m*, frac *m*.

morning sickness *n* (*U*) nausées *fpl* (matinales).

Moroccan [mə'rɒkən] ◇ *adj* marocain(e). ◇ *n* Marocain *m*, -e *f*.

Morocco [mə'rɒkəʊ] *n* Maroc *m*; **in ~** au Maroc.

moron ['mɔːrɒn] *n inf* idiot *m*, -e *f*, crétin *m*, -e *f*.

moronic [mə'rɒnɪk] *adj* idiot(e), crétin(e).

morose [mə'rəʊs] *adj* morose.

morphine ['mɔːfiːn] *n* morphine *f*.

morris dancing ['mɒrɪs-] *n* (*U*) danse folklorique anglaise.

Morse (code) [mɔːs-] *n* morse *m*.

morsel ['mɔːsl] *n* bout *m*, morceau *m*.

mortal ['mɔːtl] ◇ *adj* mortel(elle). ◇ *n* mortel *m*, -elle *f*.

mortality [mɔː'tælətɪ] *n* mortalité *f*.

mortality rate *n* taux *m* de mortalité.

mortally ['mɔːtəlɪ] *adv* mortellement.

mortar ['mɔːtəʳ] *n* mortier *m*.

mortarboard ['mɔːtəbɔːd] *n* mortier *m* (chapeau).

mortgage ['mɔːgɪdʒ] ◇ *n* emprunt-logement *m*. ◇ *vt* hypothéquer.

mortgagee [ˌmɔːgɪ'dʒiː] *n* créancier *m*, -ière *f* hypothécaire.

mortgagor [ˌmɔːgɪ'dʒɔːʳ] *n* débiteur *m*, -trice *f* hypothécaire.

mortician [mɔː'tɪʃn] *n Am* entrepreneur *m* de pompes funèbres.

mortified ['mɔːtɪfaɪd] *adj* mortifié(e).

mortise lock ['mɔːtɪs-] *n* serrure *f* encastrée.

mortuary ['mɔːtʃʊərɪ] (*pl* **-ies**) *n* morgue *f*.

mosaic [mə'zeɪɪk] *n* mosaïque *f*.

Moscow ['mɒskəʊ] *n* Moscou.

Moslem ['mɒzləm] = **Muslim**.

mosque [mɒsk] *n* mosquée *f*.

mosquito [məs'ki:təʊ] (*pl* **-es** OR **-s**) *n* moustique *m*.

mosquito net *n* moustiquaire *f*.

moss [mɒs] *n* mousse *f*.

mossy ['mɒsɪ] (*compar* **-ier**, *superl* **-iest**) *adj* moussu(e), couvert(e) de mousse.

most [məʊst] (*superl of* **many**) ◇ *adj* **-1.** [the majority of] la plupart de; ~ **tourists here are German** la plupart des touristes ici sont allemands. **-2.** [largest amount of]: **(the)** ~ le plus de; **she's got (the)** ~ **money/sweets** c'est elle qui a le plus d'argent/de bonbons.
◇ *pron* **-1.** [the majority] la plupart; ~ **of the tourists here are German** la plupart des touristes ici sont allemands; ~ **of them** la plupart d'entre eux. **-2.** [largest amount]: **(the)** ~ le plus; **at** ~ au maximum, tout au plus. **-3.** *phr*: **to make the** ~ **of sthg** profiter de qqch au maximum.
◇ *adv* **-1.** [to greatest extent]: **(the)** ~ le plus. **-2.** *fml* [very] très, fort. **-3.** *Am* [almost] presque.

mostly ['məʊstlɪ] *adv* principalement, surtout.

MOT ◇ *n* (*abbr of* **Ministry of Transport (test)**) *contrôle technique annuel obligatoire pour les véhicules de plus de trois ans.* ◇ *vt*: **to have one's car** ~**'d** soumettre sa voiture au contrôle technique.

motel [məʊ'tel] *n* motel *m*.

moth [mɒθ] *n* papillon *m* de nuit; [in clothes] mite *f*.

mothball ['mɒθbɔ:l] *n* boule *f* de naphtaline.

moth-eaten *adj* mité(e).

mother ['mʌðər] ◇ *n* mère *f*. ◇ *vt* [child] materner, dorloter.

motherboard ['mʌðəbɔ:d] *n* COMPUT carte *f* mère.

motherhood ['mʌðəhʊd] *n* maternité *f*.

Mothering Sunday ['mʌðərɪŋ-] *n* fête *f* des Mères.

mother-in-law (*pl* **mothers-in-law** OR **mother-in-laws**) *n* belle-mère *f*.

motherland ['mʌðəlænd] *n* mère patrie *f*.

motherless ['mʌðəlɪs] *adj* orphelin(e) de mère.

motherly ['mʌðəlɪ] *adj* maternel(elle).

Mother Nature *n* la nature.

mother-of-pearl ◇ *n* nacre *f*. ◇ *comp* de nacre.

Mother's day *n* fête *f* des Mères.

mother ship *n* ravitailleur *m*.

mother superior *n* mère *f* supérieure.

mother-to-be (*pl* **mothers-to-be**) *n* future maman *f*.

mother tongue *n* langue *f* maternelle.

motif [məʊ'ti:f] *n* motif *m*.

motion ['məʊʃn] ◇ *n* **-1.** [gen] mouvement *m*; **to set sthg in** ~ mettre qqch en branle; **to go through the** ~**s** [act insincerely] faire semblant de faire quelque chose. **-2.** [in debate] motion *f*. ◇ *vt*: **to** ~ **sb to do sthg** faire signe à qqn de faire qqch. ◇ *vi*: **to** ~ **to sb** faire signe à qqn.

motionless ['məʊʃənlɪs] *adj* immobile.

motion picture *n Am* film *m*.

motivate ['məʊtɪveɪt] *vt* **-1.** [act, decision] motiver. **-2.** [student, workforce]: **to** ~ **sb (to do sthg)** pousser qqn (à faire qqch).

motivated ['məʊtɪveɪtɪd] *adj* motivé(e).

motivation [,məʊtɪ'veɪʃn] *n* motivation *f*.

motive ['məʊtɪv] *n* motif *m*.

motley ['mɒtlɪ] *adj pej* hétéroclite.

motocross ['məʊtəkrɒs] *n* motocross *m*.

motor ['məʊtər] ◇ *adj Br* automobile. ◇ *n* [engine] moteur *m*. ◇ *vi dated* aller en automobile.

Motorail® ['məʊtəreɪl] *n Br* train *m* autocouchette OR autos-couchettes.

motorbike ['məʊtəbaɪk] *n inf* moto *f*.

motorboat ['məʊtəbəʊt] *n* canot *m* automobile.

motorcade ['məʊtəkeɪd] *n* cortège *m* de voitures.

motorcar ['məʊtəkɑ:r] *n Br* automobile *f*, voiture *f*.

motorcycle ['məʊtə,saɪkl] *n* moto *f*.

motorcyclist ['məʊtə,saɪklɪst] *n* motocycliste *mf*.

motoring ['məʊtərɪŋ] ◇ *adj Br* [magazine, correspondent] automobile; **a** ~ **offence** une infraction au code de la route. ◇ *n* tourisme *m* automobile.

motorist ['məʊtərɪst] *n* automobiliste *mf*.

motorize, -ise ['məʊtəraɪz] *vt* motoriser.

motor lodge *n Am* motel *m*.

motor racing *n* (U) course *f* automobile.

motor scooter *n* scooter *m*.

motor vehicle *n* véhicule *m* automobile.

motorway ['məʊtəweɪ] *Br* ◇ *n* autoroute *f*. ◇ *comp* d'autoroute.

mottled ['mɒtld] *adj* [leaf] tacheté(e); [skin] marbré(e).

motto ['mɒtəʊ] (*pl* **-s** OR **-es**) *n* devise *f*.

mould, mold *Am* [məʊld] ◇ *n* **-1.** [growth] moisissure *f*. **-2.** [shape] moule *m*. ◇ *vt* **-1.**

[shape] mouler, modeler. **-2.** *fig* [influence] former, façonner.

moulding, molding *Am* ['məʊldɪŋ] *n* **-1.** [decoration] moulure *f.* **-2.** [moulded object] moulage *m.*

mouldy, moldy *Am* ['məʊldɪ] (*compar* **-ier,** *superl* **-iest**) *adj* moisi(e).

moult, molt *Am* [məʊlt] ◇ *vt* perdre. ◇ *vi* muer.

mound [maʊnd] *n* **-1.** [small hill] tertre *m*, butte *f.* **-2.** [pile] tas *m*, monceau *m.*

mount [maʊnt] ◇ *n* **-1.** [support - for jewel] monture *f*; [- for photograph] carton *m* de montage; [- for machine] support *m.* **-2.** [horse] monture *f.* **-3.** [mountain] mont *m.* ◇ *vt* monter; **to ~ a horse** monter (sur) un cheval; **to ~ a bike** monter sur OR enfourcher un vélo; **to ~ guard over** monter la garde auprès de. ◇ *vi* **-1.** [increase] monter, augmenter. **-2.** [climb on horse] se mettre en selle.

mountain ['maʊntɪn] *n lit* & *fig* montagne *f*; **don't make a ~ out of a molehill** n'en fais pas une montagne.

mountain bike *n* V.T.T. *m.*

mountaineer [,maʊntɪ'nɪə] *n* alpiniste *mf.*

mountaineering [,maʊntɪ'nɪərɪŋ] *n* alpinisme *m.*

mountainous ['maʊntɪnəs] *adj* [region] montagneux(euse).

mountain range *n* chaîne *f* de montagnes.

mountain rescue *n* secours *m* en montagne.

mounted ['maʊntɪd] *adj* monté(e), à cheval.

Mountie ['maʊntɪ] *n inf membre de la police montée canadienne.*

mourn [mɔːn] ◇ *vt* pleurer. ◇ *vi*: **to ~ (for sb)** pleurer (qqn).

mourner ['mɔːnə] *n* [related] parent *m* du défunt; [unrelated] ami *m*, -e *f* du défunt.

mournful ['mɔːnfʊl] *adj* [face] triste; [sound] lugubre.

mourning ['mɔːnɪŋ] *n* deuil *m*; **in ~** en deuil.

mouse [maʊs] (*pl* **mice**) *n* COMPUT & ZOOL souris *f.*

mousetrap ['maʊstræp] *n* souricière *f.*

moussaka [muː'sɑːkə] *n* moussaka *f.*

mousse [muːs] *n* mousse *f.*

moustache *Br* [məs'tɑːʃ], **mustache** *Am* ['mʌstæʃ] *n* moustache *f.*

mouth [*n* maʊθ, *vt* maʊð] ◇ *n* **-1.** [of person, animal] bouche *f*; [of dog, cat, lion] gueule *f*; **to keep one's ~ shut** *inf* se taire. **-2.** [of cave] entrée *f*; [of river] embouchure *f.* ◇ *vt*

[words] former silencieusement (avec la bouche).

mouthful ['maʊθfʊl] *n* **-1.** [of food] bouchée *f*; [of drink] gorgée *f.* **-2.** *inf* [difficult name] nom *m* à coucher dehors.

mouthorgan ['maʊθ,ɔːgən] *n* harmonica *m.*

mouthpiece ['maʊθpiːs] *n* **-1.** [of telephone] microphone *m*; [of musical instrument] bec *m.* **-2.** [spokesperson] porte-parole *m inv.*

mouth-to-mouth *adj*: **~ resuscitation** bouche-à-bouche *m inv.*

mouthwash ['maʊθwɒʃ] *n* eau *f* dentifrice.

mouth-watering [-,wɔːtərɪŋ] *adj* alléchant(e).

movable ['muːvəbl] *adj* mobile.

move [muːv] ◇ *n* **-1.** [movement] mouvement *m*; **to be on the ~** [person] être en déplacement; [troops] être en marche; **to get a ~ on** *inf* se remuer, se grouiller. **-2.** [change - of house] déménagement *m*; [- of job] changement *m* d'emploi. **-3.** [in game - action] coup *m*; [- turn to play] tour *m*; *fig* démarche *f.* ◇ *vt* **-1.** [shift] déplacer, bouger. **-2.** [change - job, office] changer de; **to ~ house** déménager. **-3.** [cause]: **to ~ sb to do sthg** inciter qqn à faire qqch. **-4.** [emotionally] émouvoir. **-5.** [propose]: **to ~ sthg/that ...** proposer qqch/que .... ◇ *vi* **-1.** [shift] bouger. **-2.** [act] agir. **-3.** [to new house] déménager; [to new job] changer d'emploi.

◆ **move about** *vi* **-1.** [fidget] remuer. **-2.** [travel] voyager.

◆ **move along** ◇ *vt sep* faire avancer. ◇ *vi* se déplacer; **the police asked him to ~ along** la police lui a demandé de circuler.

◆ **move around** = **move about**.

◆ **move away** *vi* [leave] partir.

◆ **move in** ◇ *vt sep* [troops] faire intervenir. ◇ *vi* [to house] emménager.

◆ **move off** *vi* [train, car] partir, s'ébranler.

◆ **move on** ◇ *vt sep* faire circuler. ◇ *vi* **-1.** [after stopping] se remettre en route. **-2.** [in discussion] changer de sujet.

◆ **move out** ◇ *vt sep* [troops] retirer. ◇ *vi* [from house] déménager.

◆ **move over** *vi* s'écarter, se pousser.

◆ **move up** *vi* [on bench etc] se déplacer.

moveable ['muːvəbl] = **movable**.

movement ['muːvmənt] *n* mouvement *m.*

movie ['muːvɪ] *n* film *m.*

movie camera *n* caméra *f.*

moviegoer ['muːvɪ,gəʊə] *n Am* cinéphile *mf.*

movie star *n Am* star *f*, vedette *f* de cinéma.

movie theater n Am cinéma m.

moving ['muːvɪŋ] adj **-1.** [emotionally] émouvant(e), touchant(e). **-2.** [not fixed] mobile.

moving staircase n escalier m roulant.

mow [məʊ] (pt **-ed**, pp **-ed** OR **mown**) vt faucher; [lawn] tondre.

◆ **mow down** vt sep faucher.

mower ['məʊə'] n tondeuse f à gazon.

mown [məʊn] pp → **mow**.

Mozambican [,məʊzæm'biːkn] ◇ adj mozambicain(e). ◇ n Mozambicain m, -e f.

Mozambique [,məʊzæm'biːk] n Mozambique m; **in** ~ au Mozambique.

MP n **-1.** (abbr of **Military Police**) PM. **-2.** Br (abbr of **Member of Parliament**) ≃ député m. **-3.** Can abbr of **Mounted Police**.

mpg (abbr of **miles per gallon**) n miles au gallon.

mph (abbr of **miles per hour**) n miles à l'heure.

MPhil [,em'fɪl] (abbr of **Master of Philosophy**) n (titulaire d'une) maîtrise de lettres.

MPS (abbr of **Member of the Pharmaceutical Society**) n membre de l'Académie de pharmacie britannique.

Mr ['mɪstə'] n Monsieur m; [on letter] M.

MRC (abbr of **Medical Research Council**) n conseil de la recherche médicale en Grande-Bretagne.

MRCP (abbr of **Member of the Royal College of Physicians**) n membre de l'Académie de médecine britannique.

MRCS (abbr of **Member of the Royal College of Surgeons**) n membre de l'Académie de chirurgie britannique.

MRCVS (abbr of **Member of the Royal College of Veterinary Surgeons**) n membre de l'Académie de chirurgie vétérinaire britannique.

Mrs ['mɪsɪz] n Madame f; [on letter] Mme.

ms. (abbr of **manuscript**) n ms.

Ms [mɪz] n titre que les femmes peuvent utiliser au lieu de madame ou mademoiselle pour éviter la distinction entre les femmes mariées et les célibataires.

MS ◇ n **-1.** (abbr of **manuscript**) ms. **-2.** (abbr of **Master of Science**) (titulaire d'une) maîtrise de sciences américaine. **-3.** (abbr of **multiple sclerosis**) SEP f. ◇ abbr of **Mississippi**.

MSA (abbr of **Master of Science in Agriculture**) n (titulaire d'une) maîtrise en sciences agricoles.

MSB (abbr of **most significant bit/byte**) n bit/octet de poids fort.

MSc (abbr of **Master of Science**) n (titulaire d'une) maîtrise de sciences.

MSC (abbr of **Manpower Services Commission**) n agence nationale britannique pour l'emploi.

MSF (abbr of **Manufacturing Science and Finance**) n confédération syndicale britannique.

MSG abbr of **monosodium glutamate**.

Msgr (abbr of **Monsignor**) Mgr.

MSt (abbr of **Mountain Standard Time**) n heure d'hiver des montagnes Rocheuses.

MSW (abbr of **Master of Social Work**) n (titulaire d'une) maîtrise en travail social.

Mt (abbr of **mount**) Mt.

MT ◇ n (abbr of **machine translation**) TA f. ◇ abbr of **Montana**.

much [mʌtʃ] (compar **more**, superl **most**) ◇ adj beaucoup de; **there isn't ~ rice left** il ne reste pas beaucoup de riz; **as ~ money as ...** autant d'argent que ...; **too ~** trop de; **how ~ ...?** combien de ...?; **how ~ money do you earn?** tu gagnes combien?

◇ pron beaucoup; **I don't think ~ of his new house** sa nouvelle maison ne me plaît pas trop; **as ~ as** autant que; **too ~** trop; **how ~?** combien?; **I'm not ~ of a cook** je suis un piètre cuisinier; **so ~ for all my hard work** tout ce travail pour rien; **I thought as ~** c'est bien ce que je pensais; **it's not up to ~** inf ça ne vaut pas grand-chose.

◇ adv beaucoup; **I don't go out ~** je ne sors pas beaucoup OR souvent; **as ~ as** autant que; **thank you very ~** merci beaucoup; **without so ~ as ...** sans même ....

◆ **much as** conj bien que (+ subjunctive).

muchness ['mʌtʃnɪs] n: **to be much of a ~** être blanc bonnet et bonnet blanc.

muck [mʌk] n (U) inf **-1.** [dirt] saletés fpl. **-2.** [manure] fumier m.

◆ **muck about**, **muck around** Br inf ◇ vt sep: **to ~ sb about** traiter qqn par-dessus OR par-dessous la jambe. ◇ vi traîner.

◆ **muck in** vi Br inf donner un coup de main.

◆ **muck out** vt sep nettoyer.

◆ **muck up** vt sep Br inf gâcher.

muckraking ['mʌkreɪkɪŋ] n fig mise f au jour de scandales.

mucky ['mʌkɪ] (compar **-ier**, superl **-iest**) adj sale.

mucus ['mjuːkəs] n mucus m.

mud [mʌd] n boue f.

muddle ['mʌdl] ◇ n désordre m, fouillis m; **to be in a ~** [room, finances] être en désordre; [person] ne plus s'y retrouver. ◇ vt **-1.** [papers] mélanger. **-2.** [person] embrouiller.

◆ **muddle along** vi se débrouiller tant bien que mal.

◆ **muddle through** vi se tirer d'affaire, s'en sortir tant bien que mal.

◆ **muddle up** vt sep mélanger.

muddle-headed [-,hedɪd] adj [thinking] confus(e); [person] brouillon(onne).

muddy ['mʌdɪ] (compar **-ier**, superl **-iest**, pt & pp **-ied**) ⬦ adj boueux(euse). ⬦ vt fig embrouiller.

mudflap ['mʌdflæp] n pare-boue m inv.

mudflat ['mʌdflæt] n laisse f.

mudguard ['mʌdgɑːd] n garde-boue m inv.

mudpack ['mʌdpæk] n masque m de beauté.

mudslinging ['mʌd,slɪŋɪŋ] n (U) fig attaques fpl.

muesli ['mjuːzlɪ] n Br muesli m.

muff [mʌf] ⬦ n manchon m. ⬦ vt inf louper.

muffin ['mʌfɪn] n muffin m.

muffle ['mʌfl] vt étouffer.

muffled ['mʌfld] adj **-1.** [sound] sourd(e), étouffé(e). **-2.** [person]: ~ **(up)** emmitouflé(e).

muffler ['mʌflə'] n Am [for car] silencieux m.

mug [mʌg] (pt & pp **-ged**, cont **-ging**) ⬦ n **-1.** [cup] (grande) tasse f. **-2.** inf [fool] andouille f. ⬦ vt [attack] agresser.

mugger ['mʌgə'] n agresseur m.

mugging ['mʌgɪŋ] n agression f.

muggy ['mʌgɪ] (compar **-ier**, superl **-iest**) adj lourd(e), moite.

mugshot ['mʌgʃɒt] n inf photo f (de criminel).

mujaheddin [,muːdʒəheˈdiːn] npl moudjahiddin mpl.

mulatto [mjuːˈlætəʊ] (pl **-s** OR **-es**) n mûlatre m, mûlatresse f.

mulberry ['mʌlbərɪ] (pl **-ies**) n **-1.** [tree] mûrier m. **-2.** [fruit] mûre f.

mule [mjuːl] n mule f.

mull [mʌl].

◆ **mull over** vt sep ruminer, réfléchir à.

mullah ['mʌlə] n mollah m.

mulled [mʌld] adj: ~ **wine** vin m chaud.

mullet ['mʌlɪt] (pl inv OR **-s**) n mulet m.

mulligatawny [,mʌlɪgəˈtɔːnɪ] n soupe indienne au curry.

mullioned ['mʌlɪənd] adj [window] à meneaux.

multi- ['mʌltɪ] prefix multi-.

multicoloured Br, **multicolored** Am [,mʌltɪˈkʌləd] adj multicolore.

multicultural [,mʌltɪˈkʌltʃərəl] adj multiculturel(elle).

multifarious [,mʌltɪˈfeərɪəs] adj divers, très varié(e).

multilateral [,mʌltɪˈlætərəl] adj multilatéral(e).

multimedia [,mʌltɪˈmiːdjə] adj multimédia (inv).

multimillionaire ['mʌltɪ,mɪljəˈneə'] n multimillionnaire mf.

multinational [,mʌltɪˈnæʃənl] ⬦ adj multinational(e). ⬦ n multinationale f.

multiple ['mʌltɪpl] ⬦ adj multiple. ⬦ n multiple m.

multiple-choice adj à choix multiple.

multiple crash n carambolage m.

multiple injuries npl lésions fpl multiples.

multiple sclerosis [-sklɪˈrəʊsɪs] n sclérose f en plaques.

multiplex cinema ['mʌltɪpleks-] n grand cinéma m à plusieurs salles.

multiplication [,mʌltɪplɪˈkeɪʃn] n multiplication f.

multiplication sign n signe m de multiplication.

multiplication table n table f de multiplication.

multiplicity [,mʌltɪˈplɪsətɪ] n multiplicité f.

multiply ['mʌltɪplaɪ] (pt & pp **-ied**) ⬦ vt multiplier. ⬦ vi se multiplier.

multipurpose [,mʌltɪˈpɜːpəs] adj polyvalent(e), à usages multiples.

multiracial [,mʌltɪˈreɪʃl] adj multiracial(e).

multistorey Br, **multistory** Am [,mʌltɪˈstɔːrɪ] ⬦ adj à étages. ⬦ n [car park] parking m à étages.

multitude ['mʌltɪtjuːd] n multitude f.

mum [mʌm] Br inf ⬦ n maman f. ⬦ adj: **to keep** ~ ne pas piper mot.

mumble ['mʌmbl] vt & vi marmotter.

mumbo jumbo ['mʌmbəʊˈdʒʌmbəʊ] n charabia m.

mummify ['mʌmɪfaɪ] (pt & pp **-ied**) vt momifier.

mummy ['mʌmɪ] (pl **-ies**) n **-1.** Br inf [mother] mamam f. **-2.** [preserved body] momie f.

mumps [mʌmps] n (U) oreillons mpl.

munch [mʌntʃ] vt & vi croquer.

mundane [mʌnˈdeɪn] adj banal(e), ordinaire.

mung bean [mʌŋ-] n mungo m.

municipal [mjuːˈnɪsɪpl] adj municipal(e).

municipality [mjuː,nɪsɪˈpælətɪ] (pl **-ies**) n municipalité f.

munificent [mjuː'nɪfɪsənt] *adj* munificent(e).

munitions [mjuː'nɪʃnz] *npl* munitions *fpl*.

mural ['mjuːərəl] *n* peinture *f* murale.

murder ['mɜːdər] ◇ *n* meurtre *m*; **to get away with** ~ *fig* pouvoir faire n'importe quoi impunément. ◇ *vt* assassiner.

murderer ['mɜːdərər] *n* meurtrier *m*, assassin *m*.

murderess ['mɜːdərɪs] *n* meurtrière *f*.

murderous ['mɜːdərəs] *adj* meurtrier(ière).

murky ['mɜːkɪ] *(compar* -ier, *superl* -iest) *adj* -1. [place] sombre. -2. [water, past] trouble.

murmur ['mɜːmər] ◇ *n* murmure *m*; MED souffle *m* au cœur. ◇ *vt & vi* murmurer.

MusB [mjuːz'biː], **MusBac** [mjuːz'bæk] *(abbr of* **Bachelor of Music**) *n* (titulaire d'un) diplôme d'études musicales.

muscle ['mʌsl] *n* muscle *m*; *fig* [power] poids *m*, impact *m*.
◆ **muscle in** *vi* intervenir, s'immiscer.

muscleman ['mʌslmən] *(pl* -men [-men]) *n* hercule *m*.

Muscovite ['mʌskəvaɪt] ◇ *adj* moscovite. ◇ *n* Moscovite *mf*.

muscular ['mʌskjʊlər] *adj* -1. [spasm, pain] musculaire. -2. [person] musclé(e).

muscular dystrophy [-'dɪstrəfɪ] *n* myopathie *f* primitive progressive, dystrophie *f* musculaire.

MusD [mjuːz'diː], **MusDoc** [mjuːz'dɒk] *(abbr of* **Doctor of Music**) *n* (titulaire d'un) doctorat d'études musicales.

muse [mjuːz] ◇ *n* muse *f*. ◇ *vi* méditer, réfléchir.

museum [mjuː'ziːəm] *n* musée *m*.

mush [mʌʃ] *n* -1. [gunge] bouillie *f*. -2. *inf* [sentimentality] sentimentalité *f*.

mushroom ['mʌʃrʊm] ◇ *n* champignon *m*. ◇ *vi* [organization, party] se développer, grandir; [houses] proliférer.

mushroom cloud *n* champignon *m* atomique.

mushy ['mʌʃɪ] *(compar* -ier, *superl* -iest) *adj* -1. [food] en bouillie. -2. *inf* [oversentimental] à l'eau de rose, à la guimauve.

music ['mjuːzɪk] *n* musique *f*.

musical ['mjuːzɪkl] ◇ *adj* -1. [event, voice] musical(e). -2. [child] doué(e) pour la musique, musicien(ienne). ◇ *n* comédie *f* musicale.

musical box *Br*, **music box** *Am n* boîte *f* à musique.

musical chairs *n (U)* chaises *fpl* musicales.

musical instrument *n* instrument *m* de musique.

music box *Am* = **musical box**.

music centre *n* chaîne *f* compacte.

music hall *n Br* music-hall *m*.

musician [mjuː'zɪʃn] *n* musicien *m*, -ienne *f*.

music stand *n* pupitre *m* à musique.

musk [mʌsk] *n* musc *m*.

musket ['mʌskɪt] *n* mousquet *m*.

muskrat ['mʌskræt] *n* rat *m* musqué, ondatra *m*.

Muslim ['mʊzlɪm] ◇ *adj* musulman(e). ◇ *n* Musulman *m*, -e *f*.

muslin ['mʌzlɪn] *n* mousseline *f*.

musquash ['mʌskwɒʃ] *n* rat *m* musqué, ondatra *m*.

muss [mʌs] *vt Am*: **to** ~ **(up)** [clothes] chiffonner, froisser; [hair] déranger.

mussel ['mʌsl] *n* moule *f*.

must [mʌst] ◇ *modal vb* -1. [expressing obligation] devoir; **I** ~ **go** il faut que je m'en aille, je dois partir; **you** ~ **come and visit** il faut absolument que tu viennes nous voir. -2. [expressing likelihood]: **they** ~ **have known** ils devaient le savoir. ◇ *n inf*: **a** ~ un must, un impératif; **the film is a** ~ c'est un film à voir absolument.

mustache *Am* = **moustache**.

mustard ['mʌstəd] *n* moutarde *f*; ~ **and cress** *Br* moutarde blanche et cresson alénois.

mustard gas *n* gaz *m* moutarde.

muster ['mʌstər] ◇ *vt* rassembler. ◇ *vi* se réunir, se rassembler.
◆ **muster up** *vt fus* rassembler.

mustn't [mʌsnt] = **must not**.

must've ['mʌstəv] = **must have**.

musty ['mʌstɪ] *(compar* -ier, *superl* -iest) *adj* [smell] de moisi; [room] qui sent le renfermé OR le moisi.

mutant ['mjuːtənt] ◇ *adj* mutant(e). ◇ *n* mutant *m*.

mutate [mjuː'teɪt] *vi* subir une mutation, muter; **to** ~ **into sthg** se changer en qqch, se transformer en qqch.

mutation [mjuː'teɪʃn] *n* mutation *f*.

mute [mjuːt] ◇ *adj* muet(ette). ◇ *n* muet *m*, -ette *f*. ◇ *vt* étouffer, assourdir.

muted ['mjuːtɪd] *adj* -1. [colour] sourd(e). -2. [reaction] peu marqué(e); [protest] voilé(e).

mutilate ['mjuːtɪleɪt] *vt* mutiler.

mutilation [ˌmjuːtɪ'leɪʃn] *n* mutilation *f*.

mutineer [ˌmjuːtɪˈnɪəʳ] *n* mutiné *m*, mutin *m*.

mutinous [ˈmjuːtɪnəs] *adj* [crew, soldiers] mutiné(e); [person, attitude] rebelle.

mutiny [ˈmjuːtɪnɪ] (*pl* **-ies**, *pt* & *pp* **-ied**) ◇ *n* mutinerie *f*. ◇ *vi* se mutiner.

mutt [mʌt] *n inf* **-1.** [fool] andouille *f*, crétin *m*, -e *f*. **-2.** [dog] clébard *m*.

mutter [ˈmʌtəʳ] ◇ *vt* [threat, curse] marmonner. ◇ *vi* marmotter, marmonner; **to ~ to o.s.** marmotter, parler dans sa barbe.

muttering [ˈmʌtərɪŋ] *n* **-1.** [remark] marmonnement *m*, marmottement *m*. **-2.** [sound] murmure *m*.

mutton [ˈmʌtn] *n* mouton *m*; **she's ~ dressed as lamb** *Br* c'est une vieille coquette.

mutual [ˈmjuːtʊəl] *adj* **-1.** [feeling, help] réciproque, mutuel(elle). **-2.** [friend, interest] commun(e).

mutual fund *n Am* fonds *m* commun de placement.

mutually [ˈmjuːtjʊəlɪ] *adv* mutuellement, réciproquement; **~ exclusive** qui s'excluent l'un l'autre.

Muzak® [ˈmjuːzæk] *n* musique *f* d'ambiance.

muzzle [ˈmʌzl] ◇ *n* **-1.** [of dog - mouth] museau *m*; [- guard] muselière *f*. **-2.** [of gun] gueule *f*. ◇ *vt lit* & *fig* museler.

muzzy [ˈmʌzɪ] (*compar* **-ier**, *superl* **-iest**) *adj* embrouillé(e), confus(e).

MVP (*abbr of* **most valuable player**) *n Am* titre de meilleur joueur décérné dans une équipe à celui qui a réalisé la meilleure performance lors d'un match, d'une saison etc.

MW (*abbr of* **medium wave**) PO.

my [maɪ] *poss adj* **-1.** [referring to oneself] mon (ma), mes (*pl*); **~ dog** mon chien; **~ house** ma maison; **~ children** mes enfants; **~ name is Joe/Sarah** je m'appelle Joe/Sarah; **it wasn't MY fault** ce n'était pas de ma faute à moi. **-2.** [in titles]: **yes, ~ Lord** oui, monsieur le comte/duc *etc*.

mynah (bird) [ˈmaɪnə-] *n* mainate *m*.

myopic [maɪˈɒpɪk] *adj* myope.

myriad [ˈmɪrɪəd] *literary* ◇ *adj* innombrable. ◇ *n* myriade *f*.

myrrh [mɜːʳ] *n* myrrhe *f*.

myrtle [ˈmɜːtl] *n* myrte *m*.

myself [maɪˈself] *pron* **-1.** (*reflexive*) me; (*after prep*) moi. **-2.** (*for emphasis*) moi-même; **I did it ~** je l'ai fait tout seul.

mysterious [mɪˈstɪərɪəs] *adj* mystérieux(ieuse); **to be ~ about sthg** faire (un) mystère de qqch.

mysteriously [mɪˈstɪərɪəslɪ] *adv* mystérieusement.

mystery [ˈmɪstərɪ] (*pl* **-ies**) ◇ *n* mystère *m*. ◇ *comp* mystérieux(ieuse).

mystery story *n* histoire *f* à suspense.

mystery tour *n* voyage *m* surprise (*dont la destination est inconnue*).

mystic [ˈmɪstɪk] ◇ *adj* [power] occulte; [rite] mystique, ésotérique. ◇ *n* mystique *mf*.

mystical [ˈmɪstɪkl] *adj* mystique.

mysticism [ˈmɪstɪsɪzm] *n* mysticisme *m*.

mystified [ˈmɪstɪfaɪd] *adj* perplexe.

mystifying [ˈmɪstɪfaɪɪŋ] *adj* inexplicable, déconcertant(e).

mystique [mɪˈstiːk] *n* mystique *f*.

myth [mɪθ] *n* mythe *m*.

mythic [ˈmɪθɪk] *adj* légendaire.

mythical [ˈmɪθɪkl] *adj* mythique.

mythological [ˌmɪθəˈlɒdʒɪkl] *adj* mythologique.

mythology [mɪˈθɒlədʒɪ] (*pl* **-ies**) *n* mythologie *f*.

myxomatosis [ˌmɪksəməˈtəʊsɪs] *n* myxomatose *f*.

n (*pl* **n's** OR **ns**), **N** (*pl* **N's** OR **Ns**) [en] *n* [letter] n *m inv*, N *m inv*.
◆ **N** (*abbr of* **north**) N.

n/a, N/A (*abbr of* **not applicable**) s.o.

NA (*abbr of* **Narcotics Anonymous**) *n* association américaine d'aide aux toxicomanes.

NAACP (*abbr of* **National Association for the Advancement of Colored People**) *n* association nationale américaine pour la promotion de gens de couleur.

NAAFI [ˈnæfɪ] (*abbr of* **Navy, Army & Air Force Institute**) *n* organisme approvisionnant les forces armées britanniques en biens de consommation.

nab [næb] (*pt* & *pp* **-bed**, *cont* **-bing**) *vt inf* **-1.** [arrest] pincer. **-2.** [get quickly] attraper, accaparer.

NACU (*abbr of* **National Association of Colleges and Universities**) *n* association des *établissements d'enseignement supérieur américains.*

nadir ['neɪ,dɪəʳ] *n* ASTRON nadir *m*; **to be at/ reach a ~** *fig* être/tomber au plus bas.

naff [næf] *adj Br inf* nul (nulle).

nag [næg] (*pt* & *pp* **-ged**, *cont* **-ging**) ◇ *vt* harceler. ◇ *vi*: **to ~ at sb** harceler qqn; **stop nagging!** arrête de me casser les pieds! ◇ *n inf* **-1.** [person] enquiquineur *m*, -euse *f*. **-2.** [horse] canasson *m*.

nagging ['nægɪŋ] *adj* **-1.** [doubt] persistant(e), tenace. **-2.** [husband, wife] enquiquineur(euse).

nail [neɪl] ◇ *n* **-1.** [for fastening] clou *m*; **to hit the ~ on the head** mettre le doigt dessus. **-2.** [of finger, toe] ongle *m*. ◇ *vt* clouer.
◆ **nail down** *vt sep* **-1.** [lid] clouer. **-2.** *fig* [person]: **to ~ sb down to sthg** faire préciser qqch à qqn.
◆ **nail up** *vt sep* [notice] fixer avec des clous, clouer.

nail-biting *adj* plein(e) de suspense.

nailbrush ['neɪlbrʌʃ] *n* brosse *f* à ongles.

nail file *n* lime *f* à ongles.

nail polish *n* vernis *m* à ongles.

nail scissors *npl* ciseaux *mpl* à ongles.

nail varnish *n* vernis *m* à ongles.

nail varnish remover *n* dissolvant *m*.

Nairobi [naɪ'rəʊbɪ] *n* Nairobi.

naive, naïve ['naɪiːv] *adj* naïf(ïve).

naivety, naïvety [naɪ'iːvtɪ] *n* naïveté *f*.

naked ['neɪkɪd] *adj* **-1.** [body, flame] nu(e); **with the ~ eye** à l'œil nu. **-2.** [emotions] manifeste, évident(e); [aggression] non déguisé(e); **the ~ truth** la vérité toute nue.

NALGO ['nælgəʊ] (*abbr of* **National and Local Government Officers' Association**) *n ancien syndicat britannique de la fonction publique.*

Nam [næm] (*abbr of* **Vietnam**) *n Am* Vietnam *m*.

NAM (*abbr of* **National Association of Manufacturers**) *n organisation patronale américaine.*

name [neɪm] ◇ *n* **-1.** [identification] nom *m*; **what's your ~?** comment vous appelez-vous?; **to know sb by ~** connaître qqn de nom; **by the ~ of** qui répond au nom de; **in my/his ~** à mon/son nom; **in the ~ of peace** au nom de la paix; **in ~ only** de nom seulement; **to call sb ~s** traiter qqn de tous les noms, injurier qqn. **-2.** [reputation] réputation *f*; **to make a ~ for o.s.** se faire un nom. **-3.** [famous person] grand nom *m*, célébrité *f*.
◇ *vt* **-1.** [gen] nommer; **to ~ sb/sthg after** *Br*, **to ~ sb/sthg for** *Am* donner à qqn/à qqch le nom de. **-2.** [date, price] fixer.

namedropping ['neɪmdrɒpɪŋ] *n*: **I hate ~** je déteste les gens qui veulent donner l'impression de connaître tous les grands de ce monde.

nameless ['neɪmlɪs] *adj* inconnu(e), sans nom; [author] anonyme.

namely ['neɪmlɪ] *adv* à savoir, c'est-à-dire.

nameplate ['neɪmpleɪt] *n* plaque *f*.

namesake ['neɪmseɪk] *n* homonyme *m*.

Namibia [nɑː'mɪbɪə] *n* Namibie *f*; **in ~** en Namibie.

Namibian [nɑː'mɪbɪən] ◇ *adj* namibien(ienne). ◇ *n* Namibien *m*, -ienne *f*.

nan(a) [næn(ə)] *n Br inf* mamie *f*, mémé *f*.

nan bread *n* (*U*) pain *m* nan.

nanny ['nænɪ] (*pl* **-ies**) *n* nurse *f*, bonne *f* d'enfants.

nanny goat *n* chèvre *f*, bique *f*.

nap [næp] (*pt* & *pp* **-ped**, *cont* **-ping**) ◇ *n*: **to have** OR **take a ~** faire un petit somme. ◇ *vi* faire un petit somme; **to be caught napping** *inf fig* être pris au dépourvu.

NAPA (*abbr of* **National Association of Performing Artists**) *n syndicat américain des gens du spectacle.*

napalm ['neɪpɑːm] *n* napalm *m*.

nape [neɪp] *n* nuque *f*.

napkin ['næpkɪn] *n* serviette *f*.

nappy ['næpɪ] (*pl* **-ies**) *n Br* couche *f*.

nappy liner *n* change *m* (jetable).

narcissi [nɑː'sɪsaɪ] *pl* → **narcissus**.

narcissism ['nɑːsɪsɪzm] *n* narcissisme *m*.

narcissistic [,nɑːsɪ'sɪstɪk] *adj* narcissique.

narcissus [nɑː'sɪsəs] (*pl* **-cissuses** OR **-cissi**) *n* narcisse *m*.

narcotic [nɑː'kɒtɪk] *n* stupéfiant *m*, narcotique *m*.

nark [nɑːk] *Br inf* ◇ *n* police *sl* mouchard *m*, indic *m*. ◇ *vt* mettre en rogne.

narky ['nɑːkɪ] (*compar* **-ier**, *superl* **-iest**) *adj Br inf* de mauvais poil.

narrate [*Br* nə'reɪt, *Am* 'næreɪt] *vt* raconter, narrer.

narration [*Br* nə'reɪʃn, *Am* næ'reɪʃn] *n* narration *f*.

narrative ['nærətɪv] ◇ *adj* narratif(ive). ◇ *n* **-1.** [story] récit *m*, narration *f*. **-2.** [skill] art *m* de la narration.

narrator [*Br* nə'reɪtəʳ, *Am* 'næreɪtər] *n* narrateur *m*, -trice *f*.

narrow ['nærəʊ] ◇ *adj* **-1.** [gen] étroit(e); **to have a ~ escape** l'échapper belle. **-2.** [victory, majority] de justesse. ◇ *vt* **-1.** [reduce]

réduire, limiter. **-2.** [eyes] fermer à demi, plisser. ◇ *vi lit* & *fig* se rétrécir.

◆ **narrow down** *vt sep* réduire, limiter.

narrow-gauge *adj* RAIL: ~ **track** voie *f* étroite.

narrowly ['nærəʊlɪ] *adv* **-1.** [win, lose] de justesse. **-2.** [miss] de peu.

narrow-minded [-'maɪndɪd] *adj* [person] à l'esprit étroit, borné(e); [attitude] étroit(e), borné(e).

NAS (*abbr of* **National Academy of Sciences**) *n* académie américaine des sciences.

NASA ['næsə] (*abbr of* **National Aeronautics and Space Administration**) *n* NASA *f*.

nasal ['neɪzl] *adj* nasal(e).

nascent ['neɪsənt] *adj fml* naissant(e).

nastily ['nɑːstɪlɪ] *adv* **-1.** [unkindly] méchamment. **-2.** [painfully]: **to fall** ~ faire une mauvaise chute.

nastiness ['nɑːstɪnɪs] *n* [unkindness] méchanceté *f*.

nasturtium [nəs'tɜːʃəm] (*pl* -s) *n* capucine *f*.

nasty ['nɑːstɪ] (*compar* -ier, *superl* -iest) *adj* **-1.** [unpleasant - smell, feeling] mauvais(e); [- weather] vilain(e), mauvais(e). **-2.** [unkind] méchant(e). **-3.** [problem] difficile, délicat(e). **-4.** [injury] vilain(e); [accident] grave; [fall] mauvais(e).

NAS/UWT (*abbr of* **National Association of Schoolmasters/Union of Women Teachers**) *n* syndicat d'enseignants et de chefs d'établissement en Grande-Bretagne.

Natal [nə'tæl] *n* Natal *m*; **in** ~ au Natal.

nation ['neɪʃn] *n* nation *f*.

national ['næʃənl] ◇ *adj* national(e); [campaign, strike] à l'échelon national; [custom] du pays, de la nation. ◇ *n* ressortissant *m*, -e *f*.

national anthem *n* hymne *m* national.

national debt *n* dette *f* publique.

national dress *n* costume *m* national.

national grid *n Br* réseau *m* électrique national.

National Guard *n*: **the** ~ la Garde Nationale (*armée nationale américaine composée de volontaires*).

National Health Service *n*: **the** ~ *le service national de santé britannique*.

National Heritage Minister *n ministre britannique de la culture et des sports*.

National Insurance *n* (*U*) *Br* **-1.** [system] *système de sécurité sociale (maladie, retraite) et d'assurance chômage*. **-2.** [payment] ≃ contributions *fpl* à la Sécurité sociale.

nationalism ['næʃnəlɪzm] *n* nationalisme *m*.

nationalist ['næʃnəlɪst] ◇ *adj* nationaliste. ◇ *n* nationaliste *mf*.

nationality [,næʃə'nælətɪ] (*pl* -ies) *n* nationalité *f*.

nationalization [,næʃnəlaɪ'zeɪʃn] *n* nationalisation *f*.

nationalize, -ise ['næʃnəlaɪz] *vt* nationaliser.

nationalized ['næʃnəlaɪzd] *adj* nationalisé(e).

national park *n* parc *m* national.

national service *n Br* MIL service *m* national OR militaire.

National Trust *n Br*: **the** ~ ≃ la Caisse nationale des Monuments historiques et des Sites.

nation state *n* nation *f*.

nationwide ['neɪʃənwaɪd] ◇ *adj* dans tout le pays; [campaign, strike] à l'échelon national. ◇ *adv* à travers tout le pays.

native ['neɪtɪv] ◇ *adj* **-1.** [country, area] natal(e). **-2.** [language] maternel(elle); **an English** ~ **speaker** une personne de langue maternelle anglaise. **-3.** [plant, animal] indigène; ~ **to** originaire de. ◇ *n* autochtone *mf*; [of colony] indigène *mf*.

Native American *n* Indien *m*, -ienne *f* d'Amérique, Amérindien *m*, -ienne *f*.

Nativity [nə'tɪvətɪ] *n*: **the** ~ la Nativité.

nativity play *n* mystère *m* de la Nativité.

NATO ['neɪtəʊ] (*abbr of* **North Atlantic Treaty Organization**) *n* OTAN *f*.

natter ['nætə'] *Br inf* ◇ *n*: **to have a** ~ tailler une bavette, bavarder. ◇ *vi* bavarder.

natty ['nætɪ] (*compar* -ier, *superl* -iest) *adj inf* [smart] chic (*inv*).

natural ['nætʃrəl] ◇ *adj* **-1.** [gen] naturel(elle); **to die of** ~ **causes** mourir de mort naturelle. **-2.** [instinct, talent] inné(e). **-3.** [footballer, musician] né(e). **-4.** [parent] vrai(e). ◇ *n*: **she's a** ~ **at dancing** c'est une danseuse née.

natural childbirth *n* accouchement *m* sans douleur.

natural gas *n* gaz *m* naturel.

natural history *n* histoire *f* naturelle.

naturalist ['nætʃrəlɪst] *n* naturaliste *mf*.

naturalize, -ise ['nætʃrəlaɪz] *vt* naturaliser; **to be** ~**d** se faire naturaliser.

naturally ['nætʃrəlɪ] *adv* **-1.** [gen] naturellement; **to come** ~ **to sb** être naturel chez qqn. **-2.** [unaffectedly] sans affectation, avec naturel.

naturalness ['nætʃrəlnɪs] *n* naturel *m*.

natural resources *npl* ressources *fpl* naturelles.

natural science *n* sciences *fpl* naturelles.

natural wastage *n* (U) départs *mpl* volontaires.

nature ['neɪtʃəʳ] *n* nature *f*; **by** ~ [basically] par essence; [by disposition] de nature, naturellement.

nature reserve *n* réserve *f* naturelle.

nature trail *n* sentier *m* signalisé pour amateurs de la nature.

naturist ['neɪtʃərɪst] *n* naturiste *mf*.

naughty ['nɔːtɪ] (*compar* **-ier**, *superl* **-iest**) *adj* **-1.** [badly behaved] vilain(e), méchant(e). **-2.** [rude] grivois(e).

nausea ['nɔːsjə] *n* nausée *f*.

nauseam ['nɔːzɪæm] → **ad nauseam**.

nauseate ['nɔːsɪeɪt] *vt lit & fig* écœurer.

nauseating ['nɔːsɪeɪtɪŋ] *adj lit & fig* écœurant(e).

nauseous ['nɔːsjəs] *adj* **-1.** MED: **to feel** ~ avoir mal au cœur, avoir des nausées. **-2.** *fig* [revolting] écœurant(e), dégoutant(e).

nautical ['nɔːtɪkl] *adj* nautique.

nautical mile *n* mille *m* marin.

naval ['neɪvl] *adj* naval(e).

naval officer *n* officier *m* de marine.

nave [neɪv] *n* nef *f*.

navel ['neɪvl] *n* nombril *m*.

navigable ['nævɪgəbl] *adj* navigable.

navigate ['nævɪgeɪt] *vt* **-1.** [plane] piloter; [ship] gouverner. **-2.** [seas, river] naviguer sur. ◇ *vi* AERON & NAUT naviguer; AUT lire la carte.

navigation [,nævɪ'geɪʃn] *n* navigation *f*.

navigator ['nævɪgeɪtəʳ] *n* navigateur *m*.

navvy ['nævɪ] (*pl* **-ies**) *n Br inf* terrassier *m*.

navy ['neɪvɪ] (*pl* **-ies**) ◇ *n* marine *f*. ◇ *adj* [in colour] bleu marine (*inv*).

navy blue ◇ *adj* bleu marine (*inv*). ◇ *n* bleu *m* marine.

Nazareth ['næzərɪθ] *n* Nazareth.

Nazi ['nɑːtsɪ] (*pl* **-s**) ◇ *adj* nazi(e). ◇ *n* Nazi *m*, **-e** *f*.

NB -1. (*abbr of* **nota bene**) NB. **-2.** *abbr of* **New Brunswick**.

NBA *n* **-1.** (*abbr of* **National Basketball Association**) *fédération américaine de basket-ball*. **-2.** (*abbr of* **National Boxing Association**) *fédération américaine de boxe*.

NBC (*abbr of* **National Broadcasting Company**) *n chaîne de télévision américaine*.

NBS (*abbr of* **National Bureau of Standards**) *n service américain des poids et mesures*.

NC -1. *abbr of* **no charge**. **-2.** *abbr of* **North Carolina**.

NCC (*abbr of* **Nature Conservancy Council**) *n organisme britannique de protection de la nature*.

NCCL (*abbr of* **National Council for Civil Liberties**) *n ligue britannique de défense des libertés civiles*.

NCO *n abbr of* **noncommissioned officer**.

NCU (*abbr of* **National Communications Union**) *n syndicat britannique des communications*.

ND *abbr of* **North Dakota**.

NE -1. *abbr of* **Nebraska**. **-2.** *abbr of* **New England**. **-3.** (*abbr of* **north-east**) N.E.

Neanderthal [nɪ'ændətɑːl] ◇ *adj*: ~ **man** homme *m* de Néandertal. ◇ *n* homme *m* de Néandertal.

neap tide [niːp-] *n* (marée *f* de) morte-eau *f*.

near [nɪəʳ] ◇ *adj* proche; **a** ~ **disaster** une catastrophe évitée de justesse OR de peu; **in the** ~ **future** dans un proche avenir, dans un avenir prochain; **it was a** ~ **thing** il était moins cinq.
◇ *adv* **-1.** [close] près; **Christmas is drawing** ~ Noël approche. **-2.** [almost]: ~ **impossible** presque impossible; **nowhere** ~ **ready/enough** loin d'être prêt/assez.
◇ *prep*: ~ **(to)** [in space] près de; [in time] près de, vers; ~ **to tears** au bord des larmes; ~ **(to) death** sur le point de mourir; ~ **(to) the truth** proche de la vérité.
◇ *vt* approcher de; **to** ~ **completion** être près d'être fini.
◇ *vi* approcher.

nearby [nɪə'baɪ] ◇ *adj* proche. ◇ *adv* tout près, à proximité.

Near East *n*: **the** ~ le Proche-Orient.

nearly ['nɪəlɪ] *adv* presque; **I** ~ **fell** j'ai failli tomber; **I** ~ **cried** j'étais sur le point de pleurer; **not** ~ **enough/as good** loin d'être suffisant/aussi bon.

near miss *n* **-1.** SPORT coup *m* qui a raté de peu. **-2.** [between planes, vehicles] quasi-collision *f*, collision *f* évitée de justesse.

nearness ['nɪənɪs] *n* proximité *f*.

nearside ['nɪəsaɪd] ◇ *adj* [right-hand drive] de gauche; [left-hand drive] de droite. ◇ *n* [right-hand drive] côté *m* gauche; [left-hand drive] côté droit.

nearsighted [,nɪə'saɪtɪd] *adj Am* myope.

neat [niːt] *adj* **-1.** [room, house] bien tenu(e), en ordre; [work] soigné(e); [handwriting] net (nette); [appearance] soigné(e), net (nette). **-2.** [solution, manoeuvre] habile, ingénieux(ieuse). **-3.** [alcohol] pur(e), sans eau. **-4.** *Am inf* [very good] chouette, super.

neatly ['niːtlɪ] *adv* **-1.** [arrange] avec ordre; [write] soigneusement; [dress] avec soin. **-2.** [skilfully] habilement, adroitement.

neatness ['niːtnɪs] *n* [of room] bon ordre *m*; [of handwriting] netteté *f*; [of appearance] mise *f* soignée.

Nebraska [nɪ'bræskə] *n* Nebraska *m*; **in ~** dans le Nebraska.

nebulous ['nebjʊləs] *adj* nébuleux(euse).

NEC (*abbr of* **National Exhibition Centre**) *n parc d'expositions près de Birmingham en Angleterre.*

necessarily ['nesəsrəlɪ] *adv* forcément, nécessairement.

necessary ['nesəsrɪ] *adj* **-1.** [required] nécessaire, indispensable; **to make the ~ arrangements** faire le nécessaire. **-2.** [inevitable] inévitable, inéluctable.

necessitate [nɪ'sesɪteɪt] *vt* nécessiter, rendre nécessaire.

necessity [nɪ'sesətɪ] (*pl* **-ies**) *n* nécessité *f*; **of ~** inévitablement, fatalement.

neck [nek] ◇ *n* **-1.** ANAT cou *m*; **to be up to one's ~ (in sthg)** *fig* être (dans qqch) jusqu'au cou; **to breathe down sb's ~** *fig* talonner qqn, être sur le dos de qqn; **to stick one's ~ out** *fig* prendre des risques, se mouiller. **-2.** [of shirt, dress] encolure *f*. **-3.** [of bottle] col *m*, goulot *m*. ◇ *vi inf* se bécoter.

neckerchief ['nekətʃɪf] (*pl* **-chiefs** OR **-chieves** [-tʃiːvz]) *n* foulard *m*.

necklace ['neklɪs] *n* collier *m*.

neckline ['neklaɪn] *n* encolure *f*.

necktie ['nektaɪ] *n Am* cravate *f*.

nectar ['nektəʳ] *n* nectar *m*.

nectarine ['nektəriːn] *n* brugnon *m*, nectarine *f*.

NEDC (*abbr of* **National Economic Development Council**) *n agence nationale britannique de développement économique.*

Neddy ['nedɪ] *n inf surnom de la NEDC.*

née [neɪ] *adj* née.

need [niːd] ◇ *n* besoin *m*; **there's no ~ to get up** ce n'est pas la peine de te lever; **there's no ~ for such language** tu n'as pas besoin d'être grossier; **~ for sthg/to do sthg** besoin de qqch/de faire qqch; **to be in** OR **have ~ of sthg** avoir besoin de qqch; **if ~ be** si besoin est, si nécessaire; **in ~** dans le besoin. ◇ *vt* **-1.** [require]: **to ~ sthg/to do sthg** avoir besoin de qqch/de faire qqch; **I ~ to go to the doctor** il faut que j'aille chez le méde-

cin. **-2.** [be obliged]: **to ~ to do sthg** être obligé(e) de faire qqch. ◇ *modal vb*: **~ we go?** faut-il qu'on y aille?; **it ~ not happen** cela ne doit pas forcément se produire.

◆ **needs** *adv*: **if ~s must** s'il le faut.

needle ['niːdl] ◇ *n* **-1.** [gen] aiguille *f*; **it's like looking for a ~ in a haystack** c'est comme chercher une aiguille dans une botte de foin. **-2.** [stylus] saphir *m*. ◇ *vt inf* [annoy] asticoter, lancer des piques à.

needlecord ['niːdlkɔːd] *n* velours *m* mille-raies.

needlepoint ['niːdlpɔɪnt] *n* dentelle *f* à l'aiguille.

needless ['niːdlɪs] *adj* [risk, waste] inutile; [remark] déplacé(e); **~ to say** ... bien entendu ....

needlessly ['niːdlɪslɪ] *adv* inutilement, sans raison.

needlework ['niːdlwɜːk] *n* **-1.** [embroidery] travail *m* d'aiguille. **-2.** (*U*) [activity] couture *f*.

needn't ['niːdnt] = **need not**.

needy ['niːdɪ] (*compar* **-ier**, *superl* **-iest**) ◇ *adj* nécessiteux(euse), indigent(e). ◇ *npl*: **the ~** les nécessiteux *mpl*.

nefarious [nɪ'feərɪəs] *adj fml* odieux(ieuse), abominable.

negate [nɪ'geɪt] *vt fml* [efforts, achievements] annuler, détruire.

negation [nɪ'geɪʃn] *n fml* [of efforts, achievements] destruction *f*.

negative ['negətɪv] ◇ *adj* négatif(ive). ◇ *n* **-1.** PHOT négatif *m*. **-2.** LING négation *f*; **to answer in the ~** répondre négativement OR par la négative.

neglect [nɪ'glekt] ◇ *n* [of garden] mauvais entretien *m*; [of children] manque *m* de soins; [of duty] manquement *m*. ◇ *vt* négliger; [garden] laisser à l'abandon; **to ~ to do sthg** négliger OR omettre de faire qqch.

neglected [nɪ'glektɪd] *adj* [child] délaissé(e), abandonné(e); [garden] laissé(e) à l'abandon.

neglectful [nɪ'glektfʊl] *adj* négligent(e); **to be ~ of sb/sthg** négliger qqn/qqch.

negligee ['neglɪʒeɪ] *n* déshabillé *m*, négligé *m*.

negligence ['neglɪdʒəns] *n* négligence *f*.

negligent ['neglɪdʒənt] *adj* négligent(e).

negligently ['neglɪdʒəntlɪ] *adv* avec négligence.

negligible ['neglɪdʒəbl] *adj* négligeable.

negotiable [nɪ'gəʊʃjəbl] *adj* négociable; [price, conditions] à débattre.

negotiate [nɪ'gəʊʃɪeɪt] ◇ *vt* **-1.** COMM & POL négocier. **-2.** [obstacle] franchir; [bend] prendre, négocier. ◇ *vi* négocier; **to ~ with sb (for sthg)** engager des négociations avec qqn (pour obtenir qqch).

negotiation [nɪˌɡəʊʃɪ'eɪʃn] *n* négociation *f*.

negotiator [nɪ'ɡəʊʃɪeɪtəʳ] *n* négociateur *m*, -trice *f*.

Negress ['niːɡrɪs] *n* négresse *f*.

Negro ['niːɡrəʊ] (*pl* **-es**) ◇ *adj* noir(e). ◇ *n* noir *m*.

neigh [neɪ] *vi* [horse] hennir.

neighbour *Br*, **neighbor** *Am* ['neɪbəʳ] *n* voisin *m*, -e *f*.

neighbourhood *Br*, **neighborhood** *Am* ['neɪbəhʊd] *n* **-1.** [of town] voisinage *m*, quartier *m*; **in the ~** à proximité. **-2.** [approximate figure]: **in the ~ of £300** environ 300 livres, dans les 300 livres.

neighbourhood watch *n Br* système de surveillance d'un quartier par tous ses habitants (pour prévenir les cambriolages et autres crimes).

neighbouring *Br*, **neighboring** *Am* ['neɪbərɪŋ] *adj* avoisinant(e).

neighbourly *Br*, **neighborly** *Am* ['neɪbəlɪ] *adj* bon voisin (bonne voisine).

neither ['naɪðəʳ, 'niːðəʳ] ◇ *adv*: **~ good nor bad ni bon ni mauvais; that's ~ here nor there** cela n'a rien à voir. ◇ *pron & adj* ni l'un ni l'autre (ni l'une ni l'autre). ◇ *conj*: **~ do I** moi non plus.

neo- ['niːəʊ] *prefix* néo-.

neoclassical [ˌniːəʊ'klæsɪkl] *adj* néoclassique.

neolithic [ˌniːə'lɪθɪk] *adj* néolithique.

neologism [niː'ɒlədʒɪzm] *n* néologisme *m*.

neon ['niːɒn] *n* néon *m*.

neon light *n* néon *m*, lumière *f* au néon.

neon sign *n* enseigne *f* lumineuse au néon.

Nepal [nɪ'pɔːl] *n* Népal *m*; **in ~** au Népal.

Nepalese [ˌnepə'liːz] (*pl inv*) ◇ *adj* népalais(e). ◇ *n* Népalais *m*, -e *f*.

Nepali [nɪ'pɔːlɪ] *n* [language] népalais *m*, népali *m*.

nephew ['nefjuː] *n* neveu *m*.

nepotism ['nepətɪzm] *n* népotisme *m*.

Neptune ['neptjuːn] *n* [planet] Neptune *f*.

nerve [nɜːv] *n* **-1.** ANAT nerf *m*. **-2.** [courage] courage *m*, sang-froid *m*; **to lose one's ~** se dégonfler, flancher. **-3.** [cheek] culot *m*, toupet *m*; **to have the ~ to do sthg** avoir le culot OR le toupet de faire qqch.

♦ **nerves** *npl* nerfs *mpl*; **to get on sb's ~s** taper sur les nerfs OR le système de qqn.

nerve centre *n lit* & *fig* centre *m* nerveux.

nerve gas *n* gaz *m* neurotoxique.

nerve-racking [-ˌrækɪŋ] *adj* angoissant(e), éprouvant(e).

nervous ['nɜːvəs] *adj* **-1.** [gen] nerveux(euse). **-2.** [apprehensive - smile, person etc] inquiet(ète); [- performer] qui a le trac; **to be ~ about sthg** appréhender qqch.

nervous breakdown *n* dépression *f* nerveuse.

nervously ['nɜːvəslɪ] *adv* **-1.** [gen] nerveusement. **-2.** [apprehensively] avec inquiétude.

nervousness ['nɜːvəsnɪs] *n* (*U*) **-1.** [apprehension - of voice etc] inquiétude *f*; [- of performer] trac *m*. **-2.** [tenseness] nervosité *f*, tension *f*.

nervous system *n* système *m* nerveux.

nervous wreck *n*: **to be a ~** être à bout de nerfs.

nervy ['nɜːvɪ] (*compar* **-ier**, *superl* **-iest**) *adj* **-1.** *inf* [nervous] énervé(e). **-2.** *Am* [cheeky] culotté(e).

nest [nest] ◇ *n* nid *m*; **~ of tables** table *f* gigogne. ◇ *vi* [bird] faire son nid, nicher.

nest egg *n* pécule *m*, bas *m* de laine.

nestle ['nesl] *vi* se blottir.

nestling ['neslɪŋ] *n* oisillon *m*.

net [net] (*pt* & *pp* **-ted**, *cont* **-ting**) ◇ *adj* net (nette). ◇ *n* **-1.** [gen] filet *m*. **-2.** [fabric] voile *m*, tulle *m*. ◇ *vt* **-1.** [fish] prendre au filet. **-2.** [money - subj: person] toucher net, gagner net; [- subj: deal] rapporter net.

netball ['netbɔːl] *n* netball *m*.

net curtains *npl* voilage *m*.

Netherlands ['neðələndz] *npl*: **the ~** les Pays-Bas *mpl*; **in the ~** aux Pays-Bas.

net profit *n* bénéfice *m* net.

nett [net] *adj* = **net**.

netting ['netɪŋ] *n* **-1.** [metal, plastic] grillage *m*. **-2.** [fabric] voile *m*, tulle *m*.

nettle ['netl] ◇ *n* ortie *f*. ◇ *vt* piquer OR toucher au vif.

network ['netwɜːk] ◇ *n* réseau *m*. ◇ *vt* **-1.** RADIO & TV diffuser. **-2.** COMPUT interconnecter.

neuralgia [njʊə'rældʒə] *n* névralgie *f*.

neurological [ˌnjʊərə'lɒdʒɪkl] *adj* neurologique.

neurologist [ˌnjʊə'rɒlədʒɪst] *n* neurologue *mf*.

neurology [ˌnjʊə'rɒlədʒɪ] *n* neurologie *f*.

neurosis [ˌnjʊə'rəʊsɪs] (*pl* **-ses**) *n* névrose *f*.

neurosurgery [ˌnjʊərəʊ'sɜːdʒərɪ] *n* neurochirurgie *f*.

neurotic [ˌnjʊəˈrɒtɪk] ◇ *adj* névrosé(e). ◇ *n* névrosé *m*, -e *f*.

neuter ['njuːtəʳ] ◇ *adj* neutre. ◇ *vt* [cat] châtrer.

neutral ['njuːtrəl] ◇ *adj* **-1.** [gen] neutre. **-2.** [face, eyes etc] inexpressif(ive), sans expression. ◇ *n* **-1.** AUT point *m* mort. **-2.** [country] état *m* OR pays *m* neutre; [person] personne *f* neutre.

neutrality [njuːˈtrælətɪ] *n* neutralité *f*.

neutralize, -ise ['njuːtrəlaɪz] *vt* neutraliser.

neutron ['njuːtrɒn] *n* neutron *m*.

neutron bomb *n* bombe *f* à neutrons.

Nevada [nɪˈvɑːdə] *n* Nevada *m*; **in** ~ dans le Nevada.

never ['nevəʳ] *adv* jamais ... ne, ne ... jamais; ~ **ever** jamais, au grand jamais; **well I** ~ ça par exemple.

never-ending *adj* interminable.

never-never *n* Br *inf*: **on the** ~ à crédit, à tempérament.

nevertheless [ˌnevəðəˈles] *adv* néanmoins, pourtant.

new [*adj* njuː, *n* njuːz] *adj* **-1.** [gen] nouveau(elle); **to be** ~ **to** [place] être nouveau dans; [job] être neuf dans. **-2.** [not used] neuf (neuve); **as good as** ~ comme neuf.

◆ **news** *n* (U) **-1.** [information] nouvelle *f*; **a piece of** ~s une nouvelle; **that's** ~**s to me** première nouvelle; **to break the** ~**s to sb** annoncer OR apprendre la nouvelle à qqn. **-2.** RADIO informations *fpl*. **-3.** TV journal *m* télévisé, actualités *fpl*.

New Age *n* New Age *m*.

new blood *n* *fig* sang *m* neuf OR frais.

newborn ['njuːbɔːn] *adj* nouveau-né(e).

New Brunswick [-ˈbrʌnzwɪk] *n* Nouveau-Brunswick *m*; **in** ~ dans le Nouveau-Brunswick.

New Caledonia [-ˌkælɪˈdəʊnjə] *n* Nouvelle-Calédonie *f*; **in** ~ en Nouvelle-Calédonie.

New Caledonian [-ˌkælɪˈdəʊnjən] ◇ *adj* néo-calédonien(ienne). ◇ *n* Néo-Calédonien *m*, -ienne *f*.

newcomer ['njuːˌkʌməʳ] *n*: ~ **(to)** nouveau-venu *m*, nouvelle-venue *f* (dans).

New Delhi *n* New Delhi.

New England *n* Nouvelle-Angleterre *f*; **in** ~ en Nouvelle-Angleterre.

newfangled [ˌnjuːˈfæŋgld] *adj* *inf* *pej* ultramoderne, trop moderne.

new-found *adj* récent(e), de fraîche date.

Newfoundland ['njuːfəndlənd] *n* Terre-Neuve *f*; **in** ~ à Terre-Neuve.

New Guinea *n* Nouvelle-Guinée *f*; **in** ~ en Nouvelle-Guinée.

New Hampshire [-ˈhæmpʃəʳ] *n* New Hampshire *m*; **in** ~ dans le New Hampshire.

New Hebrides *npl* Nouvelles-Hébrides *fpl*; **in the** ~ aux Nouvelles-Hébrides.

New Jersey *n* le New Jersey; **in** ~ dans le New Jersey.

newly ['njuːlɪ] *adv* récemment, fraîchement.

newlyweds ['njuːlɪwedz] *npl* nouveaux OR jeunes mariés *mpl*.

New Mexico *n* Nouveau-Mexique *m*; **in** ~ au Nouveau-Mexique.

new moon *n* nouvelle lune *f*.

New Orleans [-ˈɔːlɪənz] *n* La Nouvelle-Orléans.

New Quebec *n* Nouveau-Québec *m*.

news agency *n* agence *f* de presse.

newsagent Br ['njuːzeɪdʒənt], **newsdealer** Am ['njuːzdiːlər] *n* marchand *m* de journaux.

news bulletin *n* bulletin *m* d'informations.

newscast ['njuːzkɑːst] *n* **-1.** RADIO informations *fpl*. **-2.** TV actualités *fpl*.

newscaster ['njuːzkɑːstəʳ] *n* présentateur *m*, -trice *f*.

news conference *n* conférence *f* de presse.

newsdealer Am = **newsagent**.

newsflash ['njuːzflæʃ] *n* flash *m* d'information.

newshound ['njuːzhaʊnd] *n* reporter *m*.

newsletter ['njuːzˌletəʳ] *n* bulletin *m*.

newsman ['njuːzmæn] (*pl* **-men** [-mən]) *n* journaliste *m*, reporter *m*.

New South Wales *n* Nouvelle-Galles du Sud *f*; **in** ~ en Nouvelle-Galles du Sud.

newspaper ['njuːzˌpeɪpəʳ] *n* journal *m*.

newspaperman ['njuːzˌpeɪpəmæn] (*pl* **-men** [-mən]) *n* journaliste *m*.

newsprint ['njuːzprɪnt] *n* papier *m* journal.

newsreader ['njuːzˌriːdəʳ] *n* présentateur *m*, -trice *f*.

newsreel ['njuːzriːl] *n* actualités *fpl* filmées.

newsroom ['njuːzruːm] *n* **-1.** PRESS salle *f* de rédaction. **-2.** RADIO & TV studio *m*.

newssheet ['njuːzʃiːt] *n* feuille *f* d'informations.

newsstand ['njuːzstænd] *n* kiosque *m* à journaux.

newsworthy ['njuːzˌwɜːðɪ] *adj* qui vaut la peine d'être publié OR qu'on en parle.

newt [njuːt] *n* triton *m*.

new technology *n* nouvelle technologie *f,* technologie de pointe.

New Testament *n*: **the** ~ le Nouveau Testament.

new town *n Br* ville *f* nouvelle.

new wave *n* nouvelle vague *f.*

New World *n*: **the** ~ le Nouveau Monde.

New Year *n* nouvel an *m,* nouvelle année *f;* **Happy** ~**!** bonne année!

New Year's Day *n* jour *m* de l'an, premier *m* de l'an.

New Year's Eve *n* la Saint-Sylvestre.

New York *n* **-1.** [city]; ~ **(City)** New York. **-2.** [state]: ~ **(State)** l'État *m* de New York; **in (the State of)** ~, **in** ~ **(State)** dans l'État de New York.

New Yorker [-'jɔːkəʳ] *n* New-Yorkais *m,* -e *f.*

New Zealand [-'ziːlənd] *n* Nouvelle-Zélande *f;* **in** ~ en Nouvelle-Zélande.

New Zealander [-'ziːləndəʳ] *n* Néo-Zélandais *m,* -e *f.*

next [nekst] ◇ *adj* prochain(e); [room] d'à côté; [page] suivant(e); ~ **Tuesday** mardi prochain; ~ **time** la prochaine fois; ~ **week** la semaine prochaine; **the** ~ **week** la semaine suivante OR d'après; ~ **year** l'année prochaine; ~, **please!** au suivant!; **the day after** ~ le surlendemain; **the week after** ~ dans deux semaines.
◇ *adv* **-1.** [afterwards] ensuite, après. **-2.** [again] la prochaine fois. **-3.** (*with superlatives*): ~ **best** le meilleur à part ..., le mieux après ...; ~ **biggest** le plus grand ... après.
◇ *prep Am* à côté de.
◆ **next to** *prep* à côté de; **it cost** ~ **to nothing** cela a coûté une bagatelle OR trois fois rien; **I know** ~ **to nothing** je ne sais presque OR pratiquement rien.

next door *adv* à côté.
◆ **next-door** *adj*: **next-door neighbour** voisin *m,* -e *f* d'à côté.

next of kin *n* plus proche parent *m.*

NF ◇ *n* (*abbr of* **National Front**) ≃ FN *m.* ◇ *abbr of* **Newfoundland**.

NFL (*abbr of* **National Football League**) *n* fédération nationale de football américain.

NFU (*abbr of* **National Farmers' Union**) *n* syndicat britannique d'exploitants agricoles.

NG *abbr of* **National Guard**.

NGO (*abbr of* **non-governmental organization**) *n* ONG *f.*

NH *abbr of* **New Hampshire**.

NHL (*abbr of* **National Hockey League**) *n* fédération nationale américaine de hockey sur glace.

NHS (*abbr of* **National Health Service**) *n* service national de santé en Grande-Bretagne, ≃ sécurité sociale *f.*

NI ◇ *n abbr of* **National Insurance**. ◇ *abbr of* **Northern Ireland**.

Niagara [naɪ'ægrə] *n*: ~ **Falls** les chutes *fpl* du Niagara.

nib [nɪb] *n* plume *f.*

nibble ['nɪbl] ◇ *vt* grignoter, mordiller. ◇ *vi*: **to** ~ **at sthg** grignoter qqch.

Nicaragua [,nɪkə'rægjuə] *n* Nicaragua *m;* **in** ~ au Nicaragua.

Nicaraguan [,nɪkə'rægjuən] ◇ *adj* nicaraguayen(enne). ◇ *n* Nicaraguayen *m,* -enne *f.*

nice [naɪs] *adj* **-1.** [holiday, food] bon (bonne); [day, picture] beau (belle); [dress] joli(e). **-2.** [person] gentil(ille), sympathique; **to be** ~ **to sb** être gentil OR aimable avec qqn.

nice-looking ['lʊkɪŋ] *adj* joli(e), beau (belle).

nicely ['naɪslɪ] *adv* **-1.** [made, manage etc] bien; [dressed] joliment; **that will do** ~ cela fera très bien l'affaire. **-2.** [politely - ask] poliment, gentiment; [- behave] bien.

nicety ['naɪsətɪ] (*pl* **-ies**) *n* délicatesse *f,* subtilité *f.*

niche [niːʃ] *n* [in wall] niche *f; fig* bonne situation *f,* voie *f.*

nick [nɪk] ◇ *n* **-1.** [cut] entaille *f,* coupure *f.* **-2.** *Br prison sl* [jail]: **the** ~ la taule OR tôle. **-3.** *Br inf* [condition]: **in good/bad** ~ en bon/mauvais état. **-4.** *phr*: **in the** ~ **of time** juste à temps. ◇ *vt* **-1.** [cut] couper, entailler. **-2.** *Br inf* [steal] piquer, faucher. **-3.** *Br inf* [arrest] pincer, choper.

nickel ['nɪkl] *n* **-1.** [metal] nickel *m.* **-2.** *Am* [coin] pièce *f* de cinq cents.

nickname ['nɪkneɪm] ◇ *n* sobriquet *m,* surnom *m.* ◇ *vt* surnommer.

Nicosia [,nɪkə'siːə] *n* Nicosie *f.*

nicotine ['nɪkətiːn] *n* nicotine *f.*

niece [niːs] *n* nièce *f.*

nifty ['nɪftɪ] (*compar* **-ier**, *superl* **-iest**) *adj inf* génial(e), super (*inv*).

Niger ['naɪdʒəʳ] *n* **-1.** [country] Niger *m;* **in** ~ au Niger. **-2.** [river]: **the (River)** ~ le Niger.

Nigeria [naɪ'dʒɪərɪə] *n* Nigeria *m;* **in** ~ au Nigeria.

Nigerian [naɪ'dʒɪərɪən] ◇ *adj* nigérian(e). ◇ *n* Nigérian *m,* -e *f.*

Nigerien [naɪ'dʒɪərɪən] ◇ *adj* nigérien(ienne). ◇ *n* Nigérien *m,* -ienne *f.*

niggardly ['nɪgədlɪ] *adj* [person] pingre, avare; [gift, amount] mesquin(e), chiche.

niggle ['nɪgl] ◇ *n* [worry] souci *m*, tracas *m*. ◇ *vt Br* **-1.** [worry] tracasser. **-2.** [criticize] faire des réflexions à, critiquer. ◇ *vi* **-1.** [worry]: **to ~ at sb** tracasser qqn. **-2.** [criticize] faire des réflexions, critiquer.

nigh [naɪ] *adv literary* près, proche; **well ~** presque.

night [naɪt] *n* **-1.** [not day] nuit *f*; **at ~** la nuit; **~ and day, day and ~** nuit et jour. **-2.** [evening] soir *m*; **at ~** le soir. **-3.** *phr*: **to have an early ~** se coucher de bonne heure; **to have a late ~** veiller, se coucher tard.
◆ **nights** *adv* **-1.** *Am* [at night] la nuit. **-2.** *Br* [nightshift]: **to work ~s** travailler OR être de nuit.

nightcap ['naɪtkæp] *n* **-1.** [drink] *boisson alcoolisée prise avant de se coucher*. **-2.** [hat] bonnet *m* de nuit.

nightclothes ['naɪtkləʊðz] *npl* vêtements *mpl* de nuit.

nightclub ['naɪtklʌb] *n* boîte *f* de nuit, night-club *m*.

nightdress ['naɪtdres] *n* chemise *f* de nuit.

nightfall ['naɪtfɔːl] *n* tombée *f* de la nuit OR du jour.

nightgown ['naɪtgaʊn] *n* chemise *f* de nuit.

nightie ['naɪtɪ] *n inf* chemise *f* de nuit.

nightingale ['naɪtɪŋgeɪl] *n* rossignol *m*.

nightlife ['naɪtlaɪf] *n* vie *f* nocturne, activités *fpl* nocturnes.

nightlight ['naɪtlaɪt] *n* veilleuse *f*.

nightly ['naɪtlɪ] ◇ *adj* (de) toutes les nuits OR tous les soirs. ◇ *adv* toutes les nuits, tous les soirs.

nightmare ['naɪtmeəʳ] *n lit & fig* cauchemar *m*.

nightmarish ['naɪtmeərɪʃ] *adj* cauchemardesque, de cauchemar.

night owl *n fig* couche-tard *m inv*, noctambule *mf*.

night porter *n* veilleur *m* de nuit.

night safe *n* coffre *m* de nuit.

night school *n* (*U*) cours *mpl* du soir.

night shift *n* [period] poste *m* de nuit.

nightshirt ['naɪtʃɜːt] *n* chemise *f* de nuit d'homme.

nightspot ['naɪt,spɒt] *n* boîte *f* de nuit, night-club *m*.

nightstick ['naɪt,stɪk] *n Am* matraque *f*.

nighttime ['naɪttaɪm] *n* nuit *f*.

night watchman *n* gardien *m* de nuit.

nightwear ['naɪtweəʳ] *n* (*U*) vêtements *mpl* de nuit.

nihilism ['naɪəlɪzm] *n* nihilisme *m*.

nil [nɪl] *n* néant *m*; *Br* SPORT zéro *m*.

Nile [naɪl] *n*: **the ~** le Nil.

nimble [nɪmbl] *adj* agile, leste; *fig* [mind] vif (vive).

nimbly ['nɪmblɪ] *adv* agilement, lestement.

nine [naɪn] *num* neuf; *see also* **six**.

nineteen [,naɪn'tiːn] *num* dix-neuf; *see also* **six**.

nineteenth [naɪn'tiːnθ] *num* dix-neuvième; *see also* **sixth**.

ninetieth ['naɪntɪəθ] *num* quatre-vingt-dixième; *see also* **sixth**.

ninety ['naɪntɪ] *num* quatre-vingt-dix; *see also* **sixty**.

ninny ['nɪnɪ] (*pl* **-ies**) *n inf* nigaud *m*, -e *f*.

ninth [naɪnθ] *num* neuvième; *see also* **sixth**.

nip [nɪp] (*pt & pp* **-ped**, *cont* **-ping**) ◇ *n* **-1.** [pinch] pinçon *m*; [bite] morsure *f*. **-2.** [of drink] goutte *f*, doigt *m*. ◇ *vt* [pinch] pincer; [bite] mordre. ◇ *vi Br inf*: **to ~ down the pub** faire un saut au pub.

nipper ['nɪpəʳ] *n Br inf* gamin *m*, -e *f*, gosse *mf*.

nipple ['nɪpl] *n* **-1.** ANAT bout *m* de sein, mamelon *m*. **-2.** [of bottle] tétine *f*.

nippy ['nɪpɪ] (*compar* **-ier**, *superl* **-iest**) *adj inf* **-1.** [cold] froid(e), frisquet(ette). **-2.** [quick - person] vif (vive); [- car] nerveux(euse).

Nissen hut ['nɪsn-] *n* hutte *f* préfabriquée en tôle.

nit [nɪt] *n* **-1.** [in hair] lente *f*. **-2.** *Br inf* [idiot] idiot *m*, -e *f*, crétin *m*, -e *f*.

nitpicking ['nɪtpɪkɪŋ] *n inf* ergotage *m*, pinaillage *m*.

nitrate ['naɪtreɪt] *n* nitrate *m*.

nitric acid ['naɪtrɪk-] *n* acide *m* nitrique.

nitrogen ['naɪtrədʒən] *n* azote *m*.

nitroglycerin(e) [,naɪtrəʊ'glɪsəriːn] *n* nitroglycérine *f*.

nitty-gritty [,nɪtɪ'grɪtɪ] *n inf*: **to get down to the ~** en venir à l'essentiel OR aux choses sérieuses.

nitwit ['nɪtwɪt] *n inf* imbécile *mf*, idiot *m*, -e *f*.

nix [nɪks] *Am* ◇ *n* [nothing] rien. ◇ *adv* non. ◇ *vt* [say no to] mettre son veto à.

NJ *abbr of* **New Jersey**.

NLF (*abbr of* **National Liberation Front**) *n* FLN *m*.

NLQ (*abbr of* **near letter quality**) qualité *quasi-courrier*.

NLRB (*abbr of* **National Labor Relations Board**) *n* commission américaine d'arbitrage en matière d'emploi.

NM *abbr of* **New Mexico.**

no [nəʊ] (*pl* **-es**) ◇ *adv* **-1.** [gen] non; [expressing disagreement] mais non. **-2.** [not any]: ~ **bigger/smaller** pas plus grand/petit; ~ **better** pas mieux. ◇ *adj* aucun(e), pas de; **there's** ~ **telling what will happen** impossible de dire ce qui va se passer; **he's** ~ **friend of mine** je ne le compte pas parmi mes amis. ◇ *n* non *m*; **she won't take** ~ **for an answer** elle n'accepte pas de refus OR qu'on lui dise non.

No., no. (*abbr of* **number**) No, no.

Noah's ark ['nəʊəz-] *n* l'arche *f* de Noé.

nobble ['nɒbl] *vt Br inf* **-1.** [racehorse] droguer. **-2.** [bribe] soudoyer, acheter. **-3.** [detain - person] accrocher.

Nobel prize [nəʊ'bel-] *n* prix *m* Nobel.

nobility [nə'bɪlətɪ] *n* noblesse *f*.

noble ['nəʊbl] ◇ *adj* noble. ◇ *n* noble *m*.

nobleman ['nəʊblmən] (*pl* **-men** [-mən]) *n* noble *m*, aristocrate *m*.

noblewoman ['nəʊbl,wʊmən] (*pl* **-women** [-wɪmɪn]) *n* (femme) noble *f*, aristocrate *f*.

nobly ['nəʊblɪ] *adv* noblement.

nobody ['nəʊbədɪ] (*pl* **-ies**) ◇ *pron* personne, aucun(e). ◇ *n pej* rien-du-tout *mf*, moins que rien *mf*.

no-claim bonus *n* bonus *m*.

nocturnal [nɒk'tɜːnl] *adj* nocturne.

nod [nɒd] (*pt* & *pp* **-ded**, *cont* **-ding**) ◇ *n* signe *m* OR inclination *f* de la tête. ◇ *vt*: to ~ **one's head** incliner la tête, faire un signe de tête. ◇ *vi* **-1.** [in agreement] faire un signe de tête affirmatif, faire signe que oui. **-2.** [to indicate sthg] faire un signe de tête. **-3.** [as greeting]: **to** ~ **to sb** saluer qqn d'un signe de tête.

◆ **nod off** *vi* somnoler, s'assoupir.

node [nəʊd] *n* nœud *m*.

nodule ['nɒdjuːl] *n* nodule *m*.

no-go area *n Br* zone *f* interdite.

noise [nɔɪz] *n* bruit *m*.

noiseless ['nɔɪzlɪs] *adj* silencieux(ieuse).

noiselessly ['nɔɪzlɪslɪ] *adv* sans bruit, silencieusement.

noisily ['nɔɪzɪlɪ] *adv* bruyamment.

noisy ['nɔɪzɪ] (*compar* **-ier**, *superl* **-iest**) *adj* bruyant(e).

nomad ['nəʊmæd] *n* nomade *mf*.

nomadic [nə'mædɪk] *adj* nomade.

no-man's-land *n* no man's land *m*.

nominal ['nɒmɪnl] *adj* **-1.** [in name only] de nom seulement, nominal(e). **-2.** [very small] nominal(e), insignifiant(e).

nominally ['nɒmɪnəlɪ] *adv* nominalement, de nom.

nominate ['nɒmɪneɪt] *vt* **-1.** [propose]: **to** ~ **sb (for/as sthg)** proposer qqn (pour/comme qqch). **-2.** [appoint]: **to** ~ **sb (as sthg)** nommer qqn (qqch); **to** ~ **sb (to sthg)** nominer qqn (à qqch).

nomination [,nɒmɪ'neɪʃn] *n* nomination *f*.

nominee [,nɒmɪ'niː] *n* personne *f* nommée OR désignée.

non- [nɒn] *prefix* non-.

nonaddictive [,nɒnə'dɪktɪv] *adj* qui ne provoque pas d'accoutumance OR de dépendance.

nonaggression [,nɒnə'greʃn] *n* nonagression *f*.

nonalcoholic [,nɒnælkə'hɒlɪk] *adj* nonalcoolisé(e).

nonaligned [,nɒnə'laɪnd] *adj* non-aligné(e).

nonbeliever [,nɒnbɪ'liːvə'] *n* incroyant *m*, -e *f*, athée *mf*.

nonchalant [*Br* 'nɒnʃələnt, *Am* ,nɒnʃə'lɑːnt] *adj* nonchalant(e).

nonchalantly [*Br* 'nɒnʃələntlɪ, *Am* ,nɒnʃə-'lɑːntlɪ] *adv* nonchalamment.

noncombatant [*Br* ,nɒn'kɒmbətənt, *Am* ,nɒnkəm'bætənt] *n* non-combattant *m*, -e *f*.

noncommissioned officer [,nɒnkə-'mɪʃənd-] *n* sous-officier *m*.

noncommittal [,nɒnkə'mɪtl] *adj* évasif(ive).

noncompetitive [,nɒnkəm'petɪtɪv] *adj* qui n'est pas basé(e) sur la compétition.

non compos mentis [-,kɒmpəs'mentɪs] *adj*: **to be** ~ ne pas avoir toute sa raison.

nonconformist [,nɒnkən'fɔːmɪst] ◇ *adj* non-conformiste. ◇ *n* non-conformiste *mf*.

nonconformity [,nɒnkən'fɔːmətɪ] *n* nonconformité *f*.

noncontributory [,nɒnkən'trɪbjʊtərɪ] *adj* sans versements de la part des bénéficiaires.

noncooperation ['nɒnkəʊ,ɒpə'reɪʃn] *n* refus *m* de coopération.

nondescript [*Br* 'nɒndɪskrɪpt, *Am* ,nɒndɪ'skrɪpt] *adj* quelconque, terne.

nondrinker [,nɒn'drɪŋkə'] *n* personne *f* qui ne boit pas d'alcool.

nondrip [,nɒn'drɪp] *adj* qui ne coule pas.

nondriver [,nɒn'draɪvə'] *n* personne *f* qui n'a pas le permis de conduire.

none [nʌn] ◇ *pron* **-1.** [gen] aucun(e); **there was** ~ **left** il n'y en avait plus, il n'en restait plus; **I'll have** ~ **of your nonsense** je ne tolérerai pas de bêtises de ta part. **-2.** [nobody] personne, nul (nulle). ◇ *adv:* ~ **the worse/wiser** pas plus mal/avancé; ~ **the better** pas mieux.

◆ **none too** *adv* pas tellement OR trop.

nonentity [nɒ'nentətɪ] (*pl* **-ies**) *n* nullité *f*, zéro *m*.

nonessential [ˌnɒnɪ'senʃl] *adj* nonessentiel(ielle), peu important(e).

nonetheless [ˌnʌnðə'les] *adv* néanmoins, pourtant.

non-event *n* événement *m* raté OR décevant.

nonexecutive director [ˌnɒn'ɪgsekjətɪv-] *n* administrateur *m*, -trice *f*.

nonexistent [ˌnɒnɪg'zɪstənt] *adj* inexistant(e).

nonfattening [ˌnbn'fætnɪŋ] *adj* qui ne fait pas grossir.

nonfiction [ˌnɒn'fɪkʃn] *n* (*U*) ouvrages *mpl* généraux.

nonflammable [ˌnɒn'flæməbl] *adj* ininflammable.

noninfectious [ˌnɒnɪn'fekʃəs] *adj* qui n'est pas infectieux(ieuse).

noninflammable [ˌnɒnɪn'flæməbl] = **nonflammable**.

noninterference [ˌnɒnɪntə'fɪərəns], **nonintervention** [ˌnɒnɪntə'venʃn] *n* noningérence *f*, non-intervention *f*.

non-iron *adj* qui ne se repasse pas.

nonmalignant [ˌnɒnmə'lɪgnənt] *adj* bénin(igne).

non-member *n* [of club] personne *f* qui n'est pas membre.

non-negotiable *adj* qu'on ne peut pas négocier OR débattre.

no-no *n inf*: **it's a** ~ c'est interdit OR défendu.

no-nonsense *adj* direct(e), sérieux(ieuse).

nonoperational [ˌnɒnɒpə'reɪʃənl] *adj* nonopérationnel(elle).

nonparticipation [ˌnɒnpɑːtɪsə'peɪʃən] *n* non-participation *f*.

nonpayment [ˌnɒn'peɪmənt] *n* nonpaiement *m*.

nonplussed, nonplused *Am* [ˌnɒn'plʌst] *adj* déconcerté(e), perplexe.

non-profit-making *Br*, **non-profit** *Am adj* à but non lucratif.

nonproliferation [ˈnɒnprə.lɪfə'reɪʃn] *n* non-prolifération *f*.

nonrenewable [ˌnɒnrɪ'njuːəbl] *adj* non renouvelable.

nonresident [ˌnɒn'rezɪdənt] *n* **-1.** [of country] non-résident *m*, -e *f*. **-2.** [of hotel] **client** *m*, -e *f* de passage.

nonreturnable [ˌnɒnrɪ'tɜːnəbl] *adj* [bottle] non consigné(e).

nonsense ['nɒnsəns] ◇ *n* (*U*) **-1.** [meaningless words] **charabia** *m*. **-2.** [foolish idea]: **it was** ~ **to suggest ...** il était absurde de suggérer .... **-3.** [foolish behaviour] **bêtises** *fpl*, idioties *fpl*; **to make (a)** ~ **of sthg** gâcher OR saboter qqch. ◇ *excl* quelles bêtises OR foutaises!

nonsensical [nɒn'sensɪkl] *adj* absurde, qui n'a pas de sens.

non sequitur [-'sekwɪtəʳ] *n* remarque *f* qui manque de suite.

nonshrink [ˌnɒn'ʃrɪŋk] *adj* irrétrécissable.

nonskid [ˌnɒn'skɪd] *adj* [tyre] antidérapant(e).

nonslip [ˌnɒn'slɪp] *adj* antidérapant(e).

nonsmoker [ˌnɒn'sməʊkəʳ] *n* non-fumeur *m*, -euse *f*, personne *f* qui ne fume pas.

nonstarter [ˌnɒn'stɑːtəʳ] *n* **-1.** *Br inf* [plan etc]: **this is a** ~ ceci n'a aucune chance de réussir. **-2.** [in race] non-partant *m*.

nonstick [ˌnɒn'stɪk] *adj* qui n'attache pas, téflonisé(e).

nonstop [ˌnɒn'stɒp] ◇ *adj* [flight] direct(e), sans escale; [activity] continu(e); [rain] continuel(elle). ◇ *adv* [talk, work] sans arrêt; [rain] sans discontinuer.

nontaxable [ˌnɒn'tæksəbl] *adj* non imposable.

nontoxic [ˌnɒn'tɒksɪk] *adj* non toxique.

nontransferable [ˌnɒntræns'fɜːrəbl] *adj* non transmissible.

non-U *adj Br dated* qui n'est pas très distingué(e), vulgaire.

nonviolence [ˌnɒn'vaɪələns] *n* non-violence *f*.

nonvoter [ˌnɒn'vəʊtəʳ] *n* abstentionniste *mf*, personne *f* qui ne vote pas.

nonvoting [ˌnɒn'vəʊtɪŋ] *adj* **-1.** [person] abstentionniste, qui ne vote pas. **-2.** FIN [shares] sans droit de vote.

nonwhite [ˌnɒn'waɪt] ◇ *adj* de couleur. ◇ *n* personne *f* de couleur.

noodles ['nuːdlz] *npl* nouilles *fpl*.

nook [nʊk] *n* [of room] coin *m*, recoin *m*; **every** ~ **and cranny** tous les coins, les coins et les recoins.

noon [nuːn] ◇ *n* midi *m*. ◇ *comp* de midi.

noonday ['nuːndeɪ] *literary* = **noon**.

no one *pron* = **nobody**.

noose [nuːs] *n* nœud *m* coulant.

no-place *Am* = nowhere.

nor [nɔːr] *conj*: ~ do I moi non plus; → neither.

Nordic ['nɔːdɪk] *adj* nordique.

Norf (*abbr of* **Norfolk**) *comté anglais*.

norm [nɔːm] *n* norme *f*.

normal ['nɔːml] *adj* normal(e).

normality [nɔːˈmælɪtɪ], **normalcy** *Am* ['nɔːmlsɪ] *n* normalité *f*.

normalize, -ise ['nɔːməlaɪz] ◇ *vt* normaliser. ◇ *vi* se normaliser, redevenir normal.

normally ['nɔːməlɪ] *adv* normalement.

Norman ['nɔːmən] ◇ *adj* normand(e). ◇ *n* Normand *m*, -e *f*.

Normandy ['nɔːməndɪ] *n* Normandie *f*; **in ~** en Normandie.

Norse [nɔːs] *adj* nordique, scandinave.

north [nɔːθ] ◇ *n* **-1.** [direction] nord *m*. **-2.** [region]: **the ~** le nord. ◇ *adj* nord (*inv*); [wind] du nord. ◇ *adv* au nord, vers le nord; **~ of** au nord de.

North Africa *n* Afrique *f* du Nord; **in ~** en Afrique du Nord.

North America *n* Amérique *f* du Nord.

North American ◇ *adj* nord-américain(aine). ◇ *n* Nord-Américain *m*, -aine *f*.

Northants [nɔːˈθænts] (*abbr of* **Northamptonshire**) *comté anglais*.

northbound ['nɔːθbaʊnd] *adj* en direction du nord; **~ carriageway** chaussée (du) nord.

North Carolina [-ˌkærəˈlaɪnə] *n* Caroline *f* du Nord; **in ~** en Caroline du Nord.

North Country *n*: **the ~** le Nord de l'Angleterre.

Northd (*abbr of* **Northumberland**) *comté anglais*.

North Dakota [-dəˈkəʊtə] *n* Dakota *m* du Nord; **in ~** dans le Dakota du Nord.

northeast [ˌnɔːθˈiːst] ◇ *n* **-1.** [direction] nord-est *m*. **-2.** [region]: **the ~** le nord-est. ◇ *adj* nord-est (*inv*); [wind] du nord-est. ◇ *adv* au nord-est, vers le nord-est; **~ of** au nord-est de.

northeasterly [ˌnɔːθˈiːstəlɪ] *adj* au nord-est, du nord-est; **in a ~ direction** vers le nord-est.

northerly ['nɔːðəlɪ] *adj* du nord; **in a ~ direction** vers le nord, en direction du nord.

northern ['nɔːðən] *adj* du nord, nord (*inv*).

Northerner ['nɔːðənər] *n* habitant *m*, -e *f* du Nord.

Northern Ireland *n* Irlande *f* du Nord; **in ~** en Irlande du Nord.

Northern Lights *npl*: **the ~** l'aurore *f* boréale.

northernmost ['nɔːðənməʊst] *adj* le plus au nord (la plus au nord), à l'extrême nord.

Northern Territory *n* Territoire *m* du Nord; **in ~** dans le Territoire du Nord.

North Korea *n* Corée *f* du Nord.

North Korean ◇ *adj* nord-coréen(enne). ◇ *n* Nord-Coréen *m*, -enne *f*.

North Pole *n*: **the ~** le pôle Nord.

North Sea ◇ *n*: **the ~** la mer du Nord. ◇ *comp* de la mer du Nord.

North Star *n*: **the ~** l'étoile *f* polaire.

North Vietnam *n* Nord Viêt-Nam *m*; **in ~** au Nord Viêt-Nam.

North Vietnamese ◇ *adj* nord-vietnamien(ienne). ◇ *n* Nord-Vietnamien *m*, -ienne *f*.

northward ['nɔːθwəd] ◇ *adj* au nord; **in a ~ direction** vers le nord. ◇ *adv* = **northwards**.

northwards ['nɔːθwədz] *adv* au nord, vers le nord.

northwest [ˌnɔːθˈwest] ◇ *n* **-1.** [direction] nord-ouest *m*. **-2.** [region]: **the ~** le nord-ouest. ◇ *adj* nord-ouest (*inv*); [wind] du nord-ouest. ◇ *adv* au nord-ouest, vers le nord-ouest; **~ of** au nord-ouest de.

northwesterly [ˌnɔːθˈwestəlɪ] *adj* au nord-ouest, du nord-ouest; **in a ~ direction** vers le nord-ouest.

Northwest Territories *npl Can*: **the ~** les Territoires *mpl* du Nord-Ouest.

North Yemen *n* Yemen *m* du Nord; **in ~** au Yemen du Nord.

Norway ['nɔːweɪ] *n* Norvège *f*; **in ~** en Norvège.

Norwegian [nɔːˈwiːdʒən] ◇ *adj* norvégien(ienne). ◇ *n* **-1.** [person] Norvégien *m*, -ienne *f*. **-2.** [language] norvégien *m*.

Nos., nos. (*abbr of* **numbers**) no.

nose [nəʊz] *n* nez *m*; **under one's ~** sous le nez; **you're just cutting your ~ off to spite your face** c'est toi qui en pâtis; **to have a ~ for sthg** flairer qqch, savoir reconnaître qqch; **he gets up my ~** *inf* il me tape sur les nerfs; **keep your ~ out of my business** occupe-toi OR mêle-toi de tes affaires, occupe-toi OR mêle-toi de tes oignons; **to look down one's ~ at sb** *fig* traiter qqn de haut (en bas); **to look down one's ~ at sthg** *fig* considérer qqch avec mépris; **to pay through the ~** payer les yeux de la tête; **to poke** OR **stick one's ~ into sthg** met-

tre OR fourrer son nez dans qqch; **to turn up one's ~ at** sthg dédaigner qqch.
◆ **nose about, nose around** vi fouiner, fureter.

nosebag ['nəʊzbæg] n musette f (mangeoire).

nosebleed ['nəʊzbliːd] n: **to have a ~** saigner du nez.

nosecone ['nəʊzkəʊn] n [of rocket] coiffe f; [of plane] nez m.

nosedive ['nəʊzdaɪv] ◇ n [of plane] piqué m. ◇ vi **-1.** [plane] descendre en piqué, piquer du nez. **-2.** fig [prices] dégringoler; [hopes] s'écrouler.

nosey ['nəʊzɪ] = **nosy**.

nosh [nɒʃ] n Br inf [food] bouffe f.

nosh-up n Br inf gueuleton m, bouffe f.

nostalgia [nɒ'stældʒə] n: **~ (for** sthg) nostalgie f (de qqch).

nostalgic [nɒ'stældʒɪk] adj nostalgique.

nostril ['nɒstrəl] n narine f.

nosy ['nəʊzɪ] (compar **-ier**, superl **-iest**) adj curieux(ieuse), fouinard(e).

not [nɒt] adv ne pas, pas; **I think ~** je ne crois pas; **I'm afraid ~** je crains que non; **~ always** pas toujours; **~ that** ... ce n'est pas que ..., non pas que ...; **~ at all** [no] pas du tout; [to acknowledge thanks] de rien, je vous en prie.

notable ['nəʊtəbl] ◇ adj notable, remarquable; **to be ~ for** sthg être célèbre pour qqch. ◇ n notable m.

notably ['nəʊtəblɪ] adv **-1.** [in particular] notamment, particulièrement. **-2.** [noticeably] sensiblement, nettement.

notary ['nəʊtərɪ] (pl **-ies**) n: **~ (public)** notaire m.

notation [nəʊ'teɪʃn] n notation f.

notch [nɒtʃ] n **-1.** [cut] entaille f, encoche f. **-2.** fig [on scale] cran m.
◆ **notch up** vt fus marquer.

note [nəʊt] ◇ n **-1.** [gen & MUS] note f; [short letter] mot m; **to take ~ of** sthg prendre note de qqch; **to compare ~s** échanger ses impressions OR ses vues. **-2.** [money] billet m (de banque). **-3.** [importance]: **of ~** de marque, éminent(e). ◇ vt **-1.** [notice] remarquer, constater. **-2.** [mention] mentionner, signaler.
◆ **notes** npl [in book] notes fpl.
◆ **note down** vt sep noter, inscrire.

notebook ['nəʊtbʊk] n **-1.** [for notes] carnet m, calepin m. **-2.** COMPUT ordinateur m portable compact.

noted ['nəʊtɪd] adj célèbre, éminent(e).

notepad ['nəʊtpæd] n bloc-notes m.

notepaper ['nəʊtpeɪpəʳ] n papier m à lettres.

noteworthy ['nəʊt,wɜːðɪ] (compar **-ier**, superl **-iest**) adj remarquable, notable.

nothing ['nʌθɪŋ] ◇ pron rien; **I've got ~ to do** je n'ai rien à faire; **there's ~ in it** ce n'est pas vrai du tout, il n'y a pas un brin de vérité là-dedans; **there's ~ to it** c'est facile comme tout OR simple comme bonjour; **for ~** pour rien; **~ if not** avant tout, surtout; **~ but** ne ... que, rien que; **there's ~ for it (but to do** sthg) Br il n'y a rien d'autre à faire (que de faire qqch).
◇ adv: **you're ~ like your brother** tu ne ressembles pas du tout OR en rien à ton frère; **I'm ~ like finished** je suis loin d'avoir fini.

nothingness ['nʌθɪŋnɪs] n néant m.

notice ['nəʊtɪs] ◇ n **-1.** [written announcement] affiche f, placard m. **-2.** [attention]: **it has come to my ~ that** ... mon attention a été attirée par le fait que ...; **it escaped my ~** je ne l'ai pas remarqué, je ne m'en suis pas aperçu; **to take ~ (of** sb/sthg) faire OR prêter attention (à qqn/qqch); **to take no ~ (of** sb/sthg) ne pas faire attention (à qqn/qqch); **he didn't take a blind bit of ~** il n'y a tenu aucun compte. **-3.** [warning] avis m, avertissement m; **at short ~** dans un bref délai; **until further ~** jusqu'à nouvel ordre. **-4.** [at work]: **to be given one's ~** recevoir son congé, être renvoyé(e); **to hand in one's ~** donner sa démission, demander son congé.
◇ vt remarquer, s'apercevoir de.

noticeable ['nəʊtɪsəbl] adj sensible, perceptible.

noticeably ['nəʊtɪsəblɪ] adv sensiblement, nettement.

notice board n panneau m d'affichage.

notification [,nəʊtɪfɪ'keɪʃn] n notification f, avis m.

notify ['nəʊtɪfaɪ] (pt & pp **-ied**) vt: **to ~ sb (of** sthg) avertir OR aviser qqn (de qqch).

notion ['nəʊʃn] n idée f, notion f.
◆ **notions** npl Am mercerie f.

notional ['nəʊʃənl] adj imaginaire, fictif(ive).

notoriety [,nəʊtə'raɪətɪ] n mauvaise OR triste réputation f.

notorious [nəʊ'tɔːrɪəs] adj [criminal] notoire; [place] mal famé(e); **to be ~ for** sthg être réputé pour qqch.

notoriously [nəʊ'tɔːrɪəslɪ] adv notoirement.

Notts [nɒts] (abbr of **Nottinghamshire**) comté anglais.

notwithstanding [ˌnɒtwɪθ'stændɪŋ] *fml* ◇ *prep* malgré, en dépit de. ◇ *adv* néanmoins, malgré tout.

nougat ['nuːgɑː] *n* nougat *m*.

nought [nɔːt] *num* zéro *m*; ~**s and crosses** morpion *m*.

noun [naʊn] *n* nom *m*.

nourish ['nʌrɪʃ] *vt* nourrir.

nourishing ['nʌrɪʃɪŋ] *adj* nourrissant(e).

nourishment ['nʌrɪʃmənt] *n* (*U*) nourriture *f*, aliments *mpl*.

Nov. (*abbr of* **November**) nov.

Nova Scotia [ˌnəʊvə'skəʊʃə] *n* Nouvelle-Ecosse *f*; **in** ~ en Nouvelle-Ecosse.

Nova Scotian [ˌnəʊvə'skəʊʃn] ◇ *n* Néo-Ecossais *m*, -e *f*. ◇ *adj* néo-écossais(e).

novel ['nɒvl] ◇ *adj* nouveau (nouvelle), original(e). ◇ *n* roman *m*.

novelist ['nɒvəlɪst] *n* romancier *m*, -ière *f*.

novelty ['nɒvltɪ] (*pl* **-ies**) *n* **-1.** [gen] nouveauté *f*. **-2.** [cheap object] gadget *m*.

November [nə'vembəʳ] *n* novembre *m*; *see also* **September**.

novice ['nɒvɪs] *n* novice *mf*.

Novocaine® ['nəʊvəkeɪn] *n* novocaïne® *f*.

now [naʊ] ◇ *adv* **-1.** [at this time, at once] maintenant; **any day/time** ~ d'un jour/moment à l'autre; ~ **and then** OR **again** de temps en temps, de temps à autre. **-2.** [in past] à ce moment-là, alors. **-3.** [to introduce statement]: ~ **let's just calm down** bon, on se calme maintenant. ◇ *conj*: ~ (**that**) maintenant que. ◇ *n*: **for** ~ pour le présent; **from** ~ **on** à partir de maintenant, désormais; **up until** ~ jusqu'à présent; **by** ~ déjà.

NOW [naʊ] (*abbr of* **National Organization for Women**) *n* organisation féministe américaine.

nowadays ['naʊədeɪz] *adv* actuellement, aujourd'hui.

nowhere *Br* ['nəʊwɜːʳ], **no-place** *Am adv* nulle part; **to appear out of** OR **from** ~ apparaître tout d'un coup; ~ **near** loin de; **we're getting** ~ on n'avance pas, on n'arrive à rien; **this is getting us** ~ cela ne nous avance à rien.

no-win situation *n* situation *f* où on perd à tous les coups.

noxious ['nɒkʃəs] *adj* toxique.

nozzle ['nɒzl] *n* ajutage *m*, buse *f*.

NP *abbr of* **notary public**.

NS *abbr of* **Nova Scotia**.

NSC (*abbr of* **National Security Council**) *n* conseil national américain de sécurité.

NSF ◇ *n* (*abbr of* **National Science Foundation**) fondation nationale américaine pour la science. ◇ *abbr of* **not sufficient funds**.

NSPCC (*abbr of* **National Society for the Prevention of Cruelty to Children**) *n* association britannique de protection de l'enfance.

NSU (*abbr of* **nonspecific urethritis**) *n* urétrite *f* non spécifique.

NSW *abbr of* **New South Wales**.

NT *n* **-1.** (*abbr of* **New Testament**) NT *m*. **-2.** *abbr of* **National Trust**.

nth [enθ] *adj inf* énième.

nuance [njuː'ɑːns] *n* nuance *f*.

nub [nʌb] *n* nœud *m*, fond *m*.

Nubian Desert ['njuːbjən-] *n*: **the** ~ le désert de Nubie.

nubile [*Br* 'njuːbaɪl, *Am* 'nuːbəl] *adj* nubile.

nuclear ['njuːklɪəʳ] *adj* nucléaire.

nuclear bomb *n* bombe *f* nucléaire.

nuclear disarmament *n* désarmement *m* nucléaire.

nuclear energy *n* énergie *f* nucléaire.

nuclear family *n* famille *f* nucléaire.

nuclear fission *n* fission *f* nucléaire.

nuclear-free zone *n* zone *f* antinucléaire.

nuclear fusion *n* fusion *f* nucléaire.

nuclear physics *n* physique *f* nucléaire.

nuclear power *n* énergie *f* nucléaire.

nuclear reactor *n* réacteur *m* nucléaire.

nuclear winter *n* hiver *m* nucléaire.

nucleus ['njuːklɪəs] (*pl* **-lei** [-lɪaɪ]) *n lit & fig* noyau *m*.

NUCPS (*abbr of* **National Union of Civil and Public Servants**) *n* syndicat britannique des employés de la fonction publique.

nude [njuːd] ◇ *adj* nu(e). ◇ *n* nu *m*; **in the** ~ nu(e).

nudge [nʌdʒ] ◇ *n* coup *m* de coude; *fig* encouragement *m*, incitation *f*. ◇ *vt* pousser du coude; *fig* encourager, pousser.

nudist ['njuːdɪst] ◇ *adj* nudiste. ◇ *n* nudiste *mf*.

nudity ['njuːdətɪ] *n* nudité *f*.

nugget ['nʌgɪt] *n* pépite *f*; ~ **of information** *fig* information *f* précieuse.

nuisance ['njuːsns] *n* ennui *m*, embêtement *m*; **he's such a** ~ il est vraiment casse-pieds; **to make a** ~ **of o.s.** embêter le monde; **what a** ~! quelle plaie!

NUJ (*abbr of* **National Union of Journalists**) *n* syndicat britannique des journalistes.

nuke [njuːk] *inf* ◇ *n* bombe *f* nucléaire. ◇ *vt* atomiser.

null [nʌl] *adj*: ~ **and void** nul et non avenu.

nullify ['nʌlɪfaɪ] (*pt* & *pp* **-ied**) *vt* annuler.

NUM (*abbr of* **National Union of Mine-workers**) *n syndicat britannique des mineurs.*

numb [nʌm] ◇ *adj* engourdi(e); **to be ~ with** [fear] être paralysé par; [cold] être transi de. ◇ *vt* engourdir.

number ['nʌmbər] ◇ *n* **-1.** [numeral] chiffre *m.* **-2.** [of telephone, house, car] numéro *m.* **-3.** [quantity] nombre *m*; **a ~ of** un certain nombre de, plusieurs; **any ~ of** un grand nombre de, bon nombre de. **-4.** [song] chanson *f.* ◇ *vt* **-1.** [amount to, include] compter; **to ~ among** compter parmi. **-2.** [give number to] numéroter.

number-crunching [-,krʌntʃɪŋ] *n inf* calcul *m* numérique.

numberless ['nʌmbəlɪs] *adj* sans nombre, innombrable.

number one ◇ *adj* premier(ière), principal(e). ◇ *n* **-1.** [priority] priorité *f.* **-2.** *inf* [oneself] soi, sa pomme.

numberplate ['nʌmbəpleɪt] *n* plaque *f* d'immatriculation.

Number Ten *n la résidence officielle du premier ministre britannique.*

numbness ['nʌmnɪs] *n* engourdissement *m.*

numbskull ['nʌmskʌl] = **numskull.**

numeracy ['njuːmərəsɪ] *n Br* compétence *f* en calcul.

numeral ['njuːmərəl] *n* chiffre *m.*

numerate ['njuːmərət] *adj Br* [person] qui sait compter.

numerical [njuːˈmerɪkl] *adj* numérique.

numerous ['njuːmərəs] *adj* nombreux(euse).

numskull ['nʌmskʌl] *n inf* crétin(e), imbécile *mf.*

nun [nʌn] *n* religieuse *f,* sœur *f.*

NUPE ['njuːpɪ] (*abbr of* **National Union of Public Employees**) *n ancien syndicat britannique des employés de la fonction publique.*

nuptial ['nʌpʃl] *adj fml* nuptial(e).

NURMTW (*abbr of* **National Union of Rail, Maritime and Transport Workers**) *n syndicat britannique des transports.*

nurse ['nɜːs] ◇ *n* infirmière *f*; **(male) ~** infirmier *m.* ◇ *vt* **-1.** [patient, cold] soigner. **-2.** *fig* [desires, hopes] nourrir. **-3.** [subj: mother] allaiter.

nursemaid ['nɜːsmeɪd] *n* gouvernante *f,* nurse *f.*

nursery ['nɜːsərɪ] (*pl* **-ies**) ◇ *adj* de maternelle. ◇ *n* **-1.** [for children] garderie *f.* **-2.** [for plants] pépinière *f.*

nursery nurse *n Br* puéricultrice *f.*

nursery rhyme *n* comptine *f.*

nursery school *n* (école *f*) maternelle *f.*

nursery slopes *npl* pistes *fpl* pour débutants.

nursing ['nɜːsɪŋ] *n* métier *m* d'infirmière.

nursing home *n* [for old people] maison *f* de retraite privée; [for childbirth] maternité *f* privée.

nurture ['nɜːtʃər] *vt* **-1.** [children] élever; [plants] soigner. **-2.** *fig* [hopes etc] nourrir.

NUS (*abbr of* **National Union of Students**) *n union nationale des étudiants de Grande-Bretagne.*

nut [nʌt] *n* **-1.** [to eat] *terme générique désignant les fruits tels que les noix, noisettes etc.* **-2.** [of metal] écrou *m*; **~s and bolts** *fig* rudiments *mpl.* **-3.** *inf* [mad person] cinglé *m,* -e *f.* **-4.** *inf* [enthusiast] fana *mf,* mordu *m,* -e *f.* **-5.** *inf* [head] caboche *f.*

◆ **nuts** ◇ *adj inf*: **to be ~s** être dingue. ◇ *excl Am inf* zut!

NUT (*abbr of* **National Union of Teachers**) *n syndicat britannique d'enseignants.*

nutcase ['nʌtkeɪs] *n inf* cinglé *m,* -e *f.*

nutcrackers ['nʌt,krækəz] *npl* casse-noix *m,* casse-noisettes *m.*

nutmeg ['nʌtmeg] *n* noix *f* (de) muscade.

nutrient ['njuːtrɪənt] *n* élément *m* nutritif.

nutrition [njuːˈtrɪʃn] *n* nutrition *f.*

nutritional [njuːˈtrɪʃənl] *adj* nutritif(ive).

nutritionist [njuːˈtrɪʃənɪst] *n* nutritionniste *mf.*

nutritious [njuːˈtrɪʃəs] *adj* nourrissant(e).

nutshell ['nʌtʃel] *n*: **in a ~** en un mot.

nutter ['nʌtər] *n Br inf* cinglé *m,* -e *f.*

nuzzle ['nʌzl] ◇ *vt* frotter son nez contre. ◇ *vi*: **to ~ (up) against** se frotter contre, frotter son nez contre.

NV *abbr of* **Nevada.**

NW (*abbr of* **north-west**) N.O.

NWT *abbr of* **Northwest Territories.**

NY *abbr of* **New York.**

Nyasaland [naɪˈæsəlænd] *n* Nyassaland *m.*

NYC *abbr of* **New York City.**

nylon ['naɪlɒn] ◇ *n* nylon *m.* ◇ *comp* en nylon.

◆ **nylons** *npl dated* [stockings] bas *mpl* nylon.

nymph [nɪmf] *n* nymphe *f.*

nymphomaniac [,nɪmfəˈmeɪnɪæk] *n* nymphomane *f.*

NYSE (*abbr of* **New York Stock Exchange**) *n* la bourse de New York.

NZ *abbr of* **New Zealand.**

o (*pl* **o's** OR **os**), **O** (*pl* **O's** OR **Os**) [əʊ] *n* **-1.** [letter] o *m inv*, O *m inv*. **-2.** [zero] zéro *m*.

oaf [əʊf] *n* butor *m*.

oak [əʊk] ◇ *n* chêne *m*. ◇ *comp* de OR en chêne.

OAP (*abbr of* **old age pensioner**) *n* retraité *m*, -e *f*.

oar [ɔːr] *n* rame *f*, aviron *m*; **to put** OR **stick one's ~ in** mettre son grain de sel.

oarlock ['ɔːlɒk] *n Am* [rowlock] dame *f* de nage.

oarsman ['ɔːzmən] (*pl* **-men** [-mən]) *n* rameur *m*.

oarswoman ['ɔːz,wʊmən] (*pl* **-women** [-wɪmɪn]) *n* rameuse *f*.

OAS (*abbr of* **Organization of American States**) *n* OEA *f*.

oasis [əʊ'eɪsɪs] (*pl* **oases** [əʊ'eɪsiːz]) *n* oasis *f*.

oatcake ['əʊtkeɪk] *n* galette *f* d'avoine.

oath [əʊθ] *n* **-1.** [promise] serment *m*; **on** OR **under ~** sous serment. **-2.** [swearword] juron *m*.

oatmeal ['əʊtmiːl] ◇ *n* (*U*) flocons *mpl* d'avoine. ◇ *comp* d'avoine.

oats [əʊts] *npl* [grain] avoine *m*.

OAU (*abbr of* **Organization of African Unity**) *n* OUA *f*.

OB *abbr of* **outside broadcast**.

obdurate ['ɒbdjʊrət] *adj fml* opiniâtre.

OBE (*abbr of* **Order of the British Empire**) *n distinction honorifique britannique*.

obedience [ə'biːdjəns] *n* obéissance *f*.

obedient [ə'biːdjənt] *adj* obéissant(e), docile.

obediently [ə'biːdjəntlɪ] *adv* docilement.

obelisk ['ɒbəlɪsk] *n* obélisque *m*.

obese [əʊ'biːs] *adj fml* obèse.

obesity [əʊ'biːsətɪ] *n* obésité *f*.

obey [ə'beɪ] ◇ *vt* obéir à. ◇ *vi* obéir.

obfuscate ['ɒbfʌskeɪt] *vt fml* obscurcir.

obituary [ə'bɪtjʊərɪ] (*pl* **-ies**) *n* nécrologie *f*.

object [*n* 'ɒbdʒɪkt, *vb* ɒb'dʒekt] ◇ *n* **-1.** [gen] objet *m*. **-2.** [aim] objectif *m*, but *m*. **-3.** GRAMM complément *m* d'objet. ◇ *vt* objec-

ter. ◇ *vi* protester; **to ~ to sthg** faire objection à qqch, s'opposer à qqch; **to ~ to doing sthg** se refuser à faire qqch.

objection [əb'dʒekʃn] *n* objection; **to have no ~ to sthg/to doing sthg** ne voir aucune objection à qqch/à faire qqch.

objectionable [əb'dʒekʃənəbl] *adj* [person, behaviour] désagréable; [language] choquant(e).

objective [əb'dʒektɪv] ◇ *adj* objectif(ive). ◇ *n* objectif *m*.

objectively [əb'dʒektɪvlɪ] *adv* d'une manière objective.

objectivity [,ɒbdʒek'tɪvətɪ] *n* objectivité *f*.

object lesson ['ɒbdʒɪkt-] *n*: **an ~ in sthg** une illustration de qqch.

objector [əb'dʒektər] *n* opposant *m*, -e *f*.

obligate ['ɒblɪgeɪt] *vt fml* obliger.

obligation [,ɒblɪ'geɪʃn] *n* obligation *f*.

obligatory [ə'blɪgətrɪ] *adj* obligatoire.

oblige [ə'blaɪdʒ] ◇ *vt* **-1.** [force]: **to ~ sb to do sthg** forcer OR obliger qqn à faire qqch. **-2.** *fml* [do a favour to] obliger. ◇ *vi* rendre service.

obliging [ə'blaɪdʒɪŋ] *adj* obligeant(e).

oblique [ə'bliːk] ◇ *adj* oblique; [reference, hint] indirect(e). ◇ *n* TYPO barre *f* oblique.

obliquely [ə'bliːklɪ] *adv* indirectement.

obliterate [ə'blɪtəreɪt] *vt* [destroy] détruire, raser.

obliteration [ə,blɪtə'reɪʃn] *n* destruction *f*.

oblivion [ə'blɪvɪən] *n* oubli *m*.

oblivious [ə'blɪvɪəs] *adj*: **to be ~ to** OR **of** être inconscient(e) de.

oblong ['ɒblɒŋ] ◇ *adj* rectangulaire. ◇ *n* rectangle *m*.

obnoxious [əb'nɒkʃəs] *adj* [person] odieux(ieuse); [smell] infect(e), fétide; [comment] désobligeant(e).

o.b.o. (*abbr of* **or best offer**) à déb.

oboe ['əʊbəʊ] *n* hautbois *m*.

oboist ['əʊbəʊɪst] *n* hautboïste *mf*.

obscene [əb'siːn] *adj* obscène.

obscenity [əb'senətɪ] (*pl* **-ies**) *n* obscénité *f*.

obscure [əb'skjʊər] ◇ *adj* obscur(e). ◇ *vt* **-1.** [gen] obscurcir. **-2.** [view] masquer.

obscurity [əb'skjʊərətɪ] *n* obscurité *f*.

obsequious [əb'siːkwɪəs] *adj fml & pej* obséquieux(ieuse).

observable [əb'zɜːvəbl] *adj* [appreciable] notable, sensible; [visible] qu'on peut observer.

observably [əb'zɜːvəblɪ] *adv* sensiblement.

observance [əb'zɜːvəns] *n* observation *f*.

observant [əb'zɜːvnt] *adj* observateur(trice).

observation [ˌɒbzə'veɪʃn] *n* observation *f*.

observation post *n* poste *m* d'observation.

observatory [əb'zɜːvətrɪ] (*pl* **-ies**) *n* observatoire *m*.

observe [əb'zɜːv] *vt* **-1.** [gen] observer. **-2.** [remark] remarquer, faire observer.

observer [əb'zɜːvəʳ] *n* observateur *m*, -trice *f*.

obsess [əb'ses] *vt* obséder; **to be ~ed by** OR **with sb/sthg** être obsédé par qqn/qqch.

obsession [əb'seʃn] *n* obsession *f*.

obsessional [əb'seʃənl] *adj* obsessionnel(elle).

obsessive [əb'sesɪv] *adj* [person] obsessionnel(elle); [need etc] qui est une obsession.

obsolescence [ˌɒbsə'lesns] *n* obsolescence *f*.

obsolescent [ˌɒbsə'lesnt] *adj* [system] qui tombe en désuétude; [machine] obsolescent(e).

obsolete ['ɒbsəliːt] *adj* obsolète.

obstacle ['ɒbstəkl] *n* obstacle *m*.

obstacle race *n* course *f* d'obstacles.

obstetrician [ˌɒbstə'trɪʃn] *n* obstétricien *m*, -ienne *f*.

obstetrics [ɒb'stetrɪks] *n* obstétrique *f*.

obstinacy ['ɒbstɪnəsɪ] *n* obstination *f*.

obstinate ['ɒbstənət] *adj* **-1.** [stubborn] obstiné(e). **-2.** [cough] persistant(e); [stain, resistance] tenace.

obstinately ['ɒbstənətlɪ] *adv* obstinément.

obstreperous [əb'strepərəs] *adj* turbulent(e).

obstruct [əb'strʌkt] *vt* **-1.** [block] obstruer. **-2.** [hinder] entraver, gêner.

obstruction [əb'strʌkʃn] *n* **-1.** [in road] encombrement *m*; [in pipe] engorgement *m*. **-2.** SPORT obstruction *f*.

obstructive [əb'strʌktɪv] *adj* [tactics] d'obstruction; [person] contrariant(e).

obtain [əb'teɪn] *vt* obtenir.

obtainable [əb'teɪnəbl] *adj* que l'on peut obtenir.

obtrusive [əb'truːsɪv] *adj* [behaviour] qui attire l'attention; [smell] fort(e).

obtrusively [əb'truːsɪvlɪ] *adv* de façon indiscrète.

obtuse [əb'tjuːs] *adj* obtus(e).

obverse ['ɒbvɜːs] *n* **-1.** [of coin]: **the ~** la face. **-2.** [opposite] inverse *m*.

obviate ['ɒbvɪeɪt] *vt fml* parer à.

obvious ['ɒbvɪəs] ◇ *adj* évident(e). ◇ *n*: **to state the ~** enfoncer des portes ouvertes.

obviously ['ɒbvɪəslɪ] *adv* **-1.** [of course] bien sûr. **-2.** [clearly] manifestement.

obviousness ['ɒbvɪəsnɪs] *n* évidence *f*.

OCAS (*abbr of* **Organization of Central American States**) *n* ODEAC *f*.

occasion [ə'keɪʒn] ◇ *n* **-1.** [gen] occasion *f*; **on ~** *fml* de temps en temps, quelquefois. **-2.** [important event] événement *m*; **to rise to the ~** se montrer à la hauteur de la situation. ◇ *vt* [cause] provoquer, occasionner.

occasional [ə'keɪʒənl] *adj* [showers] passager(ère); [visit] occasionnel(elle); **I have the ~ drink/cigarette** je bois un verre/je fume une cigarette de temps à autre.

occasionally [ə'keɪʒnəlɪ] *adv* de temps en temps, quelquefois.

occasional table *n* table *f* basse.

occluded front [ə'kluːdɪd-] *n* METEOR front *m* occlus.

occult [ɒ'kʌlt] ◇ *adj* occulte. ◇ *n*: **the ~** le surnaturel.

occupancy ['ɒkjupənsɪ] *n* occupation *f*.

occupant ['ɒkjupənt] *n* occupant *m*, -e *f*; [of vehicle] passager *m*.

occupation [ˌɒkju'peɪʃn] *n* **-1.** [job] profession *f*. **-2.** [pastime, by army] occupation *f*.

occupational [ˌɒkjuː'peɪʃənl] *adj* [accident, injury] du travail; [pension] professionnel(elle).

occupational hazard *n* risque *m* du métier.

occupational therapist *n* ergothérapeute *mf*.

occupational therapy *n* thérapeutique *f* occupationnelle, ergothérapie *f*.

occupied ['ɒkjupaɪd] *adj* occupé(e).

occupier ['ɒkjupaɪəʳ] *n* occupant *m*, -e *f*.

occupy ['ɒkjupaɪ] (*pt* & *pp* **-ied**) *vt* occuper; **to ~ o.s.** s'occuper.

occur [ə'kɜːʳ] (*pt* & *pp* **-red**, *cont* **-ring**) *vi* **-1.** [happen - gen] avoir lieu, se produire; [- difficulty] se présenter. **-2.** [be present] se trouver, être présent(e). **-3.** [thought, idea]: **to ~ to sb** venir à l'esprit de qqn.

occurrence [ə'kʌrəns] *n* [event] événement *m*, circonstance *f*.

ocean ['əuʃn] *n* océan *m*; *Am* [sea] mer *f*.

oceangoing ['əuʃn,gəuɪŋ] *adj* au long cours.

Oceania [ˌəuʃɪ'eɪnɪə] *n* Océanie *f*; **in ~** en Océanie.

Oceanian [ˌəuʃɪ'eɪnɪən] ◇ *adj* océanien(ienne). ◇ *n* Océanien *m*, -ienne *f*.

ochre *Br*, **ocher** *Am* ['əukəʳ] *adj* ocre (*inv*).

o'clock [ə'klɒk] *adv*: **two ~** deux heures.

OCR *n* **-1.** *abbr of* **optical character reader**. **-2.** *abbr of* **optical character recognition**.

Oct. (*abbr of* **October**) oct.

octagon ['ɒktəgən] *n* octogone *m*.

octagonal [ɒk'tægənl] *adj* octogonal(e).

octane ['ɒkteɪn] *n* octane *m*.

octane number, octane rating *n* indice *m* d'octane.

octave ['ɒktɪv] *n* octave *f*.

octet [ɒk'tet] *n* octuor *m*.

October [ɒk'təʊbər] *n* octobre *m*; *see also* **September**.

octogenarian [ˌɒktəʊdʒɪ'neərɪən] *n* octogénaire *mf*.

octopus ['ɒktəpəs] (*pl* **-puses** OR **-pi** [-paɪ]) *n* pieuvre *f*.

OD -1. *abbr of* **overdose**. **-2.** *abbr of* **overdrawn**.

odd [ɒd] *adj* **-1.** [strange] bizarre, étrange. **-2.** [leftover] qui reste. **-3.** [occasional]: **I play the ~** game of tennis je joue au tennis de temps en temps. **-4.** [not part of pair] dépareillé(e). **-5.** [number] impair(e). **-6.** *phr*: **twenty ~** years une vingtaine d'années.
♦ **odds** *npl*: **the ~s** les chances *fpl*; **the ~s are that ...** il y a des chances pour que ... (+ *subjunctive*), il est probable que ...; **against the ~s** envers et contre tout; **~s and ends** petites choses *fpl*, petits bouts *mpl*; **to be at ~s with sb** être en désaccord avec qqn; **to be at ~s with sthg** ne pas concorder avec qqch.

oddball ['ɒdbɔːl] *n inf* excentrique *mf*.

oddity ['ɒdɪtɪ] (*pl* **-ies**) *n* **-1.** [person] personne *f* bizarre; [thing] chose *f* bizarre. **-2.** [strangeness] étrangeté *f*.

odd-job man *Br*, **odd jobber** *Am n* homme *m* à tout faire.

odd jobs *npl* petits travaux *mpl*.

oddly ['ɒdlɪ] *adv* curieusement; **~ enough** chose curieuse.

oddments *npl* fins *fpl* de série.

odds-on ['ɒdz-] *adj inf*: **~ favourite** grand favori.

ode [əʊd] *n* ode *f*.

odious ['əʊdjəs] *adj* odieux(ieuse).

odometer [əʊ'dɒmɪtər] *n* odomètre *m*.

odorless *Am* = **odourless**.

odour *Br*, **odor** *Am* ['əʊdər] *n* odeur *f*.

odourless *Br*, **odorless** *Am* ['əʊdəlɪs] *adj* inodore.

odyssey ['ɒdɪsɪ] *n* odyssée *f*.

OECD (*abbr of* **Organization for Economic Cooperation and Development**) *n* OCDE *f*.

oesophagus *Br*, **esophagus** *Am* [ɪ'sɒfəgəs] *n* œsophage *m*.

oestrogen *Br*, **estrogen** *Am* [ˈiːstrədʒən] *n* œstrogène *m*.

of [*unstressed* əv, *stressed* ɒv] *prep* **-1.** [gen] de; **the cover ~ a book** la couverture d'un livre; **the King ~ England** le roi d'Angleterre; **to die ~ cancer** mourir d'un cancer. **-2.** [expressing quantity, amount, age etc] de; **thousands ~ people** des milliers de gens; **a piece ~ cake** un morceau de gâteau; **a pound ~ tomatoes** une livre de tomates; **a gang ~ criminals** une bande de malfaiteurs; **a child ~ five** un enfant de cinq ans; **a cup ~ coffee** une tasse de café. **-3.** [made from] en; **to be made ~ sthg** être en qqch. **-4.** [with dates, periods of time]: **the 12th ~ February** le 12 février; **the night ~ the disaster** la nuit de la catastrophe.

off [ɒf] ◇ *adv* **-1.** [at a distance, away]: **10 miles ~** à 16 kilomètres; **two days ~** dans deux jours; **a long time ~** encore loin; **far ~** au loin; **to keep ~** se tenir éloigné(e); **to be ~** partir, s'en aller. **-2.** [so as to remove]: **to take ~** enlever; **to cut sthg ~** couper qqch; **could you help me ~ with my coat?** pouvez-vous m'aider à enlever mon manteau? **-3.** [so as to complete]: **to finish ~** terminer; **to kill ~** achever. **-4.** [not at work etc]: **a day/week ~** un jour/une semaine de congé. **-5.** [so as to separate]: **to fence/curtain sthg ~** séparer qqch par une clôture/un rideau. **-6.** [discounted]: **£10 ~** 10 livres de remise OR réduction. **-7.** [financially]: **to be well ~** être aisé(e) OR riche; **to be badly ~** être pauvre.
◇ *prep* **-1.** [at a distance from, away from] de; **to get ~ a bus** descendre d'un bus; **to jump ~ a wall** sauter d'un mur; **to take a book ~ a shelf** prendre un livre sur une étagère; **~ the coast** près de la côte. **-2.** [so as to remove from]: **to cut a branch ~ a tree** couper une branche d'un arbre. **-3.** [not attending]: **to be ~ work** ne pas travailler; **~ school** absent de l'école. **-4.** [no longer liking]: **she's ~ her food** elle n'a pas d'appétit. **-5.** [deducted from] sur. **-6.** *inf* [from]: **to buy sthg ~ sb** acheter qqch à qqn.
◇ *adj* **-1.** [food] avarié(e), gâté(e); [milk] tourné(e). **-2.** [TV, light] éteint(e); [engine] coupé(e). **-3.** [cancelled] annulé(e). **-4.** [not at work etc] absent(e); **I'll be ~ next week** je serai absent la semaine prochaine. **-5.** *inf* [offhand]: **he was a bit ~ with me** il n'a pas été sympa avec moi.

offal ['ɒfl] *n* (*U*) abats *mpl*.

off-balance *adv*: **to throw/push sb ~** faire perdre l'équilibre à qqn.

offbeat ['ɒfbiːt] *adj inf* original(e), excentrique.

off-centre ◇ *adj* décentré(e), décalé(e). ◇ *adv* de côté.

off-chance *n*: **on the ~ that ...** au cas où ....

off colour *adj* [ill] patraque.

offcut ['ɒfkʌt] *n* chute *f*.

off-day *n inf*: **I'm having an ~ today** je ne suis pas dans mon assiette aujourd'hui.

off duty *adj* qui n'est pas de service; [doctor, nurse] qui n'est pas de garde.

offence *Br*, **offense** *Am* [ə'fens] *n* **-1.** [crime] délit *m*. **-2.** [upset]: **to cause sb ~** vexer qqn; **to take ~** se vexer.

offend [ə'fend] ◇ *vt* offenser. ◇ *vi* commettre un délit; **to ~ against** enfreindre.

offended [ə'fendɪd] *adj* offensé(e), froissé(e).

offender [ə'fendər] *n* **-1.** [criminal] criminel *m*, -elle *f*. **-2.** [culprit] coupable *mf*.

offending [ə'fendɪŋ] *adj* qui est la cause OR à l'origine du problème.

offense [*sense 2* 'ɒfens] *n Am* **-1.** = offence. **-2.** SPORT attaque *f*.

offensive [ə'fensɪv] ◇ *adj* **-1.** [behaviour, comment] blessant(e). **-2.** [weapon, action] offensif(ive). ◇ *n* offensive *f*; **to go on** OR **take the ~** passer à OR prendre l'offensive.

offensiveness [ə'fensɪvnɪs] *n* caractère *m* choquant.

offer ['ɒfər] ◇ *n* **-1.** [gen] offre *f*, proposition *f*. **-2.** [price, bid] offre *f*. **-3.** [in shop] promotion *f*; **on ~** [available] en vente; [at a special price] en réclame, en promotion. ◇ *vt* **-1.** [gen] offrir; **to ~ sthg to sb**, **to ~ sb sthg** offrir qqch à qqn; **to ~ to do sthg** proposer OR offrir de faire qqch. **-2.** [provide - services etc] proposer; [- hope] donner. ◇ *vi* s'offrir.

OFFER ['ɒfər] (*abbr of* **Office of Electricity Regulation**) *n organisme britannique chargé de contrôler les activités des compagnies régionales de la distribution d'électricité.*

offering ['ɒfərɪŋ] *n* RELIG offrande *f*.

off-guard *adj* au dépourvu.

offhand [,ɒf'hænd] ◇ *adj* cavalier(ière). ◇ *adv* tout de suite.

office ['ɒfɪs] *n* **-1.** [place, staff] bureau *m*. **-2.** [department] département *m*, service *m*. **-3.** [position] fonction *f*, poste *m*; **in ~** en fonction; **to take ~** entrer en fonction.

office automation *n* bureautique *f*.

office block *n* immeuble *m* de bureaux.

office boy *n* garçon *m* de bureau.

officeholder ['ɒfɪs,həʊldər] *n* fonctionnaire *mf*.

office hours *npl* heures *fpl* de bureau.

office junior *n Br* employé *m*, -e *f* subalterne.

Office of Fair Trading *n organisme de défense des consommateurs.*

officer ['ɒfɪsər] *n* **-1.** [in armed forces] officier *m*. **-2.** [in organization] agent *m*, fonctionnaire *mf*. **-3.** [in police force] officier *m* (de police).

office work *n* travail *m* de bureau.

office worker *n* employé *m*, -e *f* de bureau.

official [ə'fɪʃl] ◇ *adj* officiel(ielle). ◇ *n* fonctionnaire *mf*.

officialdom [ə'fɪʃəldəm] *n* bureaucratie *f*.

officially [ə'fɪʃəlɪ] *adv* **-1.** [formally] officiellement. **-2.** [supposedly] en principe.

official receiver *n* syndic *m* de faillite.

officiate [ə'fɪʃɪeɪt] *vi* officier; **to ~ at a wedding** célébrer un mariage.

officious [ə'fɪʃəs] *adj pej* trop zélé(e).

offing ['ɒfɪŋ] *n*: **in the ~** en vue, en perspective.

off-key ◇ *adj* faux (fausse). ◇ *adv* faux.

off-licence *n Br magasin autorisé à vendre des boissons alcoolisées à emporter.*

off limits *adj* interdit(e).

off-line *adj* COMPUT non connecté(e).

offload [ɒf'ləʊd] *vt inf*: **to ~ sthg (onto sb)** se décharger de qqch (sur qqn).

off-peak ◇ *adj* [electricity] utilisé(e) aux heures creuses; [fare] réduit(e) aux heures creuses. ◇ *adv* [travel] aux heures creuses.

off-putting [-putɪŋ] *adj* désagréable, rébarbatif(ive).

off sales *npl Br* vente *f* de boissons alcoolisées à emporter.

off season *n*: **the ~** la morte-saison.

♦ **off-season** *adj* hors saison.

offset ['ɒfset] (*pt* & *pp* offset, *cont* -ting) *vt* [losses] compenser.

offshoot ['ɒfʃuːt] *n*: **to be an ~ of sthg** être né(e) OR provenir de qqch.

offshore ['ɒfʃɔːr] ◇ *adj* [oil rig] offshore (*inv*); [island] proche de la côte; [fishing] côtier(ière). ◇ *adv* au large.

offside ◇ *adj* **-1.** [right-hand drive] de droite; [left-hand drive] de gauche. **-2.** SPORT hors-jeu (*inv*). ◇ *adv* SPORT hors-jeu. ◇ *n* [right-hand drive] côté *m* droit; [left-hand drive] côté gauche.

offspring ['ɒfsprɪŋ] (*pl inv*) *n* rejeton *m*.

offstage [,ɒf'steɪdʒ] *adj & adv* dans les coulisses.

off-the-cuff ◇ *adj* impromptu(e). ◇ *adv* impromptu.

off-the peg *adj Br* de prêt-à-porter.

off-the-record ◇ *adj* officieux(ieuse). ◇ *adv* confidentiellement.

off-the-wall *adj inf* loufoque.

off-white *adj* blanc cassé (*inv*).

OFGAS ['ɒfgæs] (*abbr of* Office of Gas Supply) *n* organisme britannique chargé de contrôler les activités des compagnies régionales de la distribution du gaz.

OFT *abbr of* Office of Fair Trading.

OFTEL ['ɒftel] (*abbr of* Office of Telecommunications) *n* organisme britannique chargé de contrôler les activités des compagnies de télécommunications.

often ['ɒfn, 'ɒftn] *adv* souvent, fréquemment; **how ~ do you visit her**? combien de fois est-ce que vous allez la voir?; **as ~ as not** assez souvent; **every so ~** de temps en temps; **more ~ than not** le plus souvent, la plupart du temps.

OFWAT ['ɒfwɒt] (*abbr of* Office of Water Supply) *n* organisme britannique chargé de contrôler les activités des compagnies régionales de la distribution des eaux.

ogle ['əʊgl] *vt* reluquer.

ogre ['əʊgə*r*] *n* ogre *m*.

oh [əʊ] *excl* oh!; [expressing hesitation] euh!

OH *abbr of* Ohio.

Ohio [əʊ'haɪəʊ] *n* Ohio *m*; **in ~** dans l'Ohio.

ohm [əʊm] *n* ohm *m*.

OHMS (*abbr of* On His (or Her) Majesty's Service) *expression indiquant le caractère officiel d'un document en Grande-Bretagne.*

oil [ɔɪl] ◇ *n* **-1.** [gen] huile *f*. **-2.** [for heating] mazout *m*. **-3.** [petroleum] pétrole *m*. ◇ *vt* graisser, lubrifier.

◆ **oils** *npl* ART huiles *fpl*.

oilcan ['ɔɪlkæn] *n* burette *f* d'huile.

oil change *n* vidange *f*.

oilcloth ['ɔɪlklɒθ] *n* toile *f* cirée.

oilfield ['ɔɪlfiːld] *n* gisement *m* pétrolifère.

oil filter *n* filtre *m* à huile.

oil-fired [-,faɪəd] *adj* au mazout.

oil industry *n*: **the ~** l'industrie *f* pétrolière.

oilman ['ɔɪlmən] (*pl* -men [-mən]) *n* pétrolier *m*.

oil paint *n* peinture *f* à l'huile.

oil painting *n* peinture *f* à l'huile.

oilrig ['ɔɪlrɪg] *n* [at sea] plate-forme *f* de forage OR pétrolière; [on land] derrick *m*.

oilskins ['ɔɪlskɪnz] *npl* ciré *m*.

oil slick *n* marée *f* noire.

oil tanker *n* **-1.** [ship] pétrolier *m*, tanker *m*. **-2.** [lorry] camion-citerne *m*.

oil well *n* puits *m* de pétrole.

oily ['ɔɪlɪ] (*compar* -ier, *superl* -iest) *adj* **-1.** [rag etc] graisseux(euse); [food] gras (grasse). **-2.** *pej* [smarmy] onctueux(euse), mielleux(euse).

ointment ['ɔɪntmənt] *n* pommade *f*.

oiro (*abbr of* offers in the region of): **~ £100** 100 livres à débattre.

OK¹ (*pl* OKs, *pt & pp* OKed, *cont* OKing), **okay** [,əʊ'keɪ] *inf* ◇ *adj*: **is it ~ with you**? ça vous va?, vous êtes d'accord?; **are you ~**? ça va? ◇ *n*: **to give (sb) the ~** donner le feu vert (à qqn). ◇ *excl* **-1.** [expressing agreement] d'accord, O.K. **-2.** [to introduce new topic]: **~, can we start now**? bon, on commence? ◇ *vt* approuver, donner le feu vert à.

OK² *abbr of* Oklahoma.

Oklahoma [,əʊklə'həʊmə] *n* Oklahoma *m*; **in ~** dans l'Oklahoma.

okra ['əʊkrə] *n* gombo *m*.

old [əʊld] ◇ *adj* **-1.** [gen] vieux (vieille), âgé(e); **I'm 20 years ~** j'ai 20 ans; **how ~ are you**? quel âge as-tu? **-2.** [former] ancien(enne); **in the ~ days** dans le temps, autrefois. **-3.** *inf* [as intensifier]: **any ~** n'importe quel (n'importe quelle). ◇ *npl*: **the ~** les personnes *fpl* âgées.

old age *n* vieillesse *f*.

old age pension *n Br* pension *f* de vieillesse.

old age pensioner *n Br* retraité *m*, -e *f*.

Old Bailey [-'beɪlɪ] *n*: **the ~** *la Cour d'Assise de Londres.*

olden ['əʊldn] *adj literary*: **in the ~ days** au temps jadis.

old-fashioned [-'fæʃnd] *adj* **-1.** [outmoded] démodé(e), passé(e) de mode. **-2.** [traditional] vieux jeu (*inv*).

old flame *n fig* ancien flirt *m*.

old hat *adj inf pej* dépassé(e).

old maid *n pej* vieille fille *f*.

old master *n* **-1.** [painter] maître *m*. **-2.** [painting] tableau *m* de maître.

old people's home *n* hospice *m* de vieillards.

Old Testament *n*: **the ~** l'Ancien Testament *m*.

old-time *adj* d'autrefois.

old-timer *n* **-1.** [veteran] vieux routier *m,* vétéran *m.* **-2.** [old man] vieillard *m.*

old wives' tale *n* histoires *fpl* de bonne femme.

Old World *n:* the ~ l'Ancien monde *m.*

O level *n Br* ≃ brevet *m* des collèges.

oligarchy ['ɒlɪgɑːkɪ] (*pl* **-ies**) *n* oligarchie *f.*

olive ['ɒlɪv] ◇ *adj* olive (*inv*). ◇ *n* olive *f;* ~ **(tree)** olivier *m.*

olive green *adj* vert olive (*inv*).

olive oil *n* huile *f* d'olive.

Olympic [ə'lɪmpɪk] *adj* olympique.
◆ **Olympics** *npl:* the ~s les Jeux *mpl* olympiques.

Olympic Games *npl:* the ~ les Jeux *mpl* olympiques.

OM (*abbr of* **Order of Merit**) *n* distinction honorifique britannique.

O & M (*abbr of* **organization and method**) *n* O et M.

Oman [əʊ'mɑːn] *n* Oman *m;* **in** ~ à Oman.

OMB (*abbr of* **Office of Management and Budget**) *n* organisme fédéral américain chargé de préparer le budget.

ombudsman ['ɒmbʊdzmən] (*pl* **-men** [-mən]) *n* ombudsman *m.*

omelet(te) ['ɒmlɪt] *n* omelette *f;* **mushroom** ~ omelette aux champignons.

omen ['əʊmən] *n* augure *m,* présage *m.*

ominous ['ɒmɪnəs] *adj* [event, situation] de mauvais augure; [sign] inquiétant(e); [look, silence] menaçant(e).

ominously ['ɒmɪnəslɪ] *adv* [speak] d'un ton menaçant; [happen, change] de façon inquiétante.

omission [ə'mɪʃn] *n* omission *f.*

omit [ə'mɪt] (*pt* & *pp* **-ted,** *cont* **-ting**) *vt* omettre; **to** ~ **to do sthg** oublier de faire qqch.

omnibus ['ɒmnɪbəs] *n* **-1.** [book] recueil *m.* **-2.** *Br* RADIO & TV diffusion groupée des épisodes de la semaine.

omnipotence [ɒm'nɪpətəns] *n* omnipotence *f.*

omnipotent [ɒm'nɪpətənt] *adj* tout-puissant (toute-puissante), omnipotent(e).

omnipresent [ˌɒmnɪ'prezənt] *adj* omniprésent(e).

omniscient [ɒm'nɪsɪənt] *adj* omniscient(e).

omnivorous [ɒm'nɪvərəs] *adj* omnivore.

on [ɒn] ◇ *prep* **-1.** [indicating position, location] sur; ~ **a chair/the wall** sur une chaise/le mur; **to stand** ~ **one leg** se tenir sur une jambe; ~ **the ceiling** au plafond; **the information is** ~ **disk** l'information est

sur disquette; **she had a strange look** ~ **her face** elle avait une drôle d'expression; ~ **the left/right** à gauche/droite. **-2.** [indicating means]: **the car runs** ~ **petrol** la voiture marche à l'essence; **to be shown** ~ **TV** passer à la télé; ~ **the radio** à la radio; ~ **the telephone** au téléphone; **to live** ~ **fruit** vivre OR se nourrir de fruits; **to hurt o.s.** ~ **sthg** se faire mal avec qqch. **-3.** [indicating mode of transport]: **to travel** ~ **a bus/train/ship** voyager en bus/par le train/en bateau; **I was** ~ **the bus** j'étais dans le bus; ~ **foot** à pied. **-4.** [concerning] sur; **a book** ~ **astronomy** un livre sur l'astronomie. **-5.** [indicating time, activity]: ~ **Thursday** jeudi; ~ **the 10th of February** le 10 février; ~ **my birthday** le jour de mon anniversaire; ~ **my return,** ~ **returning** à mon retour; ~ **holiday** en vacances; **to be** ~ **nightshift** être de nuit. **-6.** [indicating influence] sur; **the impact** ~ **the environment** l'impact sur l'environnement. **-7.** [indicating membership]: **to be** ~ **a committee** faire partie OR être membre d'un comité. **-8.** [using, supported by]: **to be** ~ **social security** recevoir l'aide sociale; **he's** ~ **tranquillizers** il prend des tranquillisants; **to be** ~ **drugs** se droguer. **-9.** [earning]: **to be** ~ **£25,000 a year** gagner 25 000 livres par an; **to be** ~ **a low income** avoir un faible revenu. **-10.** [obtained from]: **interest** ~ **investments** intérêts de placements; **a tax** ~ **alcohol** une taxe sur l'alcool. **-11.** [referring to musical instrument] à; **to play sthg** ~ **the violin/flute/guitar** jouer qqch au violon/à la flûte/à la guitare. **-12.** *inf* [paid by]: **the drinks are** ~ **me** c'est moi que régale, c'est ma tournée.
◇ *adv* **-1.** [indicating covering, clothing]: **put the lid** ~ mettez le couvercle; **to put a sweater** ~ mettre un pull; **what did she have** ~? qu'est-ce qu'elle portait?; **he had nothing** ~ il était tout nu. **-2.** [taking place]: **when the war was** ~ quand c'était la guerre, pendant la guerre. **-3.** [being shown]: **what's** ~ **at the Ritz?** qu'est-ce qu'on joue OR donne au Ritz? **-4.** [working - radio, TV, light] allumé(e); [- machine] en marche; [- tap] ouvert(e); **turn** ~ **the power** mets le courant. **-5.** [indicating continuing action]: **to work** ~ continuer à travailler; **we talked** ~ **into the night** nous avons parlé jusque tard dans la nuit; **he kept** ~ **walking** il continua à marcher. **-6.** [forward]: **send my mail** ~ **(to me)** faites suivre mon courrier; **later** ~ plus tard; **earlier** ~ plus tôt. **-7.** [of transport]: **the train stopped and we all got** ~ le train s'est arrêté et nous sommes tous montés. **-8.** *inf* [referring to behaviour]: **it's just not** ~! cela ne se fait pas! **-9.** *inf:* **to be**

OR **go ~ at sb (to do sthg)** harceler qqn (pour qu'il fasse qqch).

◆ **from ... on** *adv*: **from now ~** dorénavant, désormais; **from then ~** à partir de ce moment-là.

◆ **on and on** *adv*: **to go ~ and ~ (about)** parler sans arrêt (de); **the list goes ~ and ~** la liste n'en finit plus.

◆ **on and off** *adv* de temps en temps; **it happened ~ and off throughout the day** cela s'est passé par intervalles OR intermittence toute la journée.

◆ **on to, onto** *prep* (*only written as* **onto** *for senses 4 and 5*) **-1.** [to a position on top of] sur; **she jumped ~ to the chair** elle a sauté sur la chaise. **-2.** [to a position on a vehicle] dans; **she got ~ to the bus** elle est montée dans le bus; **he jumped ~ to his bicycle** il a sauté sur sa bicyclette. **-3.** [to a position attached to]: **stick the photo ~ to the page with glue** colle la photo sur la page. **-4.** [aware of wrongdoing]: **to be onto sb** être sur la piste de qqn. **-5.** [into contact with]: **get onto the factory** contactez l'usine.

ON *abbr of* **Ontario**.

ONC (*abbr of* **Ordinary National Certificate**) *n* brevet de technicien en Grande-Bretagne.

once [wʌns] ◇ *adv* **-1.** [on one occasion] une fois; **~ a day** une fois par jour; **~ again** OR **more** encore une fois; **~ and for all** une fois pour toutes; **~ in a while** de temps en temps; **~ or twice** une ou deux fois; **for ~** pour une fois. **-2.** [previously] autrefois, jadis; **~ upon a time** il était une fois. ◇ *conj* dès que.

◆ **at once** *adv* **-1.** [immediately] immédiatement. **-2.** [at the same time] en même temps; **all at ~** tout d'un coup.

once-over *n inf*: **to give sb the ~** jauger qqn d'un coup d'œil; **to give sthg the ~** jeter un coup d'œil à qqch.

oncoming ['ɒn,kʌmɪŋ] *adj* [traffic] venant en sens inverse; [danger] imminent(e).

OND (*abbr of* **Ordinary National Diploma**) *n* brevet de technicien supérieur en Grande-Bretagne.

one [wʌn] ◇ *num* [the number 1] un (une); **~ hundred** cent; **~ thousand** mille; **page ~** page un; **~ of my friends** l'un de mes amis, un ami à moi; **~ fifth** un cinquième; **in ~s and twos** par petits groupes. ◇ *adj* **-1.** [only] seul(e), unique; **it's her ~ ambition/love** c'est son unique ambition/son seul amour. **-2.** [indefinite]: **~ day** we went to Athens un jour nous sommes allés à Athènes; **~ of these days** un de ces jours. **-3.** *inf* [a]: **I've got ~ awful hangover!** j'ai

une de ces gueules de bois!; **~ hell of a bang** une détonation de tous les diables.

◇ *pron* **-1.** [referring to a particular thing or person]: **which ~ do you want?** lequel voulez-vous?; **this ~** celui-ci; **that ~** celui-là; **she's the ~ I told you about** c'est celle dont je vous ai parlé; **I'm not** OR **I've never been ~ to gossip but** ... je ne suis pas du genre à cancaner, mais .... **-2.** *inf* [blow] coup *m*; **she really thumped him ~** elle lui a flanqué un de ces coups. **-3.** *fml* [you, anyone] on; **to do ~'s duty** faire son devoir.

◆ **at one** *adv*: **to be at ~ with sb/sthg** être d'accord avec qqn/en accord avec qqch.

◆ **for one** *adv* pour ma/sa *etc* part; **I for ~ remain unconvinced** pour ma part je ne suis pas convaincu.

◆ **one up on** *adv*: **to be** OR **have ~ up on sb** avoir l'avantage sur qqn.

one-armed bandit *n* machine *f* à sous.

one-liner *n* bon mot *m*.

one-man *adj* [business] dirigé(e) par un seul homme; **~ show** one-man show *m inv*, spectacle solo *m*.

one-man band *n* **-1.** [musician] homme-orchestre *m*. **-2.** *fig* [business] entreprise *f* dirigée par un seul homme.

oneness ['wʌnnɪs] *n* (*U*) [harmony] accord *m*, harmonie *f*.

one-night stand *n* **-1.** THEATRE représentation *f* unique. **-2.** *inf* [sexual relationship] aventure *f* d'un soir.

one-off *inf* ◇ *adj* [offer, event, product] unique. ◇ *n*: **a ~** [product] un exemplaire unique; [event] un événement unique.

one-on-one *Am* = **one-to-one**.

one-parent family *n* famille *f* monoparentale.

one-piece *adj* [swimsuit] une pièce (*inv*).

onerous ['əʊnərəs] *adj* [task] pénible; [responsibility] lourd(e), pesant(e).

oneself [wʌn'self] *pron* **-1.** (*reflexive*) se; (*after prep*) soi. **-2.** (*emphatic*) soi-même.

one-sided [-'saɪdɪd] *adj* **-1.** [unequal] inégal(e). **-2.** [biased] partial(e).

onetime ['wʌntaɪm] *adj* ancien(ienne).

one-to-one *Br*, **one-on-one** *Am adj* [discussion] en tête à tête; **~ tuition** cours *mpl* particuliers.

one-upmanship [,wʌn'ʌpmənʃɪp] *n* art *m* de faire toujours mieux que les autres.

one-way *adj* **-1.** [street] à sens unique. **-2.** [ticket] simple.

ongoing ['ɒn,ɡəʊɪŋ] *adj* en cours, continu(e).

onion ['ʌnjən] *n* oignon *m*.

online ['ɒnlaɪn] *adj & adv* COMPUT en ligne, connecté(e).

onlooker ['ɒn,lʊkər] *n* spectateur *m*, -trice *f*.

only ['əʊnlɪ] ◇ *adj* seul(e), unique; **an ~ child** un enfant unique.

◇ *adv* **-1.** [gen] ne ... que, seulement; **he ~ reads science fiction** il ne lit que de la science fiction; **it's ~ a scratch** c'est juste une égratignure; **he left ~ a few minutes ago** il est parti il n'y a pas deux minutes. **-2.** [for emphasis]: **I ~ wish I could** je voudrais bien; **it's ~ natural (that) ...** c'est tout à fait normal que ...; **I was ~ too willing to help** je ne demandais qu'à aider; **not ~ ... but also** non seulement ... mais encore; **I ~ just caught the train** j'ai eu le train de justesse.

◇ *conj* seulement, mais; **he look like his brother, ~ smaller** il ressemble à son frère, mais en plus petit.

o.n.o., ono (*abbr of* **or near(est) offer**) à déb.

onrush ['ɒnrʌʃ] *n* [of emotion] vague *f*, montée *f*.

on-screen *adj & adv* COMPUT à l'écran.

onset ['ɒnset] *n* début *m*, commencement *m*.

onshore ['ɒnʃɔːr] *adj & adv* [from sea] du large; [on land] à terre.

onside [ɒn'saɪd] *adj & adv* SPORT en jeu.

Ont. *abbr of* **Ontario**.

Ontario [ɒn'teərɪəʊ] *n* Ontario *m*; **in ~** dans l'Ontario.

on-the-job *adj* [training] sur le tas.

on-the-spot *adj* [interview] sur place.

onto ['ɒntuː] = **on to**.

onus ['əʊnəs] *n* responsabilité *f*, charge *f*.

onward ['ɒnwəd] *adj & adv* en avant.

onwards ['ɒnwədz] *adv* en avant; **from now ~** dorénavant, désormais; **from then ~** à partir de ce moment-là.

onyx ['ɒnɪks] *n* onyx *m*.

oodles ['uːdlz] *npl inf*: **~ of** plein de, un tas de.

oof [ʊf] *excl inf* ouïe!, ouille!, aïe!

ooh [uː] *excl inf* oh!

oops [ʊps, uːps] *excl inf* houp!, hop là!

ooze [uːz] ◇ *vt fig* [charm, confidence] respirer. ◇ *vi*: **to ~ from** OR **out of sthg** suinter de qqch. ◇ *n* vase *f*.

opacity [ə'pæsətɪ] *n* opacité *f*; *fig* obscurité *f*.

opal ['əʊpl] *n* [gem] opale *f*.

opaque [əʊ'peɪk] *adj* opaque; *fig* obscur(e).

OPEC ['əʊpek] (*abbr of* **Organization of Petroleum Exporting Countries**) *n* OPEP *f*.

open ['əʊpn] ◇ *adj* **-1.** [gen] ouvert(e). **-2.** [receptive]: **to be ~ (to)** être réceptif(ive) (à); **to lay o.s. ~ to criticism** s'exposer aux critiques. **-3.** [view, road, space] dégagé(e). **-4.** [uncovered - car] découvert(e); **an ~ fire** un feu de cheminée. **-5.** [meeting] public(que); [competition] ouvert(e) à tous. **-6.** [disbelief, honesty] manifeste, évident(e). **-7.** [unresolved] non résolu(e).

◇ *n*: **in the ~** [sleep] à la belle étoile; [eat] au grand air; **to bring sthg out into the ~** divulguer qqch, exposer qqch au grand jour.

◇ *vt* **-1.** [gen] ouvrir. **-2.** [inaugurate] inaugurer.

◇ *vi* **-1.** [door, flower] s'ouvrir. **-2.** [shop, library etc] ouvrir. **-3.** [meeting, play etc] commencer.

◆ **open on to** *vt fus* [subj: room, door] donner sur.

◆ **open out** *vi* [road, river] s'élargir.

◆ **open up** ◇ *vt sep* [develop] exploiter, développer. ◇ *vi* **-1.** [possibilities etc] s'offrir, se présenter. **-2.** [unlock door] ouvrir.

open-air *adj* en plein air.

open-and-shut *adj* clair(e), évident(e).

opencast ['əʊpnkɑːst] *adj* [mining] à ciel ouvert.

open day *n* journée *f* portes ouvertes.

open-ended [-'endɪd] *adj* [meeting] sans limite de durée.

opener ['əʊpnər] *n* [for cans] ouvre-boîtes *m inv*; [for bottles] ouvre-bouteilles *m inv*, décapsuleur *m*.

open-handed [-'hændɪd] *adj* généreux(euse).

openhearted [,əʊpn'hɑːtɪd] *adj* franc (franche).

open-heart surgery *n* chirurgie *f* à cœur ouvert.

opening ['əʊpnɪŋ] ◇ *adj* [first] premier(ière); [remarks] préliminaire. ◇ *n* **-1.** [beginning] commencement *m*, début *m*. **-2.** [in fence] trou *m*, percée *f*; [in clouds] trouée *f*, déchirure *f*. **-3.** [opportunity - gen] occasion *f*; [- COMM] débouché *m*. **-4.** [job vacancy] poste *m*.

opening hours *npl* heures *fpl* d'ouverture.

opening night *n* première *f*.

opening time *n Br* [of pub] heure *f* d'ouverture.

open letter *n* lettre *f* ouverte.

openly ['əʊpənlɪ] *adv* ouvertement, franchement.

open market *n* marché *m* libre.

open marriage *n* mariage *m* moderne (*où chacun est libre d'avoir des aventures*).

open-minded [-'maɪndɪd] *adj* [person] qui a l'esprit large; [attitude] large.

open-mouthed [-'maʊðd] *adj & adv* bouche bée (*inv*).

open-necked [-'nekt] *adj* à col ouvert.

openness ['əʊpənnɪs] *n* [frankness] franchise *f*.

open-plan *adj* non cloisonné(e).

open prison *n* prison *f* ouverte.

open sandwich *n* canapé *m*.

open season *n* saison *f* de la chasse.

open shop *n* absence de monopole syndical.

Open University *n* Br: the ~ ≃ centre *m* national d'enseignement à distance.

open verdict *n* JUR jugement qui enregistre un décès sans en spécifier la cause.

opera ['ɒpərə] *n* opéra *m*.

opera glasses *npl* jumelles *fpl* de théâtre.

opera house *n* opéra *m*.

opera singer *n* chanteur *m*, -euse *f* d'opéra.

operate ['ɒpəreɪt] ◇ *vt* -1. [machine] faire marcher, faire fonctionner. -2. COMM diriger. ◇ *vi* -1. [rule, law, system] jouer, être appliqué(e); [machine] fonctionner, marcher. -2. COMM opérer, travailler. -3. MED opérer; to ~ on sb/sthg opérer qqn/de qqch.

operatic [,ɒpə'rætɪk] *adj* d'opéra.

operating room ['ɒpəreɪtɪŋ-] *n Am* salle *f* d'opération.

operating system ['ɒpəreɪtɪŋ-] *n* COMPUT système *m* d'exploitation.

operating theatre *Br*, **operating room** *Am* ['ɒpəreɪtɪŋ-] *n* salle *f* d'opération.

operation [,ɒpə'reɪʃn] *n* -1. [gen & MED] opération *f*; to have an ~ (for) se faire opérer (de). -2. [of machine] marche *f*, fonctionnement *m*; to be in ~ [machine] être en marche OR en service; [law, system] être en vigueur. -3. [COMM - company] exploitation *f*; [- management] administration *f*, gestion *f*.

operational [,ɒpə'reɪʃənl] *adj* -1. [machine] en état de marche. -2. [difficulty, costs] d'exploitation.

operative ['ɒprətɪv] ◇ *adj* en vigueur. ◇ *n* ouvrier *m*, -ière *f*.

operator ['ɒpəreɪtər] *n* -1. TELEC standardiste *mf*. -2. [of machine] opérateur *m*, -trice *f*. -3. COMM directeur *m*, -trice *f*.

operetta [,ɒpə'retə] *n* opérette *f*.

ophthalmic optician [ɒf'θælmɪk-] *n* opticien *m*, -ienne *f*.

ophthalmologist [,ɒfθæl'mɒlədʒɪst] *n* ophtalmologue *mf*, ophtalmologiste *mf*.

opinion [ə'pɪnjən] *n* opinion *f*, avis *m*; **to be of the** ~ **that** être d'avis que, estimer que; **in my** ~ à mon avis.

opinionated [ə'pɪnjəneɪtɪd] *adj pej* dogmatique.

opinion poll *n* sondage *m* d'opinion.

opium ['əʊpjəm] *n* opium *m*.

opponent [ə'pəʊnənt] *n* adversaire *mf*.

opportune ['ɒpətjuːn] *adj* opportun(e).

opportunism [,ɒpə'tjuːnɪzm] *n* opportunisme *m*.

opportunist [,ɒpə'tjuːnɪst] *n* opportuniste *mf*.

opportunity [,ɒpə'tjuːnətɪ] (*pl* **-ies**) *n* occasion *f*; **to take the** ~ **to do** OR **of doing sthg** profiter de l'occasion pour faire qqch; **to get the** ~ avoir l'occasion.

oppose [ə'pəʊz] *vt* s'opposer à.

opposed [ə'pəʊzd] *adj* opposé(e); **to be** ~ **to** être contre, être opposé à; **as** ~ **to** par opposition à.

opposing [ə'pəʊzɪŋ] *adj* opposé(e).

opposite ['ɒpəzɪt] ◇ *adj* opposé(e); [house] d'en face. ◇ *adv* en face. ◇ *prep* en face de. ◇ *n* contraire *m*.

opposite number *n* homologue *mf*.

opposite sex *n*: the ~ le sexe opposé.

opposition [,ɒpə'zɪʃn] *n* -1. [gen] opposition *f*. -2. [opposing team] adversaire *mf*.
◆ **Opposition** *n Br* POL: **the Opposition** l'opposition.

oppress [ə'pres] *vt* -1. [persecute] opprimer. -2. [depress] oppresser.

oppressed [ə'prest] ◇ *adj* opprimé(e). ◇ *npl*: **the** ~ les opprimés *mpl*.

oppression [ə'preʃn] *n* oppression *f*.

oppressive [ə'presɪv] *adj* -1. [unjust] oppressif(ive). -2. [weather, heat] étouffant(e), lourd(e). -3. [silence] oppressant(e).

oppressor [ə'presər] *n* oppresseur *m*.

opprobrium [ə'prəʊbrɪəm] *n* opprobre *m*.

opt [ɒpt] ◇ *vt*: to ~ to do sthg choisir de faire qqch. ◇ *vi*: to ~ for opter pour.
◆ **opt in** *vi*: to ~ in (to) choisir de participer (à).
◆ **opt out** *vi*: to ~ out (of) [gen] choisir de ne pas participer (à); [of responsibility] se dérober (à); [of NHS] ne plus faire partie (de).

optic ['ɒptɪk] *adj* optique.

optical ['ɒptɪkl] *adj* optique.

optical character reader *n* COMPUT lecteur *m* optique de caractères.

optical character recognition n COMPUT reconnaissance f optique de caractères.

optical fibre n TELEC fibre f optique.

optical illusion n illusion f d'optique.

optician [ɒp'tɪʃn] n -1. [who sells glasses] opticien m, -ienne f. -2. [ophthalmologist] ophtalmologiste mf.

optics ['ɒptɪks] n (U) optique f.

optimism ['ɒptɪmɪzm] n optimisme m.

optimist ['ɒptɪmɪst] n optimiste mf.

optimistic [,ɒptɪ'mɪstɪk] adj optimiste; to be ~ about être optimiste pour.

optimize, -ise ['ɒptɪmaɪz] vt optimaliser.

optimum ['ɒptɪməm] adj optimum.

option ['ɒpʃn] n option f, choix m; she had no ~ but to pay up elle n'a pas pu faire autrement que de payer; to have the ~ to do OR of doing sthg pouvoir faire qqch, avoir la possibilité de faire qqch.

optional ['ɒpʃənl] adj facultatif(ive); an ~ extra un accessoire.

opulence ['ɒpjʊləns] n -1. [wealth] opulence f. -2. [sumptuousness] magnificence f.

opulent ['ɒpjʊlənt] adj -1. [wealthy] opulent(e). -2. [sumptuous] magnifique.

opus ['əʊpəs] (pl -es OR opera) n MUS opus m.

or [ɔːr] conj -1. [gen] ou. -2. [after negative]: he can't read ~ write il ne sait ni lire ni écrire. -3. [otherwise] sinon. -4. [as correction] ou plutôt.

OR abbr of Oregon.

oracle ['ɒrəkl] n [prophet] oracle m.

oral ['ɔːrəl] ◇ adj -1. [spoken] oral(e). -2. [MED - medicine] par voie orale, par la bouche; [- hygiene] buccal(e). ◇ n oral m, épreuve f orale.

orally ['ɔːrəlɪ] adv -1. [in spoken form] oralement. -2. MED par voie orale, par la bouche.

orange ['ɒrɪndʒ] ◇ adj orange (inv). ◇ n -1. [fruit] orange f. -2. [colour] orange m.

orangeade [,ɒrɪndʒ'eɪd] n orangeade f.

orange blossom n (U) fleur f d'oranger.

Orangeman ['ɒrɪndʒmən] (pl -men [-mən]) n Br orangiste m.

orangutang [ɔː,ræŋuː'tæŋ] n orang-outang m.

oration [ɔː'reɪʃn] n fml discours m.

orator ['ɒrətər] n orateur m, -trice f.

oratorio [,ɒrə'tɔːrɪəʊ] (pl -s) n oratorio m.

oratory ['ɒrətrɪ] n art m oratoire, éloquence f.

orb [ɔːb] n globe m.

orbit ['ɔːbɪt] ◇ n orbite f; to be in/go into ~ (around) être/entrer sur orbite (autour de), être/entrer en orbite (autour de). ◇ vt décrire une orbite autour de.

orchard ['ɔːtʃəd] n verger m; apple ~ champ m de pommiers, pommeraie f.

orchestra ['ɔːkɪstrə] n orchestre m.

orchestral [ɔː'kestrəl] adj orchestral(e).

orchestra pit n fosse f d'orchestre.

orchestrate ['ɔːkɪstreɪt] vt lit & fig orchestrer.

orchestration [,ɔːke'streɪʃn] n lit & fig orchestration f.

orchid ['ɔːkɪd] n orchidée f.

ordain [ɔː'deɪn] vt -1. [decree] ordonner, décréter. -2. RELIG: to be ~ed être ordonné prêtre.

ordeal [ɔː'diːl] n épreuve f.

order ['ɔːdər] ◇ n -1. [gen] ordre m; to be under ~s to do sthg avoir (reçu) l'ordre de faire qqch. -2. COMM commande f; to place an ~ with sb for sthg passer une commande de qqch à qqn; on ~ commandé(e); to ~ sur commande. -3. [sequence] ordre m; in ~ dans l'ordre; in ~ of importance par ordre d'importance. -4. [fitness for use]: in working ~ en état de marche; out of ~ [machine] en panne; [behaviour] déplacé(e); in ~ [correct] en ordre. -5. (U) [discipline - gen] ordre m; [- in classroom] discipline f; to keep ~ maintenir l'ordre. -6. Am [portion] part f. ◇ vt -1. [command] ordonner; to ~ sb to do sthg ordonner à qqn de faire qqch; to ~ that ordonner que. -2. COMM commander. ◇ vi commander.

◆ **orders** npl RELIG: to take holy ~s entrer dans les ordres.

◆ **in the order of** Br, **on the order of** Am prep environ, de l'ordre de.

◆ **in order that** conj pour que, afin que.

◆ **in order to** conj pour, afin de.

◆ **order about, order around** vt sep commander.

order book n carnet m de commandes.

order form n bulletin m de commande.

orderly ['ɔːdəlɪ] (pl -ies) ◇ adj [person] ordonné(e); [crowd] discipliné(e); [office, room] en ordre. ◇ n [in hospital] garçon m de salle.

order number n numéro m de commande.

ordinal ['ɔːdɪnl] ◇ adj ordinal(e). ◇ n nombre m ordinal.

ordinarily ['ɔːdənrəlɪ] adv d'habitude, d'ordinaire.

ordinary ['ɔːdənrɪ] ◇ *adj* -1. [normal] ordinaire. -2. *pej* [unexceptional] ordinaire, quelconque. ◇ *n*: **out of the ~** qui sort de l'ordinaire, exceptionnel(elle).

ordinary level *n Br* ≃ brevet *m* des collèges.

ordinary seaman *n Br* simple matelot *m*.

ordinary shares *npl Br* FIN actions *fpl* ordinaires.

ordination [ˌɔːdɪ'neɪʃn] *n* ordination *f*.

ordnance ['ɔːdnəns] *n* (*U*) -1. [supplies] matériel *m* militaire. -2. [artillery] artillerie *f*.

Ordnance Survey *n* service cartographique national en Grande-Bretagne, ≃ IGN *m*.

ore [ɔːʳ] *n* minerai *m*.

oregano [ˌɒrɪ'gɑːnəʊ] *n* origan *m*.

Oregon ['ɒrɪgən] *n* Oregon *m*; **in ~** dans l'Oregon.

organ ['ɔːgən] *n* -1. [gen] organe *m*. -2. MUS orgue *m*.

organic [ɔː'gænɪk] *adj* -1. [of animals, plants] organique. -2. [farming, food] biologique. -3. *fig* [development] naturel(elle).

organically [ɔː'gænɪklɪ] *adv* [farm, grow] sans engrais chimiques.

organic chemistry *n* chimie *f* organique.

organism ['ɔːgənɪzm] *n* organisme *m*.

organist ['ɔːgənɪst] *n* organiste *mf*.

organization [ˌɔːgənaɪ'zeɪʃn] *n* organisation *f*.

organizational [ˌɔːgənaɪ'zeɪʃnl] *adj* -1. [structure, links] organisationnel(elle). -2. [skill] d'organisation.

organization chart *n* organigramme *m*.

organize, -ise ['ɔːgənaɪz] ◇ *vt* organiser. ◇ *vi* [workers] se syndiquer.

organized ['ɔːgənaɪzd] *adj* organisé(e).

organized crime *n* crime *m* organisé.

organized labour *n* main d'œuvre *f* syndiquée.

organizer ['ɔːgənaɪzəʳ] *n* organisateur *m*, -trice *f*.

organza [ɔː'gænzə] *n* organza *m*.

orgasm ['ɔːgæzm] *n* orgasme *m*.

orgy ['ɔːdʒɪ] (*pl* -ies) *n lit* & *fig* orgie *f*.

orient ['ɔːrɪənt] = **orientate**.

Orient ['ɔːrɪənt] *n*: **the ~** l'Orient *m*.

oriental [ˌɔːrɪ'entl] ◇ *adj* oriental(e). ◇ *n* Oriental *m*, -e *f* (*attention: le terme 'oriental' est considéré raciste*).

orientate ['ɔːrɪenteɪt] *vt*: **to be ~d towards** viser, s'adresser à; **to ~ o.s.** s'orienter.

orientation [ˌɔːrɪen'teɪʃn] *n* orientation *f*.

orienteering [ˌɔːrɪən'tɪərɪŋ] *n* (*U*) course *f* d'orientation.

orifice ['ɒrɪfɪs] *n* orifice *m*.

origami [ˌɒrɪ'gɑːmɪ] *n* origami *m*.

origin ['ɒrɪdʒɪn] *n* -1. [of river] source *f*; [of word, conflict] origine *f*. -2. [birth]: **country of ~** pays *m* d'origine.
◆ **origins** *npl* origines *fpl*.

original [ɒ'rɪdʒənl] ◇ *adj* original(e); [owner] premier(ière). ◇ *n* original *m*.

originality [əˌrɪdʒə'nælətɪ] *n* originalité *f*.

originally [ə'rɪdʒənəlɪ] *adv* à l'origine, au départ.

original sin *n* péché *m* originel.

originate [ə'rɪdʒəneɪt] ◇ *vt* être l'auteur de, être à l'origine de. ◇ *vi* [belief, custom]: **to ~ (in)** prendre naissance (dans); **to ~ from** provenir de.

origination [əˌrɪdʒə'neɪʃn] *n* (*U*) origine *f*.

originator [ə'rɪdʒəneɪtəʳ] *n* auteur *m*, initiateur *m*, -trice *f*.

Orinoco [ˌɒrɪ'nəʊkəʊ] *n*: **the (River) ~** l'Orénoque *m*.

Orkney Islands ['ɔːknɪ-], **Orkneys** ['ɔːknɪz] *npl*: **the ~** les Orcades *fpl*; **in the ~s** dans les Orcades.

Ormuz [ɔː'muːz] = **Hormuz**.

ornament ['ɔːnəmənt] *n* -1. [object] bibelot *m*. -2. (*U*) [decoration] ornement *m*.

ornamental [ˌɔːnə'mentl] *adj* [garden, pond] d'agrément; [design] décoratif(ive).

ornamentation [ˌɔːnəmen'teɪʃn] *n* décoration *f*.

ornate [ɔː'neɪt] *adj* orné(e).

ornately [ɔː'neɪtlɪ] *adv* avec beaucoup d'ornements.

ornery ['ɔːnərɪ] *adj Am inf* désagréable.

ornithologist [ˌɔːnɪ'θɒlədʒɪst] *n* ornithologue *mf*, ornithologiste *mf*.

ornithology [ˌɔːnɪ'θɒlədʒɪ] *n* ornithologie *f*.

orphan ['ɔːfn] ◇ *n* orphelin *m*, -e *f*. ◇ *vt*: **to be ~ed** devenir orphelin(e).

orphanage ['ɔːfənɪdʒ] *n* orphelinat *m*.

orthodontist [ˌɔːθə'dɒntɪst] *n* orthodontiste *mf*.

orthodox ['ɔːθədɒks] *adj* -1. [conventional] orthodoxe. -2. RELIG [traditional] traditionaliste.

Orthodox Church *n*: **the ~** l'Église *f* orthodoxe.

orthodoxy ['ɔːθədɒksɪ] *n* orthodoxie *f*.

orthopaedic [ˌɔːθə'piːdɪk] *adj* orthopédique.

orthopaedics [ˌɔːθə'piːdɪks] *n* (*U*) orthopédie *f*.

orthopaedist [ˌɔːθə'piːdɪst] *n* orthopédiste *mf*.

orthopedic [ˌɔ:θə'pi:dɪk] *etc* = **orthopaedic** *etc.*

OS ◇ *n* (*abbr of* **Ordnance Survey**) ≃ IGN *m.* ◇ *abbr of* **outsize**.

O/S *abbr of* **out of stock**.

Oscar ['ɒskər] *n* CINEMA Oscar *m.*

oscillate ['ɒsɪleɪt] *vi lit* & *fig* osciller.

oscilloscope [ɒ'sɪləskəup] *n* oscilloscope *m.*

OSD (*abbr of* **optical scanning device**) *n* lecteur optique.

OSHA (*abbr of* **Occupational Safety and Health Administration**) *n* direction de la sécurité et de l'hygiène au travail aux États-Unis.

Oslo ['ɒzləu] *n* Oslo.

osmosis [ɒz'məusɪs] *n* osmose *f.*

osprey ['ɒsprɪ] (*pl* **-s**) *n* balbuzard *m.*

Ostend [ɒ'stend] *n* Ostende.

ostensible [ɒ'stensəbl] *adj* prétendu(e).

ostensibly [ɒ'stensəblɪ] *adv* en apparence, soi-disant.

ostentation [ˌɒstən'teɪʃn] *n* ostentation *f.*

ostentatious [ˌɒstən'teɪʃəs] *adj* ostentatoire.

osteoarthritis [ˌɒstɪəuɑ:'θraɪtɪs] *n* (U) ostéoarthrose *f.*

osteopath ['ɒstɪəpæθ] *n* ostéopathe *mf.*

osteopathy [ˌɒstɪ'ɒpəθɪ] *n* ostéopathie *f.*

ostracize, -ise ['ɒstrəsaɪz] *vt* frapper d'ostracisme, mettre au ban.

ostrich ['ɒstrɪtʃ] *n* autruche *f.*

OT *n* **-1.** (*abbr of* **Old Testament**) AT *m.* **-2.** *abbr of* **occupational therapy**.

OTC (*abbr of* **Officer Training Corps**) *n* section de formation des officiers en Grande-Bretagne.

other ['ʌðər] ◇ *adj* autre; **the ~ one** l'autre; **the ~ day/week** l'autre jour/semaine. ◇ *adv*: **there was nothing to do ~ than confess** il ne pouvait faire autrement que d'avouer; **~ than John** John à part. ◇ *pron*: **~s** d'autres; **the ~** l'autre; **the ~s** les autres; **one after the ~** l'un après l'autre (l'une après l'autre); **one or ~ of you** l'un (l'une) de vous deux; **none ~ than** nul (nulle) autre que.

◆ **something or other** *pron* quelque chose, je ne sais quoi.

◆ **somehow or other** *adv* d'une manière ou d'une autre.

otherwise ['ʌðəwaɪz] ◇ *adv* autrement; **or ~** [or not] ou non. ◇ *conj* sinon.

other world *n*: **the ~** l'au-delà *m.*

otherworldly [ˌʌðə'wɜ:ldlɪ] *adj* détaché(e) des biens de ce monde.

OTT (*abbr of* **over the top**) *adj Br inf*: **it's a bit ~** c'est un peu trop.

Ottawa ['ɒtəwə] *n* Ottawa.

otter ['ɒtər] *n* loutre *f.*

OU *abbr of* **Open University**.

ouch [autʃ] *excl* aïe!, ouïe!

ought [ɔ:t] *aux vb* **-1.** [sensibly]: **I really ~ to go** il faut absolument que je m'en aille; **you ~ to see a doctor** tu devrais aller chez le docteur. **-2.** [morally]: **you ~ not to have done that** tu n'aurais pas dû faire cela; **you ~ to look after your children better** tu devrais t'occuper un peu mieux de tes enfants. **-3.** [expressing probability]: **she ~ to pass her exam** elle devrait réussir à son examen.

oughtn't [ɔ:tnt] = **ought not**.

Ouija board® ['wi:dʒə-] *n* oui-ja *m.*

ounce [auns] *n* = 28,35g, once *f.*

our ['auər] *poss adj* notre, nos (*pl*); **~ money/house** notre argent/maison; **~ children** nos enfants; **it wasn't OUR fault** ce n'était pas de notre faute à nous.

ours ['auəz] *poss pron* le nôtre (la nôtre), les nôtres (*pl*); **that money is ~** cet argent est à nous OR est le nôtre; **it wasn't their fault, it was OURS** ce n'était pas de leur faute, c'était de notre faute à nous OR de la nôtre; **a friend of ~** un ami à nous, un de nos amis.

ourselves [auə'selvz] *pron pl* **-1.** (*reflexive*) nous. **-2.** (*for emphasis*) nous-mêmes; **we did it by ~** nous l'avons fait tous seuls.

oust [aust] *vt*: **to ~ sb (from)** évincer qqn (de).

ouster ['austər] *n Am* [from country] expulsion *f*; [from office] renvoi *m.*

out [aut] *adv* **-1.** [not inside, out of doors] dehors; **we all got ~** [of car] nous sommes tous sortis; **I'm going ~ for a walk** je sors me promener; **to run ~** sortir en courant; **~ here** ici; **~ there** là-bas; **~ you go!** sors!, file! **-2.** [away from home, office, published] sorti(e); **John's ~ at the moment** John est sorti, John n'est pas là en ce moment; **don't stay ~ too late** ne rentre pas trop tard; **an afternoon ~** une sortie l'après-midi; **let's have an evening ~** et si on sortait ce soir? **-3.** [extinguished] éteint(e); **the lights went ~** les lumières se sont éteintes. **-4.** [of tides]: **the tide is ~** la marée est basse. **-5.** [out of fashion] démodé(e), passé(e) de mode. **-6.** [in flower] en fleur; **the crocuses are ~** les crocus sont sortis. **-7.** [visible - moon] levé(e); **the sun is ~** il fait du soleil; **the stars are ~** les étoiles brillent. **-8.** *inf* [on strike] en grève. **-9.** [not possible]:

sorry, that's ~ désolé, cela ne va pas OR n'est pas possible. **-10.** [determined]: **to be ~ to do sthg** être résolu(e) OR décidé(e) à faire qqch.

◆ **out of** *prep* **-1.** [outside] en dehors de; **to go ~ of the room** sortir de la pièce; **to be ~ of the country** être à l'étranger. **-2.** [indicating cause] par; **~ of spite/love/boredom** par dépit/amour/ennui. **-3.** [indicating origin, source] de, dans; **a page ~ of a book** une page d'un livre; **to drink ~ of a glass** boire dans un verre; **to get information ~ of sb** arracher OR soutirer des renseignements à qqn; **it's made ~ of plastic** c'est en plastique; **we can pay for it ~ of petty cash** on peut le payer avec l'argent des dépenses courantes. **-4.** [without] sans; **~ of petrol/money** à court d'essence/d'argent; **we're ~ of sugar** nous n'avons plus de sucre. **-5.** [sheltered from] à l'abri de; **we're ~ of the wind here** nous sommes à l'abri du vent ici. **-6.** [to indicate proportion] sur; **one ~ of ten people** une personne sur dix; **ten ~ of ten** dix sur dix.

out-and-out *adj* [liar] fieffé(e); [disgrace] complet(ète).

outback ['autbæk] *n*: **the ~** l'intérieur *m* du pays (*en Australie*).

outbid [aut'bɪd] (*pt & pp* **outbid**, *cont* **-ding**) *vt*: **to ~ sb (for)** enchérir sur qqn (pour).

outboard (motor) ['autbɔːd-] *n* (moteur *m*) hors-bord *m*.

outbound ['autbaund] *adj* [train, flight] en partance.

outbreak ['autbreɪk] *n* [of war, crime] début *m*, déclenchement *m*; [of spots etc] éruption *f*.

outbuildings ['autbɪldɪŋz] *npl* dépendances *fpl*.

outburst ['autbɜːst] *n* explosion *f*.

outcast ['autkɑːst] *n* paria *m*.

outclass [aut'klɑːs] *vt* surclasser.

outcome ['autkʌm] *n* issue *f*, résultat *m*.

outcrop ['autkrɒp] *n* affleurement *m*.

outcry ['autkraɪ] (*pl* **-ies**) *n* tollé *m*.

outdated [aut'deɪtɪd] *adj* démodé(e), vieilli(e).

outdid [aut'dɪd] *pt* → **outdo**.

outdistance [aut'dɪstəns] *vt lit & fig* distancer.

outdo [aut'duː] (*pt* **-did**, *pp* **-done** [-'dʌn]) *vt* surpasser.

outdoor ['autdɔː] *adj* [life, swimming pool] en plein air; [activities] de plein air.

outdoors [aut'dɔːz] *adv* dehors.

outer ['autə] *adj* extérieur(e); **Outer London** la grande banlieue de Londres.

Outer Mongolia *n* Mongolie-Extérieure *f*.

outermost ['autəməust] *adj* [area] le plus éloigné (la plus éloignée); [layer] le plus (la plus) à l'extérieur.

outer space *n* cosmos *m*.

outfit ['autfɪt] *n* **-1.** [clothes] tenue *f*. **-2.** *inf* [organization] équipe *f*.

outfitters *n* Br *dated* [for clothes] magasin *m* spécialisé de confection pour hommes.

outflank [aut'flæŋk] *vt* MIL déborder, prendre à revers; *fig* déjouer les manœuvres de.

outgoing ['aut,gəuɪŋ] *adj* **-1.** [chairman etc] sortant(e); [mail] à expédier; [train] en partance. **-2.** [friendly, sociable] ouvert(e).

◆ **outgoings** *npl* Br dépenses *fpl*.

outgrow [aut'grəu] (*pt* **-grew**, *pp* **-grown**) *vt* **-1.** [clothes] devenir trop grand(e) pour. **-2.** [habit] se défaire de.

outhouse ['authaus, *pl* - hauzɪz] *n* appentis *m*.

outing ['autɪŋ] *n* **-1.** [trip] sortie *f*. **-2.** [of homosexuals] *campagne, menée par des militants homosexuels, destinée à dévoiler l'homosexualité d'une personne publique.*

outlandish [aut'lændɪʃ] *adj* bizarre.

outlast [aut'lɑːst] *vt* survivre à.

outlaw ['autlɔː] ◇ *n* hors-la-loi *m inv*. ◇ *vt* **-1.** [practice] proscrire. **-2.** [person] mettre hors la loi.

outlay ['autleɪ] *n* dépenses *fpl*.

outlet ['autlet] *n* **-1.** [for emotion] exutoire *m*. **-2.** [hole, pipe] sortie *f*. **-3.** [shop]: **retail ~** point *m* de vente. **-4.** Am ELEC prise *f* (de courant).

outline ['autlaɪn] ◇ *n* **-1.** [brief description] grandes lignes *fpl*; **in ~** en gros. **-2.** [silhouette] silhouette *f*. ◇ *vt* **-1.** [describe briefly] exposer les grandes lignes de. **-2.** [silhouette]: **to be ~d against** se dessiner OR se découper sur.

outlive [aut'lɪv] *vt* **-1.** [subj: person] survivre à. **-2.** [subj: idea, object]: **it's ~d its usefulness** cela a fait son temps.

outlook ['autluk] *n* **-1.** [disposition] attitude *f*, conception *f*. **-2.** [prospect] perspective *f*.

outlying ['aut,laɪɪŋ] *adj* [village] reculé(e); [suburbs] écarté(e).

outmanoeuvre Br, **outmaneuver** Am [aut'mənəuvə] *vt* [competitor, rival] l'emporter sur.

outmoded [aut'məudɪd] *adj* démodé(e).

outnumber [aut'nʌmbə] *vt* surpasser en nombre.

out-of-date *adj* [passport] périmé(e); [clothes] démodé(e); [belief] dépassé(e).

out of doors *adv* dehors.

out-of-the-way *adj* [village] perdu(e); [pub] peu fréquenté(e).

outpace [,aʊt'peɪs] *vt* **-1.** [subj: person] devancer. **-2.** *fig* [subj: technology] dépasser.

outpatient ['aʊt,peɪʃnt] *n* malade *mf* en consultation externe.

outplay [,aʊt'pleɪ] *vt* SPORT dominer.

outpost ['aʊtpəʊst] *n* avant-poste *m*.

outpouring [,aʊt'pɔːrɪŋ] *n literary* [of emotion] effusion *f*.

output ['aʊtpʊt] ◇ *n* **-1.** [production] production *f*. **-2.** COMPUT sortie *f*. ◇ *vt* COMPUT sortir.

outrage ['aʊtreɪdʒ] ◇ *n* **-1.** [emotion] indignation *f*. **-2.** [act] atrocité *f*. ◇ *vt* outrager.

outraged ['aʊtreɪdʒd] *adj* outré(e).

outrageous [aʊt'reɪdʒəs] *adj* **-1.** [offensive, shocking] scandaleux(euse), monstrueux(euse). **-2.** [very unusual] choquant(e).

outran [,aʊt'ræn] *pt* → outrun.

outrank [aʊt'ræŋk] *vt* être le supérieur de; MIL avoir un grade supérieur à.

outrider ['aʊt,raɪdər] *n* [on motorcycle] motocycliste *m* d'escorte.

outright [*adj* 'aʊtraɪt, *adv* ,aʊt'raɪt] ◇ *adj* absolu(e), total(e). ◇ *adv* **-1.** [deny] carrément, franchement. **-2.** [win, fail] complètement, totalement; **to be killed** ~ être tué sur le coup.

outrun [,aʊt'rʌn] (*pt* **-ran**, *pp* **-run**, *cont* **-ning**) *vt* distancer.

outsell [,aʊt'sel] (*pt* & *pp* **-sold**) *vt* dépasser les ventes de.

outset ['aʊtset] *n*: **at the** ~ au commencement, au début; **from the** ~ depuis le commencement OR début.

outshine [,aʊt'ʃaɪn] (*pt* & *pp* **-shone** [-'ʃɒn]) *vt fig* éclipser, surpasser.

outside [*adv* ,aʊt'saɪd, *adj, prep* & *n* 'aʊtsaɪd] ◇ *adj* **-1.** [gen] extérieur(e); **an** ~ **opinion** une opinion indépendante. **-2.** [unlikely - chance, possibility] faible. ◇ *adv* à l'extérieur; **to go/run/look** ~ aller/courir/regarder dehors. ◇ *prep* **-1.** [not inside] à l'extérieur de, en dehors de. **-2.** [beyond] ~ **office hours** en dehors des heures de bureau. ◇ *n* extérieur *m*; **at the** ~ *fig* au plus, au maximum.
◆ **outside of** *prep Am* [apart from] à part.

outside broadcast *n Br* RADIO & TV émission *f* réalisée à l'extérieur.

outside lane *n* AUT [in UK] voie *f* de droite; [in Europe, US] voie *f* de gauche.

outside line *n* TELEC ligne *f* extérieure.

outsider [,aʊt'saɪdər] *n* **-1.** [in race] outsider *m*. **-2.** [from society] étranger *m*, -ère *f*.

outsize ['aʊtsaɪz] *adj* **-1.** [bigger than usual] énorme, colossal(e). **-2.** [clothes] grande taille (*inv*).

outsized ['aʊtsaɪzd] *adj* énorme, colossal(e).

outskirts ['aʊtskɜːts] *npl*: **the** ~ la banlieue.

outsmart [,aʊt'smɑːt] *vt* être plus malin(igne) que.

outsold [,aʊt'səʊld] *pt* & *pp* → outsell.

outspoken [,aʊt'spəʊkn] *adj* franc (franche).

outspread [,aʊt'spred] *adj* [arms, legs] écarté(e); [wings, newspaper] déployé(e).

outstanding [,aʊt'stændɪŋ] *adj* **-1.** [excellent] exceptionnel(elle), remarquable. **-2.** [example] marquant(e). **-3.** [not paid] impayé(e). **-4.** [unfinished - work, problem] en suspens.

outstay [,aʊt'steɪ] *vt*: **I don't want to** ~ **my welcome** je ne veux pas abuser de votre hospitalité.

outstretched [,aʊt'stretʃt] *adj* [arms, hands] tendu(e); [wings] déployé(e).

outstrip [,aʊt'strɪp] (*pt* & *pp* **-ped**, *cont* **-ping**) *vt* devancer.

out-take *n* CINEMA & TV prise *f* ratée.

out-tray *n* corbeille *f* pour le courrier à expédier.

outvote [,aʊt'vəʊt] *vt*: **to be** ~**d** ne pas obtenir la majorité.

outward ['aʊtwəd] ◇ *adj* **-1.** [going away]: ~ **journey** aller *m*. **-2.** [apparent, visible] extérieur(e). ◇ *adv Am* = outwards.

outwardly ['aʊtwədlɪ] *adv* [apparently] en apparence.

outwards *Br* ['aʊtwədz], **outward** *Am adv* vers l'extérieur.

outweigh [,aʊt'weɪ] *vt fig* primer sur.

outwit [,aʊt'wɪt] (*pt* & *pp* **-ted**, *cont* **-ting**) *vt* se montrer plus malin(igne) que.

outworker ['aʊt,wɜːkər] *n* travailleur *m*, -euse *f* à domicile.

oval ['əʊvl] ◇ *adj* ovale. ◇ *n* ovale *m*.

Oval Office *n*: **the** ~ *bureau du président des États-Unis à la Maison-Blanche*.

ovarian [əʊ'veərɪən] *adj* ovarien(ienne).

ovary ['əʊvərɪ] (*pl* **-ies**) *n* ovaire *m*.

ovation [əʊ'veɪʃn] *n* ovation *f*; **the audience gave her a standing** ~ le public l'a ovationnée.

oven ['ʌvn] *n* [for cooking] four *m*.

oven glove *n* gant *m* de cuisine.

ovenproof ['ʌvnpruːf] *adj* qui va au four.

oven-ready *adj* prêt(e) à cuire.

ovenware ['ʌvnweəʳ] *n* (U) plats *mpl* qui vont au four.

over ['əuvəʳ] ◇ *prep* **-1.** [above] au-dessus de. **-2.** [on top of] sur. **-3.** [on other side of] de l'autre côté de; **they live ~ the road** ils habitent en face. **-4.** [to other side of] par-dessus; **to go ~ the border** franchir la frontière. **-5.** [more than] plus de; **~ and above** en plus de. **-6.** [senior to]: **he's ~ me at work** il occupe un poste plus élevé que le mien. **-7.** [concerning] à propos de, au sujet de. **-8.** [during] pendant.
◇ *adv* **-1.** [distance away]: **~ here** ici; **~ there** là-bas. **-2.** [across]: **they flew ~ to America** ils se sont envolés pour les États-Unis; **we invited them ~** nous les avons invités chez nous. **-3.** [to the ground]: **to lean ~** se pencher; **she pushed the pile of books ~** elle a renversé la pile de livres. **-4.** [more] plus. **-5.** [remaining]: **there's nothing (left) ~** il ne reste rien. **-6.** RADIO: **~ and out!** à vous! **-7.** [involving repetitions]: **(all) ~ again** (tout) au début; **~ and ~ again** à maintes reprises, maintes fois.
◇ *adj* [finished] fini(e), terminé(e).
◇ *n* over *m*.
◆ **all over** ◇ *prep* **-1.** [covering]: **the child had chocolate all ~ her face** l'enfant avait du chocolat sur toute la figure. **-2.** [throughout] partout, dans tout; **all ~ the world** dans le monde entier. ◇ *adv* **-1.** [everywhere] partout. **-2.** [finished] fini(e).

over- ['əuvəʳ] *prefix* sur-.

overabundance [,əuvərə'bʌndəns] *n* surabondance *f*.

overact [,əuvər'ækt] *vi pej* THEATRE en faire trop.

overactive [,əuvər'æktɪv] *adj* trop actif(ive).

overall [*adj & n* 'əuvərɔːl, *adv* ,əuvər'ɔːl] ◇ *adj* [general] d'ensemble. ◇ *adv* en général. ◇ *n* **-1.** [gen] tablier *m*. **-2.** *Am* [for work] bleu *m* de travail.
◆ **overalls** *npl* **-1.** [for work] bleu *m* de travail. **-2.** *Am* [dungarees] salopette *f*.

overambitious [,əuvəræm'bɪʃəs] *adj* trop ambitieux(ieuse).

overanxious [,əuvər'æŋkʃəs] *adj* trop inquiet(iète), trop anxieux(ieuse).

overarm ['əuvərɑːm] *adj & adv* par en dessus.

overate [,əuvər'et] *pt* → overeat.

overawe [,əuvər'ɔː] *vt* impressionner.

overbalance [,əuvə'bæləns] *vi* basculer.

overbearing [,əuvə'beərɪŋ] *adj* autoritaire.

overblown [,əuvə'bləun] *adj pej* exagéré(e).

overboard ['əuvəbɔːd] *adv*: **to fall ~** tomber par-dessus bord; **to go ~** *inf fig* en faire trop; **to go ~ about** *inf fig* s'enthousiasmer pour.

overbook [,əuvə'buk] *vi* surréserver.

overburden [,əuvə'bɜːdn] *vt*: **to be ~ed with sthg** être surchargé(e) de qqch.

overcame [,əuvə'keɪm] *pt* → overcome.

overcapitalize, -ise [,əuvə'kæpɪtəlaɪz] FIN *vt & vi* surcapitaliser.

overcast [,əuvə'kɑːst] *adj* couvert(e).

overcharge [,əuvə'tʃɑːdʒ] ◇ *vt*: **to ~ sb (for sthg)** faire payer (qqch) trop cher à qqn. ◇ *vi*: **to ~ (for sthg)** demander un prix excessif (pour qqch).

overcoat ['əuvəkəut] *n* pardessus *m*.

overcome [,əuvə'kʌm] (*pt* **-came**, *pp* **-come**) *vt* **-1.** [fears, difficulties] surmonter. **-2.** [overwhelm]: **to be ~ (by** OR **with)** [emotion] être submergé(e) (de); [grief] être accablé(e) (de).

overcompensate [,əuvə'kɒmpənseɪt] *vi*: **to ~ (for sthg)** surcompenser (qqch).

overconfident [,əuvə'kɒnfɪdənt] *adj* [too certain] trop sûr(e) de soi; [arrogant] suffisant(e).

overcook [,əuvə'kuk] *vt* faire trop cuire.

overcrowded [,əuvə'kraudɪd] *adj* bondé(e).

overcrowding [,əuvə'kraudɪŋ] *n* surpeuplement *m*.

overdeveloped [,əuvə'devələpt] *adj* PHOT & *fig* trop développé(e).

overdo [,əuvə'duː] (*pt* **-did** [-'dɪd], *pp* **-done**) *vt* **-1.** [exaggerate] exagérer. **-2.** [do too much] trop faire; **to ~ it** se surmener. **-3.** [overcook] trop cuire.

overdone [,əuvə'dʌn] ◇ *pp* → overdo. ◇ *adj* [food] trop cuit(e).

overdose ◇ *n* overdose *f*. ◇ *vi*: **to ~ on** prendre une dose excessive de.

overdraft ['əuvədrɑːft] *n* découvert *m*.

overdrawn [,əuvə'drɔːn] *adj* à découvert.

overdress [,əuvə'dres] *vi* être trop bien habillé(e) (pour l'occasion).

overdrive ['əuvədraɪv] *n fig*: **to go into ~** mettre les bouchées doubles.

overdue [,əuvə'djuː] *adj* **-1.** [late]: **~ (for)** en retard (pour). **-2.** [change, reform]: **(long) ~** attendu(e) (depuis longtemps). **-3.** [unpaid] arriéré(e), impayé(e).

overeager [,əuvər'iːgəʳ] *adj* trop zélé(e).

overeat [,əuvər'iːt] (*pt* **-ate**, *pp* **-eaten**) *vi* trop manger.

overemphasize, -ise [,əuvər'emfəsaɪz] *vt* donner trop d'importance à.

overenthusiastic ['əʊvərɪn,θjuːzɪ'æstɪk] *adj* trop enthousiaste.

overestimate [,əʊvər'estɪmeɪt] *vt* surestimer.

overexcited [,əʊvər'ɪksaɪtɪd] *adj* surexcité(e).

overexpose [,əʊvərɪk'spəʊz] *vt* PHOT surexposer.

overfeed [,əʊvə'fiːd] (*pt* & *pp* **-fed**) *vt* suralimenter.

overfill [,əʊvə'fɪl] *vt* trop remplir.

overflow [*vb* ,əʊvə'fləʊ, *n* 'əʊvəfləʊ] ◇ *vi* **-1.** [gen] déborder. **-2.** [streets, box]: **to be ~ing (with)** regorger (de); **full to ~ing** plein à craquer. ◇ *vt* déborder de. ◇ *n* [pipe, hole] trop-plein *m*.

overgrown [,əʊvə'grəʊn] *adj* [garden] envahi(e) par les mauvaises herbes.

overhang [*n* 'əʊvəhæŋ, *vb* ,əʊvə'hæŋ] (*pt* & *pp* **-hung**) ◇ *n* surplomb *m*. ◇ *vt* surplomber. ◇ *vi* être en surplomb.

overhaul [*n* 'əʊvəhɔːl, *vb* ,əʊvə'hɔːl] ◇ *n* **-1.** [of car, machine] révision *f*. **-2.** *fig* [of system] refonte *f*, remaniement *m*. ◇ *vt* **-1.** [car, machine] réviser. **-2.** *fig* [system] refondre, remanier.

overhead [*adv* ,əʊvə'hed, *adj* & *n* 'əʊvəhed] ◇ *adj* aérien(ienne). ◇ *adv* au-dessus. ◇ *n* *Am* (U) frais *mpl* généraux.

◆ **overheads** *npl Br* frais *mpl* généraux.

overhear [,əʊvə'hɪər] (*pt* & *pp* **-heard** [-'hɜːd]) *vt* entendre par hasard.

overheat [,əʊvə'hiːt] ◇ *vt* surchauffer. ◇ *vi* [engine] chauffer.

overhung [,əʊvə'hʌŋ] *pt* & *pp* → **overhang**.

overindulge [,əʊvərɪn'dʌldʒ] ◇ *vi* trop gâter. ◇ *vi*: **to ~ (in)** abuser (de).

overjoyed [,əʊvə'dʒɔɪd] *adj*: **~ (at)** transporté(e) de joie (à).

overkill ['əʊvəkɪl] *n* [excess]: **that would be ~** ce serait de trop.

overladen [,əʊvə'leɪdn] ◇ *pp* → **overload**. ◇ *adj* surchargé(e).

overlaid [,əʊvə'leɪd] *pt* & *pp* → **overlay**.

overland ['əʊvəlænd] *adj* & *adv* par voie de terre.

overlap [*n* 'əʊvəlæp, *vb* ,əʊvə'læp] (*pt* & *pp* **-ped**, *cont* **-ping**) ◇ *n lit* & *fig* chevauchement *m*. ◇ *vt* [edge] dépasser de. ◇ *vi lit* & *fig* se chevaucher.

overlay [,əʊvə'leɪ] (*pt* & *pp* **-laid**) *vt*: **to be overlaid with** être recouvert(e) de.

overleaf [,əʊvə'liːf] *adv* au verso, au dos.

overload [,əʊvə'ləʊd] (*pp* **-loaded** OR **-laden**) *vt* surcharger.

overlong [,əʊvə'lɒŋ] ◇ *adj* long (trop longue). ◇ *adv* trop longtemps.

overlook [,əʊvə'lʊk] *vt* **-1.** [subj: building, room] donner sur. **-2.** [disregard, miss] oublier, négliger. **-3.** [excuse] passer sur, fermer les yeux sur.

overlord ['əʊvəlɔːd] *n* suzerain *m*.

overly ['əʊvəlɪ] *adv* trop.

overmanning [,əʊvə'mænɪŋ] *n* (U) sureffectifs *mpl*.

overnight [*adj* 'əʊvənaɪt, *adv* ,əʊvə'naɪt] ◇ *adj* **-1.** [journey, parking] de nuit; [stay] d'une nuit. **-2.** *fig* [sudden]: **~ success** succès *m* immédiat. ◇ *adv* **-1.** [stay, leave] la nuit. **-2.** [suddenly] du jour au lendemain.

overpaid [,əʊvə'peɪd] ◇ *pt* & *pp* → **overpay**. ◇ *adj* trop payé(e), surpayé(e).

overpass ['əʊvəpɑːs] *n Am* toboggan® *m*.

overpay [,əʊvə'peɪ] (*pt* & *pp* **-paid**) *vt* trop payer.

overplay [,əʊvə'pleɪ] *vt* [exaggerate] exagérer.

overpopulated [,əʊvə'pɒpjʊleɪtɪd] *adj* surpeuplé(e).

overpower [,əʊvə'paʊər] *vt* **-1.** [in fight] vaincre. **-2.** *fig* [overwhelm] accabler, terrasser.

overpowering [,əʊvə'paʊərɪŋ] *adj* [desire] irrésistible; [smell] entêtant(e).

overpriced [,əʊvə'praɪsd] *adj pej* excessivement cher (chère).

overproduction [,əʊvəprə'dʌkʃn] *n* surproduction *f*.

overprotective [,əʊvəprə'tektɪv] *adj* protecteur(trice) à l'excès.

overran [,əʊvə'ræn] *pt* → **overrun**.

overrated [,əʊvə'reɪtɪd] *adj* surfait(e).

overreach [,əʊvə'riːtʃ] *vt*: **to ~ o.s.** trop entreprendre.

overreact [,əʊvərɪ'ækt] *vi*: **to ~ (to sthg)** réagir (à qqch) de façon excessive.

override [,əʊvə'raɪd] (*pt* **-rode**, *pp* **-ridden**) *vt* **-1.** [be more important than] l'emporter sur, prévaloir. **-2.** [overrule - decision] annuler.

overriding [,əʊvə'raɪdɪŋ] *adj* [need, importance] primordial(e).

overripe [,əʊvə'raɪp] *adj* trop mûr(e).

overrode [,əʊvə'rəʊd] *pt* → **override**.

overrule [,əʊvə'ruːl] *vt* [person] prévaloir contre; [decision] annuler; [objection] rejeter.

overrun (*pt* **-ran**, *pp* **-run**, *cont* **-running**) [,əʊvə'rʌn] ◇ *vt* **-1.** MIL [occupy] occuper. **-2.** *fig* [cover, fill]: **to be ~ with** [weeds] être envahi(e) de; [rats] être infesté(e) de. ◇ *vi* dépasser (le temps alloué).

oversaw [ˌəuvə'sɔː] *pt* → **oversee**.

overseas [*adj* 'əuvəsiːz, *adv* ˌəuvə'siːz] ◇ *adj* [sales, company] à l'étranger; [market] extérieur(e); [visitor, student] étranger(ère); ~ **aid** aide *f* aux pays étrangers. ◇ *adv* à l'étranger.

oversee [ˌəuvə'siː] (*pt* **-saw**, *pp* **-seen** [-'siːn]) *vt* surveiller.

overseer ['əuvəˌsiːər] *n* contremaître *m*.

overshadow [ˌəuvə'ʃædəu] *vt* [subj: building, tree] dominer; *fig* éclipser.

overshoot [ˌəuvə'ʃuːt] (*pt* & *pp* **-shot**) *vt* dépasser, rater.

oversight ['əuvəsait] *n* oubli *m*; **through ~** par mégarde.

oversimplification ['əuvəˌsimplifi'keiʃn] *n* simplification *f* excessive.

oversimplify [ˌəuvə'simplifai] (*pt* & *pp* **-ied**) *vt* & *vi* trop simplifier.

oversleep [ˌəuvə'sliːp] (*pt* & *pp* **-slept** [-'slept]) *vi* ne pas se réveiller à temps.

overspend [ˌəuvə'spend] (*pt* & *pp* **-spent** [-'spent]) *vi* trop dépenser.

overspill ['əuvəspil] *n* [of population] excédent *m*.

overstaffed [ˌəuvə'stɑːft] *adj*: **to be ~** avoir un excédent de personnel.

overstate [ˌəuvə'steit] *vt* exagérer.

overstay [ˌəuvə'stei] *vt*: **I don't want to ~ my welcome** je ne veux pas abuser de votre hospitalité.

overstep [ˌəuvə'step] (*pt* & *pp* **-ped**, *cont* **-ping**) *vt* dépasser; **to ~ the mark** dépasser la mesure.

overstock [ˌəuvə'stɒk] *vt* stocker à l'excès.

overstrike ['əuvəstraik] COMPUT ◇ *n* surimpression *f*. ◇ *vt* surimprimer.

oversubscribed [ˌəuvəsʌb'skraibd] *adj*: **the share offer was ~** la demande d'achats a dépassé le nombre de titres émis.

overt ['əuvɜːt] *adj* déclaré(e), non déguisé(e).

overtake [ˌəuvə'teik] (*pt* **-took**, *pp* **-taken** [-'teikn]) ◇ *vt* **-1.** AUT doubler, dépasser. **-2.** [subj: misfortune, emotion] frapper. ◇ *vi* AUT doubler.

overtaking *n* dépassement *m*; "**no ~**" «défense de doubler».

overthrow [*n* 'əuvəθrəu, *vb* ˌəuvə'θrəu] (*pt* **-threw** [-'θruː], *pp* **-thrown** [-'θrəun]) ◇ *n* [of government] coup *m* d'État. ◇ *vt* **-1.** [government] renverser. **-2.** [idea] rejeter, écarter.

overtime ['əuvətaim] ◇ *n* (*U*) **-1.** [extra work] heures *fpl* supplémentaires. **-2.** Am

SPORT prolongations *fpl*. ◇ *adv*: **to work ~** faire des heures supplémentaires.

overtly ['əuvɜːtli] *adv* ouvertement.

overtones ['əuvətəunz] *npl* notes *fpl*, accents *mpl*.

overtook [ˌəuvə'tuk] *pt* → **overtake**.

overture ['əuvəˌtjuər] *n* MUS ouverture *f*.

◆ **overtures** *npl*: **to make ~s to sb** faire des ouvertures à qqn.

overturn [ˌəuvə'tɜːn] ◇ *vt* **-1.** [gen] renverser. **-2.** [decision] annuler. ◇ *vi* [vehicle] se renverser; [boat] chavirer.

overuse [ˌəuvə'juːz] *vt* abuser de.

overview ['əuvəvjuː] *n* vue *f* d'ensemble.

overweening [ˌəuvə'wiːniŋ] *adj* démesuré(e).

overweight [ˌəuvə'weit] *adj* trop gros (grosse).

overwhelm [ˌəuvə'welm] *vt* **-1.** [subj: grief, despair] accabler; **to be ~ed with joy** être au comble de la joie. **-2.** MIL [gain control of] écraser.

overwhelming [ˌəuvə'welmiŋ] *adj* **-1.** [overpowering] irrésistible, irrépressible. **-2.** [defeat, majority] écrasant(e).

overwhelmingly [ˌəuvə'welmiŋli] *adv* **-1.** [generous, happy] immensément. **-2.** [in large numbers] en masse.

overwork [ˌəuvə'wɜːk] ◇ *n* surmenage *m*. ◇ *vt* **-1.** [person, staff] surmener. **-2.** *fig* [idea] exploiter. ◇ *vi* se surmener.

overwrought [ˌəuvə'rɔːt] *adj* excédé(e) à bout.

ovulate ['ɒvjuleit] *vi* ovuler.

ovulation [ˌɒvju'leiʃn] *n* ovulation *f*.

ow [au] *excl* aïe!

owe [əu] *vt*: **to ~ sthg to sb, to ~ sb sthg** devoir qqch à qqn.

owing ['əuiŋ] *adj* dû(e).

◆ **owing to** *prep* à cause de, en raison de.

owl [aul] *n* hibou *m*.

own [əun] ◇ *adj* propre; **my ~ car** ma propre voiture; **she has her ~ style** elle a son style à elle. ◇ *pron*: **I've got my ~** j'ai le mien; **he has a house of his ~** il a une maison à lui, il a sa propre maison; **on one's ~** tout seul (toute seule); **to get one's ~ back** *inf* prendre sa revanche. ◇ *vt* posséder.

◆ **own up** *vi*: **to ~ up (to sthg)** avouer OR confesser (qqch).

own brand *n* COMM produit qui porte la marque de la maison.

owner ['əunər] *n* propriétaire *mf*.

owner-occupier *n* occupant *m* propriétaire.

ownership ['əʊnəʃɪp] *n* propriété *f*.

own goal *n* -1. FTBL: **to score an ~** marquer contre son camp. -2. *Br fig* [foolish mistake] gaffe *f*.

ox [ɒks] (*pl* **oxen**) *n* bœuf *m*.

Oxbridge ['ɒksbrɪdʒ] *n* désignation collective des universités d'Oxford et de Cambridge.

oxen ['ɒksn] *pl* → **ox**.

Oxfam ['ɒksfæm] *n* association humanitaire contre la faim.

oxide ['ɒksaɪd] *n* oxyde *m*.

oxidize, -ise ['ɒksɪdaɪz] *vi* s'oxyder.

Oxon (*abbr of* **Oxfordshire**) comté anglais.

Oxon. (*abbr of* **Oxoniensis**) de l'université d'Oxford.

oxtail soup ['ɒksteɪl] *n* soupe *f* à la queue de bœuf.

ox tongue *n* langue *f* de bœuf.

oxyacetylene [,ɒksɪə'setɪliːn] ◇ *n* mélange *m* d'oxygène et d'acétylène. ◇ *comp* [torch] oxyacétylénique.

oxygen ['ɒksɪdʒən] *n* oxygène *m*.

oxygenate [ɒk'sɪdʒəneɪt] *vt* oxygéner.

oxygen mask *n* masque *m* à oxygène.

oxygen tent *n* tente *f* à oxygène.

oyster ['ɔɪstə'] *n* huître *f*.

oz. *abbr of* **ounce**.

ozone ['əʊzəʊn] *n* ozone *m*.

ozone-friendly *adj* qui préserve la couche d'ozone.

ozone layer *n* couche *f* d'ozone.

P

p¹ (*pl* **p's** OR **ps**), **P** (*pl* **P's** OR **Ps**) [piː] p *m inv*, P *m inv*.

◆ **P** -1. *abbr of* **president**. -2. (*abbr of* **prince**) Pce.

p² -1. (*abbr of* **page**) p. -2. *abbr of* **penny**, **pence**.

pa [pɑː] *n inf* papa *m*.

p.a. (*abbr of* **per annum**) p.a.

PA ◇ *n* -1. *Br abbr of* **personal assistant**. -2. (*abbr of* **public address system**) sono *f*. -3. (*abbr of* **Press Association**) agence de presse britannique. ◇ *abbr of* **Pennsylvania**.

PABX (*abbr of* **private automatic branch exchange**) *n* autocommutateur *m* privé.

PAC (*abbr of* **political action committee**) *n* comité américain de promotion du recours à l'action politique.

pace [peɪs] ◇ *n* -1. [speed, rate] vitesse *f*, allure *f*; **at one's own ~** à son propre rythme; **to keep ~ (with sb)** marcher à la même allure (que qqn); **to keep ~ (with sthg)** se maintenir au même niveau (que qqch). -2. [step] pas *m*. ◇ *vt* [room etc] arpenter. ◇ *vi*: **to ~ (up and down)** faire les cent pas.

pacemaker ['peɪs,meɪkə'] *n* -1. MED stimulateur *m* cardiaque, pacemaker *m*. -2. SPORT meneur *m*, -euse *f*.

pacesetter ['peɪs,setə'] *n Am* SPORT meneur *m*, -euse *f*.

pachyderm ['pækɪdɜːm] *n* pachyderme *m*.

Pacific [pə'sɪfɪk] ◇ *adj* du Pacifique. ◇ *n*: **the ~ (Ocean)** l'océan *m* Pacifique, le Pacifique.

pacification [,pæsɪfɪ'keɪʃn] *n* -1. [of person, baby] apaisement *m*. -2. [of country] pacification *f*.

pacifier ['pæsɪfaɪə'] *n Am* [for child] tétine *f*, sucette *f*.

pacifism ['pæsɪfɪzm] *n* pacifisme *m*.

pacifist ['pæsɪfɪst] *n* pacifiste *mf*.

pacify ['pæsɪfaɪ] (*pt* & *pp* **-ied**) *vt* -1. [person, baby] apaiser. -2. [country] pacifier.

pack [pæk] ◇ *n* -1. [bag] sac *m*. -2. [packet] paquet *m*. -3. [of cards] jeu *m*. -4. [of dogs] meute *f*; [of wolves, thieves] bande *f*. -5. RUGBY pack *m*. ◇ *vt* -1. [clothes, belongings] emballer; **to ~ one's bags** faire ses bagages. -2. [fill] remplir; **to be ~ed into** être entassé dans. ◇ *vi* [for journey] faire ses bagages OR sa valise.

◆ **pack in** ◇ *vt sep Br inf* [stop] plaquer; **~ it in!** [stop annoying me] arrête!, ça suffit maintenant!; [shut up] la ferme! ◇ *vi* tomber en panne.

◆ **pack off** *vt sep inf* [send away] expédier.

◆ **pack up** ◇ *vt* [clothes, belongings] mettre dans une valise. ◇ *vi* -1. [for journey] faire sa valise. -2. *inf* [finish work] se casser. -3. *Br inf* [car, washing machine] tomber en panne.

package ['pækɪdʒ] ◇ *n* -1. [of books, goods] paquet *m*. -2. *fig* [of proposals etc] ensemble *m*, série *f*. -3. COMPUT progiciel *m*. ◇ *vt* [wrap up] conditionner.

package deal *n* contrat *m* global.

package holiday *n* vacances *fpl* organisées.

packager ['pækɪdʒəˈ] n -1. [person] emballeur m, -euse f. -2. COMM maison d'édition qui crée des livres sur commande pour d'autres maisons.

package tour n vacances fpl organisées.

packaging ['pækɪdʒɪŋ] n conditionnement m.

packed [pækt] adj: ~ **(with)** bourré(e) (de).

packed lunch n Br panier-repas m.

packed-out adj Br inf bourré(e).

packet ['pækɪt] n -1. [gen] paquet m. -2. Br inf [lot of money]: **their new car cost a ~** leur nouvelle voiture leur a coûté un paquet OR très cher.

packhorse ['pækhɔːs] n cheval m de charge.

pack ice n pack m.

packing ['pækɪŋ] n [material] emballage m.

packing case n caisse f d'emballage.

pact [pækt] n pacte m.

pad [pæd] (pt & pp **-ded**, cont **-ding**) ◇ n -1. [of cotton wool etc] morceau m; **shin ~** FTBL protège-tibia m; **shoulder ~s** épaulettes fpl. -2. [of paper] bloc m. -3. SPACE: **(launch) ~** pas m de tir. -4. [of cat, dog] coussin m. -5. inf [home] pénates mpl. ◇ vt [furniture, jacket] rembourrer; [wound] tamponner. ◇ vi [walk softly] marcher à pas feutrés.

♦ **pad out** vt sep fig [speech, letter] délayer.

padded ['pædɪd] adj rembourré(e).

padded cell n cellule f matelassée.

padding ['pædɪŋ] n -1. [material] rembourrage m. -2. fig [in speech, letter] délayage m.

paddle ['pædl] ◇ n -1. [for canoe etc] pagaie f. -2. [in sea]: **to have a ~** faire trempette. -3. [table-tennis bat] raquette f de ping-pong). ◇ vt pagayer. ◇ vi -1. [in canoe etc] avancer en pagayant. -2. [duck] barboter. -3. [in sea] faire trempette.

paddle boat, **paddle steamer** n bateau m à aubes.

paddling pool ['pædlɪŋ-] n Br -1. [in park etc] pataugeoire f. -2. [inflatable] piscine f gonflable.

paddock ['pædək] n -1. [small field] enclos m. -2. [at racecourse] paddock m.

paddy field ['pædɪ-] n rizière f.

paddy wagon ['pædɪ-] n Am [Black Maria] panier m à salade.

padlock ['pædlɒk] ◇ n cadenas m. ◇ vt cadenasser.

paederast ['pedəræst] = pederast.

paediatric [,piːdɪ'ætrɪk] = pediatric.

paediatrician [,piːdɪə'trɪʃn] = pediatrician.

paediatrics [,piːdɪ'ætrɪks] = pediatrics.

paedophile ['piːdəfaɪl] = pedophile.

paella [paɪ'elə] n paella f.

paeony = peony.

pagan ['peɪgən] ◇ adj païen(ïenne). ◇ n païen m, -ïenne f.

paganism ['peɪgənɪzm] n paganisme m.

page [peɪdʒ] ◇ n -1. [of book] page f. -2. [sheet of paper] feuille f. ◇ vt [in airport] appeler au micro.

pageant ['pædʒənt] n [show] spectacle m historique.

pageantry ['pædʒəntrɪ] n apparat m.

page boy n -1. Br [at wedding] garçon m d'honneur. -2. [hairstyle] coiffure f à la page.

pager ['peɪdʒəˈ] n récepteur m de poche.

pagination [,pædʒɪ'neɪʃn] n pagination f.

pagoda [pə'gəudə] n pagode f.

paid [peɪd] ◇ pt & pp → **pay**. ◇ adj [work, holiday, staff] rémunéré(e), payé(e); **badly/ well ~** mal/bien payé.

paid-up adj Br qui a payé sa cotisation.

pail [peɪl] n seau m.

pain [peɪn] ◇ n -1. [hurt] douleur f; **to be in ~** souffrir; **a ~ in the neck** inf un enquiquineur (une enquiquineuse), un casse-pieds m inv. -2. inf [annoyance]: **it's/he is such a ~** c'est/il est vraiment assommant. ◇ vt: **it ~s me (to do sthg)** je suis peiné (de faire qqch).

♦ **pains** npl [effort, care]: **to be at ~s to do sthg** vouloir absolument faire qqch; **to take ~s to do sthg** se donner beaucoup de mal OR peine pour faire qqch; **for one's ~s** pour sa peine.

pained [peɪnd] adj peiné(e).

painful ['peɪnfʊl] adj -1. [physically] douloureux(euse). -2. [emotionally] pénible.

painfully ['peɪnfʊlɪ] adv -1. [fall, hit] douloureusement. -2. [remember, feel] péniblement.

painkiller ['peɪn,kɪləˈ] n calmant m, analgésique m.

painless ['peɪnlɪs] adj -1. [without hurt] indolore, sans douleur. -2. fig [changeover] sans heurt.

painlessly ['peɪnlɪslɪ] adv sans douleur.

painstaking ['peɪnz,teɪkɪŋ] adj [worker] assidu(e); [detail, work] soigné(e).

painstakingly ['peɪnz,teɪkɪŋlɪ] adv assidûment, avec soin.

paint [peɪnt] ◇ n peinture f. ◇ vt -1. [gen] peindre. -2. [with make-up]: **to ~ one's nails** se vernir les ongles.

paintbox ['peɪntbɒks] n ART boîte f de couleurs.

paintbrush ['peɪntbrʌʃ] *n* pinceau *m*.

painted ['peɪntɪd] *adj* peint(e).

painter ['peɪntər] *n* peintre *m*.

painting ['peɪntɪŋ] *n* **-1.** (*U*) [gen] peinture *f*. **-2.** [picture] toile *f*, tableau *m*.

paint stripper *n* décapant *m*.

paintwork ['peɪntwɜːk] *n* (*U*) surfaces *fpl* peintes.

pair [peər] *n* **-1.** [of shoes, wings etc] paire *f*; **a ~ of trousers** un pantalon; **a ~ of compasses** un compas. **-2.** [couple] couple *m*.

◆ **pair off** ◇ *vt sep* mettre par paires OR deux. ◇ *vi* se mettre par paires OR deux par deux.

paisley (pattern) ['peɪzlɪ-] ◇ *n* (*U*) (motif *m*) cachemire *m*. ◇ *comp* cachemire.

pajamas [pə'dʒɑːməz] = **pyjamas.**

Paki ['pækɪ] *n Br v inf* terme raciste désignant un *Pakistanais*.

Pakistan [*Br* ˌpɑːkɪ'stɑːn, *Am* 'pækɪstæn] *n* Pakistan *m*; **in ~** au Pakistan.

Pakistani [*Br* ˌpɑːkɪ'stɑːnɪ, *Am* ˌpækɪ'stænɪ] ◇ *adj* pakistanais(e). ◇ *n* Pakistanais *m*, -e *f*.

pal [pæl] *n inf* **-1.** [friend] copain *m*, copine *f*. **-2.** [as term of address] mon vieux *m*.

PAL (*abbr of* **phase alternation line**) *n* PAL *m*.

palace ['pælɪs] *n* palais *m*.

palaeontology *Br*, **paleontology** *Am* [ˌpælɪɒn'tɒlədʒɪ] *n* paléontologie *f*.

palatable ['pælətəbl] *adj* **-1.** [food] agréable au goût. **-2.** *fig* [idea] acceptable, agréable.

palate ['pælət] *n* palais *m*.

palatial [pə'leɪʃl] *adj* pareil(eille) à un palais.

palaver [pə'lɑːvər] *n* (*U*) *inf* **-1.** [talk] palabres *fpl*. **-2.** [fuss] histoire *f*, affaire *f*.

pale [peɪl] ◇ *adj* pâle. ◇ *vi*: **to ~ into insignificance (beside)** n'être rien (à côté de).

pale ale *n Br* pale-ale *f*.

paleness ['peɪlnɪs] *n* pâleur *f*.

Palestine ['pæləˌstaɪn] *n* Palestine *f*.

Palestinian [ˌpælə'stɪnɪən] ◇ *adj* palestinien(ienne). ◇ *n* Palestinien *m*, -ienne *f*.

palette ['pælət] *n* palette *f*.

palette knife *n* ART couteau *m* à palette; CULIN spatule *f* (en métal).

palimony ['pælɪmənɪ] *n* pension alimentaire versée à un concubin.

palindrome ['pælɪndrəʊm] *n* palindrome *m*.

palings ['peɪlɪŋz] *npl* palissade *f*.

pall [pɔːl] ◇ *n* **-1.** [of smoke] voile *m*. **-2.** *Am* [coffin] cercueil *m*. ◇ *vi* perdre de son charme.

pallbearer ['pɔːlˌbeərər] *n* porteur *m* de cercueil.

pallet ['pælɪt] *n* palette *f*.

palliative ['pælɪətɪv] *n* palliatif *m*.

pallid ['pælɪd] *adj literary* pâle, blafard(e).

pallor ['pælər] *n literary* pâleur *f*.

palm [pɑːm] *n* **-1.** [tree] palmier *m*. **-2.** [of hand] paume *f*.

◆ **palm off** *vt sep inf*: **to ~ sthg off on sb** refiler qqch à qqn; **to ~ sb off with sthg** se débarrasser de qqn avec qqch; **to ~ sthg off as** faire passer qqch pour.

palmistry ['pɑːmɪstrɪ] *n* chiromancie *f*.

palm oil *n* huile *f* de palme.

Palm Sunday *n* dimanche *m* des Rameaux.

palm tree *n* palmier *m*.

palomino [ˌpælə'miːnəʊ] (*pl* **-s**) *n* cheval doré à crinière et queue blanches.

palpable ['pælpəbl] *adj* évident(e), manifeste.

palpably ['pælpəblɪ] *adv* de façon évidente, manifestement.

palpitate ['pælpɪteɪt] *vi*: **to ~ (with)** palpiter (de).

palpitations [ˌpælpɪ'teɪʃənz] *npl* palpitations *fpl*.

palsy ['pɔːlzɪ] *n* paralysie *f*.

paltry ['pɔːltrɪ] (*compar* **-ier**, *superl* **-iest**) *adj* dérisoire.

pampas ['pæmpəz] *n*: **the ~** la pampa.

pampas grass *n* herbe *f* de la pampa.

pamper ['pæmpər] *vt* choyer, dorloter.

pamphlet ['pæmflɪt] ◇ *n* brochure *f*. ◇ *vi* distribuer des brochures.

pamphleteer [ˌpæmflə'tɪər] *n* POL pamphlétaire *mf*.

pan [pæn] (*pt* & *pp* **-ned**, *cont* **-ning**) ◇ *n* **-1.** [gen] casserole *f*. **-2.** *Am* [for bread, cakes etc] moule *m*. ◇ *vt inf* [criticize] démolir. ◇ *vi* **-1.** [for gold] laver. **-2.** CINEMA faire un panoramique.

panacea [ˌpænə'sɪə] *n* panacée *f*.

panache [pə'næʃ] *n* panache *m*.

panama ['pænəmɑː] *n*: **~ (hat)** panama *m*.

Panama *n* Panama *m*; **in ~** au Panama.

Panama Canal *n*: **the ~** le canal de Panama.

Panama City *n* Panama.

Panamanian [ˌpænə'meɪnjən] ◇ *adj* panaméen(enne). ◇ *n* Panaméen *m*, -enne *f*.

pan-American *adj* panaméricain(e).

pancake ['pænkeɪk] *n* crêpe *f*.

Pancake Day *n Br* mardi gras *m*.

pancake roll *n* rouleau *m* de printemps.

Pancake Tuesday *n* mardi gras *m*.

pancreas ['pæŋkrɪəs] *n* pancréas *m*.

panda ['pændə] (*pl inv* OR **-s**) *n* panda *m*.

Panda car *n Br* voiture *f* de patrouille.

pandemonium [,pændɪ'məʊnjəm] *n* tohubohu *m inv*.

pander ['pændə'] *vi*: **to ~ to sb** se prêter aux exigences de qqn; **to ~ to sthg** se plier à qqch.

pane [peɪn] *n* vitre *f*, carreau *m*.

panel ['pænl] *n* **-1.** TV & RADIO invités *mpl*; [of experts] comité *m*. **-2.** [of wood] panneau *m*. **-3.** [of machine] tableau *m* de bord.

panel game *n Br* jeu télévisé où rivalisent des équipes d'invités célèbres.

panelling *Br*, **paneling** *Am* ['pænlɪŋ] *n* (*U*) lambris *m*.

panellist *Br*, **panelist** *Am* ['pænəlɪst] *n* invité *m*, -e *f*.

panel pin *n Br* clou *m* sans tête.

pang [pæŋ] *n* tiraillement *m*.

panic ['pænɪk] (*pt* & *pp* **-ked**, *cont* **-king**) ◇ *n* panique *f*. ◇ *vi* paniquer.

panicky ['pænɪkɪ] *adj* [person] paniqué(e); [feeling] de panique.

panic stations *n inf*: **it was ~** c'était la panique générale.

panic-stricken *adj* affolé(e), pris(e) de panique.

pannier ['pænɪə'] *n* [on horse] bât *m*; [on bicycle] sacoche *f*.

panoply ['pænəplɪ] *n* panoplie *f*.

panorama [,pænə'rɑːmə] *n* panorama *m*.

panoramic [,pænə'ræmɪk] *adj* panoramique.

pansy ['pænzɪ] (*pl* **-ies**) *n* **-1.** [flower] pensée *f*. **-2.** *inf pej* [man] tante *f*, tapette *f*.

pant [pænt] *vi* haleter.

panther ['pænθə'] (*pl inv* OR **-s**) *n* panthère *f*.

panties ['pæntɪz] *inf* culotte *f*.

pantihose ['pæntɪhəʊz] = **panty hose**.

panto ['pæntəʊ] (*pl* **-s**) *n Br inf* genre théâtral pour enfants.

pantomime ['pæntəmaɪm] *n Br* genre théâtral pour enfants; **~ dame** rôle travesti outré et ridicule dans la 'pantomime'.

PANTOMIME:
Le genre typiquement britannique de la 'pantomime' est très conventionnel; certains personnages-types ('pantomime dame', 'principal boy') et certaines rengaines ('look behind you!', 'Oh yes he is! - Oh no he isn't!') apparaissent dans toutes les pièces. Ces pièces, qui se jouent au moment des fêtes de fin d'année, sont généralement inspirées d'un conte de fées

pantry ['pæntrɪ] (*pl* **-ies**) *n* garde-manger *m inv*.

pants [pænts] *npl* **-1.** *Br* [underpants - for men] slip *m*, caleçon *m*; [- for women] culotte *f*, slip. **-2.** *Am* [trousers] pantalon *m*.

panty hose ['pæntɪhəʊz] *npl Am* collant *m*.

papa [*Br* pə'pɑː, *Am* 'pæpə] *n* papa *m*.

papacy ['peɪpəsɪ] (*pl* **-ies**) *n*: **the ~** la papauté.

papadum ['pæpədəm] = **popadum**.

papal ['peɪpl] *adj* papal(e).

paparazzi [,pæpə'rætsɪ] *npl usu pej* paparazzi *mpl*.

papaya [pə'paɪə] *n* papaye *f*.

paper ['peɪpə'] ◇ *n* **-1.** (*U*) [for writing on] papier *m*; **a piece of ~** [sheet] une feuille de papier; [scrap] un morceau de papier; **on ~** [written down] par écrit; [in theory] sur le papier. **-2.** [newspaper] journal *m*. **-3.** [in exam - test] épreuve *f*; [- answers] copie *f*. **-4.** [essay]: **~ (on)** essai *m* (sur). ◇ *adj* [hat, bag etc] en papier; *fig* [profits] théorique. ◇ *vt* tapisser.

◆ **papers** *npl* [official documents] papiers *mpl*.

◆ **paper over** *vt fus fig* dissimuler.

paperback ['peɪpəbæk] *n*: **~ (book)** livre *m* de poche; **in ~** en poche.

paperboy ['peɪpəbɔɪ] *n* livreur *m* de journaux.

paper clip *n* trombone *m*.

papergirl ['peɪpəgɜːl] *n* livreuse *f* de journaux.

paper handkerchief *n* mouchoir *m* en papier.

paper knife *n* coupe-papier *m inv*.

paper money *n* (*U*) papier-monnaie *m*.

paper shop *n Br* marchand *m* de journaux.

paperweight ['peɪpəweɪt] *n* presse-papiers *m inv*.

paperwork ['peɪpəwɜːk] *n* paperasserie *f*.

papier-mâché [,pæpjeɪ'mæʃeɪ] ◇ *n* papier mâché *m*. ◇ *comp* en papier mâché.

papist ['peɪpɪst] *n pej* papiste *mf*.

paprika ['pæprɪkə] *n* paprika *m*.

Papua ['pæpjʊə] *n* Papouasie *f*.

Papuan ['pæpjʊən] ◇ *adj* papou(e). ◇ *n* Papou *m*, -e *f*.

Papua New Guinea *n* Papouasie-Nouvelle-Guinée *f*; **in** ~ en Papouasie-Nouvelle-Guinée.

par [pɑːʳ] *n* -**1.** [parity]: **on a** ~ **with** à égalité avec. -**2.** GOLF par *m*; **under/over** ~ en-dessous/en-dessus du par. -**3.** [good health]: **below** OR **under** ~ pas en forme.

para ['pærə] *n Br inf* para *m*.

parable ['pærəbl] *n* parabole *f*.

parabola [pə'ræbələ] *n* parabole *f*.

paracetamol [,pærə'siːtəmɒl] *n* paracétamol *m*.

parachute ['pærəʃuːt] ◇ *n* parachute *m*. ◇ *vi* descendre en parachute.

parade [pə'reɪd] ◇ *n* -**1.** [celebratory] parade *f*, revue *f*. -**2.** MIL défilé *m*; **to be on** ~ défiler. -**3.** *Br* [street of shops]: **shopping** ~ rue *f* commerçante. ◇ *vt* -**1.** [people] faire défiler. -**2.** [object] montrer. -**3.** *fig* [flaunt] afficher. ◇ *vi* défiler.

parade ground *n* terrain *m* de manœuvres.

paradigm ['pærədaɪm] *n* paradigme *m*.

paradigmatic [,pærədɪg'mætɪk] *adj* paradigmatique.

paradise ['pærədaɪs] *n* paradis *m*.
◆ **Paradise** *n* Paradis *m*.

paradox ['pærədɒks] *n* paradoxe *m*.

paradoxical [,pærə'dɒksɪkl] *adj* paradoxal(e).

paradoxically [,pærə'dɒksɪklɪ] *adv* paradoxalement.

paraffin ['pærəfɪn] *n* paraffine *f*.

paraffin wax *n* paraffine *f*.

paragon ['pærəgən] *n* modèle *m*, parangon *m*.

paragraph ['pærəgrɑːf] *n* paragraphe *m*.

Paraguay ['pærəgwaɪ] *n* Paraguay *m*; **in** ~ au Paraguay.

Paraguayan [,pærə'gwaɪən] ◇ *adj* paraguayen(enne). ◇ *n* Paraguayen *m*, -enne *f*.

parakeet ['pærəkiːt] *n* perruche *f*.

parallel ['pærəlel] ◇ *adj lit* & *fig*: ~ **(to** OR **with)** parallèle (à). ◇ *n* -**1.** GEOGR & GEOM parallèle *f*. -**2.** *fig* [similar person, object] équivalent *m*; **to have no** ~ ne pas avoir d'équivalent. -**3.** [similarity] comparaison *f*, parallèle *m*. ◇ *vt fig* être semblable à.

parallel bars *npl* barres *fpl* parallèles.

paralyse *Br*, **-yze** *Am* ['pærəlaɪz] *vt lit* & *fig* paralyser.

paralysed *Br*, **paralyzed** *Am* ['pærəlaɪzd] *adj lit* & *fig* paralysé(e).

paralysis [pə'rælɪsɪs] (*pl* **-lyses** [-lɪsiːz]) *n* paralysie *f*.

paralytic [,pærə'lɪtɪk] ◇ *adj* -**1.** MED paralytique. -**2.** *Br inf* [drunk] ivre mort(e). ◇ *n* paralytique *mf*.

paramedic [,pærə'medɪk] *n* auxiliaire médical *m*, auxiliaire médicale *f*.

paramedical [,pærə'medɪkl] *adj* paramédical(e).

parameter [pə'ræmɪtəʳ] *n* paramètre *m*.

paramilitary [,pærə'mɪlɪtrɪ] *adj* paramilitaire.

paramount ['pærəmaunt] *adj* primordial(e); **of** ~ **importance** d'une importance suprême.

paranoia [,pærə'nɔɪə] *n* paranoïa *f*.

paranoiac [,pærə'nɔɪæk] ◇ *adj* paranoïaque. ◇ *n* paranoïaque *mf*.

paranoid ['pærənɔɪd] *adj* paranoïde.

paranormal [,pærə'nɔːml] *adj* paranormal(e).

parapet ['pærəpɪt] *n* parapet *m*.

paraphernalia [,pærəfə'neɪljə] *n* (*U*) attirail *m*, bazar *m*.

paraphrase ['pærəfreɪz] ◇ *n* paraphrase *f*. ◇ *vt* paraphraser. ◇ *vi* faire une paraphrase.

paraplegia [,pærə'pliːdʒə] *n* paraplégie *f*.

paraplegic [,pærə'pliːdʒɪk] ◇ *adj* paraplégique. ◇ *n* paraplégique *mf*.

parapsychology [,pærəsaɪ'kɒlədʒɪ] *n* parapsychologie *f*.

Paraquat® ['pærəkwɒt] *n* Paraquat® *m*.

parasite ['pærəsaɪt] *n lit* & *fig* parasite *m*.

parasitic [,pærə'sɪtɪk] *adj lit* & *fig* parasite.

parasol ['pærəsɒl] *n* [above table] parasol *m*; [hand-held] ombrelle *f*.

paratrooper ['pærətruːpəʳ] *n* parachutiste *mf*.

parboil ['pɑːbɔɪl] *vt* faire bouillir OR cuire à demi.

parcel ['pɑːsl] (*Br pt* & *pp* **-led**, *cont* **-ling**, *Am pt* & *pp* **-ed**, *cont* **-ing**) *n* paquet *m*.
◆ **parcel up** *vt sep* empaqueter.

parcel post *n*: **to send sthg** ~ envoyer qqch par colis postal.

parched [pɑːtʃt] *adj* -**1.** [gen] desséché(e). -**2.** *inf* [very thirsty] assoiffé(e), mort(e) de soif.

parchment ['pɑːtʃmənt] *n* parchemin *m*.

pardon ['pɑːdn] ◇ *n* -**1.** JUR grâce *f*. -**2.** (*U*) [forgiveness] pardon *m*; **I beg your** ~? [showing surprise, asking for repetition] comment?, pardon?; **I beg your** ~! [to apologize] je vous demande pardon. ◇ *vt* -**1.** [forgive] pardonner; **to** ~ **sb for sthg** pardonner qqch à qqn; ~ **me!** pardon!, excusez-moi! -**2.** JUR gracier. ◇ *excl* comment?

pardonable ['pɑːdnəbl] *adj* pardonnable.

pare [peəʳ] *vt* [apple] peler, éplucher; [fingernails] couper.

◆ **pare down** *vt sep* **-1.** [stick, fingernails] couper. **-2.** *fig* [reduce] réduire.

parent ['peərənt] *n* père *m*, mère *f*.

◆ **parents** *npl* parents *mpl*.

parentage ['peərəntɪdʒ] *n* (*U*) naissance *f*.

parental [pə'rentl] *adj* parental(e).

parent company *n* société *f* mère.

parenthesis [pə'renθɪsɪs] (*pl* **-theses** [-θɪsiːz]) *n* parenthèse *f*.

parenthetical [,pærən'θetɪkl] *adj* entre parenthèses.

parenthood ['peərənthʊd] *n* condition *f* de parent.

parenting ['peərəntɪŋ] *n* l'art *m* d'être parent.

parent-teacher association *n* association *f* des parents d'élèves et des professeurs.

pariah [pə'raɪə] *n* paria *m*.

Paris ['pærɪs] *n* Paris.

parish ['pærɪʃ] *n* **-1.** RELIG paroisse *f*. **-2.** *Br* [area of local government] commune *f*.

parish council *n Br* conseil *m* municipal.

parishioner [pə'rɪʃənəʳ] *n* paroissien *m*, -ienne *f*.

Parisian [pə'rɪzjən] ◇ *adj* parisien(ienne). ◇ *n* Parisien *m*, -ienne *f*.

parity ['pærətɪ] *n* égalité *f*.

park [pɑːk] ◇ *n* parc *m*, jardin *m* public. ◇ *vt* garer. ◇ *vi* se garer, stationner.

parka ['pɑːkə] *n* parka *f*.

parking ['pɑːkɪŋ] *n* stationnement *m*; "no ~" «défense de stationner», «stationnement interdit».

parking garage *n Am* parking *m* couvert.

parking light *n Am* feu *m* de position.

parking lot *n Am* parking *m*.

parking meter *n* parcmètre *m*.

parking place *n* place *f* de stationnement.

parking ticket *n* contravention *f*, PV *m*.

Parkinson's disease ['pɑːkɪnsnz-] *n* maladie *f* de Parkinson.

park keeper *n Br* gardien *m*, -ienne *f* de parc.

parkland ['pɑːklænd] *n* (*U*) parc *m*.

parkway ['pɑːkweɪ] *n Am* large route divisée ou bordée d'arbres.

parky ['pɑːkɪ] (*compar* **-ier**, *superl* **-iest**) *adj Br inf*: **it's** ~ il fait frisquet.

parlance ['pɑːləns] *n*: **in common/legal** *etc* ~ en langage courant/légal *etc*.

parliament ['pɑːləmənt] *n* parlement *m*.

parliamentarian [,pɑːləmen'teərɪən] *n* parlementaire *mf*.

parliamentary [,pɑːlə'mentərɪ] *adj* parlementaire.

parlour *Br*, **parlor** *Am* ['pɑːləʳ] *n dated* salon *m*.

parlour game *n* jeu *m* de salon.

parlous ['pɑːləs] *adj fml* précaire.

Parmesan (cheese) [,pɑːmɪ'zæn-] *n* parmesan *m*.

parochial [pə'rəukjəl] *adj pej* de clocher.

parody ['pærədɪ] (*pl* **-ies**, *pt & pp* **-ied**) ◇ *n* parodie *f*. ◇ *vt* parodier.

parole [pə'rəul] ◇ *n* (*U*) parole *f*; **on** ~ en liberté conditionnelle. ◇ *vt* mettre en liberté conditionnelle.

paroxysm ['pærəksɪzm] *n* [of rage] accès *m*; **a** ~ **of laughter** un fou rire.

parquet ['pɑːkeɪ] *n* parquet *m*.

parrot ['pærət] *n* perroquet *m*.

parrot fashion *adv* comme un perroquet.

parry ['pærɪ] (*pt & pp* **-ied**) *vt* **-1.** [blow] parer. **-2.** [question] éluder.

parsimonious [,pɑːsɪ'məunjəs] *adj fml & pej* parcimonieux(ieuse).

parsley ['pɑːslɪ] *n* persil *m*.

parsnip ['pɑːsnɪp] *n* panais *m*.

parson ['pɑːsn] *n* pasteur *m*.

parson's nose *n Br* croupion *m*.

part [pɑːt] ◇ *n* **-1.** [gen] partie *f*; **the best** OR **better** ~ **of** la plus grande partie de; **for the most** ~ dans l'ensemble; **in** ~ en partie; ~ **and parcel of** partie intégrante de. **-2.** [of TV serial etc] épisode *m*. **-3.** [component] pièce *f*. **-4.** [in proportions] mesure *f*. **-5.** THEATRE rôle *m*. **-6.** [involvement]: ~ **in** participation *f* à; **to play an important** ~ **in** jouer un rôle important dans; **to take** ~ **in** participer à; **to want no** ~ **in** ne pas vouloir se mêler de; **for my** ~ en ce qui me concerne; **on my/his** *etc* ~ de ma/sa *etc* part. **-7.** *Am* [hair parting] raie *f*. ◇ *adv* en partie. ◇ *vt*: **to** ~ **one's hair** se faire une raie. ◇ *vi* **-1.** [couple] se séparer. **-2.** [curtains] s'écarter, s'ouvrir.

◆ **parts** *npl*: **in these** ~**s** dans cette région.

◆ **part with** *vt fus* [money] débourser; [possession] se défaire de.

partake [pɑː'teɪk] (*pt* **-took**, *pp* **-taken**) *vi fml*: **to** ~ **of** prendre.

part exchange *n* reprise *f*; **in** ~ comme reprise en compte.

partial ['pɑːʃl] *adj* **-1.** [incomplete] partiel(ielle). **-2.** [biased] partial(e). **-3.** [fond]: **to be** ~ **to** avoir un penchant pour.

partiality [ˌpɑːʃɪˈælətɪ] n **-1.** [bias] partialité f. **-2.** [fondness]: ~ **for** prédilection f OR penchant m pour.

partially [ˈpɑːʃəlɪ] adv partiellement.

participant [pɑːˈtɪsɪpənt] n participant m, -e f.

participate [pɑːˈtɪsɪpeɪt] vi: **to** ~ **(in)** participer (à).

participation [pɑːˌtɪsɪˈpeɪʃn] n participation f.

participle [ˈpɑːtɪsɪpl] n participe m.

particle [ˈpɑːtɪkl] n particule f.

parti-coloured [ˈpɑːtɪ-] adj bariolé(e).

particular [pəˈtɪkjʊlər] adj **-1.** [gen] particulier(ière). **-2.** [fussy] pointilleux(euse); ~ **about** exigeant(e) à propos de.

◆ **particulars** npl renseignements mpl.

◆ **in particular** adv en particulier.

particularity [pəˌtɪkjʊˈlærətɪ] (pl **-ies**) n particularité f.

particularly [pəˈtɪkjʊləlɪ] adv particulièrement.

parting [ˈpɑːtɪŋ] n **-1.** [separation] séparation f. **-2.** Br [in hair] raie f.

parting shot n flèche f du Parthe.

partisan [ˌpɑːtɪˈzæn] ⋄ adj partisan(e). ⋄ n partisan m, -e f.

partition [pɑːˈtɪʃn] ⋄ n **-1.** [wall, screen] cloison f. **-2.** [of country] partition f. ⋄ vt **-1.** [room] cloisonner. **-2.** [country] partager.

partly [ˈpɑːtlɪ] adv partiellement, en partie.

partner [ˈpɑːtnər] ⋄ n **-1.** [gen] partenaire mf. **-2.** [in a business, crime] associé m, -e f. ⋄ vt être le partenaire de.

partnership [ˈpɑːtnəʃɪp] n association f; to enter into ~ **(with)** s'associer (avec).

partook [pɑːˈtʊk] pt → **partake**.

partridge [ˈpɑːtrɪdʒ] n perdrix f.

part-time adj & adv à temps partiel.

part-timer n travailleur m, -euse f à temps partiel.

party [ˈpɑːtɪ] (pl **-ies**) ⋄ n **-1.** POL parti m. **-2.** [social gathering] fête f, réception f; to have OR throw a ~ donner une fête. **-3.** [group] groupe m. **-4.** JUR partie f; to be a ~ to être complice de. ⋄ vi inf faire la fête.

party line n **-1.** POL ligne f du parti. **-2.** TELEC ligne f commune à deux abonnés.

party piece n inf numéro m habituel.

party political broadcast n Br moment d'antenne réservé à un parti politique.

party politics n (U) politique f politicienne.

party wall n mur m mitoyen.

parvenu(e) [ˈpɑːvənjuː] n pej parvenu m, -e f.

pass [pɑːs] ⋄ n **-1.** SPORT passe f. **-2.** [document - for security] laissez-passer m inv; [- for travel] carte f d'abonnement. **-3.** Br [in exam] mention f passable. **-4.** [between mountains] col m. **-5.** phr: to make a ~ at sb faire du plat à qqn.

⋄ vt **-1.** [object, time] passer; to ~ sthg to sb, to ~ sb sthg passer qqch à qqn. **-2.** [person in street etc] croiser. **-3.** [place] passer devant. **-4.** AUT dépasser, doubler. **-5.** [exceed] dépasser. **-6.** [exam] réussir (à); [driving test] passer. **-7.** [candidate] recevoir, admettre. **-8.** [law, motion] voter. **-9.** [opinion] émettre; [judgment] rendre, prononcer.

⋄ vi **-1.** [gen] passer. **-2.** AUT doubler, dépasser. **-3.** SPORT faire une passe. **-4.** [in exam] réussir, être reçu(e). **-5.** [occur] se dérouler, avoir lieu.

◆ **pass around** = **pass round**.

◆ **pass as** vt fus passer pour.

◆ **pass away** vi s'éteindre.

◆ **pass by** ⋄ vt sep: **the news ~ed him by** la nouvelle ne l'a pas affecté. ⋄ vi passer à côté.

◆ **pass for** = **pass as**.

◆ **pass off** vt sep: to ~ sb/sthg off as faire passer qqn/qqch pour.

◆ **pass on** ⋄ vt sep: to ~ sthg on (to) [object] faire passer qqch (à); [tradition, information] transmettre qqch (à). ⋄ vi **-1.** [move on] continuer son chemin. **-2.** = **pass away**.

◆ **pass out** vi **-1.** [faint] s'évanouir. **-2.** Br MIL finir OR terminer les classes.

◆ **pass over** vt fus [problem, topic] passer sous silence.

◆ **pass round** vt sep faire passer.

◆ **pass to** vt fus passer à, revenir à.

◆ **pass up** vt sep [opportunity, invitation] laisser passer.

passable [ˈpɑːsəbl] adj **-1.** [satisfactory] passable. **-2.** [road] praticable; [river] franchissable.

passably [ˈpɑːsəblɪ] adv passablement.

passage [ˈpæsɪdʒ] n **-1.** [gen] passage m. **-2.** [between rooms] couloir m. **-3.** [sea journey] traversée f.

passageway [ˈpæsɪdʒweɪ] n [between houses] passage m; [between rooms] couloir m.

passbook [ˈpɑːsbʊk] n livret m de banque.

passé [pæˈseɪ] adj pej démodé(e).

passenger [ˈpæsɪndʒər] n passager m, -ère f.

passerby [ˌpɑːsəˈbaɪ] (pl **passersby** [ˌpɑːsəzˈbaɪ]) n passant m, -e f.

passing [ˈpɑːsɪŋ] ⋄ adj [remark] en passant;

[trend] passager(ère). ◇ *n*: **with the ~ of time** avec le temps.
◆ **in passing** *adv* en passant.
passion ['pæʃn] *n* passion *f*; **to have a ~ for** avoir la passion de.
◆ **Passion** *n*: **the Passion** la Passion.
passionate ['pæʃənət] *adj* passionné(e).
passionately ['pæʃənətlɪ] *adv* avec passion.
passionfruit ['pæʃənfruːt] *n* fruit *m* de la passion.
passive ['pæsɪv] ◇ *adj* passif(ive). ◇ *n* GRAMM: **the ~** le passif.
passively ['pæsɪvlɪ] *adv* passivement.
passive resistance *n* résistance *f* passive.
passive smoking *n* tabagisme *m* passif.
passivity [pæ'sɪvətɪ] *n* passivité *f*.
passkey ['pɑːskiː] *n* passe *m*.
Passover ['pɑːs,əʊvəʳ] *n*: **(the) ~** la Pâque juive.
passport ['pɑːspɔːt] *n* **-1.** [document] passeport *m*. **-2.** *fig* [means]: **~ to** clef *f* de.
passport control *n* contrôle *m* des passeports.
password ['pɑːswɜːd] *n* mot *m* de passe.
past [pɑːst] ◇ *adj* **-1.** [former] passé(e); **for the ~ five years** ces cinq dernières années; **the ~ week** la semaine passée OR dernière. **-2.** [finished] fini(e).
◇ *adv* **-1.** [in times]: **it's ten ~** il est dix (minutes passées de l'heure). **-2.** [in front]: **to drive ~** passer (devant); **to run ~** passer (devant) en courant.
◇ *n* passé *m*; **in the ~** dans le temps.
◇ *prep* **-1.** [in times]: **it's half ~ eight** il est huit heures et demie; **it's five ~ nine** il est neuf heures cinq. **-2.** [in front of] devant; **we drove ~ them** nous les avons dépassés en voiture. **-3.** [beyond] après, au delà de; **to be ~ it** *inf* être trop vieux pour ça; **I wouldn't put it ~ him** *inf pej* cela ne m'étonnerait pas de lui.
pasta ['pæstə] *n* (*U*) pâtes *fpl*.
paste [peɪst] ◇ *n* **-1.** [gen] pâte *f*. **-2.** CULIN pâté *m*. **-3.** (*U*) [glue] colle *f*. **-4.** (*U*) [jewellery] strass *m*. ◇ *vt* coller.
pastel ['pæstl] ◇ *adj* pastel (*inv*). ◇ *n* pastel *m*.
paste-up *n* TYPO collage *m*.
pasteurize, -ise ['pɑːstʃəraɪz] *vt* pasteuriser.
pastiche [pæ'stiːʃ] *n* pastiche *m*.
pastille ['pæstɪl] *n* pastille *f*.
pastime ['pɑːstaɪm] *n* passe-temps *m inv*.
pasting ['peɪstɪŋ] *n* *inf* [beating] rossée *f*.
pastor ['pɑːstəʳ] *n* pasteur *m*.

pastoral ['pɑːstərəl] *adj* pastoral(e).
past participle *n* participe *m* passé.
pastrami [pə'strɑːmɪ] *n* viande *f* de bœuf fumée et épicée.
pastry ['peɪstrɪ] (*pl* **-ies**) *n* **-1.** [mixture] pâte *f*. **-2.** [cake] pâtisserie *f*.
past tense *n* passé *m*.
pasture ['pɑːstʃəʳ] *n* pâturage *m*, pré *m*.
pastureland ['pɑːstʃələænd] *n* pâturage *m*, herbage *m*.
pasty[1] ['peɪstɪ] (*compar* **-ier**, *superl* **-iest**) *adj* blafard(e), terreux(euse).
pasty[2] ['pæstɪ] (*pl* **-ies**) *n* *Br* petit pâté *m*, friand *m*.
pasty-faced ['peɪstɪ,feɪst] *adj* au teint blafard OR terreux.
pat [pæt] (*compar* **-ter**, *superl* **-test**, *pt* & *pp* **-ted**, *cont* **-ting**) ◇ *adj* tout prêt (toute prête), tout fait (toute faite). ◇ *n* **-1.** [light stroke] petite tape *f*; [to animal] caresse *f*. **-2.** [of butter] noix *f*, noisette *f*. ◇ *vt* [person] tapoter, donner une tape à; [animal] caresser.
Patagonia [,pætə'gəʊnjə] *n* Patagonie *f*; **in ~** en Patagonie.
Patagonian [,pætə'gəʊnjən] ◇ *adj* patagon(onne). ◇ *n* Patagon *m*, -onne *f*.
patch [pætʃ] ◇ *n* **-1.** [piece of material] pièce *f*; [to cover eye] bandeau *m*. **-2.** [small area - of snow, ice] plaque *f*. **-3.** [of land] parcelle *f*, lopin *m*; **vegetable ~** carré *m*. **-4.** [period of time]: **a difficult ~** une mauvaise passe. **-5.** *phr*: **not to be a ~ on sb** *inf* ne pas arriver OR venir à la cheville de qqn; **not to be a ~ on sthg** *inf* ne pas valoir qqch. ◇ *vt* rapiécer.
◆ **patch together** *vt sep* faire à la va-vite.
◆ **patch up** *vt sep* **-1.** [mend] rafistoler, bricoler. **-2.** *fig* [quarrel] régler, arranger; **to ~ up a relationship** se raccommoder.
patchwork ['pætʃwɜːk] ◇ *adj* en patchwork. ◇ *n* patchwork *m*.
patchy ['pætʃɪ] (*compar* **-ier**, *superl* **-iest**) *adj* [gen] inégal(e); [knowledge] insuffisant(e), imparfait(e).
pâté ['pæteɪ] *n* pâté *m*.
patent [*Br* 'peɪtənt, *Am* 'pætənt] ◇ *adj* [obvious] évident(e), manifeste. ◇ *n* brevet *m* (d'invention). ◇ *vt* faire breveter.
patented [*Br* 'peɪtəntɪd, *Am* 'pætəntɪd] *adj* breveté(e).
patentee [*Br* ,peɪtən'tiː, *Am* ,pætən'tiː] *n* titulaire *m* d'un brevet.
patent leather *n* cuir *m* verni.
patently [*Br* 'peɪtəntlɪ, *Am* 'pætəntlɪ] *adv* manifestement.
Patent Office *n* bureau *m* des brevets.

paternal [pə'tɜ:nl] *adj* paternel(elle).

paternalistic [pə,tɜ:nə'lɪstɪk] *adj pej* paternaliste.

paternity [pə'tɜ:nətɪ] *n* paternité *f.*

paternity leave *n* congé *m* parental (*pour pères*).

paternity suit *n* JUR action *f* en recherche de paternité.

path [pɑ:θ, *pl* pɑ:ðz] *n* **-1.** [track] chemin *m,* sentier *m.* **-2.** [way ahead, course of action] voie *f,* chemin *m.* **-3.** [trajectory] trajectoire *f.* **-4.** *phr:* **our ~s had crossed before** nos chemins s'étaient déjà croisés.

pathetic [pə'θetɪk] *adj* **-1.** [causing pity] pitoyable, attendrissant(e). **-2.** [useless - efforts, person] pitoyable, minable.

pathetically [pə'θetɪklɪ] *adv* **-1.** [cry, whimper] pitoyablement. **-2.** [inadequate, feeble] lamentablement.

pathological [,pæθə'lɒdʒɪkl] *adj* pathologique.

pathologist [pə'θɒlədʒɪst] *n* pathologiste *mf.*

pathology [pə'θɒlədʒɪ] *n* pathologie *f.*

pathos ['peɪθɒs] *n* pathétique *m.*

pathway ['pɑːθweɪ] *n* chemin *m,* sentier *m.*

patience ['peɪʃns] *n* **-1.** [of person] patience *f;* **to try sb's ~** mettre la patience de qqn à l'épreuve, éprouver la patience de qqn. **-2.** [card game] réussite *f.*

patient ['peɪʃnt] ◇ *adj* patient(e). ◇ *n* [in hospital] patient *m,* -e *f,* malade *mf;* [of doctor] client *m,* -e *f,* malade.

patiently ['peɪʃntlɪ] *adv* patiemment.

patina ['pætɪnə] *n* patine *f.*

patio ['pætɪəʊ] (*pl* **-s**) *n* patio *m.*

patio doors *npl* portes vitrées coulissantes.

Patna rice ['pætnə-] *n* riz *m* Patna (à grains longs).

patois ['pætwɑː] (*pl inv*) *n* patois *m.*

patriarch ['peɪtrɪɑːk] *n* patriarche *m.*

patriarchy ['peɪtrɪɑːkɪ] (*pl* **-ies**) *n* patriarcat *m.*

patrimony [*Br* 'pætrɪmənɪ, *Am* 'pætrɪməʊnɪ] *n fml* patrimoine *m,* héritage *m.*

patriot [*Br* 'pætrɪət, *Am* 'peɪtrɪət] *n* patriote *mf.*

patriotic [*Br* ,pætrɪ'ɒtɪk, *Am* ,peɪtrɪ'ɒtɪk] *adj* [gen] patriotique; [person] patriote.

patriotism [*Br* 'pætrɪətɪzm, *Am* 'peɪtrɪətɪzm] *n* patriotisme *m.*

patrol [pə'trəʊl] (*pt & pp* **-led**, *cont* **-ling**) ◇ *n* patrouille *f;* **to be on ~** être de patrouille; **to go on ~** aller en patrouille. ◇ *vt* patrouiller dans, faire une patrouille dans.

patrol car *n* voiture *f* de police.

patrolman [pə'trəʊlmən] (*pl* **-men** [-mən]) *n Am* agent *m* de police.

patrol wagon *n Am* fourgon *m* cellulaire.

patrolwoman [pə'trəʊl,wʊmən] (*pl* **-women** [-wɪmɪn]) *n Am* femme *f* agent de police.

patron ['peɪtrən] *n* **-1.** [of arts] mécène *m,* protecteur *m,* -trice *f.* **-2.** *Br* [of charity] patron *m,* -onne *f.* **-3.** *fml* [customer] client *m,* -e *f.*

patronage ['peɪtrənɪdʒ] *n* patronage *m.*

patronize, -ise ['pætrənaɪz] *vt* **-1.** [talk down to] traiter avec condescendance. **-2.** *fml* [back financially] patronner, protéger.

patronizing ['pætrənaɪzɪŋ] *adj* condescendant(e).

patron saint *n* saint patron *m,* sainte patronne *f.*

patter ['pætər] ◇ *n* **-1.** [sound - of rain] crépitement *m.* **-2.** [talk] baratin *m,* bavardage *m.* ◇ *vi* [feet, paws] trottiner; [rain] frapper, fouetter.

pattern ['pætən] *n* **-1.** [design] motif *m,* dessin *m.* **-2.** [of distribution, population] schéma *m;* [of life, behaviour] mode *m.* **-3.** [diagram]: (sewing) ~ patron *m.* **-4.** [model] modèle *m.*

patterned ['pætənd] *adj* à motifs.

patty ['pætɪ] (*pl* **-ies**) *n* petit pâté *m.*

paucity ['pɔːsətɪ] *n* indigence *f.*

paunch [pɔːntʃ] *n* bedaine *f.*

paunchy ['pɔːntʃɪ] (*compar* **-ier**, *superl* **-iest**) *adj* ventru(e), ventripotent(e).

pauper ['pɔːpər] *n* indigent *m,* -e *f,* nécessiteux *m,* -euse *f.*

pause [pɔːz] ◇ *n* **-1.** [short silence] pause *f,* silence *m.* **-2.** [break] pause *f,* arrêt *m.* ◇ *vi* **-1.** [stop speaking] marquer un temps. **-2.** [stop moving, doing] faire une pause, s'arrêter.

pave [peɪv] *vt* paver; **to ~ the way for sb/sthg** ouvrir la voie à qqn/qqch.

paved [peɪvd] *adj* pavé(e).

pavement ['peɪvmənt] *n* **-1.** *Br* [at side of road] trottoir *m.* **-2.** *Am* [roadway] chaussée *f.*

pavement artist *n Br* artiste *mf* des rues.

pavilion [pə'vɪljən] *n* pavillon *m.*

paving ['peɪvɪŋ] *n* (*U*) pavé *m.*

paving stone *n* pavé *m.*

paw [pɔː] ◇ *n* patte *f.* ◇ *vt* **-1.** [subj: animal] donner des coups de patte à. **-2.** *pej* [subj: person] tripoter, peloter.

pawn [pɔːn] ◇ *n lit & fig* pion *m.* ◇ *vt* mettre au mont-de-piété, mettre en gage.

pawnbroker ['pɔːn‚brəukə^r] *n* prêteur *m*, -euse *f* sur gages.

pawnshop ['pɔːnʃɒp] *n* mont-de-piété *m*.

pay [peɪ] (*pt* & *pp* **paid**) ◇ *vt* **-1.** [gen] payer; **to ~ sb for sthg** payer qqn pour qqch, payer qqch à qqn; **I paid £20 for that shirt** j'ai payé cette chemise 20 livres; **to ~ money into an account** *Br* verser de l'argent dans un compte; **to ~ a cheque into an account** déposer un chèque à un compte; **to ~ one's way** payer sa part. **-2.** [be profitable to] rapporter à; **it will ~ you not to say anything** *fig* tu as intérêt OR tu gagneras à ne rien dire. **-3.** [give, make]: **to ~ attention (to sb/sthg)** prêter attention (à qqn/qqch); **to ~ sb a compliment** faire un compliment à qqn; **to ~ sb a visit** rendre visite à qqn. ◇ *vi* payer; **to ~ dearly for sthg** *fig* payer qqch cher. ◇ *n* salaire *m*, traitement *m*.
◆ **pay back** *vt sep* **-1.** [return loan of money] rembourser. **-2.** [revenge oneself on] payer, revaloir; **I'll ~ you back for that** tu me le paieras, je te le revaudrai.
◆ **pay off** ◇ *vt sep* **-1.** [repay - debt] s'acquitter de, régler; [- loan] rembourser. **-2.** [dismiss] licencier, congédier. **-3.** [bribe] soudoyer, acheter. ◇ *vi* [course of action] être payant(e).
◆ **pay out** ◇ *vt sep* **-1.** [money] dépenser, débourser. **-2.** [rope] laisser filer, lâcher. ◇ *vi* dépenser, débourser.
◆ **pay up** *vi* payer.

payable ['peɪəbl] *adj* **-1.** [gen] payable. **-2.** [on cheque]: **~ to** à l'ordre de.

paybed ['peɪbed] *n Br* lit *m* privé.

pay check *n Am* paie *f*.

payday ['peɪdeɪ] *n* jour *m* de paye.

PAYE (*abbr of* **pay as you earn**) *n en Grande-Bretagne, système de retenue à la source des impôts sur le revenu.*

payee [peɪ'iː] *n* bénéficiaire *mf*.

pay envelope *n Am* salaire *m*.

payer ['peɪə^r] *n* payeur *m*, -euse *f*.

paying guest ['peɪɪŋ-] *n* hôte *m* payant.

paying-in book ['peɪɪŋ-] *n Br* carnet *m* de versements.

payload ['peɪləud] *n* charge *f* utile.

paymaster ['peɪ‚mɑːstə^r] *n* intendant *m*.

paymaster general *n* trésorier-payeur *m*.

payment ['peɪmənt] *n* paiement *m*.

payoff ['peɪɒf] *n* **-1.** [result] résultat *m*. **-2.** *Br* [redundancy payment] indemnité *f* de licenciement.

payola [peɪ'əulə] *n inf* pot-de-vin *m*, dessous *m* de table.

pay packet *n Br* **-1.** [envelope] enveloppe *f* de paie. **-2.** [wages] paie *f*.

pay phone, **pay station** *Am n* téléphone *m* public, cabine *f* téléphonique.

payroll ['peɪrəul] *n* registre *m* du personnel; **they have 100 people on the ~** ils ont 100 employés OR salariés.

payslip ['peɪslɪp] *n Br* feuille *f* OR bulletin *m* de paie.

pay station *Am* = **pay phone**.

PBS (*abbr of* **Public Broadcasting Service**) *n société américaine de production télévisuelle.*

PBX (*abbr of* **private branch exchange**) *n* autocommutateur *m* privé.

pc ◇ *n abbr of* **postcard**. ◇ (*abbr of* **per cent**) p. cent.

p/c *abbr of* **petty cash**.

PC ◇ *n* **-1.** (*abbr of* **personal computer**) PC *m*, micro *m*. **-2.** *abbr of* **police constable**. **-3.** (*abbr of* **privy councillor**) *membre du conseil privé*. ◇ *adj abbr of* **politically correct**.

PCB (*abbr of* **printed circuit board**) *n* plaquette *f* à circuits imprimés.

PCV (*abbr of* **passenger carrying vehicle**) *n véhicule de transport en commun (en Grande-Bretagne).*

pd *abbr of* **paid**.

PD *abbr of* **police department**.

pdq (*abbr of* **pretty damn quick**) *adv inf* illico presto.

PDSA (*abbr of* **People's Dispensary for Sick Animals**) *n association britannique de soins aux animaux malades.*

PDT (*abbr of* **Pacific Daylight Time**) *n heure d'été du Pacifique.*

PE (*abbr of* **physical education**) *n* EPS *f*.

pea [piː] *n* pois *m*.

peace [piːs] *n* (*U*) paix *f*; [quiet, calm] calme *m*, tranquillité *f*; **to be at ~ with sthg/sb/o.s.** être en paix avec qqch/qqn/soi-même, être en accord avec qqch/qqn/soi-même; **to make (one's) ~ with sb** faire la paix avec qqn.

peaceable ['piːsəbl] *adj* paisible, pacifique.

peaceably ['piːsəblɪ] *adv* paisiblement, pacifiquement.

Peace Corps *n organisation américaine de coopération avec les Pays en Voie de Développement.*

peaceful ['piːsful] *adj* **-1.** [quiet, calm] paisible, calme. **-2.** [not aggressive - person] pacifique; [- demonstration] non-violent(e).

peacefully ['piːsfulɪ] *adv* paisiblement.

peacefulness ['piːsfʊlnɪs] *n* paix *f*, calme *m*.

peacekeeping force ['piːs,kiːpɪŋ-] *n* force *f* de maintien de la paix.

peacemaker ['piːs,meɪkəʳ] *n* pacificateur *m*, -trice *f*.

peace offering *n inf* gage *m* de paix, cadeau *m* (pour faire la paix).

peacetime ['piːstaɪm] *n* temps *m* de paix.

peach [piːtʃ] ◇ *adj* couleur pêche (*inv*). ◇ *n* pêche *f*.

Peach Melba [-'melbə] *n* pêche *f* Melba.

peacock ['piːkɒk] *n* paon *m*.

peahen ['piːhen] *n* paonne *f*.

peak [piːk] *n* **-1.** [mountain top] sommet *m*, cime *f*. **-2.** *fig* [of career, success] apogée *m*, sommet *m*. **-3.** [of cap] visière *f*. ◇ *adj* [condition] optimum. ◇ *vi* atteindre un niveau maximum.

peaked [piːkt] *adj* [cap] à visière.

peak hours *npl* heures *fpl* d'affluence OR de pointe.

peak period *n* période *f* de pointe.

peak rate *n* tarif *m* normal.

peaky ['piːkɪ] (*compar* **-ier**, *superl* **-iest**) *adj Br inf* souffrant(e), fatigué(e).

peal [piːl] ◇ *n* [of bells] carillonnement *m*; [of laughter] éclat *m*; [of thunder] coup *m*. ◇ *vi* [bells] carillonner.

peanut ['piːnʌt] *n* cacahuète *f*.

peanut butter *n* beurre *m* de cacahuètes.

pear [peəʳ] *n* poire *f*.

pearl [pɜːl] *n* perle *f*.

pearly ['pɜːlɪ] (*compar* **-ier**, *superl* **-iest**) *adj* nacré(e).

peasant ['peznt] *n* **-1.** [in countryside] paysan *m*, -anne *f*. **-2.** *pej* [ignorant person] péquenaud *m*, -e *f*.

peasantry ['pezntrɪ] *n*: the ~ la paysannerie, les paysans *mpl*.

peashooter ['piː,ʃuːtəʳ] *n* sarbacane *f*.

peat [piːt] *n* tourbe *f*.

peaty ['piːtɪ] (*compar* **-ier**, *superl* **-iest**) *adj* tourbeux(euse).

pebble ['pebl] *n* galet *m*, caillou *m*.

pebbledash [,pebl'dæʃ] *n Br* crépi *m*.

pecan (nut) [pɪ'kæn-] *n* noix *f* de pecan OR pacane.

peck [pek] ◇ *n* **-1.** [with beak] coup *m* de bec. **-2.** [kiss] bise *f*. ◇ *vt* **-1.** [with beak] picoter, becqueter. **-2.** [kiss]: **to ~ sb on the cheek** faire une bise à qqn. ◇ *vi* picoter, donner des coups de bec.

pecking order ['pekɪŋ-] *n* hiérarchie *f*.

peckish ['pekɪʃ] *adj Br inf*: **to feel ~** avoir un petit creux.

pectin ['pektɪn] *n* pectine *f*.

pectoral ['pektərəl] *adj* pectoral(e).

peculiar [pɪ'kjuːljəʳ] *adj* **-1.** [odd] bizarre, curieux(ieuse). **-2.** [slightly ill]: **to feel ~** se sentir tout drôle (toute drôle) OR tout chose (toute chose). **-3.** [characteristic]: **~ to** propre à, particulier(ière) à.

peculiarity [pɪ,kjuːlɪ'ærətɪ] (*pl* **-ies**) *n* **-1.** [oddness] bizarrerie *f*, singularité *f*. **-2.** [characteristic] particularité *f*, caractéristique *f*.

peculiarly [pɪ'kjuːljəlɪ] *adv* **-1.** [especially] particulièrement. **-2.** [oddly] curieusement, bizarrement. **-3.** [characteristically] typiquement.

pecuniary [pɪ'kjuːnjərɪ] *adj* pécuniaire.

pedagogical [,pedə'gɒdʒɪkl] *adj* pédagogique.

pedagogy ['pedəgɒdʒɪ] *n* pédagogie *f*.

pedal ['pedl] (*Br pt & pp* **-led**, *cont* **-ling**, *Am pt & pp* **-ed**, *cont* **-ing**) ◇ *n* pédale *f*. ◇ *vi* pédaler.

pedal bin *n* poubelle *f* à pédale.

pedalo ['pedələʊ] *n Br* pédalo *m*.

pedant ['pedənt] *n* pédant *m*, -e *f*.

pedantic [pɪ'dæntɪk] *adj pej* pédant(e).

pedantry ['pedəntrɪ] *n pej* pédantisme *m*, pédanterie *f*.

peddle ['pedl] *vt* **-1.** [drugs] faire le trafic de. **-2.** [gossip, rumour] colporter, répandre.

peddler ['pedləʳ] *n* **-1.** [drug dealer] trafiquant *m* de drogue. **-2.** *Am* = **pedlar**.

pederast ['pedəræst] *n* pédéraste *m*.

pedestal ['pedɪstl] *n* piédestal *m*; **to put sb on a ~** mettre qqn sur un piédestal.

pedestrian [pɪ'destrɪən] ◇ *adj pej* médiocre, dépourvu(e) d'intérêt. ◇ *n* piéton *m*.

pedestrian crossing *n Br* passage *m* pour piétons, passage clouté.

pedestrianize, -ise [pɪ'destrɪənaɪz] *vt* transformer en zone piétonnière.

pedestrian precinct *Br*, **pedestrian zone** *Am n* zone *f* piétonnière.

pediatric [,piːdɪ'ætrɪk] *adj* de pédiatrie.

pediatrician [,piːdɪə'trɪʃn] *n* pédiatre *mf*.

pediatrics [,piːdɪ'ætrɪks] *n* pédiatrie *f*.

pedicure ['pedɪ,kjʊəʳ] *n* pédicurie *f*.

pedigree ['pedɪgriː] ◇ *adj* [animal] de race. ◇ *n* **-1.** [of animal] pedigree *m*. **-2.** [of person] ascendance *f*, généalogie *f*.

pedlar *Br*, **peddler** *Am* ['pedləʳ] *n* colporteur *m*.

pedophile ['piːdəfaɪl] *n* pédophile *m*.

pee [piː] *inf* ◇ *n* pipi *m*, pisse *f*; **to go for a ~** aller pisser un coup. ◇ *vi* faire pipi, pisser.

peek [piːk] *inf* ◇ *n* coup *m* d'œil furtif. ◇ *vi* jeter un coup d'œil furtif.

peel [piːl] ◇ *n* [of apple, potato] peau *f*; [of orange, lemon] écorce *f*. ◇ *vt* éplucher, peler. ◇ *vi* -1. [paint] s'écailler. -2. [wallpaper] se décoller. -3. [skin] peler.
◆ **peel off** *vt sep* [gen] enlever; [label] décoller, détacher.

peeler ['piːlə'] *n* couteau-éplucheur *m*.

peelings ['piːlɪŋz] *npl* épluchures *fpl*.

peep [piːp] ◇ *n* -1. [look] coup *m* d'œil OR regard *m* furtif. -2. *inf* [sound] bruit *m*. ◇ *vi* jeter un coup d'œil furtif.
◆ **peep out** *vi* apparaître, se montrer.

peephole ['piːphəul] *n* judas *m*.

peeping Tom [ˌpiːpɪŋ'tɒm] *n* voyeur *m*.

peep show *n* visionneuse *f*.

peer [pɪə'] ◇ *n* pair *m*. ◇ *vi* scruter, regarder attentivement.

peerage ['pɪərɪdʒ] *n* [rank] pairie *f*; **the ~** les pairs *mpl*.

peeress ['pɪərɪs] *n* pairesse *f*.

peer group *n* pairs *mpl*.

peer pressure *n* influence *f* de ses pairs.

peeved [piːvd] *adj inf* fâché(e), irrité(e).

peevish ['piːvɪʃ] *adj* grincheux(euse).

peg [peg] (*pt & pp* **-ged**, *cont* **-ging**) ◇ *n* -1. [hook] cheville *f*. -2. [for clothes] pince *f* à linge. -3. [on tent] piquet *m*. ◇ *vt fig* [prices] bloquer.
◆ **peg out** *vi Br inf* casser sa pipe.

pegboard ['pegbɔːd] *n* tableau *m* à trous.

PEI *abbr of* **Prince Edward Island**.

pejorative [pɪ'dʒɒrətɪv] *adj* péjoratif(ive).

pekinese [ˌpiːkə'niːz], **pekingese** [ˌpiːkɪŋ'iːz] (*pl inv* OR **-s**) *n* [dog] pékinois *m*.
◆ **Pekinese, Pekingese** ◇ *adj* pékinois(e). ◇ *n* Pékinois *m*, -e *f*.

Peking [piː'kɪŋ] *n* Pékin *m*.

pekingese = **pekinese**.

pelican ['pelɪkən] (*pl inv* OR **-s**) *n* pélican *m*.

pelican crossing *n Br* passage *m* pour piétons avec feux de circulation.

pellet ['pelɪt] *n* -1. [small ball] boulette *f*. -2. [for gun] plomb *m*.

pell-mell [ˌpel'mel] *adv* à la débandade.

pelmet ['pelmɪt] *n Br* lambrequin *m*.

Peloponnese [ˌpeləpə'niːz] *npl*: **the ~** le Péloponnèse.

pelt [pelt] ◇ *n* -1. [animal skin] peau *f*, fourrure *f*. -2. [speed]: **at full ~** à fond de train, à toute vitesse. ◇ *vt*: **to ~ sb (with sthg)** bombarder qqn (de qqch). ◇ *vi* -1. [rain] pleuvoir à verse OR à seaux. -2. [run fast]:

to ~ along courir ventre à terre; **to ~ down the stairs** dévaler l'escalier.

pelvic ['pelvɪk] *adj* pelvien(ienne).

pelvis ['pelvɪs] (*pl* **-vises** OR **-ves** [-viːz]) *n* pelvis *m*, bassin *m*.

pen [pen] (*pt & pp* **-ned**, *cont* **-ning**) ◇ *n* -1. [for writing] stylo *m*. -2. [enclosure] parc *m*, enclos *m*. ◇ *vt* -1. *literary* [write] écrire. -2. [enclose] parquer.

penal ['piːnl] *adj* pénal(e).

penalize, -ise ['piːnəlaɪz] *vt* -1. [gen] pénaliser. -2. [put at a disadvantage] désavantager.

penal settlement *n* colonie *f* pénitentiaire.

penalty ['penltɪ] (*pl* **-ies**) *n* -1. [punishment] pénalité *f*; **to pay the ~ (for sthg)** *fig* supporter OR subir les conséquences (de qqch). -2. [fine] amende *f*. -3. HOCKEY pénalité *f*; **~ (kick)** FTBL penalty *m*; RUGBY (coup *m* de pied de) pénalité *f*.

penalty area, penalty box *n Br* FTBL surface *f* de réparation.

penalty clause *n* clause *f* pénale.

penalty goal *n* RUGBY but *m* de pénalité.

penalty kick → **penalty**.

penance ['penəns] *n* -1. RELIG pénitence *f*. -2. *fig* [punishment] corvée *f*, pensum *m*.

pen-and-ink *adj* à la plume.

pence [pens] *Br pl* → **penny**.

penchant [*Br* pãʃã, *Am* 'pentʃənt] *n*: **to have a ~ for sthg** avoir un faible pour qqch; **to have a ~ for doing sthg** avoir tendance à OR bien aimer faire qqch.

pencil ['pensl] (*Br pt & pp* **-led**, *cont* **-ling**, *Am pt & pp* **-ed**, *cont* **-ing**) ◇ *n* crayon *m*; **in ~** au crayon. ◇ *vt* griffonner au crayon, crayonner.

pencil case *n* trousse *f* (d'écolier).

pencil sharpener *n* taille-crayon *m*.

pendant ['pendənt] *n* [jewel on chain] pendentif *m*.

pending ['pendɪŋ] *fml* ◇ *adj* -1. [imminent] imminent(e). -2. [court case] en instance. ◇ *prep* en attendant.

pending tray *n Br* (corbeille *f* des) affaires *fpl* en attente OR à traiter.

pendulum ['pendjuləm] (*pl* **-s**) *n* balancier *m*.

penetrate ['penɪtreɪt] ◇ *vt* -1. [gen] pénétrer dans; [subj: light] percer; [subj: rain] s'infiltrer dans. -2. [subj: spy] infiltrer. ◇ *vi* *inf* [be understood]: **it didn't ~** c'est resté sans effet sur lui/elle *etc*.

penetrating ['penɪtreɪtɪŋ] *adj* pénétrant(e); [scream, voice] perçant(e).

penetration [ˌpenɪ'treɪʃn] *n* pénétration *f*.

pen friend *n* correspondant *m*, -e *f*.

penguin ['peŋgwɪn] *n* manchot *m*.

penicillin [ˌpenɪ'sɪlɪn] *n* pénicilline *f*.

peninsula [pə'nɪnsjulə] (*pl* **-s**) *n* péninsule *f*.

penis ['piːnɪs] (*pl* **penises** ['piːnɪsɪz]) *n* pénis *m*.

penitent ['penɪtənt] *adj* repentant(e), contrit(e).

penitentiary [ˌpenɪ'tenʃərɪ] (*pl* **-ies**) *n Am* prison *f*.

penknife ['pennaɪf] (*pl* **-knives** [-naɪvz]) *n* canif *m*.

pen name *n* pseudonyme *m*.

pennant ['penənt] *n* fanion *m*, flamme *f*.

penniless ['penɪlɪs] *adj* sans le sou.

Pennines ['penaɪnz] *npl*: **the ~** les Pennines, la chaîne Pennine.

Pennsylvania [ˌpensɪl'veɪnjə] *n* Pennsylvanie *f*; **in ~** en Pennsylvanie.

penny ['penɪ] (*pl sense 1* **-ies**, *pl sense 2* **pence**) *n* **-1.** [coin] *Br* penny *m*; *Am* cent *m*. **-2.** *Br* [value] pence *m*. **-3.** *phr*: **a ~ for your thoughts** à quoi penses-tu?; **the ~ dropped** *Br inf* j'ai compris OR pigé, ça a fait tilt; **to spend a ~** *Br* aller au petit coin; **they are two** OR **ten a ~** *Br inf* il y en a à la pelle.

penny-pinching [-ˌpɪntʃɪŋ] ◇ *adj* [person] radin(e), pingre; [attitude] mesquin(e). ◇ *n* (*U*) économies *fpl* de bouts de chandelle.

pen pal *n inf* correspondant *m*, -e *f*.

pension ['penʃn] *n* **-1.** *Br* [on retirement] retraite *f*. **-2.** [from disability] pension *f*.

◆ **pension off** *vt sep* mettre à la retraite.

pensionable ['penʃənəbl] *adj*: **to be of ~ age** avoir l'âge de la retraite.

pension book *n Br* livret *m* de retraite.

pensioner ['penʃənər] *n Br*: **(old-age) ~** retraité *m*, -e *f*.

pension fund *n* caisse *f* de retraite.

pension plan, **pension scheme** *n* plan *m* OR régime *m* de retraite.

pensive ['pensɪv] *adj* songeur(euse).

pentagon ['pentəgən] *n* pentagone *m*.

◆ **Pentagon** *n Am*: **the Pentagon** le Pentagone.

PENTAGON:

Le Pentagone, immense bâtiment à cinq façades situé à Washington, abrite le ministère américain de la Défense; plus généralement, ce terme désigne le pouvoir militaire américain

pentathlon [pen'tæθlən] (*pl* **-s**) *n* pentathlon *m*.

Pentecost ['pentɪkɒst] *n* Pentecôte *f*.

penthouse ['penthaus, *pl* -hauzɪz] *n* appartement *m* de luxe (en attique).

pent up ['pent-] *adj* [emotions] refoulé(e); [energy] contenu(e).

penultimate [pe'nʌltɪmət] *adj* avant-dernier(ière).

penury ['penjurɪ] *n* indigence *f*, misère *f*.

peony ['pɪənɪ] (*pl* **-ies**) *n* pivoine *f*.

people ['piːpl] ◇ *n* [nation, race] nation *f*, peuple *m*. ◇ *npl* **-1.** [persons] personnes *fpl*; **few/a lot of ~** peu/beaucoup de monde, peu/beaucoup de gens; **there were a lot of ~ present** il y avait beaucoup de monde. **-2.** [in general] gens *mpl*; **~ say that ...** on dit que .... **-3.** [inhabitants] habitants *mpl*. **-4.** POL: **the ~** le peuple. ◇ *vt*: **to be ~d by** OR **with** être peuplé(e) de.

pep [pep] (*pt & pp* **-ped**, *cont* **-ping**) *n inf* (*U*) entrain *m*, pep *m*.

◆ **pep up** *vt sep inf* **-1.** [person] remonter, requinquer. **-2.** [party, event] animer.

PEP (*abbr of* **personal equity plan**) *n en Grande-Bretagne, plan d'épargne en actions exonéré d'impôt*.

pepper ['pepər] *n* **-1.** [spice] poivre *m*; **black/white ~** poivre noir/blanc. **-2.** [vegetable] poivron *m*; **red/green ~** poivron *m* rouge/vert.

pepperbox *n Am* = **pepper pot**.

peppercorn ['pepəkɔːn] *n* grain *m* de poivre.

peppered ['pepəd] *adj* **-1.** [essay, speech]: **~ (with)** truffé(e) (de). **-2.** [walls]: **~ (with)** criblé(e) (de).

pepper mill *n* moulin *m* à poivre.

peppermint ['pepəmɪnt] *n* **-1.** [sweet] bonbon *m* à la menthe. **-2.** [herb] menthe *f* poivrée.

pepper pot *Br*, **pepperbox** *Am* ['pepəbɒks] *n* poivrier *m*.

peppery ['pepərɪ] *adj* poivré(e).

pep talk *n inf* paroles *fpl* OR discours *m* d'encouragement.

peptic ulcer ['peptɪk-] *n* ulcère *m* gastro-duodénal.

per [pɜːr] *prep*: **~ person** par personne; **to be paid £10 ~ hour** être payé 10 livres de l'heure; **~ kilo** le kilo; **as ~ instructions** conformément aux instructions, à vos/tes *etc* instructions.

per annum *adv* par an.

P-E ratio (*abbr of* **price-earnings ratio**) *n indice de rentabilité d'une valeur*.

per capita [pə'kæpɪtə] *adj & adv* par habitant OR tête.

perceive [pə'siːv] *vt* **-1.** [notice] percevoir de. **-2.** [understand, realize] remarquer, s'apercevoir de. **-3.** [consider]: **to ~ sb/sthg as** considérer qqn/qqch comme.

per cent *adv* pour cent.

percentage [pə'sentɪdʒ] *n* pourcentage *m*.

perceptible [pə'septəbl] *adj* sensible.

perception [pə'sepʃn] *n* **-1.** perception *f*. **-2.** [insight] perspicacité *f*, intuition *f*. **-3.** [opinion] opinion *f*.

perceptive [pə'septɪv] *adj* perspicace.

perceptively [pə'septɪvlɪ] *adv* de manière perspicace.

perch [pɜːtʃ] (*pl sense 2 only inv* OR **-es**) ◇ *n* **-1.** *lit* & *fig* [position] perchoir *m*. **-2.** [fish] perche *f*. ◇ *vi* se percher.

percolate ['pɜːkəleɪt] *vi* **-1.** [coffee] passer. **-2.** *fig* [news] s'infiltrer, filtrer.

percolator ['pɜːkəleɪtə'] *n* cafetière *f* à pression.

percussion [pə'kʌʃn] *n* MUS percussion *f*; **the ~ (section)** la batterie, la percussion.

percussionist [pə'kʌʃənɪst] *n* percussionniste *mf*.

peremptory [pə'remptərɪ] *adj* péremptoire.

perennial [pə'renjəl] ◇ *adj* permanent(e), perpétuel(elle); BOT vivace. ◇ *n* BOT plante *f* vivace.

perestroika [,perə'strɔɪkə] *n* perestroïka *f*.

perfect [*adj & n* 'pɜːfɪkt, *vb* pə'fekt] ◇ *adj* parfait(e); **he's a ~ nuisance** il est absolument insupportable. ◇ *n* GRAMM: **~ (tense)** parfait *m*. ◇ *vt* parfaire, mettre au point.

perfect competition ['pɜːfɪkt-] *n* ECON concurrence *f* parfaite.

perfection [pə'fekʃn] *n* perfection *f*; **to ~** parfaitement (bien).

perfectionist [pə'fekʃənɪst] *n* perfectionniste *mf*.

perfectly ['pɜːfɪktlɪ] *adv* parfaitement; **you know ~ well** tu le sais très bien.

perforate ['pɜːfəreɪt] *vt* perforer.

perforations [,pɜːfə'reɪʃnz] *npl* [in paper] pointillés *mpl*.

perform [pə'fɔːm] ◇ *vt* **-1.** [carry out] exécuter; [- function] remplir; **to ~ an operation** MED opérer. **-2.** [play, concert] jouer. ◇ *vi* **-1.** [machine] marcher, fonctionner; [team, person]: **to ~ well/badly** avoir de bons/ mauvais résultats. **-2.** [actor] jouer; [singer] chanter.

performance [pə'fɔːməns] *n* **-1.** [carrying out] exécution *f*. **-2.** [show] représentation *f*. **-3.** [by actor, singer etc] interprétation *f*. **-4.** [of car, engine] performance *f*.

performance art *n* art *m* de représentation.

performance car *n* voiture *f* à hautes performances OR très performante.

performer [pə'fɔːmə'] *n* artiste *mf*, interprète *mf*.

performing arts [pə'fɔːmɪŋ-] *npl*: **the ~** les arts *mpl* du spectacle.

perfume ['pɜːfjuːm] *n* parfum *m*.

perfumed [*Br* 'pɜːfjuːmd, *Am* pər'fjuːmd] *adj* parfumé(e).

perfunctory [pə'fʌŋktərɪ] *adj* rapide, superficiel(ielle).

perhaps [pə'hæps] *adv* peut-être; **~ so/not** peut-être que oui/non.

peril ['perɪl] *n* danger *m*, péril *m*; **at one's ~** à ses risques et périls.

perilous ['perələs] *adj* dangereux(euse), périlleux(euse).

perilously ['perələslɪ] *adv* dangereusement.

perimeter [pə'rɪmɪtə'] *n* périmètre *m*; **~ fence** clôture *f*; **~ wall** mur *m* d'enceinte.

period ['pɪərɪəd] ◇ *n* **-1.** [gen] période *f*. **-2.** SCH ≃ heure *f*. **-3.** [menstruation] règles *fpl*. **-4.** *Am* [full stop] point *m*. ◇ *comp* [dress, house] d'époque.

periodic [,pɪərɪ'ɒdɪk] *adj* périodique.

periodical [,pɪərɪ'ɒdɪkl] ◇ *adj* = **periodic**. ◇ *n* [magazine] périodique *m*.

periodic table *n* tableau *m* de Mendéleïev.

period pains *npl* règles *fpl* douloureuses.

period piece *n* [furniture] meuble *m* d'époque.

peripatetic [,perɪpə'tetɪk] *adj* [salesman] itinérant(e); [teacher] qui enseigne dans plusieurs écoles.

peripheral [pə'rɪfərəl] ◇ *adj* **-1.** [unimportant] secondaire. **-2.** [at edge] périphérique. ◇ *n* COMPUT périphérique *m*.

periphery [pə'rɪfərɪ] (*pl* **-ies**) *n* [edge] périphérie *f*.

periscope ['perɪskəup] *n* périscope *m*.

perish ['perɪʃ] *vi* **-1.** [die] périr, mourir. **-2.** [food] pourrir, se gâter; [rubber] se détériorer.

perishable ['perɪʃəbl] *adj* périssable.
◆ **perishables** *npl* denrées *fpl* périssables.

perishing ['perɪʃɪŋ] *adj Br inf* **-1.** [cold] très froid(e). **-2.** [damn] sacré(e).

peritonitis [,perɪtə'naɪtɪs] *n* (*U*) péritonite *f*.

perjure ['pɜːdʒə'] *vt* JUR: **to ~ o.s.** se parjurer.

perjury ['pɜːdʒərɪ] *n* (*U*) JUR parjure *m*, faux serment *m*.

perk [pɜːk] *n inf* à-côté *m*, avantage *m*.
◆ **perk up** *vi* se ragaillardir.

perky ['pɜːkɪ] (*compar* -**ier**, *superl* -**iest**) *adj inf* [cheerful] guilleret(ette); [lively] plein(e) d'entrain.

perm [pɜːm] ◇ *n* permanente *f*. ◇ *vt*: **to have one's hair ~ed** se faire faire une permanente.

permanence ['pɜːmənəns] *n* permanence *f*.

permanent ['pɜːmənənt] ◇ *adj* permanent(e). ◇ *n Am* [perm] permanente *f*.

permanently ['pɜːmənəntlɪ] *adv* -**1.** [blind, damaged] définitivement, de manière permanente. -**2.** [closed, available] en permanence.

permeable ['pɜːmjəbl] *adj* perméable.

permeate ['pɜːmɪeɪt] *vt* -**1.** [subj: liquid, smell] s'infiltrer dans, pénétrer. -**2.** [subj: smell, feeling, idea] se répandre dans.

permissible [pə'mɪsəbl] *adj* acceptable, admissible.

permission [pə'mɪʃn] *n* permission *f*, autorisation *f*; **to give sb ~ to do sthg** donner à qqn la permission de faire qqch.

permissive [pə'mɪsɪv] *adj* permissif(ive).

permissiveness [pə'mɪsɪvnɪs] *n* permissivité *f*.

permit [*vb* pə'mɪt, *n* 'pɜːmɪt] (*pt* & *pp* -**ted**, *cont* -**ting**) ◇ *vt* permettre; **to ~ sb to do sthg** permettre à qqn de faire qqch, autoriser qqn à faire qqch; **to ~ sb sthg** permettre qqch à qqn; **weather permitting** si le temps le permet. ◇ *n* permis *m*.

permutation [,pɜːmjuː'teɪʃn] *n* permutation *f*.

pernicious [pə'nɪʃəs] *adj fml* [harmful] pernicieux(ieuse).

pernickety [pə'nɪkətɪ] *adj inf* [fussy] tatillon(onne), pointilleux(euse).

peroxide [pə'rɒksaɪd] *n* peroxyde *m*.

peroxide blonde *n* blonde *f* décolorée.

perpendicular [,pɜːpən'dɪkjulə⁻] ◇ *adj* perpendiculaire. ◇ *n* perpendiculaire *f*.

perpetrate ['pɜːpɪtreɪt] *vt* perpétrer, commettre.

perpetration [,pɜːpɪ'treɪʃn] *n* perpétration *f*.

perpetrator ['pɜːpɪtreɪtə⁻] *n* auteur *m*.

perpetual [pə'petʃuəl] *adj* -**1.** *pej* [continuous] continuel(elle), incessant(e). -**2.** [longlasting] perpétuel(elle).

perpetually [pə'petʃuəlɪ] *adv* -**1.** *pej* [continuously] sans cesse, continuellement. -**2.** [for ever] toujours, constamment.

perpetual motion *n* mouvement *m* perpétuel.

perpetuate [pə'petʃueɪt] *vt* perpétuer.

perpetuation [pə,petʃu'eɪʃn] *n* perpétuation *f*.

perpetuity [,pɜːpɪ'tjuːətɪ] *n*: **in ~** *fml* à perpétuité.

perplex [pə'pleks] *vt* rendre perplexe.

perplexed [pə'plekst] *adj* perplexe.

perplexing [pə'pleksɪŋ] *adj* déroutant(e), déconcertant(e).

perplexity [pə'pleksətɪ] *n* perplexité *f*.

perquisite ['pɜːkwɪzɪt] *n fml* à-côté *m*, avantage *m*.

per se [pɜː'seɪ] *adv* en tant que tel (telle), en soi.

persecute ['pɜːsɪkjuːt] *vt* persécuter, tourmenter.

persecution [,pɜːsɪ'kjuːʃn] *n* persécution *f*.

persecutor ['pɜːsɪkjuːtə⁻] *n* persécuteur *m*, -trice *f*.

perseverance [,pɜːsɪ'vɪərəns] *n* persévérance *f*, ténacité *f*.

persevere [,pɜːsɪ'vɪə⁻] *vi* -**1.** [with difficulty] persévérer, persister; **to ~ with** persévérer OR persister dans. -**2.** [with determination]: **to ~ in doing sthg** persister à faire qqch.

Persia ['pɜːʃə] *n* Perse *f*; **in ~** en Perse.

Persian ['pɜːʃn] ◇ *adj* persan(e); HISTORY perse. ◇ *n* -**1.** [person] Persan *m*, -e *f*; HISTORY Perse *mf*. -**2.** [language] persan *m*.

Persian cat *n* chat *m* persan.

Persian Gulf *n*: **the ~** le golfe Persique.

persist [pə'sɪst] *vi*: **to ~ (in doing sthg)** persister OR s'obstiner (à faire qqch).

persistence [pə'sɪstəns] *n* persistance *f*.

persistent [pə'sɪstənt] *adj* -**1.** [noise, rain] continuel(elle); [problem] constant(e). -**2.** [determined] tenace, obstiné(e).

persistently [pə'sɪstəntlɪ] *adv* -**1.** [constantly] continuellement, constamment. -**2.** [determinedly] obstinément, avec persévérance.

persnickety [pə'snɪkɪtɪ] *adj Am* tatillon(onne), pointilleux(euse).

person ['pɜːsn] (*pl* **people** OR **persons** *fml*) *n* -**1.** [man or woman] personne *f*; **in ~** en personne; **in the ~ of** en la personne de. -**2.** *fml* [body]: **about one's ~** sur soi.

persona [pə'səunə] (*pl* -**s** OR -**ae** [-iː]) *n* personnage *m*.

personable ['pɜːsnəbl] *adj* sympathique, agréable.

personage ['pɜːsənɪdʒ] *n* personnage *m*.

personal ['pɜːsənl] ◇ *adj* -**1.** [gen] personnel(elle). -**2.** *pej* [rude] désobligeant(e). ◇ *n Am* petite annonce *f* (pour rencontres).

personal account *n* compte *m* personnel.

personal allowance *n* TAX abattement *m*.

personal assistant *n* secrétaire *mf* de direction.

personal call *n* communication *f* téléphonique privée.

personal column *n* petites annonces *fpl*.

personal computer *n* ordinateur *m* personnel OR individuel.

personal estate *n* (*U*) biens *mpl* personnels.

personal hygiene *n* hygiène *f* corporelle.

personality [ˌpɜːsə'nælətɪ] (*pl* **-ies**) *n* personnalité *f*.

personalize, -ise ['pɜːsənəlaɪz] *vt* **-1.** [mark with name] personnaliser. **-2.** [make too personal] rendre trop personnel(elle).

personalized ['pɜːsənəlaɪzd] *adj* **-1.** [marked with name] personnalisé(e). **-2.** [for one person] personnel(elle).

personally ['pɜːsnəlɪ] *adv* personnellement; **to take sthg** ~ se sentir visé par qqch.

personal organizer *n* agenda *m* modulaire multifonction.

personal pension plan *n* retraite *f* personnelle.

personal pronoun *n* pronom *m* personnel.

personal property *n* (*U*) JUR biens *mpl* personnels.

personal stereo *n* baladeur *m*, Walkman® *m*.

persona non grata [-'grɑːtə] (*pl* **personae non gratae** [-'grɑːtiː]) *n* persona non grata.

personify [pə'sɒnɪfaɪ] (*pt* & *pp* **-ied**) *vt* personnifier.

personnel [ˌpɜːsə'nel] ◇ *n* (*U*) [department] service *m* du personnel. ◇ *npl* [staff] personnel *m*.

personnel department *n* service *m* du personnel.

personnel officer *n* responsable *mf* du personnel.

person-to-person *adj* avec préavis.

perspective [pə'spektɪv] *n* **-1.** ART perspective *f*; **to get sthg in** ~ *fig* mettre qqch dans son contexte. **-2.** [view, judgment] point *m* de vue, optique *f*.

Perspex® ['pɜːspeks] *n Br* ≃ plexiglas® *m*.

perspicacious [ˌpɜːspɪ'keɪʃəs] *adj* perspicace.

perspiration [ˌpɜːspə'reɪʃn] *n* **-1.** [sweat] sueur *f*. **-2.** [act of perspiring] transpiration *f*.

perspire [pə'spaɪəʳ] *vi* transpirer, suer.

persuade [pə'sweɪd] *vt*: **to** ~ **sb to do sthg** persuader OR convaincre qqn de faire qqch; **to** ~ **sb that** convaincre qqn que; **to** ~ **sb of** convaincre qqn de.

persuasion [pə'sweɪʒn] *n* **-1.** [act of persuading] persuasion *f*. **-2.** [belief - religious] confession *f*; [- political] opinion *f*, conviction *f*.

persuasive [pə'sweɪsɪv] *adj* [person] persuasif(ive); [argument] convaincant(e).

persuasively [pə'sweɪsɪvlɪ] *adv* d'un ton persuasif, d'une manière convaincante.

pert [pɜːt] *adj* mutin(e), coquin(e).

pertain [pə'teɪn] *vi fml*: ~**ing to** concernant, relatif(ive) à.

pertinence ['pɜːtɪnəns] *n* pertinence *f*.

pertinent ['pɜːtɪnənt] *adj* pertinent(e), approprié(e).

perturb [pə'tɜːb] *vt* inquiéter, troubler.

perturbed [pə'tɜːbd] *adj fml* inquiet(iète), troublé(e).

Peru [pə'ruː] *n* Pérou *m*; **in** ~ au Pérou.

perusal [pə'ruːzl] *n* lecture *f* attentive.

peruse [pə'ruːz] *vt* lire attentivement.

Peruvian [pə'ruːvjən] ◇ *adj* péruvien(ienne). ◇ *n* [person] Péruvien *m*, -ienne *f*.

pervade [pə'veɪd] *vt* [subj: smell] se répandre dans; [subj: feeling, influence] envahir.

pervasive [pə'veɪsɪv] *adj* pénétrant(e), envahissant(e).

perverse [pə'vɜːs] *adj* [contrary - person] contrariant(e); [- enjoyment] malin(igne).

perversely [pə'vɜːslɪ] *adv* [contrarily] par esprit de contradiction.

perversion [*Br* pə'vɜːʃn, *Am* pə'vɜːrʒn] *n* **-1.** [sexual] perversion *f*. **-2.** [of truth] travestissement *m*.

perversity [pə'vɜːsətɪ] *n* [contrariness] caractère *m* contrariant, esprit *m* de contradiction.

pervert [*n* 'pɜːvɜːt, *vb* pə'vɜːt] ◇ *n* pervers *m*, -e *f*. ◇ *vt* **-1.** [truth, meaning] travestir, déformer; [course of justice] entraver. **-2.** [sexually] pervertir.

perverted [pə'vɜːtɪd] *adj* **-1.** [sexually] pervers(e). **-2.** [reasoning] tordu(e).

peseta [pə'seɪtə] *n* peseta *f*.

peso ['peɪsəʊ] (*pl* **-s**) *n* peso *m*.

pessary ['pesərɪ] (*pl* **-ies**) *n* [medicine] ovule *m*.

pessimism ['pesɪmɪzm] *n* pessimisme *m*.

pessimist ['pesɪmɪst] *n* pessimiste *mf*.

pessimistic [ˌpesɪ'mɪstɪk] *adj* pessimiste.

pest [pest] *n* **-1.** [insect] insecte *m* nuisible; [animal] animal *m* nuisible. **-2.** *inf* [nuisance] casse-pieds *m inv*.

pester ['pestər] *vt* harceler, importuner.

pesticide ['pestɪsaɪd] *n* pesticide *m*.

pestle ['pesl] *n* pilon *m*.

pet [pet] (*pt* & *pp* **-ted**, *cont* **-ting**) ◇ *adj* [favourite]: ~ **subject** dada *m*; ~ **hate** bête *f* noire. ◇ *n* **-1.** [animal] animal *m* (familier). **-2.** [favourite person] chouchou *m*, -oute *f*. ◇ *vt* caresser, câliner. ◇ *vi* se peloter, se caresser.

petal ['petl] *n* pétale *m*.

peter ['piːtər]
◆ **peter out** *vi* [path] s'arrêter, se perdre; [interest] diminuer, décliner.

pethidine ['peθɪdiːn] *n* péthidine *f*.

petit bourgeois [pə,tiːʹbʊəʒwɑː] (*pl* **petits bourgeois** [pə,tiːʹbʊəʒwɑː]) ◇ *adj* petit-bourgeois (petite-bourgeoise). ◇ *n* petit-bourgeois *m*, petite-bourgeoise *f*.

petite [pəʹtiːt] *adj* menu(e).

petit four [,peti-] (*pl* **petits fours**) *n* petit-four *m*.

petition [pɪʹtɪʃn] ◇ *n* pétition *f*. ◇ *vt* adresser une pétition à. ◇ *vi* **-1.** [campaign]: **to** ~ **for/against** faire une pétition en faveur de/ contre. **-2.** JUR: **to** ~ **for divorce** faire une demande en divorce.

petitioner [pɪʹtɪʃənər] *n* pétitionnaire *mf*.

pet name *n* petit nom *m*.

petrified ['petrɪfaɪd] *adj* [terrified] paralysé(e) OR pétrifié(e) de peur.

petrify ['petrɪfaɪ] (*pt* & *pp* **-ied**) *vt* [terrify] paralyser OR pétrifier de peur.

petrochemical [,petrəʊʹkemɪkl] *adj* pétrochimique.

petrodollar ['petrəʊ,dɒlər] *n* FIN pétrodollar *m*.

petrol ['petrəl] *n* Br essence *f*.

petrolatum [,petrəʹleɪtəm] *n* Am vaseline *f*.

petrol bomb *n* Br cocktail *m* Molotov.

petrol can *n* Br bidon *m* à essence.

petroleum [pɪʹtrəʊljəm] *n* pétrole *m*.

petroleum jelly *n* Br vaseline *f*.

petrol pump *n* Br pompe *f* à essence.

petrol station *n* Br station-service *f*.

petrol tank *n* Br réservoir *m* d'essence.

petticoat ['petɪkəʊt] *n* jupon *m*.

pettiness ['petɪnɪs] *n* [small-mindedness] mesquinerie *f*, étroitesse *f* d'esprit.

petty ['petɪ] (*compar* **-ier**, *superl* **-iest**) *adj* **-1.** [small-minded] mesquin(e). **-2.** [trivial] insignifiant(e), sans importance.

petty cash *n* (U) petite caisse *f*.

petty officer *n* second maître *m*.

petulant ['petjʊlənt] *adj* irritable.

pew [pjuː] *n* banc *m* d'église.

pewter ['pjuːtər] *n* étain *m*.

PG (*abbr of* **parental guidance**) en *Grande-Bretagne, désigne un film pour lequel l'avis des parents est recommandé.*

PGA (*abbr of* **Professional Golfers' Association**) *n* association de joueurs de golf professionnels.

p & h (*abbr of* **postage and handling**) *n* Am frais *de* port.

PH (*abbr of* **Purple Heart**) *n* distinction militaire américaine.

PHA (*abbr of* **Public Housing Administration**) *n* services du logement social aux États-Unis.

phallic ['fælɪk] *adj* phallique; ~ **symbol** symbole *m* phallique.

phallus ['fæləs] (*pl* **-es** OR **phalli** ['fælaɪ]) *n* phallus *m*.

phantom ['fæntəm] ◇ *adj* fantomatique, spectral(e). ◇ *n* [ghost] fantôme *m*.

phantom pregnancy *n* grossesse *f* nerveuse, fausse grossesse.

pharaoh ['feərəʊ] *n* pharaon *m*.

Pharisee ['færɪsiː] *n* Pharisien *m*, -ienne *f*.

pharmaceutical [,fɑːməʹsjuːtɪkl] *adj* pharmaceutique.
◆ **pharmaceuticals** *npl* produits *mpl* pharmaceutiques.

pharmacist ['fɑːməsɪst] *n* pharmacien *m*, -ienne *f*.

pharmacology [,fɑːməʹkɒlədʒɪ] *n* pharmacologie *f*.

pharmacy ['fɑːməsɪ] (*pl* **-ies**) *n* pharmacie *f*.

phase [feɪz] ◇ *n* phase *f*. ◇ *vt* faire progressivement.
◆ **phase in** *vt sep* introduire progressivement.
◆ **phase out** *vt sep* supprimer progressivement.

PhD (*abbr of* **Doctor of Philosophy**) *n* (titulaire d'un) doctorat de 3e cycle.

pheasant ['feznt] (*pl inv* OR **-s**) *n* faisan *m*.

phenobarbitone Br [,fiːnəʊʹbɑːbɪtəʊn], **phenobarbitol** Am [,fiːnəʊʹbɑːbɪtl] *n* phénobarbital *m*.

phenomena [fɪʹnɒmɪnə] *pl* → **phenomenon**.

phenomenal [fɪʹnɒmɪnl] *adj* phénoménal(e), extraordinaire.

phenomenon [fɪʹnɒmɪnən] (*pl* **-mena**) *n* phénomène *m*.

phew [fjuː] *excl* ouf!

phial ['faɪəl] n fiole f.

Philadelphia [ˌfɪlə'delfjə] n Philadelphie; **in** ~ à Philadelphie.

philanderer [fɪ'lændərər] n coureur m, don Juan m.

philanthropic [ˌfɪlən'θrɒpɪk] adj philanthropique.

philanthropist [fɪ'lænθrəpɪst] n philanthrope mf.

philately [fɪ'lætəlɪ] n philatélie f.

philharmonic [ˌfɪlɑː'mɒnɪk] adj philharmonique.

Philippine ['fɪlɪpiːn] adj philippin(e); **the ~ Islands** les Philippines fpl.

◆ **Philippines** npl: **the ~s** les Philippines fpl.

philistine [Br 'fɪlɪstaɪn, Am 'fɪlɪstiːn] n philistin m, béotien m, -ienne f.

Phillips® ['fɪlɪps] comp: ~ **screw** vis f cruciforme; ~ **screwdriver** tournevis m cruciforme.

philosopher [fɪ'lɒsəfər] n philosophe mf.

philosophical [ˌfɪlə'sɒfɪkl] adj **-1.** philosophique. **-2.** [stoical] philosophe.

philosophize, -ise [fɪ'lɒsəfaɪz] vi philosopher.

philosophy [fɪ'lɒsəfɪ] (pl -ies) n philosophie f.

phlegm [flem] n flegme m.

phlegmatic [fleg'mætɪk] adj flegmatique.

Phnom Penh [ˌnɒm'pen] n Phnom Penh.

phobia ['fəubjə] n phobie f; **to have a ~ about** avoir la phobie de.

phoenix ['fiːnɪks] n phénix m.

phone [fəun] ◇ n téléphone m; **to be on the ~** [speaking] être au téléphone; Br [connected to network] avoir le téléphone. ◇ comp téléphonique. ◇ vt téléphoner à, appeler. ◇ vi téléphoner.

◆ **phone up** vt sep & vi téléphoner.

phone book n annuaire m (du téléphone).

phone booth n cabine f téléphonique.

phone box n Br cabine f téléphonique.

phone call n coup m de téléphone OR fil; **to make a ~** passer OR donner un coup de fil.

phonecard ['fəunkɑːd] n télécarte f.

phone-in n RADIO & TV programme m à ligne ouverte.

phone line n **-1.** [wire] câble m téléphonique. **-2.** [connection] ligne f téléphonique.

phone number n numéro m de téléphone.

phone-tapping [-ˌtæpɪŋ] n écoute f téléphonique.

phonetics [fə'netɪks] n (U) phonétique f.

phoney Br, **phony** Am ['fəunɪ] (compar -ier, superl -iest, pl -ies) inf ◇ adj **-1.** [passport, address] bidon (inv). **-2.** [person] hypocrite, pas franc (pas franche). ◇ n poseur m, -euse f.

phoney war n drôle de guerre f.

phony Am = **phoney**.

phosphate ['fɒsfeɪt] n phosphate m.

phosphorus ['fɒsfərəs] n phosphore m.

photo ['fəutəu] n photo f; **to take a ~ of sb/sthg** photographier qqn/qqch, prendre qqn/qqch en photo.

photocall ['fəutəukɔːl] n séance f de photos.

photocopier [ˌfəutəu'kɒpɪər] n photocopieur m, copieur m.

photocopy ['fəutəuˌkɒpɪ] (pt & pp -ied, pl -ies) ◇ n photocopie f. ◇ vt photocopier.

photoelectric cell [ˌfəutəuɪ'lektrɪk-] n cellule f photoélectrique.

photo finish n SPORT photo-finish f.

Photofit® ['fəutəufɪt] n: ~ **(picture)** portrait-robot m, photo-robot f.

photogenic [ˌfəutəu'dʒenɪk] adj photogénique.

photograph ['fəutəgrɑːf] ◇ n photographie f; **to take a ~ (of sb/sthg)** prendre (qqn/qqch) en photo, photographier (qqn/qqch). ◇ vt photographier, prendre en photo.

photographer [fə'tɒgrəfər] n photographe mf.

photographic [ˌfəutə'græfɪk] adj photographique.

photographic memory n mémoire f photographique.

photography [fə'tɒgrəfɪ] n photographie f.

photojournalism [ˌfəutəu'dʒɜːnəlɪzm] n reportage m en photos.

photon ['fəutɒn] n photon m.

photo opportunity n séance f photoprotocolaire.

photosensitive [ˌfəutəu'sensɪtɪv] adj photosensible.

Photostat® ['fəutəstæt] (pt & pp -ted, cont -ting) n photostat m, photocopie f.

◆ **photostat** vt photocopier, faire un photostat de.

photosynthesis [ˌfəutəu'sɪnθəsɪs] n photosynthèse f.

phrasal verb ['freɪzl-] n verbe m à postposition.

phrase [freɪz] ◇ n expression f. ◇ vt exprimer, tourner.

phrasebook ['freɪzbʊk] n guide m de conversation (pour touristes).

phraseology [ˌfreɪzɪ'ɒlədʒɪ] *n* phraséologie *f*.

physical ['fɪzɪkl] ◇ *adj* -1. [gen] physique. -2. [world, objects] matériel(ielle). ◇ *n* [examination] visite *f* médicale.

physical chemistry *n* chimie *f* physique.

physical education *n* éducation *f* physique.

physical examination *n* visite *f* médicale.

physical geography *n* géographie *f* physique.

physical jerks *npl Br hum* exercices *mpl*, gymnastique *f*.

physically ['fɪzɪklɪ] *adv* physiquement.

physically handicapped ◇ *adj*: to be ~ être un handicapé (une handicapée) physique. ◇ *npl*: the ~ les handicapés *mpl* physiques.

physical science *n* science *f* physique.

physical training *n* éducation *f* physique.

physician [fɪ'zɪʃn] *n* médecin *m*.

physicist ['fɪzɪsɪst] *n* physicien *m*, -ienne *f*.

physics ['fɪzɪks] *n* (U) physique *f*.

physio ['fɪzɪəʊ] (*pl* -s) *n Br inf* -1. (*abbr of* **physiotherapist**) kiné *mf*. -2. (*abbr of* **physiotherapy**) kiné *f*.

physiognomy [ˌfɪzɪ'ɒnəmɪ] (*pl* -ies) *n* physionomie *f*.

physiology [ˌfɪzɪ'ɒlədʒɪ] *n* physiologie *f*.

physiotherapist [ˌfɪzɪəʊ'θerəpɪst] *n* kinésithérapeute *mf*.

physiotherapy [ˌfɪzɪəʊ'θerəpɪ] *n* kinésithérapie *f*.

physique [fɪ'ziːk] *n* physique *m*.

pianist ['pɪənɪst] *n* pianiste *mf*.

piano [pɪ'ænəʊ] (*pl* -s) *n* piano *m*.

piano accordion *n* accordéon *m* à clavier.

Picardy ['pɪkədɪ] *n* Picardie *f*; **in** ~ en Picardie.

piccalilli [ˌpɪkə'lɪlɪ] *n* piccalilli *f*.

piccolo ['pɪkələʊ] (*pl* -s) *n* piccolo *m*.

pick [pɪk] ◇ *n* -1. [tool] pioche *f*, pic *m*. -2. [selection]: **to take one's** ~ choisir, faire son choix. -3. [best]: **the** ~ **of** le meilleur (la meilleure) de.
◇ *vt* -1. [select, choose] choisir, sélectionner; **to** ~ **one's way across** OR **through sthg** traverser avec précaution. -2. [gather] cueillir. -3. [remove] enlever. -4. [nose]: **to** ~ **one's nose** se décrotter le nez; **to** ~ **one's teeth** se curer les dents. -5. [fight, quarrel] chercher; **to** ~ **a fight (with sb)** chercher la bagarre (à qqn). -6. [lock] crocheter.
◇ *vi*: **to** ~ **and choose** faire le/la difficile.

◆ **pick at** *vt fus* [food] picorer.

◆ **pick on** *vt fus* s'en prendre à, être sur le dos de.

◆ **pick out** *vt sep* -1. [recognize] repérer, reconnaître. -2. [select, choose] choisir, désigner.

◆ **pick up** ◇ *vt sep* -1. [lift up] ramasser; **to** ~ **up the pieces** *fig* recoller les morceaux, recommencer comme avant. -2. [collect] aller chercher, passer prendre. -3. [collect in car] prendre, chercher. -4. [skill, language] apprendre; [habit] prendre; [bargain] découvrir; **to** ~ **up speed** prendre de la vitesse. -5. [subj: police]: **to** ~ **sb up for sthg** arrêter OR cueillir qqn pour qqch. -6. *inf* [sexually - woman, man] draguer. -7. RADIO & TELEC [detect, receive] capter, recevoir. -8. [conversation, work] reprendre, continuer.
◇ *vi* [improve, start again] reprendre.

pickaxe *Br*, **pickax** *Am* ['pɪkæks] *n* pioche *f*, pic *m*.

picker ['pɪkə'] *n* cueilleur *m*, -euse *f*.

picket ['pɪkɪt] ◇ *n* piquet *m* de grève. ◇ *vt* mettre un piquet de grève devant.

picketing ['pɪkətɪŋ] *n* (U) piquets *mpl* de grève.

picket line *n* piquet *m* de grève.

pickings ['pɪkɪŋz] *npl*: **there are rich** ~ **to be had** ça peut rapporter beaucoup d'argent.

pickle ['pɪkl] ◇ *n* pickles *mpl*; **to be in a** ~ être dans le pétrin. ◇ *vt* conserver dans du vinaigre OR de la saumure.

pickled ['pɪkld] *adj* -1. [food] au vinaigre. -2. *inf* [drunk] rond(e), pompette.

pick-me-up *n inf* remontant *m*.

pickpocket ['pɪkˌpɒkɪt] *n* pickpocket *m*, voleur *m* à la tire.

pick-up *n* -1. [of record player] pick-up *m*. -2. [truck] camionnette *f*.

pick-up truck *n* camionnette *f*.

picky ['pɪkɪ] (*compar* -ier, *superl* -iest) *adj* difficile.

picnic ['pɪknɪk] (*pt* & *pp* -ked, *cont* -king) ◇ *n* pique-nique *m*. ◇ *vi* pique-niquer.

picnicker ['pɪknɪkə'] *n* pique-niqueur *m*, -euse *f*.

Pict [pɪkt] *n*: **the** ~s les Pictes *mpl*.

pictorial [pɪk'tɔːrɪəl] *adj* illustré(e).

picture ['pɪktʃə'] ◇ *n* -1. [painting] tableau *m*, peinture *f*; [drawing] dessin *m*. -2. [photograph] photo *f*, photographie *f*. -3. TV image *f*. -4. CINEMA film *m*. -5. [in mind] tableau *m*, image *f*. -6. *fig* [situation] tableau *m*. -7. [epitome]: **she's the** ~ **of health** elle respire la santé. -8. *phr*: **to get the** ~ *inf* piger; **to be**

in/out of the ~ être/ne pas être au courant;
to put sb in the ~ mettre qqn au courant.
◇ vt -1. [in mind] imaginer, s'imaginer, se
représenter. -2. [in photo] photographier.
-3. [in painting] représenter, peindre.
◆ **pictures** *npl Br*: the ~s le cinéma.
picture book *n* livre *m* d'images.
picture rail *n* cimaise *f*.
picturesque [ˌpɪktʃəˈresk] *adj* pittoresque.
picture window *n* fenêtre *f* panoramique.
piddling [ˈpɪdlɪŋ] *adj inf pej* dérisoire, insi-
gnifiant(e).
pidgin [ˈpɪdʒɪn] ◇ *n* pidgin *m*. ◇ *comp*: ~
English pidgin english *m*; ~ **French** petit
nègre *m*.
pie [paɪ] *n* tourte *f*; ~ **in the sky** projet en
l'air.
piebald [ˈpaɪbɔːld] *adj* pie (*inv*).
piece [piːs] *n* -1. [gen] morceau *m*; [of string]
bout *m*; a ~ **of furniture** un meuble; a ~ **of
clothing** un vêtement; a ~ **of advice** un
conseil; a ~ **of information** un renseignement; a ~ **of work** un travail; **to fall to** ~s
tomber en morceaux; **to be smashed to** ~s
être cassé en mille morceaux; **to take sthg
to** ~s démonter qqch; **in** ~s en morceaux;
in one ~ [intact] intact(e); [unharmed] sain et
sauf; **to go to** ~s *fig* s'effondrer, craquer.
-2. [coin, item, in chess] pièce *f*; [in draughts]
pion *m*. -3. PRESS article *m*.
◆ **piece together** *vt sep* [facts] coordonner.
pièce de résistance [ˌpjesdərezisˈtɑ̃ːs]
(*pl* pièces de résistance [ˌpjesdərezisˈtɑ̃ːs]) *n*
pièce *f* de résistance.
piecemeal [ˈpiːsmiːl] ◇ *adj* fait(e) petit à
petit. ◇ *adv* petit à petit, peu à peu.
piecework [ˈpiːswɜːk] *n* (*U*) travail *m* à la
pièce OR aux pièces.
pie chart *n* camembert *m*, graphique *m*
rond.
pied-a-terre [ˌpɪeɪdæˈteəʳ] (*pl* pieds-a-terre
[ˌpɪeɪdæˈteəʳ]) *n* pied-à-terre *m inv*.
pie-eyed [-ˈaɪd] *adj inf* rond(e), gris(e).
pie plate *n Am* plat allant au four.
pier [pɪəʳ] *n* [at seaside] jetée *f*.
pierce [pɪəs] *vt* percer, transpercer; **to have
one's ears** ~d se faire percer les oreilles.
pierced [pɪəst] *adj* percé(e).
piercing [ˈpɪəsɪŋ] *adj* -1. [sound, look] per-
çant(e). -2. [wind] pénétrant(e).
piety [ˈpaɪətɪ] *n* piété *f*.
piffle [ˈpɪfl] *n* (*U*) *inf* bêtises *fpl*, balivernes *fpl*.
piffling [ˈpɪflɪŋ] *adj inf* insignifiant(e).
pig [pɪg] (*pt & pp* -ged, *cont* -ging) *n* -1. [ani-
mal] porc *m*, cochon *m*. -2. *inf pej* [greedy

eater] goinfre *m*, glouton *m*; **to make a** ~ **of
o.s.** se goinfrer. -3. *inf pej* [unkind person]
sale type *m*.
◆ **pig out** *vi inf* s'empiffrer.
pigeon [ˈpɪdʒɪn] (*pl inv* OR -s) *n* pigeon *m*.
pigeon-chested [-ˌtʃestɪd] *adj* à la poitrine
bombée.
pigeonhole [ˈpɪdʒɪnhəʊl] ◇ *n* [compartment]
casier *m*. ◇ *vt* [classify] étiqueter, cataloguer.
pigeon-toed [-ˌtəʊd] *adj* qui a les pieds en
dedans.
piggish [ˈpɪgɪʃ] *adj inf* cochon(onne), dé-
goûtant(e).
piggy [ˈpɪgɪ] (*compar* -ier, *superl* -iest, *pl*
-ies) ◇ *adj* de cochon. ◇ *n inf* cochon *m*.
piggyback [ˈpɪgɪbæk] *n*: **to give sb a** ~ porter qqn sur son dos.
piggybank [ˈpɪgɪbæŋk] *n* tirelire *f*.
pigheaded [ˌpɪgˈhedɪd] *adj* têtu(e).
piglet [ˈpɪglɪt] *n* porcelet *m*.
pigment [ˈpɪgmənt] *n* pigment *m*.
pigmentation [ˌpɪgmənˈteɪʃn] *n* pigmentation *f*.
pigmy [ˈpɪgmɪ] (*pl* -ies) = **pygmy**.
pigpen *Am* = **pigsty**.
pigskin [ˈpɪgskɪn] ◇ *n* peau *f* de porc. ◇
comp en peau de porc.
pigsty [ˈpɪgstaɪ] (*pl* -ies), **pigpen** *Am*
[ˈpɪgpen] *n lit* & *fig* porcherie *f*.
pigswill [ˈpɪgswɪl] *n lit* & *fig* pâtée *f* pour
les porcs.
pigtail [ˈpɪgteɪl] *n* natte *f*.
pike [paɪk] (*pl sense 1 only inv* OR -s) *n* -1.
[fish] brochet *m*. -2. [spear] pique *f*.
pikestaff [ˈpaɪkstɑːf] *n* manche *m* d'une pique.
pilaster [pɪˈlæstəʳ] *n* pilastre *m*.
pilchard [ˈpɪltʃəd] *n* pilchard *m*.
pile [paɪl] ◇ *n* -1. [heap] tas *m*; a ~ **of**, ~s
of un tas OR des tas de. -2. [neat stack] pile
f. -3. [of carpet] poil *m*. ◇ *vt* empiler.
◆ **piles** *npl* MED hémorroïdes *fpl*.
◆ **pile in** *vi inf* s'empiler.
◆ **pile into** *vt fus inf* s'entasser dans, s'empiler dans.
◆ **pile out** *vi inf* sortir en se bousculant.
◆ **pile up** ◇ *vt sep* empiler, entasser. ◇ *vi*
-1. [form a heap] s'entasser. -2. *fig* [work,
debts] s'accumuler.
pile driver *n* sonnette *f*.
pileup [ˈpaɪlʌp] *n* AUT carambolage *m*.
pilfer [ˈpɪlfəʳ] ◇ *vt* chaparder. ◇ *vi*: **to** ~
(from) faire du chapardage (dans).
pilgrim [ˈpɪlgrɪm] *n* pèlerin *m*.

pilgrimage ['pɪlgrɪmɪdʒ] *n* pèlerinage *m*.

pill [pɪl] *n* **-1.** [gen] pilule *f*. **-2.** [contraceptive]: **the ~** la pilule; **to be on the ~** prendre la pilule.

pillage ['pɪlɪdʒ] ◇ *n* pillage *m*. ◇ *vt* piller.

pillar ['pɪləʳ] *n* *lit* & *fig* pilier *m*.

pillar box *n* *Br* boîte *f* aux lettres.

pillbox ['pɪlbɒks] *n* **-1.** [box for pills] boîte *f* à pilules. **-2.** MIL casemate *f*.

pillion ['pɪljən] *n* siège *m* arrière; **to ride ~** monter derrière.

pillock ['pɪlək] *n* *Br inf* imbécile *mf*.

pillory ['pɪlərɪ] (*pl* **-ies**, *pt* & *pp* **-ied**) ◇ *n* pilori *m*. ◇ *vt*: **to be pilloried** être mis(e) au pilori.

pillow ['pɪləʊ] *n* **-1.** [for bed] oreiller *m*. **-2.** *Am* [on sofa, chair] coussin *m*.

pillowcase ['pɪləʊkeɪs], **pillowslip** ['pɪləʊslɪp] *n* taie *f* d'oreiller.

pilot ['paɪlət] ◇ *n* **-1.** AERON & NAUT pilote *m*. **-2.** TV émission *f* pilote. ◇ *comp* pilote. ◇ *vt* piloter.

pilot burner, **pilot light** *n* veilleuse *f*.

pilot scheme *n* projet-pilote *m*.

pilot study *n* étude *f* pilote OR expérimentale.

pimento [pɪ'mentəʊ] (*pl inv* OR **-s**) *n* piment *m*.

pimp [pɪmp] *n* *inf* maquereau *m*, souteneur *m*.

pimple ['pɪmpl] *n* bouton *m*.

pimply ['pɪmplɪ] (*compar* **-ier**, *superl* **-iest**) *adj* boutonneux(euse).

pin [pɪn] (*pt* & *pp* **-ned**, *cont* **-ning**) ◇ *n* **-1.** [for sewing] épingle *f*; **to have ~s and needles** avoir des fourmis; **to be on ~s and needles** *Am* être sur des charbons ardents. **-2.** [drawing pin] punaise *f*. **-3.** [safety pin] épingle *f* de nourrice OR de sûreté. **-4.** [of plug] fiche *f*. **-5.** TECH goupille *f*, cheville *f*. **-6.** [in grenade] goupille *f*. **-7.** GOLF: **the ~** le drapeau de trou. ◇ *vt*: **to ~ sthg to/on sthg** épingler qqch à/sur qqch; **to ~ sb against** OR **to clouer qqn contre**; **to ~ sthg on sb** [blame] mettre OR coller qqch sur le dos de qqn; **to ~ one's hopes on sb/sthg** mettre tous ses espoirs en qqn/dans qqch.

◆ **pin down** *vt sep* **-1.** [identify] définir, identifier. **-2.** [force to make a decision]: **to ~ sb down** obliger qqn à prendre une décision.

◆ **pin up** *vt sep* épingler.

PIN [pɪn] (*abbr of* **personal identification number**) *n* code *m* confidentiel.

pinafore ['pɪnəfɔːʳ] *n* **-1.** [apron] tablier *m*. **-2.** *Br* [dress] chasuble *f*.

pinball ['pɪnbɔːl] *n* flipper *m*.

pinball machine *n* flipper *m*.

pincer movement ['pɪnsəʳ-] *n* mouvement *m* de tenailles.

pincers ['pɪnsəz] *npl* **-1.** [tool] tenailles *fpl*. **-2.** [of crab] pinces *fpl*.

pinch [pɪntʃ] ◇ *n* **-1.** [nip] pincement *m*; **to feel the ~** tirer le diable par la queue. **-2.** [of salt] pincée *f*. ◇ *vt* **-1.** [nip] pincer. **-2.** [subj: shoes] serrer. **-3.** *inf* [steal] piquer, faucher.

◆ **at a pinch** *Br*, **in a pinch** *Am adv* à la rigueur.

pinched [pɪntʃt] *adj* [features] tiré(e); **to be ~ for time/money** être à court de temps/d'argent; **~ with cold** transi de froid.

pincushion ['pɪn,kʊʃn] *n* pelote *f* à épingles.

pine [paɪn] ◇ *n* pin *m*. ◇ *comp* en pin. ◇ *vi*: **to ~** to désirer ardemment.

◆ **pine away** *vi* languir.

pineapple ['paɪn,æpl] *n* ananas *m*.

pinecone ['paɪnkəʊn] *n* pomme *f* de pin.

pine needle *n* aiguille *f* de pin.

pinetree ['paɪntriː] *n* pin *m*.

pinewood ['paɪnwʊd] *n* **-1.** [forest] pinède *f*. **-2.** (*U*) [material] bois *m* de pin.

ping [pɪŋ] ◇ *n* [of bell] tintement *m*; [of metal] bruit *m* métallique. ◇ *vi* [bell] tinter; [metal] faire un bruit métallique.

Ping-Pong® [-pɒŋ] *n* ping-pong *m*.

pinhole ['pɪnhəʊl] *n* trou *m* d'épingle.

pinion ['pɪnjən] ◇ *n* pignon *m*. ◇ *vt* [person] clouer.

pink [pɪŋk] ◇ *adj* rose; **to go** OR **turn ~** rosir, rougir. ◇ *n* **-1.** [colour] rose *m*; **in ~** en rose. **-2.** [flower] mignardise *f*.

pink gin *n* *Br* boisson alcoolisée contenant du gin et de l'angusture.

pinkie ['pɪŋkɪ] *n* *Am* & *Scot* petit doigt *m*.

pinking ['pɪŋkɪŋ] *n* *Br* AUT cliquettement *m*.

pinking scissors, **pinking shears** *npl* ciseaux *mpl* à cranter.

pin money *n* argent *m* de poche.

pinnacle ['pɪnəkl] *n* **-1.** [mountain peak, spire] pic *m*, cime *f*. **-2.** *fig* [high point] apogée *m*.

pinny ['pɪnɪ] (*pl* **-ies**) *n* *inf* tablier *m*.

pinpoint ['pɪnpɔɪnt] *vt* **-1.** [cause, problem] définir, mettre le doigt sur. **-2.** [position] localiser.

pinprick ['pɪnprɪk] *n* piqûre *f* d'épingle; *fig* petit désagrément *m*.

pin-striped [-straɪpt] *adj* à très fines rayures.

pint [paɪnt] *n* **-1.** *Br* [unit of measurement] =*0,568 litre,* demi-litre *m.* **-2.** *Am* [unit of measurement] =*0,473 litre,* ≃ demi-litre *m.* **-3.** *Br* [beer] ≃ demi *m.*

pintable ['pɪnteɪbl] *n Br* flipper *m.*

pinto ['pɪntəʊ] (*pl* **-s** OR **-es**) *Am* ◇ *adj* pie (*inv*). ◇ *n* cheval *m* pie.

pint-size(d) *adj inf* minuscule.

pinup ['pɪnʌp] *n* pin-up *f inv.*

pioneer [ˌpaɪə'nɪəʳ] ◇ *n lit* & *fig* pionnier *m.* ◇ *vt:* **to** ~ **sthg** être un des premiers (une des premières) à faire qqch.

pioneering [ˌpaɪə'nɪərɪŋ] *adj* [work, research] de pionnier.

pious ['paɪəs] *adj* **-1.** RELIG pieux (pieuse). **-2.** *pej* [sanctimonious] moralisateur(trice).

piously ['paɪəslɪ] *adv* pieusement.

pip [pɪp] *n* **-1.** [seed] pépin *m.* **-2.** *Br* RADIO top *m.*

pipe [paɪp] ◇ *n* **-1.** [for gas, water] tuyau *m.* **-2.** [for smoking] pipe *f.* ◇ *vt* acheminer par tuyau.

◆ **pipes** *npl* MUS cornemuse *f.*
◆ **pipe down** *vi inf* se taire, la fermer.
◆ **pipe up** *vi inf* se faire entendre.

pipe cleaner *n* cure-pipe *m.*

piped music *n Br* musique *f* de fond.

pipe dream *n* projet *m* chimérique.

pipeline ['paɪplaɪn] *n* [for gas] gazoduc *m;* [for oil] oléoduc *m,* pipeline *m;* **to be in the** ~ *fig* être imminent OR proche.

piper ['paɪpəʳ] *n* joueur *m,* -euse *f* de cornemuse.

piping hot ['paɪpɪŋ-] *adj* bouillant(e).

pipsqueak ['pɪpskwiːk] *n pej* moins *m* que rien.

piquant ['piːkənt] *adj* piquant(e).

pique [piːk] *n* dépit *m;* **a fit of** ~ un accès de dépit.

piracy ['paɪrəsɪ] *n* **-1.** [at sea] piraterie *f.* **-2.** [of video, program] piratage *m.*

piranha [pɪ'rɑːnə] *n* piranha *m.*

pirate ['paɪrət] ◇ *adj* [video, program] pirate. ◇ *n* pirate *m.* ◇ *vt* [video, program] pirater.

pirate radio *n Br* radio *f* pirate.

pirouette [ˌpɪru'et] ◇ *n* pirouette *f.* ◇ *vi* pirouetter.

Pisces ['paɪsiːz] *n* Poissons *mpl;* **to be (a)** ~ être Poissons.

piss [pɪs] *vulg* ◇ *n* **-1.** [urine] pisse *f;* **to have a** ~ pisser. **-2.** *phr:* **to take the** ~ **out of** se foutre de. ◇ *vi* pisser.

◆ **piss down** *v impers Br vulg* pleuvoir comme vache qui pisse.
◆ **piss off** *vulg* ◇ *vt sep* emmerder. ◇ *vi Br* foutre le camp; ~ **off!** fous le camp!

pissed [pɪst] *adj vulg* **-1.** *Br* [drunk] bourré(e). **-2.** *Am* [annoyed] en boule.

pissed off *adj vulg* qui en a plein le cul.

pistachio [pɪ'stɑːʃɪəʊ] (*pl* **-s**) *n* pistache *f.*

pistol ['pɪstl] *n* pistolet *m.*

pistol-whip *vt Am* frapper avec un pistolet.

piston ['pɪstən] *n* piston *m.*

pit [pɪt] (*pt* & *pp* **-ted,** *cont* **-ting**) ◇ *n* **-1.** [hole] trou *m;* [in road] petit trou; [on face] marque *f.* **-2.** [for orchestra] fosse *f.* **-3.** [mine] mine *f.* **-4.** [quarry] carrière *f.* **-5.** *Am* [of fruit] noyau *m.* **-6.** *phr:* **the** ~ **of one's stomach** le creux de l'estomac. ◇ *vt:* **to** ~ **sb against sb** opposer qqn à qqn; **to** ~ **one's wits against sb** se mesurer avec qqn.

◆ **pits** *npl* **-1.** [in motor racing]: **the** ~**s** les stands *mpl.* **-2.** *inf* [awful]: **the** ~**s** l'horreur *f* complète OR totale.

pitch [pɪtʃ] ◇ *n* **-1.** SPORT terrain *m.* **-2.** MUS ton *m.* **-3.** [level, degree] degré *m.* **-4.** [selling place] place *f.* **-5.** *inf* [sales talk] baratin *m.* **-6.** AERON & NAUT tangage *m.* **-7.** [throw] lancement *m.* ◇ *vt* **-1.** [throw] lancer; **to be** ~**ed into sthg** être catapulté dans qqch. **-2.** [set - price] fixer; [- speech] adapter. **-3.** [tent] dresser; [camp] établir. ◇ *vi* **-1.** [ball] rebondir. **-2.** [fall]: **to** ~ **forward** être projeté(e) en avant. **-3.** AERON & NAUT tanguer.

◆ **pitch in** *vi* s'y mettre.

pitch-black *adj* noir(e) comme dans un four.

pitched [pɪtʃt] *adj* [sloping] penché(e).

pitched battle *n* bataille *f* rangée.

pitcher ['pɪtʃəʳ] *n Am* **-1.** [jug] cruche *f.* **-2.** [in baseball] lanceur *m.*

pitchfork ['pɪtʃfɔːk] *n* fourche *f.*

piteous ['pɪtɪəs] *adj* pitoyable.

piteously ['pɪtɪəslɪ] *adv* pitoyablement.

pitfall ['pɪtfɔːl] *n* piège *m.*

pith [pɪθ] *n* **-1.** [in plant] moelle *f.* **-2.** [of fruit] peau *f* blanche. **-3.** *fig* [crux] essence *f.*

pithead ['pɪthed] *n* carreau *m* de mine.

pith helmet *n* casque *m* colonial.

pithy ['pɪθɪ] (*compar* **-ier,** *superl* **-iest**) *adj* [brief] concis(e); [terse] piquant(e).

pitiable ['pɪtɪəbl] *adj* pitoyable.

pitiful ['pɪtɪfʊl] *adj* [condition] pitoyable; [excuse, effort] lamentable.

pitifully ['pɪtɪfʊlɪ] *adv* [look, cry] pitoyablement; [poor] lamentablement.

pitiless ['pɪtɪlɪs] *adj* sans pitié, impitoyable.

pitman ['pɪtmən] (*pl* **-men** [-mən]) *n* mineur *m* de fond.

pit pony *n Br* cheval *m* de mine.

pit prop *n* poteau *m* de mine.

pit stop *n* [in motor racing] arrêt *m* aux stands.

pitta bread ['pɪtə-] *n* pain *m* grec, pita *m*.

pittance ['pɪtəns] *n* [wage] salaire *m* de misère.

pitted ['pɪtɪd] *adj*: ~ **(with)** [face] grêlé(e) (par); [metal] piqué(e) (de).

pitter-patter ['pɪtə,pætər] *n* [of rain] crépitement *m*.

pituitary [pɪ'tjuɪtrɪ] (*pl* **-ies**) *n*: ~ **(gland)** glande *f* pituitaire.

pity ['pɪtɪ] (*pt & pp* **-ied**) ◇ *n* pitié *f*; **what a** ~! quel dommage!; **it's a** ~ c'est dommage; **to take** OR **have** ~ **on sb** prendre qqn en pitié, avoir pitié de qqn. ◇ *vt* plaindre.

pitying ['pɪtɪɪŋ] *adj* compatissant(e).

pivot ['pɪvət] ◇ *n lit & fig* pivot *m*. ◇ *vi*: **to** ~ **(on)** pivoter (sur).

pixel ['pɪksl] *n* COMPUT pixel *m*.

pixie, pixy ['pɪksɪ] (*pl* **-ies**) *n* lutin *m*.

pizza ['piːtsə] *n* pizza *f*.

pizzazz [pɪ'zæz] *n inf* vitalité *f*, énergie *f*.

Pl. (*abbr of* **Place**) *rue*.

P & L (*abbr of* **profit and loss**) *n pertes et profits*.

placard ['plækɑːd] *n* placard *m*, affiche *f*.

placate [plə'keɪt] *vt* calmer, apaiser.

placatory [plə'keɪtərɪ] *adj* apaisant(e).

place [pleɪs] ◇ *n* **-1.** [location] endroit *m*, lieu *m*; ~ **of birth** lieu *m* de naissance. **-2.** [proper position, seat, vacancy, rank] place *f*; **everything fell into** ~ *fig* tout s'éclaircit; **to put sb in their** ~ remettre qqn à sa place. **-3.** [home]: **at/to my** ~ chez moi. **-4.** [in book]: **to lose one's** ~ perdre la page. **-5.** MATH: **decimal** ~ décimale *f*. **-6.** [instance]: **in the first** ~ tout de suite; **in the first** ~ ... **and in the second** ~ ... premièrement ... et deuxièmement .... **-7.** *phr*: **to take** ~ avoir lieu; **to take the** ~ **of** prendre la place de, remplacer.

◇ *vt* **-1.** [position, put] placer, mettre. **-2.** [apportion]: **to** ~ **the responsibility for sthg on sb** tenir qqn pour responsable de qqch. **-3.** [identify] remettre. **-4.** [order] passer; **to** ~ **a bet** parier. **-5.** [in race]: **to be** ~**d** être placé(e).

◆ **all over the place** *adv* [everywhere] partout.

◆ **in place** *adv* **-1.** [in proper position] à sa place. **-2.** [established] mis en place.

◆ **in place of** *prep* à la place de.

◆ **out of place** *adv* pas à sa place; *fig* déplacé(e).

placebo [plə'siːbəʊ] (*pl* **-s** OR **-es**) *n* placebo *m*.

place card *n* carte *f* marque-place.

placed [pleɪst] *adj*: **how are we** ~ **for time?** est-ce qu'on a assez de temps?; **how are you** ~ **for money?** qu'est-ce que tu as comme argent?

placekick ['pleɪskɪk] *n* coup *m* de pied placé.

place mat *n* set *m* (de table).

placement ['pleɪsmənt] *n* placement *m*.

placenta [plə'sentə] (*pl* **-s** OR **-tae** [-tiː]) *n* placenta *m*.

place setting *n* couvert *m*.

placid ['plæsɪd] *adj* **-1.** [person] placide. **-2.** [sea, place] calme.

placidly ['plæsɪdlɪ] *adv* avec placidité.

plagiarism ['pleɪdʒjərɪzm] *n* plagiat *m*.

plagiarist ['pleɪdʒjərɪst] *n* plagiaire *mf*.

plagiarize, -ise ['pleɪdʒjəraɪz] *vt* plagier.

plague [pleɪg] ◇ *n* **-1.** MED peste *f*; **to avoid sb/sthg like the** ~ fuir qqn/qqch comme la peste. **-2.** *fig* [nuisance] fléau *m*. ◇ *vt*: **to be** ~**d by** [bad luck] être poursuivi(e) par; [doubt] être rongé(e) par; **to** ~ **sb with questions** harceler qqn de questions.

plaice [pleɪs] (*pl inv*) *n* carrelet *m*.

plaid [plæd] *n* plaid *m*.

Plaid Cymru [,plaɪd'kʌmrɪ] *n parti nationaliste gallois*.

plain [pleɪn] ◇ *adj* **-1.** [not patterned] uni(e). **-2.** [simple] simple. **-3.** [clear] clair(e), évident(e); **to make sthg** ~ **to sb** [bien] faire comprendre qqch à qqn. **-4.** [blunt] carré(e), franc (franche). **-5.** [absolute] pur(e) (et simple). **-6.** [not pretty] quelconque, ordinaire. ◇ *adv inf* complètement. ◇ *n* GEOGR plaine *f*.

plain chocolate *n Br* chocolat *m* à croquer.

plain-clothes *adj* en civil.

plain flour *n Br* farine *f* (sans levure).

plainly ['pleɪnlɪ] *adv* **-1.** [obviously] manifestement. **-2.** [distinctly] clairement. **-3.** [frankly] carrément, sans détours. **-4.** [simply] simplement.

plain sailing *n*: **it should be** ~ **from now on** ça devrait aller comme sur des roulettes maintenant.

plainspoken [,pleɪn'spəʊkən] *adj* au franc-parler.

plaintiff ['pleɪntɪf] *n* demandeur *m*, -eresse *f*.

plaintive ['pleɪntɪv] *adj* plaintif(ive).

plait [plæt] ◇ *n* natte *f*. ◇ *vt* natter, tresser.

plan [plæn] (*pt* & *pp* **-ned**, *cont* **-ning**) ◇ *n* plan *m*, projet *m*; **to go according to** ~ se passer OR aller comme prévu. ◇ *vt* **-1.** [organize] préparer. **-2.** [propose]: **to** ~ **to do sthg** projeter de faire qqch, avoir l'intention de faire qqch. **-3.** [design] concevoir. ◇ *vi*: **to** ~ **(for sthg)** faire des projets (pour qqch).
◆ **plans** *npl* plans *mpl*, projets *mpl*; **have you any** ~**s for tonight?** avez-vous prévu quelque chose pour ce soir?
◆ **plan on** *vt fus*: **to** ~ **on doing sthg** prévoir de faire qqch.
◆ **plan out** *vt sep* préparer dans le détail.

plane [pleɪn] ◇ *adj* plan(e). ◇ *n* **-1.** [aircraft] avion *m*. **-2.** GEOM plan *m*. **-3.** *fig* [level] niveau *m*. **-4.** [tool] rabot *m*. **-5.** [tree] platane *m*. ◇ *vt* raboter.

planet ['plænɪt] *n* planète *f*.

planetarium [,plænɪ'teərɪəm] (*pl* **-riums** OR **-ria** [-rɪə]) *n* planétarium *m*.

planetary ['plænɪtrɪ] *adj* planétaire.

plane tree *n* platane *m*.

plangent ['plændʒənt] *adj literary* retentissant(e).

plank [plæŋk] *n* **-1.** [of wood] planche *f*. **-2.** POL [policy] point *m*.

plankton ['plæŋktən] *n* plancton *m*.

planned [plænd] *adj* [crime] prémédité(e); [economy] planifié(e), dirigé(e).

planner ['plænər] *n* **-1.** [designer]: **town** ~ urbaniste *mf*. **-2.** [strategist] planificateur *m*, -trice *f*.

planning ['plænɪŋ] *n* **-1.** [designing] planification *f*. **-2.** [preparation] préparation *f*, organisation *f*.

planning permission *n* permis *m* de construire.

plan of action *n* plan *m* d'action.

plant [plɑːnt] ◇ *n* **-1.** BOT plante *f*. **-2.** [factory] usine *f*. **-3.** (*U*) [heavy machinery] matériel *m*. ◇ *vt* **-1.** [gen] planter. **-2.** [bomb] poser; **to** ~ **sthg on sb** cacher qqch sur qqn.
◆ **plant out** *vt sep* repiquer.

plantain ['plæntɪn] *n* plantain *m*.

plantation [plæn'teɪʃn] *n* plantation *f*.

planter ['plɑːntər] *n* [farmer] planteur *m*, -euse *f*.

plant pot *n* pot *m* de fleurs.

plaque [plɑːk] *n* **-1.** [commemorative sign] plaque *f*. **-2.** (*U*) [on teeth] plaque *f* dentaire.

plasma ['plæzmə] *n* plasma *m*.

plaster ['plɑːstər] ◇ *n* **-1.** [material] plâtre *m*; **in** ~ dans le plâtre. **-2.** *Br* [bandage] pansement *m* adhésif. ◇ *vt* **-1.** [wall, ceiling] plâtrer. **-2.** [cover]: **to** ~ **sthg (with)** couvrir qqch (de).

plasterboard ['plɑːstəbɔːd] *n* placoplâtre® *m*.

plaster cast *n* **-1.** [for broken bones] plâtre *m*. **-2.** [model, statue] moule *m*.

plastered ['plɑːstəd] *adj inf* [drunk] bourré(e).

plasterer ['plɑːstərər] *n* plâtrier *m*.

plastering ['plɑːstərɪŋ] *n* plâtrage *m*.

plaster of Paris *n* plâtre *m* de moulage.

plastic ['plæstɪk] ◇ *adj* plastique. ◇ *n* plastique *m*.

plastic bullet *n* balle *f* de plastique.

plastic explosive *n* plastic *m*.

Plasticine® *Br* ['plæstɪsiːn], **play dough** *Am n* pâte *f* à modeler.

plasticize, -ise ['plæstɪsaɪz] *vt* plastifier.

plastic money *n* (*U*) cartes *fpl* de crédit.

plastic surgeon *n* spécialiste *mf* en chirurgie esthétique.

plastic surgery *n* chirurgie *f* esthétique OR plastique.

plate [pleɪt] ◇ *n* **-1.** [dish] assiette *f*; **to have a lot on one's** ~ *fig* avoir du pain sur la planche; **you can't expect everything to be handed to you on a** ~ *fig* on ne peut pas tout t'apporter sur un plateau. **-2.** [sheet of metal, plaque] plaque *f*. **-3.** (*U*) [metal covering]: **gold/silver** ~ plaqué *m* or/argent. **-4.** [in book] planche *f*. **-5.** [in dentistry] dentier *m*. ◇ *vt*: **to be** ~**d (with)** être plaqué(e) (de).

Plate *n*: **the River** ~ le Rio de la Plata.

plateau ['plætəʊ] (*pl* **-s** OR **-x** [-təʊz]) *n* plateau *m*; *fig* phase *f* OR période *f* de stabilité.

plateful ['pleɪtful] *n* assiettée *f*.

plate-glass *adj* vitré(e).

plate rack *n* égouttoir *m*.

platform ['plætfɔːm] *n* **-1.** [stage] estrade *f*; [for speaker] tribune *f*. **-2.** [raised structure, of bus, of political party] plate-forme *f*. **-3.** RAIL quai *m*.

platform ticket *n Br* ticket *m* de quai.

plating ['pleɪtɪŋ] *n* placage *m*.

platinum ['plætɪnəm] ◇ *adj* [hair] platiné(e). ◇ *n* platine *m*. ◇ *comp* en platine.

platinum blonde *n* blonde *f* platinée.

platitude ['plætɪtjuːd] *n* platitude *f*.

platonic [plə'tɒnɪk] *adj* platonique.

platoon [plə'tuːn] *n* section *f*.

platter ['plætər] *n* [dish] plat *m*.

platypus ['plætɪpəs] (*pl* **-es**) *n* ornithorynque *m*.

plaudits ['plɔːdɪts] *npl* louanges *fpl*, éloges *mpl*.

plausible ['plɔːzəbl] *adj* plausible.

plausibly ['plɔːzəblɪ] *adv* de façon plausible.

play [pleɪ] ◇ *n* **-1.** (*U*) [amusement] jeu *m*, amusement *m*. **-2.** THEATRE pièce *f* (de théâtre); **a radio** ~ une pièce radiophonique. **-3.** SPORT: **in/out of** ~ en/hors jeu. **-4.** [consideration]: **to come into** ~ *fig* entrer en jeu. **-5.** [game]: ~ **on words** jeu *m* de mots. **-6.** TECH jeu *m*.
◇ *vt* **-1.** [gen] jouer; **to** ~ **a part** OR **role in** *fig* jouer un rôle dans. **-2.** [game, sport] jouer à. **-3.** [team, opponent] jouer contre. **-4.** MUS [instrument] jouer de. **-5.** *phr*: **to** ~ **it safe** ne pas prendre de risques.
◇ *vi* jouer.
◆ **play along** *vi*: **to** ~ **along (with sb)** entrer dans le jeu (de qqn).
◆ **play at** *vt fus* jouer à; **what's he** ~**ing at?** *inf* à quoi joue-t-il?
◆ **play back** *vt sep* [tape] réécouter; [film] repasser.
◆ **play down** *vt sep* minimiser.
◆ **play off** ◇ *vt sep*: **to** ~ **sb/sthg off against** monter qqn/qqch contre. ◇ *vi* SPORT jouer la belle.
◆ **play (up)on** *vt fus* jouer sur.
◆ **play up** ◇ *vt sep* [emphasize] insister sur. ◇ *vi* **-1.** [machine] faire des siennes. **-2.** [child] ne pas être sage.

playable ['pleɪəbl] *adj* [pitch] praticable.

play-act *vi* jouer la comédie.

playbill ['pleɪbɪl] *n* affiche *f*.

playboy ['pleɪbɔɪ] *n* playboy *m*.

play dough *Am* = **Plasticine®**.

player ['pleɪə'] *n* **-1.** [gen] joueur *m*, -euse *f*. **-2.** THEATRE acteur *m*, -trice *f*.

playfellow ['pleɪ,feləʊ] *n* camarade *mf*.

playful ['pleɪful] *adj* **-1.** [person, mood] taquin(e). **-2.** [kitten, puppy] joueur(euse).

playfully ['pleɪfulɪ] *adv* en badinant.

playgoer ['pleɪ,gəʊə'] *n* amateur *m* de théâtre.

playground ['pleɪgraund] *n* cour *f* de récréation.

playgroup ['pleɪgruːp] *n* jardin *m* d'enfants.

playhouse ['pleɪhaus, *pl* -hauzɪz] *n Am* maison *f* en modèle réduit (*pour jouer*).

playing card ['pleɪɪŋ-] *n* carte *f* à jouer.

playing field ['pleɪɪŋ-] *n* terrain *m* de sport.

playlist ['pleɪlɪst] *n Br* liste *f* de disques à passer (*à la radio*).

playmate ['pleɪmeɪt] *n* camarade *mf*.

play-off *n* SPORT belle *f*.

playpen ['pleɪpen] *n* parc *m*.

playroom ['pleɪrum] *n* salle *f* de jeu.

playschool ['pleɪskuːl] *n* jardin *m* d'enfants.

plaything ['pleɪθɪŋ] *n lit* & *fig* jouet *m*.

playtime ['pleɪtaɪm] *n* récréation *f*.

playwright ['pleɪraɪt] *n* dramaturge *m*.

plaza ['plɑːzə] *n* [square] place *f*; **shopping** ~ **centre** *m* commercial.

plc *abbr of* **public limited company**.

plea [pliː] *n* **-1.** [for forgiveness, mercy] supplication *f*; [for help, quiet] appel *m*. **-2.** JUR: **to enter a** ~ **of not guilty** plaider non coupable.

plea bargaining *n* possibilité pour un inculpé de se voir notifier un chef d'inculpation moins grave s'il accepte de plaider coupable.

plead [pliːd] (*pt* & *pp* OR **pled**) ◇ *vt* **-1.** JUR plaider. **-2.** [give as excuse] invoquer. ◇ *vi* **-1.** [beg]: **to** ~ **with sb (to do sthg)** supplier qqn (de faire qqch); **to** ~ **for sthg** implorer qqch. **-2.** JUR plaider.

pleading ['pliːdɪŋ] ◇ *adj* suppliant(e). ◇ *n* (*U*) supplications *fpl*.

pleasant ['pleznt] *adj* agréable.

pleasantly ['plezntlɪ] *adv* [smile, speak] aimablement; [surprised] agréablement.

pleasantry ['plezntrɪ] (*pl* **-ies**) *n*: **to exchange pleasantries** échanger des propos aimables.

please [pliːz] ◇ *vt* plaire à, faire plaisir à; **to** ~ **o.s.** faire comme on veut; ~ **yourself!** comme vous voulez! ◇ *vi* plaire, faire plaisir; **to do as one** ~**s** faire comme on veut; **if you** ~ s'il vous plaît. ◇ *adv* s'il vous plaît.

pleased [pliːzd] *adj* **-1.** [satisfied]: **to be** ~ **(with)** être content(e) (de). **-2.** [happy]: **to be** ~ **(about)** être heureux(euse) (de); ~ **to meet you!** enchanté(e) !

pleasing ['pliːzɪŋ] *adj* plaisant(e).

pleasingly ['pliːzɪŋlɪ] *adv* agréablement.

pleasurable ['pleʒərəbl] *adj* agréable.

pleasure ['pleʒə'] *n* plaisir *m*; **with** ~ avec plaisir, volontiers; **it's a** ~, **my** ~ je vous en prie.

pleat [pliːt] ◇ *n* pli *m*. ◇ *vt* plisser.

pleated ['pliːtɪd] *adj* plissé(e).

plebiscite ['plebɪsaɪt] *n* plébiscite *m*.

plectrum ['plektrəm] (*pl* **-s**) *n* plectre *m*.

pled [pled] *pt* & *pp* → **plead**.

pledge [pledʒ] ◇ *n* **-1.** [promise] promesse *f*. **-2.** [token] gage *m*. ◇ *vt* **-1.** [promise] promettre. **-2.** [make promise]: **to** ~ **o.s. to** s'engager à; **to ~ sb to secrecy** faire promettre le secret à qqn. **-3.** [pawn] mettre en gage.

plenary session ['pliːnərɪ-] *n* séance *f* plénière.

plenitude ['plenɪtjuːd] *n* plénitude *f*.

plentiful ['plentɪfʊl] *adj* abondant(e).

plenty ['plentɪ] ◇ *n* (*U*) abondance *f*. ◇ *pron*: **~ of** beaucoup de; **we've got ~ of time** nous avons largement le temps. ◇ *adv Am* [very] très.

plethora ['pleθərə] *n* pléthore *f*.

pleurisy ['plʊərəsɪ] *n* pleurésie *f*.

Plexiglas® ['pleksɪɡlɑːs] *n Am* plexiglas® *m*.

pliable ['plaɪəbl], **pliant** ['plaɪənt] *adj* **-1.** [material] pliable, souple. **-2.** *fig* [person] docile.

pliers ['plaɪəz] *npl* tenailles *fpl*, pinces *fpl*.

plight [plaɪt] *n* condition *f* critique.

plimsoll ['plɪmsəl] *n Br* tennis *m*.

Plimsoll line *n* ligne *f* de flottaison en charge.

plinth [plɪnθ] *n* socle *m*.

PLO (*abbr of* **Palestine Liberation Organization**) *n* OLP *f*.

plod [plɒd] (*pt & pp* **-ded**, *cont* **-ding**) *vi* **-1.** [walk slowly] marcher lentement OR péniblement. **-2.** [work slowly] peiner.

plodder ['plɒdə'] *n pej* bûcheur *m*, -euse *f*.

plonk [plɒŋk] *n* (*U*) *Br inf* [wine] pinard *m*, vin *m* ordinaire.

◆ **plonk down** *vt sep inf* poser brutalement.

plop [plɒp] (*pt & pp* **-ped**, *cont* **-ping**) ◇ *n* ploc *m*. ◇ *vi* faire ploc.

plot [plɒt] (*pt & pp* **-ted**, *cont* **-ting**) ◇ *n* **-1.** [plan] complot *m*, conspiration *f*. **-2.** [story] intrigue *f*. **-3.** [of land] (parcelle *f* de) terrain *m*, lopin *m*. **-4.** *Am* [house plan] plan *m*. ◇ *vt* **-1.** [plan] comploter; **to ~ to do sthg** comploter de faire qqch. **-2.** [chart] déterminer, marquer. **-3.** MATH tracer, marquer. ◇ *vi* comploter.

plotter ['plɒtə'] *n* [schemer] conspirateur *m*, -trice *f*.

plough *Br*, **plow** *Am* [plaʊ] ◇ *n* charrue *f*. ◇ *vt* [field] labourer.

◆ **plough into** ◇ *vt sep* [money] investir. ◇ *vt fus* [subj: car] rentrer dans.

◆ **plough on** *vi* continuer péniblement OR laborieusement.

◆ **plough up** *vt sep* [field] labourer.

ploughman's ['plaʊmənz-] (*pl inv*) *n Br*: **~ (lunch)** repas de pain, fromage et pickles.

ploughshare *Br* **plowshare** *Am* ['plaʊʃeə'] *n* soc *m* de charrue.

plow *etc* [plaʊ] *Am* = **plough** *etc*.

ploy [plɔɪ] *n* stratagème *m*, ruse *f*.

PLR (*abbr of* **Public Lending Right**) *n* droit d'auteur versé pour les ouvrages prêtés par les bibliothèques.

pluck [plʌk] ◇ *vt* **-1.** [flower, fruit] cueillir. **-2.** [pull sharply] arracher. **-3.** [chicken, turkey] plumer. **-4.** [eyebrows] épiler. **-5.** MUS pincer. ◇ *n* (*U*) *dated* courage *m*, cran *m*.

◆ **pluck up** *vt fus*: **to ~ up the courage to do sthg** rassembler son courage pour faire qqch.

plucky ['plʌkɪ] (*compar* **-ier**, *superl* **-iest**) *adj dated* qui a du cran, courageux(euse).

plug [plʌɡ] (*pt & pp* **-ged**, *cont* **-ging**) ◇ *n* **-1.** ELEC prise *f* de courant. **-2.** [for bath, sink] bonde *f*. **-3.** *inf* [for new book, film etc] pub *f*, publicité *f*. ◇ *vt* **-1.** [hole] boucher, obturer. **-2.** *inf* [new book, film etc] faire de la publicité pour.

◆ **plug in** *vt sep* brancher.

plughole ['plʌɡhəʊl] *n* bonde *f*, trou *m* d'écoulement.

plum [plʌm] ◇ *adj* **-1.** [colour] prune (*inv*). **-2.** [very good]: **a ~ job** un fromage. ◇ *n* [fruit] prune *f*.

plumage ['pluːmɪdʒ] *n* plumage *m*.

plumb [plʌm] ◇ *adv* **-1.** *Br* [exactly] exactement, en plein. **-2.** *Am* [completely] complètement. ◇ *vt*: **to ~ the depths of** toucher le fond de.

◆ **plumb in** *vt sep Br* raccorder.

plumber ['plʌmə'] *n* plombier *m*.

plumbing ['plʌmɪŋ] *n* (*U*) **-1.** [fittings] plomberie *f*, tuyauterie *f*. **-2.** [work] plomberie *f*.

plumb line *n* fil *m* à plomb.

plume [pluːm] *n* **-1.** [feather] plume *f*. **-2.** [on hat] panache *m*. **-3.** [column]: **a ~ of smoke** un panache de fumée.

plummet ['plʌmɪt] *vi* **-1.** [bird, plane] plonger. **-2.** *fig* [decrease] dégringoler.

plummy ['plʌmɪ] (*compar* **-ier**, *superl* **-iest**) *adj Br pej* [voice] de la haute, snob.

plump [plʌmp] *adj* bien en chair, grassouillet(ette).

◆ **plump for** *vt fus* opter pour, choisir.

◆ **plump up** *vt sep* [cushion] secouer.

plumpness ['plʌmpnɪs] *n* corpulence *f*, embonpoint *m*.

plum pudding *n* pudding *m* de Noël.

plunder ['plʌndə'] ◇ *n* (*U*) **-1.** [stealing, raiding] pillage *m*. **-2.** [stolen goods] butin *m*. ◇ *vt* piller.

plunge [plʌndʒ] ◇ *n* **-1.** [dive] plongeon *m*; **to take the ~** se jeter à l'eau. **-2.** *fig* [decrease] dégringolade *f*, chute *f*. ◇ *vt*: **to ~**

sthg into plonger qqch dans. ◇ *vi* **-1.** [dive] plonger, tomber. **-2.** *fig* [decrease] dégringoler.

plunger ['plʌndʒəʳ] *n* débouchoir *m* à ventouse.

plunging ['plʌndʒɪŋ] *adj* [neckline] plongeant(e).

pluperfect [,pluːˈpɜːfɪkt] *n*: ~ **(tense)** plusque-parfait *m*.

plural ['plʊərəl] ◇ *adj* **-1.** GRAMM pluriel(ielle). **-2.** [not individual] collectif(ive). **-3.** [multicultural] multiculturel(elle). ◇ *n* pluriel *m*.

pluralistic [,plʊərəˈlɪstɪk] *adj* pluraliste.

plurality [plʊˈrælətɪ] *n* **-1.** [large number]: a ~ of une multiplicité de. **-2.** *Am* [majority] majorité *f*.

plus [plʌs] (*pl* **-es** OR **-ses**) ◇ *adj*: 30 ~ 30 ou plus. ◇ *n* **-1.** MATH signe *m* plus. **-2.** *inf* [bonus] plus *m*, atout *m*. ◇ *prep* et. ◇ *conj* [moreover] de plus.

plus fours *npl* pantalon *m* de golf.

plush [plʌʃ] *adj* luxueux(euse), somptueux(euse).

plus sign *n* signe *m* plus.

Pluto ['pluːtəʊ] *n* [planet] Pluton *f*.

plutocrat ['pluːtəkræt] *n* ploutocrate *m*.

plutonium [pluːˈtəʊnɪəm] *n* plutonium *m*.

ply [plaɪ] (*pt* & *pp* **plied**) ◇ *adj*: **four ~** [wool] à quatre fils; [wood] à quatre plis. ◇ *n* [of wool] fil *m*; [of wood] pli *m*. ◇ *vt* **-1.** [trade] exercer. **-2.** [supply]: **to ~ sb with drink** ne pas arrêter de remplir le verre de qqn. ◇ *vi* [ship etc] faire la navette.

plywood ['plaɪwʊd] *n* contreplaqué *m*.

p.m., pm (*abbr of* **post meridiem**): **at 3 ~** à 15h.

PM *abbr of* **prime minister**.

PMS *abbr of* **premenstrual syndrome**.

PMT *abbr of* **premenstrual tension**.

pneumatic [njuːˈmætɪk] *adj* pneumatique.

pneumatic drill *n* marteau-piqueur *m*.

pneumonia [njuːˈməʊnjə] *n* (*U*) pneumonie *f*.

po = **PO²**.

Po [pəʊ] *n*: **the (River) ~** le Pô.

PO¹ *abbr of* **Post Office**.

PO², po *abbr of* **postal order**.

POA (*abbr of* **Prison Officers' Association**) *n syndicat des agents pénitentiaires en Grande-Bretagne*.

poach [pəʊtʃ] ◇ *vt* **-1.** [fish] pêcher sans permis; [deer etc] chasser sans permis. **-2.** *fig* [idea] voler. **-3.** CULIN pocher. ◇ *vi* braconner.

poacher ['pəʊtʃəʳ] *n* braconnier *m*.

poaching ['pəʊtʃɪŋ] *n* braconnage *m*.

PO Box (*abbr of* **Post Office Box**) *n* BP *f*.

pocket ['pɒkɪt] ◇ *n lit* & *fig* poche *f*; **to be out of ~** en être de sa poche; **to live in each other's ~s** être trop ensemble; **to pick sb's ~** faire les poches à qqn. ◇ *adj* de poche. ◇ *vt* empocher.

pocketbook ['pɒkɪtbʊk] *n* **-1.** [notebook] carnet *m*. **-2.** *Am* [handbag] sac *m* à main.

pocket calculator *n* calculatrice *f* de poche, calculette *f*.

pocketful ['pɒkɪtful] *n* pleine poche *f*.

pocket-handkerchief *n* mouchoir *m* de poche.

pocketknife ['pɒkɪtnaɪf] (*pl* **-knives** [-naɪvz]) *n* canif *m*.

pocket money *n* argent *m* de poche.

pocket-size(d) *adj* de poche.

pockmark ['pɒkmɑːk] *n* marque *f* de la petite vérole.

pod [pɒd] *n* **-1.** [of plants] cosse *f*. **-2.** [of spacecraft] nacelle *f*.

podgy ['pɒdʒɪ] (*compar* **-ier**, *superl* **-iest**) *adj inf* boulot(otte), rondelet(ette).

podiatrist [pəˈdaɪətrɪst] *n Am* pédicure *mf*.

podium ['pəʊdɪəm] (*pl* **-diums** OR **-dia** [-dɪə]) *n* podium *m*.

POE (*abbr of* **port of entry**) *n port d'arrivée.*

poem ['pəʊɪm] *n* poème *m*.

poet ['pəʊɪt] *n* poète *m*.

poetic [pəʊˈetɪk] *adj* poétique.

poetic justice *n* justice *f* immanente.

poet laureate *n* poète *m* lauréat.

poetry ['pəʊɪtrɪ] *n* poésie *f*.

pogo stick ['pəʊgəʊ-] *n* échasse *f* à ressort.

pogrom ['pɒgrəm] *n* pogrom *m*, pogrome *m*.

poignancy ['pɔɪnjənsɪ] *n* caractère *m* poignant.

poignant ['pɔɪnjənt] *adj* poignant(e).

poinsettia [pɔɪnˈsetɪə] *n* poinsettia *m*.

point [pɔɪnt] ◇ *n* **-1.** [tip] pointe *f*. **-2.** [place] endroit *m*, point *m*. **-3.** [time] stade *m*, moment *m*; ~ **of no return** point *m* de non retour. **-4.** [detail, argument] question *f*, détail *m*; **you have a ~** il y a du vrai dans ce que vous dites; **to make a ~** faire une remarque; **to make one's ~** dire ce qu'on a à dire, dire son mot; **it's a sore ~ with her** *fig* elle est très sensible sur ce point. **-5.** [main idea] point *m* essentiel. **-6.** [purpose]: **what's the ~?** à quoi bon?; **to get** OR **come to the ~** en venir au fait; **to miss the ~** ne pas comprendre; **beside the ~** à côté de la question; **to the ~** pertinent(e), ap-

proprié(e). **-6.** [feature]: **good** ~ qualité *f*; **bad** ~ défaut *m*. **-7.** [purpose]: **what's the** ~ **in buying a new car?** à quoi bon acheter une nouvelle voiture?; **there's no** ~ **in having a meeting** cela ne sert à rien d'avoir une réunion. **-8.** [on scale, in scores] point *m*. **-9.** MATH: **two** ~ **six** deux virgule six. **-10.** [of compass] aire *f* du vent. **-11.** *Br* ELEC prise *f* (de courant). **-12.** *Am* [full stop] point *m* (final). **-13.** *phr*: **to make a** ~ **of doing sthg** ne pas manquer de faire qqch.
◇ *vt*: **to** ~ **sthg (at)** [gun, camera] braquer qqch (sur); [finger, hose] pointer qqch (sur).
◇ *vi* **-1.** [indicate with finger]: **to** ~ **(at sb/ sthg), to** ~ **(to sb/sthg)** montrer (qqn/qqch) du doigt, indiquer (qqn/qqch) du doigt. **-2.** [face]: **to** ~ **north/south** indiquer le nord/le sud. **-3.** *fig* [suggest]: **to** ~ **to sthg** suggérer qqch, laisser supposer qqch.
◆ **points** *npl Br* RAIL aiguillage *m*.
◆ **up to a point** *adv* jusqu'à un certain point, dans une certaine mesure.
◆ **on the point of** *prep* sur le point de.
◆ **point out** *vt sep* [person, place] montrer, indiquer; [fact, mistake] signaler.

point-blank ◇ *adj* [refusal] catégorique; [question] de but en blanc; **at** ~ **range** à bout portant. ◇ *adv* **-1.** [refuse] catégoriquement; [ask] de but en blanc. **-2.** [shoot] à bout portant.

point duty *n Br* service *m* de la circulation.

pointed ['pɔɪntɪd] *adj* **-1.** [sharp] pointu(e). **-2.** *fig* [remark] mordant(e), incisif(ive).

pointedly ['pɔɪntɪdlɪ] *adv* d'un ton mordant.

pointer ['pɔɪntə'] *n* **-1.** [piece of advice] tuyau *m*, conseil *m*. **-2.** [needle] aiguille *f*. **-3.** [stick] baguette *f*. **-4.** COMPUT pointeur *m*.

pointing ['pɔɪntɪŋ] *n* [on wall] jointoiement *m*.

pointless ['pɔɪntlɪs] *adj* inutile, vain(e).

point of order (*pl* **points of order**) *n* question *f* de procédure OR de droit.

point of sale (*pl* **points of sale**) *n* point *m* de vente.

point of view (*pl* **points of view**) *n* point *m* de vue.

point-to-point *n Br* steeple-chase *m* pour cavaliers amateurs.

poise [pɔɪz] *n fig* calme *m*, sang-froid *m*.

poised [pɔɪzd] *adj* **-1.** [ready]: ~ **(for)** prêt(e) (pour); **to be** ~ **to do sthg** se tenir prêt à faire qqch. **-2.** *fig* [calm] calme, posé(e).

poison ['pɔɪzn] ◇ *n* poison *m*. ◇ *vt* **-1.** [gen] empoisonner. **-2.** [pollute] polluer.

poisoning ['pɔɪznɪŋ] *n* empoisonnement *m*; **food** ~ intoxication *f* alimentaire.

poisonous ['pɔɪznəs] *adj* **-1.** [fumes] toxique; [plant] vénéneux(euse). **-2.** [snake] venimeux(euse). **-3.** *fig* [rumours, influence] pernicieux(ieuse).

poison-pen letter *n* lettre *f* anonyme venimeuse.

poke [pəʊk] ◇ *n* [prod, jab] coup *m*. ◇ *vt* **-1.** [prod] pousser, donner un coup de coude à. **-2.** [push] fourrer. **-3.** [fire] attiser, tisonner. **-4.** [stretch]: **he** ~**d his head round the door** il a passé la tête dans l'embrasure de la porte. ◇ *vi* [protrude] sortir, dépasser.
◆ **poke about, poke around** *vi inf* fouiller, fourrager.
◆ **poke at** *vt fus* [with finger] pousser (du doigt); [with stick] pousser (avec un bâton).

poker ['pəʊkə'] *n* **-1.** [game] poker *m*. **-2.** [for fire] tisonnier *m*.

poker-faced [-,feɪst] *adj* au visage impassible.

poky ['pəʊkɪ] (*compar* **-ier**, *superl* **-iest**) *adj pej* [room] exigu(ë), minuscule.

Poland ['pəʊlənd] *n* Pologne *f*; **in** ~ en Pologne.

polar ['pəʊlə'] *adj* polaire.

polar bear *n* ours *m* polaire OR blanc.

polarity [pəʊ'lærətɪ] *n* polarité *f*.

polarization [,pəʊləraɪ'zeɪʃn] *n* polarisation *f*.

polarize, -ise ['pəʊləraɪz] *vt* polariser.

Polaroid® ['pəʊlərɔɪd] *n* **-1.** [camera] Polaroïd® *m*. **-2.** [photograph] photo *f* polaroïd.

Polaroids® ['pəʊlərɔɪdz] *npl* lunettes *fpl* polaroïd.

pole [pəʊl] *n* **-1.** [rod, post] perche *f*, mât *m*. **-2.** ELEC & GEOGR pôle *m*; ~**s apart** aux antipodes (l'un de l'autre).

Pole [pəʊl] *n* Polonais *m*, -e *f*.

poleaxed ['pəʊlækst] *adj* assommé(e).

polecat ['pəʊlkæt] *n* putois *m*.

polemic [pə'lemɪk] *n* polémique *f*.

pole position *n* pole position *f*.

Pole Star *n*: **the** ~ l'Étoile *f* Polaire.

pole vault *n*: **the** ~ le saut à la perche.
◆ **pole-vault** *vi* sauter à la perche.

pole-vaulter [-,vɔːltə'] *n* sauteur *m*, -euse *f* à la perche.

police [pə'liːs] ◇ *npl* **-1.** [police force]: **the** ~ la police. **-2.** [policemen] agents *mpl* de police. ◇ *vt* maintenir l'ordre dans.

police car *n* voiture *f* de police.

police constable *n Br* agent *m* de police.

police department n Am service m de police.

police dog n chien m policier.

police force n police f.

policeman [pə'liːsmən] (pl -men [-mən]) n agent m de police.

police officer n policier m.

police record n casier m judiciaire.

police state n état m policier.

police station n commissariat m (de police).

policewoman [pə'liːs,wumən] (pl -women [-,wimin]) n femme f agent de police.

policy ['pɒləsɪ] (pl -ies) n -1. [plan] politique f. -2. [document] police f.

policy-holder n assuré m, -e f.

polio ['pəʊlɪəʊ] n polio f.

polish ['pɒlɪʃ] ◇ n -1. [for shoes] cirage m; [for floor] cire f, encaustique f. -2. [shine] brillant m, lustre m. -3. fig [refinement] raffinement m. ◇ vt [shoes, floor] cirer; [car] astiquer; [cutlery, glasses] faire briller.
◆ **polish off** vt sep inf expédier.

Polish ['pəʊlɪʃ] ◇ adj polonais(e). ◇ n [language] polonais m. ◇ npl: **the** ~ les Polonais mpl.

polished ['pɒlɪʃt] adj -1. [refined] raffiné(e). -2. [accomplished] accompli(e), parfait(e).

polite [pə'laɪt] adj -1. [courteous] poli(e). -2. [refined] bien élevé(e), qui a du savoir-vivre.

politely [pə'laɪtlɪ] adv poliment.

politeness [pə'laɪtnɪs] n (U) politesse f.

politic ['pɒlətɪk] adj politique.

political [pə'lɪtɪkl] adj politique.

political asylum n droit m d'asile (politique).

political football n: **the abortion issue has become a** ~ les partis politiques se renvoient la balle au sujet de l'avortement.

political geography n géographie f politique.

politically [pə'lɪtɪklɪ] adv politiquement.

politically correct adj politiquement correct(e) (conforme à l'éthique du mouvement "PC").

POLITICALLY CORRECT:
Le mouvement "PC" est un mouvement intellectuel, surtout américain, qui vise à établir une nouvelle éthique, notamment en bannissant de la langue certains termes jugés discriminants. Ce mouvement prône de remplacer par exemple: 'American Indian' par 'Native American', 'Black' par 'African American', 'short' par 'vertically challenged'

political prisoner n prisonnier m politique.

political science n (U) sciences fpl politiques.

politician [,pɒlɪ'tɪʃn] n homme m, femme f politique.

politicize, -ise [pə'lɪtɪsaɪz] vt politiser.

politics ['pɒlətɪks] ◇ n (U) politique f. ◇ npl -1. [personal beliefs]: **what are his** ~? de quel bord est-il? -2. [of group, area] politique f.

polka ['pɒlkə] n polka f.

polka dot n pois m.

poll [pəʊl] ◇ n vote m, scrutin m. ◇ vt -1. [people] interroger, sonder. -2. [votes] obtenir.
◆ **polls** npl: **to go to the** ~s aller aux urnes.

pollen ['pɒlən] n pollen m.

pollen count n taux m de pollen.

pollinate ['pɒləneɪt] vt féconder avec du pollen.

pollination [,pɒlɪ'neɪʃn] n pollinisation f.

polling ['pəʊlɪŋ] n (U) élections fpl.

polling booth n isoloir m.

polling day n Br jour m du scrutin OR des élections.

polling station n bureau m de vote.

pollster ['pəʊlstər] n enquêteur m, -euse f.

poll tax n Br ≃ impôts mpl locaux.

pollutant [pə'luːtnt] n polluant m.

pollute [pə'luːt] vt polluer.

pollution [pə'luːʃn] n pollution f.

polo ['pəʊləʊ] n polo m.

polo neck n Br -1. [neck] col m roulé. -2. [jumper] pull m à col roulé.
◆ **polo-neck** adj Br à col roulé.

poltergeist ['pɒltəgaɪst] n esprit m frappeur.

poly ['pɒlɪ] (pl -s) n inf abbr of polytechnic.

polyanthus [,pɒlɪ'ænθəs] (pl -thuses OR -thi [-θaɪ]) n primevère f.

poly bag n Br inf sac m en plastique.

polyester [,pɒlɪ'estər] n polyester m.

polyethylene Am = polythene.

polygamist [pə'lɪgəmɪst] n polygame mf.

polygamy [pə'lɪgəmɪ] n polygamie f.

polygon ['pɒlɪgɒn] n polygone m.

polymer ['pɒlɪmər] n polymère m.

Polynesia [,pɒlɪ'niːzjə] n Polynésie f; **in** ~ en Polynésie; **French** ~ Polynésie française.

Polynesian [,pɒlɪ'niːzjən] ◇ adj polynésien(ienne). ◇ n -1. [person] Polynésien m, -ienne f. -2. [language] polynésien m.

polyp ['pɒlɪp] *n* polype *m*.

polyphony [pə'lɪfənɪ] *n fml* polyphonie *f*.

polystyrene [,pɒlɪ'staɪriːn] *n* polystyrène *m*.

polytechnic [,pɒlɪ'teknɪk] *n établissement d'enseignement supérieur en Grande-Bretagne.*

POLYTECHNIC:
Les conditions d'admission des 'polytechnics' sont moins rigoureuses que celles des universités à proprement parler. Ils délivrent les mêmes diplômes que les universités ('BA', 'MA' etc), mais aussi des diplômes techniques non universitaires. Certaines universités sont d'anciens 'polytechnics' ayant changé de statut

---

polythene *Br* ['pɒlɪθiːn], **polyethylene** *Am* [,pɒlɪ'eθɪliːn] *n* polyéthylène *m*.

polythene bag *n Br* sac *m* en plastique.

polyunsaturated [,pɒlɪʌn'sætʃəreɪtɪd] *adj* polyinsaturé(e).

polyurethane [,pɒlɪ'jʊərəθeɪn] *n* polyuréthane *m*.

pom [pɒm] *n Austr inf terme péjoratif désignant un Anglais.*

pomander [pə'mændə^r] *n* diffuseur *m* de parfum.

pomegranate ['pɒmɪ,grænɪt] *n* grenade *f*.

pommel ['pɒml] *n* pommeau *m*.

pomp [pɒmp] *n* pompe *f*, faste *m*.

pompom ['pɒmpɒm] *n* pompon *m*.

pompous ['pɒmpəs] *adj* **-1.** [person] fat, suffisant(e). **-2.** [style, speech] pompeux(euse).

ponce [pɒns] *n Br v inf pej* **-1.** [effeminate man] homme *m* efféminé. **-2.** [pimp] maquereau *m*.

poncho ['pɒntʃəʊ] (*pl* -s) *n* poncho *m*.

pond [pɒnd] *n* étang *m*, mare *f*.

ponder ['pɒndə^r] ◇ *vt* considérer, peser. ◇ *vi*: **to ~ (on** OR **over)** réfléchir (sur).

ponderous ['pɒndərəs] *adj* **-1.** [dull] lourd(e). **-2.** [large, heavy] pesant(e).

pong [pɒŋ] *Br inf* ◇ *n* puanteur *f*. ◇ *vi* puer, schlinguer.

pontiff ['pɒntɪf] *n* souverain *m* pontife.

pontificate [pɒn'tɪfɪkeɪt] *vi pej*: **to ~ (on)** pontifier (sur).

pontoon [pɒn'tuːn] *n* **-1.** [bridge] ponton *m*. **-2.** *Br* [game] vingt-et-un *m*.

pony ['pəʊnɪ] (*pl* -ies) *n* poney *m*.

ponytail ['pəʊnɪteɪl] *n* queue *f* de cheval.

pony-trekking [-,trekɪŋ] *n* randonnée *f* à cheval OR poney.

poodle ['puːdl] *n* caniche *m*.

poof [pʊf] *n Br v inf pej* tapette *f*, pédé *m*.

pooh [puː] *excl* berk!, pouah!

pooh-pooh *vt inf* dédaigner.

pool [puːl] ◇ *n* **-1.** [pond, of blood] mare *f*; [of rain, light] flaque *f*. **-2.** [swimming pool] piscine *f*. **-3.** SPORT billard *m* américain. ◇ *vt* [resources etc] mettre en commun.

◆ **pools** *npl Br*: **the ~s** ≃ le loto sportif.

pooped [puːpt] *adj inf* crevé(e).

poor [pɔː^r] ◇ *adj* **-1.** [gen] pauvre. **-2.** [not very good] médiocre, mauvais(e). ◇ *npl*: **the ~** les pauvres *mpl*.

poorhouse ['pɔːhaʊs, *pl* -haʊzɪz] *n* hospice *m* des pauvres.

poorly ['pɔːlɪ] ◇ *adj Br* souffrant(e). ◇ *adv* mal, médiocrement.

poorness ['pɔːnɪs] *n* médiocrité *f*.

poor relation *n fig* parent *m* pauvre.

pop [pɒp] (*pt & pp* -ped, *cont* -ping) ◇ *n* **-1.** (U) [music] pop *m*. **-2.** (U) *inf* [fizzy drink] boisson *f* gazeuse. **-3.** *inf* [father] papa *m*. **-4.** [sound] pan *m*. ◇ *vt* **-1.** [burst] faire éclater, crever. **-2.** [put quickly] mettre, fourrer. ◇ *vi* **-1.** [balloon] éclater, crever; [cork, button] sauter. **-2.** [eyes]: **his eyes popped** il a écarquillé les yeux. **-3.** [go quickly]: **I'm just popping to the newsagent's** je fais un saut chez le marchand de journaux.

◆ **pop in** *vi* entrer en passant.

◆ **pop up** *vi* surgir.

popadum ['pɒpədəm] *n* poppadum *m*.

pop art *n* pop art *m*.

pop concert *n* concert *m* pop.

popcorn ['pɒpkɔːn] *n* pop-corn *m*.

pope [pəʊp] *n* pape *m*.

pop group *n* groupe *m* pop.

poplar ['pɒplə^r] *n* peuplier *m*.

poplin ['pɒplɪn] *n* popeline *f*.

popper ['pɒpə^r] *n Br* pression *f*.

poppy ['pɒpɪ] (*pl* -ies) *n* coquelicot *m*, pavot *m*.

poppycock ['pɒpɪkɒk] *n* (U) *inf pej* idioties *fpl*, bêtises *fpl*.

Poppy Day *n Br* anniversaire *m* de l'armistice.

POPPY DAY:
Journée de commémoration pendant laquelle on porte un coquelicot en papier en souvenir des soldats britanniques morts lors des guerres mondiales

---

Popsicle® ['pɒpsɪkl] *n Am* ≃ Esquimau® *m*.

pop singer *n* chanteur *m*, -euse *f* pop.

populace ['pɒpjʊləs] *n*: **the ~** le peuple.

popular ['pɒpjʊləʳ] *adj* **-1.** [gen] populaire. **-2.** [name, holiday resort] à la mode.

popularity [,pɒpjʊ'lærəti] *n* popularité *f.*

popularize, -ise ['pɒpjʊləraɪz] *vt* **-1.** [make popular] populariser. **-2.** [simplify] vulgariser.

popularly ['pɒpjʊləlɪ] *adv* communément.

populate ['pɒpjʊleɪt] *vt* peupler.

populated ['pɒpjʊleɪtɪd] *adj* peuplé(e).

population [,pɒpjʊ'leɪʃn] *n* population *f.*

population explosion *n* explosion *f* démographique.

populist ['pɒpjʊlɪst] *n* populiste *mf.*

pop-up *adj* **-1.** [toaster] automatique. **-2.** [book] dont les images se déplient.

porcelain ['pɔːsəlɪn] *n* porcelaine *f.*

porch [pɔːtʃ] *n* **-1.** [entrance] porche *m.* **-2.** *Am* [verandah] véranda *f.*

porcupine ['pɔːkjʊpaɪn] *n* porc-épic *m.*

pore [pɔːʳ] *n* pore *m.*

◆ **pore over** *vt fus* examiner de près.

pork [pɔːk] *n* porc *m.*

pork chop *n* côtelette *f* de porc.

pork pie *n* pâté *m* de porc en croûte.

porn [pɔːn] (*abbr of* **pornography**) *n* (U) *inf* porno *m*; **hard ~** porno *m* hard, hard *m*; **soft ~** porno *m* soft, soft *m.*

pornographic [,pɔːnə'græfɪk] *adj* pornographique.

pornography [pɔː'nɒgrəfɪ] *n* pornographie *f.*

porous ['pɔːrəs] *adj* poreux(euse).

porpoise ['pɔːpəs] *n* marsouin *m.*

porridge ['pɒrɪdʒ] *n* porridge *m.*

port [pɔːt] ◇ *n* **-1.** [town, harbour] port *m.* **-2.** NAUT [left-hand side] bâbord *m*; **to ~** à bâbord. **-3.** [drink] porto *m.* **-4.** COMPUT port *m.* ◇ *comp* **-1.** [of a port] portuaire, du port. **-2.** NAUT [left-hand] de bâbord.

portable ['pɔːtəbl] *adj* portatif(ive).

Portacrib® ['pɔːtə,krɪb] *n Am* moïse *m,* porte-bébé *m.*

portal ['pɔːtl] *n literary* portail *m.*

Port-au-Prince [,pɔːtəʊ'prɪns] *n* Port-au-Prince.

portcullis [,pɔːt'kʌlɪs] *n* herse *f.*

portend [pɔː'tend] *vt* présager, augurer.

portent ['pɔːtənt] *n* présage *m.*

porter ['pɔːtəʳ] *n* **-1.** *Br* [doorman] concierge *m,* portier *m.* **-2.** [for luggage] porteur *m.* **-3.** *Am* [on train] employé *m,* -e *f* des wagons-lits.

portfolio [,pɔːt'fəʊljəʊ] (*pl* **-s**) *n* **-1.** [case] serviette *f.* **-2.** [sample of work] portfolio *m.* **-3.** ꟳIN portefeuille *m.*

porthole ['pɔːthəʊl] *n* hublot *m.*

portion ['pɔːʃn] *n* **-1.** [section] portion *f,* part *f.* **-2.** [of food] portion *f.*

portly ['pɔːtlɪ] (*compar* **-ier,** *superl* **-iest**) *adj* corpulent(e).

port of call *n* **-1.** NAUT port *m* d'escale. **-2.** *fig* [on journey] endroit *m.*

Port of Spain *n* Port of Spain.

portrait ['pɔːtreɪt] *n* portrait *m.*

portraitist ['pɔːtreɪtɪst] *n* portraitiste *mf.*

portray [pɔː'treɪ] *vt* **-1.** CINEMA & THEATRE jouer, interpréter. **-2.** [describe] dépeindre. **-3.** [paint] faire le portrait de.

portrayal [pɔː'treɪəl] *n* **-1.** CINEMA & THEATRE interprétation *f.* **-2.** [painting, photograph] portrait *m.* **-3.** [description] description *f.*

Portugal ['pɔːtʃʊgl] *n* Portugal *m*; **in ~** au Portugal.

Portuguese [,pɔːtʃʊ'giːz] ◇ *adj* portugais(e). ◇ *n* [language] portugais *m.* ◇ *npl*: **the ~** les Portugais *mpl.*

Portuguese man-of-war *n* galère *f.*

pose [pəʊz] ◇ *n* **-1.** [stance] pose *f.* **-2.** *pej* [affectation] pose *f,* affectation *f.* ◇ *vt* **-1.** [danger] présenter. **-2.** [problem, question] poser. ◇ *vi* **-1.** ART & *pej* poser. **-2.** [pretend to be]: **to ~ as** se faire passer pour.

poser ['pəʊzəʳ] *n* **-1.** *pej* [person] poseur *m,* -euse *f.* **-2.** *inf* [hard question] question *f* difficile, colle *f.*

poseur [pəʊ'zɜːʳ] *n pej* poseur *m,* -euse *f.*

posh [pɒʃ] *adj inf* **-1.** [hotel, clothes etc] chic (*inv*). **-2.** *Br* [upper class] de la haute.

posit ['pɒzɪt] *vt fml* énoncer, poser en principe.

position [pə'zɪʃn] ◇ *n* **-1.** [gen] position *f*; **in ~** en place, en position. **-2.** [job] poste *m,* emploi *m.* **-3.** [state] situation *f*; **to be in a/no ~ to do sthg** être/ne pas être à même de faire qqch. ◇ *vt* placer, mettre en position; **to ~ o.s.** se placer, se mettre.

positive ['pɒzətɪv] *adj* **-1.** [gen] positif(ive). **-2.** [sure] sûr(e), certain(e); **to be ~ about sthg** être sûr de qqch. **-3.** [optimistic] positif(ive), optimiste; **to be ~ about sthg** avoir une attitude positive au sujet de qqch. **-4.** [definite] formel(elle), précis(e). **-5.** [evidence] irréfutable, indéniable. **-6.** [downright] véritable.

positive discrimination *n* discrimination *f* positive.

positively ['pɒzətɪvlɪ] *adv* **-1.** [optimistically] avec optimisme, de façon positive. **-2.** [definitely] formellement. **-3.** [favourably] favorablement. **-4.** [irrefutably] d'une manière irréfutable. **-5.** [completely] absolument, complètement.

positive vetting *n Br* enquête *sur une personne pour des raisons de sécurité.*

positivism ['pɒzɪtɪvɪzm] *n* positivisme *m.*

posse ['pɒsɪ] *n Am* détachement *m,* troupe *f.*

possess [pə'zes] *vt* posséder.

possessed [pə'zest] *adj* [mad] possédé(e).

possession [pə'zeʃn] *n* possession *f.*
◆ **possessions** *npl* possessions *fpl,* biens *mpl.*

possessive [pə'zesɪv] ◇ *adj* possessif(ive). ◇ *n* GRAMM possessif *m.*

possessively [pə'zesɪvlɪ] *adv* d'une manière possessive.

possessor [pə'zesəʳ] *n* possesseur *m,* propriétaire *mf.*

possibility [,pɒsə'bɪlətɪ] (*pl* **-ies**) *n* **-1.** [chance, likelihood] possibilité *f,* chances *fpl*; **there is a ~ that ...** il se peut que ... (+ *subjunctive*). **-2.** [option] possibilité *f,* option *f.*

possible ['pɒsəbl] ◇ *adj* possible; **as much as ~** autant que possible; **as soon as ~** dès que possible; **the best/worst ~** le meilleur/pire possible. ◇ *n* possible *m.*

possibly ['pɒsəblɪ] *adv* **-1.** [perhaps] peut-être. **-2.** [within one's power]: **I'll do all I ~ can** je ferai tout mon possible. **-3.** [expressing surprise]: **how could he ~ have known?** mais comment a-t-il pu le savoir? **-4.** [for emphasis]: **I can't ~ accept your money** je ne peux vraiment pas accepter cet argent.

possum ['pɒsəm] (*pl inv* OR **-s**) *n Am* opossum *m.*

post [pəʊst] ◇ *n* **-1.** [service]: **the ~** la poste; **the letter is in the ~** la lettre a été postée; **by ~** par la poste. **-2.** [letters, delivery] courrier *m.* **-3.** *Br* [collection] levée *f.* **-4.** [pole] poteau *m.* **-5.** [position, job] poste *m,* emploi *m.* **-6.** MIL poste *m.* **-7.** *phr:* **to pip sb at the ~** coiffer qqn au poteau. ◇ *vt* **-1.** [by mail] poster, mettre à la poste. **-2.** [employee] muter. **-3.** *phr:* **to keep sb ~ed** tenir qqn au courant.

post- [pəʊst] *prefix* post-.

postage ['pəʊstɪdʒ] *n* affranchissement *m*; **~ and packing** frais *mpl* de port et d'emballage.

postage stamp *n* timbre-poste *m.*

postal ['pəʊstl] *adj* postal(e).

postal order *n* mandat *m* postal.

postbag ['pəʊstbæg] *n* **-1.** *Br* [bag] sac *m* postal. **-2.** *inf* [letters received] courrier *m,* lettres *fpl.*

postbox ['pəʊstbɒks] *n Br* boîte *f* aux lettres.

postcard ['pəʊstkɑːd] *n* carte *f* postale.

postcode ['pəʊstkəʊd] *n Br* code *m* postal.

postdate [,pəʊst'deɪt] *vt* postdater.

poster ['pəʊstəʳ] *n* [for advertising] affiche *f*; [for decoration] poster *m.*

poste restante [,pəʊst'restɑːnt] *n* poste *f* restante.

posterior [pɒ'stɪərɪəʳ] ◇ *adj* postérieur(e). ◇ *n hum* postérieur *m,* derrière *m.*

posterity [pɒ'sterətɪ] *n* postérité *f.*

poster paint *n* gouache *f.*

post-free *adj* franco (de port) (*inv*).

postgraduate [,pəʊst'grædjʊət] ◇ *adj* de troisième cycle. ◇ *n* étudiant *m,* -e *f* de troisième cycle.

posthaste [,pəʊst'heɪst] *adv* très vite, en toute hâte.

posthumous ['pɒstjʊməs] *adj* posthume.

posthumously ['pɒstjʊməslɪ] *adv* à titre posthume.

post-industrial *adj* post-industriel(ielle).

posting ['pəʊstɪŋ] *n* [assignment] affectation *f.*

postman ['pəʊstmən] (*pl* **-men** [-mən]) *n* facteur *m.*

postmark ['pəʊstmɑːk] ◇ *n* cachet *m* de la poste. ◇ *vt* timbrer, tamponner.

postmaster ['pəʊst,mɑːstəʳ] *n* receveur *m* des postes.

Postmaster General (*pl* **Postmasters General**) *n* ≃ ministre *m* des Postes et Télécommunications.

postmistress ['pəʊst,mɪstrɪs] *n* receveuse *f* des postes.

postmortem [,pəʊst'mɔːtəm] ◇ *adj*: **~ examination** autopsie *f.* ◇ *n lit* & *fig* autopsie *f.*

postnatal [,pəʊst'neɪtl] *adj* post-natal(e).

post office *n* **-1.** [organization]: **the Post Office** les Postes et Télécommunications *fpl.* **-2.** [building] (bureau *m* de) poste *f.*

post office box *n* boîte *f* postale.

postoperative [,pəʊst'ɒpərətɪv] *adj* postopératoire.

postpaid [,pəʊst'peɪd] *adj* port payé.

postpone [,pəʊst'pəʊn] *vt* reporter, remettre.

postponement [,pəʊst'pəʊnmənt] *n* renvoi *m,* report *m.*

postscript ['pəʊstskrɪpt] *n* post-scriptum *m*; *fig* supplément *m,* addenda *m inv.*

postulate [*n* 'pɒstjʊlət, *vb* 'pɒstjʊleɪt] ◇ *n* postulat *m.* ◇ *vt* [theory] avancer.

posture ['pɒstʃə'] ◇ *n* -1. (U) [pose] position *f*, posture *f*. -2. *fig* [attitude] attitude *f*. ◇ *vi* poser, prendre des attitudes.

posturing ['pɒstʃərɪŋ] *n* pose *f*, affectation *f*.

postviral syndrome [,pəust'vaɪərl-] *n* syndrome *m* de fatigue chronique.

postwar [,pəust'wɔːr] *adj* d'après-guerre.

posy ['pəuzɪ] (*pl* -ies) *n* petit bouquet *m* de fleurs.

pot [pɒt] (*pt* & *pp* -ted, *cont* -ting) ◇ *n* -1. [for cooking] marmite *f*, casserole *f*. -2. [for tea] théière *f*; [for coffee] cafetière *f*. -3. [for paint, jam, plant] pot *m*. -4. (U) *inf* [cannabis] herbe *f*. ◇ *vt* [plant] mettre en pot.

potash ['pɒtæʃ] *n* potasse *f*.

potassium [pə'tæsɪəm] *n* potassium *m*.

potato [pə'teɪtəu] (*pl* -es) *n* pomme *f* de terre.

potato crisps *Br*, **potato chips** *Am npl* (pommes *fpl*) chips *fpl*.

potato peeler *n* (couteau *m*) éplucheur *m*.

pot-bellied [-,belɪd] *adj* [from overeating] ventru(e); [from malnutrition] au ventre gonflé.

potboiler ['pɒt,bɔɪlə'] *n fig* œuvre *f* alimentaire.

potbound ['pɒtbaund] *adj*: **a ~ plant** *une plante qui est devenue trop grande pour son pot*.

potency ['pəutənsɪ] *n* (U) -1. [power, influence] puissance *f*. -2. [of drink] teneur *f* en alcool. -3. [of man] virilité *f*.

potent ['pəutənt] *adj* -1. [powerful, influential] puissant(e). -2. [drink] fort(e). -3. [man] viril.

potentate ['pəutənteɪt] *n* potentat *m*.

potential [pə'tenʃl] ◇ *adj* [energy, success] potentiel(ielle); [uses, danger] possible; [enemy] en puissance. ◇ *n* (U) [of person] capacités *fpl* latentes; **to have ~** [person] promettre; [company] avoir de l'avenir; [scheme] offrir des possibilités.

potentially [pə'tenʃəlɪ] *adv* potentiellement.

pothole ['pɒthəul] *n* -1. [in road] nid-de-poule *m*. -2. [underground] caverne *f*, grotte *f*.

potholer ['pɒt,həulə'] *n Br* spéléologue *mf*.

potholing ['pɒt,həulɪŋ] *n Br* spéléologie *f*; **to go ~** faire de la spéléologie.

potion ['pəuʃn] *n* [magic] breuvage *m*; **love ~** philtre *m*.

potluck [,pɒt'lʌk] *n*: **to take ~** [gen] choisir au hasard; [at meal] manger à la fortune du pot.

pot plant *n* plante *f* d'appartement.

potpourri [,pəu'puərɪ] *n* (U) [dried flowers] fleurs *fpl* séchées.

pot roast *n* rôti *m* braisé.

potshot ['pɒt,ʃɒt] *n*: **to take a ~ (at sthg)** tirer (sur qqch) sans viser.

potted ['pɒtɪd] *adj* -1. [plant]: **~ plant** plante *f* d'appartement. -2. [food] conservé(e) en pot. -3. *Br fig* [condensed] condensé(e), abrégé(e).

potter ['pɒtə'] *n* potier *m*.
◆ **potter about, potter around** *vi Br* bricoler.

Potteries ['pɒtərɪz] *npl*: **the ~** *la région des poteries dans le Staffordshire (en Angleterre)*.

potter's wheel *n* tour *m* de potier.

pottery ['pɒtərɪ] (*pl* -ies) *n* poterie *f*; **a piece of ~** une poterie.

potting compost ['pɒtɪŋ-] *n* terreau *m*.

potty ['pɒtɪ] (*compar* -ier, *superl* -iest, *pl* -ies) *Br inf* ◇ *adj*: **~ (about)** toqué(e) (de). ◇ *n* pot *m* (de chambre).

potty-trained *adj* propre.

pouch [pautʃ] *n* -1. [small bag] petit sac *m*; **tobacco ~** blague *f* à tabac. -2. [of kangaroo] poche *f* ventrale.

pouffe [puːf] *n Br* [seat] pouf *m*.

poultice ['pəultɪs] *n* cataplasme *m*.

poultry ['pəultrɪ] ◇ *n* (U) [meat] volaille *f*. ◇ *npl* [birds] volailles *fpl*.

pounce [pauns] *vi*: **to ~ (on)** [bird] fondre (sur); [person] se jeter (sur); **to ~ on** *fig* sauter sur.

pound [paund] ◇ *n* -1. *Br* [money] livre *f*. -2. [weight] = 453,6 grammes, ≃ livre *f*. -3. [for cars, dogs] fourrière *f*. ◇ *vt* -1. [strike loudly] marteler. -2. [crush] piler, broyer. ◇ *vi* -1. [strike loudly]: **to ~ on** donner de grands coups à. -2. [heart] battre fort; **my head is ~ing** j'ai des élancements dans la tête.

pounding ['paundɪŋ] *n* (U) -1. [of fists] martèlement *m*. -2. [of heart] battement *m* violent; **to get OR take a ~** [city] être pilonné(e); [team] être battu à plate couture OR à plates coutures.

pound sterling *n* livre *f* sterling.

pour [pɔːr] ◇ *vt* verser; **shall I ~ you a drink?** je te sers quelque chose à boire?; **to ~ money into sthg** *fig* investir beaucoup d'argent dans qqch. ◇ *vi* -1. [liquid] couler à flots. -2. *fig* [rush]: **to ~ in/out** entrer/sortir en foule. ◇ *v impers* [rain hard] pleuvoir à verse.
◆ **pour in** *vi* [letters, news] affluer.
◆ **pour out** *vt sep* -1. [empty] vider. -2.

[serve - drink] verser, servir. **-3.** *fig* [emotions] épancher.

pouring ['pɔːrɪŋ] *adj* [rain] torrentiel(ielle).

pout [paut] ◇ *n* moue *f*. ◇ *vi* faire la moue.

poverty ['pɒvətɪ] *n* pauvreté *f*; *fig* [of ideas] indigence *f*, manque *m*.

poverty line *n* seuil *m* de pauvreté.

poverty-stricken *adj* [person] dans la misère; [area] misérable, très pauvre.

poverty trap *n Br situation dans laquelle, du fait d'une augmentation d'un revenu faible, on ne peut plus toucher les prestations sociales.*

pow [pau] *excl inf* pan!, paf!

POW *abbr of* **prisoner of war.**

powder ['paudə'] ◇ *n* poudre *f*. ◇ *vt* [face, body] poudrer.

powder compact *n* poudrier *m*.

powdered ['paudəd] *adj* **-1.** [milk, eggs] en poudre. **-2.** [face] poudré(e).

powder puff *n* houppette *f*.

powder room *n* toilettes *fpl* pour dames.

powdery ['paudərɪ] *adj* [snow etc] poudreux(euse).

power ['pauə'] ◇ *n* **-1.** (*U*) [authority, ability] pouvoir *m*; **to have ~ over sb** avoir de l'autorité sur qqn; **to take ~** prendre le pouvoir; **to come to ~** parvenir au pouvoir; **to be in ~** être au pouvoir; **to be in** OR **within one's ~ to do sthg** être en son pouvoir de faire qqch; **~ of speech** parole *f*; **the ~s that be** les autorités *fpl*. **-2.** [strength, powerful person] puissance *f*, force *f*. **-3.** (*U*) [energy] énergie *f*. **-4.** [electricity] courant *m*, électricité *f*.

◇ *vt* faire marcher, actionner.

power base *n* support *m* politique.

powerboat ['pauəbəut] *n* hors-bord *m inv*.

power broker *n* négociateur *m*, -trice *f*.

power cut *n* coupure *f* de courant.

power failure *n* panne *f* de courant.

powerful ['pauəful] *adj* **-1.** [gen] puissant(e). **-2.** [smell, voice] fort(e). **-3.** [speech, novel] émouvant(e).

powerhouse ['pauəhaus, *pl* -hauzɪz] *n fig* personne *f* dynamique OR énergique.

powerless ['pauəlɪs] *adj* impuissant(e); **to be ~ to do sthg** être dans l'impossibilité de faire qqch, ne pas pouvoir faire qqch.

power line *n* ligne *f* à haute tension.

power of attorney *n* procuration *f*.

power plant *n* centrale *f* électrique.

power point *n Br* prise *f* de courant.

power-sharing [-ˌʃeərɪŋ] *n* partage *m* du pouvoir.

power station *n* centrale *f* électrique.

power steering *n* direction *f* assistée.

power worker *n* employé *m*, -e *f* de l'électricité.

pp (*abbr of* **per procurationem**) pp.

p & p *abbr of* **postage and packing.**

PPE (*abbr of* **philosophy, politics and economics**) *n philosophie, science politique et science économique (cours à l'université).*

ppm (*abbr of* **parts per million**) ppm.

PPS ◇ *n* (*abbr of* **parliamentary private secretary**) *parlementaire britannique assurant la liaison entre un ministre et les députés de son parti.* ◇ (*abbr of* **post postscriptum**) PPS.

PQ *abbr of* **Province of Quebec.**

Pr. (*abbr of* **Prince**) Pce.

PR ◇ *n* **-1.** *abbr of* **proportional representation. -2.** *abbr of* **public relations.** ◇ *n abbr of* **Puerto Rico.**

practicable ['præktɪkəbl] *adj* réalisable, faisable.

practical ['præktɪkl] ◇ *adj* **-1.** [gen] pratique. **-2.** [plan, solution] réalisable. ◇ *n* épreuve *f* pratique.

practicality [ˌpræktɪ'kælətɪ] *n* (*U*) aspect *m* pratique.

◆ **practicalities** *npl* détails *mpl* pratiques.

practical joke *n* farce *f*.

practically ['præktɪklɪ] *adv* **-1.** [in a practical way] d'une manière pratique. **-2.** [almost] presque, pratiquement.

practice, practise *Am* ['præktɪs] *n* **-1.** (*U*) [at sport] entraînement *m*; [at music etc] répétition *f*; **to be out of ~** être rouillé(e). **-2.** [training session - sport] séance *f* d'entraînement; [- at music etc] répétition *f*. **-3.** [act of doing]: **to put sthg into ~** mettre qqch en pratique; **in ~** [in fact] en réalité, en fait. **-4.** [habit] pratique *f*, coutume *f*. **-5.** (*U*) [of profession] exercice *m*. **-6.** [of doctor] cabinet *m*; [of lawyer] étude *f*.

practiced *Am* = **practised.**

practicing *Am* = **practising.**

practise, practice *Am* ['præktɪs] ◇ *vt* **-1.** [sport] s'entraîner à; [piano etc] s'exercer à. **-2.** [custom] suivre, pratiquer; [religion] pratiquer; **to ~ what one preaches** prêcher par l'exemple. **-3.** [profession] exercer. ◇ *vi* **-1.** SPORT s'entraîner; MUS s'exercer. **-2.** [doctor, lawyer] exercer.

practised, practiced *Am* ['præktɪst] *adj* [teacher, nurse] expérimenté(e); [liar] fieffé(e); **to be ~ at doing sthg** être expert à faire qqch; **a ~ eye** un œil exercé.

practising, practicing *Am* ['præktɪsɪŋ] *adj*

[doctor, lawyer] **en exercice**; [Christian etc] **pratiquant(e)**; [homosexual] **déclaré(e)**.

practitioner [præk'tɪʃnəʳ] n praticien m, -ienne f; **medical ~** médecin m.

pragmatic [præg'mætɪk] adj pragmatique.

pragmatism ['prægmətɪzm] n pragmatisme m.

pragmatist ['prægmətɪst] n pragmatiste mf.

Prague [prɑːg] n Prague.

prairie ['preərɪ] n prairie f.

praise [preɪz] ◇ n (U) louange f, louanges fpl, éloge m, éloges mpl; **to sing sb's ~s** chanter les louanges de qqn. ◇ vt louer, faire l'éloge de.

praiseworthy ['preɪz,wɜːðɪ] adj louable, méritoire.

praline ['prɑːliːn] n praline f.

pram [præm] n landau m.

PRAM [præm] (abbr of **programmable random access memory**) n RAM f programmable.

prance [prɑːns] vi **-1.** [person] se pavaner. **-2.** [horse] caracoler.

prang [præŋ] Br inf dated ◇ n [of car] accrochage m; [of plane] collision f. ◇ vt emboutir, bousiller.

prank [præŋk] n tour m, niche f.

prat [præt] n Br v inf pej crétin m, -e f.

prattle ['prætl] pej ◇ n (U) bavardage m, babillage m. ◇ vi babiller; **to ~ on about sthg** parler sans fin de qqch.

prawn [prɔːn] n crevette f rose.

prawn cocktail n crevettes fpl mayonnaise.

prawn cracker n genre de chips au goût de crevette.

pray [preɪ] vi: **to ~ (to sb)** prier (qqn); **to ~ for rain** prier pour qu'il pleuve.

prayer [preəʳ] n lit & fig prière f; **to say one's ~s** faire sa prière.

◆ **prayers** npl [service] office m.

prayer book n livre m de messe.

prayer meeting n réunion f pour dire des prières.

pre- [priː] prefix pré-.

preach [priːtʃ] ◇ vt [gen] prêcher; [sermon] prononcer. ◇ vi **-1.** RELIG: **to ~ (to sb)** prêcher (qqn). **-2.** pej [pontificate]: **to ~ (at sb)** sermonner (qqn).

preacher ['priːtʃəʳ] n prédicateur m, pasteur m.

preamble [priː'æmbl] n préambule m, avant-propos m inv.

prearrange [,priːə'reɪndʒ] vt organiser OR fixer à l'avance.

precarious [prɪ'keərɪəs] adj précaire.

precariously [prɪ'keərɪəslɪ] adv d'une manière précaire.

precast [,priː'kɑːst] adj: **~ concrete** béton m précoulé.

precaution [prɪ'kɔːʃn] n précaution f; **as a ~ (against)** par précaution (contre).

precautionary [prɪ'kɔːʃənərɪ] adj de précaution, préventif(ive).

precede [prɪ'siːd] vt précéder.

precedence ['presɪdəns] n: **to take ~ over sthg** avoir la priorité sur qqch; **to have** OR **take ~ over sb** avoir la préséance sur qqn.

precedent ['presɪdənt] n précédent m.

preceding [prɪ'siːdɪŋ] adj précédent(e).

precept ['priːsept] n précepte m.

precinct ['priːsɪŋkt] n **-1.** Br [area]: **pedestrian ~** zone f piétonnière; **shopping ~** centre m commercial. **-2.** Am [district] circonscription f (administrative).

◆ **precincts** npl [of institution] enceinte f.

precious ['preʃəs] adj **-1.** [gen] précieux(ieuse). **-2.** inf iro [damned] sacré(e); **~ little** très peu, bien peu. **-3.** [affected] affecté(e).

precious metal n métal m précieux.

precious stone n pierre f précieuse.

precipice ['presɪpɪs] n précipice m, paroi f à pic.

precipitate [adj prɪ'sɪpɪtət, vb prɪ'sɪpɪteɪt] fml ◇ adj hâtif(ive). ◇ vt [hasten] hâter, précipiter.

precipitation [prɪ,sɪpɪ'teɪʃn] n précipitation f.

precipitous [prɪ'sɪpɪtəs] adj **-1.** [very steep] escarpé(e), à pic. **-2.** [hasty] hâtif(ive).

précis [Br 'preɪsiː, Am 'presiː] n résumé m.

precise [prɪ'saɪs] adj précis(e); [measurement, date] exact(e); **49.5 to be ~** 49,5 pour être exact.

precisely [prɪ'saɪslɪ] adv précisément, exactement.

precision [prɪ'sɪʒn] ◇ n précision f, exactitude f. ◇ comp de précision.

preclude [prɪ'kluːd] vt fml empêcher; [possibility] écarter; **to ~ sb from doing sthg** empêcher qqn de faire qqch.

precocious [prɪ'kəʊʃəs] adj précoce.

precocity [prɪ'kɒsətɪ] n précocité f.

precognition [,priːkɒg'nɪʃn] n connaissance f anticipée.

preconceived [,priːkən'siːvd] adj préconçu(e).

preconception [,priːkən'sepʃn] n préjugé m, idée f préconçue.

precondition [ˌpriːkən'dɪʃn] *n fml* condition *f* sine qua non.

precooked [priː'kʊkt] *adj* précuit(e).

precursor [ˌpriː'kɜːsəʳ] *n fml* précurseur *m*.

predate [priː'deɪt] *vt* précéder.

predator ['predətəʳ] *n* **-1.** [animal, bird] prédateur *m*, rapace *m*. **-2.** *fig* [person] corbeau *m*.

predatory ['predətrɪ] *adj* **-1.** [animal, bird] prédateur(trice). **-2.** *fig* [person] rapace.

predecease [ˌpriːdɪ'siːs] *vt* décéder avant.

predecessor ['priːdɪsesəʳ] *n* **-1.** [person] prédécesseur *m*. **-2.** [thing] précédent *m*, -e *f*.

predestination [priːˌdestɪ'neɪʃn] *n* prédestination *f*.

predestine [ˌpriː'destɪn] *vt*: **to be ~d to sthg/to do sthg** être prédestiné(e) à qqch/à faire qqch.

predetermine [ˌpriːdɪ'tɜːmɪn] *vt* **-1.** [predestine] déterminer d'avance. **-2.** [prearrange] organiser OR fixer à l'avance.

predetermined [ˌpriːdɪ'tɜːmɪnd] *adj* **-1.** [predestined] déterminé(e) d'avance. **-2.** [prearranged] organisé(e) OR fixé(e) à l'avance.

predicament [prɪ'dɪkəmənt] *n* situation *f* difficile; **to be in a ~** être dans de beaux draps.

predict [prɪ'dɪkt] *vt* prédire.

predictable [prɪ'dɪktəbl] *adj* prévisible.

predictably [prɪ'dɪktəblɪ] *adv* [react, behave] d'une manière prévisible; **~, he was late** comme c'était à prévoir, il est arrivé en retard.

prediction [prɪ'dɪkʃn] *n* prédiction *f*.

predictor [prɪ'dɪktəʳ] *n* indicateur *m*.

predigest [ˌpriːdaɪ'dʒest] *vt fig* prédigérer.

predilection [ˌpriːdɪ'lekʃn] *n*: **~ for sthg** prédilection *f* pour qqch.

predispose [ˌpriːdɪs'pəʊz] *vt*: **to be ~d to sthg/to do sthg** être prédisposé(e) à qqch/à faire qqch.

predisposition ['priːˌdɪspə'zɪʃn] *n*: **~ to sthg/to do sthg, ~ towards sthg/towards doing sthg** prédisposition *f* à qqch/à faire qqch.

predominance [prɪ'dɒmɪnəns] *n* prédominance *f*.

predominant [prɪ'dɒmɪnənt] *adj* prédominant(e).

predominantly [prɪ'dɒmɪnəntlɪ] *adv* principalement, surtout.

predominate [prɪ'dɒmɪneɪt] *vi* prédominer.

preeminent [priː'emɪnənt] *adj* le plus en vue (la plus en vue).

preempt [ˌpriː'empt] *vt* **-1.** [action, decision] devancer, prévenir. **-2.** [land] acquérir par droit de préemption.

preemptive [ˌpriː'emptɪv] *adj* préventif(ive).

preemptive strike *n* attaque *f* préventive.

preen [priːn] *vt* **-1.** [subj: bird] lisser, nettoyer. **-2.** *fig* [subj: person]: **to ~ o.s.** se faire beau (belle).

preexist [ˌpriːɪg'zɪst] *vi* préexister.

prefab ['priːfæb] *n inf* maison *f* préfabriquée.

prefabricate [ˌpriː'fæbrɪkeɪt] *vt* préfabriquer.

preface ['prefɪs] ◇ *n*: **~ (to)** préface *f* (de), préambule *m* (de). ◇ *vt*: **to ~ sthg with sthg** faire précéder qqch de qqch.

prefect ['priːfekt] *n Br* [pupil] élève *m* de terminale qui aide les professeurs à maintenir la discipline.

prefer [prɪ'fɜːʳ] (*pt & pp* -**red**, *cont* -**ring**) *vt* préférer; **to ~ sthg to sthg** préférer qqch à qqch, aimer mieux qqch que qqch; **to ~ to do sthg** préférer faire qqch, aimer mieux faire qqch.

preferable ['prefrəbl] *adj*: **~ (to)** préférable (à).

preferably ['prefrəblɪ] *adv* de préférence.

preference ['prefərəns] *n* préférence *f*.

preference shares *Br npl*, **preferred stock** *Am n* (*U*) actions *fpl* privilégiées OR de priorité.

preferential [ˌprefə'renʃl] *adj* préférentiel(ielle).

preferred [prɪ'fɜːd] *adj* préféré(e).

preferred stock *Am* = **preference shares**.

prefigure [priː'fɪgəʳ] *vt* annoncer, préfigurer.

prefix ['priːfɪks] *n* préfixe *m*.

pregnancy ['pregnənsɪ] (*pl* -**ies**) *n* grossesse *f*.

pregnancy test *n* test *m* de grossesse.

pregnant ['pregnənt] *adj* **-1.** [woman] enceinte; [animal] pleine, gravide. **-2.** *fig* [pause] lourd(e) de sens.

preheated [ˌpriː'hiːtɪd] *adj* préchauffé(e).

prehistoric [ˌpriːhɪ'stɒrɪk] *adj* préhistorique.

prehistory [ˌpriː'hɪstərɪ] *n* préhistoire *f*.

pre-industrial *adj* pré-industriel(ielle).

prejudge [ˌpriː'dʒʌdʒ] *vt* [situation, issue] préjuger de; [person] juger d'avance.

prejudice ['predʒʊdɪs] ◇ *n* **-1.** [biased view]: **~ (in favour of/against)** préjugé *m* (en faveur de/contre), préjugés *mpl* (en faveur de/contre). **-2.** (*U*) [harm] préjudice *m*, tort *m*. ◇ *vt* **-1.** [bias]: **to ~ sb (in favour of/**

against) prévenir qqn (en faveur de/contre), influencer qqn (en faveur de/contre). **-2.** [harm] porter préjudice à.

prejudiced ['predʒudɪst] *adj* [person] qui a des préjugés; [opinion] préconçu(e); **to be ~ in favour of/against** avoir des préjugés en faveur de/contre.

prejudicial [ˌpredʒʊ'dɪʃl] *adj*: **~ (to)** préjudiciable (à), nuisible (à).

prelate ['prelɪt] *n* prélat *m*.

preliminary [prɪ'lɪmɪnərɪ] (*pl* **-ies**) *adj* préliminaire.

◆ **preliminaries** *npl* préliminaires *mpl*.

prelims ['priːlɪmz] *npl Br* [exams] examens *mpl* préliminaires.

prelude ['preljuːd] *n* [event]: **~ to sthg** prélude *m* de qqch.

premarital [ˌpriː'mærɪtl] *adj* avant le mariage.

premature ['premə,tjʊəʳ] *adj* prématuré(e).

prematurely ['premə,tjʊəlɪ] *adv* prématurément.

premeditated [ˌpriː'medɪteɪtɪd] *adj* prémédité(e).

premenstrual syndrome, premenstrual tension [priː'menstruəl-] *n* syndrome *m* prémenstruel.

premier ['premjəʳ] ◇ *adj* primordial(e), premier(ière). ◇ *n* premier ministre *m*.

premiere ['premɪeəʳ] *n* première *f*.

Premier League *n en Angleterre, ligue indépendante regroupant les meilleurs clubs de football.*

premiership ['premɪəʃɪp] *n* fonction *f* de premier ministre.

premise ['premɪs] *n* prémisse *f*; **on the ~ that** en partant du principe que.

◆ **premises** *npl* local *m*, locaux *mpl*; **on the ~s** sur place, sur les lieux.

premium ['priːmjəm] *n* prime *f*; **at a ~** [above usual value] à prix d'or; [in great demand] très recherché OR demandé; **to put** OR **place a high ~ on sthg** accorder OR attacher beaucoup d'importance à qqch.

premium bond *n Br* ≃ billet *m* de loterie.

premonition [ˌpremə'nɪʃn] *n* prémonition *f*, pressentiment *m*.

prenatal [ˌpriː'neɪtl] *adj Am* prénatal(e).

preoccupation [priːˌɒkjʊ'peɪʃn] *n* préoccupation *f*; **~ with sthg** souci de qqch.

preoccupied [priː'ɒkjʊpaɪd] *adj*: **~ (with)** préoccupé(e) (de).

preoccupy [priː'ɒkjʊpaɪ] (*pt* & *pp* **-ied**) *vt* préoccuper.

preordain [ˌpriːɔː'deɪn] *vt* décider OR déter-

miner d'avance; **to be ~ed to do sthg** être prédestiné à faire qqch.

prep [prep] *n (U) Br inf* devoirs *mpl*.

prepacked [ˌpriː'pækt] *adj* préconditionné(e).

prepaid ['priːpeɪd] *adj* payé(e) d'avance; [envelope] affranchi(e).

preparation [ˌprepə'reɪʃn] *n* préparation *f*; **in ~ for** en vue de.

◆ **preparations** *npl* préparatifs *mpl*; **to make ~s for** faire des préparatifs pour, prendre ses dispositions pour.

preparatory [prɪ'pærətrɪ] *adj* [work, classes] préparatoire; [actions, measures] préliminaire.

preparatory school *n* [in UK] école *f* primaire privée; [in US] *école privée qui prépare à l'enseignement supérieur.*

prepare [prɪ'peəʳ] ◇ *vt* préparer. ◇ *vi*: **to ~ for sthg/to do sthg** se préparer à qqch/à faire qqch.

prepared [prɪ'peəd] *adj* **-1.** [done beforehand] préparé(e) d'avance. **-2.** [willing]: **to be ~ to do sthg** être prêt(e) OR disposé(e) à faire qqch. **-3.** [ready]: **to be ~ for sthg** être prêt(e) pour qqch.

preponderance [prɪ'pɒndərəns] *n* majorité *f*.

preponderantly [prɪ'pɒndərəntlɪ] *adv* surtout, pour la plupart.

preposition [ˌprepə'zɪʃn] *n* préposition *f*.

prepossessing [ˌpriːpə'zesɪŋ] *adj fml* agréable, attrayant(e).

preposterous [prɪ'pɒstərəs] *adj* ridicule, absurde.

preppy ['prepɪ] (*pl* **-ies**) *Am inf* ◇ *adj* bon chic bon genre. ◇ *n* personne *f* bon chic bon genre.

prep school *abbr of* **preparatory school**.

Pre-Raphaelite [ˌpriː'ræfəlaɪt] ◇ *adj* préraphaélite. ◇ *n* préraphaélite *mf*.

prerecorded [ˌpriːrɪ'kɔːdɪd] *adj* enregistré(e) à l'avance, préenregistré(e).

prerequisite [ˌpriː'rekwɪzɪt] *n* condition *f* préalable.

prerogative [prɪ'rɒgətɪv] *n* prérogative *f*, privilège *m*.

presage ['presɪdʒ] *vt* présager.

Presbyterian [ˌprezbɪ'tɪərɪən] ◇ *adj* presbytérien(ienne). ◇ *n* presbytérien *m*, -ienne *f*.

presbytery ['prezbɪtrɪ] *n* [residence] presbytère *m*.

preschool [ˌpriː'skuːl] ◇ *adj* préscolaire. ◇ *n Am* école *f* maternelle.

prescient ['presɪənt] *adj* prescient(e).

prescribe [prɪ'skraɪb] *vt* **-1.** MED prescrire. **-2.** [order] ordonner, imposer.

prescription [prɪ'skrɪpʃn] *n* [MED - written form] ordonnance *f*; [- medicine] médicament *m*; **on ~** sur ordonnance.

prescription charge *n Br prix (fixe) à payer pour chaque médicament figurant sur une ordonnance.*

prescriptive [prɪ'skrɪptɪv] *adj* normatif(ive).

presence ['prezns] *n* présence *f*; **to be in sb's ~** OR **in the ~ of sb** être en la présence de qqn; **to have ~** avoir de la présence.

presence of mind *n* présence *f* d'esprit.

present [*adj & n* 'preznt, *vb* prɪ'zent] ◇ *adj* **-1.** [current] actuel(elle). **-2.** [in attendance] présent(e); **to be ~ at** assister à.
◇ *n* **-1.** [current time]: **the ~** le présent; **at ~** actuellement, en ce moment; **for the ~** pour le moment. **-2.** [gift] cadeau *m*. **-3.** GRAMM: **~ (tense)** présent *m*.
◇ *vt* **-1.** [gen] présenter; [opportunity] donner. **-2.** [give] donner, remettre; **to ~ sb with sthg, to ~ sthg to sb** donner OR remettre qqch à qqn. **-3.** [portray] représenter, décrire. **-4.** [arrive]: **to ~ o.s.** se présenter.

presentable [prɪ'zentəbl] *adj* présentable.

presentation [,prezn'teɪʃn] *n* **-1.** [gen] présentation *f*. **-2.** [ceremony] remise *f* (de récompense/prix). **-3.** [talk] exposé *m*. **-4.** [of play] représentation *f*.

presentation copy *n* exemplaire *m* offert gracieusement.

present day *n*: **the ~** aujourd'hui.

◆ **present-day** *adj* d'aujourd'hui, contemporain(e).

presenter [prɪ'zentər] *n Br* présentateur *m*, -trice *f*.

presentiment [prɪ'zentɪmənt] *n* pressentiment *m*.

presently ['prezntlɪ] *adv* **-1.** [soon] bientôt, tout à l'heure. **-2.** [at present] actuellement, en ce moment.

preservation [,prezə'veɪʃn] *n* (*U*) **-1.** [maintenance] maintien *m*. **-2.** [protection] protection *f*, conservation *f*.

preservation order *n décret ordonnant la conservation d'un monument, édifice etc.*

preservative [prɪ'zɜːvətɪv] *n* conservateur *m*.

preserve [prɪ'zɜːv] ◇ *vt* **-1.** [maintain] maintenir. **-2.** [protect] conserver. **-3.** [food] conserver, mettre en conserve. ◇ *n* [jam] confiture *f*.

◆ **preserves** *npl* [jam] confiture *f*; [vegetables] pickles *mpl*, condiments *mpl*.

preserved [prɪ'zɜːvd] *adj* conservé(e).

preset [,priː'set] (*pt & pp* **preset**, *cont* **-ting**) *vt* prérégler.

preshrunk [,priː'ʃrʌŋk] *adj* irrétrécissable.

preside [prɪ'zaɪd] *vi*: **to ~ (over** OR **at sthg)** présider (qqch).

presidency ['prezɪdənsɪ] (*pl* **-ies**) *n* présidence *f*.

president ['prezɪdənt] *n* **-1.** [gen] président *m*. **-2.** *Am* [company chairman] P-DG *m*.

President-elect *n titre du président des États-Unis nouvellement élu (en novembre) jusqu'à la cérémonie d'investiture présidentielle (le 20 janvier).*

presidential [,prezɪ'denʃl] *adj* présidentiel(ielle).

press [pres] ◇ *n* **-1.** [push] pression *f*. **-2.** [journalism]: **the ~** [newspapers] la presse, les journaux *mpl*; [reporters] les journalistes *mpl*; **to get a good/bad ~** avoir bonne/mauvaise presse. **-3.** [printing machine] presse *f*; [for wine] pressoir *m*.
◇ *vt* **-1.** [push] appuyer sur; **to ~ sthg against sthg** appuyer qqch sur qqch. **-2.** [squeeze] serrer. **-3.** [iron] repasser, donner un coup de fer à. **-4.** [urge]: **to ~ sb (to do sthg** OR **into doing sthg)** presser qqn (de faire qqch); **to ~ sb for sthg** demander qqch à qqn avec insistance. **-5.** [force]: **to ~ sthg on** OR **upon sb** offrir qqch à qqn avec insistance. **-6.** [pursue - claim] insister sur. **-7.** JUR: **to ~ charges (against sb)** porter plainte (contre qqn).
◇ *vi* **-1.** [push]: **to ~ (on)** appuyer (sur). **-2.** [squeeze]: **to ~ (on sthg)** serrer (qqch). **-3.** [crowd] se presser.

◆ **press for** *vt fus* demander avec insistance.

◆ **press on** *vi* [continue]: **to ~ on (with sthg)** continuer (qqch), ne pas abandonner (qqch).

press agency *n* agence *f* de presse.

press agent *n* agent *m* de publicité.

press baron *n Br* baron *m* OR magnat *m* de la presse.

press box *n* tribune *f* de la presse.

press conference *n* conférence *f* de presse.

press corps *n Am* journalistes *mpl*.

press cutting *n Br* coupure *f* de journal.

pressed [prest] *adj*: **to be ~ for time/ money** être à court de temps/d'argent.

press fastener *n Br* pression *f*.

press gallery *n* tribune *f* de la presse.

pressgang ['presgæŋ] ◇ *n* enrôleurs *mpl,* racoleurs *mpl.* ◇ *vt Br* **to ~ sb into doing sthg** forcer la main à qqn pour qu'il fasse qqch.

pressing ['presɪŋ] *adj* urgent(e).

pressman ['presmæn] (*pl* **-men** [-men]) *n Br* journaliste *m.*

press officer *n* attaché *m* de presse.

press release *n* communiqué *m* de presse.

press-stud *n Br* pression *f.*

press-up *n Br* pompe *f,* traction *f.*

pressure ['preʃər] ◇ *n* (*U*) **-1.** [gen] pression *f;* **to put ~ on sb (to do sthg)** faire pression sur qqn (pour qu'il fasse qqch). **-2.** [stress] tension *f.* ◇ *vt:* **to ~ sb to do** OR **into doing sthg** forcer qqn à faire qqch.

pressure cooker *n* Cocotte-minute® *f,* autocuiseur *m.*

pressure gauge *n* manomètre *m.*

pressure group *n* groupe *m* de pression.

pressurize, -ise ['preʃəraɪz] *vt* **-1.** TECH pressuriser. **-2.** *Br* [force]: **to ~ sb to do** OR **into doing sthg** forcer qqn à faire qqch.

Prestel® ['prestel] *n Br* ≃ Télétel® *m.*

prestige [pre'stiːʒ] ◇ *n* prestige *m.* ◇ *comp* de prestige.

prestigious [pre'stɪdʒəs] *adj* prestigieux(ieuse).

prestressed concrete [,priː'strest-] *n* béton *m* précontraint.

presumably [prɪ'zjuːməblɪ] *adv* vraisemblablement.

presume [prɪ'zjuːm] *vt* présumer; **to ~ (that) ... supposer que ....**

presumption [prɪ'zʌmpʃn] *n* **-1.** [assumption] supposition *f,* présomption *f.* **-2.** (*U*) [audacity] présomption *f.*

presumptuous [prɪ'zʌmptʃuəs] *adj* présomptueux(euse).

presuppose [,priːsə'pəʊz] *vt* présupposer.

pretax [,priː'tæks] *adj* avant impôts.

pretence, pretense *Am* [prɪ'tens] *n* prétention *f;* **to make a ~ of doing sthg** faire semblant de faire qqch; **under false ~s** sous des prétextes fallacieux.

pretend [prɪ'tend] ◇ *vt:* **to ~ to do sthg** faire semblant de faire qqch. ◇ *vi* faire semblant.

pretense *Am* = **pretence.**

pretension [prɪ'tenʃn] *n* prétention *f;* **to have ~s to sthg** avoir des prétentions à qqch.

pretentious [prɪ'tenʃəs] *adj* prétentieux(ieuse).

pretentiously [prɪ'tenʃəslɪ] *adv* de façon prétentieuse.

pretentiousness [prɪ'tenʃəsnɪs] *n* (*U*) prétention *f.*

preterite ['pretərət] *n* prétérit *m.*

pretext ['priːtekst] *n* prétexte *m;* **on** OR **under the ~ that ...** sous prétexte que ...; **on** OR **under the ~ of doing sthg** sous prétexte de faire qqch.

Pretoria [prɪ'tɔːrɪə] *n* Pretoria.

prettify ['prɪtɪfaɪ] (*pt* & *pp* **-ied**) *vt* enjoliver.

prettily ['prɪtɪlɪ] *adv* joliment.

pretty ['prɪtɪ] (*compar* **-ier,** *superl* **-iest**) ◇ *adj* joli(e). ◇ *adv* [quite] plutôt; **~ much** OR **well** pratiquement, presque.

pretzel ['pretsl] *n* bretzel *m.*

prevail [prɪ'veɪl] *vi* **-1.** [be widespread] avoir cours, régner. **-2.** [triumph]: **to ~ (over)** prévaloir (sur), l'emporter (sur). **-3.** [persuade]: **to ~ on** OR **upon sb to do sthg** persuader qqn de faire qqch.

prevailing [prɪ'veɪlɪŋ] *adj* **-1.** [current] actuel(elle). **-2.** [wind] dominant(e).

prevalence ['prevələns] *n* (*U*) fréquence *f.*

prevalent ['prevələnt] *adj* courant(e), répandu(e).

prevaricate [prɪ'værɪkeɪt] *vi* tergiverser.

prevent [prɪ'vent] *vt:* **to ~ sb/sthg (from doing sthg)** empêcher qqn/qqch (de faire qqch).

preventable [prɪ'ventəbl] *adj* qui peut être évité(e).

preventative [prɪ'ventətɪv] = **preventive.**

prevention [prɪ'venʃn] *n* (*U*) prévention *f.*

preventive [prɪ'ventɪv] *adj* préventif(ive).

preview ['priːvjuː] *n* avant-première *f.*

previous ['priːvjəs] *adj* **-1.** [earlier] antérieur(e). **-2.** [preceding] précédent(e).

previously ['priːvjəslɪ] *adv* avant, auparavant.

prewar [,priː'wɔːr] *adj* d'avant-guerre.

prey [preɪ] *n* proie *f;* **to fall ~ to** devenir la proie de.

◆ **prey on** *vt fus* **-1.** [live off] faire sa proie de. **-2.** [trouble]: **to ~ on sb's mind** ronger qqn, tracasser qqn.

price [praɪs] ◇ *n* **-1.** [cost] prix *m;* **at any ~** à tout prix; **she achieved fame, but at a ~** elle est devenue célèbre, mais ça lui a coûté cher. **-2.** [penalty]: **to pay the ~ for sthg** payer le prix pour qqch. ◇ *vt* fixer le prix de.

price-cutting *n* (*U*) réductions *fpl* de prix.

price-fixing [-,fɪksɪŋ] *n* (*U*) contrôle *m* des prix.

priceless ['praɪslɪs] *adj* sans prix, inestimable.

price list *n* tarif *m*.

price tag *n* [label] étiquette *f*.

price war *n* guerre *f* des prix.

pricey ['praɪsɪ] (*compar* **-ier**, *superl* **-iest**) *adj inf* chérot.

prick [prɪk] ◇ *n* **-1.** [scratch, wound] piqûre *f*. **-2.** *vulg* [stupid person] con *m*, conne *f*. ◇ *vt* piquer.

◆ **prick up** *vt fus*: **to ~ up one's ears** [animal] dresser les oreilles; [person] dresser OR tendre l'oreille.

prickle ['prɪkl] ◇ *n* **-1.** [thorn] épine *f*. **-2.** [sensation on skin] picotement *m*. ◇ *vi* picoter.

prickly ['prɪklɪ] (*compar* **-ier**, *superl* **-iest**) *adj* **-1.** [plant, bush] épineux(euse). **-2.** *fig* [person] irritable.

prickly heat *n* (*U*) boutons *mpl* de chaleur.

pride [praɪd] ◇ *n* (*U*) **-1.** [satisfaction] fierté *f*; **to take ~ in sthg/in doing sthg** être fier de qqch/de faire qqch; **it was his ~ and joy** c'était sa fierté; **to have ~ of place** avoir la place d'honneur. **-2.** [self-esteem] orgueil *m*, amour-propre *m*; **to swallow one's ~** ravaler son orgueil. **-3.** *pej* [arrogance] orgueil *m*. ◇ *vt*: **to ~ o.s. on sthg** être fier (fière) de qqch.

priest [priːst] *n* prêtre *m*.

priestess ['priːstɪs] *n* prêtresse *f*.

priesthood ['priːsthʊd] *n* **-1.** [position, office]: **the ~** le sacerdoce. **-2.** [priests]: **the ~** le clergé.

prig [prɪg] *n* petit saint *m*, petite sainte *f*.

prim [prɪm] (*compar* **-mer**, *superl* **-mest**) *adj* guindé(e).

primacy ['praɪməsɪ] *n* primauté *f*.

prima donna [ˌpriːmə'dɒnə] (*pl* **-s**) *n* prima donna *f inv*; **to be a ~** *fig* & *pej* se prendre pour le nombril du monde.

primaeval [praɪ'miːvəl] = **primeval**.

prima facie [ˌpraɪmə'feɪʃiː] *adj*: **~ evidence** commencement *m* de preuve; **~ case** affaire *f* qui, de prime abord, paraît fondée.

primal ['praɪml] *adj* **-1.** [original] primitif(ive). **-2.** [most important] primordial(e).

primarily ['praɪmərɪlɪ] *adv* principalement.

primary ['praɪmərɪ] (*pl* **-ies**) ◇ *adj* **-1.** [main] premier(ière), principal(e). **-2.** SCH primaire. ◇ *n* Am POL primaire *f*.

PRIMARIES:
Les primaires américaines sont des élections (directes ou indirectes selon les États) aboutissant à la sélection des candidats qui seront en lice pour représenter les deux partis nationaux à l'élection présidentielle

primary colour *n* couleur *f* primaire.

primary election *n* Am primaire *f*.

primary school *n* école *f* primaire.

primate ['praɪmeɪt] *n* **-1.** ZOOL primate *m*. **-2.** RELIG primat *m*.

prime [praɪm] ◇ *adj* **-1.** [main] principal(e), primordial(e). **-2.** [excellent] excellent(e); **~ quality** première qualité; **~ cut of meat** morceau de premier choix. ◇ *n*: **to be in one's ~** être dans la fleur de l'âge; **to be past one's ~** être sur le retour. ◇ *vt* **-1.** [gun, pump] amorcer. **-2.** [paint] apprêter. **-3.** [inform]: **to ~ sb about sthg** mettre qqn au courant de qqch.

prime minister *n* premier ministre *m*.

prime mover [-'muːvər] *n* *fig* instigateur *m*, -trice *f*.

prime number *n* nombre *m* premier.

primer ['praɪmər] *n* **-1.** [paint] apprêt *m*. **-2.** [textbook] introduction *f*.

prime time *n* (*U*) RADIO & TV heures *fpl* de grande écoute.

◆ **prime-time** *adj* aux heures de grande écoute.

primeval [praɪ'miːvl] *adj* [ancient] primitif(ive).

primitive ['prɪmɪtɪv] *adj* primitif(ive).

primordial [praɪ'mɔːdjəl] *adj* primordial(e).

primrose ['prɪmrəʊz] *n* primevère *f*.

Primus stove® ['praɪməs-] *n* réchaud *m* de camping.

prince [prɪns] *n* prince *m*.

◆ **Prince** *n*: **Prince of Wales** Prince de Galles.

Prince Charming *n* *hum* prince *m* charmant.

Prince Edward Island [-'edwəd-] *n* l'île *f* du Prince-Édouard.

princely ['prɪnslɪ] (*compar* **-ier**, *superl* **-iest**) *adj* princier(ière).

princess [prɪn'ses] *n* princesse *f*.

◆ **Princess** *n*: **Princess Royal** princesse royale.

principal ['prɪnsəpl] ◇ *adj* principal(e). ◇ *n* SCH directeur *m*, -trice *f*; UNIV doyen *m*, -enne *f*.

principality [ˌprɪnsɪ'pælətɪ] (*pl* **-ies**) *n* principauté *f*.

principally ['prɪnsəplɪ] *adv* principalement.

principle ['prɪnsəpl] *n* principe *m*; **on ~, as a matter of ~** par principe.

◆ **in principle** *adv* en principe.

principled ['prɪnsəpld] *adj* [behaviour] dicté(e) par des principes; [person] qui a des principes.

print [prɪnt] ◇ *n* **-1.** (*U*) [type] caractères *mpl*; **to be in** ~ être disponible; **to be out of** ~ être épuisé. **-2.** ART gravure *f*. **-3.** [photograph] épreuve *f*. **-4.** [fabric] imprimé *m*. **-5.** [mark] empreinte *f*. ◇ *vt* **-1.** [produce by printing] imprimer. **-2.** [publish] publier. **-3.** [write in block letters] écrire en caractères d'imprimerie. ◇ *vi* [printer] imprimer.
◆ **print out** *vt sep* COMPUT imprimer.

printed circuit ['prɪntɪd-] *n* circuit *m* imprimé.

printed matter ['prɪntɪd-] *n* (*U*) imprimés *mpl*.

printer ['prɪntər] *n* **-1.** [person, firm] imprimeur *m*. **-2.** COMPUT imprimante *f*.

printing ['prɪntɪŋ] *n* (*U*) **-1.** [act of printing] impression *f*. **-2.** [trade] imprimerie *f*.

printing press *n* presse *f* typographique.

printout ['prɪntaʊt] *n* COMPUT sortie *f* d'imprimante, listing *m*.

prior ['praɪər] ◇ *adj* antérieur(e), précédent(e). ◇ *n* [monk] prieur *m*.
◆ **prior to** *prep* avant; ~ **to doing sthg** avant de faire qqch.

prioritize, -ise [praɪ'ɒrɪtaɪz] *vt* donner la priorité à.

priority [praɪ'ɒrɪtɪ] (*pl* **-ies**) ◇ *adj* prioritaire. ◇ *n* priorité *f*; **to have** OR **take** ~ **(over)** avoir la priorité (sur).
◆ **priorities** *npl* priorités *fpl*.

priory ['praɪərɪ] (*pl* **-ies**) *n* prieuré *m*.

prise [praɪz] *vt*: **to** ~ **sthg away from sb** arracher qqch à qqn; **to** ~ **sthg open** forcer qqch.

prism ['prɪzm] *n* prisme *m*.

prison ['prɪzn] *n* prison *f*.

prison camp *n* camp *m* de prisonniers.

prisoner ['prɪznər] *n* prisonnier *m*, -ière *f*; **to be taken** ~ être fait prisonnier.

prisoner of war (*pl* **prisoners of war**) *n* prisonnier *m*, -ière *f* de guerre.

prissy ['prɪsɪ] (*compar* **-ier**, *superl* **-iest**) *adj* prude, guindé(e).

pristine ['prɪstiːn] *adj* [condition] parfait(e); [clean] immaculé(e).

privacy [*Br* 'prɪvəsɪ, *Am* 'praɪvəsɪ] *n* intimité *f*.

private ['praɪvɪt] ◇ *adj* **-1.** [not public] privé(e). **-2.** [confidential] confidentiel(elle). **-3.** [personal] personnel(elle). **-4.** [unsociable - person] secret(ète). ◇ *n* **-1.** [soldier] (simple) soldat *m*. **-2.** [secrecy]: **in** ~ en privé.
◆ **privates** *npl inf* parties *fpl*.

private company *n* société *f* privée.

private detective *n* détective *m* privé.

private enterprise *n* (*U*) entreprise *f* privée.

private eye *n* détective *m* privé.

private income *n* Br revenu *m* personnel.

private investigator *n* détective *m* privé.

privately ['praɪvɪtlɪ] *adv* **-1.** [not by the state]: ~ **owned** du secteur privé. **-2.** [confidentially] en privé. **-3.** [personally] intérieurement, dans son for intérieur.

private member *n* Br simple député *m*.

private parts *npl inf* parties *fpl*.

private practice *n* (*U*) Br cabinet *m* de médecin non conventionné.

private property *n* propriété *f* privée.

private school *n* école *f* privée.

private sector *n*: **the** ~ le secteur privé.

privation [praɪ'veɪʃn] *n* privation *f*.

privatization [ˌpraɪvətaɪ'zeɪʃn] *n* privatisation *f*.

privatize, -ise ['praɪvɪtaɪz] *vt* privatiser.

privet ['prɪvɪt] *n* troène *m*.

privilege ['prɪvɪlɪdʒ] *n* privilège *m*.

privileged ['prɪvɪlɪdʒd] *adj* privilégié(e).

privy ['prɪvɪ] *adj*: **to be** ~ **to sthg** être dans le secret de qqch.

Privy Council *n* Br: **the** ~ le Conseil privé.

PRIVY COUNCIL:
En font partie tous les ministres du gouvernement ainsi que d'autres personnalités du Commonwealth. Le 'Privy Council' compte environ 400 membres, mais ils ne se réunissent en plénière que dans des circonstances exceptionnelles

Privy Purse *n*: **the** ~ la cassette du souverain.

prize [praɪz] ◇ *adj* [possession] très précieux(ieuse); [animal] primé(e); [idiot, example] parfait(e). ◇ *n* prix *m*. ◇ *vt* priser.

prize day *n* Br jour *m* de la distribution des prix.

prizefight ['praɪzfaɪt] *n* combat *m* professionnel.

prize-giving *n* Br distribution *f* des prix.

prizewinner ['praɪzˌwɪnər] *n* gagnant *m*, -e *f*.

pro [prəʊ] (*pl* **-s**) *n* **-1.** *inf* [professional] pro *mf inv*. **-2.** [advantage]: **the** ~**s and cons** le pour et le contre.

pro- [prəʊ] *prefix* pro-.

PRO (*abbr of* **public relations officer**) *n* responsable des relations publiques.

pro-am ['prəʊ'æm] ⬦ *adj* pro-am. ⬦ *n* tournoi *m* pro-am.

probability [,prɒbə'bɪlətɪ] (*pl* **-ies**) *n* probabilité *f*; **in all ~** selon toute probabilité.

probable ['prɒbəbl] *adj* probable.

probably ['prɒbəblɪ] *adv* probablement.

probate ['prəʊbeɪt] JUR ⬦ *n* homologation *f*. ⬦ *vt Am* homologuer.

probation [prə'beɪʃn] *n* (*U*) **-1.** JUR mise *f* à l'épreuve; **to put sb on ~** mettre qqn en sursis avec mise à l'épreuve. **-2.** [trial period] essai *m*; **to be on ~** être à l'essai.

probationary [prə'beɪʃnrɪ] *adj* [teacher, nurse] à l'essai; [period, year] d'essai.

probationer [prə'beɪʃnə*r*] *n* **-1.** [employee] stagiaire *mf*. **-2.** JUR sursitaire *mf* avec mise à l'épreuve.

probation officer *n* agent *m* de probation.

probe [prəʊb] ⬦ *n* **-1.** [investigation]: **~ (into)** enquête *f* (sur). **-2.** MED & TECH sonde *f*. ⬦ *vt* sonder. ⬦ *vi*: **to ~ for** OR **into sthg** chercher à découvrir qqch.

probing ['prəʊbɪŋ] *adj* [question] pénétrant(e); [look] inquisiteur(trice).

probity ['prəʊbətɪ] *n* probité *f*.

problem ['prɒbləm] ⬦ *n* problème *m*; **no ~!** *inf* pas de problème! ⬦ *comp* difficile.

problematic(al) [,prɒblə'mætɪk(l)] *adj* problématique.

procedural [prə'si:dʒərəl] *adj* de procédure.

procedure [prə'si:dʒə*r*] *n* procédure *f*.

proceed [prə'si:d] ⬦ *vt* [do subsequently]: **to ~ to do sthg** se mettre à faire qqch. ⬦ *vi* **-1.** [continue]: **to ~ (with sthg)** continuer (qqch), poursuivre (qqch). **-2.** *fml* [advance] avancer.

◆ **proceeds** *npl* recette *f*.

proceedings [prə'si:dɪŋz] *npl* **-1.** [of meeting] débats *mpl*. **-2.** JUR poursuites *fpl*.

process [*n* 'prəʊses] ⬦ *n* **-1.** [series of actions] processus *m*; **in the ~** ce faisant; **to be in the ~ of doing sthg** être en train de faire qqch. **-2.** [method] procédé *m*. ⬦ *vt* [raw materials, food, data] traiter, transformer; [application] s'occuper de.

processed cheese ['prəʊsest-] *n* fromage en minces lamelles préemballé.

processing ['prəʊsesɪŋ] *n* traitement *m*, transformation *f*.

procession [prə'seʃn] *n* cortège *m*, procession *f*.

processor ['prəʊsesə*r*] *n* **-1.** COMPUT processeur *m*. **-2.** CULIN robot *m* ménager OR de cuisine.

pro-choice *adj* pour le droit d'avortement.

proclaim [prə'kleɪm] *vt* [declare] proclamer.

proclamation [,prɒklə'meɪʃn] *n* proclamation *f*.

proclivity [prə'klɪvətɪ] (*pl* **-ies**) *n* *fml*: **~ to** OR **towards sthg** propension *f* à qqch.

procrastinate [prə'kræstɪneɪt] *vi* faire traîner les choses.

procrastination [prə,kræstɪ'neɪʃn] *n* procrastination *f*.

procreate ['prəʊkrɪeɪt] *vi* procréer.

procreation [,prəʊkrɪ'eɪʃn] *n* procréation *f*.

procurator fiscal ['prɒkjʊreɪtə*r*-] *n* *Scot* ≃ procureur *m*.

procure [prə'kjʊə*r*] *vt* [for oneself] se procurer; [for someone else] procurer; [release] obtenir.

procurement [prə'kjʊəmənt] *n* obtention *f*.

prod [prɒd] (*pt* & *pp* **-ded**, *cont* **-ding**) ⬦ *n* petit coup *m*; **to give sb a ~** *fig* faire rappeler à qqn. ⬦ *vt* **-1.** [push, poke] pousser doucement. **-2.** [remind, prompt]: **to ~ sb (into doing sthg)** pousser OR inciter qqn (à faire qqch).

prodigal ['prɒdɪgl] *adj* prodigue.

prodigious [prə'dɪdʒəs] *adj* prodigieux(ieuse).

prodigy ['prɒdɪdʒɪ] (*pl* **-ies**) *n* prodige *m*.

produce [*n* 'prɒdju:s, *vb* prə'dju:s] ⬦ *n* (*U*) produits *mpl*. ⬦ *vt* **-1.** [gen] produire. **-2.** [cause] provoquer, causer. **-3.** [show] présenter. **-4.** THEATRE mettre en scène.

producer [prə'dju:sə*r*] *n* **-1.** [of film, manufacturer] producteur *m*, -trice *f*. **-2.** THEATRE metteur *m* en scène.

product ['prɒdʌkt] *n* produit *m*; **to be a ~ of sthg** être le produit OR le résultat de qqch.

production [prə'dʌkʃn] *n* **-1.** (*U*) [manufacture, of film] production *f*; **to go into ~** entrer en production; **to put sthg into ~** entreprendre la fabrication de qqch. **-2.** (*U*) [output] rendement *m*. **-3.** (*U*) THEATRE [of play] mise *f* en scène. **-4.** [show - gen] production *f*; [- THEATRE] pièce *f*.

production line *n* chaîne *f* de fabrication.

production manager *n* directeur *m*, -trice *f* de la production.

productive [prə'dʌktɪv] *adj* **-1.** [land, business, workers] productif(ive). **-2.** [meeting, experience] fructueux(euse).

productively [prə'dʌktɪvlɪ] *adv* **-1.** [operate, use] de façon productive. **-2.** [spend time] de façon fructueuse.

productivity [,prɒdʌk'tɪvətɪ] *n* productivité *f*.

productivity deal n accord m de productivité.

Prof. (abbr of Professor) Pr.

profane [prə'feɪn] adj impie.

profanity [prə'fænətɪ] (pl -ies) n impiété f.

profess [prə'fes] vt professer; **to ~ to do/be** prétendre faire/être.

professed [prə'fest] adj déclaré(e).

profession [prə'feʃn] n profession f; **by ~** de son métier.

professional [prə'feʃənl] ◇ adj **-1.** [gen] professionnel(elle). **-2.** [of high standard] de (haute) qualité. ◇ n professionnel m, -elle f.

professional foul n faute f délibérée.

professionalism [prə'feʃnəlɪzm] n professionnalisme m.

professionally [prə'feʃnəlɪ] adv **-1.** [as professional] en professionnel; **~ qualified** diplômé(e). **-2.** [skilfully] de façon professionnelle.

professor [prə'fesə'] n **-1.** Br UNIV professeur m (de faculté). **-2.** Am & Can [teacher] professeur m.

professorship [prə'fesəʃɪp] n chaire f.

proffer ['prɒfə'] vt: **to ~ sthg (to sb)** offrir qqch (à qqn); **to ~ one's hand (to sb)** tendre la main (à qqn).

proficiency [prə'fɪʃənsɪ] n: **~ (in)** compétence f (en).

proficient [prə'fɪʃənt] adj: **~ (in OR at sthg)** compétent(e) (en qqch).

profile ['prəʊfaɪl] n profil m; **in ~** de profil; **to keep a low ~** adopter un profil bas.

profit ['prɒfɪt] ◇ n **-1.** [financial] bénéfice m, profit m; **to make a ~** faire un bénéfice; **to sell sthg at a ~** vendre qqch à profit. **-2.** [advantage] profit m. ◇ vi [financially] être le bénéficiaire; [gain advantage] tirer avantage OR profit.

profitability [,prɒfɪtə'bɪlətɪ] n rentabilité f.

profitable ['prɒfɪtəbl] adj **-1.** [financially] rentable, lucratif(ive). **-2.** [beneficial] fructueux(euse), profitable.

profitably ['prɒfɪtəblɪ] adv **-1.** [at a profit] de façon rentable. **-2.** [spend time] utilement.

profiteering [,prɒfɪ'tɪərɪŋ] n affairisme m, mercantilisme m.

profit-making ◇ adj à but lucratif. ◇ n réalisation f de bénéfices.

profit margin n marge f bénéficiaire.

profit sharing [-,ʃeərɪŋ] n participation f aux bénéfices.

profligate ['prɒflɪgɪt] adj **-1.** [extravagant] prodigue. **-2.** [immoral] débauché(e).

pro forma [-'fɔːmə] adj pro forma.

profound [prə'faʊnd] adj profond(e).

profoundly [prə'faʊndlɪ] adv profondément.

profuse [prə'fjuːs] adj [apologies, praise] profus(e); [bleeding] abondant(e).

profusely [prə'fjuːslɪ] adv [sweat, bleed] abondamment; **to apologize ~** se confondre en excuses.

profusion [prə'fjuːʒn] n profusion f.

progeny ['prɒdʒənɪ] (pl -ies) n progéniture f.

progesterone [prə'dʒestərəʊn] n progestérone f.

prognosis [prɒg'nəʊsɪs] (pl -noses [-'nəʊsiːz]) n pronostic m.

prognostication [prɒg,nɒstɪ'keɪʃn] n pronostic m.

program ['prəʊgræm] (pt & pp -med OR -ed, cont -ming OR -ing) ◇ n **-1.** COMPUT programme m. **-2.** Am = programme. ◇ vt **-1.** COMPUT programmer. **-2.** Am = programme.

programer Am = programmer.

programmable [prəʊ'græməbl] adj programmable.

programme Br, **program** Am ['prəʊgræm] ◇ n **-1.** [schedule, booklet] programme m. **-2.** RADIO & TV émission f. ◇ vt programmer; **to ~ sthg to do sthg** programmer qqch pour faire qqch.

programmer Br, **programer** Am ['prəʊgræmə'] n COMPUT programmeur m, -euse f.

programming ['prəʊgræmɪŋ] n programmation f.

programming language n langage m de programmation.

progress [n 'prəʊgres, vb prəʊ'gres] ◇ n progrès m; **to make ~** [improve] faire des progrès; **to make ~ in sthg** avancer dans qqch; **in ~** en cours. ◇ vi **-1.** [improve - gen] progresser, avancer; [- person] faire des progrès. **-2.** [continue] avancer. **-3.** [move on]: **to ~ to sthg** passer à qqch.

progression [prə'greʃn] n progression f.

progressive [prə'gresɪv] adj **-1.** [enlightened] progressiste. **-2.** [gradual] progressif(ive).

progressively [prə'gresɪvlɪ] adv progressivement.

progress report n [on patient] bulletin m de santé; [on student] bulletin scolaire; [on work] compte-rendu m.

prohibit [prə'hɪbɪt] vt prohiber; **to ~ sb from doing sthg** interdire OR défendre à qqn de faire qqch.

prohibition [ˌprəʊɪ'bɪʃn] *n* **-1.** [law, rule] prohibition *f.* **-2.** (*U*) [act of prohibiting] interdiction *f,* défense *f.*

prohibitive [prə'hɪbətɪv] *adj* prohibitif(ive).

project [*n* 'prɒdʒekt, *vb* prə'dʒekt] ◇ *n* **-1.** [plan, idea] projet *m,* plan *m.* **-2.** SCH [study]: ~ (on) dossier *m* (sur), projet *m* (sur). ◇ *vt* **-1.** [gen] projeter. **-2.** [estimate] prévoir. ◇ *vi* [jut out] faire saillie.

projectile [prə'dʒektaɪl] *n* projectile *m.*

projection [prə'dʒekʃn] *n* **-1.** [estimate] prévision *f.* **-2.** [protrusion] saillie *f.* **-3.** (*U*) [display, showing] projection *f.*

projectionist [prə'dʒekʃənɪst] *n* projectionniste *mf.*

projection room *n* cabine *f* de projection.

projector [prə'dʒektəʳ] *n* projecteur *m.*

proletarian [ˌprəʊlɪ'teərɪən] *adj* prolétarien(ienne).

proletariat [ˌprəʊlɪ'teərɪət] *n* prolétariat *m.*

pro-life *adj* pour le respect de la vie.

proliferate [prə'lɪfəreɪt] *vi* proliférer.

prolific [prə'lɪfɪk] *adj* prolifique.

prologue, prolog *Am* [prəʊ'lɒg] *n* lit & fig prologue *m.*

prolong [prə'lɒŋ] *vt* prolonger.

prom [prɒm] *n* **-1.** *Br inf* (*abbr of* **promenade**) promenade *f,* front *m* de mer. **-2.** *Am* [ball] bal *m* d'étudiants. **-3.** *Br inf* (*abbr of* **promenade concert**) concert *m* promenade.

promenade [ˌprɒmə'nɑːd] *n Br* [road by sea] promenade *f,* front *m* de mer.

promenade concert *n Br* concert *m* promenade.

prominence ['prɒmɪnəns] *n* **-1.** [importance] importance *f.* **-2.** [conspicuousness] proéminence *f.*

prominent ['prɒmɪnənt] *adj* **-1.** [important] important(e). **-2.** [noticeable] proéminent(e).

prominently ['prɒmɪnəntlɪ] *adv* au premier plan, bien en vue.

promiscuity [ˌprɒmɪs'kjuːətɪ] *n* promiscuité *f.*

promiscuous [prɒ'mɪskjʊəs] *adj* [person] aux mœurs légères; [behaviour] immoral(e).

promise ['prɒmɪs] ◇ *n* promesse *f*; to make (sb) a ~ faire une promesse (à qqn); to show ~ avoir de l'avenir, promettre. ◇ *vt*: to ~ (sb) to do sthg promettre (à qqn) de faire qqch; to ~ sb sthg promettre qqch à qqn. ◇ *vi* promettre.

promising ['prɒmɪsɪŋ] *adj* prometteur(euse).

promissory note ['prɒmɪsərɪ-] *n* billet *m* à ordre.

promo ['prəʊməʊ] (*pl* -s) (*abbr of* **promotion**) *n inf* promo *f.*

promontory ['prɒməntrɪ] (*pl* -ies) *n* promontoire *m.*

promote [prə'məʊt] *vt* **-1.** [foster] promouvoir. **-2.** [push, advertise] promouvoir, lancer. **-3.** [in job] promouvoir.

promoter [prə'məʊtəʳ] *n* **-1.** [organizer] organisateur *m,* -trice *f.* **-2.** [supporter] promoteur *m,* -trice *f.*

promotion [prə'məʊʃn] *n* promotion *f,* avancement *m*; to get OR be given ~ être promu, obtenir de l'avancement.

prompt [prɒmpt] ◇ *adj* rapide, prompt(e). ◇ *adv*: at nine o'clock ~ à neuf heures précises OR tapantes. ◇ *vt* **-1.** [motivate, encourage]: to ~ sb (to do sthg) pousser OR inciter qqn (à faire qqch). **-2.** THEATRE souffler sa réplique à. ◇ *n* THEATRE réplique *f.*

prompter ['prɒmptəʳ] *n* THEATRE souffleur *m,* -euse *f.*

promptly ['prɒmptlɪ] *adv* **-1.** [immediately] rapidement, promptement. **-2.** [punctually] ponctuellement.

promptness ['prɒmptnɪs] *n* **-1.** [speediness] promptitude *f.* **-2.** [punctuality] ponctualité *f.*

promulgate ['prɒmlgeɪt] *vt* promulguer.

prone [prəʊn] *adj* **-1.** [susceptible]: to be ~ to sthg être sujet(ette) à qqch; to be ~ to do sthg avoir tendance à faire qqch. **-2.** [lying flat] étendu(e) face contre terre.

prong [prɒŋ] *n* [of fork] dent *f.*

pronoun ['prəʊnaʊn] *n* pronom *m.*

pronounce [prə'naʊns] ◇ *vt* prononcer. ◇ *vi*: to ~ on se prononcer sur.

pronounced [prə'naʊnst] *adj* prononcé(e).

pronouncement [prə'naʊnsmənt] *n* déclaration *f.*

pronunciation [prəˌnʌnsɪ'eɪʃn] *n* prononciation *f.*

proof [pruːf] *n* **-1.** [evidence] preuve *f.* **-2.** [of book etc] épreuve *f.* **-3.** [of alcohol] teneur *f* en alcool.

proofread ['pruːfriːd] (*pt* & *pp* -read [-red]) *vt* corriger les épreuves de.

proofreader ['pruːfˌriːdəʳ] *n* correcteur *m,* -trice *f* d'épreuves.

prop [prɒp] (*pt* & *pp* -ped, *cont* -ping) ◇ *n* **-1.** [physical support] support *m,* étai *m.* **-2.** *fig* [supporting thing, person] soutien *m.* **-3.** RUGBY pilier *m.* ◇ *vt*: to ~ sthg against appuyer qqch contre OR à.
♦ **props** *npl* accessoires *mpl.*

◆ **prop up** *vt sep* **-1.** [physically support] soutenir, étayer. **-2.** *fig* [sustain] soutenir.

Prop. *abbr of* **proprietor**.

propaganda [ˌprɒpə'gændə] *n* propagande *f*.

propagate ['prɒpəgeɪt] ◇ *vt* propager. ◇ *vi* se propager.

propagation [ˌprɒpə'geɪʃn] *n* propagation *f*.

propane ['prəupeɪn] *n* propane *m*.

propel [prə'pel] (*pt* & *pp* **-led**, *cont* **-ling**) *vt* propulser; *fig* pousser.

propeller [prə'pelər] *n* hélice *f*.

propelling pencil [prə'pelɪŋ-] *n Br* portemine *m inv*.

propensity [prə'pensəti] (*pl* **-ies**) *n*: ~ **(for** OR **to)** propension *f* (à).

proper ['prɒpər] *adj* **-1.** [real] vrai(e). **-2.** [correct] correct(e), bon (bonne). **-3.** [decent - behaviour etc] convenable. **-4.** *inf* [for emphasis]: **he's a** ~ **idiot!** c'est un imbécile fini!

properly ['prɒpəlɪ] *adv* **-1.** [satisfactorily, correctly] correctement, comme il faut. **-2.** [decently] convenablement, comme il faut.

proper noun *n* nom *m* propre.

property ['prɒpəti] (*pl* **-ies**) *n* **-1.** (*U*) [possessions] biens *mpl*, propriété *f*. **-2.** [building] bien *m* immobilier; [land] terres *fpl*. **-3.** [quality] propriété *f*.

property developer *n* promoteur *m* immobilier.

property owner *n* propriétaire *m* (foncier).

property tax *n* impôt *m* foncier.

prophecy ['prɒfɪsɪ] (*pl* **-ies**) *n* prophétie *f*.

prophesy ['prɒfɪsaɪ] (*pt* & *pp* **-ied**) *vt* prédire.

prophet ['prɒfɪt] *n* prophète *m*.

prophetic [prə'fetɪk] *adj* prophétique.

propitious [prə'pɪʃəs] *adj fml* propice, favorable.

proponent [prə'pəunənt] *n* adepte *mf*, partisan *m*, -e *f*.

proportion [prə'pɔːʃn] *n* **-1.** [part] part *f*, partie *f*. **-2.** [ratio] rapport *m*, proportion *f*; **in** ~ **to** proportionnellement à; **out of all** ~ **to** sans commune mesure avec. **-3.** ART: **in** ~ proportionné(e); **out of** ~ mal proportionné; **to get sthg out of** ~ *fig* exagérer qqch; **a sense of** ~ *fig* le sens de la mesure.

proportional [prə'pɔːʃənl] *adj* proportionnel(elle).

proportional representation *n* représentation *f* proportionnelle.

proportionate [prə'pɔːʃnət] *adj* proportionné(e).

proposal [prə'pəuzl] *n* **-1.** [suggestion] proposition *f*, offre *f*. **-2.** [offer of marriage] demande *f* en mariage.

propose [prə'pəuz] ◇ *vt* **-1.** [suggest] proposer. **-2.** [intend]: **to** ~ **to do** OR **doing sthg** avoir l'intention de faire qqch, se proposer de faire qqch. **-3.** [toast] porter. ◇ *vi* faire une demande en mariage; **to** ~ **to sb** demander qqn en mariage.

proposed [prə'pəuzd] *adj* proposé(e).

proposition [ˌprɒpə'zɪʃn] ◇ *n* proposition *f*; **to make sb a** ~ faire une proposition à qqn. ◇ *vt* faire des propositions à.

propound [prə'paund] *vt fml* soumettre, proposer.

proprietary [prə'praɪətrɪ] *adj* de marque déposée; ~ **brand** marque *f* déposée.

proprietor [prə'praɪətər] *n* propriétaire *mf*.

propriety [prə'praɪətɪ] *n* (*U*) *fml* [moral correctness] bienséance *f*.

propulsion [prə'pʌlʃn] *n* propulsion *f*.

pro rata [-'rɑːtə] ◇ *adj* proportionnel(elle). ◇ *adv* au prorata.

prosaic [prəu'zeɪɪk] *adj* prosaïque, banal(e).

Pros. Atty (*abbr of* **prosecuting attorney**) *avocat général*.

proscenium [prə'siːnjəm] (*pl* **-niums** OR **-nia** [-njə]) *n*: ~ **(arch)** proscenium *m*.

proscribe [prəu'skraɪb] *vt* proscrire.

prose [prəuz] ◇ *n* (*U*) prose *f*. ◇ *comp* en prose.

prosecute ['prɒsɪkjuːt] ◇ *vt* poursuivre (en justice). ◇ *vi* [police] engager des poursuites judiciaires; [lawyer] représenter la partie plaignante.

prosecution [ˌprɒsɪ'kjuːʃn] *n* poursuites *fpl* judiciaires, accusation *f*; **the** ~ la partie plaignante; [in Crown case] ≃ le ministère public.

prosecutor ['prɒsɪkjuːtər] *n* plaignant *m*, -e *f*.

prospect [*n* 'prɒspekt, *vb* prə'spekt] ◇ *n* **-1.** [hope] possibilité *f*, chances *fpl*. **-2.** [probability] perspective *f*. ◇ *vi*: **to** ~ **(for sthg)** prospecter (pour chercher qqch).

◆ **prospects** *npl*: ~**s (for)** chances *fpl* (de), perspectives *fpl* (de).

prospecting [prə'spektɪŋ] *n* prospection *f*.

prospective [prə'spektɪv] *adj* éventuel(elle).

prospector [prə'spektər] *n* prospecteur *m*, -trice *f*.

prospectus [prə'spektəs] (*pl* **-es**) *n* prospectus *m*.

prosper ['prɒspər] *vi* prospérer.

prosperity [prɒ'sperətɪ] *n* prospérité *f.*

prosperous ['prɒspərəs] *adj* prospère.

prostate (gland) ['prɒsteɪt-] *n* prostate *f.*

prosthesis [prɒs'θiːsɪs] (*pl* **-theses** [-'θiːsiːz]) *n* prothèse *f.*

prostitute ['prɒstɪtjuːt] *n* prostituée *f*; **male ~** prostitué *m.*

prostitution [,prɒstɪ'tjuːʃn] *n* prostitution *f.*

prostrate [*adj* 'prɒstreɪt, *vb* prɒ'streɪt] ◇ *adj* **-1.** [lying down] à plat ventre. **-2.** [with grief etc] prostré(e). ◇ *vt*: **to ~ o.s. (before sb)** se prosterner (devant qqn).

protagonist [prə'tægənɪst] *n* protagoniste *mf.*

protect [prə'tekt] *vt*: **to ~ sb/sthg (against), to ~ sb/sthg (from)** protéger qqn/qqch (contre), protéger qqn/qqch (de).

protection [prə'tekʃn] *n*: **~ (from OR against)** protection *f* (contre), défense *f* (contre).

protectionism [prə'tekʃənɪzm] *n* protectionnisme *m.*

protectionist [prə'tekʃənɪst] *adj* protectionniste.

protection money *n* argent versé par les victimes d'un racket.

protective [prə'tektɪv] *adj* **-1.** [layer, clothing] de protection. **-2.** [person, feelings] protecteur(trice); **to feel ~ towards sb** se montrer protecteur envers qqn.

protective custody *n* détention d'une personne pour sa propre sécurité.

protectiveness [prə'tektɪvnɪs] *n* attitude *f* protectrice.

protector [prə'tektər] *n* **-1.** [person] protecteur *m*, -trice *f.* **-2.** [object] dispositif *m* de protection.

protectorate [prə'tektərət] *n* protectorat *m.*

protégé ['prɒteʒeɪ] *n* protégé *m.*

protégée ['prɒteʒeɪ] *n* protégée *f.*

protein ['prəʊtiːn] *n* protéine *f.*

protest [*n* 'prəʊtest, *vb* prə'test] ◇ *n* protestation *f.* ◇ *vt* **-1.** [state] protester de. **-2.** *Am* [protest against] protester contre. ◇ *vi*: **to ~ (about/against)** protester (à propos de/contre).

Protestant ['prɒtɪstənt] ◇ *adj* protestant(e). ◇ *n* protestant *m*, -e *f.*

Protestantism ['prɒtɪstəntɪzm] *n* protestantisme *m.*

protestation [,prɒte'steɪʃn] *n* protestation *f.*

protester [prə'testər] *n* [on march, at demonstration] manifestant *m*, -e *f.*

protest march *n* manifestation *f*, marche *f* de protestation.

protocol ['prəʊtəkɒl] *n* protocole *m.*

proton ['prəʊtɒn] *n* proton *m.*

prototype ['prəʊtətaɪp] *n* prototype *m.*

protracted [prə'træktɪd] *adj* prolongé(e).

protractor [prə'træktər] *n* rapporteur *m.*

protrude [prə'truːd] *vi* avancer, dépasser.

protrusion [prə'truːʒn] *n* avancée *f*, saillie *f.*

protuberance [prə'tjuːbərəns] *n* protubérance *f.*

proud [praʊd] *adj* **-1.** [satisfied, dignified] fier (fière); **to be ~ to do sthg** être fier de faire qqch. **-2.** *pej* [arrogant] orgueilleux(euse), fier (fière).

proudly ['praʊdlɪ] *adv* **-1.** [with satisfaction, dignity] fièrement, avec fierté. **-2.** *pej* [arrogantly] orgueilleusement.

provable ['pruːvəbl] *adj* qui peut être prouvé(e), prouvable.

prove [pruːv] (*pp* **-d** OR **proven**) *vt* **-1.** [show to be true] prouver. **-2.** [turn out]: **to ~ (to be) false/useful** s'avérer faux/utile; **to ~ o.s. to be sthg** se révéler être qqch.

proven ['pruːvn, 'prəʊvn] ◇ *pp* → **prove.** ◇ *adj* [fact] avéré(e), établi(e); [liar] fieffé(e).

Provençal [,prɒvɒn'saːl] ◇ *adj* provençal(e). ◇ *n* **-1.** [person] Provençal *m*, -e *f.* **-2.** [language] Provençal *m.*

Provence [prɒ'vɒns] *n* Provence *f*; **in ~** en Provence.

proverb ['prɒvɜːb] *n* proverbe *m.*

proverbial [prə'vɜːbjəl] *adj* proverbial(e).

provide [prə'vaɪd] *vt* fournir; **to ~ sb with sthg** fournir qqch à qqn; **to ~ sthg for sb** fournir qqch à qqn.
◆ **provide for** *vt fus* **-1.** [support] subvenir aux besoins de. **-2.** *fml* [make arrangements for] prévoir.

provided [prə'vaɪdɪd]
◆ **provided (that)** *conj* à condition que (+ subjunctive), pourvu que (+ subjunctive).

providence ['prɒvɪdəns] *n* providence *f.*

providential [,prɒvɪ'denʃl] *adj* providentiel(ielle).

provider [prə'vaɪdər] *n* pourvoyeur *m*, -euse *f.*

providing [prə'vaɪdɪŋ]
◆ **providing (that)** *conj* à condition que (+ subjunctive), pourvu que (+ subjunctive).

province ['prɒvɪns] *n* **-1.** [part of country] province *f.* **-2.** [speciality] domaine *m*, compétence *f.*
◆ **provinces** *npl*: **the ~s** la province.

provincial [prə'vɪnʃl] *adj* **-1.** [town, newspaper] de province. **-2.** *pej* [narrow-minded] provincial(e).

provision [prə'vɪʒn] *n* **-1.** (*U*) [act of supplying]: ~ **(of)** approvisionnement *m* (en), fourniture *f* (de). **-2.** [supply] provision *f*, réserve *f*. **-3.** (*U*) [arrangements]: **to make ~ for** [the future] prendre des mesures pour; [one's family] pourvoir aux besoins de. **-4.** [in agreement, law] clause *f*, disposition *f*.
♦ **provisions** *npl* [supplies] provisions *fpl*.

provisional [prə'vɪʒənl] *adj* provisoire.

Provisional IRA *n* branche de l'IRA qui pratique le terrorisme.

provisional licence *n* Br permis *m* de conduire provisoire (*jusqu'à l'obtention du permis de conduire*).

provisionally [prə'vɪʒnəlɪ] *adv* provisoirement, à titre provisoire.

proviso [prə'vaɪzəʊ] (*pl* **-s**) *n* condition *f*, stipulation *f*; **with the ~ that** à (la) condition que (+ *subjunctive*).

Provo ['prəʊvəʊ] (*pl* **-s**) (*abbr of* **Provisional**) *n* inf membre de la branche de l'IRA pratiquant le terrorisme.

provocation [ˌprɒvə'keɪʃn] *n* provocation *f*.

provocative [prə'vɒkətɪv] *adj* provocant(e).

provocatively [prə'vɒkətɪvlɪ] *adv* d'une manière provocante.

provoke [prə'vəʊk] *vt* **-1.** [annoy] agacer, contrarier. **-2.** [cause - fight, argument] provoquer; [- reaction] susciter.

provoking [prə'vəʊkɪŋ] *adj* agaçant(e), énervant(e).

provost ['prɒvəst] *n* **-1.** Br UNIV doyen *m*. **-2.** Scot [head of town council] maire *m*.

prow [praʊ] *n* proue *f*.

prowess ['praʊɪs] *n* prouesse *f*.

prowl [praʊl] ◇ *n*: **to be on the ~** rôder. ◇ *vt* [streets etc] rôder dans. ◇ *vi* rôder.

prowl car *n* Am voiture *f* de police en patrouille.

prowler ['praʊlə'] *n* rôdeur *m*, -euse *f*.

proximity [prɒk'sɪmətɪ] *n*: ~ **(to)** proximité *f* (de); **in the ~ of** à proximité de.

proxy ['prɒksɪ] (*pl* **-ies**) *n*: **by ~** par procuration.

prude [pru:d] *n* prude *f*.

prudence ['pru:dns] *n* prudence *f*.

prudent ['pru:dnt] *adj* prudent(e).

prudently ['pru:dntlɪ] *adv* prudemment, avec prudence.

prudish ['pru:dɪʃ] *adj* prude, pudibond(e).

prune [pru:n] ◇ *n* [fruit] pruneau *m*. ◇ *vt* [tree, bush] tailler.

prurient ['prʊərɪənt] *adj* lascif(ive).

Prussian ['prʌʃn] ◇ *adj* prussien(ienne). ◇ *n* Prussien *m*, -ienne *f*.

pry [praɪ] (*pt* & *pp* **pried**) *vi* se mêler de ce qui ne vous regarde pas; **to ~ into sthg** chercher à découvrir qqch.

PS (*abbr of* **postscript**) *n* PS *m*.

psalm [sɑ:m] *n* psaume *m*.

PSBR (*abbr of* **public sector borrowing requirement**) *n* partie du budget de l'État non couverte par les impôts en Grande-Bretagne.

pseud [sju:d] *n* Br inf frimeur *m*, -euse *f*.

pseudo- [ˌsju:dəʊ] *prefix* pseudo-.

pseudonym ['sju:dənɪm] *n* pseudonyme *m*.

psi (*abbr of* **pounds per square inch**) *livres au pouce carré (mesure de pression*).

psoriasis [sɒ'raɪəsɪs] *n* psoriasis *m*.

psst [pst] *excl* psitt!

PST (*abbr of* **Pacific Standard Time**) *n* heure du Pacifique.

psych [saɪk]
♦ **psych up** *vt sep* inf préparer psychologiquement; **to ~ o.s. up** se préparer psychologiquement.

psyche ['saɪkɪ] *n* psyché *f*.

psychedelic [ˌsaɪkɪ'delɪk] *adj* psychédélique.

psychiatric [ˌsaɪkɪ'ætrɪk] *adj* psychiatrique.

psychiatric nurse *n* infirmière *f* en psychiatrie.

psychiatrist [saɪ'kaɪətrɪst] *n* psychiatre *mf*.

psychiatry [saɪ'kaɪətrɪ] *n* psychiatrie *f*.

psychic ['saɪkɪk] ◇ *adj* **-1.** [clairvoyant - person] doué(e), de seconde vue; [- powers] parapsychique. **-2.** MED psychique. ◇ *n* médium *m*.

psychoanalyse, -yze *Am* [ˌsaɪkəʊ'ænəlaɪz] *vt* psychanalyser.

psychoanalysis [ˌsaɪkəʊə'næləsɪs] *n* psychanalyse *f*.

psychoanalyst [ˌsaɪkəʊ'ænəlɪst] *n* psychanalyste *mf*.

psychological [ˌsaɪkə'lɒdʒɪkl] *adj* psychologique.

psychological warfare *n* (*U*) guerre *f* psychologique.

psychologist [saɪ'kɒlədʒɪst] *n* psychologue *mf*.

psychology [saɪ'kɒlədʒɪ] *n* psychologie *f*.

psychopath ['saɪkəpæθ] *n* psychopathe *mf*.

psychosis [saɪ'kəʊsɪs] (*pl* **-choses** [-'kəʊsi:z]) *n* psychose *f*.

psychosomatic [ˌsaɪkəʊsə'mætɪk] *adj* psychosomatique.

psychotherapy [ˌsaɪkəʊ'θerəpɪ] *n* psychothérapie *f*.

psychotic [saɪk'ɒtɪk] ◇ *adj* psychotique. ◇ *n* psychotique *mf*.

pt -1. *abbr of* **pint. -2.** *abbr of* **point.**

Pt. (*abbr of* **Point**) [on map] Pte.

PT (*abbr of* **physical training**) *n* EPS *f.*

PTA (*abbr of* **parent-teacher association**) *n* *association de parents d'élèves et de professeurs.*

Pte. *abbr of* **Private.**

PTO ◇ *n* (*abbr of* **parent-teacher organization**) *aux États-Unis, association de parents d'élèves et de professeurs.* ◇ (*abbr of* **please turn over**) TSVP.

PTV *n* **-1.** (*abbr of* **pay television**) *télévision payante.* **-2.** (*abbr of* **public television**) *programmes télévisés éducatifs.*

pub [pʌb] *n* pub *m.*

PUB:
Dans l'ensemble des îles Britanniques, le pub est un des grands foyers de la vie sociale. Ces établissements — interdits aux personnes non accompagnées de moins de 16 ans — étaient soumis à des horaires stricts, mais ceux-ci se sont beaucoup assouplis récemment (voir 'licensing hours'). De simple débit de boissons, qu'il était souvent, de plus en plus le pub évolue vers une sorte de brasserie servant des repas légers

pub. *abbr of* **published.**

pub-crawl *n Br*: **to go on a** ~ faire la tournée des pubs.

puberty ['pju:bəti] *n* puberté *f.*

pubescent [pju:'besnt] *adj* pubescent(e).

pubic ['pju:bɪk] *adj* du pubis.

public ['pʌblɪk] ◇ *adj* public(ique); [library] municipal(e); **it's** ~ **knowledge that** ... tout le monde sait que ..., il est de notoriété publique que ...; **to make sthg** ~ rendre qqch public; **to go** ~ COMM émettre des actions dans le public. ◇ *n*: **the** ~ le public; **in** ~ en public.

public-address system *n* système *m* de sonorisation.

publican ['pʌblɪkən] *n Br* gérant *m*, -e *f,* d'un pub.

publication [,pʌblɪ'keɪʃn] *n* publication *f.*

public bar *n Br* bar *m.*

public company *n* société *f* anonyme (*cotée en Bourse*).

public convenience *n Br* toilettes *fpl* publiques.

public domain *n*: **in the** ~ dans le domaine public.

public holiday *n* jour *m* férié.

public house *n Br* pub *m.*

publicist ['pʌblɪsɪst] *n* agent *m* de publicité.

publicity [pʌb'lɪsɪti] ◇ *n* (*U*) publicité *f.* ◇ *comp* de publicité.

publicity stunt *n* coup *m* publicitaire.

publicize, -ise ['pʌblɪsaɪz] *vt* faire connaître au public.

public limited company *n* société *f* anonyme (*cotée en Bourse*).

publicly ['pʌblɪklɪ] *adv* publiquement, en public.

public office *n* fonctions *fpl* officielles.

public opinion *n* (*U*) opinion *f* publique.

public ownership *n* nationalisation *f.*

public prosecutor *n* ≃ procureur *m* de la République.

public relations ◇ *n* (*U*) relations *fpl* publiques. ◇ *npl* relations *fpl* publiques.

public relations officer *n* responsable *mf* des relations publiques.

public school *n* **-1.** *Br* [private school] école *f* privée. **-2.** *Am* [state school] école *f* publique.

PUBLIC SCHOOL:
En Angleterre et au pays de Galles, le terme 'public school' désigne une école privée de type traditionnel; certaines de ces écoles (Eton et Harrow, par exemple) sont très réputées et recherchées. La 'public school' est censée former l'élite de la nation. Aux États-Unis et parfois en Écosse, le terme désigne une école publique

public sector *n* secteur *m* public.

public servant *n* fonctionnaire *mf.*

public service vehicle *n Br* autobus *m.*

public-spirited *adj* qui fait preuve de civisme.

public transport *n* (*U*) transports *mpl* en commun.

public utility *n* service *m* public.

public works *npl* travaux *mpl* publics.

publish ['pʌblɪʃ] *vt* publier.

publisher ['pʌblɪʃər] *n* éditeur *m*, -trice *f.*

publishing ['pʌblɪʃɪŋ] *n* (*U*) [industry] édition *f.*

publishing company, publishing house *n* société *f* OR maison *f* d'édition.

pub lunch *n repas de midi servi dans un pub.*

puce [pju:s] *adj* puce (*inv*).

puck [pʌk] *n* ICE HOCKEY palet *m.*

pucker ['pʌkər] ◇ *vt* plisser. ◇ *vi* se plisser.

pudding ['pʊdɪŋ] *n* **-1.** [food - sweet] entremets *m*; [- savoury] pudding *m*. **-2.** (*U*) *Br* [course] dessert *m*.

puddle ['pʌdl] *n* flaque *f*.

pudgy ['pʌdʒɪ] = podgy.

puerile ['pjʊəraɪl] *adj* puéril(e).

Puerto Rican [ˌpwɜːtəʊ'riːkən] ◇ *adj* portoricain(e). ◇ *n* Portoricain *m*, -e *f*.

Puerto Rico [ˌpwɜːtəʊ'riːkəʊ] *n* Porto Rico *f*, Puerto Rico *f*.

puff [pʌf] ◇ *n* **-1.** [of cigarette, smoke] bouffée *f*. **-2.** [gasp] souffle *m*. ◇ *vt* [cigarette etc] tirer sur. ◇ *vi* **-1.** [smoke]: **to ~ at** OR **on sthg** fumer qqch. **-2.** [pant] haleter.

◆ **puff out** *vt sep* [cheeks, chest] gonfler.

◆ **puff up** *vi* se gonfler.

puffed [pʌft] *adj* **-1.** [swollen]: **~ (up)** gonflé(e). **-2.** *Br inf* [out of breath]: **~ (out)** essoufflé(e).

puffed sleeve *n* manche *f* ballon.

puffin ['pʌfɪn] *n* macareux *m*.

puffiness ['pʌfɪnɪs] *n* gonflement *m*, bouffissure *f*.

puff pastry, **puff paste** *Am n* (*U*) pâte *f* feuilletée.

puffy ['pʌfɪ] (*compar* **-ier**, *superl* **-iest**) *adj* gonflé(e), bouffi(e).

pug [pʌg] *n* carlin *m*.

pugnacious [pʌg'neɪʃəs] *adj fml* querelleur(euse), batailleur(euse).

puke [pjuːk] *vi inf* dégobiller.

pull [pʊl] ◇ *vt* **-1.** [gen] tirer. **-2.** [strain - muscle, hamstring] se froisser. **-3.** [tooth] arracher. **-4.** [attract] attirer. **-5.** [gun] sortir. ◇ *vi* tirer. ◇ *n* **-1.** [tug with hand]: **to give sthg a ~** tirer sur qqch. **-2.** (*U*) [influence] influence *f*.

◆ **pull ahead** *vi*: **to ~ ahead (of)** prendre la tête (devant).

◆ **pull apart** *vt sep* [separate] séparer.

◆ **pull at** *vt fus* tirer sur.

◆ **pull away** *vi* **-1.** AUT démarrer. **-2.** [in race] prendre de l'avance.

◆ **pull back** *vi* reculer.

◆ **pull down** *vt sep* [building] démolir.

◆ **pull in** *vi* AUT se ranger.

◆ **pull off** *vt sep* **-1.** [take off] enlever, ôter. **-2.** [succeed in] réussir.

◆ **pull on** *vt sep* [clothes] mettre, enfiler.

◆ **pull out** ◇ *vt sep* [troops etc] retirer. ◇ *vi* **-1.** RAIL partir, démarrer. **-2.** AUT déboîter. **-3.** [withdraw] se retirer.

◆ **pull over** *vi* AUT se ranger.

◆ **pull through** ◇ *vi* s'en sortir, s'en tirer. ◇ *vt sep* tirer d'affaire.

◆ **pull together** ◇ *vt sep*: **to ~ o.s. together** se ressaisir, se reprendre. ◇ *vi fig* faire un effort.

◆ **pull up** ◇ *vt sep* **-1.** [raise] remonter. **-2.** [chair] avancer. **-3.** [stop]: **to ~ sb up short** arrêter qqn court. ◇ *vi* s'arrêter.

pull-down menu *n* COMPUT menu *m* déroulant.

pulley ['pʊlɪ] (*pl* **pulleys**) *n* poulie *f*.

pullout ['pʊlaʊt] *n* supplément *m* détachable.

pullover ['pʊlˌəʊvəʳ] *n* pull *m*.

pulp [pʌlp] ◇ *adj* [fiction, novel] de quatre sous. ◇ *n* **-1.** [for paper] pâte *f* à papier. **-2.** [of fruit] pulpe *f*. ◇ *vt* [food] réduire en pulpe.

pulpit ['pʊlpɪt] *n* chaire *f*.

pulsar ['pʌlsɑːʳ] *n* pulsar *m*.

pulsate [pʌl'seɪt] *vi* [heart] battre fort; [air, music] vibrer.

pulse [pʌls] ◇ *n* **-1.** MED pouls *m*; **to take sb's ~** prendre le pouls de qqn. **-2.** TECH impulsion *f*. ◇ *vi* battre, palpiter.

◆ **pulses** *npl* [food] légumes *mpl* secs.

pulverize, **-ise** ['pʌlvəraɪz] *vt* **-1.** [crush] pulvériser. **-2.** *fig* [destroy - town] détruire; [- person] démolir.

puma ['pjuːmə] (*pl inv* OR **-s**) *n* puma *m*.

pumice (stone) ['pʌmɪs-] *n* pierre *f* ponce.

pummel ['pʌml] (*Br pt* & *pp* **-led**, *cont* **-ling**, *Am pt* & *pp* **-ed**, *cont* **-ing**) *vt* bourrer de coups.

pump [pʌmp] ◇ *n* pompe *f*. ◇ *vt* **-1.** [water, gas etc] pomper. **-2.** *inf* [invest]: **to ~ money into sthg** injecter des capitaux dans qqch. **-3.** *inf* [interrogate] essayer de tirer les vers du nez à. ◇ *vi* [heart] battre fort.

◆ **pumps** *npl* [shoes] escarpins *mpl*.

pumpernickel ['pʌmpənɪkl] *n* pain *m* de seigle noir.

pumpkin ['pʌmpkɪn] *n* potiron *m*.

pumpkin pie *n* tarte *f* au potiron (*dessert achevant traditionnellement le dîner de Thanksgiving*).

pun [pʌn] *n* jeu *m* de mots, calembour *m*.

punch [pʌntʃ] ◇ *n* **-1.** [blow] coup *m* de poing. **-2.** [tool] poinçonneuse *f*. **-3.** [drink] punch *m*. ◇ *vt* **-1.** [hit - once] donner un coup de poing à; [- repeatedly] donner des coups de poing à; **to ~ a hole in sthg** faire un trou dans qqch. **-2.** [ticket] poinçonner; [paper] perforer.

◆ **punch in** *vi Am* pointer (en arrivant).

◆ **punch out** *vi Am* pointer (en partant).

Punch-and-Judy show [-'dʒuːdɪ-] *n* guignol *m*.

punch bag, **punch ball**, **punching bag** *Am* ['pʌntʃɪŋ-] *n* punching-ball *m*.

punch bowl *n* coupe *f* à punch.

punch-drunk *adj* sonné(e), groggy (*inv*).

punch(ed) card [pʌntʃ(t)-] *n* carte *f* perforée.

punching bag *Am* = punch bag.

punch line *n* trait *m* final (*d'une blague*).

punch-up *n* Br *inf* bagarre *f*.

punchy ['pʌntʃɪ] (*compar* **-ier**, *superl* **-iest**) *adj inf* [style] incisif(ive).

punctilious [pʌŋk'tɪlɪəs] *adj* pointilleux(euse).

punctual ['pʌŋktʃʊəl] *adj* ponctuel(elle).

punctually ['pʌŋktʃʊəlɪ] *adv* à l'heure.

punctuate ['pʌŋktʃʊəɪt] *vt* ponctuer.

punctuation [ˌpʌŋktʃʊ'eɪʃn] *n* ponctuation *f*.

punctuation mark *n* signe *m* de ponctuation.

puncture ['pʌŋktʃəʳ] ◇ *n* crevaison *f*. ◇ *vt* [tyre, ball] **crever**; [skin] **piquer**.

pundit ['pʌndɪt] *n* pontife *m*.

pungent ['pʌndʒənt] *adj* **-1.** [smell] **âcre**; [taste] **piquant(e)**. **-2.** *fig* [criticism] **caustique**, **acerbe**.

punish ['pʌnɪʃ] *vt* punir; **to ~ sb for sthg/ for doing sthg** punir qqn pour qqch/pour avoir fait qqch.

punishable ['pʌnɪʃəbl] *adj* punissable.

punishing ['pʌnɪʃɪŋ] *adj* [schedule, work] **épuisant(e)**, **éreintant(e)**; [defeat] **cuisant(e)**.

punishment ['pʌnɪʃmənt] *n* punition *f*, châtiment *m*; **to take a lot of ~** [car, furniture] **être malmené**.

punitive ['pjuːnətɪv] *adj* [action] **punitif(ive)**; [tax] **très lourd(e)**.

Punjab [ˌpʌn'dʒɑːb] *n*: **the ~** le Pendjab; **in the ~** au Pendjab.

Punjabi [ˌpʌn'dʒɑːbɪ] ◇ *adj* du Pendjab. ◇ *n* **-1.** [person] **habitant** *m*, **-e** *f* du Pendjab. **-2.** [language] **pendjabi** *m*.

punk [pʌŋk] ◇ *adj* punk (*inv*). ◇ *n* **-1.** (*U*) [music]: **~ (rock)** punk *m*. **-2. ~ (rocker)** punk *mf*. **-3.** *Am inf* [lout] **loubard** *m*.

punnet ['pʌnɪt] *n* Br barquette *f*.

punt [pʌnt] ◇ *n* [boat] **bateau** *m* à fond plat. ◇ *vi* [in boat] **se promener en bateau à fond plat**.

punter ['pʌntəʳ] *n* Br **-1.** [gambler] **parieur** *m*, **-ieuse** *f*. **-2.** *inf* [customer] **client** *m*, **-e** *f*.

puny ['pjuːnɪ] (*compar* **-ier**, *superl* **-iest**) *adj* **chétif(ive)**.

pup [pʌp] *n* **-1.** [young dog] **chiot** *m*. **-2.** [young seal] **bébé-phoque** *m*.

pupil ['pjuːpl] *n* **-1.** [student] **élève** *mf*. **-2.** [of eye] **pupille** *f*.

puppet ['pʌpɪt] *n* **-1.** [toy] **marionnette** *f*. **-2.** *pej* [person, country] **fantoche** *m*, **pantin** *m*.

puppet government *n* **gouvernement** *m* **fantoche**.

puppet show *n* **spectacle** *m* de marionnettes.

puppy ['pʌpɪ] (*pl* **-ies**) *n* **chiot** *m*.

puppy fat *n* (*U*) *inf* **rondeurs** *fpl* d'adolescence.

purchase ['pɜːtʃəs] ◇ *n* **achat** *m*. ◇ *vt* **acheter**.

purchase order *n* **bon** *m* de commande OR d'achat.

purchase price *n* **prix** *m* d'achat.

purchaser ['pɜːtʃəsəʳ] *n* **acheteur** *m*, **-euse** *f*.

purchase tax *n* Br **taxe** *f* à l'achat.

purchasing power ['pɜːtʃəsɪŋ-] *n* **pouvoir** *m* d'achat.

purdah ['pɜːdə] *n* **système qui oblige les femmes musulmanes à vivre à l'écart du monde**.

pure [pjʊəʳ] *adj* **pur(e)**.

purebred ['pjʊəbred] *adj* **de race**.

puree ['pjʊəreɪ] ◇ *n* **purée** *f*. ◇ *vt* **écraser en purée**.

purely ['pjʊəlɪ] *adv* **purement**.

pureness ['pjʊənɪs] *n* **pureté** *f*.

purgative ['pɜːgətɪv] *n* **purgatif** *m*.

purgatory ['pɜːgətrɪ] *n* (*U*) *hum* [suffering] **purgatoire** *m*.

◆ **Purgatory** *n* [place] **purgatoire** *m*.

purge [pɜːdʒ] ◇ *n* POL **purge** *f*. ◇ *vt* **-1.** POL **purger**. **-2.** [rid] **débarrasser**, **purger**.

purification [ˌpjʊərɪfɪ'keɪʃn] *n* **purification** *f*, **épuration** *f*.

purifier ['pjʊərɪfaɪəʳ] *n* **épurateur** *m*.

purify ['pjʊərɪfaɪ] (*pt* & *pp* **-ied**) *vt* **purifier**, **épurer**.

purist ['pjʊərɪst] *n* **puriste** *mf*.

puritan ['pjʊərɪtən] ◇ *adj* **puritain(e)**. ◇ *n* **puritain** *m*, **-e** *f*.

puritanical [ˌpjʊərɪ'tænɪkl] *adj pej* **puritain(e)**.

purity ['pjʊərətɪ] *n* **pureté** *f*.

purl [pɜːl] ◇ *n* (*U*) **maille** *f* à l'envers. ◇ *vt* **tricoter à l'envers**.

purloin [pɜː'lɔɪn] *vt fml* or *hum* **voler**, **dérober**.

purple ['pɜːpl] ◇ *adj* **violet(ette)**. ◇ *n* **violet** *m*.

purport [pə'pɔːt] *vi fml*: **to ~ to do/be sthg** **prétendre faire/être qqch**.

purpose ['pɜːpəs] *n* **-1.** [reason] **raison** *f*, **motif** *m*. **-2.** [aim] **but** *m*, **objet** *m*; **to no ~**

en vain, pour rien. **-3.** [determination] détermination *f*.

◆ **on purpose** *adv* exprès.

purpose-built *adj* construit(e) spécialement.

purposeful ['pɜːpəsful] *adj* résolu(e), déterminé(e).

purposely ['pɜːpəsli] *adv* exprès.

purr [pɜːr] ◇ *n* ronronnement *m*. ◇ *vi* ronronner.

purse [pɜːs] ◇ *n* **-1.** [for money] portemonnaie *m inv*, bourse *f*. **-2.** *Am* [handbag] sac *m* à main. ◇ *vt* [lips] pincer.

purser ['pɜːsər] *n* commissaire *m* de bord.

purse snatcher [-ˌsnætʃər] *n Am* voleur *m*, -euse *f* à la tire.

purse strings *npl*: **to hold the ~** tenir les cordons de la bourse.

pursue [pəˈsjuː] *vt* **-1.** [follow] poursuivre, pourchasser. **-2.** [policy, aim] poursuivre; [question] continuer à débattre; [matter] approfondir; [project] donner suite à; **to ~ an interest in sthg** se livrer à qqch.

pursuer [pəˈsjuːər] *n* poursuivant *m*, -e *f*.

pursuit [pəˈsjuːt] *n* **-1.** (*U*) *fml* [attempt to obtain] recherche *f*, poursuite *f*. **-2.** [chase, in sport] poursuite *f*; **in ~ of** à la poursuite de; **in hot ~** aux trousses. **-3.** [occupation] occupation *f*, activité *f*.

purveyor [pəˈveɪər] *n fml* fournisseur *m*.

pus [pʌs] *n* pus *m*.

push [puʃ] ◇ *vt* **-1.** [press, move - gen] pousser; [- button] appuyer sur. **-2.** [encourage]: **to ~ sb (to do sthg)** inciter OR pousser qqn (à faire qqch). **-3.** [force]: **to ~ sb (into doing sthg)** forcer OR obliger qqn (à faire qqch). **-4.** [campaign]: **to ~ for sthg** faire pression pour obtenir qqch. **-5.** *inf* [promote] faire de la réclame pour. **-6.** *drugs sl* vendre, fournir.

◇ *vi* pousser; [on button] appuyer.

◇ *n* **-1.** [with hand] poussée *f*. **-2.** [forceful effort] effort *m*. **-3.** *phr*: **to give sb the ~** *Br inf* [end relationship] plaquer qqn; [dismiss] ficher qqn à la porte.

◆ **push ahead** *vi* continuer, persévérer; **to ~ ahead with sthg** persévérer dans qqch, continuer (à faire) qqch.

◆ **push around** *vt sep inf fig* marcher sur les pieds de.

◆ **push in** *vi* [in queue] resquiller.

◆ **push off** *vi inf* filer, se sauver.

◆ **push on** *vi* continuer.

◆ **push over** *vt sep* faire tomber.

◆ **push through** *vt sep* [law, reform] faire accepter.

pushbike ['puʃbaɪk] *n Br* vélo *m*.

push-button *adj* à touches.

pushcart ['puʃkɑːt] *n* charrette *f* à bras.

pushchair ['puʃtʃeər] *n Br* poussette *f*.

pushed [puʃt] *adj inf*: **to be ~ for sthg** être à court de qqch; **to be hard ~ to do sthg** avoir du mal OR de la peine à faire qqch.

pusher ['puʃər] *n drugs sl* dealer *m*.

pushing ['puʃɪŋ] *prep inf*: **he's ~ 40** il frise la quarantaine.

pushover ['puʃˌəuvər] *n inf*: **it's a ~** c'est un jeu d'enfant.

push-start *vt* faire démarrer en poussant.

push-up *n* pompe *f*, traction *f*.

pushy ['puʃɪ] (*compar* **-ier**, *superl* **-iest**) *adj pej* qui se met toujours en avant.

puss [pus], **pussy (cat)** ['pusɪ-] *n inf* minet *m*, minou *m*.

pussy willow *n* saule *m*.

put [put] (*pt* & *pp* put, *cont* **-ting**) *vt* **-1.** [gen] mettre; **to ~ responsibility on sb** donner des responsabilités à qqn. **-2.** [place] mettre, poser, placer; **to ~ the children to bed** coucher les enfants. **-3.** [express] dire, exprimer. **-4.** [question] poser; **to ~ it to sb that ...** suggérer à qqn que .... **-5.** [estimate] estimer, évaluer. **-6.** [invest]: **to ~ money into** investir de l'argent dans; **I've ~ a lot of time into this work** j'ai passé beaucoup de temps à faire ce travail.

◆ **put across** *vt sep* [ideas] faire comprendre.

◆ **put aside** *vt sep* **-1.** [place on one side] mettre de côté, poser. **-2.** *fig* [money] mettre de côté; [differences] ne pas tenir compte de.

◆ **put away** *vt sep* **-1.** [tidy away] ranger. **-2.** *inf* [lock up] enfermer.

◆ **put back** *vt sep* **-1.** [replace] remettre (à sa place OR en place). **-2.** [postpone] remettre. **-3.** [clock, watch] retarder.

◆ **put by** *vt sep* [money] mettre de côté.

◆ **put down** *vt sep* **-1.** [lay down] poser, déposer. **-2.** [quell - rebellion] réprimer. **-3.** *inf* [criticize] humilier. **-4.** [write down] inscrire, noter. **-5.** *Br* [kill]: **to have a dog/cat ~ down** faire piquer un chien/chat.

◆ **put down to** *vt sep* attribuer à.

◆ **put forward** *vt sep* **-1.** [propose] proposer, avancer. **-2.** [meeting, clock, watch] avancer.

◆ **put in** *vt sep* **-1.** [spend - time] passer. **-2.** [submit] présenter.

◆ **put off** *vt sep* **-1.** [postpone] remettre (à plus tard). **-2.** [cause to wait] décommander. **-3.** [discourage] dissuader. **-4.** [disturb] déconcerter, troubler. **-5.** [cause to dislike] dégoûter.

◆ **put on** *vt sep* **-1.** [clothes] mettre, enfiler. **-2.** [arrange - exhibition etc] organiser; [- play] monter. **-3.** [gain]: **to ~ on weight** prendre du poids, grossir. **-4.** [switch on - radio, TV] allumer, mettre; **to ~ the light on** allumer (la lumière); **to ~ the brake on** freiner. **-5.** [record, CD, tape] passer, mettre. **-6.** [start cooking] mettre à cuire. **-7.** [pretend - gen] feindre; [- accent etc] prendre. **-8.** [bet] parier, miser. **-9.** [add] ajouter. **-10.** *inf* [tease] faire marcher.

◆ **put onto** *vt sep*: **to ~ sb onto sb/sthg** indiquer qqn/qqch à qqn.

◆ **put out** *vt sep* **-1.** [place outside] mettre dehors. **-2.** [book, statement] publier; [record] sortir. **-3.** [fire, cigarette] éteindre; **to ~ the light out** éteindre (la lumière). **-4.** [extend - hand] tendre. **-5.** *inf* [injure]: **to ~ one's back/hip out** se démettre le dos/la hanche. **-6.** [annoy, upset]: **to be ~ out** être contrarié(e). **-7.** [inconvenience] déranger; **to ~ o.s. out** se donner du mal.

◆ **put over** *vt sep* [ideas] faire comprendre.

◆ **put through** *vt sep* TELEC passer.

◆ **put together** *vt sep* **-1.** [assemble - machine, furniture] monter, assembler; [- team] réunir; [- report] composer. **-2.** [combine] mettre ensemble; **more than all the others ~ together** plus que tous les autres réunis. **-3.** [organize] monter, organiser.

◆ **put up** *vt sep* **-1.** [build - gen] ériger; [- tent] dresser. **-2.** [umbrella] ouvrir; [flag] hisser. **-3.** [fix to wall] accrocher. **-4.** [provide - money] fournir. **-5.** [propose - candidate] proposer. **-6.** [increase] augmenter. **-7.** [provide accommodation for] loger, héberger. ◇ *vt fus*: **to ~ up a fight** se défendre.

◆ **put upon** *vt fus Br*: **to be ~ upon** se laisser faire.

◆ **put up to** *vt sep*: **to ~ sb up to sthg** pousser OR inciter qqn à faire qqch.

◆ **put up with** *vt fus* supporter.

putative ['pju:tətɪv] *adj* putatif(ive).

put-down *n inf* rebuffade *f*.

putrefaction [ˌpju:trɪ'fækʃn] *n* putréfaction *f*.

putrefy ['pju:trɪfaɪ] (*pt & pp* **-ied**) *vi* se putréfier.

putrid ['pju:trɪd] *adj* putride.

putsch [pʊtʃ] *n* putsch *m*.

putt [pʌt] ◇ *n* putt *m*. ◇ *vt & vi* putter.

putter ['pʌtər] *n* [club] putter *m*.

◆ **putter about, putter around** *Am* bricoler.

putting green ['pʌtɪŋ-] *n* green *m*.

putty ['pʌtɪ] *n* mastic *m*.

put-up job *n inf* coup *m* monté.

put-upon *adj inf* qui se laisse marcher sur les pieds.

puzzle ['pʌzl] ◇ *n* **-1.** [toy] casse-tête *m inv*; [mental] devinette *f*. **-2.** [mystery] mystère *m*, énigme *f*. ◇ *vt* rendre perplexe. ◇ *vi*: **to ~ over sthg** essayer de comprendre qqch.

◆ **puzzle out** *vt sep* comprendre.

puzzled ['pʌzld] *adj* perplexe.

puzzling ['pʌzlɪŋ] *adj* curieux(ieuse).

PVC (*abbr of* **polyvinyl chloride**) *n* PVC *m*.

Pvt. *abbr of* **Private**.

pw (*abbr of* **per week**) p.sem.

PWR (*abbr of* **pressurized-water reactor**) *n* REP *m*.

PX (*abbr of* **post exchange**) *n* magasin de l'armée.

pygmy ['pɪgmɪ] (*pl* **-ies**) *n* pygmée *m*.

pyjama [pə'dʒɑ:mə] *comp* de pyjama.

◆ **pyjamas** *npl* pyjama *m*; **a pair of ~** un pyjama.

pylon ['paɪlən] *n* pylône *m*.

pyramid ['pɪrəmɪd] *n* pyramide *f*.

pyramid selling *n* vente *f* en pyramide.

pyre ['paɪər] *n* bûcher *m* funéraire.

Pyrenean [ˌpɪrə'ni:ən] *adj* pyrénéen(enne).

Pyrenees [ˌpɪrə'ni:z] *npl*: **the ~** les Pyrénées *fpl*.

Pyrex® ['paɪreks] ◇ *n* Pyrex® *m*. ◇ *comp* en Pyrex®.

pyromaniac [ˌpaɪrə'meɪnɪæk] *n* pyromane *mf*.

pyrotechnics [ˌpaɪrəʊ'teknɪks] ◇ *n* (*U*) pyrotechnie *f*. ◇ *npl fig* [skill] feu *m* d'artifice.

python ['paɪθn] (*pl inv* OR **-s**) *n* python *m*.

Q

q (*pl* **q's** OR **qs**), **Q** (*pl* **Q's** OR **Qs**) [kju:] *n* [letter] q *m inv*, Q *m inv*.

Qatar [kæ'tɑːʳ] Qatar *m*, Katar *m*; **in ~** au Qatar.

QC (*abbr of* **Queen's Counsel**) *n* ≃ bâtonnier *m* de l'ordre.

QED (*abbr of* **quod erat demonstrandum**) CQFD.

QM *abbr of* **quartermaster**.

q.t., **QT** (*abbr of* **quiet**) *inf*: **on the ~** en douce.

qty (*abbr of* **quantity**) qté.

quack [kwæk] ◇ *n* **-1.** [noise] coin-coin *m inv*. **-2.** *inf pej* [doctor] charlatan *m*. ◇ *vi* faire coin-coin.

quad [kwɒd] **-1.** *abbr of* **quadruple**. **-2.** *abbr of* **quadruplet**. **-3.** *abbr of* **quadrangle**.

quadrangle ['kwɒdræŋgl] *n* **-1.** [figure] quadrilatère *m*. **-2.** [courtyard] cour *f*.

quadrant ['kwɒdrənt] *n* quadrant *m*.

quadraphonic [,kwɒdrə'fɒnɪk] *adj* quadriphonique.

quadrilateral [,kwɒdrɪ'lætərəl] ◇ *adj* quadrilatéral(e). ◇ *n* quadrilatère *m*.

quadruped ['kwɒdrʊped] *n* quadrupède *m*.

quadruple [kwɒ'druːpl] ◇ *adj* quadruple. ◇ *vt & vi* quadrupler.

quadruplets [kwɒ'drʊplɪts] *npl* quadruplés *mpl*.

quads [kwɒdz] *npl inf* quadruplés *mpl*.

quaff [kwɒf] *vt dated* boire (à longs traits).

quagmire ['kwægmaɪəʳ] *n* bourbier *m*.

quail [kweɪl] (*pl inv* OR **-s**) ◇ *n* caille *f*. ◇ *vi literary* reculer.

quaint [kweɪnt] *adj* pittoresque.

quaintness ['kweɪntnɪs] *n* pittoresque *m*.

quake [kweɪk] ◇ *n* (*abbr of* **earthquake**) *inf* tremblement *m* de terre. ◇ *vi* trembler.

Quaker ['kweɪkəʳ] *n* quaker *m*, -eresse *f*.

qualification [,kwɒlɪfɪ'keɪʃn] *n* **-1.** [certificate] diplôme *m*. **-2.** [quality, skill] compétence *f*. **-3.** [qualifying statement] réserve *f*.

qualified ['kwɒlɪfaɪd] *adj* **-1.** [trained] diplômé(e). **-2.** [able]: **to be ~ to do sthg** avoir la compétence nécessaire pour faire qqch. **-3.** [limited] restreint(e), modéré(e).

qualify ['kwɒlɪfaɪ] (*pt & pp* **-ied**) ◇ *vt* **-1.** [modify] apporter des réserves à. **-2.** [entitle]: **to ~ sb to do sthg** qualifier qqn pour faire qqch. ◇ *vi* **-1.** [pass exams] obtenir un diplôme. **-2.** [be entitled]: **to ~ (for sthg)** avoir droit (à qqch), remplir les conditions requises (pour qqch). **-3.** SPORT se qualifier.

qualifying ['kwɒlɪfaɪɪŋ] *adj* **-1.** [modifying] nuancé(e). **-2.** [entitling]: **~ exam** examen *m* d'entrée. **-3.** SPORT [time] qui permet de se qualifier; **~ round** série *f* éliminatoire.

qualitative ['kwɒlɪtətɪv] *adj* qualitatif(ive).

quality ['kwɒlətɪ] (*pl* **-ies**) ◇ *n* qualité *f*. ◇ *comp* de qualité.

quality control *n* contrôle *m* de qualité.

quality press *n Br*: **the ~** la presse sérieuse.

qualms ['kwɑːmz] *npl* doutes *mpl*.

quandary ['kwɒndərɪ] (*pl* **-ies**) *n* embarras *m*; **to be in a ~ about** OR **over sthg** être bien embarrassé à propos de qqch.

quango ['kwæŋgəʊ] (*abbr of* **quasiautonomous non-governmental organization**) (*pl* **-s**) *n Br ușu pej* commission indépendante financée par l'État.

quantifiable [kwɒntɪ'faɪəbl] *adj* quantifiable.

quantify ['kwɒntɪfaɪ] (*pt & pp* **-ied**) *vt* quantifier.

quantitative ['kwɒntɪtətɪv] *adj* quantitatif(ive).

quantity ['kwɒntətɪ] (*pl* **-ies**) *n* quantité *f*; **in ~** en quantité; **an unknown ~** une inconnue.

quantity surveyor *n* métreur *m*, -euse *f*.

quantum leap ['kwɒntəm-] *n fig* bond *m* en avant.

quantum theory ['kwɒntəm-] *n* théorie *f* des quanta.

quarantine ['kwɒrəntiːn] ◇ *n* quarantaine *f*; **to be in ~** être en quarantaine. ◇ *vt* mettre en quarantaine.

quark [kwɑːk] *n* quark *m*.

quarrel ['kwɒrəl] (*Br pt & pp* **-led**, *cont* **-ling**, *Am pt & pp* **-ed**, *cont* **-ing**) ◇ *n* querelle *f*, dispute *f*; **I have no ~ with her** je n'ai rien contre elle. ◇ *vi*: **to ~ (with)** se quereller (avec), se disputer (avec).

quarrelsome ['kwɒrəlsəm] *adj* querelleur(euse).

quarry ['kwɒrɪ] (*pl* **-ies**, *pt & pp* **-ied**) ◇ *n* **-1.** [place] carrière *f*. **-2.** [prey] proie *f*. ◇ *vt* extraire.

quarry tile *n* carreau *m*.

quart [kwɔːt] *n* = *1,136 litre Br,* = *0,946 litre Am,* ≃ litre *m*.

quarter ['kwɔːtəʳ] *n* **-1.** [fraction, weight] quart *m;* **a ~ past two** *Br,* **a ~ after two** *Am* deux heures et quart; **a ~ to two** *Br,* **a ~ of two** *Am* deux heures moins le quart. **-2.** [of year] trimestre *m.* **-3.** *Am* [coin] pièce *f* de 25 cents. **-4.** [area in town] quartier *m.* **-5.** [direction]: **from all ~s** de tous côtés.
◆ **quarters** *npl* [rooms] quartiers *mpl.*
◆ **at close quarters** *adv* de près.

quarterback ['kwɔːtəbæk] *n* SPORT quarterback *m.*

quarterdeck ['kwɔːtədek] *n* gaillard *m* d'arrière.

quarterfinal [ˌkwɔːtəˈfaɪnl] *n* quart *m* de finale.

quarter-hour *adj* [intervals] d'un quart d'heure.

quarter light *n* *Br* AUT déflecteur *m.*

quarterly ['kwɔːtəlɪ] (*pl* **-ies**) ⋄ *adj* trimestriel(ielle). ⋄ *adv* trimestriellement. ⋄ *n* publication *f* trimestrielle.

quartermaster ['kwɔːtəˌmɑːstəʳ] *n* MIL intendant *m.*

quarter note *n* *Am* MUS noire *f.*

quarter sessions *npl* [in UK] tribunal *m* de grande instance; [in US] *dans certains États, tribunal local à compétence criminelle, pouvant avoir des fonctions administratives.*

quartet [kwɔːˈtet] *n* quatuor *m.*

quarto ['kwɔːtəʊ] (*pl* **-s**) *n* in-quarto *m inv.*

quartz [kwɔːts] *n* quartz *m.*

quartz watch *n* montre *f* à quartz.

quasar ['kweɪzɑːʳ] *n* quasar *m.*

quash [kwɒʃ] *vt* **-1.** [sentence] annuler, casser. **-2.** [rebellion] réprimer.

quasi- ['kweɪzaɪ] *prefix* quasi-.

quaver ['kweɪvəʳ] ⋄ *n* **-1.** MUS croche *f.* **-2.** [in voice] tremblement *m,* chevrotement *m.* ⋄ *vi* trembler, chevroter.

quavering ['kweɪvərɪŋ] *adj* tremblant(e), chevrotant(e).

quay [kiː] *n* quai *m.*

quayside ['kiːsaɪd] *n* bord *m* du quai.

queasy ['kwiːzɪ] (*compar* **-ier,** *superl* **-iest**) *adj:* **to feel ~** avoir mal au cœur.

Quebec [kwɪˈbek] *n* **-1.** [province] Québec *m;* **in ~** au Québec. **-2.** [city] Québec.

Quebecer, Quebecker [kwɪˈbekəʳ] *n* Québécois *m,* -e *f.*

queen [kwiːn] *n* **-1.** [gen] reine *f.* **-2.** [playing card] dame *f.*

Queen Mother *n:* **the ~** la reine mère.

Queen's Counsel *n* *Br* avocat *m* de la Couronne.

Queen's English *n* *Br:* **the ~** l'anglais *m* correct.

queen's evidence *n* *Br:* **to turn ~** témoigner contre ses complices.

queer [kwɪəʳ] ⋄ *adj* [odd] étrange, bizarre; **I'm feeling a bit ~** je ne me sens pas très bien. ⋄ *n inf pej* pédé *m,* homosexuel *m.*

quell [kwel] *vt* réprimer, étouffer.

quench [kwentʃ] *vt:* **to ~ one's thirst** se désaltérer.

querulous ['kwerʊləs] *adj* [child] ronchonneur(euse); [voice] plaintif(ive).

query ['kwɪərɪ] (*pl* **-ies,** *pt* & *pp* **-ied**) ⋄ *n* question *f.* ⋄ *vt* mettre en doute, douter de.

quest [kwest] *n literary:* **~ (for)** quête *f* (de).

question ['kwestʃn] ⋄ *n* **-1.** [gen] question *f;* **to ask (sb) a ~** poser une question (à qqn). **-2.** [doubt] doute *m;* **to call** OR **bring sthg into ~** mettre qqch en doute; **it's open to ~ whether ...** on peut se demander si ...; **without ~** incontestablement, sans aucun doute; **beyond ~** [know] sans aucun doute. **-3.** *phr:* **there's no ~ of ...** il n'est pas question de ....
⋄ *vt* **-1.** [interrogate] questionner. **-2.** [express doubt about] mettre en question OR doute.
◆ **in question** *adv:* **the ... in ~** le/la/les ... en question.
◆ **out of the question** *adv* hors de question.

questionable ['kwestʃənəbl] *adj* **-1.** [uncertain] discutable. **-2.** [not right, not honest] douteux(euse).

questioner ['kwestʃənəʳ] *n* personne *f* qui pose une question.

questioning ['kwestʃənɪŋ] ⋄ *adj* interrogateur(trice). ⋄ *n* (*U*) interrogation *f.*

question mark *n* point *m* d'interrogation.

question master, quizmaster ['kwɪzˌmɑːstəʳ] *n* meneur *m* de jeu.

questionnaire [ˌkwestʃəˈneəʳ] *n* questionnaire *m.*

question time *n* *Br* POL *heure réservée aux questions des députés.*

queue [kjuː] *Br* ⋄ *n* queue *f,* file *f;* **to jump the ~** resquiller, passer avant son tour. ⋄ *vi* faire la queue.

queue-jump *vi* *Br* resquiller.

quibble ['kwɪbl] *pej* ⋄ *n* chicane *f.* ⋄ *vi:* **to ~ (over** OR **about)** chicaner (à propos de).

quiche [kiːʃ] *n* quiche *f.*

quick [kwɪk] ◇ *adj* **-1.** [gen] rapide. **-2.** [response, decision] prompt(e), rapide. ◇ *adv* vite, rapidement.

quicken ['kwɪkn] ◇ *vt* accélérer, presser. ◇ *vi* s'accélérer.

quickly ['kwɪklɪ] *adv* **-1.** [rapidly] vite, rapidement. **-2.** [without delay] promptement, immédiatement.

quickness ['kwɪknɪs] *n* [speed] rapidité *f*.

quicksand ['kwɪksænd] *n* sable *m* mouvant.

quicksilver ['kwɪk,sɪlvər] *n* vif-argent *m*, mercure *m*.

quickstep ['kwɪkstep] *n*: **the** ~ le fox-trot.

quick-tempered *adj* emporté(e).

quick-witted [-'wɪtɪd] *adj* [person] à l'esprit vif.

quid [kwɪd] (*pl inv*) *n Br inf* livre *f*.

quid pro quo [-'kwəu] (*pl* quid pro quos) *n* contrepartie *f*.

quiescent [kwaɪ'esnt] *adj fml* immobile.

quiet ['kwaɪət] ◇ *adj* **-1.** [not noisy] tranquille; [voice] bas (basse); [engine] silencieux(ieuse). **-2.** [not busy] calme. **-3.** [silent] silencieux(ieuse); **to keep** ~ **about sthg** ne rien dire à propos de qqch, garder qqch secret. **-4.** [intimate] intime; **to have a** ~ **word with sb** dire deux mots en particulier à qqn. **-5.** [colour] discret(ète), sobre. ◇ *n* tranquillité *f*; **on the** ~ *inf* en douce. ◇ *vt Am* calmer, apaiser.
◆ **quiet down** ◇ *vt sep* calmer, apaiser. ◇ *vi* se calmer.

quieten ['kwaɪətn] *vt* calmer, apaiser.
◆ **quieten down** ◇ *vt sep* calmer, apaiser. ◇ *vi* se calmer.

quietly ['kwaɪətlɪ] *adv* **-1.** [without noise] sans faire de bruit, silencieusement; [say] doucement. **-2.** [without excitement] tranquillement, calmement. **-3.** [without fuss - leave] discrètement.

quietness ['kwaɪətnɪs] *n* (*U*) **-1.** [silence] silence *m*. **-2.** [peacefulness] calme *m*, tranquillité *f*.

quiff [kwɪf] *n Br* mèche *f*.

quill (pen) [kwɪl-] *n* plume *f* d'oie.

quilt [kwɪlt] *n* [padded] édredon *m*; (**continental)** ~ couette *f*.

quilted ['kwɪltɪd] *adj* matelassé(e).

quince [kwɪns] *n* coing *m*.

quinine [kwɪ'niːn] *n* quinine *f*.

quins *Br* [kwɪnz], **quints** *Am* [kwɪnts] *npl inf* quintuplés *mpl*.

quintessential [kwɪntə'senʃl] *adj* typique.

quintet [kwɪn'tet] *n* quintette *m*.

quints *Am* = quins.

quintuplets [kwɪn'tjuːplɪts] *npl* quintuplés *mpl*.

quip [kwɪp] (*pt* & *pp* **-ped**, *cont* **-ping**) ◇ *n* raillerie *f*. ◇ *vi* railler.

quire ['kwaɪər] *n* cahier *m*.

quirk [kwɜːk] *n* bizarrerie *f*; **a** ~ **of fate** un caprice du sort.

quirky ['kwɜːkɪ] (*compar* **-ier**, *superl* **-iest**) *adj* étrange, bizarre.

quit [kwɪt] (*Br pt* & *pp* quit OR **-ted**, *cont* **-ting**, *Am pt* & *pp* quit, *cont* **-ting**) ◇ *vt* **-1.** [resign from] quitter. **-2.** [stop]: **to** ~ **smoking** arrêter de fumer. ◇ *vi* **-1.** [resign] démissionner. **-2.** [give up] abandonner.

quite [kwaɪt] *adv* **-1.** [completely] tout à fait, complètement; **I** ~ **agree** je suis entièrement d'accord; **not** ~ pas tout à fait; **I don't** ~ **understand** je ne comprends pas bien. **-2.** [fairly] assez, plutôt. **-3.** [for emphasis]: **she's** ~ **a singer** c'est une chanteuse formidable; **it was** ~ **a surprise** c'était une drôle de surprise. **-4.** [to express agreement]: ~ **(so)!** exactement!

Quito ['kiːtəu] *n* Quito.

quits [kwɪts] *adj inf*: **to be** ~ **(with sb)** être quitte (envers qqn); **to call it** ~ en rester là.

quitter ['kwɪtər] *n inf pej* dégonflé *m*, -e *f*.

quiver ['kwɪvər] ◇ *n* **-1.** [shiver] frisson *m*. **-2.** [for arrows] carquois *m*. ◇ *vi* frissonner.

quivering ['kwɪvərɪŋ] *adj* frissonnant(e).

quixotic [kwɪk'sɒtɪk] *adj* chevaleresque.

quiz [kwɪz] (*pl* **-zes**, *pt* & *pp* **-zed**, *cont* **-zing**) ◇ *n* **-1.** [gen] quiz *m*, jeu-concours *m*. **-2.** *Am* SCH interrogation *f*. ◇ *vt*: **to** ~ **sb (about sthg)** interroger qqn (au sujet de qqch).

quizmaster = question master.

quizzical ['kwɪzɪkl] *adj* narquois(e), moqueur(euse).

quoits [kwɔɪts] *n* (*U*) jeu *m* de palet.

Quonset hut ['kwɒnsɪt-] *n Am* hutte *f* préfabriquée en tôle.

quorate ['kwɔːreɪt] *adj Br* dont le quorum est atteint.

quorum ['kwɔːrəm] *n* quorum *m*.

quota ['kwəutə] *n* quota *m*.

quotation [kwəu'teɪʃn] *n* **-1.** [citation] citation *f*. **-2.** COMM devis *m*.

quotation marks *npl* guillemets *mpl*; **in** ~ entre guillemets.

quote [kwəut] ◇ *n inf* **-1.** [citation] citation *f*. **-2.** COMM devis *m*. ◇ *vt* **-1.** [cite] citer. **-2.** COMM indiquer, spécifier. ◇ *vi* **-1.** [cite]: **to** ~ **(from sthg)** citer (qqch). **-2.** COMM: **to for sthg** établir un devis pour qqch.
◆ **quotes** *npl inf* guillemets *mpl*.

quoted company ['kwəʊtɪd-] *n Br* société *f* cotée en Bourse.

quotient ['kwəʊʃnt] *n* quotient *m*.

qv (*abbr of* **quod vide**) *expression renvoyant le lecteur à une autre entrée dans une encyclopédie.*

qwerty keyboard ['kwɜːtɪ-] *n Br* clavier *m* QWERTY.

R

r (*pl* **r's** OR **rs**), **R** (*pl* **R's** OR **Rs**) [ɑːr] *n* [letter] r *m inv*, R *m inv*.

◆ **R** -1. (*abbr of* **right**) dr. -2. *abbr of* **River**. -3. (*abbr of* **Réaumur**) R. -4. (*abbr of* **restricted**) *aux États-Unis, indique qu'un film est interdit aux moins de 17 ans.* -5. *Am abbr of* **Republican**. -6. *Br* (*abbr of* **Rex**) *suit le nom d'un roi.* -7. *Br* (*abbr of* **Regina**) *suit le nom d'une reine.*

RA (*abbr of* **Royal Academy**) *n académie britannique des beaux-arts (organisant notamment un salon annuel).*

RAAF (*abbr of* **Royal Australian Air Force**) *n armée de l'air australienne.*

Rabat [rə'bɑːt] *n* Rabat.

rabbi ['ræbaɪ] *n* rabbin *m*.

rabbit ['ræbɪt] *n* lapin *m*.

rabbit hole *n* terrier *m*.

rabbit hutch *n* clapier *m*.

rabbit warren *n* garenne *f*.

rabble ['ræbl] *n* cohue *f*.

rabble-rousing *adj* [speech] qui incite à la violence.

rabid ['ræbɪd, 'reɪbɪd] *adj lit & fig* enragé(e).

rabies ['reɪbiːz] *n* rage *f*.

RAC (*abbr of* **Royal Automobile Club**) *n club automobile britannique,* ≃ TCF *m*, ≃ ACF *m*.

raccoon [rə'kuːn] *n* raton *m* laveur.

race [reɪs] ◇ *n* -1. [competition] course *f*. -2. [people, ethnic background] race *f*. ◇ *vt* -1. [compete against] faire la course avec. -2. [horse] faire courir. ◇ *vi* -1. [compete] courir; to ~ **against sb** faire la course avec qqn. -2. [rush]: to ~ **in/out** entrer/sortir à toute allure. -3. [pulse] être très rapide. -4. [engine] s'emballer.

race car *Am* = **racing car**.

racecourse ['reɪskɔːs] *n* champ *m* de courses.

race driver *Am* = **racing driver**.

racehorse ['reɪshɔːs] *n* cheval *m* de course.

race meeting *n* courses *fpl*.

race relations *npl* relations *fpl* interraciales.

race riot *n* émeute *f* raciale.

racetrack ['reɪstræk] *n* piste *f*.

racial discrimination ['reɪʃl-] *n* discrimination *f* raciale.

racialism *etc* ['reɪʃəlɪzm] = **racism** *etc*.

racing ['reɪsɪŋ] *n* (*U*): **(horse)** ~ les courses *fpl*.

racing car *Br*, **race car** *Am n* voiture *f* de course.

racing driver *Br*, **race driver** *Am n* coureur *m* automobile, pilote *m* de course.

racism ['reɪsɪzm] *n* racisme *m*.

racist ['reɪsɪst] ◇ *adj* raciste. ◇ *n* raciste *mf*.

rack [ræk] ◇ *n* [for bottles] casier *m*; [for luggage] porte-bagages *m inv*; [for plates] égouttoir *m*; **toast** ~ porte-toasts *m inv*. ◇ *vt literary*: to be ~**ed by** OR **with sthg** être tenaillé(e) par qqch.

racket ['rækɪt] *n* -1. [noise] boucan *m*. -2. [illegal activity] racket *m*. -3. SPORT raquette *f*.

racketeering [ˌrækə'tɪərɪŋ] *n* racket *m*.

raconteur [ˌrækɒn'tɜːr] *n* conteur *m*, -euse *f*.

racquet ['rækɪt] *n* raquette *f*.

racy ['reɪsɪ] (*compar* **-ier**, *superl* **-iest**) *adj* [novel, style] osé(e).

RADA ['rɑːdə] (*abbr of* **Royal Academy of Dramatic Art**) *n conservatoire britannique d'art dramatique.*

radar ['reɪdɑːr] *n* radar *m*.

radar trap *n* piège *m* radar.

radial (tyre) ['reɪdjəl-] *n* pneu *m* à carcasse radiale.

radian ['reɪdjən] *n* radian *m*.

radiance ['reɪdjəns] *n* (*U*) rayonnement *m*, éclat *m*.

radiant ['reɪdjənt] *adj* -1. [happy] radieux(ieuse). -2. *literary* [brilliant] rayonnant(e). -3. TECH radiant(e).

radiate ['reɪdɪeɪt] ◇ *vt* -1. [heat, light] émettre, dégager. -2. *fig* [confidence, health] respirer. ◇ *vi* -1. [heat, light] irradier. -2. [roads, lines] rayonner.

radiation [ˌreɪdɪ'eɪʃn] *n* [radioactive] radiation *f*.

radiation sickness *n* mal *m* des rayons.

radiator ['reɪdɪeɪtər] *n* radiateur *m*.

radiator grille *n* calandre *f*.

radical ['rædɪkl] ◇ *adj* radical(e). ◇ *n* POL radical *m*, -e *f*.

radically ['rædɪklɪ] *adv* radicalement.

radii ['reɪdɪaɪ] *pl* → **radius**.

radio ['reɪdɪəʊ] (*pl* -s) ◇ *n* radio *f*; **on the ~** à la radio. ◇ *comp* de radio. ◇ *vt* [person] appeler par radio; [information] envoyer par radio.

radioactive [,reɪdɪəʊ'æktɪv] *adj* radioactif(ive).

radioactive waste *n* (*U*) déchets *mpl* radioactifs.

radioactivity [,reɪdɪəʊæk'tɪvətɪ] *n* radioactivité *f*.

radio alarm *n* radio-réveil *m*.

radio-controlled *adj* téléguidé(e).

radio frequency *n* radiofréquence *f*.

radiogram ['reɪdɪəʊ,græm] *n* [message] radiogramme *m*.

radiographer [,reɪdɪ'ɒgrəfəʳ] *n* radiologue *mf*.

radiography [,reɪdɪ'ɒgrəfɪ] *n* radiographie *f*.

radiology [,reɪdɪ'ɒlədʒɪ] *n* radiologie *f*.

radiopaging ['reɪdɪəʊ,peɪdʒɪŋ] *n* système d'appel par récepteur de poche.

radiotelephone [,reɪdɪəʊ'telɪfəʊn] *n* radiotéléphone *m*.

radiotherapist [,reɪdɪəʊ'θerəpɪst] *n* radiothérapeute *mf*.

radiotherapy [,reɪdɪəʊ'θerəpɪ] *n* radiothérapie *f*.

radish ['rædɪʃ] *n* radis *m*.

radium ['reɪdɪəm] *n* radium *m*.

radius ['reɪdɪəs] (*pl* **radii**) *n* -1. MATH rayon *m*. -2. ANAT radius *m*.

radon ['reɪdɒn] *n* radon *m*.

RAF [ɑːˈreɪeɪ, ræf] *n* abbr of **Royal Air Force**.

raffia ['ræfɪə] *n* raphia *m*.

raffish ['ræfɪʃ] *adj* dissolu(e).

raffle ['ræfl] ◇ *n* tombola *f*. ◇ *vt* mettre en tombola.

raft [rɑːft] *n* -1. [of wood] radeau *m*. -2. [large number] tas *m*; **a ~ of policies** POL un train de mesures.

rafter ['rɑːftəʳ] *n* chevron *m*.

rag [ræg] *n* -1. [piece of cloth] chiffon *m*; **it's like a red ~ to a bull** c'est comme la couleur rouge pour le taureau. -2. *pej* [newspaper] torchon *m*.
◆ **rags** *npl* [clothes] guenilles *fpl*; **from ~s to riches** de la misère à la richesse.

ragamuffin ['rægə,mʌfɪn] *n* galopin *m*.

rag-and-bone man *n* chiffonnier *m*.

ragbag ['rægbæg] *n* fig ramassis *m*.

rag doll *n* poupée *f* de chiffon.

rage [reɪdʒ] ◇ *n* -1. [fury] rage *f*, fureur *f*. -2. *inf* [fashion]: **to be (all) the ~** faire fureur. ◇ *vi* -1. [person] être furieux(ieuse). -2. [storm, argument] faire rage.

ragged ['rægɪd] *adj* -1. [person] en haillons; [clothes] en lambeaux. -2. [line, edge, performance] inégal(e).

raging ['reɪdʒɪŋ] *adj* [thirst, headache] atroce; [storm] déchaîné(e).

ragout ['rægu:] *n* ragoût *m*.

ragtime ['rægtaɪm] *n* ragtime *m*.

rag trade *n* inf: **the ~** la confection.

rag week *n* Br *semaine de carnaval organisée par des étudiants afin de collecter des fonds pour des œuvres charitables.*

raid [reɪd] ◇ *n* -1. MIL raid *m*. -2. [by criminals] hold-up *m* inv; [by police] descente *f*. ◇ *vt* -1. MIL faire un raid sur. -2. [subj: criminals] faire un hold-up dans; [subj: police] faire une descente dans.

raider ['reɪdəʳ] *n* -1. [attacker] agresseur *m*. -2. [thief] braqueur *m*.

rail [reɪl] ◇ *n* -1. [on ship] bastingage *m*; [on staircase] rampe *f*; [on walkway] garde-fou *m*. -2. [bar] barre *f*. -3. RAIL rail *m*; **by ~** en train. ◇ *comp* [transport, travel] par le train; [strike] des cheminots.

railcard ['reɪlkɑːd] *n* Br carte *f* de chemin de fer.

railing ['reɪlɪŋ] *n* [fence] grille *f*; [on ship] bastingage *m*; [on staircase] rampe *f*; [on walkway] garde-fou *m*.

railway *Br* ['reɪlweɪ], **railroad** *Am* ['reɪlrəʊd] *n* [system, company] chemin *m* de fer; [track] voie *f* ferrée.

railway engine *n* locomotive *f*.

railway line *n* [route] ligne *f* de chemin de fer; [track] voie *f* ferrée.

railwayman ['reɪlweɪmən] (*pl* -men [-mən]) *n* Br cheminot *m*.

railway station *n* gare *f*.

railway track *n* voie *f* ferrée.

rain [reɪn] ◇ *n* pluie *f*. ◇ *v impers* METEOR pleuvoir; **it's ~ing** il pleut. ◇ *vi* [fall like rain] pleuvoir.
◆ **rain down** *vi* pleuvoir.
◆ **rain off** *Br*, **rain out** *Am* *vt sep* annuler à cause de la pluie.

rainbow ['reɪnbəʊ] *n* arc-en-ciel *m*.

rain check *n* Am: **I'll take a ~ (on that)** une autre fois peut-être.

raincoat ['reɪnkəʊt] *n* imperméable *m*.

raindrop ['reɪndrɒp] *n* goutte *f* de pluie.

rainfall ['reɪnfɔːl] *n* [shower] chute *f* de pluie; [amount] précipitations *fpl*.

rain forest forêt *f* tropicale humide.

rain gauge n pluviomètre m.

rainproof ['reɪnpruːf] adj imperméable.

rainstorm ['reɪnstɔːm] n trombe f d'eau, pluie f torrentielle.

rainwater ['reɪn,wɔːtər] n eau f de pluie.

rainy ['reɪnɪ] (compar **-ier**, superl **-iest**) adj pluvieux(ieuse).

raise [reɪz] ◇ vt **-1.** [lift up] lever; **to ~ o.s.** se lever. **-2.** [increase - gen] augmenter; [- standards] élever; **to ~ one's voice** élever la voix. **-3.** [obtain]: **to ~ money** [from donations] collecter des fonds; [by selling, borrowing] se procurer de l'argent. **-4.** [subject, doubt] soulever; [memories] évoquer. **-5.** [children, cattle] élever. **-6.** [crops] cultiver. **-7.** [build] ériger, élever.
◇ n Am augmentation f (de salaire).

raisin ['reɪzn] n raisin m sec.

Raj [rɑːdʒ] n: **the ~** l'empire britannique aux Indes.

rajah ['rɑːdʒə] n raja m, rajah m.

rake [reɪk] ◇ n **-1.** [implement] râteau m. **-2.** dated & literary [immoral man] débauché m.
◇ vt [path, lawn] ratisser; [leaves] râteler.
◆ **rake in** vt sep inf amasser.
◆ **rake up** vt sep [past] fouiller dans.

rake-off n inf pourcentage m, commission f.

rakish ['reɪkɪʃ] adj **-1.** [dissolute] dissolu(e). **-2.** [jaunty] désinvolte.

rally ['rælɪ] (pl **-ies**, pt & pp **-ied**) ◇ n **-1.** [meeting] rassemblement m. **-2.** [car race] rallye m. **-3.** SPORT [exchange of shots] échange m. ◇ vt rallier. ◇ vi **-1.** [supporters] se rallier. **-2.** [patient] aller mieux; [prices] remonter.
◆ **rally round** ◇ vt fus apporter son soutien à. ◇ vi inf venir en aide.

rallying ['rælɪɪŋ] n (U) rallye m.

rallying cry n cri m de ralliement.

rallying point n point m de rassemblement.

ram [ræm] (pt & pp **-med**, cont **-ming**) ◇ n bélier m. ◇ vt **-1.** [crash into] percuter contre, emboutir. **-2.** [force] tasser. **-3.** phr: **to ~ sthg home** beaucoup insister sur qqch.

RAM [ræm] (abbr of **random access memory**) n RAM f.

Ramadan [,ræmə'dæn] n ramadan m.

ramble ['ræmbl] ◇ n randonnée f, promenade f à pied. ◇ vi **-1.** [walk] faire une promenade à pied. **-2.** pej [talk] radoter.
◆ **ramble on** vi pej radoter.

rambler ['ræmblər] n [walker] randonneur m, -euse f.

rambling ['ræmblɪŋ] adj **-1.** [house] plein(e) de coins et recoins. **-2.** [speech] décousu(e).

RAMC (abbr of **Royal Army Medical Corps**) n service de santé des armées britanniques.

ramekin ['ræmɪkɪn] n ramequin m.

ramification [,ræmɪfɪ'keɪʃn] n ramification f.

ramp [ræmp] n **-1.** [slope] rampe f. **-2.** AUT [to slow traffic down] ralentisseur m; "~" «dénivellation».

rampage [ræm'peɪdʒ] ◇ n: **to go on the ~** tout saccager. ◇ vi se déchaîner.

rampant ['ræmpənt] adj qui sévit.

ramparts ['ræmpɑːts] npl rempart m.

ramshackle ['ræm,ʃækl] adj branlant(e).

ran [ræn] pt → **run**.

RAN (abbr of **Royal Australian Navy**) n marine de guerre australienne.

ranch [rɑːntʃ] n ranch m.

rancher ['rɑːntʃər] n propriétaire mf de ranch.

ranch house n Am ranch m.

rancid ['rænsɪd] adj rance.

rancour Br, **rancor** Am ['ræŋkər] n rancœur f.

random ['rændəm] ◇ adj fait(e) au hasard; [number] aléatoire. ◇ n: **at ~** au hasard.

random access memory n COMPUT mémoire f vive.

randomly ['rændəmlɪ] adv au hasard.

R and R (abbr of **rest and recreation**) n Am permission f.

randy ['rændɪ] (compar **-ier**, superl **-iest**) adj inf excité(e).

rang [ræŋ] pt → **ring**.

range [reɪndʒ] (cont **rangeing**) ◇ n **-1.** [of plane, telescope etc] portée f; **at close ~** à bout portant; **to be out of ~** être hors de portée; **to be within ~ of** être à portée de. **-2.** [of subjects, goods] gamme f; **price ~** éventail m des prix. **-3.** [of mountains] chaîne f. **-4.** [shooting area] champ m de tir. **-5.** MUS [of voice] tessiture f.
◇ vt [place in row] mettre en rang.
◇ vi **-1.** [vary]: **to ~ between ... and ...** varier entre ... et ...; **to ~ from ... to ...** varier de ... à .... **-2.** [include]: **to ~ over sthg** couvrir qqch.

ranger ['reɪndʒər] n garde m forestier.

Rangoon [ræŋ'guːn] n Rangoon.

rangy ['reɪndʒɪ] (compar **-ier**, superl **-iest**) adj élancé(e).

rank [ræŋk] ◇ adj **-1.** [absolute - disgrace, stupidity] complet(ète); [- injustice] fla-

grant(e); **he's a ~ outsider** il n'a aucune chance. **-2.** [smell] fétide.
◇ *n* **-1.** [in army, police etc] grade *m*; **to pull ~** user de sa supériorité hiérarchique (pour faire faire qqch à qqn). **-2.** [social class] rang *m*. **-3.** [row] rangée *f*; **taxi ~** station *f* de taxis; **to close ~s** serrer les rangs. **-4. the ~ and file** la masse; [of union] la base.
◇ *vt* **-1.** [classify] classer. **-2.** *Am* [outrank] avoir un grade supérieur à.
◇ *vi*: **to ~ among** compter parmi; **to ~ as** être aux rangs de.
◆ **ranks** *npl* **-1.** MIL: **the ~s** le rang. **-2.** *fig* [members] rangs *mpl*.

ranking ['ræŋkɪŋ] ◇ *n* [rating] classement *m*. ◇ *adj Am* [high-ranking] du plus haut rang.

rankle ['ræŋkl] *vi*: **it ~d with him** ça lui est resté sur l'estomac OR le cœur.

ransack ['rænsæk] *vt* [search through] mettre tout sens dessus dessous dans; [damage] saccager.

ransom ['rænsəm] *n* rançon *f*; **to hold sb to ~** [keep prisoner] mettre qqn à rançon; *fig* exercer un chantage sur qqn.

rant [rænt] *vi* déblatérer.

ranting ['ræntɪŋ] *n* (*U*) invectives *fpl*.

rap [ræp] (*pt & pp* **-ped,** *cont* **-ping**) ◇ *n* **-1.** [knock] coup *m* sec. **-2.** MUS rap *m*. **-3.** *phr*: **to take the ~** *inf* trinquer, payer les pots cassés. ◇ *vt* [table] frapper sur; [knuckles] taper sur. ◇ *vi* **-1.** [knock]: **to ~ on** [door] frapper à; [table] frapper sur. **-2.** MUS rapper.

rapacious [rə'peɪʃəs] *adj* rapace.

rapacity [rə'pæsɪtɪ] *n* rapacité *f*.

rape [reɪp] ◇ *n* **-1.** [crime, attack] viol *m*. **-2.** *fig* [of countryside etc] destruction *f*. **-3.** [plant] colza *m*. ◇ *vt* violer.

rapeseed ['reɪpsiːd] *n* graine *f* de colza.

rapid ['ræpɪd] *adj* rapide.
◆ **rapids** *npl* rapides *mpl*.

rapid-fire *adj* [gun] à tir rapide; **~ questions** un feu roulant de questions.

rapidity [rə'pɪdətɪ] *n* rapidité *f*.

rapidly ['ræpɪdlɪ] *adv* rapidement.

rapidness ['ræpɪdnɪs] = **rapidity**.

rapist ['reɪpɪst] *n* violeur *m*.

rapper ['ræpər] *n* rappeur *m*, -euse *f*.

rapport [ræ'pɔːr] *n* rapport *m*.

rapprochement [ræ'prɒʃmã] *n* rapprochement *m*.

rapt [ræpt] *adj* [interest, attention] profond(e); **to be ~ in thought** être plongé dans ses pensées.

rapture ['ræptʃər] *n* ravissement *m*; **to go into ~s over** OR **about** s'extasier sur.

rapturous ['ræptʃərəs] *adj* [applause, welcome] enthousiaste.

rare [reər] *adj* **-1.** [gen] rare. **-2.** [meat] saignant(e).

rarefied ['reərɪfaɪd] *adj* **-1.** [air] raréfié(e). **-2.** *fig* [place, atmosphere] raffiné(e).

rarely ['reəlɪ] *adv* rarement.

rareness ['reənɪs] *n* rareté *f*.

raring ['reərɪŋ] *adj*: **to be ~ to go** être impatient(e) de commencer.

rarity ['reərətɪ] (*pl* **-ies**) *n* rareté *f*.

rascal ['rɑːskl] *n* polisson *m*, -onne *f*.

rash [ræʃ] ◇ *adj* irréfléchi(e), imprudent(e). ◇ *n* **-1.** MED éruption *f*. **-2.** [spate] succession *f*, série *f*.

rasher ['ræʃər] *n* tranche *f*.

rashly ['ræʃlɪ] *adv* sans réfléchir.

rashness ['ræʃnɪs] *n* imprudence *f*.

rasp [rɑːsp] ◇ *n* [harsh sound] grincement *m*. ◇ *vi* dire d'une voix âpre.

raspberry ['rɑːzbərɪ] (*pl* **-ies**) *n* **-1.** [fruit] framboise *f*. **-2.** [rude sound]: **to blow a ~** faire pfft.

rasping ['rɑːspɪŋ] *adj* [voice] âpre; [sound] grinçant(e).

rasta ['ræstə] *n inf* rasta *mf inv*.

rastafarian [ˌræstə'feərɪən] *n* rastafari *mf inv*.

rat [ræt] *n* **-1.** [animal] rat *m*; **to smell a ~** soupçonner anguille sous roche. **-2.** *inf pej* [person] ordure *f*, salaud *m*.

ratbag ['rætbæg] *n Br inf pej* salope *f*.

ratchet ['rætʃɪt] *n* rochet *m*.

rate [reɪt] ◇ *n* **-1.** [speed] vitesse *f*; [of pulse] fréquence *f*; **~ of flow** débit *m*; **at this ~** à ce train-là. **-2.** [ratio, proportion] taux *m*. **-3.** [price] tarif *m*. ◇ *vt* **-1.** [consider]: **I ~ her very highly** je la tiens en haute estime; **to ~ sb/sthg as** considérer qqn/qqch comme; **to ~ sb/sthg among** classer qqn/qqch parmi. **-2.** [deserve] mériter.
◆ **rates** *npl Br* impôts *mpl* locaux.
◆ **at any rate** *adv* en tout cas.

rateable value ['reɪtəbl-] *n Br* valeur *f* locative imposable.

rate of exchange *n* taux *m* OR cours *m* du change.

ratepayer ['reɪt,peɪər] *n Br* contribuable *mf*.

rather ['rɑːðər] *adv* **-1.** [somewhat, more exactly] plutôt. **-2.** [to small extent] un peu. **-3.** [preferably]: **I'd ~ wait** je préférerais attendre; **she'd ~ not go** elle préférerait ne pas y aller. **-4.** [on the contrary]: **(but)** ~ ... au contraire ....

◆ **rather than** *conj* plutôt que.

ratification [,rætɪfɪ'keɪʃn] *n* ratification *f*.

ratify ['rætɪfaɪ] (*pt & pp* **-ied**) *vt* ratifier, approuver.

rating ['reɪtɪŋ] *n* **-1.** [of popularity etc] cote *f*. **-2.** *Br* [sailor] matelot *m*.

◆ **ratings** *npl* RADIO & TV indice *m* d'écoute.

ratio ['reɪʃɪəʊ] (*pl* **-s**) *n* rapport *m*.

ration ['ræʃn] ◇ *n* ration *f*. ◇ *vt* rationner.

◆ **rations** *npl* vivres *mpl*.

rational ['ræʃənl] *adj* rationnel(elle).

rationale [,ræʃə'nɑːl] *n* logique *f*.

rationalization [,ræʃənəlaɪ'zeɪʃn] *n* rationalisation *f*.

rationalize, -ise ['ræʃənəlaɪz] *vt* rationaliser.

rationing ['ræʃənɪŋ] *n* rationnement *m*.

rat race *n* jungle *f*.

rattle ['rætl] ◇ *n* **-1.** [of bottles, typewriter keys] cliquetis *m*; [of engine] bruit *m* de ferraille. **-2.** [toy] hochet *m*. ◇ *vt* **-1.** [bottles] faire s'entrechoquer; [keys] faire cliqueter. **-2.** [unsettle] secouer. ◇ *vi* [bottles] s'entrechoquer; [keys, machine] cliqueter; [engine] faire un bruit de ferraille.

◆ **rattle off** *vt sep* réciter à toute vitesse.

◆ **rattle on** *vi*: to ~ on (about sthg) parler sans arrêt (de qqch).

◆ **rattle through** *vt fus* [work] expédier; [speech, list] lire à toute allure.

rattlesnake ['rætlsneɪk], **rattler** *Am* ['rætlə'] *n* serpent *m* à sonnettes.

ratty ['rætɪ] (*compar* **-ier**, *superl* **-iest**) *adj inf* **-1.** *Br* [in bad mood] de mauvais poil. **-2.** *Am* [in bad condition] pourri(e).

raucous ['rɔːkəs] *adj* [voice, laughter] rauque; [behaviour] bruyant(e).

raunchy ['rɔːntʃɪ] (*compar* **-ier**, *superl* **-iest**) *adj* d'une sensualité brute.

ravage ['rævɪdʒ] *vt* ravager.

◆ **ravages** *npl* ravages *mpl*.

rave [reɪv] ◇ *adj* [review] élogieux(ieuse). ◇ *n Br inf* [party] rave *f*. ◇ *vi* **-1.** [talk angrily]: to ~ at OR against tempêter OR fulminer contre. **-2.** [talk enthusiastically]: to ~ about parler avec enthousiasme de.

raven ['reɪvn] ◇ *adj* [hair] de jais. ◇ *n* corbeau *m*.

ravenous ['rævənəs] *adj* [person] affamé(e); [animal, appetite] vorace.

raver ['reɪvə'] *n Br inf*: she's a ~ elle aime faire la fête.

rave-up *n Br inf* fête *f*.

ravine [rə'viːn] *n* ravin *m*.

raving ['reɪvɪŋ] *adj*: ~ **lunatic** fou furieux (folle furieuse).

◆ **ravings** *npl* délire *m*.

ravioli [,rævɪ'əʊlɪ] *n* (U) ravioli *mpl*.

ravish ['rævɪʃ] *vt* [delight] ravir, enchanter.

ravishing ['rævɪʃɪŋ] *adj* ravissant(e), enchanteur(eresse).

raw [rɔː] *adj* **-1.** [uncooked] cru(e). **-2.** [untreated] brut(e). **-3.** [painful] à vif. **-4.** [inexperienced] novice; ~ **recruit** bleu *m*. **-5.** [weather] froid(e); [wind] âpre.

raw deal *n*: to get a ~ être défavorisé(e).

raw material *n* matière *f* première.

ray [reɪ] *n* [beam] rayon *m*; *fig* [of hope] lueur *f*.

rayon ['reɪɒn] *n* rayonne *f*.

raze [reɪz] *vt* raser.

razor ['reɪzə'] *n* rasoir *m*.

razor blade *n* lame *f* de rasoir.

razor-sharp *adj* coupant(e) comme un rasoir; *fig* [person, mind] vif (vive).

razzle ['ræzl] *n Br inf*: to go on the ~ faire les quatre cents coups.

razzmatazz ['ræzəmətæz] *n inf* tape-à-l'œil *m inv*.

R & B (*abbr of* **rhythm and blues**) *n* R & B *m*.

RC *abbr of* **Roman Catholic**.

RCA (*abbr of* **Royal College of Art**) *n* école de beaux-arts à Londres.

RCAF (*abbr of* **Royal Canadian Air Force**) *n* armée de l'air canadienne.

RCMP (*abbr of* **Royal Canadian Mounted Police**) *n* police montée canadienne.

RCN *n* **-1.** (*abbr of* **Royal College of Nursing**) syndicat britannique des infirmières et des infirmiers. **-2.** (*abbr of* **Royal Canadian Navy**) marine de guerre canadienne.

Rd *abbr of* **Road**.

R & D (*abbr of* **research and development**) *n* R-D *f*.

RDC (*abbr of* **rural district council**) *n* municipalité en zone rurale en Grande-Bretagne.

re [riː] *prep* concernant.

RE *n* **-1.** (*abbr of* **religious education**) instruction *f* religieuse. **-2.** (*abbr of* **Royal Engineers**) le génie militaire britannique.

reach [riːtʃ] ◇ *vt* **-1.** [gen] atteindre; [place, destination] arriver à; [agreement, decision] parvenir à. **-2.** [contact] joindre, contacter. ◇ *vi* [land] s'étendre; to ~ out tendre le bras; to ~ down to pick sthg up se pencher pour ramasser qqch. ◇ *n* [of arm, boxer] allonge *f*; **within** ~ [object] à portée; [place] à proximité; **out of** OR **beyond sb's** ~ [object]

hors de portée; [place] d'accès difficile, difficilement accessible.

◆ **reaches** *npl* étendue *f*.

reachable ['ri:tʃəbl] *adj* -1. [place] accessible; [object] à portée. -2. [contactable] joignable.

react [rɪ'ækt] *vi* -1. [gen] réagir. -2. MED: **to ~ to sthg** avoir une réaction à qqch.

reaction [rɪ'ækʃn] *n* réaction *f*.

reactionary [rɪ'ækʃənrɪ] ◇ *adj* réactionnaire. ◇ *n* réactionnaire *mf*.

reactivate [rɪ'æktɪveɪt] *vt* réactiver.

reactor [rɪ'æktər] *n* réacteur *m*.

read [ri:d] (*pt & pp* read [red]) ◇ *vt* -1. [gen] lire. -2. [subj: sign, letter] dire. -3. [interpret, judge] interpréter. -4. [subj: meter, thermometer etc] indiquer. -5. *Br* UNIV étudier. ◇ *vi* lire; **the book ~s well** le livre se lit bien. ◇ *n*: **to be a good ~** être un bon livre, être d'une lecture agréable.

◆ **read into** *vt sep*: **to ~ a lot into sthg** attacher beaucoup d'importance à qqch.

◆ **read out** *vt sep* lire à haute voix.

◆ **read up on** *vt fus* étudier.

readable ['ri:dəbl] *adj* agréable à lire.

readdress [ˌri:ə'dres] *vt* faire suivre.

reader ['ri:dər] *n* [of book, newspaper] lecteur *m*, -trice *f*.

readership ['ri:dəʃɪp] *n* [of newspaper] nombre *m* de lecteurs.

readily ['redɪlɪ] *adv* -1. [willingly] volontiers. -2. [easily] facilement.

readiness ['redɪnɪs] *n* -1. [preparation]: **to be in ~** être prêt(e). -2. [willingness] empressement *m*.

reading ['ri:dɪŋ] *n* -1. (*U*) [gen] lecture *f*. -2. [interpretation] interprétation *f*. -3. [on thermometer, meter etc] indications *fpl*.

reading lamp *n* lampe *f* de lecture OR de bureau.

reading room *n* salle *f* de lecture.

readjust [ˌri:ə'dʒʌst] ◇ *vt* [instrument] régler (de nouveau); [mirror] rajuster; [policy] rectifier. ◇ *vi* [person]: **to ~ (to)** se réadapter (à).

readmit [ˌri:əd'mɪt] *vt* réadmettre.

readout ['ri:daʊt] *n* COMPUT affichage *m*.

read-through [ri:d-] *n*: **to have a ~ of sthg** parcourir qqch.

ready ['redɪ] (*pt & pp* -ied) ◇ *adj* -1. [prepared] prêt(e); **to be ~ to do sthg** être prêt à faire qqch; **to get ~** se préparer; **to get sthg ~** préparer qqch. -2. [willing]: **to be ~ to do sthg** être prêt(e) OR disposé(e) à faire qqch. ◇ *vt* préparer.

ready cash *n* liquide *m*.

ready-made *adj lit & fig* tout fait (toute faite).

ready money *n* liquide *m*.

ready-to-wear *adj* prêt-à-porter.

reaffirm [ˌri:ə'fɜ:m] *vt* réaffirmer.

reafforest [ˌri:ə'fɒrɪst] *vt* reboiser.

reafforestation ['ri:əˌfɒrɪ'steɪʃn] *n* reboisement *m*.

real ['rɪəl] ◇ *adj* -1. [gen] vrai(e), véritable; **~ life** réalité *f*; **for ~** pour de vrai; **this is the ~ thing** [object] c'est de l'authentique; [situation] c'est pour de vrai OR de bon. -2. [actual] réel(elle); **in ~ terms** dans la pratique. ◇ *adv Am* très.

real ale *n Br* ale *f* véritable.

real estate *n* (*U*) biens *mpl* immobiliers.

realign [ˌri:ə'laɪn] *vt* POL regrouper.

realignment [ˌri:ə'laɪnmənt] *n* POL regroupement *m*.

realism ['rɪəlɪzm] *n* réalisme *m*.

realist ['rɪəlɪst] *n* réaliste *mf*.

realistic [ˌrɪə'lɪstɪk] *adj* réaliste.

realistically [ˌrɪə'lɪstɪklɪ] *adv* d'une manière réaliste, avec réalisme.

reality [rɪ'ælətɪ] (*pl* -ies) *n* réalité *f*; **in ~** en réalité.

realization [ˌrɪəlaɪ'zeɪʃn] *n* réalisation *f*.

realize, -ise ['rɪəlaɪz] *vt* -1. [understand] se rendre compte de, réaliser. -2. [sum of money, idea, ambition] réaliser.

reallocate [ˌri:'æləkeɪt] *vt* réattribuer.

really ['rɪəlɪ] ◇ *adv* -1. [gen] vraiment. -2. [in fact] en réalité. ◇ *excl* -1. [expressing doubt] vraiment? -2. [expressing surprise] pas possible! -3. [expressing disapproval] franchement!, ça alors!

realm [relm] *n* -1. *fig* [subject area] domaine *m*. -2. [kingdom] royaume *m*.

real-time *adj* COMPUT en temps réel.

realtor ['rɪəltər] *n Am* agent *m* immobilier.

ream [ri:m] *n* [of papers] rame *f*.

◆ **reams** *npl* des pages et des pages.

reap ['ri:p] *vt* -1. [harvest] moissonner. -2. *fig* [obtain] récolter.

reappear [ˌri:ə'pɪər] *vi* réapparaître, reparaître.

reappearance [ˌri:ə'pɪərəns] *n* réapparition *f*.

reapply [ˌri:ə'plaɪ] (*pt & pp* -ied) *vi*: **to ~ (for a job)** postuler de nouveau (un emploi).

reappraisal [ˌri:ə'preɪzl] *n* réévaluation *f*.

reappraise [ˌri:ə'preɪz] *vt* réévaluer.

rear [rɪər] ◇ *adj* arrière (*inv*), de derrière. ◇ *n* -1. [back] arrière *m*; **to bring up the ~** fermer la marche. **-2.** *inf* [bottom] derrière *m*. ◇ *vt* [children, animals] élever. ◇ *vi* [horse]: to ~ **(up)** se cabrer.

rear admiral *n* vice-amiral *m*.

rearguard action ['rɪəgɑːd-] *n* combat *m* d'arrière-garde.

rear light *n* feu *m* arrière.

rearm [riːˈɑːm] *vt & vi* réarmer.

rearmament [rɪˈɑːməmənt] *n* réarmement *m*.

rearmost ['rɪəməʊst] *adj* dernier(ière).

rearrange [ˌriːəˈreɪndʒ] *vt* **-1.** [furniture, room] réarranger; [plans] changer. **-2.** [meeting - to new time] changer l'heure de; [- to new date] changer la date de.

rearrangement [ˌriːəˈreɪndʒmənt] *n* **-1.** [of furniture etc] réarrangement *m*. **-2.** [of meeting - to new time] changement *m* de l'heure; [- to new date] changement de la date.

rearview mirror ['rɪəvjuː-] *n* rétroviseur *m*.

reason ['riːzn] ◇ *n* **-1.** [cause]: ~ **(for)** raison *f* (de); **by** ~ **of** *fml* en raison de; **for some** ~ pour une raison ou pour une autre. **-2.** (*U*) [justification]: **to have** ~ **to do sthg** avoir de bonnes raisons de faire qqch; **I have** ~ **to believe (that)** ... j'ai lieu de croire que .... **-3.** [common sense] **bon sens** *m*; **he won't listen to** ~ on ne peut pas lui faire entendre raison; **it stands to** ~ c'est logique. ◇ *vt* déduire. ◇ *vi* raisonner.
♦ **reason with** *vt fus* raisonner (avec).

reasonable ['riːznəbl] *adj* raisonnable.

reasonably ['riːznəblɪ] *adv* **-1.** [quite] assez. **-2.** [sensibly] raisonnablement.

reasoned ['riːznd] *adj* raisonné(e).

reasoning ['riːznɪŋ] *n* raisonnement *m*.

reassemble [ˌriːəˈsembl] ◇ *vt* **-1.** [reconstruct] remonter. **-2.** [regroup] rassembler. ◇ *vi* se rassembler.

reassess [ˌriːəˈses] *vt* réexaminer.

reassessment [ˌriːəˈsesmənt] *n* réexamen *m*.

reassurance [ˌriːəˈʃɔːrəns] *n* **-1.** [comfort] réconfort *m*. **-2.** [promise] assurance *f*.

reassure [ˌriːəˈʃɔːr] *vt* rassurer.

reassuring [ˌriːəˈʃɔːrɪŋ] *adj* rassurant(e).

reawaken [ˌriːəˈweɪkn] *vt* [interest] faire renaître.

rebate ['riːbeɪt] *n* [on product] rabais *m*; **tax** ~ ≃ dégrèvement *m* fiscal.

rebel [*n* 'rebl, *vb* rɪˈbel] (*pt & pp* -**led**, *cont* -**ling**) ◇ *n* rebelle *mf*. ◇ *vi*: **to** ~ **(against)** se rebeller (contre).

rebellion [rɪˈbeljən] *n* rébellion *f*.

rebellious [rɪˈbeljəs] *adj* rebelle.

rebirth [ˌriːˈbɜːθ] *n* renaissance *f*.

rebound [*n* 'riːbaʊnd, *vb* rɪˈbaʊnd] ◇ *n* [of ball] rebond *m*; **to be on the** ~ [person] être sous le coup d'une déception sentimentale. ◇ *vi* **-1.** [ball] rebondir. **-2.** *fig* [action, joke]: **to** ~ **on** OR **upon sb** se retourner contre qqn.

rebuff [rɪˈbʌf] ◇ *n* rebuffade *f*. ◇ *vt* repousser.

rebuild [ˌriːˈbɪld] *vt* reconstruire.

rebuke [rɪˈbjuːk] ◇ *n* réprimande *f*. ◇ *vt* réprimander.

rebut [riːˈbʌt] (*pt & pp* -**ted**, *cont* -**ting**) *vt* réfuter.

rebuttal [riːˈbʌtl] *n* réfutation *f*.

rec. *abbr of* **received**.

recalcitrant [rɪˈkælsɪtrənt] *adj* récalcitrant(e).

recall [rɪˈkɔːl] ◇ *n* **-1.** [memory] rappel *m*. **-2.** [change]: **beyond** ~ irrévocable. ◇ *vt* **-1.** [remember] se rappeler, se souvenir de. **-2.** [summon back] rappeler; **to** ~ **Parliament** convoquer le Parlement.

recant [rɪˈkænt] ◇ *vt* [statement] rétracter; RELIG abjurer. ◇ *vi* se rétracter; RELIG abjurer.

recap ['riːkæp] (*pt & pp* -**ped**, *cont* -**ping**) ◇ *n* récapitulation *f*. ◇ *vt* **-1.** [summarize] récapituler. **-2.** *Am* [tyre] rechaper. ◇ *vi* récapituler.

recapitulate [ˌriːkəˈpɪtjʊleɪt] *vt & vi* récapituler.

recapture [ˌriːˈkæptʃər] ◇ *n* reprise *f*. ◇ *vt* **-1.** [feeling] retrouver. **-2.** [territory, prisoner] reprendre.

recd, rec'd *abbr of* **received**.

recede [riːˈsiːd] *vi* **-1.** [person, car etc] s'éloigner; [hopes] s'envoler. **-2.** [hair]: **his hair is receding** son front se dégarnit.

receding [rɪˈsiːdɪŋ] *adj* [hairline] dégarni(e); [chin, forehead] fuyant(e).

receipt [rɪˈsiːt] *n* **-1.** [piece of paper] reçu *m*. **-2.** (*U*) [act of receiving] réception *f*.
♦ **receipts** *npl* recettes *fpl*.

receivable [rɪˈsiːvəbl] *adj* **-1.** [able to be received] recevable. **-2.** FIN à recevoir.

receive [rɪˈsiːv] ◇ *vt* **-1.** [gen] recevoir; [news] apprendre. **-2.** [welcome] accueillir, recevoir; **to be well/badly ~d** [film, speech etc] être bien/mal accueilli. ◇ *vi* [in tennis etc] recevoir le service.

receiver [rɪˈsiːvər] *n* **-1.** [of telephone] récepteur *m*, combiné *m*. **-2.** [radio, TV set] récepteur *m*. **-3.** [criminal] receleur *m*, -euse *f*. **-4.** FIN [official] administrateur *m*, -trice *f* judiciaire.

receivership [rɪ'siːvəʃɪp] *n*: **to go into ~** être mis(e) en liquidation.

receiving end [rɪ'siːvɪŋ-] *n*: **to be on the ~ (of sthg)** faire les frais (de qqch).

recent ['riːsnt] *adj* récent(e).

recently ['riːsntlɪ] *adv* récemment; **until ~** jusqu'à ces derniers temps.

receptacle [rɪ'septəkl] *n* récipient *m*.

reception [rɪ'sepʃn] *n* **-1.** [gen] réception *f.* **-2.** [welcome] accueil *m*, réception *f*.

reception centre *n* centre *m* d'accueil.

reception class *n Br* cours *m* préparatoire.

reception desk *n* réception *f*.

receptionist [rɪ'sepʃənɪst] *n* réceptionniste *mf*.

reception room *n* salon *m*.

receptive [rɪ'septɪv] *adj* réceptif(ive).

receptiveness [rɪ'septɪvnɪs] *n* réceptivité *f*.

recess ['riːses, *Br* rɪ'ses] *n* **-1.** [alcove] niche *f.* **-2.** [secret place] recoin *m.* **-3.** POL: **to be in ~** être en vacances. **-4.** *Am* SCH récréation *f*.

recessed ['riːsest, *Br* rɪ'sest] *adj* [window] dans un renfoncement; [door handle, light] encastré(e).

recession [rɪ'seʃn] *n* récession *f*.

recessionary [rɪ'seʃənrɪ] *adj* de récession.

recessive [rɪ'sesɪv] *adj* BIOL récessif(ive).

recharge [,riː'tʃɑːdʒ] *vt* recharger.

rechargeable [,riː'tʃɑːdʒəbl] *adj* rechargeable.

recipe ['resɪpɪ] *n lit & fig* recette *f*.

recipient [rɪ'sɪpɪənt] *n* [of letter] destinataire *mf*; [of cheque] bénéficiaire *mf*; [of award] récipiendaire *mf*.

reciprocal [rɪ'sɪprəkl] *adj* réciproque.

reciprocate [rɪ'sɪprəkeɪt] ◇ *vt* rendre, retourner. ◇ *vi* en faire autant.

recital [rɪ'saɪtl] *n* récital *m*.

recitation [,resɪ'teɪʃn] *n* récitation *f*.

recite [rɪ'saɪt] *vt* **-1.** [say aloud] réciter. **-2.** [list] énumérer.

reckless ['reklɪs] *adj* imprudent(e).

recklessness ['reklɪsnɪs] *n* imprudence *f*.

reckon ['rekn] *vt* **-1.** *inf* [think] penser. **-2.** [consider, judge] considérer. **-3.** [expect]: **to ~ to do sthg** compter faire qqch. **-4.** [calculate] calculer.

◆ **reckon on** *vt fus* compter sur.

◆ **reckon with** *vt fus* [expect] s'attendre à; **he's a person to be ~ed with** il faut compter avec lui.

◆ **reckon without** *vt fus* compter sans.

reckoning ['rekənɪŋ] *n* [calculation] (*U*) calculs *mpl*; **day of ~** jour *m* de vérité.

reclaim [rɪ'kleɪm] *vt* **-1.** [claim back] réclamer. **-2.** [land] assécher.

reclamation [,reklə'meɪʃn] *n* [of land] assèchement *m*.

recline [rɪ'klaɪn] *vi* [person] être allongé(e).

reclining [rɪ'klaɪnɪŋ] *adj* [chair] à dossier réglable.

recluse [rɪ'kluːs] *n* reclus *m*, -e *f*.

reclusive [rɪ'kluːsɪv] *adj* reclus(e).

recognition [,rekəg'nɪʃn] *n* reconnaissance *f*; **in ~ of** en reconnaissance de; **the town has changed beyond** OR **out of all ~** la ville est méconnaissable.

recognizable ['rekəgnaɪzəbl] *adj* reconnaissable.

recognize, -ise ['rekəgnaɪz] *vt* reconnaître.

recoil [*vb* rɪ'kɔɪl, *n* 'riːkɔɪl] ◇ *vi*: **to ~ (from)** reculer (devant). ◇ *n* [of gun] recul *m*.

recollect [,rekə'lekt] *vt* se rappeler.

recollection [,rekə'lekʃn] *n* souvenir *m*.

recommence [,riːkə'mens] *vt & vi* recommencer.

recommend [,rekə'mend] *vt* **-1.** [commend]: **to ~ sb/sthg (to sb)** recommander qqn/qqch (à qqn). **-2.** [advise] conseiller, recommander.

recommendation [,rekəmen'deɪʃn] *n* recommandation *f*.

recommended retail price [,rekə'mendɪd-] *n* prix *m* de vente conseillé.

recompense ['rekəmpens] ◇ *n* dédommagement *m*. ◇ *vt* dédommager.

reconcile ['rekənsaɪl] *vt* **-1.** [beliefs, ideas] concilier. **-2.** [people] réconcilier; **to be ~d with sb** se réconcilier avec qqn. **-3.** [accept]: **to ~ o.s. to sthg** se faire à l'idée de qqch.

reconciliation [,rekənsɪlɪ'eɪʃn] *n* **-1.** [of beliefs, ideas] conciliation *f.* **-2.** [of people] réconciliation *f*.

recondite ['rekəndaɪt] *adj fml* obscur(e).

reconditioned [,riːkən'dɪʃnd] *adj* remis(e) en état.

reconnaissance [rɪ'kɒnɪsəns] *n* reconnaissance *f*.

reconnect [,riːkə'nekt] *vt* rebrancher.

reconnoitre *Br*, **reconnoiter** *Am* [,rekə'nɔɪtər] ◇ *vt* reconnaître. ◇ *vi* aller en reconnaissance.

reconsider [,riːkən'sɪdər] ◇ *vt* reconsidérer. ◇ *vi* reconsidérer la question.

reconstitute [,riː'kɒnstɪtjuːt] *vt* reconstituer.

reconstruct [,riːkən'strʌkt] *vt* **-1.** [gen] reconstruire. **-2.** [crime, event] reconstituer.

reconstruction [,riːkən'strʌkʃn] *n* **-1.** [gen]

reconstruction *f.* **-2.** [of crime, event] reconstitution *f.*

reconvene [ˌriːkən'viːn] *vt* convoquer de nouveau.

record [*n & adj* 'rekɔːd, *vb* rɪ'kɔːd] ◇ *n* **-1.** [written account] rapport *m*; [file] dossier *m*; **to keep sthg on ~** archiver qqch; **to go on ~ as saying (that)** ... déclarer publiquement que ...; **(police) ~** casier *m* judiciaire; **off the ~** non officiel; **to set** OR **put the ~ straight** mettre les choses au clair. **-2.** [vinyl disc] disque *m*. **-3.** [best achievement] record *m.* ◇ *adj* record (*inv*). ◇ *vt* **-1.** [write down] noter. **-2.** [put on tape] enregistrer.

record-breaker *n* personne *f* qui bat le record.

record-breaking *adj* qui bat tous les records.

recorded delivery [rɪ'kɔːdɪd-] *n*: **to send sthg by ~** envoyer qqch en recommandé.

recorder [rɪ'kɔːdə'] *n* [musical instrument] flûte *f* à bec.

record holder *n* détenteur *m*, -trice *f* du record.

recording [rɪ'kɔːdɪŋ] *n* enregistrement *m.*

recording studio *n* studio *m* d'enregistrement.

record library *n* discothèque *f.*

record player *n* tourne-disque *m.*

recount [*n* 'riːkaʊnt, *vt sense 1* rɪ'kaʊnt, *sense 2* ˌriː'kaʊnt] ◇ *n* [of vote] deuxième dépouillement *m* du scrutin. ◇ *vt* **-1.** [narrate] raconter. **-2.** [count again] recompter.

recoup [rɪ'kuːp] *vt* récupérer.

recourse [rɪ'kɔːs] *n*: **to have ~ to** avoir recours à.

recover [rɪ'kʌvə'] ◇ *vt* **-1.** [retrieve] récupérer; **to ~ sthg from sb** reprendre qqch à qqn. **-2.** [one's balance] retrouver; [consciousness] reprendre; **to ~ o.s.** se ressaisir. ◇ *vi* **-1.** [from illness] se rétablir; [from shock, divorce] se remettre. **-2.** *fig* [economy] se redresser; [trade] reprendre.

recoverable [riː'kʌvrəbl] *adj* FIN récupérable.

recovery [rɪ'kʌvərɪ] (*pl* -ies) *n* **-1.** [from illness] guérison *f*, rétablissement *m*. **-2.** *fig* [of economy] redressement *m*, reprise *f*. **-3.** [retrieval] récupération *f.*

recovery vehicle *n* Br dépanneuse *f.*

recreate [ˌriːkrɪ'eɪt] *vt* recréer.

recreation [ˌrekrɪ'eɪʃn] *n* (*U*) [leisure] récréation *f*, loisirs *mpl.*

recreational [ˌrekrɪ'eɪʃənl] *adj* de récréation.

recreation room *n* salle *f* de récréation; *Am* [in house] salle de jeu.

recrimination [rɪˌkrɪmɪ'neɪʃn] *n* récrimination *f.*

recrudescence [ˌriːkruː'desns] *n* recrudescence *f.*

recruit [rɪ'kruːt] ◇ *n* recrue *f.* ◇ *vt* recruter; **to ~ sb to do sthg** *fig* embaucher qqn pour faire qqch. ◇ *vi* recruter.

recruitment [rɪ'kruːtmənt] *n* recrutement *m.*

rectangle ['rek,tæŋgl] *n* rectangle *m.*

rectangular [rek'tæŋgjʊlə'] *adj* rectangulaire.

rectification [ˌrektɪfɪ'keɪʃn] *n* rectification *f.*

rectify ['rektɪfaɪ] (*pt & pp* -ied) *vt* [mistake] rectifier.

rectitude ['rektɪtjuːd] *n* rectitude *f.*

rector ['rektə'] *n* **-1.** [priest] pasteur *m*. **-2.** *Scot* [head - of school] directeur *m*; [- of college, university] président élu par les étudiants.

rectory ['rektərɪ] (*pl* -ies) *n* presbytère *m.*

rectum ['rektəm] *n* rectum *m.*

recuperate [rɪ'kuːpəreɪt] *vi* se rétablir.

recuperation [rɪˌkuːpə'reɪʃn] *n* rétablissement *m.*

recur [rɪ'kɜːr] (*pt & pp* -red, *cont* -ring) *vi* [error, problem] se reproduire; [dream] revenir; [pain] réapparaître.

recurrence [rɪ'kʌrəns] *n* répétition *f.*

recurrent [rɪ'kʌrənt] *adj* [error, problem] qui se reproduit souvent; [dream] qui revient souvent.

recurring [rɪ'kɜːrɪŋ] *adj* **-1.** [error, problem] qui se reproduit souvent; [dream] qui revient souvent. **-2.** MATH périodique.

recyclable [ˌriː'saɪkləbl] *adj* recyclable.

recycle [ˌriː'saɪkl] *vt* recycler.

red [red] (*compar* -der, *superl* -dest) ◇ *adj* rouge; [hair] roux (rousse). ◇ *n* rouge *m*; **to be in the ~** *inf* être à découvert; **to see ~** voir rouge.

◆ **Red** *pej* ◇ *adj* rouge. ◇ *n* rouge *mf.*

red alert *n* alerte *f* maximale; **to be on ~** être en état d'alerte maximale.

red blood cell *n* globule *m* rouge.

red-blooded [-'blʌdɪd] *adj hum* viril(e).

red-brick *adj Br* [building] en brique rouge.

◆ **redbrick** *adj Br*: **redbrick university** université *f* moderne.

red card *n* FTBL: **to be shown the ~, to get a ~** recevoir un carton rouge.

red carpet *n*: **to roll out the ~ for sb** dérouler le tapis rouge pour qqn.

◆ **red-carpet** *adj*: **to give sb the red-**

carpet treatment recevoir qqn en grande pompe.

Red Crescent *n*: the ~ le Croissant Rouge.

Red Cross *n*: the ~ la Croix-Rouge.

redcurrant ['redkʌrənt] *n* [fruit] groseille *f*; [bush] groseillier *m*.

red deer *n* cerf *m*.

redden ['redn] *vt & vi* rougir.

redecorate [,riː'dekəreɪt] ◇ *vt* repeindre et retapisser. ◇ *vi* refaire la peinture et les papiers peints.

redeem [rɪ'diːm] *vt* **-1.** [save, rescue] racheter; to ~ **o.s.** se racheter. **-2.** [from pawnbroker] dégager.

redeeming [rɪ'diːmɪŋ] *adj* qui rachète (les défauts).

redefine [,riːdɪ'faɪn] *vt* redéfinir.

redemption [rɪ'dempʃn] *n* rédemption *f*; **beyond** OR **past** ~ *fig* irrémédiable.

redeploy [,riːdɪ'plɔɪ] *vt* MIL redéployer; [staff] réorganiser, réaffecter.

redeployment [,riːdɪ'plɔɪmənt] *n* MIL redéploiement *m*; [of staff] réorganisation *f*, réaffectation *f*.

redesign [,riːdɪ'zaɪn] *vt* [room] redessiner; [system] réorganiser.

redevelop [,riːdɪ'veləp] *vt* réaménager.

redevelopment [,riːdɪ'veləpmənt] *n* réaménagement *m*.

red-faced [-'feɪst] *adj* rougeaud(e), rubicond(e); [with embarrassment] rouge de confusion.

red-haired [-'heəd] *adj* roux (rousse).

red-handed [-'hændɪd] *adj*: **to catch sb** ~ prendre qqn en flagrant délit OR la main dans le sac.

redhead ['redhed] *n* roux *m*, rousse *f*.

red herring *n* *fig* fausse piste *f*.

red-hot *adj* **-1.** [extremely hot] brûlant(e); [metal] chauffé(e) au rouge. **-2.** [very enthusiastic] ardent(e).

redid [,riː'dɪd] *pt* → redo.

Red Indian ◇ *adj* de Peau-Rouge (*attention: le terme 'Red Indian' est considéré raciste*). ◇ *n* Peau-Rouge *mf*.

redirect [,riːdɪ'rekt] *vt* **-1.** [energy, money] réorienter. **-2.** [traffic] détourner. **-3.** [letters] faire suivre.

rediscover [,riːdɪ'skʌvər] redécouvrir.

redistribute [,riːdɪ'strɪbjuːt] *vt* redistribuer.

red-letter day *n* jour *m* mémorable, jour à marquer d'une pierre blanche.

red light *n* [traffic signal] feu *m* rouge.

red-light district *n* quartier *m* chaud.

red meat *n* viande *f* rouge.

redness ['rednɪs] *n* rougeur *f*.

redo [,riː'duː] (*pt* -did, *pp* -done) *vt* refaire.

redolent ['redələnt] *adj literary* **-1.** [reminiscent]: ~ **of** qui rappelle, évocateur(trice) de. **-2.** [smelling]: ~ **of** qui sent.

redone [,riː'dʌn] *pp* → redo.

redouble [,riː'dʌbl] *vt*: **to** ~ **one's efforts (to do sthg)** redoubler d'efforts (pour faire qqch).

redoubtable [rɪ'daʊtəbl] *adj* redoutable, formidable.

redraft [,riː'drɑːft] *vt* rédiger à nouveau.

redraw [,riː'drɔː] (*pt* -drew, *pp* -drawn) *vt* dessiner à nouveau.

redress [rɪ'dres] ◇ *n* (*U*) *fml* réparation *f*. ◇ *vt*: **to** ~ **the balance** rétablir l'équilibre.

redrew [,riː'druː] *pt* → redraw.

Red Sea *n*: the ~ la mer Rouge.

Red Square *n* la place Rouge.

red squirrel *n* écureuil *m*.

red tape *n* *fig* paperasserie *f* administrative.

reduce [rɪ'djuːs] ◇ *vt* réduire; **to be ~d to doing sthg** en être réduit à faire qqch; **to** ~ **sb to tears** faire pleurer qqn. ◇ *vi* *Am* [diet] suivre un régime amaigrissant.

reduced [rɪ'djuːst] *adj* réduit(e); **in** ~ **circumstances** dans la gêne.

reduction [rɪ'dʌkʃn] *n* **-1.** [decrease]: ~ **(in)** réduction *f* (de), baisse *f* (de). **-2.** [discount] rabais *m*, réduction *f*.

redundancy [rɪ'dʌndənsɪ] (*pl* -ies) *n* *Br* [dismissal] licenciement *m*; [unemployment] chômage *m*.

redundancy payment *n* *Br* indemnité *f* de licenciement.

redundant [rɪ'dʌndənt] *adj* **-1.** *Br* [jobless]: **to be made** ~ être licencié(e). **-2.** [not required] superflu(e).

redwood ['redwʊd] *n*: ~ **(tree)** séquoia *m*.

reecho [,riː'ekəʊ] ◇ *vt* [repeat] répéter. ◇ *vi* [echo again] retentir.

reed [riːd] ◇ *n* **-1.** [plant] roseau *m*. **-2.** MUS anche *f*. ◇ *comp* [basket etc] en roseau.

reeducate [,riː'edjʊkeɪt] *vt* rééduquer.

reedy ['riːdɪ] (*compar* -ier, *superl* -iest) *adj* [voice] flûté(e), aigu(ë).

reef [riːf] *n* récif *m*, écueil *m*.

reek [riːk] ◇ *n* relent *m*. ◇ *vi*: **to** ~ **(of sthg)** puer (qqch), empester (qqch).

reel [riːl] ◇ *n* **-1.** [roll] bobine *f*. **-2.** [on fishing rod] moulinet *m*. ◇ *vi* **-1.** [stagger] chanceler. **-2.** [whirl]: **my mind was ~ing** j'avais la tête qui tournait.

◆ **reel in** *vt sep* remonter.

◆ **reel off** *vt sep* [list] débiter.

reelect [ˌriːɪˈlekt] *vt*: **to ~ sb (as) sthg** réélire qqn qqch.

reelection [ˌriːɪˈlekʃn] *n* réélection *f*.

reemphasize [ˌriːˈemfəsaɪz] *vt* souligner de nouveau.

reenact [ˌriːɪˈnækt] *vt* [play] reproduire; [event] reconstituer.

reenter [ˌriːˈentər] *vt* [room, earth's atmosphere] rentrer dans; [country] retourner dans.

reentry [ˌriːˈentrɪ] *n* [into earth's atmosphere] rentrée *f*; [into country] retour *m*.

reexamine [ˌriːɪɡˈzæmɪn] *vt* examiner de nouveau.

reexport [ˌriːˈekspɔːt] COMM ◇ *n* réexportation *f*. ◇ *vt* réexporter.

ref [ref] *n* **-1.** *inf* (*abbr of* **referee**) arbitre *m*. **-2.** (*abbr of* **reference**) ADMIN réf. *f*.

refectory [rɪˈfektərɪ] (*pl* **-ies**) *n* réfectoire *m*.

refer [rɪˈfɜːr] (*pt & pp* **-red**, *cont* **-ring**) *vt* **-1.** [person]: **to ~ sb to** [hospital] envoyer qqn à; [specialist] adresser qqn à; ADMIN renvoyer qqn à. **-2.** [report, case, decision]: **to ~ sthg to** soumettre qqch à.

◆ **refer to** *vt fus* **-1.** [speak about] parler de, faire allusion à OR mention de. **-2.** [apply to] s'appliquer à, concerner. **-3.** [consult] se référer à, se reporter à.

referee [ˌrefəˈriː] ◇ *n* **-1.** SPORT arbitre *m*. **-2.** *Br* [for job application] répondant *m*, -e *f*. ◇ *vt* SPORT arbitrer. ◇ *vi* SPORT être arbitre.

reference [ˈrefrəns] *n* **-1.** [mention]: **~ (to)** allusion *f* (à), mention *f* (de); **with ~ to** comme suite à. **-2.** (*U*) [for advice, information]: **~ (to)** consultation *f* (de), référence *f* (à); **for future ~** à titre d'information. **-3.** COMM référence *f*. **-4.** [in book] renvoi *m*; **map ~** coordonnées *fpl*. **-5.** [for job application - letter] référence *f*; [- person] répondant *m*, -e *f*.

reference book *n* ouvrage *m* de référence.

reference library *n* bibliothèque *f* d'ouvrages à consulter.

reference number *n* numéro *m* de référence.

referendum [ˌrefəˈrendəm] (*pl* **-s** OR **-da** [-də]) *n* référendum *m*.

referral [rɪˈfɜːrəl] *n fml* **-1.** (*U*) [act of referring] envoi *m*. **-2.** [patient referred] malade envoyé *m*, malade envoyée *f*.

refill [*n* ˈriːfɪl, *vb* ˌriːˈfɪl] ◇ *n* **-1.** [for pen] recharge *f*. **-2.** *inf* [drink]: **would you like a ~?** vous voulez encore un verre? ◇ *vt* remplir à nouveau.

refillable [ˌriːˈfɪləbl] *adj* [pen] rechargeable; [bottle] qu'on peut faire remplir à nouveau.

refine [rɪˈfaɪn] *vt* raffiner; *fig* peaufiner.

refined [rɪˈfaɪnd] *adj* raffiné(e); [system, theory] perfectionné(e).

refinement [rɪˈfaɪnmənt] *n* **-1.** [improvement] perfectionnement *m*. **-2.** (*U*) [gentility] raffinement *m*.

refinery [rɪˈfaɪnərɪ] (*pl* **-ies**) *n* raffinerie *f*.

refit [*n* ˈriːfɪt, *vb* ˌriːˈfɪt] (*pt & pp* **-ted**, *cont* **-ting**) ◇ *n* [of ship] réparation *f*, remise *f* en état. ◇ *vt* [ship] réparer, remettre en état.

reflate [ˌriːˈfleɪt] ECON ◇ *vt* relancer. ◇ *vi* effectuer une relance (de l'économie).

reflation [ˌriːˈfleɪʃn] *n* ECON relance *f*.

reflationary [riːˈfleɪʃənrɪ] *adj* ECON de relance.

reflect [rɪˈflekt] ◇ *vt* **-1.** [be a sign of] refléter. **-2.** [light, image] réfléchir, refléter; [heat] réverbérer; **to be ~ed in** se refléter dans. **-3.** [think]: **to ~ that ...** se dire que .... ◇ *vi* [think]: **to ~ (on** OR **upon)** réfléchir (sur), penser (à).

reflection [rɪˈflekʃn] *n* **-1.** [sign] indication *f*, signe *m*. **-2.** [criticism]: **~ on** critique *f* de. **-3.** [image] reflet *m*. **-4.** (*U*) [of light, heat] réflexion *f*. **-5.** [thought] réflexion *f*; **on ~** réflexion faite.

reflective [rɪˈflektɪv] *adj* **-1.** [surface, material] réfléchissant(e). **-2.** [thoughtful] pensif(ive).

reflector [rɪˈflektər] *n* réflecteur *m*.

reflex [ˈriːfleks] *n*: **~ (action)** réflexe *m*.

◆ **reflexes** *npl* réflexes *mpl*.

reflex camera *n* appareil *m* reflex.

reflexive [rɪˈfleksɪv] *adj* GRAMM [pronoun] réfléchi(e); **~ verb** verbe *m* pronominal réfléchi.

reflexology [ˌriːflekˈsɒlədʒɪ] *n* réflexothérapie *f*.

reforest [ˌriːˈfɒrɪst] = **reafforest**.

reforestation [riːˌfɒrɪˈsteɪʃn] = **reafforestation**.

reform [rɪˈfɔːm] ◇ *n* réforme *f*. ◇ *vt* [gen] réformer; [person] corriger. ◇ *vi* [behave better] se corriger, s'amender.

reformat [ˌriːˈfɔːmæt] (*pt & pp* **-ted**, *cont* **-ting**) *vt* COMPUT reformater.

Reformation [ˌrefəˈmeɪʃn] *n*: **the ~** la Réforme.

reformatory [rɪˈfɔːmətrɪ] *n Am* centre *m* d'éducation surveillée (pour jeunes délinquants).

reformed [rɪˈfɔːmd] *adj* [better behaved] qui s'est corrigé(e) OR amendé(e).

reformer [rɪ'fɔːməʳ] *n* réformateur *m*, -trice *f*.

reformist [rɪ'fɔːmɪst] ◇ *adj* réformiste. ◇ *n* réformiste *mf*.

refract [rɪ'frækt] ◇ *vt* réfracter. ◇ *vi* se réfracter.

refrain [rɪ'freɪn] ◇ *n* refrain *m*. ◇ *vi*: **to ~ from doing sthg** s'abstenir de faire qqch.

refresh [rɪ'freʃ] *vt* rafraîchir, revigorer; **to ~ sb's memory** rafraîchir la mémoire de qqn.

refreshed [rɪ'freʃt] *adj* reposé(e).

refresher course [rɪ'freʃəʳ-] *n* cours *m* de recyclage OR remise à niveau.

refreshing [rɪ'freʃɪŋ] *adj* **-1.** [pleasantly different] agréable, réconfortant(e). **-2.** [drink, swim] rafraîchissant(e).

refreshments [rɪ'freʃmənts] *npl* rafraîchissements *mpl*.

refrigerate [rɪ'frɪdʒəreɪt] *vt* réfrigérer.

refrigeration [rɪ,frɪdʒə'reɪʃn] *n* réfrigération *f*.

refrigerator [rɪ'frɪdʒəreɪtəʳ] *n* réfrigérateur *m*, frigidaire *m*.

refuel [,riː'fjʊəl] (*Br pt* & *pp* **-led**, *cont* **-ling**; *Am pt* & *pp* **-ed**, *cont* **-ing**) ◇ *vt* ravitailler. ◇ *vi* se ravitailler en carburant.

refuge ['refjuːdʒ] *n* **-1.** [place of safety] refuge *m*, abri *m*. **-2.** [safety] *lit* & *fig*: **to take ~ in** se réfugier dans.

refugee [,refjʊ'dʒiː] *n* réfugié *m*, -e *f*.

refugee camp *n* camp *m* de réfugiés.

refund [*n* 'riːfʌnd, *vb* riː'fʌnd] ◇ *n* remboursement *m*. ◇ *vt*: **to ~ sthg to sb**, **to ~ sb sthg** rembourser qqch à qqn.

refurbish [,riː'fɜːbɪʃ] *vt* remettre à neuf, rénover.

refurbishment [,riː'fɜːbɪʃmənt] *n* rénovation *f*.

refurnish [,riː'fɜːnɪʃ] *vt* remeubler.

refusal [rɪ'fjuːzl] *n*: **~ (to do sthg)** refus *m* (de faire qqch).

refuse[1] [rɪ'fjuːz] ◇ *vt* refuser; **to ~ to do sthg** refuser de faire qqch. ◇ *vi* refuser.

refuse[2] ['refjuːs] *n* (*U*) [rubbish] ordures *fpl*, détritus *mpl*.

refuse collection ['refjuːs-] *n* enlèvement *m* des ordures ménagères.

refuse collector ['refjuːs-] *n* éboueur *m*.

refuse dump ['refjuːs-] *n* décharge *f* (publique).

refute [rɪ'fjuːt] *vt* réfuter.

reg., **regd.** (*abbr of* **registered**): **~ trademark** marque *f* déposée.

regain [rɪ'geɪn] *vt* [composure, health] retrouver; [leadership] reprendre.

regal ['riːgl] *adj* majestueux(euse), royal(e).

regale [rɪ'geɪl] *vt*: **to ~ sb with sthg** divertir qqn en lui racontant qqch.

regalia [rɪ'geɪljə] *n* (*U*) insignes *mpl*.

regard [rɪ'gɑːd] ◇ *n* **-1.** (*U*) [respect] estime *f*, respect *m*. **-2.** [aspect]: **in this/that ~** à cet égard. ◇ *vt* considérer; **to ~ o.s. as** se considérer comme; **to be highly ~ed** être tenu(e) en haute estime.

◆ **regards** *npl*: **(with best) ~s** bien amicalement; **give her my ~s** faites-lui mes amitiés.

◆ **as regards** *prep* en ce qui concerne.

◆ **in regard to**, **with regard to** *prep* en ce qui concerne, relativement à.

regarding [rɪ'gɑːdɪŋ] *prep* concernant, en ce qui concerne.

regardless [rɪ'gɑːdlɪs] *adv* quand même.

◆ **regardless of** *prep* sans tenir compte de, sans se soucier de.

regatta [rɪ'gætə] *n* régate *f*.

regd. = reg.

Regency ['riːdʒənsɪ] *adj* Régence (anglaise).

regenerate [rɪ'dʒenəreɪt] *vt* [economy, project] relancer.

regeneration [rɪ,dʒenə'reɪʃn] *n* [of economy, project] relance *f*.

regent ['riːdʒənt] *n* régent *m*, -e *f*.

reggae ['regeɪ] *n* reggae *m*.

regime [reɪ'ʒiːm] *n* régime *m*.

regiment ['redʒɪmənt] *n* régiment *m*.

regimental [,redʒɪ'mentl] *adj* du régiment.

regimented ['redʒɪmentɪd] *adj* [organization] trop rigide; [life] strict(e).

region ['riːdʒən] *n* région *f*; **in the ~ of** environ.

regional ['riːdʒənl] *adj* régional(e).

register ['redʒɪstəʳ] ◇ *n* [record] registre *m*. ◇ *vt* **-1.** [record officially] déclarer. **-2.** [show, measure] indiquer, montrer. **-3.** [express] exprimer. ◇ *vi* **-1.** [on official list] s'inscrire, se faire inscrire. **-2.** [at hotel] signer le registre. **-3.** *inf* [advice, fact]: **it didn't ~** je n'ai pas compris.

registered ['redʒɪstəd] *adj* **-1.** [person] inscrit(e); [car] immatriculé(e); [charity] agréé(e) par le gouvernement. **-2.** [letter, parcel] recommandé(e).

registered nurse *n* infirmier diplômé d'État *m*, infirmière diplômée d'État *f*.

registered post *Br*, **registered mail** *Am n*: **to send sthg by ~** envoyer qqch en recommandé.

registered trademark *n* marque *f* déposée.

registrar [ˌredʒɪ'strɑːʳ] n -1. [keeper of records] officier m de l'état civil. -2. UNIV secrétaire m général. -3. Br [doctor] chef m de clinique.

registration [ˌredʒɪ'streɪʃn] n -1. [gen] enregistrement m, inscription f. -2. AUT = **registration number**.

registration document n ≃ carte f grise.

registration number n AUT numéro m d'immatriculation.

registry ['redʒɪstrɪ] (pl -ies) n bureau m de l'enregistrement.

registry office n bureau m de l'état-civil.

regress [rɪ'gres] vi: to ~ (to) régresser (au stade de).

regression [rɪ'greʃn] n régression f.

regressive [rɪ'gresɪv] adj régressif(ive).

regret [rɪ'gret] (pt & pp -ted, cont -ting) ◇ n regret m. ◇ vt [be sorry about]: to ~ sthg/doing sthg regretter qqch/d'avoir fait qqch; we ~ to announce ... nons sommes au regret d'annoncer ....

regretful [rɪ'gretful] adj [person] plein(e) de regrets; [look] de regret.

regretfully [rɪ'gretfulɪ] adv à regret.

regrettable [rɪ'gretəbl] adj regrettable, fâcheux(euse).

regrettably [rɪ'gretəblɪ] adv malheureusement.

regroup [ˌriː'gruːp] vi se regrouper.

regt abbr of **regiment**.

regular ['regjʊləʳ] ◇ adj -1. [gen] régulier(ière); [customer] fidèle. -2. [usual] habituel(elle). -3. Am [normal - size] standard (inv). -4. Am [pleasant] sympa (inv). ◇ n [at pub] habitué m, -e f; [at shop] client m, -e f fidèle.

regular army n armée f de métier.

regularity [ˌregjʊ'lærətɪ] n régularité f.

regularly ['regjʊləlɪ] adv régulièrement.

regulate ['regjʊleɪt] vt régler.

regulation [ˌregjʊ'leɪʃn] ◇ adj [standard] réglementaire. ◇ n -1. [rule] règlement m. -2. (U) [control] réglementation f.

regurgitate [rɪ'gɜːdʒɪteɪt] vt régurgiter; fig & pej ressortir, répéter.

rehabilitate [ˌriːə'bɪlɪteɪt] vt [criminal] réinsérer, réhabiliter; [patient] rééduquer.

rehabilitation ['riːə,bɪlɪ'teɪʃn] n [of criminal] réinsertion f, réhabilitation f; [of patient] rééducation f.

rehash [ˌriː'hæʃ] vt inf pej remanier.

rehearsal [rɪ'hɜːsl] n répétition f.

rehearse [rɪ'hɜːs] vt & vi répéter.

rehouse [ˌriː'haʊz] vt reloger.

reign ['reɪn] ◇ n règne m. ◇ vi: to ~ (over) lit & fig régner (sur).

reigning ['reɪnɪŋ] adj [champion] actuel(elle).

reimburse [ˌriːɪm'bɜːs] vt: to ~ sb (for) rembourser qqn (de).

reimbursement [ˌriːɪm'bɜːsmənt] n remboursement m.

Reims [riːmz] n Reims.

rein [reɪn] n fig: to give (a) free ~ to sb, to give sb free ~ laisser la bride sur le cou à qqn; to keep a tight ~ on sb tenir la bride haute à qqn; to keep a tight ~ on sthg contrôler étroitement qqch.

◆ **reins** npl -1. [for horse] rênes fpl. -2. [for child] laisse f.

◆ **rein in** vt sep [horse] serrer la bride à; fig modérer.

reincarnation [ˌriːɪnkɑː'neɪʃn] n réincarnation f.

reindeer ['reɪn,dɪəʳ] (pl inv) n renne m.

reinforce [ˌriːɪn'fɔːs] vt -1. [strengthen] renforcer. -2. [back up, confirm] appuyer, étayer.

reinforced concrete [ˌriːɪn'fɔːst-] n béton m armé.

reinforcement [ˌriːɪn'fɔːsmənt] n -1. (U) [strengthening] renforcement m. -2. [strengthener] renfort m.

◆ **reinforcements** npl renforts mpl.

reinstate [ˌriːɪn'steɪt] vt [employee] rétablir dans ses fonctions, réintégrer; [policy, method] rétablir.

reinstatement [ˌriːɪn'steɪtmənt] n réintégration f, rétablissement m.

reinterpret [ˌriːɪn'tɜːprɪt] vt interpréter de nouveau (différemment).

reintroduce ['riː,ɪntrə'djuːs] vt réintroduire.

reintroduction [riː,ɪntrə'dʌkʃn] n réintroduction f.

reissue [riː'ɪʃuː] ◇ n [of book] réédition f. ◇ vt [book] rééditer; [film, record] ressortir.

reiterate [riː'ɪtəreɪt] vt réitérer, répéter.

reiteration [riː,ɪtə'reɪʃn] n réitération f.

reject [n 'riːdʒekt, vb rɪ'dʒekt] ◇ n [product] article m de rebut. ◇ vt -1. [not accept] rejeter. -2. [candidate, coin] refuser.

rejection [rɪ'dʒekʃn] n -1. [non-acceptance] rejet m. -2. [of candidate] refus m.

rejig [ˌriː'dʒɪg] (pt & pp -ged, cont -ging) vt Br inf réorganiser.

rejoice [rɪ'dʒɔɪs] vi: to ~ (at OR in) se réjouir (de).

rejoicing [rɪ'dʒɔɪsɪŋ] n (U) réjouissance f.

rejoin[1] [ˌriː'dʒɔɪn] vt rejoindre; [club] adhérer de nouveau à.

rejoin² [rɪ'dʒɔɪn] *vt* [reply] répondre, répliquer.

rejoinder [rɪ'dʒɔɪndə^r] *n* réplique *f*, riposte *f*.

rejuvenate [rɪ'dʒuːvəneɪt] *vt* rajeunir.

rejuvenation [rɪ,dʒuːvə'neɪʃn] *n* rajeunissement *m*.

rekindle [,riː'kɪndl] *vt* *fig* ranimer, raviver.

relapse [rɪ'læps] ◇ *n* rechute *f*; **to have a ~** faire une rechute, rechuter. ◇ *vi*: **to ~ into** retomber dans.

relate [rɪ'leɪt] ◇ *vt* **-1.** [connect]: **to ~ sthg to sthg** établir un lien OR rapport entre qqch et qqch. **-2.** [tell] raconter. ◇ *vi* **-1.** [be connected]: **to ~ to** avoir un rapport avec. **-2.** [concern]: **to ~ to** se rapporter à. **-3.** [empathize]: **to ~ (to sb)** s'entendre (avec qqn).
◆ **relating to** *prep* concernant.

related [rɪ'leɪtɪd] *adj* **-1.** [people] apparenté(e). **-2.** [issues, problems etc] lié(e).

relation [rɪ'leɪʃn] *n* **-1.** [connection]: **~ (to/between)** rapport *m* (avec/entre); **in ~ to** par rapport à. **-2.** [person] parent *m*, -e *f*.
◆ **relations** *npl* [relationship] relations *fpl*, rapports *mpl*.

relational [rɪ'leɪʃənl] *adj* COMPUT relationnel(elle).

relationship [rɪ'leɪʃnʃɪp] *n* **-1.** [between people, countries] relations *fpl*, rapports *mpl*; [romantic] liaison *f*. **-2.** [connection] rapport *m*, lien *m*.

relative ['relətɪv] ◇ *adj* relatif(ive). ◇ *n* parent *m*, -e *f*.
◆ **relative to** *prep* [compared with] relativement à; [connected with] se rapportant à, relatif(ive) à.

relatively ['relətɪvlɪ] *adv* relativement.

relativity [,relə'tɪvətɪ] *n* relativité *f*.

relax [rɪ'læks] ◇ *vt* **-1.** [person] détendre, relaxer. **-2.** [muscle, body] décontracter, relâcher; [one's grip] desserrer. **-3.** [rule] relâcher. ◇ *vi* **-1.** [person] se détendre, se décontracter. **-2.** [muscle, body] se relâcher, se décontracter. **-3.** [one's grip] se desserrer.

relaxation [,riːlæk'seɪʃn] *n* **-1.** [of person] relaxation *f*, détente *f*. **-2.** [of rule] relâchement *m*.

relaxed [rɪ'lækst] *adj* détendu(e), décontracté(e).

relaxing [rɪ'læksɪŋ] *adj* relaxant(e), qui détend.

relay ['riːleɪ] (*pt* & *pp* senses *1* & *2* **-ed**, *pt* & *pp* sense *3* **relaid**) ◇ *n* **-1.** SPORT: **~ (race)** course *f* de relais; **in ~s** *fig* en se relayant. **-2.** RADIO & TV [broadcast] retransmission *f*.

◇ *vt* **-1.** RADIO & TV [broadcast] relayer. **-2.** [message, information] transmettre, communiquer. **-3.** [carpet, tiles] poser à nouveau, reposer.

release [rɪ'liːs] ◇ *n* **-1.** [from prison, cage] libération *f*. **-2.** [from pain, misery] délivrance *f*. **-3.** [statement] communiqué *m*. **-4.** [of gas, heat] échappement *m*. **-5.** (*U*) [of film, record] sortie *f*; **to be on ~** CINEMA passer dans les salles de cinéma. **-6.** [film] nouveau film *m*; [record] nouveau disque *m*.
◇ *vt* **-1.** [set free] libérer. **-2.** [lift restriction on]: **to ~ sb from** dégager qqn de. **-3.** [make available - supplies] libérer; [- funds] débloquer. **-4.** [let go of] lâcher. **-5.** TECH [brake, handle] desserrer; [mechanism] déclencher. **-6.** [gas, heat]: **to be ~d (from/into)** se dégager (de/dans), s'échapper (de/dans). **-7.** [film, record] sortir; [statement, report] publier.

relegate ['relɪgeɪt] *vt* reléguer; **to be ~d** *Br* SPORT être relégué à la division inférieure.

relegation [,relɪ'geɪʃn] *n* relégation *f*.

relent [rɪ'lent] *vi* [person] se laisser fléchir; [wind, storm] se calmer.

relentless [rɪ'lentlɪs] *adj* implacable.

relentlessly [rɪ'lentlɪslɪ] *adv* implacablement.

relevance ['reləvəns] *n* (*U*) **-1.** [connection]: **~ (to)** rapport *m* (avec). **-2.** [significance]: **~ (to)** importance *f* (pour).

relevant ['reləvənt] *adj* **-1.** [connected]: **~ (to)** qui a un rapport (avec). **-2.** [significant]: **~ (to)** important(e) (pour). **-3.** [appropriate - information] utile; [- document] justificatif(ive).

reliability [rɪ,laɪə'bɪlətɪ] *n* fiabilité *f*.

reliable [rɪ'laɪəbl] *adj* [person] sur qui on peut compter, fiable; [device] fiable; [company, information] sérieux(ieuse).

reliably [rɪ'laɪəblɪ] *adv* de façon fiable; **to be ~ informed (that) ...** savoir de source sûre que ....

reliance [rɪ'laɪəns] *n*: **~ (on)** dépendance *f* (de).

reliant [rɪ'laɪənt] *adj*: **to be ~ on** être dépendant(e) de.

relic ['relɪk] *n* relique *f*; [of past] vestige *m*.

relief [rɪ'liːf] *n* **-1.** [comfort] soulagement *m*. **-2.** [for poor, refugees] aide *f*, assistance *f*. **-3.** *Am* [social security] aide *f* sociale.

relief map *n* carte *f* en relief.

relief road *n* *Br* route *f* de délestage.

relieve [rɪ'liːv] *vt* **-1.** [pain, anxiety] soulager; **to ~ sb of sthg** [take away from] délivrer qqn de qqch. **-2.** [take over from] relayer. **-3.** [give help to] secourir, venir en aide à.

relieved [rɪ'liːvd] *adj* soulagé(e).

religion [rɪ'lɪdʒn] *n* religion *f*.

religious [rɪ'lɪdʒəs] *adj* religieux(ieuse); [book] de piété.

reline [‚riː'laɪn] *vt* [clothes, bag] redoubler; [brakes] changer les garnitures de.

relinquish [rɪ'lɪŋkwɪʃ] *vt* [power] abandonner; [claim, plan] renoncer à; [post] quitter.

relish ['relɪʃ] ◇ *n* **-1.** [enjoyment]: **with (great)** ~ avec délectation. **-2.** [pickle] condiment *m*. ◇ *vt* [enjoy] prendre plaisir à; **I don't ~ the thought** OR **idea** OR **prospect of seeing him** la perspective de le voir ne m'enchante OR ne me sourit guère.

relive [‚riː'lɪv] *vt* revivre.

relocate [‚riːlə'keɪt] ◇ *vt* installer ailleurs, transférer. ◇ *vi* s'installer ailleurs, déménager.

relocation [‚rɪləʊ'keɪʃn] *n* transfert *m*, déménagement *m*.

relocation expenses *npl* frais *mpl* de déménagement.

reluctance [rɪ'lʌktəns] *n* répugnance *f*.

reluctant [rɪ'lʌktənt] *adj* peu enthousiaste; **to be ~ to do sthg** rechigner à faire qqch, être peu disposé à faire qqch.

reluctantly [rɪ'lʌktəntlɪ] *adv* à contrecœur, avec répugnance.

rely [rɪ'laɪ] (*pt* & *pp* **-ied**)
◆ **rely on** *vt fus* **-1.** [count on] compter sur; **to ~ on sb to do sthg** compter sur qqn OR faire confiance à qqn pour faire qqch. **-2.** [be dependent on] dépendre de.

REM (*abbr of* **rapid eye movement**) *n* activité oculaire intense durant le sommeil paradoxal.

remain [rɪ'meɪn] ◇ *vt* rester; **to ~ to be done** rester à faire; **it ~s to be seen ...** reste à savoir .... ◇ *vi* rester.
◆ **remains** *npl* **-1.** [remnants] restes *mpl*. **-2.** [antiquities] ruines *fpl*, vestiges *mpl*.

remainder [rɪ'meɪndə'] *n* reste *m*.

remaining [rɪ'meɪnɪŋ] *adj* qui reste; **last ~** dernier(ière).

remake [*n* 'riːmeɪk, *vb* ‚riː'meɪk] CINEMA ◇ *n* remake *m*. ◇ *vt* refaire.

remand [rɪ'mɑːnd] JUR ◇ *n*: **on ~** en détention préventive. ◇ *vt*: **to ~ sb (in custody)** placer qqn en détention préventive.

remand centre *n Br* maison *f* de détention préventive.

remark [rɪ'mɑːk] ◇ *n* [comment] remarque *f*, observation *f*. ◇ *vt* [comment]: **to ~ that ...** faire remarquer que .... ◇ *vi*: **to ~ on** faire des remarques sur.

remarkable [rɪ'mɑːkəbl] *adj* remarquable.

remarkably [rɪ'mɑːkəblɪ] *adv* remarquablement.

remarry [‚riː'mærɪ] (*pt* & *pp* **-ied**) *vi* se remarier.

remedial [rɪ'miːdjəl] *adj* **-1.** [pupil, class] de rattrapage. **-2.** [exercise] correctif(ive); [action] de rectification.

remedy ['remədɪ] (*pl* **-ies**, *pt* & *pp* **-ied**) ◇ *n*: ~ **(for)** MED remède *m* (pour OR contre); *fig* remède (à OR contre). ◇ *vt* remédier à.

remember [rɪ'membər] ◇ *vt* **-1.** [gen] se souvenir de, se rappeler; **to ~ to do sthg** ne pas oublier de faire qqch, penser à faire qqch; **to ~ doing sthg** se souvenir d'avoir fait qqch, se rappeler avoir fait qqch. **-2.** [as greeting]: **to ~ sb to sb** rappeler qqn au bon souvenir de qqn. ◇ *vi* se souvenir, se rappeler.

remembrance [rɪ'membrəns] *n*: **in ~ of** en souvenir OR mémoire de.

Remembrance Day *n* l'Armistice *m*.

remind [rɪ'maɪnd] *vt*: **to ~ sb of** OR **about sthg** rappeler qqch à qqn; **to ~ sb to do sthg** rappeler à qqn de faire qqch, faire penser à qqn à faire qqch.

reminder [rɪ'maɪndər] *n* **-1.** [to jog memory]: **to give sb a ~ (to do sthg)** faire penser à qqn (à faire qqch). **-2.** [letter, note] rappel *m*.

reminisce [‚remɪ'nɪs] *vi* évoquer des souvenirs; **to ~ about sthg** évoquer qqch.

reminiscences [‚remɪ'nɪsənsɪz] *npl* souvenirs *mpl*.

reminiscent [‚remɪ'nɪsnt] *adj*: ~ **of** qui rappelle, qui fait penser à.

remiss [rɪ'mɪs] *adj* négligent(e).

remission [rɪ'mɪʃn] *n* (*U*) **-1.** JUR remise *f*. **-2.** MED rémission *f*.

remit[1] [rɪ'mɪt] (*pt* & *pp* **-ted**, *cont* **-ting**) *vt* [money] envoyer, verser.

remit[2] ['riːmɪt] *n Br* [responsibility] attributions *fpl*.

remittance [rɪ'mɪtns] *n* **-1.** [amount of money] versement *m*. **-2.** COMM **règlement** *m*, paiement *m*.

remnant ['remnənt] *n* **-1.** [remaining part] reste *m*, restant *m*. **-2.** [of cloth] coupon *m*.

remodel [‚riː'mɒdl] (*Br pt* & *pp* **-led**, *cont* **-ling**, *Am pt* & *pp* **-ed**, *cont* **-ing**) remodeler.

remold *Am* = **remould**.

remonstrate ['remənstreɪt] *vi*: **to ~ (with sb about sthg)** faire des remontrances (à qqn au sujet de qqch).

remorse [rɪ'mɔːs] *n* (*U*) remords *m*.

remorseful [rɪ'mɔːsfʊl] *adj* plein(e) de remords.

remorseless [rɪ'mɔːslɪs] *adj* implacable.

remorselessly [rɪ'mɔːslɪslɪ] *adv* implacablement.

remote [rɪ'məʊt] *adj* -1. [far-off - place] éloigné(e); [- time] lointain(e). -2. [person] distant(e). -3. [possibility, chance] vague.

remote control *n* télécommande *f.*

remote-controlled [-kən'trəʊld] *adj* télécommandé(e).

remotely [rɪ'məʊtlɪ] *adv* -1. [in the slightest]: not ~ pas le moins du monde, absolument pas. -2. [far off] au loin.

remoteness [rɪ'məʊtnɪs] *n* -1. [of place] éloignement *m*, isolement *m*. -2. [of person] attitude *f* distante.

remould *Br*, **remold** *Am* ['riːməʊld] *n* pneu *m* rechapé.

removable [rɪ'muːvəbl] *adj* [detachable] détachable, amovible.

removal [rɪ'muːvl] *n* -1. (*U*) [act of removing] enlèvement *m*. -2. *Br* [change of house] déménagement *m*.

removal man *n Br* déménageur *m.*

removal van *n Br* camion *m* de déménagement.

remove [rɪ'muːv] *vt* -1. [take away - gen] enlever; [- stain] faire partir, enlever; [- problem] résoudre; [- suspicion] dissiper. -2. [clothes] ôter, enlever. -3. [employee] renvoyer.

removed [rɪ'muːvd] *adj*: to be far ~ from être très éloigné(e) OR différent(e) de.

remover [rɪ'muːvər] *n* [for paint] décapant *m*; [for stains] détachant *m*; [for nail-varnish] dissolvant *m.*

remuneration [rɪ,mjuːnə'reɪʃn] *n* rémunération *f.*

Renaissance [rə'neɪsns] ◇ *n*: the ~ la Renaissance. ◇ *comp* (de la) Renaissance.

rename [,riː'neɪm] *vt* rebaptiser.

rend [rend] (*pt & pp* rent) *vt* déchirer.

render ['rendər] *vt* rendre; [assistance] porter; FIN [account] présenter.

rendering ['rendərɪŋ] *n* [of play, music etc] interprétation *f.*

rendezvous ['rɒndɪvuː] (*pl inv*) *n* rendez-vous *m.*

rendition [ren'dɪʃn] *n* interprétation *f.*

renegade ['renɪgeɪd] *n* renégat *m*, -e *f.*

renege [rɪ'niːg] *vi*: to ~ on manquer à, revenir sur.

renegotiate [,riːnɪ'gəʊʃɪeɪt] ◇ *vt* renégocier. ◇ *vi* négocier à nouveau.

renew [rɪ'njuː] *vt* -1. [gen] renouveler; [negotiations, strength] reprendre; [interest] faire

renaître; **to ~ acquaintance with sb** renouer connaissance avec qqn. -2. [replace] remplacer.

renewable [rɪ'njuːəbl] *adj* renouvelable.

renewal [rɪ'njuːəl] *n* -1. [of activity] reprise *f.* -2. [of contract, licence etc] renouvellement *m.*

rennet ['renɪt] *n* présure *f.*

renounce [rɪ'naʊns] *vt* [reject] renoncer à.

renovate ['renəveɪt] *vt* rénover.

renovation [,renə'veɪʃn] *n* rénovation *f.*

renown [rɪ'naʊn] *n* renommée *f*, renom *m.*

renowned [rɪ'naʊnd] *adj*: ~ **(for)** renommé(e) (pour).

rent [rent] ◇ *pt & pp* → **rend**. ◇ *n* [for house] loyer *m*. ◇ *vt* louer.

◆ **rent out** *vt sep* louer.

rental ['rentl] ◇ *adj* de location. ◇ *n* [for car, television, video] prix *m* de location; [for house] loyer *m.*

rent book *n* carnet *m* de quittances de loyer.

rent boy *n Br inf* jeune garçon *m* qui se prostitue.

rented ['rentɪd] *adj* loué(e).

rent-free ◇ *adj* gratuit(e). ◇ *adv* sans payer de loyer.

renumber [,riː'nʌmbər] *vt* renuméroter.

renunciation [rɪ,nʌnsɪ'eɪʃn] *n* renonciation *f.*

reoccurrence [,riːə'kʌrəns] *n*: **if there's a ~** ... si cela se reproduit ...

reopen [,riː'əʊpn] ◇ *vt* rouvrir; [negotiations] reprendre. ◇ *vi* rouvrir; [negotiations] reprendre; [wound] se rouvrir.

reorganization ['riː,ɔːgənaɪ'zeɪʃn] *n* réorganisation *f.*

reorganize, -ise [,riː'ɔːgənaɪz] ◇ *vt* réorganiser. ◇ *vi* se réorganiser.

rep [rep] *n* -1. (*abbr of* **representative**) VRP *m.* -2. *abbr of* **repertory**. -3. *abbr of* **repertory company**.

Rep. *Am* -1. *abbr of* **Representative**. -2. *abbr of* **Republican**.

repaid [riː'peɪd] *pt & pp* → **repay**.

repaint [,riː'peɪnt] *vt* repeindre.

repair [rɪ'peər] ◇ *n* réparation *f*; **in good/ bad ~** en bon/mauvais état. ◇ *vt* réparer.

repair kit *n* trousse *f* à outils.

repaper [,riː'peɪpər] *vt* retapisser.

reparations [,repə'reɪʃnz] *npl* réparations *fpl.*

repartee [,repɑː'tiː] *n* repartie *f.*

repatriate [,riː'pætrɪeɪt] *vt* rapatrier.

repay [riː'peɪ] (*pt* & *pp* **repaid**) *vt* -1. [money]: **to ~ sb sthg, to ~ sthg to sb** rembourser qqch à qqn. -2. [favour] payer de retour, récompenser; **to ~ sb for sthg** récompenser qqn de OR pour qqch.

repayment [riː'peɪmənt] *n* remboursement *m*.

repeal [rɪ'piːl] ◇ *n* abrogation *f*. ◇ *vt* abroger.

repeat [rɪ'piːt] ◇ *vt* -1. [gen] répéter; **to ~ o.s.** se répéter. -2. RADIO & TV rediffuser. ◇ *n* RADIO & TV reprise *f*, rediffusion *f*.

repeated [rɪ'piːtɪd] *adj* répété(e).

repeatedly [rɪ'piːtɪdlɪ] *adv* à maintes reprises, très souvent.

repel [rɪ'pel] (*pt* & *pp* **-led**, *cont* **-ling**) *vt* repousser.

repellent [rɪ'pelənt] ◇ *adj* répugnant(e), repoussant(e). ◇ *n*: **insect ~** crème *f* anti-insecte.

repent [rɪ'pent] ◇ *vt* se repentir de. ◇ *vi*: **to ~ (of)** se repentir (de).

repentance [rɪ'pentəns] *n* (U) repentir *m*.

repentant [rɪ'pentənt] *adj* repentant(e).

repercussions [ˌriːpə'kʌʃnz] *npl* répercussions *fpl*.

repertoire ['repətwɑ'] *n* répertoire *m*.

repertory ['repətrɪ] *n* répertoire *m*.

repertory company *n* compagnie *f* OR troupe *f* de répertoire.

repetition [ˌrepɪ'tɪʃn] *n* répétition *f*.

repetitious [ˌrepɪ'tɪʃəs], **repetitive** [rɪ'petɪtɪv] *adj* [action, job] répétitif(ive); [article, speech] qui a des redites.

rephrase [ˌriː'freɪz] *vt* réécrire, tourner autrement.

replace [rɪ'pleɪs] *vt* -1. [gen] remplacer. -2. [put back] remettre (à sa place).

replacement [rɪ'pleɪsmənt] *n* -1. [substituting] remplacement *m*; [putting back] replacement *m*. -2. [new person]: **~ (for sb)** remplaçant *m*, -e *f* (de qqn).

replacement part *n* pièce *f* de rechange.

replay [*n* 'riːpleɪ, *vb* ˌriː'pleɪ] ◇ *n* match *m* rejoué. ◇ *vt* -1. [match, game] rejouer. -2. [film, tape] repasser.

replenish [rɪ'plenɪʃ] *vt*: **to ~ one's supply of sthg** se réapprovisionner en qqch.

replete [rɪ'pliːt] *adj fml* rempli(e); [person] rassasié(e).

replica ['replɪkə] *n* copie *f* exacte, réplique *f*.

replicate ['replɪkeɪt] *vt fml* reproduire.

replication [ˌreplɪ'keɪʃn] *n fml* reproduction *f*.

reply [rɪ'plaɪ] (*pl* **-ies**, *pt* & *pp* **-ied**) ◇ *n*: **~ (to)** réponse *f* (à); **in ~ (to)** en réponse (à). ◇ *vt* & *vi* répondre.

reply coupon *n* coupon-réponse *m*.

reply-paid *adj* réponse payée.

report [rɪ'pɔːt] ◇ *n* -1. [account] rapport *m*, compte-rendu *m*; PRESS reportage *m*. -2. *Br* SCH bulletin *m*. ◇ *vt* -1. [news, crime] rapporter, signaler. -2. [make known]: **to ~ that ...** annoncer que .... -3. [complain about]: **to ~ sb (to)** dénoncer qqn (à). ◇ *vi* -1. [give account]: **to ~ (on)** faire un rapport (sur); PRESS faire un reportage (sur). -2. [present oneself]: **to ~ (to sb/for sthg)** se présenter (à qqn/pour qqch).

◆ **report back** *vi*: **to ~ back (to)** présenter son rapport (à).

reportage [ˌrepɔː'tɑːʒ] *n* (U) reportage *m*.

report card *n* bulletin *m* scolaire.

reportedly [rɪ'pɔːtɪdlɪ] *adv* à ce qu'il paraît.

reported speech [rɪ'pɔːtɪd-] *n* style *m* indirect.

reporter [rɪ'pɔːtə'] *n* reporter *m*.

repose [rɪ'pəʊz] *n literary* repos *m*.

repository [rɪ'pɒzɪtrɪ] (*pl* **-ies**) *n* dépôt *m*.

repossess [ˌriːpə'zes] *vt* saisir.

repossession [ˌriːpə'zeʃn] *n* saisie *f*.

repossession order *n* ordre *m* de saisie.

reprehensible [ˌreprɪ'hensəbl] *adj* répréhensible.

represent [ˌreprɪ'zent] *vt* -1. [gen] représenter; **to be well** OR **strongly ~ed** être bien représenté. -2. [describe]: **to ~ sb/sthg as** décrire qqn/qqch comme.

representation [ˌreprɪzen'teɪʃn] *n* [gen] représentation *f*.

◆ **representations** *npl*: **to make ~s to sb** faire une démarche auprès de qqn.

representative [ˌreprɪ'zentətɪv] ◇ *adj* représentatif(ive). ◇ *n* représentant *m*, -e *f*.

repress [rɪ'pres] *vt* réprimer.

repressed [rɪ'prest] *adj* -1. [person - sexually] refoulé(e). -2. [feelings] réprimé(e), contenu(e).

repression [rɪ'preʃn] *n* répression *f*; [sexual] refoulement *m*.

repressive [rɪ'presɪv] *adj* répressif(ive).

reprieve [rɪ'priːv] ◇ *n* -1. *fig* [delay] sursis *m*, répit *m*. -2. JUR sursis *m*. ◇ *vt* accorder un sursis à.

reprimand ['reprɪmɑːnd] ◇ *n* réprimande *f*. ◇ *vt* réprimander.

reprint [*n* 'riːprɪnt, *vb* ˌriː'prɪnt] ◇ *n* réimpression *f*. ◇ *vt* réimprimer.

reprisal [rɪ'praɪzl] *n* représailles *fpl*.

reproach [rɪ'prəʊtʃ] ◇ *n* reproche *m*. ◇ *vt*: **to ~ sb (for** OR **with sthg)** reprocher qqch à qqn.

reproachful [rɪ'prəʊtʃful] *adj* [look, words] de reproche.

reprobate ['reprəbeɪt] *n hum* dépravé *m*, -e *f*.

reproduce [,ri:prə'dju:s] ◇ *vt* reproduire. ◇ *vi* se reproduire.

reproduction [,ri:prə'dʌkʃn] *n* reproduction *f*.

reproductive [,ri:prə'dʌktɪv] *adj* reproducteur(trice).

reprogram [,ri:'prəʊgræm] (*pt* & *pp* **-ed** OR **-med**, *cont* **-ing** OR **-ming**) *vt* reprogrammer.

reproof [rɪ'pru:f] *n* reproche *m*, blâme *m*.

reprove [rɪ'pru:v] *vt*: **to ~ sb (for)** blâmer qqn (pour OR de), réprimander qqn (pour).

reproving [rɪ'pru:vɪŋ] *adj* réprobateur(trice).

reptile ['reptaɪl] *n* reptile *m*.

Repub. *Am abbr of* **Republican**.

republic [rɪ'pʌblɪk] *n* république *f*.

republican [rɪ'pʌblɪkən] ◇ *adj* républicain(e). ◇ *n* républicain *m*, -e *f*.
◆ **Republican** ◇ *adj* républicain(e); **the Republican Party** *Am* le parti républicain. ◇ *n* républicain *m*, -e *f*.

repudiate [rɪ'pju:dɪeɪt] *vt fml* [offer, suggestion] rejeter; [friend] renier.

repudiation [rɪ,pju:dɪ'eɪʃn] *n fml* [of offer, suggestion] rejet *m*; [of friend] reniement *m*.

repugnant [rɪ'pʌgnənt] *adj* répugnant(e).

repulse [rɪ'pʌls] *vt* repousser.

repulsion [rɪ'pʌlʃn] *n* répulsion *f*.

repulsive [rɪ'pʌlsɪv] *adj* repoussant(e).

reputable ['repjʊtəbl] *adj* de bonne réputation.

reputation [,repjʊ'teɪʃn] *n* réputation *f*; **to have a ~ for sthg** être réputé pour qqch; **to have a ~ for being ...** avoir la réputation d'être ....

repute [rɪ'pju:t] *n*: **of ~** de renom; **of good ~** de bonne réputation.

reputed [rɪ'pju:tɪd] *adj* réputé(e); **to be ~ to be sthg** être réputé pour être qqch, avoir la réputation d'être qqch.

reputedly [rɪ'pju:tɪdlɪ] *adv* à OR d'après ce qu'on dit.

reqd *abbr of* **required**.

request [rɪ'kwest] ◇ *n*: **~ (for)** demande *f* (de); **on ~** sur demande; **at sb's ~** sur OR à la demande de qqn. ◇ *vt* demander; **to ~ sb to do sthg** demander à qqn de faire qqch.

request stop *n Br* arrêt *m* facultatif.

requiem (mass) ['rekwɪəm-] *n* messe *f* de requiem.

require [rɪ'kwaɪəʳ] *vt* [subj: person] avoir besoin de; [subj: situation] nécessiter; **to ~ sb to do sthg** exiger de qqn qu'il fasse qqch.

required [rɪ'kwaɪəd] *adj* exigé(e), requis(e).

requirement [rɪ'kwaɪəmənt] *n* besoin *m*.

requisite ['rekwɪzɪt] *adj fml* requis(e).

requisition [,rekwɪ'zɪʃn] *vt* réquisitionner.

reran [,ri:'ræn] *pt* → **rerun**.

reread [,ri:'ri:d] (*pt* & *pp* **reread** [,ri:'red]) *vt* relire.

rerecord [,ri:rɪ'kɔ:d] *vt* réenregistrer.

reroute [,ri:'ru:t] *vt* dérouter.

rerun [,ri:'rʌn] (*pt* **-ran**, *pp* **-run**, *cont* **-ning**) ◇ *n* [of TV programme] rediffusion *f*, reprise *f*; *fig* répétition *f*. ◇ *vt* **-1.** [race] réorganiser. **-2.** [TV programme] rediffuser; [tape] passer à nouveau, repasser.

resale price maintenance ['ri:seɪl-] *n Br* prix imposé aux distributeurs par le fabricant.

resat [,ri:'sæt] *pt* & *pp* → **resit**.

reschedule [*Br* ,ri:'ʃedjʊl, *Am* ,ri:'skedʒʊl] *vt* [to new date] changer la date de; [to new time] changer l'heure de; FIN rééchelonner.

rescind [rɪ'sɪnd] *vt* [contract] annuler; [law] abroger.

rescue ['reskju:] ◇ *n* **-1.** (*U*) [help] secours *mpl*; **to go/come to sb's ~** aller/venir au secours de qqn. **-2.** [successful attempt] sauvetage *m*. ◇ *vt* sauver, secourir.

rescue operation *n* opération *f* de sauvetage.

rescuer ['reskjʊəʳ] *n* sauveteur *m*.

reseal [,ri:'si:l] *vt* [letter] recacheter.

resealable [,ri:'si:ləbl] *adj* [envelope] qui peut être recacheté(e).

research [,rɪ'sɜ:tʃ] ◇ *n* (*U*): **~ (on** OR **into)** recherche *f* (sur), recherches *fpl* (sur); **~ and development** recherche et développement. ◇ *vt* faire des recherches sur. ◇ *vi*: **to ~ (into)** faire des recherches (sur).

researcher [rɪ'sɜ:tʃəʳ] *n* chercheur *m*, -euse *f*.

research work *n* (*U*) recherches *fpl*.

resell [,ri:'sel] (*pt* & *pp* **resold**) *vt* revendre.

resemblance [rɪ'zembləns] *n*: **~ (to)** ressemblance *f* (avec).

resemble [rɪ'zembl] *vt* ressembler à.

resent [rɪ'zent] *vt* être indigné(e) par; **I ~ that!** je n'apprécie pas (ça) du tout!

resentful [rɪ'zentful] *adj* plein(e) de ressentiment.

resentfully [rɪ'zentfulɪ] *adv* avec ressentiment.

resentment [rɪ'zentmənt] *n* ressentiment *m*.

reservation [,rezə'veɪʃn] *n* **-1.** [booking] réservation *f*. **-2.** [uncertainty]: **without ~** sans réserve. **-3.** *Am* [for Native Americans] réserve *f* indienne.

◆ **reservations** *npl* [doubts] réserves *fpl*.

reserve [rɪ'zɜːv] ◇ *n* **-1.** [gen] réserve *f*; **in ~** en réserve. **-2.** SPORT remplaçant *m*, -e *f*. ◇ *vt* **-1.** [save] garder, réserver. **-2.** [book] réserver. **-3.** [retain]: **to ~ the right to do sthg** se réserver le droit de faire qqch.

reserve bank *n Am* banque *f* de réserve.

reserve currency *n* monnaie *f* de réserve.

reserved [rɪ'zɜːvd] *adj* réservé(e).

reserve price *n Br* prix *m* minimum.

reserve team *n Br* deuxième équipe *f*.

reservist [rɪ'zɜːvɪst] *n* réserviste *m*.

reservoir ['rezəvwɑːr] *n* réservoir *m*.

reset [,riː'set] (*pt & pp* reset, *cont* -ting) ◇ *vt* **-1.** [clock, watch] remettre à l'heure; [meter, controls] remettre à zéro. **-2.** [bone] remettre. **-3.** COMPUT ré-initialiser. ◇ *vi* COMPUT ré-initialiser.

resettle [,riː'setl] ◇ *vt* [land] repeupler; [people] établir, implanter. ◇ *vi* [people] se fixer (ailleurs), s'établir (ailleurs).

resettlement [,riː'setlmənt] *n* [of land] repeuplement *m*; [of people] établissement *m*, implantation *f*.

reshape [,riː'ʃeɪp] *vt* [policy, thinking] réorganiser.

reshuffle [,riː'ʃʌfl] ◇ *n* remaniement *m*; **cabinet ~** remaniement ministériel. ◇ *vt* remanier.

reside [rɪ'zaɪd] *vi fml* résider.

residence ['rezɪdəns] *n* résidence *f*; **in ~** en résidence; **to take up ~** s'installer.

residence permit *n* permis *m* de séjour.

resident ['rezɪdənt] ◇ *adj* résidant(e); [chaplain, doctor] à demeure. ◇ *n* résident *m*, -e *f*.

residential [,rezɪ'denʃl] *adj* [course] qui nécessite de loger sur place; **~ institution** internat *m*.

residential area *n* quartier *m* résidentiel.

residents' association *n* association *f* de quartier.

residual [rɪ'zɪdjʊəl] *adj* restant(e); CHEM résiduel(elle).

residue ['rezɪdjuː] *n* reste *m*; CHEM résidu *m*.

resign [rɪ'zaɪn] ◇ *vt* **-1.** [job] démissionner de. **-2.** [accept calmly]: **to ~ o.s. to** se résigner à. ◇ *vi*: **to ~ (from)** démissionner (de).

resignation [,rezɪg'neɪʃn] *n* **-1.** [from job] démission *f*. **-2.** [calm acceptance] résignation *f*.

resigned [rɪ'zaɪnd] *adj*: **~ (to)** résigné(e) (à).

resilience [rɪ'zɪlɪəns] *n* [of material] élasticité *f*; [of person] ressort *m*.

resilient [rɪ'zɪlɪənt] *adj* [material] élastique; [person] qui a du ressort.

resin ['rezɪn] *n* résine *f*.

resist [rɪ'zɪst] *vt* résister à.

resistance [rɪ'zɪstəns] *n* résistance *f*.

resistant [rɪ'zɪstənt] *adj* **-1.** [opposed]: **to be ~ to** [gen] résister à; [change] s'opposer à. **-2.** [immune]: **~ (to)** rebelle (à).

resistor [rɪ'zɪstər] *n* ELEC résistance *f*.

resit [*n* 'riːsɪt, *vb* ,riː'sɪt] (*pt & pp* -sat, *cont* -ting) *Br* ◇ *n* deuxième session *f*. ◇ *vt* repasser, se représenter à.

resold [,riː'səʊld] *pt & pp* → **resell**.

resolute ['rezəluːt] *adj* résolu(e).

resolutely ['rezəluːtlɪ] *adv* résolument.

resolution [,rezə'luːʃn] *n* résolution *f*.

resolve [rɪ'zɒlv] ◇ *n* (*U*) [determination] résolution *f*. ◇ *vt* **-1.** [decide]: **to ~ (that)** ... décider que ...; **to ~ to do sthg** résoudre OR décider de faire qqch. **-2.** [solve] résoudre.

resonance ['rezənəns] *n* résonance *f*.

resonant ['rezənənt] *adj* résonnant(e).

resonate ['rezəneɪt] *vi* résonner.

resort [rɪ'zɔːt] *n* **-1.** [for holidays] lieu *m* de vacances. **-2.** [recourse] recours *m*; **as a last ~, in the last ~** en dernier ressort OR recours.

◆ **resort to** *vt fus* recourir à, avoir recours à.

resound [rɪ'zaʊnd] *vi* **-1.** [noise] résonner. **-2.** [place]: **to ~ with** retentir de.

resounding [rɪ'zaʊndɪŋ] *adj* retentissant(e).

resource [rɪ'sɔːs] *n* ressource *f*.

resourceful [rɪ'sɔːsful] *adj* plein(e) de ressources, débrouillard(e).

resourcefulness [rɪ'sɔːsfulnɪs] *n* (*U*) ressource *f*.

respect [rɪ'spekt] ◇ *n* **-1.** [gen]: **~ (for)** respect *m* (pour); **to have ~ for sb** avoir du respect à OR pour qqn; **to show ~ for sb** témoigner du respect à OR pour qqn; **with ~** avec respect; **with ~, ...** sauf votre respect, ... **-2.** [aspect]: **in this** OR **that ~** à cet égard; **in every ~** à tous égards; **in some ~s** à certains égards. ◇ *vt* respecter; **to ~ sb for sthg** respecter qqn pour qqch.

◆ **respects** *mpl* respects, hommages *mpl*; **to pay one's last ~s to sb** rendre un dernier hommage à qqn.

◆ **with respect to** *prep* en ce qui concerne, quant à.

respectability [rɪ,spektə'bɪlətɪ] *n* respectabilité *f*.

respectable [rɪ'spektəbl] *adj* **-1.** [morally correct] respectable. **-2.** [adequate] raisonnable, honorable.

respectably [rɪ'spektəblɪ] *adv* [correctly] convenablement.

respectful [rɪ'spektfʊl] *adj* respectueux(euse).

respectfully [rɪ'spektfʊlɪ] *adv* avec respect, respectueusement.

respective [rɪ'spektɪv] *adj* respectif(ive).

respectively [rɪ'spektɪvlɪ] *adv* respectivement.

respiration [,respə'reɪʃn] *n* respiration *f*.

respirator ['respəreɪtər] *n* respirateur *m*.

respiratory [*Br* rɪ'spɪrətrɪ, *Am* 'respərətɔːrɪ] *adj* respiratoire.

respire [rɪ'spaɪər] *vi* respirer.

respite ['respaɪt] *n* répit *m*.

resplendent [rɪ'splendənt] *adj* resplendissant(e).

respond [rɪ'spɒnd] ◇ *vt* répondre. ◇ *vi:* **to ~ (to)** répondre (à).

response [rɪ'spɒns] *n* réponse *f*; **in ~** en réponse.

responsibility [rɪ,spɒnsə'bɪlətɪ] (*pl* **-ies**) *n:* **~ (for)** responsabilité *f* (de); **to accept** OR **take ~ for sthg** prendre OR accepter la responsabilité de qqch.

responsible [rɪ'spɒnsəbl] *adj* **-1.** [gen]: **~ (for sthg)** responsable (de qqch); **to be ~ to sb** être responsable devant qqn. **-2.** [job, position] qui comporte des responsabilités.

responsibly [rɪ'spɒnsəblɪ] *adv* de façon responsable.

responsive [rɪ'spɒnsɪv] *adj* **-1.** [quick to react] qui réagit bien. **-2.** [aware]: **~ (to)** attentif(ive) (à).

respray [*n* 'riːspreɪ, *vb* ,riː'spreɪ] ◇ *n:* **to give a car a ~** repeindre une voiture. ◇ *vt* repeindre.

rest [rest] ◇ *n* **-1.** [remainder]: **the ~ (of)** le reste (de); **the ~ (of them)** les autres *mfpl*. **-2.** [relaxation, break] repos *m*; **to have a ~** se reposer. **-3.** [support] support *m*, appui *m*. **-4.** *phr:* **to come to ~** s'arrêter. ◇ *vt* **-1.** [relax] faire OR laisser reposer. **-2.** [support]: **to ~ sthg on/against** appuyer qqch sur/contre. **-3.** *phr:* **~ assured** soyez certain(e).

◇ *vi* **-1.** [relax] se reposer. **-2.** [be supported]: **to ~ on/against** s'appuyer sur/contre. **-3.** *fig* [argument, result]: **to ~ on** reposer sur; **the responsibility ~s with you** c'est vous qui êtes responsable; **the decision ~s with you** il vous appartient de décider.

rest area *n Am* & *Austr* aire *f* de repos.

restart [,riː'staːt] ◇ *vt* [engine] remettre en marche; [work] reprendre, recommencer. ◇ *vi* **-1.** [play, film] reprendre. **-2.** [engine] se remettre en marche.

restate [,riː'steɪt] *vt* répéter.

restaurant ['restərɒnt] *n* restaurant *m*.

restaurant car *n Br* wagon-restaurant *m*.

rest cure *n* cure *f* de repos.

rested ['restɪd] *adj* reposé(e).

restful ['restfʊl] *adj* reposant(e).

rest home *n* maison *f* de repos.

resting place ['restɪŋ-] *n* lieu *m* de repos.

restitution [,restɪ'tjuːʃn] *n* [returning] restitution *f*; [compensation] réparation *f*.

restive ['restɪv] *adj* agité(e).

restless ['restlɪs] *adj* agité(e).

restlessly ['restlɪslɪ] *adv* avec agitation.

restock [,riː'stɒk] ◇ *vt* réapprovisionner. ◇ *vi* se réapprovisionner.

restoration [,restə'reɪʃn] *n* **-1.** [of law and order, monarchy] rétablissement *m*. **-2.** [renovation] restauration *f*.

restorative [rɪ'stɒrətɪv] *adj* fortifiant(e).

restore [rɪ'stɔːr] *vt* **-1.** [law and order, monarchy] rétablir; [confidence] redonner. **-2.** [renovate] restaurer. **-3.** [give back] rendre, restituer.

restorer [rɪ'stɔːrər] *n* [person] restaurateur *m*, -trice *f*.

restrain [rɪ'streɪn] *vt* [person, crowd] contenir, retenir; [emotions] maîtriser, contenir; **to ~ o.s. from doing sthg** se retenir de faire qqch.

restrained [rɪ'streɪnd] *adj* [tone] mesuré(e); [person] qui se domine.

restraint [rɪ'streɪnt] *n* **-1.** [restriction] restriction *f*, entrave *f*. **-2.** (*U*) [self-control] mesure *f*, retenue *f*.

restrict [rɪ'strɪkt] *vt* restreindre, limiter; **to ~ o.s. to** se limiter à.

restricted [rɪ'strɪktɪd] *adj* **-1.** [limited, small] limité(e). **-2.** [not public - document] confidentiel(ielle); [- area] interdit(e).

restriction [rɪ'strɪkʃn] *n* restriction *f*, limitation *f*; **to place ~s on sthg** apporter des restrictions à qqch.

restrictive [rɪ'strɪktɪv] *adj* restrictif(ive).

restrictive practices *npl* pratiques *fpl* restrictives.

rest room *n Am* toilettes *fpl*.

restructure [ˌriːˈstrʌktʃəʳ] *vt* restructurer.

result [rɪˈzʌlt] ◇ *n* résultat *m*; **as a ~** en conséquence; **as a ~ of** [as a consequence of] à la suite de; [because of] à cause de. ◇ *vi* **-1.** [cause]: **to ~ in** aboutir à. **-2.** [be caused]: **to ~ (from)** résulter (de).

resultant [rɪˈzʌltənt] *adj fml* qui (en) résulte.

resume [rɪˈzjuːm] *vt & vi* reprendre.

résumé [ˈrezjuːmeɪ] *n* **-1.** [summary] résumé *m*. **-2.** *Am* [curriculum vitae] curriculum vitae *m inv*, CV *m*.

resumption [rɪˈzʌmpʃn] *n* reprise *f*.

resurface [ˌriːˈsɜːfɪs] ◇ *vt* [road] regoudronner. ◇ *vi* [rivalries, problems] réapparaître.

resurgence [rɪˈsɜːdʒəns] *n* réapparition *f*.

resurrect [ˌrezəˈrekt] *vt fig* ressusciter.

resurrection [ˌrezəˈrekʃn] *n fig* résurrection *f*.

◆ **Resurrection** *n*: **the Resurrection** la Résurrection.

resuscitation [rɪˌsʌsɪˈteɪʃn] *n* réanimation *f*.

retail [ˈriːteɪl] ◇ *n* (U) détail *m*. ◇ *adv* au détail.

retailer [ˈriːteɪləʳ] *n* détaillant *m*, -e *f*.

retail outlet *n* magasin *m* de détail.

retail price *n* prix *m* de détail.

retail price index *n Br* indice *m* des prix.

retain [rɪˈteɪn] *vt* conserver.

retainer [rɪˈteɪnəʳ] *n* **-1.** [fee] provision *f*. **-2.** [servant] serviteur *m*.

retaining wall [rɪˈteɪnɪŋ-] *n* mur *m* de soutènement.

retaliate [rɪˈtælɪeɪt] *vi* rendre la pareille, se venger.

retaliation [rɪˌtælɪˈeɪʃn] *n* (U) vengeance *f*, représailles *fpl*.

retarded [rɪˈtɑːdɪd] *adj* retardé(e).

retch [retʃ] *vi* avoir des haut-le-cœur.

retention [rɪˈtenʃn] *n* maintien *m*, conservation *f*; MED rétention *f*.

retentive [rɪˈtentɪv] *adj* [memory] fidèle.

rethink [*n* ˈriːθɪŋk, *vb* ˌriːˈθɪŋk] (*pt & pp* **-thought** [-ˈθɔːt]) ◇ *n*: **to have a ~ (on** OR **about sthg)** repenser (qqch). ◇ *vt & vi* repenser.

reticence [ˈretɪsəns] *n* réticence *f*.

reticent [ˈretɪsənt] *adj* peu communicatif(ive); **to be ~ about sthg** ne pas beaucoup parler de qqch.

retina [ˈretɪnə] (*pl* **retinas** OR **-nae** [-niː]) *n* rétine *f*.

retinue [ˈretɪnjuː] *n* suite *f*.

retire [rɪˈtaɪəʳ] *vi* **-1.** [from work] prendre sa retraite. **-2.** [withdraw] se retirer. **-3.** [to bed] (aller) se coucher.

retired [rɪˈtaɪəd] *adj* à la retraite, retraité(e).

retirement [rɪˈtaɪəmənt] *n* retraite *f*.

retirement age *n* âge *m* de la retraite.

retirement pension *n* retraite *f*.

retiring [rɪˈtaɪərɪŋ] *adj* **-1.** [shy] réservé(e). **-2.** [from work] sur le point de prendre sa retraite.

retort [rɪˈtɔːt] ◇ *n* [sharp reply] riposte *f*. ◇ *vt* riposter.

retouch [ˌriːˈtʌtʃ] *vt* retoucher.

retrace [rɪˈtreɪs] *vt*: **to ~ one's steps** revenir sur ses pas.

retract [rɪˈtrækt] ◇ *vt* **-1.** [statement] rétracter. **-2.** [undercarriage] rentrer, escamoter; [claws] rentrer. ◇ *vi* [undercarriage] rentrer, s'escamoter.

retractable [rɪˈtræktəbl] *adj* escamotable.

retraction [rɪˈtrækʃn] *n* [of statement] rétractation *f*.

retrain [ˌriːˈtreɪn] ◇ *vt* recycler. ◇ *vi* se recycler.

retraining [ˌriːˈtreɪnɪŋ] *n* recyclage *m*.

retread [*n* ˈriːtred, *vb* ˌriːˈtred] ◇ *n* pneu *m* rechapé. ◇ *vt* rechaper.

retreat [rɪˈtriːt] ◇ *n* retraite *f*; **to beat a hasty ~** partir en vitesse. ◇ *vi* [move away] se retirer; MIL battre en retraite.

retrenchment [rɪˈtrentʃmənt] *n* [of spending] réduction *f*.

retrial [ˌriːˈtraɪəl] *n* nouveau procès *m*.

retribution [ˌretrɪˈbjuːʃn] *n* châtiment *m*.

retrieval [rɪˈtriːvl] *n* (U) COMPUT recherche *f* et extraction *f*.

retrieve [rɪˈtriːv] *vt* **-1.** [get back] récupérer. **-2.** COMPUT rechercher et extraire. **-3.** [situation] sauver.

retriever [rɪˈtriːvəʳ] *n* [dog] retriever *m*.

retroactive [ˌretrəʊˈæktɪv] *adj* rétroactif(ive).

retrograde [ˈretrəgreɪd] *adj* rétrograde.

retrogressive [ˌretrəˈgresɪv] *adj* rétrograde.

retrospect [ˈretrəspekt] *n*: **in ~** après coup.

retrospective [ˌretrəˈspektɪv] ◇ *adj* **-1.** [mood, look] rétrospectif(ive). **-2.** JUR [law, pay rise] rétroactif(ive). ◇ *n* rétrospective *f*.

retrospectively [ˌretrəˈspektɪvlɪ] *adv* **-1.** [looking back] rétrospectivement. **-2.** JUR rétroactivement.

return [rɪˈtɜːn] ◇ *n* **-1.** (U) [arrival back, giving back] retour *m*. **-2.** TENNIS renvoi *m*. **-3.** *Br* [ticket] aller (et) retour *m*. **-4.** [profit] rapport m, rendement m. ◇ comp [journey] de retour. ◇ vt **-1.** [gen] rendre; [a loan] rembourser; [library book] rapporter. **-2.** [send back] renvoyer. **-3.** [replace] remettre. **-4.** POL élire. ◇ vi [come back] revenir; [go back] retourner.

◆ **returns** npl COMM recettes fpl; **many happy ~s (of the day)!** bon anniversaire!

◆ **in return** adv en retour, en échange.

◆ **in return for** prep en échange de.

returnable [rɪ'tɜːnəbl] adj [bottle] consigné(e).

returning officer [rɪ'tɜːnɪŋ-] n Br responsable mf du scrutin.

return key n COMPUT touche f entrée.

return match n match m retour.

return ticket n Br aller (et) retour m.

reunification [ˌriːjuːnɪfɪ'keɪʃn] n réunification f.

reunion [ˌriː'juːnjən] n réunion f.

Reunion [ˌriː'juːnjən] n: ~ **(Island)** (l'île f de) la Réunion; **in ~** à la Réunion.

reunite [ˌriːjuː'naɪt] vt: **to be ~d with sb** retrouver qqn.

reupholster [ˌriːʌp'həʊlstər] vt recouvrir.

reusable [riː'juːzəbl] adj réutilisable.

reuse [n ˌriː'juːs, vb ˌriː'juːz] ◇ n réutilisation f. ◇ vt réutiliser.

rev [rev] (pt & pp **-ved**, cont **-ving**) inf ◇ n (abbr of **revolution**) tour m. ◇ vt: **to ~ the engine (up)** emballer le moteur. ◇ vi: **to ~ (up)** s'emballer.

revalue [ˌriː'væljuː] vt FIN réévaluer.

revamp [ˌriː'væmp] vt inf [system, department] réorganiser; [house] retaper.

rev counter n compte-tours m inv.

reveal [rɪ'viːl] vt révéler.

revealing [rɪ'viːlɪŋ] adj **-1.** [clothes - low-cut] décolleté(e); [- transparent] qui laisse deviner le corps. **-2.** [comment] révélateur(trice).

reveille [Br rɪ'vælɪ Am 'revəlɪ] n réveil m.

revel ['revl] (Br pt & pp **-led**, cont **-ling**, Am pt & pp **-ed**, cont **-ing**) vi: **to ~ in sthg** se délecter de qqch.

revelation [ˌrevə'leɪʃn] n révélation f.

reveller Br, **reveler** Am ['revələr] n fêtard m, -e f.

revelry ['revlrɪ] n (U) festivités fpl.

revenge [rɪ'vendʒ] ◇ n vengeance f; **to take ~ (on sb)** se venger (de qqn). ◇ comp [killing, attack] suscité(e) par la vengeance. ◇ vt venger; **to ~ o.s. on sb** se venger de qqn.

revenue ['revənjuː] n revenu m.

reverberate [rɪ'vɜːbəreɪt] vi retentir, se répercuter; fig avoir des répercussions.

reverberations [rɪˌvɜːbə'reɪʃnz] npl réverbérations fpl; fig répercussions fpl.

revere [rɪ'vɪər] vt révérer, vénérer.

reverence ['revərəns] n révérence f, vénération f.

Reverend ['revərənd] n révérend m.

Reverend Mother n révérende mère f.

reverent ['revərənt] adj respectueux(euse).

reverential [ˌrevə'renʃl] adj révérencieux(ieuse).

reverie ['revərɪ] n rêverie f.

revers [rɪ'vɪə] (pl inv) n revers m.

reversal [rɪ'vɜːsl] n **-1.** [of policy, decision] revirement m. **-2.** [ill fortune] revers m de fortune.

reverse [rɪ'vɜːs] ◇ adj [order, process] inverse. ◇ n **-1.** AUT: ~ **(gear)** marche f arrière; **to be in ~** être en marche arrière; **to go into ~** faire marche arrière. **-2.** [opposite]: **the ~** le contraire. **-3.** [back]: **the ~** [of paper] verso m, dos m; [of coin] revers m. ◇ vt **-1.** [order, positions] inverser; [decision, trend] renverser. **-2.** [turn over] retourner. **-3.** Br TELEC: **to ~ the charges** téléphoner en P.C.V. ◇ vi AUT faire marche arrière; **to ~ into a wall** rentrer dans un mur en faisant marche arrière.

reverse-charge call n Br appel m en P.C.V.

reversible [rɪ'vɜːsəbl] adj réversible.

reversing light [rɪ'vɜːsɪŋ-] n Br feu m de marche arrière.

reversion [rɪ'vɜːʃn] n (U) retour m.

revert [rɪ'vɜːt] vi: **to ~ to** retourner à.

review [rɪ'vjuː] ◇ n **-1.** [of salary, spending] révision f; [of situation] examen m; **salaries come up for ~ in December** les salaires doivent être révisés en décembre; **the situation is under ~** on est en train d'examiner la situation. **-2.** [of book, play etc] critique f, compte rendu m. ◇ vt **-1.** [salary] réviser; [situation] examiner. **-2.** [book, play etc] faire la critique de. **-3.** [troops] passer en revue. **-4.** Am [study again] réviser.

reviewer [rɪ'vjuːər] n critique mf.

revile [rɪ'vaɪl] vt injurier.

revise [rɪ'vaɪz] ◇ vt **-1.** [reconsider] modifier. **-2.** [rewrite] corriger. **-3.** Br [study again] réviser. ◇ vi Br: **to ~ (for)** réviser (pour).

revised [rɪ'vaɪzd] adj [estimate, figure] nouveau(elle); [version] revu(e) et corrigé(e).

revision [rɪ'vɪʒn] n révision f.

revisionist [rɪ'vɪʒnɪst] ◇ adj révisionniste. ◇ n révisionniste mf.

revisit [,riː'vɪzɪt] vt visiter de nouveau.

revitalize, -ise [,riː'vaɪtəlaɪz] vt revitaliser.

revival [rɪ'vaɪvl] n [of economy, trade] reprise f; [of interest] regain m.

revive [rɪ'vaɪv] ◇ vt -1. [person] ranimer. -2. fig [economy] relancer; [interest] faire renaître; [tradition] rétablir; [musical, play] reprendre; [memories] ranimer, raviver. ◇ vi -1. [person] reprendre connaissance. -2. fig [economy] repartir, reprendre; [hopes] renaître.

revoke [rɪ'vəʊk] vt [law] abroger; [order] annuler; [licence] retirer.

revolt [rɪ'vəʊlt] ◇ n révolte f. ◇ vt révolter, dégoûter. ◇ vi se révolter.

revolting [rɪ'vəʊltɪŋ] adj dégoûtant(e); [smell] infect(e).

revolution [,revə'luːʃn] n -1. [gen] révolution f. -2. TECH tour m, révolution f.

revolutionary [,revə'luːʃnərɪ] (pl -ies) ◇ adj révolutionnaire. ◇ n révolutionnaire mf.

revolutionize, -ise [,revə'luːʃənaɪz] vt révolutionner.

revolve [rɪ'vɒlv] vi: to ~ (around) tourner (autour de).

revolver [rɪ'vɒlvə'] n revolver m.

revolving [rɪ'vɒlvɪŋ] adj tournant(e); [chair] pivotant(e).

revolving door n tambour m.

revue [rɪ'vjuː] n revue f.

revulsion [rɪ'vʌlʃn] n répugnance f.

reward [rɪ'wɔːd] ◇ n récompense f. ◇ vt: to ~ sb (for/with sthg) récompenser qqn (de/par qqch).

rewarding [rɪ'wɔːdɪŋ] adj [job] qui donne de grandes satisfactions; [book] qui vaut la peine d'être lu(e).

rewind [,riː'waɪnd] (pt & pp **rewound**) vt [tape] rembobiner.

rewire [,riː'waɪə'] vt [house] refaire l'installation électrique de.

reword [,riː'wɜːd] vt reformuler.

rework [,riː'wɜːk] vt retravailler.

rewound [,riː'waʊnd] pt & pp → **rewind**.

rewrite [,riː'raɪt] (pt **rewrote** [,riː'rəʊt], pp **rewritten** [,riː'rɪtn]) vt récrire.

REX (abbr of **real-time executive routine**) n superviseur en temps réel.

Reykjavik ['rekjəvɪk] n Reykjavik.

RFC (abbr of **Rugby Football Club**) n fédération de rugby.

RGN (abbr of **registered general nurse**) n en

Grande-Bretagne, infirmier ou infirmière diplômé(e) d'État.

Rh (abbr of **rhesus**) Rh.

rhapsody ['ræpsədɪ] (pl -ies) n rhapsodie f; to go into rhapsodies about sthg s'extasier sur qqch.

Rheims = Reims.

Rhesus ['riːsəs] n: ~ **positive/negative** rhésus m positif/négatif.

rhetoric ['retərɪk] n rhétorique f.

rhetorical question [rɪ'tɒrɪkl-] n question f pour la forme.

rheumatic [ruː'mætɪk] adj [pain, joint] rhumatismal(e); [person] rhumatisant(e).

rheumatism ['ruːmətɪzm] n (U) rhumatisme m.

rheumatoid arthritis ['ruːmətɔɪd-] n polyarthrite f rhumatoïde.

Rhine [raɪn] n: the ~ le Rhin.

Rhineland ['raɪnlænd] n Rhénanie f.

rhinestone ['raɪnstəʊn] n faux diamant m.

rhino ['raɪnəʊ] (pl inv OR -s), **rhinoceros** [raɪ'nɒsərəs] (pl inv OR -es) n rhinocéros m.

Rhode Island [rəʊd-] n Rhode Island m; in ~ dans le Rhode Island.

Rhodes [rəʊdz] n Rhodes.

Rhodesia [rəʊ'diːʃə] n Rhodésie f; in ~ en Rhodésie.

Rhodesian [rəʊ'diːʃn] ◇ adj rhodésien(ienne). ◇ n Rhodésien m, -ienne f.

rhododendron [,rəʊdə'dendrən] n rhododendron m.

Rhône [rəʊn] n: the (River) ~ le Rhône.

rhubarb ['ruːbɑːb] n rhubarbe f.

rhyme [raɪm] ◇ n -1. [word, technique] rime f; in ~ en vers. -2. [poem] poème m. ◇ vi: to ~ (with) rimer (avec).

rhyming slang ['raɪmɪŋ-] n Br sorte d'argot traditionnellement employé par les Cockneys qui consiste à remplacer un mot par un groupe de mots choisis pour la rime.

rhythm ['rɪðm] n rythme m.

rhythm and blues n rhythm and blues m.

rhythmic(al) ['rɪðmɪk(l)] adj rythmique.

RI ◇ n (abbr of **religious instruction**) instruction f réligieuse. ◇ abbr of **Rhode Island**.

rib [rɪb] n -1. ANAT côte f. -2. [of umbrella] baleine f; [of structure] membrure f.

ribald ['rɪbəld] adj paillard(e).

ribbed [rɪbd] adj [jumper, fabric] à côtes.

ribbon ['rɪbən] n ruban m.

rib cage n cage f thoracique.

rice [raɪs] n riz m.

rice field *n* rizière *f*.

rice paper *n* papier *m* de riz.

rice pudding *n* riz *m* au lait.

rich [rɪtʃ] ◇ *adj* [clothes, fabrics] somptueux(euse); **to be ~ in** être riche en. ◇ *npl*: **the ~ les riches** *mpl*.
◆ **riches** *npl* richesses *fpl*, richesse *f*.

richly ['rɪtʃlɪ] *adv* **-1.** [rewarded] largement; [provided] très bien; **~ deserved** bien mérité. **-2.** [sumptuously] richement.

richness ['rɪtʃnɪs] *n* (*U*) richesse *f*.

Richter scale ['rɪktə-] *n*: **the ~** l'échelle *f* de Richter.

rickets ['rɪkɪts] *n* (*U*) rachitisme *m*.

rickety ['rɪkətɪ] *adj* branlant(e).

rickshaw ['rɪkʃɔː] *n* pousse-pousse *m inv*.

ricochet ['rɪkəʃeɪ] (*pt* & *pp* **-ed** OR **-ted**, *cont* **-ing** OR **-ting**) ◇ *n* ricochet *m*. ◇ *vi*: **to ~** (**off**) ricocher (sur).

rid [rɪd] (*pt* **rid** OR **-ded**, *pp* **rid**, *cont* **-ding**) ◇ *adj*: **to be ~ of** être débarrassé(e) de. ◇ *vt*: **to ~ sb/sthg of** débarrasser qqn/qqch de; **to get ~ of** se débarrasser de.

riddance ['rɪdəns] *n inf*: **good ~!** bon débarras!

ridden ['rɪdn] *pp* → **ride**.

riddle ['rɪdl] *n* énigme *f*.

riddled ['rɪdld] *adj*: **to be ~ with** être criblé(e) de.

ride [raɪd] (*pt* **rode**, *pp* **ridden**) ◇ *n* promenade *f*, tour *m*; **to go for a ~** [on horse] faire une promenade à cheval; [on bike] faire une promenade à vélo; [in car] faire un tour en voiture; **to take sb for a ~** *inf fig* faire marcher qqn.
◇ *vt* **-1.** [travel on]: **to ~ a horse/a bicycle** monter à cheval/en vélo. **-2.** *Am* [travel in - bus, train, elevator] prendre. **-3.** [distance] parcourir, faire.
◇ *vi* [on horseback] monter à cheval, faire du cheval; [on bicycle] faire de la bicyclette OR du vélo; **to ~ in a car/bus** aller en voiture/bus.
◆ **ride up** *vi* remonter.

rider ['raɪdə-] *n* [of horse] cavalier *m*, -ière *f*; [of bicycle] cycliste *mf*; [of motorbike] motocycliste *mf*.

ridge [rɪdʒ] *n* **-1.** [of mountain, roof] crête *f*, arête *f*. **-2.** [on surface] strie *f*.

ridicule ['rɪdɪkjuːl] ◇ *n* ridicule *m*. ◇ *vt* ridiculiser.

ridiculous [rɪ'dɪkjʊləs] *adj* ridicule.

ridiculously [rɪ'dɪkjʊləslɪ] *adv* ridiculement.

riding ['raɪdɪŋ] ◇ *n* équitation *f*; **to go ~** faire de l'équitation OR du cheval. ◇ *comp* d'équitation.

riding crop *n* cravache *f*.

riding habit *n* habit *m* d'amazone.

riding school *n* école *f* d'équitation.

rife [raɪf] *adj* répandu(e); **the city was ~ with rumours** des bruits couraient dans toute la ville.

riffraff ['rɪfræf] *n* racaille *f*.

rifle ['raɪfl] ◇ *n* fusil *m*. ◇ *vt* [drawer, bag] vider.
◆ **rifle through** *vt fus* fouiller dans.

rifle range *n* [indoor] stand *m* de tir; [outdoor] champ *m* de tir.

rift [rɪft] *n* **-1.** GEOL fissure *f*. **-2.** [quarrel] désaccord *m*.

Rift Valley *n*: **the ~** le Rift Valley.

rig [rɪg] (*pt* & *pp* **-ged**, *cont* **-ging**) ◇ *n*: (**oil**) **~** [on land] derrick *m*; [at sea] plate-forme *f* de forage. ◇ *vt* [match, election] truquer.
◆ **rig up** *vt sep* installer avec les moyens du bord.

rigging ['rɪgɪŋ] *n* [of ship] gréement *m*.

right [raɪt] ◇ *adj* **-1.** [correct - answer, time] juste, exact(e); [- decision, direction, idea] bon (bonne); **to be ~** (**about**) avoir raison (au sujet de); **to get a question ~** donner la bonne réponse; **to get one's facts ~** être sûr de ce qu'on avance. **-2.** [morally correct] bien (*inv*); **to be ~ to do sthg** avoir raison de faire qqch. **-3.** [appropriate] qui convient. **-4.** [not left] droit(e). **-5.** *Br inf* [complete] véritable.
◇ *n* **-1.** (*U*) [moral correctness] bien *m*; **to be in the ~** avoir raison. **-2.** [entitlement, claim] droit *m*; **by ~s** en toute justice; **in one's own ~** soi-même. **-3.** [not left] droite *f*.
◇ *adv* **-1.** [correctly] correctement. **-2.** [not left] à droite. **-3.** [emphatic use]: **~ down/up** tout en bas/en haut; **~ here** ici (même); **~ in the middle** en plein milieu; **go ~ to the end of the street** allez tout au bout de la rue; **to turn ~ round** se retourner; **~ after Christmas** tout de suite après Noël; **~ now** tout de suite; **~ away** immédiatement.
◇ *vt* **-1.** [injustice, wrong] réparer. **-2.** [ship] redresser.
◇ *excl* bon!
◆ **Right** *n* POL: **the Right** la droite.

right angle *n* angle *m* droit; **to be at ~s** (**to**) faire un angle droit (avec).

righteous ['raɪtʃəs] *adj* [person] droit(e); [indignation] justifié(e).

righteousness ['raɪtʃəsnɪs] *n* vertu *f*.

rightful ['raɪtful] *adj* légitime.

rightfully ['raɪtfulɪ] *adv* légitimement.

right-hand *adj* de droite; **~ side** droite *f*, côté *m* droit.

right-hand drive *adj* avec conduite à droite.

right-handed [-'hændɪd] *adj* [person] droitier(ière).

right-hand man *n* bras *m* droit.

rightly ['raɪtlɪ] *adv* -1. [answer, believe] correctement. -2. [behave] bien. -3. [angry, worried etc] à juste titre.

right-minded [-'maɪndɪd] *adj* sensé(e).

rightness ['raɪtnɪs] *n* -1. [correctness] justesse *f*. -2. [moral correctness] droiture *f*.

righto ['raɪtəʊ] *excl inf* d'accord!

right of way *n* -1. AUT priorité *f*. -2. [access] droit *m* de passage.

right-on *adj inf* branché(e).

rights issue *n* émission *f* de droits de souscription.

right-thinking [-'θɪŋkɪŋ] *adj* sensé(e).

right wing *n*: **the ~** la droite.
◆ **right-wing** *adj* de droite.

right-winger *n* POL personne *f* qui est de droite.

rigid ['rɪdʒɪd] *adj* -1. [gen] rigide. -2. [harsh] strict(e).

rigidity [rɪ'dʒɪdətɪ] *n* rigidité *f*.

rigidly ['rɪdʒɪdlɪ] *adv* -1. [gen] rigidement. -2. [harshly] strictement.

rigmarole ['rɪgmərəʊl] *n pej* -1. [process] comédie *f*. -2. [story] galimatias *m*.

rigor *Am* = **rigour**.

rigor mortis [-'mɔːtɪs] *n* rigidité *f* cadavérique.

rigorous ['rɪgərəs] *adj* rigoureux(euse).

rigorously ['rɪgərəslɪ] *adv* rigoureusement.

rigour *Br*, **rigor** *Am* ['rɪgə*] *n* rigueur *f*.

rig-out *n Br inf* accoutrement *m*.

rile [raɪl] *vt* agacer.

rim [rɪm] *n* [of container] bord *m*; [of wheel] jante *f*; [of spectacles] monture *f*.

rind [raɪnd] *n* [of fruit] peau *f*; [of cheese] croûte *f*; [of bacon] couenne *f*.

ring [rɪŋ] (*pt* **rang**, *pp* **rung** *vt senses 1 & 2 & vi*, *pt & pp* **ringed** *vt sense 3 only*) ◇ *n* -1. [telephone call]: **to give sb a ~** donner OR passer un coup de téléphone à qqn. -2. [sound of bell] sonnerie *f*; **the name has a familiar ~** ce nom me dit quelque chose. -3. [circular object] anneau *m*; [on finger] bague *f*; [for napkin] rond *m*. -4. [of people, trees etc] cercle *m*. -5. [for boxing] ring *m*. -6. [of criminals, spies] réseau *m*.
◇ *vt* -1. *Br* [make phone call to] téléphoner à, appeler. -2. [bell] (faire) sonner; **to ~ the doorbell** sonner à la porte. -3. [draw a circle round, surround] entourer.

◇ *vi* -1. *Br* [make phone call] téléphoner. -2. [bell, telephone, person] sonner; **to ~ for sb** sonner qqn. -3. [resound]: **to ~ with** résonner de. -4. *phr*: **to ~ true** sonner juste.
◆ **ring back** *vt sep & Br* rappeler.
◆ **ring off** *vi Br* raccrocher.
◆ **ring out** *vi* -1. [sound] retentir. -2. *Br* TELEC téléphoner à l'extérieur.
◆ **ring up** *vt sep Br* téléphoner à, appeler.

ring binder *n* classeur *m* à anneaux.

ringer ['rɪŋə*] *n*: **to be a dead ~ for sb** être le sosie de qqn.

ring finger *n* annulaire *m*.

ringing ['rɪŋɪŋ] ◇ *adj* retentissant(e). ◇ *n* [of bell] sonnerie *f*; [in ears] tintement *m*.

ringing tone *n* sonnerie *f*.

ringleader ['rɪŋ,liːdə*] *n* chef *m*.

ringlet ['rɪŋlɪt] *n* anglaise *f*.

ringmaster ['rɪŋ,mɑːstə*] *n* présentateur *m*.

ring road *n Br* (route *f*) périphérique *m*.

ringside ['rɪŋsaɪd] ◇ *n*: **the ~** le premier rang. ◇ *comp* [seat] au premier rang.

ringway ['rɪŋweɪ] *n Br* (route *f*) périphérique *m*.

ringworm ['rɪŋwɜːm] *n* teigne *f*.

rink [rɪŋk] *n* [for ice skating] patinoire *f*; [for roller-skating] skating *m*.

rinse [rɪns] ◇ *n*: **to give sthg a ~** rincer qqch. ◇ *vt* rincer; **to ~ one's mouth out** se rincer la bouche.

Rio (de Janeiro) [,riːəʊ(dədʒə'nɪərəʊ)] *n* Rio de Janeiro.

Rio Grande [,riːəʊ'grændɪ] *n*: **the ~** le Rio Grande.

Rio Negro [,riːəʊ'neɪgrəʊ] *n*: **the ~** le Rio Negro.

riot ['raɪət] ◇ *n* émeute *f*; **to run ~** se déchaîner. ◇ *vi* participer à une émeute.

rioter ['raɪətə*] *n* émeutier *m*, -ière *f*.

rioting ['raɪətɪŋ] *n* (U) émeutes *fpl*.

riotous ['raɪətəs] *adj* [crowd] tapageur(euse); [behaviour] séditieux(ieuse); [party] bruyant(e).

riot police *npl* ≃ C.R.S. *mpl*.

riot shield *n* bouclier *m* anti-émeute.

rip [rɪp] (*pt & pp* **-ped**, *cont* **-ping**) ◇ *n* déchirure *f*, accroc *m*. ◇ *vt* -1. [tear] déchirer. -2. [remove violently] arracher. ◇ *vi* se déchirer.
◆ **rip off** *vt sep inf* -1. [person] arnaquer. -2. [product, idea] copier.
◆ **rip up** *vt sep* déchirer.

RIP (*abbr of* **rest in peace**) qu'il/elle repose en paix.

ripcord ['rɪpkɔːd] *n* poignée *f* d'ouverture.

ripe [raɪp] *adj* mûr(e).

ripen ['raɪpn] *vt & vi* mûrir.

ripeness ['raɪpnɪs] *n* maturité *f*.

rip-off *n inf*: that's a ~! c'est de l'escroquerie OR de l'arnaque!

ripple ['rɪpl] ◇ *n* ondulation *f*, ride *f*; a ~ of applause des applaudissements discrets. ◇ *vt* rider.

rip-roaring *adj inf* [party] de tous les diables; [success] monstre.

rise [raɪz] (*pt* rose, *pp* risen ['rɪzn]) ◇ *n* -1. *Br* [increase] augmentation *f*, hausse *f*; [in temperature] élévation *f*, hausse *f*. -2. *Br* [increase in salary] augmentation *f* (de salaire). -3. [to power, fame] ascension *f*. -4. [slope] côte *f*, pente *f*. -5. *phr*: to give ~ to donner lieu à. ◇ *vi* -1. [move upwards] s'élever, monter; to ~ to power arriver au pouvoir; to ~ to fame devenir célèbre; to ~ to a challenge/to the occasion se montrer à la hauteur d'un défi/de la situation. -2. [from chair, bed] se lever. -3. [increase - gen] monter, augmenter; [- voice, level] s'élever. -4. [rebel] se soulever.
♦ **rise above** *vt fus* [problem] surmonter; [argument] ne pas faire cas de.

riser ['raɪzər] *n*: early ~ lève-tôt *mf inv*; late ~ lève-tard *mf inv*.

risible ['rɪzəbl] *adj* risible.

rising ['raɪzɪŋ] ◇ *adj* -1. [ground, tide] montant(e). -2. [prices, inflation, temperature] en hausse. -3. [star, politician etc] à l'avenir prometteur. ◇ *n* [revolt] soulèvement *m*.

rising damp *n* humidité *f* (qui monte du sol).

risk [rɪsk] ◇ *n* risque *m*, danger *m*; at one's own ~ à ses risques et périls; to run the ~ of doing sthg courir le risque de faire qqch; to take a ~ prendre un risque; at ~ en danger; at the ~ of au risque de. ◇ *vt* [health, life etc] risquer; to ~ doing sthg courir le risque OR risquer de faire qqch; to ~ it tenter OR risquer le coup.

risk capital *n* capital *m* à risque.

risk-taking *n* (U) le fait de prendre des risques.

risky ['rɪskɪ] (*compar* -ier, *superl* -iest) *adj* risqué(e).

risotto [rɪ'zɒtəʊ] (*pl* -s) *n* risotto *m*.

risqué ['riːskeɪ] *adj* risqué(e), osé(e).

rissole ['rɪsəʊl] *n Br* rissole *f*.

rite [raɪt] *n* rite *m*.

ritual ['rɪtʃʊəl] ◇ *adj* rituel(elle). ◇ *n* rituel *m*.

rival ['raɪvl] (*Br pt & pp* -led, *cont* -ling, *Am pt & pp* -ed, *cont* -ing) ◇ *adj* rival(e),

concurrent(e). ◇ *n* rival *m*, -e *f*. ◇ *vt* rivaliser avec.

rivalry ['raɪvlrɪ] *n* rivalité *f*.

river ['rɪvər] *n* rivière *f*, fleuve *m*.

river bank *n* berge *f*, rive *f*.

riverbed ['rɪvəbed] *n* lit *m* (de rivière OR de fleuve).

riverside ['rɪvəsaɪd] *n*: the ~ le bord de la rivière OR du fleuve.

rivet ['rɪvɪt] ◇ *n* rivet *m*. ◇ *vt* -1. [fasten with rivets] river, riveter. -2. *fig* [fascinate]: to be ~ed by être fasciné(e) par.

riveting ['rɪvɪtɪŋ] *adj fig* fascinant(e).

Riviera [ˌrɪvɪ'eərə] *n*: the French ~ la Côte d'Azur; the Italian ~ la Riviera italienne.

Riyadh ['riːæd] *n* Riyad, Riad.

RN *n* -1. *abbr of* Royal Navy. -2. *abbr of* registered nurse.

RNA (*abbr of* ribonucleic acid) *n* ARN *m*.

RNLI (*abbr of* Royal National Lifeboat Institution) *n* société britannique de sauvetage en mer.

RNZAF (*abbr of* Royal New Zealand Air Force) *n* armée de l'air néo-zélandaise.

RNZN (*abbr of* Royal New Zealand Navy) *n* marine de guerre néo-zélandaise.

roach [rəʊtʃ] *n Am* [cockroach] cafard *m*.

road [rəʊd] *n* route *f*; [small] chemin *m*; [in town] rue *f*; by ~ par la route; on the ~ to *fig* sur le chemin de; on the ~ sur la route; we've been on the ~ for two days on voyage depuis deux jours.

road atlas *n* atlas *m* routier.

roadblock ['rəʊdblɒk] *n* barrage *m* routier.

road-fund licence *n Br* ≃ vignette *f*.

road hog *n inf pej* chauffard *m*.

roadholding ['rəʊdˌhəʊldɪŋ] *n* AUT tenue *f* de route.

roadie ['rəʊdɪ] *n inf* membre de l'équipe technique d'un groupe en tournée.

road map *n* carte *f* routière.

road roller [-ˌrəʊlər] *n* rouleau *m* compresseur.

road safety *n* sécurité *f* routière.

road sense *n* [of driver] notion *f* de la conduite.

roadshow ['rəʊdʃəʊ] *n* spectacle *m* de tournée.

roadside ['rəʊdsaɪd] ◇ *n*: the ~ le bord de la route. ◇ *comp* au bord de la route.

road sign *n* panneau *m* routier OR de signalisation.

roadsweeper ['rəʊdˌswiːpər] *n* [vehicle] balayeuse *f*.

road tax *n* ≃ vignette *f*.

road test *n* essai *m* sur route.

◆ **road-test** *vt* essayer sur route.

road transport *n* transport *m* routier.

roadway ['rəudweɪ] *n* chaussée *f*.

road works *npl* travaux *mpl* (de réfection des routes).

roadworthy ['rəud,wɜːðɪ] *adj* en bon état de marche.

roam [rəum] ◇ *vt* errer dans. ◇ *vi* errer.

roar [rɔːr] ◇ *vi* [person, lion] rugir; [wind] hurler; [car] gronder; [plane] vrombir; **to ~ with laughter** se tordre de rire. ◇ *vt* hurler; [of person, lion] rugissement *m*. ◇ *n* [of traffic] grondement *m*; [of plane, engine] vrombissement *m*.

roaring ['rɔːrɪŋ] *adj*: **a ~ fire** une belle flambée; **~ drunk** complètement saoul(e); **a ~ success** un succès monstre OR fou; **to do a ~ trade** faire des affaires en or.

roast [rəust] ◇ *adj* rôti(e). ◇ *n* rôti *m*. ◇ *vt* **-1.** [meat, potatoes] rôtir. **-2.** [coffee, nuts etc] griller.

roast beef *n* rôti *m* de bœuf, rosbif *m*.

roasting ['rəustɪŋ] *inf* ◇ *adj* torride. ◇ *adv*: **a ~ hot day** une journée torride.

roasting tin *n* plat *m* à rôtir.

rob [rɒb] (*pt* & *pp* **-bed**, *cont* **-bing**) *vt* [person] voler; [bank] dévaliser; **to ~ sb of sthg** [money, goods] voler OR dérober qqch à qqn; [opportunity, glory] enlever qqch à qqn.

robber ['rɒbər] *n* voleur *m*, -euse *f*.

robbery ['rɒbərɪ] (*pl* **-ies**) *n* vol *m*.

robe [rəub] *n* **-1.** [gen] robe *f*. **-2.** *Am* [dressing gown] peignoir *m*.

robin ['rɒbɪn] *n* rouge-gorge *m*.

robot ['rəubɒt] *n* robot *m*.

robotics [rəu'bɒtɪks] *n* (*U*) robotique *f*.

robust [rəu'bʌst] *adj* robuste.

robustly [rəu'bʌstlɪ] *adv* robustement.

rock [rɒk] ◇ *n* **-1.** (*U*) [substance] roche *f*. **-2.** [boulder] rocher *m*. **-3.** *Am* [pebble] caillou *m*. **-4.** [music] rock *m*. **-5.** *Br* [sweet] sucre *m* d'orge. ◇ *comp* [music, band] de rock. ◇ *vt* **-1.** [baby] bercer; [cradle, boat] balancer. **-2.** [shock] secouer. ◇ *vi* (se) balancer.

◆ **on the rocks** *adv* **-1.** [drink] avec de la glace OR des glaçons. **-2.** [marriage, relationship] près de la rupture.

rock and roll *n* rock *m*, rock and roll *m*.

rock bottom *n*: **at ~** au plus bas; **to hit ~** toucher le fond.

◆ **rock-bottom** *adj* [price] sacrifié(e).

rock cake *n* *Br* rocher *m*.

rock climber *n* varappeur *m*, -euse *f*.

rock-climbing *n* varappe *f*; **to go ~** faire de la varappe.

rock dash *n* *Am* crépi *m*.

rocker ['rɒkər] *n* **-1.** [chair] fauteuil *m* à bascule, rocking-chair *m*. **-2.** *phr*: **to be off one's ~** *inf* être fêlé.

rockery ['rɒkərɪ] (*pl* **-ies**) *n* rocaille *f*.

rocket ['rɒkɪt] ◇ *n* **-1.** [gen] fusée *f*. **-2.** MIL fusée *f*, roquette *f*. ◇ *vi* monter en flèche.

rocket launcher [-,lɔːntʃər] *n* lance-fusées *m inv*, lance-roquettes *m inv*.

rock face *n* paroi *f* rocheuse.

rockfall ['rɒkfɔːl] *n* chute *f* de pierres.

rock-hard *adj* dur(e) comme de la pierre.

Rockies ['rɒkɪz] *npl*: **the ~** les Rocheuses *fpl*.

rocking chair ['rɒkɪŋ-] *n* fauteuil *m* à bascule, rocking-chair *m*.

rocking horse ['rɒkɪŋ-] *n* cheval *m* à bascule.

rock music *n* rock *m*.

rock'n'roll [,rɒkən'rəul] = **rock and roll**.

rock pool *n* mare *f* dans les rochers.

rock salt *n* sel *m* gemme.

rocky ['rɒkɪ] (*compar* **-ier**, *superl* **-iest**) *adj* **-1.** [ground, road] rocailleux(euse), caillouteux(euse). **-2.** *fig* [economy, marriage] précaire.

Rocky Mountains *npl*: **the ~** les montagnes *fpl* Rocheuses.

rococo [rə'kəukəu] *adj* rococo (*inv*).

rod [rɒd] *n* [metal] tige *f*; [wooden] baguette *f*; (**fishing**) **~** canne *f* à pêche.

rode [rəud] *pt* → **ride**.

rodent ['rəudənt] *n* rongeur *m*.

rodeo ['rəudɪ,əu] (*pl* **-s**) *n* rodéo *m*.

roe [rəu] *n* (*U*) œufs *mpl* de poisson.

roe deer *n* chevreuil *m*.

rogue [rəug] ◇ *adj* **-1.** [animal] solitaire. **-2.** *fig* [person] dissident(e). ◇ *n* **-1.** [likeable rascal] coquin *m*. **-2.** *dated* [dishonest person] filou *m*, crapule *f*.

roguish ['rəugɪʃ] *adj* espiègle.

role [rəul] *n* rôle *m*.

roll [rəul] ◇ *n* **-1.** [of material, paper etc] rouleau *m*. **-2.** [of bread] petit pain *m*. **-3.** [list] liste *f*. **-4.** [of drums, thunder] roulement *m*. ◇ *vt* rouler; [log, ball etc] faire rouler; **to ~ one's eyes** [in fear, despair] rouler les yeux; **~ed into one** tout à la fois. ◇ *vi* rouler.

◆ **roll about**, **roll around** *vi* [person] se rouler; [object] rouler çà et là.

◆ **roll back** *vt sep* *Am* [prices] baisser.

◆ **roll in** *vi inf* [money] couler à flots.

◆ **roll over** *vi* se retourner.

◆ **roll up** ◇ *vt sep* **-1.** [carpet, paper etc] rouler. **-2.** [sleeves] retrousser. ◇ *vi inf* [arrive] s'amener, se pointer.

roll bar *n* arceau *m* de sécurité.

roll call *n* appel *m*.

rolled gold [rəuld-] *n* plaqué *m* or.

roller ['rəulər] *n* rouleau *m*.

roller blind *n* store *m*.

roller coaster *n* montagnes *fpl* russes.

roller skate *n* patin *m* à roulettes.

◆ **roller-skate** *vi* faire du patin à roulettes.

roller towel *n* essuie-main *m* à rouleau.

rollicking ['rɒlıkıŋ] *adj*: we had a ~ good time on s'est amusé comme des (petits) fous.

rolling ['rəulıŋ] *adj* **-1.** [hills] onduleux(euse). **-2.** *phr*: to be ~ in it *inf* rouler sur l'or.

rolling mill *n* laminoir *m*.

rolling pin *n* rouleau *m* à pâtisserie.

rolling stock *n* matériel *m* roulant.

rollneck ['rəulnek] *adj* à col roulé.

roll of honour *n* liste *f* des combattants morts au champ d'honneur.

roll-on *adj* [deodorant] à bille.

roll-on roll-off *adj Br*: ~ **ferry** roll on-roll off *m*, roulier *m*.

roly-poly [,rəulı'pəulı] (*pl* **-ies**) *n Br*: ~ **(pudding)** roulé *m* à la confiture.

ROM [rɒm] (*abbr of* **read only memory**) *n* ROM *f*.

romaine lettuce [rəu'meın] *n Am* romaine *f* (*laitue*).

Roman ['rəumən] ◇ *adj* romain(e). ◇ *n* Romain *m*, -e *f*.

Roman candle *n* chandelle *f* romaine.

Roman Catholic ◇ *adj* catholique. ◇ *n* catholique *mf*.

romance [rəu'mæns] *n* **-1.** (*U*) [romantic quality] charme *m*. **-2.** [love affair] idylle *f*. **-3.** [book] roman *m* (d'amour).

Romanesque [,rəumə'nesk] *adj* roman(e).

Romani ['rəumənı] = **Romany**.

Romania [ruː'meınjə] *n* Roumanie *f*; **in** ~ en Roumanie.

Romanian [ruː'meınjən] ◇ *adj* roumain(e). ◇ *n* **-1.** [person] Roumain *m*, -e *f*. **-2.** [language] roumain *m*.

Roman numerals *npl* chiffres *mpl* romains.

romantic [rəu'mæntık] *adj* romantique.

romanticism [rəu'mæntısızm] *n* romantisme *m*.

romanticize, **-ise** [rəu'mæntısaız] *vt & vi* romancer.

Romany ['rəumənı] (*pl* **-ies**) ◇ *adj* de bohémien. ◇ *n* **-1.** [person] bohémien *m*, -ienne *f*. **-2.** [language] romani *m*.

Rome [rəum] *n* Rome.

romp [rɒmp] ◇ *n* ébats *mpl*. ◇ *vi* s'ébattre.

rompers ['rɒmpəz] *npl*, **romper suit** ['rɒmpər-] *n* barboteuse *f*.

roof [ruːf] *n* toit *m*; [of cave, tunnel] plafond *m*; **the ~ of the mouth** la voûte du palais; **to have a ~ over one's head** avoir OR posséder un toit; **to go through** OR **hit the ~** *fig* exploser.

roof garden *n* jardin *m* sur le toit.

roofing ['ruːfıŋ] *n* toiture *f*.

roof rack *n* galerie *f*.

rooftop ['ruːftɒp] *n* toit *m*.

rook [rʊk] *n* **-1.** [bird] freux *m*. **-2.** [chess piece] tour *f*.

rookie ['rʊkı] *n Am inf* bleu *m*.

room [ruːm, rʊm] *n* **-1.** [in building] pièce *f*. **-2.** [bedroom] chambre *f*. **-3.** (*U*) [space] place *f*; **there is ~ for improvement** on peut faire mieux; ~ **to** OR **for manoeuvre** marge *f* de manœuvre.

rooming house ['ruːmıŋ-] *n Am* maison *f* de rapport.

roommate ['ruːmmeıt] *n* camarade *mf* de chambre.

room service *n* service *m* dans les chambres.

room temperature *n* température *f* ambiante.

roomy ['ruːmı] (*compar* **-ier**, *superl* **-iest**) *adj* spacieux(ieuse).

roost [ruːst] ◇ *n* perchoir *m*, juchoir *m*; **to rule the ~** faire la loi. ◇ *vi* se percher, se jucher.

rooster ['ruːstər] *n* coq *m*.

root [ruːt] ◇ *adj* [fundamental] principal(e), fondamental(e). ◇ *n* racine *f*; *fig* [of problem] origine *f*; **to take ~** *lit & fig* prendre racine; **to put down ~s** [person] s'enraciner. ◇ *vi*: **to ~ through** fouiller dans.

◆ **roots** *npl* racines *fpl*.

◆ **root for** *vt fus Am inf* encourager.

◆ **root out** *vt sep* [eradicate] extirper.

root beer *n Am* boisson gazeuse à base de racines de plantes.

root crop *n* racine *f*.

rooted ['ruːtıd] *adj*: **to be ~ to the spot** être cloué(e) sur place.

rootless ['ruːtlıs] *adj* sans racines.

root vegetable *n* racine *f*.

rope [rəup] ◇ *n* corde *f*; **to know the ~s** connaître son affaire, être au courant. ◇ *vt* corder; [climbers] encorder.

◆ **rope in** *vt sep inf fig* enrôler.

◆ **rope off** *vt sep* délimiter par une corde.

rop(e)y ['rəupɪ] (*compar* **-ier**, *superl* **-iest**) *adj Br inf* **-1.** [poor-quality] pas fameux(euse), pas brillant(e). **-2.** [unwell]: **I feel a bit ~ today** je me sens un peu patraque aujourd'hui.

rosary ['rəuzərɪ] (*pl* **-ies**) *n* rosaire *m*.

rose [rəuz] ◇ *pt* → **rise**. ◇ *adj* [pink] rose. ◇ *n* [flower] rose *f*.

rosé ['rəuzeɪ] *n* rosé *m*.

rosebed ['rəuzbed] massif *m* de rosiers.

rosebud ['rəuzbʌd] bouton *m* de rose.

rose bush *n* rosier *m*.

rose hip *n* gratte-cul *m*.

rosemary ['rəuzmərɪ] *n* romarin *m*.

rosette [rəu'zet] *n* rosette *f*.

rosewater ['rəuz,wɔːtəʳ] *n* eau *f* de rose.

rosewood ['rəuzwud] *n* bois *m* de rose.

ROSPA ['rɒspə] (*abbr of* **Royal Society for the Prevention of Accidents**) *n association britannique pour la prévention des accidents.*

roster ['rɒstəʳ] *n* liste *f*, tableau *m*.

rostrum ['rɒstrəm] (*pl* **-trums** OR **-tra** [-trə]) *n* tribune *f*.

rosy ['rəuzɪ] (*compar* **-ier**, *superl* **-iest**) *adj* rose.

rot [rɒt] (*pt & pp* **-ted**, *cont* **-ting**) ◇ *n* (U) **-1.** [decay] pourriture *f*. **-2.** *Br dated* [nonsense] bêtises *fpl*, balivernes *fpl*. ◇ *vt & vi* pourrir.

rota ['rəutə] *n* liste *f*, tableau *m*.

rotary ['rəutərɪ] ◇ *adj* rotatif(ive). ◇ *n Am* [roundabout] rond-point *m*.

Rotary Club *n*: **the ~** le Rotary Club.

rotate [rəu'teɪt] ◇ *vt* **-1.** [turn] faire tourner. **-2.** [alternate - jobs] faire à tour de rôle; [- crops] alterner. ◇ *vi* [turn] tourner.

rotation [rəu'teɪʃn] *n* **-1.** [turning movement] rotation *f*. **-2.** [alternation] alternance *f*; **in ~** à tour de rôle.

rote [rəut] *n*: **by ~** de façon machinale, par cœur.

rote learning *n* apprentissage *m* machinal OR par cœur.

rotor ['rəutəʳ] *n* rotor *m*.

rotten ['rɒtn] *adj* **-1.** [decayed] pourri(e). **-2.** *inf* [bad] moche. **-3.** *inf* [unwell]: **to feel ~** sentir mal fichu(e). **-4.** [unhappy]: **I feel ~ about it** ça me contrarie.

rotund [rəu'tʌnd] *adj* rondelet(ette).

rouble ['ruːbl] *n* rouble *m*.

rouge [ruːʒ] *n* rouge *m* à joues.

rough [rʌf] ◇ *adj* **-1.** [not smooth - surface] rugueux(euse), rêche; [- road] accidenté(e); [- sea] agité(e), houleux(euse); [- crossing] mauvais(e). **-2.** [person, treatment] brutal(e); [manners, conditions] rude; [area] mal fréquenté(e). **-3.** [guess] approximatif(ive); ~ **copy**, ~ **draft** brouillon *m*; ~ **sketch** ébauche *f*. **-4.** [harsh - voice, wine] âpre; [- life] dur(e); **to have a ~ time** en baver. **-5.** [tired, ill] mal fichu(e).

◇ *adv*: **to sleep ~** coucher à la dure.

◇ *n* **-1.** GOLF rough *m*. **-2.** [undetailed form]: **in ~** au brouillon.

◇ *vt phr*: **to ~ it** vivre à la dure.

◆ **rough out** *vt sep* ébaucher.

roughage ['rʌfɪdʒ] *n* (U) fibres *fpl* alimentaires.

rough and ready *adj* rudimentaire.

rough-and-tumble *n* (U) bagarre *f*.

roughcast ['rʌfkɑːst] *n* crépi *m*.

rough diamond *n Br fig*: **he's a ~** sous ses dehors frustes, il a beaucoup de qualités.

roughen ['rʌfn] *vt* rendre rugueux(euse) OR rêche.

rough justice *n* justice *f* sommaire.

roughly ['rʌflɪ] *adv* **-1.** [approximately] approximativement. **-2.** [handle, treat] brutalement. **-3.** [built, made] grossièrement.

roughneck ['rʌfnek] *n* **-1.** [oil-rig worker] *personne travaillant sur une plate-forme pétrolière.* **-2.** *Am inf* [ruffian] dur *m*.

roughness ['rʌfnɪs] *n* **-1.** [of skin, surface] rugosité *f*. **-2.** [of treatment, person] brutalité *f*.

roughshod ['rʌfʃɒd] *adv*: **to ride ~ over sthg** passer outre à qqch; **to ride ~ over sb** traiter qqn cavalièrement.

roulette [ruː'let] *n* roulette *f*.

round [raund] ◇ *adj* rond(e).

◇ *prep* autour de; ~ **here** par ici; **all ~ the country** dans tout le pays; **just ~ the corner** au coin de la rue; *fig* tout près; **to go ~ sthg** [obstacle] contourner qqch; **to go ~ a museum** visiter un musée.

◇ *adv* **-1.** [surrounding]: **all ~** tout autour. **-2.** [near]: ~ **about** dans le coin. **-3.** [in measurements]: **10 metres ~** 10 mètres de diamètre. **-4.** [to other side]: **to go ~** faire le tour; **to turn ~** se retourner; **to look ~** se retourner (pour regarder). **-5.** [at or to nearby place]: **come ~ and see us** venez OR passez nous voir; **he's ~ at her house** il est chez elle; **I'm just going ~ to the shop** je vais juste faire une course. **-6.** [approximately]: ~ **(about)** vers, environ.

◇ *n* **-1.** [of talks etc] série *f*; **a ~ of applause** une salve d'applaudissements. **-2.** [of competition] manche *f*. **-3.** [of doctor] visites *fpl*; [of postman, milkman] tournée *f*. **-4.** [of ammunition] cartouche *f*. **-5.** [of drinks] tournée *f*. **-6.** BOXING reprise *f*, round *m*. **-7.** GOLF partie *f*.
◇ *vt* [corner] **tourner**; [bend] **prendre**.

◆ **rounds** *npl* [of doctor] visites *fpl*; **to do** OR **go the ~s** [story, joke] circuler; [illness] faire des ravages.

◆ **round off** *vt sep* terminer, conclure.

◆ **round up** *vt sep* **-1.** [gather together] rassembler. **-2.** MATH arrondir.

roundabout ['raʊndəbaʊt] ◇ *adj* détourné(e). ◇ *n Br* **-1.** [on road] rond-point *m*. **-2.** [at fairground] manège *m*. **-3.** [at playground] tourniquet *m*.

rounded ['raʊndɪd] *adj* arrondi(e).

rounders ['raʊndəz] *n Br* sorte de baseball.

Roundhead ['raʊndhed] *n* Tête *f* ronde.

roundly ['raʊndlɪ] *adv* [beaten] complètement; [condemned etc] franchement, carrément.

round-shouldered [-'ʃəʊldəd] *adj* voûté(e).

round-table *adj*: **~ talks** table *f* ronde.

round the clock *adv* vingt-quatre heures sur vingt-quatre.

◆ **round-the-clock** *adj* vingt-quatre heures sur vingt-quatre.

round trip ◇ *adj Am* aller-retour. ◇ *n* aller et retour *m*.

roundup ['raʊndʌp] *n* [summary] résumé *m*.

rouse [raʊz] *vt* **-1.** [wake up] réveiller. **-2.** [impel]: **to ~ o.s. to do sthg** se forcer à faire qqch; **to ~ sb to action** pousser OR inciter qqn à agir. **-3.** [emotions] susciter, provoquer.

rousing ['raʊzɪŋ] *adj* [speech] vibrant(e), passionné(e); [welcome] enthousiaste.

rout [raʊt] ◇ *n* déroute *f*. ◇ *vt* mettre en déroute.

route [ruːt] ◇ *n* **-1.** [gen] itinéraire *m*. **-2.** *fig* [way] chemin *m*, voie *f*. ◇ *vt* [goods] acheminer.

route map *n* [for journey] croquis *m* d'itinéraire; [for buses, trains] carte *f* du réseau.

route march *n* marche *f* d'entraînement.

routine [ruː'tiːn] ◇ *adj* **-1.** [normal] habituel(elle), de routine. **-2.** *pej* [uninteresting] de routine. ◇ *n* routine *f*.

routinely [ruː'tiːnlɪ] *adv* de façon systématique.

rove [rəʊv] *literary* ◇ *vt* errer dans. ◇ *vi*: **to ~ around** errer.

roving ['rəʊvɪŋ] *adj* itinérant(e).

row¹ [rəʊ] ◇ *n* **-1.** [line] rangée *f*; [of seats] rang *m*. **-2.** *fig* [of defeats, victories] série *f*; **in a ~** d'affilée, de suite. ◇ *vt* [boat] faire aller à la rame; [person] transporter en canot OR bateau. ◇ *vi* ramer.

row² [raʊ] ◇ *n* **-1.** [quarrel] dispute *f*, querelle *f*. **-2.** *inf* [noise] vacarme *m*, raffut *m*. ◇ *vi* [quarrel] se disputer, se quereller.

rowboat ['rəʊbəʊt] *n Am* canot *m*.

rowdiness ['raʊdɪnɪs] *n* chahut *m*, tapage *m*.

rowdy ['raʊdɪ] (*compar* **-ier**, *superl* **-iest**) *adj* chahuteur(euse), tapageur(euse).

rower ['rəʊə'] *n* rameur *m*, -euse *f*.

row house [rəʊ-] *n Am* maison *f* attenante aux maisons voisines.

rowing ['rəʊɪŋ] *n* SPORT aviron *m*.

rowing boat *n Br* canot *m*.

rowing machine *n* machine *f* à ramer.

royal ['rɔɪəl] ◇ *adj* royal(e). ◇ *n inf* membre *m* de la famille royale.

Royal Air Force *n*: **the ~** l'armée *f* de l'air britannique.

royal blue *adj* bleu roi (*inv*).

royal family *n* famille *f* royale.

royalist ['rɔɪəlɪst] *n* royaliste *mf*.

royal jelly *n* gelée *f* royale.

Royal Mail *n Br*: **the ~** ≃ la Poste.

Royal Marines *n Br*: **the ~** les Marines *mpl*.

Royal Navy *n*: **the ~** la marine de guerre britannique.

royalty ['rɔɪəltɪ] *n* royauté *f*.

◆ **royalties** *npl* droits *mpl* d'auteur.

RP (*abbr of* **received pronunciation**) *n* prononciation standard de l'anglais britannique.

RPI (*abbr of* **retail price index**) *n* IPC *m*.

rpm *npl* (*abbr of* **revolutions per minute**) tours *mpl* par minute, tr/min.

RR *abbr of* **railroad**.

RRP *n abbr of* **recommended retail price**.

RSA (*abbr of* **Royal Society of Arts**) *n* société britannique pour la promotion des arts, de l'industrie et du commerce.

RSC (*abbr of* **Royal Shakespeare Company**) *n* compagnie de théâtre britannique.

RSI (*abbr of* **repetitive strain injury**) *n* douleur de poignet provoquée par les mouvements effectués au clavier d'un ordinateur.

RSPB (*abbr of* **Royal Society for the Protection of Birds**) *n* ligue britannique pour la protection des oiseaux.

RSPCA (*abbr of* **Royal Society for the Prevention of Cruelty to Animals**) *n* société britannique protectrice des animaux, ≃ SPA *f*.

RST (*abbr of* **Royal Shakespeare Theatre**) *n* célèbre théâtre à Stratford-upon-Avon.

RSVP (*abbr of* **répondez s'il vous plaît**) RSVP.

Rt Hon (*abbr of* **Right Honourable**) *expression utilisée pour des titres nobiliaires.*

Rt Rev (*abbr of* **Right Reverend**) *expression utilisée pour un évêque de l'Église anglicane.*

rub [rʌb] (*pt & pp* **-bed**, *cont* **-bing**) ◇ *vt* frotter; **to ~ sthg in** [cream etc] faire pénétrer qqch (en frottant); **to ~ one's eyes/hands** se frotter les yeux/les mains; **to ~ it in** *inf fig* remuer le couteau dans la plaie; **to ~ sb up the wrong way** *Br*, **to ~ sb the wrong way** *Am fig* prendre qqn à rebrousse-poil. ◇ *vi* frotter.

◆ **rub off on** *vt fus* [subj: quality] déteindre sur.

◆ **rub out** *vt sep* [erase] effacer.

rubber ['rʌbər] ◇ *adj* en caoutchouc. ◇ *n* **-1.** [substance] caoutchouc *m*. **-2.** *Br* [eraser] gomme *f*. **-3.** *Am inf* [condom] préservatif *m*. **-4.** [in bridge] robre *m*, rob *m*. **-5.** *Am* [overshoe] caoutchouc *m*.

rubber band *n* élastique *m*.

rubber boot *n Am* bottes *fpl* de caoutchouc.

rubber dinghy *n* canot *m* pneumatique.

rubberize, -ise ['rʌbəraɪz] *vt* caoutchouter.

rubberneck ['rʌbənek] *vi Am inf* faire le badaud.

rubber ring *n* anneau *m* en caoutchouc; [for swimmer] bouée *f*.

rubber stamp *n* tampon *m*.

◆ **rubber-stamp** *vt fig* approuver sans discussion.

rubber tree *n* hévéa *m*.

rubbery ['rʌbəri] *adj* caoutchouteux(euse).

rubbing ['rʌbɪŋ] *n* [of brass] décalque *m*.

rubbish ['rʌbɪʃ] ◇ *n* (*U*) **-1.** [refuse] détritus *mpl*, ordures *fpl*. **-2.** *inf fig* [worthless objects] camelote *f*; **the play was ~** la pièce était nulle. **-3.** *inf* [nonsense] bêtises *fpl*, inepties *fpl*. ◇ *vt inf* débiner.

rubbish bin *n Br* poubelle *f*.

rubbish dump *n Br* dépotoir *m*.

rubbishy ['rʌbɪʃi] *adj inf* qui ne vaut rien, nul (nulle).

rubble ['rʌbl] *n* (*U*) décombres *mpl*.

rubella [ruː'belə] *n* rubéole *f*.

ruby ['ruːbi] *n* (*pl* **-ies**) *n* rubis *m*.

RUC (*abbr of* **Royal Ulster Constabulary**) *n* corps de police d'Irlande du Nord.

ruched [ruːʃt] *adj* garni(e) d'un ruché.

ruck [rʌk] *n* **-1.** *inf* [fight] bagarre *f*. **-2.** RUGBY mêlée *f* ouverte.

rucksack ['rʌksæk] *n* sac *m* à dos.

ructions ['rʌkʃnz] *npl inf* grabuge *m*.

rudder ['rʌdə] *n* gouvernail *m*.

ruddy ['rʌdi] (*compar* **-ier**, *superl* **-iest**) *adj* **-1.** [complexion, face] coloré(e). **-2.** *Br inf* [dated] [damned] sacré(e).

rude [ruːd] *adj* **-1.** [impolite - gen] impoli(e); [- word] grossier(ière); [- noise] incongru(e). **-2.** [sudden]: **it was a ~ awakening** le réveil fut pénible. **-3.** *literary* [primitive] grossier(ière), rudimentaire.

rudely ['ruːdli] *adv* **-1.** [impolitely] impoliment. **-2.** [suddenly] brusquement.

rudeness ['ruːdnɪs] *n* [impoliteness] impolitesse *f*; [of joke] grossièreté *f*.

rudimentary [,ruːdɪ'mentəri] *adj* rudimentaire.

rudiments ['ruːdɪmənts] *npl* rudiments *mpl*.

rue [ruː] *vt* regretter (amèrement).

rueful ['ruːfʊl] *adj* triste.

ruff [rʌf] *n* fraise *f*.

ruffian ['rʌfjən] *n* voyou *m*.

ruffle ['rʌfl] *vt* **-1.** [hair] ébouriffer; [water] troubler. **-2.** [person] froisser; [composure] faire perdre.

rug [rʌg] *n* **-1.** [carpet] tapis *m*. **-2.** [blanket] couverture *f*.

rugby ['rʌgbi] *n* rugby *m*.

Rugby League *n* rugby *m* à treize.

Rugby Union *n* rugby *m* à quinze.

rugged ['rʌgɪd] *adj* **-1.** [landscape] accidenté(e); [features] rude. **-2.** [vehicle etc] robuste.

ruggedness ['rʌgɪdnɪs] *n* [of landscape] aspect *m* accidenté.

rugger ['rʌgə] *n Br inf* rugby *m*.

ruin ['rʊɪn] ◇ *n* ruine *f*. ◇ *vt* ruiner; [clothes, shoes] abîmer.

◆ **in ruin(s)** *adv lit & fig* en ruine.

ruination [rʊɪ'neɪʃn] *n* ruine *f*.

ruinous ['rʊɪnəs] *adj* [expensive] ruineux(euse).

rule [ruːl] ◇ *n* **-1.** [gen] règle *f*; **as a ~** en règle générale. **-2.** [regulation] règlement *m*; **to bend the ~s** faire une entorse au règlement. **-3.** (*U*) [control] autorité *f*. ◇ *vt* **-1.** [control] dominer. **-2.** [govern] gouverner. **-3.** [decide]: **to ~ (that)** ... décider que .... ◇ *vi* **-1.** [give decision - gen] décider; [- JUR] statuer. **-2.** *fml* [be paramount] prévaloir. **-3.** [king, queen] régner; POL gouverner.

◆ **rule out** *vt sep* exclure, écarter.

rulebook ['ruːlbʊk] *n*: **the ~** le règlement.

ruled [ruːld] *adj* [paper] réglé(e).

ruler ['ruːlər] *n* **-1.** [for measurement] règle *f*. **-2.** [leader] chef *m* d'État.

ruling ['ruːlɪŋ] ◇ *adj* au pouvoir. ◇ *n* décision *f*.

rum [rʌm] (*compar* **-mer**, *superl* **-mest**) ◇ *n* rhum *m*. ◇ *adj Br dated* bizarre.

Rumania [ruːˈmeɪnjə] = **Romania**.

Rumanian [ruːˈmeɪnjən] = **Romanian**.

rumba ['rʌmbə] *n* rumba *f*.

rumble ['rʌmbl] ◇ *n* **-1.** [of thunder, traffic] grondement *m*; [in stomach] gargouillement *m*. **-2.** *Am inf* [fight] bagarre *f*. ◇ *vt Br inf dated*: **to ~ sb** voir clair dans le jeu de qqn. ◇ *vi* [thunder, traffic] gronder; [stomach] gargouiller.

rumbustious [rʌmˈbʌstɪəs] *adj Br* bruyant(e).

ruminate ['ruːmɪneɪt] *vi*: **to ~ (about OR on sthg)** ruminer (qqch).

rummage ['rʌmɪdʒ] *vi* fouiller.

rummage sale *n Am* vente *f* de charité.

rummy ['rʌmɪ] *n* rami *m*.

rumour *Br*, **rumor** *Am* ['ruːmər] *n* rumeur *f*.

rumoured *Br*, **rumored** *Am* ['ruːməd] *adj*: **he is ~ to be very wealthy** le bruit court OR on dit qu'il est très riche.

rump [rʌmp] *n* **-1.** [of animal] croupe *f*. **-2.** *inf* [of person] derrière *m*. **-3.** POL restant *m*.

rumple ['rʌmpl] *vt* froisser, chiffonner.

rump steak *n* romsteck *m*.

rumpus ['rʌmpəs] *n inf* chahut *m*.

rumpus room *n Am* salle *f* de jeu.

run [rʌn] (*pt* ran, *pp* run, *cont* -ning) ◇ *n* **-1.** [on foot] course *f*; **to go for a ~** faire un petit peu de course à pied; **to break into a ~** se mettre à courir; **on the ~** en fuite, en cavale; **to make a ~ for it** se sauver. **-2.** [in car - for pleasure] tour *m*; [- journey] trajet *m*. **-3.** [series] suite *f*, série *f*; **a ~ of bad luck** une période de déveine; **in the short/long ~** à court/long terme. **-4.** THEATRE: **to have a long ~** tenir longtemps l'affiche. **-5.** [great demand]: **on ~** ruée *f* sur. **-6.** [in tights] échelle *f*. **-7.** [in cricket, baseball] point *m*. **-8.** [track - for skiing, bobsleigh] piste *f*.
◇ *vt* **-1.** [race, distance] courir; **to ~ errands (for sb)** faire des courses OR commissions (pour qqn). **-2.** [manage - business] diriger; [- shop, hotel] tenir; [- course] organiser. **-3.** [operate] faire marcher. **-4.** [car] avoir, entretenir. **-5.** [water, bath] faire couler. **-6.** [publish] publier. **-7.** *inf* [drive]: **can you ~ me to the station?** tu peux m'amener OR me conduire à la gare? **-8.** [move]: **to ~ sthg**

along/over sthg passer qqch le long de/sur qqch.
◇ *vi* **-1.** [on foot] courir; **to ~ for it** se sauver. **-2.** [pass - road, river, pipe] passer; **to ~ through sthg** traverser qqch. **-3.** *Am* [in election]: **to ~ (for)** être candidat (à). **-4.** [operate - machine, factory] marcher; [- engine] tourner; **everything is running smoothly** tout va comme sur des roulettes, tout va bien; **to ~ on sthg** marcher à qqch; **to ~ off sthg** marcher sur qqch. **-5.** [bus, train] faire le service; **trains ~ every hour** il y a un train toutes les heures; **to be running late** [person] être en retard; [bus, train] avoir du retard. **-6.** [flow] couler; **my nose is running** j'ai le nez qui coule; **to ~ dry** se tarir. **-7.** [colour] déteindre; [ink] baver. **-8.** [continue - contract, insurance policy] être valide; [THEATRE] se jouer; **output is running at 100 units a day** la production est de 100 unités par jour.

◆ **run across** *vt fus* [meet] tomber sur.

◆ **run along** *vi dated*: **~ along now!** filez maintenant!

◆ **run away** *vi* **-1.** [flee]: **to ~ away (from)** s'enfuir (de); **to ~ away from home** faire une fugue. **-2.** *fig* [avoid]: **to ~ away from sthg** éviter qqch.

◆ **run away with** *vt fus*: **don't let your enthusiasm ~ away with you!** ne t'emballe pas trop!

◆ **run down** ◇ *vt sep* **-1.** [in vehicle] renverser. **-2.** [criticize] dénigrer. **-3.** [production] restreindre; [industry] réduire l'activité de. ◇ *vi* [clock] s'arrêter; [battery] se décharger.

◆ **run into** *vt fus* **-1.** [encounter - problem] se heurter à; [- person] tomber sur; **to ~ into debt** s'endetter, faire des dettes. **-2.** [in vehicle] rentrer dans. **-3.** [amount to] se monter à, s'élever à.

◆ **run off** ◇ *vt sep* [a copy] tirer. ◇ *vi*: **to ~ off (with)** s'enfuir (avec).

◆ **run on** *vi* [meeting] durer; **time is running on** le temps passe.

◆ **run out** *vi* **-1.** [food, supplies] s'épuiser; **time is running out** il ne reste plus beaucoup de temps. **-2.** [licence, contract] expirer.

◆ **run out of** *vt fus* manquer de; **to ~ out of petrol** tomber en panne d'essence, tomber en panne sèche.

◆ **run over** *vt sep* renverser.

◆ **run through** *vt fus* **-1.** [practise] répéter. **-2.** [read through] parcourir.

◆ **run to** *vt fus* **-1.** [amount to] monter à, s'élever à. **-2.** [afford]: **I think I could ~ to a new suit** je crois bien que je pourrais me payer OR m'offrir un nouveau costume.

◆ **run up** *vt fus* [bill, debt] laisser accumuler.

◆ **run up against** *vt fus* se heurter à.

run-around *n inf:* **to give sb the** ~ faire des réponses de Normand à qqn.

runaway ['rʌnəweɪ] ◇ *adj* [train, lorry] fou (folle); [horse] emballé(e); [victory] haut la main; [inflation] galopant(e). ◇ *n* fuyard *m*, fugitif *m*, -ive *f*.

rundown ['rʌndaʊn] *n* **-1.** [report] bref résumé *m*. **-2.** [of industry] réduction *f* délibérée.

◆ **run-down** *adj* **-1.** [building] délabré(e). **-2.** [person] épuisé(e).

rung [rʌŋ] ◇ *pp* → **ring**. ◇ *n* échelon *m*, barreau *m*.

run-in *n inf* prise *f* de bec.

runnel ['rʌnl] *n* ruisseau *m*.

runner ['rʌnər] *n* **-1.** [athlete] coureur *m*, -euse *f*. **-2.** [of guns, drugs] contrebandier *m*. **-3.** [of sledge] patin *m*; [for car seat] glissière *f*; [for drawer] coulisseau *m*.

runner bean *n Br* haricot *m* à rames.

runner-up (*pl* **runners-up**) *n* second *m*, -e *f*.

running ['rʌnɪŋ] ◇ *adj* **-1.** [argument, battle] continu(e). **-2.** [consecutive]: **three weeks** ~ trois semaines de suite. **-3.** [water] courant(e). ◇ *n* **-1.** (*U*) SPORT course *f*; **to go** ~ faire de la course. **-2.** [management] direction *f*, administration *f*. **-3.** [of machine] marche *f*, fonctionnement *m*. **-4.** *phr:* **to be in the** ~ **(for)** avoir des chances de réussir (dans); **to be out of the** ~ **(for)** n'avoir aucune chance de réussir (dans); **to make the** ~ [in race] mener la course; [in relationship] prendre l'initiative. ◇ *comp* de course.

running commentary *n* commentaire *m* suivi.

running costs *npl* frais *mpl* d'exploitation.

running mate *n Am* candidat *m* à la vice-présidence.

running repairs *npl* réparations *fpl* courantes.

runny ['rʌnɪ] (*compar* **-ier**, *superl* **-iest**) *adj* **-1.** [food] liquide. **-2.** [nose] qui coule.

run-of-the-mill *adj* banal(e), ordinaire.

runt [rʌnt] *n* avorton *m*.

run-through *n* répétition *f*.

run-up *n* **-1.** [preceding time]: **in the** ~ **to** sthg dans la période qui précède qqch. **-2.** SPORT course *f* d'élan.

runway ['rʌnweɪ] *n* piste *f*.

rupture ['rʌptʃər] *n* rupture *f*.

rural ['rʊərəl] *adj* rural(e).

ruse [ruːz] *n* ruse *f*.

rush [rʌʃ] ◇ *n* **-1.** [hurry] hâte *f*; **there's no** ~ ça ne presse pas, ce n'est pas pressé. **-2.** [surge] ruée *f*, bousculade *f*; **to make a** ~ **for** sthg se ruer OR se précipiter vers qqch; **a** ~ **of air** une bouffée d'air; **a** ~ **of blood to the head** un coup de sang. **-3.** [demand]: ~ **(on OR for)** ruée *f* (sur). ◇ *vt* **-1.** [hurry - work] faire à la hâte; [- person] bousculer; [- meal] expédier; **to** ~ **sb into doing sthg** forcer qqn à faire qqch à la hâte. **-2.** [send quickly] transporter OR envoyer d'urgence. **-3.** [attack suddenly] prendre d'assaut. ◇ *vi* **-1.** [hurry] se dépêcher; **to** ~ **into sthg** faire qqch sans réfléchir. **-2.** [crowd] se précipiter, se ruer; **the blood** ~**ed to her head** le sang lui monta à la tête.

◆ **rushes** *npl* **-1.** BOT joncs *mpl*. **-2.** CINEMA épreuves *fpl* de tournage, rushes *mpl*.

rushed [rʌʃt] *adj* [person] pressé(e); [work] fait(e) à la hâte.

rush hour *n* heures *fpl* de pointe OR d'affluence.

rush job *n* travail *m* d'urgence.

rusk [rʌsk] *n* biscotte *f*.

russet ['rʌsɪt] *adj* feuille-morte (*inv*).

Russia ['rʌʃə] *n* Russie *f*; **in** ~ en Russie.

Russian ['rʌʃn] ◇ *adj* russe. ◇ *n* **-1.** [person] Russe *mf*. **-2.** [language] russe *m*.

Russian roulette *n* roulette *f* russe.

rust [rʌst] ◇ *n* rouille *f*. ◇ *vi* se rouiller.

rustic ['rʌstɪk] *adj* rustique.

rustle ['rʌsl] ◇ *n* [of leaves] bruissement *m*; [of papers] froissement *m*. ◇ *vt* **-1.** [paper] froisser. **-2.** *Am* [cattle] voler. ◇ *vi* [leaves] bruire; [papers] produire un froissement.

rustproof ['rʌstpruːf] *adj* inoxydable.

rusty ['rʌstɪ] (*compar* **-ier**, *superl* **-iest**) *adj lit* & *fig* rouillé(e).

rut [rʌt] *n* ornière *f*; **to get into a** ~ s'encroûter; **to be in a** ~ être prisonnier de la routine.

rutabaga [ˌruːtə'beɪgə] *n Am* rutabaga *m*.

ruthless ['ruːθlɪs] *adj* impitoyable.

ruthlessly ['ruːθlɪslɪ] *adv* de façon impitoyable.

ruthlessness ['ruːθlɪsnɪs] *n* caractère *m* impitoyable.

RV *n* **-1.** (*abbr of* **revised version**) *traduction de la Bible de 1611 révisée entre 1881 et 1895.* **-2.** *Am* (*abbr of* **recreational vehicle**) camping-car *m*.

Rwanda [rʊ'ændə] *n* Ruanda *m*, Rwanda *m*; **in** ~ au Ruanda.

Rwandan [rʊ'ændən] ◇ *adj* ruandais(e). ◇ *n* Ruandais *m*, -e *f*.

rye [raɪ] *n* **-1.** [grain] seigle *m*. **-2.** [bread] pain *m* de seigle.

rye bread *n* pain *m* de seigle.

rye grass *n* ivraie *f*.

rye whiskey *n* whisky *m* à base de seigle.

S

s (*pl* ss OR s's), **S** (*pl* Ss OR S's) [es] *n* [letter] s *m inv*, S *m inv*.
◆ **S** (*abbr of* south) S.

SA -1. *abbr of* **South Africa**. **-2.** *abbr of* **South America**.

Saar [sɑːr] *n*: the ~ la Sarre.

Sabbath ['sæbəθ] *n*: the ~ le sabbat.

sabbatical [sə'bætɪkl] *n* année *f* sabbatique; to be on ~ faire une année sabbatique.

saber *Am* = sabre.

sabotage ['sæbətɑːʒ] ◇ *n* sabotage *m*. ◇ *vt* saboter.

saboteur [ˌsæbə'tɜːr] *n* saboteur *m*.

sabre *Br*, **saber** *Am* ['seɪbər] *n* sabre *m*.

saccharin(e) ['sækərɪn] *n* saccharine *f*.

sachet ['sæʃeɪ] *n* sachet *m*.

sack [sæk] ◇ *n* **-1.** [bag] sac *m*. **-2.** *Br inf* [dismissal]: to get OR be given the ~ être renvoyé(e), se faire virer. ◇ *vt Br inf* [dismiss] renvoyer, virer.

sackful ['sækful] *n* sac *m*.

sacking ['sækɪŋ] *n* [fabric] toile *f* à sac.

sacrament ['sækrəmənt] *n* sacrement *m*.

sacred ['seɪkrɪd] *adj* sacré(e).

sacrifice ['sækrɪfaɪs] *lit* & *fig* ◇ *n* sacrifice *m*. ◇ *vt* sacrifier.

sacrilege ['sækrɪlɪdʒ] *n lit* & *fig* sacrilège *m*.

sacrilegious [ˌsækrɪ'lɪdʒəs] *adj* sacrilège.

sacrosanct ['sækrəʊsæŋkt] *adj* sacrosaint(e).

sad [sæd] (*compar* **-der**, *superl* **-dest**) *adj* triste.

sadden ['sædn] *vt* attrister, affliger.

saddle ['sædl] ◇ *n* selle *f*. ◇ *vt* **-1.** [horse] seller. **-2.** *fig* [burden]: to ~ sb with sthg coller qqch à qqn.
◆ **saddle up** ◇ *vt fus* seller. ◇ *vi* seller son cheval.

saddlebag ['sædlbæg] *n* sacoche *f*.

saddler ['sædlər] *n* sellier *m*.

sadism ['seɪdɪzm] *n* sadisme *m*.

sadist ['seɪdɪst] *n* sadique *mf*.

sadistic [sə'dɪstɪk] *adj* sadique.

sadly ['sædlɪ] *adv* **-1.** [unhappily] tristement. **-2.** [unfortunately] malheureusement.

sadness ['sædnɪs] *n* tristesse *f*.

s.a.e., **sae** *abbr of* **stamped addressed envelope**.

safari [sə'fɑːrɪ] *n* safari *m*; to go on ~ aller en safari.

safari park *n* réserve *f*.

safe [seɪf] ◇ *adj* **-1.** [not dangerous - gen] sans danger; [- driver, play, guess] prudent(e); it's not ~ c'est dangereux; it's ~ to say (that) ... on peut dire à coup sûr que ...; in ~ hands en bonnes mains. **-2.** [not in danger] hors de danger, en sécurité; your secret is ~ with me je saurai garder votre secret; ~ and sound sain et sauf (saine et sauve). **-3.** [not risky - bet, method] sans risque; [- investment] sûr(e); to be on the ~ side par précaution.
◇ *n* coffre-fort *m*.

safebreaker ['seɪfˌbreɪkər] *n* perceur *m* de coffre-fort.

safe-conduct *n* sauf-conduit *m*.

safe-deposit box *n* coffre-fort *m*.

safeguard ['seɪfgɑːd] ◇ *n*: ~ (against) sauvegarde *f* (contre). ◇ *vt*: to ~ sb/sthg (against) sauvegarder qqn/qqch (contre), protéger qqn/qqch (contre).

safe house *n* lieu *m* sûr.

safekeeping [ˌseɪf'kiːpɪŋ] *n* bonne garde *f*.

safely ['seɪflɪ] *adv* **-1.** [not dangerously] sans danger. **-2.** [not in danger] en toute sécurité, à l'abri du danger. **-3.** [arrive - person] à bon port, sain et sauf (saine et sauve); [- parcel] à bon port. **-4.** [for certain]: I can ~ say (that) ... je peux dire à coup sûr que ....

safe sex *n* sexe *m* sans risque, S.S.R. *m*.

safety ['seɪftɪ] ◇ *n* sécurité *f*. ◇ *comp* de sécurité.

safety belt *n* ceinture *f* de sécurité.

safety catch *n* cran *m* de sûreté.

safety curtain *n* rideau *m* de fer.

safety-deposit box = safe-deposit box.

safety island *n Am* refuge *m*.

safety match *n* allumette *f* de sûreté.

safety net *n* filet *m* (de protection).

safety pin *n* épingle *f* de sûreté OR de nourrice.

safety valve *n* soupape *f* de sûreté.

saffron ['sæfrən] *n* safran *m*.

sag [sæg] (*pt* & *pp* **-ged**, *cont* **-ging**) *vi* **-1.** [sink downwards] s'affaisser, fléchir. **-2.** *fig* [decrease] baisser.

saga ['sɑːgə] *n* saga *f*; *fig* & *pej* histoire *f*.

sage [seɪdʒ] ◇ *adj* sage. ◇ *n* **-1.** (*U*) [herb] sauge *f*. **-2.** [wise man] sage *m*.

saggy ['sægɪ] (*compar* **-gier**, *superl* **-giest**) *adj* [bed] affaissé(e); [breasts] pendant(e).

Sagittarius [,sædʒɪ'teərɪəs] *n* Sagittaire *m*; to be (a) ~ être Sagittaire.

Sahara [sə'hɑːrə] *n*: the ~ (**Desert**) le (désert du) Sahara.

Saharan [sə'hɑːrən] *adj* saharien(ienne).

said [sed] *pt* & *pp* → say.

sail [seɪl] ◇ *n* **-1.** [of boat] voile *f*; to set ~ faire voile, prendre la mer. **-2.** [journey] tour *m* en bateau. ◇ *vt* **-1.** [boat] piloter, manœuvrer. **-2.** [sea] parcourir. ◇ *vi* **-1.** [person - travel] aller en bateau. **-2.** [boat - move] naviguer; the ship ~ed into harbour le bateau est entré au port; [- leave] partir, prendre la mer. **-3.** *fig* [through air] voler.

◆ **sail through** *vt fus fig* réussir les doigts dans le nez.

sailboard ['seɪlbɔːd] *n* planche *f* à voile.

sailboat *Am* = sailing boat.

sailcloth ['seɪlklɒθ] *n* toile *f* à voile.

sailing ['seɪlɪŋ] *n* **-1.** (*U*) SPORT voile *f*; to go ~ faire de la voile. **-2.** [departure] départ *m*.

sailing boat *Br*, **sailboat** *Am* ['seɪlbəut] *n* bateau *m* à voiles, voilier *m*.

sailing ship *n* voilier *m*.

sailor ['seɪlə'] *n* marin *m*, matelot *m*; to be a good ~ avoir le pied marin.

saint [seɪnt] *n* saint *m*, -e *f*.

Saint Helena [-ɪ'liːnə] *n* Sainte-Hélène *f*; on ~ à Sainte-Hélène.

Saint Lawrence [-'lɒrəns] *n*: the ~ (**River**) le Saint-Laurent.

Saint Lucia [-'luːʃə] *n* Sainte-Lucie.

saintly ['seɪntlɪ] (*compar* **-ier**, *superl* **-iest**) *adj* [person] saint(e); [life] de saint.

sake [seɪk] *n*: for the ~ of sb par égard pour qqn, pour (l'amour de) qqn; for the children's ~ pour les enfants; for the ~ of my health pour ma santé; for the ~ of argument à titre d'exemple; to do sthg for its own ~ faire qqch pour le plaisir; for God's OR heaven's ~ pour l'amour de Dieu OR du ciel.

salad ['sæləd] *n* salade *f*.

salad bowl *n* saladier *m*.

salad cream *n Br* sorte de mayonnaise douce.

salad dressing *n* vinaigrette *f*.

salad oil *n* huile *f* de table.

salamander ['sælə,mændə'] *n* salamandre *f*.

salami [sə'lɑːmɪ] *n* salami *m*.

salaried ['sælərɪd] *adj* salarié(e).

salary ['sælərɪ] (*pl* **-ies**) *n* salaire *m*, traitement *m*.

salary scale *n* échelle *f* des salaires.

sale [seɪl] *n* **-1.** [gen] vente *f*; on ~ en vente; (**up**) for ~ à vendre. **-2.** [at reduced prices] soldes *mpl*; the shop is having a ~ le magasin fait des soldes; in a ~ en solde.

◆ **sales** ◇ *npl* **-1.** [quantity sold] ventes *fpl*. **-2.** [at reduced prices]: the ~s les soldes *mpl*. ◇ *comp* [figures, department] des ventes; ~s manager directeur commercial *m*, directrice commerciale *f*.

saleroom *Br* ['seɪlrum], **salesroom** *Am* ['seɪlzrum] *n* salle *f* des ventes.

sales assistant, salesclerk ['seɪlzklɜːrk] *Am n* vendeur *m*, -euse *f*.

sales conference *n* conférence *f* du personnel des ventes.

sales drive *n* campagne *f* de vente.

sales force *n* force *f* de vente.

salesman ['seɪlzmən] (*pl* **-men** [-mən]) *n* [in shop] vendeur *m*; [travelling] représentant *m* de commerce.

sales pitch *n* boniment *m*.

sales rep *n inf* représentant *m* de commerce.

sales representative *n* représentant *m* de commerce.

salesroom *Am* = saleroom.

sales slip *n Am* [receipt] ticket *m* de caisse.

sales tax *n* taxe *f* à l'achat.

sales team *n* équipe *f* de vente.

saleswoman ['seɪlz,wumən] (*pl* **-women** [-,wɪmɪn]) *n* [in shop] vendeuse *f*; [travelling] représentante *f* de commerce.

salient ['seɪljənt] *adj fml* qui ressort.

saline ['seɪlaɪn] *adj* salin(e); ~ drip perfusion *f* de sérum artificiel.

saliva [sə'laɪvə] *n* salive *f*.

salivate ['sælɪveɪt] *vi* saliver.

sallow ['sæləu] *adj* cireux(euse).

sally ['sælɪ] (*pl* **-ies**, *pt* & *pp* **-ied**) *n* [sortie] sortie *f*.

◆ **sally forth** *vi hum or literary* sortir.

salmon ['sæmən] (*pl inv* OR **-s**) *n* saumon *m*.

salmonella [,sælmə'nelə] *n* salmonelle *f*.

salmon pink ◇ *adj* rose saumon (*inv*). ◇ *n* rose *m* saumon.

salon ['sælɒn] *n* salon *m*.

saloon [sə'luːn] *n* **-1.** *Br* [car] berline *f*. **-2.** *Am* [bar] saloon *m*. **-3.** *Br* [in pub]: ~ (**bar**) bar *m*. **-4.** [in ship] salon *m*.

salopettes [ˌsælə'pets] *npl* combinaison *f* de ski.

salt [sɔːlt, sɒlt] ◇ *n* sel *m*; **the ~ of the earth** le sel de la terre; **to rub ~ into sb's wounds** remuer OR retourner le couteau dans la plaie; **take what he says with a pinch of ~** ne prenez pas ce qu'il dit au pied de la lettre. ◇ *comp* [food] salé(e). ◇ *vt* [food] saler; [roads] mettre du sel sur.

◆ **salt away** *vt sep* mettre de côté.

SALT [sɔːlt] (*abbr of* **Strategic Arms Limitation Talks/Treaty**) *n* SALT *m*, négociations américano-soviétiques sur la limitation des armes stratégiques.

salt cellar *Br*, **salt shaker** *Am* [-ˌʃeɪkəʳ] *n* salière *f*.

salted ['sɔːltɪd] *adj* salé(e).

saltpetre *Br*, **saltpeter** *Am* [ˌsɔːlt'piːtəʳ] *n* salpêtre *m*.

salt shaker *Am* = saltcellar.

saltwater ['sɔːlt,wɔːtəʳ] ◇ *n* eau *f* de mer. ◇ *adj* de mer.

salty ['sɔːltɪ] (*compar* -**ier**, *superl* -**iest**) *adj* [food] salé(e); [water] saumâtre.

salubrious [sə'luːbrɪəs] *adj* salubre.

salutary ['sæljʊtrɪ] *adj* salutaire.

salute [sə'luːt] ◇ *n* salut *m*. ◇ *vt* saluer. ◇ *vi* faire un salut.

Salvadorean, **Salvadorian** [ˌsælvə'dɔːrɪən] ◇ *adj* salvadorien(ienne). ◇ *n* Salvadorien *m*, -ienne *f*.

salvage ['sælvɪdʒ] ◇ *n* (*U*) -**1.** [rescue of ship] sauvetage *m*. -**2.** [property rescued] biens *mpl* sauvés. ◇ *vt* sauver.

salvage vessel *n* bateau *m* de sauvetage.

salvation [sæl'veɪʃn] *n* salut *m*.

Salvation Army *n*: **the ~** l'Armée *f* du Salut.

salve [sælv] *vt*: **to do sthg to ~ one's conscience** faire qqch pour avoir la conscience en paix.

salver ['sælvəʳ] *n* plateau *m*.

salvo ['sælvəʊ] (*pl* -**s** OR -**es**) *n* salve *f*.

Samaritan [sə'mærɪtn] *n*: **good ~** bon Samaritain *m*.

samba ['sæmbə] *n* samba *f*.

same [seɪm] ◇ *adj* même; **she was wearing the ~ jumper as I was** elle portait le même pull que moi; **at the ~ time** en même temps; **one and the ~** un seul et même (une seule et même).

◇ *pron*: **the ~** le même (la même), les mêmes (*pl*); **I'll have the ~ as you** je prendrai la même chose que toi; **she earns the ~ as I do** elle gagne autant que moi; **to do the ~** faire de même, en faire autant; **all** OR **just the ~** [anyway] quand même, tout de même; **it's all the ~ to me** ça m'est égal; **its not the ~** ce n'est pas pareil. ◇ *adv*: **the ~** [treat, spelled] de la même manière.

sameness ['seɪmnɪs] *n pej* monotonie *f*.

Samoa [sə'məʊə] *n* Samoa *m*; **in ~** à Samoa; **American ~** les Samoa américaines *fpl*.

Samoan [sə'məʊən] ◇ *adj* samoan(e). ◇ *n* Samoan *m*, -e *f*.

samosa [sə'məʊsə] *n* genre de brick indien aux légumes.

sample ['sɑːmpl] ◇ *n* échantillon *m*. ◇ *vt* -**1.** [taste] goûter. -**2.** MUS faire le sampling de.

sampler ['sɑːmpləʳ] *n* SEWING modèle *m* de broderie.

sanatorium (*pl* -**riums** OR -**ria** [-rɪə]), **sanitorium** *Am* (*pl* -**riums** OR -**ria** [-rɪə]) [ˌsænə'tɔːrɪəm] *n* sanatorium *m*.

sanctify ['sæŋktɪfaɪ] (*pt* & *pp* -**ied**) *vt* sanctifier.

sanctimonious [ˌsæŋktɪ'məʊnjəs] *adj* moralisateur(trice).

sanction ['sæŋkʃn] ◇ *n* sanction *f*. ◇ *vt* sanctionner.

◆ **sanctions** *npl* sanctions *fpl*.

sanctity ['sæŋktətɪ] *n* sainteté *f*.

sanctuary ['sæŋktʃʊərɪ] (*pl* -**ies**) *n* -**1.** [for birds, wildlife] réserve *f*. -**2.** [refuge] asile *m*. -**3.** [holy place] sanctuaire *m*.

sanctum ['sæŋktəm] (*pl* -**s**) *n* fig [private place] retraite *f*.

sand [sænd] ◇ *n* sable *m*. ◇ *vt* [wood] poncer.

◆ **sands** *npl* plage *f* de sable.

sandal ['sændl] *n* sandale *f*.

sandalwood ['sændlwʊd] *n* (bois *m* de) santal *m*.

sandbag ['sændbæg] *n* sac *m* de sable.

sandbank ['sændbæŋk] *n* banc *m* de sable.

sandblast ['sændblɑːst] *vt* décaper à la sableuse, sabler.

sandbox *Am* = sandpit.

sandcastle ['sænd,kɑːsl] *n* château *m* de sable.

sand dune *n* dune *f*.

sander ['sændəʳ] *n* ponceuse *f*.

sandpaper ['sænd,peɪpəʳ] ◇ *n* papier *m* de verre. ◇ *vt* poncer (au papier de verre).

sandpit *Br* ['sændpɪt], **sandbox** *Am* ['sændbɒks] *n* bac *m* à sable.

sandstone ['sændstəʊn] *n* grès *m*.

sandstorm ['sændstɔːm] *n* tempête *f* de sable.

sandtrap ['sændtræp] *n Am* GOLF bunker *m*.

sandwich ['sænwɪdʒ] ◇ *n* sandwich *m*. ◇ *vt fig*: **to be ~ed between** être (pris(e)) en sandwich entre.

sandwich board *n* panneau *m* publicitaire (*d'homme sandwich ou posé comme un tréteau*).

sandwich course *n Br* stage *m* de formation professionnelle.

sandy ['sændɪ] (*compar* **-ier**, *superl* **-iest**) *adj* **-1.** [beach] de sable; [earth] sableux(euse). **-2.** [sand-coloured] sable (*inv*).

sane [seɪn] *adj* **-1.** [not mad] sain(e) d'esprit. **-2.** [sensible] raisonnable, sensé(e).

sang [sæŋ] *pt* → **sing**.

sanguine ['sæŋgwɪn] *adj* optimiste.

sanitary ['sænɪtrɪ] *adj* **-1.** [method, system] sanitaire. **-2.** [clean] hygiénique, salubre.

sanitary towel, **sanitary napkin** *Am n* serviette *f* hygiénique.

sanitation [,sænɪ'teɪʃn] *n* (U) [in house] installations *fpl* sanitaires.

sanitation worker *n Am* éboueur *m*.

sanitize, -ise ['sænɪtaɪz] *vt fig* expurger.

sanitorium *Am* = **sanatorium**.

sanity ['sænɪtɪ] *n* (U) **-1.** [saneness] santé *f* mentale, raison *f*. **-2.** [good sense] bon sens *m*.

sank [sæŋk] *pt* → **sink**.

San Marino [,sænmə'riːnəʊ] *n* Saint-Marin *m*; **in ~** à Saint-Marin.

San Salvador [,sæn'sælvədɔːr] *n* San Salvador.

Sanskrit ['sænskrɪt] *n* sanskrit *m*, sanscrit *m*.

Santa (Claus) ['sæntə(,klɔːz)] *n* le père Noël.

São Paulo [,saʊ'paʊləʊ] *n* **-1.** [city] São Paulo. **-2.** [state]: **~ (State)** São Paulo *m*, l'État *m* de São Paulo; **in ~** dans le São Paulo.

sap [sæp] (*pt & pp* **-ped**, *cont* **-ping**) ◇ *n* **-1.** [of plant] sève *f*. **-2.** *Am inf* [gullible person] nigaud *m*, -e *f*. ◇ *vt* [weaken] saper.

sapling ['sæplɪŋ] *n* jeune arbre *m*.

sapphire ['sæfaɪər] *n* saphir *m*.

Sarajevo [,særə'jeɪvəʊ] *n* Sarajevo.

sarcasm ['sɑːkæzm] *n* sarcasme *m*.

sarcastic [sɑː'kæstɪk] *adj* sarcastique.

sarcophagus [sɑː'kɒfəgəs] (*pl* **-gi** [-gaɪ] OR **-guses**) *n* sarcophage *m*.

sardine [sɑː'diːn] *n* sardine *f*.

Sardinia [sɑː'dɪnjə] *n* Sardaigne *f*; **in ~** en Sardaigne.

sardonic [sɑː'dɒnɪk] *adj* sardonique.

Sargasso Sea [sɑː'gæsəʊ-] *n*: **the ~** la mer des Sargasses.

sari ['sɑːrɪ] *n* sari *m*.

sarong [sə'rɒŋ] *n* sarong *m*.

sarsaparilla [,sɑːspə'rɪlə] *n* salsepareille *f*.

sartorial [sɑː'tɔːrɪəl] *adj fml* vestimentaire.

SAS (*abbr of* **Special Air Service**) *n* commando d'intervention spéciale de l'armée britannique.

SASE *abbr of* **self-addressed stamped envelope**.

sash [sæʃ] *n* [of cloth] écharpe *f*.

sash window *n* fenêtre *f* à guillotine.

Saskatchewan [,sæs'kætʃɪ,wən] *n* Saskatchewan *m*.

sassy ['sæsɪ] *adj Am inf* culotté(e).

sat [sæt] *pt & pp* → **sit**.

Sat. (*abbr of* **Saturday**) sam.

SAT [sæt] *n* **-1.** (*abbr of* **Standard Assessment Test**) *examen national en Grande-Bretagne pour les élèves de 7 ans, 11 ans et 14 ans*. **-2.** (*abbr of* **Scholastic Aptitude Test**) *examen d'entrée à l'université aux États-Unis*.

Satan ['seɪtn] *n* Satan *m*.

satanic [sə'tænɪk] *adj* satanique.

satchel ['sætʃəl] *n* cartable *m*.

sated ['seɪtɪd] *adj* [person, hunger]: **~ (with)** rassasié(e) (de).

satellite ['sætəlaɪt] ◇ *n* satellite *m*. ◇ *comp* **-1.** [link] par satellite; **~ dish** antenne *f* parabolique. **-2.** [country, company] satellite.

satellite TV *n* télévision *f* par satellite.

satiate ['seɪʃɪeɪt] *vt* [person, hunger] rassasier.

satin ['sætɪn] ◇ *n* satin *m*. ◇ *comp* [sheets, pyjamas] de OR en satin; [wallpaper, finish] satiné(e).

satire ['sætaɪər] *n* satire *f*.

satirical [sə'tɪrɪkl] *adj* satirique.

satirist ['sætərɪst] *n* satiriste *mf*.

satirize, -ise ['sætəraɪz] *vt* faire la satire de.

satisfaction [,sætɪs'fækʃn] *n* satisfaction *f*.

satisfactory [,sætɪs'fæktərɪ] *adj* satisfaisant(e).

satisfied ['sætɪsfaɪd] *adj* **-1.** [happy]: **~ (with)** satisfait(e) (de). **-2.** [convinced]: **to be ~** that être sûr(e) que.

satisfy ['sætɪsfaɪ] (*pt & pp* **-ied**) *vt* **-1.** [gen] satisfaire. **-2.** [convince] convaincre, persuader; **to ~ sb that** convaincre qqn que; **to ~ o.s. that** s'assurer que.

satisfying ['sætɪsfaɪɪŋ] *adj* satisfaisant(e).

satsuma [,sæt'suːmə] *n* satsuma *f*.

saturate ['sætʃəreɪt] *vt*: **to ~ sthg (with)** saturer qqch (de).

saturated fat ['sætʃəreɪtɪd-] *n* matière *f* grasse saturée.

saturation [,sætʃə'reɪʃn] ◇ *n* saturation *f*. ◇ *comp* [bombing] en masse.

saturation point *n*: **to reach ~** arriver à saturation *f*.

Saturday ['sætədɪ] ◇ *n* samedi *m*; **it's ~ on** est samedi; **are you going ~?** *inf* tu y vas samedi?; **see you ~!** *inf* à samedi!; **on ~** samedi; **on ~s** le samedi; **last ~** samedi dernier; **this ~** ce samedi; **next ~** samedi prochain; **every ~** tous les samedis; **every other ~** un samedi sur deux; **the ~ before** l'autre samedi; **the ~ before last** pas samedi dernier, mais le samedi d'avant; **the ~ after next, ~ week, a week on ~** samedi en huit; **to work ~s** travailler le samedi. ◇ *comp* [paper] du OR de samedi; **I have a ~ appointment** j'ai un rendez-vous samedi; **~ morning/afternoon/evening** samedi matin/après-midi/soir; **a ~ job** un petit boulot (*le samedi pour gagner de l'argent de poche*).

Saturn ['sætən] *n* [planet] Saturne *f*.

sauce [sɔːs] *n* **-1.** CULIN sauce *f*. **-2.** *Br inf* [cheek] toupet *m*.

sauce boat *n* saucière *f*.

saucepan ['sɔːspən] *n* casserole *f*.

saucer ['sɔːsər] *n* sous-tasse *f*, soucoupe *f*.

saucy ['sɔːsɪ] (*compar* **-ier**, *superl* **-iest**) *adj inf* coquin(e).

Saudi (Arabia) ['saʊdɪ-] *n* Arabie Saoudite *f*; **in ~** en Arabie Saoudite.

Saudi (Arabian) ['saʊdɪ-] ◇ *adj* saoudien(ienne). ◇ *n* [person] Saoudien *m*, -ienne *f*.

sauna ['sɔːnə] *n* sauna *m*.

saunter ['sɔːntər] *vi* flâner.

sausage ['sɒsɪdʒ] *n* saucisse *f*.

sausage roll *n Br* feuilleté *m* à la saucisse.

sauté [*Br* 'saʊteɪ, *Am* saʊ'teɪ] (*pt* & *pp* **sautéed** OR **sautéd**) ◇ *adj* sauté(e). ◇ *vt* [potatoes] faire sauter; [onions] faire revenir.

savage ['sævɪdʒ] ◇ *adj* [fierce] féroce. ◇ *n* sauvage *mf*. ◇ *vt* attaquer avec férocité.

savageness ['sævɪdʒnɪs], **savagery** ['sævɪdʒrɪ] *n* férocité *f*.

savanna(h) [sə'vænə] *n* savane *f*.

save [seɪv] ◇ *vt* **-1.** [rescue] sauver; **to ~ sb's life** sauver la vie à OR de qqn. **-2.** [time] gagner; [strength] économiser; [food] garder; [money - set aside] mettre de côté; [- spend less] économiser; **we ~d £10 by buying in bulk** on a économisé 10 livres en achetant en grosses quantités. **-3.** [avoid]

éviter, épargner; **to ~ sb sthg** épargner qqch à qqn; **to ~ sb from doing sthg** éviter à qqn de faire qqch. **-4.** SPORT arrêter. **-5.** COMPUT sauvegarder. ◇ *vi* [save money] mettre de l'argent de côté. ◇ *n* SPORT arrêt *m*. ◇ *prep fml*: **~ (for)** sauf, à l'exception de. ◆ **save up** *vi* mettre de l'argent de côté.

save-as-you-earn *n Br* plan d'épargne national par prélèvements mensuels.

saveloy ['sævəlɔɪ] *n Br* cervelas *m*.

saver ['seɪvər] *n* **-1.** [object]: **it's a money ~** ça me fait économiser de l'argent. **-2.** FIN épargnant *m*, -e *f*.

saving grace ['seɪvɪŋ-] *n*: **its ~ was ...** ce qui le rachetait, c'était ....

savings ['seɪvɪŋz] *npl* économies *fpl*.

savings account *n Am* compte *m* d'épargne.

savings and loan association *n Am* société *f* de crédit immobilier.

savings bank *n* caisse *f* d'épargne.

saviour *Br*, **savior** *Am* ['seɪvjər] *n* sauveur *m*. ◆ **Saviour** *n*: **the Saviour** le Sauveur.

savoir-faire [,sævwɑː'feər] *n* savoir-vivre *m*.

savour *Br*, **savor** *Am* ['seɪvər] *vt lit* & *fig* savourer.

savoury *Br* (*pl* **-ies**), **savory** *Am* (*pl* **-ies**) ['seɪvərɪ] ◇ *adj* **-1.** [food] salé(e). **-2.** [respectable] recommandable. ◇ *n* petit plat *m* salé.

Savoy [sə'vɔɪ] *n* Savoie *f*; **in ~** en Savoie.

saw [sɔː] (*Br pt* **-ed**, *pp* **sawn**, *Am pt* & *pp* **-ed**) ◇ *pt* → **see**. ◇ *n* scie *f*. ◇ *vt* scier.

sawdust ['sɔːdʌst] *n* sciure *f* (de bois).

sawed-off shotgun *Am* = **sawn-off shotgun**.

sawmill ['sɔːmɪl] *n* scierie *f*.

sawn [sɔːn] *pp Br* → **saw**.

sawn-off shotgun *Br*, **sawed-off shotgun** ['sɔːd-] *Am n* carabine *f* à canon scié.

sax [sæks] *n inf* saxo *m*.

Saxon ['sæksn] ◇ *adj* saxon(onne). ◇ *n* Saxon *m*, -onne *f*.

saxophone ['sæksəfəʊn] *n* saxophone *m*.

saxophonist [*Br* ,sæks'ɒfənɪst, *Am* 'sæksə,fəʊnɪst] *n* saxophoniste *mf*.

say [seɪ] (*pt* & *pp* **said**) ◇ *vt* **-1.** [gen] dire; **could you ~ that again?** vous pouvez répéter ce que vous venez de dire?; **(let's) ~ you won a lottery ...** supposons que tu gagnes le gros lot ...; **it ~s a lot about him** cela en dit long sur lui; **she's said to be ...** on dit qu'elle est ...; **to ~ to o.s.** se dire; **~ nothing of** sans parler de; **that goes**

without ~**ing** cela va sans dire; **I'll** ~ **this for him ...** je dois lui rendre cette justice que ...; **it has a lot to be said for it** cela va beaucoup d'avantages; **she didn't have much to** ~ **for herself** *inf* elle n'avait pas grand-chose à dire. **-2.** [subj: clock, watch] indiquer.
◇ *n*: **to have a/no** ~ avoir/ne pas avoir voix au chapitre; **to have a** ~ **in sthg** avoir son mot à dire sur qqch; **to have one's** ~ dire ce que l'on a à dire, dire son mot.
◆ **that is to say** *adv* c'est-à-dire.

SAYE *n abbr of* **save as you earn**.

saying ['seɪɪŋ] *n* dicton *m*.

say-so *n inf* [permission] autorisation *f*.

SBA (*abbr of* **Small Business Administration**) *n* organisme fédéral américain d'aide aux petites entreprises.

s/c *abbr of* **self-contained**.

SC ◇ *n abbr of* **supreme court**. ◇ *abbr of* **South Carolina**.

scab [skæb] *n* **-1.** [of wound] croûte *f*. **-2.** *inf pej* [non-striker] jaune *m*.

scabby ['skæbɪ] (*compar* **-ier**, *superl* **-iest**) *adj* couvert(e) de croûtes.

scabies ['skeɪbiːz] *n* (*U*) gale *f*.

scaffold ['skæfəʊld] *n* échafaud *m*.

scaffolding ['skæfəldɪŋ] *n* échafaudage *m*.

scalaway *Am* = **scallywag**.

scald [skɔːld] ◇ *n* brûlure *f*. ◇ *vt* ébouillanter; **to** ~ **one's arm** s'ébouillanter le bras.

scalding ['skɔːldɪŋ] *adj* bouillant(e).

scale [skeɪl] ◇ *n* **-1.** [gen] échelle *f*; **to** ~ [map, drawing] à l'échelle. **-2.** [of ruler, thermometer] graduation *f*. **-3.** MUS gamme *f*. **-4.** [of fish, snake] écaille *f*. **-5.** *Am* = **scales**. ◇ *vt* **-1.** [cliff, mountain, fence] escalader. **-2.** [fish] écailler.
◆ **scales** *npl* balance *f*.
◆ **scale down** *vt fus* réduire.

scale diagram *n* plan *m* à l'échelle.

scale model *n* modèle *m* réduit.

scallion ['skæljən] *n Am* [spring onion] ciboule *f*.

scallop ['skɒləp] ◇ *n* [shellfish] coquille *f* Saint-Jacques. ◇ *vt* [edge, garment] festonner.

scallywag *Br* ['skælɪwæg], **scalawag** *Am* ['skæləwæg] *n inf* polisson *m*, -onne *f*.

scalp [skælp] ◇ *n* **-1.** ANAT cuir *m* chevelu. **-2.** [trophy] scalp *m*. ◇ *vt* scalper.

scalpel ['skælpəl] *n* scalpel *m*.

scalper ['skælpər] *n Am* [tout] revendeur *m* de billets.

scam [skæm] *n inf* arnaque *f*.

scamp [skæmp] *n inf* coquin *m*, -e *f*.

scamper ['skæmpər] *vi* trottiner.

scampi ['skæmpɪ] *n* (*U*) scampi *mpl*.

scan [skæn] (*pt & pp* **-ned**, *cont* **-ning**) ◇ *n* MED scanographie *f*; [during pregnancy] échographie *f*. ◇ *vt* **-1.** [examine carefully] scruter. **-2.** [glance at] parcourir. **-3.** TECH balayer. **-4.** COMPUT faire un scannage de. ◇ *vi* **-1.** LITERATURE se scander. **-2.** COMPUT scanner.

scandal ['skændl] *n* **-1.** [gen] scandale *m*. **-2.** [gossip] médisance *f*.

scandalize, **-ise** ['skændəlaɪz] *vt* scandaliser.

scandalous ['skændələs] *adj* scandaleux(euse).

Scandinavia [,skændɪ'neɪvjə] *n* Scandinavie *f*; **in** ~ en Scandinavie.

Scandinavian [,skændɪ'neɪvjən] ◇ *adj* scandinave. ◇ *n* [person] Scandinave *mf*.

scanner ['skænər] *n* [gen & COMPUT] scanner *m*.

scant [skænt] *adj* insuffisant(e).

scanty ['skæntɪ] (*compar* **-ier**, *superl* **-iest**) *adj* [amount, resources] insuffisant(e); [income] maigre; [dress] minuscule.

scapegoat ['skeɪpgəʊt] *n* bouc *m* émissaire.

scar [skɑːr] (*pt & pp* **-red**, *cont* **-ring**) ◇ *n* cicatrice *f*. ◇ *vt* **-1.** [skin, face] marquer d'une cicatrice; [landscape] défigurer. **-2.** *fig* [mentally] marquer.

scarce ['skeəs] *adj* rare, peu abondant(e); **to make o.s.** ~ s'esquiver.

scarcely ['skeəslɪ] *adv* à peine; ~ **anyone** presque personne; **I** ~ **ever go there now** je n'y vais presque jamais.

scarcity ['skeəsətɪ] *n* manque *m*.

scare [skeər] ◇ *n* **-1.** [sudden fear]: **to give sb a** ~ faire peur à qqn. **-2.** [public fear] panique *f*; **bomb** ~ alerte *f* à la bombe. ◇ *vt* faire peur à, effrayer.
◆ **scare away**, **scare off** *vt sep* faire fuir.

scarecrow ['skeəkrəʊ] *n* épouvantail *m*.

scared ['skeəd] *adj* apeuré(e); **to be** ~ avoir peur; **to be** ~ **stiff** OR **to death** être mort de peur.

scarey ['skeərɪ] = **scary**.

scarf [skɑːf] (*pl* **-s** OR **scarves**) *n* [wool] écharpe *f*; [silk etc] foulard *m*.

scarlet ['skɑːlət] ◇ *adj* écarlate. ◇ *n* écarlate *f*.

scarlet fever *n* scarlatine *f*.

scarves [skɑːvz] *pl* → **scarf**.

scary ['skeərɪ] (*compar* **-ier**, *superl* **-iest**) *adj* *inf* qui fait peur.

scathing ['skeɪðɪŋ] *adj* [criticism] acerbe; [reply] cinglant(e); **to be ~ about sb/sthg** critiquer qqn/qqch de manière acerbe.

scatter ['skætər] ◇ *vt* [clothes, paper etc] éparpiller; [seeds] semer à la volée. ◇ *vi* se disperser.

scatterbrained ['skætəbreɪnd] *adj inf* écervelé(e).

scattered ['skætəd] *adj* [wreckage, population] dispersé(e); [paper] éparpillé(e); [showers] intermittent(e).

scattering ['skætərɪŋ] *n* [small number] petit nombre *m*; [small amount] petite quantité *f*.

scatty ['skætɪ] *(compar* -ier, *superl* -iest) *adj Br inf* écervelé(e).

scavenge ['skævɪndʒ] ◇ *vt* [object] récupérer. ◇ *vi* [person]: **to ~ for sthg** faire les poubelles pour trouver qqch.

scavenger ['skævɪndʒə'] *n* -1. [animal] animal *m* nécrophage. -2. [person] personne *f* qui fait les poubelles.

SCE (*abbr of* **Scottish Certificate of Education**) *n certificat de fin d'études secondaires en Écosse.*

scenario [sɪ'nɑːrɪəu] *(pl* -s) *n* -1. [possible situation] hypothèse *f*, scénario *m*. -2. [of film, play] scénario *m*.

scene [siːn] *n* -1. [in play, film, book] scène *f*; **to make a ~** *fig* faire une scène; **behind the ~s** dans les coulisses. -2. [sight] spectacle *m*, vue *f*; [picture] tableau *m*. -3. [location] lieu *m*, endroit *m*; **on the ~** sur les lieux; **a change of ~** un changement de décor. -4. [area of activity]: **the political ~** la scène politique; **the music ~** le monde de la musique; **it's not my ~** *inf* ce n'est pas mon truc. -5. *phr*: **to set the ~ for sb** mettre qqn au courant de la situation; **to set the ~ for sthg** préparer la voie à qqch.

scenery ['siːnərɪ] *n* (*U*) -1. [of countryside] paysage *m*. -2. THEATRE décor *m*, décors *mpl*.

scenic ['siːnɪk] *adj* [tour] touristique; **a ~ view** un beau panorama.

scenic route *n* route *f* touristique.

scent [sent] ◇ *n* -1. [smell - of flowers] senteur *f*, parfum *m*; [- of animal] odeur *f*, fumet *m*. -2. *fig* [track] piste *f*. -3. (*U*) [perfume] parfum *m*. ◇ *vt lit* & *fig* sentir.

scented ['sentɪd] *adj* parfumé(e).

scepter *Am* = sceptre.

sceptic *Br*, **skeptic** *Am* ['skeptɪk] *n* sceptique *mf*.

sceptical *Br*, **skeptical** *Am* ['skeptɪkl] *adj*: **~ (about)** sceptique (sur).

scepticism *Br*, **skepticism** *Am* ['skeptɪsɪzm] *n* scepticisme *m*.

sceptre *Br*, **scepter** *Am* ['septə'] *n* sceptre *m*.

SCF (*abbr of* **Save the Children Fund**) *n* association caritative britannique s'occupant des enfants.

schedule [*Br* 'ʃedjul, *Am* 'skedʒul] ◇ *n* -1. [plan] programme *m*, plan *m*; **(according) to ~** selon le programme, comme prévu; **on ~** [at expected time] à l'heure (prévue); [on expected day] à la date prévue; **ahead of/behind ~** en avance/en retard (sur le programme). -2. [list - of times] horaire *m*; [- of prices] tarif *m*. ◇ *vt*: **to ~ sthg (for)** prévoir qqch (pour).

scheduled flight [*Br* 'ʃedjuld-, *Am* 'skedʒuld-] *n* vol *m* régulier.

schematic [skɪ'mætɪk] *adj* schématique.

scheme [skiːm] ◇ *n* -1. [plan] plan *m*, projet *m*. -2. *pej* [dishonest plan] combine *f*. -3. [arrangement] arrangement *m*; **colour ~** combinaison *f* de couleurs; **the ~ of things** l'ordre des choses. ◇ *vt pej*: **to ~ to do sthg** conspirer pour faire qqch. ◇ *vi pej* conspirer.

scheming ['skiːmɪŋ] *adj* intrigant(e).

schism ['sɪzm, 'skɪzm] *n* schisme *m*.

schizophrenia [ˌskɪtsə'friːnjə] *n* schizophrénie *f*.

schizophrenic [ˌskɪtsə'frenɪk] ◇ *adj* schizophrène. ◇ *n* schizophrène *mf*.

schlepp [ʃlep] *Am inf* ◇ *vt* trimbaler. ◇ *vi*: **to ~ (around)** se trimbaler.

schmal(t)z [ʃmɔːlts] *n inf* sentimentalité *f* à la guimauve.

schmuck [ʃmʌk] *n Am inf* rigolo *m*.

scholar ['skɒlə'] *n* -1. [expert] érudit *m*, -e *f*, savant *m*, -e *f*. -2. *dated* [student] écolier *m*, -ière *f*, élève *mf*. -3. [holder of scholarship] boursier *m*, -ière *f*.

scholarship ['skɒləʃɪp] *n* -1. [grant] bourse *f* (d'études). -2. [learning] érudition *f*.

scholastic [skə'læstɪk] *adj fml* scolaire.

school [skuːl] *n* -1. [gen] école *f*; [secondary school] lycée *m*, collège *m*. -2. [university department] faculté *f*. -3. *Am* [university] université *f*. -4. [of fish] banc *m*.

school age *n* âge *m* scolaire.

schoolbook ['skuːlbuk] *n* livre *m* scolaire OR de classe.

schoolboy ['skuːlbɔɪ] *n* écolier *m*, élève *m*.

schoolchild ['skuːltʃaɪld] *(pl* -children [-tʃɪldrən]) *n* écolier *m*, -ière *f*, élève *mf*.

schooldays ['skuːldeɪz] *npl* années *fpl* d'école.

school dinner *n* déjeuner *m* à la cantine (de l'école).

school district *n Am aux États-Unis,* autorité locale décisionnaire dans le domaine de l'enseignement primaire et secondaire.

school friend *n* camarade *mf* d'école.

schoolgirl ['sku:lgɜ:l] *n* écolière *f,* élève *f.*

schooling ['sku:lɪŋ] *n* instruction *f.*

schoolkid ['sku:lkɪd] *n inf* écolier *m,* -ière *f,* élève *mf.*

school-leaver [-,li:vəʳ] *n Br* élève *qui a fini ses études secondaires.*

school-leaving age [-'li:vɪŋ-] *n Br* âge *m* de fin de scolarité.

schoolmarm ['sku:lmɑ:m] *n Am* institutrice *f.*

schoolmaster ['sku:l,mɑ:stəʳ] *n* [primary] instituteur *m,* maître *m* d'école; [secondary] professeur *m.*

schoolmistress ['sku:l,mɪstrɪs] *n* [primary] institutrice *f,* maîtresse *f* d'école; [secondary] professeur *m.*

school of thought *n* école *f* (de pensée).

school report *n* bulletin *m.*

schoolroom ['sku:lrum] *n* salle *f* de classe.

schoolteacher ['sku:l,ti:tʃəʳ] *n* [primary] instituteur *m,* -trice *f;* [secondary] professeur *m.*

school uniform *n* uniforme *m* scolaire.

schoolwork ['sku:lwɜ:k] *n* (*U*) travail *m* scolaire or de classe.

school year *n* année *f* scolaire.

schooner ['sku:nəʳ] *n* -1. [ship] schooner *m,* goélette *f.* -2. *Br* [sherry glass] grand verre *m* à xérès.

sciatica [saɪ'ætɪkə] *n* sciatique *f.*

science ['saɪəns] ◇ *n* science *f.* ◇ *comp* [student] en sciences; [degree] de OR ès sciences; [course] de sciences.

science fiction *n* science-fiction *f.*

science park *n* parc *m* scientifique.

scientific [,saɪən'tɪfɪk] *adj* scientifique.

scientist ['saɪəntɪst] *n* scientifique *mf.*

sci-fi [,saɪ'faɪ] (*abbr of* **science fiction**) *n inf* science-fiction *f,* S.F. *f.*

Scilly Isles ['sɪlɪ-], **Scillies** ['sɪlɪz] *npl:* **the ~** les îles *fpl* Sorlingues; **in the ~** aux îles Sorlingues.

scintillating ['sɪntɪleɪtɪŋ] *adj* brillant(e).

scissors ['sɪzəz] *npl* ciseaux *mpl;* **a pair of ~** une paire de ciseaux.

sclerosis ➤ **multiple sclerosis.**

scoff [skɒf] ◇ *vt Br inf* bouffer, boulotter. ◇ *vi:* **to ~ (at)** se moquer (de).

scold [skəʊld] *vt* gronder, réprimander.

scone [skɒn] *n* scone *m.*

scoop [sku:p] ◇ *n* -1. [for sugar] pelle *f* à main; [for ice cream] cuiller *f* à glace. -2. [of

ice cream] boule *f.* -3. [news report] exclusivité *f,* scoop *m.* ◇ *vt* [with hands] prendre avec les mains; [with scoop] prendre avec une pelle à main.

◆ **scoop out** *vt sep* évider.

scoot [sku:t] *vi inf* filer.

scooter ['sku:təʳ] *n* -1. [toy] trottinette *f.* -2. [motorcycle] scooter *m.*

scope [skəʊp] *n* (*U*) -1. [opportunity] occasion *f,* possibilité *f.* -2. [of report, inquiry] étendue *f,* portée *f.*

scorch [skɔ:tʃ] ◇ *vt* [clothes] brûler légèrement, roussir; [skin] brûler; [land, grass] dessécher. ◇ *vi* roussir.

scorched earth policy [skɔ:tʃt-] *n* politique *f* de la terre brûlée.

scorcher ['skɔ:tʃəʳ] *n inf* [day] journée *f* torride.

scorching ['skɔ:tʃɪŋ] *adj inf* [day] torride; [sun] brûlant(e).

score [skɔ:ʳ] ◇ *n* -1. SPORT score *m.* -2. [in test] note *f.* -3. *dated* [twenty] vingt. -4. MUS partition *f.* -5. [subject]: **on that ~** à ce sujet, sur ce point. ◇ *vt* -1. [goal, point etc] marquer; **to ~ 100%** avoir 100 sur 100. -2. [success, victory] remporter. -3. [cut] entailler. ◇ *vi* -1. SPORT marquer (un but/point etc). -2. [in an argument]: **to ~ over sb** marquer un point contre qqn.

◆ **scores** *npl:* **~s of** des tas de, plein de.

◆ **score out** *vt sep Br* barrer, rayer.

scoreboard ['skɔ:bɔ:d] *n* tableau *m.*

scorecard ['skɔ:kɑ:d] *n* carte *f* de score.

scorer ['skɔ:rəʳ] *n* marqueur *m.*

scorn [skɔ:n] ◇ *n* (*U*) mépris *m,* dédain *m;* **to pour ~ on sb** accabler qqn de mépris. ◇ *vt* -1. [person, attitude] mépriser. -2. [help, offer] rejeter, dédaigner.

scornful ['skɔ:nful] *adj* méprisant(e); **to be ~ of sthg** mépriser qqch, dédaigner qqch.

Scorpio ['skɔ:pɪəʊ] (*pl* -s) *n* Scorpion *m;* **to be (a) ~** être Scorpion.

scorpion ['skɔ:pjən] *n* scorpion *m.*

Scot [skɒt] *n* Écossais *m,* -e *f.*

scotch [skɒtʃ] *vt* [rumour] étouffer; [plan] faire échouer.

Scotch [skɒtʃ] ◇ *adj* écossais(e). ◇ *n* scotch *m,* whisky *m.*

Scotch egg *n Br* œuf dur enrobé de chair à saucisse et recouvert de chapelure.

Scotch (tape)® *n Am* scotch® *m.*

scot-free *adj inf:* **to get off ~** s'en tirer sans être puni(e).

Scotland ['skɒtlənd] *n* Écosse *f;* **in ~** en Écosse.

Scotland Yard *n* ancien nom du siège de la police à Londres (aujourd'hui New Scotland Yard).

Scots [skɒts] ◇ *adj* écossais(e). ◇ *n* [dialect] écossais *m*.

Scotsman ['skɒtsmən] (*pl* **-men** [-mən]) *n* Écossais *m*.

Scotswoman ['skɒtswʊmən] (*pl* **-women** [-,wɪmɪn]) *n* Écossaise *f*.

Scottish ['skɒtɪʃ] *adj* écossais(e).

Scottish National Party *n*: **the** ~ le Parti national écossais.

scoundrel ['skaʊndrəl] *n dated* gredin *m*.

scour [skaʊəʳ] *vt* **-1.** [clean] récurer. **-2.** [search - town etc] parcourir; [- countryside] battre.

scourer ['skaʊrəʳ] *n* [pad] tampon *m* à récurer; [powder] poudre *f* à récurer.

scourge [skɜːdʒ] *n* fléau *m*.

Scouse [skaʊs] *n inf* **-1.** [person] habitant *m*, -e *f* de Liverpool. **-2.** [accent] accent *m* de Liverpool.

scout [skaʊt] *n* MIL éclaireur *m*.
◆ **Scout** *n* [boy scout] Scout *m*.
◆ **scout around** *vi*: **to** ~ **around (for)** aller à la recherche (de).

scoutmaster ['skaʊt,mɑːstəʳ] *n* chef *m* scout.

scowl [skaʊl] ◇ *n* regard *m* noir, air *m* renfrogné. ◇ *vi* se renfrogner, froncer les sourcils; **to** ~ **at sb** jeter des regards noirs à qqn.

SCR (*abbr of* **senior common room**) *n Br* salle des étudiants de 3e cycle.

scrabble ['skræbl] *vi* **-1.** [scrape]: **to** ~ **at sthg** gratter qqch. **-2.** [feel around]: **to** ~ **around for sthg** tâtonner pour trouver qqch.

Scrabble® ['skræbl] *n* Scrabble® *m*.

scraggy ['skrægɪ] (*compar* **-ier**, *superl* **-iest**) *adj* décharné(e), maigre.

scram [skræm] (*pt & pp* **-med**, *cont* **-ming**) *vi inf* filer, ficher le camp.

scramble ['skræmbl] ◇ *n* [rush] bousculade *f*, ruée *f*. ◇ *vi* **-1.** [climb]: **to** ~ **up a hill** grimper une colline en s'aidant des mains OR à quatre pattes. **-2.** [compete]: **to** ~ **for sthg** se disputer qqch.

scrambled eggs ['skræmbld-] *npl* œufs *mpl* brouillés.

scrambler ['skræmbləʳ] *n* COMPUT brouilleur *m*.

scrap [skræp] (*pt & pp* **-ped**, *cont* **-ping**) ◇ *n* **-1.** [of paper, material] bout *m*; [of information] fragment *m*; [of conversation] bribe *f*; **it won't make a** ~ **of difference** cela ne chan-

gera absolument rien. **-2.** [metal] ferraille *f*. **-3.** *inf* [fight, quarrel] bagarre *f*. ◇ *vt* [car] mettre à la ferraille; [plan, system] abandonner, laisser tomber.
◆ **scraps** *npl* [food] restes *mpl*.

scrapbook ['skræpbʊk] *n* album *m* (*de coupures de journaux etc*).

scrap dealer *n* ferrailleur *m*, marchand *m* de ferraille.

scrape [skreɪp] ◇ *n* **-1.** [scraping noise] raclement *m*, grattement *m*. **-2.** *dated* [difficult situation]: **to get into a** ~ se fourrer dans le pétrin. ◇ *vt* **-1.** [clean, rub] gratter, racler; **to** ~ **sthg off sthg** enlever qqch de qqch en grattant OR raclant. **-2.** [surface, car, skin] érafler. ◇ *vi* gratter.
◆ **scrape through** *vt fus* réussir de justesse.
◆ **scrape together**, **scrape up** *vt sep*: **to** ~ **some money together** réunir de l'argent en raclant les fonds de tiroirs.

scraper ['skreɪpəʳ] *n* grattoir *m*, racloir *m*.

scrap heap *n* tas *m* de ferraille; **on the** ~ *fig* au rebut, au placard.

scrapings ['skreɪpɪŋz] *npl* raclures *fpl*.

scrap merchant *n Br* ferrailleur *m*, marchand *m* de ferraille.

scrap metal *n* ferraille *f*.

scrap paper *Br*, **scratch paper** *Am n* (papier *m*) brouillon *m*.

scrappy ['skræpɪ] (*compar* **-ier**, *superl* **-iest**) *adj* [work, speech] décousu(e).

scrapyard ['skræpjɑːd] *n* parc *m* à ferraille.

scratch [skrætʃ] ◇ *n* **-1.** [wound] égratignure *f*, éraflure *f*. **-2.** [on glass, paint etc] éraflure *f*. **-3.** *phr*: **to be up to** ~ être à la hauteur; **to do sthg from** ~ faire qqch à partir de rien. ◇ *vt* **-1.** [wound] écorcher, égratigner. **-2.** [mark - paint, glass etc] rayer, érafler. **-3.** [rub] gratter; **to** ~ **o.s.** se gratter. ◇ *vi* [gratter; person] se gratter.

scratchpad ['skrætʃpæd] *n Am* bloc-notes *m*.

scratch paper *Am* = **scrap paper**.

scratchy ['skrætʃɪ] (*compar* **-ier**, *superl* **-iest**) *adj* **-1.** [record] qui grésille, qui craque. **-2.** [material] qui gratte.

scrawl [skrɔːl] ◇ *n* griffonnage *m*, gribouillage *m*. ◇ *vt* griffonner, gribouiller.

scrawny ['skrɔːnɪ] (*compar* **-ier**, *superl* **-iest**) *adj* [person] efflanqué(e); [body, animal] décharné(e).

scream [skriːm] ◇ *n* **-1.** [cry] cri *m* perçant, hurlement *m*; [of laughter] éclat *m*. **-2.** *inf* [funny person]: **he's a** ~ il est tordant. ◇ *vt* hurler. ◇ *vi* [cry out] crier, hurler.

scree [skri:] *n* éboulis *m*.

screech [skri:tʃ] ◇ *n* -1. [cry] cri *m* perçant. -2. [of tyres] crissement *m*. ◇ *vt* hurler. ◇ *vi* -1. [cry out] pousser des cris perçants. -2. [tyres] crisser.

screen [skri:n] ◇ *n* -1. [gen] écran *m*. -2. [panel] paravent *m*. ◇ *vt* -1. CINEMA projeter, passer; TV téléviser, passer. -2. [hide] cacher, masquer. -3. [shield] protéger. -4. [candidate, employee] passer au crible, filtrer. -5. MED: **to ~ sb for sthg** faire subir à qqn un test de dépistage pour qqch.

◆ **screen off** *vt sep* séparer par un paravent.

screen door *n* porte *f* avec moustiquaire.

screen dump *n* COMPUT vidage *m* d'écran.

screening ['skri:nɪŋ] *n* -1. CINEMA projection *f*; TV passage *m* à la télévision. -2. [for security] sélection *f*, tri *m*. -3. MED dépistage *m*.

screenplay ['skri:npleɪ] *n* scénario *m*.

screen print *n* sérigraphie *f*.

screen saver *n* COMPUT circuit *m* économiseur (d'écran).

screen test *n* bout *m* d'essai.

screenwriter ['skri:n,raɪtər] *n* scénariste *mf*.

screw [skru:] ◇ *n* [for fastening] vis *f*. ◇ *vt* -1. [fix with screws]: **to ~ sthg to sthg** visser qqch à OR sur qqch. -2. [twist] visser. -3. *vulg* [woman] baiser. ◇ *vi* se visser.

◆ **screw up** *vt sep* -1. [crumple up] froisser, chiffonner. -2. [eyes] plisser; [face] tordre. -3. *v inf* [ruin] gâcher, bousiller.

screwball ['skru:bɔ:l] *n Am inf* [person] cinglé *m*, -e *f*.

screwdriver ['skru:,draɪvər] *n* [tool] tournevis *m*.

screwtop jar ['skru:tɒp-] *n* pot *m* à couvercle à pas de vis.

screwy ['skru:ɪ] *adj Am inf* fou (folle), cinglé(e).

scribble ['skrɪbl] ◇ *n* gribouillage *m*, griffonnage *m*. ◇ *vt & vi* gribouiller, griffonner.

scribe [skraɪb] *n* scribe *m*.

scrimp [skrɪmp] *vi*: **to ~ and save** économiser OR lésiner sur tout.

script [skrɪpt] *n* -1. [of play, film etc] scénario *m*, script *m*. -2. [writing system] écriture *f*. -3. [handwriting] (écriture *f*) script *m*.

scripted ['skrɪptɪd] *adj* préparé(e) à l'avance.

Scriptures ['skrɪptʃəz] *npl*: **the ~** les (Saintes) Écritures *fpl*.

scriptwriter ['skrɪpt,raɪtər] *n* scénariste *mf*.

scroll [skrəʊl] ◇ *n* rouleau *m*. ◇ *vt* COMPUT faire défiler.

◆ **scroll down** *vi* COMPUT défiler vers le bas.

◆ **scroll up** *vi* COMPUT défiler vers le haut.

scroll bar *n* COMPUT barre *f* de défilement.

scrooge [skru:dʒ] *n inf pej* grippe-sou *m*.

scrotum ['skrəʊtəm] (*pl* -ta [-tə] OR -tums) *n* scrotum *m*.

scrounge [skraʊndʒ] *inf* ◇ *vt*: **to ~ money off sb** taper qqn; **can I ~ a cigarette off you?** je peux te piquer une cigarette? ◇ *vi* faire le parasite; **to ~ off sb** *Br* vivre aux crochets de qqn.

scrounger ['skraʊndʒər] *n inf* parasite *m*.

scrub [skrʌb] (*pt & pp* -**bed**, *cont* -**bing**) ◇ *n* -1. [rub]: **to give sthg a ~** nettoyer qqch à la brosse. -2. (*U*) [undergrowth] broussailles *fpl*. ◇ *vt* [floor, clothes etc] laver OR nettoyer à la brosse; [hands, back] frotter; [saucepan] récurer.

scrubbing brush *Br* ['skrʌbɪŋ-], **scrub brush** *Am n* brosse *f* dure.

scruff [skrʌf] *n*: **by the ~ of the neck** par la peau du cou.

scruffy ['skrʌfɪ] (*compar* -**ier**, *superl* -**iest**) *adj* mal soigné(e), débraillé(e).

scrum(mage) ['skrʌm(ɪdʒ)] *n* RUGBY mêlée *f*.

scrumptious ['skrʌmpʃəs] *adj inf* délicieux(ieuse), fameux(euse).

scrunch [skrʌntʃ] ◇ *vt* écraser, faire craquer. ◇ *vi* craquer, crisser.

scruples ['skru:plz] *npl* scrupules *mpl*.

scrupulous ['skru:pjʊləs] *adj* scrupuleux(euse).

scrupulously ['skru:pjʊləslɪ] *adv* scrupuleusement; **~ clean** d'une propreté méticuleuse; **~ honest** d'une honnêteté scrupuleuse.

scrutinize, -ise ['skru:tɪnaɪz] *vt* scruter, examiner attentivement.

scrutiny ['skru:tɪnɪ] *n* (*U*) examen *m* attentif.

scuba diving ['sku:bə-] *n* plongée *f* sous-marine autonome.

scud [skʌd] (*pt & pp* -**ded**, *cont* -**ding**) *vi literary* [clouds] courir.

scuff [skʌf] *vt* -1. [damage] érafler. -2. [drag]: **to ~ one's feet** traîner les pieds.

scuffle ['skʌfl] ◇ *n* bagarre *f*, échauffourée *f*. ◇ *vi* se bagarrer, se battre.

scull [skʌl] ◇ *n* aviron *m*. ◇ *vi* ramer.

scullery ['skʌlərɪ] (*pl* -**ies**) *n* arrière-cuisine *f*.

sculpt [skʌlpt] *vt* sculpter.

sculptor ['skʌlptər] *n* sculpteur *m*.

sculpture ['skʌlptʃəʳ] ◇ *n* sculpture *f*. ◇ *vt* sculpter.

scum [skʌm] *n* **-1.** (*U*) [froth] écume *f*, mousse *f*. **-2.** *v inf pej* [person] salaud *m*. **-3.** (*U*) *v inf pej* [people] déchets *mpl*.

scupper ['skʌpəʳ] *vt* **-1.** NAUT couler. **-2.** *Br fig* [plan] saboter, faire tomber à l'eau.

scurf [skɜːf] *n* (*U*) pellicules *fpl*.

scurrilous ['skʌrələs] *adj* calomnieux(ieuse).

scurry ['skʌrɪ] (*pt* & *pp* **-ied**) *vi* se précipiter; **to ~ away** OR **off** se sauver, détaler.

scurvy ['skɜːvɪ] *n* scorbut *m*.

scuttle ['skʌtl] ◇ *n* seau *m* à charbon. ◇ *vi* courir précipitamment OR à pas précipités.

scythe [saɪð] ◇ *n* faux *f*. ◇ *vt* faucher.

SD *abbr of* **South Dakota**.

SDI (*abbr of* **Strategic Defense Initiative**) *n* IDS *f*.

SDLP (*abbr of* **Social Democratic and Labour Party**) *n* parti travailliste d'Irlande du Nord.

SDP (*abbr of* **Social Democratic Party**) *n* parti social-démocrate en Grande-Bretagne.

SE (*abbr of* **south-east**) S-E.

sea [siː] ◇ *n* **-1.** [gen] mer *f*; **at ~** en mer; **by ~** par mer; **by the ~** au bord de la mer; **out to ~** au large. **-2.** *phr*: **to be all at ~** nager complètement. **-3.** *fig* [large number] multitude *f*. ◇ *comp* [voyage] en mer; [animal] marin(e), de mer.
◆ **seas** *npl*: **the ~s** les mers *fpl*.

sea air *n* air *m* marin OR de la mer.

sea anemone *n* anémone *f* de mer.

seabed ['siːbed] *n*: **the ~** le fond de la mer.

seabird ['siːbɜːd] *n* oiseau *m* marin OR de mer.

seaboard ['siːbɔːd] *n* littoral *m*, côte *f*.

sea breeze *n* brise *f* de mer.

seafaring ['siːˌfeərɪŋ] *adj* [nation] maritime; **a ~** un marin.

seafood ['siːfuːd] *n* (*U*) fruits *mpl* de mer.

seafront ['siːfrʌnt] *n* front *m* de mer.

seagoing ['siːˌgəʊɪŋ] *adj* [boat] de mer.

seagull ['siːgʌl] *n* mouette *f*.

seahorse ['siːhɔːs] *n* hippocampe *m*.

seal [siːl] (*pl inv* OR **-s**) ◇ *n* **-1.** [animal] phoque *m*. **-2.** [official mark] cachet *m*, sceau *m*; **~ of approval** approbation *f*; **to put** OR **set the ~ on sthg** sceller qqch. **-3.** [official fastening] cachet *m*. **-4.** [TECH - device] joint *m* d'étanchéité; [- join] joint *m* étanche. ◇ *vt* **-1.** [envelope] coller, fermer. **-2.** [document, letter] sceller, cacheter. **-3.** [block off] obturer, boucher.
◆ **seal off** *vt sep* [area, entrance] interdire l'accès de.

sealable ['siːlɪbl] *adj* qui peut être fermé(e) hermétiquement.

sea lane *n* couloir *m* maritime.

sealant ['siːlənt] *n* enduit *m* étanche.

sea level *n* niveau *m* de la mer.

sealing wax ['siːlɪŋ-] *n* cire *f* à cacheter.

sea lion (*pl inv* OR **-s**) *n* otarie *f*.

sealskin ['siːlskɪn] *n* peau *f* de phoque.

seam [siːm] *n* **-1.** SEWING couture *f*; **to be bursting at the ~s** *fig* être plein à craquer. **-2.** [of coal] couche *f*, veine *f*.

seaman ['siːmən] (*pl* **-men** [-mən]) *n* marin *m*.

seamanship ['siːmənʃɪp] *n* habileté *f* de marin.

sea mist *n* brume *f* de mer.

seamless ['siːmlɪs] *adj* **-1.** SEWING sans coutures. **-2.** *fig* [faultless] parfait(e), irréprochable.

seamstress ['semstrɪs] *n* couturière *f*.

seamy ['siːmɪ] (*compar* **-ier**, *superl* **-iest**) *adj* sordide.

séance ['seɪɒns] *n* séance *f* de spiritisme.

seaplane ['siːpleɪn] *n* hydravion *m*.

seaport ['siːpɔːt] *n* port *m* de mer.

search [sɜːtʃ] ◇ *n* [of person, luggage, house] fouille *f*; [for lost person, thing] recherche *f*, recherches *fpl*; **~ for** recherche de; **in ~ of** à la recherche de.
◇ *vt* [house, area, person] fouiller; [memory, mind, drawer] fouiller dans; **to ~ one's bag/pocket for sthg** fouiller dans son sac/sa poche pour essayer de retrouver qqch; **to ~ a house/an area for sthg** fouiller une maison/un quartier pour essayer de retrouver qqch.
◇ *vi*: **to ~ (for sb/sthg)** chercher (qqn/qqch).
◆ **search out** *vt sep* découvrir.

searcher ['sɜːtʃəʳ] *n* chercheur *m*, -euse *f*.

searching ['sɜːtʃɪŋ] *adj* [question] poussé(e), approfondi(e); [look] pénétrant(e); [review, examination] minutieux(ieuse).

searchlight ['sɜːtʃlaɪt] *n* projecteur *m*.

search party *n* équipe *f* de secours.

search warrant *n* mandat *m* de perquisition.

searing ['sɪərɪŋ] *adj* **-1.** [pain] fulgurant(e); [heat] torride. **-2.** *fig* [exposure, attack] virulent(e).

sea salt *n* sel *m* marin OR de mer.

seashell ['siːʃel] *n* coquillage *m*.

seashore ['siːʃɔːr] *n*: **the** ~ le rivage, la plage.

seasick ['siːsɪk] *adj*: **to be** OR **feel** ~ avoir le mal de mer.

seaside ['siːsaɪd] *n*: **the** ~ le bord de la mer.

seaside resort *n* station *f* balnéaire.

season ['siːzn] ◇ *n* -**1.** [gen] saison *f*; **in** ~ [food] de saison; **out of** ~ [holiday] hors saison; [food] hors de saison. -**2.** [of films] cycle *m*. ◇ *vt* assaisonner, relever.

seasonal ['siːzənl] *adj* saisonnier(ière).

seasoned ['siːznd] *adj* [traveller, campaigner] chevronné(e), expérimenté(e); [soldier] aguerri(e).

seasoning ['siːznɪŋ] *n* assaisonnement *m*.

season ticket *n* carte *f* d'abonnement.

seat [siːt] ◇ *n* -**1.** [gen] siège *m*; [in theatre] fauteuil *m*; **take a** ~! asseyez-vous! -**2.** [place to sit - in bus, train] place *f*. -**3.** [of trousers] fond *m*. ◇ *vt* -**1.** [sit down] faire asseoir, placer; **please be** ~**ed** veuillez vous asseoir; **to** ~ **o.s.** s'asseoir. -**2.** [have room for]: **the car** ~**s five** on tient à cinq dans cette voiture; **the hall** ~**s 200** il y a 200 places assises dans cette salle.

seat belt *n* ceinture *f* de sécurité.

seated ['siːtɪd] *adj* assis(e).

-seater ['siːtər] *suffix*: **a two** ~ **(car)** une voiture à deux places.

seating ['siːtɪŋ] ◇ *n* (U) [capacity] sièges *mpl*, places *fpl* (assises). ◇ *comp* [plan] de table; ~ **capacity** nombre *m* de places assises.

SEATO ['siːtəʊ] (*abbr of* **Southeast Asia Treaty Organization**) *n* OTASE *f*.

sea urchin *n* oursin *m*.

seawall ['siːˈwɔːl] *n* digue *f*.

seawater ['siːˌwɔːtər] *n* eau *f* de mer.

seaweed ['siːwiːd] *n* (U) algue *f*.

seaworthy ['siːˌwɜːðɪ] *adj* en bon état de navigabilité.

sebaceous [sɪˈbeɪʃəs] *adj* sébacé(e).

sec. *abbr of* **second**.

SEC (*abbr of* **Securities and Exchange Commission**) *n commission américaine des opérations de Bourse*, ≃ COB *f*.

secateurs [ˌsekəˈtɜːz] *npl Br* sécateur *m*.

secede [sɪˈsiːd] *vi fml*: **to** ~ **(from)** se séparer (de), faire sécession (de).

secession [sɪˈseʃn] *n fml* sécession *f*.

secluded [sɪˈkluːdɪd] *adj* retiré(e), écarté(e).

seclusion [sɪˈkluːʒn] *n* solitude *f*, retraite *f*.

second¹ ['sekənd] ◇ *n* -**1.** [gen] seconde *f*; **wait a** ~! une seconde!, (attendez) un instant!; ~ **(gear)** seconde. -**2.** *Br* UNIV ≃ licence *f* avec mention assez bien. ◇ *num* deuxième, second(e); **his score was** ~ **only to hers** il n'y a qu'elle qui a fait mieux que lui OR qui l'a surpassé; *see also* **sixth**. ◇ *vt* [proposal, motion] appuyer.

◆ **seconds** *npl* -**1.** COMM articles *mpl* de second choix. -**2.** [of food] rabiot *m*.

second² [sɪˈkɒnd] *vt Br* [employee] affecter temporairement.

secondary ['sekəndrɪ] *adj* secondaire; **to be** ~ **to** être moins important(e) que.

secondary modern *n Br* ≃ collège *m*.

secondary picketing *n* (U) piquets *mpl* de grève de solidarité.

secondary school *n* école *f* secondaire, lycée *m*.

second best ['sekənd-] *adj* deuxième; **to come off** ~ se faire battre, perdre; **don't settle for** ~ ne choisis que ce qu'il y a de mieux.

second-class ['sekənd-] *adj* -**1.** *pej* [citizen] de deuxième zone; [product] de second choix. -**2.** [ticket] de seconde OR deuxième classe. -**3.** [stamp] à tarif réduit. -**4.** *Br* UNIV [degree] ≃ avec mention assez bien.

second cousin ['sekənd-] *n* petit cousin *m*, petite cousine *f*.

second-degree burn ['sekənd-] *n* brûlure *f* du deuxième degré.

seconder ['sekəndər] *n personne qui appuie une proposition*.

second floor ['sekənd-] *n Br* troisième étage *m*; *Am* deuxième étage.

second-guess ['sekənd-] *vt inf* -**1.** [with hindsight] juger avec le recul. -**2.** [predict] anticiper, prévoir.

second hand ['sekənd-] *n* [of clock] trotteuse *f*.

second-hand ['sekənd-] ◇ *adj* -**1.** [goods, shop] d'occasion. -**2.** *fig* [information] de seconde main. ◇ *adv* -**1.** [not new] d'occasion. -**2.** *fig* [indirectly]: **to hear sthg** ~ apprendre qqch de seconde main OR indirectement.

second-in-command ['sekənd-] *n* commandant *m* en second.

secondly ['sekəndlɪ] *adv* deuxièmement, en second lieu.

secondment [sɪˈkɒndmənt] *n Br* affectation *f* temporaire.

second nature ['sekənd-] *n* seconde nature *f*.

second-rate ['sekənd-] *adj pej* de deuxième ordre, médiocre.

second thought ['sekənd-] *n*: **to have ~s about sthg** avoir des doutes sur qqch; **on ~s** *Br*, **on ~** *Am* réflexion faite, tout bien réfléchi.

secrecy ['si:krəsɪ] *n* (U) secret *m*.

secret ['si:krɪt] ◇ *adj* secret(ète). ◇ *n* secret *m*; **in ~** en secret.

secret agent *n* agent *m* secret.

secretarial [,sekrə'teərɪəl] *adj* [course, training] de secrétariat, de secrétaire; **~ staff** secrétaires *mpl*.

secretariat [,sekrə'teərɪət] *n* secrétariat *m*.

secretary [*Br* 'sekrətrɪ, *Am* 'sekrə,terɪ] (*pl* -ies) *n* -1. [gen] secrétaire *mf*. -2. POL [minister] ministre *m*.

secretary-general (*pl* **secretaries-general**) *n* secrétaire *m* général.

Secretary of State *n* -1. *Br*: **~ (for)** ministre *m* (de). -2. *Am* ≃ ministre *m* des Affaires étrangères.

secrete [sɪ'kri:t] *vt* -1. [produce] sécréter. -2. *fml* [hide] cacher.

secretion [sɪ'kri:ʃn] *n* sécrétion *f*.

secretive ['si:krətɪv] *adj* secret(ète), dissimulé(e).

secretly ['si:krɪtlɪ] *adv* secrètement.

secret police *n* police *f* secrète.

secret service *n* [in UK] ≃ Deuxième Bureau *m*; [in US] *service de protection du président, du vice-président et de leur famille.*

sect [sekt] *n* secte *f*.

sectarian [sek'teərɪən] *adj* [killing, violence] d'ordre religieux.

section ['sekʃn] ◇ *n* -1. [portion - gen] section *f*, partie *f*; [- of road, pipe] tronçon *m*; [- of document, law] article *m*; **the sports ~** PRESS la rubrique des sports. -2. GEOM coupe *f*, section *f*. ◇ *vt* sectionner.

sector ['sektər] *n* secteur *m*.

secular ['sekjʊlər] *adj* [life] séculier(ière); [education] laïque; [music] profane.

secure [sɪ'kjʊər] ◇ *adj* -1. [fixed - gen] fixe; [- windows, building] bien fermé(e). -2. [safe - job, future] sûr(e); [- valuable object] en sécurité, en lieu sûr. -3. [free of anxiety - childhood] sécurisant(e); [- marriage] solide; **to feel ~** se sentir en sécurité. ◇ *vt* -1. [obtain] obtenir. -2. [fasten - gen] attacher; [- door, window] bien fermer. -3. [make safe] assurer la sécurité de.

securely [sɪ'kjʊəlɪ] *adv* [fixed, locked] solidement, bien.

security [sɪ'kjʊərətɪ] (*pl* -ies) ◇ *n* sécurité *f*. ◇ *comp* de sécurité.

◆ **securities** *npl* FIN titres *mpl*, valeurs *fpl*.

security blanket *n* doudou *m*.

Security Council *n*: **the ~** le Conseil de Sécurité.

security forces *npl* forces *fpl* de sécurité.

security guard *n* garde *m* de sécurité.

security risk *n* personne qui présente un risque pour la sécurité nationale ou d'une organisation.

secy (*abbr of* **secretary**) secr.

sedan [sɪ'dæn] *n Am* berline *f*.

sedan chair *n* chaise *f* à porteurs.

sedate [sɪ'deɪt] ◇ *adj* posé(e), calme. ◇ *vt* donner un sédatif à.

sedation [sɪ'deɪʃn] *n* (U) sédation *f*; **under ~** sous calmants.

sedative ['sedətɪv] ◇ *adj* sédatif(ive). ◇ *n* sédatif *m*, calmant *m*.

sedentary ['sedntrɪ] *adj* sédentaire.

sediment ['sedɪmənt] *n* sédiment *m*, dépôt *m*.

sedition [sɪ'dɪʃn] *n* sédition *f*.

seditious [sɪ'dɪʃəs] *adj* séditieux(ieuse).

seduce [sɪ'dju:s] *vt* séduire; **to ~ sb into doing sthg** amener OR entraîner qqn à faire qqch.

seduction [sɪ'dʌkʃn] *n* séduction *f*.

seductive [sɪ'dʌktɪv] *adj* séduisant(e).

see [si:] (*pt* **saw**, *pp* **seen**) ◇ *vt* -1. [gen] voir; **~you!** au revoir!; **~ you soon/later/ tomorrow** *etc*! à bientôt/tout à l'heure/ demain *etc*!; **I'll ~ what I can do** je vais voir ce que je peux faire. -2. [accompany]: **I saw her to the door** je l'ai accompagnée OR reconduite jusqu'à la porte; **I saw her onto the train** je l'ai accompagnée au train. -3. [like]: **what do you ~ in him?** qu'est-ce que tu lui trouves? -4. [make sure]: **to ~ (that)** ... s'assurer que ....
◇ *vi* voir; **you ~,** ... voyez-vous, ...; **I ~** je vois, je comprends; **let's ~, let me ~** voyons, voyons voir.

◆ **seeing as, seeing that** *prep inf* vu que, étant donné que.

◆ **see about** *vt fus* [arrange] s'occuper de.

◆ **see off** *vt sep* -1. [say goodbye to] accompagner (pour dire au revoir). -2. *Br* [chase away] faire partir OR fuir.

◆ **see through** ◇ *vt fus* [scheme] voir clair dans; **to ~ through sb** voir dans le jeu de qqn. ◇ *vt sep* [deal, project] mener à terme, mener à bien.

◆ **see to** *vt fus* s'occuper de, se charger de.

seed [si:d] *n* -1. [of plant] graine *f*. -2. SPORT: **fifth ~** joueur classé cinquième *m*, joueuse classée cinquième *f*.

◆ **seeds** *npl fig* germes *mpl,* semences *fpl.*

seedless ['si:dlɪs] *adj* sans pépins.

seedling ['si:dlɪŋ] *n* jeune plant *m,* semis *m.*

seedy ['si:dɪ] (*compar* **-ier,** *superl* **-iest**) *adj* miteux(euse).

seek [si:k] (*pt* & *pp* **sought**) *vt* **-1.** [gen] chercher; [peace, happiness] rechercher; **to ~ to do sthg** chercher à faire qqch; **to ~ revenge** chercher à se venger. **-2.** [advice, help] demander.

◆ **seek out** *vt sep* chercher.

seem [si:m] ◇ *vi* sembler, paraître; **to ~ bored** avoir l'air de s'ennuyer; **to ~ sad/tired** avoir l'air triste/fatigué; **I ~ to remember ...** je crois me rappeler .... ◇ *v impers:* **it ~s (that) ...** il semble OR paraît que ....

seeming ['si:mɪŋ] *adj fml* apparent(e).

seemingly ['si:mɪŋlɪ] *adv* apparemment.

seemly ['si:mlɪ] (*compar* **-ier,** *superl* **-iest**) *adj dated* & *literary* convenable.

seen [si:n] *pp* → **see.**

seep [si:p] *vi* suinter.

seersucker ['sɪə,sʌkər] *n* crépon *m* de coton.

seesaw ['si:sɔ:] *n* bascule *f.*

seethe [si:ð] *vi* **-1.** [person] bouillir, être furieux(ieuse). **-2.** [place]: **to be seething with** grouiller de.

seething ['si:ðɪŋ] *adj* [furious] furieux(ieuse).

see-through *adj* transparent(e).

segment ['segmənt] *n* **-1.** [section] partie *f,* section *f.* **-2.** [of fruit] quartier *m.*

segregate ['segrɪgeɪt] *vt* séparer.

segregation [,segrɪ'geɪʃn] *n* ségrégation *f.*

Seine [seɪn] *n:* **the (River) ~** la Seine.

seismic ['saɪzmɪk] *adj* sismique.

seize [si:z] *vt* **-1.** [grab] saisir, attraper. **-2.** [capture] s'emparer de, prendre. **-3.** [arrest] arrêter. **-4.** *fig* [opportunity, chance] saisir, sauter sur.

◆ **seize (up)on** *vt fus* saisir, sauter sur.

◆ **seize up** *vi* **-1.** [body] s'ankyloser. **-2.** [engine, part] se gripper.

seizure ['si:ʒər] *n* **-1.** MED crise *f,* attaque *f.* **-2.** (*U*) [of town] capture *f;* [of power] prise *f.*

seldom ['seldəm] *adv* peu souvent, rarement.

select [sɪ'lekt] ◇ *adj* **-1.** [carefully chosen] choisi(e). **-2.** [exclusive] de premier ordre, d'élite. ◇ *vt* sélectionner, choisir.

select committee *n* commission *f* d'enquête.

selected [sɪ'lektɪd] *adj* choisi(e).

selection [sɪ'lekʃn] *n* sélection *f,* choix *m.*

selective [sɪ'lektɪv] *adj* sélectif(ive); [person] difficile.

selector [sɪ'lektər] *n* [person] sélectionneur *m,* -euse *f.*

self [self] (*pl* **selves**) *n* moi *m;* **she's her old ~ again** elle est redevenue elle-même.

self- [self] *prefix* auto-.

self-addressed envelope [-ə'drest-] *n* enveloppe *f* portant ses propres nom et adresse.

self-addressed stamped envelope [-ə'drest-] *n Am* enveloppe *f* affranchie pour la réponse.

self-adhesive *adj* autocollant(e).

self-appointed [-ə'pɔɪntɪd] *adj pej:* **she's the ~ leader** elle se pose en chef.

self-assembly *adj Br* qu'on monte OR assemble soi-même.

self-assertive *adj* qui sait s'affirmer.

self-assurance *n* confiance *f* en soi, assurance *f.*

self-assured *adj* sûr(e) de soi, plein(e) d'assurance.

self-catering *adj* [holiday - in house] en maison louée; [- in flat] en appartement loué.

self-centred [-'sentəd] *adj* égocentrique.

self-cleaning *adj* autonettoyant(e).

self-coloured *adj Br* uni(e).

self-confessed [-kən'fest] *adj* de son propre aveu.

self-confident *adj* sûr(e) de soi, plein(e) d'assurance.

self-conscious *adj* timide, embarrassé(e).

self-contained *adj* [flat] indépendant(e), avec entrée particulière; [person] qui se suffit à soi-même.

self-control *n* maîtrise *f* de soi.

self-controlled *adj* maître (maîtresse) de soi.

self-defence *n* autodéfense *f;* **in ~** JUR en légitime défense; [reply] pour sa défense.

self-denial *n* abnégation *f.*

self-destruct [-dɪs'trʌkt] ◇ *adj* autodestructeur(trice). ◇ *vi* s'autodétruire.

self-determination *n* autodétermination *f.*

self-discipline *n* autodiscipline *f.*

self-doubt *n* manque *m* de confiance en soi.

self-drive *adj Br* sans chauffeur.

self-educated *adj* autodidacte.

self-effacing [-ɪ'feɪsɪŋ] *adj* qui cherche à s'effacer.

self-employed [-ɪm'plɔɪd] *adj* qui travaille à son propre compte.

self-esteem *n* respect *m* de soi, estime *f* de soi.

self-evident *adj* qui va de soi, évident(e).

self-explanatory *adj* évident(e), qui ne nécessite pas d'explication.

self-expression *n* libre expression *f*.

self-focusing [-'fəʊkəsɪŋ] *adj* autofocus (*inv*), à mise au point automatique.

self-government *n* autonomie *f*.

self-help *n* (*U*) initiative *f* personnelle.

self-important *adj* suffisant(e).

self-imposed [-ɪm'pəʊzd] *adj* que l'on s'impose à soi-même.

self-indulgent *adj pej* [person] qui ne se refuse rien; [film, book, writer] nombriliste.

self-inflicted [-ɪn'flɪktɪd] *adj* que l'on s'inflige à soi-même, volontaire.

self-interest *n* (*U*) *pej* intérêt *m* personnel.

selfish ['selfɪʃ] *adj* égoïste.

selfishness ['selfɪʃnɪs] *n* égoïsme *m*.

selfless ['selflɪs] *adj* désintéressé(e).

self-locking [-'lɒkɪŋ] *adj* à fermeture automatique.

self-made *adj*: ~ **man** self-made-man *m*.

self-opinionated *adj* opiniâtre.

self-perpetuating [-pə'petʃʊeɪtɪŋ] *adj* qui se perpétue indéfiniment.

self-pity *n* apitoiement *m* sur soi-même.

self-portrait *n* autoportrait *m*.

self-possessed *adj* maître (maîtresse) de soi.

self-proclaimed [-prə'kleɪmd] *adj pej* soi-disant (*inv*), prétendu(e).

self-raising flour *Br* [-,reɪzɪŋ-], **self-rising flour** *Am n* farine *f* avec levure incorporée.

self-regard *n* (*U*) **-1.** *pej* [self-interest] intérêt *m* personnel. **-2.** [self-respect] respect *m* de soi.

self-regulating [-'regjʊleɪtɪŋ] *adj* qui se réglemente soi-même.

self-reliant *adj* indépendant(e), qui ne compte que sur soi.

self-respect *n* respect *m* de soi.

self-respecting [-rɪs'pektɪŋ] *adj* qui se respecte.

self-restraint *n* (*U*) retenue *f*, mesure *f*.

self-righteous *adj* satisfait(e) de soi.

self-rising flour *Am* = **self-raising flour**.

self-rule *n* autonomie *f*.

self-sacrifice *n* abnégation *f*.

selfsame ['selfseɪm] *adj* exactement le même (exactement la même).

self-satisfied *adj* suffisant(e), content(e) de soi.

self-sealing [-'siːlɪŋ] *adj* [envelope] autocollant(e).

self-seeking [-'siːkɪŋ] *adj* égoïste.

self-service ◇ *n* libre-service *m*, self-service *m*. ◇ *comp* libre-service, self-service.

self-starter *n* AUT démarreur *m* automatique.

self-styled [-'staɪld] *adj pej* soi-disant (*inv*), prétendu(e).

self-sufficient *adj* autosuffisant(e); **to be ~ in** satisfaire à ses besoins en.

self-supporting [-sə'pɔːtɪŋ] *adj* [business, industry] financièrement indépendant(e).

self-taught *adj* autodidacte.

self-test *vi* COMPUT faire un autotest.

self-will *n* obstination *f*.

sell [sel] (*pt & pp* **sold**) ◇ *vt* **-1.** [gen] vendre; **to ~ sthg for £100** vendre qqch 100 livres; **to ~ sthg to sb, to ~ sb sthg** vendre qqch à qqn. **-2.** *fig* [make acceptable]: **to ~ sthg to sb, to ~ sb sthg** faire accepter qqch à qqn; **to ~ o.s.** se faire valoir. ◇ *vi* **-1.** [person] vendre. **-2.** [product] se vendre; **it ~s for OR at £10** il se vend 10 livres.

◆ **sell off** *vt sep* vendre, liquider.

◆ **sell out** ◇ *vt sep*: **the performance is sold out** il ne reste plus de places, tous les billets ont été vendus. ◇ *vi* **-1.** [shop]: **we're sold out** on n'en a plus. **-2.** [betray one's principles] être infidèle à ses principes.

◆ **sell up** *vi* vendre son affaire.

sell-by date *n Br* date *f* limite de vente.

seller ['selər] *n* vendeur *m*, -euse *f*.

seller's market *n* marché *m* à la hausse.

selling ['selɪŋ] *n* (*U*) vente *f*.

selling price *n* prix *m* de vente.

Sellotape® ['seləteɪp] *n Br* ≃ Scotch® *m*, ruban *m* adhésif.

◆ **sellotape** *vt* scotcher.

sell-out *n*: **the match was a ~** on a joué à guichets fermés.

seltzer ['seltsər] *n Am* eau *f* de seltz.

selves [selvz] *pl* → **self**.

semantic [sɪ'mæntɪk] *adj* sémantique.

semantics [sɪ'mæntɪks] *n* (*U*) sémantique *f*.

semaphore ['seməfɔːr] *n* (*U*) signaux *mpl* à bras.

semblance ['sembləns] *n* semblant *m*.

semen ['siːmen] *n* (*U*) sperme *m*, semence *f*.

semester [sɪ'mestər] *n* semestre *m*.

semi ['semɪ] *n* **-1.** *Br inf* (*abbr of* **semidetached house**) maison *f* jumelée. **-2.** *Am abbr of* **semitrailer**.

semi- [‚semɪ] *prefix* semi-, demi-.

semiautomatic [‚semɪ‚ɔːtə'mætɪk] *adj* semi-automatique.

semicircle ['semɪ‚sɜːkl] *n* demi-cercle *m*.

semicircular [‚semɪ'sɜːkjʊlər] *adj* semi-circulaire, demi-circulaire.

semicolon [‚semɪ'kəʊlən] *n* point-virgule *m*.

semiconscious [‚semɪ'kɒnʃəs] *adj* à demi conscient(e).

semidetached [‚semɪdɪ'tætʃt] ◇ *adj* jumelé(e). ◇ *n Br* maison *f* jumelée.

semifinal [‚semɪ'faɪnl] *n* demi-finale *f*.

semifinalist [‚semɪ'faɪnəlɪst] *n* demi-finaliste *mf*.

seminal ['semɪnl] *adj* **-1.** [of semen] séminal(e). **-2.** [influential] qui fait école.

seminar ['semɪnɑːr] *n* séminaire *m*.

seminary ['semɪnərɪ] (*pl* **-ies**) *n* RELIG séminaire *m*.

semiotics [‚semɪ'ɒtɪks] *n* (U) sémiotique *f*.

semiprecious ['semɪ‚preʃəs] *adj* semi-précieux(ieuse).

semiskilled [‚semɪ'skɪld] *adj* spécialisé(e).

semi-skimmed [-skɪmd] *adj* [milk] demi-écrémé.

semitrailer [‚semɪ'treɪlər] *n* **-1.** [trailer] semi-remorque *f*. **-2.** *Am* [lorry] semi-remorque *m*.

semolina [‚semə'liːnə] *n* semoule *f*.

Sen. **-1.** *abbr of* **senator**. **-2.** *abbr of* **Senior**.

SEN (*abbr of* **State Enrolled Nurse**) *n* en Grande-Bretagne, infirmier ou infirmière diplômé(e) d'État.

Senate ['senɪt] *n* POL: **the ~** le sénat; **the United States ~** le Sénat américain.

SENATE:
Le Sénat constitue, avec la Chambre des Représentants, l'organe législatif américain; composé de 100 membres (deux par État), il détient l'exclusivité du droit d'impeachment

senator ['senətər] *n* sénateur *m*.

send [send] (*pt* & *pp* **sent**) *vt* **-1.** [gen] envoyer; [letter] expédier, envoyer; **to ~ sb sthg, to ~ sthg to sb** envoyer qqch à qqn; **~ her my love** embrasse-la pour moi; **to ~ sb for sthg** envoyer qqn chercher qqch; **to ~ sb home** renvoyer qqn (chez lui); **to ~ sb to the doctor's/to prison** envoyer qqn chez le médecin/en prison. **-2.** [cause to move]: **the explosion sent glass everywhere**

l'explosion a projeté des débris de verre partout.

◆ **send down** *vt sep* [send to prison] coffrer.

◆ **send for** *vt fus* **-1.** [person] appeler, faire venir. **-2.** [by post] commander par correspondance.

◆ **send in** *vt sep* [report, application] envoyer, soumettre.

◆ **send off** *vt sep* **-1.** [by post] expédier. **-2.** SPORT expulser.

◆ **send off for** *vt fus* commander par correspondance.

◆ **send up** *vt sep* **-1.** *inf Br* [imitate] parodier, ridiculiser. **-2.** *Am* [send to prison] coffrer.

sender ['sendər] *n* expéditeur *m*, -trice *f*.

send-off *n* fête *f* d'adieu.

send-up *n Br inf* parodie *f*.

Senegal [‚senɪ'gɔːl] *n* Sénégal *m*; **in ~** au Sénégal.

Senegalese [‚senɪgə'liːz] ◇ *adj* sénégalais(e). ◇ *npl*: **the ~** les Sénégalais *mpl*.

senile ['siːnaɪl] *adj* sénile.

senile dementia *n* démence *f* sénile.

senility [sɪ'nɪlətɪ] *n* sénilité *f*.

senior ['siːnjər] ◇ *adj* **-1.** [highest-ranking] plus haut placé(e). **-2.** [higher-ranking]: **~ to sb** d'un rang plus élevé que qqn. **-3.** SCH [pupils, classes] grand(e); **~ year** *Am* dernière année. ◇ *n* **-1.** [older person] aîné *m*, -e *f*. **-2.** SCH grand *m*, -e *f*.

senior citizen *n* personne *f* âgée OR du troisième âge.

senior high school *n Am* ≃ lycée *m*.

seniority [‚siːnɪ'ɒrətɪ] *n* [in rank] supériorité *f*, ancienneté *f*.

sensation [sen'seɪʃn] *n* sensation *f*.

sensational [sen'seɪʃənl] *adj* **-1.** [gen] sensationnel(elle). **-2.** [pej] PRESS à sensation.

sensationalist [sen'seɪʃnəlɪst] *adj pej* à sensation.

sense [sens] ◇ *n* **-1.** [ability, meaning] sens *m*; **to make ~** [have meaning] avoir un sens; **to make ~ of sthg** comprendre qqch; **~ of humour** sens de l'humour; **~ of smell** odorat *m*. **-2.** [feeling] sentiment *m*. **-3.** [wisdom] bon sens *m*, intelligence *f*; **to make ~** [be sensible] être logique; **to talk ~** parler raison; **there's no ~ in arguing/fighting** cela ne sert à rien de discuter/se battre. **-4.** *phr*: **to come to one's ~s** [be sensible again] revenir à la raison; [regain consciousness] reprendre connaissance.
◇ *vt* [feel] sentir.

◆ **in a sense** *adv* dans un sens.

senseless ['senslɪs] *adj* -1. [stupid] stupide. -2. [unconscious] sans connaissance.

sensibilities [,sensɪ'bɪlətɪz] *npl* susceptibilité *f*.

sensible ['sensəbl] *adj* [reasonable] raisonnable, judicieux(ieuse).

sensibly ['sensəblɪ] *adv* raisonnablement, judicieusement.

sensitive ['sensɪtɪv] *adj* -1. [gen]: ~ (to) sensible (à). -2. [subject] délicat(e). -3. [easily offended]: ~ (about) susceptible (en ce qui concerne).

sensitivity [,sensɪ'tɪvətɪ] *n* sensibilité *f*.

sensor ['sensər] *n* détecteur *m*.

sensual ['sensjʊəl] *adj* sensuel(elle).

sensuous ['sensjʊəs] *adj* qui affecte les sens.

sent [sent] *pt & pp* → **send**.

sentence ['sentəns] ◇ *n* -1. GRAMM phrase *f*. -2. JUR condamnation *f*, sentence *f*. ◇ *vt*: to ~ sb (to) condamner qqn (à).

sententious [sen'tenʃəs] *adj* sentencieux(ieuse).

sentiment ['sentɪmənt] *n* -1. [feeling] sentiment *m*. -2. [opinion] opinion *f*, avis *m*. -3. *pej* [sentimentality] sentimentalité *f*, sensiblerie *f*.

sentimental [,sentɪ'mentl] *adj* sentimental(e).

sentimentality [,sentɪmen'tælətɪ] *n pej* sentimentalité *f*, sensiblerie *f*.

sentinel ['sentɪnl] *n* sentinelle *f*.

sentry ['sentrɪ] (*pl* -**ies**) *n* sentinelle *f*.

Seoul [səʊl] *n* Séoul.

separable ['seprəbl] *adj*: ~ (from) séparable (de).

separate [*adj & n* 'seprət, *vb* 'sepəreɪt] ◇ *adj* -1. [not joined]: ~ (from) séparé(e) (de). -2. [individual, distinct] distinct(e). ◇ *vt* -1. [gen]: to ~ sb/sthg (from) séparer qqn/qqch. (de); to ~ sthg into diviser OR séparer qqch en. -2. [distinguish]: to ~ sb/sthg (from) distinguer qqn/qqch. (de). ◇ *vi* se séparer; to ~ into se diviser OR se séparer en.
◆ **separates** *npl Br* coordonnés *mpl*.

separated ['sepəreɪtɪd] *adj* [not living together] séparé(e).

separately ['seprətlɪ] *adv* séparément.

separation [,sepə'reɪʃn] *n* séparation *f*.

separatist ['seprətɪst] *n* séparatiste *mf*.

sepia ['siːpjə] *adj* sépia (*inv*).

Sept. (*abbr of* **September**) sept.

September [sep'tembər] ◇ *n* septembre *m*; when are you going? - ~ quand partez-vous? - en septembre; one of the hottest

~s on record un des mois de septembre les plus chauds qu'on ait connus; in ~ en septembre; last ~ septembre dernier; this ~ septembre de cette année; next ~ septembre prochain; by ~ en septembre, d'ici septembre; every ~ tous les ans en septembre; during ~ pendant le mois de septembre; at the beginning of ~ au début du mois de septembre, début septembre; at the end of ~ à la fin du mois de septembre, fin septembre; in the middle of ~ au milieu du mois de septembre, à la mi-septembre.
◇ *comp* (du mois) de septembre; [election] au mois de septembre, en septembre.

septet [sep'tet] *n* septuor *m*.

septic ['septɪk] *adj* infecté(e).

septicaemia *Br*, **septicemia** *Am* [,septɪ-'siːmɪə] *n* septicémie *f*.

septic tank *n* fosse *f* septique.

sepulchre *Br* ['sepəlkər], **sepulcher** *Am* ['sepəlkər] *n literary* sépulcre *m*, tombeau *m*.

sequel ['siːkwəl] *n* -1. [book, film]: ~ (to) suite *f* (de). -2. [consequence]: ~ (to) conséquence *f* (de).

sequence ['siːkwəns] *n* -1. [series] suite *f*, succession *f*. -2. [order] ordre *m*; in ~ par ordre. -3. [of film] séquence *f*.

sequester [sɪ'kwestər], **sequestrate** [sɪ'kwestreɪt] *vt* séquestrer, mettre sous séquestre.

sequin ['siːkwɪn] *n* paillette *f*.

Serb = **Serbian**.

Serbia ['sɜːbjə] *n* Serbie *f*; in ~ en Serbie.

Serbian ['sɜːbjən], **Serb** [sɜːb] ◇ *adj* serbe. ◇ *n* -1. [person] Serbe *mf*. -2. [dialect] serbe *m*.

Serbo-Croat [,sɜːbəʊ'krəʊæt], **Serbo-Croatian** [,sɜːbəʊkrəʊ'eɪʃn] ◇ *adj* serbo-croate. ◇ *n* [language] serbo-croate *m*.

serenade [,serə'neɪd] ◇ *n* sérénade *f*. ◇ *vt* donner la sérénade à.

serene [sɪ'riːn] *adj* [calm] serein(e), tranquille.

serenely [sɪ'riːnlɪ] *adv* sereinement, avec sérénité.

serenity [sɪ'renətɪ] *n* sérénité *f*, tranquillité *f*.

serf [sɜːf] *n* serf *m*, serve *f*.

serge [sɜːdʒ] *n* serge *f*.

sergeant ['sɑːdʒənt] *n* -1. MIL sergent *m*. -2. [in police] brigadier *m*.

sergeant major *n* sergent-major *m*.

serial ['sɪərɪəl] *n* feuilleton *m*.

serialize, **-ise** ['sɪərɪəlaɪz] *vt* [on TV] diffuser en feuilleton; [in newspaper etc] publier en feuilleton.

serial killer *n* meurtrier *m* en série.

serial number *n* numéro *m* de série.

series ['sɪəriːz] (*pl inv*) *n* série *f*.

serious ['sɪərɪəs] *adj* sérieux(ieuse); [illness, accident, trouble] **grave; to be ~ about doing sthg** songer sérieusement à faire qqch.

seriously ['sɪərɪəslɪ] *adv* sérieusement; [ill] gravement; [wounded] grièvement, gravement; **to take sb/sthg ~** prendre qqn/qqch au sérieux.

seriousness ['sɪərɪəsnɪs] *n* **-1.** [of mistake, illness] gravité *f*; **in all ~** en toute sincérité. **-2.** [of person, speech] sérieux *m*.

sermon ['sɜːmən] *n* sermon *m*.

serpent ['sɜːpənt] *n literary* serpent *m*.

serrated [sɪ'reɪtɪd] *adj* en dents de scie.

serum ['sɪərəm] (*pl* **serums** OR **sera** ['sɪərə]) *n* sérum *m*.

servant ['sɜːvənt] *n* domestique *mf*.

serve [sɜːv] ◇ *vt* **-1.** [work for] servir. **-2.** [have effect]: **to ~ to do sthg** servir à faire qqch; **to ~ a purpose** [subj: device etc] servir à un usage; **it ~s my purpose** cela fait l'affaire. **-3.** [provide for] desservir. **-4.** [meal, drink, customer] servir; **to ~ sthg to sb, to ~ sb sthg** servir qqch à qqn. **-5.** JUR: **to ~ sb with a summons/writ, to ~ a summons/writ on sb** signifier une assignation/une citation à qqn, notifier une assignation/une citation à qqn. **-6.** [prison sentence] purger, faire; [apprenticeship] faire. **-7.** SPORT servir. **-8.** *phr*: **it ~s him/you right** c'est bien fait pour lui/toi.
◇ *vi* servir; **to ~ as** servir de; **to ~ on a committee** être membre d'un comité.
◇ *n* SPORT service *m*.
◆ **serve out, serve up** *vt sep* [food] servir.

server ['sɜːvəʳ] *n* COMPUT serveur *m*.

service ['sɜːvɪs] ◇ *n* **-1.** [gen] service *m*; **in/out of ~** en/hors service; **to be of ~ (to sb)** être utile (à qqn), rendre service (à qqn). **-2.** [of car] révision *f*; [of machine] entretien *m*. ◇ *vt* **-1.** [car] réviser; [machine] assurer l'entretien de. **-2.** FIN [debt] rembourser.
◆ **services** ◇ *npl* **-1.** [on motorway] aire *f* de services. **-2.** [armed forces]: **the ~s** les forces *fpl* armées. **-3.** [help] service *m*.

serviceable ['sɜːvɪsəbl] *adj* pratique.

service area *n* aire *f* de services.

service charge *n* service *m*.

service industries *npl*: **the ~** le secteur tertiaire.

serviceman ['sɜːvɪsmən] (*pl* **-men** [-mən]) *n* soldat *m*, militaire *m*.

service station *n* station-service *f*.

servicewoman ['sɜːvɪs,wʊmən] (*pl* **-women** [-,wɪmɪn]) *n* femme *f* soldat.

serviette [,sɜːvɪ'et] *n* serviette *f* (de table).

servile ['sɜːvaɪl] *adj* servile, obséquieux(ieuse).

servility [sɜː'vɪlətɪ] *n* servilité *f*.

serving ['sɜːvɪŋ] ◇ *adj* [spoon, dish] de service. ◇ *n* [of food] portion *f*.

sesame ['sesəmɪ] *n* sésame *m*.

session ['seʃn] *n* **-1.** [gen] séance *f*; **in ~** en séance. **-2.** *Am* [shool term] trimestre *m*.

set [set] (*pt & pp* **set**, *cont* **-ting**) ◇ *adj* **-1.** [fixed - gen] fixe; [- phrase] figé(e). **-2.** *Br* SCH [book] au programme. **-3.** [ready]: **~ (for sthg/to do sthg)** prêt(e) (à qqch/à faire qqch). **-4.** [determined]: **to be ~ on sthg** vouloir absolument qqch; **to be ~ on doing sthg** être résolu(e) à faire qqch; **to be dead ~ against sthg** s'opposer formellement à qqch. **-5.** *phr*: **to be ~ in one's ways** tenir à ses habitudes.
◇ *n* **-1.** [of keys, tools, golf clubs etc] jeu *m*; [of stamps, books] collection *f*; [of saucepans] série *f*; [of tyres] train *m*; **a ~ of teeth** [natural] une dentition, une denture; [false] un dentier. **-2.** [television, radio] poste *m*. **-3.** CINEMA plateau *m*; THEATRE scène *f*. **-4.** TENNIS manche *f*, set *m*.
◇ *vt* **-1.** [place] placer, poser, mettre; [jewel] sertir, monter; **to be ~ back from sthg** être en retrait de qqch. **-2.** [cause to be]: **to ~ sb free** libérer qqn, mettre qqn en liberté; **to ~ sthg in motion** mettre qqch en branle OR en route; **to ~ sb's mind at rest** tranquilliser qqn; **to ~ sthg on fire** mettre le feu à qqch. **-3.** [prepare - trap] tendre; [- table] mettre. **-4.** [adjust] régler. **-5.** [fix - date, deadline, target] fixer. **-6.** [establish - example] donner; [- trend] lancer; [- record] établir. **-7.** [homework, task] donner; [problem] poser. **-8.** MED [bone, leg] remettre. **-9.** [arrange]: **to ~ sthg to music** mettre qqch en musique. **-10.** [story]: **to be ~** se passer, se dérouler.
◇ *vi* **-1.** [sun] se coucher. **-2.** [jelly] prendre; [glue, cement] durcir.
◆ **set about** *vt fus* [start] entreprendre, se mettre à; **to ~ about doing sthg** se mettre à faire qqch.
◆ **set against** *vt sep* **-1.** [compare] mettre en balance; **to ~ expenses against tax** déduire les dépenses des impôts. **-2.** [cause to oppose]: **to ~ sb against sb** monter qqn contre qqn.

◆ **set ahead** *vt sep Am* [clock] avancer.

◆ **set apart** *vt sep* [distinguish] distinguer.

◆ **set aside** *vt sep* **-1.** [save] mettre de côté. **-2.** [not consider] rejeter, écarter.

◆ **set back** *vt sep* **-1.** [delay] retarder. **-2.** *inf* [cost]: **it ~ me back £300** cela m'a coûté 300 livres.

◆ **set down** *vt sep* **-1.** [write down]: **to ~ sthg down (in writing)** coucher qqch par écrit. **-2.** [put down] déposer.

◆ **set in** *vi* [weather, feeling] commencer, s'installer; [infection] se déclarer.

◆ **set off** ◇ *vt sep* **-1.** [cause] déclencher, provoquer. **-2.** [bomb] faire exploser; [firework] faire partir. ◇ *vi* se mettre en route, partir.

◆ **set on** *vt sep*: **to ~ a dog on sb** lâcher un chien contre OR sur qqn.

◆ **set out** ◇ *vt sep* **-1.** [arrange] disposer. **-2.** [explain] présenter, exposer. ◇ *vt fus* [intend]: **to ~ out to do sthg** entreprendre OR tenter de faire qqch. ◇ *vi* [on journey] se mettre en route, partir.

◆ **set up** *vt sep* **-1.** [organization] créer, fonder; [committee, procedure] constituer, mettre en place; [meeting] arranger, organiser; **to ~ o.s. up** s'établir à son compte; **to ~ up house** OR **home** s'installer. **-2.** [statue, monument] dresser, ériger; [roadblock] placer, installer. **-3.** [equipment] préparer, installer. **-4.** *inf* [make appear guilty] monter un coup contre. ◇ *vi* [in business] s'établir.

setback ['setbæk] *n* contretemps *m*, revers *m*.

set menu *n* menu *m* fixe.

set piece *n* ART & LITERATURE morceau *m* traditionnel.

setsquare ['setskweə'] *n Br* équerre *f*.

settee [se'ti:] *n* canapé *m*.

setter ['setə'] *n* [dog] setter *m*.

setting ['setɪŋ] *n* **-1.** [surroundings] décor *m*, cadre *m*. **-2.** [of dial, machine] réglage *m*.

settle ['setl] ◇ *vt* **-1.** [argument] régler; **that's ~d then** (c'est) entendu. **-2.** [bill, account] régler, payer. **-3.** [calm - nerves] calmer; **to ~ one's stomach** calmer les douleurs d'estomac. **-4.** [make comfortable] installer; **to ~ o.s.** s'installer. ◇ *vi* **-1.** [make one's home] s'installer, se fixer. **-2.** [make oneself comfortable] s'installer. **-3.** [dust] retomber; [sediment] se déposer; [bird, insect] se poser.

◆ **settle down** *vi* **-1.** [give one's attention]: **to ~ down to sthg/to doing sthg** se mettre à qqch/à faire qqch. **-2.** [make oneself comfortable] s'installer. **-3.** [become respectable] se ranger. **-4.** [become calm] se calmer.

◆ **settle for** *vt fus* accepter, se contenter de.

◆ **settle in** *vi* s'adapter.

◆ **settle on** *vt fus* [choose] fixer son choix sur, se décider pour.

◆ **settle up** *vi*: **to ~ up (with sb)** régler (qqn).

settled ['setld] *adj* [weather] au beau fixe.

settlement ['setlmənt] *n* **-1.** [agreement] accord *m*. **-2.** [colony] colonie *f*. **-3.** [payment] règlement *m*.

settler ['setlə'] *n* colon *m*.

set-to *n inf* bagarre *f*.

set-up *n inf* **-1.** [system]: **what's the ~?** comment est-ce que c'est organisé? **-2.** [deception to incriminate] coup *m* monté.

seven ['sevn] *num* sept; *see also* **six**.

seventeen [,sevn'ti:n] *num* dix-sept; *see also* **six**.

seventh ['sevnθ] *num* septième; *see also* **sixth**.

seventh heaven *n*: **to be in (one's) ~** être au septième ciel.

seventieth ['sevntjəθ] *num* soixante-dixième; *see also* **sixth**.

seventy ['sevntɪ] *num* soixante-dix; *see also* **sixty**.

sever ['sevə'] *vt* **-1.** [cut through] couper. **-2.** *fig* [relationship, ties] rompre.

several ['sevrəl] ◇ *adj* plusieurs. ◇ *pron* plusieurs *mfpl*.

severance ['sevrəns] *n* [of relations] rupture *f*.

severance pay *n* indemnité *f* de licenciement.

severe [sɪ'vɪə'] *adj* **-1.** [weather] rude, rigoureux(euse); [shock] gros (grosse), dur(e); [pain] violent(e); [illness, injury] grave. **-2.** [person, criticism] sévère.

severely [sɪ'vɪəlɪ] *adv* **-1.** [injured] grièvement; [damaged] sérieusement. **-2.** [sternly] sévèrement.

severity [sɪ'verətɪ] *n* **-1.** [of storm] violence *f*; [of problem, illness] gravité *f*. **-2.** [sternness] sévérité *f*.

sew [səʊ] (*Br pp* **sewn**, *Am pp* **sewed** OR **sewn**) *vt & vi* coudre.

◆ **sew up** *vt sep* **-1.** [join] recoudre. **-2.** *inf* [deal]: **it's (all) sewn up!** c'est dans la poche!

sewage ['su:ɪdʒ] *n* (*U*) eaux *fpl* d'égout, eaux usées.

sewage farm *n* champs *mpl* d'épandage.

sewer ['suə'] *n* égout *m*.

sewerage ['suərɪdʒ] *n* système *m* d'égouts.

sewing ['səʊɪŋ] n (U) **-1.** [activity] couture f. **-2.** [work] ouvrage m.

sewing machine n machine f à coudre.

sewn [səʊn] pp → **sew**.

sex [seks] n **-1.** [gender] sexe m. **-2.** (U) [sexual intercourse] rapports mpl (sexuels); **to have ~ with** avoir des rapports (sexuels) avec.

sex appeal n sex-appeal m.

sex education n éducation f sexuelle.

sexism ['seksɪzm] n sexisme m.

sexist ['seksɪst] ◇ adj sexiste. ◇ n sexiste mf.

sex life n vie f sexuelle.

sex object n objet m sexuel.

sex shop n sex-shop m.

sextet [seks'tet] n sextuor m.

sextuplet [seks'tjuːplɪt] n sextuplé m, -e f.

sexual ['sekʃʊəl] adj sexuel(elle).

sexual assault n agression f sexuelle, tentative f de viol.

sexual harassment n harcèlement m sexuel.

sexual intercourse n (U) rapports mpl (sexuels).

sexuality [,sekʃʊ'ælətɪ] n sexualité f.

sexy ['seksɪ] (compar -ier, superl -iest) adj inf sexy (inv).

Seychelles [seɪ'ʃelz] npl: **the ~** les Seychelles fpl; **in the ~** aux Seychelles.

SF, sf (abbr of science fiction) n SF f.

SFO (abbr of Serious Fraud Office) n service britannique de la répression des fraudes.

SG (abbr of Surgeon General) n directeur fédéral américain de la santé publique.

Sgt (abbr of sergeant) Sgt.

sh [ʃ] excl chut!

shabby ['ʃæbɪ] (compar -ier, superl -iest) adj **-1.** [clothes] élimé(e), râpé(e); [furniture] minable; [person, street] miteux(euse). **-2.** [behaviour] moche, méprisable.

shack [ʃæk] n cabane f, hutte f.

shackle ['ʃækl] vt enchaîner; fig entraver.
◆ **shackles** npl fers mpl; fig entraves fpl.

shade [ʃeɪd] ◇ n **-1.** (U) [shadow] ombre f. **-2.** [lampshade] abat-jour m inv. **-3.** [colour] nuance f, ton m. **-4.** [of meaning, opinion] nuance f. ◇ vt [from light] abriter; **to ~ one's eyes** s'abriter les yeux. ◇ vi: **to ~ into** se fondre en.
◆ **shades** npl inf [sunglasses] lunettes fpl de soleil.

shading ['ʃeɪdɪŋ] n (U) ombres fpl.

shadow ['ʃædəʊ] ◇ adj Br POL fantôme, de l'opposition. ◇ n ombre f; **to be a ~ of one's former self** n'être plus que l'ombre de soi-même; **there's not a** OR **the ~ of a doubt** il n'y a pas l'ombre d'un doute.

shadow cabinet n cabinet m fantôme.

shadowy ['ʃædəʊɪ] adj **-1.** [dark] ombreux(euse). **-2.** [hard to see] indistinct(e). **-3.** [sinister] mystérieux(ieuse).

shady ['ʃeɪdɪ] (compar -ier, superl -iest) adj **-1.** [garden, street etc] ombragé(e); [tree] qui donne de l'ombre. **-2.** inf [dishonest] louche.

shaft [ʃɑːft] ◇ n **-1.** [vertical passage] puits m; [of lift] cage f. **-2.** TECH arbre m. **-3.** [of light] rayon m. **-4.** [of tool, golf club] manche m. ◇ vt v inf **-1.** [dupe] avoir, baiser. **-2.** Am [treat unfairly] s'en prendre à.

shaggy ['ʃægɪ] (compar -ier, superl -iest) adj hirsute.

shaggy-dog story n histoire f farfelue OR à dormir debout.

shake [ʃeɪk] (pt shook, pp shaken) ◇ vt **-1.** [move vigorously - gen] secouer; [- bottle] agiter; **to ~ sb's hand** serrer la main de OR à qqn; **to ~ hands** se serrer la main; **to ~ one's head** secouer la tête; [to say no] faire non de la tête. **-2.** [shock] ébranler, secouer. ◇ vi trembler. ◇ n [tremble] tremblement m; **to give sthg a ~** secouer qqch.
◆ **shake down** vt sep Am inf **-1.** [rob] racketter. **-2.** [search] fouiller.
◆ **shake off** vt sep [police, pursuers] semer; [illness] se débarrasser de.

shakedown ['ʃeɪkdaʊn] n Am inf **-1.** [extortion] racket m. **-2.** [search] fouille f.

shaken ['ʃeɪkn] pp → **shake**.

shakeout ['ʃeɪkaʊt] n FIN récession f.

Shakespearean [ʃeɪk'spɪərɪən] adj shakespearien(ienne).

shake-up n inf remaniement m.

shaky ['ʃeɪkɪ] (compar -ier, superl -iest) adj [building, table] branlant(e); [hand] tremblant(e); [person] faible; [argument, start] incertain(e).

shale [ʃeɪl] n schiste m.

shall [weak form ʃəl, strong form ʃæl] aux vb **-1.** (1st person sg & 1st person pl) (to express future tense): **I ~ be ....** je serai .... **-2.** (esp 1st person sg & 1st person pl) (in questions): **~ we have lunch now?** tu veux qu'on déjeune maintenant?; **where ~ I put this?** où est-ce qu'il faut mettre ça? **-3.** [will definitely]: **we ~ succeed** nous réussirons. **-4.** (in orders): **you ~ tell me!** tu vas OR dois me le dire!

shallot [ʃə'lɒt] n échalote f.

shallow ['ʃæləʊ] adj **-1.** [water, dish, hole] peu profond(e). **-2.** pej [superficial] superficiel(ielle).

◆ **shallows** *npl* bas-fond *m*.

sham [ʃæm] (*pt & pp* **-med**, *cont* **-ming**) ◇ *adj* feint(e), simulé(e). ◇ *n* comédie *f*. ◇ *vi* faire semblant, jouer la comédie.

shambles ['ʃæmblz] *n* désordre *m*, pagaille *f*.

shame [ʃeɪm] ◇ *n* **-1.** (*U*) [remorse, humiliation] honte *f*; **to bring ~ on** OR **upon sb** faire la honte de qqn. **-2.** [pity]: **it's a ~ (that ...)** c'est dommage (que ... (+ *subjunctive*)); **what a ~!** quel dommage! ◇ *vt* faire honte à, mortifier; **to ~ sb into doing sthg** obliger qqn à faire qqch en lui faisant honte.

shamefaced [,ʃeɪm'feɪst] *adj* honteux(euse), penaud(e).

shameful ['ʃeɪmfʊl] *adj* honteux(euse), scandaleux(euse).

shameless ['ʃeɪmlɪs] *adj* effronté(e), éhonté(e).

shammy ['ʃæmɪ] (*pl* **-ies**) *n*: **~ (leather)** peau *f* de chamois.

shampoo [ʃæm'puː] (*pl* **-s**, *pt & pp* **-ed**, *cont* **-ing**) ◇ *n* shampooing *m*. ◇ *vt*: **to ~ sb** OR **sb's hair** faire un shampooing à qqn.

shamrock ['ʃæmrɒk] *n* trèfle *m*.

shandy ['ʃændɪ] (*pl* **-ies**) *n* panaché *m*.

shan't [ʃɑːnt] = **shall not**.

shantytown ['ʃæntɪtaʊn] *n* bidonville *m*.

shape [ʃeɪp] ◇ *n* **-1.** [gen] forme *f*; **in the ~ of a T** en forme de T; **to take ~** prendre forme OR tournure. **-2.** [guise]: **in the ~ of** sous forme de; **in any ~ or form** de n'importe quelle sorte. **-3.** [health]: **to be in good/bad ~** être en bonne/mauvaise forme; **to lick** OR **knock sb into ~** dresser qqn. ◇ *vt* **-1.** [pastry, clay etc]: **to ~ sthg (into)** façonner OR modeler qqch (en). **-2.** [ideas, project, character] former.

◆ **shape up** *vi* [person, plans] se développer, progresser; [job, events] prendre tournure OR forme.

SHAPE [ʃeɪp] (*abbr of* **Supreme Headquarters Allied Powers, Europe**) *n* quartier général des forces alliées en Europe.

-shaped ['ʃeɪpt] *suffix*: **egg~** en forme d'œuf; **L~** en forme de L.

shapeless ['ʃeɪplɪs] *adj* informe.

shapely ['ʃeɪplɪ] (*compar* **-ier**, *superl* **-iest**) *adj* bien fait(e).

shard [ʃɑːd] *n* tesson *m*.

share [ʃeə] ◇ *n* [portion, contribution] part *f*; **to have a ~ in the profits** participer aux bénéfices. ◇ *vt* partager; **to ~ the news with sb** faire part d'une nouvelle à qqn. ◇ *vi*: **to ~ (in sthg)** partager (qqch).

◆ **shares** *npl* actions *fpl*.

◆ **share out** *vt sep* partager, répartir.

share capital *n* capital *m* actions.

share certificate *n* titre *m* OR certificat *m* d'actions.

shareholder ['ʃeə,həʊldə] *n* actionnaire *mf*.

share index *n* indice *m* des valeurs boursières.

share-out *n* partage *m*, répartition *f*.

shareware ['ʃeəweə] *n* COMPUT shareware *m*.

shark [ʃɑːk] (*pl inv* OR **-s**) *n* **-1.** [fish] requin *m*. **-2.** *fig* [dishonest person] escroc *m*, pirate *m*.

sharp [ʃɑːp] ◇ *adj* **-1.** [knife, razor] tranchant(e), affilé(e); [needle, pencil, teeth] pointu(e). **-2.** [image, outline, contrast] net (nette). **-3.** [person, mind] vif (vive); [eyesight] perçant(e). **-4.** [sudden - change, rise] brusque, soudain(e); [- hit, tap] sec (sèche). **-5.** [words, order, voice] cinglant(e). **-6.** [cry, sound] perçant(e); [pain, cold] vif (vive); [taste] piquant(e). **-7.** MUS: **C/D ~** do/ré dièse.

◇ *adv* **-1.** [punctually]: **at 8 o'clock ~** à 8 heures pile OR tapantes. **-2.** [immediately]: **~ left/right** tout à fait à gauche/droite. ◇ *n* MUS dièse *m*.

sharpen ['ʃɑːpn] ◇ *vt* **-1.** [knife, tool] aiguiser; [pencil] tailler. **-2.** *fig* [senses] aiguiser; [mind] affiner; [disagreement, conflict] aviver, envenimer. ◇ *vi* [senses] s'aiguiser.

sharp end *n Br fig*: **to be at the ~** être en première ligne.

sharpener ['ʃɑːpnə] *n* [for pencil] taille-crayon *m*; [for knife] aiguisoir *m* (pour couteaux).

sharp-eyed [-'aɪd] *adj*: **she's very ~** elle remarque tout, rien ne lui échappe.

sharply ['ʃɑːplɪ] *adv* **-1.** [distinctly] nettement. **-2.** [suddenly] brusquement. **-3.** [harshly] sévèrement, durement.

sharpness ['ʃɑːpnɪs] *n* **-1.** [of image, outline] netteté *f*. **-2.** [of mind] vivacité *f*. **-3.** [of remarks, criticism] dureté *f*, sévérité *f*.

sharpshooter ['ʃɑːp,ʃuːtə] *n* tireur *m* d'élite.

sharp-tongued [-'tʌŋd] *adj* qui a la langue acérée.

sharp-witted [-'wɪtɪd] *adj* à l'esprit vif.

shat [ʃæt] *pt & pp* → **shit**.

shatter ['ʃætə] ◇ *vt* **-1.** [window, glass] briser, fracasser. **-2.** *fig* [hopes, dreams] détruire. **-3.** *fig* [upset]: **to be ~ed (by)** être bouleversé(e) (par). ◇ *vi* se fracasser, voler en éclats.

shattered ['ʃætəd] *adj* **-1.** [upset] bouleversé(e). **-2.** *Br inf* [very tired] flapi(e).

shattering ['ʃætərɪŋ] *adj* **-1.** [upsetting] bouleversant(e). **-2.** *Br* [tiring] crevant(e), épuisant(e).

shatterproof ['ʃætəpruːf] *adj* anti-éclats.

shave [ʃeɪv] ◇ *n*: **to have a ~** se raser; **that was a close ~** *fig* on l'a échappé belle, il était moins cinq. ◇ *vt* **-1.** [remove hair from] raser; **to ~ one's legs** se raser les jambes. **-2.** [wood] planer, raboter. ◇ *vi* se raser.

◆ **shave off** *vt sep* [beard, hair] se raser.

shaven ['ʃeɪvn] *adj* rasé(e).

shaver ['ʃeɪvər] *n* rasoir *m* électrique.

shaving brush ['ʃeɪvɪŋ-] *n* blaireau *m*.

shaving cream ['ʃeɪvɪŋ-] *n* crème *f* à raser.

shaving foam ['ʃeɪvɪŋ-] *n* mousse *f* à raser.

shavings ['ʃeɪvɪŋz] *npl* [of wood, metal] copeaux *mpl*.

shaving soap ['ʃeɪvɪŋ-] *n* savon *m* à barbe.

shawl [ʃɔːl] *n* châle *m*.

she [ʃiː] ◇ *pers pron* **-1.** [referring to woman, girl, animal] elle; **~'s tall** elle est grande; **SHE can't do it** elle, elle ne peut pas le faire; **there ~ is** la voilà; **if I were OR was ~** *fml* si j'étais elle, à sa place. **-2.** [referring to boat, car, country] *follow the gender of your translation.* ◇ *n*: **it's a ~** [animal] c'est une femelle; [baby] c'est une fille. ◇ *comp*: **~-elephant** éléphant *m* femelle; **~-wolf** louve *f*.

sheaf [ʃiːf] (*pl* **sheaves**) *n* **-1.** [of papers, letters] liasse *f*. **-2.** [of corn, grain] gerbe *f*.

shear [ʃɪər] (*pt* **-ed**, *pp* **-ed** OR **shorn**) *vt* [sheep] tondre.

◆ **shears** *npl* **-1.** [for garden] sécateur *m*, cisaille *f*. **-2.** [for dressmaking] ciseaux *mpl*.

◆ **shear off** ◇ *vt fus* [branch] couper; [piece of metal] cisailler. ◇ *vi* se détacher.

sheath [ʃiːθ] (*pl* **-s**) *n* **-1.** [for knife, cable] gaine *f*. **-2.** *Br* [condom] préservatif *m*.

sheathe [ʃiːð] *vt* **-1.** [knife] engainer, rengainer. **-2.** [cover - gen] recouvrir; [- cable] gainer.

sheath knife *n* couteau *m* à gaine.

sheaves [ʃiːvz] *pl* → **sheaf**.

shed [ʃed] (*pt* & *pp* **shed**, *cont* **-ding**) ◇ *n* [small] remise *f*, cabane *f*; [larger] hangar *m*. ◇ *vt* **-1.** [hair, skin, leaves] perdre. **-2.** [tears] verser, répandre; **to ~ blood** verser le sang. **-3.** [employees] se défaire de, congédier. **-4.** [load - subj: lorry] déverser, perdre.

she'd [weak form ʃɪd, strong form ʃiːd] = **she had, she would**.

sheen [ʃiːn] *n* lustre *m*, éclat *m*.

sheep [ʃiːp] (*pl inv*) *n* mouton *m*.

sheepdog ['ʃiːpdɒg] *n* chien *m* de berger.

sheepfold ['ʃiːpfəʊld] *n* parc *m* à moutons.

sheepish ['ʃiːpɪʃ] *adj* penaud(e).

sheepishly ['ʃiːpɪʃlɪ] *adv* d'un air penaud.

sheepskin ['ʃiːpskɪn] *n* peau *f* de mouton.

sheepskin jacket *n* veste *f* en mouton.

sheepskin rug *n* (petit tapis *m* en) peau *f* de mouton.

sheer [ʃɪər] *adj* **-1.** [absolute] pur(e). **-2.** [very steep] à pic, abrupt(e). **-3.** [material] fin(e).

sheet [ʃiːt] *n* **-1.** [for bed] drap *m*; **as white as a ~** blanc (blanche) comme un linge. **-2.** [of paper, glass, wood] feuille *f*; [of metal] plaque *f*.

sheet feed *n* COMPUT alimentation *f* feuille à feuille.

sheet ice *n* verglas *m*.

sheeting ['ʃiːtɪŋ] *n* (*U*) [metal] tôles *fpl*; [plastic etc] feuilles *fpl*.

sheet lightning *n* (*U*) éclair *m* diffus.

sheet metal *n* (*U*) tôle *f*.

sheet music *n* (*U*) partition *f*.

sheik(h) [ʃeɪk] *n* cheik *m*.

shelf [ʃelf] (*pl* **shelves**) *n* [in building] rayon *m*, étagère *f*.

shelf life *n* durée *f* de conservation.

shell [ʃel] ◇ *n* **-1.** [of egg, nut, snail] coquille *f*. **-2.** [of tortoise, crab] carapace *f*. **-3.** [on beach] coquillage *m*. **-4.** [of building, car] carcasse *f*. **-5.** MIL obus *m*. ◇ *vt* **-1.** [peas] écosser; [nuts, prawns] décortiquer; [eggs] enlever la coquille de, écaler. **-2.** MIL bombarder.

◆ **shell out** *inf* ◇ *vt sep* débourser. ◇ *vi*: **to ~ out (for)** casquer (pour).

she'll [ʃiːl] = **she will, she shall**.

shellfish ['ʃelfɪʃ] (*pl inv*) *n* **-1.** [creature] crustacé *m*, coquillage *m*. **-2.** (*U*) [food] fruits *mpl* de mer.

shelling ['ʃelɪŋ] *n* MIL bombardement *m*.

shellshock ['ʃelʃɒk] *n* (*U*) psychose *f* traumatique.

shell suit *n Br* survêtement *m* (*en nylon imperméabilisé*).

shelter ['ʃeltər] ◇ *n* abri *m*. ◇ *vt* **-1.** [protect] abriter, protéger. **-2.** [refugee, homeless person] offrir un asile à; [criminal, fugitive] cacher. ◇ *vi* s'abriter, se mettre à l'abri.

sheltered ['ʃeltəd] *adj* **-1.** [from weather] abrité(e). **-2.** [life, childhood] protégé(e), sans soucis; **~ housing** foyers-logements *mpl* (*pour personnes âgées ou handicapées*).

shelve [ʃelv] ◇ *vt fig* mettre au frigidaire, mettre en sommeil. ◇ *vi* descendre en pente.

shelves [ʃelvz] *pl* → **shelf**.

shelving ['ʃelvɪŋ] *n* (U) étagères *fpl*, rayonnages *mpl*.

shenanigans [ʃɪ'nænɪɡənz] *npl inf* [trickery] micmacs *mpl*, manigances *fpl*.

shepherd ['ʃepəd] ◇ *n* berger *m*. ◇ *vt fig* conduire.

shepherd's pie ['ʃepədz-] *n* ≃ hachis *m* Parmentier.

sherbet ['ʃɜːbət] *n* -1. *Br* [sweet powder] poudre *f* aromatisée. -2. *Am* [sorbet] sorbet *m*.

sheriff ['ʃerɪf] *n Am* shérif *m*.

sherry ['ʃerɪ] (*pl* -ies) *n* xérès *m*, sherry *m*.

she's [ʃiːz] = she is, she has.

Shetland ['ʃetlənd] *n*: (the) ~ (Islands) les (îles) Shetland *fpl*; in (the) ~ (Islands) dans les Shetland.

sh(h) [ʃ] *excl* chut!

shield [ʃiːld] ◇ *n* -1. [armour] bouclier *m*. -2. *Br* [sports trophy] plaque *f*. ◇ *vt*: to ~ sb (from) protéger qqn (de OR contre).

shift [ʃɪft] ◇ *n* -1. [change] changement *m*, modification *f*. -2. [period of work] poste *m*; [workers] équipe *f*. ◇ *vt* -1. [move] déplacer, changer de place; to ~ the blame onto sb rejeter la responsabilité sur qqn. -2. [change] changer, modifier. ◇ *vi* -1. [move - gen] changer de place; [- wind] tourner, changer. -2. [change] changer, se modifier. -3. *Am* AUT changer de vitesse.

shift key *n* [on typewriter] touche *f* de majuscules.

shiftless ['ʃɪftlɪs] *adj* fainéant(e), paresseux(euse).

shift stick *n Am* levier *m* de vitesse.

shifty ['ʃɪftɪ] (*compar* -ier, *superl* -iest) *adj inf* sournois(e), louche.

Shiite ['ʃiːaɪt] ◇ *adj* chiite. ◇ *n* Chiite *mf*.

shilling ['ʃɪlɪŋ] *n* shilling *m*.

shilly-shally ['ʃɪlɪˌʃælɪ] (*pt* & *pp* -ied) *vi* hésiter, être indécis(e).

shimmer ['ʃɪmər] ◇ *n* reflet *m*, miroitement *m*. ◇ *vi* miroiter.

shin [ʃɪn] (*pt* & *pp* -ned, *cont* -ning) *n* tibia *m*;.

◆ **shin up** *Br*, **shinny up** *Am vt fus* grimper à.

shinbone ['ʃɪnbəʊn] *n* tibia *m*.

shine [ʃaɪn] (*pt* & *pp* shone) ◇ *n* brillant *m*. ◇ *vt* -1. [direct]: to ~ a torch on sthg éclairer qqch. -2. [polish] faire briller, astiquer. ◇ *vi* briller; to ~ at sthg *fig* briller dans qqch.

shingle ['ʃɪŋɡl] *n* (U) [on beach] galets *mpl*.
◆ **shingles** *n* (U) zona *m*.

shining ['ʃaɪnɪŋ] *adj* -1. [gleaming] brillant(e), luisant(e). -2. [achievement] extraordinaire; to be a ~ example of sthg être un modèle de qqch.

shinny ['ʃɪnɪ] *Am*
◆ **shinny up** = shin up.

shiny ['ʃaɪnɪ] (*compar* -ier, *superl* -iest) *adj* brillant(e).

ship [ʃɪp] (*pt* & *pp* -ped, *cont* -ping) ◇ *n* bateau *m*; [larger] navire *m*. ◇ *vt* [goods] expédier par bateau; [troops, passengers] transporter.

shipbuilder ['ʃɪpˌbɪldər] *n* constructeur *m* de navires.

shipbuilding ['ʃɪpˌbɪldɪŋ] *n* construction *f* navale.

ship canal *n* canal *m* maritime.

shipment ['ʃɪpmənt] *n* [cargo] cargaison *f*, chargement *m*.

shipper ['ʃɪpər] *n* affréteur *m*, chargeur *m*.

shipping ['ʃɪpɪŋ] *n* (U) -1. [transport] transport *m* maritime. -2. [ships] navires *mpl*.

shipping agent *n* agent *m* maritime.

shipping company *n* compagnie *f* de navigation.

shipping forecast *n* météo *f* marine.

shipping lane *n* voie *f* de navigation.

shipshape ['ʃɪpʃeɪp] *adj* bien rangé(e), en ordre.

shipwreck ['ʃɪprek] ◇ *n* -1. [destruction of ship] naufrage *m*. -2. [wrecked ship] épave *f*. ◇ *vt*: to be ~ed faire naufrage.

shipwrecked ['ʃɪprekt] *adj* naufragé(e).

shipyard ['ʃɪpjɑːd] *n* chantier *m* naval.

shire [ʃaɪər] *n* [county] comté *m*.
◆ **Shire** *n*: the Shires les Comtés du centre de l'Angleterre.

shire horse *n* cheval *m* de gros trait.

shirk [ʃɜːk] *vt* se dérober à.

shirker ['ʃɜːkər] *n* tire-au-flanc *m*.

shirt [ʃɜːt] *n* chemise *f*.

shirtsleeves ['ʃɜːtsliːvz] *npl*: to be in (one's) ~ être en manches OR en bras de chemise.

shirttail ['ʃɜːtteɪl] *n* pan *m* de chemise.

shirty ['ʃɜːtɪ] (*compar* -ier, *superl* -iest) *adj Br inf* de mauvais poil, de mauvaise humeur.

shit [ʃɪt] (*pt* & *pp* shit OR -ted OR shat, *cont* -ting) *vulg* ◇ *n* -1. [excrement] merde *f*. -2. (U) [nonsense] conneries *fpl*. -3. [person] salaud *m*. ◇ *vi* chier. ◇ *excl* merde!

shiver ['ʃɪvər] ◇ *n* frisson *m*; to give sb the ~s *fig* donner le frisson OR la chair de poule à qqn. ◇ *vi*: to ~ (with) trembler (de), frissonner (de).

shoal [ʃəʊl] *n* [of fish] banc *m*.

shock [ʃɒk] ◇ *n* **-1.** [surprise] choc *m*, coup *m*. **-2.** (*U*) MED: **to be suffering from ~, to be in (a state of) ~** être en état de choc. **-3.** [impact] choc *m*, heurt *m*. **-4.** ELEC décharge *f* électrique. ◇ *vt* **-1.** [upset] bouleverser. **-2.** [offend] choquer, scandaliser.

shock absorber [-əb,zɔːbəʳ] *n* amortisseur *m*.

shocked [ʃɒkt] *adj* **-1.** [upset] bouleversé(e). **-2.** [offended] choqué(e), scandalisé(e).

shocking ['ʃɒkɪŋ] *adj* **-1.** [very bad] épouvantable, terrible. **-2.** [outrageous] scandaleux(euse).

shockproof ['ʃɒkpruːf] *adj* antichoc (*inv*).

shock tactics *npl* tactique *f* de choc.

shock therapy, **shock treatment** *n* traitement *m* par électrochocs.

shock troops *npl* troupes *fpl* de choc.

shock wave *n* onde *f* de choc.

shod [ʃɒd] ◇ *pt & pp* → **shoe**. ◇ *adj* chaussé(e).

shoddy ['ʃɒdɪ] (*compar* **-ier**, *superl* **-iest**) *adj* [goods, work] de mauvaise qualité; [treatment] indigne, méprisable.

shoe [ʃuː] (*pt & pp* **-ed** OR **shod**, *cont* **-ing**) ◇ *n* chaussure *f*, soulier *m*. ◇ *vt* [horse] ferrer.

shoebrush ['ʃuːbrʌʃ] *n* brosse *f* à chaussures.

shoe cleaner *n* produit *m* pour chaussures.

shoehorn ['ʃuːhɔːn] *n* chausse-pied *m*.

shoelace ['ʃuːleɪs] *n* lacet *m* de soulier.

shoemaker ['ʃuː,meɪkəʳ] *n* [repairer] cordonnier *m*; [manufacturer] fabricant *m* de chaussures.

shoe polish *n* cirage *m*.

shoe repairer [-rɪ,peərəʳ] *n* cordonnier *m*.

shoe shop *n* magasin *m* de chaussures.

shoestring ['ʃuːstrɪŋ] ◇ *adj* [budget] étroit(e). ◇ *n* *fig*: **on a ~** à peu de frais.

shoetree ['ʃuːtriː] *n* embauchoir *m*.

shone [ʃɒn] *pt & pp* → **shine**.

shoo [ʃuː] ◇ *vt* chasser. ◇ *excl* ouste!

shook [ʃʊk] *pt* → **shake**.

shoot [ʃuːt] (*pt & pp* **shot**) ◇ *vt* **-1.** [kill with gun] tuer d'un coup de feu; [wound with gun] blesser d'un coup de feu; **to ~ o.s.** [kill o.s.] se tuer avec une arme à feu. **-2.** *Br* [hunt] chasser. **-3.** [arrow] décocher, tirer. **-4.** [direct - glance, look] lancer, décocher; **to ~ questions at sb** bombarder qqn de questions. **-5.** CINEMA tourner. **-6.** *Am* [play - pool] jouer à.

◇ *vi* **-1.** [fire gun]: **to ~ (at)** tirer (sur). **-2.** *Br* [hunt] chasser. **-3.** [move quickly]: **to ~ in/out/past** entrer/sortir/passer en trombe, entrer/sortir/passer comme un bolide. **-4.** CINEMA tourner. **-5.** SPORT tirer, shooter.

◇ *n* **-1.** *Br* [hunting expedition] partie *f* de chasse. **-2.** [of plant] pousse *f*.

◇ *excl* *Am* *inf* **-1.** [go ahead] vas-y! **-2.** [damn] zut!

◆ **shoot down** *vt sep* **-1.** [aeroplane] descendre, abattre. **-2.** [person] abattre. **-3.** *fig* [proposal] démolir; [person] descendre en flammes.

◆ **shoot up** *vi* **-1.** [child, plant] pousser vite. **-2.** [price, inflation] monter en flèche. **-3.** *drugs sl* se shooter.

shooting ['ʃuːtɪŋ] *n* **-1.** [killing] meurtre *m*. **-2.** (*U*) [hunting] chasse *f*.

shooting range *n* champ *m* de tir.

shooting star *n* étoile *f* filante.

shooting stick *n* canne-siège *f*.

shoot-out *n* fusillade *f*.

shop [ʃɒp] (*pt & pp* **-ped**, *cont* **-ping**) ◇ *n* **-1.** [store] magasin *m*, boutique *f*; **to talk ~** parler métier OR boutique. **-2.** [workshop] atelier *m*. ◇ *vi* faire ses courses; **to go shopping** aller faire les courses OR commissions.

◆ **shop around** *vi* comparer les prix.

shop assistant *n* *Br* vendeur *m*, -euse *f*.

shop floor *n*: **the ~** *fig* les ouvriers *mpl*.

shopkeeper ['ʃɒp,kiːpəʳ] *n* commerçant *m*, -e *f*.

shoplifter ['ʃɒp,lɪftəʳ] *n* voleur *m*, -euse *f* à l'étalage.

shoplifting ['ʃɒp,lɪftɪŋ] *n* (*U*) vol *m* à l'étalage.

shopper ['ʃɒpəʳ] *n* personne *f* qui fait ses courses.

shopping ['ʃɒpɪŋ] *n* (*U*) [purchases] achats *mpl*.

shopping bag *n* sac *m* à provisions.

shopping centre *Br*, **shopping mall** *Am*, **shopping plaza** *Am* *n* centre *m* commercial.

shopping list *n* liste *f* des commissions.

shopping mall *Am*, **shopping plaza** *Am* = **shopping centre**.

shopsoiled *Br* ['ʃɒpsɔɪld], **shopworn** *Am* ['ʃɒpwɔːn] *adj* qui a fait l'étalage, abîmé(e) (en magasin).

shop steward *n* délégué syndical *m*, déléguée syndicale *f*.

shopwalker ['ʃɒp,wɔːkəʳ] *n* *Br* surveillant *m*, -e *f* de magasin.

shopwindow [,ʃɒp'wɪndəʊ] *n* vitrine *f*.

shopworn *Am* = shopsoiled.

shore [ʃɔːʳ] *n* rivage *m*, bord *m*; **on ~** à terre.

◆ **shore up** *vt sep* étayer, étançonner; *fig* consolider.

shore leave *n* permission *f* à terre.

shoreline ['ʃɔːlaɪn] *n* côte *f*.

shorn [ʃɔːn] ◇ *pp* → **shear.** ◇ *adj* tondu(e).

short [ʃɔːt] ◇ *adj* **-1.** [not long - in time] court(e), bref (brève); [- in space] court. **-2.** [not tall] petit(e). **-3.** [curt] brusque, sec (sèche). **-4.** [lacking]: **time/money is ~** nous manquons de temps/d'argent; **we're £10 ~** il nous manque 10 livres; **to be ~ of** manquer de; **to be ~ of breath** être essoufflé(e). **-5.** [abbreviated]: **to be ~ for** être le diminutif de.
◇ *adv*: **to be running ~ of** [running out of] commencer à manquer de, commencer à être à court de; **to cut sthg ~** [visit, speech] écourter qqch; [discussion] couper court à qqch; **to stop ~** s'arrêter net; **to bring** OR **pull sb up ~** arrêter qqn net.
◇ *n* **-1.** *Br* [alcoholic drink] alcool *m* fort. **-2.** [film] court métrage *m*.
◆ **for short** *adv*: **he's called Bob for ~** Bob est son diminutif.
◆ **in short** *adv* (enfin) bref.
◆ **nothing short of** *prep* rien moins que, pratiquement.
◆ **short of** *prep* [unless, without]: **~ of doing sthg** à moins de faire qqch, à part faire qqch.
◆ **shorts** *npl* **-1.** [gen] short *m*. **-2.** *Am* [underwear] caleçon *m*.

shortage ['ʃɔːtɪdʒ] *n* manque *m*, insuffisance *f*.

short back and sides *n Br* coupe *f* bien dégagée.

shortbread ['ʃɔːtbred] *n* sablé *m*.

short-change *vt* **-1.** [subj: shopkeeper]: **to ~ sb** ne pas rendre assez à qqn. **-2.** *fig* [cheat] tromper, rouler.

short circuit *n* court-circuit *m*.
◆ **short-circuit** ◇ *vt* court-circuiter. ◇ *vi* se mettre en court-circuit.

shortcomings [,ʃɔːt'kʌmɪŋz] *npl* défauts *mpl*.

shortcrust pastry ['ʃɔːtkrʌst-] *n* pâte *f* brisée.

short cut *n* **-1.** [quick route] raccourci *m*. **-2.** [quick method] solution *f* miracle.

shorten ['ʃɔːtn] ◇ *vt* **-1.** [holiday, time] écourter. **-2.** [skirt, rope etc] raccourcir. ◇ *vi* [days] raccourcir.

shortening ['ʃɔːtnɪŋ] *n* (*U*) CULIN matière *f* grasse.

shortfall ['ʃɔːtfɔːl] *n* déficit *m*.

shorthand ['ʃɔːthænd] *n* (*U*) **-1.** [writing system] sténographie *f*. **-2.** [abbreviation] forme *f* abrégée.

shorthanded [,ʃɔːt'hændɪd] *adj*: **to be ~** manquer de personnel.

shorthand typist *n Br* sténodactylo *f*.

short-haul *adj* court-courrier (*inv*).

short list *n Br* liste *f* des candidats sélectionnés.
◆ **short-list** *vt Br* **to be short-listed (for)** être au nombre des candidats sélectionnés (pour).

short-lived [-'lɪvd] *adj* de courte durée.

shortly ['ʃɔːtlɪ] *adv* **-1.** [soon] bientôt. **-2.** [curtly] d'une manière brusque, sèchement.

shortness ['ʃɔːtnɪs] *n* **-1.** [of visit etc] brièveté *f*. **-2.** [of person] petite taille *f*; [of skirt, hair] peu *m* de longueur.

short-range *adj* à courte portée.

short shrift [-'ʃrɪft] *n*: **to give sb ~** envoyer promener qqn.

shortsighted [,ʃɔːt'saɪtɪd] *adj* myope; *fig* imprévoyant(e).

short-staffed [-'stɑːft] *adj*: **to be ~** manquer de personnel.

short story *n* nouvelle *f*.

short-tempered [-'tempəd] *adj* emporté(e), irascible.

short-term *adj* [effects, solution] à court terme; [problem] de courte durée.

short time *n Br*: **on ~** en chômage partiel.

short wave *n* (*U*) ondes *fpl* courtes.

shot [ʃɒt] ◇ *pt & pp* → **shoot.** ◇ *n* **-1.** [gunshot] coup *m* de feu; **like a ~** sans tarder, sans hésiter. **-2.** [marksman] tireur *m*. **-3.** SPORT coup *m*. **-4.** [photograph] photo *f*; CINEMA plan *m*. **-5.** *inf* [attempt]: **to have a ~ at sthg** essayer de faire qqch. **-6.** [injection] piqûre *f*. **-7.** [of alcohol] coup *m*.

shotgun ['ʃɒtgʌn] *n* fusil *m* de chasse.

shot put *n* [event] lancer *m* du poids; [object] poids *m*.

should [ʃʊd] *aux vb* **-1.** [indicating duty]: **we ~ leave now** il faudrait partir maintenant. **-2.** [seeking advice, permission]: **~ I go too?** est-ce que je devrais y aller aussi? **-3.** [as suggestion]: **I ~ deny everything** moi, je nierais tout. **-4.** [indicating probability]: **she ~ be home soon** elle devrait être de retour bientôt, elle va bientôt rentrer. **-5.** [was or were expected]: **they ~ have won the match** ils auraient dû gagner le match. **-6.** [indicating intention, wish]: **I ~ like to come with**

you j'aimerais bien venir avec vous. **-7.** (*as conditional*): **you ~ go if you're invited** tu devrais y aller si tu es invité. **-8.** (*in subordinate clauses*): **we decided that you ~ meet him** nous avons décidé que ce serait toi qui irais le chercher. **-9.** [expressing uncertain opinion]: **I ~ think he's about 50 (years old)** je pense qu'il doit avoir dans les 50 ans.

shoulder ['ʃəʊldər] ◇ *n* épaule *f*; **to look over one's ~** se retourner; **he needed a ~ to cry on** il avait besoin de réconfort; **to rub ~s with sb** *fig* côtoyer qqn. ◇ *vt* **-1.** [carry] porter. **-2.** [responsibility] endosser.

shoulder bag *n* sac *m* en bandoulière.

shoulder blade *n* omoplate *f*.

shoulder-length *adj*: **~ hair** cheveux mi-longs.

shoulder strap *n* **-1.** [on dress] bretelle *f*. **-2.** [on bag] bandoulière *f*.

shouldn't ['ʃʊdnt] = should not.

should've ['ʃʊdəv] = should have.

shout [ʃaʊt] ◇ *n* [cry] cri *m*. ◇ *vt & vi* crier.
◆ **shout down** *vt sep* huer, conspuer.
◆ **shout out** *vt sep* crier.

shouting ['ʃaʊtɪŋ] *n* (U) cris *mpl*.

shove [ʃʌv] ◇ *n*: **to give sb/sthg a ~** pousser qqn/qqch. ◇ *vt* pousser; **to ~ sb about** bousculer qqn; **to ~ clothes into a bag** fourrer des vêtements dans un sac.
◆ **shove off** *vi* **-1.** [in boat] pousser au large. **-2.** *inf* [go away] ficher le camp, filer.

shovel ['ʃʌvl] (*Br pt & pp* -led, *cont* -ling, *Am pt & pp* -ed, *cont* -ing) ◇ *n* [tool] pelle *f*. ◇ *vt* enlever à la pelle, pelleter.

show [ʃəʊ] (*pt* -ed, *pp* shown OR -ed) ◇ *n* **-1.** [display] démonstration *f*, manifestation *f*. **-2.** [at theatre] spectacle *m*; [on radio, TV] émission *f*. **-3.** CINEMA séance *f*. **-4.** [exhibition] exposition *f*; **on ~** exposé(e); **for ~** pour (faire de) l'effet; **flower ~** floralies *fpl*. ◇ *vt* **-1.** [gen] montrer; [profit, loss] indiquer; [respect] témoigner; [courage, mercy] faire preuve de; **he has nothing to ~ for all his hard work** tout son travail n'a rien donné; **to ~ sb sthg, to ~ sthg to sb** montrer qqch à qqn; **to ~ sb how to do sthg** montrer OR faire voir à qqn comment faire qqch; **it just goes to ~ that ...** cela prouve que .... **-2.** [escort]: **to ~ sb to his seat/table** conduire qqn à sa place/sa table. **-3.** [film] projeter, passer; [TV programme] donner, passer. ◇ *vi* **-1.** [indicate] indiquer, montrer. **-2.** [be visible] se voir, être visible. **-3.** CINEMA: **what's ~ing tonight?** qu'est-ce qu'on joue comme film ce soir?
◆ **show around** = show round.

◆ **show off** ◇ *vt sep* exhiber. ◇ *vi* faire l'intéressant.
◆ **show round** *vt sep*: **to ~ sb round a town/a house** faire visiter une ville/une maison à qqn.
◆ **show up** ◇ *vt sep* [embarrass] embarrasser, faire honte à. ◇ *vi* **-1.** [stand out] se voir, ressortir. **-2.** [arrive] s'amener, rappliquer.

showbiz ['ʃəʊbɪz] *n inf* show-biz *m*.

show business *n* (U) monde *m* du spectacle, show-business *m*.

showcase ['ʃəʊkeɪs] *n lit & fig* vitrine *f*.

showdown ['ʃəʊdaʊn] *n*: **to have a ~ with sb** s'expliquer avec qqn, mettre les choses au point avec qqn.

shower ['ʃaʊər] ◇ *n* **-1.** [device, act] douche *f*; **to have OR take a ~** prendre une douche, se doucher. **-2.** [of rain] averse *f*. **-3.** *fig* [of questions, confetti] avalanche *f*, déluge *m*. **-4.** *Am* [party] fête organisée en l'honneur d'une femme qui va se marier, par exemple, et à laquelle chacun des invités offre un petit cadeau. ◇ *vt*: **to ~ sb with** couvrir qqn de. ◇ *vi* [wash] prendre une douche, se doucher.

shower cap *n* bonnet *m* de douche.

showerproof ['ʃaʊəpruːf] *adj* imperméable.

showery ['ʃaʊərɪ] *adj* pluvieux(ieuse).

showing ['ʃəʊɪŋ] *n* CINEMA projection *f*.

show jumping [-,dʒʌmpɪŋ] *n* jumping *m*.

showman ['ʃəʊmən] (*pl* -men [-mən]) *n* **-1.** [at fair, circus] forain *m*. **-2.** *fig* [publicity-seeker]: **he's a real ~** il a le sens du spectacle.

showmanship ['ʃəʊmənʃɪp] *n* sens *m* du spectacle.

shown [ʃəʊn] *pp* → show.

show-off *n inf* m'as-tu-vu *m*, -e *f*.

show of hands *n*: **to have a ~** voter à main levée.

showpiece ['ʃəʊpiːs] *n* [main attraction] joyau *m*, trésor *m*.

showroom ['ʃəʊrʊm] *n* salle *f* OR magasin *m* d'exposition; [for cars] salle de démonstration.

showy ['ʃəʊɪ] (*compar* -ier, *superl* -iest) *adj* voyant(e); [person] prétentieux(ieuse).

shrank [ʃræŋk] *pt* → shrink.

shrapnel ['ʃræpnl] *n* (U) éclats *mpl* d'obus.

shred [ʃred] (*pt & pp* -ded, *cont* -ding) ◇ *n* **-1.** [of material, paper] lambeau *m*, brin *m*. **-2.** *fig* [of evidence] parcelle *f*; [of truth] once *f*, grain *m*. ◇ *vt* [food] râper; [paper] déchirer en lambeaux.

shredder ['ʃredər] *n* [machine] destructeur *m* de documents.

shrew [ʃruː] n [animal] musaraigne f.

shrewd [ʃruːd] adj fin(e), astucieux(ieuse).

shrewdness ['ʃruːdnɪs] n finesse f, perspicacité f.

shriek [ʃriːk] ◇ n cri m perçant, hurlement m; [of laughter] éclat m. ◇ vt hurler, crier. ◇ vi pousser un cri perçant; **to ~ with laughter** éclater de rire.

shrill [ʃrɪl] adj [sound, voice] aigu(ë); [whistle] strident(e).

shrimp [ʃrɪmp] n crevette f.

shrine [ʃraɪn] n [place of worship] lieu m saint.

shrink [ʃrɪŋk] (pt **shrank**, pp **shrunk**) ◇ vt rétrécir. ◇ vi **-1.** [cloth, garment] rétrécir; [person] rapetisser; fig [income, popularity etc] baisser, diminuer. **-2.** [recoil]: **to ~ away from sthg** reculer devant qqch; **to ~ from doing sthg** rechigner OR répugner à faire qqch.

shrinkage ['ʃrɪŋkɪdʒ] n rétrécissement m; fig diminution f, baisse f.

shrink-wrap vt emballer sous film plastique.

shrivel ['ʃrɪvl] (Br pt & pp **-led**, cont **-ling**, Am pt & pp **-ed**, cont **-ing**) ◇ vt: **to ~ (up)** rider, flétrir. ◇ vi: **to ~ (up)** se rider, se flétrir.

shroud [ʃraud] ◇ n [cloth] linceul m. ◇ vt: **to be ~ed in** [darkness, fog] être enseveli(e) sous; [mystery] être enveloppé(e) de.

Shrove Tuesday ['ʃrəʊv-] n Mardi m gras.

shrub [ʃrʌb] n arbuste m.

shrubbery ['ʃrʌbərɪ] n massif m d'arbustes.

shrug [ʃrʌg] (pt & pp **-ged**, cont **-ging**) ◇ n haussement m d'épaules. ◇ vt: **to ~ one's shoulders** hausser les épaules. ◇ vi hausser les épaules.
- **shrug off** vt sep ignorer.

shrunk [ʃrʌŋk] pp → shrink.

shrunken ['ʃrʌŋkn] adj [person] ratatiné(e).

shucks [ʃʌks] excl Am inf **-1.** [it was nothing] de rien! **-2.** [damn] zut!

shudder ['ʃʌdər] ◇ n frisson m, frémissement m. ◇ vi **-1.** [tremble]: **to ~ (with)** frémir (de), frissonner (de); **I ~ to think** je n'ose pas y penser. **-2.** [shake] vibrer, trembler.

shuffle ['ʃʌfl] ◇ n **-1.** [of feet] marche f traînante. **-2.** [of cards]: **to give the cards a ~** battre les cartes. ◇ vt **-1.** [drag]: **to ~ one's feet** traîner les pieds. **-2.** [cards] mélanger, battre. ◇ vi **-1.** [walk]: **to ~ in/out** entrer/sortir en traînant les pieds. **-2.** [fidget] remuer.

shun [ʃʌn] (pt & pp **-ned**, cont **-ning**) vt fuir, éviter.

shunt [ʃʌnt] vt **-1.** RAIL aiguiller. **-2.** fig [move] transférer, déplacer.

shunter ['ʃʌntər] n RAIL [engine] locomotive f de manœuvre.

shush [ʃuʃ] excl chut!

shut [ʃʌt] (pt & pp **shut**, cont **-ting**) ◇ adj [closed] fermé(e). ◇ vt fermer; **~ your mouth** OR **face !** v inf ta gueule!, la ferme! ◇ vi **-1.** [door, window] se fermer. **-2.** [shop] fermer.
- **shut away** vt sep [valuables, papers] mettre sous clef; **to ~ o.s. away** s'enfermer.
- **shut down** vt sep & vi fermer.
- **shut in** vt sep enfermer; **to ~ o.s. in** s'enfermer.
- **shut out** vt sep **-1.** [noise] supprimer; [light] ne pas laisser entrer; **to ~ sb out** laisser qqn à la porte. **-2.** [feelings, thoughts] chasser.
- **shut up** inf ◇ vt sep [silence] faire taire. ◇ vi se taire.

shutdown ['ʃʌtdaun] n fermeture f.

shutter ['ʃʌtər] n **-1.** [on window] volet m. **-2.** [in camera] obturateur m.

shuttle ['ʃʌtl] ◇ adj: **~ service** (service m de) navette f. ◇ n [train, bus, plane] navette f. ◇ vi faire la navette.

shuttlecock ['ʃʌtlkɒk] n volant m.

shy [ʃaɪ] (pt & pp **shied**) ◇ adj **-1.** [timid] timide. **-2.** [wary]: **to be ~ of doing sthg** avoir peur de faire qqch, hésiter à faire qqch. ◇ vi [horse] s'effaroucher.
- **shy away from** vt fus: **to ~ away from sthg** reculer devant qqch; **to ~ away from doing sthg** répugner à faire qqch.

shyly ['ʃaɪlɪ] adv timidement.

shyness ['ʃaɪnɪs] n timidité f.

Siam [,saɪ'æm] n Siam m; **in ~** au Siam.

Siamese [,saɪə'miːz] (pl inv) ◇ adj siamois(e). ◇ n **-1.** [person] Siamois m, -e f. **-2.** **~ (cat)** chat m siamois.

Siamese twins npl [brothers] frères mpl siamois; [sisters] sœurs fpl siamoises.

SIB (abbr of **Securities and Investment Board**) n organisme britannique qui fait appliquer la réglementation concernant les investissements.

Siberia [saɪ'bɪərɪə] n Sibérie f; **in ~** en Sibérie.

Siberian [saɪ'bɪərɪən] ◇ adj sibérien(ienne). ◇ n Sibérien m, -ienne f.

sibling ['sɪblɪŋ] n [brother] frère m; [sister] sœur f.

Sicilian [sɪˈsɪljən] ◇ *adj* sicilien(ienne). ◇ *n* [person] Sicilien *m*, -ienne *f*.

Sicily [ˈsɪsɪlɪ] *n* Sicile *f*; **in** ~ en Sicile.

sick [sɪk] *adj* **-1.** [ill] malade. **-2.** [nauseous]: **to feel** ~ avoir envie de vomir, avoir mal au cœur; **to be** ~ *Br* [vomit] vomir; **to make sb** ~ *fig* écœurer qqn, dégoûter qqn. **-3.** [fed up]: **to be** ~ **of** en avoir assez OR marre de. **-4.** [joke, humour] macabre.

sickbay [ˈsɪkbeɪ] *n* infirmerie *f*.

sickbed [ˈsɪkbed] *n* lit *m* de malade.

sicken [ˈsɪkn] ◇ *vt* écœurer, dégoûter. ◇ *vi Br*: **to be** ~**ing for sthg** couver qqch.

sickening [ˈsɪknɪŋ] *adj* [disgusting] écœurant(e), dégoûtant(e).

sickle [ˈsɪkl] *n* faucille *f*.

sick leave *n* (*U*) congé *m* de maladie.

sickly [ˈsɪklɪ] (*compar* -**ier**, *superl* -**iest**) *adj* **-1.** [unhealthy] maladif(ive), souffreteux(euse). **-2.** [smell, taste] écœurant(e).

sickness [ˈsɪknɪs] *n* **-1.** [illness] maladie *f*. **-2.** *Br* (*U*) [nausea] nausée *f*, nausées *fpl*; [vomiting] vomissement *m*, vomissements *mpl*.

sickness benefit *n* (*U*) prestations *fpl* en cas de maladie.

sick pay *n* (*U*) indemnité *f* OR allocation *f* de maladie.

sickroom [ˈsɪkrum] *n* chambre *f* de malade.

side [saɪd] ◇ *n* **-1.** [gen] côté *m*; **at** OR **by my/her** *etc* ~ à mes/ses *etc* côtés; **to stand to one** ~ se tenir sur le côté; **on every** ~, **on all** ~**s** de tous côtés; **from** ~ **to** ~ d'un côté à l'autre; ~ **by** ~ côte à côte; **to put sthg to** OR **on one** ~ mettre qqch de côté. **-2.** [of table, river] bord *m*. **-3.** [of hill, valley] versant *m*, flanc *m*. **-4.** [in war, debate] camp *m*, côté *m*; SPORT équipe *f*, camp *m*; [of argument] point *m* de vue; **to be on sb's** ~ être avec qqn, soutenir qqn; **to take sb's** ~ prendre le parti de qqn. **-5.** [aspect - gen] aspect *m*; [- of character] facette *f*; **to be on the safe** ~ pour plus de sûreté, par précaution. **-6.** *phr*: **on the large/small** ~ plutôt grand/petit, un peu trop grand/petit; **to do sthg on the** ~ faire qqch en plus; **to keep** OR **stay on the right** ~ **of sb** se faire bien voir de qqn.
◇ *adj* [situated on side] latéral(e).
◆ **side with** *vt fus* prendre le parti de, se ranger du côté de.

sideboard [ˈsaɪdbɔːd] *n* [cupboard] buffet *m*.

sideboards *Br* [ˈsaɪdbɔːdz], **sideburns** *Am* [ˈsaɪdbɜːnz] *npl* favoris *mpl*, rouflaquettes *fpl*.

sidecar [ˈsaɪdkɑːr] *n* side-car *m*.

side dish *n* accompagnement *m*, garniture *f*.

side effect *n* **-1.** MED effet *m* secondaire OR indésirable. **-2.** [unplanned result] effet *m* secondaire, répercussion *f*.

sidekick [ˈsaɪdkɪk] *n inf* [friend] copain *m*, copine *f*; *pej* acolyte *mf*.

sidelight [ˈsaɪdlaɪt] *n* AUT feu *m* de position.

sideline [ˈsaɪdlaɪn] *n* **-1.** [extra business] activité *f* secondaire. **-2.** SPORT ligne *f* de touche; **on the** ~ *fig* dans la coulisse.

sidelong [ˈsaɪdlɒŋ] *adj & adv* de côté.

side-on *adj & adv* de côté.

side plate *n* assiette *f* à pain, petite assiette.

side road *n* [not main road] route *f* secondaire; [off main road] route transversale.

sidesaddle [ˈsaɪdˌsædl] *adv*: **to ride** ~ monter en amazone.

sideshow [ˈsaɪdʃəu] *n* spectacle *m* forain.

sidestep [ˈsaɪdstep] (*pt & pp* -**ped**, *cont* -**ping**) *vt* faire un pas de côté pour éviter OR esquiver; *fig* éviter.

side street *n* [not main street] petite rue *f*; [off main street] rue transversale.

sidetrack [ˈsaɪdtræk] *vt*: **to be** ~**ed** se laisser distraire.

sidewalk [ˈsaɪdwɔːk] *n Am* trottoir *m*.

sideways [ˈsaɪdweɪz] *adj & adv* de côté.

siding [ˈsaɪdɪŋ] *n* voie *f* de garage.

sidle [ˈsaɪdl]
◆ **sidle up** *vi*: **to** ~ **up to sb** se glisser vers qqn.

SIDS (*abbr of* **sudden infant death syndrome**) *n* mort subite du nourrisson.

siege [siːdʒ] *n* siège *m*.

Sierra Leone [sɪˈerə lɪˈəun] *n* Sierra Leone *f*; **in** ~ en Sierra Leone.

Sierra Leonean [sɪˈerə lɪˈəunjən] ◇ *adj* de la Sierra Leone. ◇ *n* habitant *m*, -e *f* de la Sierra Leone.

sieve [sɪv] ◇ *n* [for flour, sand etc] tamis *m*; [for liquids] passoire *f*; **I've got a head** OR **memory like a** ~ ma mémoire est une passoire. ◇ *vt* [flour etc] tamiser; [liquid] passer.

sift [sɪft] ◇ *vt* **-1.** [flour, sand] tamiser. **-2.** *fig* [evidence] passer au crible. ◇ *vi*: **to** ~ **through** examiner, éplucher.

sigh [saɪ] ◇ *n* soupir *m*; **to heave a** ~ **of relief** pousser un soupir de soulagement. ◇ *vi* [person] soupirer, pousser un soupir.

sight [saɪt] ◇ *n* **-1.** [seeing] vue *f*; **in** ~ en vue; **in/out of** ~ en/hors de vue; **to catch** ~ **of** apercevoir; **to know sb by** ~ connaître qqn de vue; **to lose** ~ **of** perdre de vue; **to**

shoot on ~ tirer à vue; **at first** ~ à première vue, au premier abord. **-2.** [spectacle] spectacle *m.* **-3.** [on gun] mire *f*; **to set one's** ~**s on sthg** décider d'obtenir qqch, viser qqch; **to set one's** ~**s on doing sthg** décider de faire qqch. **-4.** [a lot]: **a** ~ **better/worse** bien mieux/pire. ◇ *vt* apercevoir.

◆ **sights** *npl* [of city] curiosités *fpl*, monuments *mpl*; [of country] sites *mpl* pittoresques.

sighting ['saɪtɪŋ] *n*: **there has been a** ~ **of the escaped criminal** on a vu le fugitif.

sightseeing ['saɪt,si:ɪŋ] *n* tourisme *m*; **to go** ~ faire du tourisme.

sightseer ['saɪt,si:ər] *n* touriste *mf*.

sign [saɪn] ◇ *n* **-1.** [gen] signe *m*; **no** ~ **of** aucune trace de; **there's no** ~ **of him yet** il n'est pas encore arrivé. **-2.** [notice] enseigne *f*; AUT panneau *m.* ◇ *vt* signer; **to** ~ **one's name** signer.

◆ **sign away** *vt sep* signer la renonciation à.

◆ **sign for** *vt fus* **-1.** [letter, parcel] signer à la réception de. **-2.** SPORT [team] signer un contrat avec.

◆ **sign in** *vi* signer à l'arrivée OR en arrivant.

◆ **sign on** *vi* **-1.** [enrol - MIL] s'engager; [- for course] s'inscrire. **-2.** [register as unemployed] s'inscrire au chômage.

◆ **sign out** *vi* signer à la sortie OR en sortant.

◆ **sign up** ◇ *vt sep* [worker] embaucher; [soldier] engager. ◇ *vi* MIL s'engager; [for course] s'inscrire.

signal ['sɪgnl] (*Br pp* & *pt* **-led**, *cont* **-ling**, *Am pp* & *pt* **-ed**, *cont* **-ing**) ◇ *n* signal *m.* ◇ *adj fml* remarquable. ◇ *vt* **-1.** [indicate] indiquer. **-2.** [gesture to]: **to** ~ **sb (to do sthg)** faire signe à qqn (de faire qqch). ◇ *vi* **-1.** AUT clignoter, mettre son clignotant. **-2.** [gesture]: **to** ~ **to sb (to do sthg)** faire signe à qqn (de faire qqch).

signal box *Br*, **signal tower** *Am n* poste *m* d'aiguillage.

signally ['sɪgnəlɪ] *adv fml* remarquablement, singulièrement.

signalman ['sɪgnlmən] (*pl* **-men** [-mən]) *n* RAIL aiguilleur *m*.

signal tower *Am* = **signal box**.

signatory ['sɪgnətrɪ] (*pl* **-ies**) *n* signataire *mf*.

signature ['sɪgnətʃər] *n* [name] signature *f*.

signature tune *n* indicatif *m*.

signet ring ['sɪgnɪt-] *n* chevalière *f*.

significance [sɪg'nɪfɪkəns] *n* **-1.** [importance] importance *f*, portée *f*. **-2.** [meaning] signification *f*.

significant [sɪg'nɪfɪkənt] *adj* **-1.** [considerable] considérable. **-2.** [important] important(e). **-3.** [meaningful] significatif(ive).

significantly [sɪg'nɪfɪkəntlɪ] *adv* **-1.** [considerably] considérablement, énormément. **-2.** [meaningfully] d'une manière significative.

signify ['sɪgnɪfaɪ] (*pt* & *pp* **-ied**) *vt* signifier, indiquer.

signing ['saɪnɪŋ] *n Br* SPORT footballeur etc qui a signé un contrat avec un club.

sign language *n* langage *m* par signes.

signpost ['saɪnpəʊst] *n* poteau *m* indicateur.

Sikh [si:k] ◇ *adj* sikh (*inv*). ◇ *n* [person] Sikh *mf*.

Sikhism ['si:kɪzm] *n* sikhisme *m*.

silage ['saɪlɪdʒ] *n* fourrage *m* ensilé.

silence ['saɪləns] ◇ *n* silence *m.* ◇ *vt* réduire au silence, faire taire.

silencer ['saɪlənsər] *n* silencieux *m*.

silent ['saɪlənt] *adj* **-1.** [person, place] silencieux(ieuse); **to be** ~ **about sthg** garder le silence sur qqch. **-2.** CINEMA & LING muet(ette).

silently ['saɪləntlɪ] *adv* silencieusement.

silent partner *n Am* (associé *m*) commanditaire *m*, bailleur *m* de fonds.

silhouette [,sɪlu:'et] ◇ *n* silhouette *f.* ◇ *vt*: **to be** ~**d against** se profiler sur, se silhouetter sur.

silicon ['sɪlɪkən] *n* silicium *m*.

silicon chip *n* puce *f*, pastille *f* de silicium.

silicone ['sɪlɪkəʊn] *n* silicone *f*.

Silicon Valley *n* Silicon Valley *f* (*centre de l'industrie électronique américaine*).

silk [sɪlk] ◇ *n* soie *f.* ◇ *comp* en OR de soie.

silk screen printing *n* sérigraphie *f*.

silkworm ['sɪlkwɜ:m] *n* ver *m* à soie.

silky ['sɪlkɪ] (*compar* **-ier**, *superl* **-iest**) *adj* soyeux(euse).

sill [sɪl] *n* [of window] rebord *m*.

silliness ['sɪlɪnɪs] *n* (*U*) stupidité *f*, bêtise *f*.

silly ['sɪlɪ] (*compar* **-ier**, *superl* **-iest**) *adj* stupide, bête.

silo ['saɪləʊ] (*pl* **-s**) *n* silo *m*.

silt [sɪlt] *n* vase *f*, limon *m*.

◆ **silt up** *vi* s'envaser.

silver ['sɪlvər] ◇ *adj* [colour] argenté(e). ◇ *n* (*U*) **-1.** [metal] argent *m.* **-2.** [coins] pièces *fpl* d'argent. **-3.** [silverware] argenterie *f.* ◇ *comp* en argent, d'argent.

silver foil, **silver paper** *n* papier *m* d'argent OR d'étain.

silver-plated [-'pleɪtɪd] *adj* plaqué(e) argent.

silver screen *n inf*: the ~ le grand écran.

silversmith ['sɪlvəsmɪθ] *n* orfèvre *mf*.

silverware ['sɪlvəweəʳ] *n* (U) **-1.** argenterie *f*. **-2.** *Am* [cutlery] couverts *mpl*.

silver wedding *n* noces *fpl* d'argent.

similar ['sɪmɪləʳ] *adj*: ~ (to) semblable (à), similaire (à).

similarity [,sɪmɪ'lærətɪ] (*pl* -ies) *n*: ~ (between/to) similitude *f* (entre/avec), ressemblance *f* (entre/avec).

similarly ['sɪmɪləlɪ] *adv* de la même manière, pareillement.

simile ['sɪmɪlɪ] *n* comparaison *f*.

simmer ['sɪməʳ] ◇ *vt* faire cuire à feu doux, mijoter. ◇ *vi* cuire à feu doux, mijoter.
◆ **simmer down** *vi inf* se calmer.

simper ['sɪmpəʳ] ◇ *n* sourire *m* affecté. ◇ *vi* minauder.

simpering ['sɪmpərɪŋ] *adj* affecté(e).

simple ['sɪmpl] *adj* **-1.** [gen] simple. **-2.** *dated* [mentally retarded] simplet(ette), simple d'esprit.

simple-minded [-'maɪndɪd] *adj* simplet(ette), simple d'esprit.

simpleton ['sɪmpltən] *n dated* niais *m*, -e *f*.

simplicity [sɪm'plɪsətɪ] *n* simplicité *f*.

simplification [,sɪmplɪfɪ'keɪʃn] *n* simplification *f*.

simplify ['sɪmplɪfaɪ] (*pt* & *pp* -ied) *vt* simplifier.

simplistic [sɪm'plɪstɪk] *adj* simpliste.

simply ['sɪmplɪ] *adv* **-1.** [gen] simplement. **-2.** [for emphasis] absolument.

simulate ['sɪmjʊleɪt] *vt* simuler.

simulation [,sɪmjʊ'leɪʃn] *n* simulation *f*.

simulator ['sɪmjʊleɪtəʳ] *n* simulateur *m*.

simultaneous [*Br* ,sɪml'teɪnjəs, *Am* ,saɪməl'teɪnjəs] *adj* simultané(e).

simultaneously [*Br* ,sɪml'teɪnjəslɪ, *Am* ,saɪməl'teɪnjəslɪ] *adv* simultanément, en même temps.

sin [sɪn] (*pt* & *pp* -ned, *cont* -ning) ◇ *n* péché *m*; **to live in** ~ vivre en concubinage. ◇ *vi*: **to** ~ (**against**) pécher (contre).

sin bin *n inf* ICE HOCKEY prison *f*.

since [sɪns] ◇ *adv* depuis; **long** ~ il y a longtemps. ◇ *prep* depuis. ◇ *conj* **-1.** [in time] depuis que. **-2.** [because] comme, puisque.

sincere [sɪn'sɪəʳ] *adj* sincère.

sincerely [sɪn'sɪəlɪ] *adv* sincèrement; **Yours** ~ [at end of letter] veuillez agréer,

Monsieur/Madame, l'expression de mes sentiments les meilleurs.

sincerity [sɪn'serətɪ] *n* sincérité *f*.

sinecure ['saɪnɪ,kjʊəʳ] *n* sinécure *f*.

sinew ['sɪnjuː] *n* tendon *m*.

sinewy ['sɪnjuːɪ] *adj* musclé(e).

sinful ['sɪnfʊl] *adj* [thought] mauvais(e); [desire, act] coupable; ~ **person** pécheur *m*, -eresse *f*.

sing [sɪŋ] (*pt* sang, *pp* sung) *vt* & *vi* chanter.

Singapore [,sɪŋə'pɔːʳ] *n* Singapour *m*.

Singaporean [,sɪŋə'pɔːrɪən] ◇ *adj* singapourien(ienne). ◇ *n* [person] Singapourien *m*, -ienne *f*.

singe [sɪndʒ] (*cont* singeing) ◇ *n* légère brûlure *f*. ◇ *vt* brûler légèrement; [cloth] roussir.

singer ['sɪŋəʳ] *n* chanteur *m*, -euse *f*.

Singhalese [,sɪŋhə'liːz] ◇ *adj* cingalais(e), ceylanais(e). ◇ *n* **-1.** [person] Cingalais *m*, -e *f*, Ceylanais *m*, -e *f*. **-2.** [language] cingalais *m*.

singing ['sɪŋɪŋ] ◇ *adj* [lesson, teacher] de chant. ◇ *n* (U) chant *m*.

singing telegram *n* télégramme *m* chanté.

single ['sɪŋgl] ◇ *adj* **-1.** [only one] seul(e), unique; **every** ~ chaque. **-2.** [unmarried] célibataire. **-3.** *Br* [ticket] simple. ◇ *n* **-1.** *Br* [one-way ticket] billet *m* simple, aller *m* (simple). **-2.** MUS (disque *m*) 45 tours *m*.
◆ **singles** *npl* TENNIS simples *mpl*.
◆ **single out** *vt sep*: **to** ~ **sb out (for)** choisir qqn (pour).

single bed *n* lit *m* à une place.

single-breasted [-'brestɪd] *adj* [jacket] droit(e).

single cream *n Br* crème *f* liquide.

single-decker (bus) [-'dekəʳ-] *n Br* bus *m* sans impériale.

Single European Market *n*: the ~ le Marché unique.

single file *n*: in ~ en file indienne, à la file.

single-handed [-'hændɪd] *adv* tout seul (toute seule).

single-minded [-'maɪndɪd] *adj* résolu(e); **to be** ~ **about sthg** concentrer toute son attention sur qqch.

single-parent family *n* famille *f* monoparentale.

single quotes *npl* guillemets *mpl*.

single room *n* chambre *f* pour une personne OR à un lit.

singles bar *n* club *m* pour célibataires.

singlet ['sɪŋglɪt] *n* Br tricot *m* de peau; SPORT maillot *m*.

single ticket *n* Br billet *m* simple, aller *m* (simple).

singsong ['sɪŋsɒŋ] ◇ *adj* [voice] chantant(e). ◇ *n* Br *inf*: **to have a ~** chanter en chœur.

singular ['sɪŋgjʊlər] ◇ *adj* singulier(ière). ◇ *n* singulier *m*.

singularly ['sɪŋgjʊləlɪ] *adv* singulièrement.

Sinhalese ['sɪnəliːz] = **Singhalese**.

sinister ['sɪnɪstər] *adj* sinistre.

sink [sɪŋk] (*pt* **sank**, *pp* **sunk**) ◇ *n* [in kitchen] évier *m*; [in bathroom] lavabo *m*. ◇ *vt* **-1.** [ship] couler. **-2.** [teeth, claws]: **to ~ sthg into** enfoncer qqch dans. ◇ *vi* **-1.** [in water - ship] couler, sombrer; [- person, object] couler. **-2.** [ground] s'affaisser; [sun] baisser; **his spirits sank** il a été pris de découragement; **to ~ into a chair** se laisser tomber dans un fauteuil; **to ~ to one's knees** tomber à genoux; **to ~ into poverty/despair** sombrer dans la misère/le désespoir. **-3.** [value, amount] baisser, diminuer; [voice] faiblir.

◆ **sink in** *vi*: **it hasn't sunk in yet** je n'ai pas encore réalisé.

sink board *n* Am égouttoir *m*.

sinking ['sɪŋkɪŋ] *n* naufrage *m*.

sinking fund *n* fonds *m* OR caisse *f* d'amortissement.

sink unit *n* bloc-évier *m*.

sinner ['sɪnər] *n* pécheur *m*, -eresse *f*.

Sinn Féin [ˌʃɪn'feɪn] *n* Sinn Féin *m*.

sinuous ['sɪnjʊəs] *adj* sinueux(euse).

sinus ['saɪnəs] (*pl* **-es**) *n* sinus *m inv*.

sip [sɪp] (*pt* & *pp* **-ped**, *cont* **-ping**) ◇ *n* petite gorgée *f*. ◇ *vt* siroter, boire à petits coups.

siphon ['saɪfn] ◇ *n* siphon *m*. ◇ *vt* **-1.** [liquid] siphonner. **-2.** *fig* [money] canaliser.

◆ **siphon off** *vt sep* **-1.** [liquid] siphonner. **-2.** *fig* [money] canaliser.

sir [sɜːr] *n* **-1.** [form of address] monsieur *m*. **-2.** [in titles]: **Sir Phillip Holden** sir Phillip Holden.

siren ['saɪərən] *n* sirène *f*.

sirloin (steak) ['sɜːlɔɪn] *n* bifteck *m* dans l'aloyau OR d'aloyau.

sissy ['sɪsɪ] (*pl* **-ies**) *n inf* poule *f* mouillée, dégonflé *m*, -e *f*.

sister ['sɪstər] ◇ *adj* [organization] sœur; ~**ship** sister-ship *m*. ◇ *n* **-1.** [sibling] sœur *f*. **-2.** [nun] sœur *f*, religieuse *f*. **-3.** Br [senior nurse] infirmière *f* chef.

sisterhood ['sɪstəhʊd] *n* RELIG communauté *f* religieuse.

sister-in-law (*pl* **sisters-in-law** OR **sister-in-laws**) *n* belle-sœur *f*.

sisterly ['sɪstəlɪ] *adj* de sœur, fraternel(elle).

sit [sɪt] (*pt* & *pp* **sat**, *cont* **-ting**) ◇ *vt* Br [exam] passer. ◇ *vi* **-1.** [person] s'asseoir; **to be sitting** être assis(e); **to ~ on a committee** faire partie OR être membre d'un comité. **-2.** [court, parliament] siéger, être en séance. **-3.** [be situated] se trouver, être. **-4.** *phr*: **to ~ tight** ne pas bouger.

◆ **sit about, sit around** *vi* rester assis(e) à ne rien faire.

◆ **sit back** *vi* [relax] se détendre; **to ~ back in a chair** se caler dans un fauteuil; **we can't just ~ back and do nothing!** il faut que nous fassions quelque chose!

◆ **sit down** ◇ *vt sep* asseoir. ◇ *vi* s'asseoir.

◆ **sit in on** *vt fus* assister à.

◆ **sit out** *vt sep* **-1.** [meeting, play etc] rester jusqu'à la fin de. **-2.** [dance]: **to ~ out a dance** ne pas danser.

◆ **sit through** *vt fus* rester jusqu'à la fin de.

◆ **sit up** *vi* **-1.** [sit upright] se redresser, s'asseoir. **-2.** [stay up] veiller.

sitcom ['sɪtkɒm] *n inf* sitcom *f*.

sit-down ◇ *adj* [meal] servi(e) à la table; [protest] sur le tas. ◇ *n* Br *inf*: **to have a ~** (s'asseoir pour) se reposer.

site [saɪt] ◇ *n* [of town, building] emplacement *m*; [archaeological] site *m*; CONSTR chantier *m*. ◇ *vt* situer, placer.

sit-in *n* sit-in *m*, occupation *f* des locaux.

sitter ['sɪtər] *n* **-1.** ART modèle *m*. **-2.** [baby-sitter] baby-sitter *mf*.

sitting ['sɪtɪŋ] *n* **-1.** [of meal] service *m*. **-2.** [of court, parliament] séance *f*.

sitting duck *n inf* cible *f* OR proie *f* facile.

sitting room *n* salon *m*.

sitting tenant *n* Br locataire *mf* en possession des lieux.

situate ['sɪtjʊeɪt] *vt* situer.

situated ['sɪtjʊeɪtɪd] *adj*: **to be ~** être situé(e), se trouver.

situation [ˌsɪtjʊ'eɪʃn] *n* **-1.** [gen] situation *f*. **-2.** [job] situation *f*, emploi *m*; **"Situations Vacant"** Br «offres d'emploi».

situation comedy *n* sitcom *f*.

sit-up *n* redressement *m* assis.

six [sɪks] ◇ *num adj* six (*inv*); **she's ~ (years old)** elle a six ans. ◇ *num pron* six *mfpl*; **I want ~** j'en veux

six; ~ **of us went** six d'entre nous sont allés; **there were ~ of us** nous étions six.
◇ *num n* **-1.** [gen] six *m inv*; **two hundred and ~** deux cent six; **we sell them in ~es** on les vend par paquets de six. **-2.** [six o'clock]: **it's ~** il est six heures; **we arrived at ~** nous sommes arrivés à six heures. **-3.** [six degrees]: **it's ~ below** il fait moins six.

six-shooter [-'ʃuːtəʳ] *n Am* revolver *m* à six coups.

sixteen [sɪks'tiːn] *num* seize; *see also* **six**.

sixth [sɪksθ] ◇ *num adj* sixième. ◇ *num adv* **-1.** [in race, competition] sixième, en sixième place. **-2.** [in list] sixièmement. ◇ *num pron* sixième *mf*. ◇ *n* **-1.** [fraction] sixième *m*. **-2.** [in dates]: **the ~ (of September)** le six (septembre).

sixth form *n Br* SCH ≃ (classe *f*) terminale *f*.

sixth form college *n Br établissement préparant aux A-levels.*

sixth sense *n* sixième sens *m*.

sixtieth ['sɪkstɪəθ] *num* soixantième; *see also* **sixth**.

sixty ['sɪkstɪ] *(pl* **-ies)** *num* soixante ; *see also* **six**.

◆ **sixties** *npl* **-1.** [decade]: **the sixties** les années *fpl* soixante. **-2.** [in ages]: **to be in one's sixties** être sexagénaire. **-3.** [in temperatures]: **in the sixties** ≃ entre 15 et 20 degrés.

size [saɪz] *n* [of person, clothes, company] taille *f*; [of building] grandeur *f*, dimensions *fpl*; [of problem] ampleur *f*, taille; [of shoes] pointure *f*; **to cut sb down to ~** rabattre le caquet à qqn.

◆ **size up** *vt sep* [person] jauger; [situation] apprécier, peser.

sizeable ['saɪzəbl] *adj* assez important(e).

-sized [-saɪzd] *suffix*: **medium~** de taille moyenne.

sizzle ['sɪzl] *vi* grésiller.

SK *abbr of* **Saskatchewan.**

skate [skeɪt] *(pl sense 2 only inv* OR **-s)** ◇ *n* **-1.** [ice skate, roller skate] patin *m*. **-2.** [fish] raie *f*. ◇ *vi* [on ice skates] faire du patin sur glace, patiner; [on roller skates] faire du patin à roulettes.

◆ **skate over, skate round** *vt fus* [problem] éluder, éviter.

skateboard ['skeɪtbɔːd] *n* planche *f* à roulettes, skateboard *m*, skate *m*.

skateboarder ['skeɪtbɔːdəʳ] *n* personne *f* qui fait du skateboard OR du skate OR de la planche à roulettes.

skater ['skeɪtəʳ] *n* [on ice] patineur *m*, -euse *f*; [on roller skates] patineur à roulettes.

skating ['skeɪtɪŋ] *n* [on ice] patinage *m*; [on roller skates] patinage à roulettes.

skating rink *n* patinoire *f*.

skein [skeɪn] *n* [of thread] écheveau *m*.

skeletal ['skelɪtl] *adj* [emaciated] squelettique.

skeleton ['skelɪtn] ◇ *adj* [crew, service] squelettique, réduit(e). ◇ *n* squelette *m*; **to have a ~ in the cupboard** *fig* avoir un secret honteux.

skeleton key *n* passe *m*, passe-partout *m inv*.

skeleton staff *n* personnel *m* réduit.

skeptic *etc Am* = **sceptic** *etc*.

sketch [sketʃ] ◇ *n* **-1.** [drawing] croquis *m*, esquisse *f*. **-2.** [description] aperçu *m*, résumé *m*. **-3.** [by comedian] sketch *m*. ◇ *vt* **-1.** [draw] dessiner, faire un croquis de. **-2.** [describe] donner un aperçu de, décrire à grands traits. ◇ *vi* dessiner.

◆ **sketch in** *vt sep* [details] ajouter, donner.

◆ **sketch out** *vt sep* esquisser, décrire à grands traits.

sketchbook ['sketʃbʊk] *n* carnet *m* à dessins.

sketchpad ['sketʃpæd] *n* bloc *m* à dessins.

sketchy ['sketʃɪ] *(compar* **-ier,** *superl* **-iest)** *adj* incomplet(ète).

skew [skjuː] ◇ *n Br*: **on the ~** de travers, en biais. ◇ *vt* [distort] fausser.

skewer ['skjuəʳ] ◇ *n* brochette *f*, broche *f*. ◇ *vt* embrocher.

skew-whiff [,skjuː'wɪf] *adj Br inf* de guingois, de traviole.

ski [skiː] *(pt & pp* **skied,** *cont* **skiing)** ◇ *n* ski *m*. ◇ *comp* de ski. ◇ *vi* skier, faire du ski.

ski boots *npl* chaussures *fpl* de ski.

skid [skɪd] *(pt & pp* **-ded,** *cont* **-ding)** ◇ *n* dérapage *m*; **to go into a ~** déraper. ◇ *vi* déraper.

skid mark *n* trace *f* de frein OR dérapage.

skid row *n Am inf*: **to be on ~** être sur le pavé.

skier ['skiːəʳ] *n* skieur *m*, -ieuse *f*.

skies [skaɪz] *pl* → **sky**.

skiing ['skiːɪŋ] ◇ *n (U)* ski *m*; **to go ~** faire du ski. ◇ *comp* de ski.

ski instructor *n* moniteur *m*, -trice *f* de ski.

ski jump *n* [slope] tremplin *m*; [event] saut *m* à OR en skis.

skilful, skillful *Am* ['skɪlful] *adj* habile, adroit(e).

skilfully, skillfully *Am* ['skɪlfʊlɪ] *adv* habilement, adroitement.

ski lift *n* remonte-pente *m.*

skill [skɪl] *n* -1. (*U*) [ability] habileté *f,* adresse *f.* -2. [technique] technique *f,* art *m.*

skilled [skɪld] *adj* -1. [skilful]: ~ (**in** OR **at doing sthg**) habile OR adroit(e) (pour faire qqch). -2. [trained] qualifié(e).

skillet ['skɪlɪt] *n Am* poêle *f* à frire.

skillful *etc Am* = **skilful** *etc.*

skim [skɪm] (*pt & pp* **-med**, *cont* **-ming**) ◇ *vt* -1. [cream] écrémer; [soup] écumer. -2. [move above] effleurer, raser. -3. [newspaper, book] parcourir. ◇ *vi*: **to ~ through sthg** [newspaper, book] parcourir qqch.

skim(med) milk [skɪm(d)-] *n* lait *m* écrémé.

skimp [skɪmp] ◇ *vt* lésiner sur. ◇ *vi*: **to ~ on** lésiner sur.

skimpy ['skɪmpɪ] (*compar* **-ier**, *superl* **-iest**) *adj* [meal] maigre; [clothes] étriqué(e); [facts] insuffisant(e).

skin [skɪn] (*pt & pp* **-ned**, *cont* **-ning**) ◇ *n* peau *f*; **by the ~ of one's teeth** de justesse; **to jump out of one's ~** *Br* sursauter, sauter au plafond; **to make sb's ~ crawl** donner la chair de poule à qqn; **to save** OR **protect one's own ~** sauver sa peau. ◇ *vt* -1. [dead animal] écorcher, dépouiller; [fruit] éplucher, peler. -2. [graze]: **to ~ one's knee** s'érafler OR s'écorcher le genou.

skin-deep *adj* superficiel(ielle).

skin diver *n* plongeur sous-marin *m,* plongeuse sous-marine *f.*

skin diving *n* plongée *f* sous-marine.

skinflint ['skɪnflɪnt] *n inf* grippe-sou *m,* avare *mf.*

skin graft *n* greffe *f* de la peau.

skinhead ['skɪnhed] *n Br* skinhead *m,* skin *m.*

skinny ['skɪnɪ] (*compar* **-ier**, *superl* **-iest**) *adj* maigre.

skint [skɪnt] *adj Br v inf* fauché(e), à sec.

skin test *n* cuti *f,* cutiréaction *f.*

skin-tight *adj* moulant(e), collant(e).

skip [skɪp] (*pt & pp* **-ped**, *cont* **-ping**) ◇ *n* -1. [jump] petit saut *m.* -2. *Br* [container] benne *f.* ◇ *vt* [page, class, meal] sauter. ◇ *vi* -1. [gen] sauter, sautiller. -2. *Br* [over rope] sauter à la corde.

ski pants *npl* fuseau *m.*

ski pole *n* bâton *m* de ski.

skipper ['skɪpə*r*] *n* NAUT & SPORT capitaine *m.*

skipping ['skɪpɪŋ] *n Br* (*U*) saut *m* à la corde.

skipping rope *n Br* corde *f* à sauter.

ski resort *n* station *f* de ski.

skirmish ['skɜːmɪʃ] ◇ *n* escarmouche *f.* ◇ *vi* s'engager dans une escarmouche; *fig* avoir une escarmouche.

skirt [skɜːt] ◇ *n* [garment] jupe *f.* ◇ *vt* -1. [town, obstacle] contourner. -2. [problem] éviter.
◆ **skirt round** *vt fus* -1. [town, obstacle] contourner. -2. [problem] éviter.

skirting board ['skɜːtɪŋ-] *n Br* plinthe *f.*

ski stick *n* bâton *m* de ski.

skit [skɪt] *n* sketch *m.*

skittish ['skɪtɪʃ] *adj* [person] frivole; [animal] ombrageux(euse).

skittle ['skɪtl] *n Br* quille *f.*
◆ **skittles** *n* (*U*) [game] quilles *fpl.*

skive [skaɪv] *vi Br inf*: **to ~ (off)** s'esquiver, tirer au flanc.

skivvy ['skɪvɪ] (*pl* **-ies**, *pt & pp* **-ied**) *Br inf* ◇ *n* boniche *f,* bonne *f* à tout faire. ◇ *vi* faire la boniche.

skulduggery [skʌl'dʌgərɪ] *n* (*U*) magouilles *fpl.*

skulk [skʌlk] *vi* [hide] se cacher; [prowl] rôder.

skull [skʌl] *n* crâne *m.*

skullcap ['skʌlkæp] *n* calotte *f.*

skunk [skʌŋk] *n* [animal] mouffette *f.*

sky [skaɪ] (*pl* **skies**) *n* ciel *m.*

skycap ['skaɪkæp] *n Am* porteur *m* (*dans un aéroport*).

skydiver ['skaɪdaɪvə*r*] *n* parachutiste *mf* qui fait de la chute libre.

skydiving ['skaɪdaɪvɪŋ] *n* parachutisme *m* en chute libre.

sky-high *inf* ◇ *adj* [prices] astronomique, exorbitant(e). ◇ *adv*: **to blow sthg ~** [building etc] faire sauter qqch; [argument, theory] démolir qqch; **to go ~** [prices] monter en flèche.

skylark ['skaɪlɑːk] *n* alouette *f.*

skylight ['skaɪlaɪt] *n* lucarne *f.*

skyline ['skaɪlaɪn] *n* ligne *f* d'horizon.

skyscraper ['skaɪˌskreɪpə*r*] *n* gratte-ciel *m inv.*

slab [slæb] *n* [of concrete] dalle *f*; [of stone] bloc *m*; [of cake] pavé *m.*

slack [slæk] ◇ *adj* -1. [not tight] lâche. -2. [not busy] calme. -3. [person] négligent(e), pas sérieux(ieuse). ◇ *n* [in rope] mou *m.*
◆ **slacks** *npl* pantalon *m.*

slacken ['slækn] ◇ *vt* [speed, pace] ralentir; [rope] relâcher. ◇ *vi* [speed, pace] ralentir.

slag [slæg] *n* (*U*) [waste material] scories *fpl.*

slagheap ['slæghiːp] *n* terril *m.*

slain [sleɪn] *pp* → slay.

slalom ['slɑːləm] *n* slalom *m*.

slam [slæm] (*pt* & *pp* -med, *cont* -ming) ◇ *vt* -1. [shut] claquer. -2. [criticize] éreinter. -3. [place with force]: **to ~ sthg on** OR **onto** jeter qqch brutalement sur, flanquer qqch sur. ◇ *vi* claquer.

slander ['slɑːndə^r] ◇ *n* calomnie *f*; JUR diffamation *f*. ◇ *vt* calomnier; JUR diffamer.

slanderous ['slɑːndrəs] *adj* calomnieux(ieuse); JUR diffamatoire.

slang [slæŋ] ◇ *adj* argotique. ◇ *n* (U) argot *m*.

slant [slɑːnt] ◇ *n* -1. [angle] inclinaison *f*; **on** OR **at a ~** de biais. -2. [perspective] point *m* de vue, perspective *f*. ◇ *vt* [bias] présenter d'une manière tendancieuse. ◇ *vi* [slope] être incliné(e), pencher.

slanting ['slɑːntɪŋ] *adj* [roof] en pente.

slap [slæp] (*pt* & *pp* -ped, *cont* -ping) ◇ *n* claque *f*, tape *f*; [on face] gifle *f*; **a ~ in the face** *fig* une gifle. ◇ *vt* -1. [person, face] gifler; [back] donner une claque OR une tape à. -2. [place with force]: **to ~ sthg on** OR **onto** jeter qqch brutalement sur, flanquer qqch sur. ◇ *adv inf* [directly] en plein.

slapdash ['slæpdæʃ], **slaphappy** ['slæp,hæpɪ] *adj inf* [work] bâclé(e); [person, attitude] insouciant(e).

slapstick ['slæpstɪk] *n* (U) grosse farce *f*.

slap-up *adj Br inf* [meal] fameux(euse).

slash [slæʃ] ◇ *n* -1. [long cut] entaille *f*. -2. [oblique stroke] oblique *f*. ◇ *vt* -1. [cut] entailler. -2. *inf* [prices] casser; [budget, unemployment] réduire considérablement.

slat [slæt] *n* lame *f*; [wooden] latte *f*.

slate [sleɪt] ◇ *n* ardoise *f*. ◇ *vt inf* [criticize] descendre en flammes.

slatted ['slætɪd] *adj* à lames; [wooden] en lattes de bois.

slaughter ['slɔːtə^r] ◇ *n* -1. [of animals] abattage *m*. -2. [of people] massacre *m*, carnage *m*. ◇ *vt* -1. [animals] abattre. -2. [people] massacrer.

slaughterhouse ['slɔːtəhaus, *pl* -hauzɪz] *n* abattoir *m*.

Slav [slɑːv] ◇ *adj* slave. ◇ *n* Slave *mf*.

slave [sleɪv] ◇ *n* esclave *mf*; **to be a ~ to sthg** *fig* être esclave de qqch. ◇ *vi* travailler comme un nègre; **to ~ over sthg** peiner sur qqch.

slaver ['sleɪvə^r] *vi* [salivate] baver.

slavery ['sleɪvərɪ] *n* esclavage *m*.

slave trade *n*: **the ~** la traite des noirs.

Slavic ['slɑːvɪk] ◇ *adj* slave. ◇ *n* [language] slave *m*; HISTORY slavon *m*.

slavish ['sleɪvɪʃ] *adj* servile.

Slavonic [slə'vɒnɪk] = Slavic.

slay [sleɪ] (*pt* slew, *pp* slain) *vt literary* tuer.

sleazy ['sliːzɪ] (*compar* -ier, *superl* -iest) *adj* [disreputable] mal famé(e).

sledge [sledʒ], **sled** *Am* [sled] *n* luge *f*; [larger] traîneau *m*.

sledgehammer ['sledʒ,hæmə^r] *n* masse *f*.

sleek [sliːk] *adj* -1. [hair, fur] lisse, luisant(e). -2. [shape] aux lignes pures.

sleep [sliːp] (*pt* & *pp* slept) ◇ *n* sommeil *m*; **to go to ~** s'endormir; **my foot has gone to ~** j'ai le pied engourdi OR endormi; **to put an animal to ~** *euphemism* piquer un animal. ◇ *vi* -1. [be asleep] dormir. -2. [spend night] coucher.

◆ **sleep around** *vi inf pej* coucher à droite et à gauche.

◆ **sleep in** *vi* faire la grasse matinée.

◆ **sleep off** *vt sep* dormir pour faire passer.

◆ **sleep through** *vt fus*: **I slept through the alarm** je n'ai pas entendu le réveil.

◆ **sleep together** *vi euphemism* coucher ensemble.

◆ **sleep with** *vt fus euphemism* coucher avec.

sleeper ['sliːpə^r] *n* -1. [person]: **to be a heavy/light ~** avoir le sommeil lourd/léger. -2. [RAIL - berth] couchette *f*; [- carriage] wagon-lit *m*; [- train] train-couchettes *m*. -3. *Br* [on railway track] traverse *f*.

sleepily ['sliːpɪlɪ] *adv* d'un air endormi.

sleeping bag ['sliːpɪŋ-] *n* sac *m* de couchage.

sleeping car ['sliːpɪŋ-] *n* wagon-lit *m*.

sleeping partner ['sliːpɪŋ-] *n Br* (associé *m*) commanditaire *m*, bailleur *m* de fonds.

sleeping pill ['sliːpɪŋ-] *n* somnifère *m*.

sleeping policeman ['sliːpɪŋ-] *n Br inf* ralentisseur *m*.

sleeping tablet ['sliːpɪŋ-] *n* somnifère *m*.

sleepless ['sliːplɪs] *adj*: **to have a ~ night** passer une nuit blanche.

sleeplessness ['sliːplɪsnɪs] *n* insomnie *f*.

sleepwalk ['sliːpwɔːk] *vi* être somnambule.

sleepy ['sliːpɪ] (*compar* -ier, *superl* -iest) *adj* -1. [person] qui a envie de dormir. -2. [place] endormi(e).

sleet [sliːt] ◇ *n* neige *f* fondue. ◇ *v impers*: **it's ~ing** il tombe de la neige fondue.

sleeve [sliːv] *n* -1. [of garment] manche *f*; **to have sthg up one's ~** *fig* avoir qqch en réserve. -2. [for record] pochette *f*.

sleeveless ['sliːvlɪs] *adj* sans manches.

sleigh [sleɪ] *n* traîneau *m*.

sleight of hand [ˌslaɪt-] *n* (U) **-1.** [skill] habileté *f*. **-2.** [trick] tour *m* de passe-passe.

slender ['slendər] *adj* **-1.** [thin] mince. **-2.** *fig* [resources, income] modeste, maigre; [hope, chance] faible.

slept [slept] *pt & pp* → **sleep**.

sleuth [sluːθ] *n inf hum* limier *m*.

slew [sluː] ◇ *pt* → **slay**. ◇ *vi* [car] déraper.

slice [slaɪs] ◇ *n* **-1.** [thin piece] tranche *f*. **-2.** *fig* [of profits, glory] part *f*. **-3.** SPORT slice *m*. ◇ *vt* **-1.** [cut into slices] couper en tranches. **-2.** [cut cleanly] trancher. **-3.** SPORT slicer. ◇ *vi*: to ~ **through sthg** trancher qqch.

sliced bread [slaɪst-] *n* (U) pain *m* en tranches.

slick [slɪk] ◇ *adj* **-1.** [skilful] bien mené(e), habile. **-2.** *pej* [superficial - talk] facile; [- person] rusé(e). ◇ *n* nappe *f* de pétrole, marée *f* noire.

slicker ['slɪkər] *n Am* [raincoat] ciré *m*.

slide [slaɪd] (*pt & pp* slid) ◇ *n* **-1.** [in playground] toboggan *m*. **-2.** PHOT diapositive *f*, diapo *f*. **-3.** [for microscope] porte-objet *m*. **-4.** *Br* [for hair] barrette *f*. **-5.** [decline] déclin *m*; [in prices] baisse *f*. ◇ *vt* faire glisser. ◇ *vi* glisser; **to let things ~** *fig* laisser les choses aller à vau-l'eau.

slide projector *n* projecteur *m* de diapositives.

slide rule *n* règle *f* à calcul.

sliding door ['slaɪdɪŋ-] *n* porte *f* coulissante.

sliding scale ['slaɪdɪŋ-] *n* échelle *f* mobile.

slight [slaɪt] ◇ *adj* **-1.** [minor] léger(ère); the ~**est** le moindre (la moindre); **not in the** ~**est** pas du tout. **-2.** [thin] mince. ◇ *n* affront *m*. ◇ *vt* offenser, faire un affront à.

slightly ['slaɪtlɪ] *adv* **-1.** [to small extent] légèrement. **-2.** [slenderly]: ~ **built** mince.

slim [slɪm] (*compar* -mer, *superl* -mest, *pt & pp* -med, *cont* -ming) ◇ *adj* **-1.** [person, object] mince. **-2.** [chance, possibility] faible. ◇ *vi* maigrir; [diet] suivre un régime amaigrissant.

slime [slaɪm] *n* (U) substance *f* visqueuse; [of snail] bave *f*.

slimmer ['slɪmər] *n* personne *f* suivant un régime amaigrissant.

slimming ['slɪmɪŋ] ◇ *n* amaigrissement *m*. ◇ *adj* [product] amaigrissant(e), pour maigrir.

slimness ['slɪmnɪs] *n* minceur *f*.

slimy ['slaɪmɪ] (*compar* -ier, *superl* -iest) *adj lit & fig* visqueux(euse).

sling [slɪŋ] (*pt & pp* slung) ◇ *n* **-1.** [for arm] écharpe *f*. **-2.** NAUT [for loads] élingue *f*. ◇ *vt*

-1. [hammock etc] suspendre; **to ~, a bag over one's shoulder** mettre son sac en bandoulière. **-2.** *inf* [throw] lancer.

slingback ['slɪŋbæk] *n* chaussure *f* à talon ouvert.

slingshot ['slɪŋʃɒt] *n Am* lance-pierres *m inv*.

slink [slɪŋk] (*pt & pp* slunk) *vi*: **to ~ away** OR **off** s'en aller furtivement.

slip [slɪp] (*pt & pp* -ped, *cont* -ping) ◇ *n* **-1.** [mistake] erreur *f*; **a ~ of the pen** un lapsus; **a ~ of the tongue** un lapsus. **-2.** [of paper - gen] morceau *m*; [- strip] bande *f*. **-3.** [underwear] combinaison *f*. **-4.** *phr*: **to give sb the ~** *inf* fausser compagnie à qqn.
◇ *vt* glisser; **to ~ sthg on** enfiler qqch.
◇ *vi* **-1.** [slide] glisser; **to ~ into sthg** se glisser dans qqch. **-2.** [decline] décliner; **to let things ~** laisser les choses aller à vau-l'eau. **-3.** *phr*: **to let sthg ~** laisser échapper qqch.
 ◆ **slip up** *vi fig* faire une erreur.

slip-on *adj*: ~ **shoes** mocassins *mpl*.
 ◆ **slip-ons** *npl* mocassins *mpl*.

slippage ['slɪpɪdʒ] *n* baisse *f*.

slipped disc [slɪpt-] *n* hernie *f* discale.

slipper ['slɪpər] *n* pantoufle *f*, chausson *m*.

slippery ['slɪpərɪ] *adj* glissant(e).

slip road *n Br* bretelle *f*.

slipshod ['slɪpʃɒd] *adj* peu soigné(e).

slipstream ['slɪpstriːm] *n* sillage *m*.

slip-up *n inf* gaffe *f*.

slipway ['slɪpweɪ] *n* cale *f* de lancement.

slit [slɪt] (*pt & pp* slit, *cont* -ting) ◇ *n* [opening] fente *f*; [cut] incision *f*. ◇ *vt* [make opening in] faire une fente dans, fendre; [cut] inciser.

slither ['slɪðər] *vi* [person] glisser; [snake] onduler.

sliver ['slɪvər] *n* [of glass, wood] éclat *m*; [of meat, cheese] lamelle *f*.

slob [slɒb] *n inf* [in habits] saligaud *m*; [in appearance] gros lard *m*.

slobber ['slɒbər] *vi* baver.

slog [slɒg] (*pt & pp* -ged, *cont* -ging) *inf* ◇ *n* **-1.** [tiring work] corvée *f*. **-2.** [tiring journey] voyage *m* pénible. ◇ *vi* **-1.** [work] travailler comme un bœuf OR un nègre. **-2.** [move] avancer péniblement.

slogan ['sləʊgən] *n* slogan *m*.

sloop [sluːp] *n* sloop *m*.

slop [slɒp] (*pt & pp* -ped, *cont* -ping) ◇ *vt* renverser. ◇ *vi* déborder.

slope [sləʊp] ◇ *n* pente *f*; **to be on a slippery ~** *fig* être sur une pente savonneuse.

◇ *vi* [land] être en pente; [handwriting, table] pencher.

sloping ['sləupɪŋ] *adj* [land, shelf] en pente; [handwriting] penché(e).

sloppy ['slɒpɪ] (*compar* **-ier**, *superl* **-iest**) *adj* **-1.** [careless] peu soigné(e). **-2.** *inf* [sentimental] sentimental(e), à l'eau de rose.

slosh [slɒʃ] ◇ *vt* renverser. ◇ *vi*: **to ~ about** [liquid] clapoter; [person] patauger.

sloshed [slɒʃt] *adj inf* bourré(e).

slot [slɒt] (*pt* & *pp* **-ted**, *cont* **-ting**) *n* **-1.** [opening] fente *f*. **-2.** [groove] rainure *f*. **-3.** [in schedule] créneau *m*.

◆ **slot in** ◇ *vt sep* [part] insérer. ◇ *vi* [part] s'emboîter.

sloth [sləʊθ] *n* **-1.** [animal] paresseux *m*. **-2.** *literary* [laziness] paresse *f*.

slot machine *n* **-1.** [vending machine] distributeur *m* automatique. **-2.** [for gambling] machine *f* à sous.

slot meter *n* *Br* compteur *m* à pièces.

slouch [slautʃ] ◇ *n* [posture] allure *f* avachie. ◇ *vi* être avachi(e).

slough [slʌf]

◆ **slough off** *vt sep* **-1.** [skin]: **to ~ off one's skin** muer. **-2.** *fig* [get rid of] se débarrasser de.

Slovak ['sləʊvæk] ◇ *adj* slovaque. ◇ *n* **-1.** [person] Slovaque *mf*. **-2.** [language] slovaque *m*.

Slovakia [slə'vækɪə] *n* Slovaquie *f*; **in ~** en Slovaquie.

Slovakian [slə'vækɪən] ◇ *adj* slovaque. ◇ *n* Slovaque *mf*.

Slovenia [slə'viːnjə] *n* Slovénie *f*; **in ~** en Slovénie.

Slovenian [slə'viːnjən] ◇ *adj* slovène. ◇ *n* Slovène *mf*.

slovenly ['slʌvnlɪ] *adj* négligé(e).

slow [sləʊ] ◇ *adj* **-1.** [gen] lent(e). **-2.** [clock, watch]: **to be ~** retarder. **-3.** [not busy] calme. ◇ *adv* lentement; **to go ~** [driver] aller lentement; [workers] faire la grève perlée. ◇ *vt* & *vi* ralentir.

◆ **slow down, slow up** *vt sep* & *vi* ralentir.

slow-acting *adj* à action lente.

slowcoach ['sləʊkəʊtʃ], **slow-poke** *Am n inf* lambin *m*, -e *f*.

slowdown ['sləʊdaʊn] *n* ralentissement *m*.

slow handclap *n* applaudissements *mpl* rythmés (*pour montrer sa désapprobation*).

slowly ['sləʊlɪ] *adv* lentement; **~ but surely** lentement mais sûrement.

slow motion *n*: **in ~** au ralenti *m*.

◆ **slow-motion** *adj* au ralenti.

slow-poke ['sləʊpəʊk] *Am* = **slowcoach**.

SLR (*abbr of* **single-lens reflex**) *n* reflex *m*.

sludge [slʌdʒ] *n* boue *f*.

slug [slʌg] (*pt* & *pp* **-ged**, *cont* **-ging**) ◇ *n* **-1.** [animal] limace *f*. **-2.** *inf* [of alcohol] rasade *f*. **-3.** *Am inf* [bullet] balle *f*. ◇ *vt inf* donner un coup de poing violent à.

sluggish ['slʌgɪʃ] *adj* [person] apathique; [movement, growth] lent(e); [business] calme, stagnant(e).

sluice [sluːs] ◇ *n* écluse *f*. ◇ *vt*: **to ~ sthg down** OR **out** laver qqch à grande eau.

slum [slʌm] (*pt* & *pp* **-med**, *cont* **-ming**) ◇ *n* [area] quartier *m* pauvre. ◇ *vt*: **to ~ it** *inf* hum s'encanailler.

slumber ['slʌmbər] *literary* ◇ *n* sommeil *m*. ◇ *vi* dormir paisiblement.

slump [slʌmp] ◇ *n* **-1.** [decline]: **~ (in)** baisse *f* (de). **-2.** [period of poverty] crise *f* (économique). ◇ *vi* lit & *fig* s'effondrer.

slung [slʌŋ] *pt* & *pp* → **sling**.

slunk [slʌŋk] *pt* & *pp* → **slink**.

slur [slɜːr] (*pt* & *pp* **-red**, *cont* **-ring**) ◇ *n* **-1.** [of voice]: **to speak with a ~** mal articuler. **-2.** [slight]: **~ (on)** atteinte *f* (à). **-3.** [insult] affront *m*, insulte *f*. ◇ *vt* mal articuler.

slurp [slɜːp] *vt* boire avec bruit.

slurred [slɜːd] *adj* mal articulé(e).

slurry ['slʌrɪ] *n* AGR purin *m*.

slush [slʌʃ] *n* [snow] neige *f* fondue.

slush fund, slush money *Am n* fonds *mpl* secrets, caisse *f* noire.

slut [slʌt] *n* **-1.** *inf* [dirty, untidy] souillon *f*. **-2.** *v inf* [sexually immoral] salope *f*.

sly [slaɪ] (*compar* **slyer** OR **slier**, *superl* **slyest** OR **sliest**) ◇ *adj* **-1.** [look, smile] entendu(e). **-2.** [person] rusé(e), sournois(e). ◇ *n*: **on the ~** en cachette.

slyness ['slaɪnɪs] *n* (*U*) ruse *f*.

smack [smæk] ◇ *n* **-1.** [slap] claque *f*; [on face] gifle *f*. **-2.** [impact] claquement *m*. ◇ *vt* **-1.** [slap] donner une claque à; [face] gifler. **-2.** [place violently] poser violemment. **-3.** *phr*: **to ~ one's lips** se lécher les babines. ◇ *adv inf* [directly] en plein; **~ in the middle** en plein milieu.

small [smɔːl] ◇ *adj* **-1.** [gen] petit(e). **-2.** [trivial] petit, insignifiant(e). ◇ *n*: **the ~ of the back** le creux OR le bas des reins.

◆ **smalls** *npl Br inf dated* dessous *mpl*.

small ads *npl Br* petites annonces *fpl*.

small arms *npl* armes *fpl* (à feu) portatives.

small change *n* petite monnaie *f*.

small fry *n* menu fretin *m*.

smallholder ['smɔːl,həʊldəʳ] *n Br* petit cultivateur *m*, petit exploitant *m* agricole.

smallholding ['smɔːl,həʊldɪŋ] *n Br* petite exploitation *f* agricole.

small hours *npl*: **in the ~** au petit jour OR matin.

smallness ['smɔːlnɪs] *n* [of building, person] petite taille *f*; [of amount, income] modicité *f*, petitesse *f*.

smallpox ['smɔːlpɒks] *n* variole *f*, petite vérole *f*.

small print *n*: **the ~** les clauses *fpl* écrites en petits caractères.

small-scale *adj* [activity, organization] peu important(e).

small talk *n* (*U*) papotage *m*, bavardage *m*.

small-time *adj* de second ordre.

smarmy ['smɑːmɪ] (*compar* **-ier**, *superl* **-iest**) *adj* mielleux(euse).

smart [smɑːt] ◇ *adj* **-1.** [stylish - person, clothes, car] élégant(e). **-2.** [clever] intelligent(e). **-3.** [fashionable - club, society, hotel] à la mode, in (*inv*). **-4.** [quick - answer, tap] vif (vive), rapide. ◇ *vi* **-1.** [eyes, skin] brûler, piquer. **-2.** [person] être blessé(e).

smart card *n* carte *f* à mémoire.

smarten ['smɑːtn]
♦ **smarten up** *vt sep* [room] arranger; **to ~ o.s. up** se faire beau (belle).

smash [smæʃ] ◇ *n* **-1.** [sound] fracas *m*. **-2.** *inf* [car crash] collision *f*, accident *m*. **-3.** *inf* [success] succès *m* fou. **-4.** SPORT smash *m*. ◇ *vt* **-1.** [glass, plate etc] casser, briser. **-2.** *fig* [defeat] détruire. ◇ *vi* **-1.** [glass, plate etc] se briser. **-2.** [crash]: **to ~ through sthg** défoncer qqch; **to ~ into sthg** s'écraser contre qqch.
♦ **smash up** *vt sep* casser, briser; [car] bousiller.

smash-and-grab (raid) *n Br* vol *effectué après avoir brisé une vitrine.*

smashed [smæʃt] *adj inf* bourré(e).

smash hit *n* succès *m* fou.

smashing ['smæʃɪŋ] *adj inf* super (*inv*).

smash-up *n* collision *f*, accident *m*.

smattering ['smætərɪŋ] *n*: **to have a ~ of** German savoir quelques mots d'allemand.

SME (*abbr of* **small and medium-sized enterprise**) *n* PME *f*.

smear [smɪəʳ] ◇ *n* **-1.** [dirty mark] tache *f*. **-2.** MED frottis *m*. **-3.** [slander] diffamation *f*. ◇ *vt* **-1.** [smudge] barbouiller, maculer. **-2.** [spread]: **to ~ sthg onto sthg** étaler qqch sur qqch; **to ~ sthg with sthg** enduire qqch de qqch. **-3.** [slander] calomnier.

smear campaign *n* campagne *f* de diffamation.

smear test *n* frottis *m*.

smell [smel] (*pt & pp* **-ed** OR **smelt**) ◇ *n* **-1.** [odour] odeur *f*. **-2.** [sense of smell] odorat *m*. ◇ *vt* sentir. ◇ *vi* **-1.** [flower, food] sentir; **I can't ~** je ne sens rien du tout; **to ~ of sthg** sentir qqch; **to ~ good/bad** sentir bon/mauvais. **-2.** [smell unpleasantly] sentir (mauvais), puer.

smelly ['smelɪ] (*compar* **-ier**, *superl* **-iest**) *adj* qui sent mauvais, qui pue.

smelt [smelt] ◇ *pt & pp* → **smell**. ◇ *vt* [metal] extraire par fusion; [ore] fondre.

smile [smaɪl] ◇ *n* sourire *m*. ◇ *vi* sourire. ◇ *vt*: **to ~ one's agreement** acquiescer d'un sourire.

smiling ['smaɪlɪŋ] *adj* souriant(e).

smirk [smɜːk] ◇ *n* sourire *m* narquois. ◇ *vi* sourire d'un air narquois.

smith [smɪθ] *n* forgeron *m*.

smithereens [ˌsmɪðə'riːnz] *npl inf*: **to be smashed to ~** être brisé(e) en mille morceaux.

smithy ['smɪðɪ] (*pl* **-ies**) *n* forge *f*.

smitten ['smɪtn] *adj hum*: **to be ~ (with)** être fou (folle) (de).

smock [smɒk] *n* blouse *f*.

smog [smɒg] *n* smog *m*.

smoke [sməʊk] ◇ *n* **-1.** (*U*) [from fire] fumée *f*. **-2.** [act of smoking]: **to have a ~** [cigarette] fumer une cigarette; [cigar] fumer un cigare. ◇ *vt & vi* fumer.

smoked [sməʊkt] *adj* [food] fumé(e).

smokeless fuel ['sməʊklɪs-] *n* combustible *qui ne produit pas de fumée.*

smokeless zone ['sməʊklɪs-] *n* zone *où la combustion de matériaux est réglementée.*

smoker ['sməʊkəʳ] *n* **-1.** [person] fumeur *m*, -euse *f*. **-2.** RAIL compartiment *m* fumeurs.

smokescreen ['sməʊkskriːn] *n fig* couverture *f*.

smoke shop *n Am* bureau *m* de tabac.

smokestack ['sməʊkstæk] *n* cheminée *f*.

smokestack industry *n Am* industrie *f* lourde.

smoking ['sməʊkɪŋ] *n* tabagisme *m*; **"no ~"** «défense de fumer».

smoking compartment *Br*, **smoking car** *Am n* compartiment *m* fumeurs.

smoky ['sməʊkɪ] (*compar* **-ier**, *superl* **-iest**) *adj* **-1.** [room, air] enfumé(e). **-2.** [taste] fumé(e).

smolder *Am* = **smoulder**.

smooch [smuːtʃ] *vi inf* se bécoter et se peloter.

smooth [smuːð] ◇ *adj* **-1.** [surface] lisse. **-2.** [sauce] homogène, onctueux(euse). **-3.** [movement] régulier(ière). **-4.** [taste] moelleux(euse). **-5.** [flight, ride] confortable; [landing, take-off] **en douceur. -6.** *pej* [person, manner] doucereux(euse), mielleux(euse). **-7.** [operation, progress] sans problèmes. ◇ *vt* [hair] lisser; [clothes, tablecloth] défroisser; **to ~ the way** aplanir les difficultés OR les obstacles.
◆ **smooth out** *vt sep* défroisser.
◆ **smooth over** *vt fus* [difficulties] aplanir; [disagreements] arranger.

smoothly ['smuːðlɪ] *adv* **-1.** [move] sans heurt. **-2.** *pej* [suavely] d'un ton doucereux. **-3.** [without problems] sans problèmes.

smoothness ['smuːðnɪs] *n* (*U*) **-1.** [of surface] aspect *m* lisse. **-2.** [of mixture] onctuosité *f.* **-3.** [of movement] régularité *f.* **-4.** [of flight, ride] confort *m.* **-5.** *pej* [of person] caractère *m* doucereux.

smooth-talking [-,tɔːkɪŋ] *adj* doucereux(euse), mielleux(euse).

smother ['smʌðər] *vt* **-1.** [cover thickly]: **to ~ sb/sthg with** couvrir qqn/qqch de. **-2.** [person, fire] étouffer. **-3.** *fig* [emotions] cacher, étouffer.

smoulder *Br*, **smolder** *Am* ['sməuldər] *vi lit & fig* couver.

smudge [smʌdʒ] ◇ *n* tache *f*; [of ink] bavure *f.* ◇ *vt* [drawing, painting] maculer; [paper] faire une marque OR trace sur; [face] salir.

smug [smʌg] (*compar* **-ger**, *superl* **-gest**) *adj* suffisant(e).

smuggle ['smʌgl] *vt* **-1.** [across frontiers] faire passer en contrebande. **-2.** [against rules]: **to ~ sthg in/out** faire entrer/sortir qqch clandestinement.

smuggler ['smʌglər] *n* contrebandier *m*, -ière *f.*

smuggling ['smʌglɪŋ] *n* (*U*) contrebande *f.*

smugness ['smʌgnɪs] *n* suffisance *f.*

smut [smʌt] *n* **-1.** [dirty mark] tache *f* de suie. **-2.** (*U*) *pej* [books, talk etc] obscénités *fpl.*

smutty ['smʌtɪ] (*compar* **-ier**, *superl* **-iest**) *adj pej* [book, language] cochon(onne).

snack [snæk] ◇ *n* casse-croûte *m inv.* ◇ *vi Am* manger un morceau.

snack bar *n* snack *m*, snack-bar *m.*

snag [snæg] (*pt & pp* **-ged**, *cont* **-ging**) ◇ *n* [problem] inconvénient *m*, écueil *m.* ◇ *vt* accrocher. ◇ *vi*: **to ~ (on)** s'accrocher (à).

snail [sneɪl] *n* escargot *m.*

snake [sneɪk] ◇ *n* serpent *m.* ◇ *vi* serpenter.

snap [snæp] (*pt & pp* **-ped**, *cont* **-ping**) ◇ *adj* [decision, election] **subit(e)**; [judgment] irréfléchi(e).
◇ *n* **-1.** [of branch] craquement *m*; [of fingers] claquement *m.* **-2.** [photograph] photo *f.* **-3.** [card game] ≃ bataille *f.*
◇ *vt* **-1.** [break] casser net. **-2.** [move]: **to ~ sthg open/shut** ouvrir/fermer qqch avec un bruit sec; **to ~ one's fingers** claquer des doigts. **-3.** [speak sharply] dire d'un ton sec.
◇ *vi* **-1.** [break] se casser net. **-2.** [move]: **to ~ into place** s'emboîter avec un bruit sec. **-3.** [dog]: **to ~ at** essayer de mordre. **-4.** [speak sharply]: **to ~ (at sb)** parler (à qqn) d'un ton sec. **-5.** *phr*: **to ~ out of it** *inf* réagir, se secouer.
◆ **snap up** *vt sep* [bargain] sauter sur.

snap fastener *n* pression *f.*

snappish ['snæpɪʃ] *adj* hargneux(euse).

snappy ['snæpɪ] (*compar* **-ier**, *superl* **-iest**) *adj inf* **-1.** [stylish] chic. **-2.** [quick] prompt(e); **make it ~!** dépêche-toi!, et que ça saute!

snapshot ['snæpʃɒt] *n* photo *f.*

snare [sneər] ◇ *n* piège *m*, collet *m.* ◇ *vt* prendre au piège, attraper.

snarl [snɑːl] ◇ *n* grondement *m.* ◇ *vi* gronder.

snarl-up *n* enchevêtrement *m*; [of traffic] embouteillage *m.*

snatch [snætʃ] ◇ *n* [of conversation] bribe *f*; [of song] extrait *m.* ◇ *vt* **-1.** [grab] saisir. **-2.** *fig* [time] réussir à avoir; [opportunity] saisir; **to ~ a look at sthg** regarder qqch à la dérobée. ◇ *vi*: **to ~ at sthg** essayer de saisir qqch.

snazzy ['snæzɪ] (*compar* **-ier**, *superl* **-iest**) *adj inf* [clothes, car] beau (belle), super (*inv*); [dresser] qui s'habille chic.

sneak [sniːk] (*Am pt* **snuck**) ◇ *n Br inf* rapporteur *m*, -euse *f.* ◇ *vt*: **to ~ a look at sb/ sthg** regarder qqn/qqch à la dérobée. ◇ *vi* [move quietly] se glisser; **to ~ up on sb** s'approcher de qqn sans faire de bruit.

sneakers ['sniːkəz] *npl Am* tennis *mpl*, baskets *fpl.*

sneaking ['sniːkɪŋ] *adj* secret(ète).

sneak preview *n* avant-première *f.*

sneaky ['sniːkɪ] (*compar* **-ier**, *superl* **-iest**) *adj inf* sournois(e).

sneer [snɪər] ◇ *n* [smile] sourire *m* dédaigneux; [laugh] ricanement *m.* ◇ *vi* **-1.** [smile] sourire dédaigneusement. **-2.** [ridicule]: **to ~ at sthg** tourner qqch en ridicule.

sneeze [sniːz] ◇ n éternuement m. ◇ vi éternuer; **it's not to be ~d at!** inf il ne faut pas cracher dessus!

snicker ['snɪkə] vi Am ricaner.

snide [snaɪd] adj sournois(e).

sniff [snɪf] ◇ n reniflement m. ◇ vt **-1.** [smell] renifler. **-2.** [inhale - drug] sniffer. ◇ vi **-1.** [to clear nose] renifler. **-2.** [to show disapproval] faire la grimace.
◆ **sniff out** vt sep **-1.** [detect by sniffing] flairer. **-2.** inf [seek out] rechercher.

sniffer dog ['snɪfə-] n chien m renifleur.

sniffle ['snɪfl] vi renifler.

snigger ['snɪgə] ◇ n rire m en dessous. ◇ vi ricaner.

snip [snɪp] (pt & pp **-ped**, cont **-ping**) ◇ n inf [bargain] bonne affaire f. ◇ vt couper.

snipe [snaɪp] vi **-1.** [shoot]: **to ~ at sb/sthg** canarder qqn/qqch. **-2.** [criticize]: **to ~ at sb** critiquer qqn sournoisement.

sniper ['snaɪpə] n tireur m isolé.

snippet ['snɪpɪt] n fragment m.

snivel ['snɪvl] (Br pt & pp **-led**, cont **-ling**, Am pt & pp **-ed**, cont **-ing**) vi geindre.

snob [snɒb] n snob mf.

snobbery ['snɒbərɪ] n snobisme m.

snobbish ['snɒbɪʃ], **snobby** ['snɒbɪ] (compar **-ier**, superl **-iest**) adj snob (inv).

snooker ['snuːkə] ◇ n [game] ≈ jeu m de billard. ◇ vt Br inf fig: **to be ~ed** être coincé(e).

snoop [snuːp] vi inf fureter.

snooper ['snuːpə] n inf fouineur m, -euse f.

snooty ['snuːtɪ] (compar **-ier**, superl **-iest**) adj inf prétentieux(ieuse).

snooze [snuːz] ◇ n petit somme m. ◇ vi faire un petit somme.

snore [snɔːr] ◇ n ronflement m. ◇ vi ronfler.

snoring ['snɔːrɪŋ] n (U) ronflement m, ronflements mpl.

snorkel ['snɔːkl] n tuba m.

snorkelling Br, **snorkeling** Am ['snɔːklɪŋ] n: **to go ~** faire de la plongée avec un tuba.

snort [snɔːt] ◇ n [of person] grognement m; [of horse, bull] ébrouement m. ◇ vi [person] grogner; [horse] s'ébrouer. ◇ vt drugs sl sniffer.

snotty ['snɒtɪ] (compar **-ier**, superl **-iest**) adj inf **-1.** [snooty] prétentieux(ieuse). **-2.** [face, child] morveux(euse).

snout [snaʊt] n groin m.

snow [snəʊ] ◇ n neige f. ◇ v impers neiger.
◆ **snow in** vt sep: **to be ~ed in** être bloqué(e) par la neige.
◆ **snow under** vt sep fig: **to be ~ed under (with)** être submergé(e) (de).

snowball ['snəʊbɔːl] ◇ n boule f de neige. ◇ vi fig faire boule de neige.

snow blindness n cécité f des neiges.

snowbound ['snəʊbaʊnd] adj bloqué(e) par la neige.

snow-capped [-kæpt] adj couronné(e) de neige.

snowdrift ['snəʊdrɪft] n congère f.

snowdrop ['snəʊdrɒp] n perce-neige m inv.

snowfall ['snəʊfɔːl] n chute f de neige.

snowflake ['snəʊfleɪk] n flocon m de neige.

snowman ['snəʊmæn] (pl **-men** [-men]) n bonhomme m de neige.

snow pea n Am mange-tout m inv.

snowplough Br, **snowplow** Am ['snəʊplaʊ] n chasse-neige m inv.

snowshoe ['snəʊʃuː] n raquette f.

snowstorm ['snəʊstɔːm] n tempête f de neige.

snowy ['snəʊɪ] (compar **-ier**, superl **-iest**) adj neigeux(euse).

SNP (abbr of **Scottish National Party**) n parti nationaliste écossais.

Snr, snr abbr of **senior**.

snub [snʌb] (pt & pp **-bed**, cont **-bing**) ◇ n rebuffade f. ◇ vt snober, ignorer.

snuck [snʌk] pt → **sneak**.

snuff [snʌf] n tabac m à priser.

snuffle ['snʌfl] vi renifler.

snuff movie n film porno où l'acteur est tué à la fin.

snug [snʌg] (compar **-ger**, superl **-gest**) adj **-1.** [person] à l'aise, confortable; [in bed] bien au chaud. **-2.** [place] douillet(ette). **-3.** [close-fitting] bien ajusté(e).

snuggle ['snʌgl] vi se blottir.

so [səʊ] ◇ adv **-1.** [to such a degree] si, tellement; **~ difficult (that)** ... si OR tellement difficile que ...; **don't be ~ stupid!** ne sois pas si bête!; **he's not ~ stupid as he looks** il n'est pas si OR aussi bête qu'il en a l'air; **we're ~ glad you could come** nous sommes si contents que vous ayez pu venir; **he's ~ sweet/kind** il est tellement mignon/gentil; **we had ~ much work!** nous avions tant de travail!; **I've never seen ~ much money/many cars** je n'ai jamais vu autant d'argent/de voitures. **-2.** [in referring back to previous statement, event etc]: **~ what's the point then?** alors à quoi bon?; **~ you knew already?** alors tu le savais déjà?; **I don't think ~** je ne crois pas; **I'm**

afraid ~ je crains bien que oui; **if** ~ si oui;
is that ~? vraiment? **-3.** [also] aussi; ~
can/do/would *etc* **I** moi aussi; **she speaks
French and** ~ **does her husband** elle parle
français et son mari aussi; **as with** ..., ~
with il en va pour ... comme pour; **just as
some people like family holidays,** ~ **others
prefer to holiday alone** de même que certains aiment des vacances en famille, de
même d'autres préfèrent passer leurs vacances tout seuls. **-4.** [in this way]: **(like)** ~
comme cela OR ça, de cette façon; **hold
your arm out,** ~ étendez votre bras,
comme cela OR ça. **-5.** [in expressing agree-
ment]: ~ **there is** en effet, c'est vrai; ~ **I see**
c'est ce que je vois. **-6.** [unspecified amount,
limit]: **they pay us** ~ **much a week** ils nous
payent tant par semaine; **not** ~ **much ... as**
pas tant ... que; **it's not** ~ **much the money
as the time involved** ce n'est pas tant l'argent que le temps que ça demande; **or** ~
environ, à peu près; **a year/week or** ~ **ago**
il y a environ un an/une semaine.
◇ *conj* alors; **he said yes and** ~ **we got
married** il a dit oui, alors on s'est mariés;
I'm away next week ~ **I won't be there** je
suis en voyage la semaine prochaine donc
OR par conséquent je ne serai pas là; ~
what have you been up to? alors, qu'est-ce
que vous devenez?; ~ **what?** *inf* et alors?,
et après?; ~ **there!** *inf* là!, et voilà!
◆ **and so on, and so forth** *adv* et ainsi
de suite.
◆ **so as** *conj* afin de, pour; **we didn't
knock** ~ **as not to disturb them** nous
n'avons pas frappé pour ne pas les déranger.
◆ **so that** *conj* [for the purpose that] pour
que (+ *subjunctive*); **he lied** ~ **that she
would go free** il a menti pour qu'elle soit
relâchée.
SO *abbr of* **standing order.**
soak [səʊk] ◇ *vt* laisser OR faire tremper.
◇ *vi* **-1.** [become thoroughly wet]: **to leave
sthg to** ~, **to let sthg** ~ laisser OR faire
tremper qqch. **-2.** [spread]: **to** ~ **into sthg**
tremper dans qqch; **to** ~ **through (sthg)**
traverser (qqch).
◆ **soak up** *vt sep* absorber.
soaked [səʊkt] *adj* trempé(e); **to be** ~
through être trempé (jusqu'aux os).
soaking ['səʊkɪŋ] *adj* trempé(e).
so-and-so *n inf* **-1.** [to replace a name]: **Mr**
~ Monsieur un tel. **-2.** [annoying person] enquiquineur *m*, -euse *f*.
soap [səʊp] ◇ *n* **-1.** (*U*) [for washing] savon
m. **-2.** TV soap opera *m*. ◇ *vt* savonner.
soap bubble *n* bulle *f* de savon.

soap flakes *npl* savon *m* en paillettes.
soap opera *n* soap opera *m*.
soap powder *n* lessive *f*.
soapsuds ['səʊpsʌdz] *npl* mousse *f* de savon.
soapy ['səʊpɪ] (*compar* -ier, *superl* -iest) *adj*
[water] savonneux(euse); [taste] de savon.
soar [sɔːʳ] *vi* **-1.** [bird] planer. **-2.** [balloon,
kite] monter. **-3.** [prices, temperature] monter
en flèche. **-4.** [building, tree, mountain] s'élever, s'élancer. **-5.** [music, voice] monter.
soaring ['sɔːrɪŋ] *adj* **-1.** [prices, temperature]
qui monte en flèche. **-2.** [building, tree,
mountain] qui s'élève. **-3.** [music, voice] qui
monte.
sob [sɒb] (*pt* & *pp* **-bed**, *cont* **-bing**) ◇ *n*
sanglot *m*. ◇ *vt* dire en sanglotant. ◇ *vi*
sangloter.
sobbing ['sɒbɪŋ] *n* (*U*) sanglots *mpl*.
sober ['səʊbəʳ] *adj* **-1.** [not drunk] qui n'est
pas ivre. **-2.** [serious] sérieux(ieuse). **-3.**
[plain - clothes, colours] sobre.
◆ **sober up** *vi* dessoûler.
sobering ['səʊbərɪŋ] *adj* qui donne à réfléchir.
sobriety [səʊ'braɪətɪ] *n fml* [seriousness] sérieux *m*.
Soc. *abbr of* **Society.**
so-called [-kɔːld] *adj* **-1.** [misleadingly
named] soi-disant (*inv*). **-2.** [widely known as]
ainsi appelé(e).
soccer ['sɒkəʳ] *n* football *m*.
sociable ['səʊʃəbl] *adj* sociable.
social ['səʊʃl] *adj* social(e).
social climber *n pej* arriviste *mf*.
social club *n* club *m*.
social conscience *n* conscience *f* sociale.
social democracy *n* social-démocratie *f*.
social event *n* événement *m* social.
social fund *n* fonds *m* d'entraide.
socialism ['səʊʃəlɪzm] *n* socialisme *m*.
socialist ['səʊʃəlɪst] ◇ *adj* socialiste. ◇ *n*
socialiste *mf*.
socialite ['səʊʃəlaɪt] *n* mondain *m*, -e *f*.
socialize, -ise ['səʊʃəlaɪz] *vi* fréquenter des
gens; **to** ~ **with sb** fréquenter qqn, frayer
avec qqn.
socialized medicine ['səʊʃəlaɪzd-] *n Am*
soins médicaux payés par les impôts.
social life *n* vie *f* sociale.
socially ['səʊʃəlɪ] *adv* **-1.** [in society] socialement, en société. **-2.** [outside business] en
dehors du travail.
social order *n* ordre *m* social.
social science *n* sciences *fpl* humaines.

social security *n* aide *f* sociale.

social services *npl* services *mpl* sociaux.

social studies *n* sciences *fpl* sociales.

social work *n* (*U*) assistance *f* sociale.

social worker *n* assistant social *m*, assistante sociale *f*.

society [sə'saɪətɪ] (*pl* -ies) *n* -1. [gen] société *f*. -2. [club] association *f*, club *m*.

socioeconomic ['səʊsɪəʊ,iːkə'nɒmɪk] *adj* socio-économique.

sociological [,səʊsjə'lɒdʒɪkl] *adj* sociologique.

sociologist [,səʊsɪ'ɒlədʒɪst] *n* sociologue *mf*.

sociology [,səʊsɪ'ɒlədʒɪ] *n* sociologie *f*.

sock [sɒk] *n* chaussette *f*; **to pull one's ~s up** *inf fig* se secouer.

socket ['sɒkɪt] *n* -1. ELEC douille *f*, prise *f* de courant. -2. [of eye] orbite *f*; [for bone] cavité *f* articulaire.

sod [sɒd] *n* -1. [of turf] motte *f* de gazon. -2. *v inf* [person] con *m*.

soda ['səʊdə] *n* -1. CHEM soude *f*. -2. [soda water] eau *f* de Seltz. -3. *Am* [fizzy drink] soda *m*.

soda syphon *n* siphon *m* d'eau de Seltz.

soda water *n* eau *f* de Seltz.

sodden ['sɒdn] *adj* trempé(e), détrempé(e).

sodium ['səʊdɪəm] *n* sodium *m*.

sofa ['səʊfə] *n* canapé *m*.

sofa bed *n* canapé-lit *m*.

Sofia ['səʊfjə] *n* Sofia.

soft [sɒft] *adj* -1. [not hard] doux (douce), mou (molle). -2. [smooth, not loud, not bright] doux (douce). -3. [without force] léger(ère). -4. [caring] tendre. -5. [lenient] faible, indulgent(e).

soft-boiled *adj* à la coque.

soft drink *n* boisson *f* non alcoolisée.

soft drugs *npl* drogues *fpl* douces.

soften ['sɒfn] ◇ *vt* -1. [fabric] assouplir; [substance] ramollir; [skin] adoucir. -2. [shock, blow] atténuer, adoucir. -3. [attitude] modérer, adoucir. ◇ *vi* -1. [substance] se ramollir. -2. [attitude, person] s'adoucir, se radoucir.

◆ **soften up** *vt sep inf* [persuade] amadouer.

softener ['sɒfnə] *n* [for washing] adoucissant *m*.

soft focus *n* flou *m*; **in ~** en flou.

soft furnishings *npl Br* tissus *mpl* d'ameublement.

softhearted [,sɒft'hɑːtɪd] *adj* au cœur tendre.

softly ['sɒftlɪ] *adv* -1. [gently, quietly] douce-

ment. -2. [not brightly] faiblement. -3. [leniently] avec indulgence.

softness ['sɒftnɪs] *n* -1. [of bed, ground, substance] mollesse *f*, moelleux *m*. -2. [of skin, sound, light] douceur *f*. -3. [lenience] indulgence *f*.

soft-pedal *vi inf* y aller doucement.

soft sell *n inf* méthode *f* de vente discrète OR non agressive.

soft toy *n* jouet *m* en peluche.

soft-spoken *adj* à la voix douce.

software ['sɒftweə] *n* (*U*) COMPUT logiciel *m*.

software package *n* COMPUT logiciel *m*, progiciel *m*.

softwood ['sɒftwʊd] *n* bois *m* tendre.

softy ['sɒftɪ] (*pl* -ies) *n inf* -1. *pej* [weak person] mauviette *f*, poule *f* mouillée. -2. [sensitive person]: **he's a big ~** c'est un tendre.

soggy ['sɒgɪ] (*compar* -ier, *superl* -iest) *adj* trempé(e), détrempé(e).

soil [sɔɪl] ◇ *n* (*U*) -1. [earth] sol *m*, terre *f*. -2. *fig* [territory] sol, territoire *m*. ◇ *vt* souiller, salir.

soiled [sɔɪld] *adj* sale.

solace ['sɒləs] *n literary* consolation *f*, réconfort *m*.

solar ['səʊlə] *adj* solaire.

solarium [sə'leərɪəm] (*pl* -riums OR -ria [-rɪə]) *n* solarium *m*.

solar panel *n* panneau *m* solaire.

solar plexus [-'pleksəs] *n* plexus *m* solaire.

solar system *n* système *m* solaire.

sold [səʊld] *pt & pp* → **sell**.

solder ['səʊldə] ◇ *n* (*U*) soudure *f*. ◇ *vt* souder.

soldering iron ['səʊldərɪŋ-] *n* fer *m* à souder.

soldier ['səʊldʒə] *n* soldat *m*.

◆ **soldier on** *vi Br* persévérer.

sold-out *adj* [tickets] qui ont tous été vendus; [play, concert] qui joue à guichets fermés.

sole [səʊl] (*pl sense 2 only inv* OR -s) ◇ *adj* -1. [only] seul(e), unique. -2. [exclusive] exclusif(ive). ◇ *n* -1. [of foot] semelle *f*. -2. [fish] sole *f*.

solely ['səʊllɪ] *adv* seulement, uniquement; **~ responsible** seul OR entièrement responsable.

solemn ['sɒləm] *adj* solennel(elle); [person] sérieux(ieuse).

solemnly ['sɒləmlɪ] *adv* -1. [speak, behave] avec solennité, sérieusement. -2. [promise, swear] solennellement.

sole trader *n* Br COMM entreprise *f* uni-personnelle OR individuelle.

solicit [sə'lɪsɪt] ◇ *vt* [request] solliciter. ◇ *vi* [prostitute] racoler.

solicitor [sə'lɪsɪtər] *n* Br JUR notaire *m*.

solicitous [sə'lɪsɪtəs] *adj* -1. [caring] plein(e) de sollicitude. -2. [anxious]: ~ **about** OR **for** préoccupé(e) de, soucieux(ieuse) de.

solid ['sɒlɪd] ◇ *adj* -1. [not fluid, sturdy, reliable] solide. -2. [not hollow - tyres] plein(e); [- wood, rock, gold] massif(ive). -3. [without interruption]: **two hours** ~ deux heures d'affilée. ◇ *n* solide *m*.

solidarity [,sɒlɪ'dærətɪ] *n* solidarité *f*.

solid fuel *n* combustible *m* solide.

solidify [sə'lɪdɪfaɪ] (*pt* & *pp* -ied) *vi* se solidifier.

solidly ['sɒlɪdlɪ] *adv* -1. [sturdily] solidement. -2. [completely] tout à fait, absolument. -3. [without interruption] sans s'arrêter, sans interruption.

soliloquy [sə'lɪləkwɪ] (*pl* -ies) *n* soliloque *m*.

solitaire [,sɒlɪ'teər] *n* -1. [jewel, board game] solitaire *m*. -2. Am [card game] réussite *f*, patience *f*.

solitary ['sɒlɪtrɪ] *adj* -1. [lonely, alone] solitaire. -2. [just one] seul(e).

solitary confinement *n* isolement *m* cellulaire.

solitude ['sɒlɪtjuːd] *n* solitude *f*.

solo ['səʊləʊ] (*pl* -s) ◇ *adj* solo (*inv*). ◇ *n* solo *m*. ◇ *adv* en solo.

soloist ['səʊləʊɪst] *n* soliste *mf*.

Solomon Islands ['sɒləmən-] *npl*: **the** ~ les îles *fpl* Salomon; **in the** ~ dans les îles Salomon.

solstice ['sɒlstɪs] *n* solstice *m*.

soluble ['sɒljʊbl] *adj* soluble.

solution [sə'luːʃn] *n* -1. [to problem]: ~ **(to)** solution *f* (de). -2. [liquid] solution *f*.

solve [sɒlv] *vt* résoudre.

solvency ['sɒlvənsɪ] *n* solvabilité *f*.

solvent ['sɒlvənt] ◇ *adj* FIN solvable. ◇ *n* dissolvant *m*, solvant *m*.

solvent abuse *n* usage *m* de solvants.

Som. (*abbr of* **Somerset**) *comté anglais*.

Somali [sə'mɑːlɪ] ◇ *adj* somali(e), somalien(ienne). ◇ *n* -1. [person] Somali *m*, -e *f*, Somalien *m*, -ienne *f*. -2. [language] somali *m*.

Somalia [sə'mɑːlɪə] *n* Somalie *f*; **in** ~ en Somalie.

sombre Br, **somber** Am ['sɒmbər] *adj* sombre.

some [sʌm] ◇ *adj* -1. [a certain amount, number of]: ~ **meat/money** de la viande/l'argent; ~ **coffee** du café; ~ **sweets** des bonbons. -2. [fairly large number or quantity of] quelque; **I had** ~ **difficulty getting here** j'ai eu quelque mal à venir ici; **I've known him for** ~ **years** je le connais depuis plusieurs années OR pas mal d'années; **we haven't seen them for** ~ **time** ça fait quelque temps qu'on ne les a pas vus. -3. (*contrastive use*) [certain]: ~ **jobs are better paid than others** certains boulots sont mieux rémunérés que d'autres; ~ **people like his music** il y en a qui aiment sa musique. -4. [in imprecise statements] quelque, quelconque; **she married** ~ **writer or other** elle a épousé un écrivain quelconque OR quelque écrivain; **there must be** ~ **mistake** il doit y avoir erreur. -5. *inf* [very good]: **that was** ~ **party!** c'était une soirée formidable!, quelle soirée! -6. *inf iro* [not very good]: ~ **party that was!** tu parles d'une soirée!; ~ **help you are!** tu parles d'une aide!, beaucoup tu m'aides!
◇ *pron* -1. [a certain amount]: **can I have** ~? [money, milk, coffee etc] est-ce que je peux en prendre?; ~ **of it is mine** une partie est à moi. -2. [a certain number] quelques-unes (quelques-unes), certains (certaines); **can I have** ~? [books, pens, potatoes etc] est-ce que je peux en prendre (quelques-uns)?; ~ **(of them) left early** quelques-uns d'entre eux sont partis tôt; ~ **say he lied** certains disent OR il y en a qui disent qu'il a menti.
◇ *adv* quelque, environ; **there were** ~ **7,000 people there** il y avait quelque OR environ 7 000 personnes.

somebody ['sʌmbədɪ] ◇ *pron* quelqu'un. ◇ *n*: **he really thinks he's** ~ il se prend pour OR se croit quelqu'un.

someday ['sʌmdeɪ] *adv* un jour, un de ces jours.

somehow ['sʌmhaʊ], **someway** Am ['sʌmweɪ] *adv* -1. [by some action] d'une manière ou d'une autre. -2. [for some reason] pour une raison ou pour une autre.

someone ['sʌmwʌn] *pron* quelqu'un.

someplace Am = **somewhere**.

somersault ['sʌməsɔːlt] ◇ *n* cabriole *f*, culbute *f*. ◇ *vi* faire une cabriole OR culbute.

something ['sʌmθɪŋ] ◇ *pron* -1. [unknown thing] quelque chose; ~ **odd/interesting** quelque chose de bizarre/d'intéressant; **or** ~ *inf* ou quelque chose comme ça. -2. [useful thing]: **(at least) that's** ~ c'est toujours ça, c'est déjà quelque chose; **there's** ~ **in what you say** il y a du vrai dans ce que vous dites. -3. *phr*: **that's really** ~! ce n'est

pas rien!; **she's** ~ **of a cook** elle est assez bonne cuisinière.
◇ *adv*: ~ **like,** ~ **in the region of** environ, à peu près.

sometime ['sʌmtaɪm] ◇ *adj* ancien(ienne).
◇ *adv* un de ces jours: ~ **last week** la semaine dernière.

sometimes ['sʌmtaɪmz] *adv* quelquefois, parfois.

someway *Am* = **somehow.**

somewhat ['sʌmwɒt] *adv* quelque peu.

somewhere *Br* ['sʌmweəʳ], **someplace** *Am* ['sʌmpleɪs] *adv* **-1.** [unknown place] quelque part: ~ **else** ailleurs; ~ **near here** près d'ici. **-2.** [used in approximations] environ, à peu près. **-3.** *phr*: **to be getting** ~ avancer, faire des progrès.

son [sʌn] *n* fils *m*.

sonar ['səʊnɑːʳ] *n* sonar *m*.

sonata [sə'nɑːtə] *n* sonate *f*.

song [sɒŋ] *n* chanson *f*; [of bird] chant *m*, ramage *m*: **for a** ~ *inf* [cheaply] pour une bouchée de pain; **to make a** ~ **and dance about sthg** *inf* faire toute une histoire OR tout un plat à propos de qqch.

songbook ['sɒŋbʊk] *n* recueil *m* de chansons.

sonic ['sɒnɪk] *adj* sonique.

sonic boom *n* bang *m*.

son-in-law (*pl* **sons-in-law** OR **son-in-laws**) *n* gendre *m*, beau-fils *m*.

sonnet ['sɒnɪt] *n* sonnet *m*.

sonny ['sʌnɪ] *n inf* fiston *m*.

soon [suːn] *adv* **-1.** [before long] bientôt; ~ **after** peu après. **-2.** [early] tôt; **write back** ~ réponds-moi vite; **how** ~ **will it be ready?** ce sera prêt quand?, dans combien de temps est-ce que ce sera prêt?; **as** ~ **as** dès que, aussitôt que. **-3.** *phr*: **I'd just as** ~ ... je préférerais ..., j'aimerais autant ....

sooner ['suːnəʳ] *adv* **-1.** [in time] plus tôt; **no** ~ ... **than** ... à peine ... que ...; ~ **or later** tôt ou tard; **the** ~ **the better** le plus tôt sera le mieux. **-2.** [expressing preference]: **I would** ~ ... je préférerais ..., j'aimerais mieux ....

soot [sʊt] *n* suie *f*.

soothe [suːð] *vt* calmer, apaiser.

soothing ['suːðɪŋ] *adj* **-1.** [pain-relieving] lénifiant(e), lénitif(ive). **-2.** [music, words] apaisant(e).

sooty ['sʊtɪ] (*compar* **-ier,** *superl* **-iest**) *adj* couvert(e) de suie.

sop [sɒp] *n pej*: ~ **(to)** concession *f* (à).

SOP (*abbr of* **standard operating procedure**) *n* marche à suivre normale.

sophisticated [sə'fɪstɪkeɪtɪd] *adj* **-1.** [stylish] raffiné(e), sophistiqué(e). **-2.** [intelligent] averti(e). **-3.** [complicated] sophistiqué(e), très perfectionné(e).

sophistication [sə,fɪstɪ'keɪʃn] *n* **-1.** [stylishness] raffinement *m*, sophistication *f*. **-2.** [intelligence] intelligence *f*. **-3.** [complexity] sophistication *f*, perfectionnement *m*.

sophomore ['sɒfəmɔːʳ] *n Am* étudiant *m*, -e *f* de seconde année.

soporific [,sɒpə'rɪfɪk] *adj* soporifique.

sopping ['sɒpɪŋ] *adj*: ~ **(wet)** tout trempé (toute trempée).

soppy ['sɒpɪ] (*compar* **-ier,** *superl* **-iest**) *adj inf* **-1.** [sentimental - book, film] à l'eau de rose; [- person] sentimental(e). **-2.** [silly] bêta(asse), bête.

soprano [sə'prɑːnəʊ] (*pl* **-s**) *n* [person] soprano *mf*; [voice] soprano *m*.

sorbet ['sɔːbeɪ] *n* sorbet *m*.

sorcerer ['sɔːsərəʳ] *n* sorcier *m*.

sordid ['sɔːdɪd] *adj* sordide.

sore [sɔːʳ] ◇ *adj* **-1.** [painful] douloureux(euse); **to have a** ~ **throat** avoir mal à la gorge. **-2.** *Am* [upset] fâché(e), contrarié(e). **-3.** *literary* [great]: **to be in** ~ **need of sthg** avoir grandement besoin de qqch. ◇ *n* plaie *f*.

sorely ['sɔːlɪ] *adv literary* [needed] grandement.

sorority [sə'rɒrətɪ] *n Am* club *m* d'étudiantes.

sorrel ['sɒrəl] *n* oseille *f*.

sorrow ['sɒrəʊ] *n* peine *f*, chagrin *m*.

sorrowful ['sɒrəfʊl] *adj* triste, affligé(e).

sorry ['sɒrɪ] (*compar* **-ier,** *superl* **-iest**) ◇ *adj* **-1.** [expressing apology, disappointment, sympathy] désolé(e); **to be** ~ **about sthg** s'excuser pour qqch; **to be** ~ **for sthg** regretter qqch; **to be** ~ **to do sthg** être désolé OR regretter de faire qqch; **to be** OR **feel** ~ **for sb** plaindre qqn; **to be** OR **feel** ~ **for o.s.** s'apitoyer sur son sort. **-2.** [poor]: **in a** ~ **state** en piteux état, dans un triste état.
◇ *excl* **-1.** [expressing apology] pardon!, excusez-moi! **-2.** [asking for repetition] pardon?, comment? **-3.** [to correct oneself] non, pardon OR je veux dire.

sort [sɔːt] ◇ *n* genre *m*, sorte *f*, espèce *f*; **what** ~ **of car have you got?** qu'est-ce que tu as comme voiture?; ~ **of** [rather] plutôt, quelque peu; **a** ~ **of** une espèce OR sorte de. ◇ *vt* trier, classer.
◆ **sorts** *npl*: **of** ~**s** si on veut, si on peut dire; **to be out of** ~**s** ne pas être dans son assiette, être patraque.

◆ **sort out** vt sep -1. [classify] ranger, classer. -2. [solve] résoudre.

sortie ['sɔːtiː] n sortie f.

sorting office ['sɔːtɪŋ-] n centre m de tri.

sort-out n Br inf: **to have a** ~ faire du rangement.

SOS (abbr of save our souls) n SOS m.

so-so inf ◇ adj quelconque. ◇ adv comme ci comme ça.

soufflé ['suːfleɪ] n soufflé m.

sought [sɔːt] pt & pp → **seek**.

sought-after adj recherché(e), demandé(e).

soul [səʊl] n -1. [gen] âme f; **I didn't see a** ~ je n'ai pas vu âme qui vive. -2. [music] soul m.

soul-destroying [-dɪ,strɔɪɪŋ] adj abrutissant(e).

soulful ['səʊlfʊl] adj [look] expressif(ive); [song etc] sentimental(e).

soulless ['səʊllɪs] adj [job] abrutissant(e); [place] sans âme.

soul mate n âme f sœur.

soul music n soul m.

soul-searching n (U) examen m de conscience.

sound [saʊnd] ◇ adj -1. [healthy · body] sain(e), en bonne santé; [- mind] sain. -2. [sturdy] solide. -3. [reliable · advice] judicieux(ieuse), sage; [- investment] sûr(e).
◇ adv: **to be** ~ **asleep** dormir à poings fermés, dormir d'un sommeil profond.
◇ n son m; [particular sound] bruit m, son m; **I don't like the** ~ **of that** fig cela ne me dit rien qui vaille; **by the** ~ **of it** ... d'après ce que j'ai compris ....
◇ vt [alarm, bell] sonner; **to** ~ **one's horn** klaxonner.
◇ vi -1. [make a noise] sonner, retentir; **to** ~ **like sthg** ressembler à qqch. -2. [seem] sembler, avoir l'air; **to** ~ **like sthg** avoir l'air de qqch, sembler être qqch.

◆ **sound out** vt sep: **to** ~ **sb out (on** OR **about)** sonder qqn (sur).

sound barrier n mur m du son.

sound bite n petite phrase f (prononcée par un homme politique etc à la radio ou à la télévision pour frapper les esprits).

sound effects npl bruitage m, effets mpl sonores.

sounding ['saʊndɪŋ] n NAUT & fig sondage m.

sounding board n -1. THEATRE abat-voix m inv. -2. fig [person] personne sur laquelle on peut essayer une nouvelle idée.

soundly ['saʊndlɪ] adv -1. [beaten] à plates coutures. -2. [sleep] profondément.

soundness ['saʊndnɪs] n [of argument] solidité f, validité f; [of theory, method] fiabilité f.

soundproof ['saʊndpruːf] adj insonorisé(e).

soundtrack ['saʊndtræk] n bande f sonore.

sound wave n onde f sonore.

soup [suːp] n soupe f, potage m.

◆ **soup up** vt sep inf [car] gonfler le moteur de.

soup kitchen n soupe f populaire.

soup plate n assiette f creuse OR à soupe.

soup spoon n cuiller f à soupe.

sour ['saʊər] ◇ adj -1. [taste, fruit] acide, aigre. -2. [milk] aigre; **to go** OR **turn** ~ tourner à l'aigre, fig [relationship] mal tourner, tourner au vinaigre. -3. [ill-tempered] aigre, acerbe. ◇ vt fig faire tourner au vinaigre, faire mal tourner. ◇ vi tourner au vinaigre, mal tourner.

source [sɔːs] n -1. [gen] source f. -2. [cause] origine f, cause f.

sour cream n crème f aigre.

sour grapes n (U) inf: **what he said was just** ~ il a dit ça par dépit.

sourness ['saʊənɪs] n -1. [of taste, fruit] aigreur f, acidité f. -2. [of milk, person] aigreur f.

south [saʊθ] ◇ n -1. [direction] sud m. -2. [region]: **the** ~ le sud; **the South of France** le Sud de la France, le Midi (de la France). ◇ adj sud (inv); [wind] du sud. ◇ adv au sud, vers le sud; ~ **of** au sud de.

South Africa n Afrique f du Sud; **in** ~ en Afrique du Sud; **the Republic of** ~ la République d'Afrique du Sud.

South African ◇ adj sud-africain(e). ◇ n [person] Sud-Africain m, -e f.

South America n Amérique f du Sud; **in** ~ en Amérique du Sud.

South American ◇ adj sud-américain(e). ◇ n [person] Sud-Américain m, -e f.

southbound ['saʊθbaʊnd] adj qui se dirige vers le sud; [carriageway] sud (inv).

South Carolina [-,kærə'laɪnə] n Caroline f du Sud; **in** ~ en Caroline du Sud.

South Dakota [-də'kəʊtə] n Dakota m du Sud; **in** ~ dans le Dakota du Sud.

southeast [,saʊθ'iːst] ◇ n -1. [direction] sud-est m. -2. [region]: **the** ~ le sud-est. ◇ adj au sud-est, du sud-est; [wind] du sud-est. ◇ adv au sud-est, vers le sud-est; ~ **of** au sud-est de.

Southeast Asia n Asie f du Sud-Est; **in** ~ en Asie du Sud-Est.

southeasterly [ˌsaʊθ'iːstəlɪ] *adj* au sud-est, du sud-est; [wind] du sud-est; **in a ~ direction** vers le sud-est.

southeastern [ˌsaʊθ'iːstən] *adj* du sud-est, au sud-est.

southerly ['sʌðəlɪ] *adj* au sud, du sud; [wind] du sud; **in a ~ direction** vers le sud.

southern ['sʌðən] *adj* du sud; [France] du Midi.

Southern Africa *n* Afrique *f* australe; **in ~** en Afrique australe.

Southerner ['sʌðənəʳ] *n* habitant *m*, -e *f* du Sud.

South Korea *n* Corée *f* du Sud; **in ~** en Corée du Sud.

South Korean ◇ *adj* sud-coréen(enne). ◇ *n* Sud-Coréen *m*, -enne *f*.

South Pole *n*: **the ~** le pôle Sud.

South Vietnam *n* Sud Viêt-Nam *m*; **in ~** au Sud Viêt-Nam.

South Vietnamese ◇ *adj* sud-vietnamien(ienne). ◇ *n* Sud-Vietnamien *m*, -ienne *f*.

southward ['saʊθwəd] ◇ *adj* au sud, du sud. ◇ *adv* = **southwards**.

southwards ['saʊθwədz] *adv* vers le sud.

southwest [ˌsaʊθ'west] ◇ *n* **-1.** [direction] sud-ouest *m*. **-2.** [region]: **the ~** le sud-ouest. ◇ *adj* au sud-ouest, du sud-ouest; [wind] du sud-ouest. ◇ *adv* au sud-ouest, vers le sud-ouest; **~ of** au sud-ouest de.

southwesterly [ˌsaʊθ'westəlɪ] *adj* au sud-ouest, du sud-ouest; [wind] du sud-ouest; **in a ~ direction** vers le sud-ouest.

southwestern [ˌsaʊθ'westən] *adj* au sud-ouest, du sud-ouest.

South Yemen *n* Yémen *m* du Sud; **in ~** au Yémen du Sud.

souvenir [ˌsuːvə'nɪəʳ] *n* souvenir *m*.

sou'wester [saʊ'westəʳ] *n* [hat] suroît *m*.

sovereign ['sɒvrɪn] ◇ *adj* souverain(e). ◇ *n* **-1.** [ruler] souverain *m*, -e *f*. **-2.** [coin] souverain *m*.

sovereignty ['sɒvrɪntɪ] *n* souveraineté *f*.

soviet ['səʊvɪət] *n* soviet *m*.

◆ **Soviet** ◇ *adj* soviétique. ◇ *n* [person] Soviétique *mf*.

Soviet Union *n*: **the (former) ~** l'(ex-) Union *f* soviétique.

sow¹ [səʊ] (*pt* **-ed**, *pp* **sown** OR **-ed**) *vt lit* & *fig* semer.

sow² [saʊ] *n* truie *f*.

sown [səʊn] *pp* → **sow¹**.

sox [sɒks] → **bobby sox**.

soya ['sɔɪə] *n* soja *m*, soya *m*.

soy(a) bean ['sɔɪ(ə)-] *n* graine *f* de soja OR soya.

soy sauce [sɔɪ-] *n* sauce *f* au soja.

sozzled ['sɒzld] *adj Br inf* rond(e), pompette.

spa [spɑː] *n* station *f* thermale.

space [speɪs] ◇ *n* **-1.** [gap, roominess, outer space] espace *m*; [on form] blanc *m*, espace; **to stare into ~** regarder dans le vide. **-2.** [room] place *f*. **-3.** [of time]: **within** OR **in the ~ of ten minutes** en l'espace de dix minutes; **~ of time** laps *m* de temps. ◇ *comp* spatial(e). ◇ *vt* espacer.

◆ **space out** *vt sep* espacer.

space age *n*: **the ~** l'ère *f* spatiale.

◆ **space-age** *adj* de l'an 2000.

space bar *n* barre *f* d'espacement.

space capsule *n* capsule *f* spatiale.

spacecraft ['speɪskrɑːft] (*pl inv*) *n* vaisseau *m* spatial.

spaceman ['speɪsmæn] (*pl* **-men** [-men]) *n* astronaute *m*, cosmonaute *m*.

space probe *n* sonde *f* spatiale.

spaceship ['speɪsʃɪp] *n* vaisseau *m* spatial.

space shuttle *n* navette *f* spatiale.

space station *n* station *f* orbitale OR spatiale.

spacesuit ['speɪssuːt] *n* combinaison *f* spatiale.

spacewoman ['speɪsˌwʊmən] (*pl* **-women** [-ˌwɪmɪn]) *n* astronaute *f*, cosmonaute *f*.

spacing ['speɪsɪŋ] *n* TYPO espacement *m*.

spacious ['speɪʃəs] *adj* spacieux(ieuse).

spade [speɪd] *n* **-1.** [tool] pelle *f*. **-2.** [playing card] pique *m*.

◆ **spades** *npl* pique *m*; **the six of ~s** le six de pique.

spadework ['speɪdwɜːk] *n inf* gros *m* du travail.

spaghetti [spə'getɪ] *n* (*U*) spaghettis *mpl*.

Spain [speɪn] *n* Espagne *f*; **in ~** en Espagne.

span [spæn] (*pt* & *pp* **-ned**, *cont* **-ning**) ◇ *pt* → **spin**. ◇ *n* **-1.** [in time] espace *m* de temps, durée *f*. **-2.** [range] éventail *m*, gamme *f*. **-3.** [of bird, plane] envergure *f*. **-4.** [of bridge] travée *f*; [of arch] ouverture *f*. ◇ *vt* **-1.** [in time] embrasser, couvrir. **-2.** [subj: bridge] franchir.

spandex ['spændeks] *n Am textile proche du Lycra®*.

spangled ['spæŋgld] *adj*: **~ (with)** pailleté(e) (de).

Spaniard ['spænjəd] *n* Espagnol *m*, -e *f*.

spaniel ['spænjəl] *n* épagneul *m*.

Spanish ['spænɪʃ] ◇ *adj* espagnol(e). ◇ *n* [language] espagnol *m*. ◇ *npl*: **the ~** les Espagnols.

Spanish America *n* Amérique *f* hispanophone.

Spanish American ◇ *adj* **-1.** [in US] hispanique. **-2.** [in Latin America] hispano-américain(e). ◇ *n* **-1.** [in US] Hispanique *mf*. **-2.** [in Latin America] Hispano-Américain *m*, -e *f*.

spank [spæŋk] ◇ *n* fessée *f*. ◇ *vt* donner une fessée à, fesser.

spanner ['spænər] *n* clé *f* à écrous.

spar [spɑːr] (*pt* & *pp* **-red**, *cont* **-ring**) ◇ *n* espar *m*. ◇ *vi* **-1.** BOXING s'entraîner à la boxe. **-2.** [verbally]: **to ~ (with)** se disputer (avec).

spare [speər] ◇ *adj* **-1.** [surplus] de trop; [component, clothing etc] de réserve, de rechange. **-2.** [available - seat, time, tickets] disponible.
◇ *n* **-1.** [tyre] pneu *m* de rechange OR de secours. **-2.** [part] pièce *f* détachée OR de rechange.
◇ *vt* **-1.** [make available - staff, money] se passer de; [- time] disposer de; **to have an hour to ~** avoir une heure de battement OR de libre; **with a minute to ~** avec une minute d'avance; **with £2 to ~** et il nous/lui *etc* reste encore deux livres. **-2.** [not harm] épargner. **-3.** [not use] épargner, ménager; **to ~ no expense** ne pas regarder à la dépense. **-4.** [save from]: **to ~ sb sthg** épargner qqch à qqn, éviter qqch à qqn.

spare part *n* pièce *f* détachée OR de rechange.

spare room *n* chambre *f* d'amis.

spare time *n* (*U*) temps *m* libre, loisirs *mpl*.

spare tyre *n* **-1.** AUT pneu *m* de rechange OR de secours. **-2.** *hum* [fat waist] bourrelet *m* (de graisse).

spare wheel *n* roue *f* de secours.

sparing ['speərɪŋ] *adj*: **to be ~ with** OR **of sthg** être économe de qqch, ménager qqch.

sparingly ['speərɪŋlɪ] *adv* [use] avec modération; [spend] avec parcimonie.

spark [spɑːk] ◇ *n* *lit* & *fig* étincelle *f*. ◇ *vt* [interest] susciter, éveiller; [scandal] provoquer; [debate] déclencher.

sparking plug *Br* ['spɑːkɪŋ-] = spark plug.

sparkle ['spɑːkl] ◇ *n* (*U*) [of eyes, jewel] éclat *m*; [of stars] scintillement *m*. ◇ *vi* étinceler, scintiller.

sparkler ['spɑːklər] *n* [firework] cierge *m* merveilleux.

sparkling wine ['spɑːklɪŋ-] *n* vin *m* mousseux.

spark plug *n* bougie *f*.

sparrow ['spærəʊ] *n* moineau *m*.

sparse [spɑːs] *adj* clairsemé(e), épars(e).

spartan ['spɑːtn] *adj* austère, de spartiate.

spasm ['spæzm] *n* **-1.** MED spasme *m*; [of coughing] quinte *f*. **-2.** [of emotion] accès *m*.

spasmodic [spæz'mɒdɪk] *adj* spasmodique.

spastic ['spæstɪk] MED ◇ *adj* handicapé(e) moteur. ◇ *n* handicapé *m*, -e *f* moteur.

spat [spæt] *pt* & *pp* → spit.

spate [speɪt] *n* [of attacks etc] série *f*.

spatial ['speɪʃl] *adj* spatial(e).

spatter ['spætər] ◇ *vt* éclabousser. ◇ *vi* gicler.

spatula ['spætjʊlə] *n* spatule *f*.

spawn [spɔːn] ◇ *n* (*U*) frai *m*, œufs *mpl*. ◇ *vt* *fig* donner naissance à, engendrer. ◇ *vi* [fish, frog] frayer.

spay [speɪ] *vt* châtrer.

SPCA (*abbr* of **Society for the Prevention of Cruelty to Animals**) *n* société américaine protectrice des animaux, ≃ SPA *f*.

SPCC (*abbr* of **Society for the Prevention of Cruelty to Children**) *n* société américaine pour la protection de l'enfance.

speak [spiːk] (*pt* **spoke**, *pp* **spoken**) ◇ *vt* **-1.** [say] dire; **to ~ ill of sb** dire du mal de qqn. **-2.** [language] parler. ◇ *vi* parler; **to ~ to** OR **with sb** parler à qqn; **to ~ to sb about sthg** parler de qqch à qqn; **to ~ about sb/sthg** parler de qqn/qqch; **to ~ well/highly of sb** dire du bien/beaucoup de bien de qqn; **nobody to ~ of** pas grand-monde; **nothing to ~ of** pas grand-chose.
◆ **so to speak** *adv* pour ainsi dire.
◆ **speak for** *vt fus* [represent] parler pour, parler au nom de; **~ for yourself!** parle pour toi!; **it ~s for itself** cela tombe sous le sens, c'est évident.
◆ **speak out** *vi* oser prendre la parole; **to ~ out against** s'élever contre, se dresser contre.
◆ **speak up** *vi* **-1.** [speak out] oser prendre la parole; **to ~ up for sb/sthg** parler en faveur de qqn/qqch, soutenir qqn/qqch. **-2.** [speak louder] parler plus fort.

speaker ['spiːkər] *n* **-1.** [person talking] personne *f* qui parle. **-2.** [person making speech] orateur *m*. **-3.** [of language]: **a German ~** une personne qui parle allemand. **-4.** [loudspeaker] haut-parleur *m*.

speaking ['spiːkɪŋ] ◇ *adv*: **relatively/politically ~** relativement/politiquement parlant; **~ as** [in the position of] en tant que;

~ of [on the subject of] à propos de. ◇ *n* (*U*) discours *m*, parole *f*.

speaking clock *n Br* horloge *f* parlante.

spear [spɪə] ◇ *n* lance *f*. ◇ *vt* transpercer d'un coup de lance.

spearhead ['spɪəhed] ◇ *n* fer *m* de lance. ◇ *vt* [campaign] **mener;** [attack] être le fer de lance de.

spec [spek] *n Br inf*: **on ~** à tout hasard.

special ['speʃl] ◇ *adj* -1. [gen] spécial(e). -2. [needs, effort, attention] particulier(ière). ◇ *n* -1. [on menu] **plat** *m* du jour. -2. TV émission *f* spéciale.

special agent *n* [spy] agent *m* secret.

special constable *n Br* auxiliaire *m* de police.

special correspondent *n* envoyé *m* spécial.

special delivery *n* (*U*) [service] exprès *m*, envoi *m* par exprès; **by ~** en exprès.

special effects *npl* effets *mpl* spéciaux.

specialist ['speʃəlɪst] ◇ *adj* spécialisé(e). ◇ *n* spécialiste *mf*.

speciality [ˌspeʃɪ'ælətɪ] (*pl* -ies), **specialty** *Am* ['speʃəltɪ] (*pl* -ies) *n* spécialité *f*.

specialize, -ise ['speʃəlaɪz] *vi*: **to ~ (in)** se spécialiser (dans).

specially ['speʃəlɪ] *adv* -1. [specifically] spécialement; [on purpose] exprès. -2. [particularly] particulièrement.

special offer *n* promotion *f*.

special school *n* école *f* pour enfants handicapés, établissement *m* spécialisé.

specialty *n Am* = **speciality.**

species ['spiːʃiːz] (*pl inv*) *n* espèce *f*.

specific [spə'sɪfɪk] *adj* -1. [particular] particulier(ière), précis(e). -2. [precise] précis(e). -3. [unique]: **~ to** propre à.

◆ **specifics** *npl* détails *mpl*.

specifically [spə'sɪfɪklɪ] *adv* -1. [particularly] particulièrement, spécialement. -2. [precisely] précisément.

specification [ˌspesɪfɪ'keɪʃn] *n* stipulation *f*.

◆ **specifications** *npl* TECH caractéristiques *fpl* techniques, spécification *f*.

specify ['spesɪfaɪ] (*pt & pp* -ied) *vt* préciser, spécifier.

specimen ['spesɪmən] *n* -1. [example] exemple *m*, spécimen *m*. -2. [of blood] prélèvement *m*; [of urine] échantillon *m*.

specimen copy *n* spécimen *m*.

specimen signature *n* spécimen *m* de signature.

speck [spek] *n* -1. [small stain] toute petite tache *f*. -2. [of dust] grain *m*.

speckled ['spekld] *adj*: **~ (with)** tacheté(e) de.

specs [speks] *npl inf* [glasses] lunettes *fpl*.

spectacle ['spektəkl] *n* spectacle *m*.

◆ **spectacles** *npl Br* lunettes *fpl*.

spectacular [spek'tækjʊlə] ◇ *adj* spectaculaire. ◇ *n* pièce *f* OR revue *f* à grand spectacle.

spectate [spek'teɪt] *vi* regarder, être là en tant que spectateur.

spectator [spek'teɪtə] *n* spectateur *m*, -trice *f*.

spectator sport *n* sport *m* que l'on regarde en tant que spectateur.

spectre *Br*, **specter** *Am* ['spektə] *n* spectre *m*.

spectrum ['spektrəm] (*pl* -tra [-trə]) *n* -1. PHYSICS spectre *m*. -2. *fig* [variety] gamme *f*.

speculate ['spekjʊleɪt] ◇ *vt*: **to ~ that ...** émettre l'hypothèse que .... ◇ *vi* -1. [wonder] faire des conjectures. -2. FIN spéculer.

speculation [spekjʊ'leɪʃn] *n* -1. [gen] spéculation *f*. -2. [conjecture] conjectures *fpl*.

speculative ['spekjʊlətɪv] *adj* spéculatif(ive).

speculator ['spekjʊleɪtə] *n* FIN spéculateur *m*, -trice *f*.

sped [sped] *pt & pp* → **speed.**

speech [spiːtʃ] *n* -1. (*U*) [ability] parole *f*. -2. [formal talk] discours *m*; **to give** OR **make a ~** faire un discours. -3. THEATRE texte *m*. -4. [manner of speaking] façon *m* de parler. -5. [dialect] parler *m*.

speech day *n Br* distribution *f* des prix.

speech impediment *n* défaut *m* d'élocution.

speechless ['spiːtʃlɪs] *adj*: **~ (with)** muet(ette) (de).

speech processing *n* traitement *m* de la parole.

speech therapist *n* orthophoniste *mf*.

speech therapy *n* orthophonie *f*.

speed [spiːd] (*pt & pp* -ed OR sped) ◇ *n* vitesse *f*; [of reply, action] vitesse, rapidité *f*. ◇ *vi* -1. [move fast]: **to ~ along** aller à toute allure OR vitesse; **to ~ away** démarrer à toute allure. -2. AUT [go too fast] rouler trop vite, faire un excès de vitesse.

◆ **speed up** ◇ *vt sep* [person] faire aller plus vite; [work, production] **accélérer.** ◇ *vi* aller plus vite; [car] **accélérer.**

speedboat ['spiːdbəʊt] *n* hors-bord *m inv*.

speeding ['spiːdɪŋ] *n* (*U*) excès *m* de vitesse.

speed limit *n* limitation *f* de vitesse.

speedo ['spiːdəʊ] (*pl* -s) *n Br inf* compteur *m* (de vitesse).

speedometer [spɪ'dɒmɪtər] *n* compteur *m* (de vitesse).

speed trap *n* radar *m* de contrôle.

speedway ['spiːdweɪ] *n* -1. (U) SPORT course *f* de motos. -2. *Am* [road] voie *f* express.

speedy ['spiːdɪ] (*compar* -ier, *superl* -iest) *adj* rapide.

speleology [,spiːlɪ'ɒlədʒɪ] *n* spéléologie *f*.

spell [spel] (*Br pt & pp* spelt OR -ed, *Am pt & pp* -ed) ◇ *n* -1. [period of time] période *f*. -2. [enchantment] charme *m*; [words] formule *f* magique; **to cast** OR **put a ~ on sb** jeter un sort à qqn, envoûter qqn. ◇ *vt* -1. [word, name] écrire. -2. *fig* [signify] signifier. ◇ *vi* épeler.

◆ **spell out** *vt sep* -1. [read aloud] épeler. -2. [explain]: **to ~ sthg out (for** OR **to sb)** expliquer qqch clairement (à qqn).

spellbound ['spelbaʊnd] *adj* subjugué(e).

spelling ['spelɪŋ] *n* orthographe *f*.

spelt [spelt] *Br pt & pp → spell.*

spend [spend] (*pt & pp* spent) *vt* -1. [pay out]: **to ~ money (on)** dépenser de l'argent (pour). -2. [time, life] passer; [effort] consacrer.

spender ['spendər] *n*: **to be a big ~** être très dépensier(ière), dépenser beaucoup.

spending ['spendɪŋ] *n* (U) dépenses *fpl*.

spending money *n* argent *m* de poche.

spending power *n* (U) pouvoir *m* d'achat.

spendthrift ['spendθrɪft] *n* dépensier *m*, -ière *f*.

spent [spent] ◇ *pt & pp → spend.* ◇ *adj* [fuel, match, ammunition] utilisé(e); [patience, energy] épuisé(e).

sperm [spɜːm] (*pl inv* OR -s) *n* sperme *m*.

spermicidal cream [,spɜːmɪ'saɪdl-] *n* crème *f* spermicide.

sperm whale *n* cachalot *m*.

spew [spjuː] *vt & vi* vomir.

sphere [sfɪər] *n* sphère *f*.

spherical ['sferɪkl] *adj* sphérique.

sphincter ['sfɪŋktər] *n* sphincter *m*.

sphinx [sfɪŋks] (*pl* -es) *n* sphinx *m*.

spice [spaɪs] ◇ *n* -1. CULIN épice *f*. -2. (U) *fig* [excitement] piment *m*. ◇ *vt* -1. CULIN épicer. -2. *fig* [add excitement to] pimenter, relever.

spick-and-span ['spɪkən,spæn] *adj* impeccable, nickel (*inv*).

spicy ['spaɪsɪ] (*compar* -ier, *superl* -iest) *adj* -1. CULIN épicé(e). -2. *fig* [story] pimenté(e), piquant(e).

spider ['spaɪdər] *n* araignée *f*.

spider's web, spiderweb *Am* ['spaɪdəweb] *n* toile *f* d'araignée.

spidery ['spaɪdərɪ] *adj* en pattes d'araignée.

spiel [ʃpiːl] *n inf* baratin *m*.

spike [spaɪk] *n* [metal] pointe *f*, lance *f*; [of plant] piquant *m*; [of hair] épi *m*.

◆ **spikes** *npl Br* chaussures *fpl* à pointes.

spiky ['spaɪkɪ] (*compar* -ier, *superl* -iest) *adj* [branch, plant] hérissé(e) de piquants; [hair] en épi.

spill [spɪl] (*Br pp & pt* spilt OR -ed, *Am pt & pp* -ed) ◇ *vt* renverser. ◇ *vi* -1. [liquid] se répandre. -2. [people]: **to ~ out of a building** sortir d'un bâtiment en masse.

spillage ['spɪlɪdʒ] *n* [of oil] déversement *m*.

spilt [spɪlt] *Br pt & pp → spill.*

spin [spɪn] (*pt* span OR spun, *pp* spun, *cont* -ning) ◇ *n* -1. [turn]: **to give sthg a ~** faire tourner qqch. -2. AERON vrille *f*. -3. *inf* [in car] tour *m*. -4. SPORT effet *m*. ◇ *vt* -1. [wheel] faire tourner; **to ~ a coin** jouer à pile ou face. -2. [washing] essorer. -3. [thread, wool, cloth] filer. -4. SPORT [ball] donner de l'effet à. ◇ *vi* tourner, tournoyer; **my head is spinning** j'ai la tête qui tourne.

◆ **spin out** *vt sep* [money, story] faire durer.

spina bifida [,spaɪnə'bɪfɪdə] *n* spina-bifida *m*.

spinach ['spɪnɪdʒ] *n* (U) épinards *mpl*.

spinal column ['spaɪnl-] *n* colonne *f* vertébrale.

spinal cord ['spaɪnl-] *n* moelle *f* épinière.

spindle ['spɪndl] *n* -1. TECH broche *f*, axe *m*. -2. [for textiles] fuseau *m*.

spindly ['spɪndlɪ] (*compar* -ier, *superl* -iest) *adj* grêle, chétif(ive).

spin doctor *n pej* expression désignant une personne chargée de relations avec la presse qui manipule et filtre les informations fournies à celle-ci.

spin-dry *vt Br* essorer.

spin-dryer *n Br* essoreuse *f*.

spine [spaɪn] *n* -1. ANAT colonne *f* vertébrale. -2. [of book] dos *m*. -3. [of plant, hedgehog] piquant *m*.

spine-chilling *adj* qui glace le sang.

spineless ['spaɪnlɪs] *adj* [feeble] faible, qui manque de cran.

spinner ['spɪnər] *n* [of thread] fileur *m*, -euse *f*.

spinning ['spɪnɪŋ] *n* [of thread] filage *m*.

spinning top *n* toupie *f*.

spin-off *n* [by-product] dérivé *m*, retombée *f*.

spinster ['spɪnstər] *n* célibataire *f*; *pej* vieille fille *f*.

spiral ['spaɪərəl] (*Br pt* & *pp* **-led**, *cont* **-ling**, *Am pt* & *pp* **-ed**, *cont* **-ing**) ◇ *adj* spiral(e). ◇ *n* spirale *f*. ◇ *vi* **-1.** [staircase, smoke] monter en spirale. **-2.** [amount, prices] monter en flèche; **to ~ downwards** descendre en flèche.

spiral staircase *n* escalier *m* en colimaçon.

spire ['spaɪər] *n* flèche *f*.

spirit ['spɪrɪt] ◇ *n* **-1.** [gen] esprit *m*; **to enter into the ~ of sthg** participer à qqch de bon cœur. **-2.** (*U*) [determination] caractère *m*, courage *m*. ◇ *vt*: **to ~ sb out of a building** faire sortir qqn d'un bâtiment de façon secrète.
◆ **spirits** *npl* **-1.** [mood] humeur *f*; **to be in high ~s** être gai(e); **to be in low ~s** être déprimé(e). **-2.** [alcohol] spiritueux *mpl*.

spirited ['spɪrɪtɪd] *adj* fougueux(euse); [performance] interprété(e) avec brio.

spirit level *n* niveau *m* à bulle d'air.

spiritual ['spɪrɪtʃʊəl] *adj* spirituel(elle).

spiritualism ['spɪrɪtʃʊəlɪzm] *n* spiritisme *m*.

spiritualist ['spɪrɪtʃʊəlɪst] *n* spirite *mf*.

spit [spɪt] (*Br pt* & *pp* **spat**, *cont* **-ting**, *Am pt* & *pp* **spit**, *cont* **-ting**) ◇ *n* **-1.** (*U*) [spittle] crachat *m*; [saliva] salive *f*. **-2.** [skewer] broche *f*. ◇ *vi* cracher. ◇ *v impers Br*: **it's spitting** il tombe quelques gouttes.
◆ **spit out** *vt sep* cracher; **~ it out!** *inf* accouche!

spite [spaɪt] ◇ *n* rancune *f*; **to do sthg out of** OR **from ~** faire qqch par malice. ◇ *vt* contrarier.
◆ **in spite of** *prep* en dépit de, malgré; **to do sthg in ~ of o.s.** faire qqch malgré soi.

spiteful ['spaɪtfʊl] *adj* malveillant(e).

spitting image ['spɪtɪŋ-] *n*: **to be the ~ of sb** être le portrait (tout) craché de qqn.

spittle ['spɪtl] *n* (*U*) crachat *m*.

splash [splæʃ] ◇ *n* **-1.** [sound] plouf *m*. **-2.** [small quantity] goutte *f*. **-3.** [of colour, light] tache *f*. ◇ *vt* éclabousser. ◇ *vi* **-1.** [person]: **to ~ about** OR **around** barboter. **-2.** [liquid] jaillir en éclaboussures.
◆ **splash out** *inf* ◇ *vt sep* [money] claquer. ◇ *vi*: **to ~ out (on)** dépenser une fortune (pour).

splashdown ['splæʃdaʊn] *n* amerrissage *m*.

splashguard ['splæʃgɑːd] *n Am* garde-boue *m inv*.

splay [spleɪ] ◇ *vt* écarter. ◇ *vi*: **to ~ (out)** s'écarter.

spleen [spliːn] *n* **-1.** ANAT rate *f*. **-2.** (*U*) *fig* [anger] mauvaise humeur *f*.

splendid ['splendɪd] *adj* splendide; [work, holiday, idea] excellent(e).

splendidly ['splendɪdlɪ] *adv* **-1.** [marvellously] de façon splendide, splendidement. **-2.** [magnificently] magnifiquement.

splendour *Br*, **splendor** *Am* ['splendər] *n* splendeur *f*.

splice [splaɪs] *vt* [join - gen] coller; [- rope] épisser.

splint [splɪnt] *n* attelle *f*.

splinter ['splɪntər] ◇ *n* éclat *m*. ◇ *vt* [wood] fendre en éclats; [glass] briser en éclats. ◇ *vi* [wood] se fendre en éclats; [glass] se briser en éclats.

splinter group *n* groupe *m* dissident.

split [splɪt] (*pt* & *pp* **split**, *cont* **-ting**) ◇ *n* **-1.** [in wood] fente *f*; [in garment - tear] déchirure *f*; [- by design] échancrure *f*. **-2.** POL: **~ (in)** division *f* OR scission *f* (au sein de). **-3.** [difference]: **~ between** écart *m* entre.
◇ *vt* **-1.** [wood] fendre; [clothes] déchirer. **-2.** POL diviser. **-3.** [share] partager; **to ~ the difference** partager la différence.
◇ *vi* **-1.** [wood] se fendre; [clothes] se déchirer. **-2.** POL se diviser; [road, path] se séparer. **-3.** *Am inf* [leave] se casser.
◆ **splits** *npl*: **to do the ~s** faire le grand écart.
◆ **split off** ◇ *vt sep*: **to ~ sthg off (from)** enlever OR détacher qqch (de). ◇ *vi*: **to ~ off (from)** se détacher (de).
◆ **split up** ◇ *vt sep*: **to ~ sthg up (into)** diviser OR séparer qqch (en). ◇ *vi* [group, couple] se séparer.

split end *n* [in hair] fourche *f*.

split-level *adj* [house] à deux niveaux.

split pea *n* pois *m* cassé.

split personality *n*: **to have a ~** souffrir d'un dédoublement de la personnalité.

split screen *n* écran *m* divisé.

split second *n* fraction *f* de seconde.

splitting ['splɪtɪŋ] *adj*: **I've got a ~ headache** j'ai un mal de tête épouvantable OR atroce.

splutter ['splʌtər] ◇ *n* [of person] bafouillage *m*. ◇ *vi* [person] bredouiller, bafouiller; [engine] tousser, bafouiller; [fire] crépiter.

spoil [spɔɪl] (*pt* & *pp* **-ed** OR **spoilt**) *vt* **-1.** [ruin - holiday] gâcher, gâter; [- view] gâter; [- food] gâter, abîmer. **-2.** [over-indulge, treat well] gâter; **to ~ o.s.** s'offrir une gâterie, se faire plaisir.

◆ **spoils** *npl* butin *m*.

spoiled ['spɔɪld] *adj* = **spoilt**.

spoilsport ['spɔɪlspɔːt] *n* trouble-fête *mf inv*.

spoilt [spɔɪlt] ◇ *pt & pp* → **spoil**. ◇ *adj* [child] gâté(e).

spoke [spəʊk] ◇ *pt* → **speak**. ◇ *n* rayon *m*.

spoken ['spəʊkn] *pp* → **speak**.

spokesman ['spəʊksmən] (*pl* -**men** [-mən]) *n* porte-parole *m inv*.

spokesperson ['spəʊks,pɜːsn] *n* porte-parole *m inv*.

spokeswoman ['spəʊks,wʊmən] (*pl* -**women** [-,wɪmɪn]) *n* porte-parole *m inv*.

sponge [spʌndʒ] (*cont* **spongeing** *Br*, **sponging** *Am*) ◇ *n* -**1.** [for cleaning, washing] éponge *f*. -**2.** [cake] gâteau *m* OR biscuit *m* de Savoie. ◇ *vt* éponger. ◇ *vi inf*: **to ~ off sb** taper qqn.

sponge bag *n Br* trousse *f* de toilette.

sponge cake *n* gâteau *m* OR biscuit *m* de Savoie.

sponge pudding *n Br* pudding *m*.

sponger ['spʌndʒəʳ] *n inf pej* parasite *m*.

spongy ['spʌndʒɪ] (*compar* -**ier**, *superl* -**iest**) *adj* spongieux(ieuse).

sponsor ['spɒnsəʳ] ◇ *n* sponsor *m*. ◇ *vt* -**1.** [finance, for charity] sponsoriser, parrainer. -**2.** [support] soutenir.

sponsored walk *n* marche *f* parrainée.

SPONSORED WALK:
Les 'sponsored walks' sont destinées à rassembler des fonds, chaque marcheur établissant une liste de personnes ayant accepté de donner une certaine somme d'argent par kilomètre parcouru. Le terme 'sponsored' s'applique également à d'autres activités, sportives ou non: 'sponsored swim', 'sponsored parachute jump', etc

sponsorship ['spɒnsəʃɪp] *n* sponsoring *m*, parrainage *m*.

spontaneity [,spɒntə'neɪətɪ] *n* spontanéité *f*.

spontaneous [spɒn'teɪnjəs] *adj* spontané(e).

spontaneously [spɒn'teɪnjəslɪ] *adv* spontanément.

spoof [spuːf] *n*: ~ (**of** OR **on**) parodie *f* (de).

spook [spuːk] *vt Am* faire peur à.

spooky ['spuːkɪ] (*compar* -**ier**, *superl* -**iest**) *adj inf* qui donne la chair de poule.

spool [spuːl] ◇ *n* [gen & COMPUT] bobine *f*. ◇ *vi* faire un spooling.

spoon [spuːn] ◇ *n* cuillère *f*, cuiller *f*. ◇ *vt*: **to ~ sthg onto a plate** verser qqch dans une assiette avec une cuiller.

spoon-feed *vt* nourrir à la cuillère; **to ~ sb** *fig* mâcher le travail à qqn.

spoonful ['spuːnfʊl] (*pl* -**s** OR **spoonsful**) *n* cuillerée *f*.

sporadic [spə'rædɪk] *adj* sporadique.

sport [spɔːt] ◇ *n* -**1.** [game] sport *m*. -**2.** *dated* [cheerful person] chic type *m*/fille *f*. ◇ *vt* arborer, exhiber.

◆ **sports** ◇ *npl Br* [sports day] réunion *f* sportive scolaire. ◇ *comp* de sport.

sporting ['spɔːtɪŋ] *adj* -**1.** [relating to sport] sportif(ive). -**2.** [generous, fair] chic (*inv*); **to have a ~ chance of doing sthg** avoir des chances de faire qqch.

sports car *n* voiture *f* de sport.

sports day *n Br* réunion *f* sportive scolaire.

sports jacket *n* veste *f* sport.

sportsman ['spɔːtsmən] (*pl* -**men** [-mən]) *n* sportif *m*.

sportsmanship ['spɔːtsmənʃɪp] *n* sportivité *f*, esprit *m* sportif.

sports pages *npl* pages *fpl* des sports.

sports personality *n* personnalité *f* sportive.

sportswear ['spɔːtsweəʳ] *n* (*U*) vêtements *mpl* de sport.

sportswoman ['spɔːts,wʊmən] (*pl* -**women** [-,wɪmɪn]) *n* sportive *f*.

sporty ['spɔːtɪ] (*compar* -**ier**, *superl* -**iest**) *adj inf* -**1.** [person] sportif(ive). -**2.** [car, clothes etc] chic (*inv*).

spot [spɒt] (*pt & pp* -**ted**, *cont* -**ting**) ◇ *n* -**1.** [mark, dot] tache *f*. -**2.** [pimple] bouton *m*. -**3.** [drop] goutte *f*. -**4.** *inf* [small amount]: **to have a ~ of lunch** manger un morceau; **to have a ~ of bother** avoir quelques ennuis. -**5.** [place] endroit *m*; **on the ~** sur place; **to do sthg on the ~** faire qqch immédiatement OR sur-le-champ. -**6.** RADIO & TV numéro *m*. -**7.** *phr*: **to have a soft ~ for sb** avoir un faible pour qqn; **to put sb on the ~** embarrasser qqn par des questions. ◇ *vt* [notice] apercevoir.

spot check *n* contrôle *m* au hasard OR intermittent.

spotless ['spɒtlɪs] *adj* [clean] impeccable.

spotlight ['spɒtlaɪt] *n* [in theatre] projecteur *m*, spot *m*; [in home] spot *m*; **to be in the ~** *fig* être en vedette.

spot-on *adj Br inf* absolument exact(e) OR juste, dans le mille.

spot price *n* prix *m* comptant.

spotted ['spɒtɪd] *adj* [pattern, material] à pois.

spotty ['spɒtɪ] (*compar* -ier, *superl* -iest) *adj* -1. *Br* [skin] boutonneux(euse). -2. *Am* [patchy] irrégulier(ière).

spouse [spaʊs] *n* époux *m*, épouse *f*.

spout [spaʊt] ◇ *n* bec *m*. ◇ *vt pej* débiter. ◇ *vi*: to ~ from OR out of jaillir de.

sprain [spreɪn] ◇ *n* entorse *f*. ◇ *vt*: to ~ one's ankle/wrist se faire une entorse à la cheville/au poignet, se fouler la cheville/le poignet.

sprang [spræŋ] *pt* → spring.

sprat [spræt] *n* sprat *m*.

sprawl [sprɔ:l] ◇ *n* (U) étendue *f*. ◇ *vi* -1. [person] être affalé(e). -2. [city] s'étaler.

sprawling ['sprɔ:lɪŋ] *adj* [city] tentaculaire.

spray [spreɪ] ◇ *n* -1. (U) [of water] gouttelettes *fpl*; [from sea] embrun *m*. -2. [container] bombe *f*, pulvérisateur *m*. -3. [of flowers] gerbe *f*. ◇ *vt* pulvériser; [plants, crops] pulvériser de l'insecticide sur. ◇ *vi*: to ~ over sb/sthg asperger qqn/qqch.

spray can *n* bombe *f*.

spray paint *n* peinture *f* en bombe.

spread [spred] (*pt & pp* spread) ◇ *n* -1. (U) [food] pâte *f* à tartiner. -2. [of fire, disease] propagation *f*. -3. [of opinions] gamme *f*. -4. PRESS double page *f*.
◇ *vt* -1. [map, rug] étaler, étendre; [fingers, arms, legs] écarter. -2. [butter, jam etc]: to ~ sthg (over) étaler qqch (sur). -3. [disease, rumour, germs] répandre, propager. -4. [in time]: to be ~ over s'étaler sur. -5. [wealth, work] distribuer, répartir.
◇ *vi* -1. [disease, rumour] se propager, se répandre. -2. [water, cloud] s'étaler.
◆ **spread out** ◇ *vt sep* -1. [distribute]: to be ~ out [people, houses etc] être dispersé(e); [city, forest] être étendu(e). -2. [map, rug] étaler, étendre. -3. [fingers, arms, legs] écarter. ◇ *vi* se disperser.

spread-eagled [-,i:gld] *adj* affalé(e).

spreadsheet ['spredʃi:t] *n* COMPUT tableur *m*.

spree [spri:] *n*: to go on a spending OR shopping ~ faire des folies.

sprig [sprɪg] *n* brin *m*.

sprightly ['spraɪtlɪ] (*compar* -ier, *superl* -iest) *adj* alerte, fringant(e).

spring [sprɪŋ] (*pt* sprang, *pp* sprung) ◇ *n* -1. [season] printemps *m*; in ~ au printemps. -2. [coil] ressort *m*. -3. [jump] saut *m*, bond *m*. -4. [water source] source *f*.
◇ *comp* de printemps.

◇ *vt* -1. [make known suddenly]: to ~ sthg on sb annoncer qqch à qqn de but en blanc; to ~ a surprise on sb surprendre qqn. -2. [develop]: to ~ a leak faire eau.
◇ *vi* -1. [jump] sauter, bondir. -2. [move suddenly]: to ~ to one's feet se lever d'un bond; to ~ into action passer à l'action; to ~ to life se mettre en marche. -3. [originate]: to ~ from provenir de.
◆ **spring up** *vi* [problem] surgir, se présenter; [friendship] naître; [wind] se lever.

springboard ['sprɪŋbɔ:d] *n lit & fig* tremplin *m*.

spring-clean ◇ *vt* nettoyer de fond en comble. ◇ *vi* faire le nettoyage de printemps.

spring onion *n Br* ciboule *f*.

spring roll *n Br* rouleau *m* de printemps.

spring tide *n* marée *f* de vive-eau.

springtime ['sprɪŋtaɪm] *n*: in (the) ~ au printemps.

springy ['sprɪŋɪ] (*compar* -ier, *superl* -iest) *adj* [carpet] moelleux(euse); [mattress, rubber] élastique.

sprinkle ['sprɪŋkl] *vt*: to ~ water over OR on sthg, to ~ sthg with water asperger qqch d'eau; to ~ salt etc over OR on sthg, to ~ sthg with salt etc saupoudrer qqch de sel etc.

sprinkler ['sprɪŋklər] *n* [for water] arroseur *m*.

sprinkling ['sprɪŋklɪŋ] *n* [of water] quelques gouttes *fpl*; [of sand] couche *f* légère; a ~ of people quelques personnes.

sprint [sprɪnt] ◇ *n* sprint *m*. ◇ *vi* sprinter.

sprinter ['sprɪntər] *n* sprinter *m*.

sprite [spraɪt] *n* lutin *m*.

spritzer ['sprɪtsər] *n*: a white wine ~ du vin blanc additionné d'eau de Seltz.

sprocket ['sprɒkɪt] *n* pignon *m*.

sprout [spraʊt] ◇ *n* -1. [vegetable]: (Brussels) ~s choux *mpl* de Bruxelles. -2. [shoot] pousse *f*. ◇ *vt* [leaves] produire; to ~ shoots germer. ◇ *vi* -1. [grow] pousser. -2. *fig* [buildings]: to ~ (up) surgir.

spruce [spru:s] ◇ *adj* net (nette), pimpant(e). ◇ *n* épicéa *m*.
◆ **spruce up** *vt sep* astiquer, briquer; to ~ o.s. up se faire tout beau.

sprung [sprʌŋ] *pp* → spring.

spry [spraɪ] (*compar* -ier, *superl* -iest) *adj* vif (vive).

SPUC (*abbr of* **Society for the Protection of the Unborn Child**) *n* ligue contre l'avortement.

spud [spʌd] *n inf* patate *f*.

spun [spʌn] *pt & pp* → spin.

spunk [spʌŋk] n (U) inf [courage] cran m.

spur [spɜːʳ] (pt & pp **-red**, cont **-ring**) ◇ n **-1.** [incentive] incitation f. **-2.** [on rider's boot] éperon m. ◇ vt **-1.** [encourage]: **to ~ sb to do sthg** encourager OR inciter qqn à faire qqch. **-2.** [bring about] provoquer.
◆ **on the spur of the moment** adv sur un coup de tête, sous l'impulsion du moment.
◆ **spur on** vt sep encourager.

spurious ['spʊərɪəs] adj **-1.** [affection, interest] feint(e). **-2.** [argument, logic] faux (fausse).

spurn [spɜːn] vt repousser.

spurt [spɜːt] ◇ n **-1.** [gush] jaillissement m. **-2.** [of activity, energy] sursaut m. **-3.** [burst of speed] accélération f; **to put on a ~** sprinter. ◇ vi **-1.** [gush]: **to ~ (out of** OR **from)** jaillir (de). **-2.** [run] foncer, sprinter.

sputter ['spʌtəʳ] vi [engine] tousser, bafouiller; [fire] crépiter.

spy [spaɪ] (pl **spies**, pt & pp **spied**) ◇ n espion m. ◇ vt inf apercevoir. ◇ vi espionner, faire de l'espionnage; **to ~ on sb** espionner qqn.

spying ['spaɪɪŋ] n (U) espionnage m.

spy satellite n satellite m espion.

Sq., sq. abbr of **square**.

squabble ['skwɒbl] ◇ n querelle f. ◇ vi: **to ~ (about** OR **over)** se quereller (à propos de).

squad [skwɒd] n **-1.** [of police] brigade f. **-2.** MIL peloton m. **-3.** SPORT [group of players] équipe f (de laquelle la sélection sera faite).

squad car n voiture f de police.

squadron ['skwɒdrən] n escadron m.

squadron leader n Br commandant m.

squalid ['skwɒlɪd] adj sordide, ignoble.

squall [skwɔːl] n [storm] bourrasque f.

squalor ['skwɒləʳ] n (U) conditions fpl sordides.

squander ['skwɒndəʳ] vt gaspiller.

square [skweəʳ] ◇ adj **-1.** [in shape] carré(e); **one ~ metre** Br un mètre carré; **three miles ~** cinq kilomètres sur cinq. **-2.** [not owing money]: **to be ~** être quitte. **-3.** inf [unfashionable] vieux jeu (inv). ◇ n **-1.** [shape] carré m. **-2.** [in town] place f. **-3.** inf [unfashionable person]: **he's a ~** il est vieux jeu. **-4.** phr: **to be back to ~ one** se retrouver au point de départ. ◇ vt **-1.** MATH élever au carré. **-2.** [reconcile] accorder.
◆ **square up** vi **-1.** [settle up]: **to ~ up with sb** régler ses comptes avec qqn. **-2.** [for fight]: **to ~ up to sb** se mettre en pos-

ture de combat face à qqn; **to ~ up to a problem** faire face à un problème.

squared ['skweəd] adj quadrillé(e).

square dance n quadrille m.

square deal n arrangement m équitable.

squarely ['skweəlɪ] adv **-1.** [directly] carrément. **-2.** [honestly] honnêtement.

square meal n bon repas m.

square root n racine f carrée.

squash [skwɒʃ] ◇ n **-1.** SPORT squash m. **-2.** Br [drink]: **orange ~** orangeade f. **-3.** Am [vegetable] courge f. ◇ vt écraser.

squat [skwɒt] (compar **-ter**, superl **-test**, pt & pp **-ted**, cont **-ting**) ◇ adj courtaud(e), ramassé(e). ◇ n Br [building] squat m. ◇ vi **-1.** [crouch]: **to ~ (down)** s'accroupir. **-2.** [in building] squatter.

squatter ['skwɒtəʳ] n Br squatter m.

squawk [skwɔːk] ◇ n cri m strident OR perçant. ◇ vi pousser un cri strident OR perçant.

squeak [skwiːk] ◇ n **-1.** [of animal] petit cri m aigu. **-2.** [of door, hinge] grincement m. ◇ vi **-1.** [mouse] pousser un petit cri aigu. **-2.** [door, hinge] grincer.

squeaky ['skwiːkɪ] (compar **-ier**, superl **-iest**) adj [voice, door] grinçant(e); [shoes] qui craquent.

squeal [skwiːl] ◇ n **-1.** [of person, animal] cri m aigu. **-2.** [of brakes] grincement m; [of tyres] crissement m. ◇ vi **-1.** [person, animal] pousser des cris aigus. **-2.** [brakes] grincer; [tyres] crisser.

squeamish ['skwiːmɪʃ] adj facilement dégoûté(e).

squeeze [skwiːz] ◇ n **-1.** [pressure] pression f. **-2.** inf [squash]: **it was a ~** on était serrés comme des sardines. ◇ vt **-1.** [press firmly] presser. **-2.** [liquid, toothpaste] exprimer; **to ~ information out of sb** soutirer OR arracher des informations à qqn. **-3.** [cram]: **to ~ sthg into sthg** entasser qqch dans qqch. ◇ vi: **to ~ into/under** se glisser dans/sous.

squeezebox ['skwiːzbɒks] n Br accordéon m.

squeezer ['skwiːzəʳ] n: **orange/lemon ~** presse-citron m inv.

squelch [skweltʃ] vi: **to ~ through mud** patauger dans la boue.

squib [skwɪb] n [firework] pétard m; **it was a damp ~** ça a été une déception.

squid [skwɪd] (pl inv OR **-s**) n calmar m.

squiffy ['skwɪfɪ] (compar **-ier**, superl **-iest**) adj Br inf dated pompette.

squiggle ['skwɪgl] n gribouillis m.

squint [skwɪnt] ◇ *n*: to have a ~ loucher, être atteint(e) de strabisme. ◇ *vi*: to ~ at sthg regarder qqch en plissant les yeux.

squire ['skwaɪəʳ] *n* [landowner] propriétaire *m*.

squirm [skwɜːm] *vi* -1. [wriggle] se tortiller. -2. *fig* [wince] avoir des haut-le-cœur; to ~ with embarrassment ne plus savoir où se mettre.

squirrel [*Br* 'skwɪrəl, *Am* 'skwɜːrəl] *n* écureuil *m*.

squirt [skwɜːt] ◇ *vt* [water, oil] faire jaillir, faire gicler; to ~ sb/sthg with sthg asperger qqn/qqch de qqch. ◇ *vi*: to ~ (out of) jaillir (de), gicler (de).

Sr -1. *abbr of* **senior**. -2. *abbr of* **sister**.

SRC *n* -1. (*abbr of* **Students' Representative Council**) comité étudiant. -2. (*abbr of* **Science Research Council**) conseil britannique de la recherche scientifique.

Sri Lanka [,sriː'læŋkə] *n* Sri Lanka *m*; in ~ au Sri Lanka.

Sri Lankan [,sriː'læŋkn] ◇ *adj* sri lankais(e). ◇ *n* [person] Sri Lankais *m*, -e *f*.

SRN (*abbr of* **State Registered Nurse**) *n* en Grande-Bretagne, infirmier ou infirmière diplômé(e) d'État.

SS (*abbr of* **steamship**) SS.

SSA (*abbr of* **Social Security Administration**) *n* sécurité sociale américaine.

ssh [ʃ] *excl* chut!

SSSI (*abbr of* **Site of Special Scientific Interest**) *n* en Grande-Bretagne, site déclaré d'intérêt scientifique.

St -1. (*abbr of* **saint**) St, Ste. -2. *abbr of* **Street**.

ST (*abbr of* **Standard Time**) *n* heure légale.

stab [stæb] (*pt* & *pp* **-bed**, *cont* **-bing**) ◇ *n* -1. [with knife] coup *m* de couteau. -2. *inf* [attempt]: to have a ~ (at sthg) essayer (qqch), tenter (qqch). -3. [twinge]: ~ of pain élancement *m*; ~ of guilt remords *m*. ◇ *vt* -1. [person] poignarder; to ~ sb to death tuer qqn d'un coup/à coups de poignard. -2. [food] piquer. ◇ *vi*: to ~ at sthg frapper qqch.

stabbing ['stæbɪŋ] ◇ *adj* [pain] lancinant(e). ◇ *n* agression *f* à coups de couteau.

stability [stə'bɪlətɪ] *n* stabilité *f*.

stabilize, -ise ['steɪbəlaɪz] ◇ *vt* stabiliser. ◇ *vi* se stabiliser.

stabilizer ['steɪbəlaɪzəʳ] *n* stabilisateur *m*.

stable ['steɪbl] ◇ *adj* stable. ◇ *n* écurie *f*.

stable lad *n* garçon *m* d'écurie.

staccato [stə'kɑːtəʊ] *adj* [note] piqué(e); [sound, voice] saccadé(e).

stack [stæk] ◇ *n* -1. [pile] pile *f*. -2. *inf* [large amount]: ~s OR a ~ of des tas de, un tas de. ◇ *vt* -1. [pile up] empiler. -2. [fill]: to be ~ed with être encombré de.

◆ **stack up** *vi Am inf* être à la hauteur.

stadium ['steɪdjəm] (*pl* **-diums** OR **-dia** [-djə]) *n* stade *m*.

staff [stɑːf] ◇ *n* [employees] personnel *m*; [of school] personnel enseignant, professeurs *mpl*. ◇ *vt* pourvoir en personnel.

staffing ['stɑːfɪŋ] *n* dotation *f* en personnel; ~ levels les besoins *mpl* en personnel.

staff nurse *n Br* infirmier *m*, -ière *f*.

staff room *n* salle *f* des professeurs.

Staffs [stæfs] (*abbr of* **Staffordshire**) comté anglais.

stag [stæg] (*pl inv* OR **-s**) *n* cerf *m*.

stage [steɪdʒ] ◇ *n* -1. [phase] étape *f*, phase *f*, stade *m*. -2. [platform] scène *f*; on ~ sur scène; to set the ~ for sthg préparer la voie à qqch. -3. [acting profession]: the ~ le théâtre. ◇ *vt* -1. THEATRE monter, mettre en scène. -2. [organize] organiser.

stagecoach ['steɪdʒkəʊtʃ] *n* diligence *f*.

stage door *n* entrée *f* des artistes.

stage fright *n* trac *m*.

stagehand ['steɪdʒhænd] *n* machiniste *m*.

stage-manage *vt lit* & *fig* mettre en scène.

stage name *n* nom *m* de scène.

stagflation [stæg'fleɪʃn] *n* stagflation *f*.

stagger ['stægəʳ] ◇ *vt* -1. [astound] stupéfier. -2. [working hours] échelonner; [holidays] étaler. ◇ *vi* tituber.

staggering ['stægərɪŋ] *adj* stupéfiant(e).

staging ['steɪdʒɪŋ] *n* mise *f* en scène.

stagnant ['stægnənt] *adj* stagnant(e).

stagnate [stæg'neɪt] *vi* stagner.

stagnation [stæg'neɪʃn] *n* stagnation *f*.

stag party *n* soirée *f* entre hommes; [before wedding] soirée où un futur marié enterre sa vie de garçon avec ses amis.

staid [steɪd] *adj* guindé(e), collet monté.

stain [steɪn] ◇ *n* [mark] tache *f*. ◇ *vt* [discol'] tacher.

stained [steɪnd] *adj* -1. [marked] taché(e). -2. [coloured] coloré(e).

stained glass *n* (U) [windows] vitraux *mpl*.

stainless steel ['steɪnlɪs-] *n* acier *m* inoxydable, inox *m*.

stain remover *n* détachant *m*.

stair [steəʳ] *n* marche *f*.

◆ **stairs** *npl* escalier *m*.

staircase ['steəkeɪs] *n* escalier *m*.

stairway ['steəweɪ] *n* escalier *m*.

stairwell ['steəwel] *n* cage *f* d'escalier.

stake [steɪk] ◇ *n* **-1.** [share]: **to have a ~ in sthg** avoir des intérêts dans qqch. **-2.** [wooden post] **poteau** *m*. **-3.** [in gambling] enjeu *m*. ◇ *vt*: **to ~ money (on** OR **upon)** jouer OR miser de l'argent (sur); **to ~ one's reputation (on)** jouer OR risquer sa réputation (sur); **to ~ a claim to sthg** revendiquer qqch.
◆ **stakes** *npl* enjeux *mpl*.
◆ **at stake** *adv* en jeu.

stakeout ['steɪkaʊt] *n* [police surveillance] surveillance *f*.

stalactite ['stæləktaɪt] *n* stalactite *f*.

stalagmite ['stæləgmaɪt] *n* stalagmite *f*.

stale [steɪl] *adj* **-1.** [food, water] pas frais (fraîche); [bread] rassis(e); [air] qui sent le renfermé. **-2.** [person] qui manque d'entrain.

stalemate ['steɪlmeɪt] *n* **-1.** [deadlock] impasse *f*. **-2.** CHESS pat *m*.

staleness ['steɪlnɪs] *n* [of food] manque *m* de fraîcheur.

stalk [stɔːk] ◇ *n* **-1.** [of flower, plant] tige *f*. **-2.** [of leaf, fruit] queue *f*. ◇ *vt* [hunt] traquer. ◇ *vi*: **to ~ in/out** entrer/sortir d'un air hautain.

stall [stɔːl] ◇ *n* **-1.** [in street, market] éventaire *m*, étal *m*; [at exhibition] stand *m*. **-2.** [in stable] stalle *f*. ◇ *vt* **-1.** AUT caler. **-2.** [delay - person] faire patienter. ◇ *vi* **-1.** AUT caler. **-2.** [delay] essayer de gagner du temps.
◆ **stalls** *npl Br* [in cinema, theatre] orchestre *m*.

stallholder ['stɔːl,həʊldə'] *n Br* marchand *m* qui possède un éventaire.

stallion ['stæljən] *n* étalon *m*.

stalwart ['stɔːlwət] ◇ *adj* [loyal] fidèle. ◇ *n* pilier *m*.

stamen ['steɪmən] *n* étamine *f*.

stamina ['stæmɪnə] *n* (*U*) résistance *f*.

stammer ['stæmə'] ◇ *n* bégaiement *m*. ◇ *vi* bégayer.

stamp [stæmp] ◇ *n* **-1.** [for letter] timbre *m*. **-2.** [tool] tampon *m*. **-3.** *fig* [of authority etc] marque *f*. ◇ *vt* **-1.** [mark by stamping] tamponner. **-2.** [stomp]: **to ~ one's foot** taper du pied. **-3.** [envelope, postcard] timbrer, affranchir. ◇ *vi* **-1.** [stomp] taper du pied. **-2.** [tread heavily]: **to ~ on sthg** marcher sur qqch.
◆ **stamp out** *vt sep* [fire] éteindre en piétinant; [opposition] éliminer; [corruption, crime] supprimer; [disease] éradiquer.

stamp album *n* album *m* de timbres.

stamp-collecting *n* philatélie *f*.

stamp collector *n* collectionneur *m*, -euse *f* de timbres, philatéliste *mf*.

stamp duty *n Br* droit *m* de timbre.

stamped addressed envelope ['stæmpt ə,drest-] *n Br* enveloppe *f* affranchie pour la réponse.

stampede [stæm'piːd] ◇ *n* débandade *f*. ◇ *vi* s'enfuir à la débandade.

stamp machine *n* distributeur *m* de timbres-poste.

stance [stæns] *n lit & fig* position *f*.

stand [stænd] (*pt & pp* **stood**) ◇ *n* **-1.** [stall] stand *m*; [selling newspapers] kiosque *m*. **-2.** [supporting object]: **umbrella ~** porte-parapluies *m inv*; **hat ~** porte-chapeaux *m inv*. **-3.** SPORT tribune *f*. **-4.** MIL résistance *f*; **to make a ~** résister. **-5.** [public position] position *f*; **to take a ~ on sthg** prendre position sur qqch. **-6.** *Am* JUR barre *f*; **to take the ~** comparaître à la barre.
◇ *vt* **-1.** [place] mettre (debout), poser (debout). **-2.** [withstand, tolerate] supporter. **-3.** [treat]: **to ~ sb a meal/a drink** payer à déjeuner/à boire à qqn. **-4.** JUR: **to ~ trial** comparaître en jugement.
◇ *vi* **-1.** [be upright - person] être OR se tenir debout; [- object] se trouver; [- building] se dresser; **~ still!** ne bouge pas!, reste tranquille! **-2.** [stand up] se lever. **-3.** [liquid] reposer. **-4.** [offer] tenir toujours; [decision] demeurer valable. **-5.** [be in particular state]: **as things ... ...** vu l'état actuel des choses ...; **unemployment/production ~s at ...** le nombre de chômeurs/la production est de .... **-6.** [have opinion]: **where do you ~ on ...?** quelle est votre position sur ...? **-7.** [be likely]: **to ~ to do sthg** risquer de faire qqch. **-8.** *Br* POL se présenter. **-9.** *Am* [park car]: **"no ~ing"** «stationnement interdit».
◆ **stand aside** *vi* s'écarter.
◆ **stand back** *vi* reculer.
◆ **stand by** ◇ *vt fus* **-1.** [person] soutenir. **-2.** [statement, decision] s'en tenir à. ◇ *vi* **-1.** [in readiness]: **to ~ by (for sthg/to do sthg)** être prêt(e) (pour qqch/pour faire qqch). **-2.** [remain inactive] rester là.
◆ **stand down** *vi* [resign] démissionner.
◆ **stand for** *vt fus* **-1.** [signify] représenter. **-2.** [tolerate] supporter, tolérer.
◆ **stand in** *vi*: **to ~ in for sb** remplacer qqn.
◆ **stand out** *vi* ressortir.
◆ **stand up** ◇ *vt sep inf* [boyfriend, girlfriend] poser un lapin à. ◇ *vi* **-1.** [rise from seat] se lever. **-2.** [claim, evidence] être accepté(e).
◆ **stand up to** *vt fus* **-1.** [weather, heat etc] résister à. **-2.** [person, boss] tenir tête à.
◆ **stand up for** *vt fus* défendre.

standard ['stændəd] ⬥ *adj* **-1.** [normal - gen] normal(e); [- size] standard (*inv*). **-2.** [accepted] correct(e). **-3.** [basic] de base. ⬥ *n* **-1.** [level] niveau *m*. **-2.** [point of reference] critère *m*; TECH norme *f*. **-3.** [flag] étendard *m*.
◆ **standards** *npl* [principles] valeurs *fpl*.

standard-bearer *n fig* porte-drapeau *m*.

standardize, -ise ['stændədaız] *vt* standardiser.

standard lamp *n Br* lampadaire *m*.

standard of living (*pl* standards of living) *n* niveau *m* de vie.

standard time *n* heure *f* légale.

standby ['stændbaı] (*pl* standbys) ⬥ *n* [person] remplaçant *m*, -e *f*; on ~ prêt à intervenir. ⬥ *comp* [ticket, flight] stand-by (*inv*).

stand-in *n* remplaçant *m*, -e *f*.

standing ['stændıŋ] ⬥ *adj* [invitation, army] permanent(e); [joke] continuel(elle). ⬥ *n* **-1.** [reputation] importance *f*, réputation *f*. **-2.** [duration]: **of long** ~ de longue date; **we're friends of 20 years'** ~ nous sommes amis depuis 20 ans.

standing committee *n* comité *m* permanent.

standing order *n* prélèvement *m* automatique.

standing ovation *n*: to give sb a ~ se lever pour applaudir qqn.

standing room *n* (*U*) places *fpl* debout.

standoffish [,stænd'ɒfıʃ] *adj* distant(e).

standpipe ['stændpaıp] *n* colonne *f* d'alimentation.

standpoint ['stændpoınt] *n* point *m* de vue.

standstill ['stændstıl] *n*: **at a** ~ [traffic, train] à l'arrêt; [negotiations, work] paralysé(e); **to come to a** ~ [traffic, train] s'immobiliser; [negotiations, work] cesser.

stank [stæŋk] *pt* → **stink**.

stanza ['stænzə] *n* strophe *f*.

staple ['steıpl] ⬥ *adj* [principal] principal(e), de base. ⬥ *n* **-1.** [for paper] agrafe *f*. **-2.** [principal commodity] produit *m* de base. ⬥ *vt* agrafer.

staple diet *n* nourriture *f* de base.

staple gun *n* agrafeuse *f* (professionnelle).

stapler ['steıplə*r*] *n* agrafeuse *f*.

star [stɑː*r*] (*pt* & *pp* **-red**, *cont* **-ring**) ⬥ *n* **-1.** [gen] étoile *f*. **-2.** [celebrity] vedette *f*, star *f*. **-3.** [asterisk] astérisque *m*. ⬥ *comp* [quality] de star; ~ **performer** vedette *f*. ⬥ *vt* CINEMA & THEATRE avoir pour vedette. ⬥ *vi*: **to** ~ **(in)** être la vedette (de).
◆ **stars** *npl* horoscope *m*.

star attraction *n* attraction *f* principale, clou *m*.

starboard ['stɑːbəd] ⬥ *adj* de tribord. ⬥ *n*: **to** ~ à tribord.

starch [stɑːtʃ] *n* amidon *m*.

starched [stɑːtʃt] *adj* amidonné(e).

starchy ['stɑːtʃı] (*compar* **-ier**, *superl* **-iest**) *adj* [food] féculent(e).

stardom ['stɑːdəm] *n* (*U*) célébrité *f*.

stare [steə*r*] ⬥ *n* regard *m* fixe. ⬥ *vi*: **to** ~ **at sb/sthg** fixer qqn/qqch du regard.

starfish ['stɑːfıʃ] (*pl inv* OR **-es**) *n* étoile *f* de mer.

stark [stɑːk] ⬥ *adj* **-1.** [room, decoration] austère; [landscape] désolé(e). **-2.** [reality, fact] à l'état brut; [contrast] dur(e). ⬥ *adv*: ~ **naked** tout nu (toute nue), à poil.

starlight ['stɑːlaıt] *n* lumière *f* des étoiles.

starling ['stɑːlıŋ] *n* étourneau *m*.

starlit ['stɑːlıt] *adj* [night] étoilé(e); [countryside] illuminé(e) par les étoiles.

starry ['stɑːrı] (*compar* **-ier**, *superl* **-iest**) *adj* étoilé(e).

starry-eyed [-'aıd] *adj* innocent(e).

Stars and Stripes *n*: **the** ~ le drapeau des États-Unis, la bannière étoilée.

star sign *n* signe *m* du zodiaque.

star-studded *adj* avec de nombreuses vedettes.

start [stɑːt] ⬥ *n* **-1.** [beginning] début *m*; **to make a good/bad** ~ bien/mal commencer; **for a** ~ pour commencer, d'abord. **-2.** [jump] sursaut *m*. **-3.** [starting place] départ *m*. **-4.** [time advantage] avance *f*. ⬥ *vt* **-1.** [begin] commencer; **to** ~ **doing** OR **to do sthg** commencer à faire qqch. **-2.** [turn on - machine] mettre en marche; [- engine, vehicle] démarrer, mettre en marche. **-3.** [set up - business, band] créer. ⬥ *vi* **-1.** [begin] commencer, débuter; **to** ~ **with** pour commencer, d'abord. **-2.** [function - machine] se mettre en marche; [- car] démarrer. **-3.** [begin journey] partir. **-4.** [jump] sursauter. **-5.** *inf* [be annoying]: **don't (you)** ~! ne commence pas, toi!
◆ **start off** ⬥ *vt sep* [meeting] ouvrir, commencer; [rumour] faire naître; [discussion] entamer, commencer. ⬥ *vi* **-1.** [begin] commencer; [begin job] débuter. **-2.** [leave on journey] partir.
◆ **start on** *vt fus* entamer.
◆ **start out** *vi* **-1.** [in job] débuter. **-2.** [leave on journey] partir.
◆ **start up** ⬥ *vt sep* **-1.** [business] créer; [shop] ouvrir. **-2.** [car, engine] mettre en marche. ⬥ *vi* **-1.** [begin] commencer. **-2.**

[machine] se mettre en route; [car, engine] démarrer.

starter ['stɑːtər] n -1. Br [of meal] hors-d'œuvre m inv. -2. AUT démarreur m. -3. [to begin race] starter m.

starter motor n démarreur m.

starter pack n [information] informations de base nécessaires pour commencer une activité; [equipment] kit m de base.

starting block ['stɑːtɪŋ-] n starting-block m, bloc m de départ.

starting point ['stɑːtɪŋ-] n point m de départ.

starting price ['stɑːtɪŋ-] n cote f de départ.

startle ['stɑːtl] vt faire sursauter.

startling ['stɑːtlɪŋ] adj surprenant(e).

starvation [stɑːˈveɪʃn] n faim f.

starve [stɑːv] ◇ vt -1. [deprive of food] affamer. -2. fig [deprive]: to ~ sb of sthg priver qqn de qqch. ◇ vi -1. [have no food] être affamé(e); to ~ to death mourir de faim. -2. inf [be hungry] avoir très faim, crever OR mourir de faim.

Star Wars n la Guerre des Étoiles (nom populaire de l'Initiative de Défense Stratégique, programme militaire spatial du Président Reagan).

state [steɪt] ◇ n état m; he's not in a fit ~ to drive il n'est pas en état de conduire; to be in a ~ être dans tous ses états. ◇ comp d'État. ◇ vt -1. [express - reason] donner; [- name and address] décliner; to ~ that ... déclarer que .... -2. [specify] préciser.
◆ **State** n: the State l'État m.
◆ **States** npl: the States les États-Unis mpl.

state-controlled adj étatisé(e), sous contrôle de l'État.

State Department n Am ≃ ministère m des Affaires étrangères.

state education n Br enseignement m public.

stateless ['steɪtlɪs] adj apatride.

stately ['steɪtlɪ] (compar -ier, superl -iest) adj majestueux(euse).

stately home n Br château m.

statement ['steɪtmənt] n -1. [declaration] déclaration f. -2. JUR déposition f. -3. [from bank] relevé m de compte.

state of affairs n état m des choses.

state of emergency n état m d'urgence.

state of mind (pl states of mind) n humeur f.

state-of-the-art adj tout dernier (toute dernière); [technology] de pointe.

state-owned [-ˈəund] adj national(e), d'État.

state school n école f publique.

state secret n secret m d'État.

state's evidence n Am: to turn ~ témoigner contre ses complices.

stateside ['steɪtsaɪd] Am ◇ adj des États-Unis. ◇ adv aux États-Unis.

statesman ['steɪtsmən] (pl -men [-mən]) n homme m d'État.

statesmanship ['steɪtsmənʃɪp] n (U) habileté f politique.

static ['stætɪk] ◇ adj statique. ◇ n (U) parasites mpl.

static electricity n électricité f statique.

station ['steɪʃn] ◇ n -1. RAIL gare f; [for buses, coaches] gare routière. -2. RADIO station f. -3. [building] poste m. -4. fml [rank] rang m. ◇ vt -1. [position] placer, poster. -2. MIL poster.

stationary ['steɪʃnərɪ] adj immobile.

stationer ['steɪʃnər] n papetier m, -ière f; ~'s (shop) papeterie f.

stationery ['steɪʃnərɪ] n (U) [equipment] fournitures fpl de bureau; [paper] papier m à lettres.

station house n Am poste m de police.

stationmaster ['steɪʃn,mɑːstər] n chef m de gare.

station wagon n Am break m.

statistic [stəˈtɪstɪk] n statistique f.
◆ **statistics** n (U) [science] statistique f.

statistical [stəˈtɪstɪkl] adj statistique; [expert] en statistiques; [report] de statistiques.

statistician [,stætɪˈstɪʃn] n statisticien m, -ienne f.

statue ['stætʃuː] n statue f.

statuesque [,stætjʊˈesk] adj sculptural(e).

statuette [,stætjʊˈet] n statuette f.

stature ['stætʃər] n -1. [height, size] stature f, taille f. -2. [importance] envergure f.

status ['steɪtəs] n (U) -1. [legal or social position] statut m. -2. [prestige] prestige m.

status quo [-ˈkwəu] n: the ~ le statu quo.

status symbol n signe m extérieur de richesse.

statute ['stætʃuːt] n loi f.

statute book n: the ~ ≃ le code, les textes mpl de loi.

statutory ['stætjʊtrɪ] adj statutaire.

staunch [stɔːntʃ] ◇ adj loyal(e). ◇ vt [flow] arrêter; [blood] étancher.

stave [steɪv] (pt & pp -d OR **stove**) n MUS portée f.
◆ **stave off** vt sep [disaster, defeat] éviter; [hunger] tromper.

stay [steɪ] ◇ *vi* **-1.** [not move away] **rester**; **to ~ put** ne pas bouger. **-2.** [as visitor - with friends] **passer quelques jours**; [- in town, country] **séjourner**; **to ~ in a hotel** descendre à l'hôtel. **-3.** [continue, remain] **rester**, **demeurer**; **to ~ away from sb** ne pas s'approcher de qqn; **to ~ away from a place** ne pas aller à un endroit; **to ~ out of sthg** ne pas se mêler de qqch. **-4.** *Scot* [reside] **habiter.** ◇ *n* [visit] **séjour** *m*.

◆ **stay in** *vi* **rester chez soi, ne pas sortir.**

◆ **stay on** *vi* **rester** (plus longtemps).

◆ **stay out** *vi* **-1.** [from home] **ne pas rentrer.** **-2.** [strikers] **rester en grève.**

◆ **stay up** *vi* **ne pas se coucher, veiller**; **to ~ up late** se coucher tard.

stayer ['steɪə'] *n Br* [horse] **stayer** *m*; [person] **personne** *f* qui a de l'endurance.

staying power ['steɪɪŋ-] *n* **endurance** *f*.

St Bernard [*Br* -'bɜːnəd, *Am* -bər'nɑːrd] *n* **saint-bernard** *m inv*.

STD *n* **-1.** (*abbr of* **subscriber trunk dialling**) **téléphone** *interurbain*. **-2.** (*abbr of* **sexually transmitted disease**) **MST** *f*.

stead [sted] *n*: **to stand sb in good ~** être utile à qqn.

steadfast ['stedfɑːst] *adj* **ferme, résolu(e)**; [supporter] **loyal(e)**.

steadily ['stedɪlɪ] *adv* **-1.** [gradually] **progressivement.** **-2.** [regularly - breathe] **régulièrement**; [- move] **sans arrêt.** **-3.** [calmly] **de manière imperturbable.**

steady ['stedɪ] (*compar* **-ier**, *superl* **-iest**, *pt* & *pp* **-ied**) ◇ *adj* **-1.** [gradual] **progressif(ive).** **-2.** [regular] **régulier(ière).** **-3.** [not shaking] **ferme**; **to hold sthg ~** tenir qqch bien OR sans bouger. **-4.** [calm - voice] **calme**; [- stare] **imperturbable.** **-5.** [stable - job, relationship] **stable.** **-6.** [sensible] **sérieux(ieuse).** ◇ *vt* **-1.** [stop from shaking] **empêcher de bouger**; **to ~ o.s.** se remettre d'aplomb. **-2.** [control - nerves] **calmer**; **to ~ o.s.** retrouver son calme.

steak [steɪk] *n* **steak** *m*; [of fish] **darne** *f*.

steakhouse ['steɪkhaus, *pl* -hauzɪz] *n* **grill** *m*, **grill-room** *m*.

steal [stiːl] (*pt* **stole**, *pp* **stolen**) ◇ *vt* **voler**, **dérober**; **to ~ a look at** jeter un regard furtif à. ◇ *vi* **-1.** [take illegally] **voler.** **-2.** [move secretly] **se glisser.**

stealing ['stiːlɪŋ] *n* (*U*) **vol** *m*.

stealth [stelθ] *n*: **by ~** en secret, discrètement.

stealthy ['stelθɪ] (*compar* **-ier**, *superl* **-iest**) *adj* **furtif(ive).**

steam [stiːm] ◇ *n* (*U*) **vapeur** *f*; **to let off ~** *fig* se défouler; **to run out of ~** *fig* s'essouf-

fler. ◇ *comp* à vapeur. ◇ *vt* CULIN **cuire à la vapeur.** ◇ *vi* **-1.** [give off steam] **fumer.** **-2.** [ship] **avancer.**

◆ **steam up** ◇ *vt sep* **-1.** [mist up] **embuer.** **-2.** *fig* [get angry]: **to get ~ed up (about)** s'énerver (pour). ◇ *vi* se couvrir de buée.

steamboat ['stiːmbəut] *n* (bateau *m* à) vapeur *m*.

steam engine *n* locomotive *f* à vapeur.

steamer ['stiːmə'] *n* **-1.** [ship] (bateau *m* à) vapeur *m*. **-2.** CULIN **cuiseur-vapeur** *m*.

steam iron *n* **fer** *m* à vapeur.

steamroller ['stiːm,rəulə'] *n* **rouleau** *m* **compresseur.**

steam shovel *n Am* **bulldozer** *m*.

steamy ['stiːmɪ] (*compar* **-ier**, *superl* **-iest**) *adj* **-1.** [full of steam] **embué(e).** **-2.** *inf* [erotic] **érotique.**

steel [stiːl] ◇ *n* (*U*) **acier** *m*. ◇ *comp* en acier, d'acier. ◇ *vt*: **to ~ o.s. (for)** s'armer de courage (pour).

steel industry *n* **industrie** *f* **sidérurgique, sidérurgie** *f*.

steel wool *n* **paille** *f* de fer.

steelworker ['stiːl,wɜːkə'] *n* **sidérurgiste** *mf*.

steelworks ['stiːlwɜːks] (*pl inv*) *n* **aciérie** *f*.

steely ['stiːlɪ] (*compar* **-ier**, *superl* **-iest**) *adj* **-1.** [steel-coloured] **acier** (*inv*). **-2.** [strong - person] **dur(e)**; [- determination, will] **de fer.**

steep [stiːp] *adj* **-1.** [hill, road] **raide**, **abrupt(e).** **-2.** [increase, decline] **énorme.** **-3.** *inf* [expensive] **excessif(ive).**

steeped [stiːpt] *adj fig*: **~ in** **imprégné(e)** de.

steeple ['stiːpl] *n* **clocher** *m*, **flèche** *f*.

steeplechase ['stiːpltʃeɪs] *n* **-1.** [horse race] **steeple-chase** *m*. **-2.** [athletics race] **steeple** *m*.

steeplejack ['stiːpldʒæk] *n* **réparateur** *m* de cheminées industrielles et de clochers.

steeply ['stiːplɪ] *adv* **-1.** [at steep angle] **en pente raide.** **-2.** [considerably] **en flèche.**

steer ['stɪə'] ◇ *n* **bœuf** *m*. ◇ *vt* **-1.** [ship] **gouverner**; [car, aeroplane] **conduire, diriger.** **-2.** [person] **diriger, guider.** ◇ *vi*: **to ~ well** [ship] **gouverner bien**; [car] **être facile à manœuvrer**; **to ~ clear of sb/sthg** éviter qqn/qqch.

steering ['stɪərɪŋ] *n* (*U*) **direction** *f*.

steering column *n* **colonne** *f* de direction.

steering committee *n* **comité** *m* d'organisation.

steering lock *n* **rayon** *m* de braquage.

steering wheel *n* **volant** *m*.

stellar ['stelə'] *adj* **stellaire.**

stem [stem] (*pt* & *pp* **-med**, *cont* **-ming**) ◇ *n*
-1. [of plant] tige *f*. **-2.** [of glass] pied *m*. **-3.**
[of pipe] tuyau *m*. **-4.** GRAMM radical *m*. ◇ *vt*
[stop] arrêter.
◆ **stem from** *vt fus* provenir de.

stench [stentʃ] *n* puanteur *f*.

stencil ['stensl] (*Br pt* & *pp* **-led**, *cont* **-ling**,
Am pt & *pp* **-ed**, *cont* **-ing**) ◇ *n* pochoir *m*.
◇ *vt* faire au pochoir.

stenographer [stə'nɒgrəfər] *n Am* sténographe *mf*.

stenography [stə'nɒgrəfi] *n Am* sténographie *f*.

step [step] (*pt* & *pp* **-ped**, *cont* **-ping**) ◇ *n*
-1. [pace] pas *m*; **in/out of** ~ **with** *fig* en
accord/désaccord avec; **to watch one's** ~
faire attention où l'on marche; *fig* faire attention à ce que l'on fait. **-2.** [action] mesure *f*. **-3.** [stage] étape *f*; ~ **by** ~ petit à petit, progressivement. **-4.** [stair] marche *f*.
-5. [of ladder] barreau *m*, échelon *m*. **-6.** *Am*
MUS ton *m*.
◇ *vi* **-1.** [move foot]: **to** ~ **forward** avancer;
to ~ **off** OR **down from sthg** descendre de
qqch; **to** ~ **back** reculer. **-2.** [tread]: **to** ~
on/in sthg marcher sur/dans qqch.
◆ **steps** *npl* **-1.** [stairs] marches *fpl*. **-2.** *Br*
[stepladder] escabeau *m*.
◆ **step aside** *vi* **-1.** [move away] s'écarter.
-2. [leave job] démissionner.
◆ **step back** *vi* [pause to reflect] prendre du
recul.
◆ **step down** *vi* [leave job] démissionner.
◆ **step in** *vi* intervenir.
◆ **step up** *vt sep* intensifier.

stepbrother ['step,brʌðər] *n* demi-frère *m*.

stepchild ['steptʃaɪld] (*pl* **-children** [-,tʃɪl-
drən]) *n* beau-fils *m*, belle-fille *f*.

stepdaughter ['step,dɔːtər] *n* belle-fille *f*.

stepfather ['step,fɑːðər] *n* beau-père *m*.

stepladder ['step,lædər] *n* escabeau *m*.

stepmother ['step,mʌðər] *n* belle-mère *f*.

stepping-stone ['stepɪŋ-] *n* pierre *f* de gué;
fig tremplin *m*.

stepsister ['step,sɪstər] *n* demi-sœur *f*.

stepson ['stepsʌn] *n* beau-fils *m*.

stereo ['steriəʊ] (*pl* **-s**) ◇ *adj* stéréo (*inv*). ◇
n **-1.** [appliance] chaîne *f* stéréo. **-2.** [sound]:
in ~ en stéréo.

stereophonic [,steriə'fɒnɪk] *adj* stéréopho-
nique.

stereotype ['steriətaɪp] ◇ *n* stéréotype *m*.
◇ *vt* stéréotyper.

sterile ['steraɪl] *adj* stérile.

sterility [ste'rɪləti] *n* stérilité *f*.

sterilization [,sterəlaɪ'zeɪʃn] *n* stérilisation
f.

sterilize, -ise ['sterəlaɪz] *vt* stériliser.

sterilized milk ['sterəlaɪzd-] *n* lait *m* stérili-
sé.

sterling ['stɜːlɪŋ] ◇ *adj* **-1.** [of British money]
sterling (*inv*). **-2.** [excellent] exception-
nel(elle). ◇ *n* (*U*) livre *f* sterling. ◇ *comp*
[traveller's cheques] en livres sterling.

sterling silver *n* argent *m* fin.

stern [stɜːn] ◇ *adj* sévère. ◇ *n* NAUT arrière
m.

sternly ['stɜːnli] *adv* sévèrement.

steroid ['stɪərɔɪd] *n* stéroïde *m*.

stethoscope ['steθəskəʊp] *n* stéthoscope *m*.

stetson ['stetsn] *n* chapeau *m* de cow-boy.

stevedore ['stiːvədɔːr] *n Am* docker *m*.

stew [stjuː] ◇ *n* ragoût *m*. ◇ *vt* [meat] cuire
en ragoût; [fruit] faire cuire. ◇ *vi*: **to let sb**
~ *fig* laisser mariner qqn.

steward ['stjuəd] *n* **-1.** [on plane, ship, train]
steward *m*. **-2.** *Br* [at demonstration, meeting]
membre *m* du service d'ordre.

stewardess ['stjuədɪs] *n* hôtesse *f*.

stewing steak *Br* ['stjuːɪŋ-], **stewbeef** *Am*
['stjuːbiːf] *n* (*U*) bœuf *m* à braiser.

St. Ex. *abbr of* **stock exchange**.

stg *abbr of* **sterling**.

stick [stɪk] (*pt* & *pp* **stuck**) ◇ *n* **-1.** [of
wood, dynamite, candy] bâton *m*. **-2.** [walking
stick] canne *f*. **-3.** SPORT crosse *f*. **-4.** *phr*: **to
get the wrong end of the** ~ mal compren-
dre.
◇ *vt* **-1.** [push]: **to** ~ **sthg in** OR **into** planter
qqch dans; **to** ~ **sthg through sthg** transpercer qqch avec qqch. **-2.** [with glue, sello-
tape]: **to** ~ **sthg (on** OR **to)** coller qqch (sur).
-3. *inf* [put] mettre. **-4.** *Br inf* [tolerate] supporter; **to** ~ **it** tenir le coup.
◇ *vi* **-1.** [adhere]: **to** ~ **(to)** coller (à). **-2.**
[jam] se coincer. **-3.** [remain]: **to** ~ **in sb's
mind** marquer qqn.
◆ **stick around** *vi inf* rester dans les parages.
◆ **stick at** *vt fus* [activity] persévérer dans;
to ~ **at a job** rester dans un emploi.
◆ **stick by** *vt fus* [statement] s'en tenir à;
[person] ne pas abandonner.
◆ **stick out** ◇ *vt sep* **-1.** [head] sortir;
[hand] lever; [tongue] tirer. **-2.** *inf* [endure]: **to**
~ **it out** tenir le coup. ◇ *vi* **-1.** [protrude]
dépasser. **-2.** *inf* [be noticeable] se remarquer.
◆ **stick out for** *vt fus Br* exiger.
◆ **stick to** *vt fus* **-1.** [follow closely] suivre.

-2. [principles] rester fidèle à; [decision] s'en tenir à; [promise] tenir.

◆ **stick together** *vi* rester ensemble; *fig* se serrer les coudes.

◆ **stick up** ◇ *vt sep* **-1.** [poster, notice] afficher. **-2.** [with gun] attaquer à main armée. ◇ *vi* dépasser.

◆ **stick up for** *vt fus* défendre.

◆ **stick with** *vt fus* **-1.** [decision, choice] s'en tenir à. **-2.** [follow closely] rester avec.

sticker ['stɪkə'] *n* [label] autocollant *m*.

sticking plaster ['stɪkɪŋ-] *n* sparadrap *m*.

stick insect *n* phasme *m*.

stick-in-the-mud *n inf* réac *mf*.

stickleback ['stɪklbæk] *n* épinoche *f*.

stickler ['stɪklə'] *n*: **to be a ~ for** être à cheval sur.

stick-on *adj* autocollant(e), adhésif(ive).

stickpin ['stɪkpɪn] *n Am* épingle *f* de cravate. '

stick shift *n Am* levier *m* de vitesses.

stick-up *n inf* vol *m* à main armée.

sticky ['stɪkɪ] (*compar* **-ier**, *superl* **-iest**) *adj* **-1.** [hands, sweets] poisseux(euse); [label, tape] adhésif(ive). **-2.** *inf* [awkward] délicat(e). **-3.** [humid] humide.

stiff [stɪf] ◇ *adj* **-1.** [rod, paper, material] rigide; [shoes, brush] dur(e); [fabric] raide. **-2.** [door, drawer, window] dur(e) (à ouvrir/fermer); [joint] ankylosé(e); **to have a ~ back** avoir des courbatures dans le dos; **to have a ~ neck** avoir un torticolis. **-3.** [formal] guindé(e). **-4.** [severe - penalty] sévère; [- resistance] tenace; [- competition] serré(e). **-5.** [difficult - task] difficile. **-6.** [drink] bien tassé(e); [wind] fort(e).
◇ *adv inf*: **to be bored ~** s'ennuyer à mourir; **to be frozen/scared ~** mourir de froid/peur.

stiffen ['stɪfn] ◇ *vt* **-1.** [material] raidir; [with starch] empeser. **-2.** [resolve] renforcer. ◇ *vi* **-1.** [body] se raidir; [joints] s'ankyloser. **-2.** [competition, resistance] s'intensifier. **-3.** [wind] devenir plus fort, fraîchir.

stiffener ['stɪfnə'] *n* **-1.** [starch] amidon *m*. **-2.** TECH raidisseur *m*.

stiffness ['stɪfnɪs] *n* (*U*) **-1.** [inflexibility] raideur *f*, rigidité *f*. **-2.** [of body, joint] ankylose *f*. **-3.** [formality] froideur *f*.

stifle ['staɪfl] *vt & vi* étouffer.

stifling ['staɪflɪŋ] *adj* étouffant(e).

stigma ['stɪgmə] *n* **-1.** [disgrace] honte *f*, stigmate *m*. **-2.** BOT stigmate *m*.

stigmatize, -ise ['stɪgmətaɪz] *vt* stigmatiser.

stile [staɪl] *n* échalier *m*.

stiletto heel [stɪ'letəu-] *n Br* talon *m* aiguille.

still [stɪl] ◇ *adv* **-1.** [up to now, up to then] encore, toujours; **I've ~ got £5 left** il me reste encore 5 livres. **-2.** [even now] encore. **-3.** [nevertheless] tout de même. **-4.** (*with comparatives*): **~ bigger/more important** encore plus grand/plus important.
◇ *adj* **-1.** [not moving] immobile.
-2. [calm] calme, tranquille. **-3.** [not windy] sans vent. **-4.** [not fizzy - gen] non gazeux(euse); [- mineral water] plat(e).
◇ *n* **-1.** PHOT photo *f*. **-2.** [for making alcohol] alambic *m*.

stillborn ['stɪlbɔːn] *adj* mort-né(e).

still life (*pl* **-s**) *n* nature *f* morte.

stillness ['stɪlnɪs] *n* [calmness] tranquillité *f*.

stilted ['stɪltɪd] *adj* emprunté(e), qui manque de naturel.

stilts ['stɪlts] *npl* **-1.** [for person] échasses *fpl*. **-2.** [for building] pilotis *mpl*.

stimulant ['stɪmjʊlənt] *n* stimulant *m*.

stimulate ['stɪmjʊleɪt] *vt* stimuler.

stimulating ['stɪmjʊleɪtɪŋ] *adj* stimulant(e).

stimulation [ˌstɪmjʊ'leɪʃn] *n* stimulation *f*.

stimulus ['stɪmjʊləs] (*pl* **-li** [-laɪ]) *n* **-1.** [encouragement] stimulant *m*. **-2.** BIOL & PSYCH stimulus *m*.

sting [stɪŋ] (*pt & pp* **stung**) ◇ *n* **-1.** [by bee] piqûre *f*; [of bee] dard *m*. **-2.** [sharp pain] brûlure *f*; **to take the ~ out of sthg** adoucir OR atténuer qqch. ◇ *vt* **-1.** [gen] piquer. **-2.** [subj: criticism] blesser. ◇ *vi* piquer.

stinging nettle ['stɪŋɪŋ-] *n Br* ortie *f*.

stingray ['stɪŋreɪ] *n* pastenague *f*.

stingy ['stɪndʒɪ] (*compar* **-ier**, *superl* **-iest**) *adj inf* radin(e).

stink [stɪŋk] (*pt* **stank** OR **stunk**, *pp* **stunk**) ◇ *n* puanteur *f*. ◇ *vi* **-1.** [smell] puer, empester. **-2.** *inf fig* [be worthless] ne rien valoir.

stink-bomb *n* boule *f* puante.

stinking ['stɪŋkɪŋ] *inf* ◇ *adj* [cold] gros (grosse); [weather] pourri(e); [place] infect(e). ◇ *adv*: **to be ~ rich** être plein(e) aux as.

stint [stɪnt] ◇ *n* [period of work] part *f* de travail. ◇ *vi*: **to ~ on** lésiner sur.

stipend ['staɪpend] *n* traitement *m*, salaire *m*.

stipulate ['stɪpjʊleɪt] *vt* stipuler.

stipulation [ˌstɪpjʊ'leɪʃn] *n* **-1.** [statement] stipulation *f*. **-2.** [condition] condition *f*.

stir [stɜːr] (*pt & pp* **-red**, *cont* **-ring**) ◇ *n* **-1.** [act of stirring]: **to give sthg a ~** remuer qqch. **-2.** [public excitement] sensation *f*. ◇ *vt* **-1.** [mix] remuer. **-2.** [move gently] agiter.

-3. [move emotionally] émouvoir. **-4.** [move]: **to ~ o.s.** se remuer. ◇ *vi* bouger, remuer.

◆ **stir up** *vt sep* **-1.** [dust] soulever. **-2.** [trouble] provoquer; [resentment, dissatisfaction] susciter; [rumour] faire naître.

stir-fry *vt* faire sauter à feu très vif.

stirring ['stɜːrɪŋ] ◇ *adj* excitant(e), émouvant(e). ◇ *n* [of interest, emotion] éveil *m*.

stirrup ['stɪrəp] *n* étrier *m*.

stitch [stɪtʃ] ◇ *n* **-1.** SEWING point *m*; [in knitting] maille *f*. **-2.** MED point *m* de suture. **-3.** [stomach pain]: **to have a ~** avoir un point de côté. **-4.** *phr*: **to be in ~es** être plié(e) en deux (de rire), se tenir les côtes. ◇ *vt* **-1.** SEWING coudre. **-2.** MED suturer.

stitching ['stɪtʃɪŋ] *n* (*U*) points *mpl*, piqûres *fpl*.

stoat [stəʊt] *n* hermine *f*.

stock [stɒk] ◇ *n* **-1.** [supply] réserve *f*. **-2.** (*U*) COMM stock *m*, réserve *f*; **in ~** en stock; **out of ~** épuisé(e). **-3.** FIN valeurs *fpl*; **~s and shares** titres *mpl*. **-4.** [ancestry] souche *f*. **-5.** CULIN bouillon *m*. **-6.** [livestock] cheptel *m*. **-7.** *phr*: **to take ~ (of)** faire le point (de). ◇ *adj* classique. ◇ *vt* **-1.** COMM vendre, avoir en stock. **-2.** [fill - shelves] garnir; [- lake] empoissonner.

◆ **stock up** *vi*: **to ~ up (with)** faire des provisions (de).

stockade [stɒ'keɪd] *n* palissade *f*.

stockbroker ['stɒk,brəʊkəʳ] *n* agent *m* de change.

stockbroking ['stɒk,brəʊkɪŋ] *n* commerce *m* des valeurs en Bourse.

stockcar ['stɒkkɑːʳ] *n* stock-car *m*.

stock company *n Am* société *f* anonyme par actions.

stock control *n* contrôle *m* des stocks.

stock cube *n Br* bouillon-cube *m*.

stock exchange *n* Bourse *f*.

stockholder ['stɒk,həʊldəʳ] *n Am* actionnaire *mf*.

Stockholm ['stɒkhəʊm] *n* Stockholm.

stocking ['stɒkɪŋ] *n* [for woman] bas *m*.

stock-in-trade *n* rudiments *mpl* du métier.

stockist ['stɒkɪst] *n Br* dépositaire *m*, stockiste *m*.

stock market *n* Bourse *f*.

stock phrase *n* cliché *m*.

stockpile ['stɒkpaɪl] ◇ *n* stock *m*. ◇ *vt* [weapons] amasser; [food] stocker.

stockroom ['stɒkrʊm] *n* réserve *f*.

stock-still *adv* sans bouger.

stocktaking ['stɒk,teɪkɪŋ] *n* (*U*) inventaire *m*.

stocky ['stɒkɪ] (*compar* **-ier**, *superl* **-iest**) *adj* trapu(e).

stodgy ['stɒdʒɪ] (*compar* **-ier**, *superl* **-iest**) *adj* **-1.** [food] lourd(e) (à digérer). **-2.** *pej* [book] indigeste.

stoic ['stəʊɪk] ◇ *adj* stoïque. ◇ *n* stoïque *mf*.

stoical ['stəʊɪkl] *adj* stoïque.

stoicism ['stəʊɪsɪzm] *n* stoïcisme *m*.

stoke [stəʊk] *vt* [fire] entretenir.

stole [stəʊl] ◇ *pt* → **steal**. ◇ *n* étole *f*.

stolen ['stəʊln] *pp* → **steal**.

stolid ['stɒlɪd] *adj* impassible.

stomach ['stʌmək] ◇ *n* [organ] estomac *m*; [abdomen] ventre *m*. ◇ *vt* [tolerate] encaisser, supporter.

stomachache ['stʌməkeɪk] *n* mal *m* de ventre, douleurs *fpl* d'estomac.

stomach pump *n* pompe *f* stomacale.

stomach ulcer *n* ulcère *m* de l'estomac.

stomach upset *n* embarras *m* gastrique.

stomp [stɒmp] *vi*: **to ~ in/out** entrer/sortir d'un pas bruyant, entrer/sortir d'un pas lourd.

stone [stəʊn] (*pl sense 3 only inv* OR **-s**) ◇ *n* **-1.** [rock] pierre *f*; [smaller] caillou *m*; **a ~'s throw from** à deux pas de. **-2.** [seed] noyau *m*. **-3.** *Br* [unit of measurement] = 6,348 *kg*. ◇ *comp* de OR en pierre. ◇ *vt* [person, car etc] jeter des pierres sur.

Stone Age *n*: **the ~** l'âge *m* de pierre.

stone-cold *adj* complètement froid(e) OR glacé(e).

stoned [stəʊnd] *adj inf* **-1.** *drugs sl* défoncé(e). **-2.** [drunk] soûl(e), bourré(e).

stonemason ['stəʊn,meɪsn] *n* tailleur *m* de pierre OR pierres.

stonewall [,stəʊn'wɔːl] *vi* être évasif(ive).

stoneware ['stəʊnweəʳ] *n* poterie *f* en grès.

stonewashed ['stəʊnwɒʃt] *adj* délavé(e).

stonework ['stəʊnwɜːk] *n* maçonnerie *f*.

stony ['stəʊnɪ] (*compar* **-ier**, *superl* **-iest**) *adj* **-1.** [ground] pierreux(euse). **-2.** [unfriendly] froid(e).

stood [stʊd] *pt & pp* → **stand**.

stooge [stuːdʒ] *n* [in comedy act] comparse *m*; *fig* pantin *m*, fantoche *m*.

stool [stuːl] *n* [seat] tabouret *m*.

stoop [stuːp] ◇ *n* **-1.** [bent back]: **to walk with a ~** marcher le dos voûté. **-2.** *Am* [of house] porche *m*. ◇ *vi* **-1.** [bend down] se pencher. **-2.** [hunch shoulders] être voûté(e).

-3. *fig* [debase oneself]: **to ~ to doing sthg** s'abaisser jusqu'à faire qqch.

stop [stɒp] (*pt* & *pp* **-ped,** *cont* **-ping**) ◇ *n*
-1. [gen] arrêt *m*; **to come to a ~** [car, train etc] s'arrêter; [production, growth] cesser; **to put a ~ to sthg** mettre un terme à qqch.
-2. [full stop] point *m*.
◇ *vt* **-1.** [gen] arrêter; [end] mettre fin à; **to ~ doing sthg** arrêter de faire qqch; **to ~ work** arrêter de travailler, cesser le travail.
-2. [prevent]: **to ~ sb/sthg (from doing sthg)** empêcher qqn/qqch (de faire qqch). **-3.** [wages] retenir; [cheque] faire opposition à. **-4.** [block] boucher.
◇ *vi* s'arrêter, cesser; **to ~ at nothing (to do sthg)** ne reculer devant rien (pour faire qqch).
◆ **stop off** *vi* s'arrêter, faire halte.
◆ **stop over** *vi* s'arrêter un jour/quelques jours.
◆ **stop up** ◇ *vt sep* [block] boucher. ◇ *vi* *Br* veiller.

stopcock ['stɒpkɒk] *n* robinet *m* d'arrêt.

stopgap ['stɒpgæp] *n* bouche-trou *m*.

stopover ['stɒp,əʊvər] *n* halte *f*.

stoppage ['stɒpɪdʒ] *n* **-1.** [strike] grève *f*. **-2.** *Br* [deduction] retenue *f*.

stopper ['stɒpər] *n* bouchon *m*.

stopping ['stɒpɪŋ] *adj* *Br*: **~ train** train *m* omnibus.

stop press *n* nouvelles *fpl* de dernière heure.

stopwatch ['stɒpwɒtʃ] *n* chronomètre *m*.

storage ['stɔːrɪdʒ] *n* **-1.** [of goods] entreposage *m*, emmagasinage *m*; [of household objects] rangement *m*. **-2.** COMPUT stockage *m*, mémorisation *f*.

storage heater *n* *Br* radiateur *m* à accumulation.

store [stɔːr] ◇ *n* **-1.** [shop] magasin *m*. **-2.** [supply] provision *f*. **-3.** [place of storage] réserve *f*. **-4.** *phr*: **to set great ~ by** OR **on** accorder OR attacher beaucoup d'importance à, faire grand cas de. ◇ *vt* **-1.** [save] mettre en réserve; [goods] entreposer, emmagasiner. **-2.** COMPUT stocker, mémoriser.
◆ **in store** *adv*: **who knows what the future holds in ~?** qui sait ce que nous réserve l'avenir?; **there's a shock in ~ for him** un choc l'attend.
◆ **store up** *vt sep* [provisions] mettre en réserve; [goods] emmagasiner; [information] mettre en mémoire, noter.

store detective *n* surveillant *m*, -e *f* de magasin.

storehouse ['stɔːhaʊs, *pl* -haʊzɪz] *n* entrepôt *m*; *fig* mine *f*.

storekeeper ['stɔː,kiːpər] *n* *Am* commerçant *m*, -e *f*.

storeroom ['stɔːrʊm] *n* magasin *m*.

storey *Br* (*pl* **storeys**), **story** *Am* (*pl* **-ies**) ['stɔːrɪ] *n* étage *m*.

stork [stɔːk] *n* cigogne *f*.

storm [stɔːm] ◇ *n* **-1.** [bad weather] orage *m*; **a ~ in a teacup** une tempête dans un verre d'eau. **-2.** *fig* [of abuse] torrent *m*; [of applause] tempête *f*. ◇ *vt* MIL prendre d'assaut. ◇ *vi* **-1.** [go angrily]: **to ~ in/out** entrer/sortir comme un ouragan. **-2.** [speak angrily] fulminer.

storm cloud *n* nuage *m* orageux.

storming ['stɔːmɪŋ] *n* prise *f* d'assaut.

stormy ['stɔːmɪ] (*compar* **-ier,** *superl* **-iest**) *adj* *lit* & *fig* orageux(euse).

story ['stɔːrɪ] (*pl* **-ies**) *n* **-1.** [gen] histoire *f*; **it's the (same) old ~** c'est toujours la même histoire, c'est toujours pareil; **to cut a long ~ short** bref. **-2.** PRESS article *m*; RADIO & TV nouvelle *f*. **-3.** *Am* = **storey**.

storybook ['stɔːrɪbʊk] *adj* [romance etc] de conte de fées.

storyteller ['stɔːrɪ,telər] *n* **-1.** [narrator] conteur *m*, -euse *f*. **-2.** *euphemism* [liar] menteur *m*, -euse *f*.

stout [staʊt] ◇ *adj* **-1.** [rather fat] corpulent(e). **-2.** [strong] solide. **-3.** [resolute] ferme, résolu(e). ◇ *n* (*U*) stout *m*, bière *f* brune.

stoutness ['staʊtnɪs] *n* [fatness] corpulence *f*.

stove [stəʊv] ◇ *pt* & *pp* → **stave.** ◇ *n* [for cooking] cuisinière *f*; [for heating] poêle *m*.

stow [stəʊ] *vt*: **to ~ sthg (away)** ranger qqch.
◆ **stow away** *vi* embarquer clandestinement.

stowaway ['stəʊəweɪ] *n* passager *m* clandestin.

straddle ['strædl] *vt* enjamber; [chair] s'asseoir à califourchon sur.

strafe [strɑːf] *vt* MIL mitrailler.

straggle ['strægl] *vi* **-1.** [buildings] s'étendre, s'étaler; [hair] être en désordre. **-2.** [person] traîner, lambiner.

straggler ['stræglər] *n* traînard *m*, -e *f*.

straggly ['strægli] (*compar* **-ier,** *superl* **-iest**) *adj* [hair] en désordre.

straight [streɪt] ◇ *adj* **-1.** [not bent] droit(e); [hair] raide. **-2.** [frank] franc (franche), honnête. **-3.** [tidy] en ordre. **-4.** [choice, exchange] simple. **-5.** [alcoholic drink] sec, sans eau. **-6.** *inf* [conventional] normal(e). **-7.** *gay sl* hétéro (*inv*). **-8.** *phr*: **let's get this ~** entendons-nous bien.

◇ *adv* **-1.** [in a straight line] **droit. -2.** [directly, immediately] **droit, tout de suite. -3.** [frankly] **carrément, franchement. -4.** [undiluted] **sec, sans eau. -5.** *phr:* **to go ~** [criminal] **rester dans le droit chemin.**
◇ *n* SPORT: **the ~ la ligne droite.**
◆ **straight off** *adv* **tout de suite, sur-le-champ.**
◆ **straight out** *adv* **sans mâcher ses mots.**

straightaway [ˌstreɪtəˈweɪ] *adv* **tout de suite, immédiatement.**

straighten ['streɪtn] ◇ *vt* **-1.** [tidy - hair, dress] **arranger;** [- room] **mettre de l'ordre dans. -2.** [make straight - horizontally] **rendre droit(e);** [- vertically] **redresser.** ◇ *vi* [person]: **to ~ (up) se redresser.**
◆ **straighten out** *vt sep* [problem] **résoudre; to ~ things out arranger les choses.**

straight face *n:* **to keep a ~ garder son sérieux.**

straightforward [ˌstreɪtˈfɔːwəd] *adj* **-1.** [easy] **simple. -2.** [frank] **honnête, franc (franche).**

strain [streɪn] ◇ *n* **-1.** [mental] **tension** *f,* **stress** *m.* **-2.** MED **foulure** *f;* **back ~ tour** *m* **de reins. -3.** TECH **contrainte** *f,* **effort** *m.* **-4.** [type - of plant] **variété** *f;* [- of virus] **souche** *f.*
◇ *vt* **-1.** [work hard - eyes] **plisser fort; to ~ one's ears tendre l'oreille. -2.** [MED - muscle] **se froisser;** [- eyes] **se fatiguer; to ~ one's back se faire un tour de reins. -3.** [patience] **mettre à rude épreuve;** [budget] **grever. -4.** [drain] **passer. -5.** TECH **exercer une contrainte sur.**
◇ *vi* [try very hard]: **to ~ to do sthg faire un gros effort pour faire qqch, se donner du mal pour faire qqch.**
◆ **strains** *npl* [of music] **accords** *mpl,* **airs** *mpl.*

strained [streɪnd] *adj* **-1.** [worried] **contracté(e), tendu(e). -2.** [relations, relationship] **tendu(e). -3.** [unnatural] **forcé(e).**

strainer ['streɪnə'] *n* **passoire** *f.*

strait [streɪt] *n* **détroit** *m.*
◆ **straits** *npl:* **in dire** OR **desperate ~s dans une situation désespérée.**

straitened ['streɪtnd] *adj fml:* **in ~ circumstances dans la gêne, dans le besoin.**

straitjacket ['streɪtˌdʒækɪt] *n* **camisole** *f* **de force.**

straitlaced [ˌstreɪtˈleɪst] *adj* **collet monté** *(inv).*

Strait of Gibraltar *n:* **the ~ le détroit de Gibraltar.**

Strait of Hormuz *n:* **the ~ le détroit d'Hormuz** OR **Ormuz.**

strand [strænd] *n* **-1.** [of cotton, wool] **brin** *m,* **fil** *m;* [of hair] **mèche** *f.* **-2.** [theme] **fil** *m.*

stranded ['strændɪd] *adj* [boat] **échoué(e);** [people] **abandonné(e), en rade.**

strange [streɪndʒ] *adj* **-1.** [odd] **étrange, bizarre. -2.** [unfamiliar] **inconnu(e).**

strangely ['streɪndʒlɪ] *adv* **étrangement, bizarrement; ~ (enough) chose curieuse.**

stranger ['streɪndʒə'] *n* **-1.** [unfamiliar person] **inconnu** *m,* **-e** *f;* **to be a ~ to sthg ne pas connaître qqch; to be no ~ to sthg bien connaître qqch. -2.** [from another place] **étranger** *m,* **-ère** *f.*

strangle ['stræŋgl] *vt* **étrangler;** *fig* **étouffer.**

stranglehold ['stræŋglhəʊld] *n* **-1.** [round neck] **étranglement** *m.* **-2.** *fig* [control]: **~ (on) domination** *f* **(de).**

strangulation [ˌstræŋgjʊˈleɪʃn] *n* **strangulation** *f.*

strap [stræp] *(pt & pp* **-ped,** *cont* **-ping)** ◇ *n* [for fastening] **sangle** *f,* **courroie** *f;* [of bag] **bandoulière** *f;* [of rifle, dress, bra] **bretelle** *f;* [of watch] **bracelet** *m.* ◇ *vt* [fasten] **attacher.**

strapless ['stræplɪs] *adj* **sans bretelles.**

strapping ['stræpɪŋ] *adj* **bien bâti(e), robuste.**

Strasbourg ['stræzbɜːg] *n* **Strasbourg.**

strata ['strɑːtə] *pl* **→ stratum.**

stratagem ['strætədʒəm] *n* **stratagème** *m.*

strategic [strəˈtiːdʒɪk] *adj* **stratégique.**

strategist ['strætɪdʒɪst] *n* **stratège** *m.*

strategy ['strætɪdʒɪ] *(pl* **-ies)** *n* **stratégie** *f.*

stratified ['strætɪfaɪd] *adj* **-1.** GEOL **stratifié(e). -2.** *fig* [society] **divisé(e) en différentes couches sociales.**

stratosphere ['strætəˌsfɪə'] *n:* **the ~ la stratosphère.**

stratum ['strɑːtəm] *(pl* **-ta)** *n* **-1.** GEOL **strate** *f,* **couche** *f.* **-2.** *fig* [of society] **couche** *f.*

straw [strɔː] ◇ *n* **-1.** [gen] **paille** *f;* **to clutch at ~s se raccrocher à n'importe quoi; the last ~ la goutte qui fait déborder le vase; that's the last ~! ça c'est le comble!** ◇ *comp* **de** OR **en paille.**

strawberry ['strɔːbərɪ] *(pl* **-ies)** ◇ *n* [fruit] **fraise** *f.* ◇ *comp* [tart, yoghurt] **aux fraises;** [jam] **de fraises.**

straw poll *n* **sondage** *m* **d'opinion.**

stray [streɪ] ◇ *adj* **-1.** [animal] **errant(e), perdu(e). -2.** [bullet] **perdu(e);** [example] **isolé(e).** ◇ *n* [animal] **animal** *m* **errant.** ◇ *vi* **-1.** [person, animal] **errer, s'égarer. -2.** [thoughts] **vagabonder, errer.**

streak [striːk] *n* **-1.** [line] **bande** *f,* **marque** *f;* **~ of lightning éclair** *m.* **-2.** [in character] **côté** *m;* **a ~ of cruelty une propension à**

la cruauté. **-3.** [period]: **a winning/losing** ~ une période de succès/d'échecs, une série de succès/d'échecs. ◇ *vi* [move quickly] se déplacer comme un éclair.

streaked [striːkt] *adj* [marked]: **to be** ~ **with** être maculé(e) de, porter des traces de.

streaky ['striːkɪ] (*compar* **-ier**, *superl* **-iest**) *adj* [paint] qui n'est pas uniforme; [surface] couvert(e) de traces.

streaky bacon *n Br* bacon *m* assez gras.

stream [striːm] ◇ *n* **-1.** [small river] ruisseau *m*. **-2.** [of liquid, gas, light] flot *m*, jet *m*. **-3.** [of people, cars] flot *m*; [of complaints, abuse] torrent *m*. **-4.** *Br* SCH classe *f* de niveau. ◇ *vi* **-1.** [liquid, gas] couler à flots, ruisseler; [light] entrer à flots. **-2.** [people, cars] affluer; **to** ~ **past** passer à flots. ◇ *Br* SCH répartir par niveau.

streamer ['striːməʳ] *n* [for party] serpentin *m*.

streamline ['striːmlaɪn] *vt* **-1.** [make aerodynamic] caréner, donner un profil aérodynamique à. **-2.** [make efficient] rationaliser.

streamlined ['striːmlaɪnd] *adj* **-1.** [aerodynamic] au profil aérodynamique. **-2.** [efficient] rationalisé(e).

street [striːt] *n* rue *f*; **it's right up his** ~ *Br inf* c'est son rayon; **to be** ~**s ahead of sb** *Br* devancer OR dépasser qqn de loin.

streetcar ['striːtkɑːʳ] *n Am* tramway *m*.

street-credibility *n* (*U*) *inf* image *f* (de marque).

street lamp, **street light** *n* réverbère *m*.

street lighting *n* éclairage *m* des rues.

street map *n* plan *m*.

street market *n* marché *m* en plein air.

street plan *n* plan *m*.

street value *n* [of drugs] valeur *f* à la revente.

streetwise ['striːtwaɪz] *adj inf* averti(e), futé(e).

strength [streŋθ] *n* **-1.** [gen] force *f*; **on the** ~ **of** [evidence] sur la foi de; [advice] en s'appuyant sur, en vertu de. **-2.** [power, influence] puissance *f*; **to go from** ~ **to** ~ connaître un succès de plus en plus éclatant, prospérer. **-3.** [solidity, of currency] solidité *f*. **-4.** [number] effectif *m*; **in** ~ en force, en grand nombre; **at full** ~ au (grand) complet; **to be below** ~ avoir un effectif insuffisant.

strengthen ['streŋθn] ◇ *vt* **-1.** [structure, team, argument] renforcer. **-2.** [economy, currency, friendship] consolider. **-3.** [resolve, dislike] fortifier, affermir. **-4.** [person] enhardir. ◇ *vi* **-1.** [sales, economy] s'améliorer. **-2.**

[opposition] s'affermir, se renforcer. **-3.** [friendship] se cimenter, se consolider. **-4.** [currency] se raffermir.

strenuous ['strenjʊəs] *adj* [exercise, activity] fatigant(e), dur(e); [effort] vigoureux(euse), acharné(e).

stress [stres] ◇ *n* **-1.** [emphasis]: ~ **(on)** accent *m* (sur). **-2.** [mental] stress *m*, tension *f*; **to be under** ~ être stressé(e). **-3.** TECH: ~ **(on)** contrainte *f* (sur), effort *m* (sur). **-4.** LING accent *m*. ◇ *vt* **-1.** [emphasize] souligner, insister sur. **-2.** LING accentuer.

stressed [strest] *adj* [tense] stressé(e).

stressful ['stresfʊl] *adj* stressant(e).

stretch [stretʃ] ◇ *n* **-1.** [of land, water] étendue *f*; [of road, river] partie *f*, section *f*. **-2.** [of time] période *f*. **-3.** [effort]: **by no** ~ **of the imagination** même avec beaucoup d'imagination.
◇ *vt* **-1.** [arms] allonger; [legs] se dégourdir; [muscles] distendre. **-2.** [pull taut] tendre, étirer. **-3.** [overwork - person] surmener; [- resources, budget] grever. **-4.** [challenge]: **to** ~ **sb** pousser qqn à la limite de ses capacités. ◇ *vi* **-1.** [area]: **to** ~ **over** s'étendre sur; **to** ~ **from ... to** s'étendre de ... à. **-2.** [person, animal] s'étirer. **-3.** [material, elastic] se tendre, s'étirer.
◇ *adj* extensible.

◆ **at a stretch** *adv* d'affilée, sans interruption.

◆ **stretch out** ◇ *vt sep* [arm, leg, hand] tendre. ◇ *vi* [lie down] s'étendre, s'allonger.

stretcher ['stretʃəʳ] *n* brancard *m*, civière *f*.

stretcher party *n* équipe *f* de brancardiers.

stretchmarks ['stretʃmɑːks] *npl* vergetures *fpl*.

stretchy ['stretʃɪ] (*compar* **-ier**, *superl* **-iest**) *adj* extensible, élastique.

strew [struː] (*pt* **-ed**, *pp* **strewn** [struːn] OR **-ed**) *vt*: **to be strewn on** OR **over** être éparpillé(e) sur; **to be strewn with** être jonché(e) de.

stricken ['strɪkn] *adj*: **to be** ~ **by** OR **with panic** être pris(e) de panique; **to be** ~ **by an illness** souffrir OR être atteint(e) d'une maladie.

strict [strɪkt] *adj* **-1.** [gen] strict(e). **-2.** [faithful]: **she's a** ~ **Catholic** elle observe rigoureusement la foi catholique.

strictly ['strɪktlɪ] *adv* **-1.** [gen] strictement; ~ **speaking** à proprement parler. **-2.** [severely] d'une manière stricte, sévèrement.

strictness ['strɪktnɪs] *n* sévérité *f*.

stride [straɪd] (*pt* **strode**, *pp* **stridden** ['strɪdn]) ◇ *n* **-1.** [long step] grand pas *m*, enjambée f. **-2.** phr: **to take sthg in one's ~** ne pas se laisser démonter par qqch. ◇ vi marcher à grandes enjambées OR à grands pas.

◆ **strides** npl [progress]: **to make (great) ~s** faire des progrès rapides.

strident ['straɪdnt] adj **-1.** [voice, sound] strident(e). **-2.** [demand, attack] véhément(e), bruyant(e).

strife [straɪf] n (U) conflit m, lutte f.

strike [straɪk] (pt & pp **struck**) ◇ n **-1.** [by workers] grève f; **to be (out) on ~** être en grève; **to go on ~** faire grève, se mettre en grève. **-2.** MIL raid m. **-3.** [of oil, gold] découverte f.
◇ comp de grève.
◇ vt **-1.** [hit - deliberately] frapper; [- accidentally] heurter. **-2.** [subj: thought] venir à l'esprit de; **she ~s me as (being) very capable** elle me fait l'impression d'être très capable, elle me paraît très capable. **-3.** [impress]: **to be struck by** OR **with** être frappé(e) par. **-4.** [conclude - deal, bargain] conclure. **-5.** [light - match] frotter. **-6.** [find] découvrir, trouver; **to ~ a balance (between)** trouver le juste milieu (entre); **to ~ a serious/happy etc note** adopter un ton sérieux/gai etc. **-7.** phr: **to be struck blind** être frappé(e) de cécité, devenir aveugle; **to be struck dumb** rester muet; **to ~ fear** OR **terror into sb** frapper qqn de terreur; **to ~ (it) lucky** avoir de la veine; **to ~ it rich** trouver le filon.
◇ vi **-1.** [workers] faire grève. **-2.** [hit] frapper. **-3.** [attack] attaquer. **-4.** [chime] sonner.

◆ **strike back** vi se venger, exercer des représailles.

◆ **strike down** vt sep terrasser.

◆ **strike off** vt sep: **to be struck off** être radié(e) OR rayé(e).

◆ **strike out** ◇ vt sep rayer, barrer. ◇ vi [head out] se mettre en route, partir; **to ~ out on one's own** [in business] se mettre à son compte.

◆ **strike up** ◇ vt fus **-1.** [conversation] commencer, engager; **to ~ up a friendship (with)** se lier d'amitié (avec). **-2.** [music] commencer à jouer. ◇ vi commencer à jouer.

strikebound ['straɪkbaʊnd] adj paralysé(e) par la grève.

strikebreaker ['straɪk,breɪkər] n briseur m de grève.

strike pay n (U) allocation f de grève, allocation-gréviste f.

striker ['straɪkər] n **-1.** [person on strike] gréviste mf. **-2.** FTBL buteur m.

striking ['straɪkɪŋ] adj **-1.** [noticeable] frappant(e), saisissant(e). **-2.** [attractive] d'une beauté frappante.

striking distance n: **to be within ~ (of)** être à deux pas (de); **to be within ~ of doing sthg** fig être à deux doigts de faire qqch.

string [strɪŋ] (pt & pp **strung**) ◇ n **-1.** (U) [thin rope] ficelle f; [piece of thin rope] bout m de ficelle; **(with) no ~s attached** sans conditions; **to pull ~s** faire jouer le piston. **-3.** [of beads, pearls] rang m. **-4.** [series] série f, suite f. **-5.** [of musical instrument] corde f. ◇ comp: **~ vest** tricot m de peau à grosses mailles; **~ bag** filet m à provisions.

◆ **strings** npl MUS: **the ~s** les cordes fpl.

◆ **string along** vt sep inf [deceive] faire marcher, tromper.

◆ **string out** vt fus échelonner.

◆ **string together** vt sep fig aligner.

◆ **string up** vt sep inf [kill by hanging] pendre.

string bean n haricot m vert.

stringed instrument ['strɪŋd-] n instrument m à cordes.

stringent ['strɪndʒənt] adj strict(e), rigoureux(euse).

string quartet n quatuor m à cordes.

strip [strɪp] (pt & pp **-ped**, cont **-ping**) ◇ n **-1.** [narrow piece] bande f; **to tear a ~ off sb, to tear sb off a ~** Br passer un bon savon à qqn, sonner les cloches à qqn. **-2.** Br SPORT tenue f. ◇ vt **-1.** [undress] déshabiller, dévêtir. **-2.** [paint, wallpaper] enlever. **-3.** [take away from]: **to ~ sb of sthg** dépouiller qqn de qqch. ◇ vi **-1.** [undress] se déshabiller, se dévêtir. **-2.** [do a striptease] faire du strip-tease.

◆ **strip off** ◇ vt sep enlever, ôter. ◇ vi se déshabiller, se dévêtir.

strip cartoon n Br bande f dessinée.

stripe [straɪp] n **-1.** [band of colour] rayure f. **-2.** [sign of rank] galon m.

striped [straɪpt] adj à rayures, rayé(e).

strip lighting n éclairage m au néon.

stripper ['strɪpər] n **-1.** [performer of striptease] strip-teaseuse f, effeuilleuse f. **-2.** [for paint] décapant m.

strip-search ◇ n fouille f d'une personne dévêtue. ◇ vt: **to ~ sb** obliger qqn à se déshabiller pour le fouiller.

strip show n (spectacle m de) strip-tease m.

striptease ['striptiːz] n strip-tease m.

stripy ['straɪpɪ] (compar **-ier**, superl **-iest**) adj à rayures, rayé(e).

strive [straɪv] (*pt* **strove**, *pp* **striven** ['strɪvn]) *vi*: to ~ **for sthg** essayer d'obtenir qqch; to ~ **to do sthg** s'efforcer de faire qqch.

strobe (light) ['strəʊb-] *n* lumière *f* stroboscopique.

strode [strəʊd] *pt* → **stride**.

stroke [strəʊk] ◇ *n* -**1.** MED attaque *f* cérébrale. -**2.** [of pen, brush] trait *m*. -**3.** [in swimming - movement] mouvement *m* des bras; [- style] nage *f*; [in rowing] coup *m* d'aviron; [in golf, tennis etc] coup *m*. -**4.** [of clock]: **on the third** ~ ≃ au quatrième top; **at the** ~ **of 12** sur le coup de minuit. -**5.** *Br* TYPO [oblique] barre *f*. -**6.** [piece]: **a** ~ **of genius** un trait de génie; **a** ~ **of luck** un coup de chance OR de veine; **not to do a** ~ **of work** ne pas en ficher une datte OR rame, ne rien faire; **at a** ~ d'un seul coup. ◇ *vt* caresser.

stroll [strəʊl] ◇ *n* petite promenade *f*, petit tour *m*. ◇ *vi* se promener sans hâte, flâner.

stroller ['strəʊlər] *n Am* [for baby] poussette *f*.

strong [strɒŋ] *adj* -**1.** [gen] fort(e); **to be** ~ **at sthg** être fort en qqch; ~ **point** fort *m*. -**2.** [structure, argument, friendship] solide. -**3.** [healthy] robuste, vigoureux(euse); **to be still going** ~ [person, group] être toujours d'attaque, être solide au poste; [machine] marcher toujours bien. -**4.** [policy, measures] énergique. -**5.** [in numbers]: **the crowd was 2,000** ~ la foule était au nombre de 2000. -**6.** [team, candidate] sérieux(ieuse), qui a des chances de gagner.

strongarm ['strɒŋɑːm] *adj*: ~ **tactics** la méthode forte.

strongbox ['strɒŋbɒks] *n* coffre-fort *m*.

stronghold ['strɒŋhəʊld] *n fig* bastion *m*.

strong language *n* (*U*) *euphemism* grossièretés *fpl*.

strongly ['strɒŋlɪ] *adv* -**1.** [gen] fortement. -**2.** [solidly] solidement.

strong man *n* [in circus] homme *m* fort, hercule *m*.

strong-minded [-'maɪndɪd] *adj* résolu(e).

strong room *n* chambre *f* forte.

strong-willed [-'wɪld] *adj* têtu(e), volontaire.

stroppy ['strɒpɪ] (*compar* -**ier**, *superl* -**iest**) *adj Br inf* difficile.

strove [strəʊv] *pt* → **strive**.

struck [strʌk] *pt & pp* → **strike**.

structural ['strʌktʃərəl] *adj* de construction.

structurally ['strʌktʃərəlɪ] *adv* du point de vue de la construction.

structure ['strʌktʃər] ◇ *n* -**1.** [organization] structure *f*. -**2.** [building] construction *f*. ◇ *vt* structurer.

struggle ['strʌgl] ◇ *n* -**1.** [great effort]: ~ **(for sthg/to do sthg)** lutte *f* (pour qqch/pour faire qqch). -**2.** [fight] bagarre *f*. ◇ *vi* -**1.** [make great effort]: **to** ~ **(for)** lutter (pour); **to** ~ **to do sthg** s'efforcer de faire qqch. -**2.** [to free oneself] se débattre; [fight] se battre. -**3.** [move with difficulty]: **to** ~ **to one's feet** se lever avec difficulté.

♦ **struggle on** *vi*: **to** ~ **on (with)** persévérer (dans).

struggling ['strʌglɪŋ] *adj* qui a du mal OR des difficultés.

strum [strʌm] (*pt & pp* -**med**, *cont* -**ming**) *vt* [guitar] gratter de; [tune] jouer.

strung [strʌŋ] *pt & pp* → **string**.

strut [strʌt] (*pt & pp* -**ted**, *cont* -**ting**) ◇ *n* -**1.** CONSTR étai *m*, support *m*. -**2.** AERON pilier *m*. ◇ *vi* se pavaner.

strychnine ['strɪkniːn] *n* strychnine *f*.

stub [stʌb] (*pt & pp* -**bed**, *cont* -**bing**) ◇ *n* -**1.** [of cigarette] mégot *m*; [of pencil] morceau *m*. -**2.** [of ticket, cheque] talon *m*. ◇ *vt*: **to** ~ **one's toe** se cogner le doigt de pied.

♦ **stub out** *vt sep* écraser.

stubble ['stʌbl] *n* (*U*) -**1.** [in field] chaume *m*. -**2.** [on chin] barbe *f* de plusieurs jours.

stubborn ['stʌbən] *adj* -**1.** [person] têtu(e), obstiné(e). -**2.** [stain] qui ne veut pas partir, rebelle.

stubbornly ['stʌbənlɪ] *adv* obstinément.

stubby ['stʌbɪ] (*compar* -**ier**, *superl* -**iest**) *adj* boudiné(e).

stucco ['stʌkəʊ] *n* stuc *m*.

stuck [stʌk] ◇ *pt & pp* → **stick**. ◇ *adj* -**1.** [jammed, trapped] coincé(e). -**2.** [stumped]: **to be** ~ sécher. -**3.** [stranded] bloqué(e), en rade.

stuck-up *adj inf pej* bêcheur(euse).

stud [stʌd] *n* -**1.** [metal decoration] clou *m* décoratif. -**2.** [earring] clou *m* d'oreille. -**3.** *Br* [on boot, shoe] clou *m*; [on sports boots] crampon *m*. -**4.** [of horses] haras *m*; **to be put out to** ~ être utilisé comme étalon.

studded ['stʌdɪd] *adj*: ~ **(with)** parsemé(e) (de), constellé(e) (de).

student ['stjuːdnt] ◇ *n* étudiant *m*, -e *f*. ◇ *comp* [life] estudiantin(e); [politics] des étudiants; [disco] pour étudiants; ~ **nurse** élève-infirmière *f*; ~ **teacher** professeur *m* stagiaire.

students' union *n* -**1.** [organization] union *f* des étudiants. -**2.** [building] club *m* (des étudiants).

stud farm *n* haras *m.*

studied ['stʌdɪd] *adj* étudié(e), calculé(e).

studio ['stjuːdɪəu] (*pl* **-s**) *n* studio *m*; [of artist] atelier *m.*

studio apartment *n Am* = **studio flat.**

studio audience *n* public *m* invité.

studio flat *Br*, **studio apartment** *Am n* studio *m.*

studious ['stjuːdjəs] *adj* studieux(ieuse).

studiously ['stjuːdjəslɪ] *adv* studieusement.

study ['stʌdɪ] (*pl* **-ies**, *pt & pp* **-ied**) ◇ *n* **-1.** [gen] étude *f.* **-2.** [room] bureau *m.* ◇ *vt* **-1.** [learn] étudier, faire des études de. **-2.** [examine] examiner, étudier. ◇ *vi* étudier, faire ses études.

stuff [stʌf] ◇ *n* (*U*) **-1.** *inf* [things] choses *fpl*; **and all that** ~ et tout ça; **to know one's** ~ **s**'y connaître. **-2.** [substance] substance *f.* **-3.** *inf* [belongings] affaires *fpl.* ◇ *vt* **-1.** [push] fourrer. **-2.** [fill]: **to** ~ **sthg (with)** remplir OR bourrer qqch (de). **-3.** *inf* [with food]: **to** ~ **o.s. (with** OR **on)** se gaver (de), s'empiffrer (de). **-4.** CULIN farcir.

stuffed [stʌft] *adj* **-1.** [filled]: ~ **with** bourré(e) de. **-2.** *inf* [with food] gavé(e). **-3.** CULIN farci(e). **-4.** [preserved - animal] empaillé(e). **-5.** *phr*: **get** ~! *Br inf* va te faire foutre!

stuffing ['stʌfɪŋ] *n* (*U*) **-1.** [filling] bourre *f,* rembourrage *m.* **-2.** CULIN farce *f.*

stuffy ['stʌfɪ] (*compar* **-ier**, *superl* **-iest**) *adj* **-1.** [room] mal aéré(e), qui manque d'air. **-2.** [person, club] vieux jeu (*inv*).

stumble ['stʌmbl] *vi* trébucher.

◆ **stumble across, stumble on** *vt fus* tomber sur.

stumbling block ['stʌmblɪŋ-] *n* pierre *f* d'achoppement.

stump [stʌmp] ◇ *n* [of tree] souche *f*; [of arm, leg] moignon *m.* ◇ *vt* [subj: question, problem] dérouter, rendre perplexe. ◇ *vi*: **to** ~ **in/out** entrer/sortir à pas lourds.

◆ **stumps** *npl* CRICKET piquets *mpl.*

◆ **stump up** *vt fus Br inf* cracher, payer.

stun [stʌn] (*pt & pp* **-ned**, *cont* **-ning**) *vt* **-1.** [knock unconscious] étourdir, assommer. **-2.** [surprise] stupéfier, renverser.

stung [stʌŋ] *pt & pp* → **sting.**

stun grenade *n* grenade *f* cataplexiante.

stunk [stʌŋk] *pt & pp* → **stink.**

stunning ['stʌnɪŋ] *adj* **-1.** [very beautiful] ravissant(e); [scenery] merveilleux(euse). **-2.** [surprising] stupéfiant(e), renversant(e).

stunt [stʌnt] ◇ *n* **-1.** [for publicity] coup *m.* **-2.** CINEMA cascade *f.* ◇ *vt* retarder, arrêter.

stunted ['stʌntɪd] *adj* rabougri(e).

stunt man *n* cascadeur *m.*

stupefy ['stjuːpɪfaɪ] (*pt & pp* **-ied**) *vt* **-1.** [tire] abrutir. **-2.** [surprise] stupéfier, abasourdir.

stupendous [stjuːˈpendəs] *adj* extraordinaire, prodigieux(ieuse).

stupid ['stjuːpɪd] *adj* **-1.** [foolish] stupide, bête. **-2.** *inf* [annoying] fichu(e).

stupidity [stjuːˈpɪdətɪ] *n* (*U*) bêtise *f,* stupidité *f.*

stupidly ['stjuːpɪdlɪ] *adv* stupidement.

stupor ['stjuːpər] *n* stupeur *f,* hébétude *f.*

sturdy ['stɜːdɪ] (*compar* **-ier**, *superl* **-iest**) *adj* [person] robuste; [furniture, structure] solide.

sturgeon ['stɜːdʒən] (*pl inv*) *n* esturgeon *m.*

stutter ['stʌtər] ◇ *n* bégaiement *m.* ◇ *vi* bégayer.

sty [staɪ] (*pl* **sties**) *n* [pigsty] porcherie *f.*

stye [staɪ] *n* orgelet *m,* compère-loriot *m.*

style [staɪl] ◇ *n* **-1.** [characteristic manner] style *m.* **-2.** (*U*) [elegance] chic *m,* élégance *f.* **-3.** [design] genre *m,* modèle *m.* ◇ *vt* [hair] coiffer.

styling mousse ['staɪlɪŋ-] *n* mousse *f* coiffante.

stylish ['staɪlɪʃ] *adj* chic (*inv*), élégant(e).

stylist ['staɪlɪst] *n* [hairdresser] coiffeur *m,* -euse *f.*

stylized, -ised ['staɪlaɪzd] *adj* stylisé(e).

stylus ['staɪləs] (*pl* **-es**) *n* [on record player] pointe *f* de lecture, saphir *m.*

stymie ['staɪmɪ] *vt inf* [plan] contrarier, contrecarrer; **to be** ~**d** [person] être coincé(e).

styrofoam® ['staɪrəfəum] *n Am* polystyrène *m.*

suave [swɑːv] *adj* doucereux(euse).

sub [sʌb] *n inf* **-1.** SPORT (*abbr of* **substitute**) remplaçant *m,* -e *f.* **-2.** (*abbr of* **submarine**) sous-marin *m.* **-3.** *Br* (*abbr of* **subscription**) cotisation *f.* **-4.** *Am* [sandwich] sandwich *m* (de baguette).

sub- [sʌb] *prefix* sous-, sub-.

subcommittee ['sʌbkəˌmɪtɪ] *n* sous-comité *m.*

subconscious [ˌsʌbˈkɒnʃəs] ◇ *adj* inconscient(e). ◇ *n*: **the** ~ l'inconscient *m.*

subconsciously [ˌsʌbˈkɒnʃəslɪ] *adv* inconsciemment.

subcontinent [ˌsʌbˈkɒntɪnənt] *n* sous-continent *m.*

subcontract [ˌsʌbkənˈtrækt] *vt* sous-traiter.

subculture ['sʌbˌkʌltʃər] *n* sous-culture *f.*

subdivide [ˌsʌbdɪˈvaɪd] *vt* subdiviser.

subdue [səbˈdjuː] *vt* **-1.** [control - rioters, enemy] soumettre, subjuguer; [- temper, anger] maîtriser, réprimer. **-2.** [light, colour] adoucir, atténuer.

subdued [səb'djuːd] *adj* **-1.** [person] abattu(e). **-2.** [anger, emotion] contenu(e). **-3.** [colour] doux (douce); [light] tamisé(e).

subeditor [ˌsʌb'edɪtər] *n* secrétaire *mf* de rédaction.

subgroup ['sʌbgruːp] *n* sous-groupe *m*.

subheading ['sʌbˌhedɪŋ] *n* sous-titre *m*.

subhuman [ˌsʌb'hjuːmən] *adj pej* moins qu'humain(e).

subject [*adj, n & prep* 'sʌbdʒekt, *vt* səb'dʒekt] ◇ *adj* soumis(e); **to be ~ to** [tax, law] être soumis à; [disease, headaches] être sujet (sujette) à. ◇ *n* **-1.** [gen] sujet *m*. **-2.** SCH & UNIV matière *f.* ◇ *vt* **-1.** [control] soumettre, assujettir. **-2.** [force to experience]: **to ~ sb to sthg** exposer OR soumettre qqn à qqch.
♦ **subject to** *prep* sous réserve de.

subjection [səb'dʒekʃn] *n* sujétion *f,* soumission *f.*

subjective [səb'dʒektɪv] *adj* subjectif(ive).

subjectively [səb'dʒektɪvlɪ] *adv* subjectivement.

subject matter *n* (*U*) sujet *m*.

sub judice [-'dʒuːdɪsɪ] *adj* JUR en train de passer devant le tribunal.

subjugate ['sʌbdʒugeɪt] *vt* [people, country] conquérir, subjuguer.

subjunctive [səb'dʒʌŋktɪv] *n* GRAMM: **~ (mood)** (mode *m*) subjonctif *m*.

sublet [ˌsʌb'let] (*pt & pp* **sublet**, *cont* **-ting**) *vt* sous-louer.

sublime [sə'blaɪm] *adj* sublime; **from the ~ to the ridiculous** du sublime au ridicule OR grotesque.

sublimely [sə'blaɪmlɪ] *adv* suprêmement, souverainement.

subliminal [ˌsʌb'lɪmɪnl] *adj* subliminal(e).

submachine gun [ˌsʌbmə'ʃiːn-] *n* mitraillette *f.*

submarine [ˌsʌbmə'riːn] *n* sous-marin *m*.

submerge [səb'mɜːdʒ] ◇ *vt* immerger, plonger; **to ~ o.s. in sthg** *fig* se plonger dans qqch. ◇ *vi* s'immerger, plonger.

submission [səb'mɪʃn] *n* **-1.** [obedience] soumission *f.* **-2.** [presentation] présentation *f,* soumission *f.*

submissive [səb'mɪsɪv] *adj* soumis(e), docile.

submit [səb'mɪt] (*pt & pp* **-ted**, *cont* **-ting**) ◇ *vt* soumettre. ◇ *vi*: **to ~ (to)** se soumettre (à).

subnormal [ˌsʌb'nɔːml] *adj* arriéré(e), attardé(e).

subordinate [*adj & n* sə'bɔːdɪnət, *vt* sə'bɔːdɪneɪt] ◇ *adj fml* [less important]: **~ (to)** secondaire (à), moins important(e) (que). ◇ *n* subordonné *m,* -e *f.* ◇ *vt* subordonner, faire passer après.

subordinate clause [sə'bɔːdɪnət-] *n* proposition *f* subordonnée.

subordination [sə,bɔːdɪ'neɪʃn] *n* subordination *f.*

subpoena [səb'piːnə] (*pt & pp* **-ed**) JUR ◇ *n* citation *f,* assignation *f.* ◇ *vt* citer OR assigner à comparaître.

sub-post office *n* Br petit bureau *m* de poste.

subroutine ['sʌbruːˌtiːn] *n* COMPUT sous-programme *m*.

subscribe [səb'skraɪb] ◇ *vi* **-1.** [to magazine, newspaper] s'abonner, être abonné(e). **-2.** [to view, belief]: **to ~ to** être d'accord avec, approuver. ◇ *vt* [money] donner.

subscriber [səb'skraɪbər] *n* **-1.** [to magazine, service] abonné *m,* -e *f.* **-2.** [to charity, campaign] souscripteur *m,* -trice *f.*

subscription [səb'skrɪpʃn] *n* **-1.** [to magazine] abonnement *m.* **-2.** [to charity, campaign] souscription *f.* **-3.** [to club] cotisation *f.*

subsection ['sʌbˌsekʃn] *n* subdivision *f,* paragraphe *m*.

subsequent ['sʌbsɪkwənt] *adj* ultérieur(e), suivant(e).

subsequently ['sʌbsɪkwəntlɪ] *adv* par la suite, plus tard.

subservient [səb'sɜːvjənt] *adj* [servile]: **~ (to)** servile (vis-à-vis de), obséquieux(ieuse) (envers).

subset ['sʌbset] *n* MATH sous-ensemble *m*.

subside [səb'saɪd] *vi* **-1.** [pain, anger] se calmer, s'atténuer; [noise] diminuer. **-2.** [CONSTR - building] s'affaisser; [- ground] se tasser.

subsidence [səb'saɪdns, 'sʌbsɪdns] *n* [CONSTR - of building] affaissement *m*; [- of ground] tassement *m*.

subsidiarity [səbsɪdɪ'ærɪtɪ] *n* subsidiarité *f.*

subsidiary [səb'sɪdjərɪ] (*pl* **-ies**) ◇ *adj* subsidiaire. ◇ *n*: **~ (company)** filiale *f.*

subsidize, -ise ['sʌbsɪdaɪz] *vt* subventionner.

subsidy ['sʌbsɪdɪ] (*pl* **-ies**) *n* subvention *f,* subside *m*.

subsist [səb'sɪst] *vi*: **to ~ (on)** vivre (de).

subsistence [səb'sɪstəns] *n* subsistance *f,* existence *f.*

subsistence allowance *n* (*U*) Br frais *mpl* de subsistance.

subsistence farming n agriculture f d'autoconsommation.

subsistence level n minimum m vital.

substance ['sʌbstəns] n -1. [gen] substance f. -2. [importance] importance f.

substandard [ˌsʌb'stændəd] adj de qualité inférieure.

substantial [səb'stænʃl] adj -1. [considerable] considérable, important(e); [meal] substantiel(ielle). -2. [solid, well-built] solide.

substantially [səb'stænʃəlɪ] adv -1. [considerably] considérablement; ~ **better** bien mieux; ~ **bigger** beaucoup plus grand. -2. [mainly] en grande partie.

substantiate [səb'stænʃɪeɪt] vt fml prouver, établir.

substantive [sʌb'stæntɪv] adj fml [meaningful] positif(ive), constructif(ive).

substitute ['sʌbstɪtjuːt] ◇ n -1. [replacement]: ~ **(for)** [person] remplaçant m, -e f (de); [thing] succédané m (de); **to be no ~ for sthg** ne pas pouvoir remplacer qqch. -2. SPORT remplaçant m, -e f. ◇ vt: **to ~ A for B** substituer A à B, remplacer B par A. ◇ vi: **to ~ for sb/sthg** remplacer qqn/qqch.

substitute teacher n Am suppléant m, -e f.

substitution [ˌsʌbstɪ'tjuːʃn] n substitution f, remplacement m.

subterfuge ['sʌbtəfjuːdʒ] n subterfuge m.

subterranean [ˌsʌbtə'reɪnjən] adj souterrain(e).

subtitle ['sʌbˌtaɪtl] n sous-titre m.

subtle ['sʌtl] adj subtil(e).

subtlety ['sʌtltɪ] n subtilité f.

subtly ['sʌtlɪ] adv subtilement.

subtotal ['sʌbˌtəʊtl] n total m partiel.

subtract [səb'trækt] vt: **to ~ sthg (from)** soustraire qqch (de).

subtraction [səb'trækʃn] n soustraction f.

subtropical [ˌsʌb'trɒpɪkl] adj subtropical(e).

suburb ['sʌbɜːb] n faubourg m.
◆ **suburbs** npl: **the ~s** la banlieue.

suburban [sə'bɜːbn] adj -1. [of suburbs] de banlieue. -2. pej [life] étriqué(e); [person] à l'esprit étroit.

suburbia [sə'bɜːbɪə] n (U) la banlieue.

subversion [səb'vɜːʃn] n subversion f.

subversive [səb'vɜːsɪv] ◇ adj subversif(ive). ◇ n personne f qui agit de façon subversive.

subvert [səb'vɜːt] vt subvertir, renverser.

subway ['sʌbweɪ] n -1. Br [underground walkway] passage m souterrain. -2. Am [underground railway] métro m.

sub-zero adj au-dessous de zéro.

succeed [sək'siːd] ◇ vt succéder à. ◇ vi réussir; **to ~ in doing sthg** réussir à faire qqch.

succeeding [sək'siːdɪŋ] adj fml [in future] à venir; [in past] suivant(e).

success [sək'ses] n succès m, réussite f.

successful [sək'sesful] adj -1. [attempt] couronné(e) de succès. -2. [film, book etc] à succès; [person] qui a du succès.

successfully [sək'sesfulɪ] adv avec succès.

succession [sək'seʃn] n succession f; **in (quick OR close) ~** coup sur soup.

successive [sək'sesɪv] adj successif(ive).

successor [sək'sesər] n successeur m.

success story n réussite f.

succinct [sək'sɪŋkt] adj succinct(e).

succinctly [sək'sɪŋktlɪ] adv succinctement, de façon succincte.

succour Br, **succor** Am ['sʌkər] n (U) literary secours m.

succulent ['sʌkjulənt] adj succulent(e).

succumb [sə'kʌm] vi: **to ~ (to)** succomber (à).

such [sʌtʃ] ◇ adj tel (telle), pareil(eille); ~ **nonsense** de telles inepties; **do you have ~ a thing as a tin-opener?** est-ce que tu aurais un ouvre-boîtes par hasard?; ~ **money/books as I have** le peu d'argent/de livres que j'ai; ~ ... **that** tel ... que. ◇ adv -1. [for emphasis] si, tellement; **it's ~ a horrible day** quelle journée épouvantable!; ~ **a lot of books** tellement de livres; ~ **a long time** si OR tellement longtemps. -2. [in comparisons] aussi. ◇ pron: **and ~ (like)** et autres choses de ce genre; **this is my car, ~ as it is** voilà ma voiture, pour ce qu'elle vaut; **have some wine, ~ as there is** prenez un peu de vin, il en reste un petit fond.
◆ **as such** adv en tant que tel (telle), en soi.
◆ **such and such** adj tel et tel (telle et telle).

suchlike ['sʌtʃlaɪk] ◇ adj de ce genre, de la sorte. ◇ pron: **and ~** [people] et autres gens de ce genre; [things] et autres choses de ce genre.

suck [sʌk] vt -1. [with mouth] sucer. -2. [draw in] aspirer. -3. fig [involve]: **to be ~ed into sthg** être impliqué(e) dans qqch.
◆ **suck up** vi inf: **to ~ up (to sb)** faire de la lèche (à qqn).

sucker ['sʌkər] n -1. [suction pad] ventouse f. -2. inf [gullible person] poire f.

suckle ['sʌkl] ◇ vt allaiter. ◇ vi téter.

sucrose ['su:krəʊz] *n* saccharose *m*.

suction ['sʌkʃn] *n* succion *f*.

suction pump *n* pompe *f* aspirante.

Sudan [su:'dɑːn] *n* Soudan *m*; **in (the) ~** au Soudan.

Sudanese [,su:də'ni:z] ◇ *adj* soudanais(e). ◇ *npl*: **the ~** les Soudanais *mpl*.

sudden ['sʌdn] *adj* soudain(e), brusque; **all of a ~** tout d'un coup, soudain.

sudden death *n* SPORT jeu pour départager les ex aequo (le premier point perdu entraîne l'élimination immédiate).

suddenly ['sʌdnlı] *adv* soudainement, tout d'un coup.

suddenness ['sʌdnnıs] *n* soudaineté *f*.

suds [sʌdz] *npl* mousse *f* de savon.

sue [su:] *vt*: **to ~ sb (for)** poursuivre qqn (pour).

suede [sweıd] ◇ *n* daim *m*. ◇ *comp* en daim.

suet ['suıt] *n* graisse *f* de rognon.

Suez ['suız] *n* Suez.

Suez Canal *n*: **the ~** le canal de Suez.

suffer ['sʌfər] ◇ *vt* **-1.** [pain, injury] souffrir de. **-2.** [consequences, setback, loss] subir. ◇ *vi* souffrir; **to ~ from** MED souffrir de.

sufferance ['sʌfrəns] *n*: **on ~** par tolérance.

sufferer ['sʌfrər] *n* MED malade *mf*.

suffering ['sʌfrıŋ] *n* souffrance *f*.

suffice [sə'faıs] *vi fml* suffire.

sufficient [sə'fıʃnt] *adj* suffisant(e).

sufficiently [sə'fıʃntlı] *adv* suffisamment.

suffix ['sʌfıks] *n* suffixe *m*.

suffocate ['sʌfəkeıt] *vt & vi* suffoquer.

suffocation [,sʌfə'keıʃn] *n* suffocation *f*.

suffrage ['sʌfrıdʒ] *n* suffrage *m*.

suffuse [sə'fju:z] *vt* baigner.

sugar ['ʃʊɡər] ◇ *n* sucre *m*. ◇ *vt* sucrer.

sugar beet *n* betterave *f* à sucre.

sugar bowl *n* sucrier *m*.

sugarcane ['ʃʊɡəkeın] *n* (U) canne *f* à sucre.

sugar-coated [-'kəʊtıd] *adj* dragéifié(e).

sugared ['ʃʊɡəd] *adj* sucré(e).

sugar lump *n* morceau *m* de sucre.

sugar refinery *n* raffinerie *f* de sucre.

sugary ['ʃʊɡərı] *adj* **-1.** [food] sucré(e). **-2.** *pej* [sentimental] doucereux(euse).

suggest [sə'dʒest] *vt* **-1.** [propose] proposer, suggérer. **-2.** [imply] suggérer.

suggestion [sə'dʒestʃn] *n* **-1.** [proposal] proposition *f*, suggestion *f*. **-2.** (U) [implication] suggestion *f*.

suggestive [sə'dʒestıv] *adj* suggestif(ive); **to be ~ of sthg** suggérer qqch.

suicidal [suı'saıdl] *adj* suicidaire.

suicide ['suısaıd] *n* suicide *m*; **to commit ~** se suicider.

suicide attempt *n* tentative *f* de suicide.

suit [su:t] ◇ *n* **-1.** [for man] costume *m*, complet *m*; [for woman] tailleur *m*. **-2.** [outfit]: **ski/diving ~** combinaison *f* de ski/de plongée. **-3.** [in cards] couleur *f*. **-4.** JUR procès *m*, action *f*. **-5.** *phr*: **to follow ~** *fig* faire de même. ◇ *vt* **-1.** [subj: clothes, hairstyle] aller à. **-2.** [be convenient, appropriate to] convenir à; **to ~ o.s.** faire comme on veut. ◇ *vi* convenir, aller.

suitability [,su:tə'bılətı] *n* convenance *f*; [of candidate] aptitude *f*.

suitable ['su:təbl] *adj* qui convient, qui va.

suitably ['su:təblı] *adv* convenablement; **~ impressed** favorablement impressionné.

suitcase ['su:tkeıs] *n* valise *f*.

suite [swi:t] *n* **-1.** [of rooms] suite *f*. **-2.** [of furniture] ensemble *m*.

suited ['su:tıd] *adj* **-1.** [suitable]: **to be ~ to/for** convenir à/pour, aller à/pour. **-2.** [couple]: **well ~** très bien assortis; **ideally ~** faits l'un pour l'autre.

suitor ['su:tər] *n* dated soupirant *m*.

sulfate Am = **sulphate**.

sulfur Am = **sulphur**.

sulfuric acid Am = **sulphuric acid**.

sulk [sʌlk] ◇ *n* bouderie *f*. ◇ *vi* bouder.

sulky ['sʌlkı] (*compar* -**ier**, *superl* -**iest**) *adj* boudeur(euse).

sullen ['sʌlən] *adj* maussade.

sulphate Br, **sulfate** Am ['sʌlfeıt] *n* sulfate *m*.

sulphur Br, **sulfur** Am ['sʌlfər] *n* soufre *m*.

sulphuric acid Br, **sulfuric acid** Am [sʌl'fjʊərık-] *n* acide *m* sulfurique.

sultan ['sʌltən] *n* sultan *m*.

sultana [səl'tɑːnə] *n* Br [dried grape] raisin *m* sec.

sultry ['sʌltrı] (*compar* -**ier**, *superl* -**iest**) *adj* **-1.** [weather] lourd(e). **-2.** [sexual] sensuel(elle).

sum [sʌm] (*pt & pp* -**med**, *cont* -**ming**) *n* **-1.** [amount of money] somme *f*. **-2.** [calculation] calcul *m*.

◆ **sum up** ◇ *vt sep* [summarize] résumer. ◇ *vi* récapituler.

Sumatra [,sʊ'mɑːtrə] *n* Sumatra *f*; **in ~** à Sumatra.

Sumatran [sʊ'mɑːtrən] ◇ *adj* sumatranais(e). ◇ *n* Sumatranais *m*, -e *f*.

summarily ['sʌmərəlɪ] *adv* sommairement.

summarize, -ise ['sʌməraɪz] ◇ *vt* résumer. ◇ *vi* récapituler.

summary ['sʌmərɪ] (*pl* **-ies**) ◇ *adj* sommaire. ◇ *n* résumé *m*.

summation [sʌ'meɪʃn] *n* **-1.** [total] addition *f*. **-2.** [summary] résumé *m*.

summer ['sʌmər] ◇ *n* été *m*; **in ~** en été. ◇ *comp* d'été; **the ~ holidays** les grandes vacances *fpl*.

summer camp *n Am* colonie *f* de vacances.

summerhouse ['sʌməhaʊs, *pl* -haʊzɪz] *n* pavillon *m* (de verdure).

summer school *n* université *f* d'été.

summertime ['sʌmətaɪm] ◇ *adj* d'été. ◇ *n* été *m*.

Summer Time *n Br* heure *f* d'été.

summery ['sʌmərɪ] *adj* estival(e).

summing-up [ˌsʌmɪŋ-] (*pl* **summings-up**) *n* JUR résumé *m*.

summit ['sʌmɪt] *n* sommet *m*.

summon ['sʌmən] *vt* appeler, convoquer.
◆ **summon up** *vt sep* rassembler.

summons ['sʌmənz] (*pl* **summonses**) JUR ◇ *n* assignation *f*. ◇ *vt* assigner.

sumo (wrestling) ['suːməʊ-] *n* sumo *m*.

sump [sʌmp] *n* carter *m*.

sumptuous ['sʌmptʃʊəs] *adj* somptueux(euse).

sum total *n* somme *f* totale.

sun [sʌn] (*pt* & *pp* **-ned**, *cont* **-ning**) ◇ *n* soleil *m*; **in the ~** au soleil. ◇ *vt*: **to ~ o.s.** se chauffer au soleil.

Sun. (*abbr of* **Sunday**) dim.

sunbathe ['sʌnbeɪð] *vi* prendre un bain de soleil.

sunbather ['sʌnbeɪðər] *n* personne *f* qui prend un bain de soleil.

sunbeam ['sʌnbiːm] *n* rayon *m* de soleil.

sunbed ['sʌnbed] *n* lit *m* à ultra-violets.

sunburn ['sʌnbɜːn] *n* (*U*) coup *m* de soleil.

sunburned ['sʌnbɜːnd], **sunburnt** ['sʌnbɜːnt] *adj* brûlé(e) par le soleil, qui a attrapé un coup de soleil.

sun cream *n* crème *f* solaire.

sundae ['sʌndeɪ] *n* glace avec des fruits, des noix et de la Chantilly.

Sunday ['sʌndɪ] *n* dimanche *m*; **~ lunch** déjeuner *m* du dimanche OR dominical; *see also* **Saturday.**

Sunday paper *n Br* journal hebdomadaire paraissant le dimanche.

SUNDAY PAPERS:
Les principaux hebdomadaires britanniques paraissent le dimanche sont les suivants:
The Independent on Sunday
The Mail on Sunday (tendance conservatrice)
The News of the World (à sensation)
The Observer (tendance centre-gauche)
the People (à sensation)
the Sunday Express (tendance conservatrice)
the Sunday Mirror (tendance centre-gauche)
the Sunday Telegraph (tendance conservatrice)
the Sunday Times

Sunday school *n* catéchisme *m*.

sundial ['sʌndaɪəl] *n* cadran *m* solaire.

sundown ['sʌndaʊn] *n* coucher *m* du soleil.

sundries ['sʌndrɪz] *npl fml* articles *mpl* divers, objets *mpl* divers.

sundry ['sʌndrɪ] *adj fml* divers; **all and ~** tout le monde, n'importe qui.

sunflower ['sʌnˌflaʊər] *n* tournesol *m*.

sung [sʌŋ] *pp* → **sing.**

sunglasses ['sʌnˌglɑːsɪz] *npl* lunettes *fpl* de soleil.

sunhat ['sʌnhæt] *n* chapeau *m* de soleil.

sunk [sʌŋk] *pp* → **sink.**

sunken ['sʌŋkən] *adj* **-1.** [in water] coulé(e), submergé(e). **-2.** [garden] en contrebas; [cheeks, eyes] creux(euse).

sunlamp ['sʌnlæmp] *n* lampe *f* à ultra-violets.

sunlight ['sʌnlaɪt] *n* lumière *f* du soleil.

Sunni ['sʊnɪ] (*pl* **-s**) *n* Sunnite *mf*.

sunny ['sʌnɪ] (*compar* **-ier**, *superl* **-iest**) *adj* **-1.** [day, place] ensoleillé(e). **-2.** [cheerful] radieux(ieuse), heureux(euse). **-3.** *phr*: **~ side up** *Am* [egg] sur le plat.

sunray lamp *n* lampe *f* à ultra-violets.

sunrise ['sʌnraɪz] *n* lever *m* du soleil.

sunroof ['sʌnruːf] *n* toit *m* ouvrant.

sunset ['sʌnset] *n* coucher *m* du soleil.

sunshade ['sʌnʃeɪd] *n* parasol *m*.

sunshine ['sʌnʃaɪn] *n* lumière *f* du soleil.

sunspot ['sʌnspɒt] *n* tache *f* solaire.

sunstroke ['sʌnstrəʊk] *n* (*U*) insolation *f*.

suntan ['sʌntæn] ◇ *n* bronzage *m*. ◇ *comp* [lotion, cream] solaire.

suntanned ['sʌntænd] *adj* bronzé(e).

suntrap ['sʌntræp] *n* endroit très ensoleillé.

sunup ['sʌnʌp] *n Am inf* lever *m* du soleil.

super ['suːpər] *adj inf* génial(e), super (*inv*).

superabundance [ˌsuːpərəˈbʌndəns] *n* surabondance *f*.

superannuation [ˈsuːpəˌrænjʊˈeɪʃn] *n* (*U*) pension *f* de retraite.

superb [suːˈpɜːb] *adj* superbe.

superbly [suːˈpɜːblɪ] *adv* superbement.

Super Bowl *n Am*: **the ~** le Super Bowl, *finale du championnat des États-Unis de football américain.*

supercilious [ˌsuːpəˈsɪlɪəs] *adj* hautain(e).

superficial [ˌsuːpəˈfɪʃl] *adj* superficiel(ielle).

superfluous [suːˈpɜːflʊəs] *adj* superflu(e).

superglue [ˈsuːpəgluː] *n* colle *f* forte.

superhuman [ˌsuːpəˈhjuːmən] *adj* surhumain(e).

superimpose [ˌsuːpərɪmˈpəʊz] *vt*: **to ~ sthg (on)** superposer qqch (à).

superintend [ˌsuːpərɪnˈtend] *vt* diriger.

superintendent [ˌsuːpərɪnˈtendənt] *n* **-1.** *Br* [of police] ≃ commissaire *m*. **-2.** [of department] directeur *m*, -trice *f*.

superior [suːˈpɪərɪər] ◇ *adj* **-1.** [gen]: **~ (to)** supérieur(e) (à). **-2.** [goods, craftsmanship] de qualité supérieure. ◇ *n* supérieur *m*, -e *f*.

superiority [suːˌpɪərɪˈɒrətɪ] *n* supériorité *f*.

superlative [suːˈpɜːlətɪv] ◇ *adj* exceptionnel(elle), sans pareil(eille). ◇ *n* GRAMM superlatif *m*.

supermarket [ˈsuːpəˌmɑːkɪt] *n* supermarché *m*.

supernatural [ˌsuːpəˈnætʃrəl] ◇ *adj* surnaturel(elle). ◇ *n*: **the ~** le surnaturel *m*.

superpower [ˈsuːpəˌpaʊər] *n* superpuissance *f*.

superscript [ˈsuːpəskrɪpt] *adj* écrit(e)/ imprimé(e) au-dessus de la ligne.

supersede [ˌsuːpəˈsiːd] *vt* remplacer.

supersonic [ˌsuːpəˈsɒnɪk] *adj* supersonique.

superstar [ˈsuːpəstɑːr] *n* superstar *f*.

superstition [ˌsuːpəˈstɪʃn] *n* superstition *f*.

superstitious [ˌsuːpəˈstɪʃəs] *adj* superstitieux(ieuse).

superstore [ˈsuːpəstɔːr] *n* hypermarché *m*.

superstructure [ˈsuːpəˌstrʌktʃər] *n* superstructure *f*.

supertanker [ˈsuːpəˌtæŋkər] *n* supertanker *m*.

supertax [ˈsuːpətæks] *n* tranche *f* supérieure de l'impôt.

supervise [ˈsuːpəvaɪz] *vt* surveiller; [work] superviser.

supervision [ˌsuːpəˈvɪʒn] *n* surveillance *f*; [of work] supervision *f*.

supervisor [ˈsuːpəvaɪzər] *n* surveillant *m*, -e *f*.

supper [ˈsʌpər] *n* **-1.** [evening meal] dîner *m*. **-2.** [before bedtime] collation *f*.

supplant [səˈplɑːnt] *vt* supplanter.

supple [ˈsʌpl] *adj* souple.

supplement [*n* ˈsʌplɪmənt, *vb* ˈsʌplɪment] ◇ *n* supplément *m*. ◇ *vt* compléter.

supplementary [ˌsʌplɪˈmentərɪ] *adj* supplémentaire.

supplementary benefit *n Br ancien nom des allocations supplémentaires accordées aux personnes ayant un faible revenu.*

supplier [səˈplaɪər] *n* fournisseur *m*.

supply [səˈplaɪ] (*pl* **-ies**, *pt* & *pp* **-ied**) ◇ *n* **-1.** [store] réserve *f*, provision *f*; **to be in short ~** manquer. **-2.** [system] alimentation *f*. **-3.** (*U*) ECON offre *f*. ◇ *vt* **-1.** [provide]: **to ~ sthg (to sb)** fournir qqch (à qqn). **-2.** [provide to]: **to ~ sb (with)** fournir qqn (en), approvisionner qqn (en); **to ~ sthg with sthg** alimenter qqch en qqch.
◆ **supplies** *npl* [food] vivres *mpl*; MIL approvisionnements *mpl*; **office supplies** fournitures *fpl* de bureau.

supply teacher *n Br* suppléant *m*, -e *f*.

support [səˈpɔːt] ◇ *n* **-1.** (*U*) [physical help] appui *m*. **-2.** (*U*) [emotional, financial help] soutien *m*. **-3.** [object] support *m*, appui *m*. ◇ *vt* **-1.** [physically] soutenir, supporter; [weight] supporter. **-2.** [emotionally] soutenir. **-3.** [financially] subvenir aux besoins de; **to ~ o.s.** subvenir à ses propres besoins. **-4.** [theory] être en faveur de, être partisan de; [political party, candidate] appuyer; SPORT être un supporter de.

supporter [səˈpɔːtər] *n* **-1.** [of person, plan] partisan *m*, -e *f*. **-2.** SPORT supporter *m*.

supportive [səˈpɔːtɪv] *adj* qui est d'un grand secours, qui soutient.

suppose [səˈpəʊz] ◇ *vt* supposer; **I don't ~ you could ...?** [in polite requests] vous ne pourriez pas ... par hasard?; **you don't ~ ...?** [asking opinion] vous ne pensez pas que ...? ◇ *vi* supposer; **I ~ (so)** je suppose que oui; **I ~ not** je suppose que non. ◇ *conj* et si, à supposer que (+ *subjunctive*).

supposed [səˈpəʊzd] *adj* **-1.** [doubtful] supposé(e). **-2.** [reputed, intended]: **to be ~ to** be être censé(e) être.

supposedly [səˈpəʊzɪdlɪ] *adv* soi-disant.

supposing [səˈpəʊzɪŋ] *conj* et si, à supposer que (+ *subjunctive*).

supposition [ˌsʌpəˈzɪʃn] *n* supposition *f*.

suppository [səˈpɒzɪtrɪ] (*pl* **-ies**) *n* suppositoire *m*.

suppress [səˈpres] *vt* **-1.** [uprising] réprimer.

-2. [information] supprimer. **-3.** [emotions] réprimer, étouffer.

suppression [sə'preʃn] n **-1.** [of uprising, emotions] répression f. **-2.** [of information] suppression f.

suppressor [sə'presər] n ELEC dispositif m antiparasite.

supranational [,su:prə'næʃənl] adj supranational(e).

supremacy [sʊ'preməsɪ] n suprématie f.

supreme [sʊ'pri:m] adj suprême.

Supreme Court n [in US]: **the ~** la Cour suprême.

SUPREME COURT:

La Cour suprême est l'organe supérieur du pouvoir judiciaire, et est composée de membres nommés par le président des États-Unis; elle détient le pouvoir de décision finale ainsi que le droit d'interpréter la Constitution

---

supremely [sʊ'pri:mlɪ] adv suprêmement.

supremo [sʊ'pri:məʊ] (pl **-s**) n Br inf grand chef m.

Supt. abbr of **superintendent**.

surcharge ['sɜ:tʃɑ:dʒ] ◇ n [extra payment] surcharge f; [extra tax] surtaxe f. ◇ vt surcharger.

sure [ʃʊər] ◇ adj **-1.** [gen] sûr(e); **to be ~ of o.s.** être sûr de soi. **-2.** [certain]: **to be ~ (of sthg/of doing sthg)** être sûr(e) (de qqch/de faire qqch), être certain(e) (de qqch/de faire qqch); **to make ~ (that)** ... s'assurer OR vérifier que .... **-3.** phr: **to be ~ to do sthg** [remember] s'assurer de faire qqch; **I am** OR **I'm ~ (that)** ... je suis bien certain que ..., je ne doute pas que .... ◇ adv **-1.** inf [yes] bien sûr. **-2.** Am [really] pour sûr, vraiment.

◆ **for sure** adv sans aucun doute.

◆ **sure enough** adv en effet, effectivement.

surefire ['ʃʊəfaɪər] adj inf certain(e), infaillible.

surefooted ['ʃʊə,fʊtɪd] adj d'un pied sûr.

surely ['ʃʊəlɪ] adv sûrement.

sure thing excl Am inf d'accord!

surety ['ʃʊərətɪ] n (U) caution f.

surf [sɜ:f] ◇ n ressac m. ◇ vi surfer.

surface ['sɜ:fɪs] ◇ n surface f; **on the ~** fig à première vue, vu de l'extérieur; **below** OR **beneath the ~** fig au fond; **to scratch the ~** fig [of problem] effleurer le problème; [of subject] effleurer le sujet. ◇ vi **-1.** [diver] remonter à la surface; [submarine] faire sur-

face. **-2.** [problem, rumour] apparaître OR s'étaler au grand jour. **-3.** inf hum [after absence] refaire surface.

surface mail n courrier m par voie de terre/de mer.

surface-to-air adj sol-air (inv).

surfboard ['sɜ:fbɔ:d] n planche f de surf.

surfeit ['sɜ:fɪt] n fml excès m.

surfer ['sɜ:fər] n surfeur m, -euse f.

surfing ['sɜ:fɪŋ] n surf m.

surge [sɜ:dʒ] ◇ n **-1.** [of people, vehicles] déferlement m; ELEC surtension f. **-2.** [of emotion, interest] vague f, montée f; [of anger] bouffée f; [of sales, applications] afflux m. ◇ vi **-1.** [people, vehicles] déferler. **-2.** [emotion] monter.

surgeon ['sɜ:dʒən] n chirurgien m.

surgery ['sɜ:dʒərɪ] (pl **-ies**) n **-1.** (U) MED [performing operations] chirurgie f. **-2.** Br MED [place] cabinet m de consultation. **-3.** Br MED & POL [consulting period] consultation f.

surgical ['sɜ:dʒɪkl] adj chirurgical(e); **~ stocking** bas m orthopédique.

surgical spirit n Br alcool m à 90°.

Surinam [,sʊərɪ'næm] n Surinam m, Suriname m; **in ~** au Surinam.

surly ['sɜ:lɪ] (compar **-ier**, superl **-iest**) adj revêche, renfrogné(e).

surmise [sɜ:'maɪz] vt fml présumer.

surmount [sɜ:'maʊnt] vt surmonter.

surname ['sɜ:neɪm] n nom m de famille.

surpass [sə'pɑ:s] vt fml dépasser.

surplus ['sɜ:pləs] ◇ adj en surplus. ◇ n surplus m.

surprise [sə'praɪz] ◇ n surprise f; **to take sb by ~** prendre qqn au dépourvu. ◇ vt surprendre.

surprised [sə'praɪzd] adj surpris(e); **I wouldn't be ~ (if ...)** ça ne m'étonnerait pas (que ...).

surprising [sə'praɪzɪŋ] adj surprenant(e).

surprisingly [sə'praɪzɪŋlɪ] adv étonnamment.

surreal [sə'rɪəl] adj surréaliste.

surrealism [sə'rɪəlɪzm] n surréalisme m.

surrealist [sə'rɪəlɪst] ◇ adj surréaliste. ◇ n surréaliste mf.

surrender [sə'rendər] ◇ n reddition f, capitulation f. ◇ vt fml [weapons, passport] rendre; [claim, rights] renoncer à. ◇ vi **-1.** [stop fighting]: **to ~ (to)** se rendre (à). **-2.** fig [give in]: **to ~ (to)** se laisser aller (à), se livrer (à).

surreptitious [,sʌrəp'tɪʃəs] adj subreptice.

surrogate ['sʌrəgeɪt] ◇ adj de substitution. ◇ n substitut m.

surrogate mother *n* mère-porteuse *f.*

surround [sə'raʊnd] ◇ *n* bordure *f.* ◇ *vt* entourer; [subj: police, army] cerner.

surrounding [sə'raʊndɪŋ] *adj* environnant(e).

surroundings [sə'raʊndɪŋz] *npl* environnement *m.*

surtax ['sɜːtæks] *n* surtaxe *f.*

surveillance [sɜː'veɪləns] *n* surveillance *f.*

survey [*n* 'sɜːveɪ, *vb* sə'veɪ] ◇ *n* -1. [investigation] étude *f*; [of public opinion] sondage *m.* -2. [of land] levé *m*; [of building] inspection *f.* ◇ *vt* -1. [contemplate] passer en revue. -2. [investigate] faire une étude de, enquêter sur. -3. [land] faire le levé de; [building] inspecter.

surveyor [sə'veɪər] *n* [of building] expert *m*; [of land] géomètre *m.*

survival [sə'vaɪvl] *n* -1. [continuing to live] survie *f.* -2. [relic] vestige *m.*

survive [sə'vaɪv] ◇ *vt* survivre à. ◇ *vi* survivre.
◆ **survive on** *vt fus* vivre de.

survivor [sə'vaɪvər] *n* survivant *m*, -e *f*; *fig* battant *m*, -e *f.*

susceptible [sə'septəbl] *adj*: ~ **(to)** sensible (à).

suspect [*adj & n* 'sʌspekt, *vb* sə'spekt] ◇ *adj* suspect(e). ◇ *n* suspect *m*, -e *f.* ◇ *vt* -1. [distrust] suspecter, douter de. -2. [think likely, consider guilty] soupçonner; **to** ~ **sb of sthg** soupçonner qqn de qqch.

suspend [sə'spend] *vt* -1. [gen] suspendre. -2. [from school] renvoyer temporairement.

suspended animation [sə'spendɪd-] *n* hibernation *f.*

suspended sentence [sə'spendɪd-] *n* condamnation *f* avec sursis.

suspender belt [sə'spendər-] *n Br* portejarretelles *m inv.*

suspenders [sə'spendəz] *npl* -1. *Br* [for stockings] jarretelles *fpl.* -2. *Am* [for trousers] bretelles *fpl.*

suspense [sə'spens] *n* suspense *m*; **to keep sb in** ~ tenir qqn en suspens.

suspension [sə'spenʃn] *n* -1. [gen & AUT] suspension *f.* -2. [from school] renvoi *m* temporaire.

suspension bridge *n* pont *m* suspendu.

suspicion [sə'spɪʃn] *n* soupçon *m*; **to be under** ~ être considéré comme suspect; **to have one's** ~s **(about)** avoir des soupçons OR des doutes (sur).

suspicious [sə'spɪʃəs] *adj* -1. [having suspicions] soupçonneux(euse). -2. [causing suspicion] suspect(e), louche.

suspiciously [sə'spɪʃəslɪ] *adv* -1. [with suspicious attitude] de façon soupçonneuse, avec méfiance. -2. [causing suspicion] de façon suspecte OR louche.

suss [sʌs]
◆ **suss out** *vt sep Br inf* piger, comprendre.

sustain [sə'steɪn] *vt* -1. [maintain] soutenir. -2. [nourish] nourrir. -3. *fml* [suffer - damage] subir; [- injury] recevoir. -4. *fml* [weight] supporter.

sustenance ['sʌstɪnəns] *n* (U) *fml* nourriture *f.*

suture ['suːtʃər] *n* suture *f.*

svelte [svelt] *adj* svelte.

SW -1. (*abbr of* **short wave**) OC. -2. (*abbr of* **south-west**) S-O.

swab [swɒb] *n* MED tampon *m.*

swagger ['swægər] ◇ *n* air *m* de parade. ◇ *vi* parader.

Swahili [swɑː'hiːlɪ] ◇ *adj* swahili(e). ◇ *n* [language] swahili *m.*

swallow ['swɒləʊ] ◇ *n* -1. [bird] hirondelle *f.* -2. [of food] bouchée *f*; [of drink] gorgée *f.* ◇ *vt* avaler; *fig* [anger, tears] ravaler. ◇ *vi* avaler.

swam [swæm] *pt* → **swim.**

swamp [swɒmp] ◇ *n* marais *m.* ◇ *vt* -1. [flood] submerger. -2. [overwhelm] déborder, submerger.

swan [swɒn] *n* cygne *m.*

swap [swɒp] (*pt & pp* **-ped**, *cont* **-ping**) ◇ *n* [exchange] échange *m.* ◇ *vt*: **to** ~ **sthg (with sb/for sthg)** échanger qqch (avec qqn/contre qqch). ◇ *vi* échanger.

swap meet *n Am* foire *f* au troc.

SWAPO ['swɑːpəʊ] (*abbr of* **South West Africa People's Organization**) *n* SWAPO *f.*

swarm [swɔːm] ◇ *n* essaim *m.* ◇ *vi* -1. [bees] essaimer. -2. *fig* [people] grouiller; **to be** ~**ing (with)** [place] grouiller (de).

swarthy ['swɔːðɪ] (*compar* **-ier**, *superl* **-iest**) *adj* basané(e).

swashbuckling ['swɒʃˌbʌklɪŋ] *adj* de cape et d'épée.

swastika ['swɒstɪkə] *n* croix *f* gammée.

swat [swɒt] (*pt & pp* **-ted**, *cont* **-ting**) *vt* écraser.

swatch [swɒtʃ] *n* échantillon *m.*

swathe [sweɪð] ◇ *n* [large area] étendue *f.* ◇ *vt literary* emmailloter, envelopper.

swathed [sweɪðd] *adj literary*: ~ **(in)** emmailloté(e) (de), enveloppé(e) (de).

swatter ['swɒtər] *n* tapette *f.*

sway [sweɪ] ◇ vt -1. [cause to swing] balancer. -2. [influence] influencer. ◇ vi se balancer. ◇ n fml: **to hold ~ over sb** tenir qqn sous son empire; **to come under the ~ of** se laisser influencer par.

Swazi ['swɑːzɪ] n Swazi mf.

Swaziland ['swɑːzɪlænd] n Swaziland m; **in ~** au Swaziland.

swear [sweəʳ] (pt **swore**, pp **sworn**) ◇ vt jurer; **to ~ to do sthg** jurer de faire qqch; **to ~ an oath** prêter serment. ◇ vi jurer.
◆ **swear by** vt fus [have confidence in] jurer par.
◆ **swear in** vt sep JUR assermenter.

swearword ['sweəwɜːd] n juron m, gros mot m.

sweat [swet] ◇ n -1. [perspiration] transpiration f, sueur f; **to be in a cold ~** avoir des sueurs froides. -2. (U) inf [hard work] corvée f. ◇ vi -1. [perspire] transpirer, suer. -2. inf [worry] se faire du mouron.

sweatband ['swetbænd] n SPORT bandeau m; [of hat] cuir m intérieur.

sweater ['swetəʳ] n pullover m.

sweatshirt ['swetʃɜːt] n sweat-shirt m.

sweatshop ['swetʃɒp] n atelier m où les ouvriers sont exploités.

sweaty ['swetɪ] (compar **-ier**, superl **-iest**) adj -1. [skin, clothes] mouillé(e) de sueur. -2. [place] chaud(e) et humide; [activity] qui fait transpirer.

swede [swiːd] n Br rutabaga m.

Swede [swiːd] n Suédois m, -e f.

Sweden ['swiːdn] n Suède f; **in ~** en Suède.

Swedish ['swiːdɪʃ] ◇ adj suédois(e). ◇ n [language] suédois m. ◇ npl: **the ~** les Suédois mpl.

sweep [swiːp] (pt & pp **swept**) ◇ n -1. [sweeping movement] grand geste m. -2. [with brush]: **to give sthg a ~** donner un coup de balai à qqch, balayer qqch. -3. [electronic] balayage m. -4. [chimney sweep] ramoneur m.
◇ vt -1. [gen] balayer; [scan with eyes] parcourir des yeux. -2. [move]: **to ~ sthg off sthg** enlever qqch de qqch d'un grand geste; **to be swept out to sea** être emporté vers le large.
◇ vi -1. [wind] s'engouffrer. -2. [emotion]: **to ~ through sb** s'emparer de qqn. -3. [person]: **to ~ along/in** avancer/entrer rapidement.
◆ **sweep aside** vt sep écarter, rejeter.
◆ **sweep away** vt sep [destroy] emporter, entraîner.
◆ **sweep up** ◇ vt sep [with brush] balayer.
◇ vi balayer.

sweeper ['swiːpəʳ] n FTBL libero m.

sweeping ['swiːpɪŋ] adj -1. [effect, change] radical(e). -2. [statement] hâtif(ive). -3. [curve] large.

sweepstake ['swiːpsteɪk] n sweepstake m.

sweet [swiːt] ◇ adj -1. [gen] doux (douce); [cake, flavour, pudding] sucré(e). -2. [kind] gentil(ille). -3. [attractive] adorable, mignon(onne). ◇ n Br -1. [candy] bonbon m. -2. [dessert] dessert m.

sweet-and-sour adj aigre-doux (aigre-douce).

sweet corn n maïs m.

sweeten ['swiːtn] vt sucrer.

sweetener ['swiːtnəʳ] n -1. [substance] édulcorant m. -2. inf [bribe] pot-de-vin m.

sweetheart ['swiːthɑːt] n -1. [term of endearment] chéri m, -e f, mon cœur m. -2. [boyfriend, girlfriend] petit ami m, petite amie f.

sweetness ['swiːtnɪs] n -1. [gen] douceur f; [of taste] goût m sucré, douceur f. -2. [attractiveness] charme m.

sweet pea n pois m de senteur.

sweet potato n patate f douce.

sweet shop n Br confiserie f.

sweet tooth n: **to have a ~** aimer les sucreries.

swell [swel] (pt **-ed**, pp **swollen** OR **-ed**) ◇ vi -1. [leg, face etc] enfler; [lungs, balloon] se gonfler; **to ~ with pride** se gonfler d'orgueil. -2. [crowd, population etc] grossir, augmenter; [sound] grossir, s'enfler. ◇ vt grossir, augmenter. ◇ n [of sea] houle f. ◇ adj Am inf chouette, épatant(e).

swelling ['swelɪŋ] n enflure f.

sweltering ['sweltərɪŋ] adj étouffant(e), suffocant(e); **I'm ~** j'étouffe.

swept [swept] pt & pp → **sweep**.

swerve [swɜːv] vi faire une embardée.

swift [swɪft] ◇ adj -1. [fast] rapide. -2. [prompt] prompt(e). ◇ n [bird] martinet m.

swiftly ['swɪftlɪ] adv -1. [quickly] rapidement, vite. -2. [promptly] promptement.

swiftness ['swɪftnɪs] n -1. [quickness] rapidité f. -2. [promptness] promptitude f.

swig [swɪg] (pt & pp **-ged**, cont **-ging**) inf ◇ vt lamper. ◇ n lampée f.

swill [swɪl] ◇ n (U) [pig food] pâtée f. ◇ vt Br [wash] laver à grande eau.

swim [swɪm] (pt **swam**, pp **swum**, cont **-ming**) ◇ n: **to have a ~** nager; **to go for a ~** aller se baigner, aller nager. ◇ vi -1. [person, fish, animal] nager. -2. [room] tourner; **my head was swimming** j'avais la tête qui tournait, la tête me tournait.

swimmer ['swimə'] *n* nageur *m*, -euse *f*.

swimming ['swimiŋ] ◇ *n* natation *f*; **to go ~** aller nager. ◇ *comp* [club, competition] de natation.

swimming baths *npl Br* piscine *f*.

swimming cap *n* bonnet *m* de bain.

swimming costume *n Br* maillot *m* de bain.

swimming pool *n* piscine *f*.

swimming trunks *npl* maillot *m* OR slip *m* de bain.

swimsuit ['swimsuːt] *n* maillot *m* de bain.

swindle ['swindl] ◇ *n* escroquerie *f*. ◇ *vt* escroquer, rouler; **to ~ sb out of sthg** escroquer qqch à qqn.

swine [swain] *n inf* [person] salaud *m*.

swing [swiŋ] (*pt* & *pp* swung) ◇ *n* -1. [child's toy] balançoire *f*. -2. [change - of opinion] revirement *m*; [- of mood] changement *m*, saute *f*. -3. [sway] balancement *m*. -4. *inf* [blow]: **to take a ~ at sb** lancer OR envoyer un coup de poing à qqn. -5. *phr*: **to be in full ~** battre son plein; **to get into the ~ of things** se mettre dans le bain. ◇ *vt* -1. [move back and forth] balancer. -2. [move in a curve] faire virer. ◇ *vi* -1. [move back and forth] se balancer. -2. [turn - vehicle] virer, tourner; **to ~ round** [person] se retourner. -3. [hit out]: **to ~ at sb** lancer OR envoyer un coup de poing à qqn. -4. [change] changer.

swing bridge *n* pont *m* tournant.

swing door *n* porte *f* battante.

swingeing ['swindʒiŋ] *adj* très sévère.

swinging ['swiŋiŋ] *adj inf* -1. [lively] animé(e), plein(e) d'entrain. -2. [uninhibited] dans le vent.

swipe [swaip] ◇ *n*: **to take a ~ at** envoyer OR donner un coup à. ◇ *vt inf* [steal] faucher, piquer. ◇ *vi*: **to ~ at** envoyer OR donner un coup à.

swirl [swɜːl] ◇ *n* tourbillon *m*. ◇ *vt* agiter, remuer. ◇ *vi* tourbillonner, tournoyer.

swish [swiʃ] ◇ *n* [of tail] battement *m*; [of dress] froufrou *m*. ◇ *vt* [tail] battre l'air de. ◇ *vi* bruire, froufrouter.

Swiss [swis] ◇ *adj* suisse. ◇ *n* [person] Suisse *m*, Suisse *f* OR, Suissesse *f*. ◇ *npl*: **the ~** les Suisses *mpl*.

swiss roll *n Br* gâteau *m* roulé.

switch [switʃ] ◇ *n* -1. [control device] interrupteur *m*, commutateur *m*; [on radio, stereo etc] bouton *m*. -2. [change] changement *m*. -3. *Am* RAIL aiguillage *m*. ◇ *vt* -1. [change] reporter; **to ~ position** changer de posi-

tion. -2. [swap] échanger; [jobs] changer de. ◇ *vi*: **to ~ to/from** passer à/de.

◆ **switch off** ◇ *vt sep* éteindre. ◇ *vi inf fig* décrocher.

◆ **switch on** *vt sep* allumer.

switchblade ['switʃbleid] *n Am* couteau *m* à cran d'arrêt.

switchboard ['switʃbɔːd] *n* standard *m*.

switchboard operator *n* standardiste *mf*.

switched-on ['switʃt-] *adj inf* branché(e).

Switzerland ['switsələnd] *n* Suisse *f*; **in ~** en Suisse.

swivel ['swivl] (*Br pt* & *pp* -led, *cont* -ling, *Am pt* & *pp* -ed, *cont* -ing) ◇ *vt* [chair] faire pivoter; [head, eyes] faire tourner. ◇ *vi* [chair] pivoter; [head, eyes] tourner.

swivel chair *n* fauteuil *m* pivotant OR tournant.

swollen ['swəuln] ◇ *pp* → swell. ◇ *adj* [ankle, face] enflé(e); [river] en crue.

swoon [swuːn] *vi literary* s'évanouir; *hum* se pâmer.

swoop [swuːp] ◇ *n* -1. [downward flight] descente *f* en piqué; **in one fell ~** d'un seul coup. -2. [raid] descente *f*. ◇ *vi* -1. [bird, plane] piquer. -2. [police, army] faire une descente.

swop [swɒp] = swap.

sword [sɔːd] *n* épée *f*; **to cross ~s (with sb)** croiser le fer (avec qqn).

swordfish ['sɔːdfiʃ] (*pl inv* OR -es) *n* espadon *m*.

swordsman ['sɔːdzmən] (*pl* -men [-mən]) *n* tireur *m* d'épée.

swore [swɔː'] *pt* → swear.

sworn [swɔːn] ◇ *pp* → swear. ◇ *adj* -1. [committed]: **to be ~ enemies** être ennemis jurés. -2. JUR sous serment.

swot [swɒt] (*pt* & *pp* -ted, *cont* -ting) *Br inf* ◇ *n pej* bûcheur *m*, -euse *f*. ◇ *vi*: **to ~ (for)** bûcher (pour).

◆ **swot up** *vt sep* & *vi inf* potasser, bûcher.

swum [swʌm] *pp* → swim.

swung [swʌŋ] *pt* & *pp* → swing.

sycamore ['sikəmɔː'] *n* sycomore *m*.

sycophant ['sikəfænt] *n* flagorneur *m*, -euse *f*, lèche-bottes *mf inv*.

Sydney ['sidni] *n* Sydney.

syllable ['siləbl] *n* syllabe *f*.

syllabub ['siləbʌb] *n* ≈ sabayon *m*.

syllabus ['siləbəs] (*pl* -buses OR -bi [-bai]) *n* programme *m*.

symbol ['simbl] *n* symbole *m*.

symbolic [sɪm'bɒlɪk] *adj* symbolique; **to be ~ of** être le symbole de.

symbolism ['sɪmbəlɪzm] *n* symbolisme *m*.

symbolize, -ise ['sɪmbəlaɪz] *vt* symboliser.

symmetrical [sɪ'metrɪkl] *adj* symétrique.

symmetry ['sɪmətrɪ] *n* symétrie *f*.

sympathetic [,sɪmpə'θetɪk] *adj* **-1.** [understanding] compatissant(e), compréhensif(ive). **-2.** [willing to support]: ~ **(to)** bien disposé(e) (à l'égard de). **-3.** [likable] sympathique.

sympathize, -ise ['sɪmpəθaɪz] *vi* **-1.** [feel sorry] compatir; **to ~ with sb** plaindre qqn; [in grief] compatir à la douleur de qqn. **-2.** [understand]: **to ~ with sthg** comprendre qqch. **-3.** [support]: **to ~ with sthg** approuver qqch, soutenir qqch.

sympathizer, -iser ['sɪmpəθaɪzəʳ] *n* sympathisant *m*, -e *f*.

sympathy ['sɪmpəθɪ] *n* (U) **-1.** [understanding]: ~ **(for)** compassion *f* (pour), sympathie *f* (pour). **-2.** [agreement] approbation *f*, sympathie *f*; **to be in ~ (with sthg)** être d'accord (avec qqch). **-3.** [support]: **in ~ (with sb)** en solidarité (avec qqn).

♦ **sympathies** *npl* **-1.** [support] soutien *m*, loyauté *f*. **-2.** [to bereaved person] condoléances *fpl*.

symphonic [sɪm'fɒnɪk] *adj* symphonique.

symphony ['sɪmfənɪ] (*pl* **-ies**) *n* symphonie *f*.

symphony orchestra *n* orchestre *m* symphonique.

symposium [sɪm'pəʊzjəm] (*pl* **-siums** OR **-sia** [-zjə]) *n* symposium *m*.

symptom ['sɪmptəm] *n* symptôme *m*.

symptomatic [,sɪmptə'mætɪk] *adj* symptomatique.

synagogue ['sɪnəgɒg] *n* synagogue *f*.

sync [sɪŋk] *n inf*: **out of ~** mal synchronisé(e); **in ~** bien synchronisé.

synchromesh gearbox ['sɪŋkrəʊmeʃ-] *n* boîte *f* de vitesses synchronisées.

synchronize, -ise ['sɪŋkrənaɪz] ◇ *vt* synchroniser. ◇ *vi* être synchronisés(es).

synchronized swimming ['sɪŋkrənaɪzd-] *n* natation *f* synchronisée.

syncopated ['sɪŋkəpeɪtɪd] *adj* syncopé(e).

syncopation [,sɪŋkə'peɪʃn] *n* syncope *f*.

syndicate [*n* 'sɪndɪkət, *vb* 'sɪndɪkeɪt] ◇ *n* syndicat *m*, consortium *m*. ◇ *vt* PRESS publier dans plusieurs journaux.

syndrome ['sɪndrəʊm] *n* syndrome *m*.

synod ['sɪnəd] *n* synode *m*.

synonym ['sɪnənɪm] *n*: ~ **(for** OR **of)** synonyme *m* (de).

synonymous [sɪ'nɒnɪməs] *adj*: ~ **(with)** synonyme (de).

synopsis [sɪ'nɒpsɪs] (*pl* **-ses** [-siːz]) *n* résumé *m*.

syntax ['sɪntæks] *n* syntaxe *f*.

synthesis ['sɪnθəsɪs] (*pl* **-ses** [-siːz]) *n* synthèse *f*.

synthesize, -ise ['sɪnθəsaɪz] *vt* synthétiser; CHEM faire la synthèse de.

synthesizer ['sɪnθəsaɪzəʳ] *n* MUS synthétiseur *m*.

synthetic [sɪn'θetɪk] *adj* **-1.** [man-made] synthétique. **-2.** *pej* [insincere] artificiel(ielle), forcé(e).

syphilis ['sɪfɪlɪs] *n* syphilis *f*.

syphon ['saɪfən] = **siphon**.

Syria ['sɪrɪə] *n* Syrie *f*; **in ~** en Syrie.

Syrian ['sɪrɪən] ◇ *adj* syrien(ienne). ◇ *n* [person] Syrien *m*, -ienne *f*.

syringe [sɪ'rɪndʒ] (*cont* **syringeing**) ◇ *n* seringue *f*. ◇ *vt* [wound] seringuer; [ear] nettoyer à l'aide d'une seringue.

syrup ['sɪrəp] *n* (U) **-1.** [sugar and water] sirop *m*. **-2.** *Br* [golden syrup] mélasse *f* raffinée.

system ['sɪstəm] *n* **-1.** [gen] système *m*; **road/railway ~** réseau *m* routier/de chemins de fer; **transport ~** réseau *m* des transports; **digestive ~** appareil *m* digestif. **-2.** [equipment - gen] installation *f*; [- electric, electronic] appareil *m*. **-3.** (U) [methodical approach] système *m*, méthode *f*. **-4.** *phr*: **to get sthg out of one's ~** *inf* laisser OR donner libre cours à qqch; **to get it out of one's ~** *inf* se défouler.

systematic [,sɪstə'mætɪk] *adj* systématique.

systematize, -ise ['sɪstəmətaɪz] *vt* systématiser.

system disk *n* COMPUT disque *m* système.

systems analyst ['sɪstəmz-] *n* COMPUT analyste fonctionnel *m*, analyste fonctionnelle *f*.

systems engineer ['sɪstəmz-] *n* COMPUT ingénieur *m* de système.

system software *n* (U) COMPUT logiciel *m* d'exploitation.

T

t (*pl* **t's** OR **ts**), **T** (*pl* **T's** OR **Ts**) [tiː] *n* [letter]
t *m inv,* T *m inv.*

ta [tɑː] *excl Br inf* merci!

TA (*abbr of* **Territorial Army**) *n armée de réserve britannique.*

tab [tæb] *n* -**1.** [of cloth] étiquette *f.* -**2.** [of
metal] languette *f.* -**3.** *Am* [bill] addition *f.*
-**4.** (*abbr of* **tabulator**) [on typewriter] tabulateur *m.* -**5.** *phr:* **to keep ~s on sb** tenir OR
avoir qqn à l'œil, surveiller qqn.

Tabasco sauce® [tə'bæskəʊ-] *n* sauce *f* Tabasco.

tabby ['tæbɪ] (*pl* -**ies**) *n:* ~ **(cat)** chat tigré
m, chatte tigrée *f.*

tabernacle ['tæbənækl] *n* tabernacle *m.*

tab key *n* touche *f* de tabulation.

table ['teɪbl] ◇ *n* table *f;* **to turn the ~s on
sb** *fig* renverser les rôles, retourner la situation. ◇ *vt* -**1.** *Br* [propose] présenter,
proposer. -**2.** *Am* [postpone] ajourner la discussion de.

tableau ['tæbləʊ] (*pl* -**x** [-z] OR -**s**) *n* tableau
m vivant.

tablecloth ['teɪblklɒθ] *n* nappe *f.*

table d'hôte ['tɑːbl,dəʊt] *n:* **the ~** le menu
à prix fixe.

table lamp *n* lampe *f.*

table licence *n licence autorisant la vente de
boissons alcoolisées seulement aux repas.*

table linen *n* linge *m* de table.

table manners *npl:* **to have good/bad ~**
savoir/ne pas savoir se tenir à table.

tablemat ['teɪblmæt] *n* dessous-de-plat *m
inv.*

table salt *n* sel *m* fin.

tablespoon ['teɪblspuːn] *n* -**1.** [spoon] cuiller
f de service. -**2.** [spoonful] cuillerée *f* à
soupe.

tablet ['tæblɪt] *n* -**1.** [pill] comprimé *m,* cachet *m.* -**2.** [of stone] plaque *f* commémora-
tive. -**3.** [of soap] savonnette *f,* pain *m* de
savon.

table tennis *n* ping-pong *m,* tennis *m* de
table.

tableware ['teɪblweəʳ] *n* vaisselle *f.*

table wine *n* vin *m* de table.

tabloid ['tæblɔɪd] *n:* ~ **(newspaper)** tabloïd
m, tabloïde *m;* **the ~ press** la presse populaire.

TABLOID:

Dans les pays anglo-saxons, le format tabloïde est caractéristique des journaux populaires. Les principaux journaux populaires
britanniques sont: the Daily Express, the
Daily Mail, the Daily Mirror, The Star, The
Sun et Today

---

taboo [tə'buː] (*pl* -**s**) ◇ *adj* tabou(e). ◇ *n*
tabou *m.*

tabulate ['tæbjʊleɪt] *vt* mettre sous forme
de table.

tachograph ['tækəgrɑːf] *n* tachygraphe *m.*

tachometer [tæ'kɒmɪtəʳ] *n* tachymètre *m.*

tacit ['tæsɪt] *adj* tacite.

taciturn ['tæsɪtɜːn] *adj* taciturne.

tack [tæk] ◇ *n* -**1.** [nail] clou *m.* -**2.** NAUT
bord *m,* bordée *f.* -**3.** *fig* [course of action]
tactique *f,* méthode *f;* **to change ~** changer
de tactique. ◇ *vt* -**1.** [fasten with nail - gen]
clouer; [- notice] punaiser. -**2.** SEWING faufiler. ◇ *vi* NAUT tirer une bordée.

◆ **tack on** *vt sep inf* ajouter, rajouter.

tackle ['tækl] ◇ *n* -**1.** FTBL tacle *m;* RUGBY
plaquage *m.* -**2.** [equipment] équipement *m,*
matériel *m.* -**3.** [for lifting] palan *m,* appareil
m de levage. ◇ *vt* -**1.** [deal with] s'attaquer
à. -**2.** FTBL tacler; RUGBY plaquer. -**3.** [attack]
empoigner. -**4.** [talk to]: **to ~ sb about** OR
on sthg parler franchement à qqn de qqch,
entreprendre qqn sur qqch.

tacky ['tækɪ] (*compar* -**ier**, *superl* -**iest**) *adj*
-**1.** *inf* [film, remark] d'un goût douteux; [je-
wellery] de pacotille. -**2.** [sticky] collant(e),
pas encore sec (sèche).

taco ['tækəʊ] (*pl* -**s**) *n galette de maïs fourrée à
la viande et au fromage.*

tact [tækt] *n* (*U*) tact *m,* délicatesse *f.*

tactful ['tæktfʊl] *adj* [remark] plein(e) de
tact; [person] qui a du tact OR de la délicatesse.

tactfully ['tæktfʊlɪ] *adv* avec tact, avec délicatesse.

tactic ['tæktɪk] *n* tactique *f.*

◆ **tactics** *n* (*U*) MIL tactique *f.*

tactical ['tæktɪkl] *adj* tactique.

tactical voting *n Br* vote *m* tactique.

tactless ['tæktlɪs] *adj* qui manque de tact
OR délicatesse.

tactlessly ['tæktlɪslɪ] *adv* sans tact, sans délicatesse.

tadpole ['tædpəʊl] *n* têtard *m*.

Tadzhikistan [tɑː,dʒɪkɪ'stɑːn] *n* Tadjikistan *m*; **in** ~ au Tadjikistan.

taffeta ['tæfɪtə] *n* (*U*) taffetas *m*.

taffy ['tæfɪ] (*pl* **-ies**) *n Am* caramel *m*.

tag [tæg] (*pt* & *pp* **-ged**, *cont* **-ging**) ◇ *n* **-1.** [of cloth] marque *f*. **-2.** [of paper] étiquette *f*. **-3.** (*U*) [game] jeu *m* du chat. **-4.** COMPUT balise *f*. ◇ *vt* marquer, étiqueter.
◆ **tag along** *vi inf* suivre.

Tagus ['teɪgəs] *n*: **the** ~ le Tage.

Tahiti [tɑː'hiːtɪ] *n* Tahiti *m*; **in** ~ à Tahiti.

Tahitian [tɑː'hiːʃn] ◇ *adj* tahitien(ienne). ◇ *n* Tahitien *m*, -ienne *f*.

tail [teɪl] ◇ *n* **-1.** [gen] queue *f*; **with one's** ~ **between one's legs** *fig* la queue entre les jambes. **-2.** [of coat] basque *f*, pan *m*; [of shirt] pan. ◇ *comp* arrière. ◇ *vt inf* [follow] filer.
◆ **tails** *npl* **-1.** [formal dress] queue-de-pie *f*, habit *m*. **-2.** [side of coin] pile *f*.
◆ **tail off** *vi* **-1.** [voice] s'affaiblir; [noise] diminuer. **-2.** [figures, sales] diminuer, baisser.

tailback ['teɪlbæk] *n Br* retenue *f*.

tailcoat [,teɪl'kəʊt] *n* habit *m*, queue-de-pie *f*.

tail end *n* fin *f*.

tailgate ['teɪlgeɪt] *n* AUT hayon *m*.

taillight ['teɪllaɪt] *n* feu *m* arrière.

tailor ['teɪlər] ◇ *n* tailleur *m*. ◇ *vt fig* adapter.

tailored ['teɪləd] *adj* ajusté(e), cintré(e).

tailor-made *adj fig* sur mesure.

tail pipe *n Am* tuyau *m* d'échappement.

tailplane ['teɪlpleɪn] *n* plan *m* fixe horizontal.

tailwind ['teɪlwɪnd] *n* vent *m* arrière.

taint [teɪnt] ◇ *n* souillure *f*. ◇ *vt* [reputation] souiller, entacher.

tainted ['teɪntɪd] *adj* **-1.** [reputation] souillé(e), entaché(e). **-2.** *Am* [food] avarié(e).

Taiwan [,taɪ'wɑːn] *n* Taiwan; **in** ~ à Taiwan.

Taiwanese [,taɪwə'niːz] ◇ *adj* taiwanais(e). ◇ *n* Taiwanais *m*, -e *f*.

take [teɪk] (*pt* **took**, *pp* **taken**) ◇ *vt* **-1.** [gen] prendre; **to** ~ **a seat** prendre un siège, s'asseoir; **to** ~ **control/command** prendre le contrôle/le commandement; **to** ~ **an exam** passer un examen; **to** ~ **a walk** se promener, faire une promenade; **to** ~ **a bath/photo** prendre un bain/une photo; **to** ~ **a lot of criticism** être très critiqué(e); **to** ~

pity on sb prendre qqn en pitié, avoir pitié de qqn; **to** ~ **offence** se vexer, s'offenser; **to** ~ **an interest in** s'intéresser à. **-2.** [lead, drive] emmener. **-3.** [accept] accepter. **-4.** [contain] contenir, avoir une capacité de. **-5.** [tolerate] supporter. **-6.** [require] demander; **how long will it** ~? combien de temps cela va-t-il prendre? **-7.** [wear]: **what size do you** ~? [clothes] quelle taille faites-vous?; [shoes] vous chaussez du combien? **-8.** [assume]: **I** ~ **it (that)** ... je suppose que ..., je pense que .... **-9.** [rent] prendre, louer. ◇ *vi* [dye, vaccine, fire] prendre.
◇ *n* CINEMA prise *f* de vues.
◆ **take aback** *vt sep* surprendre, décontenancer; **to be taken aback** être décontenancé(e) OR surpris(e).
◆ **take after** *vt fus* tenir de, ressembler à.
◆ **take apart** *vt sep* [dismantle] démonter.
◆ **take away** *vt sep* **-1.** [remove] enlever. **-2.** [deduct] retrancher, soustraire.
◆ **take back** *vt sep* **-1.** [return] rendre, rapporter. **-2.** [accept] reprendre. **-3.** [statement, accusation] retirer.
◆ **take down** *vt sep* **-1.** [dismantle] démonter. **-2.** [write down] prendre. **-3.** [lower] baisser.
◆ **take in** *vt sep* **-1.** [deceive] rouler, tromper. **-2.** [understand] comprendre. **-3.** [include] englober, couvrir. **-4.** [provide accommodation for] recueillir.
◆ **take off** ◇ *vt sep* **-1.** [remove] enlever, ôter. **-2.** [have as holiday]: **to** ~ **a week/day off** prendre une semaine/un jour de congé; **to** ~ **time off** prendre un congé. **-3.** *Br* [imitate] imiter. **-4.** [go away suddenly]: **to** ~ **o.s. off** s'en aller, partir. ◇ *vi* **-1.** [plane] décoller. **-2.** [go away suddenly] partir. **-3.** [be successful] démarrer.
◆ **take on** ◇ *vt sep* **-1.** [accept] accepter, prendre. **-2.** [employ] embaucher, prendre. **-3.** [confront] s'attaquer à; [competitor] faire concurrence à; SPORT jouer contre. ◇ *vt fus* [assume] prendre.
◆ **take out** *vt sep* **-1.** [from container] sortir; [from pocket] prendre. **-2.** [delete] enlever, supprimer. **-3.** [go out with] emmener, sortir avec; **to** ~ **it** OR **a lot out of sb** *inf* épuiser qqn, vider qqn.
◆ **take out on** *vt sep*: **to** ~ **sthg out on sb** passer qqch sur qqn; **don't** ~ **it out on me!** ne t'en prends pas à moi!
◆ **take over** ◇ *vt sep* **-1.** [take control of] reprendre, prendre la direction de. **-2.** [job]: **to** ~ **over sb's job** remplacer qqn, prendre la suite de qqn. ◇ *vi* **-1.** [take control] prendre le pouvoir. **-2.** [in job] prendre la relève.
◆ **take to** *vt fus* **-1.** [person] éprouver de la

sympathie pour, sympathiser avec; [activity] prendre goût à. **-2.** [begin]: **to ~ to doing sthg** se mettre à faire qqch.

◆ **take up** *vt sep* **-1.** [begin - job] prendre; **to ~ up singing** se mettre au chant. **-2.** [continue - story] reprendre, continuer. **-3.** [discuss]: **to ~ an issue up with sb** aborder une question avec qqn. **-4.** [use up] prendre, occuper.

◆ **take up on** *vt sep* **-1.** [accept]: **to ~ sb up on an offer** accepter l'offre de qqn. **-2.** [ask to explain]: **to ~ sb up on sthg** demander à qqn d'expliquer qqch.

◆ **take upon** *vt sep*: **to ~ it upon o.s. to do sthg** prendre sur soi de faire qqch.

takeaway *Br* ['teɪkə,weɪ], **takeout** *Am* ['teɪkaʊt] *n* **-1.** [shop] restaurant *m* qui fait des plats à emporter. **-2.** [food] plat *m* à emporter.

take-home pay *n* salaire *m* net (après déductions).

taken ['teɪkn] ◇ *pp* → **take**. ◇ *adj*: **she was very ~ with him/the idea** il/l'idée lui plaisait beaucoup.

takeoff ['teɪkɒf] *n* [of plane] décollage *m*.

takeout *Am* = **takeaway**.

takeover ['teɪk,əʊvə'] *n* **-1.** [of company] prise *f* de contrôle, rachat *m*. **-2.** [of government] prise *f* de pouvoir.

takeover bid *n* offre *f* publique d'achat, OPA *f*.

taker ['teɪkə'] *n* preneur *m*, -euse *f*.

takeup ['teɪkʌp] *n* [of shares] souscription *f*.

taking ['teɪkɪŋ] *adj dated* charmant(e), séduisant(e).

◆ **takings** *npl* recette *f*.

talc [tælk], **talcum (powder)** ['tælkəm-] *n* talc *m*.

tale [teɪl] *n* **-1.** [fictional story] histoire *f*, conte *m*. **-2.** [anecdote] récit *m*, histoire *f*.

talent ['tælənt] *n*: **~ (for)** talent *m* (pour).

talented ['tæləntɪd] *adj* qui a du talent, talentueux(euse).

talent scout *n* dénicheur *m*, -euse *f* de talents.

talisman ['tælɪzmən] (*pl* **-s**) *n* talisman *m*.

talk [tɔːk] ◇ *n* **-1.** [conversation] discussion *f*, conversation *f*. **-2.** (*U*) [gossip] bavardages *mpl*, racontars *mpl*. **-3.** [lecture] conférence *f*, causerie *f*. ◇ *vi* **-1.** [speak]: **to ~ (to sb)** parler (à qqn); **to ~ about** parler de; **~ing of Lucy, ...** à propos de Lucy, ...; **to ~ big** se vanter. **-2.** [gossip] bavarder, jaser. **-3.** [make a speech] faire un discours, parler; **to ~ on** OR **about** parler de. ◇ *vt* parler.

◆ **talks** *npl* entretiens *mpl*, pourparlers *mpl*.

◆ **talk down to** *vt fus* parler avec condescendance à.

◆ **talk into** *vt sep*: **to ~ sb into doing sthg** persuader qqn de faire qqch.

◆ **talk out of** *vt sep*: **to ~ sb out of doing sthg** dissuader qqn de faire qqch.

◆ **talk over** *vt sep* discuter de.

talkative ['tɔːkətɪv] *adj* bavard(e), loquace.

talker ['tɔːkə'] *n* causeur *m*, -euse *f*, bavard *m*, -e *f*.

talking point ['tɔːkɪŋ-] *n* sujet *m* de conversation OR discussion.

talking-to ['tɔːkɪŋ-] *n inf* savon *m*, réprimande *f*; **to give sb a good ~** passer un bon savon à qqn.

talk show *Am n* talk-show *m*, causerie *f*.

tall [tɔːl] *adj* grand(e); **how ~ are you?** combien mesurez-vous?; **she's 5 feet ~** elle mesure 1,50 m.

tallboy ['tɔːlbɔɪ] *n* commode *f*.

tall order *n*: **that's a ~** c'est demander beaucoup, cela va être difficile.

tall story *n* histoire *f* à dormir debout.

tally ['tælɪ] (*pl* **-ies**, *pt* & *pp* **-ied**) ◇ *n* compte *m*. ◇ *vi* correspondre, concorder.

talon ['tælən] *n* serre *f*, griffe *f*.

tambourine [,tæmbə'riːn] *n* tambourin *m*.

tame [teɪm] ◇ *adj* **-1.** [animal, bird] apprivoisé(e). **-2.** *pej* [person] docile; [party, story, life] terne, morne. ◇ *vt* **-1.** [animal, bird] apprivoiser. **-2.** [people] mater, dresser.

tamely ['teɪmlɪ] *adv* [accept, agree] docilement.

tamer ['teɪmə'] *n* dompteur *m*, -euse *f*.

Tamil ['tæmɪl] ◇ *adj* tamoul(e), tamil(e). ◇ *n* **-1.** [person] Tamoul *m*, -e *f*, Tamil *m*, -e *f*. **-2.** [language] tamoul *m*, tamil *m*.

tamper ['tæmpə']

◆ **tamper with** *vt fus* [machine] toucher à; [records, file] altérer, falsifier; [lock] essayer de crocheter.

tampon ['tæmpɒn] *n* tampon *m*.

tan [tæn] (*pt* & *pp* **-ned**, *cont* **-ning**) ◇ *adj* brun clair (*inv*). ◇ *n* bronzage *m*, hâle *m*. ◇ *vi* bronzer.

tandem ['tændəm] *n* [bicycle] tandem *m*; **in ~** en tandem.

tandoori [tæn'dʊərɪ] ◇ *n* tandouri *m*, tandoori *m*. ◇ *comp* tandouri, tandoori.

tang [tæŋ] *n* [taste] saveur *f* forte OR piquante; [smell] odeur *f* forte OR piquante.

tangent ['tændʒənt] *n* GEOM tangente *f*; **to go off at a ~** *fig* changer de sujet, faire une digression.

tangerine [ˌtænˈdʒəriːn] n mandarine f.

tangible [ˈtændʒəbl] adj tangible.

Tangier [tænˈdʒɪər] n Tanger.

tangle [ˈtæŋgl] ◇ n -1. [mass] enchevêtrement m, emmêlement m. -2. fig [confusion] embrouillamini m; **to get into a ~** s'empêtrer, s'embrouiller. ◇ vt: **to get ~d (up)** s'emmêler. ◇ vi s'emmêler, s'enchevêtrer.
◆ **tangle with** vt fus inf se frotter à.

tangled [ˈtæŋgld] adj emmêlé(e); fig embrouillé(e).

tango [ˈtæŋgəʊ] (pl **-es**) ◇ n tango m. ◇ vi danser le tango.

tangy [ˈtæŋɪ] (compar **-ier**, superl **-iest**) adj piquant(e), fort(e).

tank [tæŋk] n -1. [container] réservoir m; **fish ~** aquarium m. -2. MIL tank m, char m (d'assaut).

tankard [ˈtæŋkəd] n chope f.

tanker [ˈtæŋkər] n -1. [ship - for oil] pétrolier m. -2. [truck] camion-citerne m. -3. [train] wagon-citerne m.

tankful [ˈtæŋkfʊl] n [of petrol] réservoir m plein d'essence.

tanned [tænd] adj bronzé(e), hâlé(e).

tannin [ˈtænɪn] n tannin m, tanin m.

Tannoy® [ˈtænɔɪ] n système m de haut-parleurs.

tantalize, -ise [ˈtæntəlaɪz] vt mettre au supplice.

tantalizing [ˈtæntəlaɪzɪŋ] adj [smell] très appétissant(e); [possibility, thought] très tentant(e).

tantamount [ˈtæntəmaʊnt] adj: **~ to** équivalent(e) à.

tantrum [ˈtæntrəm] (pl **-s**) n crise f de colère; **to have** OR **throw a ~** faire OR piquer une colère.

Tanzania [ˌtænzəˈnɪə] n Tanzanie f; **in ~** en Tanzanie.

Tanzanian [ˌtænzəˈnɪən] ◇ adj tanzanien(ienne). ◇ n Tanzanien m, -ienne f.

tap [tæp] (pt & pp **-ped**, cont **-ping**) ◇ n -1. [device] robinet m. -2. [light blow] petite tape f, petit coup m. ◇ vt -1. [hit] tapoter, taper. -2. [resources, energy] exploiter, utiliser. -3. [telephone, wire] mettre sur écoute. ◇ vi taper, frapper.

tap dance n claquettes fpl.

tap dancer n danseur m, -euse f de claquettes.

tape [teɪp] ◇ n -1. [magnetic tape] bande f magnétique; [cassette] cassette f. -2. [strip of cloth, adhesive material] ruban m. -3. SPORT bande f d'arrivée. ◇ vt -1. [record] enregistrer; [on video] magnétoscoper, enregistrer

au magnétoscope. -2. [stick] scotcher. -3. Am [bandage] bander.

tape deck n dérouleur m de bande magnétique.

tape measure n centimètre m, mètre m.

taper [ˈteɪpər] ◇ n [candle] bougie f fine. ◇ vi s'effiler; [trousers] se terminer en fuseau.
◆ **taper off** vi diminuer.

tape-record [-rɪˌkɔːd] vt enregistrer (au magnétophone).

tape recorder n magnétophone m.

tape recording n enregistrement m (au magnétophone).

tapered [ˈteɪpəd] adj [fingers] effilé(e), fuselé(e); [trousers] en fuseau.

tapestry [ˈtæpɪstrɪ] (pl **-ies**) n tapisserie f.

tapeworm [ˈteɪpwɜːm] n ténia m.

tapioca [ˌtæpɪˈəʊkə] n tapioca m.

tapir [ˈteɪpər] (pl inv OR **-s**) n tapir m.

tappet [ˈtæpɪt] n poussoir m.

tar [tɑːr] n (U) goudron m.

tarantula [təˈræntjʊlə] n tarentule f.

target [ˈtɑːgɪt] ◇ n -1. [of missile, bomb] objectif m; [for archery, shooting] cible f. -2. fig [for criticism] cible f. -3. fig [goal] objectif m; **on ~** dans les temps. ◇ vt -1. [city, building] viser. -2. fig [subj: policy] s'adresser à, viser; [subj: advertising] cibler.

tariff [ˈtærɪf] n -1. [tax] tarif m douanier. -2. [list] tableau m OR liste f des prix.

Tarmac® [ˈtɑːmæk] n [material] macadam m.
◆ **tarmac** n AERON: **the tarmac** la piste.

tarnish [ˈtɑːnɪʃ] ◇ vt lit & fig ternir. ◇ vi se ternir.

tarnished [ˈtɑːnɪʃt] adj lit & fig terni(e).

tarot [ˈtærəʊ] n: **the ~** le tarot, les tarots mpl.

tarot card n tarot m.

tarpaulin [tɑːˈpɔːlɪn] n [material] toile f goudronnée; [sheet] bâche f.

tarragon [ˈtærəgən] n estragon m.

tart [tɑːt] ◇ adj -1. [bitter] acide. -2. [sarcastic] acide, acerbe. ◇ n -1. CULIN tarte f. -2. v inf [prostitute] pute f, grue f.
◆ **tart up** vt sep Br inf pej [room] retaper, rénover; **to ~ o.s. up** se faire beau (belle).

tartan [ˈtɑːtn] ◇ n tartan m. ◇ comp écossais(e).

tartar(e) sauce [ˈtɑːtər-] n sauce f tartare.

tartness [ˈtɑːtnɪs] n acidité f.

task [tɑːsk] n tâche f, besogne f.

task force n MIL corps m expéditionnaire.

taskmaster [ˈtɑːskˌmɑːstər] n: **hard ~** tyran m.

Tasmania [tæzˈmeɪnjə] n Tasmanie f.

Tasmanian [tæz'meɪnjən] ◇ adj tasmanien(ienne). ◇ n Tasmanien m, -ienne f.

tassel ['tæsl] n pompon m, gland m.

taste [teɪst] ◇ n **-1.** [gen] goût m; **have a ~!** goûte!; **in bad/good ~** de bon/mauvais goût. **-2.** fig [liking]: **~ (for)** penchant m (pour), goût m (pour). **-3.** fig [experience] aperçu m; **to have had a ~ of sthg** avoir tâté OR goûté de qqch. ◇ vt **-1.** [sense - food] sentir. **-2.** [test, try] déguster, goûter. **-3.** fig [experience] tâter de, goûter de. ◇ vi: **to ~ of/like** avoir le goût de; **to ~ good/odd** etc avoir bon goût/un drôle de goût etc.

taste bud n papille f gustative.

tasteful ['teɪstful] adj de bon goût.

tastefully ['teɪstfulɪ] adv avec goût.

tasteless ['teɪstlɪs] adj **-1.** [object, decor, remark] de mauvais goût. **-2.** [food] qui n'a aucun goût, fade.

taster ['teɪstə'] n dégustateur m, -trice f.

tasty ['teɪstɪ] (compar **-ier**, superl **-iest**) adj [delicious] délicieux(ieuse), succulent(e).

tat [tæt] n (U) Br inf pej camelote f.

tattered ['tætəd] adj en lambeaux.

tatters ['tætəz] npl: **in ~** [clothes] en lambeaux; [confidence] brisé(e); [reputation] ruiné(e).

tattoo [tə'tu:] (pl **-s**) ◇ n **-1.** [design] tatouage m. **-2.** Br [military display] parade f OR défilé m militaire. ◇ vt tatouer.

tattooist [tə'tu:ɪst] n tatoueur m.

tatty ['tætɪ] (compar **-ier**, superl **-iest**) adj Br inf pej [clothes] défraîchi(e), usé(e); [flat, area] miteux(euse), minable.

taught [tɔ:t] pt & pp → **teach**.

taunt [tɔ:nt] ◇ vt railler, se moquer de. ◇ n raillerie f, moquerie f.

Taurus ['tɔ:rəs] n Taureau m; **to be (a) ~** être Taureau.

taut [tɔ:t] adj tendu(e).

tauten ['tɔ:tn] ◇ vt tendre. ◇ vi se tendre.

tautology [tɔ:'tɒlədʒɪ] n tautologie f.

tavern ['tævn] n taverne f.

tawdry ['tɔ:drɪ] (compar **-ier**, superl **-iest**) adj pej [jewellery] clinquant(e); [clothes] voyant(e), criard(e).

tawny ['tɔ:nɪ] adj fauve.

tax [tæks] ◇ n taxe f, impôt m. ◇ vt **-1.** [goods] taxer. **-2.** [profits, business, person] imposer. **-3.** [strain] mettre à l'épreuve.

taxable ['tæksəbl] adj imposable.

tax allowance n abattement m fiscal.

taxation [tæk'seɪʃn] n (U) **-1.** [system] imposition f. **-2.** [amount] impôts mpl.

tax avoidance [-ə'vɔɪdəns] n évasion f fiscale.

tax collector n percepteur m.

tax cut n baisse f de l'impôt.

tax-deductible [-dɪ'dʌktəbl] adj déductible des impôts.

tax disc n Br vignette f.

tax evasion n fraude f fiscale.

tax-exempt Am = **tax-free**.

tax exemption n exonération f d'impôt.

tax exile n Br personne qui vit à l'étranger pour échapper au fisc.

tax-free Br, **tax-exempt** Am adj exonéré(e) (d'impôt).

tax haven n paradis m fiscal.

taxi ['tæksɪ] ◇ n taxi m. ◇ vi [plane] rouler au sol.

taxicab ['tæksɪkæb] n taxi m.

taxidermist ['tæksɪdɜ:mɪst] n taxidermiste mf.

taxi driver n chauffeur m de taxi.

taximeter ['tæksɪ,mi:tə'] n taximètre m.

taxing ['tæksɪŋ] adj éprouvant(e).

tax inspector n inspecteur m des impôts.

taxi rank Br, **taxi stand** n station f de taxis.

taxman ['tæksmæn] (pl **-men** [-men]) n percepteur m.

taxpayer ['tæks,peɪə'] n contribuable mf.

tax relief n allègement m OR dégrèvement m fiscal.

tax return n déclaration f d'impôts.

tax year n année f fiscale.

TB n abbr of **tuberculosis**.

T-bone steak n steak m dans l'aloyau.

tbs., tbsp. (abbr of **tablespoon(ful)**) cs.

TD n **-1.** (abbr of **Treasury Department**) ministère américain de l'économie et des finances. **-2.** abbr of **touchdown**.

tea [ti:] n **-1.** [drink, leaves] thé m. **-2.** Br [afternoon meal] goûter m; [evening meal] dîner m.

teabag ['ti:bæg] n sachet m de thé.

tea ball n Am boule f à thé.

tea break n Br pause-café f.

tea caddy [-,kædɪ] n boîte f à thé.

teacake ['ti:keɪk] n Br petit pain rond avec des raisins secs.

teach [ti:tʃ] (pt & pp **taught**) ◇ vt **-1.** [instruct] apprendre; **to ~ sb sthg, to ~ sthg to sb** apprendre qqch à qqn; **to ~ sb to do sthg** apprendre à qqn à faire qqch; **to ~ (sb) that ...** apprendre (à qqn) que .... **-2.** [subj: teacher] enseigner; **to ~ sb sthg, to ~**

sthg to sb enseigner qqch à qqn. ◇ *vi* enseigner.

teacher ['tiːtʃər] *n* professeur *m*.

teachers college *Am* = **teacher training college**.

teacher's pet *n pej* chouchou *m*, chouchoute *f*.

teacher training college *Br*, **teachers college** *Am n* ≃ institut *m* universitaire de formation de maîtres, ≃ IUFM *m*.

teaching ['tiːtʃɪŋ] *n* enseignement *m*.

teaching aids *npl* outils *mpl* pédagogiques.

teaching hospital *n Br* centre *m* hospitalo-universitaire, C.H.U. *m*.

teaching practice *n* (U) stage *m* de formation.

teaching staff *npl* enseignants *mpl*.

tea cloth *n Br* **-1.** [tablecloth] nappe *f*. **-2.** [tea towel] torchon *m*.

tea cosy *Br*, **tea cozy** *Am n* couvre-théière *m*, cosy *m*.

teacup ['tiːkʌp] *n* tasse *f* à thé.

teak [tiːk] ◇ *n* teck *m*. ◇ *comp* en teck.

tea leaves *npl* feuilles *fpl* de thé.

team [tiːm] *n* équipe *f*.
◆ **team up** *vi*: to ~ **up** (**with sb**) faire équipe (avec qqn).

team games *npl* jeux *mpl* d'équipe.

teammate ['tiːmmeɪt] *n* co-équipier *m*, -ière *f*.

team spirit *n* esprit *m* d'équipe.

teamster ['tiːmstər] *n Am* routier *m*, camionneur *m*.

teamwork ['tiːmwɜːk] *n* (U) travail *m* d'équipe, collaboration *f*.

tea party *n* thé *m*.

teapot ['tiːpɒt] *n* théière *f*.

tear¹ [tɪər] *n* larme *f*; **in ~s** en larmes.

tear² [teər] (*pt* **tore**, *pp* **torn**) ◇ *vt* **-1.** [rip] déchirer; to ~ **sthg open** ouvrir qqch (en le déchirant); to ~ **sb/sthg to pieces** *fig* éreinter qqn/qqch. **-2.** [remove roughly] arracher. **-3.** *phr*: to be torn between être tiraillé(e) entre. ◇ *vi* **-1.** [rip] se déchirer. **-2.** [move quickly] foncer, aller à toute allure. **-3.** *phr*: to ~ **loose** s'échapper. ◇ *n* déchirure *f*, accroc *m*.
◆ **tear apart** *vt sep* **-1.** [rip up] déchirer, mettre en morceaux. **-2.** *fig* [country, company] diviser; [person] déchirer.
◆ **tear at** *vt fus* déchirer.
◆ **tear away** *vt sep*: to ~ **o.s. away** (**from**) s'arracher (de OR à).
◆ **tear down** *vt sep* [building] démolir; [poster] arracher.
◆ **tear off** *vt sep* [clothes] enlever à la hâte.

◆ **tear up** *vt sep* déchirer.

tearaway ['teərəˌweɪ] *n Br inf* casse-cou *mf inv*.

teardrop ['tɪədrɒp] *n* larme *f*.

tearful ['tɪəful] *adj* **-1.** [person] en larmes. **-2.** [event] larmoyant(e).

tear gas [tɪər-] *n* (U) gaz *m* lacrymogène.

tearing ['teərɪŋ] *adj inf* terrible, fou (folle).

tearjerker ['tɪəˌdʒɜːkər] *n hum* roman *m*/film *m* qui fait pleurer dans les chaumières.

tearoom ['tiːrʊm] *n* salon *m* de thé.

tease [tiːz] ◇ *n* taquin *m*, -e *f*. ◇ *vt* [mock]: to ~ **sb** (**about sthg**) taquiner qqn (à propos de qqch).

tea service, tea set *n* service *m* à thé.

tea shop *n* salon *m* de thé.

teasing ['tiːzɪŋ] *adj* taquin(e).

Teasmaid® ['tiːzmeɪd] *n Br* théière *f* automatique avec horloge incorporée.

teaspoon ['tiːspuːn] *n* **-1.** [utensil] petite cuillère *f*, cuillere à café. **-2.** [amount] cuillerée *f* à café.

tea strainer *n* passoire *f*.

teat [tiːt] *n* tétine *f*.

teatime ['tiːtaɪm] *n Br* l'heure *f* du thé.

tea towel *n* torchon *m*.

tea urn *n* fontaine *f* à thé.

technical ['teknɪkl] *adj* technique.

technical college *n Br* collège *m* technique.

technical drawing *n* (U) dessin *m* industriel.

technicality [ˌteknɪ'kælətɪ] (*pl* **-ies**) *n* **-1.** [intricacy] technicité *f*. **-2.** [detail] détail *m* technique.

technically ['teknɪklɪ] *adv* **-1.** [gen] techniquement. **-2.** [theoretically] en théorie.

technician [tek'nɪʃn] *n* technicien *m*, -ienne *f*.

Technicolor® ['teknɪˌkʌlər] *n* (U) Technicolor® *m*.

technique [tek'niːk] *n* technique *f*.

technocrat ['teknəkræt] *n* technocrate *mf*.

technological [ˌteknə'lɒdʒɪkl] *adj* technologique.

technologist [tek'nɒlədʒɪst] *n* technologue *mf*.

technology [tek'nɒlədʒɪ] (*pl* **-ies**) *n* technologie *f*.

teddy ['tedɪ] (*pl* **-ies**) *n*: ~ (**bear**) ours *m* en peluche, nounours *m*.

tedious ['tiːdjəs] *adj* ennuyeux(euse).

tedium ['tiːdjəm] *n fml* ennui *m*.

tee [tiː] *n* GOLF tee *m*.

◆ **tee off** *vi* GOLF partir du tee.

teem [tiːm] *vi* **-1.** [rain] pleuvoir à verse. **-2.** [place]: **to be ~ing with** grouiller de.

teen [tiːn] *adj inf* [fashion] pour ados; [music, problems] d'ados.

teenage ['tiːneɪdʒ] *adj* adolescent(e).

teenager ['tiːn,eɪdʒəʳ] adolescent *m*, -e *f*.

teens [tiːnz] *npl* adolescence *f*.

teeny (weeny) [,tiːnɪ('wiːnɪ)], **teensy (weensy)** [,tiːnzɪ('wiːnzɪ)] *adj inf* minuscule, tout petit (toute petite).

tee shirt *n* tee-shirt *m*.

teeter ['tiːtəʳ] *vi* vaciller; **to ~ on the brink of** *fig* être au bord de.

teeter-totter *n Am* bascule *f*.

teeth [tiːθ] *pl* → **tooth**.

teethe [tiːð] *vi* [baby] percer ses dents.

teething ring ['tiːðɪŋ-] *n* anneau *m* de dentition.

teething troubles ['tiːðɪŋ-] *npl fig* difficultés *fpl* initiales.

teetotal [tiː'təʊtl] *adj* qui ne boit jamais d'alcool.

teetotaller *Br*, **teetotaler** *Am* [tiː'təʊtləʳ] *n* personne *f* qui ne boit jamais d'alcool.

TEFL ['tefl] (*abbr of* **teaching of English as a foreign language**) *n enseignement de l'anglais langue étrangère.*

Teflon® ['teflɒn] ◇ *n* Téflon® *m*. ◇ *comp* en Téflon®.

Tehran, Teheran [,teə'rɑːn] *n* Téhéran.

tel. (*abbr of* **telephone**) tél.

Tel-Aviv [,telə'viːv] *n*: **~(-Jaffa)** Tel-Aviv(-Jaffa).

tele- ['telɪ] *prefix* télé-.

telecast ['telɪkɑːst] *n* émission *f* de télévision.

telecom ['telɪkɒm] *n*, **telecoms** ['telɪkɒmz] *npl Br inf* télécommunications *fpl*.

telecommunications ['telɪkə,mjuːnɪ'keɪʃnz] *npl* télécommunications *fpl*.

telegram ['telɪgræm] *n* télégramme *m*.

telegraph ['telɪgrɑːf] ◇ *n* télégraphe *m*. ◇ *vt* télégraphier.

telegraph pole, telegraph post *Br n* poteau *m* télégraphique.

telepathic [,telɪ'pæθɪk] *adj* télépathique.

telepathy [tɪ'lepəθɪ] *n* télépathie *f*.

telephone ['telɪfəʊn] ◇ *n* téléphone *m*; **to be on the ~** *Br* [connected] avoir le téléphone; [speaking] être au téléphone. ◇ *vt* téléphoner à. ◇ *vi* téléphoner.

telephone book *n* annuaire *m*.

telephone booth *n* cabine *f* téléphonique.

telephone box *n Br* cabine *f* téléphonique.

telephone call *n* appel *m* téléphonique, coup *m* de téléphone.

telephone directory *n* annuaire *m*.

telephone exchange *n* central *m* téléphonique.

telephone kiosk *n Br* cabine *f* téléphonique.

telephone number *n* numéro *m* de téléphone.

telephone operator *n* standardiste *mf*.

telephone tapping [-'tæpɪŋ] *n* mise *f* sur écoute.

telephonist [tɪ'lefənɪst] *n Br* téléphoniste *mf*.

telephoto lens [,telɪ'fəʊtəʊ-] *n* téléobjectif *m*.

teleprinter ['telɪ,prɪntəʳ], **teletypewriter** *Am* [,telɪ'taɪp,raɪtəʳ] *n* téléscripteur *m*.

Teleprompter® [,telɪ'prɒmptəʳ] *n* téléprompteur *m*.

telesales ['telɪseɪlz] *npl* vente *f* par téléphone.

telescope ['telɪskəʊp] *n* télescope *m*.

telescopic [,telɪ'skɒpɪk] *adj* télescopique.

teletext ['telɪtekst] *n* télétexte *m*.

telethon ['telɪθɒn] *n* téléthon *m*.

teletypewriter *Am* = **teleprinter**.

televise ['telɪvaɪz] *vt* téléviser.

television ['telɪ,vɪʒn] *n* **-1.** (U) [medium, industry] télévision *f*; **on ~** à la télévision. **-2.** [apparatus] (poste *m* de) télévision *f*, téléviseur *m*.

television licence *n Br* redevance *f*.

television programme *n* émission *f* de télévision.

television set *n* poste *m* de télévision, téléviseur *m*.

telex ['teleks] ◇ *n* télex *m*. ◇ *vt* [message] envoyer par télex, télexer; [person] envoyer un télex à.

tell [tel] (*pt & pp* **told**) ◇ *vt* **-1.** [gen] dire; [story] raconter; **to ~ sb (that)** ... dire à qqn que ...; **to ~ sb sthg, to ~ sthg to sb** dire qqch à qqn; **to ~ sb to do sthg** dire OR ordonner à qqn de faire qqch; **I told you so!** je te l'avais bien dit! **-2.** [judge, recognize] savoir, voir; **he can't ~ the time** il ne sait pas lire l'heure; **could you ~ me the time?** tu peux me dire l'heure (qu'il est)?; **there's no ~ing ...** on ne peut pas savoir .... ◇ *vi* **-1.** [speak] parler. **-2.** [judge] savoir. **-3.** [have effect] se faire sentir.

◆ **tell apart** *vt sep* distinguer.

◆ **tell off** *vt sep* gronder.

teller ['telər] n -1. [of votes] scrutateur m, -trice f. -2. [in bank] caissier m, -ière f.

telling ['telɪŋ] adj [remark] révélateur(trice).

telling-off (pl tellings-off) n réprimande f.

telltale ['telteɪl] ◇ adj révélateur(trice). ◇ n rapporteur m, -euse f, mouchard m, -e f.

telly ['telɪ] (pl -ies) (abbr of **television**) n Br inf télé f; **on ~** à la télé.

temerity [tɪ'merətɪ] n témérité f.

temp [temp] inf ◇ n (abbr of **temporary (employee)**) intérimaire mf. ◇ vi travailler comme intérimaire.

temp. (abbr of **temperature**) temp.

temper ['tempər] ◇ n -1. [angry state]: **to be in a ~** être en colère; **to lose one's ~** se mettre en colère; **to have a short ~** être emporté. -2. [mood] humeur f. -3. [temperament] tempérament m. ◇ vt [moderate] tempérer.

temperament ['temprəmənt] n tempérament m.

temperamental [,temprə'mentl] adj [volatile, unreliable] capricieux(ieuse).

temperance ['temprəns] n (U) [moderation] modération f; [from alcohol] tempérance f.

temperate ['temprət] adj tempéré(e).

temperature ['temprətʃər] n température f; **to take sb's ~** prendre la température de qqn; **to have a ~** avoir de la température OR de la fièvre.

tempered ['tempəd] adj -1. [steel] trempé(e). -2. [moderated] tempéré(e), modéré(e).

tempest ['tempɪst] n literary tempête f.

tempestuous [tem'pestjuəs] adj lit & fig orageux(euse).

tempi ['tempiː] pl → tempo.

template ['templɪt] n gabarit m.

temple ['templ] n -1. RELIG temple m. -2. ANAT tempe f.

templet ['templɪt] = **template**.

tempo ['tempəu] (pl -pos OR -pi) n tempo m.

temporarily [,tempə'rerəlɪ] adv temporairement, provisoirement.

temporary ['tempərərɪ] adj temporaire, provisoire.

tempt [tempt] vt tenter; **to ~ sb to do sthg** donner à qqn l'envie de faire qqch; **to be OR feel ~ed to do sthg** être tenté OR avoir envie de faire qqch.

temptation [temp'teɪʃn] n tentation f.

tempting ['temptɪŋ] adj tentant(e).

ten [ten] num dix; see also **six**.

tenable ['tenəbl] adj -1. [argument, position] défendable. -2. [job, post]: **~ for** auquel on est nommé(e) pour.

tenacious [tɪ'neɪʃəs] adj tenace.

tenacity [tɪ'næsətɪ] n (U) ténacité f.

tenancy ['tenənsɪ] (pl -ies) n location f.

tenant ['tenənt] n locataire mf.

Ten Commandments npl: **the ~** les dix commandements mpl.

tend [tend] vt -1. [have tendency]: **to ~ to do sthg** avoir tendance à faire qqch; **I ~ to think (that)** ... j'ai tendance à penser que .... -2. [look after] s'occuper de, garder.

tendency ['tendənsɪ] (pl -ies) n: **~ (to do sthg)** tendance f (à faire qqch); **a ~ towards fascism** une tendance fasciste.

tender ['tendər] ◇ adj tendre; [bruise, part of body] sensible, douloureux(euse). ◇ n COMM soumission f. ◇ vt fml [apology, money] offrir; [resignation] donner.

tenderize, -ise ['tendəraɪz] vt attendrir.

tenderly ['tendəlɪ] adv [caringly] tendrement.

tenderness ['tendənɪs] n (U) -1. [compassion] tendresse f. -2. [soreness] sensibilité f.

tendon ['tendən] n tendon m.

tendril ['tendrəl] n vrille f.

tenement ['tenəmənt] n immeuble m.

Tenerife [,tenə'riːf] n Tenerife; **in ~** à Tenerife.

tenet ['tenɪt] n fml principe m.

tenner ['tenər] n Br inf [amount] dix livres; [note] billet m de dix livres.

Tennessee [,tenə'siː] n Tennessee m; **in ~** dans le Tennessee.

tennis ['tenɪs] ◇ n (U) tennis m. ◇ comp de tennis.

tennis ball n balle f de tennis.

tennis court n court m de tennis.

tennis racket n raquette f de tennis.

tenor ['tenər] ◇ adj [saxophone, recorder] ténor (inv); [voice] de ténor. ◇ n -1. [singer] ténor m. -2. fml [meaning] sens m, substance f.

tenpin bowling Br ['tenpɪn-], **tenpins** Am ['tenpɪnz] n (U) bowling m (à dix quilles).

tense [tens] ◇ adj tendu(e). ◇ n temps m. ◇ vt tendre. ◇ vi se contracter.

tensed up [tenst-] adj contracté(e), tendu(e).

tension ['tenʃn] n tension f.

ten-spot n Am billet m de dix dollars.

tent [tent] n tente f.

tentacle ['tentəkl] n tentacule m.

tentative ['tentətɪv] *adj* **-1.** [hesitant] hésitant(e). **-2.** [not final] provisoire.

tentatively ['tentətɪvlɪ] *adv* **-1.** [hesitantly] de façon hésitante. **-2.** [not finally] provisoirement.

tenterhooks ['tentəhʊks] *npl*: **to be on ~** être sur des charbons ardents.

tenth [tenθ] *num* dixième; *see also* **sixth**.

tent peg *n* piquet *m* de tente.

tent pole *n* montant *m* OR mât *m* de tente.

tenuous ['tenjʊəs] *adj* ténu(e).

tenuously ['tenjʊəslɪ] *adv* de façon ténue.

tenure ['tenjər] *n* (*U*) *fml* **-1.** [of property] bail *m*. **-2.** [of job]: **to have ~** être titulaire.

tepee ['tiːpiː] *n* tipi *m*.

tepid ['tepɪd] *adj* tiède.

tequila [tɪ'kiːlə] *n* tequila *f*.

Ter., Terr. *abbr of* **Terrace.**

term [tɜːm] ◇ *n* **-1.** [word, expression] terme *m*. **-2.** SCH & UNIV trimestre *m*. **-3.** [period of time] durée *f*, période *f*; **a prison ~** une peine de prison; **in the long/short ~** à long/court terme. ◇ *vt* appeler.

◆ **terms** *npl* **-1.** [of contract, agreement] conditions *fpl*. **-2.** [basis]: **in international/real ~s** en termes internationaux/réels; **on equal** OR **the same ~s** d'égal à égal; **to be on good ~s (with sb)** être en bons termes (avec qqn); **to be on speaking ~s** s'adresser la parole, se parler; **to be on speaking ~s with sb** adresser la parole à qqn, parler à qqn; **to come to ~s with sthg** accepter qqch. **-3.** *phr*: **to think in ~s of doing sthg** envisager de OR penser faire qqch.

◆ **in terms of** *prep* sur le plan de, en termes de.

terminal ['tɜːmɪnl] ◇ *adj* MED en phase terminale. ◇ *n* **-1.** AERON, COMPUT & RAIL terminal *m*. **-2.** ELEC borne *f*.

terminally ['tɜːmɪnəlɪ] *adv*: **to be ~ ill** être en phase terminale.

terminate ['tɜːmɪneɪt] ◇ *vt* **-1.** *fml* [end - gen] terminer, mettre fin à; [- contract] résilier. **-2.** [pregnancy] interrompre. ◇ *vi* **-1.** [bus, train] s'arrêter. **-2.** [contract] se terminer.

termination [,tɜːmɪ'neɪʃn] *n* **-1.** (*U*) *fml* [ending - gen] conclusion *f*; [- of contract] résiliation *f*. **-2.** [of pregnancy] interruption *f* (volontaire) de grossesse.

termini ['tɜːmɪnaɪ] *pl* → **terminus**.

terminology [,tɜːmɪ'nɒlədʒɪ] *n* terminologie *f*.

terminus ['tɜːmɪnəs] (*pl* **-ni** OR **-nuses**) terminus *m*.

termite ['tɜːmaɪt] *n* termite *m*.

Terr. = Ter.

terrace ['terəs] *n* **-1.** [patio, on hillside] terrasse *f*. **-2.** *Br* [of houses] rangée *f* de maisons.

◆ **terraces** *npl* FTBL: **the ~s** les gradins *mpl*.

terraced ['terəst] *adj* [hillside] en terrasses.

terraced house *n Br* maison *f* attenante aux maisons voisines.

terracotta [,terə'kɒtə] *n* terre *f* cuite.

terrain [te'reɪn] *n* terrain *m*.

terrapin ['terəpɪn] (*pl inv* OR **-s**) *n* tortue *f* d'eau douce.

terrestrial [tə'restrɪəl] *adj fml* terrestre.

terrible ['terəbl] *adj* terrible; [holiday, headache, weather] affreux(euse), épouvantable.

terribly ['terəblɪ] *adv* terriblement; [sing, write, organized] affreusement mal; [injured] affreusement.

terrier ['terɪər] *n* terrier *m*.

terrific [tə'rɪfɪk] *adj* **-1.** [wonderful] fantastique, formidable. **-2.** [enormous] énorme, fantastique.

terrified ['terɪfaɪd] *adj* terrifié(e); **to be ~ of** avoir une terreur folle OR peur folle de.

terrify ['terɪfaɪ] (*pt & pp* **-ied**) *vt* terrifier.

terrifying ['terɪfaɪɪŋ] *adj* terrifiant(e).

terrine [te'riːn] *n* terrine *f*.

territorial [,terɪ'tɔːrɪəl] *adj* territorial(e).

Territorial Army *n Br*: **the ~** l'armée territoriale.

territorial waters *npl* eaux *fpl* territoriales.

territory ['terətrɪ] (*pl* **-ies**) *n* territoire *m*.

terror ['terər] *n* terreur *f*.

terrorism ['terərɪzm] *n* terrorisme *m*.

terrorist ['terərɪst] *n* terroriste *mf*.

terrorize, -ise ['terəraɪz] *vt* terroriser.

terror-stricken *adj* épouvanté(e).

terry(cloth) ['terɪ(klɒθ)] *n* tissu *m* éponge.

terse [tɜːs] *adj* brusque.

tersely ['tɜːslɪ] *adv* avec brusquerie.

tertiary ['tɜːʃərɪ] *adj* tertiaire.

tertiary education *n* enseignement *m* supérieur.

Terylene® ['terəliːn] *n* Térylène *m*®.

TESL ['tesl] (*abbr of* **teaching of English as a second language**) *n* enseignement *m* de l'anglais seconde langue.

TESSA ['tesə] (*abbr of* **tax-exempt special savings account**) *n* en Grande-Bretagne, plan d'épargne exonéré d'impôt.

test [test] ◇ *n* **-1.** [trial] essai *m*; [of friendship, courage] épreuve *f*; **to put sb/sthg to the ~** mettre qqn/qqch à l'épreuve. **-2.** [examination - of aptitude, psychological] test *m*; [- SCH & UNIV] interrogation *f* écrite/orale; [- of driving] (examen *m* du) permis *m* de conduire. **-3.** [MED - of blood, urine] analyse *f*; [- of eyes] examen *m*. ◇ *vt* **-1.** [try] essayer; [determination, friendship] mettre à l'épreuve. **-2.** SCH & UNIV faire faire une interrogation écrite/orale à; **to ~ sb on sthg** interroger qqn sur qqch. **-3.** [MED - blood, urine] analyser; [- eyes, reflexes] faire un examen de.

testament ['testəmənt] *n* **-1.** [will] testament *m*. **-2.** [proof]: **~ to** témoignage *m* de.

test ban *n* interdiction *f* d'essais nucléaires.

test card *n Br* mire *f*.

test case *n* JUR affaire-test *f*.

test-drive *vt* essayer.

tester ['testər] *n* **-1.** [person] contrôleur *m*, -euse *f*. **-2.** [sample] échantillon *m*.

test flight *n* vol *m* d'essai.

testicles ['testɪklz] *npl* testicules *mpl*.

testify ['testɪfaɪ] (*pt* & *pp* **-ied**) ◇ *vt*: **to ~ that ...** témoigner que .... ◇ *vi* **-1.** JUR témoigner. **-2.** [be proof]: **to ~ to sthg** témoigner de qqch.

testimonial [,testɪ'məʊnjəl] *n* **-1.** [character reference] recommandation *f*. **-2.** [tribute] témoignage *m* d'estime.

testimony ['testɪmənɪ] *n* témoignage *m*.

testing ['testɪŋ] *adj* éprouvant(e).

testing ground *n* banc *m* d'essai.

test match *n Br* match *m* international.

test paper *n* **-1.** SCH interrogation *f* écrite. **-2.** CHEM papier *m* réactif.

test pattern *n Am* mire *f*.

test pilot *n* pilote *m* d'essai.

test tube *n* éprouvette *f*.

test-tube baby *n* bébé-éprouvette *m*.

testy ['testɪ] (*compar* **-ier**, *superl* **-iest**) *adj* [person] irritable; [remark] désobligeant(e).

tetanus ['tetənəs] *n* tétanos *m*.

tetchy ['tetʃɪ] (*compar* **-ier**, *superl* **-iest**) *adj* ombrageux(euse), qui prend ombrage facilement.

tête-à-tête [,teɪtɑː'teɪt] *n* tête-à-tête *m inv*.

tether ['teðər] ◇ *vt* attacher. ◇ *n*: **to be at the end of one's ~** être au bout du rouleau.

Texan ['teksn] *n* Texan *m*, -e *f*.

Texas ['teksəs] *n* Texas *m*; **in ~** au Texas.

Tex-Mex [,teks'meks] *adj* Tex-Mex (*inv*).

text [tekst] *n* texte *m*.

textbook ['tekstbʊk] *n* livre *m* OR manuel *m* scolaire.

textile ['tekstaɪl] ◇ *n* textile *m*. ◇ *comp* textile.

◆ **textiles** *npl* [industry] textile *m*.

texture ['tekstʃər] *n* texture *f*; [of paper, wood] grain *m*.

TGIF *inf* (*abbr of* **thank God it's Friday!**) *encore une semaine de tirée!*

TGWU (*abbr of* **Transport and General Workers' Union**) *n le plus grand syndicat interprofessionnel britannique.*

Thai [taɪ] ◇ *adj* thaïlandais(e). ◇ *n* **-1.** [person] Thaïlandais *m*, -e *f*. **-2.** [language] thaï *m*.

Thailand ['taɪlænd] *n* Thaïlande *f*; **in ~** en Thaïlande.

thalidomide [θə'lɪdəmaɪd] *n* thalidomide *f*.

Thames [temz] *n*: **the ~** la Tamise.

than [*weak form* ðən, *strong form* ðæn] *conj* que; **Sarah is younger ~ her sister** Sarah est plus jeune que sa sœur; **more ~ three days/50 people** plus de trois jours/50 personnes.

thank [θæŋk] ◇ *vt*: **to ~ sb (for)** remercier qqn (pour OR de); **~ God** OR **goodness** OR **heavens!** Dieu merci!

◆ **thanks** ◇ *npl* remerciements *mpl*. ◇ *excl* merci!

◆ **thanks to** *prep* grâce à.

thankful ['θæŋkfʊl] *adj* **-1.** [grateful]: **~ (for)** reconnaissant(e) (de). **-2.** [relieved] soulagé(e).

thankfully ['θæŋkfʊlɪ] *adv* **-1.** [with relief] avec soulagement. **-2.** [with gratitude] avec reconnaissance.

thankless ['θæŋklɪs] *adj* ingrat(e).

thanksgiving ['θæŋks,gɪvɪŋ] *n* action *f* de grâce.

◆ **Thanksgiving (Day)** *n fête nationale américaine.*

THANKSGIVING:

Thanksgiving commémore, le 4ème jeudi de novembre, l'installation des premiers colons en Amérique; le dîner en famille qui a généralement lieu à cette occasion est traditionnellement composé d'une dinde aux airelles accompagnée de patates douces, et se termine par une tarte au potiron

thank you *excl*: **~ (for)** merci (pour OR de).

◆ **thankyou** *n* merci *m*.

that [ðæt, *weak form of pron sense 2* & *conj* ðət] (*pl* **those**) ◇ *pron* **-1.** (*demonstrative use: pl 'those'*) ce, cela, ça; (*as opposed to 'this'*) celui-là (celle-là); **who's ~?** qui est-ce?; **is ~ Maureen?** c'est Maureen?; **what's ~?** qu'est-ce que c'est que ça?; **~'s a shame**

c'est dommage; **I had never seen ~ before** je n'avais jamais vu cela OR ça auparavant; **which shoes are you going to wear, these or those?** quelles chaussures vas-tu mettre, celles-ci ou celles-là?; **those who** ceux (celles) qui. **-2.** *(to introduce relative clauses - subject)* qui; (- *object)* que; (- *with prep)* lequel (laquelle), lesquels (lesquelles) *(pl)*; **we came to a path ~ led into the woods** nous arrivâmes à un sentier qui menait dans les bois; **show me the book ~ you bought** mentre-moi le livre que tu as acheté; **on the day ~ we left** le jour où nous sommes partis.

◇ *adj (demonstrative: pl 'those')* ce (cette), cet *(before vowel or silent "h")*, ces *(pl)*; *(as opposed to 'this')* ce (cette) ... -là, ces ... -là *(pl)*; **those chocolates are delicious** ces chocolats sont délicieux; **later ~ day** plus tard ce jour-là; **I prefer ~ book** je préfère ce livre-là; **I'll have ~ one** je prendrai celui-là.

◇ *adv* aussi, si; **it wasn't ~ bad/good** ce n'était pas si mal/bien que ça.

◇ *conj* que; **tell him ~ the children aren't coming** dites-lui que les enfants ne viennent pas; **he recommended ~ I phone you** il m'a conseillé de vous appeler.

◆ **at that** *adv* en plus, par surcroît.

◆ **that is (to say)** *adv* c'est-à-dire.

◆ **that's it** *adv* [that's all] c'est tout; ~**'s it, I'm leaving** ça y est, je m'en vais.

◆ **that's that** *adv*: **and ~'s ~** un point c'est tout.

thatched [θætʃt] *adj* de chaume.

Thatcherism ['θætʃərɪzm] *n* thatcherisme *m*.

that's [ðæts] = **that is**.

thaw [θɔː] ◇ *vt* [ice] faire fondre OR dégeler; [frozen food] décongeler. ◇ *vi* **-1.** [ice] dégeler, fondre; [frozen food] décongeler. **-2.** *fig* [people, relations] se dégeler. ◇ *n* dégel *m*.

the [weak form ðə, before vowel ðɪ, strong form ðiː] *def art* **-1.** [gen] le (la), l' (+ vowel or silent "h"), les *(pl)*; ~ **book** le livre; ~ **sea** la mer; ~ **man** l'homme; ~ **boys/girls** les garçons/filles; ~ **highest mountain in ~ world** la montagne la plus haute du monde; **has ~ postman been?** est-ce que le facteur est passé?; ~ **monkey is a primate** le singe est un primate; ~ **Joneses are coming to supper** les Jones viennent dîner; **you're not THE John Smith, are you?** vous n'êtes pas le célèbre John Smith, si?; **it's THE place to go to in Paris** c'est l'endroit à la mode OR l'endroit chic de Paris (où il faut aller); **to play ~ piano** jouer du piano. **-2.** *(with an adjective to form a noun)*: ~ **Brit**ish les Britanniques; ~ **old/young** les vieux/jeunes; ~ **impossible** l'impossible. **-3.** [in dates]: ~ **twelfth of May** le douze mai; ~ **forties** les années quarante. **-4.** [in comparisons]: ~ **more ... ~ less** plus ... moins; ~ **sooner ~ better** le plus tôt sera le mieux. **-5.** [in titles]: **Alexander ~ Great** Alexandre le Grand; **George ~ First** Georges Premier.

theatre, theater *Am* ['θɪətər] *n* **-1.** THEATRE théâtre *m*. **-2.** *Br* MED salle *f* d'opération. **-3.** *Am* [cinema] cinéma *m*.

theatregoer, theatergoer *Am* ['θɪətə,gəʊər] *n* habitué *m*, -e *f* du théâtre.

theatrical [θɪ'ætrɪkl] *adj* théâtral(e); [company] de théâtre.

theft [θeft] *n* vol *m*.

their [ðeər] *poss adj* leur, leurs *(pl)*; ~ **house** leur maison; ~ **children** leurs enfants; **it wasn't THEIR fault** ce n'était pas de leur faute à eux.

theirs [ðeəz] *poss pron* le leur (la leur), les leurs *(pl)*; **that house is ~** cette maison est la leur, cette maison est à eux/elles; **it wasn't our fault, it was THEIRS** ce n'était pas de notre faute, c'était de la leur; **a friend of ~** un de leurs amis, un ami à eux/elles.

them [weak form ðəm, strong form ðem] *pers pron pl* **-1.** *(direct)* les; **I know ~** je les connais; **if I were** OR **was ~** si j'étais eux/elles, à leur place. **-2.** *(indirect)* leur; **we spoke to ~** nous leur avons parlé; **she sent ~ a letter** elle leur a envoyé une lettre; **I gave it to ~** je le leur ai donné. **-3.** *(stressed, after prep, in comparisons etc)* eux (elles); **you can't expect THEM to do it** tu ne peux pas exiger que ce soit eux qui le fassent; **with ~** avec eux/elles; **without ~** sans eux/elles; **we're not as wealthy as ~** nous ne sommes pas aussi riches qu'eux/qu'elles.

thematic [θɪ'mætɪk] *adj* thématique.

theme [θiːm] *n* **-1.** [topic, motif] thème *m*, sujet *m*. **-2.** MUS thème *m*; [signature tune] indicatif *m*.

theme park *n* parc *m* à thème.

theme song *n* chanson *f* principale, thème *m* principal.

theme tune *n* chanson *f* principale, thème *m* principal.

themselves [ðem'selvz] *pron* **-1.** *(reflexive)* se; *(after prep)* eux (elles). **-2.** *(for emphasis)* eux-mêmes *mpl*, elles-mêmes *fpl*; **they did it ~** ils l'ont fait tout seuls.

then [ðen] *adv* **-1.** [not now] alors, à cette époque. **-2.** [next] puis, ensuite. **-3.** [in that case] alors, dans ce cas. **-4.** [therefore] donc. **-5.** [also] d'ailleurs, et puis.

thence [ðens] *adv fml* & *literary* de là.

theologian [θɪə'ləʊdʒən] *n* théologien *m*.

theology [θɪ'ɒlədʒɪ] *n* théologie *f*.

theorem ['θɪərəm] *n* théorème *m*.

theoretical [θɪə'retɪkl] *adj* théorique.

theoretically [θɪə'retɪklɪ] *adv* théoriquement.

theorist ['θɪərɪst] *n* théoricien *m*, -ienne *f*.

theorize, -ise ['θɪəraɪz] *vi*: **to ~ (about)** émettre une théorie (sur), théoriser (sur).

theory ['θɪərɪ] (*pl* **-ies**) *n* théorie *f*; **in ~** en théorie.

therapeutic [θerə'pjuːtɪk] *adj* thérapeutique.

therapist ['θerəpɪst] *n* thérapeute *mf*, psychothérapeute *mf*.

therapy ['θerəpɪ] *n* (*U*) thérapie *f*.

there [ðeəʳ] ◇ *pron* **-1.** [indicating existence of sthg]: **~ is/are** il y a; **~'s someone at the door** il y a quelqu'un à la porte; **~ must be some mistake** il doit y avoir erreur. **-2.** *fml* (*with vb*): **~** followed an ominous silence un silence lourd de menaces suivit.
◇ *adv* **-1.** [in existence, available] y, là; **is anybody ~?** il y a quelqu'un?; **is John ~, please?** [when telephoning] est-ce que John est là, s'il vous plaît? **-2.** [referring to place] y, là; **I'm going ~ next week** j'y vais la semaine prochaine; **~ it is** c'est là; **~ he is!** le voilà!; **over ~** là-bas; **it's six kilometres ~ and back** cela fait six kilomètres aller-retour. **-3.** [point in conversation, particular stage] là; **can I stop you ~?** est-ce que je peux vous arrêter là?; **we're getting ~** on y arrive. **-4.** *inf phr*: **all/not all ~** qui a/n'a plus toute sa tête.
◇ *interj*: **~, I knew he'd turn up** tiens OR voilà, je savais bien qu'il s'amènerait; **~, ~** allons, allons.
◆ **there and then, then and there** *adv* immédiatement, sur-le-champ.
◆ **there you are** *adv* **-1.** [handing over something] voilà. **-2.** [emphasizing that one is right] vous voyez bien; **~ you are, what did I tell you!** tu vois, qu'est-ce que je t'avais dit! **-3.** [expressing reluctant acceptance] c'est comme ça, que voulez-vous?

thereabouts ['ðeərəbaʊts], **thereabout** *Am* ['ðeərəbaʊt] *adv*: **or ~** [nearby] par là; [approximately] environ.

thereafter [ðeər'ɑːftəʳ] *adv fml* après cela, par la suite.

thereby [ðeər'baɪ] *adv fml* ainsi, de cette façon.

therefore ['ðeəfɔːʳ] *adv* donc, par conséquent.

therein [ðeər'ɪn] *adv fml* [inside] dedans; [in that matter] en cela.

there's [ðeəz] = **there is**.

thereupon [ðeərə'pɒn] *adv fml* sur ce, sur quoi.

thermal ['θɜːml] *adj* thermique; [clothes] en thermolactyl.

thermal reactor *n* réacteur *m* thermique.

thermal underwear *n* (*U*) sous-vêtements *mpl* en thermolactyl.

thermodynamics [θɜːməʊdaɪ'næmɪks] *n* (*U*) thermodynamique *f*.

thermoelectric [θɜːməʊɪ'lektrɪk] *adj* thermoélectrique.

thermometer [θə'mɒmɪtəʳ] *n* thermomètre *m*.

thermonuclear [θɜːməʊ'njuːklɪəʳ] *adj* thermonucléaire.

thermoplastic [θɜːməʊ'plæstɪk] ◇ *adj* thermoplastique. ◇ *n* thermoplastique *m*, thermoplaste *m*.

Thermos (flask)® ['θɜːmɒs-] *n* bouteille *f* thermos, thermos *m* or *f*.

thermostat ['θɜːməstæt] *n* thermostat *m*.

thesaurus [θɪ'sɔːrəs] (*pl* **-es**) *n* dictionnaire *m* de synonymes.

these [ðiːz] *pl* → **this**.

thesis ['θiːsɪs] (*pl* **theses** ['θiːsiːz]) *n* thèse *f*.

they [ðeɪ] *pers pron pl* **-1.** [people, things, animals - unstressed] ils (elles); [- stressed] eux (elles); **~'re pleased** ils sont contents (elles sont contentes); **~'re pretty earrings** ce sont de jolies boucles d'oreille; **THEY can't do it** eux (elles), ils (elles) ne peuvent pas le faire; **there ~ are** les voilà. **-2.** [unspecified people] on, ils; **~ say it's going to snow** on dit qu'il va neiger; **~'re going to put up petrol prices** ils vont augmenter le prix de l'essence.

they'd [ðeɪd] = **they had**, **they would**.

they'll [ðeɪl] = **they shall**, **they will**.

they're [ðeəʳ] = **they are**.

they've [ðeɪv] = **they have**.

thick [θɪk] ◇ *adj* **-1.** [gen] épais (épaisse); [forest, hedge, fog] dense; [voice] indistinct(e); **to be 6 inches ~** avoir 15cm d'épaisseur. **-2.** *inf* [stupid] bouché(e). **-3.** [full, covered]: **to be ~ with** [dust] être couvert(e) de; [people] être plein(e) de; **~ with smoke** [from cigarettes] enfumé(e); [from fire] plein d'une fumée épaisse. ◇ *n*: **in the ~ of** au plus fort de, en plein OR au beau milieu de.

◆ **thick and fast** *adv*: **questions came ~ and fast** les questions pleuvaient.
◆ **through thick and thin** *adv* envers et contre tout, quoi qu'il advienne.

thicken ['θɪkn] ◇ *vt* épaissir. ◇ *vi* s'épaissir.

thickening ['θɪknɪŋ] *n* épaississant *m*.

thicket ['θɪkɪt] *n* fourré *m*.

thickly ['θɪklɪ] *adv* **-1.** [not thinly - spread] en couche épaisse; [- cut] en tranches épaisses. **-2.** [densely - wooded, populated] très. **-3.** [speak, say] d'une voix indistincte.

thickness ['θɪknɪs] *n* épaisseur *f*.

thickset [,θɪk'set] *adj* trapu(e).

thick-skinned [-'skɪnd] *adj* qui a la peau dure.

thief [θiːf] (*pl* **thieves**) *n* voleur *m*, -euse *f*.

thieve [θiːv] *vt & vi* voler.

thieves [θiːvz] *pl* → **thief**.

thieving ['θiːvɪŋ] ◇ *adj* voleur(euse). ◇ *n* (*U*) vol *m*.

thigh [θaɪ] *n* cuisse *f*.

thighbone ['θaɪbəʊn] *n* fémur *m*.

thimble ['θɪmbl] *n* dé *m* (à coudre).

thin [θɪn] (*compar* **-ner**, *superl* **-nest**, *pt & pp* **-ned**, *cont* **-ning**) ◇ *adj* **-1.** [slice, layer, paper] mince; [cloth] léger(ère); [person] maigre. **-2.** [liquid, sauce] clair(e), peu épais (peu épaisse). **-3.** [sparse - crowd] épars(e); [- vegetation, hair] clairsemé(e); **to be ~ on top** [person] se dégarnir.
◇ *adv*: **to be wearing ~** [joke] n'être plus amusant(e); **my patience is wearing ~** je suis à bout de patience.
◇ *vi* [hair]: **to be thinning** s'éclaircir, se dégarnir.
◆ **thin down** *vt sep* [liquid, paint] délayer, diluer; [sauce] éclaircir.

thin air *n*: **to appear out of ~** apparaître tout d'un coup; **to disappear into ~** disparaître complètement, se volatiliser.

thing [θɪŋ] *n* **-1.** [gen] chose *f*; **the (best) ~ to do would be ...** le mieux serait de ...; **for one ~** en premier lieu, pour commencer; **(what) with one ~ and another** pour plusieurs raisons; **the ~ is ...** le problème, c'est que ...; **it's just one of those ~s** *inf* c'est comme ça, ce sont des choses qui arrivent; **to have a ~ about sb/sthg** *inf* [like] adorer qqn/qqch, être fou de qqn/qqch; [dislike] avoir qqn/qqch en horreur; **to make a ~ (out) of** *inf* faire tout un plat OR toute une histoire de. **-2.** [anything]: **I don't know a ~** je n'y connais absolument rien. **-3.** [object] chose *f*, objet *m*. **-4.** [person]:

you poor ~! mon pauvre! **-5.** *inf* [fashion]: **the ~** la mode.
◆ **things** *npl* **-1.** [clothes, possessions] affaires *fpl*. **-2.** *inf* [life]: **how are ~s?** comment ça va?

thingamabob ['θɪŋəmə,bɒb], **thingamajig** ['θɪŋəmədʒɪg], **thingummy (jig)** *Br* ['θɪŋəmɪ-], **thingie** *Br*, **thingy** *Br* ['θɪŋɪ] *n* truc *m*, machin *m*.

think [θɪŋk] (*pt & pp* **thought**) ◇ *vt* **-1.** [believe]: **to ~ (that)** croire que, penser que; **I ~ so/not** je crois que oui/non, je pense que oui/non. **-2.** [have in mind] penser à. **-3.** [imagine] s'imaginer; **I can't ~ why** je ne comprends pas OR je me demande bien pourquoi tu as accepté de le faire. **-4.** [remember]: **did you ~ to bring any money?** avez-vous pensé à apporter de l'argent? **-5.** [in polite requests]: **do you ~ you could help me?** tu pourrais m'aider?
◇ *vi* **-1.** [use mind] réfléchir, penser. **-2.** [have stated opinion]: **what do you ~ of** OR **about his new film?** que pensez-vous de son dernier film?; **to ~ a lot of sb/sthg** penser beaucoup de bien de qqn/qqch. **-3.** *phr*: **to ~ better of sthg/of doing sthg** décider après tout de ne pas faire qqch; **to ~ nothing of doing sthg** trouver tout à fait normal OR tout naturel de faire qqch; **to ~ twice** y réfléchir à deux fois.
◇ *n inf*: **to have a ~ (about sthg)** réfléchir (à qqch).
◆ **think about** *vt fus*: **to ~ about sb/sthg** songer à OR penser à qqn/qqch; **to ~ about doing sthg** songer à faire qqch; **I'll ~ about it** je vais y réfléchir.
◆ **think back** *vi*: **to ~ back (to)** repenser (à).
◆ **think of** *vt fus* **-1.** [consider] = **think about. -2.** [remember] se rappeler. **-3.** [conceive] penser à, avoir l'idée de; **to ~ of doing sthg** avoir l'idée de faire qqch. **-4.** [show consideration for] penser à.
◆ **think out**, **think through** *vt sep* bien étudier, bien considérer.
◆ **think over** *vt sep* réfléchir à.
◆ **think up** *vt sep* imaginer.

thinker ['θɪŋkər] *n* penseur *m*.

thinking ['θɪŋkɪŋ] ◇ *adj* qui pense, qui réfléchit. ◇ *n* (*U*) opinion *f*, pensée *f*; **to do some ~** réfléchir; **to my way of ~** à mon avis.

think tank *n* comité *m* d'experts.

thinly ['θɪnlɪ] *adv* **-1.** [not thickly - spread] en couche mince; [- cut] en tranches minces. **-2.** [sparsely - wooded, populated] peu.

thinner ['θɪnər] *n* diluant *m*.

thinness ['θɪnnɪs] *n* (U) [of slice, layer, paper] minceur *f*; [of person] maigreur *f*; [of cloth] légèreté *f*.

thin-skinned [-'skɪnd] *adj* susceptible, très sensible.

third [θɜːd] ◇ *num* troisième; *see also* **sixth**. ◇ *n* UNIV ≃ licence *f* mention passable.

third-class *adj Br* UNIV: ~ **degree** ≃ licence *f* mention passable.

third-degree burns *npl* brûlures *fpl* du troisième degré.

thirdly [θɜːdlɪ] *adv* troisièmement, tertio.

third party *n* tiers *m*, tierce personne *f*.

third party insurance *n* assurance *f* de responsabilité civile.

third-rate *adj pej* de dernier OR troisième ordre.

Third World *n*: **the** ~ le Tiers-Monde.

thirst [θɜːst] *n* soif *f*; ~ **for** *fig* soif de.

thirsty ['θɜːstɪ] (*compar* -**ier**, *superl* -**iest**) *adj* [person]: **to be** OR **feel** ~ avoir soif; [work] qui donne soif.

thirteen [,θɜː'tiːn] *num* treize; *see also* **six**.

thirteenth [,θɜː'tiːnθ] *num* treizième; *see also* **sixth**.

thirtieth ['θɜːtɪəθ] *num* trentième; *see also* **sixth**.

thirty ['θɜːtɪ] (*pl* -**ies**) *num* trente; *see also* **sixty**.

thirty-something *adj* caractéristique de certaines personnes ayant la trentaine et issues d'un milieu aisé.

this [ðɪs] (*pl* **these**) ◇ *pron* (*demonstrative use*) ce, ceci (*as opposed to 'that'*) celui-ci (celle-ci); ~ **is for you** c'est pour vous; **who's** ~? qui est-ce?; **what's** ~? qu'est-ce que c'est?; **which sweets does she prefer, these or those**? quels bonbons préfère-t-elle, ceux-ci ou ceux-là?; ~ **is Daphne Logan** [introducing another person] je vous présente Daphne Logan; [introducing oneself on phone] ici Daphne Logan, Daphne Logan à l'appareil; **to talk about** ~ **and that** parler de choses et d'autres; **to do** ~ **and that** faire toutes sortes de choses.
◇ *adj* -**1.** (*demonstrative use*) ce (cette), cet (*before vowel or silent "h"*), ces (*pl*); (*as opposed to 'that'*) ce (cette) ... -ci, ces ... -ci (*pl*); **these chocolates are delicious** ces chocolats sont délicieux; **I prefer** ~ **book** je préfère ce livre-ci; **I'll have** ~ **one** je prendrai celui-ci; ~ **afternoon** cet après-midi; ~ **morning** ce matin; ~ **week** cette semaine. -**2.** *inf* [a certain] un certain (une certaine).
◇ *adv* aussi; **it was** ~ **big** c'était aussi

grand que ça; **you'll need about** ~ **much** il vous en faudra à peu près comme ceci.

thistle ['θɪsl] *n* chardon *m*.

thither ['ðɪðər] → **hither**.

tho' [ðəʊ] = **though**.

thong [θɒŋ] *n* -**1.** [of leather] lanière *f*. -**2.** *Am* [flip-flop] tong *f*.

thorn [θɔːn] *n* épine *f*; **to be a** ~ **in sb's flesh** OR **side** être une source continuelle d'exaspération pour qqn.

thorny ['θɔːnɪ] (*compar* -**ier**, *superl* -**iest**) *adj lit* & *fig* épineux(euse).

thorough ['θʌrə] *adj* -**1.** [exhaustive - search, inspection] minutieux(ieuse); [- investigation, knowledge] approfondi(e). -**2.** [meticulous] méticuleux(euse). -**3.** [complete, utter] complet(ète), absolu(e).

thoroughbred ['θʌrəbred] *n* pur-sang *m inv*.

thoroughfare ['θʌrəfeər] *n fml* rue *f*, voie *f* publique.

thoroughly ['θʌrəlɪ] *adv* -**1.** [fully, in detail] à fond. -**2.** [completely, utterly] absolument, complètement.

thoroughness ['θʌrənɪs] *n* (U) -**1.** [exhaustiveness] minutie *f*. -**2.** [meticulousness] soin *m* méticuleux.

those [ðəʊz] *pl* → **that**.

though [ðəʊ] ◇ *conj* bien que (+ *subjunctive*), quoique (+ *subjunctive*). ◇ *adv* pourtant, cependant.

thought [θɔːt] ◇ *pt* & *pp* → **think**. ◇ *n* -**1.** [gen] pensée *f*; [idea] idée *f*, pensée; **after much** ~ après avoir mûrement réfléchi. -**2.** [intention] intention *f*.
◆ **thoughts** *npl* -**1.** [reflections] pensées *fpl*, réflexions *fpl*; **to collect one's** ~**s** rassembler ses idées. -**2.** [views] opinions *fpl*, idées *fpl*.

thoughtful ['θɔːtfʊl] *adj* -**1.** [pensive] pensif(ive). -**2.** [considerate - person] prévenant(e), attentionné(e); [- remark, act] plein(e) de gentillesse.

thoughtfulness ['θɔːtfʊlnɪs] *n* (U) -**1.** [pensiveness] air *m* pensif. -**2.** [considerateness - of person] prévenance *f*; [- of remark, act] délicatesse *f*.

thoughtless ['θɔːtlɪs] *adj* [person] qui manque d'égards (pour les autres); [remark, behaviour] irréfléchi(e).

thoughtlessness ['θɔːtlɪsnɪs] *n* (U) manque *m* d'égards OR de prévenance.

thousand ['θaʊznd] *num* mille; **a** OR **one** ~ mille; ~**s of** des milliers de; *see also* **six**.

thousandth ['θaʊzntθ] *num* millième; *see also* **sixth**.

thrash [θræʃ] *vt* **-1.** [hit] battre, rosser. **-2.** *inf* [defeat] écraser, battre à plates coutures.
◆ **thrash about, thrash around** *vi* s'agiter.
◆ **thrash out** *vt sep* [problem] débrouiller, démêler; [idea] débattre, discuter.

thrashing ['θræʃɪŋ] *n* **-1.** [hitting] rossée *f*, correction *f*. **-2.** *inf* [defeat] défaite *f*.

thread [θred] ◇ *n* **-1.** [gen] fil *m*. **-2.** [of screw] filet *m*, pas *m*. ◇ *vt* **-1.** [needle] enfiler. **-2.** [move]: **to ~ one's way through the crowd** se faufiler parmi la foule.

threadbare ['θredbeə'] *adj* usé(e) jusqu'à la corde.

threat [θret] *n*: **~ (to)** menace *f* (pour).

threaten ['θretn] ◇ *vt*: **to ~ sb (with)** menacer qqn (de); **to ~ to do sthg** menacer de faire qqch. ◇ *vi* menacer.

threatening ['θretnɪŋ] *adj* menaçant(e); [letter] de menaces.

three [θriː] *num* trois; *see also* **six**.

three-D *adj* [film, picture] en relief.

three-day event *n* concours *m* complet d'équitation.

three-dimensional *adj* [film, picture] en relief; [object] à trois dimensions.

threefold ['θriːfəʊld] ◇ *adj* triple. ◇ *adv*: **to increase ~** tripler.

three-legged race [-'legɪd-] *n* course *f* à trois pieds.

three-piece *adj*: **~ suit** (costume *m*) trois pièces *m*; **~ suite** canapé *m* et deux fauteuils assortis.

three-ply *adj* [wool] à trois fils.

three-point turn *n Br* demi-tour *m* en trois manœuvres.

three-quarters *npl* [fraction] trois quarts *mpl*.

threesome ['θriːsəm] *n* trio *m*, groupe *m* de trois personnes.

three-star *adj* trois étoiles.

three-wheeler [-'wiːlə'] *n* voiture *f* à trois roues.

thresh [θreʃ] *vt* battre.

threshing machine ['θreʃɪŋ-] *n* batteuse *f*.

threshold ['θreʃhəʊld] *n* seuil *m*; **to be on the ~ of** *fig* être au bord OR seuil de.

threshold agreement *n* accord *m* d'indexation des salaires sur le coût de la vie.

threw [θruː] *pt* → **throw**.

thrift [θrɪft] *n* **-1.** [gen] (*U*) économie *f*, épargne *f*. **-2.** *Am* [savings bank] = **thrift institution**.

thrift institution *n Am* caisse *f* d'épargne.

thrifty ['θrɪftɪ] (*compar* **-ier**, *superl* **-iest**) *adj* économe.

thrill [θrɪl] ◇ *n* **-1.** [sudden feeling] frisson *m*, sensation *f*. **-2.** [enjoyable experience] plaisir *m*. ◇ *vt* transporter, exciter. ◇ *vi*: **to ~ to a story/the music** être transporté(e) par une histoire/la musique.

thrilled [θrɪld] *adj*: **~ (with sthg/to do sthg)** ravi(e) (de qqch/de faire qqch), enchanté(e) (de qqch/de faire qqch).

thriller ['θrɪlə'] *n* thriller *m*.

thrilling ['θrɪlɪŋ] *adj* saisissant(e), palpitant(e).

thrive [θraɪv] (*pt* **-d** OR **throve**, *pp* **-d**) *vi* [person] bien se porter; [plant] pousser bien; [business] prospérer.

thriving ['θraɪvɪŋ] *adj* [person] bien portant(e); [plant] qui pousse bien; [business] prospère.

throat [θrəʊt] *n* gorge *f*; **to ram** OR **force sthg down sb's ~** *fig* rebattre les oreilles de qqn avec qqch; **it stuck in my ~** *fig* ça m'est resté en travers de la gorge; **to be at each other's ~s** se disputer, se battre.

throaty ['θrəʊtɪ] (*compar* **-ier**, *superl* **-iest**) *adj* guttural(e).

throb [θrɒb] (*pt* & *pp* **-bed**, *cont* **-bing**) ◇ *n* [of drums] battement *m*; [of pulse] pulsation *f*; [of engine] vibration *f*. ◇ *vi* [heart] palpiter, battre fort; [engine] vibrer; [music] taper; **my head is throbbing** j'ai des élancements dans la tête.

throes [θrəʊz] *npl*: **to be in the ~ of** [war, disease] être en proie à; **to be in the ~ of an argument** être en pleine dispute.

thrombosis [θrɒm'bəʊsɪs] (*pl* **-boses** ['bəʊsiːz]) *n* thrombose *f*.

throne [θrəʊn] *n* trône *m*.

throng [θrɒŋ] ◇ *n* foule *f*, multitude *f*. ◇ *vt* remplir, encombrer. ◇ *vi* affluer.

throttle ['θrɒtl] ◇ *n* [valve] papillon *m* des gaz; [lever] commande *f* des gaz. ◇ *vt* [strangle] étrangler.

through [θruː] ◇ *adj* [finished]: **are you ~?** tu as fini?; **to be ~ with sthg** avoir fini qqch.
◇ *adv*: **to let sb ~** laisser passer qqn; **to read sthg ~** lire qqch jusqu'au bout; **to sleep ~ till ten** dormir jusqu'à dix heures.
◇ *prep* **-1.** [relating to place, position] à travers; **to travel ~ sthg** traverser qqch; **to cut ~ sthg** couper qqch. **-2.** [during] pendant. **-3.** [because of] à cause de. **-4.** [by means of] par l'intermédiaire de, par l'entremise de. **-5.** *Am* [up till and including]: **Monday ~ Friday** du lundi au vendredi.

◆ **through and through** adv [completely] jusqu'au bout des ongles; [thoroughly] par cœur, à fond.

throughout [θruː'aut] ◇ prep **-1.** [during] pendant, durant; ~ **the meeting** pendant toute la réunion. **-2.** [everywhere in] partout dans. ◇ adv **-1.** [all the time] tout le temps. **-2.** [everywhere] partout.

throve [θrəuv] pt → **thrive.**

throw [θrəu] (pt **threw**, pp **thrown**) ◇ vt **-1.** [gen] jeter; [ball, javelin] lancer; **to ~ one's arms around sb** jeter ses bras autour de qqn; **to ~ o.s. into sthg** fig se jeter à corps perdu dans qqch. **-2.** [rider] désarçonner. **-3.** [have suddenly - tantrum, fit] piquer. **-4.** fig [confuse] déconcerter, décontenancer. ◇ n lancement m, jet m.

◆ **throw away** vt sep **-1.** [discard] jeter. **-2.** fig [money] gaspiller; [opportunity] perdre.

◆ **throw in** vt sep [include] donner en plus OR en prime.

◆ **throw out** vt sep **-1.** [discard] jeter. **-2.** fig [reject] rejeter. **-3.** [from house] mettre à la porte; [from army, school] expulser, renvoyer.

◆ **throw up** ◇ vt sep [dust, water] jeter, projeter. ◇ vi inf [vomit] dégobiller, vomir.

throwaway ['θrəuə,weɪ] adj **-1.** [disposable] jetable, à jeter. **-2.** [remark] désinvolte.

throwback ['θrəubæk] n: ~ **(to)** retour m (à).

throw-in n Br FTBL rentrée f en touche, remise f en jeu.

thrown [θrəun] pp → **throw.**

thru [θruː] Am inf = **through.**

thrush [θrʌʃ] n **-1.** [bird] grive f. **-2.** MED muguet m.

thrust [θrʌst] ◇ n **-1.** [forward movement] poussée f; [of knife] coup m. **-2.** [main aspect] idée f principale, aspect m principal. ◇ vt **-1.** [shove] enfoncer, fourrer. **-2.** [jostle]: **to ~ one's way** se frayer un passage.

◆ **thrust upon** vt sep: **to ~ sthg upon sb** imposer qqch à qqn.

thrusting ['θrʌstɪŋ] adj [person] qui se met en avant.

thruway ['θruːweɪ] n Am voie f express.

thud [θʌd] (pt & pp **-ded**, cont **-ding**) ◇ n bruit m sourd. ◇ vi tomber en faisant un bruit sourd.

thug [θʌg] n brute f, voyou m.

thumb [θʌm] ◇ n pouce m; **to twiddle one's ~s** se tourner les pouces. ◇ vt inf [hitch]: **to ~ a lift** faire du stop OR de l'auto-stop.

◆ **thumb through** vt fus feuilleter, parcourir.

thumb index n répertoire m à onglets.

thumbnail ['θʌmneɪl] ◇ adj bref (brève), concis(e). ◇ n ongle m du pouce.

thumbnail sketch n croquis m rapide.

thumbs down n: **to get** OR **be given the ~** être rejeté(e).

thumbs up n [go-ahead]: **to give sb the ~** donner le feu vert à qqn.

thumbtack ['θʌmtæk] n Am punaise f.

thump [θʌmp] ◇ n **-1.** [blow] grand coup m. **-2.** [thud] bruit m sourd. ◇ vt **-1.** [hit] cogner, taper sur. **-2.** [place heavily] poser violemment. ◇ vi **-1.** [move heavily]: **to ~ in/out** entrer/sortir à pas pesants. **-2.** [heart] battre fort.

thunder ['θʌndər] ◇ n (U) **-1.** METEOR tonnerre m. **-2.** fig [of traffic] vacarme m; [of applause] tonnerre m. ◇ vt tonner, tonitruer. ◇ v impers METEOR tonner. ◇ vi fig [traffic] tonner, gronder.

thunderbolt ['θʌndəbəult] n coup m de foudre.

thunderclap ['θʌndəklæp] n coup m de tonnerre.

thundercloud ['θʌndəklaud] n nuage m orageux.

thundering ['θʌndərɪŋ] adj terrible, monstre.

thunderous ['θʌndərəs] adj [noise] assourdissant(e); ~ **applause** un tonnerre d'applaudissements.

thunderstorm ['θʌndəstɔːm] n orage m.

thunderstruck ['θʌndəstrʌk] adj fig stupéfait(e), sidéré(e).

thundery ['θʌndərɪ] adj orageux(euse).

Thur, Thurs (abbr of **Thursday**) jeu.

Thursday ['θɜːzdɪ] n jeudi m; see also **Saturday.**

thus [ðʌs] adv fml **-1.** [therefore] par conséquent, donc. **-2.** [in this way] de cette façon, comme ceci.

thwart [θwɔːt] vt contrecarrer, contrarier.

thyme [taɪm] n thym m.

thyroid ['θaɪrɔɪd] n thyroïde f.

tiara [tɪ'ɑːrə] n [worn by woman] diadème m.

Tiber ['taɪbər] n: **the (River)** ~ le Tibre.

Tibet [tɪ'bet] n Tibet m; **in** ~ au Tibet.

Tibetan [tɪ'betn] ◇ adj tibétain(e). ◇ n **-1.** [person] Tibétain m, -e f. **-2.** [language] tibétain m.

tibia ['tɪbɪə] (pl **-biae** [-biiː] OR **-s**) n tibia m.

tic [tɪk] n tic m.

tick [tɪk] ◇ n **-1.** [written mark] coche f; **to put a ~ beside sthg** cocher qqch. **-2.** [sound] tic-tac m. **-3.** [insect] tique f. ◇ vt cocher. ◇ *vi* faire tic-tac; **what makes him ~?** *fig* je me demande comment il fonctionne.

◆ **tick away, tick by** *vi* passer.

◆ **tick off** *vt sep* **-1.** [mark off] cocher. **-2.** [tell off] passer un savon à, enguirlander.

◆ **tick over** *vi* [engine, business] tourner au ralenti.

ticked [tɪkt] *adj Am* en rogne.

tickertape ['tɪkəteɪp] *n* (*U*) bande *f* de téléimprimeur.

ticket ['tɪkɪt] *n* **-1.** [for access, train, plane] billet *m*; [for bus] ticket *m*; [for library] carte *f*; [label on product] étiquette *f*. **-2.** [for traffic offence] P.-V. *m*, papillon *m*. **-3.** POL liste *f*.

ticket agency *n* billetterie *f*.

ticket collector *n Br* contrôleur *m*, -euse *f*.

ticket holder *n* personne *f* munie d'un billet.

ticket inspector *n Br* contrôleur *m*, -euse *f*.

ticket machine *n* distributeur *m* de billets.

ticket office *n* bureau *m* de vente des billets.

ticking off ['tɪkɪŋ-] (*pl* **tickings off**) *n*: to give sb a ~ passer un savon à qqn, enguirlander qqn; to get a ~ recevoir un savon, se faire enguirlander.

tickle ['tɪkl] ◇ *vt* **-1.** [touch lightly] chatouiller. **-2.** *fig* [amuse] amuser. ◇ *vi* chatouiller.

ticklish ['tɪklɪʃ] *adj* **-1.** [person] qui craint les chatouilles, chatouilleux(euse). **-2.** *fig* [delicate] délicat(e), difficile.

tick-tack-toe *n Am* [game] ≃ morpion *m*.

tidal ['taɪdl] *adj* [force] de la marée; [river] à marées; [barrier] contre la marée.

tidal wave *n* raz-de-marée *m inv*.

tidbit *Am* = **titbit**.

tiddler ['tɪdlər] *n Br* [fish] petit poisson *m*.

tiddly ['tɪdlɪ] (*compar* -ier, *superl* -iest) *adj Br inf* **-1.** [tipsy] pompette, gai(e). **-2.** [tiny] minuscule.

tiddlywinks ['tɪdlɪwɪŋks], **tiddledywinks** *Am* ['tɪdldɪwɪŋks] *n* jeu *m* de puce.

tide [taɪd] *n* **-1.** [of sea] marée *f*. **-2.** *fig* [of opinion, fashion] courant *m*, tendance *f*; [of protest] vague *f*.

◆ **tide over** *vt sep* dépanner.

tidemark ['taɪdmɑːk] *n* **-1.** [of sea] ligne *f* de marée haute. **-2.** *Br* [round bath, neck] ligne *f* de crasse.

tidily ['taɪdɪlɪ] *adv* soigneusement, avec ordre.

tidiness ['taɪdɪnɪs] *n* (*U*) ordre *m*.

tidings ['taɪdɪŋz] *npl literary* nouvelles *fpl*.

tidy ['taɪdɪ] (*compar* -ier, *superl* -iest, *pt & pp* -ied) ◇ *adj* **-1.** [room, desk] en ordre, bien rangé(e); [hair, dress] soigné(e). **-2.** [person - in habits] ordonné(e); [- in appearance] soigné(e). **-3.** *inf* [sizeable] coquet(ette), rondelet(ette). ◇ *vt* ranger, mettre de l'ordre dans.

◆ **tidy away** *vt sep* ranger.

◆ **tidy up** ◇ *vt sep* ranger, mettre de l'ordre dans. ◇ *vi* ranger.

tie [taɪ] (*pt & pp* tied, *cont* tying) ◇ *n* **-1.** [necktie] cravate *f*. **-2.** [string, cord] cordon *m*. **-3.** *fig* [link] lien *m*. **-4.** [in game, competition] égalité *f* de points. **-5.** *Am* RAIL traverse *f*. ◇ *vt* **-1.** [fasten] attacher. **-2.** [shoelaces] nouer, attacher; to ~ a knot faire un nœud. **-3.** *fig* [link]: to be ~d to être lié(e) à. **-4.** *fig* [restricted]: to be ~d to être cloué(e) à. ◇ *vi* [draw] être à égalité.

◆ **tie down** *vt sep fig* [restrict] restreindre la liberté de.

◆ **tie in with** *vt fus* concorder avec, coïncider avec.

◆ **tie up** *vt sep* **-1.** [with string, rope] attacher. **-2.** [shoelaces] nouer, attacher. **-3.** *fig* [money, resources] immobiliser. **-4.** *fig* [link]: to be ~d up with être lié(e) à.

tiebreak(er) ['taɪbreɪk(ər)] *n* **-1.** TENNIS tiebreak *m*. **-2.** [in game, competition] question *f* subsidiaire.

tied [taɪd] *adj* SPORT: **a ~ match** un match nul.

tied cottage *n Br* logement *m* de fonction (*mis à la disposition d'un employé agricole etc*).

tied up *adj* [busy] occupé(e), pris(e).

tie-dye *vt* nouer et teindre.

tie-in *n* **-1.** [link] lien *m*, rapport *m*. **-2.** [product]: **the book is a ~ with the TV series** le livre est tiré de la série télévisée.

tiepin ['taɪpɪn] *n* épingle *f* de cravate.

tier [tɪər] *n* [of seats] gradin *m*; [of cake] étage *m*.

Tierra del Fuego [tɪ,erədel'fweɪgəʊ] *n* Terre de Feu *f*; **in ~** en Terre de Feu.

tie-up *n* **-1.** [link] lien *m*, rapport *m*. **-2.** *Am* [interruption] interruption *f*, arrêt *m*.

tiff [tɪf] *n* bisbille *f*, petite querelle *f*.

tiger ['taɪgər] *n* tigre *m*.

tiger cub *n* petit *m* du tigre.

tight [taɪt] ◇ *adj* **-1.** [clothes, group, competition, knot] serré(e); **the dress was a ~** fit la robe était un peu juste. **-2.** [taut] tendu(e). **-3.** [painful - chest] oppressé(e); [- stomach] noué(e). **-4.** [schedule] serré(e), minuté(e). **-5.** [strict] strict(e), sévère. **-6.** [corner, bend] raide. **-7.** *inf* [drunk] soûl(e), rond(e). **-8.** *inf* [miserly] radin(e), avare.

◇ *adv* **-1.** [firmly, securely] bien, fort; **to hold ~** tenir bien; **hold ~!** tiens bon!; **to shut** OR **close sthg ~** bien fermer qqch. **-2.** [tautly] à fond.

◆ **tights** *npl* collant *m*, collants *mpl*.

tighten ['taɪtn] ◇ *vt* **-1.** [belt, knot, screw] resserrer; **to ~ one's hold** OR **grip on** resserrer sa prise sur. **-2.** [pull tauter] tendre. **-3.** [make stricter] renforcer. ◇ *vi* **-1.** [rope] se tendre. **-2.** [grip, hold] se resserrer.

◆ **tighten up** *vt sep* **-1.** [belt, screw] resserrer. **-2.** [make stricter] renforcer.

tightfisted [,taɪt'fɪstɪd] *adj pej* radin(e), pingre.

tightknit [,taɪt'nɪt] *adj* [family, community] uni(e).

tight-lipped [-'lɪpt] *adj* **-1.** [in anger] les lèvres serrées. **-2.** [silent] qui ne dit rien, qui garde le silence.

tightly ['taɪtlɪ] *adv* **-1.** [closely]: **to fit ~** être juste; **to pack ~** entasser, tasser. **-2.** [firmly] bien, fort. **-3.** [tautly] à fond.

tightness ['taɪtnɪs] *n* **-1.** [of clothes] étroitesse *f*. **-2.** [in chest] oppression *f*. **-3.** [strictness] sévérité *f*, rigueur *f*.

tightrope ['taɪtrəʊp] *n* corde *f* raide; **to be on** OR **walking a ~** *fig* être sur la corde raide.

tightrope walker *n* funambule *mf*.

Tigré ['tiːɡreɪ] *n* Tigré *m*; **in ~** dans le Tigré.

tigress ['taɪɡrɪs] *n* tigresse *f*.

Tigris ['taɪɡrɪs] *n*: **the (River) ~** le Tigre.

tilde ['tɪldə] *n* tilde *m*.

tile [taɪl] *n* [on roof] tuile *f*; [on floor, wall] carreau *m*.

tiled [taɪld] *adj* [floor, wall] carrelé(e); [roof] couvert de tuiles.

tiling ['taɪlɪŋ] *n* [of floor, wall] carrelage *m*; [of roof - action] pose *f* de tuiles; [- tuiles] tuiles *fpl*.

till [tɪl] ◇ *prep* jusqu'à; **from six ~ ten** o'clock de six heures à dix heures. ◇ *conj* jusqu'à ce que (+ *subjunctive*); **wait ~ I come back** attends que je revienne; *(after negative)* avant que (+ *subjunctive*); **it won't be ready ~ tomorrow** çe ne sera pas prêt avant demain. ◇ *n* tiroir-caisse *m*.

tiller ['tɪlər] *n* NAUT barre *f*.

tilt [tɪlt] ◇ *n* inclinaison *f*. ◇ *vt* incliner, pencher. ◇ *vi* s'incliner, pencher.

timber ['tɪmbər] *n* **-1.** (*U*) [wood] bois *m* de charpente OR de construction. **-2.** [beam] poutre *f*, madrier *m*.

timbered ['tɪmbəd] *adj* en bois.

time [taɪm] ◇ *n* **-1.** [gen] temps *m*; **a long ~** longtemps; **in a short ~** dans peu de temps, sous peu; **to take ~** prendre du temps; **to be ~ for sthg** être l'heure de qqch; **to get the ~ to do sthg** prendre le temps de faire qqch; **it's a good ~ to do sthg** c'est le moment de faire qqch; **to have a good ~** s'amuser bien; **to have a hard ~ doing sthg** avoir du mal à faire qqch; **in good ~** de bonne heure; **ahead of ~** en avance, avant l'heure; **on ~** à l'heure; **it's high ~ (that) ...** il est grand temps que ...; **~ and a half** une fois et demie le tarif normal; **to have no ~ for sb/sthg** ne pas supporter qqn/qqch; **to make good ~** [on journey] bien rouler OR marcher; [in schedule] bien avancer; **to pass the ~** passer le temps; **to play for ~** essayer de gagner du temps; **to take one's ~ (doing sthg)** prendre son temps (pour faire qqch). **-2.** [as measured by clock] heure *f*; **what's the ~?** quelle heure est-il?; **in a week's/year's ~** dans une semaine/un an; **to keep ~** être toujours à l'heure; **to lose ~** retarder. **-3.** [point in time in past] époque *f*; **to be ahead of one's ~** être en avance sur son temps; **before my ~** avant que j'arrive ici. **-4.** [occasion] fois *f*; **from ~ to ~** de temps en temps, de temps à autre; **~ after ~, ~ and again** à maintes reprises, maintes et maintes fois; **at the best of ~s** même quand tout va bien. **-5.** MUS mesure *f*. ◇ *vt* **-1.** [schedule] fixer, prévoir. **-2.** [race, runner] chronométrer. **-3.** [arrival, remark] choisir le moment de.

◆ **times** ◇ *npl* fois *fpl*; **four ~s as much as me** quatre fois plus que moi. ◇ *prep* MATH fois.

◆ **at a time** *adv* d'affilée; **one at a ~** un par un, un seul à la fois; **months at a ~** des mois et des mois.

◆ **at (any) one time** *adv* à la fois.

◆ **at times** *adv* quelquefois, parfois.

◆ **at the same time** *adv* en même temps.

◆ **about time** *adv*: **it's about ~ (that) ...** il est grand temps que ...; **about ~ too!** ce n'est pas trop tôt!

◆ **for the time being** *adv* pour le moment.

◆ **in time** *adv* **-1.** [not late]: **in ~ (for)** à l'heure (pour). **-2.** [eventually] à la fin, à la longue; [after a while] avec le temps, à la longue.

time-and-motion study *n* étude *f* de productivité (*qui se concentre sur l'efficacité des employés*).

time bomb *n lit* & *fig* bombe *f* à retardement.

time-consuming [-kən,sjuːmɪŋ] *adj* qui prend beaucoup de temps.

timed [taɪmd] *adj* [race, test] chronométré(e); **well ~ opportun(e); badly ~** inopportun(e).

time difference *n* décalage *m* horaire.

time-honoured [-,ɒnəd] *adj* consacré(e).

timekeeping ['taɪm,kiːpɪŋ] *n* ponctualité *f*.

time lag *n* décalage *m*.

time-lapse *adj*: **~ photography** accéléré *m*.

timeless ['taɪmlɪs] *adj* éternel(elle).

time limit *n* délai *m*.

timely ['taɪmlɪ] (*compar* -**ier**, *superl* -**iest**) *adj* opportun(e).

time machine *n* machine *f* à voyager dans le temps.

time off *n* temps *m* libre.

time out *n* **-1.** SPORT temps *m* mort. **-2.** [break]: **to take ~ to do sthg** trouver le temps de faire qqch.

timepiece ['taɪmpiːs] *n dated* [watch] montre *f*; [clock] horloge *f*.

timer ['taɪmə'] *n* minuteur *m*.

timesaving ['taɪm,seɪvɪŋ] *adj* qui fait gagner du temps.

time scale *n* période *f*; [of project] délai *m*.

time-share *n Br* logement *m* en multipropriété.

time sheet *n* feuille *f* de présence.

time signal *n* top *m* horaire.

time switch *n* minuterie *f*.

timetable ['taɪm,teɪbl] *n* **-1.** SCH emploi *m* du temps. **-2.** [of buses, trains] horaire *m*. **-3.** [schedule] calendrier *m*.

time zone *n* fuseau *m* horaire.

timid ['tɪmɪd] *adj* timide.

timidly ['tɪmɪdlɪ] *adv* timidement.

timing ['taɪmɪŋ] *n* (*U*) **-1.** [of remark] à-propos *m*. **-2.** [scheduling]: **the ~ of the election** le moment choisi pour l'élection. **-3.** [measuring] chronométrage *m*.

timing device *n* mouvement *m* d'horlogerie.

timpani ['tɪmpənɪ] *npl* timbales *fpl*.

tin [tɪn] ◇ *n* **-1.** (*U*) [metal] étain *m*; [in sheets] fer-blanc *m*. **-2.** *Br* [can] boîte *f* de conserve. **-3.** [small container] boîte *f*; **cake ~** [for baking] moule *m* à gâteau; [for storing] boîte à gâteaux. ◇ *comp* en étain, d'étain.

tin can *n* boîte *f* de conserve.

tinder ['tɪndə'] *n* petit bois *m*.

tinfoil ['tɪnfɔɪl] *n* (*U*) papier *m* (d')aluminium.

tinge [tɪndʒ] *n* **-1.** [of colour] teinte *f*, nuance *f*. **-2.** [of feeling] nuance *f*.

tinged [tɪndʒd] *adj*: **~ with** teinté(e) de.

tingle ['tɪŋgl] *vi* picoter; **to ~ with** brûler de.

tingling ['tɪŋglɪŋ] *n* (*U*) picotement *m*.

tinker ['tɪŋkə'] ◇ *n Br* **-1.** *pej* [gypsy] romanichel *m*, -elle *f*. **-2.** [rascal] polisson *m*, -onne *f*. ◇ *vi*: **to ~ (with sthg)** bricoler (qqch).

tinkle ['tɪŋkl] ◇ *n* **-1.** [sound] tintement *m*. **-2.** *Br inf* [phone call]: **to give sb a ~** passer un coup de fil à qqn. ◇ *vi* [ring] tinter.

tin mine *n* mine *f* d'étain.

tinned [tɪnd] *adj Br* en boîte.

tinnitus [tɪ'naɪtəs] *n* acouphène *m*.

tinny ['tɪnɪ] (*compar* -**ier**, *superl* -**iest**) *adj* **-1.** [sound] métallique. **-2.** *inf pej* [badly made]: **a ~ car** un tas de ferraille, une vraie casserole.

tin opener *n Br* ouvre-boîtes *m inv*.

tin-pot *adj Br inf pej* [country, dictator] de rien du tout.

tinsel ['tɪnsl] *n* (*U*) guirlandes *fpl* de Noël.

tint [tɪnt] ◇ *n* teinte *f*, nuance *f*; [in hair] rinçage *m*. ◇ *vt* teinter.

tinted ['tɪntɪd] *adj* [glasses, windows] teinté(e).

tiny ['taɪnɪ] (*compar* -**ier**, *superl* -**iest**) *adj* minuscule.

tip [tɪp] (*pt* & *pp* -**ped**, *cont* -**ping**) ◇ *n* **-1.** [end] bout *m*; **it's on the ~ of my tongue** je l'ai sur le bout de la langue. **-2.** *Br* [dump] décharge *f*. **-3.** [to waiter etc] pourboire *m*. **-4.** [piece of advice] tuyau *m*. ◇ *vt* **-1.** [tilt] faire basculer. **-2.** [spill] renverser. **-3.** [waiter etc] donner un pourboire à. ◇ *vi* **-1.** [tilt] basculer. **-2.** [spill] se renverser. **-3.** [give money to waiter etc] laisser un pourboire.

◆ **tip off** *vt sep* prévenir.

◆ **tip over** ◇ *vt sep* renverser. ◇ *vi* se renverser.

tip-off *n* tuyau *m*; [to police] dénonciation *f*.

tipped ['tɪpt] *adj* qui a un embout; [cigarette] à bout filtre.

Tipp-Ex® ['tɪpeks] *Br* ◇ *n* Tipp-ex® *m*. ◇ *vt* tippexer.

tipple ['tɪpl] *n inf*: **what's your ~?** qu'est-ce que tu aimes boire d'habitude?

tipsy ['tɪpsɪ] (*compar* -**ier**, *superl* -**iest**) *adj inf* gai(e).

tiptoe ['tɪptəʊ] ◇ *n*: **on ~** sur la pointe des pieds. ◇ *vi* marcher sur la pointe des pieds.

tip-top *adj inf dated* excellent(e).

TIR (*abbr of* **Transports Internationaux Routiers**) TIR.

tirade [taɪ'reɪd] *n* diatribe *f*.

Tirana, Tiranë [tɪ'rɑːnə] *n* Tirana.

tire ['taɪə'] ◇ *n Am* = **tyre**. ◇ *vt* fatiguer.
◇ *vi* **-1.** [get tired] se fatiguer. **-2.** [get fed
up]: **to ~ of** se lasser de.
◆ **tire out** *vt sep* épuiser.

tired ['taɪəd] *adj* **-1.** [sleepy] fatigué(e), las
(lasse). **-2.** [fed up]: **to be ~ of sthg/of doing
sthg** en avoir assez de qqch/de faire qqch.

tiredness ['taɪədnɪs] *n* fatigue *f*.

tireless ['taɪəlɪs] *adj* infatigable.

tiresome ['taɪəsəm] *adj* ennuyeux(euse).

tiring ['taɪərɪŋ] *adj* fatigant(e).

Tirol = **Tyrol**.

tissue ['tɪʃuː] *n* **-1.** [paper handkerchief] mouchoir *m* en papier. **-2.** (*U*) BIOL tissu *m*. **-3.**
phr: **a ~ of lies** un tissu de mensonges.

tissue paper *n* (*U*) papier *m* de soie.

tit [tɪt] *n* **-1.** [bird] mésange *f*. **-2.** *vulg*
[breast] nichon *m*, néné *m*.

titbit *Br* ['tɪtbɪt], **tidbit** *Am* ['tɪdbɪt] *n* **-1.** [of
food] bon morceau *m*. **-2.** *fig* [of news] pe-
tite nouvelle *f*; **a ~ of gossip** un petit potin.

tit for tat *n* un prêté pour un rendu.

titillate ['tɪtɪleɪt] ◇ *vt* titiller. ◇ *vi* titiller
les sens.

titivate ['tɪtɪveɪt] *vt* pomponner.

title ['taɪtl] *n* titre *m*.

titled ['taɪtld] *adj* titré(e).

title deed *n* titre *m* de propriété.

titleholder ['taɪtl,həʊldə'] *n* SPORT tenant *m*,
-e *f* du titre.

title page *n* page *f* de titre.

title role *n* rôle *m* principal.

titter ['tɪtə'] *vi* rire bêtement.

tittle-tattle ['tɪtl,tatl] *n* (*U*) *inf pej* ragots
mpl, cancans *mpl*.

titular ['tɪtjʊlə'] *adj* nominal(e).

T-junction *n* intersection *f* en T.

TLS (*abbr of* **Times Literary Supplement**) *n*
édition littéraire du *Times*.

TM ◇ *n* (*abbr of* **transcendental meditation**) MT *f*. ◇ *abbr of* **trademark**.

TN *abbr of* **Tennessee**.

TNT (*abbr of* **trinitrotoluene**) *n* TNT *m*.

to [unstressed before consonant tə, unstressed
before vowel tʊ, stressed tuː] ◇ *prep* **-1.** [indica-
ting place, direction] à; **to go ~ Liverpool/
Spain/school** aller à Liverpool/en Espagne/
à l'école; **to go ~ the butcher's** aller chez
le boucher; **~ the left/right** à gauche/
droite. **-2.** (to express indirect object) à; **to
give sthg ~ sb** donner qqch à qqn; **we
were listening ~ the radio** nous écoutions

la radio; **he refused to give an answer ~
my question** il refusa de répondre à ma
question. **-3.** [indicating reaction, effect] à; **~
my delight/surprise** à ma grande joie/
surprise; **it worked ~ our advantage** cela a
tourné à notre avantage; **to be ~ sb's liking** être au goût de qqn. **-4.** [in stating opin-
ion]: **~ me, ...** à mon avis, ...; **it seemed
quite unnecessary ~ me/him** *etc* cela me/lui
etc semblait tout à fait inutile. **-5.** [indica-
ting state, process]: **to drive sb ~ drink** pousser qqn à boire; **to shoot ~ fame** devenir
célèbre du jour au lendemain; **it could lead
~ trouble** cela pourrait causer des ennuis.
-6. [as far as] à, jusqu'à; **to count ~ 10**
compter jusqu'à 10; **we work from 9 ~ 5**
nous travaillons de 9 heures à 17 heures.
-7. [in expressions of time] moins; **it's ten ~
three/quarter ~ one** il est trois heures
moins dix/une heure moins le quart. **-8.**
[per] à; **40 miles ~ the gallon** ≃ 7 litres aux
cent (km). **-9.** [accompanied by]: **a poem set
~ music** un poème mis en musique; **we
danced ~ the sound of guitars** on a dansé
au son des guitares. **-10.** [of, for] de; **the
key ~ the car** la clef de la voiture; **a letter
~ my daughter** une lettre à ma fille.
◇ *adv* [shut]: **push the door ~** fermez la
porte.
◇ *with infinitive* **-1.** (forming simple infinitive):
~ walk marcher; **~ laugh** rire. **-2.** (following
another verb): **to begin ~ do sthg** commencer à faire qqch; **to try ~ do sthg** essayer
de faire qqch; **to want ~ do sthg** vouloir
faire qqch. **-3.** (following an adjective): **difficult ~ do** difficile à faire; **ready ~ go** prêt à
partir. **-4.** (indicating purpose): **he
worked hard ~ pass his exam** il a travaillé
dur pour réussir son examen. **-5.** (substi-
tuting for a relative clause): **I have a lot ~ do**
j'ai beaucoup à faire; **he told me ~ leave** il
m'a dit de partir. **-6.** (to avoid repetition of
infinitive): **I meant to call him but I forgot ~**
je voulais l'appeler, mais j'ai oublié. **-7.** [in
comments]: **~ be honest ...** en toute franchise ...; **~ sum up ...** en résumé, ..., pour
récapituler, ...
◆ **to and fro** *adv*: **to go ~ and fro** aller et
venir; **to walk ~ and fro** marcher de long
en large.

toad [təʊd] *n* crapaud *m*.

toadstool ['təʊdstuːl] *n* champignon *m* vénéneux.

toady ['təʊdɪ] (*pl* **-ies**, *pt* & *pp* **-ied**) *pej* ◇ *n*
lèche-bottes *mf inv*. ◇ *vi*: **to ~ (to sb)** lé-
cher les bottes (de qqn).

to-and-fro *adj* de va-et-vient.

◆ **to and fro** *adv* avec un mouvement de va-et-vient; **to walk to and fro** marcher de long en large.

toast [təʊst] ◇ *n* **-1.** (U) [bread] pain *m* grillé, toast *m*. **-2.** [drink] toast *m*; **to drink a ~ to sb/sthg** lever son verre en l'honneur de qqn/à qqch. ◇ *vt* **-1.** [bread] (faire) griller. **-2.** [person] porter un toast à.

toasted sandwich ['təʊstɪd-] *n* sandwich *m* grillé.

toaster ['təʊstər] *n* grille-pain *m inv*.

toast rack *n* porte-toasts *m inv*.

tobacco [tə'bækəʊ] *n* (U) tabac *m*.

tobacconist [tə'bækənɪst] *n* buraliste *mf*; **~'s (shop)** bureau *m* de tabac.

Tobago [tə'beɪgəʊ] → **Trinidad and Tobago.**

toboggan [tə'bɒgən] ◇ *n* luge *f*. ◇ *vi* faire de la luge.

today [tə'deɪ] ◇ *n* aujourd'hui *m*. ◇ *adv* aujourd'hui.

toddle ['tɒdl] *vi* [child] marcher d'un pas hésitant.

toddler ['tɒdlər] *n* tout-petit *m* (*qui commence à marcher*).

toddy ['tɒdɪ] (*pl* **-ies**) *n* grog *m*.

to-do (*pl* **-s**) *n inf dated* histoire *f*.

toe [təʊ] ◇ *n* [of foot] orteil *m*, doigt *m* de pied; [of sock, shoe] bout *m*. ◇ *vt*: **to ~ the line** se plier.

toehold ['təʊhəʊld] *n* prise *f*; **to have a ~ in a market** *fig* avoir un pied dans un marché.

toenail ['təʊneɪl] *n* ongle *m* d'orteil.

toffee ['tɒfɪ] *n* caramel *m*.

toffee apple *n Br* pomme *f* caramélisée.

tofu ['təʊfuː] *n* tofu *m*.

toga ['təʊgə] *n* toge *f*.

together [tə'geðər] ◇ *adv* **-1.** [gen] ensemble. **-2.** [at the same time] en même temps. ◇ *adj inf* équilibré(e).

◆ **together with** *prep* ainsi que.

togetherness [tə'geðənɪs] *n* (U) unité *f*.

toggle ['tɒgl] *n* bouton *m* de duffle-coat.

toggle switch *n* ELECTRON & COMPUT interrupteur *m* à bascule.

Togo ['təʊgəʊ] *n* Togo *m*; **in ~** au Togo.

Togolese [,təʊgə'liːz] ◇ *adj* togolais(e). ◇ *n* Togolais *m*, -e *f*.

togs [tɒgz] *npl inf* fringues *fpl*.

toil [tɔɪl] *literary* ◇ *n* labeur *m*. ◇ *vi* travailler dur.

◆ **toil away** *vi*: **to ~ away (at sthg)** travailler dur (à qqch).

toilet ['tɔɪlɪt] *n* [lavatory] toilettes *fpl*, cabinets *mpl*; **to go to the ~** aller aux toilettes OR aux cabinets.

toilet bag *n* trousse *f* de toilette.

toilet paper *n* (U) papier *m* hygiénique.

toiletries ['tɔɪlɪtrɪz] *npl* articles *mpl* de toilette.

toilet roll *n* rouleau *m* de papier hygiénique.

toilet soap *n* savonnette *f*.

toilet tissue *n* (U) papier *m* hygiénique.

toilet-trained [-,treɪnd] *adj* propre.

toilet water *n* eau *f* de toilette.

to-ing and fro-ing [,tuːɪŋən'frəʊɪŋ] *n* (U) allées *fpl* et venues.

token ['təʊkn] ◇ *adj* symbolique. ◇ *n* **-1.** [voucher] bon *m*. **-2.** [symbol] marque *f*.

◆ **by the same token** *adv* de même.

Tokyo ['təʊkjəʊ] *n* Tokyo.

told [təʊld] *pt & pp* → **tell.**

tolerable ['tɒlərəbl] *adj* passable.

tolerably ['tɒlərəblɪ] *adv* passablement.

tolerance ['tɒlərəns] *n* tolérance *f*.

tolerant ['tɒlərənt] *adj* tolérant(e).

tolerate ['tɒləreɪt] *vt* **-1.** [put up with] supporter. **-2.** [permit] tolérer.

toleration [,tɒlə'reɪʃn] *n* (U) tolérance *f*.

toll [təʊl] ◇ *n* **-1.** [number] nombre *m*. **-2.** [fee] péage *m*. **-3.** *phr*: **to take its ~** se faire sentir. ◇ *vt & vi* sonner.

tollbooth ['təʊlbuːθ] *n* poste *m* de péage.

toll bridge *n* pont *m* à péage.

toll-free *Am* ◇ *adj*: **~ number** numéro *m* vert. ◇ *adv*: **to call ~** appeler un numéro vert.

tomato [*Br* tə'mɑːtəʊ, *Am* tə'meɪtəʊ] (*pl* **-es**) *n* tomate *f*.

tomb [tuːm] *n* tombe *f*.

tombola [tɒm'bəʊlə] *n* tombola *f*.

tomboy ['tɒmbɔɪ] *n* garçon *m* manqué.

tombstone ['tuːmstəʊn] *n* pierre *f* tombale.

tomcat ['tɒmkæt] *n* matou *m*.

tomfoolery [tɒm'fuːlərɪ] *n* (U) bêtises *fpl*.

tomorrow [tə'mɒrəʊ] ◇ *n* demain *m*. ◇ *adv* demain.

ton [tʌn] (*pl inv* OR **-s**) *n* **-1.** [imperial] = 1016 kg *Br*, = 907,2 kg *Am*, ≃ tonne *f*. **-2.** [metric] = 1000 kg, tonne *f*. **-3.** *phr*: **to weigh a ~** *inf* peser une tonne; **to come down on sb like a ~ of bricks** tomber sur qqn à bras raccourcis.

◆ **tons** *npl inf*: **~s (of)** des tas (de), plein (de).

tonal ['təʊnl] *adj* tonal(e).

tone [təun] *n* **-1.** [gen] ton *m*. **-2.** [on phone] tonalité *f*. **-3.** *phr*: **to lower the ~ (of)** rabaisser le ton (de).

◆ **tone down** *vt sep* modérer.

◆ **tone in** *vi*: **to ~ in (with)** s'harmoniser (avec).

◆ **tone up** *vt sep* tonifier.

tone-deaf *adj* qui n'a aucune oreille.

toner ['təunər] *n* **-1.** [for photocopier, printer] toner *m*. **-2.** [cosmetic] astringent *m*, lotion *f* tonique.

Tonga ['tɒŋgə] *n* Tonga; **in ~** à Tonga.

tongs [tɒŋz] *npl* pinces *fpl*; [for hair] fer *m* à friser.

tongue [tʌŋ] *n* **-1.** [gen] langue *f*; **to have a sharp ~** avoir la langue bien acérée OR affilée; **to have one's ~ in one's cheek** *inf* ne pas être sérieux; **to hold one's ~** *fig* tenir sa langue; **~s will wag** on va jaser. **-2.** [of shoe] languette *f*.

tongue-in-cheek *adj* ironique.

tongue-tied [-,taɪd] *adj* muet(ette).

tongue twister [-,twɪstər] *n* phrase *f* difficile à dire.

tonic ['tɒnɪk] *n* **-1.** [tonic water] Schweppes® *m*. **-2.** [medicine] tonique *m*; **the holiday was a real ~** *fig* ces vacances m'ont fait beaucoup de bien.

tonic water *n* Schweppes® *m*.

tonight [tə'naɪt] ⋄ *n* ce soir *m*; [late] cette nuit *f*. ⋄ *adv* ce soir; [late] cette nuit.

tonnage ['tʌnɪdʒ] *n* tonnage *m*.

tonne [tʌn] (*pl inv* OR **-s**) *n* tonne *f*.

tonsil ['tɒnsl] *n* amygdale *f*.

tonsil(l)itis [,tɒnsɪ'laɪtɪs] *n* (*U*) amygdalite *f*.

too [tuː] *adv* **-1.** [also] aussi. **-2.** [excessively] trop; **~ many people** trop de gens; **it was over all ~ soon** ça s'était terminé bien trop tôt; **I'd be only ~ happy to help** je serais trop heureux de vous aider; **I wasn't ~ impressed** ça ne m'a pas impressionné outre mesure.

took [tuk] *pt* → **take**.

tool [tuːl] *n lit* & *fig* outil *m*; **to ~ down ~s** *Br* cesser le travail; **the ~s of sb's trade** les outils du métier de qqn.

◆ **tool around** *vi Am inf* traîner.

tool box *n* boîte *f* à outils.

tool kit *n* trousse *f* à outils.

toot [tuːt] ⋄ *n* coup *m* de klaxon. ⋄ *vt*: **to ~ one's horn** klaxonner. ⋄ *vi* klaxonner.

tooth [tuːθ] (*pl* teeth) *n* dent *f*; **to be long in the ~** *Br pej* n'être plus tout jeune; **to be fed up to the back teeth with** *Br inf* en avoir ras le bol de; **to grit one's teeth** serrer les dents; **to lie through one's teeth** mentir comme un arracheur de dents.

◆ **teeth** *npl fig* [power]: **to have no teeth** être impuissant.

toothache ['tuːθeɪk] *n* mal *m* OR rage *f* de dents; **to have ~** avoir mal aux dents.

toothbrush ['tuːθbrʌʃ] *n* brosse *f* à dents.

toothless ['tuːθlɪs] *adj* édenté(e).

toothpaste ['tuːθpeɪst] *n* (pâte *f*) dentifrice *m*.

toothpick ['tuːθpɪk] *n* cure-dents *m inv*.

tooth powder *n* poudre *f* dentifrice.

tootle ['tuːtl] *vi inf*: **to ~ off** se sauver.

top [tɒp] (*pt* & *pp* **-ped**, *cont* **-ping**) ⋄ *adj* **-1.** [highest] du haut. **-2.** [most important, successful - officials] important(e); [- executives] supérieur(e); [- pop singer] fameux(euse); [- sportsman, sportswoman] meilleur(e); [- in exam] premier(ière). **-3.** [maximum] maximum; **at ~ speed** à toute vitesse.

⋄ *n* **-1.** [highest point - of hill] sommet *m*; [- of page, pile] haut *m*; [- of tree] cime *f*; [- of list] début *m*, tête *f*; **at the ~ of the stairs/ the street** en haut de l'escalier/la rue; **on ~** dessus; **to go over the ~** *Br* en faire un peu trop, exagérer; **at the ~ of one's voice** à tue-tête. **-2.** [lid - of bottle, tube] bouchon *m*; [- of pen] capuchon *m*; [- of jar] couvercle *m*. **-3.** [of table, box] dessus *m*. **-4.** [clothing] haut *m*. **-5.** [toy] toupie *f*. **-6.** [highest rank - in league] tête *f*; [- in scale] haut *m*; [- SCH] premier *m*, -ière *f*.

⋄ *vt* **-1.** [be first in] être en tête de. **-2.** [better] surpasser; **to ~ an offer** surenchérir. **-3.** [exceed] dépasser.

◆ **on top of** *prep* **-1.** [in space] sur. **-2.** [in addition to] en plus de. **-3.** [in control of]: **to be on ~ of one's work** avoir son travail bien en main. **-4.** *phr*: **my work is getting on ~ of me** je me suis laissé dépasser par mon travail; **things are getting on ~ of me** je suis complètement dépassé.

◆ **top up** *Br*, **top off** *Am vt sep* remplir.

topaz ['təupæz] *n* topaze *f*.

top brass *n* (*U*) *inf*: **the ~** les gros bonnets *mpl*.

topcoat ['tɒpkəut] *n* **-1.** [item of clothing] manteau *m*. **-2.** [paint] dernière couche *f*.

top dog *n inf* chef *m*.

top-flight *adj* de premier ordre.

top floor *n* dernier étage *m*.

top gear *n* quatrième/cinquième vitesse *f*.

top hat *n* haut-de-forme *m*.

top-heavy *adj* mal équilibré(e).

topic ['tɒpɪk] *n* sujet *m*.

topical ['tɒpɪkl] *adj* d'actualité.

topknot ['tɒpnɒt] *n* [in hair] houppe *f*.

topless ['tɒplɪs] *adj* [woman] aux seins nus; ~ **swimsuit** monokini *m*.

top-level *adj* au plus haut niveau.

topmost ['tɒpməʊst] *adj* le plus haut (la plus haute).

top-notch *adj inf* de premier choix.

topographer [tə'pɒgrəfəʳ] *n* topographe *mf*.

topography [tə'pɒgrəfɪ] *n* topographie *f*.

topped [tɒpt] *adj*: ~ **by** OR **with** recouvert(e) de.

topping ['tɒpɪŋ] *n* garniture *f*.

topple ['tɒpl] ◇ *vt* renverser. ◇ *vi* basculer.
◆ **topple over** *vi* tomber.

top-ranking [-'ræŋkɪŋ] *adj* [official] haut placé(e); [player] haut classé(e).

TOPS [tɒps] (*abbr of* **Training Opportunities Scheme**) *n programme du recyclage professionnel en Grande-Bretagne*.

top-secret *adj* top secret (top secrète).

top-security *adj* de haute surveillance.

topsoil ['tɒpsɔɪl] *n* terre *f*.

topspin ['tɒpspɪn] *n* lift *m*.

topsy-turvy [,tɒpsɪ'tɜːvɪ] ◇ *adj* -1. [messy] sens dessus dessous. -2. [confused]: **to be ~** ne pas tourner rond. ◇ *adv* [messily] sens dessus dessous.

tor [tɔːʳ] *n* [hill] colline *f* rocheuse.

torch [tɔːtʃ] *n* -1. *Br* [electric] lampe *f* électrique. -2. [burning] torche *f*.

tore [tɔːʳ] *pt* → **tear**.

torment [*n* 'tɔːment, *vb* tɔː'ment] ◇ *n* tourment *m*. ◇ *vt* tourmenter.

tormentor [tɔː'mentəʳ] *n* bourreau *m*.

torn [tɔːn] *pp* → **tear**.

tornado [tɔː'neɪdəʊ] (*pl* **-es** OR **-s**) *n* tornade *f*.

Toronto [tə'rɒntəʊ] *n* Toronto.

torpedo [tɔː'piːdəʊ] (*pl* **-es**) ◇ *n* torpille *f*. ◇ *vt* torpiller.

torpedo boat *n* torpilleur *m*.

torpor ['tɔːpəʳ] *n* torpeur *f*.

torque [tɔːk] *n* couple *m* (de torsion).

torrent ['tɒrənt] *n* torrent *m*.

torrential [tə'renʃl] *adj* torrentiel(ielle).

torrid ['tɒrɪd] *adj* -1. [hot] torride. -2. *fig* [passionate] ardent(e).

torso ['tɔːsəʊ] (*pl* **-s**) *n* torse *m*.

tortoise ['tɔːtəs] *n* tortue *f*.

tortoiseshell ['tɔːtəʃel] ◇ *adj*: ~ **cat** chat *m* roux tigré. ◇ *n* (*U*) [material] écaille *f*. ◇ *comp* en écaille.

tortuous ['tɔːtʃʊəs] *adj* -1. [winding] tortueux(euse). -2. [over-complicated] alambiqué(e).

torture ['tɔːtʃəʳ] ◇ *n* torture *f*. ◇ *vt* torturer.

torturer ['tɔːtʃərəʳ] *n* tortionnaire *mf*.

Tory ['tɔːrɪ] (*pl* **-ies**) ◇ *adj* tory, conservateur(trice). ◇ *n* tory *mf*, conservateur *m*, -trice *f*.

toss [tɒs] ◇ *vt* -1. [throw] jeter; **to ~ a coin** jouer à pile ou face; **to ~ one's head** rejeter la tête en arrière. -2. [salad] remuer; [pancake] faire sauter. -3. [throw about] ballotter. ◇ *vi* -1. [with coin] jouer à pile ou face. -2. [move about]: **to ~ and turn** se tourner et se retourner. ◇ *n* -1. [of coin] coup *m* de pile ou face. -2. [of head] mouvement *m* brusque.
◆ **toss up** *vi* jouer à pile ou face.

toss-up *n inf*: **it was a ~ who'd win** il était impossible de savoir qui allait gagner.

tot [tɒt] (*pt* & *pp* **-ted**, *cont* **-ting**) *n* -1. *inf* [small child] tout petit *m*, toute petite *f*. -2. [of drink] larme *f*, goutte *f*.
◆ **tot up** *vt sep inf* additionner.

total ['təʊtl] (*Br pt* & *pp* **-led**, *cont* **-ling**, *Am pt* & *pp* **-ed**, *cont* **-ing**) ◇ *adj* total(e); [disgrace, failure] complet (complète); **a ~ fool** un abruti fini. ◇ *n* total *m*; **in ~** au total. ◇ *vt* -1. [add up] additionner. -2. [amount to] s'élever à. -3. *Am inf* [wreck] bousiller, détruire.

totalitarian [,təʊtælɪ'teərɪən] *adj* totalitaire.

totality [təʊ'tælətɪ] *n* totalité *f*.

totally ['təʊtəlɪ] *adv* totalement; **I ~ agree** je suis entièrement d'accord.

tote bag [təʊt-] *n Am* sac *m* (à provisions).

totem pole ['təʊtəm-] *n* mât *m* totémique.

toto ['təʊtəʊ]
◆ **in toto** *adv fml* entièrement, complètement.

totter ['tɒtəʳ] *vi lit* & *fig* chanceler.

toucan ['tuːkən] *n* toucan *m*.

touch [tʌtʃ] ◇ *n* -1. (*U*) [sense] toucher *m*. -2. [detail] touche *f*; **to put the finishing ~es to sthg** mettre la dernière main à qqch. -3. (*U*) [skill] marque *f*, note *f*. -4. [contact]: **to keep in ~ (with sb)** rester en contact (avec qqn); **to get in ~ with sb** entrer en contact avec qqn; **to lose ~** [friends] se perdre de vue; **to lose ~ with sb** perdre qqn de vue; **to be out of ~ with** ne plus être au courant de. -5. SPORT: **in ~** en touche. -6. [small amount]: **a ~** un petit peu. -7. *phr*: **it was ~ and go** c'était tangent; **it was ~ and go whether ...** il n'était pas sûr que ...; **he's**

a soft ~ [for money] on peut le taper facilement.
◇ *vt* toucher.
◇ *vi* **-1.** [with fingers etc] toucher. **-2.** [be in contact] se toucher.
◆ **a touch** *adv* [loud, bright] un peu trop.
◆ **touch down** *vi* [plane] atterrir.
◆ **touch on** *vt fus* effleurer.

touch-and-go *adj* incertain(e).

touchdown ['tʌtʃdaun] *n* **-1.** [of plane] atterrissage *m*. **-2.** [in American football] but *m*.

touched [tʌtʃt] *adj* **-1.** [grateful] touché(e). **-2.** *inf* [slightly mad] fêlé(e).

touching ['tʌtʃɪŋ] *adj* touchant(e).

touch judge *n* RUGBY juge *m* de touche.

touchline ['tʌtʃlaɪn] *n* ligne *f* de touche.

touchpaper ['tʌtʃ,peɪpər] *n* papier *m* nitraté.

touch-type *vi* taper au toucher.

touchy ['tʌtʃɪ] (*compar* -ier, *superl* -iest) *adj* **-1.** [person] susceptible; **to be ~ about sthg** ne pas aimer parler de qqch. **-2.** [subject, question] délicat(e).

tough [tʌf] *adj* **-1.** [material, vehicle, person] solide; [character, life] dur(e). **-2.** [meat] dur(e). **-3.** [decision, problem, task] difficile. **-4.** [rough - area of town] dangereux(euse). **-5.** [strict] sévère. **-6.** *inf* [unfortunate]: **~ luck!** pas de veine!; **that's ~!** c'est vache!, c'est malheureux!

toughen ['tʌfn] *vt* **-1.** [character] endurcir. **-2.** [material] renforcer.

toughened ['tʌfnd] *adj* [glass] trempé(e).

toughness ['tʌfnɪs] *n* (*U*) **-1.** [resilience] dureté *f*. **-2.** [of material] solidité *f*. **-3.** [of decision, problem, task] difficulté *f*. **-4.** [strictness] sévérité *f*.

toupee ['tu:peɪ] *n* postiche *m*.

tour [tuər] ◇ *n* **-1.** [journey] voyage *m*; [by pop group etc] tournée *f*. **-2.** [of town, museum] visite *f*, tour *m*. ◇ *vt* visiter. ◇ *vi*: **to ~ round a country** visiter un pays.

tourer ['tuərər] *n* voiture *f* de tourisme.

touring ['tuərɪŋ] ◇ *adj* [show, theatre group] en tournée; [exhibition] ambulant(e). ◇ *n* tourisme *m*; **to go ~** faire du tourisme.

tourism ['tuərɪzm] *n* tourisme *m*.

tourist ['tuərɪst] *n* touriste *mf*.

tourist class *n* classe *f* touriste.

tourist (information) office *n* office *m* de tourisme.

touristy ['tuərɪstɪ] *adj pej* touristique.

tournament ['tɔ:nəmənt] *n* tournoi *m*.

tourniquet ['tuənɪkeɪ] *n* tourniquet *m*.

tour operator *n* voyagiste *m*.

tousle ['tauzl] *vt* ébouriffer.

tout [taut] ◇ *n* revendeur *m* de billets. ◇ *vt* [tickets] revendre; [goods] vendre. ◇ *vi*: **to ~ for trade** racoler les clients.

tow [təu] ◇ *n*: **to give sb a ~** remorquer qqn; **"on ~"** *Br* «véhicule en remorque»; **with sb in ~** à la suite de qqn. ◇ *vt* remorquer.

towards *Br* [tə'wɔ:dz], **toward** *Am* [tə'wɔ:d] *prep* **-1.** [gen] vers; [movement] vers, en direction de. **-2.** [in attitude] envers. **-3.** [for the purpose of] pour.

towaway zone ['təuəweɪ-] *n Am* zone de stationnement interdit sous peine de mise à la fourrière.

towbar ['təubɑ:] *n* barre *f* de remorquage.

towel ['tauəl] *n* serviette *f*; [tea towel] torchon *m*.

towelling *Br*, **toweling** *Am* ['tauəlɪŋ] *n* (*U*) tissu *m* éponge.

towel rail *n* porte-serviettes *m inv*.

tower ['tauər] ◇ *n* tour *f*; **a ~ of strength** *Br* un appui solide. ◇ *vi* s'élever; **to ~ over sb/sthg** dominer qqn/qqch.

tower block *n Br* tour *f*.

towering ['tauərɪŋ] *adj* imposant(e).

town [taun] *n* ville *f*; **to go out on the ~** faire la tournée des grands ducs; **to go to ~ on sthg** *fig* ne pas lésiner sur qqch.

town centre *n* centre-ville *m*.

town clerk *n* ≃ secrétaire *m* de mairie.

town council *n* conseil *m* municipal.

town hall *n* mairie *f*.

town house *n* [fashionable house] hôtel *m* particulier.

town plan *n* plan *m* de ville.

town planner *n* urbaniste *mf*.

town planning *n* urbanisme *m*.

townsfolk ['taunzfəuk], **townspeople** ['taunz,pi:pl] *npl* citadins *mpl*.

township ['taunʃɪp] *n* **-1.** [in South Africa] township *f*. **-2.** [in US] ≃ canton *m*.

towpath ['təupɑ:θ, *pl* -ɑ:ðz] *n* chemin *m* de halage.

towrope ['təurəup] *n* câble *m* de remorquage.

tow truck *n Am* dépanneuse *f*.

toxic ['tɒksɪk] *adj* toxique.

toxin ['tɒksɪn] *n* toxine *f*.

toy [tɔɪ] *n* jouet *m*.
◆ **toy with** *vt fus* **-1.** [idea] caresser. **-2.** [coin etc] jouer avec; **to ~ with one's food** manger du bout des dents.

toy boy *n inf* étalon *m*, jeune amant d'une femme plus âgée.

toy shop *n* magasin *m* de jouets.

trace [treɪs] ◇ *n* trace *f*; **without ~** sans laisser de traces. ◇ *vt* **-1.** [relatives, criminal] retrouver; [development, progress] suivre; [history, life] retracer. **-2.** [on paper] tracer.

trace element *n* oligo-élément *m*.

tracer bullet ['treɪsəʳ-] *n* balle *f* traçante.

tracing ['treɪsɪŋ] *n* [copy] calque *m*.

tracing paper *n* (*U*) papier-calque *m*.

track [træk] ◇ *n* **-1.** [path] chemin *m*; **off the beaten ~** hors des sentiers battus. **-2.** SPORT piste *f*. **-3.** RAIL voie *f* ferrée. **-4.** [of animal, person] trace *f*; **to hide** OR **cover one's ~s** brouiller les pistes; **to stop dead in one's ~s** s'arrêter net. **-5.** [on record, tape] piste *f*. **-6.** *phr*: **to keep ~ of sb** rester en contact avec qqn; **to keep ~ of** [events] suivre; **to lose ~ of sb** perdre contact avec qqn; **to lose ~ of** [events] ne plus suivre; **to lose ~ of time** perdre la notion du temps; **to be on the right~** être sur la bonne voie; **to be on the wrong ~** être sur la mauvaise piste.
◇ *vt* suivre la trace de.
◇ *vi* [camera] faire un travelling.
◆ **track down** *vt sep* [criminal, animal] dépister; [object, address etc] retrouver.

tracker dog ['trækəʳ-] *n* chien *m* policier.

track event *n* épreuve *f* sur piste.

tracking station ['trækɪŋ-] *n* station *f* d'observation.

track record *n* palmarès *m*.

track shoes *npl* chaussures *fpl* à pointes.

tracksuit ['træksuːt] *n* survêtement *m*.

tract [trækt] *n* **-1.** [pamphlet] tract *m*. **-2.** [of land, forest] étendue *f*. **-3.** MED appareil *m*, système *m*.

traction ['trækʃn] *n* (*U*) **-1.** PHYSICS traction *f*. **-2.** MED extension *f*; **in ~** en extension.

traction engine *n* locomobile *f*.

tractor ['træktəʳ] *n* tracteur *m*.

tractor-trailer *n* Am semi-remorque *m*.

trade [treɪd] ◇ *n* **-1.** (*U*) [commerce] commerce *m*. **-2.** [job] métier *m*; **by ~** de son état. ◇ *vt* [exchange]: **to ~ sthg (for)** échanger qqch (contre). ◇ *vi* **-1.** COMM: **to ~ (with sb)** commercer (avec qqn). **-2.** Am [shop]: **to ~ at** OR **with** faire ses courses à OR chez.
◆ **trade in** *vt sep* [exchange] échanger, faire reprendre.

trade barrier *n* barrière *f* douanière.

trade deficit *n* déficit *m* commercial.

trade discount *n* remise *f* confraternelle OR à la profession.

trade fair *n* exposition *f* commerciale.

trade gap *n* déficit *m* commercial.

trade-in *n* reprise *f*.

trademark ['treɪdmɑːk] *n* **-1.** COMM marque *f* de fabrique. **-2.** *fig* [characteristic] marque *f*.

trade name *n* nom *m* de marque.

trade-off *n* compromis *m*.

trade price *n* prix *m* de gros.

trader ['treɪdəʳ] *n* marchand *m*, -e *f*, commerçant *m*, -e *f*.

trade route *n* route *f* commerciale.

trade secret *n* secret *m* de fabrication.

tradesman ['treɪdzmən] (*pl* **-men** [-mən]) *n* commerçant *m*.

tradespeople ['treɪdz,piːpl] *npl* commerçants *mpl*.

trade(s) union *n* Br syndicat *m*.

Trades Union Congress *n* Br: **the ~** la Confédération des syndicats britanniques.

trade(s) unionist *n* Br syndicaliste *mf*.

trade wind *n* alizé *m*.

trading ['treɪdɪŋ] *n* (*U*) commerce *m*.

trading estate *n* Br zone *f* industrielle.

trading stamp *n* timbre-prime *m*.

tradition [trə'dɪʃn] *n* tradition *f*.

traditional [trə'dɪʃənl] *adj* traditionnel(elle).

traditionally [trə'dɪʃnəlɪ] *adv* traditionnellement.

traffic ['træfɪk] (*pt* & *pp* **-ked**, *cont* **-king**) ◇ *n* (*U*) **-1.** [vehicles] circulation *f*. **-2.** [illegal trade]: **~ (in)** trafic *m* (de). ◇ *vi*: **to ~ in** faire le trafic de.

traffic circle *n* Am rond-point *m*.

traffic island *n* refuge *m*.

traffic jam *n* embouteillage *m*.

trafficker ['træfɪkəʳ] *n*: **~ (in)** trafiquant *m*, -e *f* (de).

traffic lights *npl* feux *mpl* de signalisation.

traffic offence Br, **traffic violation** Am *n* infraction *f* au code de la route.

traffic sign *n* panneau *m* de signalisation.

traffic violation Am = **traffic offence**.

traffic warden *n* Br contractuel *m*, -elle *f*.

tragedy ['trædʒədɪ] (*pl* **-ies**) *n* tragédie *f*.

tragic ['trædʒɪk] *adj* tragique.

tragically ['trædʒɪklɪ] *adv* tragiquement, de façon tragique.

trail [treɪl] ◇ *n* **-1.** [path] sentier *m*; **to blaze a ~** *fig* faire œuvre de pionnier. **-2.** [trace] piste *f*; **on the ~ of** sur la piste de. ◇ *vt* **-1.** [drag] traîner. **-2.** [follow] suivre. ◇ *vi* **-1.** [drag, move slowly] traîner. **-2.** SPORT [lose]: **to be ~ing** être mené(e).
◆ **trail away**, **trail off** *vi* s'estomper.

trailblazing ['treɪl,bleɪzɪŋ] *adj* de pionnier.

trailer ['treɪlə'] n -1. [vehicle - for luggage] remorque f; [- for living in] **caravane** f. -2. CINEMA bande-annonce f.

trailer park n Am terrain aménagé pour les camping-cars.

train [treɪn] ◇ n -1. RAIL train m. -2. [of dress] traîne f. ◇ vt -1. [teach]: **to ~ sb to do sthg** apprendre à qqn à faire qqch. -2. [for job] former; **to ~ sb as/in** former qqn comme/dans. -3. SPORT: **to ~ sb (for)** entraîner qqn (pour). -4. [plant] faire grimper. -5. [gun, camera] braquer. ◇ vi -1. [for job]: **to ~ (as)** recevoir OR faire une formation (de). -2. SPORT: **to ~ (for)** s'entraîner (pour).

trained [treɪnd] adj formé(e).

trainee [treɪ'niː] ◇ adj stagiaire, apprenti(e). ◇ n stagiaire mf.

trainer ['treɪnə'] n -1. [of animals] dresseur m, -euse f. -2. SPORT entraîneur m.
◆ **trainers** npl Br chaussures fpl de sport.

training ['treɪnɪŋ] n (U) -1. [for job]: ~ **(in)** formation f (de). -2. SPORT entraînement m.

training college n Br école f professionnelle.

training course n cours m OR stage m de formation.

training shoes npl Br chaussures fpl de sport.

train of thought n: **my/his ~** le fil de mes/ses pensées.

train set n train m électrique.

train spotter [-,spɒtə'] n passionné m, -e f de trains.

train station n Am gare f.

traipse [treɪps] vi traîner.

trait [treɪt] n trait m.

traitor ['treɪtə'] n traître m.

trajectory [trə'dʒektərɪ] (pl **-ies**) n trajectoire f.

tram [træm], **tramcar** ['træmkɑː'] n Br tram m, tramway m.

tramlines ['træmlaɪnz] npl Br -1. [for trams] voies fpl de tram. -2. TENNIS lignes fpl de côté.

tramp [træmp] ◇ n -1. [homeless person] clochard m, -e f. -2. Am inf [woman] traînée f. ◇ vt [countryside] parcourir, battre; **to ~ the streets** battre le pavé. ◇ vi marcher d'un pas lourd.

trample ['træmpl] ◇ vt piétiner. ◇ vi: **to ~ on sthg** piétiner qqch; **to ~ on sb** fig bafouer qqn.

trampoline ['træmpəliːn] n trampoline m.

trance [trɑːns] n transe f; **in a ~** en transe.

tranquil ['træŋkwɪl] adj tranquille.

tranquility Am = tranquillity.

tranquilize Am = tranquillize.

tranquilizer Am = tranquillizer.

tranquillity Br, **tranquility** Am [træŋ'kwɪlətɪ] n tranquillité f.

tranquillize, **-ise** Br, **tranquilize** Am ['træŋkwɪlaɪz] vt mettre sous tranquillisants OR calmants.

tranquillizer Br, **tranquilizer** Am ['træŋkwɪlaɪzə'] n tranquillisant m, calmant m.

transact [træn'zækt] vt traiter, régler.

transaction [træn'zækʃn] n transaction f.

transatlantic [,trænzət'læntɪk] adj [flight, crossing] transatlantique; [politics] d'outre-Atlantique.

transceiver [træn'siːvə'] n émetteur-récepteur m.

transcend [træn'send] vt transcender.

transcendental meditation [,trænsen-'dentl-] n méditation f transcendantale.

transcribe [træn'skraɪb] vt transcrire.

transcript ['trænskrɪpt] n transcription f.

transept ['trænsept] n transept m.

transfer [n 'trænsfɜː', vb træns'fɜː'] (pt & pp **-red**, cont **-ring**) ◇ n -1. [gen] transfert m; [of power] passation f; [of money] virement m. -2. [design] décalcomanie f. -3. Am [ticket] ticket permettant de changer de train ou de bus sans payer de supplément. ◇ vt -1. [gen] transférer; [power, control] faire passer; [money] virer. -2. [employee] transférer, muter. ◇ vi être transféré.

transferable [træns'fɜːrəbl] adj transférable, transmissible; **not ~** [ticket] non cessible.

transference ['trænsfərəns] n [of power] passation f.

transfer fee n Br SPORT prix m d'un transfert.

transfigure [træns'fɪgə'] vt transfigurer.

transfix [træns'fɪks] vt: **to be ~ed with fear** être paralysé(e) par la peur.

transform [træns'fɔːm] vt: **to ~ sb/sthg (into)** transformer qqn/qqch (en).

transformation [,trænsfə'meɪʃn] n transformation f.

transformer [træns'fɔːmə'] n ELEC transformateur m.

transfusion [træns'fjuːʒn] n transfusion f.

transgress [træns'gres] fml ◇ vt transgresser. ◇ vi pécher.

transgression [træns'greʃn] n fml -1. [fault] faute f. -2. (U) [doing wrong] transgression f.

transient ['trænzɪənt] ◇ *adj* passager(ère). ◇ *n Am* [person] voyageur *m*, -euse *f* en transit.

transistor [træn'zɪstər] *n* transistor *m*.

transistor radio *n* transistor *m*.

transit ['trænsɪt] *n*: **in** ~ en transit.

transit camp *n* camp *m* volant.

transition [træn'zɪʃn] *n* transition *f*; **in** ~ en transition.

transitional [træn'zɪʃənl] *adj* de transition.

transitive ['trænzɪtɪv] *adj* GRAMM transitif(ive).

transit lounge *n* salle *f* de transit.

transitory ['trænzɪtrɪ] *adj* transitoire.

translate [træns'leɪt] ◇ *vt* traduire. ◇ *vi* [person] traduire; [expression, word] se traduire.

translation [træns'leɪʃn] *n* traduction *f*.

translator [træns'leɪtər] *n* traducteur *m*, -trice *f*.

translucent [trænz'luːsnt] *adj* translucide.

transmission [trænz'mɪʃn] *n* **-1.** [gen] transmission *f*. **-2.** RADIO & TV [programme] émission *f*.

transmit [trænz'mɪt] (*pt* & *pp* **-ted**, *cont* **-ting**) *vt* transmettre.

transmitter [trænz'mɪtər] *n* émetteur *m*.

transparency [trans'pærənsɪ] (*pl* **-ies**) *n* **-1.** PHOT diapositive *f*; [for overhead projector] transparent *m*. **-2.** (*U*) [quality] transparence *f*.

transparent [træns'pærənt] *adj* transparent(e).

transpire [træn'spaɪər] *fml* ◇ *vt*: **it** ~**s that** ... on a appris que .... ◇ *vi* [happen] se passer, arriver.

transplant [*n* 'trænsplɑːnt] ◇ *n* MED greffe *f*, transplantation *f*. ◇ *vt* **-1.** MED greffer, transplanter. **-2.** [seedlings] repiquer. **-3.** [move] transplanter.

transport [*n* 'trænspɔːt, *vb* træn'spɔːt] ◇ *n* transport *m*. ◇ *vt* transporter.

transportable [træn'spɔːtəbl] *adj* transportable.

transportation [,trænspɔː'teɪʃn] *n* transport *m*.

transport cafe *n Br* restaurant *m* de routiers, routier *m*.

transporter [træn'spɔːtər] *n* [for cars] transporteur *m* de voitures.

transpose [træns'pəʊz] *vt* transposer.

transsexual [træns'sekʃʊəl] *n* transsexuel(elle).

transvestite [trænz'vestaɪt] *n* travesti *m*, -e *f*.

trap [træp] (*pt* & *pp* **-ped**, *cont* **-ping**) ◇ *n* piège *m*. ◇ *vt* prendre au piège; **to be trapped** être coincé; **to be trapped in a relationship** être piégé dans une relation.

trapdoor [,træp'dɔːr] *n* trappe *f*.

trapeze [trə'piːz] *n* trapèze *m*.

trapper ['træpər] *n* trappeur *m*.

trappings ['træpɪŋz] *npl* signes *mpl* extérieurs.

trash [træʃ] *n* (*U*) **-1.** *Am* [refuse] ordures *fpl*. **-2.** *inf pej* [poor-quality thing] camelote *f*.

trashcan ['træʃkæn] *n Am* poubelle *f*.

trashy ['træʃɪ] (*compar* **-ier**, *superl* **-iest**) *adj* *inf* qui ne vaut rien, nul (nulle).

trauma ['trɔːmə] *n* MED trauma *m*; *fig* traumatisme *m*.

traumatic [trɔː'mætɪk] *adj* traumatisant(e).

traumatize, -ise ['trɔːmətaɪz] *vt* traumatiser.

travel ['trævl] (*Br pt* & *pp* **-led**, *cont* **-ling**, *Am pt* & *pp* **-ed**, *cont* **-ing**) ◇ *n* (*U*) voyage *m*, voyages *mpl*. ◇ *vt* parcourir. ◇ *vi* **-1.** [make journey] voyager. **-2.** [move - current, signal] aller, passer; [- news] se répandre, circuler.

◆ **travels** *npl* voyages *mpl*.

travel agency *n* agence *f* de voyages.

travel agent *n* agent *m* de voyages; **to/at the** ~**'s** à l'agence *f* de voyages.

travel brochure *n* dépliant *m* touristique.

traveler *etc Am* = **traveller** *etc*.

travelled *Br*, **traveled** *Am* ['trævld] *adj* **-1.** [person] qui a beaucoup voyagé. **-2.** [road, route]: **much** ~ très fréquenté(e).

traveller *Br*, **traveler** *Am* ['trævlər] *n* **-1.** [person on journey] voyageur *m*, -euse *f*. **-2.** [sales representative] représentant *m*.

traveller's cheque *n* chèque *m* de voyage.

travelling *Br*, **traveling** *Am* ['trævlɪŋ] *adj* **-1.** [theatre, circus] ambulant(e). **-2.** [clock, bag etc] de voyage; [allowance] de déplacement; ~ **time** durée *f* du voyage.

travelling expenses *npl* frais *mpl* de déplacement.

travelling salesman *n* représentant *m*.

travelogue, travelog *Am* ['trævəlɒg] *n* **-1.** [talk] compte-rendu *m* OR récit *m* de voyage. **-2.** [film] documentaire *m*.

travelsick ['trævəlsɪk] *adj*: **to be** ~ avoir le mal de la route/de l'air/de mer.

traverse ['trævəs, trə'vɜːs] *vt fml* traverser.

travesty ['trævəstɪ] (*pl* **-ies**) *n* parodie *f*.

trawl [trɔːl] ◇ *n* [fishing net] chalut *m*. ◇ *vt* [area of sea] pêcher au chalut dans. ◇ *vi*: **to**

~ **for cod/mackerel** pêcher la morue/le hareng au chalut.

trawler ['trɔːlə'] n chalutier m.

tray [treɪ] n plateau m.

treacherous ['tretʃərəs] adj traître (traîtresse).

treachery ['tretʃərɪ] n traîtrise f.

treacle ['triːkl] n Br mélasse f.

tread [tred] (pt **trod**, pp **trodden**) ◇ n **-1.** [on tyre] **bande** f de roulement; [of shoe] **semelle** f. **-2.** [way of walking] **pas** m; [sound] **bruit** m de pas. ◇ vt [crush]: **to ~ sthg into** écraser qqch dans. ◇ vi: **to ~ (on)** marcher (sur); **to ~ carefully** fig y aller doucement.

treadle ['tredl] n pédale f.

treadmill ['tredmɪl] n **-1.** [wheel] trépigneuse f. **-2.** fig [dull routine] routine f, train-train m.

treas. (abbr of **treasurer**) trés.

treason ['triːzn] n trahison f.

treasure ['treʒə'] ◇ n trésor m. ◇ vt [object] garder précieusement; [memory] chérir.

treasure hunt n chasse f au trésor.

treasurer ['treʒərə'] n trésorier m, -ière f.

treasure trove n JUR trésor m, objets de valeur trouvés et que personne n'a réclamés.

treasury ['treʒərɪ] (pl **-ies**) n [room] trésorerie f.

◆ **Treasury** n: **the Treasury** le Ministère des Finances.

treasury bill n bon m du Trésor.

treat [triːt] ◇ vt **-1.** [gen] traiter; **to ~ sb like a child** traiter qqn en enfant; **to ~ sthg as a joke** prendre qqch à la rigolade. **-2.** [on special occasion]: **to ~ sb to sthg** offrir OR payer qqch à qqn; **to ~ o.s. to sthg** s'offrir qqch, se payer qqch. ◇ n **-1.** [gift] cadeau m; **to give sb a ~** faire plaisir à qqn; **this is my ~** [pay for meal, drink] c'est moi qui régale. **-2.** [delight] plaisir m.

treatise ['triːtɪz] n: **~ (on)** traité m (de).

treatment ['triːtmənt] n traitement m.

treaty ['triːtɪ] (pl **-ies**) n traité m.

treble ['trebl] ◇ adj **-1.** [MUS - voice] de soprano; [- recorder] aigu (aiguë). **-2.** [triple] triple. ◇ n [on stereo control] aigu m; [boy singer] soprano m. ◇ vt & vi tripler.

treble clef n clef f de sol.

tree [triː] n **-1.** [gen] arbre m; **to be barking up the wrong ~** fig se tromper d'adresse. **-2.** COMPUT arbre m, arborescence f.

tree-lined adj bordé(e) d'arbres.

tree surgeon n arboriculteur m, -trice f.

treetop ['triːtɒp] n cime f.

tree-trunk n tronc m d'arbre.

trek [trek] (pt & pp **-ked**, cont **-king**) ◇ n randonnée f. ◇ vi faire une randonnée; fig se traîner.

trellis ['trelɪs] n treillis m.

tremble ['trembl] vi trembler.

tremendous [trɪ'mendəs] adj **-1.** [size, success, difference] énorme; [noise] terrible. **-2.** inf [really good] formidable.

tremendously [trɪ'mendəslɪ] adv [exciting, expensive, big] extrêmement; [loud] terriblement.

tremor ['tremə'] n tremblement m.

tremulous ['tremjʊləs] adj literary [voice] tremblant(e); [smile] timide.

trench [trentʃ] n tranchée f.

trenchant ['trentʃənt] adj mordant(e), incisif(ive).

trench coat n trench-coat m.

trench warfare n (U) guerre f de tranchées.

trend [trend] n [tendency] tendance f.

trendsetter ['trend,setə'] n personne f qui lance une mode.

trendy [trendɪ] (compar **-ier**, superl **-iest**, pl **-ies**) inf ◇ adj branché(e), à la mode. ◇ n personne f branchée.

trepidation [,trepɪ'deɪʃn] n fml: **in** OR **with ~** avec inquiétude.

trespass ['trespəs] vi [on land] entrer sans permission; **"no ~ing"** «défense d'entrer».

trespasser ['trespəsə'] n intrus m, -e f; **"~s will be prosecuted"** «défense d'entrer sous peine de poursuites».

trestle ['tresl] n tréteau m.

trestle table n table f à tréteaux.

trial ['traɪəl] n **-1.** JUR procès m; **to be on ~ (for)** passer en justice (pour). **-2.** [test, experiment] essai m; **on ~** à l'essai; **by ~ and error** en tâtonnant. **-3.** [unpleasant experience] épreuve f; **~s and tribulations** tribulations fpl.

trial basis n: **on a ~** à l'essai.

trial period n période f d'essai.

trial run n essai m.

trial-size(d) adj [pack, box] d'essai.

triangle ['traɪæŋgl] n **-1.** [gen] triangle m. **-2.** Am [set square] équerre f.

triangular [traɪ'æŋgjʊlə'] adj triangulaire.

triathlon [traɪ'æθlɒn] (pl **-s**) n triathlon m.

tribal ['traɪbl] adj tribal(e).

tribe [traɪb] n tribu f.

tribulation [,trɪbjʊ'leɪʃn] n → **trial**.

tribunal [traɪ'bjuːnl] n tribunal m.

tribune ['trɪbjuːn] n HISTORY tribun m.

tributary ['trɪbjʊtrɪ] (pl **-ies**) n affluent m.

tribute ['trɪbjuːt] *n* tribut *m,* hommage *m;* **to pay ~ to** rendre hommage à; **to be a ~ to sthg** témoigner de qqch.

trice [traɪs] *n:* **in a ~** en un clin d'œil.

triceps ['traɪseps] (*pl inv* OR **-cepses**) *n* triceps *m.*

trick [trɪk] ◇ *n* **-1.** [to deceive] tour *m,* farce *f;* **to play a ~ on sb** jouer un tour à qqn. **-2.** [to entertain] tour *m.* **-3.** [knack] truc *m;* **that will do the ~** *inf* ça fera l'affaire. ◇ *comp* [knife, moustache etc] truqué(e), faux (fausse). ◇ *vt* attraper, rouler; **to ~ sb into doing sthg** amener qqn à faire qqch (par la ruse).

trickery ['trɪkərɪ] *n* (*U*) ruse *f.*

trickle ['trɪkl] ◇ *n* [of liquid] filet *m;* **a ~ of people/letters** quelques personnes/lettres. ◇ *vi* [liquid] dégouliner; **to ~ in/out** [people] entrer/sortir par petits groupes.

trick or treat *n* une gâterie ou une farce, *phrase rituelle des enfants déguisés qui font la quête la veille de Halloween.*

trick question *n* question-piège *f.*

tricky ['trɪkɪ] (*compar* **-ier,** *superl* **-iest**) *adj* [difficult] difficile.

tricycle ['traɪsɪkl] *n* tricycle *m.*

trident ['traɪdnt] *n* trident *m.*

tried [traɪd] ◇ *pt & pp* → **try.** ◇ *adj:* **~ and tested** [method, system] qui a fait ses preuves.

trier ['traɪəʳ] *n:* **to be a ~** être persévérant(e).

trifle ['traɪfl] ◇ *n* **-1.** *Br* CULIN ≃ diplomate *m.* **-2.** [unimportant thing] bagatelle *f.*
◆ **a trifle** *adv* un peu, un tantinet.
◆ **trifle with** *vt fus* badiner avec; [sb's affections] se jouer de.

trifling ['traɪflɪŋ] *adj* insignifiant(e).

trigger ['trɪgəʳ] ◇ *n* [on gun] détente *f,* gâchette *f.* ◇ *vt* déclencher, provoquer.
◆ **trigger off** *vt sep* déclencher, provoquer.

trigonometry [,trɪgə'nɒmətrɪ] *n* trigonométrie *f.*

trilby ['trɪlbɪ] (*pl* **-ies**) *n Br* feutre *m.*

trill [trɪl] ◇ *n* trille *m.* ◇ *vi* triller.

trillions ['trɪljənz] *npl inf:* **~ (of)** tout un tas (de), plein (de).

trilogy ['trɪlədʒɪ] (*pl* **-ies**) *n* trilogie *f.*

trim [trɪm] (*compar* **-mer,** *superl* **-mest,** *pt & pp* **-med,** *cont* **-ming**) ◇ *adj* **-1.** [neat and tidy] net (nette). **-2.** [slim] svelte. ◇ *n* **-1.** [of hair] coupe *f.* **-2.** [on clothes] garniture *f;* [inside car] garniture intérieure. ◇ *vt* **-1.** [cut gen] couper; [- hedge] tailler. **-2.** [decorate]: **to ~ sthg (with)** garnir OR orner qqch (de).

◆ **trim away, trim off** *vt sep* couper.

trimmed [trɪmd] *adj:* **~ with** [clothes] orné(e) de.

trimming ['trɪmɪŋ] *n* **-1.** [on clothing] parement *m.* **-2.** CULIN garniture *f.*

Trinidad and Tobago ['trɪnɪdæd-] *n* Trinité-et-Tobago *f;* **in ~** à Trinité-et-Tobago.

Trinidadian [,trɪnɪ'dædɪən] ◇ *adj* trinidadien(ienne). ◇ *n* Trinidadien *m,* -ienne *f.*

Trinity ['trɪnɪtɪ] *n* RELIG: **the ~** la Trinité.

trinket ['trɪŋkɪt] *n* bibelot *m.*

trio ['triːəʊ] (*pl* **-s**) *n* trio *m.*

trip [trɪp] (*pt & pp* **-ped,** *cont* **-ping**) ◇ *n* **-1.** [journey] voyage *m.* **-2.** drugs *sl* trip *m.* ◇ *vt* [make stumble] faire un croche-pied à. ◇ *vi* [stumble]: **to ~ (over)** trébucher (sur).
◆ **trip up** *vt sep* **-1.** [make stumble] faire un croche-pied à. **-2.** [catch out] prendre en défaut.

tripartite [,traɪ'pɑːtaɪt] *adj* triparti(e), tripartite.

tripe [traɪp] *n* (*U*) **-1.** CULIN tripe *f.* **-2.** *inf* [nonsense] bêtises *fpl,* idioties *fpl.*

triple ['trɪpl] ◇ *adj* triple. ◇ *vt & vi* tripler.

triple jump *n:* **the ~** le triple saut.

triplets ['trɪplɪts] *npl* triplés *mpl,* triplées *fpl.*

triplicate ['trɪplɪkət] ◇ *adj* en trois exemplaires. ◇ *n:* **in ~** en trois exemplaires.

tripod ['traɪpɒd] *n* trépied *m.*

Tripoli ['trɪpəlɪ] *n* Tripoli.

tripper ['trɪpəʳ] *n Br* excursionniste *mf.*

tripwire ['trɪpwaɪəʳ] *n* fil *m* de détente.

trite [traɪt] *adj pej* banal(e).

triumph ['traɪəmf] ◇ *n* triomphe *m.* ◇ *vi:* **to ~ (over)** triompher (de).

triumphal [traɪ'ʌmfl] *adj* triomphal(e).

triumphant [traɪ'ʌmfənt] *adj* [exultant] triomphant(e).

triumphantly [traɪ'ʌmfəntlɪ] *adv* de façon triomphante, triomphalement.

triumvirate [traɪ'ʌmvɪrət] *n* HISTORY triumvirat *m.*

trivet ['trɪvɪt] *n* **-1.** [over fire] trépied *m.* **-2.** [to protect table] dessous-de-plat *m.*

trivia ['trɪvɪə] *n* (*U*) [trifles] vétilles *fpl,* riens *mpl.*

trivial ['trɪvɪəl] *adj* insignifiant(e).

triviality [,trɪvɪ'ælətɪ] (*pl* **-ies**) *n* banalité *f.*

trivialize, -ise ['trɪvɪəlaɪz] *vt* banaliser.

trod [trɒd] *pt* → **tread.**

trodden ['trɒdn] *pp* → **tread.**

Trojan ['trəʊdʒən] ◇ *adj* troyen(enne). ◇ *n* Troyen *m,* -enne *f;* **to work like a ~** travailler comme un nègre OR une bête de somme.

troll [trəʊl] n troll m.

trolley ['trɒlɪ] (pl **trolleys**) n **-1.** Br [for shopping, luggage] chariot m, caddie m. **-2.** Br [for food, drinks] chariot m, table f roulante. **-3.** Am [tram] tramway m, tram m.

trolleybus ['trɒlɪbʌs] n trolleybus m.

trombone [trɒm'bəʊn] n MUS trombone m.

troop [truːp] ◇ n bande f, troupe f. ◇ vi: **to ~ in/out/off** entrer/sortir/partir en groupe.

◆ **troops** npl troupes fpl.

trooper ['truːpər] n **-1.** MIL soldat m. **-2.** Am [policeman] policier m (appartenant à la police d'un État).

troopship ['truːpʃɪp] n transport m.

trophy ['trəʊfɪ] (pl **-ies**) n trophée m.

tropical ['trɒpɪkl] adj tropical(e).

Tropic of Cancer ['trɒpɪk-] n: **the ~** le tropique du Cancer.

Tropic of Capricorn ['trɒpɪk-] n: **the ~** le tropique du Capricorne.

tropics ['trɒpɪks] npl: **the ~** les tropiques mpl.

trot [trɒt] (pt & pp **-ted**, cont **-ting**) ◇ n [of horse] trot m. ◇ vi trotter.

◆ **on the trot** adv inf de suite, d'affilée.

◆ **trot out** vt sep pej débiter.

Trotskyism ['trɒtskɪɪzm] n trotskisme m.

trotter ['trɒtər] n [pig's foot] pied m de porc.

trouble ['trʌbl] ◇ n (U) **-1.** [difficulty] problème m, difficulté f; **to be in ~** avoir des ennuis; **to get into ~** s'attirer des ennuis; **the ~ (with sb/sthg) is** ... l'ennui (avec qqn/qqch), c'est que .... **-2.** [bother] peine f, mal m; **to take the ~ to do sthg** se donner la peine de faire qqch; **it's no ~!** ça ne me dérange pas!; **to be asking for ~** chercher les ennuis. **-3.** [pain, illness] mal m, ennui m. **-4.** [fighting] bagarre f; POL troubles mpl, conflits mpl.

◇ vt **-1.** [worry, upset] peiner, troubler. **-2.** [bother] déranger. **-3.** [give pain to] faire mal à.

◆ **troubles** npl **-1.** [worries] ennuis mpl. **-2.** POL troubles mpl, conflits mpl.

troubled ['trʌbld] adj **-1.** [worried] inquiet(ète). **-2.** [disturbed - period] de troubles, agité(e); [- country] qui connaît une période de troubles.

trouble-free adj sans problèmes.

troublemaker ['trʌbl,meɪkər] n fauteur m, -trice f de troubles.

troubleshooter ['trʌbl,ʃuːtər] n expert m, spécialiste mf.

troublesome ['trʌblsəm] adj [job] pénible; [cold] gênant(e); [back, knee] qui fait souffrir.

trouble spot n point m chaud.

trough [trɒf] n **-1.** [for animals - with water] abreuvoir m; [- with food] auge f. **-2.** [low point - of wave] creux m; fig point m bas. **-3.** METEOR dépression f.

trounce [traʊns] vt inf écraser.

troupe [truːp] n troupe f.

trouser press ['traʊzə-] n presse f à pantalons.

trousers ['traʊzəz] npl pantalon m.

trouser suit ['traʊzə-] n Br tailleur-pantalon m.

trousseau ['truːsəʊ] (pl **-x** [-z] OR **-s**) n trousseau m.

trout [traʊt] (pl inv OR **-s**) n truite f.

trove [trəʊv] → **treasure trove.**

trowel ['traʊəl] n [for gardening] déplantoir m; [for cement, plaster] truelle f.

truancy ['truːənsɪ] n absentéisme m.

truant ['truːənt] n [child] élève mf absentéiste; **to play ~** faire l'école buissonnière.

truce [truːs] n trêve f.

truck [trʌk] ◇ n **-1.** [lorry] camion m. **-2.** RAIL wagon m à plate-forme. ◇ vt Am transporter par camion.

truck driver n routier m.

trucker ['trʌkər] n Am routier m.

truck farm n Am jardin m maraîcher.

trucking ['trʌkɪŋ] n Am camionnage m.

truck stop n Am relais m routier.

truculent ['trʌkjʊlənt] adj agressif(ive).

trudge [trʌdʒ] ◇ n marche f pénible. ◇ vi marcher péniblement.

true ['truː] adj **-1.** [factual] vrai(e); **to come ~** se réaliser. **-2.** [genuine] vrai(e), authentique; **~ love** le grand amour. **-3.** [exact] exact(e). **-4.** [faithful] fidèle, loyal(e). **-5.** TECH droit(e); [wheel] dans l'axe.

true-life adj vrai(e), vécu(e).

truffle ['trʌfl] n truffe f.

truism ['truːɪzm] n truisme m.

truly ['truːlɪ] adv **-1.** [gen] vraiment. **-2.** [sincerely] vraiment, sincèrement. **-3.** phr: **yours ~** [at end of letter] croyez à l'expression de mes sentiments distingués.

trump [trʌmp] ◇ n atout m. ◇ vt couper.

trump card n fig atout m.

trumped-up [trʌmpt-] adj pej inventé(e) de toutes pièces.

trumpet ['trʌmpɪt] ◇ n trompette f. ◇ vi [elephant] barrir.

trumpeter ['trʌmpɪtər] n trompettiste mf.

truncate [trʌŋ'keɪt] *vt* tronquer.

truncheon ['trʌntʃən] *n* matraque *f*.

trundle ['trʌndl] ◇ *vt* [cart, wheelbarrow] pousser lentement. ◇ *vi* aller lentement.

trunk [trʌŋk] *n* -1. [of tree, person] tronc *m*. -2. [of elephant] trompe *f*. -3. [box] malle *f*. -4. *Am* [of car] coffre *m*.
◆ **trunks** *npl* maillot *m* de bain.

trunk call *n Br* communication *f* interurbaine.

trunk road *n* (route *f*) nationale *f*.

truss [trʌs] *n* -1. MED bandage *m* herniaire. -2. CONSTR ferme *f*.

trust [trʌst] ◇ *vt* -1. [have confidence in] avoir confiance en, se fier à; **to ~ sb to do sthg** compter sur qqn pour faire qqch. -2. [entrust]: **to ~ sb with sthg** confier qqch à qqn. -3. *fml* [hope]: **to ~ (that)** ... espérer que .... ◇ *n* -1. (*U*) [faith]: **~ (in sb/sthg)** confiance *f* (en qqn/dans qqch); **to take sthg on ~** accepter qqch les yeux fermés; **to put** OR **place one's ~ in sb** faire confiance à qqn. -2. (*U*) [responsibility] responsabilité *f*; **a position of ~** un poste de confiance. -3. FIN: **in ~** en dépôt. -4. COMM trust *m*.

trust company *n* société *f* fiduciaire.

trusted ['trʌstɪd] *adj* [person] de confiance; [method] qui a fait ses preuves.

trustee [trʌs'tiː] *n* FIN & JUR fidéicommissaire *mf*; [of institution] administrateur *m*, -trice *f*.

trusteeship [,trʌs'tiːʃɪp] *n* FIN & JUR fidéicommis *m*; [of institution] fonction *f* d'administrateur.

trust fund *n* fonds *m* en fidéicommis.

trusting ['trʌstɪŋ] *adj* confiant(e).

trustworthy ['trʌst,wɜːðɪ] *adj* digne de confiance.

trusty ['trʌstɪ] (*compar* -**ier**, *superl* -**iest**) *adj hum* fidèle.

truth [truːθ] *n* vérité *f*; **in (all) ~** à dire vrai, en vérité.

truth drug *n* sérum *m* de vérité.

truthful ['truːθful] *adj* [person, reply] honnête; [story] véridique.

try [traɪ] (*pt* & *pp* -**ied**, *pl* -**ies**) ◇ *vt* -1. [attempt, test] essayer; [food, drink] goûter; **to ~ to do sthg** essayer de faire qqch. -2. JUR juger. -3. [put to the test] éprouver, mettre à l'épreuve. ◇ *vi* essayer; **to ~ for sthg** essayer d'obtenir qqch. ◇ *n* -1. [attempt] essai *m*, tentative *f*; **to have a ~ at sthg** essayer de faire qqch; **to give sthg a ~** essayer qqch. -2. RUGBY essai *m*.
◆ **try on** *vt sep* [clothes] essayer.
◆ **try out** *vt sep* essayer.

trying ['traɪɪŋ] *adj* pénible, éprouvant(e).

try-out *n inf* essai *m*.

tsar [zɑːʳ] *n* tsar *m*.

T-shirt *n* tee-shirt *m*.

tsp. (*abbr of* **teaspoon**) cc.

T-square *n* té *m*.

TT *abbr of* **teetotal**.

Tuareg ['twɑːreg] *n* [person] Touareg *m*, -ègue *f*.

tub [tʌb] *n* -1. [of ice cream - large] boîte *f*; [- small] petit pot *m*; [of margarine] barquette *f*. -2. [bath] baignoire *f*.

tuba ['tjuːbə] *n* tuba *m*.

tubby ['tʌbɪ] (*compar* -**ier**, *superl* -**iest**) *adj inf* rondouillard(e), boulot(otte).

tube [tjuːb] *n* -1. [cylinder, container] tube *m*. -2. ANAT: **bronchial ~s** bronches *fpl*. -3. *Br* [underground train] **métro** *m*; **the ~** [system] le métro; **by ~** en métro.

tubeless ['tjuːblɪs] *adj* [tyre] sans chambre à air.

tuber ['tjuːbəʳ] *n* tubercule *m*.

tuberculosis [tjuː,bɜːkjʊ'ləusɪs] *n* tuberculose *f*.

tube station *n Br* station *f* de métro.

tubing ['tjuːbɪŋ] *n* (*U*) tubes *mpl*, tuyaux *mpl*.

tubular ['tjuːbjʊləʳ] *adj* tubulaire.

TUC *n abbr of* **Trades Union Congress**.

tuck [tʌk] ◇ *n* SEWING rempli *m*. ◇ *vt* [place neatly] ranger.
◆ **tuck away** *vt sep* [store] mettre de côté OR en lieu sûr; **to be ~ed away** [village, house] être caché(e) OR blotti(e).
◆ **tuck in** ◇ *vt* -1. [child, patient] border. -2. [clothes] rentrer. ◇ *vi inf* boulotter; **~ in!** allez-y, mangez!
◆ **tuck up** *vt sep* [child, patient] border.

tuck shop *n Br* [at school] petite boutique qui vend des bonbons et des gâteaux.

Tudor ['tjuːdəʳ] *adj* -1. HISTORY des Tudors. -2. ARCHIT Tudor (*inv*).

Tue., Tues. (*abbr of* **Tuesday**) mar.

Tuesday ['tjuːzdɪ] *n* mardi *m*; *see also* **Saturday**.

tuft [tʌft] *n* touffe *f*.

tug [tʌg] (*pt* & *pp* -**ged**, *cont* -**ging**) ◇ *n* -1. [pull]: **to give sthg a ~** tirer sur qqch. -2. [boat] remorqueur *m*. ◇ *vt* tirer. ◇ *vi*: **to ~ (at)** tirer (sur).

tugboat ['tʌgbəut] *n* remorqueur *m*.

tug-of-love *n Br inf* conflit entre des parents pour obtenir la garde des enfants.

tug-of-war *n* lutte *f* de traction à la corde; *fig* lutte acharnée.

tuition [tjuːˈɪʃn] *n* (*U*) cours *mpl*.

tulip [ˈtjuːlɪp] *n* tulipe *f*.

tulle [tjuːl] *n* tulle *m*.

tumble [ˈtʌmbl] ◇ *vi* **-1.** [person] tomber, faire une chute; [water] tomber en cascades. **-2.** *fig* [prices] tomber, chuter. ◇ *n* chute *f*, culbute *f*.

◆ **tumble to** *vt fus Br inf* piger.

tumbledown [ˈtʌmbldaʊn] *adj* délabré(e), qui tombe en ruines.

tumble-dry *vt* faire sécher en machine.

tumble-dryer [-ˌdraɪəʳ] *n* sèche-linge *m inv*.

tumbler [ˈtʌmbləʳ] *n* [glass] verre *m* (droit).

tummy [ˈtʌmɪ] (*pl* **-ies**) *n inf* ventre *m*.

tumour *Br*, **tumor** *Am* [ˈtjuːməʳ] *n* tumeur *f*.

tumult [ˈtjuːmʌlt] *n* tumulte *m*.

tumultuous [ˈtjuːmʌltjʊəs] *adj* tumultueux(euse); [applause] frénétique.

tuna [*Br* ˈtjuːnə, *Am* ˈtuːnə] (*pl inv* OR **-s**) *n* thon *m*.

tundra [ˈtʌndrə] *n* toundra *f*.

tune [tjuːn] ◇ *n* **-1.** [song, melody] air *m*. **-2.** [harmony]: **in ~** [MUS - instrument] accordé(e), juste; [- play, sing] juste; **out of ~** [MUS - instrument] mal accordé(e); [- play, sing] faux; **to the ~ of** *fig* d'un montant de; **to be in/out of ~ (with)** *fig* être en accord/désaccord (avec); **to change one's ~** *inf* changer de ton.
◇ *vt* **-1.** MUS accorder. **-2.** RADIO & TV régler. **-3.** [engine] régler.
◇ *vi* RADIO & TV: **to ~ to a channel** se mettre sur une chaîne.

◆ **tune in** *vi* RADIO & TV être à l'écoute; **to ~ in to** se mettre sur.

◆ **tune up** *vi* MUS accorder son instrument.

tuneful [ˈtjuːnfʊl] *adj* mélodieux(ieuse).

tuneless [ˈtjuːnlɪs] *adj* discordant(e).

tuner [ˈtjuːnəʳ] *n* **-1.** RADIO & TV syntoniseur *m*, tuner *m*. **-2.** MUS [person] accordeur *m*.

tuner amplifier *n* ampli-tuner *m*.

tungsten [ˈtʌŋstən] ◇ *n* tungstène *m*. ◇ *comp* au tungstène.

tunic [ˈtjuːnɪk] *n* tunique *f*.

tuning fork [ˈtjuːnɪŋ-] *n* diapason *m*.

Tunis [ˈtjuːnɪs] *n* Tunis.

Tunisia [tjuːˈnɪzɪə] *n* Tunisie *f*; **in ~** en Tunisie.

Tunisian [tjuːˈnɪzɪən] ◇ *adj* tunisien(ienne). ◇ *n* [person] Tunisien *m*, -ienne *f*.

tunnel [ˈtʌnl] (*Br pt* & *pp* **-led**, *cont* **-ling**, *Am pt* & *pp* **-ed**, *cont* **-ing**) ◇ *n* tunnel *m*. ◇ *vi* faire OR creuser un tunnel.

tunnel vision *n* rétrécissement *m* du champ visuel; *fig* & *pej* vues *fpl* étroites.

tunny [ˈtʌnɪ] (*pl inv* OR **-ies**) *n* thon *m*.

tuppence [ˈtʌpəns] *n Br dated* deux pence *mpl*.

turban [ˈtɜːbən] *n* turban *m*.

turbid [ˈtɜːbɪd] *adj* trouble.

turbine [ˈtɜːbaɪn] *n* turbine *f*.

turbo [ˈtɜːbəʊ] (*pl* **-s**) *n* turbo *m*.

turbocharged [ˈtɜːbəʊtʃɑːdʒd] *adj* turbo (*inv*).

turbojet [ˌtɜːbəʊˈdʒet] *n* [engine] turboréacteur *m*; [plane] avion *m* à turboréacteur.

turboprop [ˌtɜːbəʊˈprɒp] *n* [engine] turbopropulseur *m*; [plane] avion *m* à turbopropulseur.

turbot [ˈtɜːbət] (*pl inv* OR **-s**) *n* turbot *m*.

turbulence [ˈtɜːbjʊləns] *n* (*U*) **-1.** [in air, water] turbulence *f*. **-2.** *fig* [unrest] agitation *f*.

turbulent [ˈtɜːbjʊlənt] *adj* **-1.** [air, water] agité(e). **-2.** *fig* [disorderly] tumultueux(euse), agité(e).

tureen [təˈriːn] *n* soupière *f*.

turf [tɜːf] (*pl* **-s** OR **turves**) ◇ *n* [grass surface] gazon *m*; [clod] motte *f* de gazon. ◇ *vt* gazonner.

◆ **turf out** *vt sep Br inf* [person] virer; [old clothes] balancer, bazarder.

turf accountant *n Br* bookmaker *m*.

turgid [ˈtɜːdʒɪd] *adj fml* [style, writing] pompeux(euse), ampoulé(e).

Turk [tɜːk] *n* Turc *m*, Turque *f*.

Turkestan, Turkistan [ˌtɜːkɪˈstɑːn] *n* Turkistan *m*; **in ~** au Turkistan.

turkey [ˈtɜːkɪ] (*pl* **turkeys**) *n* dinde *f*.

Turkey [ˈtɜːkɪ] *n* Turquie *f*; **in ~** en Turquie.

Turkish [ˈtɜːkɪʃ] ◇ *adj* turc (turque). ◇ *n* [language] turc *m*. ◇ *npl*: **the ~** les Turcs *mpl*.

Turkish bath *n* bain *m* turc.

Turkish delight *n* loukoum *m*.

Turkmenian [ˌtɜːkˈmenɪən] *adj* turkmène.

Turkmenistan [ˌtɜːkmenɪˈstɑːn] *n* Turkménistan *m*.

turmeric [ˈtɜːmərɪk] *n* curcuma *m*.

turmoil [ˈtɜːmɔɪl] *n* agitation *f*, trouble *m*.

turn [tɜːn] ◇ *n* **-1.** [in road] virage *m*, tournant *m*; [in river] méandre *m*. **-2.** [revolution, twist] tour *m*. **-3.** [change] tournure *f*, tour *m*. **-4.** [in game] tour *m*; **in ~** tour à tour, chacun son tour; **to take (it in) ~s to do sthg** faire qqch à tour de rôle. **-5.** [end - of

year, century] fin *f*. **-6.** [performance] numéro *m*. **-7.** MED crise *f*, attaque *f*. **-8.** *phr*: **to do sb a good** ~ rendre (un) service à qqn.
◇ *vt* **-1.** [gen] tourner; [omelette, steak etc] retourner; **to** ~ **sthg inside out** retourner qqch; **to** ~ **one's thoughts/attention to sthg** tourner ses pensées/son attention vers qqch. **-2.** [change]: **to** ~ **sthg into** changer qqch en. **-3.** [become]: **to** ~ **red** rougir; **his hair is** ~**ing grey** ses cheveux grisonnent; **the demonstration** ~**ed nasty** la manifestation a mal tourné.
◇ *vi* **-1.** [gen] tourner; [person] se tourner, se retourner. **-2.** [in book]: **to** ~ **to a page** se reporter OR aller à une page. **-3.** [for consolation]: **to** ~ **to sb/sthg** se tourner vers qqn/qqch. **-4.** [change]: **to** ~ **into** se changer en, se transformer en.
◆ **turn against** *vt fus* se retourner contre.
◆ **turn around** = **turn round**.
◆ **turn away** ◇ *vt sep* [refuse entry to] refuser. ◇ *vi* se détourner.
◆ **turn back** ◇ *vt sep* [sheets] replier; [person, vehicle] refouler. ◇ *vi* rebrousser chemin.
◆ **turn down** *vt sep* **-1.** [reject] rejeter, refuser. **-2.** [radio, volume, gas] baisser.
◆ **turn in** *vi inf* [go to bed] se pieuter.
◆ **turn off** ◇ *vt fus* [road, path] quitter. ◇ *vt sep* [radio, TV, engine, gas] éteindre; [tap] fermer. ◇ *vi* [leave path, road] tourner.
◆ **turn on** ◇ *vt sep* **-1.** [radio, TV, engine, gas] allumer; **to** ~ **the light on** allumer la lumière. **-2.** *inf* [excite sexually] exciter. ◇ *vt fus* [attack] attaquer.
◆ **turn out** ◇ *vt sep* **-1.** [light, gas fire] éteindre. **-2.** [produce] produire. **-3.** [eject - person] mettre dehors. **-4.** [empty - pocket, bag] retourner, vider. ◇ *vt fus*: **to** ~ **out to be** s'avérer; **it** ~**ed out to be a success** en fin de compte, cela a été une réussite; **it** ~**s out that** ... il s'avère OR se trouve que .... ◇ *vi* **-1.** [end up] finir. **-2.** [arrive - person] venir.
◆ **turn over** ◇ *vt sep* **-1.** [consider] retourner dans sa tête. **-2.** [hand over] rendre, remettre. ◇ *vi Br* TV changer de chaîne.
◆ **turn round** ◇ *vt sep* **-1.** [reverse] retourner. **-2.** [wheel, words] tourner. ◇ *vi* [person] se retourner.
◆ **turn up** ◇ *vt sep* [TV, radio] mettre plus fort; [gas] monter. ◇ *vi* **-1.** [arrive - person] se pointer. **-2.** [be found - person, object] être retrouvé; [- opportunity] se présenter.

turnabout ['tɜːnəbaʊt] *n* [of situation] revirement *m*; [of policy] changement *m*.

turnaround *Am* = **turnround**.

turncoat ['tɜːnkəʊt] *n pej* renégat *m*.

turning ['tɜːnɪŋ] *n* [off road] route *f* latérale; **take the first** ~ **on the left** prenez la première à gauche.

turning circle *n* rayon *m* de braquage.

turning point *n* tournant *m*, moment *m* décisif.

turnip ['tɜːnɪp] *n* navet *m*.

turnout ['tɜːnaʊt] *n* [at election] taux *m* de participation; [at meeting] assistance *f*.

turnover ['tɜːn,əʊvər] *n* (*U*) **-1.** [of personnel] renouvellement *m*. **-2.** FIN chiffre *m* d'affaires.

turnpike ['tɜːnpaɪk] *n Am* autoroute *f* à péage.

turnround *Br* ['tɜːnraʊnd], **turnaround** *Am* ['tɜːnəraʊnd] *n* **-1.** COMM: ~ **(time)** délai *m*. **-2.** [change] retournement *m*.

turn signal lever *n Am* (manette *f* de) clignotant *m*.

turnstile ['tɜːnstaɪl] *n* tourniquet *m*.

turntable ['tɜːn,teɪbl] *n* platine *f*.

turn-up *n Br* [on trousers] revers *m inv*; **a** ~ **for the books** *inf* une sacrée surprise.

turpentine ['tɜːpəntaɪn] *n* térébenthine *f*.

turps [tɜːps] *n Br inf* térébenthine *f*.

turquoise ['tɜːkwɔɪz] ◇ *adj* turquoise (*inv*). ◇ *n* **-1.** [mineral, gem] turquoise *f*. **-2.** [colour] turquoise *m*.

turret ['tʌrɪt] *n* tourelle *f*.

turtle ['tɜːtl] (*pl inv* OR **-s**) *n* tortue *f* de mer.

turtledove ['tɜːtldʌv] *n* tourterelle *f*.

turtleneck ['tɜːtlnek] *n* [garment] pull *m* à col montant; [neck] col *m* montant.

turves [tɜːvz] *Br pl* → **turf**.

tusk [tʌsk] *n* défense *f*.

tussle ['tʌsl] ◇ *n* lutte *f*. ◇ *vi* se battre; **to** ~ **over sthg** se disputer qqch.

tut [tʌt] *excl* mais non!, allons donc!

tutor ['tjuːtər] ◇ *n* **-1.** [private] professeur *m* particulier. **-2.** UNIV directeur *m*, -trice *f* d'études. ◇ *vt*: **to** ~ **sb (in sthg)** donner à qqn des cours particuliers (de qqch).

tutorial [tjuː'tɔːrɪəl] ◇ *adj* [group, class] de travaux dirigés. ◇ *n* travaux *mpl* dirigés.

tutu ['tuːtuː] *n* tutu *m*.

tux [tʌks] *n inf* smoking *m*.

tuxedo [tʌk'siːdəʊ] (*pl* **-s**) *n* smoking *m*.

TV (*abbr of* **television**) ◇ *n* **-1.** (*U*) [medium, industry] télé *f*; **on** ~ à la télé. **-2.** [apparatus] (poste *m* de) télé *f*. ◇ *comp* de télé.

TV dinner *n* repas *m* surgelé (*sur un plateau*).

twaddle ['twɒdl] *n* (*U*) *inf* bêtises *fpl*, fadaises *fpl*.

twang [twæŋ] ◇ n -1. [sound] bruit m de pincement. -2. [accent] nasillement m. ◇ vt [guitar] pincer. ◇ vi [wire, string] vibrer.

tweak [twi:k] vt inf [ear] tirer; [nose] tordre.

twee [twi:] adj Br pej mièvre.

tweed [twi:d] ◇ n tweed m. ◇ comp de OR en tweed.

tweet [twi:t] vi gazouiller.

tweezers ['twi:zəz] npl pince f à épiler.

twelfth [twelfθ] num douzième; see also sixth.

Twelfth Night n la fête des Rois.

twelve [twelv] num douze; see also six.

twentieth ['twentɪəθ] num vingtième; see also sixth.

twenty ['twentɪ] (pl -ies) num vingt; see also six.

twenty-twenty vision n vision f de dix dixièmes à chaque œil.

twerp [twɜːp] n inf crétin m, -e f, andouille f.

twice [twaɪs] adv deux fois; ~ a day deux fois par jour; he earns ~ as much as me il gagne deux fois plus que moi OR le double de moi; ~ as big deux fois plus grand; ~ my size/age le double de ma taille/mon âge.

twiddle ['twɪdl] ◇ vt jouer avec. ◇ vi: to ~ with sthg jouer avec qqch.

twig [twɪg] n brindille f, petite branche f.

twilight ['twaɪlaɪt] n crépuscule m.

twill [twɪl] n sergé m.

twin [twɪn] ◇ adj jumeau (jumelle); [town] jumelé(e); ~ beds lits mpl jumeaux. ◇ n jumeau m, jumelle f.

twin-bedded [-'bedɪd] adj à deux lits.

twin carburettor n carburateur m double-corps.

twine [twaɪn] ◇ n (U) ficelle f. ◇ vt: to ~ sthg round sthg enrouler qqch autour de qqch.

twin-engined [-'endʒɪnd] adj bimoteur.

twinge [twɪndʒ] n [of pain] élancement m; a ~ of guilt un remords.

twinkie ['twɪŋkɪ] n Am [cake] petit gâteau fourré à la crème.

twinkle ['twɪŋkl] ◇ n [of stars, lights] scintillement m; [in eyes] pétillement m. ◇ vi [star, lights] scintiller; [eyes] briller, pétiller.

twin room n chambre f à deux lits.

twin set n Br twin-set m.

twin town n ville f jumelée.

twin tub n machine f à double tambour.

twirl [twɜːl] ◇ vt faire tourner. ◇ vi tournoyer.

twist [twɪst] ◇ n -1. [in road] zigzag m, tournant m; [in river] méandre m, coude m; [in rope] entortillement m. -2. [turn]: to give the lid a ~ [to open] dévisser le couvercle; [to close] visser le couvercle. -3. fig [in plot] tour m. ◇ vt -1. [wind, curl] entortiller. -2. [contort] tordre. -3. [turn] tourner; [lid - to open] dévisser; [- to close] visser. -4. [sprain]: to ~ one's ankle se tordre OR se fouler la cheville. -5. [words, meaning] déformer. ◇ vi -1. [river, path] zigzaguer. -2. [be contorted] se tordre. -3. [turn]: to ~ round se retourner.

twisted ['twɪstɪd] adj pej tordu(e).

twister ['twɪstər] n Am tornade f.

twisty ['twɪstɪ] (compar -ier, superl -iest) adj inf sinueux(euse), en zigzag.

twit [twɪt] n Br inf crétin m, -e f.

twitch [twɪtʃ] ◇ n tic m. ◇ vt [rope] tirer d'un coup sec; [ears - subj: animal] remuer. ◇ vi [muscle, eye, face] se contracter.

twitter ['twɪtər] vi -1. [bird] gazouiller. -2. pej [person] jacasser.

two [tu:] num deux; in ~ en deux; see also six.

two-bit adj pej de pacotille.

two-dimensional adj à deux dimensions; pej superficiel(ielle), simpliste.

two-door adj [car] à deux portes.

twofaced [,tu:'feɪst] adj pej fourbe.

twofold ['tu:fəʊld] ◇ adj double. ◇ adv doublement; to increase ~ doubler.

two-handed [-'hændɪd] adj à deux poignées.

two-piece adj: ~ swimsuit deux-pièces m inv; ~ suit [for man] costume m (deux-pièces).

two-ply adj [yarn] à deux fils; [wood] à deux épaisseurs.

two-seater n [car] voiture f à deux places; [plane] biplace m.

twosome ['tu:səm] n inf couple m.

two-stroke ◇ adj à deux temps. ◇ n deux-temps m inv.

two-time vt inf tromper.

two-tone adj de deux tons.

two-way adj [traffic, trade] dans les deux sens; ~ radio poste m émetteur-récepteur.

TX abbr of Texas.

tycoon [taɪ'ku:n] n magnat m.

type [taɪp] ◇ n -1. [sort, kind] genre m, sorte f; [model] modèle m; [in classification] type m. -2. [person]: he's not the marrying ~ il n'est pas du genre à se marier; he's/she's not my ~ inf lui/elle, ce n'est pas mon genre OR type. **-3.** (*U*) TYPO caractères *mpl.* ◇ *vt* [letter, reply] **taper** (à la machine); **to ~ data into a computer** introduire des données dans un ordinateur. ◇ *vi* taper (à la machine).

◆ **type up** *vt sep* taper.

typecast ['taɪpkɑːst] (*pt* & *pp* **typecast**) *vt*: **to be ~ as** être cantonné dans le rôle de; **to be ~** être cantonné aux mêmes rôles.

typeface ['taɪpfeɪs] *n* TYPO œil *m* de caractère.

typescript ['taɪpskrɪpt] *n* texte *m* dactylographié.

typeset ['taɪpset] (*pt* & *pp* **typeset**, *cont* **-ting**) *vt* composer.

typewriter ['taɪp,raɪtə'] *n* machine *f* à écrire.

typhoid (fever) ['taɪfɔɪd-] *n* typhoïde *f*.

typhoon [taɪ'fuːn] *n* typhon *m*.

typhus ['taɪfəs] *n* typhus *m*.

typical ['tɪpɪkl] *adj*: **~ (of)** typique (de), caractéristique (de); **that's ~ (of him/her)!** c'est bien de lui/d'elle!

typically ['tɪpɪklɪ] *adv* typiquement.

typify ['tɪpɪfaɪ] (*pt* & *pp* **-ied**) *vt* **-1.** [characterize] être caractéristique de. **-2.** [represent] représenter.

typing ['taɪpɪŋ] *n* dactylo *f*, dactylographie *f*.

typing error *n* faute *f* de frappe.

typing pool *n* bureau *m* OR pool *m* des dactylos.

typist ['taɪpɪst] *n* dactylo *mf*, dactylographe *mf*.

typo ['taɪpəʊ] *n inf* coquille *f*.

typographic(al) error [,taɪpə'græfɪk(l)-] *n* faute *f* typographique.

typography [taɪ'pɒgrəfɪ] *n* typographie *f*.

tyrannical [tɪ'rænɪkl] *adj* tyrannique.

tyranny ['tɪrənɪ] *n* tyrannie *f*.

tyrant ['taɪrənt] *n* tyran *m*.

tyre *Br*, **tire** *Am* ['taɪə'] *n* pneu *m*.

tyre pressure *n* pression *f* (de gonflage).

Tyrol, Tirol ['tɪrɒl] *n* Tyrol *m*.

Tyrolean [tɪrə'liːən], **Tyrolese** [,tɪrə'liːz] ◇ *adj* tyrolien(ienne). ◇ *n* Tyrolien *m*, -ienne *f*.

Tyrrhenian Sea [tɪ'riːnɪən-] *n*: **the ~** la mer Tyrrhénienne.

tzar [zɑː'] = **tsar**.

U

u (*pl* **u's** OR **us**), **U** (*pl* **U's** OR **Us**) [juː] *n* [letter] u *m inv*, U *m inv*.

◆ **U** (*abbr of* **universal**) *en Grande-Bretagne désigne un film tous publics.*

UAW (*abbr of* **United Automobile Workers**) *n syndicat américain de l'industrie automobile.*

UB40 (*abbr of* **unemployment benefit form 40**) *n en Grande-Bretagne, carte de pointage pour bénéficier de l'allocation de chômage.*

U-bend *n* siphon *m*.

ubiquitous [juː'bɪkwɪtəs] *adj* omniprésent(e).

UCATT [juːkæt] (*abbr of* **Union of Construction, Allied Trades and Technicians**) *n syndicat britannique des employés du bâtiment.*

UCCA ['ʌkə] (*abbr of* **Universities Central Council on Admissions**) *n organisme centralisant les demandes d'inscription dans les universités britanniques.*

UCL (*abbr of* **University College, London**) *n université londonienne.*

UCW (*abbr of* **The Union of Communication Workers**) *n syndicat britannique des communications.*

UDA (*abbr of* **Ulster Defence Association**) *n ancienne organisation paramilitaire protestante en Irlande du Nord.*

UDC (*abbr of* **Urban District Council**) *n conseil d'une communauté urbaine.*

udder ['ʌdə'] *n* mamelle *f*.

UDI (*abbr of* **unilateral declaration of independence**) *n déclaration unilatérale d'indépendance.*

UDR (*abbr of* **Ulster Defence Regiment**) *n régiment de réservistes en Irlande du Nord.*

UEFA [juː'eɪfə] (*abbr of* **Union of European Football Associations**) *n* UEFA *f*.

UFC (*abbr of* **Universities Funding Council**) *n organisme répartissant les crédits entre les universités en Grande-Bretagne.*

UFO (*abbr of* **unidentified flying object**) *n* OVNI *m*, ovni *m*.

Uganda [juː'gændə] *n* Ouganda *m*; **in ~** en Ouganda.

Ugandan [juːˈgændən] ◇ *adj* ougandais(e). ◇ *n* [person] Ougandais *m*, -e *f*.

ugh [ʌg] *excl* pouah!, beurk!

ugliness [ˈʌglɪnɪs] *n* (*U*) **-1.** [unattractiveness] laideur *f*. **-2.** *fig* [unpleasantness] caractère *m* pénible OR désagréable.

ugly [ˈʌglɪ] (*compar* **-ier**, *superl* **-iest**) *adj* **-1.** [unattractive] laid(e). **-2.** *fig* [unpleasant] pénible, désagréable.

UHF (*abbr of* **ultra-high frequency**) *n* UHF.

UHT (*abbr of* **ultra-heat treated**) UHT.

UK (*abbr of* **United Kingdom**) *n* Royaume-Uni *m*, R.U. *m*.

Ukraine [juːˈkreɪn] *n*: **the** ~ l'Ukraine *f*; **in the** ~ en Ukraine.

Ukrainian [juːˈkreɪnjən] ◇. *adj* ukrainien(ienne). ◇ *n* **-1.** [person] Ukrainien *m*, -ienne *f*. **-2.** [language] ukrainien *m*.

ukulele [ˌjuːkəˈleɪlɪ] *n* guitare *f* hawaïenne, ukulélé *m*.

Ulan Bator [uˈlɑːnˈbɑːtə] *n* Oulan-Bator.

ulcer [ˈʌlsə] *n* ulcère *m*.

ulcerated [ˈʌlsəreɪtɪd] *adj* ulcéré(e).

Ulster [ˈʌlstə] *n* Ulster *m*; **in** ~ dans l'Ulster.

Ulsterman [ˈʌlstəmən] (*pl* **-men** [-mən]) *n* habitant *m* OR natif *m* de l'Ulster.

Ulster Unionist Party *n* parti politique essentiellement protestant favorable au maintien de l'Ulster au sein du Royaume-Uni.

ulterior [ʌlˈtɪərɪə] *adj*: ~ **motive** arrière-pensée *f*.

ultimata [ˌʌltɪˈmeɪtə] *pl* → ultimatum.

ultimate [ˈʌltɪmət] ◇ *adj* **-1.** [final] final(e), ultime. **-2.** [most powerful] ultime, suprême. ◇ *n*: **the** ~ **in** le fin du fin dans.

ultimately [ˈʌltɪmətlɪ] *adv* [finally] finalement.

ultimatum [ˌʌltɪˈmeɪtəm] (*pl* **-tums** OR **-ta** [-tə]) *n* ultimatum *m*.

ultra- [ˈʌltrə] *prefix* ultra-.

ultramarine [ˌʌltrəməˈriːn] *adj* (bleu) outre-mer (*inv*).

ultrasonic [ˌʌltrəˈsɒnɪk] *adj* ultrasonique.

ultrasound [ˈʌltrəsaʊnd] *n* (*U*) ultrasons *mpl*.

ultraviolet [ˌʌltrəˈvaɪələt] *adj* ultra-violet(ette).

um [ʌm] *excl* heu!

umbilical cord [ʌmˈbɪlɪkl-] *n* cordon *m* ombilical.

umbrage [ˈʌmbrɪdʒ] *n*: **to take** ~ **(at)** prendre ombrage (de).

umbrella [ʌmˈbrelə] ◇ *n* [portable] para-

pluie *m*; [fixed] parasol *m*. ◇ *adj* [organization] qui en regroupe plusieurs autres.

UMIST [ˈjuːmɪst] (*abbr of* **University of Manchester Institute of Science and Technology**) *n* institut de science et de technologie de l'université de Manchester.

umpire [ˈʌmpaɪə] ◇ *n* arbitre *m*. ◇ *vt* arbitrer. ◇ *vi* être l'arbitre.

umpteen [ˌʌmpˈtiːn] *num adj inf* je ne sais combien de.

umpteenth [ˌʌmpˈtiːnθ] *num adj inf* énième.

UMW (*abbr of* **United Mineworkers of America**) *n* syndicat américain de mineurs.

UN (*abbr of* **United Nations**) *n*: **the** ~ l'ONU *f*, l'Onu *f*.

unabashed [ˌʌnəˈbæʃt] *adj* nullement décontenancé(e).

unabated [ˌʌnəˈbeɪtɪd] *adj*: **the rain continued** ~ la pluie continua de tomber sans répit.

unable [ʌnˈeɪbl] *adj*: **to be** ~ **to do sthg** ne pas pouvoir faire qqch, être incapable de faire qqch.

unabridged [ˌʌnəˈbrɪdʒd] *adj* intégral(e).

unacceptable [ˌʌnəkˈseptəbl] *adj* inacceptable.

unaccompanied [ˌʌnəˈkʌmpənɪd] *adj* **-1.** [child] non accompagné(e); [luggage] sans surveillance. **-2.** [song] a cappella, sans accompagnement.

unaccountable [ˌʌnəˈkauntəbl] *adj* **-1.** [inexplicable] inexplicable. **-2.** [not responsible]: **to be** ~ **for sthg** ne pas être responsable de qqch; **to be** ~ **to sb** ne pas être responsable envers OR devant qqn.

unaccountably [ˌʌnəˈkauntəblɪ] *adv* [inexplicably] de façon inexplicable, inexplicablement.

unaccounted [ˌʌnəˈkauntɪd] *adj*: **to be** ~ **for** manquer.

unaccustomed [ˌʌnəˈkʌstəmd] *adj* **-1.** [unused]: **to be** ~ **to sthg/to doing sthg** ne pas être habitué(e) à qqch/à faire qqch. **-2.** [not usual] inaccoutumé(e), inhabituel(elle).

unacquainted [ˌʌnəˈkweɪntɪd] *adj*: **to be** ~ **with sb/sthg** ne pas connaître qqn/qqch.

unadulterated [ˌʌnəˈdʌltəreɪtɪd] *adj* **-1.** [unspoilt - wine] non frelaté(e); [- food] naturel(elle). **-2.** [absolute - joy] sans mélange; [- nonsense, truth] pur et simple (pure et simple).

unadventurous [ˌʌnədˈventʃərəs] *adj* qui manque d'audace.

unaffected [ˌʌnəˈfektɪd] *adj* **-1.** [unchanged]: ~ **(by)** non affecté(e) (par). **-2.** [natural] naturel(elle).

unafraid [ˌʌnəˈfreɪd] *adj* sans crainte, sans peur.

unaided [ˌʌnˈeɪdɪd] *adj* sans aide.

unambiguous [ˌʌnæmˈbɪgjʊəs] *adj* non équivoque.

un-American [ˈʌn-] *adj* anti-américain(e).

unanimity [ˌjuːnəˈnɪmətɪ] *n* unanimité *f*.

unanimous [juːˈnænɪməs] *adj* unanime.

unanimously [juːˈnænɪməslɪ] *adv* à l'unanimité.

unannounced [ˌʌnəˈnaʊnst] *adj* sans tambour ni trompette.

unanswered [ˌʌnˈɑːnsəd] *adj* qui reste sans réponse.

unappealing [ˌʌnəˈpiːlɪŋ] *adj* peu attirant(e).

unappetizing, **-ising** [ˌʌnˈæpɪtaɪzɪŋ] *adj* peu appétissant(e).

unappreciated [ˌʌnəˈpriːʃɪeɪtɪd] *adj* peu apprécié(e).

unappreciative [ˌʌnəˈpriːʃɪətɪv] *adj*: ~ **(of)** indifférent(e) (à).

unapproachable [ˌʌnəˈprəʊtʃəbl] *adj* inabordable, d'un abord difficile.

unarmed [ˌʌnˈɑːmd] *adj* non armé(e).

unarmed combat *n* combat *m* sans armes.

unashamed [ˌʌnəˈʃeɪmd] *adj* [luxury] insolent(e); [liar, lie] effronté(e), éhonté(e).

unassisted [ˌʌnəˈsɪstɪd] *adj* sans aide.

unassuming [ˌʌnəˈsjuːmɪŋ] *adj* modeste, effacé(e).

unattached [ˌʌnəˈtætʃt] *adj* **-1.** [not fastened, linked]: ~ **(to)** indépendant(e) (de). **-2.** [without partner] libre, sans attaches.

unattainable [ˌʌnəˈteɪnəbl] *adj* inaccessible.

unattended [ˌʌnəˈtendɪd] *adj* [luggage, shop] sans surveillance; [child] seul(e).

unattractive [ˌʌnəˈtræktɪv] *adj* **-1.** [not beautiful] peu attrayant(e), peu séduisant(e). **-2.** [not pleasant] déplaisant(e).

unauthorized, **-ised** [ʌnˈɔːθəraɪzd] *adj* non autorisé(e).

unavailable [ˌʌnəˈveɪləbl] *adj* qui n'est pas disponible, indisponible.

unavoidable [ˌʌnəˈvɔɪdəbl] *adj* inévitable.

unavoidably [ˌʌnəˈvɔɪdəblɪ] *adj* inévitablement; to be ~ detained être retardé pour des raisons indépendantes de sa volonté.

unaware [ˌʌnəˈweəʳ] *adj* ignorant(e), inconscient(e); to be ~ of sthg ne pas avoir conscience de qqch, ignorer qqch.

unawares [ˌʌnəˈweəz] *adv*: to catch OR take sb ~ prendre qqn au dépourvu.

unbalanced [ˌʌnˈbælənst] *adj* **-1.** [biased] tendancieux(ieuse), partial(e). **-2.** [deranged] déséquilibré(e).

unbearable [ʌnˈbeərəbl] *adj* insupportable.

unbearably [ʌnˈbeərəblɪ] *adv* insupportablement; it's ~ hot il fait une chaleur insupportable.

unbeatable [ˌʌnˈbiːtəbl] *adj* imbattable.

unbecoming [ˌʌnbɪˈkʌmɪŋ] *adj* [unattractive] peu seyant(e).

unbeknown(st) [ˌʌnbɪˈnəʊn(st)] *adv*: ~ to à l'insu de.

unbelievable [ˌʌnbɪˈliːvəbl] *adj* incroyable.

unbelievably [ˌʌnbɪˈliːvəblɪ] *adv* incroyablement; to be ~ stupid être d'une bêtise incroyable.

unbend [ˌʌnˈbend] (*pt & pp* **unbent**) *vi* [relax] se détendre.

unbending [ˌʌnˈbendɪŋ] *adj* inflexible, intransigeant(e).

unbent [ˌʌnˈbent] *pt & pp* → **unbend**.

unbia(s)sed [ˌʌnˈbaɪəst] *adj* impartial(e).

unblemished [ˌʌnˈblemɪʃt] *adj* *fig* sans tache.

unblock [ˌʌnˈblɒk] *vt* déboucher.

unbolt [ˌʌnˈbəʊlt] *vt* déverrouiller.

unborn [ˌʌnˈbɔːn] *adj* [child] qui n'est pas encore né(e).

unbreakable [ˌʌnˈbreɪkəbl] *adj* incassable.

unbridled [ˌʌnˈbraɪdld] *adj* effréné(e), débridé(e).

unbuckle [ˌʌnˈbʌkl] *vt* déboucler.

unbutton [ˌʌnˈbʌtn] *vt* déboutonner.

uncalled-for [ˌʌnˈkɔːld-] *adj* [remark] déplacé(e); [criticism] injustifié(e).

uncanny [ʌnˈkænɪ] (*compar* **-ier**, *superl* **-iest**) *adj* étrange, mystérieux(ieuse); [resemblance] troublant(e).

uncared-for [ˌʌnˈkeəd-] *adj* délaissé(e), négligé(e).

uncaring [ˌʌnˈkeərɪŋ] *adj* qui ne se soucie pas des autres.

unceasing [ˌʌnˈsiːsɪŋ] *adj* *fml* incessant(e), continuel(elle).

unceremonious [ˈʌnˌserɪˈməʊnjəs] *adj* brusque.

unceremoniously [ˈʌnˌserɪˈməʊnjəslɪ] *adj* brusquement.

uncertain [ʌnˈsɜːtn] *adj* incertain(e); in no ~ terms sans mâcher ses mots.

unchain [ˌʌnˈtʃeɪn] *vt* désenchaîner.

unchallenged [ˌʌnˈtʃælɪndʒd] *adj* incontesté(e), indiscuté(e).

unchanged [ˌʌnˈtʃeɪndʒd] *adj* inchangé(e).

unchanging [ˌʌnˈtʃeɪndʒɪŋ] *adj* invariable, immuable.

uncharacteristic [ˈʌnˌkærəktəˈrɪstɪk] *adj* inhabituel(elle).

uncharitable [ˌʌnˈtʃærɪtəbl] *adj* peu charitable.

uncharted [ˌʌnˈtʃɑːtɪd] *adj* [land, sea] qui n'est pas sur la carte; ~ **territory** *fig* domaine inexploré.

unchecked [ˌʌnˈtʃekt] *adj* non maîtrisé(e), sans frein.

uncivilized, -ised [ˌʌnˈsɪvɪlaɪzd] *adj* non civilisé(e), barbare.

unclassified [ˌʌnˈklæsɪfaɪd] *adj* [documents] non classé(e); [information] non secret(ète).

uncle [ˈʌŋkl] *n* oncle *m*.

unclean [ˌʌnˈkliːn] *adj* **-1.** [dirty] sale. **-2.** RELIG impur(e).

unclear [ˌʌnˈklɪəʳ] *adj* **-1.** [message, meaning, motive] qui n'est pas clair(e). **-2.** [uncertain - person, future] incertain(e).

Uncle Sam l'Oncle Sam (*personnage représentant les États-Unis dans la propagande pour l'armée*).

unclothed [ˌʌnˈkləʊðd] *adj* nu(e), sans vêtements.

uncomfortable [ˌʌnˈkʌmftəbl] *adj* **-1.** [shoes, chair, clothes etc] inconfortable; *fig* [fact, truth] désagréable. **-2.** [person - physically] qui n'est pas à l'aise; [- ill at ease] mal à l'aise.

uncomfortably [ˌʌnˈkʌmftəblɪ] *adv* **-1.** [in physical discomfort] inconfortablement. **-2.** *fig* [uneasily] avec gêne.

uncommitted [ˌʌnkəˈmɪtɪd] *adj* non engagé(e).

uncommon [ʌnˈkɒmən] *adj* **-1.** [rare] rare. **-2.** *fml* [extreme] extraordinaire.

uncommonly [ʌnˈkɒmənlɪ] *adv* *fml* extraordinairement.

uncommunicative [ˌʌnkəˈmjuːnɪkətɪv] *adj* peu expansif(ive), peu communicatif(ive).

uncomplicated [ˌʌnˈkɒmplɪkeɪtɪd] *adj* simple, peu compliqué(e).

uncomprehending [ˈʌnˌkɒmprɪˈhendɪŋ] *adj* qui ne comprend pas.

uncompromising [ʌnˈkɒmprəmaɪzɪŋ] *adj* intransigeant(e).

unconcerned [ˌʌnkənˈsɜːnd] *adj* [not anxious] qui ne s'inquiète pas.

unconditional [ˌʌnkənˈdɪʃənl] *adj* inconditionnel(elle).

uncongenial [ˌʌnkənˈdʒiːnjəl] *adj* *fml* peu agréable.

unconnected [ˌʌnkəˈnektɪd] *adj* [facts, events] sans rapport.

unconquered [ˌʌnˈkɒŋkəd] *adj* qui n'a pas été conquis(e).

unconscious [ʌnˈkɒnʃəs] ◇ *adj* **-1.** [having lost consciousness] sans connaissance. **-2.** *fig* [unaware]: **to be ~ of** ne pas avoir conscience de, ne pas se rendre compte de. **-3.** [unnoticed - desires, feelings] inconscient(e). ◇ *n* PSYCH inconscient *m*.

unconsciously [ʌnˈkɒnʃəslɪ] *adv* inconsciemment.

unconstitutional [ˈʌnˌkɒnstɪˈtjuːʃənl] *adj* inconstitutionnel(elle), anticonstitutionnel(elle).

uncontested [ˌʌnkənˈtestɪd] *adj* incontesté(e); [election] sans opposition.

uncontrollable [ˌʌnkənˈtrəʊləbl] *adj* **-1.** [unrestrainable - emotion, urge] irrépressible, irrésistible; [- increase, epidemic] qui ne peut être enrayé(e). **-2.** [unmanageable - person] impossible, difficile.

uncontrolled [ˌʌnkənˈtrəʊld] *adj* [emotion, urge] non contenu(e); [increase] effréné(e); [inflation, epidemic] galopant(e).

unconventional [ˌʌnkənˈvenʃənl] *adj* peu conventionnel(elle), original(e).

unconvinced [ˌʌnkənˈvɪnst] *adj* qui n'est pas convaincu(e), sceptique.

unconvincing [ˌʌnkənˈvɪnsɪŋ] *adj* peu convaincant(e).

uncooked [ˌʌnˈkʊkt] *adj* non cuit(e), cru(e).

uncooperative [ˌʌnkəʊˈɒpərətɪv] *adj* peu coopératif(ive).

uncork [ˌʌnˈkɔːk] *vt* déboucher.

uncorroborated [ˌʌnkəˈrɒbəreɪtɪd] *adj* non corroboré(e).

uncouth [ʌnˈkuːθ] *adj* grossier(ière).

uncover [ʌnˈkʌvəʳ] *vt* découvrir.

uncurl [ˌʌnˈkɜːl] *vi* [hair] se défriser, se déboucler; [wire, snake] se dérouler.

uncut [ˌʌnˈkʌt] *adj* **-1.** [film] intégral(e), sans coupures. **-2.** [jewel] brut(e), non taillé(e).

undamaged [ˌʌnˈdæmɪdʒd] *adj* non endommagé(e), intact(e).

undaunted [ˌʌnˈdɔːntɪd] *adj* non découragé(e).

undecided [ˌʌndɪˈsaɪdɪd] *adj* [person] indécis(e), irrésolu(e); [issue] indécis(e).

undemanding [ˌʌndɪˈmɑːndɪŋ] *adj* [task] peu astreignant(e), peu exigeant(e); [person] peu exigeant(e).

undemonstrative [ˌʌndɪˈmɒnstrətɪv] *adj* peu expansif(ive), peu démonstratif(ive).

undeniable [ˌʌndɪˈnaɪəbl] *adj* indéniable, incontestable.

under ['ʌndər] ◇ *prep* **-1.** [gen] sous. **-2.** [less than] moins de; **children** ~ **five** les enfants de moins de cinq ans. **-3.** [subject to - effect, influence] sous; ~ **the circumstances** dans ces circonstances, étant donné les circonstances; **to be** ~ **an obligation to sb** être redevable à qqn, avoir une dette de reconnaissance envers qqn; **to be** ~ **the impression that** ... avoir l'impression que .... **-4.** [undergoing]: ~ **discussion** en discussion; ~ **consideration** à l'étude, à l'examen; ~ **review** qui doit être révisé. **-5.** [according to] selon, conformément à. ◇ *adv* **-1.** [underneath] dessous; [underwater] sous l'eau; **to go** ~ [company] couler, faire faillite. **-2.** [less] au-dessous.

under- ['ʌndər] *prefix* sous-.

underachiever [,ʌndərə'tʃiːvər] *n* *personne dont les résultats ne correspondent pas à ses possibilités.*

underage [ʌndər'eɪdʒ] *adj* mineur(e); ~ **drinking** consommation *f* d'alcool par les mineurs; ~ **sex** rapports *mpl* sexuels entre des mineurs.

underarm ['ʌndərɑːm] ◇ *adj* [deodorant] pour les aisselles. ◇ *adv* [throw, bowl] par en-dessous.

underbrush ['ʌndərbrʌʃ] *n* (U) *Am* sous-bois *m inv.*

undercarriage ['ʌndə,kærɪdʒ] *n* train *m* d'atterrissage.

undercharge [,ʌndə'tʃɑːdʒ] *vt* ne pas faire assez payer à.

underclothes ['ʌndəkləʊðz] *npl* sous-vêtements *mpl.*

undercoat ['ʌndəkəʊt] *n* [of paint] couche *f* de fond.

undercook [,ʌndə'kʊk] *vt* ne pas assez cuire.

undercover ['ʌndə,kʌvər] ◇ *adj* secret(ète). ◇ *adv* clandestinement.

undercurrent ['ʌndə,kʌrənt] *n* *fig* [tendency] courant *m* sous-jacent.

undercut [,ʌndə'kʌt] (*pt & pp* **undercut**, *cont* **-ting**) *vt* [in price] vendre moins cher que.

underdeveloped [,ʌndədɪ'veləpt] *adj* [country] sous-développé(e); [person] qui n'est pas complètement développé(e) OR formé(e).

underdog ['ʌndədɒg] *n*: **the** ~ l'opprimé *m*; SPORT celui (celle) que l'on donne perdant(e).

underdone [,ʌndə'dʌn] *adj* [food] pas assez cuit(e); [steak] saignant(e).

underemployment [,ʌndərɪm'plɔɪmənt] *n* sous-emploi *m.*

underestimate [*n* ,ʌndər'estɪmət, *vb* ,ʌndər'estɪmeɪt] ◇ *n* sous-estimation *f.* ◇ *vt* sous-estimer.

underexposed [,ʌndərɪk'spəʊzd] *adj* PHOT sous-exposé(e).

underfinanced [,ʌndə'faɪnænst] *adj* insuffisamment financé(e).

underfoot [,ʌndə'fʊt] *adv* sous les pieds; **to trample sthg** ~ fouler qqch aux pieds; **the ground** ~ le sol.

undergo [,ʌndə'gəʊ] (*pt* **-went**, *pp* **-gone** [-'gɒn]) *vt* subir; [pain, difficulties] éprouver.

undergraduate [,ʌndə'grædjuət] ◇ *adj* [course, studies] pour étudiants de licence. ◇ *n* étudiant *m*, -e *f* qui prépare la licence.

underground [*adj & n* 'ʌndəgraʊnd, *adv* ,ʌndə'graʊnd] ◇ *adj* **-1.** [below the ground] souterrain(e). **-2.** *fig* [secret] clandestin(e). ◇ *adv*: **to go/be forced** ~ entrer dans la clandestinité. ◇ *n* **-1.** *Br* [subway] métro *m.* **-2.** [activist movement] résistance *f.*

undergrowth ['ʌndəgrəʊθ] *n* (U) sous-bois *m inv.*

underhand [,ʌndə'hænd] *adj* sournois(e), en dessous.

underinsured [,ʌndərɪn'ʃʊəd] *adj* sous-assuré(e).

underlay ['ʌndəleɪ] *n* [for carpet] thibaude *f.*

underline [,ʌndə'laɪn] *vt* souligner.

underlying [,ʌndə'laɪɪŋ] *adj* sous-jacent(e).

undermanned [,ʌndə'mænd] *adj* à court de personnel OR de main d'œuvre.

undermentioned [,ʌndə'menʃnd] *adj* *fml* (cité(e)) ci-dessous.

undermine [,ʌndə'maɪn] *vt* *fig* [weaken] saper, ébranler.

underneath [,ʌndə'niːθ] ◇ *prep* **-1.** [beneath] sous, au-dessous de. **-2.** [in movements] sous. ◇ *adv* **-1.** [beneath] en dessous, dessous. **-2.** *fig* [fundamentally] au fond. ◇ *adj inf* d'en dessous. ◇ *n* [underside]: **the** ~ le dessous.

undernourished [,ʌndə'nʌrɪʃt] *adj* sous-alimenté(e).

underpaid [*pt & pp* ,ʌndə'peɪd, *adj* 'ʌndəpeɪd] ◇ *pt & pp* → **underpay**. ◇ *adj* sous-payé(e).

underpants ['ʌndəpænts] *npl* slip *m.*

underpass ['ʌndəpɑːs] *n* [for cars] passage *m* inférieur; [for pedestrians] passage *m* souterrain.

underpay [,ʌndə'peɪ] (*pt & pp* **-paid**) *vt* sous-payer.

underpin [ˌʌndə'pɪn] (*pt* & *pp* **-ned**, *cont* **-ning**) *vt* étayer.

underplay [ˌʌndə'pleɪ] *vt* réduire l'importance de, minimiser.

underprice [ˌʌndə'praɪs] *vt* mettre un prix trop bas à

underprivileged [ˌʌndə'prɪvɪlɪdʒd] *adj* défavorisé(e), déshérité(e).

underproduction [ˌʌndəprə'dʌkʃn] *n* sous-production *f*.

underrated [ˌʌndə'reɪtɪd] *adj* sous-estimé(e).

underscore [ˌʌndə'skɔːʳ] *vt lit* & *fig* souligner.

undersea ['ʌndəsiː] *adj* sous-marin(e).

undersecretary [ˌʌndə'sekrətərɪ] (*pl* **-ies**) *n* sous-secrétaire *m*.

undersell [ˌʌndə'sel] (*pt* & *pp* **-sold**) *vt* COMM vendre moins cher que; **to ~ o.s.** *fig* ne pas se mettre assez en valeur.

undershirt ['ʌndəʃɜːt] *n Am* maillot *m* de corps.

underside ['ʌndəsaɪd] *n*: **the ~** le dessous.

undersigned ['ʌndəsaɪnd] *n fml*: **I, the ~** je soussigné(e).

undersize(d) [ˌʌndə'saɪz(d)] *adj* trop petit(e).

underskirt ['ʌndəskɜːt] *n* jupon *m*.

undersold [ˌʌndə'səʊld] *pt* & *pp* → **undersell**.

understaffed [ˌʌndə'stɑːft] *adj* à court de personnel.

understand [ˌʌndə'stænd] (*pt* & *pp* **-stood**) ◇ *vt* **-1.** [gen] comprendre; **to make o.s. understood** se faire comprendre. **-2.** *fml* [be informed]: **I ~ (that)** ... je crois comprendre que ..., il paraît que .... ◇ *vi* comprendre.

understandable [ˌʌndə'stændəbl] *adj* compréhensible.

understandably [ˌʌndə'stændəblɪ] *adv* **-1.** [speak] de façon compréhensible. **-2.** [naturally] naturellement.

understanding [ˌʌndə'stændɪŋ] ◇ *n* **-1.** [knowledge, sympathy] compréhension *f*; **it was my ~ that ...** j'avais compris que .... **-2.** [agreement] accord *m*, arrangement *m*; **to come to an ~ (over)** s'entendre (sur); **on the ~ that ...** à condition que ... (+ *subjunctive*). ◇ *adj* [sympathetic] compréhensif(ive).

understate [ˌʌndə'steɪt] *vt* réduire l'importance de, minimiser.

understatement [ˌʌndə'steɪtmənt] *n* **-1.** [inadequate statement] affirmation *f* en dessous de la vérité. **-2.** (*U*) [quality of understating] euphémisme *m*.

understood [ˌʌndə'stʊd] *pt* & *pp* → **understand**.

understudy ['ʌndəˌstʌdɪ] (*pl* **-ies**) *n* doublure *f*.

undertake [ˌʌndə'teɪk] (*pt* **-took**, *pp* **-taken** [-'teɪkn]) *vt* **-1.** [take on - gen] entreprendre; [- responsibility] assumer. **-2.** [promise]: **to ~ to do sthg** promettre de faire qqch, s'engager à faire qqch.

undertaker ['ʌndəˌteɪkəʳ] *n* entrepreneur *m* des pompes funèbres.

undertaking [ˌʌndə'teɪkɪŋ] *n* **-1.** [task] entreprise *f*. **-2.** [promise] promesse *f*.

undertone ['ʌndətəʊn] *n* **-1.** [quiet voice] voix *f* basse. **-2.** [vague feeling] courant *m*.

undertook [ˌʌndə'tʊk] *pt* → **undertake**.

undertow ['ʌndətəʊ] *n* courant *m* sous-marin.

undervalue [ˌʌndə'væljuː] *vt* [house, antique etc] sous-évaluer; [person] sous-estimer, mésestimer.

underwater [ˌʌndə'wɔːtəʳ] ◇ *adj* sous-marin(e). ◇ *adv* sous l'eau.

underwear ['ʌndəweəʳ] *n* (*U*) sous-vêtements *mpl*.

underweight [ˌʌndə'weɪt] *adj* qui ne pèse pas assez, qui est trop maigre.

underwent [ˌʌndə'went] *pt* → **undergo**.

underworld [ˌʌndə'wɜːld] *n* [criminal society]: **the ~** le milieu, la pègre.

underwrite ['ʌndəraɪt] (*pt* **-wrote**, *pp* **-written**) *vt* **-1.** FIN garantir. **-2.** [in insurance] garantir, assurer contre.

underwriter ['ʌndəˌraɪtəʳ] *n* assureur *m*.

underwritten [ˌʌndəˌrɪtn] *pp* → **underwrite**.

underwrote ['ʌndərəʊt] *pt* → **underwrite**.

undeserved [ˌʌndɪ'zɜːvd] *adj* immérité(e).

undesirable [ˌʌndɪ'zaɪərəbl] *adj* indésirable.

undeveloped [ˌʌndɪ'veləpt] *adj* [land] non exploité(e), inexploité(e).

undid [ˌʌn'dɪd] *pt* → **undo**.

undies ['ʌndɪz] *npl inf* dessous *mpl*, lingerie *f*.

undignified [ʌn'dɪgnɪfaɪd] *adj* peu digne, qui manque de dignité.

undiluted [ˌʌndaɪ'ljuːtɪd] *adj* **-1.** [quality, emotion] sans mélange. **-2.** [liquid] non dilué(e).

undiplomatic [ˌʌndɪplə'mætɪk] *adj* peu diplomate.

undischarged [ˌʌndɪs'tʃɑːdʒd] *adj* [debt] non acquitté(e), non liquidé(e); **~ bankrupt** [person] failli *m* non réhabilité.

undisciplined [ʌn'dɪsɪplɪnd] *adj* indiscipliné(e).

undiscovered [ˌʌndɪ'skʌvəd] *adj* non découvert(e).

undisputed [ˌʌndɪ'spjuːtɪd] *adj* incontesté(e).

undistinguished [ˌʌndɪ'stɪŋgwɪʃt] *adj* médiocre, quelconque.

undivided [ˌʌndɪ'vaɪdɪd] *adj* indivisé(e), entier(ière).

undo [ˌʌn'duː] (*pt* -did, *pp* -done) *vt* -1. [unfasten] défaire. -2. [nullify] annuler, détruire.

undoing [ˌʌn'duːɪŋ] *n* (*U*) *fml* perte *f*, ruine *f*.

undone [ˌʌn'dʌn] ◇ *pp* → undo. ◇ *adj* -1. [unfastened] défait(e). -2. [task] non accompli(e).

undoubted [ʌn'daʊtɪd] *adj* indubitable, certain(e).

undoubtedly [ʌn'daʊtɪdlɪ] *adv* sans aucun doute.

undreamed-of [ʌn'driːmdɒv], **undreamt-of** [ʌn'dremtɒv] *adj* inimaginable.

undress [ˌʌn'dres] ◇ *vt* déshabiller. ◇ *vi* se déshabiller.

undressed [ˌʌn'drest] *adj* déshabillé(e); to get ~ se déshabiller.

undrinkable [ˌʌn'drɪŋkəbl] *adj* [unfit to drink] non potable; [disgusting] imbuvable.

undue [ˌʌn'djuː] *adj fml* excessif(ive).

undulate ['ʌndjʊleɪt] *vi* onduler.

unduly [ˌʌn'djuːlɪ] *adv fml* trop, excessivement.

undying [ʌn'daɪɪŋ] *adj literary* éternel(elle).

unearned income [ˌʌn'ɜːnd-] *n* (*U*) rentes *fpl*.

unearth [ˌʌn'ɜːθ] *vt* -1. [dig up] déterrer. -2. *fig* [discover] découvrir, dénicher.

unearthly [ʌn'ɜːθlɪ] *adj* -1. [ghostly] mystérieux(ieuse). -2. *inf* [uncivilized - time of day] indu(e), impossible.

unease [ʌn'iːz] *n* (*U*) malaise *m*.

uneasy [ʌn'iːzɪ] (*compar* -ier, *superl* -iest) *adj* [person, feeling] mal à l'aise, gêné(e); [peace] troublé(e), incertain(e); [silence] gêné(e).

uneatable [ˌʌn'iːtəbl] *adj* [not fit to eat] non comestible; [disgusting] immangeable.

uneaten [ˌʌn'iːtn] *adj* non mangé(e).

uneconomic ['ʌnˌiːkə'nɒmɪk] *adj* peu économique, peu rentable.

uneducated [ˌʌn'edjʊkeɪtɪd] *adj* [person] sans instruction.

unemotional [ˌʌnɪ'məʊʃənl] *adj* qui ne montre OR trahit aucune émotion.

unemployable [ˌʌnɪm'plɔɪəbl] *adj* inapte au travail.

unemployed [ˌʌnɪm'plɔɪd] ◇ *adj* au chômage, sans travail. ◇ *npl*: the ~ les sans-travail *mpl*, les chômeurs *mpl*.

unemployment [ˌʌnɪm'plɔɪmənt] *n* chômage *m*.

unemployment benefit *Br*, **unemployment compensation** *Am n* allocation *f* de chômage.

unenviable [ˌʌn'envɪəbl] *adj* peu enviable.

unequal [ˌʌn'iːkwəl] *adj* -1. [different] inégal(e). -2. [unfair] injuste.

unequalled *Br*, **unequaled** *Am* [ˌʌn'iːkwəld] *adj* inégalé(e).

unequivocal [ˌʌnɪ'kwɪvəkl] *adj* sans équivoque.

unerring [ˌʌn'ɜːrɪŋ] *adj* sûr(e), infaillible.

UNESCO [juː'neskəʊ] (*abbr of* **United Nations Educational, Scientific and Cultural Organization**) *n* UNESCO *f*, Unesco *f*.

unethical [ʌn'eθɪkl] *adj* immoral(e).

uneven [ˌʌn'iːvn] *adj* -1. [not flat - surface] inégal(e); [- ground] accidenté(e). -2. [inconsistent] inégal(e). -3. [unfair] injuste.

uneventful [ˌʌnɪ'ventful] *adj* sans incidents.

unexceptional [ˌʌnɪk'sepʃənl] *adj* qui n'a rien d'exceptionnel.

unexpected [ˌʌnɪk'spektɪd] *adj* inattendu(e), imprévu(e).

unexpectedly [ˌʌnɪk'spektɪdlɪ] *adv* subitement, d'une manière imprévue.

unexplained [ˌʌnɪk'spleɪnd] *adj* inexpliqué(e).

unexploded [ˌʌnɪk'spləʊdɪd] *adj* [bomb] non explosé(e), non éclaté(e).

unexpurgated [ˌʌn'ekspəgeɪtɪd] *adj* non expurgé(e), intégral(e).

unfailing [ʌn'feɪlɪŋ] *adj* qui ne se dément pas, constant(e).

unfair [ˌʌn'feər] *adj* injuste.

unfair dismissal *n* licenciement *m* injuste OR abusif.

unfairness [ˌʌn'feənɪs] *n* injustice *f*.

unfaithful [ˌʌn'feɪθful] *adj* infidèle.

unfamiliar [ˌʌnfə'mɪljər] *adj* -1. [not well-known] peu familier(ière), peu connu(e). -2. [not acquainted]: to be ~ with sthg/sb mal connaître qqch/qqn, ne pas connaître qqch/qqn.

unfashionable [ʌn'fæʃnəbl] *adj* démodé(e), passé(e) de mode; [person] qui n'est plus à la mode.

unfasten [ˌʌn'fɑːsn] *vt* défaire.

unfavourable *Br*, **unfavorable** *Am* [ˌʌnˈfeɪvrəbl] *adj* défavorable.

unfeeling [ʌnˈfiːlɪŋ] *adj* impitoyable, insensible.

unfinished [ˌʌnˈfɪnɪʃt] *adj* inachevé(e).

unfit [ˌʌnˈfɪt] *adj* -1. [not in good health] qui n'est pas en forme. -2. [not suitable]: ~ **(for)** impropre (à); [person] inapte (à).

unflagging [ˌʌnˈflægɪŋ] *adj* inlassable, infatigable.

unflappable [ˌʌnˈflæpəbl] *adj* imperturbable, flegmatique.

unflattering [ˌʌnˈflætərɪŋ] *adj* peu flatteur(euse).

unflinching [ʌnˈflɪntʃɪŋ] *adj* inébranlable.

unfold [ʌnˈfəʊld] ◇ *vt* -1. [map, newspaper] déplier. -2. [explain - plan, proposal] exposer. ◇ *vi* [become clear] se dérouler.

unforeseeable [ˌʌnfɔːˈsiːəbl] *adj* imprévisible.

unforeseen [ˌʌnfɔːˈsiːn] *adj* imprévu(e).

unforgettable [ˌʌnfəˈgetəbl] *adj* inoubliable.

unforgivable [ˌʌnfəˈgɪvəbl] *adj* impardonnable.

unformatted [ˌʌnˈfɔːmætɪd] *adj* COMPUT non formaté(e).

unfortunate [ʌnˈfɔːtʃnət] *adj* -1. [unlucky] malheureux(euse), malchanceux(euse). -2. [regrettable] regrettable, fâcheux(euse).

unfortunately [ʌnˈfɔːtʃnətlɪ] *adv* malheureusement.

unfounded [ˌʌnˈfaʊndɪd] *adj* sans fondement, dénué(e) de tout fondement.

unfriendly [ˌʌnˈfrendlɪ] *(compar* -ier, *superl* -iest) *adj* hostile, malveillant(e).

unfulfilled [ˌʌnfʊlˈfɪld] *adj* -1. [ambition, potential, prophecy] non réalisé(e), inaccompli(e); [promise] non tenu(e). -2. [person, life] insatisfait(e), frustré(e).

unfurl [ʌnˈfɜːl] *vt* déployer.

unfurnished [ˌʌnˈfɜːnɪʃt] *adj* non meublé(e).

ungainly [ʌnˈgeɪnlɪ] *adj* gauche.

ungenerous [ˌʌnˈdʒenərəs] *adj* -1. [mean - person] peu généreux(euse); [- amount] mesquin(e). -2. [unkind] peu charitable, mesquin(e).

ungodly [ˌʌnˈgɒdlɪ] *adj* -1. [irreligious] impie, irréligieux(ieuse). -2. *inf* [unreasonable] indu(e), impossible.

ungrateful [ʌnˈgreɪtfʊl] *adj* ingrat(e), peu reconnaissant(e).

ungratefulness [ʌnˈgreɪtfʊlnɪs] *n* ingratitude *f*.

unguarded [ˌʌnˈgɑːdɪd] *adj* -1. [house, camp etc] sans surveillance. -2. [careless]: **in an ~ moment** dans un moment d'inattention.

unhappily [ʌnˈhæpɪlɪ] *adv* -1. [sadly] tristement. -2. [unfortunately] malheureusement.

unhappiness [ʌnˈhæpɪnɪs] *n* (*U*) tristesse *f*, chagrin *m*.

unhappy [ʌnˈhæpɪ] *(compar* -ier, *superl* -iest) *adj* -1. [sad] triste, malheureux(euse). -2. [uneasy]: **to be ~ (with OR about)** être inquiet(iète) (au sujet de). -3. [unfortunate] malheureux(euse), regrettable.

unharmed [ˌʌnˈhɑːmd] *adj* indemne, sain et sauf (saine et sauve).

UNHCR *(abbr of* **United Nations High Commission for Refugees)** *n* HCR *m*.

unhealthy [ʌnˈhelθɪ] *(compar* -ier, *superl* -iest) *adj* -1. [person, skin] maladif(ive); [conditions, place] insalubre, malsain(e); [habit] malsain. -2. *fig* [undesirable] malsain(e).

unheard [ˌʌnˈhɜːd] *adj*: **her warning went ~** on n'a pas tenu compte de son avertissement.

unheard-of *adj* -1. [unknown] inconnu(e). -2. [unprecedented] sans précédent, inouï(e).

unheeded [ˌʌnˈhiːdɪd] *adj*: **his advice went ~** on n'a pas suivi OR écouté ses conseils.

unhelpful [ˌʌnˈhelpfʊl] *adj* -1. [person, attitude] peu serviable, peu obligeant(e). -2. [advice, book] qui n'aide en rien, peu utile.

unhindered [ʌnˈhɪndəd] *adj* sans obstacles, sans encombre.

unhook [ˌʌnˈhʊk] *vt* -1. [dress, bra] dégrafer. -2. [coat, picture, trailer] décrocher.

unhurt [ˌʌnˈhɜːt] *adj* indemne, sain et sauf (saine et sauve).

unhygienic [ˌʌnhaɪˈdʒiːnɪk] *adj* non hygiénique.

UNICEF [ˈjuːnɪˌsef] *(abbr of* **United Nations International Children's Emergency Fund)** *n* UNICEF *m*, Unicef *m*.

unicorn [ˈjuːnɪkɔːn] *n* licorne *f*.

unicycle [ˈjuːnɪsaɪkl] *n* monocyle *m*.

unidentified [ˌʌnaɪˈdentɪfaɪd] *adj* non identifié(e).

unidentified flying object *n* objet *m* volant non identifié.

unification [ˌjuːnɪfɪˈkeɪʃn] *n* unification *f*.

uniform [ˈjuːnɪfɔːm] ◇ *adj* [rate, colour] uniforme; [size] même. ◇ *n* uniforme *m*.

uniformity [ˌjuːnɪˈfɔːmətɪ] *n* uniformité *f*.

uniformly [ˈjuːnɪfɔːmlɪ] *adv* uniformément.

unify [ˈjuːnɪfaɪ] *(pt & pp* -ied) *vt* unifier.

unifying [ˈjuːnɪfaɪɪŋ] *adj* qui unifie, unificateur(trice).

unilateral [,juːnɪ'lætərəl] *adj* unilatéral(e).

unimaginable [,ʌnɪ'mædʒɪnəbl] *adj* inimaginable, inconcevable.

unimaginative [,ʌnɪ'mædʒɪnətɪv] *adj* qui manque d'imagination, peu imaginatif(ive).

unimpaired [,ʌnɪm'peəd] *adj* intact(e).

unimpeded [,ʌnɪm'piːdɪd] *adj* sans entrave.

unimportant [,ʌnɪm'pɔːtənt] *adj* sans importance, peu important(e).

unimpressed [,ʌnɪm'prest] *adj* qui n'est pas impressionné(e).

uninhabited [,ʌnɪn'hæbɪtɪd] *adj* inhabité(e).

uninhibited [,ʌnɪn'hɪbɪtɪd] *adj* sans inhibitions, qui n'a pas d'inhibitions.

uninitiated [,ʌnɪ'nɪʃɪeɪtɪd] *npl*: the ~ les non-initiés, les profanes.

uninjured [,ʌn'ɪndʒəd] *adj* qui n'est pas blessé(e), indemne.

uninspiring [,ʌnɪn'spaɪrɪŋ] *adj* qui n'a rien d'inspirant.

unintelligent [,ʌnɪn'telɪdʒent] *adj* inintelligent(e).

unintentional [,ʌnɪn'tenʃənl] *adj* involontaire, non intentionnel(elle).

uninterested [,ʌn'ɪntrəstɪd] *adj* indifférent(e).

uninterrupted ['ʌn,ɪntə'rʌptɪd] *adj* ininterrompu(e), continu(e).

uninvited [,ʌnɪn'vaɪtɪd] *adj* qui n'a pas été invité(e).

union ['juːnjən] ◇ *n* **-1.** [trade union] syndicat *m*. **-2.** [alliance] union *f*. ◇ *comp* syndical(e).

Unionist ['juːnjənɪst] *n* Br POL unioniste *mf*.

unionize, -ise ['juːnjənaɪz] *vt* syndiquer.

Union Jack *n*: the ~ l'Union Jack *m*, le drapeau britannique.

union shop *n* Am atelier *m* d'ouvriers syndiqués.

unique [juː'niːk] *adj* **-1.** [exceptional] unique, exceptionnel(elle). **-2.** [exclusive]: ~ **to** propre à. **-3.** [very special] unique.

uniquely [juː'niːklɪ] *adv* **-1.** [exclusively] uniquement. **-2.** [exceptionally] exceptionnellement.

unisex ['juːnɪseks] *adj* unisexe.

unison ['juːnɪzn] *n* unisson *m*; **in** ~ à l'unisson; [say] en chœur, en même temps.

UNISON ['juːnɪzn] *n* «supersyndicat» britannique des services publics.

unit ['juːnɪt] *n* **-1.** [gen] unité *f*. **-2.** [machine part] élément *m*, bloc *m*. **-3.** [of furniture] élément *m*; **storage** ~ meuble *m* de rangement. **-4.** [department] service *m*. **-5.** [chapter] chapitre *m*.

unit cost *n* prix *m* de revient unitaire.

unite [juː'naɪt] ◇ *vt* unifier. ◇ *vi* s'unir.

united [juː'naɪtɪd] *adj* **-1.** [in harmony] uni(e); **to be** ~ **in** sthg être uni dans qqch. **-2.** [unified] unifié(e).

United Arab Emirates *npl*: the ~ les Émirats *mpl* arabes unis.

united front *n*: **to present a** ~ montrer un front uni.

United Kingdom *n*: the ~ le Royaume-Uni.

United Nations *n*: the ~ les Nations *fpl* Unies.

United States *n*: the ~ les États-Unis *mpl*; **in the** ~ aux États-Unis; **the** ~ **of America** les États-Unis d'Amérique.

unit price *n* prix *m* unitaire.

unit trust *n* Br société *f* d'investissement à capital variable.

unity ['juːnətɪ] *n* (U) unité *f*.

Univ. *abbr of* **University**.

universal [,juːnɪ'vɜːsl] *adj* universel(elle).

universal joint *n* joint *m* universel OR de cardan.

universe ['juːnɪvɜːs] *n* univers *m*.

university [,juːnɪ'vɜːsətɪ] (*pl* **-ies**) ◇ *n* université *f*. ◇ *comp* universitaire; [lecturer] d'université; ~ **student** étudiant *m*, -e *f* à l'université.

unjust [,ʌn'dʒʌst] *adj* injuste.

unjustifiable [ʌn'dʒʌstɪfaɪəbl] *adj* injustifiable.

unjustified [ʌn'dʒʌstɪfaɪd] *adj* injustifié(e).

unkempt [,ʌn'kempt] *adj* [clothes, person] négligé(e), débraillé(e); [hair] mal peigné(e).

unkind [ʌn'kaɪnd] *adj* **-1.** [uncharitable] méchant(e), pas gentil(ille). **-2.** *fig* [weather, climate] rude, rigoureux(euse).

unkindly [,ʌn'kaɪndlɪ] *adv* méchamment.

unknown [,ʌn'nəʊn] ◇ *adj* inconnu(e). ◇ *n* [person] inconnu *m*, -e *f*; **the** ~ l'inconnu *m*.

unlace [,ʌn'leɪs] *vt* défaire, délacer.

unladen [,ʌn'leɪdn] *adj* sans charge; ~ **weight** poids *m* à vide.

unlawful [,ʌn'lɔːful] *adj* illégal(e).

unleaded [,ʌn'ledɪd] *adj* sans plomb.

unleash [,ʌn'liːʃ] *vt* literary déchaîner.

unleavened [,ʌn'levnd] *adj* sans levain, azyme.

unless [ən'les] *conj* à moins que (+ *subjunctive*); ~ **I'm mistaken** à moins que je (ne) me trompe; ~ **otherwise informed** sauf avis contraire.

unlicensed, unlicenced Am [,ʌn'laɪsənst] *adj* [person] qui ne détient pas de licence;

[activity] **non autorisé(e), illicite;** [vehicle] **sans vignette;** [restaurant, premises] **qui ne détient pas de licence de débit de boissons.**

unlike [ˌʌn'laɪk] *prep* **-1.** [different from] **différent(e) de. -2.** [in contrast to] **contrairement à, à la différence de. -3.** [not typical of]: **it's ~ you to complain cela ne te ressemble pas de te plaindre.**

unlikely [ʌn'laɪklɪ] **-1.** [event, result] **peu probable, improbable;** [story] **invraisemblable. -2.** [bizarre - clothes etc] **invraisemblable.**

unlimited [ʌn'lɪmɪtɪd] *adj* **illimité(e).**

unlisted [ʌn'lɪstɪd] *adj Am* [phone number] **qui est sur la liste rouge.**

unlit [ˌʌn'lɪt] *adj* **-1.** [lamp, fire, cigarette] **non allumé(e). -2.** [street, building] **non éclairé(e).**

unload [ˌʌn'ləʊd] *vt* **décharger; to ~ sthg on** OR **onto sb** *fig* **se décharger de qqch sur qqn.**

unlock [ˌʌn'lɒk] *vt* **ouvrir.**

unloved [ˌʌn'lʌvd] *adj* **qui n'est pas aimé(e); to feel ~ ne pas se sentir aimé.**

unluckily [ʌn'lʌkɪlɪ] *adv* **malheureusement.**

unlucky [ʌn'lʌkɪ] *(compar* **-ier,** *superl* **-iest)** *adj* **-1.** [unfortunate - person] **malchanceux(euse), qui n'a pas de chance;** [- experience, choice] **malheureux(euse). -2.** [object, number etc] **qui porte malheur.**

unmanageable [ʌn'mænɪdʒəbl] *adj* [vehicle, parcel] **peu maniable;** [hair] **difficiles à coiffer.**

unmanly [ˌʌn'mænlɪ] *(compar* **-ier,** *superl* **-iest)** *adj* **qui n'est pas viril.**

unmanned [ˌʌn'mænd] *adj* **sans équipage.**

unmarked [ˌʌn'mɑːkt] *adj* **-1.** [uninjured - body, face] **sans marque. -2.** [unidentified - box, suitcase] **sans marque d'identification;** [- police car] **banalisé(e).**

unmarried [ˌʌn'mærɪd] *adj* **célibataire, qui n'est pas marié(e).**

unmask [ˌʌn'mɑːsk] *vt* **démasquer;** [truth, hypocrisy] **dévoiler.**

unmatched [ˌʌn'mætʃt] *adj* **sans pareil(eille).**

unmentionable [ʌn'menʃnəbl] *adj* [subject] **dont il ne faut pas parler;** [word] **qu'il ne faut pas dire.**

unmistakable [ˌʌnmɪ'steɪkəbl] *adj* **qu'on ne peut pas ne pas reconnaître.**

unmitigated [ʌn'mɪtɪgeɪtɪd] *adj* [disaster] **total(e);** [evil] **non mitigé(e).**

unmoved [ˌʌn'muːvd] *adj*: **~ (by) indifférent(e) (à).**

unnamed [ˌʌn'neɪmd] *adj* [person] **anonyme;** [object] **sans dénomination.**

unnatural [ʌn'nætʃrəl] *adj* **-1.** [unusual] **anormal(e), qui n'est pas naturel(elle). -2.** [affected] **peu naturel(elle);** [smile] **forcé(e).**

unnecessary [ʌn'nesəsərɪ] *adj* [remark, expense, delay] **inutile; it's ~ to do sthg ce n'est pas la peine de faire qqch.**

unnerving [ˌʌn'nɜːvɪŋ] *adj* **troublant(e).**

unnoticed [ˌʌn'nəʊtɪst] *adj* **inaperçu(e).**

UNO *(abbr of* **United Nations Organization)** *n* **ONU** *m,* **Onu** *m.*

unobserved [ˌʌnəb'zɜːvd] *adj* **inaperçu(e).**

unobtainable [ˌʌnəb'teɪnəbl] *adj* **impossible à obtenir.**

unobtrusive [ˌʌnəb'truːsɪv] *adj* [person] **effacé(e);** [object] **discret(ète);** [building] **que l'on remarque à peine.**

unoccupied [ˌʌn'ɒkjʊpaɪd] *adj* [house] **inhabité(e);** [seat] **libre.**

unofficial [ˌʌnə'fɪʃl] *adj* **non officiel(ielle).**

unopened [ˌʌn'əʊpənd] *adj* **non ouvert(e), qui n'a pas été ouvert(e).**

unorthodox [ˌʌn'ɔːθədɒks] *adj* **peu orthodoxe.**

unpack [ˌʌn'pæk] ◇ *vt* [suitcase] **défaire;** [box] **vider;** [clothes] **déballer.** ◇ *vi* **défaire ses bagages.**

unpaid [ˌʌn'peɪd] *adj* **-1.** [person] **bénévole;** [work] **sans rémunération, bénévole. -2.** [rent] **non acquitté(e);** [bill] **impayé(e).**

unpalatable [ʌn'pælətəbl] *adj* **d'un goût désagréable;** *fig* **dur(e) à avaler.**

unparalleled [ʌn'pærəleld] *adj* [success, crisis] **sans précédent;** [beauty] **sans égal.**

unpatriotic ['ʌnˌpætrɪ'ɒtɪk] *adj* [person] **peu patriote;** [act] **antipatriotique.**

unpick [ˌʌn'pɪk] *vt* **découdre.**

unpin [ˌʌn'pɪn] *(pt & pp* **-ned,** *cont* **-ning)** *vt* [sewing, hair] **retirer les épingles de.**

unplanned [ˌʌn'plænd] *adj* **imprévu(e);** [pregnancy] **accidentel(elle).**

unpleasant [ʌn'pleznt] *adj* **désagréable.**

unpleasantness [ʌn'plezntnɪs] *n* **caractère** *m* **désagréable.**

unplug [ʌn'plʌg] *(pt & pp* **-ged,** *cont* **-ging)** *vt* **débrancher.**

unpolished [ˌʌn'pɒlɪʃt] *adj* **-1.** [not shined - floor] **non poli(e);** [- furniture, shoes] **non ciré(e). -2.** [not accomplished] **peu raffiné(e).**

unpolluted [ˌʌnpə'luːtɪd] *adj* **non pollué(e).**

unpopular [ˌʌn'pɒpjʊlər] *adj* **impopulaire.**

unprecedented [ʌn'presɪdəntɪd] *adj* **sans précédent.**

unpredictable [ˌʌnprɪ'dɪktəbl] *adj* imprévisible.

unprejudiced [ˌʌn'predʒudɪst] *adj* sans préjugés.

unprepared [ˌʌnprɪ'peəd] *adj* non préparé(e); **to be ~ for sthg** ne pas s'attendre à qqch.

unprepossessing [ˈʌnˌpriːpə'zesɪŋ] *adj* peu avenant(e).

unpretentious [ˌʌnprɪ'tenʃəs] *adj* sans prétention.

unprincipled [ʌn'prɪnsəpld] *adj* sans scrupules.

unprintable [ˌʌn'prɪntəbl] *adj fig* qu'on ne peut pas répéter.

unproductive [ˌʌnprə'dʌktɪv] *adj* improductif(ive).

unprofessional [ˌʌnprə'feʃənl] *adj* [person, work] peu professionnel(elle); [attitude] contraire à l'éthique de la profession.

unprofitable [ˌʌn'prɒfɪtəbl] *adj* peu rentable.

unprompted [ˌʌn'prɒmptɪd] *adj* spontané(e).

unpronounceable [ˌʌnprə'naunsəbl] *adj* imprononçable.

unprotected [ˌʌnprə'tektɪd] *adj* sans protection.

unprovoked [ˌʌnprə'vəukt] *adj* sans provocation.

unpublished [ˌʌn'pʌblɪʃt] *adj* inédit(e).

unpunished [ˌʌn'pʌnɪʃt] *adj*: **to go ~** rester impuni(e).

unqualified [ˌʌn'kwɒlɪfaɪd] *adj* **-1.** [person] non qualifié(e); [teacher, doctor] non diplômé(e). **-2.** [success] formidable; [support] inconditionnel(elle).

unquestionable [ʌn'kwestʃənəbl] *adj* [fact] incontestable; [honesty] certain(e).

unquestioning [ʌn'kwestʃənɪŋ] *adj* aveugle, absolu(e).

unravel [ʌn'rævl] (*Br pt & pp* **-led**, *cont* **-ling**, *Am pt & pp* **-ed**, *cont* **-ing**) **-1.** [undo - knitting] défaire; [- fabric] effiler; [- threads] démêler. **-2.** *fig* [solve] éclaircir.

unreadable [ˌʌn'riːdəbl] *adj* illisible.

unreal [ˌʌn'rɪəl] *adj* [strange] irréel(elle).

unrealistic [ˌʌnrɪə'lɪstɪk] *adj* irréaliste.

unreasonable [ʌn'riːznəbl] *adj* qui n'est pas raisonnable, déraisonnable.

unrecognizable [ˌʌn'rekəgnaɪzəbl] *adj* méconnaissable.

unrecognized [ˌʌn'rekəgnaɪzd] *adj* **-1.** [person] non reconnu(e). **-2.** [achievement, talent] méconnu(e).

unrecorded [ˌʌnrɪ'kɔːdɪd] *adj* non enregistré(e).

unrefined [ˌʌnrɪ'faɪnd] *adj* **-1.** [not processed] non raffiné(e), brut(e). **-2.** [vulgar] peu raffiné(e).

unrehearsed [ˌʌnrɪ'hɜːst] *adj* [performance] sans répétition; [speech, response] improvisé(e).

unrelated [ˌʌnrɪ'leɪtɪd] *adj*: **to be ~ (to)** n'avoir aucun rapport (avec).

unrelenting [ˌʌnrɪ'lentɪŋ] *adj* implacable.

unreliable [ˌʌnrɪ'laɪəbl] *adj* [machine, method] peu fiable; [person] sur qui on ne peut pas compter.

unrelieved [ˌʌnrɪ'liːvd] *adj* [pain, gloom] constant(e).

unremarkable [ˌʌnrɪ'mɑːkəbl] *adj* quelconque.

unremitting [ˌʌnrɪ'mɪtɪŋ] *adj* inlassable.

unrepeatable [ˌʌnrɪ'piːtəbl] *adj* [comment] qu'on ne peut pas répéter.

unrepentant [ˌʌnrɪ'pentənt] *adj* impénitent(e).

unrepresentative [ˌʌnreprɪ'zentətɪv] *adj*: **~ (of)** peu représentatif(ive) (de).

unrequited [ˌʌnrɪ'kwaɪtɪd] *adj* non partagé(e).

unreserved [ˌʌnrɪ'zɜːvd] *adj* **-1.** [support, admiration] sans réserve. **-2.** [seat] non réservé(e).

unresolved [ˌʌnrɪ'zɒlvd] *adj* non résolu(e).

unresponsive [ˌʌnrɪ'spɒnsɪv] *adj*: **to be ~ to** ne pas réagir à.

unrest [ˌʌn'rest] *n* (*U*) troubles *mpl*.

unrestrained [ˌʌnrɪ'streɪnd] *adj* effréné(e).

unrestricted [ˌʌnrɪ'strɪktɪd] *adj* sans restriction, illimité(e).

unrewarding [ˌʌnrɪ'wɔːdɪŋ] *adj* ingrat(e).

unripe [ˌʌn'raɪp] *adj* qui n'est pas mûr(e).

unrivalled *Br*, **unrivaled** *Am* [ʌn'raɪvld] *adj* sans égal(e).

unroll [ˌʌn'rəul] *vt* dérouler.

unruffled [ˌʌn'rʌfld] *adj* [person] imperturbable.

unruly [ʌn'ruːlɪ] (*compar* **-ier**, *superl* **-iest**) *adj* [crowd, child] turbulent(e); [hair] indisciplinés.

unsafe [ˌʌn'seɪf] *adj* **-1.** [dangerous] dangereux(euse). **-2.** [in danger]: **to feel ~** ne pas se sentir en sécurité.

unsaid [ˌʌn'sed] *adj*: **to leave sthg ~** passer qqch sous silence.

unsaleable, **unsalable** *Am* [ˌʌn'seɪləbl] *adj* invendable.

unsatisfactory [ˈʌnˌsætɪsˈfæktərɪ] *adj* qui laisse à désirer, peu satisfaisant(e).

unsavoury, **unsavory** *Am* [ˌʌnˈseɪvərɪ] *adj* [person] peu recommandable; [district] mal famé(e).

unscathed [ˌʌnˈskeɪðd] *adj* indemne.

unscheduled [*Br* ˌʌnˈʃedjʊld, *Am* ˌʌnˈskedʒʊld] *adj* non prévu(e).

unscientific [ˈʌnˌsaɪən'tɪfɪk] *adj* peu scientifique.

unscrew [ˌʌnˈskruː] *vt* dévisser.

unscripted [ˌʌnˈskrɪptɪd] *adj* improvisé(e).

unscrupulous [ʌnˈskruːpjʊləs] *adj* sans scrupules.

unseat [ˌʌnˈsiːt] *vt* **-1.** [rider] désarçonner. **-2.** *fig* [MP] faire perdre son siège à; [leader] faire perdre sa position à.

unseeded [ˌʌnˈsiːdɪd] *adj* qui n'est pas classé(e) en tête de série.

unseemly [ʌnˈsiːmlɪ] (*compar* **-ier**, *superl* **-iest**) *adj* inconvenant(e).

unseen [ˌʌnˈsiːn] *adj* [not observed] inaperçu(e).

unselfish [ˌʌnˈselfɪʃ] *adj* désintéressé(e).

unselfishly [ˌʌnˈselfɪʃlɪ] *adv* de manière désintéressée.

unsettle [ˌʌnˈsetl] *vt* perturber.

unsettled [ˌʌnˈsetld] *adj* **-1.** [person] perturbé(e), troublé(e). **-2.** [weather] variable, incertain(e). **-3.** [argument] qui n'a pas été résolu(e); [situation] incertain(e).

unsettling [ˌʌnˈsetlɪŋ] *adj* inquiétant(e).

unshak(e)able [ʌnˈʃeɪkəbl] *adj* inébranlable.

unshaven [ˌʌnˈʃeɪvn] *adj* non rasé(e).

unsheathe [ˌʌnˈʃiːð] *vt* dégainer.

unsightly [ʌnˈsaɪtlɪ] *adj* laid(e).

unskilled [ˌʌnˈskɪld] *adj* non qualifié(e).

unsociable [ʌnˈsəʊʃəbl] *adj* sauvage.

unsocial [ˌʌnˈsəʊʃl] *adj*: **to work ~ hours** travailler en dehors des heures normales.

unsold [ˌʌnˈsəʊld] *adj* invendu(e).

unsolicited [ˌʌnsəˈlɪsɪtɪd] *adj* non sollicité(e).

unsolved [ˌʌnˈsɒlvd] *adj* non résolu(e).

unsophisticated [ˌʌnsəˈfɪstɪkeɪtɪd] *adj* simple.

unsound [ˌʌnˈsaʊnd] *adj* **-1.** [theory] mal fondé(e); [decision] peu judicieux(ieuse). **-2.** [building, structure] en mauvais état.

unspeakable [ʌnˈspiːkəbl] *adj* indescriptible.

unspeakably [ʌnˈspiːkəblɪ] *adv* indescriptiblement.

unspecified [ˌʌnˈspesɪfaɪd] *adj* non spécifié(e).

unspoiled [ˌʌnˈspɔɪld], **unspoilt** [ˌʌnˈspɔɪlt] *adj* intact(e); [countryside] qui n'a pas été défiguré(e).

unspoken [ˌʌnˈspəʊkən] *adj* [thought, wish] inexprimé(e); [agreement] tacite.

unsporting [ˌʌnˈspɔːtɪŋ] *adj* qui n'est pas fair-play.

unstable [ˌʌnˈsteɪbl] *adj* instable.

unstated [ˌʌnˈsteɪtɪd] *adj* non déclaré(e).

unsteady [ˌʌnˈstedɪ] (*compar* **-ier**, *superl* **-iest**) *adj* [hand] tremblant(e); [table, ladder] instable.

unstinting [ˌʌnˈstɪntɪŋ] *adj* [praise, support] sans réserve; [person] généreux(euse), prodigue.

unstoppable [ˌʌnˈstɒpəbl] *adj* qu'on ne peut pas arrêter.

unstrap [ˌʌnˈstræp] (*pt* & *pp* **-ped**, *cont* **-ping**) *vt* défaire les attaches de.

unstructured [ˌʌnˈstrʌktʃəd] *adj* non structuré(e).

unstuck [ˌʌnˈstʌk] *adj*: **to come ~** [notice, stamp, label] se décoller; *fig* [plan, system] s'effondrer; *fig* [person] essuyer un échec.

unsubstantiated [ˌʌnsəbˈstænʃɪeɪtɪd] *adj* sans fondement.

unsuccessful [ˌʌnsəkˈsesfʊl] *adj* [attempt] vain(e); [meeting] infructueux(euse); [candidate] refusé(e).

unsuccessfully [ˌʌnsəkˈsesfʊlɪ] *adv* en vain, sans succès.

unsuitable [ˌʌnˈsuːtəbl] *adj* qui ne convient pas; [clothes] peu approprié(e); **to be ~ for** ne pas convenir à.

unsuited [ˌʌnˈsuːtɪd] *adj* **-1.** [not appropriate]: **to be ~ to/for** ne pas convenir à/pour. **-2.** [not compatible]: **to be ~ (to each other)** ne pas aller ensemble.

unsung [ˌʌnˈsʌŋ] *adj* [hero] méconnu(e).

unsure [ˌʌnˈʃɔːr] *adj* **-1.** [not certain]: **to be ~ (about/of)** ne pas être sûr(e) (de). **-2.** [not confident]: **to be ~ (of o.s.)** ne pas être sûr(e) de soi.

unsurpassed [ˌʌnsəˈpɑːst] *adj* non surpassé(e).

unsuspecting [ˌʌnsəˈspektɪŋ] *adj* qui ne se doute de rien.

unsweetened [ˌʌnˈswiːtnd] *adj* non sucré(e).

unswerving [ʌnˈswɜːvɪŋ] *adj* [loyalty, determination] inébranlable.

unsympathetic [ˈʌnˌsɪmpəˈθetɪk] *adj* [unfeeling] indifférent(e).

untamed [ˌʌn'teɪmd] adj [animal] sauvage; fig [person] farouche.

untangle [ˌʌn'tæŋgl] vt [string, hair] démêler.

untapped [ˌʌn'tæpt] adj inexploité(e).

untaxed [ˌʌn'tækst] adj non imposé(e).

untenable [ˌʌn'tenəbl] adj indéfendable.

unthinkable [ʌn'θɪŋkəbl] adj impensable.

unthinkingly [ʌn'θɪŋkɪŋlɪ] adv sans réfléchir.

untidy [ʌn'taɪdɪ] (compar -ier, superl -iest) adj [room, desk] en désordre; [work, handwriting] brouillon (inv); [person, appearance] négligé(e).

untie [ˌʌn'taɪ] (cont untying) vt [knot, parcel, shoelaces] défaire; [prisoner] détacher.

until [ən'tɪl] ◇ prep -1. [gen] jusqu'à; ~ now jusqu'ici. -2. (after negative) avant; not ~ tomorrow pas avant demain; we weren't told the news ~ four o'clock on ne nous a appris la nouvelle qu'à quatre heures. ◇ conj -1. [gen] jusqu'à ce que (+ subjunctive). -2. (after negative) avant que (+ subjunctive); don't sign ~ you've checked everything ne signe rien avant d'avoir tout vérifié.

untimely [ʌn'taɪmlɪ] adj [death] prématuré(e); [arrival] intempestif(ive); [remark] mal à propos; [moment] mal choisi(e).

untiring [ʌn'taɪərɪŋ] adj infatigable.

untold [ˌʌn'təʊld] adj [amount, wealth] incalculable; [suffering, joy] indescriptible.

untouched [ˌʌn'tʌtʃt] adj -1. [unharmed - person] indemne; [- thing] intact(e). -2. [uneaten - meal] auquel on n'a pas touché.

untoward [ˌʌntə'wɔːd] adj malencontreux(euse).

untrained [ˌʌn'treɪnd] adj -1. [person, worker] sans formation. -2. [voice] non travaillé(e); [mind] non formé(e).

untrammelled Br, **untrammeled** Am [ʌn'træməld] adj fml libre.

untranslatable [ˌʌntræns'leɪtəbl] adj intraduisible.

untreated [ˌʌn'triːtɪd] adj -1. MED non soigné(e). -2. [sewage, chemical] non traité(e).

untried [ˌʌn'traɪd] adj [method] qui n'a pas été mis(e) à l'épreuve; [product] qui n'a pas été essayé(e).

untroubled [ˌʌn'trʌbld] adj [undisturbed]: to be ~ by sthg rester impassible devant qqch.

untrue [ˌʌn'truː] adj -1. [not accurate] faux (fausse), qui n'est pas vrai(e). -2. [unfaithful]: to be ~ to sb être infidèle à qqn.

untrustworthy [ˌʌn'trʌst,wɜːðɪ] adj [person] qui n'est pas digne de confiance.

untruth [ˌʌn'truːθ] n mensonge m.

untruthful [ˌʌn'truːθfʊl] adj [person] menteur(euse); [statement] mensonger(ère).

untutored [ˌʌn'tjuːtəd] adj [person] peu instruit(e).

unusable [ˌʌn'juːzəbl] adj inutilisable.

unused [sense 1 ʌn'juːzd, sense 2 ʌn'juːst] adj -1. [clothes] neuf (neuve); [machine] qui n'a jamais servi; [land] qui n'est pas exploité. -2. [unaccustomed]: to be ~ to sthg/to doing sthg ne pas avoir l'habitude de qqch/de faire qqch.

unusual [ʌn'juːʒl] adj rare, inhabituel(elle).

unusually [ʌn'juːʒəlɪ] adv exceptionnellement.

unvarnished [ʌn'vɑːnɪʃt] adj fig [truth] tout nu (toute nue); [account] sans embellissement.

unveil [ˌʌn'veɪl] vt lit & fig dévoiler.

unwaged [ˌʌn'weɪdʒd] adj Br non salarié(e).

unwanted [ˌʌn'wɒntɪd] adj [object] dont on ne se sert pas; [child] non désiré(e); to feel ~ se sentir mal-aimé(e).

unwarranted [ʌn'wɒrəntɪd] adj injustifié(e).

unwavering [ʌn'weɪvərɪŋ] adj [determination] inébranlable.

unwelcome [ʌn'welkəm] adj [news, situation] fâcheux(euse); [visitor] importun(e); to make sb feel ~ faire sentir à qqn qu'il dérange.

unwell [ˌʌn'wel] adj: to be/feel ~ ne pas être/se sentir bien.

unwholesome [ˌʌn'həʊlsəm] adj malsain(e).

unwieldy [ʌn'wiːldɪ] (compar -ier, superl -iest) adj -1. [cumbersome] peu maniable. -2. fig [system] lourd(e); [method] trop complexe.

unwilling [ˌʌn'wɪlɪŋ] adj: to be ~ to do sthg ne pas vouloir faire qqch; to be an ~ helper aider à contrecœur.

unwind [ˌʌn'waɪnd] (pt & pp -wound) ◇ vt dérouler. ◇ vi fig [person] se détendre.

unwise [ˌʌn'waɪz] adj imprudent(e), peu sage.

unwitting [ʌn'wɪtɪŋ] adj fml involontaire.

unwittingly [ʌn'wɪtɪŋlɪ] adv fml involontairement.

unworkable [ˌʌn'wɜːkəbl] adj impraticable.

unworldly [ˌʌn'wɜːldlɪ] adj détaché(e) de ce monde.

unworthy [ʌn'wɜːðɪ] (compar -ier, superl -iest) adj [undeserving]: ~ (of) indigne (de).

unwound [ˌʌn'waʊnd] pt & pp → unwind.

unwrap [ˌʌn'ræp] (*pt* & *pp* **-ped**, *cont* **-ping**) *vt* défaire.

unwritten law [ˌʌn'rɪtn-] *n* droit *m* coutumier.

unyielding [ʌn'jiːldɪŋ] *adj* inflexible.

unzip [ˌʌn'zɪp] (*pt* & *pp* **-ped**, *cont* **-ping**) *vt* ouvrir la fermeture éclair de.

up [ʌp] (*pt* & *pp* **-ped**, *cont* **-ping**) ◇ *adv* **-1.** [towards or in a higher position] en haut; **she's ~ in her bedroom** elle est en haut dans sa chambre; **we walked ~ to the top** on est montés jusqu'en haut; **a house ~ in the mountains** une maison à la montagne; **pick it ~!** ramasse-le!; **the sun came ~** le soleil s'est levé; **prices are going ~** les prix augmentent; **~ there** là-haut. **-2.** [into an upright position]: **to stand ~** se lever; **to sit ~** s'asseoir (bien droit); **~ you get!** allez, lève-toi! **-3.** [northwards]: **I'm coming ~ to York next week** je viens à York la semaine prochaine; **~ north** dans le nord. **-4.** [along a road, river]: **their house is a little further ~** leur maison est un peu plus loin. **-5.** [close up, towards]: **to come ~ to sb** s'approcher de qqn. ◇ *prep* **-1.** [towards or in a higher position] en haut de; **~ a hill/mountain** en haut d'une colline/d'une montagne; **~ a ladder** sur une échelle; **I went ~ the stairs** j'ai monté l'escalier. **-2.** [at far end of]: **they live ~ the road from us** ils habitent un peu plus haut OR loin que nous (dans la même rue); **her flat is just ~ the corridor** son appartement est juste au bout du couloir. **-3.** [against current of river]: **to sail ~ the Amazon** remonter l'Amazone en bateau. ◇ *adj* **-1.** [out of bed] levé(e); **I was ~ at six today** je me suis levé à six heures aujourd'hui. **-2.** [at an end]: **the five weeks are ~ next Monday** les cinq semaines finissent OR se terminent lundi prochain; **time's ~** c'est l'heure. **-3.** [under repair]: **"road ~"** «attention travaux». **-4.** *inf* [wrong]: **is something ~?** il y a quelque chose qui ne va pas?; **what's ~?** qu'est-ce qui ne va pas?, qu'est-ce qu'il y a? ◇ *n*: **~s and downs** hauts et bas *mpl*. ◇ *vt inf* [price, cost] augmenter.

◆ **up against** *prep*: **we came ~ against a lot of opposition** nous nous sommes heurtés à une forte opposition; **to be ~ against it** avoir beaucoup de mal (à s'en sortir).

◆ **up and down** ◇ *adv*: **to jump ~ and down** sauter; **to walk ~ and down** faire les cent pas. ◇ *prep*: **she's ~ and down the stairs all day** elle n'arrête pas de monter et descendre l'escalier toute la journée; **she looked ~ and down the ranks of soldiers** elle passa les troupes en revue; **we walked ~ and down the avenue** nous avons arpenté l'avenue.

◆ **up to** *prep* **-1.** [indicating level] jusqu'à; **it could take ~ to six weeks** cela peut prendre jusqu'à six semaines; **it's not ~ to standard** ce n'est pas de la qualité voulue, ceci n'a pas le niveau requis. **-2.** [well or able enough for]: **to be ~ to doing sthg** [able to] être capable de faire qqch; [well enough for] être en état de faire qqch; **my French isn't ~ to much** mon français ne vaut pas grand'chose OR n'est pas fameux. **-3.** *inf* [secretly doing something]: **what are you ~ to?** qu'est-ce que tu fabriques?; **they're ~ to something** ils mijotent quelque chose, ils préparent un coup. **-4.** [indicating responsibility]: **it's not ~ to me to decide** ce n'est pas moi qui décide, il ne m'appartient pas de décider; **it's ~ to you** c'est à vous de voir.

◆ **up to, up until** *prep* jusqu'à.

up-and-coming *adj* à l'avenir prometteur.

up-and-up *n*: **to be on the ~** *Br* [improving] aller de mieux en mieux; **on the ~** *Am* [honest] honnête.

upbeat ['ʌpbiːt] *adj* optimiste.

upbraid [ʌp'breɪd] *vt*: **to ~ sb (for sthg/for doing sthg)** réprimander qqn (pour qqch/pour avoir fait qqch).

upbringing ['ʌpˌbrɪŋɪŋ] *n* éducation *f*.

update [ˌʌp'deɪt] *vt* mettre à jour.

upend [ʌp'end] *vt* [object] mettre debout.

upfront [ˌʌp'frʌnt] ◇ *adj*: **~ (about)** franc (franche) (au sujet de). ◇ *adv* [in advance] d'avance.

upgrade [ˌʌp'greɪd] *vt* [facilities] améliorer; [employee] promouvoir; [pay] augmenter.

upheaval [ʌp'hiːvl] *n* bouleversement *m*.

upheld [ʌp'held] *pt* & *pp* → **uphold**.

uphill [ˌʌp'hɪl] ◇ *adj* **-1.** [slope, path] qui monte. **-2.** *fig* [task] ardu(e). ◇ *adv*: **to go ~** monter.

uphold [ʌp'həʊld] (*pt* & *pp* **-held**) *vt* [law] maintenir; [decision, system] soutenir.

upholster [ʌp'həʊlstər] *vt* rembourrer.

upholstery [ʌp'həʊlstəri] *n* rembourrage *m*; [of car] garniture *f* intérieure.

upkeep ['ʌpkiːp] *n* entretien *m*.

upland ['ʌplənd] *adj* des hautes terres.

◆ **uplands** *npl* hautes terres *fpl*.

uplift [ʌp'lɪft] *vt* élever; [person] élever l'âme de.

uplifting [ʌp'lɪftɪŋ] *adj* édifiant(e).

uplighter ['ʌplaɪtər] *n* sorte d'applique (qui diffuse une lumière dirigée vers le haut).

up-market *adj* haut de gamme (*inv*).

upon [ə'pɒn] *prep fml* sur; ~ **hearing the news ...** à ces nouvelles ...; **summer/the weekend is** ~ **us** l'été/le week-end approche.

upper ['ʌpəʳ] ◇ *adj* supérieur(e). ◇ *n* [of shoe] empeigne *f*.

upper class *n*: **the** ~ la haute société.

◆ **upper-class** *adj* [accent, person] aristocratique.

uppercut ['ʌpəkʌt] *n* uppercut *m*.

upper hand *n*: **to have the** ~ avoir le dessus; **to gain** OR **get the** ~ prendre le dessus.

uppermost ['ʌpəməʊst] *adj* le plus haut (la plus haute); **it was** ~ **in his mind** c'était sa préoccupation majeure.

Upper Volta [-'vɒltə] *n* Haute-Volta *f*; **in** ~ en Haute-Volta.

uppity ['ʌpətɪ] *adj inf* prétentieux(ieuse).

upright [*adj sense 1 & adv* ,ʌp'raɪt, *adj sense 2 & n* 'ʌpraɪt] ◇ *adj* **-1.** [person] droit(e); [structure] vertical(e); [chair] à dossier droit; ~ **freezer** congélateur *m* armoire; ~ **vacuum cleaner** aspirateur *m* balai. **-2.** *fig* [honest] droit(e). ◇ *adv* [stand, sit] droit. ◇ *n* montant *m*.

upright piano *n* piano *m* droit.

uprising ['ʌp,raɪzɪŋ] *n* soulèvement *m*.

uproar ['ʌprɔːʳ] *n* **-1.** (*U*) [commotion] tumulte *m*. **-2.** [protest] protestations *fpl*.

uproarious [ʌp'rɔːrɪəs] *adj* **-1.** [noisy] tumultueux(euse). **-2.** [amusing] tordant(e).

uproot [ʌp'ruːt] *vt lit* & *fig* déraciner.

upset [ʌp'set] (*pt* & *pp* **upset**, *cont* **-ting**) ◇ *adj* **-1.** [distressed] peiné(e), triste; [offended] vexé(e). **-2.** MED: **to have an** ~ **stomach** avoir l'estomac dérangé. ◇ *n*: **to have a stomach** ~ avoir l'estomac dérangé. ◇ *vt* **-1.** [distress] faire de la peine à. **-2.** [plan, operation] déranger. **-3.** [turn upside down] renverser.

upsetting [ʌp'setɪŋ] *adj* [distressing] bouleversant(e).

upshot ['ʌpʃɒt] *n* résultat *m*.

upside down ['ʌpsaɪd-] ◇ *adj* à l'envers. ◇ *adv* à l'envers; **to turn sthg** ~ *fig* mettre qqch sens dessus dessous.

upstage [,ʌp'steɪdʒ] *vt* éclipser.

upstairs [,ʌp'steəz] ◇ *adj* d'en haut, du dessus. ◇ *adv* en haut. ◇ *n* étage *m*.

upstanding [,ʌp'stændɪŋ] *adj* droit(e).

upstart ['ʌpstɑːt] *n* parvenu *m*, -e *f*.

upstate [,ʌp'steɪt] *Am* ◇ *adj*: ~ **New York** la partie nord de l'État de New York. ◇ *adv* dans/vers le nord de l'État.

upstream [,ʌp'striːm] ◇ *adj* d'amont; **to be** ~ **(from)** être en amont (de). ◇ *adv* vers l'amont; [swim] contre le courant.

upsurge ['ʌpsɜːdʒ] *n*: ~ **(of/in)** recrudescence *f* (de).

upswing ['ʌpswɪŋ] *n*: ~ **(in)** [popularity] remontée *f* (de); **an** ~ **in economic activity** une reprise de l'activité économique.

uptake ['ʌpteɪk] *n*: **to be quick on the** ~ saisir vite; **to be slow on the** ~ être lent(e) à comprendre.

uptight [ʌp'taɪt] *adj inf* tendu(e).

up-to-date *adj* **-1.** [modern] moderne. **-2.** [most recent - news] tout dernier (toute dernière). **-3.** [informed]: **to keep** ~ **with** se tenir au courant de.

up-to-the-minute *adj* de dernière minute.

uptown [,ʌp'taʊn] *Am* ◇ *adj* [area] résidentiel(ielle). ◇ *adv* dans/vers les quartiers résidentiels.

upturn [ʌp'tɜːn] *n*: ~ **(in)** reprise *f* (de).

upturned [ʌp'tɜːnd] *adj* [car, cup] renversé(e); [nose] retroussé(e).

upward ['ʌpwəd] ◇ *adj* [movement] ascendant(e); [look, rise] vers le haut. ◇ *adv Am* = **upwards**.

upwardly-mobile ['ʌpwədlɪ-] *adj* susceptible de promotion sociale.

upwards ['ʌpwədz] *adv* vers le haut.

◆ **upwards of** *prep* plus de.

upwind ['ʌp'wɪnd] *adj*: **to be** ~ **of sthg** être dans le vent OR au vent par rapport à qqch.

URA (*abbr of* **Urban Renewal Administration**) *n administration américaine des rénovations urbaines*.

Urals ['jʊərəlz] *npl*: **the** ~ l'Oural *m*; **in the** ~ dans l'Oural.

uranium [jʊ'reɪnjəm] *n* uranium *m*.

Uranus ['jʊərənəs] *n* [planet] Uranus *f*.

urban ['ɜːbən] *adj* urbain(e).

urbane [ɜː'beɪn] *adj* courtois(e).

urbanize, -ise ['ɜːbənaɪz] *vt* urbaniser.

urban renewal *n* réaménagement *m* des zones urbaines.

urchin ['ɜːtʃɪn] *n dated* gamin *m*, -e *f*.

Urdu ['ʊəduː] *n* ourdou *m*.

urge [ɜːdʒ] ◇ *n* forte envie *f*; **to have an** ~ **to do sthg** avoir une forte envie de faire qqch. ◇ *vt* **-1.** [try to persuade]: **to** ~ **sb to do sthg** pousser qqn à faire qqch, presser qqn de faire qqch. **-2.** [advocate] conseiller.

urgency ['ɜːdʒənsɪ] *n* (*U*) urgence *f*.

urgent ['ɜːdʒənt] *adj* [letter, case, request] urgent(e); [plea, voice, need] pressant(e).

urgently ['ɜːdʒəntlɪ] *adv* d'urgence; [appeal] d'une manière pressante.

urinal [ˌjʊəˈraɪnl] *n* urinoir *m*.

urinary ['jʊərɪnərɪ] *adj* urinaire.

urinate ['jʊərɪneɪt] *vi* uriner.

urine ['jʊərɪn] *n* urine *f*.

urn [ɜːn] *n* **-1.** [for ashes] urne *f*. **-2.** [for tea]: tea ~ fontaine *f* à thé.

Uruguay ['jʊərəgwaɪ] *n* Uruguay *m*; in ~ en Uruguay.

Uruguayan [ˌjʊərəˈgwaɪən] ◇ *adj* uruguayen(enne). ◇ *n* Uruguayen *m*, -enne *f*.

us [ʌs] *pers pron* nous; **can you see/hear** ~? vous nous voyez/entendez?; **it's** ~ c'est nous; **you can't expect** US **to do it** vous ne pouvez pas exiger que ce soit nous qui le fassions; **she gave it to** ~ elle nous l'a donné; **with/without** ~ avec/sans nous; **they are more wealthy than** ~ ils sont plus riches que nous; **some of** ~ quelques-uns d'entre nous.

US *n abbr of* United States.

USA *n* **-1.** *abbr of* United States of America. **-2.** (*abbr of* United States Army) *armée de terre américaine.*

usable ['juːzəbl] *adj* utilisable.

USAF (*abbr of* United States Air Force) *n armée de l'air américaine.*

usage ['juːzɪdʒ] *n* **-1.** LING usage *m*. **-2.** (*U*) [handling, treatment] traitement *m*.

USCG (*abbr of* United States Coast Guard) *n service de surveillance côtière américain.*

USDA (*abbr of* United States Department of Agriculture) *n ministère américain de l'agriculture.*

USDAW ['ʌzdɔː] (*abbr of* Union of Shop, Distributive and Allied Workers) *n syndicat britannique des personnels de la distribution.*

USDI (*abbr of* United States Department of the Interior) *n ministère américain de l'intérieur.*

use [*n & aux vb* juːs, *vt* juːz] ◇ *n* **-1.** [act of using] utilisation *f*, emploi *m*; **to be in** ~ être utilisé; **to be out of** ~ être hors d'usage; **to make** ~ **of sthg** utiliser qqch. **-2.** [ability to use] usage *m*; **to let sb have the** ~ **of sthg** prêter qqch à qqn. **-3.** [usefulness]: **to be of** ~ être utile; **it's no** ~ ça ne sert à rien; **what's the** ~ **(of doing sthg)?** à quoi bon (faire qqch)?

◇ *aux vb*: **I** ~**d to live in London** avant j'habitais à Londres; **he didn't** ~ **to be so fat** il n'était pas si gros avant; **there** ~**d to be a tree here** (autrefois) il y avait un arbre ici.

◇ *vt* **-1.** [gen] utiliser, se servir de, employer. **-2.** *pej* [exploit] se servir de.

◆ **use up** *vt sep* [supply] épuiser; [food] finir; [money] dépenser.

used [*senses 1 and 2* juːzd, *sense 3* juːst] *adj* **-1.** [handkerchief, towel] sale. **-2.** [car] d'occasion. **-3.** [accustomed]: **to be** ~ **to sthg/to doing sthg** avoir l'habitude de qqch/de faire qqch; **to get** ~ **to sthg** s'habituer à qqch.

useful ['juːsful] *adj* utile; **to come in** ~ être utile.

usefulness ['juːsfulnɪs] *n* (*U*) utilité *f*.

useless ['juːslɪs] *adj* **-1.** [gen] inutile. **-2.** *inf* [person] incompétent(e), nul (nulle).

uselessness ['juːslɪsnɪs] *n* (*U*) inutilité *f*.

user ['juːzər] *n* [of product, machine] utilisateur *m*, -trice *f*; [of service] usager *m*.

user-friendly *adj* convivial(e), facile à utiliser.

USES (*abbr of* United States Employment Service) *n services américains de l'emploi.*

usher ['ʌʃər] ◇ *n* placeur *m*. ◇ *vt*: **to** ~ **sb in/out** faire entrer/sortir qqn.

usherette [ˌʌʃəˈret] *n* ouvreuse *f*.

USIA (*abbr of* United States Information Agency) *n agence américaine de renseignements.*

USM *n* **-1.** (*abbr of* United States Mail) ≃ la Poste. **-2.** (*abbr of* United States Mint) ≃ la Monnaie.

USN (*abbr of* United States Navy) *n marine de guerre américaine.*

USPHS (*abbr of* United States Public Health Service) *n aux États-Unis, direction des affaires sanitaires et sociales.*

USS (*abbr of* United States Ship) *expression précédant le nom d'un bâtiment de la marine américaine.*

USSR (*abbr of* Union of Soviet Socialist Republics) *n*: **the (former)** ~ l'(ex-)URSS *f*; **in the** ~ en URSS.

usu. *abbr of* usually.

usual ['juːʒəl] *adj* habituel(elle); **as** ~ comme d'habitude.

usually ['juːʒəlɪ] *adv* d'habitude, d'ordinaire.

usurp [juːˈzɜːp] *vt* usurper.

usury ['juːʒʊrɪ] *n* (*U*) usure *f*.

UT *abbr of* Utah.

Utah ['juːtɑː] *n* Utah *m*; in ~ dans l'Utah.

utensil [juːˈtensl] *n* ustensile *m*.

uterus ['juːtərəs] (*pl* **-ri** [-raɪ] OR **-ruses**) *n* utérus *m*.

utilitarian [ˌjuːtɪlɪˈteərɪən] *adj* utilitaire.

utility [juːˈtɪlətɪ] (*pl* **-ies**) *n* **-1.** (*U*) [usefulness] utilité *f*. **-2.** [public service] service *m* public. **-3.** COMPUT utilitaire *m*.

utility room *n* buanderie *f*.

utilize, -ise [ˈjuːtəlaɪz] *vt* utiliser; [resources] exploiter, utiliser.

utmost [ˈʌtməʊst] ◇ *adj* le plus grand (la plus grande). ◇ *n*: **to do one's** ~ faire tout son possible, faire l'impossible; **to the** ~ au plus haut point.

utopia [juːˈtəʊpjə] *n* utopie *f*.

utter [ˈʌtəʳ] ◇ *adj* total(e), complet(ète). ◇ *vt* prononcer; [cry] pousser.

utterly [ˈʌtəlɪ] *adv* complètement.

U-turn *n* demi-tour *m*; *fig* revirement *m*.

UV (*abbr of* **ultra-violet**) UV.

UV-A, UVA (*abbr of* **ultra-violet-A**) UVA.

UV-B, UVB (*abbr of* **ultra-violet-B**) UVB.

UWIST [ˈjuːwɪst] (*abbr of* **University of Wales Institute of Science and Technology**) *n institut de science et de technologie de l'université du pays de Galles.*

Uzbek [ˈʊzbek] ◇ *adj* ouzbek. ◇ *n* **-1.** [person] Ouzbek *mf*. **-2.** [language] ouzbek *m*.

Uzbekistan [ʊz,bekɪˈstɑːn] *n* Ouzbékistan *m*; **in** ~ en Ouzbékistan.

v¹ (*pl* **v's** OR **vs**), **V** (*pl* **V's** OR **Vs**) [viː] *n* [letter] v *m inv*, V *m inv*.

v² **-1.** (*abbr of* **verse**) v. **-2.** (*abbr of* **vide**) [cross-reference] v. **-3.** *abbr of* **versus**. **-4.** (*abbr of* **volt**) v.

VA *abbr of* **Virginia**.

vac (*abbr of* **vacation**) *n Br inf* vacances *fpl*.

vacancy [ˈveɪkənsɪ] (*pl* **-ies**) *n* **-1.** [job] poste *m* vacant. **-2.** [room available] chambre *f* à louer; **"vacancies"** «chambres à louer»; **"no vacancies"** «complet».

vacant [ˈveɪkənt] *adj* **-1.** [room] inoccupé(e); [chair, toilet] libre. **-2.** [job, post] vacant(e). **-3.** [look, expression] distrait(e).

vacant lot *n* terrain *m* inoccupé; [for sale] terrain *m* à vendre.

vacantly [ˈveɪkəntlɪ] *adv* d'un air distrait.

vacate [vəˈkeɪt] *vt* quitter.

vacation [vəˈkeɪʃn] *n Am* vacances *fpl*.

vacationer [vəˈkeɪʃənəʳ] *n Am* vacancier *m*, -ière *f*.

vacation resort *n Am* camp *m* de vacances.

vaccinate [ˈvæksɪneɪt] *vt* vacciner.

vaccination [,væksɪˈneɪʃn] *n* vaccination *f*.

vaccine [Br ˈvæksiːn, Am vækˈsiːn] *n* vaccin *m*.

vacillate [ˈvæsəleɪt] *vi* hésiter.

vacuum [ˈvækjʊəm] ◇ *n* **-1.** TECH & *fig* vide *m*. **-2.** [cleaner] aspirateur *m*. ◇ *vt* [room] passer l'aspirateur dans; [carpet] passer à l'aspirateur.

vacuum cleaner *n* aspirateur *m*.

vacuum-packed *adj* emballé(e) sous vide.

vacuum pump *n* pompe *f* à vide.

vagabond [ˈvægəbɒnd] *n literary* vagabond *m*, -e *f*.

vagaries [ˈveɪgərɪz] *npl* caprices *mpl*.

vagina [vəˈdʒaɪnə] *n* vagin *m*.

vagrancy [ˈveɪgrənsɪ] *n* vagabondage *m*.

vagrant [ˈveɪgrənt] *n* vagabond *m*, -e *f*.

vague [veɪg] *adj* **-1.** [gen] vague, imprécis(e). **-2.** [absent-minded] distrait(e).

vaguely [ˈveɪglɪ] *adv* vaguement.

vain [veɪn] *adj* **-1.** [futile, worthless] vain(e). **-2.** *pej* [conceited] vaniteux(euse).
◆ **in vain** *adv* en vain, vainement.

vainly [ˈveɪnlɪ] *adv* **-1.** [in vain] en vain, vainement. **-2.** [conceitedly] avec vanité.

valance [ˈvæləns] *n* **-1.** [on bed] tour *m* de lit. **-2.** *Am* [over window] cantonnière *f*.

vale [veɪl] *n literary* val *m*.

valedictory [,vælɪˈdɪktərɪ] *adj fml* d'adieu.

valentine card [ˈvæləntaɪn-] *n* carte *f* de la Saint-Valentin.

Valentine's Day [ˈvæləntaɪnz-] *n*: **(St)** ~ la Saint-Valentin.

valet [ˈvæleɪ, ˈvælɪt] *n* valet *m* de chambre.

valet parking *n*: **"~"** «voiturier».

valet service *n* **-1.** [for clothes] service *m* pressing. **-2.** [for cars] nettoyage *m* complet.

Valetta, Valleta [vəˈletə] *n* la Valette.

valiant [ˈvæljənt] *adj* vaillant(e).

valid [ˈvælɪd] *adj* **-1.** [reasonable] valable. **-2.** [legally usable] valide.

validate [ˈvælɪdeɪt] *vt* valider.

validity [vəˈlɪdətɪ] *n* validité *f*.

Valium® [ˈvælɪəm] *n* valium® *m*.

Valletta = **Valetta**.

valley [ˈvælɪ] (*pl* **valleys**) *n* vallée *f*.

valour *Br*, **valor** *Am* [ˈvæləʳ] *n* (*U*) *fml* & *literary* bravoure *f*.

valuable ['væljuəbl] *adj* -1. [advice, time, information] **précieux(ieuse)**. -2. [object, jewel] de valeur.

◆ **valuables** *npl* objets *mpl* de valeur.

valuation [,vælju'eɪʃn] *n* -1. (U) [pricing] estimation *f*, expertise *f*. -2. [estimated price] valeur *f* estimée. -3. [opinion] opinion *f*.

value ['vælju:] ◇ *n* valeur *f*; **to be good ~** être d'un bon rapport qualité-prix; **to place a high ~ on sthg** accorder beaucoup de valeur à qqch; **to get ~ for money** en avoir pour son argent; **to take sb/sthg at face ~** prendre qqn/qqch au pied de la lettre. ◇ *vt* -1. [estimate price of] expertiser. -2. [cherish] apprécier.

◆ **values** *npl* [morals] valeurs *fpl*.

value-added tax [-'ædɪd-] *n* taxe *f* sur la valeur ajoutée.

valued ['vælju:d] *adj* précieux(ieuse).

value judg(e)ment *n* jugement *m* de valeur.

valuer ['væljuə'] *n* expert *m*.

valve [vælv] *n* [on tyre] valve *f*; TECH soupape *f*.

vamoose [və'mu:s] *vi inf* s'éclipser.

vampire ['væmpaɪə'] *n* vampire *m*.

van [væn] *n* -1. AUT camionnette *f*. -2. *Br* RAIL fourgon *m*.

V and A (*abbr of* **Victoria and Albert Museum**) *n* grand musée londonien des arts décoratifs.

vandal ['vændl] *n* vandale *mf*.

vandalism ['vændəlɪzm] *n* vandalisme *m*.

vandalize, -ise ['vændəlaɪz] *vt* saccager.

vanguard ['vænga:d] *n* avant-garde *f*; **in the ~ of** à l'avant-garde de.

vanilla [və'nɪlə] ◇ *n* vanille *f*. ◇ *comp* [ice cream, yoghurt] à la vanille.

vanish ['vænɪʃ] *vi* disparaître.

vanishing point ['vænɪʃɪŋ-] *n* point *m* de fuite.

vanity ['vænətɪ] *n* (U) *pej* vanité *f*.

vanity unit *n* élément de salle de bains avec lavabo encastré.

vanquish ['væŋkwɪʃ] *vt literary* vaincre.

vantagepoint ['va:ntɪdʒ,pɔɪnt] *n* [for view] bon endroit *m*; *fig* position *f* avantageuse.

vapour *Br*, **vapor** *Am* ['veɪpə'] *n* (U) vapeur *f*; [condensation] buée *f*.

vapour trail *n* traînée *f* de vapeur.

variable ['veərɪəbl] ◇ *adj* variable; [mood] changeant(e). ◇ *n* variable *f*.

variance ['veərɪəns] *fml*: **at ~ (with)** en désaccord (avec).

variant ['veərɪənt] ◇ *adj* différent(e). ◇ *n* variante *f*.

variation [,veərɪ'eɪʃn] *n*: **~ (in)** variation *f* (de).

varicose veins ['værɪkəus-] *npl* varices *fpl*.

varied ['veərɪd] *adj* varié(e).

variety [və'raɪətɪ] (*pl* -ies) *n* -1. [gen] variété *f*. -2. [type] variété *f*, sorte *f*.

variety show *n* spectacle *m* de variétés.

various ['veərɪəs] *adj* -1. [several] plusieurs. -2. [different] divers.

varnish ['va:nɪʃ] ◇ *n* vernis *m*. ◇ *vt* vernir.

varnished ['va:nɪʃt] *adj* verni(e).

vary ['veərɪ] (*pt* & *pt* -ied) ◇ *vt* varier. ◇ *vi*: **to ~ (in/with)** varier (en/selon), changer (en/selon).

varying ['veərɪŋ] *adj* qui varie, variable.

vascular ['væskjulə'] *adj* vasculaire.

vase [*Br* va:z, *Am* veɪz] *n* vase *m*.

vasectomy [və'sektəmɪ] (*pl* -ies) *n* vasectomie *f*.

Vaseline® ['væsəli:n] *n* vaseline® *f*.

vast [va:st] *adj* vaste, immense.

vastly ['va:stlɪ] *adv* extrêmement, infiniment.

vastness ['va:stnɪs] *n* immensité *f*.

vat [væt] *n* cuve *f*.

VAT [væt, vi:eɪ'ti:] (*abbr of* **value added tax**) *n* ≃ TVA *f*.

Vatican ['vætɪkən] *n*: **the ~** le Vatican.

Vatican City *n* l'État *m* de la cité du Vatican, le Vatican; **in ~** au Vatican.

vault [vɔ:lt] ◇ *n* -1. [in bank] chambre *f* forte. -2. [roof] voûte *f*. -3. [jump] saut *m*. -4. [in church] caveau *m*. ◇ *vt* sauter. ◇ *vi*: **to ~ over sthg** sauter (par-dessus) qqch.

vaulted ['vɔ:ltɪd] *adj* voûté(e).

vaulting horse ['vɔ:ltɪŋ-] *n* cheval-d'arçons *m inv*.

vaunted ['vɔ:ntɪd] *adj fml*: **much ~** tant vanté(e).

VC *n* -1. (*abbr of* **vice-chairman**) vice-président *m*. -2. (*abbr of* **Victoria Cross**) *la plus haute distinction militaire britannique*.

VCR (*abbr of* **video cassette recorder**) *n* magnétoscope *m*.

VD *n abbr of* **venereal disease**.

VDU (*abbr of* **visual display unit**) *n* moniteur *m*.

veal [vi:l] *n* (U) veau *m*.

veer [vɪə'] *vi* virer.

veg [vedʒ] *n inf* -1. (*abbr of* **vegetable**) légume *m*. -2. (U) (*abbr of* **vegetables**) légumes *mpl*.

vegan ['viːgən] ◇ *adj* végétalien(ienne). ◇ *n* végétalien *m*, -ienne *f*.

vegetable ['vedʒtəbl] ◇ *n* légume *m*. ◇ *adj* [matter, protein] végétal(e); [soup, casserole] de OR aux légumes.

vegetable garden *n* jardin *m* potager.

vegetable knife *n* couteau *m* à légumes.

vegetable oil *n* huile *f* végétale.

vegetarian [ˌvedʒɪ'teərɪən] ◇ *adj* végétarien(ienne). ◇ *n* végétarien *m*, -ienne *f*.

vegetarianism [ˌvedʒɪ'teərɪənɪzm] *n* végétarisme *m*.

vegetate ['vedʒɪteɪt] *vi pej* végéter.

vegetation [ˌvedʒɪ'teɪʃn] *n* (*U*) végétation *f*.

veggie ['vedʒɪ] (*abbr of* **vegetarian**) *Br inf* ◇ *adj* végétarien(ienne). ◇ *n* végétarien *m*, -ienne *f*.

vehement ['viːəmənt] *adj* véhément(e).

vehemently ['viːəməntlɪ] *adv* avec véhémence.

vehicle ['viːəkl] *n lit* & *fig* véhicule *m*.

vehicular [vɪ'hɪkjʊləʳ] *adj fml* [transport] de véhicules; ~ **traffic** circulation *f*.

veil [veɪl] *n lit* & *fig* voile *m*.

veiled [veɪld] *adj* [threat, reference] voilé(e).

vein [veɪn] *n* **-1.** ANAT veine *f*. **-2.** [of leaf] nervure *f*. **-3.** [of mineral] filon *m*. **-4.** [mood]: **in the same** ~ dans le même style.

Velcro® ['velkrəu] *n* Velcro® *m*.

vellum ['veləm] *n* vélin *m*.

velocity [vɪ'lɒsətɪ] (*pl* **-ies**) *n* vélocité *f*.

velour [və'lʊəʳ] *n* velours *m*.

velvet ['velvɪt] ◇ *n* velours *m*. ◇ *comp* de OR en velours.

vend [vend] *vt fml* & JUR vendre.

vendetta [ven'detə] *n* vendetta *f*.

vending machine ['vendɪŋ-] *n* distributeur *m* automatique.

vendor ['vendɔʳ] **-1.** *fml* [salesperson] marchand *m*, -e *f*. **-2.** JUR vendeur *m*, -eresse *f*.

veneer [və'nɪəʳ] *n* placage *m*; *fig* apparence *f*.

venerable ['venərəbl] *adj* vénérable.

venerate ['venəreɪt] *vt* vénérer.

venereal disease [vɪ'nɪərɪəl-] *n* maladie *f* vénérienne.

Venetian [vɪ'niːʃn] ◇ *adj* vénitien(ienne). ◇ *n* Vénitien *m*, -ienne *f*.

venetian blind *n* store *m* vénitien.

Venezuela [ˌvenɪz'weɪlə] *n* Venezuela *m*; **in** ~ au Venezuela.

Venezuelan [ˌvenɪz'weɪlən] ◇ *adj* vénézuélien(ienne). ◇ *n* Vénézuélien *m*, -ienne *f*.

vengeance ['vendʒəns] *n* vengeance *f*; **it began raining with a** ~ il a commencé à pleuvoir très fort; **she's back with a** ~ elle fait un retour en force.

vengeful ['vendʒfʊl] *adj* vengeur(eresse).

Venice ['venɪs] *n* Venise.

venison ['venɪzn] *n* venaison *f*.

venom ['venəm] *n lit* & *fig* venin *m*.

venomous ['venəməs] *adj lit* & *fig* venimeux(euse).

vent [vent] ◇ *n* [pipe] tuyau *m*; [opening] orifice *m*; **to give** ~ **to** donner libre cours à. ◇ *vt* [anger, feelings] donner libre cours à; **to** ~ **sthg on sb** décharger qqch sur qqn.

ventilate ['ventɪleɪt] *vt* ventiler.

ventilation [ˌventɪ'leɪʃn] *n* ventilation *f*.

ventilator ['ventɪleɪtəʳ] *n* ventilateur *m*.

Ventimiglia [ˌventɪ'mɪljə] *n* Vintimille.

ventriloquist [ven'trɪləkwɪst] *n* ventriloque *mf*.

venture ['ventʃəʳ] ◇ *n* entreprise *f*. ◇ *vt* risquer; **to** ~ **to do sthg** se permettre de faire qqch. ◇ *vi* s'aventurer.

venture capital *n* capital-risque *m*.

venturesome ['ventʃəsəm] *adj* **-1.** [person] téméraire. **-2.** [action] risqué(e).

venue ['venjuː] *n* lieu *m*.

Venus ['viːnəs] *n* [planet] Vénus *f*.

veracity [və'ræsətɪ] *n* véracité *f*.

veranda(h) [və'rændə] *n* véranda *f*.

verb [vɜːb] *n* verbe *m*.

verbal ['vɜːbl] *adj* verbal(e).

verbally ['vɜːbəlɪ] *adv* verbalement.

verbatim [vɜː'beɪtɪm] *adj* & *adv* mot pour mot.

verbose [vɜː'bəus] *adj* verbeux(euse).

verdict ['vɜːdɪkt] *n* **-1.** JUR verdict *m*. **-2.** [opinion]: ~ **(on)** avis *m* (sur).

verge [vɜːdʒ] *n* **-1.** [of lawn] bordure *f*; [of road] bas-côté *m*, accotement *m*. **-2.** [brink]: **on the** ~ **of sthg** au bord de qqch; **on the** ~ **of doing sthg** sur le point de faire qqch.
◆ **verge (up)on** *vt fus* friser, approcher de.

verger ['vɜːdʒəʳ] *n* bedeau *m*.

verification [ˌverɪfɪ'keɪʃn] *n* vérification *f*.

verify ['verɪfaɪ] (*pt* & *pp* **-ied**) *vt* vérifier.

veritable ['verɪtəbl] *adj hum or fml* véritable.

vermilion [və'mɪljən] ◇ *adj* vermillon (*inv*). ◇ *n* vermillon *m*.

vermin ['vɜːmɪn] *npl* vermine *f*.

Vermont [vɜː'mɒnt] *n* Vermont *m*; **in** ~ dans le Vermont.

vermouth ['vɜːməθ] *n* vermouth *m*.

vernacular [vəˈnækjʊləʳ] ◇ *adj* vernaculaire. ◇ *n* dialecte *m*.

verruca [vəˈruːkə] (*pl* **-cas** OR **-cae** [-kaɪ]) *n* verrue *f* plantaire.

versa → **vice versa**.

versatile [ˈvɜːsətaɪl] *adj* [person, player] aux talents multiples; [machine, tool, food] souple d'emploi.

versatility [ˌvɜːsəˈtɪlətɪ] *n* [of person] variété *f* de talents; [of machine, tool] souplesse *f* d'emploi.

verse [vɜːs] *n* **-1.** (*U*) [poetry] vers *mpl*. **-2.** [stanza] strophe *f*. **-3.** [in Bible] verset *m*.

versed [vɜːst] *adj*: **to be well ~ in sthg** être versé(e) dans qqch.

version [ˈvɜːʃn] *n* version *f*.

versus [ˈvɜːsəs] *prep* **-1.** SPORT contre. **-2.** [as opposed to] par opposition à.

vertebra [ˈvɜːtɪbrə] (*pl* **-brae** [-briː]) *n* vertèbre *f*.

vertebrate [ˈvɜːtɪbreɪt] *n* vertébré *m*.

vertical [ˈvɜːtɪkl] *adj* vertical(e).

vertical integration *n* FIN intégration *f* verticale.

vertically [ˈvɜːtɪklɪ] *adv* verticalement.

vertigo [ˈvɜːtɪgəʊ] *n* (*U*) vertige *m*; **to suffer from ~** avoir le vertige.

verve [vɜːv] *n* verve *f*.

very [ˈverɪ] ◇ *adv* **-1.** [as intensifier] très; **~ much** beaucoup. **-2.** [as euphemism]: **not ~** pas très. ◇ *adj*: **the ~ room/book** la pièce/ le livre même; **the ~ man/thing I've been looking for** juste l'homme/la chose que je cherchais; **at the ~ least** tout au moins; **~ last/first** tout dernier/premier; **of one's ~ own** bien à soi.
◆ **very well** *adv* très bien; **I can't ~ well tell him ...** je ne peux tout de même pas lui dire que ....

vespers [ˈvespəz] *n* (*U*) vêpres *fpl*.

vessel [ˈvesl] *n fml* **-1.** [boat] vaisseau *m*. **-2.** [container] récipient *m*.

vest [vest] *n* **-1.** *Br* [undershirt] maillot *m* de corps. **-2.** *Am* [waistcoat] gilet *m*.

vested interest [ˈvestɪd-] *n*: **~ (in)** intérêt *m* particulier (à).

vestibule [ˈvestɪbjuːl] *n* **-1.** *fml* [entrance hall] vestibule *m*. **-2.** *Am* [on train] sas *m*.

vestige [ˈvestɪdʒ] *n* vestige *m*.

vestry [ˈvestrɪ] (*pl* **-ies**) *n* sacristie *f*.

Vesuvius [vɪˈsuːvjəs] *n* le Vésuve.

vet [vet] (*pt* & *pp* **-ted**, *cont* **-ting**) ◇ *n* **-1.** *Br* (*abbr of* **veterinary surgeon**) vétérinaire *mf*. **-2.** *Am* (*abbr of* **veteran**) ancien combattant *m*, vétéran *m*. ◇ *vt* [candidates] examiner avec soin.

veteran [ˈvetrən] ◇ *adj* [experienced] chevronné(e). ◇ *n* **-1.** MIL ancien combattant *m*, vétéran *m*. **-2.** [experienced person] vétéran *m*.

veteran car *n Br* voiture *f* d'époque (*construite avant 1905*).

Veteran's Day *n* aux États-Unis, fête nationale en l'honneur des anciens combattants (le 11 novembre).

veterinarian [ˌvetərɪˈneərɪən] *n Am* vétérinaire *mf*.

veterinary science [ˈvetərɪnrɪ-] *n* science *f* vétérinaire.

veterinary surgeon [ˈvetərɪnrɪ-] *n Br fml* vétérinaire *mf*.

veto [ˈviːtəʊ] (*pl* **-es**, *pt* & *pp* **-ed**, *cont* **-ing**) ◇ *n* veto *m*. ◇ *vt* opposer son veto à.

vetting [ˈvetɪŋ] *n* (*U*) [of candidates] examen *m* minutieux.

vex [veks] *vt* contrarier.

vexed question [vekst-] *n* question *f* controversée.

VFD (*abbr of* **voluntary fire department**) *n* pompiers bénévoles aux États-Unis.

vg (*abbr of* **very good**) tb.

vgc (*abbr of* **very good condition**) TBE, tbe.

VHF (*abbr of* **very high frequency**) VHF.

VHS (*abbr of* **video home system**) *n* VHS *m*.

VI *abbr of* **Virgin Islands**.

via [ˈvaɪə] *prep* **-1.** [travelling through] via, par. **-2.** [by means of] au moyen de.

viability [ˌvaɪəˈbɪlətɪ] *n* viabilité *f*.

viable [ˈvaɪəbl] *adj* viable.

viaduct [ˈvaɪədʌkt] *n* viaduc *m*.

vibrant [ˈvaɪbrənt] *adj* vibrant(e).

vibrate [vaɪˈbreɪt] *vi* vibrer.

vibration [vaɪˈbreɪʃn] *n* vibration *f*.

vicar [ˈvɪkəʳ] *n* [in Church of England] pasteur *m*.

vicarage [ˈvɪkərɪdʒ] *n* presbytère *m*.

vicarious [vɪˈkeərɪəs] *adj*: **to take a ~ pleasure in sthg** retirer du plaisir indirectement de qqch.

vice [vaɪs] *n* **-1.** [immorality, fault] vice *m*. **-2.** [tool] étau *m*.

vice- [vaɪs] *prefix* vice-.

vice-admiral *n* vice-amiral *m*.

vice-chairman *n* vice-président *m*, -e *f*.

vice-chancellor *n* UNIV président *m*, -e *f*.

vice-president *n* vice-président *m*, -e *f*.

vice squad *n* brigade *f* des mœurs.

vice versa [ˌvaɪsɪˈvɜːsə] *adv* vice versa.

vicinity [vɪ'sɪnətɪ] *n*: **in the ~ (of)** aux alentours (de), dans les environs (de).

vicious ['vɪʃəs] *adj* violent(e), brutal(e).

vicious circle *n* cercle *m* vicieux.

viciousness ['vɪʃəsnɪs] *n* violence *f*, brutalité *f*.

vicissitudes [vɪ'sɪsɪtjuːdz] *npl fml* vicissitudes *fpl*.

victim ['vɪktɪm] *n* victime *f*.

victimize, -ise ['vɪktɪmaɪz] *vt* faire une victime de.

victor ['vɪktər] *n* vainqueur *m*.

Victoria Cross [vɪk'tɔːrɪə-] *n* Croix *f* de Victoria.

Victoria Falls [vɪk'tɔːrɪə-] *npl* les chutes *fpl* Victoria.

Victorian [vɪk'tɔːrɪən] *adj* victorien(ienne).

Victoriana [ˌvɪktɔːrɪ'ɑːnə] *n* (*U*) objets *mpl* de l'époque victorienne.

victorious [vɪk'tɔːrɪəs] *adj* victorieux(ieuse).

victory ['vɪktərɪ] (*pl* **-ies**) *n*: **~ (over)** victoire *f* (sur).

video ['vɪdɪəʊ] (*pl* **-s**, *pt* & *pp* **-ed**, *cont* **-ing**) ◇ *n* **-1.** [medium, recording] vidéo *f*. **-2.** [machine] **magnétoscope** *m*. **-3.** [cassette] vidéocassette *f*. ◇ *comp* vidéo (*inv*). ◇ *vt* **-1.** [using video recorder] **magnétoscoper. -2.** [using camera] faire une vidéo de, filmer.

video camera *n* caméra *f* vidéo.

video cassette *n* vidéocassette *f*.

videodisc *Br*, **videodisk** *Am* ['vɪdɪəʊdɪsk] *n* vidéodisque *m*.

video game *n* jeu *m* vidéo.

video machine *n* magnétoscope *m*.

videophone ['vɪdɪəʊfəʊn] *n* vidéophone *m*, visiophone *m*.

video player, videorecorder ['vɪdɪəʊrɪˌkɔːdər] *n* magnétoscope *m*.

video recording *n* enregistrement *m* vidéo.

video shop *n* vidéoclub *m*.

videotape ['vɪdɪəʊteɪp] *n* **-1.** [cassette] vidéocassette *f*. **-2.** (*U*) [ribbon] **bande** *f* vidéo.

vie [vaɪ] (*pt* & *pp* **vied**, *cont* **vying**) *vi*: **to ~ for sthg** lutter pour qqch; **to ~ with sb (for sthg/to do sthg)** rivaliser avec qqn (pour qqch/pour faire qqch).

Vienna [vɪ'enə] *n* Vienne.

Viennese [ˌvɪə'niːz] ◇ *adj* viennois(e). ◇ *n* Viennois *m*, -e *f*.

Vietnam [ˌvjet'næm] *n* Viêt-Nam *m*; **in ~** au Viêt-Nam.

Vietnamese [ˌvjetnə'miːz] ◇ *adj* vietnamien(ienne). ◇ *n* [language] vietnamien *m*. ◇ *npl*: **the ~** les Vietnamiens.

view [vjuː] ◇ *n* **-1.** [opinion] opinion *f*, avis *m*; **~ on sthg** opinion sur qqch; **in my ~** à mon avis; **to take the ~ that ...** être d'avis que .... **-2.** [scene, ability to see] vue *f*; **to come into ~** apparaître. ◇ *vt* **-1.** [consider] considérer. **-2.** [examine - gen] examiner; [- house] visiter.
◆ **in view of** *prep* vu, étant donné.
◆ **with a view to** *conj* dans l'intention de, avec l'idée de.

viewdata ['vjuːˌdeɪtə] *n* vidéotex *m*.

viewer ['vjuːər] *n* **-1.** TV téléspectateur *m*, -trice *f*. **-2.** [for slides] visionneuse *f*.

viewfinder ['vjuːˌfaɪndər] *n* viseur *m*.

viewpoint ['vjuːpɔɪnt] *n* point *m* de vue.

vigil ['vɪdʒɪl] *n* veille *f*; RELIG vigile *f*.

vigilance ['vɪdʒɪləns] *n* vigilance *f*.

vigilant ['vɪdʒɪlənt] *adj* vigilant(e).

vigilante [ˌvɪdʒɪ'læntɪ] *n* membre *m* d'un groupe d'autodéfense.

vigor *Am* = **vigour**.

vigorous ['vɪgərəs] *adj* vigoureux(euse).

vigour *Br*, **vigor** *Am* ['vɪgər] *n* vigueur *f*.

Viking ['vaɪkɪŋ] ◇ *adj* viking (*inv*). ◇ *n* Viking *mf*.

vile [vaɪl] *adj* [mood] massacrant(e), exécrable; [person, act] vil(e), ignoble; [food] infect(e), exécrable.

vilify ['vɪlɪfaɪ] (*pt* & *pp* **-ied**) *vt* calomnier.

villa ['vɪlə] *n* villa *f*; [bungalow] pavillon *m*.

village ['vɪlɪdʒ] *n* village *m*.

villager ['vɪlɪdʒər] *n* villageois *m*, -e *f*.

villain ['vɪlən] *n* **-1.** [of film, book] méchant *m*, -e *f*; [of play] traître *m*. **-2.** [criminal] bandit *m*.

Vilnius ['vɪlnɪəs] *n* Vilnious.

VIN (*abbr* of **vehicle identification number**) *n* numéro d'immatriculation.

vinaigrette [ˌvɪnɪ'gret] *n* vinaigrette *f*.

vindicate ['vɪndɪkeɪt] *vt* justifier.

vindication [ˌvɪndɪ'keɪʃn] *n* justification *f*.

vindictive [vɪn'dɪktɪv] *adj* vindicatif(ive).

vine [vaɪn] *n* vigne *f*.

vinegar ['vɪnɪgər] *n* vinaigre *m*.

vine leaf *n* feuille *f* de vigne.

vineyard ['vɪnjəd] *n* vignoble *m*.

vintage ['vɪntɪdʒ] ◇ *adj* **-1.** [wine] de grand cru. **-2.** [classic] typique. ◇ *n* année *f*, millésime *m*.

vintage car *n* Br voiture *f* d'époque (*construite entre 1919 et 1930*).

vintage wine *n* vin *m* de grand cru.

vintner ['vɪntnəʳ] *n* négociant *m* en vins.

vinyl ['vaɪnɪl] ◇ *n* vinyle *m*. ◇ *comp* de OR en vinyle.

viola [vɪ'əʊlə] *n* alto *m*.

violate ['vaɪəleɪt] *vt* violer.

violation [,vaɪə'leɪʃn] *n* violation *f*.

violence ['vaɪələns] *n* violence *f*.

violent ['vaɪələnt] *adj* -1. [gen] violent(e). -2. [colour] criard(e).

violently ['vaɪələntlɪ] *adv* violemment; [die] de mort violente.

violet ['vaɪələt] ◇ *adj* violet(ette). ◇ *n* -1. [flower] violette *f*. -2. [colour] violet *m*.

violin [,vaɪə'lɪn] *n* violon *m*.

violinist [,vaɪə'lɪnɪst] *n* violoniste *mf*.

VIP (*abbr of* **very important person**) *n* VIP *mf*.

viper ['vaɪpəʳ] *n* vipère *f*.

viral ['vaɪrəl] *adj* viral(e).

virgin ['vɜːdʒɪn] ◇ *adj literary* [land, forest, soil] vierge. ◇ *n* [woman] vierge *f*; [man] garçon *m*/ homme *m* vierge.

Virginia [və'dʒɪnjə] *n* Virginie *f*; **in** ~ en Virginie.

Virgin Islands *n*: **the** ~ les îles *fpl* Vierges; **in the** ~ dans les îles Vierges.

virginity [və'dʒɪnətɪ] *n* virginité *f*.

Virgo ['vɜːgəʊ] (*pl* -s) *n* Vierge *f*; **to be (a)** ~ être Vierge.

virile ['vɪraɪl] *adj* viril(e).

virility [vɪ'rɪlətɪ] *n* virilité *f*.

virtual ['vɜːtʃʊəl] *adj* virtuel(elle); **it's a** ~ **certainty** c'est quasiment OR pratiquement certain.

virtually ['vɜːtʃʊəlɪ] *adv* virtuellement, pratiquement.

virtual memory *n* COMPUT mémoire *f* virtuelle.

virtual reality *n* réalité *f* virtuelle.

virtue ['vɜːtjuː] *n* -1. [good quality] vertu *f*. -2. [benefit]: ~ **(in doing sthg)** mérite *m* (à faire qqch).

◆ **by virtue of** *prep fml* en vertu de.

virtuoso [,vɜːtjʊ'əʊzəʊ] (*pl* -sos OR -si [-siː]) *n* virtuose *mf*.

virtuous ['vɜːtʃʊəs] *adj* vertueux(euse).

virulent ['vɪrʊlənt] *adj* virulent(e).

virus ['vaɪrəs] *n* COMPUT & MED virus *m*.

visa ['viːzə] *n* visa *m*.

vis-à-vis [,viːzɑː'viː] *prep fml* par rapport à.

viscose ['vɪskəʊs] *n* viscose *f*.

viscosity [vɪ'skɒsətɪ] *n* viscosité *f*.

viscount ['vaɪkaʊnt] *n* vicomte *m*.

viscous ['vɪskəs] *adj* visqueux(euse).

vise [vaɪs] *n Am* étau *m*.

visibility [,vɪzɪ'bɪlətɪ] *n* visibilité *f*.

visible ['vɪzəbl] *adj* visible.

visibly ['vɪzəblɪ] *adv* visiblement.

vision ['vɪʒn] *n* -1. (*U*) [ability to see] vue *f*. -2. [foresight, dream] vision *f*. -3. (*U*) TV image *f*.

visionary ['vɪʒənrɪ] (*pl* -ies) ◇ *adj* visionnaire. ◇ *n* visionnaire *mf*.

visit ['vɪzɪt] ◇ *n* visite *f*; **on a** ~ en visite. ◇ *vt* [person] rendre visite à; [place] visiter.

◆ **visit with** *vt fus Am* -1. [go and see] aller voir. -2. [chat to] parler avec.

visiting card ['vɪzɪtɪŋ-] *n* carte *f* de visite.

visiting hours ['vɪzɪtɪŋ-] *npl* heures *fpl* de visite.

visitor ['vɪzɪtəʳ] *n* [to person] invité *m*, -e *f*; [to place] visiteur *m*, -euse *f*; [to hotel] client *m*, -e *f*.

visitors' book *n* livre *m* d'or; [in hotel] registre *m*.

visitor's passport *n Br* passeport *m* temporaire.

visor ['vaɪzəʳ] *n* visière *f*.

vista ['vɪstə] *n* [view] vue *f*.

VISTA ['vɪstə] (*abbr of* **Volunteers in Service to America**) *n programme américain d'aide aux personnes les plus défavorisées*.

visual ['vɪʒʊəl] *adj* visuel(elle).

visual aids *npl* supports *mpl* visuels.

visual display unit *n* écran *m* de visualisation.

visualize, -ise ['vɪʒʊəlaɪz] *vt* se représenter, s'imaginer.

visually ['vɪʒʊəlɪ] *adv* visuellement; ~ **handicapped** malvoyant(e).

vital ['vaɪtl] *adj* -1. [essential] vital(e). -2. [full of life] plein(e) d'entrain.

vitality [vaɪ'tælətɪ] *n* vitalité *f*.

vitally ['vaɪtəlɪ] *adv* absolument.

vital statistics *npl inf* [of woman] mensurations *fpl*.

vitamin [*Br* 'vɪtəmɪn, *Am* 'vaɪtəmɪn] *n* vitamine *f*.

vitriolic [,vɪtrɪ'ɒlɪk] *adj* au vitriol.

viva ['vaɪvə] = **viva voce**.

vivacious [vɪ'veɪʃəs] *adj* enjoué(e).

vivacity [vɪ'væsətɪ] *n* vivacité *f*.

viva voce [,vaɪvə'vəʊsɪ] *n* examen *m* oral.

vivid ['vɪvɪd] *adj* -1. [bright] vif (vive). -2. [clear - description] vivant(e); [- memory] net (nette), précis(e).

vividly ['vɪvɪdlɪ] *adv* [describe] d'une manière vivante; [remember] clairement.

vivisection [,vɪvɪ'sekʃn] *n* vivisection *f*.

vixen ['vɪksn] *n* [fox] renarde *f*.

viz [vɪz] (*abbr of* **vide licet**) c.-à-d.

VLF (*abbr of* **very low frequency**) *n* très basse fréquence.

V-neck *n* [neck] décolleté *m* en V; [sweater] pull *m* à décolleté en V.

VOA (*abbr of* **Voice of America**) *n* station radiophonique américaine à destination de l'étranger.

vocabulary [və'kæbjʊlərɪ] (*pl* **-ies**) *n* vocabulaire *m*.

vocal ['vəʊkl] *adj* **-1.** [outspoken] qui se fait entendre. **-2.** [of the voice] vocal(e).

◆ **vocals** *npl* chant *m*.

vocal cords *npl* cordes *fpl* vocales.

vocalist ['vəʊkəlɪst] *n* chanteur *m*, -euse *f* (*dans un groupe*).

vocation [vəʊ'keɪʃn] *n* vocation *f*.

vocational [vəʊ'keɪʃənl] *adj* professionnel(elle).

vociferous [və,sɪfərəs] *adj* bruyant(e).

vodka ['vɒdkə] *n* vodka *f*.

vogue [vəʊg] ◇ *adj* en vogue, à la mode. ◇ *n* vogue *f*, mode *f*; **in** ~ en vogue, à la mode.

voice [vɔɪs] ◇ *n* **-1.** [gen] voix *f*; **to raise/lower one's** ~ élever/baisser la voix; **to keep one's** ~ **down** parler bas. **-2.** [influence]: **to have a** ~ **in** avoir son mot à dire dans. ◇ *vt* [opinion, emotion] exprimer.

voice box *n* larynx *m*.

voice-over *n* voix *f* off.

void [vɔɪd] ◇ *adj* **-1.** [invalid] nul (nulle); → **null**. **-2.** *fml* [empty]: ~ **of** dépourvu(e) de, dénué(e) de. ◇ *n* vide *m*.

voile [vɔɪl] *n* (*U*) voile *m*.

vol. (*abbr of* **volume**) vol.

volatile [*Br* 'vɒlətaɪl, *Am* 'vɒlətl] *adj* [situation] explosif(ive); [person] lunatique, versatile; [market] instable.

vol-au-vent ['vɒləʊvɑ̃] *n* vol-au-vent *m inv*.

volcanic [vɒl'kænɪk] *adj* volcanique.

volcano [vɒl'keɪnəʊ] (*pl* **-es** OR **-s**) *n* volcan *m*.

vole [vəʊl] *n* campagnol *m*.

Volga ['vɒlgə] *n*: **the (River)** ~ la Volga.

volition [və'lɪʃn] *n fml*: **of one's own** ~ de son propre gré.

volley ['vɒlɪ] (*pl* **volleys**) ◇ *n* **-1.** [of gunfire] salve *f*. **-2.** *fig* [of questions, curses] torrent *m*; [of blows] volée *f*, pluie *f*. **-3.** SPORT volée *f*. ◇ *vt* frapper à la volée, reprendre de volée.

volleyball ['vɒlɪbɔːl] *n* volley-ball *m*.

volt [vəʊlt] *n* volt *m*.

Volta ['vɒltə] *n* Volta *f*.

voltage ['vəʊltɪdʒ] *n* voltage *m*, tension *f*.

voluble ['vɒljʊbl] *adj* volubile, loquace.

volume ['vɒljuːm] *n* **-1.** [gen] volume *m*. **-2.** [of work, letters] quantité *f*; [of traffic] densité *f*.

volume control *n* réglage *m* du volume.

voluminous [və'luːmɪnəs] *adj fml* **-1.** [garment] immense. **-2.** [container] volumineux(euse).

voluntarily [*Br* 'vɒləntrɪlɪ, *Am* ,vɒlən'terəlɪ] *adv* volontairement.

voluntary ['vɒləntrɪ] *adj* **-1.** [not obligatory] volontaire. **-2.** [unpaid] bénévole.

voluntary liquidation *n* liquidation *f* volontaire.

voluntary redundancy *n Br* départ *m* volontaire.

volunteer [,vɒlən'tɪər] ◇ *n* **-1.** [gen & MIL] volontaire *mf*. **-2.** [unpaid worker] bénévole *mf*. ◇ *vt* **-1.** [offer]: **to** ~ **to do sthg** se proposer OR se porter volontaire pour faire qqch. **-2.** [information, advice] donner spontanément. ◇ *vi* **-1.** [offer one's services]: **to** ~ **(for)** se porter volontaire (pour), proposer ses services (pour). **-2.** MIL s'engager comme volontaire.

voluptuous [və'lʌptʃʊəs] *adj* voluptueux(euse).

vomit ['vɒmɪt] ◇ *n* vomi *m*. ◇ *vi* vomir.

voracious [və'reɪʃəs] *adj* vorace.

vortex ['vɔːteks] (*pl* **-texes** OR **-tices** [-tɪsiːz]) *n* vortex *m*; *fig* [of events] tourbillon *m*.

vote [vəʊt] ◇ *n* **-1.** [individual decision]: ~ **(for/against)** vote *m* (pour/contre), voix *f* (pour/contre). **-2.** [ballot] vote *m*; **to put sthg to the** ~ procéder à un vote sur qqch. **-3.** [right to vote] droit *m* de vote. ◇ *vt* **-1.** [declare] élire. **-2.** [choose]: **to** ~ **to do sthg** voter OR se prononcer pour faire; **they** ~**d to return to work** ils ont voté le retour au travail. ◇ *vi*: **to** ~ **(for/against)** voter (pour/contre).

◆ **vote in** *vt sep* élire.

◆ **vote out** *vt sep* évincer par un vote.

vote of confidence (*pl* **votes of confidence**) *n* vote *m* de confiance.

vote of no confidence (*pl* **votes of no confidence**) *n* motion *f* de censure.

vote of thanks (*pl* **votes of thanks**) *n* discours *m* de remerciement.

voter ['vəʊtər] *n* électeur *m*, -trice *f*.

voting ['vəʊtɪŋ] *n* scrutin *m*.

vouch [vaʊtʃ]

◆ **vouch for** *vt fus* répondre de, se porter garant de.

voucher ['vautʃər] n bon m, coupon m.

vow [vau] ◇ n vœu m, serment m. ◇ vt: to ~ to do sthg jurer de faire qqch; to ~ (that) ... jurer que ....

vowel ['vauəl] n voyelle f.

voyage ['vɔɪɪdʒ] n voyage m en mer; [in space] vol m.

voyeur [vwɑːˈjɜːr] n voyeur m, -euse f.

voyeurism [vwɑːˈjɜːrɪzm] n voyeurisme m.

VP n abbr of **vice-president**.

vs abbr of **versus**.

VSO (abbr of **Voluntary Service Overseas**) n organisation britannique envoyant des travailleurs bénévoles dans des pays en voie de développement pour contribuer à leur développement technique.

VSOP (abbr of **very special old pale**) appellation réservée à certains cognacs et armagnacs.

VT abbr of **Vermont**.

VTOL ['viːtɒl] (abbr of **vertical takeoff and landing**) n ADAV m.

VTR (abbr of **video tape recorder**) n magnétoscope m.

vulgar ['vʌlgər] adj **-1.** [in bad taste] vulgaire. **-2.** [offensive] grossier(ère).

vulgarity [vʌlˈgærətɪ] n (U) **-1.** [poor taste] vulgarité f. **-2.** [offensiveness] grossièreté f.

vulnerability [ˌvʌlnərəˈbɪlətɪ] n vulnérabilité f.

vulnerable ['vʌlnərəbl] adj vulnérable; ~ to [attack] exposé(e) à; [colds] sensible à.

vulture ['vʌltʃər] n lit & fig vautour m.

w (pl **w's** OR **ws**), **W** (pl **W's** OR **Ws**) ['dʌbljuː] n w m inv, W m inv.
◆ **W -1.** (abbr of **west**) O, W. **-2.** (abbr of **watt**) w.

WA abbr of **Washington**.

wacky ['wækɪ] (compar **-ier**, superl **-iest**) adj inf farfelu(e).

wad [wɒd] n **-1.** [of cotton wool, paper] tampon m. **-2.** [of banknotes, documents] liasse f. **-3.** [of tobacco] chique f; [of chewing-gum] boulette f.

wadding ['wɒdɪŋ] n rembourrage m, capitonnage m.

waddle ['wɒdl] vi se dandiner.

wade [weɪd] vi patauger.
◆ **wade through** vt fus fig se taper.

wadge [wɒdʒ] n Br inf morceau m; [of papers] tas m.

wading pool ['weɪdɪŋ-] n Am pataugeoire f.

wafer ['weɪfər] n [thin biscuit] gaufrette f.

wafer-thin adj mince comme du papier à cigarette OR une pelure d'oignon.

waffle ['wɒfl] ◇ n **-1.** CULIN gaufre f. **-2.** Br inf [vague talk] verbiage m. ◇ vi parler pour ne rien dire.

waft [wɑːft, wɒft] vi flotter.

wag [wæg] (pt & pp **-ged**, cont **-ging**) ◇ vt remuer, agiter. ◇ vi [tail] remuer.

wage [weɪdʒ] ◇ n salaire m, paie f, paye f. ◇ vt: to ~ war against faire la guerre à.
◆ **wages** npl salaire m.

wage claim n revendication f salariale.

wage differential n écart m des salaires.

wage earner n salarié m, -e f.

wage freeze n blocage m des salaires.

wage packet n Br **-1.** [envelope] enveloppe f de paye. **-2.** fig [pay] paie f, paye f.

wager ['weɪdʒər] n pari m.

wage rise n Br augmentation f de salaire.

waggish ['wægɪʃ] adj inf facétieux(ieuse), plaisant(e).

waggle ['wægl] inf ◇ vt agiter, remuer; [ears] remuer. ◇ vi remuer.

waggon ['wægən] Br = **wagon**.

wagon ['wægən] n **-1.** [horse-drawn] chariot m, charrette f. **-2.** Br RAIL wagon m.

waif [weɪf] n enfant abandonné m, enfant abandonnée f.

wail [weɪl] ◇ n gémissement m. ◇ vi gémir.

wailing ['weɪlɪŋ] n (U) gémissements mpl, plaintes fpl.

waist [weɪst] n taille f.

waistband ['weɪstbænd] n ceinture f.

waistcoat ['weɪskəut] n gilet m.

waistline ['weɪstlaɪn] n taille f.

wait [weɪt] ◇ n attente f; to have a long ~ attendre longtemps. ◇ vi attendre; I can't ~ to do sthg je brûle d'impatience de faire qqch; (just) you ~! tu ne perds rien pour attendre!; ~ and see! tu vas voir bien!; ~ a minute OR second OR moment! [interrupting person] minute (papillon)!; [interrupting oneself] attends voir! ◇ vt Am [delay] retarder.

◆ **wait about, wait around** *vi* attendre; [waste time] perdre son temps à attendre.

◆ **wait for** *vt fus* attendre; **to ~ for sb to do sthg** attendre que qqn fasse qqch.

◆ **wait on** *vt fus* [serve food to] servir.

◆ **wait up** *vi* veiller, ne pas se coucher.

waiter ['weɪtər] *n* garçon *m*, serveur *m*.

waiting game ['weɪtɪŋ-] *n* politique *f* d'attente.

waiting list ['weɪtɪŋ-] *n* liste *f* d'attente.

waiting room ['weɪtɪŋ-] *n* salle *f* d'attente.

waitress ['weɪtrɪs] *n* serveuse *f*.

waive [weɪv] *vt* [fee] renoncer à; [rule] prévoir une dérogation à.

waiver ['weɪvər] *n* JUR dérogation *f*.

wake [weɪk] (*pt* **woke** OR **-d**, *pp* **woken** OR **-d**) ◇ *n* [of ship] sillage *m*; **in one's ~** *fig* dans son sillage; **in the ~ of** *fig* à la suite de. ◇ *vt* réveiller. ◇ *vi* se réveiller.

◆ **wake up** ◇ *vt sep* réveiller. ◇ *vi* **-1.** [wake] se réveiller. **-2.** *fig* [become aware]: **to ~ up (to sthg)** prendre conscience (de qqch), se sensibiliser (à qqch).

waken ['weɪkən] *fml* ◇ *vt* réveiller. ◇ *vi* se réveiller.

waking hours ['weɪkɪŋ-] *npl* heures *fpl* de veille.

Wales [weɪlz] *n* pays *m* de Galles; **in ~** au pays de Galles.

walk [wɔːk] ◇ *n* **-1.** [action] démarche *f*, façon *f* de marcher. **-2.** [journey - for pleasure] promenade *f*; [- long distance] marche *f*; **it's a long ~** c'est loin à pied; **to go for a ~** aller se promener, aller faire une promenade. **-3.** [route] promenade *f*.
◇ *vt* **-1.** [accompany - person] accompagner; [- dog] promener. **-2.** [distance] faire à pied; **to ~ the streets** [homeless] être sur le pavé; [in search] arpenter la ville; [prostitute] faire le trottoir.
◇ *vi* **-1.** [gen] marcher. **-2.** [for pleasure] se promener.

◆ **walk away with** *vt fus inf fig* gagner OR remporter haut la main.

◆ **walk in on** *vt fus* [interrupt] déranger; [in embarrassing situation] prendre en flagrant délit.

◆ **walk off** *vt sep* [headache, cramp] faire une promenade pour se débarrasser de.

◆ **walk off with** *vt fus inf* **-1.** [steal] faucher. **-2.** [win easily] gagner OR remporter haut la main.

◆ **walk out** *vi* **-1.** [leave suddenly] partir. **-2.** [go on strike] se mettre en grève, faire grève.

◆ **walk out on** *vt fus* quitter.

walkabout ['wɔːkə,baut] *n* *Br* [by president etc] bain *m* de foule.

walker ['wɔːkər] *n* [for pleasure] promeneur *m*, -euse *f*; [long-distance] marcheur *m*, -euse *f*.

walkie-talkie [,wɔːkɪ'tɔːkɪ] *n* talkie-walkie *m*.

walk-in *adj* **-1.** [cupboard] assez grand(e) pour qu'on puisse y entrer. **-2.** *Am* [easy] facile.

walking ['wɔːkɪŋ] *n* (*U*) marche *f* à pied, promenade *f*.

walking shoes *npl* chaussures *fpl* de marche.

walking stick *n* canne *f*.

Walkman® ['wɔːkmən] *n* baladeur *m*, Walkman® *m*.

walk of life (*pl* **walks of life**) *n* milieu *m*.

walk-on *adj* [part, role] de figurant(e).

walkout ['wɔːkaut] *n* [strike] grève *f*, débrayage *m*.

walkover ['wɔːk,əuvər] *n* victoire *f* facile.

walkway ['wɔːkweɪ] *n* passage *m*; [between buildings] passerelle *f*.

wall [wɔːl] *n* **-1.** [of room, building] mur *m*; [of rock, cave] paroi *f*; **to come up against a brick ~** se heurter à un mur; **to drive sb up the ~** rendre qqn fou, taper sur le système de qqn. **-2.** ANAT paroi *f*.

wallchart ['wɔːltʃɑːt] *n* planche *f* murale.

wall cupboard *n* placard *m* mural.

walled [wɔːld] *adj* fortifié(e).

wallet ['wɒlɪt] *n* portefeuille *m*.

wallflower ['wɔːl,flauər] *n* **-1.** [plant] giroflée *f*. **-2.** *inf fig* [person]: **to be a ~** faire tapisserie.

Walloon [wɒ'luːn] ◇ *adj* wallon(onne). ◇ *n* **-1.** [person] Wallon *m*, -onne *f*. **-2.** [language] wallon *m*.

wallop ['wɒləp] *inf* ◇ *n* gros coup *m*. ◇ *vt* [person] flanquer un coup à; [ball] taper fort dans.

wallow ['wɒləu] *vi* **-1.** [in liquid] se vautrer. **-2.** [in emotion]: **to ~ in** se complaire dans.

wall painting *n* peinture *f* murale.

wallpaper ['wɔːl,peɪpər] ◇ *n* papier *m* peint. ◇ *vt* tapisser.

Wall Street *n* Wall Street *m*.

WALL STREET:
Wall Street est le quartier de la finance à New York et le nom est souvent employé pour désigner le monde américain de la finance

wall-to-wall *adj*: ~ **carpet** moquette *f.*

wally ['wɒlɪ] (*pl* -**ies**) *n Br inf* idiot *m*, -e *f*, andouille *f.*

walnut ['wɔːlnʌt] *n* -**1.** [nut] noix *f.* -**2.** [tree, wood] noyer *m.*

walrus ['wɔːlrəs] (*pl inv* OR -**es**) *n* morse *m.*

waltz [wɔːls] ◇ *n* valse *f.* ◇ *vi* -**1.** [dance] valser, danser la valse. -**2.** *inf* [walk confidently] marcher d'un air dégagé OR de façon désinvolte.

wan [wɒn] (*compar* -**ner**, *superl* -**nest**) *adj* pâle, blême.

wand [wɒnd] *n* baguette *f.*

wander ['wɒndər] *vi* -**1.** [person] errer. -**2.** [mind] divaguer; [thoughts] vagabonder.

wanderer ['wɒndərər] *n* vagabond *m*, -e *f.*

wandering ['wɒndərɪŋ] *adj* ambulant(e).

wanderlust ['wɒndəlʌst] *n* bougeotte *f*, envie *f* de voyager.

wane [weɪn] ◇ *n*: **on the ~** en déclin; [power, interest] faiblissant(e). ◇ *vi* -**1.** [influence, interest] diminuer, faiblir. -**2.** [moon] décroître.

wangle ['wæŋgl] *vt inf* se débrouiller pour obtenir.

wanna ['wɒnə] = **want a**, **want to**.

want [wɒnt] ◇ *n* -**1.** [need] besoin *m.* -**2.** [lack] manque *m*; **for ~ of** faute de, par manque de. -**3.** [deprivation] pauvreté *f*, besoin *m.* ◇ *vt* -**1.** [desire] vouloir; **to ~ to do sthg** vouloir faire qqch; **to ~ sb to do sthg** vouloir que qqn fasse qqch. -**2.** *inf* [need] avoir besoin de; **you ~ to be more careful** tu devrais être plus prudent.

want ad *n Am inf* petite annonce *f.*

wanted ['wɒntɪd] *adj*: **to be ~ (by the police)** être recherché(e) (par la police).

wanting ['wɒntɪŋ] *adj*: **to be ~ in** manquer de; **to be found ~** ne pas être à la hauteur; **not to be found ~** être à la hauteur.

wanton ['wɒntən] *adj* [destruction, neglect] gratuit(e).

war [wɔːr] (*pt* & *pp* -**red**, *cont* -**ring**) ◇ *n* guerre *f*; **to go to ~** entrer OR se mettre en guerre; **to have been in the ~s** *Br* être dans un sale état. ◇ *vi* se battre.

War., **Warks.** (*abbr of* **Warwickshire**) comté anglais.

warble ['wɔːbl] *vi* [bird] gazouiller.

war crime *n* crime *m* de guerre.

war criminal *n* criminel *m* de guerre.

war cry *n* cri *m* de guerre.

ward [wɔːd] *n* -**1.** [in hospital] salle *f.* -**2.** *Br*

POL circonscription *f* électorale. -**3.** JUR pupille *mf.*

◆ **ward off** *vt fus* [danger] écarter; [disease, blow] éviter; [evil spirits] éloigner.

war dance *n* danse *f* guerrière.

warden ['wɔːdn] *n* -**1.** [of park etc] gardien *m*, -ienne *f.* -**2.** *Br* [of youth hostel, hall of residence] directeur *m*, -trice *f.* -**3.** *Am* [of prison] directeur *m*, -trice *f.*

warder ['wɔːdər] *n* [in prison] gardien *m*, -ienne *f.*

ward of court *n* pupille *mf* sous tutelle judiciaire.

wardrobe ['wɔːdrəʊb] *n* garde-robe *f.*

wardrobe mistress *n Br* costumière *f.*

warehouse ['weəhaʊs, *pl* -haʊzɪz] *n* entrepôt *m*, magasin *m.*

wares [weəz] *npl* marchandises *fpl.*

warfare ['wɔːfeər] *n* (*U*) guerre *f.*

war game *n* -**1.** [military exercise] manœuvres *fpl* militaires. -**2.** [game of strategy] jeu *m* de stratégie militaire.

warhead ['wɔːhed] *n* ogive *f*, tête *f.*

warily ['weərəlɪ] *adj* avec précaution OR circonspection.

warlike ['wɔːlaɪk] *adj* belliqueux(euse).

warm [wɔːm] ◇ *adj* -**1.** [gen] chaud(e); **are you ~ enough?** tu as assez chaud?; **it's ~ today** il fait chaud aujourd'hui. -**2.** [friendly] chaleureux(euse). ◇ *vt* chauffer.

◆ **warm over** *vt sep Am lit* & *fig* resservir.

◆ **warm to** *vt fus* [person] se prendre de sympathie pour; [idea, place] se mettre à aimer.

◆ **warm up** ◇ *vt sep* réchauffer. ◇ *vi* -**1.** [person, room] se réchauffer. -**2.** [machine, engine] chauffer. -**3.** SPORT s'échauffer.

warm-blooded [-'blʌdɪd] *adj* à sang chaud.

war memorial *n* monument *m* aux morts.

warm front *n* METEOR front *m* chaud.

warm-hearted [-'hɑːtɪd] *adj* chaleureux(euse), affectueux(euse).

warmly ['wɔːmlɪ] *adv* -**1.** [in warm clothes]: **to dress ~** s'habiller chaudement. -**2.** [in a friendly way] chaleureusement.

warmness ['wɔːmnɪs] *n* chaleur *f.*

warmonger ['wɔːˌmʌŋgər] *n* belliciste *mf.*

warmth [wɔːmθ] *n* chaleur *f.*

warm-up *n* SPORT échauffement *m.*

warn [wɔːn] ◇ *vt* avertir, prévenir; **to ~ sb of sthg** avertir qqn de qqch; **to ~ sb not to do sthg** conseiller à qqn de ne pas faire qqch, déconseiller à qqn de faire qqch. ◇ *vi*: **to ~ of sthg** annoncer un risque de qqch.

warning ['wɔːnɪŋ] ◇ *adj* d'avertissement. ◇ *n* avertissement *m*.

warning light *n* voyant *m*, avertisseur *m* lumineux.

warning triangle *n Br* triangle *m* de signalisation.

warp [wɔːp] ◇ *vt* **-1.** [wood] gauchir, voiler. **-2.** [personality] fausser, pervertir. ◇ *vi* [wood] gauchir, se voiler. ◇ *n* [of cloth] chaîne *f*.

warpath ['wɔːpɑːθ] *n*: to be on the ~ *fig* être sur le sentier de la guerre.

warped [wɔːpt] *adj* **-1.** [wood] gauchi(e). **-2.** [personality, idea] perverti(e).

warrant ['wɒrənt] ◇ *n* JUR mandat *m*. ◇ *vt* **-1.** [justify] justifier. **-2.** [guarantee] garantir.

warrant officer *n* adjudant *m*.

warranty ['wɒrəntɪ] (*pl* **-ies**) *n* garantie *f*.

warren ['wɒrən] *n* terrier *m*.

warring ['wɔːrɪŋ] *adj* en guerre.

warrior ['wɒrɪəʳ] *n* guerrier *m*, -ière *f*.

Warsaw ['wɔːsɔː] *n* Varsovie; **the** ~ **Pact** le pacte de Varsovie.

warship ['wɔːʃɪp] *n* navire *m* de guerre.

wart [wɔːt] *n* verrue *f*.

wartime ['wɔːtaɪm] ◇ *adj* de guerre. ◇ *n*: in ~ en temps de guerre.

war widow *n* veuve *f* de guerre.

wary ['weərɪ] (*compar* **-ier**, *superl* **-iest**) *adj* prudent(e), circonspect(e); to be ~ of se méfier de; to be ~ of doing sthg hésiter à faire qqch.

was [wɒz] *pt* → **be**.

wash [wɒʃ] ◇ *n* **-1.** [act] lavage *m*; to have a ~ se laver; to give sthg a ~ laver qqch. **-2.** [clothes] lessive *f*. **-3.** [from boat] remous *m*. ◇ *vt* **-1.** [clean] laver; to ~ one's hands se laver les mains. **-2.** [carry]: the waves ~ed the oil/body onto the beach les vagues ont rejeté le pétrole/corps sur la plage. ◇ *vi* se laver.

◆ **wash away** *vt sep* emporter.

◆ **wash down** *vt sep* **-1.** [food] arroser. **-2.** [clean] laver à grande eau.

◆ **wash out** *vt sep* **-1.** [stain, dye] faire partir, enlever. **-2.** [container] laver.

◆ **wash up** ◇ *vt sep* **-1.** *Br* [dishes]: to ~ the dishes up faire OR laver la vaisselle. **-2.** [subj: sea, river] rejeter. ◇ *vi* **-1.** *Br* [wash dishes] faire OR laver la vaisselle. **-2.** *Am* [wash oneself] se laver.

washable ['wɒʃəbl] *adj* lavable.

wash-and-wear *adj* qui ne nécessite aucun repassage.

washbasin *Br* ['wɒʃˌbeɪsn], **washbowl** *Am* ['wɒʃbəʊl] *n* lavabo *m*.

washcloth ['wɒʃˌklɒθ] *n Am* gant *m* de toilette.

washed-out [ˌwɒʃt-] *adj* **-1.** [pale] délavé(e). **-2.** [exhausted] lessivé(e).

washed-up [ˌwɒʃt-] *adj inf* [person] fini(e); [project] fichu(e).

washer [wɒʃəʳ] *n* **-1.** TECH rondelle *f*. **-2.** [washing machine] machine *f* à laver.

washer-dryer *n* machine *f* à laver séchante.

washing ['wɒʃɪŋ] *n* (*U*) **-1.** [action] lessive *f*. **-2.** [clothes] linge *m*, lessive *f*.

washing line *n* corde *f* à linge.

washing machine *n* machine *f* à laver.

washing powder *n Br* lessive *f*, détergent *m*.

Washington ['wɒʃɪŋtən] *n* **-1.** [state]: ~ **State** l'État *m* de Washington. **-2.** [city]: ~ **D.C.** Washington.

washing-up *n Br* vaisselle *f*.

washing-up liquid *n Br* liquide *m* pour la vaisselle.

washout ['wɒʃaʊt] *n inf* fiasco *m*.

washroom ['wɒʃrʊm] *n Am* toilettes *fpl*.

wasn't [wɒznt] = **was not**.

wasp [wɒsp] *n* guêpe *f*.

Wasp, WASP [wɒsp] (*abbr of* **White Anglo-Saxon Protestant**) *n inf* personne *de* race blanche, d'origine anglo-saxonne et protestante.

waspish ['wɒspɪʃ] *adj* revêche, grincheux(euse).

wastage ['weɪstɪdʒ] *n* gaspillage *m*.

waste [weɪst] ◇ *adj* [material] de rebut; [fuel] perdu(e); [area of land] en friche. ◇ *n* **-1.** [misuse] gaspillage *m*; it's a ~ of money [extravagance] c'est du gaspillage; [bad investment] c'est de l'argent perdu; to go to ~ [gen] être gaspillé; [food] se perdre; [work] ne servir à rien; a ~ of time une perte de temps. **-2.** (*U*) [refuse] déchets *mpl*, ordures *fpl*. ◇ *vt* [money, food, energy] gaspiller; [time, opportunity] perdre.

◆ **wastes** *npl literary* étendues *fpl* désertes.

wastebasket *Am* = **wastepaper basket**.

waste disposal unit *n* broyeur *m* d'ordures.

wasteful ['weɪstfʊl] *adj* [person] gaspilleur(euse); [activity] peu économique.

waste ground *n* (*U*) terrain *m* vague.

wasteland ['weɪstˌlænd] *n* [in country] terre *f* à l'abandon; [in city] terrain *m* vague.

waste paper *n* papier *m* de rebut.

wastepaper basket [ˌweɪst'peɪpəʳ-], **wastepaper bin** [ˌweɪst'peɪpəʳ-], **waste-**

basket *Am* ['weɪst,bɑːskɪt] *n* corbeille *f* à papier.

watch [wɒtʃ] ◇ *n* -1. [timepiece] montre *f*. -2. [act of watching]: **to keep ~** faire le guet, monter la garde; **to keep ~ on sb/sthg** surveiller qqn/qqch. -3. [guard] garde *f*; NAUT [shift] **quart** *m*. ◇ *vt* -1. [look at] regarder. -2. [spy on, guard] surveiller. -3. [be careful about] faire attention à; **~ your language!** surveille ton langage!; **~ it!** *inf* attention! ◇ *vi* regarder.

◆ **watch out** *vi* faire attention, prendre garde.

◆ **watch over** *vt fus* veiller sur.

watchdog ['wɒtʃdɒg] *n* -1. [dog] chien *m* de garde. -2. *fig* [organization] organisation *f* de contrôle.

watchful ['wɒtʃʊl] *adj* vigilant(e).

watchmaker ['wɒtʃ,meɪkəʳ] *n* horloger *m*.

watchman ['wɒtʃmən] (*pl* **-men** [-mən]) *n* gardien *m*.

watchword ['wɒtʃwɜːd] *n* mot *m* d'ordre.

water ['wɔːtəʳ] ◇ *n* -1. [liquid] eau *f*; **to pour** OR **throw cold ~ on sthg** *fig* se montrer négatif à l'égard de qqch; **to tread ~** flotter; **that's all ~ under the bridge** tout ça, c'est du passé. -2. [urine]: **to pass ~** uriner. ◇ *vt* arroser. ◇ *vi* -1. [eyes] pleurer, larmoyer. -2. [mouth]: **my mouth was ~ing** j'en avais l'eau à la bouche; **it made my mouth ~** cela m'a fait venir l'eau à la bouche.

◆ **waters** *npl* [sea] eaux *fpl*.

◆ **water down** *vt sep* -1. [dilute] diluer; [alcohol] couper d'eau. -2. *usu pej* [plan, demand] atténuer, modérer; [play, novel] édulcorer.

water bed *n* lit *m* d'eau.

water bird *n* oiseau *m* aquatique.

water biscuit *n* cracker *m*, craquelin *m*.

waterborne ['wɔːtəbɔːn] *adj* [disease] d'origine hydrique.

water bottle *n* gourde *f*, bidon *m* (à eau).

water buffalo *n* karbau *m*, kérabau *m*.

water cannon *n* canon *m* à eau.

water chestnut *n* châtaigne *f* d'eau.

water closet *n* *dated* toilettes *fpl*, waters *mpl*.

watercolour ['wɔːtə,kʌləʳ] *n* -1. [picture] aquarelle *f*. -2. [paint] peinture *f* à l'eau, couleur *f* pour aquarelle.

water-cooled [-,kuːld] *adj* à refroidissement par eau.

watercourse ['wɔːtəkɔːs] *n* cours *m* d'eau.

watercress ['wɔːtəkres] *n* cresson *m*.

watered-down [,wɔːtəd-] *adj usu pej* modéré(e), atténué(e); [version] édulcoré(e).

waterfall ['wɔːtəfɔːl] *n* chute *f* d'eau, cascade *f*.

waterfront ['wɔːtəfrʌnt] *n* quais *mpl*.

water heater *n* chauffe-eau *m inv*.

waterhole ['wɔːtəhəʊl] *n* mare *f*, point *m* d'eau.

watering can ['wɔːtərɪŋ-] *n* arrosoir *m*.

water jump *n* brook *m*.

water level *n* niveau *m* de l'eau.

water lily *n* nénuphar *m*.

waterline ['wɔːtəlaɪn] *n* NAUT ligne *f* de flottaison.

waterlogged ['wɔːtəlɒgd] *adj* -1. [land] détrempé(e). -2. [vessel] plein(e) d'eau.

water main *n* conduite *f* principale d'eau.

watermark ['wɔːtəmɑːk] *n* -1. [in paper] filigrane *m*. -2. [showing water level] laisse *f*.

watermelon ['wɔːtə,melən] *n* pastèque *f*.

water pipe *n* conduite *f* d'eau.

water pistol *n* pistolet *m* à eau.

water polo *n* water-polo *m*.

waterproof ['wɔːtəpruːf] ◇ *adj* imperméable. ◇ *n* imperméable *m*. ◇ *vt* imperméabiliser.

water rates *npl Br* taxe *f* sur l'eau.

water-resistant *adj* qui résiste à l'eau.

watershed ['wɔːtəʃed] *n fig* [turning point] tournant *m*, moment *m* critique.

waterside ['wɔːtəsaɪd] ◇ *adj* au bord de l'eau. ◇ *n*: **the ~** le bord de l'eau.

water skiing *n* ski *m* nautique.

water softener *n* adoucisseur *m* d'eau.

water-soluble *adj* soluble dans l'eau.

waterspout ['wɔːtəspaut] *n* trombe *f*.

water supply *n* alimentation *f* en eau, approvisionnement *m* d'eau.

water table *n* niveau *m* hydrostatique.

water tank *n* réservoir *m* d'eau, citerne *f*.

watertight ['wɔːtətaɪt] *adj* -1. [waterproof] étanche. -2. *fig* [excuse, contract] parfait(e); [argument] irréfutable; [plan] infaillible.

water tower *n* château *m* d'eau.

waterway ['wɔːtəweɪ] *n* voie *f* navigable.

waterworks ['wɔːtəwɜːks] (*pl inv*) *n* [building] installation *f* hydraulique, usine *f* de distribution d'eau.

watery ['wɔːtərɪ] *adj* -1. [food, drink] trop dilué(e); [tea, coffee] pas assez fort(e). -2. [pale] pâle.

watt [wɒt] *n* watt *m*.

wattage ['wɒtɪdʒ] *n* puissance *f* OR consommation *f* en watts.

wave [weɪv] ◇ *n* **-1.** [of hand] geste *m*, signe *m*. **-2.** [of water, emotion, nausea] vague *f*. **-3.** [of light, sound] onde *f*; [of heat] bouffée *f*. **-4.** [in hair] cran *m*, ondulation *f*. ◇ *vt* **-1.** [arm, handkerchief] agiter; [flag, stick] brandir. **-2.** [signal to]: **he ~d the car on** il a fait signe à la voiture d'avancer. ◇ *vi* **-1.** [with hand] faire signe de la main; **to ~ at** OR **to sb** faire signe à qqn, saluer qqn de la main. **-2.** [flags, trees] flotter.

◆ **wave aside** *vt sep* *fig* [dismiss] écarter, rejeter.

◆ **wave down** *vt sep*: **to ~ down a vehicle** faire signe à un véhicule de s'arrêter.

wave band *n* bande *f* de fréquences, gamme *f* d'ondes.

wavelength ['weɪvleŋθ] *n* longueur *f* d'ondes; **to be on the same ~** *fig* être sur la même longueur d'ondes.

waver ['weɪvər] *vi* **-1.** [falter] vaciller, chanceler. **-2.** [hesitate] hésiter, vaciller. **-3.** [fluctuate] fluctuer, varier.

wavy ['weɪvɪ] (*compar* **-ier**, *superl* **-iest**) *adj* [hair] ondulé(e); [line] onduleux(euse).

wax [wæks] ◇ *n* (*U*) **-1.** [in candles, polish] cire *f*; [for skis] fart *m*. **-2.** [in ears] cérumen *m*. ◇ *vt* cirer; [skis] farter. ◇ *vi* **-1.** *dated or hum* [become] devenir; **to ~ and wane** connaître des hauts et des bas. **-2.** [moon] croître.

waxen ['wæksən] *adj* cireux(euse).

wax paper *n* *Am* papier *m* sulfurisé.

waxworks ['wækswɜːks] (*pl inv*) *n* [museum] musée *m* de cire.

way [weɪ] ◇ *n* **-1.** [means; method] façon *f*; **~s and means** moyens *mpl*; **to get** OR **have one's ~** obtenir ce qu'on veut; **she expects to have everything her own ~** elle s'attend à ce qu'on lui fasse ses quatre volontés. **-2.** [manner, style] façon *f*, manière *f*; **in the same ~** de la même manière OR façon; **this/that ~** comme ça, de cette façon; **in a ~** d'une certaine manière, en quelque sorte; **in a big/small ~** à un haut/moindre degré. **-3.** [skill]: **to have a ~ with** savoir comment s'y prendre avec; **to have a ~ of doing sthg** avoir le chic pour faire qqch. **-4.** [route, path] chemin *m*; **~ in** entrée *f*; **~ out** sortie *f*; **to be out of one's ~** [place] ne pas être sur sa route; **on the** OR **one's ~** sur le OR son chemin; **across** OR **over the ~** juste en face; **to be under ~** [ship] faire route; *fig* [meeting] être en cours; **to get under ~** [ship] se mettre en route; *fig* [meeting] démarrer; **"give ~"** *Br* «vous n'avez pas la priorité»; **to be in the ~** gêner; **to be out of the ~** [finished] être fini; [not blocking] ne

pas gêner; **to go out of one's ~ to do sthg** se donner du mal pour faire qqch; **to keep out of sb's ~** éviter qqn; **keep out of the ~!** restez à l'écart!; **to make one's ~** aller; **to make one's ~ towards** se diriger vers; **to make ~ for** faire place à; **to stand in sb's ~** *fig* [subj: obstacle] gêner qqn; [subj: person] s'opposer à la volonté de qqn; **to work one's ~** progresser. **-5.** [direction]: **to go/ look/come this ~** aller/regarder/venir par ici; **the right/wrong ~ round** [in sequence] dans le bon/mauvais ordre; **she had her hat on the wrong ~ round** elle avait mis son chapeau à l'envers; **the right/wrong ~ up** dans le bon/mauvais sens. **-6.** [distance]: **all the ~** tout le trajet; *fig* [support etc] jusqu'au bout; **most of the ~** presque tout le trajet OR chemin; **a long ~** loin; **to go a long ~ towards doing sthg** *fig* contribuer largement à faire qqch. **-7.** *phr*: **to give ~** [under weight, pressure] céder; **no ~!** pas question!

◇ *adv* *inf* [a lot] largement; **~ better** bien mieux.

◆ **ways** *npl* [customs, habits] coutumes *fpl*.

◆ **by the way** *adv* au fait.

◆ **by way of** *prep* **-1.** [via] par. **-2.** [as a sort of] en guise de.

◆ **in the way of** *prep* comme.

waylay [,weɪ'leɪ] (*pt* & *pp* **-laid** [-'leɪd]) *vt* arrêter (au passage).

way of life *n* façon *f* de vivre.

way-out *adj* *inf* excentrique.

wayside ['weɪsaɪd] *n* [roadside] bord *m* (de la route); **to fall by the ~** *fig* tomber à l'eau.

wayward ['weɪwəd] *adj* qui n'en fait qu'à sa tête; [behaviour] capricieux(ieuse).

WC (*abbr of* **water closet**) *n* W.-C. *mpl*.

WCC (*abbr of* **World Council of Churches**) *n* assemblée mondiale des Églises.

we [wiː] *pers pron* nous; **WE can't do it** nous, nous ne pouvons pas le faire; **as ~ say in France** comme on dit en France; **~ British** nous autres Britanniques.

weak [wiːk] *adj* **-1.** [gen] faible. **-2.** [delicate] fragile. **-3.** [unconvincing] peu convaincant(e). **-4.** [drink] léger(ère).

weaken ['wiːkn] ◇ *vt* **-1.** [undermine] affaiblir. **-2.** [reduce] diminuer. **-3.** [physically - person] affaiblir; [- structure] fragiliser. ◇ *vi* faiblir.

weak-kneed [-niːd] *adj* *inf* *pej* lâche.

weakling ['wiːklɪŋ] *n* *pej* mauviette *f*.

weakly ['wiːklɪ] *adv* faiblement.

weak-minded [-'maɪndɪd] *adj* [weak-willed] faible de caractère.

weakness ['wiːknɪs] n -1. (U) [physical - of person] faiblesse f; [- of structure] fragilité f. -2. [liking]: **to have a ~ for sthg** avoir un faible pour qqch. -3. [imperfect point] point m faible, faiblesse f.

weal [wiːl] n marque f.

wealth [welθ] n -1. (U) [riches] richesse f. -2. [abundance]: **a ~ of** une profusion de.

wealth tax n Br impôt m sur la fortune.

wealthy ['welθɪ] (compar -ier, superl -iest) adj riche.

wean [wiːn] vt -1. [baby, lamb] sevrer. -2. [discourage]: **to ~ sb from** OR **off sthg** [interest, habit] faire perdre qqch à qqn; [drugs, alcohol] détourner qqn de qqch.

weapon ['wepən] n arme f.

weaponry ['wepənrɪ] n (U) armement m.

wear [weəʳ] (pt wore, pp worn) ◇ n (U) -1. [type of clothes] tenue f. -2. [damage] usure f; **~ and tear** usure. -3. [use]: **these shoes have had a lot of ~** ces chaussures ont fait beaucoup d'usage; **to be the worse for ~** être fatigué; [drunk] être mûr.
◇ vt -1. [clothes, hair] porter; **she ~s her hair in a bun** elle porte un chignon. -2. [damage] user.
◇ vi -1. [deteriorate] s'user. -2. [last]: **to ~ well** durer longtemps, faire de l'usage; **to ~ badly** ne pas durer longtemps. -3. phr: **to ~ thin** [excuse] ne plus marcher.
◆ **wear away** ◇ vt sep [rock, wood] user; [grass] abîmer. ◇ vi [rock, wood] s'user; [grass] s'abîmer.
◆ **wear down** ◇ vt sep -1. [material] user. -2. [person, resistance] épuiser. ◇ vi s'user.
◆ **wear off** vi disparaître.
◆ **wear on** vi [time] passer lentement; [evening, afternoon] se traîner; [discussion] traîner en longueur.
◆ **wear out** ◇ vt sep -1. [shoes, clothes] user. -2. [person] épuiser. ◇ vi s'user.

wearable ['weərəbl] adj mettable.

wearily ['wɪərɪlɪ] adv péniblement; **to sigh ~** pousser un soupir de lassitude.

weariness ['wɪərɪnɪs] n lassitude f.

wearing ['weərɪŋ] adj [exhausting] épuisant(e).

weary ['wɪərɪ] (compar -ier, superl -iest) adj -1. [exhausted] las (lasse); [sigh] de lassitude. -2. [fed up]: **to be ~ of sthg/of doing sthg** être las de qqch/de faire qqch.

weasel ['wiːzl] n belette f.

weather ['weðəʳ] ◇ n temps m; **what's the ~ like?** quel temps fait-il?; **good ~** beau temps; **to make heavy ~ of it** se compliquer la tâche; **to be under the ~** être patra-

que. ◇ vt [crisis, problem] surmonter. ◇ vi [rock] s'éroder; [wood] s'user.

weather-beaten adj -1. [face, skin] tanné(e). -2. [building, stone] abîmé(e) par les intempéries.

weathercock ['weðəkɒk] n girouette f.

weathered ['weðəd] adj [stone] érodé(e); [building, wood] qui a souffert des intempéries.

weather forecast n météo f, prévisions fpl météorologiques.

weatherman ['weðəmæn] (pl -men [-men]) n météorologue m.

weather map n carte f météorologique.

weatherproof ['weðəpruːf] adj [clothing] imperméable; [building] à l'épreuve des intempéries.

weather report n bulletin m météorologique.

weather ship n navire m météo.

weather vane [-veɪn] n girouette f.

weave [wiːv] (pt wove, pp woven) ◇ n tissage m. ◇ vt -1. [using loom] tisser. -2. [move]: **to ~ one's way** se faufiler. ◇ vi [move] se faufiler.

weaver ['wiːvəʳ] n tisserand m, -e f.

web [web] n -1. [cobweb] toile f (d'araignée). -2. fig [of lies] tissu m.

webbed [webd] adj palmé(e).

webbing ['webɪŋ] n (U) sangles fpl.

web-footed [-'fʊtɪd] adj aux pieds palmés.

wed [wed] (pt & pp wed OR -ded) literary ◇ vt épouser. ◇ vi se marier.

we'd [wiːd] = we had, we would.

Wed. (abbr of Wednesday) mer.

wedded ['wedɪd] adj [committed]: **~ to** dévoué(e) à.

wedding ['wedɪŋ] n mariage m.

wedding anniversary n anniversaire m de mariage.

wedding cake n pièce f montée.

wedding dress n robe f de mariée.

wedding reception n réception f de mariage.

wedding ring n alliance f.

wedge [wedʒ] ◇ n -1. [for steadying] cale f. -2. [for splitting] coin m; **to drive a ~ between** fig semer la discorde entre; **the thin end of the ~** fig le commencement de la fin. -3. [of cake, cheese] morceau m. ◇ vt caler.

wedlock ['wedlɒk] n (U) literary mariage m.

Wednesday ['wenzdɪ] n mercredi m; see also **Saturday**.

wee [wiː] ◇ *adj Scot* petit(e). ◇ *n v inf* pipi *m.* ◇ *vi v inf* faire pipi.

weed [wiːd] ◇ *n* **-1.** [plant] mauvaise herbe *f.* **-2.** *Br inf* [feeble person] mauviette *f.* ◇ *vt* désherber.

◆ **weed out** *vt sep* éliminer.

weeding ['wiːdɪŋ] *n* désherbage *m.*

weedkiller ['wiːd,kɪlə'] *n* désherbant *m.*

weedy ['wiːdɪ] (*compar* **-ier**, *superl* **-iest**) *adj Br inf* [feeble] qui agit comme une mauviette.

week [wiːk] *n* semaine *f*; **Saturday ~, a ~ on Saturday** samedi en huit.

weekday ['wiːkdeɪ] *n* jour *m* de semaine.

weekend [,wiːk'end] *n* week-end *m*; **on** OR **at the ~** le week-end.

weekend bag *n* sac *m* de voyage.

weekly ['wiːklɪ] ◇ *adj* hebdomadaire. ◇ *adv* chaque semaine. ◇ *n* hebdomadaire *m.*

weeny ['wiːnɪ] *adj Br inf* tout petit (toute petite).

weep [wiːp] (*pt* & *pp* **wept**) ◇ *n*: **to have a ~** pleurer. ◇ *vt* & *vi* pleurer.

weeping willow ['wiːpɪŋ-] *n* saule *m* pleureur.

weepy [wiːpɪ] (*compar* **-ier**, *superl* **-iest**) *adj* [person] pleurnicheur(euse); [film] sentimental(e).

wee-wee *n* & *vi* = **wee**.

weft [weft] *n* trame *f.*

weigh [weɪ] ◇ *vt* **-1.** [gen] peser. **-2.** NAUT: **to ~ anchor** lever l'ancre.

◆ **weigh down** *vt sep* **-1.** [physically]: **to be ~ed down with sthg** plier sous le poids de qqch. **-2.** [mentally]: **to be ~ed down by** OR **with sthg** être accablé par qqch.

◆ **weigh (up)on** *vt fus* peser à.

◆ **weigh out** *vt sep* peser.

◆ **weigh up** *vt sep* **-1.** [consider carefully] examiner; **to ~ up the pros and cons** peser le pour et le contre. **-2.** [size up] juger, évaluer.

weighbridge ['weɪbrɪdʒ] *n Br* pont-bascule *m.*

weighing machine ['weɪŋ-] *n* balance *f.*

weight [weɪt] ◇ *n lit* & *fig* poids *m*; **to put on** OR **gain ~** prendre du poids, grossir; **to lose ~** perdre du poids, maigrir; **to pull one's ~** faire sa part du travail, participer à la tâche; **to ~ off one's feet** se reposer, s'asseoir; **to throw one's ~ about** faire l'important; **to carry ~** avoir du poids. ◇ *vt*: **to ~ sthg (down)** [hold in place] maintenir qqch avec un poids; [make heavier] alourdir qqch.

weighted ['weɪtɪd] *adj*: **to be ~ in favour of/against** être favorable/défavorable à.

weighting ['weɪtɪŋ] *n* indemnité *f.*

weightlessness ['weɪtlɪsnɪs] *n* apesanteur *f.*

weightlifter ['weɪt,lɪftə'] *n* haltérophile *m.*

weightlifting ['weɪt,lɪftɪŋ] *n* haltérophilie *f.*

weight training *n* musculation *f.*

weighty ['weɪtɪ] (*compar* **-ier**, *superl* **-iest**) *adj* [serious] important(e), de poids.

weir [wɪə'] *n* barrage *m.*

weird [wɪəd] *adj* bizarre.

weirdo ['wɪədəu] (*pl* **-s**) *n inf* drôle de type *m.*

welcome ['welkəm] ◇ *adj* **-1.** [guest, help etc] bienvenu(e); **to make sb ~** faire bon accueil à qqn. **-2.** [free]: **you're ~ to ...** n'hésitez pas à .... **-3.** [in reply to thanks]: **you're ~** il n'y a pas de quoi, de rien. ◇ *n* accueil *m.* ◇ *vt* **-1.** [receive] accueillir. **-2.** [approve of] se réjouir de. ◇ *excl* bienvenue!

welcoming ['welkəmɪŋ] *adj* accueillant(e).

weld [weld] ◇ *n* soudure *f.* ◇ *vt* souder.

welder [weldə'] *n* soudeur *m.*

welfare ['welfeə'] ◇ *adj* social(e). ◇ *n* **-1.** [well-being] bien-être *m.* **-2.** *Am* [income support] assistance *f* publique.

welfare state *n* État-providence *m.*

well [wel] (*compar* **better**, *superl* **best**) ◇ *adj* bien; **I'm very ~, thanks** je vais très bien, merci; **all is ~** tout va bien; **(all) ~ and good** très bien; **just as ~** aussi bien.

◇ *adv* bien; **the team was ~ beaten** l'équipe a été battue à plates coutures; **to go ~** aller bien; **~ done!** bravo!; **~ and truly** bel et bien; **to be ~ in with sb** *inf* être bien avec qqn; **you're ~ out of it** *inf* c'est mieux comme ça pour toi.

◇ *n* [for water, oil] puits *m.*

◇ *excl* **-1.** [in hesitation] heu!, eh bien! **-2.** [to correct oneself] bon!, enfin! **-3.** [to express resignation]: **oh ~!** eh bien! **-4.** [in surprise] tiens!

◆ **as well** *adv* **-1.** [in addition] aussi, également. **-2.** [with same result]: **I/you** *etc* **may** OR **might as ~ (do sthg)** je/tu *etc* ferais aussi bien (de faire qqch).

◆ **as well as** *conj* en plus de, aussi bien que.

◆ **well up** *vi*: **tears ~ed up in her eyes** les larmes lui montaient aux yeux.

we'll [wiːl] = **we shall, we will**.

well-adjusted *adj* bien dans sa peau.

well-advised [-əd'vaɪzd] *adj* sage; **you would be ~ to do sthg** tu ferais bien de faire qqch.

well-appointed [-ə'pɔɪntɪd] *adj* bien équipé(e).

well-balanced *adj* (bien) équilibré(e).

well-behaved [-bɪ'heɪvd] *adj* sage.

wellbeing [ˌwel'biːɪŋ] *n* bien-être *m*.

well-bred [-'bred] *adj* bien élevé(e).

well-built *adj* bien bâti(e).

well-chosen *adj* bien choisi(e).

well-disposed *adj*: to be ~ to OR towards sb être bien disposé(e) envers qqn; to be ~ towards sthg être favorable à qqch.

well-done *adj* CULIN bien cuit(e).

well-dressed [-'drest] *adj* bien habillé(e).

well-earned [-ɜːnd] *adj* bien mérité(e).

well-established *adj* bien établi(e).

well-fed *adj* bien nourri(e).

well-groomed [-'gruːmd] *adj* soigné(e).

wellhead ['welhed] *n* source *f*.

well-heeled [-hiːld] *adj inf* nanti(e).

wellies ['welɪz] *npl Br inf* = **wellington boots**.

well-informed *adj*: to be ~ (about/on) être bien informé(e) (sur).

Wellington ['welɪŋtən] *n* Wellington.

wellington boots ['welɪŋtən-], **wellingtons** ['welɪŋtənz] *npl* bottes *fpl* de caoutchouc.

well-intentioned [-ɪn'tenʃnd] *adj* bien intentionné(e).

well-kept *adj* -1. [building, garden] bien tenu(e). -2. [secret] bien gardé(e).

well-known *adj* bien connu(e).

well-mannered *adj* bien élevé(e).

well-meaning *adj* bien intentionné(e).

well-nigh *adv* presque, pratiquement.

well-off *adj* -1. [rich] riche. -2. [well-provided]: to be ~ for sthg être bien pourvu(e) en qqch; he doesn't know when he is ~ *inf* il ne connaît pas son bonheur.

well-paid *adj* bien payé(e).

well-preserved *adj fig* bien conservé(e).

well-proportioned [-prə'pɔːʃnd] *adj* bien proportionné(e).

well-read *adj* cultivé(e).

well-rounded [-'raundɪd] *adj* [education, background] complet(ète).

well-spoken *adj* qui parle bien.

well-thought-of *adj* qui a une bonne réputation.

well-thought-out *adj* bien conçu(e).

well-timed *adj* bien calculé(e), qui vient à point nommé.

well-to-do *adj* riche.

wellwisher ['wel,wɪʃəʳ] *n* admirateur *m*, -trice *f*.

well-woman clinic *n Br* centre *m* de santé pour femmes.

Welsh [welʃ] ◇ *adj* gallois(e). ◇ *n* [language] gallois *m*. ◇ *npl*: the ~ les Gallois *mpl*.

Welshman ['welʃmən] (*pl* -men [-mən]) *n* Gallois *m*.

Welsh rarebit [-'reəbɪt] *n* toast *m* au fromage chaud.

Welshwoman ['welʃ,wumən] (*pl* -women [-,wɪmɪn]) *n* Galloise *f*.

welter ['weltəʳ] *n* [of ideas, emotions] confusion *f*.

welterweight ['weltəweɪt] *n* poids *m* welter.

wend [wend] *vt literary*: to ~ one's way homewards [set off] se mettre en route pour rentrer à la maison; [be on one's way] être sur le chemin de la maison.

wendy house ['wendɪ-] *n Br* maison *f* en modèle réduit (*pour jouer*).

went [went] *pt* → **go**.

wept [wept] *pt & pp* → **weep**.

were [wɜːʳ] → **be**.

we're [wɪəʳ] = **we are**.

weren't [wɜːnt] = **were not**.

werewolf ['wɪəwulf] (*pl* -wolves [-wulvz]) *n* loup-garou *m*.

west [west] ◇ *n* -1. [direction] ouest *m*. -2. [region]: the ~ l'ouest *m*. ◇ *adj* ouest (*inv*); [wind] d'ouest. ◇ *adv* de l'ouest, vers l'ouest; ~ of à l'ouest de.
◆ **West** *n* POL: the West l'Occident *m*.

West Bank *n*: the ~ la Cisjordanie; on the ~ en Cisjordanie.

westbound ['westbaund] *adj* en direction de l'ouest.

West Country *n Br*: the ~ le sud-ouest de l'Angleterre.

West End *n Br*: the ~ le West-End (*quartier des grands magasins et des théâtres, à Londres*).

westerly ['westəlɪ] *adj* à l'ouest; [wind] de l'ouest; in a ~ direction vers l'ouest.

western ['westən] ◇ *adj* -1. [gen] de l'ouest. -2. POL occidental(e). ◇ *n* [book, film] western *m*.

Westerner ['westənəʳ] *n* -1. POL Occidental *m*, -e *f*. -2. [inhabitant of west of country] personne *f* de l'ouest.

westernize, -ise ['westənaɪz] *vt* occidentaliser.

Western Samoa *n* Samoa *fpl* occidentales; in ~ dans les Samoa occidentales.

West German ◇ *adj* allemand(e) de l'Ouest. ◇ *n* Allemand *m*, -e *f* de l'Ouest.

West Germany *n*: (former) ~ (ex-)Allemagne *f* de l'Ouest; **in** ~ en Allemagne de l'Ouest.

West Indian ◇ *adj* antillais(e). ◇ *n* Antillais *m*, -e *f*.

West Indies [-'ındiːz] *npl* Antilles *fpl*; **in the** ~ aux Antilles.

Westminster ['westmınstər] *n quartier du centre de Londres.*

WESTMINSTER:

C'est dans ce quartier que se trouvent le Parlement et le palais de Buckingham. Le nom 'Westminster' est également employé pour désigner le Parlement lui-même

---

West Virginia *n* Virginie-Occidentale *f*; **in** ~ en Virginie-Occidentale.

westward ['westwəd] *adj* & *adv* vers l'ouest.

westwards ['westwədz] *adv* vers l'ouest.

wet [wet] (*compar* -ter, *superl* -test, *pt* & *pp* **wet** OR -ted, *cont* -ting) ◇ *adj* -1. [damp, soaked] mouillé(e). -2. [rainy] pluvieux(ieuse). -3. [not dry - paint, cement] frais (fraîche). -4. *Br inf pej* [weak, feeble] ramolli(e). ◇ *n inf* POL modéré *m*, -e *f*. ◇ *vt* mouiller; **to** ~ **o.s.** [child] mouiller sa culotte; *inf* [be terrified] pisser dans son froc.

wet blanket *n inf pej* rabat-joie *m inv*.

wet-look *adj* brillant(e).

wetness ['wetnıs] *n* -1. [dampness] humidité *f*. -2. *Br inf pej* [feebleness] faiblesse *f*.

wet nurse *n* nourrice *f*.

wet rot *n* pourriture *f* humide.

wet suit *n* combinaison *f* de plongée.

WEU (*abbr of* **Western European Union**) *n* UEO *f*.

we've [wiːv] = **we have**.

whack [wæk] *inf* ◇ *n* -1. [share] part *f*. -2. [hit] grand coup *m*. ◇ *vt* donner un grand coup à, frapper fort.

whacked [wækt] *adj Br inf* [exhausted] crevé(e).

whacky ['wækı] *adj* = **wacky**.

whale [weıl] *n* baleine *f*; **to have a** ~ **of a time** *inf* drôlement bien s'amuser.

whaling ['weılıŋ] *n* pêche *f* à la baleine.

wham [wæm] *excl inf* vlan!

wharf [wɔːf] (*pl* -s OR **wharves** [wɔːvz]) *n* quai *m*.

what [wɒt] ◇ *adj* -1. (*in direct, indirect questions*) quel (quelle), quels (quelles) (*pl*); ~ **colour is it?** c'est de quelle couleur?; **he**

asked me ~ **colour it was** il m'a demandé de quelle couleur c'était. -2. (*in exclamations*) quel (quelle), quels (quelles) (*pl*); ~ **a surprise!** quelle surprise!; ~ **an idiot I am!** ce que je peux être bête!
◇ *pron* -1. (*interrogative - subject*) qu'est-ce qui; (- *object*) qu'est-ce que, que; (- *after prep*) quoi; ~ **are they doing?** qu'est-ce qu'ils font?, que font-ils?; ~ **is going on?** qu'est-ce qui se passe?; ~ **are they talking about?** de quoi parlent-ils?; ~ **about another drink/going out for a meal?** et si on prenait un autre verre/allait manger au restaurant?; ~ **about the rest of us?** et nous alors?; ~ **if ...?** et si ...? -2. (*relative - subject*) ce qui; (- *object*) ce que; **I saw** ~ **happened/fell** j'ai vu ce qui s'était passé/ était tombé; **you can't have** ~ **you want** tu ne peux pas avoir ce que tu veux.
◇ *excl* [expressing disbelief] comment!, quoi!

whatever [wɒt'evər] ◇ *adj* quel (quelle) que soit; **any book** ~ n'importe quel livre; **no chance** ~ pas la moindre chance; **nothing** ~ rien du tout. ◇ *pron* quoi que (+ *subjunctive*); **I'll do** ~ **I can** je ferai tout ce que je peux; ~ **can this be?** qu'est-ce que cela peut-il bien être?; ~ **that may mean** quoi que cela puisse bien vouloir dire; **or** ~ ou n'importe quoi d'autre.

whatnot ['wɒtnɒt] *n inf* -1. [thing] machin *m*. -2. [other things]: **and** ~ et d'autres bricoles.

whatsoever [,wɒtsəʊ'evər] *adj*: **I had no interest** ~ je n'éprouvais pas le moindre intérêt; **nothing** ~ rien du tout.

wheat [wiːt] *n* blé *m*.

wheat germ *n* germe *m* de blé.

wheatmeal ['wiːtmiːl] *n* farine *f* de blé.

wheedle ['wiːdl] *vt*: **to** ~ **sb into doing sthg** enjôler qqn pour qu'il fasse qqch; **to** ~ **sthg out of sb** enjôler qqn pour obtenir qqch.

wheel [wiːl] ◇ *n* -1. [gen] roue *f*. -2. [steering wheel] volant *m*. ◇ *vt* pousser. ◇ *vi*: **to** ~ **(round)** se retourner brusquement.

wheelbarrow ['wiːl,bærəʊ] *n* brouette *f*.

wheelbase ['wiːlbeıs] *n* empattement *m*.

wheelchair [,wiːl'tʃeər] *n* fauteuil *m* roulant.

wheelclamp ['wiːlklæmp] ◇ *n* sabot *m* de Denver. ◇ *vt*: **my car was** ~ed on a mis un sabot à ma voiture.

wheeler-dealer ['wiːlə-] *n pej* combinard *m*.

wheeling and dealing ['wiːlıŋ-] *n U pej* combines *fpl*.

wheeze [wiːz] ◇ *n* [sound] respiration *f* sifflante. ◇ *vi* respirer avec un bruit sifflant.

wheezy ['wiːzɪ] (*compar* -ier, *superl* -iest) *adj* [person] **poussif(ive)**; [cough] **sifflant(e)**; [voice, chest] **d'asthmatique**.

whelk [welk] *n* bulot *m*, buccin *m*.

when [wen] ◇ *adv* (*in direct, indirect questions*) quand; ~ **does the plane arrive?** quand OR à quelle heure arrive l'avion?; **he asked me ~ I would be in London** il m'a demandé quand je serais à Londres. ◇ *conj* **-1.** [referring to time] quand, lorsque; **he came to see me ~ I was abroad** il est venu me voir quand j'étais à l'étranger; **one day ~ I was on my own** un jour que OR où j'étais tout seul; **on the day ~ it happened** le jour où cela s'est passé. **-2.** [whereas, considering that] alors que.

whenever [wen'evər] ◇ *conj* quand; [each time that] chaque fois que. ◇ *adv* n'importe quand.

where [weər] ◇ *adv* (*in direct, indirect questions*) où; ~ **do you live?** où habitez-vous?; **do you know ~ he lives?** est-ce que vous savez où il habite? ◇ *conj* **-1.** [referring to place, situation] où; **this is ~ ...** c'est là que .... **-2.** [whereas] alors que.

whereabouts [,weərə'baʊts] ◇ *adv* où. ◇ *npl*: **their ~ are still unknown** on ne sait toujours pas où ils se trouvent.

whereas [weər'æz] *conj* alors que.

whereby [weə'baɪ] *conj fml* par lequel (laquelle), au moyen duquel (de laquelle).

wheresoever [,weəsəʊ'evər] *conj* = **wherever**.

whereupon [,weərə'pɒn] *conj fml* après quoi, sur quoi.

wherever [weər'evər] ◇ *conj* où que (+ *subjunctive*). ◇ *adv* **-1.** [no matter where] n'importe où. **-2.** [where] où donc; ~ **did you hear that?** mais où donc as-tu entendu dire cela?

wherewithal ['weəwɪðɔːl] *n fml*: **to have the ~ to do sthg** avoir les moyens de faire qqch.

whet [wet] (*pt* & *pp* **-ted**, *cont* **-ting**) *vt*: **to ~ sb's appetite for sthg** donner à qqn envie de qqch.

whether ['weðər] *conj* **-1.** [indicating choice, doubt] si. **-2.** [no matter if]: ~ **I want to or not** que je le veuille ou non.

whew [hwjuː] *excl* ouf!

whey [weɪ] *n* petit-lait *m*.

which [wɪtʃ] ◇ *adj* **-1.** (*in direct, indirect questions*) quel (quelle), quels (quelles) (*pl*); ~ **house is yours?** quelle maison est la

tienne?; ~ **one?** lequel (laquelle)? **-2.** [to refer back to sthg]: **in ~ case** auquel cas. ◇ *pron* **-1.** (*in direct, indirect questions*) lequel (laquelle), lesquels (lesquelles) (*pl*); ~ **do you prefer?** lequel préférez-vous?; **I can't decide ~ to have** je ne sais vraiment pas lequel prendre. **-2.** (*in relative clauses - subject*) qui; (- *object*) que; (- *after prep*) lequel (laquelle), lesquels (lesquelles) (*pl*); **take the slice ~ is nearer to you** prends la tranche qui est le plus près de toi; **the television ~ we bought** le téléviseur que nous avons acheté; **the settee on ~ I am sitting** le canapé sur lequel je suis assis; **the film of ~ you spoke** le film dont vous avez parlé. **-3.** (*referring back - subject*) ce qui; (- *object*) ce que; **why did you say you were ill, ~ nobody believed?** pourquoi as-tu dit que tu étais malade, ce que personne n'a cru?

whichever [wɪtʃ'evər] ◇ *adj* quel (quelle) que soit; **choose ~ colour you prefer** choisissez la couleur que vous préférez, n'importe laquelle. ◇ *pron* n'importe lequel (laquelle).

whiff [wɪf] *n* **-1.** [of perfume, smoke] bouffée *f*; [of food] odeur *f*. **-2.** *fig* [sign] signe *m*.

while [waɪl] ◇ *n* moment *m*; **let's stay here for a ~** restons ici un moment; **we've been waiting for a ~** nous attendons depuis un moment; **for a long ~** longtemps; **after a ~** après quelque temps; **to be worth one's ~** valoir la peine. ◇ *conj* **-1.** [during the time that] pendant que. **-2.** [whereas] alors que.

◆ **while away** *vt sep* passer.

whilst [waɪlst] *conj* = **while**.

whim [wɪm] *n* lubie *f*.

whimper ['wɪmpər] ◇ *n* gémissement *m*. ◇ *vt* & *vi* gémir.

whimsical ['wɪmzɪkl] *adj* saugrenu(e).

whine [waɪn] ◇ *n* gémissement *m*, longue plainte *f*. ◇ *vi* **-1.** [make sound] gémir. **-2.** [complain]: **to ~ (about)** se plaindre (de).

whinge [wɪndʒ] (*cont* **whingeing**) *vi Br*: **to ~ (about)** se plaindre (de).

whip [wɪp] (*pt* & *pp* **-ped**, *cont* **-ping**) ◇ *n* **-1.** [for hitting] fouet *m*. **-2.** *Br* POL chef *m* de file (*d'un groupe parlementaire*). ◇ *vt* **-1.** [gen] fouetter. **-2.** [take quickly]: **to ~ sthg out** sortir qqch brusquement; **to ~ sthg off** ôter OR enlever qqch brusquement.

◆ **whip up** *vt sep* [provoke] stimuler, attiser.

whiplash injury ['wɪplæʃ-] *n* coup *m* du lapin.

whipped cream [wɪpt-] *n* crème *f* fouettée.

whippet ['wɪpɪt] *n* whippet *m*.

whip-round *n Br inf*: **to have a** ~ faire une collecte.

whirl [wɜːl] ◇ *n* **-1.** *lit* & *fig* tourbillon *m*; **I/my mind was in a** ~ tout tourbillonnait en moi/dans ma tête. **-2.** *phr*: **let's give it a** ~ *inf* tentons le coup. ◇ *vt*: **to** ~ **sb/sthg round** [spin round] faire tourbillonner qqn/ qqch. ◇ *vi* tourbillonner; *fig* [head, mind] tourner.

whirlpool ['wɜːlpuːl] *n* tourbillon *m*.

whirlwind ['wɜːlwɪnd] ◇ *adj fig* éclair (*inv*). ◇ *n* tornade *f*.

whirr [wɜːr] ◇ *n* [of engine] ronronnement *m*. ◇ *vi* [engine] ronronner.

whisk [wɪsk] ◇ *n* CULIN fouet *m*, batteur *m* (à œufs). ◇ *vt* **-1.** [move quickly] emmener OR emporter rapidement. **-2.** CULIN battre.

whisker ['wɪskər] *n* moustache *f*.
♦ **whiskers** *npl* favoris *mpl*.

whisky *Br* (*pl* **-ies**), **whiskey** *Am* & *Irish* (*pl* **-s**) ['wɪskɪ] *n* whisky *m*.

whisper ['wɪspər] ◇ *n* murmure *m*. ◇ *vt* murmurer, chuchoter. ◇ *vi* chuchoter.

whispering ['wɪspərɪŋ] *n* chuchotement *m*.

whist [wɪst] *n* whist *m*.

whistle ['wɪsl] ◇ *n* **-1.** [sound] sifflement *m*. **-2.** [device] sifflet *m*. ◇ *vt* & *vi* siffler.

whistle-stop tour *n*: **to make a** ~ **of** [subj: politician] faire une tournée éclair dans.

whit [wɪt] *n* brin *m*.

Whit [wɪt] *n Br* Pentecôte *f*.

white [waɪt] ◇ *adj* **-1.** [in colour] blanc (blanche); **to go** OR **turn** ~ [hair] blanchir; [face] pâlir. **-2.** [coffee, tea] au lait. ◇ *n* **-1.** [colour, of egg, eye] blanc *m*. **-2.** [person] blanc *m*, blanche *f*.
♦ **whites** *npl* **-1.** SPORT tenue *f* blanche. **-2.** [washing] linge *m* blanc.

white blood cell *n* globule *m* blanc.

whiteboard ['waɪtbɔːd] *n* tableau *m* blanc.

white Christmas *n* Noël *m* blanc.

white-collar *adj* de bureau.

white elephant *n fig* objet *m* coûteux et inutile.

white goods *npl* **-1.** [linen] articles *mpl* de blanc. **-2.** [household machines] électroménager *m*.

white-haired [-'heəd] *adj* aux cheveux blancs.

Whitehall ['waɪthɔːl] *n* rue du centre de Londres.

WHITEHALL:
Cette rue réunit de nombreux services gouvernementaux, et le nom est souvent em-

ployé pour désigner le gouvernement lui-même

---

white horses *npl Br* [of waves] moutons *mpl*.

white-hot *adj* chauffé(e) à blanc.

White House *n*: **the** ~ la Maison Blanche.

white knight *n* chevalier *m* blanc.

white lie *n* pieux mensonge *m*.

white light *n* lumière *f* blanche.

white magic *n* magie *f* blanche.

white meat *n* viande *f* blanche.

whiten ['waɪtn] *vt* & *vi* blanchir.

whitener ['waɪtnər] *n* agent *m* blanchissant.

whiteness ['waɪtnɪs] *n* blancheur *f*.

white noise *n* son *m* blanc.

whiteout ['waɪtaut] *n* jour *m* blanc.

white paper *n* POL livre *m* blanc.

white sauce *n* sauce *f* blanche.

White Sea *n*: **the** ~ la mer Blanche.

white spirit *n Br* white spirit *m*.

white-tie *adj* [dinner] en habit.

whitewash ['waɪtwɒʃ] ◇ *n* **-1.** (*U*) [paint] chaux *f*. **-2.** *pej* [cover-up]: **a government** ~ une combine du gouvernement pour étouffer l'affaire. ◇ *vt* **-1.** [paint] blanchir à la chaux. **-2.** *pej* [cover up] blanchir.

whitewater rafting ['waɪt,wɔːtər-] *n* raft *m*, rafting *m*.

white wedding *n* mariage *m* en blanc.

white wine *n* vin *m* blanc.

whiting ['waɪtɪŋ] (*pl inv* OR **-s**) *n* merlan *m*.

Whit Monday [wɪt-] *n* le lundi *m* de Pentecôte.

Whitsun ['wɪtsn] *n* Pentecôte *f*.

whittle ['wɪtl] *vt* [reduce]: **to** ~ **sthg away** OR **down** réduire qqch.

whiz, **whizz** (*pt* & *pp* **-zed**, *cont* **-zing**) [wɪz] ◇ *n inf*: **to be a** ~ **at sthg** être un as de qqch. ◇ *vi* [go fast] aller à toute allure.

whiz(z) kid *n inf* petit prodige *m*.

who [huː] *pron* **-1.** (*in direct, indirect questions*) qui; ~ **are you?** qui êtes-vous?; **I didn't know** ~ **she was** je ne savais pas qui c'était. **-2.** (*in relative clauses*) qui; **he's the doctor** ~ **treated me** c'est le médecin qui m'a soigné; **I don't know the person** ~ **came to see you** je ne connais pas la personne qui est venue vous voir.

WHO (*abbr of* **World Health Organization**) *n* OMS *f*.

who'd [huːd] = **who had**, **who would**.

whodu(n)nit [,huː'dʌnɪt] *n inf* polar *m*.

whoever [huːˈevəʳ] *pron* **-1.** [unknown person] quiconque. **-2.** [indicating surprise, astonishment] qui donc. **-3.** [no matter who] qui que (+ *subjunctive*); ~ **you are** qui que vous soyez; ~ **wins** qui que ce soit qui gagne.

whole [həʊl] ⋄ *adj* **-1.** [entire, complete] entier(ère). **-2.** [for emphasis]: **a** ~ **lot of questions** toute une série de questions; **a** ~ **lot bigger** bien plus gros; **a** ~ **new idea** une idée tout à fait nouvelle. ⋄ *n* **-1.** [all]: **the** ~ **of the school** toute l'école; **the** ~ **of the summer** tout l'été. **-2.** [unit, complete thing] tout *m*.
◆ **as a whole** *adv* dans son ensemble.
◆ **on the whole** *adv* dans l'ensemble.

wholefood [ˈhəʊlfuːd] *n* Br aliments *mpl* complets.

whole-hearted [-ˈhɑːtɪd] *adj* sans réserve, total(e).

wholemeal [ˈhəʊlmiːl] *Br*, **whole wheat** *Am adj* complet(ète).

wholemeal bread *n* Br (*U*) pain *m* complet.

whole note *n* Am ronde *f*.

wholesale [ˈhəʊlseɪl] ⋄ *adj* **-1.** [buying, selling] en gros; [price] de gros. **-2.** *pej* [excessive] en masse. ⋄ *adv* **-1.** [in bulk] en gros. **-2.** *pej* [excessively] en masse.

wholesaler [ˈhəʊlˌseɪləʳ] *n* marchand *m* de gros, grossiste *mf*.

wholesome [ˈhəʊlsəm] *adj* sain(e).

whole wheat *Am* = **wholemeal**.

who'll [huːl] = **who will**.

wholly [ˈhəʊlɪ] *adv* totalement.

whom [huːm] *pron fml* **-1.** (*in direct, indirect questions*) qui; ~ **did you phone?** qui avez-vous appelé au téléphone?; **for/of/to** ~ pour/de/à qui. **-2.** (*in relative clauses*) que; **the girl** ~ **he married** la jeune fille qu'il a épousée; **the man of** ~ **you speak** l'homme dont vous parlez; **the man to** ~ **you were speaking** l'homme à qui vous parliez.

whoop [wuːp] ⋄ *n* cri *m*. ⋄ *vi* pousser des cris (de joie/de triomphe).

whoopee [wʊˈpiː] *excl* youpi!

whooping cough [ˈhuːpɪŋ-] *n* coqueluche *f*.

whoops [wʊps] *excl* oups!

whoosh [wʊʃ] *inf* ⋄ *n* [of water, air] jet *m*. ⋄ *vi* [water] jaillir.

whop [wɒp] *vt inf* battre à plates coutures.

whopper [ˈwɒpəʳ] *n inf* **-1.** [something big]: **it's a real** ~ c'est absolument énorme. **-2.** [lie] mensonge *m* énorme.

whopping [ˈwɒpɪŋ] *inf* ⋄ *adj* énorme. ⋄ *adv*: **a** ~ **great lorry/lie** un camion/mensonge absolument énorme.

whore [hɔːʳ] *n offensive* putain *f*.

who're [ˈhuːəʳ] = **who are**.

whose [huːz] ⋄ *pron* **-1.** (*in direct, indirect questions*) à qui; ~ **is this?** à qui est ceci? **-2.** (*in relative clauses*) dont; **that's the boy** ~ **father's an MP** c'est le garçon dont le père est député; **the girl** ~ **mother you phoned yesterday** la fille à la mère de qui OR à laquelle tu as téléphoné hier. ⋄ *adj* à qui; **car is that?** à qui est cette voiture?; ~ **son is he?** de qui est-il le fils?

whosoever [ˌhuːsəʊˈevəʳ] *pron dated* quiconque.

who's who [huːz-] *n* [book] bottin *m* mondain.

who've [huːv] = **who have**.

why [waɪ] ⋄ *adv* (*in direct questions*) pourquoi; ~ **did you lie to me?** pourquoi m'as-tu menti?; ~ **don't you all come?** pourquoi ne pas tous venir?, pourquoi est-ce que vous ne viendriez pas tous?; ~ **not?** pourquoi pas? ⋄ *conj* pourquoi; **I don't know** ~ **he said that** je ne sais pas pourquoi il a dit cela. ⋄ *pron*: **there are several reasons** ~ **he left** il est parti pour plusieurs raisons, les raisons pour lesquelles il est parti sont nombreuses; **I don't know the reason** ~ je ne sais pas pourquoi. ⋄ *excl* tiens!
◆ **why ever** *adv* pourquoi donc.

WI ⋄ *n abbr of* **Women's Institute**. ⋄ **-1.** *abbr of* **West Indies**. **-2.** *abbr of* **Wisconsin**.

wick [wɪk] *n* **-1.** [of candle, lighter] mèche *f*. **-2.** *phr*: **to get on sb's** ~ *Br inf* taper sur les nerfs de qqn.

wicked [ˈwɪkɪd] *adj* **-1.** [evil] mauvais(e). **-2.** [mischievous, devilish] malicieux(ieuse). **-3.** *inf* [very good] génial(e), super (*inv*).

wicker [ˈwɪkəʳ] *adj* en osier.

wickerwork [ˈwɪkəwɜːk] ⋄ *n* vannerie *f*. ⋄ *comp* en osier.

wicket [ˈwɪkɪt] *n* CRICKET **-1.** [stumps, dismissal] guichet *m*. **-2.** [pitch] terrain *m* entre les guichets.

wicket keeper *n* CRICKET gardien *m* de guichet.

wide [waɪd] ⋄ *adj* **-1.** [gen] large; **how** ~ **is the room?** quelle est la largeur de la pièce?; **to be six metres** ~ faire six mètres de large OR de largeur. **-2.** [gap, difference] grand(e). **-3.** [experience, knowledge, issue] vaste. **-4.** [eyes] écarquillé(e). **-5.** [off-target] qui passe à côté. ⋄ *adv* **-1.** [broadly] largement; **open** ~! ouvrez grand! **-2.** [off-target]:

the shot went ~ le coup est passé loin du but OR à côté.

wide-angle lens n PHOT objectif m grand angle.

wide-awake adj tout à fait réveillé(e).

wide boy n Br inf pej escroc m.

wide-eyed [-'aɪd] adj **-1.** [surprised, frightened] aux yeux écarquillés. **-2.** [innocent] aux yeux grands ouverts.

widely ['waɪdlɪ] adv **-1.** [smile, vary] largement. **-2.** [extensively] beaucoup; **to be ~ read** avoir beaucoup lu; **it is ~ believed that** ... beaucoup pensent que ..., nombreux sont ceux qui pensent que ...; **~ known** largement OR bien connu(e).

widen ['waɪdn] ◇ vt **-1.** [make broader] élargir. **-2.** [gap, difference] agrandir, élargir. ◇ vi **-1.** [become broader] s'élargir. **-2.** [gap, difference] s'agrandir, s'élargir. **-3.** [eyes] s'agrandir.

wide open adj grand ouvert (grande ouverte); **the ~ spaces** les grands espaces.

wide-ranging [-'reɪndʒɪŋ] adj varié(e); [consequences] de grande envergure.

widespread ['waɪdspred] adj très répandu(e).

widow ['wɪdəʊ] n veuve f.

widowed ['wɪdəʊd] adj veuf (veuve).

widower ['wɪdəʊəʳ] n veuf m.

width [wɪdθ] n largeur f; **in ~** de large.

widthways ['wɪdθweɪz] adv en largeur.

wield [wi:ld] vt **-1.** [weapon] manier. **-2.** [power] exercer.

wife [waɪf] (pl **wives**) n femme f, épouse f.

wig [wɪg] n perruque f.

wiggle ['wɪgl] inf ◇ n **-1.** [movement] tortillement m. **-2.** [wavy line] ondulation f. ◇ vt remuer. ◇ vi se tortiller.

wiggly ['wɪglɪ] (compar **-ier**, superl **-iest**) adj inf [line] ondulé(e).

wigwam ['wɪgwæm] n wigwam m.

wild [waɪld] ◇ adj **-1.** [animal, attack, scenery, flower] sauvage. **-2.** [weather, sea] déchaîné(e). **-3.** [laughter, hope, plan] fou (folle); **the crowd went ~** la foule s'est déchaînée; **to run ~** être déchaîné. **-4.** [eyes] de fou (de folle); [hair] en bataille. **-5.** [random - estimate] fantaisiste; **I made a ~ guess** j'ai dit ça au hasard. **-6.** inf [very enthusiastic]: **to be ~ about** être dingue de. ◇ n: **in the ~** dans la nature.

◆ **wilds** npl: **the ~s of** le fin fond de; **to live in the ~s** habiter en pleine nature.

wild card n COMPUT caractère m joker.

wildcat ['waɪldkæt] n [animal] chat m sauvage.

wildcat strike n grève f sauvage.

wildebeest ['wɪldɪbiːst] (pl inv OR **-s**) n gnou m.

wilderness ['wɪldənɪs] n étendue f sauvage; **to be in the ~** fig faire une traversée du désert.

wildfire ['waɪld,faɪəʳ] n: **to spread like ~** se répandre comme une traînée de poudre.

wild flower n fleur f sauvage.

wild-goose chase n inf: **it turned out to be a ~** ça s'est révélé être totalement inutile.

wildlife ['waɪldlaɪf] n (U) faune f et flore f.

wildly ['waɪldlɪ] adv **-1.** [enthusiastically, fanatically] frénétiquement. **-2.** [guess, suggest] au hasard; [shoot] dans tous les sens. **-3.** [very - different, impractical] tout à fait. **-4.** [menacingly] farouchement.

wild rice n riz m sauvage.

wild West n inf: **the ~** le Far West.

wiles [waɪlz] npl artifices mpl.

wilful Br, **willful** Am ['wɪlfʊl] adj **-1.** [determined] obstiné(e). **-2.** [deliberate] délibéré(e).

will[1] [wɪl] ◇ n **-1.** [mental] volonté f; **against one's ~** contre son gré; **at ~** à volonté. **-2.** [document] testament m. ◇ vt: **to ~ sthg to happen** prier de toutes ses forces pour que qqch se passe; **to ~ sb to do sthg** concentrer toute sa volonté sur qqn pour qu'il fasse qqch.

will[2] [wɪl] modal vb **-1.** (to express future tense): **I ~ see you next week** je te verrai la semaine prochaine; **when ~ you have finished it?** quand est-ce que vous l'aurez fini?; **I'll be arriving at six** j'arriverai à six heures; **~ you be here next week?** — yes I ~/no I won't est-ce que tu seras là la semaine prochaine? — oui/non. **-2.** [indicating willingness]: **~ you have some more tea?** voulez-vous encore du thé?; **I won't do it** je refuse de le faire, je ne veux pas le faire. **-3.** [in commands, requests]: **you ~ leave this house at once** tu vas quitter cette maison tout de suite; **close that window, ~ you?** ferme cette fenêtre, veux-tu?; **~ you be quiet!** veux-tu te taire!, tu vas te taire! **-4.** [indicating possibility, what usually happens]: **the hall ~ hold up to 1000 people** la salle peut abriter jusqu'à 1000 personnes; **this ~ stop any draughts** ceci supprimera tous les courants d'air; **pensions ~ be paid monthly** les pensions sont payées tous les mois. **-5.** [expressing an assumption]: **that'll be your father** cela doit être ton père. **-6.** [indicating irritation]: **well, if you ~ leave your toys everywhere** ... que veux-tu, si tu t'obstines à laisser traîner tes jouets partout ...; she ~ **keep phoning** me elle n'arrête pas de me téléphoner.

willful *Am* = **wilful**.

willing ['wɪlɪŋ] *adj* **-1.** [prepared]: **if you're ~ si vous voulez bien; to be ~ to do sthg** être disposé(e) OR prêt(e) à faire qqch. **-2.** [eager] enthousiaste.

willingly ['wɪlɪŋlɪ] *adv* volontiers.

willingness ['wɪlɪŋnɪs] *n* **-1.** [preparedness]: **~ to do sthg** bonne volonté *f* à faire qqch. **-2.** [keenness] enthousiasme *m*.

willow (tree) ['wɪləʊ-] *n* saule *m*.

willowy ['wɪləʊɪ] *adj* svelte.

willpower ['wɪl,paʊə] *n* volonté *f*.

willy ['wɪlɪ] (*pl* **-ies**) *n* Br inf zizi *m*.

willy-nilly [,wɪlɪ'nɪlɪ] *adv* **-1.** [at random] n'importe comment. **-2.** [wanting to or not] bon gré mal gré.

wilt [wɪlt] *vi* [plant] se faner; *fig* [person] dépérir.

Wilts [wɪlts] *abbr of* **Wiltshire**.

wily ['waɪlɪ] (*compar* **-ier**, *superl* **-iest**) *adj* rusé(e).

wimp [wɪmp] *n pej inf* mauviette *f*.

win [wɪn] (*pt & pp* **won**, *cont* **-ning**) ◇ *n* victoire *f*. ◇ *vt* **-1.** [game, prize, competition] gagner. **-2.** [support, approval] obtenir; [love, friendship] gagner. ◇ *vi* gagner; **you/I** *etc* **can't ~** il n'y a rien à faire.
◆ **win over, win round** *vt sep* convaincre, gagner à sa cause.

wince [wɪns] ◇ *vi*: **to ~ (at/with)** [with body] tressaillir (à/de); [with face] grimacer (à/de). ◇ *n* tressaillement *m*.

winch [wɪntʃ] ◇ *n* treuil *m*. ◇ *vt* hisser à l'aide d'un treuil.

Winchester disk ['wɪntʃestə-] *n* disque *m* (dur) Winchester.

wind[1] [wɪnd] ◇ *n* **-1.** METEOR vent *m*. **-2.** [breath] souffle *m*. **-3.** (*U*) [in stomach] gaz *mpl*; **to break ~** *euphemism* lâcher un vent. **-4.** [in orchestra]: **the ~** les instruments *mpl* à vent. **-5.** *phr*: **to get ~ of sthg** *inf* avoir vent de qqch. ◇ *vt* **-1.** [knock breath out of] couper le souffle à. **-2.** Br [baby] faire faire son rot à.

wind[2] [waɪnd] (*pt & pp* **wound**) ◇ *vt* **-1.** [string, thread] enrouler. **-2.** [clock] remonter. **-3.** *phr*: **to ~ its way** [river, road] serpenter. ◇ *vi* [river, road] serpenter.
◆ **wind back** *vt sep* [tape] rembobiner.
◆ **wind down** ◇ *vt sep* **-1.** [car window] baisser. **-2.** [business] cesser graduellement. ◇ *vi* **-1.** [clock] ralentir. **-2.** [relax] se détendre.
◆ **wind forward** *vt sep* [tape] embobiner.

◆ **wind up** ◇ *vt sep* **-1.** [finish - meeting] clôturer; [- business] liquider. **-2.** [clock, car window] remonter. **-3.** Br inf [deliberately annoy] faire marcher. **-4.** *inf* [end up]: **to ~ up doing sthg** finir par faire qqch. ◇ *vi inf* [end up] finir.

windbreak ['wɪndbreɪk] *n* pare-vent *m inv*.

windcheater Br ['wɪnd,tʃiːtə], **windbreaker** *Am* ['wɪnd,breɪkə] *n* coupe-vent *m inv*.

windchill ['wɪndtʃɪl] *n* abaissement *m* de la température dû au vent.

winded ['wɪndɪd] *adj* essoufflé(e).

windfall ['wɪndfɔːl] *n* **-1.** [fruit] fruit *m* que le vent a fait tomber. **-2.** [unexpected gift] aubaine *f*.

winding ['waɪndɪŋ] *adj* sinueux(euse).

wind instrument [wɪnd-] *n* instrument *m* à vent.

windmill ['wɪndmɪl] *n* moulin *m* à vent.

window ['wɪndəʊ] *n* **-1.** [gen & COMPUT] fenêtre *f*. **-2.** [pane of glass, in car] vitre *f*. **-3.** [of shop] vitrine *f*.

window box *n* jardinière *f*.

window cleaner *n* laveur *m*, -euse *f* de vitres.

window dressing *n* (*U*) **-1.** [in shop] étalage *m*. **-2.** *fig* [non-essentials] façade *f*.

window envelope *n* enveloppe *f* à fenêtre.

window frame *n* châssis *m* de fenêtre.

window ledge *n* rebord *m* de fenêtre.

window pane *n* vitre *f*.

window shade *n Am* store *m*.

window-shopping *n* lèche-vitrines *m*; **to go ~** (aller) faire du lèche-vitrines.

windowsill ['wɪndəʊsɪl] *n* [outside] rebord *m* de fenêtre; [inside] appui *m* de fenêtre.

windpipe ['wɪndpaɪp] *n* trachée *f*.

windscreen Br ['wɪndskriːn], **windshield** *Am* ['wɪndʃiːld] *n* pare-brise *m inv*.

windscreen washer *n* lave-glace *m*.

windscreen wiper *n* essuie-glace *m*.

windshield *Am* = **windscreen**.

windsock ['wɪndsɒk] *n* manche *f* à air.

windsurfer ['wɪnd,sɜːfə] *n* **-1.** [person] véliplanchiste *mf*. **-2.** [board] planche *f* à voile.

windsurfing ['wɪnd,sɜːfɪŋ] *n*: **to go ~** faire de la planche à voile.

windswept ['wɪndswept] *adj* **-1.** [scenery] balayé(e) par les vents. **-2.** [person] échevelé(e); [hair] ébouriffé(e).

wind tunnel [wɪnd-] *n* soufflerie *f*, tunnel *m* aérodynamique.

Windward Islands ['wɪndwəd-] *n*: **the ~** les îles *fpl* du Vent.

windy ['wɪndɪ] (*compar* **-ier**, *superl* **-iest**) *adj* venteux(euse); **it's ~** il fait du vent.

wine [waɪn] *n* vin *m*.

wine bar *n* Br bar *m* à vin.

wine bottle *n* bouteille *f* à vin.

wine box *n* Cubitainer® *m*.

wine cellar *n* cave *f* (à vin).

wineglass ['waɪnglɑːs] *n* verre *m* à vin.

wine list *n* carte *f* des vins.

wine merchant *n* Br marchand *m* de vins.

winepress ['waɪnpres] *n* pressoir *m*.

wine tasting [-,teɪstɪŋ] *n* dégustation *f* (de vins).

wine waiter *n* sommelier *m*.

wing [wɪŋ] *n* aile *f*.
◆ **wings** *npl* **-1.** THEATRE: **the ~s** les coulisses *fpl*. **-2.** [pilot's badge] galons *mpl*.

wing commander *n* Br lieutenant-colonel *m*.

winger ['wɪŋə'] *n* SPORT ailier *m*.

wing nut *n* vis *f* à ailettes.

wingspan ['wɪŋspæn] *n* envergure *f*.

wink [wɪŋk] ◇ *n* clin *m* d'œil; **to have forty ~s** *inf* faire un petit roupillon; **not to sleep a ~, not to get a ~ of sleep** *inf* ne pas fermer l'œil. ◇ *vi* **-1.** [with eyes]: **to ~ (at sb)** faire un clin d'œil (à qqn). **-2.** *literary* [lights] clignoter.

winkle ['wɪŋkl] *n* bigorneau *m*.
◆ **winkle out** *vt sep* extirper; **to ~ sthg out of sb** arracher qqch à qqn.

winner ['wɪnə'] *n* [person] gagnant *m*, -e *f*.

winning ['wɪnɪŋ] *adj* **-1.** [victorious, successful] gagnant(e). **-2.** [pleasing] charmeur(euse).
◆ **winnings** *npl* gains *mpl*.

winning post *n* poteau *m* d'arrivée.

Winnipeg ['wɪnɪ,peg] *n* Winnipeg.

winsome ['wɪnsəm] *adj literary* séduisant(e).

winter ['wɪntə'] ◇ *n* hiver *m*; **in ~** en hiver. ◇ *comp* d'hiver.

winter sports *npl* sports *mpl* d'hiver.

wintertime ['wɪntətaɪm] *n* (*U*) hiver *m*; **in ~** en hiver.

wint(e)ry ['wɪntrɪ] *adj* d'hiver.

wipe [waɪp] ◇ *n*: **to give sthg a ~** essuyer qqch, donner un coup de torchon à qqch. ◇ *vt* essuyer.
◆ **wipe away** *vt sep* [tears] essuyer.
◆ **wipe out** *vt sep* **-1.** [erase] effacer. **-2.** [eradicate] anéantir.
◆ **wipe up** *vt sep & vi* essuyer.

wiper ['waɪpə'] *n* [windscreen wiper] essuie-glace *m*.

wire ['waɪə'] ◇ *n* **-1.** (*U*) [metal] fil *m* de fer. **-2.** [cable etc] fil *m*. **-3.** [telegram] télégramme *m*. ◇ *comp* en fil de fer. ◇ *vt* **-1.** [fasten, connect]: **to ~ sthg to sthg** relier qqch à qqch avec du fil de fer. **-2.** [ELEC - plug] installer; [- house] faire l'installation électrique de. **-3.** [send telegram to] télégraphier à.

wire brush *n* brosse *f* métallique.

wire cutters *npl* cisaille *f*.

wireless ['waɪəlɪs] *n dated* T.S.F. *f*.

wire netting *n* (*U*) grillage *m*.

wire-tapping [-,tæpɪŋ] *n* (*U*) écoute *f* téléphonique.

wire wool *n* Br paille *f* de fer.

wiring ['waɪərɪŋ] *n* (*U*) installation *f* électrique.

wiry ['waɪərɪ] (*compar* **-ier**, *superl* **-iest**) *adj* **-1.** [hair] crépu(e). **-2.** [body, man] noueux(euse).

Wisconsin [wɪs'kɒnsɪn] *n* Wisconsin *m*; **in ~** dans le Wisconsin.

wisdom ['wɪzdəm] *n* sagesse *f*.

wisdom tooth *n* dent *f* de sagesse.

wise [waɪz] *adj* sage; **to get ~ to sthg** *inf* piger qqch; **to be no ~r, to be none the ~r** ne pas en savoir plus (pour autant), ne pas être plus avancé.
◆ **wise up** *vi* piger.

wisecrack ['waɪzkræk] *n pej* vanne *f*.

wish [wɪʃ] ◇ *n* **-1.** [desire] souhait *m*, désir *m*; **~ for sthg/to do sthg** désir de qqch/de faire qqch. **-2.** [magic request] vœu *m*. ◇ *vt* **-1.** [want]: **to ~ to do sthg** souhaiter faire qqch; **I ~ (that) he'd come** j'aimerais bien qu'il vienne; **I ~ I could** si seulement je pouvais. **-2.** [expressing hope]: **to ~ sb sthg** souhaiter qqch à qqn. ◇ *vi* [by magic]: **to ~ for sthg** souhaiter qqch.
◆ **wishes** *npl*: **best ~es** meilleurs vœux; **(with) best ~es** [at end of letter] bien amicalement.
◆ **wish on** *vt sep*: **to ~ sthg on sb** souhaiter qqch à qqn.

wishbone ['wɪʃbəʊn] *n* bréchet *m*.

wishful thinking ['wɪʃful-] *n*: **that's just ~** c'est prendre mes/ses *etc* désirs pour des réalités.

wishy-washy ['wɪʃɪ,wɒʃɪ] *adj inf pej* [person] sans personnalité; [ideas] vague.

wisp [wɪsp] *n* **-1.** [tuft] mèche *f*. **-2.** [small cloud] mince filet *m* OR volute *f*.

wispy ['wɪspɪ] (*compar* **-ier**, *superl* **-iest**) *adj* [hair] fin(e).

wistful ['wɪstfʊl] *adj* nostalgique.

wit [wɪt] *n* **-1.** [humour] esprit *m*. **-2.** [funny person] homme *m* d'esprit, femme *f* d'esprit. **-3.** [intelligence]: **to have the ~ to do sthg** avoir l'intelligence de faire qqch.
◆ **wits** *npl*: **to have** OR **keep one's ~s about one** être attentif(ive) OR sur ses gardes; **to be scared out of one's ~s** *inf* avoir une peur bleue; **to be at one's ~s' end** ne plus savoir que faire.

witch [wɪtʃ] *n* sorcière *f*.

witchcraft ['wɪtʃkrɑːft] *n* sorcellerie *f*.

witchdoctor ['wɪtʃ,dɒktəʳ] *n* sorcier *m*.

witch-hazel *n* hamamélis *m*.

witch-hunt *n pej* chasse *f* aux sorcières.

with [wɪð] *prep* **-1.** [in company of] avec; **I play tennis ~ his wife** je joue au tennis avec sa femme; **we stayed ~ them for a week** nous avons passé une semaine chez eux; **you can leave it ~ me** je m'en occupe, laissez-moi faire. **-2.** [indicating opposition] avec; **to argue ~ sb** disputer avec qqn; **the war ~ Germany** la guerre avec OR contre l'Allemagne. **-3.** [indicating means, manner, feelings] avec; **I washed it ~ detergent** je l'ai lavé avec un détergent; **the room was hung ~ balloons** la pièce était ornée de ballons; **"All right", she said ~ a smile** «Très bien», dit-elle en souriant OR avec un sourire; **she was trembling ~ fright** elle tremblait de peur; **~ care** avec soin. **-4.** [having] avec; **a man ~ a beard** un homme avec une barbe, un barbu; **the man ~ the moustache** l'homme à la moustache; **a city ~ many churches** une ville qui a de nombreuses églises; **the computer comes ~ a printer** l'ordinateur est vendu avec une imprimante. **-5.** [regarding]: **he's very mean ~ money** il est très près de ses sous, il est très avare; **what will you do ~ the house?** qu'est-ce que tu vas faire de la maison?; **the trouble ~ her is that** ... l'ennui avec elle OR ce qu'il y a avec elle c'est que .... **-6.** [indicating simultaneity]: **I can't do it ~ you watching me** je ne peux pas le faire quand OR pendant que tu me regardes. **-7.** [because of]: **~ the weather as it is, we've decided to stay at home** vu le temps qu'il fait OR étant donné le temps, nous avons décidé de rester à la maison; **~ my luck, I'll probably lose** avec ma chance habituelle, je suis sûr de perdre. **-8.** *phr*: **I'm ~ you** [I understand] je vous suis; [I'm on your side] je suis des vôtres; [I agree] je suis d'accord avec vous.

withdraw [wɪð'drɔː] (*pt* **-drew**, *pp* **-drawn**) ◇ *vt* **-1.** *fml* [remove]: **to ~ sthg (from)** enlever qqch (de). **-2.** [money, troops, remark] retirer. ◇ *vi* **-1.** *fml* [leave]: **to ~ (from)** se retirer (de). **-2.** MIL se replier; **to ~ from** évacuer; **to ~ to safety** se mettre à l'abri. **-3.** [quit, give up]: **to ~ (from)** se retirer (de).

withdrawal [wɪð'drɔːəl] *n* **-1.** [gen]: **~ (from)** retrait *m* (de). **-2.** MIL repli *m*. **-3.** MED manque *m*.

withdrawal symptoms *npl* crise *f* de manque.

withdrawn [wɪð'drɔːn] ◇ *pp* → **withdraw**. ◇ *adj* [shy, quiet] renfermé(e).

withdrew [wɪð'druː] *pt* → **withdraw**.

wither ['wɪðəʳ] ◇ *vt* flétrir. ◇ *vi* **-1.** [dry up] se flétrir. **-2.** [weaken] mourir.

withered ['wɪðəd] *adj* flétri(e).

withering ['wɪðərɪŋ] *adj* [look] foudroyant(e).

withhold [wɪð'həʊld] (*pt* & *pp* **-held**) *vt* [services] refuser; [information] cacher; [salary] retenir.

within [wɪ'ðɪn] ◇ *prep* **-1.** [inside] à l'intérieur de, dans; **~ her** en elle, à l'intérieur d'elle-même. **-2.** [budget, comprehension] dans les limites de; [limits] dans. **-3.** [less than - distance] à moins de; [- time] d'ici, en moins de; **~ the week** avant la fin de la semaine. ◇ *adv* à l'intérieur.

without [wɪð'aʊt] ◇ *prep* sans; **~ a coat** sans manteau; **I left ~ seeing him** je suis parti sans l'avoir vu; **I left ~ him seeing me** je suis parti sans qu'il m'ait vu; **to go ~ sthg** se passer de qqch. ◇ *adv*: **to go** OR **do ~** s'en passer.

withstand [wɪð'stænd] (*pt* & *pp* **-stood**) *vt* résister à.

witness ['wɪtnɪs] ◇ *n* **-1.** [gen] témoin *m*; **to be ~ to sthg** être témoin de qqch. **-2.** [testimony]: **to bear ~ to sthg** témoigner de qqch. ◇ *vt* **-1.** [accident, crime] être témoin de. **-2.** *fig* [changes, rise in birth rate] assister à. **-3.** [countersign] contresigner.

witness box *Br*, **witness stand** *Am n* barre *f* des témoins.

witter ['wɪtəʳ] *vi Br inf pej* radoter, parler pour ne rien dire.

witticism ['wɪtɪsɪzm] *n* mot *m* d'esprit.

witty ['wɪtɪ] (*compar* **-ier**, *superl* **-iest**) *adj* plein(e) d'esprit, spirituel(elle).

wives [waɪvz] *pl* → **wife**.

wizard ['wɪzəd] *n* magicien *m*; *fig* as *m*, champion *m*, -ionne *f*.

wizened ['wɪznd] *adj* ratatiné(e).

wk (*abbr of* **week**) sem.

Wm. (*abbr of* **William**) *Guillaume*.

WO *n abbr of* **warrant officer**.

wobble ['wɒbl] *vi* [hand, wings] trembler; [chair, table] branler.

wobbly ['wɒblɪ] (*compar* **-ier**, *superl* **-iest**) *adj inf* [jelly] tremblant(e); [table] branlant(e).

woe [wəʊ] *n literary* malheur *m*.

wok [wɒk] *n* wok *m*.

woke [wəʊk] *pt* → **wake**.

woken ['wəʊkn] *pp* → **wake**.

wolf [wʊlf] (*pl* **wolves**) *n* [animal] loup *m*.
◆ **wolf down** *vt sep inf* engloutir.

wolf whistle *n* sifflement *m* admiratif.

wolves ['wʊlvz] *pl* → **wolf**.

woman ['wʊmən] (*pl* **women**) ◇ *n* femme *f*. ◇ *comp*: ~ **doctor** femme *f* médecin; ~ **footballer** footballeuse *f*; ~ **taxi driver** femme *f* chauffeur de taxi; ~ **teacher** professeur *m* femme.

womanhood ['wʊmənhʊd] *n* (*U*) **-1.** [adult life]: **to reach** ~ devenir une femme. **-2.** [women] femmes *fpl*.

womanize, -ise ['wʊmənaɪz] *vi pej* courir les femmes.

womanly ['wʊmənlɪ] *adj* féminin(e).

womb [wuːm] *n* utérus *m*.

wombat ['wɒmbæt] *n* wombat *m*.

women ['wɪmɪn] *pl* → **woman**.

women's group *n* groupe *m* féministe.

Women's Institute *n Br*: **the** ~ l'association locale des femmes.

women's liberation *n* libération *f* de la femme.

won [wʌn] *pt & pp* → **win**.

wonder ['wʌndər] ◇ *n* **-1.** (*U*) [amazement] étonnement *m*. **-2.** [cause for surprise]: **it's a** ~ **(that)** ... c'est un miracle que ...; **it's no** OR **little** OR **small** ~ **(that)** ... il n'est pas étonnant que .... **-3.** [amazing thing, person] merveille *f*; **to work** OR **do** ~s faire des merveilles.
◇ *vt* **-1.** [speculate]: **to** ~ **(if** OR **whether)** se demander (si). **-2.** [in polite requests]: **I** ~ **whether you would mind shutting the window?** est-ce que cela ne vous ennuierait pas de fermer la fenêtre?
◇ *vi* **-1.** [speculate] se demander; **to** ~ **about sthg** s'interroger sur qqch. **-2.** *literary* [be amazed]: **to** ~ **at sthg** s'étonner de qqch.

wonderful ['wʌndəfʊl] *adj* merveilleux(euse).

wonderfully ['wʌndəfʊlɪ] *adv* **-1.** [very well] merveilleusement, à merveille. **-2.** [for emphasis] extrêmement.

wonderland ['wʌndəlænd] *n* pays *m* merveilleux.

wonky ['wɒŋkɪ] (*compar* **-ier**, *superl* **-iest**) *adj Br inf* bancal(e).

won't [wəʊnt] = **will not**.

wont [wəʊnt] ◇ *adj*: **to be** ~ **to do sthg** avoir l'habitude de faire qqch. ◇ *n dated or literary*: **as is one's** ~ comme à son habitude OR à l'accoutumée.

woo [wuː] *vt* **-1.** *literary* [court] courtiser. **-2.** [try to win over] chercher à rallier (à soi OR à sa cause).

wood [wʊd] ◇ *n* bois *m*; **touch** ~! touchons du bois!; **you can't see the** ~ **for the trees** *Br* ce sont les arbres qui cachent la forêt. ◇ *comp* en bois.
◆ **woods** *npl* bois *mpl*.

wooded ['wʊdɪd] *adj* boisé(e).

wooden ['wʊdn] *adj* **-1.** [of wood] en bois. **-2.** *pej* [actor] gauche.

wooden spoon *n* cuillère *f* de bois; **to win** OR **get the** ~ *Br fig* être classé dernier.

woodland ['wʊdlənd] *n* région *f* boisée.

woodpecker ['wʊd,pekər] *n* pivert *m*.

wood pigeon *n* ramier *m*.

woodshed ['wʊdʃed] *n* bûcher *m*.

woodwind ['wʊdwɪnd] *n*: **the** ~ les bois *mpl*.

woodwork ['wʊdwɜːk] *n* menuiserie *f*.

woodworm ['wʊdwɜːm] *n* ver *m* du bois; **to have** ~ être piqué par les vers.

woof [wʊf] ◇ *n* aboiement *m*. ◇ *excl* ouah!

wool [wʊl] *n* laine *f*; **to pull the** ~ **over sb's eyes** *inf* rouler qqn (dans la farine).

woollen *Br*, **woolen** *Am* ['wʊlən] *adj* en laine, de laine.
◆ **woollens** *npl* lainages *mpl*.

woolly ['wʊlɪ] (*compar* **-ier**, *superl* **-iest**, *pl* **-ies**) ◇ *adj* **-1.** [woollen] en laine, de laine. **-2.** *inf* [idea, thinking] confus(e). ◇ *n inf* lainage *m*.

woolly-headed [-'hedɪd] *adj inf pej* confus(e).

woozy ['wuːzɪ] (*compar* **-ier**, *superl* **-iest**) *adj inf* sonné(e).

Worcester sauce ['wʊstər-] *n* (*U*) sauce épicée à base de soja et de vinaigre.

Worcs (*abbr of* **Worcestershire**) ancien comté anglais.

word [wɜːd] ◇ *n* **-1.** LING mot *m*; **in your own** ~s dans vos mots à vous; **too stupid for** ~s vraiment trop bête; ~ **for** ~ [repeat, copy] mot pour mot; [translate] mot à mot; **in other** ~s en d'autres mots OR termes; **not in so many** ~s pas exactement; **in a** ~ en un mot; **by** ~ **of mouth** de bouche à oreille; **to put in a (good)** ~ **for sb** glisser un mot en faveur de qqn; **just say the** ~

vous n'avez qu'un mot à dire; **to have a ~ (with sb)** parler (à qqn); **to have ~s with sb** *inf* avoir des mots avec qqn; **to have the last ~** avoir le dernier mot; **she doesn't mince her ~s** elle ne mâche pas ses mots; **to weigh one's ~s** peser ses mots; **I couldn't get a ~ in edgeways** je n'ai pas réussi à placer un seul mot. **-2.** (*U*) [news] nouvelles *fpl*. **-3.** [promise] parole *f*; **to give sb one's ~** donner sa parole à qqn; **to be as good as one's ~, to be true to one's ~** tenir (sa) parole.
◇ *vt* [letter, reply] rédiger.

word game *n* jeu *m* avec les mots.

wording ['wɜːdɪŋ] *n* (*U*) termes *mpl*.

word-perfect *adj*: **he had his lines ~** il connaissait ses répliques au mot près.

wordplay ['wɜːdpleɪ] *n* (*U*) jeux *mpl* de mots.

word processing *n* (*U*) COMPUT traitement *m* de texte.

word processor *n* COMPUT machine *f* à traitement de texte.

wordwrap ['wɜːdræp] *n* COMPUT retour *m* à la ligne automatique.

wordy ['wɜːdɪ] (*compar* **-ier**, *superl* **-iest**) *adj pej* verbeux(euse).

wore [wɔːʳ] *pt* → **wear**.

work [wɜːk] ◇ *n* **-1.** (*U*) [employment] travail *m*, emploi *m*; **to be in ~** avoir un emploi; **out of ~** sans emploi, au chômage; **at ~** au travail. **-2.** [activity, tasks] travail *m*; **at ~** au travail; **to have one's ~ cut out doing sthg** OR **to do sthg** avoir du mal OR de la peine à faire qqch. **-3.** ART & LITERATURE œuvre *f*. *loc*: **he's a nasty piece of ~** *inf* c'est un salaud.
◇ *vt* **-1.** [person, staff] faire travailler. **-2.** [machine] faire marcher. **-3.** [wood, metal, land] travailler. **-4.** [cause to become]: **to ~ o.s. into a rage** se mettre en rage. **-5.** [make]: **to ~ one's way through a crowd** se frayer un chemin à travers une foule; **to ~ one's way along** avancer petit à petit; **he ~ed his way to the top** il est parvenu au sommet à la force du poignet.
◇ *vi* **-1.** [do a job] travailler; **to ~ on sthg** travailler à qqch. **-2.** [function, be successful] marcher. **-3.** [have effect]: **to ~ against sb** jouer contre qqn; **to ~ against sthg** aller à l'encontre de qqch. **-4.** [become]: **to ~ loose** se desserrer.
◆ **works** ◇ *n* [factory] usine *f*. ◇ *npl* **-1.** [mechanism] mécanisme *m*. **-2.** [digging, building] travaux *mpl*. **-3.** *inf* [everything]: **the ~s** tout le tralala.
◆ **work off** *vt sep* [anger etc] passer.

◆ **work on** *vt fus* **-1.** [pay attention to] travailler à. **-2.** [take as basis] se baser sur.

◆ **work out** ◇ *vt sep* **-1.** [plan, schedule] mettre au point. **-2.** [total, answer] trouver. ◇ *vi* **-1.** [figure, total]: **to ~ out at se** monter à. **-2.** [turn out] se dérouler. **-3.** [be successful] (bien) marcher. **-4.** [train, exercise] s'entraîner.

◆ **work up** ◇ *vt sep* **-1.** [excite]: **to ~ o.s. up into** se mettre dans. **-2.** [generate]: **to ~ up an appetite** s'ouvrir l'appétit; **to ~ up enthusiasm** s'enthousiasmer; **to ~ up courage** trouver du courage.

workable ['wɜːkəbl] *adj* [plan] réalisable; [system] fonctionnel(elle).

workaday ['wɜːkədeɪ] *adj pej* ordinaire, commun(e).

workaholic [,wɜːkə'hɒlɪk] *n* bourreau *m* de travail.

workbasket ['wɜːk,bɑːskɪt] *n* corbeille *f* à ouvrage.

workbench ['wɜːkbentʃ] *n* établi *m*.

workbook ['wɜːkbʊk] *n* cahier *m* d'exercices.

workday ['wɜːkdeɪ] *n* **-1.** [day's work] journée *f* de travail. **-2.** [not weekend] jour *m* ouvrable.

worked up [wɜːkt-] *adj* dans tous ses états.

worker ['wɜːkəʳ] *n* travailleur *m*, -euse *f*, ouvrier *m*, -ière *f*; **to be a hard/fast ~** travailler dur/vite; **to be a good ~** bien travailler.

workforce ['wɜːkfɔːs] *n* main *f* d'œuvre.

workhouse ['wɜːkhaʊs] *n* **-1.** *Br* [poorhouse] hospice *m*. **-2.** *Am* [prison] maison *f* de correction.

working ['wɜːkɪŋ] *adj* **-1.** [in operation] qui marche. **-2.** [having employment] qui travaille. **-3.** [conditions, clothes] de travail.
◆ **workings** *npl* [of system, machine] mécanisme *m*; **I'll never understand the ~s of his mind** *fig* je ne comprendrai jamais ce qui se passe dans sa tête.

working capital *n* (*U*) **-1.** [assets minus liabilities] fonds *mpl* de roulement. **-2.** [available money] capital *m* d'exploitation.

working class *n*: **the ~** la classe ouvrière.
◆ **working-class** *adj* ouvrier(ière).

working day *n* = **workday**.

working group *n* groupe *m* de travail.

working knowledge *n* connaissance *f* pratique.

working man *n* ouvrier *m*.

working model *n* modèle *m* opérationnel.

working order *n*: **in ~** en état de marche.

working party n groupe m de travail.

working week n semaine f de travail.

work-in-progress n travail m en cours.

workload ['wɜːkləʊd] n quantité f de travail.

workman ['wɜːkmən] (pl **-men** [-mən]) n ouvrier m.

workmanship ['wɜːkmənʃɪp] n (U) travail m.

workmate ['wɜːkmeɪt] n camarade mf OR collègue mf de travail.

work of art n lit & fig œuvre f d'art.

workout ['wɜːkaʊt] n séance f d'entraînement.

work permit [-,pɜːmɪt] n permis m de travail.

workplace ['wɜːkpleɪs] n lieu m de travail.

workroom ['wɜːkrʊm] n salle f de travail.

works council n comité m d'entreprise.

workshop ['wɜːkʃɒp] n atelier m.

workshy ['wɜːkʃaɪ] adj Br fainéant(e).

workstation ['wɜːk,steɪʃn] n COMPUT poste m de travail.

work surface n plan m de travail.

worktable ['wɜːk,teɪbl] n table f de travail.

worktop ['wɜːktɒp] n Br plan m de travail.

work-to-rule n Br grève f du zèle.

world [wɜːld] ◇ n **-1.** [gen] monde m; what/where in the ~ ...? que/où diable ...?; the ~ over dans le monde entier. **-2.** loc: to be dead to the ~ dormir profondément; to get the best of both ~s gagner sur tous les plans; to think the ~ of sb admirer qqn énormément, ne jurer que par qqn; to do sb the ~ of good faire un bien fou à qqn, faire énormément de bien à qqn; a ~ of difference une énorme différence.
◇ comp [power] mondial(e); [language] universel(elle); [tour] du monde.

World Bank n: the ~ la Banque mondiale.

world-class adj de niveau international.

World Cup ◇ n: the ~ la Coupe du monde. ◇ comp de Coupe du monde.

world-famous adj de renommée mondiale; to become ~ acquérir une renommée mondiale.

worldly ['wɜːldlɪ] adj de ce monde, matériel(ielle); ~ goods literary biens mpl.

world music n world music f.

world power n puissance f mondiale.

World Series n Am: the ~ le championnat américain de baseball.

World War I n la Première guerre mondiale.

World War II n la Deuxième guerre mondiale.

world-weary adj [person] las (lasse) du monde; [cynicism, sigh] blasé(e).

worldwide ['wɜːldwaɪd] ◇ adj mondial(e). ◇ adv dans le monde entier.

worm [wɜːm] ◇ n [animal] ver m. ◇ vt: to ~ one's way [move] avancer à plat ventre OR en rampant; to ~ one's way into sb's affections gagner insidieusement l'affection de qqn.
◆ **worms** npl [parasites] vers mpl.
◆ **worm out** vt sep: to ~ sthg out of sb soutirer qqch à qqn.

worn [wɔːn] ◇ pp → **wear.** ◇ adj **-1.** [threadbare] usé(e). **-2.** [tired] las (lasse).

worn-out adj **-1.** [old, threadbare] usé(e). **-2.** [tired] épuisé(e).

worried ['wʌrɪd] adj soucieux(ieuse), inquiet(iète); you really had me ~ vous m'avez fait faire bien du souci; to be ~ (about) se faire du souci (à propos de); to be ~ sick se faire un sang d'encre.

worrier ['wʌrɪəʳ] n anxieux m, -ieuse f.

worry ['wʌrɪ] (pl **-ies,** pt & pp **-ied**) ◇ n **-1.** [feeling] souci m. **-2.** [problem] souci m, ennui m. ◇ vt inquiéter, tracasser. ◇ vi: to ~ about se faire du souci au sujet de; not to ~! ne vous en faites pas!

worrying ['wʌrɪɪŋ] adj inquiétant(e).

worse [wɜːs] ◇ adj **-1.** [not as good] pire; to get ~ [situation] empirer. **-2.** [more ill]: he's ~ today il va plus mal aujourd'hui. ◇ adv plus mal; they're even ~ off c'est encore pire pour eux; ~ off [financially] plus pauvre. ◇ n pire m; for the ~ pour le pire; a change for the ~ une détérioration.

worsen ['wɜːsn] vt & vi empirer.

worsening ['wɜːsnɪŋ] adj qui va en empirant.

worship ['wɜːʃɪp] (Br pt & pp **-ped,** cont **-ping,** Am pt & pp **-ed,** cont **-ing**) ◇ vt adorer. ◇ n **-1.** (U) RELIG culte m. **-2.** [adoration] adoration f.
◆ **Worship** n: Your/Her/His Worship Votre/Son Honneur m.

worshipper Br, **worshiper** Am ['wɜːʃɪpəʳ] n **-1.** RELIG fidèle mf. **-2.** [admirer] adorateur m, -trice f.

worst [wɜːst] ◇ adj: the ~ le pire (la pire), le plus mauvais (la plus mauvaise); his ~ enemy son pire ennemi. ◇ adv le plus mal; the ~ affected area la zone la plus touchée. ◇ n: the ~ le pire; to get the ~ of it [in fight] avoir le dessous; if the ~ comes to the ~ au pire.
◆ **at (the) worst** adv au pire.

worsted ['wʊstɪd] *n* laine *f* peignée.

worth [wɜːθ] ◇ *prep* **-1.** [in value]: **to be ~ sthg** valoir qqch; **how much is it ~?** combien cela vaut-il? **-2.** [deserving of]: **it's ~ a visit** cela vaut une visite; **it's/she is ~** it cela/elle en vaut la peine; **to be ~ doing sthg** valoir la peine de faire qqch. ◇ *n* valeur *f*; **a week's/£20 ~ of groceries** pour une semaine/20 livres d'épicerie.

worthless ['wɜːθlɪs] *adj* **-1.** [object] sans valeur, qui ne vaut rien. **-2.** [person] qui n'est bon à rien.

worthwhile [,wɜːθ'waɪl] *adj* [job, visit] qui en vaut la peine; [charity] louable.

worthy ['wɜːðɪ] (*compar* **-ier**, *superl* **-iest**) *adj* **-1.** [deserving of respect] digne. **-2.** [deserving]: **to be ~ of sthg** mériter qqch. **-3.** *pej* [good but unexciting] méritant(e).

would [wʊd] *modal vb* **-1.** (*in reported speech*): **she said she ~ come** elle a dit qu'elle viendrait. **-2.** [indicating likelihood]: **what ~ you do?** que ferais-tu?; **what ~ you have done?** qu'aurais-tu fait?; **I ~ be most grateful** je vous en serais très reconnaissant. **-3.** [indicating willingness]: **she ~n't go** elle ne voulait pas y aller; **he ~ do anything for her** il ferait n'importe quoi pour elle. **-4.** (*in polite questions*): **~ you like a drink?** voulez-vous OR voudriez-vous à boire?; **~ you mind closing the window?** cela vous ennuierait de fermer la fenêtre? **-5.** [indicating inevitability]: **he ~ say that** j'étais sûr qu'il allait dire ça, ça ne m'étonne pas de lui. **-6.** [giving advice]: **I ~ report it if I were you** si j'étais vous je préviendrais les autorités. **-7.** [expressing opinions]: **I ~ prefer** je préférerais; **I ~ have thought (that)** ... j'aurais pensé que ....

would-be *adj* prétendu(e).

wouldn't ['wʊdnt] = would not.

would've ['wʊdəv] = would have.

wound¹ [wuːnd] ◇ *n* blessure *f*; **to lick one's ~s** *fig* panser ses plaies. ◇ *vt* blesser.

wound² [waʊnd] *pt & pp* → **wind²**.

wounded ['wuːndɪd] ◇ *adj* blessé(e). ◇ *npl*: **the ~** les blessés *mpl*.

wounding ['wuːndɪŋ] *adj* blessant(e).

wove [wəʊv] *pt* → **weave**.

woven ['wəʊvn] *pp* → **weave**.

wow [waʊ] *excl inf* oh là là!

WP ◇ *n* (*abbr of* **word processing, word processor**) TTX *m*. ◇ (*abbr of* **weather permitting**) *si le temps le permet*.

WPC (*abbr of* **woman police constable**) *n* *Br* femme *agent de police*; **~ Roberts** l'agent Roberts.

wpm (*abbr of* **words per minute**) mots/min.

WRAC [ræk] (*abbr of* **Women's Royal Army Corps**) *n* section féminine de l'armée de terre britannique.

WRAF [ræf] (*abbr of* **Women's Royal Air Force**) *n* section féminine de l'armée de l'air britannique.

wrangle ['ræŋgl] ◇ *n* dispute *f*. ◇ *vi*: **to ~ (with sb over sthg)** se disputer (avec qqn à propos de qqch).

wrap [ræp] (*pt & pp* **-ped**, *cont* **-ping**) ◇ *vt* **-1.** [cover in paper, cloth]: **to ~ sthg (in)** envelopper OR emballer qqch (dans); **to ~ sthg around** OR **round sthg** enrouler qqch autour de qqch. **-2.** [encircle]: **to ~ one's hands around** OR **round sthg** entourer qqch de ses mains; **to wrap one's fingers around** OR **round sthg** entourer qqch de ses doigts; **to ~ one's arms around** OR **round sb** enlacer qqn. ◇ *n* [garment] châle *m*.

◆ **wrap up** ◇ *vt sep* **-1.** [cover in paper or cloth] envelopper, emballer. **-2.** *inf* [complete] conclure, régler. ◇ *vi* [put warm clothes on]: **~ up well** OR **warmly!** couvrez-vous bien!

wrapped up [ræpt-] *adj inf*: **to be ~ in sthg** être absorbé(e) par qqch; **to be ~ in sb** ne penser qu'à qqn.

wrapper ['ræpəʳ] *n* papier *m*; *Br* [of book] jaquette *f*, couverture *f*.

wrapping ['ræpɪŋ] *n* emballage *m*.

wrapping paper *n* (*U*) papier *m* d'emballage.

wrath [rɒθ] *n* (*U*) *literary* courroux *m*.

wreak [riːk] *vt* [destruction, havoc] entraîner.

wreath [riːθ] *n* couronne *f*.

wreathe [riːð] *vt literary* couronner.

wreck [rek] ◇ *n* **-1.** [car, plane, ship] épave *f*. **-2.** *inf* [person] loque *f*; **I feel a ~** je me sens épuisé; **I look a ~** j'ai l'air d'une véritable loque. ◇ *vt* **-1.** [destroy] détruire. **-2.** NAUT provoquer le naufrage de; **to be ~ed** s'échouer. **-3.** [spoil - holiday] gâcher; [- health, hopes, plan] ruiner.

wreckage ['rekɪdʒ] *n* (*U*) débris *mpl*.

wrecker ['rekəʳ] *n Am* [vehicle] dépanneuse *f*.

wren [ren] *n* roitelet *m*.

wrench [rentʃ] ◇ *n* **-1.** [tool] clef *f* anglaise. **-2.** [injury] entorse *f*. **-3.** [emotional] déchirement *m*. ◇ *vt* **-1.** [pull violently] tirer violemment; **to ~ sthg off** arracher qqch. **-2.** [arm, leg, knee] se tordre.

wrest [rest] *vt literary*: **to ~ sthg from sb** arracher violemment qqch à qqn.

wrestle ['resl] ◇ *vt* lutter. ◇ *vi* **-1.** [fight]: **to ~ (with sb)** lutter (contre qqn). **-2.** *fig* [struggle]: **to ~ with sthg** se débattre OR lutter contre qqch.

wrestler ['reslə] *n* lutteur *m*, -euse *f*.

wrestling ['resliŋ] *n* lutte *f*.

wretch [retʃ] *n* pauvre diable *m*.

wretched ['retʃid] *adj* **-1.** [miserable] misérable. **-2.** *inf* [damned] fichu(e), maudit(e).

wriggle ['rɪgl] ◇ *vt* remuer, tortiller. ◇ *vi* remuer, se tortiller.

◆ **wriggle out of** *vt fus*: **to ~ out of sthg** se tirer de qqch; **to ~ out of doing sthg** éviter de faire qqch.

wring [rɪŋ] (*pt & pp* **wrung**) *vt* **-1.** [washing] essorer, tordre. **-2.** [hands, neck] tordre.

◆ **wring out** *vt sep* essorer, tordre.

wringing ['rɪŋɪŋ] *adj*: **~ (wet)** [person] trempé(e); [clothes] mouillé(e), à tordre.

wrinkle ['rɪŋkl] ◇ *n* **-1.** [on skin] ride *f*. **-2.** [in cloth] pli *m*. ◇ *vt* plisser. ◇ *vi* se plisser, faire des plis.

wrinkled ['rɪŋkld], **wrinkly** ['rɪŋklɪ] *adj* **-1.** [skin] ridé(e). **-2.** [cloth] froissé(e).

wrist [rɪst] *n* poignet *m*.

wristband ['rɪstbænd] *n* [of watch] bracelet *m*.

wristwatch ['rɪstwɒtʃ] *n* montre-bracelet *f*.

writ [rɪt] *n* acte *m* judiciaire.

write [raɪt] (*pt* **wrote**, *pp* **written**) ◇ *vt* **-1.** [gen & COMPUT] écrire; **to ~ sb a letter** écrire une lettre à qqn. **-2.** *Am* [person] écrire à. **-3.** [cheque, prescription] faire. ◇ *vi* [gen & COMPUT] écrire; **to ~ to sb** *Br* écrire à qqn.

◆ **write back** ◇ *vt sep*: **to ~ a letter back** répondre par une lettre. ◇ *vi* répondre.

◆ **write down** *vt sep* écrire, noter.

◆ **write in** *vi* écrire.

◆ **write into** *vt sep*: **to ~ a clause into a contract** insérer une clause dans un contrat.

◆ **write off** ◇ *vt sep* **-1.** [project] considérer comme fichu, abandonner pour non-viabilité. **-2.** [debt, investment] passer aux profits et pertes. **-3.** [person] considérer comme fini. **-4.** *Br inf* [vehicle] bousiller. ◇ *vi* écrire pour demander des renseignements; **to ~ off to sb** écrire à qqn; **to ~ off for sthg** écrire pour demander qqch.

◆ **write up** *vt sep* [notes] mettre au propre.

write-off *n* [vehicle]: **to be a ~** être complètement démoli(e).

write-protect *vt* COMPUT protéger en écriture.

writer ['raɪtə] *n* **-1.** [as profession] écrivain *m*. **-2.** [of letter, article, story] auteur *m*.

write-up *n inf* critique *f*.

writhe [raɪð] *vi* se tordre.

writing ['raɪtɪŋ] *n* (*U*) **-1.** [handwriting, activity] écriture *f*; **in ~** par écrit. **-2.** [something written] écrit *m*.

◆ **writings** *npl* écrits *mpl*.

writing case *n Br* nécessaire *m* de correspondance.

writing desk *n* secrétaire *m*.

writing paper *n* (*U*) papier *m* à lettres.

written ['rɪtn] ◇ *pp* → **write**. ◇ *adj* écrit(e).

WRNS (*abbr of* **Women's Royal Naval Service**) *n* section féminine de la marine de guerre britannique.

wrong [rɒŋ] ◇ *adj* **-1.** [not normal, not satisfactory] qui ne va pas; **is something ~?** y a-t-il quelque chose qui ne va pas?; **what's ~?** qu'est-ce qui ne va pas?; **there's something ~ with the switch** l'interrupteur ne marche pas bien. **-2.** [not suitable] qui ne convient pas. **-3.** [not correct - answer, decision, turning] mauvais(e); **to be ~** [person] avoir tort; **to be ~ to do sthg** avoir tort de faire qqch. **-4.** [morally bad]: **it's ~ to ....** c'est mal de ....

◇ *adv* [incorrectly] mal; **to get sthg ~** se tromper à propos de qqch; **to go ~** [make a mistake] se tromper, faire une erreur; [stop functioning] se détraquer; **don't get me ~** *inf* comprenez-moi bien.

◇ *n* mal *m*; **to be in the ~** être dans son tort.

◇ *vt* faire du tort à.

wrong-foot *Br vt* **-1.** SPORT prendre à contre-pied. **-2.** *fig* [surprise] prendre par surprise OR au dépourvu.

wrongful ['rɒŋful] *adj* [unfair] injuste; [arrest, dismissal] injustifié(e).

wrongly ['rɒŋlɪ] *adv* **-1.** [unsuitably] mal. **-2.** [mistakenly] à tort.

wrong number *n* faux numéro *m*.

wrote [rəut] *pt* → **write**.

wrought iron [rɔːt-] *n* fer *m* forgé.

wrung [rʌŋ] *pt & pp* → **wring**.

WRVS (*abbr of* **Women's Royal Voluntary Service**) *n* association de femmes au service des déshérités.

wry [raɪ] *adj* **-1.** [amused - smile, look] amusé(e); [- humour] ironique. **-2.** [displeased] désabusé(e).

wt. (*abbr of* **weight**) pds.

WV *abbr of* **West Virginia**.

WW *abbr of* **world war**.

WY *abbr of* **Wyoming**.

Wyoming [waɪ'əʊmɪŋ] *n* Wyoming *m*; **in** ~ dans le Wyoming.

WYSIWYG ['wɪzɪwɪg] (*abbr of* **what you see is what you get**) WYSIWYG, tel écran, tel écrit.

x (*pl* **x's** OR **xs**), **X** (*pl* **X's** OR **Xs**) [eks] *n* -**1.** [letter] x *m inv*, X *m inv*. -**2.** [unknown thing] x *m inv*. -**3.** [to mark place] **croix** *f*. -**4.** [at end of letter]: **XXX grosses bises**.

xenophobia [,zenə'fəʊbjə] *n* xénophobie *f*.

Xerox® ['zɪərɒks] ◇ *n* -**1.** [machine] photocopieuse *f*. -**2.** [copy] photocopie *f*. ◇ *vt* photocopier.

Xmas ['eksməs] ◇ *n* Noël *m*. ◇ *comp* de Noël.

X-ray ◇ *n* -**1.** [ray] rayon *m* X. -**2.** [picture] radiographie *f*, radio *f*. ◇ *vt* radiographier.

xylophone ['zaɪləfəʊn] *n* xylophone *m*.

y (*pl* **y's** OR **ys**), **Y** (*pl* **Y's** OR **Ys**) [waɪ] *n* -**1.** [letter] y *m inv*, Y *m inv*. -**2.** MATH y *m inv*.

yacht [jɒt] *n* yacht *m*.

yachting ['jɒtɪŋ] *n* yachting *m*.

yachtsman ['jɒtsmən] (*pl*. **-men** [-mən]) *n* yachtman *m*.

yachtswoman ['jɒts,wʊmən] (*pl* **-women** [-,wɪmɪn]) *n* yachtwoman *f*.

yahoo [jɑː'huː] *n* rustre *m*.

yak [jæk] *n* yack *m*.

Yale lock® [jeɪl-] *n* serrure *f* à barillet.

yam [jæm] *n* patate *f* douce.

Yangtze ['jæŋtsɪ] *n*: **the** ~ le Yang-tseu-kiang, le Yangzi Jiang *m*.

yank [jæŋk] *vt* tirer d'un coup sec.

Yank [jæŋk] *n Br inf* terme péjoratif désignant un Américain, Amerloque *mf*.

Yankee ['jæŋkɪ] *n* -**1.** *Br inf* [American] terme péjoratif désignant un Américain, Amerloque *mf*. -**2.** *Am* [citizen] Yankee *mf*.

yap [jæp] (*pt* & *pp* **-ped**, *cont* **-ping**) *vi* -**1.** [dog] japper. -**2.** *pej* [person] jacasser.

yard [jɑːd] *n* -**1.** [unit of measurement] = *91,44 cm*, yard *m*. -**2.** [walled area] cour *f*. -**3.** [area of work] chantier *m*. -**4.** *Am* [attached to house] jardin *m*.

yardstick ['jɑːdstɪk] *n* mesure *f*.

yarn [jɑːn] *n* -**1.** [thread] fil *m*. -**2.** *inf* [story] histoire *f*; **to spin sb a** ~ raconter une histoire à qqn.

yashmak ['jæʃmæk] *n* litham *m*.

yawn [jɔːn] ◇ *n* -**1.** [when tired] bâillement *m*; **to give a** ~ bâiller. -**2.** *Br inf* [boring event]: **it was a real** ~ c'était vraiment ennuyeux. ◇ *vi* -**1.** [when tired] bâiller. -**2.** [gape] s'ouvrir, béer.

yd *abbr of* **yard**.

yeah [jeə] *adv inf* ouais.

year [jɪəʳ] *n* -**1.** [calendar year] année *f*; **all (the)** ~ **round** toute l'année; ~ **in** ~ **out** année après année. -**2.** [period of 12 months] année *f*, an *m*; **to be 21** ~**s old** avoir 21 ans. -**3.** [financial year] année *f*; **the** ~ **1992-93** l'exercice 1992-93.
◆ **years** *npl* [long time] années *fpl*.

yearbook ['jɪəbʊk] *n* annuaire *m*, almanach *m*.

yearling ['jɪəlɪŋ] *n* yearling *m*.

yearly ['jɪəlɪ] ◇ *adj* annuel(elle). ◇ *adv* -**1.** [once a year] annuellement. -**2.** [every year] chaque année; **twice** ~ deux fois par an.

yearn [jɜːn] *vi*: **to** ~ **for sthg/to do sthg** aspirer à qqch/à faire qqch.

yearning ['jɜːnɪŋ] *n*: ~ **(for sb/sthg)** désir *m* ardent (pour qqn/de qqch).

yeast [jiːst] *n* levure *f*.

yell [jel] ◇ *n* hurlement *m*. ◇ *vi* & *vt* hurler.

yellow ['jeləʊ] ◇ *adj* -**1.** [colour] jaune. -**2.** [cowardly] lâche. ◇ *n* jaune *m*. ◇ *vi* jaunir.

yellow card *n* FTBL carton *m* jaune.

yellow fever *n* fièvre *f* jaune.

yellow lines *n* bandes *fpl* jaunes.

YELLOW LINES:
En Grande-Bretagne, une ligne jaune parallèle au trottoir signifie 'arrêt autorisé réglementé'; une double ligne jaune signifie 'stationnement interdit'

---

yellowness ['jeləʊnɪs] *n* (*U*) couleur *f* jaune.

Yellow Pages® *n*: the ~ les pages *fpl* jaunes.

Yellow River *n*: the ~ le fleuve Jaune.

Yellow Sea *n*: the ~ la mer Jaune.

yelp [jelp] ◇ *n* jappement *m*. ◇ *vi* japper.

Yemen ['jemən] *n* Yémen *m*; **in** ~ au Yémen.

Yemeni ['jemənɪ] ◇ *adj* yéménite. ◇ *n* Yéménite *mf*.

yen [jen] (*pl sense 1 inv*) *n* **-1.** [Japanese currency] yen *m*. **-2.** [longing]: **to have a** ~ **for sthg/to do sthg** avoir une forte envie de qqch/de faire qqch.

yeoman of the guard ['jəʊmən-] (*pl* yeomen of the guard) *n* hallebardier *m* de la garde royale.

yep [jep] *adv inf* ouais.

yes [jes] ◇ *adv* **-1.** [gen] oui; ~, **please** oui, s'il te/vous plaît. **-2.** [expressing disagreement] si. ◇ *n* oui *m inv*.

yes-man *n pej* béni-oui-oui *m inv*.

yesterday ['jestədɪ] ◇ *n* hier *m*; **the day before** ~ avant-hier. ◇ *adv* hier.

yet [jet] ◇ *adv* **-1.** [gen] encore; ~ **faster** encore plus vite; **not** ~ pas encore; ~ **again** encore une fois; **as** ~ jusqu'ici. **-2.** déjà; **have they finished** ~? est-ce qu'ils ont déjà fini? ◇ *conj* et cependant, mais.

yeti ['jetɪ] *n* yéti *m*.

yew [juː] *n* if *m*.

Y-fronts *npl Br* slip *m*.

YHA (*abbr of* Youth Hostels Association) *n* association britannique des auberges de jeunesse.

Yiddish ['jɪdɪʃ] ◇ *adj* yiddish (*inv*). ◇ *n* [language] yiddish *m*.

yield [jiːld] ◇ *n* rendement *m*. ◇ *vt* **-1.** [produce] produire. **-2.** [give up] céder. ◇ *vi* **-1.** [gen]: **to** ~ (**to**) céder (à). **-2.** *Am* AUT [give way]: "~" «cédez le passage».

yippee [*Br* jɪ'piː, *Am* 'jɪpɪ] *excl* hourra!

YMCA (*abbr of* Young Men's Christian Association) *n* union chrétienne de jeunes gens (*proposant notamment des services d'hébergement*).

yo [jəʊ] *excl inf* salut!

yob(bo) ['jɒb(əʊ)] *n Br inf* voyou *m*, loubard *m*.

yodel ['jəʊdl] (*Br pt* & *pp* **-led**, *cont* **-ling**, *Am pt* & *pp* **-ed**, *cont* **-ing**) *vi* iodler, jodler.

yoga ['jəʊgə] *n* yoga *m*.

yoghourt, yoghurt, yogurt [*Br* 'jɒgət, *Am* 'jəʊgərt] *n* yaourt *m*.

yoke [jəʊk] *n lit* & *fig* joug *m*.

yokel ['jəʊkl] *n pej* péquenaud *m*, -e *f*.

yolk [jəʊk] *n* jaune *m* (d'œuf).

yonder ['jɒndər] *adv literary* là-bas.

Yorks. [jɔːks] (*abbr of* Yorkshire) *comté anglais*.

Yorkshire pudding ['jɔːkʃər-] *n* yorkshire pudding *m*, *pâte à choux cuite qui accompagne le rosbif*.

Yorkshire terrier ['jɔːkʃər-] *n* Yorkshire-terrier *m*.

you [juː] *pers pron* **-1.** (*subject - sg*) tu (- *polite form, pl*) vous; ~'**re a good cook** tu es/vous êtes bonne cuisinière; **are** ~ **French?** tu es/vous êtes français?; ~ **French** vous autres Français; ~ **idiot!** espèce d'idiot!; **if I were** OR **was** ~ si j'étais toi/vous, à ta/votre place; **there** ~ **are** [you've appeared] te/vous voilà; [have this] voilà, tiens/tenez; **that jacket really isn't** ~ cette veste n'est pas vraiment ton/votre style. **-2.** (*object - unstressed, sg*) te; (- *polite form, pl*) vous; **I can see** ~ je te/vous vois; **I gave it to** ~ je te/vous l'ai donné. **-3.** (*object - stressed, sg*) toi (- *polite form, pl*) vous; **I don't expect** YOU **to do it** je n'exige pas que ce soit toi qui le fasses/vous qui le fassiez. **-4.** (*after prep, in comparisons etc, sg*) toi; (- *polite form, pl*) vous; **we shall go without** ~ nous irons sans toi/vous; **I'm shorter than** ~ je suis plus petit que toi/vous. **-5.** [anyone, one] on; ~ **have to be careful** on doit faire attention; **exercise is good for** ~ l'exercice est bon pour la santé.

you'd [juːd] = **you had**, **you would**.

you'll [juːl] = **you will**.

young [jʌŋ] ◇ *adj* jeune. ◇ *npl* **-1.** [young people]: **the** ~ les jeunes *mpl*. **-2.** [baby animals] les petits *mpl*.

younger ['jʌŋgər] *adj* plus jeune.

youngish ['jʌŋɪʃ] *adj* assez jeune.

young man *n* jeune homme *m*.

youngster ['jʌŋstər] *n* jeune *m*.

young woman *n* jeune femme *f*.

your [jɔːr] *poss* **-1.** (*referring to one person*) ton (ta), tes (*pl*); (*polite form, pl*) votre, vos (*pl*); ~ **dog** ton/votre chien; ~ **house** ta/votre maison; ~ **children** tes/vos enfants; **what's** ~ **name?** comment t'appelles-tu/vous appelez-vous?; **it wasn't** YOUR **fault** ce n'était pas de ta faute à toi/de votre faute à vous. **-2.** (*impersonal - one's*) son (sa), ses (*pl*); ~ **attitude changes as you get older** on change sa manière de voir en vieillissant; **it's good for** ~ **teeth/hair** c'est bon pour les dents/les cheveux; ~ **average Englishman** l'Anglais moyen.

you're [jɔːr] = you are.

yours [jɔːz] *poss pron (referring to one person)* le tien (la tienne), les tiens (les tiennes); (*pl*); (*polite form, pl*) le vôtre (la vôtre), les vôtres (*pl*); **that desk is** ~ ce bureau est à toi/à vous, ce bureau est le tien/le vôtre; **it wasn't her fault, it was** YOURS ce n'était pas de sa faute, c'était de ta faute à toi/de votre faute à vous; **a friend of** ~ un ami à toi/vous, un de tes/vos amis.
◆ **Yours** *adv* [in letter] → **faithfully, sincerely** *etc.*

yourself [jɔːˈself] (*pl* **-selves** [-ˈselvz]) *pron* **-1.** (*reflexive - sg*) te; (*- polite form, pl*) vous; (*after preposition - sg*) toi; (*- polite form, pl*) vous. **-2.** (*for emphasis - sg*) toi-même; (*- polite form*) vous-même; (*- pl*) vous-mêmes; **did you do it** ~? tu l'as/vous l'avez fait tout seul?

youth [juːθ] *n* **-1.** (*U*) [period, quality] jeunesse *f.* **-2.** [young man] jeune homme *m.* **-3.** (*U*) [young people] jeunesse *f,* jeunes *mpl.*

youth club *n* centre *m* de jeunes.

youthful [ˈjuːθful] *adj* **-1.** [eager, innocent] de jeunesse, juvénile. **-2.** [young] jeune.

youthfulness [ˈjuːθfulnɪs] *n* jeunesse *f.*

youth hostel *n* auberge *f* de jeunesse.

youth hostelling [-ˈhɒstəlɪŋ] *n Br*: **to go** ~ voyager en dormant dans des auberges de jeunesse.

you've [juːv] = you have.

yowl [jaul] ◇ *n* [of dog, person] hurlement *m*; [of cat] miaulement *m.* ◇ *vi* [dog, person] hurler; [cat] miauler.

yo-yo [ˈjəujəu] *n* yo-yo *m.*

yr *abbr of* **year.**

YTS (*abbr of* **Youth Training Scheme**) *n programme gouvernemental britannique d'insertion des jeunes dans la vie professionnelle.*

Yucatan [ˌjʌkəˈtɑːn] *n* Yucatan *m.*

yuck [jʌk] *excl inf* berk!

Yugoslav = Yugoslavian.

Yugoslavia [ˌjuːgəˈslɑːvjə] *n* Yougoslavie *f*; **in** ~ en Yougoslavie.

Yugoslavian [ˌjuːgəˈslɑːvɪən], **Yugoslav** [ˌjuːgəˈslɑːv] ◇ *adj* yougoslave. ◇ *n* Yougoslave *mf.*

yule log [juːl-] *n* **-1.** [piece of wood] bûche *f.* **-2.** [cake] bûche *f* de Noël.

yuletide [ˈjuːltaɪd] *n* (*U*) *literary* époque *f* de Noël.

yummy [ˈjʌmɪ] (*compar* **-ier,** *superl* **-iest**) *adj inf* délicieux(ieuse).

yuppie, yuppy [ˈjʌpɪ] (*pl* **-ies**) *n inf* yuppie *mf.*

YWCA (*abbr of* **Young Women's Christian Association**) *n union chrétienne de jeunes filles (proposant notamment des services d'hébergement).*

Z

z (*pl* **z's** OR **zs**), **Z** (*pl* **Z's** OR **Zs**) [*Br* zed, *Am* ziː] *n* [letter] z *m inv,* Z *m inv.*

Zagreb [ˈzɑːgreb] *n* Zagreb.

Zaïre [zɑːˈɪər] *n* Zaïre *m*; **in** ~ au Zaïre.

Zaïrese [zɑːˈɪəriːz] ◇ *adj* zaïrois(e). ◇ *n* Zaïrois *m,* -e *f.*

Zambesi, Zambezi [zæmˈbiːzɪ] *n*: **the** ~ le Zambèze.

Zambia [ˈzæmbɪə] *n* Zambie *f*; **in** ~ en Zambie.

Zambian [ˈzæmbɪən] ◇ *adj* zambien(ienne). ◇ *n* Zambien *m,* -ienne *f.*

zany [ˈzeɪnɪ] (*compar* **-ier,** *superl* **-iest**) *adj inf* dingue.

Zanzibar [ˌzænzɪˈbɑː] *n* Zanzibar *m.*

zap [zæp] (*pt* & *pp* **-ped,** *cont* **-ping**) *inf* ◇ *vt* [kill] descendre, tuer. ◇ *vi*: **to** ~ **(off)** somewhere foncer quelque part.

zeal [ziːl] *n* zèle *m.*

zealot [ˈzelət] *n fml* fanatique *mf.*

zealous [ˈzeləs] *adj* zélé(e).

zebra [*Br* ˈzebrə, *Am* ˈziːbrə] (*pl inv* OR **-s**) *n* zèbre *m.*

zebra crossing *n Br* passage *m* pour piétons.

zenith [*Br* ˈzenɪθ, *Am* ˈziːnəθ] *n lit* & *fig* zénith *m.*

zeppelin [ˈzepəlɪn] *n* zeppelin *m.*

zero [*Br* ˈzɪərəu, *Am* ˈziːrəu] (*pl inv* OR **-es**) ◇ *adj* zéro, aucun(e). ◇ *n* zéro *m.*
◆ **zero in on** *vt fus* **-1.** [subj: weapon] se diriger droit sur. **-2.** [subj: person] s'attaquer (d'entrée de jeu) à.

zero-rated [-ˌreɪtɪd] *adj Br* exempt(e) de TVA.

zest [zest] *n* (*U*) **-1.** [excitement] piquant *m.* **-2.** [eagerness] entrain *m.* **-3.** [of orange, lemon] zeste *m.*

zigzag [ˈzɪgzæg] (*pt* & *pp* **-ged,** *cont* **-ging**) ◇ *n* zigzag *m.* ◇ *vi* zigzaguer.

zilch [zɪltʃ] *n Am inf* zéro *m*, que dalle.

Zimbabwe [zɪm'bɑːbwɪ] *n* Zimbabwe *m*; **in ~** au Zimbabwe.

Zimbabwean [zɪm'bɑːbwɪən] ◇ *adj* zimbabwéen(enne). ◇ *n* Zimbabwéen *m*, -enne *f*.

Zimmer frame® ['zɪmər-] *n* déambulateur *m*.

zinc [zɪŋk] *n* zinc *m*.

Zionism ['zaɪənɪzm] *n* sionisme *m*.

Zionist ['zaɪənɪst] ◇ *adj* sioniste. ◇ *n* Sioniste *mf*.

zip [zɪp] (*pt* & *pp* **-ped**, *cont* **-ping**) *n Br* [fastener] fermeture *f* éclair®.

◆ **zip up** *vt sep* [jacket] remonter la fermeture éclair de; [bag] fermer la fermeture éclair de.

zip code *n Am* code *m* postal.

zip fastener *n Br* = **zip**.

zipper ['zɪpər] *n Am* = **zip**.

zit [zɪt] *n inf* bouton *m*.

zither ['zɪðər] *n* cithare *f*.

zodiac ['zəʊdɪæk] *n*: **the ~** le zodiaque; **sign of the ~** signe *m* du zodiaque.

zombie ['zɒmbɪ] *n fig* & *pej* zombi *m*.

zone [zəʊn] *n* zone *f*.

zoo [zuː] *n* zoo *m*.

zoological [,zəʊə'lɒdʒɪkl] *adj* zoologique.

zoologist [zəʊ'ɒlədʒɪst] *n* zoologiste *mf*.

zoology [zəʊ'ɒlədʒɪ] *n* zoologie *f*.

zoom [zuːm] ◇ *vi inf* **-1.** [move quickly] aller en trombe. **-2.** [rise rapidly] monter en flèche. ◇ *n* PHOT zoom *m*.

◆ **zoom in** *vi* CINEMA: **to ~ in (on)** faire un zoom (sur).

◆ **zoom off** *vi inf* partir en trombe.

zoom lens *n* zoom *m*.

zucchini [zuː'kiːnɪ] (*pl inv*) *n Am* courgette *f*.

Zulu ['zuːluː] ◇ *adj* zoulou(e). ◇ *n* **-1.** [person] Zoulou *m*, -e *f*. **-2.** [language] zoulou *m*.

Zürich ['zjʊərɪk] *n* Zurich.

CONJUGAISONS

Auxiliaires

[1] avoir

Indicatif présent

j'	**ai**
tu	**as**
il, elle	**a**
nous	av**ons**
vous	av**ez**
ils, elles	**ont**

Indicatif imparfait

j'	av**ais**
tu	av**ais**
il, elle	av**ait**
nous	av**ions**
vous	av**iez**
ils, elles	av**aient**

Indicatif futur

j'	au**rai**
tu	au**ras**
il, elle	au**ra**
nous	au**rons**
vous	au**rez**
ils, elles	au**ront**

Indicatif passé simple

j'	**eus**
tu	**eus**
il, elle	**eut**
nous	**eûmes**
vous	**eûtes**
ils, elles	**eurent**

Subjonctif présent

que j'	**aie**
que tu	**aies**
qu'il, elle	**ait**
que nous	**ayons**
que vous	**ayez**
qu'ils, elles	**aient**

Conditionnel présent

j'	au**rais**
tu	au**rais**
il, elle	au**rait**
nous	au**rions**
vous	au**riez**
ils, elles	au**raient**

Impératif

aie
ayons
ayez

Participe présent

ayant

Participe passé

eu, e

[2] être

Indicatif présent

je	**suis**
tu	**es**
il, elle	**est**
nous	**sommes**
vous	**êtes**
ils, elles	**sont**

Indicatif imparfait

j'	ét**ais**
tu	ét**ais**
il, elle	ét**ait**
nous	ét**ions**
vous	ét**iez**
ils, elles	ét**aient**

Indicatif futur

je	se**rai**
tu	se**ras**
il, elle	se**ra**
nous	sé**rons**
vous	se**rez**
ils, elles	se**ront**

Indicatif passé simple

je	**fus**
tu	**fus**
il, elle	**fut**
nous	**fûmes**
vous	**fûtes**
ils, elles	**furent**

Subjonctif présent

que je	**sois**
que tu	**sois**
qu'il, elle	**soit**
que nous	**soyons**
que vous	**soyez**
qu'ils, elles	**soient**

Conditionnel présent

je	se**rais**
tu	se**rais**
il, elle	se**rait**
nous	se**rions**
vous	se**riez**
ils, elles	se**raient**

Impératif

sois
soyons
soyez

Participe présent

étant

Participe passé

été

Verbes réguliers

[3] chanter   chant-

Indicatif présent
je	chant**e**
tu	chant**es**
il, elle	chant**e**
nous	chant**ons**
vous	chant**ez**
ils, elles	chant**ent**

Indicatif passé simple
je	chant**ai**
tu	chant**as**
il, elle	chant**a**
nous	chant**âmes**
vous	chant**âtes**
ils, elles	chant**èrent**

Impératif
chant**e**
chant**ons**
chant**ez**

Participe présent
chant**ant**

Indicatif imparfait
je	chant**ais**
tu	chant**ais**
il, elle	chant**ait**
nous	chant**ions**
vous	chant**iez**
ils, elles	chant**aient**

Subjonctif présent
que je	chant**e**
que tu	chant**es**
qu'il, elle	chant**e**
que nous	chant**ions**
que vous	chant**iez**
qu'ils, elles	chant**ent**

Participe passé
chant**é, e**

Indicatif futur
je	chant**erai**
tu	chant**eras**
il, elle	chant**era**
nous	chant**erons**
vous	chant**erez**
ils, elles	chant**eront**

Conditionnel présent
je	chant**erais**
tu	chant**erais**
il, elle	chant**erait**
nous	chant**erions**
vous	chant**eriez**
ils, elles	chant**eraient**

[32] finir   fin-

Indicatif présent
je	fin**is**
tu	fin**is**
il, elle	fin**it**
nous	fin**issons**
vous	fin**issez**
ils, elles	fin**issent**

Indicatif passé simple
je	fin**is**
tu	fin**is**
il, elle	fin**it**
nous	fin**îmes**
vous	fin**îtes**
ils, elles	fin**irent**

Impératif
fin**is**
fin**issons**
fin**issez**

Participe présent
fin**issant**

Indicatif imparfait
je	fin**issais**
tu	fin**issais**
il, elle	fin**issait**
nous	fin**issions**
vous	fin**issiez**
ils, elles	fin**issaient**

Subjonctif présent
que je	fin**isse**
que tu	fin**isses**
qu'il, elle	fin**isse**
que nous	fin**issions**
que vous	fin**issiez**
qu'ils, elles	fin**issent**

Participe passé
fin**i, e**

Indicatif futur
je	fin**irai**
tu	fin**iras**
il, elle	fin**ira**
nous	fin**irons**
vous	fin**irez**
ils, elles	fin**iront**

Conditionnel présent
je	fin**irais**
tu	fin**irais**
il, elle	fin**irait**
nous	fin**irions**
vous	fin**iriez**
ils, elles	fin**iraient**

Premier groupe : verbes en -er,

participe présent -ant,

terminaisons de l'indicatif présent **-e, -es, -e, -ons, -ez, -ent**

Pour les formes non indiquées, se reporter au verbe chanter (page précédente)

[4] **baisser** baiss-

Indicatif présent		Participe présent	Participe passé
je	baisse	baissant	baissé, e
nous	baissons		

[5] **pleurer** pleur-

Indicatif présent		Participe présent	Participe passé
je	pleure	pleurant	pleuré, e
nous	pleurons		

[6] **jouer** jou-

Indicatif présent		Participe présent	Participe passé
je	joue	jouant	joué, e
nous	jouons		

[7] **saluer** salu-

Indicatif présent		Participe présent	Participe passé
je	salue	saluant	salué, e
nous	saluons		

[8] **arguer** argu-, argu-ë

Indicatif présent		Indicatif futur		Participe présent
j'	argue	j'	arguerai	arguant
	ou arguë		ou arguërai	
nous	arguons			Participe passé
ils, elles	arguent			argué, e
	ou arguënt			

[9] **copier** copi-

Indicatif imparfait		Indicatif futur		Participe présent
nous	copiions	je	copierai	copiant
				Participe passé
				copié, e

• Le conditionnel a le même radical que le futur mais comporte les terminaisons de l'imparfait (**rais**, etc.)

[10] prier   pri-

Indicatif imparfait	**Indicatif futur**	**Participe présent**
nous pri**ions**	je pri**erai**	pri**ant**

Participe passé
pri**é, e**

[11] payer   pay-
                pay- / pai- (devant e)

Indicatif présent	**Indicatif futur**	**Participe présent**
je pai**e**	je pai**erai**	pay**ant**
ou pay**e**	ou pay**erai**	
nous pay**ons**		

Participe passé
pay**é, e**

Indicatif imparfait
je   pay**ais**
nous   pay**ions**

[13] ployer   ploy- / ploi- (devant e)

Indicatif présent	**Indicatif futur**	**Participe présent**
je ploi**e**	je ploi**erai**	ploy**ant**
nous ploy**ons**		

Participe passé
ploy**é, e**

Indicatif imparfait
je   ploy**ais**
nous   ploy**ions**

[14] essuyer   essuy- / essui- (devant e)

Indicatif présent	**Indicatif futur**	**Participe présent**
j' essui**e**	j' essui**erai**	essuy**ant**
nous essuy**ons**	nous essui**erons**	

Participe passé
essuy**é, e**

Indicatif imparfait
j'   essuy**ais**
nous   essuy**ions**

[15] créer   cré-

Indicatif présent	**Indicatif futur**	**Participe présent**
je cré**e**	je cré**erai**	cré**ant**
nous cré**ons**	nous cré**erons**	

Participe passé
cré**é**, cré**ée**

Indicatif imparfait
je   cré**ais**
nous   cré**ions**

• Le conditionnel a le même radical que le futur mais comporte les terminaisons de l'imparfait (r**ais**, etc.)

[16] avancer   avanc- / avanç- (devant a, o)

Indicatif présent		**Participe présent**
j'	avanc**e**	avanç**ant**
nous	avanç**ons**	

		Participe passé
Indicatif imparfait		avanc**é, e**
j'	avanç**ais**	
nous	avanc**ions**	

[17] manger   mang- / mange- (devant a, o)

Indicatif présent		**Participe présent**
je	mang**e**	mange**ant**
nous	mange**ons**	

		Participe passé
Indicatif imparfait		mang**é, e**
je	mange**ais**	
nous	mang**ions**	

[18] céder   céd- / cèd-

Indicatif présent		Indicatif passé simple		**Participe présent**
je	cèd**e**	je	céd**ai**	céd**ant**
nous	céd**ons**	nous	céd**âmes**	

				Participe passé
Indicatif futur				céd**é, e**
je	céd**erai**			
nous	céd**erons**			

[19] semer   sem- / sèm-

Indicatif présent		Indicatif futur		**Participe présent**
je	sèm**e**	je	sèm**erai**	sem**ant**
nous	sem**ons**	nous	sèm**erons**	

				Participe passé
Indicatif imparfait				sem**é, e**
je	sem**ais**			
nous	sem**ions**			

[20] rapiécer   rapiéc- / rapièc-
rapiéç- / rapièç- (devant a, o)

Indicatif présent		Indicatif futur		**Participe présent**
je	rapièc**e**	je	rapiéc**erai**	rapiéç**ant**
nous	rapiéç**ons**	nous	rapiéc**erons**	

				Participe passé
Indicatif imparfait		**Indicatif passé simple**		rapiéc**é, e**
je	rapiéç**ais**	je	rapiéç**ai**	
nous	rapiéc**ions**	nous	rapiéç**âmes**	

• Le conditionnel a le même radical que le futur mais comporte les terminaisons de l'imparfait (r**ais**, etc.)

[21] acquiescer acquiesc- /
acquiesç- (devant a, o)

Indicatif présent
j'   acquiesce
nous   acquiesçons

Participe présent
acquiesçant

Participe passé
acquiescé

[22] siéger siég- / sièg-
siége- / siège- (devant a, o)

Indicatif présent
je   siège
nous   siégeons

Indicatif passé simple
je   siégeai
nous   siégeâmes

Participe passé
siégé

Indicatif imparfait
je   siégeais
nous   siégions

Participe présent
siégeant

Indicatif futur
je   siégerai
nous   siégerons

[23] déneiger déneig- /
déneige- (devant a, o)

Indicatif présent
je   déneige
nous   déneigeons

Indicatif passé simple
je   déneigeai
nous   déneigeâmes

Participe passé
déneigé, e

Indicatif imparfait
je   déneigeais
nous   déneigions

Participe présent
déneigeant

Indicatif futur
je   déneigerai
nous   déneigerons

[24] appeler appel- / appell-

Indicatif présent
j'   appelle
nous   appelons

Indicatif passé simple
j'   appelai
ils, elles appelèrent

Participe passé
appelé, e

Indicatif imparfait
j'   appelais
nous   appelions

Participe présent
appelant

Indicatif futur
j'   appellerai
nous   appellerons

• Le conditionnel a le même radical que le futur mais comporte les terminaisons de l'imparfait (**rais**, etc.)

[25] peler   pel- / pèl- (devant e)

Indicatif présent		**Participe présent**	**Participe passé**
je	pèle	pelant	pelé, e
nous	pelons		

[26] interpeller   interpell-

Indicatif présent		**Participe présent**	**Participe passé**
j'	interpelle	interpellant	interpellé, e
nous	interpellons		

[27] jeter   jet- / jett- (devant e)

Indicatif présent		**Participe présent**	**Participe passé**
je	jette	jetant	jeté, e
nous	jetons		

[28] acheter   achet- / achèt-

Indicatif présent		**Participe présent**	**Participe passé**
j'	achète	achetant	acheté, e
nous	achetons		

[29] dépecer   dépec- / dépeç- (devant a, o) / dépèc- (devant e)

Indicatif présent		**Participe présent**	**Participe passé**
je	dépèce	dépeçant	dépecé, e
nous	dépeçons		

Indicatif imparfait
je	dépeçais
nous	dépecions

• Le conditionnel a le même radical que le futur mais comporte les terminaisons de l'imparfait (**rais**, etc.)

[30] envoyer   envoy- / envoi- (devant e) /
                 enver-

Indicatif présent		**Indicatif passé simple**		**Participe présent**
j'	envoie	j'	envoyai	envoyant
nous	envoyons	ils, elles	envoyèrent	

Participe passé
envoyé, **e**

Indicatif imparfait
j'   envoyais
nous   envoyions

Indicatif futur
j'   enverrai
nous   enverrons

[31] aller   all- / v- / i- / aill-

Indicatif présent		**Indicatif passé simple**		**Impératif**
je	vais	j'	allai	va
tu	vas	ils, elles	allèrent	allons
il, elle	va			allez
nous	allons	**Subjonctif présent**		
ils, elles	vont	que j'	aille	**Participe présent**
		qu'il, elle	aille	allant
Indicatif imparfait		que nous	allions	
j'	allais	qu'ils, elles	aillent	**Participe passé**
nous	allions			allé, **e**

Indicatif futur
j'   irai
ils, elles   iront

• Le conditionnel a le même radical que le futur mais comporte les terminaisons de l'imparfait (**rais**, etc.)

Deuxième groupe : verbes en -ir,
parcipe présent **-issant**

[32] finir

voir tableau des verbes réguliers p II

[33] haïr   ha-ï / ha-i

Indicatif présent
je   hais
tu   hais
il, elle   hait
nous   haïssons
ils, elles   haïssent

Indicatif imparfait
je   haïssais
ils, elles   haïssaient

Indicatif futur
je   haïrai
ils, elles   haïront

Indicatif passé simple
je   haïs
ils, elles   haïrent

Subjonctif présent
que je   haïsse
qu'ils, elles   haïssent

Participe présent
haïssant

Participe passé
haï, e

Troisième groupe :
parcipe présent **-ant**,
terminaisons de l'indicatif présent en **-e, -es, -e, -ons, -ez, -ent**
et en **-s, -s, -t, -ons, -ez, -ent**
a) verbes en -ir

[34] ouvrir   ouvr- / ouv-

Indicatif présent
j'   ouvre
il, elle   ouvre
nous   ouvrons
ils, elles   ouvrent

Indicatif imparfait
j'   ouvrais
nous   ouvrions

Indicatif futur
j'   ouvrirai
nous   ouvrirons

Indicatif passé simple
j'   ouvris
ils, elles   ouvrirent

Subjonctif présent
que j'   ouvre
qu'il, elle   ouvre
que nous   ouvrions
qu'ils, elles   ouvrent

Impératif
ouvre
ouvrons
ouvrez

Participe présent
ouvrant

Participe passé
ouvert, e

• Le conditionnel a le même radical que le futur mais comporte les terminaisons de l'imparfait (**rais**, etc.)

[35] fuir   fuy- / fui-

Indicatif présent

je	fuis
il, elle	fuit
nous	fuyons
ils, elles	fuient

Indicatif imparfait

je	fuyais
nous	fuyions

Indicatif futur

je	fuirai
ils, elles	fuiront

Indicatif passé simple

je	fuis
ils, elles	fuirent

Subjonctif présent

que je	fuie
qu'il, elle	fuie
que nous	fuyions
qu'ils, elles	fuient

Impératif

fuis
fuyons
fuyez

Participe présent
fuyant

Participe passé
fui, e

[36] endormir   endorm- / endor-

Indicatif présent

j'	endors
il, elle	endort
nous	endormons
ils, elles	endorment

Indicatif imparfait

j'	endormais
nous	endormions

Indicatif futur

j'	endormirai
ils, elles	endormiront

Indicatif passé simple

j'	endormis
ils, elles	endormirent

Subjonctif présent

que j'	endorme
qu'il, elle	endorme
que nous	endormions
qu'ils, elles	endorment

Impératif

endors
endormons
endormez

Participe présent
endormant

Participe passé
endormi, e

[37] démentir   dément- / démen-

Indicatif présent

je	démens
il, elle	dément
nous	démentons
ils, elles	démentent

Indicatif imparfait

je	démentais
nous	démentions

Indicatif futur

je	démentirai
ils, elles	démentiront

Indicatif passé simple

je	démentis
ils, elles	démentirent

Subjonctif présent

que je	démente
qu'il, elle	démente
que nous	démentions
qu'ils, elles	démentent

Impératif

démens
démentons
démentez

Participe présent
démentant

Participe passé
démenti, e

• Le conditionnel a le même radical que le futur mais comporte les terminaisons de l'imparfait (**rais**, etc.)

[38] servir   serv- / ser-

Indicatif présent

je	sers
il, elle	sert
nous	servons
ils, elles	servent

Indicatif imparfait

je	servais
nous	servions

Indicatif futur

je	servirai
nous	servirons

Indicatif passé simple

je	servis
il, elle	servit
nous	servîmes
ils, elles	servirent

Subjonctif présent

que je	serve
qu'il, elle	serve
que nous	servions
qu'ils, elles	servent

Impératif

sers
servons
servez

Participe présent
servant

Participe passé
servi, e

[39] acquérir   acquér- / acquer- / acquier- / acquièr- / acqu-

Indicatif présent

j'	acquiers
il, elle	acquiert
nous	acquérons
ils, elles	acquièrent

Indicatif imparfait

j'	acquérais
nous	acquérions

Indicatif futur

j'	acquerrai
nous	acquerrons

Indicatif passé simple

j'	acquis
il, elle	acquit
nous	acquîmes
ils, elles	acquirent

Subjonctif présent

que j'	acquière
qu'il, elle	acquière
que nous	acquérions
qu'ils, elles	acquièrent

Impératif

acquiers
acquérons
acquérez

Participe présent
acquérant

Participe passé
acquis, e

[40] venir   ven- / vien- / vienn- / viend- / vin-

Indicatif présent

je	viens
il, elle	vient
nous	venons
ils, elles	viennent

Indicatif imparfait

je	venais
nous	venions

Indicatif futur

je	viendrai
nous	viendrons

Indicatif passé simple

je	vins
il, elle	vint
nous	vînmes
ils, elles	vinrent

Subjonctif présent

que je	vienne
qu'il, elle	vienne
que nous	venions
qu'ils, elles	viennent

Impératif

viens
venons
venez

Participe présent
venant

Participe passé
venu, e

• Le conditionnel a le même radical que le futur mais comporte les terminaisons de l'imparfait (**rais**, etc.)

[41] cueillir   cueill-

Indicatif présent
je   cueill**e**
il, elle   cueill**e**
nous   cueill**ons**
ils, elles   cueill**ent**

Indicatif imparfait
je   cueill**ais**
nous   cueill**ions**

Indicatif futur
je   cueill**erai**
nous   cueill**erons**

Indicatif passé simple
je   cueill**is**
il, elle   cueill**it**
nous   cueill**îmes**
ils, elles   cueill**irent**

Subjonctif présent
que je   cueill**e**
qu'il, elle   cueill**e**
que nous   cueill**ions**
qu'ils, elles   cueill**ent**

Impératif
cueill**e**
cueill**ons**
cueill**ez**

Participe présent
cueill**ant**

Participe passé
cueill**i, e**

[42] mourir   mour- / meur- / mor-

Indicatif présent
je   meur**s**
il, elle   meur**t**
nous   mour**ons**
ils, elles   meur**ent**

Indicatif imparfait
je   mour**ais**
nous   mour**ions**

Indicatif futur
je   mour**rai**
nous   mour**rons**

Indicatif passé simple
je   mour**us**
il, elle   mour**ut**
nous   mour**ûmes**
ils, elles   mour**urent**

Subjonctif présent
que je   meur**e**
qu'il, elle   meur**e**
que nous   mour**ions**
qu'ils, elles   meur**ent**

Impératif
meur**s**
mour**ons**
mour**ez**

Participe présent
mour**ant**

Participe passé
mor**t, e**

[43] partir   part- / par-

Indicatif présent
je   par**s**
il, elle   par**t**
nous   part**ons**
ils, elles   part**ent**

Indicatif imparfait
je   part**ais**
nous   part**ions**

Indicatif futur
je   part**irai**
nous   part**irons**

Indicatif passé simple
je   part**is**
il, elle   part**it**
nous   part**îmes**
ils, elles   part**irent**

Subjonctif présent
que je   part**e**
qu'il, elle   part**e**
que nous   part**ions**
qu'ils, elles   part**ent**

Impératif
par**s**
part**ons**
part**ez**

Participe présent
part**ant**

Participe passé
part**i, e**

• Le conditionnel a le même radical que le futur mais comporte les terminaisons de l'imparfait (**rais**, etc.)

[44] revêtir   revêt-

Indicatif présent
je	revê**ts**
il, elle	revê**t**
nous	revê**tons**
ils, elles	revê**tent**

Indicatif imparfait
je	revê**tais**
nous	revê**tions**

Indicatif futur
je	revê**tirai**
nous	revê**tirons**

Indicatif passé simple
je	revê**tis**
il, elle	revê**tit**
nous	revê**tîmes**
ils, elles	revê**tirent**

Subjonctif présent
que je	revê**te**
qu'il, elle	revê**te**
que nous	revê**tions**
qu'ils, elles	revê**tent**

Impératif
revê**ts**
revê**tons**
revê**tez**

Participe présent
revê**tant**

Participe passé
revê**tu, e**

[45] courir   cour-

Indicatif présent
je	cour**s**
il, elle	cour**t**
nous	cour**ons**
ils, elles	cour**ent**

Indicatif imparfait
je	cour**ais**
nous	cour**ions**

Indicatif futur
je	cour**rai**
nous	cour**rons**

Indicatif passé simple
je	cour**us**
il, elle	cour**ut**
nous	cour**ûmes**
ils, elles	cour**urent**

Subjonctif présent
que je	cour**e**
qu'il, elle	cour**e**
que nous	cour**ions**
qu'ils, elles	cour**ent**

Impératif
cour**s**
cour**ons**
cour**ez**

Participe présent
cour**ant**

Participe passé
cour**u, e**

• Le conditionnel a le même radical que le futur mais comporte les terminaisons de l'imparfait (**rais**, etc.)

[46] faillir faill- / failliss- / fau- / faud-

Indicatif présent
je	faill**e**
	ou fau**x**
il, elle	faill**e**
	ou fau**t**
nous	faillss**ons**
	ou faill**ons**
ils, elles	faillss**ent**
	ou faill**ent**

Indicatif imparfait
je	faillss**ais**
	ou faill**ais**
nous	faillss**ions**
	ou faill**ions**

Indicatif futur
je	faill**irai**
	ou faud**rai**
nous	faill**irons**
	ou faud**rons**

Indicatif passé simple
je	faill**is**
il, elle	faill**it**
nous	faill**îmes**
ils, elles	faill**irent**

Subjonctif présent
que je	faillss**e**
	ou faill**e**
qu'il, elle	faillss**e**
	ou faill**e**
que nous	faillss**ions**
	ou faill**ions**
qu'ils, elles	faillss**ent**
	ou faill**ent**

Impératif
faill**is** ou fau**x**
faillss**ons** ou faill**ons**
faillss**ez** ou faill**ez**

Participe présent
faillss**ant** ou faill**ant**

Participe passé
faill**i**

[47] défaillir défaill-

Indicatif présent
je	défaill**e**
il, elle	défaill**e**
nous	défaill**ons**
ils, elles	défaill**ent**

Indicatif imparfait
| je | défaill**ais** |
| nous | défaill**ions** |

Indicatif futur
je	défaill**irai**
	ou défaill**erai**
nous	défaill**irons**
	ou défaill**erons**

Indicatif passé simple
je	défaill**is**
il, elle	défaill**it**
nous	défaill**îmes**
ils, elles	défaill**irent**

Subjonctif présent
que je	défaill**e**
qu'il, elle	défaill**e**
que nous	défaill**ions**
qu'ils, elles	défaill**ent**

Impératif
défaill**e**
défaill**ons**
défaill**ez**

Participe présent
défaill**ant**

Participe passé
défaill**i**

• Le conditionnel a le même radical que le futur mais comporte les terminaisons de l'imparfait (**rais**, etc.)

[48] bouillir bouill- / bou-

Indicatif présent		**Indicatif passé simple**		**Impératif**
je	bous	je	bouillis	bous
il, elle	bout	il, elle	bouillit	bouillons
nous	bouillons	nous	bouillîmes	bouillez
ils, elles	bouillent	ils, elles	bouillirent	

Participe présent
bouillant

Indicatif imparfait		**Subjonctif présent**	
je	bouillais	que je	bouille
nous	bouillions	qu'il, elle	bouille
		que nous	bouillions
		qu'ils, elles	bouillent

Participe passé
bouilli, e

Indicatif futur	
je	bouillirai
nous	bouillirons

[49] gésir gi- / gis-

Indicatif présent		**Participe présent**
je	gis	gisant
tu	gis	
il, elle	gît	
nous	gisons	
vous	gisez	
ils, elles	gisent	

Indicatif imparfait	
je	gisais
nous	gisions
ils, elles	gisaient

Remarque : Gésir est défectif aux autres temps et modes.

[50] saillir "faire saillie" saill-

Indicatif présent		**Indicatif passé simple**		**Impératif**
il, elle	saille	il, elle	saillit	inusité
ils, elles	saillent	ils, elles	saillirent	

Participe présent
saillant

Indicatif imparfait		**Subjonctif présent**	
il, elle	saillait	qu'il, elle	saille
ils, elles	saillaient	qu'ils, elles	saillent

Participe passé
sailli, e

Indicatif futur	
il, elle	saillera
ils, elles	sailleront

Remarque : Dans le sens de "s'accoupler", saillir se conjugue sur le modèle de finir et n'est guère usité qu'à l'infinitif et à la 3e personne du singulier ou du pluriel.

• Le conditionnel a le même radical que le futur mais comporte les terminaisons de l'imparfait (**rais**, etc.)

Troisième groupe :
b) verbes en -oir

[52] recevoir   recev- / reçoiv- / reçoi- / reç-

Indicatif présent
je	reçois
il, elle	reçoit
nous	recevons
ils, elles	reçoivent

Indicatif imparfait
je	recevais
nous	recevions

Indicatif futur
je	recevrai
nous	recevrons

Indicatif passé simple
je	reçus
il, elle	reçut
nous	reçûmes
ils, elles	reçurent

Subjonctif présent
que je	reçoive
qu'il, elle	reçoive
que nous	recevions
qu'ils, elles	reçoivent

Impératif
reçois
recevons
recevez

Participe présent
recevant

Participe passé
reçu, e

[53] devoir   dev- / doiv- / doi- / d-

Indicatif présent
je	dois
il, elle	doit
nous	devons
ils, elles	doivent

Indicatif imparfait
je	devais
nous	devions

Indicatif futur
je	devrai
nous	devrons

Indicatif passé simple
je	dus
il, elle	dut
nous	dûmes
ils, elles	durent

Subjonctif présent
que je	doive
qu'il, elle	doive
que nous	devions
qu'ils, elles	doivent

Impératif
dois
devons
devez

Participe présent
devant

Participe passé
dû, due
dus, dues

[54] mouvoir   mouv- / meuv- / meu- / m-

Indicatif présent
je	meus
il, elle	meut
nous	mouvons
ils, elles	meuvent

Indicatif imparfait
je	mouvais
nous	mouvions

Indicatif futur
je	mouvrai
nous	mouvrons

Indicatif passé simple
je	mus
il, elle	mut
nous	mûmes
ils, elles	murent

Subjonctif présent
que je	meuve
qu'il, elle	meuve
que nous	mouvions
qu'ils, elles	meuvent

Impératif
meus
mouvons
mouvez

Participe présent
mouvant

Participe passé
mû, mue
mus, mues

• Le conditionnel a le même radical que le futur mais comporte les terminaisons de l'imparfait (**rais**, etc.)

[55] **émouvoir**   émouv- / émeuv- / émeu- / ém-

Indicatif présent
j'   émeus
il, elle   émeut
nous   émouvons
ils, elles   émeuvent

Indicatif imparfait
j'   émouvais
nous   émouvions

Indicatif futur
j'   émouvrai
nous   émouvrons

Indicatif passé simple
j'   émus
il, elle   émut
nous   émûmes
ils, elles   émurent

Subjonctif présent
que j'   émeuve
qu'il, elle   émeuve
que nous   émouvions
qu'ils, elles émeuvent

Impératif
émeus
émouvons
émouvez

Participe présent
émouvant

Participe passé
ému, e

[56] **promouvoir**   promouv- / promeuv- / promeu- / prom-

Indicatif présent
je   promeus
il, elle   promeut
nous   promouvons
ils, elles   promeuvent

Indicatif imparfait
je   promouvais
nous   promouvions

Indicatif futur
je   promouvrai
nous   promouvrons

Indicatif passé simple
je   promus
il, elle   promut
nous   promûmes
ils, elles   promurent

Subjonctif présent
que je   promeuve
qu'il, elle   promeuve
que nous   promouvions
qu'ils, elles promeuvent

Impératif
promeus
promouvons
promouvez.

Participe présent
promouvant

Participe passé
promu, e

[57] **vouloir**   voul- / veul- / veu- / voud- / veuill-

Indicatif présent
je   veux
il, elle   veut
nous   voulons
ils, elles   veulent

Indicatif imparfait
je   voulais
nous   voulions

Indicatif futur
je   voudrai
nous   voudrons

Indicatif passé simple
je   voulus
il, elle   voulut
nous   voulûmes
ils, elles   voulurent

Subjonctif présent
que je   veuille
qu'il, elle   veuille
que nous   voulions
qu'ils, elles veuillent

Impératif
veux ou veuille
voulons ou veuillons
voulez ou veuillez

Participe présent
voulant

Participe passé
voulu, e

• Le conditionnel a le même radical que le futur mais comporte les terminaisons de l'imparfait (**rais**, etc.)

[58] **pouvoir**   pouv- / peuv- / peu- / pour- / pui- / puiss- / p-

Indicatif présent

je	peux
	ou puis
il, elle	peut
nous	pouvons
ils, elles	peuvent

Indicatif imparfait

| je | pouvais |
| nous | pouvions |

Indicatif futur

| je | pourrai |
| nous | pourrons |

Indicatif passé simple

je	pus
il, elle	put
nous	pûmes
ils, elles	purent

Subjonctif présent

que je	puisse
qu'il, elle	puisse
que nous	puissions
qu'ils, elles	puissent

Impératif
inusité

Participe présent
pouvant

Participe passé
pu

[59] **savoir**   sav- / sai- / sau- / sach- / s-

Indicatif présent

je	sais
il, elle	sait
nous	savons
ils, elles	savent

Indicatif imparfait

| je | savais |
| nous | savions |

Indicatif futur

| je | saurai |
| nous | saurons |

Indicatif passé simple

je	sus
il, elle	sut
nous	sûmes
ils, elles	surent

Subjonctif présent

que je	sache
qu'il, elle	sache
que nous	sachions
qu'ils, elles	sachent

Impératif
sache
sachons
sachez

Participe présent
sachant

Participe passé
su, e

[60] **valoir**   val- / vau- / vaud- / vaill-

Indicatif présent

je	vaux
il, elle	vaut
nous	valons
ils, elles	valent

Indicatif imparfait

| je | valais |
| nous | valions |

Indicatif futur

| je | vaudrai |
| nous | vaudrons |

Indicatif passé simple

je	valus
il, elle	valut
nous	valûmes
ils, elles	valurent

Subjonctif présent

que je	vaille
qu'il, elle	vaille
que nous	valions
qu'ils, elles	vaillent

Impératif
vaux
valons
valez

Participe présent
valant

Participe passé
valu, e

• Le conditionnel a le même radical que le futur mais comporte les terminaisons de l'imparfait (**rais**, etc.)

[61] **prévaloir** préval- / prévau- / prévaud-

Indicatif présent
je	prévau**x**
il, elle	prévau**t**
nous	préval**ons**
ils, elles	préval**ent**

Indicatif imparfait
je	préval**ais**
nous	préval**ions**

Indicatif futur
je	prévaud**rai**
nous	prévaud**rons**

Indicatif passé simple
je	préval**us**
il, elle	préval**ut**
nous	préval**ûmes**
ils, elles	préval**urent**

Subjonctif présent
que je	préval**e**
qu'il, elle	préval**e**
que nous	préval**ions**
qu'ils, elles	préval**ent**

Impératif
prévau**x**
préval**ons**
préval**ez**

Participe présent
préval**ant**

Participe passé
préval**u, e**

[62] **voir** voi- / voy- / ver- / v-

Indicatif présent
je	voi**s**
il, elle	voi**t**
nous	voy**ons**
ils, elles	voi**ent**

Indicatif imparfait
je	voy**ais**
nous	voy**ions**

Indicatif futur
je	ver**rai**
nous	ver**rons**

Indicatif passé simple
je	vi**s**
il, elle	vi**t**
nous	v**îmes**
ils, elles	vi**rent**

Subjonctif présent
que je	voi**e**
qu'il, elle	voi**e**
que nous	voy**ions**
qu'ils, elles	voi**ent**

Impératif
voi**s**
voy**ons**
voy**ez**

Participe présent
voy**ant**

Participe passé
v**u, e**

[63] **prévoir** prévoi- / prévoy- / prév-

Indicatif présent
je	prévoi**s**
il, elle	prévoi**t**
nous	prévoy**ons**
ils, elles	prévoi**ent**

Indicatif imparfait
je	prévoy**ais**
nous	prévoy**ions**

Indicatif futur
je	prévoi**rai**
nous	prévoi**rons**

Indicatif passé simple
je	prév**is**
il, elle	prév**it**
nous	prév**îmes**
ils, elles	prév**irent**

Subjonctif présent
que je	prévoi**e**
qu'il, elle	prévoi**e**
que nous	prévoy**ions**
qu'ils, elles	prévoi**ent**

Impératif
prévoi**s**
prévoy**ons**
prévoy**ez**

Participe présent
prévoy**ant**

Participe passé
prév**u, e**

• Le conditionnel a le même radical que le futur mais comporte les terminaisons de l'imparfait (**rais**, etc.)

[64] pourvoir   pourvoi- / pourvoy- / pourv-

Indicatif présent
je	pourvois
il, elle	pourvoit
nous	pourvoyons
ils, elles	pourvoient

Indicatif imparfait
| je | pourvoyais |
| nous | pourvoyions |

Indicatif futur
| je | pourvoirai |
| nous | pourvoirons |

Indicatif passé simple
je	pourvus
il, elle	pourvut
nous	pourvûmes
ils, elles	pourvurent

Subjonctif présent
que je	pourvoie
qu'il, elle	pourvoie
que nous	pourvoyions
qu'ils, elles	pourvoient

Impératif
pourvois
pourvoyons
pourvoyez

Participe présent
pourvoyant

Participe passé
pourvu, e

[65] asseoir   assie- / assié- / assey- / assoi- / assoy- / ass-

Indicatif présent
j'	assieds
	ou assois
il, elle	assied
	ou assoit
nous	asseyons
	ou assoyons
ils, elles	asseyent
	ou assoient

Indicatif imparfait
j'	asseyais
	ou assoyais
nous	asseyions
	ou assoyions

Indicatif futur
j'	assiérai
	ou assoirai
nous	assiérons
	ou assoirons

Indicatif passé simple
j'	assis
il, elle	assit
nous	assîmes
ils, elles	assirent

Subjonctif présent
que j'	asseye
	ou assoie
qu'il, elle	asseye
	ou assoie
que nous	asseyions
	ou assoyions
qu'ils, elles	asseyent
	ou assoient

Impératif
assieds ou assois
asseyons ou assoyons
asseyez ou assoyez

Participe présent
asseyant ou assoyant

Participe passé
assis, e

Remarque : L'usage tend à écrire avec -eoi- les formes avec -oi-, je m'asseois, il asseoira...

• Le conditionnel a le même radical que le futur mais comporte les terminaisons de l'imparfait (**rais**, etc.)

[66] surseoir   sursoi- / sursoy- / surseoi- / surs-

Indicatif présent

je	sursois
il, elle	sursoit
nous	sursoyons
ils, elles	sursoient

Indicatif imparfait

je	sursoyais
nous	sursoyions

Indicatif futur

je	surseoirai
nous	surseoirons

Indicatif passé simple

je	sursis
il, elle	sursit
nous	sursîmes
ils, elles	sursirent

Subjonctif présent

que je	sursoie
qu'il, elle	sursoie
que nous	sursoyions
qu'ils, elles	sursoient

Impératif

sursois
sursoyons
sursoyez

Participe présent

sursoyant

Participe passé

sursis, e

[67] seoir   sie- / sié- / sey-

Indicatif présent

il, elle	sied
ils, elles	siéent

Indicatif imparfait

il, elle	seyait
ils, elles	seyaient

Indicatif futur

il, elle	siéra
ils, elles	siéront

Subjonctif présent

qu'il, elle	siée
qu'ils, elles	siéent

Conditionnel présent

il, elle	siérait
ils, elles	siéraient

Participe présent

seyant

Participe passé

inusité

Remarque : Inusité aux autres temps et formes. Seoir a ici le sens de "convenir".

[68] pleuvoir   pleuv- / pleu- / pl-

Indicatif présent

il	pleut

Indicatif imparfait

il	pleuvait

Indicatif futur

il	pleuvra

Indicatif passé simple

il	plut

Subjonctif présent

qu'il	pleuve

Impératif

inusité

Participe présent

pleuvant

Participe passé

plu

Remarque : La 3e personne du pluriel est possible au figuré : les injures pleuvaient.

• Le conditionnel a le même radical que le futur mais comporte les terminaisons de l'imparfait (**rais**, etc.)

[69] falloir   fall- / fau- / faud- / faill-

Indicatif présent		**Indicatif passé simple**		**Impératif**
il	fau**t**	il	fall**ut**	inusité

Indicatif imparfait		**Subjonctif présent**		**Participe présent**
il	fall**ait**	qu'il	faill**e**	inusité

Indicatif futur			**Participe passé**
il	fau**dra**		fall**u**

[70] échoir   échoi- / échoy- / éch- / éché- / écher-

Indicatif présent		**Indicatif passé simple**		**Impératif**
il, elle	échoi**t**	il, elle	éch**ut**	inusité
ils, elles	échoi**ent**	ils, elles	éch**urent**	

Indicatif imparfait		**Subjonctif présent**		**Participe présent**
il, elle	échoy**ait**	qu'il, elle	échoi**e**	échéa**nt**
ils, elles	échoy**aient**	qu'ils, elles	échoi**ent**	

Indicatif futur			**Participe passé**
il, elle	échoi**ra**		éch**u, e**
	ou écher**ra**		
ils, elles	échoi**ront**		
	ou écher**ront**		

[71] déchoir   déchoi- / déchoy- / déch-

Indicatif présent		**Indicatif passé simple**		**Impératif**
je	déchoi**s**	je	déch**us**	inusité
il, elle	déchoi**t**	il, elle	déch**ut**	
nous	déchoy**ons**	nous	déch**ûmes**	**Participe présent**
ils, elles	déchoi**ent**	ils, elles	déch**urent**	inusité

Indicatif imparfait		**Subjonctif présent**		**Participe passé**
inusité		que je	déchoi**e**	déch**u, e**
		qu'il, elle	déchoi**e**	
Indicatif futur		que nous	déchoy**ions**	
je	déchoi**rai**	qu'ils, elles	déchoi**ent**	
nous	déchoi**rons**			

• Le conditionnel a le même radical que le futur mais comporte les terminaisons de l'imparfait (**rais**, etc.)

[72] choir   choi- / cher- / ch-

Indicatif présent		**Indicatif passé simple**		**Impératif**
je	chois	je	chus	inusité
tu	chois	il, elle	chut	
il, elle	choit	nous	chûmes	**Participe présent**
ils, elles	choient	ils, elles	churent	inusité

Indicatif imparfait	**Subjonctif présent**	**Participe passé**
inusité	inusité	chu, e

Indicatif futur

je	choirai
	ou cherrai
nous	choirons
	ou cherrons

Remarque : Choir se conjugue à tous les temps composés avec l'auxiliaire être.

Troisième groupe :
c) verbes en -re

[73] vendre   vend-

Indicatif présent		**Indicatif passé simple**		**Impératif**
je	vends	je	vendis	vends
il, elle	vend	il, elle	vendit	vendons
nous	vendons	nous	vendîmes	vendez
ils, elles	vendent	ils, elles	vendirent	

Indicatif imparfait		**Subjonctif présent**		**Participe présent**
				vendant
je	vendais	que je	vende	
nous	vendions	qu'il, elle	vende	
		que nous	vendions	**Participe passé**
Indicatif futur		qu'ils, elles	vendent	vendu, e
je	vendrai			
nous	vendrons			

• Le conditionnel a le même radical que le futur mais comporte les terminaisons de l'imparfait (**rais**, etc.)

[74] répandre répand-

Indicatif présent
je répands
il, elle répand
nous répandons
ils, elles répandent

Indicatif imparfait
je répandais
nous répandions

Indicatif futur
je répandrai
nous répandrons

Indicatif passé simple
je répandis
il, elle répandit
nous répandîmes
ils, elles répandirent

Subjonctif présent
que je répande
qu'il, elle répande
que nous répandions
qu'ils, elles répandent

Impératif
répands
répandons
répandez

Participe présent
répandant

Participe passé
répandu, e

[75] répondre répond-

Indicatif présent
je réponds
il, elle répond
nous répondons
ils, elles répondent

Indicatif imparfait
je répondais
nous répondions

Indicatif futur
je répondrai
nous répondrons

Indicatif passé simple
je répondis
il, elle répondit
nous répondîmes
ils, elles répondirent

Subjonctif présent
que je réponde
qu'il, elle réponde
que nous répondions
qu'ils, elles répondent

Impératif
réponds
répondons
répondez

Participe présent
répondant

Participe passé
répondu, e

[76] mordre mord-

Indicatif présent
je mords
il, elle mord
nous mordons
ils, elles mordent

Indicatif imparfait
je mordais
nous mordions

Indicatif futur
je mordrai
nous mordrons

Indicatif passé simple
je mordis
il, elle mordit
nous mordîmes
ils, elles mordirent

Subjonctif présent
que je morde
qu'il, elle morde
que nous mordions
qu'ils, elles mordent

Impératif
mords
mordons
mordez

Participe présent
mordant

Participe passé
mordu, e

• Le conditionnel a le même radical que le futur mais comporte les terminaisons de l'imparfait (**rais**, etc.)

[77] perdre   perd-

Indicatif présent
je	perd**s**
il, elle	perd
nous	perd**ons**
ils, elles	perd**ent**

Indicatif imparfait
| je | perd**ais** |
| nous | perd**ions** |

Indicatif futur
| je | perd**rai** |
| nous | perd**rons** |

Indicatif passé simple
je	perd**is**
il, elle	perd**it**
nous	perd**îmes**
ils, elles	perd**irent**

Subjonctif présent
que je	perd**e**
qu'il, elle	perd**e**
que nous	perd**ions**
qu'ils, elles	perd**ent**

Impératif
perd**s**
perd**ons**
perd**ez**

Participe présent
perd**ant**

Participe passé
perd**u, e**

[78] rompre   romp-

Indicatif présent
je	romp**s**
il, elle	romp**t**
nous	romp**ons**
ils, elles	romp**ent**

Indicatif imparfait
| je | romp**ais** |
| nous | romp**ions** |

Indicatif futur
| je | romp**rai** |
| nous | romp**rons** |

Indicatif passé simple
je	romp**is**
il, elle	romp**it**
nous	romp**îmes**
ils, elles	romp**irent**

Subjonctif présent
que je	romp**e**
qu'il, elle	romp**e**
que nous	romp**ions**
qu'ils, elles	romp**ent**

Impératif
romp**s**
romp**ons**
romp**ez**

Participe présent
romp**ant**

Participe passé
romp**u, e**

[79] prendre   prend- / pren- / prenn- / pr-

Indicatif présent
je	prend**s**
il, elle	prend
nous	pren**ons**
ils, elles	prenn**ent**

Indicatif imparfait
| je | pren**ais** |
| nous | pren**ions** |

Indicatif futur
| je | prend**rai** |
| nous | prend**rons** |

Indicatif passé simple
je	pr**is**
il, elle	pr**it**
nous	pr**îmes**
ils, elles	pr**irent**

Subjonctif présent
que je	prenn**e**
qu'il, elle	prenn**e**
que nous	pren**ions**
qu'ils, elles	prenn**ent**

Impératif
prend**s**
pren**ons**
pren**ez**

Participe présent
pren**ant**

Participe passé
pr**is, e**

• Le conditionnel a le même radical que le futur mais comporte les terminaisons de l'imparfait (**rais**, etc.)

[80] **craindre**   craind- / crain- / craign-

Indicatif présent

je	crain**s**
il, elle	crain**t**
nous	craign**ons**
ils, elles	craign**ent**

Indicatif imparfait

| je | craign**ais** |
| nous | craign**ions** |

Indicatif futur

| je | craind**rai** |
| nous | craind**rons** |

Indicatif passé simple

je	craign**is**
il, elle	craign**it**
nous	craign**îmes**
ils, elles	craign**irent**

Subjonctif présent

que je	craign**e**
qu'il, elle	craign**e**
que nous	craign**ions**
qu'ils, elles	craign**ent**

Impératif

crain**s**
craign**ons**
craign**ez**

Participe présent

craign**ant**

Participe passé

crain**t, e**

[81] **peindre**   peind- / pein- / peign-

Indicatif présent

je	pein**s**
il, elle	pein**t**
nous	peign**ons**
ils, elles	peign**ent**

Indicatif imparfait

| je | peign**ais** |
| nous | peign**ions** |

Indicatif futur

| je | peind**rai** |
| nous | peind**rons** |

Indicatif passé simple

je	peign**is**
il, elle	peign**it**
nous	peign**îmes**
ils, elles	peign**irent**

Subjonctif présent

que je	peign**e**
qu'il, elle	peign**e**
que nous	peign**ions**
qu'ils, elles	peign**ent**

Impératif

pein**s**
peign**ons**
peign**ez**

Participe présent

peign**ant**

Participe passé

pein**t, e**

[82] **joindre**   joind- / join- / joign-

Indicatif présent

je	join**s**
il, elle	join**t**
nous	joign**ons**
ils, elles	joign**ent**

Indicatif imparfait

| je | joign**ais** |
| nous | joign**ions** |

Indicatif futur

| je | joind**rai** |
| nous | joind**rons** |

Indicatif passé simple

je	joign**is**
il, elle	joign**it**
nous	joign**îmes**
ils, elles	joign**irent**

Subjonctif présent

que je	joign**e**
qu'il, elle	joign**e**
que nous	joign**ions**
qu'ils, elles	joign**ent**

Impératif

join**s**
joign**ons**
joign**ez**

Participe présent

joign**ant**

Participe passé

join**t, e**

• Le conditionnel a le même radical que le futur mais comporte les terminaisons de l'imparfait (**rais**, etc.)

[83] **battre** batt- / bat-

Indicatif présent		Indicatif passé simple		Impératif	
je	bat**s**	je	batt**is**	bat**s**	
il, elle	bat	il, elle	batt**it**	batt**ons**	
nous	batt**ons**	nous	batt**îmes**	batt**ez**	
ils, elles	batt**ent**	ils, elles	batt**irent**		

Participe présent
batt**ant**

Indicatif imparfait		Subjonctif présent	
je	batt**ais**	que je	batt**e**
nous	batt**ions**	qu'il, elle	batt**e**
		que nous	batt**ions**

Participe passé
batt**u, e**

Indicatif futur
que nous batt**ions**
qu'ils, elles batt**ent**

Indicatif futur	
je	batt**rai**
nous	batt**rons**

[84] **mettre** mett- / met- / m-

Indicatif présent		Indicatif passé simple		Impératif	
je	met**s**	je	m**is**	met**s**	
il, elle	met	il, elle	m**it**	mett**ons**	
nous	mett**ons**	nous	m**îmes**	mett**ez**	
ils, elles	mett**ent**	ils, elles	m**irent**		

Participe présent
mett**ant**

Indicatif imparfait		Subjonctif présent	
je	mett**ais**	que je	mett**e**
nous	mett**ions**	qu'il, elle	mett**e**
		que nous	mett**ions**
		qu'ils, elles	mett**ent**

Participe passé
m**is, e**

Indicatif futur	
je	mett**rai**
nous	mett**rons**

[85] **moudre** moud- / moul-

Indicatif présent		Indicatif passé simple		Impératif	
je	moud**s**	je	moul**us**	moud**s**	
il, elle	moud	il, elle	moul**ut**	moul**ons**	
nous	moul**ons**	nous	moul**ûmes**	moul**ez**	
ils, elles	moul**ent**	ils, elles	moul**urent**		

Participe présent
moul**ant**

Indicatif imparfait		Subjonctif présent	
je	moul**ais**	que je	moul**e**
nous	moul**ions**	qu'il, elle	moul**e**
		que nous	moul**ions**
		qu'ils, elles	moul**ent**

Participe passé
moul**u, e**

Indicatif futur	
je	moud**rai**
nous	moud**rons**

• Le conditionnel a le même radical que le futur mais comporte les terminaisons de l'imparfait (**rais**, etc.)

[86] coudre   coud- / cous-

Indicatif présent
je	couds
il, elle	coud
nous	cousons
ils, elles	cousent

Indicatif imparfait
je	cousais
nous	cousions

Indicatif futur
je	coudrai
nous	coudrons

Indicatif passé simple
je	cousis
il, elle	cousit
nous	cousîmes
ils, elles	cousirent

Subjonctif présent
que je	couse
qu'il, elle	couse
que nous	cousions
qu'ils, elles	cousent

Impératif
couds
cousons
cousez

Participe présent
cousant

Participe passé
cousu, e

[87] absoudre   absoud- / absou- / absolv- / absol-

Indicatif présent
j'	absous
il, elle	absout
nous	absolvons
ils, elles	absolvent

Indicatif imparfait
j'	absolvais
nous	absolvions

Indicatif futur
j'	absoudrai
nous	absoudrons

Indicatif passé simple
j'	absolus
il, elle	absolut
nous	absolûmes
ils, elles	absolurent

Subjonctif présent
que j'	absolve
qu'il, elle	absolve
que nous	absolvions
qu'ils, elles	absolvent

Impératif
absous
absolvons
absolvez

Participe présent
absolvant

Participe passé
absout, e

[88] résoudre   résoud- / résou- / résolv- / résol-

Indicatif présent
je	résous
il, elle	résout
nous	résolvons
ils, elles	résolvent

Indicatif imparfait
je	résolvais
nous	résolvions

Indicatif futur
je	résoudrai
nous	résoudrons

Indicatif passé simple
je	résolus
il, elle	résolut
nous	résolûmes
ils, elles	résolurent

Subjonctif présent
que je	résolve
qu'il, elle	résolve
que nous	résolvions
qu'ils, elles	résolvent

Impératif
résous
résolvons
résolvez

Participe présent
résolvant

Participe passé
résolu, e

• Le conditionnel a le même radical que le futur mais comporte les terminaisons de l'imparfait (**rais**, etc.)

[89] suivre   suiv- / sui-

Indicatif présent

je	suis
il, elle	suit
nous	suivons
ils, elles	suivent

Indicatif imparfait

je	suivais
nous	suivions

Indicatif futur

je	suivrai
nous	suivrons

Indicatif passé simple

je	suivis
il, elle	suivit
nous	suivîmes
ils, elles	suivirent

Subjonctif présent

que je	suive
qu'il, elle	suive
que nous	suivions
qu'ils, elles	suivent

Impératif

suis
suivons
suivez

Participe présent

suivant

Participe passé

suivi, e

[90] vivre   viv- / vi- / véc-

Indicatif présent

je	vis
il, elle	vit
nous	vivons
ils, elles	vivent

Indicatif imparfait

je	vivais
nous	vivions

Indicatif futur

je	vivrai
nous	vivrons

Indicatif passé simple

je	vécus
il, elle	vécut
nous	vécûmes
ils, elles	vécurent

Subjonctif présent

que je	vive
qu'il, elle	vive
que nous	vivions
qu'ils, elles	vivent

Impératif

vis
vivons
vivez

Participe présent

vivant

Participe passé

vécu, e

[91] paraître   paraît- / paraiss- / parai- / par- (-î- devant t)

Indicatif présent

je	parais
il, elle	paraît
nous	paraissons
ils, elles	paraissent

Indicatif imparfait

je	paraissais
nous	paraissions

Indicatif futur

je	paraîtrai
nous	paraîtrons

Indicatif passé simple

je	parus
il, elle	parut
nous	parûmes
ils, elles	parurent

Subjonctif présent

que je	paraisse
qu'il, elle	paraisse
que nous	paraissions
qu'ils, elles	paraissent

Impératif

parais
paraissons
paraissez

Participe présent

paraissant

Participe passé

paru, e

• Le conditionnel a le même radical que le futur mais comporte les terminaisons de l'imparfait (**rais**, etc.)

[92] naître (auxiliaire être)
naît- / naiss- / nai- / naqu- / n-

Indicatif présent		**Indicatif passé simple**		**Impératif**
je	nais	je	naquis	nais
il, elle	naît	il, elle	naquit	naissons
nous	naissons	nous	naquîmes	naissez
ils, elles	naissent	ils, elles	naquirent	

Participe présent
naissant

Indicatif imparfait		**Subjonctif présent**	
je	naissais	que je	naisse
nous	naissions	qu'il, elle	naisse
		que nous	naissions

Participe passé
né, e

Indicatif futur		qu'ils, elles	naissent
je	naîtrai		
nous	naîtrons		

[93] croître   croît- / croiss- / croî- / cr-

Indicatif présent		**Indicatif passé simple**		**Impératif**
je	croîs	je	crûs	croîs
il, elle	croît	il, elle	crût	croissons
nous	croissons	nous	crûmes	croissez
ils, elles	croissent	ils, elles	crûrent	

Participe présent
croissant

Indicatif imparfait		**Subjonctif présent**	
je	croissais	que je	croisse
nous	croissions	qu'il, elle	croisse
		que nous	croissions

Participe passé
crû, crue
crus, crues

Indicatif futur		qu'ils, elles	croissent
je	croîtrai		
nous	croîtrons		

Remarque : L'accent circonflexe sur le i apparaît devant un t, ainsi que dans les formes qui peuvent être confondues avec celles du verbe croire.

[94] accroître   accroît- / accroiss- / accroi- / accr- (-î- devant t)

Indicatif présent		**Indicatif passé simple**		**Impératif**
j'	accrois	j'	accrus	accrois
il, elle	accroît	il, elle	accrut	accroissons
nous	accroissons	nous	accrûmes	accroissez
ils, elles	accroissent	ils, elles	accrurent	

Participe présent
accroissant

Indicatif imparfait		**Subjonctif présent**	
j'	accroissais	que j'	accroisse
nous	accroissions	qu'il, elle	accroisse
		que nous	accroissions

Participe passé
accru, e

Indicatif futur		qu'ils, elles	accroissent
j'	accroîtrai		
nous	accroîtrons		

• Le conditionnel a le même radical que le futur mais comporte les terminaisons de l'imparfait (**rais**, etc.)

[95] rire   ri- / r-

Indicatif présent		**Indicatif passé simple**		**Impératif**
je	ris	je	ris	ris
il, elle	rit	il, elle	rit	rions
nous	rions	nous	rîmes	riez
ils, elles	rient	ils, elles	rirent	

Participe présent
riant

Indicatif imparfait		**Subjonctif présent**	
je	riais	que je	rie
nous	riions	qu'il, elle	rie

Participe passé
ri

que nous   riions
qu'ils, elles   rient

Indicatif futur	
je	rirai
nous	rirons

[96] conclure   conclu- / concl-

Indicatif présent		**Indicatif passé simple**		**Impératif**
je	conclus	je	conclus	conclus
il, elle	conclut	il, elle	conclut	concluons
nous	concluons	nous	conclûmes	concluez
ils, elles	concluent	ils, elles	conclurent	

Participe présent
concluant

Indicatif imparfait		**Subjonctif présent**	
je	concluais	que je	conclue
nous	concluions	qu'il, elle	conclue

Participe passé
conclu, e

que nous   concluions
qu'ils, elles   concluent

Indicatif futur	
je	conclurai
nous	conclurons

Remarque : Inclure *se conjugue comme* conclure *mais son participe passé est* inclus, e.

[97] nuire   nui- / nuis- / nu-

Indicatif présent		**Indicatif passé simple**		**Impératif**
je	nuis	je	nuisis	nuis
il, elle	nuit	il, elle	nuisit	nuisons
nous	nuisons	nous	nuisîmes	nuisez
ils, elles	nuisent	ils, elles	nuisirent	

Participe présent
nuisant

Indicatif imparfait		**Subjonctif présent**	
je	nuisais	que je	nuise
nous	nuisions	qu'il, elle	nuise

Participe passé
nui

que nous   nuisions
qu'ils, elles   nuisent

Indicatif futur	
je	nuirai
nous	nuirons

Remarque : Luire et reluire *connaissent une autre forme de passé simple :* je luis , je reluis.

• Le conditionnel a le même radical que le futur mais comporte les terminaisons de l'imparfait (**rais**, etc.)

[98] conduire   condui- / conduis-

Indicatif présent

je	conduis
il, elle	conduit
nous	conduisons
ils, elles	conduisent

Indicatif imparfait

je	conduisais
nous	conduisions

Indicatif futur

je	conduirai
nous	conduirons

Indicatif passé simple

je	conduisis
il, elle	conduisit
nous	conduisîmes
ils, elles	conduisirent

Subjonctif présent

que je	conduise
qu'il, elle	conduise
que nous	conduisions
qu'ils, elles	conduisent

Impératif

conduis
conduisons
conduisez

Participe présent
conduisant

Participe passé
conduit, e

[99] écrire   écri- / écriv-

Indicatif présent

j'	écris
il, elle	écrit
nous	écrivons
ils, elles	écrivent

Indicatif imparfait

j'	écrivais
nous	écrivions

Indicatif futur

j'	écrirai
nous	écrirons

Indicatif passé simple

j'	écrivis
il, elle	écrivit
nous	écrivîmes
ils, elles	écrivirent

Subjonctif présent

que j'	écrive
qu'il, elle	écrive
que nous	écrivions
qu'ils, elles	écrivent

Impératif

écris
écrivons
écrivez

Participe présent
écrivant

Participe passé
écrit, e

[100] suffire   suffi- / suffis- / suff-

Indicatif présent

je	suffis
il, elle	suffit
nous	suffisons
ils, elles	suffisent

Indicatif imparfait

je	suffisais
nous	suffisions

Indicatif futur

je	suffirai
nous	suffirons

Indicatif passé simple

je	suffis
il, elle	suffit
nous	suffîmes
ils, elles	suffirent

Subjonctif présent

que je	suffise
qu'il, elle	suffise
que nous	suffisions
qu'ils, elles	suffisent

Impératif

suffis
suffisons
suffisez

Participe présent
suffisant

Participe passé
suffi

• Le conditionnel a le même radical que le futur mais comporte les terminaisons de l'imparfait (**rais**, etc.)

[102] dire di- / dis- / d-

Indicatif présent

je	dis
il, elle	dit
nous	disons
vous	dites
ils, elles	disent

Indicatif imparfait

| je | disais |
| nous | disions |

Indicatif futur

| je | dirai |
| nous | dirons |

Indicatif passé simple

je	dis
il, elle	dit
nous	dîmes
ils, elles	dirent

Subjonctif présent

que je	dise
qu'il, elle	dise
que nous	disions
qu'ils, elles	disent

Impératif

dis
disons
dites

Participe présent

disant

Participe passé

dit, e

[103] contredire contredi- / contredis- / contred-

Indicatif présent

je	contredis
il, elle	contredit
nous	contredisons
vous	contredisez
ils, elles	contredisent

Indicatif imparfait

| je | contredisais |
| nous | contredisions |

Indicatif futur

| je | contredirai |
| nous | contredirons |

Indicatif passé simple

je	contredis
il, elle	contredit
nous	contredîmes
ils, elles	contredirent

Subjonctif présent

que je	contredise
qu'il, elle	contredise
que nous	contredisions
qu'ils, elles	contredisent

Impératif

contredis
contredisons
contredisez

Participe présent

contredisant

Participe passé

contredit, e

[104] maudire maudi- / maudiss- / maud-

Indicatif présent

je	maudis
il, elle	maudit
nous	maudissons
ils, elles	maudissent

Indicatif imparfait

| je | maudissais |
| nous | maudissions |

Indicatif futur

| je | maudirai |
| nous | maudirons |

Indicatif passé simple

je	maudis
il, elle	maudit
nous	maudîmes
ils, elles	maudirent

Subjonctif présent

que je	maudisse
qu'il, elle	maudisse
que nous	maudissions
qu'ils, elles	maudissent

Impératif

maudis
maudissons
maudissez

Participe présent

maudissant

Participe passé

maudit, e

• Le conditionnel a le même radical que le futur mais comporte les terminaisons de l'imparfait (**rais**, etc.)

[105] **bruire** brui- / bruy-

Indicatif présent
je   bru**is**
tu   bru**is**
il, elle   bru**it**
inusité aux personnes
du pluriel

Indicatif imparfait
je   bruy**ais**
nous   bruy**ions**

Indicatif futur
je   brui**rai**
nous   brui**rons**

Indicatif passé simple
inusité

Subjonctif présent
inusité

Impératif
inusité

Participe présent
inusité

Participe passé
brui**t**

[106] **lire** li- / lis- / l-

Indicatif présent
je   l**is**
il, elle   l**it**
nous   lis**ons**
ils, elles   lis**ent**

Indicatif imparfait
je   lis**ais**
nous   lis**ions**

Indicatif futur
je   li**rai**
nous   li**rons**

Indicatif passé simple
je   l**us**
il, elle   l**ut**
nous   l**ûmes**
ils, elles   l**urent**

Subjonctif présent
que je   l**ise**
qu'il, elle   l**ise**
que nous   lis**ions**
qu'ils, elles   lis**ent**

Impératif
l**is**
lis**ons**
lis**ez**

Participe présent
lis**ant**

Participe passé
l**u**, **e**

[107] **croire** croi- / croy- / cr-

Indicatif présent
je   cro**is**
il, elle   cro**it**
nous   croy**ons**
ils, elles   croi**ent**

Indicatif imparfait
je   croy**ais**
nous   croy**ions**

Indicatif futur
je   croi**rai**
nous   croi**rons**

Indicatif passé simple
je   cr**us**
il, elle   cr**ut**
nous   cr**ûmes**
ils, elles   cr**urent**

Subjonctif présent
que je   cro**ie**
qu'il, elle   cro**ie**
que nous   croy**ions**
qu'ils, elles   croi**ent**

Impératif
cro**is**
croy**ons**
croy**ez**

Participe présent
croy**ant**

Participe passé
cr**u**, **e**

• Le conditionnel a le même radical que le futur mais comporte les terminaisons de l'imparfait (**rais**, etc.)

[108] boire   boi- / boiv- / buv- / b-

Indicatif présent
je	bois
il, elle	boit
nous	buvons
ils, elles	boivent

Indicatif imparfait
je	buvais
nous	buvions

Indicatif futur
je	boirai
nous	boirons

Indicatif passé simple
je	bus
il, elle	but
nous	bûmes
ils, elles	burent

Subjonctif présent
que je	boive
qu'il, elle	boive
que nous	buvions
qu'ils, elles	boivent

Impératif
bois
buvons
buvez

Participe présent
buvant

Participe passé
bu, e

[109] faire   fai- / fais- / fe- / fass- / f-

Indicatif présent
je	fais
il, elle	fait
nous	faisons
vous	faites
ils, elles	font

Indicatif imparfait
je	faisais
nous	faisions

Indicatif futur
je	ferai
nous	ferons

Indicatif passé simple
je	fis
il, elle	fit
nous	fîmes
ils, elles	firent

Subjonctif présent
que je	fasse
qu'il, elle	fasse
que nous	fassions
qu'ils, elles	fassent

Impératif
fais
faisons
faites

Participe présent
faisant

Participe passé
fait, e

[110] plaire   plai- / plais- / pl- (-î- devant t)

Indicatif présent
je	plais
il, elle	plaît
nous	plaisons
ils, elles	plaisent

Indicatif imparfait
je	plaisais
nous	plaisions

Indicatif futur
je	plairai
nous	plairons

Indicatif passé simple
je	plus
il, elle	plut
nous	plûmes
ils, elles	plurent

Subjonctif présent
que je	plaise
qu'il, elle	plaise
que nous	plaisions
qu'ils, elles	plaisent

Impératif
plais
plaisons
plaisez

Participe présent
plaisant

Participe passé
plu

• Le conditionnel a le même radical que le futur mais comporte les terminaisons de l'imparfait (**rais**, etc.)

[111] taire   tai- / tais- / t-

Indicatif présent
je	tais
il, elle	tait
nous	taisons
ils, elles	taisent

Indicatif imparfait
je	taisais
nous	taisions

Indicatif futur
je	tairai
nous	tairons

Indicatif passé simple
je	tus
il, elle	tut
nous	tûmes
ils, elles	turent

Subjonctif présent
que je	taise
qu'il, elle	taise
que nous	taisions
qu'ils, elles	taisent

Impératif

tais
taisons
taisez

Participe présent

taisant

Participe passé

tu, e

[112] extraire   extrai- / extray-

Indicatif présent
j'	extrais
il, elle	extrait
nous	extrayons
ils, elles	extraient

Indicatif imparfait
j'	extrayais
nous	extrayions

Indicatif futur
j'	extrairai
nous	extrairons

Indicatif passé simple

inusité

Subjonctif présent
que j'	extraie
qu'il, elle	extraie
que nous	extrayions
qu'ils, elles	extraient

Impératif

extrais
extrayons
extrayez

Participe présent

extrayant

Participe passé

extrait, e

[113] clore   clo- / clos- (-ô- devant t)

Indicatif présent
je	clos
il, elle	clôt
nous	closons
ils, elles	closent

Indicatif imparfait

inusité

Indicatif futur
je	clorai
nous	clorons

Indicatif passé simple

inusité

Subjonctif présent
que je	close
qu'il, elle	close
que nous	closions
qu'ils, elles	closent

Impératif

clos
inusité aux personnes
du pluriel

Participe présent

closant

Participe passé

clos, e

Remarque : Éclore se conjugue comme clore, mais l'Académie préconise il, elle éclot sans accent circonflexe.

• Le conditionnel a le même radical que le futur mais comporte les terminaisons de l'imparfait (**rais**, etc.)

[114] vaincre   vainc- / vainqu-

Indicatif présent
je	vaincs
il, elle	vainc
nous	vainquons
ils, elles	vainquent

Indicatif imparfait
| je | vainquais |
| nous | vainquions |

Indicatif futur
| je | vaincrai |
| nous | vaincrons |

Indicatif passé simple
je	vainquis
il, elle	vainquit
nous	vainquîmes
ils, elles	vainquirent

Subjonctif présent
que je	vainque
qu'il, elle	vainque
que nous	vainquions
qu'ils, elles	vainquent

Impératif
vaincs
vainquons
vainquez

Participe présent
vainquant

Participe passé
vaincu, e

[115] frire   fri-

Indicatif présent
je	fris
tu	fris
il, elle	frit

inusité aux personnes
du pluriel

Indicatif imparfait
inusité

Indicatif futur
| je | frirai |
| nous | frirons |

Indicatif passé simple
inusité

Subjonctif présent
inusité

Conditionnel présent
| je | frirais |
| nous | fririons |

Impératif
fris
inusité aux personnes
du pluriel

Participe présent
inusité

Participe passé
frit, e

[116] foutre   fout- / fou-

Indicatif présent
je	fous
tu	fous
il, elle	fout
nous	foutons
ils, elles	foutent

Indicatif imparfait
| je | foutais |
| nous | foutions |

Indicatif futur
| je | foutrai |
| nous | foutrons |

Indicatif passé simple
inusité

Subjonctif présent
que je	foute
qu'il, elle	foute
que nous	foutions
qu'ils, elles	foutent

Impératif
fous
foutons
foutez

Participe présent
foutant

Participe passé
foutu, e

• Le conditionnel a le même radical que le futur mais comporte les terminaisons de l'imparfait (**rais**, etc.)

ENGLISH IRREGULAR VERBS

Infinitive	Past Tense	Past Participle
arise	arose	arisen
awake	awoke	awoken
be	was, were	been
bear	bore	born(e)
beat	beat	beaten
become	became	become
befall	befell	befallen
begin	began	begun
behold	beheld	beheld
bend	bent	bent
beseech	besought	besought
beset	beset	beset
bet	bet (also betted)	bet (also betted)
bid	bid (also bade)	bid (also bidden)
bind	bound	bound
bite	bit	bitten
bleed	bled	bled
blow	blew	blown
break	broke	broken
breed	bred	bred
bring	brought	brought
build	built	built
burn	burnt (also burned)	burnt (also burned)
burst	burst	burst
buy	bought	bought
can	could	-
cast	cast	cast
catch	caught	caught
choose	chose	chosen
cling	clung	clung
come	came	come
cost	cost	cost
creep	crept	crept
cut	cut	cut
deal	dealt	dealt
dig	dug	dug
do	did	done
draw	drew	drawn
dream	dreamed (also dreamt)	dreamed (also dreamt)
drink	drank	drunk
drive	drove	driven
dwell	dwelt	dwelt
eat	ate	eaten
fall	fell	fallen
feed	fed	fed
feel	felt	felt

Infinitive	Past Tense	Past Participle
fight	fought	fought
find	found	found
flee	fled	fled
fling	flung	flung
fly	flew	flown
forbid	forbade	forbidden
forecast	forecast	forecast
forego	forewent	foregone
foresee	foresaw	foreseen
foretell	foretold	foretold
forget	forgot	forgotten
forgive	forgave	forgiven
forsake	forsook	forsaken
freeze	froze	frozen
get	got	got (Am gotten)
give	gave	given
go	went	gone
grind	ground	ground
grow	grew	grown
hang	hung (also hanged)	hung (also hanged)
have	had	had
hear	heard	heard
hide	hid	hidden
hit	hit	hit
hold	held	held
hurt	hurt	hurt
keep	kept	kept
kneel	knelt (also kneeled)	knelt (also kneeled)
know	knew	known
lay	laid	laid
lead	led	led
lean	leant (also leaned)	leant (also leaned)
leap	leapt (also leaped)	leapt (also leaped)
learn	learnt (also learned)	learnt (also learned)
leave	left	left
lend	lent	lent
let	let	let
lie	lay	lain
light	lit (also lighted)	lit (also lighted)
lose	lost	lost
make	made	made
may	might	-
mean	meant	meant
meet	met	met
mistake	mistook	mistaken
mow	mowed	mown (also mowed)
pay	paid	paid
put	put	put

Big Dipper ['-dipər] *n* **-1.** *Br* [rollercoaster] montagnes *fpl* russes. **-2.** *Am* ASTRON : **the ~** la Grande Ourse.

Black Maria [-mə'raɪə] *n inf* panier m à salade.

city ['sɪtɪ] (*pl* **-ies**) *n* ville *f*, cité *f*.

◆ **City** *n Br* : **the City** la City.

THE CITY:

La City, quartier financier de la capitale, est une circonscription administrative autonome de Londres ayant sa propre police. Le terme « The City » est souvent employé pour désigner le monde britannique de la finance

civil list *n Br* liste *f* civile *(allouée à la famille royale par le parlement britannique)*.

gynaecological *Br*, **gynecological** *Am* [sitɪ] *adj* gynécologique.

hadn't ['hædnt] = **had not**.

make [meɪk] (*pt & pp* **made**) - *vt* **-1.** [gen - produce] faire; [-manufacture] faire, fabriquer; **to ~ a meal** préparer un repas; **to ~ a film** tourner OR réaliser un film. **-2.** [perform an action] faire.

parent ['peərənt] *n* père m, mère f.

◆ **parents** *npl* parents *mpl*.

PAYE (*abbr of* **pay as you earn**) *n* en Grande-Bretagne, système de retenue à la source des impôts sur le revenu.

step [step] (*pt & pp* **-ped**, *cont* **-ping**) ◇ *vi* **-1.** [pace] pas *m*; **in/out of ~ with** en accord/désaccord avec; **to watch one's ~** faire attention où l'on marche; *fig* faire attention à ce que l'on fait. **-2.** [action] mesure *f*. **-3.** [stage] étape *f*; **~ by ~** petit à petit, progressivement. **-4.** [stair] marche *f*. **-5.** [of ladder] barreau *m*, échelon *m*. **-6.** *Am* MUS ton *m*. ◇ *vi* **-1.** [move foot]: **to ~ forward** avancer; **to ~ off** or **down from sthg** descendre de qqch; **to ~ back** reculer. **-2.** [tread]: **to ~ on/in sthg** marcher sur/dans qqch.

◆ **steps** *npl* **-1.** [stairs] marches *fpl*. **-2.** *Br* [stepladder] escabeau *m*.

◆ **step aside** *vi* **-1.** [move away] s'écarter. **-2.** [leave job] démissionner.